MW01641598

Webster
Comprehensive
Dictionary

Encyclopedic Edition

Volume One

STANDARD EDUCATIONAL CORPORATION
LAKE BLUFF, ILLINOIS

Webster Comprehensive Dictionary
ENCYCLOPEDIC EDITION
Editorial Board

Funk & Wagnalls New International Dictionary of the English Language
was previously published as
Funk & Wagnalls New Comprehensive International Dictionary of the English Language
and is also published as
Webster Comprehensive Dictionary

ISBN 0-89434-428-5

Z-4

Printed in the United States of America.

TABLE OF CONTENTS

Volume One

Volume Two

SPECIAL SUPPLEMENTARY FEATURES

Editorial Advisory Board

Consulting Editors

Consultants

Editorial Staff

Introduction

The *Webster Comprehensive Dictionary: Encyclopedic Edition* is backed by three quarters of a century of experience in dictionary-making and, like its predecessors, is designed to serve the practical and professional needs of all who speak or use the English language. No resource of lexicographical skill has been spared to fulfil this purpose.

Throughout their work, the editors, with the valued cooperation of many of the nation's eminent leaders in education, industry, the arts, sciences, and professions, have been guided by the following objectives:

TO PRESENT the fundamental facts and characteristics of the language accurately, fully, and interestingly. The definitions, and the wealth of additional material here presented, are the result of years of scholarly research into the many facets of word-meaning and usage, combined with an editorial awareness of the wide-ranging developments of our expanding world. Details of syllabication, spelling, pronunciation, morphological forms, and grammatical usage have been included without stint. Etymologies, or short word-histories, are provided for the interesting insight they give into the richness and versatility of the English vocabulary. Particular attention is given to the word builders—the indispensable prefixes, suffixes, and combining forms in which English is so rich and which are constantly at work supplying new words to the language. An innovation in dictionary practice—the inclusion of hundreds of homophones and collateral adjectives under their appropriate entries—has been effected to highlight two of the more interesting and valuable, but seldom considered, features of the language.

TO PRESENT adequately the significant contributions to English made in the United States, with requisite definitions, usage notes, and discriminative comment. Similar treatment is accorded to such areas of speech as slang, dialects, colloquialisms, and various forms of English as modified or influenced by Scottish, Irish, Canadian, Australian, and other sources — all of these being properly labeled for ready identification.

TO SECURE the widest possible coverage of both the established word stock of English and of the rapidly expanding vocabularies of the arts, sciences, trades and professions. In the first group, selection has depended upon the overriding factors of usage, word-frequency counts, and sound historical judgment, reinforced by the consensus of the many authorities consulted in the course of preparation. In the second, choice of entries has been determined by a conscientious and extensive review of the appropriate sources in every technical field.

These, then, have been the major, but by no means the only, objectives of the editors and their many specialist consultants. A fuller discussion of the what, how, why, and wherefore of the contents of this book is given in the following pages of the Introduction and in the Explanatory Notes at page xvi.

Definition & Semantic Change

DEFINITIONS in this dictionary are adapted to the nature of the word. Any effort to tailor all words to fit a rigid pattern of definition would result in distortion rather than clarification of meaning. Instead of following a standard formula for defining, the editors have constantly kept in mind the need to study the meanings of words in phrases, compounds, and sentences and the processes of meaning-change which words have undergone and are still undergoing. This semantic approach enables the definer to stress variety rather than uniformity. It leads to a frank acceptance of the policy of different techniques of defining for different types of words. Our basic aim has been to formulate a definition that can substitute for the word itself in the context in which the user reads or hears it. The context, too, is often shown, in the form of illustrative phrases and sentences following many of the definitions. Pictures are used at points where a visual aid tells a fuller story about an object or process than words can.

Either the most relevant or the most general meaning is given first, depending on the sequence which will best convey to the user the interrelations between the various meanings of the entry. Historical order is not usually followed, for it is of more practical value to the user to start with the word as it is today. Where the current sense of a word is more meaningful in the light of its history, however, the original sense is given first. (Note, for example, the flow of semantic development in the entry **scapegoat** in the vocabulary section.)

A different approach in defining is needed for words that are far removed from concrete, picturable things, and that deal with concepts or abstract ideas of a complex nature. Terms dealing with theology, politics, economics, psychology, and sociology are often packed with different meanings for different people. It is desirable to give space and time coordinates, so that the meaning of the word at different times and places is thrown into strong relief; its various interpretations and applications are then more readily evident if the coverage is detailed and complete. Every user will thus find the particular reference he is looking for. For examples of the application of this pattern of defining, see the entries **dean** and **fusion.**

The user will often find in this, as in most dictionaries, definitions or parts of definitions that are introduced by such qualifying words as "specifically," "figuratively," "loosely," and the like. (See **disinterested, gale, seasoning.**) He will also find following others such limiting or warning signs after a colon as "in derogatory use," "a term of contempt," "a genteelism," or "used ironically." (See **smart** or **canicular.**) These added qualifying notes indicate that the word or phrase in question has acquired certain overtones of meaning that are conveyed either by the intonation of the voice, or by the habitual association of the word with a certain kind of situation. Its literal or primary meaning is thus specialized, bettered, worsened, or figuratively extended, as the case may be.

Specialization and Generalization Many words that now have very general meanings started life as the names of specific things. At one time the nineteen animals chiefly hunted as game were each blessed with an individual term for the tail, but, as the general word *tail* came into vogue, most of these special names disappeared. The *brush* of the fox, however, still survives.

Often the processes of specialization and generalization of meaning work like a shuttle service. A word will shift from a specific to a general sense and then back again in the course of centuries of use. The word *gear,* for example, in early Middle English meant habits or manners. By 1500 it acquired a more generalized sense: property or equipment, comprising clothing, arms, armor, harness, or any tool or apparatus — a fairly comprehensive coverage. Then, with the increasing use of machinery in the Renaissance period, *gear* came to mean "an arrangement of fixed and moving parts in a machine for any special purpose." Finally, in modern mechanics, *gear* is now further specialized to mean "a wheel having teeth that fit into another wheel of the same kind, usually of a different size, to make the second wheel turn at a different speed from the first."

Radiation One of the most interesting ways in which words extend meaning is by radiation. In this case the word does not change its basic meaning, but it radiates out from this central core of meaning a variety of extended senses. Take the word *action,* for example. Its primary meaning is "doing." In an extended sense it may mean (1) an acting; a state of activity (*thought* vs. *action*), (2) the natural or usual motion of an organ (the *action* of the heart), (3) the movements of a mechanism (the valve *action* in an engine), (4) a thing done; a deed (the *actions* of a fool), (5) the sequence of events in a play, (6) a military or naval battle, (7) a legal proceeding (a court *action*), (8) attitude or position expressing some kind of emotion (the *action* of a painting). In all of these senses of *action,* the primary notion of "doing" is the underlying factor. According to dictionary convention, the meanings are given in sequence, but they may be envisaged as radiating from the central sense.

Transference This is another way in which words change meaning or enlarge in scope. It applies particularly to words involving feeling attitudes or value judgments. A kind of projection occurs whereby an emotion in the speaker is transferred to the objects or persons represented. If a poet speaks of "the cruel, crawling foam," a moment's reflection will tell us that the foam is not cruel, nor does it crawl. Rather, the speaker has projected his own very human feeling as to the cruelty of the sea, and imagines that the movement of the foam is an encroaching one. The attributing of human emotions and motivation to inanimate objects is an example of a semantic process whereby a word may be greatly extended in use.

Melioration and Deterioration Here are two additional processes by which words reflect attitudes either complimentary or contemptuous. For example, the social standing of a word seems to depend very closely on the status of the class, group, or profession which it describes. Since the rise of the city-state in ancient Greece and Rome, and the predominance of urban culture as the supposed center of civilization, words that have to do with the city usually have a favorable aura; thus the word *urbane* — a variant of *urban* — has to do not merely with a person who lives in a city, but one who supposedly has polish, manners, tact, and a pleasing manner. This process of elevation in the status of a word is called melioration.

In contrast, words associated with farming and the farmer have shown a tendency to come down in the world. Deterioration of meaning has set in again and again. To be sure, in any agrarian society where farming is the basic occupation, words associated with the lord of the manor, or even with a country squire who has sizable land holdings, usually give evidence of the high esteem with which landowners are held in the community. Serfs who worked on a villa or manorial estate in the late Roman Imperial period, or in the early Middle Ages, were described by the word *villanus* meaning "one attached to the villa or manor." Such a person was considered part of the property of the lord, and went with the villa when it was sold. When these "villeins," as they were called in early medieval France, went to visit in a nearby city, they were at once recognized as coming from the country. They often got into rows and quarrels, and were considered to have rough and uncouth manners. The name by which they were known was "villain" in Norman French, and the word passed into English, where it later acquired something close to its modern sense of a rascally person of evil intentions. Finally, the word took on the meaning of arch scoundrel, wicked opponent of the hero.

Genteelisms A genteelism constitutes a special case of deterioration. The word itself is a case in point, for genteelism originally meant the possession of qualities expected in well-bred and well-mannered persons, and was thus synonymous with gentility. But it went downhill as changing economic conditions made it increasingly difficult for many people in this group to maintain their standards of living. The novelists, noting the prevalence of "shabby genteel" characters in run-down urban areas and suburbs, associated them with an unsuccessful effort to maintain status, so that the word *genteelism* itself acquired rather a contemptuous or ironic flavor, as have *genteel* and *gentility.* (See these entries in the vocabulary section.)

Adulteration Adulteration of meaning occurs when a word is corrupted in sense by adroit manipulation of the context in which it appears, so that by association it takes on a flavor and feeling which subtly and gradually shift it from its primary sense. It can then be used as a clever weapon in propaganda in whatever direction the manipulator wants it to go. This fate has overtaken the word *semantics* itself. It is necessarily concerned with the processes of meaning shift, and the transition to a loose sense of "verbal shiftiness" or "verbal trickery" is one that is easily made. This process very nearly negates the proper meaning of the word and makes suspect the integrity and rigor of semantic analysis.

Euphemisms Polite substitutes for words that have an unpleasant or somehow embarrassing connotation are called euphemisms. Euphemistic replacement is, by its nature, a continual process, for the euphemism loses its power to conceal once it becomes too closely connected with the thing it represents. Thus, each age has its own euphemisms. The Victorian era is considered to have seen the height of verbal prudishness, and today we smile at conventions which made shocking such words as *leg* and *shirt* when used in the presence of ladies. With the reaction against Victorianism and the revolt against convention that marked the Jazz Age, blunt speaking became the fashion and the old euphemisms were rapidly discarded. Today, one finds in wide use words which would have been considered gross or obscene fifty years ago. The modern tendency is indeed toward the use of straightforward language, but the essence of the euphemistic process is still preserved in such commonly encountered substitutions as *rest-room, criminal assault,* and *social disease.*

Hyperbole The tendency to exaggeration in speech and writing has remained a constant throughout most periods of the language. Particularly has this been true of the United States, beginning with the time of the tall tale of the frontier. This tendency flourished richly in the field of slang, but it was very far from being confined to that area. Some once strong adjectives have, in informal speech, lost most of their original potency (see the definitions labeled *Colloq.* under **awful** and **terrible**), and many adjectives of size, such as *colossal, gigantic,* and *mammoth,* have been considerably reduced in stature. The constant caution in the use of superlatives finally had its effect upon many of these terms, and today the understatement is esteemed in principle if not always in practice by American speakers and writers.

Figurative extension The use of a word in a figurative sense is perhaps the commonest way of extending meaning. When in the mid-thirties the study of allergies came into fashion in medicine, the adjective *allergic,* with a precise technical meaning, soon came into use in the sense of "adversely sensitive to," but it was picked up by around 1940 as at first a slang translation for "antipathetic." It became fashionable to say, "I'm allergic to crooners — or boring lectures" or any other pet aversion that the speaker harbored. This figurative sense is now accepted as having good colloquial standing.

This process has left many deposits in the language. The *flag* symbolizes the power of a country, just as the Roman *eagles,* the standard of the Roman legions, came to stand for the legions themselves, and by further extension, for the power of the Roman Empire. This type of figure of speech is called a metonomy, or sign for the thing signified. Next to metaphor, a comparison made without the use of the word *like* or *as,* it is one of the commonest devices for giving a figurative meaning to an individual word.

The process of adapting proper names — historical or mythological personification — for the purpose of describing qualities or conditions, is also a way in which new meaning is brought into play. One who admires himself inordinately is called a *Narcissus,* a man of great wisdom is a *Solomon,* one of prodigious strength is a *Hercules,* and a woman of great beauty is called a *Venus.*

The various methods used to extend the meanings of words exhibit the long poetic tradition of our language. Words are constantly acquiring new figurative senses, and the lexicographer must continually consider whether or not to add the new meanings to his treatment of the words in question. If the extended meaning is not self-evident, it must be supplied. The word *extrapolation* is a case in point. In the last ten years this mathematical term, which means extending a graph or table by projecting values beyond the point for which data are known, has acquired a quite natural figurative sense: projection of known scientific data into the realm of conjecture; in short, something close to legitimate scientific prophecy. The user of a dictionary, if he finds only the technical mathematical sense, may not be able to infer the figurative meaning in which he finds "extrapolation" in a magazine or newspaper. Here, and in many similar cases, the dictionary must include the figurative sense (see **extrapolation,** definition 2). Since this process has been going on in the language for nearly a millennium, constantly reinforcing and interplaying with the several other processes of meaning-change, it is not surprising that English is perhaps the richest of all languages in words with multiple meanings.

Usage Levels and Labels

In this dictionary the most important label is one that is not here. As the best style is the absence of it, so the "best" words in our language are those needing no label that make up general-purpose English. A writer who is a general practitioner will usually stick to this level of standard English.

Colloquialisms The words or phrases labeled *Colloq.* in this dictionary belong to the informal, comfortable language of everyday social life. The line between standard English and colloquial is hard to draw because expressions labeled *Colloq.* are usually understood just as well as if they were standard words, and the company they keep means that, unlike slang, they are in good repute among cultivated speakers. They would not be usable in full-dress, formal discourse but neither would they lower the tone to the level of slang.

Slang Slang consists either of words in themselves substandard and in bad repute or of standard words and phrases that are used in something less than a reputable sense. Slang may be highly colorful and bold, but very often it is derogatory or irreverent. As one of its basic characteristics is its daring newness, ninety-five percent of it is ephemeral.

Dialect The label *Dial.* (for *Dialectal*) in this dictionary indicates a word or usage that occurs in a local or regional dialect: a type of language that deviates from the standard language in vocabulary and often also in idiom, pronunciation, morphology, and syntactical construction. Sometimes words that are peculiar to a particular dialect are understood in other areas, but they are still felt as belonging to a distinctive type of local speech. A dialect that exists as an enclave within a country that uses an entirely different language is a *patois,* as, for example, the French Canadian spoken in Quebec, and its offshoot, the Cajun dialect of the descendants of the Acadians, who came down from Nova Scotia to Louisiana.

Americanisms American English came fully of age between the two World Wars and acquired its official chronicler in H. L. Mencken, who produced, in 1919, a book called *The American Language,* later much revised and supplemented. Initially, Mencken made too large claims for the American variety of English, basing his case for an American language on distinctive differences, and deemphasizing the total pattern of basic similarity between the language of this country and that of England. In this dictionary the label *U.S.* indicates words, phrases, and usages current in the United States and usually, though not always, originating here. In this way an attempt has been made to meet the needs of foreign users and those in other parts of the English-speaking world who want to be at home with American literature and its idioms. Often this has meant applying to the label *U. S.* the further label *Slang* or *Colloq.*

Briticisms The label *Brit.* (for *British*) in this dictionary denotes words, idioms, phrases, verb forms, and usages current in Great Britain (often also in other parts of the Commonwealth) but not in the United States. How it is that a monkey wrench is a *spanner* in England, a windshield is a *windscreen,* a baby carriage a *perambulator* ("pram"), suspenders *braces,* and a motor truck a *lorry*; and why a "close call" or "close shave" should be " a near thing" in British English, is anybody's guess. Sometimes the distinction between British and American usage involves a grammatical form. Such is the case with *gotten,* quite obsolete in standard British speech, but widely used in this country as a past participle of *get* when a completed action is expressed ("I've *gotten* much accomplished today").

Gotten is accordingly labeled *U.S.* in this book when it appears as one of the inflected forms in the entry **get,** and a short discussion of American and British usage is given under the main entry **gotten.**

Scottish There is a certain condescension in labeling words in Burns's poems and the novels of Sir Walter Scott by what is in effect a dialect label: *Scot.* (for *Scottish*). Such a label, however, is the fashion and it is used here with the note that the language of the Court of Scotland was in a sense merged with the Queen's English of Elizabeth I when the son of Mary Stuart, James VI of Scotland, became James I of England and launched the Authorized Version of the Bible known by his name.

Australian, Canadian, etc. In the overseas members of the Commonwealth new words have come into the English language just as they have in the United States. Local fauna and flora, the objects and processes peculiar to each area, have required new terms. In Australia, particularly, there have been additions in the way of riming slang, words from the language of the aborigines, and some modifications of British usage — the whole resulting in what may be properly called Australian English. To a lesser degree, Canadian English may also be differentiated. In all such cases, however, the departure from the English current in Great Britain is far less than in the case of the United States.

Archaic, Obsolete, Rare, or Poetic Words go out of fashion or fall into disuse, rapidly in the case of slang, at a more leisurely pace for clichés and informal words, while the jargons of pseudo-science, outmoded science, or mannered literary criticism decay more slowly, but none the less surely. When, therefore, an unusual word turns up in prose meant for the general reader, it is natural to ask about its status. If the word happens to be encased in a well-known quotation, it is likely to be labeled *Archaic* by the lexicographer. In "I'll make a ghost of him that lets me," the use of *let* in the sense of "hinder" is thus labeled *Archaic,* meaning that it is known and understood in our older literature, ranging from Elizabethan writing down through the works of Milton and Dryden but ordinarily not usable in present everyday writing or speaking. So in effect the label *Archaic* means "current from around 1500 until 1700," and hence turning up in quotations from that period but no longer used much, if at all, in writing subsequent to that stretch of about two hundred years.

Another group of words is labeled *Obs.* (for *Obsolete*). This is a more final verdict. It means that a word has gone so far out of use that it is quite forgotten. It has somehow failed to meet the test of survival, even to the extent of leading the somewhat ghostly life of an archaic word. Some such words died very early in the history of the language, failing to make their way from Old English to Middle English, and, while they had some slight and sporadic use in occasional writings, they did not really become established. One such word is *wanhope,* a native compound replaced by the Old French borrowing *despair.*

The lexicographer also has to take into account a borderline area of words that, once current, are now in the process of becoming obsolete. The best solution in the way of a label for these waifs and strays is *Rare.* More often the dictionary must be content to say of such locutions "Formerly," or "In the early —th century," or some such phrasing which will indicate a definite period when the objects to which they referred were in active use, without labeling the word itself as obsolete — for often the word survives the object.

Lastly, there are the words that are closely associated with poetry — at least with traditional old-fashioned poetry — but which are felt as out of place in prose, even in that "other music of prose" which Landor described as producing a poetic effect without being avowedly poetic in form, diction, or outward aspect. The label *Poetic* is employed to suggest to the user of this dictionary that if he is writing traditional verse the word may do well enough, but that if he is writing prose discretion is indicated.

Field Labels An important part of the lexicographer's task is not only the correct defining of the words in a dictionary but also the assignment of many of the definitions to specific areas of knowledge. In a great many cases this can be done by so phrasing the definition that the reader can immediately see the bearing of the word in any one of a large number of special areas, ranging from Aeronautics and Architecture to Theology and Zoology. Where this procedure can be applied simply and without loss of clarity, it has been used in this dictionary; but, for the further assistance of both layman and specialist, some sixty special fields of knowledge have been represented by appropriate labels for the purpose of indicating that a term, or a particular sense of it, has a restricted or specialized meaning within the designated area.

Conspicuous in this group of labels are those that pertain to the sciences, in both their fundamental and applied aspects. It is here that the language is being expanded with hundreds of new terms or of new meanings attached to old, often venerable words. Such terms as *automation, cybernetics, motivation research, nucleonics, information theory,* and hundreds of others in the physical, biological, medical, and social sciences have been given particular attention in the preparation of this dictionary. The editors have utilized all dependable sources of information and checked their findings with those of carefully chosen authorities in specified fields.

Synonyms and Antonyms

Synonyms Full advantage is taken of the dual nature of the English language, by giving not only the long literary synonyms that derive mainly from classical and Romance sources but also the short, sinewy words which come into play with such force in speech, and which, aptly used in writing, make the discourse sound like a man speaking, not like a book. However, the user will not find in the synonymies in this work any undue stress on the notion, first given currency by Herbert Spencer, that the so-called Saxon element in the language should be favored over the classical, for many of the short, pithy, highly expressive words in the language are from Greek and Latin, either directly or through Romance channels. The view taken throughout in treating synonyms is that each member of a group of related words has equal validity and usefulness in its own context, regardless of its origin. The only criterion by which they have been considered is the suitability of the word to the context.

Thus, we might speak of a thief as having *stolen* a wallet, but a child *filches* candy from a store, and a soldier *pilfers* army supplies. Similarly, a valuable document is *purloined,* while funds are *embezzled.* Bandits may *rob* all whom they meet, but they *plunder* the countryside.

The synonymy under the entry for **steal** will enable the reader to see why the above distinctions were made and to judge for himself the extent to which the words can be interchanged without complete loss either of sense or of shading. A great many ample synonymies such as these will be found throughout the vocabulary section of this book.

Antonyms In further pursuit of a sharper sense of word meaning, the reader may then look at the antonyms, which are listed immediately following most synonym entries. Words that are opposed or contrasted in meaning furnish, oddly enough, a valuable extension of the definitions of the words involved. To be sure, it is definition by contraries, but teachers who understand the art of testing know that the surest proof of a student's knowledge of the meaning of a word is his ability to give its antonym.

As the synonymies show, a key word in English may have a dozen synonyms that approximate it or overlap with it in meaning; but there are few words that have more than one exact antonym, as *black* has *white,* and *wet* has *dry*. The juxtaposition of the synonyms and the antonyms for a given word makes it possible for the user to carry out for himself a further refinement of interpretation. The user can check whether the antonyms given negate one or more of the synonyms as well as the key word.

The Pronunciations

THE PRONUNCIATIONS in this dictionary have been compiled by editors trained in phonetics and acquainted with the facts of the spoken language. There is, however, no single authority on pronunciation in this country, and no standard dialect. In the case of major regional variations in speech, the editors have recorded first the patterns of pronunciation of the largest region, that of the great midwestern section that was formerly called "General American." Work on a linguistic atlas for the United States has indicated that the large speech areas are far from homogeneous, but the method of recording used in this book is suited to the purposes of a dictionary where the aim is to provide reference rather than extensive linguistic data. It is not intended, of course, that if you are in a speech community where words like *forest* and *orange* are pronounced with the vowel of *stop,* or where *four* and *explore* are pronounced with the vowel of *stone,* you are to change your speech pattern to that of the first pronunciation here recorded, that is (fôr′ist) and (fôr). It has not been possible or practicable to record the speech of all dialect areas in this country. (Not recorded, for example, is the speech of those parts of the country where *r* is not pronounced when in final or pre-consonantal position, as in *car, better,* and *part.*) You may not, then, find your particular dialect recorded, but your mode of speech, if it is normal for your area, is right for you.

There are, of course, other variations in pronunciation apart from those of regional speech patterns. Whether you say (ab′də·mən) or (ab·dō′mən), (ser′ə·brəl) or (sə·rē′brəl) is purely a matter of personal choice; both variants are recorded. It is sometimes impossible to determine the most frequent pronunciation in such cases, and a second or third variant shown is to be regarded as equally acceptable.

Although the words in a dictionary must be pronounced in isolation, the editors have attempted to record them as they would be uttered in the flow of speech. In accordance with this policy, the symbol (ə), called *schwa,* was borrowed from the International Phonetic Alphabet to record the unstressed neutral vowel heard in the first syllable of *about* and in the second syllables of *comma, barren,* and *lemon.*

Some variant pronunciations are restricted to particular fields or professions, such as the medical or military. These have been labeled in this book as follows:

ob·lique (ə·blēk′, *in military usage* ə·blīk′)

Foreign pronunciations, when pertinent, are duly recorded and labeled, although an established Anglicization is always shown first:

a·dieu (ə·dōō′, ə·dyōō′; *Fr.* à·dyœ′)

It sometimes occurs that a word will differ in its pronunciation depending on its use as a noun, verb, etc., or in some particular sense. The differing pronunciation is ordinarily shown immediately before the particular use or uses to which it applies, as follows:

en·sign (en′sīn) *n.* **1** A distinguished flag or banner; especially, a national standard or naval flag. **2** (en′sən) In the U.S. Navy or Coast Guard, a commissioned officer of the lowest grade, ranking with a second lieutenant in the U.S. Army, Air Force, or Marine Corps.

The Key The system used for the recording of pronunciation in this book is one which has been determined to be the simplest, most meaningful, and accurate one for the purposes of dictionary transcription. It utilizes, with a few exceptions, the letters of the alphabet, combined with certain standard diacritical marks, such as the macron for the so-called "long vowels" (ā), (ē), (ī), (ō), (yōō). The conventional breve for the "short vowels" (a), (e), (i), (o), (u), has been eliminated from this key in all but one case, as these symbols are generally understood to be "short" when unmarked. The breve is retained in the one symbol (ŏŏ), the vowel in *book,* to avoid confusion with the vowel in *pool.* The elimination of the breve in all other cases, and the use of the one symbol (ə) for the unstressed neutral vowel however spelled, has resulted in a key for this dictionary in which only twelve characters, excluding the special symbols for foreign sounds, require special marking.

The Etymologies

THE ETYMOLOGIES in this dictionary present a concise history of the word with reference to origin, form changes, and semantic development. Native words that existed in the earliest period of the language are shown in their Old English form:

bedridden . . . [OE *bedrida* < *bed* bed + *rida* rider]

For borrowings, the immediate source is indicated first, followed by as many intermediate forms and languages as are necessary to show significant changes, and the word is then traced back to its earliest recorded forms or components in Latin, Greek, etc.:

diameter . . . [<OF *diametre* <L *diametrus* <Gk. *diametros* <*dia-* through + *metron* measure]

Where the ultimate language of origin cannot be determined, and the general provenance is known, a linguistic family is cited as the source:

garden . . . [<AF *gardin* <Gmc.]

or a geographical area is indicated:

banana . . . [<Sp. < native African name]

In the case of words of obscure origin, it has sometimes been possible to cite likely cognates in related languages:

gloat . . . [Cf. ON *glotta* grin]
groom . . . [ME *grom.* Cf. OF *gromet* a servant.]

Otherwise, such words are marked "origin uncertain" or "origin unknown," and the Middle English form is cited where one exists:

boy . . . [ME *boi*; origin unknown]

Of special interest to the student of words are the many other informative facts also given in the etymologies. Pairs or sets of words which have entered English through different intermediate languages or dialects, but can be traced back to the same ultimate source word, have been marked as "doublets." The etymologies of such words will show a common form, indicating the point at which the divergence of form and meaning first occurred and the necessary intermediate forms needed to show clearly the development of the modern words.

zero . . . [<F *zéro* <Ital. *zero* <Arabic *sifr.* Doublet of CIPHER.]
cipher . . . [<OF *cyfre* <Arabic *sifr.* Doublet of ZERO.]

A similar situation occurs when two or more words may be traced to the same primitive root; the divergence in meaning is much earlier than in the case of doublets, and so these words have no common recorded form. Such cognates are indicated by the phrase "Akin to . . .".

language . . . [<OF *langage* <*langue* tongue <L *lingua* tongue, language. Akin to TONGUE.]
tongue . . . [OE *tunge.* Akin to LANGUAGE.]

Another class of words may be derived from variants or different stems of the same recorded word in an ancient language, as Old English or Latin. This type of relationship is shown by the phrase "Related to . . ." in the etymologies.

hale[2] . . . [OE *hāl.* Related to WHOLE.]
whole . . . [OE (Northumbrian) *hōl,* var. of *hāl.* Related to HALE[2].]

The use of numerous cross-references has made it possible to present a large amount of information in a small space and without unnecessary repetition. The etymologies of many compound words, such as *acrophobia, hydrophone, transoceanic* may be found under the main entries for each of their components, where complete histories are given: *acro-, -phobia*; *hydro-, -phone*; *trans-, -oceanic.* In other compound words where the identity of the components may be obscure, the break-down is made in the form of cross-references to the source of additional information.

morphology . . . [<MORPHO- + -LOGY]
azine . . . [<AZ- + -INE[2]]

Etymologies of special interest, connecting words with important people, places, or events, are recorded with additional notes explaining the historic background of the word. (See **gerrymander, buncombe.**)

Many etymologies provide interesting insights into the cultural and social history of other times and places which still influence our thoughts and speech.

Usage

by Albert H. Marckwardt

Every society places its stamp of approval upon certain forms or modes of social behavior and looks askance upon deviations from them. In our culture, applause for a fine musical performance would be considered out of place at a church service, but entirely appropriate and in fact praiseworthy in a concert hall. The particular mode of behavior which is accorded such prestige may vary according to geography and social class. The English and European continentals recognize one manner of manipulating a knife and fork to convey food to the mouth; Americans employ a quite different technique. The American way seems needlessly awkward to the European; the European way seems crude to the Americans. When they entertain at dinner, upper middle-class Americans are likely to eat by candlelight and to have flowers on the table. This is regarded as ostentatious, or at best superfluous, in working-class circles.

The use of language is one of many kinds of social behavior. Here, as in other matters, certain forms of speech and writing have acquired prestige, whereas others are looked upon with disfavor. Moreover, differentiations on the basis of geography and social class are readily apparent. The past tense of the verb *eat (et),* used by many speakers of British English of unquestioned social standing, would be considered rustic or uneducated by most Americans; conversely, the Americanism *donate* has not yet gained thorough acceptance in Britain. "Bring them crates over here," is a sentence calculated to produce cooperation and a speedy result when addressed to a group of factory workmen; the substitution of *those containers* in that particular social context would produce suspicion, resentment, and probably not the desired result.

Standard English

That form of the English language which has acquired prestige from its use by those educated persons who are carrying on the affairs of the English-speaking community (whether narrowly or broadly conceived) is known as Standard English. In short, the standard language is that which possesses social utility and social prestige. History bears out this observation with remarkable fidelity. All we know of the earliest stage of our language, that which we refer to as Old English, spoken on the island between the mid-fifth century incursions of Germanic-speaking Angles, Saxons, and Jutes and the mid-11th century Norman Conquest, was that there were decided regional differences, resulting in four major dialects. During the first two of these six centuries the center of power was clearly in the kingdom of Northumbria, and that dialect constituted the standard. At the time of the powerful King Offa, political and cultural influence shifted southward, and the dialect of Mercia acquired prestige. From the mid-ninth century onward, the West Saxon dynasty assumed political leadership; King Alfred fathered a cultural renaissance and a major educational program; and this time the standard moved westward, remaining there through the period of religious reform, also centered in the same area. Thus it is that most of the Old English literature which has come down to us is in West Saxon. Even the early selections originally written in other dialects were finally recopied in the prestige dialect.

The development of the language during the Middle English period (1050–1475) bears out the same principle. By the time the English language had recovered from its temporary subjugation to Norman French, London was firmly established as the political, economic, and cultural center of the island. It is interesting to observe that by the end of the 14th century the dialect of London was used by many of the major literary figures irrespective of where they were born. Chaucer, a native Londoner, employed it in his poetry, which is possibly no surprise, but so too did Gower, born in Kent, and Wycliffe, who hailed from Lincolnshire. One acute observer has pointed out that Standard English had its origin in the kind of language employed in the courts of law and the governmental offices at Westminster, that it was essentially administrative English. This is another telling bit of evidence of the close relationship between the standard language and the bases of influence.

The emergence of the London dialect as a standard for the entire country first won formal recognition in Puttenham's *The Arte of English Poesie* (1589) in which the language of London and of the shires within a radius of sixty miles, "and not much beyond," was recommended as a model for aspiring writers to follow. This was accompanied by the statement that educated gentlemen in the outlying portions of England had adopted London English as a standard and were speaking it as well as people living in the capital.

It was just at this point in time that the English language entered on its worldwide career. It was transported first across the Atlantic to the American mainland and the Caribbean islands. The spread to the Asian subcontinent followed in the 18th century; to Australia and South Africa in the 19th. At the outset the colonies were generally willing and eager to follow the standard of the mother country, even though it was at times less than ideally suited to all aspects of the local situation, but as they acquired more and more independence, economic and cultural as well as political, new national forms of the language tended to emerge and to develop their own standard norms.

Today English is spoken as a native language by vast numbers of people—approximately 300,000,000—distributed over four continents of the globe. The standard reveals a considerable amount of variation from one country to another, and even in one part of some countries as compared with another. Thus, Standard West Indian English differs from both Standard British and Standard American English, and Standard South African differs from all of these. Standard Canadian English is distinct from Standard Australian. It is even possible to speak of standard forms of English in areas where it is not the native language, notably India and the Philippines. In the United Kingdom itself there is a standard form of Scots and a standard Northern English, both of which differ from the Received Standard of the London area.

The Role of the Dictionary

Ideally a dictionary is an accurate record of a language as it is employed by those who speak and write it. But as we have already seen, the English language, even in terms of just its present use, to say nothing of its past, exists on such a vast scale that no single work is likely to do justice to it in its entirety. Inevitably the task has had to be broken up into smaller segments. Some dictionaries deal with pronunciation only, at times even confined to a particular country—England or America. Others confine themselves to particular segments of the language: dialect, slang, or one or another technical vocabulary. More ambitious is the attempt by the historical dictionary to include within the bounds of a single work evidence of both the present and earlier stages of the language, although sometimes a dictionary may be confined to just one early period—Old or Middle English, for example. There are dictionaries which concentrate on the language as it is, and has been, used in England, in Scotland, in the United States, and in Canada. Consequently, in the face of this inescapable specialization and division of labor, a dictionary which purports to be general in its purpose must of necessity exercise a high degree of selective reporting on those aspects of the language which will best serve the needs of those who consult it.

The editors of this dictionary have assumed that it will be used principally in the United States, by persons who are familiar with American English. Only rarely have they felt it necessary to identify features of the language which are characteristic of this country. For example, the past participial form *gotten* is identified in a note as an American usage, and the peculiarly American use of *integrate* as used in "to integrate schools" bears the label *U.S.* The editors have taken on the responsibility of identifying usages peculiar to Britain, Canada, or Australia, indicating these with the appropriate label. Any item not so identified is in current use in the United States. In this connection it should be realized that despite all that has been said here about differences throughout the world, the unity of the English language in the many countries in which it is spoken far outweighs the diversity.

The obligation of the dictionary to record the state of the language or some segment of it as accurately as possible has already been mentioned. This may properly be termed a descriptive function, and it reflects the way in which the editors approach their task. But the nonprofessional, the layman who consults the dictionary, does so from other motives. Either he is seeking information on some particular facet of the language about which he knows nothing—the most obvious instance being the meaning of a word he has not previously encountered—or to discover which of several possible uses of the language, relative to spelling, pronunciation, word division, word meaning, or grammatical form, has acquired a sufficient degree of prestige and propriety to justify his employment of it. In short, his view of the dictionary function is essentially prescriptive. He hopes to be told what to say and to write, or more accurately perhaps, how to say and how to write.

In the light of all that has been said up to this point, these two concepts, the descriptive and the prescriptive, should not be in conflict with each other. It has already been pointed out that the standard language *is* the language of the socially and culturally dominant group within a speech community. There can be no other source upon which to base it. Accordingly, if the dictionary records that language accurately and faithfully, it should constitute a reliable guide and preceptor.

Unfortunately, the problem is not so simple as it seems on the surface. For a number of reasons too complicated to explain here, many people, Americans in particular, are reluctant to accept this simple and straightforward view of the matter. For one thing, experience has taught them that some persons of position and influence have little feeling for or command of the niceties of the language, and accordingly they are led to question the reliability and usefulness of an accurate exercise of the descriptive technique. Second, they are committed to a rigid and monolithic view of what constitutes the standard language and expect to find a single answer as to what is linguistically approved or appropriate, irrespective of the circumstances in which it may occur. The facts of the case are quite at variance with this assumption. Again, language like any form of social behavior varies in response to the demands of the particular social situation. Many of us would not hesitate to pick up a chicken drumstick with our fingers at a picnic but would feel constrained to use a knife and fork at a formal dinner. Neither form of behavior is superior or inferior to the other; it is a question of adaptation to the circumstances. Differences in regional standards prevail as well. In some parts of the country, for the host at a cocktail party to employ a bartender smacks of ostentation, whereas a hired caterer is accepted as the norm. Elsewhere just the reverse set of values prevails.

Varieties of Usage

It is precisely for this reason that dictionaries find it necessary to employ various kinds of labels to indicate the sphere of usage in which a particular word or expression is or is not acceptable. Those labels which are most often misunderstood have to do with the degree of formality which characterizes the communication. No dictionary has found it possible to recognize more than a dichotomy here, namely a formal and an informal type of speech. Clearly, each one of us in the course of a day's use of the language communicates much more in an informal manner than in a formal. The differences are pervasive, including pronunciation and structure as well as vocabulary. To take just a few obvious instances: the clipped form *dorm* is a frequent informal equivalent for *dormitory;* the phrase *all in* often serves for *exhausted, catch on* for *understand,* to cover at least three of the four major parts of speech. There is a whole battery of adverbs such as *consequently* and *accordingly* which may find *so* as their normal equivalent in less formal discourse. The same distinction extends to such phrase structures as *at all events* and *needless to say.* In the negative-interrogative form of the verb, *isn't he, can't he, won't he* are the informal expressions corresponding to *is he not, can he not, will he not,* a consideration affecting both syntax and pronunciation.

Actually we are faced with more than a dichotomy here. Some observers recognize at least four distinct linguistic styles, including the formal *(This is not the man whom we seek),* the consultative *(This is not the man we're looking for),* the casual *(He's not our man)* and the intimate *('Fraid you picked a lemon).* It is beyond the bounds of practicality or serviceability for the dictionary to recognize more than two broad types of situation, the formal and the informal. Moreover, in terms of the expectations of most of the people who consult a dictionary, it is more to the point to label the justifiably informal than it would be to signalize the formal. Generally the length and stylistic aura of a word will identify it as being primarily confined to formal use.

Distinctions drawn on the basis of formality often cut across differences in the mode of communication, speech or writing. Much, but not all, of our speech activity in the course of a day is informal. Some of our writing at least is more likely to be formal, although many personal letters, memoranda, the private writing contained in diaries and journals, may well fall into the informal category.

The point is that these are matters of the function of language, not of acceptability or correctness. A person whose informal speech may be characterized as "talking like a book" or "talking as if he had swallowed the dictionary," has simply failed to sort out the styles properly. One may rest assured that whatever a dictionary labels as *informal* is not less correct than an unlabeled item but that it is appropriate to an informal situation or purpose. Dictionaries usually do not affix a label to those words appropriate only for formal use on the ground that the social penalties for excessive formality of speech, though very real, seem somehow less onerous than those for misplaced informality.

Slang

Somewhat akin to informality, but differing from it in several important respects, is the use of language we have come to call slang. Slang is difficult to define, partly because the term itself has changed in meaning over the centuries. Originally it referred to thieves' argot, and today the term is still applied to the special terminology of certain occupations and other groups, including oil drillers, baseball players, rock or jazz musicians, college students, shoe salesmen, tramps, drug addicts, and prison inmates, but it has also taken on a much broader application. It includes clipped forms like *benny* and *frag,* echoic terms like *slurp,* meaningless tag phrases of the class of *twenty-three skidoo* from the early years of the century, *so's your old man, and how, you better believe it,* all of which have had their fleeting currency, only to be replaced by what will undoubtedly be the equally temporary *got to (He's got to be the best ball player in the league)* and the interjection *Wow!* which appears to be the stock in trade of the younger generation and the mindless consumer pictured on television commercials.

Not included in the concept of slang are dialect, localisms, profanity, and the so-called four-letter words once taboo in polite society, now increasingly accepted. It is also important to recognize that most slang is colloquial in nature in that it occurs in speech much more frequently than in writing; on the other hand, it would be a grave error to think of all colloquial or informal language as slang. Nor is slang to be confused with nonstandard language; it is at times consciously employed for a particular effect by persons of unquestioned cultivation.

Dictionaries are far from uniform in what they label as slang; even the special dictionaries of slang include many entries which do not at all fit the concept as it has been set forth here. The label *slang* after a word or a particular meaning of a word is an indication of its general unsuitability for formal communication; it suggests moreover that when used informally, it may have something of a slight shock value in a serious context; at the very least it will call attention to itself. This would be true, for example, of *boss* used adjectivally in the sense of "great, wonderful," of *bug off* for "go away!" and of *bug out,* "to escape, run away." Each country where English is a native language has its own variety of slang. *Wizard* is often used in England as a blanket term of approval; *dinkum* is confined to Australia. Both are relatively unknown in the United States. In this dictionary, slang terms found in other English-speaking countries will be labeled as to their place of origin. If an item is simply characterized as *slang* with no additional qualifying term, it may be assumed to be current in this country.

Regional Variation

In no English-speaking country is the language uniform over the entire area. In certain fields of the vocabulary, terminology differs from one part of the country to the other. This is especially true of words having to do with the more homelike and intimate aspects of life: the physical environment, the home, foods and cooking, the farm and farm operations, the fauna and flora. The literary term *earthworm* is called an *angleworm* in certain regions and a *fishworm* or *fishing worm* in others, and in addition there are several terms which have a much more restricted currency: *eaceworm, angle dog,* and *dewworm. Skillet* and *spider,* though now somewhat old-fashioned, are still used for *frying pan* or *fry pan* in some areas. Limited access highways have developed a highly varied terminology: *turnpike, freeway, expressway, parkway,* to mention only a few.

It is impossible in a general dictionary such as this to include all such variants, nor would it be helpful to label as *Regional* every term limited to extensive regions. Nevertheless, in terms of its function as an accurate recorder of the language, the dictionary must inform its users when a term, limited geographically, differs from a more commonly preferred synonym. There is a problem here in that dialect research in this country is still going on and that reliable information about the regional incidence of many terms is not yet readily available. In general the policy of this dictionary will be to indicate that a word is regional when that is known to be the case and when the word is not likely to be familiar to others outside the region of its use, but there will be no attempt to delimit the precise areas of its occurrence.

Nonstandard English

The very fact that a painstaking attempt has been made to clarify the concept of Standard English should be evidence in itself that there are features of the language which do not meet these requirements. Most of the aberrations are matters of grammatical form: *hisself* instead of *himself, hisn* instead of *his, growed* instead of *grew* or *grown, anyways* instead of *anyway,* and so on. Occasionally these are matters which pertain wholly to the vocabulary, like *irregardless,* or to the pronunciation, as with the dropping of the first *r* in *secretary* and *library.*

At one time it was the custom for dictionaries to employ the label *illiterate* for such deviations from standard usage. For several reasons the term is far from satisfactory. The percentage of actual illiterates in the United States is relatively small, even if so-called functional illiteracy is to be used as a criterion. The type of expressions so labeled often extended to many persons who had experienced some schooling. Because of these and other considerations dictionaries have recently tended to use *nonstandard* as the preferred designation for deviations from the linguistic norm which tend to be matters of social rather than regional dialect. It is rare, of course, for anyone to consult the dictionary for the meanings of words so labeled. The principal service that the dictionary performs is to indicate their status.

Usage Notes

It must be recognized, however, that there is no immediately definable hard-and-fast line separating the standard from the nonstandard. There is, indeed, a gray area, a zone of disputed items about which there may be considerable difference of opinion, even among authorities of equal experience and eminence. In connection with some of the locutions falling within this zone of uncertainty, not only must the extent of use by speakers of the standard language be considered but also the attitude toward the word or construction in question. For example, there can be no doubt that many react with aversion to the terms *lady doctor* and *cleaning lady*. They regard *lady* here as an example of false gentility, and much prefer *woman* to signify gender. Logical or illogical, informed or uninformed, this fairly widespread feeling is part of the total record, the total history of the word, and as such, it is the function of the dictionary to take note of that fact. Clearly no single label would suffice in this instance; an explanation of some sort is called for. This dictionary, along with many other reference works on language, copes with problems such as this through the device of a usage note, which, although necessarily brief and concise, does explain the nature of the problem that has arisen in connection with this particular word.

Further issues about usage may arise from mistaken grammatical analysis on the one hand, or the failure to distinguish what is current in informal as opposed to the formal standard language on the other. An instance of the latter is the use of *like* as a conjunction introducing a subordinate clause ("He didn't work like his father worked.") Reliable measures of the incidence of this construction indicate that it has a high frequency in informal English but that it occurs only rarely in the formal written language. But again there are some who are reluctant to accept it. Labeling the construction *informal* would probably satisfy the purely factual requirements of the situation, but it would fail to warn the reader of the dictionary that his use of the construction might give offense in some quarters. Again a brief statement is more helpful than a single unmodified categorization.

As one compares the usage notes in various dictionaries, he is likely to find a wide divergence of attitude and philosophy, ranging from a fairly broad permissiveness to a nervous reluctance to admit any deviation from the most rigid adherence to approved formal usage of a century ago. It is the considered opinion of the editors of this work that neither of these extremes is well calculated to serve the needs of those who look to the dictionary for help in matters of this kind.

Language changes from century to century and from generation to generation. To the extent that these changes have affected the usage of Standard English it is the responsibility of the dictionary to acknowledge them. There is often a discrepancy, as well, between what is in actual fact current as Standard English and what many opinionated or ill-informed persons believe that usage to be. The responsibility of the dictionary here is to set the record straight, to report and interpret the facts as accurately as possible. At the same time the dictionary must be equally perceptive in distinguishing, for the person who consults it, between standard usage which is acceptable beyond a shadow of doubt and that about which there is some qualification or question. Unfortunately, there is a great lack of awareness on the part of the general public about the services which dictionaries do perform with respect to matters of usage. As dictionaries improve in their faithfulness to fact and the nicety of their discrimination, it is reasonably certain that readers will take fuller advantage of the service which only a carefully and conscientiously edited dictionary is capable of offering.

The English of Canada, Australia, and New Zealand

by H. Rex Wilson

As the language of the greatest colonizing nation in modern times, English has spread to widely separated parts of the world and has evolved on its own as the first language of the dominant peoples of several now-independent nations. The largest of these is the United States, but just as inhabitants of both sides of the Atlantic recognize the difference between American English and that of the Old Country, so Canadians, Australians, and New Zealanders are conscious of respectable varieties of English within their boundaries which differ in various degrees and ways from the language used by the residents of Great Britain or the United States.

Canadian English

Scholarly interest in Canadian English has developed real strength only since World War II, although the bibliography of writings on the English spoken in Canada goes back over a hundred years. This literature is disproportionately loaded with alarm and indignation over the unfortunate spread of "Americanisms." Because Canada evolved by gradual stages from a group of colonies to an independent nation, the long-held British connection has led to false linguistic expectations on the part of some Englishmen and Canadians, and even of a few residents of the United States. To the majority of visitors from the U.S. who come from the states just south of the border from New York and on westward, Canadians speak "just like us." And indeed even the most exacting students of Canadian English would have to admit that superficially this remark is justified.

Origins

In its origins Canadian English is predominantly American. It descends directly from the language of pre-Revolutionary War settlers on the seaboard and immediate hinterland of the present United States. In the uprootings, both forced and voluntary, which followed the Revolution, Canada received an English-speaking population drawn almost entirely from the old American colonies. It is estimated that by 1830 eighty percent of the English-speaking population of Canada could be traced back to the United States. Upon the language of this majority the relative handful of governors, administrators, military officers and clergy of English origin could not be expected to make any substantial impression, although as members of a highly prestigious group they were bound to have some effect.

Some time before the settlement of the American colonies, some groups in England began to lose the *r*-sound between a vowel and a following consonant (as in *art*). This sort of pronunciation and the one which retained the older *r* were rivals both in England and in some of the settlement areas of the U.S. The "*r*-droppers" prevailed in eastern New England and in the coastal South, but the *r*-sound was retained throughout the rest of the colonies, and it was largely from these areas that the basic post-Revolutionary population of Canada was drawn. Meanwhile, the *r*-dropping became the dominant speech fashion in England. These easily-noted features are the main ones which cause superficial observers from England to identify Canadian speakers as "American" and U.S. visitors to find that Canadians talk "just like us."

But subsequent settlement, independent patterns of pronunciation, the distinctive experience of the physical environment, contact with other linguistic groups, and the prestige of the colonial administration have imposed upon Canadian English features which set it off from other types of English.

Pronunciation

The first difference in language that most people notice when they meet someone from another speech area is in pronunciation. Strangers have accents. But this is just what Canadians seem to lack when they are first heard by many residents of the U.S., and even visitors from the South and Southwest will find Canadian speech little different from that of the "Yankees." The origins of Canadian English just mentioned will help account for this.

Sooner or later the visitor to Canada will notice that Canadians say *oot* and *aboot* for *out* and *about*, but if he asks about it Canadians will deny it. And, strictly speaking, they are right. However, what has been heard is something different from the vowel in *down* and *mountain*. This tendency to have a different vowel before sounds like *t* and *s* than before sounds like *d*, *z*, *n* is very widespread. In the verb *house* (where the vowel is followed by a *z* sound) the vowel sound will be the same as the one in *down*, and although it may sound different in various places in Canada the range of difference will be about the same as in the U.S. But the vowel sound of the noun *house* (where the vowel is followed by an *s* sound) is different. This pronunciation varies quite a bit from place to place and even in the pronunciations of one speaker, but the general characteristic of most Canadian speech is to have a difference between the vowels in these different situations, and Americans are left with the impression that Canadians say *oot* and *aboot*.

The pronunciation of vowels varying on the basis of the following sound is not unique and can be found in scattered parts of the United States. In these areas and in Canada the vowels of *write* and *ride* show a similar pattern.

The pronunciation of a few individual words may also catch the visitor's ear. The words *either* and *neither* have first syllables which rhyme with *eye* with far greater frequency than is found in the United States. Some longer words, such as *controversy*, may have the main stress on the second rather than the first syllable, reflecting the prestige of British pronunciation supported by private schools set up on the British model and by returning Canadians who have studied at British universities. Although not unknown before World War II, the British pronunciation of *schedule* (shed′yo͞ol) has gained ground in recent years, apparently under the influence of the Canadian Broadcasting Corporation.

The pronunciation of the word *clerk* like that of the family name *Clark*, once a striking feature of Ontario speech, has now died out except in official usage (*County Clerk*) and in the Presbyterian Church (*Clerk of Session*).

Regional accents are not prominent in Canada, probably because of a large amount of movement within the country and relatively few isolated homogeneous settlements of native speakers of English. The island provinces of Newfoundland and Prince Edward Island are notable exceptions, while the imprint of New England continues to set parts of Nova Scotia and New Brunswick off from Ontario and from the Scottish-settled areas of Nova Scotia. Some areas originally settled by non-English-speakers have produced distinctive varieties of English as the result of earlier bilingualism.

Spelling Differences

For the most part, differences in spelling between England and the United States are traceable to Noah Webster, America's first great lexicographer. Canadians understandably did not come under the influence of Webster's spelling reforms in the early 19th century, and British spelling conventions have persisted. Words like *traveller* and *jeweller* continued to have double *l*, and *-our* spellings persisted in words like *honour* and *flavour*. The noun *practice* continued to be set off from the verb *practise*. Today these spellings are no longer insisted upon in most school systems, although consistency in usage by the individual is expected. This "loss of standards," especially in the *-our* spellings, can still raise furious condemnation in the editorial pages of some newspapers in Canada. In their own style these pages and the advertisements in the paper may tend to be conservative, while the news columns tend toward "American" spellings.

The spellings *tyre* and *kerb(stone)* are as strange to Canadians as to Americans and must be explained in Canadian dictionaries as *Brit.* for *tire* and *curb(stone)*. The spelling *gaol* for *jail* was once common in newspapers but began disappearing even before World War II.

Vocabulary

The words which a nation uses to conduct its business are great reflectors of its discovery of its environment and its historical development. In 1967 a group of scholars under Professor Walter S. Avis produced *A Dictionary of Canadianisms on Historical Principles* which provides a comprehensive view of the growing and changing vocabulary of Canadian life. This vocabulary has been drawn from many sources, and much of it belongs to experiences shared with settlers of the northern states in the common development of North America. It is not surprising, therefore, that many words reflecting this early experience have passed out of use or are found only in writings referring to specific historical periods.

An American would be puzzled, to say the least, by a reference to an alligator in the forests of Ontario. In the movement of logs by water the lumber industry was greatly helped by *alligators*, amphibious paddle-wheel scows, equipped with a winching arrangement for travel overland.

An equally puzzling term, but in this case a contemporary one, might be found in the statement, "We went to separate schools together." In many parts of Canada religious groups have the legal right to set up their own schools supported by public funds. These are usually referred to as *separate schools*, and a statement such as the one mentioned may be made without suspicion of humorous intent or mental deficiency.

In the Arctic (usually pronounced *Artic*) the term *white-out* has been formed on the model of *black-out* to describe a condition where reflected light from snow or haze or fine blowing snow obscures the horizon and features of the landscape.

Canadian coiners of words have sometimes shown a fine sense of irony as in the now obsolete *Nova Scotia nightingale* for a "singing" marsh frog, and *CPR strawberries* for prunes, which were a prominent item of diet during the building of the Canadian Pacific Railway. On the whole, Canadians have not been distinguished in coining regional names. Most are obviously derivative, like Winipegger or Newfie (Newfoundlander), but Maritimers may be called *Bluenoses* (from Nova Scotia), *Herringchokers* (from New Brunswick) and *Spud Islanders* (a reference to the importance of the potato in the economy of Prince Edward Island).

The *Dictionary of Canadianisms* shows a surprising number of words which have long been accepted in the United States but apparently first gained currency in Canada. In recent times the most striking exports have been in the vocabulary of lacrosse and hockey. *Lacrosse* is of Canadian French origin from a fancied resemblance between the stick used in the game and a Bishop's crozier. While U.S. fans are familiar with the whole standard terminology of hockey, including the penitential seat known as the *penalty box*, they may not know the journalistic coinage *sin bin*.

Because of an administrative history different from that of the United States, Canadian government offers a large number of distinctive terms of British origin. The title *Prime Minister* is, of course, widely used in other countries, but the names of some other positions may be surprising and even a little quaint, such as the term *Reeve* for the council chairman of a village, township, or municipal district council in Ontario and the West. In Ontario the County Council composed of Reeves and Deputy Reeves is presided over by a *Warden*. The familiar title *Sheriff* in Canada signifies a court officer and not a man charged with general law enforcement and peacekeeping duties. A Lieutenant- (pronounced *leftenant*) Governor is not a person who acts for a Governor but the official and ceremonial head of the government of a Province, representing the Crown.

Since colonial times Canadian English has imported virtually its whole technological vocabulary from the United States. Visitors from England have problems in discussing automobile maintenance until they have learned the American words for parts of their motor cars. Canadian railroading, established in large part by American engineers, uses the terminology they brought augmented by later imports. The term *sleeper* for a railway tie held its own until the 1920's at least, but now is rarely heard and one Canadian dictionary labels it *British*.

Canada made its first contribution to the jet age in 1854 by the invention and naming of kerosene in Nova Scotia. Oddly, in Ontario a term of apparent Pennsylvania origin, *coal oil*, is preferred. So widely accepted has *kerosene* become in the U.S. that it has even raised objections in New Zealand as an "Americanism" displacing the British *paraffin (oil)*.

Canadians have borrowed words from languages with which they have had contact. *Woodchuck*, although it looks and sounds English, is derived from an Algonquian word which was first imitated by English speakers as *wejack*. The Canada jay has a name that goes one step further. A Cree name was first imitated as *Whisky John* and then familiarized to *whiskyjack*.

Naturally the long French sojourn in Canada before English settlement has left its marks and, as far as place names go, this extends beyond the border of Canada. The word *portage* is classically representative of the early years, and it has never been displaced by *carry* or *carrying place*. In politics the old terms *Bleu* (or *Parti Bleu*, Conservative) and *Rouge* (or *Parti Rouge*, Liberal) may occasionally appear in English newspaper accounts of politics in Quebec. Sometimes these are Anglicized to *Blue* and *Red*.

Influenced by the special economics of printing in a bilingual country, no passenger train of the Canadian National Railways has "left" its station for many years, although most have "departed" fairly close to schedule. The abbreviations *Arr.* and *Dep.* in the timetable require no translation. Similarly, the two telegraph companies in the country have settled on *telecommunications* in their names.

In its modest space program Canada has named its first communications satellite *Alouette* (French, lark) and a more recent one *anik* (Eskimo, brother).

The English of Australia and New Zealand

The English of Australia and New Zealand is much more satisfyingly exotic to the American ear than that of Canada. The first impression is that the language of these countries is very much like British English, and, although extended observation will show that these dialects do have some very distinctive characteristics of their own, the initial impression is justified by history. The time of separation from the mother country is much shorter for both of these countries; there are still members of the older generation who refer to England as "Home" although not born there themselves. Australia did not begin to receive English-speaking settlers until after the American Revolution, and New Zealand not until about fifty years later. Further, the origin of the population was much more predominantly English in the formative years of Australian and New Zealand society than it was in North America in a similar period, with a much lower proportion of Scots and Irish. Apparently the majority of the settlers were from the south rather than the north of England. Australian and New Zealand speakers tend to be "*r*-droppers."

Australian English

Australian English became well known to United States servicemen during the Second World War. Although the song "Waltzing Matilda" with its baffling vocabulary had made its way across the Pacific some time before, wartime contacts first made Americans aware of the peculiarities of Australian pronunciation, and a considerable collection of teasing jokes developed—such as the one about the USAAF Major who was brought unconscious to an Australian hospital in Port Moresby, New Guinea. Regaining consciousness and feeling more dead than alive, he asked a nursing sister:

"Was I brought here to die?"

"Oh, no, sir," she replied, "You were brought here yesterday."

Like most such jokes this exploits the so-called Cockney feature in which the vowel of *day* as pronounced by most Americans and Canadians is replaced by the vowel of *die*. Australians themselves seem to enjoy humor based on their speech peculiarities, as is evidenced by the success of a slim volume called *Let Stalk Strine* by Afferbeck Lauder, who claims to be Professor of Strine Studies at the University of Sinny. (The title and author are stated, appropriately, in Strine and are translated as follows: *Let's Talk Australian* by Alphabetical Order, Professor of Australian Studies at the University of Sydney.)

The form of language on which this book is based is what is usually called "Broad" Australian, a term also used in New Zealand. Australians and New Zealanders often modify their speech toward the standard British "Received Pronunciation" (RP), although the tendency seems stronger in New Zealand than in Australia. Accordingly it is not unusual to find an Australian Ph.D. at a North American university happily doin' what comes naturally as far as pronunciation is concerned, although his professional writing would show no marked difference, beyond personal style, from that of his colleagues who speak other dialects of English.

English speakers did not originally come voluntarily to Australia. English law had provided "transportation" as a punishment as early as the reign of Queen Elizabeth, and a substantial amount of the labor on early American plantations was performed by convicts shipped out from England. After the American Revolution attention turned to Australia as a place to send these undesirables. These "unwilling emigrants" were a very mixed group, and included many who had been convicted of such crimes as petty theft or poaching, or had been imprisoned for debt. Such constructive skills as they brought with them were chiefly those most useful in an urban setting. The unskilled often learned trades to supplement these. Their language was that of the city, so that Australian rural vocabulary had to be supplied from new sources, thus distinguishing the agricultural and cattle-raising vocabulary from that of the Old Country (although some technical terms, like *drover* for a cattle herder, have had currency in England, Australia, and America).

Australians have been, almost from the beginning, very mobile. Originally the population was confined between the sea and the Great Dividing Range on the east coast, but in 1813 a pass was found through the range, and free settlers, who had begun to arrive in 1793, began moving into the rest of the continent. As cattle and sheep raising and mining developed, convict labor was assigned to free settlers on contract, so that even they became mobile—often more so than the free settler who held land. Under varying special arrangements some convicts were free to move about within certain territorial limits and make their own working contracts with employers. As a result, Australia appears to have few dialect differences, except in local borrowings from the languages of the native peoples and the distribution of the vowel of *bat* and that of *father* in certain words.

Pronunciation The most obvious difference between Australian and most American English, after *r*-dropping, is the apparent *day/die* confusion. When an Australian pronounces *day* he does not quite rhyme it with an American's pronunciation of *die*, but it is close enough to cause confusion to the American, at least on first meeting. This parallels roughly the initial impression that Canadians say *oot* for *out*. A characteristic less apparent to Americans, unless they come from New England, lies in the vowels of *path, grass, contrast* which have the sound of the vowel in *bat* rather than of *father* in the areas of oldest settlement, but may be found with the vowel of *father* in the state of South Australia, and there *dance* may also be found with this pronunciation.

Whenever a vowel in any English dialect becomes too much like another, the speakers of that dialect tend to shift the second one to keep distinctions between words which otherwise would come to sound too nearly alike. Thus, other vowels in Australian English also seem displaced to the American ear. The distinction between *day* and *die* is maintained by a vowel in *die* which approaches that of *boy* in American speech, and *boy* in turn has a vowel which is difficult for "foreigners" to hear and impossible to represent without using phonetic notation.

Vocabulary Once a jolly swagman camped by a billabong,
Under the shade of a coolibah tree;
And he sang as he watched and waited
till his billy boiled,
"You'll come a-waltzing matilda with me."

This verse and several equally incomprehensible ones following it are well known to participants in American community sings. Much of the diction is now rather old-fashioned in Australia. The *a-waltzing* is quite common to many older varieties of English and certainly is not typical of today's Australian speech. *Waltzing matilda* is probably preserved only because of this song. *Matilda* is not capitalized, nor is "she" surrounded by commas—although more than one tank and possibly some aircraft received "her" name in World War II. The *swagman*, roughly equivalent to the older American *bindlestiff*, an itinerant who carried his belongings rolled up in a bundle or *swag (bindle)*, is gone from the scene. Carrying the swag or *matilda* was known as *waltzing matilda*. The *billabong* is a name given by native people to a blind channel of a river, roughly equivalent to a bayou; *coolibah* is a native tree name. The *billy* is a cylindrical metal cooking pot assumed to be derived from the native word *billa* (water, as in *billabong)*.

In the vocabulary of daily use Australians unexpectedly use the word *station* for what animal raisers in the United States would call a ranch, and they have adapted words of international currency to special uses, such as calling a shopping cart a *jeep*.

Among the borrowings from the native languages the word *kangaroo* appeared in print in the reports of Captain James Cook before actual settlement had begun. It has been borrowed for the American coinage *kangaroo court* which in turn has been reborrowed into Australian English. The word *boomerang* has developed many figurative meanings throughout the English-speaking world, starting, apparently, with Oliver Wendell Holmes' use of it in 1845.

New Zealand English

New Zealand English shares some features with Australian, partly through exchange of population and partly through being settled from the same general area of England. Although from a distance the two countries seem close together, New Zealand is not a group of islands off the Australian coast, as it has sometimes been described. The Tasman Sea which separates them is 1,200 miles wide. Nevertheless, some of the earliest settlers of New Zealand were escaped convicts from Australia. In the period before organized settlement began in 1839 there were also deserters from ships, particularly whaling vessels, so that there may have been a small contribution to the population from New England.

Pronunciation Some of the vowel features of Australian English which have been discussed are reflected in New Zealand speech. The vowels in words of the type *dance, path*, and *grass* have the vowel of *father* (as in South Australia) rather than that of *bat*. Greek compounds ending in *-graph*, however, have the vowel of *bat*.

The vowels of *day, die*, and *boy* follow the Australian pattern, and some speakers even have a vowel for *die* which could sound like a short "o" to visitors, who might look in vain on a map for a place called Crosschurch, not knowing that the mapmakers spell it *Christchurch*.

The most striking feature of New Zealand pronunciation is the shift of short vowels so that *bet* might sound like *bit* (and a parade might be described as a *precision*). The vowel of *bat* meanwhile gets close to that of *bet* so that the main mountain range of the country, the Southern Alps, would seem to rhyme with *helps*.

Vocabulary Except for borrowings from the native languages and obvious recent imports, it is often very difficult to tell which of the items of the New Zealand vocabulary that it shares with Australia are the products of these islands. Because of its slightly earlier settlement and its role as the source of some of the early New Zealand population, Australia is usually assumed to be the source of the common vocabulary, but scholars in that part of the world are engaged in sorting these words out. As yet neither Australia nor New Zealand possesses the equivalent of the *Dictionary of Americanisms* or the *Dictionary of Canadianisms*, but an absorbing collection of essays on the English of the two countries and related territories has been published in Australia under the title *English Transported*, edited by W. S. Ramson. One of its important themes is the need for such works.

Whatever their origin, some terms have a specific New Zealand meaning. To an Australian the term *bush* may merely mean undeveloped scrub country, but to the New Zealander it is dense forest.

Recent American influence is easier to trace. The adoption of the term *cent* in both Australian and New Zealand as a unit of decimal coinage reflects this, although the term *dollar* was long known as a slang name for five shillings.

Borrowings from the native population, particularly for the names of plants and animals, have been very important. The *kiwi*, a flightless bird, has given its name not only as a term for New Zealander, but for nonflying personnel in air forces and airlines outside of New Zealand, especially former American stewardesses who have been assigned to ground duties.

The interplay of English and the native language (Maori) has been beset by some interesting pronunciation problems, particularly in the matter of the type of "r" used by each. One apparent borrowing from Maori, *taipo*, meaning *devil*, has been reinterpreted as a possible Maori borrowing from English *tripod*, for the support for the land-surveyor's theodolite which the Maori saw as a "land-stealing devil." On their side, English speakers have had their problems pronouncing some Maori words, particularly in interpreting "r"s as "d"s. Thus to find a burr referred to as a *biddybid* might seem to a visitor like a too-cute joke, but actually this is a distortion of the Maori word *piripiri*.

New Zealanders seem to share some words with other parts of the English-speaking world but with surprisingly different meanings. The term *section* for a city building lot might give a western American farmer an exaggerated idea of the spaciousness of New Zealand real estate developments. An Englishman, to whom *lay-by* is a recess at the roadside suitable for parking, would be startled to find that this refers to a purchase plan known in America as *layaway*.

Do We Speak the Same Language?

Not even the most extreme differences in the dialects of English justify calling any two of them different languages, and yet the ways in which we use what are apparently the same words can seem a barrier rather than an aid to understanding. Not only would the New Zealand use of *section* surprise a North American wheat farmer, but his use of *block* for a large tract of land in a rural area seems to carry confusion to extremes.

The Australian use of *jeep* as the name for a shopping cart is merely whimsical to the American, and if he were a trotting fan he would be surprised a few years ago to learn that mothers in Dunedin, New Zealand, wheeled their young children about in *sulkies*.

Sometimes we sort out sets of words in peculiar ways. The American *checks* his *baggage*, the Englishman *registers* his *luggage*, the New Zealander *checks* his *luggage*. The American gets his *mail* from the *mailman* or *letter carrier*, the Canadian may be served by a *mailman* or *postman* who brings his *mail*, and the New Zealander gets his *mail* or *letters* from a *postman*.

The quality of a meaning may be very different, too. In the north of England *homely* is complimentary, and in Australia a *squatter* or a descendant of one has a certain prestige. Early settlement of the interior was rather haphazard and settlers merely occupied land, having their titles regularized later. In the history of the United States the nearest equivalent is *homesteader*, which is in distinct contrast with the American use of the term *squatter*.

Even a word so closely associated with Old England as *tea* is highly unreliable. To most Americans it is either a beverage or an afternoon social event (at which, in some regions, only coffee is served). In England it can be a daily or twice-daily occurrence and range, in the latter part of the day, from a light meal to a rather heavy one in the form known as Scottish High Tea. In Australia and the Maritime Provinces of Canada *tea* is apt to be another name for *supper*. And in New Zealand *supper* is a bedtime snack.

Explanatory Notes

See pronunciation key on page xx.

Syllabication
Pronunciation
Trade name
Combining form
Geographic entry
Abbreviation
Prefix
Cross-reference
Part of speech
Taxonomic classification
Idiomatic phrase
Usage label
Field label
Homograph
Illustrative example
Inflected forms
Phrasal entry
Variant
Hyphenation

Car·bo·run·dum (kär′bə·run′dəm) *n.* An abrasive of silicon carbide: a trade name.

-cidal *combining form* Killing; able to kill: *homicidal.* [<L *caedere* kill]

Col·o·ra·do (kol′ə·rä′dō, -rad′ō) A western State of the United States; 103,967 square miles; capital, Denver; entered the Union Aug. 1, 1876: nicknamed *Centennial State*: abbr. *Colo.*

com- *prefix* With; together: *combine, compare.* Also: *co-* before *gn, h,* and vowels; *col-* before *l*, as in *collide*; *con-* before *c, d, f, g, j, n, q, s, t, v,* as in *concur, confluence, connect, conspire*; *cor-* before *r*, as in *correspond.* [<L *com-* < *cum* with]

craal (kräl) See KRAAL.

crab[1] (krab) *n.* **1** Any of various species of ten-footed crustaceans of the suborder *Brachyura* in the order *Decapoda,* characterized by a small abdomen folded under the body, a flattened carapace, and short antennae. They can walk in any direction without turning, but usually move sideways. **2** The hermit crab. **3** The horseshoe crab. **4** A crab louse, *Phthirus pubis.* **5** *Aeron.* The lateral slant in an airplane needed to maintain a flight line in a cross-wind. **6** A form of windlass. **7** *pl.* The lowest throw of a pair of dice. **— to catch a crab** In rowing, to sink an oar blade too deeply; also, to miss the water entirely or skim the surface in making a stroke, and thus fall backward. **—** *v.* **crabbed, crab·bing** *v.i.* **1** To take or fish for crabs. **2** *U.S. Colloq.* To back out: to *crab* out of an agreement. **3** *Naut.* To drift sideways, as a ship. **—** *v.t.* **4** *Aeron.* To head (an airplane) across a contrary wind so as to compensate for drift. [OE *crabba.* Akin to CRAB[3].]

crab[2] (krab) *n.* **1** A crab apple. **2** A crab-apple tree. **3** An ill-tempered, surly, or querulous person. **—** *v.* **crabbed, crab·bing** *v.t.* **1** *Colloq.* To disparage; belittle; complain about. **2** *Colloq.* To ruin or spoil: *He crabbed the entire act.* **3** *Obs.* To make surly or sour; irritate. **4** *Brit. Dial.* To cudgel or beat, as with a crabstick. **—** *v.i.* **5** To be ill-tempered. [? <Scand. Cf. dial. Sw. *scrabba* wild apple.]

crab[3] (krab) *v.i.* **crabbed, crab·bing** To seize each other fiercely, as hawks when fighting; claw. [<MDu. *crabben* scratch. Akin to CRAB[1].]

Crab A constellation and sign of the Zodiac; Cancer.

crab angle The angle between the direction of movement of an airplane, rocket, or guided missile and the direction in which the nose points, resembling . . . .

crab apple A kind of small, sour apple: also called *crab.*

deep-seat·ed (dēp′sē′tid) *adj.* So far in as to be ineradicable or almost ineradicable: said of emotions, diseases, etc.

Deep South The southernmost parts of Alabama, Georgia, Louisiana, and Mississippi, conventionally regarded as typifying Southern culture and traditions.

deer (dir) *n. pl.* **deer** **1** A ruminant (family *Cervidae*) having deciduous antlers, usually in the male only, as the moose, elk, and reindeer. Popularly, *deer* is used mainly of the smaller species. ◆ Collateral adjective: *cervine.* See FALLOW DEER, VENISON. **2** A deerlike animal. **3** Formerly, any quadruped; a wild animal. ◆ Homophone: *dear.* [OE *dēor* beast]

deer·fly (dir′flī′) *n. pl.* **·flies** A bloodsucking fly (genus *Chrysops*), similar to a horsefly but smaller and with banded wings. For illustration see INSECTS (injurious).

di·eth·y·lene glycol (dī·eth′ə·lēn) *Chem.* An organic compound, $O(CH_2CH_2OH)_2$, used as an anti-freeze mixture and as an agent in many chemical processes for the . . . .

di·eth·yl·stil·bes·trol (dī·eth′əl·stil·bes′trōl) *n. Biochem.* Stilbestrol.

di·e·ti·tian (dī′ə·tish′ən) *n.* One skilled in the principles of dietetics and in their practical application in health and disease. Also **di·e·tet·ist** (dī′ə·tet′ist), **di′e·ti′cian.**

Dieu vous garde (dyœ′ vōō′ gȧrd′) *French* God protect you.

Diez (dēts), **Friedrich Christian,** 1794–1876, German philologist.

dif·fer (dif′ər) *v.i.* **1** To be unlike in quality, degree, form, etc.: often with *from.* **2** To disagree; dissent: often with *with.* **3** To quarrel: sometimes with *over* or *about.* [<OF *differer* <L *differre* < *dis-* apart + *ferre* carry. Doublet of DEFER[1].]

dif·fer·ence (dif′ər·əns, dif′rəns) *n.* **1** The state or quality of being other or unlike, or that in which two things are unlike; . . . . . . **8** *Her.* A device in blazons to distinguish persons bearing the same arms. **—** *v.t.* **·enced, ·enc·ing** **1** To make or mark as different; distinguish; discriminate. **2** *Her.* To add a mark of difference to.

Synonyms (noun): contrariety, contrast, disagreement, discrepancy, dissimilarity, disparity, dissimilarity, dissimilitude, distinction, divergence, diversity, inconsistency, inequality, unlikeness, variation. A *difference* is in the things compared; . . . . *Diversity* involves more than two objects; *variation* is a *difference* in the condition or action of the same object at different times. *Antonyms:* agreement, consonance, harmony, identity, likeness, resemblance, sameness, similarity, uniformity, unity.

dif·fer·ent (dif′ər·ənt, dif′rənt) *adj.* **1** Not the same; distinct; other: *A different clerk is there now.* **2** Marked by a difference; completely or partly unlike; dissimilar. **3** Unusual. See synonyms under CONTRARY. [<F *différent* <L *differens, -entis,* ppr. of *differre.* See DIFFER.] **— dif′fer·ent·ly** *adv.* **— dif′fer·ent·ness** *n.*

◆ **different from, than, to** In American usage, *from* is established as the idiomatic preposition to follow *different*; when, however, a clause follows the connective, *than* is gaining increasing acceptance: a result *different than* (= *from that which* or *from what*) had been expected. This last is established British usage, which also accepts *to* . . . .

-dom *suffix of nouns* **1** State or condition of being: *freedom.* **2** Rank of; domain of: *kingdom.* **3** The totality of those having a certain rank, state or condition: *Christendom.* [OE *-dōm* < *dōm* state]

Collateral adjective
Homophone
Inflected form
Chemical formula
Cross-reference
Variants
Foreign language label
Biographic entry
Usage notes
Definition numbers
Synonyms
Antonyms
Illustrative example
Run-on entries
Usage note
Suffix
Etymology

Syllabication Division of words into syllables — as an indication of the points at which a word may be broken at the end of a line — is indicated by a centered dot (·) in the main bold-faced entries, as **ad·jec·ti·val.** In the secondary entries (run-on derivatives and variant forms) the centered dot is eliminated wherever the primary and secondary syllable stresses are marked, as in **ad'jec·ti'val·ly.** In hyphened compounds the hyphen takes the place of a centered dot. Phrasal entries of two or more words are not syllabified when each element is entered elsewhere, as in **caballine fountain.**

Pronunciations The pronunciation is shown in parentheses immediately following the bold-faced entry, as **di·chot·o·my** (dī·kot'ə·mē). When more than one pronunciation is recorded, the first given is usually the most widely used wherever it has been possible to determine extent of usage; often, however, usage may be almost equally divided. The order of the pronunciations is not intended to be an indication of preference; all pronunciations shown are valid for educated American speech.

The syllabication of the pronunciations follows, in general, the syllabic breaks heard in speech, rather than the conventional division of the bold-faced entry, as **bod·ing** (bō'ding), **grat·er** (grā'tər), **ju·di·cial** (jōō·dish'əl), **an·es·the·tize** (ə·nes'thə·tīz).

When a variant pronunciation differs merely in part from the first pronunciation recorded, only the differing syllable or syllables are shown, provided that there is no possibility of misinterpretation, as **eq·ua·bil·i·ty** (ek'wə·bil'ə·tē, ē'kwə-). Phrasal entries (those which consist of two or more words) are not pronounced if the individual elements are separately entered in proper alphabetic place.

Parts of speech These are shown in italics following the pronunciation for main entries, and are abbreviated as follows: *n.* (noun), *v.* (verb), *pron.* (pronoun), *adj.* (adjective), *adv.* (adverb), *prep.* (preposition), *conj.* (conjunction), *interj.* (interjection). When more than one part of speech is entered under a main entry, the additional designations are run in and preceded by a bold-faced dash, as **cor·ner** (kôr'·nər) *n.* . . . **—** *v.t.* . . . **—** *v.i.* . . . **—** *adj.* . . .

Verbs used transitively are identified as *v.t.*, those intransitively as *v.i.*; those used both transitively and intransitively in all senses are designated *v.t.* & *v.i.*

Inflected forms These include the past tense, past participle, and present participle of verbs, the plural of nouns, and the comparative and superlative of adjectives and adverbs. The inflected forms are entered wherever there is some irregularity in spelling or form. They are shown in boldface type, with syllabication, immediately after the part of speech designation. Only the syllable affected is shown, provided there is no ambiguity possible, as **com·pute** (kəm·pyōōt') *v.t.* **·put·ed, ·put·ing.** An inflected form that requires pronunciation or is alphabetically distant from the main entry may also be separately entered and pronounced in its proper vocabulary place.

Principal parts of verbs The order in which the principal parts are shown is past tense, past participle, and present participle, as **come** (kum) *v.* **came, come, com·ing.** Where the past tense and past participle are identical, only two forms are entered, as **bake** (bāk) *v.* **baked, bak·ing.** When alternative forms are given, the first form indicated is usually the one preferred, as **grov·el** (gruv'əl, grov'-) *v.i.* **grov·eled** or **grov·elled, grov·el·ing** or **grov·el·ling.** Variant forms not in the standard vocabulary are shown in parentheses and labeled, as **drink** (dringk) *v.* **drank** (*Obs.* **drunk**), **drunk** (*Obs.* **drunk·en**), **drink·ing.** Principal parts entirely regular in formation — those that add *-ed* and *-ing* directly to the infinitive without spelling modification — are not shown.

Plural of nouns Irregular forms are here preceded by the designation *pl.*, as **a·lum·nus** (ə·lum'nəs) *n. pl.* **·ni** (-nī); **co·dex** (kō'deks) *n. pl.* **co·di·ces** (kō'də·sēz, kod'ə-); **deer** (dir) *n. pl.* **deer.** When alternative plurals are given, the first shown is the preferred form, as **buf·fa·lo** (buf'ə·lō) *n. pl.* **·loes** or **·los; chrys·a·lis** (kris'ə·lis) *n. pl.* **chrys·a·lis·es** or **chry·sal·i·des** (kri·sal'ə·dēz). Words that have different plural forms for specific senses are shown as follows:

an·ten·na (an·ten'ə) *n. pl.* **an·ten·nae** (an·ten'ē) *for def.* **1, an·ten·nas** *for def.* **2. 1** *Entomol.* One of the paired, lateral, movable, jointed appendages on the head of an insect or other arthropod. **2** *Telecom.* A system of wires upheld in a vertical or horizontal position by a mast or tower, for transmitting or receiving electromagnetic waves in wireless telegraphy, telephony, and radio. . . . .

Comparison of adjectives and adverbs The comparatives and superlatives of adjectives and adverbs are shown immediately after the part of speech when there is some spelling modification or a complete change of form, as **mer·ry** (mer'ē) *adj.* **·ri·er, ·ri·est; bad**[1] (bad) *adj.* **worse, worst; well**[2] (wel) *adv.* **bet·ter, best.**

Definition numbers In entries for words having several senses, the order in which the definitions appear is, wherever possible, that of frequency of use, rather than semantic evolution. Each such definition is distinguished by a bold-faced number, the numbering starting anew after each part-of-speech designation when it is followed by more than one sense. Closely related meanings, especially those within a specific field or area of study, are defined under the same number and set apart by small bold-faced letters.

bol·ster (bōl'stər) *n.* **1** A long, narrow pillow as wide as a bed. **2** A pad used as a support or . . . . **3** Anything shaped like . . . . **4** *Archit.* **a** The lateral part of the volute of an Ionic capital. **b** A crosspiece of an arch centering . . . . **5** *Mech.* A steel block . . . . **—** *v.t.* **1** To support with a pillow. **2** To prop up . . . . **3** To furnish with padding. . . .

Restrictive labels Entries or particular senses of words and terms having restricted application are variously labeled according to: (1) usage level, as *Slang, Colloq.* (colloquial), *Dial.* (dialectal), *Poetic,* etc.; (2) localization, as *U.S.* (United States), *Brit.* (British), *Austral.* (Australian), *Scot.* (Scottish English), etc.; (3) field or subject, as *Astron.* (astronomy), *Geom.* (geometry), *Mining* (mining), *Naut.* (nautical), *Surg.* (surgery), etc.; (4) language of origin, as *Afrikaans, French, German, Latin,* etc.

These labels serve as a guide in the ready identification of special aspects of a word or term as a whole or of one or more of its parts. The usage labels qualify a word in terms of its relationship to standard English; the localized area designations identify the geographical region of the English-speaking world in which a word has originated or where it has particular application; the subject labels indicate that a word or definition has a specialized use in some field of work or study; and the foreign language labels reflect the fact that a word or phrase, although used in English speech and writing, has not yet undergone the process of Anglicization of pronunciation, meaning, or usage, and is still felt to be foreign (these foreign terms are usually italicized in writing).

Restrictive labels that apply to only one sense of a word are entered after the definition number, as:

beat (bēt) *v.* . . . . **9** *Music* To mark or measure with or as with a baton: to *beat* time. . . . . **13** *Colloq.* To baffle; perplex: It *beats* me. **14** *Slang* To defraud; swindle. . . . . **20** *Physics* To alternate in intensity so as to pulsate . . . . **24** *Naut.* To work against contrary winds or currents by tacking.

Labels entered immediately after the part of speech designation apply to all the senses for that part of speech; those shown directly after the pronunciation and before the first part-of-speech designation refer to the entire entry, as:

hal·i·dom (hal'ə·dəm) *n. Archaic* **1** Holiness. **2** A holy relic. **3** A holy place; sanctuary. . . . **grouch** (grouch) *U.S. Colloq. v.i.* To grumble; be surly or discontented. **—** *n.* **1** A discontented, grumbling person. **2** A grumbling, sulky mood. . . . .

A complete list of the label abbreviations used in this dictionary will be found on page xx.

Variant forms In the case of words having more than one approved spelling (as *esthetic, aesthetic*; *center, centre*), the main entry is made under what is considered to be the form in more general use in the United States. The alternate form is cross-referred when it is not within close range of the alphabetic position of the main entry, and is also shown in italic type at the end of the main entry or after all the definitions for a particular part of speech to which it applies. Variant forms that do not require cross-reference are shown in the same position in the main entry but in boldface type with syllabication, stress marks, and, when necessary, pronunciation. A variant that applies to but one of several senses of a word is attached with a colon to the definition to which it pertains.

bach·e·lor (bach'ə·lər, bach'lər) *n.* . . . . **3** A young knight serving under another's banner: also **bach'e·lor-at-arms'.** . . . . **5** A young male fur seal kept from the breeding grounds by the older males: also called *holluschick.* . . . .

Forms that have some restricted usage are labeled accordingly, as **hon·or** . . . Also *Brit.* **hon'our.**

Phrasal entries Numerous phrases are entered and defined in the vocabulary section of this book in alphabetic place according to the first word of the phrase, as **bird of paradise, earth inductor, free verse, right of search.** In many other instances, however, it has been more expedient to enter and define such phrases under the main element. Thus, *Old English* and *Middle English* are run in as subordinate entries under **English,** preceded by a heavy dash; *alternating current, direct current,* and *eddy current* are entered and defined under **current.** All such entries are cross-referred in alphabetic place.

In some entries, particularly those for plants and animals, varying combinations of the word being defined are given within the main entry in boldface type and not entered in alphabetic place, as **leop·ard** · · · **2** Any similar cat, such as the **American leopard** or jaguar, the **hunting leopard** or cheetah, the **snow leopard** or ounce.

Encyclopedic entries A similar device has been employed where it has been advisable to bring together in one place as much logically related information as possible. Certain groups of terms are fully treated in an alphabetic boldface listing under the primary word common to each group. This treatment points up significant relationships between terms, facilitates comparison and selection of the term desired, and allows for the presentation of a range of information ordinarily characteristic of encyclopedias. For example, the entry for **time** contains a listing, with full definitions, of the various classifications from *astronomical time* through *zone time.* Similar listings have been included under the following entries: *angle, calendar, court, cross, current (ocean currents), diamond, fraction, glass, law, number, school, spaniel,* and *terrier.* All terms so entered are separately cross-referred.

Idiomatic phrases Often a main-entry word, when in conjunction with various prepositions, adverbs, adjectives, etc., will form a phrase distinct in sense from the meaning of the combined elements. Such idiomatic phrases are shown in smaller boldface type within the entry for the principal word in the phrase; they are preceded by a heavy dash, and follow all the definitions for the particular part of speech involved. Thus, under the verb **carry** will be found subordinate entries for the phrases *carry arms, carry away, carry off, carry on,* etc.; under the entry for the noun **hand** such phrases as *at first hand, by hand, to have one's hands full,* *to lend a hand,* etc., are set apart and defined in detail.

Collateral adjectives Because of the grafting of Norman French and late Renaissance Latin idioms on early English we find a good many English nouns which have adjectives closely connected with them in sense but not in form, such as *brachial* with *arm, cervical* with *neck, lacustrine* with *lake, hibernal* with *winter, diurnal* with *day, reticular* with *net,* and the like. Such adjectives which, through a collateral line of meaning, have come to express certain special adjectival senses, are, of course, listed in their regular alphabetic place, but, as a convenience for those who do not know or cannot recall them, a large number of such functionally related adjectives have been entered with their associated nouns, attached to the particular meaning of the noun to which they apply, in the form ◆ Collateral adjective: *brachial.*

Homophones Words identical in sound but different in spelling and meaning, such as the groups *altar / alter, filter / philter, hail / hale, principal / principle, right / rite / write,* and several hundred others, often lead to confusion in the writing of English. A large number of these have been listed just before the etymology of every relevant entry, in the form ◆ Homophone: *altar.* No entries have been made for such groups as *horse / hoarse, burrow / burro* which, because of variant pronunciations, are homophonic for some speakers but not for others.

Etymologies The etymologies are shown in brackets after the definitions and before the run-on derivatives. The following examples show the manner of entry and the use of cross-references: (1) **spe·cial** . . . [<OF *especial* <L *specialis* < *species* kind, species]; the etymology is to be read: derived from (<) the Old French (OF) word *especial* from the Latin (L) word *specialis* which in turn is from Latin *species* meaning "kind, species"; (2) **arroyo** . . . [<Sp.]; here the reading is to be: derived from (<) a Spanish (Sp.) word of the same form and meaning; (3) **has·sle** . . . [? <HAGGLE + TUSSLE]; this etymology is to be read: perhaps (?) derived from (<) a blending of "haggle" and (+) "tussle," the small capital letters indicating that the etymologies of these words will be found under their main entries; (4) **de·cep·tion** . . . [<L *deceptio, -onis* < *decipere.* See DECEIVE.]; (5) **bul·wark** . . . [<MHG *bolwerc.* Akin to BOULEVARD.]; (6) **a·dult** . . . [<L *adultus,* pp. of *adolescere* grow up < *ad-* + *alescere* grow. Related to ADOLESCENT.]; (7) **jour·nal** . . . [<OF <L *diurnalis.* Doublet of DIURNAL.]

Cross-references In (4), "See" directs attention to the etymology under "deceive" for further information; in (5), "Akin to" points to the fact that "boulevard" and "bulwark" are cognate words; in (6), "Related to" indicates that these words derive from different recorded stems of the same word; in (7), "Doublet of" marks the fact that "journal" and "diurnal" are ultimately derived from the same Latin word, but have come into English by different paths, in this case, the former through Old French and the latter directly from Latin.

For the complete list of the abbreviations which are used in the etymologies in this work, see page xx.

Run-on entries Words that are actually or ostensibly derived from other words by the addition or replacement of a suffix, and whose sense can be inferred from the meaning of the main word, are run on, in smaller boldface type, at the end of the appropriate main entries. The run-on entries are preceded by a heavy dash and followed by a part-of-speech designation. They are syllabified and stressed, and, when necessary, a full or partial pronunciation is indicated, as **in·sip·id** (in·sip′id) *adj.* . . . **— in·si·pid·i·ty** (in′si·pid′ə·tē), **in·sip′id·ness** *n.* **— in·sip′id·ly** *adv.*

Usage notes Points of grammar and idiom, when an integral part of definition, are included, following a colon, after the particular sense of a word to which they apply, as **anx·ious** . . . **3** Intent; eagerly desirous; solicitous: with *for* or the infinitive with *to*: *anxious* for success; *anxious* to succeed . . .

More extensive notes consisting of supplementary information on grammar, accepted usage, the relative status of variant forms, etc., are entered at the end of the relevant entries and prefaced with the symbol ◆. (See **anyone, Asiatic, can, have.**)

Synonyms and antonyms Extended discussions of the differentiation in shades of meaning within a group of related words, or in some cases simple lists of synonyms, are given at the end of relevant entries in paragraphed form after the run-on derivatives. Lists of antonyms are often added as well to point up further distinctions in meaning.

Alphabetization All entries in this dictionary (general vocabulary, affixes, geographical and biographical entries, foreign words and phrases, etc.) are in one alphabetic list, with the exception of an extended list of abbreviations given, for the sake of ready reference, in one section at the back of the book. Thus, the entry for **ampere (the electrical unit)** immediately precedes that for **André Marie Ampère,** for whom it was named; the entry for **Bridge of Sighs** precedes **Bridgeport** and follows **bridgehead**; the prefix **pro–** is entered immediately after the word **pro** (a professional) and before the word **proa** (a sailing vessel).

Hyphens The hyphen used in the spelling of hyphemes (hyphened words) in this dictionary is printed with extra length to distinguish it as a spelling characteristic, as **cap–a–pie, battle–scarred.** This lengthened hyphen is also used in the entries for prefixes, suffixes, and combining forms, as **un–, –less, hydro–.** The standard hyphen is utilized at the ends of lines to indicate syllabic breaks in words ordinarily written solid, as *com-prehensive,* while the lengthened hyphen is retained for the end–of–line breaks in hyphemes.

Homographs These words, which are identical in spelling but differ in meaning and origin (and often in pronunciation), are separately entered and differentiated by the following superior figure, as **bushel**[1] (measure), **bushel**[2] (mend); **pink**[1] (color), **pink**[2] (stab), **pink**[3] (sailing vessel), **pink**[4] (fade). The numbering also serves to simplify cross–reference to such words.

Cross–references Cross–references are directions to see another entry for additional information. They direct the reader from a variant spelling, inflected form, subentry, etc., to a main entry. The entry to be sought is generally indicated in small capital letters, as **car·a·cul** . . . See KARAKUL; **aes·thete** . . . , **aes·thet·ic** . . . See ESTHETE, etc.; **cor·po·ra** . . . Plural of CORPUS; **Old English** See under ENGLISH.

Sometimes a cross–reference is made to a homograph entry or to a particular definition or part of speech of the main entry, as

flied (flīd) Past tense and past participle of FLY[1] (def. 7).
taps (taps) See TAP[2] (*n.* def. 3).

Some entries are defined by citing another form, as

se·pi·o·lite . . . *n.* Meerschaum.

This is a type of cross–reference. Complete information will be found under the word or term used in the definition.

See the note on **Etymologies,** for the system of cross–referring there used.

Prefixes, suffixes, and combining forms These are entered and defined in regular alphabetic order. The prefix is followed by the lengthened hyphen, the suffix preceded by it, as **anti–** *prefix*; **–ical** *suffix.*

Similarly, the combining form is followed or preceded by the lengthened hyphen depending on its position in combination, as **proto–** *combining form*; **–cide** *combining form.*

Word lists The meaning of many combinations of words (hyphemes, solidemes, and two word phrases) is easily deduced by combining the senses of their component parts. Such self–explaining compounds have been entered in list form under the first element — that is, under prefixes (**bi–, co–, non–, re–,** etc.) combining forms (**auto–, counter–, mid–,** etc.), and words (**corn, heart, man, peace,** etc.). These lists serve to indicate the preferred form of a compound — whether written solid, with a hyphen, or as a two–word phrase. The listings are not intended to be all–inclusive; most of the prefixes and combining forms so entered combine freely in English in the formation of new compounds based on existing forms.

Chemical formulas As an integral part of the definitions of the large number of chemical substances listed in this dictionary, the reader will find the formulas which, in the chemist's shorthand, indicate what constituents enter into a compound, and in what proportions. These formulas, though usually of the simple empirical type, help to prevent confusion in the identification of hundreds of the substances used in medicine, industry, and the arts, and are particularly useful in recognizing distinctions between the two broad fields of inorganic and organic chemicals.

Taxonomic classification Essential technical information regarding the many plants and animals described under their common names is provided by the listing, usually in italic type enclosed in parentheses, of one or more of the principal taxonomic categories — phylum or division, class, order, family, genus, and species — by which they are correctly identified in botanical and zoological usage. This information, checked against the latest and most reliable sources, is especially useful in showing relationships between seemingly very different types and in discriminating within and between deceptively similar groups, such as toads and frogs, spruce and hemlock, and moths and butterflies.

Trade names Of the thousands of words used to identify trademarked or proprietary articles, drugs, processes, and services, a generous number have been entered and defined in this book because of their wide public acceptance. In every such case the word is entered as though it were a proper name: that is, with an initial capital letter, and the added notation, "a trade name" or — chiefly for the pharmaceutical products — "a proprietary name (or brand) . . ." This technique is employed to alert the reader to the commercial status of a word and, by implication, to caution him against employing it in a generic sense that might involve him in legal difficulties with those claiming a prescriptive or legal right to its use. This treatment of proprietary names is in no sense to be interpreted as establishing a formal status within the meaning of any of the various statutes involving the protection and use of trade names, registered or otherwise.

Illustrations, maps, and tables The illustrations in this book — all of them carefully prepared line drawings — have been selected with the emphasis on their explanatory value rather than their pictorial or decorative effect. They often include informative captions, and are intended to supplement the definitions.

A certain number of geographic entries are accompanied by small, precise spot maps which show at a glance just how a given place, region, lake, island, or other feature is related to its immediate surroundings — as under *Congo* (river system), *English Channel, Holy Roman Empire, Suez.*

For a selected group of entries supplementary information has been provided in the form of charts and tables, as for foreign alphabets (see **alphabet**), the geological time scale (see **geology**), chemical elements (see **periodic table**), the major wars of history (see **war**), constellations, clouds, the endocrine glands, etc.

Abbreviations The abbreviations used in the body of this book (in labeling within entries, in etymologies, etc.) will be found listed on page xx. Where abbreviations of main-entry words are entered, they are shown at the end of the entry, as Abbr. *B.A., A.B.* (Bachelor of Arts); Abbr. *AWOL, awol, A.W.O.L., a.w.o.l.* (absent without leave); Abbr. *Dan.* (Danish). Biblical references are to the King James Bible and indicate book, chapter, and verse, in that order, as *Matt.* v 3–12. An extended list of standard abbreviations will be found at the end of the dictionary, following the vocabulary section.

TABLE OF ENGLISH SPELLINGS

FOLLOWING is a list of words exemplifying the possible spellings for the sounds of English. The sounds represented by these spellings are shown in the pronunciation symbols used in this dictionary, followed by their equivalents in the International Phonetic Alphabet.

a	æ	cat, plaid, calf, laugh
ā	eɪ,e	mate, bait, gaol, gauge, pay, steak, skein, weigh, prey
â(r)	ɛ,ɛr	dare, fair, prayer, where, bear, their
ä	ɑ	dart, ah, calf, laugh, sergeant, heart
b	b	boy, rubber
ch	tʃ	chip, batch, righteous, bastion, structure
d	d	day, ladder, called
e	ɛ	many, aesthete, said, says, bet, steady, heifer, leopard, friend, foetid
ē	i	Caesar, quay, scene, meat, see, seize, people, key, ravine, grief, phoebe
f	f	fake, coffin, cough, half, phase
g	g	gate, beggar, ghoul, guard, vague
h	h	hot, whom
hw	hw, ʍ	whale
i	ɪ	pretty, been, tin, sieve, women, busy, guilt, lynch
ī	aɪ	aisle, aye, sleight, eye, dime, pie, sigh, guile, buy, try, lye
j	dʒ	edge, soldier, modulate, rage, exaggerate, joy
k	k	can, accost, saccharine, chord, tack, acquit, king, talk, liquor
l	l	let, gall
m	m	drachm, phlegm, palm, make, limb, grammar, condemn
n	n	gnome, know, mnemonic, note, banner, pneumatic
ng	ŋ	sink, ring, meringue
o	ɑ, ɒ	watch, pot
ō	oʊ,o	beau, yeoman, sew, over, soap, roe, oh, brooch, soul, though, grow
ô	ɔ	ball, balk, fault, dawn, cord, broad, ought
oi	ɔɪ	poison, toy
ou	aʊ	out, bough, cow
o͞o	u	rheum, drew, move, canoe, mood, group, through, fluke, sue, fruit
o͝o	ʊ	wolf, foot, could, pull
p	p	map, happen
r	r	rose, rhubarb, marry, diarrhea, wriggle
s	s	cite, dice, psyche, saw, scene, schism, mass
sh	ʃ	ocean, chivalry, vicious, pshaw, sure, schist, prescience, nauseous, shall, pension, tissue, fission, potion
t	t	walked, thought, phthisic, ptarmigan, tone, Thomas, butter
th	θ	thick
th	ð	this, bathe
u	ʌ	some, does, blood, young, sun
yo͞o	ju,ɪu	beauty, eulogy, queue, pew, ewe, adieu, view, fuse, cue, youth, yule
û(r)	ɜr,ɝ	yearn, fern, err, girl, worm, journal, burn, guerdon, myrtle
v	v	of, Stephen, vise, flivver
w	w	choir, quilt, will
y	j	onion, hallelujah, yet
z	z	was, discern, scissors, xylophone, zoo, muzzle
zh	ʒ	rouge, pleasure, incision, seizure, glazier
ə	ə	above, fountain, darken, clarity, parliament, cannon, porpoise, vicious, locus
ər	ər,ɚ	mortar, brother, elixir, donor, glamour,augur, nature, zephyr

SPELLING:
Plurals and Participles

BASICALLY, plurals in English are formed by the addition of *-s* or *-es* (depending on the preceding sound) to the complete word; past participles are formed by the addition of *-ed,* and present participles by adding *-ing.* There are, however, many exceptions. In this book, all such exceptions (the "irregular" inflected forms) are indicated within the entry, in boldface immediately following the part-of-speech label.

fly (flī) *n. pl.* **flies . . .**
sheep (shēp) *n. pl.* **sheep . . .**
cal·ci·fy (kal′sə·fī) *v.t.* & *v.i.* **·fied, ·fy·ing . . .**
go (gō) *v.i.* **went, gone, go·ing . . .**

Some rules for the spelling of these forms (with the exception of nouns which form their plurals by some internal change and the so-called strong verbs) are listed below:

PLURALS

1. Nouns ending in *y* preceded by a consonant change *y* to *i* and add *-es.*

baby babies story stories

2. Nouns ending in *y* preceded by a vowel add *-s* without change.

chimney chimneys valley valleys

Note, however, that *money* may have either form in the plural — *moneys, monies.*

3. Some nouns ending in *f* or *fe* change this to *v* and add *-es.*

knife knives shelf shelves
BUT: roof roofs safe safes

Note: Some words may have alternate plural forms.

scarf scarfs or scarves

4. Most words ending in *o* form a plural in *-os.*

cameo cameos folio folios halo halos

A few words ending in *o* (*echo, hero, Negro,* etc.) form the plural only in *-oes (echoes, heroes, Negroes),* but many others in this category have alternative plurals in both forms.

buffalo buffalos or buffaloes
mosquito mosquitos or mosquitoes
volcano volcanoes or volcanos

PAST AND PRESENT PARTICIPLES

1. The final consonant is doubled for monosyllables or words accented on the final syllable when they end in a *single* consonant preceded by a *single* vowel.

control, controlled, controlling
hop, hopped, hopping
occur, occurred, occurring
quit, quitted, quitting *(Note: a* u *following* q *is not to be counted as an additional vowel.)*
BUT: help, helped, helping *(two consonants)*
seed, seeded, seeding *(two vowels)*

Some words *not* accented on the final syllable have a variant participial form with a doubled consonant; the single consonant form is preferred in the United States.

travel, traveled or travelled, traveling or travelling
worship, worshiped or worshipped, worshiping or worshipping

2. Words ending in silent or mute *e* drop the *e* before *-ed* and *-ing,* unless it is needed to avoid confusion with another word.

change, changed, changing love, loved, loving
singe, singed, singeing dye, dyed, dyeing

3. Verbs ending in *ie* usually change this to *y* before adding *-ing.*

die, died, dying lie, lied, lying

4. Verbs ending in *c* add a *k* before *-ed* and *-ing.*

mimic, mimicked, mimicking
picnic, picnicked, picnicking

PRONUNCIATION KEY

The primary stress mark (′) is placed after the syllable bearing the heavier stress or accent; the secondary stress mark (′) follows a syllable having a somewhat lighter stress, as in **com·men·da·tion** (kom′ən·dā′shən).

a	add, map
ā	ace, rate
â(r)	care, air
ä	palm, father
b	bat, rub
ch	check, catch
d	dog, rod
e	end, pet
ē	even, tree
f	fit, half
g	go, log
h	hope, hate
i	it, give
ī	ice, write
j	joy, ledge
k	cool, take
l	look, rule
m	move, seem
n	nice, tin
ng	ring, song
o	odd, hot
ō	open, so
ô	order, jaw
oi	oil, boy
ou	out, now
o͞o	pool, food
o͝o	took, full
p	pit, stop
r	run, poor
s	see, pass
sh	sure, rush
t	talk, sit
th	thin, both
t͟h	this, bathe
u	up, done
û(r)	urn, term
yo͞o	use, few
v	vain, eve
w	win, away
y	yet, yearn
z	zest, muse
zh	vision, pleasure
ə	the schwa, an unstressed vowel representing the sound of *a* in *above*, *e* in *sicken*, i in *clarity*, *o* in *melon*, *u* in *focus*

FOREIGN SOUNDS

à as in French *ami, patte.* This is a vowel midway in quality between (a) and (ä).

œ as in French *peu,* German *schön.* Round the lips for (ō) and pronounce (ā).

ü as in French *vue,* German *grün.* Round the lips for (o͞o) and pronounce (ē).

kh as in German *ach,* Scottish, *loch.* Pronounce a strongly aspirated (h) with the tongue in position for (k) as in *cool* or *keep.*

ṅ This symbol indicates that the preceding vowel is nasal. The nasal vowels in French are œṅ *(brun),* aṅ *(main),* äṅ *(chambre),* ôṅ *(dont).* This symbol indicates that a preceding (l) or (r) is voiceless, as in French *débâcle* (dā·bä′kl′) or *fiacre* (fyà′kr′), or that a preceding (y) is pronounced consonantly in a separate syllable followed by a slight schwa sound, as in French *fille* (fē′y′).

Note on the accentuation of foreign words: Many languages do not employ stress in the manner of English; only an approximation can be given of the actual situation in such languages. As it is not possible to reproduce the tones of Chinese in a work of this kind, Chinese names have been here recorded with primary stress on each syllable and may be so pronounced. Japanese and Korean have been shown without stress and may be pronounced with a level accent throughout. French words are shown conventionally with a primary stress on the last syllable; however, this stress tends to be evenly divided among the syllables (except for those that are completely unstressed), with slightly more force and higher pitch on the last syllable.

ABBREVIATIONS USED IN THIS WORK

abbr.	abbreviation(s)
A.D.	year of our Lord
adj.	adjective
adv.	adverb
Aeron.	Aeronautics
AF	Anglo-French
Agric.	Agriculture
Alg.	Algebra
alter.	alteration
Am. Ind.	American Indian
Anat.	Anatomy
Anthropol.	Anthropology
appar.	apparently
Archeol.	Archeology
Archit.	Architecture
assoc.	association
Astron.	Astronomy
aug.	augmentative
Austral.	Australian
Bacteriol.	Bacteriology
B.C.	Before Christ
Biochem.	Biochemistry
Biol.	Biology
Bot.	Botany
Brit.	British
c.	century
Can.	Canadian
cf.	compare
Chem.	Chemistry
Chron.	Chronicles
Col.	Colossians
Colloq.	Colloquial
compar.	comparative
conj.	conjunction
Cor.	Corinthians
Dan.	Daniel, Danish
def.	definition
Dent.	Dentistry
Deut.	Deuteronomy
Dial.	Dialect, Dialectal
dim.	diminutive
Du.	Dutch
E	English
Eccl.	Ecclesiastical
Eccles.	Ecclesiastes
Ecclus.	Ecclesiasticus
Ecol.	Ecology
Econ.	Economics
Electr.	Electricity
Engin.	Engineering
Entomol.	Entomology
Eph.	Ephesians
esp.	especially
Esth.	Esther
Ex., Exod.	Exodus
Ezek.	Ezekiel
F, Fr.	French
fem.	feminine
freq.	frequentative
G, Ger.	German
Gal.	Galatians
Gen.	Genesis
Geog.	Geography
Geol.	Geology
Geom.	Geometry
Gk.	Greek (Homer—A.D. 200)
Gmc.	Germanic
Govt.	Government
Gram.	Grammar
Hab.	Habakkuk
Hag.	Haggai
Heb.	Hebrews
Her.	Heraldry
HG	High German
Hind.	Hindustani
Hos.	Hosea
Icel.	Icelandic
Illit.	Illiterate
imit.	imitative
infl.	influence, influenced
intens.	intensive
interj.	interjection
Is., Isa.	Isaiah
Ital.	Italian
Jas.	James
Jer.	Jeremiah
Jon.	Jonah
Josh.	Joshua
Judg.	Judges
L, Lat.	Latin (Classical, 80 B.C.–A.D. 200)
Lam.	Lamentations
Lev., Levit.	Leviticus
LG	Low German
LGk.	Late Greek (200–600)
Ling.	Linguistics
lit.	literally
LL	Late Latin (200–600)
M	Middle
Mal.	Malachi
masc.	masculine
Math.	Mathematics
Matt.	Matthew
MDu.	Middle Dutch
ME	Middle English (1150–1500)
Mech.	Mechanics
Med.	Medicine, Medieval
Med. Gk.	Medieval Greek (600–1500)
Med. L	Medieval Latin (600–1500)
Metall.	Metallurgy
Meteorol.	Meteorology
MF	Middle French (1400–1600)
MHG	Middle High German (1100–1450)
Mic.	Micah
Mil.	Military
MLG	Middle Low German (1100–1450)
n.	noun
Nah.	Nahum
Naut.	Nautical
Nav.	Naval
N. Am. Ind.	North American Indian
NE	Northeast
Neh.	Nehemiah
neut.	neuter
NL	New Latin (after 1500)
Norw.	Norwegian
Num., Numb.	Numbers
NW	Northwest
O	Old
Ob., Obad.	Obadiah
Obs.	Obsolete
OE	Old English (before 1150)
OF	Old French (before 1400)
OHG	Old High German (before 1100)
ON	Old Norse (before 1500)
orig.	original, originally
Ornithol.	Ornithology
OS	Old Saxon (before 1100)
Paleontol.	Paleontology
Pet.	Peter
Pg.	Portuguese
Phil.	Philippians
Philem.	Philemon
Philos.	Philosophy
Phonet.	Phonetics
Phot.	Photography
Physiol.	Physiology
pl.	plural
pp.	past participle
ppr.	present participle
prep.	preposition
prob.	probably
pron.	pronoun
Prov.	Proverbs
Ps., Psa.	Psalms
Psychoanal.	Psychoanalysis
Psychol.	Psychology
pt.	preterit
ref.	reference
Rev.	Revelation
Rom.	Romans
Sam., Saml.	Samuel
Scand.	Scandinavian
Scot.	Scottish
SE	Southeast
sing.	singular
Skt.	Sanskrit
Sociol.	Sociology
S. of Sol.	Song of Solomon
S. Am. Ind.	South American Indian
Sp.	Spanish
Stat.	Statistics
superl.	superlative
Surg.	Surgery
Sw.	Swedish
SW	Southwest
Technol.	Technology
Telecom.	Telecommunication
Theol.	Theology
Thess.	Thessalonians
Tim.	Timothy
Tit.	Titus
trans.	translation
Trig.	Trigonometry
ult.	ultimate, ultimately
U.S.	United States
v.	verb
var.	variant
v.i.	verb intransitive
v.t.	verb transitive
WGmc.	West Germanic
Zech.	Zechariah
Zeph.	Zephaniah
Zool.	Zoology

◆ Usage note; Homophone; Collateral adjective < from + plus ? possibly

Webster
COMPREHENSIVE
Dictionary

Encyclopedic Edition

a, A (ā) *n. pl.* **a's, A's** or **As, aes** (āz) **1** The first letter of the English alphabet: from Phoenician *aleph,* through the Hebrew *aleph,* Greek *alpha,* and Roman *A.* **2** Any sound of the letter *a.* See ALPHABET. — *symbol* **1a** Primacy in class or order: grade *A* beef. **b** a grade denoting the superior work of a student, or a student so rated. **2** A substitute for the numeral 1: section *A.* **3** *Music* **a** One of a series of tones, the sixth in the natural diatonic scale of C, or the first note in the related minor scale. **b** A standard for tuning instruments: the pitch of this tone. **c** The written note representing this tone. **d** The scale built upon A. **3** *Chem.* Formerly the symbol for argon.

a¹ (ə, *stressed* ā) *indefinite article* or *adj.* In each; to each; for each: twice *a* year; one dollar *a* bushel: equivalent to *per.* ◆**a, per** *A* is preferred to *per,* except where *per* is required in business and statistical writing. [OE *an, on* in, on, at; orig. a prep.]

a² (ə, *stressed* ā) *indefinite article* or *adj.* One; any; some; each: before a vowel, *an.* See AN, ARTICLE.

Special uses: before plural nouns with *few, great many,* or *good many;* with *on, at,* or *of,* denoting oneness, sameness: birds of *a* feather; before proper names referring to the qualities or character of an individual: He is *a* Hercules in strength. [Reduced form of AN used before consonant sounds]

◆a, an *A* is used before a word beginning with a consonant sound, now including *h* when pronounced: *a* history, *a* hotel (*Brit.* often *an* hotel). Before an unaccented syllable beginning with *h* many writers prefer the older usage: *an* historical novel, *an* hysterical cry. *An* is used before a word beginning with a vowel sound, including one which is pronounced though not written: *an* X ray, *an* *n*-dimensional figure.

a³ (ə, ä) *v. Brit. Dial.* Have.

a⁴ (ā, ô, ə) *pron. Brit. Dial.* He, she, it, they: an unstressed form.

a-¹ *prefix* On; in; at: *aboard, asleep, agog, agoing.* [OE *an, on* in, on, at]

a-² *prefix* Used as an intensive or without added meaning: *arise, abide.* [OE *ā-*]

a-³ *prefix* Of; from: *athirst, akin, anew.* [OE *of* off, of]

a-⁴ *prefix* **1** Without; not: *achromatic.* **2** Apart from; unconcerned with: *amoral.* See note under ALPHA PRIVATIVE. [Reduced form of AN- used before consonant sounds]

a-⁵ Reduced var. of AB- before *m, p,* and *v.*

a-⁶ Reduced var. of AD- before *sc, sp,* and *st.*

a·a (ä′ä′) *n.* A brittle, scoriaceous substance consisting of sand, earth, stones, and melted lava, cooled and broken up. [<Hawaiian]

Aa (ä) Any of several small rivers of Europe, especially one in NW France and one in NW Germany.

Aa·chen (ä′kən, *Ger.* ä ′khən) A city in western Germany on the Belgian border; capital of Charlemagne's empire: French *Aix-la-Chapelle.*

aal (äl) *n.* **1** An East Indian shrub *(Morinda royoc),* the root of which yields a red dye. **2** The dye. Also called *Indian mulberry.* [<Hind.]

Aa·land Islands (ō′län) A Finnish archipelago at the entrance of the Gulf of Bothnia; 551 square miles; chief town, Mariehamn: also *Åland Islands. Finnish* **Ah·ve·nan·maa** (ä′ve·nän·mä′).

Aal·borg (ôl′bôr) A port in northern Denmark; also *Ålborg.*

a·a·li·i (ä′ä·lē′ē) *n.* A small tropical tree *(Dodo-naea viscosa),* native to Australia, Hawaii, Jamaica, and Madagascar, valued for its dark, hard, and durable timber. [<Hawaiian]

Aar (är) The longest river that is entirely in Switzerland, flowing 183 miles to the Rhine. Also **Aa·re** (ä′rə).

Aa·rau (ä′rou) A city in north central Switzerland.

aard·vark (ärd′värk′) *n.* A burrowing, ant-eating African mammal *(Orycteropus afer)* about the size of the pig, with long protrusile, sticky tongue to which the ants adhere, and strong, digging forefeet; an ant bear. [<Afrikaans < Du. *aarde* earth + *vark* pig]

AARDVARK
(4 to 5½ feet from nose to tail; tail 2 to 2½ feet)

aard·wolf (ärd′wŏŏlf′) *n.* A hyenalike, nocturnal, carnivorous mammal *(Proteles cristatus)* of southern and eastern Africa, living chiefly on carrion and termites. [<Afrikaans <Du. *aarde* earth + *wolf* wolf]

Aar·hus (ôr′hōōs) A port in eastern Jutland, the second largest city in Denmark.

Aar·on (âr′ən, ar′ən) A masculine personal name. [<Hebrew *Aharōn?* enlightener] **—Aaron** The first Jewish high priest; brother of Moses. *Ex.* iv 14.

Aa·ron·ic (â·ron′ik) *adj.* **1** Of or pertaining to Aaron, the high priest, or his descendants; of or pertaining to a high priest. **2** relating to the lower order of Mormon priesthood. Also **Aa·ron′i·cal.**

Aaron's rod **1** The rod cast by Aaron before Pharaoh, which became a serpent (*Ex.* vii 9–15), and later blossomed (*Num.* xvii 8). **2** *Archit.* A rod-shaped molding, ornamented with sprouting leaves or with a single serpent twined about it. **3** A plant that flowers on long stems, as the mullein.

aas·vo·gel (äs′fō′gəl) *n.* A vulture. [<Afrikaans]

Ab (ab, äb) A Hebrew month; 11th of civil calendar; 5th of ecclesiastical year. The 9th day of Ab is a fast day to commemorate the destruction of Jerusalem and the Temple, 586 B.C. and A.D. 70. The 15th day is a secular festival. See CALENDAR (Hebrew).

ab-¹ *prefix* Off; from; away: *absolve, abduct, abrogate.* Also: *a-* before *m, p, v,* as in *avocation; abs-* before *c, t,* as in *abscess, abstract.* [<L < *ab* from]

ab-² Assimilated var. of AD-.

ab-³ *prefix* (in the centimeter-gram-second system of measurement) for theoretical electromagnetic units, as *abampere, abhenry.*

a·ba (ä′bə) *n.* A sleeveless garment of camel's- or goat's-hair cloth worn in the middle East; also, the cloth. [<Arabic *abā′*]

ab·a·ca (ab′ə·kä, ä′bə·kä′) *n.* **1** A banana plant *(Musa textilis)* of the Philippine Islands. **2** The inner fiber of this plant, used for cordage. Also called Manila hemp. [<Tagalog]

ab·a·cis·cus (ab′ə·sis′kəs) *n.* **1** A square tile in a mosaic floor or pavement. **2** *Obs.* An abacus. [<L <Gk. *abakiskos,* dim. of *abax* a slab]

ab·a·cist (ab′ə·sist) *n.* One who uses an abacus.

a·back (ə·bak′) *adv.* So as to be pressed backward, as sails; backward; aloof. **—taken aback** **1** *Naut.* Caught by a sudden change of wind so as to reverse the sails. **2** Disconcerted, as by a sudden check. [OE *on bæc* to or on the back]

ab·a·cus (ab′ə·kəs) *n. pl.* **cus·es** or **·ci** (-sī) **1** An ancient calculating device with counters sliding on wires or in grooves. **2** *Archit.* A slab forming the top of a capital. For illustration see CAPITAL. [<L <Gk. *abax* counting table]

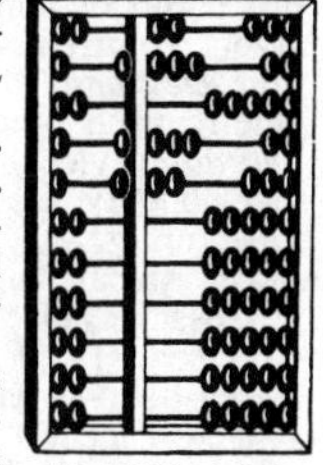

ABACUS *(def. 1)*

A·ba·dan (ä′bä·dän′, ab′ə·dan′) Chief town on **Abadan Island** in the Shatt-al-Arab delta of SW Iran: oil refining and shipping center.

A·bad·don (ə·bad′ən) In the Old Testament: **1** The bottomless pit; hell; the place of destruction. **2** The angel of the bottomless pit; Apollyon. [<Hebrew *ăbaddōn* destruction]

a·baft (ə·baft′, ə·bäft′) *adv. Naut.* Toward the stern; back; behind. — *prep.* Further aft than; astern of: *abaft* the mainmast. [OE *on beæftan* <*on* on, at + *be* about + *æftan,* adv., behind, back]

ab·a·lo·ne (ab′ə·lō′nē) *n.* A marine gastropod mollusk (genus *Haliotis*) having a perforated ear-shaped shell lined with mother-of-pearl. Its meat is used for food. [<Sp.]

ab·am·pere (ab·am′pir) *n.* The cgs electromagnetic unit of current, equal to 10 absolute amperes. [<AB(SOLUTE) + AMPERE]

a·ban·don (ə·ban′dən) *v.t.* **1** To give up wholly; desert; forsake, as an effort or attempt. **2** To surrender or give over: with *to:* He *abandoned* his share to his partner. **3** To yield (oneself) without restraint, as to a feeling or pastime. —*n.* **1** Utter surrender to one's feelings or natural impulses. **2** Freedom. [<OF *abandoner* <*abandon* under one's own control] **—a·ban′don·er** *n.* **—a·ban′don·ment** *n.*

Synonyms (verb): abdicate, abjure, cease, cede, desert, discontinue, forgo, forsake, forswear, leave, quit, recant, relinquish, renounce, repudiate, resign, retract, surrender, vacate. *Abandon* denotes the complete and final giving up, letting go, or withdrawal from persons or things of any kind; *abdicate* and *resign* apply to office, authority, or power; *cede* to territorial possessions; *surrender* especially to military force, and more generally to any demand, claim, passion, etc. *Quit* carries an idea of suddenness or abruptness not necessarily implied in *abandon,* and may not have the same suggestion of finality. *Relinquish* commonly implies reluctance. *Abandon* implies previous association with responsibility for or control of; *forsake* implies previous association with inclination or attachment. *Forsake,* like *abandon,* may be used either in the favorable or unfavorable sense; *desert* is commonly unfavorable, except when used of localities; as "The *Deserted* Village"; a soldier *deserts* his post. While a monarch *abdicates,* a president or other elected or appointed officer *resigns.* See also RENOUNCE. *Antonyms:* adopt, advocate, assert, cherish, claim, court, defend, favor, haunt, hold, keep, maintain, occupy, prosecute, protect, pursue, retain, seek, support, undertake, uphold, vindicate.

a·ban·doned (ə·ban′dənd) *adj.* **1** Deserted; left behind; forsaken. **2** Unrestrained; without moderation. **3** Given over to dissolute practices; profligate; shameless. See synonyms under ADDICTED, BAD.

à bas (à bä′) *French* Down with: an expression indicating disapproval of a person or thing: opposed to *vive.*

a·base (ə·bās′) *v.t.* **a·based, a·bas·ing 1** To lower in position, rank, prestige, or estimation; cast down; humble. **2** *Obs.* To reduce in value, as coinage; debase. [<OF *abaissier* < *a* to + *baissier* to lower <L *ad-* + LL *bassus* low] **—a·bas·ed·ly** (ə·bā′sid·lē) *adv.* **—a·bas′ed·ness** *n.* **—a·bas′er** *n.* **—a·base′ment** *n.*
Synonyms: debase, degrade, depress, discredit, disgrace, dishonor, humble, humiliate, lower, reduce, sink. *Abase* generally refers to outward conditions, *debase* to quality or character: The coinage is *debased* by excess of alloy, the person by vice. *Humble* refers chiefly to the feelings, *humiliate* to outward conditions. To *disgrace* is chiefly applied to deserved moral odium: he *disgraced* himself by his conduct. To *dishonor* a person is to deprive him of honor that should or might be given. To *discredit* one is to injure his reputation. *Degrade* may refer to station, but is now chiefly used of character: drunkenness is a *degrading* vice. *Antonyms:* advance, aggrandize, dignify, elevate, exalt, honor, promote, raise, uplift.

a·bash (ə·bash′) *v.t.* To deprive of self-possession; disconcert; make ashamed or confused. [<OF *esbaïss-,* stem of *esbaïr* astonish] **—a·bash·ed·ly** (ə·bash′id·lē) *adv.* **—a·bash′ment** *n.*
Synonyms: bewilder, chagrin, confound, confuse, daunt, discompose, disconcert, dishearten, embarrass, humble, humiliate, mortify, overawe, shame. Any sense of inferiority *abashes,* with or without the sense of wrong. The children are *abashed* at their parents' reproof. To *confuse* is to bring into a state of mental bewilderment; to *confound* is to overwhelm the mental faculties; to *daunt* is to subject to a certain degree of fear. Confusion generally refers to the intellect, embarrassment to the feelings. A witness may be *embarrassed* by annoying remarks or questions so as to become *confused* in statements. To *mortify* a person is to bring on a painful sense of humiliation: The parent is *mortified* by the child's rudeness. The *embarrassed* speaker finds it difficult to proceed. The mob is *overawed* by the military, the hypocrite *shamed* by exposure. See EMBARRASS. Compare CHAGRIN. *Antonyms:* animate, assure, buoy, cheer, embolden, encourage, inspirit, rally, uphold.

a·bate (ə·bāt′) *v.* **a·bat·ed, a·bat·ing** *v.t.* **1** To make less; reduce in size, number, degree, amount, importance, speed, or force. **2** To deduct, as part of a payment. **3** *Law* To do away with; annul. *—v.i.* **4** To become less, as in strength or degree. **5** *Law* To fail; become void. [< OF *abatre* beat down < *a-* to (<L *ad-*) + *batre* beat <L *batuere*] **—a·bat·a·ble** (ə·bā′tə·bəl) *adj.* **—a·bat·er** (ə·bāt′·ər) *n.*
Synonyms: decline, decrease, diminish, ebb, lessen, lower, mitigate, moderate, reduce, relax, subside. See ABOLISH, ALLAY, ALLEVIATE.) *Antonyms:* aggravate, augment, enhance, increase, intensify.

a·bate·ment (ə·bāt′mənt) *n.* **1** An abating or the amount abated. **2** *Law* A doing away with; annulment.

ab·a·tis (ab′ə·tis, ab′ə ·tē′) *n. Mil.* An obstruction of felled trees or bent saplings pointed in the direction of expected enemy attack, often interwoven with barbed wire. Also **ab′at·tis.** [<F < *abattre* to fell]

a·ba·tor (ə·bā′tər) *n. Law* **1** One who removes a nuisance. **2** One who unlawfully seizes an inheritance in the place of the rightful heir. **3** The agent or cause in effecting an abatement. [<AF < *abatre.* See ABATE.]

A battery *Electr.* A battery that supplies the power for the filaments of a vacuum tube.

ab·at·toir (ab′ə·twär′) *n.* A slaughterhouse. [<F]

ab·ax·i·al (ab·ak′sē·əl) *adj.* Situated or facing away from the axis. [<AB-[1] + AXIAL]

abb (ab) *n.* In weaving, the warp or the yarn for it. [OE *āweb*]

Ab·ba (ab′ə) *n.* **1** Father: a title used with the names of patriarchs and bishops in the Syrian, the Coptic, and the Ethiopian churches. **2** God: a form of address used in the New Testament: *Mark* xiv 36. [<Aramaic]

ab·ba·cy (ab′ə·sē) *n. pl.* **·cies** The office, term of office, dignity, or jurisdiction of an abbot. [<LL *abbatia* <L *abbas* ABBOT]

Ab·bas (ä′bäs), 566–652, the uncle of Mohammed.

Ab·bas·sid (ə·bas′īd, ab′ə·sīd) *n.* Any of the caliphs of the dynasty ruling at Baghdad, 749–1258, and claiming descent from Abbas. *—adj.* Of or pertaining to this dynasty. Also **Ab·bas·side** (ə·bas′id, ab′ə·sid).

ab·ba·tial (ə·bā′shəl) *adj.* Of or pertaining to an abbot or an abbey. Also **ab·bat·i·cal** (ə·bat′i·kəl).

ab·bé (ab′ā, *Fr.* à·ā′) *n.* **1** A title of respect in France given to a priest or any person entitled to wear ecclesiastical dress. **2** An abbot. [<F]

Ab·bé (à·bā′), **Lake** A salt lake on the border between Ethiopia and Somalia.

ab·bess (ab′is) *n.* A woman superior of a community of nuns connected with an abbey. [<OF *abbesse* <LL *abbatissa* <L *abbas* ABBOT]

Ab·be·ville (ab′ə·vil, *Fr.* àb·vēl′) A town in northern France.

Ab·be·vil·li·an (ab′ə·vil′ē·ən) *adj. Anthropol.* Designating a culture stage of the Lower Paleolithic period, represented by crude handaxes of the core type. [from *Abbeville,* France, where artifacts were found]

ab·bey (ab′ē) *n. pl.* **ab·beys 1** The monastic establishment of a society of monks under the jurisdiction of an abbot or of nuns under an abbess. **2** The buildings of such a society; its monastery or convent. **3** The church attached to a monastery or convent. See synonyms under CLOISTER. [<OF *abaie* <LL *abbatia* <L *abbas* ABBOT]

Ab·bey (ab′ē), **Edwin Austin,** 1852–1911, U.S. artist.

Abbey Theatre A repertory theater in Dublin, associated since 1904 with the Irish literary revival.

ab·bot (ab′ət) *n.* The superior of a community of monks connected with an abbey. [OE *abbod* <L <Gk. *abbas* <Aramaic *abba* father] **—ab′bot·cy, ab′bot·ship** *n.*

Abbot of Misrule The leader of festivities in medieval Christian revels.

Ab·bott (ab′ət), **Jacob,** 1803–79, U.S. clergyman and author of juvenile literature. **—Lyman,** 1835–1922, son of Jacob, U.S. clergyman, editor, and author.

Ab·bots·ford (ab′əts·fərd) An estate on the Tweed in SE Scotland: residence of Sir Walter Scott.

ab·bre·vi·ate (ə·brē′vē ·āt) *v.t.* **·at·ed, ·at·ing 1** To condense or make briefer. **2** To shorten, as a word or expression, especially by omission or contraction: Mistress is *abbreviated* to Mrs. [<L *abbreviatus,* pp. of *abbreviare* <*ad-* to + *breviare* shorten < *brevis* short. Doublet of ABRIDGE.] **—ab·bre′vi·a′tor** *n.*
Synonyms: abridge, compress, condense, contract, curtail, epitomize, prune, reduce, shorten. Compare ABBREVIATIONS, ABRIDGMENT. *Anatonyms:* amplify, enlarge, expand, extend, lengthen.

ab·bre·vi·a·tion (ə·brēvē·ā′shən) *n.* **1** A shortened form or contraction, as of a word or phrase; abridgment. **2** A making shorter or the state of being shortened. **3** *Music* A notation indicating repeated notes, chords, etc., by a single symbol.
Synonyms: abridgment, abstract, compendium, condensation, contraction, curtailment, epitome, reduction, shortening, summary. An *abbreviation* is a shortening by any method; a *contraction* is a *reduction* of size by the drawing together of the parts. A *contraction* of a word is made by omitting certain letters or syllables and bringing together the first and last letters or elements; a *contraction* is an *abbreviation,* but an *abbreviation* is not necessarily a *contraction. Abbreviation* and *contraction* are used of words and phrases, *abridgment* of books, paragraphs, sentences, etc. See ABRIDGMENT. *Antonyms:* amplification, dilation, dilution, elongation, enlargement, expansion, expatiation, explication, extension, prolongation.

ABBREVIATION *(def. 3)*

Ab·by (ab′ē) Diminutive of ABIGAIL.

ABC (ā′bē′sē′) *pl.* **ABC's 1** The alphabet: usually plural. **2** The rudiments, elements, or basic facts (of a subject). **3** *Obs.* A primer.

ab·cou·lomb (ab′ko͞o·lom′) *n.* The cgs electromagnetic unit of charge, equal to 10 absolute coulombs. [<AB(SOLUTE) + COULOMB]

ABC powers A former diplomatic grouping, consisting of Argentina, Brazil, and Chile.

ABD (ā′bē′dē′) *n.* A candidate for a doctoral program who has completed all required courses and examinations but not a dissertation. [*a*ll *b*ut *d*issertation]

Abd- A word element meaning "servant," "slave," used as a prefix before names for the Deity to form proper names in Semitic languages; as, *Abdallah* servant of God.

Ab·dal·lah·ibn·Ya·sin (äb′däl·lä′ib′ən·y ä·sēn′), died c. 1058, Arab scholar; founder of the Almoravides. Also **Ab·dul·lah·ibn·Ya·sin** (äb′·do͝ol·lä′-).

Abd-el-Ka·der (äb′del·kä′dir), 1807?–83, Algerian tribal emir. Also **Abd′-el-Ka′dir.**

Abd-er Rah·man Khan (äb′dər rə·män′ khän′), 1830?–1901, emir of Afghanistan 1880–1901.

ab·di·cate (ab′də·kāt) *v.* **·cat·ed, ·cat·ing** *v.t.* To give up formally; renounce, as claims to or possession of a throne, power, or rights. *—v.i.* To renounce a throne, power, or rights: His subjects forced the king to *abdicate.* See synonyms under ABANDON. [<L *abdicatus,* pp. of *abdicare* renounce < *ab-* away + *dicare* proclaim] **—ab·di·ca·ble** (ab′di·kə·bəl) *adj.* **—ab′di·ca′tion** *n.* **—ab′di·ca′tor** *n.*

Ab·di·el (ab′dē·əl) A masculine personal name. [<Hebrew, servant of God] **—Abdiel** An angel who opposed Satan's revolt, in Milton's *Paradise Lost.*

ab·do·men (ab′də·mən, ab·dō′mən) *n.* **1** In mammals, the visceral cavity between the diaphragm and the pelvic floor; the belly: in human anatomy often restricted to the cavity above the true pelvis. **2** In vertebrates other than mammals, the region or cavity that contains the viscera. **3** *Entomol.* The hindmost of the main divisions of the arthropod body. [<L]

ABDOMINAL REGIONS
1. Right hypochondriac region.
2. Left hypochondriac.
3. Epigastric.
4. Umbilical.
5. Right lumbar.
6. Left lumbar.
7. Right inguinal.
8. Left inguinal.
9. Hypogastric.

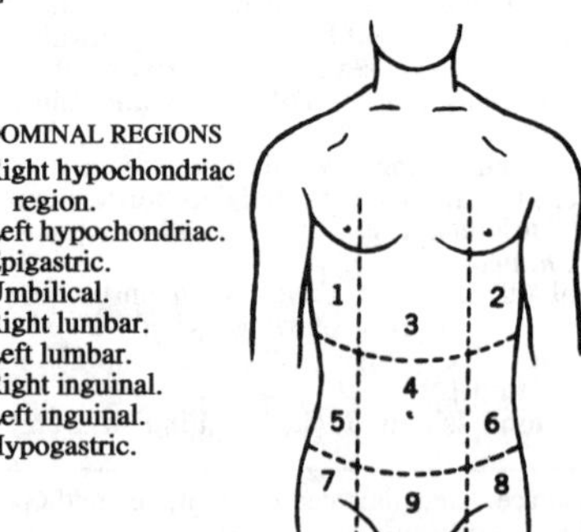

ab·dom·i·nal (ab·dom′ə·nəl) *adj.* Of, pertaining to, or situated on or in the abdomen. **—ab·dom′i·nal·ly** *adv.*

ab·duce (ab·do͞os′, -dyo͞os′) *v.t. Physiol.* To draw or lead away, as by muscular action. [<L *abducere.* See ABDUCT.] **—ab·du′cent** *adj.*

ab·duct (ab·dukt′) *v.t.* **1** To carry away wrongfully, as by force or fraud; kidnap. **2** *Physiol.* To draw or move away from the median plane of the body or from the axis of a limb. [<L *abductus,* pp. of *abducere* <*ab-* away + *ducere* lead] **—ab·duc′tion** *n.* **—ab·duc′tor** *n.*

Ab·dul-A·ziz (äb′do͞ol·ä·zēz′), 1830–76, Turkish sultan 1861–76.

Ab·dul Ba·ha (äb′do͞ol bä·hä′), 1844–1921, Persian leader. Also **Ab·bas Ef·fen·di** (äb·bäs′ e·e·fen′dē).

Ab·dul-Ha·mid II (äb′do͞ol·hä ·mēd′), 1842–1918, sultan of Turkey 1876–1909.

Ab·dul ibn-Hu·sein (äb′do͞ol ib′ən·hoo·sīn′), 1882–1951, ruler of Transjordania, emir 1921–46; king 1946–51; assassinated.

Ab·dul-Me·jid (äb′do͞ol·me·jēd′), 1823–61, Turkish sultan 1839–61. Also **Ab′dul-Me·djid′.**

Ab·dul-Wah·hab (äb′do͞ol·wä·hôb′), 1691–1787, Mohammedan reformer; founder of Wahabiism.

Abd-ur-Rah·man (äb′do͞or·rä′män), died 788, founder of the Ommiad Moslem dynasty in Spain in 756.

Abe (āb) Diminutive of ABRAHAM or ABRAM.

a·beam (ə·bēm′) *adj. & adv.* At right angles to the line of a vessel's keel; opposite the middle of a ship.

a·be·ce·dar·i·an (ā′bē·sē·dâr′ē·ən) *adj.* **1** Pertaining to or formed by the alphabet; alphabetically arranged. **2** Pertaining to a learner of the alphabet; rudimentary; ignorant. —*n.* **1** A teacher of the alphabet or one who is learning it. **2** A novice; beginner. Also **a·be·ce·da·ry** (ā′bē·sē′dar·ē). [<Med.L *abecedarius*]

A·bé·ché (á·bā·shā′) Capital of Ouaddaï prefecture in east-central Chad: Arabic *Abeshr.* Also **A·bé·cher** (á·bā·shā′).

a·bed (ə·bed′) *adv.* In bed; on a bed; to bed.

A·bed·ne·go (ə·bed′ni·gō) Babylonian captive. *Dan.* iii. See SHADRACH.

A·bel (ā′bəl) A masculine personal name. [<L <Gk. *Abel* <Hebrew *Hebel,* lit., breath] **—Abel** Second son of Adam. *Gen.* iv 2.

A·bel (ā′bəl), **John Jacob,** 1857–1938, U.S. pharmacologist.

Ab·e·lard (ab′ə·lärd), **Pierre,** 1079–1142, French scholastic philosopher; husband of Héloïse. Also **Ab′ai·lard.**

a·bele (ə·bēl′, ā′bəl) *n.* The white poplar (*Populus alba*). [<Du. *abeel* <OF *abel* <LL *albellus,* dim. of L *albus* white]

a·be·li·a (ə·be′lē·ə, -lyə) *n.* A shrub having small glossy leaves and bell-like flowers ranging from pink to white.

Abe·na·ki (a′bə·nä′kē) *n. pl:* **Abenaki, Abenakis. 1** The people of an American Indian group of Northern New England and the adjoining parts of Quebec. **2** Both of the Algonquian languages spoken by the Abenaki.

Ab·er·corn (ab′ər·kôrn), **James Albert,** 1869–1953, third duke of Abercorn, governor of Northern Ireland 1922–45.

Ab·er·crom·bie (ab′ər·krom′bē, -krum′bē), **James,** 1706–81, British general.

Ab·er·deen (ab′ər·dēn′) A district in and capital of the Grampian region in NE Scotland.

Ab·er·deen (ab′ər·dēn) A town in NE Maryland near Chesapeake Bay.

Aberdeen An·gus (ang′gəs) A breed of hornless black cattle of Scottish origin.

ab·er·rance (ab·er′əns) *n.* A wandering from the right way; deviation from the path of rectitude. Also **ab·er′ran·cy.**

ab·er·rant (ab·er′ənt) *adj.* **1** Straying from the right way or usual course; wandering. **2** Varying from type; abnormal; exceptional. [<L *aberrans, -antis,* ppr. of *aberrare* <*ab-* from + *errare* wander]

ab·er·ra·tion (ab′ə·rā′shən) *n.* **1** Deviation from a right, customary, prescribed, or natural course or condition; wandering; error. **2** Partial mental derangement. **3** *Optics* The failure of a lens or mirror to bring all light rays to the same focus: called **chromatic aberration** when due to different refrangibility of light of different colors, and **spherical aberration** when due to the form of lens or mirror. **4** *Astron.* An apparent displacement of a heavenly body, due to the effect of relative motion upon the light coming from it. **5** An abnormal structure; a deviation from a standard type: a chromosomal *aberration.* [<L *aberratio, -onis* <*aberrare.* See ABERRANT.]

Ab·er·yst·wyth (ab′ə·rist′with) A port in Dyfed County, Wales.

A·beshr (a·besh′ər) Arabic name for ABÉCHÉ.

a·bet (ə·bet′) *v.t.* **a·bet·ted, a·bet·ting** To encourage and support, especially wrong-doing or a wrong-doer; instigate; countenance. [<OF *abeter* incite, arouse < *a-* to (<L *ad-*) + *beter* tease, bait <ON *beita* cause to bite] **—a·bet′ment, a·bet·tal** *n.*

Synonyms: aid, assist, countenance, embolden, encourage, help, incite, instigate, promote, sanction, support, uphold. *Abet* and *instigate* are used almost without exception in a bad sense; one may *incite* either to good or evil. One *incites* or *instigates* to the doing of something not yet done, or to increased activity or further advance in the doing of it; one *abets* by giving sympathy, countenance, or substantial aid to the doing of that which is already projected or in process of commission. See AID. *Antonyms:* baffle, confound, counteract, denounce, deter, disapprove, disconcert, discourage, dissuade, frustrate, hinder, impede, obstruct.

a·bet·tor (ə·bet′ər) *n.* One who abets. See synonyms under ACCESSORY. Also **a·bet′ter.**

a·bey·ance (ə·bā′əns) *n.* **1** Suspension or temporary inaction. **2** *Law* An undetermined condition, as of an estate awaiting an owner. Also **a·bey′an·cy.** [< AF *abeiance* <OF *beer* gape <LL *badare*] **—a·bey′ant** *adj.*

ab·far·ad (ab·far′əd, -ad) *n.* The cgs electromagnetic unit of capacitance, equal to 1 abcoulomb per abvolt, or 1,000,000,000 farads. [<AB(SOLUTE) + FARAD]

Ab·ha (ab·hä′) The chief town of Southern Province, Saudi Arabia.

ab·hen·ry (ab·hen′rē) *n.* The cgs electromagnetic unit of inductance, equal to 10^{-9} henry. [<AB(SOLUTE) + HENRY]

ab·he·sive (ab·hē′siv) *adj.* Not sticking to another material.

ab·hor (ab·hôr′) *v.t.* **ab·horred, ab·hor·ring** To regard with repugnance; feel horror of; detest; loathe. [<L *abhorrere* <) *ab-* from + *horrere* shrink] **—ab·hor′rer** *n.*

Synonyms: abominate, despise, detest, dislike, hate, loathe, scorn, shun. *Abhor* is stronger than *despise,* implying a shuddering recoil, especially a moral recoil. *Detest* expresses indignation, with something of contempt. *Loathe* implies disgust, physical or moral. We *abhor* a traitor, *despise* a coward, *detest* a liar. We *dislike* an uncivil person. We *abhor* cruelty, *hate* tyranny. Compare ABOMINATION. *Antonyms:* admire, approve, covet, crave, desire, enjoy, esteem, like, love, relish.

ab·hor·rence (ab·hôr′əns, -hor′-) *n.* The act of abhorring, or that which is abhorred. See synonyms under ABOMINATION, ANTIPATHY, HATRED.

ab·hor·rent (ab·hôr′ənt, -hor′-) *adj.* **1** Detestable or horrible: with *to.* **2** Feeling abhorrence. **—ab·hor′rent·ly** *adv.*

A·bib (ā·bib′, *Hebrew* ä ·vēv′) See NISAN.

a·bi·dance (ə·bīd′ns) *n.* **1** An abiding; dwelling. **2** Continuance; adherence to or an abiding by (rules, methods, etc.).

a·bide (ə·bīd′) *v.* **a·bode** or **a·bid·ed, a·bid·ing** *v.i.* **1** To continue in a place; stay. **2** To have one's abode; dwell; reside. **3** To continue in some condition or state; remain faithful or unchanging. —*v.t.* **4** To look for; wait for: to *abide* the event. **5** To await expectantly or defiantly. **6** To endure; put up with. **—to abide by 1** To behave in accordance with; be faithful to, as a promise or rule. **2** To accept the consequences of; submit to. [OE *abidan*] **—a·bid′er** *n.* **—a·bid′ing** *adj.* **—a·bid′ing·ly** *adv.*

Synonyms: anticipate, await, bear, bide, continue, dwell, endure, expect, inhabit, live, lodge, remain, reside, rest, sojourn, stand, stay, stop, tarry, tolerate, wait, watch. To *abide* is to remain continuously without limit of time unless expressed by the text. *Lodge, sojourn, stay, tarry,* and *wait,* always imply a limited time; *lodge,* to pass the night; *sojourn,* to *remain* temporarily; *live, dwell, reside,* to have a permanent home. *Stop,* in the sense of *stay* or *sojourn,* is colloquial. Compare ENDURE, REST. *Antonyms:* abandon, avoid, depart, forfeit, forfend, journey, migrate, move, proceed, reject, resist, shun.

Ab·i·djan (ab′i·jän′) A port in west Africa, administrative center of the Ivory Coast.

A·bi·el (ā′bē·el, ə·bī′el) A masculine personal name. [<Hebrew, father of strength] **—Abiel** One of David's thirty mighty men. I *Chron.* xi 32.

ab·i·et·ic acid (ab′ē·et′ik) *Chem.* An acid, $C_{20}H_{30}O_2$, isolated from pine rosin in the form of a slightly yellow crystalline powder; it is used in lacquers, varnishes, soaps, and driers. [<L *abies* fir]

Ab·i·gail (ab′ə·gāl) A feminine personal name. [<Hebrew, my father's joy] **—Abigail** The wife of Nabal and afterward of David. I *Sam.* xxv 14.

ab·i·gail (ab′ə·gāl) *n.* A lady's maid: from a character in Beaumont and Fletcher's *The Scornful Lady.*

A·bi·hu (ə·bī′hyo͞o) Second son of Aaron. *Lev.* x 1.

A·bi·jah (ə·bī′jə) King of Judah. I *Kings* xiv 1. [<Hebrew, whose father is Jehovah]

a·bil·i·ty (ə·bil′ə·tē) *n. pl.* **·ties 1** The state of being able; physical, mental, legal, or financial power to do. **2** *pl.* Natural or acquired aptitude. **3** *Psychol.* That which a person can actually do on the basis of present development and training. [<OF *ablete* <L *habilitas* <*habilis.* See ABLE.]

Synonyms: aptitude, capability, capacity, cleverness, competence, competency, dexterity, efficiency, expertness, faculty, power, qualification, readiness, skill, talent. *Ability* includes every form of *power. Capacity* is power to receive. *Dexterity* and *skill* are readiness and facility in action, having a special end, and are largely acquired. *Efficiency* brings all one's *ability* to bear promptly on the thing to be done. Compare POWER. *Antonyms:* awkwardness, imbecility, inability, incapacity, incompetency, inefficiency, stupidity.

A·bim·e·lech (ə·bim′ə·lek) Son of Gideon; king of Shechem. *Judges* viii 31.

ab in·con·ve·ni·en·ti (ab in′kən·vē′nē·en′tē) *Latin* From the inconvenience involved: a legal phrase signifying that an argument based on such grounds carries much weight.

ab in·i·ti·o (ab i·nish′ē·ō) *Latin* From the beginning.

ab in·tra (ab in′trə) *Latin* From within.

ab·i·o·gen·e·sis (ab′ē·ō·jen′ə·sis) *n.* The springing up of living from non-living matter; especially, the old doctrine of the generation of new organisms from putrid and decomposing organic matter; spontaneous generation. Compare BIO-GENESIS. [<A-[4] + BIO- + GENESIS] **—ab·i·o·ge·net·ic** (ab′ē·ō·jə·net′ik) or **·i·cal** *adj.* **—ab·i·og·e·nist** (ab′ē·oj′ə·nist) *n.*

ab·i·o·sis (ab′ē·ō′sis) *n.* Absence of life; a lifeless state. [<GK. *abios* lifeless] **—ab·i·ot·ic** (ab′ē·ot′ik) *adj.*

ab·i·ot·ro·phy (ab′ē·ot′rə·fē) *n.* Premature or abnormal degeneration or wasting away of the body. [<A-[4] + BIO- + -TROPHY]

ab·ir·ri·tant (ab·ir′ə·tənt) *n.* A soothing agent; a medicine that eases irritation. —*adj.* Relieving irritation; soothing.

ab·ir·ri·tate (ab·ir′ə·tāt) *v.t.* **·tat·ed, ·tat·ing** To diminish sensibility in; relieve irritation in. **—ab·ir′ri·ta′·tion** *n.*

A·bi·shai (ä·bē′shī) A Jewish general. II *Sam.* xxiii 18.

ab·ject (ab′jekt, ab·jekt′) *adj.* Sunk to a low condition; groveling; mean; despicable; also, downcast in spirit; servile. See synonyms under PITIFUL. [<L *abjectus,* pp. of *abjicere*

throw away < *ab-* away + *jacere* throw] **—ab·jec′tive** *adj.* **—ab′ject·ly** *adv.* **—ab′ject·ness, ab·jec′tion** *n.*

ab·ju·ra·tion (ab′jo͞o·rā′shən) *n.* The act of abjuring or state of being abjured; repudiation.

ab·jure (ab·jo͝or′) *v.t.* **ab·jured, ab·jur·ing 1** To renounce under oath; forswear. **2** To retract or recant, as an opinion; repudiate; abandon. See synonyms under ABANDON, RENOUNCE. [<L *abjurare* deny on oath < *ab-* away + *jurare* swear] **—ab·jur·a·to·ry** (ab·jo͝or′a·tôr′ ē, -tō′rē) *adj.* **—ab·jur′er** *n.*

Ab·khaz Autonomous Republic (ab·kaz′) An administrative division of the Republic of Georgia, between the Black Sea and the Greater Caucasus; 3,300 square miles; capital, Sukhumi. Also **Ab·kha·zia, Ab·kha·sia** (ab·kā′zhə).

ab·late (ab·lāt′) *v.t.* **·lat·ed, ·lat·ing 1** To remove, as by cutting away, eroding, etc. **2** To undergo ablation.

ab·la·tion (ab·lā′shən) *n.* **1** The surgical removal of tissues or organs from the body. **2** *Geol.* The wearing away of rocks. **3** *Aerospace* The disintegration of part of the nose cone on a missile or spacecraft when it reenters the atmosphere. [<L *ablatio, -onis* a carrying away < *ablatus,* pp. of *auferre* <*ab-* away + *ferre* carry] **—ab·la·ti·tious** *adj.*

ab·la·tive (ab′lə·tiv) *adj.* **1** *Gram.* Pertaining to a grammatical case expressing separation or instrumentality. **2** *Obs.* Subtractive. —*n.* *Gram.* **1** A case of Latin and Sanskrit nouns, denoting *from, with, in, by,* etc. **2** A word in this case. [<L *ablativus* <*ablatus* carried away. See ABLATIDON.]

ablative absolute In Latin grammar, the construction in the ablative case of a noun and participle, a noun and an adjective, or two nouns, constituting an adverbial phrase which stands apart in syntax from the rest of the sentence; as, *sole oriente,* nox fugit (*the sun rising,* night flees).

ab·laut (äb′lout, ab′-; *Ger.* äp′lout) *n.* The change of one root vowel into another to show a variation of tense, part of speech, or meaning, as in *swim, swam, swum.* Compare UMLAUT. [<G < *ab* off + *laut* sound]

a·blaze (ə·blāz′) *adj.* & *adv.* On fire; in a blaze; hence, in a glow of excitement; zealous; ardent.

a·ble (ā′bəl) *adj.* **a·bler** (ā′blər), **a·blest** (ā′blist) **1** Having adequate power; competent; qualified. **2** Having superior abilities; capable. See synonyms under ADEQUATE, CLEVER, COMPETENT, GOOD, SAGACIOUS. [<OF *hable* able <L *habilis* manageable, suitable, fit < *habere* have, hold]

-able *or* **-ible** *suffix* **1** Given to; tending to; like to: *peaceable, changeable.* **2** Fit to; able to; capable of; worthy of: *eatable, salable, solvable.* The *-able* ending is extended in English to form adjectives from native verbs, nouns, and phrases, as *answerable, plowable, get-at-able,* etc. [<F <L *-abilis, -ibilis, -bilis*]

a·ble-bod·ied (ā′bəl·bod′ēd) *adj.* Having a sound strong body; competent for physical service; robust.

able-bodied seaman An experienced and skilled seaman, receiving higher pay than an ordinary seaman: usually abbreviated *A.B.*

ab·le·gate (ab′li·gāt) *n.* A special papal envoy charged with various missions, such as the bearing of the official insignia to newly appointed cardinals. [<L *ablegatus,* pp. of *ablegare* <*ab-* away + *legare* dispatch]

a·bloom (ə·blo͞om′) *adj.* & *adv.* Blooming; in blossom.

ab·lu·ent (ab′lo͞o·ənt) *adj.* Cleansing. —*n.* A cleansing agent; a detergent. [<L *abluens, -entis,* ppr. of *abluere* <*ab-* away + *luere* wash]

a·blush (ə·blush′) *adj.* Blushing.

ab·lu·tion (ab·lo͞o′shən) *n.* **1** A washing or cleansing, especially of the body; a bath. **2** A ceremonial or symbolic washing; especially, in the Roman Catholic Church, the wine and water used to remove any trace of the eucharistic elements from the chalice and the priest's fingers after communion. **3** The washing of the hands of the priest before, during, and after the celebration of the Mass. **4** Any liquid used in washing or cleansing. [<L *ablutio, -onis* <*abluere* wash away. See ABLUENT.] **—ab·lu′tion·ar′y** *adj.*

a·bly (ā′blē) *adv.* With ability; capably.

-ably *suffix* Like; in the manner of: *peaceably:* used to form adverbs from adjectives ending in *-able.*

ab·mho (ab′mō) *n.* The cgs electromagnetic unit of conductance, equal to a current in a conductor of one abampere when the potential difference between the ends of the conductor is one abvolt. [<AB(SOLUTE) + MHO]

ab·ne·gate (ab′nə·gāt) *v.t.* **·gat·ed, ·gat·ing** To deny to oneself, as a right or privilege; renounce. [<L *abnegatus,* pp. of *abnegare* <*ab-* away + *negare* deny] **—ab′ne·ga′tor** *n.*

ab·ne·ga·tion (ab′nə·gā′shən) *n.* Renunciation: denial; self-denial.

Ab·ner (ab′nər) A masculine personal name. [<Hebrew, father of light] **—Abner** A Jewish general; slain by Joab. I *Sam.* xiv 50.

ab·net (ab′net) *n.* A long girdle or sash, usually of linen, worn around the body by ancient Jewish priests. [<Hebrew]

ab·nor·mal (ab·nôr′məl) *adj.* Not according to rule; different from the usual or average; unnatural; irregular. See synonyms under IRREGULAR. [Earlier *anormal* <F <Med.L *anormalus,* alter. of *anomalus* <Gk. *anōmalos* irregular; re-formed on Latin *ab* away, from] **—ab·nor′mal·ly** *adv.*

ab·nor·mal·i·ty (ab′nôr·mal′ə·tē) *n. pl.* **·ties 1** Irregularity. **2** That which is abnormal.

ab·nor·mi·ty (ab·nôr′mə·tē) *n. pl.* **·ties** An irregularity; malformation; a monstrosity. [<L *abnormitas, -tatis* <*abnormis* irregular < *ab-* from + *norma* rule]

ab·o (ab′ō) *n. pl.* **·bos** *Austral.* An Australian aborigine. [Short for *aboriginal*].

Å·bo (ō′bo͞o) Swedish name for TURKU, Finland.

a·board (ə·bôrd′, ə·bōrd′) *adv.* **1** On board; into, in, or on a conveyance. **2** Alongside; on one side. **—all aboard** Get on board or in!: a warning to passengers that their conveyance is about to start. —*prep.* **1** On board of; upon or within, as a conveyance: *aboard* the train. **2** Across or alongside of.

a·bode[1] (ə·bōd′) *n.* **1** A place of abiding; dwelling; home. **2** The state or act of abiding; sojourn; stay. See synonyms under HOME, HOUSE. —*v.* Past tense and past participle of ABIDE. [OE *abad*]

a·bode[2] (ə·bōd′) *Obs. v.t.* & *v.i.* **a·bod·ed, a·bod·ing 1** To forebode; be ominous. **2** To wait or delay. —*n.* An omen. Also *Obs.* **a·bode′ment** *n.* [ME *abeden* announce, OE *abeodan*]

ab·ohm (ab·ōm′) *n.* The cgs electromagnetic unit of resistance, equal to one millionth of an ohm. [<AB(SOLUTE) + OHM]

a·boi·deau (á·bwä·dō′) *n. pl.* **·deaus** -dōz′) or **·deaux** (-dō′) *Canadian* A sluicegate in the dikes along the Bay of Fundy; also, a dike with sluicegates. Also **a·boi·teau′.** [<dial F (Canadian)]

a·bol·ish (ə·bol′ish) *v.t.* To do away with; put an end to; annul; destroy. [<F *aboliss-,* stem of *abolir* <L *abolescere* decay, vanish, inceptive of *abolere* destroy] **—a·bol′ish·a·ble** *adj.* **—a·bol′·ish·er** *n.* **—a·bol′ish·ment** *n.*

Synonyms: abate, abrogate, annihilate, annul, destroy, end, eradicate, exterminate, extirpate, nullify, obliterate, overthrow, prohibit, remove, repeal, reverse, revoke, subvert, supplant, suppress, terminate. *Abolish* is now used only of institutions, customs, and conditions, especially those wide-spread and long-existing; as, to *abolish* poverty. A building that is burned to the ground is said to be *destroyed* by fire. *Annihilate* signifies to put absolutely out of existence. Matter is never *annihilated,* but only changes its form. *Abolish* is not said of laws. There we use *repeal, abrogate, nullify,* etc.; *repeal* by the enacting body, *nullify* by revolutionary proceedings; a later statute *abrogates,* without formally *repealing,* any earlier law with which it conflicts. An appellate court may *reverse* or set aside the decision of an inferior court. *Overthrow* may be used in either a good or a bad sense; *suppress* is commonly in a good, *subvert* always in a bad sense; as to *subvert* our liberties; to *suppress* a rebellion. The law *prohibits* what may never have existed; it *abolishes* an existing evil. We *abate* a nuisance, *terminate* a controversy. Compare CANCEL, DEMOLISH, EXTERMINATE. *Antonyms:* authorize, cherish, confirm, continue, enact, establish, institute, introduce, legalize, promote, reinstate, renew, repair, restore, revive, support, sustain.

ab·o·li·tion (ab′ə·lish′ən) *n.* The act of abolishing; extinction; the state or fact of being abolished; specifically, the abolishing of slavery in the United States. [<L *abolitio, -onis* <*abolere* destroy] **—ab′o·li′tion·al** *adj.*

ab·o·li·tion·ar·y (ab′ə·lish′ən·er′ē) *adj.* Destructive; subversive.

ab·o·li·tion·ism (ab′ə·lish′ən·iz′əm) *n.* The movement of opposition to slavery in the United States. **—ab′o·li′tion·ist** *n.*

a·bol·la (ə·bol′ə) *n. pl.* **a·bol·lae** (-ē) A Roman cloak. [<L]

a·bo·ma (ə·bō′mə) *n.* The ringed boa or one of other large South American snakes of the family *Boidae.* [<Pg.]

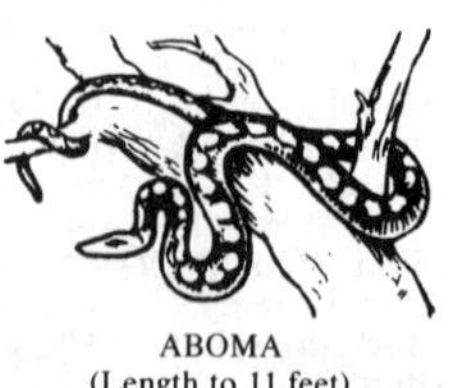
ABOMA
(Length to 11 feet)

ab·o·ma·sum (ab′ə·mā′səm) *n. pl.* **·sa** (-sə) The fourth or true digestive stomach of a ruminant. [<NL <L *ab-* away from + *omasum* bullock's tripe]

A-bomb (ā′bom′) See ATOMIC BOMB under BOMB.

a·bom·i·na·ble (ə·bom′ə·nə·bəl) *adj.* Very hateful; loathsome; detestable; horrible. See synonyms under BAD, CRIMINAL. [<OF <L *abominabilis* <) *abominari.* See ABOMINATE.] **—a·bom′i·na·bly** *adv.*

abominable snowman A legendary humanoid creature supposed to inhabit the Himalayas and reported to leave giant footprints in the snow. Also called *yeti.*

a·bom·i·nate (ə·bom′ə·nāt) *v.t.* **·nat·ed, ·nat·ing 1** To regard with horror or loathing; abhor. **2** To dislike strongly. See synonyms under ABHOR. [<L *abominatus,* pp. of *abominari* abhor as an ill omen < *ab-* off + *omen* omen] **—a·bom′i·na′tor** *n.*

a·bom·i·na·tion (ə·bom′ə·nā′shən) *n.* **1** Strong aversion or loathing; extreme disgust and hatred. **2** Anything that excites disgust, hatred, or loathing; any detestable act or practice; anything vile or shamefully wicked.

Synonyms: abhorrence, abuse, annoyance, aversion, crime, curse, detestation, disgust, evil, execration, hatred, horror, iniquity, nuisance, offense, plague, shame, villainy, wickedness. *Abomination* was originally applied to anything held in religious or ceremonial *aversion* or *abhorrence.* The word is now more often applied to the object of such *aversion* or *abhorrence* than to the state of mind that so regards it; in common use *abomination* signifies something loathed, or that deserves to be. A toad is to many an object of *disgust;* a foul sewer is an *abomination. Antonyms:* affection, appreciation, approval, benefit, blessing, delight, desire, enjoyment, esteem, gratification, joy.

à bon droit (á′ bôn′ drwá′) *French* With justice; rightfully.

à bon mar·ché (á′ bôn ′ már·shā′) *French* At a good bargain; inexpensively.

a·boon (ə·bo͞on′) *adv.* & *prep. Scot.* & *Brit. Dial.* Above.

ab·o·ral (ab·ôr′əl, -ō′rəl) *adj. Zool.* Pertaining to or situated away from the mouth. **—ab·o′ral·ly** *adv.*

ab·o·rig·i·nal (ab′ə·rij′ə·nəl) *adj.* **1** Of or pertaining to the aborigines. **2** Native to the soil; indigenous. —*n.* **1** *pl.* **·nes** (-nēz) *Austral.* An Australian aborigine. **2** An original inhabitant. **—ab′o·rig′i·nal·ly** *adv.*

ab o·rig·i·ne (ab ō·rij′ə·nē) *Latin* From the origin.

ab·o·rig·i·ne (ab′ə·rij′ə·nē) *n.* **1** One of the original native inhabitants of a country, especially Australia. **2** *pl.* Flora and fauna indigenous to a geographical area. [<L *aborigines* earliest inhabitants < *ab origine* from the beginning]

a·born·ing (ə·bôr′ning) *adv.* While being born or produced: to die *aborning.*

a·bort (ə·bôrt′) *v.i.* **1** To bring forth young prematurely; miscarry. **2** *Biol.* To fail of complete development. **3** *Mil.* To fail to carry out a mission. — *v.t.* **4** To cause to have a miscarriage. **5** To bring to a premature or unsuccessful conclusion. [<L *abortus,* pp. of *aboriri* miscarry < *ab-* off, away + *oriri* arise, be born]

a·bor·ti·fa·cient (ə·bôr′tə·fā′shənt) *adj.* Causing abortion. —*n.* Anything used to cause abortion. [<L *abortus* (see ABORT) + *-i-* + -FACIENT]

a·bor·tion (ə·bôr′shən) *n.* **1** The expulsion of a fetus prematurely, when non-viable; miscarriage. **2** A miscarriage produced artificially. **3** The defective result of a premature birth; a monstrosity. **4** *Biol.* Partial or complete arrest of development, as of an embryo. **5** Failure of anything to progress or develop normally or as expected. [<L *abortio, -onis* < *aboriri.* See ABORT.] — **a·bor′tion·al** *adj.*

a·bor·tion·ist (ə·bôr′shən·ist) *n.* One who causes or performs abortion.

a·bor·tive (ə·bôr′tiv) *adj.* **1** Brought forth or born prematurely. **2** Imperfectly developed. **3** Rudimentary, as an organ or stamen. **4** Coming to naught; failing, as an effort. **5** Causing abortion. **6** *Med.* Shortened in its course: an *abortive* fever. See synonyms under USELESS, VAIN. —**a·bor′tive·ly** *adv.* —**a·bor′tive·ness** *n.*

A·bou·kir (ä′bo͞o·kir′, ə·bo͞o′kər) See ABUKIR.

a·bou·li·a (ə·bo͞o′lē·ə), **a·bou·lic** (ə·bo͞o′lik) See ABULIA, etc.

a·bound (ə·bound′) *v.i.* **1** To be in abundance; be plentiful. **2** To have plenty of; be rich in: with *in:* The book *abounds* in humorous incidents. **3** To be full of; teem: with *with:* The lakes *abound* with fish. See synonyms under FLOW. Compare AMPLE. [<OF *abunder* <L *abundare* overflow < *ab-* from + *undare* flow in waves < *unda* wave]

a·bout (ə·bout′) *adv.* **1** Around the outside; on every side: Blessings compass thee *about.* **2** Almost: *about* finished; approximately: in *about* an hour. **3** Around, in revolution or rotation: turn and turn *about.* **4** In any direction; toward any, every, or the opposite side: to look or move *about.* **5** Here and there, as without direction: to wander *about.* —*prep.* **1** On the outside or on every side of; encircling: walls *about* the city. **2** Here and there in; to and fro upon: lambs running *about* the fields. **3** Somewhere near or within; on some side of: Stay *about* the house today. **4** Attached to as an attribute: an aura of sanctity *about* her. **5** Approximating to; not far from, as in quantity or time: leaving *about* midnight; troops numbering *about* four thousand. **6** Engaged in; concerned with: Go on *about* your business; He goes *about* his work skilfully. **7** In reference to; concerning: a book *about* Napoleon. **8** In possession of; at hand: I do not have the money *about* me. See synonyms under AT. [OE *onbūtan, ābūtan*]

a·bout-face (ə·bout′fās′) *n.* **1** *Mil.* A drill movement and command for pivoting about to face in exactly the opposite direction. **2** Any turning around or reversal, as of opinion or point of view, especially if sudden. —*v.i.* (ə) ·bout′fās′) **-faced, -fac·ing 1** To perform an about-face. **2** To change one's opinions, ways, etc.

about-ship (ə·bout′ship′) *v.i.* **-shipped, -ship·ping** *Naut.* To change a ship's course by going on the opposite tack.

a·bove (ə·buv′) *adv.* **1** Vertically up or in a higher place; overhead; on the upper side. **2** Superior in rank or position. **3** In a previous or an earlier place: in the paragraph *above.* **4** In heaven. —*adj.* Given, said, placed, etc., in what is above; preceding. —*n.* That which precedes or is just before; something above. —*prep.* **1** Vertically over; higher than; rising beyond: books piled *above* one another; mountains towering *above* the plain. **2** *Geog.* Farther north than: *above* the fortieth parallel. **3** Exceeding a specific period; more than: a show lasting *above* three hours. **4** More than; in excess of: He ran *above* 500 yards. **5** Surpassing in volume, clearness, or intensity: a voice heard *above* the din. **6** Surpassing in authority, quality, or power: a moral law *above* the civil law. **6** Beyond the reach or influence of: conduct *above* suspicion. [OE *abufen*]

Above may appear as a combining form in open, hyphenated, or closed two-word phrases:

above all	**above measure**
above-cited	**above-mentioned**
above deck	**above-named**
above-given	**above-quoted**
aboveground	**above-said**
above-listed	**above-written**

Synonyms (prep.): on, over, upon. *Above* is the most inclusive of these prepositions. It can ordinarily be substituted for *on, upon,* or *over;* as, the boards were piled one *on* or *upon* another (one *above* another), the hawk flies *over* the wood (*above* the wood). But it will be seen that while *above* is more inclusive it is less definite; the boards laid one *on* another are in contact, but when laid one *above* another, they may not touch. *Over* often contains an intimation of extension or motion across, while *above* may simply imply greater elevation. If we say, the mountain towers *above* the plain, we think only of its height; but if we say, the mountain towers *over* the plain, we think of the plain as in the shadow of the mountain and dominated by it. So we say the mountain is 7,000 feet *above* the sea, where it would be impossible to say 7,000 feet *over* the sea. *Upon* is practically identical with *on,* preference being generally for euphonic reasons. *Antonyms:* see BENEATH.

a·bove·board (ə·buv′bôrd′, -bōrd′) *adj. & adv.* In open sight; hence, without concealment, fraud, or trickery; honest. See synonyms under CANDID.

a·bove·ground (a·buv′ground′) *adj. & adv.* **1** Above the surface of the ground: *aboveground* nuclear testing. **2** In the open; not secret. **3** Not buried; alive.

a·bove·men·tioned (ə·buv′men′shənd) *adj.* mentioned before: the *abovementioned* data.

ab o·vo (ab ō′vō) *Latin* From the beginning; literally, from the egg.

ab·ra·ca·dab·ra (ab′rə·kə·dab′rə) *n.* A cabalistic word written in triangular form, anciently used as a preventive or curative charm; a spell; hence, any jargon of conjuring or nonsensical words. [<L]

a·brade (a·brād′) *v.t.* **a·brad·ed, a·brad·ing** To rub or wear off by friction; scrape away. [<L *abradere* <*ab-* away + *radere* scrape] —**a·bra′dant** *adj. & n.* —**a·brad′er** *n.*

A·bra·ham (ā′brə·ham; *Dan., Du., Ger., Sw.* ä′brä·häm) A masculine personal name. Also *Fr.* **A·bra·ham** (à·brà·àm′), *Ital.* **A·bra·ha·mo** (ä′brä·ä′mō), *Lat.* **A·bra·ha·mus** (ä′brə·hä ′·məs), *Pg.* **A·bra·hão** (ä ′brä·oun′), *Sp.* **A·bra·han** (ä′brä·än′). [<Hebrew, ? father of a multitude (of nations)] —**Abraham** The progenitor of the Hebrews; first called Abram.

Abraham, Plains of The plateau in the SW part of the city of Quebec, Canada: battlefield where the British defeated the French in 1759, establishing British control of Canada.

Abraham Lincoln Birthplace National Historical Site A park near Hodgenville, central Kentucky, containing a memorial that encloses a 19th century cabin replicating the one in which Lincoln was born.

A·bram (ā′brəm; *Fr.* à·brän′; *Sp.* ä·bräm′) A masculine personal name. Also *Ital.* **A·bra·mo** (ä·brä′mō), *Lat.* **A·bra·mus** (ä·brä′məs). [<Hebrew, ? exalted father] —**Abram** Abraham, before God changed his name. *Gen.* xvii 5.

a·bran·chi·al (ə·brang′kē·əl, ā-) *adj.* Without gills. Also **a·bran·chi·ate** (ə·brang′kē·it, -āt, ā-), **a·bran·chi·ous** (ə·brang′kē·əs, ā-). [<A-[4] without + Gk. *branchia* gills]

a·bra·sion (ə·brā′zhən) *n.* **1** The act or result of abrading. **2** *Geol.* A wearing away, as of rocks by glaciers. **3** An abraded place. See synonyms under FRICTION. [<L *abrasio, -onis* <*abradere.* See ABRADE.]

a·bra·sive (ə·brā′siv, -ziv) *adj.* Abrading or tending to abrade. —*n.* An abrading substance.

ab·re·act (ab′rē·akt′) *v.t. Psychoanal.* To produce abreaction. [< *abreaction*]

ab·re·ac·tion (ab′rē·ak′shən) *n. Psychoanal.* The releasing of pent-up emotion or disagreeable memories by reliving them through words, feelings, or actions: a form of catharsis. [<AB-[1] from + REACTION, after G *abreagierung*]

ab·re·ac·tive (ab′rē·ak′tiv) *adj.* Pertaining to or causing abreaction.

a·breast (ə·brest′) *adv.* Side by side and equally advanced. —**abreast of** (or **with**) Side by side with; not behind or ahead of.

a·bri (ə·brē′, *Fr.* à ·brē′) *n. pl.* **a·bris** (ə·brēz′, *Fr.* à·brē′) A refuge or shelter; specifically, a dug-out or an air-raid shelter. [<F]

a·bridge (ə·brij′) *v.t.* **a·bridged, a·bridg·ing 1** To give the substance of in fewer words; condense; epitomize. **2** To shorten, as in time. **3** To curtail or lessen, as rights. **4** To deprive; stint, as a person of privileges: with *of.* See synonyms under ABBREVIATE, RESTRAIN, RETRENCH. [<OF *abregier* <L *abbreviare.* Doublet of ABBREVIATE]

a·bridg·ment (ə·brij′mənt) *n.* **1** The act of abridging; the state of being abridged. **2** Something that has been abridged; an epitome or abstract. **3** *Obs.* That which causes time to pass quickly. Also **a·bridge′ment.**

Synonyms: abbreviation, abstract, analysis, compend, compendium, conspectus, digest, epitome, outline, *précis,* summary, synopsis. An *abridgment* gives the most important portions of a work substantially as they stand. An *outline* or *synopsis* is a kind of sketch closely following the plan. An *abstract, digest* or *précis* is an independent statement of what a book or an article contains, the *abstract* closely following the main heads, the *digest* or *précis* giving the substance with careful consideration of all. An *analysis* draws out the chief thoughts or arguments, expressed or implied. An *epitome, compend,* or *compendium* is a condensed view of a subject, whether derived from a previous publication or not. See ABBREVIATION. *Antonyms:* amplification, expansion, paraphrase.

a·brim (ə·brim′) *adj.* Brimming: eyes *abrim* with tears.

a·broach (ə·brōch′) *adj.* & adv. In a condition to let out the liquor; on tap; in circulation; astir. [<A-[1] on. + BROACH]

a·broad (ə·brôd′) *adv.* **1** Out of one's home or abode; out of doors. **2** Out of one's own country; in or into foreign lands. **3** Broadly; widely; at large; in circulation. **4** Wide of the mark; astray. [ME *abroad.* See A-[1] and BROAD.]

ab·ro·gate (ab′rə·gāt) *v.t.* **·gat·ed, ·gat·ing** To annul by authority, as a law; abolish; repeal. See synonyms under ABOLISH, ANNUL, CANCEL. [<L *abrogatus,* pp. of *abrogare* <*ab-* away + *rogare* ask, propose] —**ab·ro·ga·ble** (ab′rə) ·gə·bəl) *adj.* —**ab′ro·ga′ tive** *adj.* —**ab′ro·ga′tor** *n.*

ab·ro·ga·tion (ab′rə·gā′shən) *n.* The act or process of abrogating; authoritative repeal.

a·brupt (ə·brupt′) *adj.* **1** Beginning, ending, or changing suddenly; broken off. **2** Unceremonious; sudden, as a departure. **3** Changing subject suddenly; unconnected, as style. **4** Steep, as a cliff. See synonyms under BLUFF[2], STEEP[1]. [<L *abruptus,* pp. of *abrumpere* <*ab-* off + *rumpere* break] —**a·brup′tion** *n.* **a·brupt′ly** *adv.* —**a·brupt′ness** *n.*

A·bruz·zi (ä·bro͞ot′tsē), **Duke of the,** Prince Luigi of Savoy-Aosta, 1873–1933, Italian naval officer and explorer.

A·bruz·zi (ä·bro͞ot′tsē) A region of central Italy on the Adriatic, including the most rugged part of the Apennines.

abs- Var. of AB-.

Ab·sa·lom (ab′sə·ləm) A masculine personal name. [<Hebrew, the father is peace] —**Absalom** The favorite and rebellious son of David. II *Sam.* xiii–xix.

ab·scess (ab′ses) *n.* A collection of pus in a body cavity formed by tissue disintegration; it may be caused by bacteria and is often accompanied by painful inflammation. —*v.i.* to form an abscess. [<L *abscessus* <*absceddere* go away < *ab-* away + *cedere* go; with ref. to the flowing of humors into the area] —**ab′scessed** *adj.*

ab·scind (ab·sind′) *v.t.* To cut off. [<L *absindere* <*ab-* off + *scindere* cut]

ABSCISSA
AB: X-axis. AC: Y-axis. *df* or *Ae*: abscissa of point *f*.

ab·scis·sa (ab·sis′ə) *n. pl.* **ab·scis·sas** or **ab·scis·sae** (-ē) The distance of any point from the vertical Y-axis of ordinates in a two-dimensional system of reference, measured on a line parallel to the horizontal X-axis of abscissas. [<L *(linea) abscissa* (line) cut off, fem. of *abscissus,* pp. of *abscindere.* See ABSCIND.]

ab·scis·sion (ab·sizh′ən, sish′ən) *n.* **1** The act of cutting off or the state of being cut off or removed. **2** *Bot.* The shedding of parts of a plant by the action of certain cells located in the branch or bark; also, the freeing of a fungus spore through breakdown of a portion of its stalk. **3** In rhetoric, an abrupt breaking off for effect, as in the middle of a sentence. Compare APOSIOPESIS. [<L *abscissio, -onis* < *abscindere.* See ABSCIND.]

ab·sciss layer (ab′sis) *Bot.* A layer of cells formed in autumn at the base of the petiole, permitting the leaf to fall. Also **abscission layer.**

ab·scond (ab·skond′) *v.i.* To depart suddenly and secretly; to escape and hide oneself. See synonyms under ESCAPE. [<L *abscondere* <*ab-* away + *condere* store] **—ab·scon′dence** *n.* **—ab·scond′er** *n.*

ab·scond·ee (ab·skon′dē) *n.* One who absconds; absconder.

ab·sence (ab′səns) *n.* **1** The state, fact, or time of not being present. **2** Lack; want. **3** Mental abstraction; lack of attention. See synonyms under WANT. [<F <L *absentia* <*absens.* See ABSENT.]

ab·sent (ab′sənt) *adj.* **1** Not present. **2** Lacking; missing; nonexistent: In some fishes the ribs are *absent.* **3** Inattentive; absent-minded. See synonyms under INATTENTIVE. *—v.t.* (ab·sent′) To take or keep (oneself) away; not be present. [<L *absens, -entis,* ppr. of *abesse* <*ab-* away + *esse* be] **—ab·sen·ta·tion** (ab′sən·tā′shən) *n.* **—ab·sent′er** *n.* **—ab′sent·ly** *adv.* **—ab′sent·ness** *n.*

ab·sen·tee (ab′sən·tē′) *n.* One who is absent, as from a job. *—adj.* **1** Relating to one who is temporarily absent: an *absentee* voter. **2** Nonresident: an *absentee* landlord. **—ab′·sen·tee′ism** *n.*

ab·sen·te re·o (ab·sen′tē rē′ō) *Law Latin* In the absence of the defendant.

ab·sent-mind·ed (ab′sənt·mīn′did) *adj.* Lacking in attention to immediate demands or business because of preoccupation. See synonyms under ABSTRACTED. **—ab′sent-mind′ed·ly** *adv.* **—ab′sent-mind′ed·ness** *n.*

absent without leave Absent from a military duty or post without permission from the proper authority, but not intending to desert. Abbr. *AWOL, awol, A.W.O.L., a.w.o.l.*

ab·sinthe (ab′sinth) *n.* **1** Wormwood or absinthium. **2** A green, bitter, alcoholic liqueur having the flavor of licorice, made from oils of wormwood and other aromatics. Also **ab′sinth.** [<F <L *absinthium* wormwood <Gk. *apsinthion*] **—ab·sin′thi·al, ab·sin′thi·an** *adj.*

ab·sin·thi·um (ab·sin′thē·əm) *n.* **1** Common wormwood; the aromatic bitter herb *Artemisia absinthium.* **2** The dried leaves and flowers of this herb, used in medicine as a gastric tonic and cardiac stimulant. [<L. See ABSINTHE.]

ab·so·lute (ab′sə·lo͞ot) *adj.* **1** Free from restriction or relation; unlimited; independent; unconditional: an *absolute* monarchy. **2** Complete; perfect. **3** Unadulterated; pure. **4** Postive; entire; total; unquestionable. **5** *Gram.* **a** Free from the usual relations of syntax or construction with other words in the sentence, as *It being late* in *It being late, we started home.* **b** Of a transitive verb, having no object expressed and, hence, functioning as intransitive, as *He writes well.* **c** Of an adjective standing without a noun, as *Only the brave deserve the fair.* **6** *Physics* Not dependent on any arbitrary standard; non-relative; specifically determined or measured only by the fundamental notions of space, mass, and time: *absolute* measurement; also, relating to the absolute-temperature scale: 15° *absolute.* *—n.* That which is absolute or perfect. **—the Absolute** The ultimate basis of all thought, reasoning, or being; God. [<L *absolutus,* pp. of *absolvere.* See ABSOLVE.] **—ab′so·lute′ness** *n.*

Synonyms (adj.): arbitrary, autocratic, despotic, infinite, perfect, pure, supreme, tyrannical, unconditional, unequivocal. As used of human authorities, *absolute* signifies free from limitation by other authority and *supreme* exalted over all other; as, an *absolute* monarch, the *supreme* court. As *absolute* power in human hands is usually abused, the unfavorable meaning of the word predominates. *Autocratic* power is *absolute* power self-established and self-maintained. *Despotic* is commonly applied to a masterful or severe use of power, which is expressed more decidedly by *tyrannical. Arbitrary* may be used in good sense; as, the pronunciation of proper names is *arbitrary;* but the bad sense is the prevailing one; as, an *arbitrary* proceeding, *arbitrary* power. Compare ARBITRARY, FLAT[1], IMPERIOUS, INFINITE, PERFECT. *Antonyms:* accountable, conditional, conditioned, constitutional, limited, responsible, restrained.

absolute alcohol Ethyl alcohol containing not more than 1 percent alcohol.

ab·so·lute·ly (ab′sə·lo͞ot′lē, *emphatic* ab′sə·lo͞ot′lē) *adv.* **1** Completely; unconditionally. **2** *Colloq.* Positively. **3** *Gram.* So as not to take an object: to use a verb *absolutely.*

absolute magnitude A measure of the intrinsic, as distinguished from the apparent, brightness of a star. It is equal to the luminosity a star would have if located at the standard distance of 10 parsecs from the sun.

absolute music See under MUSIC.

absolute pitch **1** The pitch of a musical tone determined by the number of its vibrations per second in relation to the frequency of a basic or standard tone (usually middle C). **2** The inherent ability to discriminate an isolated note. Also called *perfect pitch.*

absolute temperature Temperature reckoned from absolute zero.

absolute zero That temperature at which a body would be wholly deprived of heat, and at which a perfect gas would exert no pressure: equivalent to about −273°C, −459°F, or −219° Réaumur.

ab·so·lu·tion (ab′sə·lo͞o′shən) *n.* **1** An absolving, or a being absolved; forgiveness. **2** In the Roman Catholic Church, the act of a priest in pronouncing the remission of sin, its eternal punishment, or the canonical penalties attached to it; the act of releasing from censure without the sacrament of penance; or a solemn rite performed at the end of a requiem mass. **3** In other churches, the declaration or imploring of God's forgiveness by a priest or minister; also, the forgiveness itself. [<L *absolutio, -onis* <*absolvere.* See ABSOLVE.]

ab·so·lu·tism (ab′sə·lo͞o·tiz′əm) *n.* **1** The doctrine or practice of unlimited authority and control; despotism; predestination. **2** Absoluteness; positiveness. **—ab′so·lu′tist** *n.* **—ab′so·lu·tis′tic** *adj.*

ab·sol·u·to·ry (ab·sol′yə·tôr′ē, -tō′rē) *adj.* Having power to absolve; absolving. [<L *absolutorius* < *absolvere.* See ABSOLVE.]

ab·solve (ab·solv′, -zolv′) *v.t.* **ab·solved, ab·solv·ing** **1** To pronounce free from the penalties or consequences of an action: His excuses do not *absolve* him from blame. **2** To acquit, as of guilt or complicity. **3** To release from an obligation, liability, or promise. **4** *Eccl.* To grant a remission of sin, its punishment, or the canonical penance attached to it; pardon. [<L *absolvere* <*ab-* from + *solvere* loose. Doublet of ASSOIL.] **—ab·solv′a·ble** *adj.* **—ab·sol′vent** *adj. & n.* **—ab·solv′er** *n.*

Synonyms: acquit, clear, discharge, exculpate, exempt, exonerate, forgive, free, justify, liberate, pardon, release. To *absolve,* in the strict sense, is to *set free* from any bond. One may be *absolved* from a promise by a breach of faith on the part of one to whom the promise was made. To *absolve* from sins is formally to remit their condemnation and penalty. To *acquit* of sin or crime is to *free* from the accusation of it; the innocent are rightfully *acquitted;* the guilty may be mercifully *absolved.* Compare JUSTIFY, PARDON. *Antonyms:* accuse, bind, charge, compel, condemn, convict, impeach, inculpate, obiligate, oblige.

ab·so·nant (ab′sə·nənt) *adj.* Discordant; unreasonable. [<AB-[1] + L *sonans.* See SONANT.]

ab·sorb (ab·sôrb′, -zôrb′) *v.t.* **1** To drink in or suck up, as through or into pores: A sponge *absorbs* water. **2** To engross completely; occupy wholly: Study *absorbs* me. **3** *Physics, Chem.* To take up or in by chemical or molecular action, as gases, heat, liquid, light, etc.: distinguished from *adsorb.* **4** To assimilate, as in the processes of nutrition and growth. **5** To take in and incorporate so as to swallow up identity or individuality: The city *absorbs* the suburbs. **6** To receive the force or action of; intercept: A spring *absorbs* a jar or jolt. **7** To take up entirely by purchase or use, as an issue of bonds or the output of a factory. [<L *absorbere* < *ab-* from + *sorbere* suck in] **—ab·sorb′a·bil′i·ty** *n.* **—ab·sorb′a·ble** *adj.* **—ab·sorb′ing** *adj.* **—ab·sorb′ing·ly** *adv.*

Synonyms: consume, engross, exhaust, imbibe, swallow. A fluid that is *absorbed* is taken up into the mass of the *absorbing* body, with which it may or may not permanently combine. A substance is *consumed* which is appropriated by some other substance, being, or agency, so that it ceases to exist or to be recognized as existing in its original condition; fuel is *consumed* in the fire, food in the body; *consume* also means to buy and use up, as an individual or the public *consumes* coal. A great talker *engrosses* the listeners. A credulous person *swallows* the most preposterous statement. A busy student is *absorbed* in a subject that takes his whole attention. *Antonyms:* disgorge, disperse, dissipate, distract, eject, emit, exude, radiate.

ab·sorbed (ab·sôrbd′, -zôrbd′) *adj.* **1** Deeply engrossed; rapt. **2** Sucked up or sunken in, as paint on a porous surface. See synonyms under ABSTRACTED. **—ab·sorb·ed·ly** (ab·sôr′·bid·lē,-zôr′-) *adv.* **—ab·sorb′ed·ness** *n.*

ab·sor·be·fa·cient (ab·sôr′bə·fā′shənt, -zôr′-) *adj.* Causing absorption or drying up. *—n.* A substance causing or promoting absorption. [<L *absorbere* (see ABSORB) + -FACIENT]

ab·sor·bent (ab·sôr′bənt, -zôr′-) *adj.* Absorbing or tending to absorb. *— n.* A substance, duct, etc., that absorbs. [<L *absorbens, -entis,* ppr. of *absorbere.* See ABSORB.] **—ab·sor′·ben·cy** *n.*

ab·sorb·er (ab·sôr′bər, -zôr′-) *n.* **1** One who or that which absorbs. **2** *Mech.* A part, as in a caloric engine, having the function of absorbing heat and giving it out later; a regenerator. **3** In an automobile spring, a device for absorbing the shock or jar of a machine in motion; a shock absorber.

ab·sorp·tance (ab·sôrp′təns, -zôrp′-) *n.* The ratio of the light absorbed by a body to the light that enters it.

ab·sorp·tion (ab·sôrp′shən, -zôrp′-) *n.* **1** The act of absorbing or the condition of being absorbed. **2** *Physics* **a** The process by which a liquid or gas is taken into the interstices of a porous substance and held there. **b** The transformation of any emission as it passes through a material substance. **3** Engrossment of the mind; preoccupation. **4** Assimilation, as by incorporation or by the digestive process. **—ab·sorp′tive** *adj.* **—ab·sorp′tive·ness, ab′·sorp·tiv′i·ty** *n.* [<L *absorptio, -onis* <*absorbere.* See ABSORB.]

absorption spectrum A spectrum which, by characteristic dark lines, indicates the presence of a substance absorbing certain wavelengths of a continuous spectrum: distinguished from *emission spectrum.*

abs·que hoc (abz′kwē hok′) *Latin* Without this.

ab·stain (ab·stān′) *v.i.* To keep oneself back; refrain voluntarily: with *from.* See synonyms under CEASE, REFRAIN[1]. [<F *abstenir* <L *abstinere a*<*ab-* from + *tenere* hold]

ab·stain·er (ab·stā′nər) *n.* One who abstains; especially a teetotaler.

ab·ste·mi·ous (ab·stē′mē·əs) *adj.* **1** Eating and drinking sparingly. **2** Characterized by or spent in abstinence; avoiding excess; self-denying; temperate. See synonyms under SOBER. <L *abstemius* temperate < *ab-* from + root of *temetum* intoxicating drink] **—ab·ste′mi·ous·ly** *adv.* **—ab·ste′mi·ous·ness** *n.*

ab·sten·tion (ab·sten′shən) *n.* A refraining or abstaining. [<L *abstentio, -onis* < *abstinere.* See ABSTAIN.] **— ab·sten′tious** *adj.*

ab·sterge (ab·stûrj′) *v.t.* **·sterged, ·sterg·ing** **1** To wipe away; cleanse. **2** To purge. [<L *abstergere* < *ab-* away + *tergere* wipe] **— ab·ster·sion** (ab·stûr′shən, -zhən) *n.* **— ab·ster·sive** (ab·stûr′siv) *adj.*

ab·ster·gent (ab·stûr′jənt) *adj.* Cleansing. *— n.* A cleansing substance.

ab·sti·nence (ab′stə·nəns) *n.* The act or practice of abstaining; forbearing voluntarily, especially from intoxicating drinks or sexual activity; self–denial. [<F <L *abstinentia* < *abstinere.* See ABSTAIN.]

Synonyms: abstemiousness, continence, fasting, frugality, moderation, self–control, self–denial, self–restraint, sobriety, temperance. *Abstinence* from food commonly signifies going without; *abstemiousness,* partaking moderately; *abstinence* may be for a single occasion, *abstemiousness* is habitual *moderation. Self–denial* is giving up what one wishes; *abstinence* may be refraining from what one does not desire. *Fasting* is *abstinence* from food for a limited time, and generally for religious reasons. *Sobriety* and *temperance* signify moderate indulgence. Total *abstinence* has come to signify the entire abstaining from intoxicating liquors or sexual activity. *Antonyms:* drunkness, excess, gluttony, greed, intemperance, intoxication, reveling, revelry, self–indulgence sensuality, wantonness.

ab•sti•nent (ab′stə•nənt) *adj.* Abstemious. See synonyms under SOBER. — **ab′sti•nent•ly** *adv.*

ab•stract (ab•strakt′, ab′strakt) *adj.* **1** Considered apart from the concrete; general, as opposed to particular. **2** Theoretical; ideal, as opposed to practical. **3** Considered or expressed without reference to particular example, as numbers, attributes, or qualities: 8 is an *abstract* number; Redness and valor are *abstract* nouns. **4** Withdrawn from contemplation of present objects; abstracted. **5** *Philos.* Dissociated from closely applied perceptions or ideas: *abstract* truth. **6** In art, generalized or universal, as opposed to concrete, specific, or representational; tending away from the realistic or literal. —*n.* (ab′•strakt) **1** A summary or epitome. **2** *Law* A compendium. **3** *Logic* An abstract idea or term. **4** *Gram.* An abstract noun. See under NOUN. **5** In pharmacy, the preparation of a drug in powder form. See synonyms under ABBREVIATION, ABRIDGMENT. — **in the abstract** Apart from concrete relation or embodiment; in its general reference or meaning; abstractly. —*v.t.* (ab•strakt′) **1** To take away; remove. **2** To take away secretly; purloin. **3** To withdraw or disengage (the attention, interest, etc.). **4** To consider apart from particular or material instances; form a general notion of: to *abstract* the idea of humanity from a crowd of men. **5** (ab′strakt) To make an abstract of, as a book or treatise; summarize; abridge. [<L *abstractus,* pp. of *abstrahere* < *ab-* away + *trahere* draw] — **ab•stract′er** *n.* — **ab•stract′ly** *adv.* — **ab•stract′ness** *n.*

Synonyms (verb): detach, disengage, divide, draw, purloin, remove, separate, steal, withdraw. The central idea of *withdrawing* makes *abstract* in common speech a euphemism for *purloin, steal.* In mental processes, we *separate* some one element from all that does not necessarily belong to it, *abstract* it, and view it alone. The mind is *abstracted* when it is *withdrawn* from all other subjects and concentrated upon one. *Antonyms:* add, increase, insert, interpose, restore, unite.

ab•stract•ed (ab•strak′tid) *adj.* **1** Absent–minded. **2** Separated from all else; apart; abstruse. — **ab•stract′ed•ly** *adv.* — **ab•stract′ed•ness** *n.*

Synonym: absent, absent–minded, absorbed, heedless, inattentive, oblivious, preoccupied. As regards mental action, *absorbed, abstracted,* and *preoccupied* refer to the cause, *absent* or *absent–minded* to the effect. The person *absorbed* in one thing will appear *absent* in others. The *absent–minded* person is *oblivious* of ordinary matters. One who is *preoccupied* is intensely busy in thought; one may be *absent–minded* simply through inattention, with fitful and aimless wandering of thought. Compare ABSTRACT. *Antonyms:* alert, attentive, ready.

abstract idea A mental representation or concept that isolates and generalizes an aspect or quality of an object or of a group of experiences, from which relationships may be or are perceived.

ab•strac•tion (ab•strak′shən) *n.* **1** State of being abstracted; an abstracting. **2** An abstract idea; a theory. **3** Separation; removal; theft. **4** Absence of mind; preoccupation. **5** Seclusion of life, as by a hermit; withdrawal from worldly objects. **6** The quality that makes a work of art generalized or universal, as distinguished from literal or concrete, present in varying degrees in widely differing art forms. **7** An art form or a work of art in which the qualities are either predominantly or totally abstract: opposed to *naturalism, realism.* Compare NON–OBJECTIVE ART. [<L *abstractio, -onis* < *abstractus.* See ABSTRACT.]

ab•strac•tive (ab•strak′tiv) *adj.* Of, pertaining to, or tending to abstraction; having the power of abstraction; epitomizing. — **ab•strac′tive•ly** *adv.* — **ab•strac′tive•ness** *n.*

abstract of title A document containing a brief and orderly statement of the original grant and subsequent conveyances and encumbrances relating to the title and ownership of real estate.

ab•stric•tion (ab•strik′shən) *n. Bot.* A process of spore–formation in certain fungi, in which the sporophore becomes constricted by septa at the place of division. [<AB-[1] + L *strictio, -onis* a binding < *stringere* bind]

ab•struse (ab•stro͞os′) *adj.* **1** Hard to understand. **2** *Obs.* Hidden; concealed. See synonyms under COMPLEX, MYSTERIOUS, OBSCURE. [<L *abstrusus,* pp. of *abstrudere* < *ab-* away + *trudere* thrust] — **ab•struse′ly** *adv.* — **ab•struse′ness** *n.*

ab•surd (ab•sûrd′, -zûrd′) *adj.* Opposed to manifest reason or truth; irrational; preposterous; ridiculous. — *n.* a literary and philosophical term suggesting the illogicality or pointlessness of the human condition from an existential point of view. [<F *absurde* <L *absurdus* out of tune, incongruous, senseless < *ab-* completely + *surdus* deaf] — **ab•surd′ly** *adv.* — **ab•surd′ness** *n.*

Synonyms: anomalous, foolish, incorrect, irrational, ludicrous, mistaken, monstrous, nonsensical, paradoxical, preposterous, ridiculous, senseless, stupid, unreasonable, wild. That is *absurd* which is contrary to the first principles of reasoning; as, that a part should be greater than the whole is *absurd.* A *paradoxical* statement appears at first thought contradictory or *absurd,* while it may be really true. Anything is *irrational* when clearly contrary to sound reason, *foolish* when contrary to practical good sense, *unreasonable* when there seems a perverse bias or an intent to go wrong. *Monstrous* and *preposterous* refer to what is overwhelmingly *absurd.* The *ridiculous* or the *nonsensical* is worthy only to be laughed at. Compare INCONGRUOUS. *Antonyms:* consistent, demonstrable, established, incontestable, incontrovertible, indisputable, indubitable, logical, rational, reasonable, sagacious, sensible, sound, substantial, true, undeniable, unquestionable, wise.

ab•surd•i•ty (ab•sûr′də•tē, -zûr′-) *n. pl.* **•ties 1** The quality of being absurd. **2** Something absurd.

A•bu–Bek•r (ə•bo͞o′•bek′ər), 573–634, first Moslem caliph of Mecca and Mohammed's successor.

A•bu•kir (ä′bo͞o•kir′, ə•bo͞o′kər) A village in northern Egypt on the western limit of **Abukir Bay** on the Mediterranean, site of the Battle of the Nile, 1798, where the British defeated the Napoleonic naval forces: also *Aboukir.*

a•bu•li•a (ə•bo͞o′lē•ə, ə•byo͞o′-) *n. Psychiatry* A form of mental derangement in which the will power is lost or impaired: also *aboulia.* [< *NL* < *Gk. aboulia* < *a-* without + *boulē* will] — **a•bu′lic** *adj.*

A•bul Ka•sim (ə•bo͝ol′ kä′sim), died 1013? Arab surgeon and medical encyclopedist. Also *Albucasis.*

a•bun•dance (ə•bun′dəns) *n.* A plentiful supply; a great quantity or number; copiousness; plenty. See synonyms under COMFORT. [<OF <L *abundantia* < *abundans.* See ABUNDANT.]

a•bun•dant (ə•bun′dənt) *adj.* Affording a plentiful supply; abounding; ample; copious. See synonyms under AMPLE. [<OF <L *abundans, -antis,* ppr. of *abundare.* See ABOUND.] — **a•bun′dant•ly** *adv.*

ab ur•be con•di•ta (ab ûr′bē kon′di•tə) *Latin* From the founding of the city (of Rome, about 753 B.C.). Abbr. *A.U.C.*

a•buse (ə•byo͞oz′) *v.t.* **a•bused, a•bus•ing 1** use improperly or injuriously; misuse. **2** To hurt by treating wrongly; injure: to *abuse* friendship. **3** To speak in coarse or bad terms of; revile; malign. **4** *Obs.* To deceive. —*n.* (ə•byo͞os′) **1** Improper or injurious use; perversion; misuse. **2** Ill–treatment; cruel treatment; injury. **3** Vicious conduct, practice, or act. **4** Vituperation; slander. See synonyms under ABOMINATION, OUTRAGE. [<F *abuser* <L *abusus,* pp. of *abuti* misuse < *ab-* away + *uti* use] — **a•bus′er** *n.*

Synonyms (verb): damage, defame, defile, harm, ill–treat, ill–use, injure, malign, maltreat, misemploy, misuse, molest, oppress, persecute, pervert, pollute, prostitute, ravish, reproach, revile, ruin, slander, victimize, vilify, violate, vituperate, wrong. *Abuse* covers all unreasonable or improper use or treatment by word or act. A tenant does not *abuse* rented property by reasonable wear, even if that may *damage* the property and *injure* its sale; he may *abuse* it by needless defacement or neglect. *Defame, malign, revile, slander, vilify,* and *vituperate* are used always in a bad sense. One may be justly *reproached.* To *persecute* one is to *ill–treat* him for opinion's sake, commonly for religious belief; to *oppress* is generally for political or pecuniary motives. *Misemploy, misuse,* and *pervert* are commonly applied to objects rather than to persons. Compare POLLUTE. *Antonyms:* applaud, benefit, cherish, conserve, consider, eulogize, extol, favor, laud, panegyrize, praise, protect, respect, shield, sustain, uphold, vindicate.

A•bu Sim•bel (ä′bo͞o sim′bel) Site of ancient rock temples on the west bank of the Nile in southern Egypt: also *Ipsambul.*

ABU SIMBEL
Colossal statues of Rameses II.

a•bu•sive (ə•byo͞o′siv) *adj.* **1** Of the nature of or characterized by abuse; harsh; vituperative. **2** Using wrongly or improperly; misapplying. — **a•bu′sive•ly** *adv.* — **a•bu′sive•ness** *n.*

a•but (ə•but′) *v.* **a•but•ted, a•but•ting** *v.i.* To touch, join, or cause to adjoin or touch at the end or side; border: with *on, upon,* or *against.* —*v.t.* To border on; end at: This building *abuts* the park. See synonyms under ADJACENT. [<OF *abouter* border on (< *a-* to + *bout* end); infl. by OF *abuter* touch with an end (< *a-* to + *but* end)] — **a•but′ter** *n.* — **a•but′ting** *adj.*

a•bu•ti•lon (ə•byo͞o′tə•lon) *n.* Any plant of a genus (*Abutilon*) of the mallow family having single bell–shaped flowers: some cultivated varieties are called *flowering maple.* [<NL <Arabic *aubūtīlūn*]

a•but•ment (ə•but′mənt) *n.* **1** The act of abutting. **2** That which abuts, or the place which is abutted upon. **3** A supporting or buttressing structure, as at the end of a bridge or wall; also, that part of an arch that takes the thrust or strain. For illustration see ARCH. **4** *Mil.* The block at the rear end of a gun that receives the rearward pressure of explosion or detonation.

a•but•tal (ə•but′l) *n.* **1** An abutting or abutment. **2** An abutting part; a boundary.

ab•volt (ab•vōlt′) *n.* The cgs electromagnetic unit of electromotive force, equal to one one–hundred–millionth of a volt. [<AB(SOLUTE) + VOLT]

a•by (ə•bī′) *v.t.* **a•bought** *Obs.* **1** To pay the penalty for. **2** To endure; suffer, as a fate. Also **a•bye′.** [OE *ābycgan* pay for]

A•by•dos (ə•bī′dos) **1** An ancient Greek city of Asia Minor opposite Sestos at the narrowest point of the Hellespont. **2** The site of a group of ancient temples in central Egypt.

a•bysm (ə•biz′əm) *n.* An abyss; an unfathomable depth. [<OF *abisme* <L *abyssus* ABYSS]

a•bys•mal (ə•biz′məl) *adj.* Unfathomable; hence, extreme: an *abysmal* ignorance. —**a•bys′mal•ly** *adv.*

a•byss (ə•bis′) *n.* **1** A bottomless gulf. **2** Hell. **3** Any vast depth; hence, a great moral or intellectual depth: an *abyss* of degradation and humiliation. **4** The lowest depths of the sea. [<L *abyssus* <Gk. *abyssos* < *a-* without + *byssos* bottom]

a•bys•sal (ə•bis′əl) *adj.* **1** Pertaining to an

abyss. 2 Designating those ocean depths beyond the continental shelf. Also **a·bys′sic.** (ə·bis′ik).

Ab·ys·sin·i·a (ab′ə·sin′ē·ə) Ethiopia. —**Ab′ys·sin·i·an** *adj. & n.*

Abyssinian cat Any of a breed of medium-sized cats with long, tapering tails, small paws, and short, silky hair with dark-colored tips.

ac- Assimilated var. of AD-.

-ac *suffix* 1 Having; affected by: *demoniac.* 2 Pertaining to; of: *cardiac.* [<Gk. *-akos* or L *-acus* or F *-aque*]

Ac *Chem.* Actinium (symbol Ac).

a·ca·cia (ə·kā′shə) *n.* 1 Any of a large genus (*Acacia*) of flowering trees and shrubs of the bean family found in the tropics and warm temperate regions, especially the green wattle acacia (*A. decurrens*) of Australia. 2 The common locust tree. 3 Gum arabic or gummy exudation of certain acacias. [<L <Gk. *akakia* a thorny tree of Egypt < *akē* point]

Ac·a·deme (ak′ə·dēm′, ak′ə·dēm) The garden or grove near ancient Athens where Plato taught. — *n.* 1 A school. 2 The scholarly life. [<L *academia.* See ACADEMY.]

a·cad·e·mese (ə·kad′ə·mēz′) *n.* The jargon characteristic of academia.

ac·a·dem·i·a (ak′ə·dē′mē·ə) *n. Often cap.* Academic institutions collectively; the academic world. [<L. See ACADEMY.]

ac·a·dem·ic (ak′ə·dem′ik) *adj.* 1 Pertaining to an academy, college, or university; scholarly. 2 Classical and literary rather than technical; formal or theoretical, as opposed to practical. 3 According to scholastic rules or usage; conventional; traditional. Also **ac′ a·dem′i·cal.** — *n.* 1 A college or university student. 2 A member of a learned society. [<L *academicus* < *academia.* See ACADEMY.] —**ac′a·dem′i·cal·ly** *adv.*

ac·a·dem·i·cals (ak′ə·dem′i·kəlz) *n. pl.* The prescribed dress of an academy, college, etc.; cap and gown.

a·cad·e·mi·cian (ə·kad′ə·mish′ən, ak′ə·də-) *n.* A member of an academy of art, science, or literature.

ac·a·dem·i·cism (ak′ə·dem′ə·siz′əm) *n.* 1 The state or quality of being academic in style or procedure. 2 Pedantic formalism, as in art or literature. Also **a·cad·e·mism** (ə·kad′ə·miz′əm).

a·cad·e·my (ə·kad′ə·mē) *n.* pl. **·mies** 1 A school, especially one intermediate between a common school and a college. 2 A learned society for the advancement of arts or sciences. [<F *académie* <L *academia* <Gk. *akadēmeia* the grove of *Akadēmos* where Plato taught] —**ac′a·dem′ic** *adj. & n.*

Academy Award One of the awards made annually by the Academy of Motion Picture Arts and Sciences.

A·ca·di·a (ə·kān′dē·ə) 1 A former name for the Atlantic coast region of North America, including Nova Scotia and New Brunswick, settled originally by the French. 2 A parish in southern Louisiana settled by deported Acadians.

A·ca·di·an (ə·kā′dē·ən) *adj.* Of or pertaining to Acadia. — *n.* One of the early French settlers of Acadia, or a descendant. See CAJUN.

Acadia National Park A rocky, mountainous area mainly on Mount Desert Island off the southern coast of Maine; 44 square miles.

ac·a·jou (ak′ə·zho͞o) *n.* 1 A tropical American wood, valued for fine furniture and interior trim. 2 The cashew tree or its fruits; also the gum which exudes from its bark. 3 French mahogany; also, the color of the finished wood. [<F. See CASHEW.]

ac·a·leph (ak′ə·lef) *n.* A jellyfish. Also **ac·a·lephe** (ak′ə·lē f). [<Gk. *akalēphē* nettle] —**ac·a·le·phan** (ak′ə·lē′fən) *adj.* & n. —**ac·a·le·phoid** (ak′ ə·lē′foid) *adj.*

a·can·thine (ə·kan′thin) *adj.* 1 Pertaining to or like an acanthus. 2 Decorated with the acanthus leaf.

acantho- *combining form* Thorn or thorny; spine, point, prickle: *acanthocephalan.* Also, before vowels, **acanth-**, as in *acanthoid.* [<Gk. *akantha* thorn]

a·can·tho·ceph·a·lan (ə·kan′thō·sef′ə·lən) *n.* Any of a phylum (*Acanthocephala*) of worms that are parasitic as adults in the intestines of fishes and other vertebrates, having a proboscis covered with hooks. Also **a·can′tho·ceph′a·lid.** [<ACANTHO- + Gk. *kephalē* head]

a·can·thoid (ə·kan′thoid) *adj.* Spiny.

ac·an·thop·ter·yg·i·an (ak′an·thop′tə·rij′ē·ən) *n.* Any of a superorder (Acanthopterygii) of teleost fishes, including most fishes having spines in the fins, as the mackerel, bass, etc. [<ACANTHO- + Gk. *pterygion* fin]

a·can·thus (ə·kan′thəs) *n. pl.* **·thus·es** or **·thi** (-thī) 1 Any plant of the genus *Acanthus* having large spinous leaves: common in the Mediterranean region. 2 A conventionalized architectural and decorative representation of its leaf, characteristic of the Corinthian capital. Also **acanthus leaf.** [<L <Gk. *akanthos* <*akē* thorn]

ACANTHUS *(def. 2)*

a cap·pel·la (ä′kə·pel′ə, *Ital.* ä′käp·pel′lä) *Music* Sung without instrumental accompaniment. [<Ital. <L *ad* according to + *cappella* chapel]

a ca·pric·cio (ä′kä·prēt′chō) *Music* At the performer's pleasure with regard to tempo and expression; capriciously. [<Ital.]

A·ca·pul·co (ä′kä·po͝ol′kō) A port and resort city of SW Mexico on the Pacific.

ac·a·ri·a·sis (ak′ə·rī′ə·sis) *n.* An itch caused by mites.

a·car·i·cide (ə·kar′ə·sīd, ak′ə·rə-) *n.* Miticide. [<ACARID + -CIDE]

ac·a·rid (ak′ə·rid) *n.* Any of an order (*Acarina*) of arachnids, including the mites and ticks. — *adj.* Of or pertaining to the acarids. [Gk. *akari* mite]

Ac·ar·na·ni·a (ak′ər·nā′nē·ə) A region on the Ionian Sea, a part of Aetolia and Acarnania Department of modern Greece; 2,137 square miles. Also, Akarnania.

ac·a·roid (ak′ə·roid) *adj.* Of or like the acarids; mitelike. [<Gk. *akari* mite, + -OID]

acaroid gum A yellow, fragrant, alcohol-soluble resin from Australian grass trees. Also **acaroid resin.**

a·car·pel·ous (ā·kär′pəl·əs) *adj. Bot.* Having no carpels. Also **a·car′pel·lous.**

a·car·pous (ā·kär′pəs) *adj. Bot.* Not bearing fruit. [<A-[4] without + Gk. *karpos* fruit]

ac·a·rus (ak′ər′əs) *n. pl.* **·a·ri** (-ə·rī) Any of the numerous mites of the genus *Acarus.* [<Gk. *akari* mite]

a·cat·a·lec·tic (ā·kat′ə·lek′tik) *adj.* Metrically complete; not catalectic; having the required number of feet or of syllables, especially in the last foot. — *n.* A full or metrically complete verse.

a·cat·a·lep·si·a (ə·kat′ə·lep′sē·ə) *n.* Impairment of the reasoning faculty; abnormal inability to comprehend. [<NL]

a·cat·a·lep·sy (ə·kat′ə·lep′sē) *n. Philos.* The incomprehensibility of all things; specifically, among the Skeptics, the doctrine that all human knowledge is only probable and that all positive judgment should be suspended. [<Gk. *akatalē psia* <*a-* not + *kata-* thoroughly + *lēpsis* a seizing. See CATALEPSY.]

a·cau·date (ā·kô′dāt) *adj. Zool.* Having no tail; tailless. Also **a·cau′dal.** [<A-[4] not + CAUDATE]

ac·au·les·cence (ak′ô·les′əns) *n. Bot.* Absence, real or apparent, of the stem. —**ac′au·les′cent,** *adj.*

a·caus·al (ā′kôz′əl) *adj.* not causal; not having to do with cause and effect.

Ac·cad (ak′ad, ä′käd), **Ac·ca·di·an** (ə·kā′dē·ən, ə ·kä′-) See AKKAD, etc.

ac·cede (ak·sēd′) *v.i.* **ac·ced·ed, ac·ced·ing** 1 To give one's consent or adherence; agree; assent: with *to.* 2 To come into or enter upon an office or dignity: with *to.* See synonyms under AGREE, ASSENT. [<L *accedere* <*ad-* to + *cedere* yield, go]

ac·ced·ence (ak·sē′dəns) *n.* The act of acceding; agreeing to.

ac·cel·er·an·do (ak·sel′ə·ran′dō; *Ital.* ät·che′·le·rän′dō) *adj. & adv. Music* With gradual quickening of the time. [<Ital.]

ac·cel·er·ant (ak·sel′ər·ənt) *adj.* Accelerating; hastening. — *n.* That which accelerates.

ac·cel·er·ate (ak·sel′ə·rāt) *v.* **·at·ed, ·at·ing** *v.t.* 1 To cause to act or move faster; increase the speed of. 2 *Physics* To increase the rate of change of (the linear or angular velocity of a body). 3 To hasten the natural or usual course of: to *accelerate* combustion. 4 To cause to happen ahead of time. —*v.i.* 5 To move or become faster; to increase in speed. See synonyms under QUICKEN. [<L *acceleratus,* pp. of *accelerare* < *ad-* to + *celerare* hasten < *celer* quick] —**ac·cel·er·a·ble** (ak·sel′ər·ə·bəl) *adj.*

ac·cel·er·a·tion (ak·sel′ə·rā′shən) *n.* 1 The act of accelerating, or the process of being accelerated; a quickening, as of progress, action, functional activity, etc. 2 The rate at which the speed of a body increases. 3 *Physics* The rate at which the velocity of a body increases per unit of time: used also of decrease of velocity, which is expressed as a **negative acceleration.**

acceleration of gravity An increase in the velocity of a body due to the force of gravity. At sea level it is about 32.17 feet per second.

ac·cel·er·a·tive (ak·sel′ə·rā′tiv) *adj.* Of, pertaining to, or causing acceleration; tending to accelerate. Also **ac·cel′er·a·to′ry.**

ac·cel·er·a·tor (ak·sel′ə·rā′tər) *n.* 1 One who or that which accelerates. 2 *Phot.* Any chemical or device for hastening the appearance or development of the picture on an exposed sensitized plate or print. 3 *Mech.* A device for increasing the speed of a machine. 4 *Chem.* A substance or agent that quickens the speed of a chemical reaction; a catalyst. 5 *Physiol.* A muscle or nerve that acts to increase the speed of a function. 6 *Physics* Any of various devices for accelerating the velocity of subatomic particles by subjecting them to the force of a synchronized electromagnetic field, as a cyclotron or synchrotron.

ac·cel·er·o·graph (ak·sel′ər·ə·graf′, -gräf′) *n.* A device for measuring the pressures developed by the combustion of an explosive in an enclosed or nearly enclosed space. [<ACCELER(ATE) + -O- + -GRAPH]

ac·cel·er·om·e·ter (ak·sel′ə·rom′ə·tər) *n.* An instrument designed to measure and record the acceleration of an aircraft.

ac·cent (ak′sent) *n.* 1 A stress of voice on a particular syllable in pronouncing a word. 2 A mark used to indicate such stress: known as **primary** (noting the chief stress) and **secondary** (noting weaker stress on some other syllable or syllables) **accents.** In ə·brē′vē·ā′shən, the primary accent is on the fourth syllable, and the secondary accent is on the second syllable. 3 One of three marks, used chiefly in the Romance languages, to indicate the quality of a vowel or diphthong: acute (´), grave (`), and circumflex (ˆ) accents. 4 *Music* Stress of voice or instrument. 5 A modulation of the voice; mode of utterance; pronunciation. 6 *Math.* A mark or marks to distinguish the value or order of similar symbols: a′ *(a prime),* a′′ *(a second),* a′′′ *(a third),* etc.; also to denote minutes and seconds in geometry, trigonometry, etc.: ′ = minutes, ″ = seconds. 8 In mensuration, a similar mark or marks to denote feet and inches, as ′ = feet; ″ = inches. 9 In prosody, the stress determining the rhythm of poetry; ictus. — *v.t.* (ak′ sent, ak·sent′) 1 To speak or pronounce with an accent; stress. 2 To write or print with a mark indicating accent or stress. 3 To call attention to; accentuate. [<L *accentus,* lit., song added to speech (a trans. of Gk. *prosōidia* PROSODY) < *ad-* to + *cantus* a singing < *canere* sing]

ac·cen·tu·al (ak·sen′cho͞o·əl) *adj.* . Of, pertaining to, having, or made by accent. —**ac·cen′tu·al·ly** *adv.*

ac·cen·tu·ate (ak·sen′cho͞o·āt) *v.t.* **·at·ed, ·at·ing** 1 To strengthen or heighten the effect of; emphasize. 2 To speak or pronounce with an accent. 3 To write or print with a mark indicating accent. [<Med.L *accentuatus,* pp. of *accentuare* <L *accentus* ACCENT] —**ac·cen′tu·a′tion** *n.*

ac·cept (ak·sept′) *v.t.* 1 To take when offered; receive with favor or willingness, as a gift. 2 To give an affirmative answer to: to *accept* an invitation, an offer of marriage, etc. 3 To agree to; admit: to *accept* an apology. 4 To take with good grace; submit to: to *accept* the inevitable. 5 To agree to pay, as a draft. 6 To believe in: to *accept* Christianity. **7** *Law* To acknowledge as valid or received: I *accepted* the subpoena. — *v.i.* **8** To agree or promise to fulfil an engagement; receive favorably. See synonyms under ACKNOWLEDGE, AGREE, ASSENT, ASSUME, CONFESS, RATIFY. [<L *acceptare,* freq. of *accipere* take < *ad-* to + *capere* take] **—ac·cept′er** *n.*

ac·cept·a·ble (ak·sep′tə·bəl) *adj.* **1** That is worthy of being accepted or capable of acceptance; pleasing; welcome. **2** Tolerable; detrimental, though not judged to require corrective measures: *acceptable* air pollution. See synonyms under AGREEABLE, DELIGHTFUL. **—ac·cept′a·ble·ness, ac·cept′a·bil′i·ty** *n.* **—ac·cept′a·bly** *adv.*

ac·cep·tance (ak·sep′təns) *n.* **1** The act of accepting; state of being accepted or acceptable; also, consent to receive. **2** An agreement to pay a bill of exchange, draft, order, or the like, according to its terms; also, the paper itself when endorsed is accepted." **3** *Law* Any form or act by which one positively or constructively acknowledges the validity or sufficiency of an act done by another, agrees to the terms of a contract, or the like. Also **ac·cep′tan·cy.**

ac·cep·tant (ak·sep′tənt) *adj.* Ready or willing to accept; receptive.

ac·cep·ta·tion (ak′sep·tā′shən) *n.* **1** The accepted meaning of a word or expression; general interpretation. **2** The state of being accepted or acceptable.

ac·cept·ed (ak·sep′tid) *adj.* Commonly recognized, believed, or approved; popular.

ac·cep·tor (ak·sep′tər) *n.* *Law* One who has given acceptance on a check or draft.

ac·cess (ak′ses) *n.* **1** The act, opportunity, or means of approaching; admittance; approach; passage; path. **2** Increase; addition; accession: an *access* of territory. **3** An attack, as of disease; a fit of passion or zeal; outburst. **4** *Eccl.* Approach to God: *access* by faith (*Rom.* v 2): used especially in the titles of certain prayers. See synonyms under ENTRANCE, INCREASE. [<L *accessus* an approach < *accedere.* See ACCEDE].

ac·ces·sa·ry (ak·ses′ər·ē) *adj., n. pl.* **·ries** *Law* Accessory. ◆ **accessary, accessory** The earlier form is *accessary* (see -ARY[1]), now retained primarily in legal usage. Later the adjective was refashioned to *accessory* (on analogy with *promissory, amatory, illusory,* etc.), which also influenced the form of the noun. *Accessory* is now the preferred common and legal spelling.

ac·ces·si·ble (ak·ses′ə·bəl) *adj.* **1** Easy of access. **2** That can be approached. **3** Attainable; that can be obtained. **4** Open to the influence of: with *to:* His heart is *accessible* to pity. See synonyms under FRIENDLY. **—ac·ces′si·bil′i·ty** *n.* **—ac·ces′si·bly** *adv.*

ac·ces·sion (ak·sesh′ən) *n.* **1** One who or that which is added; addition. **2** Attainment, as of office; succession to a throne; induction or elevation. **3** Access; admittance; approach: the *accession* of light. **4** Assent; agreement; consent. **5** *Law* The acquisition of property of a concomitant nature by virtue of the ownership of the principal, to which it is accessory as an incident. **6** A beginning, increase, or paroxysm, of disease, anger, folly, etc. See ACCESS. —*v.t.* To record, as additions to a library or museum. [<L *accessio, -onis* <*accedere.* See ACCEDE.] **—ac·ces′sion·al** *adj.*

Synonyms (*noun*): addition, arrival augmentation, enlargement, extension, inauguration, increase, influx. See ENTRANCE.

ac·ces·so·ri·al (ak′sə·sôr′ē·əl, -sō′rē·əl) *adj.* Pertaining to an accessory.

ac·ces·so·ry (ak·ses′ər·ē) *n. pl.* **·ries 1** A person or thing that aids subordinately; an adjunct; appurtenance; accompaniment. **2** *pl.* Such items of apparel as complete an outfit, as gloves, scarf, hat, or handbag. **3** *Law* A person who, even if not present, is concerned, either before or after, in the perpetration of a felony below the crime of treason. See also note under ACCESSARY. —*adj.* **1** Aiding the principal design, or assisting subordinately the chief agent, as in the commission of a crime. **2** Contributory; supplemental; additional: *accessory* nerves. Also *accessary.* [<L *accessorius* <*accessus,* pp. of *accedere.* See ACCEDE.] **—ac·ces′ so·ri·ly** *adv.* **—ac·ces′so·ri·ness** *n.*

Synonyms (*noun*): abetter or abettor, accomplice, ally, assistant, associate, attendant, coadjutor, colleague, companion, confederate, follower, helper, henchman, participator, partner, retainer. *Colleague* is used always in a good sense, *associate* and *coadjutor* generally so; *ally, assistant, associate, attendant, companion, helper,* either in a good or a bad sense; *abettor, accessory, accomplice, confederate,* almost always in a bad sense. In law, an *abettor* (the general legal spelling) is always present, either actively or constructively, at the commission of the crime; an *accessory* never. An *accomplice* is usually a principal; an *accessory* never. If present, though only to stand outside and keep watch against surprise, one is an *abettor,* and not an *accessory.* At common law, an *accessory* implies a principal, and cannot be convicted until after the conviction of the principal; the *accomplice* or *abettor* can be convicted as a principal. *Accomplice* and *abettor* have nearly the same meaning, but the former is the popular, the latter the legal term. Compare APPENDAGE, AUXILIARY. *Antonyms:* adversary, antagonist, betrayer, chief, commander, enemy, foe, hinderer, instigator, leader, opponent, principal, rival.

accessory after the fact A person who, knowing a felony to have been committed, comforts, conceals, or assists the felon.

accessory before the fact One who instigates, aids, or encourages another to commit a felony, but is not present at its perpetration.

accessory fruit Pseudocarp.

access time *Electronics* **1** The time required for a unit of information to be released from the memory or storage element of an computer. **2** The time required for the effective storage of such information in the computer.

ac·ciac·ca·tu·ra (ät·chäk′kä·to͞o′rä) *n.* *Music* **1** A short clear appoggiatura. **2** In old organ music, a grace note in which the principal note is sustained while the note below is struck for an instant only. [<Ital. < *acci-* + *accare* crush]

ac·ci·dence (ak′sə·dəns) *n.* **1** *Gram.* That part of grammar that treats of the accidents or inflections of words. **2** A book dealing with the rudiments of grammar. **3** The rudiments or elements of any art or science. [< *accidents,* pl. of (ACCIDENT (def. 3)]

ac·ci·dent (ak′sə·dənt) *n.* **1** Anything that happens by chance; anything occurring unexpectedly, undesignedly, or without known or assignable cause; a contingency; especially, any unpleasant or unfortunate occurrence involving injury, loss, suffering, or death; a casualty; mishap. **2** Any non-essential circumstance or attribute. **3** *Gram.* An inflection, as of case, gender, number, etc. **4** *Logic* Any feature, element, or accompaniment of an object not essential to the conception of it. [<L *accidens, -entis,* ppr. of *accidere* happen < *ad-* upon + *cadere* fall]

Synonyms: adventure, calamity, casualty, chance, contingency, disaster, fortuity, hap, happening, hazard, incident, misadventure, misfortune, mishap, possibility. An *accident* is that which happens without anyone's direct intention; a *chance* that which happens without any known cause. An *incident* is viewed as occurring in the regular course of things, but subordinate to the main purpose, or aside from the main design. *Fortune* and *chance* are nearly equivalent, but *chance* can be used of human effort and endeavor as *fortune* cannot; we say "there is one *chance* in a thousand" ; as personified, we speak of fickle *Fortune,* blind *Chance.* Since the unintended is often the undesirable, *accident* tends to signify some *calamity* or *disaster,* but we may speak of a fortunate or happy *accident.* An *adventure* is that which may turn out ill, a *misadventure* that which does turn out ill. A slight disturbing *accident* is a *mishap.* Compare CATASTROPHE, EVENT, HAZARD. *Antonyms:* Appointment, calculation, certainty, decree, fate, foreordination, intention, law, necessity, ordainment, ordinance, plan, preparation, provision, purpose.

ac·ci·den·tal (ak′sə·den′təl) *adj.* **1** Happening or coming by chance or without design; casual; fortuitous; taking place unexpectedly, unintentionally, or out of the usual course. **2** Non-essential; subordinate; incidental: said of any attribute or feature not entering into the very nature of a thing. **3** *Music* Pertaining to or indicating a sharp, natural, flat, etc., elsewhere than in the signature. —*n.* **1** A casual, incidental, or non-essential feature or property. **2** *Music* A sharp, flat, or natural elsewhere than in the signature. There are five *accidentals* or signs of chromatic alteration to show that the notes to which they are applied have to be raised or lowered a semitone or a tone: the sharp, double-sharp, flat, double-flat, and the natural. **—ac′ci·den′tal·ness** *n.*

Synonyms (adj.): chance, uncontemplated, undesigned, unexpected, unforeseen, unintended, unpremediated. See INCIDENTAL. *Antonyms:* calculated, contemplated, deliberate, designed, intended, planned, preconcerted, purposed, studied.

ac·ci·den·tal·ism (ak′sə·den′təl·iz′əm) *n.* **1** An accidental condition or effect. **2** *Med.* A theory that ignores the causes of disease and deals only with symptoms. **3** *Philos.* The theory that events occur by accident or without cause. **—ac′ ci·den′tal·ist** *n.*

ac·ci·den·tal·ly (ak′sə·den′təl·ē) *adv.* **1** By accident or chance; unintentionally; casually. **2** As an accidental or subsidiary feature or effect; incidentally.

ac·ci·dent·ed (ak′sə·den′tid) *adj.* Marked by unevenness in the surface: an *accidented* field.

ac·ci·die (ak′sə·dē) See ACEDIA.

ac·cip·i·ter ak·sip′ə·tər) *n.* **1** Any of the birds of prey belonging to the genus *Accipiter,* characterized by short rounded wings and a long tail, such as a goshawk. **2** Any member of the family Accipitridae, such as an eagle, hawk, or kite. [<L *accipiter* hawk]

ac·cip·i·trine (ak·sip′ə·trin, -trīn) *adj.* **1** Belonging to birds of prey; of or pertaining to a family of hawks (*Accipitridae*); resembling a hawk. **2** Raptorial.

ac·claim (ə·klām′) *v.t.* **1** To proclaim by acclamation; hail as: to *acclaim* him victor. **2** To shout approval of; show enthusiasm for. **3** To shout; call out: *acclaim* one's sorrow. —*v.i.* **4** To applaud; shout approval. —*n.* Applause; pronouncement. See synonyms under APPLAUSE. [<L *acclamare* <*ad-* to + *clamare* shout] **—ac·claim′a·ble** *adj.* **—ac·claim′er** *n.*

ac·cla·ma·tion (ak′lə·mā′shən) *n.* **1** The act of acclaiming; that which is expressed in the act; a shout, as of applause. **2** A loud and general viva-voce vote of approval, as in public assembly. **3** In the Roman Catholic Church, the elevation to an ecclesiastical dignity by the unanimous voice of the electors, without voting: one of the ways of electing a pope. **4** *Music* The responsive chant in antiphonal singing. **5** *Archeol.* A short inscription containing a wish or injunction, found on tombs, amultes, etc.; also, a representation, in sculpture or on a medal, of persons expressing joy or approval. See synonyms under APPLAUSE. [<L *acclamatio, -onis* < *acclamare.* See ACCLAIM.]

ac·clam·a·to·ry (ə·klam′ə·tôr′ē, -tō′rē) *adj.* Relating to or expressing joy and acclamation.

ac·cli·mate (ə·klī′mit, ak′lə·māt) *v.t.* & *v.i.* **·mat·ed, ·mat·ing** To adapt or become adapted to a foreign climate or new environment: said of persons, plants, or animals; acclimatize. [<F *acclimater* < *à* to (<L *ad-*) + *climat* CLIMATE] **—ac·cli·ma·ta·ble** (ə·klī′mə·tə·bəl) *adj.* **—ac·cli·ma·tion** (ak′lə·mā′shən), **ac·cli·ma·ta·tion** (ə·klī′mə′tā′shən) *n.*

ac·cli·ma·tize (ə·klī′mə·tīz) *v.t. v.i.* **·tized, ·tiz·ing** Acclimate. **—ac·cli′ma·tiz′a·ble** *adj.* **—ac·cli′ma·ti·za′tion** *n.* **—ac·cli′ma·tiz′er** *n.*

ac·cliv·i·ty (ə·kliv′ə·tē) *n. pl.* **·ties** An upward slope: opposed to *declivity.* See synonyms under HEIGHT. [<L *acclivatas, -tatis* steepness < *ad-* to + *clivus* hill]

ac·cli·vous (ə·klī′vəs) *adj.* Sloping upward. Also **ac·cliv·i·tous** (əkliv′ə·təs).

ac·co·lade (ak′ə·lād′, -läd′) *n.* **1** A mark of praise or expression of appreciation. **2** The salutation, at first an embrace, later a light blow with a sword, in conferring knighthood; hence, an honor conferred. 3 *Music* A vertical brace or heavy bar. 4 *Archit.* A curved ornamental molding. [<F <Ital. *accollata* < *accollare* embrace about the neck < L *ad* to + *collum* neck]

ACCOLADE *(def. 4)*

ac·com·mo·date (ə·kom′ə·dāt) *v.* **·dat·ed, ·dat·ing** *v.t.* 1 To do a favor for; oblige; help. 2 To provide for; give lodging to. 3 To be suitable for; to contain comfortably: The hall *accommodates* large numbers. 4 To adapt or modify; adjust: He *accommodated* his needs to our capacity to fulfil them. 5 To reconcile or settle, as conflicting opinions. —*v.i.* 6 To be or become adjusted or conformed, as the eye to distance. [<L *accommodatus,* pp. of *accommodare* < *ad-* to + *commodare* make fit, suit < *com-* with + *modus* measure] —**ac·com′mo·da′tive** *adj.* —**ac·com′mo·da′tive·ness** *n.*

Synonyms: adapt, adjust, entertain, fit, furnish, harmonize, lodge, oblige, receive, reconcile, serve, suit, supply. See ADAPT, ADJUST.

ac·com·mo·dat·ing (ə·kom′ə·dā′ting) *adj.* Disposed to accommodate; obliging. —**ac·com′mo·dat′ing·ly** *adv.*

ac·com·mo·da·tion (ə·kom′ ə·dā′shən) *n.* 1 The act of accomodating, or the state of being accommodated; adjustment; adaptation. 2 A convenience; entertainment; specifically, lodging, board, etc. 3 A loan or other help or favor; specifically, an accommodation bill. 4 Obligingness. 5 An accommodation train. 6 The adjustment of the eye to vision at different distances.

accommodation bill or **note** A note given or bill of exchange accepted, not for value received but as an accommodation or favor in the course of business.

accommodation ladder A ladder or stairway hung at the side of a ship or boat.

accommodation train A railway train that stops at all or at most of the stations.

ac·com·pa·ni·ment (ə·kum′pə·ni·mənt, ə·kump′ni-) *n.* 1 Anything that accompanies. 2 *Music* A subordinate part, vocal or instrumental, accompanying, enriching, or supporting a leading part. See synonyms under APPENDAGE, CIRCUMSTANCE.

ac·com·pa·nist (ə·kum′pə·nist, ə·kump′nist) *n.* A musician who plays or sings the accompaniment.

ac·com·pa·ny (ə·kum′pə·nē) *v.t.* **·nied, ·ny·ing** 1 To go with; attend; escort. 2 To be or occur with; coexist with: Weakness often *accompanies* disease. 3 To supplement with: He *accompanied* his insults with blows. 4 To play a musical accompaniment to or for. See synonyms under FOLLOW. [<F *accompagner* < *à* to + *compagne* COMPANION] —**ac·com′pa·ni·er** *n.*

ac·com·plice (ə·kom′plis) *n.* 1 An associate in wrong or crime, whether as principal or accessory. 2 *Obs.* One who cooperates; an associate. See synonyms under ABETTOR, ACCESSORY. [< *a,* indefinite article + F *complice* accomplice <LL *complex* accomplice. See COMPLEX.]

ac·com·plish (ə·kom′plish) *v.t.* 1 To bring to pass; perform; effect. 2 To bring to completion; finish. 3 *Obs.* To make complete; perfect, as in external acquirements or mental polish. [<OF *acompliss-,* stem of *acomplir* <LL *accomplere* <L *ad-* to + *complere* fill up, complete] —**ac·com′plish·a·ble** *adj.* —**ac·com′plish·er** *n.*

Synonyms: achieve, complete, consummate, discharge, do, effect, execute, finish, fulfil, perform, realize. *Perform* and *accomplish* both imply working toward the end; but *perform* always allows a possibility of not attaining, while *accomplish* carries the thought of full completion. See ATTAIN , EFFECT.

ac·com·plished (ə·kom′plisht) *adj.* 1 Proficient; polite; polished; having accomplishments. 2 Completed; consummated. See synonyms under POLITE.

ac·com·plish·ment (ə·kom′plish·mənt) *n.* 1 An accomplishment; fulfilment; performance; completion. 2 An acquirement or attainment that tends to perfect or equip in character, manners, or person. See synonyms under ACT, ATTAINMENT, END.

ac·cord (ə·kôrd′) *v.t.* 1 To render as due; grant; concede: to *accord* merited honor. 2 To bring into agreement; make harmonize or correspond, as opinions. 3 To reconcile; literally, to bring heart to heart, as former enemies. —*v.i.* 4 To agree; harmonize: Those colors *accord* well together. See synonyms under AGREE, ASSENT. —*n.* 1 Harmony, especially of sounds; agreement. 2 Spontaneous impulse; choice: of one's own *accord.* 3 A settlement of any difference; reconciliation; specifically, an agreement between governments. See synonyms under HARMONY. [<OF *acorder* <LL *accordare* be of one mind, agree <L *ad-* to + *cor* heart] —**ac·cord′a·ble** *adj.* —**ac·cord′er** *n.*

ac·cord·ance (ə·kôr′dəns) *n.* Agreement; conformity. See synonyms under HARMONY.

ac·cord·ant (ə·kôr′dənt) *adj.* Consonant; agreeing; corresponding. —**ac·cord′ant·ly** *adv.*

ac·cord·ing (ə·kôr′ding) *adj.* Being in accordance or agreement; harmonizing. —*adv.* Agreeably; conformably; just.

according as 1 In proportion as, in accordance with. 2 Depending on whether.

ac·cord·ing·ly (ə·kôr′ding·lē) *adv.* In a conformable manner; suitably; consequently. See synonyms under CONSEQUENTLY, HENCE, THEREFORE, WHEREFORE.

according to 1 In accordance with; in conformity with. 2 As stated or believed by; on the authority of. 3 In proportion to.

ac·cor·di·on (ə·kôr′dē ·ən) *n.* A portable free-reed musical wind-instrument with from 5 to 50 keys, the air for which is furnished by a bellows alternately pulled apart and pressed together by the performer. [<Ital. *accordare* accord, harmonize] —**ac·cor′di·on·ist** *n.*

accordion pleating Pleating that resembles the folds of the bellows part of an accordion.

ac·cost (ə·kôst′, ə·kost′) *v.t.* 1 To speak to first; address; greet. 2 To approach for sexual purposes; proposition. See synonyms under ADDRESS. — *n.* Manner or act of addressing; greeting. [<F *accoster* <LL *accostare* be side to side <L *ad-* to + *costa* rib]

ac·couche·ment (ə·ko͞osh′mənt, *Fr.* á·ko͞osh·mäṅ′) *n.* Delivery in childbed; confinement. [<F *accoucher* put to bed, give birth < *à* to (<L *ad-*) + *coucher* put to bed. See COUCH.]

ac·cou·cheur (á·ko͞o·shœr′) *n.* *French* A professional obstetrician; a male physician who practices obstetrics.

ac·cou·cheuse (á·ko͞o·shœz′) *n.* *French* A midwife.

ac·count (ə·kount′) *v.t.* 1 To hold to be; consider; estimate. —*v.i.* 2 To provide a reckoning, as of funds paid or received: with *to* or *with* (someone) *for* (something). 3 To give a rational explanation; refer to some cause or natural law: with *for.* 4 To be responsible; answer: with *for.* 5 To cause death, capture or incapacitation: with *for.* See synonyms under CALCULATE. —*n.* 1 A record of a transaction; reckoning; computation 2 Any narrative, statement, report, or description; notice; explanation. 3 The act or time of rendering a reckoning; judgment. 4 Consideration, as of value; importance; concern; estimation; esteem. 5 A record of debits and credits, receipts and expenditures; any methodical enumeration, score, or reckoning; to render an *account,* charge to one's *account,* an *account* at a bank. See synonyms under HISTORY, REASON, REPORT.—**on account of** Because of; for the sake of. [<OF *aconter* <LL *accomptare* <L *ad-* to + *computare* COUNT]

ac·count·a·ble (ə·koun′tə·bəl) *adj.* 1 Liable to be called to account; responsible. 2 Capable of being accounted for or explained. —**ac·count′a·bil′i·ty** *n.* —**ac·count′a·bly** *adv.*

ac·count·an·cy (ə·koun′tən·sē) *n.* The work, art, or business of an accountant.

ac·count·ant (ə·koun′tənt) *n.* 1 One whose business is to keep or examine books, as of a mercantile or banking house or in a public office. 2 One who keeps, examines, or is skilled in accounts. 3 One who is accountable or responsible. —**certified public accountant** In the United States, a public accountant who has been granted a certificate of proficiency by a State examining body, and is allowed to use the designation C.P.A. —**chartered accountant** In Great Britain, a member of an Institute of Chartered Accountants. —**public accountant** An accountant whose services, for a compensation, are available to the public.

ac·count·ing (ə·koun′ting) *n.* The art or system of recording, classifying, and summarizing commercial transactions in monetary terms. Compare BOOKKEEPING.

account rendered An account or bill presented by the creditor for examination by the debtor, to be paid if correct.

account stated An account presented by the creditor and assented to as correct by the debtor.

ac·cou·ter (ə·ko͞o′tər) *v.t.* **·tered** or **·tred** (-tərd), **·ter·ing** or **·tring** To furnish with dress or trappings; equip, as for military service. Also **ac·cou′tre.** [<F *accoutrer;* ult. origin uncertain]

ac·cou·ter·ment (ə·ko͞o′tər·mənt) *n.* 1 Equipment; apparel; dress; trappings: chiefly used in plural; also, the act of accoutering. 2 *Mil.* The equipment of a soldier other than arms and dress. Also **ac·cou′tre·ment.** See synonyms under CAPARISON.

Ac·cra (ak′rə) A port on the Gulf of Guinea, capital of Ghana: also *Akkra.*

ac·cred·it (ə·kred′it) *v.t.* 1 To furnish or send with credentials, as an ambassador; authorize. 2 To vouch for officially; certify as fulfilling requirements. 3 To enter on the credit side of the ledger; give credit for. 4 To attribute to: with *with:* I *accredited* my foes with as much wit as my friends. 5 To accept as true; believe. 6 To confer acceptance or favor on: Her actions do not tend to *accredit* her words. [<F *accréditer* < *à* to (<L *ad-*) + *crédit* CREDIT]

ac·cred·i·ta·tion (ə·kred′ə·tā′shən) *n.* *U.S.* The grant to an academic institution, by an accrediting body, of status indicating valuation of its course credits and degrees as in accord with the standards set by the accrediting body.

ac·cre·men·ti·tion (ak′rə·men·tish′ən) *n.* *Biol.* Growth by division of cells; accretion. —**ac′cre·men·ti′tious** *adj.*

ac·cresce (ə·kres′) *v.i.* **·cresced, ·cresc·ing** *Obs.* 1 To accrue. 2 To increase. [<L *accrescere* < *ad-* to + *crescere* grow]

ac·cres·cence (ə·kres′əns) *n.* Gradual growth; an accretion. Also **ac·cres′cen·cy.**

ac·cres·cent (ə·kres′ənt) *adj.* 1 *Bot.* Continuing to grow after flowering: said of a calyx or other part of the flower. 2 Growing continuously; expanding with age.

ac·crete (ə·krēt′) *v.* **ac·cret·ed, ac·cret·ing** *v.i.* 1 To grow together or be united by adhesion: with *to.* 2 To increase by a series of additions. —*v.t.* 3 To cause to grow together or be added: with *to:* The student should *accrete* discretion to the other qualities of mind. —*adj.* 1 Formed or marked be accretions. 2 *Bot.* Grown together: said of parts normally separate. [<L *accretus,* pp. of *accrescere.* See ACCRESCE.]

ac·cre·tion (ə·krē′shən) *n.* 1 Growth or formation by external additions; increase by adhesion or inclusion; an accumulation or external addition; matter added. 2 *Pathol.* Abnormal adhesion or growing together. 3 *Law* Increase, as of land along the seashore or a river, by deposit of alluvium. 4 Increase by natural growth. 5 *Geol.* The enlargement of rock masses and inorganic bodies by the addition of new material. —**ac·cre′tive** *adj.*

ac·croach (ə·krōch′) *v.t.* *Rare* To usurp, as royal prerogatives. [<OF *accrocher* < *a* to + *croc* hook]

ac·cru·al (ə·kro͞o′əl) *n.* 1 The act of accruing; increase. 2 The amount of increase. Also **ac·crue′ment.**

accrual basis The keeping of accounts in such

manner as to show accrued earned income and accrued expense without regard to actual paid income and actual disbursements: opposed to *cash basis*.

ac·crue (ə·kro͞o′) *v.i.* **·crued, ·cru·ing 1** To come as a natural result or increment, as by growth: with *to*. **2** To arise as an addition, accession, or advantage; accumulate, as the interest on money: used with *from*. **3** *Law* To become established as a permanent right. [<obs. n. *accrue* an accession <F *accrû*, pp. of *accroître* increase <L *accrescere*. See ACCRESCE.]

ac·cu·ba·tion (ak′yo͞o·bā′shən) *n. Archaic* The act or position of reclining, as the ancient Romans at meals. [<L *accubatio, -onis <accubare* lie near to < *ad-* to + *cubare* lie down]

ac·cul·tur·a·tion (ə·kul′ chə·rā′shən) *n. Sociol.* The modification of culture traits induced by contacts between peoples having different ways of life; culture change. ʼ

ac·cum·bent (ə·kum′bənt) *adj.* **1** Lying down; recumbent. **2** *Bot.* Lying against something, as a; cotyledon against a radicle. [<L *accumbens,-entis*, ppr. of *accumbere* lie down] **—ac·cum′ben·cy** *n.*

ac·cu·mu·late (ə·kyo͞om′yə·lāt) *v.* **·lat·ed, ·lat·ing v.t. 1** To heap or pile up; amass; collect. — *v.i.* . **2** To become greater in quantity or number; increase. [<L *accumulatus*, pp. of *accumulare <ad-* to + *cumulare* heap < cumulus a heap] **—ac·cu·mu·la·ble** (ə·kyo͞om′yə·lə·bəl) *adj.*

ac·cu·mu·la·tion (ə·kyo͞omyə·lā′shən) *n.* **1** An amassing; increase; a collected mass. **2** A surplus accumulated in excess of all liabilities and credited to the active capital of a corporation. **3** *Geol.* The underground movement of oil and gas into porous rock formations, where large reserves may collect.

ac·cu·mu·la·tive (ə·kyo͞om′yə·lā′tiv) *adj.* Serving or tending to accumulate; characterized by accumulation; given to amassing; cumulative; collective. **—ac·cu′mu·la′tive·ly** *adv.* **—ac·cu′mu·la′tive·ness** *n.*

ac·cumu·la·tor (ə·kyo͞om′yə·lā′tər) *n.* **1** A person or thing that accumulates. **2** A power-storing hydraulic apparatus. **3** *Electr.* A storage battery or cell utilizing the energy of reversible chemical reactions. **4** A Leyden jar, or a condenser. **5** A resilient insert in a trace or in a chain or rope used in dredging, to prevent parting by too sudden strain.

ac·cu·ra·cy (ak′yər·ə·sē) *n.* The quality of being accurate; exactness; precision; correctness.

ac·cu·rate (ak′yər·it) *adj.* Conforming exactly to truth or to a standard; without error; precise; exact; correct. See synonyms under CORRECT, JUST, PARTICULAR, PRECISE. [<L *accuratus* done with care, pp. of *accurare* take care of < *ad-* to + cura care] **—ac′cu·rate·ly** *adv.* **—ac′cu·rate·ness** *n.*

ac·curs·ed (ə·kûr′sid, ə·kûrst′) *adj.* **1** Doomed to, deserving, or causing a curse. **2** Cursed; detestable; miserable. Also **ac·curst′**. **—ac·curs′ed·ly adv. —ac·curs′ed·ness** *n.*

ac·cu·sa·tion (ak′yo͞o·zā′shən) *n.* **1** A charge of crime or misconduct; an indictment. **2** The act of accusing; arraignment. **3** The crime or act with which one is charged. Also **ac·cu·sal** (ə·kyo͞o′zəl). **—ac·cu·sa·to·ry** (ə·kyo͞o′zə·tôr′ē, -tō′rē) *adj.*

ac·cu·sa·tive (ə·kyo͞o′zə·tiv) *adj. Gram.* Denoting, in inflected languages, the relation of the direct object of a verb or preposition, or the goal toward which an action is directed; objective. Also **ac·cu·sa·ti·val** (ə·kyo͞o′ zə·tī′vəl). —*n.* **1** The case of Latin and Greek nouns corresponding to the English objective. **2** A word in this case. [<L *accusativus*, trans. of Gk. *ptōsis aitiatikē* (the case) of accusing or pertaining to that which is caused < *aitiatos* produced by a cause] **—ac·cu′sa·tive·ly** *adv.*

ac·cu·sa·tori·al (ə·kyo͞o′zə·tôr′ē·əl, -tō′rē·əl) *adj.* Pertaining to an accuser.

ac·cuse (ə·kyo͞oz′) *v.* **ac·cused, ac·cus·ing** *v.t.* **1** To charge with fault or error; blame; censure. **2** To bring charges against, as of a crime or an offense: with *of*. —*v.i.* **3** To make accusation; utter charges. See synonyms under ARRAIGN, BLAME. [<OF *acuser* <L *accusare* call to account < *ad-* 5 to + *causa* cause, lawsuit] **—ac·cus′er** *n.* **—ac·cus′ing·ly** *adv.*

ac·cused (ə·kyo͞ozd′) *n. Law* The defendant or defendants in a criminal case: The judge ordered the *accused* to be brought before the bench.

ac·cus·tom (ə·kus′təm) *v.t.* To make familiar by use; habituate or inure, as oneself: with *to*. [<OF *acostumer <a-* to (<L *ad-*) + *costume* CUSTOM]

ac·cus·tomed (ə·kus′təmd) *adj.* **1** Habitual; usual: my *accustomed* haunts. **2** Used; in the habit: with the infinitive or *to:* He is *accustomed* to rising early. See synonyms under ADDICTED, (HABITUAL, USUAL. 3

ac·cus·tom·ize (ə·kus′təm·īz) *v.t. & v.i.* **·ized, ·iz·ing** To adapt or become adapted to the conditions and requirements of a new environment. **—ac·cus′tom·i·za′tion** *n.*

ACD An anticoagulant solution of acid, citrate, and dextrose, used to prolong the period during which whole blood can be stored for use in transfusions.

ace (ās) *n.* **1** A single spot, as on a playing card or die; a card or side of a die so marked. **2** A very small amount, distance, or degree; a unit; particle. **3** Something excellent or first-rate; hence, one who excels in any field. **4** A military aviator who has destroyed five or more enemy aircraft. **5** In tennis and similar games, a point won by a single stroke, as upon the service. **—within an ace** Within a hair's breadth; on the very point or verge. —*v.t.* aced (āst), **ac·ing 1** To score a point against in a single stroke, as upon the service in tennis. 2 *Slang* To get the better of, as by a timely move or act. [<OF *as* <L *as* unity, unit]

-acea *suffix Zool.* Used in forming names of classes and orders of animals: *Crustacea* (class), *Cetacea* (order). [<L, neut. pl. of *-aceus*]

-aceae *suffix Bot.* Used in forming names of families of plants: *Vitaceae*, the vine family. [<L, fem. pl. of *-aceus*]

-acean *suffix* **1** Forming adjectives equivalent to those in -ACEOUS. **2** FORMING SINGULAR NOUNS TO COLLECTIVE PLURALS IN *-acea: crustacean*. [<L *-aceus* + -AN]

a·ce·di·a (ə·sē′dē·ə) *n.* **1** Listlessness; mental depression. **2** Sloth, the fourth of the seven deadly sins. Also *accidie*. [<LL <Gk. *akēdia <a-* without + *kēdos* care]

A·cel·da·ma (ə·sel′də·mə) The field of blood; the potter's field near Jerusalem; hence, any place of bloody or murderous associations. *Matt.* xxvii 8 and *Acts* i 18. [<L <Gk. *Akeldama* <Aramaic *hakal damā* the field of blood]

a·cel·lu·lar (ā′sel′yə·lər) *adj.* Lacking cells; not composed of cells.

a·cen·tric (ā·sen′trik) *adj.* Without a center; not in, or directed from, a center. —*n. Genetics* A fragment of a chromosome without a centromere.

-aceous *suffix* Of the nature of; belonging or pertaining to; like: *cretaceous* chalky: *herbaceous* herblike: used in botany and zoology to form adjectives corresponding to nouns in *-acea, -aceae*. [<L *-aceus* of the nature of]

a·ceph·a·lous (ā·sef′ə·ləs) *adj.* **1** Headless. **2** *Zool.* Without a clearly defined head, as certain mollusks. **3** Having no rule. **4** Lacking proper beginning, as a line of verse. [<L *acephalus* <Gk. *akephalos* headless < *a-* without + *kephalē* head]

a·ce·qui·a (ä·sā′kē·ə) *n. SW U.S.* A canal for irrigation. [<Sp.]

ac·e·rate (as′ə·rāt) *adj. Bot.* Acerose. Also **ac′e·rat′ed.**

a·cerb′ic (a·sûrb′ik) *adj.* Sour and astringent; harsh; sharp. See synonyms under BITTER. [<L *acerbus* < *acer* sharp] Also **a·cerb′**.

ac·er·bate (as′ər·bāt) *v.t.* **·bat·ed, ·bat·ing 1** To make sour; embitter. **2** To irritate; exasperate.

a·cer·bi·ty (ə·sûr′bə·tē) *n. pl.* **·ties 1** Sourness, bitterness, or astringency of flavor, as that of unripe fruit. **2** Severity, as of temper, etc.; harshness; sharpness. See synonyms under ACRIMONY. Also **a·cer·bi·tude** (ə·sûr′bə·to͞od,-tyo͞od) [<F *acerbité* <L *acerbitas, -tatis <acerbus* sharp]

a·cer·ic (a·ser′ik) *adj.* Pertaining to the maple. [<NL *acericus* <L *acer* maple]

ac·e·rose (as′ə·rōs) *adj. Bot.* Needle-shaped, like pine leaves. [<L *acerosus* ACEROSE; later erroneously derived from L *acus* needle]

a·cer·vate (ə·sûr′vit, -vāt, as′ər·vāt) *adj. Bot.* Massed or heaped together; growing compactly in clusters. [<L *acervatus*, pp. of *acervare* heap up < *acervus* heap] **—a·cer′vate·ly** *adv.*

a·cer·vu·lus (ə·sûr′vyo͞o ·ləs) *n. pl.* **·li** (·lī) *Bot.* An open, saucer-shaped, non-sexual, spore producing fruit body appearing in some parasitic, imperfectly known fungi. [<NL, dim. of L *acervus* heap]

a·ces·cent (ə·ses′ənt) *adj.* Becoming or tending to become sour; slightly sour. —*n.* That which is slightly sour. [<L *acescens, -entis*, ppr. of *acescere* become sour]

acet- Var. of ACETO-.

ac·e·tab·u·lum (as′ə·tab′yə·ləm) *n. pl.* **·la** (-lə) **1** *Anat.* The socket in the hip in which the head of the femur rests and revolves. **2** A sucker, as on a tapeworm, leech, or other invertebrate. **3** Any of the depressions in an insect's exoskeleton into which a leg fits. [<L, (a small vinegar cup < *acetum* vinegar]

ac·e·tal (as′ə·tal) *n.* **1** A volatile, flammable liquid, CH_3 $CH(OC_2H_5)_2$, used as a solvent and in perfumery. **2** Any of a class of compounds formed from alcohol and aldehydes.

ac·et·al·de·hyde (as′ə·tal′də·hīd) *n.* A flammable, colorless, fuming liquid, used chiefly in organic synthesis.

ac·et·am·ide (as′ə·tam′īd, -id; ə·set′ə·mīd, -mid) *n.* The amide of acetic acid; a white crystalline compound, C_2H_5NO, formed by heating acetic ether with ammonia.

ac·e·ta·min·o·phen (as′ə·tə·min′ə·fən) *n.* A synthetic crystalline compound, $C_8H_9NO_2$, used in chemical synthesis and in medicine as an analgesic and antipyretic drug.

ac·et·an·i·lide (as′ə·tan′ə·līd, -lid) *n.* An acetyl derivative of aniline, C_8H_9ON, consisting of white shining crystalline scales, and used as a sedative and antipyretic.

ac·e·tate (as′ə·tāt) *n.* **1** A salt or ester of acetic acid. **2** A fiber formed of partially hydrolyzed cellulose acetate, used in the textile industry. Also called *acetate rayon* or *rayon*.

acetate rayon Acetate.

a·ce·tic (ə·sē′tik, ə·set′ik) *adj.* Pertaining to vinegar or acetic acid; sour. [<L *acetum* vinegar]

acetic acid A colorless, pungent liquid or deliquescent crystalline solid acid, $C_2H_4O_2$, used industrially and constituting in dilute solution the chief component of vinegar.

acetic anhydride A pungent liquid, $(CH_3CO)_2O$, that combines with water to form acetic acid, used in the manufacture of acetyl compounds.

a·cet·i·fy (ə·set′ə·fī) *v.* **·fied, ·fy·ing** *v.t.* To convert into acid or vinegar. —*v.i.* To become acid or vinegar. **—a·cet′i·fi·ca′tion** *n.* **—a·cet′i·fi′er** *n.*

aceto- *combining form* Of, pertaining to, or from acetic acid or acetyl. Also, before vowels, *acet*. [<L *acetum* vinegar]

ac·e·to·a·ce·tic acid (as′ə·to·ə·se′tik) A colorless product of fat metabolism, CH_3 $COCH_2$ COOH, present in abnormal amounts in the urine of diabetics.

ac·e·tone (as′ə·tōn) *n.* A colorless, volatile, flammable liquid ketone, CH_3 $COCH_3$, used mainly as a solvent. [<ACET- + -ONE] **—ac·e·ton·ic** (as′ə·ton′ik) *adj.*

acetone body Ketone body.

ac·e·to·phe·net·i·din (as′ə·tō·fə·net′ə·din) *n.* A white, crystalline, phenol derivative $C_{10}H_{13}NO_2$, used as an analgesic and anti-pyretic drug. Also called *phenacetin*.

ac·e·to·phe·none (as′ə·tō ·fē′nōn) *n.* Transparent crystals or a colorless liquid, C_8H_8O, obtained by distilling calcium acetate and calcium benzoate, used as a hypnotic. [<ACETO- + PHEN(YL) + -ONE]

ac·e·tous (as′ə·təs) *adj.* 1 Of, pertaining to, or producing vinegar or acetic acid. 2 Tasting like vinegar; sour. See synonyms under BITTER. Also **ac·e·tose** (as′ə·tōs). —**ac·e·tos·i·ty** (as′ə·tos′ə·tē) *n.*

a·ce·tum (ə·sē′təm) *n.* Vinegar. [<L]

ac·e·tyl (as′ə·til) *n.* The univalent radical, CH_3CO, of acetic acid. [<ACET- + -YL] —**ac′e·tyl′ic** *adj.*

a·cet·y·late (ə·set′ə·lāt) *v.t.* **·lat·ed, ·lat·ing** *Chem.* To introduce an acetyl group into (the molecule of an organic compound), as by treatment with acetic anhydride. —**a·cet′y·la′tion** *n.*

ac·e·tyl·cho·line (as′ə·til·kō′lēn, -kol′in) *n.* A compound, $C_7H_{17}O_3N$, released at certain nerve endings where it facilitates transmission of autonomous nerve impulses, and also present in many tissues and species of organisms, including ergot, from which it is obtained for medical uses.

ac·e·tyl·cho·lin·es·ter·ase (as′ə·təl·kō′lə·nes′·tə·rās, -kol′ə-) *n.* An enzyme that inactivates acetylcholine.

a·cet·y·lene (ə·set′ə·lēn) *n.* A colorless flammable, gaseous hydrocarbon, C_2H_2, obtainable by the action of water on calcium carbide, and used in organic syntheses and as a fuel for welding, cutting metals, etc. [<ACETYL + -ENE] .

acetylene series The series of alkynes, of which the simplest member is acetylene.

ac·e·tyl·sal·i·cyl·ic acid (as′ə·til·sal′ə·sil′ik, ə·sē′təl-) Aspirin.

A·chae·a (ə·kē′ə) A department of the northern Peloponnesian peninsula, Greece. Also **A·chæ′a, A·cha·ia** (ə·kā′ə, ə·kī′ə).

A·chae·an (əkē′ən) *adj* . Pertaining to Achaea, its people, or their culture. — *n.* 1 A member of one of the four major tribes of ancient Greece. The Achaeans migrated into Greece about 1300 B.C. 2 A Greek. Also **A·chæ′an, A·cha′ian.**

A·cha·tes (ə·kā′tēz) In Vergil's *Aeneid,* the faithful friend of Aeneas; hence, any loyal companion.

ache (āk) *v.i.* **ached** (ākt), **ach·ing** 1 To suffer dull, continued pain; be in pain or distress. 2 *Colloq.* To yearn; be eager; followed by *for* or the infinitive. [Orig. *ake,* OE *acan;* present spelling due to infl. of the n.] — *n.* A local, dull, and protracted pain. See synonyms under AGONY. [OE *æce* <the v.; pron. before 1700 (āch), present pron. due to infl. of the v.] —**ach′er** *n.* —**ach′ing** *adj.* & *n.* —**ach′ing·ly** *adv.*

a·chene (ā·kēn′) *n. Bot.* A small, dry, indehiscent pericarp containing one seed, as in the dandelion, buttercup, etc.: also spelled *akene.* Also **a·che·ni·um** (ā·kē′·nē·əm) *pl.* **·ni·a** (-nē·ə). [<NL *achenium* <A-[4] not + Gk. *chainein* gape, recoil] —**a·che′·ni·al** *adj.*

ACHENE (Of dandelion: actual size)

A·cher·nar (ā′kər·när) One of the 20 brightest stars, 0.60 magnitude; Alpha in the constellation Eridanus. See STAR. [<Arabic *ākhir al-nahr* end of the river]

Ach·e·ron (ak′ə·ron) 1 In Greek and Roman mythology, the river of woe, one of the five rivers surrounding Hades, across which Charon ferried the dead. 2 Hades.

Ach·e·son (ach′ə·sən), **Dean Gooderham,** 1893–1971, lawyer and statesman; U.S. secretary of state 1949–53.

A·cheu·le·an (ə·shōō′lē·ən) *adj. Anthropol.* Describing a cultural stage following the second glacial epoch of the Pleistocene and noted chiefly for a superior working of stone implements and weapons. Also **A·cheu′li·an.** [from *St. Acheul,* France, where artifacts were found]

à che·val (à shə·vàl′) *French* On horseback; astride.

a·chieve (ə·chēv′), *v.* **a·chieved, a·chiev·ing** *v.t.* 1 To accomplish; finish successfully. 2 To win or attain, as by effort, skill, or perseverance; He *achieved* a position of eminence. —*v.i.* 3 To accomplish something; to attain an object. See synonyms under ACCOMPLISH, ATTAIN, EFFECT, GAIN, GET, SUCCEED. [<OF *achever* < *a chief (venir)* (come) to a head, finish <LL *ad caput (venire)*] —**a·chiev′a·ble** *adj.* —**a·chiev′er** *n.*

a·chieve·ment (ə·chēv′mənt) *n.* 1 The act of achieving; an accomplishment or attainment. 2 A thing achieved; a noteworthy and successful action or a distinguished feat. 3 *Her.* An escutcheon. See synonyms under ACT, CAREER, END, VICTORY, WORK.

achievement age *Psychol.* A measure of performance on an achievement test, expressed in terms of an empirically determined average age for the same performance.

achievement quotient *Psychol.* A number expressing the ratio of the achievement age to the chronological age. Abbr. *A.Q.*

achievement test *Psychol.* A standardized test for measuring an individual's progress in the mastery of a subject to be learned. Compare INTELLIGENCE TEST.

Ach·il·le·an (ak′ə·lē′ən) *adj.* Of or like Achilles; all but invulnerable; wrathful; valiant; swift.

A·chil·les (ə·kil′ēz) In the *Iliad,* the son of Peleus and Thetis, foremost Greek hero of the Trojan War who killed Hector and was killed by the arrow Paris shot into his right heel, the only vulnerable spot on his body.

Achilles' heel A vulnerable point.

Achilles' tendon The large tendon for the superficial muscles of the calf of the leg, attached to the bone of the heel.

A·chit·o·phel (ə·kit′ə·fel) In Dryden's satire *Absalom and Achitophel,* a caricature of Lord Shaftesbury: in allusion to a counselor of King David who joined with Absalom in rebelling against him. II *Sam.* xv–xvii. Also spelled *Ahithophel.*

ach·la·myd·e·ous (ak′lə·mid′ē·əs) *adj. Bot.* Lacking both calyx and corolla. [<A-[4] without + Gk. *chlamys, chlamydos* cloak]

a·chlor·hy·dri·a (ā′klôr·hī′drē·ə) *n.* Absence of hydrochloric acid in the gastric juice. —**a′chlor·hy·dric** *adj.*

a·chon·dro·pla·si·a (ə·kon′drō·plā′zhē·ə) *n.* A congenital, hereditary disease characterized by failure in development of the long bones, resulting in a form of dwarfism. Also **a·chon·dro·plas·ty** [<NL<A -[4] not + Gk. *chondros* cartilage + -PLASIA] —**a·chon·dro·plas·tic** *adj.*

ach·ro·mat·ic (ak′rə·mat′ik) *adj.* 1 *Optics* Free from color or iridescence; transmitting light without showing or separating it into its constituent colors, as a lens. 2 *Biol.* Resisting the usual staining agents; also, containing achromatin. 3 *Music* Unmodulated; without accidentals. [<Gk. *achrō matos* <*a-* without + *chrōma* color] —**ach′ro·mat′i·cal·ly** *adv.* —**a·chro·ma·tism** (ə·krō′mə·tiz′ əm), **a·chro·ma·tic·i·ty** (ə·krō′mə·tis′ə·tē) *n.*

a·chro·ma·tin (ə·krō′mə·tin) *n.* The substance in the cell nucleus that does not readily take color from basic stains.

a·chro·ma·tize (ə·krō′mə·tīz) *v.t.* **·tized, ·tiz·ing** To make achromatic.

a·chro·ma·top·si·a (ə·krō ′mə·top′sē·ə) *n.* Total lack of color vision. [<Gk. *achrōmatos* without color + *opsis* sight]

a·chro·ma·tous (ə·krō′mə·təs) *adj.* Having less than the normal color; colorless.

a·chro·mic (ə·krō′mik) *adj.* Colorless. Also **a·chro′mous.**

a·cic·u·la (ə·sik′yə·lə) *n. pl.* **·lae** (-lē) 1 A slender needlelike process; a bristle or prickle, as on a plant or animal. 2 A needle-shaped body, as some crystals. [<L, dim. of *acus* needle] —**a·cic′u·lar, a·cic′u·late** (-lit, -lā t), **a·cic′u·lat′ed** *adj.*

ac·id (as′id) *adj.* 1 Sharp and biting to the taste, as vinegar; sour. 2 Pertaining to, yielding, like, or reacting like, an acid. 3 Acidic. 4 Sharp-tempered; biting. —*n.* 1 Any sour substance. **2a** Any of a class of compounds that in aqueous solution turns blue litmus red and reacts with bases and with certain metals to form salts. **b** A compound that dissociates in water to yield hydrogen ions. **c** A compound that dissociates in a solvent to produce the positive ion of the solvent. **d** A molecule or ion that can attach itself to another molecule or ion by a covalent bond with an unshared pair of electrons. 3 *Slang.* LSD. See synonyms under BITTER. [<L *acidus* sharp, sour] — **ac′id·ly** *adv.* —**ac′id·ness** *n.*

ac·id–fast (as′id·fast′, -fäst′) *adj.* Not readily decolorized by acids when stained: said of bacteria, epithelial tissue, etc.

ac·id–form·ing (as′id·fôr′ming) *adj.* Pertaining to or designating foods which in metabolism yield a large acid residue.

ac·id·head (as′id·hed′) *n. Slang.* One who uses or is addicted to LSD.

a·cid·ic (ə·sid′ik) *adj.* 1 Acid; having properties of an acid. 2 Forming an acid as a result of a chemical or metabolic process; acid-forming.

a·cid·i·fy (ə·sid′ə·fī) *v.* **·fied, ·fy·ing** *v.t.* 1 To render acid. 2 To change into an acid. —*v.i.* 3 To become acid. —**a·cid′i·fi′a·ble** *adj.* —**a·cid′i·fi·ca′tion** *n.* —**a·cid′i·fi′er** *n.*

ac·i·dim·e·ter (as′i·dim′ə·tər) *n.* Any apparatus or device for estimating or measuring the amount of acid in a sample. See HYDROMETER. —**ac·i·di·met·ric** (as′i·di·met′rik), **ac′i·di·met′ri·cal** *adj.* —**ac′i·dim′e·try** *n.*

a·cid·i·ty (ə·sid′ə·tē) *n.* 1 The state or quality of being acid. 2 Degree of acid strength. 3 Hyperacidity.

a·cid·o·phil (a·sid′ə·fil) *n.* Any acidophilic substance, organism, or tissue. Also **a·cid·o·phile.**

ac·i·doph·i·lic (as′ə·dof′ə·lik) *adj.* 1 Having an affinity for acid stains. 2 Having a preference for an acid environment.

ac·i·doph·i·lus milk (as′ə·dof′ə·ləs) Milk that has been fermented by certain bacteria *(Lactobacillus acidophilus)* to improve its qualities as an intestinal tonic.

ac·i·do·sis (as′ə·dō′sis) *n.* An abnormal condition of depleted alkaline reserves in the blood and other body fluids. —**as·i·dot·ic** *adj.*

acid rain Atmospheric precipitation with a pH of 5.6 or lower due to dissolved air pollutants such as oxides of nitrogen and sulfur.

acid rock A kind of rock-and-roll music with sound and lyrics which suggest drug-taking or psychedelic experiences.

acid test A definite test of value, quality, truth, virtue, etc.: from the alchemists' method of testing metals after attempting transmutation to gold.

a·cid·u·late (ə·sij′ōō·lāt) *v.t.* **·lat·ed, ·lat·ing** To make somewhat acid or sour. —**a·cid′·u·la′tion** *n.*

a·cid·u·lous (ə·sij′ōō·ləs) *adj.* Slightly acid; sub-acid; sour. Also **a·cid′u·lent.** See synonyms under BITTER) [<L *acidulus* slightly sour, dim. of *acidus* sour]

ac·i·er·ate (as′ē·ə·rāt) *v.t.* **·at·ed, ·at·ing** To turn into steel. [<F *acier* steel] —**ac′ i·er·a′tion** *n.*

ac·i·form (as′ə·fôrm) *adj.* Needle-shaped. [<L *acus* needle + -FORM]

ac·i·nac·i·form (as′ə·nas′ə·fôrm, ə·sin′ə·sə-) *adj. Bot.* Scimitar-shaped; having one edge thick and slightly concave, the other thin and convex: said of a leaf. [<L *acinaces* scimitar (<Gk. *akinakēs*) M + -FORM]

ac·i·nar (as′ə·nər) *adj.* Pertaining to, constituting an acinus.

a·cin·i·form (ə·sin′ə·fôrm) *adj.* 1 Having a clustered structure like that of a bunch of grapes. 2 Like a grape. [<L *acinus* grape + -FORM]

ac·i·nose (as′ə·nōs) *adj. Geol.* Consisting of minute granular concretions, as certain ores.

ac·i·nous (as′ə·nəs) *adj.* Composed of small racemose lobules or acini.

ac·i·nus (as′ə·nəs) *n. pl.* **·ni** (-nī) 1 *Bot.* One of the drupelets of an aggregate baccate fruit, as a raspberry; also, a grape seed. 2 A berry, as a grape, growing in bunches; a bunch of such berries. 3 *Anat.* The terminal division of the secreting portion of a racemose gland. [<L, ape]

-acious *suffix of adjectives* Abounding in; characterized by; given to: *pugnacious, vivacious.* [<L *-ax, -acis* + -OUS]

-acity *suffix* Quality or state of: *tenacity, pugnacity:* used to form abstract nouns corresponding to adjectives in *-acious.* [<L *-acitas, -acitatis*]

ack-ack (ak′ak′) *n. Slang.* Anti-aircraft fire. [British radio operator's code for *A.A.* (anti-aircraft)]

Ack·ia Battleground National Monument (ak′yə) A site near Tupelo in NE Mississippi where Chickasaw Indians and English forces defeated French troops and Choctaw Indians in 1736; established 1938.

ac·knowl·edge (ak·nol′ij) *v.* **·edged, ·edg·ing** *v.t.* **1** To own or admit as true; confess: He *acknowledged* his ignorance. **2** To recognize as or avow to be: The savages *acknowledged* the idol as their god. **3** To declare or admit the authority of, as a claim or right. **4** *Law* To assent to the validity of; certify: She *acknowledged* the service of a writ. **5** To own or admit as implying obligation or incurring responsibility: He *acknowledged* his debts to all his creditors. **6** To show appreciation of; thank for: I *acknowledged* the favor graciously. **7** To report and respond to the receipt or arrival of: Her secretary *acknowledged* our letter. —*v.i.* **8** In card games, to respond to a partner's bid so as to indicate a weak hand. [Earlier *aknowledge* < obs. *aknow* admit, confess (OE *oncnāwan*) + *knowledge,* v., admit] —**ac·knowl′edge·a·ble** *adj.* —**ac·knowl′edg·er** *n.*

Synonyms: accept, admit, avow, certify, concede, confess, endorse, grant, own, profess, recognize. See AVOW, CONFESS. *Antonyms:* deny, disavow, disclaim, disown, repudiate.

ac·knowl·edg·ment (ak·nol′ij·mənt) *n.* **1** The act of acknowledging; avowal; confession; recognition; report or admission of receipt. **2** *Law* A formal declaration before competent authority, or the official certificate of such declaration. Also *Brit.* **ac·knowl′edge·ment.** See synonyms under APOLOGY.

a·clas·tic (ā·klas′tic) *adj. Physics* Not refracting. [<GK. *aklastos* unbroken + -IC]

a·cline (ā′klīn) *n. Geol.* A rock bed without any dips or folds, lying in a horizontal position.

a·clin·ic (ā·klin′ik) *adj.* Having no inclination or dip: said of the magnetic equator, where the compass needle does not dip. [<Gk. *aklinēs* <*a-* not + *klinein* bend]

ac·me (ak′mē) *n.* The highest point, or summit; perfection; climax. [<Gk. *akmē* point]

ac·ne (ak′nē) *n.* A chronic skin affliction seen chiefly in adolescents and characterized by inflammation of the sebaceous glands and hair follicles and the development of blackheads and pimples on the face, chest, and back. —**ac·ned** (-nēd) *adj.* [? Alter. of Gk. *akmē* point]

ac·node (ak′nōd) *n. Math.* A point outside a curve whose coordinates satisfy the equation of the curve; a conjugate point. [<L *acus* needle + NODE]

a·cock (ə·kok′) *adj.* **1** In cocked fashion or position. **2** Alert; vigilant. —*adv.* In a cocked manner or position: He set his hat *acock.*

a·coe·lo·mate (ā·sē′lə·māt, -mit) *adj.* Lacking either a true or false body cavity, as the flatworms. —*n.* Flatworm.

ac·o·lyte (ak′ə·līt) *n.* **1** An attendant or assistant. **2** *Eccl.* An attendant for subordinate duties on the ministers officiating at a sacred rite; especially, a member of the highest of the four minor orders of the Roman Catholic Church. [<Med. L *acolitus* < Gk. *akolouthos* follower, attendant]

à compte (à kôṅt′) *French* On account; in part payment.

A·con·ca·gua (ä′kôn·kä′gwä) An extinct volcano in west central Argentina; 22,834 feet; highest peak in the Western Hemisphere.

ac·o·nite (ak′ə·nīt) *n.* **1** The monkshood or any of the generally poisonous plants of the genus *Aconitum.* Also **ac′o·ni′tum.** **2** A very toxic drug obtained from the root of *Aconitum napellus.* [<F. *aconit* <L *aconitum* <Gk. *akoniton*]

a·corn (ā′kôrn, ā′kərn) *n.* **1** The fruit of the oak, a one-seeded nut, fixed in a woody cup. **2** *Aeron.* A special type of fitting used to preventabrasion of intersecting wires in the cross-bracing of an aircraft. [OE *æcern*]

acorn squash A variety of winter squash of acornlike shape having a dark green, ridged rind and yellow flesh.

ACORNS
a. Red oak. *b.* Scarlet oak. *c.* Pin oak. *d.* Black oak. *e.* White oak.

acorn tube A small thermionic radio tube for use at high frequencies. Also *Brit.* **acorn valve.**

à corps per·du (à kôr per·dü′) *French* Headlong; impetuously; literally, with lost body.

a·cot·y·le·don (ā′kot·ə·lē′dən) *n. Bot.* A plant without cotyledons or seed lobes. [<A-[4] without + COTYLEDON] —**a′cot·y·le′do·nous** *adj.*

a·cou·me·ter (ə·ko͞o ′mi·tər, ə·kou′-) *n.* An instrument for testing the acuity of the sense of hearing. [<Gk. *akouein* hear + -METER]

a·cous·ma (ə·ko͞os′mə) *n. Psychiatry* An auditory hallucination. [<Gk. *akousma* a thing heard]

a·cous·tic (ə·ko͞os′tik, ə·kous′-) *adj.* **1** Pertaining to the act or sense of hearing, the science of sound, or the sound heard. **2** Designed to deaden, enhance, or otherwise modify sound. **3** Having no electronic amplification, as a musical instrument. Also **a·cous′ti·cal.** [<F *acoustique* <Gk. *akoustikos* pertaining to hearing < *akouein* hear] —**a·cous′ti·cal·ly** *adv.*

acoustic distortion The discrepancy between the acoustic values of sounds as transmitted over a telecommunication system and as received by the listener.

acoustic phonetics See under PHONETICS.

a·cous·tics (ə·ko͞os′tiks, ə·kous′-) *n.* **1** That branch of physics which treats of the phenomena and laws of sound: construed as singular. **2** The sound-producing qualities of an auditorium: construed as plural. See -ICS.

acoustic saturation The auditory effectiveness of one source of sound as compared with other sources: used in determining the instrumental composition of an orchestra or band playing under specified conditions.

acoustic wind A theoretical wind of constant velocity whose effects on a sound wave are assumed to be identical to the actual winds of varying velocities.

à cou·vert (à ko͞o·vâ′) *French* Under cover; sheltered.

ac·quaint (ə·kwānt′) *v.t.* **1** To make familiar or conversant: with *with: Acquaint* yourself with the court routine. **2** To cause to know; inform: with *with:* She *acquainted* her son with the circumstances of his birth. [<OF *acointer* <LL *adcognitare* make known <L *ad-* to + *cognitus,* pp. of *cognoscere* know < *com-* with + *gnoscere* come to know]

ac·quain·tance (ə·kwān′təns) *n.* **1** Knowledge of any person or thing. **2** A person or persons with whom one is acquainted. —**ac·quain′tance·ship** *n.*

Synonyms: association, companionship, experience, familiarity, fellowship, friendship, intimacy, knowledge. *Acquaintance* between persons is mutual, assuming that each knows the other. *Acquaintance* is less than *familiarity* or *intimacy;* it does not involve *friendship,* for one may be well acquainted with an enemy. *Fellowship* involves not merely *acquaintance* and *companionship,* but sympathy as well. Compare FRIENDSHIP, LOVE. As regards studies, pursuits, etc., *acquaintance* is less than *familiarity,* which supposes minute *knowledge* of particulars, arising often from long *experience* or *association. Antonyms:* ignorance, ignoring, inexperience, unfamiliarity.

ac·quaint·ed (ə·kwān′tid) *adj.* Having acquaintance; having personal knowledge of: with *with.*

ac·quest (ə·kwest′) *n.* **1** An act of acquiring; also, the thing acquired. **2** *Law* Property acquired by means other than inheritance, as by gift or purchase. [<MF <LL *acquistum* for L *acquisitum* <*acquirere.* See ACQUIRE.]

ac·qui·esce (ak′wē·es′) *v.i.* **·esced** (-est′), **·esc·ing** To consent or concur tacitly; assent; comply; with *in* (formerly with *to*): The candidate *acquiesced* in all the party's plans. See synonyms under AGREE, ASSENT. [<MF *acquiescer* <L *acquiescere* <*ad-* to + *quiescere* rest] — **ac′qui·es′cent** *adj.* —**ac′qui·esc′ing·ly** *adv.*

ac·qui·es·cence (ak′wē·es′əns) *n.* Quiet submission; passive consent: with *in* (formerly with *to*). Also **ac′qui·es′cen·cy.**

ac·quire (ə·kwīr′) *v.t.* **·quired, ·quir·ing** **1** To obtain or receive by one's endeavor or purchase. **2** To get as one's own; gain. See synonyms under ATTAIN, GAIN, GET, LEARN. [<L *acquirere* <*ad-* to + *quaerere* seek] —**ac·quir′a·ble** *adj.* —**ac·quir′er** *n.*

acquired character or **characteristic** A structural or functional modification of an organism considered as a result of the activities of the organism or of the postnatal influences exerted by the environment: distinguished from *inherited character.*

acquired immune deficiency syndrome See AIDS

ac·quire·ment (ə·kwīr′mənt) *n.* **1** The act of acquiring. **2** An acquired power or attainment. See synonyms under ATTAINMENT.

ac·qui·si·tion (ak′wə·zish′ən) *n.* **1** The act of acquiring. **2** Anything gained or won; a power or possession. See synonyms under ATTAINMENT. [<L *acquisitio, -onis* <*acquirere.* See ACQUIRE.]

ac·quis·i·tive (ə·kwiz′ə·tiv) *adj.* Able or inclined to acquire, as money or property. —**ac·quis′i·tive·ly** *adv.* —**ac·quis′i·tive·ness** *n.*

ac·quit (ə·kwit′) *v.t.* **ac·quit·ted, ac·quit·ting** **1** To free or clear, as from an accusation; declare innocent; exonerate. **2** To relieve, as of an obligation; absolve: Your generosity *acquits* you of all further duties toward me. **3** To repay or return, as a favor; discharge, as a debt. **4** To conduct (oneself); perform one's part: He *acquitted* himself like a man. See synonyms under ABSOLVE, JUSTIFY, PARDON. [<OF *aquiter* <L *ad-* to + *quietare* settle, quiet] —**ac·quit′ter** *n.*

ac·quit·tal (ə·kwit′l) *n.* **1** The act of acquitting, or the state of being acquitted or found innocent of a charge or accusation. **2** The performance of a duty. Also **ac·quit′ment.**

ac·quit·tance (ə·kwit′ns) *n.* Release or discharge, as from indebtedness; satisfaction of indebtedness or obligation; a receipt; an acquittal.

a·cra·si·a (ə·krā′zhē·ə) *n.* Extreme lack of self-control. [< Med.L <Gk. *akrasia* bad mixture < *akratos* unmixed (of drinks), intemperate]

a·cre (ā′kər) *n.* **1** A measure of land, commonly 160 square rods; also 43,560 square feet, 4,840 square yards, or 0.404 hectare. The Scottish acre contains about 6,150 square yards and the Irish acre, 7,840. **2** A field. **3** *pl.* Lands. —**God's acre** A churchyard or burial ground. [OE *æcer* field]

A·cre (ä′kər, ā′kər) A resort town NE of Haifa, Israel, on the **Bay of Acre** of the eastern Mediterranean: Old Testament *Accho;* New Testament *Ptolemais:* called **Saint Jean d'A·cre** (saṅ zhäṅ dä′kr′) during the Crusades. Hebrew: Akko.

A·cre (ä′kri) A federal state in western Brazil; 59,139 square miles; capital, Rio Branco.

a·cre·age (ā′kər·ij) *n.* Area in acres; acres collectively.

a·cred (ā′kərd) *adj.* Comprising or owning many acres of land.

a·cre-foot (ā′kər·fo͝ot′) *n.* The amount of water required to cover one level acre to a depth of 1 foot; 43,560 cubic feet: used by irrigation engineers.

a·cre-inch (ā′kər·inch′) *n.* One twelfth of an acre-foot, or 3,630 cubic feet.

ac·rid (ak′rid) *adj.* Of a cutting, burning taste or odor; pungent. See synonyms under BITTER. [<L *acer, acris;* infl. by *acid*] —**ac′rid·ly** *adv.* —**ac′rid·ness** *n.*

ac·ri·dine (ak′rə·dēn, -din) *n.* A crystalline compound, $C_{13}H_9N$, obtained from coal tar and used in the synthesis of an important series of dyes and antiseptics. [<ACRID + -INE]

a•crid•i•ty (ə•krid′ə•tē) *n.* The quality of being acrid; acrimony of speech or temper.

ac•ri•fla•vine (ak′rə•flā′ vēn, -vin) *n.* An odorless brownish-red, granular compound, $C_{14}H_{14}N_3Cl$, derived from acridine; used as an antiseptic and disinfectant.

Ac•ri•lan (ak′rə•lan) *n.* A synthetic fiber consisting of a copolymer of acrylonitrile and vinyl acetate: a trade name.

ac•ri•mo•ni•ous (ak′rə•mō ′nē•əs) *adj.* Full of bitterness; sarcastic; caustic; sharp. See synonyms under BITTER, MOROSE. **—ac′ri•mo′ni•ous•ly** *adv.* **—ac′ri•mo′ni•ous•ness** *n.*

ac•ri•mo•ny (ak′rə•mō′nē) *n. pl.* **•nies** Sharpness or bitterness of speech or temper; acridity. [<L *acrimonia* <*acer* sharp]

acro- *combining form* **1** At the top; highest; topped with; at the tip or end of: *acrogen.* **2** *Med.* Pertaining to the extremities: *acromegaly.* [<Gk. *akros* at the top or end]

ac•ro•bat (ak′rə•bat) *n.* **1** One who is skilled in feats requiring muscular coordination, as in tight-rope walking, tumbling, trapeze performing, etc.; a gymnast. **2** One who makes surprising political or other changes. [<F *acrobate* <Gk. *akrobatos* walking on tiptoe < *akros* tip + *bainein* walk, go] **—ac′ ro•bat′ic** or **•i•cal** *adj.* **—ac′ro•bat′i•cal•ly** *adv.*

ac•ro•car•pous (ak′rō•kä r′pəs) *adj. Bot.* Bearing fruit at the end of a stem, as some mosses.

ac•ro•cen•tric (ak′ro•sen′trik) *adj.* Having the centromere located close to one end: said of a chromosome.

ac•ro•dont (ak′rə•dont) *adj.* Having rootless teeth firmly ankylosed at the base with the bony edge of the jaw. —*n.* An acrodont creature.

ac•ro•drome (ak′rə•drōm) *adj. Bot.* Running to the point: said of leaves in which the nerves in running through the blade all point to or reach the apex. Also **a•crod•ro•mous** (ə•krod′ rə•məs).

ac•ro•gen (ak′rə•jən) *n. Bot.* An organism growing at the apex only, as ferns, mosses, etc. [<ACRO- + -GEN]

ac•ro•gen•ic (ak′rə•jen′ik) *adj. Bot.* Growing at the apex, as certain cryptogams and zoophytes; also, of or pertaining to an acrogen. Also **a•crog•e•nous** (ə•kroj′ə•nə s). **—a•crog′e•nous•ly** *adv.*

a•cro•le•in (ə•krō′lē•in) *n.* A volatile colorless liquid C_3H_4, intensely irritating to the nose and eyes, and obtained variously, as by dehydrating glycerol or destructively distilling fats: used as a tear gas. [<ACR) (ID) + L *olere* smell + -IN]

ac•ro•lith (ak′rə•lith) *n.* A statue with stone head and extremities, the trunk being usually of wood and draped. [<ACRO- + -LITH[1]] **—a•crol•i•than** (ə•krol′ə•thən), **ac′ro•lith′ic** *adj.*

ac•ro•log•ic (ak′rə•loj′ik) *adj.* Relating to or based on initials. [<ACRO- + Gk. *logos* word]

ac•ro•meg•a•ly (ak′rō•meg′ə•lē) *n.* A chronic disorder caused by oversecretion of pituitary growth hormone, characterized by enlargement of the face, extremities, and viscera, including both soft and bony tissue. [<F *acromégalie* <Gk. *akros* ACRO- + *megas, megalon* big] **—ac•ro•me•gal•ic** (ak′rō•mi•gal′ik) *adj.*

a•cro•mi•on (ə•krō′mē•ən) *n. pl.* **•mi•a** (-mē•ə) *Anat.* The projecting prolongation of the scapula or shoulder blade forming the point of the shoulder. Also **acromial process.** [<NL <Gk. *akrōmion* < *akros* at the tip + *ōmos* shoulder] **—a•cro′mi•al** *adj.*

ac•ro•nym (ak′rə•nim) *n.* A word formed by the combining of initial letters *(Eniac, Unesco)* or syllables and letters (*radar* and *sonar*) of a series of words or a compound term. [<ACRO- + *-nym* name, as in HOMONYM]

a•crop•e•tal (ə•krop′ə•təl) *adj. Bot.* Developing from the base upward toward the apex, as certain forms of inflorescence. [<ACRO- + L *petere* seek, go toward] **—a•crop′e•tal•ly** *adv.*

ac•ro•pho•bi•a (ak′rə•fō′bē•ə) *n.* Dread stimulated by being at a great height: also called *hypsophobia.*

a•crop•o•lis (ə•krop′ə•lis) *n.* The citadel of an ancient Greek city, especially **the Acropolis,** that of Athens. [<Gk. *akropolis* <*akros* top, highest part + *polis* city]

ac•ro•some (ak′rə•som) *n.* A tiny structure at the front of a sperm cell that releases egg-penetrating enzymes. [<ACRO- + Gk. *soma* body]

ac•ro•spire (ak′rə•spīr) *n. Bot.* The first sprout from a germinating seed of grain. [<ACRO- + Gk. *speira* anything twisted]

a•cross (ə•krôs′, ə•kros′) *adv.* **1** From one side to the other. **2** On or at the other side. **3** Crosswise; crossed, as arms. —*prep.* **1** On or from the other side of; beyond; over: the music from *across* the street. **2** Through or over the surface of: riding *across* the field; A tree fell *across* the road. [<A-[1] on, in + CROSS]

a•cros•tic (ə•krôs′tik, ə•kros′-) *n.* A poem or other composition in which initial or other letters, taken in order, form a word or phrase. [<L *acrostichis* <Gk. *akrostichis* <*akros* end + *stichos* line of verse] **—a•cros′ti•cal•ly** *adv.*

ac•ry•late (ak′rə•lāt) *n.* A slat of acrylic acid.

acrylate resin Acrylic resin.

a•cryl•ic (ə•kril′ik) *adj.* Designating an acid, $C_3H_4O_2$, having a sharp, acrid odor, prepared from acrolein or from certain derivatives of propionic acid, used in making commercial transparent resins and plastics. —*n.* **1** A paint having a base of acrylic resin. **2** A painting made with such a paint. **3** Acrylic resin. **4** Acrylic fiber. [<ACR (OLEIN) + -YL + -IC]

acrylic adic A colorless, corrosive, easily polymerized liquid, $C_3H_4O_2$, used in the manufacture of acrylic resins.

acrylic fiber Any of various synthetic fibers made by polymerizing acnylonitrile, often combined with a copolymer.

acrylic resin Any of numerous tough, transparent, thermoplastic resins made by polymerizing acrylic acid or its derivatives, used to fashion various molded objects and as a component of protective coatings, adhesives, etc.

ac•ry•lo•ni•trile (ak′rə•lō•nī′trəl, -tril) *n.* A colorless, liquid compound, CH_2CHCN, used in the manufacture of synthetic rubber and fiber.

act (akt) *v.t.* **1** To play the part of; impersonate, as in a drama: She *acted* Juliet well. **2** To perform on the stage, as a play: The company *acted* most of Shaw's works. **3** To perform as if on a stage; feign the character of: Don't *act* the martyr. **4** To behave as suitable to: *Act* your age. **5** *Obs.* To actuate. —*v.i.* **5** To behave or conduct oneself: He knows how to *act* in society. **6** To carry out a purpose or function; perform: The brake refused to *act.* **7** To carry out a purpose or function in a particular way: with *as:* The test *acted* as a check. **8** To put forth power; produce an effect: often with *on:* The poison *acted* on his stomach at once. **9** To serve temporarily or as a substitute, as in some office or capacity: with *for:* The corporal *acted* for her commanding officer. **10** To perform on or as on the stage: She *acts* for a living. **11** To pretend; play a part so as to appear: He concealed his real feelings and *acted* friendly. **12** To serve for theatrical performance or use: This scene *acts* well. **—to act on** (or **upon**) To order one's conduct in accordance with; obey: to *act on* someone's advice. **—to act up** *Colloq.* To behave mischievously; appear troublesome. [<L *actus,* pp. of *agere* do, infl. in development by the n.] —*n.* **1** The exertion of power, bodily or mental; something done; a deed. **2** A section of a drama; the largest division of a play or opera. **3** An enactment or edict; a formal transaction, as of a legislative body. **4** A formal written statement. **5** The performance of a natural function or process. [<L *actus* a doing, and *actum* a thing done < *agere* do]

Synonyms (noun): accomplishment, achievement, action, consummation, deed, doing, effect, execution, exercise, exertion, exploit, feat, motion, movement, operation, performance, proceeding, transaction, work. *Act* is single, individual, momentary; *action* a complex of *acts,* or a process, state, or habit of exerting power. *Act* and *deed* are both used for the thing done, but *act* refers to the power put forth, *deed* to the result accomplished. *Deed* is commonly used of great, notable, and impressive *acts,* as are *achievement, exploit,* and *feat.* A *feat* exhibits strength, skill, personal power, whether mental or physical; as, a *feat* of arms, a *feat* of memory. *Achievement* is the doing of something great and noteworthy; an *exploit* is brilliant, but its effect may be transient; an *achievement* is solid, and its effect enduring. See EXERCISE, MOTION. *Antonyms:* cessation, deliberation, endurance, immobility, inaction, inactivity, inertia, passion (in philosophic sense), quiescence, quiet, repose, rest, suffering, suspension.

ac•ta (ak′tə) *n.* Acts; especially, proceedings or minutes of proceedings kept on record in a court. [<L, pl. of *actum* a thing done]

act•a•ble (ak′tə•bəl) *adj.* That can be acted, as a role in a play. **—act′ a•bil′i•ty** *n.*

Ac•tae•on (ak•tē′ən) In Greek mythology, a hunter who surprised Diana bathing and was turned by her into a stag and killed by his own dogs. Also **Ac•tæ′on.**

Ac•te (ak′tē) See AKTI.

ACTH A hormone that is secreted by the anterior lobe of the pituitary gland and that stimulates the secretion of cortisone and other hormones by the cortex of the adrenal glands. [< *a(dreno)c(ortico)t(ropic) h(ormone)*]

Ac•ti•an (ak′shē•ən) *adj.* Of or relating to Actium in Greece.

actin- Var. of ACTINO-.

ac•tin (ak′tin) *n.* A protein component of muscle fibrils that interacts with myosin in muscular contraction.

ac•ti•nal (ak′tə•nəl, ak•tī′-) *adj. Zool.* **1** Bearing tentacles or rays. **2** Of or pertaining to the tentacle-bearing oral region of certain radially symmetrical animals, as the sea anemone.

act•ing (ak′ting) *adj.* **1** Operating or officiating, especially in place of another: *acting* secretary. **2** Functioning; in working order. **3** Containing directions for actors: the *acting* script. —*n.* **1** Performance, especially of a part in a play. **2** Pretense or simulation.

ac•tin•i•a (ak•tin′ē•ə) *n. pl.* **•i•ae** (-i•ē) or **•i•as** A sea anemone. [<NL <Gk. *aktis, aktinos* ray] **—ac•tin′i•an** *adj.* & n.

ac•tin•ic (ak•tin′ik) *adj.* **1** Pertaining to actinism. **2** Potent to effect chemical changes by radiant energy. — **ac•tin′•i•cal•ly** *adv.*

actinic rays Radiation in the violet and ultraviolet part of the spectrum capable of effecting chemical changes, as in photography.

ac•ti•nide series (ak′ti•nīd) *Chem.* A transition series of radioactive elements arranged within the periodic table on the analogy of the lanthanide or rare-earth series: it begins with actinium, atomic number 89, and continues to lawrencium, atomic number 103.

ac•tin•i•form (ak•tin′ə•fôrm) *adj.* Having a radiate form, as actinia.

ac•tin•ism (ak′tin•iz′əm) *n.* **1** The property of electromagnetic radiation, especially in the violet and ultra-violet range, to effect chemical change. **2** The production of such change. [<ACITIN(O) + -ISM]

ac•petin•i•um (ak•tin′ē•əm) *n.* A short-lived radioactive element (symbol Ac, atomic number 89), occurring naturally in uranium and radium ores and produced synthetically in nuclear reactors, the most stable isotope having an atomic mass of 227 and a half-life of 21.6 years. See PERIODIC TABLE.

actinium series The succession of radioactive elements resulting from the stepwise disintegration of uranium of mass number 235 to the stable isotope of lead of mass number 207.

actino- *combining form* **1** Pertaining to a radiate structure or the presence of tentacles: *actinozoan.* **2** Pertaining to the action of light or other electromagnetic radiation: *actinograph.* Also **actin-, actini-.** [<Gk. *aktis, aktinos* ray]

ac•tin•o•graph (ak•tin′ə•graf, -gräf) *n.* A recording actinometer.

ac•ti•noid (ak′ti•noid) *adj.* Having the form of rays; radiate, as a starfish. [<ACTIN(O)- + -OID]

ac•tin•o•lite (ak•tin′ə•līt) *n.* A variety of amphibole.

ac•ti•nol•o•gy (ak′ti•nol′ə•jē) *n.* The science of the chemical action of light.

ac•tin•o•mere (ak•tin′ə•mir) See ANTIMERE.

ac•ti•nom•e•ter (ak′ti•nom′ə•tər) *n.* **1** An instrument for measuring the heat intensity of the sun's rays and for determining the actinic effect of light rays. **2** An instrument for determining the power of radiation by its chemical effect on gases, acids, etc. **—ac•ti•no•met•ric**

(ak′ti·nō·met′rik) or **·ri·cal** *adj.* —**ac′ti·nom′e·try** *n.*

ac·ti·no·mor·phic (ak′ti·nō·môr′fik) *adj. Biol.* Exhibiting radial symmetry in structure. Also **ac′ti·no·mor′phous.** —**ac′ti·no·mor′phy** *n.*

ac·ti·no·my·cete (ak′ti·nō ·mī·sēt′) *n.* Any of an order (Actinomycetales) of filamentous or rod-shaped bacteria, including many animal and plant pathogens as well as saprophytes in soil, water, and decaying organic matter. —**ac·ti·no·my·cet·ous** *adj.*

ac·ti·no·my·co·sis (ak′ti·nō·mī·kō′sis) *n.* An infectious disease of cattle, hogs, and occasionally humans, caused by an actinomycete *(Actinomyces bovis)* and characterized by tumors about the jaws and neck: also called *lumpy jaw.* —**ac′ti·no·my·cot′ic** (-kot′ik) *adj.*

ac·ti·non (ak′ti·non) *n.* An isotope of radon emanating from actinium, having mass number 219 and a half-life of nearly four seconds.

ac·tin·o·ther·a·py (ak′tin·ō·ther′ə·pē) *n.* Radiotherapy.

ac·tin·o·u·ra·ni·um (ak′tin·ō·yo͞o·rā′nē·əm) *n.* The uranium isotope of mass 238.

ac·ti·no·zo·an (ak′ti·nə·zō′ən) *n.* An anthozoan. [<ACTINO- + Gk. *zōon* life] —**ac′ti·no·zo′an** *adj.*

ac·tion (ak′shən) *n.* **1** The putting forth or exerting of power; an acting, doing, or working; operation; activity. **2** The performance by any organ of its proper function: The *action* of the heart was normal. **3** The movement of the parts or mechanism of something: the *action* of the *engine.* **4** The result of putting forth power; the thing done; especially, any act of volition; deed: the rational *actions* of men. **5** In literature, the connected series of events on which the interest depends. **6** A military conflict; battle: a general *action.* **7** *Rel.* A devotional exercise or religious function. **8** *Law* The lawful demand of one's right through judicial proceedings; a judicial proceeding for the enforcement of rights, the redress of wrongs, or the punishment of public offenses. **9** In sculpture or painting, gesture or attitude represented as expressing passion or sentiment. **10** *Physics* A magnitude describing the condition of any dynamic system, expressible as twice the mean kinetic energy of the system during a given interval, multiplied by the duration of the interval. **11** *Slang.* Lively or exciting social activity; excitement: where the *action* is. **12** *Slang.* Money wagered; betting. See synonyms under ACT, BATTLE, BEHAVIOR, EXERCISE, MOTION, OPERATION, TRANSACTION, WORK. [<F <L *actio, -onis* <*agere* do]

ac·tion·a·ble (ak′shən·ə·bəl) *adj.* Affording ground for prosecution, as a trespass or a libel. —**ac′tion·a·bly** *adv.*

Ac·ti·um (ak′tē·əm, ak′shē·əm) An ancient Greek town and promontory in NW Acarnania: site of the naval victory of Octavian (later, Augustus Caesar) over Mark Antony, 31 B.C.

ac·ti·vate (ak′tə·vāt) *v.t.* **·vat·ed, ·vat·ing 1** To make active. **2** To put into or make capable of action, as a military unit. **3** To make radioactive. **4** To promote or hasten chemical reactivity, as by heat or other agency. **5** To purify sewage by aeration or other means of facilitating bacterial action. —**ac′ti·va′tion** *n.*

activated carbon Amorphous carbon specially prepared in finely divided or porous form and highly adsorptive owing to the very large surface area per unit volume. Also **activated charcoal.**

activation analysis A method of chemical analysis by the identification of characteristic radioactive disintegration patterns following neutron bombardment of the sample.

ac·ti·va·tor (ak′tə·vā′tər) *n.* **1** *Biochem.* A substance that renders active an enzyme that is secreted in an inactive form. **2** *Chem.* A catalyst.

ac·tive (ak′tiv) *adj.* **1** Abounding in action; agile; lively; quick; brisk; busy. **2** *Gram.* **a** Designating a voice of the verb which indicates that the subject of the sentence is performing the action, as *fires* is in the active voice in *The soldier fires the gun:* opposed to *passive* **b** Describing verbs expressing action as distinguished from being and state, as *run, hit, jump.* **3** Being in or pertaining to a state of action: opposed to *quiescent, extinct,* or *latent:* an *active* volcano. **4** Causing or promoting action, or manifested in action; practical. **5** Bearing interest; also, consisting of cash or of property easily exchanged for cash. **6** Radioactive. — *n. Gram.* The active voice. [<F *actif,* fem. *active* <L *activus* <*agere* do] —**ac′tive·ly** *adv.* —**ac′tive·ness** *n.*

Synonyms: agile, alert, brisk, bustling, busy, diligent, energetic, expeditious, industrious, lively, mobile, nimble, prompt, quick, ready, restless, sprightly, spry, supple, vigorous. *Active* refers to both quickness and constancy of action; in the former sense it is allied with *agile, alert, brisk,* etc.; in the latter, with *busy, diligent, industrious.* The *active* enjoy employment, the *busy* are actually employed, the *diligent* and the *industrious* are habitually *busy.* The *restless* are *active* from inability to keep quiet; their activity may be without purpose, or out of all proportion to the purpose contemplated. The *officious* are undesirably *active* in the affairs of others. Compare ALERT, ALIVE, BUSY, MEDDLESOME. *Antonyms:* dull, heavy, idle, inactive, indolent, inert, lazy, quiescent, quiet, slow, sluggish, stupid.

active account An account against which many checks are drawn and deposited.

active component *Electr.* The component of an alternating current that is in phase with the electromotive force.

active duty 1 Full military or naval status with full pay and allowances. **2** Service or action in the field or at sea in time of war. Also **active service.**

active euthanasia Euthanasia (def. 2).

active immunity Resistance to a disease due to antibodies produced by the body in response to exposure to or inoculation with a pathogenic antigen.

active list 1 A list of officers of the regular United States military establishment who are in a permanent legal active status entitling them to promotion by seniority. **2** Officers of other components of the United States Army on active duty.

active transport Movement of a substance across a cell membrane in a direction contrary to diffusion, from a lower to a higher concentration.

ac·tiv·i·ty (ak·tiv′ə·tē) *n. pl.* **·ties 1** The state or quality of being active; action; vigorous movement; active force or operation. **2** *Mech.* Mechanical work done in a unit of time. **3** *Physics* **a** The degree of emission from a radioactive substance in terms of observed effects. **b** The excitability of a gas subject to ionization. **4** *Optics* Capacity of a substance to rotate the plane of polarized light to left or right, measured by a polariscope. See synonyms under EXERCISE.

Act of Congress A bill that has passed both houses of the United States Congress and has become law either with or without the approval of the President, in accordance with the provisions of the Constitution.

act of God *Law* An inevitable event occurring by reason of the operations of nature unmixed with human agency or human negligence.

act of war An act of armed aggression by a nation without a formal declaration of war.

ac·to·my·o·sin (ak′tə·mī′ə·sin) *n.* A protein complex of actin and myosin forming the principal contractile constituent of muscle.

Ac·ton (ak′tən), **Lord, John Emerich Edward Dalberg-Acton,** 1834–1902, English historian.

ac·tor (ak′tər) *n.* **1** One who acts; specifically, a player on the stage, motion pictures, etc. **2** Any doer. See synonyms under AGENT, CAUSE. [<L, a doer < *agere* do]

ac·tress (ak′tris) *n.* A woman who acts, as on the stage, in television, motion pictures, etc.

Acts of the Apostles The fifth book of the New Testament. Also **Acts.**

ac·tu·al (ak′cho͞o·əl) *adj.* **1** Existing in fact; real. **2** Being in existence or action now; existent; present. See synonyms under SURE. —*n.* **1** Something real or actually existing; a reality. **2** In finance, actual assets or receipts. **3** A drama based on actual persons or events. [<F *actuel* <LL *actualis* <L *actus* a doing. See ACT.]

ac·tu·al·i·ty (ak′cho͞o·al′ə·tē) *n. pl.* **·ties 1** The quality of being actual; reality; realism. **2** A documentary film or broadcast.

ac·tu·al·ize (ak′cho͞o·əl·īz) *v.t.* **·ized, ·iz·ing 1** To make real; realize in action, as a possibility. **2** To make seem real; describe or represent realistically. —**ac′tu·al·i·za′tion** *n.*

ac·tu·al·ly (ak′cho͞o·əl·ē) *adv.* In act or fact; as a matter of fact; in reality; really; truly.

ac·tu·ar·y (ak′cho͞o·er′ē) *n. pl.* **·ar·ies** One who specializes in the mathematics of insurance, mortality rates, and the like; especially, the official statistician of an insurance company, who calculates and states risks, premiums, etc. [<L *actuarius* clerk < *actus.* See ACT.] —**ac·tu·ar·i·al** (ak′cho͞o·â r′ē·əl) *adj.* —**ac′tu·ar′i·al·ly** *adv.*

ac·tu·ate (ak′cho͞o·āt) *v.t.* **·at·ed, ·at·ing 1** To move to action; impel, as a mechanism. **2** To incite or influence, as the will: I was *actuated* by motives of kindness. [<Med.L *actuatus,* pp. of *actuare* <L *actus* a doing. See ACT).] —**ac′tu·a′tion** *n.*

Synonyms: activate, compel, dispose, draw, drive, excite, impel, incite, incline, induce, influence, lead, move, persuade, prompt, stir, urge. One is *urged* from without, *actuated* or *impelled* from within. See INFLUENCE. *Antonyms:* deter, dissuade, hinder, restrain.

ac·tu·a·tor (ak′cho͞o·ā ′tər) *n.* **1** One who or that which actuates. **2** The mechanism that releases the trigger of an automatic weapon.

acu- *combining form* Needle; point. [<L *acus*]

ac·u·ate (ak′yo͞o·it, -āt) *adj.* Pointed; sharp.

a·cu·i·ty (ə·kyo͞o′ə·tē) *n.* Acuteness; sharpness. [<MF *acuité* <Med.L *acuitas* <L *acus* needle]

a·cu·le·ate (ə·kyo͞o′lē·it, -āt) *adj.* **1** Armed with a sting. **2** *Bot.* Provided with prickles; prickly. [<L *aculeatus* <*aculeus,* dim. of *acus* needle]

a·cu·le·o·late (ə·kyo͞o′ lē·ə·lit) *adj. Bot.* Provided with very tiny prickles.

a·cu·men (ə·kyo͞o′mən) *n.* Quickness of insight or discernment; keenness of intellect. [<L, point, sharpness (of the mind) < *acuere* sharpen]

Synonyms: acuteness, cleverness, discernment, insight, keenness, perception, perspicacity, sagacity, sharpness, shrewdness. *Sharpness, acuteness,* and *insight,* however keen, and *perception,* however deep, fall short of the meaning of *acumen,* which belongs to an astute and discriminating mind. *Cleverness* is a practical aptitude for study or learning. *Perspicacity* is the power to see clearly and quickly through that which is difficult or involved. Compare SAGACIOUS. *Antonyms:* dullness, obtuseness, stupidity.

a·cu·mi·nate (ə·kyo͞o′mə·nāt) *v.t.* **·nat·ed, ·nat·ing** To sharpen; make pointed. *adj.* (ə·kyo͞o′mə·nit, -nāt) Ending in a long tapering point, as a leaf, feather, fin, etc. Compare ACUTE, and see illustration under LEAF. [<L *acuminatus,* pp. of *acuminare* point <acumen. See ACUMEN.] —**a·cu′ mi·na′tion** *n.*

a·cu·mi·nous (ə·kyo͞o′mə·nəs) *adj.* Having acumen.

ac·u·punc·ture (ak′yo͞o·pungk′chər) *n.* A traditional Chinese treatment for pain or disease in which numerous long, fine needles are inserted at predetermined points on the body. [<ACU- + PUNCTURE]

ac·u·punc·tur·ist (ak′yo͞o·pungk′chər·ist) *n.* One who practices acupuncture.

a·cush·la (ä·ko͝osh′lə) *n.* Dear one; darling. [<Irish *ac* oh + *cuisle* pulse of the heart]

a·cute (ə·kyo͞ot′) *adj.* **1** Keenly discerning or sensitive: an *acute* thinker. **2** Keenly discerning or sensitive: *acute* hearing. **3** Affecting keenly; poignant; intense. **4** Of rapid onset and short duration: an *acute* illness. **5** *Music* Shrill; high. **6** Threatening; critical: an *acute* shortage of water. [<L *acutus,* pp. of *acuere* sharpen] —**a·cute′ly** *adv.* —**a·cute′ness** *n.*

Synonyms: astute, cunning, discerning, intelligent, keen, penetrating, perspicacious, piercing, pointed, sagacious, sharp, shrewd, subtile, subtle. See ASTUTE, SAGACIOUS. *Antonyms:* blunt, chronic, dull, grave, obtuse, stolid, stupid.

acute accent See under ACCENT.

acute angle See under ANGLE.

-acy *suffix* of nouns Forming nouns of quality, state or condition from adjectives in *-acious* , and nouns and adjectives in *-ate: fallacy, celibacy, curacy.* [<F *-atie* <L *-acia, -atia* <Gk. *-ateia;* or directly <L or <Gk.]

a·cy·clic (ə-sī′klik, ə-sik′lik) *adj.* **1** *Bot.* Arranged in spirals rather than whorls. **2** *Chem.* Having atoms in the molecule connected in an open chain rather than a ring.

a·cy·clo·vir (ā-sī-klə-vir) *n.* A synthetic drug used in the treatment of virus infections, such as the genital type of herpes simplex.

ac·yl (as′əl) *n.* A radical derived from an organic acid by removal of the hydroxyl (OH) group.

ad[1] (ad) *n. Colloq.* An advertisement.

ad[2] (ad) *prep. Latin* To; toward; as to.

ad- *prefix* To; toward; near: *adhere, advert, adrenal;* often, in English, without perceptible force. Also: *a-* before *sc, sp, st,* as in *ascribe; ab-* before *b,* as in *abbreviate; ac-* before *c, q,* as in *acquire; af-* before *f,* as in *afferent; ag-* before *g,* as in *agglutinate; al-* before *l,* as in *allude; an-* before *n,* as in *annex; ap-* before *p,* as in *append; ar-* before *r,* as in *arrive; as-* before *s,* as in *associate; at-* before *t,* as in *attract.* [<L *ad-* <*ad* to]

-ad[1] *suffix* Of or pertaining to; used to form: **1** Collective numerals: *triad.* **2** Names of poems: *Iliad, Dunciad.* **3** *Bot.* Names of some plants: *cycad.* [<Gk. *-as, -ados*]

-ad[2] *suffix of adverbs Anat., Zool.* To; toward; in the direction of: *dorsad,* toward the back. [<L *ad* to, toward]

A·da (ā′də) A feminine personal name. [<Hebrew, beauty]

A·da·ba·zar (ä′dä·bä ·zär′) See ADAPAZARI.

a·dac·tyl·i·a (ā′dak-til′ē-ə) *n.* Congenital absence of fingers or toes. Also **adactyly** [<NL <Gk. *a-* without + *daktylos* finger] **—a·dac·ty·lous** (ə-dak′tə-ləs) *adj.*

ad·age (ad′ij) *n.* A saying that has obtained credit or force by long use; a proverb. [<F < L *adagium* <*ad-* to + root of *aio* I say]

Synonyms: aphorism, apothegm, axiom, byword, dictum, maxim, motto, precept, proverb, saw, saying. See PROVERB.

a·da·gio (ə-dä′jō, -zhē-ō) *adj. Music* Slow: faster than *largo* but slower than *andante.* —*n.* A musical composition, movement, etc. in adagio time. — *adv.* Slowly. [<Ital. *adagio,* lit., at ease]

adagio dance A ballet dance in slow tempo.

A·dak (ā′dak) One of the Aleutian Islands in the central Andreanof group.

A·dal·bert (ä′däl-bert) German form of ALBERT.

A·da·li·a (ä-dä′lē-ä) See ANTALYA.

Ad·a·line (ad′ə-līn) See ADELINE.

Ad·am (ad′əm) A masculine personal name. [<Hebrew, man] **—Adam** The first man, progenitor of the human race, *Gen.* ii 7. Hence, mankind collectively. **—the old Adam** Unregenerate or depraved human nature. **—A·dam·ic** (ə-dam′ik) *adj.*

Ad·am (ad′əm) Of or pertaining to a neoclassic style of architecture, furniture, etc., originated in England by the **Adam** brothers, **Robert,** 1728–92, and **James,** 1730–94.

Ad·am-and-Eve (ad′əm-ənd-ēv′) *n.* The puttyroot.

ad·a·mant (ad′ə-mant, -mənt) *n.* **1** A very hard imaginary mineral. **2** Formerly, the diamond or lodestone. **3** *Archaic* Exceeding hardness; impenetrability. — *adj.* Immovable; unyielding. [<OF *adamaunt* < L *adamas, -antis* the hardest metal (hence, unyielding) <Gk. *adamas* <*a-* not + *damaein* conquer. Doublet of DIAMOND.]

ad·a·man·tine (ad′ə-man′tin, -tēn, -tīn) *adj.* **1** Made of or like adamant; of impenetrable hardness. **2** Having a diamondlike luster. Also **ad·a·man·te·an** (ad′ə-man-tē′ən).

Ad·a·mic (ad′ə-mik), **Louis,** 1899–1951, U.S. author born in Slovenia.

Ad·am·ite (ad′əm-īt) *adj.* Descended from Adam. —*n.* **1** A descendant of Adam; a human being. **2** One who goes naked in imitation of Adam. **—Ad·am·it·ic** (ad′əm-it′ik) or **·i·cal** *adj.*

A·da·mo (ä-dä′mō) Italian form of ADAM.

Ad·ams (ad′əmz) A prominent Massachusetts family, including **John,** 1735–1826, second president of the United States 1797–1801; his son **John Quincy,** 1767–1848, sixth president of the United States 1825–29; **Charles Francis,** 1807–86), son of John Quincy, diplomat; **Henry Brooks,** 1838–1918, son of Charles Francis, author; **Samuel,** 1722–1803, cousin of John, patriot, signer of the Declaration of Independence. **—Franklin Pierce,** ("F.P.A"), 1881–1960, U.S. journalist. **—James Truslow,** 1878–1949, U.S. historian. **—John Couch,** 1819–92, English astronomer. **—Maude,** stage name of Maude Kiskadden, 1872–1953, U.S. actress.

Ad·ams (ad′əmz), **Mount 1** A peak of the White Mountains in New Hampshire; 5,805 feet. **2** A peak of the Cascade Range in Washington; 12,307 feet.

Adam's ale Water.

Adam's apple *Anat.* The prominence made by the thyroid cartilage on the front of the human throat, conspicuous in males.

ad·ams·ite (ad′əmz-īt) *n.* A yellow, crystalline, arsenical compound, $(C_6H_4)_2$ NHAsCl, used dispersed in air as a poison gas causing skin, eye, and lung irritation and nausea. [after Major Roger *Adams,* born 1889, American discoverer]

Ad·am's nee·dle (ad′əmz-nēd′l) *n.* Any of various species of yucca.

A·dan (ä-dän′) Spanish form of ADAM.

A·da·na (ä′dä-nä) A city in southern Turkey on the Seyhan River.

A·dão (ä-douń′) Portuguese form of ADAM.

A·da·pa·za·ri (ä-dä-pä-zä′ri) A town in NW Turkey: also *Adabazar.*

a·dapt (ə-dapt′) *v.t.* **1** To make suitable, as by remodeling: with *for:* to *adapt* a novel for the theater. **2** To modify (oneself) to conform to a situation or environment. —*v.i.* **3** To become adjusted to a circumstance or environment: with *to:* Some plants *adapt* well to high altitudes. [<F *adapter* < L *adaptare* <*ad-* to + *aptare* fit]

Synonyms: accommodate, adjust, arrange, attune, conform, fashion, fit, harmonize, prepare, proportion, set, suit. *Fit* and *adapt* refer to the bringing about of agreement; *fit* applies especially to original purpose; as, the key is *fitted* to the lock; *adapt* often applies to the securing of agreement by partial change; a novel is *adapted* for the stage by changing it from the narrative to the dramatic form. *Adjust* refers chiefly to relative position; the parts of a typewriter, already *fitted* and *adapted* to each other, must be *adjusted* for perfect alinement. To *suit* is to make one thing or person in all respects agreeable to another. *Conform* implies external agreement, as of a glacier to a rock surface, or of dissenters to an established church. *Accommodate* implies some concession or yielding to secure harmony; as, to *accommodate* oneself to circumstances. *Arrange* refers to position and order, commonly of detached objects; as, to *arrange* the furniture of a room, or the heads of a discourse. See ACCOMMODATE. Compare SET.

a·dapt·a·ble (ə-dap′tə-bəl) *adj.* Capable of being adapted. **—a·dapt′a·bil′i·ty, a·dapt′a·ble·ness** *n.*

ad·ap·ta·tion (ad′əp-tā′shən) *n.* **1** The act of adapting or fitting one thing to another; the state of being suited or fitted. **2** The process of adapting or adjusting to new conditions. **3** Anything adapted. **4** *Biol.* An advantageous conformation of an organism to changes in its environment. **5** *Physiol.* The change in the response of an organ of sense owing to prolonged or repeated stimulation. **—ad′ap·ta′tion·al** *adj.* **—ad′ap·ta′tion·al·ly** *adv.*

a·dapt·er (ə-dap′tər) *n.* **1** A person or thing that adapts. **2** *Mech.* Any device that serves to connect or fit together two parts of an apparatus, or to permit the use of an apparatus for a purpose for which it was not intended. **3** A device for converting available electric current to a form required to power a given device. Also **a·dap′tor.**

a·dap·tive (ə-dap′tiv) *adj.* Capable of, pertaining to, fit for, or manifesting adaptation. **—a·dap′tive·ly** *adv.* **—a·dap′tive·ness** *n.*

adaptive radiation An evolutionary process by which a single relatively unspecialized type of organism gives rise to a variety of specialized forms by adaptation to different environmental conditions.

A·dar (ə-där′, ā′där) A Hebrew month. See CALENDAR (Hebrew).

ad ar·bit·ri·um (ad är-bit′rē-əm) *Latin* At will; arbitrarily.

ad·ax·i·al (ad-ak′sē-əl) *adj.* Toward or beside the axis of an organism or an organ.

a·days (ə-dāz′) *adv.* By day; on each day; during the day: now only in *nowadays.*

add (ad) *v.t.* **1** To join or unite, so as to increase the importance, size, quantity or number: to *add* more weight to the load; *add* insult to injury. **2** To find the sum of, as a column of figures; unite in a total. **3** To say or write further. —*v.i.* **4** To produce an increase in: with *to:* My new duties *added* to my worries. **5** To perform the arithmetical process of addition. **—to add up 1** To accumulate to a total. **2** *Colloq.* To make sense. [<L *addere* <*ad-* to + *dare* give] **— add′a·bil′i·ty, add′i·bil′i·ty** *n.* **—add′a·ble, add′i·ble** *adj.*

Synonyms: adjoin, affix, amplify, annex, append, attach, augment, enlarge, extend, increase, subjoin. To *add* is to *increase* by *adjoining* or *uniting:* in distinction from *multiply,* which is to *increase* by repeating. To *augment* a thing is to *increase* it by any means, but this word chiefly indicates an extension of volume. We may *enlarge* a house, a farm, or an empire, *extend* influence or dominion, *augment* a stream, power, or influence, *attach* or *annex* a building to one that it *adjoins,* or *annex* a territory, *affix* a seal or a signature, *attach* a condition to a promise. A speaker may amplify a discourse by a fuller treatment throughout than was originally planned, or he may *append* or *subjoin* certain remarks without change of what has gone before. *Antonyms:* abstract, deduct, diminish, dissever, lessen, reduce, remove, subtract, withdraw.

Ad·dams (ad′əmz), **Jane,** 1860–1935, U.S. social worker.

ad·dax (ad′aks) *n.* A North African and Arabian antelope *(Addax nasomaculata)* with shaggy hair on the throat and forehead, long and twisted horns, a white spot on the face, and a whitish body. [<L <native African word]

ADDAX
(3 feet high at shoulder; 3 to 4 feet long)

ad·dend (ad′end, ə-dend′) *n. Math.* A quantity or number that is to be united in one sum with another quantity or number called the *augend.* [See ADDENDUM]

ad·den·dum (ə-den′dəm) *n. pl.* **·da** (-də) **1** A thing added, or to be added. **2** *Mech.* The radial distance between the pitch circle and the outer ends of the teeth on a geared wheel; also, the part of a tooth outside the pitch circle. See synonyms under APPENDAGE, INCREASE. [<L, neut. gerundive of *addere* add]

ad·der[1] (ad′ər) *n.* **1** A viper, especially the common European viper *(Vipera berus),* about two feet long, of a brownish color variegated with black. **2** One of various other snakes, as the harmless puff adder of the United States. [OE *nædre* (*a nadder* in ME becoming *an adder*)]

add·er[2] (ad′ər) *n.* **1** A person or thing that adds. **2** An adding machine.

ad·ders·mouth (ad′ərz-mouth′) *n.* Any of vari-

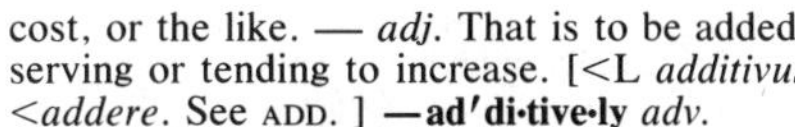

ous delicate terrestrial orchids (genus *Malaxis*), having small greenish flowers.

ADDER'S-TONGUE *(def. 2)*

ad·der's-tongue (ad′ərz·tung′) *n.* **1** A fern (genus *Ophio-glossum*), so named from the form of its spore-bearing spike. **2** Any of various flowering plants, as the dog's-tooth violet.

ad·dict (ə·dikt′) *v.t.* **1** To apply or devote (oneself) persistently or habitually: with *to.* **2** To cause to pursue or practice continuously: with *to:* This task *addicted* me to obscure research. —*n.* (ad′ikt) One who is habituated to some practice such as using alcohol or drugs. [<L *addictus,* pp. of *addicere* assign, devote to < *ad-* to + *dicere* say]

ad·dict·ed (ə·dik′tid) *adj.* Accustomed; inclined to the pursuit, practice, or taking of anything: *addicted* to drugs.

Synonyms: abandoned, accustomed, attached, devoted, disposed, given, habituated, inclined, predisposed, prone, wedded. One is *addicted* to that which has been allowed to gain a strong, habitual, and enduring hold upon action, inclination, or involuntary tendency. A person may be *accustomed* to labor, *attached* to a profession, *devoted* to his religion, *given* to study or to gluttony (in the bad sense). One *inclined* to luxury may become *habituated* to poverty. One is *wedded* to that which has become a second nature, as to science or to art. *Prone* is used only in a bad sense, and generally of natural tendencies; as, our hearts are *prone* to evil. *Abandoned* tells of acquired viciousness to which one has surrendered oneself. *Addicted* is used in a bad sense; *devoted,* chiefly in the good sense; as, a mother's *devoted* affection. *Antonyms:* averse, disinclined, indisposed, unaccustomed.

ad·dic·tion (ə·dik′shən) *n.* **1** Habitual inclination; bent. **2** A condition of compulsive psychological or physiological dependence on a drug.

ad·dic·tive (ə·dik′tiv) *adj.* Of, pertaining to, or causing addiction; habit-forming.

adding machine A keyboard machine that automatically manipulates a series of numbers and processess input by the operator.

Ad·dis A·ba·ba (ä′dis ä′bə·bä, ad′is ab′ə·bə) The capital of Ethiopia. Also **A′dis A′ba·ba.**

Ad·di·son (ad′ə·sən), **Joseph,** 1672–1719, English essayist and poet.

Ad·di·so·ni·an (ad′ə·sō′nē·ən) *adj.* Of or pertaining to Joseph Addison; especially, like his literary style, characterized by clarity, urbanity, etc.

Addison's disease A syndrome resulting from insufficient hormonal secretion by the adrenal cortex, characterized by brownish pigmentation of the skin, anemia, and chronic fatigue. [after Thomas *Addison,* 1793–1860, English physician]

ad·dit·a·ment (ə·dit′ə·mənt) *n.* A thing added; addition. Also **ad·dit′i·ment.** [<L *additamentum*]

ad·di·tion (ə·dish′ən) *n.* **1** The act of adding, or that which is added; an increase; annex; accession. **2** *Math.* The uniting of two or more arithmetical or algebraic quantities in one sum, indicated by the plus sign (+). **3** *Law* A title or mark of designation attached to a man's name. See synonyms under ACCESSION, APPENDAGE, INCREASE. [<F <L *additio, -onis* <*addere.* See ADD.]

ad·di·tion·al (ə·dish′ən·əl) *adj.* Being in addition, supplementary. —*n.* An addition. —**ad·di′tion·al·ly** *adv.*

additional tax A surtax.

ad·di·tive (ad′ə·tiv) *n.* An extra ingredient added in small quantity to a product for the purpose of altering or improving some characteristic, such as stability, flavor, performance, cost, or the like. — *adj.* That is to be added; serving or tending to increase. [<L *additivus* <*addere.* See ADD.] —**ad′di·tive·ly** *adv.*

ad·dle (ad′l) *v.* **ad·dled, ad·dling** *v.i.* **1** To become spoiled, as eggs. **2** To become muddled or mixed up, as a discourse. —*v.t.* **3** To cause to spoil. **4** To cause to become confused. —*adj.* **1** Spoiled, as eggs; rotten. **2** Confused; mixed up, as discourse: now generally in compounds: *addle-pated.* [OE *adela* liquid filth]

ad·dle-brained (ad′l·brānd′) *adj.* Confused; mixed up. Also **ad′dle-head′ed, ad′dle-pat′ed, ad′dle-wit′ted.**

add·on (ad′on′, -ôn′) —*n.* An additional or added sum, quantity, or item. —*adj.* Additional; accessory: *add-on* units for air conditioning.

ad·dress (ə·dres′) *v.t.* **ad·dressed, ad·dress·ing 1** To speak to; accost: She *addressed* the bystanders fiercely. **2** To deliver a set discourse to: The president *addressed* the council every third week. **3** To direct, as spoken or written words, to the attention of: with *to:* He *addressed* his letters to his wife. **4** To devote the energy or force of (oneself): with *to:* He *addressed* himself to the task. **5** To superscribe or mark with a destination, as a letter. **6** To consign, as a cargo to a merchant. **7** To aim or direct, as a ball by a golf club. **8** To pay court to, as a lover; woo. —*n.* (ə) ·dres′, *esp. for* **2** *and* **3** (ad′res) **1** A set or formal discourse; a speaking to or accosting; an appeal; application; petition. **2** The writing on an envelope, etc. directing something to a person or place. **3** The name, place, residence, etc. of a person. **4** Consignment, as of a vessel or cargo. **5** The manner of a person; delivery; bearing. **6** *Chiefly pl.* Any courteous or devoted attention; wooing. **7** Skillful conduct or action; adroitness; tact. **8** *Electronics* **a** A particular location in the memory or storage element of a computer, as indicated by a number or other symbol. **b** a designation referring to a person for the purpose of sending or receiving electronic mail. **9** *Obs.* Preparation or that which is prepared. [<OF *adresser* <VL *addrictiare, addirectiare* <L *ad-* to + *directus* straight] —**ad·dress·er, ad·dress·or** *n.*

Synonyms (verb): accost, apostrophize, appeal, approach, court, greet, hail, inscribe, salute, woo. To *accost* is to speak first to; *greet* is not so distinctly limited; to *salute* is to *greet* with special token of respect; to *hail* is to *greet* in a loud-voiced and commonly hearty and joyous way. *Address* is slightly more formal than *accost* or *greet,* though it may often be interchanged with them. One may *address* another at considerable length in a speech or in writing; one *accosts* orally and briefly. *Antonyms:* avoid, cut, elude, ignore, overlook, pass, shun.

Synonyms (noun): adroitness, courtesy, dexterity, discretion, ingenuity, manners, politeness, readiness, speech, tact. *Address,* as here considered, is a general power to direct to the matter in hand whatever qualities are most needed for it at the moment. It includes *adroitness* and *discretion* to know what to do or say and what to avoid; *ingenuity* to devise; *readiness* to speak or act; the *dexterity* that comes of practice; and *tact,* which is the power of fine touch as applied to human character and feeling. *Courtesy* and *politeness* are indispensable elements of good *address.* Compare SPEECH. *Antonyms:* awkwardness, boorishness, clownishness, clumsiness, fatuity, folly, rudeness, stupidity, unmannerliness, unwisdom.

ad·dress·ee (ad′res·ē′, ə·dres′ē′) *n.* One who is addressed.

Ad·dres·so·graph (ə·dres′ə·graf, -gräf) *n.* A machine for printing addresses from stencils: a trade name.

ad·duce (ə·do͞os′, ə·dyo͞os′) *v.t.* **ad·duced, ad·duc·ing** To bring forward for proof or consideration, as an example; cite; allege. See synonyms under ALLEGE. [<L *adducere* <*ad-* to + *ducere* lead] —**ad·duce′a·ble, ad·duc′i·ble** *adj.*

ad·du·cent (ə·do͞o′sənt, ə·dyo͞o′-) *adj.* Drawing together; adducting.

ad·duct (ə·dukt′) *v.t. Physiol.* To draw toward the axis: said of muscles. [<L *adductus,* pp. of *adducere.* See ADDUCE.] —**ad·duc′tion** *n.*

ad·duc·tive (ə·duk′tiv) *adj.* **1** Adducing. **2** Tending to adduct.

ad·duc·tor (ə·duk′tər) *n.* An adducting muscle.

Ad·dy (ad′ē) Diminutive of ADELINE.

-ade [1] *suffix* of nouns **1** Act or action: *cannonade.* **2** A person or group concerned in an action or process: *cavalcade.* **3** Product of an action or process: *lemonade.* [<F *-ade* <Provençal, Pg., or Sp. *-ada* or Ital. *-ata* <L *-ata,* fem. pp. ending]

-ade [2] *suffix* of nouns Relating to; pertaining to: *decade.* The more common English form of this suffix is *-ad.* See -AD[1] [<F -ade <Gk. *-as,-ados*]

Ade (ād), **George,** 1866–1944, U.S. humorist.

a·deem (ə·dēm′) *v.t.* **1** To take away. **2** *Law* To revoke, as the bequest of a legacy. [<L adimere <ad- to (oneself) + *emere* take]

Ad·e·la (ad′ə·lə) A feminine personal name. Also *Fr.* **A·dèle** (à·del′), *Ger.* **A·de·le** (ä·dā′lə). See ADELINE.)

Ad·e·laide (ad′ə·lād) A feminine personal name. Also *Fr.* **A·dé·la·ïde** (à·dā·là·ēd′), *Ger.* **A·del·heid** (ä′del·hīt), *Ital.* **A·de·la·i·da** (ä′dā · lä′i·dä). See ADELINE. [< OHG, nobility]— **Adelaide, Queen,** 1792–1849, wife of William IV of England.

Ad·e·laide (ad′ə·lād) The capital of South Australia.

A·dé·lie Coast (ad′ə·lē, *Fr.* à·dā·lē′) A region on the coast of Wilkes Land, Antarctica, under French sovereignty; 150,000 square miles. *French* **Terre A·dé·lie** (târ à·dā·ē′).

Ad·e·line (ad′ə·līn; *Dan.* ä′di·lē′ni, *Fr.* àd· lē n′, *Ger.* ä′de·lē′nə) A feminine personal name. Also **Ad·e·li·cia** (ad′ə·lish′ə), **Ad·e·li·na** (ad′ə·lī′nə, *Du.* ä′di·lēə). [<OHG, of noble birth]

a·del·phous (ə·del′fəs) *adj. Bot.* Having stamens with clustered or coalescent filaments: used mainly as a suffix. [<Gk. *adelphos* brother]

a·demp·tion (ə·demp′shən) *n. Law* Disposal by a testator in his lifetime of specific property bequeathed in his will so that the bequest is adeemed. [<L *ademptio, -onis* <*adimere.* See ADEEM.]

A·den (äd′n, ād′n) A former British colony at the SW tip of the Arabian peninsula, now a part of Yemen; principal city **Aden,** pop. about 417,000.

Aden, Gulf of A western inlet of the Arabian Sea, between Yemen and Somalia.

Ad·en·au·er (ad′ən·ou′ər, *Ger.* ä′dən·ou′ər), **Konrad,** 1876–1967, German statesman; first chancellor of the West German republic 1949–63.

A·den·i (ä′den·ē) *n. pl.* **A·den·is** A native or inhabitant of Aden. — *adj.* Of or pertaining to Aden. Also **A·den·ese** (ä′dən·ēz′, -ēs′, ä′dən-).

ad·e·nine (ad′ə·nin, -nēn,-nīn) *n.* A purine base, $C_5H_5N_5$, occurring as a constituent of DNA and RNA and of various nucleotides essential in cellular metabolism. [<ADEN(O)- + -INE[2]]

adeno- *combining form* Gland: *adenology.* Also, before vowels, **aden-.** [<Gk. *adēn* gland]

ad·e·no·hy·poph·y·sis (ad′ə·nō·hī·pof′ə·sis) *n. pl.* **·y·ses** (·ə·sēz) The anterior and principal hormone-secreting lobe of the pituitary gland. —ad·e·no·hy·po·phys·e·al (ad′ə·nō·hī·pō·fiz′ē·əl) *adj.*

ADENOIDS *(a)*

ad·e·noid (ad′ə·noid) *adj.* Of or like a gland;

glandular: also **ad′e·noi′dal.** —*n. Usually pl.* An enlarged mass of lymphoid tissue in the nasopharynx, in severe cases obstructing breathing and speech. [<ADEN (O)- + -OID]

ad·e·no·ma (ad′ə·nō′mə) *n. pl.* **-ma·ta** (-mə·tə) or **-mas** *Pathol.* A usually benign tumor of glandular origin or structure. [<ADEN(O)- + -OMA] —**ad·e·nom·a·tous** (ad′ə·nom′ə·təs) *adj.*

a·den·o·sine (ə·den′ə·sēn, -sin) *n.* A nucleoside, $C_{10}H_{13}N_5O_4$, composed of adenine and ribose.

adenosine diphosphate A compound of adenosine and two phosphate groups resulting from the hydrolysis of adenosine triphosphate. Symbol ADP.

adenosine monophosphate Any of several isomers of a coenzyme consisting of adenosine with an attached phosphate group and playing a major part in energy transfer and hormonal action in living cells. Also called *adenylic acid.* Symbol AMP.

adenosine triphosphate The major energy-carrying molecule in cellular metabolism, consisting of an adenosine nucleotide with three phosphate groups attached by bonds that release large amounts of energy when the compound is hydrolyzed. Symbol ATP.

ad·e·no·vi·rus (ad′ə·nō·vī′rəs) *n.* Any of a group of viruses found in humans and other mammals and producing infections chiefly of the respiratory system.

Aden Protectorate Formerly, a group of Arab tribal districts on the southern coast of the Arabian Peninsula comprising a British protectorate, now a part of Yemen.

ad·e·nyl·ic acid (ad′ə·nil′ ik) Adenosine monophosphate.

a·dept (ə·dept′) *adj.* Highly skillful; proficient. —**ad·ept** (ad′ept, ə·dept′) *n.* **1** One fully skilled in any art; an expert. **2** *Archaic* An alchemist who professed to have discovered how to convert base metals into gold. [<L *adeptus* having attained, pp. of *adipisci* attain < *ad-* to + *apisci* get] —**a·dept′ly** *adv.* —**a·dept′ness** *n.*

ad·e·quate (ad′ə·kwit) *adj* . **1** Equal to what is required; suitable to the case or occasion; fully sufficient. **2** Equal in size, extent, value, etc. [<L *adaequatus,* pp. of *adaequare* <ad- to + *aequus* equal] —**ad·e·qua·cy** (ad′ə·kwə·sē), **ad′e·quate·ness** *n.* —**ad′e·quate·ly** *adv.*

Synonyms: commensurate, enough, equal, fit, fitting, plentiful, satisfactory, sufficient. *Adequate, commensurate, enough,* and *sufficient* signify *equal* to some given occasion or work. *Commensurate* is the more precise and learned word, signifying that which exactly measures the matter in question. Work is *satisfactory* if it satisfies those for whom it is done, while it may be very poor work judged by some higher standard. Compare AMPLE, COMPETENT. *Antonyms:* inadequate, insufficient, unequal, unfit, unsatisfactory.

ad ex·tre·mum (ad eks·trē′məm) *Latin* To the extreme; finally.

ad·fect·ed (ad·fek′tid) *adj. Math.* Containing different powers of an unknown quantity. [Specialized var. of AFFECTED]

ad fin. (ad fin′) At, to, or toward the end (L *ad finem*).

ad fi·nem (ad fī′nem) *Latin* To the end.

ad·here (ad·hir′) *v.i.* **ad·hered, ad·her·ing 1** To stick fast or together. **2** To be attached or devoted, as a follower or disciple, to a party or faith: with *to.* **3** To follow closely or without deviation: with *to:* I *adhered* to the plan. **4** *Obs.* To be consistent, as an alibi. [<L *adhaerere* <*ad-* to + *haerere* stick]

ad·her·ence (ad·hir′əns) *n* . The act or state of adhering; attachment; adhesion. Also **ad·her′en·cy.** See synonyms under ATTACHMENT.

ad·her·ent (ad·hir′ənt) *adj.* **1** Clinging or sticking fast. **2** *Bot.* Adnate; grown together. — *n.* One who is devoted or attached, as to a cause or leader; a follower: also **ad·her′er.** —**ad·her′ent·ly** *adv.*

Synonyms (noun): aid, aider, ally, backer, disciple, follower, partisan, supporter. An *adherent* is one who is devoted or attached to a person, party, principle, cause, creed, or the like. *Allies* may differ on every point except the specific ground of union. *Allies* are regarded as equals; *adherents* and *disciples* are followers. *Partisan* has the narrow sense of adhesion to a party. One may be an *adherent* or *supporter* of a party and not a *partisan. Backer* usually indicates a financial *supporter.* Compare ACCESSORY. *Antonyms:* adversary, antagonist, betrayer, deserter,enemy, hater, opponent, renegade, traitor.

ad·he·sion (ad·hē′zhən) *n.* **1** The act of adhering; the state of being attached; adherence. **2** Assent; concurrence. **3** Close connection, as of ideas. **4** *Physics* The binding force exerted by molecules of unlike substances when brought in contact, as wood and glue. **5** The union of normally separate tissues in the body by proliferating fibrous tissue. See synonyms under ATTACHMENT. [<F *adhésion* <L *adhaesio, -onis* <*adhaerere.* See ADHERE.]

ad·he·sive (ad·hē′siv) *adj* . **1** Having the quality of adhering; tending or causing to adhere; sticky; clinging. **2** Prepared to adhere; gummed. — *n.* A substance that causes adhesion. —**ad·he′sive·ly** *adv.* —**ad·he′sive·ness** *n.*

Synonyms (adj.): cohesive, glutinous, gummy, sticking, sticky, viscid, viscous. *Adhesive* is the scientific, *sticky* the popular word. That which is *adhesive* tends to join itself to the surface of any other body with which it is placed in contact; *cohesive* expresses the tendency of particles of the same substance to hold together. *Antonyms:* free, inadhesive, loose, separable.

adhesive tape A piece or strip of fabric coated with adhesive material, used for bandages, dressings, etc.

ad·hib·it (ad·hib′it) *v.t.* **1** To let in; admit, as to a court of law. **2** To affix; fasten, as a label. **3** To apply; administer, as a medicine. [<L *adhibitus,* pp. of *adhibere* hold towards, apply to < *ad-* to + *habere* have, hold] — **ad·hi·bi·tion** (ad′hi·bish′ən) *n.*

ad hoc (ad hok′) *Latin* With respect to this (particular thing); up to this time.

ad hoc committee A committee formed for a specific purpose in a specific situation.

ad hom·i·nem (ad hom′ə·nem) *Latin* To the man; to one's individual passions and prejudices.

ad·i·a·bat·ic (ad′ē·ə·bat′ik, ā′dē·ə-) *adj. Physics.* Pertaining to a closed thermodynamic system in which changes are effected without gain or loss of heat, as in the insulated cylinder of an engine. [<Gk. *adiabatos* impassable < *a-* not + *dia-* through + *bainein* go]

ad·i·aph·o·rous (ad′ē·af′ər·əs) *adj.* Not included under the essential tenets or principles of religion and morality. [<Gk. *adiaphoros* <*a-* not + *diaphoros* different < *dia-* through + *pherein* carry]

ad·i·a·ther·man·cy (ad′ē·ə·thûr′mən·sē) *n. Physics.* The quality of being impervious to radiant heat. [<Gk. *a-* not + *dia* through + *thermē* heat]

a·dieu (ə·do͞o, ə·dyo͞o′; *Fr.* à·dyœ′) *n. pl.* **a·dieus,** *Fr.* **a·dieux** (à·dyœ′) A farewell. — *interj.* Good-by; farewell: literally, "to God (I commend you)." See synonyms under FAREWELL.<F < *à* to + *dieu* God]

A·di·ge (ä′dē·ā) A river of northern Italy, flowing 220 miles to the Adriatic.

ad in·fi·ni·tum (ad in′fə·nī′təm) To infinity; hence, limitlessly. [<L]

ad in·ter·im (ad in′tər·im) Meanwhile; in the meantime. [<L]

a·di·os (ä′dē·ōs′, ad′ē·ōs′; *Sp.* ä·dyōs′) *interj.* Farewell; good-by: literally, "to God (I commend you)." [<Sp. < *a* to + *dios* God]

ad·i·po·cere (ad′ə·pō·sir′) *n.* A waxy substance formed in decomposing human or animal corpses under moist and airless conditions. [<F *adipocire* <L *adeps, adipis* fat + *cera* wax] —**ad·i·poc·er·ous** (ad′ə·pos′ər·əs) *adj.*

ad·i·pose (ad′ə·pōs) *adj.* Of or pertaining to fat; fatty. See synonyms under CORPULENT. [<NL *adiposus* <L *adeps* fat] —**ad′i·pose′ness, ad·i·pos·i·ty** (ad′ə·pos′ə·tē) *n.*

adipose tissue A type of connective tissue containing many cells specialized for storing fat.

Ad·i·ron·dack Mountains (ad′ə·ron′dak) A mountain range in NE New York; highest peak, 5,344 feet. Also **Ad′i·ron′dacks.**

ad·it (ad′it) *n.* **1** An approach; entrance; passage. **2** A nearly horizontal entrance to a mine. **3** Access; admission. See synonyms under ENTRANCE. [<L *aditus,* pp. of *adire* approach < *ad-* to + *ire* go]

ad·ja·cen·cy (ə·jā′sən·sē) *n. pl.* **·cies** That which is contiguous or adjacent; contiguity. Also **ad·ja′cence.**

ad·ja·cent (ə·jā′sənt) *adj.* Lying near or close at hand; adjoining, contiguous. [<L *adjacens, -entis,* ppr. of *adjacere* < *ad-* near + *jacere* lie] —**ad·ja′cent·ly** *adv.*

Synonyms: abutting, adjoining, attached, bedside, bordering, close, conterminous, contiguous, near, neighboring, next, nigh. *Adjacent* farms may not be connected; if *adjoining,* they meet at the boundary line. *Conterminous* would imply that their dimensions were exactly equal on the side where they adjoin. *Contiguous* may be used for either *adjacent* or *adjoining. Near* is a relative word, places being called *near* upon the railroad which would elsewhere be deemed remote. *Neighboring* always implies such proximity that the inhabitants may be neighbors. *Next* views some object as the nearest of several or many. *Antonyms:* detached, disconnected, disjoined, distant, remote, separate.

adjacent angle See under ANGLE.

ad·jec·ti·val (aj′ik·tī′vəl, aj′ik·ti·vəl) *adj.* **1** Pertaining to or like an adjective. **2** Used as an adjective. —*n.* A word or group of words used as an adjective. —**ad′jec·ti′val·ly** *adv.*

ad·jec·tive (aj′ik·tiv) *n.* **1** *Gram.* A word used to limit or qualify a noun: one of the eight traditional parts of speech. **2** A dependent or corollary. —*adj.* **1** Pertaining to an adjective. **2** *Gram.* Depending upon or standing in adjunct relation to a noun. **3** Of the nature of an adjunct; dependent; procedural: *adjective* law. **4** *Chem* . Requiring the use of a mordant, as in dyeing. [<L *adjectivus* that is added < *adjicere* add to < *ad-* to + *jacere* throw] —**ad′jec·tive·ly** *adv.*

ad·join (ə·join′) *v.t.* **1** To be next to; border upon. **2** *Obs.* To join to; append; unite: with *to.* —*v.i.* **3** To lie close together; be in contact. See synonyms under ADD. [<OF *ajoindre* <L *adjungere* <*ad-* to + *jungere* join]

ad·join·ing (ə·joi′ning) *adj.* Lying next; bordering; contiguous. See synonyms under ADJACENT

ad·journ (ə·jûrn′) *v.t.* **1** To put off to another day or place, as a meeting or session; postpone. **2** To put off to the next session, as the decision of a council. —*v.i.* **3** To postpone or suspend proceedings for a specified time: The court *adjourned* for three days. **4** To move or go to another place: Shall we *adjourn* to the porch? See synonyms under PROCRASTINATE, POSTPONE. [<OF *ajorner, ajurner* <LL *adjurnare* set a day <L *ad-* to + *diurnus* daily < *dies* day]

ad·journ·ment (ə·jûrn′mənt) *n.* The act of adjourning, or the period for which anything is adjourned; postponement.

ad·judge (ə·juj′) *v.t.* **1** To determine or decide judicially, as a case. **2** To pronounce or order by law: The testimony was *adjudged* perjury. **3** To condemn or sentence: with *to:* The defendant was *adjudged* to imprisonment. **4** To award by law, as damages. **5** *Obs.* To regard or consider. [<OF *ajugier* <L *adjudicare* <*ad-* to + *judicare* judge. Doublet of ADJUDICATE.]

ad·ju·di·catè (ə·jo͞o′də·kāt) *v.* **·cat·ed, ·cat·ing** *v.t.* To determine judicially, as a case; adjudge. — *v.i.* To act as a judge. [<L *adjudicatus* , pp. of *adjudicare.* Doublet of ADJUDGE.] —**ad·ju′di·ca′tor** *n.*

ad·ju·di·ca·tion (ə·jo͞o′ də·kā′shən) *n.* The act or process of adjudicating or adjudging; judicial decision.

ad·junct (aj′ungkt) *adj.* Joined subordinately; auxiliary. —*n.* **1** Something connected subordinately; an auxiliary. **2** A person associated with another person in an auxiliary or subordinate relation; a helper; associate; assistant. **3** *Gram.* A word or words added to define, limit, qualify, or modify other words. **4** *Logic* Any non-essential quality of a thing, as distinguished from its essence or substance. See synonyms under APPENDAGE, HELP. [<L *adjunctus,* pp. of *adjungere.* See ADJOIN.]

ad·junc·tive (ə·jungk′tiv) *adj.* Constituting or contributing to form an adjunct. —**ad·junc′tive·ly** *adv.*

ad·ju·ra·tion (aj′o͞o·rā′shən) *n.* The act of adjuring; a solemn oath.

ad·jur·a·to·ry (ə·jo͞or′ə·tôr′ē, -tō′rē) *adj* . Of, pertaining to, or containing an adjuration or command.

ad·jure (ə·jo͞or′) *v.t.* **ad·jured, ad·jur·ing 1** To

charge or entreat solemnly, as under oath or penalty. 2 To appeal to earnestly. [<L *adjurare* <*ad-* to + *jurare* swear] **—ad·jur′er, ad·ju′ror** *n.*

ad·just (ə·just′) *v.t.* 1 To arrange so as to fit or match; make correspond, as to a standard. 2 To harmonize or compose, as differences. 3 To arrange in order; systematize. 4 To regulate or make accurate, as a compass. 5 To make allowance for elevation and deflection, as of a gun in firing. 6 To determine an amount to be paid, as in settling an insurance claim. —*v.i.* 7 To adapt oneself; conform, as to a new environment. See synonyms under ACCOMMODATE, ADAPT, PREPARE, REGULATE, SET, SETTLE. [<OF *ajouster* <L *ad-* to + *juxta* near; refashioned on F *juste* right <L *justus*] **—ad·just′a·ble** *adj.* **—ad·just′er, ad·jus′tor** *n.* **—ad·jus′tive** *adj.*

ad·just·ment (ə·just′mənt) *n.* 1 The act, process, means, or result of adjusting; regulation; arrangement; settlement. 2 *Mech.* **a** An instrument or means whereby something may be adjusted; that which regulates; as, the *adjustments* of a watch, telescope, or microscope. **b** A device, as a screw or wedge, for raising or adjusting a part so as to take up wear or lost motion. 4 The determining of the just amount of insurance payable for losses, as in fire or shipping; also, of the just amount payable for the failure of an article to fulfil a guarantee made of its reasonable wear and use.

ad·ju·tage (aj′ə·tij) *n.* 1 *Mech.* A tube or nozzle for the discharge of liquid, so shaped as to offer the least friction. 2 A spout or tube, as of a fountain. [<F *ajutage*, var. of *ajoutage* <*ajouter* add, join to]

ad·ju·tant (aj′ə·tənt) *n.* 1 *Mil.* A military staff officer who issues the administrative orders of a command. 2 Any of various large storks of the genus *Leptoptilus*. Also called **adjutant bird,** *marabou*. [<L *adjutans, -antis*, ppr. of *adjutare* assist, freq. of *adjuvare*. See AID.] **—ad′ju·tan·cy, ad′ju·tant·ship** *n.*

adjutant general The adjutant of a division or larger military unit. **—The Adjutant General** The officer, holding the rank of major general, in charge of the administrative branch of the United States Army.

ad·ju·vant (aj′ə·vənt) *adj.* Assisting; helpful. —*n.* 1 A helper. 2 Any substance that heightens the action of an antigen or a drug. [<L *adjuvans, -antis* , ppr. of *adjuvare*. See AID.]

Ad·ler (äd′lər), **Alfred,** 1870–1937, Austrian psychiatrist.

Ad·ler (ad′lər), **Cyrus** 1863–1940, U.S. educator and reformer. **—Felix,** 1851–1933, U.S. educator; founder of the Ethical Culture Society.

ad·lib (ad′lib′) *v.t.* & *v.i.* **·libbed, ·lib·bing** *Colloq.* To improvise, as words, gestures, or music not called for in the original script or score. —*adj.* Made up on the spot: *adlib* comments. —*adv.* On the spur of the moment: to dictate *adlib*. [<AD LIBITUM)]

ad lib·i·tum (ad lib′ə·təm) *Latin* 1 At will; as one pleases. 2 *Music* Freely: a direction indicating that a section or passage may be omitted or varied as the performer wishes.

ad li·tem (ad lī′təm) *Latin* For the particular suit or action.

ad·man (ad′man′) *n. U.S. Colloq.* A person who writes advertisement.

ad·meas·ure (ad·mezh′ər) *v.t.* **·ured, ·ur·ing** To assign a share of or to; apportion. [<OF *amesurer* <LL *admensurare* <*ad-* to + *mensurare* MEASURE] **—ad·meas′ur·er** *n.*

ad·meas·ure·ment (ad·mezh′ər·mənt) *n.* 1 An admeasuring. 2 Measure; size; dimensions. Also **ad·men·su·ra·tion** (ad·men′shə·rā′shən).

Ad·me·tus (ad·mē′təs) In Greek mythology, a king of Thessaly, husband of Alcestis.

ad·min·i·cle (ad·min′i·kəl) *n.* 1 Anything that helps or supports; an auxiliary. 2 *Law* Corroborative or explanatory evidence. [<L *adminiculum* a prop, orig., a support for the hand < *ad-* to + *manus* hand]**—ad·mi·nic·u·lar** (ad′mə·nik′yə·lər) *adj.* **—ad′mi·nic′u·la′tion** *n.*

ad·mi·nic·u·late (ad′mə·nik′yə·lāt) *v.t.* **·lat·ed, ·lat·ing** *Law* To furnish corroborative evidence.

ad·min·is·ter (ad·min′is·tər) *v.t.* 1 To have the charge or direction of; manage. 2 To supply or provide with; apply, as medicine or treatment. 3 To inflict; mete out; dispense, as punishment or the sacraments. 4 *Law* To settle by testamentary or official appointment; act as executor of, as an estate. 5 To tender, as an oath. —*v.i.* 6 To contribute toward an end; minister: with *to*. 7 To carry out the functions of an administrator. See synonyms under EXECUTE. [<OF *aministrer* (F *administrer*) <L *administrare* minister to < *ad-* to + *ministrare* serve] **—ad·min·is·te·ri·al** (ad·min′is·tir′ē·əl) *adj.* **—ad·min·is·tra·ble** (ad·min′is·trə·bəl) *adj.*

ad·min·is·trant (ad·min′is·trənt) *adj.* Managing affairs; executive. — *n.* One who administers.

ad·min·is·trate (ad·min′is·trāt) *v.t.* **·trat·ed, ·trat·ing** To administer.

ad·min·is·tra·tion (ad·min′is·trā′shən) *n.* 1 The act of administering, or the state of being administered; management of public affairs. 2 The government as existing, or the persons collectively who compose it, especially its executive department; also, the official tenure of such government. 3 *Law* The legal management and settlement of the estate of a deceased person, as by an executor, or of a minor, lunatic, or one otherwise incompetent, as by a trustee or administrator.

ad·min·is·tra·tive (ad·min′is·trā′tiv) *adj.* Pertaining to administration; executive. **—ad·min′is·tra′tive·ly** *adv.*

ad·min·is·tra·tor (ad·min′is·trā′tər) *n.* 1 One who administers something. 2 *Law* One commissioned by a competent court to administer upon the personal property of a deceased person. [<L] **—ad·min′is·tra′ tor·ship** *n.*

ad·min·is·tra·trix (ad·min′is·trā′triks) *n. pl.* **·tra·trix·es** or **·tra·tri·ces** (-trā′trə·sē z, -trə·trī′sēz) A woman administrator.

ad·mi·ra·ble (ad′mər·ə·bəl) *adj.* 1 Worthy of admiration; excellent. 2 Wonderful; praiseworthy. See synonyms under EXCELLENT, GOOD. [<F <L *admirabilis* <*admirari*. See ADMIRE.] — **ad′mi·ra·ble·ness, ad′mi·ra·bil′i·ty** *n.* **—ad′mi·ra·bly** *adv.*

ad·mi·ral (ad′mər·əl) *n.* 1 A naval officer of the highest rank, in the United States Navy equivalent in rank to a general in the United States Army; also, loosely, a rear admiral in the United States Navy, and a rear admiral or vice admiral in other navies. 2 The flagship of a fleet. 3 Any of various showy butterflies of Europe and North America, such as the red admiral *(Vanessa atalanta)* and the white admiral *(Limenitis sybilla)*. **—rear admiral** A naval officer ranking next below a vice admiral: in the United States Navy, equivalent in rank to a major general. **—vice admiral** A naval officer ranking next below an admiral: in the United States Navy, equivalent in rank to a lieutenant general. See table under GRADE. [<OF *amiral, admiral* < Arabic *amīr-al* commander of the (as in *amī) r-albahr* commander of the sea); influenced by L *admirabilis* admirable]

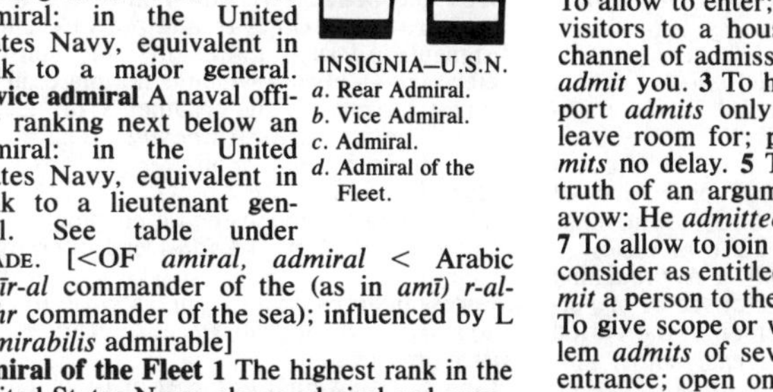

INSIGNIA—U.S.N.
a. Rear Admiral.
b. Vice Admiral.
c. Admiral.
d. Admiral of the Fleet.

Admiral of the Fleet 1 The highest rank in the United States Navy, above admiral and corresponding to General of the Army. 2 Any officer entitled to hold that rank. Also, as a form of address, *Fleet Admiral*.

ad·mi·ral·ship (ad′mər·əl·ship′) *n.* The office or rank of an admiral.

Ad·mi·ral·ty (ad′mər·əl·tē′) *n.* Until 1964 a department of the British government having supreme charge of naval affairs. Since 1964 the Defence Council carries this responsibility, acting through the Admiralty Board.

ad·mi·ral·ty *n.* 1 The office or functions of an admiral. 2 The branch of jurisprudence or of the judiciary that takes cognizance of maritime affairs, civil and criminal.

Admiralty Island An island of the Alexander Archipelago of SE Alaska; 1,664 square miles.

Admiralty Islands An island group in the Bismarck Archipelago; 800 square miles; capital, Lorengau, on Manus. Also **Admiralties.**

admiralty law The code or system of law and procedure relating to maritime affairs; maritime law.

Admiralty Range The mountains on the north coast of Victoria Land, Antarctica.

ad·mi·ra·tion (ad′mə·rā′shən) *n.* 1 Wonder combined with approbation in view of anything rare, great, excellent, beautiful, sublime; hence, pleased and gratified observation and contemplation. 2 That which is admired or excites pleased approval; anything marvelous or prodigious. 3 *Obs.* Wonder. See synonyms under AMAZEMENT.

ad·mire (ad·mīr′) *v.* **ad·mired, ad·mir·ing** *v.t.* 1 To regard with wonder, pleasure, and approbation. 2 To have respect or esteem for. 3 *Obs.* To wonder or marvel at. —*v.i.* 4 To feel or express admiration. [<L *admirari* <*ad-* at + *mirari* wonder] **—ad·mir′er** *n.* **—ad·mir′ing** *adj.* **—ad·mir′ing·ly** *adv.*

Synonyms: adore, applaud, approve, enjoy, esteem, extol, honor, love, respect, revere, venerate. We *admire* beauty in nature and art, *enjoy* books or society. We *approve* what is excellent, *applaud* heroic deeds, *esteem* the good, *love* our friends. We *honor* and *respect* noble character wherever found; we *revere* and *venerate* it in the aged. We *extol* or *adore* the goodness, majesty, and power of God. *Antonyms:* abhor, abominate, contemn, despise, detest, dislike, execrate, hate, ridicule, scorn.

ad·mis·si·ble (ad·mis′ə·bəl) *adj.* 1 Such as may be admitted; allowable, as proof. 2 Worthy of being considered, as an idea. **—ad·mis′si·bil′i·ty, -ad·mis′si·ble·ness** *n.* **—ad·mis′si·bly** *adv.*

ad·mis·sion (ad·mish′ən) *n.* 1 The act of admitting, or the state of being admitted; entrance. 2 A conceding, or that which is conceded; acknowledging or confessing: an *admission* of guilt. 3 The price charged or paid to be admitted; entrance fee. 4 *Rel.* A formal act, by ecclesiastical authority, admitting a candidate to a benefice or church. 5 *Mech.* **a** Entrance of steam or other motive fluid into a cylinder. **b** The point in the stroke or rotation at which such entrance takes place. **c** The period between entrance of motive force and expansion or exhaust thereof. See synonyms under BELIEF, ENTRANCE[1]. [<L *admissio, -onis* <*admissus*, pp. of *admittere*. See ADMIT.]

Admission Day A legal holiday to commemorate the admission of a State into the Union.

ad·mis·sive (ad·mis′iv) *adj.* Characterized by, tending to, implying, or granting admission. Also **ad·mis·so·ry** (ad·mis′ər·ē).

ad·mit (ad·mit′) *v.* **ad·mit·ted, ad·mit·ting** *v.t.* 1 To allow to enter; grant entrance to: to *admit* visitors to a house. 2 To be the means or channel of admission to; let in: This key will *admit* you. 3 To have room for; contain: The port *admits* only two ships at once. 4 To leave room for; permit: Her impatience *admits* no delay. 5 To concede or grant, as the truth of an argument. 6 To acknowledge or avow: He *admitted* his part in the conspiracy. 7 To allow to join or become associated with; consider as entitled to the privileges of: to *admit* a person to the bar as an attorney. —*v.i.* 8 To give scope or warrant: with *of:* This problem *admits* of several solutions. 9 To afford entrance; open on: with *to:* This gate *admits* to the garden. [<L *admittere* <*ad-* to + *mittere* send, let go] **—ad·mit′ ta·ble, ad·mit′ti·ble** *adj.*

ad·mit·tance (ad·mit′ns) *n.* 1 The act of admitting, or the state or fact of being admitted; entrance; right or permission to enter; actual entrance; admission. 2 *Electr.* The reciprocal of the impedance of an alternating-current circuit. 3 In English law, the last stage, or perfection, of copyhold assurances of title. See synonyms under ACCESS, ENTRANCE[1].

ad·mit·ta·tur (ad′mi·tā′tər) *n.* A certificate of admission granted by some colleges. [<L, let him be admitted]

ad·mit·ted (ad·mit′id) *adj.* Accepted as valid or true; acknowledged; conceded. See synonyms under AUTHENTIC.

ad·mit·ted·ly (ad·mit′id·lē) *adv.* Confessedly.

ad·mix (ad·miks′) *v.t.* **ad·mixed** or **ad·mixt, ad·mix·ing** To mingle or mix with something else. [Back formation from ME *admixt* mixed with <L *admixtus*, pp. of *admiscere* <*ad-* to + *miscere* mix]

ad·mix·ture (ad·miks′chər) *n.* **1** That which is formed by admixing; a mixture. **2** The ingredient added to the principal substance in forming a mixture. **3** The act of mingling or mixing, or the state of being mixed. See synonyms under ALLOY. [<L *admixtus*, pp. of *admiscere* mix with. See ADMIX.]

ad·mon·ish (ad·mon′ish) *v.t.* **1** To advise of a fault; administer mild reproof to. **2** To caution against danger or error; warn, as of something to be avoided: The gallows *admonished* the citizens against a life of crime. **3** To charge authoritatively; exhort; urge: He *admonished* me to follow him. [<OF *amonester* <LL *admonestare* <L *admonere* <*ad-* to + *monere* warn] —**ad·mon′ish·er** *n.*

ad·mo·ni·tion (ad′mə·nish′ən) *n.* The act of admonishing; gentle reproof. Also **ad·mon′ish·ment.** [<L *admonitio, -onis* <*admonere*. See ADMONISH.]

ad·mon·i·tor (ad·mon′ə·tər) *n.* One who admonishes; a monitor. [<L]

ad·mon·i·to·ry (ad·mon′ə·tôr′ē, -tō′rē) *adj.* Giving admonition. Also **ad·mon′i·tive.**

ad·nate (ad′nāt) *adj. Biol.* Grown together; fused: said esp. of unlike parts not typically joined, as the calyx and ovary of a flower. [<L *adnatus*, pp. of *adnasci*. See ADNASCENT.] —**ad·na′tion** *n.*

ad nau·se·am (ad nô′shē·am, -sē-) *Latin* To the degree of disgust; so as to nauseate or produce disgust.

ad·nex·a (ad·nek′sə) *n. pl. Anat.* The structures accessory to a main organ or part, as the eyelids and lacrimal glands that serve the eyeball. —**ad·nex′al** *adj.*

ad·noun (ad′noun′) *n. Gram.* An adjective; especially, an adjective used as a noun. [<AD- + NOUN; modeled on *adverb*] —**ad·nom·i·nal** (ad·nom′ə·nəl) *adj.*

a·do (ə·do͞o′) *n.* Unnecessary activity; bustle; fuss; trouble. [ME *at do*, northern dial. form for the infinitive *to do*]

a·do·be (ə·dō′bē) *n.* **1** A sun-dried brick or a structure of such material. **2** The mixed earth or sandy, calcareous clay of which such bricks are made. **3** A brick of clay material with which pulverized ore may be combined. **4** *U.S. Dial.* A Mexican silver dollar. — *adj.* Composed of adobe: often used figuratively to denote things made in Mexico. [<Sp. <Arabic *at-tub* the brick]

adobe flat *Geol.* A smooth, gently sloping, and usually narrow plain composed of clay deposited by an ephemeral stream.

a·do·bo (ə·dō′bō) *n.* A Philippine stew of meat, fish, or chicken marinated in a sauce, browned in fat, and simmered in the marinade. [Sp.]

ad·o·les·cence (ad′ə·les′əns) *n.* **1** The process of growing up. **2** The state or period of growth from the onset of puberty to the stage of adult development. Also **ad′ o·les′cen·cy.**

ad·o·les·cent (ad′ə·les′ənt) *adj.* **1** Approaching adult development. **2** Characteristic of or pertaining to youth. —*n.* A person in the period of adolescence. [<L *adolescens, -entis*, ppr. of *adolescere* grow up. See ADULT.]

Ad·olph (ad′olf, ā′dolf) A masculine personal name. Also *Dan., Du., Ger.* **A·dolf** (ä′dôlf), *Fr.* **A·dolphe** (à·dôlf′), *Ital., Sp.* **A·dol·fo** (ä·dôl′fō), *Pg.* **A·dol·pho** (ä·dôl′fō), *Lat.* **A·dol·phus** (ə·dol′fəs). [<OHG, noble wolf]

Ad·o·na·i (ad′ə·nā′ī, -nī′) In the Old Testament, Lord: a name for God. [<Hebrew, my Lord]

A·don·ic (ə·don′ik) *adj.* **1** Pertaining to Adonis. **2** In prosody, designating a verse consisting of a dactyl and a spondee, supposedly first used in laments for Adonis. —*n.* An Adonic verse.

A·don·is (ə·don′is, ə·dō′nis) **1** In Greek mythology, a youth beloved by Venus for his beauty: killed by a wild boar. **2** Any youth of rare beauty.

a·dopt (ə·dopt′) *v.t.* **1** To take into a new relationship; accept and treat as a member of one's family. **2** To take into one's family or as one's child by legal measures. **3** To take and follow as one's own, as a course of action. **4** To take up from someone else and use as one's own, as a phrase, practice, or creed. **5** To vote to accept, as a motion or committee report See synonyms under EMBRACE. [<F *adopter* <L *adoptare* <*ad-* to + *optare* choose] —**a·dopt′er** *n.*

a·dopt·ee (ə·dop′tē′) *n.* One who is adopted.

a·dop·tion (ə·dop′shən) *n.* **1** The act of adopting, or the condition of being adopted. **2** The legal act whereby an adult person takes a minor into the relation of a child. **3** The acceptance of a word unchanged in form from a foreign language. **4** The receiving into a clan or tribe of one from outside, and treating him as one of the same blood.

A·dop·tion·ist (ə·dop′shən·ist) *n.* One of a Spanish sect (8th century) maintaining that Christ was the son of God by adoption only. Also **A·dop′tian·ist.** —**A·dop′tion·ism** *n.*

a·dop·tive (ə·dop′tiv) *adj.* Pertaining or tending to adoption; characterized by adoption. —**a·dop′tive·ly** *adv.*

a·dor·a·ble (ə·dôr′ə·bəl, ə·dōr′-) *adj.* **1** Worthy of adoration. **2** Worthy of or calling forth devoted affection or attachment. —**a·dor′a·bil′i·ty, a·dor′a·ble·ness** *n.* —**a·dor′a·bly** *adv.*

ad·o·ra·tion (ad′ə·rā′shən) *n.* **1** The act of adoring; worship of God or reverence of the divine. **2** An emotion composed of profound admiration, utmost love, and devotion. **3** Formerly, a method of electing a pope by an act of homage from two thirds of the cardinals present, now, the homage given by the cardinals after his election. **4** A representation of homage to or worship of a person or object, especially of a divine person, as the infant Jesus. See synonyms under PRAYER, REVERENCE, VENERATION. [<F <L *adoratio, -onis* <*adorare*. See ADORE.]

a·dore (ə·dôr′, ə·dōr′) *v.* **a·dored, a·dor·ing** *v.t.* **1** To render divine honor to; worship as divine. **2** To love or honor with intense devotion. **3** *Colloq.* To like especially. —*v.i.* **4** To worship. See synonyms under ADMIRE, PRAISE, VENERATE. [<F *adorer* <L *adorare* <*ad-* to + *orare* speak, pray] —**a·dor′er** *n.* —**a·dor′ing** *adj.*

a·dorn (ə·dôrn′) *v.t.* **1** To be an ornament to; increase the beauty of. **2** To furnish or decorate with ornaments. [<F *adorner* <L *adornare* <*ad-* to + *ornare* furnish, deck out] —**a·dorn′ing** *adj. & n.* —**a·dorn′ment** *n.*

Synonyms: beautify, bedeck, decorate, embellish, garnish, gild, illustrate, ornament. An author *embellishes* a narrative with fine descriptions, the artist *illustrates* it with beautiful engravings, the binder *glids* and *decorates* the volume. A feast is *garnished* with flowers. *Deck* and *bedeck* are commonly said of apparel. To *ornament* is to add outward embellishment. *Adorn* is more lofty and spiritual, referring to a beauty which is not material and cannot be put on by ornaments or decorations. See GARNISH. *Antonyms:* deface, deform, disfigure, mar, spoil.

A·do·wa (ä′dō·wä) See ADUWA.

ADP Symbol for adenosine diphosphate.

ad pa·tres (ad pā′trēz) *Latin* Dead; literally, to his fathers.

ad·press (ad·pres′) *v.t.* To press close to. [<L *adpressus*, pp. of *adprimere* <*ad-* to + *premere* press]

ad quem (ad kwem′) *Latin* At or to which.

A·dras·tus (ə·dras′təs) In Greek legend, a king of Argos who led the Seven against Thebes, of whom he was the only survivor. See SEVEN AGAINST THEBES.

ad ref·er·en·dum (ad ref′ə·ren′dəm) *Latin* For further consideration.

ad rem (ad rem′) *Latin* To the point; direct; pertinent.

ad·re·nal (ə·drē′nəl) *adj.* **1** Near the kidneys. **2** Of or from the adrenal glands. —*n.* Either of the adrenal glands. [<AD- + L *renes* kidneys]

adrenal gland Either of the two endocrine glands located on the upper end of each kidney and consisting of a medulla, which secretes epinephrine and norepinephrine, and a cortex, which secretes various steroidal hormones. Also called *suprarenal gland.*

ad·ren·a·line (ə·dren′a·lin) *n.* **1** *Brit.* Epinephrine. **2** An internal stimulant popularly adduced as the initiator of energetic reactions to danger, challenge, etc. **3** *Colloq.* Used in nontechnical contexts: My *adrenaline* was pumping when we won the game.

Ad·ren·a·lin (ə·dren′ə·lin) Proprietary name for a pharmaceutical preparation of epinephrine.

ad·ren·er·gic (ad′rə·nėr′gik) *adj.* **1** Having chemical activity similar to that of epinephrine or related substances. **2** Stimulating the release of epinephrine or similar hormones.

ad·re·no·cor·ti·cal (ə·drē′no·kôr′tə·kəl) *adj.* Pertaining to or secreted by the cortex of the adrenal gland.

ad·re·no·cor·ti·co·tro·pic (ə·drē′nō·kôr′ti·ko·trō′pik) *adj.* Acting upon the cortex of the adrenal gland. Also **adrenocorticotrophic.**

adrenocorticotropic hormone ACTH.

A·dri·an (ā′drē·ən) **1** A masculine personal name. Also *Fr.* **A·dri·en** (à·drē·aṅ′), *Ital.* **A·dri·a·no** (ä′drē·ä′nō), *Lat.* **A·dri·a·nus** (ā′drē ā′nəs). **2** Appellation of six popes. [<L] —**Adrian** See HADRIAN. —**Adrian IV,** 1100?–59, real name Nicholas Breakspear, pope 1154–59; the only English pope.

A·dri·a·no·ple (ā′drē·ə·nō′pəl) An ancient city of Europe. See EDIRNE.

A·dri·at·ic (ā′drē·at′·ik) *adj.* Of or pertaining to the Adriatic Sea or to the inhabitants of its coastal regions.

Adriatic race See DINARIC RACE.

Adriatic Sea An arm of the Mediterranean Sea, east of Italy; 500 miles long.

a·drift (ə·drift′) *adv. & adj.* In a drifting state; drifting.

a·droit (ə·droit′) *adj.* Skillful in varied situations dexterous; expert. See synonyms under CLEVER. [<F < *à* to (<L *ad-*) + *droit* right (<L *directus*)] —**a·droit′ly** *adv.* —**a·droit′ness** *n.*

à droite (à drwát′) *French* To, toward, or on the right.

ad·sci·ti·tious (ad′sə·tish′əs) *adj.* Supplemental; adventitious; added from without; not essential. [<L *adscitus*, pp. of *adsciscere* admit, accept < *ad-* to + *sciscere* acknowledge]

ad·script (ad′skript) *adj.* Written after: distinguished from *subscript.* [<L *adscriptus*, pp. of *adscribere, ascribere*. See ASCRIBE.] —**ad·scrip′tion** *n.*

ad·sorb (ad·sôrb′, -zôrb′) *v.t. Chem.* To condense and hold by adsorption: distinguished from *absorb.* [<AD- + L *sorbere* suck in] —**ad·sor′bent** *n.*

ad·sor·bate (ad·sôr′bāt, -zôr′-) *n.* A substance that has been or is being adsorbed.

ad·sorp·tion (ad·sôrp′shən, -zôrp′-) *n.* The retention of molecules or ions of a gas or liquid on the surface of a different substance. [<ADSORB; modeled on *absorption*] —**ad·sorp′tive** *adj.*

ad·su·ki bean (ad·so͞o′kē, -zo͞o′-) **1** A leguminous plant *(Phaseolus angularis)* widely cultivated in East Asia. **2** The edible seed of this plant. Also *adzuki bean.* [<Japanese *adzuki*]

ad·sum (ad′sum) *Latin* I am present: an answer to a roll call.

ad sum·mum (ad sum′əm) *Latin* To the highest point or amount.

ad·u·la·res·cence (aj′ə·lə·res′əns) *n.* The peculiar sheen of the ordinary moonstone. [<ADULARIA + -ESCENCE]

ad·u·lar·i·a (aj′ə·lâr′ē·ə) *n. Mineral.* A transparent or translucent form of orthoclase; moonstone. [from Mt. *Adula*, in Switzerland]

ad·u·late (aj′ə·lāt) *v.t.* **·lat·ed, ·lat·ing** To flatter servilely; praise extravagantly. [<L *adulatus*, pp. of *adulari* fawn] —**ad′u·la′tor** *n.*

ad·u·la·tion (aj′ə·lā′shən) *n.* Servile flattery;

extravagant and hypocritical praise; fulsome compliment.

ad·u·la·to·ry (aj′ə·lə·tôr′ē, -tō′rē) *adj.* Obsequiously flattering.

A·dul·lam·ite (ə·dul′əm·īt) *n.* **1** A native or inhabitant of Adullam. *Gen.* xxxviii 1. **2** In English history, a seceder (1866) from the Liberal party. Compare I *Sam.* xxii 1, 2.

a·dult (ə·dult′, ad′ult) *n.* **1** A person who has attained the age of maturity or legal majority. **2** *Biol.* A fully developed animal or plant. —*adj.* **1** Grown-up; full-grown: an *adult* person. **2** Of or for grown-up persons: *adult* behavior, *adult* education. **3** Pertaining to or of a sexual nature. [<L *adultus,* pp. of *adolescere* grow up < *ad-* to + *alescere* grow. Related to ADOLESCENT.] —**a·dult′ness** *n.*

a·dul·ter·ant (ə·dul′tər·ənt) *n.* An adulterating substance. See synonyms under ALLOY.)

a·dul·ter·ate (ə·dul′tər·āt) *v.t.* **·at·ed, ·at·ing** To make impure or inferior by admixture of other or baser ingredients; corrupt. —*adj.* (ə·dul′tər·it) **1** Adulterated; corrupted; debased; spurious. **2** Adulterous. [<L *adulteratus,* pp. of *adulterare* corrupt < *ad-* to + *alter* other, different] —**a·dul′ter·a′tion** *n.* —**a·dul′ter·a′tor** *n.*

a·dul·ter·ine (ə·dul′tər·in, -īn) *adj.* **1** Originating in, or pertaining to, adultery: *adulterine* children. **2** Unauthorized; spurious.

a·dul·ter·ous (ə·dul′tər·əs) *adj.* Of, pertaining to, or given to adultery; illicit. —**a·dul′ter·ous·ly** *adv.*

a·dul·ter·y (ə·dul′tər·ē) *n. pl.* **·ter·ies** **1** The sexual intercourse of two persons, either of whom is married to a third person; unchastity; unfaithfulness. **2** Any lewdness or unchastity of act or thought, as in violation of the divine commandments. *Matt.* v 27, 28. **3** *Eccl.* A marriage not approved by ecclesiastical authority. [<L *adulterium*] —**a·dul′ ter·er** *n.* —**a·dul′ter·ess** *n. fem.*

a·dult·hood (ə·dult′ho͝od) *n.* The state of being an adult.

ad·um·bral (ad·um′brəl) *adj.* Overshadowing; shady.

ad·um·brant (ad·um′brənt) *adj.* Dimly shadowing.

ad·um·brate (ad·um′brāt) *v.t.* **·brat·ed, ·brat·ing** **1** To represent the mere shadow of; to outline sketchily. **2** To foreshadow; prefigure. **3** To shade or overshadow; darken. [<L *adumbratus,* pp. of *adumbrare* < *ad-* to + *umbrare* shade < *umbra* shade]

ad·um·bra·tion (ad′əm·brā ′shən) *n.* **1** A slight sketch. **2** A foreshadowing. **3** An overshadowing; obscuration.

ad·um·bra·tive (ad·um′brə·tiv) *adj.* Faintly indicative.

a·dust (ə·dust′) *adj.* **1** Burning; hot; seared. **2** Browned; sunburnt. **3** Parched and dry; formerly said of the body or blood. **4** Melancholy; gloomy. [<L *adustus,* pp. of *adurere* burn up < *ad-* to + *urere* burn]

A·du·wa (ä′do͞o·wä) A town in Eritrea: also *Adowa.*

ad va·lo·rem (ad və·lôr′əm, -lō′rəm) According or in proportion to the value: *Ad valorem* duties are based on a percentage of the value of the goods imported. [<L]

ad·vance (ad·vans′, -väns′) *v.* **ad·vanced, ad·vanc·ing** *v.t.* **1** To cause to go forward or upward; move forward in position or place. **2** To put in a better or more advantageous situation. **3** To further; promote: to *advance* the progress of science. **4** To make occur earlier; accelerate. **5** To offer; propose: to *advance* a suggestion. **6** To raise in rate or price: to *advance* a discount to five percent. **7** To pay, as money or interest, before legally due. **8** To lend: Can you *advance* me some money? **9** *Law* To provide, as financial support, for children, especially before the distribution of an estate. —*v.i.* **10** To move or go forward: The armies *advance* on all fronts. **11** To make progress; rise or improve: The stock market *advanced* three points. See synonyms under ACCELERATE, AMEND, FLOURISH, INCREASE, PROMOTE, SERVE. —*adj.* Of, pertaining to, or being an advance; being before in time or place: an *advance* payment. —*n.* **1** The act of advancing, or the state of being advanced; forward movement; progress; improvement; also, an increase or rise, as of prices. **2** One who or that which is at the head; the foremost part. **3** Anything supplied or paid beforehand; also, the act of so supplying or paying. **4** An act of personal approach; overture; proposal: His *advances* were rejected. **5** The place at the front, or in the lead. **6** *Naut.* The distance made by a vessel in the line of a previous course after putting down the helm, as for a tack: distinguished from *transfer.* **7** In fencing, a swift, short step forward with the right foot, promptly followed by the left, in such a manner as to enable the fencer to retain balance and be in readiness for parry, etc. See synonyms under PROGRESS. [ME *avancen* <OF *avancier* <L *ab-* away + *ante* before; the initial *a-* was later altered to *ad-* as if from L *ad-* to, toward]—**in advance** **1** In front. **2** Before due; beforehand. —**ad·vanc′er** *n.*

ad·vanced (ad·vanst′, -vänst′) *adj.* **1** Being ranged at the front, or in advance of others, as in progress or thought: *advanced* ideas. **2** Having arrived at a somewhat late or forward stage, as of life, time, etc.: an *advanced* age.

advanced standing Credit allowed a student by one college for courses taken at another.

advance guard A detachment of troops marching ahead of the main body to insure its security and progress, and to locate the main body of enemy troops.

ad·vance·ment (ad·vans′mənt, -väns′-) *n.* **1** The act of advancing, or the state of being advanced; progression; furtherance; promotion; preferment; uplift: the *advancement* of knowledge. **2** A payment of money before it is due.

advance post One of the positions of a detachment of troops in advance of the main body, occupied for its security, from which information about the enemy is sent back to headquarters.

advance signal A signal, in the block system, indicating that a train may pass a block even when the entire block is not clear.

ad·vanc·ing (ad·vans′ing, -väns′-) *adj.* Forward-moving; increasing; progressive. —**ad·vanc′ing·ly** *adv.*

ad·van·tage (ad·van′tij, -vän′-) *n.* **1** Anything favorable to success; superiority; favoring circumstance. **2** Gain or benefit; profit. See synonyms under PROFIT, RIGHT, UTILITY, VICTORY. —**to advantage** So as to reveal the best of or bring about the best results. —*v.t.* **·taged, ·tag·ing** To give advantage or profit to; be a benefit or service to. [<OF *avantage* <*avant* before <L *ab ante* from before. See ADVANCE.]

ad·van·ta·geous (ad′vən·tā ′jəs) *adj.* Affording advantage; profitable; favorable; beneficial. See synonyms under EXPEDIENT, GOOD. —**ad′van·ta′geous·ly** *adv.* — **ad′van·ta′geous·ness** *n.*

ad·vec·tion (ad·vek′shən) *n. Meteorol.* Heat-transference by the horizontal motion of air currents. [<L *advectio, -onis* <*advehere* convey < *ad-* to + *vehere* carry]

ad·vent (ad′vent) *n.* A coming or arrival, as of any important event or person. [<L *adventus,* pp. of *advenire* <*ad-* to + *venire* come]

Ad·vent (ad′vent) *n.* **1** The birth of Christ. **2** The second coming of Christ. **3** The season including the four Sundays before Christmas.

Ad·vent·ist (ad′ven·tist, ad·ven′-) *n.* One who believes in the second coming of Christ, the Last Judgment, and the end of the world are at hand: the term is now applied to a member of any of the following sects, all descended from the church founded by William Miller: **Advent Christian Church, Seventh-Day Adventists, Church of God (Seventh Day).** See MILLERITE. —**Ad′vent·ism** *n.*

ad·ven·ti·ti·a (ad′ven·tish′ē·ə) *n.* The outermost covering of an organ or a blood vessel, composed of extrinsic connective tissue. —**ad′ven·ti′tial** *adj.*

ad·ven·ti·tious (ad′ven·tish′əs) *adj.* **1** Not inherent; extrinsic; accidental; casual. **2** Accidental; acquired, not inherited. **3** *Biol.* **a** Occurring in an unusual location: an *adventitious* root. **b** Adventitial. **c** Adventive. [<L *adventicius* coming from abroad, foreign. See ADVENT.] —**ad′ven·ti′tious·ly** *adv.* —**ad′ven·ti′tious·ness** *n.*

ad·ven·tive (ad·ven′tiv) *adj. Biol.* Exotic; not firmly established in a new environment. —*n.* An adventive organism.

Advent Sunday The Sunday nearest to St. Andrew's Day, the last day of November.

ad·ven·ture (ad·ven′chər) *v.* **·tured, ·tur·ing** *v.t.* **1** To venture upon; take the chance of. **2** To risk the loss of; imperil. —*v.i.* **3** To run risks. **4** To venture upon daring or dangerous undertakings. —*n.* **1** A hazardous or exciting experience; daring feat. **2** A commercial venture; speculation. **3** *Obs.* Danger; hazard; chance; fortune. See synonyms under ACCIDENT. [<OF *aventure* <L *adventura (res)* (a thing) about to happen < *advenire.* See ADVENT.]

ad·ven·tur·er (ad·ven′chər·ər) *n.* A seeker of adventures or fortune in new fields or by questionable means.

ad·ven·tur·ous (ad·ven′chər·əs) *adj.* **1** Disposed to seek adventures or take risks; venturesome. Also **ad·ven′ture·some** (-səm). **2** Attended with risk; hazardous. See synonyms under BRAVE. —**ad·ven′tur·ous·ly** *adv.* —**ad·ven′tur·ous·ness** *n.*

ad·verb (ad′vûrb) *n.* **1** Any of a class of words used to modify the meaning of a verb, adjective, or other adverb, in regard to time, place, manner, means, cause, degree, etc.: one of the eight traditional parts of speech. **2** Any word or phrase having this function. [<L *adverbium* <*ad-* to + *verbum* verb]

ad·ver·bi·al (ad·vûr′bē·əl) *adj.* Of, pertaining to, containing, used like an adverb, or tending to use adverbs. —**ad·ver·bi·al·i·ty** (ad·vûr′bē·al′ə·tē) *n.* —**ad·ver′bi·al·ly** *adv.*

ad·ver·sar·y (ad′vər·ser′ ē) *n. pl.* **·sar·ies** One actively hostile; an opponent; enemy. See synonyms under ANTAGONIST, ENEMY. —**the Adversary** Satan. [<L *adversarius,* lit., one turned towards < *adversus.* See ADVERSE.]

ad·ver·sa·tive (ad·vûr′sə·tiv) *adj.* Expressing opposition or antithesis. — *n.* An antithetic word or proposition. —**ad·ver′ sa·tive·ly** *adv.*

ad·verse (ad·vûrs′, ad′vûrs) *adj.* **1** Opposing or opposed; antagonistic; also, unpropitious; detrimental. **2** *Bot.* Turned toward the stem or main axis. **3** Opposite. See synonyms under INIMICAL. [<L *adversus* turned against, pp. of *advertere* <*ad-* to + *vertere* turn] —**ad·verse′ly** *adv.* —**ad·verse′ness** *n.*

ad·ver·si·ty (ad·vûr′sə·tē) *n. pl.* **·ties** A condition of hardship or affliction; misfortune; calamity. See synonyms under CATASTROPHE, MISFORTUNE. [<OF *aversite* <L *adversitas* <*adversus.* See ADVERSE.]

ad·vert (ad·vûrt′) *v.i.* To turn the attention; take notice; refer: with *to.* See synonyms under ALLUDE. [<L *advertere* <*ad-* to + *vertere* turn] —**ad·ver′tence, ad·ver′ten·cy** *n.*

ad·ver·tent (ad·vûr′tənt) *adj.* Giving attention; heedful. —**ad·ver′tent·ly** *adv.*

ad·ver·tise (ad′vər·tīz, ad′vər·tīz′) *v.* **·tised, ·tis·ing** *v.t.* **1** To make known by public notice; to proclaim the qualities of, as by publication or broadcasting, generally in order to sell. **2** *Obs.* To notify or warn. —*v.i.* **3** To inquire by public notice, as in a newspaper: with *for:* to *advertise* for a house. **4** To distribute or publish advertisements: The company *advertised* widely in national magazines. See synonyms under ANNOUNCE, INFORM, PUBLISH. Also **ad′ver·tize.** [<MF *advertiss-,* stem of *advertir* warn, give notice to <L *advertere.* See ADVERT.] —**ad′ver·tis′er** *n.*

ad·ver·tise·ment (ad′vər·tīz′mənt, ad·vûr′tis·mənt, -tiz-) *n.* **1** A public notice, as in a newspaper or on a radio or television program. **2** A giving notice; notification; information. Also **ad′ver·tize′ment.**

ad·ver·tis·ing (ad′vər·tī′zing) *n.* **1** Any system or method of attracting public notice to an event to be attended, or the desirability of commercial products for sale; promotion; also, advertisements collectively. **2** The business of writing and publicizing advertisements; promoting. Also **ad′ver·tiz′ing.**

ad·ver·tor·i·al (ad·vər·tôr′ē·əl; -tō′rē-) *n.* An editorial that includes elements of a commercial advertising message. [Blend of ADVERT(ISING) + (EDIT) ORIAL]

ad·vice (ad·vīs′) *n.* **1** Encouragement or dissuasion; counsel; suggestion. **2** *Often pl.* Information; notification. **3** *Obs.* Deliberation; fore-thought; hence, opinion. See synonyms under COUNSEL. [<OF *avis* view, opinion <L *ad-* to + *visum,* pp. of *videre* see]

ad·vis·a·ble (ad·vī′zə·bəl) *adj.* Proper to be advised or recommended; expedient. **—ad·vis′a·bil′i·ty, ad·vis′a·ble·ness** *n.* **—ad·vis′·a·bly** *adv.*

ad·vise (ad·vīz′) *v.* **ad·vised, ad·vis·ing** *v.t.* **1** To give advice to; counsel. **2** To recommend: to *advise* a course of action. **3** To notify; inform, as of a transaction. **4** *Obs.* To consider; observe. —*v.i.* **5** To take counsel: with *with:* He *advised* with his lawyer. **6** To give advice. See synonyms under ADMONISH, INFORM[1]. [<OF *aviser* <*avis.* See ADVICE.]

ad·vised (ad·vīzd′) *adj.* **1** Done with advice or counsel, or with deliberation and forethought; intended; deliberate; prudent. **2** Counseled. **3** Informed. See synonyms under CONSCIOUS.

ad·vis·ed·ly (ad·vī′zid·lē) *adv.* With forethought or advice; not hastily.

ad·vis·ee (ad·vī′zē, ad′vī·zē′) *n.* **1** One who is advised. **2** A student assigned to an advisor.

ad·vise·ment (ad·vīz′mənt) *n.* Consultation; deliberation.

ad·vis·er (ad·vī′zər) *n.* One who advises; specifically, a teacher in a school or college to whom certain students are assigned for periodic counsel. Also **ad·vi′sor.**

ad·vi·so·ry (ad·vī′zər·ē) *adj.* Having power to advise; containing or given as advice; not mandatory. —*n.* **1** A bulletin or report that advises about certain developments: a weather *advisory.* **2** A recommendation.

ad·vo·ca·cy (ad′və·kə·sē) *n.* The act of advocating or pleading a cause; a vindication; defense.

advocacy journalism Journalism that promotes a certain point of view, especially in news articles.

ad·vo·cate (ad′və·kāt) *v.t.* **·cat·ed, ·cat·ing** To speak or write in favor of; defend; recommend. [< *n.*] — *n.* (ad′və·kit, -kāt) One who pleads the cause of another; an intercessor; defender; counselor. See synonyms under PLEAD. [<OF *avocat* <L *advocatus* one summoned to another < *advocare* <*ad-* to + *vocare* call] **—ad′vo·ca′ tor** *n.* **—ad·voc·a·to·ry** (ad·vok′ə·tôr′ē, -tō′rē) *adj.*

ad·vo·ca·tion (ad′və·kā′shən) *n.* **1** A process in Scots law by which an action may be transferred from an inferior to a superior court without final judgment in the former. **2** Pleading; advocacy.

ad·vo·ca·tus di·ab·o·li (ad′ və·kā′təs dī·ab′ə·lī) *Latin* The devil's advocate.

ad·vow·son (ad·vou′zən) *n.* In English law, the right of presentation to a vacant ecclesiastical benefice; patronage. [<OF *avoeson* <L *advocatio.* See ADVOCATE.]

ad·y·na·mi·a (ad′ə·nā′mē·ə) *n. Pathol.* Lack of physical strength, resulting from disease. [<NL <Gk. *a-* without + *dynamis* strength]

ad·y·tum (ad′ə·təm) *n. pl.* **·ta** (-tə) **1** An inner or secret shrine in some ancient places of worship. **2** Hence, a sanctum. [<L <Gk. *adyton,* neut. of *adytos* not to be entered < *a-* no + *dyein* enter]

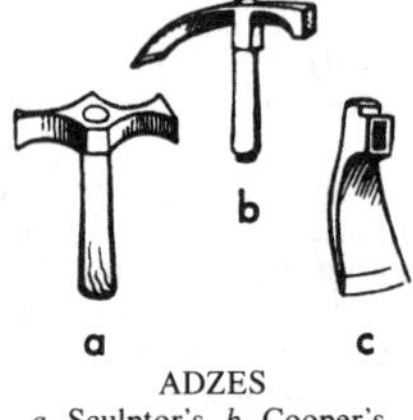

ADZES
a. Sculptor's. *b.* Cooper's. *c.* Carpenter's.

adze (adz) *n.* A hand cutting tool having its blade at right angles with its handle and usually curved: used for dressing timber, etc. —*v.t.* **adzed, adz·ing** To hew or dress with an adze. Also **adz.** [OE *adesa*]

A·dzhar Autonomous Republic (ə·jär′, ä′jär) An administrative division of the Republic of Georgia; 1,100 square miles; capital, Batum. Also **Adzharia** and **Adjaria.**

ad·zu·ki bean (ad·zo͞o′kē) See ADSUKI BEAN.

ae- For words not found here, see under E-.

æ **1** A digraph of Latin origin, equivalent to Greek *ai:* sometimes retained in the spelling of Greek and Latin proper names and used in certain scientific terms. **2** A digraph in Old English, symbolizing the sound of *a* in *hat.* Also printed as **ae.**

Æ (ā′ē′) Pen name of **George William Russell,** 1867– 1935, Irish poet and artist.

Ae·a·cus (ē′ə·kəs) In Greek mythology, a son of Zeus and king of Aegina who ruled so justly that after his death he was made a judge in Hades. Also **Æ′a·cus.**

Ae·ae·a (ē·ē′ə) A legendary island between Italy and Sicily, mentioned in the *Odyssey* as the home of Circe. Also **Æ·æ′a. —Ae·ae′an** *adj.*

ae·ci·al stage (ē′shē·əl) The phase in the life stage of certain rust fungi in which aecia (spores) are formed.

ae ·cid·i·um (ē·sid′ē·əm) *n. pl.* **·i·a** (-ē·ə) *Bot.* An aecium. [<NL <Gk. *aikia* injury] **—ae·cid′·i·al** *adj.*

ae·ci·um (ē′sē·əm) *n. Bot.* The sorus developed from the haploid mycelium of certain rust fungi *(Uridinales)* and usually bearing spores in a chainlike formation. **—ae′ci·al** *adj.* [<NL <Gk. *aikia* injury]

a·e·des (ā·ē′dēz) *n.* Any of a genus *(Aëdes)* of mosquitoes which includes species that are vectors for yellow fever, dengue, and other diseases. [<NL <Gk. *aēdēs* unpleasant < *a-* not + *hēdys* sweet] **—a·e·dine** *adj.*

ae·dile (ē′dīl) *n.* A magistrate of ancient Rome who had charge of public lands, buildings, public spectacles, etc.: also spelled *edile.* Also **æ′dile.** [<L *ædilis* < *æ) des* building]**— ae·dile·ship** *n.*

Ae·e·tes (ē·ē′tēz) In Greek mythology, king of Colchis; father of Medea and possessor of the Golden Fleece. Also **Æ·e′tes.**

Ae·ga·di·an Islands (ē·gā′dē·ən) The Egadi Islands. Also **Æ·ga′di·an; Ae·ga′de·an, Æ·.**

Ae·ga·tes (ē·gā′tēz) The Egadi Islands. Also **Æ·ga′tes.**

Ae·ge·an (i·jē′ən) *adj.* Of or pertaining to the Aegean Islands or the Aegean Sea; specifically, of or pertaining to the ancient civilization of this region: also *Egean.* Also **Æ·ge′an.**

Aegean Islands General name for the islands in the Aegean Sea comprising the Greek Regions of Aegean North; capital, Mytilene: and Aegean South; capital, Hermoupolis.

Aegean Sea An arm of the Mediterranean Sea between Greece and Asia Minor.

Ae·geus (ē′jo͞os, ē′jē·əs) In Greek mythology, a king of Athens, father of Theseus. Also **Æ′·geus.**

Ae·gid·i·us (ē·jid′·ē·əs) Latin form of GILES. Also **Æ·gid′i·us.**

Ae·gi·na (ē·jī′nə) An island and its chief town in the Saronic Gulf (also **Gulf of Aegina**) of the Aegean Sea off eastern central Greece. Also **Æ·gi′na. —Ae·gi·ne·tan** (ē′jə·nē′tən) *adj. & n.*

Aegina marbles or **sculptures** A collection of sculptures, the most important of which originally decorated the pediments of the temple of Aphaea, on the island of Aegina, built about 475 B.C. They were discovered in 1811.

Æ·gir (ē′jər, ā′jər) The Norse god of the sea. Also **Æ′ger.** [<ON]

ae·gis (ē′jis) *n.* **1** In Greek mythology, an attribute of Zeus used in various forms by several other gods, as Athena's goatskin cloak bearing Medusa's head. **2** Any shield or defensive armor. **3** A protecting influence or power; sponsorship: also spelled *egis.* Also **æ′gis.**

Ae·gis·thus (ē·jis′thəs) In Greek legend, the lover of Clytemnestra and her accomplice in the murder of Agamemnon. Also **Æ·gis′thus.**

Ae·gle (ē′glē) One of the Hesperides. Also **Æ′gle.**

Ae·gos·pot·a·mi (ē′gəs·pot′ə·mī) A river in ancient Thrace flowing into the Hellespont: at its mouth the Spartans destroyed the Athenian fleet (405 B.C.), resulting in the end of the Peloponnesian War. Also **Æ′gos·pot′a·mi; Ae′gos·pot′a·mos** (-məs), **Æ·.**

Ae·gyp·tus (ē·jip′təs) In Greek mythology, king of Egypt; brother of Danaus, whose daughters his sons married. See DANAIDES. Also **Æ·gyp′tus.**

Ae·gyp·tus (ē·jip′təs) An ancient name for Egypt. Also **Æ·gyp′tus.**

Æl·fric (al′frik), died 1020?, English monk and writer; abbot of Eynsham.

A·el·lo (ā·el′ō) One of the Harpies.

-aemia See -EMIA.

Ae·mil·i·us (ē·mil′ē·əs) Latin form of EMIL. Also **Æ·mil′i·us.**

Ae·ne·as (i·nē′əs) In Greek and Roman legend, a Trojan, son of Anchises and Venus, hero of the *Aeneid:* after the sack of Troy he wandered for seven years before reaching Latium where he founded the city of Lavinium. See ASCANIUS, DIDO. Also **Æ·ne′as.**

Ae·ne·as Sil·vi·us (i·nē′əs sil′vē·əs) See PIUS II. Also **Ae·ne′as Syl′vi·us.**

Ae·ne·id (i·nē′id) *n.* A Latin epic poem by Vergil narrating the adventures of Aeneas. Also **Æ·ne′ id.**

a·e·ne·ous (ā·ē′nē·əs) *adj.* Having a golden-green or lustrous brassy color: said especially of insects. Also **a·e′ne·us.** [<L *aeneus* <*aes* copper, bronze]

ae·o·li·an (ē·ō′lē·ən) *adj.* Pertaining to or caused by the winds; wind-borne: also *eolian.*

Ae·o·li·an (ē·ō′lē·ən) *adj.* **1** Of or pertaining to ancient Aeolis in Asia Minor, its people, or their language; Aeolic. **2** Pertaining to Aeolus, Greek god of the winds. —*n.* **1** A member of one of the four major tribes of ancient Greece. The Aeolians settled in central Greece, Lesbos, and Aeolis. **2** Aeolic. Also spelled *Eolian.* Also **Æ·o′li·an.**

Aeolian harp A stringed instrument so constructed as to produce musical sounds when exposed to a current of air.

Aeolian Islands See LIPARI ISLANDS.

Ae·ol·ic (ē·ol′ik) *n.* A dialect of ancient Greek spoken in Aeolis (including Lesbos), Thessaly, and Boeotia, represented by the poetry of Sappho and Alcaeus. —*adj.* Aeolian. Also spelled *Eolic.* Also **Æ·ol′ic.**

ae·ol·i·pile (ē·ol′ə·pīl) See EOLIPILE.

Ae·o·lis (ē′ə·lis) A region in ancient Greece and NW Asia Minor. Also **Æ′o·lis; Ae·o·li·a** (ē·ō′lē·ə).

ae·o·lo·trop·ic (ē′ə·lō·trop′ik) *adj. Physics* Anisotropic. [<Gk. *aiolos* varying + -TROPIC]

Ae·o·lus (ē′ə·ləs) **1** In Greek mythology, the god of the winds. **2** In Greek legend, a Thessalian king, son of Helen and ancestor of the Aeolians. Also **Æ′o·lus.**

ae·on (ē′ən, ē′on), **ae·o·ni·an** (ē·ō′nē·ən) See EON, etc.

Ae·qui·an (ē′kwē·ən) *n.* The Indo-European language of an early Italic people inhabiting Latium. [<L *Aequi,* pl.]

ae·quum (ē′kwəm) *n.* That quantity of food which is barely adequate to sustain an organism doing work. [<L < *aequus* even]

aer- Var. of AERO-.

ae·rar·i·an (ē·râr′ē·ən) *adj.* Fiscal; pertaining to the ancient Roman treasury. —*n.* A Roman citizen of the lowest rank, who had no right to vote, and paid only a poll tax. [<L *aerarius* <*aerarium* treasury < *aes, aeris* copper, money]

aer·as·the·ni·a (âr′əs·thē′nē·ə, ā′ər·əs-) *n.* Aeroneurosis. [<NL <AER- + Gk. *astheneia* weakness]

aer·ate (âr′āt, ā′ə·rāt) *v.t.* **·at·ed, ·at·ing** **1** To supply or charge with air or gas. **2** To purify by exposure to air. **3** To oxygenate, as blood. [<AER- + -ATE[2]] **—aer·a′tion** *n.*

aer·a·tor (âr′ā·tər, ā′ə·rā′tər) *n.* **1** An apparatus for charging liquids with gas under pressure. **2** A device for supplying a stream of gas or air, as for fumigating, destroying fungi, etc.

aer·en·chy·ma (âr·eng′kə·mə, ā′ə·reng′kə·mə) *n. Bot.* A specialized tissue serving in some aquatic plants for buoyancy and aeration, and consisting of thin-walled cells with intercellular air spaces.

aeri- Var. of AERO-.

aer·i·al (âr′ē·əl, ā·ir′ē·əl) *adj.* **1** Of or in the air. **2** Like air; atmospheric. **3** *Bot.* Growing or living in the air and not in the soil or in water.

4 Airy; insubstantial; spiritual. 5 Existing or performed in the air. 6 Of, by, or for aircraft: *aerial* bombardment. See synonyms under AIRY. —*n.* (âr′ē·əl) An antenna, as in television and radio. [<L *aerius* airy < *aer* air] —**aer′i·al·ly** *adv.*

aerial bomb See under BOMB.

aer·i·al·ist (âr′ē·əl·ist, ā·ir′ē·əl-) *n.* One who performs feats of skill in the air, as a tightrope walker, trapeze artist, etc.

aer·i·al·i·ty (âr′ē·al′ə·tē, ā·ir′ē-) *n.* Tenuity, or want of substance; airiness.

aerial ladder An extension ladder commonly mounted on a truck, and operated by levers: used by firefighters in saving life or property.

aerial train An airplane towing behind it one or more gliders.

aer·ie (âr′ē, ir′ē) *n.* 1 The nest of a predatory bird, as the eagle, on a crag. 2 The brood or young of such a bird. Also spelled *aery, eyry, eyrie.* [<Med.L *aeria* <OF *aire?* <L *area* open space] —**aer′ied** *adj.*

aer·if·er·ous (âr·if′ər·əs, ā′ə·rif′-) *adj.* Containing or conveying air. [<AERI- + -FEROUS]

aer·i·fi·ca·tion (âr′ə·fi·kā′shən, ā′ər·ə-) *n.* 1 The act or process of converting into air, gas, or vapor; the process of becoming air, gas, or vapor. 2 Purification by exposure to, air; aeration. Also **aer′i·fac′tion.**

aer·i·form (âr′ə·fôrm, ā′ər·ə·fôrm′) *adj.* Like air; gaseous; unsubstantial; intangible.

aer·i·fy (âr′ə·fī, ā ′ər·ə·fī) *v.t.* **·fied, ·fy·ing** 1 To aerate. 2 To change into a gaseous form.

aero- *combining form* 1 Air; of the air: *aerobiology.* 2 Of aircraft or flying: *aeromarinegs.* 3 Gas; of gases: *aerogen.* Also *aer-, aeri-.* [<Gk. *aēr* air]

aer·o·al·ler·gen (âr′ō·al′ər·jən, ā′ər·ō-) *n.* An airborne substance that is capable of producing an allergenic response in a sensitized subject. — **aer′o·al·ler·gen′ic** *adj.*

aer·o·bal·lis·tics (âr′ō·bə·lis′tiks, ā′ər·ō-) *n.* The ballistics of missiles dropped, launched, or fired from aircraft in flight. —**aer′o·bal·lis′tic** *adj.*

aer·o·bat·ics (âr′ə·bat′iks, ā′ər·ə-) *n.* Aerial maneuvers that are not necessary to normal flight voluntarily performed in aircraft; trick or stunt flying. [<AERO- + (ACRO)BATICS]

aer·o·ba·tion (âr′ə·bā ′shən, ā′ər·ə-) *n. Aeron.* The performance of aerial feats; stunt flying; exhibition flying.

aer·obe (âr′ōb, ā′ər·ōb) *n.* A microorganism that can live only in the presence of free oxygen: opposed to *anaerobe.* [<AERO- + Gk. *bios* life]

aer·o·bic (âr·ō′bik, ā·ə·rō′-) *adj.* 1 Living in air. 2 Pertaining to aerobics. —**aer·o′ bi·cal·ly** *adv.*

aer·o·bics (âr′ō′biks) *n. pl.* A system of calisthenics and other strenuous physical activities designed to improve the functioning of the lungs and heart by speeding up oxygen consumption and circulation.

aer·o·bi·ol·o·gy (âr′ō ·bī·ol′ə·jē, ā′ər·ō -) *n.* The study of the dispersal of airborne bacteria, pollen grains, fungal spores, etc., and of airborne pollutants having biological effects. —**aer′o·bi′o·log′i·cal** *adj.*

aer·o·bi·o·scope (âr′ō·bī′ə·skōp, ā′ər·ō-) *n.* An instrument for the determination of the bacterial content of air.

aer·o·car·to·graph (âr′ō·kär′tə·graf, -gräf, ā′ər·ō-) *n.* A mapmaking device that utilizes air photographs to show the contour and elevation of ground features.

aer·o·cy·cle (âr′ə·sī′kəl, ā′ər·ə-) *n.* A flying machine constructed on the helicopter principle but intended to carry only one person at low altitude and over a short flight range.

aer·o·do·net·ics (âr′ō·ə·net′iks, ā′ər·ō-) *n* . The branch of dynamics that treats of gliding and soaring flight. [<AERO- + Gk. *donētos* shaken < *donein* shake]

aer·o·drome (âr′ə·drōm, ā′ər·ə-) *n.* Airdrome.

aer·o·dy·nam·ics (âr′ō·dī·nam′iks, ā′ər·ō-) *n.* The branch of physics that treats of the laws of motion of gases, especially atmospheric, under the influence of gravity and other mechanical forces, and of the mechanical effects produced by such motion. —**aer′o·dy·nam′ic** *adj.*

aer·o·dyne (âr′ə·dīn, ā′ər·ə-) *n.* Any aircraft which is heavier than air, as an airplane, glider, helicopter, etc. [<AERO- + Gk. *dynamis* power]

aer·o·e·las·tic·i·ty (âr′ō·i·las′tis′ə·tē, ā′ər·ō-) *n. Eng.* The effect of aerodynamic forces on elastic materials and structures exposed to the wind, especially steel and other metals, aircraft, bridges, and buildings. —**aer′o·e·las′tic** *adj.*

aer·o·e·las·tics (âr′ō·i·las′tiks, ā′ər·ō-) *n.* The study of the elastic deformations in the structural elements of aircraft and of the aerodynamic conditions leading to the maximum stability and control of these elements. —**aer′o·e·las′tic** *adj.*

aer·o·em·bo·lism (âr′ō·em′bə·liz′əm, ā′ər·ō-) *n.* 1 A bubble of air or other gas in the heart or in blood vessels. 2 Decompression sickness. Compare CAISSON DISEASE.

aer·o·foil (âr′ə·foil, ā ′ər·ə-) *n.* Airfoil.

aer·o·gel (âr′ə·jel, ā′ər·ə-) *n.* A porous substance obtained from a gel by replacing the dispersed liquid phase with a gas.

aer·o·gen (âr′ə·jen, ā′ər·ə-) *n.* A microorganism that forms gas.

aer·o·gen·ic (âr′ə·jen′ik, ā′ər·ə-) *adj.* 1 Gas-producing: *aerogenic* bacteria. 2 Having the form of gas: *aerogenic* vaccine spray.

aer·o·gram (âr′ə·gram, ā ′ər·ə-) *n.* 1 A wireless message; radiogram. 2 The record traced by a meteorograph.

aer·o·gramme (âr′ə·gram, ā′ər·ə-) *n.* An international airmail letter consisting of a single folded sheet: also, *Brit., air letter.* [<F]

aer·o·graph (âr′ə·graf, -gräf, ā′ər·ə-) *n.* A meteorograph.

aer·og·ra·phy (âr·og′rə·fē, ā′ə·rog′-) *n.* A description of or treatise on the atmosphere and its phenomena. —**aer′o·graph′ic** or **·i·cal** *adj.* —**aer′o·graph′i·cal·ly** *adv.*

aer·o·hy·dro·plane (âr′ə·hī′drə·plān, ā′ər·ə-) See HYDROPLANE.

aer·o·lite (âr′ə·līt, ā ′ər·ə-) *n.* A mass falling on the earth from celestial space and containing more stone than iron. See METEORITE. Also **aer′o·lith** (-lith). [<AERO- + Gk. *lithos* stone] —**aer′o·lit′ic** (-lit′ik) *adj.*

aer·ol·o·gy (âr·ol′ə·jē, ā′ə·rol′-) *n.* 1 *Physics* The science of the laws and phenomena of the atmosphere. 2 *Meteorol.* The study of the atmosphere in its vertical extent. —**aer·o·log·ic** (âr′ə·loj′ik, ā′ər·ə-) or **·i·cal** *adj.* —**aer·ol′o·gist** *n.*

aer·o·mag·net·ic (âr′ō·mag·net′ik, ā′ə·ō-) *adj.* Pertaining to magnetism in, or the action of magnetic force on, portions of the atmosphere, esp. the upper layers: an *aeromagnetic* survey.

aer·o·man·cy (âr′ə·man′ sē, ā′ər·ə-) *n.* The art of divination or augury by atmospheric phenomena; hence, a forecasting of atmospheric changes. [<AERO- + Gk. *manteia* divination]

aer·o·ma·rine (âr′ō·mə·rēn′, ā′ər·ō-) *adj.* Pertaining to the navigation of aircraft over the ocean.

aer·o·me·chan·ics (âr′ō·mə·kan′iks, ā′ər·ō-) *n.* 1 The science that treats of equilibrium and motion of air and gases, including *aerostatics* and *aerodynamics.* 2 Pneumatics. —**aer′o·me·chan′ic** *adj. & n.*

aer·o·med·i·cine (âr′ō·med′ə·sən, ā′ər·ō-) *n.* 1 Aviation medicine. 2 Space medicine. —**aer′o·med′i·cal** *adj.*

aer·o·me·te·or·o·graph (âr′ō·mē′ē·ôr′ə·graf, -gräf, ā′ər·ō-) *n.* A device for recording atmospheric conditions, as temperature, pressure and moisture, wind velocities, etc.

aer·om·e·ter (âr·om′ə·tər, ā′ə·rom′ə·tər) *n.* An apparatus for weighing and estimating the density of air or other gases.

aer·om·e·try (âr·om′ə·trē, ā′ə·rom′-) *n.* The science of weighing and measuring air and other gases. —**aer·o·met·ric** (âr′ə·met′rik, ā′ər·ə-) *adj.*

aer·o·naut (âr′ə·nôt, ā′ər·ə-) *n.* 1 One who navigates the air; a balloonist or aviator. 2 A space traveler. [<F *aéronaute* <Gk. *aēr* air + *nautēs* sailor]

aer·o·nau·tic (âr′ə·nô′tik, ā′ər·ə-) *adj.* 1 Pertaining to, floating in, or navigating the air. 2 Pertaining to aeronautics. Also **aer′o·nau′ti·cal.**

aer·o·nau·tics (âr′ə·nô′tiks, ā′ə·ə-) *n.* 1 The science or art of navigating aircraft. 2 That branch of engineering which deals with the design, construction, operation, and performance characteristics of aircraft.

aer·o·neu·ro·sis (âr′ō·nŏŏ·rō′sis, -nyŏŏq-, ā′ər·ō-) *n. Pathol.* A condition of nervous exhaustion sometimes affecting airplane pilots, characterized by emotional tension, irritability, gastric distress, and insomnia. Also called **aerasthenia, flying fatigue.**

aer·on·o·my (âr·on′ə·mē , ā′ər·on′-) *n.* The scientific study of the physics and chemistry of the earth or other orbiting body. —**aer′o·nom′i·cal** *adj.*

aer·o·pause (âr′ə·pôz, ā′ər·ə-) *n. Meteorol.* The region of the atmosphere where the conditions of outer space are gradually approached: it is believed to extend from about 12 to 125 miles above the earth.

aer·o·pha·gi·a (âr′ə·fā′jē·ə, ā′ər·ə-) *n. Med.* The swallowing of air.

aer·o·phi·lat·e·ly (âr′ō·fi·lat′ə·lē, ā′ər·ō-) *n.* The collecting of air-mail stamps, covers, etc. —**aer′o·phi·lat′e·list** *n.*

aer·o·phobe (âr′ə·fōb, ā ′ər·ə-) *n.* A person or organism evincing or affected by aerophobia.

aer·o·pho·bi·a (âr′ə·fō′bē·ə, ā′ər·ə-) *n.* 1 A morbid fear of fresh air and of airborne infection. 2 A morbid fear of flying. 3 *Biol.* Movement of an organism away from air or oxygen.

aer·o·phore (âr′ə·ôr, ā′ər·ə-) *n.* 1 An apparatus for inflating the lungs of a newborn infant to stimulate breathing. 2 A device for delivering air as needed to firefighters, aviators, etc.

aer·o·pho·tog·ra·phy (âr′ ō·fə·tog′rə·fē, ā′ər·ō-) *n.* Photography from aircraft.

aer·o·phys·ics (âr′ō·fiz′iks, ā′ər·ō-) *n.* Physical science considered with reference to the design, construction, and operation of aircraft, rockets, guided missiles, etc.: the physics of aeronautics and aviation.

aer·o·phyte (âr′ə·fīt, ā′ər·ə-) *n. Bot.* An epiphyte (def. 1).

aer·o·plane (âr′ə·plān, ā′ər·ə) See AIRPLANE.

aer·o·scope (âr′ə·skōp, ā′ər·ə-) *n.* An instrument for collecting the minute particles in the atmosphere for microscopic examination. —**aer′o·scop′ic** (-skop′ik) *adj.*

aer·o·sid·er·ite (âr′ō·sid′ə·rīt, ā′ər·ō-) *n.* A meteorite of which iron is the chief constituent.

aer·o·sid·er·o·lite (âr′ō ·sid′ər·ə·līt′, ā′ər·ō-) *n.* A meteorite that is both metallic and stony.

aer·o·sol (âr′ə·sōl, -sol, ā′ər·ə-) *n.* 1 A colloidal dispersion of solid or liquid particles in a gaseous medium. 2 A substance packaged under pressure along with a volatile propellant which, upon release through a nozzle, disperses fine particles of the substance in the air. —*adj.* Pertaining to, resembling, dispensing, or dispensed as an aerosol. Also **aer′o·sol′ic.** [<AERO- + SOL(UTION)]

aer·o·sol·ize (âr′ə·sol·īz, ā′ər·ə-) *v.t.* **·ized, ·iz·ing** To package with a propellant under pressure for dispersion as an aerosol. —**aer′o·sol′i·za′tion** *n.*

aer·o·space (âr′ō·spās, ā′ər·ō-) *n.* 1 The earth's atmosphere and outer space, considered as a single region in the operation of rockets, guided missiles, and spacecraft. 2 The study and investigation of this region, especially with reference to space travel.

aer·o·sphere (âr′ə·sfir, ā′ər·ə-) *n.* The entire atmosphere considered as a single gaseous shell surrounding the earth.

aer·o·stat (âr′ə·stat, ā′ər·ə-) *n.* Any aircraft which is lighter than air, as a balloon or dirigible. [<F *aé rostat* <Gk *aēr* air + *statos* standing] —**aer′o·stat′ic** or **·i·cal** *adj.*

aer·o·stat·ics (â′ə·stat′iks, ā′ər·ə-) *n.* 1 The branch of physics that treats of the mechanical properties of air and gases not in motion. 2 The art and science of operating lighter-than-air aircraft, as balloons and dirigibles: distinguished from *aviation.*

aer·o·sta·tion (âr′ə·stā′shən, ā′ər·ə-) *n.* **1** The art of raising and supporting bodies, as balloons, by means of fluids lighter than air: opposed to *aviation.* **2** *Obs.* Aerostatics. Compare AEROSTATICS.

aer·o·tax·is (âr′ə·tak′sis, ā′ər·ə-) *n. Biol.* Movement of an organism away from or toward a source of air or oxygen.

aer·o·ther·a·peu·tics (âr′ō·ther′ə·pyōō′tiks, ā′ə r·ō-) *n. Med.* A system of treating disease by varying the atmospheric pressure upon the patient or by changing the composition of the air. Also **aer′o·ther′a·py** (-ther′ə·pē).

aer·o·ther·mo·dy·nam·ics (âr′o·thûr′mō·dī·nam′ iks, ā′ər·ō-) *n.* The branch of thermodynamics that deals with the relations between heat and mechanical energy in gases, especially in their applications to changes induced by the motions of bodies in the medium.

aer·ot·ro·pism (âr·ot′rə·piz′əm, ā′ə·rot′-) *n. Biol.* A change in orientation of a plant affected by differential growth of tissues in response to the presence of air or oxygen. **—aer·o·trop·ic** (âr′ə·trop′ik, ā′ər·ə-) *adj.*

ae·ru·gi·nous (i·rōō′jə·nəs) Resembling verdigris; bluish green. Also spelled *eruginous.* [<Latin *aerugo* <*aes* brass, copper]

aer·y [1] (âr′ē, ā′ər·ē) *adj.* Airy; aerial.

aer·y [2] (âr′ē, ir′ē) See AERIE.

aes (ēz) *n.* Money made of copper or bronze. [<L]

Aes·chi·nes (es′kə·nēz), 389–314 B.C., Athenian orator; rival of Demosthenes. Also **Æs′chi·nes.**

Aes·chy·le·an (es′kə·lē′ən) *adj.* Similar to, or in the style of, the tragedies of Aeschylus; hence, majestic; stately. Also **Æs′chy·le′an.**

Aes·chy·lus (es′kə·ləs), 525–456 B.C., Greek tragic dramatist. Also **Æs′chy·lus.**

Aes·cu·la·pi·an (es′kyə·lā′pē·ən) *adj.* Relating to Aesculapius; hence, pertaining to the art of healing; medical. *—n.* A disciple of Aesculapius; hence, a physician. Also spelled *Esculapian.*

Aes·cu·la·pi·us (es′kyə·lā′pē·əs) In Roman mythology, the god of medicine: identified with the Greek *Asclepius.* Also **Æs′cu·la′pi·us.**

Æ·sir (ā′sir, ē′-) *sing.* The gods of the Teutonic pantheon collectively. See VAN[2].

Ae·sop (ē′səp, ē′sop) Greek author of fables, sixth century B.C. Also **Æ′sop.**

Ae·so·pi·an (ē·sō′pē·ən) *adj.* **1** Of or pertaining to Aesop; resembling the fables of Aesop. **2** Cryptic; phrased in figurative language or fable to carry a special meaning to the initiated: also spelled *Esopian.* Also **Æ·so′pi·an.**

aes·thete (es′thēt), **aes·thet·ic** (es·thet′ik) See ESTHETE, etc.

ae·ta·tis su·ae (ē·tā′tis sōō′ē) *Latin* Of his or her age; at a specified age. Also **æ·ta′tis su′æ.**

Æth·el·bert (ath′əl·bûrt) See ETHELBERT.

æth·el·ing (ath′əl·ing) See ATHELING.

Æth·el·red (ath′əl·red) See ETHELRED.

Ae·thi·o·pi·a (ē′thē·ō′pē·ə) See ETHIOPIA.

ae·thri·o·scope (ē′thrē·ə·skōp′) *n.* A thermometric instrument for measuring minute changes in the heat radiated from the sky. [<Gk. *aithria* clear sky + -SCOPE]

A·e·tian (ā·ē′shən) *n.* One of the party of practioners of extreme Arianism that flourished in the latter half of the fourth century: so called from its leader, Aetius of Antioch.

Aet·na (et′nə) See ETNA. Also **Æt′na.**

Ae·to·li·a (ē·tō′lē·ə) A part of the Aetolia and Acarnania Department of modern Greece. Also **Æ·to′li·a.** *Greek* **Ai·to·li·a** (â′tô·lē′ä). **—Ae·to′li·an,** *adj. & n.*

af- Assimilated var. of AD-.

a·far (ə·fär′) *adv.* At, from, or to a distance; remotely. [<A-[1] on + FAR]

a·feard (ə·fird ′) *adj. Dial.* Afraid; fearful. Also **a·feared′.**

a·fe·brile (ā·fē′brəl, ā·feb′rəl) *adj.* Free from fever.

aff (af) *adv. & prep. Scot.* Off; off from.

af·fa·ble (af′ə·bəl) *adj.* **1** Easy and courteous in manner; approachable. **2** Benign; mild. See synonyms under BLAND, FRIENDLY. [<F <L *affabilis,* lit., able to be spoken to < *affari* <*ad-* to + *fari* speak] **—af′fa·bil′i·ty, af′fa·ble·ness** *n.* **—af′fa·bly** *adv.*

af·fair (ə·fâr′) *n.* **1** Anything done or to be done; business; concern: often in plural. **2** An unimportant event, as a skirmish; matter; thing. **3** A vague or indefinite object or fact: The first ship was a rude *affair.* **4** See LOVE AFFAIR. See synonyms under BATTLE, BUSINESS, TRANSACTION. [<OF *afaire* <*a faire* to do <L *ad* to + *facere* do]

af·faire (à·fâr′) *n. French* Short for **affaire d'a·mour** (dà·mōōr′), a love affair, or **affaire de coeur** (də·kœr′), affair of the heart.

af·faire d'hon·neur (à·fâr′dô·nœr′) *French* A matter of honor; a duel.

af·fect[1] (ə·fekt′) *v.t.* **1** To act upon or have an effect upon; impress; influence. **2** To touch or move emotionally. **3** To attack or attaint: A disease *affects* the body. See synonyms under CONCERN, INFLUENCE. Compare EFFECT. *—n.* **1** (af′ekt) *Psychol.* **a** That which tends to arouse emotion rather than to stimulate thought or perception. **b** The diffuse mental condition thus produced. **c** The fundamental controlling element in an emotional state. **2** *Obs.* Inward disposition; inclination. [<L *affectus,* pp. of *afficere* influence, attack < *ad-* to + *facere* do; def 1 of noun <G *affekt*]

af·fect[2] (ə·fekt′) *v.t.* **1** To have a liking for; show a preference for; fancy: to *affect* large hats. **2** To imitate or counterfeit for effect; make a show of one's liking or aptitude for: to *affect* a British accent; to *affect* omniscience. **3** To tend toward naturally; haunt; frequent: said of animals and plants. **4** *Obs.* To aim at; to aspire for or to. See synonyms under ASSUME, LIKE, PRETEND. [<F *affecter* <L *affectare* aim at, freq. of *afficere.* See AFFECT[1] .]

af·fec·ta·tion (af′ek·tā′shən) *n.* **1** A studied pretense; shallow display: with *of:* an *affectation* of wealth. **2** Artificiality of manner or behavior; affectedness. See synonyms under HYPOCRISY, PRETENSE. [<L *affectatio, -onis* <*affectare.* See AFFECT[2].]

af·fect·ed[1] (ə·fek′tid) *adj.* **1** Acted upon, as by a drug. **2** Moved emotionally; influenced. **3** Attacked, as by disease; diseased. **4** *Math.* Affected. [pp. of AFFECT[1]]

af·fect·ed[2] (ə·fek′tid) *adj.* **1** Assumed falsely or in outward semblance only; showing affectation. **2** Having a liking, inclination, or affection; inclined. **3** Fondly cherished; loved; frequented. See synonyms under FACTITIOUS, SQUEAMISH. [pp. of AFFECT[2]] **—af·fect′ed·ly** *adv.* **—af·fect′ed·ness** *n.*

af·fect·er (ə·fek′tər) *n.* One who affects or pretends.

af·fect·ing[1] (ə·fek′ting) *adj.* Having power to move the feelings; pathetic. **—af·fect′ing·ly** *adv.*

af·fect·ing[2] (ə·fek′ting) *adj. Obs.* **1** Showing love. **2** Pretending; falsely displaying.

af·fec·tion (ə·fek′shən) *n.* **1** *Often pl.* Good disposition, as toward another; fond attachment; kind feelings: usually distinguished from *love* as less powerful or intense. **2** *Often pl.* A mental state brought about by any influence; an emotion or feeling: to influence people by playing on their *affections.* **3** An abnormal state of the body; disease. **4** The act of affecting or influencing or the state of being influenced. **5** A property or attribute: Thought is said to be an *affection* of matter. **6** *Psychol.* Conscious perception of feeling or emotion: distinguished from *cognition.* **7** *Obs.* Constitutional inclination; tendency. See synonyms under ATTACHMENT, FRIENDSHIP, LOVE, INFLUENCE, DISEASE.

af·fec·tion·al (ə·fek′shən·əl) *adj.* Of or pertaining to affections. **—af·fec′tion·al·ly** *adv.*

af·fec·tion·ate (ə·fek′shən·it) *adj.* **1** Having or expressing love; loving; fond. **2** *Obs.* Favorably inclined. See synonyms under FRIENDLY. **—af·fec′tion·ate·ly** *adv.* **—af·fec′tion·ate·ness** *n.*

af·fec·tive (ə·fek′tiv) *adj.* **1** Pertaining to or exciting affection; emotional or stirring emotion. **2** *Psychol.* Pertaining to or arising from feeling or emotional reactions rather than from thought.

af·fec·tiv·i·ty (af′ek·tiv′ə·tē) *n. Psychol.* The relative intensity of response to a feeling or emotion.

af·fect·less (ə·fekt′lis) *adj.* Unfeeling; unemotional. **—af·fect′less·ly** *adv.* **—af·fect′less·ness** *n.*

af·fen·pin·scher (ä′fən·pin′shər) *n.* A toy terrier of monkeylike appearance, having a hard, wiry coat, usually black, a round head, a short, pointed muzzle, and a short tail. [<G monkey terrier]

af·fer·ent (af′ər·ənt) *adj.* Conducting inward, or toward the center: said of those nerve processes which transmit sensory stimuli from receptory organs to the central nervous system: opposed to *efferent.* [<L *afferens, -entis,* ppr. of *afferre* <*ad-* to + *ferre* bear]

af·fet·tu·o·so (äf·fet′tōō ·ō′sō) *adj. Music.* Tender; soft; pathetic: designating a passage or piece to be rendered with feeling. [<Ital.]

af·fi·ance (ə·fī′əns) *v.t.* **·anced, ·anc·ing** **1** To promise in marriage; betroth. **2** *Archaic* To pledge. *—n.* **1** A betrothal; pledge of faith. **2** *Obs.* Confidence. [<OF *afiancer* <*afiance* trust, confidence < *after* trust < Med.L *affidare* <L *ad-* to + *fidus* faithful]

af·fi·ant (ə·fī′ənt) *n. Law* One who makes an affidavit.

af·fi·da·vit (af′ə·dā′vit) *n.* **1** A voluntary sworn declaration, in writing, made before competent authority. **2** Any solemn or formal declaration. [<Med.L, he has stated on oath, perfect tense of *affidare.* See AFFIANCE.]

af·fil·i·ate (ə·fil′ē·āt) *v.* **·at·ed, ·at·ing** *v.t.* **1** To associate or unite, as a member or branch to a larger or principal body: with *to* or *with.* **2** To join or associate (oneself): with *with.* **3** To receive as a child; adopt. **4** To fix the legal paternity of. **5** To determine relations of, as the sources or branches of a field of study. *—v.i.* **6** To associate or ally oneself: with *with.* *—adj.* Affiliated. *—n.* Something affiliated. [<L *affiliatus,* pp. of *affiliare* adopt < *ad-* to + *filius* son]

af·fil·i·a·tion (ə·fil′ē ·ā′shən) *n.* **1** The act of affiliating, or the state of being affiliated; association; friendly relationship; connection; adoption. **2** Combination; union.

af·fine (ə·fīn′) *n. Obs.* **1** A relative by marriage. **2** A kinsman. [<F *affin* <L *affinis.* See AFFINITY.]

af·fined (ə·fīnd′) *adj.* **1** Joined by artificial ties; allied; related by marriage. **2** *Obs.* Under obligation, due to some close relation. [<F *affiné* related < *affin.* See AFFINE.]

af·fin·i·ty (ə·fin′ə·tē) *n. pl.* **·ties** **1** Any natural drawing or inclination; close relation or agreement. **2** *Biol.* A structural or physiologic likeness in different organisms indicative of a common origin. **3** Structural likenesses indicating a common origin, as in languages. **4** *Chem.* The force of attraction by which differing chemical elements unite to form compounds. **5** Connection through certain relations formed, as by church or state; especially, relationship through marriage (as opposed to blood relationship). **6** A Platonic or spiritual attraction held to exist between certain persons, especially between those of opposite sexes; also, the person exerting such attraction. [<L *affinitas, -tatis* <*affinis* adjacent, related < *ad-* to + *finis* end]

Synonyms: alliance, analogy, birth, blood, consanguinity, descent, family, kin, kind, kindred, race, relationship. *Kind* is broader than *kin,* denoting the most general *relationship,* as one of the whole human species in man *kind,* human *kind,* etc.; *kin* and *kindred* denote direct *relationship* that can be traced through either blood or marriage, especially the former; either of these words may signify collectively all persons of the same blood or members of the same family, relatives or relations. *Affinity* is *relationship* by marriage, *consanguinity* is *relationship* by blood. *Antonyms:* See ANTIPATHY.

af·firm (ə·fûrm′) *v.t.* **1** To declare or state positively; assert and maintain to be true; aver. **2** To confirm or ratify, as a judgment or law. *—v.i.* **3** *Law* To make a formal judicial declaration, but not under oath. [<OF *afermer* < *affirmare* <*ad-* to + *firmare* make firm < *firmus* strong] **—af·firm′a·ble** *adj.* **—af·firm′a·bly** *adv.* **—af·firm′ance** *n.* **—af·firm′ant** *adj. & n.* **—af·firm′er** *n.*

Synonyms: assert, asseverate, aver, declare, depose, endorse, maintain, predicate, propound, protest, state, swear, tell, testify. *Affirm* has less of egotism than *assert,* more solemnity than *declare,* and more composure than *asseverate*, which is to *assert* emphatically. In legal usage, *affirm* differs from *affirmation* after *swear* in not invoking the name of God. See ALLEGE, ASSERT, STATE. *Antonyms:* contradict, deny, dispute, gainsay, negative, oppose, refute.

af•fir•ma•tion (af′ər•mā′shən) *n.* **1** The act of affirming, or that which is affirmed. **2** A declaration; statement; predication. **3** A solemn declaration made before a competent officer, in place of a judicial oath. **4** Confirmation; ratification. See synonyms under TESTIMONY.

af•firm•a•tive (ə•fûr′mə•tiv) *adj.* **1** Characterized by affirmation; asserting that the fact is so; ratifying; confirmative. **2** *Math.* Positive: an *affirmative* quantity. Also **af•firm•a•to•ry** (ə•fûr′mə•tôr′ē, -tō′re). —*n.* **1** A word or expression of affirmation or assent; that which affirms or asserts: to answer in the *affirmative*. **2** That side in a debate which affirms the proposition debated.

affirmative action *U.S.* A program that promotes the employment and education of women and of minority groups.

af•firm•a•tive•ly (ə•fûr′mə•tiv•lē) *adv.* In an affirmative manner; positively; on the affirmative side.

af•fix (ə•fiks′) *v.t.* **1** To fix or attach; fasten, as a seal; append, as a signature at the end of a document. **2** To connect with or lay upon, as blame, responsibility, etc. See synonyms under ADD. —*n.* (af′iks) **1** That which is attached, appended, or added. **2** *Ling.* A prefix, suffix, or infix. [<L *affixus*, pp. of *affigere* <*ad-* to + *figere* fasten]

af•fla•tus (ə•flā′təs) *n.* **1** The communication of supernatural knowledge, as in a state of exaltation: the divine *afflatus*. **2** Any creative inspiration or impulse. [<L, a breathing upon < *afflare* blow on < *ad-* to + *flare* blow] .

af•flict (ə•flikt′) *v.t.* **1** To distress with continued suffering; trouble. **2** *Obs.* To cast down; overthrow. See synonyms under CHASTEN, HURT. [<obs. *afflict*, adj., afflicted <L *afflictus*, pp. of *affligere* dash against, strike down < *ad-* to + *fligere* dash, strike]

af•flic•tion (ə•flik′shən) *n.* **1** The state of being afflicted; sore distress of body or mind. **2** That which causes great suffering or distress; misfortune; calamity. See synonyms under GRIEF, MISFORTUNE.

af•flic•tive (ə•flik′tiv) *adj.* Causing or involving pain or distress; grievous. See synonyms under TROUBLESOME. **—af•flic′tive•ly** *adv.*

af•flu•ence (af′lo͞o•əns) *n.* **1** A profuse or abundant supply, as of riches; wealth; abundance; opulence. **2** A flowing toward; concourse. [<F <L *affluentia* <*affluere*. See AFFLUENT.]

af•flu•ent (af′lo͞o•ənt) *adj.* **1** Abounding; abundant. **2** Wealthy; opulent. **3** Flowing freely; fluent. See synonyms under AMPLE. —*n.* A stream that flows into another; a tributary. [<L *affluens, -entis*, ppr. of *affluere* <*ad* - to + *fluere* flow] **—af′flu•ent•ly** *adv.*

af•flux (af′luks) *n.* A flowing toward a point, as blood to a tissue or organ; congestion. Also **af•flux′ion** [<Med.L *affluxus* < *affluere*. See AFFLUENT.]

af•force (ə•fôrs′, ə•fōrs′) *v.t.* **af•forced, af•forc•ing** To reinforce, as a jury by the addition of new members. [<OF *aforcer* <L *ex* out + *fortis* strong] **—af•force′ment** *n.*

af•ford (ə•fôrd′, ə•fōrd′) *v.t.* **1** To have sufficient means for; be able to meet the expense of: Can you *afford* to go to Europe? **2** To incur without detriment: He can *afford* to suffer now. **3** To produce or furnish, as in behalf of; confer, as pleasure or profit: It *affords* me great delight to tell you this. [OE *geforthian* further, promote] **—af•ford′a•ble** *adj.*

af•for•est (ə•fôr′ist, ə•for′ist) *v.t.* To convert into a forest, as barren land. [<AD- + FOREST] **—af•for•es•ta•tion** (ə•fôr′is•tā′shən, ə•for′-) *n.*

af•fran•chise (ə•fran′chīz) *v.t.* **•chised, •chis•ing** To enfranchise; liberate. [<F *affranchiss-*, stem of *affranchir* <*à* to + *franchir* free. See FRANCHISE.]

af•fray (ə•frā′) *n.* **1** A public brawl or fight; a disturbance of the peace. **2** *Law* The fighting in public of two or more persons in a manner that will naturally produce terror in others. See synonyms under ALTERCATION, QUARREL. —*v.t.* *Archaic* To cause to feel sudden fear; terrify; startle. [<OF *effrei, esfrei*, ult. <L *ex-* out + a Gmc. word for "peace" (cf. OHG *fridu*)]

af•fri•cate (af′ri•kit) *n.* *Phonet.* A complex sound consisting of a stop followed by the fricative release of breath at the point of contact, as *ch* (t + sh) in *church*. [<L *affricatus*, pp. of *affricare* <*ad-* against + *fricare* rub] **—af•fric•a•tive** (ə•frik′ə•tiv) *adj.*, *n.*

af•fright (ə•frīt′) *v.t.* *Obs.* To strike with sudden fear; frighten. See synonyms under FRIGHTEN. —*n.* Sudden fear; also, a cause of terror. See synonyms under ALARM, FEAR, FRIGHT. [OE *āfyrhtan*] **—af•fright′ment** *n.*

af•front (ə•frunt′) *v.t.* **1** To insult openly; treat with insolence; offend by word or act. **2** To confront in defiance; accost. **3** *Archaic* To front in position; face toward. — *n.* **1** An open insult or indignity. **2** *Obs.* A meeting. See synonyms under OUTRAGE. [<OF *afronter* strike on the forehead <LL *affrontare* strike against <L *ad-* to + *frons* forehead] **—af•front′er** *n.* **—af•fron′tive** *adj.*

Synonyms (verb): aggravate, annoy, displease, exasperate, insult, irritate, offend, provoke, tease, vex, wound. *Aggravate* in the sense of *offend* is not in approved use. To *provoke*, literally to call out or challenge, is to begin a contest; one *provokes* another to violence. To *affront* is to offer some defiant offense or indignity, as it were to one's face. Compare PIQUE[1]. *Antonyms:* conciliate, content, gratify, honor, please.

af•fuse (ə•fyo͞oz′) *v.t.* **af•fused, af•fus•ing** *Archaic.* To pour on, as water. [<L *affusus*, pp. of *affundere* <*ad-* to + *fundere* pour]

af•fu•sion (ə•fyo͞o′zhən) *n.* A pouring on or into; a sprinkling, as in baptism.

af•ghan (af′gən, -gan) *n.* A soft wool coverlet, knitted or crocheted, often in many-colored geometrical patterns.

Af•ghan (af′gən, -gan) *n.* **1** A native of Afghanistan. **2** The dominant language of Afghanistan: also called *Pushtu*. **3** An Afghan hound. —*adj.* Of or pertaining to Afghanistan, its inhabitants, or their language.

Afghan hound An ancient breed of large hound originally from Egypt, having long, thick, silky hair and a narrow muzzle.

Af•ghan•i•stan (af•gan′ə•stan) An independent country of south central Asia; 250,000 square miles; capital, Kabul.

a•fi•cio•na•do (ə•fish′ə•nä′dō, ə•fis′ē-) *n. pl.* **•dos** (-dōz) An avid follower or fan, as of a sport or activity; devotee: an *aficionado* of horse racing. [<Sp.]

a•field (ə•fēld′) *adv.* **1** In or to the field; abroad. **2** Off the track; astray.

a•fire (ə•fīr′) *adv. & adj* . On fire.

a•flame (ə•flām′) *adv. & adj.* Flaming; glowing.

af•la•tox•in (af′lə•tok′san) *n.* Any of several toxic carcinogens produced by certain strains of a fungus *(Aspergillus flavus)* growing on peanuts, corn, beans, etc.

AFL-CIO A United States labor organization with a membership of about 14 million workers, created in 1955 as a result of a merger between the *American Federation of Labor* and the *Congress of Industrial Organizations*.

a•float (ə•flōt′) *adv. & adj.* **1** Floating on the surface of a liquid or a body of water. **2** Not aground or ashore. **2** In motion or circulation, as a rumor. **3** Adrift; unfixed. **4** Overflowed; flooded, as the deck of a ship.

à fond (á fôn′) *French* To the bottom; thoroughly.

a•foot (ə•fo͝ot′) *adv.* **1** On foot. **2** Able to walk. **3** In motion or progress; on the move; astir. [ME *on fot*]

a•fore (ə•fôr′, ə•fōr′) *adv., prep., & conj.* Before. [OE *onforan*, blended with *æt-foran* before. See ON, AT, and FORE.]

a•fore•hand (ə•fôr′hand′, ə•fōr′-) *adv. & adj.* Beforehand; prepared; supplied with what is needed for the future.

a•fore•said (ə•fôr′sed′, ə•fōr′-) *adj.* Said or mentioned before.

a•fore•thought (ə•fôr′thôt′, ə•fōr′-) *adj.* Intended, devised, contrived, or planned beforehand; premeditated. —*n.* Premeditation.

a•fore•time (ə•fôr′tīm′, ə•fōr′-) *adv.* At a previous time; formerly.

a for•ti•o•ri (ā fôr′shē •ôr′ī, ā fōr′shē•ō′rī, -rē) *Latin* By a stronger reason; all the more.

a•foul (ə•foul′) *adv. & adj.* In entanglement or collision; entangled. — **to run (or fall) afoul of** To become entangled with; get into difficulties with.

a•fraid (ə•frād′) *adj.* Filled with fear or apprehension; apprehensive; fearful. [Orig. pp. of AFFRAY]

A–frame (ā′frām′) *n.* A framework in the shape of the letter A, as that supporting a slanted roof.

a•fresh (ə•fresh′) *adv.* Once more; anew; again: We started *afresh*.

Af•ri•ca (af′ri•kə) *n.* The second largest continent, located in the eastern hemisphere south of Europe and joined to Asia by the Sinai peninsula; 11,500,000 square miles.

Af•ri•can (af′ri•kən) *adj.* Of or pertaining to Africa or to the black race. —*n.* **1** A native or naturalized inhabitant of Africa. **2** One of the African races.

African American *n.* An American of black African descent.

Af•ri•can•ize (af′rə•kən•īz′) *v.t.* **•ized, •iz•ing 1** To make African in character or nature. **2** To place under the control of Africans, especially of black Africans. **—Af′ri•can•i•za′tion** *n.*

African lily *n.* A greenhouse potted plant *(Agapanthus africanus)* from Africa, with deep blue or white flowers growing in umbellate clusters.

African sleeping sickness *n.* A disease confined to tropical Africa, caused by either of two species of trypanosomes *(Trypanosoma gambiense* or *T. rhodesiense)* usually transmitted by the bite of the tsetse fly and marked by recurrent fever and headaches, progressive lethargy, somnolence and death. Also called *sleeping sickness*. Also **African trypanosomiasis.**

African violet *n.* Any of a genus *(Saintpaulia)* of tropical African perennial herbs with purple, pink, or white flowers.

Af•ri•kaans (af′ri•käns′, -känz′) *n.* A South African language that developed from the speech of the 17th–century Dutch settlers in this region, containing many words of English, French, and Malay origin: also called *Taal, South African Dutch, Cape Dutch*.

Af•ri•ka•ner (af′ri•kä′nər) *n.* A person born in South Africa of European blood.

Af•ro (af′rō) *n. pl.* **Af•ros** A hair style in which tightly curled hair is shaped into a full, rounded mass. —*adj.* Of, pertaining to, or influenced by African culture.

Afro- *combining form* Africa; African. [<L *Afer* an African]

Af•ro–A•mer•i•can (af′rō•ə•mer′ə•kən) *adj.* Of or pertaining to Americans of black African descent. —*n.* An Afro-American person.

aft (aft, äft) *adj.* Of or near the stern, or rear, of a vessel. — *adv.* Toward the rear; astern. [OE *æftan* behind]

af•ter (af′tər, äf′-) *adj.* **1** *Naut.* Farther aft; toward the stern. **2** Following in time or place; subsequent; later. —*adv.* **1** At a later time. **2** In the rear; behind. —*prep.* **1** In the rear of; farther back than; following: The prisoners followed *after* the soldiers. **2** Subsequently to; at a later period than: His will was read *after* his death. **3** In succession to; following repeatedly: the same routine day *after* day. **4** As a result of; subsequently to and because of: *After* their quarrel they decided to separate. **5** Notwithstanding; subsequently to and in spite of: *After* the best endeavors, one may fail. **6** Next below in order or importance: This office comes right *after* the president in power. **7** In search or pursuit of: to strive *after* wisdom. **8** According to the nature, wishes, or customs of; in conformity with: a woman *after* my own heart. **9** In imitation of; in the manner of: a painting *after* Vermeer. **10** In honor, remembrance, or observance of: I was named *after* Lincoln. **11** In relation to; concerning: to inquire *after* someone's health. —*conj.* Following the time that: *After* I went home, I went to bed. [OE *æfter* behind]

After may appear as a combining form in

open, hyphenated, or closed two-word phrases with the following meanings:

1 Following in place, order, or time:

after-acquired	**after-mentioned**
after-age	**after-named**
after-ages	**aftersails**
after-described	**after-specified**
after-designed	**after-supper**
after-knowledge	**after-written**
aftermast	**after-years**

2 Secondary; following the main occurrence:

aftercrop	**after-mass**
aftergrowth	

3 Following not at once; eventual; after delay:

aftereffect	**after-reckoning**
after-penitence	**after-remedy**

after all All things considered; on the whole.

af·ter·birth (af′tər·bûrth′, äf′-) *n.* The placenta and fetal membranes expelled from the uterus following delivery of mammalian offspring.

af·ter·bod·y (af′tər·bod′ ē, äf′-) *n.* In rocketry, a section of a rocket or missile that continues to trail the nose cone or satellite from which it separates.

af·ter·brain (af′tər·brān′, äf′-) *n.* Hindbrain.

af·ter·burn·er (af′tər·bûr′nər, äf′-) *n. Aeron.* A device for injecting extra fuel into the exhaust system of a jet engine as a means of increasing the thrust.

af·ter·burn·ing (af′tər·bûr′ning, äf′-) *n. Aeron.* **1** An irregular burning of fuel occurring subsequently to the normal combustion of fuel in a rocket or jet engine. **2** The technique of using an afterburner.

af·ter·care (af′tər·kâr′, äf′-) *n.* Supplementary observation and treatment as needed of a person discharged from a program or a hospital or other institution.

af·ter·cool·er (af′tər·ko͞o′ lər, äf′-) *n. Aeron.* A radiator designed to reduce the temperature of the fuel mixture in the supercharging system of a jet airplane flying at extreme altitudes.

af·ter·damp (af′tər·damp′, äf′-) *n.* A suffocating mixture of gases, chiefly nitrogen and carbon dioxide, found in mines after a fire or an explosion of firedamp.

af·ter·deck (af′tər·dek′, äf′-) *n. Naut.* That part of a deck aft of amidships.

af·ter-din·ner (af′tər·din′ər, äf′-) *adj.* **1** Occurring, made, or done after dinner: an *after-dinner* speech. **2** Served after dinner: *after-dinner* coffee.

af·ter·ef·fect (af′tər·ə·fekt′, äf′-) *n.* **1** An effect succeeding its cause after an interval. **2** A result following the initial effects of an agent, as a drug, X-rays, etc.

af·ter·glow (af′tər·glō′, äf′-) *n.* **1** A glow after a light has disappeared, as in metals cooling after being heated to incandescence or in the western sky after sunset. **2** The luminosity of a rarefied gas after the passage of an electric charge through it. **3** An agreeable feeling occurring after a pleasant or profitable experience.

af·ter·im·age (af′tər·im′ij, äf′-) *n.* **1** *Psychol.* The persistence of a visual sensation after the direct stimulus has been withdrawn from the retina. Also called *photogene.* **2** A similar effect of other senses.

af·ter·life (af′tər·līf′, äf′-) *n.* Life after death.

af·ter·math (af′tər·math, äf′-) *n.* **1** Results; consequences; especially, ill consequences. **2** *Agric.* The second grass crop of the season, after the first has been cut for hay; a second mowing. [<AFTER + MATH[1]]

af·ter·most (af′tər·mōst, äf′-) *adj.* **1** *Naut.* Nearest the stern: also **aft′most. 2** Last.

af·ter·noon (af′tər·no͞on′, äf′-) *n.* That part of the day between noon and sunset; hence, the closing part: the *afternoon* of life. —*adj.* Of, for, or occurring in the afternoon.

af·ter·pain (af′tər·pān′, äf′-) *n.* **1** A subsequent pain. **2** *pl.* The pains succeeding childbirth, due to contraction of the womb.

af·ter·piece (af′tər·pēs′, äf′-) *n.* **1** A farce or other short piece after a play. **2** *Naut.* The heel of a rudder.

af·ter·sen·sa·tion (af′tər·sen·sā′shən, äf′-) *n. Psychol.* Any sensory persistence after direct stimulation has ceased, as an afterimage, aftertaste, etc.

af·ter·shaft (af′tər·shaft′, äf′tər·shäft′) *n.* A secondary shaft of the feather in many birds, springing from near the junction of the quill with the rachis.

af·ter·shock (af′tər·shäk) *n.* A minor tremor following a major earthquake.

af·ter·taste (af′tər·tāst′, äf′-) *n.* A taste persisting in the mouth, as after a meal.

af·ter·thought (af′tər·thôt′, äf′-) *n.* **1** A later or more deliberate thought, as after decision or action. **2** A thought occurring too late to affect action in the matter to which it refers.

af·ter·time (af′tər·tīm′, äf′-) *n.* Time following the present; the future.

af·ter·ward (af′tər·wərd, äf′-) *adv.* In time following; subsequently. Also **af′ter·wards.** [OE *æfterweard*]

af·ter·world (af′tər·wûrld′, äf′-) *n.* The future world; also, the world after death.

af·to·sa (af·tō′sə) *n. SW U.S.* Foot-and-mouth disease. [<Sp., fem., aphthous]

ag- Assimilated var. of AD-.

Ag *chem.* Silver (symbol Ag). [L *argentum*]

a·ga (ä′gə) *n.* An officer of high military or civil rank in Mohammedan countries: also spelled *agha.* [<Turkish]

A·ga·des (ä′gə·des, ag′ə·dēz) A city in the Republic of the Niger. Also **A·ga·dez** (ä′gə·dēz, ag′ə-).

A·ga·dir (ä′gə·dir′, ag′ə-) A port in SW Morocco.

a·gain (ə·gen′, *esp. Brit.* ə·gān′) *adv.* **1** At a second or another time; once more; anew; afresh: to bring a subject to life *again.* **2** Once repeated: half as much *again.* **3** To the same place or over the same course; back, as in a previous condition: Here we are *again!* **4** In correspondence with something previous or preceding; in reply; in return: The valley echoed *again* to the sound of horns. **5** In the next place; further; moreover: *Again,* since the weather is uncertain, I may not be able to come. **6** On the other hand; from another point of view. [OE *ongegn*]

again and again Repeatedly.

a·gainst (ə·genst′, *esp. Brit.* ə·gānst′) *prep.* **1** In contact with and pressing upon: leaning *against* the wall. **2** In collision with: The ship was dashed *against* the rocks. **3** In front of; directly opposite: *against* the background of the sky. **4** In anticipation of; in preparation for: to be ready *against* the third day; to hoard wealth *against* old age. **5** In opposition to; contrary to: *against* my wishes. **6** In hostility to: fighting *against* the invader. **7** To the debit of: Charge it *against* my account. **8** In comparison with; contrasted with: my word *against* yours. [OE *ongegn* + *-es,* adverbial genitive suffix + inorganic *-t*]

A·ga Khan (ä′gə kän′) A hereditary Mohammedan title passing to the heads of families descended from Ali. —**Aga Khan III,** 1877–1957, leader of Ismaelian Mohammedans, succeeding his father, Aga Khan II, in 1885.

a·gal (ä·gäl′) *n. Arabic* A thick cord worn by Bedouins over the kaffiyeh to keep it in place.

ag·a·lac·ti·a (ag′ə·lak′shē·ə) *n. Pathol.* The failure or deficiency of milk secretion. [<NL <Gk. *agalaktia* <*a-* without + *gala, galaktos* milk]

a·gal·loch (ə·gal′ək, ag′ə·lok) *n.* The fragrant wood of a tree *(Aquilaria agallocha)* of Indochina and neighboring regions; the aloes or lign-aloes of the Scriptures (*Num.* xxiv:5). Also called *aloes, lignaloes.* Also **a·gal·wood** (ä′gəl·wo͝od′, ag′əl-). [<NL *agallochum* <Gk. *agallochon* bitter aloe]

ag·al·mat·o·lite (ag′əl·mat′ə·līt) *n.* One of various soft waxy minerals, pagodite, pinite, or steatite, used for carvings by the Chinese. [<Gk. *agalma* statue, image + *lithos* stone]

ag·a·ma (ag′ə·mə) *n.* Any of various small terrestrial lizards of the family Agamidae, found in Africa, southeastern Europe, and central India. [<Carib]

Ag·a·mem·non (ag′ə·mem′non, -nən) In Greek legend, king of Mycenae, brother of Menelaus and father of Orestes, Electra, and Iphigenia: chief of the Greek army in the Trojan war, he was killed on his return by his wife Clytemnestra and her lover Aegisthus.

a·gam·ete (ä·gam′ēt) *n.* Any unicellular organism that reproduces asexually, as certain protozoans.

a·gam·ic (ə·gam′ik) *adj.* Reproducing without the union of two sexes; parthenogenic; asexual. Also **ag·a·mous** (ag′ə·məs). [<Gk. *agamos* unmarried < *a-* without + *gamos* marriage] —**a·gam′i·cal·ly** *adv.*

a·gam·ma·glob·u·li·ne·mi·a (ä·gam′ə·glob′yə·lə·nē′mē·ə) *n.* Any congenital, acquired, or transient condition in which gamma globulins and antibodies are deficient or lacking in the blood.

ag·a·mo·gen·e·sis (ag′ə·mō·jen′ə·sis) *n.* Reproduction without the union of opposite sexual elements, as by budding, cell division, or parthenogenesis. [<NL <Gk. *agamos* unmarried + GENESIS] —**ag′a·mo·ge·net′ic** (-jə·net′ik) *adj.*

A·ga·ña (ä·gä′nyä) The capital of Guam.

Ag·a·nip·pe (ag′ə·nip′ē) A spring on Mount Helicon, Greece, traditionally sacred to the Muses.

ag·a·pan·thus (ag′ə·pan′thəs) *n.* Any of a genus *(Agapanthus)* of South African plants of the lily family, bearing umbels of blue or white flowers; the African lily. [<NL <Gk. *agapē* love + *anthos* flower]

a·gape[1] (ə·gāp′, ə·gap′) *adv. & adj.* In a gaping state; gaping.

ag·a·pe [2] (ag′ə·pē) *n. pl.* **·pae** (-pē) The social meal or love feast of the early Christians. [<Gk. *agapē* love]

a·gar (ā′gär, ā′gər, ä ′gär) *n.* A gelatinous substance obtained from certain red algae and used as a gelling material in culture media and in the food industry. Also **a·gar-a·gar.** [<Malay *agar-agar*]

ag·a·ric (ag′ə·rik, ə·gar′ik) *n.* **1** Any of the various fungi (order Agaricales) bearing an umbrellalike fruiting body with gills on the underside, including the common edible mushroom *Agaricus campestris.* **2** The dried fruiting body of various fungi, used as touchwood, in medicine, etc. [<L *agaricum* <Gk. *agarikon,* named after *Agaria,* in Sarmatia] —**a·gar′i·ca·ceous** (ə·gar′i·kā′shəs) *adj.*

ag·a·ric·ic acid (ag′ə·ris′ik) The active principle of agaric, a white, odorless, tasteless crystalline powder, $C_{22}H_{40}O_7$, formerly used in medicine for the relief of night sweats.

agaric mineral Rock milk.

A·gar·ta·la (ə·gûr′tə·lə) The capital of Tripura state, India.

Ag·as·siz (ag′ə·sē, *Fr.* à·gà·sē′), **Alexander,** 1835–1910, U.S. zoologist, born in Switzerland; son of **(Jean) Louis (Rodolphe),** 1807–73, U.S. naturalist and teacher, born in Switzerland.

ag·ate (ag′it) *n.* **1** A variegated waxy quartz or chalcedony, SiO_2, in which the colors are usually in bands. **2** A child's playing marble. **3** *Printing* 5 1/2 point type. See TYPOGRAPHY. **4** Any of several instruments, as the drawplate of gold-wire drawers. **5** *Obs.* A very diminutive person; in allusion to the figures cut upon agates for rings. [<F <L *achates* <Gk. *achatēs* <*Achatēs,* a river in Sicily]

ag·ate·ware (ag′it·wâr′) *n.* **1** Pottery veined and mottled to resemble agate. **2** A kind of steel or iron kitchenware, enameled and grained to resemble agate pottery.

Ag·a·tha (ag′ə·thə; *Dan.* ä·gä′thə, *Du.* a·ga′ta) A feminine personal name. Also *Fr.* **A·gathe** (à·gàt′), *Ger.* **A·ga·the** (ä·gä′tə), *Ital., Sp.* **A·ga·ta** (ä ′gä·tä), *Pg.* **A·ga·tha** (ä ′gä·tä), *Sw.* **A·ga·ta** (ä·gä′tä), *Lat.* **Ag·a·the** (ag′ə·thē). [<Gk. *Agathē* good, kind]

A·gath·o·cles (ə·gath′ə·klēz), 361–289 B.C., tyrant of Syracuse.

ag·a·tho·de·mon (ag′ə·thō·dē′mən) *n.* A benevolent spirit; a good genius: opposed to *cacodemon.* [<Gk. *agathodaimōn* <*agathos* good + *daimōn* spirit]

ag·a·tize (ag′ə·tīz) *v.t.* **·tized, ·tiz·ing** To make into or cause to resemble agate or agateware.

à gauche (à gōsh′) *French* To, toward, or on the left (hand).

a·ga·ve (ə·gä′vē *or* ə·gä′vē) *n.* Any of a genus *(Agave)* of fleshy-leaved plants native to hot, desert areas of the Americas, as the century plant and the sisal. [<NL <Gk. *Agauē,* proper n., fem. of *agauos* noble]

a·gaze (ə·gāz′) *adv.* In the posture or attitude of gazing.

age (āj) *n.* **1** The entire period of life or existence, as of a person, thing, nation, etc. **2** The period or stage of life as measured by the time already or previously passed. **3** The closing period of life; decline of life; the state of being old. **4** Any period of life that fits or unfits for any function, office, duty, etc.; specifically, that time of life at which one legally becomes mature, independent, and responsible, usually 21 years; majority: used especially in the phrase **of age.** **5** Any period of life naturally distinct; stage of life. **6** Any great and distinct period of time in the history of humanity, of the earth, etc.; era; epoch; generation. **7** A century. **8** A long time; protracted period: They have been gone an *age.* **9** *Psychol.* The physical and mental development of a person, measured in years, in relation to the normal physical and mental development of an average child. —*v.* **aged, ag·ing** or **age·ing** *v.t.* **1** To make or cause to grow old. **2** In dyeing, to fix and distribute the mordant in, as fabric, by exposure to air or chemicals. —*v.i.* **3** To assume or show some characteristics of age; ripen: wine *ages* in barrels. [<OF *aage* <L *aetas* age, a span of life]

-age *suffix* of nouns **1** Collection or aggregate of: *baggage, leafage.* **2** Condition, office, service, or other relation or connection of: *drayage; pilgrimage.* [<OF <L *-aticum,* neut. adj. suffix]

a·ged (ā′jid *for defs.* 1, 2, 4; ājd *for def.* 3) *adj.* **1** Advanced in years; very old. **2** Of, like, or characteristic of old age. **3** Of or at the age of: a child, *aged* five. **4** *Geol.* Nearing base level reduction: said of configuration of ground. See synonyms under ANCIENT. —**a′ged·ly** *adv.* —**a′ged·ness** *n.*

a·gee (ə·jē′) *adv.* & *adj.* Awry; askew. [<A-[1] + GEE[2]]

age·ing (ā′jing) See AGING.

age-in-grade (āj′in·grād′) *n.* A military officer's age in relation to rank: a consideration in qualification for field service.

age·ism (ā′jiz·əm) *n.* Discrimination or prejudice, esp. as directed against elderly people. —**age′ist** *n., adj.*

age·less (āj′lis) *adj.* **1** Not seeming to grow old. **2** Having no limits of duration.

age·long (āj′long′, -long′) *adj.* Lasting a long time; everlasting: *agelong* myths.

a·gen·cy (ā′jən·sē) *n.* pl. **·cies 1** Active power or operation; activity. **2** Means; instrumentality. **3** The relation of an agent to his principal. **4** The business, office, or place of business, of an agent. **5** Any establishment where business is done for others. See synonyms under OPERATION. [<L *agentia* <*agere* do]

a·gen·da (ə·jen′də) *n. pl.* of **agendum** A record of things to be done, as items of business; a memorandum; specifically, a program of business to be done or papers to be read at a meeting: What's on the *agenda* for today?

a·gen·dum (ə·jen′dəm) *n.* pl. **·da** *Eccl.* A thing to be done, as a liturgical detail: opposed to *credendum,* a matter of belief. [<L, neut. gerundive of *agere* do]

a·gen·e·sis (ə·jen′ə·sis) *n.* The absence of a tissue or organ due to a failure in development. Also **ag·e·ne·sia** (aj′ə·nē′zhə, -zhē·ə). [<A-[4] without + GENESIS]

age norm *Psychol.* The average score made on a standard set of tests by a random group of children of given age; the score typical for a child of stated age.

a·gent (ā′jənt) *n.* **1** One who or that which acts or has power to act; an efficient cause of anything; actor; doer. **2** One who or that which acts for another; a factor; steward; deputy. **3** Any force or substance having power to effect a material change in bodies, as a chemical, drug, or earth movement. **4** A means by which something is done. **5** One who transacts business for another: a literary *agent.* **6** A traveling salesman or canvasser. —*adj.* Obs. Acting: opposed to *passive.* [<L *agens, agentis,* ppr. of *agere* Ado]

Synonyms (noun): actor, cause, doer, factor, instrument, means, mover, operator, performer, promoter. In strict philosophical usage, the prime *mover* or *doer* of an act is the *agent.* Thus we speak of someone as a free *agent.* But in common usage, especially in business, an *agent* is not the prime *actor,* but only an *instrument* or *factor,* acting under orders or instructions. Compare CAUSE. *Antonyms:* chief, inventor, originator, principal.

a·gen·tial (ā·jen′shəl) *adj.* Of or pertaining to an agent or agency.

Agent Orange A toxic herbicidal and defoliant mixture containing dioxin used extensively by the United States in military operations in Vietnam before its use was banned in early 1970.

a·gent pro·vo·ca·teur (á·zhäṅ′ prô·vô·kȧ·tœr′) *pl.* **a·gents pro·vo·ca·teurs** (á·zhä ṅ′ prô·vô·kȧ·tœr′) *French* A secret agent implanted in an organization, as a trade union or political party, to incite its members to actions or declarations that will incur penalties or punishment.

age of consent The age before which sexual relations, regardless of consent, constitute statutory rape.

age-old (āj′ōld′) *adj.* Extremely old; ancient: *age-old* traditions.

ag·e·ot·ro·pism (aj′ē·ot′rə·piz′əm) *n. Bot.* Apogeotropism. —**ag·e·o·trop·ic** (aj′ē·ō·trop′ik) *adj.*

ag·er (ā′jər) *n.* **1** That which promotes age or produces an effect of age. **2** A boxlike vessel in which fabrics are treated with steam or ammonia fumes to fix the colors.

ag·e·ra·tum (aj′ə·rā′təm, ə·jer′ə·təm) *n.* **1** Any of a large genus (*Ageratum*) of tropical American herbs of the family Compositae or Asteraceae with opposite petioled leaves and terminal cymes or panicles of blue or white flowers in small heads. **2** Any of several plants having similar heads of blue flowers. [<NL <Gk. *agē raton,* a kind of plant < *agēratos* ageless < *a-* not + *gēras* old age]

A·ges·i·la·us (ə·jes′ə·lā′əs) 444?–360 B.C., Spartan king.

a·geu·si·a (ə·gyo͞o′sē·ə) *n.* Loss or impairment of the sense of taste. Also **a·geus·ti·a** (ə·gyo͞os′tē ·ə). [<NL <Gk. *a-* without + *geusis* taste] —**a·geu′sic** *adj.*

ag·ger (aj′ər) *n.* **1** A mound or heap; an earthwork; especially, in ancient Rome, the rampart of a fortified camp; a bank against a wall that overtops the defenses. **2** A military road. [<L]

Ag·gie (ag′ē) Diminutive of AGATHA.

ag·glom·er·ate (ə·glom′ə·rāt) *v.t.* & *v.i.* **·at·ed, ·at·ing** To gather, form, or grow into a ball or rounded mass. —*adj.* (ə·glom′ər·it, -ə·rāt) Gathered into a mass or heap; clustered densely. —*n.* (ə·glom′ər·it, -ə·rāt) **1** A heap or mass of things thrown together indiscriminately. **2** *Geol.* An unstratified mass of compacted volcanic debris with fragments of all sizes. [<L *agglomeratus,* pp. of *agglomerare* <*ad-* to + *glomerare* gather into a ball < *glomus* ball] —**ag·glom·er·at·ic** (ə·glom′ə·rat′ik), **ag·glom′er·a′tive** *adj.*

ag·glom·er·a·tion (ə·glom′ə·rā′shən) *n.* **1** The process of agglomerating. **2** The state or condition of being agglomerated. **3** A jumbled heap or mass.

ag·glu·ti·nant (ə·glo͞o′tə·nənt) *adj.* Tending to cause adhesion; sticky. —*n.* An adhesive substance.

ag·glu·ti·nate (ə·glo͞o′tə·nāt) *v.t.* & *v.i.* **·nat·ed, ·nat·ing 1** To unite, as with glue; join by adhesion. **2** *Ling.* To form (words) by agglutination. **3** To mass together, as living cells or bacteria, by agglutination. —*adj.* (ə·glo͞o′tə · nit, -nāt) Joined by adhesion. [<L *agglutinatus,* pp. of *agglutinare* glue to < *ag-* to + *glutinare* <*gluten* glue]

ag·glu·ti·na·tion (ə·glo͞o′ tə·nā′shən) *n.* **1** Adhesion of distinct parts; a mass formed by adhesion. **2** *Ling.* In some languages, a combination of word elements without change of form or meaning to form new compound word elements. **3** The clumping together of particles, as red blood cells, bacteria, etc., suspended in blood serum or other medium.

ag·glu·ti·na·tive (ə·glo͞o′tə·nā′tiv) *adj.* **1** Tending toward, pertaining to, or characterized by agglutination. **2** *Ling.* Denoting a language, such as Turkish or Hungarian, in which words are formed by adding to a word root other word roots or simple words without change of form or loss of original meaning of the various elements.

ag·glu·ti·nin (ə·glo͞o′tə·nin) *n.* An antibody formed in blood serum that causes clumping of particles, as red corpuscles or bacteria, bearing the corresponding antigen.

ag·glu·tin·o·gen (ag′lo͞o·tin′ə·jən) *n.* An antigen that stimulates the formation of a specific corresponding antibody (agglutinin) when introduced into an animal body. —**ag′glu·tin′o·gen′ic** *adj.*

ag·grade (ə·grād′) *v.t.* **ag·grad·ed, ag·grad·ing** *Geol.* To add to or raise, as the bed of a river by the deposition of silt. [<AD- + GRADE] —**ag·gra·da·tion** (ag′rə·dā′shən) *n.*

ag·gran·dize (ə·gran′dīz, ag′rən·dīz) *v.t.* **·dized, ·diz·ing 1** To make great or greater; increase. **2** To increase the power or rank of (oneself): to *aggrandize* oneself at another's expense. **3** To make appear greater; exalt. [<F *agrandiss-,* stem of *agrandir* <L *ad-* to + *grandire* make great] —**ag·gran·dize·ment** (ə·gran′diz·mənt) *n.* —**ag·gran′diz·er** *n.*

ag·gra·vate (ag′rə·vāt) *v.t.* **·vat·ed, ·vat·ing 1** To make worse; increase, intensify, as an offense. **2** To make heavier or more burdensome, as a duty. **3** *Colloq.* To provoke or exasperate; arouse to anger. [<L *aggravatus,* pp. of *aggravare* make heavy or burdensome < *ad-* to + *gravare* make heavy < *gravis* heavy. Doublet of AGGRIEVE.] —**ag′gra·vat′ing** *adj.* —**ag′gra·vat′ing·ly** *adv.* **ag′gra·va′tive** *adj.*

Synonyms: affront, enhance, heighten, increase, intensify, magnify. *Enhance* and *magnify* are most often used in the lofty and good sense; as, to *enhance* the glory of God; "I *magnify* mine office," *Rom.* xi 13. *Aggravate* is used always in the bad sense meaning to make worse what is already bad; as, to *aggravate* a fever or an enmity. See AFFRONT, INCREASE. *Antonyms:* alleviate, assuage, attenuate, diminish, lessen, palliate, reduce, soften.

aggravated assault *Law* Assault committed with the intention of committing an additional offense.

ag·gra·va·tion (ag′rə·vā′shən) *n.* **1** A making heavier or worse or the state of being aggravated. **2** Some extrinsic circumstance considered as increasing the atrocity of a crime. **3** *Colloq.* Exasperation; irritation.

ag·gre·gate (ag′rə·gāt) *v.t.* **·gat·ed, ·gat·ing 1** To bring or gather together, as into a mass, sum, or body; collect; mass. **2** To amount to; form a total of. See synonyms under AMASS. —*adj.* (ag′rə·git) **1** Collected into a sum, mass, or total; gathered into a whole; formed by collection; collective. **2** *Bot.* **a** Crowded close together in a dense cluster, as a flower head. **b** Formed of a coherent mass of drupelets, as a fruit. **3** *Geol.* Composed of distinct minerals separable by mechanical means, as granite. —*n.* (ag′rə·git) **1** The entire number, sum, mass, or quantity of something; amount; total, collection. **2** Material for making concrete. —**in the aggregate** Collectively; as a whole. [<L *aggregatus,* pp. of *aggregare,* lit., bring to the flock < *ad-* to + *gregare* collect < *grex* flock] —**ag′gre·ga′tive** *adj.* —**ag′gre·ga′ tor** *n.*

Synonyms (noun): agglomeration, aggregation, amount, collection, entirety, heap, mass, sum, total, totality, whole. An *aggregate* of financial items is an *amount, sum,* or *total.* An *aggregate* or *aggregation* of material objects is a *collection, mass,* or *whole;* an *agglomeration* is a heterogeneous *mass. Collection* points rather to the differences, *mass* to the unity. We say a *collection* of minerals, a *mass* of rock. The result of multiplication is a product, the result of addition a *sum, total,* or *aggregate.*

ag·gre·ga·tion (ag′rə·gā′shən) *n.* **1** A collection into a whole; a mass; aggregate; whole. **2** The act of aggregating, or the state of being aggregated.

ag·gress (ə·gres′) *v.i.* To undertake an attack; begin a quarrel. [<L *aggressus,* pp. of *aggredi* approach, attack < *ad-* to + *gradi* step, go < *gradus* a step]

ag·gres·sion (ə·gresh′ən) *n.* **1** An unprovoked attack; encroachment. **2** Habitual aggressive action or practices. **3** *Psychoanal.* A primary instinct, generally associated with emotional states, to carry out action in a forceful way.

Synonyms: assault, attack, encroachment, incursion, intrusion, invasion, onslaught, trespass. An *attack* may be by word; an *aggression* is always by deed. An *assault* may be upon the person, an *aggression* is upon rights, possessions, etc. An *invasion* of a nation's territories is an act of *aggression;* an *intrusion* upon a neighboring estate is a *trespass. On-*

slaught signifies intensely violent *assault,* as by an army or a desperado, yet it is sometimes used of violent speech. *Antonyms:* defense, repulsion, resistance, retreat.

ag·gres·sive (ə·gres′iv) *adj.* **1** Disposed to begin an attack or encroachment. **2** Disposed to vigorous activity; assertive. **—ag·gres′sive·ly** *adv.* **—ag·gres′sive·ness** *n.*

ag·gres·sor (ə·gres′ər) *n.* One who commits an aggression or begins a quarrel.

ag·grieve (ə·grēv′) *v.t.* **ag·grieved, ag·griev·ing** **1** To cause sorrow to; distress or afflict. **2** To give cause for just complaint, as by injustice. See synonyms under ABUSE. [<OF *agrever* <L *aggravare.* Doublet of AGGRAVATE.]

ag·grieved (ə·grēvd′) *adj.* **1** Subjected to ill-treatment; feeling an injury or injustice. **2** Injured, as by legal decision adversely infringing upon one's rights. **—ag·griev·ed·ness** (ə·grē′vid·nis) *n.*

a·gha (ä′gə) See AGA.

a·ghast (ə·gast′, ə·gäst′) *adj.* Struck dumb with horror. [pp. of obs. *agast* frighten, OE *ā-* A-[1] + *gæstan* terrify; spelling infl. by *ghost*]

ag·ile (aj′əl, aj′īl) *adj.* **1** Able to move or act quickly and easily; active; nimble. **2** Characterized by quickness of perception or response; alert: an *agile* mind. See synonyms under ACTIVE, NIMBLE. [<F <L *agilis* <*agere* do, move] **—ag′ile·ly** *adv.* **—ag′ile·ness** *n.*

a·gil·i·ty (ə·jil′ə·tē) *n.* Quickness and readiness in movement or mind; nimbleness. [<F *agilité* <L *agilitas* <*agilis.* See AGILE.]

Ag·in·court (aj′in·kôrt, -kōrt; *Fr.* à·zhań·ko͝or′) A village in northern France: site of an English victory over the French, 1415.

ag·ing (ā′jing) *n.* **1** The process of acquiring characteristics of age. **2** *Biol.* The progressive breakdown of an organism or any of its parts through the cumulative effects of irreversible physicochemical changes acting over a period of time. **3** The effects of time on the properties of materials or substances. **4** Any means for obtaining such effects artificially, as the weathering of clay for bricks, or the acid treatment of bronze to obtain a patina. **5** *Metall.* A change in the properties of certain metals, as hardness and tensile strength, caused by heat treatment and cold working. **6** A method of steaming fabrics to develop and fix the colors. Also spelled *ageing.*

ag·i·o (aj′ē·ō) *n. pl.* **ag·i·os** **1** The premium payable for the exchange of one kind or quality of money into another; exchange premium. **2** An allowance for depreciation of coin by wear. [<Ital. *aggio* exchange]

ag·i·o·tage (aj′ē·ə·tij) *n.* Brokerage; stockjobbing. [<F]

a·gist (ə·jist′) *v.t. Law* **1** To feed and care for, as horses or cattle, for hire. **2** To assess, as land or its owner, for a public purpose. [<OF *agister* <*a-* to (<L *ad-*) + *gister* lodge, ult. <L *jacere* lie] **—a·gist′ment** *n.*

ag·i·tate (aj′ə·tāt) *v.* **·tat·ed, ·tat·ing** *v.t.* **1** To shake or move irregularly. **2** To set or keep moving, as a fan. **3** To excite or endeavor to excite, as a crowd; perturb. **4** To discuss publicly and incessantly, as a controversial question. **5** *Archaic* To revolve in the mind; plan. *—v.i.* **6** To keep a subject or cause under continuous discussion, in order to excite public interest. [<L *agitatus,* pp. of *agitare* set in motion, freq. of *agere* move]

ag·i·ta·tion (aj′ə·tā′shən) *n.* **1** Violent motion. **2** Open, active discussion; urgent consideration. **3** Strong or tumultuous emotion. See synonyms under TUMULT.

a·gi·ta·to (ä′jē·tä′tō) *adj.* & *adv. Music* Stirring; restless; agitated: a direction in musical execution. [<Ital.]

ag·i·ta·tor (aj′ə·tā′tər) *n.* One who or that which agitates; specifically, one who promotes social change.

ag·it·prop (aj′it·prop′) *n.* **1** Communist political propaganda, as in a play, film, etc. **2** Any political propaganda. — *adj.* Pertaining to or of the nature of agitprop. [<Russ., Former Communist Party agency for agitation and propaganda]

A·gla·ia (ə·glā′ə) One of the three Graces.

a·glare (ə·glâr′) *adv.* In a glare.

a·gleam (ə·glēm′) *adv.* & *adj.* Bright; gleaming.

ag·let (ag′lit) *n.* A metal sheath or tag at the end of a lace or ribbon to facilitate threading; hence, any ornamental pendant: also spelled *aiglet.* [<F *aiguillette,* dim. of *aiguille* needle, ult. <L *acus*]

a·gley (ə·glē′, ə·glī′) *adv. Scot.* Aside; askew. Also **a·glee** (ə·glē′).

A·glos·sa (ə·glos′ə) *n.* pl. **1** A suborder of tailless amphibians without a tongue and with the Eustachian tubes confluent. **2** A group of headless and tongueless mollusks, including the clams, oysters, mussels, etc. [<NL <Gk. *aglō ssos* without a tongue < *a-* without + *glōssa* tongue]

a·glow (ə·glō′) *adv.* & *adj.* In a glow; glowing.

ag·mi·nate (ag′mə·nit, -nāt) *adj.* Grouped in clusters. Also **ag′mi·nat′ed.** [<L *agmen, agminis* troop, crowd + -ATE[1]]

ag·nail (ag′nāl′) *n.* **1** A hangnail. **2** A painful swelling under or about a nail; whitlow. [OE *angnægl* <*ange* narrow, painful + *nægl* nail]

ag·nate (ag′nāt) *adj.* **1** Related on the male or the father's side. **2** Akin; similar. *—n.* A relative in the male line only. Compare COGNATE, ENATE. [<F *agnat* <L *agnatus* a relation (on the father's side), orig., added by birth, pp. of *agnasci* be born in addition to < *ad-* to + *nasci* be born] **—ag·nat·ic** (ag·nat′ik) *adj.* **—ag·nat′i·cal·ly** *adv.* **—ag·na·tion** (ag·nā′shən) *n.*

Ag·nes (ag′nis; *Dan., Du., Ger.* äg′nes) A feminine personal name. Also *Fr.* **A·gnès** (à·nyes′), *Ital.* **A·gne·se** (ä·nyā′zä). [<Gk., pure, sacred, or chaste]

Ag·ni (ug′nē, ag′nē) In Hindu mythology, the god of fire, representing also lightning and sun, according to the Vedas. Also **Ag′nis.** [<Skt.]

ag·no·men (ag·nō′mən) *n.* pl. **ag·nom·i·na** (ag·nom′ə·nə) An added name due to some special achievement; a nickname. [<L < *ad-* to + (*g*) *nomen* name] **—ag·nom′i·nal** *adj.*

ag·no·si·a (ag·nō′sē·ə) *n.* Impairment or loss of the ability to recognize or interpret sensory perceptions of familiar persons or things. [<NL <Gk. *at-* without + *gnōsis* knowing, knowledge] **—ag·no′sic** *adj.*

ag·nos·tic (ag·nos′tik) *adj.* Professing ignorance or the inability to know, especially in religion. *—n.* One who holds the theory of agnosticism. See synonyms under SKEPTIC. [<Gk. *agnōstos* unknowing, unknown < *a-* not + *gignōskein* know]

ag·nos·ti·cism (ag·nos′tə·siz′əm) *n.* **1** The doctrine of nescience, or the theory which maintains that humans cannot have, and have not, any real or valid knowledge, but can know only impressions. **2** The theory that first truths, substance, cause, the human soul, and a First Cause, can neither be proved nor disproved, and must remain unknown or unknowable. **3** *Theol.* The theory that God is unknown or unknowable: distinguished from *atheism.*

ag·nus (ag′nəs) *n. pl.* **ag·ni** (ag′nī) The lamb as a Christian emblem; an Agnus Dei. [<L, lamb]

Ag·nus bell (ag′nəs) *Eccl.* The bell rung while the *Agnus Dei* is recited.

Ag·nus De·i (ag′nəs dē′ī, dā′ē) **1** *Eccl.* A figure of a lamb, as an emblem of Christ, often bearing a cross and banner. **2** In the Roman Catholic Church, a medallion or cake of wax stamped with this emblem and blessed by the Pope. **3** *Eccl.* **a** A prayer in the mass, beginning with the words *Agnus Dei.* **b** In Anglican and some other churches, a translation of this prayer, beginning "O Lamb of God." **4** A musical setting for this prayer. [<LL, Lamb of God. See *John* i 29.]

a·go (ə·gō′) *adv.* In the past; in time gone by; since. *—adj.* Gone by; past. [OE *āgān* past, gone away]

a·gog (ə·gog′) *adv.* & *adj.* In a state of eager curiosity; excited with interest or expectation. [<MF *en gogues* in a merry mood]

-agog *combining form* Leading, promoting, or inciting: *demagog, pedagog.* Also **-agogue.** [<Gk. *agōgos* leading]

ag·on (ag′ōn, -on) *n. pl.* **a·go·nes** (ə·gō′nēz) **1** One of the great national game festivals of ancient Greece, or the assembly at such a festival. **2** A division of the Greek drama in which the introduction or dramatized argument is carried on by the principal characters. [<Gk. *agōn* assembly, contest]

a·gone (ə·gôn′, ə·gon′) *adj.* & *adv. Obs.* Ago.

a·gon·ic (ə·gon′ik) *adj.* Having or forming no angle. [<Gk. *agōnos* <*a-* without + *gōnia* angle]

agonic line *Geog.* One of several lines on the earth's surface on which the direction of the magnetic needle is truly north and south; a line of no magnetic declination.

ag·o·nist (ag′ə·nist) *n.* A contestant for a prize. [<AGON]

ag·o·nis·tic (ag′ə·nis′tik) *adj.* **1** Pertaining to athletic or polemic contest. **2** Striving for effect; strained. **3** Combative; polemic. Also **ag′o·nis′ti·cal.** **—ag′o·nis′ti·cal·ly** *adv.*

ag·o·nis·tics (ag′ə·nis′tiks) *n.* The art or science of athletic contests.

ag·o·nize (ag′ə·nīz) *v.* **·nized, ·niz·ing** *v.i.* **1** To be in or suffer extreme pain or anguish. **2** To make convulsive efforts, as in wrestling; strive. *—v.t.* **3** To subject to agony; torture. [<F *agoniser* <Med.L *agonizare* <Gk. *agōnizesthai* contend, strive < *agōn* contest]

ag·o·ny (ag′ə·nē) *n. pl.* **·nies** **1** Intense suffering of body or mind; anguish; struggle. **2** Violent or very earnest contest or striving. **3** The suffering or struggle that precedes death. [<L *agonia* <Gk. *agōnia* <*agōn* contest]

Synonyms: ache, anguish, distress, pain, pang, paroxysm, suffering, throe, torment, torture. *Agony* and *anguish* express the uttermost *pain* or *suffering* of body or mind; *agony* that with which the sufferer struggles; *anguish,* that by which he is crushed. Compare AFFLICTION, GRIEF.

ag·o·ra (ag′ər·ə) *n.* pl. **ag·o·rae** (-ər·ē) or **ag·o·ras** **1** In ancient Greece, a popular assembly for political or other purposes. **2** A place of popular assembly; especially, the market place. [<Gk.]

ag·o·ra·pho·bi·a (ag′ər·ə·fō′bē·ə) *n.* Morbid fear of open spaces; fear of exposure to unidentified dangers.

A·gos·ti·no (ä′gōs·tē′nō) Italian form of AUGUSTINE.

a·gou·ti (ə·go͞o′tē) *n. pl.* **·tis** or **·ties** **1** A tropical American rodent (genus *Dasyprocta* or *Myoprocta*), of grizzly color, little larger than a rabbit, with three hind toes. **2** A grizzled appearance of fur resulting from bands of light and dark coloration on each hair. Also **a·gou′ty.** [<F <Sp. *aguti* <Tupian]

AGOUTI *(def. 1)*

A·gra (ä′grä, ä′grə) **1** A district of western Uttar Pradesh state, India; 1,816 square miles; formerly a province of northern India. **2** A city, capital of Agra district, on the Jumna SE of Delhi: site of the Taj Mahal.

a·graffe (ə·graf′) *n.* **1** A hook or clasp; especially, an ornamental clasp used on armor or for fastening rich clothing. **2** A builders' cramp iron. Also **a·grafe′.** [<F]

A·gram (ä′gräm) The German name for ZAGREB.

a·gran·u·lo·cyte (ə·gran′yo͞o·lō·sīt) *n.* A type of leukocyte having the cytoplasm clear of granules.

a·gran·u·lo·cy·to·sis (ə·gran′yo͞o ·lō′sī·tō′sis) *n.* An acute febrile disease characterized by the absence or drastic reduction of granulocytes in the blood, often resulting from hypersensitivity to an administered drug.

ag·ra·pha (ag′rə·fə) *n.* pl. A collection of sayings ascribed to Jesus Christ, but not found in the Bible. See LOGIA. [<Gk. *agraphos* unwritten]

a·graph·i·a (ā·graf′ē·ə) *n.* A partial or total loss of the ability to write. [<NL <Gk. *a-* without + *graphein* write] **—a·graph′ic** *adj.*

a·grar·i·an (ə·grâr′ē·ən) *adj.* **1** Pertaining to land or its tenure or to a general distribution of lands. **2** Organizing or furthering agricultural interests and aid to farmers: an *agrarian* investment. *—n.* One who advocates agrarianism. [<L *agrarius* <*ager* field]

a·grar·i·an·ism (ə·grâr′ē·ən·iz′əm) *n.* **1** The theory or practice of equal distribution of lands. **2** Agitation or political dissension with the view of redistributing tenure of lands or of equalizing farm income, especially by the use of government controls.

a·gree (ə·grē′) *v.* **a·greed, a·gree·ing** *v.i.* **1** To give consent; accede: with *to.* **2** To come into or be in harmony. **3** To be of one mind; concur: with *with.* **4** To come to terms, as in the details of a transaction: with *about* or *on.* **5** To be acceptable or favorable; suit: with *with:* This food does not *agree* with us. **6** To conform or match, as scales of measurement. **7** *Gram.* To correspond in person, number, case, or gender. —*v.t.* **8** To grant as a concession: with a noun clause: I *agree* that the choice is difficult, but you must choose. [<OF *agreer* <*a gre* to one's liking <L *ad* to + *gratus* pleasing]

Synonyms: accede, accept, accord, acquiesce, admit, approve, assent, coincide, combine, comply, concur, consent, harmonize. *Agree* is the most general term of this group; to *concur* is to *agree* in general; to *coincide* is to *agree* in every particular. One *accepts* another's terms, *complies* with her wishes, *admits* her statement, *approves* her plan, *conforms* to her views of doctrine or duty, *accedes* or *consents* to her proposal. *Accede* expresses the more formal agreement, *consent* the more complete. One may silently *acquiesce* in that which does not meet his views, but which he does not care to contest. See ASSENT. *Antonyms:* contend, contradict, decline, demur, deny, differ, disagree, dispute, dissent, oppose, protest, refuse.

a·gree·a·ble (ə·grē′ə ·bəl) *adj.* **1** Agreeing with or suited to the mind or senses; pleasurable; especially, of persons, giving pleasure by manner, bearing, or conversation. **2** Naturally or logically corresponding; suitable; correspondent; conformable: a truth *agreeable* to human reason. **3** Ready to agree; favorably inclined; giving assent; willing. **4** Being in accordance or conformity; conforming. **—a·gree′ a·bil′i·ty, a·gree′a·ble·ness** *n.* **—a·gree′a·bly** *adv.*

Synonyms: acceptable, amiable, comfortable, delightful, good, grateful, gratifying, pleasant, pleasing, welcome. See AMIABLE. *Antonyms:* disagreeable, hateful, obnoxious, offensive.

a·greed (ə·grēd′) *adj.* **1** Brought into or being in harmony; united. **2** Settled by consent, bargain, or contract. **3** Admitted or conceded; granted.

a·gree·ment (ə·grē′mənt) *n.* **1** The act of coming into accord, or the state of being in accord; conformity. **2** An arrangement or understanding between two or more parties as to a course of action; a covenant or treaty. **3** *Law* A contract. See synonyms under CONTRACT, HARMONY. **4** *Gram.* CONCORD (def. 3).

a·gres·tial (ə·gres′chəl) *adj.* Growing wild on cultivated ground, as weeds. Also **a·gres·tal** (ə·gres′təl).

a·gres·tic (ə·gres′tik) *adj.* Rural; unpolished. Also **a·gres′ti·cal.** [<L *agrestis* <*ager* field]

ag·ri·bus·i·ness (ag′rə·biz′nis, -niz) *n.* All those commercial activities associated with agriculture, including the production, processing, and distribution of farm products and the manufacture of farm equipment. [<AGRI(CULTURE) + BUSINESS]

A·gric·o·la (ə·grik′ə·lə), **Gnaeus Julius,** A.D. 37–93, Roman governor of Britain.

ag·ri·cul·ture (ag′rə·kul′chər) *n.* **1** The cultivation of the soil; the raising of food crops, breeding and raising of livestock, etc.; tillage; farming. **2** The science that treats of the cultivation of the soil. **—Department of Agriculture** An executive department of the U.S. government since 1899 (originally established 1862), headed by the Secretary of Agriculture, that acquires and distributes information on agricultural subjects and administers laws to protect the farmer and consuming public. [<F<L *agricultura*<*ager* field + *cultura* cultivation] **—ag′ri·cul′tur·al** *adj.* **— ag′ri·cul′tur·al·ly** *adv.*

Synonyms: cultivation, culture, farming, floriculture, gardening, horticulture, husbandry, tillage. *Agriculture* is the generic term, including the science, the art, and the process of supplying human wants by raising the products of the soil, and by the associated industries; *farming* is the practice of *agriculture* as a business. We speak of the science of *agriculture,* the business of *farming:* scientific *agriculture* may be wholly in books; scientific *farming* is practiced upon the land.

ag·ri·cul·tur·ist (ag′rə·kul′chər·ist) *n.* One engaged in agriculture; a farmer. Also **ag′ri·cul′tur·al·ist.**

A·gri·gen·to (ä′grē·jen′tō) A town in SW Sicily; site of Greek temples: formerly *Girgenti.* Ancient **Ag·ri·gen·tum** (ag′ri·jen′təm).

ag·ri·mo·ny (ag′rə·mō′nē) *n.* **1** Any of several erect, perennial, rosaceous herbs (genus *Agrimonia*) having small yellow flowers on a long stalk and fruit covered with hooked hairs. **2** Any of several composite herbs of similar habit, as hemp agrimony, etc. [<L *agrimonia,* var. of *aragemonia* <Gk. *argemōnē*]

A·grip·pa (ə·grip′ə) **Cornelius,** 1486–1535, German cabalistic philosopher and professor of magic. **—Agrippa, Herod** See HEROD AGRIPPA. **—Agrippa, Marcus Vipsanius,** 63–12 B.C., Roman statesman, geographer, and general.

Ag·rip·pi·na (ag′ri·pī′nə), 13? B.C.—A.D. 33, wife of Germanicus and mother of Caligula. **—Agrippina,** A.D. 15–59, daughter of preceding, mother of Nero.

Ag·rip·pin·i·an (ag′ri·pin′ē·ən) *n.* A follower of **Ag·rip·pi·nus** (ag′ri·pī′nəs), second-century bishop of Carthage who taught rebaptism of heretics.

agro- *combining form* Of or pertaining to fields or agriculture: *agronomy.* [<Gk. < *agros* field]

ag·ro·bi·ol·o·gy (ag′rō·bī·ol′ə·jē) *n.* The quantitative study of plant life, especially in relation to the genetic and environmental factors that determine the vitality, growth, and yields of cultivated plants. **—ag·ro·bi·o·log·ic** (ag′rō·bī′ə·loj′ik) or **·i·cal** *adj.* **—ag′ro·bi′ o·log′i·cal·ly** *adv.* **—ag′ro·bi·ol′o·gist** *n.*

ag·ro·chem·i·cal (ag′rō·kem′ə·kəl) *n.* Any chemical product, such as fertilizers or insecticides, used in agriculture. — *adj.* Pertaining to agrochemicals: the *agrochemical* industry.

ag·ro·cli·ma·tol·o·gy (ag′rō·klī′mə·tol′ə·jē) *n.* The branch of climatology concerned with the effects of weather upon agricultural crops.

a·grol·o·gy (ə·grol′ə·jē) *n.* The science of soils, especially in its practical applications. **—ag·ro·log·ic** (ag′rə·loj′ik) or **·i·cal** *adj.* **—ag′ro·log′i·cal·ly** *adv.*

ag·ro·ma·ni·a (ag′rō·mā′nē·ə) *n.* A morbid desire to live in open country, and especially in solitude.

ag·ro·nom·ic (ag′rə·nom′ik) *adj.* Of or pertaining to agronomy or agronomics. Also **ag′ro·nom′i·cal.**

ag·ro·nom·ics (ag′rə·nom′iks) *n.* **1** In political economy, the science that treats of the distribution and management of land, especially as a source of the wealth of a nation. **2** AGRONOMY.

a·gron·o·my (ə·gron′ə·mē) *n.* The application of scientific principles to the cultivation of land; scientific husbandry, especially in production of field crops. **—a·gron′o·mist** *n.* [<Gk. *agronomos* an overseer of lands < *agros* field + *nemein* distribute, manage]

Synonyms: agriculture. *Agronomy* differs from *agriculture* in that it is concerned only with crop-production, while *agriculture* includes the improvement and care of animals and their products.

ag·ros·tol·o·gy (ag′rē·stol′ə·jē) *n.* That branch of botany which treats of grasses. [<Gk. *agrōstis,* a kind of grass + -LOGY] **—a·gros·to·log·ic** (ə·gros′tə·loj′ik) **or ·i·cal** *adj.*

ag·ro·tech·ny (ag′rə·tek′ nē) *n.* The science of preserving farm products and processing them into manufactured edible foods.

a·ground (ə·ground′) *adv. & adj.* On the shore or bottom, as a vessel; stranded.

a·guar·di·en·te (ä·gwär′dē·en′tā) *n.* **1** A brandy made in Spain and Portugal. **2** Any common distilled liquor, as pulque or whisky. **3** A wood spirit drawn from cane refuse after the rum has been extracted: used as a drink by Cubans. [<Sp. < *agua ardiente* burning water]

A·guas·ca·li·en·tes (ä′gwäs·kä·lē·en′tes) A state in central Mexico; 2,499 square miles; capital, Aguascalientes.

a·gue (ā′gyōō) *n.* **1** *Pathol.* A periodic malarial fever; intermittent fever; chills and fever. **2** A chill or paroxysm of violent shivering. [<OF <L *(febbris) acuta* an acute fever]

a·gue·weed (ā′gyōō·wēd′) *n.* A tall, slender gentian *(Gentiana quinquefolia)* with clusters of bluish purple or white tubular flowers.

A·gui·nal·do (ä′gē·näl′dō), **Emilio,** 1869–1964, Filipino rebel leader.

a·gu·ish (ā′gyōō·ish) *adj.* Like, producing, or tending to produce ague; chilly; subject to ague. **—a′gu·ish·ly** *adv.* **—a′gu·ish·ness** *n.*

A·gul·has (ə·gul′əs, *Pg.* ə·gōōl′yəs), **Cape** The southernmost point of Africa, in the Republic of South Africa, on the dividing line between the Indian and Atlantic Oceans.

a·gush (ə·gush′) *adj. & adv.* Gushing.

A·gus·tín (ä′gōōs·tēn′) Spanish form of AUGUSTINE.

ah (ä) *interj.* An exclamation expressive of various emotions, as surprise, triumph, satisfaction, contempt, compassion, or complaint.

a·ha (ä·hä′) *interj.* An exclamation expressing surprise, triumph, or mockery.

A·hab (ā′hab), died 897 B.C., seventh king of Israel.

A·has·u·e·rus (ə·haz′yōō ·ir′əs, ə·has′-) One of several Median and Persian kings mentioned in the Old Testament, specifically, in the book of Esther; generally identified with Xerxes. See WANDERING JEW under JEW.

a·head (ə·hed′) *adv.* **1** At the head or front. **2** In advance. **3** Onward; forward: I pressed *ahead.* **4** Without restraint; headlong. **—ahead of** In advance of, as in time, rank, achievement, etc. **—to get ahead** To make one's way socially, financially, etc. [<A-[1] + HEAD]

a·heap (ə·hēp′) *adv.* In or into a heap.

a·hem (ə·hem′) *interj.* An exclamation to attract attention.

a·him·sa (ə·him′sä) *n.* The doctrine that all life is sacred, exemplified in the Jainist, Brahman, and Buddhist philosophies by strict nonviolence to all living things. [<Skt. *ahimsā* non-injury]

a·his·tor·i·cal (ā′his·tôr′ə·kəl, -tər′-) *adj.* Not historical; without regard for history.

Ah·mad·nag·ar (ä′məd·nug′ər) A district of Maharashtra State, India; 6,646 square miles; capital, Ahmadnagar. Also **Ah′med·nag′ar.**

Ah·med·a·bad (ä′məd·ä ·bäd′) A district of Gujarat State, India; 3,800 square miles; capital, Ahmedabad. Also **Ah′mad·a·bad′.**

Ah·med Fu·ad (ä′med fōō·äd′) See FUAD.

a·hold[1] (ə·hōld′) *adv.* Close to the wind: to lay a ship *ahold.*

a·hold [2] (ə·hōld) *U.S. Dialect* A hold (of): to get *ahold* of one's arm.

a·hoy (ə·hoi′) *interj.* Ho there! a call used in hailing: ship *ahoy!* [Var. of HOY]

Ah·ri·man (ä′ri·mən) In Zoroastrian religion, the principle of evil, source of death, disease, and disorder: opponent of Ormuzd.

a·hull (ə·hul′) *adv. Naut.* So as to lie under bare poles, helm lashed alee, and the bow nearly into the wind: said of a ship in heavy weather.

A·hu·ra Maz·da (ä′hōō·rä mäz′dä) See ORMUZD.

Ah·vaz (ä·wäz′) A city on the Karun River in SW Iran.

ai·blins (ā′blinz) See ABLINS.

aid (ād) *v.t.* & v.i. To render assistance (to); help; succor. —*n.* **1** The act or result of helping or succoring, or the means employed; cooperation; assistance. **2** A person or thing that affords assistance; a helper; assistant; aide-de-camp. **3** *Law* A remedy; correction; also, a subsidy. **4** In medieval law, a pecuniary contribution by a feudal vassal to his lord, limited by Magna Carta to three special occasions. See synonyms under ADHERENT, AUXILIARY, HELP, SUBSIDY. [<OF *aider* <L royal prerogatives. [<OF *accrocher* <*a* to + *croc* hook]

Synonyms (verb): abet, assist, befriend, cooperate, encourage, foster, help, second, serve, succor, support, sustain, uphold. *Help* expresses greater dependence and deeper need than *aid.* To *aid* is to *second* another's exertions, but may fall short of the meaning of *help.* In law, to *aid* or *abet* makes one a principal. (Compare synonyms for ACCESSORY). To *cooperate* or *collaborate* implies complete or approximate equality, *collaborate* being used chiefly of literary or scientific work; to *assist* implies a subordinate and secondary relation. One *assists* a fallen friend to rise and *cooperates* in helping others. We *encourage* the timid or despondent, *succor* those in danger, *support* the weak, *uphold* those who else might be shaken or cast down. Compare ABET, ACCESSORY, PROMOTE. *Antonyms:* counteract, discourage, hinder, obstruct, oppose, resist, thwart, withstand.

A·ï·da (ä·ē′də) The heroine and title of an opera (1871) by Giuseppe Verdi.

aid·ance (ād′ns) *n.* The act of aiding; assistance; help. **—aid′ant** *adj.*

aide (ād) *n.* **1** An officer of the personal staff of the head of a government. **2** An aide-de-camp. **3** A naval officer assisting a superior officer. [<F, assistant]

aide-de-camp (ād′də·kamp′) *n.* pl. **aides-de-camp** An officer of the personal staff of a general, who transmits orders and attends to matters of etiquette and protocol. Also **aid-de-camp, aide.** [<F *aide de camp,* lit., field assistant]

Ai·din (ī·din′) See AYDIN.

AIDS (ādz) *n.* A disease that impairs the human immune system, caused by infection with the human immunodeficiency virus (HIV), transmitted through blood and bodily fluids; characterized by development of recurrent or chronic opportunistic infections with an increased incidence of certain cancers. [acronym for *a*cquired *i*mmune *d*eficiency *s*yndrome].

AIDS-related complex *n.* A collection of symptoms, including fever, weakness, weight loss, and swelling of the lymph nodes, associated with the presence of antibodies to the human immunodeficiency or AIDS virus; frequently followed by the development of AIDS. Also **ARC.**

AIDS virus *n.* HIV

ai·glet (ā′glit) See AGLET.

ai·gret (ā′gret, ā·gret′) *n.* **1** A heron, the egret. **2** A tuft of feathers or gems, worn on a helmet, headdress, etc. See EGRET. Also **ai′grette.** [<F *aigrette.* See EGRET.]

ai·guille (ā·gwēl′, ā′gwēl) *n.* **1** *Geol.* A sharp rocky mountain peak, as those of the Italian Alps near Mont Blanc. **2** A slender rock-perforating drill. [<F, needle]

ai·guil·lette (ā′gwi·let′) *n.* An ornamental shoulder tag; aglet; specifically, such a decoration on a uniform, consisting of bullion cord, loops, knots, and tassels. [<F, *aiguille* needle]

Ai·ken (ā′kin), **Conrad,** 1889–1973, U.S. poet.

ai·ki·do (ī·ki·dō′, -ki′dō) *n.* A self-defense discipline from Japan based on nonresistance and use of the opponent's own momentum.

ail (āl) *v.t.* To cause uneasiness or pain to; trouble; make ill. —*v.t.* To be somewhat ill; feel pain. ◆Homophone: *ale.* [OE *eglan*] **—ail′ing** *adj.*

ai·lan·thus (ā·lan′thəs) *n.* **1** Any of a small genus *(Ailanthus)* of tall, deciduous trees, native to Asia and Australia, having pinnate leaves and staminate and pistillate flowers often on separate trees. **2** Tree of heaven. [<NL <) Amboina *ailanto* tree of heaven]

Ai·leen (ī·lēn′, ā·lē*Brit var of*
n′) Irish form of HELEN

ai·le·ron (ā′lə·ron) *n.* **1** *Archit.* A wing wall shaped like a scroll to conceal the aisle of a church, or a half-gable formed by a penthouse roof. **2** *Aeron.* Any of several types of hinged and movable auxiliary surfaces of an airplane, usually located near the trailing edge of a wing and operated by the pilot to give a rolling motion about the longitudinal axis. [<F, dim. of *aile* wing]

ail·ment (āl′mənt) *n.* Indisposition of body or mind; slight illness.

Ail·sa Craig (āl′səkrāg) A basaltic columnar islet at the entrance of the Firth of Clyde, Scotland; 1,097 feet high.

ai·lu·ro·pho·bi·a (ā·lo͞or′ə·fō′bē·ə) *n.* Morbid fear of cats. Also called *galeophobia, gatophobia.* [<Gk. *ailouros* cat + -PHOBIA]

aim (ām) *v.t.* **1** To direct, as a missile, blow, weapon, word, or act, toward or against some thing or person; point or level: to *aim* a gun at someone; to *aim* a speech at an offender. —*v.i.* **2** To have a purpose; endeavor earnestly: with the infinitive: to *aim* to please. **3** To direct a missile, weapon, etc.: We *aimed* and fired. — *n.* **1** The act of aiming, directing, or pointing a weapon, missile, remark, etc., at anything. **2** The line of direction of anything aimed. **3** The object or point aimed at or to be aimed at; a mark or target. **4** Design; purpose. **5** Conjecture; guess. [<OF *aesmer* <*a-* to (<L *ad-*) + *esmer* <L *aestimare* estimate]

Synonyms (noun): aspiration, design, determination, direction, end, endeavor, goal, inclination, intent, intention, mark, object, purpose, reason, tendency. The *aim* is the direction in which one shoots, or that which is aimed at. The *mark* is that at which one shoots; the *goal,* that toward which one moves or works. All indicate the direction of *endeavor.* The *end* is the point at which people expect or hope to close their labors; the *object,* that which they would grasp as the reward. *Aspiration, design, endeavor, purpose,* referring to the mental acts by which the *aim* is attained, are often used as interchangeable with *aim.* Compare AMBITION, DESIGN, DIRECTION, PURPOSE. *Antonyms:* aimlessness, avoidance, carelessness, heedlessness, neglect, negligence, oversight, purposelessness, thoughtlessness.

Ai·mée (ā·mā′) French form of AMY.

aim·less (ām′lis) *adj.* Wanting in aim or purpose. **—aim′less·ly** *adv.* **—aim′less·ness** *n.*

a·in [1] (ä′yēn) See AYIN.

ain [2] (ān) *adj: Scot.* Own.

Ain (an̄) A river in eastern France, flowing south 118 miles to the Rhône.

ain·sel' (ān·sel′) *n. Scot.* Own self. Also **ain·sell′.**

Ains·worth (ānz′wûrth), **William Harrison,** 1805–82, English novelist.

ain't (ānt) *Illit. & Dial.* Am not; also used for *are not, is not, has not,* and *have not.* ◆**ain't, aren't I** *Ain't* is used in many literary contexts to emphasize or authenticate the dialect of a character or to provide emphasis and garner attention in prose. Often used in fixed phrases (say it *ain't* so), *ain't* is well established in common American and British usage. Frequently labeled nonstandard.

Ain·tab (īn·täb′) A former name for GAZIANTEP.

Ai·nu (ī′no͞o) *n.* **1** One of an aboriginal people of Japan, now found only in the northern parts. **2** The unclassified, unrelated language of the Ainu. Also **Ai·no** (ī′nō).

air (âr) *n.* **1** The atmosphere of the earth, consisting of a mixture of gases containing approximately 79 percent nitrogen, 19 percent oxygen, and small amounts of other gases including carbon dioxide, hydrogen, helium, argon, and methane. **2** The open space around and above the earth. **3** An atmospheric movement or current; breeze; wind. **4** Utterance abroad; publicity: to give *air* to one's views. **5** The medium through which radio waves are transmitted; airways. **6** The representation of atmosphere in painting; atmospheric perspective. **7** Something light and ethereal; wind. **8** Peculiar or characteristic appearance; mien; manner. **9** Assumed manner; affectation: to put on *airs.* **10** *Music* A melody as contrasted with a harmony; tune; especially, the leading or soprano part in a harmonized piece. **11** *Obs.* Breath. See synonyms under TUNE, WIND. **—in the air 1** Prevalent; abroad, as gossip; astir; in the making, as plans. **2** Without foundation in fact; unformed: The project is still *in the air.* **3** Excited; mentally upset. **—on the air** Broadcasting by radio; being broadcast. —*v.t.* **1** To expose to the air; admit air into so as to purify or dry; ventilate. **2** To make public; show off; display; exhibit. **3** *Colloq.* To broadcast by radio or television. ◆Homophone: *heir.* [<OF <L *aer* <) Gk. *aer* air, mist]

Air may appear as a combining form in open hyphenated, or closed two-word phrases, with the following meanings:

1 By means of air or the air:

air-bred	**air-dropped**
air-blasted	**air-filled**
air-blown	**air-formed**
air-cooling	**air-insulated**
air-cured	**air-slacked**
air-dried	**air-spun**
air-driven	

2 Of or pertaining to the atmospheric air:

air-breathing	**airlike**
air-conveying	**air-swallowing**
air-defiling	**airward**
air-heating	**airwise**

3 Conducting, confining, or regulating air:

air compressor	**air filter**
airduct	**air regulator**

4 Operating or operated by air, especially by power of heated or compressed air:

air condenser	**air hammer**
air drill	**air motor**

5 Performed by or suitable for aircraft:

air action	**air navigation**
air armament	**air park**
air assault	**air pickup**
air attack	**air race**
air cover	**air refueling**
air echelon	**air rescue**
air express	**air show**
air evacuation	**air squadron**
air freight	**air strike**
air group	**air terminal**
air landing	**air unit**
air meet	**air war**

Synonyms (noun): appearance, bearing, behavior, carriage, demeanor, deportment, expression), fashion, look, manner, mien, port, pretense, sort, style, way. *Air* is that combination of qualities which makes the entire impression we receive in a person's presence; we say he has the *air* of a scholar, or the *air* of a villain. *Appearance* refers more to dress and other externals. *Expression* and *look* especially refer to the face. *Expression* is more often applied to that which is habitual; as, a pleasant *expression; look* may be momentary; as, a *look* of dismay passed over your face. We may, however, speak of the *look* or *looks* as indicating all that we look at; as, she had the *look* of an adventurer. *Bearing* indicates often the expression of feeling or state of mind through bodily pose; as, a noble *bearing; port,* practically identical in meaning with *bearing,* is more exclusively a literary word. *Carriage,* the manner of holding the body, as in walking, is more completely physical than *bearing. Mien* is closely synonymous with *air,* but is a somewhat stilted or literary usage. Compare BEHAVIOR, PRETENSE.

A·ïr (ä·ir′) A mountainous region in northern Niger: also *Asben, Azben.*

air alert A signal warning of the expected or imminent approach of enemy aircraft.

air·bag (âr′bag′) *n.* An automatically inflatable safety device installed beneath the dashboard of an automobile and designed to cushion passengers in case of a collision.

air base A base for operations by aircraft.

air bladder 1 An air-filled sac situated under the spinal column of most fishes and serving as a hydrostatic device. Also called *swim bladder.* **2** Any sac filled with air or gas, as the flotation devices on bladderwrack and other seaweeds.

air·boat (âr′bōt′) *n.* A swamp boat.

air·borne (âr′bôrn′, -bōrn′) *adj.* **1** Transported in aircraft; specifically, designating specialized units of infantry or parachute troops so carried. **2** Aloft; no longer in contact with the ground. **3** Transported by air currents, as pollen, dust, etc.

air·bound (âr′bound′) *adj.* Impeded or stopped up by air, as an airplane motor.

air brake A brake operated by compressed air.

air·bra·sive (âr′brā′siv, -ziv) *adj.* Of or pertaining to a method of drilling teeth by means of a finely powdered abrasive pinpointed against the surface in a minute, controlled jet of air or other gas under high pressure.

air•brush (âr′brush′) *n.* An implement for spraying liquids by compressed air, especially one used by commercial artists and photographers for coating surfaces with a film of color.

air•burst (âr′bûrst′) *n.* An explosion in the air, as of a bomb or projectile.

air carrier An aircraft that carries freight.

air chamber An enclosed space containing, or designed to contain, air for various mechanical or vital uses. Also **air cavity, air cell.**

air•cock (âr′kok′) *n. Mech.* A valve specially designed to control the flow of air.

air-con•di•tion (âr′kən•dish′ən) *v.t.* To equip with or ventilate by air-conditioning. **—air′-con•di′tioned** *adj.*

air-con•di•tion•ing (âr′kən•dish′ən•ing) *n.* A system for treating air in buildings, dwellings, and other enclosed structures so as to regulate temperature, humidity, and purity for personal comfort.

air-cool (âr′ko͞ol′) *v.t.* To cool, as the cylinders of an engine, with a flow of air instead of water or other medium. **—air′-cooled′** *adj.*

air corridor An air lane, especially one established by international agreement.

air cover 1 A protection given by aircraft in military operations. **2** The aircraft giving this protection.

air•craft (âr′kraft′, -kräft′) *n.* Any form of craft designed for flight through or navigation in the air, as airplanes, dirigibles, balloons, helicopters, kites, and gliders.

aircraft carrier A large ship designed to carry aircraft, with a level upper flight deck usually extending beyond the bow and stern, serving as a mobile air base at sea: also called *flattop.*

air•craft•man (âr′kraft′mən, -kräft′-) *n. pl.* **•men** *Brit.* **1** Any of the four lower grades in the Royal Air Force. **2** One holding this rank.

air•crafts•man (âr′krafts′mən, -kräfts′-) *n. pl.* **•men** A skilled aircraft designer or builder.

air cushion 1 A bag inflated with air, especially one used as a pillow. **2** An air spring.

air cylinder 1 A nearly airtight cylinder having a piston playing in it: used to check the recoil of a gun. **2** A cylinder beneath a railway car, in which is compressed air which operates brakes. See BRAKE[1].

air defense All the measures taken to counter act aerial attack, including the use of fighter aircraft, surface-to-air missiles, anti-aircraft artillery, blackouts, radar networks, etc.

air•dock (âr′dok′) *n. Aeron.* A hangar equipped with ramps, bridges, conveyor belts, and hydraulic lifts for the rapid unloading of passengers and freight from large airliners.

air•drome (âr′drōm′) *n. Archaic* An airport.

air•drop (âr′drop′) *n.* Personnel, food, equipment, and other supplies dropped by parachute from an aircraft. —*v.t.* & *v.i.* **•dropped, •drop•ping** To drop (personnel, supplies, etc.) by parachute from an aircraft.

air-dry (âr′drī′) *v.t.* **•dried, •dry•ing** To dry by exposing to the air.

Aire (âr) A river in north Yorkshire, England.

Aire•dale (âr′dāl) *n.* A large terrier with a wiry tan coat and black markings. See TERRIER. [from *Airedale,* the valley of the Aire River]

air embolism Aeroembolism (def. 1).

air engine An engine operated by the rapid thermal expansion of a controlled stream of compressed air.

air•er (âr′ər) *n. Brit.* A frame on which clothes are stretched to be aired or dried.

air•field (âr′fēld′) *n.* An airport; specifically, the field or course of an airport.

air•flow (âr′flō′) *n.* **1** A flow of air. **2** The air currents developed by the motion of an automobile, aircraft, etc.

air•foil (âr′foil′) *n. Aeron.* A winglike surface designed to provide the maximum aerodynamic advantage for an airplane in flight.

air force The air arm of a country's defense forces. **—United States Air Force** The air force of the United States, administered by the Department of the Air Force under the Department of Defense; established in 1947 and organized in 1951 to consist of the Regular Air Force, the Air Force Reserve, and the Air National Guard of the United States. Until 1947 it was part of the Army, under the title of the United States Army Air Force. See ROYAL AIR FORCE, ROYAL CANADIAN AIR FORCE, ROYAL AUSTRALIAN AIR FORCE.

air force academy A training school for service in the air force; specifically, the United States Air Force Academy, Colorado Springs, Colo.

air•frame (âr′frām′) *n.* An airplane complete except for the engine and its controls; a glider.

air gun A gun impelling a missile by compressed air.

air•head (âr′hed′) *n.* **1** A position established in enemy territory that can be supplied and reinforced by air. **2** *Slang* A brainless person.

air•hole (âr′hōl′) *n.* **1** A hole containing, or made by or for, gas or air. **2** A flaw in a casting. **3** An opening in the ice over a body of water. **4** *Aeron.* An air pocket. Also **air hole.**

air•i•ly (âr′ə•lē) *adv.* **1** In a light or airy manner; delicately. **2** In light spirits; jauntily; gaily.

air•i•ness (âr′ē•nis) *n.* The quality of being airy.

air•ing (âr′ing) *n.* **1** An exposure to the air, as for drying. **2** Public exposure or discussion. **3** Exercise in the air.

air jacket *Mech.* An air-filled compartment around some part of a machine, usually designed to control the transmission of heat.

air lane A lane for air traffic, especially one characterized by steady winds.

airles (ârlz), **air-penny** (âr′pen′ē) See ARLES.

air•less (âr′lis) *adj.* Destitute of air or of fresh air.

air letter 1 An airmail letter. **2** A sheet of lightweight writing paper for use in airmail letters. **3** *Brit.* An aérogramme.

air•lift (âr′lift′) *n.* **1** An operation of transporting foodstuffs and other commodities into a blockaded area. **2** The load carried by such a transport method. —*v.t.* & *v.i.* To transport (food and supplies) by airplane, especially during a land blockade.

air•line (âr′līn′) *n.* **1** A regular route traveled by aircraft carrying freight and passengers. **2** The business organization operating such a transport system.

air•lin•er (âr′lī′nər) *n.* A large, passenger aircraft operated by an airline.

air layering A method of vegetative propagation in which part of a branch or shoot is enclosed in a moist wrapping until roots form and then detached and planted it in earth.

air•lock (âr′lok′) *n.* **1** An airtight chamber, as of a submarine or spacecraft, for passage between areas of unequal air pressure.

air•log (âr′lôg′, -log′) *n.* An instrument for recording the linear travel of aircraft and guided missiles through the air.

air mail 1 Mail carried by airplane. **2** A system of carrying mail by airplane; particularly, a postal system in charge of forwarding of mail by aircraft. **—air′-mail′, air′mail′** *adj.*

air•man (âr′mən) *n. pl.* **air′men 1** Any person who is occupied with the navigation of an aircraft, whether as a pilot, mechanic, or other member of the operating crew. **2** An enlisted grade in the United States Air Force.

air mass *Meteorol.* Any extensive portion of the earth's atmosphere characterized by essentially uniform conditions of temperature, pressure, moisture, etc., along a horizontal plane.

Air Medal A decoration in the form of a bronze compass rose on which is an eagle carrying two lightning flashes in its talons: awarded by the United States Air Force for meritorious achievement while participating in an aerial flight: instituted in 1942.

air meter A device for measuring the rate of flow of air or gas.

air mile A nautical mile by air.

airn (ârn) *n. Scot.* Iron; also, an iron tool.

air•plane (âr′plān′) *n.* A heavier-than-air flying craft, supported by aerodynamic forces acting upon fixed wings, and kept in flight by propellers or jet propulsion.

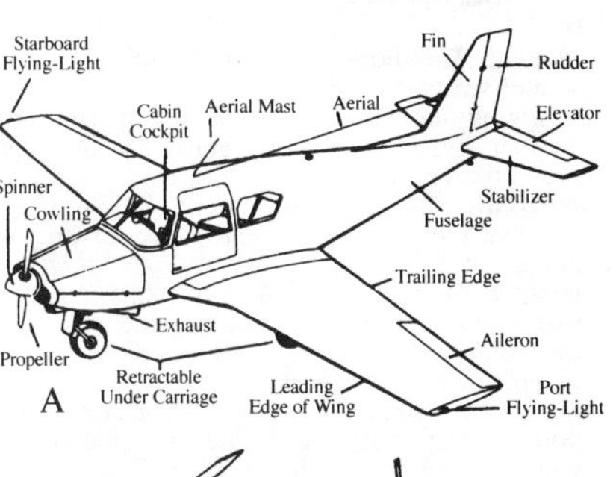

AIRPLANE SHOWING FUNCTIONAL PARTS
A. Four-passenger light plane.
B. Helicopter. *C.* Turbojet.

airplane cloth A cotton fabric plain-woven in varying weights, used for luggage, sportswear, etc.: originally made of unbleached linen for airplane wings.

air plant an epiphyte (def. 1).

air pocket *Aeron.* A sudden downward air current due to the sinking of a mass of heavy cooled air.

air pollution The contamination of the air, esp. by industrial waste gases, fuel exhaust, or smoke.

air•port (âr′pôrt′, -pōrt′) *n.* A field laid out as a base for aircraft, including all structures and appurtenances necessary for operation, housing, storage, repair, and maintenance: also called *airdrome.*

air•post (âr′pōst′) *n.* Air mail.

air power The strength of a nation in terms of its command of the air in peace and war.

air•proof (âr′pro͞of′) *adj.* Impenetrable by air.

air pump A pump for exhausting, compressing, or transmitting air.

air raid An attack by military aircraft, especially bombers in mass formation.

air-raid shelter A place set aside and equipped for the protection of people during an air raid.

air rifle A rifle utilizing compressed air to propel a pellet or BB.

air sac 1 *Ornithol.* One of the membranous sacs filled with air located in different parts of the body in birds, often extending through the bones and communicating with the lungs. **2** *Entomol.* Any of the large, thin-walled structures connected to the tracheal system in some insects. **3** An alveolus of the lungs.

air-scoop (âr′sko͞op′) *n.* A device for utilizing the air stream to maintain pressure and furnish ventilation within an airship.

air•screw (âr′skro͞o) *n. Brit.* A power-driven propeller for use on aircraft, consisting of two or more helical blades.

air shaft An open shaft intended to secure proper ventilation of a building or other structure.

air•ship (âr′ship′) *n.* **1** An aircraft, generally of large size, mechanically propelled and depending upon gases for flotation; a dirigible balloon. **2** Loosely, an airplane.

air•sick•ness (âr′sik′nis) Motion sickness experienced while flying. **—air′sick** *adj.*

air•space (âr′spās′) *n.* **1** The atmosphere. **2** That portion of the atmosphere overlying a designated geographical area, considered as subject to territorial jurisdiction or international law in respect to its use by aircraft, guided missiles, rockets, etc.

air speed The speed of an airplane with relation to the air: distinguished from *ground speed.*

air-speed meter An instrument for measuring the speed of aircraft in flight.

air-spray (âr′sprā′) *n.* **1** A compressed-air device for spraying liquids on a prepared surface. 2 The liquid used in such a device. **—air′-sprayed′** *adj.*

air·spring (âr′spring′) *n.* A device for resisting sudden pressure by the elasticity of compressed air.

air·stream (âr′trē′) *n.* A current or flow of air, especially one set up by the propeller or propellers of an aircraft.

air·strip (âr′strip′) *n.* A makeshift airfield, usually prepared from prefabricated materials for temporary use, as for landing fighter planes: also called *fighter strip.*

airt (ârt) *v.t. Scot.* To guide. —*n.* **1** A cardinal point of the compass. **2** The direction of the wind, or, poetically, the wind.

air thermometer A thermometer in which temperature differences are measured by the expansion and contraction of enclosed air or gas.

air·tight (âr′tīt′) *adj.* **1** Not allowing air to escape or enter. **2** Hence, having no weak places; flawless: an *airtight* argument.

air turbine A turbine operated by air currents fed to the vanes under pressure.

air umbrella A heavy concentration of military aircraft sent out to cover the movements and support the action of ground forces.

air valve *Mech.* **1** A valve, usually automatic, for the control of the flow of air. **2** An air cock.

air vesicle *Bot.* A large air chamber serving as a float in many water plants, especially in certain seaweeds.

air·way (âr′wā′) *n.* **1** Any passageway for air, as the windpipe, a ventilator shaft, etc. **2** *Aeron.* A specific route of travel selected for aircraft. **3** *pl. U.S. Colloq.* Channels for radio or television broadcasting.

air·wor·thi·ness (âr′wûr′thē·nis) *n.* **1** Fitness for flight. **2** The status of one who has met certain requirements for flying an airplane.

air·wor·thy (âr′wûr′thē) *adj.* Being in fit condition for flight.

air·y (âr′ē) *adj.* **air·i·er, air·i·est** **1** Of or pertaining to the air; in the air. **2** Open to or pervaded by the free air; breezy: an *airy* retreat. **3** Like or of the nature of air; as light as air; hence, immaterial; delicate; graceful; ethereal; buoyant: an *airy* evening dress, *airy* music, *airy* nothings. **4** Without reality, or dealing in unreal things or fancies; visionary; speculative. **5** Putting on airs; affected. **6** Light or quick of mood; vivacious; gay. **7** In painting, having transparent atmospheric effect. **8** Pertaining to the soul; spiritual.

Synonyms: aerial, animated, ethereal, fairy-like, frolicsome, gay, joyous, light, lively, sprightly. *Aerial* and *airy* both signify of or belonging to the air, but *airy* describes that which seems as if made of air; we speak of *airy* shapes where we could not well say *aerial; ethereal* describes its objects as belonging to the upper air, the pure ether, and so, often, heavenly. *Sprightly,* spiritlike, refers to light, free, cheerful activity of mind and body. That which is *lively* or *animated* may be agreeable or the reverse; as, an *animated* discussion; a *lively* company. *Antonyms:* clumsy, heavy, inert, ponderous, slow.

A·i·sha (ä′i·shä), 611–678, Mohammed's favorite wife: also spelled *Ayesha.*

aisle (īl) *n.* **1** A passageway, as in a church, theater, or other audience-room, by which the pews or seats may be reached or the room traversed. **2** Originally, a lateral division or wing of a church, flanking the main structure or nave, from which it usually is divided by a range of columns or piers. **3** Any similar wing or passage, as in a forest. ◆Homophone: *isle.* [<OF *aile, ele* wing (of a building) <) L *ala* wing; spelling infl. by *isle*]

aisled (īld) *adj.* **1** Provided with aisles. **2** Placed in an aisle.

Aisne (ān, *Fr.* en) A river in northern France, flowing west 175 miles to the Oise.

ait (āt) *n. Brit. Dial.* A little island, especially one in a river. [OE *īggath, ī geoth*]

aitch (āch) *n.* The letter *H, h.*

aitch·bone (āch′bōn′) *n.* **1** The rump bone in cattle. **2** The cut of beef with this bone. [<OF *nache* buttock + BONE; ME *a nache bone* became *anache bone;*]

aith (āth) *n. Scot.* An oath. Also **aithe.**

aits (āits) *n. pl. Scot.* Oats.

Ai·tu·ta·ki (ī′tōō·tä′kē) One of the Cook Islands in the South Pacific; 7 square miles.

ai·ver (ā′vər) *n. Scot.* A draft horse.

Aix-en-Pro·vence (eks′äṅ·prô ·väṅs′) A city in SE France.

Aix-la-Cha·pelle (āks′lä·shä·pel′, *Fr.* eks′lȧ·shȧ·pel′) French name for AACHEN.

ai·zle (ā′zəl) *n. Scot.* A hot cinder.

A·jac·cio (ä·yät′chō) A port in western Corsica; birthplace of Napoleon I.

a·jar [1] (ə·jär′) *adv. & adj.* Partly open, as a door. [ME *a-* on + *char,* OE *cerr* turn]

a·jar [2] (ə·jär′) *adv. & adj.* In a jarring or discordant condition; wanting in harmony. [<A + JAR[2]]

A·jax (ā′jaks) In the *Iliad,* the son of Telamon and the bravest of all the Greeks who besieged Troy except Achilles.

Ajax the Lesser In the *Iliad,* son of the king of Locris, and one of Helen's suitors.

a·jee (ə·jē′) *adv. & adj. Scot.* Awry; askew; also, ajar: also spelled *agee.*

Aj·mer (uj·mir′) or **Aj·mer-Mer·wa·ra** (-mer·wä′rə) **1** Formerly, a chief commissioner's state in NW India, now a district of Rajasthan state. **2** A city in central Rajasthan, India, former capital of the state of Ajmer.

aj·o·wan (aj′ō·wən) *n.* The ripe fruit of a plant *(Trachyspermum ammi)* grown in Egypt, India, and Iran, cultivated as a source of thymol and cymene. [<native name]

a·kar·y·ote (ā·kar′ē·ōt) *n.* A cell having no nucleus, as a human erythrocyte. —*adj.* Lacking a nucleus.

Ak·bar (ak′bär), 1542–1605, Mogul emperor of Hindustan. Also **Ak·ber** (ak′bər).

Ak·bar Khan (ak′bär kän′), died 1849, Afghan leader.

a·kene (ā·kēn′) See ACHENE.

A·ken·side (ā′kən·sīd), **Mark,** 1721–70, English poet and physician.

Akh·na·ten (äk·nä′tən) See IKHNATON.

a·kim·bo (ə·kim′bō) *adv.* With the hands on hips and the elbows outward. [ME *in kene bowe* in a sharp bow]

a·kin (ə·kin′) *adj. & adv.* **1** Of the same kin; related by blood. **2** Of similar nature or qualities. See synonyms under ALIKE. [<A-[2] + KIN]

ak·i·ne·sis (ak′ə·nē′sis) *n.* **1** Impairment or loss of motor function. **2** Immobility due to any cause. Also **ak·i·ne·si·a** (ak′ə·nē′sē ·ə). [<NL <Gk. *a-* without + *kinēsis* motion]**—ak′i·ne′sic** *adj.*

ak·i·nete (ak′ə·nēt) *n. Bot.* A non-motile, thickwalled resting spore in certain green algae. [<Gk. *akinētos* motionless] **—ak·i·net·ic** (ak′ə·net′ik) *adj.*

A·ki·ta (ä·kē·tä) A city on northern Honshu island, Japan.

Ak·kad (ak′ad, ä′käd) **1** A region of Mesopotamia occupying the northern part of Babylonia. **2** A city of Nimrod's kingdom. *Gen.* x 10. Also *Accad.*

Ak·ka·di·an (ə·kā′dē·ən, ə·kä′-) *n.* **1** One of the inhabitants of ancient Akkad. **2** The extinct group of East Semitic languages of Akkad, Assyria, and Babylonia, or any language of this group. —*adj.* **1** Of Akkad or its inhabitants. **2** Of the extinct Semitic languages of the Assyrians and Babylonians. Also spelled *Accadian.*

Ak·ker·man (ä·kir·män′) The former Russian and Turkish name for BELGOROD DNESTROVSKI.

Ak·kra (ak′rə) See ACCRA.

Ak·ron (ak′rən) A city in NE Ohio.

Ak·sum (äk·sōōm′) A town in northern Ethiopia, site of the ancient capital of Ethiopia: also *Axum.*

Ak·ti (ak′tē) The eastern prong of the Chalcidice peninsula of Greek Macedonia on the Aegean Sea; coextensive with Mount Athos: also *Acte.*

Ak·yab (ak·yab′, ak′yab) A port of southern Burma at the mouth of the Kaladan River on the Bay of Bengal. Also: Sittwe.

al- [1] *prefix* The: Arabic definite article, as in *Alkoran, algebra.*

al- [2] Assimilated var. of AD-.

-al [2] *suffix* of adjectives and nouns Of or pertaining to; characterized by; connected with: *per-sonal, musical;* also in some nouns that were originally adjectives: *animal, rival.* [<L *-alis*]

-al [2] *suffix* of nouns The act of doing or the state of suffering that which is expressed by the verb stem: *betrayal, refusal.* [<OF *-aille* <L *-alia,* neut. pl. of *-alis*]

-al [3] *suffix* Chem. Denoting a compound having the properties of or derived from an aldehyde: *chloral.* [<AL(DEHYDE)]

Al *Chem.* Aluminum (symbol Al).

Al (al) Diminutive of ALBERT, ALFRED.

a·la (ā′lə) *n. pl.* **a·lae** (ā′lē) *Biol.* Any wing or winglike structure, as one of the lateral projections of the nose, one of the two side petals of a papilionaceous flower, a projection found on certain seeds, etc. [<L, wing]

à la (ä′lä, ä′lə; *Fr.* ȧ lȧ) **1** After the manner of: hair dressed *à la* Pompadour. **2** In cooking; according to or prepared after the manner of: lobster *à la* Newburg. Also **a la.** [<F]

Al·a·bam·a (al′ə·bam′ə) A State in the SE United States, bordering on the Gulf of Mexico; 51,609 square miles; capital, Montgomery; entered the Union Dec. 14, 1819: nickname, *Cotton State:* abbr. **AL** **—Al·a·bam·i·an** (al′ə·bam′ē·ən), **Al′a·bam′an** *adj. & n.*

Alabama River A river in Alabama, flowing SW 320 miles to the Mobile river.

al·a·bas·ter (al′ə·bas′ tər, -bäs′-) *n.* **1** A white or (delicately tinted fine-grained gypsum. **2** A dense, translucent variety of calcite, sometimes banded like marble. —*adj.* Made of or like alabaster; smooth and white. [<L <Gk. *alabast(r)os* an alabaster box, ? from the name of a town in Egypt] **—al′a·bas′trine** (-trin) *adj.*

al·a·bas·ter-stone (al′ə·bas′ tər·stōn′, -bäs′-) *n.* A hot-spring or cave deposit of aragonite.

à la bonne heure (ȧ lȧ bôn œ′) *French* Good; well done; literally, at a good hour.

à la carte (ä′lə kärt′) By the card; in accordance with the bill of fare: said of meals at hotels, etc., each item having a separate price: contrasted with *table d'hôte.* [<F]

a·la·cha (ä·lä′chä) *n.* A lightweight Asian fabric of silk or cotton. [<Turkish *ālājah*]

a·lack (ə·lak′) *interj. Archaic* An exclamation of regret or sorrow. Also **a·lack·a·day** (ə·lak′ə·dā′). [< *ah* oh + *lack* failure, disgrace]

a·lac·ri·ty (ə·lak′rə·tē) *n.* Cheerful willingness and promptitude; facility. [<L *alacritas, -tatis* < *alacer* lively] **—a·lac′ri·tous** *adj.*

A·la Dagh (ä′lä däkh′) A mountain range north of Ankara, Turkey; highest point, 11,000 feet. Also **A·la Dag** (ä′lä däg′).

A·lad·din (ə·lad′n) A boy in the *Arabian Nights* who is able to cause one jinni to appear and do his bidding whenever he rubs a magic lamp, and another whenever he rubs a magic ring.

à la fin (ȧ lȧ faṅ′) *French* To or at the end; finally.

à la fran·çaise (ȧ lȧ frä ṅ·sez′) *French* In the French style.

A·la·gez (ä′lə·gez′) An extinct volcano of Erivan, Armenia; 13,435 feet: also *Aragats.* Also **A·la·göz** (ä ·lä·œz′).

A·la·go·as (ä′lə·gō′əs) A state in eastern Brazil; 11,016 square miles; capital, Maceió.

Al Ah·sa See HASA, EL.

A·lai (ä·lī′) A mountain range of Kyrgyzstan, in the Tien Shan system.

a·la·li·a (ə·lā′lē·ə) *n.* Inability to speak, whether due to impairment or paralysis of the organs of speech or to brain damage. [<Gk. *a-* without + *lalia* talking] **—a·la·lic** *adj.*

A·la·mein (ä′lə·män′, al′ə-), **El** A village of northern Egypt; site of a decisive British recovery and victory against Axis forces (1942) in World War II. Also **A′la·mein′.**

Al·a·man·ni (al′ə·man′ī) See ALEMANNI.

al·a·me·da (al′ə·mē′də, -mā′-) *n. SW U.S.* A shaded walk: so called because generally planted with *alamos* or poplar trees. [<Sp. < *álamo* poplar]

al·a·mo (al′ə·mō, ä′lə·mō) *n. pl.* **-mos** Any of various species of cottonwood. [<Sp.]

Al·a·mo (al′ə·mō) A Franciscan mission building, San Antonio, Texas; besieged and taken by Mexicans, 1836. **—Remember the Alamo!** A rallying cry for United States forces in the Mexican War (1848).

à la mode (ä′lə mōd′, al′ ə·mōd′) **1** Literally, according to the mode; in the fashion. **2** Served with ice cream: pie *à la mode.* [<F]

Al·a·mo·gor·do (al′ə·mə·gôr′dō) A town in southern New Mexico: site of the first atomic bomb trial explosion, July 16, 1945.

à la mort (á lá môr′) *French* Literally, to the death; hence, mortally ill in mind or body; mortally.

al·an (al′ən) *n.* **1** *Her.* A short-eared mastiff. **2** *Obs.* A wolfhound. Also **al·and** (al′ənd), **al·ant** (al′ənt). [<OF]

Å·land Islands (ō′län) See AALAND ISLANDS.

à la New·burg (ä′ lənōō′bûrg, nyōō′bûrg) Cooked with a sauce made of egg yolks, cream, sherry, and butter.

a·lang (ə·lang′) *adv. prep. Scot.* Along.

à l'an·glaise (á läṅ·glez′) *French* In the English style.

al·a·nine (al′ə·nēn, -nin) *n.* An amino acid, $C_3H_7NO_2$, occurring as a constituent of most proteins. [<AL(DEHYDE) + infix *-an* + -INE$_2$]

a·lar (ā′lər) *adj.* Pertaining to an ala or wing; wing-shaped. [<L *alaris* <*ala* wing]

A·lar·cón (ä′lär·kōn′), **Pedro Antonio de,** 1833–91, Spanish poet.

Al·a·ric (al′ə·rik), 370?–410 A.D., king of the Visigoths who sacked Rome. **—Alaric II,** died 507, Visigoth king; issued legal code.

a·larm (ə·lärm′) *n.* **1** Sudden fear or apprehension arousing to defense or escape. **2** Any sound or signal to apprise of danger or arouse from 'sleep. **3** A mechanism, as of a clock, giving such signal. **4** A call to arms, to meet danger. **5** *Obs.* A sudden attack. *—v.t.* **1** To strike with sudden fear. **2** To arouse to a sense of danger; give warning to. See synonyms under FRIGHTEN. [<OF *alarme* <Ital. *all' arme* to arms]) **—a·larm′a·ble** *adj.*

Synonyms (noun): affright, apprehension, consternation, dismay, disquiet, dread, fear, fright, panic, terror, timidity. *Alarm,* according to its derivation, is a sudden arousal to meet and repel danger and may be quite consistent with true courage. *Apprehension, disquiet,* and *dread* are in anticipation of danger; *consternation, dismay,* and *terror* are overwhelming *fear,* generally in the actual presence of that which is terrible. Compare FEAR. *Antonyms:* assurance, calmness, confidence, repose, security.

alarm clock A clock that rings at a predetermined hour.

a·larm·ing (ə·lär′ming) *adj.* Exciting alarm; causing fear and apprehension; disturbing: an *alarming* symptom. **—a·larm′ ing·ly** *adv.*

a·larm·ist (ə·lär′mist) *n.* **1** One who needlessly excites or tries to excite alarm. **2** One who is easily or overeasily alarmed. **—a·larm′ism** *n.*

a·lar·um (ə·lar′əm, ə·lär′əm) *n. Obs.* An alarm.

a·la·ry (ā′lər·ē, al′ər·ē) *adj.* Pertaining to alae or wings; wing-shaped. [<L *alarius* <*ala* wing]

a·las (ə·las′, ə·läs′) *interj.* An exclamation of disappointment, regret, sorrow, etc. [<OF *a* ah! + *las* wretched <L *lassus* weary]

A·la·she·hir (ä′lä·she·hir′) A city in western Turkey, on the site of ancient *Philadelphia.* Also **A′la·se·hir′.**

a·las·aka (ə·las′kə) *n.* **1** A heavy rubber-topped overshoe. **2** A specially prepared yarn of wool and cotton, used as material for women's dresses and coats.

A·las·ka (ə·las′kə) A State of the United States in NW North America, including the Aleutian Islands and the Alexander Archipelago; 586,400 square miles; capital, Juneau; entered the Union Jan. 3, 1959; **—A·las′kan** *adj.* & n.

Alaska, Gulf of A broad northern inlet of the Pacific on the south coast of Alaska between Alaska Peninsula and the Alexander Archipelago.

Alaska cod A species of cod found in the northern Pacific Ocean.

Alaska Highway A road from Dawson Creek, British Columbia, through the Yukon to Fairbanks, Alaska: built in 1942 as a United States military supply route; 1,527 miles: unofficially called *Alcan Highway.*

Alaskan malamute Any of a breed of working dog of arctic regions, having a strong, compact body, a coarse, heavy coat, and standing about two feet high at the shoulder.

Alaska Peninsula A long, narrow promontory of SW Alaska, extending about 400 miles between the Bering Sea and the Pacific.

Alaska Range A mountain range in south central Alaska; highest peak, 20,320 feet.

a·las·tor (ə·las′tər) *n.* Any avenging or relentless deity. [<Gk. *alastōr* <*a-* not + *lathein* forget]

A·la Tau (ä′lä tou′) The generic name for several series of mountain ranges in the Tien Shan system between Turkestan and Mongolia.

a·late (ā′lāt) *adj.* Having wings or structures resembling wings. Also **a′lat·ed.** [<L *alatus* <*ala* wing]

a·la·tion (ā·lā′shən) *n.* **1** The condition of being winged. **2** *Entomol.* The way in which an insect's wings are arranged.

Al·a·va (al′ə·və), **Cape** A promontory on the Pacific Ocean in NW Washington; westernmost point on the United States mainland.

alb (alb) *n. Eccl.* A white linen vestment, reaching to the ankles, close-sleeved and girded at the waist, worn over the cassock and amice. [OE *albe* <L *alba (vestis)* white garment)]

ALB

al·ba[1] (al′bə) *n. Physiol.* The white tissues or structures of the central nervous system. [<NL <L, white]

al·ba[2] (äl′bə, al′bə) *n.* A short, formal lyric in Provençal troubadour literature, originally evoked by the necessity for lovers to separate when a watchman announced the dawn; aubade. [<Provençal, dawn]

Al·ba (äl′bä), **Duke of,** 1508–82, Fernando Álvarez de Toledo, Spanish general: also spelled *Alva.*

Al·ba·ce·te (äl′vä·thā′tā) A province of SE central Spain; 5,738 square miles; capital, Albacete.

al·ba·core (al′bə·kôr, -kōr) *n. pl.* **·core** or **·cores** Any of various large scombroid fishes, especially a commercially important food and game fish (*Thunnus alalunga*) having very long pectoral fins. [<Pg. *albacor* <Arabic *al* the + *bukr* young camel]

Al·ba Lon·ga (al′bə lông′g·ə, long′gə) A city of ancient Latium, SE of Rome; traditional birthplace of Romulus and Remus.

Al·ba·ni·a (al·bā′nē·ə, -bān′yə) **1** A Balkan republic northwest of Greece; 10,629 square miles; capital, Tirana. *Albanian* Shqip·ni (shkyip·nē′). **2** *Obs.* Scotland. **3** An ancient country corresponding approximately to Azerbaijan.

Al·ba·ni·an (al·bā′nē·ən, -bān′yən) *adj.* Of or pertaining to Albania, its people, or their language. *—n.* **1** A native or inhabitant of Albania. **2** The language of Albania, belonging to the Albanian subfamily of Indo-European languages.

Al·ba·ny (ôl′bə·nē) The capital of New York, a port on the Hudson River.

Albany River A river in north central Ontario, Canada, flowing about 600 miles eastward to James Bay.

al·ba·ta (al·bā′tə) *n.* A white German silver, consisting of nickel, copper, and zinc. [<NL, fem. pp. of *albare* make white < *albus* white]

al·ba·tross (al′bə·trôs, -tros) *n. pl.* **·tros·ses** or **·tross** Any of a small family (Diomedeidae) of large web-footed sea birds with long, narrow wings and hooked beaks, confined mostly to the Southern Hemisphere. [Orig. *alcatras* frigate bird <Pg. *alcatraz* pelican <Arabic *al-ghaṭṭas* a sea eagle]

ALBATROSS (Wing span up to 12 feet)

albatross cloth A smooth-faced woolen textile fabric of medium weight.

al·be·do (al·bē′dō) *n.* **1** *Astron.* The percentage of the total illumination of a planet or satellite that is reflected from its surface: the albedo of the moon is 7.2; of the planet Mars, 14.8. **2** Reflectivity. **3** The white, spongy portion of the inner rind of citrus fruit that contains the substance pectin. [<L <*albus* white]

al·be·it (ôl·bē′it) *conj.* Even though; even if; notwithstanding; although. [ME *al be it* although it be]

Al·be·marle (al′bə·märl), **Duke of** See MONK.

Albemarle Sound An inlet of the Atlantic in NE North Carolina.

Al·bé·niz (äl·vā′nēth), **Isaac,** 1860–1909, Spanish composer and pianist.

al·ber·ca (äl·ber′kə) *n. SW U.S.* A pond; pool; also, a sink to carry off waste or dirty water. [<Sp.]

Al·ber·ich (äl′bər·ikh) **1** In Norse mythology, the king of the gnomes. **2** In the *Nibelungenlied,* the dwarf who guards the treasure of the Nibelungs.

Al·bert (al′bərt; *Fr.* äl·bâr′; Ger., Sw. äl′bert) A masculine personal name. Also *Ital., Sp.* **Al·ber·to** (äl·ber′tō), *Lat.* **Al·ber·tus** (al·bûr′təs). [<F <OHG *Adalbrecht* nobly bright] **—Albert I,** 1875–1934, king of the Belgians 1909–34. —Albert, Prince, 1819–61, Prince of Saxe-Coburg-Gotha, consort of Victoria of England. —Albert of Brandenburg, 1490–1545, archbishop of Magdeburg and elector of Mainz.

Albert, Lake A lake on the Zaire-Uganda border. Also **Albert Nyanza.**

Al·ber·ta (al·bûr′tə) Feminine of ALBERT.

Al·ber·ta (al·bûr′tə) A province in western Canada; 255,285 square miles; capital, Edmonton.

Al·ber·tan (al·bûr′tən) *n.* One from or living in Alberta.

Albert Edward, Mount A peak of the Owen Stanley Range, New Guinea; 13,000 feet.

al·bert·ite (al′bər·tīt) *n.* A jet-black, brittle hydrocarbon resembling coal and used as fuel. [from *Albert* County, New Brunswick + -ITE[1]]

Albert Memorial A monument to Prince Albert in Kensington Gardens, London.

Al·ber·tus Mag·nus (al·bûr′təs mag′nəs), 1200?–80, Swabian medieval philosopher and theologian.

al·ber·type (al′bər·tīp) *n.* A picture printed in ink from a photographic plate of gelatin and albumin sensitized with potassium bichromate; also, the process by which the picture is produced. Also **albert type,** [after Joseph *Albert,* 1825–86, German inventor]

al·bes·cent (al·bes′ənt) *adj.* Growing white or moderately white; becoming whitish. [<L *albescens, -entis,* ppr. of *albescere* become white < *albus* white] **—al·bes′cence** *n.*

al·bi·ca·tion (al′bi·kā′shən) *n.* **1** The process of growing or becoming white. **2** *Bot.* The development of light patches or streaks on the foliage of plants. [<L *albicatus,* pp. of *albicare* whiten < *albus* white]

al·bi·fi·ca·tion (al′bə·fi·kā′shən) *n.* The process of making or changing to white. [<F <Med. L *albificatio, -onis,* <*albificare* make white < *albus* white]

Al·bi·gen·ses (al′bə·jen′sēz) *n. pl.* A sect of religious reformers during the 11th to 13th centuries in the south of France; suppressed for their heretical doctrines. Also *French* **Al·bi·geois** (äl·bē·zhwá′). [<Med. L. from *Albi,* a town in southern France]

Al·bi·gen·si·an (al′bə·jen′sē·ən, -shən) *adj.* Pertaining to the Albigenses. *—n.* One of the Albigenses.

al·bin·ism (al′bə·niz′əm) *n.* **1** An abnormal condition in human beings characterized by a genetically determined lack of pigment in certain cells of the skin, hair, and eyes, and giving a very white or pale appearance. **2** Deficient pigmentation in an animal or plant. **3** The state or condition of being an albino. **—al·bin·ic** (al·bin′ik) *adj.*

al·bi·no (al·bī′nō) *n. pl.* **·nos** A person, animal, or plant lacking normal pigmentation. [<Pg. < *albo* <L *albus* white]

Al·bi·on (al′bē·ən) England: an ancient name now generally only in literary use. [<L]

al·bite (al′bīt) *n.* A triclinic white feldspar, $NaAlSi_3O_8$, a common constituent of granite and other rocks. See FELDSPAR. [<L *albus*

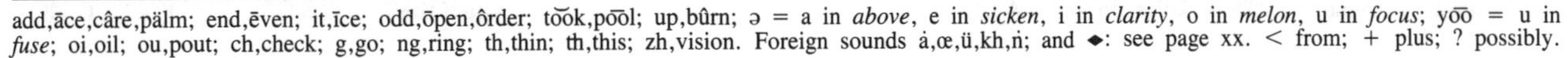
add, āce, câre, pälm; end, ēven; it, īce; odd, ōpen, ôrder; tŏŏk, pōōl; up, bûrn; ə = a in *above,* e in *sicken,* i in *clarity,* o in *melon,* u in *focus;* yōō = u in *fuse;* oi, oil; ou, pout; ch, check; g, go; ng, ring; th, thin; th, this; zh, vision. Foreign sounds á, œ, ü, kh, ṅ; and ◆: see page xx. < from; + plus; ? possibly.

white + -ITE[1]] **—al·bit·i·cal** (al·bit′i·kəl) *adj.*

Al·boin (al′boin, -bō·in), died 573, founder and king of the Lombard dominion in Italy.

Al·bo·rak (al′bə·rak) The white mule on which Mohammed is said to have visited the seven heavens. [< Arabic *al-burāq*]

Å·borg (ôl′bôr) See AALBORG.

al·bor·noz (äl′bōr·nōth′) *n.* A burnoose. [< Sp.]

Al·brecht (äl′brekht) German form of ALBERT.

Al·bu·ca·sis (al′byo͞o·kā′sis). See ABUL KASIM.

al·bum (al′bəm) *n.* **1** A book for holding photographs or the like. **2** A blank book for registering names or preserving autographs, stamps, poetical selections, etc. **3** A printed compilation. **4** A single long-playing phonograph record. **5** A set of phonograph records or tape recordings. [< L, white tablet]

al·bu·men (al·byo͞o′mən) *n.* **1** The white of an egg. **2** *Bot.* The nutritive material that fills the space in a seed between the embryo and the seed coats; endosperm or perisperm. **3** Albumin. [< L, white of an egg < *albus* white]

al·bu·men·ize (al·byo͞o′mən·īz) *v.t.* **·ized, ·iz·ing** To treat with albumen.

al·bu·min (al·byo͞o′mən) *n.* Any of a group of simple proteins which are common in plant and animal tissues and which are soluble in water and coagulable by heat. [< F *albumine* < L *albumen, -inis.* See ALBUMEN.]

al·bu·min·ize (al·byo͞o′mən·īz) *v.t.* **·ized, ·iz·ing 1** To convert into albumin. **2** To coat or saturate with albumin. Also spelled *albumenize.* **—al·bu′min·i·za′tion** *n.* **—al·bu′min·iz′er** *n.*

al·bu·mi·noid (al·byo͞o′mə·noid) *adj.* Of or like albumen or albumin. *—n.* One of a diversified subclass of the simple proteins derived mainly from the supporting and connective animal tissues. Also **al·bu′me·noid. —al·bu′mi·noi′dal** *adj.*

al·bu·mi·nous (al·byo͞o′mə·nəs) *adj.* Of, pertaining to, like, or consisting of albumen or albumin. Also **al·bu′mi·nose** (-nōs).

al·bu·mi·nu·ri·a (al·byo͞o′mə·no͝or′ē·ə, -nyo͝or′-) *n.* The presence of albumin in the urine. [< NL < ALBUMIN + Gk. *ouron* urine] **—al·bu′mi·nu′ric** *adj.*

al·bu·mose (al·byo͞o′mōs, al′byo͞o·mōs) *n.* Any of various albuminous products of the enzymatic hydrolysis of proteins during digestion.

Al·bu·quer·que (äl′bo͞o·ker′kə), **Affonso de,** 1453–1515, Portuguese navigator.

Al·bu·quer·que (al′bə·kûr′kē) A resort city on the Rio Grande in NW New Mexico.

al·bur·num (al·bûr′nəm) *n.* Sapwood. [< L < *albus* white]

Al·cae·us (al·sē′əs) A Greek poet of Mitylene; lived about 600 B.C. See ALCAIC. Also **Al·cæ′us. —Alcaeus** In Greek mythology, a king of Tiryns, son of Perseus and Andromeda; father of Amphitryon.

Al·ca·ic (al·kā′ik) *adj.* Of or pertaining to the poet Alcaeus or to his favorite meter, consisting of four strophes, each of four verses having four accents apiece. *—n.* Verse written in Alcaic strophes.

al·caide (al·kād′, *Sp.* äl·kä′ē·thä) *n.* **1** The governor of a Spanish, Portuguese, or Moorish castle or fortress. **2** The warden of a prison; a jailer. Also **al·cayde′.** [< Sp. < Arabic *al-qā'id* the leader]

al·cal·de (al·kal′dē, *Sp.* äl·käl′dā) *n.* A magistrate in a Spanish or Spanish-American pueblo or town; later, a chief magistrate or mayor. [< Sp. < Arabic *al-qāḍī* the judge]

Al·can Highway (al′kan) See ALASKA HIGHWAY.

Al·ca·traz (al′kə·traz) A small island in San Francisco Bay, California; former site of a Federal prison.

al·caz·ar (al·kaz′ər, al′kə·zär; *Sp.* äl·kä′thär) *n.* A Moorish castle in Spain; especially, **The Alcazar,** a Moorish palace in Seville, later used by the Spanish kings. [< Sp. < Arabic *al-qaṣr* the castle]

Al·ces·tis (al·ses′tis) In Greek mythology, the heroic wife of Admetus; she volunteered to die to save her husband's life but was rescued from Hades by Hercules.

al·che·mist (al′kə·mist) *n.* One skilled in or practicing alchemy.

al·che·mis·tic (al′kə·mis′tik) *adj.* Of or pertaining to alchemy or alchemists; practicing alchemy. Also **al′che·mis′ti·cal.**

al·che·mize (al′kə·mīz) *v.t.* **·mized, ·miz·ing** To transmute by or as by alchemy.

al·che·my (al′kə·mē) *n.* **1** An ancient quasi-magical art through which practitioners sought a formula to cure any disease, confer eternal youth, and transmute base metals into gold. **2** Any cunning, mysterious, or preternatural process of changing the structure or appearance of things. [< OF *alkemie* < Med.L *alchimia* < Arabic *al-kīmiyā* < L Gk. *chēmeia* transmutation of metals, later prob. confused with *chymeia* pouring, infusion < *cheein* pour] **—al·chem·ic** (al·kem′ik) *adj.* **—al·chem′i·cal·ly** *adv.*

Al·ci·bi·a·des (al′sə·bī′ə·dēz), 450–404 B.C., Athenian general.

Al·ci·des (al·sī′dēz) Hercules: so named because he was the grandson of Alcaeus.

al·ci·dine (al′sə·dīn, -din) *n.* Any of a family (Alcidae) of web-footed sea birds of the Northern Hemisphere, including the auks, puffins, guillemots, etc. Also **al·cid.** *—adj.* Pertaining to or resembling an alcidine.

Alc·man (alk′mən) Spartan poet of the seventh century B.C.

Alc·me·ne (alk·mē′nē) In Greek mythology, the mother of Hercules by Zeus, who seduced her in the guise of her husband Amphitryon.

al·co·hol (al′kə·hôl, -hol) *n.* **1** A colorless, volatile, inflammable liquid, C_2H_5OH, produced commercially by the fermentation of cereal grains, molasses, and fruits, widely used as a solvent in industry and medicine, and as the intoxicating principle in beer, wine, and distilled liquor. Also called *ethanol, ethyl alcohol, grain alcohol.* **2** Any of a group of organic compounds containing one or more functional hydroxyl (OH) groups. **3** Any liquor containing ethyl alcohol. [< Med.L, orig., fine powder < Arabic *al-koh'l* the powdered antimony]

al·co·hol·ate (al′kə·hôl·āt, -hol-) *n.* **1** A type of alcohol in which the hydrogen of the hydroxyl is replaced by a metal. **2** An alcoholic compound or solution.

alcohol dehydrogenase An enzyme found in yeast and liver, necessary for the metabolism and production of alcohols.

al·co·hol·ic (al′kə·hôl′ik, -hol′-) *adj.* **1** Of, pertaining to, or containing alcohol. **2** Produced by alcohol: an *alcoholic* stupor. **3** Afflicted with alcoholism. *—n.* One who consumes alcohol compulsively. **—al·co·hol·i·cal·ly** *adv.*

al·co·hol·ic·i·ty (al′kə·hôl·is′ə·tē, -hol-) *n.* The quality of being alcoholic; alcoholic strength: the *alcoholicity* of a wine.

al·co·hol·ism (al′kə·hôl′iz·əm, -hol′-) *n.* Compulsive and habitual consumption of alcohol accompanied by varying degrees of deterioration, especially of the nervous and digestive systems.

al·co·hol·ize (al′kə·hôl·īz′, -hol-) *v.t.* **·ized, ·iz·ing 1** To change into alcohol. **2** To mix or saturate with alcohol. **—al′co·hol′i·za′tion** *n.*

al·co·hol·om·e·ter (al′kə·hôl·om′ə·tər, -hol-) *n.* An instrument, such as a modified hydrometer, for ascertaining the concentration of alcohol in a liquid. **—al′co·hol·om′e·try** *n.*

al·co·hol·y·sis (al′kə·hôl′ə·sis, -hol-) *n.* A decomposing by the action of alcohol.

Al·cor (al′kôr) See under MIZAR.

Al·co·ran (al′kō·rän′, -ran′) *n.* The Koran. **—Al′co·ran′ic** (-ran′ik) *adj.*

al·co·sol (al′kə·sōl, -sol) *n.* An alcoholic colloidal solution.

Al·cott (ôl′kət, -kot), **Amos Bronson,** 1799–1888, U.S. educator. **—Louisa May,** 1832–88, U.S. novelist; daughter of Amos B.

al·cove (al′kōv) *n.* **1** A recess connected with or at the side of a larger room, as to contain a bed. **2** Any embowered or secluded spot. **3** A niche in the face of a cliff or the wall of a building. [< F *alcôve* < Sp. *alcoba* < Arabic *al-qobbah* the vaulted chamber]

Al·cuin (al′kwin), 735–804, English scholar and ecclesiastical reformer; friend and adviser of Charlemagne: in Old English spelled *Ealhwine.* Also **Al′cwin.**

Al·cy·o·ne (al·sī′ə·nē) **1** In Greek mythology: **a** The daughter of Aeolus who, mourning her husband Ceyx, cast herself into the sea and was changed into a kingfisher: also *Halcyone.* **b** One of the Pleiades. **2** *Astron.* The brightest star in the Pleiades.

Al·da (äl′də), **Frances,** 1885–1952, U.S. soprano born in New Zealand.

Al·dan (äl·dän′) A river in the Yakut Republic, U.S.S.R.; flowing north 1,767 miles to the Lena.

Al·deb·a·ran (al·deb′ə·rən) A red star, Alpha in the constellation Taurus; one of the 20 brightest stars, 1.06 magnitude. See STAR. [< Arabic *al-dabarān* the follower (i.e., of the Pleiades)]

al·de·hyde (al′də·hīd) *n.* **1** *Chem.* Any one of a group of aliphatic compounds derived from the alcohols, and intermediate between the alcohols and the acids; they have the general formula R-CHO. **2** Acetaldehyde. [< AL(COHOL) + DEHYD(ROGENIZED)]

Al·den (ôl′dən), **John,** 1599–1687, one of the original Pilgrim settlers of Plymouth Colony, 1620; the chief character in Longfellow's *Courtship of Miles Standish.*

al den·te (äl·den′tā) *Ital.* Cooked so as to be chewy; firm to the tooth.

al·der (ôl′dər) *n.* **1** Any of a genus (Alnus) of catkin-bearing shrubs and trees usually growing in moist areas in the Northern Hemisphere. **2** Any of various unrelated species resembling *Alnus* species. [OE *alor*]

al·der·man (ôl′dər·mən) *n. pl.* **·men 1** A member of a municipal legislative body, who usually also exercises certain judicial functions. **2** In England and Ireland, a member of the higher branch of a town council, as in a borough, whose office corresponds to that of the *bailie* in Scotland. [OE *ealdorman* head man]**—al′der·man·cy** (-mən·sē), **al′der·man·ship′** *n.***—al′der·man′ic** (-man′ik) *adj.*

al·der·man·ate (ôl′dər·mən·āt) *n.* **1** The position, dignity, or term of office of alderman. **2** Aldermen collectively.

Al·der·ney (ôl′dər·nē) The northernmost of the Channel Islands; 3 square miles: French *Aurigny.*

Alderney *n.* One of a breed of cattle originally peculiar to the island of Alderney.

Al·der·shot (ôl′dər·shot) A borough and permanent military camp, Hampshire, England.

Al·dine (ôl′dīn, al′-, -dēn) *adj.* Pertaining to or printed by the press of Aldus Manutius, Venetian editor and printer, or to his family (1494–1597): applied also to a modern series of books, and a style of display types. *—n.* A book printed by the Aldine press, noted for fine typography.

al·dol (al′dôl, -dol) *n. Chem.* A colorless liquid, $C_4H_8O_2$, a condensation product of acetaldehyde, or any of a group of similar aldehyde condensates. [< ALD(EHYDE) + (ALCOH)OL]

al·dol·ase (al′də·lās) *n.* An enzyme that appears in muscle tissue.

al·dose (al′dōs) *n. Chem.* Any of a class of monosaccharides containing in the molecule a group (CHO) that is characteristic of aldehydes.

al·dos·te·rone (al·dos′·tə·rōn) *n.* An adrenocortical steroid hormone, $C_{21}H_{28}O_5$, which regulates the metabolism of potassium and sodium.

al·dos·te·ron·ism (al·dos′tər·ə·niz′əm) *n.* Excessive secretion of aldosterone resulting in hypertension and loss of potassium through the kidneys.

Al·drich (ôl′drich), **Thomas Bailey,** 1836–1907, U.S. poet and novelist.

Al·drin (ôl′drin), **Edwin Eugene, Jr.,** born 1930, U.S. astronaut; one of the first two men to walk on the moon, July 20, 1969.

al·drin (al′drin) *n.* A powerful insecticide, $C_{12}H_8Cl_6$, derived from naphthalene, useful against insects that infest the soil, such as locusts and grasshoppers.

ale (āl) *n.* **1** A beverage made from a fermented infusion of malt, usually flavored with hops: ale resembles beer but generally has more body. **2** An English rural ale-drinking festival. ◆ Homophone: *ail.* [OE *ealu*]

a·le·a·tor·ic (ā′lē·ə·tôr′ik, -tōr′-) *adj. Music* Made up of chance or random elements: *aleatoric* melodies.

a·le·a·to·ry (ā′lē·ə·tôr′ē, -tō′rē) *adj.* **1** Of or

pertaining to gambling or luck. 2 Dependent upon contingency. [< L *aleatorius* < *aleator* gambler < *alea* a die, chance]

a·lec·i·thal (ə·les′i·thəl) *adj.* Having no yolk, as the eggs of placental mammals. [< Gk. *a-* without + *lekithos* yolk]

Al·eck (al′ik) Diminutive of ALEXANDER.

A·lec·to (ə·lek′tō) One of the three Furies.

a·lee (ə·lē′) *adv. Naut.* At, on, or to the lee side of a vessel.

al·e·gar (al′ə·gər, ā′lə-) *n.* Sour ale; a vinegar produced by the fermentation of malt. [< ALE + (VINE)GAR]

ale·house (āl′hous′) *n.* A place where ale is sold to the public.

A·le·jan·dro (ä′lā·hän′drō) Spanish form of ALEXANDER. Also *fem.* **A′le·jan′dra** (-drä) or **A·le·jan·dri·na** (ä′lā·hän·drē′nä).

A·le·khine (ä·lyu′khin), **Alexander,** 1892–1946, French world chess champion born in Russia. Also **A·lje′chin.**

A·lek·san·dro·pol (ä·lyik·sän·drô′pəl) The former name of LENINAKAN.

A·lek·san·drovsk (ä·lyik·sän′drôfsk) 1 A port near Murmansk, NW U.S.S.R. 2 A Russian port in western Sakhalin Island. 3 Former name of ZAPOROZHE.

A·le·mán (ä′lā·män′), **Mateo,** 1547?–1610?, Spanish novelist. **—Miguel,** 1902–1983 Mexican lawyer; president of Mexico 1946–52.

Al·e·man·ni (al′ə·man′ī) *n.* A group of South Germanic tribes that fought against Rome in the third to fifth centuries: also spelled *Alamanni, Allemanni.*

Al·e·man·nic (al′ə·man′ik) *adj.* Of or pertaining to the Alemanni or their language. Also **Al′e·man′ni·an.** *—n.* The language of the ancient Alemanni: a dialect of Old High German. Also spelled *Alamannic, Allemannic.*

A·lem·bert (dà·läṅ·bâr′), **Jean le Rond d′,** 1717–83, French mathematician and philosopher.

a·lem·bic (ə·lem′bik) *n.* 1 An apparatus of glass or metal formerly used in distilling. 2 Anything that tests, purifies, or transforms. [< OF *alambic* < L *alambicus* < Arabic *al-anbīq* the still < Gk. *ambix* a cup]

a·lem·bi·cate (ə·lem′bə·kāt) *v.t.* **·cat·ed, ·cat·ing** To distill in an alembic.

A·len·çon (à·läṅ·sôṅ′) A town in NW France.

A·len·çon lace (ə·len′sən, *Fr.* à·läṅ·sôṅ′) A fine, needlepoint lace originally made in Alençon.

a·leph (ä′lif) *n.* The first letter in the Hebrew alphabet. Also **a′lef.** See ALPHABET.

A·lep·po (ə·lep′ō) A city of NW Syria, largest in the country. *French* **A·lep** (à·lep′).

a·lert (ə·lûrt′) *adj.* 1 Keenly watchful; on the look-out; ready for sudden action; vigilant. 2 Lively; nimble.
—n. 1 A warning against sudden attack; especially, a signal to prepare for an air raid or gas attack. 2 An alert attitude; guard; the period of preparedness for defense. 3 *Aeron.* The condition of an airplane which is manned and equipped to make a sortie. **—on the alert** On the look-out; ready. *—v.t.* To prepare for action; warn, as of a threatened attack or raid. [< F *alerte* < Ital. *all'erta* on the watch] **—a·lert′ly** *adv.* **—a·lert′ness** *n.*
Synonyms (adj.): active, alive, brisk, bustling, nimble, prepared, prompt, ready, vigilant, watchful, wide-awake. *Alert, ready,* and *wide-awake* refer to a watchful promptness for action. *Ready* suggests preparation; the wandering Indian is *alert,* the trained soldier is *ready. Ready* expresses more life and vigor than *prepared.* The gun is *prepared;* the man is *ready. Prompt* expresses readiness for appointment or demand at the required moment. The good general is *ready* for emergencies, *alert* to perceive opportunity or peril, *prompt* to seize occasion. Compare ACTIVE, ALIVE, NIMBLE. *Antonyms*: drowsy, dull, heavy, inactive, slow, sluggish, stupid.

-ales *suffix Bot.* A feminine plural used to form the scientific names of plant orders. [< L, pl. of -ALIS]

A·les·san·dri·a (ä′les·sän′drē·ä) A city in northern Italy.

A·les·san·dro (ä′les·sän′drō) Italian form of ALEXANDER. Also *fem.* **A′les·san′dra** (-drä).

a·leu·ro·man·cy (ə·lo͝or′ə·man′sē) *n.* Divination by means of flour or meal. [< F *aleuromancie* < Gk. *aleuron* flour + *manteia* divination]

a·leu·rone (ə·lo͝or′ōn) *n. Bot.* An albuminoid substance found in minute solid granules in the seeds of some plants. In seeds of wheat and other cereals they form the outermost or **aleurone layer** of the endosperm. [< Gk. *aleuron* flour] **—al·eu·ron·ic** (al′yo͞o·ron′ik) *adj.*

Al·e·ut (al′ē·o͞ot) *n. pl.* **Al·e·uts** or **Al·e·ut** 1 A native of the Aleutian Islands belonging to either of two Eskimoan tribes called *Unungun.* 2 A subfamily of the Eskimo-Aleut family of languages, comprising the Aleutian Island dialects. **—A·leu·tian** (ə·lo͞o′shən), **A·leu′tic** *adj.*

A·leu·tian Islands (ə·lo͞o′shən) A chain of volcanic islands, extending some 1,100 miles from the tip of the Alaska Peninsula between the North Pacific and the Bering Sea. Also **A·leu′tians.**

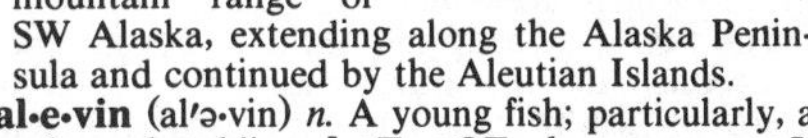

Aleutian Range A mountain range of SW Alaska, extending along the Alaska Peninsula and continued by the Aleutian Islands.

al·e·vin (al′ə·vin) *n.* A young fish; particularly, a salmon hatchling. [< F < OF *alever* to rear < L *ad-* to + *levare* raise]

ale·wife (āl′wīf′) *n. pl.* **·wives** A small North American anadromous fish of the herring family (*Pomolobus pseudoharengus*). [? < Am. Ind.]

Al·ex·an·der (al′ig·zan′dər, -zän′-; *Du., Ger.* ä′lek·sän′dər) 1 A masculine personal name. Also *Fr.* **A·lex·an·dre** (à·lek·säṅ′dr′), *Gk.* **A·lex·an·dros** (ä·leks′än·drōs), *Pg.* **A·lex·an·dre** (ä′leg·zäṅ′drə)). 2 Name of many kings of Bulgaria, Greece, Russia, Scotland, Serbia, Yugoslavia, etc. 3 Appellation of eight popes. [< Gk., helper of men]
—Alexander I, 1888–1934, king of Yugoslavia 1921–34.
—Alexander II, 1818–81, czar of Russia 1855–81.
—Alexander III, died 1181, real name Orlando Bandinelli, pope 1159–81.
—Alexander VI, 1431?–1503, real name Rodrigo Borgia, pope 1492–1503.
—Alexander Nev·ski (nev′skē, nef′-), 1220?–63, Russian hero.
—Alexander Se·ve·rus (sə·vir′əs), 208?–235; Roman emperor 222–235.
—Alexander the Great, 356–323 B.C., king of Macedon 336–323, conqueror of Asia.

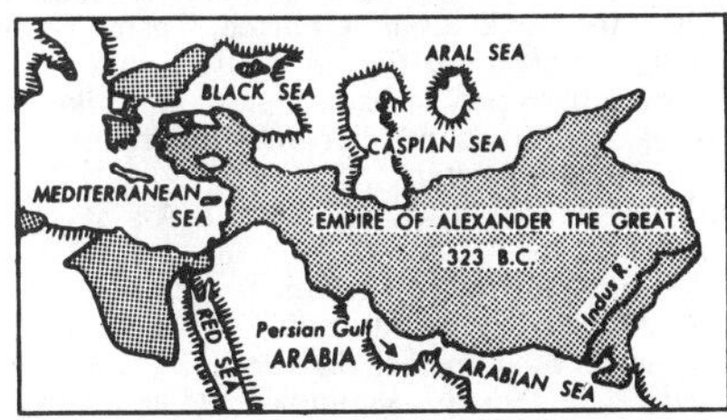

Al·ex·an·der (al′ig·zan′dər, -zän′-), **Sir Harold Rupert Leofric George,** 1891–1969, first Viscount Alexander of Tunis, British field marshal; governor general of Canada 1946–1952.

Alexander Archipelago A group of more than 1,000 islands, SE Alaska. Also **Alexander Islands.**

Al·ex·an·dra (al′ig·zan′drə, -zän′-) A feminine personal name: feminine of ALEXANDER. Also **Al·ex·an·dri·na** (al′ig·zan·drē′nə, -zän-), *Fr.* **A·lex·an·drine** (à·lek·säṅ·drēn′).
—Alexandra, Queen, 1844–1925, wife of Edward VII of England.

Alexandra Nile See KAGERA.

Al·ex·an·dret·ta (al′ig·zan·dret′ə, -zän-) A former name for ISKENDERUN.

Al·ex·an·dri·a (al′ig·zan′drē·ə, -zän′-) The chief port and ancient capital of Egypt. *Arabic* **Al Is·kan·da·ri·ya** (al is·kan·da·rē′yə).

Al·ex·an·dri·an (al′ig·zan′drē·ən, -zän′-) *adj.* 1 Of or pertaining to Alexander the Great, his reign, or his conquests. 2 Of or pertaining to the Alexandrian school or its influence. 3 In prosody, Alexandrine. *—n.* 1 A native or inhabitant of Alexandria. 2 In prosody, an Alexandrine verse.

Alexandrian school 1 A late Hellenic school of literature, science, and philosophy, at Alexandria, Egypt, during the last three centuries B.C. 2 The school of Christian philosophers and theologians at Alexandria during the first five centuries A.D., which sought to combine Christianity and Greek philosophy, and so gave rise to Neoplatonism and Gnosticism.

Al·ex·an·drine (al′ig·zan′drin, -drēn, -zän′-) *n.* In prosody, a line of verse having six iambic feet with the caesura generally after the third. *—adj.* Of, composed of, or characterized by Alexandrines. Also *Alexandrian.*

al·ex·an·drite (al′ig·zan′drīt, -zän′-) *n.* A green variety of chrysoberyl, red by artificial light. [after *Alexander* II, czar of Russia]

A·lex·an·drou·po·lis (ä′lek·sän·dro͞o′pô·lēs) A port on the Aegean, NE Greece: formerly *Dedeagach.*

A·le·xan·drovsk (u·lyi·ksän′drôfsk) The former name for ZAPOROZHE.

a·lex·i·a (ə·lek′sē·ə) *n.* Loss of ability to grasp the significance of written or printed matter. Also called *word blindness.* [< NL < Gk. *a-* without + *lexis* speech < *legein* speak]

a·lex·ic (ə·lek′sik) *adj.* 1 Suffering from alexia. 2 Pertaining to alexin.

a·lex·in (ə·lek′sin) *n. Immunology* Complement. [< Gk. *alexein* ward off]

a·lex·i·phar·mic (ə·lek′si·fär′mik) *Med. adj.* Serving to ward off or resist poison; antidotal. *—n.* An antidote or poison preventive. [< Gk. *alexipharmakos* < *alexein* ward off + *pharmakon* poison]

A·lex·is Mi·khai·lo·vich (ə·lek′sis mē·khī′lə·vich), 1629–76, czar of Russia; father of Peter the Great.

Alexis Pe·tro·vich (pi·trô′vich), 1690–1718, Russian prince; son of Peter the Great.

A·lex·i·us I Com·ne·nus (ə·lek′sē·əs, kom·nē′nəs), 1048–1118, Byzantine emperor 1081–1118.

al·fal·fa (al·fal′fə) *n.* A perennial leguminous herb (*Medicago sativa*) having deep roots, compound pinnate leaves, and clusters of small purple flowers, widely grown for fodder. Also called *lucerne, purple medic.* [< Sp. < Arabic *al-faṣfaṣah* the best kind of fodder]

al·fa·qui (al′fə·kē′) *n.* A teacher of Mohammedan law or of the Koran; a priest of Islam. Also **al′fa·ki′** or **al′fa·quin′** (-kēn′). [< Sp. < Arabic *al-faqīh*]

Al·fie·ri (äl·fyâ′rē), **Vittorio,** 1749–1803, Italian dramatic poet.

al·fil·e·ri·a (al·fil′ə·rē′ə) *n.* A biennial European weed *(Erodium cicutarium)* naturalized in North America, having leafy stems and rose or purple umbellate flowers. Alse **alfilaria.** Also called *pin clover.* [< Am. Sp. < Sp. *alfiler* pin < Arabic *al-khilāl* the thorn]

Al·föld (ôl′fœld) The fertile central plain of Hungary.

Al·fon·so (äl·fôn′sō) 1 Italian and Spanish form of ALPHONSO. 2 One of many Spanish and Portuguese kings. Also *Dan., Ger.* **Alfons** (äl′fôns).
—Alfonso XIII, 1886–1941, king of Spain 1886–1931; deposed.

al·for·ja (al·fôr′jə, *Sp.* äl·fôr′hä) *n.* 1 A leather pouch; saddle bag. 2 A cheek pouch, especially of the baboon. [< Sp. < Arabic *al-khorj*]

Al·fred (al′frid; *Dan.* äl′fred; *Du., Ger.* äl′fret; *Fr.* àl·fred′) A masculine personal name. Also *Ital., Pg., Sp.* **Al·fre·do** (äl·frā′dō), *Lat.* **Al·fre·dus** (al·frē′dəs), *fem.* **Al·fre′da.** [OE *ælfred,* lit., elf counsel (i.e., good counselor)]
—Alfred the Great, 849–901, king of the West Saxons; defeated the Danish invaders, built the first English navy, and is known as the father of English prose literature.

al·fres·co (al·fres′kō) *adv.* In the open air.

—*adj.* Occurring outdoors, as a meal. Also **al fresco.** [< Ital.]

al·gae (al′jē) *n. pl.* A large group of primitive, mostly aquatic, chlorophyll-bearing plants lacking specialized tissues and organs such as roots, stems, leaves, and flowers, and including forms ranging from giant seaweeds to single-celled diatoms and pond scums. [< L, seaweed] **—al·gal** (al′gəl) *adj.*

al·gar·ro·ba (al′gə·rō′bə) *n.* **1** The carob tree or its fruit, the carob bean. **2** A species of mesquite or its edible pods. Also **al′ga·ro′ba.** [< Sp. < Arabic *al-kharrūbah* the carob]

Al·gar·ve (äl·gär′və) The southernmost province of Portugal; 1,958 square miles; capital, Faro; formerly a Moorish kingdom.

al·ge·bra (al′jə·brə) *n.* **1** The branch of mathematics which treats of quantity and number in the abstract, and in which calculations are performed by means of letters and symbols: it includes the solution of equations of any degree. **2** A treatise on this subject. [< Ital. < Arabic *al-jebr* the reunion of broken parts, bone-setting]

al·ge·bra·ic (al′jə·brā′ik) *adj.* Pertaining to algebra. Also **al′ge·bra′i·cal.** **—al′ge·bra′i·cal·ly** *adv.*

al·ge·bra·ist (al′jə·brā′ist) *n.* One skilled in algebra.

Al·ge·cir·as (al′jə·sir′əs, *Sp.* äl′hā·thē′räs) A port in southern Spain, opposite Gibraltar.

al·ge·don·ic (al′jə·don′ik) *adj.* Characterized by or relating to the agreeable and the disagreeable. [< Gk. *algos* pain + *hēdonikos* pleasurable]

al·ge·don·ics (al′jə·don′iks) *n. Psychol.* The study of pain and pleasure in relation to human life.

Al·ger (al′jər), **Horatio,** 1834–99, U.S. writer of boys' stories.

Al·ge·ri·a (al·jir′ē·ə) A republic in NW Africa, formerly a dependency of France; 919,352 square miles; capital, Algiers. *French* **Al·gé·rie** (ál·zhā·rē′). **—Al·ge′ri·an** *adj. & n.*

Al·ge·rine (al′jə·rēn′) *n.* **1** An inhabitant or native of Algeria, especially a native Berber, Arab, or Moor; an Algerian. **2** A pirate.

al·ge·rine (al′jə·rēn′) *n.* A soft woolen fabric or shawl with bright stripes.

Algerine War The war between the United States and the pirates of the Algerian coast, 1815.

Al·ger·non (al′jər·nən) A masculine personal name [? < OF *al grenon* with a mustache]

al·ge·si·a (al·jē′zē·ə) *n.* Sensitiveness to pain. [< Gk. *algos* pain]

al·get·ic (al·jet′ik) *adj.* Relating to or causing pain. [< Gk. *algein* feel pain]

-algia *suffix* Pain or disease of: *neuralgia.* [< Gk. *algos* pain]

al·gi·cide (al′jə·sīd) *n.* Any chemical agent used to kill algae. Also **al·gae·cide.** **—al·gi·cid·al** (al′jə·sī′dəl) *adj.*

al·gid (al′jid) *adj.* Cold; chilly: the *algid* stage of ague. [< F *algide* < L *algidus* cold < *algere* be cold] **—al·gid′i·ty** *n.*

Al·giers (al·jirz′) The capital of Algeria, a major port on the Mediterranean.

al·gin (al′jin) *n.* An insoluble, gelatinous acid obtained from various seaweeds, especially the giant kelp, used as an emulsifier and thickening agent. Also **alginic acid.** [< ALGA]

al·gi·nate (al′jə·nāt) *n.* Any of various salts of algin. —*adj.* Denoting any of various synthetic yarns or textile fibers made from algin or alginates.

al·goid (al′goid) *adj.* Of or like algae.

Al·gol (al′gol) The variable star Beta in Perseus: also called *Demon Star.* [< Arabic *al-ghūl* the ghoul, the demon]

al·go·lag·ni·a (al′gə·lag′nē·ə) *n. Psychiatry* Pleasure, specifically of a sexual nature, aroused by the infliction or the experiencing of pain. See MASOCHISM and SADISM. [< NL < Gk. *algos* pain + *lagneia* lust] **—al′go·lag′nic** *adj.* **—al′go·lag′nist** *n.*

al·gol·o·gy (al·gol′ə·jē) *n.* That branch of botany which treats of algae. [< L *alga* seaweed + -(O)LOGY] **—al·go·log·i·cal** (al′gə·loj′i·kəl) *adj.* **—al·gol′o·gist** *n.*

al·gom·e·ter (al·gom′ə·tər) *n.* An instrument to measure the intensity of pain. Also called *algesimeter.* [< Gk. *algos* pain + -METER] **—al·go·met·ric** (al′gə·met′·rik) or **·ri·cal** *adj.* **—al·gom′e·try** *n.*

Al·gon·ki·an (al·gong′kē·ən) *adj.* **1** *Geol.* Of, pertaining to, or characterized by a series of rock strata between the Archaean and the Cambrian; Proterozoic. **2** Former spelling of ALGONQUIAN.

Al·gon·qui·an (al·gong′kē·ən, -kwē·ən) *n.* **1** A large linguistic stock of North American Indians, formerly inhabiting the territory from Hudson Bay south to North Carolina and Tennessee, east of the Mississippi, including the Algonquin, Arapaho, Blackfoot, Cheyenne, Cree, Ojibwa, Micmac, Sauk, Delaware, Massachuset, and Shawnee tribes. **2** A member of one of the tribes belonging to this stock. —*adj.* Of or pertaining to the Algonquian family.

Al·gon·quin (al·gong′kin, -kwin) *n.* **1** A member of certain Algonquian tribes formerly inhabiting territory near the mouth of the Ottawa river, and of certain other tribes north of the St. Lawrence river. **2** The language spoken by these tribes, belonging to the East Central subfamily of Algonquian Indian languages. Also **Al·gon·kin** (al·gong′kin).

Algonquin Provincial Park A national park in SE Ontario, Canada; 2,740 square miles.

al·go·pho·bi·a (al′gə·fō′bē·ə) *n. Psychiatry* A morbid fear of pain. [< Gk. *algos* pain + -PHOBIA] **—al′go·pho′bic** *adj.*

al·gor (al′gôr) *n. Pathol.* Cold; chilliness; especially, an abnormal coldness, as in the early stages of a fever. [< L]

al·go·rism (al′gə·riz′əm) *n.* **1** The Arabic or decimal system of numeration. **2** Any method of computation using Arabic notation. **3** Arithmetic. Also **al·go·rithm** (al′gə·rith′əm). [< OF *algorisme* < Med.L *algorismus* < Arabic *al-Khowārazmī,* lit., the native of Khwārazm (Khiva), surname of a 9th cent. Arab mathematician]

al·gous (al′gəs) *adj.* Of, like, or filled with algae.

al·gua·zil (al′gwä·zēl′) *n.* A Spanish officer of justice. [< Sp. < Arabic *al-wazīr* the vizier]

al·gum (al′gum) See ALMUG.

Al·ham·bra (al·ham′brə) The medieval palace of the Moorish kings at Granada, Spain. [< Sp. < Arabic *al-hamrā′* the red (house)]

Al·ham·bresque (al′ham·bresk′) *adj.* Like the Alhambra or its peculiar and delicate type of Moorish architecture.

a·li·as (ā′lē·əs) *n. pl.* **a·li·as·es** **1** An assumed name. **2** *Law* A second writ to the same effect as a former one, issued after the first has failed. —*adv.* Otherwise called; called by an assumed name. [< L, at another time or place]

A·li (ä′lē), 600?–661, son-in-law and adopted son of Mohammed; fourth Arabian calif.

A·li Ba·ba (ä′lē bä′bä) In the *Arabian Nights,* the hero of the tale *Ali Baba and the Forty Thieves,* who gains entrance to a robbers' cave by crying out the magic words "Open sesame."

al·i·bi (al′ə·bī) *n.* **1** A form of defense by which the accused, in order to establish his innocence, undertakes to show that he was elsewhere when the crime was committed: He had a perfect *alibi.* **2** *Colloq.* Any excuse; especially, a poor and flimsy excuse. —*v.i. Colloq.* To make excuses for oneself. [< L, elsewhere]

al·i·bil·i·ty (al′ə·bil′ə·tē) *n.* Nutritive quality or value.

al·i·ble (al′ə·bəl) *adj.* Nourishing; nutritive. [< L *alibilis* < *alere* nourish]

A·li·can·te (ä′lē·kän′tā) A port in SE Spain; center of a wine-producing region.

Al·ice (al′is; *Fr.* á·lēs′; *Ger.* ä·lē′sə) A feminine personal name. Also *Ital.* **A·li·cia** (ä·lē′chä), *Lat.* **A·li·ci·a** (ə·lē′shē·ə), *Sp.* **A·lí·ci·a** (ä·lē′·thē·ä). [< Gmc. See ADELINE.]

Alice blue A light-blue color of slightly dusty hue. [after *Alice* Roosevelt Longworth, daughter of Theodore Roosevelt] **—Al′ice-blue′** *adj.*

al·i·cy·clic (al′i·sī′klik, -sik′lik) *adj.* Having both aliphatic and cyclic molecular structure or chemical properties. [< ALI(PHATIC) + CYCLIC]

al·i·dade (al′i·dād) *n.* **1** An auxiliary circle, frame, or movable arm, carrying microscopes or verniers, for reading the divisions of a graduated circle or arc. **2** A theodolite having such an arm. Also **al·i·dad** (al′i·dad). [< F < Med.L. *alhidada* < Arabic *al-'idādah* the revolving radius of a graduated circle]

al·ien (āl′yən, ā′lē·ən) *adj.* **1** Of another country; foreign. **2** Of foreign character; not similar; incongruous; inconsistent; also, unsympathetic. —*n.* **1** An unnaturalized foreign resident. **2** One of another race. **3** One estranged or excluded. **4** *Bot.* A plant native to one region maintaining itself under conditions prevailing in another. —*v.t.* **1** To transfer to another, as property. **2** To estrange. [< L *alienus* belonging to another]

Synonyms (adj.): conflicting, contradictory, contrary, contrasted, distant, foreign, hostile, opposed, remote, strange, unconnected, unlike. *Foreign* refers to difference of birth, *alien* to difference of allegiance. In their figurative use, that is *foreign* which is *remote, unlike,* or *unconnected;* that is *alien* which is *conflicting, hostile,* or *opposed. Antonyms*: akin, appropriate, apropos, essential, germane, pertinent, proper, relevant.

Synonyms (noun): foreigner, stranger. A naturalized citizen is not an *alien,* even if a *foreigner* by birth, and perhaps a *stranger* in the place where he resides. A person of foreign birth not naturalized is an *alien,* though he may have been long resident in the country, and ceased to be a stranger. He is an *alien* in one country if his allegiance is to another. *Antonyms*: citizen, countryman, native.

al·ien·a·ble (āl′yən·ə·bəl, ā′lē·ən-) *adj.* That can be made over or transferred, as property to the ownership of another. **—al′ien·a·bil′i·ty** *n.*

al·ien·age (āl′yən·ij, ā′lē·ən-) *n.* The state of being alien.

al·ien·ate (āl′yən·āt, ā′lē·ən-) *v.t.* **·at·ed, ·at·ing** **1** To make indifferent or unfriendly; estrange: to *alienate* a friend. **2** To cause to feel estranged or withdrawn from society. **3** To make over; transfer, as property to the ownership of another. **4** To turn away, as affection or interest. **—al′ien·a′tor** *n.*

al·ien·a·tion (āl′yən·ā′shən, ā′lē·ən-) *n.* **1** The act of alienating, or the state of being alienated. **2** An anxious or resentful feeling of not belonging to or having a fit place in society. **3** An abnormal condition of indifference to or estrangement from others. **4** *Law* The transfer of property, or title, to another.

al·ien·ee (āl′yən·ē′, ā′lē·ən·ē′) *n.* One who takes over tranferred property.

al·ien·ism (āl′yən·iz′əm, ā′lē·ən-) *n.* Alienage.

al·ien·ist (āl′yən·ist, ā′lē·ən-) *n.* One skilled in the study or treatment of mental disorders: term used chiefly in medical jurisprudence. [< F *aliéniste,* ult. < L *alienus* foreign, strange]

al·ien·or (āl′yən·ər, ā′lē·ən·ôr′) *n. Law* One who alienates property to another; a vender. Also **al′ien·er.** [< AF]

a·lif (ä′lif) *n.* The first letter in the Arabic alphabet.

al·i·form (al′ə·fôrm, ā′lə·fôrm) *adj.* Wing-shaped; alar. [< L *ala* a wing + -FORM]

Al·i·garh (al′i·gûr′) A city in western Uttar Pradesh state, India.

a·light[1] (ə·līt′) *v.i.* **a·light·ed** or **a·lit, a·light·ing** **1** To descend and come to rest; settle, as after flight. **2** To dismount, as from a horse or vehicle. **3** To come or fall upon by accident: with *on* or *upon.* [< OE *ālīhtan* < *ā-* out, off + *līhtan* alight, orig., make light]

a·light[2] (ə·līt′) *adj. & adv.* Lighted; lighted up; on fire; kindled. [ME *aliht,* pp. of *alihten* light up]

a·lign (ə·līn′), *v.t.* To arrange or place in a line; bring into line. —*v.i.* To fall into line. Also spelled *aline.* [< F *aligner* < *a-* to (< L *ad-*) + *ligne* line < L *linea*] **—a·lign·ment** *n.*

a·like (ə·līk′) *adj.* Having resemblance; like

one another; resembling, wholly or in part. —*adv.* In like manner. [OE *gelic, onlic*] **—a·like′ness** *n.*

Synonyms (adj.): akin, analogous, equal, equivalent, homogeneous, identical, kindred, like, resembling, similar, synonymous, uniform. Two or more objects are *alike* when each resembles the other or others; by modifiers *alike* may be made to express more or less resemblance; as, these houses are somewhat (that is, partially) *alike*; or, exactly (that is, in all respects) *alike*; or *alike* in color or structure. Substances are *homogeneous* which are made up of elements of the same kind, or which are the same in structure. To say "this is the *identical* man" is to say not merely that he is *similar* to the one in mind, but that he is the very *same* person. Things are *analogous* when they are *similar* in idea, plan, use, or character, but perhaps quite unlike in appearance; as, the gills of fishes are said to be *analogous* to the lungs in terrestrial animals. Compare IDENTICAL. *Antonyms*: different, dissimilar, distinct, heterogeneous, unlike.

al·i·ment (al′ə·mənt) *n.* Food; nutriment; sustenance. See synonyms under FOOD. —*v.t.* To furnish with food; nourish. [<L *alimentum* <*alere* nourish]**—al·i·men·tal** (al′ə·men′təl) *adj.* **—al′i·men′tal·ly** *adv.*

al·i·men·ta·ry (al′ə·men′tər·ē) *adj.* Supplying nourishment; connected with the function of nutrition.

alimentary canal The continuous digestive tube leading from the mouth through the esophagus, stomach, and intestines, having muscular walls which absorb nutrients and by peristalsis propel waste material to be discharged at the anus.

al·i·men·ta·tion (al′ə·men·tā′shən) *n.* **1** The act or process of supplying nutrition. **2** The act, process, or capacity of receiving nourishment or being nourished. **3** Maintenance; support.

al·i·men·ta·tive (al′ə·men′tə·tiv) *adj.* Of or pertaining to alimentation; nutritive.

al·i·mo·ny (al′ə·mō′nē) *n.* **1** *Law* The allowance made to a woman by order of court, from her husband's estate or income, for her maintenance after her divorce or legal separation from him, or during a suit therefor. The allowance made during suit is called **alimony pendente lite.** **2** Maintenance; means of living or sustenance. [<L *alimonia* food, support <*alere* nourish]

a·line (ə·līn′) *v.* **a·lined, a·lin·ing** *v.t.* To arrange or place in a line; bring into line. —*v.i.* To fall into line. Also spelled *align.* [<F *aligner* <*a-* to (<L *ad-*) + *ligne* line <L *linea*]

a·line·ment (ə·līn′mənt) *n.* **1** Position or place in line; formation in line. **2** A straight line through two or more points. **3** *Eng.* The ground plan, as of a railroad. Also spelled *alignment.*

A·li Pa·sha (ä′lē pä·shä′), 1741–1822, Albanian warrior and leader: called the "Lion of Janina."

al·i·ped (al′ə·ped) *adj.* Having winglike membranes connecting the digits and the front and hind feet on each side, as a bat. —*n.* An aliped animal; a bat. [<L *alipes, -pedis* wing-footed <*ala* wing + *pes* foot]

al·i·phat·ic (al′ə·fat′ik) *adj.* Pertaining to or designating any organic compound of carbon and hydrogen having the carbon atoms connected in a straight or branched chain. [<Gk. *aleiphar, aleiphatos* fat, oil]

al·i·quant (al′ə·kwənt) *adj.* Contained in another number, but with remainder. [<L *aliquantus* some, somewhat <*alius* other + *quantus* how large, how much]

al·i·quot (al′ə·kwət) *adj.* Contained in another quantity an exact number of times. —*n.* A small aliquot portion of a measured volume or weight of a substance taken as a sample representing the whole. [<L *aliquot* <*alius* other + *quot* how many]

a·list (ə·list′) *adv. & adj.* In a canted or inclined position; listed over.

a·lit (ə·lit′) Past tense and past participle of ALIGHT[1].

a·lite (ā′līt) *n.* A component, consisting largely of calcium silicate, of the clinker produced in making portland cement. [<*A*, a rating + -LITE]

a·li·un·de (ā′lē·un′dē) *adv. Law Latin* From a source extrinsic to the principal matter; from elsewhere: Testimony to explain or contradict a written instrument from other sources than itself is evidence *aliunde.*

a·live (ə·līv′) *adj.* **1** In a living state, or a state in which the organs perform their functions; having life: said of organisms: opposed to *dead.* **2** In action, motion, or existence; in force, or operation; in full vigor. **3** In lively action; in an animated state; sprightly: *alive* with enthusiasm. **4** In a condition of attentiveness, sensitiveness, or susceptibility; open to impressions. **5** Abounding in life or living things, or in evidences of life: The hive was *alive* with bees. [OE *on līfe* in life]

Synonyms: active, alert, animate, animated, breathing, brisk, existent, existing, live, lively, living, quick, subsisting, vivacious. *Alive* applies to all degrees of life, from that which shows one to be barely *existing* or *existent* as a living thing, as when we say he is barely *alive,* to that which implies the utmost of vitality and power. So the word *quick,* which began by signifying "having life," is now mostly applied to energy of life as shown in swiftness of action. *Breathing* is capable of like contrast. We say of a dying man, "he is still *breathing*"; or we speak of a *breathing* statue, where we mean having, or seeming to have breath and life. Compare ACTIVE, ALERT, NIMBLE. *Antonyms*: dead, deceased, defunct, dispirited, dull, inanimate, lifeless, spiritless.

a·liz·a·rin (ə·liz′ə·rin) *n.* A basic orange-red crystalline coloring compound, $C_{14}H_8O_4$; used to dye cotton, wool, and silks various shades of red: formerly prepared from madder, now manufactured from anthraquinone. —*adj.* Designating any organic compound derived from anthraquinone: *alizarin* blue, *alizarin* crimson, *alizarin* green. Also **a·liz·a·rine** (ə·liz′ə·rin, -rēn). [<F *alizerine* <*alizari* madder]

al·ka·hest (al′kə·hest) *n.* The hypothetical universal solvent sought by the ancient alchemists. [A pseudo-Arabic word coined by Paracelsus]

al·ka·le·mi·a (al′kə·lē′mē·ə) *n. Pathol.* A reduction to below normal or safe limits of acidity in the blood; increased alkalinity. [<NL <ALKALI + -EMIA]

al·ka·les·cen·cy (al′kə·les′ən·sē) *n.* A tendency to become alkaline; slight alkalinity. Also **al′ka·les′cence.**

al·ka·les·cent (al′kə·les′ənt) *adj.* Becoming or tending to become alkaline. —*n.* An alkalescent compound.

al·ka·li (al′kə·lī) *n. pl.* **·lis** or **·lies** **1** *Chem.* A compound of hydrogen and oxygen with any one of the elements lithium, sodium, potassium, rubidium, and cesium, or the ammonium radical, characterized by great solubility in water and capability of neutralizing acids and of turning red litmus paper blue. **2** Anything that will neutralize an acid, as lime, magnesia, etc. **3** Sodium carbonate. **4** Mineral matter, not including sodium chloride, found in natural waters and in soils. [<MF *alcali* <Arabic *al-qalīy* the ashes of saltwort]

al·kal·ic (al·kal′ik) *adj.* Containing or characterized by a considerable amount of the alkaline bases, especially soda and potash.

alkali flat *Geol.* An arid plain, permeated or incrusted with alkaline salts; the bed of an evaporated lake.

al·ka·li·fy (al′kə·lə·fī, al·kal′ə·fī) *v.t. & v.i.* **·fied, ·fy·ing** To change into or become alkaline or an alkali.

alkali metals Any of the metallic elements of group Ia of the periodic table, including lithium, sodium, potassium, rubidium, cesium, and francium.

al·ka·lim·e·ter (al′kə·lim′ə·tər) *n.* **1** An instrument for measuring the concentration or the amount of alkali in a solid or liquid. **2** An instrument for measuring the amount of carbon dioxide evolved in a reaction.

al·ka·lim·e·try (al′kə·lim′ə·trē) *n.* The determination of the percentage of alkali in a solution by a volumetric or other method.

al·ka·line (al′kə·līn, -lin) *adj.* **1** Of, pertaining to, or having the characteristics of an alkali; containing or produced by an alkali. **2** Having a pH greater than 7.

alkaline earth The oxide of any of the alkaline-earth metals.

al·ka·line-earth metals (al′kə·līn ûrth, -lin) A group of elements resembling the alkali metals but somewhat less reactive, usually including calcium, strontium, magnesium, and barium, and sometimes also other elements of group IIa of the periodic table.

al·ka·lin·i·ty (al′kə·lin′ə·tē) *n.* The state or quality of being alkaline.

al·ka·lize (al′kə·līz) *v.t. & v.i.* **·lized, ·liz·ing** To convert into or become alkali or alkaline. **—al′ka·li·za′tion** *n.*

al·ka·loid (al′kə·loid) *n.* Any of various nitrogenous bases of vegetable origin, usually having a toxic effect on animals, as strychnine, nicotine, or cocaine. **—al′ka·loi′dal** *adj.*

al·ka·lo·sis (al′kə·lō′sis) *n.* A higher concentration than normal of carbonate in body fluids.

al·kane (al′kān) *n.* Any of a homologous series of saturated aliphatic hydrocarbons having the general formula C_nH_{2n+2}, as methane, ethane, etc.

alkane series Methane series.

al·ka·net (al′kə·net) *n.* **1** A perennial plant *(Alkanna tinctoria)* or its roots, which yield a red dye. **2** The dye obtained from this plant, used as a chemical indicator. **3** Bugloss. **4** Puccoon. [<Sp. *alcaneta,* dim. of *alcana* henna <Arabic *al-hinnā′* the henna]

al·kene (al′kēn) *n.* Any of a series of unsaturated aliphatic hydrocarbons having the general formula C_nH_{2n} and containing a carbon-to-carbon double bond, as ethylene, propylene, etc. Also called *olefin.* [<ALK(YL) + -ENE]

Alk·maar (älk′mär) A city in NW Netherlands.

Al·ko·ran (al′kō·rän′, -ran′) *n.* The Koran. **—Al′ko·ran′ic** (-ran′ik) *adj.*

al·kyd (al′kid) Any of a group of adhesive resins made by combining an unsaturated organic acid and a polyhydric alcohol, used for paints and other surface coatings. Also **alkyd resin.**

al·kyl (al′kil) *n.* A univalent hydrocarbon radical having the general formula C_nH_{2n+1}, equivalent to an alkane molecule minus a hydrogen atom. Also **alkyl radical.** [<ALK(ALI) + -YL]

al·kyl·ate (al′kə·lāt) *v.t.* **·at·ed, ·at·ing** To introduce one or more alkyl groups into. —*n.* A product of alkylation, as a high-octane gasoline.

al·kyl·a·tion (al′kə·lā′shən) *n.* **1** The process of introducing one or more alkyl radicals into a compound by substitution or addition. **2** A refinery process for producing high-octane gasoline by forcing the combination of constituent alkanes and alkenes by the action of heat, pressure, and catalysts.

al·kyne (al′kīn) *n.* Any of a series of unsaturated aliphatic hydrocarbons having the general formula C_nH_{2n-2} and containing a carbon-to-carbon triple bond, as ethyne (acetylene) etc. Also **alkine.** [<ALKY(L) + -INE]

all (ôl) *adj.* **1** The entire substance or extent of: *all* Europe; *all* wisdom. **2** The entire number of; the individual components of, without exception: to be known to *all* men. **3** The greatest possible: in *all* haste. **4** Any whatever: beyond *all* doubt. **5** Every: used in phrases with *manner, sorts,* and *kinds*: *all* manner of men. **6** Nothing except: He was *all* skin and bones. See synonyms under EVERY. —*n.* **1** Everything that one has; entire interest or possession: to give one's *all.* **2** Whole being; totality. —*pron.* **1** Everyone: *All* are condemned. **2** Each one: When he questioned his students, *all* were ready with an answer. **3** Everything: *All* is in readiness. **4** Every part, as of a whole: *All* of it is gone. ◆Homophone; *awl.* [OE] **—above all** Primarily; of the first importance. **—after all** **1** On the other hand. **2** In the long run; in spite of everything. **—all in all** All things considered; taken as a whole. **—at all.** **1** In any way: I can't come *at all.* **2** To any degree or extent; no luck *at all.* **—for all** To the degree that: *For all* I care, you can go without me. **—for all of (me, you, him, her,** or **us)** As for: You can leave now, *for all of* me.**—in all** Including everything; all told. **—onceand for all** Once and no more; finally. —*adv.* **1** Wholly; entirely: fallen *all* to bits; running*all* the way; traveling *all* through the night. **2** Exclusively; only: That portion is *all* three *all.* **—all along** All the time: I knew it *all along.* **—all but 1** Almost; on the verge of: I was *all but* exhausted by my trip. **2** Every one except: He took *all but* six. **—all in** *Colloq.* Wearied, as from exertion. **—all of** No less than; quite: It's *all of* ten miles. **—all out** Making every effort: They went *all out* for victory. **—all over 1** Finished; past and gone: The love affair is *all over* between us. **2** Everywhere; in all parts: He's been *all over.* **3** Typically; in every way: That's George *all over.* **—all the (better, more,** etc.) So much the (better, more, etc.) **—all up with** *Colloq.* Ended; without power to continue: It's *all up with* him.

al·la bre·ve (ä′lə brev′ā, *Ital.* äl′lä brā′vā) *Music* A measure of duple or quadruple time in which the beat is represented by the half note: performed twice as quickly as common time. Symbol C. [< Ital., lit., according to the breve]

all·ach·es·the·sia (al′ak·is·thē′zhə, -zhē·ə) *n.* A tactile sensation localized elsewhere than at the point of stimulation. Also *allesthesia.* [< Gk. *allachē* elsewhere + *aisthēsis* feeling]

Al·lah (al′ə, ä′lə) In the Moslem religion, the one supreme being; God. [< Arabic]

Al·la·ha·bad (al′ə·hə·bad′, ä′lə·hä·bäd′) A city on the Jumna River, capital of Uttar Pradesh state, India.

all-A·mer·i·can (ôl′ə·mer′ə·kən) *adj.* **1** Representative of America or of the United States. **2** Composed of the best in America: an *all-American* football team. **3** Of or composed of Americans exclusively. **4** Of all the Americas. **5** Within or confined to America or the United States. —*n.* **1** An imaginary or ideal team, as of football players, selected from the college players considered best in a season. **2** A player selected for such a team. **3** One of the best in America.

Al·lan-a-Dale (al′ən·ə·dāl′) In English legend, an outlaw of Robin Hood's band.

al·lan·toid (ə·lan′toid) *adj.* **1** Sausage-shaped. **2** Resembling or possessing an allantois. Also **al·lan·toi·dal** (al′ən·toi′dəl). [Gk. *allantoeidēs* < *allas* sausage + *eidos* form]

al·lan·to·in (ə·lan′tō·in) *n.* An oxidation product of uric acid, $C_4H_6N_4O_3$, occurring in allantoic fluid, fetal urine, and elsewhere, which promotes healing when applied to wounds.

al·lan·to·is (ə·lan′tō·is) *n.* A membranous, fluid-filled sac that develops from the hindgut in the embryos of reptiles, birds, and mammals. [< NL < *allantoides* < GK. See ALLANTOID.] —**al·lan·to·ic** (al′ən·tō′ik) *adj.*

all-a·round (ôl′ə·round′) *adj.* All-round.

al·la vos·tra sa·lu·te (äl′lä vôs′trä sä·lōō′tä) *Italian* To your health.

al·lay (ə·lā′) *v.t.* **al·layed, al·lay·ing 1** To lessen the violence or reduce the intensity of. **2** To lay to rest, as fears; pacify; calm. [OE *ālecgan* < *ā-* away + *lecgan* lay] —**al·lay′er** *n.*

Synonyms: abate, alleviate, appease, assuage, calm, compose, lessen, lighten, mitigate, moderate, mollify, pacify, palliate, quiet, reduce, relieve, soften, soothe, still, tranquilize. We *allay* suffering by using means to *soothe* and *tranquilize* the sufferer; we *alleviate* suffering by doing something toward removal of the cause. *Pacify* and *appease* signify to bring to peace; to *mollify* is to soften; to *mitigate* is to make mild; we *mollify* a temper, *mitigate* rage or pain. To *calm, quiet,* or *tranquilize* is to make still; *compose,* to adjust to a calm and settled condition; to *soothe* is to bring to pleased quietude. We *allay* excitement, *calm* agitation, *compose* our feelings, *pacify* the quarrelsome, *quiet* the clamorous, *soothe* grief or distress. Compare ALLEVIATE. *Antonyms*: agitate, arouse, excite, fan, kindle, provoke, rouse, stir.

all-clear (ôl′klir′) *n.* The signal indicating that an air raid is over.

al·le·cret (al′ə·kret) *n. Archaic* A breastplate with tassets, worn by light cavalry and infantry about the 16th century: also spelled *halecret.* [< MF *allecret, halcret*]

al·le·ga·tion (al′ə·gā′shən) *n.* The act of alleging. **2** That which is alleged; a formal assertion. **3** Something alleged without proof. **4** *Law* The assertion of a party to a suit, which he undertakes to prove. [< L *allegatio, -onis* < *allegare* send a message < *ad-* to + *legare* commission]

al·lege (ə·lej′) *v.t.* **al·leged, al·leg·ing 1** To assert to be true without proving; affirm. **2** To plead as an excuse, in support of or in opposition to a claim or accusation. **3** *Archaic* To cite or quote. [< AF *alegier,* OF *esligier* < L *ex-* out + *litigare* sue; infl. by L *allegare* (see ALLEGATION) and *lex* law] —**al·lege′a·ble** *adj.* —**al·leged′** *adj.* —**al·leg′er** *n.*

Synonyms: adduce, advance, affirm, assert, asseverate, assign, aver, cite, claim, declare, introduce, maintain, offer, plead, produce, say, state. To *allege* is formally to state as true, without proving. *Adduce* is a secondary word; nothing can be *adduced* in evidence until something has been *stated* or *alleged,* which the evidence is to sustain. An *alleged* fact stands open to question or doubt. When an *alleged* criminal is brought to trial, the counsel on either side are accustomed to *advance* a theory, and *adduce* the strongest possible evidence in its support; they will *produce* documents and witnesses, *cite* precedents, *assign* reasons, *introduce* suggestions, *offer* pleas. The accused will usually *assert* his innocence. Compare STATE. *Antonyms*: see AFFIRM.

al·leg·ed·ly (ə·lej′id·lē) *adv.* According to allegation.

Al·le·ghe·ny (al′ə·gā′nē) *adj.* Of or pertaining to the Allegheny Mountains or River. Also **Al′le·gha′ny.**

Allegheny Mountains A mountain range of the Appalachian system, extending from Pennsylvania to Virginia.

Allegheny River A river in western New York and Pennsylvania; flowing SW 325 miles to join with the Monongahela, forming the Ohio River.

Allegheny Series *Geol.* The middle Coal Measures of the eastern United States.

al·le·giance (ə·lē′jəns) *n.* **1** Fidelity, or an obligation of fidelity, to a government from a citizen, to a superior, or to a principle. **2** The obligation of fidelity in general. **3** *Archaic* The duty and obligation of a vassal holding lands by fealty to the superior lord. [ME *alegeaunce* < *a-* to (< L *ad-*) + OF *ligeance* < *liege.* See LIEGE.]

Synonyms: devotion, faithfulness, fealty, fidelity, homage, loyalty, obedience, subjection. The feudal uses of these words have mostly passed away with the state of society that gave them birth; but their origin still colors their present meaning. A patriotic American feels an enthusiastic *loyalty* to the Republic; he takes an oath of *allegiance* to the government, but his *loyalty* will lead him to do more than mere *allegiance* could demand; he pays *homage* to God or to those principles of right that are supreme; he acknowledges the duty of *obedience* to all rightful authority; he resents the idea of *subjection. Fealty,* except in poetic style, has given place to *faithfulness* or *fidelity. Antonyms*: disaffection, disloyalty, rebellion, sedition, treason.

al·le·giant (ə·lē′jənt) *adj. Obs.* Loyal; faithful.

al·le·gor·ic (al′ə·gôr′ik, -gor′-) *adj.* Pertaining to, appearing in, or containing allegory; figurative. Also **al′le·gor′i·cal.** —**al′le·gor′i·cal·ly** *adv.* —**al′le·gor′i·cal·ness** *n.*

al·le·go·rist (al′ə·gôr′ist, -gō′rist, al′ə·gər·ist) *n.* One who composes or uses allegories.—**al′le·go·ris′tic** *adj.*

al·le·go·rize (al′ə·gə·rīz) *v.* **·rized, ·riz·ing** *v.t.* **1** To turn into an allegory; relate in the manner of an allegory. **2** To explain or interpret as an allegory. —*v.i.* **3** To make or use allegory. —**al·le·go·ri·za·tion** (al′ə·gôr′ə·zā′shən, -gor′-) *n.* —**al′le·go·riz′er** *n.*

al·le·go·ry (al′ə·gôr′ē, -gō′rē) *n. pl.* **·ries 1** The setting forth of a subject or the telling of a story in figurative or symbolic language requiring interpretation; especially, a narrative veiling a moral by symbolic devices, such as personification, metaphor, etc. **2** Any subject or story so presented. **3** Loosely, any symbolic representation in literature or art; an emblem. [< L *allegoria* < Gk. *allēgoria,* lit., a speaking otherwise < *allos* other + *agoreuein* speak in public assembly < *agora* forum]

Synonyms: fable, fiction, illustration, metaphor, parable, simile, story. The *allegory, parable,* or *fable* tells its story as if true, leaving the reader or hearer to discover its fictitious character and learn its lesson. The word *fiction* is applied almost exclusively to novels, short stories, or romances. An *allegory* or *parable* is a moral or religious tale, of which the moral lesson is the substance and all descriptions and incidents but accessories; the *parable* is generally briefer and less adorned than the *allegory.* A *fable* is generally brief, representing animals as the speakers and actors, and conveying some lesson of practical wisdom or shrewdness. Compare SIMILE, STORY. *Antonyms*: chronicle, fact, history, narrative, record.

al·le·gret·to (al′ə·gret′ō, *Ital.* äl′lā·gret′tō) *adj. & adv. Music* Rather fast; faster than *andante* but slower than *allegro.* —*n. pl.* **·tos** A movement in allegretto time. [< Ital.]

al·le·gro (ə·lā′grō, ə·leg′rō; *Ital.* äl·lā′grō) *adj. & adv. Music* Quick; lively: faster than *allegretto* but slower than *presto.* —*n. pl.* **·gros** A musical composition, movement, etc., in such tempo. [< Ital.]

allegro non tan·to (nōn tän′tō) *Music* Moderately lively. [< Ital.]

al·lele (ə·lēl′) *n. Genetics* An allelomorph.

al·le·lo·morph (ə·lē′lə·môrf, ə·lel′ə-) *n. Genetics* In Mendel's law, one of a pair of contrasted characters which become segregated in the formation of reproductive cells. [< Gk. *allēlōn* of one another + *morphē* form] —**al·le′lo·mor′phic** *adj.* —**al·le′lo·mor′phism** *n.*

al·le·lu·ia (al′ə·lōō′yə) *n. & interj.* Hallelujah. Also **al′le·lu′iah.** [< L. See HALLELUJAH.] —**al·le·lu·iat·ic** (al′ə·lōō·yat′ik) *adj.*

Al·le·magne (âl·màn′y′) The French name for GERMANY.

al·le·mande (al′ə·mand′, *Fr.* âl·mänd′) *n.* **1** A stately processional dance in duple rhythm, originating in Germany. **2** The music for this. **3** *Music* A formal movement in various suites, resembling the dance chiefly in its duple rhythm. [< F, lit., German]

Al·le·man·ni (al′ə·man′ī) See ALEMANNI.

Al·len (al′ən), **Ethan,** 1737–89, American soldier, leader of the "Green Mountain Boys," a body of Vermont soldiers in the Revolution. —**Grant,** 1848–99, English author. —**Ira,** 1751–1814, American soldier and legislator; brother of Ethan.

—**(William) Her·vey** (hûr′vē), 1889–1949, U.S. novelist.

Al·len·by (al′ən·bē), **Edmund Henry,** 1861–1936, first viscount, British field marshal; commanded forces in Egypt and Palestine, 1917–18.

Al·len·stein (ä′len·shtīn) See OLSZTYN.

Al·len·town (al′ən·toun) A city in eastern Pennsylvania.

al·ler·gen (al′ər·jən) *n.* Any substance capable of producing allergy. —**al·ler·gen·ic** (al′ər·jen′ik) *adj.*

al·ler·gic (ə·lûr′jik) *adj.* **1** Characteristic of or pertaining to allergy. **2** Highly susceptible to. **3** *Colloq.* Having an aversion to.

al·ler·gist (al′ər·jist) *n.* A specialist in the treatment of allergies.

al·ler·gy (al′ər·jē) *n. pl.* **·gies 1** A condition of exaggerated sensibility, as manifested by various physiologic reactions to an environmental substance or sensory stimulus that produces no reaction in nonsensitive individuals. **2** Anaphylaxis. [< NL *allergia* < Gk. *allos* other + *ergon* work]

al·les·the·sia (al′is·thē′zhə, -zhē·ə) See ALLACHESTHESIA.

al·leth·rin (ə·leth′rin) *n.* A synthetic liquid compound, used as an insecticide.

al·le·vi·ate (ə·lē′vē·āt) *v.t.* **·at·ed, ·at·ing** To make lighter or easier to bear; relieve, as pain; mitigate. [< L *alleviatus,* pp. of *alleviare* < *ad-* to + *levis* light]

Synonyms: abate, allay, assuage, lessen, lighten, mitigate, moderate, reduce, relieve, remove, soften. *Alleviate* is less than *relieve; relieve,* ordinarily, less than *remove. Assuage* is to sweeten; *mitigate,* to make milder; *moderate,* to bring within measure; *abate,* to beat down and so make less. We *abate* a fever; *lessen* anxiety; *moderate* passions or desires; *lighten* burdens; *mitigate* or *alleviate* pain; *reduce* inflammation; *soften, assuage,* or *moderate* grief; we *lighten* or *mitigate* punishments; we *relieve* suffering. Compare ALLAY. *Antonyms*: aggravate, augment, embitter, enhance, heighten, increase, intensify, magnify. —**al·le′vi·a′tion** *n.* —**al·le′vi·a′tor** *n.*

al·le·vi·a·tive (ə·lē′vē·ā′tiv, ə·lē′vē·ə·tiv) *adj.*

Tending to alleviate. Also **al·le·vi·a·to·ry** (ə·lē′·vē·ə·tôr′ē, -tō′rē). —*n.* Anything that alleviates.

al·ley[1] (al′ē) *n.* **1** A narrow passageway, street, path, or walk; especially, a narrow way behind city buildings, running parallel to a street. **2** A long narrow space for bowling, or the building containing it. See synonyms under WAY. [< OF *alee* a going, passage < *aler* go, ? < L *ambulare*]

al·ley[2] (al′ē) *n.* A large playing marble. [< ALABASTER]

alley cat A cat which forages for food in alleys, etc.

al·leyed (al′ēd) *adj.* Having an alley or alleys; having the form or nature of an alley.

Al·leyn (al′in), **Edward,** 1566–1626, English actor and producer.

al·ley·way (al′ē·wā′) *n.* A short or narrow passageway between buildings.

al·lez-vous-en (à·lā·vo͞o·zäṅ′) *French* Go away! Off with you!

all-fired (ôl′fird′) *U.S. Slang adj.* Excessive: an *all-fired* shame. —*adv.* Inordinately: He walked *all-fired* slow. [Alter. of *hell-fired*]

All Fools' Day The first of April: a day on which jokes and tricks are commonly practiced.

all fours 1 The four legs of a quadruped, or the arms and legs of a person. **2** Seven-up, a card game. **—to go** (or **be**) **on all fours 1** To move or crawl on all four limbs, as a baby. **2** To run smoothly, as a machine. **—to be on all fours with** To present an exact comparison or analogy with.

all hail All health! an exclamation in friendly salutation.

All-hal·low·mas (ôl′hal′ō·məs) *n.* The feast of All Saints.

All-hal·lows (ôl′hal′ōz) *n.* All Saints' Day, Nov. 1.

All-hal·low·tide (ôl′hal′ō·tīd) *n.* The season near Nov. 1.

all·heal (ôl′hēl′) *n.* Any of various plants reputed to have healing properties, as the selfheal and the garden heliotrope.

al·li·a·ceous (al′ē·ā′shəs) *adj.* **1** Pertaining to or belonging to a genus *(Allium)* of liliaceous herbs with a pungent odor, including the various species of onions, leeks, and garlic. **2** Having the taste or smell of onions or garlic. [< ALLIUM]

al·li·ance (ə·lī′əns) *n.* **1** A formal treaty or agreement between states or other parties. **2** The union so formed; any intimate relationship. [< OF *aliance* (MF *alliance*) < L *alligantia* < *alligare.* See ALLY.]

Synonyms: affinity, coalition, compact, confederacy, confederation, federation, fusion, kin, league, partnership, union. Commonly, *alliance* is a connection formed by treaty between sovereign states for mutual aid in war; *partnership* is a mercantile word. We speak of an alliance *with* a neighboring people; *against* the common enemy; *for* offense and defense; alliance *of, between,* or *among* nations. *Coalition* is oftenest used of political parties; *fusion* is now the more common word in this sense. In a *confederacy* or *confederation* there is an attempt to unite separate states in a general government without surrender of sovereignty. *Union* makes the separate states substantially one. *Federation* is a poetic and rhetorical word expressing something of the same thought. The United States is a federal *union.* See ASSOCIATION. *Antonyms*: antagonism, discord, disunion, divorce, enmity, hostility, schism, secession, separation, war.

Al·lie (al′ē) Diminutive of ALICE. Also **Al′ly.**

al·lied (ə·līd′) *adj.* **1** United, confederated, or leagued. **2** Morphologically, genetically, or otherwise related.

Al·lier (à·lyā′) **1** A river in central France, flowing NW 250 miles to the Loire. **2** A department of central France; 2,850 square miles; capital, Moulins.

Al·lies (al′īz, ə·līz′) See under ALLY.

al·li·ga·tion (al′ə·gā′shən) *n.* Formerly, the method of finding or rule for finding the relation between the prices of the ingredients in a mixture, their proportions, quality, and the price of the mixture. In **alligation alternate** the proportion is required, the other two quantities being given: in **alligation medial** the cost of the mixture is required. [< L *alligatio, -onis* < *alligare* < *ad-* to + *ligare* bind]

al·li·ga·tor (al′ə·gā′tər) *n.* **1** Either of two species of large, crocodilian reptiles *(genus Alligator),* found only in rivers and swamps of the southern United States and in the Yangtze River in China, having a shorter, blunter head than the crocodile and no lower teeth protruding when the jaw is closed. **2** Any crocodilian. **3** Leather made from the hide of an alligator. **4** A machine for squeezing ore, etc. [Earlier *alligarta* < Sp. *el lagarto* the lizard < L *lacertus*]

ALLIGATOR
(Length up to 18 feet)

alligator pear The avocado.

alligator snapping turtle A very large freshwater turtle *(Macrochelys temmincki)* having the head covered with plates and a fleshy extension on the tongue. Also **alligator snapper.**

all-im·por·tant (ôl′im·pôr′tənt) *adj.* Very important; crucial; necessary.

all-in·clu·sive (ôl′in·klo͞o′siv) *adj.* Including everything; general.

all-in-one (ôl′in·wun′) *n.* A woman's foundation garment, consisting of a brassière and girdle, with or without panties.

all in the wind 1 *Naut.* In line with the wind, so as not to draw, as the sails of a ship. **2** *Colloq.* Puzzled; nonplused; confused.

al·li·sion (ə·lizh′ən) *n. Naut.* The act of a vessel's striking or dashing against another: distinguished from *collision.* [< L *allisio, -onis* < *allidere* < *ad-* against + *lidere* strike violently]

Al·li·son (al′ə·sən), **Samuel King,** born 1900, U.S. physicist.

al·lit·er·ate (ə·lit′ə·rāt) *v.* **·at·ed, ·at·ing** *v.i.* **1** To speak alliteratively; use alliteration, as in the writing of verse. **2** To constitute alliteration: These two lines of verse *alliterate.* —*v.t.* **3** To make alliterative: to *alliterate* verses. [< AL-[2] to + L *littera* a letter (of the alphabet)]

al·lit·er·a·tion (ə·lit′ə·rā′shən) *n.* **1** The use or repetition of a succession of words with same initial letter or sound: Langland uses *alliteration* in his line "A fair field full of folk." **—al·lit·er·a·tive** (ə·lit′ə·rā′tiv, -ər·ə·tiv) *adj.* **—al·lit′er·a′tive·ly** *adv.* **—al·lit′er·a′tive·ness** *n.*

al·li·um (al′ē·əm) *n.* Any of a large genus *(Allium)* of liliaceous plants having a tunicate bulb, leafless scapes with flowers in a terminal umbel, and a pungent, onionlike smell, as onions, leeks, garlic, shallots, chives, etc. [< L]

allo- *combining form* **1** Other; alien: *allotheism,* worship of strange gods. **2** Variant; different: *allogeneic,* differing genetically. [< Gk. *allos* other]

al·lo·bar (al′ə·bär) *n. Meteorol.* An area above which the barometric pressure has changed during a specified interval. [ALLO- + Gk. *baros* weight, pressure] **—al·lo·bar·ic** (al′ə·bar′ik) *adj.*

al·lo·cate (al′ə·kāt) *v.t.* **·cat·ed, ·cat·ing 1** To set apart for a special purpose, as funds. **2** To apportion; assign, as a share or in shares. **3** To locate or localize, as a person or event. [< Med.L *allocatus,* pp. of *allocare* < L *ad-* to + *locare* place < *locus* a place] **—al·lo·ca·ble** (al′ə·kə·bəl) *adj.*

al·lo·ca·tion (al′ə·kā′shən) *n.* **1** An allocating or being allocated. **2** Something allocated.

al·lo·ca·tur (al′ō·kā′tər) *n. Law* The judicial indorsement of a writ or order. [< Med.L, lit., it is allowed]

al·loch·tho·nous (ə·lok′thə·nəs) *adj.* Originating, formed, or developed elsewhere: distinguished from *autochthonous.* [< ALLO- + Gk. *chthōn* earth, land]

al·lo·cu·tion (al′ə·kyo͞o′shən) *n.* A formal, official, or authoritative exhortation or address. [< L *allocutio, -onis* < *alloqui* < *ad-* to + *loqui* speak]

al·lo·di·al (ə·lō′dē·əl) *adj. Law* Pertaining to the absolute ownership of land, free from rent or service: opposed to *feudal.* Also spelled *alodial.*

al·lo·di·um (ə·lō′dē·əm) *n. pl.* **·di·a** (-dē·ə) *Law* **1** The interest or estate in lands held in absolute ownership; estates in fee simple. **2** Land so held. Also spelled *alodium.* [< Med.L *allodium, alodium* < OHG *alōd, allōd* entire property < *all* all + *ōt* property]

al·log·a·my (ə·log′ə·mē) *n. Bot.* Fecundation of a flower by pollen from another flower of the same species; cross-fertilization: opposed to *autogamy.* [< ALLO- + Gk. *gamos* marriage] **—al·log′a·mous** *adj.*

al·lo·ge·ne·ic (al′ə·jə·nē′ik) *adj.* Differing genetically to the extent of having the potential to initiate an immune reaction. Also **al·lo·gen·ic** (al′ə·jen′ik) *adj.*

al·lo·graft (al′ə·graft, -gräft) *n.* A graft of tissue from a donor who differs genetically but is of the same species as the recipient; homograft.

al·lom·er·ism (ə·lom′ər·iz′əm) *n.* Constancy of crystalline form with variation in chemical constitution. [< ALLO-[2] + Gk. *meros* a part] **—al·lom′er·ous** *adj.*

al·lom·e·try (ə·lom′ə·trē) *n.* The relative changes in dimension of organs and parts of the body during development and growth of the organism as a whole. **—al·lo·met·ric** (al′ə·met′rik) *adj.*

al·lo·morph (al′ə·môrf) *n.* **1** *Mineral.* **a** A pseudomorph formed without change of chemical composition, as calcite after aragonite. Compare PARAMORPHISM. **b** A variety of pseudomorph the constituents of which have been partially or totally changed, or one which has assumed a substitute constituent. **2** *Ling.* Any of the positional variants of a morpheme. [< ALLO- + Gk. *morphē* form] **—al′lo·mor′phic** *adj.* **—al′lo·mor′phism** *n.*

al·lons (à·lôṅ′) *French* Let's go! Come on!

al·lo·nym (al′ə·nim) *n.* **1** The name of one person taken by another, especially by an author; a false name. **2** A book under such a name. [< ALLO- + Gk. *onyma* name] **—al·lon·y·mous** (ə·lon′ə·məs) *adj.*

al·lo·path·ic (al′ə·path′ik) *adj.* Pertaining to, favoring, or practicing allopathy. **—al′lo·path′i·cal·ly** *adv.*

al·lop·a·thy (ə·lop′ə·thē) *n. Med.* The system of remedial treatment in which it is sought to cure a disease by producing a condition different from or incompatible with the effects of the disease: opposed to *homeopathy.* [< ALLO- + Gk. *pathos* suffering] **—al·lop′a·thist, al·lo·path** (al′ə·path) *n.*

al·lo·pat·ric (al′ə·pat′rik) *adj.* Occurring in isolated areas, as organisms of the same species; separated geographically.

al·lo·phane (al′ə·fān) *n.* An amorphous, translucent mineral of variable color, composed mainly of a hydrated aluminum silicate. [< Gk. *allophanēs* appearing otherwise < *allos* other + *phainesthai* appear; with ref. to its change of appearance under the blowpipe]

al·lo·phone (al′ə·fōn) *n. Phonet.* Any of the nondistinctive variants of a phoneme: The velar (k) of *coop* and the palatal (k) of *keep* are *allophones* of the phoneme /k/. [< ALLO- + Gk. *phōnē* a sound, voice]

al·lo·some (al′ə·sōm) *n.* **1** Sex chromosome. **2** Any aberrant chromosome. [< ALLO- + Gk. *sōma* body]

al·lot (ə·lot′) *v.t.* **al·lot·ted, al·lot·ting 1** To assign by lot; distribute so that the recipients have no choice: to *allot* duties. **2** To apportion or assign, as to a special function, person, or place: with *to*: to *allot* ten years to the acquisition of knowledge. [< OF *aloter* < *a-* to (< L *ad-*) + *lot.* See LOT.]

Synonyms: appoint, apportion, assign, award, destine, distribute, divide, give, grant, select. *Allot* applies to the giving of a definite thing; a portion or extent of time or space is *allotted. Appoint* may be used of time, space, or person; as the *appointed* day; the *appointed* place; an officer was *appointed* to this station. *Destine* fixes or assumes to fix what is considerably in the future; as, he *destines* his son to follow his own profession. *Assign* is rarely used of time, but rather of places, persons, or things. That which is *alloted, appointed,* or *assigned* is more or less arbitrary; that which is *awarded* is the due return for something the receiver has done, and he has right and claim to it, as, the medal was *awarded* for valor. *Antonyms*: appropriate, confiscate, deny, refuse, resume, retain, seize, withhold.

al·lot·ment (ə·lot′mənt) *n.* **1** The act of allotting or that which is allotted. **2** *U.S. Mil.* A portion of one's pay assigned to a member of the family. **3** A plot of land. **4** Destiny.

al·lo·trope (al′ə·trōp) *n.* One of the forms assumed by an allotropic substance: The diamond is an *allotrope* of carbon.

al·lo·trop·ic (al′ə·trop′ik) *adj.* Of, pertaining to, or having the property of allotropy: Ozone is an *allotropic* form of oxygen. Also **al′lo·trop′i·cal.** **—al′lo·trop′i·cal·ly** *adv.*

al·lot·ro·pism (ə·lot′rə·piz′əm) *n.* Allotropy.

al·lot·ro·py (ə·lot′rə·pē) *n.* The property shown by certain elements of having more than one physical form, usually due to different groupings of atoms stable under different conditions, especially different temperatures. [< Gk. *allotropia* variation < *allos* other + *tropos* turn, manner]

all′ ot·ta·va (äl ôt·tä′vä) *Music* A direction placed above or below the staff to indicate that the music is to be performed an octave higher or lower than written. Abbr. *8va.* [< Ital., lit., at the octave]

al·lot·tee (ə·lot′ē′) *n.* One to whom anything is allotted.

al·lot·ter·y (ə·lot′ər·ē) *n. Obs.* Allotment; share; portion.

all-out (ôl′out′) *adj.* Complete and entire; to the fullest extent.

all-o·ver (ôl′ō′vər) *adj.* Having, resembling, or pertaining to a pattern extending over the entire surface. —*n.* (ôl′ō′vər) A fabric or other substance having such a pattern.

all-o·ver·ish (ôl′ō′vər·ish) *adj. Colloq.* Ill; sick; vaguely apprehensive and unwell.

al·low (ə·lou′) *v.t.* **1** To put no obstacle in the way of; permit to occur or do: Children are *allowed* in the park; He *allowed* the flowers to wither. **2** To admit; grant, as something claimed; acknowledge as true or valid: I *allow* her ability, but not her right to exercise it. **3** To make an addition, deduction, or concession of, as for a consideration not formally appearing in the reckoning: to *allow* three pounds extra for waste; to *allow* customers a month to pay. **4** To grant; allot, as a share or portion: The emperor *allowed* him one hundred pounds a year. **5** *U.S. Dial.* To maintain; declare. **6** *Archaic* Approve; sanction. —*v.i.* **7** To permit the occurrence or realization of: with *of*: Your remark *allows* of several interpretations. **8** To bear in mind as a modifying or extenuating circumstance; make due allowance for: with *for*: to *allow* for traffic conditions in getting to the train on time. [< OF *alouer* place, use, assign < Med.L *allocare* (see ALLOCATE) and OF *alouer, aloer* approve < L *allaudare* extol < *ad-* to + *laudare* praise] **—al·lowed′** *adj.*

Synonyms: admit, concede, confess, endure, grant, let, permit, sanction, suffer, tolerate, yield. We *allow* that which we do not attempt to hinder; we *permit* that to which we give express authorization; we *concede* a right; *grant* a request; *permit* an inspection of accounts; *sanction* a marriage; *tolerate* the rudeness of a well-meaning clerk; *submit* to a surgical operation; *yield* to a demand or necessity against our wish or will. *Suffer,* in the sense of mild concession, is now becoming rare. Compare PERMISSION. *Antonyms*: deny, disallow, disapprove, forbid, protest, refuse, reject, resist, withstand. See synonyms for PROHIBIT.

al·low·a·ble (ə·lou′ə·bəl) *adj.* That can be allowed; permissible; admissible. **—al·low′a·ble·ness** *n.* **—al·low′a·bly** *adv.*

al·low·ance (ə·lou′əns) *n.* **1** An allowing or being allowed. **2** That which is allowed. **3** A limited amount or portion, as of an income or food, granted at regular intervals. **4** A sum or item put to one's credit in a transaction, as in consideration of the exchange of the used article or a purchase in volume; discount: The dealer will give you an *allowance* on your old car. **5** A difference permitted in excess or abatement, as of a specification: to make *allowances* for haste. **6** *Obs.* Acknowledgment. See synonyms under PERMISSION, SALARY, SUBSIDY. —*v.t.* **·anced, ·anc·ing 1** To put on an allowance; limit to a regular amount. **2** To supply in limited or meager quantities.

Al·lo·way (al′ə·wā) A village near Ayr, Scotland; birthplace of Robert Burns.

al·low·ed·ly (ə·lou′id·lē) *adv.* By general allowance or admission; admittedly.

al·loy (al′oi, ə·loi′) *n.* Any of numerous substances having metallic properties and consisting of two or more elements of which at least one is a metal. **2** Anything that reduces purity. —*v.t.* (ə·loi′) **1** To reduce the purity of, as a metal, by mixing with an alloy. **2** To combine (substances) to form an alloy. **3** To modify or debase, as by mixture with something inferior. —*v.i.* To become a constituent of an alloy: Carbon *alloys* with iron to form steel. [< F *aloi,* OF *alei* < *aleier* combine < L *alligare ad-* to + *ligare* bind]

Synonyms (noun): admixture, adulteration, debasement, deterioration. *Adulteration, debasement,* and *deterioration* are always used in the bad sense; *admixture* is neutral, and may be good or bad; *alloy* is commonly good in the literal sense, as for giving hardness to coin, etc. An excess of *alloy* virtually amounts to *adulteration*; but *adulteration* is commonly restricted to articles used for food, drink, medicine, and kindred uses.

Al·loy steel A steel having special properties due to a constituent in addition to carbon and iron.

all-purpose (ôl′pûr′pəs) *adj.* Generally useful; answering every purpose.

all-right (ôl′rīt′) *adj. Slang* **1** Dependable; honest; loyal. **2** Good; excellent.

all right 1 Satisfactory: His work is *all right.* **2** Correct, as a result in addition. **3** Uninjured; not hurt: Were you *all right* after your fall? **4** Certainly; without a doubt: I'll be there *all right!* **5** Yes: usually in answer to a question: May I leave now? *All right.* See ALRIGHT.

all-round (ôl′round′) *adj.* **1** Of comprehensive range or scope; complete in action or effect. **2** Excelling in all or many aspects or departments of the same business or ability; many-sided; versatile. Also *all-around.*

All Saints The festival of the Church commemorative of all saints and martyrs, occurring Nov. 1; All-hallows; All-hallowmas. In the Greek Church it is observed on the first Sunday after Pentecost. Also **All Saints' Day.**

all·seed (ôl′sēd′) *n.* Any of various small many-seeded plants, as knotgrass, goosefoot, flaxwort, etc.

All Souls In the Roman Catholic Church, a day of commemoration, occurring Nov. 2, on which special intercession is made for the souls of all the faithful departed. Also **All Souls' Day.**

all·spice (ôl′spīs′) *n.* **1** The aromatic dried berry of a West Indian tree; the pimento. **2** The sharply flavored, fragrant spice made from it. [So called because thought to combine the flavors of several spices]

all-star (ôl′stär′) *adj.* Consisting wholly of star performers, as the cast of a play.

All·ston (ôl′stən), **Washington,** 1779–1843, U.S. painter.

all the same Without difference, notwithstanding.

all-time (ôl′tīm′) *adj.* Perennially popular; likely to endure for all time: an *all-time* favorite.

all told When all are counted.

al·lude (ə·lōōd′) *v.i.* **al·lud·ed, al·lud·ing** To refer without express mention; make indirect or casual reference: with *to.* [< L *alludere* play with, joke < *ad-* to + *ludere* play]

Synonyms: advert, hint, imply, indicate, insinuate, intimate, mention, point, refer, signify, suggest. *Allude* is erroneously used in the general sense of *mention* or *speak of.* We *allude* to a matter slightly, in passing; we *advert* to it when we turn from our path to treat it; we *refer* to it by any clear utterance or expression. One may *hint* at a thing in a friendly way, but what is *insinuated* is always unfavorable, generally both hostile and cowardly. One may *indicate* his wishes, *intimate* his plans, *imply* his opinion, *signify* his will, *suggest* a course of action. Compare SUGGESTION.

al·lure (ə·lōōr′) *v.t. & v.i.* **al·lured, al·lur·ing** To draw with or as with a lure; attract or exercise attraction; entice. —*n.* That which allures; allurement. [< OF *alurer, aleurrer* < *a-* to (< L *ad-*) + *leurre* lure. See LURE.] **—al·lur′er** *n.*

Synonyms (verb): attract, cajole, captivate, coax, decoy, draw, entice, inveigle, lure, seduce, tempt, win. One may *attract* without intent. One may *allure* to evil, but ordinarily to good. *Lure* is more akin to the physical nature and commonly used in an unfavorable sense. To *tempt* is to endeavor to lead one wrong; to *seduce* is to succeed in *winning* one from good to ill. *Win* may be used in a good sense, in which it surpasses the highest sense of *allure,* because it succeeds in that which *allure* attempts. *Coax* expresses the attraction of the person, not of the thing. A man may be *coaxed* to that which is by no means *alluring. Cajole* and *decoy* carry the idea of deceiving and ensnaring. To *inveigle* is to lead one blindly, as into folly or wrong. See DRAW, PERSUADE. *Antonyms*: chill, damp, deter, dissuade, repel, warn.

al·lure·ment (ə·lōōr′mənt) *n.* **1** Enticement; fascination; attraction. **2** A charm or bait. **3** The act of alluring, as by some charm or bait.

al·lur·ing (ə·lōōr′ing) *adj.* That draws as with a lure; attractive; fascinating. **—al·lur′ing·ly** *adv.* **—al·lur′ing·ness** *n.*

al·lu·sion (ə·lōō′zhən) *n.* **1** An alluding; indirect reference; suggestion. **2** A figure of speech consisting of a passing, but significant, reference to a well-known person, place, event etc. [< L *allusio, -onis* < *allusus,* pp. of *alludere.* See ALLUDE.]

al·lu·sive (ə·lōō′siv) *adj.* Having allusion to; suggestive; figurative. **—al·lu′sive·ly** *adv.* **—al·lu′sive·ness** *n.*

al·lu·vi·al (ə·lōō′vē·əl) *adj.* Pertaining to or composed of alluvium. —*n.* Alluvium.

alluvial cone *Geol.* The fan-shaped accumulation of detritus deposited where a river issues from a steep course upon flatland. Also called **alluvial fan.**

al·lu·vi·on (ə·lōō′vē·ən) *n.* **1** A flood deposit of earth; alluvium. **2** Inundation; flood. **3** The wash or flow of waves against the shore or banks. **4** *Law* The gradual increase of land by the action of flowing water. **5** *Geol.* A downpour of volcanic cinder mud. [< F < L *alluvio, -onis* a washing against, a flooding < *alluere* < *ad-* to + *luere* wash]

al·lu·vi·um (ə·lōō′vē·əm) *n. pl.* **·vi·a** (-vē·ə) or **·vi·ums** *Geol.* Deposits, as of sand or mud, transported and laid down by flowing water in river beds, flood-plains, lakes, and estuaries. [< L]

all wet *U.S. Slang* Completely wrong.

all wool *Colloq.* Absolutely genuine. **—all′-wool′** *adj.*

al·ly (ə·lī′) *v.* **al·lied, al·ly·ing** *v.t.* To unite or combine in an affinity, marriage, or association, by relationship, similarity of structure, treaty, or compact: generally in the passive with *to* or *with,* or used reflexively: The minister hoped to *ally* France with Spain against England; He *allied* himself with all liberal thinkers. —*v.i.* To enter into alliance; become allied. —*n.* (al′ī, ə·lī′) *pl.* **al·lies 1** A person or thing connected with another, usually in some relation of helpfulness or kinship; a state, sovereign, or chief leagued with another, as by treaty or common action. **2** Any friendly associate or helper. **3** An organism or substance associated with another by similarity of structure or properties. See synonyms under ACCESSORY, ADHERENT, ASSOCIATE, AUXILIARY. **—the Allies 1** The twenty-seven nations allied against the Central Powers in World War I; specifically, Russia, France, Great Britain, Italy, and Japan, adhering to the Declaration of London; the **Allied and Associated Powers** included twenty-two other nations, co-belligerent but not adhering to the Declaration. **2** The nations and governments-in-exile known as the United Nations in World War II. [< OF *alier* < L *alligare* < *ad-* to + *ligare* bind]

al·lyl (al′il) *n.* A univalent unsaturated radical, C_3H_5. [< L *allium* garlic + -YL] **—al·lyl·ic** (ə·lil′ik) *adj.*

allyl alcohol A pungent, flammable, poisonous liquid. CH_2:CH·CH_2OH.

allyl resin Any of a group of thermosetting synthetic resins derived from allyl compounds and used in laminated and molded plastic products.

allyl sulfide A colorless liquid, $(C_3H_5)_2S$, contained in garlic, onions, and other vegetables, giving them their characteristic taste and odor.

Al·ma (al′mə) A feminine personal name.

Al·ma A·ta (äl′mä ä′tä) The capital of Kazakh S.S.R.: formerly *Vyernyi.*

al·ma·cén (äl′mä·sän′) *n. pl.* **·ce·nes** (-sä′näs) *SW U.S.* **1** A warehouse. **2** A dockyard. [< Sp.]

Al·ma·dén (äl′mä·ᵺän′) A city in south central Spain; site of several rich mercury mines.

Al·ma·gest (al′mə·jest) *n.* **1** Ptolemy's huge work on astronomy, explaining the celestial motions on the geocentric system: named from the title of the Arabian translation of this work made in 827. **2** In medieval science, any authoritative treatise, as upon astrology or alchemy. Also **al′ma·gest.** [<OF *almageste* <Arabic *al-majistī* <*al* the + Gk. *megistē (syntaxis)* the greatest (work)]

al·mah (al′mə) *n.* An Egyptian dancing and singing girl: also spelled *alme, almeh.* Also **al′ma.** [<Arabic *'ālimah* learned]

al·ma ma·ter (al′mə mä′tər, al′mə mā′tər, äl′mə mä′tər) The institution of learning which one has attended. [<L, fostering mother]

al·ma·nac (ôl′mə·nak) *n.* A yearly calendar giving the days of the week and month through the year, with weather forecasts, astronomical information, times of high and low tides, and other tabulated data. [<Med.L <Sp. <Arabic *al-manākh*]

al·man·dine (al′mən·dēn, -din) *n.* A deep red to brownish variety of garnet composed of iron aluminum silicate. Also **al′man·dite** (-dīt). [for *alabandine,* from *Alabanda,* city in Asia Minor]

Al·ma-Tad·e·ma (al′mə·tad′ə·mə), **Sir Lawrence,** 1836–1912, English painter; born in the Netherlands.

al·me, al·meh (al′me) See ALMAH.

al·me·mar (al·mē′mär) *n.* In a Jewish synagog, the platform from which the Pentateuch and the Prophets are read. [<Arabic *al-minbar* the pulpit]

Al·me·rí·a (äl′mā·rē′ä) A seaport in SE Spain on the **Gulf of Almería,** an arm of the Mediterranean.

Al·me·ri·cus (al′mə·rī′kəs) Latin form of EMERY.

al·might·y (ôl·mī′tē) *adj.* **1** Able to do all things; omnipotent. **2** Great; remarkable. —*adv. Slang* Exceedingly: *almighty* mad. **—the Almighty** God; the Supreme Being. [OE *ealmihtig* <*eal* all + *mihtig* mighty]**—al·might′i·ly** *adv.* **—al·might′i·ness** *n.*

almighty dollar *Colloq.* Money conceived of as having or imparting great power.

Al·mi·ra (al·mī′rə) A feminine personal name. [<Arabic, lofty, a princess]

Al·mo·hades (al′mə·hādz, -hadz) *n. pl.* **1** Followers of a strictly monotheistic reform among the Moslems of North Africa, founded by Mohammed ibn Tumart (died 1128). **2** The Moslem dynasty in North Africa and Spain founded by them, which lasted from 1145 to 1269. **—Al′mo·hade** *adj. & n.* [<Arabic *al-muwahhid* the one who professes monotheism]

Al·mon (al′mən) A masculine personal name. [<Hebrew, hidden]

al·mond (ä′mənd, am′ənd) *n.* **1** A small rosaceous tree *(Prunus amygdalus)* widely cultivated in warm temperate regions. **2** The nutlike edible seed of this tree. **3** Anything having a flattened oval shape resembling the almond seed. **4** A pale brown, the color of an almond shell. [<OF *almande, amande* <L *amygdala* <Gk. *amygdalē*]

al·mon·er (al′mən·ər, ä′mən-) *n.* An official dispenser of alms; formerly, a household chaplain, as of a prince. Also **alm·ner** (alm′·nər, äm′nər). [<OF *almosnier* <LL *eleemosynarius* pertaining to alms <L *eleemosyna* alms. See ALMS.]

al·mon·ry (al′mən·rē, ä′mən-) *n. pl.* **·ries** The residence of an almoner; a place where alms are dispensed.

Al·mo·ra·vides (al·môr′ə·vīdz, -mō′rə-) *n. pl.* A Moslem dynasty in Africa and Spain in the 11th and 12th centuries which began as a religious revival under Abdallah-ibn-Yasin and lasted from 1056 to 1145. [<Arabic *al-murābit*] **Al·mo′ra·vide** *adj* & *n.*

al·most (ôl′mōst′ ôl·mōst′) *adv.* Approximately; very nearly; all but. —*adj.* not quite: to have *almost* nothing. [OE *ealmæst.* See ALL, MOST.]

al·mous (al′məs, ä′məs, ô′məs) See AWMOUS.

alms (ämz) *n. sing. & pl.* A gift or gifts for the poor; charitable offerings; charity. Some self-explaining compounds have *alms* as their first element: **almsgiver, almsgiving, almsmoney,** etc. Collateral adjective: *eleemosynary.* [OE *ælmesse* <L *eleemosyna* alms <Gk. *eleēmosynē* <*eleos* pity]

alms·deed (ämz′dēd′) *n.* An act of charity.

alms·house (ämz′hous′) *n.* **1** A house where paupers are supported; a poorhouse. **2** In England, a house where deserving poor people are supported by charity, generally on a charitable foundation.

alms·man (ämz′mən) *n. pl.* **·men** (-mən) **1** One supported by charity. **2** *Obs.* A giver of alms. **—alms′wom′an** *n. fem.*

al·muce (al′myōōs) *n.* A hood or hooded cape lined with fur, formerly worn by clergymen and monks: also spelled *amice.* [<OF *aumuce* <Med.L *almutia*]

ALMUCE
From tomb of Philip the Bold 13th Cent., French.

al·mud (al·mōōd′) *n.* A liquid and dry measure of Turkey, Spain, and some other countries, varying from about 2 to 32 quarts. Also **al·mude′.** [<Sp. <Arabic *al-mudd*]

al·mug (al′mug) *n.* A precious wood used for the making of harps, psalteries, etc.: also *algum.* [<Hebrew]

al·ni·co (al′nə·kō) *n.* Any of a group of ferrous alloys containing aluminum, nickel, and cobalt and having persistent magnetic properties.

a·lo·di·al (ə·lō′dē·əl), **a·lo·di·um** (-əm) See ALLODIAL, etc.

al·oe (al′ō) *n. pl.* **·oes 1** Any member of a genus *(Aloe)* of Old World plants of the lily family, some species of which furnish a drug, and others valuable fiber. **2** *pl. (construed as singular)* A bitter cathartic obtained from the juice of certain species of aloe. **3** *pl. (construed as singular)* Agalloch. [OE *aluwe* <L *aloe* <Gk. *aloē*]**—al·o·et·ic** (al′ō·et′ik) *adj.*

A·lo·fi (ä·lō′fē) See WALLIS AND FUTUNA ISLANDS.

a·loft (ə·lôft′, ə·loft′) *adv.* **1** In or to a high or higher place; on high; high up. **2** *Naut.* At or to the higher parts of a ship's rigging. [<ON *a lopt* in (the) air]

A·lo·gi·an (ə·lō′jē·ən) *n. pl.* **Al·o·gi** (al′ə·jī) or **A·lo·gi·ans** One of a sect of the second and third centuries that rejected the doctrine that Jesus is the Logos, and denied the authenticity of the Fourth Gospel and the Apocalypse. [<Med.L *alogiani* <Gk. *alogioi* <*a-* not + *logos* word]

a·lo·ha (ə·lō′ə, ä·lō′hä) *n. Hawaiian* Love: used also as a salutation and a farewell.

al·o·in (al′ō·in) *n.* A bitter crystalline substance of varying composition, obtained from aloes and forming its purgative principle.

A·lois (ə·lois′) See ALOYSIUS.

al·o·man·cy (al′ə·man′sē) See HALOMANCY.

a·lone (ə·lōn′) *adv. & adj.* **1** Without company; solitary. **2** Without equal; unique; unparalleled. **3** Excluding all others; solely; only. [ME *al one* all alone]

a·long (ə·lông′, ə·long′) *adv.* **1** Over, through, or following the length of in time or space; lengthwise. **2** Progressively onward in the course of motion. **3** In company or association: with *with:* I came *along* with my cousins. **4** Together; side by side: The donkey came *along* all the way. **5** Advanced in age or duration: well *along* in years. **—all along** The whole time; from the outset. **—along with** As well as; in addition to. **—right along** Continuously. **—to get along 1** To manage in spite of difficulties. **2** To go away: *Get along* with you! **3** To exist together in harmony: Her cat and dog *get along* very well. —*prep.* **1** In the line of; through or over the length of: The ship sailed *along* the coast. **2** At points throughout or over the length of: Trees are planted *along* the road. **3** During the course of; throughout: *along* the track of centuries. [OE *andlang*]

along of *Illit. & Dial.* Because of.

a·long·shore (ə·lông′shôr′, ə·long′-, -shōr′) *adv.* Along the shore, either on the water or on the land.

a·long·side (ə·lông′sīd′, ə·long′-) *adv.* Close to or along the side. —*prep.* Side by side with; at the side of.

A·lon·zo (ə·lon′zō) See ALPHONSO. Also *Sp.* **A·lon·so** (ä·lōn′sō).

a·loof (ə·lōōf′) *adj.* Distant, especially in manner or interest; not in sympathy with or desiring to associate with others. —*adv.* At a distance; apart: to stand, keep, or hold *aloof.* [<A-[1] + *loof* <Du. *loef* LUFF] **—a·loof′ly** *adv.*

al·o·pe·ci·a (al′ə·pē′shē·ə, -sē·ə) *n.* Loss of hair; partial or total baldness. [<L, baldness, fox mange <Gk. *alōpekia* <*alōpēx* fox]

A·lost (ȧ·lôst′) A town in central Belgium NW of Brussels. *Flemish* **Aalst** (älst).

a·loud (ə·loud′) *adv.* Loudly or audibly.

a·low[1] (ə·lō′) *adv.* In or to a lower position; below: opposed to *aloft.*

a·low[2] (ə·lou′) *adv. Scot.* In a blaze; on fire. Also **a·lowe′.**

Al·o·ys·ius (al′ō·ish′əs, -is′ē·əs) A masculine personal name: also *Alois.* [See LOUIS.]

alp (alp) *n.* **1** Any peak of the Alps. **2** An alpine pasture. **3** A lofty mountain. [<L *Alpes* the Alps]

al·pac·a (al·pak′ə) *n.* **1** A domesticated ruminant *(Lama pacos)* of South America related to the guanaco and llama. **2** Its long, silky wool. **3** Cloth made from the wool of the alpaca. **4** A glossy, usually black fabric made of various fiber combinations other than alpaca wool. [<Sp. <Arabic *al* the + Peruvian *paco* name of the animal]

ALPACA
(About 3½ feet high at the shoulder)

al·pen·glow (al′pən·glō′) *n.* **1** The rosy light of the rising or setting sun, seen on the Alps or other mountains. **2** The reappearance of the sunset colors on a mountain summit after the original colors have faded. **3** A similar phenomenon preceding the regular sunrise coloration. [Trans. of G *Alpenglühen*]

al·pen·horn (al′pən·hôrn′) See ALPHORN.

al·pen·stock (al′pən·stok′) *n.* A long, iron-pointed staff, used by mountain-climbers. [<G, lit., alps stick]

al·pes·trine (al·pes′trin) *adj.* **1** Of, pertaining to, or growing on mountain heights below the limit of forest growth. **2** Subalpine. [<L *alpestris* <L *Alpes* Alps]

al·pha (al′fə) *n.* **1** The first letter and vowel in the Greek alphabet (Α, α); corresponding to English a. As a numeral it denotes 1. **2** The beginning or first of anything. **—the alpha and omega** Both the first and the last; beginning and end; the sum total: used of Christ. *Rev.* i 8. —*adj.* **1** Designating the first in order of importance or discovery: *alpha* test. **2** *Chem.* Denoting a carbon atom next to a designated carbon in an organic molecule. **3** *Physics* Denoting the first of a series of radiations or emissions arranged in order of increasing frequency: *alpha* rays, *alpha* particle. [<Gk. <Hebrew *aleph* OX]

Al·pha (al′fə) *n. Astron.* The principal or brightest star in a constellation.

al·pha·bet (al′fə·bet) *n.* **1** The letters that form the elements of written language, in order as fixed by usage: in English, 26 in number. **2** Any system of characters or symbols representing the simple sounds of speech. See TABLE OF FOREIGN ALPHABETS on next page. **3** The simplest elements or rudiments of anything. —*v.t.* To alphabetize. [<L *alphabetum* <Gk. *alpha* a + *bēta* b]

al·pha·bet·ic (al′fə·bet′ik) *adj.* **1** Pertaining to, having, or expressed by an alphabet. **2** Arranged in the order of the alphabet. Also **al′pha·bet′i·cal.** **—al′pha·bet′i·cal·ly** *adv.*

al·pha·bet·ize (al·fə·bə·tīz′) *v.t.* **·ized, ·iz·ing 1** To put in alphabetical order. **2** To express by or furnish with an alphabet or alphabetic symbols. **—al·pha·bet·i·za·tion** (al′fə·bet′ə·zā′shən) *n.* **—al′pha·bet·iz′er** *n.*

Alpha Cen·tau·ri (sen·tôr′ē) *Astron.* The principal star in the constellation of Centaurus; the third brightest star in the heavens.

alpha helix A spiral arrangement of amino acids in certain protein molecules, forming a cylinder with side groups projecting outward.

TABLE OF FOREIGN ALPHABETS

(1) ARABIC

ا	alif	—[1]
ب	ba	b
ت	ta	t
ث	sa	th
ج	jim	j
ح	ha	h
خ	kha	kh
د	dal	d
ذ	zal	t͟h
ر	ra	r
ز	za	z
س	sin	s
ش	shin	sh
ص	sad	s
ض	ḍad	d
ط	ta	t
ظ	za	z
ع	ain	—[2]
غ	ghain	gh[3]
ف	fa	f
ق	qaf	k[4]
ك	kaf	k[5]
ل	lam	l
م	mim	m
ن	nun	n
ه	ha	h
و	waw	w
ي	ya	y

(2) HEBREW

א	aleph	—[6]
בּ, ב	beth	b, v
גּ, ג	gimel	g, gh[3]
דּ, ד	daleth	d, t͟h
ה	he	h
ו	vav	v
ז	zayin	z
ח	ḥeth	kh
ט	ṭeth	t
י	yod	y
כּ, כ, ך[8]	kaph	k[5], kh
ל	lamed	l
מ, ם[8]	mem	m
נ, ן[8]	nun	n
ס	samek	s
ע	ayin	—[7]
פּ, פ, ף[8]	pe	p, f
צ, ץ[8]	sade	s
ק	koph	k[4]
ר	resh	r
שׁ, שׂ	sin, shin	s, sh
תּ, ת	tav	t, th

(3) GREEK

Α	α	alpha	ä
Β	β	beta	b
Γ	γ	gamma	g
Δ	δ	delta	d
Ε	ε	epsilon	e
Ζ	ζ	zeta	z
Η	η	eta	ā
Θ	θ	theta	th[9]
Ι	ι	iota	ē
Κ	κ	kappa	k
Λ	λ	lambda	l
Μ	μ	mu	m
Ν	ν	nu	n
Ξ	ξ	xi	ks
Ο	ο	omicron	o
Π	π	pi	p
Ρ	ρ	rho	r
Σ	σ, ς[8]	sigma	s
Τ	τ	tau	t
Υ	υ	upsilon	ü, o͞o
Φ	φ	phi	f[10]
Χ	χ	chi	kh[11]
Ψ	ψ	psi	ps
Ω	ω	omega	ō

(4) RUSSIAN

А	а	ä
Б	б	b
В	в	v
Г	г	g
Д	д	d
Е	е	e, ye
Ж	ж	zh
З	з	z
И	и	ē, yē
Й	й	e[12]
К	к	k
Л	л	l
М	м	m
Н	н	n
О	о	ô, o
П	п	p
Р	р	r
С	с	s
Т	т	t
У	у	o͞o
Ф	ф	f
Х	х	kh
Ц	ц	ts
Ч	ч	ch
Ш	ш	sh
Щ	щ	shch
Ъ	ъ	—[13]
Ы	ы	œ
Ь	ь	—[14]
Э	э	e
Ю	ю	yo͞o
Я	я	yä

(5) GERMAN

𝔄	𝔞	ä
𝔄̈	𝔞̈	e
𝔅	𝔟	b
ℭ	𝔠	k, ts, s
𝔇	𝔡	d
𝔈	𝔢	e, ā
𝔉	𝔣	f
𝔊	𝔤	g
ℌ	𝔥	h
ℑ	𝔦	i, ē
ℑ	𝔧	y
𝔎	𝔨	k
𝔏	𝔩	l
𝔐	𝔪	m
𝔑	𝔫	n
𝔒	𝔬	ŏ, ô
𝔒	𝔬̈	œ
𝔓	𝔭	p
𝔔(u)	𝔮(u)	k(v)
ℜ	𝔯	r
𝔖	ſ, 𝔰[8]	s, z
𝔗	𝔱	t
𝔘	𝔲	o͞o, o͝o
𝔘̈	𝔲̈	ü
𝔙	𝔳	f
𝔚	𝔴	v
𝔛	𝔵	ks
𝔜	𝔶	ē, ü
ℨ	𝔷	ts

In each column the characters of the alphabet are given first, followed by the names of the characters in Arabic, Hebrew, and Greek. The last row in each column shows the approximate English sound represented by each character. Columns 3, 4, and 5 show the upper- and lower-case forms. The Arabic characters are given in their final, unconnected forms. The German style of letter, called *fraktur*, has, since the 1880's, been gradually replaced in German printing by the Latin letter.

[1] Functions as the bearer of hamza (the glottal stop), or as a lengthener of short *a*. [2] A voiced pharyngeal fricative. [3] A voiced velar fricative. [4] A uvular stop. [5] A voiceless velar stop. [6] A glottal stop, now usually silent, or pronounced according to the accompanying vowel points. [7] A pharyngeal fricative, now usually silent, or pronounced according to the accompanying vowel points. [8] The alternate form is restricted to the ends of words. [9, 10, 11] In classical Greek these were pronounced as aspirated stops similar to the sounds in foo*th*ill, ha*ph*azard, and bloc*kh*ouse. [12] Appears only as the second vowel in a diphthong. [13] Formerly, a sign of non-palatalization of consonants at the ends of words; since 1918, used only between two syllables to indicate that they are separately pronounced. [14] A sign of palatalization of a preceding consonant.

---

alpha iron The common allotrope of iron, stable below 770° and having a cubic crystalline structure and magnetic properties.

al·pha·nu·mer·ic (al′fə·no͞o·mer′ik, -nyo͞o-) *adj.* Able to use both letters and numbers: an *alphanumeric* computer.

alpha particle *Physics* The positively charged nucleus of the helium atom (H^4), consisting of two protons and two neutrons; it is a product of disintegration of various isotopes of both natural and artificial radioactive elements.

alpha privative In Greek grammar, a prefix having negative or privative force, as in *atheos* godless. See A-[4], AN-[1]. ◆ The term is also applied to this prefix as naturalized in English, where it is sometimes used to express a shade of meaning different from that of the other negative prefixes, the Latin-derived *in-* and *non-*, and the native *un-*. *A-*, *an-*, as prefixed to terms or stems of Greek or Latin origin, often means "apart from" or "not concerned with,": An *amoral* approach to economics is one not concerned with moral issues.

alpha ray *Physics* A stream of alpha particles, emitted with an initial velocity and over a mean range varying with the source and method of production.

alpha rhythm A frequency of 8 to 18 per second in brain waves, characteristic of a relaxed resting state in normal human adults.

alpha star *Physics* A starlike formation in a photographic emulsion, consisting of short heavy tracks identifying the paths of slow alpha particles emitted from a radioactive element.

al·pha·to·coph·er·ol (al′fə·tō·kof′ər·ōl, -ol) *n.* A light-yellow oily liquid obtained from wheat germ oil or produced synthetically and having potent vitamin E activity.

Al·phe·ratz (al′fə·rats′) The brightest star in the constellation Andromeda: also called *Sirrah.*

Al·phe·us (al·fē′əs) In Greek mythology, a river god who fell in love with the nymph Arethusa, changing into a river to mingle with her when she had become a fountain to escape him.

Al·phe·us (al·fē′əs) The chief river of the Peloponnesus, Greece, flowing NW 69 miles: formerly *Rouphia. Greek* **Al·fiós** (äl·fyôs′).

Al·phon·so (al·fon′zō, -sō) A masculine personal name. Also *Fr.* **Al·phonse** (äl·fôns′), *Lat.* **Al·phon·sus** (al·fon′səs). See also ALFONSO.

alp·horn (alp′hôrn′) *n.* A slightly curved, very sonorous horn, made of wood and from 7 to 12 feet long, used by cowherds in the Alps and formerly by Swiss soldiers: also *alpenhorn.* [<Gk. *alpenhorn* horn of the Alps]

Al·pine (al′pīn, -pin) *adj.* **1** Pertaining to or characteristic of the Alps. **2** Designating a European racial stock found in the Alps and adjacent districts, and marked by medium height, broad short skull and face, and brunette coloring. [<L *Alpinus*]

al·pine (al′pīn, -pin) *adj.* **1** Like an alp or mountain; lofty and towering: alpine *terrian.* **2** Occurring in regions above the timberline in mountains or tundra. —*n.* A plant native to treeless tundra or mountain tops.

habiting or growing in mountain regions above the limits of forest growth.
alpine garden A garden for alpine plants, especially a rock garden.
al·pi·nist (al′pə·nist) *n.* A climber of alps; a mountaineer. **—al′pi·nism** *n.*
Al·pi·no (äl·pē′nō) *n.* pl. **Al·pi·ni** (-pē′nē) A member of a body of Italian troops trained for Alpine or mountain warfare. [<Ital.]
Alps (alps) A mountain system of southern Europe, extending 680 miles from the Mediterranean coast of southern France to the Adriatic coast of Yugoslavia, separating the Po valley of northern Italy from the lowlands of France, Germany, and the Danubian plain; highest peak, 15,781 feet.
al·read·y (ôl·red′ē) *adv.* Before or by this time or the time mentioned; even now. [<ALL + READY]
al·right (ôl·rīt′) All right: a spelling not yet considered acceptable.
Al·sace (al·sās′, al′sas; *Fr.* àl·zàs′) A region and former province of France along the Rhine border of Germany: ancient **Al·sa·tia** (al·sā′shə): German *Elass.*
Al·sace-Lor·raine (al′sās·lə) ·rān′, al′ ·sas-; *Fr.* àl·zà s′· lô·ren′) A disputed (border region between NE France and SW Germany; ceded to Germany in 1871, regained by France in 1919, annexed by Germany in 1940, regained by France in 1945: German *Elsass-Lothringen.*

Al·sa·tia (al·sā′shə) A section of London, formerly a sanctuary for insolvent debtors and criminals: also called *Whitefriars.* [<Med.L <G *Elsass,* lit., foreign settlement]
Al·sa·tian (al·sā′shən) *adj.* **1** Of or pertaining to Alsace. **2** Of or pertaining to Alsatia. —*n.* **1** A native or inhabitant of Alsace. **2** A resident of Alsatia; hence, a debtor or criminal in sanctuary. **3** A German shepherd.
al·sike (al′sīk, -sik, ôl′-) *n.* A leguminous forage plant *(Trifolium hybridum)* with pink or white flowers. Also **Alsike clover.** [from *Alsike,* Swedish town]
Al·si·rat (al′sē·rät′) **1** In the Moslem religion, the bridge and only way to paradise over the abyss of hell: said to be finer than a hair and sharper than a razor. **2** In the Koran, the narrow path or correct way of religion. [<Arabic *al-ṣirāt* the road]
al·so (ôl′sō) *adv.* & conj. **1** As something further tending in the same direction; besides; in addition: They *also* serve who only stand and wait. **2** In like manner; likewise: to provide for the pupils and *also* for the teachers. [OE *alswā, ealswā* all (wholly) so.]
al·so-ran (ôl′so·ran′) *n.* U.S. Colloq. **1** A horse that fails to win, place, or show in a race. **2** Hence, an unsuccessful candidate in an election or competition.
alt (alt) *Music adj.* Alto; high-pitched in the musical scale. —*n.* The octave next above the treble staff. **—in alt** In this octave. [<Ital. *alto* <L *al-tus* high]
Al·tai Mountains (al·tī′, äl-) A mountain system of central Asia at the juncture of China, Mongolia, and the U.S.S.R.; highest peak, 15,157 feet. Also **Al·tay′.**
Altai Territory A region of SW Siberia; 101,000 square miles; capital, Barnaul.
Al·ta·ian (al·tā′ən, -tī) ′-) *n.* One of the peoples of the Altai Mountains or of the Ural-Altaic linguistic group. —*adj.* Altaic.
Al·ta·ic (al·tā′ik) *n.* A family of agglutinative languages of Europe and Asia, generally considered to comprise the Turkic, Mongolian, and Manchu-Tungusic subfamilies: sometimes classified with Uralic in a Ural-Altaic family. —*adj.* **1** Of the Altai Mountains. **2** Pertaining to the peoples and languages of the Ural-Altaic stock; Turanian. Also *Altaian.*
Al·ta·ir (al·tä′ir, al·târ′) The brightest star in the constellation Aquila; one of the 20 brightest stars. See STAR. [<Arabic *al-ṭā′ir* the bird]
Al·ta·ma·ha River (ôl′tə·mə·hô′) A river in SE Georgia, flowing 137 miles SE to the Atlantic Ocean.
Al·ta·mi·ra (äl′tä·mē ′rä) A cave near Santander, in Spain, noted for the early Stone Age drawings on its walls.

ALTAMIRA
A cave drawing.

al·tar (ôl′tər) *n.* **1** Any raised place or structure on which sacrifices may be offered or incense burned as an act of worship. **2** *Eccl.* The structure of wood or stone on which the elements are consecrated in the Eucharist; the communion table. **—to lead to the altar** To marry. ◆) Homophone: *alter.*([OE <L *altare* high altar <*altus* high]
Al·tar (ôl′tər) The constellation Ara.
al·tar·age (ôl′tər·ij) *n.* Eccl. **1** A revenue from altar offerings. **2** The endowment of an altar for general or special masses.
altar boy An attendant at the altar; acolyte.
altar bread *Eccl.* Bread used in the Eucharist, especially the unleavened wafer used in some churches.
al·tar·piece (ôl′tər·pē s′) *n.* A painting, mosaic, or bas-relief over and behind the altar; a reredos.
alt·az·i·muth (alt·az′ə·məth) *n.* Astron. An instrument with two graduated circles, one vertical and one horizontal, for measuring the altitude and azimuth of celestial bodies.
Alt·dorf (ält′dôrf) The capital of Uri canton in central Switzerland; scene of traditional exploits of William Tell.
Al·ten·burg (äl′tən·bo͝org) A city in eastern Thuringia, Germany.
al·ter (ôl′tər) *v.t.* **1** To cause to be different; change; modify; transform. **2** To castrate or spay. —*v.i.* **3** To become different; change, as in character or appearance. See synonyms under CHANGE. ◆Homophone: *altar.* [<MF *altérer* <Med.L *alterare* <L *alter* other]
al·ter·a·bil·i·ty (ôl′tə) r·ə·bil′ə·tē) *n.* Liability to or capacity for change.
al·ter·a·ble (ôl′tər·ə) ·bəl) *adj.* Capable of alteration. **—al·ter·a·bil·i·ty** (ôl′tər·ə·bil′ə·tē), **al′ter·a·ble·ness** *n.* **—al′ter·a·bly** *adv.*
al·ter·a·tion (ôl′tə·rā ′shən) *n.* **1** The act or result of altering; or the state of being altered; modification; change. **2** *Geol.* Any change in the composition or texture of a rock occurring subsequent to its formation but not due to a cementing or induration of its original constituents. —*adj.* Of or pertaining to a geological alteration: Can *alteration* product. See synonyms under CHANGE.
al·ter·a·tive (ôl′tə·rā ′tiv) *adj.* **1** Tending to produce change. **2** *Med.* Tending to change gradually the bodily condition to a normal state. —*n.* An alterative medicine or treatment. Also **al·ter·ant** (ôl′tər·ənt).
al·ter·cate (ôl′tər·kāt, al′-) *v.i.* **·cat·ed, ·cat·ing** To dispute vehemently; wrangle. [<L *altercatus,* pp. of *altercari* <*alter* other]
al·ter·ca·tion (ôl′tər·kā′shən, al′-) *n.* Angry controversy; disputing; wrangling.
Synonyms: affray, brawl, broil, contention, controversy, debate, discussion, disputation, dispute, dissension, disturbance, fracas, quarrel, wrangle, wrangling. *Dispute* is preferably used of rights and claims; as, the title or the will is in *dispute; debate* and *discussion* refer rather to abstract matters, and may be entirely amicable. *Disputation* has a touch of bitterness. *Altercation, contention, controversy,* and *wrangle* are all words signifying more or less of ill-feeling; so is *dispute* in common speech; as, a sharp *dispute. Contention* and *controversy* are capable of a good sense in the learned or elevated style. See QUARREL. *Antonyms:* agreement, concord, consonance, harmony, unanimity, unity.
al·ter e·go (ôl′tər ē′gō, al′tər eg′ō) **1** Another self; a double. **2** An intimate friend. [<L, lit., other I]
al·ter i·dem (al′tər ī′dem) *Latin* Another self; a duplicate.
al·ter·nate (ôl′tər·nāt, al′-) *v.* **·nat·ed, ·nat·ing** *v.t.* **1** To arrange, use, or perform in alternation. **2** To cause to succeed and be succeeded by continuously: with *by* or *with:* to *alternate* a passive with an active style. —*v.i.* **3** To occur or appear alternately. **4** To take turns: to *alternate* on a job. **5** To pass from one thing or condition to another and back again repeatedly: Cycles of depression and inflation *alternate.* **6** *Electr.* To change from the positive to the negative direction and back rapidly; vibrate; pulsate. —*adj.* (ôl′tər·nit, al′-) **1** Existing, occurring, or following by turns; reciprocal. **2** Referring or pertaining to every other (of a series). **3** Alternative: an *alternate* method. **4** *Bot.* **a** Placed singly at regular intervals on opposite sides of the stem, as leaves. **b** Disposed by turn among other parts, as stamens opposite the intervals between petals. —*n.* (ô l′tər·nit, al′-) A substitute or second; especially, one substituting for another in the performance of a duty or in the filling of a position; a second choice. [<L *alternatus,* pp. of *alternare* <*alternus* every second one < *alter* other] **—al′ter·nate·ness** *n.*
alternate angle See under ANGLE.
al·ter·nate·ly (ôl′tər·nit·lē, al′-) *adv.* In alternate order or position; by turns.
alternating current See under CURRENT.
al·ter·na·tion (ôl′tər·nā′shən, al′-) *n.* Occurrence or action of two things or series of things in turn; passage from one place, state, or condition to another and back again: *alternation* between day and night.
alternation of generations Metagenesis.
al·ter·na·tive (ôl·tûr′nə·tiv, al-) *adj.* **1** Affording a choice between two things. **2** Of or pertaining to alternation; implying or involving an alternative: *alternative* conjunctions. **3** Occurring outside the boundaries of the established social, economic, or medical systems. —*n.* **1** Something that may or must be instead of something else; a choice between two things: used sometimes, loosely, of more than two. **2** One of the things to be chosen. **—al·ter′na·tive·ly** *adv.* **—al·ter′na·tive·ness** *n.*
Synonyms: choice, election, option, pick, preference, resource. A *choice* may be among many things; an *alternative* is in the strictest sense of *choice* between two things, but the usage is often extended to more than two. *Option* is the right or privilege of choosing; *choice* may be either the right to choose, the act of choosing, or the thing chosen. A *choice, pick, election,* or *preference* is that which suits one best; an *alternative* is that to which one is restricted; a *resource,* that to which one is glad to betake oneself. *Antonyms:* compulsion, necessity.
al·ter·na·tor (ôl′tər·nā ′tər, al′-) *n.* **1** One who or that which alternates. **2** *Electr.* A dynamo giving an alternating current. Also **al′ter·nat′ er.**
al·the·a (al·thē′ə) *n.* Any of a small but widely distributed genus *(Althaea)* of herbs with large flowers, including the hollyhock and the marshmallow. **2** The rose of Sharon (def. 2). Also **althaea.** [<L <Gk. *althaia* wild mallow]
Al·the·a (al·thē′ə) A feminine personal name. [<Gk., wholesome] **—Althaea** In Greek mythology, the wife of Oeneus and mother of Meleager.
alt·horn (alt′hôrn′) *n.* A wind instrument of the saxhorn class: used by military bands. [<ALT + HORN]
al·though (ôl·thō′) *conj.* Admitting or granting that; though: *Although* I believe the contrary, I accept your explanation. Also **al·tho′.** [<ALL + THOUGH]
alti- *combining from* High: *altiscope.* Also *alto-.* [<L < *altus* high]
al·ti·graph (al′tə·graf, -grä f) *n.* A recording altimeter.
al·tim·e·ter (al·tim′ə·tə) r, al′tə·mē′tər) *n.* **1** An aneroid barometer calibrated to permit accurate determination of altitudes above sea level, especially by aircraft pilots. **2** Any similar instrument operating by radio waves, etc. **—al·tim·ee·try** (al·tim′ə) ·trē) *n.*
al·ti·pla·no (äl′ti·plä′nō) *n.* High upland plateaus, especially in Andean countries. [<Sp. <Latin *altus* high + *planus* level]
al·ti·scope (al′tə·skōp) *n.* A periscope.
al·tis·o·nant (al·tis′ə·nənt) *adj.* High-sounding; pompous.
al·ti·tude (al′tə·to͞od; -tyo͞o d) *n.* **1** Vertical elevation above any given point, especially

above mean sea level; height. 2 *Astron.* Angular elevation above the horizon. 3 *Geom.* The vertical distance from the base of a figure to its highest point. 4 A high or the highest point. See synonyms under HEIGHT. [<L *altitudo* <*altus* high]

altitude sickness A syndrome of varying severity due to inadequate atmospheric oxygen at the low barometric pressures obtaining at high altitudes and including hyperventilation, dizziness, nausea, etc.

al·ti·tu·di·nal (al′tə·to͞o′də·nəl, -tyo͞o′-) *adj.* Relating to altitude.

al·to (al′tō) *adj.* Sounding or ranging between tenor and treble. —*n. pl.* **·tos** 1 The lowest female voice; contralto. 2 The highest male voice, or countertenor. 3 A singer who has an alto voice. 4 A tenor violin. 5 An althorn. [<Ital. <L *altus* high]

alto- See ALTI-.

al·to·cu·mu·lus (al′tō·kyo͞o′myə·ləs) *n.* Meteorol. A fleecy cloud, usually a rounded mass: also called *cumulocirrus*.

al·to·geth·er (ôl′tə·geth′ər, ôl′tə·geth′ər) *n.* A whole; also, the general effect; tout ensemble. —**in the altogether** *Colloq.* In the nude. —*adv.* 1 Completely; wholly; entirely. 2 With everything included; in all; all told. [<ALL + TOGETHER]

Al·to·na (äl′tō·nä) The major fishing port of Hamburg, Germany.

Al·too·na (al·to͞o′nə) A city in central Pennsylvania.

al·to-re·lie·vo (al′tō·ri·lē′vō) *n. pl.* **·vos** High relief; sculptured or carved work in which the carving, figures, etc., stand out very strongly from the background: contrasted with *bas-relief*. See RELIEF. [<Ital.]

al·to-ri·lie·vo (äl′tō·rē·lyâ′vō) *n. pl.* **al·ti·ri·lie·vi** (äl′tē·rē·lyâ′vē) *Italian* Alto-relievo.

al·to·stra·tus (al′tō·strā ′təs) *n.* Meteorol. A gray to bluish-gray cloud, usually forming a compact mass.

al·toun (ôl′to͞on) *n.* Scot. Old town.

al·tri·cial (al·trish′əl) *adj.* Having young that hatch in a naked and helpless state requiring care by one or both parent birds. Compare *precocial*. [<L *altrices*, pl. of *altrix* a nurse + -IAL]

al·tru·ism (al′tro͞o·iz′əm) *n.* 1 Devotion to the interests of others; disinterested benevolence: opposed to *egoism*. 2 *Biol.* Consistent behavior by individual organisms that tends to decrease the total reproductive output of the individual while enhancing that of other members of the group or species. [<F *altruisme*, ult. <L *alter* other]

al·tru·ist (al′tro͞o·ist) *n.* One devoted to or professing altruism.

al·tru·is·tic (al′tro͞o·is′tik) *adj.* Pertaining to altruism or altruists. —**al′tru·is′ti·cal·ly** *adv.*

al·u·del (al′yə·del) *n.* Chem. One of a series of pear-shaped vessels of glass or earthenware fitted one into another and used for condensation, as in subliming mercury. [<F <Sp. <Arabic *al-uthāl* the utensil]

A·luin (à·lwaṅ′) French form of ALVIN. Also *Sp.* **A·lui·no** (ä·lwē′nō).

al·u·la (al′yə·lə) *n. pl.* **·lae** (lē) 1 *Ornithol.* A tuft of feathers on that part of a bird's wing homologous to the thumb. Also called *bastard wing*. 2 *Entomol.* A membranous lobe separated from the wing base in certain flies. [<NL, dim. of L *ala* wing] —**al′u·lar** *adj.*

al·um (al′əm) *n.* 1 An astringent white crystalline double salt of potassium and aluminum sulfates ($KAl(SO_4)_2 \cdot 12H_2O$) widely used in medicine, manufacturing and the arts. 2 Any of a class of double sulfates of a univalent metal such as potassium or sodium and a trivalent metal such as aluminum, chromium, iron, etc. [<OF <L *alumen*]

A·lum·bra·do (ä′lo͞om·brä ′dō) *n.* One of a Spanish sect of the 16th century. See ILLUMINATI. [<Sp., lit., illuminated]

a·lu·mi·na (ə·lo͞o′mə·nə) *n.* A native aluminum oxide (Al_2O_3), occurring as corundum and, in hydrated or impure form, as bauxite. [<NL <L *alumen, -minis* alum]

a·lu·min·ate (ə·lo͞o′mə) ·nāt) *n.* Any of several salts derived from aluminum hydroxide in which aluminum and oxygen together form a negative ion.

alumina trihydrate Aluminum hydroxide.

a·lu·mi·nif·er·ous (ə·lo͞o ′mə·nif′ər·əs) *adj.* Containing or yielding alum, alumina, or aluminum.

a·lu·mi·nize (ə·lo͞o′mə) ·nīz) *v.t.* **·nized, ·niz·ing** To cover with a film or coat of aluminum or an aluminum compound.

a·lu·mi·no·sil·i·cate (ə·lo͞o′mə·no·sil′ə·kit, -kāt) *n.* A compound of aluminum and silicon with a metal oxide or other radical.

a·lu·mi·no·ther·my (ə·lo͞o ′mə·nō·thûr′mē) *n.* The process of generating heat by the chemical combination of aluminum with a metallic oxide.

a·lu·mi·num (ə·lo͞o′mə) ·nəm) *n.* An abundant metallic element (symbol Al, atomic number 13) found only in combination, chiefly with oxygen, and having the useful properties of lightness and resistance to oxidation. Also *Brit.* **al·u·min·i·um** (al′yə·min′ē·əm). See PERIODIC TABLE. [<NL <L *alumen, -minis* alum] —**a·lu′mi·nous** *adj.*

aluminum bronze An alloy of aluminum and copper resembling pale gold: used in cheap jewelry, etc.

aluminum hydroxide The hydrated form of alumina, $Al_2O_3 \cdot 3H_2O$ or $Al(OH)_3$, formed as a gelatinous white precipitate when a soluble aluminum salt is treated with a soluble base. Also called *alumina trihydrate*.

aluminum oxide Alumina, Al_2O_3, specifically in the form of a white powder or colorless crystals.

aluminum sulfate A colorless, water-soluble salt, $Al_2(SO_4)_3$, used in water purification and in various manufacturing processes.

a·lum·na (ə·lum′nə) *n. pl.* **·nae** (-nē) A female graduate of a college or school. [<L, fem. of *alumnus*]

a·lum·nus (ə·lum′nəs) *n.* pl. **·ni** (-nī) 1 A male graduate of a college or school. 2 Originally, any pupil. [<L, foster son, pupil < *alere* nourish]

al·um·root (al′əm·ro͞ot′, -ro͝ot′) *n.* 1 Any of a genus *(Heuchera)* of North American perennial herbs having small clusters of greenish or purplish flowers, especially *H. americana*, or its astringent root. 2 The spotted cranesbill.

A·lun·dum (ə·lun′dəm) *n.* A fused crystalline alumina used as an abrasive: a trade name.

al·u·nite (al′yə·nīt) *n.* A mineral consisting chiefly of a basic potassium aluminum sulfate, used in the production of alum. Also **al′um·stone′**. [<F < *alun* <L *alumen* alum]

Al·u·re·dus (al′yo͞o·rē′dəs) Latin form of ALFRED.

al·u·ta·ceous (al′yə·tā′shəs) *adj.* Resembling tawed leather, as in its soft and pliable qualities or its pale-brown color; leathery. [<L *alutacius* <*aluta* soft leather]

Al·va (al′və, *Sp.* äl′vä), **Duke of** See ALBA.

Al·va·ra·do (äl′vä·rä ′thō), **Alonso de,** 1490?–) 1554, Spanish soldier, fought in Peru, and under Cortez in Mexico. —**Pedro de,** 1495–1541, Spanish officer, companion of Cortez in Mexico.

Al·va·rez (al′və·rez), **Luis Walter,** born 1911, U.S. physicist.

Ál·va·rez Quin·te·ro (äl′vä·räth kēn·tā′rō), **Joa·quín,** 1873–1944, and Serafí) n, 1871–1938, brothers, Spanish dramatists and journalists.

al·ve·o·lar (al·vē′ə·lər) *adj.* 1 Pertaining to or contining an alveolus or alveoli. 2 *Anat.* Denoting that part of the jaws in which the teeth are set. 3 *Phonet.* Formed with the tongue touching or near the alveolar ridge, as (t), (d), and (s) in English. —*n. Phonet.* A sound so produced.

alveolar arch *Anat.* The arch of the upper jawbone in vertebrates.

alveolar point In craniometry, the point situated between the two middle incisors of the upper jaw.

alveolar ridge *Anat.* The inwardly projecting bony ridge of the jaw just above the upper front teeth.

al·ve·o·late (al·vē′ə·lit, al′vē·ə-) *adj.* Having alveoli arranged like the cells of a honeycomb; deeply pitted. Also **al·ve·o·lat·ed** (al·vē′ə·lā′ tid). —**al·ve′o·la′tion** *n.*

al·ve·o·lus (al·vē′ə·ləs) *n. pl.* **·li** (-lī) 1 A minute air sac at the end of each bronchiole in the lungs. 2 A tooth socket. 3 An acinus in a racemose gland. 4 One of the cells of a honeycomb. [<L, dim. of *alveus* a hollow]

al·ve·o·pal·a·tal (al·ve′ə) ·pal′ə·təl) *adj.* Intermediate between alveolar and palatal: *alveopalatal* sounds.

Al·vin (al′vin) A masculine personal name. Also *Ital.* **Al·vi·no** (äl·vē′nō).

al·vine (al′vin, -vīn) *adj.* Pertaining to the abdomen and the intestines. [<L *alvus* belly]

al·ways (ôl′wiz, -wāz) *adv.* 1 Perpetually; for all time; ceaselessly. 2 At every time; on all occasions: opposed to *sometimes*. Also *Archaic* or *Poetic* **al·way** (ôl′wā). [<ALL + WAY + adverbial genitive ending *-s*]

Al·win (al′win, *Ger.* äl′vin) See ALVIN.

a·lys·sum (ə·lis′əm) *n.* 1 Any of a large genus *(Alyssum)* of cruciferous plants bearing white or yellow flowers. 2 Sweet alyssum. [<NL <Gk. *alysson*, name of a plant, ? < *alyssos* curing madness < *a-* not + *lyssa* madness]

Alz·hei·mer's disease (älts′hī·mərz) *n.* A disease affecting mental stability by premature degeneration of the central nervous system.

am (am, *unstressed* əm) Present tense, first person singular, of BE. [OE *eom, am*]

Am *Chem.* Americium (symbol Am).

Am·a·bel (am′ə·bel) A feminine personal name. Also **A·mab·i·lis** (ə·mab′i·lis). [<L, fem., lovable]

am·a·bil·i·ty (am′ə·bil′ə·tē) *n.* Lovableness. [<L *amabilitas, -tatis* <*amabilis* lovely]

am·a·da·vat (am′ə·də·vat′) *n.* A small singing bird of India *(Estrelda amandava)*, having red and black plumage flecked with white, and a red beak. [<East Indian]

Am·a·dis (am′ə·dis) A masculine personal name. [<Sp. <L, love of God]

—**Amadis of Gaul** The hero in a Spanish romance of this title by Vasco de Lobeira, 1360–1403.

am·a·dou (am′ə·do͞o) *n.* A soft spongy combustible substance, prepared from several species of fungus (as *Boletus, Polyporus*, or *Hernandia*), found on old trees: used as tinder, especially after being steeped in a solution of saltpeter, and also as a styptic. [<F]

A·ma·ga·sa·ki (ä·mä·gä·sä·kē) A city on Osaka Bay in southern Honshu island, Japan.

a·mah (ä′mə, am′ə) *n.* In India and the Orient, a female attendant for children; especially, a wet-nurse. Also **a′ma.** [<Anglo-Indian]

A·mai·mon (ə·mā′mən, ə) ·mī′-) In medieval demonology, the devil of the East. Also **A·ma·mon** (ə·mā′mə) n), **A·may′mon.**

a·main (ə·mān′) *adv.* Vehemently; forcibly; exceedingly; without delay; at full speed. [<A-[1] + MAIN[1]) strength]

à main ar·mée (à maṅ nà r·mā′) *French* By force of arms.

a·maist (ə·māst′) *adv.* Scot. Almost.

Am·a·lek (am′ə·lek) 1 Grandson of Esau. *Gen.* xxxvi 12. 2 The descendants of Amalek, a nation hostile to Israel. *Ex.* xvii 8–13. Also **Am′a·lech** (-lek).

Am·a·lek·ite (am′ə·lek·ī) t, ə·mal′ə·kīt) *n.* One of a nomad people dwelling in the desert south of Judah; a marauding tribe that warred against Israel. *Num.* xiii 29.

A·mal·fi (ä·mäl′fē) A town in southern Italy on the Gulf of Salerno.

a·mal·gam (ə·mal′gəm) *n.* 1 An alloy of mercury and one or more metals. 2 Any mixture or combination of two or more bodies, substances, or things. [<MF *amalgame* <) Med.L *amalgama* <Arabic *al-malgham* <) Gk. *malagma* an emollient < *malassein* soften]

a·mal·gam·a·ble (ə·mal′gə) ·mə·bəl) *adj.* Capable of forming an amalgam.

a·mal·ga·mate (ə·mal′gə·māt) *v.t.* & v.i. **·mat·ed, ·mat·ing** 1 To form an amalgam; unite in an alloy with mercury, as a metal. 2 To unite or combine: The four parts of the original are *amalgamated* into two. See synonyms under MIX, UNITE. —**a·mal·ga·ma·tive** (ə·mal′gə·mā′ tiv) *adj.* —**a·mal·ga·ma·tor** (ə·mal′gə·mā′tər) *n.*

a·mal·ga·ma·tion (ə·mal′ gə·mā′shən) *n.* 1 The forming of an amalgam. 2 A mingling of racial or ethnic stocks. 3 The removal of metals from their ores by treatment with mercury. 4 A substance formed by mixture.

A·ma·li·a (*Du., Ger.* ä·mä′lē·ä; *Ital.* ä·mä′lyä) Dutch, German, and Italian form of AMELIA.

Am·al·the·a (am′əl·thē′ə) In Greek mythology, the goat on whose milk Zeus was bred, one of whose horns, the **horn of Amalthea,** broken off by the god, became the *cornucopia*, or horn of plenty. Also **Am′al·thae′a, Am′·al·thæ′a.**

A·man·da (ə·man′də) A feminine personal name. Also *Fr.* **A·man·dine** (á·mäṅ·dēn′). [<L, lovable]

am·a·ni·ta (am′ə·nī′tə) *n.* Any of a genus *(Amanita)* of fleshy fungi that includes highly poisonous species sometimes mistaken for edible mushrooms. [<Gk. *amanitai,* a kind of fungus]

a·man·ta·dine (ə·man′tə·dēn) *n.* A compound, $C_{10}H_{17}N$, used to treat Parkinsonism and as an antiviral prophylactic against epidemic influenza.

a·man·u·en·sis (ə·man′yōō·en′sis) *n. pl.* **·ses** (-sēz) One who copies manuscript or takes dictation; a secretary. [<L <*a-* *(ab-)* from + *manus* hand]

A·ma·pá (ä·mə·pä′) A federal territory in northern Brazil; 53,057 square miles; capital, Macapá.

am·a·ranth (am′ə·ranth) *n.* **1** Any of a genus *(Amaranthus)* of weedy, mostly annual herbs, having spikes of small green or purplish flowers with a dry, persistent calyx. **2** A deep purplish hue. **3** An imaginary never-fading flower. [<L *amarantus* <Gk. *amarantos,* lit., unfading <*a-* not + *marainein* wither]

am·a·ran·thine (am′ə·ran′thin) *adj.* **1** Pertaining to, like, or containing amaranth. **2** Unfading; everlasting. **3** Of purplish hue.

Am·a·ryl·lis (am′ə·ril′is) In pastoral poetry, a country girl or shepherdess.

am·a·ryl·lis (am′ə·ril′is) *n.* **1** Any one of various bulbous South African plants of the genus *Amaryllis,* often cultivated for their large, lilylike flowers, as the belladonna lily. **2** Any of several similar liliaceous plants. [<L <Gk. *Amaryllis,* fem. personal name]

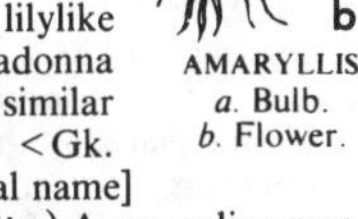

AMARYLLIS
a. Bulb.
b. Flower.

Am·a·sa (am′ə·sə, ə·mā′sə) A masculine personal name. [<Hebrew, a burden]

—Amasa Nephew of David; captain of the host of Absalom; slain by Joab. II *Sam.* xx 4.

a·mass (ə·mas′) *v.t.* To heap up; accumulate, especially as wealth or possessions for oneself. [<OF *amasser* <*a-* to (<L *ad-*) + *masser* pile up <L *massa* mass] **—a·mass′a·ble** *adj.* **—a·mass′er** *n.* **—a·mass′ment** *n.*

Synonyms: accumulate, aggregate, collect, gather. To *amass* is to bring together materials that make a mass, a great bulk or quantity, *accumulate* being commonly applied to the more gradual, *amass* to the more rapid gathering of money or materials. We say interest is *accumulated* rather than is *amassed;* a fortune may be rapidly *amassed* by shrewd speculations. *Aggregate* is now most commonly used of numbers and amounts; as, the expenses will *aggregate* a round million. Compare AGGREGATE, *n. Antonyms*: disperse, dissipate, divide, parcel, portion, scatter, spend, squander, waste.

A·ma·ta (ä·mä′tä) Italian form of AMY.

am·a·teur (am′ə·chōōr, -tōōr, -tyōōr, am′ə·tûr′) *adj.* **1** Pertaining to or done by an amateur. **2** Composed of amateurs: an *amateur* cast. **3** Not expert or professional. *—n.* **1** One who practices an art or science, not professionally, but for his own pleasure. **2** An athlete who has not engaged in contests for money, or used any athletic art as a means of livelihood. **3** One who does something without professional skill or ease. [<F <L *amator* lover <*amare* love]**—am′a·teur·ism** *n.*

Synonyms (noun): connoisseur, critic, dilettante, novice, tyro. Etymologically, the *amateur* is one who loves, the *connoisseur* one who knows. The *amateur* practices to some extent that in regard to which he may not be well informed; the *connoisseur* is well informed in regard to that which he may not practice at all. *Dilettante,* which had originally the sense of *amateur,* has come to denote one who is superficial, pretentious, and affected, whether in theory or practice.

am·a·teur·ish (am′ə·chōōr′ish, -tōōr′-, -tyōōr′-, -tûr′-) *adj.* Lacking the skill or perfection of an expert or professional. **—am′a·teur′ish·ly** *adv.* **—am′a·teur′ish·ness** *n.*

A·ma·ti (ä·mä′tē) *n.* A violin made by any of the Amati, a family of violinmakers at Cremona, Italy, in the 16th and 17th centuries, notably **Nicola** or **Nicolò**, 1596–1684.

am·a·tive (am′ə·tiv) *adj.* Pertaining to sexual love; amorous. [<L *amatus,* pp. of *amare* love] **—am′a·tive·ly** *adv.*

am·a·tive·ness (am′ə·tiv·nis) *n.* The propensity to love or to sexual passion.

am·a·tol (am′ə·tol, -tōl) *n.* An explosive mixture of variable proportions of ammonium nitrate and trinitrotoluene. [<AM(MONIUM) + TOL(UENE)]

Am·a·ton·ga·land (am′ə·tong′gə·land′) See TONGALAND.

am·a·to·ry (am′ə·tôr′ē, -tō′rē) *adj.* Characterized by or designed to excite love; expressing or given to sexual love; erotic, as a poem. Also **am′a·to′ri·al.** [<L *amatorius* <*amare* love]

am·au·ro·sis (am′ô·rō′sis) *n.* Total or partial loss of sight without apparent organic defect. [<Gk. *amaurōsis* <*amauros* dark] **—am·au·rot·ic** (am′ô·rot′ik) *adj.*

a·maze (ə·māz′) *v.t.* **a·mazed, a·maz·ing 1** To overwhelm, as by wonder or surprise; astonish greatly. **2** *Obs.* To puzzle; bewilder. [OE *āmasian*] **—a·mazed′** *adj.* **—a·maz·ed·ly** (ə·mā′zid·lē) *adv.* **—a·maz′ed·ness** *n.*

a·maze·ment (ə·māz′mənt) *n.* **1** Wonder; surprise; astonishment. **2** *Obs.* Stupefaction; frenzy; dementia. Also *Archaic* **a·maze′.**

Synonyms: admiration, astonishment, awe, bewilderment, confusion, consternation, perplexity, surprise, wonder. *Amazement* and *astonishment* both express the momentary overwhelming of the mind by that which is beyond expectation. *Awe* is the yielding of the mind to something supremely grand in character or formidable in power, and ranges from apprehension or dread to reverent worship. *Surprise* lies midway between *astonishment* and *amazement,* and usually concerns slighter matters. *Consternation* adds terror to *astonishment* or *amazement.* Compare PERPLEXITY. *Antonyms*: anticipation, calmness, composure, coolness, expectation, indifference, preparation, self-possession, steadiness.

a·maz·ing (ə·mā′zing) *adj.* Causing amazement; astonishing; wonderful. See synonyms under EXTRAORDINARY. **—a·maz′ing·ly** *adv.*

Am·a·zon (am′ə·zon, -zən) *n.* **1** In Greek mythology, one of a race of female warriors, said to have lived in Scythia, near the Black Sea. **2** A female warrior. **3** Any large, strong or athletic woman or girl. Also **am′a·zon** *n.* [<L <Gk. *Amazōn*; derived by the Greeks as <*a-* without + *mazos* breast, because of the fable that they cut off the right breast to facilitate the use of the bow]

Am·a·zon (am′ə·zon, -zən) A river in South America, carrying the largest volume of water of any in the world and flowing about 3,300 miles from the Andes through northern Brazil to the Atlantic. *Spanish & Portugese* **A·ma·zo·nas** (*Sp.* ä′mä·sō′näs, *Pg.* ä·mə·zō′nəs).

Amazon ant Any of several species of ants of the genus *Polyergus* that capture the larvae or pupae of other species and raise them as workers.

A·ma·zo·nas (*Sp.* ä′mä·sō′näs, *Pg.* ä·mə·zō′·nəs) **1** A state in NW Brazil; 614,913 square miles; capital, Manaus. **2** A commissary of SE Colombia; 48,008 square miles; capital, Letica. **3** A department of northern Peru; 13,948 square miles. **4** A territory of southern Venezuela; 67,857 square miles; capital, Puerto Ayacucho.

Am·a·zo·ni·an (am′ə·zō′nē·ən) *adj.* **1** Pertaining to the Amazons; warlike; masculine: said of women. **2** Pertaining to the Amazon River. *—n.* An Amazon.

am·a·zon·ite (am′ə·zən·īt) *n.* A green variety of microcline often used as a gemstone. Also **Amazon stone.** [from the *Amazon* River]

am·bage (am′bij) *n. pl.* **am·bag·es** (am′bə·jiz, *Lat.* am·bā′jēz) **1** A winding or circuitous path. **2** *Usually pl.* An indirect method of proceeding. [<OF *ambages* <L *ambi-* around + *agere* go] **—am·ba·gious** (am·bā′jəs) *adj.* **—am·ba′gious·ly** *adv.* **—am·ba′gious·ness** *n.*

Am·ba·la (um·bä′lə) A city in eastern Punjab, India.

am·ba·ry (am·bä′rē) *n.* **1** A tropical malvaceous plant *(Hibiscus cannabinus)* cultivated in Asia for its tough fiber. **2** The hemplike fiber of this plant, used for sacking, cordage, etc. Also **am·ba′ri.** Also called *kenaf.* [<Hind. *ambārā*]

am·bas·sa·dor (am·bas′ə·dər, -dôr) *n.* **1** An accredited diplomatic agent of the highest rank, appointed as the representative of one government or state to another **(ambassador extraordinary and plenipotentiary)** or to represent a government or state at a particular function, as the wedding of a king **(ambassador extraordinary on special mission). 2** Any personal representative or messenger. Also *embassador.* See synonyms under HERALD. **—ambassador-at-large** An ambassador accredited to no specific country or government. **—goodwill ambassador** Any person traveling in a foreign country to promote friendly relations and understanding. [<F *ambassadeur* <Ital. *ambasciatore*] **—am·bas·sa·do·ri·al** (am·bas′ə·dôr′ē·əl, -dō′rē-) *adj.* **—am·bas′·sa·dor·ship** *n.*

am·bas·sa·dress (am·bas′ə·dris) *n.* **1** A woman ambassador. **2** The wife of an ambassador.

am·ber (am′bər) *n.* **1** A translucent yellow to reddish brown fossil resin of an extinct coniferous tree, used mainly as an ornament. **2** Anything the color of amber. **3** An amber-colored light used to produce the effect of sunlight, as on a stage. *—v.t.* **1** To encase or preserve in amber. **2** To give an amber color to. *—adj.* Pertaining to, like, or of the color of amber. [<F *ambre* <Arabic *'anbar* ambergris]

am·ber·gris (am′bər·grēs, -gris) *n.* An opaque, grayish, waxy morbid secretion from the intestines of the sperm whale, sometimes found floating on the ocean or lying on the shore: used in perfumery. [<F *ambre gris* gray amber]

am·ber·jack (am′bər·jak′) *n.* Any of several species of large carangoid food and game fishes (genus *Seriola)* found in warm areas of the western Atlantic.

am·ber·oid (am′bər·oid) See AMBROID.

ambi- *combining form* Both: *ambidextrous.* [<L *ambo* both]

am·bi·ance (am′bē·əns) *n.* Ambience. [<F]

am·bi·dex·ter (am′bə·dek′stər) *adj.* Ambidextrous. *—n.* **1** One who uses both hands equally well. **2** A double-dealer; hypocrite. [<Med. L <L *ambo* both + *dexter* right (hand)] **—am′bi·dex′tral** (-dek′strəl) *adj.*

am·bi·dex·ter·i·ty (am′bə·dek·ster′ə·tē) *n.* **1** The state or quality of being ambidextrous. **2** Duplicity; trickery.

am·bi·dex·trous (am′bə·dek′strəs) *adj.* **1** Able to use both hands equally well. **2** Very dexterous or skilful. **3** Dissembling; double-dealing. **—am′bi·dex′trous·ly** *adv.* **—am′bi·dex′trous·ness** *n.*

am·bi·ence (am′bē·əns) *n.* The environment or pervading atmosphere of a place, situation, etc. Also *ench* **am·bi·ance** *(äṅ·be·aṅs′).* [<L *ambiens* AMBIENT]

am·bi·ent (am′bē·ənt) *adj.* **1** Surrounding; encircling; encompassing. **2** Circulating. *—n.* Anything that encompasses. [<L *ambiens, -entis,* ppr. of *ambire* <*ambi-* around + *ire* go]

am·bi·gu·i·ty (am′bə·gyōō′ə·tē) *n. pl.* **·ties 1** The quality of being ambiguous; doubtfulness. **2** An expression or statement that can be variously interpreted.

am·big·u·ous (am·big′yōō·əs) *adj.* **1** Capable of being understood in more senses than one; having a double meaning; equivocal. **2** Doubtful or uncertain: a liquid of *ambiguous* nature. **3** Obscure, indistinct, as shadows. See synonyms under EQUIVOCAL, OBSCURE. [< L *ambiguus* < *ambigere* wander about < *ambi-* around + *agere* go] **—am·big′u·ous·ly** *adv.* **—am·big′u·ous·ness** *n.*

am·bit (am′bit) *n.* **1** That which bounds; a boundary. **2** Circumference; circuit. **3** Extent or sphere, as of actions or words; scope. [< L *ambitus* circuit < *ambire.* See AMBIENT.]

am·bi·ten·den·cy (am′bə·ten′dən·sē) *n. Psychol.* The state of having conflicting tendencies.

am·bi·tion (am·bish′ən) *n.* **1** Eager or inordinate desire, as for power, wealth, or distinction. **2** A strong desire to achieve something considered great or good: with *of* or the infinitive. **3** An object so desired or striven for. **4** *Obs.* A canvassing for an office or the like. *—v.t.* To desire and seek eagerly. [< L *ambitio, -onis* a going about (to solicit votes) < *ambire.* See AMBIENT.] **—am·bi′tion·less** *adj.*

Synonyms (noun): aspiration, competition, emulation, opposition, rivalry. *Aspiration* is the desire for excellence, pure and simple. *Ambition,* literally a going around to solicit votes, has primary reference to the award or approval of others, and is the eager desire for power, fame, or something deemed great and eminent. *Emulation* is not so much to win any excellence or success for itself as to equal or surpass other persons. Compare EMULATION. *Antonyms*: carelessness, contentment, humility, indifference, satisfaction.

am·bi·tious (am·bish′əs) *adj.* **1** Actuated or characterized by ambition. **2** Greatly desiring; eager for: with *of* or the infinitive. **3** Aspiring, as to a high or imposing position. **—am·bi′tious·ly** *adv.* **—am·bi′tious·ness** *n.*

am·biv·a·lence (am·biv′ə·ləns) *n. Psychol.* The state of being ambivalent.

am·biv·a·lent (am·biv′ə·lənt) *adj.* **1** Uncertain or subject to change, especially because affected by contradictory emotions or ideas: an *ambivalent* attitude. **2** *Psychol.* Experiencing contradictory and opposing emotions toward the same person at the same time, especially love and hate. [< AMBI- + L *valens, -entis,* ppr. of *valere* be strong, be worth]

am·bi·ver·sion (am′bə·vûr′zhən, -shən) *n. Psychol.* A condition intermediate between introversion and extroversion. [< AMBI- + *-version,* as in *introversion*]

am·bi·vert (am′bə·vûrt) *n. Psychol.* A personality type which is intermediate between the introvert and extrovert.

am·ble (am′bəl) *v.i.* **am·bled** (-bəld), **am·bling 1** To move, as a horse, by lifting the two feet on one side together, alternately with the two feet on the other. **2** To move with an easy, swaying motion resembling this gait; proceed leisurely. *—n.* **1** The single-foot. **2** An ambling movement, like that of a horse. [< OF *ambler* < L *ambulare* walk] **—am′bling** *adj.* **—am′bling·ly** *adv.*

am·bler (am′blər) *n.* One that ambles, especially an ambling horse.

am·blyg·o·nite (am·blig′ə·nīt) *n.* A white or greenish mineral found in cleavable masses consisting largely of basic lithium aluminum phosphate and constituting an important source of lithium. [< G *amblygonit* < Gk. *amblygōnios* having obtuse angles]

am·bly·o·pi·a (am′blē·ō′pē·ə) *n.* Dimness of vision, without discoverable disease or errors of refraction in the eye. [< NL < Gk. *amblys* dull + *ōps* eye] **—am·bly·op·ic** (am′blē·op′ik) *adj.*

am·bo (am′bō) *n. pl.* **am·bos** (am′bōz) or **am·bo·nes** (am·bō′nēz) In early Christian churches, a raised pulpitlike stand or desk, where parts of the service were read or chanted: usually two, one on each side of the nave. [< Gk. *ambōn* a rising ground]

am·bo·cep·tor (am′bə·sep′tər) *n. Bacteriol.* A thermostable agent supposed by Ehrlich to exist in blood serum and to assist in the destruction of pathogenic organisms by uniting them to another substance (the complement) also present in the blood. [< L *ambo* both + (RE)CEPTOR]

Am·boi·na (am·boi′nə) See AMBON. Also **Am·boy′na.**

Amboina wood A mottled wood obtained from any of several leguminous trees (genus *Pterocarpus*) of Asia and Africa, used in cabinetwork. Also **am·boy′na.** Also called *padauk.*

Am·boise (däṅ·bwȧz′), **George d′,** 1460–1510, French cardinal and statesman.

Am·boise (äṅ·bwȧz′) A town in west central France on the Loire; residence of the Valois kings from Charles VIII to Francis II.

Am·bon (äm′bôn) An Indonesian island SW of Ceram; 314 square miles; chief town, Amboina: also *Amboina, Amboyna.*

am·broid (am′broid) *n.* A reconstructed or imitation amber consisting of fragments of amber and sometimes other resins united by pressure and heat. Also *amberoid.*

Am·brose (am′brōz) A masculine personal name. Also *Dan., Du., Ger.* **Am·bro·si·us** (äm·brō′zē·ōōs), *Fr.* **Am·broise** (äṅ·brwȧz′), *Ital.* **Am·bro·gio** (äm·brō′jō), *Sp., Pg.* **Am·bro·sio** (*Sp.* äm·brō′syō, *Pg.* äṅ·brō′zyōō), *Lat.* **Am·bro·si·us** (am·brō′zhē·əs, -zē·əs). [< Gk., divine, immortal] **—Ambrose, Saint,** 340?–397, bishop of Milan; one of the Latin fathers.

Ambrose Channel An entrance to New York Harbor: reckoning point for the time of a voyage in or out of New York.

am·bro·sia (am·brō′zhə, -zhē·ə) *n.* **1** The food of the gods, giving immortality. **2** Hence, any very delicious food or drink. **3** A richly perfumed salve or unguent. **4** *Bot.* Any of a genus *(Ambrosia)* of coarse herbs, weedy composite herbs comprising the ragweeds. [< L < Gk. *ambrosia* < *ambrotos* immortal < *a-* not + *brotos* mortal]

AMBROSIA (def. 4) (3 to 6 feet high)

am·bro·si·a·ceous (am·brō·zē·ā′shəs) *adj.* Belonging to the genus *Ambrosia,* comprising weedy herbs of the composite family, as the ragweeds.

am·bro·sial (am·brō′zhəl, -zhē·əl) *adj.* **1** Of or like ambrosia; fragrant; delicious. **2** Worthy of the gods; heavenly. Also **am·bro·sian** (am·brō′zhən, -zhē·ən). **—am·bro′sial·ly** *adv.*

Am·bro·sian (am·brō′zhən, -zhē·ən) *adj.* Of or attributed to St. Ambrose or resembling his style.

Ambrosian chant The mode of singing or chanting divine service introduced by St. Ambrose in the cathedral at Milan, but afterward superseded by the Gregorian system.

Ambrosian hymn Any metrical hymn written by St. Ambrose or characterized by his style.

Ambrosian liturgy *Eccl.* An ancient liturgy compiled by St. Ambrose, somewhat different from the Roman liturgy.

am·bro·type (am′brə·tīp′) *n.* A photograph made by an obsolete method in which a negative on a glass plate backed by a black surface appears positive because of light reflected from the silver in the negative. [< (James) *Ambro(se* Cutting), 1814–67, inventor + -TYPE]

am·bry (am′brē) *n. pl.* **·bries 1** A depository for goods, food, or money; pantry; cupboard; closet. **2** *Eccl.* A closet near the altar for the sacred vessels. **3** *Obs.* A library. Also **am·ber·y** (am′bər·ē). [ME *almarie, amerie, ambrie* < L *armarium* a chest, orig., a place for storing arms]

ambs·ace (āmz′ās′, amz′-) *n.* **1** Both aces, the lowest throw at dice. **2** Bad luck; misfortune. **3** Worthlessness; that which is next to nothing. [< OF *ambes as* < L *ambas as* double ace]

am·bu·cy·cle (am′byə·sī′kəl) *n.* A small ambulance attached like a side-car to a motorcycle. [< AMBU(LANCE) + (MOTOR)CYCLE]

am·bu·la·cral (am′byə·lā′krəl) *adj.* Of, pertaining to, or situated near an ambulacrum.

ambulacral feet The tube feet of echinoderms.

ambulacral groove A furrow on the oral surface of the radii of a starfish.

ambulacral ossicle An ossicle of which the sides of the ambulacral groove are formed.

ambulacral pore The aperture piercing the ambulacral plates of echinoids or between the contiguous ambulacral ossicles of asteroids, admitting the ducts of the pedicels or tube feet.

am·bu·la·crum (am′byə·lā′krəm) *n. pl.* **·cra** (-krə) Any of the radial series of perforated plates on the oral surface of echinoderms through which the tube feet are thrust. [< L, a covered walk < *ambulare* walk]

am·bu·lance (am′byə·ləns) *n.* **1** A covered vehicle for conveying the sick and wounded. **2** A moving or field hospital. **3** A boat or airplane for conveying sick and wounded personnel. [< F < *(hôpital) ambulant* walking (hospital) < L *ambulare* walk]

am·bu·lance-chas·er (am′byə·ləns·chā′sər) *n. U.S. Slang* A lawyer or his agent who seeks the victim of an accident to persuade him to institute a suit at law for damages.

am·bu·lant (am′byə·lənt) *adj.* Walking or moving about from place to place; shifting. [< L *ambulans, -antis,* ppr. of *ambulare* walk]

am·bu·late (am′byə·lāt) *v.i.* **·lat·ed, ·lat·ing** To walk about; move from place to place. [< L *ambulatus,* pp. of *ambulare* walk] **—am′·bu·la′tion** *n.* **—am·bu·la·tive** (am′byə·lā′tiv, -lə·tiv) *adj.*

am·bu·la·to·ry (am′byə·lə·tôr′ē, -tō′rē) adj. **1** Pertaining to or for walking or walkers. **2** Able to walk, as an invalid. **3** Shifting; not fixed or stationary. **4** *Law* Alterable, as a writ or pleading until filed, or a will at any time during the testator's life. *—n. pl.* **·ries** A place, as a corridor, for walking.

am·bus·cade (am′bəs·kād′) *n.* **1** The act of hiding, or the state of being hidden, to surprise adversaries. **2** The place of hiding, or persons hidden; an ambush. *—v.t. & v.i.* **·cad·ed, ·cad·ing** To ambush. Also *Archaic* **am·bus·ca·do** (am′bəs·kā′dō). [< F *embuscade* < Ital. *imboscata* an ambush < *imboscare.* See AMBUSH.] **—am′bus·cad′er** *n.*

am·bush (am′bōōsh) *n.* **1** The act or condition of lying in wait to surprise or attack an enemy. **2** The hiding place or the persons hidden. Also **am′bush·ment.** *—v.t. & v.i.* **1** To hide in order to attack unexpectedly. **2** To attack from a hidden place; waylay. [< OF *embusche* < *embuschier* < Ital. *imboscare* place in a bush, set an ambush < L *in-* in + *boscus* a wood] **—am′bush·er** *n.*

Am·chit·ka (am·chit′kə) Easternmost of the Rat Islands in the Aleutian Islands group.

a·me·ba (ə·mē′bə) *n. pl.* **·bas** or **·bae** (-bē) Any of various naked protozoans of the genus *Amoeba* and other genera in the order Amoebidae, typically of indefinite shape, moving and feeding by the action of pseudopodia, and reproducing by fission. Also *amoeba.* [< NL < Gk. *amoibē* change] **—a·me′bic** *adj.*

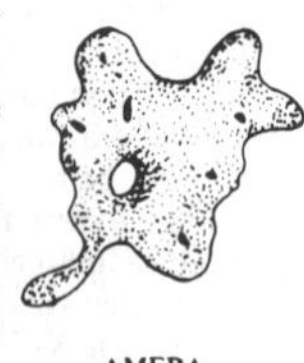

AMEBA

am·e·be·an (am′ə·bē′ən) *adj.* Alternately or reciprocally responsive: also spelled *amoebaean, amoebean.* [< L *amoebaeum (carmen)* < Gk. *(asma) amoibaion* responsive (song) < *amoibē* change]

am·e·bi·a·sis (am′ə·bī′ə·sis) *n.* Infection by a parasitic ameba, especially *Entamoeba histolytica,* usually manifested by severe intestinal symptoms. Also *amoebiasis.* [< NL < AMEBA + -IASIS]

amebic dysentery Severe amebiasis involving ulceration and bleeding of the colon and painful diarrhea.

a·me·bo·cyte (ə·mē′bō·sīt) *n.* Any wandering ameboid cell of a multicellular organism, as a leukocyte. Also *amoebocyte.*

a·me·boid (ə·mē′boid) *adj.* Resembling an ameba, as in its change of form: also spelled *amoeboid.*

a·meer (ə·mir′) *n.* **1** The sovereign of Afghanistan. **2** A Mohammedan prince or governor. Also **a·mir′.** [< Arabic *amīr* ruler]

am·el·corn (am′əl·kôrn′) *n.* An inferior kind of wheat *(Triticum sativum dicoccum)* cultivated in Europe mainly for the manufacture of starch; emmer. [< G *amelkorn* starch corn]

A·mel·ia (ə·mēl′yə, ə·mē′lē·ə; *Ital., Pg., Sp.* ä·mā′lyä) A feminine personal name. Also *Fr.* **A·mé·lie** (ȧ·mā·lē′). [< Gmc., lit., industrious]

a·mel·io·rate (ə·mēl′yə·rāt) *v.t.* & *v.i.* **·rat·ed, ·rat·ing** To make or become better; meliorate; improve. See synonyms under AMEND. [<F *améliorer* <L *ad-* to + *meliorare* to better <*melior* better] —**a·mel·io·ra·ble** (ə·mēl′·yə·rə·bəl) *adj.* —**a·mel′io·rant** (-rənt) *n.* —**a·mel·io·ra·tive** (ə·mēl′yə·rā′tiv, -rə·tiv) *adj.* —**a·mel′io·ra′tor** *n.*

a·mel·io·ra·tion (ə·mēl′yə·rā′shən) *n.* The act, process, or result of ameliorating, or the state of being ameliorated; improvement.

a·mel·o·blast (ə·mel′ə·blast) *n.* An epithelial cell, one of those producing the enamel of the teeth. [<OF *amail* enamel + -BLAST]

a·men (ā′men′, ä′-) *interj.* So it is; so be it. —*n.* **1** The word *amen* at the end of a prayer or hymn, meaning *so be it.* **2** Any expression of hearty assent or conviction. **3** A concluding act or word; termination. —*v.t.* **1** To say amen to; express hearty concurrence in or approval of. **2** To say or write that last word of; make an end of. —*adv. Obs.* Verily; truly. [<L <Gk. <Hebrew *āmēn* verily]

A·men (ā·men′) Christ, the true and faithful witness. *Rev.* iii 14.

A·men (ä′mən) In Egyptian mythology, the god of life and procreation, represented as having a ram's head; later identified with the sun-god, as the supreme deity, and called **Amen-Ra** (-rä′). Also spelled *Ammon, Amon.*

a·me·na·ble (ə·mē′nə·bəl, ə·men′ə-) *adj.* **1** Liable to be called to account; responsible to authority. **2** Submissive; tractable. **3** Capable of being tested or judged by rule or law. See synonyms under DOCILE. [<F *amener* bring to <*a-* to (<L *ad-*) + *mener* lead <L *minare* drive (with threats) <*minari* threaten] —**a·me′na·bil′i·ty, a·me′na·ble·ness** *n.* —**a·me′na·bly** *adv.*

amen corner *U.S.* The corner of a church laterally facing the pulpit, where, as in provincial regions of the United States, the deacons, who lead the responsive amens, usually sit.

a·mend (ə·mend′) *v.t.* **1** To change for the better; improve. **2** To free from faults; correct; reform. **3** To change or alter by authority: to *amend* a bill. **4** *Obs.* To mend or repair. —*v.i.* **5** To become better in conduct. [<OF *amender* <L *emendare* to free from faults <*ex-* from + *mendum* fault] —**a·mend′a·ble** *adj.*—**a·mend′a·ble·ness***n.* —**a·mend′er** *n.*

Synonyms: advance, ameliorate, better, cleanse, correct, emend, improve, meliorate, mend, mitigate, purify, reclaim, rectify, reform, repair. To *amend* is to change for the better by removing faults, errors, or defects; it always refers to that which at some point falls short of a standard of excellence. *Advance, better,* and *improve* may refer either to what is quite imperfect or to what has reached a high degree of excellence. We *correct* evils, *reform* abuses, *rectify* incidental conditions of evil or error; we *ameliorate* poverty and misery, which we cannot wholly remove. We *mend* a tool, *repair* a building, *correct* proof; we *amend* character or conduct that is faulty, or a statement or law that is defective. Compare ALLAY, ALLEVIATE, EMEND. *Antonyms:* aggravate, blemish, corrupt, debase, depress, deteriorate, harm, impair, injure, mar, spoil, tarnish, vitiate.

a·mend·a·to·ry (ə·men′də·tôr′ē, -tō′rē) *adj.* Tending to amend; corrective.

a·mende (ə·mend′, *Fr.* à·mäṅd′) *n.* A reparation or recantation. [<F]

a·mende ho·no·ra·ble (à·mäṅd′ ô·nô·rà′bl′) *French* Public reparation or apology.

a·mend·ment (ə·mend′mənt) *n.* **1** Change for the better. **2** A removal of faults; correction. **3** The changing, as of a law, bill, or motion. **4** The statement of such a change, as in a clause or paragraph.

a·mends (ə·mendz′) *n. pl.* Reparation, as in satisfaction or compensation for loss, damage, or injury. See synonyms under RECOMPENSE. [<OF *amendes,* pl. of *amende* a fine <*amender.* See AMEND.]

A·men·ho·tep (ä′mən·hō′tep) Name of four Egyptian pharaohs.
—**Amenhotep III,** 1411–1375 B.C., conqueror, built temple at Karnak.
—**Amenhotep IV** See IKHNATON.

a·men·i·ty (ə·men′ə·tē) *n. pl.* **·ties 1** Agreeableness; pleasantness. **2** *pl.* Agreeable features or aspects, as of a place or scene. **3** *Often pl.* Any of the pleasant acts and courtesies of polite behavior. [<L *amoenitas, -tatis* <*amoenus* pleasant]

a·men·or·rhe·a (ā·men′ə·rē′ə) *n.* Abnormal suppression or absence of menstruation. [<NL <Gk. *a-* not + *mēn* month + *rheein* flow] —**a·men′·or·rhe′·ic, a·men′or·rhoe′ic** *adj.*

a men·sa et tho·ro (ā men′sə et thō′rō) *Latin* In law, a partial suspension by law of the marriage relations for some cause arising after marriage that renders it impossible for the parties to live together; a judicial separation; literally, from board and bed.

am·ent (am′ənt, ā′mənt) *n.* A catkin. [<L *amentum* a thong]

am·en·ta·ceous (am′ən·tā′shəs) *adj. Bot.* Like, pertaining to, or bearing catkins.

a·men·tia (ā·men′shə, -shē·ə) *n.* **1** Congenital lack of normal mental development; feeblemindedness. **2** Temporary insanity. [<L <*a-* (*ab-*) away + *mens* mind]

am·en·tif·er·ous (am′ən·tif′ər·əs) *adj. Bot.* Bearing aments, or catkins.

Am·er·a·sian (am′ər·ā′zhen) *adj.* Having both American and Asian parentage. —*n.* A person of American and Asian parentage.

a·merce (ə·mûrs′) *v.t.* **a·merced, a·merc·ing 1** To punish by an assessment or fine. **2** To punish, as by deprivation. [<AF *amercier* to fine <*a merci* at the mercy of] —**a·merce′a·ble** *adj.* —**a·merce′·ment** *n.* —**a·merc′er** *n.*

A·mer·i·ca (ə·mer′ə·kə) **1** The lands in the Western Hemisphere; specifically, either of the two continents, North America or South America. Also **the Americas. 2** The United States of America.

America A popular patriotic hymn written by S. F. Smith; also, the tune to which it is sung, that of the English "God Save the King."

A·mer·i·can (ə·mer′ə·kən) *adj.* **1** Pertaining to the continent or people of North or South America, or of the Western Hemisphere. **2** Pertaining to the United States of America, its history, government, people, etc. —*n.* **1** A citizen of the United States. **2** The English language as spoken and written in the United States; American English. **3** An inhabitant of America.

A·mer·i·ca·na (ə·mer′ə·kä′nə, -kan′ə, -kā′nə) *n. pl.* Things American, collectively; any collection of American literary papers, sayings, or other data, especially relating to American history and traditions.

American aloe The century plant.

American Beauty A hybrid perennial rose with large, deep red blossoms on long stems.

American cheese Any of several cheeses popular in the United States; especially, a mild yellow kind of Cheddar.

American crawl See under CRAWL[1].

American eagle The bald eagle, especially in reference to its symbolic function as the national emblem of The United States of America.

American Empire An American style of furniture popular in the first half of the 19th century, influenced by the neo-classical decorative art of the First French Empire.

American English The English language as used in the United States, with especial reference to pronunciation and vocabulary: also called *American.*

American Expeditionary Forces The United States Army troops in Europe during World War I. Abbr. *A.E.F.*

American Federation of Labor A federation of trade unions, founded in 1886, which merged in 1955 with the Congress of Industrial Organizations. Abbr. *AFL* or *A.F. of L.*

American Indian A member of one of the aboriginal races of America.

A·mer·i·can·ism (ə·mer′ə·kən·iz′əm) *n.* **1** A word, phrase, usage, or a trait, custom, or tradition peculiar to the people of the United States or to some of them. **2** Attachment to America or its institutions, traditions, and way of life.

A·mer·i·can·ist (ə·mer′ə·kən·ist) *n.* One who makes a special study of subjects pertaining to America, as its history, geography, or resources.

American ivy The Virginia creeper.

A·mer·i·can·ize (ə·mer′ə·kən·īz) *v.t.* & *v.i.* **·ized, ·iz·ing** To become or cause to become American in spirit or methods; imitate or become like the Americans, as in speech, customs, etc. —**A·mer·i·can·i·za′tion** *n.*

American Legion An organization of veterans of World War I and World War II, founded in 1919.

American Library Association An organization of librarians and libraries, founded in 1876. Abbr. *A.L.A.*

American plan At a hotel, the system of paying for room, meals, and other services at a fixed, inclusive rate. Compare EUROPEAN PLAN.

American Revolution See under REVOLUTION.

American Samoa See SAMOA.

American Veterans Committee An organization of veterans of World War II. Abbr. *AVC, A.V.C.*

American Veterans of World War II, Korea, and Vietnam An organization of veterans: also called *Amvets.*

America's Cup A trophy, won in England in 1851 by the schooner-yacht *America* in a race with British yachts, which has since become the chief trophy of international yacht racing, the races being held by custom when a challenge is issued by certain British or Canadian yacht clubs.

am·er·ic·i·um (am′ə·rish′ē·əm) *n.* A transuranium element (symbol Am, atomic number 95) produced in nuclear reactors by neutron bombardment of plutonium, the most stable isotope having mass number 243 and a half-life of 7370 years. See PERIODIC TABLE. [<NL, after *America*]

A·me·ri·go (ä′mā·rē′gō) Italian form of EMERY.

Amerigo Vespucci See VESPUCCI.

Am·er·in·di·an (am′ə·rin′dē·ən) *adj.* Of or pertaining to the American Indians or the Eskimos, individually or collectively. Also **Am′er·in′dic.** —*n.* An American Indian or Eskimo. Also **Am·er·ind** (am′ə·rind). [<AMER(ICAN) + INDIAN]

Ames (āmz), **Winthrop,** 1871–1937, U.S. theater producer.

ames·ace (āmz′ās′) See AMBSACE.

am·e·thyst (am′ə·thist) *n.* A violet to purple gemstone consisting of either quartz or corundum. **2** A violet to purple color. —*adj.* Violet or purple. [<OF *ametiste* <L *amethystus* <Gk. *amethystos* not drunken <*a-* not + *methystos* drunken <*methy* wine; from the ancient belief that a wearer of the stone would be unaffected by wine]

am·e·thys·tine (am′ə·this′tin, -tīn) *adj.* Of the color of an amethyst; violet; purple.

am·e·tro·pi·a (am′ə·trō′pē·ə) *n.* Any condition of the eye in which errors of refraction prevent focusing of images on the retina. [<NL <Gk. *ametros* irregular + *ōps* eye] —**am·e·trop·ic** (am′ə·trop′ik) *adj.*

Am·for·tas (äm·fôr′täs) In Wagner's *Parsifal,* chief knight of the Holy Grail. See PARSIFAL.

Am·ha·ra (äm·hä′rä) A former province of Ethiopia; divided in 1942 into two northern provinces.

Am·har·ic (am·har′ik, äm·hä′rik) *n.* A Southwest Semitic language spoken officially in Ethiopia. —*adj.* Of or pertaining to the inhabitants of Amhara, or to their language.

Am·herst (am′ûrst), **Baron Jeffrey,** 1717–1797, English general in French and Indian War; appointed governor general of British North America.

a·mi (à·mē′) *n. pl.* **a·mis** (à·mē′) *French* A friend.

am·i·a (am′ē·ə) *n.* A ganoid fish belonging to the genus *Amia,* of which it is the sole representative; the bowfin *(A. calva).* [<NL <Gk. *amia* kind of tunny]

a·mi·a·bil·i·ty (ā′mē·ə·bil′ə·tē) *n.* Sweetness of disposition; lovableness. Also **a′mi·a·ble·ness.**

a·mi·a·ble (ā′mē·ə·bəl) *adj.* **1** Pleasing in disposition, kind-hearted. **2** Free from irritation; friendly: an *amiable* rivalry. [<OF <L *amicabilis* friendly <*amicus* friend. Doublet of AMICABLE.] —**a′mi·a·bly** *adv.*

Synonyms: agreeable, attractive, benignant, charming, engaging, gentle, good-natured, kind, lovable, lovely, loving, pleasant, pleasing, sweet, winning, winsome. *Amiable* combines the senses of *lovable* or *lovely* and *loving; amiable* is a higher and stronger word than *good-natured* or *agreeable. Lovely* is often applied to externals; as, a *lovely* face. *Amiable* denotes a disposition desirous to cheer, please, and make happy. A selfish man of the world may have the art to be *agreeable;* a handsome, brilliant, and witty person may be *charming* or even *attractive,* while by no means *amiable. Antonyms*: acrimonious, churlish, crabbed, cruel, crusty, disagreeable, dogged, gruff, hateful, ill-conditioned, ill-humored, ill-natured, ill-tempered, morose, sour, sullen, surly, unamiable.

am·i·an·thus (am′ē·an′thəs) *n.* **1** A fine, silky asbestos. Also **am·i·an·tus.** [<L *amianthus* <Gk. *amiantos (lithos),* lit., unsoiled (stone), a stone like asbestos]

am·i·ca·ble (am′i·kə·bəl) *adj.* Showing or promoting good will; friendly; peaceable. [<L *amicabilis* <*amicus* friend. Doublet of AMIABLE.] —**am·i·ca·bil·i·ty** (am′i·kə·bil′ə·tē), **am′i·ca·ble·ness** *n.* —**am′i·ca·bly** *adv.*

Synonyms: cordial, favorable, friendly, hearty, kind, neighborly, sociable. The Anglo-Saxon *friendly* is stronger than the Latin *amicable;* that which is *amicable* may be merely formal; that which is *friendly* is from the heart. *Antonyms*: adverse, antagonistic, hostile, unfriendly.

amicable number See under NUMBER.

am·ice[1] (am′is) *n.* An ecclesiastical vestment consisting of a rectangular piece of fine white linen upon which a small cross is embroidered. It is the first garment put around the shoulders by the priest in vesting for mass. [<OF *amit* <L *amictus* cloak]

am·ice[2] See ALMUCE.

a·mid (ə·mid′) *prep.* **1** In the midst of; among: He continued working *amid* the clamor of the crowd. **2** Mingled with or surrounded by: villages *amid* the woodlands. Also *amidst.* [OE *amiddan,* for *on middan* in the middle]

Synonyms: amidst, among, amongst, between, betwixt. *Amid* or *amidst* denotes surrounded by; *among* or *amongst,* mingled with. *Between* is said of two persons or objects, or of two groups of persons or objects. *Amid* denotes mere position; *among,* some active relation, as of companionship, hostility, etc. We say *among* (never *amid*) friends, or *among* (sometimes *amid*) enemies. *Antonyms*: beyond, outside, without.

am·ide (am′īd, -id) *n.* Any of a group of organic compounds containing the radical $CONH_2$. [<AM(MONIA) + -IDE] —**a·mid·ic** (ə·mid′ik) *adj.*

am·i·din (am′ə·din) *n.* A transparent gelatinous solution of starch in hot water. [<F *amidon* starch]

a·mid·most (ə·mid′mōst′) *adv.* In the very middle. —*prep.* In the center of.

amido- *combining form Chem.* Used to indicate a compound containing both the NH_2 radical and an acid radical. [<AMIDE]

a·mi·do·gen (ə·mē′də·jən, ə·mid′ə-) *n.* The univalent radical, NH_2, known from its existence in various organic compounds.

am·i·dol (am′ə·dol, -dōl) *n.* A white crystalline powder, $C_6H_3(NH_2)_2OH{\cdot}HCl$, used chiefly as a photographic developer.

a·mi·do·py·rine (ə·mē′dō·pī′rēn, am′ə·dō·pī′·rēn, -rin) See AMINOPYRINE.

a·mid·ships (ə·mid′ships) *adv. Naut.* Halfway between stem and stern of a ship.

a·midst (ə·midst′) *prep.* Amid. [ME *amidde* + adverbial genitive suffix *-s* + inorganic *t*]

Am·i·ens (am′ē·ənz, *Fr.* à·myaṅ′) A city of northern France on the Somme. —**Treaty of Amiens** An agreement among England, Holland, France, and Spain (1802), marking a period of peace in the Napoleonic Wars.

a·mi·go (ə·mē′gō) *n. pl.* **·gos** A friend; comrade. [<Sp.]

am·ine (am′in, ə·mēn′) *n.* Any of a class of organic compounds theoretically derived from ammonia by replacement of one or more hydrogen atoms by organic radicals. [<AM(MONIA) + -INE] —**am·in′ic** *adj.*

-amine *combining form Chem.* Used to denote an amine: *methylamine.*

a·mi·no (ə·mē′nō, am′ə·nō) *adj.* Containing the NH_2 group attached to a nonacid radical. [<AMINE]

amino- *combining form* Indicating a compound containing the group NH_2 attached to a nonacid radical.

amino acid Any of a group of some 80 organic compounds which contain one or more basic amino and acid carboxyl groups and which in some cases polymerize to form peptides and proteins.

am·i·no·ben·zo·ic acid Any of three isomeric derivatives of benzoic acid having the formula $C_7H_7O_2N$. See PARAAMINOBENZOIC ACID.

a·mi·no·plast (ə·mē′nə·plast) *n.* Any of a class of synthetic resins made from amido or amino compounds, as urea-formaldehyde.

a·mi·no·py·rine (ə·mē′nō·pī′rēn, am′ə·nō·pī′·rēn, -rin) *n.* A colorless synthetic drug, $C_{13}H_{17}ON_3$, used as an anodyne and antipyretic in colds, rheumatism, neuritis, etc.: also called *amidopyrine.*

a·mir (ə·mir′) See AMEER.

Am·ish (am′ish, ä′mish) *adj.* Relating to or designating the adherents of Jacob Ammann, a 17th century Mennonite. —*n. pl.* A sect of Mennonites, founded by Jacob Ammann: also spelled *Omish.*

a·miss (ə·mis′) *adj.* Out of order or relation; wrong; improper: used predicatively: Something is *amiss.* —*adv.* **1** Improperly. **2** Erroneously. **3** Defectively. —**to take amiss** To take offense at; feel resentment toward. [ME *amis* <*a-* at + *mis* miss[2]]

am·i·to·sis (am′ə·tō′sis) *n.* Cell division by simple fission of the nucleus and cytoplasm without the formation and splitting of chromosomes. [<NL <A-[4] without + MITOSIS] —**am·i·tot·ic** (am′ə·tot′ik) *adj.* —**am′i·tot′i·cal·ly** *adv.*

am·i·ty (am′ə·tē) *n. pl.* **·ties** Peaceful relations; mutual good will; friendship. See synonyms under FRIENDSHIP, HARMONY. [<MF *amitié,* ult. <L *amicus* friend]

Am·man (äm′män) The capital of Jordan.

am·me·ter (am′mē′tər) *n. Electr.* An amperemeter, an instrument for measuring the amperage of an electric current. [<AM(PERE) + -METER]

am·mine (am′ēn) *n. Chem.* **1** The ammonia molecule NH_3 in combination. **2** Any of various complex compounds containing the ammonia molecule. [<AMM(ONIA) + -INE]

am·mo·cete (am′ə·sēt) *n.* The prolonged larval stage of the lamprey, represented by an eyeless, transparent, wormlike filter feeder living in muddy river bottoms. Also **ammocoete.** [<Gk. *ammos* sand + *koitē* bed]

Am·mon (am′ən) The Greek and the Roman name for the Egyptian god AMEN: also *Zeus-Ammon, Jupiter-Ammon.*

Am·mon (am′ən) *n. pl.* A people descended from Ben Ammi, the son of Lot: chiefly in the phrase **children of Ammon.** *Deut.* ii 19. Also **Am·mon·ites** (am′ən·īts).

am·mo·nal (am′ə·nal) *n.* An explosive mixture containing TNT, ammonium nitrate, and aluminum powder. [<AMMON(IUM) + AL(UMINUM)]

am·mo·nia (ə·mōn′yə, ə·mō′nē·ə) *n.* **1** A colorless, pungent gas, NH_3, readily soluble in water to form an alkaline solution, produced in the decomposition of many organic nitrogenous compounds. **2** Ammonium hydroxide. [<SAL AMMONIAC]

am·mo·ni·ac[1] (ə·mō′nē·ak) *adj.* Of, containing, or resembling ammonia. Also **am·mo·ni·a·cal** (am′ə·nī′ə·kəl).

am·mo·ni·ac[2] (ə·mō′nē·ak) *n.* A gum resin obtained from an umbelliferous plant *(Dorema ammoniacum)* of Asia. Also called *gum ammoniac.* [<F <L *ammoniacum* <Gk. *ammōniakon,* a resinous gum said to come from a plant growing near the temple of *Ammon* in Libya]

am·mo·ni·ate (ə·mō′nē·āt) *v.t.* **·at·ed, ·at·ing** To treat or combine with ammonia. —*n.* (ə·mō′nē·it) A compound containing ammonia. —**am·mo′ni·a′tion** *n.*

am·mon·i·fi·ca·tion (ə·mon′ə·fi·kā′shən) *n.* **1** The addition of ammonia or ammonium salts, as in the form of fertilizer added to the soil. **2** The stage in the nitrogen cycle in which nitrogenous compounds are decomposed to form ammonia by the action of bacteria, fungi, etc.

am·mon·i·fy (ə·mon′ə·fī) *v.t.* & *v.i.* **·fied, ·fy·ing** To bring about or undergo ammonification.

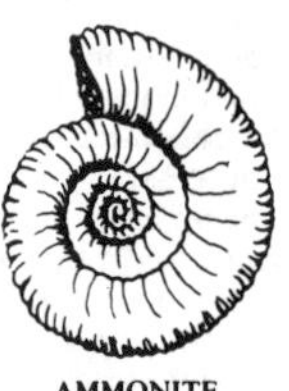
AMMONITE (European)

am·mon·ite[1] (am′ən·īt) *n.* Any of various flat spiral shells of an extinct order (Ammonoidea) of cephalopods that flourished in the Mesozoic era. Also **am′·mon·oid.** [<L *cornu Ammonis* horn of Ammon]

am·mon·ite[2] (am′ən·īt) *n.* **1** A fertilizer composed of animal wastes. **2** An explosive containing ammonium nitrate as the principal component. [<AMMON(IA) + -ITE[1]]

Am·mon·ite (am′ən·īt) *n.* One of the people of Ammon.

am·mo·ni·um (ə·mō′nē·əm) *n. Chem.* The univalent radical NH_4, which in compounds formed from ammonia acts as an alkali metal. [<NL <AMMONIA]

ammonium chloride A white, crystalline salt, NH_4Cl, used as a flux in soldering and galvanizing and as an electrolyte in dry cells. Also called *sal ammoniac.*

ammonium hydroxide A compound, NH_4OH, formed in ordinary aqueous or caustic ammonia.

ammonium nitrate A colorless, crystalline, soluble salt, NH_4NO_3, used as an ingredient of explosives and in freezing mixtures.

ammonium sulfate A commercial salt, $(NH_4)_2SO_4$, manufactured from the ammoniac liquor produced in the manufacture of gas. It is used as a nitrogenous fertilizer.

am·mu·ni·tion (am′yə·nish′ən) *n.* **1** *Mil.* Any one of various articles used in the discharge of firearms and ordnance, as cartridges, shells, shot, rockets, primers, fuses, grenades, and chemicals. **2** Any resources for attack or defense. —*v.t.* To supply with ammunition. [<MF *amunition,* for *munition (la munition* taken as *l'amunition)* <L *munitio, -onis* <*munire* fortify]

am·ne·sia (am·nē′zhə, -zhē·ə) *n.* Loss or impairment of memory; morbid forgetfulness. [<NL <Gk. *amnēsia* forgetfulness <*a-* not + *mnasthai* remember] —**am·ne·sic** (am·nē′sik, -zik) *adj.*

am·ne·si·ac (am·nē′zhē·ak, -zē-) *n.* One suffering from amnesia. —*adj.* Pertaining to or causing loss of memory.

am·nes·tic (am·nes′tik) *n.* Any agent that produces amnesia. —*adj.* Amnesiac.

am·nes·ty (am′nəs·tē) *n. pl.* **·ties** **1** An official act of oblivion or pardon on the part of a government, absolving without trial all offenders or groups of offenders. **2** Intentional forgetfulness or overlooking, especially of wrongdoing. —*v.t.* **·tied, ·ty·ing** To pardon; grant amnesty to. [<F *amnestie* <L *amnestia* <Gk. *amnēstia* <*a-* not + *mnasthai* remember]

am·ni·o·cen·te·sis (am′nē·ō·sen·tē′sis) *n.* The sampling of amniotic fluid of a pregnant woman, as to detect chromosomal anomalies or to determine the sex of the fetus. [<AMNION + Gk. *kentein* to prick]

am·ni·on (am′nē·ən) *n. pl.* **·ni·ons** or **·ni·a** (-nē·ə) A tough, membranous, fluid-containing sac enclosing the embryo of birds, reptiles, and mammals. [<Gk. *amnion* the fetal envelope, dim. of *amnos* lamb] —**am·ni·on·ic** (am′nē·on′ik), **am·ni·ot·ic** (am′nē·ot′ik) *adj.*

am·ni·ote (am′nē·ōt) *n.* Any member of the three classes of animals (Reptilia, Aves, and Mammalia) in which the embryo is protected by an amnion. —*adj.* Of or pertaining to amniotes.

am·o·bar·bi·tal (am′o·bär′bə·tôl) *n.* A bitter crystalline barbiturate, $C_{11}H_{18}N_2O_3$, used as a sedative and hypnotic.

am·o·di·a·quin (am′ō·dī′ə·kwin) *n.* A synthetic drug, $C_{20}H_{22}ClN_3O$, used chiefly to treat malaria.

a·mock, a·mok (ə·muk′, ə·mok′), **a·moke** (ə·mōk′), etc. See AMUCK.

a·moe·ba (ə·mē′bə), **a·moe·bic** (ə·mē′bik), **a·moe·boid** (ə·mē′boid), etc. See AMEBA, etc.

am·oe·bae·an, am·oe·be·an (am′ə·bē′ən) See AMEBEAN.

a·mo·le (ə·mō′lā) *n.* **1** The roots or parts of certain plants, employed in Mexico and the

SW United States as a substitute for soap. 2 Any plant that produces such roots, as the century plant and the soap plant. [<Am. Sp. <Nahuatl]

A·mon (ä′mən) See AMEN.

among (ə·mung′) *prep.* 1 In the midst of: a house *among* the trees. 2 Mingled with; included within a mass or multitude: He was just one *among* hundreds. 3 In the class, group, number, or company of: one example *among* many. 4 In association with; connected with: Some truth may be found *among* many errors. 5 Shared by; affecting all of: money divided *among* the poor. 6 According to the customs of; in the country or time of: usage *among* educated people; a practice *among* the French. Also **amongst**. See synonyms under AMID, BETWEEN. [OE *on gemong* in the crowd]

a·mon·til·la·do (ə·mon′tə·lä′dō, *Sp.* ä·môn′tē·lyä′thō) *n.* A pale, dry kind of sherry. [<Sp., from *Montilla,* a town in southern Spain]

a·mor·al (ā·môr′əl, ā·mor′əl) *adj.* 1 Not subject to or concerned with moral or ethical judgment or distinctions. 2 Lacking a sense of right or wrong; lacking moral responsibility. [<A-[4] not + MORAL] **—a·mo·ral·i·ty** (ā′mə·ral′ə·tē) *n.***—a·mor′al·ly** *adv.*

am·o·ret·to (am′ə·ret′ō) *n. pl.* **·ret·ti** (-ret′ē) A cupid. [<Ital., dim of *amore* love <L *amor*]

a·mo·ri·no (ä′mō·rē′nō) *n.* **·ni** (-nē) An amoretto.

am·o·rist (am′ə·rist) *n.* 1 A lover; one given to amours. 2 One who writes about romantic love. **—am′o·ris′tic** *adj.*

Am·o·rites (am′ə·rīts) One of the chief nations in the land of Canaan before its conquest by the Israelites. *Gen.* xv 16.

a·mo·ro·so (ä′mō·rō′sō) *adj. Music* Tender. —*adv. Music* Tenderly. —*n. pl.* **·si** (-sē) A gallant; lover. [<Ital., amorous]

am·o·rous (am′ə·rəs) *adj.* 1 Having a propensity for falling in love; influenced by sexual affection or appetite; loving; ardent in affection. 2 Of or pertaining to love; showing, springing from, or exciting to love or sexual desire. 3 In love; enamored: usually with *of.* [<OF <LL *amorosus* <L *amor* love] **—am′orous·ly** *adv.* **—am′o·rous·ness** *n.*

a·mor pa·tri·ae (ā′môr pā′tri·ē) *Latin* Love of native country; patriotism.

a·mor·phism (ə·môr′fiz·əm) *n.* The state or quality of being amorphous.

a·mor·phous (ə·môr′fəs) *adj.* 1 Without definite form or shape; structureless. 2 *Geol.* Found or occurring in masses lacking definite stratification. 3 Anomalous; unorganized. 4 Having no apparent fine structure; not crystalline. [<Gk. *amorphos* <*a-* without + *morphē* form] **—a·mor′phous·ly** *adv.* **—a·mor′phous·ness** *n.*

a·mort (ə·môrt′) *adj. & adv. Archaic* Without life or animation; dejected, as if dead.

am·or·ti·za·tion (am′ər·tə·zā′shən, ə·môr′tə·zā′shən) *n.* 1 An amortizing or being amortized. 2 The sum of money set aside or devoted to amortizing a debt.

am·or·tize (am′ər·tīz, ə·môr′tīz) *v.t.* **·tized, ·tiz·ing** 1 To extinguish, as a debt or liability, by payments to a sinking fund or creditor. 2 *Law* To sell and convey, as land, to a corporation having perpetual succession; alienate in mortmain. Also *Brit.* **am′or·tise.** [<OF *amortiss-,* stem of *amortir* extinguish, sell in mortmain <L *ad-* to + *mors, mortis* death] **—am·or·tiz·a·ble** (am′ər·tīz′ə·bəl, a·môr′tiz·ə·bəl) *adj.*

a·mor·tize·ment (ə·môr′tiz·mənt) *n.* 1 Amortization. 2 *Archaic* The finishing portion at the top of any part of a structure.

A·mos (ā′məs) A masculine personal name. [<Hebrew, ? borne by God]
—**Amos** A minor prophet, eighth century B.C., or the Old Testament book bearing his name.

a·mo·tion (ə·mō′shən) *n. Archaic.* A removal, as from office; deprivation of ownership. [<L *amotio, -onis* <*amotus,* pp. of *amovere.* See AMOVE.]

a·mount (ə·mount′) *n.* 1 A sum total; aggregate. 2 The value of the principal with the interest upon it, as in a loan. 3 The entire significance, value, or effect. 4 Quantity: a considerable *amount* of discussion. See synonyms under AGGREGATE. [<*v.*] —*v.i.* 1 To rise in number of quantity so as to reach: with *to*: This bill *amounts* to ten dollars. 2 To be equivalent in effect or importance: He doesn't *amount* to a row of beans. [<OF *amonter* <*amont* upward <*a mont* to the mountain <L *ad* to + *mons, montis* mountain]

a·mour (ə·mo͞or′) *n.* A love affair; intrigue. [<F]

a·mour-pro·pre (à·mo͞or′prô′pr′) *n. French* Self-love; self-esteem.

a·move (ə·mo͞ov′) *v.t.* **a·moved, a·mov·ing** *Law* To remove from a position or office. [<L *amovere* remove <*ab-* from + *movere* move]

A·moy (ə·moi′) 1 An island in Formosa Strait, Fukien Province, SE China. 2 A leading port and industrial center on Amoy island. Formerly *Szeming.*

amp (amp) *n. Colloq.* 1 Ampere. 2 An electrically amplified guitar.

AMP Symbol for adenosine monophosphate.

am·pe·lid·e·ous (am′pə·lid′ē·əs) *adj.* Of or relating to the vine family. [<NL *Ampelideae* the vine family <Gk. *ampelos* vine]

am·pe·lop·sis (am′pə·lop′sis) *n.* 1 Any member of a genus *(Ampelopsis)* of woody vines with small greenish flowers and alternate simple or compound leaves. [<NL <Gk. *ampelos* vine + *opsis* appearance]

am·per·age (am·pir′ij, am′pər·ij) *n.* The strength of an electric current in amperes.

am·pere (am′pir, am·pir′) *n. Electr.* The practical unit of electric-current strength; such a current as would be given with an electromotive force of one volt through a wire having a resistance of one ohm. **—international ampere** The current which on passing through a silver-nitrate solution will deposit silver at the rate of 0.001118 gram a second. [after A. M. *Ampère*]

Am·père (äṅ·pâr′), **André Marie,** 1775–1836, French physicist.

am·pere-hour (am′pir·our′) *n. Electr.* A quantity of electricity sufficient to furnish a current of an ampere for an hour.

am·pere-me·ter (am′pir·mē′tər) *n.* An ammeter. Also **am·pe·rom·e·ter** (am′pə·rom′ə·tər).

am·pere-turn (am′pir·tûrn′) *n. Electr.* An ampere flowing through one turn of a coil, considered with reference to electromagnetic effect. An electromagnet with 1,000 convolutions and a current of 5 amperes would have 5,000 ampere-turns.

am·per·sand (am′pər·sand, am′pər·sand′) *n.* The character (& or &) meaning *and.* [<*and per se and,* lit., & by itself = and]

am·phet·a·mine (am·fet′ə·mēn, -min) *n.*— 1 A colorless liquid, $C_9H_{13}N$, used as a stimulant of the central nervous system. 2 any of the various crystalline compounds of amphetamine used as drugs. [<*a(lpha)-m(ethyl)-ph(enyl)-et(hyl)-amine*]

amphi- *prefix* 1 On both or all sides; at both ends: *amphicoelous.* 2 Around: *amphigean.* 3 Of both kinds; in two ways: *amphibious.* [<Gk. <*amphi* around]

Am·phi·a·ra·us (am′fē·ə·rā′əs) See under SEVEN AGAINST THEBES.

am·phi·ar·thro·sis (am′fē·är·thrō′sis) *n. pl.* **·ses** (-sēz) *Anat.* An articulation in which bones are connected by intervening fibrocartilage permitting limited movement, as between adjacent vertebrae.

am·phi·as·ter (am′fē·as′tər) *n.* 1 *Biol.* That stage of cell division in which the chromatin filaments assume a radiate appearance at each end of the nuclear spindle; also, the figure so formed. 2 *Zool.* A spicule with two whorls of spines connected by a vertical axis, as in certain sponges. [<NL <AMPHI- + Gk. *astēr* star]

am·phib·i·an (am·fib′ē·n) *n. pl.* **·bi·ans** or **·bi·a** (def. 1) 1 Any of a class *(Amphibia)* of cold-blooded vertebrate organisms with smooth, moist skin, whose life cycle typically comprises tadpoles which hatch from eggs as aquatic, gilled, limbless forms and which metamorphose into terrestrial air-breathing adults with four limbs, as frogs, toads, newts, salamanders, etc. 2 Any amphibious organism. 3 An airplane constructed to rise from and alight on either land or water. 4 A craft capable of self-propulsion upon land and upon water. —*adj.* Amphibious.

am·phib·i·ol·o·gy (am·fib′ē·ol′ə·jē) *n. pl.* **·gies** 1 The scientific study of amphibians. 2 A treatise relating to this subject.

am·phib·i·ot·ic (am·fib′ē·ot′ik, am′fə·bī·ot′ik) *adj.* Having a life cycle with successive aquatic and terrestrial cycles.

am·phib·i·ous (am·fib′ē·əs) *adj.* 1 Living or adapted to life on land or in water. 2 Capable of operating on land or water: an *amphibious* tank. 3 Capable of operating on water and in the air: an *amphibious* airplane. 4 Of a mixed nature; connected with two ranks, classes, etc. [<Gk. *amphibios* having a double life <*amphi-* of two kinds + *bios* life] **—am·phib′i·ous·ly** *adv.* **—am·phib′i·ous·ness** *n.*

am·phi·blas·tu·la (am′fə·blas′cho͞o·lə) *n. Biol.* A blastula wherein the cells of one hemisphere differ from those of the other hemisphere, as in certain sponges.

am·phi·bole (am′fə·bōl) *n. Mineral.* Any of a class of variously colored hydrous silicates, consisting chiefly of calcium, magnesium, iron, aluminum, and sodium; tremolite, actinolite, asbestos, and hornblende are important varieties. [<F <L *amphibolus* ambiguous <Gk. *amphibolos* <*amphiballein* to throw around, to doubt <*amphi-* around + *ballein* throw]

am·phi·bol·ic (am′fə·bol′ik) *adj.* Pertaining to or like amphiboly; ambiguous. Also **am·phib·o·lous** (am·fib′ə·ləs).

am·phib·o·lite (am·fib′ə·līt) *n.* A rock consisting chiefly of amphibole and plagioclase, often with inclusions of garnet and quartz.

am·phi·bol·o·gy (am′fə·bol′ə·jē) *n. pl.* **·gies** An ambiguous phrase or sentence; ambiguity. [<F *amphibologie* <LL *amphibologia,* for L *amphibolia* <Gk. *amphibolia* ambiguity <*amphiballein.* See AMPHIBOLE.] **—am·phib·o·log·i·cal** (am·fib′ə·loj′i·kəl) *adj.*

am·phib·o·ly (am·fib′ə·lē) *n. pl.* **·lies** An ambiguous construction of language; a group of words admitting of two meanings. [<L *amphibolia.* See AMPHIBOLOGY.]

am·phi·brach (am′fə·brak) *n.* In prosody, a metrical foot, consisting of a long or accented syllable between two short or unaccented ones (˘ ¯ ˘). [<L *amphibrachys* <Gk. <*amphi-* at both ends + *brachys* short]

am·phi·car·pous (am′fə·kär′pəs) *adj. Bot.* Having fruit of two kinds, either in form or in period of ripening. Also **am′phi·car′pic.** [<AMPHI- + Gk. *karpos* fruit]

am·phi·chro·ic (am′fə·krō′ik) *adj.* Exhibiting either of two colors, as certain substances when subjected to tests with acids or alkalis. Also **am·phi·chro·mat·ic** (am′fə·krō·mat′ik). [<AMPHI- + Gk. *chroa* color]

am·phi·coe·lous (am′fə·sē′ləs) *adj. Zool.* Concave at both ends; biconcave, as the vertebrae of fishes and of certain extinct reptiles and birds. [<AMPHI- + Gk. *koilos* hollow]

am·phic·ty·on (am·fik′tē·ən) *n.* 1 A delegate to one of the ancient Greek amphictyonic councils. 2 The council as a body. [<L *amphictyones* <Gk. *amphiktyones* neighbors]

am·phic·ty·on·ic (am·fik′tē·on′ik) *adj.* Of or pertaining to an amphictyony.

am·phic·ty·o·ny (am·fik′tē·ə·nē) *n. pl.* **·nies** A league of ancient Greek states, allied in the worship of a common deity, as around a religious center or shrine, such as Delphi.

am·phi·cyr·tic (am′fə·sûr′tik) *adj.* Convex at both ends; biconvex. [<AMPHI- + Gk. *kyrtos* convex]

am·phi·dip·loid (am′fə·dip′loid) *n. Genetics* An interspecific hybrid having two diploid sets of chromosomes, one from each parent.**—am·phi·dip·loid·al** (am′f·dip′loi·dl) *adj.* **—am′phi·dip′loi·dy** *n.*

am·phi·ge·an (am′fə·jē′ən) *adj. Bot.* Extending around the globe in nearly the same latitude, as certain species of plants. [<AMPHI- + Gk. *gē* earth]

am·phi·gas·tri·um (am′fə·gas′trē·əm) *n. pl.* **·tri·a** (-tre·) A small, rudimentary leaf on the under surface of the stem of certain liverworts. [<AMPHI- + Gk. *gastēr* belly]

am·phi·gen·e·sis (am′fə·jen′ə·sis) *n.* 1 *Biol.* The merging of two gametes to form a fertilized cell or zygote. 2 *Psychol.* Sexual response of a predominantly homosexual person in regard to members of the opposite sex. **—am·phi·gen·ic** (am′fə·jen′ik) *adj.*

am·phig·e·nous (am·fij′ə·nəs) *adj. Bot.* Growing all around an object, as certain parasitic fungi; capable of developing in any direction permitted by the environment.

am·phi·go·ry (am′fə·gôr′ē, -gō′rē) *n. pl.* **·ries** A meaningless rigmarole with a semblance of sense; a burlesque, as one written in nonsensical verse.. Also **am·phi·gou·ri** (am′fə·go͞o′·rē) *pl.* **·ris** (-rēz). [<F *amphigouri;* ult. origin unknown] **—am·phi·gor·ic** (am′fə·gôr′ik, -gor′-) *adj.*

am·phil·o·gism (am·fil′ə·jiz′əm) *n. Obs.* A circumlocution. [<Gk. *amphilogos* <*amphi-* around + *logos* word]

am·phim·a·cer (am·fim′ə·sər) In prosody, a metrical foot consisting of one short or unaccented syllable between two long or accented ones (- ⌣ -): opposed to *amphibrach.* Also called *cretic.* [<L *amphimacrus* <Gk. *amphimakros* <*amphi-* on both sides + *makros* long]

am·phi·mix·is (am′fə·mik′sis) *n. Biol. The fusion of ovum and sperm in sexual reproduction.* [<NL AMPHI- + Gk. *mixis* a mingling] **—am·phi·mic·tic** (am′fə·mik′tik) *adj.* **—am′phi·mic′ti·cal·ly** *adv.*

am·phi·neur·an (am′fə·no͝or′ən, -nyo͝or′-) *n.* Any of a class of marine mollusks having bilateral symmetry and calcareous spicules that lie embedded in the cuticle, as the chitons.

Am·phi·on (am·fī′ən) In Greek mythology, a son of Jupiter and Antiope and husband of Niobe, who with his twin brother Zethus walled Thebes by the music of a magical lyre given him by Hermes.

am·phi·ox·us (am′fē·ok′səs) *n.* The lancelet. [<AMPHI- + Gk. *oxys* sharp]

am·phi·pod (am′fə·pod) *n.* Any of an order of small crustaceans *(Amphipoda)* having legs adapted to swimming and others adapted to walking and jumping, as the sand fleas. *—adj.* Of or pertaining to the amphipods. [<AMPHI- + Gk. *pous, podos* foot] **—am·phip·o·dan, am·phip′o·dous** *adj.*

am·phip·ro·style (am·fip′rə·stīl, am′fə·prō′stīl) *n.* A temple or other building of the classical period having at each end a columned portico but with no columns at the sides. *—adj.* Built like such a building: also **am·phip·ro·sty·lar** (am·fip′rə·stī′lər, am′fə·prō·stī′-). [<L *amphiprostylus* <Gk. *amphiprostylos*<*amphi-* on both sides + *prostylos* PROSTYLE]

am·phis·bae·na (am′fis·bē′nə) *n.* **1** A mythical serpent having a head at each end of the body and moving in either direction. **2** *Zool.* A tropical, legless lizard (family *Amphisbaenidae*) having head and tail much alike. [<L <Gk. *amphisbaina* <*amphis, amphi-* at both ends + *bainein* go] **—am′phis·bae′nic** *adj.*

am·phis·cians (am·fish′ənz) *n. pl. Archaic* The inhabitants of the torrid zone, whose shadows fall at one season to the north, at the other to the south. Also **am·phis·ci·i** (am·fish′ē·ī). [<Med.L *amphiscii* <Gk. *amphiskios* throwing a shadow both ways <*amphi-* on both sides + *skia* shadow]

am·phi·sty·lar (am′fə·stī′lər) *adj. Archit.* With columns at each end or on each side. [<AMPHI- + Gk. *stylos* pillar]

am·phi·the·a·ter (am′fə·thē′ə·tər) *n.* **1** An edifice of elliptical shape, constructed about a central open space or arena, with tiers of seats sloping upward. **2** Any structure of similar shape, as a natural area or theater having slopes or tiers of seats entirely surrounding a central space. **3** The place where a spectacle or battle takes place; scene of action. Also **am′phi·the′a·tre.** [<L *amphitheatrum* <Gk. *amphitheatron* <*amphi-* around + *theatron* theater]

am·phi·the·at·ri·cal (am′fə·thē·at′ri·kəl) *adj.* Of, pertaining to, resembling, or performed in an amphitheater. Also **am·phi·the·a·tral** (am′fə·thē′ə·trəl), **am·phi·the·at·ric** (am′fə·thē·at′rik). **—am′phi·the·at′ri·cal·ly** *adv.*

am·phi·the·ci·um (am′fə·thē′shē·əm, -sē·əm) *n. pl.* **·ci·a** (-shē·ə, -sē·ə) *Bot.* The outer layer of cells surrounding the endothecium in the spore case of mosses. [<NL <AMPHI- + Gk. *thēkion,* dim. of *thēkē* a case, container]

am·phit·ri·chous (am·fit′rə·kəs) *adj.* Having flagella at both ends, as certain bacteria. [<AMPHI- + Gk. *thrix, trichos* hair]

Am·phi·tri·te (am′fə·trī′tē) In Greek mythology, one of the Nereids, who became wife of Poseidon and goddess of the sea.

am·phit·ro·pous (am·fit′rə·pəs) *adj. Bot.* Half inverted with the hilum lateral: said of an ovule or seed. [<AMPHI- + -TROPOUS]

Am·phit·ry·on (am·fit′rē·ən) In Greek mythology, the husband of Alcmene.

am·phi·u·ma (am′fē·yo͞o′mə) *n. Zool.* Any of a genus *(Amphiuma)* of salamanders typical of the congo-snake family *(Amphiumidae).* [<NL <AMPHI- + Gk. *pneuma* breath]

am·pho·ra (am′fə·rə) *n. pl.* **·rae** (-rē) In ancient Greece, a tall, two-handled earthenware jar for wine or oil, narrow at the neck and the base. [<L <Gk. *amphoreus* <*amphi-* on both sides + *phoreus* bearer <*pherein* bear] — **am′pho·ral** *adj.*

AMPHORAE

am·phor·ic (am·fôr′ik, -for′-) *adj.* **1** Having a sound like that made by blowing into the mouth of an amphora. **2** Amphoral.

am·pho·ter·ic (am′fə·ter′ik) *adj.* Capable of reacting chemically as either an acid or a base. [<Gk. *amphoteros* both]

am·pho·ter·i·cin (am′fə·ter′ə·sin) *n.* An antibiotic produced by a soil actinomycete *(Streptomyces nodosus)* and having a component, amphotericin B, that is effective as a systemic fungicide.

am·pi·cil·lin (am′pə·sil′ən) *n.* A kind of penicillin that is especially effective against Gram-negative bacteria

am·ple (am′pəl) *adj.* **1** Of great dimensions or capacity; large; great in amount of degree. **2** More than enough; abundant; liberal. **3** Fully sufficient to meet all needs or requirements; adequate. [<F <L *amplus* large, abundant] **—am′ple·ness** *n.*

Synonyms: abundant, affluent, bountiful, complete, copious, enough, full, large, liberal, plenteous, plentiful, sufficient. That is *enough* which just meets a given demand; that is *ample* which gives a safe, but not a large, margin beyond; that is *abundant, affluent, bountiful, liberal, plentiful,* which is largely in excess of manifest need. Compare ENOUGH, LARGE, PLENTIFUL. *Antonyms*: deficient, inadequate, insufficient, niggardly, scant, small, stingy.

am·plex·i·caul (am̀·plek′si·kôl) *adj. Bot.* Clasping a stem, as the base of some leaves. [<NL *amplexicaulis* <L *amplexus* embracing + *caulis* stem]

am·pli·a·tive (am′plē·ā′tiv) *adj.* Supplementing, or adding to.

am·pli·fi·ca·tion (am′plə·fi·kā′shən) *n.* **1** An amplifying or being amplified; augmentation; addition. **2** An extended statement; the matter added to amplify a subject; details. **3** *Electr.* An increase in the voltage or power of an electric current. See synonyms under INCREASE.

am·pli·fi·er (am′plə·fī′ər) *n.* **1** One who or that which amplifies or increases. **2** A megaphonelike device for increasing the volume of sound. **3** *Electr.* A device for increasing the intensity of electric impulses by the control of power supplied by a local source, usually by means of vacuum tubes or dynamos. **4** A loudspeaker.

am·pli·fy (am′plə·fī) *v.* **·fied, ·fy·ing** *v.t.* **1** To enlarge or increase in scope, significance, or power. **2** To add to so as to make more complete, as by illustrations. **3** To exaggerate; magnify. **4** *Electr.* To increase the strength or amplitude of, as electromagnetic impulses. *—v.i.* **5** To make additional remarks; expatiate. [<F *amplifier* <L *amplificare* <*amplus* large + *facere* make] — **am·pli·fi·ca·tive** (am′plə·fi·kā′tiv, am·plif′i·kə·tiv), **am·plif·i·ca·to·ry** (am·plif′i·kə·tôr′ē, -tō′rē) *adj.*

Synonyms: augment, develop, dilate, enlarge, expand, expatiate, extend, increase, unfold, widen. *Amplify* is now chiefly applied to discourse or writing, signifying to make fuller in statement, as by stating fully what was before only implied, or by adding illustrations to make the meaning more readily apprehended, etc. We may *develop* a thought, *expand* an illustration, *extend* a discussion, *expatiate* on a hobby, *dilate* on some theme or incident, *enlarge* a volume, *unfold* a scheme, *widen* the range of treatment. Compare ADD. *Antonyms*: abbreviate, abridge, amputate, compress, condense, curtail, delete, epitomize, reduce, retrench, shorten, summarize, contract, tighten.

am·pli·tude (am′plə·to͞od, -tyo͞od) *n.* **1** Greatness of extent; largeness; breadth; the state or quality of being ample: the *amplitude* of the oceans. **2** Fullness or completeness; abundance or richness: the *amplitude* of life. **3** Broad range or scope, as of mental capacity: an *amplitude* of talent. **4** *Astron.* The arc of the horizon between true east and west and the center of the sun, moon, or any star at its rising or setting. **5** *Physics* The extent of the swing of a vibrating body on each side of the mean position. **6** *Electr.* The peak value attained by an alternating current during one complete cycle. [<L *amplitudo* <*amplus* large]

amplitude modulation That form of radio transmission in which the carrier wave is modulated by varying the amplitude above and below a standard value in accordance with the signals to be transmitted. Compare FREQUENCY MODULATION.

am·ply (am′plē) *adv.* In an ample manner; largely; liberally; sufficiently.

am·poule (am·po͞ol) *n. Med.* A small, hermetically sealed vial, usually made of glass, containing a medicament for injection or other use. Also **am·pule** (am′pyo͞ol), **am·pul** (am′pul). [<F <L *ampulla* ampulla (def. 3)]

am·pul·la (am·pul′ə) *n. pl.* **am·pul·lae** (-pul′ē) **1** *Eccl.* A flask for holding the consecrated oil used in confirmation, ordination, and extreme unction; specifically, that used in England at the consecration of kings. **2** The cruet used for the wine or water at mass. **3** An ancient Roman bottle or vase with a slender neck and flattened mouth, used to hold perfumes and oils and for carrying wine. **4** *Anat.* A small sac or dilated segment of a tube or gland. [<L, dim. of *amphora* jar] **—am·pul′lar** *adj.*

am·pul·la·ceous (am′pə·lā′shəs) *adj.* Of, pertaining to, or like an ampulla; bladder-shaped; inflated.

am·pu·tate (am′pyo͞o·tāt) *v.t.* **·tat·ed, ·tat·ing 1** *Surg.* To remove by cutting, as a limb; cut off the whole or a part of. **2** To reduce; prune: to *amputate* funds for a project. [<L *amputatus,* pp. of *amputare* <*ambi-* around + *putare* trim, prune] **—am′·pu·ta′tion** *n.* **—am′pu·ta′tor** *n.*

am·pu·tee (am′pyo͞o·tē′) *n.* One who has had a limb or limbs removed by amputation.

am·ri·ta (um·rē′tə) *n.* In Hindu mythology: **1** The ambrosia of immortality, sometimes represented as the fruit of a tree or the cream of the ocean churned by the gods. **2** Immortality. Also **am·ree′ta.** [<Skt. *amṛta*]

Am·rit·sar (um·rit′sər) A city in western Punjab, India.

Am·ster·dam (am′stər·dam) A port on the Zuider Zee; constitutional capital and largest city of the Netherlands.

amt (ämt) *n.* An administrative territorial division of Denmark or Norway. [<G]

Am·trak (am′trak) *n.* A government-controlled public corporation, officially known as the National Railroad Passenger Corporation, created in 1970 to run the essential passenger service linking major U.S. cities which private enterprise is unable to provide.

a·muck (ə·muk′) *adj.* Possessed with murderous frenzy. *—adv.* In a violent or frenzied manner. **—to run amuck** To run about attacking everybody one meets. Also spelled *amock, amok, amoke.* [<Malay *amoq* engaging furiously in battle]

A·mu Dar·ya (ä·mo͞o′ där′yä) A principal river of central Asia, flowing 872 miles to the Aral Sea from the U.S.S.R.-Afghanistan border: ancient *Oxus:* Arabic *Jaihun.*

am·u·let (am′yə·lit) *n.* Anything worn about one's person to protect from witchcraft, accident, or ill luck; a charm. See synonyms under TALISMAN. [<L *amuletum* charm]

A·mund·sen (ä′mo͝on·sən), **Ro·ald** (rō′äl), 1872–1928, Norwegian explorer; discovered South Pole, 1911.

A·mur (ä·mo͞or′) A river in eastern Asia, flowing 1,767 miles to the Gulf of Sákhalin and forming the boundary between Manchuria and the U.S.S.R.

a·muse (ə·myo͞oz′) *v.t.* **a·mused, a·mus·ing 1** To occupy pleasingly; entertain; divert: to *amuse* oneself by playing the guitar. **2** To cause to laugh or smile, as with pleasure. **3** *Archaic* To beguile; delude. [<F *amuser*

<*à* at (<L *ad-*) + OF *muser* stare] **—a·mus′·a·ble** *adj.* **—a·mus′er** *n.*

a·muse·ment (ə·myōōz′mənt) *n.* **1** The state of being amused; the feeling of delight or joy, as in some diversion. **2** That which amuses, as an entertainment, game, or spectacle. See synonyms under COMFORT, ENTERTAINMENT, FROLIC, SPORT.

a·mus·ing (ə·myōō′zing) *adj.* **1** Entertaining or diverting. **2** Arousing laughter.

a·mu·sive (ə·myōō′ziv, -siv) *adj.* Having power to amuse; amusing.

Am·vets (am′vets′) American Veterans of World War II, Korea, and Vietnam.

A·my (ā′mē) A feminine personal name. [<L, beloved]

a·myg·da·la (ə·mig′də·lə) *n. pl.* **·lae** (-lē) **1** An almond. **2** An almond-shaped mass of gray matter in the anterior part of the temporal lobe of the brain. [<L <Gk. *amygdalē* almond]

a·myg·da·la·ceous (ə·mig′də·lā′shəs) *adj.* Allied to the almond.

a·myg·da·late (ə·mig′də·lit, -lāt) *adj.* Pertaining to or like almonds.

a·myg·dale (ə·mig′dāl) *n. Geol.* An almond-shaped cavity formed by expanding steam in volcanic and intrusive rocks, filled with mineral secretions which are often of commercial importance and of value in the determination of geologic time. [<Gk. *amygdalē* almond]

a·myg·dal·ic (am′ig·dal′ik) Of or pertaining to almonds.

a·myg·da·lin (ə·mig′də·lin) *n.* A white crystalline compound, $C_{20}H_{27}O_{11}N$, obtained from the kernel of bitter almonds and related plants and yielding on hydrolysis glucose, benzaldehyde, and hydrocyanic acid.

a·myg·da·line (ə·mig′də·lin, -līn) *adj.* Pertaining to or like almonds.

a·myg·da·loid (ə·mig′də·loid) *adj.* **1** Almond-shaped. **2** Pertaining to or of an amygdala. **3** *Geol.* Containing amygdales or resembling an amygdaloid rock. Also **a·myg′da·loi′dal.** *—n.* An igneous rock, usually basaltic, containing amygdales.

a·myg·dule (ə·mig′dyōōl) *n. Geol.* One of the mineral cavities in an amygdale.

am·yl (am′il) *n.* A univalent hydrocarbon radical, C_5H_{11}, having eight isomeric forms and entering into many organic compounds. Also called *pentyl.* [<Gk. *amylon* starch + -YL]

am·y·la·ceous (am′ə·lā′shəs) *adj.* Pertaining to or like starch; starchy.

amyl acetate A colorless, sweet-smelling, oily compound, $C_7H_{14}O_2$, used as a solvent and in flavors and perfumes. Also called *banana oil.*

amyl alcohol **1** A colorless liquid, $C_5H_{11}OH$, consisting of any one or a combination of any of eight isomeric alcohols.

am·y·lase (am′ə·lās) *n.* Any of several enzymes occurring in plants and animals which promote the conversion of starch and glycogen to sugar. [<AMYL + -ASE]

am·y·lene (am′ə·lēn) *n.* **1** A colorless volatile liquid, consisting of several olefins, obtained by distilling amyl alcohol with zinc chloride, and used as an anesthetic. **2** Any of the isomeric hydrocarbons, C_5H_{10}, belonging to the ethylene series. [<AMYL + -ENE]

a·myl·ic (ə·mil′ik) *adj.* Of, pertaining to, or derived from amyl.

amyl nitrite A volatile yellow liquid, $C_5H_{11}NO_2$, having a fruity odor, used by inhalation to relieve arterial spasms, as in angina pectoris.

amylo- *combining form* **1** Of starch: *amyloplast.* **2** Of amyl. Also, before vowels, **amyl-.** [def. 1 <AMYLUM; def. 2 <AMYL]

am·y·lo·dex·trin (am′ə·lo·dek′strən) *n.* A white, odorless powder formed by hydrolysis of starch, becoming reddish-brown in iodine solutions.

a·myl·o·gen (ə·mil′ə·jən) *n.* Starch granulose or granules that are soluble in water.

am·y·lo·gen·ic (am′ə·lō·jen′ik) *adj.* Pertaining to the biosynthesis of starch.

am·y·loid (am′ə·loid) *n.* **1** *Bot.* A gummy or starchlike substance formed in woody tissues in the process of lignification. **2** *Pathol.* Waxy matter formed in certain diseased tissues of the body, but not chemically related to starch. — *adj.* Like or containing starch. **—am′y·loi′dal** *adj.*

am·y·loi·do·sis (am′ə·loi·dō′sis) *n.* Deterioration of organic tissues with deposition of amyloids.

am·y·lol·y·sis (am′ə·lol′ə·sis) *n.* The hydrolysis of starch to sugar by the action of enzymes. **—am·y·lo·lyt·ic** (am′ə·lō·lit′ik) *adj.*

am·y·lo·pec·tin (am′ə·lō·pek′tin) *n.* An almost insoluble branched-chain carbohydrate polymer occurring on the surface of starch granules and staining violet with iodine.

am·y·lo·plast (am′ə·lō·plast′) *n. Bot.* **1** A starch-forming cell. **2** A leucoplastid or amylogenic body. Also **am′y·lo·plas′tid** (-plas′·tid),**am′y·lo·plas′tide** (-plas′tid, tīd).

am·y·lop·sin (am′ə·lop′sin) *n.* A constituent of pancreatic juice which promotes the conversion of starch to sugar. [<AMYLO- + (TRY)PSIN]

am·y·lose (am′ə·lōs) *n.* An unbranched carbohydrate polymer occurring as a water-soluble component of starch which turns blue in iodine.

am·y·lum (am′ə·ləm) *n.* Starch. [<L <Gk. *amylon* starch]

a·my·o·to·ni·a (ə·mī′ə·tō′nē·ə) *n.* Abnormal muscular flaccidity. [<NL <Gk. *a-* without + *mys, myos* muscle + *tonos* tone]

am·y·ot·ro·phy (am′e-ot′rə·fē) *n.* Atrophy of a muscle or muscles. [<Gk. *a-* without + *mys, myos* muscle + *trophē* nourishment]

Am·y·tal (am′ə·tal, -tôl) *n.* A proprietary name for amobarbital.

an[1] (an, *unstressed* ən) *indefinite article & adj.* **1** Each or any. **2** One; one kind of; one single. Used like the article *a,* but before words beginning with a vowel sound; as, *an* acorn, *an* honest man. **3** For each: The price is a dollar *an* apple. [OE *an* one]

an[2] (an, *unstressed* ən) *conj. Archaic* And, especially in the sense *and if,* or *if*: often written **an'.** See AND.

an-[1] *prefix* Without; not: *anacid, anarchy.* Also, before consonants except *h, a-* (called *alpha privative*). [<Gk.]

an-[2] Var. of ANA-.

an-[3] Assimilated var. of AD-.

-an *suffix* Used to form adjectives and nouns denoting connection with a country, person, group, doctrine, etc., as follows: **1** Pertaining to; belonging to: *human, sylvan.* **2** Originating in; living in: *Italian.* **3** Adhering to; following: *Lutheran.* [<L *-anus*]

a·na[1] (ā′nə, ä′nə) *n.* **1** A collection of notes, sketches, or scraps of literature bearing on some particular person, place, or subject. **2** The information in such a collection. See -ANA.

an·a[2] (an′ə) *adv. Med.* Of each a like amount: used in prescriptions. [<Gk. *ana* throughout]

A·na (ä′nä) Spanish form of ANN.

ana- *prefix* **1** Up; upward: *anadromous.* **2** Back; backward: *anapest.* **3** Anew: sometimes capable of being rendered *re-,* as *anabaptism,* rebaptism. **4** Throughout; thoroughly: *analysis.* Also, before vowels or *h, an-,* as in *anode.* [<Gk. <*ana* on]

-ana *suffix* Pertaining to: added to the names of notable persons, places, etc., to indicate a collection of materials, such as writings or anecdotes, about the subject: *Americana, Johnsoniana.* Also *-iana.* [<L, neut. pl. of *-anus.* See -AN]

an·a·bae·na (an′ə·bē′nə) *n. pl.* **·nas** Any of various blue-green algae of the genus *Anabaena,* sometimes imparting a disagreeable taste and odor to water supplies. [<NL <Gk. *anabainein.* See ANABASIS.]

An·a·bap·tist (an′ə·bap′tist) *n.* One of a sect that arose in Zurich in 1523 among the followers of Zwingli, who started the Reformation in Switzerland and advocated opposition to infant baptism, and believed that only such persons as had been baptized after a confession of faith in Christ constituted a real church. *—adj.* Of or pertaining to Anabaptists or Anabaptism. [<NL *anabaptista* <L *anabaptismus* <Gk. *anabaptismos* rebaptism <*anabaptizein* rebaptize <*ana-* anew + *baptizein* baptize] **—An′a·bap′tism***n.*

an·a·bas (an′ə·bas) *n.* Any of a genus *(Anabas)* of freshwater fishes of Africa and Asia adapted to using oxygen both in water and in the atmosphere, as the climbing perch, which *(Anabas scandens),* called the *climbing fish,* can travel on land and climb trees by means of its spinous gill covers. [<NL <Gk. *anabas* <*anabainein.* See ANABASIS.]

a·nab·a·sis (ə·nab′ə·sis) *n. pl.* **·ses** (-sēz) A military advance or incursion, as that of Cyrus the Younger, with 10,000 Greek auxiliaries, against Artaxerxes II in 401 B.C., described in Xenophon's *Anabasis.* [<Gk. <*anabainein* go up <*ana-* up + *bainein* go]

an·a·bat·ic (an′ə·bat′ik) *adj.* **1** Of or pertaining to an anabasis. **2** *Meteorol.* Rising upwards, as air currents.

an·a·bi·o·sis (an′ə·bī·ō′sis) *n.* A suspension of animation susceptible of resuscitation. [<NL <ANA- + Gk. *bios* life]

an·a·bi·ot·ic (an′ə·bī·ot′ik) *adj.* Lifeless, but capable of resuscitation.

an·a·bleps (an′ə·bleps) *n.* A fresh-water cyprinodont fish of tropical America having each eye divided into two segments, the upper portion adapted for vision in air, the lower for vision in water. Also called *four-eyed fish.* [<NL <Gk. *anablepein* look up]

ANABLEPS

an·a·bol·ic steroid (an′ə·bol′ik) Any of various synthetic drugs that stimulate the development of large and strong muscles.

a·nab·o·lism (ə·nab′ə·liz′əm) *n.* The phase of metabolism in which large and complex molecules are built up from smaller, simpler compounds. [<Gk. *anabolē* a heaping up <*ana-* up + *bolē* a stroke] **—an·a·bol·ic** (an′ə·bol′ik) *adj.*

an·a·branch (an′ə·branch, -bränch) *n. Geog.* An effluent of a stream which rejoins the main stream, forming an island between the two watercourses. [<*ana(stomosing) branch*]

an·a·car·di·a·ceous (an′ə·kär′dē·ā′shəs) *adj. Bot.* Designating a large family *(Anacardiaceae)* of trees or shrubs of the order *Sapindales,* the sumac family, with resinous, milky, acrid juice, alternate leaves, and small flowers. [<NL <ANA- similar to + Gk. *kardia* heart; with ref. to the shape of the fruit]

an·a·ca·thar·sis (an′ə·kə·thär′sis) *n. Med.* **1** Regurgitation; vomiting. **2** Expectoration. [<NL <Gk. *anakatharsis* <*ana-* up + *katharsis* purification]

a·nach·o·rism (ə·nak′ə·riz′əm) *n.* Something foreign to a country or unsuited to local conditions; a geographical error: compare with *anachronism.* [<ANA- + Gk. *chōros* country, place]

a·nach·ro·nism (ə·nak′rə·niz′əm) *n.* **1** A chronological error. **2** Something occurring or represented as occurring out of its proper time. [<F *anachronisme* <L *anachronismus* <Gk. *anachronismos* <*anachronizein* refer to a wrong time <*ana-* against + *chronos* time] **—an·a·chron·ic** (an′ə·kron′ik), **a·nach′·ro·nis′tic, a·nach′ro·nis′ti·cal, a·nach′ro·nous** *adj.*

an·ac·id (an·as′id) *adj. Med.* Lacking the normal degree of acidity: said especially of gastric secretions. **—an·a·cid·i·ty** (an′ə·sid′·ə·tē) *n.*

a·nac·la·sis (ə·nak′lə·sis) *n.* In prosody, the exchange of place of a short syllable with a preceding long one; thus, -⏑⏑- for --⏑⏑. [<NL <Gk. *anaklasis* <*anaklaein* bend back <*ana-* back + *klaein* break]

an·a·clas·tic (an′ə·klas′tik) *adj.* **1** *Optics* Pertaining to refraction or bending; caused by or causing refraction. **2** In prosody, characterized by anaclasis.

an·a·cli·nal (an′ə·klī′nəl) *adj. Geol.* Transverse to the course of underlying rocks and against the dip, as a valley. [<ANA- on + Gk. *klinein* lean]

an·a·cli·sis (an′ə·klī′sis, ə·nak′lə·sis) *n. Psychoanal.* A strong emotional dependence upon others, especially those who typify a child's first object of love or source of protection and support. [<NL <Gk. *anaklisis* <*anaklinein* lean upon <*ana-* upon + *klinein* lean]

an·a·clit·ic (an′ə·klit′ik) *adj.* **1** Needing support; dependent. **2** Exhibiting anaclisis.

an·a·co·lu·thon (an′ə·kə·lōō′thon) *n. pl.* **·thons** or **·tha** (-thə) **1** Violation of grammatical sequence, as for the sake of energy or to express strong emotion. 2 An instance of this; a sentence in which anacoluthon occurs. [<Gk. *anakolouthos* lacking sequence <*an-* not + *akolouthos* following] **—an'a·co·lu'thic** *adj.*

an·a·con·da (an'ə·kon'də) *n.* 1 A very large nonvenomous, semiaquatic snake, *Eunectes murinus,* of tropical South America, which crushes its prey in its coils. 2 Any of very large constrictors. [Origin unknown]

An·a·con·da (an'ə·kon'də) A copper-mining city in SW Montana; site of the world's largest copper smelter.

A·nac·re·on (ə·nak'rē·ən, -on), 563?–478 B.C., Greek erotic poet.

A·nac·re·on·tic (ə·nak'rē·on'tik) *adj.* 1 Pertaining to or like the lyrics of Anacreon. 2 Praising love and wine; convivial; amatory. *—n.* A poem in the manner of Anacreon; amatory or convivial verse.

an·a·cru·sis (an'ə·kroo͞'sis) *n.* 1 In prosody, one or more unemphatic introductory syllables in a line of verse that would properly begin with a stressed syllable. 2 *Music* An upbeat. [<NL <Gk. *anakrousis* <*anakrouein* push back <*ana-* back + *krouein* strike] **—an·a·crus·tic** (an'ə·krus'tik) *adj.*

an·a·dem (an'ə·dem) *n.* A wreath for the head; garland; fillet. [<L *anadema* <Gk. *anadēma* <*anadein* wreathe <*ana-* up + *dein* bind]

an·a·di·plo·sis (an'ə·di·plō'sis) *n.* Rhetorical repetition, in which the ending of a sentence, line, or clause is repeated and emphasized at the beginning of the next. [<L <Gk. *anadiplōsis* <*ana-* again + *diploein* to double <*diploos* double]

a·nad·ro·mous (ə·nad'rə·məs) *adj.* Ascending upriver from the sea to spawn: said of fishes such as salmon. Compare *catadromous.* [<Gk. *anadromos* <*ana-* up + *dromos* a running <*dramein* run]

a·nae·mi·a (ə·nē'mē·ə), etc. See ANEMIA, etc.

an·aer·obe (an·âr'ōb, an·ā'ə·rōb) *n.* A microorganism that thrives in the absence of free oxygen. [<AN-[1] without + AERO- + Gk. *bios* life]

an·aer·o·bic (an'âr·ō'bik, -ob'ik, an'ā·ə·rō'bik, -rob'ik) *adj.* Living or functioning in the absence of free oxygen: *anaerobic* bacteria. 2 Containing no uncombined oxygen: an *anaerobic* environment. **—an'aer·o'bi·cal·ly** *adv.*

an·aer·o·phyte (an·âr'ə·fit, an·ā'ər·ə-) *n. Bot.* A plant not requiring uncombined oxygen for respiration.

an·aes·the·sia (an'is·thē'zhə, -zhē·ə), **an·aes·thet·ic** (an'is·thet'ik), etc. See ANESTHESIA, etc.

an·a·glyph (an'ə·glif) *n.* 1 An ornament in low relief, as a cameo. 2 *Optics* A stereoscopic picture of an object produced in two colors, red and green, and from two angles, as from the right and the left eye: used to determine abnormal binocular vision. [<Gk. *anaglyphē* <*ana-* up + *glyphein* carve]

an·a·glyph·ic (an'ə·glif'ik) *adj.* Pertaining to, ornamented with, or executed in anaglyph. Also **an'a·glyph'i·cal, an·a·glyp·tic** (an'ə·glip'tik).

an·a·glyph·ics (an'ə·glif'iks) *n.* The art of carving anaglyphic decoration. Also **an·a·glyp·tics** (an'ə·glip'tiks).

an·a·glyph·o·scope (an'ə·glif'ə·skōp) *n. Optics* A device consisting of paired lenses or eyeglasses, one red and the other green, adapted to produce anaglyphs and to give ordinary pictures a stereoscopic effect.

an·a·go·ge (an'ə·gō'jē) *n.* Spiritual or mystical significance or interpretation of words, especially of the Scriptures. [<NL <Gk. *anagōgē* a leading up <*ana-* up + *agein* lead]

an·a·gog·ic (an'a·goj'ik) *adj.* 1 Pertaining to or using anagoge; mystical: also **an'a·gog'i·cal.** 2 *Psychoanal.* Pertaining to material from the psyche expressive of constructive ideals. **—an'·a·gog'i·cal·ly** *adv.*

an·a·gram (an'ə·gram) *n.* 1 A word or phrase formed by transposing the letters of another word or phrase. 2 *pl.* A game in which the players make words by transposing or adding letters. [<NL *anagramma* <Gk. *ana-* anew + *gramma* a letter <*graphein* write] **—an·a·gram·mat·ic** (an'ə·grə·mat'ik) or **·i·cal** *adj.* **—an'a·gram·mat'i·cal·ly** *adv.*

an·a·gram·ma·tize (an'ə·gram'ə·tīz) *v.t.* **·tized, ·tiz·ing** To arrange as an anagram.

a·nal (ā'nəl) *adj.* 1 **a** Of, pertaining to, or situated in the region of the anus. **b** Situated near the anus. 2 *Psychoanal.* **a** Of or relating to the second stage of psychosexual development of the child in which interest in excretion is dominant. **b** Of, pertaining to, or characterized by qualities in the adult, as orderliness or an inclination to hoard, regarded as typifying this stage of development. Compare GENITAL, ORAL.

a·nal·cime (a·nal'sim, -sīm) *n. Mineral.* An isometric white or pale zeolite. Also **a·nal'cite** (-sīt, -sit). [<AN-[1] not + Gk. *alkimos* strong]

an·a·lect (an'ə·lekt) *n. pl.* **an·a·lec·ta** (an'ə·lek'tə) or **·lects** A selection or fragment from a literary work or group of works: usually in the plural. [<L *analecta,* pl. <Gk. *analekta* <*analegein* collect <*ana-* up + *legein* gather] **—an'a·lec'tic** *adj.*

an·a·lep·tic (an'ə·lep'tik) *adj. Med.* Restorative or stimulating, especially to the central nervous system. *—n.* A medicine with analeptic properties. [<Gk. *analēptikos* restorative <*analambanein* recover <*ana-* up + *lambanein* take]

anal fin *Zool.* The unpaired median ventral fin just behind the anus in fishes: opposed to *dorsal fin.*

an·al·ge·si·a (an'əl·jē'zē·ə, -sē·ə) *n.* Insensibility to pain without loss of consciousness. [<NL <Gk. *analgēsia* <*an-* without + *algos* pain]

an·al·ge·sic (an'əl·jē'zik, -sik) *n.* A drug that prevents or relieves pain. *—adj.* Pertaining to or promoting analgesia.

an·a·log (an'ə·lôg, -log) *n.* 1 Anything analogous to something else. 2 *Biol.* An organ analogous to one in another species or group: distinguished from *homolog.* Also **an'a·logue.** [<F *analogue* <L *analogus.* See ANALOGY.]

analog computer A computing machine so designed and constructed as to provide information in terms of physical quantities analogous to those in which the problems are formulated. Compare DIGITAL COMPUTER.

an·a·log·i·cal (an'ə·loj'i·kəl) *adj.* Pertaining to, containing, or based on analogy. Also **an'·a·log'ic. —an'a·log'i·cal·ly** *adv.*

a·nal·o·gist (ə·nal'ə·jist) *n.* One who uses or reasons from analogy.

a·nal·o·gize (ə·nal'ə·jīz) *v.* **·gized, ·giz·ing** *v.i.* To use or reason by analogy. *—v.t.* To show to be analogous.

a·nal·o·gous (ə·nal'ə·gəs) *adj.* 1 Resembling in certain respects. 2 *Biol.* Having a similar function but different in origin and structure, as the wings of birds and insects. See synonyms under ALIKE. **—a·nal'o·gous·ly** *adv.* **—a·nal'o·gous·ness** *n.*

a·nal·o·gy (ə·nal'ə·jē) *n. pl.* **·gies** 1 Resemblance of properties or relations; similarity without identity. 2 Any similarity or agreement. 3 *Biol.* A similarity in function and superficial appearance, but not in origin: opposed to *homology.* 4 *Logic* Reasoning in which from certain observed and known relations or parallel resemblances others are inferred; reasoning that proceeds from the individual or particular to a coordinate individual or particular, thus involving both induction and deduction. 5 *Ling.* The formative process by which words take on inflections or constructions that are imitative of more familiar words and existing patterns without having undergone the same true linguistic development; as, the past tense of *climb* changed from the strong form *clomb* to the weak form *climbed* on analogy with the weak verbs. [<F *analogie* <L *analogia* <Gk. *analogia* <*analogos* proportionate, conformable <*ana-* according to + *logos* proportion]

Synonyms: coincidence, comparison, likeness, parity, proportion, relation, resemblance, semblance, similarity, simile, similitude. *Analogy* is specifically a *resemblance* of relations; a *resemblance* that may be reasoned from, so that from the *likeness* in certain respects we may infer that other and perhaps deeper relations exist. *Parity* of reasoning is said of an argument equally conclusive on subjects not strictly analogous. *Coincidence* is complete agreement in some one or more respects. *Similitude* is a rhetorical comparison of one thing to another with which it has some points in common. *Resemblance* and *similarity* are external or superficial, and may involve no deeper relation. Compare ALLEGORY. *Antonyms*: disagreement, disproportion, dissimiliarity, incongruity, unlikeness.

an·al·pha·bet·ic (an·al'fə·bet'ik) *adj. & n.* Illiterate.

a·nal·y·sand (ə·nal'ə·sand) *n. Psychoanal.* The person who is being analyzed.

an·a·lyse (an'ə·līz) British spelling of ANALYZE.

a·nal·y·sis (ə·nal'ə·sis) *n. pl.* **·ses** (-sēz) 1 The resolution of a whole into its parts or elements: opposed to *synthesis.* 2 A statement of the results of this; logical synopsis. 3 A method of determining or describing the nature of a thing by resolving it into its parts: to study literature by the *analysis* of texts. 4 *Math.* **a** The process of resolving a problem into its first elements. **b** The investigation of the relations of variable or indeterminate quantities by means of symbols, including some branches of algebra and the differential and integral calculus. 5 *Chem.* **a** The identification of constituents of a compound, solution, mixture, or the like. See *qualitative analysis.* **b** The determination of the quantity or proportion of such constituents. See *quantitative analysis.* **c** A statement of the results of an analysis. 6 Psychoanalysis. See synonyms under ABRIDGMENT. Compare SYNTHESIS. [<Med.L <Gk. *analysis* <*ana-* throughout + *lysis* a loosing <*lyein* to loose]

analysis si·tus (sī'təs) Topology. [<NL, analysis of region]

an·a·lyst (an'ə·list) *n.* 1 One who analyzes or is skilled in analysis. 2 A psychoanalyst. ◆ Homophone: *annalist.*

an·a·lyt·ic (an'ə·lit'ik) *adj.* 1 Pertaining to, skilled in, or proceeding by analysis. 2 Resolving into constituent parts or first principles. 3 *Ling.* Describing a language, such as Modern English, that expresses grammatical relationships and the modification of word meanings by means of particles, auxiliaries, etc., rather than by inflection: opposed to *synthetic* or *inflectional.* Also **an'a·lyt'i·cal. —an'a·lyt'i·cal·ly** *adv.*

analytical balance An electronic or mechanical instrument for weighing substances to the nearest 0.1 milligram or less.

analytical psychology 1 The analysis of psychological phenomena by systematic introspection. 2 The systematic psychology and psychoanalytic methods originated by and associated with C. G. Jung.

analytic geometry Geometry in which position is represented analytically by a system of coordinates and the procedure by which solutions are obtained is largely algebraic.

an·a·lyt·ics (an'ə·lit'iks) *n.* 1 The science or use of analysis. 2 The part of logic concerned with analysis.

an·a·lyze (an'ə·līz) *v.t.* **·lyzed, ·lyz·ing** 1 To resolve into constituent parts or elements. 2 To make an analysis of, as a chemical compound or a mathematical problem. 3 *Gram.* To separate (a sentence) into its grammatical elements. 4 To examine minutely or critically, as a text. Also *Brit.* **an'a·lyse.** [<F *analyser* <*analyse* <Med. L *analyses.* See ANALYSIS.] **—an'a·lyz'a·ble** *adj.* **—an'a·ly·za'tion** *n.* **—an'a·lyz'er** *n.*

A·nam (ə·nam', an'am) See ANNAM.

an·am·ne·sis (an'am·nē'sis) *n. pl.* **·ses** (·sēz) 1 *Psychol.* A reproducing in memory; recollection. 2 The complete medical history of a patient as obtained from all available sources. [<Gk. *anamnēsis* <*ana-* back + *mimnēskein* call to mind]

an·am·nes·tic (an'am·nes'tik) *adj.* 1 Stimulating the faculty of memory. 2 Pertaining to anamnesis.

anamnestic analysis Investigation of the mental history of a neurotic individual, particularly by the psychoanalytic methods developed by C. G. Jung.

anamnestic reaction A rapid increase in antibodies in an organism upon exposure to an antigen which had been encountered at some prior time. Also **anamnestic response.**

an·a·mor·phism (an'ə·môr'fiz·əm) *n.* 1 Distortion of shape. 2 *Biol.* Anamorphosis. [<ANA- up + Gk. *morphē* form]

an·a·mor·pho·scope (an'ə·môr'fə·skōp) *n.*

Optics A vertical cylindrical mirror for viewing an anamorphosis.

an·a·mor·pho·sis (an′ə·môr′fə·sis, -môr·fō′sis) *n.* **1** *Optics* A distorted representation of an object, unrecognizable except when viewed through a polyhedron or from a particular point, or when reflected from a specially constructed mirror, as an anamorphoscope. **2** *Biol.* An increase in complexity during the course of the evolution of an organism. Also call *anamorphism.* [<NL <Gk. *anamorphōsis* <Gk. *anamorphoein* <*ana-* again + *morphoein* form]

A·nan·da Ma·hi·dol (ä·nän′dä mä′hē·dôl′), 1925–46, king of Siam 1935–46.

an·an·drous (an·an′drəs) *adj. Bot.* Destitute of stamens, as a female flower.

An·a·ni·as (an′ə·nī′əs) **1** The husband of Sapphira; both fell dead after lying (*Acts* v 1–6); hence, any liar. **2** A disciple in Damascus who restored Paul's sight. *Acts* ix 10–18. **3** A high priest in Jerusalem who tried Paul. *Acts* xxiii 2–5.

an·an·thous (an·an′thəs) *adj. Bot.* Flowerless. [<AN-[1] without + Gk. *anthos* flower]

an·a·nym (an′ə·nim) *n.* A pseudonym consisting of a name written backwards, as *Niamert* for *Tremain.* [<Gk. *ana-* back + *onoma, onyma* name]

an·a·pest (an′ə·pest) *n.* **1** In prosody, a metrical foot consisting of two short or unaccented syllables followed by one long or accented syllable. **2** A line of verse made up of or characterized by such feet. Also **an′a·paest.** [<L *anapaestus* <Gk. *anapaistos* <*ana-* back + *paiein* strike] — **an′a·pes′tic** or **·ti·cal, an′a·paes′tic** or **·ti·cal** *adj.*

an·a·phase (an′ə·fāz) *n. Biol.* The stage of mitosis or meiosis in which the corresponding parts of the divided chromosomes move to opposite poles of the spindle. **an′a·pha′sic** *adj.* [ANA- up + PHASE]

a·naph·o·ra (ə·naf′ə·rə) *n.* The rhetorical device of repeating a word or phrase in the beginning of several successive verses, clauses, or sentences. [<L <Gk. *anaphora* <*ana-* back + *pherein* carry]

an·aph·ro·dis·i·a (an·af′rə·diz′ē·ə) *n.* Absence or impairment of sexual desire. [<NL <AN-[1] without + Gk. *aphrodisia* sexual pleasure <*Aphroditē,* the goddess of love]

an·aph·ro·dis·i·ac (an·af′rə·diz′ē·ak) *adj.* Of, pertaining to, or tending to produce anaphrodisia. —*n.* An anaphrodisiac agent or treatment.

an·a·phy·lac·toid (an′ə·fə·lak′toid) *adj.* Similar to anaphylaxis.

an·a·phy·lax·is (an′ə·fə·lak′sis) *n.* Hypersensitivity to a foreign protein following injection of a small sensitizing dose. Also called *allergy.* [<NL <ANA- + (PRO)PHYLAXIS] —**an′a·phy·lac′tic** (-lak′tik) *adj.*

an·a·pla·sia (an′ə·plā′zhə, -zhē·ə) *n. Biol.* A reversion of cells to an undifferentiated or more primitive form, destroying their capacity for full development and functioning. [<NL <ANA- + -PLASIA]

an·a·plas·mo·sis (an′ə·plaz·mō′sis) *n.* A disease of domestic cattle and other ruminants due to a protozoan (genus *Anaplasma*) that inhabits red blood cells of the vertebrate host. [<NL <ANA- + PLASMA + -OSIS]

an·a·plas·tic (an′ə·plas′tik) *adj.* **1** *Surg.* Restoring lost or absent parts, as by transplanting tissue. **2** *Biol.* Of or pertaining to anaplasia.

an·a·plas·ty (an′ə·plas′tē) *n.* Plastic surgery. [<NL <Gk. *anaplastos* <*ana-* anew + *plassein* form]

an·ap·tot·ic (an′ap·tot′ik) *adj. Ling.* Losing or having lost inflections by phonetic decay: said of a language, as English. [<ANA- back + Gk. *ptōtikos* belonging to case < *ptōsis* a case]

an·ap·tyx·is (an′ap·tik′sis) *n.* The insertion of an extra vowel in a word so as to create another syllable, as in (fil′əm) for *film.* [<Gk. *anaptyxis* an unfolding <*ana-* back + *ptyssein* to fold]

A·na·pur·na (ä′nə·po͝or′nə) A mountain of the Himalaya range in north central Nepal; 26,502 feet: also *Annapurna.*

an·ar·chic (an·är′kik) *adj.* **1** Pertaining to or like anarchy. **2** Advocating anarchy. **3** Inducing anarchy; lawless. Also **an·ar′chi·cal.** —**an·ar′chi·cal·ly** *adv.*

an·ar·chism (an′ər·kiz′əm) *n.* **1** The theory that all forms of government are incompatible with individual and social liberty and should be abolished. **2** The methods, especially terroristic ones, of anarchists. —**philosophic anarchism** The advocacy of voluntary cooperation and mutual aid as a substitute for the coercive power of the state.

an·ar·chist (an′ər·kist) *n.* **1** One who believes in and advocates anarchism. **2** One who encourages or furthers anarchy. Also **an·arch** (an′ärk). —**an′ar·chis′tic** *adj.*

an·ar·chy (an′ər·kē) *n.* **1** Absence of government. **2** Lawless confusion and political disorder. **3** General disorder. See synonyms under DISORDER, REVOLUTION. [<Gk. *anarchia* <*anarchos* without a leader <*an-* without + *archos* leader, chief]

an·ar·thri·a (an·är′thrē·ə) *n.* Inability to utter articulate speech as a result of neural damage. —**an·ar′thric** *adj.*

an·ar·throus (an·är′thrəs) *adj.* **1** *Gram.* Used without the article: said of some Greek nouns in certain cases. **2** *Zool.* Lacking distinct joints. [<Gk. *anarthros* unjointed <*an-* without + *arthron* joint]

an·a·sar·ca (an′ə·sär′kə) *n.* A generalized swelling due to infiltration of serous fluid into body cavities and subcutaneous connective tissue. [<NL <Gk. *ana-* throughout + *sarx* flesh] —**an′a·sar′cous** *adj.*

An·as·ta·si·us I (an′ə·stā′shē·əs), 430?–518, Byzantine emperor 491–518.

—**Anastasius II,** died 721?, Byzantine emperor 713–716.

Anastasius IV, died 1154, real name Conrad, pope 1153–54.

an·as·tig·mat·ic (an·as′tig·mat′ik) *adj. Optics* **1** Not astigmatic; specifically, corrected for astigmatism, as a lens. **2** Pertaining to a compound photographic lens, each element of which is adapted to correct the astigmatism of the other. [<AN-[1] + ASTIGMATIC]

a·nas·to·mose (ə·nas′tə·mōz) *v.* **·mosed, ·mos·ing** *v.t.* To create an anastomosis. —*v.i.* To be connected by one or more anastomoses.

a·nas·to·mo·sis (ə·nas′tə·mō′sis) *n. pl.* **·ses** (-sēz) A natural or artificial connection, interlacing, or union of parts or branches of a system of blood vessels, leaf veins, rivers, or the like. Also called *inosculation.* [<NL <Gk. *anastomōsis* opening <*ana-* again + *stoma* mouth] — **a·nas′to·mot′ic** (-mot′ik) *adj.*

a·nas·tro·phe (ə·nas′trə·fē) *n.* In rhetoric, the inversion of the natural or usual order of words, as "homeward directly he went." Also **a·nas′·tro·phy.** [<Gk. *anastrophē* <*ana strephein* <*ana-* back + *strephein* turn]

an·a·tase (an′ə·tās, -tāz) *n.* A variously colored mineral consisting of tetragonal crystals of titanium oxide, TiO_2. Also called *octahedrite.* [<F <Gk. *anatasis* extension]

a·nath·e·ma (ə·nath′ə·mə) *n. pl.* **·mas** or **·ma·ta** (-mətə) **1** A formal ecclesiastical ban or curse, excommunicating a person or damning something, as a book or heresy. **2** Any curse or imprecation. **3** A person or thing excommunicated or damned. **4** A person or thing greatly disliked or detested. See synonyms under IMPRECATION. [<L <Gk. *anathema* a thing devoted (to evil) <*anatithenai* dedicate <*ana-* up + *tithenai* set, place]

anathema mar·a·nath·a (mar′ə·nath′ə) A formula formerly interpreted as an extreme curse: now considered an incorrect reading of I *Cor.* xvi 22. [<Gk. *anathema* a curse + Aramaic *Maranā′thā* Our Lord, come]

a·nath·e·ma·tize (ə·nath′ə·mə·tīz) *v.* **·tized, ·tiz·ing** *v.t.* To pronounce an anathema against. —*v.i.* To utter or express anathemas. —**a·nath′e·ma·ti·za′tion** *n.*

An·a·to·li·a (an′ə·tō′lē·ə) A mountainous peninsula comprising the westernmost part of Asia and almost all of Turkey; 287,117 square miles; formerly synonymous with Asia Minor. — **An′a·to′lic** *adj.*

An·a·to·li·an (an′ə·tō′lē·ən) *adj.* Pertaining to Anatolia or its people. —*n.* A family of languages of which Cuneiform Hittite is the best known: related to or descended from Indo-European. See INDO-HITTITE.

an·a·tom·i·cal (an′ə·tom′i·kəl) *adj.* **1** Pertaining to the structure of an organism. **2** Structural, especially as distinguished from functional. Also **an′a·tom′ic.** —**an′a·tom′i·cal·ly** *adv.*

a·nat·o·mist (ə·nat′ə·mist) *n.* One skilled in or a student of anatomy; a dissector.

a·nat·o·mize (ə·nat′ə·mīz) *v.t.* **·mized, ·miz·ing** **1** To dissect an animal or plant for the purpose of investigating the structure, position, and interrelationships of its parts. **2** To examine critically or minutely; analyze. —**a·nat′o·mi·za′·tion** *n.*

a·nat·o·my (ə·nat′ə·mē) *n. pl.* **·mies** **1** The science of the structure of organisms, as of the human body, and of the interrelations of their parts. **2** The art or practice of dissection in order to investigate the structure, position, and interrelationship of organs. **3** A textbook or treatise dealing with the art or practice of dissection. **4** A skeleton. **5** An anatomical model, showing the structure, position, and interrelationship of organs. **6** Any kind of analysis or close examination. [<F *anatomie* <L *anatomia* <Gk. *anatomia,* earlier *anatomē* dissection <*anatemnein* cut up <*ana-* up + *temnein* cut]

a·nat·ro·pous (ə·nat′rə·pəs) *adj. Bot.* Inverted, with the micropyle next to the hilum and the radicle inferior: said of an ovule. [<NL <ANA- + -TROPOUS]

a·nat·to (ä·nä′tō) *n.* Annatto. [<Cariban]

An·ax·ag·o·ras (an′ak·sag′ə·rəs), 500–428 B.C., Greek philosopher.

An·ax·i·man·der (an·ak′sə·man′dər), 610–546? B.C., Greek philosopher and astronomer.

An·ax·im·e·nes (an′ak·sim′ə·nēz), sixth century B.C. Greek philosopher.

An·cae·us (an·sē′əs) In Greek mythology, a son of Neptune who was told he would never drink the wine of his own vineyard. He scornfully started to drink, but was told there was a wild boar nearby, went out to kill it, and was killed himself; hence the proverb "There's many a slip between the cup and the lip."

-ance *suffix of nouns* Forming nouns of action, quality, state, or condition from adjectives in *-ant,* and also directly from verbs, as in abundance, resistance, forbearance. Compare -ANCY. [<F *-ance* <L *-antia, -entia,* a suffix used to form nouns from present participles; or directly from Latin]

◆ **-ance, -ence** The modern spelling of words in this group is unpredictable. The confusion arose originally in borrowings from Old French *(resistance, assistance)* where *-ance* had come to represent Latin *-entia,* as well as *-antia.* Since 1500, however, some of these have been altered back to *-ence* on the Latin model, as in the case of *dependence,* earlier *dependance.* Later Latin borrowings in French and in English (through French or directly from Latin) discriminate between *-ance* and *-ence* according to the vowel of the Latin original.

an·ces·tor (an′ses·tər) *n.* **1** One from whom descent is derived; especially, such person further back in the line than a grandparent; forefather; progenitor; forebear. **2** *Law* One who precedes another in the line of legal inheritance, whether or not a direct progenitor: correlative of *heir.* **3** *Biol.* An actual or hypothetical organism from which subsequent types have developed; a prototype. [<OF *ancestre* <L *antecessor* <*antecedere* <*ante-* before + *cedere* go]

an·ces·tral (an·ses′trəl) *adj.* Of, pertaining to, or inherited from an ancestor. —**an·ces′tral·ly** *adv.*

an·ces·tress (an′ses·tris) *n.* A female ancestor.

an·ces·try (an′ses·trē) *n. pl.* **·tries** **1** The line or body of ancestors; ancestors collectively. **2** Descent; ancestral lineage. **3** Noble or worthy lineage.

An·chi·ses (an·kī′sēz) In Roman legend, the father of Aeneas, rescued from burning Troy on his son's shoulders.

an·chor[1] (ang′kər) *n.* 1 A heavy implement, usually of iron or steel and having a long shank and two or more hooks or flukes that grip the sea bottom: used for holding fast a vessel by means of a connecting cable. 2 Any similar object used in such a manner for such a purpose. 3 Anything that makes stable or secure; anything depended on for support or security. 4 A military base from which an army operates. —**at anchor** Anchored, as a ship. —**to cast** (or **drop**) **anchor** To put down the anchor in order to hold fast a vessel. —**to ride at anchor** To be anchored, as a ship. —**to weigh anchor** To take up the anchor so as to sail away. —*v.t.* 1 To secure or make secure by an anchor. 2 To fix firmly. —*v.i.* 3 To come to anchor; lie at anchor, as a ship. 4 To become fixed; to hold oneself fast, as to a place. [OE *ancor* < L *ancora* < Gk. *ankyra*]

ANCHORS
1. Fluke 2. Mushroom 3. Grapnel
r. Ring *e.* Eye *h.* Hoops *st.* Stock *sh.* Shank *b.* Bills or pees *f.* Flukes or palms *a.* Arms *c.* Crown

an·chor[2] (ang′kər) *n.* An anchorite.

an·chor·age (ang′kər·ij) *n.* 1 A place fit for or used for anchoring. 2 A coming to or lying at anchor. 3 That to which something is anchored; a means of support or security. 4 The fee charged for anchoring or the right to anchor, as in a harbor.

An·chor·age (ang′kər·ij) A southern Alaskan port, the largest city in Alaska.

an·cho·ress (ang′kə·ris) *n.* A woman anchorite.

anchor hold 1 The strength or grip with which an anchor holds. 2 The chief ground of trust; security; fixedness.

an·cho·rite (ang′kə·rīt) *n.* One who has withdrawn from the world; a religious recluse; hermit. Also **an′cho·ret** (-rit, -ret). [< L *anachoreta* < Gk. *anachōrētēs* < *anachōreein* retire, retreat < *ana-* back + *chōreein* withdraw] —**an′cho·rit′ic** (-rit′ik) *adj.*

an·chor·less (ang′kər·lis) *adj.* 1 Without an anchor. 2 Not settled or stable; drifting; insecure; without roots.

anchor man 1 An athlete, as in a relay race, who competes last for his team. 2 A television or radio broadcaster who coordinates the coverage of an event or program.

anchor watch *Naut.* The part of a crew set to watch while a vessel lies at anchor.

an·cho·vy (an′chō·vē, -chə·vē, an·chō′vē) *n. pl.* **·vies** Any of several very small, herring-like marine fishes (family Engraulidae) including some of commercial value as food or as a source of fishmeal. [< Sp., Pg. *anchova*, ? < Basque *anchua* < *antzua* dry]

an·cho·vy pear 1 A West Indian fruit tasting like the mango. 2 The tall unbranched tree *(Grias cauliflora)* of the myrtle family that bears this fruit.

an·chu·sa (ang·kyōō′sə, an·chōō′zə) *n.* Any plant of a genus *(Anchusa)* of hairy-stemmed plants, including various species of bugloss. [< NL < L < Gk. *anchousa*]

an·chu·sin (ang·kyōō′sin, an·chōō′zin) *n.* A red resinous substance obtained from the root of various anchusas and other plants, used in dyeing.

an·chy·lose (ang′kə·los) *v.* **·losed, ·los·ing** To ankylose.

an·chy·lo·sis (ang′kə·lō′sis) *n.* Ankylosis.

an·cienne no·blesse (äṅ·syen′ nô·bles′) *French* The old nobility; especially, that prior to the French Revolution.

an·cien ré·gime (äṅ·syaṅ′ rā·zhēm′) *French* A former political and social system; specifically, that system prevailing in France before the Revolution of 1789. Also **Ancient Regime.**

an·cient[1] (ān′shənt) *adj.* 1 Existing or occurring in times long gone by, especially before the fall of the Roman Empire of the West, in 476: opposed to *modern: ancient* history, *ancient* authors. 2 Belonging to or having existed from a remote antiquity; of great age: *ancient* relics. 3 *Archaic* Venerable; sage. —*n.* 1 One who lived in ancient times. 2 An ancient or venerable person. —**the ancients** 1 The ancient Greeks, Romans, Hebrews, or other civilized nations of antiquity. 2 The ancient authors of Greece and Rome. [< OF *ancien*, ult. < L *ante* before] —**an′cient·ness** *n.*

Synonyms (adj.): aged, antiquated, antique, gray, hoary, immemorial, old, olden, time-honored, time-worn, venerable. *Ancient*, from the French, is the more stately; *old*, from the Anglo-Saxon, the more familiar word. *Venerable* expresses the involuntary reverence that we yield to the majestic and the long-enduring. See ANTIQUE, OLD. *Antonyms*: fresh, modern, new, novel, recent.

an·cient[2] (ān′shənt) *n.* An ensign, standard, or flag. 2 A flag standard-bearer. [Alter. of ENSIGN]

ancient light *Law* A window facing toward the property of another, which having been unobstructed for 20 years, gives the owner the right to its light and which, therefore, may not be obstructed by the erection of a building: a law in England and in some parts of the United States.

an·cient·ly (ān′shənt·lē) *adv.* In the distant past; of old.

Ancient of Days God. *Dan.* vii 9.

an·cil·lar·y (an′sə·ler′ē) *adj.* 1 Subordinate. 2 Auxiliary; serving to help. [< L *ancillaris* < *ancilla* maid]

an·cip·i·tal (an·sip′ə·təl) *adj. Bot.* Two-edged, as the stems of certain plants. Also **an·cip′i·tous.** [< L *anceps, ancipitis* two-headed < *an- (ambi-)* on both sides + *caput* head]

an·cis·troid (an·sis′troid) *adj.* Hook-shaped. [< Gk. *ankistron* a hook + -OID]

an·con (ang′kon) *n. pl.* **an·co·nes** (ang·kō′nēz) *Archit.* An elbow-shaped projection; a console, as for an ornament on a keystone. [< L < Gk. *ankōn* a bend, the elbow] —**an·co·nal** (ang′kə·nəl), **an·co·ne·al** (ang·kō′nē·əl) *adj.*

ANCON
(def. 2)

An·co·na (äng·kō′nä) A city in central Italy, on the Adriatic.

-ancy *suffix of nouns* A modern variant of -ANCE: *infancy, vacancy*: used to form new words expressing quality, state, or condition, or to refashion older nouns of quality in *-ance*, the latter being largely reserved for nouns of action: *constancy*. [< L *-antia*]

an·cy·los·to·mi·a·sis (an′sə·los′tə·mī′ə·sis) *n. pl.* **·ses** (·sēz) A condition in humans and some other mammals due to infestation by hookworms. Also called *hookworm disease.* [< NL < Gk. *ankylos* crooked + *stoma* mouth]

An·cy·ra (an·sī′rə) See ANKARA.

and (and, *unstressed* ənd, ən) *conj.* 1 Also; added to; as well as: a particle denoting addition, emphasis, or union, used as a connective between words, phrases, clauses, and sentences: shoes *and* ships *and* sealing wax; walking miles *and* miles; a horse both swift *and* strong. 2 As a result or consequence: Speak one word *and* you are a dead man! 3 To: in idiomatic use with *come, go, try*, etc.: Try *and* stop me; Come *and* see us; Go *and* find the answer. 4 *Archaic* Then: *And* she answered unto him. 5 *Obs.* If; in addition. See synonyms under BUT[1]. [OE]

an·dab·a·ta (an·dab′ə·tə) *n. pl.* **·tae** (-tē) One who fights blindly, or acts as if blindfolded; originally, in ancient Rome, a gladiator who fought wearing a helmet without eye openings. For illustration, see under GLADIATOR. Also **an·da·bate** (an′də·bāt). [< L]

an·dab·a·tar·i·an (an·dab′ə·târ′ē·ən) *adj.* Like the fights of a blindfolded gladiator or andabata; hence, misdirected, or blindly ineffectual.

An·da·lu·sia (an′də·lōō′zhə, -shə) A region of southern Spain bordering on the Atlantic, the Strait of Gibraltar, and the Mediterranean. *Spanish* **An·da·lu·cí·a** (än′dä·lōō·thē′ä).

An·da·lu·sian (an′də·lōō′zhən, -shən) *adj.* Of or pertaining to Andalusia or its inhabitants. —*n.* 1 One of the inhabitants of Andalusia. 2 A dialect of southern Spain.

an·da·lu·site (an′də·lōō′sīt) *n.* A variously colored orthorhombic aluminum silicate, Al_2SiO_5, occurring in metamorphic rock. [from *Andalusia*, region in Spain, where it was discovered]

An·da·man and Nic·o·bar Islands (an′də·mən; nik′ə·bär′) A chief commissioner's state of India in the east Bay of Bengal; 3,143 square miles; capital, Port Blair on South Andaman: comprising the northerly **Andaman Islands**; 2,508 square miles; and the southerly **Nicobar Islands**; 635 square miles.

An·da·ma·nese (an′də·mə·nēz′, -nēs′) *n. pl.* **-nese** 1 Any of the Negrito people of the Andaman and Nicobar Islands. 2 The language of these people. —*adj.* Of or pertaining to this people or their language.

Andaman Sea An easterly part of the Bay of Bengal between the Malay Peninsula and the Andaman and Nicobar Islands.

an·dan·te (an·dan′tē, än·dän′tā) *adj. & adv. Music* Moderately slowly; slower than allegretto but faster than larghetto. —*n.* Music in andante tempo. [< Ital., lit., walking]

an·dan·ti·no (an′dan·tē′nō, än′dän-) *adj. & adv. Music* Slightly quicker than andante: originally, slower than andante, but now generally meaning not so slow as andante. —*n.* Music in andantino tempo. [< Ital., dim. of *andante*]

An·de·an (an·dē′ən, an′dē·ən) *adj.* Of or pertaining to the Andes Mountains.

An·der·lecht (än′dər·lekht) A city in central Belgium SW of Brussels.

An·ders (än′ders), **Wła·dy·sław** (vlä·di′släf), born 1892, Polish general.

An·der·sen (an′dər·sən), **Hans Christian,** 1805–75, Danish writer of fairy tales.

An·der·son (an′dər·sən), **Carl David,** born 1905, U.S. physicist. —**Marian,** born 1908, U.S. Negro contralto. —**Maxwell,** 1888–1959, U.S. playwright. —**Sherwood,** 1876–1941, U.S. author.

An·der·son·ville (an′dər·sən·vil) A village in SW Georgia; site of a Confederate prison for Union soldiers during the Civil War.

An·des (an′dēz) A mountain range in western South America, extending over 4,000 miles from Venezuela southward to Tierra del Fuego; highest peak, Aconcagua, 22,835 feet. *Spanish* **Los An·des** (lōs än′dās).

an·de·site (an′də·zīt) *n.* A volcanic rock, containing essentially plagioclase with biotite, hornblende, or augite. [from the *Andes* Mountains]

and·i·ron (and′ī′ərn) *n.* One of two iron, steel, etc., supports for wood to be burned in an open fireplace. Also called *firedog.* [< OF *andier;* infl. by IRON]

An·di·zhan (än·dē·zhän′) A city in eastern Uzbek S.S.R.

and/or Either *and* or *or*, according to the meaning intended: Place bills *and/or* coins in this container: a business and legal usage.

An·dor·ra (an·dôr′ə, -dor′ə) A republic between France and Spain, subject to the joint suzerainty of the president of France and the Bishop of Urgel, Spain; 191 square miles; capital, Andorra la Vella.

andr- *combining form* Variant of ANDRO-.

an·dra·dite (an′drə·dīt) *n.* A variety of garnet composed of calcium iron silicate, varying in color from green to brown or black. [after J. B. de *Andrada* e Silva, 1763?–1838, Brazilian geologist]

An·drás·sy (än′drä·shē), **Count Gyu·la** (dy·ōō′lä), father 1823–90, son, 1860–1929, Hungarian statesmen.

An·dré (än′drā, an′drē), **John,** 1751–80, British major, hanged as a spy during the American Revolution.

An·dre·a·nof Islands (än′drā·ä′nôf) An island group in the central Aleutians between Rat and Fox Islands.

An·dre·ev (än·drā′yef), **Leonid Nikolaievich,** 1871–1919, Russian writer.

An·drew (an′drōō) A masculine personal name. Also **An·dre·as** (an·drē′əs; *Dan.* än·dres′; *Du., Ger.* än·drā′äs; *Lat.* an′drē·əs), *Fr.* **An·dré** (äṅ·drā′), *Ital.* **An·dre·a** (än·drā′ä), *Pg.* **An·dre** (äṅ·drā′), *Sp.* **An·drés** (än·drās′). [< Gk., man] —**Andrew, Saint,** One of the twelve Apostles; brother of Peter; martyred in Greece.

An·drewes (an′drōōz), **Lancelot,** 1555–1626, English bishop and scholar.

An·drews (an′drōōz), **Charles McLean,** 1863–1943, U.S. educator and historian. —**Roy Chapman,** 1884–1960, U.S. naturalist, explorer, and archeologist.

An·dri·a (än′drē·ä) A city in Apulia, southern Italy.

andro- *combining form* 1 Human: *androcephalous.* 2 Male; masculine: *andromorphous.* 3 *Bot.* Stamen; anther: *androecium.* [< Gk. *anēr, andros* man]

an·dro·cen·trism (an′drə·sen′triz·əm) *n.* Preoccupation with men and the activities of men to the exclusion of women in human affairs. —**an·dro·cen·tric** (an′drə·sen′trik) *adj.*

an·dro·ceph·a·lous (an′drə·sef′ə·ləs) *adj.* Having a human head, especially when joined to the body of an animal, as the Egyptian sphinx. [< ANDRO- + Gk. *kephalē* head]

An·dro·cles (an′drə·klēz) A Roman slave, first century A.D., whose life, according to legend, was spared in the arena by a lion that remembered him as the man who had once drawn a thorn from its paw. Also **An′dro·clus.**

an·dro·clin·i·um (an′drə·klin′ē·əm) *n. Bot.* Clinandrium. [< NL < ANDRO- + Gk. *klinē* a bed]

an·droc·ra·cy (an·drok′rə·sē) *n.* The rule of males; male supremacy. [< Greek *anēr, andros* man + *kratos* rule] —**an·dro·crat·ic** (an′drə·krat′ik) *adj.*

an·droe·ci·um (an·drē′shē·əm, -sē·əm) *n. pl.* **·ci·a** (-shē·ə, -sē·ə) *Bot.* The stamens of a flower collectively. [< NL < ANDRO- + Gk. *oikos* house] —**an·droe·cial** (an·drē′shəl) *adj.*

an·dro·gen (an′drə·jən) *n.* Any of various steroid hormones produced in the testes and the adrenal cortex which affect the development of masculine sexual characteristics.—**an·dro·gen·ic** (an′drə·jen′ik) *adj.*

an·drog·en·ize (an·droj′ə·nīz) *v.* **·ized, ·iz·ing.** To effect the development of masculine characteristics in, as by treatment with androgens. —**an′dro·gen·i·za′tion** *n.*

an·drog·e·nous (an·droj′ə·nəs) *adj.* Pertaining to or characterized by the production of male offspring.

An·dro·ge·us (an·drō′jē·əs) In Greek mythology, the son of Minos and Pasiphae, killed at Athens; to avenge him, Minos forced the Athenians to send a tribute of seven boys and seven girls every year, or every ninth year according to some traditions, to be thrown to the Minotaur. See MINOTAUR, THESEUS.

an·dro·gyne (an′drə·jin, -jīn) *n.* 1 A hermaphrodite. 2 *Bot.* An androgynous plant. [< MF < L *androgynus* < Gk. *androgynos* having the characteristics of both sexes < *anēr, andros* man + *gynē* woman]

an·drog·y·noid (an·droj′ə·noid) *adj.* Designating a male with hermaphroditic characteristics. [< ANDRO- + Gk. *gynē* woman]

an·drog·y·nous (an·droj′ə·nəs) *adj.* 1 Uniting the characteristics of both sexes; hermaphrodite. 2 *Bot.* Having the male and female flowers in the same cluster. 3 Undifferentiated as to sex, as in dress, bearing, etc.; unisex. Also **an·drog·y·nal** (an·droj′ə·nəl), **an·dro·gyn·ic** (an′·drə·jin′ik).

an·drog·y·ny (an·droj′ə·nē) *n.* Hermaphroditism.

an·droid (an′droid) *adj.* Having a human shape. —*n.* An automaton made to simulate a human being; a humanoid robot. [< NL *androides* < Gk. *androeidēs* manlike]

an·drol·o·gy (an·drol′ə·jē) *n.* The study of the male reproductive system and the disorders peculiar to it. —**an·drol′o·gist** *n.*

An·drom·a·che (an·drom′ə·kē) In Greek legend, the wife of Hector and mother of Astyanax, taken captive to Greece after the fall of Troy.

An·dro·med (an′drə·med) *n.* One of a system of meteors that seem to radiate from a point in the constellation Andromeda, called *Bielids,* because supposed to be the remains of Biela's comet. Also **An·dro·mede** (an′drə·mēd), **An·drom·e·did** (an·drom′ə·did).

An·drom·e·da (an·drom′ə·də) 1 In Greek mythology, the daughter of Cepheus and Cassiopeia, rescued from a sea monster and married by Perseus. 2 *Astron.* A northern constellation: see CONSTELLATION.

an·dro·mor·phous (an′drə·môr′fəs) *adj.* Having masculine shape or appearance. [< ANDRO- + Gk. *morphē* form]

An·dros (an′dros) The northernmost island of the Cyclades in the Aegean Sea; 145 square miles.

An·dros (an′drəs), **Sir Edmund,** 1637–1714, English colonial governor in America.

An·dros·cog·gin River (an′drə·skog′in) A river in New Hampshire and Maine; flowing SE 175 miles to the Kennebec River.

An·dros Island (an′dros) An island in the western Bahamas, largest of the group; 1,600 square miles.

an·dro·sphinx (an′drə·sfingks′) *n.* A sphinx with a man's head and a lion's body. See SPHINX.

an·dro·spore (an′drə·spôr′, -spōr′) *n. Bot.* Microspore.

an·dros·ter·one (an·dros′tə·rōn) *n.* An androgenic sex hormone, $C_{19}H_{30}C_2$, typically present in the urine of men and women. [< ANDRO- + STER(OL) + -ONE]

-androus *suffix* 1 *Bot.* Having a stamen or stamens: *monandrous, diandrous.* 2 Pertaining to men: *polyandrous.* [< Gk. *anēr, andros* man]

and so forth Together with more of the same kind, or along the same line; et cetera.

An·dva·re (än′dwä·rē) In Norse mythology, the dwarf from whom Loki stole the Nibelung treasure and the ring that carried the curse. Also **An′dwa·ri.**

An·dy (an′dē) Diminutive of ANDREW.

ane (ān) *adj.* & *n. Scot.* One.

-ane[1] *suffix* Used primarily to differentiate words that have a corresponding form in -AN, as *human, humane.* [< L *-anus*]

-ane[2] *suffix Chem.* Denoting an open-chain saturated hydrocarbon compound of the methane series: *pentane.* [An arbitrary formation]

a·near (ə·nir′) *v., adv.* & *prep. Poetic* or *Archaic* Near.

an·ec·do·ta (an′ik·dō′tə) *n. pl.* Unpublished historical details.

an·ec·dot·age (an′ik·dō′tij) *n.* 1 Anecdotes collectively. 2 *Colloq.* Old age: humorously considered the age for anecdotes.

an·ec·do·tal (an′ik·dōt′l) *adj.* Pertaining to, characterized by, or consisting of anecdotes. —**an′ec·do′tal·ly** *adv.*

an·ec·dote (an′ik·dōt) *n.* A brief account of some incident; a short narrative of an interesting or entertaining nature. See synonyms under STORY. [< Med.L *anecdota* < Gk. *anekdota,* neut. pl. of *anekdotos* unpublished < *an-* not + *ekdotos* published < *ekdidonai* give out, publish < *ek-* out + *didonai* give]

an·ec·dot·ic (an′ik·dot′ik) *adj.* 1 Anecdotal. 2 Habitually telling or given to anecdotes. Also **an′ec·dot′i·cal.** —**an′ec·dot′i·cal·ly** *adv.*

an·ec·dot·ist (an′ik·dō′tist) *n.* One who collects, publishes, or is given to telling anecdotes.

an·e·cho·ic (an′e·kō′ik) *adj.* 1 Without echoes. 2 Completely devoid of sound-wave reverberations: applied especially to researches in the problems of sound and acoustics.

a·nele (ə·nēl′) *v.t.* **a·neled, a·nel·ing** *Archaic* To anoint, as in administering extreme unction or some other rite. [ME *anelien* < *an-* on + *ele* oil, OE *ele* oil < L *oleum*]

an·e·lec·tric (an′ə·lek′trik) *adj.* Non-electric. —*n. Obs.* A non-electric substance.

a·ne·mi·a (ə·nē′mē·ə) *n.* A general or local deficiency in the amount or quality of red blood corpuscles or of hemoglobin in the blood or of both. Also spelled *anaemia.* [< NL < Gk. *anaimia* < *an-* without + *haima* blood]

a·ne·mic (ə·nē′mik) *adj.* 1 Of, having, or characterized by anemia. 2 Pale; without strength or vigor. Also spelled *anaemic.*

anemo- *combining form* Wind: *anemometer.* [< Gk. *anemos*]

a·nem·o·chore (ə·nem′ə·kôr, -kōr) *n. Bot.* A plant distributed by the wind.

a·nem·o·gram (ə·nem′ə·gram) *n.* A record made by an anemograph.

a·nem·o·graph (ə·nem′ə·graf, -gräf) *n. Meteorol.* An instrument that makes an automatic record of the velocity, force, or direction of the wind. —**a·nem′o·graph′ic** *adj.*

an·e·mog·ra·phy (an′ə·mog′rə·fē) *n. pl.* **·phies** *Meteorol.* 1 The art or act of recording automatically the velocity and direction of winds. 2 A description of or treatise on winds or their phenomena.

an·e·mol·o·gy (an′ə·mol′ə·jē) *n.* The branch of meteorological science that deals with the winds and related phenomena. —**an·e·mo·log·ic** (an′ə·mō·loj′ik) or **·i·cal** *adj.*

ANEMOMETER

an·e·mom·e·ter (an′·ə·mom′ə·tər) *n. Meteorol.* An instrument for measuring the force or velocity of wind. —**an·e·mo·met·ric** (an′ə·mō·met′rik) or **·ri·cal** *adj.*

an·e·mo·met·ro·graph (an′ə·mō·met′rə·graf, -gräf) *n. Meteorol.* An anemograph, especially one that records both force and direction.

an·e·mom·e·try (an′ə·mom′ə·trē) *n. Meteorol.* The act or art of determining the velocity, force, and direction of the winds.

SEA ANEMONE (*def. 2*)
(3 to 5 inches in height)

a·nem·o·ne (ə·nem′·ə·nē) *n.* 1 Any of a genus (*Anemone*) of perennial herbs of cool and temperate regions having petal-like sepals instead of petals. 2 The sea anemone. [< Gk. *anemōnē* < *anemos* wind]

an·e·moph·i·lous (an′ə·mof′ə·ləs) *adj.* Pollinated by wind-borne pollen. [< ANEMO- + Gk. *philos* loving]

an·e·moph·i·ly (an′ə·mof′ə·lē) *n.* Pollination by the wind.

a·nem·o·scope (ə·nem′ə·skōp) *n. Meteorol.* An instrument for determining the presence and direction of the wind.

an·e·mot·ro·pism (an′ə·mot′rə·piz′əm) *n.* The tropism of an organism with respect to the wind. —**an·e·mo·trop·ic** (an′ə·mō·trop′ik) *adj.*

an·en·ce·phal·ic (an·en′sə·fal′ik) *adj.* Lacking a brain. —*n.* A fetus with a rudimentary brain or none. [< Gk. *an-* without + *enkephalos* brain]

a·nent (ə·nent′) *prep.* 1 *Archaic* & *Scot.* Concerning; in regard to. 2 *Obs.* On a line with. 3 *Obs.* Facing toward. [OE *onefen, onemn* near to + inorganic *-t*]

an·er·gy (an′ər·jē) *n.* 1 Lack of energy; inactivity. 2 Absent or reduced sensitivity to a specific allergen or antigen. [< NL *anergia* < Gk. *an-* without + *ergon* work] —**an·er·gic** (an·ûr′jik) *adj.*

an·er·oid (an′ə·roid) *adj.* Not containing or using a fluid. —*n.* An aneroid barometer. [< Gk. *a-* not + *nēros* wet + -OID]

aneroid altimeter An altimeter that uses air pressure to measure altitude.

aneroid barometer An instrument showing atmospheric pressure and approximate altitude above sea level by the movements of the elastic top of a chamber equipped with a calibrated dial and from which almost all the air has been removed.

an·es·the·sia (an′is·thē′zhə, -zhē·ə) *n.* 1 Partial or total loss of physical sensation, particularly of touch, due to disease or psychic disturbances. 2 Local or general insensibility to pain induced by the injection of an anesthetic drug, or the inhaling of an anesthetic gas. Also **an·es·the·sis** (an′is·thē′·sis): also spelled *anaesthesia* [< NL < Gk. *anaisthēsia* insensibility < *an-* without + *aisthēsis* sensation]

an·es·the·si·ol·o·gy (an′is·thē′zē·ol′ə·jē) *n.* The branch of medicine that deals with the study and administration of anesthetics. Also spelled *anaesthesiology.* —**an′es·the′si·ol′o·gist** *n.*

an·es·thet·ic (an′is·thet′ik) *adj.* 1 Pertaining to or like anesthesia. 2 Producing anesthesia; making insensible to pain. —*n.* A drug or gas that causes unconsciousness or deadens sensation, as morphine, ether, chloroform, etc. Also spelled *anaesthetic.*

an·es·the·tist (ə·nes′thə·tist) *n.* A person trained to administer anesthetics: also spelled *anaesthetist.*

an·es·the·tize (ə·nes′thə·tīz) *v.t.* **·tized, ·tiz·ing** To induce anesthesia in; to render insensible, especially to pain: also spelled *anaesthetize.* —**an·es·the·ti·za·tion** (ə·nes′thə·tə·zā′shən, an′is·thet′ə-) *n.*

an·es·trus (an·es′trəs) *n.* The interval of sexual quiescence between successive periods of estrus. **—an·es·trous** *adj.*

an·e·thole (an′ə·thôl, -thol) *n.* A colorless crystalline compound, $C_{10}H_{12}O$, obtained from anise and fennel oils: used in perfumery and in medicine as an aromatic carminative. [<L *anethum* anise + -OLE]

an·eu·rysm (an′yə·riz′əm) *n.* A blood-filled, pulsating sac due to a localized abnormal dilatation of the wall of an artery. Also spelled **an′eu·rism.** [<Gk. *aneurysma* <*ana-* up + *eurys* wide] —**an·eu·rys·mal** (an′yə·riz′məl) or **·ris′mal** *adj.*

a·new (ə·nōō′, ə·nyōō′) *adv.* **1** As a new act; in a new way. **2** Again; over again in a different way.

an·frac·tu·os·i·ty (an·frak′chōō·os′ə·tē) *n. pl.* **·ties 1** The state or quality of being anfractuous. **2** A tortuous channel, depression, or process.

an·frac·tu·ous (an·frak′chōō·əs) *adj.* Tortuous; having many winding passages or grooves; sinuous. [<L *anfractuosus* <*anfractus* a winding <*an-* *(ambi-)* around + *frangere* break]

an·ga·ry (ang′gə·rē) *n.* In international law, the right of a warring nation, in case of need, to seize and use, or to destroy, neutral property, especially ships, the exercise of this right being subject to claim for compensation. Also **an·gar·i·a** (ang·gâr′ē·ə). [<F *angarie* <L *angaria* forced service to a lord <Gk. *angaros* courier]

an·gel (ān′jəl) *n.* **1** *Theol.* One of an order of spiritual beings endowed with immortality, attendant upon the Deity; a heavenly guardian, ministering spirit, or messenger. **2** A fallen spiritual being, also immortal. **3** In traditional and popular thought, the glorified spirit of a deceased person. **4** A pastor or bishop. *Rev.* ii 1. **5** A person of real or fancied angelic qualities. **6** In Christian Science, a message from Truth and Love; the inspiration of goodness, purity, and immortality, counteracting all evil, sensuality, and mortality. **7** A conventional representation of an angel, usually a youthful winged human figure in white robes with a halo. **8** A former English gold coin with the archangel Michael shown on it. **9** A guardian spirit or attendant. **10** *Colloq.* The financial backer of a play or of any enterprise. —*adj.* Angelic. [OE *engel* <L *angelus* <Gk. *angelos* messenger]

angel dust *Slang* Phencyclidine, especially when used illegally for psychedelic effect.

An·ge·le·no (an′jə·lē′nō) *n.* A native or inhabitant of Los Angeles.

An·gel Fall (ān′jəl) A waterfall in SE Venezuela, said to be the world's highest uninterrupted waterfall; 3,212 feet.

an·gel·fish (ān′jəl·fish′) *n. pl.* **·fish** or **·fish·es 1** Any of various species of small, colorful, reef-dwelling fishes (family Chaetodontidae) with laterally compressed bodies. **2** The scalare.

ANGELFISH *(def. 3)* (3 to 6 inches long)

angel food cake A delicate, spongy cake made without shortening or egg yolks. Also **angel cake.**

an·gel·hood (ān′jəl·hŏŏd) *n.* The state or nature of an angel.

an·gel·ic (an·jel′ik) *adj.* **1** Pertaining to, of, or consisting of angels; celestial. **2** Like an angel; pure; beautiful; saintly. Also **an·gel′i·cal.** [<L *angelicus* <Gk. *angelikos* <*angelos* messenger] **—an·gel′i·cal·ly** *adv.*

An·gel·i·ca (an·jel′i·kə; *Ger.* äng·gä′lē·kä, *Ital.* än·je′lē·kä) See ANGELINA.

an·gel·i·ca (an·jel′i·kə) *n.* **1** Any of various plants of a genus *(Angelica)* widely distributed in the northern hemisphere, especially a species *(A. archangelica)* that yields an oil used as a flavoring agent. **2** A confection of candied angelica stalks. **3** A sweet white or pale-yellow fortified wine. [<Med.L *(herba) angelica* the angelic (herb); so called from its use against poisons]

an·gel·i·ca-tree (an·jel′i·kə·trē′) *n.* A shrub or small tree *(Aralia spinosa)* with prickly trunk and leaves, native to the eastern United States. Also called *Hercules'-club.*

An·gel·i·co (än·jel′i·kō), **Fra,** 1387–1455, Giovanni da Fiesole, Italian painter and monk: original name *Guidi di Pietro.*

An·ge·li·na (an′jə·lī′nə, *Ger.* äng′gā·lē′nä) A feminine personal name. Also *Fr.* **An·gé·lique** (äṅ·zhā·lēk′) or **An·gé·line** (äṅ·zhā·lēn′). See also ANGELICA. [<Gk., angel]

an·gel·ol·a·try (ān′jəl·ol′ə·trē) *n.* Angel-worship.

an·gel·ol·o·gy (ān′jəl·ol′ə·jē) *n.* The doctrine concerning angels; the branch of theology that treats of angels. **—an·gel·o·log·ic** (ān′·jəl·ə·loj′·ik) or **·log′i·cal** *adj.*

angel shark A raylike shark of temperate seas (genus *Squatina)* having very large winglike pectoral fins.

an·ge·lus (an′jə·ləs) *n.* **1** In the Roman Catholic Church, a prayer said to commemorate the Annunciation: named from its first word. **2** A bell rung at morning, noon, and night as a call to recite this prayer: also called **angelus bell.** Also **An′ge·lus.** [<L]

an·ger (ang′gər) *n.* Violent vindictive passion; sudden and strong displeasure, as a result of injury, opposition, or mistreatment; wrath; ire. —*v.t.* **1** To make angry; enrage. **2** *Dial.* To inflame; make painful. See synonyms under INCENSE[1]. [<ON *angr* grief]

Synonyms (noun): animosity, choler, displeasure, exasperation, fury, hatred, impatience, indignation, ire, irritation, offense, passion, rage, resentment, temper, wrath. *Anger* is sharp, sudden, and, like all violent passions, necessarily brief. *Resentment* (a feeling back or feeling over again) is persistent brooding over injuries. *Rage* drives one beyond the bounds of prudence or discretion: *fury* is stronger yet, and sweeps one away into uncontrollable violence. *Anger* is personal and usually selfish. *Wrath* is deeper, more enduring than *anger,* and may be vengeful. *Indignation* is impersonal and unselfish *displeasure* at unworthy acts (L *indigna*), that is, at wrong as wrong. Pure *indignation* is not followed by regret, and is often a duty. See HATRED. *Antonyms:* forbearance, gentleness, long-suffering, patience, peace, peaceableness, peacefulness, self-control.

An·gers (an′jərz, ang′gərz; *Fr.* äṅ·zhā′) A city of western France on the Maine.

An·ge·vin (an′jə·vin) *adj.* **1** Of or pertaining to Anjou. **2** Of or pertaining to the Plantagenet kings of England from 1154 to 1204. —*n.* **1** A native or inhabitant of Anjou. **2** A member of the royal house of Anjou. Also **An′ge·vine** (-vin, -vīn). [<F]

an·gi·na (an·jī′nə, an′jə·nə) *n.* **1** Any disease characterized by spasmodic suffocating pain, as quinsy, croup, etc. **2** Angina pectoris. [<L, quinsy <*angere* choke] **—an·gi′nal** *adj.* **—an·gi·nose** (an′jə·nōs) *adj.*

angina pec·to·ris (pek′tə·ris) Paroxysmal pain below the sternum and sometimes extending to the left shoulder and arm, due to inadequate blood and oxygen supplied to the heart. [<NL, angina of the chest]

angio- *combining form* **1** *Bot.* Seed vessel: *angiosperm.* **2** *Med.* Blood vessel; lymph vessel: *angiology.* Also, before vowels, **angi-.** [<Gk. *angeion* case, vessel, capsule]

an·gi·o·car·di·og·ra·phy (an′jē·ō·kär′dē·og′rə·fē) *n.* Radiography of the heart and connecting blood vessels of the chest following injection of a substance opaque to radiation. **—an′gi·o·car′·di·o·graph′ic** *adj.*

an·gi·o·car·pous (an′jē·ə·kär′pəs) *adj. Bot.* **1** Having the fruit covered by a distinct envelope. **2** Having the fruit-bearing surface disposed inside the tissue of the sporocarp, as certain fungi, or lining the interior of cavities, as certain lichens. Also **—an′gi·o·car′pic. —an·gi·o·car·py** (an′jē·ō·kär′pē) *n.*

an·gi·og·ra·phy (an′jē·og′rə·fē) *n.* Radiography of blood vessels following injection of a radiopaque substance. **—an·gi·o·gram** (an′jē·ō·gram) **—an·gi·o·graph·ic** (an′jē·ō·graf′ik) *adj.*

an·gi·ol·o·gy (an′jē·ol′ə·jē) *n.* That part of systematic anatomy which relates to blood and lymph vessels.

an·gi·o·ma (an′jē·ō′mə) *n. pl.* **·mas** or **·ma·ta** (-mə·tə) A tumor consisting of blood vessels and/or lymph vessels. [<NL <ANGI(O)- + -OMA] **—an·gi·om·a·tous** (an′jē·om′ə·təs) *adj.*

an·gi·o·sperm (an′jē·ə·spûrm′) *n.* Any plant of a division (Magnoliophyta, formerly Angiospermae) of vascular seed plants in which the ovules are enclosed in an ovary. Also called *flowering plant.* **an′gi·o·sper′mous** *adj.*

an·gi·o·ten·sin (an′jē·ō·ten′sin) *n.* **1** Either of two peptide hormones that influence the constriction of blood vessels and the secretion of aldosterone. **2** A synthetic amide used in medicine as a pressor agent.

an·gi·ot·o·my (an′jē·ot′ə·mē) *n.* Incision into an artery or vein.

Ang·kor (ang′kôr) An assemblage of ruins in NW Cambodia; site of **Angkor Thom** (tôm), an ancient Khmer capital, and **Angkor Wat** or **Angkor Vat** (wät), the best preserved Khmer temple.

an·gle[1] (ang′gəl) *v.i.* **an·gled, an·gling 1** To fish with a hook and line. **2** To try to get slyly or artfully: with *for.* [<*n.*] —*n. Obs.* A fish hook; fishing tackle. [OE *angel* fish hook]

an·gle[2] (ang′gəl) *n.* **1** *Geom.* **a** The figure formed by the meeting of two lines or of two or more surfaces; corner; point. **b** The figure, concept, or relation of two straight lines (sides) emanating from one point (the vertex).

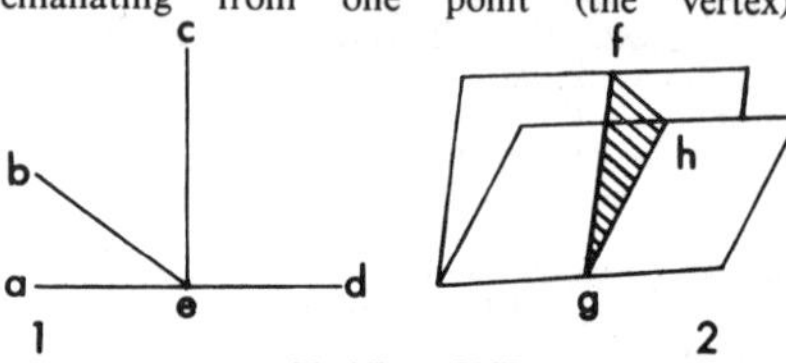

PLANE ANGLES

c The figure formed by the intersection of two straight lines or of two or more planes. See list of geometric angles below. **2** A secluded place resembling a corner; nook. **3** The point of view or aspect from which any object, question, or situation may be regarded. **—critical angle 1** The least angle of incidence at which a ray is totally reflected. **2** *Aeron.* The angle of attack at which the airflow striking the under surface of an airplane changes abruptly, causing similar changes in lift and drag. **—gliding angle** *Aeron.* The angle the flight path of an airplane makes with the horizontal when flying in still air under the influence of gravity alone. —*v.* **an·gled, an·gling** *v.t.* **1** To move or turn at an angle or by angles: to *angle* a ball to avoid a hazard. **2** *Colloq.* To impart a particular bias or interpretation, as to a story or report. —*v.i.* **3** To proceed or turn itself at an angle or by angles: The road *angled* up the hill. [<F <L *angulus* a corner, angle]

PRINCIPAL GEOMETRIC ANGLES

—acute angle An angle less than a right angle.

—adjacent angle An angle having a common side with another angle and the same vertex.

—alternate angle Either of two non-adjacent interior or exterior angles formed on opposite sides of a line which crosses two other lines.

—central angle An angle whose vertex is the center of a circle and whose sides are radii.

—complementary angle One of two angles whose sum is a right angle.

—conjugate angle Either of two angles whose sum is a perigon.

—dihedral angle The relation of two intersecting planes, as measured by the difference in direction of perpendiculars to them.

—exterior angle 1 Any of four angles formed on the outside of two straight lines cut by a third line. **2** The angle formed between any side of a polygon and the extension of an adjacent side.

—interior angle 1 One of the four angles formed between two straight lines cut by a third line. **2** The angle formed in the interior of a polygon by two adjacent sides.

—obtuse angle An angle greater than a right angle.

—plane angle An angle made by lines lying in one plane.

—reflex angle An angle greater than a straight angle.

—right angle An angle whose sides are perpendicular to each other; an angle of 90°.
—solid angle The angle formed at the vertex of a cone or subtended at the point of intersection of three or more planes; equal to 4π steradians.
—spherical angle The angle formed at the intersection of two great circles on a sphere: its value is a measure of the difference in direction of the arcs of the intersecting circles.
—straight angle An angle of 180°, generated by two straight lines extending in opposite directions from the vertex.
—supplementary angle One of two angles whose sum is a straight angle.

An•gle (ang′gəl) *n.* **1** A member of a Germanic tribe which migrated from southern Denmark to Britain in the fifth and sixth centuries and founded the kingdoms of East anglia, Mercia, and Northumbria. **2** A national of any of the kingdoms in the parts of Britain settled by this tribe: from its descendants the country came to be called England (Angle-land). [<L *Anglus*, sing. of *Angli* <Gmc.]

an•gled (ang′gəld) *adj.* **1** Having angles. **2** Set or placed at an angle.

an•gle•doz•er (ang′gəl•dō ′zər) *n.* A tractorlike machine for leveling ground, scraping roads, etc., with its scraper adjusted to push the dirt off to one side.

angle iron A piece of iron in the form of an angle, especially a right angle, for joining or strengthening beams, girders, and corners, or as a component member of an iron structure. Also **an′gle-i′ron** *n.*

an•gle•me•ter (ang′gəl•mē ′tər) *n.* **1** A clinometer. **2** *Mech.* A device for determining the differences in angular velocity of the crank shaft of an engine during a revolution.

angle of attack *Aeron.* The acute angle between movement relative to air or wind and the chord of an airfoil, or the fore-and-aft axis of a body.

angle of incidence **1** *Optics* The angle at which a beam of light or sound strikes a surface relative to the perpendicular. **2** *Aeron.* The angle of attack.

angle of repose The inclination to the horizontal assumed by a heap of sand, gravel, or other loose particulate material when in equilibrium with gravity. Also called **angle of friction.**

angle of view *Optics* The angle formed by two lines drawn from the extremities of an object or scene to the center of a lens.

angle of yaw *Aeron.* The acute angle between the direction of the relative wind and the plane of symmetry of an aircraft.

angle plate *Mech.* One of two metal plates which may be securely bolted at right angles to each other as a support for tools or in machine-working.

an•gle•pod (ang′gəl•pod′) *n.* A vine (genus *Vincetoxicum*) of the milkweed family, especially *V. gonocarpos* of the southern United States, bearing angular pods.

an•gler (ang′glər) *n.* **1** One of a family *(Lophiidae)* of fishes having a wide, froglike mouth and antennalike filaments attached to the head with which it angles for its prey: also called *frogfish*. **2** One who fishes with rod, hook, and line.

An•gle•sey (ang′gəl•sē) An island county of NW Wales; 275 square miles. Also **An′gle•sea.**

an•gle•site (ang′glə•sīt) *n.* A highly lustrous, white orthorhombic lead sulfate, $PbSO_4$. [from *Anglesey*, where first found]

an•gle•tube (ang′gəl•tŏŏb′, -tyŏŏb′) *n.* The tube which connects the facepiece of a gas mask to the hose.

an•gle•worm (ang′gəl•wûrm′) *n.* An earthworm commonly used as bait in angling.

An•gli•a (ang′glē•ə) The Latin name for ENGLAND.

An•gli•an (ang′glē•ən) *adj.* Pertaining to the Angles or their country. — *n.* The Northumbrian and Mercian dialects of Old English.

An•glic (ang′glik) *n.* A simplified form of English evolved for use as an auxiliary international language by R. E. Zachrisson, 1880–1937, Swedish linguist. — *adj.* Anglian.

An•gli•can (ang′glə•kən) *adj.* **1** Pertaining to the Church of England, the churches derived from it, or the High-Church party in any of these. **2** Pertaining to England or that which is English. — *n.* A member of the Church of England or of any church derived from it; also, a High-Churchman. [<Med. L *Anglicanus* < *Anglicus* English <L *Angli* the Angles, the English]

An•gli•can•ism (ang′gli•kən•iz′əm) *n.* The doctrine, discipline, and practice of the Church of England.

Anglican orders Holy orders, as administered in the Church of England.

An•gli•ce (ang′glə•sē) *adv.* In English; according to the usage of the English language: Napoli, *Anglice* Naples. [<Med. L]

An•gli•cism (ang′glə•siz′ə) m) *n.* **1** Any word, phrase, or idiom peculiarly English. **2** A word, phrase, or sense used in England, but not in accepted use in the United States; a Briticism. **3** Any trait or usage peculiarly English. **4** The state or quality of being English.

An•gli•cist (ang′glə•sist) *n.* An authority on or student of English language and literature.

An•gli•ci•za•tion (ang′glə•sə•zā′shən, -sī•zā′shən) *n.* **1** The act of making or becoming English in quality, character, or form. **2** The result or effect of Anglicizing.

An•gli•cize (ang′glə•sīz) *v.* **•cized, •ciz•ing** *v.t.* To give an English form, style, or idiom to. — *v.i.* To acquire some English trait or peculiarity; become like the English. Also *Brit.* **An′gli•cise.**

An•gli•form (ang′glə•fôrm) *adj.* Having English form.

An•gli•fy (ang′glə•fī) *v.t. v.i.* **•fied, •fy•ing** To Anglicize.

an•gling (ang′gling) *n.* The act or art of fishing with a hook, line, and rod.

An•glist (ang′glist) *n.* An authority of England.

Anglo- *combining form* English; English and: used in various adjectives and nouns indicating relations of language, interests, etc., between the countries concerned or natives of them: *Anglo-Asiatic, Anglo-Irish*. [<L *Anglus* an Angle, an Englishman]

An•glo (ang′glō) *n.* pl. **•glos** *U.S.* An Anglo-American, especially as distinguished from a Mexican-American.

An•glo-Af•ri•can (ang′glō•af′rə•kən) *adj.* Designating a native of Africa of English descent.

An•glo-A•mer•i•can (ang′glō•ə•mer′ə•kən) *adj.* **1** Of or pertaining to England and America or the relations of the peoples of the two countries: *Anglo-American* trade. **2** Of or pertaining to the English people who have settled in America. — *n.* A native of England or a descendant of a native of England who has settled in the United States or in America.

An•glo-Boer War (ang′glō•bōr′, -bor′, -bŏŏr′) See BOERWAR in table under WAR.

An•glo-Cath•o•lic (ang′glō•kath′ə•lik, -kath′•lik) *adj.* **1** Of the Anglican Church, but emphasizing Catholic rather than Protestant tendencies. **2** Pertaining to the High-Church party in the Church of England or allied bodies. **—An•glo-Ca•thol•i•cism** (ang′•glō•kə•thol′ə•siz′əm) *n.*

An•glo-Chi•nese (ang′glō•chī) •nēz′, -chī•nēs′) *adj.* Of or pertaining to persons or things in China that are of English origin.

An•glo-French (ang′glō•french′) *adj.* **1** Pertaining to the English and French jointly or to their countries. **2** Relating to Anglo-French. — *n.* The Norman dialect of Old French current in England from the Norman Conquest to the end of the 13th century: also called *Anglo-Norman, Norman French*. Abbr. *A.F., AF.*

An•glo-In•di•an (ang′glō•in′dē•ən) *adj.* **1** Pertaining to or between England and India. **2** Of the Anglo-Indians. **3** Having both English and East Indian characteristics: the *Anglo-Indian* style of living. — *n.* **1** An Englishman living in India. **2** A person of mixed English and Indian parentage. **3** The vocabulary, consisting of Anglicized native words, developed by British citizens in civil and military service in India: also called *Hobson-Jobson*.

An•glo•ma•ni•a (ang′glō•mā′nē•ə) *n.* Overfondness for or imitation of English manners,speech, institutions, or customs. **—An′glo•ma′ni•ac** (-ak) *n.*

An•glo-Nor•man (ang′glō•nô r′mən) *adj.* **1** English and Norman. **2** Pertaining to the Normans who settled in England after the Norman Conquest, their descendants, or their language. —*n.* **1** One of the Norman settlers in England after the Norman Conquest. **2** Anglo-French.

An•glo•phile (ang′glə•fīl, -fil) *n.* A lover of England or its people, customs, institutions, or manners. — *adj.* Of or like Anglophiles. Also **An′glo•phil** (-fil).

An•glo•phobe (ang′glə•fōb) *n.* One who hates or distrusts England or English manners, people, institutions, or customs. — *adj.* Of or like Anglophobes. Also **An•glo•pho•bi•ac** (ang′glə•fō′bē•ak).

An•glo•pho•bi•a (ang′glə•fō′bē•ə) *n.* Hatred or dread of England or English customs, people, manners, or institutions. **—An′glo•pho′bic** (-fō′bik, -fob′ik) *adj.*

An•glo-Sax•on (ang′glō•sak′sən) *n.* **1** A member of one of the Germanic tribes (Angles, Saxons, and Jutes) that conquered Britain in the fifth and sixth centuries. **2** A member of the nation descended from these peoples which dominated England until the Norman Conquest. **3** Their West Germanic language; Old English. **4** Any one of English nationality or descent. **5** *Colloq.* Simple, pithy, unadorned English, free of scholarly borrowings or circumlocutions: the native element in the language being considered more forceful and direct. **6** *Colloq.* The short, vulgar words of the language, as used for their pungency. **7** Loosely, the modern English language. — *adj.* Of or pertaining to the Anglo-Saxons, their language, customs, or descendants. **—An′glo-Sax′on•ism** *n.*

Anglo-Saxon Chronicle A chronological prose history of England in Old English from early Christian times to 1154; especially those recensions to 892 usually accredited to Alfred.

An•go•la (ang•gō′lə) A country in western Africa; 481,351 square miles; capital, Loanda; formerly *Portuguese West Africa*.

An•go•ra (ang•gôr′ə, -gō ′rə, ang′gə•rə) See ANKARA.

An•go•ra (ang•gôr′ə, -gō ′rə) *n.* **1** An Angora goat. **2** The long, silky hair of this goat: when manufactured, often called *mohair*. **3** An imitation of Angora cloth made of rabbit hair. **4** A shawl, cloth, etc., made of Angora material or its imitations. **5** An Angora cat.

Angora cat A variety of cat, originally from Angora, with long, silky hair.

Angora goat A goat, originally from Angora, reared for its long, silky hair, known as **Angora wool.**

an•gos•tu•ra bark (ang′gəs•tŏŏr′ə, -tyŏŏr′ə) A bark from a South American tree *(Galipea officinalis)*, used in the preparation of a tonic and flavoring. Also **An′gos•tu′ra.** [from *Angostura*, former name of Ciudad Bolívar]

Angostura bitters A bitter aromatic infusion, used as a flavoring, prepared from angostura bark and other roots, etc.: a trade name.

An•gou•l ême (äṅ•gōō•lem′) A city in western France.

An•gra do He•ro•ís•mo (äng′grə dōō ē•rōō•ēz′mōō) One of three districts in the Azores, comprising Terceira, S;atao Jorge, and Graciosa islands; 268 square miles; capital, Angra do Heroísmo, on Terceira.

An•gra Pe•que•na (ang′grə pē •kwē′nə) The former name for LÅU/U DERITZ.

an•gry (ang′grē) *adj.* **an•gri•er, an•gri•est** **1** Feeling, showing, or excited by anger; indignant. **2** Showing signs of anger; appearing to threaten: *angry* skies. **3** Badly inflamed: an *angry* sore. **—an•gri•ly** (ang′grə•lē) *adv.* **—an•gri•nessn.**

angst (ängst) *n.* Anxiety; dread. [<G]

ang•strom (ang′strəm) *n.* A unit for the measurement of wavelength, equal to a hundred millionth of a centimeter, or 0.003937 millionths of an inch. Also **angstrom unit.** [after A. J. Ångströ m]

Ång•ström (ang′strəm, *Sw.* ōng′strœm), **Anders Jonas,** 1814–74, Swedish physicist.

an•gui•form (ang′gwə•fôrm) *adj.* Shaped like a snake. [<L *anguis* snake + -FORM]

An·guil·la (ang·gwil′ə) See ST. CHRISTOPHER, NEVIS AND ANGUILLA.

an·guil·li·form (ang·gwil′ə·fôrm) *adj.* Having the form of an eel. [<L *anguilla* eel + -FORM]

an·guine (ang′gwin) *adj.* Of, pertaining to, or like a snake. [<L *anguinus* <*anguis* snake]

an·guish (ang′gwish) *n.* Excruciating mental or bodily pain; agony; torture. See synonyms under AGONY, ANXIETY. —*v.t.* & *v.i.* To affect or suffer with anguish. [OF *anguisse* <L *angustia* tightness, difficulty <*angustus* narrow, tight]

an·gu·lar (ang′gyə·lər) *adj.* **1** Having, forming, or constituting an angle or angles; sharp-cornered; pointed. **2** Measured by an angle: *angular* motion. **3** Pertaining to angles. **4** Bony; gaunt and with little flesh, so as to be awkward or ungraceful. **5** Of a crabbed or unaccommodating disposition. [<L *angularis* <*angulus* corner, angle] **—an′gu·lar·ly** *adv.*

an·gu·lar·i·ty (ang′gyə·lar′ə·tē) *n. pl.* **·ties 1** The state or condition of being angular. **2** *pl.* Angular outlines or corners. Also **an′gu·lar·ness.**

an·gu·late (ang′gyə·lit, -lāt) *adj.* Having angles; angular: used chiefly in botany: *angulate* leaves. Also **an′gu·lat′ed.** —*v.t.* & *v.i.* **·lat·ed, ·lat·ing** To make or become angular. [<L *angulatus,* pp. of *angulare* make angular <*angulus* corner, angle] **—an′gu·late·ly** *adv.*

an·gu·la·tion (ang′gyə·lā′shən) *n.* **1** The making of angles. **2** An angular formation or position.

An·gus (ang′gəs) A county in eastern Scotland; 874 square miles: formerly *Forfar.*

Angus Og (ōg) In Irish mythology, Angus the Young, god of love and beauty; son of Dagda.

an·gus·tate (ang·gus′tāt) *adj.* Compressed; narrowed. [<L *angustatus,* pp. of *angustare* narrow <*angustus* narrow]

ang·wan·ti·bo (äng′wän·tē′bō) *n.* A small, tailed primate *(Arctocebus calabarensis)* of African forests, having a small, pointed face.

An·halt (än′hält) A former state and duchy of central Germany; 898 square miles.

an·he·la·tion (an′hi·lā′shən) *n. Pathol.* Shortness of breath; difficult respiration; dyspnoea. [<F *anhélation* <L *anhelatio, -onis* <*anhelare* pant]

an·he·lous (an·hē′ləs) *adj.* Short-breathed; panting.

an·hi·dro·sis (an′hi·drō′sis) *n. Pathol.* Partial or complete lack of perspiration. Also **an·i·dro·sis** (an′i·drō′sis). [<NL <Gk. *an-* without + *hidrōs* perspiration] **—an·hi·drot·ic** (an′hi·drot′ik) *adj.*

an·hin·ga (an·hing′gə) *n.* The snakebird. [<Tupian]

An·hwei (än′hwā′) A province of eastern China; 54,000 square miles; divided after 1949 into **North Anhwei;** 40,000 square miles; capital, Hofei; and **South Anhwei;** 14,000 square miles; capital, Wuhu. Also **An·hui** (än′hwā′).

an·hy·drate (an·hī′drāt) *v.t.* **·drat·ed, ·drat·ing** To dehydrate.

an·hy·dride (an·hī′drīd, -drid) *n. Chem.* **1** Any organic or inorganic compound from which the water has been removed. **2** A non-metallic oxide to which water has been added, with formation of an *acid anhydride.* **3** A metallic oxide which forms a *basic anhydride* upon the addition of water. [See ANHYDROUS]

an·hy·drite (an·hī′drīt) *n.* An orthorhombic calcium sulfate, $CaSO_4$, found as a whitish or light-colored mineral.

an·hy·drous (an·hī′drəs) *adj. Chem.* Pertaining to or designating a compound which has no water in its composition, especially one having no water of crystallization. [<Gk. *anydros* waterless <*an-* without + *hydōr* water]

a·ni (ä′nē) *n.* Any of several species of birds of the cuckoo family (genus *Crotophaga*), generally black with metallic reflections, ranging from Florida southward. [<Tupian]

An·i·ak·chak (an′ē·ak′chak) A volcano in the Aleutian Range, SW Alaska; crater diameter, 6 miles.

a·nigh (ə·nī′) *adv.* & *prep.* Near; nigh; nigh to.

a·night (ə·nīt′) *adv.* At night; nightly. Also **a·nights′.**

an·il (an′il) *n.* **1** A West Indian indigo plant *(Indigofera suffruticosa).* **2** The indigo dye made from this plant. [<F <Pg. <Arabic *al-nīl* the blue]

an·ile (an′īl, ā′nīl, an′il) *adj.* Like an old woman; weak or feeble-minded. [<L *anilis* <*anus* old woman] **—a·nil·i·ty** (ə·nil′ə·tē) *n.*

an·i·line (an′ə·lin, -līn) *n.* A colorless oily compound, $C_6H_5NH_2$, the base from which many of the coal-tar dyes, resins, and varnishes are made. It may be regarded as derived from ammonia, NH_3, by replacing one molecule of hydrogen with the radical phenyl, C_6H_5, and is hence considered chemically as *phenylamine.* Aniline was originally obtained in the distillation of indigo, but is now chiefly made from nitrobenzene. —*adj.* Made of, derived from, or pertaining to aniline. Also **an·i·lin** (an′ə·lin). [<ANIL + -INE]

aniline red See MAGENTA.

an·i·mad·ver·sion (an′ə·mad·vûr′zhən, -shən) *n.* Criticism or censure; a censorious comment or reflection: with *on* or *upon.* [<L *animadversio, -onis* <*animadvertere.* See ANIMADVERT.] **—an′i·mad·ver′sive** (-siv) *adj.* **—an′i·mad·ver′sive·ness** *n.*

Synonyms: aspersion, blame, censure, chiding, comment, criticism, disapproval, rebuke, reflection, reprehension, reproof. *Comment* and *criticism* may be favorable as well as censorious; they imply no superiority or authority on the part of him who utters them; nor do *reflection* and *reprehension,* which are simply turning the mind back upon what is disapproved. *Reprehension* is calm and just, and with good intent; it is therefore a serious matter, however mild, and is capable of great force, as expressed in the phrase severe *reprehension. Reflection* is often from mere ill feeling, and is likely to be more personal and less impartial than *reprehension;* we often speak of unkind or unjust *reflections. Rebuke,* literally a stopping of the mouth, is administered to a forward or hasty person; *reproof* is administered to one intentionally or deliberately wrong; both words imply authority in the reprover. *Antonyms*: approbation, approval, commendation, encomium, eulogy, panegyric, praise.

an·i·mad·vert (an′ə·mad·vûrt′) *v.i.* **1** To comment critically, usually in an adverse sense: with *upon.* **2** *Obs.* To notice. [<L *animadvertere* take notice of <*animus* mind + *advertere* turn to. See ADVERT.]

an·i·mal (an′ə·məl) *n.* **1** A sentient living organism typically endowed with voluntary motion and sensation: distinguished from *plant.* **2** Any such creature as distinguished from man; a beast or brute. **3** A debased and bestial human being. **4** *pl.* Domestic quadrupeds. **5** Any creature but a bird, fish, or insect. —*adj.* **1** Of or pertaining to animals. **2** Bestial.

Synonyms (noun): beast, brute, fauna. An *animal* is a sentient being, distinct from inanimate matter and from vegetable life on the one side and from purely mental and spiritual existence on the other. Man is properly classified as an *animal,* but to call any individual man an *animal* is to imply that the animal nature has undue supremacy. The *brute* is the *animal* viewed as dull to all finer feeling; the *beast* is looked upon as a being of appetites. *Creature* is a word of wide signification, including inanimate objects, plants, animals, angels, or men as *divinely* created. The *animals* of a region are collectively called its *fauna. Antonyms*: angel, man, matter, mind, mineral, soul, spirit, vegetable.

animal act Any entertainment or demonstration featuring one or more performing animals.

animal charcoal Charcoal made from bones; bone-black.

animal crackers Small, sweetened cookies made in the shape of various animals.

an·i·mal·cu·la (an′ə·mal′kyə·lə) Plural of ANIMALCULUM.

an·i·mal·cu·lae (an′ə·mal′kyə·lē) Erroneous plural of *animalcula,* thought of as a feminine singular noun.

an·i·mal·cule (an′ə·mal′kyōōl) *n.* **1** A microscopic, usu. motile organism, as a paramecium, ameba, etc. **2** *Obs.* Any small animal, as a gnat. [<L *animalculum,* dim. of *animal* animal] **an′i·mal′cu·lar** (-kyə·lər) *adj.*

an·i·mal·cu·lism (an′ə·mal′kyə·liz′əm) *n.* An old biological theory that animalcules are the cause or source of vital phenomena and also of disease.

an·i·mal·cu·lum (an′ə·mal′kyə·ləm) *n. pl.* **·la** (-lə) An animalcule.

animal heat Heat generated by the chemical processes constantly going on in an animal organism: sustained at nearly uniform temperatures.

animal husbandry That branch of agriculture specializing in the breeding, raising, and care of farm animals.

an·i·mal·ism (an′ə·məl·iz′əm) *n.* **1** The state or condition of mere animals; the state of being actuated by sensual appetites only. **2** The belief or doctrine that man is entirely animal, having no soul or spirit.

an·i·mal·ist (an′ə·məl·ist) *n.* **1** An adherent to the doctrine of animalism. **2** A painter or sculptor of animals. **—an′i·mal·is′tic** *adj.*

an·i·mal·i·ty (an′ə·mal′ə·tē) *n.* **1** The animal qualities. **2** Animal life; the animal kingdom. **3** The merely animal nature, as distinguished from the moral and spiritual.

an·i·mal·i·za·tion (an′ə·məl·ə·zā′shən, -ī·zā′-) *n.* **1** The act of animalizing, or the state of being animalized. **2** *Ecol.* The number and kinds of animals, as horses, cattle, etc., in a country or district.

an·i·mal·ize (an′ə·məl·īz′) *v.t.* **·ized, ·iz·ing 1** To render brutal; sensualize. **2** To change into animal matter, especially by digestive assimilation. **3** *Obs.* To give animal form to.

animal kingdom One of the three great divisions of nature, embracing all animal organisms: contrasted with the *mineral* and *vegetable kingdoms;* also, all animals, collectively.

an·i·mal·ly (an′ə·məl·ē) *adv.* **1** In an animal manner; with respect to the body; corporally, as distinguished from mentally. **2** With respect to the animal or animal spirits; physically, as distinguished from spiritually.

animal magnetism 1 Mesmerism. **2** Magnetic personal qualities. **3** Sensualism: usually with opprobrious implications.

animal spirits Vivaciousness; energy; the buoyancy of good health.

animal starch Glycogen.

an·i·mate (an′ə·māt) *v.t.* **·mat·ed, ·mat·ing 1** To impart life to; make alive. **2** To move to action; incite; inspire: What motives *animated* him? **3** To produce activity or energy in: The wind *animated* the flags. See synonyms under ENCOURAGE, STIMULATE, STIR[1]. —*adj.* (an′ə·mit) **1** Possessing animal life; living. **2** Vivacious; lively. Also **an′i·mat′ed.** See synonyms under AIRY, ALIVE, EAGER, SANGUINE, VIVID. [<L *animatus,* pp. of *animare* to fill with breath, make alive <*anima* breath, soul] **—an′i·mat′ed·ly** *adv.*

animated cartoon See under CARTOON.

an·i·mat·er (an′ə·mā′tər) *n.* An animator.

an·i·mat·ing (an′ə·mā′ting) *adj.* Imparting life or animation; inspiring. **—an′i·mat′ing·ly** *adv.*

an·i·ma·tion (an′ə·mā′shən) *n.* **1** The act of imparting or the state of possessing life. **2** The state of being animated; liveliness; vivacity. **3** The process and technique of preparing the set of drawings to be filmed and exhibited as an animated cartoon. See synonyms under WARMTH.

an·i·ma·tive (an′ə·mā′tiv) *adj.* Enlivening; inspiring.

a·ni·ma·to (ä′nē·mä′tō) *adv. Music* With animation; in an animated manner: also *con anima.* [<Ital.]

an·i·ma·tor (an′ə·mā′tər) *n.* **1** One who or that which animates. **2** An artist who prepares a given set of drawings to be filmed as an animated cartoon.

an·i·mé (an′ə·mā, -mē) *n.* A hard fossilized resin obtained from the stem of an East African tree *(Hymenaea courbaril),* used in making flavorings, varnishes and lacquers. [<F <Sp., prob. <native name]

an·i·mism (an′ə·miz′əm) *n.* **1** The doctrine that the phenomena of animal life are produced by a soul or spiritual force distinct from matter. **2** The belief in the existence of spirit or soul, as distinct from matter. **3** The doctrine that inanimate objects and natural phenomena possess a personal life or soul. [<L *anima* soul] **—an′i·mist** *n.* **—an′i·mis′tic** *adj.*

an·i·mos·i·ty (an′ə·mos′ə·tē) *n. pl.* **·ties** Active and vehement enmity; hatred; ill will. See synonyms under ANGER, ENMITY, FEUD[1], HATRED, HOSTILITY. [<L *animositas, -tatis* high spirit, boldness <*animus* soul, mind, spirit]

an·i·mus (an′ə·məs) *n.* **1** Hostile feeling or intent; animosity. **2** The animating thought or purpose; disposition; temper. **3** Purpose; intention. [<L]

an·i·on (an′ī′ən) *n. Chem.* The electronegative constituent of an electrolyte, appearing at the anode of a voltaic cell; a negative ion: opposed to *cation.* [<Gk. *anion* (thing) going up, neut. of ppr. of *anienai* <*ana-* up + *ienai* go]

an·ise (an′is) *n.* **1** A small South European and North African plant *(Pimpinella anisum)* that furnishes aniseed. **2** Aniseed. Compare DILL. [<OF *anis* <L *anisum* <Gk. *anison*]

an·i·seed (an′i·sēd′) *n.* The fragrant seed of the anise plant, used in cookery and medicine.

an·i·sei·ko·ni·a (an·ī′si·kō′nē·ə, an·is′i-) *n. Pathol.* A disorder of vision in which the image perceived by one eye differs in form and size from that perceived by the other. [<Gk. *anisos* unequal + *eikōn* image]

an·i·sei·kon·ic (an·ī′si·kon′ik, an·is′i-) *adj.* **1** Pertaining to, characterized by, or serving to correct aniseikonia. **2** *Optics* Describing lenses designed to produce distorted images, especially in connection with the testing of vision.

an·i·sette (an′ə·zet′, -set′) *n.* A cordial made from or flavored with aniseed. [<F]

aniso- *combining form* Unequal; dissimilar: *anisogamy.* See ISO-. [<Gk. *anisos* unequal]

an·i·so·ga·mete (an·ī′sə·gə·mēt′) *n.* Heterogamete.

an·i·sog·a·my (an′ī·sog′ə·mē) *n. Biol.* A union of gametes similar in general type but unequal in size: opposed to *isogamy.* —**an′i·sog′a·mous** *adj.*

an·i·sole (an′ə·sōl) *n.* A colorless liquid compound, C_7H_8O, used as an insecticide and in the manufacture of perfumes. [<L *anisum* anise + -OLE[1]]

an·i·so·mer·ic (an·ī′sə·mer′ik) *adj. Chem.* Composed of the same elements but in different proportions: opposed to *isomeric.*

an·i·som·er·ous (an′ī·som′ər·əs) *adj.* **1** *Bot.* Having an unequal number of parts in different floral whorls; unsymmetrical. **2** *Zool.* Having the ridges of contiguous molar teeth increasing by more than one, as in mastodons.

an·i·so·met·ric (an·ī′sə·met′rik) *adj. Mineral.* Not isometric; specifically, dissimilar in the direction of the different axes, as some crystals.

an·i·so·me·tro·pi·a (an·ī′sə·mə·trō′pē·ə) *n. Pathol.* Inequality in the refracting power of the eyes.

an·i·so·phyl·lous (an·ī′sə·fil′əs) *adj. Bot.* Having leaves of unequal size or unlike form.

an·i·so·phyl·ly (an·ī′sə·fil′ē) *n. Bot.* The property of having different leaves; particularly, the possession of leaves of different size and character on different sides of plagiotropic shoots.

an·i·so·spore (an·ī′sə·spôr′, -spōr′) *n. Zool.* A form of spore developed by colonial radiolarians, consisting of microspores and macrospores which probably copulate: opposed to *isospore.*

an·i·so·trop·ic (an·ī′sə·trop′ik) *adj.* **1** *Physics* Having different properties in different directions, as when a fibrous substance conducts heat more rapidly along its fibers than across them. **2** *Bot.* Responding unequally to external influences, as plant organs. **3** *Optics* Exhibiting double refraction, as a lens or mineral. Also *eolitropic.* Compare ISOTROPIC.

an·i·sot·ro·py (an′ī·sot′rə·pē) *n.* The property or state of being anisotropic. Also **an′i·sot′ro·pism** (-piz′əm).

A·ni·ta (ə·nē′tə) Diminutive of ANA.

An·jou (an′jōō, *Fr.* äṅ·zhōō′) A former province of western France; divided in 1790 into several departments.

Anjou A family of French nobles, originally ruling the duchy of Anjou, who succeeded to the English throne in 1154 upon the accession of Henry II, son of Geoffrey of Anjou. See PLANTAGENET.

An·ka·ra (äng′kə·rə, ang′-) The capital of Turkey since 1923, located in central Anatolia: ancient *Ancyra:* formerly *Angora.*

An·ka·ra·tra Highlands (äng′kä·rä′·trä) A mountainous region of central Madagascar; highest point, 8,552 feet.

an·ker (ang′kər) *n.* A liquid measure of about 10 gallons. [<Du.]

an·ker·ite (ang′kər·īt) *n.* A mineral resembling dolomite, composed of a white, red, or grayish calcium-magnesium-iron carbonate crystallizing in the hexagonal system. [after Prof. *Anker,* Austrian mineralogist]

ankh (angk) *n.* In Egyptian art and mythology, a tau cross having a looped top: an emblem of generation; the ansate cross. For illustration see under CROSS. [<Egyptian *ānkh* life, soul]

An·king (än′king′) A city on the Yangtze River; former capital of Anhwei Province, China: formerly *Hwaining.*

an·kle (ang′kəl) *n. Anat.* **1** The joint connecting the foot and the leg. **2** The part of the leg between the foot and the calf near the ankle joint. [Prob. <ON, replacing OE *ancleōw*]

an·kle·bone (ang′kəl·bōn′) *n. Anat.* The talus or astragalus. Also **ankle bone.**

an·klet (ang′klit) *n.* **1** An ornament or fetter for the ankle. **2** A short sock reaching just above the ankle.

an·kus (ang′kəs, -kəsh) *n.* An elephant goad consisting of a sharp spike and hook set on a short staff. Also **an·kush** (ang′kəsh). [<Hind.]

an·ky·lose (ang′kə·lōs) *v.t. & v.i.* **·losed, ·los·ing** To unite or join by ankylosis: also spelled *anchylose.*

an·ky·lo·sis (ang′kə·lō′sis) *n.* **1** *Anat.* The knitting together or consolidation of two bones or parts of bones. **2** *Pathol.* The abnormal adhesion of bones, especially those forming a joint; stiffening of a joint. Also spelled *anchylosis.* [<NL <Gk. *ankylōsis* <*ankylos* crooked] — **an′ky·lot′ic** (-lot′ik) *adj.*

an·ky·los·to·mi·a·sis (ang′kə·los′tə·mī′ə·sis) See ANCYLOSTOMIASIS.

an·lace (an′lis) *n.* A broad two-edged dagger or short sword. Also **an′las.** [<OF *alenas, alenaz* dagger <*alesne* awl <Gmc.]

an·la·ge (än′lä·gə) *n.* **1** *Biol.* The first recognizable traces of an organ or part seen as an accumulation of cells in a developing embryo. **2** Basis; foundation; rudiment. Also **An′la·ge.** [<G, a laying on, foundation]

Ann (an) A feminine personal name. Also **Anne, An′na.** See HANNAH. [<Hebrew, grace]

Ann, Cape A cape of NE Massachusetts.

an·na (an′ə) *n.* A copper coin of India, equal to one-sixteenth of a rupee. [<Hind. *ānā*]

An·na (an′ə; *Dan., Du., Ger., Lat.* ä′nä; *Ital.* än′nä) A feminine personal name. See ANN.

an·na·berg·ite (an′ə·bûr′gīt) *n.* An apple-green hydrous nickel arsenate crystallizing in the monoclinic system; nickelbloom. [from *Annaberg,* town in eastern Germany]

an·nal (an′əl) *n.* The record of a single year; an item or entry in a book of annals.

an·nal·ist (an′əl·ist) *n.* A writer of annals; a historian. ◆Homophone: *analyst.* —**an′nal·is′tic** *adj.*

an·nals (an′əlz) *n. pl.* **1** A record of events in their chronological order, year by year. **2** A narrative of events in which the order of time, rather than the causal relation, is followed or made prominent; chronicles. **3** A periodical publication of discoveries, transactions, etc. **4** History or records in general: the *annals* of crime. **5** In the Roman Catholic Church, masses said at stated intervals during the year. See synonyms under HISTORY. [<L *annales (libri)* yearly (record), chronicles <*annus* year]

An·nam (ə·nam′, an′am) A former empire and French protectorate. See CENTRAL VIETNAM.

An·na·mese (an′ə·mēz′, -mēs′) *n. pl.* **An·na·mese** **1** A native or inhabitant of Annam, or the people of Annam collectively. **2** The language of Annam, including the Tonkinese and Cochin Chinese dialects: a member of the Mon-Khmer subfamily of the Austro-Asiatic family of languages. Also spelled *Anamese.* —*adj.* **1** Of Annam. **2** Of or pertaining to the inhabitants of Annam, their language, or their culture.

An·na·mite (an′ə·mīt) *adj. & n.* Annamese.

An·nap·o·lis (ə·nap′ə·lis) The capital of Maryland; seat of the United States Naval Academy.

Annapolis Royal A port on an arm of the Bay of Fundy, Nova Scotia.

An·na·pur·na (ä′nə·pōōr′nə) See ANAPURNA.

Ann Ar·bor (an′ är′bər) A city in SE Michigan.

an·nates (an′āts, -its) *n. pl.* In the Roman Catholic Church, the first fruits, or the first year's revenue of bishops and certain other ecclesiastics, paid to the Pope on their appointment to a see or benefice. [<F *annate* <Med.L *annata* <L *annus* year]

an·nat·to (ä·nä′tō) **1** A small evergreen tree *(Bixa orellana)* of Central America, cultivated for its seeds. **2** A yellowish red dyestuff obtained from the pulp enclosing the seeds of the annatto tree, used to color foods, textiles, varnishes. Also *anatto, arnatto.*

Anne (an, *Fr.* än) A feminine personal name. See ANN.

—**Anne,** 1665–1714, English queen; last of the Stuarts.

—**Anne of Austria,** 1601–66, consort of Louis XIII of France; regent 1643–61 for her son, Louis XIV.

—**Anne of Bohemia,** 1366–94, wife of Richard II of England.

—**Anne Boleyn** See BOLEYN.

—**Anne of Cleves** (klēvz), 1515–57, fourth wife of Henry VIII.

—**Anne of Denmark,** 1574–1619, wife of James I of England.

an·neal (ə·nēl′) *v.t.* **1** To render tough, as something formerly brittle, by heating and then slowly cooling. **2** To toughen; render enduring, as the will. **3** *Archaic* To fix in place by heating and then cooling, as colors or enamel. [OE *anǣlan* burn]

an·nec·tent (ə·nek′tənt) *adj.* Connecting; joining on. [<L *annectens, -entis,* ppr. of *annectere.* See ANNEX.]

an·ne·lid (an′ə·lid) *n. Zool.* Any of a phylum *(Annelida)* of segmented invertebrates, including the earthworms, leeches, marine worms, etc. —*adj.* Of or pertaining to this phylum. [<NL <F *annélide* <*anneler* arrange in rings <OF *annel* a ring <L *annellus* for *anellus,* dim. of *anulus* a ring]

an·nel·i·dan (ə·nel′ə·dən) *adj. & n.* Annelid.

An·nette (ə·net′, *Fr.* à·net′) Diminutive of ANN.

an·nex (ə·neks′) *v.t.* **1** To add or append, as an additional or minor part, to existing possessions; affix. **2** To attach, as an attribute, condition, or consequence: What punishment is *annexed* to vice? **3** *Archaic:* To join; unite. —*n.* (an′eks) **1** An addition to a building; also, a nearby building used in addition to the main building. **2** A supplementary service or department. **3** An addition to a document; addendum. **4** *Mil.* An appendix to a combat order specifying the details prescribed in a given field or subject: an artillery *annex.* [<F *annexer* <L *annexus,* pp. of *annectere* tie together <*ad-* to + *nectere* tie] — **an·nex′·a·ble** *adj.* —**an·nex′ive** *adj.*

an·nex·a·tion (an′ek·sā′shən) *n.* **1** An annexing or being annexed. **2** That which is annexed. **3** The permanent incorporation of newly acquired territory with the national domain. Also **an·nex′ment.**

An·nie (an′ē) Diminutive of ANN.

An·nie Oak·ley (an′ē ōk′lē) *U.S. Slang* A free pass to a theater, etc.: in allusion to the practice of punching a pass, which then resembled a small target after use by **Annie Oakley,** 1860–1926, U.S. markswoman.

an·ni·hi·late (ə·nī′ə·lāt) *v.t.* **·lat·ed, ·lat·ing** **1** To destroy absolutely. **2** To annul; abolish; make void. See synonyms under ABOLISH, EXTERMINATE. [<L *annihilatus,* pp. of *annihilare* <*ad-* to + *nihil* nothing] —**an·ni·hi·la·able** (ə·nī′·ə·lə·bəl) *adj.* —**an·ni′hi·la′tor** *n.*

an·ni·hi·la·tion (ə·nī′ə·lā′shən) *n.* An annihilating or being annihilated; extinction.

an·ni·hi·la·tion·ism (ə·nī′ə·lā′shən·iz′əm) *n. Theol.* The doctrine that the finally impenitent will be totally annihilated after death.

an·ni·hi·la·tion·ist (ə·nī′ə·lā′shən·ist) *n.* A believer in annihilation or annihilationism.

an·ni·hi·la·tive (ə·nī′ə·lā′tiv) *adj.* Tending to annihilate. Also **an·ni·hi·la·to·ry** (ə·nī′ə·lə·tôr′ē, -tō′rē).

an·ni·ver·sa·ry (an′ə·vûr′sər·ē) *n. pl.* **·ries 1** A day separated by a year or by an exact number of years from some past event. **2** A commemorative observance or celebration on such occasion. Wedding anniversaries are popularly named from the character of the presents regarded as appropriate to their celebration: **paper anniversary** (1st), **wooden anniversary** (5th), **tin anniversary** (10th), **crystal anniversary** (15th), **china anniversary** (20th), **silver anniversary** (25th), **golden anniversary** (50th), **diamond anniversary** (60th and 75th). —*adj.* **1** Recurring annually or at the same date every year. **2** Pertaining to or occurring on an anniversary. [< L *anniversarius* < *annus* year + *versus,* pp. of *vertere* turn]

Anniversary Day Australia Day.

an·no Chris·ti (an′ō kris′tī) *Latin* In the year of Christ.

an·no Dom·i·ni (an′ō dom′ə·nī) *Latin* In the year of our Lord or of the Christian era: abbr. *A.D.*

an·no mun·di (an′ō mun′dī) *Latin* In the year of the world: used in chronology, with the supposititious date of creation at 4004 B.C.

An·no·na (ə·nō′nə) In Roman mythology, the personification of fruitfulness and abundance, symbolized by a cornucopia and ears of grain.

an·no·tate (an′ō·tāt) *v.t.* **·tat·ed, ·tat·ing** To make explanatory or critical notes on or upon; to provide a commentary for, as a text. [< L *annotatus,* pp. of *annotare* < *ad-* to + *notare* note, mark < *nota* a mark] —**an′no·ta′tor** *n.*

an·no·ta·tion (an′ō·tā′shən) *n.* **1** An annotating or being annotated. **2** A critical or explanatory note; a comment.

an·no·ta·tive (an′ō·tā′tiv) *adj.* Of or marked by annotations. Also **an·no·ta·to·ry** (ə·nō′tə·tôr′ē, -tō′rē).

an·nounce (ə·nouns′) *v.t.* **an·nounced, an·nounc·ing 1** To make known publicly or officially; proclaim; publish. **2** To give notice of the approach or appearance of, as by a signal. **3** To make known to the senses: A roar *announced* the presence of the avalanche. **4** To serve as the announcer for, as a radio program. [< OF *anoncier* < L *annuntiare* < *ad-* to + *nuntiare* report < *nuntius* messenger]

Synonyms: advertise, communicate, declare, enunciate, herald, notify, proclaim, promulgate, propound, publish, report, reveal, speak. *Announce* is chiefly anticipatory; we *announce* a forthcoming book, a guest when he arrives. We *advertise* our business, *communicate* our intentions, *enunciate* our views; we *notify* an individual of a matter. We *propound* a question or an argument, *promulgate* the views of a sect or party. We *report* an interview, *reveal* a secret, *herald* the coming of some great event. *Declare* has often been an authoritative force; to *declare* war is to cause war to be. We *declare* war, *proclaim* peace. *Antonyms*: bury, conceal, hide, hush, secrete, suppress, withhold.

an·nounce·ment (ə·nouns′mənt) *n.* **1** An announcing or being announced. **2** That which is announced. **3** A printed declaration or publication.

an·nounc·er (ə·noun′sər) *n.* **1** One who announces. **2** A person who identifies the station from which a radio or television program is broadcast, introduces the performers and the program, etc.

an·noy (ə·noi′) *v.t.* **1** To be troublesome to; bother; irritate. **2** To do harm to or injure continuously or by repeated acts: Guerrilla fire *annoyed* the regiment. See synonyms under AFFRONT, HARASS. —*n. Obs.* Annoyance. [< OF *anuier, anoier* < L *in odio* in hatred] —**an·noy′er** *n.*

an·noy·ance (ə·noi′əns) *n.* **1** An annoying or being annoyed. **2** One who or that which annoys. See synonyms under ABOMINATION.

an·noy·ing (ə·noi′ing) *adj.* Vexatious, troublesome. See synonyms under TROUBLESOME. —**an·noy′ing·ly** *adv.* —**an·noy′ing·ness** *n.*

an·nu·al (an′yōō·əl) *adj.* **1** Returning, performed, or occurring every year. **2** Pertaining to the year; reckoned by the year. **3** *Bot.* Lasting or living only one year. —*n.* **1** A book or pamphlet issued once a year. **2** *Bot.* A plant living for a single year or season. **3** In the Roman Catholic Church, a yearly mass for a deceased person; also, the offering made for it. **4** *Archaic* A yearly payment. [< OF *annuel* < L *annualis* yearly < *annus* year]

an·nu·al·ly (an′yōō·əl·ē) *adv.* Year by year; yearly.

annual parallax See under PARALLAX.

annual ring Any of the concentric rings in a cross section of a tree trunk resulting from seasonal alternations of growth and quiescence. Also called *growth ring.*

an·nu·i·tant (ə·nōō′ə·tənt, ə·nyōō′-) *n.* One receiving, or entitled to receive, an annuity.

an·nu·it coep·tis (an′yōō·it sep′tis) *Latin* He (God) has favored our undertakings: motto on the reverse of the great seal of the United States.

an·nu·i·ty (ə·nōō′ə·tē, ə·nyōō′-) *n. pl.* **·ties 1** An annual allowance or income; also, the right to receive such an allowance or the duty of paying it. **2** The return from an investment of capital, with interest, in a series of yearly payments; especially, an agreed amount paid by an insurance company at stated intervals, usually monthly, in consideration of either a single premium or premiums paid over a period of years. [< F *annuité* < Med.L *annuitas, -tatis* < L *annus* year]

an·nul (ə·nul′) *v.t.* **an·nulled, an·nul·ling 1** To destroy the force of; declare void or invalid, as a law. **2** To reduce to nothing; extinguish: One loyalty may *annul* another in the mind. **3** To put an end or stop to, as a practice. [< OF *anuller* < LL *annullare* < L *ad-* to + *nullus* none] —**an·nul′la·ble** *adj.*

Synonyms: abolish, abrogate, cancel, destroy, extinguish, nullify, obliterate, quash, repeal, rescind, revoke. See ABOLISH, CANCEL. *Antonyms*: confirm, enact, establish, institute, maintain, preserve, sustain, uphold.

an·nu·lar (an′yə·lər) *adj.* **1** Pertaining to or formed like a ring; ring-shaped. **2** Marked with rings. [< L *annularis* < *annulus, anulus* ring] —**an′nu·lar·ly** *adv.*

annular eclipse *Astron.* A solar eclipse in which a narrow circular strip of the sun is visible beyond the dark mass of the moon.

annular ligament *Anat.* A ligament encircling the wrist or ankle.

an·nu·late (an′yə·lit, -lāt) *adj.* Furnished with rings; ringed. Also **an′nu·lat′ed.**

an·nu·la·tion (an′yə·lā′shən) *n.* **1** The act of forming rings. **2** A ringlike formation or segment, as in an annelid.

an·nu·let (an′yə·lit) *n.* **1** A small ring. **2** *Archit.* A small projecting circular molding, specifically, around the capital of a pillar. [< L *annulus* a ring + -ET]

an·nul·ment (ə·nul′mənt) *n.* **1** An annulling or being annulled. **2** An invalidation, as of a marriage.

an·nu·lose (an′yə·lōs) *adj.* Composed of or furnished with rings. [< L *annulus* a ring + -OSE]

an·nu·lus (an′yə·ləs) *n. pl.* **·li** (-lī) or **·lus·es 1** A ringlike body or figure. **2** *Geom.* The area between the circumferences of two concentric circles. **3** *Astron.* The thin, visible edge of the sun's disk as it appears around the body of the moon in an annular eclipse. [< L, a ring]

an·nun·ci·ate (ə·nun′shē·āt, -sē-) *v.t.* **·at·ed, ·at·ing** To announce. [< L *annuntiatus,* pp. of *annuntiare. See* ANNOUNCE.]

an·nun·ci·a·tion (ə·nun′sē·ā′shən, -shē-) *n.* **1** The act of announcing, or that which is announced; a proclamation.

An·nun·ci·a·tion (ə·nun′sē·ā′shən, -shē-) *n.* **1** The announcement of the Incarnation to the Virgin by an angel. *Luke* i 28–38. **2** The festival (March 25) commemorating this event.

annunciation lily The white or Madonna lily *(Lilium candidum),* often shown in pictures of the Annunciation.

an·nun·ci·a·tor (ə·nun′shē·ā′tər, -sē-) *n.* **1** A person or thing that announces. **2** An electrical indicator that shows a number or name when a bell is rung.

an·nus mi·rab·i·lis (an′əs mə·rab′ə·lis) *Latin* Wonderful year: used especially of the year 1666, notable in English history for the Dutch War and the Great Fire of London.

a·no·ci–as·so·ci·a·tion (ə·nō′sē·ə·sō′sē·ā′shən, -shē·ā′shən) *n. Surg.* A method in which the effects of surgical shock and exhaustion have been eliminated by the use of anesthetics, general and local. Also **a·no·ci·a·tion** (ə·nō′·sē·ā′shən, -shē-). See NOCI-ASSOCIATION. [< A-[4] not + L *nocere* harm + ASSOCIATION]

an·o·dal (an·ō′dəl) *adj.* Pertaining to an anode.

an·ode (an′ōd) *n. Electr.* The electrode through which current enters a non-metallic conductor and toward which electrons or anions flow from the cathode. It is positive for an electrolytic bath or vacuum tube, negative for a voltaic cell. [< Gk. *anodos* a way up < *ana-* up + *hodos* road, way]

an·od·ic (an·od′ik) *adj.* **1** Pertaining to an anode. **2** Proceeding upward.

an·o·dize (an′ə·dīz) *v.t.* **·dized, ·diz·ing** To oxidize or coat the surface of (a metal) by making it the anode of an electrolytic bath containing sodium phosphate or other suitable electrolyte.

an·o·dyne (an′ə·dīn) *adj.* Having power to allay pain; soothing. —*n.* Any drug that relieves pain or soothes. [< L *anodynus* < Gk. *anōdynos* < *an-* without + *odynē* pain]

a·noint (ə·noint′) *v.t.* **1** To smear with oil or any soft substance; pour or rub oil upon; apply ointment to. **2** To put oil on as a sign of consecration, as in a religious ceremony. [< OF *enoint,* pp. of *enoindre* < L *inungere* < *in-* on + *ungere* smear] —**a·noint′er** *n.* —**a·noint′ment** *n.*

an·o·lyte (an′ə·līt) *n.* In electrolysis, that portion of the electrolyte which is nearest the anode. [< ANO(DE) + (ELECTRO)LYTE]

a·nom·a·lism (ə·nom′ə·liz′əm) *n.* **1** That which is anomalous; an anomaly. **2** *Rare* The state or fact of being anomalous.

a·nom·a·lous (ə·nom′ə·ləs) *adj.* Deviating from the common rule; irregular; exceptional; abnormal. See synonyms under ABSURD, IRREGULAR, ODD. [< L *anomalus* < Gk. *anōmalos* < *an-* not + *homalos* even < *homos* same]—**a·nom′a·lous·ly** *adv.* —**a·nom′a·lous·ness** *n.*

a·nom·a·ly (ə·nom′ə·lē) *n. pl.* **·lies 1** Deviation from rule, type, or form; irregularity; anything abnormal. **2** *Astron.* **a** The angular distance of a planet from its perihelion, as seen from the sun. **b** The angle which measures apparent irregularities in the movement of a planet. [< L *anomalia* < Gk. *anōmalia* < *anōmalos.* See ANOMALOUS.] —**a·nom·a·lis·tic** (ə·nom′ə·lis′tik) or **·ti·cal** *adj.*

an·o·mie (an′ə·mē) *n.* An anxious awareness that the prevailing values of society have little or no personal relevance to one's condition; also, a condition of society characterized by the relative absence of norms or moral standards. [< F < Gk. *anomia* lawlessness < *a-* without (See A-[4]) + *nomos* law] —**a·nom·ic** (ə·nom′ik) *adj.*

a·non (ə·non′) *Archaic adv.* **1** In a little while; soon; presently. **2** Immediately. **3** At another time; again. —**ever and anon** Now and again. —*interj.* At once! [OE *on an* in one]

Anon. Abbreviation for ANONYMOUS.

an·o·nym (an′ə·nim) *n.* **1** An anonymous person or writer. **2** A pseudonym.

a·non·y·mous (ə·non′ə·məs) *adj.* Having no acknowledged name; bearing no name; of unknown authorship or agency. [< Gk. *anōnymos* < *an-* without + *onoma, onyma* name] —**an·o·nym·i·ty** (an′ə·nim′ə·tē), **a·non′y·mous·ness** *n.* —**a·non′y·mous·ly** *adv.*

a·noph·e·les (ə·nof′ə·lēz) *n.* Any of a genus *(Anopheles)* of mosquitoes of mostly tropical and subtropical distribution including numerous species that carry the malaria parasite and transmit the disease among humans. [< NL < Gk. *anōphelēs* harmful] —**a·noph·e·line** (ə·nof′ə·līn, -lin) *adj.*

a·no·rak (ä′nə·räk) *n.* A warm, hooded jacket, worn in arctic climates. [< Eskimo *anoraq*]

an·o·rec·tic (an′ə·rek′tik) *n.* A person having anorexia. —*adj.* of or pertaining to anorexia.

an·o·rex·i·a (an′ə·rek′sē·ə) *n.* Absence of appetite, especially when accompanied by emotional stress and resulting in malnutrition and emaciation. Also **anorexia nervosa.** [< NL < Gk. *anorexia* < *an-* without + *orexis* appetite]

an·o·rex·ic (an′ə·rek′sik) *adj.* Avoiding food; suffering from anorexia. —*n.* An anorexic person.

an·or·thic (an·ôr′thik) *adj.* Triclinic. [< Gk. *an-* not + *orthos* straight]

an·or·thite (an·ôr′thīt) *n.* A triclinic feldspar, $CaAl_2Si_2O_8$, found in igneous rocks. [<AN-[1] + Gk. *orthos* straight + -ITE[1]] **—an·or·thit·ic** (an′ôr·thit′ik) *adj.*

an·or·tho·scope (an·ôr′thə·skōp) *n.* An instrument by which distorted figures drawn on one of two revolving disks can be seen as normal images through slits in the other. [<AN-[1] + ORTHO- + -SCOPE]

an·or·tho·site (an·ôr′thə·sīt) *n. Geol.* A granular igneous rock composed essentially or wholly of plagioclase, which in the typical anorthosite is labradorite. [<AN-[1] + Gk. *orthos* straight + -ITE[1]]

an·os·mi·a (an·oz′mē·ə, -os′-) *n. Pathol.* Loss of the sense of smell. [<NL <Gk. *an-* without + *osmē* smell] **—an·os′mic** *adj.*

an·oth·er (ə·nuth′ər) *adj.* & *pron.* **1** Not the same; distinct; different: often used as the correlative of *one*: One man's meat is *another* man's poison. **2** Different in character while of the same or similar substance: From that time I became *another* man. **3** Different in substance while of the same or similar character. **4** A further; an additional; one more. ◆ *Another* was originally written as two words, *an other.* As a pronoun its plural is *others.*

an·ox·e·mi·a (an′ok·sē′mē·ə) *n. Pathol.* Lack of oxygen in the blood. [<NL <AN-[1] + OX(YGEN) + -EMIA] **—an′ox·e′mic** *adj.*

an·ox·i·a (an·ok′sē·ə) *n. Pathol.* Oxygen deficiency; any condition characterized by defective or insufficient oxidation of the body tissues. [<AN-[1] + OX(YGEN) + -IA] **—an·ox′ic** *adj.*

an·sa (an′sə) *n. pl.* **·sae** (-sē) **1** *pl. Astron.* The apparent ends of Saturn's rings, which, seen obliquely, seem to project from the sides of the planet like handles. **2** A handle, as of a pitcher. [<L, a handle]

an·sate (an′sāt) *adj.* Having a handle. Also **an′sat·ed.** [<L *ansatus* <*ansa* a handle]

ansate cross See under CROSS.

An·schluss (än′shlo͞os) *n. German* Political union.

An·selm (an′selm, *Ger.* än′selm) A masculine personal name. Also **An·sel** (an′səl), *Fr.* **An·selme** (äṅ·selm′), *Ital., Sp.* **An·sel·mo** (än·sel′mō), *Pg.* **An·sel·mo** (äṅ·sel′mo͞o), *Lat.* **An·sel·mus** (an·sel′məs). [<Gmc., divine helmet] **—Anselm, Saint,** 1033–1109, archbishop of Canterbury.

An·ser (an′sər) *n.* **1** *Ornithol.* A genus of birds typical of *Anserinae,* a subfamily including the geese. **2** *Astron.* A small star in the constellation of the Fox and Goose (Vulpecula cum Ansere). See CONSTELLATION. [<L, goose]

an·ser·ine (an′sə·rīn, -sər·in) *adj.* **1** Pertaining to a goose; gooselike, as the human skin when chilled. **2** Silly; stupid. **3** Pertaining or belonging to the subfamily *Anserinae* of birds; the geese. Also **an′ser·ous.** *—n.* An organic substance, $C_{10}H_{16}O_3N_4$, obtained from the muscles of birds, fishes, and reptiles. [<L *anserinus* <*anser* a goose]

An·shan (än′shän′) A city in southern Manchuria, China.

An·stey (an′stē), **F.** Pseudonym of Thomas Anstey Guthrie, 1856–1934, English writer.

an·swer (an′sər, än′-) *v.i.* **1** To reply or respond, as by words or actions. **2** To serve the purpose; prove successful: This solution *answers* best. **3** To be responsible or accountable: with *for.* I will *answer* for his honesty. **4** To correspond or match, as in appearance: with *to*: This man *answers* to your description. *—v.t.* **5** To speak, write, or act in response or reply to: to *answer* a letter. **6** To be sufficient for; fulfil: This rod *answers* the purpose. **7** To pay for; discharge, as a debt or liability: to *answer* damages. **8** To conform or correspond to; match: to *answer* a description. **9** *Law* To reply favorably to, as a petition or petitioner. **—to answer back** To reply emphatically or rudely; talk back, as in contradiction. *—n.* **1** A reply, especially one that is definite and final. **2** Any action in return or in kind; retaliation. **3** The result of a calculation or solution of a problem in mathematics. **4** *Law* The written defense of a defendant in an action to charges filed against him by the plaintiff in which he sets up matters of *fact* as defense in contradistinction to a *demurrer.* **5** *Music* The restatement of a musical theme or phrase by a different voice or instrument. [OE *andswerian*] **—an′swer·er** *n.*

Synonyms (noun): rejoinder, repartee, reply, response, retort. Anything said or done in return for some word, action, or suggestion of another may be called an *answer,* as the blow of an angry man, the movement of a bolt in a lock, an echo, etc. A *reply* is an unfolding, and ordinarily implies thought and intelligence. An *answer* to a charge or an argument effectually meets or disposes of it, as a *reply* may not do. See RESPONSE.

an·swer·a·ble (an′sər·ə·bəl, än′-) *adj.* **1** Liable to be called to account (*for* anything or *to* someone); responsible. **2** Requiring or admitting of answer; also, obligated to answer. **3** Corresponding; adequate; suitable. **—an′swer·a·ble·ness** *n.* **—an′swer·a·bly** *adv.*

ant (ant) *n.* A small social hymenopterous insect (family *Formicidae*); an emmet. The communities of ants are made up of winged males, females winged till after pairing, and wingless neuters or workers. For illustration see under INSECT (injurious). [OE *ǣmete*]

an't (ant, änt, ānt) **1** Are not. **2** *Brit.* Am not. **3** *Illit.* & *Dial.* Is not; has not; have not.

ant- Var. of ANTI-.

-ant *suffix* **1** In the act or process of doing (what is denoted by the stem): used to form adjectives with nearly the meaning of the present participle: *militant, litigant,* etc. **2** One who or that which does (what is indicated by the stem): forming nouns of participial origin: *servant* one who serves. [<F *-ant* <L *-ans (-antis), -ens(-entis),* present participial suffixes]

an·ta (an′tə) *n. pl.* **·tae** (-tē) *Archit.* A pilaster, especially when forming the termination of a side wall continued beyond a transverse wall, or when placed on a wall to form a range of columns. [<L]

ant·ac·id (ant·as′id) *n. Med.* An alkaline remedy for stomach acidity. *—adj.* Correcting acidity. Also **an′ti·ac′id.**

An·tae·us (an·tē′əs) In Greek legend, a wrestler, invincible while in contact with the earth: crushed by Hercules, who lifted him into the air. Also **An·tæ′us. —An·tae′an** *adj.*

an·tag·o·nism (an·tag′ə·niz′əm) *n.* Mutual resistance; opposition; hostility. See synonyms under ANTIPATHY, ENMITY. [<Gk. *antagōnisma* <*antagōnizesthai.* See ANTAGONIZE.]

an·tag·o·nist (an·tag′ə·nist) *n.* **1** An adversary; opponent. See synonyms under ENEMY. **2** Any agent having an effect contrary to that of a similar agent, as a drug, muscle, hormone, etc.

an·tag·o·nis·tic (an·tag′ə·nis′tik) *adj.* Opposed; hostile. Also **an·tag′o·nis′ti·cal.** See synonyms under CONTRARY, INIMICAL. **—an·tag′o·nis′·ti·cal·ly** *adv.*

an·tag·o·nize (an·tag′ə·nīz) *v.* **·nized, ·niz·ing** *v.t.* **1** To oppose, contend with, or struggle against. **2** To make unfriendly; to make an antagonist of. **3** To counteract; neutralize, as a force or action. *—v.i.* **4** To act antagonistically. See synonyms under CONTEND. [<Gk. *antagōnizesthai* struggle against <*anti-* against + *agōnizesthai* struggle, strive]

An·ta·ki·ya (än′tä·kē′yä) The Turkish and Arabic name for ANTIOCH. Also **An·ta·kya** (än′tä·kyä′).

ant·al·gic (ant·al′jik) *adj.* Tending to alleviate pain. *—n.* An anodyne. [<ANT- + Gk. *algos* pain]

ant·al·ka·li (ant·al′kə·lī) *n. pl.* **·lis** or **·lies** Any substance able to neutralize alkalis, or counteract an alkaline tendency in the system. [<ANT- + ALKALI] **—ant·al′ka·line** (-līn, -lin) *adj.* & *n.*

An·tal·ya (än·täl′yä) A port in SW Anatolia, Turkey, on the **Gulf of Antalya,** an inlet of the Mediterranean: also *Adalia.*

An·ta·na·na·ri·vo (an′tə·na′nə·rē′vō) The English name for TANANARIVE.

ant·arc·tic (ant·ärk′tik, -är′tik) *adj.* Pertaining to or designating the South Pole or the regions near it. [<L *antarcticus* <Gk. *antarktikos* southern <*anti-* opposite + *arktos* the Bear (a northern constellation), the north]

Ant·arc·ti·ca (ant·ärk′tə·kə, -är′-) A continent surrounding the South Pole of the earth, extending at certain points north of the antarctic circle and almost entirely covered by a vast ice sheet; over 5,000,000 square miles. Also **Antarctic Continent.**

Antarctic Archipelago See PALMER ARCHIPELAGO.

Antarctic Circle The boundary of the South Frigid Zone, 23°30′ from the South Pole, including most of Antarctica.

Antarctic Ocean The ocean within the Antarctic Circle and bordering Antarctica.

Antarctic Zone The region, including most of Antarctica, enclosed by the Antarctic Circle.

An·tar·es (an·târ′ēz) A giant red star, Alpha in the constellation Scorpio; one of the 20 brightest stars, 1.22 magnitude. [<Gk. *Antarēs* <*anti-* similar to + *Arēs* Mars; with ref. to its color]

ant bear **1** The giant ant-eater *(Myrmecophaga jubata),* a large edentate mammal of tropical America that feeds wholly or chiefly on ants; it has a long snout, protrusible tongue, powerful digging claws, and a shaggy, black-banded coat. **2** The aardvark.

ant bird Any of numerous small birds of the family *Formicarlidae,* of South America, which feed upon ants. Also called **ant′-catch′er.**

ant cow An aphid insect kept by ants as a source of food. The aphids yield a honeylike fluid on being stroked on the abdomen by the antennae of the ants.

an·te (an′tē) *v.t.* & *v.i.* **an·teed** or **an·ted, an·te·ing** **1** In poker, to put up, as a stake, before the cards are dealt. **2** *Slang* To pay (one's share). **—to ante up** *Slang* To ante. *—n.* **1** The stake put up in a game of poker. **2** A stake put up after the cards are dealt, but before drawing new ones. [<L, before]

ante- *prefix* **1** Before in time or order: *antenatal.* **2** Before in position; in front of: *antechamber.* [<L *ante* before]

The words in the following list are self-explanatory:

antebaptismal	**anteporch**
antebridal	**anteresurrection**
ante-Christian	**anterevolutionary**
antehuman	**antespring**
antemarital	**ante-Victorian**
ante-Norman	**ante-war**

an·te·a (an′tē·ə) *adv. Law Latin* Formerly; heretofore.

ant·eater (ant′ē′tər) *n.* **1** The ant bear. **2** One of several other mammals that feed partly on ants, as the tamandua, echidna, or aardvark. **3** An ant bird.

THE GIANT ANT-EATER (8 feet long over-all; 2 feet tall)

an·te·bel·lum (an′·tē·bel′əm) *adj.* Of the time before the war, especially, before the Civil War in the United States. [<L *ante bellum* before the war]

an·te·bra·chi·um (an′tē·brā′kē·əm) *n. pl.* **·chi·a** (-kē·ə) *Anat.* The forearm. [<NL <ANTE- + L *brachium* arm]

an·te·cede (an′tə·sēd′) *v.t.* & *v.i.* **·ced·ed, ·ced·ing** To go or come before, as in rank, place, or time; precede. [<L *antecedere* <*ante* before + *cedere* go]

an·te·ce·dence (an′tə·sēd′ns) *n.* **1** Precedence; going before; priority. **2** *Astron.* The apparent retrograde motion of a planet. Also **an′te·ce′den·cy.**

an·te·ce·dent (an′tə·sēd′nt) *adj.* **1** Going before; prior in time, place, or order; preceding; anterior: often with *to.* **2** *Geol.* Having a course across a fold or fault of the earth's surface: contrasted with *consequent.* *—n.* **1** One who or that which precedes or goes before. **2** *Gram.* The word, phrase, or clause to which a pronoun, especially a relative pronoun, refers. **3** *pl.* The facts, collectively, that have gone before in the history of a person or thing; also, ancestry. **4** *Math.* The first term of a ratio; in a proportion, the first and third terms. **5** *Logic* That upon which something else is based. See synonyms under CAUSE, PRECEDENT. [<L *antecedens, -entis,* ppr. of *antecedere.* See ANTECEDE.] **—an′te·ce′dent·ly** *adv.*

Synonyms (adj.): anterior, earlier, foregoing, former, introductory, precedent, preceding, preliminary, previous, prior. When used simply of time, *antecedent* and *previous* refer to that which happens at any prior time; *preceding* to that which is immediately or next before. See PREVIOUS. *Antonyms*: consequent, following, later, posterior, subsequent, succeeding.

an·te·ces·sor (an'tə·ses'ər) *n.* One who precedes or goes before; a leader; pioneer. [< L < *antecedere.* See ANTECEDE.]

an·te·cham·ber (an'ti·chām'bər) *n.* A room serving as an entranceway to another apartment.

an·te·chap·el (an'ti·chap'əl) *n.* The portion of a chapel outside of the rood screen; a vestibule or narthex.

an·te·choir (an'ti·kwīr') *n.* A portion of a chapel set apart just in front of the choir, enclosed, or partially enclosed, by a screen.

an·te·date (an'ti·dāt' *v.t.* **·dat·ed, ·dat·ing 1** To assign to a date earlier than the actual one, as a document; date back. **2** To be or occur earlier than; precede. **3** To cause to happen at or return to an earlier date; accelerate.

an·te·di·lu·vi·an (an'ti·di·lōō'vē·ən) *adj.* **1** Pertaining to the times, events, etc., before the Flood. **2** Antiquated; primitive. —*n.* **1** A person, animal, or plant that lived before the Flood. **2** An old or old-fashioned person. [< ANTE- + L *diluvium* deluge]

an·te·fix (an'ti·fiks) *n. pl.* **·fix·es** or **·fix·a** (-fik'sə) *Archit.* An upright ornament at the eaves of a tiled roof, to hide the joints between two adjacent rows of tiles, or at the edge of a frieze: sometimes also at the ridge, forming part of a cresting. [< L *antefixus.* See ANTE- and FIX.] —**an'te·fix'al** *adj.*

ANTEFIX

an·te·lope (an'tə·lōp) *n. pl.* **·lope** or **·lopes 1** Any one of various Old World hollow-horned ruminants of the family *Bovidae,* including the gazelle, chamois, gnu, etc. **2** The hide of such an animal. **3** *U.S.* The pronghorn. [< OF *antelop* < Med.L *antalopus* < LGk. *antholops*]

an·te·me·rid·i·an (an'ti·mə·rid'ē·ən) *adj.* Before noon; between midnight and the next noon.

an·te me·rid·i·em (an'tē mə·rid'ē·em) *Latin* Before the sun reaches the meridian, counted from the preceding midnight; before noon. Abbr. *a.m.* or *A.M.*

an·te mor·tem (an'tē môr'təm) *Latin* Before or immediately preceding death.

an·te·mun·dane (an'ti·mun'dān) *adj.* Pertaining to, existing, or occurring before the world's creation. [< ANTE- + L *mundus* world]

an·te·na·tal (an'ti·nāt'l) *adj.* Occurring or existing before birth; pertaining to conditions before birth.

an·ten·na (an·ten'ə) *n. pl.* **an·ten·nae** (an·ten'ē) *for def.* **1, an·ten·nas** *for def.* **2. 1** *Entomol.* One of the paired, lateral, movable, jointed appendages on the head of an insect or other arthropod. **2** *Telecom.* A system of wires upheld in a vertical or horizontal position by a mast or tower, for transmitting or receiving electromagnetic waves in wireless telegraphy, telephony, and radio. —**cage antenna** A radio antenna consisting of several wires arranged in parallel around a series of loops between two uprights and converging at each end. [< NL < L, a yard on which a sail is spread]

an·ten·nule (an·ten'yōōl) *n. Zool.* A small antenna or antennalike appendage. Also **an·ten·nu·la** (an·ten'yə·lə).

an·te·nup·tial (an'ti·nup'shəl, -chəl) *adj.* Previous to marriage; occurring or being before marriage.

an·te·pas·chal (an'ti·pas'kəl) *adj.* Occurring before the Passover or Easter.

an·te·past (an'ti·past, -päst) *n.* **1** Foretaste. **2** *Obs.* An appetizer. See synonyms under ANTICIPATION. [< ANTE- + L *pastus* food]

an·te·pen·di·um (an'ti·pen'dē·əm) *n. pl.* **·di·a** (-dē·ə) A covering, usually embroidered, for the front of the altar. [< Med.L < L *ante* before + *pendere* hang]

an·te·pe·nult (an'ti·pē'nult, -pi·nult') *n.* The last syllable but two of a word. Also **an·te·pe·nul·ti·ma** (an'ti·pi·nul'tə·mə).

an·te·pe·nul·ti·mate (an'ti·pi·nul'tə·mit) *adj.* Pertaining to the last but two of any series. —*n.* The antepenult.

an·te·pran·di·al (an'ti·pran'dē·əl) *adj.* Occurring or being before dinner.

an·te·ri·or (an·tir'ē·ər) *adj.* **1** Antecedent in time; prior; earlier: ages *anterior* to the Flood. **2** Farther front or forward, in space: an *anterior* cavity. **3** *Biol.* Situated in front: opposed to *posterior,* in the lower animals, relatively near the head; in man, toward the ventral side of the body. **4** *Bot.* Turned away from the main axis or stem, as the side of a leaf or flower; lower. [< L, compar. of *ante* before] —**an·te'ri·or·ly** *adv.*

Synonyms: former, forward, front, prior. *Anterior* is employed chiefly with reference to place. *Prior* bears exclusive reference to time. *Former* is used of time, or of position in written or printed matter, not of space in general. Compare ANTECEDENT, PREVIOUS. *Antonyms*: after, hind, hinder, hindmost, later, latter, posterior, subsequent, succeeding.

antero- *combining form* Anterior; placed in front. [< L *anterus* (assumed form)]

an·ter·o·in·fe·ri·or (an'tər·ō·in·fir'ē·ər) *adj.* Situated in front and below.

an·te·room (an'ti·rōōm', -rŏŏm') *n.* A waiting-room; antechamber.

an·ter·o·pos·te·ri·or (an'tər·ō·pos·tir'ē·ər) *adj.* **1** Of or pertaining to the front and rear; extending from front to rear. **2** Median.

an·te·type (an'ti·tīp') *n.* A preceding type; prototype.

an·te·ver·sion (an'ti·vûr'zhən, -shən) *n. Pathol.* A turning or tipping forward, as of the uterus.

an·te·vert (an'ti·vûrt') *v.t. Pathol.* To displace by turning or tipping forward, as an internal organ. [< L *antevertere* < *ante* before + *vertere* turn]

anth- Var. of ANTI-.

ant·he·li·on (ant·hē'lē·ən, an·thē'-) *n. pl.* **·li·a** (-lē·ə) *Astron.* A faint glory or series of diffraction rings about the shadow of an object cast by a low sun upon a cloud or fog bank; a mock sun. [< NL < Gk. *anthēlion* < *anti-* against + *hēlios* sun]

ant·he·lix (ant·hē'liks, an·thē'-) *n. pl.* **ant·hel·i·ces** (ant·hel'ə·sēz, an·thel'-) *Anat.* The inner curved ridge on the cartilage of the external ear: also *antihelix.* [< ANT- + HELIX]

an·thel·min·tic (an'thel·min'tik) *adj. Med.* Tending to expel intestinal worms. —*n.* A vermifuge. Also **an'thel·min'thic** (-thik). [< ANT- + Gk. *helmins, -inthos* worm]

an·them (an'thəm) *n.* **1** A musical composition, usually set to words from the Bible. **2** A joyous or triumphal song or hymn, or the music to which it is set. —*v.t.* To celebrate with, or sing as, an anthem. [OE *antefn* < LL *antiphona* < Gk. *antiphōna,* lit., things sounding in response < *anti-* against + *phōnē* voice. Doublet of ANTIPHON.]

an·the·mi·on (an·thē'mē·ən) *n. pl.* **·mi·a** (-mē·ə) The honeysuckle or palm-leaf pattern in decorative designs: common in Greek art. [< Gk., flower]

ANTHEMION

an·ther (an'thər) *n. Bot.* The pollen-bearing part of a stamen. [< F *anthère* < L *anthera,* a medicine obtained from flowers < Gk. *anthēra,* fem. of *antherōs* flowery < *anthos* flower]

an'ther·id·i·o·phore (an'thə·rid'ē·ə·fôr', -fōr') *n. Bot.* An outgrowing part of a sexual plant bearing antheridia only, as in hepatic mosses.

an·ther·id·i·um (an'thə·rid'ē·əm) *n. pl.* **·ther·id·i·a** (-thə·rid'ē·ə) *Bot.* The male sexual organ in cryptogams, the analog of the anther in flowering plants. Also **an·ther·id** (an'thər·id). [< NL, dim. of Gk. *antherōs* flowery] —**an'ther·id'i·al** *adj.*

an·ther·o·zo·id (an'thər·ə·zō'id, an'thər·ə·zoid') *n. Bot.* The male fecundating cell in cryptogams. It is a minute mass of protoplasm, provided with vibratory cilia, and produced in an antheridium. Also **an'ther·o·zo'oid** (-zō'oid). [< ANTHER + ZOOID] —**an'ther·o·zo'i·dal** (-zō'ə·dəl), **an'ther·o·zo·oi'dal** (-zō·oid'l) *adj.*

an·the·sis (an·thē'sis) *n. Bot.* The time or process of expansion in a flower; full bloom of a flower. [< NL < Gk. *anthēsis* full bloom < *antheein* bloom]

An·thes·te·ri·a (an'thes·tir'ē·ə) *n. pl.* A three days' festival in honor of Dionysus formerly held at Athens from the 11th to the 13th of **An'thes·te'ri·on** (-tir'ē·ən), a month nearly corresponding to February. [< Gk. *anthestēria* < *anthos* flower]

antho- *combining form* Flower: *anthophorous.* [< Gk. *anthos* a flower]

an·tho·ceph·a·lous (an'thō·sef'ə·ləs) *adj.* Having a head like a flower. [< ANTHO- + Gk. *kephalē* head]

An·thoc·er·os (an·thos'ər·əs) *n.* A genus of liverworts, especially the horned liverworts, the type of the order *Anthocerotales.* [< NL < ANTHO- + Gk. *keras* horn]

an·tho·cy·a·nin (an'thō·sī'ə·nin) *n.* The water-soluble coloring-matter of flowers, leaves, and other parts of plants which imparts red, violet, blue, blue-green, or green colors, dependent on the acidity or alkalinity of the cell sap: also called *cyanin, erythrophyll.* [< ANTHO- + Gk. *kyanos* blue]

an·tho·di·um (an·thō'dē·əm) *n. pl.* **·di·a** (-dē·ə) *Bot.* The flowering head of plants of the composite family: so called from the resemblance of the involucre to a calyx and of the ray florets, when present, to petals. [< NL < Gk. *anthōdēs* flowerlike < *anthos* a flower]

an·thoid (an'thoid) *adj.* Like a flower.

an·thol·o·gize (an·thol'ə·jīz) *v.* **·gized, ·giz·ing** *v.i.* To make an anthology or anthologies. —*v.t.* To put into an anthology or make an anthology of.

an·thol·o·gy (an·thol'ə·jē) *n. pl.* **·gies** A collection of choice or representative literary extracts. [< L *anthologia* < Gk. *anthologia* a garland, collection of poems < *anthos* flower + *legein* gather] —**an·tho·log·i·cal** (an'thə·loj'i·kəl) *adj.* —**an·thol'o·gist** *n.*

An·tho·ny (an'thə·nē, -tə-) A masculine personal name. See also ANTONY. [< L *Antonius,* the name of a Roman gens]

—**Anthony, Saint,** 251–356, one of the Christian fathers; founder of monastic life; born in Egypt.

—**Anthony of Padua, Saint,** 1195–1231, Franciscan monk.

An·tho·ny (an'thə·nē), **Susan Brownell,** 1820–1906, U.S. suffragist.

an·tho·phore (an'thə·fôr, -fōr) *n. Bot.* A stipe formed by the prolongation of an internode between the calyx and the corolla.

an·thoph·o·rous (an·thof'ər·əs) *adj.* Flower-bearing. [< Gk. *anthophoros* < *anthos* flower + *pherein* bear]

an·tho·tax·y (an'thə·tak'sē) *n. Bot.* The arrangement of flowers on the axis of inflorescence. [< ANTHO- + Gk. *taxis* arrangement]

an·tho·zo·an (an'thə·zō'ən) *n.* Any of a class (Anthozoa) of sessile, usually cylindrical, marine coelenterates, growing singly or in colonies, and including the sea anemones and corals. Also **anthozoon.** Also called *actinozoan.* —*adj.* Of or pertaining to the class *Anthozoa.* [< NL < ANTHO- + Gk. *zōein* live] —**an'tho·zo'ic** *adj.*

an·tho·zo·oid (an'thə·zō'oid) *n.* An individual polyp in a compound colony.

an·thra·cene (an'thrə·sēn) *n. Chem.* A blue fluorescent crystalline compound, $C_{14}H_{10}$, obtained in the last products of coal-tar distillation and used largely in the manufacture of alizarin and related dyes. [< Gk. *anthrax, -akos* coal + -ENE]

an·thra·cite (an'thrə·sīt) *n.* Mineral coal of nearly pure carbon which burns slowly and with little flame; hard coal. [< L *anthracites* < Gk. *anthrakitēs* coallike < *anthrax* coal] —**an·thra·cit·ic** (an'thrə·sit'ik) *adj.*

an·thrac·nose (an·thrak'nōs) *n.* A destructive disease of plants usually manifested by sharply defined discolored spots and caused by various fungi. [< Gk. *anthrax, -akos* coal, carbuncle + *nosos* disease]

an·thra·coid (an'thrə·koid) *adj.* **1** Resembling anthrax. **2** Like the precious carbuncle or like carbon.

an·thra·qui·none (an'thrə·kwi·nōn') *n.* A yellow crystalline compound, $C_{14}H_8O_2$, made from anthracene by oxidation with chromic and sulfuric acid: used in the manufacture of alizarin dyes and certain laxatives. [< Gk. *anthrax* coal + QUINONE]

an·thrax (an'thraks) *n. pl.* **·thra·ces** (-thrə·

sēz) **1** A carbuncle. **2** *Pathol.* An infectious and malignant febrile disease of man and some animals, caused by *Bacillus anthracis,* often with carbuncular swellings; splenic fever. **3** A bacillus found in the blood of those affected with splenic fever. **4** A gem stone of the ancients: probably the carbuncle. [<Gk., coal, carbuncle]

an·throp·ic (an·throp′ik) *adj.* Pertaining to the human species or the period of its existence. Also **an·throp′i·cal.**

anthropo- *combining form* Man; human: *anthropometry.* Also, before vowels, **anthrop-**, as in *anthropoid.* [<Gk. *anthrōpos* man]

an·thro·po·cen·tric (an′thrə·pō·sen′trik) *adj.* **1** Centering in man; regarding man as the central fact or final aim and end of the universe, or of any system: an *anthropocentric* philosophy. **2** Based on comparison with man: *anthropocentric* analysis of animal instincts.

an·thro·pog·e·ny (an′thrə·poj′ə·nē) *n.* The branch of anthropology that treats of the origin and development of man, either individually (ontogeny) or ethnically (phylogeny). See ANTHROPOLOGY. Also **an·thro·po·gen·e·sis** (an′thrə·pō·jen′ə·sis).

an·thro·pog·ra·phy (an′thrə·pog′rə·fē) *n.* The branch of anthropology that treats of the geographic distribution, variations, and peculiarities of the human race or its component parts; descriptive anthropology.

an·thro·poid (an′thrə·poid) *adj.* **1** Like a human being in form or other characteristics; manlike: said of the highest apes, as the gorilla, chimpanzee, and orang. **2** *Zool.* Of or pertaining to a suborder of primate mammals, including man, apes, and monkeys *(Anthropoidea).* Also **an′thro·poid′al.** —*n.* An anthropoid ape.

an·thro·pol·o·gy (an′thrə·pol′ə·jē) *n.* **1** The science of man in his physical, social, material, and cultural development, including the study of his origins, evolution, geographic distribution, ethnology, and communal forms. **2** The detailed study of the customs, beliefs, folkways, and superstitions of an ethnic group, especially on a comparative basis. **—an·thro·po·log·i·cal** (an′thrə·pə·loj′i·kəl) or **·log′ic** *adj.* **—an′thro·po·log′i·cal·ly** *adv.* **—an′thro·pol′o·gist** *n.*

an·thro·pom·e·try (an′thrə·pom′ə·trē) *n.* The science and technique of human measurements, specifically of anatomical and physiological features; also, the analysis and interpretation of the data so obtained. **—an·thro·po·met·ric** (an′thrə·pō·met′rik) or **·met′ri·cal** *adj.*

an·thro·po·mor·phic (an′thrə·pō·môr′fik) *adj.* Of or pertaining to anthropomorphism; having human form or human characteristics; manshaped.

an·thro·po·mor·phism (an′thrə·pō·môr′fiz·əm) *n.* The ascription of human attributes, feelings, conduct, or characteristics to God or any spiritual being, or to the powers of nature, etc. **—an′thro·po·mor′phist** *n.*

an·thro·po·mor·phize (an′thrə·pō·môr′fīz) *v.t.* & *v.i.* **·phized, ·phiz·ing** To endow (gods or natural objects) with human characteristics or qualities.

an·thro·po·mor·pho·sis (an′thrə·pō·môr′fə·sis) *n.* Transformation into human shape.

an·thro·po·mor·phous (an′thrə·pō·môr′fəs) *adj.* Having or resembling human form.

an·thro·pon·o·my (an′thrə·pon′ə·mē) *n.* The science of the laws that regulate the development of man in relation to environment and to other organisms. Also **an′thro·po·nom′ics**(-pō·nom′·iks). **—an′thro·po·nom′i·cal** *adj.*

an·thro·pop·a·thism (an′thrə·pop′ə·thiz′əm) *n.* **1** Anthropopathy. **2** An expression used in anthropopathy.

an·thro·pop·a·thy (an′thrə·pop′ə·thē) *n.* The attributing of human emotions, passions, suffering, etc., to God or to gods. [<Med. L *anthropopathia* <Gk. *anthrōpopatheia* humanity < *anthrōpos* man + *pathos* feeling]

an·thro·poph·a·gi (an′thrə·pof′ə·jī) *n. pl. sing.* **a·gus** (-ə·gəs) Eaters of human flesh; cannibals. [<L, pl. of *anthropophagus* <Gk. *anthrōpophagos* <*anthrōpos* man + *phagein* eat]

an·thro·po·phag·ic (an′thrə·pō·faj′ik) *adj.* Pertaining to the anthropophagi; man-eating. Also **an′thro·po·phag′i·cal.**

an·thro·poph·a·gite (an′thrə·pof′ə·jīt) *n.* A cannibal. Also **an′thro·poph′a·gist.**

an·thro·poph·a·gous (an′thrə·pof′ə·gəs) *adj.* Cannibalistic.

an·thro·poph·a·gy (an′thrə·pof′ə·jē) *n.* The eating of human flesh; cannibalism.

an·thro·po·zo·ic (an′thrə·pō·zō′ik) *adj. Geol.* Characterized by the existence of man: applied to the Quaternary period.

an·thu·ri·um (an·thŏŏr′ē·əm) *n.* Any of a genus *(Anthurium)* of tropical American perennials of the arum family, with heart-shaped or lōbed leaves and densely flowered spathes. [<NL <Gk. *anthos* flower + *oura* tail]

an·ti (an′tī, an′tē) *n. pl.* **·tis** *Colloq.* One opposed to any proposed or enacted policy.

anti- *prefix*

1 Against; opposed to:

anti-abrasion
anti-agglutinating
anti-aggression
anti-alien
anti-Americanism
anti-anarchic
anti-aquatic
anti-Aristotelian
anti-ascetic
antibigotry
anticaste
anticensorship
anti-chafing
antichurch
anticivic
anticlogging
anticoagulating
anticombination
anticommercial
anticommunist
anticonductor
anticonscription
anticontagion
anticontagious
anticorrosive
anti-Darwinism
antidemocratic
antidiastase
antidogmatic
antidraft
antidumping
antidynamic
antidynastic
anti-empirical
anti-episcopal
anti-erosion
anti-evangelical
anti-evolutionist
anti-expansionist
antifaction
antifanatic
anti-Fascism
anti-Fascist
antifat
antifeminism
antifeminist
antiferment
antifeudalism
antiflash
antiforeign
antiforeignism
antigambling
antigrowth
antihierarchist
antihuman
antihypnotic
anti-imperialism
anti-imperialist
anti-imperialistic
anti-intellectual
antilabor
anti-Lamarckian
antileveling
antilipase
antiliturgical
antilottery
antimachine
anti-Malthusian
antimaterialist
antimerger
antimiasmatic
antimilitarism
antimilitarist
antimiscegenation
antimonarchist
antimonopolist
antimoral
antimusical
antinational
antinepotism
antinicotine
antinoise
anti-oxidase
anti-oxidizer
anti-oxygenating
antiparasitic
anti-Platonic
antiplethoric
antipolitical
antipollution
antipuritan
antiradical
antiradiation
antirationalism
antireformist
antireligious
antirevolutionary
antiromantic
antiroyalist
antitrust
antischolastic
antiscientific
antisensitizer
antisimoniacal
antiskid
antismoking
antistalling
antistatism
antisubmarine
antisuffragist
antitarnish
antitartaric
antitax
antitobacco
antitorpedo
anti-union
antivaccinationist
antivibratory
antivivisection
antivivisectionist
anti-war
antiwaste
antizealot
anti-Zionism

2 Opposite to; reverse:

anticyclic
antihero
antilogic
antipole

3 Rivaling; spurious:

anti-Caesar
anticritic
anti-emperor
anti-king
anti-Messiah
antiprophet

4 *Med.* Counteracting; curative; neutralizing:

anti-aphrodisiac
anti-apoplectic
anti-arthritic
anti-asthmatic
antibilious
antibubonic
anticachectic
anticarious
antibacterial
antibacteriolytic
anticolic
anticonvulsive
antidysenteric
anti-emetic
anti-epileptic
anti-erysipelas
antihemorrhoidal
antihydrophobic
antiluetic
antimalarial
antimephitic
antimicrobic
antimycotic
antinarcotic
anticatalase
anticatarrhal
antipathogen
antipneumococcic
antipruritic
antirheumatic
antiscrofulous
antiserum
antispirochetic
antistaphylococcic
antistreptococcal
antisudorific
antitetanic
antithrombin
antityphoid
antivirus

Anti- usually changes to *ant-* before words beginning with a vowel, as in *antacid,* and to *anth-* before the aspirate in words of Greek formation or analogy, as *anthelmintic.* [<Gk. <*anti* against]

an·ti·aer·i·al (an′tē·âr′ē·əl, -ā·ir′ē·əl) *adj.* Opposing attack from the air, as by parachute or glider troops.

an·ti·air·craft (an′tē·âr′kraft′, -âr′kräft′) *adj.* Opposed to or directed against aircraft: said especially of a type of gun or defense.

anti-aircraft artillery Fixed or mobile equipment used to spot, illuminate, and shoot at enemy aircraft, including sound locators, radar, searchlights, guns, etc.

an·ti·ar (an′tē·är) *n.* **1** The upas tree. **2** The acrid, virulent poison found in the gum of this tree, the glucoside antiarin, $C_{27}H_{42}O_{10}\cdot 4H_2O$, used as an arrow poison [<Javanese *antjar*]

an·ti·bi·o·sis (an′ti·bī·ō′sis) *n.* The condition of associated organisms in which one is detrimental to the other; antipathy.

an·ti·bi·ot·ic (an′ti·bī·ot′ik) *n.* **1** That which is antagonistic toward or destructive of life. **2** *Biochem.* **a** Any of a large class of substances produced by various micro-organisms and fungi that have the power of arresting the growth of other micro-organisms or of destroying them: some, as penicillin and streptomycin, are of value in the treatment of certain infectious diseases. **b** A chemical having similar properties produced by higher plants, some animals, and synthetically.

an·ti·bod·y (an′ti·bod′ē) *n. pl.* **·bod·ies** A globulin formed in the body in response to a foreign substance, as a protein or polysaccharide, and serving to neutralize the foreign substance.

an·tic (an′tik) *n.* **1** A prank; caper. **2** A clown; buffoon. **3** A grotesque figure or play. —*adj.* Odd; fantastic; ludicrous; incongruous. —*v.i.* **an·ticked, an·tick·ing** To play the clown; perform antics. Also *Obs.* **an′tick.** [<Ital. *antico* old (but used in the sense of grotesque) <L *antiquus.* Doublet of ANTIQUE.] **—an′tic·ly** *adv.*

an·ti·cat·a·lyst (an′ti·kat′ə·list) *n. Chem.* A catalyst which stops or retards a chemical reaction; a negative catalyst.

an·ti·cath·ode (an′ti·kath′ōd) *n.* The electrode in a vacuum or X-ray tube which receives and reflects the rays emitted from the cathode.

an·ti·chlor (an′ti·klôr, -klōr) *n.* Any substance, as sodium hyposulfite, used to neutralize the chlorine left in fabrics or the like after bleaching with hypochlorites. **—an′ti·chlo·ris′tic** *adj.*

An·ti·christ (an′ti·krīst′) *n.* Any opponent or enemy of Christ, whether a person or a power; specifically, a great enthroned antagonist, foretold in the Scriptures, who, as some have understood, is to precede the second coming of Christ: by some considered as evil personified. See I *John* ii 18.

an·ti·christ (an′ti·krīst′) *n.* **1** A false claimant of the attributes and characteristics of Christ. **2** A denier or opponent of Christ or Christianity. **—an·ti·chris·tian** (an′ti·kris′chən) *adj.*

an·tic·i·pant (an·tis′ə·pənt) *adj.* Coming or acting in advance; anticipating; expectant. —*n.* One who anticipates or expects.

an·tic·i·pate (an·tis′ə·pāt) *v.t.* **·pat·ed, ·pat·ing** **1** To experience or realize beforehand; expect; foresee: to *anticipate* a successful season. **2** To act or arrive sooner than. **3** To act or arrive sooner than so as to prevent; forestall: to *anticipate* an opponent's tactics. **4** To foresee and fulfil beforehand, as expectations.

5 To take or make use of beforehand, as income not yet available. 6 To discharge, as a debt or liability before it is due. 7 To cause to happen earlier; accelerate. [< L *anticipatus*, pp. of *anticipare* < *ante-* before + *capere* take] —**an·tic′i·pa′tor** *n.*

Synonyms: abide, apprehend, expect, forecast, foretaste, hope. We *expect* that which we have good reason to believe will happen. We *hope* for that which we much desire and somewhat *expect.* We *apprehend* what we both *expect* and fear. *Anticipate* is commonly used now, like *foretaste,* of that which we *expect* both with confidence and pleasure. In this use it is a stronger word than *hope;* I *hope* for a visit from my friend; I *expect* it when he writes that he is coming; and as the time draws near I *anticipate* it with pleasure. Compare ABIDE, PREVENT. *Antonyms*: distrust, doubt, dread, fear, recall, recollect, remember.

an·tic·i·pa·tion (an·tis′ə·pā′shən) *n.* **1** The act of anticipating; especially, a foreseeing or foretaste; expectation. **2** An instinctive prevision. **3** *Music* The introduction of a note

ANTICIPATION (*def. 3*)

before its expected place in the harmony.

Synonyms: antepast, apprehension, expectancy, expectation, foreboding, forecast, foresight, foretaste, forethought, hope, presentiment, prevision. *Expectation* may be either of good or evil; *presentiment* almost always, *apprehension* and *foreboding* always, of evil; *anticipation* and *antepast,* commonly of good. Thus, we speak of the pleasures of *anticipation.* A *foretaste* may be of good or evil, and is more than imaginary; it is a part actually received in advance. *Foresight* and *forethought* prevent future evil and secure future good by timely looking forward, and acting upon what is foreseen. Compare ANTICIPATE. *Antonyms*: astonishment, consummation, despair, doubt, dread, enjoyment, fear, realization, surprise, wonder.

an·tic·i·pa·tive (an·tis′ə·pā′tiv) *adj.* Anticipating; having the nature, quality, or habit of anticipation. —**an·tic′i·pa′tive·ly** *adv.*

an·tic·i·pa·to·ry (an·tis′ə·pə·tôr′ē, -tō′rē) *adj.* Pertaining to, showing, or embodying anticipation. —**an·tic′i·pa·to′ri·ly** *adv.*

an·ti·clas·tic (an′ti·klas′tik) *adj. Math.* Having opposite curvature in different directions; convex in one direction and concave in another. Compare SYNCLASTIC. [< ANTI- + Gk. *klastos* broken < *klaein* break]

an·ti·cler·i·cal (an′ti·kler′i·kəl) *adj.* Opposed to clerical influence; specifically, opposed to the Roman Catholic Church.

an·ti·cli·max (an′ti·klī′maks) *n.* **1** A real, apparent, or ludicrous decrease in the importance or impressiveness of what is said: opposed to *climax.* **2** Any sudden descent or fall contrasted with a previous rise. —**an′ti·cli·mac′tic** (-klī·mak′tik) *adj.*

an·ti·cli·nal (an′ti·klī′nəl) *adj. Geol.* Forming a bend with the convex side upward, as a rock stratum or group of strata: also **an′ti·clin′ic** (-klin′ik). —*n.* An anticlinal line, fold, or disposition of strata; a saddleback: also **an′ti·cline.** See SYNCLINAL. [< ANTI- + Gk. *klinein* slope]

an·ti·cli·no·ri·um (an′ti·klī·nôr′ē·əm, -nō′rē·əm) *n. pl.* **·no·ri·a** (-nôr′ē·ə, -nō′rē·ə) *Geol.* A system of roughly parallel folds in stratified rocks, having on the whole an anticlinal

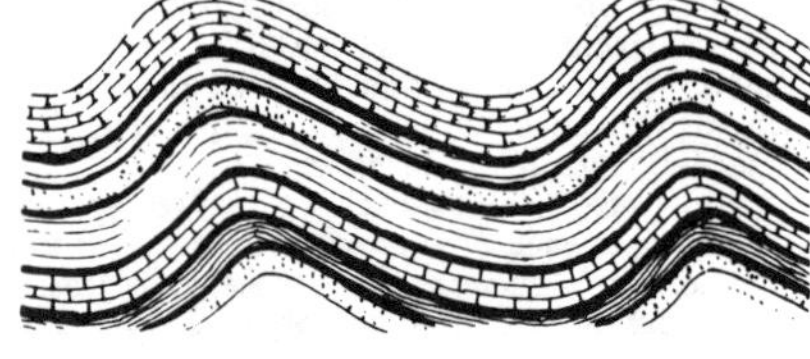

ANTICLINORIUM

structure and forming a great compound arch. [<NL <ANTI- + Gk. *klinein* slope + *oros* mountain]

antic mask See ANTIMASK.

an·ti·co·her·er (an′ti·kō·hir′ər) *n. Electr.* A wave-sensitive device which differs from the coherer in that its resistance increases, instead of decreases, under the action of electromagnetic waves. See DE-COHERER.

an·ti·cos·mon (an′ti·koz′mon) *n. Physics* The supposed fundamental particle from which the anticosmos developed, characterized by a nucleonic charge opposite to that of the cosmon.

an·ti·cos·mos (an′ti·koz′məs) *n. Physics* A cosmos composed entirely of antimatter and supposed to have been formed by the splitting of the universon into two distinct parts existing independently of each other in a condition of metastable equilibrium.

An·ti·cos·ti (an′ti·kôs′tē, -kos′-) An island in the Gulf of St. Lawrence, Quebec, Canada; about 3,043 square miles.

an·ti·cy·clone (an′ti·sī′klōn) *n. Meteorol.* An atmospheric condition of high central pressure relative to the surrounding area, with horizontal spiral currents flowing clockwise in the northern hemisphere, counterclockwise in the southern; also, the region subject to this condition.

an·ti·cy·clon·ic (an′ti·sī·klon′ik) *adj.* **1** Of or pertaining to an anticyclone. **2** Opposed to the cyclonic theory in meteorology.

an·ti·dote (an′ti·dōt) *n.* Anything that will counteract or remove the effects of poison, disease, or any evil. [<L *antidotum* <Gk. *antidoton* <*antidotos* given against <*anti-* against + *didonai* give] —**an′ti·do′tal** *adj.* —**an′ti·do′tal·ly** *adv.*

an·ti·drom·ic (an′ti·drom′ik) *adj. Physiol.* Denoting a movement or course opposed to the normal, as of a nerve impulse. [<ANTI- + Gk. *dromos* a running]

an·ti·en·er·gis·tic (an′tē·en′ər·jis′tik) *adj.* Resisting applied energy: contrasted with *synergistic.*

An·tie·tam (an·tē′təm) A village near Sharpsburg in western Maryland at the mouth of **Antietam Creek**; site of the fiercest day's battle of the Civil War, September 17, 1862.

an·ti·fe·brile (an′ti·fē′brəl, -feb′rəl) *adj.* Having the power to allay fever; antipyretic. —*n.* An antifebrile agent.

an·ti·fed·er·al (an′ti·fed′ər·əl, -fed′rəl) *adj.* Opposed to federalism: capitalized when used historically to mean opposed to the adoption of the U.S. Constitution in 1787–89.

an·ti·fed·er·al·ism (an′ti·fed′ər·əl·iz′əm, -fed′·rəl-) *n.* Opposition to federalism, especially to the Federal party. —**an′ti·fed′er·al·ist** *n.*

An·ti·fed·er·al·ist (an′ti·fed′ər·əl·ist, -fed′rəl-) *n.* A member of the political party that opposed the ratification of the U.S. Constitution. After it was ratified, the Antifederalists, led by Jefferson, opposed any extension of the powers of the Federal government.

an·ti·freeze (an′ti·frēz′) *n.* A liquid of low freezing point, added to or substituted for the cooling agent in combustion-engine radiators, to prevent freezing.

an·ti·fric·tion (an′ti·frik′shən) *adj.* Lessening or tending to lessen friction, as by lubricants or rollers. —*n.* **1** A lubricant. **2** A roller or other device for lessening friction. —**antifriction metal** Any alloy having a low coefficient of friction: used for bearing-surfaces.

an·ti·gen (an′tə·jən) *n.* Any of several substances, such as toxins, enzymes, proteins, which, injected into an organism, cause the development of antibodies. Also **an′ti·gene** (-jēn). —**an·ti·gen·ic** (an′tə·jen′ik) *adj.*

An·tig·o·ne (an·tig′ə·nē) In Greek legend, a daughter of Oedipus and Jocasta who accompanied her blinded father into exile and later was sentenced to death by her uncle Creon for illegally burying her brother Polynices.

An·tig·o·nus I (an·tig′ə·nəs), 382–301 B.C., general of Alexander the Great and king of Macedonia 306–301 B.C.: called "the Cyclops."

An·ti·gua (an·tē′gwə, -gə) A presidency of the Leeward Islands, comprising the island of Antigua (108 square miles) and its dependencies: Barbuda; 62 square miles; and Redonda; 1/2 square mile; capital, St. John's, on Antigua.

Antigua Guatemala A resort city in south central Guatemala; former capital of Guatemala. Also **Antigua.**

an·ti·he·lix (an′ti·hē′liks) See ANTHELIX.

an·ti·his·ta·mine (an′ti·his′tə·mēn, -min) *n. Med.* Any of certain drugs which neutralize the vasoconstrictor action of histamine in the body: used especially in the treatment of allergic conditions, as hay fever, asthma, etc., and of thecommon cold. —**an′ti·his′ta·min′ic** (-min′ik) *adj.*

an·ti·ic·er (an′tē·ī′sər) *n. Aeron.* A device for preventing the formation of ice on airplane wings and other exposed surfaces by the use of a spray delivering warm air or a special liquid preparation. Compare DE-ICER.

an·ti·ke·to·gen·e·sis (an′ti·kē′tə·jen′ə·sis) *n. Biochem.* The reduction or prevention of ketosis by the oxidation of sugar or allied substances in the body.

an·ti·knock (an′ti·nok′) *adj.* Tending to prevent detonation or pinging in an internal-combustion engine —*n.* Any agent, as tetraethyllead, having antiknock properties.

An·ti-Leb·a·non (an′ti·leb′ə·nən) A mountain range east of the Lebanon Mountains, on the Syria-Lebanon border.

an·ti·le·gal·ist (an′ti·lē′gəl·ist) *n.* One who repudiates law as the guide of human conduct.

an·ti·lip·oid (an′ti·lip′oid) *n.* An antibody which reacts with fatlike substances.

an·ti·lith·ic (an′ti·lith′ik) *Med. adj.* Efficacious against stones or calculi. —*n.* An agent which prevents or destroys urinary calculi. [< ANTI- + Gk. *lithos* stone]

An·til·les (an·til′ēz) The islands of the West Indies, except the Bahamas; divided into the **Greater Antilles**: Cuba, Hispaniola, Jamaica, and Puerto Rico; and the **Lesser Antilles**: Trinidad, the Leeward and Windward Islands, Barbados, and other islands: also *Caribbees.*

an·ti·log·a·rithm (an′ti·lôg′ə·rith′əm, -log′-) *n. Math.* The number corresponding to a given logarithm.

an·til·o·gous (an·til′ə·gəs) *adj. Physics* Designating that pole of a pyro-electric crystal which is negative while the crystal is being heated and positive as it cools. Compare ANALOGOUS. [<Gk. *antilogos* contradictory <*anti-* against + *legein* speak]

an·til·o·gy (an·til′ə·jē) *n. pl.* **·gies** Inconsistency in terms or ideas; contradiction.

an·ti·ma·cas·sar (an′ti·mə·kas′ər) *n.* A covering to prevent the soiling of the backs of chairs or sofas by contact with the hair; a tidy. [< ANTI- + MACASSAR (OIL)]

an·ti·mask (an′ti·mask′, -mäsk′) *n.* A grotesque interlude between the acts of a mask, often burlesquing it: also called *antic mask.* Also **an′ti·masque′.**

an·ti·mat·ter (an′ti·mat′ər) *n. Physics* Matter composed of antiparticles.

an·ti·mere (an′tə·mir) *n. Biol.* A part symmetrical with, or corresponding to, a part on the opposite side of the main axis; an opposite, symmetrical, or homotypic part, as an arm of a starfish, or the right or left half of a bilaterally symmetrical animal: also called *actinomere.* [<ANTI- + Gk. *meros* part] —**an·ti·mer·ic** (an′·tə·mer′ik) *adj.* —**an·tim·er·ism** (an·tim′ə·riz′·əm) *n.*

an·ti·mol·e·cule (an′ti·mol′ə·kyōōl) *n.* A molecule of antimatter.

an·ti·mo·nar·chic (an′ti·mə·när′kik) *adj.* Opposed to monarchism. Also **an′ti·mo·nar′chi·cal.**

an·ti·mo·ni·al (an′tē·mō′nē·əl) *adj.* Of or containing antimony. —*n.* A medicine, one of whose ingredients is antimony.

an·ti·mo·nic (an′tə·mō′nik, -mon′ik) *adj.* Of, pertaining to, or containing antimony, especially when combined in its higher or pentad valence: *antimonic* sulfide, Sb_2S_5.

an·ti·mo·nous (an′tə·mō′nəs) *adj.* Of, pertaining to, or containing antimony, especially in its lower valence: *antimonous* oxide, Sb_4O_6. Also **an′ti·mo′ni·ous.**

an·ti·mon·soon (an′ti·mon·sōōn′) *n. Meteorol.* The atmospheric current moving over a monsoon in an opposite direction to it.

an·ti·mo·ny (an′tə·mō′nē) *n.* A silver-white, brittle, flaky metallic element (symbol Sb, atomic number 51), sometimes found native, used chiefly in alloys. See PERIODIC TABLE. ◆ Collateral adjective: *stibial.* [<Med.L *antimonium,* ? <Arabic]

an·ti·mo·ny-glance (an′tə·mō′nē·glans′, -gläns′) *n.* Stibnite.

an·ti·mo·nyl (an′tə·mə·nil′) *n.* A univalent radical SbO, forming the base of several salts.

antimonyl potassium tartrate See TARTAR EMETIC.

an·ti·mu·ta·gen (an′ti·myōō′tə·jən) *n.* A chemical regarded as having the property of inhibiting or decreasing the hereditary variability of micro-organisms and germ cells. [<ANTI- + L *mutare* alter + -GEN] — **an'ti·mu'ta·gen'ic** (-myōō'tə·jen'ik) *adj.*

an·ti·neu·tron (an'ti·nōō'tron, -nyōō'-) *n. Physics* An antiparticle having the same mass as a neutron, but having a reversed magnetic moment of equal magnitude.

an·tin·i·on (an·tin'ē·on) *n. Anat.* That point in the median line of the glabellum furthest removed from the inion: a craniometrical term. [<NL <ANTI- + INION]

an·ti·node (an'ti·nōd') *n. Physics* The section that lies midway between the nodal points of a vibrating medium; a loop.

an·ti·no·mi·an (an'ti·nō'mē·ən) *n. Theol.* One holding that faith frees the Christian from the obligations of the moral law. —*adj.* Of or pertaining to this doctrine. —**an'ti·no'mi·an·ism** *n.*

an·tin·o·my (an·tin'ə·mē) *n. pl.* **·mies 1** Self-contradiction in a law; opposition of one law or rule to another. **2** Irreconcilability of seemingly necessary inferences or conclusions; paradox. [<L *antinomia* <Gk. *antinomia* <*anti-* against + *nomos* law]

An·tin·o·us (an·tin'ō·əs) In the *Odyssey*, the most insistent of Penelope's suitors and the first to be slain by Odysseus.

An·ti·och (an'tē·ok) An ancient city on the Orontes in southern Turkey; former capital of Syria: Arabic and Turkish *Antakiya* or *Antakya*, Roman *Caesarea.*

An·ti·o·chi·an (an'tē·ō'kē·ən) *adj.* **1** Of or pertaining to **Antiochus of Ascalon**, died 68 B.C., the founder of an eclectic school of philosophy uniting Platonic, Aristotelian, and Stoic doctrines. **2** Of or pertaining to Antioch.

An·ti·o·chus (an·tī'ə·kəs) Name of thirteen kings of the Seleucid dynasty in Syria, third to first century B.C.

—**Antiochus III,** 242–187 B.C., conquered Egypt and much of the Near East; defeated by the Romans at Magnesia, 190 B.C.: known as *Antiochus the Great.*

—**Antiochus IV,** died 163 B.C., attempted to suppress Judaism and brought on the Maccabean revolt: called "Epiphanes."

An·ti·o·pe (an·tī'ə·pē) **1** In Greek mythology, a maiden loved by Zeus in the form of a satyr, to whom she bore two sons, Amphion and Zethus. **2** Hippolyta, queen of the Amazons.

an·ti·par·ti·cle (an'ti·pär'ti·kəl) *n. Physics* An elementary particle, as a positron, antiproton, antineutron, etc., equal in mass to another elementary particle, as an electron, proton, neutron, etc., but opposite to it in charge and in magnetic properties. Contact between a particle and its opposite results in mutual annihilation and the release of energy.

an·ti·pas·to (än'tē·päs'tō) *n.* A course of smoked or salted meat, fish, vegetables, etc., served as an appetizer. [<Ital. <*anti-* before (<L *ante*) + *pasto* food <L *pastus*]

An·tip·a·ter (an·tip'ə·tər), 398–319 B.C., regent of Macedonia.

—**Antipater,** died 43 B.C., procurator of Judea; father of Herod the Great.

an·tip·a·thet·ic (an·tip'ə·thet'ik, an'ti·pə-) *adj.* Having antipathy; naturally repugnant or opposed. Also **an·tip'a·thet'i·cal.** —**an·tip'a·thet'i·cal·ly** *adv.*

an·tip·a·thy (an·tip'ə·thē) *n. pl.* **·thies 1** An instinctive feeling of aversion or dislike. **2** One who or that which excites aversion. [<Gk. *antipatheia* <*anti-* against + *pathein* feel, suffer]

Synonyms: abhorrence, antagonism, aversion, detestation, disgust, dislike, distaste, hatred, hostility, loathing, opposition, repugnance, uncongeniality. *Antipathy, repugnance,* and *uncongeniality* are instinctive; other forms of *dislike* may be acquired or cherished for cause. Compare ACRIMONY, ANGER, HATRED. *Antonyms*: affinity, agreement, attraction, congeniality, harmony, kindliness, partiality, predilection, regard, sympathy.

an·ti–Pe·la·gi·an (an'ti·pi·lā'jē·ən) *Theol. adj.* Against Pelagius and his beliefs, as certain creeds or church decrees. —*n.* One who opposed Pelagius or his doctrines.

an·ti·pe·ri·od·ic (an'ti·pir'ē·od'ik) *Med. adj.* Remedial of periodic diseases, as quinine for malaria. —*n.* A remedy for such diseases.

an·ti–per·son·nel (an'ti·pûr'sə·nel') *adj. Mil.* Designating weapons, such as bombs, mines, etc., which are employed against individuals rather than against defenses or mechanized equipment.

an·ti·per·spi·rant (an'ti·pûr'spə·rənt) *n.* A preparation which acts to diminish or prevent perspiration: an astringent applied to the skin.

an·ti·phlo·gis·tic (an'ti·flō·jis'tik) *Med. adj.* Capable of reducing inflammation. —*n.* A remedy for inflammation.

an·ti·phon (an'tə·fon) *n.* **1** A verse of a psalm or hymn said or chanted in response to another. **2** A composition consisting of passages for alternate singing or chanting. **3** A versicle chanted before, and often after, a psalm or canticle, and varying with the church season or feast. [<LL *antiphona* <Gk. *antiphona.* Doublet of ANTHEM.] —**an'ti·phon'ic** or **·i·cal** *adj.*

an·tiph·o·nal (an·tif'ə·nəl) *adj.* Of or pertaining to an antiphon. —*n.* An antiphonary. —**an·tiph'o·nal·ly** *adv.*

an·tiph·o·nar·y (an·tif'ə·ner'ē) *n. pl.* **·nar·ies** A book of antiphons. Also **an·tiph'o·nar** (-nər). —*adj.* Of or pertaining to a book of antiphons.

an·tiph·o·ny (an·tif'ə·nē) *n. pl.* **·nies 1** An anthem or other composition to be sung antiphonally. **2** Antiphonal singing. **3** In ancient Greek music, accompaniment in the octave.

an·tiph·ra·sis (an·tif'rə·sis) *n. pl.* **·ses** (-sēz) The use of a term in a sense opposite to its meaning; irony. [<L <Gk. *antiphrasis* <*antiphrazein* express by antithesis <*anti-* against + *phrazein* speak]

an·tip·o·dal (an·tip'ə·dəl) *adj.* **1** Pertaining to or situated on the opposite side of the earth. **2** Diametrically opposed. Also **an·tip·o·de·an** (an·tip'ə·dē'ən).

an·ti·pode (an'ti·pōd) *n.* An exact opposite.

an·tip·o·des (an·tip'ə·dēz) *n. pl.* **1** A place or region on the opposite side of the earth, or its inhabitants. **2** Any person or thing diametrically opposed to another, or at the opposite extreme from another. [<L <Gk. *antipodes,* pl. of *antipous* having the feet opposite <*anti-* opposite + *pous* foot]

An·tip·o·des (an·tip'ə·dēz) **1** A group of uninhabited islands SE of and belonging to New Zealand; 24 square miles: so called from their antipodal position to Greenwich, England. **2** Australasia.

an·ti·pope (an'ti·pōp') *n.* A usurping pope or one not canonically elected.

an·ti·pro·ton (an'ti·prō'ton) *n. Physics* An antiparticle having the same mass as the proton, an equal but opposite charge, and a reversed magnetic moment of equal magnitude; its collision with a proton or neutron results in the liberation of energy equivalent to both particles.

an·ti·py·ic (an'ti·pī'ik) *Med. adj.* Preventive of suppuration. —*n.* A remedy against suppuration. [<ANTI- + Gk. *pyon* pus]

an·ti·py·ret·ic (an'ti·pī·ret'ik) *Med. adj.* Preventive or alleviative of fever. —*n.* A medicine to allay fever. [<ANTI- + Gk. *pyretos* fever]

an·ti·py·rine (an'ti·pī'rin, -rēn) *n.* A white crystalline compound, $C_{11}H_{12}N_2O$, used in medicine as an antipyretic. Also **an'ti·py'rin** (-rin).

an·ti·quar·i·an (an'ti·kwâr'ē·ən) *adj.* Pertaining to antiquity or to the knowledge of or collecting of antiquities. —*n.* An antiquary. —**an'ti·quar'i·an·ism** *n.*

an·ti·quar·y (an'ti·kwer'ē) *n. pl.* **·quar·ies** One who collects, examines, deals in, or studies ancient objects; one versed in ancient things, as relics, monuments, old manuscripts, etc. [<L *antiquarius* <*antiquus* ancient]

an·ti·quate (an'ti·kwāt) *v.t.* **·quat·ed, ·quat·ing 1** To make old, out of date, or obsolete. **2** To cause to look antique; give an old-fashioned air or style to. —**an'ti·qua'tion** *n.*

an·ti·quat·ed (an'ti·kwā'tid) *adj.* **1** Out of date; old-fashioned; obsolete. **2** Ancient; superannuated. See synonyms under ANCIENT, ANTIQUE.

an·tique (an·tēk') *adj.* **1** Of, pertaining to, or having come down from ancient times. **2** In the style of ancient times. **3** Old; old-fashioned. **4** Pertaining or belonging to ancient Greece or Rome. —*n.* **1** The style of ancient art, or a specimen of it. **2** Any ancient object, as a piece of furniture, glass, etc. **3** A Roman-faced type with all the lines of nearly the same thickness. —*v.t.* **an·tiqued, an·ti·quing** To make seemingly old; give the appearance of antiquity to. [<F <L *antiquus* ancient <*ante* before. Doublet of ANTIC.] —**an·tique'ly** *adv.* —**an·tique'ness** *n.*

Synonyms (adj.): ancient, antiquated, old-fashioned, quaint, superannuated. *Antique* refers to an *ancient, antiquated* to a discarded style. The *antique* is that which is either *ancient* in fact or *ancient* in style. The *antiquated* is not so much out of date as out of vogue. *Old-fashioned* may be used approvingly or contemptuously. In the latter case it becomes a synonym for *antiquated;* in the good sense it approaches the meaning of *antique,* but indicates less duration. *Quaint* combines the idea of age with a pleasing oddity. The *antiquated* person is out of style and out of sympathy with the present generation by reason of age; the *superannuated* person is incapacitated for present activities by reason of age. Compare ANCIENT, OLD. *Antonyms*: fashionable, fresh, modern, modish, new, recent, stylish.

an·tiq·ui·ty (an·tik'wə·tē) *n. pl.* **·ties 1** The state or quality of being ancient. **2** Ancient times, people, or civilization. **3** Anything belonging to ancient times.

an·ti·re·mon·strant (an'ti·ri·mon'strənt) *n.* An opponent of remonstrance. —*adj.* Opposed to remonstrance.

An·ti·re·mon·strant (an'ti·ri·mon'strənt) *n.* A Dutch Calvinist who opposed the Arminian Remonstrance. —*adj.* Pertaining to such opposition.

an·ti–rent (an'ti·rent') *adj.* **1** Opposed to payment of land rent. **2** Designating a concerted movement in Ireland in 1881, opposing the payment of rent to absentee landlords. —**an'ti–rent'er** *n.* —**an'ti–rent'ism** *n.*

An·ti–rent (an'ti·rent') *adj.* Designating a political party in New York State (1839–47) opposed to paying farm rents to patroons.

an·tir·rhi·num (an'tə·rī'nəm) *n.* Any of a genus (*Antirrhinum*) of chiefly Old World herbs of the figwort family, including the common American snapdragon. [<NL <Gk. *antirrhinon* <*anti-* resembling + *rhis* nose]

an·ti–sab·ba·tar·i·an (an'ti·sab'ə·târ'ē·ən) *adj.* Of or pertaining to one who opposes the observance of the Sabbath. —*n.* One who denies the moral obligation to observe the Sabbath, or opposes its strict or puritanical observance.

An·ti–Sa·loon League (an'ti·sə·lōōn') An organization, founded nationally in 1895, aiming to abolish the sale and use of liquor.

An·ti·sa·na (än'tē·sä'nä) A volcano in the Andes, north central Ecuador; 18,714 feet.

an·tis·cians (an·tish'ənz) *n. pl.* Dwellers on the same meridian on opposite sides of the equator, whose shadows at noon fall in opposite directions. Also **an·tis·ci·i** (an·tish'ē·ī). [<L *antiscii* <Gk. *antiskioi* <*anti-* opposite + *skia* shadow]

an·ti·scor·bu·tic (an'ti·skôr·byōō'tik) *Med. adj.* Relieving or preventing scurvy. —*n.* A remedy for scurvy.

an·ti–Sem·i·tism (an'ti·sem'ə·tiz'əm) *n.* Opposition to, prejudice or discrimination against, or intolerance of Jews, Jewish culture, etc. —**an'ti–Sem'ite** *n.* —**an'ti–Se·mit'ic** (-sə·mit'ik) *adj.* —**an'ti–Se·mit'i·cal·ly** *adv.*

an·ti·sep·sis (an'tə·sep'sis) *n.* **1** The condition in or method by which a substance, or organism, is kept sterile against the growth of pathogenic or putrefactive bacteria. **2** Listerism. [<NL <ANTI- + Gk. *sēpsis* putrefaction]

an·ti·sep·tic (an'tə·sep'tik) *adj.* **1** Of, pertaining to, or used in antisepsis. **2** Preventing or counteracting putrefaction, etc. Also **an'ti·sep'ti·cal.** —*n.* Any substance having antiseptic qualities, as solutions of carbolic acid and of corrosive sublimate. —**an'ti·sep'ti·cal·ly** *adv.* —**an'ti·sep'ti·cism** (-sep'tə·siz'əm) *n.*

an·ti·sep·ti·cize (an'tə·sep'tə·sīz) *v.t.* **·cized, ·ciz·ing** To render antiseptic; treat by the application of antiseptics.

an·ti·se·rum (an′ti·sir′əm) *n.* A serum which contains antibodies, the injection of which into the blood stream provides immunity from specific diseases.

an·ti–slav·er·y (an′ti·slā′vər·ē, -slāv′rē) *adj.* Opposed to human slavery. —*n.* Opposition to human slavery.

an·ti·so·cial (an′ti·sō′shəl) *adj.* **1** Averse to social intercourse or society. **2** Opposed to treating society as a unit; anarchistic. **3** Obstructive or disruptive of social good.

an·ti·so·cial·ist (an′ti·sō′shəl·ist) *n.* One hostile to socialistic teachings. —**an′ti·so′cial·is′·tic** *adj.*

an·ti·so·lar (an′tī·sō′lər) *adj.* **1** Situated or occurring at a point in the heavens 180 degrees from the sun in azimuth. **2** Diametrically opposite the sun, as the center of a rainbow.

an·ti·spas·mod·ic (an′ti·spaz·mod′ik) *adj.* Relieving or checking spasms. —*n.* An antispasmodic preparation, as ammonia, camphor, etc.

An·tis·the·nes (an·tis′thə·nēz) 444?–371? B.C., Greek philosopher; reputed founder of Cynic school.

an·tis·tro·phe (an·tis′trə·fē) *n.* **1** In ancient Greek poetry, the verses sung by the chorus in a play while returning from left to right, in answer to the previous strophe. **2** In classical prosody, the lines of an ode comprising a stanza and alternating with the strophe. **3** The second of two alternating metrical systems in a poem. [<Gk. *antistrophē* <*antistrephein* turn against <*anti-* against, opposite + *strephein* turn] —**an·ti·stroph·ic** (an′ti·strof′ik) *adj.*

an·ti–tank (an′ti·tangk′) *adj. Mil.* Designed to combat tanks and other mechanized equipment: *anti–tank* guns.

an·ti·te·tan·ic (an′tī·te·tan′ik) *Med. adj.* Relieving or preventing tetanus. —*n.* A remedy for tetanus.

an·ti·the·ism (an′ti·thē′iz·əm) *n.* **1** Opposition to belief in God. **2** In philosophy and religion, opposition to theism.

an·tith·e·sis (an·tith′ə·sis) *n. pl.* **·ses** (-sēz) **1** The balancing of contrasted words or ideas against each other. **2** The direct contrary; a strong contrast. [<L <Gk. <*antitithenai* oppose <*anti-* against + *tithenai* place]

an·ti·thet·i·cal (an′tə·thet′i·kəl) *adj.* Directly opposed; strongly contrasted. Also **an′ti·thet′·ic.** —**an′ti·thet′i·cal·ly** *adv.*

an·ti·tox·in (an′ti·tok′sin) *n.* A substance, usually a protein, formed in the living tissues of a plant or animal, which neutralizes the bacterial poison that produced it. Also **an′ti·tox′ine** (-tok′sin, -sēn) —**an′ti·tox′ic** *adj.*

an·ti·trade (an′ti·trād′) *Meteorol. n.* One of the upper air currents in the tropics, moving contrary to the trade winds. —*adj.* Pertaining to or designating such an air current.

an·tit·ra·gus (an·tit′rə·gəs) *n. pl.* **·gi** (-jī) *Anat.* The conical eminence behind the opening of the ear. [<ANTI- + TRAGUS]

an·ti–Trin·i·tar·i·an (an′ti·trin′ə·târ′ē·ən) *adj. Theol.* Opposing the doctrine of the Trinity. —*n.* One who opposes the doctrine of the Trinity.

an·ti·trust (an′ti·trust′) *adj.* Pertaining to the regulation of or opposition to trusts, cartels, pools, monopolies, and other organizations and practices in restraint of trade.

an·ti·twi·light (an′ti·twī′līt) *n. Meteorol.* A pink or purplish light sometimes seen after sunset or before sunrise in the part of the sky opposite the sun.

an·ti·type (an′ti·tīp′) *n.* **1** That which a type or symbol represents; the original of a type. **2** A person or event in the New Testament prefigured by one in the Old. [<Gk. *antitypos* <*anti-* corresponding to, against + *typos* stamp, type] —**an·ti·ty·pal** (an′ti·tī′pəl), **an·ti·typ·ic** (an′ti·tip′ik) or **·i·cal** *adj.*

an·ti·ven·in (an′ti·ven′in) *n.* **1** The active principle of a serum which protects animals against snake poison or venom. **2** The serum. Also **an·ti·ven·ene, an·ti·ven·ine** (an′ti·ven′ēn, -və·nēn′). [<ANTI- + L *venenum* poison]

an·ti·vi·ral (an′ti·vī′rəl) *adj.* **1** Injurious to or destructive of viruses. **2** Counteracting a virus, as certain drugs.

an·ti·vi·rot·ic (an′ti·vī·rot′ik) *n.* A substance which destroys viruses or inhibits their development. —*adj.* Antiviral.

an·ti·world (an′ti·wûrld′) *n. Physics* A hypothetical world or universe composed only of antimatter: sometimes called *contra–terrene.*

ant·ler (ant′lər) *n.* **1** A deciduous bony outgrowth or horn on the head of various members of the deer family, usually branched. **2** Any one of its branches or tines. [<OF *antoillier,* ult. <L *ante-* before + *oculus* eye] —**ant′lered** *adj.*

ANTLERS
A. Rusine.
B., C., D. Rucervine: normal, intermediate, extreme.
E. Subelaphine.
F. Elaphine.
Tine: *a.* Brow *b.* Bez *c.* Royal

Ant·li·a (ant′lē·ə) A southern constellation near Argo. See CONSTELLATION.

ant–li·on (ant′lī′ən) *n.* **1** An insect (family *Myrmeleontidae*) resembling a dragonfly; especially, its long-jawed, louselike larva, usually called *doodle–bug,* which buries itself in a funnel–shaped pit with only its jaws projecting and preys on ants and other insects. For illustration see under INSECT (beneficial). **2** A mythical animal, half lion, half ant.

An·to·fa·gas·ta (än′tō·fä·gäs′·tä) A port in northern Chile.

An·toine (äṅ·twȧn′) French form of ANTHONY.

An·toine (äṅ·twȧn′), **Père** (pâr) See ANTONIO DE SEDILLA.

An·toi·nette (an′twə·net′, -tə-; *Fr.* äṅ·twȧ·net′) French form of ANTONIA. Also *Ger.* **An·to·niet·te** (än′tō·nyet′ə), *Ital.* **An·to·niet·ta** (än′tō·nyet′tä).

An·ton (än′tōn) Danish, Dutch, German, and Swedish form of ANTHONY.

An·to·nes·cu (än′tō·nes′ko͞o), **Ion** (yon), 1882–1946, Rumanian general and political leader 1940–44; executed.

An·to·ni·a (an·tō′nē·ə) A feminine personal name; feminine of ANTHONY. Also *Fr.* **An·to·nie** (äṅ·tô·nē′), *Ger.* **An·to·nie** (än·tō′nye), *Ital., Sp.* **An·to·ni·na** (än′tō·nē′nä).

An·to·ni·nus (an′tə·nī′nəs) See AURELIUS, MARCUS.

Antoninus Pi·us (pī′əs), A.D. 86–161; emperor of Rome A.D. 131–61.

An·to·nio (än·tō′nyō) Italian, Portuguese, and Spanish form of ANTHONY.
—**An·to·ni·o** (an·tō′nē·ō, -tōn′yō) One of several characters in Shakespeare's plays: in the *Merchant of Venice,* the merchant; in *Two Gentlemen of Verona,* father of Proteus; in *The Tempest,* Prospero's brother, who has usurped his dukedom; in *Twelfth Night,* a sea–captain; in *Much Ado About Nothing,* brother of Leonato, governor of Messina.

Antonio de Se·dil·la (thā sā·thē′lyä) 1748–1829, Spanish Capuchin priest in New Orleans, accused of trying to introduce the Inquisition: called *Père Antoine.*

An·to·ni·us (*Ger.* än·tō′nē·o͝os, *Lat.* an·tō′nē·əs) German and Latin form of ANTHONY.

an·to·no·ma·sia (an′tə·nō·mā′zhə, -zhē·ə) *n.* **1** The substitution of a title or epithet for a proper name, as *his Honor,* for a judge. **2** The use of the name of a representative individual for a class, as a *Cicero,* for an orator. [<L <Gk. <*antonomazein* name instead < *anti-* instead of + *onoma* name]

An·to·ny (an′tə·nē) See ANTHONY.
—**Antony, Mark,** 83–30 B.C., Roman general and triumvir: also *Marcus Antonius.*

an·to·nym (an′tə·nim) *n.* A word directly opposed to another in meaning: contrasted with *synonym.* [<Gk. *antōnymia* <*anti-* opposite + *onoma, onyma* name]

an·tre (an′tər) *n. Obs.* A cavern. [<F <L *antrum* <Gk. *antron* cave]

An·trim (an′trim) A county of Ulster province in NE Northern Ireland; 1,098 square miles; county seat, Belfast.

an·trorse (an·trôrs′) *adj. Biol.* Directed forward or upward, as the short feathers hiding the nostrils in corvine birds. [<NL *antrorsus* <ANTERO- + L *versus,* pp. of *vertere* turn] —**an·trorse′ly** *adv.*

an·trum (an′trəm) *n. pl.* **·tra** (-trə) *Anat.* A cavity, usually in a bone. [<L <Gk. *antron* cave]

antrum of High·more (hī′môr, -mōr) *Anat.* A cavity in the upper jaw opening into the nose. [after Nathaniel *Highmore,* 1613–85, English anatomist]

an·trus·tion (an·trus′chən) *n.* A vassal follower and companion of the early Frankish princes. Compare THANE. [<F <Med. L *antrustio, -onis* <OHG *trōst* trust, protection] —**an·trus′tion·ship** *n.*

An·try·cide (an′tri·sīd) *n.* Proprietary name for a synthetic crystalline compound developed as a drug for use against trypanosomiasis in cattle, especially in tropical Africa.

An·tung (an′to͝ong′, *Chinese* än′do͝ong′) A port on the Yalu in southern Manchuria, capital of Liaotung province.

Ant·werp (ant′wûrp) A port on the Scheldt in northern Belgium: French *Anvers. Flemish* **Ant·wer·pen** (änt′ver·pən).

A·nu (ä′no͞o) In Babylonian mythology, the sky god.

A·nu·bis (ə·no͞o′bis, ə·nyo͞o′-) In Egyptian mythology, the jackal–headed conductor of the dead to judgment: identified with the Greek *Hermes.*

ANUBIS

A·nu·ra·dha·pu·ra (ə·no͞o′rä·də·po͝or′ə) A Buddhist pilgrimage center in north central Ceylon; former capital of Ceylon.

a·nu·ran (ə·no͝or′ən, ə·nyo͝or′-) *adj.* & *n. Zool.* Salientian. [<AN-[1] without + Gk. *oura* tail] —**a·nu′rous** *adj.*

an·u·re·sis (an′yo͞o·rē′sis) *n.* Anury. —**an′u·ret′ic** (-ret′·ik) *adj.*

an·u·ry (an′yo͞o·rē) *n. Pathol.* Suppression or defective excretion of the urine. Also **a·nu·ri·a** (ə·no͝or′ē·ə, ə·nyo͝or′-). [<NL *anuria* <Gk. *an-* without + *ouron* urine] —**a·nu·ric** (ə·no͝or′·ik, ə·nyo͝or′-) *adj.*

a·nus (ā′nəs) *n. Anat.* The opening at the lower extremity of the alimentary canal. [<L, orig. a ring]

An·vers (äṅ·vâr′) The French name for ANTWERP.

an·vil (an′vil) *n.* **1** A heavy block of iron or steel on which metal may be forged. **2** Anything similar to an anvil, as the lower contact of a telegraph key, etc. **3** *Anat.* The incus of the inner ear. **4** That part of the primer in a cartridge or shell which receives the impact of the firing pin and detonates the charge. **5** *Mech.* The fixed element of a measuring device, as in calipers. —*v.t.* & *v.i.* **an·viled** or **·villed, an·vil·ing** or **·vil·ling** To work at or shape on an anvil. [OE *anfilte*]

DOUBLE–BEAK ANVIL
a. Rounded beak. *b.* Flat beak. *c.* Cutter, or chisel hole.

an·vil·top (an′vil·top′) *n. Meteorol.* A large, dense, anvil–shaped mass of cloud usually formed at the top of a cumulonimbus cloud preceding heavy showers or thunderstorms; incus (def. 2). For illustration see CLOUD.

anx·i·e·ty (ang·zī′ə·tē) *n. pl.* **·ties** **1** Disturbance of mind regarding some uncertain event; misgiving; worry. **2** Strained or solicitous desire, as for some object or purpose; eagerness. [<L *anxietas, -tatis* <*anxius.* See ANXIOUS.]

Synonyms: anguish, apprehension, care, concern, disquiet, disturbance, dread, fear, foreboding, fretfulness, fretting, misgiving, perplexity, solicitude, trouble, worry. *Anxiety* refers to some future event, always suggesting hopeful possibility, and thus differing from *apprehension, fear, dread, foreboding, terror,* all of which may be quite despairing. *Worry* is a more petty, restless, and manifest *anxiety; anxiety* may be quiet and silent; *worry* is communicated to all around. *Solicitude* is a milder *anxiety. Fretting* or *fretfulness* is a weak complaining without thought of accomplishing or changing anything, but merely as a relief to one's own *disquiet. Perplexity* often involves *anxiety,* but may be quite free from it. One feels anxiety *for* a friend's return; anxiety *about, for, in regard to,* or *concerning* the future. *Antonyms*: apathy, assurance, calmness, carelessness, confidence, ease, lightheartedness, nonchalance, satisfaction, tranquillity.

anx·ious (angk′shəs, ang′-) *adj.* **1** Troubled in mind respecting some uncertain matter; having anxiety: often with *about, at,* or *over:*

anxious about health; *anxious* at the delay; *anxious* over her safety. **2** Fraught with or causing anxiety; worrying; distressing: an *anxious* matter. **3** Intent; eagerly desirous; solicitous: with *for* or the infinitive with *to: anxious* for success; *anxious* to succeed. See synonyms under EAGER. [<L *anxius* < *angere* choke, distress] — **anx′·ious·ly** *adv.* — **anx′ious·ness** *n.*

anxious seat *U.S.* The mourner's bench.

an·y (an′ē) *adj.* **1** One (person, thing, or part) indefinitely and indifferently; a; an; some; no matter what: at *any* price. **2** Some (individuals) of a number, class, or total. See synonyms under EVERY. —*pron.* One or more persons, things, or portions out of a number. —*adv.* Somewhat; in the least; at all: doing *any* better today. ◆ *Any,* in colloquial negative and interrogative sentences, is used absolutely to mean noticeably, at all: Did you hurt yourself *any?* [OE *ænig* < *ān* one]

an·y·bod·y (en′i·bod′ē, -bud′ē) *pron.* Any person whatever; anyone. —*n. pl.* **·bod·ies 1** Any common or ordinary person. **2** A person of prestige or importance: He isn't *anybody.*

an·y·how (en′i·hou′) *adv.* **1** In any way whatever; by any means. **2** Notwithstanding; in any case: *Anyhow,* we did the best we could. **3** Carelessly.

any more 1 Anything added: Do not give me *any more.* **2** Now; from now on: He's not welcome *any more.*

any more than With more reason or likelihood than: I couldn't do that *any more than* I could fly.

an·y·one (en′i·wun′, -wən) *pron.* Any person. ◆ **any one, anyone** *Any one* is used to distinguish one person from others in the same group or class: *Any one* of these men may be guilty. *Anyone* (indefinite pronoun) means any person at all: Can *anyone* identify the culprit?

an·y·thing (en′i·thing′) *pron.* Any thing, event, or matter of any sort. —*n.* A thing of any kind. —*adv. Archaic* To any degree; in any way.

anything but By no means; far from: *anything but* safe.

an·y·way (en′i·wā′) *adv.* **1** No matter what happens; in any event. **2** Nevertheless; anyhow. **3** Carelessly; haphazardly.

an·y·ways (en′i·wāz′) *adv. Dial.* In any way; at all.

an·y·where (en′i·hwâr′) *adv.* In, at, or to any place whatever.

an·y·wise (en′i·wīz′) *adv.* In any manner.

An·zac (an′zak) *adj.* Pertaining to the *A* ustralian and *N* ew *Z* ealand *A* rmy *C* orps during World War I. —*n.* **1** A member of this army corps. **2** Any soldier from Australian or New Zealand.

An·zi·o (an′zē·ō, *Ital.* än′tsyō) A town on the west coast of Italy south of Rome; site of Allied beachhead in the invasion of Italy, World War II, January, 1944.

A-OK (ā′ō·kā′) *adj. Colloq.* Perfectly all right; just fine. Also **A′-o·kay′.**

A-one (ā′wun′) *n.* **1** First or highest class: said of a vessel to denote condition of its hull and equipment. Written **A-1. 2** *Colloq.* Excellent; first-rate; superior.

A·o·ni·a (ā·ō′nē·ə) A district in ancient Greece including Mount Helicon, sacred to the Muses. — **A·o′ni·an** *adj.*

A·o·ran·gi (ä′ō·räng′gē) See COOK, MOUNT.

a·o·rist (ā′ə·rist) *n.* A tense of Greek verbs simply expressing past action without further limitation as to completion, continuance, or repetition. Abbr. *aor.* [<Gk. *aoristos* indefinite < *a-* without + *horos* boundary]

a·o·ris·tic (ā′ə·ris′tik) *adj.* **1** Relating to the aorist tense. **2** Indefinite; undefined.

a·or·ta (ā·ôr′tə) *n. pl.* **·tas** or **·tae** (-tē) *Anat.* The great artery springing from the left ventricle of the heart and forming the main arterial trunk which distributes blood to all of the body except the lungs. [<NL <Gk. *aortē* < *aeirein* raise, heave] — **a·or′tal, a·or′tic** *adj.*

A·os·ta (ä·ôs′tä), **Duke of,** 1869–1931, Emanuele Filiberto, Italian general in World War I. — **Duke of,** 1898–1942, Amedeo Umberto, Italian general in World War II; son of preceding.

A·os·ta (ä·ôs′tä) A city in Piedmont, NW Italy, regional capital of Val d'Aosta.

a·ou·dad (ä′o͞o·dad) *n.* The bearded argali (genus *Ammotragus*), a wild sheep of North Africa: also spelled *audad.* [<F <Berber *audad*]

ap-[1] Assimilated var. of AD-.

ap-[2] Var. of APO-.

a·pace (ə·pās′) *adv.* Rapidly; fast. [<A-[1] on + PACE]

A·pach·e (ə·pach′ē) *n. pl.* **A·pach·es** or **A·pach·e** One of a tribe of fierce North American Indians of Athapascan stock.

a·pache (ə·päsh′, ə·pash′; *Fr.* à·pàsh′) *n.* One of a band of lawless persons formerly frequenting the streets of Paris by night. [<F < *Apache*]

Apache State Nickname of ARIZONA.

ap·a·go·ge (ap′ə·gō′jē) *n.* **1** *Math.* The use of one proposition already demonstrated to prove another. **2** *Logic* Establishment of a thesis by showing its contrary to be absurd. [<Gk. *apagōgē* a leading away < *apagein* < *apo-* away + *agein* lead] — **ap′a·gog′ic** (-goj′ik) or **·i·cal** *adj.*

Ap·a·lach·ee Bay (ap′ə·lach′ē) A bay of the Gulf of Mexico in NW Florida.

Ap·a·lach·i·co·la River (ap′ə·lach′i·kō′lə) A river in NW Florida, flowing south 112 miles to the Gulf of Mexico.

ap·a·nage (ap′ə·nij) See APPANAGE.

a·pa·re·jo (ä′pä·rā′hō) *n. pl.* **·jos** (-hōz) *SW U.S.* A type of packsaddle with stuffed leather cushions. [<Sp.]

A·par·ri (ä·pä′rē) A port on Babuyan Channel in northern Luzon, Philippines.

a·part (ə·pärt′) *adv.* **1** So as to be separated in space or time, or from companionship, sympathy, or the like; aside. **2** So as to be isolated or separated for use of purpose. **3** So as to be independent logically or in thought. **4** Part from part; in pieces or to pieces; asunder. [<F *à part* <L *ad* to + *pars, partis* part]

a·part·heid (ə·pärt′hīt, -hāt) *n.* Racial segregation, especially as supported by law as an instrument of government policy. Specifically, enforced in the Republic of South Africa, was repealed after 1994 democratic elections. [<Afrikaans, apartness]

a·part·ment (ə·pärt′mənt) *n.* **1** A room or suite of rooms. **2** One of several similar suites of rooms in one building, equipped for housekeeping; a flat. [<F *appartement* <Ital. *appartamento,* ult. <L *ad* to + *pars, partis* part]

apartment house A multiple-dwelling building divided into a number of apartments.

a·pas·ti·a (ə·pas′tē·ə) *n. Psychiatry* Morbid abstention from food. [<Gk.] — **a·pas′tic** *adj.*

ap·as·tron (ap·as′tron) *n. Astron.* That point in the orbit of either member of a double star when the stars are at maximum distance from each other: opposed to *periastron.* [<AP- away from + Gk. *astron* star]

ap·a·tet·ic (ap′ə·tet′ik) *adj. Zool.* Having natural camouflage of imitative coloration or form. [<Gk. *apatētikos* deceiving < *apatē* deceit]

ap·a·thet·ic (ap′ə·thet′ik) *adj.* **1** Without emotion or feeling. **2** Indifferent; unconcerned; stolid. Also **ap′a·thet′i·cal.** — **ap′a·thet′i·cal·ly** *adv.*

ap·a·thy (ap′ə·thē) *n. pl.* **·thies 1** Lack of feeling, emotion, or sensation; insensibility. **2** Indifference; lack of interest. [<L *apathia* <Gk. *apatheia* < *a-* without + *pathos* feeling < *pathein* feel]

Synonyms: calmness, composure, immobility, impassibility, indifference, insensibility, lethargy, phlegm, quietness, quietude, sluggishness, stillness, stoicism, tranquillity, unconcern, unfeelingness. *Composure* results ordinarily from force of will, or from perfect confidence in one's own resoures. *Indifference* is a want of interest; *insensibility* is a want of feeling; *unconcern* has reference to consequences. *Stoicism* is an intentional suppression of feeling and deadening of sensibilities, while *apathy* is involuntary, denoting a simple absence of emotion. Compare CALM, REST, STUPOR. *Antonyms:* agitation, alarm, anxiety, care, distress, disturbance, eagerness, emotion, excitement, feeling, frenzy, fury, passion, sensibility, sensitiveness, storm, susceptibility, sympathy, turbulence, vehemence, violence.

ap·a·tite (ap′ə·tīt) *n. Mineral.* A hexagonal, usually brown or green calcium phosphate of chlorine or fluorine. [<Gk. *apatē* deceit + -ITE[1]; because it was mistaken for other minerals]

ape (āp) *n.* **1** A large, tailless, Old World primate, as a gorilla or chimpanzee. **2** Loosely, any monkey. **3** A mimic. —*v.t.* **aped, ap·ing** To imitate; mimic. See synonyms under IMITATE. [OE *apa*]

a·peak (ə·pēk′) *adv. Naut.* In or nearly in a vertical position, as an anchor.

A·pel·doorn (ä′pəl·dōrn) A town in east central Netherlands.

A·pel·les (ə·pel′ēz) Greek painter of the fourth century B.C.

ape man Any of various primates resembling man, as Pithecanthropus.

Ap·en·nines (ap′ə·nīnz) A mountain range constituting most of the Italian peninsula south of the Po valley; highest peak, 9,560 feet.

a·pep·si·a (ā·pep′sē·ə, ə-) *n. Med.* Lack of capacity to digest. Also **a·pep′sy.** [<NL <Gk. *a-* not + *peptein* digest] — **a·pep′tic** (-tik) *adj.*

a·per·çu (à·per·sü′) *n. pl.* **a·per·çus** (-sü′) *French* **1** A glance. **2** An insight or perception. **3** An outline or conspectus.

a·pe·ri·ent (ə·pir′ē·ənt) *Med. adj.* Tending mildly to stimulate the action of the bowels; laxative. —*n.* A gently purgative remedy. Also **a·per·i·tive** (ə·per′ə·tiv). [<L *aperiens, -entis,* ppr. of *aperire* open]

a·pe·ri·od·ic (ā′pir·ē·od′ik) *adj.* **1** *Pathol.* Not manifesting periodicity, as some diseases. **2** *Physics* **a** Without cyclic vibrations; not periodic. **b** Pertaining to any vibrating system whose oscillations are reduced or eliminated by sufficient damping, as the pointer of an indicating device which comes to a full stop without terminal vibration.

aperiodic antenna A radio antenna responding with a high degree of constancy to a wide range of frequencies.

aperiodic compass A magnetic compass whose needle assumes its final position in one movement and without any further fluctuation.

a·pe·ri·o·dic·i·ty (ā·pir′ē·ə·dis′ə·tē) *n.* Aperiodic condition.

a·pé·ri·tif (à·pā·rē·tēf′) *n. French* A drink of alcoholic liquor or wine taken as an appetizer.

a·pert (ə·pûrt′) *adj. Archaic* Open; undisguised. [<OF <L *apertus,* pp. of *aperire* open] — **a·pert′ly** *adv.* — **a·pert′ness** *n.*

ap·er·ture (ap′ər·cho͝or, -chər) *n.* **1** An open passage; orifice; hole; cleft. **2** An opening, often adjustable in diameter, through which light enters the lens of a camera or other optical instrument. See synonyms under HOLE. [<L *apertura* < *apertus,* pp. of *aperire* open] — **ap′er·tur·al** *adj.* — **ap′er·tured** *adj.*

ap·er·y (ā′pər·ē) *n. pl.* **·er·ies** The act of aping; mimicry.

a·pet·al·ous (ā·pet′əl·əs) *adj. Bot.* **1** Without petals. **2** Pertaining to the *Apetalae,* a division of plants in which the flowers are without petals.

a·pex (ā′peks) *n. pl.* **·a·pex·es** or **ap·i·ces** (ap′ə·sēz, ā′pə-) **1** The highest point; tip; top. **2** *Geom.* The vertex (of an angle). **3** Climax. **4** *Phonet.* The tip of the tongue. [<L]

aph- Var. of APO-.

a·pha·gi·a (ə·fā′jē·ə) *n. Pathol.* Loss of the power to swallow. [<NL <Gk. *a-* not + *phagein* eat]

a·pha·ki·a (ə·fā′kē·ə) *n. Pathol.* A condition of the eye marked by absence of the lens. Also **a·pha′ci·a.** [<NL <Gk. *a-* without + *phakē* lentil, lens of the eye]

a·phan·i·sis (ə·fan′ə·sis) *n. Psychoanal.* The fear of losing sexual potency. [<Gk., obliteration < *aphanizein* make unseen, destroy < *a-* not + *phainein* show]

aph·a·nite (af′ə·nīt) *n. Mineral.* A dense, fine-grained diabase with a compact texture. [<Gk. *aphanēs* unseen + -ITE[1]; so called because its grains are invisible to the naked eye] — **aph′·a·nit′ic** (-nit′ik) *adj.*

a·pha·sia (ə·fā′zhə, zhē·ə) *n.* Partial or total loss of the ability to articulate or understand language due to damage to the cerebral cortex. See

[<NL <Gk. *aphasia* <*aphatos* speechless <*a-* not + *phanai* speak] **—a·pha·sic** (ə·fā′zik, -sik), **a·pha·si·ac** (ə·fā′·zē·ak) *adj.* & *n.*

a·phe·li·on (ə·fē′lē·ən). *n. pl.* **·li·ons** or **·li·a** (-lē·ə). *Astron.* The point in an orbit of a planet or comet, farthest from the sun: opposed to *perihelion.* [<APH-(APO-) away from + Gk. *hēlios* sun] **—a·phe′li·an** (-ən) *adj.*

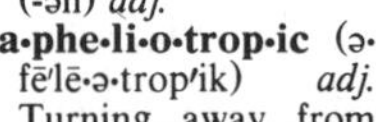

APHELION
P. Perihelion. *S.* Sun. *A.* Aphelion.

a·phe·li·o·trop·ic (ə·fē′lē·ə·trop′ik) *adj.* Turning away from the source of light; having negative heliotropism. [<APH- (APO-)+ HELIOTROPIC] **—a·phe′·li·o·trop′i·cal·ly** *adv.* **—a·phe·li·ot·ro·pism** (ə·fē′lē·ot′rə·piz′əm) *n.*

a·phe·mi·a (ə·fē′mē·ə) *n. Pathol.* A form of aphasia characterized by inability to name objects by speech, while retaining power to name them by writing. See SPEECH DISORDER. [<NL <Gk. *a-* without + *phēmē* voice] **—a·phem·ic** ə·fem′ik) *adj.*

a·phen·go·scope (ə·feng′gə·skōp) *n.* A epidiascope. [<Gk. *aphengēs* without light (<*a-* without + *phengos* light) + -SCOPE]

a·pher·e·sis (ə·fer′ə·sis) *n.* The dropping of an unaccented syllable or sound from the beginning of a word, as in *squire* for *esquire*: opposite of *apocope.* Also **a·phaer′e·sis.** [<L *aphaeresis* <Gk. *aphairesis* <*aphairein* take away <*apo-* away + *hairein* take] **—aph·e·ret·ic** (af′ə·ret′ik) *adj.*

aph·e·sis (af′ə·sis) *n.* The gradual, developmental loss of a short or unaccented vowel at the beginning of a word, as in *mend* for *amend*: a form of apheresis. [< NL <Gk., a letting go <*aphienai* <*apo-* from + *hienai* send] **—a·phet·ic** (ə·fet′ik) *adj.*

a·phid (ā′fid, af′id) *n.* Any of a family *(Aphididae)* of numerous, small, juice-sucking insects, injurious to plants; a plant louse. [<APHIS]

a·phis (ā′fis, af′is) *n. pl.* **aph·i·des** (af′ə·dēz) A member of a genus *(Aphis)* especially injurious to fruits and vegetables. [<NL; origin uncertain]

aph·lo·gis·tic (af′lō·jis′tik, ā′flō-) *adj.* Flameless; giving light by incandescence, as a lamp. [<Gk. *aphlogistos* not flammable]

a·pho·ni·a (ə·fō′nē·ə, ā-) *n. Pathol.* Loss of voice, especially when due to organic or structural causes; hoarseness. [<NL <Gk. *aphōnia* <*a-* without + *phōnē* voice]

a·phon·ic (ə·fon′ik, ā-) *adj.* **1** *Pathol.* Affected with or characterized by aphonia. **2** *Phonet.* **a** Not representing a sound; lacking pronunciation. **b** Voiceless.

aph·o·rism (af′ə·riz′əm) *n.* **1** A brief, sententious statement of a truth or principle. **2** A proverb; maxim; precept. See synonyms under ADAGE. [<F *aphorisme* <Med. L *aphorismus* <Gk. *aphorismos* definition <*aphorizein* mark off, define <*apo-* from + *horizein* divide <*horos* boundary]

aph·o·ris·mic (af′ə·riz′mik) *adj.* Having the form of an aphorism; containing or abounding in aphorisms. Also **—aph·o·ris·mat·ic** (af′ə·riz·mat′ik).

aph·o·rist (af′ə·rist) *n.* A maker or user of aphorisms. **—aph′o·ris′tic** or **·ti·cal** *adj.* **—aph′o·ris′ti·cal·ly** *adv.*

aph·o·rize (af′ə·rīz) *v.i.* **·rized, ·riz·ing** To write or speak in aphorisms.

a·pho·tic (ā·fō′tik) *adj.* Without light; dark. [<Gk. *aphōs, aphōtos* <*a-* without + *phōs* light]

aphotic region That portion of any body of water lying at a depth beyond the reach of sunight.

aph·ro·dis·i·a (af′rə·diz′ē·ə) *n. Pathol.* Excessive sexual desire.

aph·ro·dis·i·ac (af′rə·diz′ē·ak) *adj.* Arousing or increasing sexual desire or potency. *—n.* An aphrodisiac drug, food, etc. [<Gk. *aphrodisiakos* <*Aphroditē* goddess of love]

Aph·ro·di·te (af′rə·dī′tē) In Greek mythology, the daughter of Zeus and Dione, the goddess of love and beauty, said to have been born from the foam of the sea: identified with the Phoenician *Astarte* and the Roman *Venus.* [<Gk. *Aphroditē* the foam-born]

aph·ro·di·te (af′rə·dī′tē) *n.* A brilliantly colored butterfly *(Argynnis aphrodite)* of the United States.

aph·tha (af′thə) *n. pl.* **·thae** (-thē) *Pathol.* A small vesicle or speck, appearing in the mouth or stomach, caused by a fungous parasite. [<L <Gk.] **—aph′thous** *adj.*

aph·thoid (af′thoid) *adj.* Having the nature of or like an aphtha.

aph·tho·sis (af·thō′sis) *n. Pathol.* Any morbid condition marked by the presence of aphthae.

a·phyl·lous (ə·fil′əs, ā-) *adj. Bot.* Without leaves. Also **a·phyl·lose** (ə·fil′ōs, ā-). [<Gk. *aphyllos* <*a-* without + *phyllon* leaf]

a·phyl·ly (ə·fil′ē, ā-) *n. Bot.* Leaflessness.

A·pi·a (ä·pē′ä, ä′pē·ä) A port on Upolu Island, capital of Western Samoa.

a·pi·an (ā′pē·ən) *adj.* Of or pertaining to bees.

a·pi·ar·i·an (ā′pē·âr′ē·ən) *adj.* Of or relating to bees or the keeping of bees. *—n.* An apiarist.

a·pi·a·rist (ā′pē·ə·rist) *n.* A beekeeper.

a·pi·ar·y (ā′pē·er′ē) *n. pl.* **·ar·ies** **1** A place where bees are kept. **2** A set of hives, bees, and equipment. [<L *apiarium* <*apis* bee]

ap·i·cal (ap′i·kəl, ā′pi-) *adj.* **1** Situated at or belonging to the apex or top, as of a conical figure. **2** *Phonet.* Describing those consonants produced with the tip of the tongue, as (t), (d), and (s). Also **a·pi·cial** (ə·pish′əl). [<L *apex, apicis* tip]

apical cell *Bot.* In many cryptogamous plants, the cell which terminates the apex of roots and stems.

ap·i·ces (ap′ə·sēz, ā′pə-) A plural of APEX.

a·pi·cul·ture (ā′pi·kul′chər) *n.* Beekeeping. [<L *apis* bee + CULTURE] **—a′pi·cul′tur·ist** *n.*

a·pic·u·lus (ə·pik′yə·ləs) *n. pl.* **·li** (-lī) *Bot.* The point terminating a leaf. [<NL, dim. of L *apex* tip] **—a·pic′u·late** (-lit, -lāt) *adj.*

a·piece (ə·pēs′) *adv.* For each person or thing; to each one; each.

à pied (à pye′) *French* On foot.

a·pi·ol·o·gy (ā′pē·ol′ə·jē) *n.* The study of bees. [<L *apis* bee + -(O)LOGY]

A·pis (ā′pis) A sacred bull worshiped by the ancient Egyptians. See SERAPIS.

ap·ish (ā′pish) *adj.* Like an ape; servilely imitative; foolish and tricky. **—ap′ish·ly** *adv.* **—ap′ish·ness** *n.*

A·pi·um (ā′pē·əm, ap′ē·əm) *n.* A genus of umbelliferous succulent herbs; celery. [<L, parsley]

a·piv·o·rous (ā·piv′ər·əs) *adj. Zool.* Bee-eating. [<L *apis* bee + -VOROUS]

a·pla·cen·tal (ā′plə·sen′təl, ap′lə-) *adj. Zool.* Without a placenta; implacental, as the monotremes and marsupials.

ap·la·nat·ic (ap′lə·nat′ik) *adj. Optics* Free from spherical or chromatic aberration. [<A-[4] not + *planatikos* wandering]

a·pla·sia (ə·plā′zhə, -zhē·ə) *n. Pathol.* **1** Partial or complete failure of tissue to grow. **2** Arrested development of parts of the body; congenital atrophy. [<NL <Gk. *a-* without + *plasis* a molding]

a·plas·tic (ā·plas′tik) *adj. Pathol.* Lacking the power of normal growth.

a·plomb (ə·plom′, *Fr.* à·plôṅ′) *n.* Assurance; self-confidence. [<F, perpendicularity, assurance <*à* according to + *plomb* plummet]

ap·noe·a (ap·nē′ə) *n. Pathol.* Suspension of respiration, partial or entire; suffocation. Also **ap·ne′a.** [<NL <Gk. *apnoia* <*a-* without + *pnoiē, pnoē* breath] **—ap·noe′al, ap·noe′ic** *adj.*

A·po (ä′pō), **Mount** A volcano in SE Mindanao; highest peak in the Philippines; 9,690 feet.

apo- *prefix* **1** Off; from; away: *apostasy.* **2** *Chem.* Used to indicate a derived compound: *apomorphine.* Also: *ap-* before vowels, as in *apagoge*; *aph-* before an aspirate, as in *aphelion.* [<Gk. <*apo* from, off]

a·poc·a·lypse (ə·pok′ə·lips) *n.* A prophecy or disclosure; any remarkable revelation. [<L *apocalypsis* <Gk. *apokalypsis* <*apokalyptein* disclose <*apo-* from + *kalyptein* cover] **—a·poc′·a·lyp′tic** (-lip′tik) or **·ti·cal** *adj.* **—a·poc′·a·lyp′ti·cal·ly** *adv.*

A·poc·a·lypse (ə·pok′ə·lips) The book of Revelation, the last book of the New Testament.

ap·o·carp (ap′ə·kärp) *n. Bot.* A gynoecium having separate carpels, as the distinct ovaries of the crowfoot family. [<APO- distinct + Gk. *karpos* fruit] **—ap′o·car′pous** *adj.*

ap·o·chro·mat·ic (ap′ə·krō·mat′ik) *adj. Optics* More exactly achromatic than an ordinary achromatic lens. **—ap′o·chro′ma·tism** (-krō′·mə·tiz′əm) *n.*

a·poc·o·pate (ə·pok′ə·pāt) *v.t.* **·pat·ed, ·pat·ing** To shorten by apocope. *—adj.* (ə·pok′ə·pit) Shortened by apocope. Also **a·poc′o·pat′ed** (-pā′·tid). **—a·poc′o·pa′tion** *n.*

a·poc·o·pe (ə·pok′ə·pē) *n.* A cutting off or elision of the last sound or syllable of a word. [<Gk. *apokopē* <*apokoptein* cut off <*apo-* off + *koptein* cut]

ap·o·crus·tic (ap′ə·krus′tik) *adj.* Having the power to repel; astringent. [<NL *apocrusticus* <Gk. *apokroustikos* <*apokrouein* beat off, repel]

A·poc·ry·pha (ə·pok′rə·fə) *n. pl.* **1** Fourteen books of the Septuagint in the Vulgate but not in the canonical Hebrew Scriptures nor in the Authorized Version. **2** One of the various collections of unauthenticated writings that abounded in the first and second centuries, proposed as additions to, but not admitted to the New Testament Gospels. [<LL, neut. pl. of *apocryphus* <Gk. *apokryphos* hidden <*apokryptein* <*apo-* away + *kryptein* hide] **—A·poc′ry·phal** *adj.*

a·poc·ry·phal (ə·pok′rə·fəl) *adj.* Of doubtful authenticity; spurious. **—a·poc′ry·phal·ly** *adv.* **—a·poc′ry·phal·ness** *n.*

a·poc·y·na·ceous (ə·pos′ə·nā′shəs) *adj. Bot.* Belonging to the dogbane family of herbaceous or woody plants *(Apocynaceae),* mainly tropical, with milky, mostly acrid juice and simple leaves, as Indian hemp, oleander, and periwinkle. [<NL *Apocynaceae* <Gk. *apokynon* dogbane <*apo-* from + *kyōn* dog]

a·poc·y·nin (ə·pos′ə·nin) *n. Chem.* An organic compound, $C_9H_{10}O_3$, forming one of the active principles of hemp dogbane. [<APOCYN(UM) + -IN]

A·poc·y·num (ə·pos′ə·nəm) *n.* Any of a genus of perennial herbs with a tough, fibrous bark and a milky juice, whose roots have medicinal qualities. [<NL, dogbane <Gk. *apo-* away + *kyōn, kynos* a dog]

ap·od (ap′əd) *n. Zool.* An animal without feet. Also **ap·o·dan** (ap′ə·dən). [<Gk. *apous, apodos* footless <*a-* without + *pous* foot]

ap·o·dac·tyl·ic (ap′ō·dak·til′ik) *adj. Pathol.* Without the use of the fingers. [<Gk. *apo-* away + *dactylos* a finger]

ap·o·dal (ap′ə·dəl) *adj. Zool.* **1** Without ventral fins. **2** Of or relating to an animal lacking distinct footlike appendages. **3** Of or relating to an order *(Apoda)* of holothurians without ambulacral feet.

ap·o·deic·tic (ap′ə·dīk′tik) *adj.* Apodictic. Also **ap′o·deic′ti·cal. —ap′o·deic′ti·cal·ly** *adv.*

ap·o·dic·tic (ap′ə·dik′tik) *adj.* Clearly demonstrable; indisputable. Also **ap′o·dic′ti·cal.** [<L *apodicticus* <Gk. *apodeiktikos* <*apodeiknynai* show by argument <*apo-* from + *deiknynai* show] **—ap′o·dic′ti·cal·ly** *adv.*

a·pod·o·sis (ə·pod′ə·sis) *n. pl.* **·ses** (-sēz) The conclusion in a conditional sentence; also, the clause expressing result in a sentence not conditional. [<Gk., a giving back <*apo-* back + *didonai* give]

a·pog·a·my (ə·pog′ə·mē) *n.* **1** *Bot.* **a** Absence of the sexual function in plants. **b** The development of the mature plant from the prothallium without intervention of sexual organs, as in certain of the higher cryptogams. **2** *Biol.* In evolution, the mating and interbreeding of segregated groups that do not differ significantly in character from other groups of their kind. [<APO- + Gk. *gamos* marriage] **—ap·o·gam·ic** (ap′ə·gam′ik) *adj.* **—a·pog′a·mous** *adj.*

ap·o·gee (ap′ə·jē) *n.* **1** *Astron.* The point in the orbit of the moon or of an artificial satellite where it is farthest from the earth; opposed to *perigee.* **2** The highest point; climax. [<F *apogée* <Gk. *apogaiou* <*apo-* away from + *gē, gaia* earth] **—ap·o·ge·al** (ap′ə·jē′əl), **ap′·o·ge′an** *adj.*

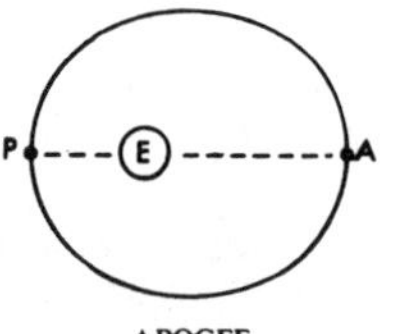

APOGEE
P. Perigee. *E.* Earth. *A.* Apogee.

ap·o·ge·ot·ro·pism (ap′ə·jē·ot′rə·piz′əm) *n. Bot.* The tendency to grow away from the earth, in opposition to gravitation, as plant stems and tree trunks; negative geotropism: also called *ageotropism.* [<APO- + GEOTRO-

PISM] — **ap·o·ge·o·trop·ic** (ap′ə·jē′ə·trop′ik) *adj.*

à point (à pwaṅ′) *French* To the point; exactly; just enough.

A·pol·lo (ə·pol′ō) **1** In Greek and Roman mythology, the god of music, poetry, prophecy, and medicine; the type of manly youth and beauty, later identified with *Helios.* **2** Any handsome young man. [<L <Gk. *Apollōn*]

APOLLO
After the Apollo Belvedere in the Vatican.

Ap·ol·lo·ni·a (ap′ə·lō′nē·ə) An ancient port of western Cyrenaica on the Mediterranean.

Ap·ol·lo·ni·us Rho·di·us (ap′·ə·lō′nē·əs rō′dē·əs), late third to early second century B.C., Greek poet and grammarian.

A·pol·los (ə·pol′əs) First century Alexandrian Jew who continued the work of St. Paul at Corinth and Ephesus. *Acts* xviii 24.

A·pol·lyon (ə·pol′yən) The angel of the bottomless pit. *Rev.* ix 11. See also ABADDON. [<Gk. *apollyōn* destroying <*apollyein* destroy completely]

ap·o·log (ap′ə·lôg, -log) *n.* A fable or moral tale. Also **ap′o·logue.** See synonyms under FICTION. [<L *apologus* <Gk. *apologos* <*apo-* from + *logos* speech]

a·pol·o·get·ic (ə·pol′ə·jet′ik) *adj.* **1** Of the nature of an apology; excusing. **2** Defending or explaining. Also **a·pol′o·get′i·cal.** —*n.* An apology or defense. [<F *apologétique* <L *apologeticus* <Gk. *apologētikos* <*apologia* a speech in defense. See APOLOGY.] — **a·pol′o·get′i·cal·ly** *adv.*

a·pol·o·get·ics (ə·pol′ə·jet′iks) *n.* That branch of theology which deals with the defensive facts and proofs of Christianity.

ap·o·lo·gi·a (ap′ə·lō′jē·ə) *n.* A justification or defense. [<L <Gk.]

a·pol·o·gist (ə·pol′ə·jist) *n.* One who argues in defense of any person or cause.

a·pol·o·gize (ə·pol′ə·jīz) *v.i.* **·gized, ·giz·ing** **1** To offer or make excuse; acknowledge, with regret, any fault or offense. **2** To make a justification or formal defense in speech or writing. — **a·pol′o·giz′er** *n.*

a·pol·o·gy (ə·pol′ə·jē) *n. pl.* **·gies** **1** A formal acknowledgment, as of error, offense, or incivility. **2** Originally, a justification or defense. **3** A poor substitute. [<L *apologia* <Gk. *apologia* a speech in defense <*apo-* from + *logos* speech]

Synonyms: acknowledgment, confession, defense, exculpation, excuse, justification, plea, vindication. According to its present meaning, he who offers an *apology* admits himself, at least technically and seemingly, in the wrong. An *excuse* for a fault is an attempt at partial justification; as, one alleges haste as an *excuse* for carelessness. *Acknowledgment* is neutral, and may be either of fact, duty, obligation, etc., or of error or fault. *Confession* is a full *acknowledgment* of wrong, generally of a grave wrong, with or without *apology* or *excuse.* Compare CONFESS, DEFENSE. *Antonyms*: accusation, censure, charge, complaint, condemnation, imputation, injury, insult, offense, wrong.

ap·o·mix·is (ap′ə·mik′sis) *n.* **1** *Biol.* Parthenogenesis. **2** *Bot.* Reproduction from cells other than ovules. [<NL <APO- from + Gk. *mixis* a mingling] — **ap′o·mic′tic** (-mik′·tik) *adj.*

ap·o·mor·phine (ap′ə·môr′fēn, -fin) *n. Med.* A crystalline alkaloid, $C_{17}H_{17}O_2N$, obtained from morphine by removing one molecule of water: used as an emetic and expectorant.

ap·o·neu·ro·sis (ap′ə·nōō·rō′sis, -nyōō-) *n. pl.* **·ses** (-sēz) *Anat.* The white fibrous tissue investing or forming the end or attachment of certain muscles. [<Gk. *aponeurōsis* <*apo-* from + *neuron* a nerve] — **ap′o·neu·rot′ic** (-rot′ik) *adj.*

ap·o·pemp·tic (ap′ə·pemp′tik) *adj.* Bidding farewell; valedictory. —*n.* A farewell hymn or ode. [<Gk. *apopemptikos* <*apopempein* send away <*apo-* away + *pempein* send]

ap·o·pet·al·ous (ap′ə·pet′əl·əs) *adj. Bot.* Polypetalous; having separated petals.

a·poph·a·sis (ə·pof′ə·sis) *n.* A mentioning of something by denying that it will be mentioned. *Example*: I will not remind you of the following instance of his heroism. [<NL <Gk. *apophasis* denial <*apophanai* speak out, deny <*apo-* away + *phanai* speak]

ap·o·phthegm (ap′ə·them), etc. See APOTHEGM, etc.

a·poph·y·ge (ə·pof′ə·jē) *n. Archit.* **1** A concave curve in a column where the shaft rises from the base or joins the capital. **2** A hollow molding immediately below the echinus of some Doric capitals. [<Gk. *apophygē* escape <*apopheugein* flee away <*apo-* away + *pheugein* flee]

a·poph·yl·lite (ə·pof′ə·līt, ap′ə·fil′īt) *n. Chem.* A white, crystalline silicate of calcium and hydrogen, sometimes containing potassium and calcium. [<APO- + Gk. *phyllon* leaf + -ITE[1]]

ap·o·phyl·lous (ap′ə·fil′əs) *adj. Bot.* Composed of distinct floral leaves: said of a perianth. [<APO- + Gk. *phyllon* leaf]

a·poph·y·sis (ə·pof′ə·sis) *n. pl.* **·ses** (-sēz) **1** *Anat.* A bony protuberance, as of a vertebra. **2** *Zool.* In arthropods, any hardened process of the body wall. **3** *Geol.* A branching offshoot from an intrusion of igneous rock. [<NL <Gk. *apophysis* branch, offshoot <*apo-* from + *phyein* grow]

ap·o·plec·tic (ap′ə·plek′tik) *adj.* Pertaining to, affected with, or tending toward apoplexy. Also **ap′o·plec′ti·cal.** —*n.* A person subject to apoplexy.

ap·o·plex (ap′ə·pleks) *v.t. Obs.* To strike with apoplexy.

ap·o·plex·y (ap′ə·plek′sē) *n. Pathol.* **1** Sudden loss or diminution of sensation and of the power of voluntary motion, due to an acute vascular lesion of the brain, as from hemorrhage; a stroke of paralysis. **2** A sudden discharge of blood within an organ. [<OF *apoplexie* <L *apoplexia* <Gk. *apoplēxia* <*apoplēssein* disable by a stroke <*apo-* from, off + *plēssein* strike]

a·port (ə·pôrt′, ə·pōrt′) *adj. Naut.* On or toward the left or port side of a ship.

ap·o·sep·al·ous (ap′ə·sep′əl·əs) *adj. Bot.* Polysepalous.

ap·o·si·o·pe·sis (ap′ə·sī′ə·pē′sis) *n.* A sudden interruption of a thought in the middle of a sentence, as if the speaker or writer were unable or unwilling to continue. *Example*: When I perceived the delights of paradise — but who could describe them? [<L <Gk. *aposiōpēsis* <*aposiōpaein* <*apo-* from + *siōpaein* be silent] — **ap′o·si′o·pet′ic** (-pet′ik) *adj.*

a·pos·po·ry (ə·pos′pər·ē) *n. Bot.* **1** A loss of the sporogenous function. **2** The development of a new organism from or near the spore-producing organ without the intervention of spores, as in some ferns. [<APO- + SPORE] — **a·pos′po·rous** *adj.*

a·pos·ta·sy (ə·pos′tə·sē) *n. pl.* **·sies** Desertion of one's faith, religion, party, or principles. Also **a·pos′ta·cy.** [<L *apostasia* <Gk. *apostasia* a standing off, desertion <*apo-* away + *stasis* a standing]

a·pos·tate (ə·pos′tāt, -tit) *adj.* Guilty of apostasy; false. —*n.* One who apostatizes.

a·pos·ta·tize (ə·pos′tə·tīz) *v.i.* **·tized, ·tiz·ing** To forsake one's faith or principles.

ap·o·stem (ap′ə·stem) *n. Pathol.* An abscess. Also **ap′o·steme** (-stēm). [<Gk. *apostēma* separation (i.e., of pus) <*apostēnai* stand off <*apo-* from + *stēnai* stand]

a·pos·te·mate (ə·pos′tə·māt) *v.i.* **·mat·ed, ·mat·ing** *Obs.* To form an abscess.

a pos·te·ri·o·ri (ā′ pos·tir′ē·ôr′ī, -ō′rī) **1** Reasoning from facts to principles or from effect to cause: opposed to *a priori.* **2** Inductive; empirical. [<L, from what comes after]

a·pos·til (ə·pos′til) *n.* A marginal note; annotation. Also **a·pos′tille.** [<F *apostille*]

a·pos·tle (ə·pos′əl) *n.* **1** One of the twelve disciples originally commissioned by Christ to preach the gospel (*Matt.* x 2–4); later also denoting Matthias, who replaced Judas Iscariot (*Acts* i 26), and Paul (*Rom.* i 1). **2** One of a class of missionaries or preachers in the early church (1 *Cor.* xii 28). **3** A Christian missionary who first evangelizes a nation or place. **4** The earliest or foremost advocate of a cause. **5** In the Mormon Church, one of the twelve members of the church's administrative council. See PRESIDENCY (def. 4). [OE *apostol* <L *apostolus* <Gk. *apostolos* one sent forth, a messenger <*apostellein* <*apo-* from + *stellein* send] — **a·pos′tle·ship, a·pos·to·late** (ə·pos′tə·lit, -lāt) *n.*

Apostles' Creed A traditional and still widely accepted Christian confession of faith, beginning "I believe in God the Father Almighty": originally attributed to the twelve apostles, but now assigned to the fourth or fifth century.

ap·os·tol·ic (ap′ə·stol′ik) *adj.* **1** Of or pertaining to an apostle, the apostles, or their times. **2** According to the doctrine or practice of the apostles. **3** *Often cap.* Papal. Also **ap′os·tol′i·cal.** — **ap′os·tol′i·cism** (-ə·siz′·əm) *n.* — **a·pos·to·lic·i·ty** (ə·pos′tə·lis′ə·tē) *n.*

Apostolic Constitutions A fourth century collection of writings on ecclesiastical matters, claiming apostolic authorship, its final section comprising a collection of 85 regulations on church discipline and worship, the **Apostolic Canons.**

Apostolic Fathers **1** A group of early Christian writers, including Clement of Rome, Ignatius, Polycarp, and others who were younger contemporaries of the apostles. **2** An ancient collection of writings attributed to them.

Ap·os·tol·i·ci (ap′ə·stol′ə·sī) *n. pl.* **1** A third century Gnostic sect practicing a strict asceticism for which they claimed apostolic precedent. **2** A similar German sect of the 12th century. **3** An Italian sect of the 13th and 14th centuries which advocated absolute poverty and attacked the worldliness of the church. **4** An Anabaptist sect which practiced ceremonially the washing of feet. [<L, apostolic <*apostolus* APOSTLE]

apostolic see Any church or bishopric originally founded by an apostle.

Apostolic See **1** The Church of Rome, regarded as having been founded by St. Peter. **2** The papacy.

apostolic succession The regular and uninterrupted transmission of spiritual authority from the apostles, claimed for their bishops by the Anglican, Greek, Roman Catholic, and some other churches.

a·pos·tro·phe[1] (ə·pos′trə·fē) *n.* **1** A symbol (') above the line, to mark the omission of a letter or letters from a word, to indicate the possessive case, the end of a quotation, or the plural of figures or letters. **2** The omission so indicated. [<F <L *apostrophus* <Gk. *apostrophos*] — **ap·os·troph·ic** (ap′ə·strof′ik) *adj.*

a·pos·tro·phe[2] (ə·pos′trə·fē) *n.* **1** A digression from a discourse; specifically, a turning aside, as from an audience, to speak to an imaginary or absent person, an attribute, or the Deity. **2** *Bot.* The arrangement of chlorophyll granules (as on the lateral walls of leaf cells) when exposed to strong light: opposed to *epistrophe.* [<L <Gk. *apostrophē* a turning away <*apostrephein* <*apo-* from + *strephein* turn] — **ap·os·troph·ic** (ap′ə·strof′ik) *adj.*

a·pos·tro·phize[1] (ə·pos′trə·fīz) *v.i.* **·phized, ·phiz·ing** To use the apostrophe; shorten a word by omission.

a·pos·tro·phize[2] (ə·pos′trə·fīz) *v.t. & v.i.* **·phized, ·phiz·ing** To address by or in a rhetorical apostrophe; to speak or write an apostrophe. See synonyms under ADDRESS.

apothecaries' measure A system of liquid measure used in pharmacy. Units and values as used in the United States are as follows:

60 minims	=	1 fluid dram
8 fluid drams	=	1 fluid ounce
4 fluid ounces	=	1 gill
4 gills	=	1 pint
2 pints	=	1 quart
4 quarts	=	1 gallon

a·poth·e·car·y (ə·poth′ə·ker′ē) *n. pl.* **·car·ies** One who keeps drugs for sale and puts up prescriptions; a druggist; pharmacist. [<LL *apothecarius* storekeeper <L *apotheca* storehouse <Gk. *apothēkē* <*apotithenai* put away <*apo-* away + *tithenai* put]

ap·o·the·ci·um (ap′ə·thē′shē·əm, -sē·əm) *n. pl.* **·ci·a** (-shē·ə, -sē·ə) *Bot.* An open, more or less cup-shaped fruit body in which the asci–

bearing layer lies exposed during the maturing of the asci; an ascocarp. Also **ap·o·the·ce** (ap′ə·thē′sē, ap′ə·thēs). [<NL <Gk. *apothēkē* storehouse] —**ap′o·the′cial** (-shəl) *adj.*

ap·o·thegm (ap′ə·them) *n.* A terse, instructive, practical saying; a sententious maxim: also spelled *apophthegm.* See synonyms under ADAGE. [<Gk. *apophthegma* a thing uttered, a terse saying < *apophthengesthai* < *apo-* from + *phthengesthai* speak, utter] —**ap·o·theg·mat·ic** (ap′ə·theg·mat′ik) or **·i·cal** *adj.*

ap·o·them (ap′ə·them) *n. Geom.* The perpendicular from the center to any side of a regular polygon. [<APO- + Gk. *thema* that which is placed < *tithenai* place]

a·poth·e·o·sis (ə·poth′ē·ō′sis, ap′ə·thē′ə·sis) *n. pl.* **·ses** (-sēz) **1** Exaltation to divine honors; deification. **2** Supreme exaltation of any person, principle, etc., as if to divine honor. [<L <Gk. *apotheōsis* < *apo-* from + *theos* a god]

a·poth·e·o·size (ə·poth′ē·ə·sīz′, ap′ə·thē′ə·sīz) *v.t.* **·sized, ·siz·ing** **1** To deify. **2** To glorify.

ap·o·tro·pa·ism (ap′ə·trō·pā′iz·əm) *n.* In folklore, the warding off of evil by incantations or ritual acts. [<Gk. *apotropaios* averting evil < *apo-* away + *trepein* turn]

ap·pal (ə·pôl′) *v.t.* **ap·palled, ap·pal·ling** To fill with dismay or horror; terrify; shock. Also **ap·pall′.** See synonyms under FRIGHTEN. [<OF *apallir* become or make pale < *a-* to (<L *ad-*) + *pale* pale <L *pallidus.* See PALE, PALLID.]

Ap·pa·la·chi·an (ap′ə·lā′chē·ən, -chən, -lach′ən) *adj.* Of or pertaining to the Appalachian Mountains.

Appalachian Mountains A mountain system of eastern North America extending from Quebec to Alabama; highest peak, 6,684 feet.

Appalachian tea **1** The leaves of either of two shrubs, the inkberry and the withe rod, used for tea in some localities of the United States. **2** Either of these two plants.

Appalachian Trail A footpath for hikers, extending 2,050 miles along the crests of the Appalachian system from Maine to Georgia.

ap·pall·ing (ə·pô′ling) *adj.* Causing or apt to cause dismay or terror. —**ap·pall′ing·ly** *adv.*

ap·pa·loo·sa (ap′əlōō′sə) *n. Often cap.* One of a breed of Western saddle horses having a characteristically mottled appearance. [Prob. after *Palouse* Indians of the northwest]

ap·pa·nage (ap′ə·nij) *n.* **1** A dependent territory or property. **2** A natural accompaniment, attribute, or endowment. **3** A portion of land assigned by a king for support of his younger sons; the public allowance to the prince of a reigning house: also *apanage.* [<F *apanage* <OF *apaner* nourish <L *ad-* to + *panis* bread]

ap·pa·ra·tus (ap′ə·rā′təs, -rat′əs) *n. pl.* **·tus** or (rarely) **·tus·es** **1** A complex device or machine for a particular purpose: an X-ray *apparatus.* **2** An integrated assembly of tools, appliances, instruments, etc., operating to achieve a specified result. **3** *Physiol.* Those organs and parts of the body by means of which natural processes are carried on: digestive *apparatus.* [<L, preparation < *apparare* make ready < *ad-* to + *parare* prepare]

ap·pa·ra·tus bel·li (ap′ə·rā′təs bel′ī) *Latin* Materials of war.

apparatus crit·i·cus (krit′i·kəs) *Latin* Books, etc., used in literary work.

ap·par·el (ə·par′əl) *n.* **1** Raiment; clothing. **2** *Eccl.* Any oblong piece of embroidery ornamenting the alb and amice. **3** Things provided for special use; arrangements or furnishings, especially for a ship or a house. See synonyms under DRESS. —*v.t.* **·eled** or **·elled, ·el·ing** or **·el·ling** **1** To clothe; dress. **2** *Archaic* To deck or equip. [<OF *apareil* preparation, provision < *apareiller* prepare, ult. <L *ad-* to + *par* equal]

ap·par·ent (ə·par′ənt, ə·pâr′-) *adj.* **1** Clearly perceived or perceivable; clear; evident; obvious; manifest; also, visible. **2** Seeming, in distinction from real or true. [<OF *aparant,* ppr. of *aparoir* appear <L *apparere.* See APPEAR.] —**ap·par′en·cy** *n.*

Synonyms: likely, presumable, probable, seeming. The *apparent* is that which appears, either that which is manifest, visible, certain, or that which is merely in seeming; as, the *apparent* motion of the sun around the earth. *Apparent* indicates less assurance than *probable* and more than *seeming.* See EVIDENT. *Antonyms*: doubtful, dubious, improbable, unimaginable, unlikely.

ap·par·ent·ly (ə·par′ənt·lē, ə·pâr′-) *adv.* Obviously or seemingly. Abbr. *appar.*

ap·pa·ri·tion (ap′ə·rish′ən) *n.* **1** A specter; phantom; ghost. **2** Any appearance, especially if remarkable; a phenomenon. **3** The act of appearing, or the state of being visible. **4** *Astron.* The period for most favorable observation of a planet, comet, or other heavenly body. [<MF <L *apparitio, -onis* < *apparere.* See APPEAR.] —**ap′pa·ri′tion·al** *adj.*

ap·par·i·tor (ə·par′ə·tər, ə·pâr′-) *n.* **1** Formerly, an official of a civil court. **2** In ecclesiastical law, an official who serves summonses and executes the processes of an ecclesiastical court. **3** *Brit.* The beadle of a university. [<L < *apparere* appear]

ap·par·te·ment (à·pàrt·mäṅ′) *French* Living quarters; an apartment.

ap·peach (ə·pēch′) *v.t. Obs.* To impeach; accuse. [ME *apechen,* var. of *empechen* <OF *empechier.* See IMPEACH.]

ap·peal (ə·pēl′) *n.* **1** An earnest entreaty for aid, sympathy, or the like; prayer; supplication. **2** A quality or manner which elicits sympathy or attraction. **3** A resort to some higher power or final means, for sanction, proof, or aid. **4** *Law* **a** The carrying of a cause from a lower to a higher tribunal for a rehearing (see COURT OF APPEALS under COURT). **b** The right to do this. **c** A request to do this. **d** A case so carried. **4** In old English law, the accusation of a criminal by an accomplice. **5** In any parliamentary body, a reference to the house of a disputed decision made by the chairman. See synonyms under ADDRESS, PLEA, SUIT. —*v.t.* **1** *Law* To refer or remove, as a case, to a higher court. **2** *Archaic* To challenge. —*v.i.* **3** To make an earnest supplication or request, as for sympathy, corroboration, or aid. **4** To awaken a favorable response; be interesting: Does this idea *appeal* to you? **5** *Law* To remove a case, or request that a case be moved, to a higher court. **6** To resort to or have recourse: with *to*: to *appeal* to reason to solve a difficulty. [<OF *apeler* <L *appellare* accost, call upon, var. of *appellere* < *ad-* to + *pellere* drive] —**ap·peal′a·ble** *adj.* —**ap·peal′er** *n.* —**ap·peal′ing·ly** *adv.*

ap·pear (ə·pir′) *v.i.* **1** To come forth into view or public notice; become visible, plain, public, or certain. **2** To be visible. **3** To be published, as a book or other writing. **4** To seem, or seem likely. **5** *Law* To come into court in person or by attorney, and submit or object to its jurisdiction in a given cause. [<OF *aparoir* <L *apparere* < *ad-* to + *parere* come forth, appear]

ap·pear·ance (ə·pir′əns) *n.* **1** External show or aspect. **2** That which appears or seems; semblance. **3** *pl.* Circumstances or indications collectively. **4** A becoming manifest or public; advent; publication. **5** A coming formally into court. **6** A phenomenon. See synonyms under AIR[1], MANNER.

ap·pease (ə·pēz′) *v.t.* **ap·peased, ap·peas·ing** **1** To reduce or bring to peace; placate; soothe, as by making concessions or yielding to demands. **2** To bribe, as an aggressor nation, with territorial or political concessions in order to avoid war or a break in diplomatic relations. **3** To satisfy or allay: *Appease* your hunger with this bread. See synonyms under ALLAY. [<OF *apaisier* < *a-* to (<L *ad-*) + *pais* peace <L *pax*] —**ap·peas′a·ble** *adj.* —**ap·peas′a·bly** *adv.* —**ap·peas′er** *n.* —**ap·peas′ing·ly** *adv.* —**ap·pea·sive** (ə·pē′siv) *adj.*

ap·pease·ment (ə·pēz′mənt) *n.* **1** The act of placating or pacifying. **2** The policy of making territorial or other concessions to potential aggressors in order to maintain peace.

ap·pel (à·pel′) *n.* **1** In fencing, a feint, often accompanied by a stamp of the foot, to procure an opening. **2** In diplomatic correspondence, the salutation of the person addressed, as Sire, Excellency, etc. [<F, lit., a call]

ap·pel·la·ble (ə·pel′ə·bəl) *adj.* Appealable. —**ap·pel′la·bil′i·ty, ap·pel·lan·cy** (ə·pel′ən·sē) *n.*

ap·pel·lant (ə·pel′ənt) *adj. Law* Of or pertaining to an appeal; appellate. —*n.* One who appeals, in any sense.

ap·pel·late (ə·pel′it) *adj. Law* Pertaining to or having jurisdiction of appeals: an *appellate* court. [<L *appellatus,* pp. of *appellare.* See APPEAL.]

ap·pel·la·tion (ap′ə·lā′shən) *n.* **1** A name or title. **2** The act of calling or naming. See synonyms under NAME.

ap·pel·la·tive (ə·pel′ə·tiv) *adj.* **1** Serving to designate or name. **2** Denoting a class, as common nouns. —*n.* **1** A title; appellation. **2** A common noun. —**ap·pel′la·tive·ly** *adv.* —**ap·pel′la·tive·ness** *n.*

ap·pel·la·to·ry (ə·pel′ə·tôr′ē, -tō′rē) *adj.* Containing an appeal.

ap·pel·lee (ap′ə·lē′) *n. Law* One against whom an appeal is taken; a defendant. [<F *appelé,* pp. of *appeler* appeal]

ap·pel·lor (ə·pel′ôr, ap′ə·lôr′) *n.* In old English law, a confessed criminal who accused an accomplice. [<AF *apelour,* OF *apeleor* <L *appellator* one who appeals < *appellare.* See APPEAL.]

ap·pend (ə·pend′) *v.t.* **1** To add, as something subordinate or supplemental. **2** To hang or attach: to *append* a seal. See synonyms under ADD. [<L *appendere* < *ad-* to + *pendere* hang]

ap·pend·age (ə·pen′dij) *n.* **1** Anything appended; a subordinate addition or adjunct: a mere *appendage.* **2** *Biol.* **a** Any part joined to or diverging from the axial trunk or from any adjunct of it. **b** A subordinate or subsidiary part, as a limb, tail, leaf, hair, etc.

Synonyms: accessory, accompaniment, addendum, addition, adjunct, appendix, appurtenance, attachment, auxiliary, concomitant, extension, increase, supplement. An *adjunct* constitutes no real part of the thing or system to which it is joined; an *appendage* is commonly a real, but not an essential or necessary, part of that with which it is connected; an *appurtenance* belongs subordinately to something by which it is employed, especially as an instrument to accomplish some purpose. An *attachment* in machinery is some mechanism that can be brought into optional connection with the principal movement; a hemmer is an *attachment* of a sewing machine. An *extension,* as of a railroad or of a franchise, adds to something already existing. See SUPPLEMENT.

ap·pen·dant (ə·pen′dənt) *adj.* **1** Hanging; attached; adjunct. **2** Associated with in a subordinate capacity. **3** Related by cause or purpose; consequent. **4** *Law* Belonging to a land grant or tenure as an added but lesser right. —*n. Law* A subsidiary right attached to one more important. Also **ap·pen′dent.**

ap·pen·dec·to·my (ap′ən·dek′tə·mē) *n. pl.* **·mies** *Surg.* The excision of the vermiform appendix. Also **ap·pen·di·cec·to·my** (ə·pen′də·sek′tə·mē). [<APPENDIX + -ECTOMY]

ap·pen·di·ceal (ap′ən·dish′əl, ə·pen′də·se′əl) *adj. Anat.* Of or relating to the vermiform appendix.

ap·pen·di·ces (ə·pen′də·sēz) A plural of APPENDIX.

ap·pen·di·ci·tis (ə·pen′də·sī′tis) *n. Pathol.* Inflammation of the vermiform appendix.

ap·pen·di·cle (ə·pen′di·kəl) *n.* A small appendage. [<L *appendicula,* dim. of *appendix*]

ap·pen·dic·u·lar (ap′ən·dik′yə·lər) *adj.* **1** Of, pertaining to, or being an appendage or appendicle; appendiculate. **2** *Anat.* Of or pertaining to the limbs or appendages.

ap·pen·dic·u·late (ap′ən·dik′yə·lit, -lāt) *adj.* **1** Having appendages, as a leaf. **2** Of the nature of or forming an appendage.

ap·pen·dix (ə·pen′diks) *n. pl.* **·dix·es** or **·di·ces** (-də·sēz) **1** An addition or appendage, as of supplementary matter at the end of a book. **2** An appendage. **3** *Anat.* **a** The vermiform appendix. **b** A process or projection; an outgrowth or prolongation. **4** *Aeron.* A large tube hanging from a spherical balloon, through which the gas passes in or out. [<L, an appendage < *appendere.* See APPEND.]

Synonyms: addendum, addition, supplement. We add an *appendix* to a book, as a dictionary, to contain names, dates, lists, etc., which would encumber the text; we add a *supplement* to supply omissions, as, for instance, to bring it up to date. An *addition* might be matter interwoven in the body of the work, an index, plates, editorial notes, etc., which might be valuable *additions,* but are not within the meaning of *appendix* or *supplement.* See APPENDAGE.

appendix ver·mi·for·mis (vûr′mə·fôr′mis) See VERMIFORM APPENDIX.

ap·per·ceive (ap′ər·sēv′) *v.t.* **·ceived, ·ceiv·ing** *Psychol.* To perceive with conscious attention, integrating new experiences, concepts, ideas, etc., with the old. [<F *apercevoir* <L *ad-* to + *percipere.* See PERCEIVE.]

ap·per·cep·tion (ap′ər·sep′shən) *n.* **1** *Psychol.* **a** That kind of perception in which the mind is conscious of the act of perceiving. **b** The adding of other mental acts to perception proper, as interpretation, recognition, and classification. **c** An act of voluntary consciousness accompanied by self-consciousness; also, the coalescence of part of a new idea with an old one by modification. **2** The powers of intellect involved in the acquisition, conservation, and elaboration of knowledge; the understanding. [<F *aperception* <*apercevoir.* See APPERCEIVE.] **—ap′per·cep′tive** *adj.*

ap·per·son·a·tion (ə·pûr′sə·nā′shən) *n. Psychiatry* The compulsive identification with or impersonation of another person: noted in many mental disorders, especially dementia precox.

ap·per·tain (ap′ər·tān′) *v.i.* To pertain or belong as by custom, function, nature, right, or fitness; relate: with *to.* See synonyms under PERTAIN. [<OF *apertenir* <LL *appertinere* <*ad-* to + *pertinere.* See PERTAIN.]

ap·pe·tence (ap′ə·təns) **1** Strong craving or propensity. **2** Instinct or tendency: the *appetence* of ducks for water. **3** *Chem.* Affinity, as in atoms and molecules. Also **ap′pe·ten·cy.** See synonyms under APPETITE, DESIRE. [<L *appetentia* <*appetere.* See APPETITE.] **—ap′pe·tent** *adj.*

ap·pe·tite (ap′ə·tīt) *n.* **1** A desire for food or drink. **2** A craving or desire; strong liking. [<OF *appetit* <L *appetitus* <*appetere* strive for <*ad-* to + *petere* seek] **—ap′pe·ti′tive** *adj.*

Synonyms: appetence, craving, desire, disposition, impulse, inclination, liking, longing, lust, passion, proclivity, proneness, propensity, relish, thirst, zest. *Appetite* is used only of the demands of the physical system, unless otherwise expressly stated, as when we say an *appetite* for knowledge; *passion* includes all excitable impulses of our nature, as anger, fear, love, hatred, etc. *Appetite* is thus more animal than *passion*; we say an *appetite* for food, a *passion* for fame. Compare DESIRE. *Antonyms*: antipathy, aversion, detestation, disgust, dislike, disrelish, distaste, hatred, indifference, loathing, repugnance, repulsion. Compare ANTIPATHY.

ap·pe·tize (ap′ə·tīz) *v.t.* **·tized, ·tiz·ing** *Rare* To excite appetite or hunger in.

ap·pe·tiz·er (ap′ə·tī′zər) *n.* Anything that excites appetite or gives relish; specifically, food or drink served before a meal to stimulate the appetite. Also *Brit.* **ap′pe·tis′er.**

ap·pe·tiz·ing (ap′ə·tī′zing) *adj.* Giving relish; tempting to the appetite. Also *Brit.* **ap′pe·tis′ing. —ap′pe·tiz′ing·ly** *adv.*

Ap·pi·an (ap′ē·ən) *adj.* Pertaining to the Appii, a Roman family, or to any of its members.

Appian Way A paved road extending from Rome to Brundisium (modern *Brindisi*), begun in 312 B.C. by **Appius Claudius Caecus,** Roman consul, and still existing in part: Latin *Via Appia.*

Ap·pi·us Clau·di·us (ap′ē·əs klô′dē·əs) Roman consul and decemvir 451 B.C.

ap·plaud (ə·plôd′) *v.t.* & *v.i.* **1** To express approval, as of a performer, particularly by clapping the hands. **2** To commend; praise in an audible or visible manner. See synonyms under ADMIRE, PRAISE. [<L *applaudere* <*ad-* to + *plaudere* clap hands, strike] **—ap·plaud′er** *n.* **—ap·plaud′ing·ly** *adv.*

ap·plause (ə·plôz′) *n.* Acclamation; approval; praise; especially as shown by clapping the hands, shouting, etc. [<L *applausus,* pp. of *applaudere.* See APPLAUD.] **—ap·plau·sive** (ə·plô′siv) *adj.* **—ap·plau′sive·ly** *adv.*

Synonyms: acclaim, acclamation, cheering, cheers, eulogy, laudation, plaudit, praise. *Praise* is the expressed and hearty approval of an individual, or of a number or multitude, one by one; *applause,* the spontaneous outburst of many at once. *Applause* is expressed in any way, by clapping of hands, etc., as well as by the voice; *acclamation* is strictly by the voice alone. *Acclaim* is the more poetic term for *acclamation,* commonly understood in a loftier sense. *Plaudit* is a shout of *applause,* and is commonly used in the plural. See EULOGY, PRAISE. *Antonyms*: denunciation, derision, hissing, obloquy, scorn, vituperation.

ap·ple (ap′əl) *n.* **1** The fleshy edible fruit or pome of any variety of a widely distributed tree (*Malus malus*) of the rose family, usually of a roundish or conical shape with a depression at each end. **2** The similar fruit of several allied species of *Malus,* as *M. prunifolia* and *M. baccata,* the Siberian crab apple, and *M. coronaria,* the American crab apple. **3** A tree of any one of the species bearing apples as its natural fruit. **4** One of several fruits or plants with little or no resemblance to the apple: May *apple,* love *apple,* oak *apple,* etc. **5** In the Bible, the apple proper; also, a citron, apricot, pear, quince, or other fruit. [OE *æppel*]

apple blossom The flower of any species of the genus *Malus*: state flower of Arkansas and Michigan.

apple butter A thick, brown, spiced applesauce made from stewed apples.

apple cart A two-wheeled hand cart used for peddling apples, etc. **—to upset the apple cart** To ruin one's plans.

apple green A clear, light yellowish green.

ap·ple·jack (ap′əl·jak′) *n.* Brandy made from fermented cider.

ap·ple·john (ap′əl·jon′) *n. Obs.* A variety of apple considered to taste best when shriveled: said to ripen about St. John's Day: also called *John apple.*

apple of discord In Greek mythology, the golden apple inscribed "for the fairest," thrown among the gods by Eris; claimed by Hera, Aphrodite, and Athena, it was awarded by Paris to Aphrodite after she promised him Helen, fairest of women.

apple of Peru **1** An annual herb (*Nicandra physaloides*) of the nightshade family. **2** Jimsonweed.

apple of Sodom **1** The fruit of a plant said to have grown in the vicinity of the Dead Sea, of fair appearance, but disintegrating into ashes when plucked. **2** Hence, any bitter disappointment or disillusionment. Also called *Dead Sea fruit.*

apple of the eye **1** The pupil of the eye. **2** Something precious.

apple polisher *U.S. Slang* One who seeks favor by obsequious behavior, flattery, etc.

ap·ple·sauce (ap′əl·sôs′) *n.* **1** Apples stewed to a pulp. **2** *U.S. Slang* Nonsense; bunk.

Ap·ple·seed (ap′əl·sēd), **Johnny** Nickname of John Chapman, 1775?–1847, American pioneer, famous for distributing seeds to establish orchards in the Middle West.

Ap·ple·ton (ap′əl·tən), **Sir Edward Victor,** 1892–1965, English physicist.

Appleton layer A region of ionized air about 150 miles above sea level which acts as a reflector of certain wavelengths of sound: also called *F-layer.* [after E. V. *Appleton*]

ap·pli·ance (ə·plī′əns) *n.* **1** Something applied to effect a result; a machine or device; an instrument. **2** *Rare* An applying or being applied. **3** *Obs.* Compliance.

ap·pli·ca·ble (ap′li·kə·bəl) *adj.* Capable of or suitable for application; relevant; fitting. [<L *applicare* apply + -ABLE] **—ap′pli·ca·bil′i·ty, ap′pli·ca·ble·ness** *n.* **—ap′pli·ca·bly** *adv.*

ap·pli·cant (ap′li·kənt) *n.* One who applies, as for a position; a candidate.

ap·pli·ca·tion (ap′li·kā′shən) *n.* **1** The act of applying. **2** That which is applied, as a remedial agent. **3** That by which one applies; especially, a formal written request or demand; a requisition; request. **4** Appropriation to a particular use. **5** The testing or carrying into effect of a general law, truth, or precept by bringing it into relation with practical affairs; also, the capacity of being thus used. **6** The act, habit, or faculty of close and continuous attention. **7** The denoting or extending of a term, or the presenting of a proposition in a manner that combines logical strength with correctness of form. See synonyms under EXERCISE, INDUSTRY. [<L *applicatio, -onis* a joining to <*applicare.* See APPLY.]

ap·pli·ca·tive (ap′li·kā′tiv) *adj.* Applying or capable of being applied; pertaining to application; applicatory; practical.

ap·pli·ca·tor (ap′li·kā′tər) *n.* An instrument or utensil for applying medication, etc., in the form of liquids or pastes.

ap·pli·ca·to·ry (ap′li·kə·tôr′ē, -tō′rē) *adj.* **1** Fit for application. **2** Making application; practical.

ap·plied (ə·plīd′) *adj.* **1** Put in practice; utilized: opposed to *abstract* or *pure*: *applied* science. **2** Dealing with certain data or problems in a practical manner as opposed to a merely theoretical one: *applied* ethics.

ap·pli·er (ə·plī′ər) *n.* A person or thing that applies.

ap·pli·qué (ap′li·kā′) *adj.* Applied: said of ornaments, as in needlework, wood, metal, etc., cut out from one material and fastened to the surface of another. **—***n.* Decoration or ornaments so applied. **—***v.t.* **·quéd** (-kād′), **·qué·ing** (-kā′ing) To sew or decorate by sewing, as ornaments of one material to the surface of another. [<F]

ap·ply (ə·plī′) *v.* **ap·plied, ap·ply·ing** *v.t.* **1** To bring into contact with something; attach, as surfaces. **2** To devote or put to a particular use: to *apply* steam to navigation. **3** To connect, as an epithet, with a particular person or thing. **4** To give (oneself) wholly to; devote: to *apply* oneself to study. **—***v.i.* **5** To make a request or petition; ask: with *for*: to *apply* for a position. **6** To have reference or appropriate relation; belong naturally: Your orders don't *apply* in an emergency. [<OF *aplier* <L *applicare* join to <*ad-* to + *plicare* fold]

ap·pog·gia·tu·ra (ə·poj′ə·to͝or′ə, -tyo͝or′ə; *Ital.* äp·pôd′jä·to͞o′rä) *n. Music* An ornament consisting of a single note preceding another note. [<Ital. <*appoggiare* lean upon, rest]

ap·point (ə·point′) *v.t.* **1** To name or select, as a person for a position, a time and place for an act or meeting, etc. **2** To ordain, as by decree; command; prescribe: These laws are *appointed* by God. **3** To fit out; equip; furnish: used chiefly in the past participle: a *well-appointed* yacht. **4** *Law* To establish as a trustee or guardian. See synonyms under ALLOT, APPORTION, INSTITUTE, SET. [<OF *apointer* arrange, settle <LL *appunctare* <L *ad-* to + *punctum* a point]

ap·point·ee (ə·poin′tē′) *n.* One appointed to an office or position.

ap·point·ment (ə·point′mənt) *n.* **1** An appointing or being appointed; position or service to which one is or may be appointed; station; office. **2** An agreement, as for meeting at a given time; an engagement. **3** Something agreed upon; direction; decree. **4** Anything for use or adornment; equipment. **5** *Law* A power or right to control or designate the disposition of property. **6** *Obs.* Preparation.

Ap·po·mat·tox (ap′ə·mat′əks) A village and county in central Virginia. At **Appomattox Court House,** established in 1940 as a national monument, Lee surrendered to Grant, April 9, 1865, virtually ending the Civil War.

Appomattox River A river of central Virginia, flowing east 137 miles to the James River.

ap·por·tion (ə·pôr′shən, ə·pōr′-) *v.t.* To divide and assign proportionally; allot. [<OF *apportionner* <LL *apportionare* <L *ad-* to + *portio, -onis* portion]

Synonyms: allot, appoint, appropriate, assign, deal, dispense, distribute, divide, grant, share. To *allot* or *assign* may be to make an arbitrary division; the same is true of *distribute* or *divide.* That which is *apportioned* is given by some fixed rule, which is meant to be uniform and fair. To *dispense* is to give out freely; as, the sun *dispenses* light and heat. One may *apportion* what he only holds in trust; he *shares* what is his own. Compare ALLOT. *Antonyms*: collect, consolidate, receive, retain.

ap·por·tion·ment (ə·pôr′shən·mənt, ə·pōr′-) *n.* **1** An apportioning or being apportioned; any proportional division or allotment. **2** *U.S.* The decision by law as to the number of representatives that a state may have in the Federal House of Representatives, or that a county or other political subdivision may have in a state legislature.

ap·pose (ə·pōz′) *v.t.* **ap·posed, ap·pos·ing 1** To apply or put, as one thing to another: with *to*: *appose* a seal to a document. **2** To arrange side by side. [<F *apposer* <*a-* to (<L *ad-*) + *poser* put. See POSE[1].] **—ap·pos′a·ble** *adj.*

ap·po·site (ap′ə·zit) *adj.* **1** Fit for or well adapted to the purpose; appropriate; pertinent; relevant: an *apposite* simile. **2** Placed or being in apposition; apposed. [<L *appositus*, pp. of *apponere* put near to <*ad-* to + *ponere* put] **—ap′po·site·ly** *adv.* **—ap′po·site·ness** *n.*

ap·po·si·tion (ap′ə·zish′ən) *n.* **1** *Gram.* The placing of one substantive beside another to add to or explain the first, as in *John, president* of the class. **2** A placing or being in immediate connection; application; addition. **3** *Biol.* Growth or increase by juxtaposition, as of tissue. **—ap′po·si′tion·al** *adj.* **—ap′po·si′tion·al·ly** *adv.*

ap·pos·i·tive (ə·poz′ə·tiv) *adj.* In or pertaining to a state of apposition. **—***n.* A word or phrase in apposition. **—ap·pos′i·tive·ly** *adv.*

ap·prais·al (ə·prā′zəl) *n.* An appraising; official valuation. Also **ap·praise′ment.**

ap·praise (ə·prāz′) *v.t.* **ap·praised, ap·prais·ing 1** To make an official valuation of; set a price or value on, especially by authority of law or agreement of interested parties. **2** To estimate the amount, quality, or worth of; judge. [<AP-[1] + PRAISE] **—ap·prais′a·ble** *adj.* **—ap·prais′er** *n.*

ap·pre·ci·a·ble (ə·prē′shē·ə·bəl, -shə·bəl) *adj.* Capable of being valued or estimated. **—ap·pre′ci·a·bly** *adv.*

ap·pre·ci·ate (ə·prē′shē·āt) *v.* **·at·ed, ·at·ing** *v.t.* **1** To form an estimate of, as to quality, etc. **2** To estimate correctly or adequately. **3** To consider highly; be keenly aware of or sensitive to. **4** To show gratitude for. **5** To raise or increase the price or value of. **—***v.i.* **6** To rise in value. [<L *appretiatus*, pp. of *appretiare* appraise <*ad-* to + *pretium* price]

Synonyms: esteem, estimate, prize, value. A jeweler *estimates* an old ring as worth so much cash; the owner may *value* it beyond price, as a family heirloom, or he may *prize* it as the gift of an *esteemed* friend, without *appreciating* its commercial value. *Antonyms*: depreciate, despise, flout, misjudge, scorn, undervalue.

ap·pre·ci·a·tion (ə·prē′shē·ā′shən) *n.* **1** An appreciating; true or adequate estimation or recognition. **2** Increase in value.

ap·pre·ci·a·tive (ə·prē′shē·ā′tiv, -shə·tiv) *adj.* Capable of showing appreciation; manifesting appreciation. **—ap·pre′ci·a′tive·ly** *adv.* **—ap·pre′ci·a′tive·ness** *n.*

ap·pre·ci·a·tor (ə·prē′shē·ā′tər) *n.* **1** One who appreciates. **2** An apparatus by means of which the proportion of gluten in flour is determined.

ap·pre·ci·a·to·ry (ə·prē′shē·ə·tôr′ē, -tō′rē, -shə-) *adj.* Appreciative. **—ap·pre′ci·a·to′ri·ly** *adv.*

ap·pre·hend (ap′ri·hend′) *v.t.* **1** To lay hold of or grasp mentally; grasp a truth or statement; perceive. **2** To expect with anxious foreboding; look forward with fear or anxiety. **3** To arrest; seize in the name of the law. **4** *Obs.* To take hold of. [<L *apprehendere* <*ad-* to + *prehendere* seize] **—ap′pre·hend′er** *n.*

Synonyms: anticipate, arrest, catch, comprehend, conceive, grasp, imagine, know, perceive, understand. In strictness we *perceive* only what is presented through the senses. We *apprehend* what is presented to the mind by any means whatever. A child can *apprehend* the distinction between right and wrong, yet the philosopher cannot *comprehend* it in its fulness. Compare ALARM, IDEA. *Antonyms*: ignore, lose, misapprehend, miss, misunderstand, overlook.

ap·pre·hen·si·ble (ap′ri·hen′sə·bəl) *adj.* Capable of being apprehended. **—ap′pre·hen′si·bil′i·ty** *n.*

ap·pre·hen·sion (ap′ri·hen′shən) *n.* **1** Distrust or dread concerning the future; foreboding; misgiving; presentiment. **2** The power of apprehending; cognition; conception. **3** An estimate; idea; opinion. **4** Legal arrest. See synonyms under ALARM, ANTICIPATION, ANXIETY, FEAR, IDEA, KNOWLEDGE, UNDERSTANDING. [<L *apprehensio, -onis* < *apprehendere*. See APPREHEND.]

ap·pre·hen·sive (ap′ri·hen′siv) *adj.* **1** Anticipative of evil; anxious; fearful; suspicious. **2** Quick to apprehend. **3** Responsive to sense impressions. **4** Having cognizance; conscious. **—ap′pre·hen′sive·ly** *adv.* **—ap′pre·hen′sive·ness** *n.*

ap·pren·tice (ə·pren′tis) *n.* **1** One who is bound by a legal agreement to serve another for an agreed period of time in order to learn a trade or business. **2** Any learner or beginner. **—***v.t.* **·ticed, ·tic·ing** To bind or take on as an apprentice. [<OF *aprentis* < *aprendre* teach <L *apprehendere* comprehend. See APPREHEND.] **—ap·pren′tice·ship** *n.*

ap·pressed (ə·prest′) *adj. Bot.* Pressed or applied closely against something, as leaves against a stem. [<L *appressus*, pp. of *apprimere* <*ad-* to + *premere* press]

ap·pres·sor (ə·pres′ər) *n. Bot.* The expansion at the tip of the hyphae of certain parasitic fungi, by means of which they fasten on to the host. Also **ap·pres·so·ri·um** (ap′rə·sôr′ē·əm, -sō′rē-).

ap·prise (ə·prīz′) *v.t.* **ap·prised, ap·pris·ing** To notify, as of an event; inform: also spelled *apprize*. See synonyms under INFORM. [<F *appris*, pp. of *apprendre* teach, inform <L *apprehendere*. See APPREHEND.] **—ap·prise′ment** *n.* **—ap·pris′er** *n.*

ap·prize[1] (ə·prīz′) *v.t.* **ap·prized, ap·priz·ing** Appraise. Also **ap·prise′.**

ap·prize[2] (ə·prīz′) *v.t.* **ap·prized, ap·priz·ing** Apprise. **—ap·prize′ment** *n.* **—ap·priz′er** *n.*

ap·proach (ə·prōch′) *v.i.* **1** To come near or nearer in time or space. **—***v.t.* **2** To come or cause to come near or nearer to. **3** To make advances to; offer a solicitation, proposal, or bribe to. **4** To come close to; almost reach; approximate: to *approach* a solution; to *approach* Bluebeard in cruelty. **—***n.* **1** The act of approaching; a coming nearer. **2** Nearness; approximation. **3** Opportunity, means, or way of approaching; access. **4** Advances, as to acquaintance, etc.; also, the manner in which any advance is made: a kindly *approach*. **5** In golf, the stroke made after the tee shot, which lands the player's ball on the putting green. **6** *pl. Mil.* Constructed works, trenches, etc., by which besiegers attack a fortified position. See synonyms under APPROXIMATION. [<OF *aprochier* <LL *appropiare* <L *ad-* to + *prope* near] **—ap·proach′a·bil′i·ty, ap·proach′a·ble·ness** *n.* **—ap·proach′a·ble** *adj.*

ap·pro·bate (ap′rə·bāt) *v.t.* **·bat·ed, ·bat·ing 1** To approve. **2** To sanction formally or officially. See synonyms under PRAISE. [<L *approbatus*, pp. of *approbare*. See APPROVE.]

ap·pro·ba·tion (ap′rə·bā′shən) *n.* **1** The act of approving; approval; commendation. **2** *Eccl.* **a** Papal official approval of a religious order. **b** A bishop's official approval of a priest as confessor. **3** *Obs.* Proof; probation. See synonyms under PRAISE.

ap·pro·ba·tive (ap′rə·bā′tiv) *adj.* Expressing or implying approbation. Also **ap·pro·ba·to·ry** (ə·prō′bə·tôr′ē, -tō′rē). **—ap′pro·ba′tive·ness** *n.*

ap·pro·pri·a·ble (ə·prō′prē·ə·bəl) *adj.* That can be appropriated.

ap·pro·pri·ate (ə·prō′prē·it) *adj.* Suitable for or belonging to the person, circumstance, or place; fit; proper; relevant. **—***v.t.* (ə·prō′prē·āt) **·at·ed, ·at·ing 1** To set apart for a particular use. **2** To take for one's own use. See synonyms under ABSTRACT, APPORTION, ASSUME. [<L *appropriatus*, pp. of *appropriare* <*ad-* to + *proprius* one's own] **—ap·pro′pri·ate·ly** *adv.* **—ap·pro′pri·ate·ness** *n.* **—ap·pro′·pri·a′tive** *adj.* **—ap·pro′pri·a′tor** *n.*

Synonyms (adj.): adapted, apt, becoming, befitting, congruous, fit, meet, pertinent, proper, suitable. *Antonyms*: inappropriate, incongruous, irrelevant, unfit, unsuitable.

ap·pro·pri·a·tion (ə·prō′prē·ā′shən) *n.* **1** Something, as money, appropriated, or set apart, as by a legislature, for a special use. **2** An appropriating or being appropriated.

ap·prov·al (ə·prōō′vəl) *n.* **1** An approving or being approved; approbation. **2** Official consent; sanction. **3** Favorable opinion; praise; commendation. See synonyms under PRAISE. **—on approval** For (a customer's) examination without obligation to purchase.

ap·prove[1] (ə·prōōv′) *v.* **ap·proved, ap·prov·ing** *v.t.* **1** To regard as worthy, proper, or right; be favorably disposed toward. **2** To confirm formally or authoritatively; sanction; ratify. **3** To show or prove (oneself) worthy of approval. **4** *Obs.* To prove by trial; test. **—***v.i.* **5** To show or state approval: with *of*: He *approved* of my desire. See synonyms under ADMIRE, AGREE, ASSENT, JUSTIFY, LIKE, PRAISE, RATIFY. [<OF *aprover* <L *approbare* <*ad-* to + *probare* approve, prove <*probus* good] **—ap·prov′a·ble** *adj.* **—ap·prov′er** *n.* **—ap·prov′ing·ly** *adv.*

ap·prove[2] (ə·prōōv′) *v.t. Law* To turn to one's profit; appropriate, as waste or common land. [<OF *approuer* profit <*a* to + *pro* profit]

ap·prox·i·mal (ə·prok′sə·məl) *adj. Anat.* Close together: said of the surfaces of teeth.

ap·prox·i·mate (ə·prok′sə·mit) *adj.* **1** Nearly, but not exactly, accurate or complete. **2** Near. **—***v.* (ə·prok′sə·māt) **·mat·ed, ·mat·ing** *v.t.* **1** To bring close to or cause to approach closely, as in time, space, or condition, without exact coincidence. **2** *Math.* To calculate a value progressively closer to exactitude: to *approximate* the square root of 6. **—***v.i.* **3** To come near or close; be similar; That watch isn't the same as mine, but it *approximates*. [<L *approximatus*, pp. of *approximare* come near <*ad-* to + *proximus*, superl. of *prope* near] **—ap·prox′i·mate·ly** *adj.*

ap·prox·i·ma·tion (ə·prok′sə·mā′shən) *n.* **1** The act or process of approximating. **2** *Math.* A result sufficiently exact for a specified purpose.

Synonyms: approach, contiguity, likeness, nearness, neighborhood, propinquity, resemblance, similarity. *Approximation* expresses as near an approach to accuracy and certainty as the conditions in any given case make possible. *Resemblance* and *similarity* may be but superficial and apparent; *approximation* is real. *Approach* is a relative term, indicating that one has come nearer than before; *approximation* brings one really near. *Nearness, neighborhood,* and *propinquity* are commonly used of place; *approximation,* of mathematical calculations and abstract reasoning; we speak of *approach* to the shore, *nearness* to the town, *approximation* to the truth. *Antonyms*: difference, distance, error, remoteness, unlikeness, variation.

ap·prox·i·ma·tive (ə·prok′sə·mā′tiv, -mə·tiv) *adj.* Approaching almost to, but not quite; obtained by or involving approximation; approximate. **—ap·prox′i·ma′tive·ly** *adv.*

ap·pulse (ə·puls′) *n. Astron.* The approach of a heavenly body toward the meridian. [<L *appulsus* < *appellere* drive to <*ad-* to + *pellere* drive] **—ap·pul′sive** (-siv) *adj.*

ap·pul·sion (ə·pul′shən) *n.* The act of striking against.

ap·pur·te·nance (ə·pûr′tə·nəns) *n.* Something belonging or attached to something else as an accessory or adjunct. See synonyms under APPENDAGE. [<AF *apurtenance*, OF *apertenance* <L *appertinere*. See APPERTAIN.]

ap·pur·te·nant (ə·pûr′tə·nənt) *adj.* Appertaining or belonging, as by right; accessory. **—***n.* An appurtenance.

A·pra Harbor (ä′prä) A harbor on the west coast of Guam: site of a United States naval base: also *Port Apra*.

a·prax·i·a (ə·prak′sē·ə, ā-) *n. Psychiatry* The inability to use or to understand the uses of things or to make purposeful movements, due to lesions in the cortical area of the brain. [<NL <Gk. *apraxia* inaction <*a-* not + *prassein* do]

a·près moi le dé·luge (à·pre mwà′ lə dā·lüzh′) *French* After me the deluge: attributed to Louis XV.

après-ski (äp′rā-skē′) *adj.* After skiing: usually applied to clothes or activities: *après-ski* boots; an *après-ski* fireside chat. [<F]

a·pri·cot (ā′pri·kot, ap′ri·kot) *n.* **1** A fruit (genus *Prunus*) of the rose family, intermediate between the peach and the plum. **2** The tree bearing this fruit. **3** A reddish-yellow color. [Earlier *apricock* (prob. directly <Pg.), *abricot* <F *abricot* <Pg. *albricoque* or Sp. *albaricoque* <Arabic *al-barqūq* <Med. Gk. *praikokion* <L *praecoquus* early ripe <*prae-* before + *coquere* cook]

A·pril (ā′prəl) The fourth month of the year, containing 30 days. [<L *Aprilis*]

April fool The subject of a practical joke on April 1, known as **April** (or **All**) **Fools' Day.**

a pri·o·ri (ā′ prī·ō′rī, ä′ prē·ôr′ē) **1** *Logic* Proceeding, as an argument, from cause to effect, or from an assumption to its logical conclusion: opposed to *a posteriori*. **2** Prior to, and thus independent of, experience; innate. **3** Previous to, or with insufficient, examination. See TRANSCENDENTAL. [<L, from what is before]

a·pri·or·i·ty (ā′prī·ôr′ə·tē, -or′-) *n.* The quality of being a priori, or not derived from experience.

a·pron (ā′prən, ā′pərn) *n.* **1** A covering to protect or adorn the front of a person's clothes, or any similar covering. **2** A part of the dress of a bishop or of the regalia of Masonic orders or other societies. **3** *Mech.* **a** Any of various overlapping pieces protecting parts of machines. **b** An endless band, as of cloth or leather, usually inclined, for conducting loose moving material, as grain in a separator. **4** *Eng.* **a** The platform or sill at the entrance to a dock. **b** The platform below a dam or in a sluiceway, or hinged to the river side of a fishing float. **5** *Geol.* A sheet of sand or gravel lying for some distance in front of the terminal moraines of a glacier. **6** *Aeron.* A hard-surfaced area in front of and around a hangar or aircraft shelter, to facilitate the handling of aircraft. **7** The part of a theater stage in front of the curtain. **8** *Mil.* **a** A movable screen of camouflage material, used to conceal artillery. **b** A network of barbed wire surrounding a post or stake in an entanglement. **9** A band of leather composing that part of an Oxford shoe which extends from the shank up and over the instep. — *v.t.* To cover or furnish with or as with an apron. [<OF *naperon,* dim. of *nape* cloth <L *mappa* cloth, napkin; in ME *a napron* became *an apron*] **—a′pron·like′** *adj.*

ap·ro·pos (ap′rə·pō′) *adj.* **1** Suited to the time, place, or occasion; pertinent; opportune: an *apropos* remark. *—adv.* **1** With reference or regard; in respect; as suggested by: with *of*: *apropos* of spring. **2** To the purpose; at the proper time; in the proper way; pertinently; appropriately: He spoke quite *apropos.* **3** By the way; incidentally: used to introduce a remark or observation. [<F *à propos* <*à* to + *propos* purpose]

ap·ro·sex·i·a (ap′rə·sek′sē·ə) *n. Psychiatry* Lack of power to concentrate the mind. [<NL <Gk. *aprosexia* lack of attention]

apse (aps) *n. Archit.* **1** An extending portion of an edifice, from the interior a recess and from the exterior a projection, usually semicircular with a half dome. **2** The eastern or altar end of a church. [<L *apsis* arch <Gk. *hapsis* a fastening, loop, wheel <*haptein* fasten]

Ap·she·ron (äp′shi·rôn′) A peninsula extending about 40 miles into the Caspian Sea from eastern Azerbaijan S.S.R.; site of the Baku oil fields.

ap·si·dal (ap′sə·dəl) *adj.* Of, pertaining to, like, or having an apse, apses, or apsides.

ap·sis (ap′sis) *n. pl.* **ap·si·des** (ap′sə·dēz) **1** *Astron.* A point of an eccentric orbit that is nearest to or farthest from the center of attraction, as the aphelion or perihelion of a planet. **2** *Geom.* The line joining these points to form the major axis of an ellipse. **3** An apse. **4** A reliquary. [<L. See APSE.]

apt (apt) *adj.* **1** Having a natural or habitual tendency; liable; likely. **2** Quick to learn; skilful. **3** Pertinent; apposite. [<L *aptus* fitted, suited] **—apt′ly** *adv.* **—apt′ness** *n.*

Synonyms: liable, likely. *Apt* inclines toward the meaning of *likely* and indicates an inherent inclination or ability. The distinction between *likely* and *liable* is that *likely* looks upon the probable event as favorable, *liable* as unfavorable; *likely* to succeed; *liable* to fail. See APPROPRIATE, CLEVER, LIKELY, SAGACIOUS.

Ap·ter·a (ap′tər·ə) *n. pl.* An order of small, primitive, wingless insects, formerly inclusive of many species now assigned to other orders. [<NL <Gk. *apteros* wingless <*a-* without + *pteron* wing]

ap·ter·al (ap′tər·əl) *adj.* **1** *Entomol.* Apterous. **2** *Archit.* Having no lateral ranges of columns, as a temple.

ap·ter·ous (ap′tər·əs) *adj.* **1** *Entomol.* Lacking wings, as the silverfish and other thysanurans. **2** *Bot.* Having no winglike expansions, as on a petiole or stem.

ap·ter·yx (ap′tər·iks) *n.* A New Zealand bird (genus *Apteryx*) with undeveloped wings, now nearly extinct. See KIWI. [<NL <Gk. *a-* without + *pteryx* wing] **—ap·ter·yg·i·al** (ap′tə·rij′ē·əl) *adj.*

ap·ti·tude (ap′tə·tōōd, -tyōōd) *n.* **1** Natural or acquired adaptation, bent, or gift: an *aptitude* for being a gracious host. **2** General fitness. **3** Quickness of understanding; readiness: an *aptitude* for spelling. Also **apt′ness.** See synonyms under ABILITY, DEXTERITY. [<F <LL *aptitudo* <L *aptus* fitted, suited. Doublet of ATTITUDE.]

aptitude test *Psychol.* A test designed to indicate the ability or fitness of an individual to engage successfully in any of a number of specialized activities.

Ap·u·lei·us (ap′yə·lē′əs), **Lucius,** second century Roman satirist and philosopher.

A·pu·lia (ə·pyōō′lyə) A region of SE Italy; 7,469 square miles. *Italian* **Pu·glia** (pōō′lyä).

A·pu·re (ä·pōō′rā) A river in west central Venezuela, flowing east 350 miles to the Orinoco.

A·pu·rí·mac (ä′pōō·rē′mäk) A river in southern Peru, flowing NW 550 miles to the Ucayali.

A·pus (ā′pəs) A southern constellation. See CONSTELLATION. [<NL <Gk. *apous* footless]

a·py·ret·ic (ā′pī·ret′ik, ap′ī-) *adj. Pathol.* Without fever. [<Gk. *apyretos* <*a-* without + *pyretos* fever]

A·qa·ba (ä′kä·bä) A town of south Jordan on the **Gulf of Aqaba,** the NE arm of the Red Sea. Ancient *Elath.*

aq·ua (ak′wə· ā′kwə) *n. pl. for def.* 1 **aq·uae** (ak′wē, ā′kwē) or **aq·uas,** *for def.* 2 **aq·uas** **1** Water. **2** A light bluish-green color; aquamarine. *—adj.* Light bluish-green. [<L]

aq·ua·cul·ture (ak′wə·kul′chər) *n.* The growing of plants or animals, especially fish or shellfish, in a body of water.

aqua for·tis (fôr′tis) Commercial nitric acid. Also **aq′ua·for′tis** *n.* [<L, strong water]

Aq·ua·lung (ak′wə·lung′) *n.* An underwater breathing apparatus or scuba: a trade name. Also **aq′ua·lung′.**

aq·ua·ma·rine (ak′wə·mə·rēn′) *n.* **1** A sea-green variety of precious beryl. **2** A bluish-green color. *—adj.* Bluish-green. [<L *aqua marina* sea water]

aq·ua·naut (ak′wə·nôt) *n.* One who explores or performs tasks underwater and is trained and equipped to live underwater over a period of time. [<L *aqua* water + *-naut* (<Gk. *nautēs* sailor), on analogy with *aeronaut, astronaut*]

aq·ua·plane (ak′wə·plān′) *n.* A board on which one stands while being towed over water by a motorboat. *—v.i.* **·planed, ·plan·ing** To ride an aquaplane.

aqua re·gi·a (rē′jē·ə) Nitrohydrochloric acid, a solvent for gold and platinum, and a powerful oxidizing agent. [<L, royal water]

aq·ua·relle (ak′wə·rel′) *n.* A kind of painting in transparent water colors. [<F <Ital. *acquerella* water color, dim. of *acqua* water <L *aqua*] **— aq′ua·rel′list** *n.*

a·quar·ium (ə·kwâr′ē·əm) *n. pl.* **a·quar·i·ums** or **a·quar·i·a** (ə·kwâr′ē·ə) **1** A tank, pond, or the like for the exhibition or study of aquatic animals or plants. **2** A public building containing such an exhibition. [<L, neut. sing. of *aquarius* pertaining to water <*aqua* water]

A·quar·i·us (ə·kwâr′ē·əs) **1** The eleventh sign of the zodiac; the Water-bearer. **2** A constellation of the zodiac. See CONSTELLATION. [<L]

a·quat·ic (ə·kwat′ik, ə·kwot′-) *adj.* Pertaining to, living in, growing in, or adapted to water. Also **a·quat′i·cal.** *—n.* **1** An aquatic animal or plant. **2** *pl.* Aquatic sports, as boating, etc. [<L *aquaticus* <*aqua* water]

aq·ua·tint (ak′wə·tint′) *n.* A form of engraving differing from an etching in that spaces instead of, or as well as, lines are bitten in by acid to give the effect of washes or tints in monochrome; also, an engraving printed from a plate so prepared. [<F *aquatinte* <Ital. *acqua tinta* dyed water <L *aqua tincta*]

a·qua·vit (ä′kwə·vēt) *n.* A Scandinavian liquor distilled from a grain or potato mash and flavored with caraway seed. Also **ak·va·vit** (äk′vä·vēt).

aqua vi·tae (vī′tē) **1** Alcohol. **2** Distilled spirits; whisky; brandy. [<L, water of life]

aq·ue·duct (ak′wə·dukt) *n.* **1** A water-conduit, particularly one for supplying a community from a distance. **2** A structure supporting a canal carried across a river or over low ground. **3** *Anat.* Any of several canals through which body liquids are conducted: the Fallopian *aqueduct.* [<L *aquaeductus* <*aqua* water + *ductus,* pp. of *ducere* lead]

aqueduct of Syl·vi·us (sil′vē·əs) *Anat.* The passage from the third to the fourth ventricle of the brain; the ventricle of the midbrain. Also called **a·quae·duc·tus cer·e·bri** (ak′wə·duk′təs ser′ə·brī).

a·que·ous (ā′kwē·əs, ak′wē-) *adj.* Pertaining to, made with, formed by, or containing water; watery.

aqueous humor *Physiol.* A clear, limpid, alkaline fluid that fills the anterior chamber of the eye from the cornea to the crystalline lens.

aqueous tension *Physics* The partial pressure due to the water vapor mixed with a gas measured over water. It is definite for each temperature.

aqui- *combining form* Water: *aquiferous.* [<L *aqua*]

aq·ui·cul·ture (ak′wi·kul′chər, ā′kwi-) *n.* Aquaculture.

aq·ui·fer (ak′wə·fər) *n. Geol.* Any water-bearing formation or group of formations, especially one that supplies ground water, wells, or springs.

a·quif·er·ous (ə·kwif′ər·əs) *adj.* Conveying or supplying water or watery fluid.

aq·ui·form (ak′wə·fôrm, ā′kwə-) *adj.* Like water; liquid.

aq·ui·fuge (ak′wə·fyōōj) *n. Geol.* A rock formation or structure which will neither absorb nor transmit water. [<AQUI- + L *fugere* flee]

Aq·ui·la (ak′wə·lə) A northern constellation, the Eagle. See CONSTELLATION. [<L, eagle]

aq·ui·le·gi·a (ak′wə·lē′jē·ə) *n.* Any of a genus *(Aquilegia)* of erect perennial plants of the crowfoot family; the columbine. [<NL <Med. L]

A·qui·le·ia (ä′kwē·lā′yä) A town in NE Italy; one of the chief cities of the Roman empire.

aq·ui·line (ak′wə·līn, -lin) *adj.* **1** Of or like an eagle. **2** Curving; hooked like an eagle's beak: an *aquiline* nose. [<L *aquilinus* <*aquila* eagle]

Aq·ui·lo (ak′wə·lō) In Roman mythology, the north or northeast wind. [<OF <L *Aquilo*]

A·qui·nas (ə·kwī′nəs), **Saint Thomas,** 1225?–1274, Italian Dominican monk and theologian.

Aq·ui·taine (ak′wə·tān′) A region of SW France; formerly a duchy, an independent kingdom, and the province of Guienne. Ancient **Aq·ui·ta·ni·a** (ak′wə·tā′nē·ə).

a·quose (ā′kwōs, ə·kwōs′) *adj.* Aqueous; watery.

a·quos·i·ty (ə·kwos′ə·tē) *n.* Moistness; wateriness.

ar (är) See ARE[2].

Ar *Chem.* Argon (symbol Ar).

ar- Assimilated var. of AD-.

-ar[1] *suffix* **1** Pertaining to; like: *regular, singular.* **2** The person or thing pertaining to: *scholar.* [ME *-er* <OF *-er, -aire, -ier* <L *-aris* (in nouns *-are*), used for *-alis* when preceded by *l*]

-ar[2] *suffix* A form of -ARY, -ER[2]: refashioned in imitation of -AR[1]: *vicar,* ME *vicary, viker.*

-ar[3] *suffix* A form of -ER[1]: refashioned in imitation of -AR[2]: *pedlar.*

A·ra (ā′rə) A southern constellation, the Altar. See CONSTELLATION. [<L, altar]

Ar·ab (ar′əb) *n.* **1** A native or inhabitant of Arabia. **2** One of a Semitic people inhabiting Arabia from ancient times, commonly the nomadic Bedouins: now scattered and admixed with various other native peoples. **3** A horse of a graceful, intelligent breed originally native to Arabia. **4** A homeless street wanderer, especially a child; a street Arab. *—adj.* Arabian.

Ar·a·bel·la (ar′ə·bel′ə, *Ital.* ä′rä·bel′lä) A feminine personal name. Also **A·ra·belle** (*Fr.* à·rà·bel′, *Ger.* ä′rä·bel′ə), *Sp.* **A·ra·be·la** (ä′rä·bā′lä). [? <Gmc.]

ar·a·besque (ar′ə·besk′) *n.* **1** An ornament or design, as those used in Arabian or Moorish architecture, employing patterns of intertwined scrollwork, conventionalized leaves or flowers, etc., painted or sculptured in low relief. **2** In ballet, a position in which the

ARABESQUE

dancer extends one leg straight backward, one arm forward, and the other arm backward. 3 *Music* A short, lively composition in rondo form. — *adj.* Relating to, executed in, or resembling arabesque; fanciful; ornamental. Also **ar'a·besk'.** [<F <Ital. *arabesco* <*Arabo* Arab]

A·ra·bi·a (ə·rā'bē·ə) A peninsula of SW Asia, between the Red Sea and the Persian Gulf; 1,000,000 square miles; anciently divided into **Arabia De·ser·ta** (di·zûr'tə), northern Arabia, **Arabia Fe·lix** (fē'liks), generally restricted to Yemen, and **Arabia Pe·trae·a** (pe·trē'ä), NW Arabia.

A·ra·bi·an (ə·rā'bē·ən) *adj.* Of or pertaining to Arabia or the Arabs. — *n.* 1 A native or inhabitant of Arabia. 2 An Arab (def. 3).

Arabian Desert 1 The desert in eastern Egypt between the Nile and the Gulf of Suez. 2 Popularly, the desert in northern Arabia.

Arabian millet Johnson grass.

Arabian Nights A collection of stories from Arabia, India, Persia, etc., dating from the tenth century A.D.: also called *The Thousand and One Nights.*

Arabian Sea A broad arm of the Indian Ocean, between Arabia and India.

Ar·a·bic (ar'ə·bik) *adj.* Of or pertaining to Arabia, the Arabs, their language, culture, etc. — *n.* The Southwest Semitic language of the Arabians, now widely spread among Moslem nations.

ar·a·bic acid (ar'ə·bik) *Chem.* A white amorphous powder, $C_5H_{10}O \cdot H_2O$, contained in gum arabic and other gums.

Arabic numerals The figures 1, 2, 3, 4, 5, 6, 7, 8, 9, and the zero (0). See NUMERAL.

a·rab·i·nose (ə·rab'ə·nōs, ar'ə·bə-) *n.* A colorless crystalline sugar of the pentose class, $C_5H_{10}O_5$, obtained from the gums of certain plants or by synthesis from glucose. [<ARAB(IC) + -IN + -OSE]

Ar·a·bist (ar'ə·bist) *n.* A student of or one versed in Arabic, Arabic literature, science, medicine, etc.

A·ra·bi·stan (ä·rä'bē·stän') A former name for KHUZISTAN.

ar·a·ble (ar'ə·bəl) *adj.* Capable of being plowed or cultivated. — *n.* Land fit for cultivation. [<L *arabilis* < *arare* plow] — **ar'a·bil'i·ty** *n.*

Arab League A confederation, established 1945, of the states of Iraq, Jordan (then *Trans-Jordan*), Lebanon, Saudi Arabia, the United Arab Republic (then *Egypt* and *Syria*), and Yemen; joined by 1959 by Libya, Morocco, Sudan, and Tunisia, and in 1961 by Kuwait.

Ar·a·by (ar'ə·bē) *Archaic* or *Poetic* Arabia.

A·ra·ca·jú (ä·rə·kə·zhōō') A port of eastern Brazil, capital of Sergipe state.

a·ra·ceous (ə·rā'shəs) *adj.* Belonging to the arum family *(Araceae)* of plants, mainly tropical, and bearing flowers on a spadix which is usually surrounded by a spathe. [<AR(UM) + -ACEOUS]

A·rach·ne (ə·rak'nē) In Greek mythology, a Lydian girl who challenged Athena to a weaving contest and was changed by the goddess into a spider. [<L <Gk. *Arachnē* < *arachnē* spider]

a·rach·nid (ə·rak'nid) *n.* Any of a class *(Arachnida)* of arthropods, embracing the spiders, scorpions, harvestmen, mites, etc. [<NL *Arachnida* <Gk. *arachnē* spider] — **a·rach·ni·dan** (ə·rak'nə·dən) *adj.* & *n.*

a·rach·noid (ə·rak'noid) *adj.* 1 Like a spider's web; thin and fine. 2 Of or pertaining to the arachnoid membrane or to the *Arachnida.* 3 *Bot.* Composed of slender entangled hairs; cobwebby. — *n.* One of the *Arachnida.* [<Gk. *arachnē* spider + -OID]

arachnoid membrane *Anat.* The midmost of the three membranes enveloping the brain and the spinal cord: between the dura mater and the pia mater. Also **arachnoid tissue.**

ar·ach·nol·o·gy (ar'ak·nol'ə·jē) *n.* The branch of zoology which treats of the arachnids.

A·rad (ä·räd') A city on the Mures in western Rumania.

A·ra·fu·ra Sea (ä'rä·fōō'rä) A part of the Pacific Ocean between northern Australia and New Guinea.

A·ra·gats (ä'rä·gäts') See ALAGEZ.

Ar·a·gon (ar'ə·gon) A region of NE Spain; 18,382 square miles; formerly an independent kingdom. *Spanish* **A·ra·gón** (ä'rä·gōn').

Ar·a·go·nese (ar'ə·gə·nēz', -nēs') *adj.* Of or pertaining to Aragon, its people, or their language. — *n. pl.* **·nese** 1 A native or inhabitant of Aragon. 2 The dialect of Spanish spoken in Aragon.

a·rag·o·nite (ə·rag'ə·nīt, ar'ə·gə-) *n.* A form of calcite crystallizing in the orthorhombic system. [from *Aragon,* Spain]

A·ra·guai·a (ä'rə·gwī'ə) A river in central Brazil, flowing north over 1,100 miles to the Atlantic. Also **A'ra·guay'a.**

A·ra·kan (ä'rä·kän') An administrative division of SW Burma on the Bay of Bengal, containing the **Arakan Yo·ma** (yō'mə), a mountain range.

A·ral·do (ä·räl'dō) Italian form of HAROLD.

a·ra·li·a·ceous (ə·rā'lē·ā'shəs) *adj. Bot.* Relating to a family of polypetalous plants *(Araliaceae),* having more than two carpels and a drupaceous fruit, the English ivy and ginseng being the best-known species. [<NL]

Ar·al Sea A salt inland sea, bordered by Kazakhstan and Uzbekistan in Asia; one of the world's largest inland seas; 24,635 square miles. Also **Lake of Aral.**

Ar·am (âr'əm), **Eugene,** 1704–59, English philologist; executed for murder.

Ar·am (âr'əm) The Biblical name of an ancient country of SW Asia, generally identified with Syria. Also **Ar·a·me·a** (ar'ə·mē'ə).

Ar·a·ma·ic (ar'ə·mā'ik) *n.* 1 Any of a group of Northwest Semitic languages, embracing Biblical Aramaic (erroneously, Chaldee), Syriac, etc. 2 The language of the Jews in Palestine after the captivity and that spoken by Christ and his disciples. Also *Aramean.* — *adj.* Aramean.

Ar·a·me·an (ar'ə·mē'ən) *adj.* Of or pertaining to ancient Aram or Aramea, or its peoples, languages, etc. — *n.* 1 An inhabitant of Aram. 2 The Aramaic language, especially in the broad sense. See ARAMAIC. Also **Ar'a·mae'an.**

A·ra·ne·ae (ə·rā'ni·ē) *n. pl.* An order of arachnids; the spiders. [<L *aranea* spider]

a·ra·ne·ous (ə·rā'nē·əs) *adj.* Made up of or covered with slender tangled hairs; cobwebby. Also **a·ra'ne·ose** (-ōs).

A·ra·nha (ə·ru'nyə), **Oswaldo,** 1894–1960, Brazilian lawyer and diplomat; minister of foreign affairs 1938–44.

Ar·an Islands (ar'ən) A group of three islands off the SW coast of County Galway, Ireland, at the entrance to Galway Bay; 18 square miles: also *Arran Islands.*

A·ran·da (ə·ran'də) *n.* A native Australian language, spoken in an extensive area of central Australia.

A·ran·sas Pass (ə·ran'səs) A channel connecting **Aransas Bay,** an inlet of the Gulf of Mexico, with the Gulf Intracoastal Waterway in southern Texas.

Ar·an·y (ôr'ôn·y'), **Janos,** 1817–82, Hungarian poet.

A·rap·a·ho (ə·rap'ə·hō) *n. pl.* **·ho** or **·hoes** An Indian of a nomadic tribe of Algonquian stock. Also **A·rap'a·hoe.**

ar·a·pai·ma (ar'ə·pī'mə) *n.* A large South American fresh-water food fish *(Arapaima gigas)* sometimes over 400 pounds in weight and 15 feet long. [<Pg. <Tupian]

Ar·a·rat (ar'ə·rat), **Mount** The highest peak in eastern Turkey; 16,945 feet; traditional resting place of Noah's ark. *Gen* viii 4. *Turkish* **Ağ·ri Da·ği** (ä·ri' dä·i').

ar·a·ro·ba (ar'ə·rō'bə) *n.* 1 Chrysarobin. 2 Zebrawood. [<Pg. <Tupian]

A·ras (ä·räs') A river forming the border between the U.S.S.R. and Turkey and Iran, flowing east 666 miles to the Kara: ancient *Araxes. Russian* **A·raks** (ä·räks').

A·rau·can (ə·rô'kən) *n.* 1 An Araucanian. 2 The language of the Araucanians.

Ar·au·ca·ni·a (ar'ô·kā'nē·ə) A region of central Chile inhabited by the Araucanians.

Ar·au·ca·ni·an (ar'ô·kā'nē·ən) *n.* 1 One of the aboriginal Indian inhabitants of Araucania. 2 A family of South American Indian languages spoken in southern and central Chile and northern Argentina. — *adj.* Of or pertaining to these people, their culture, or their language.

ar·au·ca·ri·a (ar'ô·kā'rē·ə) *n.* Any of a genus *(Araucaria)* of usually South American or Australian evergreen trees. [<NL <Sp. *Araucano* Araucanian]

A·ra·wak (ä'rä·wäk) *n.* Arawakan.

A·ra·wa·kan (ä'rä·wä'kən) *n.* 1 The most widely spread South American Indian linguistic stock, found from the headwaters of the Paraguay River, in southern Bolivia, to the northernmost part of the South American continent, and throughout the Antilles. 2 A member of any of the tribes speaking these languages. Also *Arawak.* — *adj.* Of or pertaining to this linguistic stock.

A·rax·es (ə·rak'sēz) The ancient name for the ARAS.

ar·ba·lest (är'bə·list) *n.* A medieval crossbow requiring a mechanical appliance to bend it.

ARBALEST
With windlass for winding back bowstring.

Also **ar'ba·list.** [<OF *arbaleste* <L *arcuballista* < *arcus* a bow + *ballista.* See BALLISTA.] — **ar'ba·lest'er** *n.*

Ar·be·la (är·bē'lə) A city in ancient Assyria on the site of modern Erbil, near which, at Gaugamela, Alexander the Great defeated Darius in 331 B.C.

Ar·ber (är'bər), **Edward,** 1836–1912, English scholar and editor.

ar·bi·ter (är'bə·tər) *n.* 1 A chosen or appointed judge or umpire, as between parties in a dispute. 2 One who has matters under his sole control; an absolute and final judge. See synonyms under JUDGE. [<L, one who goes to see, a witness, judge < *ad-* to + *bitere,* *betere* go]

ar·bi·ter el·e·gan·ti·ae (är'bə·tər el'ə·gan'shi·ē) *Latin* A judge in matters of style. Also **arbiter el·e·gan·ti·a·rum** (el'ə·gan'shē·ā'rəm).

ar·bi·tra·ble (är'bə·trə·bəl) *adj.* Subject to, capable of, or suitable for arbitration.

ar·bi·trage (är'bə·trij, är'bə·träzh') *n.* 1 The simultaneous buying and selling of the same thing, as stocks or bonds, in different markets, in order to profit by the difference between the prices ruling in such markets. 2 Arbitration. [<F < *arbitrer* arbitrate] — **ar·bi·trag·ist** (är'bə·trə·jist) *n.*

ar·bi·tral (är'bə·trəl) *adj.* Pertaining to an arbitrator or arbitration; subject to arbitration.

ar·bit·ra·ment (är·bit'rə·mənt) *n.* 1 The act of deciding by arbitration, or the decision of an arbitrator; an award. 2 Absolute and final decision by any power or authority to which a contest has been or may be appealed; also, the power or right to make such decision. Also **ar·bit're·ment.** [<OF *arbitrement* < *arbitrer.* See ARBITRATE.]

ar·bi·trar·y (är'bə·trer'ē) *adj.* 1 Based on mere opinion or prejudice; capricious. 2 Absolute; despotic. 3 *Law* Not determined by statute; discretionary. [<L *arbitrarius* < *arbiter.* See ARBITER.] — **ar'bi·trar'i·ly** *adv.* — **ar'bi·trar'i·ness** *n.*

Synonyms: absolute, despotic, dictatorial, domineering, harsh, imperious, irresponsible, overbearing, peremptory, tyrannical, tyrannous. See ABSOLUTE, IMPERIOUS. *Antonyms*: constitutional, equitable, free, lenient, limited, mild, obliging, restrained, restricted.

ar·bi·trate (är'bə·trāt) *v.t.* & *v.i.* **·trat·ed, ·trat·ing** 1 To submit to or settle by arbitration. 2 To act as judge or arbitrator, as for a case. [<L *arbitratus,* pp. of *arbitrari* < *arbiter.* See ARBITER.] — **ar'bi·tra'tive** *adj.*

ar·bi·tra·tion (är'bə·trā'shən) *n.* The hearing and settlement of a dispute between two parties by the decision of a third party or court to which the matter is referred by the contestants as a means of avoiding war, a strike, a lawsuit, etc. See CONCILIATION, MEDIATION.

ar·bi·tra·tor (är'bə·trā'tər) *n.* 1 A person

chosen by agreement of parties to decide a dispute between them. 2 One empowered to decide a matter; an arbiter. See synonyms under JUDGE. [<L]

ar·bi·tress (är′bə·tris) *n.* A woman arbiter. Also **ar·bi·tra·trix** (är′bə·trā′triks).

Ar·blay (där′blā), **Madame d'** See BURNEY, FANNY.

ar·bo·lo·co (är′bō·lō′kō) *n.* A central American tree *(Montanoa lehmannii)* of the composite family, having a hard durable wood used for making billiard cues. [<Sp. *árbol* tree]

ar·bor[1] (är′bər) *n.* 1 A bower, as of latticework, supporting vines or trees; a place shaded by trees. 2 *Obs.* An orchard. Also *Brit.* **ar′bour.** [Earlier *erber, herber* <AF, var. of OF *erbier, herbier* <L *herbarium* a collection of herbs <*herba* grass, herb]

ar·bor[2] (är′bər) *n. pl.* **ar·bo·res** (är′bər·ēz) *for defs.* 1 and 3, **ar·bors** *for def.* 2. 1 A tree: used chiefly in botanical names. 2 *Mech.* a A shaft, mandrel, spindle, or axle, as of a circular saw, lathe, or watch wheel. b A principal support of a machine. 3 A pictured genealogical tree. [<L, tree]

Arbor Day A U.S. spring holiday observed in some States by planting trees.

ar·bo·re·al (är·bôr′ē·əl, -bō′rē-) *adj.* 1 Of or pertaining to a tree or trees; arborescent. 2 Living or situated among trees.

ar·bo·re·ous (är·bôr′ē·əs, -bō′rē-) *adj.* 1 Of the nature of or like a tree. 2 Forming a tree trunk, as distinguished from a shrub. 3 Having many trees; wooded.

ar·bo·res·cent (är′bə·res′ənt) *adj.* Treelike in character, appearance, or size; branching. —**ar′bo·res′cence** *n.*

ar·bo·re·tum (är′bə·rē′təm) *n. pl.* **·tums** or **·ta** (-tə) A botanical garden exhibiting trees for their scientific interest and educational value, and in association with appropriate wildlife features. [<L <*arbor* tree]

arbori- *combining form* Tree: *arboriform.* [<L *arbor* tree]

ar·bo·ri·cul·ture (är′bə·ri·kul′chər) *n.* The cultivation of trees or shrubs. —**ar′bo·ri·cul′tur·al** *adj.* —**ar′bo·ri·cul′tur·ist** *n.*

ar·bo·ri·form (är′ber·ə·fôrm, är·bôr′ə-, är·bor′·ə-) *adj.* Formed like a tree.

ar·bor·i·za·tion (är′bər·ə·zā′shən, -ī·zā′-) *n.* The formation of a treelike arrangement or figure, as in some minerals and fossils.

ar·bor·ous (är′bər·əs) *adj.* Of, pertaining to, or formed by trees.

ar·bor·vi·tae (är′bər·vī′tē) *n.* 1 An evergreen shrub or tree of the genus *Thuya* or *Thuja,* of the pine family, especially *T. orientalis.* 2 *Anat.* The branching appearance of the white matter shown in a section of the cerebellum. [<L, tree of life]

ar·bus·cle (är′bus·əl) *n.* 1 A dwarf tree, or one between a shrub and a tree in size. 2 An arbuscule. [<L *arbuscula,* dim. of *arbor* tree]

ar·bus·cule (är·bus′kyōōl) *n. Zool.* A tuft, as of cilia, etc.

ar·bute (är′byōōt) *n.* 1 The European strawberry tree. 2 The arbutus. [<L *arbutus*]

Ar·buth·not (är′bəth·not, är·buth′nət), **John,** 1667–1735, Scottish satirist and physician.

ar·bu·tus (är·byōō′təs) *n.* 1 Any member of a small genus *(Arbutus)* of evergreen trees or shrubs of the heath family, whose bark, leaves, and fruit are used in drugs. 2 The trailing arbutus. [<L, strawberry tree]

arc (ärk) *n.* 1 Anything in the shape of an arch, of a curve, or of a part of a circle; a bow; arch. 2 *Geom.* A part of any algebraic curve, especially of a circle. 3 *Electr.* The bow of flame occurring in an arc light. 4 *Astron.* A part of the apparent path of a heavenly body. —*v.i.* **arcked** or **arced** (ärkt), **arck·ing** or **arc·ing** (är′king) *Electr.* To form a voltaic arc. ◆ Homophone: *ark.* [<L *arcus* bow, arch. Doublet of ARCH[1].]

Arc, Jeanne d' (zhän dárk) See JOAN OF ARC.

ar·cade (är·kād′) *n.* 1 *Archit.* a A vaulted roof. b An ornamental series or range of arches with their supporting columns or piers, standing against the face of a wall **(blind arcade)** or free, as a support of a ceiling, roof, etc. 2 A roofed passageway or street, especially one having shops, etc., opening from it. 3 An avenue of trees, statues, etc. —*v.t.* **·cad·ed, ·cad·ing** To furnish with or form into an arcade or arcades. [<F <Med.L *arcata* <L *arcus* bow, arch]

Ar·ca·di·a (är·kā′dē·ə) 1 A nome of central Peloponnesus, Greece, traditionally associated with the pastoral pursuits of its ancient inhabitants. 2 Hence, any region of ideal rustic simplicity and contentment. *Modern Greek* **Ar·ka·dhi·a** (är′kä·thē′ä).

Ar·ca·di·an (är·kā′dē·ən) *adj.* 1 Of or pertaining to Arcadia. 2 Ideally rural or simple; pastoral. —*n.* 1 A native of or dweller in Arcadia. 2 One with simple, pastoral tastes.

Ar·ca·dy (är′kə·dē) *Archaic* or *Poetic* Arcadia.

ar·cane (är·kān′) *adj.* Secret; hidden. [<L *arcanus. See* ARCANUM.]

ar·ca·num (är·kā′nəm) *n. pl.* **·na** (-nə) 1 An inner secret or mystery. 2 One of the great secrets of nature which the alchemists sought to discover. 3 A secret remedy; an elixir. [<L, neut. of *arcanus* hidden <*arca* chest]

ar·ca·ture (är′kə·chŏŏr) *n.* 1 A small arcade formed by a series of little arches. 2 A blind arcade, used merely for ornament.

arc-bou·tant (ȧr·bōō·täṅ′) *n. pl.* **arcs-bou·tants** (ȧr·bōō·täṅ′) *French* An arched buttress.

arch[1] (ärch) *n.* 1 A curved structure spanning an opening, formed of wedge-shaped parts resting on supports at the two extremities. 2 Any similar structure or object; an archway.

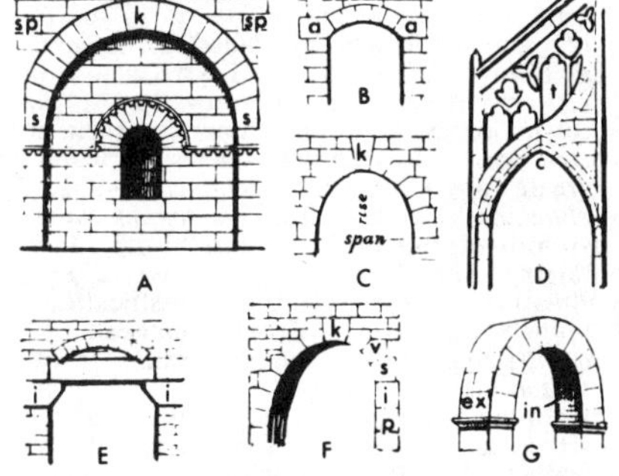

TYPES OF ARCHES

3 The form of an arch; a bowlike curve. 4 *Mech.* The height within the curve of an arched body, as through the central portion of a leaf spring. 5 *Aeron.* a The curve of a surface from front to rear. b A curved wing tip. 6 *Anat.* A curved or archlike part: the dental arch. 7 One of the major patterns into which all fingerprints are divided: subclassed as *plain, tented,* and *exceptional.* —*v.t.* 1 To cause to form an arch or arches. 2 To furnish with an arch or arches. 3 To span; extend over, as an arch. —*v.i.* 4 To form an arch or arches. [<OF *arche* <Med. L. *arca* <L *arcus* bow, arch. Doublet of ARC.]

arch[2] (ärch) *adj.* 1 Cunning; roguish; sly; coy. 2 Most eminent; chief. [<ARCH-] —**arch′ly** *adv.* —**arch′ness** *n.*

arch- *prefix* 1 Chief; principal: *archchancellor.* 2 Very great; extreme: *archknave.* Also *archi-,* as in *archidiaconal.* [OE *arce-, erce-* <L *arch-, arche-, archi-* <Gk. *archos* ruler]

Ar·chae·an (är·kē′ən) See ARCHEAN.

archaeo- See ARCHEO-.

ar·chae·ol·o·gy (är′kē·ol′ə·jē), etc. See ARCHEOLOGY, etc.

ar·chae·op·ter·yx (är′kē·op′tər·iks) *n.* A representative of a genus *(Archaeopteryx)* of fossil reptilian birds of the Upper Jurassic period, combining reptilian and avian characteristics. Also **ar′che·op′ter·yx.** [<NL <ARCHAEO- + Gk. *pteryx* wing]

Ar·chae·o·zo·ic (är′kē·ə·zō′ik) See ARCHEOZOIC.

ar·cha·ic (är·kā′ik) *adj.* 1 Belonging to a former period; no longer in use; antiquated. 2 Characterizing a word, an inflectional form, or a phrase found only in the older literature and in the Bible, but no longer in current use. Also **ar·cha′i·cal.** [<Gk. *archaikos* <*archaios* ancient]

ar·cha·ism (är′kē·iz′əm, -kā-)*n.* 1 An archaic word, idiom, or expression. 2 Archaic style or usage.

ar·cha·ist (är′kē·ist, -kā-) *n.* 1 One who uses or affects archaisms or the archaic. 2 One who studies antiquities; an archeologist.

ar·cha·is·tic (är′kē·is′tik, -kā-) *adj.* Of, pertaining to, or imitating the archaic; inclined to, characterized by, or affecting archaism.

ar·cha·ize (är′kē·īz, -kā-) *v.* **·ized, ·iz·ing** *v.t.* To make archaic or archaistic. —*v.i.* To use archaisms. Also *Brit.* **ar′cha·ise.** —**ar′cha·iz′er** *n.*

Ar·cham·bault (ȧr·shäṅ·bō′) French form of ARCHIBALD.

arch·an·gel (ärk′ān′jəl) *n.* 1 An angel of highest rank; in Christian legend one of seven, in the Koran one of four, chief angels. 2 The garden angelica. —**the Archangel** In Christian legend, usually Michael. [<L *archangelus* <Gk. *archangelos* <*arch-* chief + *angelos* angel] —**arch·an·gel·ic** (ärk′an·jel′ik) or **·i·cal** *adj.*

Arch·an·gel (ärk′ān′jəl) See ARKHANGELSK.

Archangel Bay See DVINA BAY.

arch·bish·op (ärch′bish′əp) *n.* The chief bishop of an ecclesiastical province.

arch·bish·op·ric (ärch′bish′əp·rik) *n.* 1 The office, rank, term of office, or jurisdiction of an archbishop. 2 The ecclesiastical province over which an archbishop has jurisdiction.

arch·dea·con (ärch′dē′kən) *n. Eccl.* A church official who administers the property, temporal affairs, missionary work, etc., of a diocese under powers delegated from the bishop: chiefly an Anglican usage.

arch·dea·con·ate (ärch′dē′kən·it) *n.* The jurisdiction of an archdeacon.

arch·dea·con·ry (ärch′dē′kən·rē) *n. pl.* **·ries** 1 The title, office, or dignity of an archdeacon. 2 An archdeacon's residence. Also **arch′dea′·con·ship.**

arch·di·o·cese (ärch′dī′ə·sēs, -sis) *n.* The diocese or jurisdiction of an archbishop.

arch·du·cal (ärch′dōō′kəl, -dyōō′-) *adj.* Of or pertaining to an archduke or an archduchy.

arch·duch·ess (ärch′duch′is) *n.* 1 A princess of the former imperial family of Austria. 2 The wife or widow of an archduke.

arch·duch·y (ärch′duch′ē) *n. pl.* **·duch·ies** The territory ruled by an archduke. Also **arch′·duke′dom.**

arch·duke (ärch′dōōk′, -dyōōk′) *n.* A chief duke, especially a prince of the former imperial family of Austria.

Ar·che·an (är·kē′ən) *adj. Geol.* Pertaining to a rock group associated with the Archeozoic era of earth's history, consisting of the oldest stratified rocks, predominantly igneous and without fossil remains. Also **Ar·chae′an.** [<Gk. *archaios* ancient <*archē* beginning]

arched (ärcht) *adj.* 1 Having the form of an arch; characterized by arches. 2 Covered or furnished with arches.

ar·che·go·ni·o·phore (ar′kə·gō′nē·ə·fôr′, -fōr′) *n. Bot.* A multicellular outgrowth of the thalloid shoot of liverworts bearing archegonia.

ar·che·go·ni·um (är′kə·gō′nē·əm) *n. pl.* **·ni·a** (-ne·ə) *Bot.* The female sexual organ of the higher cryptogams, the analog of the pistil of flowering plants, which has, when ready for fertilization, the form of a cellular sac or flask containing an egg-cell. Also **ar·che·gone** (är′kə·gōn). [<NL <Gk. *archegonos* primitive parent <*archos* chief, first + *gonos* offspring] —**ar′che·go′ni·al** *adj.* —**ar′che·go′ni·ate** (-it, -āt) *adj.*

Ar·che·la·us (är′kə·lā′əs) Ruler of Judea, son and successor of Herod. *Matt.* ii 22.

arch·en·e·my (ärch′en′ə·mē) *n. pl.* **·mies** 1 Satan. 2 The principal enemy.

ar·chen·ter·on (är·ken′tər·on) *n. Biol.* The primitive enteron or alimentary cavity. [<ARCH(I)- + Gk. *enteron* intestine] —**ar·chen·ter·ic** (är′ken·ter′ik) *adj.*

archeo- *combining form* Ancient: *Archeozoic.* Also *archaeo-* [<Gk. *archaios* ancient]

ar·che·o·as·tron·o·my (är′kē·o·ə·stron′ə·mē) *n.* The astronomy of ancient cultures as deduced from archeological evidence.

ar·che·ol·o·gy (är′kē·ol′ə·jē) *n.* The science or study of history from the evidence of the relics and remains of early human cultures as discovered chiefly by systematic excavations: also spelled *archaeology.* —**ar·che·o·log·i·cal** (är′kē·ə·loj′i·kəl) or ·**log′ic** *adj.* —**ar′che·ol′o·gist** (-jist) *n.*

ar·che·op·ter·yx (är′kē·op′tər·iks) See ARCHAEOPTERYX.

Ar·che·o·zo·ic (är′kē·ə·zō′ik) *n. Geol.* The oldest of the eras making up the geological record. See chart under GEOLOGY. —*adj.* Belonging to or indicating this era. Also spelled *Archaeozoic* [<ARCHEO- + Gk. *zōon* animal]

arch·er (är′chər) *n.* One who shoots with a bow and arrow. [<OF *archier* <L *arcarius* bowman <*arcus* bow]

Arch·er (är′chər) The tenth sign of the zodiac. See SAGITTARIUS.

Ar·cher (är′chər), **William,** 1856–1924, Scottish critic and dramatist.

arch·er·fish (är′chər·fish′) *n. pl.* ·**fish** or ·**fish·es** A percomorph fish (*Toxotes jaculator*) of India and Polynesia, with the ability to shoot drops of water to bring down its insect prey.

arch·er·y (är′chər·ē) *n.* **1** The art or sport of shooting with the bow and arrows. **2** The weapons and outfit of the archer. **3** Archers collectively.

Arch·es National Monument (är′chiz) A group of wind-eroded rock formations in SE Utah, established as a national monument in 1929; 53 square miles.

ar·che·spore (är′kə·spôr, -spōr) *n. Bot.* The cell, or group of cells, from which the pollen mother cells are formed within a pollen sac, or the spore mother cells within a sporangium. Also **ar′che·spo′ri·um** (-spôr′ē·əm, spō′rē·əm). [<NL *archesporium* <ARCHI- + Gk. *sporos* seed] —**ar′che·spo′ri·al** *adj.*

ar·che·type (är′kə·tīp) *n.* An original or standard pattern or model; a prototype. See synonyms under EXAMPLE, IDEA, IDEAL, MODEL. [<L *archetypum* <Gk. *archetypon* pattern, model <*arche-* first + *typos* stamp, pattern] —**ar′che·typ′al** *adj.* —**ar′che·typ′ic** (-tip′ik) or ·**i·cal** *adj.*

arch·fiend (ärch′fēnd′) *n.* A chief fiend; specifically, Satan.

archi– *prefix* **1** Var. of ARCH–. **2** *Biol.* Original; primitive: *archiblast.* [See ARCH-]

Ar·chi·bald (är′chə·bôld) A masculine personal name. Also *Lat.* **Ar·chi·bal·dus** (är′kə·bôl′dəs). [<Gmc., nobly bold]

ar·chi·blast (är′kə·blast) *n. Biol.* **1** The primitive portion of the blastoderm or germinal disk. **2** The epiblast. [<ARCHI- + Gk. *blastos* germ]

ar·chi·carp (är′kə·kärp) *n. Bot.* A female sex organ of certain fungi; an ascogonium. [<ARCHI- + Gk. *karpos* fruit]

ar·chi·di·ac·o·nal (är′ki·dī·ak′ə·nəl) *adj.* Pertaining to an archdeacon or an archdeaconry.

ar·chi·di·ac·o·nate (är′ki·dī·ak′ə·nāt) *n.* The office of an archdeacon.

Ar·chie (är′chē) Diminutive of ARCHIBALD. Also **Ar′chy.**

ar·chi·e·pis·co·pa·cy (är′kē·i·pis′kə·pə·sē) *n. pl.* ·**cies** The rank and rule of an archbishop. Also **ar′chi·e·pis′co·pate** (-pāt).

ar·chi·e·pis·co·pal (är′kē·i·pis′kə·pəl) *adj.* Of or pertaining to an archbishop, his office, or residence.

ar·chil (är′kil) *n.* **1** A lichen of the Cape Verde and Canary Islands (*Rocella tinctoria*), yielding the dyestuff orchil. **2** The dyestuff obtained from this lichen; orchil. Also spelled *orchil.* [earlier *orchil* <OF *orchel, orcheil* <Ital. *orcello*]

Ar·chi·lo·chi·an (är′kə·lō′kē·ən) *adj.* Characteristic of or pertaining to the early Greek satiric poet Archilochus or the verse named after him. —*n.* The dactylic trimeter or tetrameter as used by Archilochus.

ar·chi·mage (är′kə·māj) *n.* **1** A chief magician; great wizard. **2** The chief priest of the Persian fire-worshipers. Also **ar·chi·ma·gus** (är′kə·mā′gəs). [<ARCHI- + Gk. *magos* magician]

ar·chi·man·drite (är′kə·man′drīt) *n.* In the Greek Orthodox Church: **1** The head of a monastery or of several monasteries. **2** A title of honor granted to distinguished celibate priests. [<L *archimandrita* <LGk. *archimandritēs* <*archi-* chief + *mandra* enclosure, monastery]

Ar·chim·bald (är′khim·bält) German form of ARCHIBALD.

Ar·chi·me·de·an (är′kə·mē′dē·ən, -mə·dē′ən) *adj.* Of, discovered by, or pertaining to Archimedes.

ARCHIMEDEAN SCREW

Archimedean screw *Mech.* A spiral conduit about an inclined axis, for raising liquid by rotation. Also **Archimedes' screw.**

Ar·chi·me·des (är′kə·mē′dēz), 287?–212 B.C., Greek mathematician; born in Sicily.

ar·chi·mime (är′kə·mīm) *n.* In ancient Rome, the actor who impersonated the leading roles of satirical dramas.

ar·chine (är·shēn′) *n.* A Russian unit of linear measure, about 28 inches long.

arch·ing (är′ching) *n.* **1** An arch or series of arches. **2** The building of arches. **3** Any curve.

ar·chi·pel·a·go (är′kə·pel′ə·gō) *n. pl.* ·**goes** or ·**gos** A sea studded with many islands, or the islands collectively. [<Ital. *arcipelago,* ult. <Gk. *archi-* chief + *pelagos* sea; orig., with ref. to the Aegean Sea] —**ar·chi·pe·lag·ic** (är′kə·pə·laj′ik) *adj.*

Ar·chi·pel·a·go (är′kə·pel′ə·gō) The ancient name for the AEGEAN SEA.

Ar·chi·pen·ko (är′ki·peng′kō), **Alexander,** 1887–1964, Russian sculptor.

ar·chi·pho·neme (är′ki·fō′nēm) *n. Ling.* The total of relevant features common to two phonemes after neutralization.

ar·chi·plasm (är′kə·plaz′əm) *n. Biol.* The permanent substance of the spindle fibers and astral rays of the cell, dispersed in the form of granules: originally called *archoplasm.*

ar·chi·tect (är′kə·tekt) *n.* **1** One whose profession is to design and draw up the plans for buildings, etc., and supervise their construction. **2** One who devises, plans, or creates anything. [<L *architectus* <Gk. *architektōn* <*archi-* chief + *tektōn* worker]

ar·chi·tec·ton·ic (är′kə·tek·ton′ik) *adj.* **1** Pertaining to architecture; constructive. **2** *Philos.* Relating to the scientific classification of knowledge. Also **ar′chi·tec·ton′i·cal.** [<L *architectonicus* <Gk. *architektonikos* <*architektōn.* See ARCHITECT.]

ar·chi·tec·ton·ics (är′kə·tek·ton′iks) *n. pl.* (construed as singular) **1** The science of architecture. **2** *Philos.* The scientific arrangement and construction of systems of knowledge. **3** Structural design, as in works of music or art.

ar·chi·tec·ture (är′kə·tek′chər) *n.* **1** The science, art, or profession of designing and constructing buildings or other structures. **2** A style or system of building: Gothic *architecture.* **3** Construction or structure generally; any ordered arrangement of the parts of a system: the *architecture* of the universe. **4** A building, or buildings collectively. [<F <L *architectura* <*architectus.* See ARCHITECT.] —**ar′chi·tec′tur·al** *adj.* —**ar′·chi·tec′tur·al·ly** *adv.*

ar·chi·trave (är′kə·trāv) *n. Archit.* **1** A chief beam; that part of an entablature which rests upon the column heads and supports the frieze. See illustration under ENTABLATURE. **2** A molded ornament, as of an arch; the archivolt, or the ornament skirting the head and sides of a door or window. [<F <Ital. <*archi-* chief (<Gk.) + *trave* beam <L *trabs*]

ar·chi·val (är·kī′vəl) *adj.* Of, pertaining to, or contained in archives.

ar·chives (är′kīvz) *n. pl.* **1** A place where public records and historical documents are kept. **2** Public records, documents, etc., as kept in such a depository. See synonyms under HISTORY. [<F *archives,* pl. of *archif* <L *archivum* <Gk. *archeion* a public office <*archē* government]

ar·chi·vist (är′kə·vist) *n.* A keeper of archives.

ar·chiv·ol·o·gy (är′kiv·ol′ə·jē) *n.* The science of maintaining and cataloging public documents. —**ar′chiv·ol′o·gist** *n.*

ar·chi·volt (är′kə·vōlt) *n. Archit.* **1** An ornamental molding following the outer curve of an arch. **2** An arch considered as supporting superincumbent weight. Also **ar′chi·vault** (-vôlt). [<Ital. *archivolto* an arched vault]

arch·let (ärch′lit) *n.* A little arch.

ar·chon (är′kon) *n.* **1** One of the nine chief magistrates of ancient Athens. **2** One of various magistrates or other officials in the Byzantine empire and modern Greece. **3** Any ruler or supreme commander. [<Gk. *archōn* <*archein* rule]

ar·chon·ship (är′kon·ship) *n.* The office or official term of an archon. Also **ar·chon·tate** (är′kən·tāt).

ar·cho·plasm (är′kə·plaz′əm) See ARCHIPLASM.

arch·priest (ärch′prēst′) *n.* **1** Formerly, the chief or senior priest of a cathedral chapter, serving as assistant to a bishop: later called a *dean.* **2** A rural dean. **3** A papal delegate appointed in 1598 as superior of Roman Catholic clergy in England: succeeded in 1623 by a vicar apostolic. —**arch′priest′hood, arch′priest′ship** *n.*

arch·way (ärch′wā′) *n.* An entrance or passage under an arch.

-archy *combining form* Rule; government: *heptarchy,* government by seven. [<Gk. *-archia* <*archos* ruler]

Ar·ci·bal·do (är′chē·bäl′dō) Italian form of ARCHIBALD.

ar·ci·form (är′sə·fôrm) *adj.* Shaped like an arc or bow. [<L *arcus* bow + -FORM]

arc light A lamp in which light of high intensity is produced between two adjacent electrodes connected with a powerful source of electricity. Also **arc lamp.**

ar·co·graph (är′kə·graf, -gräf) *n.* An instrument for drawing curves without striking them from a center point. [<L *arcus* arc + -GRAPH]

Ar·co·le (är′kō·lā) A village in northern Italy; scene of Napoleon's victory over the Austrians, 1796.

Ar·cot (är·kot′) A town in east central Madras state, India.

Arc·tal·pine (ärk·tal′pin) *adj.* **1** *Geog.* Of or pertaining to northern regions beyond the limits of tree growth; also, to mountain heights above the timber line. **2** *Ecol.* Designating those plant and animal forms which live beyond or above the limits of tree growth.

arc·tic (ärk′tik, är′tik) *adj.* **1** Pertaining to, suitable for, or characteristic of the North Pole or the regions, etc., near it. **2** Extremely cold; frigid. —*n.* **1** The region around the North Pole. **2** The Arctic Circle. **3** *pl. U.S.* Warm, waterproof overshoes. [Earlier *artik* <OF *artique* <L *articus, arcticus* <Gk. *arktikos* of the Bear (the northern constellation *Ursa Major*), northern <*arktos* bear]

Arctic Archipelago A north Canadian island group in the Arctic Ocean, comprising most of Franklin District, Northwest Territories. Also **Arctic Islands.**

Arctic char A salmonoid fish (*Salvelinus alpinus*) of Canada and Europe.

Arctic Circle The boundary of the North Frigid Zone, 23° 28′ from the North Pole.

Arctic Ocean An almost landlocked sea north of the Arctic Circle and surrounding the North Pole; 5,440,000 square miles.

Arc·tu·rus (ärk·tŏŏr′əs, -tyŏŏr′) One of the 20 brightest stars, 0.24 magnitude and of an orange color; Alpha in the constellation Boötes. See STAR. [<L <Gk. *Arktouros* guardian of the bear <*arktos* a bear + *ouros* a guard]

ar·cu·ate (är′kyōō·it, -āt) *adj.* Bent or curved like a bow; arched. Also **ar′cu·at′ed.** [<L *arcuatus,* pp. of *arcuare* curve like a bow <*arcus* a bow]

ar·cu·a·tion (är′kyōō·ā′shən) *n.* **1** The act of curving or bending, or the state of being bent. **2** *Archit.* The use of arches; arched work.

ar·cus (är′kəs) *n. Meteorol.* A cloud resembling an arch: seen usually in cumulonimbus clouds. [<L, arch]

-ard *suffix of nouns* One who does something to excess or who is to be disparaged: *drunkard, coward;* sometimes changed to *-art: braggart.* [<OF *-ard, -art* <G *-hard, -hart* hardy]

ar·deb (är′deb) *n.* A unit of capacity for dry measure, used in Egypt and neighboring Moslem countries, varying from about 4 quarts to 8 bushels. [<Arabic]

Ar·de·bil (är′də·bēl′) A city in Azerbaijan, NW Iran. Also **Ar′da·bil′.**

Ar·den (är′dən), **Forest of** Formerly, a large wooded tract in Warwickshire, England.

ar·den·cy (är′dən·sē) *n.* The quality of being ardent; ardor; intensity; warmth.

Ar·dennes (är·den′) A wooded plateau, mostly in SW Belgium, extending into NE France. Also **Ardennes Forest.**

ar·dent (är′dənt) *adj.* **1** Vehement in emotion or action; passionate; zealous; intense. **2** Red;

glowing; flashing. **3** On fire; burning. [<L *ardens, -entis,* ppr. of *ardere* burn] **—ar′dent·ly** *adv.* **—ar′dent·ness.** n.

Synonyms: burning, eager, excitable, fervent, fervid, fierce, fiery, glowing, hot, impassioned, inflammable, intense, keen, longing, passionate, sanguine, vehement. See EAGER[1]. *Antonyms*: apathetic, calm, cold, cool, dispassionate, frigid, icy, indifferent, listless, phlegmatic, stolid, stony.

ardent spirits Alcoholic distilled liquors.

ar·dor (är′dər) *n.* **1** Warmth or intensity of passion or affection; eagerness; vehemence; zeal. **2** Great heat, as of fire, sun, or fever. Also *Brit.* **ar′dour.** See synonyms under ENTHUSIASM, WARMTH. [<L, a flame, fire <*ardere* burn]

ar·du·ous (är′joo·əs) *adj.* **1** Involving great labor, hardship, or difficulty; difficult. **2** Toiling strenuously; energetic. **3** Steep; hard to climb or surmount. [<L *arduus* steep] **—ar′·du·ous·ly** *adv.* **—ar′du·ous·ness** *n.*

Synonyms: difficult, exhausting, hard, laborious, onerous, severe, toilsome, trying. *Hard* may be active or passive; a thing may be *hard* to do or *hard* to bear. *Arduous* is always active. That which is *difficult* may require labor, or simply skill and address, as a *difficult* problem or puzzle. That which is *arduous* always requires persevering toil. *Antonyms*: easy, facile, light, pleasant, slight, trifling, trivial.

are[1] (är) *v.* First, second, and third person plural, present indicative, of the verb BE; also used as second person singular. [OE (Northumbrian) *aron*]

are[2] (âr, är) *n.* A measure of area in the metric system comprising a square dekameter or one hundred square meters. See METRIC SYSTEM. [<F <L *area.* Doublet of AREA.]

ar·e·a (âr′ē·ə) *n. pl.* **ar·e·as;** *for def.* 6, *often* **ar·e·ae** (âr′i·ē) **1** Any open space. **2** A tract or portion of the earth's surface; region. **3** Superficial extent; total outside surface. See SQUARE MEASURE. **4** A yard of a building; areaway. **5** Figuratively, the extent of anything; scope. **6** *Anat.* A section of the cerebral cortex with a specific motor or sensory function. [<L, an open space of level ground. Doublet of ARE[2].] **—ar′e·al** *adj.*

area bombing The bombing of a general region with no attempt to hit specific targets within that region. Compare PATTERN BOMBING, PRECISION BOMBING.

area code A three-digit number that identifies one of the telephone areas into which the United States is divided.

area fire Artillery fire or bombing designed to cover an entire area, either all at once or part by part: distinguished from *precision fire.*

area rule *Aeron.* A design principle for improving the performance of supersonic air-craft by narrowing the fuselage in the area where the wings are attached.

area target A target for artillery fire or bombing that extends over a large area. Compare POINT TARGET.

ar·e·a·way (âr′ē·ə·wā′) *n.* **1** A small sunken court before basement windows or passageway to a basement door. **2** A passageway, as from one building or part of a building to another.

ar·e·ca (ar′i·kə, ə·rē′kə) *n.* **1** Any tree of a genus *(Areca)* of tropical palms, including the betel nut palm. **2** The fruit of such a tree. [<Pg. <Malayalam *ādekka*]

A·re·ci·bo (ä′rä·sē′bō) A port of NW Puerto Rico.

ar·e·ic (ar′ē·ik) *adj. Geog.* Pertaining to or designating a region of the earth contributing little or no surface drainage, as the Sahara. [<L *arere* be dry]

a·re·na (ə·rē′nə) *n.* **1** The central space for contestants in a Roman amphitheater. **2** Any place like this: The football players came into the *arena.* **3** A sphere of action or contest. [<L, sand, sandy place]

ar·e·na·ceous (ar′ə·nā′shəs) *adj.* **1** Pertaining to or like sand. **2** Full of or growing in sand; sandy. [<L *arenaceus* <*arena* sand]

arena theater A stage in the center of a room or auditorium, surrounded by seats and with out proscenium: also called *theater-in-the-round, central staging.*

ar·ene (ar′ēn) *n. Chem.* Any compound belonging to the class of aromatic hydrocarbon compounds. [<AR(OMATIC) + -ENE]

ar·e·nic·o·lous (ar′ə·nik′ə·ləs) *adj.* Living in sand. [<L *arena* sand + *colere* dwell]

aren't (ärnt) A contraction of *are not.* ◆ **Aren't I?** is condoned as a genteel colloquial substitute for the illiterate *Ain't I?,* though it is at variance with grammar.

areo- *combining form* Mars: *areography.* [<Gk. *Arēs*]

ar·e·o·cen·tric (âr′ē·ō·sen′trik) *adj.* Having reference to the planet Mars as a center or origin.

ar·e·og·ra·phy (âr′ē·og′rə·fē) *n.* A description of the physical features of the planet Mars.

a·re·o·la (ə·rē′ə·lə) *n. pl.* **·lae** (-lē) or **·las 1** *Bot.* A small space or interstice in a network of veins or vessels, as on leaves. **2** *Anat.* The colored circle about a nipple or about a vesicle; a depressed spot. Also **ar·e·ole** (âr′ē·ōl). [<L, dim. of *area* open space] **—a·re′o·lar** *adj.*

areolar tissue *Anat.* Connective tissue composed of loose meshes of fibers enclosing irregular cavities; cellular tissue.

a·re·o·late (ə·rē′ə·lit, -lāt) *adj.* Marked off into areolae. Also **a·re′o·lat′ed.**

a·re·o·la·tion (ə·rē′ə·lā′shən) *n.* **1** The state of being areolate. **2** The arrangement of areolae. **3** A space containing areolae.

ar·e·ol·o·gy (âr′ē·ol′ə·jē) *n.* The scientific study of the planet Mars in all its aspects.

ar·e·om·e·ter (âr′ē·om′ə·tər) *n.* A hydrometer. [<Gk. *araios* thin + -METER]

Ar·e·op·a·gite (ar′ē·op′ə·jīt, -gīt) *n.* A member of the court of the Areopagus.

Ar·e·op·a·gus (ar′ē·op′ə·gəs) A hill NW of the Acropolis on which the highest court of ancient Athens held its sessions; hence, the court itself. [<L <Gk. *Areiopagos* <*Arēs* Mars + *pagos* hill]

A·re·qui·pa (ä′rā·kē′pä) A city in southern Peru.

Ar·es (âr′ēz) In Greek mythology, the god of war: identified with the Roman *Mars.*

a·rête (ə·rāt′) *n. Geog.* A sharp mountain spur or ridge. [<F <L *arista* awn of wheat, fishbone]

ar·e·thu·sa (ar′ə·thōō′zə, -sə) *n.* Any plant of a bulbous genus *(Arethusa)* of North American orchids, having a leafless or one-leaved scape and rose-colored flowers.

Ar·e·thu·sa (ar′ə·thōō′zə, -sə) In Greek mythology, a nymph who was changed into a fountain so that she might escape her pursuer Alpheus.

A·re·ti·no (ä′rā·tē′nō), **Pietro,** 1492–1556, Italian poet and courtier.

A·rez·zo (ä·ret′tsō) A town in central Italy: ancient *Arretium.*

Ar·gae·us (är·jē′əs) The ancient name for ERCIYAS DAGI. Also **Ar·gæ′us.**

ar·gal[1] (är′gəl) See ARGOL.

ar·gal[2] (är′gəl) See ARGALI.

ar·gal[3] (är′gəl) *conj. Obs.* Therefore. [Alter. of L *ergo*]

ar·ga·la (är′gə·lə) *n.* **1** An adjutant bird. **2** A marabou. [<Hind. *hargilā*]

ar·ga·li (är′gə·lē) *n. pl.* **·lis** or **·li 1** An Asiatic wild sheep *(Ovis ammon)* with large, thick, horns curved spirally **2** Any of several other wild sheep, as the **bearded argali** or aoudad; the **American argali** or big horn. [<Mongolian]

ARGALI
(4 feet tall at the shoulder; horn spread, about 3 feet)

Ar·gall (är′gôl, -gəl), **Sir Samuel,** died 1625, English mariner.

Ar·gand (ar·gän′), **Aimé,** 1755–1803, Swiss physician and chemist.

Ar·gand burner (är′gənd) An oil or gas burner having a cylindrical wick supplied with air within as well as without to provide a maximum area of contact between the fuel and the flame. [after A. *Argand*]

Argand lamp A lamp using an Argand burner.

ar·gent (är′jənt) *n.* **1** *Her.* The white color of armorial bearings, symbolic of purity, innocence, etc. **2** Silver. **3** Silvery quality or color; whiteness. *—adj.* Like or made of silver; white; silvery: also **ar·gen·tal** (är·jen′təl). [<F <L *argentum* silver] **—ar·gen·te·ous** (är·jen′tē·əs).

ar·gen·tan (är′jən·tən) *n.* German silver. [<L *argentum* silver]

Ar·gen·tan (år·zhäṅ·täṅ′) A town in Normandy, NW France; scene of a strategic battle of World War II, August, 1944.

ar·gen·tate (är′jən·tāt) *adj.* Silvery or shining white.

ar·gen·ta·tion (är′jən·tā′shən) *n.* A coating or plating with silver.

Ar·gen·teuil (år·zhäṅ·tœ′y′) A city on the NW outskirts of Paris, France.

ar·gen·tic (är·jen′tik) *adj.* Containing or pertaining to silver, especially in its higher valence or ordinary proportion: *argentic* chloride, AgCl.

ar·gen·tif·er·ous (är′jən·tif′ər·əs) *adj.* Containing or producing silver: *argentiferous* ore.

Ar·gen·ti·na (är′jən·tē′nə) A republic of southern South America between the Andes and the Atlantic; 1,073,699 square miles; capital, Buenos Aires. Also **Argentine Republic** or **the Argentine.**

ar·gen·tine (är′jən·tin, -tīn) *n.* **1** Silver-white metal. **2** A precipitate of tin and zinc. **3** A pearly calcite. **4** The silvery substance obtained from fish scales and used in making artificial pearls. **5** Silver. *—adj.* Silvery. [<F *argentin* < <*argentum* silver]

Ar·gen·tine (är′jən·tēn, -tīn) *adj.* Of or pertaining to Argentina. *—n.* A native or citizen of Argentina. **—Ar·gen·tin·an** (är′jən·tin′·ē·ən) *n.*

ar·gen·tite (är′jən·tīt) *n.* An isometric, lead-gray, sectile silver sulfide, Ag_2S; silver glance; argyrite. [<L *argentum* silver + -ITE[1]]

ar·gen·tol (är′jən·tōl, -tol) *n.* A silver salt, $C_9N_5N(OH)SO_3Ag$, used as an antiseptic and astringent. [<L *argentum* silver + -OL]

ar·gen·tous (är·jen′təs) *adj.* Of or pertaining to a compound containing univalent silver.

ar·gen·tum (är·jen′təm) *n. Chem.* Silver. [<L]

Ar·ges (är′jesh) A river of southern Rumania, flowing SE 180 miles to the Danube.

ar·gil (är′jil) *n.* **1** Potters' clay; white clay. **2** Aluminite. [<F *argile* <L *argilla* white clay <Gk. *argilla* <*argos* white] **—ar·gil·lif·er·ous** (är′·jə·lif′ər·əs) *adj.*

ar·gil·la·ceous (är′jə·lā′shəs) *adj.* Containing, consisting of, or like clay; clayey.

ar·gil·lite (är′jə·līt) *n.* An argillaceous sedimentary rock, with or without slaty cleavage; mudrock: sometimes called *pelite* [<L *argilla* white clay + -ITE[1]]

ar·gil·lous (är·jil′əs) *adj.* Argillaceous; clayey.

ar·gi·nine (är′jə·nēn, -nin, -nīn) *n.* One of the amino acids essential to nutrition, $C_6H_{14}O_2N_4$, obtained from animal and vegetable proteins by hydrolysis or bacterial action. [<L *argentum* silver + -INE[2]]

Ar·gi·nu·sae (är′jə·nōō′sē, -nyōō′-) The ancient name of three islands between Lesbos and Asia Minor; site of a naval battle in which the Athenians defeated the Spartans in 406 B.C. Also **Ar′gi·nu′sæ.**

Ar·give (är′jīv, -gīv) *adj.* **1** Of or pertaining to Argos or Argolis. **2** Greek. *—n.* **1** An inhabitant of Argos or Argolis. **2** A Greek, as in Homer.

ar·gle (är′gəl) *v.i. Scot.* To wrangle; argue. Also **ar′gle-bar′gle.**

Ar·go (är′gō) **1** In Greek legend, the ship in which Jason and the Argonauts sailed for the Golden Fleece. **2** *Astron.* A large southern constellation, the Ship, now generally divided into four parts.

ar·gol (är′gəl) *n.* Crude cream of tartar: the base of tartaric acid: also spelled *argal.* [ME *argoile;* origin unknown]

Ar·go·lis (är′gə·lis) A region of Greece in the NE Peloponnesus around the city of Argos, bordering on the **Gulf of Argolis,** an inlet of the Aegean.

ar·gon (ar′gon) *n.* An inert gaseous element (symbol Ar, atomic number 18), constituting about 0.94% of the atmosphere. See PERIODIC TABLE. [<NL <Gk., neuter of *argos* idle, inert]

ar·go·naut (är′gə·nôt) *n. Zool.* The paper nautilus.

Ar·go·naut (är′gə·nôt) *n.* **1** In Greek legend, one who sailed with Jason in the ship Argo to find the Golden Fleece. **2** A gold-seeker who went to California in 1849. [< L *Argonauta* < Gk. *Argonautēs* < *Argo,* the ship + *nautēs* sailor] — **ar′go·nau′tic** *adj.*

Ar·gonne (är′gon, *Fr.* ȧr·gôn′) A wooded ridge in northern France; site of several major battles of World War I. Also **Argonne Forest.**

Ar·gos (är′gos, -gəs) A city of NE Peloponnesus, traditionally the oldest city in Greece.

ar·go·sy (är′gə·sē) *n. pl.* **·sies 1** A large merchant ship. **2** A fleet of merchant vessels. [Earlier *ragusy* < *Ragusa,* Italian port which carried on extensive trade with England in the 16th C.]

ar·got (är′gō, -gət) *n.* **1** The secret language of the underworld. **2** The phraseology peculiar to any class or group. [< F] **—ar·got·ic** (är·got′ik) *adj.*

ar·gue (är′gyo͞o) *v.* **ar·gued, ar·gu·ing** *v.i.* **1** To urge reasons to support or contest a measure or opinion; reason. **2** To dispute or quarrel: Are you trying to *argue* with me? **3** To reason in opposition; raise objections: Don't stand there *arguing*—do as I say! —*v.t.* **4** To urge reasons for or against; discuss, as a proposal. **5** To contend or maintain, as by giving reasons: to *argue* that all men are equal. **6** To prove or indicate, as from evidence: His manner of speaking *argued* a good education. **7** To influence or convince, as by argument: to *argue* someone into buying a house. [< OF *arguer* < L *argutare,* freq. of *arguere* make clear, prove] **—ar′gu·a·ble** *adj.* — **ar·gu·er** *n.*

Synonyms: debate, demonstrate, discuss, dispute, prove, question, reason. To *argue* is to show the reasons for or against, so as to make a matter clear by reasoning; to *discuss* is to shake a matter apart for examination or analysis: One may *argue* or *discuss* a matter by himself; or with advocates, to make all clear; or with opponents, to *prove* his position and answer objections. We *argue* a case, *dispute* a bill. One side may do all the *arguing*; in *debating* both sides take part. See DISPUTE, PLEAD, REASON.

ar·gu·fy (är′gyə·fī) *v.* **·fied, ·fy·ing** *Colloq.* or *Dial.*—*v.t.* **1** To worry with arguing. —*v.i.* **2** To signify. **3** To argue, especially obstinately or merely for the sake of the argument. [< ARGUE + -FY]

ar·gu·ment (är′gyə·mənt) *n.* **1** A reason offered for or against something. **2** Something offered in proof; evidence. **3** A process of reasoning to establish or refute a position by the use of evidence; demonstration. **4** A contest in reasoning; debate; discussion. **5** *Logic* The middle term of a syllogism. **6** The plot or gist of a literary work. **7** *Stat.* A number given on the margin of a table to facilitate finding any of the included values. **8** *Math.* An independent variable from which another quantity can be deduced or on which its calculation depends. **9** *Obs.* The subject matter of a discourse or discussion; theme. See synonyms under REASON, REASONING. [< F < L *argumentum* < *arguere* make clear, prove]

ar·gu·men·ta·tion (är′gyə·men·tā′shən) *n.* **1** The methodical or logical setting forth of premises and the drawing of conclusions therefrom. **2** Interchange of argument; discussion; debate. **3** A sequence of arguments; process of reasoning.

ar·gu·men·ta·tive (är′gyə·men′tə·tiv) *adj.* Pertaining to, consisting of, or marked by argument; given to argumentation: an *argumentative* style. **—ar′gu·men′ta·tive·ly** *adv.* **—ar′gu·men′ta·tive·ness** *n.*

ar·gu·men·tum ad hom·i·nem (är′gyə·men′·təm ad hom′ə·nem) *Latin* Literally, an argument to the man; an argument addressed to feelings and prejudices rather than to reason.

Ar·gun (är′go͞on′) A river in NE Asia between the U.S.S.R. and Manchuria, flowing west 950 miles to the Shilka.

ar·gus (är′gəs) *n.* An East Indian pheasant (genus *Argus).*

Ar·gus (är′gəs) In Greek mythology, a giant with a hundred eyes: killed by Hermes, after which his eyes were put into the peacock's tail.

Ar·gus-eyed (är′gəs·īd′) *adj.* Sharp-sighted; vigilant.

ar·gute (är·gyo͞ot′) *adj.* **1** Quick or subtle; sharp; shrewd. **2** Shrill of sound. **3** *Bot.* Sharp-toothed, as a serrate leaf. [< L *argutus,* pp. of *arguere* make clear, prove]

Ar·gyle plaid (är′gīl) Plaid design of solid blocks or diamonds overlaid by a contrasting plaid. [from the tartan of the clan Campbell of *Argyll*]

Ar·gyll (är·gīl′) A country of western Scotland; 3,110 square miles. Also **Ar·gyll·shire** (är·gīl′·shir).

Ar·gyll (är·gīl′), **Duke of,** 1845–1914, John Douglas Sutherland Campbell, governor general of Canada 1878–83.

ar·gyr·o·dite (är·jir′ə·dīt) *n.* A steel-gray metallic silver mineral, Ag_6GeS_5, that crystallizes in the monoclinic system. [< Gk. *argyrōdēs* rich in silver < *argyros* silver]

Ar·gy·rol (är′jə·rōl, -rol) *n.* A compound of silver oxide and a protein, used as a local antiseptic in membranous infections: a trade name. [< Gk. *argyros* silver + -OL]

a·ri·a (ä′rē·ə, âr′ē·ə) *n.* **1** An air; melody. **2** An elaborate solo for single voice, as in an opera or oratorio, often with instrumental accompaniment. [< Ital. < L *aer* air]

-aria *suffix* Used in forming new Latin names, especially in zoological and botanical classifications. [< NL < L *-arius*]

Ar·i·ad·ne (ar′ē·ad′nē) In Greek mythology, the daughter of Minos and Pasiphae, who gave Theseus the thread by which he found his way out of the Labyrinth: when he fled Crete, Theseus took her with him, but later abandoned her on Naxos.

Ar·i·an (âr′ē·ən) *adj.* Of or pertaining to Arius or Arianism. —*n.* A believer in Arianism.

Ar·i·an (âr′ē·ən, ar′-, är′yən) See ARYAN.

-arian *suffix* Used in forming adjectives and adjectival nouns denoting occupation, age, sect, beliefs, etc.: *nonagenarian, predestinarian.* [< L *-arius* -ary + *-anus* -an]

Ar·i·an·ism (âr′ē·ən·iz′əm) *n.* The doctrines of Arius (fourth century) and his followers, denying that Christ is one substance with the Father.

A·ri·ca (ä·rē′kä) A port in northern Chile.

ar·id (ar′id) *adj.* **1** Parched with heat; dry. **2** Unfruitful; barren. **3** Without interest; dull. **4** Profitless. [< L *aridus* < *arere* be dry] **—a·rid·i·ty** (ə·rid′ə·tē), **ar′id·ness** *n.* **—ar′id·ly** *adv.*

ar·i·el (âr′ē·əl) *n.* An African gazelle *(Gazella dama).* Also **ariel gazelle.** [< Arabic *aryal*]

Ar·i·el (âr′ē·əl) A masculine personal name. [< Hebrew, lion of God]

—Ariel In medieval folklore, a spirit of the air.

—Ariel In Shakespeare's *Tempest,* an airy spirit employed by Prospero.

Ar·i·el (âr′ē·əl) The inner satellite of Uranus.

Ar·ies (âr′ēz, âr′ē·iz) **1** *Astron.* A constellation, the Ram. **2** In astrology, the first sign of the zodiac, which the sun enters on or about March 21st, the vernal equinox. See CONSTELLATION. [< L, the Ram]

ar·i·et·ta (ar′ē·et′ə) *n.* A short aria. Also **ar·i·ette** (ar′ē·et′). [< Ital.]

a·right (ə·rīt′) *adv.* In a right way; correctly; rightly; exactly.

A·ri·ka·ra (ə·rē′kər·ə) *n.* A member of a North American Indian tribe of Caddoan linguistic stock, formerly inhabiting the Dakotas.

ar·il (ar′il) *n. Bot.* An accessory covering of a seed, orginating at or around the funiculus, [< NL *arillus* < Med. L *arilli* dried grapes] **—ar·il·late** (ar′ə·lāt), **ar′il·lat′ed** *adj.*

ar·il·lode (ar′ə·lōd) *n. Bot.* A false aril; an outgrowth originating at or around the micropyle. [< NL *arillus* (see ARIL) + -ODE[2]]

Ar·i·ma·the·a (ar′ə·mə·thē′ə) A town of ancient Palestine, the home of Joseph, a disciple of Jesus, *Matt.* xxvii 57. Also **Ar′i·ma·thae′a. —Ar′·i·ma·the′an** *adj.*

A·rim·i·num (ə·rim′ə·nəm) The ancient name for RIMINI.

A·ri·on (ə·rī′on) Greek poet and musician of Lesbos, about 700 B.C.; reputed inventor of dithyrambic poetry.

ar·iose (ar′ē·ōs, ar′ē·ōs′) *adj. Music* Characteristic of a melody; songlike. [< Ital. *arioso* < *aria* air]

a·rio·so (ä·ryō′sō) *adj.* & *adv. Music* Of the nature or in the manner of both recitative and aria: said of a passage of dramatic or declamatory character emphasized by the libretto. [< Ital.]

A·ri·os·to (ä′rē·ôs′tō), **Lodovico,** 1474–1533, Italian poet.

-arious *suffix of adjectives* Connected with; pertaining to: *gregarious.* [< L *-arius* -ary + -OUS]

Ar·i·o·vis·tus (ar′ē·ō·vis′təs) Germanic chieftain of the first century B.C.; an opponent of Julius Caesar.

A·ri·pua·ña (ä′rē·pwa·nañ′) A river in western Brazil, flowing 400 miles north to the Madeira.

a·rise (ə·rīz′) *v.i.* **a·rose** (ə·rōz), **a·ris·en** (ə·riz′·ən), **a·ris·ing 1** To get up, as from a prone position. **2** To rise; ascend, as the sun above the horizon. **3** To spring forth; originate, as a river from its source. **4** To be born; come into being; appear. **5** *Poetic* To revive from death. [OE *ārīsan* < *ā-* up + *rīsan* rise]

a·ris·ta (ə·ris′tə) *n. pl.* **·tae** (-tē) *Bot.* An awn or any similar bristly or beardlike appendage. [< L. Doublet of ARRIS.]

Ar·is·tae·us (ar′is·tē′əs) In Greek mythology, a son of Apollo, the tutelary deity of herdsmen and beekeepers. Also **Ar′is·tæ′us.**

Ar·is·tar·chus (ar′is·tär′kəs), 220–142 B.C., grammarian and critic of Alexandria.

—Aristarchus of Samos Greek astronomer of the third century B.C.

a·ris·tate (ə·ris′tāt) *adj. Bot.* Having a beard-like appendage; awned.

Ar·is·ti·des (ar′is·tī′dēz) Greek statesman and general in the fifth century B.C.: called "the Just."

Ar·is·tip·pus (ar′is·tip′əs), 435–366? B.C., Greek philosopher of Cyrene.

aristo- *combining form* Best, finest: *aristocracy.* [< Gk. *aristos*]

ar·is·toc·ra·cy (ar′is·tok′rə·sē) *n. pl.* **·cies 1** A hereditary nobility or privileged class, preeminent by birth or privilege and having prescriptive rank and rights. **2** The chief persons of a country; hence, any group preeminent in any way, as by virtue of wealth, talent, etc. **3** A state ruled by its best citizens. **4** The ruling class in such a state. [< L *aristocratia* < Gk. *aristokratia* < *aristos* best + *krateein* rule]

a·ris·to·crat (ə·ris′tə·krat, ar′is·tə·krat′) *n.* **1** A member of an aristocracy. **2** A proud and exclusive person. **3** One who prefers an aristocratic form of government. **—a·ris′to·crat′ic** or **·i·cal** *adj.* **—a·ris′to·crat′i·cal·ly** *adv.*

Ar·is·tol (ar′is·tōl, -tol) *n.* Proprietary name of a brand of thymol iodide. [< ARISTO- + -OL]

a·ris·to·lo·chi·a·ceous (ə·ris′tə·lō′kē·ā′shəs) *adj. Bot.* Belonging to a family *(Aristolochiaceae)* of tropical climbing plants with apetalous, irregular, pungent-smelling flowers. [< NL < L *aristolochia,* a plant deemed useful in childbirth < Gk. *aristolocheia* < *aristos* best + *locheia* childbirth]

Ar·is·toph·a·nes (ar′is·tof′ə·nēz), 450–380? B.C., Greek comic dramatist.

Ar·is·to·te·li·an (ar′is·tə·tē′lē·ən, -tə·tēl′yən, ə·ris′tə-) *adj.* Pertaining to or characteristic of Aristotle or his philosophy. —*n.* An adherent of Aristotle or of Aristotelianism.

Ar·is·to·te·li·an·ism (ar′is·tə·tē′lē·ən·iz′əm, -tēl′yən-, ə·ris′tə-) *n.* The philosophy or doctrines of Aristotle, especially as distinguished from Platonism by empirical or deductive reasoning.

Aristotelian logic 1 The deductive logic of Aristotle, characterized by the syllogism. **2** Logic considered from the standpoint of the form, rather than the content, of propositions.

Ar·is·tot·le (ar′is·tot′l), 384–322 B.C., Greek philosopher; pupil of Plato.

Aristotle's lantern *Zool.* The skeleton of the mouth parts of a sea urchin.

a·ris·to·type (ə·ris′tə·tīp) *n. Phot.* A print made on paper treated with mixed collodion and gelatin. [< ARISTO- + -TYPE]

a·ris·tu·late (ə·ris′cho͞o·lit, -lāt) *adj. Bot.* Having a small awn. [< L *arista* beard of grain]

ar·ith·man·cy (ar′ith·man′sē) *n.* Divination by numbers. [< Gk. *arithmos* number + *manteia* divination]

a·rith·me·tic (ə·rith′mə·tik) *n.* **1** The science of numbers and of computing with numbers under the four operations of addition, subtraction, multiplication, and division. **2** A treatise upon this science.

—ar·ith·met·ic (ar′ith·met′ik) *adj.* Of or pertaining to arithmetic: also **ar′ith·met′i·cal.**

[<L *arithmetica* <Gk. *(hē) arithmetikē (technē)* (the) counting (art) <*arithmeein* count, number <*arithmos* number] —**ar′ith·met′i·cal·ly** *adv.*

a·rith·me·ti·cian (ə·rith′mə·tish′ən, ar′ith-) *n.* One who uses or is skilled in arithmetic.

ar·ith·met·ic mean (ar′ith·met′ik) The sum of a group of measures, observations, magnitudes, scores, etc., divided by the total number of items in the group.

ar·ith·met·ic progression (ar′ith·met′ik) A sequence of terms such that each except the first differs from the preceding one by a constant quantity, either plus or minus, as 2, 4, 6, 8. See GEOMETRIC PROGRESSION. Also **arithmetical progression, arithmetic series, arithmetic sequence.**

a·rith·mo·ma·ni·a (ə·rith′mō·mā′nē·ə, -mān′yə) *n.* The impulse or desire to count everything. [<NL <Gk. *arithmos* number + -MANIA]

ar·ith·mom·e·ter (ar′ith·mom′ə·tər) *n.* A calculating machine.

-arium *suffix of nouns* **1** A place for: *herbarium.* **2** Connected with: *honorarium.* [<L <*-arius.* See -ARY.]

A·ri·us (ə·rī′əs, âr′ē·əs), 280?–336, Greek theologian; patriarch of Alexandria. See ARIANISM.

a ri·ve·der·ci (ä rē′vā·dâr′chē) *Italian* Until we meet again; so long.

Ar·i·zo·na (ar′ə·zō′nə) A State of the SW United States, bordering on Mexico; 113,909 square miles; capital, Phoenix; entered the Union Feb. 14, 1912: nickname *Apache State*: abbr. AZ —**Ar′i·zo′nan, Ar′i·zo′ni·an** (-nē·ən) *adj. & n.*

ark (ärk) *n.* **1** The ship of Noah (*Gen.* vi 14–22). **2** The chest containing the tables of the law (*Ex.* xxv 10): also called the **ark of the covenant. 3** The papyrus cradle of Moses (*Ex.* ii 3). **4** A flat–bottomed freight boat or scow; also, a large farm wagon. **5** *Dial.* A coffer, chest, or bin. ◆ Homophone: *arc.* [OE *arc* <L *arca* chest]

Ar·kan·san (är·kan′zən) *n.* A native or inhabitant of Arkansas.

Ar·kan·sas (är′kən·sô) **1** A State of the south central United States, just west of the Mississippi River; 53,102 square miles; capital, Little Rock; entered the Union June 15, 1836: nickname *Wonder State* or *Bear State*: abbr. AR **2** See QUAPAW.

Ar·kan·sas River (är′kən·sô, är·kan′zəs) A river rising in the Rocky Mountains of central Colorado and flowing SE 1,450 miles to the Mississippi in Arkansas.

Arkansas Traveler 1 Colonel Sandy Faulkner, 1803–74, an Arkansas cotton planter: alleged author of a famous dialog between a squatter and himself, the traveler. **2** Also, the dialog and the tune entitled *Arkansas Traveler.*

Ar·khan·gelsk (är·khän′gelsk) A city on the Dvina in NW Russian S.F.S.R.: also *Archangel.*

Ark·wright (ärk′rīt), **Sir Richard,** 1732–92, English cotton–manufacturer; invented the spinning jenny.

Arl·berg (ärl′berkh) An Alpine peak, 5,910 feet, in western Austria; winter sports center and site of the **Arlberg Tunnel,** 6⅜ miles.

Ar·len (är′lən), **Michael,** 1895–1956, English novelist born in Armenia: original name *Dikran Kouyoumdjian.*

arles (ärlz) *n. Brit. Dial.* **1** Money given in confirmation of a bargain: also **arles′–pen′ny. 2** An earnest or foretaste.

Arles (ärlz, *Fr.* árl) A city in SE France; site of Roman ruins. Ancient **Ar·e·las** (ar′ə·las).

Ar·ling·ton (är′ling·tən) An urban county of NE Virginia on the Potomac River opposite Washington, D.C.; site of a national cemetery containing the tomb of the Unknown Soldier.

Ar·liss (är′lis), **George,** 1868–1946, English actor.

Ar·lon (ár·lôṅ′) A city in SE Belgium, capital of Luxemburg province.

arm[1] (ärm) *n.* **1** *Anat.* **a** The upper limb of the human body, from the shoulder to the hand or wrist. **b** The part from the shoulder joint to the elbow joint. **2** The fore limb of vertebrates other than man. ◆ Collateral adjective: *brachial.* **3** An armlike part or appendage. **4** The part in contact with the human arm: *arm* of a chair. **5** Anything branching out like an arm from the main body, or set apart or considered as a distinct part or branch; a subdivision: an *arm* of the sea. **6** *Naut.* **a** One of the projecting members of an anchor, ending in a fluke. **b** An end of a spar. **7** Strength to accomplish or aid; might: the *arm* of the law. —**arm in arm** With arms enlaced, as two persons walking together. —**at arm's length** At a distance, so as to keep from being friendly or intimate. —**with open arms** Cordially; warmly. [OE *arm, earm*]

arm[2] (ärm) *n.* **1** A weapon. **2** A distinct branch of the naval or military service: the air *arm.* —*v.t.* **1** To supply with instruments of warfare; equip, as with weapons or tools. **2** To make secure, as with a protective covering. —*v.i.* **3** To supply or equip oneself with weapons or other defensive means. **4** To supply oneself with the means necessary for an undertaking. [See ARMS]

ar·ma·da (är·mä′də, -mā′-) *n.* A fleet of war–vessels. —**the Armada** The fleet sent against England by Spain in 1588. It was defeated by the English navy and almost entirely destroyed by storms: also called **Invincible Armada, Spanish Armada.** [<Sp. <L *armata* <*armare* arm. Doublet of ARMY.]

ar·ma·dil·lo (är′mə·dil′ō) *n. pl.* **·los** An American burrowing nocturnal mammal (family *Dasypodidae*) of the Edentate order, having an armorlike covering of jointed plates; especially, the nine–banded armadillo *(Dasypus novemcinctus)* of Mexico and Texas. [<Sp., dim. of *armado* armed <L *armatus,* pp. of *armare* arm]

ARMADILLO
(1 1/2 feet from head to tail; tail about 1 foot)

Ar·ma·ged·don (är′mə·ged′n) **1** In Biblical prophecy, the scene of a great battle between the forces of good and evil, to occur at the end of the world. *Rev.* xvi 16. **2** Any great or decisive conflict. [<LL *Armagedon* <Gk. *Armageddon,* prob. <Hebrew *Megiddon* the plain of Megiddo, a perennial battlefield]

Ar·magh (är·mä′) A county of Ulster province, southern Northern Ireland; 489 square miles; county seat, Armagh.

Ar·ma·gnac (ár·má·nyák′) *n.* Brandy distilled from wine in the Armagnac region of SW France.

ar·ma·ment (är′mə·mənt) *n.* **1** A land or naval force. **2** The guns, munitions, and other military equipment of a fortification, military unit, airplane, vehicle, or vessel. **3** Equipment or the act of arming or equipping for war or battle. **4** The body of naval, air, and ground forces equipped for war, engaged in an expedition, or present in a given command area. **5** The aggregate of a nation's organized war power. See synonyms under ARMY. [<L *armamenta* implements, ship's tackle <*armare* arm]

Ar·mand (ár·mäṅ′) French form of HERMAN.

ar·ma·ture (är′mə·choo͝r) *n.* **1** A piece of soft iron joining the poles of a magnet to prevent the loss of magnetic power. **2** *Electr.* **a** In a dynamo or motor, the cylindrical, laminated iron core carrying the coils of insulated wire to be revolved through the magnetic field. **b** The part of a relay, as a buzzer or bell, that vibrates when activated by a magnetic field. **3** *Biol.* **a** Protective covering for defense or offense, as the shells of animals, prickles on plants, etc. **b** A set of organs: the gastric *armature.* **4** *Archit.* Framing used to stiffen or brace. **5** In sculpture, a framework to support the clay or other substance used in modeling. **6** Arms; armor. —*v.t.* **·tured, ·tur·ing** To furnish or provide with an armature. [<F <L *armatura* armor <*armare* arm. Doublet of ARMOR.]

arm·band (ärm′band′) *n.* A brassard. Also **arm band.**

arm·chair (ärm′châr′) *n.* A chair with side supports for the arms or elbows.

armed (ärmd) *adj.* Equipped with arms; provided with or bearing weapons.

armed forces The combined military and naval forces of a nation; in the United States, the Army, Navy, Air Force, Marine Corps, and Coast Guard.

Ar·me·ni·a (är·mē′nē·ə, -mēn′yə) **1** A former kingdom of NE Asia Minor; generally understood to include eastern Turkey and the Armenian S.S.R. **2** A constituent republic (**Armenian S.S.R.**) of Transcaucasian U.S.S.R.; 11,500 square miles; capital, Erivan. *Armenian* **Ha·yas·dan** (hä′yäs·tän′, -dän′).

Ar·me·ni·an (är·mē′nē·ən, -mēn′yən) *adj.* Of or pertaining to the country, people, or language of Armenia. —*n.* **1** A native of Armenia. **2** The language of Armenia, belonging to the Armenian subfamily of Indo–European languages.

Ar·men·tières (ár·mäṅ·tyâr′) A town in northern France, near Lille; destroyed in heavy World War I fighting, 1918.

arm·er (är′mər) *n.* One who arms.

ar·met (är′met) *n.* A light steel helmet of the 15th and 16th centuries, with vizor and neck-guard. [<F <OF *armette,* dim. of *arme* arm[2]]

arm·ful (ärm′fo͝ol′) *n. pl.* **·fuls** That which is held, or as much as can be held, in the arm or arms.

arm·hole (ärm′hōl′) *n.* An opening for the arm in a garment.

ar·mi·ger (är′mə·jər) *n.* **1** An armorbearer attending a knight; a squire. **2** A person entitled to bear heraldic arms. Also **ar·mig·e·ro** (är·mij′ə·rō). [<L <*arma* weapons + *gerere* bear]

ar·mil·lar·y (är′mə·ler′ē, är·mil′ə·rē) *adj.* Pertaining to or consisting of a ring or rings. [<L *armilla* arm ring, bracelet]

armillary sphere *Astron.* An arrangement of concentric rings in the form of a skeleton sphere, representing the relative positions of the ecliptic and other celestial circles.

arm·ing (är′ming) *n.* **1** The act of supplying with or taking arms. **2** That with which anything is armed. **3** *Naut.* Tallow on a sounding plummet to bring up matter from sea bottom. **4** *Her.* A coat of arms.

Ar·min·i·an·ism (är·min′ē·ən·iz′əm) *n. Theol.* The doctrines of Jacobus Arminius and his followers, opposed to Calvinism chiefly as holding a less rigorous view of predestination. —**Ar·min′i·an** *adj. & n.*

Ar·min·i·us (är·min′ē·əs) Latin form of HERMAN. —**Arminius,** 17 B.C.–A.D. 21, German national hero, defeated Roman governor Varus at battle of Teutoburger Wald, A.D. 9: sometimes called "Hermann."

Arminius, Jacobus, 1560–1609, Dutch Protestant theologian.

ar·mip·o·tent (är·mip′ə·tənt) *adj.* Mighty in arms. [<L *armipotens, -entis* <*arma* arms + *potens.* See POTENT.] —**ar·mip′o·tence** *n.*

ar·mi·stice (är′mə·stis) *n.* A temporary cessation, by mutual agreement, of hostilities; a truce. [<F <L *arma* arms + *stare* stand still]

Armistice Day See VETERANS DAY.

arm·let (ärm′lit) *n.* **1** A little arm, as of the sea. **2** An ornamental band worn around the upper arm. **3** A small, short sleeve. **4** *Archaic* A piece of armor for the arm.

ar·moire (är·mwär′) *n.* A large, movable, often ornate cabinet or cupboard; ambry. [<F <OF *aumoire* <L *armarium* a chest, orig., a place for storing arms]

ar·mor (är′mər) *n.* **1** A defensive covering, as of mail for a warrior, or of metallic plates for a war vessel, a tank, a deep–sea diver's suit, etc. **2** The aggregate of armored assault vehicles available to a military command. **3** *Biol.* The protective covering of various animals, as turtles, armadillos, and some fishes. See synonyms under ARMS. —*v.t. & v.i.* To furnish with or put on armor. Also *Brit.* **ar′mour.** [<OF *armeüre* <L *armatura.* Doublet of ARMATURE.]

ar·mor·bear·er (är′mər·bâr′ər) *n.* One bearing the arms of a warrior; a squire; armiger.

ar·mor–clad (är′mər·klad′) *adj.* Covered or plated with armor.

ar·mored (är′mərd) *adj.* **1** Protected by armor, as an automobile, a cruiser, or train. **2** Equipped with armored vehicles, as a military unit. Also *Brit.* **ar′moured.**

armored car 1 *Mil.* A motor vehicle protected by armor plate and used for reconnaissance, carrying ammunition or personnel, or as a self-propelled mount for machine-guns, anti-aircraft artillery, etc. 2 A small truck or other vehicle protected by light armor plate, used for transporting money, etc.

armored force A combination of tanks, armored cars, and other armored vehicles functioning as an offensive unit in modern warfare.

ar·mor·er (är′mər·ər) *n.* 1 A maker, repairer, or custodian of arms or armor. 2 A manufacturer of arms. 3 *Mil.* An enlisted man in charge of the repair, maintenance, and supply of small arms. Also *Brit.* **ar′mour·er.**

ar·mo·ri·al (är·môr′ē·əl, -mō′rē-) *adj.* Pertaining to heraldry or heraldic arms. —*n.* A treatise on heraldry.

Ar·mor·ic (är·môr′ik, -mor′-) *adj.* Of Armorica, its people, or their language. —*n.* Armorican.

Ar·mor·i·ca (är·môr′ə·kə, -mor′-) An ancient name for the NW part of France, later identified with Brittany.

Ar·mor·i·can (är·môr′ə·kən, -mor′-) *adj.* Armoric. —*n.* 1 A native or inhabitant of Armorica. 2 The language of Armorica, belonging to the Brythonic branch of Celtic languages; Breton. Also *Armoric.*

ar·mor-pierc·ing (är′mər·pir′sing) *adj.* Designating a type of projectile with a hard-shelled nose, designed to penetrate heavy armor and burst on the far side.

armor plate A protective covering of special high carbon steel alloy containing variable proportions of nickel, chrome, and manganese, forged under great pressure and given a hard surface. **—ar′mor-plat′ed** *adj.*

ar·mor·y[1] (är′mər·ē) *n. pl.* **·mor·ies** 1 A place for the safekeeping of arms. 2 A building for the use of a body of militia, including general storage for arms and equipment, drill-rooms, etc. 3 *U.S.* A factory for making firearms. 4 *Archaic* Arms collectively; armor. 5 *Archaic* The craft or trade of the armorer. Also *Brit.* **ar′mour·y.** [Prob. < ARMOR]

ar·mor·y[2] (är′mər·ē) *n. Archaic* 1 Armorial bearings; heraldic arms. 2 Heraldry; the science of blazoning arms. [< OF *armoirie* < *armoier* blazoner < *armoier* blazon, publish a coat of arms]

ar·mour (är′mər), etc. See ARMOR, etc.

Ar·mour (är′mər), **Philip Danforth,** 1832–1901, U.S. meat packer.

ar·mo·zine (är′mə·zēn′) *n. Archaic* A plain silk, often used for clerical robes, etc. Also **armo·zeen′** [< F *armoisin*]

arm·pit (ärm′pit′) *n.* The cavity under the arm at the shoulder; axilla.

arms (ärmz) *n. pl.* 1 Weapons collectively. 2 Warfare. 3 The official insignia or device of a state, person, or family. 4 Heraldic symbols. —**small arms** Firearms of small caliber, carried by hand, as pistols, rifles, machine-guns, etc. **—to arms!** Arm yourselves! Make ready for battle! **—to bear arms** 1 To be provided with arms. 2 To serve as a member of the armed forces. **—under arms** Provided with weapons; ready for war. **—up in arms** Aroused and ready to fight. [< F *armes* < L *arma* weapons]

Synonyms: armor; weapons. *Arms* are implements of attack; *armor* is a defensive covering. Any vessel provided with cannon is an *armed* vessel; an *armored* ship is steel-clad. Anything that can be wielded in fight may be a *weapon; arms* are especially made and designed for conflict.

Arm·strong (ärm′strông, -strong), **Edwin Howard,** 1890–1954, U.S. electrical engineer. **—Neil Alden,** born 1930, U.S. astronaut; first man to walk on the moon, July 20, 1969. **—William George,** 1810–1900, Baron Armstrong of Cragside, English inventor and industrialist.

ar·mure (är′myŏŏr) *n.* A twilled fabric woven in ridges to resemble chain mail. [< F < OF *armeüre.* See ARMOR.]

ar·my (är′mē) *n. pl.* **ar·mies** 1 A large organized body of men armed for military service on land. 2 The largest organized autonomous unit of the U.S. land forces, consisting of a headquarters, a variable number of corps, and auxiliary troops and trains: also called **field army.** 3 Any large, united body: an *army* of ants. 4 A host. **—United States Army** 1 The U.S. land military forces administered by the Department of the Army under the Department of Defense and including the Regular Army, the Army Reserve, and the National Guard of the United States. 2 Loosely, the Regular Army. [< OF *armee* < L *armata.* Doublet of ARMADA.]

Synonyms: armament, force, forces, host, legions, military, multitude, phalanx, soldiers, soldiery, troops. *Host* is used for any vast and orderly assemblage; as, the stars are called the heavenly *host. Multitude* expresses number without order or organization. Organization and unity rather than numbers are the essentials of an *army. Legion* and *phalanx* are applied by a kind of poetic license to modern *forces*; the plural *legions* is preferred to the singular. Any organized body of men by whom law is executed is a *force.*

Ar·my (är′mē) *n.* The total military land forces of a specified country, exclusive in some countries of the air forces: the British *Army,* the French *Army,* the American *Army,* etc.

Army Air Forces The air arm of the U.S. Army before establishment of the separate U.S. Air Force in 1947.

army ant A foraging ant.

army of occupation An army maintained in a defeated country to enforce the terms of surrender, keep the peace, etc.

Army of the United States 1 The body of personnel on active service in the United States Army, usually during wartime, composed of persons from the Regular Army appointed to a higher grade than their regular commissions, draftees, personnel or units of the Army Reserve and National Guard, and other components created for special purposes. 2 Loosely, United States Army.

army worm The larva of a moth (family *Phalaenidae*) which moves at times in vast destructive hosts, especially the larva of *Leucania unipuncta.*

ar·nat·to (är·nat·ō) *n.* Annatto.

Arne (ärn), **Thomas Augustine,** 1710–78, English composer.

Arn·hem (ärn′hem) The capital of Gilderland province on the lower Rhine, eastern Netherlands. *German* **Arn·heim** (ärn′hīm).

Arn·hem Land (är′nəm) A coastal region of Northern Territory, Australia; designated as an aboriginal reservation in 1931; about 31,200 square miles.

ar·ni·ca (är′ni·kə) *n.* 1 Any of a genus *(Arnica)* of widely distributed herbaceous perennials of the composite family, especially the common European arnica *(A. montana).* 2 A tincture prepared from the flower heads and roots of this herb, extensively used for sprains and bruises. [< NL]

Ar·no (är′nō) A river of central Italy, flowing 150 miles west to the Mediterranean.

Ar·nold (är′nəld, *Ger.* är′nôlt) A masculine personal name. Also *Fr.* **Ar·naud** (år·nō′), *Ital.* **Ar·nol·do** (är·nôl′dō), *Sp.* **Ar·nal·do** (är·näl′dō). [< Gmc., eagle power]

—Ar·nold von Win·kel·ried (är′nôlt fôn ving′·kəl·rēt) Swiss hero said to have led the charge against the Austrians at the battle of Sempach, 1386.

Arnold, Benedict, 1741–1801, American Revolutionary general who became a traitor. **—Sir Edwin,** 1832–1904, English poet and Orientalist. **—Henry Harky,** 1886–1950, commanding general of United States Army Air Forces in World War II. **—Matthew,** 1822–88, English poet and critic. **—Thomas,** 1795–1842, English educator, father of preceding.

A·roe Islands (är′rōō) See ARU ISLANDS.

ar·oid (är′oid) *adj.* Araceous. Also **a·roi·de·ous** (ə·roi′dē·əs). —*n.* Any araceous plant. [< AR(UM) + -OID]

a·roint (ə·roint′) *v.i. Archaic* Avaunt! Begone!: used in the imperative, with reflexive *thee* or *ye.* Also **a·roynt′.** [Origin uncertain]

a·ro·ma (ə·rō′mə) *n.* 1 Fragrance, as from plants; agreeable odor. 2 Characteristic quality or style. [< L < Gk. *arōma* spice] **—a·ro·ma·tous** (ə·rō′mə·təs) *adj.*

ar·o·mat·ic (ar′ə·mat′ik) *adj.* 1 Having an aroma; fragrant; spicy. 2 *Chem.* Pertaining to a group of hydrocarbon compounds of the closed-ring formation and derived chiefly from benzene, as naphthalene: distinguished from *aliphatic.* Also **ar′o·mat′i·cal.** —*n.* 1 Any vegetable or drug of agreeable odor. 2 An aromatic chemical compound. **—ar′o·mat′i·cal·ly** *adv.*

a·ro·ma·tic·i·ty (ə·rō′mə·tis′ə·tē) *n. Chem.* The aromatic character of certain hydrocarbons as determined by their molecular structure rather than by their smell.

a·ro·ma·tize (ə·rō′mə·tīz) *v.t.* **·tized, ·tiz·ing** 1 To make fragrant or aromatic. 2 *Chem.* To convert (an aliphatic hydrocarbon) into one of the aromatic group.

A·roos·took River (ə·rōōs′tŏŏk) A river in northern Maine, flowing east 140 miles to the St. John River.

Aroostook War A series of border skirmishes between citizens of Maine and of New Brunswick, leading to the settlement of the NE boundary of the United States in 1842.

a·rose (ə·rōz′) Past tense of ARISE.

A·rou·et (å·rwe′), **François Marie** see VOLTAIRE.

a·round (ə·round′) *adv.* 1 So as to encompass or encircle all sides; in various directions. 2 So as to face the opposite way or different ways successively. 3 *U.S.* From place to place; here and there: to walk *around.* 4 *U.S. Colloq.* Nearby; in the vicinity: Wait *around* until I call. 5 In or to a particular place: Come *around* to see us again. 6 *U.S. Colloq.* Approximately; about: *around* fifty dollars. **—to come around** 1 To revive; regain consciousness. 2 To become convinced, as of an opinion. **—to get around** 1 To coax; wheedle; cajole. 2 To overcome; as an obstacle; hence, to evade or circumvent, as a law or rule. **—to get around to** To give attention to or accomplish: He'll *get around to* it in time. **—to have been around** *Colloq.* To be experienced in the ways of the world. —*prep.* 1 About the circuit of; encircling: to travel *around* the world. 2 In all or many directions about: a field of force *around* either magnetic pole. 3 On the other side of; to be reached or found by passing to the left or right of: the church *around* the corner. 4 Here and there in; in the region of; in various parts of: He wandered *around* the city. 5 Somewhere near or within: You'll find me *around* the house. 6 Approximately: The train leaves *around* midnight. [< A-[1] on + ROUND]

a·rous·al (ə·rou′zəl) *n.* An arousing; awakening.

a·rouse (ə·rouz′) *v.* **a·roused, a·rousing** *v.t.* 1 To stir up, as from sleep; awaken. 2 To excite, as to a state of high emotion; animate. —*v.i.* 3 To arouse oneself. See synonyms under ENCOURAGE, STIR. [< ROUSE, on analogy with *arise*]

a·row (ə·rō′) *adv.* In a row.

Arp (ärp), **Hans,** 1888–1966, German painter and sculptor: also **Jean Arp.**

Ar·pád (är′päd), died 907, Hungarian national hero.

ar·peg·gi·o (är·pej′·ē·ō, -pej′ō) *n. pl.* **·gi·os** *Music* 1 The sounding or playing of the notes of a chord in rapid succession instead of simultaneously, as in playing the harp. 2 A chord so played. [< Ital. < *arpeggiare* play on a harp < *arpa* a harp]

ARPEGGIO

ar·peg·gi·oed (är·pej′ē·ōd) *adj.* Sounded in the manner of an arpeggio.

ar·pent (är′pənt, *Fr.* år·pän′) *n.* An old French measure of land, equivalent to about an acre: still used in Louisiana and in Quebec. Also **ar·pen** (är′pən). [< F]

ar·que·bus (är′kwə·bəs), etc. See HARQUEBUS, etc.

ar·rack (ar′ək) *n.* A strong Oriental liquor distilled from rice, molasses, etc. [< Arabic *'araq* sweat, juice]

ar·raign (ə·rān′) *v.t.* 1 *Law* To call into court and cause to answer to an indictment. 2 To call upon for an answer; accuse. —*n.* Accusation; indictment. [< AF *arainer,* OF *araisnier* < LL *arrationare* call to account < L *ad-* to + *ratio* reason] **—ar·raign′ment** *n.*

Synonyms (verb): accuse, censure, charge, cite, impeach, indict, summon. One may *charge* another with any fault, great or trifling, privately or publicly, formally or informally. *Accuse* suggests more of the formal and criminal. *Indict* and *arraign* apply strictly to judicial proceedings; an alleged criminal is *indicted* by the grand jury and *arraigned* before the court. *Censure* carries the idea of fault but not of crime; it may be private and individual, or public and official. A judge, a president, or other officer of high rank may be *impeached* before the appropriate tribunal for high crimes; the veracity of a witness may be *impeached* by damaging evidence. One is arraigned *at* the bar, *before* the tribunal, *of* or *for* a crime, *on* or *upon* an indictment. *Antonyms*: acquit, condone, discharge, excuse, exonerate, forgive, overlook, pardon, release.

Ar·ran (ar′ən) An island in the Firth of Clyde, Buteshire, Scotland; 166 square miles.

ar·range (ə·rānj′) *v.* **ar·ranged, ar·rang·ing** *v.t.* **1** To put in definite or proper order. **2** To adjust, as a conflict or dispute; settle. **3** To change or adapt, as a musical composition for other instruments or voices than those originally intended. —*v.i.* **4** To come to an agreement or understanding: often with *with*. **5** To see about the details; make plans: I was late, but he *arranged* accordingly. See synonyms under ADAPT, ADJUST, CLASSIFY, PREPARE, RANGE, REGULATE, SET, SETTLE. [< OF *arangier* < *a-* to (< L *ad-*) + *rangier* put in order < *rang* rank[1]. See RANK[1].]

ar·range·ment (ə·rānj′mənt) *n.* **1** An arranging or that which is arranged; disposition; order. **2** A preparation, measure, or plan. **3** Settlement, as of a dispute; adjustment. **4** The style in which something is arranged, as a stage scene or combination of colors; a system of parts arranged: the *arrangement* of a library or museum. **5** *Music* **a** The adaptation of a composition to other voices or instruments than those for which it was originally composed. **b** The composition so adapted.

Ar·ran Islands (ar′ən) See ARAN ISLANDS.

ar·rant (ar′ənt) *adj.* **1** Notoriously bad; unmitigated. **2** *Obs.* Wandering about. [Var. of ERRANT] —**ar′rant·ly** *adv.*

ar·ras (ar′əs) *n.* **1** A tapestry. **2** A hanging for the walls of a room, especially one made of tapestry. [from *Arras*, France]

Ar·ras (ar′əs, *Fr.* à·räs′) A city of northern France.

ar·ra·sene (ar′ə·sēn′) *n.* An embroidery material of wool or silk. [< ARRAS]

ar·ras·tre (ä·räs′trā) *n.* **1** A crude apparatus for grinding and mixing ores. **2** In the Philippine Islands, lighterage, storage, and haulage, as of cargo. Also **ar·ras·tra** (ä·räs′trə). [< Sp.]

ar·ray (ə·rā′) *n.* **1** Regular or proper order; arrangement, as for a battle, display, etc. **2** The persons or things arrayed, especially a military force. **3** Clothing; fine dress. **4** An orderly arrangement, as of brilliant objects, or a series of values in a statistical table. **5** In English history, the arming of militia: commission of *array*. —*v.t.* **1** To draw up in order of battle, as troops; set in order. **2** To adorn; dress, as for display. See synonyms under DRESS. [< AF *arai*, OF *arei* < *a-* to (< L *ad-*) + *rei* order < Gmc.]

ar·ray·al (ə·rā′əl) *n.* **1** The act or process of arraying; mustering of a force. **2** Anything arrayed; an array.

ar·rear·age (ə·rir′ij) *n.* **1** The state of being in arrears. **2** The amount in arrears. **3** *Rare* A thing kept in reserve.

ar·rear (ə·rir′) *n.* **1** The state of being behind or behindhand, as with obligations, business, etc. **2** *Usually pl.* That which is behindhand; a part, as of a debt, overdue and unpaid. —**in arrears** (or **arrear**) Behind in meeting payment, fulfilling an obligation, etc. [< OF *arere* < L *ad-* to + *retro* backward]

ar·rest (ə·rest′) *v.t.* **1** To stop suddenly; check, as the course, movement, or development of. **2** To take into custody by legal authority. **3** To attract and fix, as the attention; engage. —*n.* **1** An arresting or being arrested; especially, seizure by legal authority. **2** A device for arresting motion, as in a machine. [< OF *arester* < LL *arrestare* < L *ad-* to + *restare* stop, remain]

Synonyms (verb): apprehend, capture, catch, delay, hold, obstruct, restrain, secure, seize, stop. *Antonyms*: discharge, dismiss, free, liberate, release.

ar·rest·er (ə·res′tər) *n.* **1** One who or that which arrests. **2** In Scots law, one who makes an arrestment.

ar·rest·ing (ə·res′ting) *adj.* Notable; compelling attention.

arresting gear *Aeron.* A contrivance for bringing an airplane to an abrupt halt when landing in a small area, as on an aircraft carrier.

ar·rest·ment (ə·rest′mənt) *n.* **1** A stoppage, as of growth. **2** In Scots law, an attachment or garnishment of property or credits in the hands of a third party.

ar·rêt (ə·rā′, ə·ret′, *Fr.* à·re′) *n. French* **1** An edict. **2** An arrest.

Ar·re·ti·um (ə·rē′shē·əm, -shəm) The ancient name for AREZZO.

Ar·rhe·ni·us (är·rā′nē·o͞os), **Svante A.**, 1859–1927, Swedish chemist.

ar·rhi·zal (ə·rī′zəl) *adj.* Rootless. Also **ar·rhi′zous** (-zəs). [< Gk. *arrhizos* < *a-* without + *rhiza* a root]

ar·rhyth·mi·a (ə·rith′mē·ə, ə·rith′-) *n. Pathol.* Irregularity of the heart or pulse. [< NL < Gk. *arrhythmia* lack of rhythm < *a-* without + *rhythmos* measure] —**ar·rhyth·mic** (ə·rith′·mik, ə·rith′-) *adj.*

ar·ri·ère (ar′ē·âr, ə·rir′) *n.* The rear: often used adjectively in the sense of dependent or subordinate: *arrière*-vassal. [< F. See ARREAR.]

ar·ri·ère-ban (ar′ē·âr·ban′, *Fr.* à·ryâr·bäṅ′) *n.* **1** In the Middle Ages, the edict of a king summoning his vassals to military service. **2** The vassals thus summoned. [< F, ult. < OHG *hari, heri* army + *ban* edict]

ar·rière-guard (ə·rir′gärd′) *n.* Rear guard. Also *French* **ar·rière-garde** (à·ryâr·gàrd′).

ar·rière-pen·sée (à·ryâr·päṅ·sā′) *n. French* A mental reservation; concealed motive.

arrière tenant A tenant of a mesne lord.

ar·rie·ro (är·ryâ′rō) *n. Spanish* A muleteer.

Ar Ri·mal (är rē·mäl′) See RUB AL KHALI.

ar·ris (ar′is) *n. Archit.* The sharp edge or ridge formed by the meeting of two surfaces, especially the sharp ridge between two channels of a Doric column. Also **ar′is.** [< OF *areste* < L *arista* awn, fishbone. Doublet of ARISTA.]

ar·ri·val (ə·rī′vəl) *n.* **1** The act of arriving. **2** One who or that which arrives or has arrived. See synonyms under ACCESSION.

ar·rive (ə·rīv′) *v.i.* **ar·rived, ar·riv·ing** **1** To reach or come to a destination or place. **2** To come at length, by any stage or process: often with *at*: to *arrive* at an idea, fatherhood, etc. **3** To attain the circumstances of success or fame in the world. [< OF *ariver* < LL *arripare* come to shore < L *ad-* to + *ripa* shore]

Synonyms: attain, come, enter, land, reach. See ATTAIN. *Antonyms*: depart, embark, go, leave, start.

ar·ri·viste (à·rē·vēst′) *n. French* A social climber or careerist.

ar·ro·ba (ä·rō′bä) *n.* **1** A liquid measure used in Spain, Mexico, etc., varying from 3.32 to 4.26 U.S. gallons. **2** A Spanish weight, equivalent to 25.37 pounds avoirdupois. **3** A Brazilian weight equivalent to 32.38 pounds avoirdupois. [< Sp. < Arabic *al-rub'* the quarter (part)]

Ar·roe Islands (ä′ro͞o) See ARU ISLANDS.

ar·ro·gance (ar′ə·gəns) *n.* The quality or state of being arrogant; haughtiness; overbearing pride. Also **ar′ro·gan·cy**. [< OF < L *arrogantia*. See ARROGANT.]

Synonyms: assumption, assurance, disdain, haughtiness, insolence, presumption, pride, superciliousness, vanity. *Arrogance* claims much for itself and concedes little to others. *Pride* is an absorbing sense of one's own greatness. *Disdain* sees contemptuously the inferiority of others to oneself. *Presumption* claims place or privilege above one's right. *Assumption* quietly takes for granted superiority and privilege which others might or might not concede. *Vanity* intensely craves admiration and applause. *Superciliousness* silently manifests mingled *haughtiness* and *disdain*. *Insolence* is open and rude expression of contempt and hostility, generally from an inferior to a superior, as from a clerk to a customer. See ASSURANCE, IMPERTINENCE.

ar·ro·gant (ar′ə·gənt) *adj.* **1** Unduly or excessively proud; overbearing; haughty. **2** Characterized by or due to arrogance: *arrogant* proposals. See synonyms under DOGMATIC, IMPERIOUS. [< OF < L *arrogans, -antis*, ppr. of *arrogare*. See ARROGATE.] —**ar′ro·gant·ly** *adv.*

ar·ro·gate (ar′ə·gāt) *v.t.* **·gat·ed, ·gat·ing** **1** To claim, demand, or take unreasonably or presumptuously; assume; usurp. **2** To attribute or ascribe without reason: to *arrogate* a privilege. See synonyms under ASSUME. [< L *arrogatus*, pp. of *arrogare* claim for oneself < *ad-* to + *rogare* ask] —**ar′ro·ga′tion** *n.*

ar·ron·disse·ment (à·rôṅ·dēs·mäṅ′) *n. pl.* **·ments** (-mäṅ′) *French* **1** The chief subdivision of a French department. **2** A district: Paris is divided into 20 *arrondissements*.

ar·row (ar′ō) *n.* **1** A straight, slender shaft generally feathered at one end and with a pointed head at the other, to be shot from a bow. **2** Anything resembling an arrow in shape, function, speed, etc. **3** A sign or figure in the shape of an arrow, used to indicate directions, as on maps, charts, etc. ◆ Collateral adjective: *sagittal*. [OE *earh, arwe*]

Ar·row (ar′ō) The constellation Sagitta. See CONSTELLATION.

ar·row·head (ar′ō·hed′) *n.* **1** The sharp-pointed head of an arrow. **2** Something resembling an arrowhead, as a mark used to point direction, etc. **3** *Archit.* The dart or tongue of an egg-and-dart molding. **4** *Bot.* Any aquatic plant of the genus *Sagittaria*, of the water-plantain family *(Alismaceae)*, with arrow-shaped leaves. —**ar′row·head′ed** *adj.*

ar·row·root (ar′ō·ro͞ot′, -root′) *n.* **1** A nutritious starch obtained from the rhizomes of a tropical American plant *(Maranta arundinacea)*. **2** The plant. **3** A similar starchy product from other tropical plants.

ar·row·wood (ar′ō·wood′) *n.* One of various North American shrubs or small trees with many straight shoots or branches, used by the Indians for making arrows, as certain species of viburnum, flowering dogwood *(Cornus florida)*, etc.

ar·row·worm (ar′ō·wûrm′) *n. Zool.* A chaetognath, especially a pelagic species *(Sagitta bipunctata)* with a transparent body, capable of descent to great depths: also called *glassworm*.

ar·row·y (ar′ō·ē) *adj.* **1** Resembling an arrow or arrows in shape, appearance, or motion; swift; sharp; darting. **2** Full of or abounding in arrows.

ar·roy·o (ə·roi′ō) *n. pl.* **·os** (-ōz) *SW U.S.* **1** The steep-sided, flat channel of an intermittent stream. **2** The stream itself. **3** A deep, dry gulch. [< Sp.]

Ar·ru Islands (ä′ro͞o). See ARU ISLANDS.

Ar·sac·id (är·sas′id) *n. pl.* **·ids** or **·i·dae** (-ə·dē) Any ruler styled Arsaces of a dynasty in Parthia and Armenia, dating from about 250 B.C. to A.D. 224 in Parthia and to 428 in Armenia.

ar·se·nal (är′sə·nəl) *n.* A public repository or manufactory of arms and munitions of war. [< Ital. *arsenale* < Arabic *dār aṣ-ṣinā'ah* workshop]

ar·se·nate (är′sə·nāt, -nit) *n. Chem.* A salt of arsenic acid containing the trivalent radical AsO_4. Also **ar·se·ni·ate** (är·sē′nē·āt, -it).

ar·se·nic (är′sə·nik) *n.* **1** A poisonous element (symbol As, atomic number 33), existing in several allotropic forms, commonly as a gray, very brittle, crystalline, semimetallic substance. See PERIODIC TABLE. **2** A tasteless, poisonous compound, arsenic trioxide, As_2O_3, used in agricultural pesticides. **3** White arsenic or arsenic trioxide, As_2O_3, a tasteless, poisonous compound. —**ar·sen·ic** (är·sen′ik) *adj.* Arsenical. [< OF < L *arsenicum* < Gk. *arsenikon* yellow orpiment]

ar·sen·i·cal (är·sen′i·kəl) *adj.* Of, pertaining to, or containing arsenic. —*n.* Any preparation of arsenic used as an insecticide or drug.

ar·se·nide (är′sə·nīd, -nid) *n.* A compound of arsenic, in which arsenic is the electronegative constituent.

ar·se·nite (är′sə·nīt) *n.* A salt of arsenous acid.

ar·se·niu·ret·ed (är·sēn′yə·ret′id, -sen′-) *adj.* Chemically combined with arsenic to form an arsenide: *arseniureted* hydrogen. Also **ar·se′niu·ret′ted.**

ar·se·no·py·rite (är′sə·nō·pī′rīt, är·sen′ə-) *n.* A silver-white, orthorhombic, iron sulfarsenide, FeAsS: also called *mispickel*. [< ARSENIC + PYRITE]

ar·se·nous (är′sə·nəs) *adj.* Of, pertaining to, or containing arsenic, especially when combined in its triad valence: *arsenous* oxide, As_2O_3; *arsenous* sulfide, As_2S_3. Also **ar·se·ni·ous** (är·sē′nē·əs).

ars gra·ti·a ar·tis (ärz grā′shē·ə är′tis) *Latin* Art for art's sake.

ar·sine (är·sēn′, är′sēn, är′sin) *n.* **1** A poisonous, inflammable, gaseous compound, AsH_3, with a nauseous odor, used as an agent of chemical warfare in shells, etc. **2** Any of various derivatives of this compound in which the hydrogen atom is replaced by a radical. [<ARS(ENIC) + -INE[2]]

Ar·sin·o·ë (är·sin′ō·ē) An ancient city of Upper Egypt west of the Nile.

ar·sis (är′sis) *n. pl.* **·ses** (-sēz) **1** In prosody: **a** The syllable that receives the ictus or stress of voice. **b** The stress itself. **c** In the original Greek usage, the raising of the foot in beating time, and hence the metrically unaccented part of the foot: the reverse of modern usage. **2** *Music* The unaccented part of a bar. [<L <Gk. *arsis* a lifting, raising < *airein* raise]

ars lon·ga, vi·ta bre·vis (ärz lông′gə vī′tə brev′is) *Latin* Art (is) long, life short.

ar·son (är′sən) *n. Law* The malicious burning of a dwelling or other structure belonging to another; also the similar burning of other property, including one's own, when insured, with the intent to defraud the insurers. [<OF <LL *arsio, -onis* a burning <L *arsus,* pp. of *ardere* burn]

Ar·son·val (dȧr·sôṅ·vȧl′), **Jacques Arsène d'** See D'ARSONVAL, JACQUES.

ars·phen·a·mine (ärs′fen·ə·mēn′, ärs′fen·am′in) *n.* A yellow, crystalline arsenic compound, $C_{12}H_{14}O_2N_2Cl_2As_2{\cdot}2H_2O$, first prepared by Paul Ehrlich as a treatment for syphilis and other spirillum infections, as relapsing fever, frambesia, etc.: also called *Salvarsan.* [<AR-S(ENIC) + PHEN(YL) + AMINE]

ars po·et·i·ca (ärz pō·et′i·kə) *Latin* The art of poetry.

art[1] (ärt) *n.* **1** The skilful, systematic arrangement or adaptation of means for the attainment of some end, especially by human endeavor as opposed to natural forces. **2** The practical application of knowledge or natural ability; skilled workmanship; mastery; dexterity. **3** A set or system of rules, principles, etc., devised for procuring some scientific, esthetic, or practical result, as by exercise; a branch of learning to be studied in order to be applied. **4 a** The application, or the principles of application, of skill, knowledge, etc., in a creative effort to produce works that have form or beauty, esthetic expression of feeling, etc., as in music, painting, sculpture, literature, architecture, and the dance. **b** Any particular branch of this, especially painting, drawing, etc. **c** The works thus created; statues; paintings, etc. **5** *Usually pl.* Any of certain branches of academic learning, as rhetoric, grammar, music, mathematics, etc.; the liberal arts, especially as distinguished from the sciences. **6** An illustration, as in a magazine or newspaper. **7** Craft; cunning; artfulness. **8** *Usually pl.* Stratagem; wiles; tricks. **9** An organized body of men trained in some trade or vocation; guild. **—fine arts** Those arts considered purely esthetic or expressive, as distinguished from the "useful arts": painting, drawing, sculpture, ceramics, architecture, literature, music, and the dance. **—household arts** The duties involved in managing a household. **—industrial arts** The technical skills used in industry, especially as subjects of study in schools. **—liberal arts** The course of study, including literature, philosophy, languages, history, etc., distinguished from professional or technical subjects, offered by an academic college: also called *arts*: a translation of Latin *artes liberales,* arts suitable for ***liberi,*** **or free men.** [<OF<L *ars, artis* **skill]**

Synonyms: address, aptitude, artifice, business, cleverness, dexterity, esthetics, ingenuity, knack, science, skill, tact. In the highest sense, *art* has no synonym. The term *esthetics* denotes the theory of the beautiful which furnishes the basis of *art.* For subordinate senses, see ARTIFICE, BUSINESS. For the distinction between *science* and *art,* see synonyms for SCIENCE.

art[2] (ärt) Archaic or poetic second person singular present tense of BE: used with *thou.*

Ar·ta·xerx·es (är′tə·zûrk′sēz) Name of three Persian kings.

—Artaxerxes II, king of Persia 404–359 B.C., defeated his brother Cyrus at Cunaxa, 401.

art de·co (ärt de′kō) A style of decorative design characterized by ornateness, geometrical forms, asymmetry, and bold colors. Also **Art De′co.**

ar·tel (är·tel′) *n.* **1** In pre–revolutionary Russia, an association of persons to carry out work in common. **2** In Soviet Russia, a cooperative organization of producers under government supervision: An agricultural *artel* is the same as a collective farm or kolkhoz. [<Russian]

Ar·te·mas (är′tə·məs) A masculine personal name.[<Gk.]

Ar·te·mis (är′tə·mis) In Greek mythology, the goddess of the chase and of the moon; twin sister of Apollo: identified with the Roman *Diana.*

ARTEMIS
After a statue of Artemis and the Hind in the Louvre.

ar·te·mis·i·a (är′tə·miz′ē·ə, -mish′ē·ə) *n.* **1** Any of a large genus *(Artemisia)* of bitter aromatic herbs of the composite family. **2** The sagebrush. [<L, mugwort <Gk.]

Ar·te·movsk (är·tyô′môfsk) A city in the eastern Ukrainian S.S.R.: formerly *Bakhmut.*

Ar·te·mus Ward (är′tə·məs wôrd) Pen name of Charles Farrar Browne, 1834–67, U.S. humorist.

ar·ten·kreis (är′tən·krīs) *n. Ecol.* A group of species having a common origin and replacing each other within a given area; a polytypic species. [<G]

ar·te·ri·al (är·tir′ē·əl) *adj.* **1** Pertaining to, like, or contained or carried in the arteries or an artery. **2** *Physiol.* Pertaining to the blood which has undergone aeration in the lungs, distinguished by its bright red color. **3** Resembling an artery in having a main channel and a system of secondary branches: an *arterial* highway.

ar·te·ri·al·ize (är·tir′ē·əl·īz′) *v.t.* **·ized, ·iz·ing** *Physiol.* To convert venous blood into arterial blood by oxygenation during its passage through the lungs in respiration. Also *Brit.* **ar·te′ri·al·ise′.** **—ar·te′ri·al·i·za′tion** *n.*

arterio– *combining form* Artery. [<Gk. *artēria*]

ar·te·ri·og·ra·phy (är·tir′ē·ogr′ə·fē) *n.* **1** The anatomy, description, etc., of the arteries or the arterial system. **2** The production of graphic representations of the action and state of the pulse.

ar·te·ri·ol·o·gy (är·tir′ē·ol′ə·jē) *n.* **1** The scientific study of the arteries in health and disease. **2** A treatise on the subject.

ar·te·ri·o·scle·ro·sis (är·tir′ē·ō·sklə·rō′sis) *n. Pathol.* The thickening and hardening of the walls of an artery, with impairment of blood circulation, as in old age. [<NL <ARTERIO- + SCLEROSIS] **—ar·te′ri·o·scle·rot′ic** (-rot′ik) *adj.*

ar·te·ri·ot·o·my (är·tir′ē·ot′ə·mē) *n.* **1** Dissection of arteries. **2** Any cutting or opening of an artery, as for letting blood.

ar·te·ri·tis (är′tə·rī′tis) *n. Pathol.* Inflammation of an artery or of its external coat.

ar·ter·y (är′tər·ē) *n. pl.* **·ter·ies 1** *Anat.* Any of a large number of muscular vessels conveying blood away from the heart to every part of the body. **2** Any principal channel in a communication or transportation network. *—v.t.* **·ter·ied, ·ter·y·ing** To supply with or as if with arteries; flow through, like an artery: Rivers *artery* the land. [<L *arteria* artery, windpipe <Gk. *artēria*]

ar·te·sian well (är·tē′zhən) A well bored down to a water–bearing stratum between impermeable strata, from a surface lower than the source of the water supply, so that the water pressure is great enough to force a flow of water out at the surface. [<F *artésien,* from *Artois,* town in France]

Ar·te·vel·de (är′tə·vel′də), **Jacob van,** 1290–1345, Flemish patriot; led insurgents at Ghent. **—Philip van,** 1340?–82, Flemish leader; son of Jacob. Also **Ar·te·veld** (är′tə·veld).

art·ful (ärt′fəl) *adj.* **1** Crafty; cunning; tricky. **2** Artificial; imitative. **3** Skilful; ingenious. See synonyms under INSIDIOUS. **—art′ful·ly** *adv.* **—art′ful·ness** *n.*

art history The study of the history of art, including painting, sculpture, and architecture. **—art historian**

ar·thral·gia (är·thral′jə) *n. Pathol.* Neuralgic pain in a joint. **—ar·thral′gic** (-jik) *adj.*

ar·thrit·ic (är·thrit′ik) *adj.* Pertaining to, having, or affected by arthritis.

ar·thri·tis (är·thrī′tis) *n. Pathol.* Inflammation of a joint. [<L <Gk. *arthritis* <*arthron* joint]

arthro– *combining form* Joint: *arthrography.* Also, before vowels, **arthr–,** as in *arthralgia.* [<Gk. *arthron*]

ar·thro·branch (är′thrə·brangk) *n. Zool.* A branchial plume grown to the membranous articulation between the coxa and body in crustaceans. Also **ar·thro·bran·chi·a** (är′thrə·brang′kē·ə). [<ARTHRO- + Gk. *branchia* gill]

ar·throc·a·ce (är·throk′ə·sē) *n.* **1** Disease of the joints, characterized by caries or dead bone. **2** An endemic disease that attacks very young animals, as calves, colts, etc. [<ARTHRO- + Gk. *kakē* illness]

ar·throd·e·sis (är·throd′ə·sis) *n. Surg.* The operation of fusing of the surfaces of joints; artificial ankylosis. [<NL<ARTHRO- + Gk. *desis* a joining]

ar·throg·ra·phy (är·throg′rə·fē) *n.* A scientific description of the joints.

ar·thro·mere (är′thrə·mir) *n. Zool.* Any typical segment in the body of an articulate invertebrate. [<ARTHRO- + -MERE]

ar·throp·a·thy (är·throp′ə·thē) *n.* Any disease of the joints.

ar·thro·plas·ty (är′thrə·plas′tē) *n. Surg.* A plastic operation on a joint or the formation of an artificial joint. **—ar′thro·plas′tic** *adj.*

ar·thro·pod (är′thrə·pod) *n. Zool.* Any of a large phylum *(Arthropoda)* of invertebrate animals characterized by jointed legs, chitinous exoskeletons, and segmented body parts, including insects, spiders, and crabs. *—adj.* Of or pertaining to the *Arthropoda.* [<ARTHRO- + Gk. *pous, podos* foot] **—ar·throp·o·dous** (är·throp′ə·dəs), **ar·throp′o·dal** *adj.*

ar·thro·sis (är·thrō′sis) *n. pl.* **·ses** (-sēz) **1** Articulation; connection of parts by joints. **2** *Pathol.* A degenerative condition of the joints.

ar·thro·spore (är′thrə·spôr, -spōr) *n.* **1** *Bot.* One of a series of spores in some algae and fungi, formed by fission and resembling a string of beads. **2** *Bacteriol.* An isolated vegetative cell in a resting state. **—ar′thro·spor′ic** (-spôr′ik, -spor′ik), **ar·thros·po·rous** (är·thros′·pə·rəs) *adj.*

Ar·thur (är′thər, *Fr.* ȧr·tür′) A masculine personal name. Also *Lat.* **Ar·thu·rus** (är·thŏŏr′·əs.

—Arthur A legendary British king of the sixth century A.D., hero of the Round Table and subject of many romances. [? <Celtic, high admirable]

Ar·thur (är′thər), **Chester Alan,** 1830–86, president of the United States 1881–85, following the assassination of President Garfield.

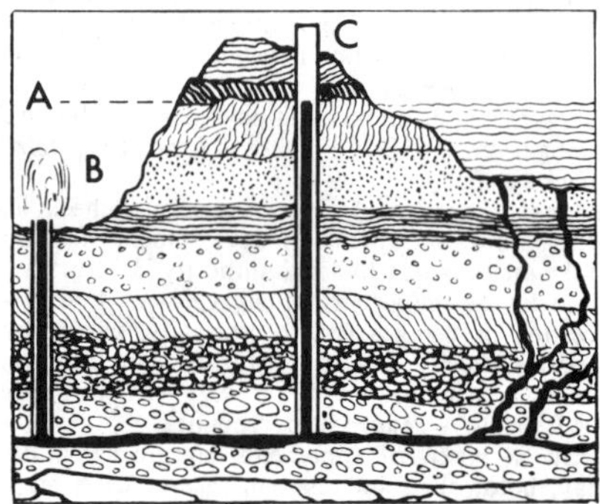

ARTESIAN WELL
THROUGH GEOLOGICAL STRATA
A. Water level. *B.* Artesian well. *C.* Ordinary well.

Ar·thu·ri·an (är·thŏŏr′ē·ən) *adj.* Of or pertaining to King Arthur and his knights. See ROUND TABLE.

ar·ti·choke (är′tə·chōk) *n.* **1** A thistlelike garden plant *(Cynara scolymus).* **2** Its succulent flower head, used as a vegetable. 3 The Jerusalem artichoke. [<Ital. *articiocco* <Arabic *al-kharshūf*]

ar·ti·cle (är′ti·kəl) *n.* 1 A particular object or substance; a material thing or class of things: an *article* of food; an *article* for sale. 2 A literary composition forming an independent part of a publication: an *article* in a newspaper. 3 A definite division; a distinct proposition, statement, or stipulation in a series of such, as in a constitution, an impeachment, or a treaty. 4 A complete item of religious belief; a point of doctrine, especially when forming a part of a statement of religious beliefs: the Thirty-nine *Articles.* 5 *Gram.* One of a class of auxiliary words inserted before a noun or a word used as a noun, or, in some languages, prefixed or suffixed to it, to limit or modify it in some way; as, English *a, an (indefinite article)* and *the (definite article).* 6 A definite part, as of a system; item; point. 7 *Archaic* A point of time; exact instant: the *article* of death. — *v.* ·cled, ·cling *v.t.* 1 To bind by a written contract, as to an attorney for instruction in law; especially, to bind to service: to *article* a seaman for a voyage. 2 To set forth in articles; specify. 3 To charge specifically; accuse by formal articles. — *v.i.* 4 To make accusations: with *against.* [<F <L *articulus,* dim. of *artus* a joint]

Articles of Confederation The constitution of the 13 original American colonies, adopted by Congress in 1781 and replaced in 1788 by the Constitution.

Articles of War, Articles for the Government of the Navy See under UNIFORM CODE OF MILITARY JUSTICE.

ar·tic·u·lar (är·tik′yə·lər) *adj.* Pertaining to a joint or the joints.

ar·tic·u·late (är·tik′yə·lit) *adj.* 1 Jointed; segmented. 2 Particularized in articles; specific; distinct. 3 Divided into consecutive syllables so as to form speech. 4 Able to speak, especially to speak well or clearly. 5 Arranged with coherence; interrelated. Also **ar·tic′u·lat′ed** (-lā′tid). — *v.* (är·tik′yə·lāt) ·lat·ed, ·lat·ing. *v.t.* 1 To utter distinctly, enunciate. 2 To give utterance to; express in words: to *articulate* your wrongs. 3 *Phonet.* To produce, as a speech sound, by the movement of the organs of speech. 4 To joint together; unite by joints. — *v.i.* 5 To speak distinctly. 6 *Phonet.* To produce a speech sound. 7 *Anat.* To form a joint: used with *with.* 8 *Obs.* To make terms. See synonyms under SPEAK. [<L *articulatus,* pp. of *articulare* divide into joints, utter distinctly <*articulus.* See ARTICLE.] — **ar·tic′u·late·ly** *adv.*

ar·tic·u·la·tion (är·tik′yə·lā′shən) *n.* 1 A jointing or being jointed together; also the manner or method of this. 2 A joint between two bones. 3 *Anat.* The union forming a joint, as of bones. 4 The utterance of articulate sounds; enunciation. 5 A speech sound, especially a consonant. 6 *Phonet.* The movements of the organs of speech in producing an articulate sound. 7 *Bot.* a A joint between two separable parts, as a leaf and a stem. b A node or the space between two nodes. — **ar·tic·u·la·to·ry** (är·tik′yə·lə·tôr′ē, -tō′rē) *adj.*

ar·tic·u·la·tor (är·tik′yə·lā′tər) *n.* 1 One who or that which articulates. 2 *Dent.* A device to secure proper articulation. 3 *Phonet.* A movable organ of speech, as the tongue.

articulatory phonetics See under PHONETICS.

ar·ti·fact (är′tə·fakt) *n.* 1 Anything made by human work or art. 2 *Biol.* A structure or appearance which is not normally present in a cell or tissue but is produced by artificial means. Also **ar′te·fact.** [<L *ars, artis* art, skill + *factus,* pp. of *facere* make]

ar·ti·fice (är′tə·fis) *n.* 1 Subtle or deceptive craft; trickery. 2 Skill; ingenuity. 3 An ingenious expedient; stratagem; maneuver. [<F <L *artificium* handicraft, skill <*ars* art + *facere* make]

Synonyms: art, blind, cheat, contrivance, craft, cunning, device, dodge, finesse, fraud, guile, imposture, invention, machination, maneuver, ruse, strategem, subterfuge, trick, wile. An *artifice, contrivance,* or *device* may be either good or bad. An *artifice* is a carefully and delicately prepared *contrivance* for doing indirectly what one could not well do directly. A *device* is something studied out for promoting an end, as in a mechanism. *Finesse* is especially subtle *contrivance,* delicate *artifice,* whether for good or evil. A *cheat* is a mean advantage in a bargain; a *fraud,* any form of covert robbery or injury. *Imposture* is a deceitful *contrivance* for securing charity, credit, or consideration. A *strategem* or *maneuver* may be good or bad. A *wile* is often but not necessarily evil. A *trick* is commonly low, injurious, and malicious, but the word is used playfully with less than its full meaning. A *ruse* or a *blind* may be quite innocent and harmless. *Antonyms*: artlessness, candor, fairness, frankness, guilelessness, honesty, ingenuousness, innocence, openness, simplicity, sincerity, truth.

ar·tif·i·cer (är·tif′ə·sər) *n.* 1 One who constructs with skill; a craftsman. 2 *Mil.* A worker in an artillery laboratory. 3 A skilful designer; an inventor.

ar·ti·fi·cial (är′tə·fish′əl) *adj.* 1 Produced by human art rather than by nature. 2 Made in imitation of or as a substitute for something natural: an *artificial* leg. 3 Not genuine or natural; affected. See synonyms under FACTITIOUS. [<L *artificialis* <*artificium.* See ARTIFICE.] — **ar′ti·fi′cial·ly** *adv.* — **ar′ti·fi′cial·ness** *n.*

artificial horizon 1 *Aeron.* An instrument like a gyroscope, providing a surface always parallel to the true horizon and indicating the deviations of an aircraft from level flight. 2 *Astron.* A level reflector, as a surface of mercury, used to determine the altitude of celestial bodies.

artificial insemination Impregnation of the female with semen from the male without direct sexual contact: also called *eutelegenesis.*

ar·ti·fi·ci·al·i·ty (är′tə·fish′ē·al′ə·tē) *n. pl.* ·ties 1 The character, fact, or state of being artificial. 2 Something artificial.

artificial language An arbitrary, auxiliary language devised for use in international communication.

ar·til·ler·y (är·til′ə·rē) *n.* 1 Guns of larger caliber than machine-guns: usually classified according to caliber as *light, medium,* and *heavy.* 2 Military units armed with such guns. 3 Branches of the United States Army composed of such units: Field *Artillery,* Coast *Artillery* Corps. 4 *U.S. Colloq.* Any small firearm. 5 The science of gunnery. 6 *Obs.* Implements of war. [<OF *artillerie* <*artiller* fortify]

ar·til·ler·y·man (är·til′ə·rē·mən) *n. pl.* ·men (-mən) 1 One who studies artillery. 2 A soldier in the artillery. Also **ar·til′ler·ist.**

ar·ti·o·dac·tyl (är′tē·ō·dak′təl) *n.* A member of a mammalian order or suborder *(Artiodactyla)* of ungulate quadrupeds with two or four equal-hoofed digits to each foot, including the ruminants, hogs, etc. — *adj.* Of or pertaining to the *Artiodactyla;* having two or four digits to each foot. [<NL <Gk. *artios* even + *daktylos* finger, toe] — **ar′ti·o·dac′ty·lous** (-ləs) *adj.*

ar·ti·san (är′tə·zən) *n.* A trained or skilled workman; superior mechanic. [<F <Ital. *artigiano,* ult. <L *ars* art]

art·ist (är′tist) *n.* 1 One who is skilled in or who makes a profession of any of the fine arts. 2 Any professional public performer, as an actor, singer, etc. 3 One who does anything particularly well, as with a feeling for form, effect, etc. [<F *artiste* <Ital. *artista* <L *ars* art]

Synonyms: artificer, artisan, mechanic, operative, workman. The work of the *artist* is creative; that of the *artisan* mechanical. The *artificer* is between the two, putting more thought, intelligence, and taste into his work than the *artisan,* but less of the idealizing, creative power than the *artist.* The man who constructs anything by mere routine and rule is a *mechanic.* The man whose work involves thought, skill, and constructive power is an *artificer.* Those who operate machinery which is nearly automatic are *operators* or *operatives.*

ar·tiste (är·tēst′) *n.* A professional dancer, singer, or entertainer. [<F]

ar·tis·tic (är·tis′tik) *adj.* 1 Of or pertaining to art or artists. 2 Conforming or conformable to the principles of art; tastefully executed. 3 Fond of or sensitive to art. Also **ar·tis′ti·cal.** — **ar·tis′ti·cal·ly** *adv.*

art·ist·ry (är′tis·trē) *n.* 1 The pursuits or occupation of an artist. 2 Artistic characteristics or ability.

Ar·ti·um Bac·ca·lau·re·us (är′shē·əm bak′ə·lô′rē·əs) *Latin* Bachelor of Arts. Abbr. *A.B.* or *B.A.*

Ar·ti·um Ma·gis·ter (är′shē·əm mə·jis′tər) *Latin* Master of Arts. Abbr. *A.M.* or *M.A.*

art·less (ärt′lis) *adj.* 1 Without craft or deceit; unaffected. 2 Natural; simple. 3 Without art or skill; clumsy. 4 Without taste; ignorant. See synonyms under CANDID, INNOCENT, RUSTIC. — **art′less·ly** *adv.* — **art′less·ness** *n.*

Art Nou·veau (ärt nōō·vō′, *Fr.* àr nōō·vō′) A style of art and design of the late 19th and early 20th centuries characterized by curved and twisting shapes often representing natural objects. [<F, lit., new art]

Ar·tois (àr·twà′) A region and former province of northern France.

Ar·tu·ro (är·tōō′rō) Italian form of ARTHUR.

art·work (art′wûrk′) *n.* Illustrations, calligraphy, or other decorative elements accompanying printed text.

art·y (är′tē) *adj.* Pretending to be artistic; ostentatiously claiming artistic worth. — **art′i·ness** *n.*

Ar·tzy·ba·sheff (är′tsi·bä′shif), **Boris,** born 1899, U.S. illustrator born in Russia.

A·ru·ba (ä·rōō′bə) An island in the western group of the Netherlands West Indies; 69 square miles.

A·ru Islands (ä′rōō) An Indonesian island group in the Arafura Sea; 3,306 square miles: also *Aroe, Arro, Arru.*

ar·um (âr′əm) *n.* 1 Any of a genus *(Arum)* of araceous Old World herbs, especially the cuckoo pint. 2 One of various related plants, as the calla lily. [<L <Gk. *aron*]

Ar·un·del (ar′ən·dəl) A municipal borough in southern Sussex, England.

a·run·di·na·ceous (ə·run′də·nā′shəs) *adj. Bot.* Pertaining to a reed or reeds; reedlike. [<L *arundinaceus* <*arundo* reed]

ar·un·din·e·ous (ar′ən·din′ē·əs) *adj. Bot.* Abounding in or like reeds; reedy.

a·rus·pex (ə·rus′peks) See HARUSPEX.

A·ru·wi·mi (ä′rōō·wē′mē) A river in NE Belgian Congo, flowing 620 miles SW to the Congo.

ar·val[1] (är′vəl) *adj.* Of or pertaining to plowed land. [<L *arvalis* <*arare* plow]

ar·val[2] (är′vəl) *n. Brit. Archaic* & *Dial.* A funeral feast. Also **ar′vel.** [appar. <Scand.]

Arval Brethren In ancient Rome, a college of 12 priests who offered sacrifices to the goddess of the fields. [Trans. of L *Fratres Arvales*]

ar·y (âr′ē) *adj. Dial.* Any: opposite of *nary.*

-ary[1] *suffix of adjectives and nouns* 1 Connected with or pertaining to what is expressed in the root word: *elementary, honorary, secondary.* 2 A person employed as or engaged in: *apothecary, antiquary, secretary.* 3 A thing connected with or a place dedicated to: *dictionary, diary, sanctuary.* [<L *-arius, -arium*]

-ary[2] *suffix of adjectives* Of or pertaining to; belonging to: *military, salutary.* See -AR[1]. [<L *-aris*]

Ar·y·an (âr′ē·ən, ar′-, är′yən) *n.* 1 A member or descendant of a prehistoric people who spoke Indo-European. 2 In Nazi ideology, a Caucasian gentile, especially one of Nordic stock. 3 *Ling.* a The Indo-Iranian subfamily of Indo-European. b A former name for the parent language of the Indo-European family. — *adj.* 1 Of or pertaining to the Aryans or their languages. 2 In Nazi ideology, of or pertaining to Caucasian gentiles. Also spelled *Arian.* [<Skt. *ārya* noble]

Ar·y·an·ize (âr′ē·ən·īz′, ar′-, är′yən-) *v.t.* ·ized, ·iz·ing 1 To make characteristically Aryan. 2 To free of all so-called non-Aryan elements or influences: a Nazi concept. Also **Ar′i·an·ize.**

ar·yl (ar′il) *adj. Chem.* Pertaining to any of a group of monovalent radicals derived from the aromatic hydrocarbon compounds, as phenyl, C_6H_5–. [<AR(OMATIC) + -YL]

ar·y·te·noid (ar′ə·tē′noid) *adj. Anat.* Of, connected with, or pertaining to two small cartilages in the larynx mounted on the cricoid cartilage and attached posteriorly to the vocal bands, for the action of which they are largely responsible. Also **ar'y·te·noi'dal.** —*n.* An arytenoid cartilage. [< Gk. *arytainoeidēs* pitcher-shaped < *arytaina* pitcher + *eidos* form]

as[1] (az, *unstressed* əz) *adv.* **1** To the same extent or degree; equally: Do I look *as* pretty? **2** For instance; thus: to release, *as* prisoners, from confinement. —*conj.* **1** To the same extent, degree, or amount: Such a man *as* he cannot fail. **2** To the degree in which; in proportion to which: He became gentler *as* he grew older. **3** In the manner of; in the way that: Do *as* I tell you. **4** At the same time that; while: They sang *as* we left. **5** Because; considering that: *As* the weather was bad, the game was postponed. **6** However; though: Bad *as* it was, it might have been worse. See synonyms under BECAUSE. —*pron.* Who, which, or that, after *such, many,* and *same*: Such people *as* like sports will enjoy the game; He lost the same kind of pen *as* you have; As many *as* are here will receive tickets. [ME *as, als, alse,* OE *ealswā* entirely so, just as. See ALSO.] **—as . . . as** A correlative construction that indicates identity or equality of two things: *as* much *as, as* good *as.* **—as for** Concerning; in the case of. **—as if.** As it would if. Also **as though. —as is** *Colloq.* Just as it is; not guaranteed perfect: said of an article or commodity somewhat shopworn or damaged. **—as it were** So to speak; in a manner; in some sort. **—as to** Concerning. **—as well** Besides. **—as well as** Equally; just as much; in addition to. **—as yet** Up to the present time; hitherto; so far.

as[2] (as) *n. pl.* **as·ses** (as'iz) **1** An early Roman coin of copper or copper alloy: originally weighing about a pound. **2** An ancient Roman unit of weight of about one pound. [< L]

As (äs) In Norse mythology, any one of the gods *(Æsir)* who dwelt in Asgard.

As *Chem.* Arsenic (symbol As).

as- Assimilated var. of AD-.

A·sa (ā'sə) A masculine personal name. [< Hebrew, ·healer]

as·a·fet·i·da (as'ə·fet'ə·də) *n.* A fetid substance prepared from the juice of certain plants of the fennel family: used in medicine as an antispasmodic: also spelled *assafoetida.* Also **as'a·foet'·i·da.** [< Med.L *asa* mastic (< Persian *azā*) + L *foetida,* fem., ill-smelling]

As·a·hel (as'ə·hel, ā'sə-) A masculine personal name. [< Hebrew, made of God]

A·sa·hi·ga·wa (ä·sä·hē·gä·wä) A city on central Hokkaido island, Japan. Also **A·sa·hi·ka·wa** (-kä·wä).

A·sa·ma (ä·sä·mä) The highest and most violent of Japan's active volcanos, on central Honshu island; 8,200 feet.

A·saph (ā'saf, ā'səf) A Levite chief singer and musician of David's court. I *Chron.* xvi 7. [< Hebrew, collector] **—A·saph·ic** (ā·saf'ik) *adj.*

as·a·rum (as'ə·rəm) *n.* **1** The dried rootstock of a North American perennial herb *(Asarum canadense)* of the birthwort family; used as an aromatic and carminative. **2** The herb itself. [< L, hazelwort, wild spikenard < Gk. *asaron*]

As·ben (az·ben') See AIR.

as·bes·tos (as·bes'təs, az-) *n.* **1** A white or light-gray mineral, obtained chiefly from actinolite and amphibole, occurring in long slender needles or fibrous masses which may be woven or shaped into acid-resisting, nonconducting, and fireproof articles: also called *earthflax, mountain cork.* **2** A fireproof curtain, as in a theater. —*adj.* Pertaining to, containing, or made of asbestos. Also **as·bes'·tus.** [< L < Gk., unquenchable < *a-* not + *sbennynai* quench; orig. applied to quicklime] **—as·bes·ti·form** (as·bes'tə·fôrm, az-) *adj.* **—as·bes·tine** (as·bes'tin, az-), **as·bes'tic** *adj.*

as·bes·to·sis (as'bes·tō'sis, az'-) *n. Pathol.* Pneumoconiosis caused by inhaling particles of asbestos.

as·bo·lin (as'bə·lin, az'-) *n.* A yellowish, acrid, oily organic compound obtained from wood soot. [< Gk. *asbolos* soot + -IN]

As·bur·y (az'ber'ē, -bər-ē), **Francis,** 1745–1816, English Methodist missionary and organizer in America.

As·ca·lon (as'kə·lon) See ASHKELON.

As·ca·ni·us (as·kā'nē·əs) In Roman legend, son of Aeneas and Creusa: reputed ancestor of the Caesars: also called *Iulus.*

as·ca·rid (as'kə·rid) *n. Zool.* A nematode worm of the genus *Ascaris,* as a roundworm or pinworm. [< Gk. *askaris, -idos* worm in the intestines]

as·cend (ə·send') *v.i.* **1** To go or move upward; rise. **2** To rise by degrees, as from particulars to generals, from the present to the past, from the lower to the higher notes of a musical scale, etc. **3** To lie along an ascending slope: The path *ascends* sharply here. —*v.t.* **4** To move or slope upward on: to *ascend* a mountain. [< L *ascendere* < *ad-* to + *scandere* climb] **—as·cend'a·ble** or **·i·ble** *adj.*

as·cen·dence (ə·sen'dəns) *n.* Ascendency. Also **as·cen'dance.**

as·cen·den·cy (ə·sen'dən·sē) *n.* The quality, fact, or state of being in the ascendent; domination; sway. Also **as·cen'dan·cy.**

as·cen·dent (ə·sen'dənt) *adj.* **1** Ascending; rising. **2** Superior; dominant. **3** *Astron.* Coming to or above the horizon. **4** *Bot.* Ascending. See synonyms under PREDOMINANT. —*n.* **1** A position of supreme power; preeminence; domination. **2** In astrology: **a** The point of the ecliptic that is rising above the eastern horizon at any instant. **b** Horoscope. **3** *Rare* An ancestor: opposed to *descendant.* Also **as·cen'dant. —to be in the ascendent** To approach or occupy a predominating position; have controlling power, fame, influence, etc.

as·cend·er (ə·sen'dər) *n.* **1** One who or that which ascends. **2** *Printing* **a** The part of a letter that reaches into the top of the body of the type. **b** Any of such letters, as *b, d, h,* etc.

as·cend·ing (ə·sen'ding) *adj.* **1** Rising or. directed upward. **2** *Bot.* Slanting or curving upward.

as·cen·sion (ə·sen'shən) *n.* **1** The act of ascending. **2** *Astron.* The elevating or rising of a star above the horizon in the celestial sphere. **—the Ascension** *Theol.* The bodily ascent of Christ into heaven after the Resurrection, commemorated on **Ascension Day** (also *Holy Thursday*), the fortieth day after Easter. [< L *ascensio, -onis* < *ascendere.* See ASCEND.] **—as·cen'sion·al** *adj.*

As·cen·sion (ə·sen'shən) **1** A British island in the South Atlantic, administered with St. Helena; 34 square miles. **2** A former name for PONAPE.

as·cen·sion·ist (ə·sen'shən·ist) *n.* One who makes ascensions, as a balloonist or a mountaineer.

as·cen·sive (ə·sen'siv) *adj.* **1** Tending upward. **2** Causing to rise. [< L *ascensus,* pp. of *ascendere. See* ASCEND.]

as·cent (ə·sent') *n.* **1** The act of ascending or going up; a rising or soaring. **2** The act of climbing or traveling up, as a mountain. **3** The method or way of ascending; that by which one ascends, as the upward slope of a hill. **4** The amount or degree of upward slope: an *ascent* of 30°. **5** A rise in state, rank, or station; advancement, as in esteem or succession. **6** *Rare* A going back in time or genealogy. ◆ Homophone: *assent.* [< ASCEND, on analogy with *descent*]

as·cer·tain (as'ər·tān') *v.t.* **1** To learn with certainty about; find out. **2** *Obs.* To make certain; determine; define. See synonyms under DISCOVER, KNOW. [< OF *acertener* < *a-* to (< L *ad-*) + *certain.* See CERTAIN.] **—as'cer·tain'·a·ble** *adj.* **—as'cer·tain'a·ble·ness** *n.* **—as'·cer·tain'a·bly** *adv.* **—as'cer·tain'ment** *n.*

as·cet·ic (ə·set'ik) *n.* **1** Originally, in the early church, one who renounced social life and comfort for solitude, self-mortification, and religious devotion; a hermit; recluse. **2** Hence, one who leads a very austere and self-denying life. —*adj.* Given to severe self-denial and austerity; practicing rigid abstinence and devotion. Also **as·cet'i·cal.** [< Gk. *askētikos* exercised, industrious, athletic < *askētēs* one who exercises (self-denial), a monk < *askeein* exercise] **—as·cet'i·cal·ly** *adv.*

as·cet·i·cism (ə·set'ə·siz'əm) *n.* **1** Ascetic belief and conduct. **2** The belief that one can attain to a high intellectual or spiritual level through solitude, mortification of the flesh, and devotional contemplation.

Asch (äsh), **Sholem,** 1880–1957, U.S. novelist and playwright in Yiddish, born in Poland.

As·cham (as'kəm), **Roger,** 1515–68, English classical scholar; tutor of Queen Elizabeth I.

as·ci (as'ī) Plural of ASCUS.

as·cians (ash'yənz) *n. pl.* Shadowless men: applied to inhabitants of the torrid zone, who twice in the year cast no shadow at noon. Also **as·ci·i** (ash'ē·ī). [< L *ascius* < Gk. *askios* without shadow < *a-* without + *skia* shadow]

as·cid·i·an (ə·sid'ē·ən) *n. Zool.* Any of a class (Ascidiacea) of solitary and colonial forms of tunicates in which the adults are sessile filter feeders that secrete a tunic of cellulose. Also called *sea squirt.—adj.* Of or pertaining to this class of animals. [< NL < ASCIDIUM]

as·cid·i·um (ə·sid'ē·əm) *n. pl.* **·cid·i·a** (-sid'ē·ə) *Bot.* A flask-shaped plant appendage. [< NL < Gk. *askidion,* dim. of *askos* bag, wine-skin]

as·cif·er·ous (ə·sif'ər·əs) *adj. Bot.* Bearing large cells or spore cases, as some ascomycetous fungi. Also **as·cig·er·ous** (ə·sij'ər·əs). [< ASCI + L *ferere* bear]

as·ci·tes (ə·sī'tēz) *n. Pathol.* Abdominal dropsy. [< L < Gk. *askitēs* < *askos* bag] **—as·cit·ic** (ə·sit'ik) or **·i·cal** *adj.*

as·cle·pi·a·da·ceous (as·klē'pē·ə·dā'shəs) *adj. Bot.* Belonging to a large family *(Asclepiadaceae)* of erect or twining plants, the milkweed family, having milky juice. [< NL *Asclepias,* a genus of plants < Gk. *asklēpias;* named after *Aesculapius*]

As·cle·pi·a·de·an (as·klē'pē·ə·dē'ən) *adj.* Of, pertaining to, or denoting a variety of classical verse, usually consisting of a spondee, two or three choriambi, and an iambus. —*n.* An Asclepiadean verse. [after *Asclepiades* of Samos, 3rd c. B.C. Greek lyric poet]

As·cle·pi·us (as·klē'pē·əs) In Greek mythology, the son of Apollo and god of medicine: identified with the Roman *Aesculapius.*

as·co·carp (as'kə·kärp) *n. Bot.* The sporocarp or fruit of ascomycetous fungi. [< Gk. *askos* bag + -CARP]

as·cog·e·nous (as·koj'ə·nəs) *adj. Bot.* Producing asci.

as·co·go·ni·um (as'kə·gō'nē·əm) *n. pl.* **·ni·a** (-nē·ə) *Bot.* The female reproductive organ before fertilization in certain of the lower cryptogams. [< NL < Gk. *askos* bag + *gonos* offspring]

as·co·my·ce·tous (as'kə·mī·sē'təs) *adj. Bot.* Belonging to a large class *(Ascomycetes)* of fungi having the spores formed in asci, including mildews and yeasts: many of the species cause destructive diseases of plants. [< NL *Ascomycetes* < ASCUS + -MYCETES]

a·scor·bic (ə·skôr'bik) See ANTISCORBUTIC.

ascorbic acid The scurvy-preventing vitamin C, a white, odorless, crystalline compound, $C_6H_8O_6$, present in citrus and other fresh fruits, tomatoes, potatoes, and green leafy vegetables, and also made synthetically from glucose.

as·co·spore (as'kə·spôr, -spōr) *n. Bot.* A spore developed within an ascus. **—as·cos·po·rous** (as·kos'pə·rəs), **as·co·spor·ic** (as'kə·spôr'ik, -spor'-) *adj.*

as·cot (as'kət, -kot) *n.* A kind of scarf or necktie, knotted so that the broad ends are laid one across the other. [from *Ascot*]

As·cot (as'kət, -kot) A village in Berkshire, England, near Windsor; site of annual races instituted in 1711.

as·cribe (ə·skrīb') *v.t.* **as·cribed, as·crib·ing 1** To refer, as to a cause or source; attribute; impute. **2** To consider or declare as belonging or being due or appropriate; assign as a quality or attribute. See synonyms under ATTRIBUTE. [< L *ascribere* < *ad-* to + *scribere* write] **—as·crib·a·ble** (ə·skrī'bə·bəl) *adj.*

as·crip·tion (ə·skrip'shən) *n.* **1** An ascribing or being ascribed. **2** An expression ascribing, or that which is ascribed. **3** A text or sentence ascribing praise and glory to the Almighty. [< L *ascriptio, -onis* < *ascribere.* See ASCRIBE.]

As·cu·lum (as'kyə·ləm) An ancient town of southern Italy; scene of a Roman defeat by Pyrrhus of Epirus, 279 B.C.; modern **As·co·li Sa·tri·a·no** (äs'kô·lē sä'trē·ä'nō).

as·cus (as'kəs) *n. pl.* **as·ci** (as'ī) *Bot.* A large cell or spore case in ascomycetous fungi and lichens. [< NL < Gk. *askos* bag, wine-skin]

as·dic (az'dik) *n.* A hydrophone, operating through the reflection of sound waves under water. Also **AS'DIC.** [< A(LLIED) S(UBMARINE) D(ETECTION) I(NVESTIGATION) C(OMMITTEE)]

-ase *suffix Chem.* Used in naming enzymes, chiefly of vegetable origin: sometimes added to a part or the whole of the name of the compound which the enzyme decomposes: *amylase, casease,* etc. [<(DIAST)ASE]

a·sea (ə·sē′) *adv.* To or toward the sea; at sea.

a·se·mi·a (ə·sē′mē·ə) *n. Psychiatry* Loss of power to understand signs of communication. [<NL <A-[4] without + Gk. *sēma* sign]

a·sep·sis (ə·sep′sis, ā-) *n. Med.* **1** Absence of or freedom from putrefactive infection. **2** The prevention of septic infection by the use of sterilized instruments, dressings, etc.

a·sep·tic (ə·sep′tik, ā-) *adj.* **1** Exempt from septic or blood poisoning conditions and from pathogenic micro-organisms. **2** Characterizing processes tending to remove such conditions. **3** Free from disease germs or tendency to putrefaction. —*n.* An aseptic preparation. —**a·sep′·ti·cal·ly** *adv.*

a·sep·ti·cism (ə·sep′tə·siz′əm, ā-) *n.* The theory and practice of aseptic surgery.

a·sep·ti·cize (ə·sep′tə·sīz, ā-) *v.t.* **·cized, ·ciz·ing** To make aseptic.

a·sex·u·al (ā·sek′shōō·əl) *adj. Biol.* **1** Having no distinct sexual organs; without sex. **2** Occurring or performed without commerce of the sexes; agamic: *asexual* methods of reproduction. —**a·sex·u·al·i·ty** (ā·sek′shōō·al′ə·tē) *n.* —**a·sex′·u·al·ly** *adv.*

a·sex·u·al·i·za·tion (ā·sek′shōō·əl·ə·zā′shən, -ī·zā′-) *n.* The act of unsexing, as by castration.

As·gard (as′gärd, äs′-) In Norse mythology, the home of the Æsir; the residence of heroes slain in battle. See BIFROST. Also **As·garth** (äs′gärth), **As·gar·dhr** (äs′gär′thr′).

ash[1] (ash) *n.* **1** The powdery, whitish-gray residue of a substance that has been burnt. See ASHES. **2** *Geol.* Comminuted lava as ejected by a volcano. [OE *asce, æsce*]

ash[2] (ash) *n.* **1** Any of a widely distributed genus *(Fraxinus)* of trees of the olive family, as the American white ash *(F. alba)* and the European ash *(F. excelsior)*. **2** Its light, tough, elastic wood. —*adj.* Made of ash wood. [OE *æsc*]

a·shamed (ə·shāmd′) *adj.* **1** Feeling shame; confused by consciousness of fault or impropriety; abashed. **2** Deterred by fear of shame; reluctant. [Orig. pp. of obs. v. *ashame* to shame or feel shame] —**a·sham·ed·ly** (ə·shā′·mid·lē) *adv.* —**a·sham′ed·ness** *n.*

A·shan·ti (ə·shan′tē, ə·shän′-) **1** A former native kingdom and British protectorate in western Africa, included since 1957 in Ghana. **2** A native of this region. **3** The Sudanic language spoken there: also called *Twi.* Also **A·shan′tee.**

Ash·bel (ash′bel) A masculine personal name. [<Hebrew, man of Baal]

Ash·bur·ton (ash′bûr′tən) A river in NW Australia, flowing 220 miles NW to Exmouth Gulf.

Ash·bur·ton (ash′bûr′tən), **Lord,** 1774–1848, Alexander Baring, English statesman and banker.

ash·cake (ash′kāk′) *n.* A cake, especially cornbread, baked in hot ashes.

ash·can (ash′kan′) *n.* **1** A large can or metal receptacle for cinders and ashes. **2** *U.S. Slang* A depth bomb.

ash·en[1] (ash′ən) *adj.* Of, pertaining to, or like ashes: pale in color; gray.

ash·en[2] (ash′ən) *adj.* Pertaining to or made of the wood of the ash tree.

Ash·er (ash′ər) The eighth son of Jacob. *Gen.* xxx 13.

ash·er·y (ash′ər·ē) *n. pl.* **·er·ies** **1** A place of deposit for ashes. **2** A place where potash is made.

ash·es (ash′iz) *n. pl.* **1** The grayish-white, powdery particles, often intermixed with charred fragments, remaining after something has been burned. **2** The remains of the human body after cremation. **3** Any dead body; corpse. **4** Remains or ruins, as after destruction. **5 The Ashes** A symbol of victory in international cricket matches between Australia and England. See ASH[1].

Ashe·ville (ash′vil) A resort city of western North Carolina.

a·shine (ə·shīn′) *adv.* Luminously. —*adj.* Shining.

Ash·ke·lon (ash′kə·lon) An ancient city on the Mediterranean coast of southern Palestine: also *Ascalon, Askalon.*

Ash·ke·naz·im (ash′kə·naz′im, äsh′kə·nä′zim) *n. pl.* The Jews settled in northern and central Europe: distinguished from the *Sephardim.* [<Hebrew] —**Ash′ke·naz′ic** *adj.*

Ash·kha·bad (äsh′khä·bäd′) The capital and largest city of Turkmen S.S.R., near the Iran border.

ash·lar (ash′lər) *n.* **1** In masonry, a rough-hewn block of stone. **2** A thin, dressed, squared stone, used for facing a wall. **3** Masonwork made of either kind of ashlar. Also **ash′ler.** [<OF *aiseler* <L *axilla,* dim. of *axis* board, plank]

ash·lar·ing (ash′lər·ing) *n.* **1** In carpentry, upright wooden plaster studs running from the floor of a garret to the rafters. **2** Ashlar masonry. Also **ash′ler·ing.**

ash·man (ash′man′) *n. pl.* **·men** (-men′) A man who collects and removes ashes.

a·shore (ə·shôr′, ə·shōr′) *adv.* **1** To or on the shore. **2** On land; aground.

ash·ram (äsh′rəm) *n.* **1** In India, a Hindu hermitage or religious retreat. **2** A religious commune. **3** A commune of hippies. [<Skt. *āśrama* <*ā* toward + *śrama* exertion]

Ash·to·reth (ash′tə·reth) An ancient Phoenician and Syrian goddess of love and fertility: identified with *Astarte.*

ash·tray (ash′trā′) *n.* A receptacle for the ashes and butts of cigars, cigarettes, and pipes. Also **ash tray.**

A·shur (ä′shōōr, ash′ər) In Assyrian mythology, the chief deity, god of war and empire: also spelled *Asshur.*

A·shur (ä′shōōr, ash′ər) See ASSYRIA.

A·shur·ba·ni·pal (ä′shoor·bä′ni·päl) Assyrian king 668–625 B.C.: known as *Sardanapalus.*

Ash Wednesday The first day of Lent: from the sprinkling of ashes on the heads of penitents.

ash·y (ash′ē) *adj.* **ash·i·er, ash·i·est** **1** Of, pertaining to, or like ashes; ash-covered. **2** Ash-colored; ashen.

A·sia (ā′zhə, ā′shə) The world's largest continent, bounded by Europe and the Pacific, Arctic, and Indian Oceans; 16,900,000 square miles.

Asia Minor The peninsula of extreme western Asia between the Black and the Mediterranean Seas, comprising most of Turkey in Asia: also *Anatolia.*

A·sian (ā′zhən, ā′shən) *adj.* Of, pertaining to, or characteristic of Asia or its peoples. —*n.* A native or inhabitant of Asia.

A·sian·ism (ā′zhən·iz′əm, ā′shən-) *n.* A florid literary and oratorical style of pre-Christian Hellenistic Asia. Compare ATTICISM.

A·si·arch (ā′shē·ärk) *n.* In the ancient Roman Empire, an official who presided over the religious rites and public games in the province of Asia. [<L *Asiarcha* <Gk. *Asiarchēs* <*Asia* Asia + *archos* ruler]

A·si·at·ic (ā′zhē·at′ik, ā′shē-) *adj. & n.* Asian. ◆ Especially in the ethnic sense *Asian* is now preferred to *Asiatic,* because of the supposed derogatory implications of the latter term.

Asiatic beetle A scarabaeid beetle *(Anomala orientalis)* destructive of sugarcane and grass roots, introduced from Japan into Hawaii and the NE United States.

Asiatic cholera See under CHOLERA.

a·side (ə·sīd′) *adv.* **1** On or to one side; apart; away. **2** Out of thought or use. **3** Away from the general company; in seclusion: He drew his friend *aside* to speak more intimately. **4** Away from one's person; down: He cast his weapon *aside.* **5** In reserve: Keep some *aside* for me. —**aside from 1** Excepting. **2** *U.S.* Apart from. —**to set aside** *Law* To declare of no authority, as a verdict, judgment, etc. —*n.* Something spoken privately, as a remark or speech by an actor supposed to be heard by the audience but not by the other actors. [<A-[1] on + SIDE]

as·i·nine (as′ə·nīn) *adj.* Pertaining to or like an ass, characterized as a stupid, silly animal. [<L *asininus* <*asinus* ass] —**as′i·nine′ly** *adv.* —**as·i·nin·i·ty** (as′ə·nin′ə·tē) *n.*

A·sir (ä·sir′) A mountainous region in western Arabia on the Red Sea between Hejaz and Yemen.

ask (ask, äsk) *v.t.* **1** To put a question to: Don't *ask* me. **2** To put a question about; inquire after: to *ask* someone the time. **3** To make a request for; solicit: to *ask* advice. **4** To need or require: This job *asks* more of me than I can give. **5** To state the price of; demand: They are *asking* three dollars a plate. **6** To invite: Were many guests *asked?* **7** *Archaic* To publish or proclaim, as the banns of marriage in a church. —*v.i.* **8** To make inquiries: with *for, after,* or *about.* **9** To make a request: How often must I *ask?* [OE *āscian*] —**ask′er** *n.* —**ask′ing** *n.*

Synonyms: beg, beseech, crave, demand, entreat, implore, petition, plead, pray, request, require, solicit, supplicate. One *asks* what he feels that he may fairly claim and reasonably expect; he *begs* for that to which he advances no claim but pity. *Entreat* implies a special earnestness of asking, and *beseech,* a still added and more humble intensity. To *supplicate* is to *ask,* as it were, on bended knees; to *implore,* with the added force of tears. *Crave* and *request* are somewhat formal terms; *crave* has almost disappeared from conversation. *Pray* is now used chiefly of address to the Supreme Being; *petition* is used of written request to persons in authority. *Beg* and *pray* are often used in polite forms of slight request; *beseech* was formerly so used. Compare DEMAND, INQUIRE. *Antonyms:* claim, command, deny, enforce, exact, extort, insist, refuse.

Ask (äsk) In Norse mythology, the first man, made from a tree by Odin, Hœner, and Loder.

As·ka·lon (as′kə·lon) See ASHKELON.

a·skance (ə·skans′) *adv.* **1** With a side glance; sidewise. **2** Disdainfully; distrustfully. Also **a·skant′.** [Origin unknown]

a·skew (ə·skyōō′) *adj.* Oblique. —*adv.* In an oblique position or manner; to one side. [<A-[1] on + SKEW]

Ask·ja (äsk′yä) An inactive volcano in east central Iceland; 4,754 feet.

a·slant (ə·slant′, ə·slänt′) *adj.* Slanting; oblique. —*adv.* In a slanting direction or position; obliquely. —*prep.* Across or over in a slanting direction or position; athwart.

a·sleep (ə·slēp′) *adj.* **1** In a state of sleep; sleeping. **2** Dormant; inactive. **3** Benumbed. **4** Dead. —*adv.* Into a sleeping condition: to fall *asleep.*

a·slope (ə·slōp′) *adj.* Sloping. —*adv.* In a sloping position.

As·ma·ra (äs·mä′rə) The capital of Eritrea.

As·mo·de·us (az′mə·dē′əs, as′-) In Jewish demonology, an evil, destructive spirit.

As·nières (ä·nyâr′) A northern suburb of Paris. Also **As·nières-sur-Seine** (-sür·sân′).

a·so·cial (ā·sō′shəl) *adj.* **1** Avoiding society; not gregarious. **2** Regardless of one's fellow beings; self-centered.

A·so·ka (ə·sō′kə), died 232 B.C., Buddhist king in India 273–232 B.C.

a·so·ma·tous (ā·sō′mə·təs, ə-) *adj.* Not having bodily form; disembodied; incorporeal. [<L *asomatus,* <Gk. *asōmatos* <*a-* without + *sōma* body]

A·so·san (ä·sō·sän) A group of five extinct volcanic cones on central Kyushu island, Japan; 5,223 feet; world's largest crater, 10 by 15 miles. Also **Mount A·so** (ä·sō).

asp[1] (asp) *n.* **1** The common European viper. **2** The haje. **3** The uraeus. [<OF *aspe* <L *aspis* <Gk.]

asp[2] (asp) *n.* The aspen.

as·par·a·gine (ə·spar′ə·jēn, -jin) *n.* An amino acid, $C_4H_8N_2O_3$, occurring as a constituent of many proteins.

as·par·a·gus (ə·spar′ə·gəs) *n.* **1** The succulent edible shoots of a cultivated variety of a perennial herb *(Asparagus officinalis)* of the lily family. **2** Any plant of this genus. [<L <Gk. *asparagos, aspharogos*]

asparagus beetle A beetle *(Crioceris asparagi)* harmful to asparagus shoots. See illustration under INSECT (injurious).

as·par·tame (as·pär′tām) *n.* A synthetic combination of the amino acids aspartic acid and phenylalanine, used as a sweetener in foods.

as·par·tic acid (as·pär′tik) A white crystalline amino acid, $C_4H_7O_4N$, found in plant and animal proteins. [<ASPARAGUS]

As·pa·sia (as·pā′zhə, -shə), 470?–410 B.C., Athenian courtesan, mistress of Pericles.

as·pect (as′pekt) *n.* **1** The look a person has; expression of countenance. **2** Appearance presented to the eye by something; look. **3** Appearance presented to the mind by circumstances, etc.; interpretation. **4** A looking or facing in a given direction. **5** The side or surface facing in a certain direction. **6** In astrology: **a** Any configuration of the planets. **b** The supposed resulting influence of this for good or evil. **7** *Gram.* A categorizing of the verb indicating, primarily, the nature of the action performed in regard to the passage of time, as in English *he ran* (perfective), *he was running* (imperfective or durative), and, in certain languages, the manner in which the action is performed, the intent of the subject, etc., as in Hebrew *'ākhal* he eats, *'ikkēl* he eats greedily. Aspect is shown in the various languages by means of auxiliaries, affixes, root changes, etc. **8** *Obs.* A look; glance. See synonyms under MANNER. [<L *aspectus,* pp. of *aspicere* look at <*ad-* at + *specere* look]

aspect ratio **1** *Telecom.* The numerical ratio of the width of a television frame to the height. **2** *Aeron.* The ratio of the square of the maximum span of an airfoil to the total wing area.

asp·en (as′pən) *n.* Any of several kinds of poplar of North America or Europe with leaves that tremble in the slightest breeze, especially the **quaking aspen** *(Populus tremuloides)* of North America: also *asp.* —*adj.* Of, like, or pertaining to the aspen; hence, shaking; tremulous. [OE *aspe*]

As·pen (as′pən) A resort and cultural center in west central Colorado.

as·per[1] (as′pər) *n.* A former Turkish silver coin, now only a money of account; equal to 1/120 of a piaster. [<F *aspre* <MGk. *aspron*]

as·per[2] (as′pər) *n.* In Greek grammar, a rough breathing (see under BREATHING). [<L *asper* rough]

as·per·ate (as′pə·rāt) *v.t.* **·at·ed, ·at·ing** To make harsh or uneven, as in sound or contour. [<L *asperatus,* pp. of *asperare* roughen <*asper* rough]

as·per·ges (ə·spûr′jēz) *n.* **1** A short service before the high mass on Sundays during which the celebrant sprinkles the altar and congregation with holy water. **2** An anthem, beginning "Asperges me", sung during this service. [<L, thou shalt sprinkle]

as·per·gill (as′pər·jil) *n.* In the Roman Catholic Church, a brush or other instrument used for sprinkling holy water: also *aspergillum.* See ASPERSORIUM. [<LL *aspergillum* <L *aspergere.* See ASPERSE.]

ASPERGILL

as·per·gil·lo·sis (as·pûr′jə·lō′sis) *n.* An infectious disease of animals and man, caused by any fungus of the genus *Aspergillus.*

as·per·gil·lum (as′pər·jil′əm) *n. pl.* **·gil·la** (-jil′ə) or **·gil·lums** Aspergill.

as·per·gil·lus (as′pər·jil′əs) *n. pl.* **·gil·li** (-jil′ī) *Bot.* Any of a genus *(Aspergillus)* of fungi belonging to the *Ascomycetes,* including the common mold fungus found on decaying vegetables, jellies, etc. [<NL; so named because of its resemblance to the ASPERGILL]

as·per·i·ty (as·per′ə·tē) *n. pl.* **·ties** **1** Roughness or harshness, as of surface, sound, style, etc. **2** Something uneven, harsh, or rough. **3** Bitterness or sharpness of temper; harsh feelings. See synonyms under ACRIMONY. [<OF *asprete* <L *asperitas, -tatis* roughness <*asper* rough]

a·sper·mous (ā·spûr′məs) *adj. Bot.* Without seeds. Also **a·sper·ma·tous** (ā·spûr′mə·təs). [<Gk. *aspermos* <*a-* without + *sperma* seed]

As·pern (äs′pûrn) A suburb of Vienna, Austria; site of Napoleon's defeat by the Austrians, 1809.

as·perse (ə·spûrs′) *v.t.* **as·persed** (ə·spûrst′), **as·pers·ing** **1** To spread false charges against; slander. **2** To besprinkle; bespatter. [<L *aspersus,* pp. of *aspergere* sprinkle on <*ad-* to + *spargere* sprinkle] —**as·pers′er, as·per′sor** *n.* —**as·per′sive** (-siv) *adj.*

Synonyms: backbite, calumniate, decry, defame, depreciate, disparage, libel, malign, revile, slander, traduce, vilify. To *asperse* is to bespatter with injurious charges; to *defame* is to assail one's good name; to *malign* is to circulate studied and malicious attacks upon character; to *traduce* is to exhibit real or assumed traits in an odious light. *Antonyms*: defend, eulogize, extol, laud, praise.

as·per·sion (ə·spûr′zhən, -shən) *n.* **1** A slandering. **2** Slander; a slanderous report or charge. See synonyms under SCANDAL. **3** Sprinkling; specifically, baptism by sprinkling.

as·per·so·ri·um (as′pər·sôr′ē·əm, -sō′rē-) *n. pl.* **·so·ri·a** (-sôr′ē·ə, -sō′rē·ə) or **·so·ri·ums** **1** A font for holy water. **2** An aspergill. Also **as·per·so·ry** (as·pûr′sə·rē). [<LL <L *aspersus.* See ASPERSE.]

as·phalt (as′fôlt, -falt) *n.* **1** A bituminous, solid, brownish-black, odorous combustible mixture of different hydrocarbons occurring in superficial deposits in various parts of the world and also obtained as a residue in the refining of petroleum; mineral pitch. **2** A mixture of this with sand or gravel, used for paving, etc. Also **as·phal·tum** (as·fal′·təm), **as·phal′tus.** —*v.t.* To pave or cover with asphalt. [<LL *asphaltum* <Gk. *asphaltos,* ? <Semitic] —**as·phal·tic** (as·fôl′tik, -fal′-) *adj.*

as·pho·del (as′fə·del) *n.* **1** A plant (genus *Asphodelus)* of the lily family, bearing white or yellow flowers. **2** Any one of certain somewhat similar plants. [<L *asphodelus* <Gk. *asphodelos.* Doublet of DAFFODIL.]

as·phyx·i·a (as·fik′sē·ə) *n. Pathol.* A condition, characterized by loss of consciousness, caused by too little oxygen and too much carbon dioxide in the blood, generally as a result of suffocation. Also **as·phyx·y** (as·fik′sē). [<NL <Gk. *asphyxia* <*a-* not + *sphyzein* beat] —**as·phyx′i·al** *adj.*

as·phyx·i·ant (as·fik′sē·ənt) *adj.* Producing or tending to produce asphyxia. —*n.* An asphyxiant agent or condition.

as·phyx·i·ate (as·fik′sē·āt) *v.* **·at·ed, ·at·ing** *v.t.* **1** To cause asphyxia in. **2** To suffocate, as by drowning or causing to breathe noxious gases. —*v.i.* To undergo asphyxia. —**as·phyx′i·a′tion** *n.* —**as·phyx′i·a′tor** *n.*

as·pic[1] (as′pik) *n. Poetic* The asp. Also **as′pis.** [<F <L *aspis*]

as·pic[2] (as′pik) *n.* The spike lavender. See under LAVENDER. [<F <Provençal *espic* <L *spica* spike, ear of corn]

as·pic[3] (as′pik) *n.* A savory jelly of meat juice or vegetable juices, served as a relish or mold for meat, vegetables, etc. [<F; ult. origin uncertain]

as·pi·dis·tra (as′pə·dis′trə) *n.* Any of a small genus *(Aspidistra)* of smooth, stemless, Chinese and Japanese herbs of the lily family, with large, glossy, evergreen leaves: widely cultivated as a house plant. [<NL <Gk. *aspis, aspidos* shield + *astron* star]

As·pin·wall (as′pin·wôl) Former name of COLÓN, Panama.

as·pir·ant (ə·spīr′ənt, as′pər·ənt) *n.* One who aspires, as after honors or place; a candidate. —*adj.* Aspiring.

as·pi·rate (as′pə·rāt) *v.t.* **·rat·ed, ·rat·ing** **1** *Phonet.* **a** To utter with a breathing or as if preceded by the letter *h.* **b** In the articulation of a stop consonant, to follow with an explosive release of breath, as (p), (t), and (k) when in initial position. **2** *Med.* To draw out, as gas or fluid, from a vessel or cavity. —*n.* (as′pər·it) **1** *Phonet.* **a** The glottal fricative represented in English and many other languages by the letter *h.* **b** The sudden expulsion of breath in the release of a stop consonant before a vowel, as after the (p) in *pat.* **2** The rough breathing in Greek or the symbol (ʻ) indicating it. **3** Any consonant pronounced with a puff of breath. —*adj.* (as′pər·it) *Phonet.* Uttered with an aspirate or strong *h* sound: also **as′pi·rat′ed.** [<L *aspiratus,* pp. of *aspirare.* See ASPIRE.]

as·pi·ra·tion (as′pə·rā′shən) *n.* **1** The act of aspiring; exalted desire; high ambition. **2** The act or effect of aspirating; a breath. **3** *Med.* The use of an aspirator for remedial purposes. **4** *Phonet.* **a** The pronunciation of a consonant with an aspirate. **b** An aspirate. See synonyms under AIM, AMBITION, DESIRE.

as·pi·ra·tor (as′pə·rā′tər) *n.* **1** An appliance for producing a suction current of air or other gas. **2** *Med.* A device for drawing off fluid matter or gases from the body by suction.

as·pir·a·to·ry (ə·spīr′ə·tôr′ē, -tō′rē) *adj.* Of, pertaining to, or adapted for breathing or suction.

as·pire (ə·spīr′) *v.i.* **as·pired, as·pir·ing** **1** To have an earnest desire or ambition, as for something high and good: with *to.* **2** To long for; seek after: with *after.* **3** *Obs.* To reach or rise upward. [<L *aspirare* breathe on, attempt to reach <*ad-* to + *spirare* breathe] —**as·pir′ing** *adj.* —**as·pir′er** *n.*

as·pi·rin (as′pər·in) *n.* A white crystalline compound, the acetyl derivative of salicylic acid, $C_9H_8O_4$, having antipyretic and antirheumatic properties. [<A(CETYL) + SPIR(AEIC ACID), former name of salicylic acid, + -IN]

a·squint (ə·skwint′) *adj.* & *adv.* With sidelong glance. [<A-[1] on + SQUINT (of uncertain origin)]

As·quith (as′kwith), **Herbert Henry,** 1852–1928, English premier 1908–16; created Earl of Oxford and Asquith 1925.

ass[1] (as) *n.* **1** A long-eared equine quadruped *(Equus asinus)* smaller than the ordinary horse. **2** The Mongolian onager. **3** An obstinate or stupid person. [OE *assa,* ? <OIrish *assan* <L *asinus*]

ass[2] (äs) *n. Scot.* Ashes: also spelled *aise.*

ass[3] (as) *n. Slang* The buttocks: usually considered vulgar. [ME *ars* <OE *ærs, ears*]

as·sa·fet·i·da (as′ə·fet′ə·də) See ASAFETIDA.

as·sa·gai (as′ə·gī) *n.* **1** A light spear, used by Zulus, Kafirs, etc. **2** The assagai tree. —*v.t.* To pierce with an assagai. Also *assegai.* [<Sp. *azagaya* or Pg. *azagaia* <Arabic *az-zaghāyah* <*al* the + *zaghāyah* spear <native Berber word]

ASSAGAI

assagai tree A South African tree *(Curtisia faginea)* of the dogwood family, used for making spears.

as·sai[1] (ä·sä′ē) *n.* **1** A palm of the genus *Euterpe,* especially *E. edulis,* bearing a purple, fleshy fruit. **2** A drink made from this fruit. [<Pg. *assahy* <Tupian]

as·sai[2] (äs·sä′ē) *adv. Music* Very: Adagio *assai* means very slowly. [<Ital.]

as·sail (ə·sāl′) *v.t.* **1** To attack violently, as by force, argument, or censure; assault. **2** To approach, as a difficulty, with the intention of mastering. See synonyms under ATTACK. [<OF *asalir, asaillir* <LL *adsalire* leap upon <L *ad-* to + *salire* leap] —**as·sail′a·ble** *adj.* —**as·sail′a·ble·ness** *n.* —**as·sail′er** *n.*

as·sail·ant (ə·sā′lənt) *adj.* Attacking; hostile. —*n.* One who assails.

As·sam (a·sam′) A state in NE India; 54,951 square miles; capital, Shillong.

As·sa·mese (as′ə·mēz′, -mēs′) *adj.* Of or pertaining to Assam. —*n.* **1** A native or inhabitant of Assam. **2** The Indo-European, Indic language of the Assamese people.

Assam States A former political agency, comprising a number of small states, situated within Assam, India.

as·sas·sin (ə·sas′in) *n.* **1** One who kills, or tries to kill, secretly or treacherously. **2** One who undertakes to commit murder, particularly of a political figure, for a reward.

As·sas·sin (ə·sas′in) *n.* One of a secret order of hashish-eating Moslem fanatics who murdered Christian leaders in the time of the Crusades. [<F <Med. L *assassinus* <Arabic *hashshāshīn* hashish-eaters <*hashīsh* hashish]

as·sas·si·nate (ə·sas′ə·nāt) *v.t.* **·nat·ed, ·nat·ing** **1** To kill by secret or surprise assault. **2** To destroy or wound by treachery, as a reputation. See synonyms under KILL. —**as·sas′si·na′tion** *n.* —**as·sas′si·na′tor** *n.*

assassin bug Any of a predatory species of hemipterous insects (family *Reduviidae)* having a short curved beak: some species suck the blood of warm-blooded animals. See illustration under INSECT (beneficial).

assassin fly A hairy, predatory fly (family *Asilidae),* especially the common robber fly (genus *Erax)* of the United States. See illustration under INSECT (beneficial).

as·sault (a·sôlt′) *n.* **1** Any violent attack, as an act, speech, or writing assailing a person or institution. **2** *Law* An unlawful attempt or offer to do bodily injury to another: distinguished from *battery.* **3** A rape. **4** *Mil.* A violent attack by troops, as upon a fortified place. See synonyms under AGGRESSION,

ATTACK. — *v.t.* & *v.i.* To attack with violence; make an assault (upon). [<OF *asaut* <L *ad-* to + *salire* leap] — **as·sault'er** *n.*

assault and battery *Law* The carrying out of an assault with force and violence; a beating.

assault boat *Mil.* A small craft used to transport attacking soldiers and their equipment across water.

as·say (ə·sā', as'ā) *n.* **1** The chemical analysis or testing of an alloy or ore, to ascertain the ingredients and their proportions. **2** The substance to be so examined. **3** The result of such a test. **4** Any examination or testing. **5** *Obs.* Attempt; trial. — *v.t.* (ə·sā') **1** To subject to chemical analysis; make an assay of. **2** To prove; test. **3** *Obs.* To attempt. — *v.i.* **4** To show by analysis a certain value or proportion, as of a precious metal: to *assay* low in platinum. [<OF *assai*, var. of *essai* trial <L *exagium* a weighing < *exigere* prove < *ex-* out + *agere* drive, do. Doublet of ESSAY.] — **as·say'er** *n.*

as·say·ing (ə·sā'ing) *n.* The process of making an assay.

as·se·gai (as'ə·gī) See ASSAGAI.

as·sem·blage (ə·sem'blij, *for def.* 4, *also Fr.* à·säṅ·bläzh') *n.* **1** An assembling or being assembled. **2** Any gathering of persons or things; collection; assembly. **3** A fitting together, as parts of a machine. **4** A work of art created by assembling materials and objects; also, the technique of making such works. See synonyms under ASSEMBLY, COMPANY. [<F]

as·sem·ble (ə·sem'bəl) *v.t.* & *v.i.* **·bled, ·bling** **1** To collect or convene; come together; congregate, as a group or meeting. **2** To fit or join together, as the parts of a mechanism. See synonyms under CONVOKE. [<OF *as(s)embler* <L *assimulare* < *ad-* to + *simul* together] — **as·sem'bler** *n.*

as·sem·bly (ə·sem'blē) *n. pl.* **·blies** **1** An assembling or being assembled. **2** A number of persons met together for a common purpose. **3** The act or process of fitting together the parts of a machine, etc., especially where such parts are machine-made in great numbers so as to be interchangeable. **4** A unit made up of such parts. **5** The parts themselves, before or after being fitted together. **6** *Mil.* The signal calling troops to form ranks. [<OF *as(s)emblee* < *as(s)embler*. See ASSEMBLE.]

Synonyms: assemblage, collection, company, conclave, concourse, conference, congregation, convention, convocation, crowd, gathering, group, host, meeting, multitude. An *assemblage* may be of persons or of objects and is promiscuous and unorganized, an *assembly* is always of persons and is organized and united in some common purpose.

As·sem·bly (ə·sem'blē) *n.* In some states of the United States, the lower house of the legislature.

assembly line An arrangement of machines and workers in a factory, as along a moving track or belt, so that a number of specialized operations may be performed on a unit of work as it passes from one to another.

as·sem·bly·man (ə·sem'blē·mən) *n. pl.* **·men** (-men', -mən) *U.S.* A member of a legislative assembly, especially of the lower house of a state legislature.

as·sent (ə·sent') *v.i.* To express agreement, as with an abstract proposition; acquiesce; concur: usually with *to*. — *n.* **1** Mental concurrence or agreement. **2** Consent of will; acquiescence. ◆ Homophone: *ascent*. [<OF *as(s)enter* <L *assentare*, freq. of *assentire* < *ad-* to + *sentire* feel] — **as·sent'er** *n.*

Synonyms (verb): accede, accept, accord, acquiesce, admit, agree, approve, coincide, concur, consent, ratify, sustain, uphold. To *assent* is an act of the understanding; to *consent*, of the will. *Assent* is sometimes used for a mild or formal *consent*. See BELIEF. *Antonyms*: contradict, demur, deny, differ, disagree, disavow, disclaim, dissent, object, protest, question, refuse.

as·sen·ta·tion (as'en·tā'shən) *n.* Obsequious assent, as to the opinions of another.

as·sen·tor (ə·sen'tər) *n.* An assenter; specifically, in Great Britain, one who, as required by law, endorses the nomination of a candidate for Parliament.

as·sert (ə·sûrt') *v.t.* **1** To state positively; affirm; declare. **2** To maintain as a right or claim, as by words or force. **3** To insist on the recognition of (oneself): He *asserted* himself at the conference. [<L *assertus*, pp. of *asserere* bind to, claim < *ad-* to + *serere* bind] — **as·sert'er, as·ser'tor** *n.*

Synonyms: affirm, allege, asseverate, aver, avouch, avow, claim, declare, maintain, pronounce, protest, say, state, tell. One may *assert* himself, his right, his belief, etc. *Assert* is controversial; *affirm*, *state*, and *tell* are simply declarative. See AFFIRM, ALLEGE. *Antonyms*: contradict, contravene, controvert, deny, disprove, dispute, gainsay, oppose, repudiate, retract, waive.

as·ser·tion (ə·sûr'shən) *n.* **1** The act of asserting. **2** A positive declaration without attempt at proof. **3** Insistence upon a right or claim. See synonyms under ASSURANCE.

as·ser·tive (ə·sûr'tiv) *adj.* **1** Of, pertaining to, or characterized by assertion. **2** Characterized by excessive assertion; overly insistent. — **as·ser'tive·ly** *adv.* — **as·ser'tive·ness** *n.*

as·ser·to·ry (ə·sûr'tər·ē) *adj.* Tending to assert.

asses' bridge The fifth proposition of the first book of Euclid, stating that the angles opposite the equal sides of an isosceles triangle are equal: so called from the difficulty beginners are supposed to have in comprehending it: also called *pons asinorum*.

as·sess (ə·ses') *v.t.* **1** To charge with a tax, fine, or other payment, as a person or property. **2** To determine the amount of, as a tax or other fine on a person or property. **3** To value, as property, for taxation. **4** To take stock of; evaluate: to *assess* the situation. See synonyms under TAX. [<OF *assesser* <LL *assessare* fix a tax <L *assidere* sit by (as a judge in court) < *ad-* to + *sedere* sit] — **as·sess'a·ble** *adj.*

as·sess·ment (ə·ses'mənt) *n.* **1** An assessing. **2** Apportionment or amount assessed. **3** The valuation of property for taxation.

as·ses·sor (ə·ses'ər) *n.* **1** One who makes assessments, as for taxation. **2** A specialist assisting a judge. **3** Any adviser or assistant. [<L, lit., one who sits beside, an assistant judge (in LL, an assessor of taxes) < *assidere*. See ASSESS.] — **as·ses·so·ri·al** (as'ə·sôr'ē·əl, -sō'rē-) *adj.*

as·set (as'et) *n.* **1** An item of property. **2** A person, thing, or quality regarded as useful or valuable: Her intelligence is an *asset*.

as·sets (as'ets) *n. pl.* **1** *Law* The property of a deceased person that is convertible into money and held for the payment of debts or legacies. **2** All the property, real and personal, of a person, of a corporation, or of a partnership, which is or may be chargeable with the debts or legacies of such parties or persons. **3** In accounting, the entries in a balance sheet showing all the property or resources of a person or business, as accounts receivable, inventory, deferred charges, and plant: opposed to *liabilities*. — **liquid assets** Such securities and assets as can be realized immediately. — **working assets** Non-permanent convertible invested funds. [<AF *asetz*, OF *asez* enough <L *ad-* to + *satis* enough]

as·sev·er·ate (ə·sev'ə·rāt) *v.t.* **·at·ed, ·at·ing** To affirm or aver emphatically or solemnly. See synonyms under AFFIRM, ALLEGE, ASSERT. [<L *asseveratus*, pp. of *asseverare* < *ad-* to + *severus* serious] — **as·sev'er·a'tion** *n.*

As·shur (ä'shŏŏr, ash'ər) **1** Ashur. **2** Assyria.

as·sib·i·late (ə·sib'ə·lāt) *v.t.* **·lat·ed, ·lat·ing** To utter with a sibilant or hissing sound; change into a sibilant. [<L *assibilatus*, pp. of *assibilare* < *ad-* to + *sibilare* hiss] — **as·sib'i·la'tion** *n.*

as·si·du·i·ty (as'ə·dōō'ə·tē, -dyōō'-) *n. pl.* **·ties** **1** Close and continuous application or effort. **2** *Usually pl.* Faithful personal attentions; carefulness; watchfulness. See synonyms under INDUSTRY.

as·sid·u·ous (ə·sij'ōō·əs) *adj.* **1** Devoted or constant, as a person. **2** Unremitting; persistent, as an action. See synonyms under BUSY, INDUSTRIOUS. [<L *assiduus* < *assidere* sit by < *ad-* to + *sedere* sit] — **as·sid'u·ous·ly** *adv.* — **as·sid'u·ous·ness** *n.*

as·sign (a·sīn') *v.t.* **1** To set apart, as for a particular function; designate. **2** To appoint or station: to *assign* a soldier to a post. **3** To allot: to *assign* a share to a participant. **4** To ascribe or attribute: to *assign* a date to an event. **5** *Law* To make over or transfer, as personal property, to another. **6** *Mil.* To allocate, as personnel, units or materiel, to a military unit as an integral unit thereof: distinguished from *attach*. See synonyms under ALLEGE, ALLOT, APPORTION, ATTRIBUTE, COMMIT, SET. — *n.* *Law Usually pl.* Assignee. [<OF *as(s)igner* <L *assignare* < *ad-* to + *signare* make a sign < *signum* sign]

as·sign·a·ble (ə·sī'nə·bəl) *adj.* **1** Capable of being assigned or allotted. **2** Legally transferable. **3** Attributable: Volcanoes are *assignable* to these geographical conditions. — **as·sign'a·bil'i·ty** *n.* — **as·sign'a·bly** *adv.*

as·sig·nat (as'ig·nat, *Fr.* à·sē·nyà') *n.* A promissory note of the French revolutionary government circulated as currency (1789–96) against the security of confiscated lands. [<F <L *assignatus*, pp. of *assignare*. See ASSIGN.]

as·sig·na·tion (as'ig·nā'shən) *n.* **1** An assigning or being assigned. **2** Something assigned; assignment. **3** An appointment for meeting, especially a secret or illicit one as made by lovers. **4** *Law* An assignment. [<OF *assignacion* <L *assignatio, -onis* < *assignare*. See ASSIGN.]

as·sign·ee (ə·sī'nē', as'ə·nē') *n.* **1** *Law* A person to whom property, rights, or powers are transferred by another. **2** *Obs.* An agent or trustee.

as·sign·ment (ə·sīn'mənt) *n.* **1** An assigning or being assigned. **2** Anything assigned, as a lesson or task. **3** *Law* **a** The transfer of a claim, right, or property or the instrument or writing of transfer. **b** The claim, right, or property transferred.

assignment of error *Law* A specification of the errors contained in the complaint, made by the plaintiff on a writ of error.

as·sign·or (ə·sī'nôr', as'ə·nôr') *n.* *Law* One who assigns or makes an assignment of any property, right, or interest. Also **as·sign·er** (ə·sī'nər).

as·sim·i·la·ble (ə·sim'ə·lə·bəl) *adj.* Capable of being assimilated. — **as·sim'i·la·bil'i·ty** *n.*

as·sim·i·late (ə·sim'ə·lāt) *v.* **·lat·ed, ·lat·ing** *v.t.* **1** *Physiol.* To take up and incorporate, as food. **2** To make into a homogeneous part, as of a substance or system. **3** To make alike or similar; cause to resemble: to *assimilate* British law to the laws of Scotland. **4** *Phonet.* To cause (a sound) to undergo assimilation. — *v.i.* **5** To become alike or similar. **6** To become absorbed or assimilated. See synonyms under COMPARE. [<L *assimilatus*, pp. of *assimilare* < *ad-* to + *similare* make like < *similis* like]

as·sim·i·la·tion (ə·sim'ə·lā'shən) *n.* **1** The act or process of assimilating. **2** *Physiol.* The transformation of digested nutriment into an integral and homogeneous part of the solids or fluids of the organism. **3** *Bot.* The starch-making function of plants. Compare ANABOLISM. **4** *Phonet.* The process whereby a sound is changed or modified to cause it to approach, or become identical with, a neighboring sound, as in the pronunciation (hôrsh'shōō') for *horseshoe*. **5** *Psychol.* The process by which all new experience, when received into consciousness, is modified so as to be incorporated with the results of previous conscious processes. **6** *Sociol.* The acceptance by one social group or community of cultural traits normally associated with another.

as·sim·i·la·tive (ə·sim'ə·lā'tiv) *adj.* Assimilating; characterized by or tending to assimilation. Also **as·sim·i·la·to·ry** (ə·sim'ə·lə·tôr'ē, -tō'rē).

As·sin·i·boin (ə·sin'ə·boin) *n. pl.* **·boins** or **·boin** **1** A member of a tribe of North American Indians of Siouan stock, formerly inhabiting parts of Montana, North Dakota, and Saskatchewan. **2** The language of this tribe.

As·sin·i·boine (ə·sin'ə·boin) **1** A river in eastern Saskatchewan, Canada, flowing SE 600 miles to Red River at Winnipeg. **2** A mountain of the Canadian Rockies, in Banff National Park; 11,870 feet.

As·si·si (ə·sē'zē, *Ital.* äs·sē'zē) A town in

Umbria, central Italy; birthplace of St. Francis.

as·sist (ə·sist′) *v.t.* **1** To give succor or support to; render help or service to; relieve. **2** To act as subordinate or deputy to. —*v.i.* **3** To give help or support. **4** In baseball, to aid a teammate or partner in a play. —**to assist at** To be present at (a ceremony, entertainment, etc.). —*n.* In baseball, a play that helps to put out a runner. See synonyms under ABET, AID, HELP, SERVE. [<F *assister* <L *assistere* < *ad-* to + *sistere* cause to stand] —**as·sist′er, as·sis′tor** *n.*

as·sis·tance (ə·sis′təns) *n.* Help; aid; support; relief. See synonyms under HELP.

as·sis·tant (ə·sis′tənt) *adj.* **1** Holding a subordinate or auxiliary place, office, or rank. **2** Affording aid; assisting. —*n.* One who or that which assists; a deputy or subordinate; helper. See synonyms under ACCESSORY, AUXILIARY.

assistant professor A teacher in a college who ranks immediately below an associate professor.

As·siut (ä·syōōt′) See ASYUT.

as·size (ə·sīz′) *n.* **1** Originally, a session of a court. **2** *pl.* **a** One of the regular sessions of the judges of a superior court for the trial of cases by jury in any county of England or Wales. **b** The time and place of such sessions. **3 a** A judicial inquest. **b** The writ by which it is instituted. **c** An action to be decided by such an inquest. **4** In Scots law, a trial by jury; also, the jury. **5** A statute or ordinance, or a rule prescribed by law or authority, as for the regulation of weights and measures or prices of commodities, etc. **6** A standard of weight, measure, price, etc. —**grand assize** In early English law, a trial by a jury of 12 knights instead of a trial by combat. —**great** (or **last**) **assize** The Last Judgment. [<OF *as(s)ise* < *aseeir* sit at, settle <L *assidere.* See ASSESS.]

assize of arms An English enactment of 1181 that every freeman should maintain arms suitable to his rank and station.

as·so·ci·a·ble (ə·sō′shē·ə·bəl, -shə·bəl) *adj.* Capable of being associated, connected, or joined. —**as·so′ci·a·bil′i·ty** *n.*

as·so·ci·ate (ə·sō′shē·it, -āt) *n.* **1** A companion; one who is habitually or frequently in the company or society of another. **2** A partner; one who is connected with another, as in some business, act, interest, office, or position. **3** Anything that habitually or frequently accompanies or is associated with something else; a concomitant. **4** One admitted to partial membership in an association, society, or institution. **5** In some educational institutions, one who has finished a course shorter than that set for a degree: an *associate* in arts. —*adj.* **1** Joined with another or others; united; allied; existing or occurring together; concomitant. **2** Having subordinate or secondary status or privileges: an *associate* professor; also, entitled to a limited or specified participation, as in rights, privileges, and functions: an *associate* member of a society. —*v.* (ə·sō′shē·āt) **·at·ed, ·at·ing** *v.t.* **1** To bring into company or relation; combine together. **2** To unite (oneself) with another or others, as in friendship or partnership. **3** To connect mentally: to *associate* poetry with madness. —*v.i.* **4** To join or be in company or relation: with *with*: She *associates* chiefly with musicians. **5** To unite, as nations in a league; combine. See synonyms under ATTRIBUTE, MIX, UNITE. [<L *associatus,* pp. of *associare* join to < *ad-* to + *sociare* join < *socius* ally]

Synonyms (noun): ally, chum, coadjutor, colleague, companion, comrade, consort, fellow, friend, helpmate, mate, partner, peer. An *associate,* as used officially, implies a chief, leader, or principal, to whom the *associate* is not fully equal in rank. *Associate* is popularly used for mere friendly relations, but oftener implies some work, enterprise, or pursuit in which the associated persons unite. We rarely speak of *associates* in crime or wrong, using *confederates* or *accomplices* instead. *Companion* gives itself with equal readiness to the good or the evil sense. *Peer* implies equality rather than companionship; as, a jury of his *peers. Comrade* expresses more fellowship and good feeling than *companion. Consort* is a word of equality and dignity, as applied especially to the marriage relation. Compare ACCESSORY, ACQUAINTANCE, FRIENDSHIP. *Antonyms*: antagonist, enemy, foe, hinderer, opponent, opposer, rival, stranger.

Associated Press An organization for collecting news and distributing it to member newspapers. Abbr. *AP, A.P.*

associate professor A teacher in a college who ranks immediately above an assistant professor and immediately below a professor or adjunct professor.

as·so·ci·a·tion (ə·sō′sē·ā′shən, -shē-) *n.* **1** An associating or the act of associating. **2** The state of being associated; fellowship; companionship. **3** A body of persons associated for some common purpose; corporation; society; partnership. **4** *U.S.* An organized, unchartered body of persons analogous to but distinguished legally from a corporation. **5** *Chem.* An aggregate, as of molecules: $(H_2O)_2$ is an *association* of two molecules of water. **6** *Ecol.* A grouping of many plant species over a wide area, sharing a common habitat and similar geographic conditions: a forest *association.* **7** *Psychol.* **a** The connection or relation of ideas, feelings, etc., with each other, with objects suggesting them, or with subjects of thought, by means of which their succession in the mind is determined. **b** The process of establishing such a connection. **8** *Brit.* Association football. —**as·so′ci·a′·tion·al** *adj.*

Synonyms: alliance, club, community, companionship, company, confederacy, confederation, conjunction, connection, corporation, familiarity, federation, fellowship, fraternity, friendship, lodge, partnership, society, union. We speak of an *alliance* of nations, a *club* of pleasure-seekers, a *community* of Shakers, a *company* of soldiers or of friends, a *confederacy, confederation, federation,* or *union* of states, a *partnership, corporation,* or *company* in business, a *conjunction* of planets, a religious, literary, or scientific *association* or *society.* See ACQUAINTANCE, ALLIANCE, ASSOCIATE, CLASS, FRIENDSHIP, INTERCOURSE. *Antonyms*: disconnection, disunion, independence, isolation, separateness, separation, severance, solitude.

association football Soccer.

as·so·ci·a·tive (ə·sō′shē·ā′tiv, -shē·ə-) *adj.* **1** Of, pertaining to, or characterized by association. **2** Causing association. —**as·so′ci·a′·tive·ly** *adv.*

as·soil (ə·soil′) *v.t. Archaic* **1** To absolve; acquit. **2** To atone for; remove. [<OF *assoil,* present indicative of *assoldre* <L *absolvere.* Doublet of ABSOLVE.]

as·so·nance (as′ə·nəns) *n.* **1** Resemblance in sound; specifically, in prosody, correspondence of the accented vowels, but not of the consonants, as in *main, came.* **2** Rough likeness; approximation. [<F <L *assonans,* ppr. of *assonare* sound to, respond to < *ad-* to + *sonare* sound] —**as′so·nant** *adj.* & *n.*

as·sort (ə·sôrt′) *v.t.* **1** To distribute into groups or classes according to kinds; classify. **2** To furnish, as a warehouse, with a variety of goods, etc. —*v.i.* **3** To fall into groups or classes of the same kind. **4** To associate; consort: with *with.* [<OF *assorter* < *a-* to (<L *ad-*) + *sorte* sort <L *sors* lot] —**as·sort·a·tive** (ə·sôr′tə·tiv) *adj.*

as·sort·ed (ə·sôr′tid) *adj.* **1** Consisting of or arranged in various sorts or kinds; varied; miscellaneous. **2** Sorted out; classified. **3** Matched; suited.

as·sort·ment (ə·sôrt′mənt) *n.* **1** The act of assorting or a being assorted; classification. **2** A collection or group of various things; miscellany.

As·sou·an, As·su·an (äs·wän′) See ASWAN.

as·suage (ə·swāj′) *v.* **as·suaged, as·suag·ing** *v.t.* **1** To make less harsh or violent; soothe; calm, as an excited person. **2** To alleviate; allay, as feelings. —*v.i.* **3** *Obs.* To grow less; abate; subside. Also *Obs.* **as·swage′.** See synonyms under ALLAY, ALLEVIATE. [<OF *as(s)ouagier,* ult. <L *ad-* to + *suavis* sweet] —**as·suage′ment** *n.*

as·sua·sive (ə·swā′siv) *adj.* Soothing; alleviating. —*n.* An alleviative.

as·sume (ə·sōōm′) *v.t.* **as·sumed, as·sum·ing** **1** To take up or adopt, as a style of dress, aspect, or character: to *assume* a haughty mien. **2** To undertake, as an office or duty. **3** To arrogate to oneself; usurp, as powers of state. **4** To take for granted; suppose to be a fact: to *assume* the sun will shine tomorrow. **5** To affect; pretend to have. [<L *assumere* take up, adopt < *ad-* to + *sumere* take] —**as·sum·a·ble** (ə·sōō′mə·bəl) *adj.*

Synonyms: accept, affect, appropriate, arrogate, claim, feign, postulate, presume, pretend, take, usurp. The distinctive idea of *assume* is to *take* by one's own independent volition, whether well or ill, rightfully or wrongfully. One may *accept* an obligation or *assume* an authority that properly belongs to him; if he *assumes* what does not belong to him, he is said to *arrogate* or *usurp* it. A man may *usurp* the substance of *power* in the most unpretending way; what he *arrogates* to himself he *assumes* with a haughty and overbearing manner. If he *takes* to himself the credit and appearance of qualities he does not possess, he is said to *affect* or *feign,* or to *pretend* to, the character he thus *assumes.* What a debater *postulates* he openly states and *takes* for granted without proof; what he *assumes* he may *take* for granted without mention. What a man *claims* he asserts his right to *take;* what he *assumes* he *takes.* See PRETEND. *Antonyms*: see synonyms for RENOUNCE.

as·sumed (ə·sōōmd′) *adj.* **1** Taken for granted. **2** Pretended; fictitious.

as·sum·ing (ə·sōō′ming) *adj.* Presumptuous; arrogant.

as·sump·sit (ə·sump′sit) *n. Law* **1** A promise or contract not under seal. **2** An action to enforce this, or to recover damages for a breach of this. [<L, he undertook]

as·sump·tion (ə·sump′shən) *n.* **1** An assuming, or that which is assumed. **2** A taking for granted; supposition. **3** Presumption; arrogance. **4** *Logic* A minor premise. See synonyms under ARROGANCE, ASSURANCE, PRETENSE. —**the Assumption 1** *Theol.* The doctrine that the Virgin Mary was bodily taken up into heaven at her death. **2** A church feast, observed on August 15, commemorating this event. [<L *assumptio, -onis* < *assumere.* See ASSUME.]

as·sump·tive (ə·sump′tiv) *adj.* **1** Characterized by assumption. **2** That can be assumed. **3** Presumptuous. —**as·sump′tive·ly** *adv.*

as·sur·ance (ə·shŏŏr′əns) *n.* **1** The act of assuring; a being assured. **2** A positive or encouraging declaration. **3** Full confidence; undoubting conviction. **4** Self-confidence; firmness of mind. **5** Boldness; effrontery. **6** *Brit.* Insurance.

Synonyms: arrogance, assertion, assumption, boldness, confidence, effrontery, impudence, presumption, self-assertion, self-confidence, self-reliance, trust. *Confidence* is founded upon reasons; *assurance* is largely a matter of feeling. In the bad sense, *assurance* is a vicious courage, with belief of one's ability to outwit or defy others; it is less gross than *impudence,* which is (according to its etymology) a shameless *boldness. Assurance* appears in act or manner; *impudence,* in speech. *Effrontery* is *impudence* defiantly displayed. Compare BELIEF, CERTAINTY, EFFRONTERY, FAITH, IMPUDENCE, PRIDE. *Antonyms*: bashfulness, confusion, consternation, dismay, distrust, doubt, hesitancy, misgiving, shyness, timidity.

as·sure (ə·shŏŏr′) *v.t.* **as·sured, as·sur·ing** **1** To make sure or secure; establish against change: His poems *assured* his immortality. **2** To give confidence to; convince: His success *assured* him of the validity of his mission. **3** To offer assurances concerning; guarantee, as something risky. **4** To promise confidently: He *assured* his friends he would return. **5** To insure. See synonyms under CONFIRM. [<OF *aseurer* <LL *assecurare* <L *ad-* to + *securus* safe] —**as·sur′a·ble** *adj.*

as·sured (ə·shŏŏrd′) *adj.* **1** Made certain; undoubted; sure. **2** Self-possessed; confident. **3** Insured. See synonyms under CONSCIOUS, SECURE, SURE. —*n.* An insured person or persons. —**as·sur·ed·ly** (ə·shŏŏr′id·lē) *adv.* —**as·sur′ed·ness** *n.*

as·sur·er (ə·shŏŏr′ər) *n.* **1** One who or that which assures. **2** *Brit.* An insurance underwriter. Also **as·sur′or.**

as·sur·gent (ə·sûr′jənt) *adj.* **1** Rising or tending to rise. **2** *Her.* Rising out of the sea. **3** *Bot.* Curving upward. [<L *assurgens,*

-entis. ppr. of *assurgere* < *ad-* to + *surgere* rise] **—as·sur′gen·cy** *n.*

As·syr·i·a (ə·sir′ē·ə) An ancient empire of western Asia: capital, Nineveh. Also *Ashur, Asshur.*

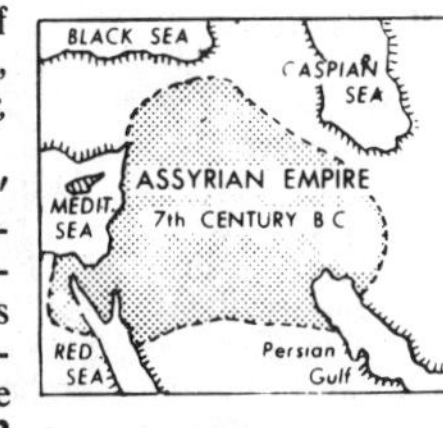

As·syr·i·an (ə·sir′ē·ən) *adj.* Of, pertaining to, or characteristic of Assyria or its people. *—n.* **1** A native of Assyria or the Assyrian empire. **2** The Semitic language spoken by the Assyrians.

As·syr·i·ol·o·gist (ə·sir′ē·ol′ə·jist) *n.* A student of Assyriology. Also **As·syr·i·o·log** (ə·sir′ē·ə·lôg, -log) or **·logue.**

As·syr·i·ol·o·gy (ə·sir′ē·ol′ə·jē) *n.* The study of Assyrian civilization, history, and language; Assyrian archeology.

As·tar·te (as·tär′tē) In Phoenician mythology, the goddess of love: identified with *Ashtoreth* and the Greek *Aphrodite.* [<L <Gk. *Astartē* <Semitic]

a·sta·si·a (ə·stā′zhē·ə, -zhə) *n. Pathol.* Inability to stand erect. [<NL <A-[4] without + Gk. *stasis* a standing]

a·stat·ic (ā·stat′ik, ə-) *adj.* **1** *Physics* Being in neutral equilibrium; having no tendency toward any change of position. **2** Unsteady. **—a·stat′i·cal·ly** *adv.* **—a·stat·i·cism** (ā·stat′ə· siz′əm, ə-) *n.*

as·ta·tine (as′tə·tēn, -tin) *n.* An unstable element (symbol At, atomic number 85) belonging to the halogen group, produced by bombarding bismuth with alpha particles, the most stable isotope having mass number 210 and a half-life of 8.3 hours. See PERIODIC TABLE. [<Gk. *astatos* unstable + -INE[2]]

as·ter (as′tər) *n.* **1** Any of a large genus *(Aster)* of plants of the composite family, having alternate leaves, and flowers with white, purple, or blue rays and yellow disk. **2** One of various allied plants, as the China aster. **3** *Biol.* The star-shaped figure appearing in the cytoplasm of a cell during mitosis and associated with the centrosome and spindle fibers. See OVUM. [<L <Gk. *astēr* star]

aster- *combining form* Star: *asteroid.* Also **asteri-, astero-.** [<Gk. *astēr*]

-aster *suffix* A contemptuous diminutive: *poetaster, criticaster.* [<L *-aster,* dim. *suffix*]

As·ter·a·ce·ae (as′tə·rā′sē·ē) Former name of the COMPOSITAE.

as·ter·a·ceous (as′tə·rā′shəs) *adj.* Of, pertaining to, or resembling an aster.

as·te·ri·a (as·tir′ē·ə) *n.* Any gemstone which when properly cut exhibits asterism. [<L, a precious stone <Gk. *asterios* starry]

as·te·ri·al·ite (as·tir′ē·əl·īt′) *n.* A fossil starfish. [<NL *Asterias* a starfish + Gk. *lithos* a rock, stone]

as·te·ri·at·ed (as·tir′ē·ā′tid) *adj.* **1** Grouped like stars. **2** Radiating, as the rays of a star. **3** *Mineral.* Exhibiting asterism, as certain sapphires.

as·te·ri·on (as·tir′ē·on) *n. Anat.* The point behind the ear marking the junction of the temporal, occipital, and parietal bones. [<Gk., neut. of *asterios* starry]

as·ter·isk (as′tər·isk) *n.* **1** *Printing* A starlike figure (*) used to indicate omissions, footnotes, references, etc. **2** Anything shaped like a star. *—v.t.* To mark with an asterisk. [<L *asteriscus* <Gk. *asteriskos,* dim. of *astēr* star]

as·ter·ism (as′tə·riz′əm) *n.* **1** *Printing* **a** A group of asterisks (***, ****). **b** A group of three asterisks set in front of a passage in the form of a triangle to call attention to it. **2** *Astron.* **a** A cluster of stars. **b** A constellation. **3** *Mineral.* The property of some crystals of showing a starlike figure by reflected or transmitted light.

a·stern (ə·stûrn′) *adv. Naut.* **1** In or at the stern. **2** In the rear; at any point behind a vessel. **3** To the rear; backward.

a·ster·nal (ā·stûr′nəl) *adj. Anat.* **1** Not attached to the sternum. **2** Not having a sternum.

as·ter·oid (as′tə·roid) *adj.* **1** Star-shaped. **2** *Bot.* Pertaining to or like an aster. *—n.* **1** *Astron.* Any of several hundred small planets between Mars and Jupiter: also called *planetoid.* **2** *Zool.* A starfish. **—as′ter·oi′dal** *adj.*

As·ter·oi·de·a (as′tə·roi′dē·ə) *n. pl.* A class of echinoderms, comprising the true starfishes. [<NL <ASTEROID] **—as′ter·oi′de·an** *adj.* & *n.*

As·ter·o·pe (as·ter′ə·pē) See STEROPE.

as·the·ni·a (as·thē′nē·ə, as′thə·nī′ə) *n. Pathol.* General debility; lack of bodily strength; weakness. Also **as·the·ny** (as′thə·nē). [<NL <Gk. *astheneia* <*a-* without + *sthenos* strength]

as·then·ic (as·then′ik) *n.* **1** One who is physically weak or undeveloped. **2** *Anthropol.* One who is characterized by a lean, generally tall figure, and light muscular development. *—adj.* **1** Of or pertaining too an asthenic person or type. **2** Of, pertaining to, or characterized by asthenia. Also **as·then′i·cal** *adj.*

as·the·no·pi·a (as′thə·nō′pē·ə) *n. Patho.* Weakness or fatigue of the visual organs. [<NL <Gk. *asthenēs* weak + -OPIA]

as·then·o·sphere (as·then′ə·sfir) *n. Geol.* A layer of dense, mobile, plastic rock underlying the lithosphere of the earth. **—as·then·o·spher·ic** (as·then′ə·sfer′ik) *adj.*

asth·ma (az′mə, as′-) *n. Pathol.* A chronic respiratory disorder characterized by recurrent paroxysmal coughing, and a sense of constriction due to spasmodic contractions of the bronchi. [<Gk., a panting <*azein* breathe hard]

asth·mat·ic (az·mat′ik, as-) *adj.* Of, pertaining to, or affected with asthma. Also **asth·mat′i·cal.** *—n.* A person suffering from or subject to asthma. **—asth·mat′i·cal·ly** *adv.*

As·ti (äs′tē) A town in Piedmont, NW Italy.

a·stig·ma·tism (ə·stig′mə·tiz′əm) *n.* A structural defect of the eye or a lens such that the rays of light from an object do not converge to a focus, thus causing imperfect vision or images. [<A-[4] without + Gk. *stigma* mark]

as·tig·mat·ic (as′tig·mat′ik) *adj.* **1** Of, having, or characterized by astigmatism. **2** Correcting astigmatism.

a·stir (ə·stûr′) *adv.* & *adj.* Stirring; moving about.

As·ti spu·man·te (äs′tē spōō·män′tā) An Italian sparkling wine, originally made in Asti.

As·to·lat (as′tə·lät, -lat) An English town in Arthurian legend.

a·stom·a·tous (ā·stom′ə·təs, ā·stō′mə-) *adj. Biol.* Without a mouth or breathing pores. Also **as·to·mous** (as′tə·məs). [<A-[4] without + Gk. *stoma, stomatos* mouth]

As·ton (as′tən), **Francis William,** 1877–1945, English physicist.

a·ston·ish (ə·ston′ish) *v.t.* **1** To affect with wonder and surprise; amaze; confound. **2** *Obs.* To stun or paralyze, as by a shock. [<OF *estoner* <L *ex-* out + *tonare* thunder] **—a·ston′ish·er** *n.* **—a·ston′ish·ing** *adj.* **—a·ston′ish·ing·ly** *adv.*

a·ston·ish·ment (ə·ston′ish·mənt) *n.* **1** An act of astonishing or the state of being astonished; surprise; amazement. **2** An object or cause of such emotion. See synonyms under AMAZEMENT, PERPLEXITY.

a·ston·y (ə·ston′ē) *v.t.* **a·ston·ied, a·ston·y·ing** *Obs.* **1** To astound; astonish. **2** To stun. [See ASTONISH] **—a·ston′ied** *adj.*

As·tor (as′tər), **John Jacob,** 1763–1848, U.S. fur merchant and capitalist. **—Lady,** 1879–1964, *née* Nancy Langhorne, Viscountess Astor, first woman member of the British House of Commons, born in the United States.

As·to·ri·a (as·tôr′ē·ə, -tō′rē·ə) A port at the mouth of the Columbia River in NW Oregon.

a·stound (ə·stound′) *v.t.* To overwhelm or shock with wonder or surprise; confound. *—adj. Obs.* Amazed; astonished. [ME *astoned* stunned, pp. of *astonien* <OF *estoner. See* ASTONISH.]

As·tra·chan (as′trə·kan, -kən) *n.* A variety of apple of Russian origin.

a·strad·dle (ə·strad′l) *adv.* & *adj.* In a straddling position; astride.

As·trae·a (as·trē′ə) In Greek mythology, the goddess of justice.

as·tra·gal (as′trə·gəl) *n.* **1** *Archit.* A small convex molding in the form of a string of beads. **2** *Anat.* The ankle bone or tarsus. **3** *pl.* Dice: originally made from such bones. [<L *astragalus* <Gk. *astragalos*]

as·trag·a·lus (as·trag′ə·ləs) *n. pl.* **·li** (-lī) *Anat.* The proximal bone of the foot, as in man or other vertebrates; talus; anklebone. [<L <Gk. *astragalos*] **—as·trag′a·lar** (-lər) *adj.*

as·tra·khan (as′trə·kan, -kən) *n.* **1** The pelts of very young lambs, with tightly curled wool, from the region near Astrakhan. **2** A fabric with a curled pile imitative of these pelts. Also **as′tra·chan.**

As·tra·khan (as′trə·kan, -kən) A city in SE Russian S.F.S.R., on the Volga Basin.

as·tral (as′trəl) *adj.* **1** Of, pertaining to, coming from, or like the stars; starry. **2** *Biol.* Of, pertaining to, or exhibiting an aster: an *astral* phase. **3** In alchemy, susceptible to influences from the stars: *astral* gold. **4** In theosophy, pertaining to or consisting of a supersensible substance supposed to pervade all space and to be refined beyond the tangible world. *—n.* **1** An astral body. **2** An astral lamp. [<LL *astralis* <L *astrum* star <Gk. *astron*] **—as′tral·ly** *adv.*

astral body **1** Any fantasmal appearance of the human body. **2** In theosophy, a counterpart of the human body, composed of astral substance, accompanying it in life, and surviving its death.

astral lamp An oil lamp with a ring-shaped reservoir so placed that its shadow is not cast directly below the flame.

a·strand (ə·strand′) *adv.* & *adj.* Aground; stranded.

as·tra·pho·bi·a (as′trə·fō′bē·ə) *n.* Morbid fear of thunder and lightning. Also **as·tra·po·pho·bi·a** (as′trə·pə·fō′bē·ə). [<NL <Gk. *astrapē* lightning + -PHOBIA]

a·stray (ə·strā′) *adv.* & *adj.* Away from the right path; wandering in or into error or evil. [<OF *estraie,* pp. of *estraier* <L *extra-* beyond + *vagare* wander]

as·trict (ə·strikt′) *v.t.* **1** To bind; restrict; limit. **2** To bind by moral or legal obligation, as an inheritance. [<L *astrictus,* pp. of *astringere.* See ASTRINGE.] **—as·tric′tion** *n.*

as·tric·tive (ə·strik′tiv) *adj.* **1** Astringent; styptic. **2** *Obs.* Restrictive; obligatory. *—n.* An astringent. **—as·tric′tive·ly** *adv.* **—as·tric′·tive·ness** *n.*

a·stride (ə·strīd′) *adv.* & *adj.* **1** With one leg on each side. **2** With the legs far apart. *—prep.* With one leg on each side of: *astride* a horse.

as·tringe (ə·strinj′) *v.t.* **as·tringed, as·tring·ing** To bind or draw together; compress; constrict. [<L *astringere* <*ad-* to + *stringere* bind fast]

as·trin·gent (ə·strin′jənt) *adj.* **1** *Med.* Tending to contract or draw together organic tissues; binding; styptic. **2** Harsh; stern; austere. *—n.* An astringent substance, as alum, tannin, etc. [<L *astringens, -entis,* ppr. of *astringere.* See ASTRINGE.] **—as·trin′gen·cy** *n.* **—as·trin′gent·ly** *adv.*

astro- *combining form* Star: *astrometry.* [<Gk. *astron* star]

as·tro·bot·a·ny (as′trō·bot′ə·nē) *n.* The investigation of plant life on planets other than the earth, especially on Mars. Also **as′tro·bo·tan′ics.** **—as′tro·bot′an·ist** *n.*

as·tro·cyte (as′trə·sīt) *n. Biol.* **1** A star-shaped cell, as of the neuroglia. **2** A bone corpuscle; osteoblast.

as·tro·dome (as′trə·dōm) *n.* A transparent domelike structure incorporated in some aircraft to facilitate observation of celestial bodies.

as·tro·ga·tion (as′trə·gā′shən) *n.* In space travel, navigation by the stars. [<ASTRO- + (NAVI)GATION] **—as′tro·ga′tor** *n.*

as·tro·labe (as′trə·lāb) *n.* An instrument formerly used for obtaining the altitudes of planets and stars. [<OF *astrelabe* <Med.L *astrolabium* <Gk. *astrolabon,* orig., star-taking <*astron* star + *lambanein* take]

as·trol·o·ger (ə·strol′ə·jər) *n.* **1** One who studies astrology. **2** *Obs.* An astronomer.

as·trol·o·gy (ə·strol′ə·jē) *n.* **1** Originally, the practical application of astronomy to human uses. **2** The study professing to fortell the future and interpret the influence of the heavenly bodies upon the destinies of men.

[<L *astrologia* <Gk. *astrologia* <*astron* star + *logos* discourse <*legein* speak] **—as·tro·log·ic** (as′trə·loj′ik) or **·i·cal, as·trol′o·gous** (-gəs) *adj.* **—as′tro·log′i·cal·ly** *adv.*

as·tro·me·te·or·ol·o·gy (as′trō·mē′tē·ə·rol′ə·jē) *n.* The study of the supposed influence of the heavenly bodies on our atmosphere.

as·trom·e·try (ə·strom′ə·trē) *n.* That branch of astronomy which determines the apparent positions, motions, and magnitudes of the heavenly bodies.

as·tro·naut (as′trə·nôt) *n.* One who travels in space. [<ASTRO- + *(aero)naut*]

as·tro·nau·tics (as′trə·nô′tiks) *n.* The science of space travel.

as·tro·nav·i·ga·tion (as′trō·nav′ə·gā′shən) *n.* That part of navigation in which position is determined by observation of celestial bodies; nautical astonomy. **—as′tro·nav′i·ga′tor** *n.*

as·tron·o·mer (ə·stron′ə·mər) *n.* One learned or expert in astronomy; a skilled observer of the heavenly bodies.

as·tro·nom·ic (as′trə·nom′ik) *adj.* **1** Of or pertaining to astronomy. **2** Enormously or inconceivably large, like the quantities used in astronomy. Also **as′tro·nom′i·cal. —as′tro·nom′i·cal·ly** *adv.*

astronomical time (or **day**) See under TIME.

astronomical unit A space unit for expressing the distances of the stars, equal to the mean distance of the earth from the sun. Compare PARSEC.

astronomical year See under YEAR.

as·tron·o·my (ə·stron′ə·mē) *n.* **1** The science that treats of the heavenly bodies, their motions, magnitudes, distances, and physical constitution. **2** A treatise on this science. [<OF *astronomie* <L *astronomia* <Gk. *astronomia* <*astron* star + *nomos* law <*nemein* distribute, arrange]

as·tro·pho·tog·ra·phy (as′trō·fə·tog′rə·fē) *n.* The art or practice of photographing heavenly bodies. **—as·tro·pho·to·graph·ic** (as′trō·fō′tə·graf′ik) *adj.*

as·tro·pho·tom·e·ter (as′trō·fō·tom′ə·tər) *n.* An instrument for determining the brightness of stars by comparing them with a light source of standard brightness. **—as′tro·pho·tom′e·try** *n.* **—as·tro·pho·to·met·ri·cal** (as′trō·fō′tə·met′ri·kəl) *adj.*

as·tro·phys·ics (as′trō·fiz′iks) *n.* That branch of astronomy which treats of the physical constitution and properties of the heavenly bodies, especially as revealed by spectrum analysis. **—as′tro·phys′i·cal** *adj.* **—as·tro·phys·i·cist** (as′trō·fiz′ə·sist) *n.*

as·tro·sphere (as′trə·sfir) *n. Biol.* **1** That part of the aster which does not include the rays; the attraction sphere or centrosphere. **2** The whole aster excluding the centrosome.

As·tu·ri·as (as·to͝or′ē·əs, *Sp.* äs·to͞o′ryäs) A region and former kingdom of NW Spain; 4,207 square miles.

as·tute (ə·sto͞ot′, ə·styo͞ot′) *adj.* Keen in discernment; acute; shrewd; sagacious, cunning. Also **as·tu·cious** (ə·sto͞o′shəs, ə·styo͞o′-), **as·tu′tious.** [<L *astutus* <*astus* cunning] **—as·tute′ly** *adv.* **—as·tute′ness** *n.*

Synonyms: acute, clear-sighted, crafty, cunning, discerning, discriminating, keen, knowing, penetrating, penetrative, perspicacious, sagacious, sharp, shrewd, subtile, subtle. *Acute* suggests the sharpness of the needle's point; *keen* the sharpness of the cutting edge. The *astute* mind adds to *acuteness* and *keenness* an element of cunning or finesse. *Knowing* has often a slightly invidious sense. See ACUTE, INTELLIGENT, KNOWING. *Antonyms*: blind, dull, idiotic, imbecile, shallow, short-sighted, stolid, stupid, undiscerning, unintelligent.

As·ty·a·nax (as·tī′ə·naks) In the *Iliad*, the son of Hector and Andromache, hurled from the battlements of Troy by the Greeks.

a·sty·lar (ā·stī′lər) *adj. Archit.* Having neither column nor pilaster. [<A-[4] without + Gk. *stylos* pillar]

A·sun·ción (ä·so͞on·syôn′) The capital of Paraguay and principal port on the Paraguay River.

a·sun·der (ə·sun′dər) *adv.* **1** In or into a different place or direction. **2** Apart; into pieces. *—adj.* Separated; apart. [OE *on sundran.* See SUNDER.]

As·wan (äs·wän′) A city on the Nile in southern Egypt; site of the **Aswan Dam** (1 1/4 miles long; 176 feet high): also *Assouan, Assuan*: ancient *Syene.*

a·swim (ə·swim′) *adv.* & *adj.* Afloat; swimming.

a·swoon (ə·swo͞on′) *adv.* & *adj.* In a swooning state.

a·syl·lab·ic (ā′si·lab′ik) *adj.* Not syllabic.

a·sy·lum (ə·sī′ləm) *n. pl.* **·lums** or **·la** (-lə) **1** An institution for the care of some class of afflicted, unfortunate, aged, or destitute persons; a retreat. **2** A place of refuge; retreat; shelter. **3** An inviolable shelter from arrest or punishment, as a temple or church in ancient times. **4** The protection afforded by a sanctuary or refuge. See synonyms under REFUGE. **—right of asylum** In international law: **1** The right to protection from arrest, subject to the will of the official in charge, enjoyed by a person who takes refuge in a foreign embassy or ministry or on a foreign warship. **2** The right to sanctuary enjoyed by troops or naval vessels taking refuge in neutral territory or waters. **3** Formerly, the right to shelter from extradition granted a political refugee in a foreign country. [<L <Gk. *asylon* <*a-* without + *sylon* right of seizure]

a·sym·met·ric (ā′si·met′rik, as′i-) *adj.* **1** Not symmetrical. **2** *Chem.* Designating an atom with optical activity, each of whose valences is held by a different atom or radical. Also **a′·sym·met′ri·cal. —a′sym·met′ri·cal·ly** *adv.*

asymmetric carbon atom A carbon atom combined with four atoms or groups, no two of which are alike, as in the lactic acids.

a·sym·me·try (ā·sim′ə·trē) *n.* Lack of symmetry or proportion. [<Gk. *asymmetria* <*a-* without + *symmetria* symmetry]

a·symp·to·mat·ic (ā′simp·tə·mat′ik) *adj.* Without symptoms: an *asymptomatic* patient.

as·ymp·tote (as′im·tōt) *n. Math.* A straight line which an indefinitely extended curve continually approaches as a limit. [<Gk. *asymptōtos* not falling together <*a-* not + *syn-* together + *piptein* fall] **—as′ymp·tot′ic** (-tot′·ik) or **·i·cal** *adj.* **—as′ymp·tot′i·cal·ly** *adv.*

a·syn·chro·nism (ā·sing′krə·niz′əm) *n.* Lack of synchronism, or coincidence in time. **—a·syn′chro·nous** (-nəs) *adj.*

as·yn·det·ic (as′in·det′ik) *adj.* **1** Of or pertaining to asyndeton. **2** Without cross-references: said of a library catalog. **—as′yn·det′i·cal·ly** *adv.*

a·syn·de·ton (ə·sin′də·ton) *n.* In rhetoric, the omission of conjunctions between parts of a sentence, as "On your mark, get set, go!" Compare POLYSYNDETON. [<L <Gk. *asyndeton* <*a-* not + *syn-* together + *deein* bind]

a·syn·tac·tic (ā′sin·tak′tik) *adj.* Not according to syntax; ungrammatical.

as you were A drill command which directs soldiers to assume the position or resume the movement preceding the last command, or which cancels an earlier command that has not yet been executed.

As·yut (äs·yo͞ot′) A city on the Nile, the largest of Upper Egypt: also *Assiut.*

at (at, *unstressed* ət) *prep.* **1** In the exact position of: the point *at* the center of the circle. **2** On or near the coming of: the train leaving *at* two; a man *at* sixty. **3** During the course or lapse of: *At* the moment the matter is uncertain. **4** In contact with; on; upon: *at* the bottom of the sea. **5** To or toward: Look *at* that sunset! **6** Through; by way of: smoke coming out *at* the windows. **7** Within the limits of; present in: to be *at* the ball grounds. **8** Engaged or occupied in: to be *at* work. **9** Attending: He was *at* the party. **10** In the state or condition of: a nation *at* war. **11** In the region or vicinity of; in proximity to: The car is *at* the door. **12** Viewed from; with an interval of: a target *at* sixty paces. **13** Having reference to: He winced *at* the thought. **14** In the manner of: *at* a trot. **15** In pursuit or quest of; in the direction of: to catch *at* straws. **16** Dependent upon: to be *at* an enemy's mercy. **17** According to: Proceed *at* your discretion. **18** To the extent of; amounting to: paying interest *at* two per cent; pencils *at* a dime apiece. [OE *æt*]

Synonyms: about, by, during, in, near, on, to, toward, with, within. As regards place, *at* is not used with names of countries; we say *in* England, *in* France, etc.; with names of cities and towns we use *at* when we think merely of the local or geographical point; when we think of inclusive space, we employ *in;* as, we arrived *at* Liverpool; there are few rich men *in* this village. As regards time, *at* is used of a point of time, as of the hour, minute, or second; as, the train leaves *at* 10:30 a.m.; *at* is also used of indefinite divisions of time involving some duration; as, *at* morning, noon, or night; to lie awake *at* night. We say *at* the hour, *on* the day, *in* the year. *On* with certain divisions of time has a special precision, signifying exactly *at,* neither before nor after; as, the train leaves *on* the hour.

At *Chem.* Astatine (symbol At).

at- Assimilated var. of AD-.

at·a·bal (at′ə·bal) *n.* A Moorish tabor or kettledrum. [<Sp. <Arabic *at-tabl* the drum]

At·a·brine (at′ə·brin, -brēn) *n.* Proprietary name for a brand of quinacrine.

A·ta·ca·ma Desert (ä′tä·kä′mä) An arid region of northern Chile, rich in natural nitrate deposits, extending 600 miles south from the border of Peru.

a·tac·a·mite (ə·tak′ə·mīt) *n.* A dark-green basic chloride of copper, crystallizing in the orthorhombic system. [from Atacama Desert]

at·a·ghan (at′ə·gan) See YATAGHAN.

A·ta·hual·pa (ä′tä·wäl′pä), died 1533, last Inca king of Peru.

a·ta·jo (ä·tä′hō) *n. SW U.S.* **1** A string of mules. **2** A cross-path shortening a road. [<Sp. *hatajo*]

At·a·lan·ta (at′ə·lan′tə) In Greek mythology, a maiden who agreed to marry any suitor who could outrun her, the losers being put to death. She was won by Hippomenes, who outwitted her by dropping three golden apples which she paused to pick up allowing him to outrun her.

at·a·man (at′ə·man) *n.* A Cossack chief; hetman. [<Russian *atamanu* <Polish *hetman* <G *hauptmann* captain <*haupt* head + *mann* man]

at·a·mas·co (at′ə·mas′kō) *n.* A low North American plant (genus *Zephyranthes*) of the amaryllis family, bearing a large white and pink flower. [<Algonquian]

atamasco lily The atamasco or an allied plant.

at·a·rac·tic (at′ə·rak′tik) *adj.* **1** Conducive to peace of mind. **2** *Med.* Having the power to tranquilize and to lessen nervous tension: said of certain drugs, as reserpine. Also **at′a·rax′ic** (-rak′sik). [<NL <Gk. *ataraktos* untroubled <*atarakteein* be calm. See ATARAXIA.]

at·a·rax·i·a (at′ə·rak′sē·ə) *n.* Freedom from anxiety; peace of mind. Also **at·a·rax·y** (at′ə·rak′sē). [<NL <Gk. *ataraxia* <*atarakteein* be calm <*a-* not + *tarattein* disturb, trouble]

A·ta·türk (ä·tä·türk′) SEE KEMAL ATATÜRK.

a·taunt (ə·tônt′) *adv. Naut.* **1** With all sails set; in full-rigged condition. **2** In order; shipshape. [<F *autant* as much (as possible)]

at·a·vism (at′ə·viz′əm) *n.* **1** Reversion to an earlier or primitive type. **2** *Biol.* Reversion. [<F *atavisme* <L *atavus* ancestor <*at-* beyond + *avus* grandfather] **—a·tav·ic** (ə·tav′ik) *adj.* **—at′a·vist** *n.* **—at′a·vis′tic** *adj.*

a·tax·i·a (ə·tak′sē·ə) *n. Pathol.* **1** Irregularity in muscular action through failure of muscular coordination. **2** Locomotor ataxia. Also **a·tax·y** (ə·tak′sē). [<NL <Gk. *ataxia* lack of order <*a-* not + *tattein* arrange]

a·tax·ic (ə·tak′sik) *adj.* Characteristic of or caused by ataxia. *—n.* One afflicted with ataxia.

a·tax·it·ic (ā′tak·sit′ik) *adj. Geol.* Of or pertaining to ore deposits occurring in unstratified form: opposed to *eutaxitic.*

a·tax·o·phe·mi·a (ə·tak′sə·fē′me·ə) *n. Pathol.* Defective coordination of the muscles of speech.

At·ba·ra (ät′bä·rä) A river in Ethiopia and NE Sudan, flowing 500 miles NE to the Nile.

A·tchaf·a·lay·a River (ə·chaf′ə·lī′ə) A river of southern Louisiana constituting an outlet of the Red and Mississippi Rivers during high water and flowing SE 170 miles to **Atchafalaya Bay,** an arm of the Gulf of Mexico.

ate[1] (āt, *chiefly Brit.* et) Past tense of EAT.

a·te[2] (ā′tē) *n.* In ancient Greek culture, the fatal and reckless blindness inciting men to crime. [<GK. *atē*]

A·te (ā′tē) In Greek mythology, a goddess, variously regarded as a daughter of Zeus or of Eris, personifying men's reckless blindness, later associated with the punishment of crime.

-ate[1] *suffix* Forming: **1** Participial adjectives equivalent to those in *-ated*: *desolate, separate.* **2** Adjectives from nouns with the meaning "possessing or characterized by": *caudate, foliate.* **3** Verbs, originally from stems of Latin verbs of the first conjugation, and, by analogy, extended to other stems: *fascinate, assassinate.* **4** *Chem.* Verbs with the meaning "combine or treat with": *chlorinate.* [<L *-atus,* pp. ending of 1st conjugation verbs]

-ate[2] *suffix* Forming: **1** Nouns denoting office, function, or agent: *magistrate.* **2** Nouns denoting the object or result of an action: *mandate.* [<L *-atus,* suffix of nouns]

-ate[3] *suffix Chem.* Used to form the names of salts and esters derived from acids whose names end in *-ic: carbonate, nitrate.* [<L *-atum,* neut. of *-atus* -ATE[1]]

at ease A drill command authorizing soldiers to relax but not to talk or leave their places; also, the position assumed at this command.

a·tech·nic (ā·tek′nik) *adj.* Without technical knowledge. [<Gk. *atechnos* unskilled <*a-* without + *technē* skill]

at·el·ier (at′əl·yā, *Fr.* à·tə·lyā′) *n.* A workshop, especially of an artist; studio. [<F, orig., pile of chips <OF *astele* chip <LL *astella* <L *astula* chip, splinter]

a·te·li·o·sis (ə·tē′lē·ō′sis, ə·tel′ē-) *n. Pathol.* An incomplete development of body or mind; infantilism. [<Gk. *atelēs* imperfect + -OSIS] **—a·tel·ic** (ə·tel′ik) *adj.*

a tem·po (ä tem′pō) *Music* In the regular time; resuming the rate of speed originally indicated. [<Ital.]

a·tem·po·ral (ā·tem′pə·rəl) *adj.* Timeless; outside of or apart from time.

Ath·a·bas·can (ath′ə·bas′kən) See ATHAPASCAN.

Ath·a·bas·ka River (ath′ə·bas′kə) A river in Alberta, Canada, flowing 765 miles to **Lake Athabaska** in northern Alberta and Saskatchewan; 3,058 square miles.

Ath·a·li·ah (ath′ə·lī′ə) The wife of Jehoram who usurped the throne of Judah on the death of her husband and on that of his successor. II *Kings* xi 1–16.

Ath·a·mas (ath′ə·mas) In Greek legend, king of Thessaly, husband of Nephele, who, seized with madness, killed his own son.

ath·a·na·sia (ath′ə·nā′zhə, -zhē·ə) *n.* Deathlessness; immortality. Also **a·than·a·sy** (ə·than′·ə·sē). [<Gk. <*a-* without + *thanatos* death]

Ath·a·na·sian creed (ath′ə·nā′zhən) A formulary of Christian belief called after Athanasius and formerly ascribed to his authorship, but now assigned to a later date.

Ath·a·na·sian·ist (ath′ə·nā′zhən·ist) *n.* An adherent of Athanasius or of the Athanasian creed.

Ath·a·na·sius (ath′ə·nā′shəs, -shē·əs), 298?–373, one of the fathers of the church; patriarch of Alexandria; opponent of Arianism.

Ath·a·pas·can (ath′ə·pas′kən) *n.* **1** A large North American Indian linguistic stock, including languages of Alaska and NW Canada, the Pacific coast (especially in Oregon and California), and the Apache and Navaho tribes of the southern SW United States. **2** A member of a tribe speaking these languages. Also *Athabascan.*

a·thart (ə·thôrt′) *adv.* & *prep.* Athwart. Also **a·thort′.**

a·the·ism (ā′thē·iz′əm) *n.* **1** The belief that there is no God. **2** The disbelief in the existence of God. **3** Godlessness in life or conduct. [<F *athéisme* <Gk. *atheos* <*a-* without + *theos* god]

a·the·ist (ā′thē·ist) *n.* One who denies or disbelieves in the existence of God. See synonyms under SKEPTIC.

a·the·is·tic (ā′thē·is′tik) *adj.* **1** Of or pertaining to atheism or atheists. **2** Given to atheism; godless. Also **a′the·is′ti·cal. —a′the·is′ti·cal·ly** *adv.*

ath·e·ling (ath′ə·ling) *n. Archaic* **1** A crown prince. **2** Any member of a noble family. Also spelled *ætheling.* [OE *ætheling* <*æthelu* noble ancestry]

Ath·el·stan (ath′əl·stan) A masculine personal name. Also **Ath′el·stane** (-stān). [OE *Æthelstan,* lit., noble stone]

—Athelstan, 895–940, Anglo-Saxon king; grandson of Alfred.

a·the·mat·ic (ā′thē·mat′ik) *adj. Ling.* Not attached to or not constituting a stem.

A·the·na (ə·thē′nə) In Greek mythology, the goddess of wisdom, war, and patroness of arts and crafts: identified with the Roman *Minerva.* Also **A·the·ne** (ə·thē′·nē). [<Gk. *Athēnē*]

ATHENA
After a gold and ivory statuette; possibly by Phidias.

ath·e·ne·um (ath′ə·nē′əm) *n.* **1** A literary club, academy, or other institution for the promotion of learning. **2** A reading room, library, etc. Also **ath′e·nae′um.**

Ath·e·ne·um (ath′ə·nē′əm) *n.* **1** The temple of Athena at Athens. **2** An academy founded by Hadrian at Rome for the promotion of learning. Also **Ath′e·nae′um.** [<L <Gk. *Athenaion*]

A·the·ni·an (ə·thē′nē·ən) *adj.* Of or pertaining to Athens, or to its art or culture. *—n.* A native or citizen of Athens.

Ath·ens (ath′ənz) An ancient city in Attica and the present capital of Greece. *Greek* **A·the·nai, A·thi·nai** (ä·thē′ne).

a·ther·man·cy (ā·thûr′mən·sē) *n.* The state or quality of being athermanous.

a·ther·ma·nous (ā·thûr′mə·nəs) *adj.* Impervious to radiant heat. [<A-[4] without + Gk. *thermainein* heat <*thermos* hot]

ath·er·o·ma (ath′ə·rō′mə) *n. Pathol.* **1** A sebaceous cyst. **2** Arteriosclerosis accompanied by pronounced degenerative changes. [<L <Gk. *atherōma* <*atherē* gruel; with ref. to the encysted matter]

ath·er·o·scle·ro·sis (ath′ər·ō·sklə·rō′sis) *n. Pathol.* Hardening of the arteries, accompanied by degenerative tissue changes in the arterial walls. [<NL <Gk. *atherē* gruel + *sklēros* hard]

Ath·er·ton (ath′ər·tən), **Gertrude Franklin,** 1857–1948, *née* Horn, U.S. novelist.

ath·e·to·sis (ath′ə·tō′sis) *n. Pathol.* A derangement of the nervous system, in which the hands and feet, especially the fingers and toes, keep moving or twitching. [<Gk. *athetos* without position, unfixed <*a-* not + *tithenai* place]

a·thirst (ə·thûrst′) *adj.* **1** Wanting water; thirsty. **2** Keenly desirous; longing. [OE *ofthyrsted,* pp. of *ofthyrstan* <*of-,* intensive + *thyrstan* thirst]

ath·lete (ath′lēt) *n.* **1** One trained in acts or feats of physical strength and agility, as rowing, wrestling, etc. **2** In classical antiquity, a contestant in the public games. [<L *athleta* <Gk. *athlētēs* a contestant in the games <*athleein* contend for a prize <*athlos* a contest <*athlon* a prize]

athlete's foot Ringworm of the foot, caused by a parasitic fungus; dermophytosis.

ath·let·ic (ath·let′ik) *adj.* **1** Of, pertaining to, or like an athlete. **2** Strong; vigorous; muscular. — **ath·let′i·cal·ly** *adv.* **—ath·let·i·cism** (ath·let′ə·siz′əm) *n.*

ath·let·ics (ath·let′iks) *n. pl.* **1** Athletic games and exercises collectively. **2** A system of athletic training: usually construed as singular.

ath·o·dyd (ath′ō·did) *n.* Former name for a ramjet engine. [<A(ERO) TH(ERM)ODY(NAMIC) D(UCT)]

at-home (ət·hōm′) *n.* An informal party or reception given at one's home. *—adj.* For use at home; informal: *at-home* clothing.

Ath·os (ath′os, ā′thos), **Mount** The highest point on Chalcidice peninsula in Greek Macedonia, coextensive with the Akte prong; 6,670 feet; site of an autonomous monastic district; 131 square miles. *Greek* **Ha·gi·on O·ros** (ä′yē·ôn ô′rôs).

a·threp·si·a (ā·threp′sē·ə, -shə) *n.* **1** *Bacteriol.* Immunity from malignant tumors due to lack of food substance of tumor cells: also called *atrepsy.* **2** *Pathol.* Marasmus. [<NL <Gk. *a-* without + *threpsis* nourishment]

a·thrill (ə·thril′) *adj.* Thrilled.

a·thwart (ə·thwôrt′) *adv.* **1** From side to side; across. **2** So as to thwart; perversely. *—prep.* **1** Across the course of; from side to side of: The ship sailed *athwart* our course. **2** Contrary to; in opposition to: His action went *athwart* our plans. [<A-[1] on + THWART]

-atic *suffix* Of; of the kind of: used in adjectives of Latin or Greek origin: *erratic.* [<F *-atique* or <L *-aticus* <Gk. *-atikos*]

a·tilt (ə·tilt′) *adv.* & *adj.* **1** In a tilted manner; tilted up. **2** Like one tilting or making a lance thrust; hence, in spirited opposition.

at·i·my (at′ə·mē) *n.* Public dishonor or disgrace; deprivation of civic rights. [<Gk. *atimia* <*a-* without + *timē* honor]

-ation *suffix of nouns* **1** Action or process of: *creation.* **2** Condition or quality of: *affectation.* **3** Result of: *reformation.* Also *-ion, -tion.* ◆**-ation** was originally found in English nouns borrowed from Latin, and is now used by analogy to form nouns on any stem, as in *starvation, thunderation.* [<F *-ation* or L *-atio, -ationis* <*-atus* -ATE[1] + *-io* -ION]

a·tip·toe (ə·tip′tō′) *adv.* On the tips of the toes.

A·ti·tlán (ä′tē·tlän′) **1** A town in SW Guatemala, on the south shore of **Lake Atitlán** (53 square miles). **2** An inactive volcano near Lake Atitlán; 11,565 feet.

-ative *suffix* Denoting relation, tendency, or characteristic: *tentative, remunerative, laxative.* [<F *-atif,* masc., *-ative,* fem. or <L *-ativus*]

At·ka (at′kə) The largest island of the Andreanof group in the Aleutian Islands.

At·kins (at′kinz), **Tommy** See TOMMY ATKINS.

At·lan·ta (at·lan′tə) A city in NW central Georgia; the state capital.

At·lan·te·an (at′lan·tē′ən) *adj.* **1** Pertaining to Atlas. **2** Pertaining to Atlantis. Also **At·lan·ti·an** (at·lan′tē·ən).

at·lan·tes (at·lan′tēz) *n. pl. Archit.* Male human figures, used in place of columns or pilasters. [<L <Gk. *Atlantes,* pl. of *Atlas*]

At·lan·tic (at·lan′tik) *adj.* **1** Of, near, in, or pertaining to the Atlantic Ocean. **2** Pertaining to or derived from Mount Atlas or the Atlas Mountains in NW Africa. *—n.* The Atlantic Ocean. [<L *Atlanticus* <Gk. *Atlantikos* pertaining to Atlas]

Atlantic Charter A statement resulting from a meeting at sea and issued in August 1941 by Churchill and Roosevelt, in which were set forth the basic aims of the Allied Nations for the peace after World War II.

Atlantic City A resort city on the Atlantic coast of SE New Jersey.

Atlantic Ocean The world's second largest ocean, extending from the Arctic to the Antarctic regions between the Americas and Europe and Africa; 31,500,000 square miles; divided by the equator into the **North Atlantic Ocean** and the **South Atlantic Ocean.**

At·lan·ti·des (at·lan′tə·dēz) *n. pl.* **1** The children of Atlas: the Pleiades, the Hesperides, etc. **2** The inhabitants of Atlantis.

At·lan·tis (at·lan′tis) A legenday island described by Plato as a center of civilization that was engulfed by the sea.

at·las (at′ləs) *n.* **1** A volume of maps usually bound together. **2** Hence, any bound collection of plates or engravings showing systematically the development of a subject, or any work producing such effect by tabular arrangement. **3** A large size of paper, 26 by 33 (34) inches. **4** *Anat.* The first cervical vertebra: so called after Atlas, who bore the world on his shoulders. **5** *Archit.* Any of the Atlantes. [def. 1 <ATLAS; because some early collections of maps contained a picture of Atlas supporting the heavens]

At·las (at′ləs) **1** In Greek mythology, a Titan supporting the pillars of heaven on his shoulders. **2** Anyone bearing a great burden. **3** An intercontinental ballistic missile of the U.S. Air Force. [<L <Gk. *Atlas* <*tlaein* bear]

Atlas beetle A large, olive-green Oriental beetle *(Chalcosoma atlas)* with two long, curved horns.

atlas grid A network of lines dividing an aerial photograph into squares to facilitate locating of points.

Atlas Mountains A range in NW Africa; highest peaks, over 15,000 feet.

at·latl (ät′lät·l) *n.* A throwing stick used to hurl a spear or harpoon at birds or aquatic animals. [<Nahuatl]

At·li (ät′lē) In the *Volsunga Saga,* a king who

married Gudrun and later murdered her brothers: identified with *Attila.*

at·man (ät′mən) *n.* In Hinduism, the soul, or selfhood; the spark in man emanating from divinity. **—Atman** The supreme soul from which all individual souls are derived and to which they return. [< Skt.]

atmo- *combining form* Vapor: *atmometer.* [< Gk. *atmos*]

at·mol·o·gy (at·mol′ə·jē) *n.* The science that treats of the laws of aqueous vapor. — **at·mo·log·ic** (at′mə·loj′ik) or **·i·cal** *adj.* — **at·mol′o·gist** *n.*

at·mol·y·sis (at·mol′ə·sis *n.* The act or process of partially separating mixtures of gases into their ingredients by virtue of their different diffusibility through porous substances. [< ATMO- + Gk. *lysis* a loosing]

at·mo·lyze (at′mə·līz) *v.t.* **·lyzed, ·lyz·ing** To separate by atmolysis. Also *Brit.* **at′mo·lyse.** — **at′mo·ly·za′tion** *n.* **—at′mo·lyz′er** *n.*

at·mom·e·ter (at·mom′ə·tər) *n.* An instrument for measuring rate of evaporation. **—at·mo·met·ric** (at′mə·met′rik) *adj.* **—at·mom′e·try** *n.*

at·mos·phere (at′məs·fir) *n.* **1** The mass or body of gases that surrounds the earth or any heavenly body. **2** The particular climatic condition of any place or region regarded as dependent on the air. **3** Any surrounding or pervasive element or influence: an *atmosphere* of gloom. **4** The prevailing tone of a poem, novel, painting, etc. **5** *Colloq.* An indefinable aura regarded as especially characteristic: This café has *atmosphere.* **6** *Physics* A conventional unit of pressure, the equivalent of the weight of a column of mercury 1 centimeter in diameter and 29.92 inches high at sea level, at a temperature of 0° C.: one atmosphere equals a pressure of 14.69 pounds per square inch. [< NL *atmosphaera* < Gk. *atmos* vapor + *sphaira* sphere]

at·mos·pher·ic (at′məs·fer′ik) *adj.* **1** Pertaining or belonging to or existing in atmosphere. **2** Dependent on, caused by, or resulting from the atmosphere. **3** Giving or creating atmosphere: *atmospheric* music. Also **at′mos·pher′i·cal.** See STATIC. **—at′mos·pher′i·cal·ly** *adv.*

at·mos·pher·ics (at′məs·fer′iks) *n.* Atmospheric conditions due to electromagnetic disturbances, especially as they affect radio transmission: also called *sferics, spherics.*

a·to·le (ä·tō′lā) *n. SW U.S.* Cornmeal mush. [< Sp. < Nahuatl]

at·oll (at′ôl, -ol, ə·tol′) *n.* A ring-shaped coral island and its associated reef, nearly or quite enclosing a lagoon. [< Malayalam *adal* closing, uniting]

ATOLL
a. Islets. *b.* Barrier reef *c.* Fringing reef. *d.* Lagoon *e.* Passage.

at·om (at′əm) *n.* **1** *Chem.* The smallest part of an element capable of existing alone or in combination and which cannot be changed or destroyed in any chemical reaction: an *atom* of sulfur, carbon, etc.: distinguished from *molecule.* **2** *Physics* The electrically neutral combination of a nucleus and its complement of electrons to form a relatively stable, distinguishable unit, regarded as a unitary system. **3** A hypothetical entity admitting of no division into smaller parts. **4** An exceedingly small quantity or particle; iota. [< L *atomus* < Gk. *atomos* indivisible < *a-* not + *temnein* cut]

a·tom·ic (ə·tom′ik) *adj.* **1** Of or pertaining to an atom or atoms: also **a·tom′i·cal. 2** Very minute; infinitesimal. **3** Of, characterized by or employing atomic energy: an *atomic* power plant. — **a·tom′i·cal·ly** *adv.*

atomic age The era characterized by the use and growing importance of atomic energy as a factor in human and social development. Also **Atomic Age.**

atomic bomb See under BOMB. Also **atom bomb.**

atomic clock A high-precision instrument for the measurement of time by a constant frequency associated with a selected line in the spectrum of ammonia gas or other suitable vibrator.

atomic energy The energy contained within the nucleus of the atom; especially, such energy when made available for human use by controlled nuclear fission or thermonuclear reactions.

Atomic Energy Commission A U.S. board formed in 1946 for the domestic control of atomic energy.

at·o·mic·i·ty (at′ə·mis′ə·tē) *n. Chem.* **1** The number of atoms in a molecule. **2** Valence. **3** In the molecule of a compound, the number of replaceable atoms or groups.

atomic mass unit *Physics* **1** A unit arbitrarily defined as $^1/_{12}$ the mass of an atom of the carbon isotope of mass 12; a dalton. Abbr. *amu*

atomic number *Physics* A number which represents the unit positive charges (protons) in the atomic nucleus of each element and corresponds to the number of extra-nuclear electrons. Hydrogen is assigned an atomic number of 1; on this basis, carbon is 6, oxygen 8, iron 26, gold 79, etc.

atomic philosophy The philosophy, anciently expounded by Democritus, Epicurus, and Lucretius, which attempts to account for all material existence, or for the entire universe, as being composed of simple, indivisible atoms.

atomic pile Reactor.

atomic power Atomic energy as a source of power.

atomic structure *Physics* **1** The configuration of the atom. **2** The arrangement of atoms in a molecule or in bulk matter.

atomic submarine A nuclear submarine.

atomic theory 1 *Chem.* The doctrine that elements unite with one another, atom by atom, and in definite simple proportions by weight. **2** *Physics* The concept that all bulk matter is composed of atoms, and that the properties of matter are ultimately to be understood in terms of the properties and interactions of the component atoms.

atomic weight *Chem.* **a** Since 1961, the weight of an atom of an element relative to that of an atom of carbon, taken as 12.01115. **b** Formerly, the weight of an atom of an element relative to that of an atom of oxygen, taken as 16.

at·om·ism (at′əm·iz′əm) *n.* **1** The atomic philosophy. **2** The atomic theory. **—at′om·ist** *n.* — **at′om·is′tic** or **·ti·cal** *adj.*

at·om·ize (at′əm·īz) *v.t.* **·ized, ·iz·ing 1** To reduce to or separate into atoms; pulverize. **2** To spray or reduce to a spray, as by an atomizer. Also *Brit.* **at′om·ise. —at′om·i·za′tion** *n.*

at·om·iz·er (at′əm·ī′zər) *n.* **1** An apparatus for reducing a liquid, especially medicine or perfume, to a spray.

at·om-me·ter (at′əm·mē′tər) *n.* The angstrom unit.

at·om·ol·o·gy (at′əm·ol′ə·jē) *n.* The study of atoms.

at·o·my[1] (at′ə·mē) *n. pl.* **·mies** *Archaic* **1** An atom. **2** A pigmy. [< L *atomi,* pl. of *atomus* atom]

at·o·my[2] (at′ə·mē) *n. pl.* **·mies** *Obs.* A skeleton or an emaciated person. [< ANATOMY (misunderstood as *an atomy*)]

a·to·nal (ā·tō′nəl) *adj. Music* Without tonality; lacking key. **—a·to′nal·ly** *adv.*

a·to·nal·ism (ā·tō′nəl·iz′əm) *n.* The theory of atonally composed music. **—a·to′nal·is′tic** *adj.*

a·to·nal·i·ty (ā′tō·nal′ə·tē) *n. Music* Lack of tonality; absence of key.

a·tone (ə·tōn′) *v.* **a·toned, a·ton·ing** *v.i.* **1** To make an expiation, as for sin or a sinner; make amends, reparation, or satisfaction. **2** *Obs.* To be at one, agree, *—v.t.* **3** *Rare* To expiate. **4** *Obs.* To propitiate; reconcile. [< earlier adverbial phrase *at one* in accord, short for *to set at one,* i.e., reconcile] **—a·ton′a·ble, a·tone′a·ble** *adj.* **—a·ton′er** *n.*

a·tone·ment (ə·tōn′mənt) *n.* **1** Satisfaction, reparation, or expiation made for wrong or injury; amends. **2** *Theol. Usually cap.* **a** The redemptive work of Christ. **b** The reconciliation between God and man effected by Christ's life, passion, and death. **3** In Christian Science, the exemplification of man's unity with God, whereby man reflects divine Truth, Life, and Love. **4** *Obs.* Reconciliation.

a·ton·ic (ə·ton′ik, ā-) *adj.* **1** Not accented, as a word or syllable. **2** Lacking tone or vigor. *—n.* An unaccented syllable or word. [< Gk. *atonos* slack < *a-* not + *teinein* stretch]

at·o·ny (at′ə·nē) *n.* **1** *Pathol.* Want of tone or power; abnormal relaxation, as of a muscle. **2** Lack of stress, as in a syllable. [< Gk. *atonia* slackness < *a-* not + *teinein* stretch]

a·top (ə·top′) *adv.* & *adj.* On or at the top. — *prep.* On the top of.

-atory *suffix of adjectives* Of or pertaining to; producing or produced by; of the nature of; expressing: *exclamatory.* [< L *-atorius* adj. suffix]

à toute force (à to͞ot fôrs′) *French* With all one's might.

à tout prix (à to͞o prē′) *French* At any price; whatever the cost.

ATP Symbol for adenosine triphosphate.

A·T·P·ase (ā′tē′pē′ās′) Adenosine triphosphatase.

at·ra·bil·ious (at′rə·bil′yəs) *adj.* Disposed to hypochondria; melancholy; splenetic. Also **at′ra·bil′i·ar** (-bil′ē·ər) [< L *atra bilis* black bile, a trans. of Gk. *melancholia.* See MELANCHOLY.] — **at′ra·bil′ious·ness** *n.*

at·ra·men·tal (at′rə·men′təl) *adj.* Of the nature of ink; inklike; inky. Also **at′ra·men′tous.** [< L *atramentum* ink < *ater* black]

A·trek (ä·trek′) A river in NE Iran, flowing west over 300 miles to its confluence with the Sumbar. Also **A·trak** (ä·trak′).

a·tre·ol (ā′trē·ōl, -ol) *n.* An aqueous solution of ammonium salts derived from organic acids, obtained as a black sirupy liquid, and used as a mild antiseptic. [< L *ater, atri* black + -OL]

at·rep·sy (at′rep·sē) See ATHREPSIA.

A·treus (ā′tro͞os, ā′trē·əs) In Greek legend, the son of Pelops and father of Agamemnon and Menelaus: to avenge the treachery of his brother Thyestes, who had seduced his wife and planned to murder him, Atreus killed his brother's sons and served them to their father at a banquet.

a·tri·al (ā′trē·əl) *adj.* Of or pertaining to an atrium.

at·ri·cho·sis (at′ri·kō′sis) *n. Pathol.* Loss of or failure to develop hair. [< NL < Gk. *atrichos* hairless (< *a-* without + *thrix* hair) + -OSIS]

at·ri·chous (at′ri·kəs) *adj. Biol.* Destitute of cilia.

a·tri·o·ven·tric·u·lar (ā′trē·ō·ven·trik′yə·lər) *adj.* Pertaining to the auricles and ventricles of the heart.

a·trip (ə·trip′) *adv.* & *adj. Naut.* **1** In a position for motion; just started from the bottom, as an anchor. **2** Properly hoisted and ready for trimming: said of a sail or a yard. **3** Freed from the fid and ready for lowering: said of a topmast. [< A-[1] on + TRIP]

a·tri·um (ā′trē·əm) *n. pl.* **a·tri·a** (ā′trē·ə) **1** The entrance hall or central open court of an ancient Roman house. **2** A court or hall. **3** *Anat.* One of the upper chambers of the heart through which venous blood is transmitted to the ventricles: also called *auricle.* **4** *Zool.* A cavity or sac. — **atrium of infection** *Med.* Any opening affording bacterial infection. [< L (def. 1)]

a·tro·cious (ə·trō′shəs) *adj.* **1** Outrageously wicked, criminal, vile, or cruel; heinous. **2** *Colloq.* Very bad or in bad taste: an *atrocious* remark. See synonyms under BARBAROUS, FLAGRANT, INFAMOUS. [< L *atrox, atrocis* harsh, cruel < *ater* black] **—a·tro′cious·ly** *adv.* **—a·tro′cious·ness** *n.*

a·troc·i·ty (ə·tros′ə·tē) *n. pl.* **·ties 1** The state or quality of being atrocious. **2** An atrocious deed or act; cruelty or wickedness. **3** *Colloq.* A bad piece of work; something in very bad taste. [< L *atrocitas, -tatis* cruelty < *atrox.* See ATROCIOUS.]

at·ro·phied (at′rə·fēd) *adj.* Wasted away; withered.

at·ro·phy (at′rə·fē) *n. pl.* **·phies** *Pathol.* **1** A wasting or withering of the body or any of its parts. **2** A stoppage of growth or development, as of a part. *—v.* **·phied, ·phy·ing** *v.t.* To cause to waste away or wither; affect with atrophy. *—v.i.* To waste away; wither. [< F *atrophie* < L *atrophia* < Gk. *atrophia* < *a-* not + *trephein* nourish] — **a·troph·ic** (ə·trof′·ik), **at·ro·phous** (at′rə·fəs) *adj.*

at·ro·pine (at′rə·pēn, -pin) *n.* A crystalline, bitter, poisonous alkaloid, $C_{17}H_{23}O_3N$, found in the deadly nightshade and in the seeds of the thorn apple or jimsonweed: used in medicine as an antispasmodic and having the power of enlarging the pupil of the eye. Also **at′ro·pin** (-pin). [< NL *Atropa* the genus of belladonna < Gk. *Atropos.* See ATROPOS]

at·ro·pism (at′rə·piz′əm) *n.* A morbid state produced by overdoses of atropine.

At·ro·pos (at′rə·pos) One of the three Fates. [<Gk., inflexible <*a-* not + *trepein* turn]

at·ro·pous (at′rə·pəs) *adj. Bot.* Not inverted; erect, as an ovule. [<Gk. *atropos.* See ATROPOS.]

at·tac·ca (ät·täk′kä) *Music* Continue without pause. [<Ital.]

at·tach (ə·tach′) *v.t.* **1** To make fast to something; affix; fasten on. **2** To connect or join on as a part of something: He *attached* himself to the expedition. **3** To add or append, as a word or signature. **4** To attribute; add as appropriate to: to *attach* great importance to the outcome of an event. **5** *Law* To secure for legal jurisdiction; seize or arrest by legal process: to *attach* an employee's salary. **6** *Mil.* To allocate, as personnel, units, or materiel, to a military organization temporarily or as a non–integral part: The regiment *attached* a medical officer. **7** *Obs.* To seize. — *v.i.* **8** To be united in sympathy or affection: with *to*: to be *attached* to someone out of sympathy. **9** To belong, as a quality or circumstance; be incidental to: with *to*: Much interest *attaches* to this opinion. See synonyms under ADD, UNITE. [<OF *atachier* <*a-* to (<L *ad-*) + *tache* nail <Gmc. Related to ATTACK.] — **at·tach′a·ble** *adj.*

at·ta·ché (at′ə·shā′, *esp. Brit.* ə·tash′ā) *n.* A person regularly and officially attached to a diplomatic mission or staff: military *attaché*, naval *attaché.* [<F, pp. of *attacher* attach]

at·tach·ment (ə·tach′mənt) *n.* **1** An attaching or a being attached; adherence; affection. **2** That by which, or the point at which, anything is attached; a bond; band; tie. **3** Affection; devoted regard. **4** An appendage or adjunct. **5** *Law* **a** Seizure of a person or property. **b** The writ commanding this.

Synonyms: adherence, adhesion, affection, devotion, esteem, estimation, friendship, inclination, love, regard, tenderness, union. An *attachment* is an affection that binds a person to another person or thing; we speak of a man's *adherence* to his purpose, his *adhesion* to his party, or to anything to which he clings tenaciously, but with no special tenderness; of his *attachment* to his church, to the old homestead, or to any persons or objects that he may hold dear. *Inclination* expresses simply a tendency, which may be good or bad, yielded to or overcome; as, an *inclination* to study. *Regard* is more distant than *affection* or *attachment*, but closer and warmer than *esteem*; we speak of high esteem, kind *regard.* Compare ACQUAINTANCE, APPENDAGE, FRIENDSHIP, LOVE, UNION. *Antonyms*: alienation, animosity, antipathy, aversion, coolness, dislike, distance, divorce, enmity, estrangement, indifference, opposition, repugnance, separation, severance.

at·tack (ə·tak′) *v.t.* **1** To set upon suddenly; begin battle or conflict with. **2** To assail with hostile words; criticize, censure. **3** To begin work on; set about, as an undertaking, with the intention of completing. **4** To begin to affect seriously or injuriously; seize: Acid *attacks* metal; Disease *attacks* a person. — *v.i.* **5** To make an attack; begin battle: The enemy *attacked* at dawn. — *n.* **1** The act of assaulting: with *on* or *upon.* **2** The first movement toward any undertaking. **3** Any hostile, offensive part or action, as with troops. **4** A seizure, as by disease. **5** *Music* The manner of beginning a phrase or passage with decision and spirit. [<F *attaquer* <Ital. *attaccare,* ult. <same source as ATTACH]

Synonyms (verb): assail, assault, beleaguer, beset, besiege, charge, combat, encounter, invade. To *attack* is to begin hostilities of any kind. *Assail* and *assault,* while of the same original etymology, have diverged in meaning, so that *assault* alone retains the meaning of direct personal violence. One may *assail* another with reproaches; he *assaults* him with a blow, a brandished weapon, etc. To *encounter* is to meet face to face, and may be said either of the *attacking* or of the resisting force or person, or of both. *Antonyms*: aid, befriend, cover, defend, preserve, protect, resist, shelter, shield, support, sustain, uphold, withstand.

Synonyms (noun): aggression, assault, encroachment, incursion, infringement, intrusion, invasion, onset, onslaught, trespass. An *attack* may be by word; an *aggression* is always by deed, upon rights, possessions, etc. An *invasion* of a nation's territories is an act of *aggression*; an *intrusion* upon a neighboring estate is a *trespass. Onslaught* signifies intensely violent *assault,* as by an army or a desperado, but it is sometimes used of violent speech. See AGGRESSION. *Antonyms*: defense, repulsion, resistance, retreat, submission, surrender.

at·tain (ə·tān′) *v.t.* **1** To achieve, accomplish or gain, as a desired purpose or state. **2** To come to, as in time; arrive at: He *attained* a ripe old age. — **to attain to** To arrive at with effort; succeed in reaching: Few men have *attained to* power such as his. [<OF *ataindre* <L *attingere* reach <*ad-* to + *tangere* touch]

at·tain·a·ble (ə·tā′nə·bəl) *adj.* That can be attained; practicable; feasible. — **at·tain′a·bil′i·ty, at·tain′a·ble·ness** *n.*

at·tain·der (ə·tān′dər) *n.* **1** The loss of all civil rights of a person, as one dead in law, upon the pronouncing of sentence of death or of outlawry against him for a capital offense. **2** *Obs.* Dishonor. — **bill of attainder** A legal act making certain crimes punishable by attainder. [<OF *ataindre* attain, strike, accuse; infl. in meaning by F *taindre* stain]

at·tain·ment (ə·tān′mənt) *n.* **1** The act of attaining. **2** That which is attained; an acquisition, as of skill.

Synonyms: accomplishment, acquirement, acquisition. These words are oftenest used in the plural. *Accomplishments* are showy, graceful, pleasing; *acquirements* are substantial and useful; *attainments* are lofty and ennobling. *Acquisitions,* unless otherwise expressly stated, are understood to be of money or property. Compare WISDOM.

at·taint (ə·tānt′) *v.t.* **1** To inflict attainder upon; condemn. **2** To disgrace; taint; sully. **3** To touch or affect, as disease. **4** *Obs.* To accuse: with *of.* **5** *Obs.* To touch; hit, as in tilting. — *n.* **1** Imputation; stigma. **2** Attainder. [<OF *ataint*, pp. of *ataindre.* See ATTAIN.]

at·tain·ture (ə·tān′chər) *n. Obs.* **1** Imputation of dishonor. **2** Attainder.

at·tar (at′ər) *n.* The fragrant essential oil extracted from the petals of flowers, especially roses: also called *ottar.* [<Persian *'aṭar* <Arabic *'iṭr* perfume]

at·tem·per (ə·tem′pər) *v.t.* **1** To reduce or modify by or as by mixture. **2** To modify the temperature of. **3** To moderate or appease, as excited feelings. **4** To adapt (oneself) so as to harmonize. **5** *Obs.* To control; regulate. [<OF *atemprer* <L *attemperare* adjust <*ad-* to + *temperare* regulate]

at·tempt (ə·tempt′) *v.t.* **1** To make an effort or trial to perform or get; endeavor to effect; try. **2** *Archaic* To try to overcome, master, win, seduce, or take by force; attack; assault: to *attempt* the life of someone. **3** *Archaic* To attract by allurements; tempt. See synonyms under ENDEAVOR. — *n.* **1** A putting forth of effort; a trial; endeavor; essay. **2** An attack. See synonyms under ENDEAVOR [<OF *attenter, attempter* <L *attentare, attemptare* try <*ad-* toward + *tentare, temptare,* freq. of *tendere* stretch] — **at·tempt′a·ble** *adj.* — **at·tempt′a·bil′i·ty** *n.*

at·tend (ə·tend′) *v.t.* **1** To wait upon; minister to; visit or care for professionally. **2** To be present at or in, as a meeting. **3** To follow as a result. **4** To accompany. **5** *Archaic* To give heed; listen. **6** *Archaic* To await. See synonyms under FOLLOW, LISTEN, SERVE. [<OF *atendre* wait, expect <L *attendere* give heed to, consider <*ad-* toward + *tendere* stretch]

at·ten·dance (ə·ten′dəns) *n.* **1** An attending. **2** Those who attend; an audience or congregation; retinue. [<OF *atendance* <*atendre.* See ATTEND.]

at·ten·dant (ə·ten′dənt) *n.* **1** One who attends, especially as a servant; also, one who is present at a ceremony. **2** A concomitant; consequent. — *adj.* Following or accompanying; waiting upon.

at·tent (ə·tent′) *adj. Archaic* Eagerly attentive; intent. [<L *attentus*, pp. of *attendere.* See ATTEND.]

at·ten·tion (ə·ten′shən) *n.* **1** The act or faculty of attending. **2** Active consciousness; the power or faculty of mental concentration. **3** An act of courtesy or gallantry. **4** Practical consideration; care. **5** *Mil.* The prescribed position of readiness to obey orders; also, the order to assume this position. See synonyms under CARE, INDUSTRY. [<L *attentio, -onis* <*attendere.* See ATTEND.]

at·ten·tive (ə·ten′tiv) *adj.* **1** Of, pertaining to, giving, or showing attention; observant; thoughtful. **2** Courteous; gallant; polite. See synonyms under OBSEQUIOUS, THOUGHTFUL. — **at·ten′tive·ly** *adv.* — **at·ten′tive·ness** *n.*

at·ten·u·ant (ə·ten′yoo͞·ənt) *adj.* Making thin; diluting. — *n.* A medicine that dilutes the body fluids or thins the blood. [<L *attenuans, -antis,* ppr. of *attenuare.* See ATTENUATE.]

at·ten·u·ate (ə·ten′yoo͞·āt) *v.* **·at·ed, ·at·ing** *v.t.* **1** To make thin, small, or fine; draw out, as a wire. **2** To reduce in value, quantity, size, or strength; weaken; impair. **3** To reduce in density; rarefy, as a liquid or gas. **4** *Bacteriol.* To weaken the virulence of a micro–organism. — *v.i.* **5** To become thin, weak, rarefied, etc. — *adj.* (a·ten′yoo͞·it) **1** Made thin; slender; rarefied; diluted. **2** *Bot.* Slender and tapering; narrow. [<L *attenuatus*, pp. of *attenuare* weaken <*ad-* + *tenuare* make thin <*tenuis* thin]

at·ten·u·a·tion (ə·ten′yoo͞·ā′shən) *n.* **1** The act or process of attenuating, or the state of being attenuated. **2** *Bacteriol.* Reduction of the virulence of micro–organisms by repeated cultivation in artificial media, exposure to light, etc.

at·test (ə·test′) *v.t.* **1** To confirm as accurate, true, or genuine; vouch for. **2** To certify, as by signature or oath. **3** To be proof of: His many works *attest* his industry. **4** To put upon oath. — *v.i.* **5** To bear witness; testify: with *to.* — *n.* One who or that which certifies or confirms; attestation. [<F *attester* <L *attestari* confirm <*ad-* to + *testari* bear witness]

at·tes·ta·tion (at′es·tā′shən) *n.* **1** A presenting (of something) as testimony. **2** Testimony; something presented as evidence.

at·tic (at′ik) *n.* **1** A half–story next the roof; a garret. **2** A low, decorative wall or structure, in classical style, above a cornice or entablature. [<F *attique,* orig. Athenian; from the false supposition that the attic was of Athenian origin]

At·tic (at′ik) *adj.* **1** Of or pertaining to Attica in ancient Greece. **2** Of, characteristic of, or pertaining to Athens; Athenian; characteristic of the Athenians; pertaining to the language, literature, art, or literary style of the Athenians. **3** Graceful; delicate; refined: *Attic* wit. — *n.* The dialect of Attica, closely related to Ionic, representing ancient Greek in its most refined form as used by Aeschylus, Sophocles, Euripides, and most of the great Greek writers. [<L *Atticus* <Gk. *Attikos* Athenian <*Attikē* Attica]

At·ti·ca (at′i·kə) A nome of east central Greece; 1,310 square miles; capital, Athens; formerly an ancient kingdom and republic of Greece.

Attic faith Inviolable faith.

At·ti·cism (at′ə·siz′əm) *n.* **1** An Attic idiom or characteristic. **2** A clear, concise, elegant expression. **3** A siding with the Athenians. **4** In Greek and Roman oratory, a style marked by simplicity of language and avoidance of rhetorical periods: contrasted with *Asianism.*

At·ti·cize (at′ə·sīz) *v.* **·cized, ·ciz·ing** *v.i.* **1** To conform to or copy Attic idiom, literary style, or customs. **2** To favor or to take the part of the Athenians. — *v.t.* **3** To cause to conform to or copy Athenian idiom, style, or customs. Also *Brit.* **At′ti·cise.**

Attic salt Delicate, refined, graceful wit. Also **Attic wit.**

At·ti·la (at′ə·lə), 406?–453, king of the Huns: called "the scourge of God."

at·tire (ə·tīr′) *v.t.* **at·tired, at·tir·ing** **1** To dress; array; adorn. **2** *Obs.* To equip. — *n.* **1** Dress or clothing; apparel; garments; costume; adornment. **2** *Her.* Antlers or horns.

as of a stag. See synonyms under DRESS. [<OF *atirer* arrange, adorn <*a-* in (<L *ad-*) + *tire* row, order (of uncertain origin)]

at·tire·ment (ə·tīr′mənt) *n.* Apparel; garb; attire.

At·tis (at′is) In classical mythology, a vegetation god worshipped with the Great Mother: an annual spring festival commemorated his death and resurrection. Also *Atys.*

at·ti·tude (at′ə·tōōd, -tyōōd) *n.* **1** Position of the body, as suggesting some thought, feeling, or action. **2** State of mind, behavior, or conduct regarding some matter, as indicating opinion or purpose. **3** *Aeron.* The position of an airplane with reference to some plane, as the earth or the horizon; tilt or tip. **4** *Med.* The position of the fetus in the womb. [<F <Ital. *attitudine* <LL *aptitudo* fitness <L *aptus* fitted, suited. Doublet of APTITUDE.] **—at·ti·tu·di·nal** (at′ə·tōō′də·nəl, -tyōō′-) *adj.*

Synonyms: pose, position, posture. A *posture* is assumed without any special reference to expression of feeling; *attitude* is the *position* appropriate to the expression of some feeling, whether consciously or unconsciously assumed. A *pose* is a *position* studied for artistic effect or considered with reference to such effect.

at·ti·tu·di·nize (at′ə·tōō′də·nīz, -tyōō′-) *v.i.* **·nized, ·niz·ing** To pose for effect; strike an attitude. Also *Brit.* **at′ti·tu′di·nise.**

Att·lee (at′lē), **Clement Richard,** 1883–1967, Earl Attlee, British Labour Party leader; prime minister 1945–51.

at·torn (ə·tûrn′) *v.i.* **1** *Law* To agree to recognize a new owner of a property or estate and promise payment of rent to him. **2** In feudal law, to consent to the transfer of land by the lord of the fee and to the continuance of one's own holding under the new lord; also, to accord homage to a lord. [<OF *atorner* turn to, assign, appoint <*a-* to (<L *ad-*) + *torner* turn. See TURN.]

at·tor·ney (ə·tûr′nē) *n.* **1** A person empowered by another to act in his stead; especially, one legally qualified to prosecute and defend actions in a court of law; an attorney at law; a lawyer. **2** *Obs.* An agent. **—by attorney** By proxy. **—power of attorney** Legal written authority to transact business for another. **—prosecuting attorney** *U.S.* The law officer empowered to act in behalf of the government, whether state, county, or national, in prosecutions for penal offenses: also called **district attorney.** [<OF *atorné,* pp. of *atorner.* See ATTORN.] **—at·tor′ney·ship** *n.*

attorney at law An attorney who is qualified to prosecute and defend actions in a court of law: also called *public attorney.*

attorney general *pl.* **attorneys general, attorney generals** The chief law officer of a government.

Attorney General *U.S.* A cabinet officer who heads the Department of Justice and is chief legal adviser to the President.

attorney in fact An attorney who is limited to business out of court: also called *private attorney.*

at·torn·ment (ə·tûrn′mənt) *n.* In feudal law, the acknowledgment by the tenant of a new lord on the alienation of land; also, the acknowledgment by a bailee that he holds property for a new party. Compare ATTORN.

at·tract (ə·trakt′) *v.t.* **1** To draw to or cause to come near by some physical force, as magnetism, and without apparent mechanical connection. **2** To draw, as the admiration or attention of, by some winning influence; allure; entice. See synonyms under ALLURE, DRAW, INTEREST. [<L *attractus,* pp. of *attrahere* <*ad-* toward + *trahere* draw, drag] **—at·tract′a·ble** *adj.* **—at·tract′a·ble·ness, at·tract′a·bil′i·ty** *n.* **—at·tract′er, at·trac′tor** *n.*

at·trac·tile (ə·trak′təl) *adj.* Having power to attract.

at·trac·tion (ə·trak′shən) *n.* **1** The act or process of attracting, or that which attracts. **2** A physical force which, exerted between or among bodies, tends to make them approach each other or prevents their separating. Compare REPULSION. **3** Anything pleasing or alluring. See synonyms under INCLINATION, LOVE.

attraction sphere *Biol.* A minute spherical mass observed near the nucleus of many cells, that appears to control the phenomena of indirect division; centrosphere.

at·trac·tive (ə·trak′tiv) *adj.* Having the power or quality of attracting; drawing; pleasing; winning. See synonyms under AMIABLE, BEAUTIFUL, PLEASANT. **—at·trac′tive·ly** *adv.* **—at·trac′tive·ness** *n.*

at·tra·hent (at′rə·hənt) *adj.* **1** Drawing to or toward something. **2** *Anat.* Drawing a part forward. *—n.* **1** An external application that draws fluids to the place where it is applied. **2** A muscle that acts by drawing forward. [<L *attrahens, -entis,* ppr. of *attrahere.* See ATTRACT.]

at·trib·ute (ə·trib′yōōt) *v.t.* **·ut·ed, ·ut·ing** To consider or ascribe as belonging to, resulting from, owing to, or caused by; assign; refer: to *attribute* the invention of music to Orpheus; to *attribute* wisdom to gray hair.

—at·tri·bute (at′rə·byōōt) *n.* **1** That which is assigned or ascribed; a characteristic. **2** *Gram.* An adjective or its equivalent. **3** In art and mythology, a distinctive mark or symbol. [<L *attributus,* pp. of *attribuere* bestow, assign <*ad-* to + *tribuere* allot, give over] **—at·trib′u·ta·ble** *adj.*

Synonyms (verb): ascribe, assign, associate, charge, connect, impute, refer. We may *attribute* to a person either that which belongs to him or that which we merely suppose to be his. Where we are quite sure, we simply *refer* a matter to the cause or class to which it belongs or *ascribe* to one what is surely his, etc. We *associate* things which may have no necessary or causal relations; as, we may *associate* the striking of a clock with the serving of dinner. We *charge* a person with what we deem blameworthy. We may *impute* good or evil, but more commonly evil. *Antonyms*: deny, disconnect, dissociate, separate, sever, sunder.

Synonyms (noun): property, quality. A *quality* denotes what a thing really is in some one respect; an *attribute* is what we conceive a thing to be in some one respect; thus, while *attribute* may, *quality* must, express something of the real nature of that to which it is ascribed; we speak of the *attributes* of God, the *qualities* of matter. A *property* is what belongs especially to one thing as its own peculiar possession, in distinction from all other things; when we speak of the *qualities* or the *properties* of matter, *quality* is the more general, *property* the more limited term. Compare CHARACTERISTIC, EMBLEM, FIGURE. *Antonyms*: being, essence, nature, substance.

at·tri·bu·tion (at′rə·byōō′shən) *n.* **1** An attributing or being attributed. **2** An ascribed characteristic or quality; attribute.

at·trib·u·tive (ə·trib′yə·tiv) *adj.* **1** Pertaining to or of the nature of an attribute; expressing or assigning an attribute. **2** So ascribed, as a work of art: That canvas is an *attributive* Vermeer. **3** *Gram.* Expressing an attribute; in English, designating an adjective or its equivalent which stands before the noun it modifies, as opposed to a predicate adjective which follows a linking verb; as, in the expression "a silver watch," silver is an *attributive* adjective. *—n. Gram.* An attributive word. **—at·trib′u·tive·ly** *adj.* **—at·trib′u·tive·ness** *n.*

at·trite (ə·trīt′) *adj.* **1** Worn down by rubbing or friction. **2** *Theol.* Having attrition. Also **at·trit·ed** (ə·trī′tid). [<L *attritus,* pp. of *atterere.* See ATTRITION.]

at·tri·tion (ə·trish′ən) *n.* **1** A rubbing out or grinding down, as by friction. **2** A gradual wearing down or weakening: a war of *attrition.* **3** *Theol.* Repentance for sin, arising from inferior motives; imperfect contrition (see under CONTRITION). [<L *attritio, -onis* rubbing, friction <*atterere* rub away <*ad-* to, against + *terere* rub]

At·tu (at′tōō) The westernmost island of the Aleutians, largest of the Near Islands.

at·tune (ə·tōōn′, ə·tyōōn′) *v.t.* **at·tuned, at·tun·ing** **1** To bring into accord with; harmonize. **2** To adjust to the right pitch, as a musical instrument; tune. See synonyms under ADAPT. [<AD- + TUNE]

A·tu·o·na (ä′tōō·ō′nä) Capital of the Marquesas Islands, on Hiva Oa.

a·twain (ə·twān′) *adv.* In two; asunder. [<A-[1] on + TWAIN]

a·tween (ə·twēn′) *prep. Obs.* Between. [<A-[1] on + (BE)TWEEN]

a·twirl (ə·twûrl′) *adj.* & *adv.* In a twirl; twirling.

a·typ·ic (ā·tip′ik) *adj.* Not typical; without typical character; differing from the type; irregular. Also **a·typ′i·cal. —a·typ′i·cal·ly** *adv.*

Au *Chem.* Gold (symbol Au).

au·bade (ō·bäd′) *n. French* Morning music, as to announce the dawn. Compare SERENADE.

Aube (ōb) A river of north central France, flowing 140 miles NW to the Seine.

Au·ber (ō·bâr′), **Daniel François,** 1782–1871, French composer.

au·berge (ō·berzh′) *n. French* An inn.

Au·ber·vil·liers (ō·ber·vē·lyā′) An industrial suburb NE of Paris, France.

Au·bi·gné (dō·bē·nyā′), **Théodore Agrippa d'** 1552–1630, French poet and Huguenot soldier.

Au·brey (ô′brē) A masculine personal name. [<G *Alberich,* lit., elf-king]

Au·brey (ô′brē), **John,** 1626–97, English antiquary.

au·burn (ô′bûrn) *adj.* Reddish-brown: *auburn* hair. *—n.* An auburn color; a reddish-brown. [<OF *auborne, alborne* <LL *alburnus* whitish <L *albus* white; infl. in meaning by ME *brun* brown]

Au·bus·son (ō·bü·sôn′) A town in central France on the Creuse, noted for its tapestries and for a carpet of tapestry weave known as **Aubusson carpet.**

Au·chin·leck (ô′kin·lek), **Sir Claude John Eyre,** born 1884, British general in World War II.

Auck·land (ôk′lənd) A chief port and former capital of New Zealand, on North Island.

Auckland Islands A group of uninhabited islands south of and belonging to New Zealand; 234 square miles.

au con·traire (ō kôn·trâr′) *French* On the contrary.

au cou·rant (ō kōō·räN′) *French* Up to date; fashionable.

auc·tion (ôk′shən) *n.* **1** A public sale of property in which the price offered for individual items is increased by bids, until the highest bidder becomes the purchaser. **2** The bidding in bridge. **3** Auction bridge (see under BRIDGE[2]). *—v.t.* To sell by or at auction. **—to auction off** To sell by or at auction. [<L *auctio, -onis* an increase, a public sale (with increasing bids) <*augere* increase]

auction block *U.S.* A stand or block on which a slave was placed to be sold at auction. **—on the auction block** Up for forced or compulsory sale.

auc·tion·eer (ôk′shən·ir′) *n.* One who conducts an auction, usually as a business. *—v.t.* To sell by auction.

au·da·cious (ô·dā′shəs) *adj.* **1** Having or exhibiting an unabashed or fearless spirit; defiant of ordinary restraint, as of law or decorum. **2** Presumptuous; shameless; insolent. [<F *audacieux* <L *audacia.* See AUDACITY.] **—au·da′cious·ly** *adv.* **—au·da′cious·ness** *n.*

au·dac·i·ty (ô·das′ə·tē) *n. pl.* **·ties** **1** The quality or state of being audacious. **2** An audacious act, remark, etc. See synonyms under EFFRONTERY, TEMERITY. [<L *audacia* boldness <*audax* bold, rash <*audere* dare]

Au·den (ô′dən), **W(ystan) H(ugh),** 1907–1973, U.S. poet born in England.

au·di·bil·i·ty (ô′də·bil′ə·tē) *n.* **1** Ability to be heard. **2** *Telecom.* The ratio of the strength of a transmitted signal to that of a barely audible signal.

au·di·ble (ô′də·bəl) *adj.* Perceptible by the ear; loud enough to be heard. [<Med. L *audibilis* <L *audire* hear] **—au′di·ble·ness** *n.* **—au′di·bly** *adv.*

au·di·ence (ô′dē·əns) *n.* **1** An assembly gathered to hear and see, as at a concert. **2** Those who are reached by a book, television program, etc. **3** The act of hearing; attention. **4** A formal hearing, interview, or conference. **5** Opportunity to be heard. [<OF <L *audientia* a hearing <*audire* hear]

au·di·ent (ô′dē·ənt) *adj.* Listening; hearing. [<L *audiens, -entis,* ppr. of *audire* hear]

au·dile (ô′dil, ô′dīl) *n. Psychol.* An individual having a tendency to form mental images derived from auditory sensations. *—adj.* Auditory. [<L *audire* hear + -ILE]

au·di·o (ô′dē·ō) *adj. Telecom.* **1** Of or pertaining to characteristics associated with sound waves. **2** Designating devices used in transmission or reception of sound waves: in television, distinguished from *video.* [<L *audire* hear]

audio- *combining form* Pertaining to hearing: *audiogram*. Also **audi-**. [<L *audire* hear]

au·di·o·cas·sette (ô′dē·ō·kə·set′; -ka·set′) *n.* Electronics. A cassette for the storage of audio material.

au·di·o·com·mu·ni·ca·tion (ô′dē·ō·kə·myo͞o′nə·kā′shən) *n.* **1** Vocal communication. **2** Any form of communication which utilizes electro-acoustic methods in the transmission, recording, and amplification of sound waves.

audio frequency A frequency of electrical, sound, or other wave vibrations coming within the range of normal human hearing, or from about 20 to 20,000 cycles a second.

au·di·o·gram (ô′dē·ō ·gram′) *n.* A graph to show the hearing level of a subject in relation to the minimum intensity of sounds perceptible to the normal ear.

au·di·om·e·ter (ô′dē·om′ə·tər) *n.* An instrument to gage and record the acuteness of hearing. **—au′di·o·met·ric** (ô′dē·ə·met′rik) *adj.* **— au′di·om′e·try** *n.*

au·di·o·phile (ô′dē·ə·fīl′) *n.* A specialist in or enthusiast of high-fidelity sound reproduction on radio, phonograph and tape recordings, etc.

au·di·o·vis·u·al (ô′dē·ō·vizh′o͞o·əl) *adj.* Pertaining to forms of instruction and entertainment other than books, as radio, television, motion pictures, photographs, recordings, etc.: *audio-visual* aids.

au·di·phone (ô′də·fōn) *n.* A device for directing sound through the bones of the head to the auditory nerve.

au·dit (ô′dit) *v.t.* **1** To examine, adjust, and certify, as accounts. **2** To attend as a listener: to *audit* a course in college. [< *n.*] *—n.* **1** An examination of an accounting document and of the evidence in support of its correctness. **2** A calling to account. **3** A settlement of accounts. **4** A balance sheet. **5** *Obs.* A hearing. [<L *auditus* a hearing < *audire* hear]

au·di·tion (ô·dish′ən) *n.* **1** The act or sense of hearing. **2** An audience or hearing; especially, a trial test or hearing, as of an actor or singer *—v.t.* To try out, as an actor or singer for a special role. *—v.i.* To demonstrate one's ability or talent when applying for an acting or singing job. [<L *auditio, -onis* a hearing < *audire* hear]

au·di·tor (ô′də·tər) *n.* **1** One who audits accounts. **2** One who listens; a hearer. **3** One who audits classes. —au′di·tress *n.* fem.

au·di·to·ri·um (ô′də·tôr′ē·əm), -tō′rē·əm *n. pl.* **·to·ri·ums** or **·to·ri·a** (-tôr′ē·ə, -tō′rē·ə) **1** The room or part of a building, as a church, theater, etc., occupied by the audience. **2** A building for concerts, public meetings, etc. [<L, lecture room, courtroom, orig. neut. of *auditorius*. See AUDITORY.]

au·di·to·ry (ô′də·tôr′ē, -tō′rē) *adj.* Of or pertaining to hearing or the organs or sense of hearing. *—n. pl.* **·ries** **1** An assembly of hearers; an audience. **2** An auditorium, particularly the nave of a church. [<L *auditorius* < *audire* hear] —au′di·to′ri·ly *adv.*

auditory canal *Anat.* The passage leading from the auricle to the tympanic membrane. See illustration under EAR.

Au·drey (ô′drē) A feminine personal name. —Saint Audrey See ETHELDREDA, SAINT. [<OF, ult. <Gmc., noble might]

Au·du·bon (ô′də·bon), **John James,** 1785–1851, U.S. ornithologist and painter.

Au·er (ou′ər), **Leopold,** 1845–) 1930, Hungarian violinist and teacher.

Au·er·bach (ou′ər·bäkh), **Berthold,** 1812–82, German novelist.

Au·er·städt (ou′ər·shtet) A village in east central Germany; scene of a French victory over the Prussians, 1806.

au fait (ō fe′) *French* Skilled, expert; well informed; literally, to the fact.

Auf·klä·rung (ouf′klâ′ro͞o ng) *n.* German The Enlightenment.

au fond (ô fôṅ′) *French* Fundamentally; at bottom; essentially.

auf Wie·der·seh·en (ouf vē′dər·zā′ən) *German* Till we meet again; good-by for now.

Au·ge·an (ô·jē′ən) *adj.* **1** Of or pertaining to Augeas or his stables. **2** Exceedingly filthy; corrupt.

Augeän stables In Greek mythology, the stables in which Augeas kept 3,000 oxen and which, uncleaned for 30 years, were cleaned in a day when Hercules turned the river Alpheus through them.

Au·ge·as (ô′jē·əs, ô·jē′əs) In Greek mythology, a king of Elis.

au·gen (ou′gən) *n. pl. Geol.* A rock formation which contains packed masses of eye-shaped particles. [<G, eyes]

au·gend (ô′jend) *n. Math.* A quantity or number to which another is to be added. See ADDEND. [<L *augendum*, neut. gerundive of *augere* increase]

au·ger (ô′gər) n. **1** A large tool with a spiral groove for boring holes in wood, etc. **2** An earth-boring tool. ◆Homophone: *augur*. [OE *nafugār*, lit., nave-borer < *nafu* nave of a wheel + *gār* borer, spear (*a nauger in ME becoming an auger*)]

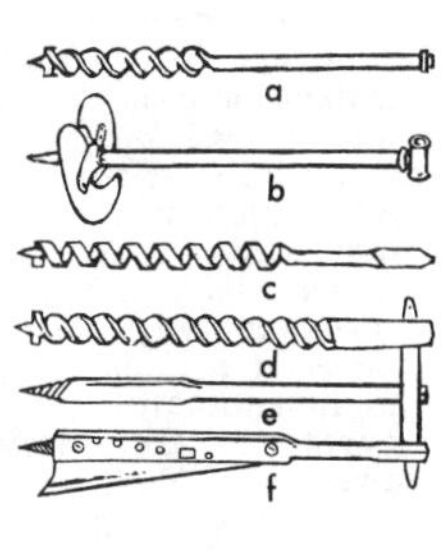

AUGERS
a. Twisted. *b.* Posthole. *c.* Ship. *d.* Chuck–shanked. *e.* Gimlet. *f.* Expanding.

Au·ghra·bies Falls (ō·khrä′bēs, ō·grä′-) A waterfall in the Orange River, in Northern Cape Province, Republic of South Africa; 480 feet: also *King George's Falls*.

aught¹ (ôt) *n.* Anything; any part or item. *—adv.* By any chance; at all; in any respect. Also spelled *ought*. ◆Homophone: *ought*. [OE *āwiht* < *ā* ever + *wiht* thing]

aught² (ôt) *n.* The figure 0; cipher; a naught; nothing. ◆Homophone: *ought*. [*a naught* taken as an *aught*]

aught·lins (ôkht′linz) *adv. Scot.* In any measure; in the least.

Au·gier (ō·zhyā′), **Guillaume Victor Émile,** 1820–89, french dramatist.

au·gite (ô′jīt) *n. Mineral.* A dark-colored variety of aluminous rock-making pyroxene. [<L *augites*, a precious stone <Gk. *augitē s* < *augē* brightness, gleam (of a gem)] —au·git·tic (ô·jit′ik) *adj.*

aug·ment (ôg·ment′) *v.t.* **1** To make greater, as in size, number, or amount; enlarge; intensify. **2** In Greek and Sanskrit grammar, to add the augment to. *—v.i.* To become greater, as in size, number, or amount. See synonyms under ADD, INCREASE. *—n.* (ôg′·ment) **1** Increase; enlargement. **2** In Greek and Sanskrit grammar, a vowel prefixed to a verb, or a lengthening of the initial vowel, to indicate past time. [<F *augmenter* <L *augmentare* < *augmentum* an increase < *augere* increase] **— aug·ment′a·ble** *adj.* **— aug·ment′er** *n.*

aug·men·ta·tion (ôg′men·tā ′shən) *n.* **1** An augmenting or being augmented. **2** The result of augmenting; enlargement; increase; an addition. **2** *Music* The repetition of a theme in notes of twice the time value of those first used; opposite of *diminution*. See synonyms under ACCESSION, INCREASE.

aug·men·ta·tive (ôg·men′tə·tiv) *adj.* **1** Having the quality or power of augmenting. **2** *Gram.* Denoting greater size or intensity, as the suffix *-agne* in French *montagne* a mountain (from *mont* a hill). *—n. Gram.* An augmentative form. Also **aug·men′tive.** Abbr. *aug.*

aug·men·ted (ôg·men′tid) *adj. Music* Increased by a half step more than the corresponding major interval.

aug·men·tor (ôg·men′tər) *n. Aeron.* A duct for increasing the thrust of a jet engine by forcing the air-fuel mixture through a narrowed channel just behind the exit nozzle.

au gra·tin (ō grät′n, grat′n; *Fr.* ō grȧ·taṅ′) Sprinkled with breadcrumbs or grated cheese and baked until brown. [<F]

Augs·burg (ôgz′bûrg, *Ger.* ouks′bo͝orkh) The capital of Swabia, SW Germany. Ancient **Au·gus·ta Vin·de·li·co·rum** (ô ·gus′tə vin·del′i·kō′rəm).

au·gur (ô′gər) *n.* **1** A religious official of ancient Rome whose duty it was to foretell future events by interpreting omens, such as the flights of birds, and to give advice on public affairs accordingly. **2** Hence, a prophet; soothsayer. Also *Obs.* **au′gur·er.** *—v.t.* **1** To predict; divine; prognosticate from or as from signs and omens; also, to conjecture from indications. **2** To betoken; portend; to be an omen of. *—v.i.* **3** To conjecture from signs and omens. **4** To be an augury or omen. ◆Homophone: *auger*. [<L *augur* < *avis* bird + *-gar* (? akin to *garrire* talk, interpret)]

Synonyms (verb): betoken, bode, forbode, forecast, foretell, foretoken, portend, predict, pre- sage, prognosticate, prophesy. Persons only *divine, forecast, foretell, predict,* or *prophesy;* things only *betoken, foretoken,* or *portend;* either persons or things *augur, bode, forebode, presage,* or *prognosticate*. As regards the outcome, *bode, forebode,* and *portend* always refer to evil or misfortune; the other words are neutral, applying equally to good or ill. One may *augur* or *divine* from indications too slight to be explained; to *forecast* always denotes calculation. See PROPHESY. *Antonyms:* assure, demonstrate, determine, establish, insure, prove, warrant.

au·gu·ral (ô′gyə·rəl) *adj.* Of or pertaining to augurs or auguries.

au·gu·ry (ô′gyə·rē) *n. pl.* **·ries** **1** The art or practice of foretelling by signs or omens; divination. **2** A portent or omen; presage. **3** The rite or ceremony conducted by an augur.

au·gust (ô·gust′) *adj.* **1** Majestic; grand; imposing. **2** Of high birth or rank; venerable; eminent. See synonyms under AWFUL) , GRAND, KINGLY. [<L *augustus* < *augere* increase, exalt] **— au·gust′ly** *adv.* **— au·gust′ness** *n.*

Au·gust (ô′gəst; *Dan., Ger., Sw.* ou′go͝ost) A masculine personal name; variant of AUGUSTUS.

Au·gust (ô′gəst) The eighth month of the year, containing 31 days. [<L, after AUGUSTUS CAESAR]

Au·gus·ta (ô·gus′tə; *Ger.* ou·go͝os′tə, *Ital.* ou·go͝os′tä) A feminine personal name; feminine of AUGUSTUS) . Also *Dan., Du., Ger.* **Au·gus·te** (ou·go͝os′tə). [<L, venerable] **— Augusta Victoria,** 1858–1921, German empress; wife of William II.

Au·gus·ta (ô·gus′tə) A city in south central Maine on the Kennebec River; the State capital.

Au·gus·tan (ô·gus′tən) *adj.* **1** Of or pertaining to the emperor Augustus or to his times. **2** Pertaining to any era which resembles that of Augustus in refinement and taste. **3** Classical; refined. **4** Pertaining to Augsburg. *—n.* A writer or artist of an Augustan age.

Augustan age **1** The period of the reign of Augustus, 27 B.C. to A.D. 14, the golden age of Roman literature. **2** A corresponding period in other literatures, as in England during the reign of Queen Anne.

Au·gus·tan·ism (ô·gus′tən·iz′əm) *n.* A characteristic or quality resembling those of the reign of Augustus, especially as shown by the literature of that period.

Au·gus·tine (ô′gəs·tēn, ô·gus′tin) A masculine personal name. Also **Au·gus·tin** (ô·gus′tən; *Fr.* ō·güs·taṅ′, *Ger.* ou′go͞o·stēn), *Lat.* **Au·gus·ti·nus** (ô′gəs·tī′nəs). [<L, venerable] **— Augustine, Saint,** 354–430, bishop of Hippo and a father of the church. **— Augustine, Saint,** died 604?, brought Christianity to England: also known as *Saint Austin*.

Au·gus·tin·i·an (ô′gəs·tin′ē·ən) *adj.* **1** Of or pertaining to St. Augustine or his doctrines. **2** Belonging to a monastic order named after St. Augustine or following his rule. *—n.* **1** A disciple of St. Augustine. **2** A member of any of the mendicant monastic orders named after St. Augustine: also **Au·gus·tin** (ô·gus′tin). **—Au′gus·tin′i·an·ism, Au·gus′tin·ism** *n.*

Augustinian canons An order of regular canons, originally of the Lateran Basilica in Rome, formerly numerous in England and Ireland.

Augustinian Hermits An order of mendicant friars, established in 1256 by Pope Alexander IV under an Augustinian rule: also called *Austin Friars*.

Au·gus·tus (ô·gus′təs) A masculine personal name. Also *Fr.* **Au·guste** (ō·güst′). [<L, venerable]

---

add,āce,câre,pälm; end,ēven; it,īce; odd,ōpen,ôrder; to͝ok,po͞ol; up,bûrn; ə = a in *above*, e in *sicken*, i in *clarity*, o in *melon*, u in *focus*; yo͞o = u in *fuse*; oi,oil; ou,pout; ch,check; g,go; ng,ring; th,thin; th,this; zh,vision. Foreign sounds ȧ,œ,ü,kh,ṅ; and ◆: see page xx. < from; + plus; ? possibly.

— Augustus Caesar, 63 B.C.–A.D. 14, Gaius Julius Caesar Octavianus, the first Roman emperor 27 B.C.–A.D. 14: before 27 B.C. called *Octavian.*
au jus (ō zhü′) *French* Served with its natural juice or gravy: said of meats.
auk (ôk) *n.* A short-winged, web-footed diving bird (family *Alcidae*) of northern seas. The **great auk** *(Plautus impennis)*, now extinct, was black above and white below, had an oval white patch between the eyes and bill, and stood erect, two feet tall. The **razor-billed auk** *(Alca torda)* is smaller, with a white line extending between the eyes and bill. [<ON *ālka*]

GREAT AUK

auk·let (ôk′lit) *n.* One of the smaller auks; especially, the crested auklet.
au lait (ō le′) *French* With milk.
auld (ôld) *adj. Scot.* Old.
Auld Cloot·ie (klōōt′ē, klōō′tē) *Scot.* The devil.
auld-far·rant (ôld′far′ənt) *adj. Scot.* Wise beyond one's years; sagacious. Also **auld-far·ran** (-far′ən).
Auld Horn·ie (hôr′nē) *Scot.* The devil.
auld lang syne (ôld′ lang sīn′, zīn′) *Scot.* Literally, old long since; hence, long ago.
au·lic (ô′lik) *adj.* Pertaining to a royal court. [<F *aulique* <L *aulicus* <Gk. *aulikos* < *aulē* a court]
Aulic Council In the Holy Roman Empire, the emperor's privy council: later the Austrian Council of State.
Au·lis (ô′lis) An ancient town in Boeotia, central Greece, on the Gulf of Euboea; traditional site for the sacrifice of Iphigenia and the embarkation of the Greeks for the Trojan War.
au na·tu·rel (ō nà·tü·rel′) *French* **1** Ungarnished; plainly cooked, as food. **2** In the nude.
aunt (ant, änt) *n.* **1** The sister of one's father or mother, or the wife of one's uncle. **2** An elderly woman: familiar or affectionate use. [<OF *aunte, ante* <L *amita* paternal aunt]
aunt·y (an′tē, än′-) *n.* A familiar, diminutive form of AUNT. Also **aunt′ie.**
au pair (ō pâr) *Chiefly Brit.* **1** An arrangement whereby one receives room and board in a foreign household in exchange for doing certain chores, as housekeeping and the care of children: often used attributively: *au pair* girls. **2** *Colloq.* A girl participating in such an arrangement. [<F, lit., at par]
au·ra (ôr′ə) *n. pl.* **au·ras** or **au·rae** (ôr′ē) **1** An invisible emanation or exhalation. **2** A distinctive air or quality enveloping or characterizing a person or thing: an *aura* of wealth. **3** A gentle breeze. **4** *Electr.* **a** *Obs.* A subtile fluid supposed to surround an electrified body. **b** The current of air caused by a convective discharge from a sharp point. **5** *Pathol.* The sensory, motor, or psychic manifestations preceding an epileptic attack or other paroxysm. **6** In psychic research, the hypothetical emanations from living organisms. [<L, breeze <Gk. *aurē* breath]
au·ral[1] (ôr′əl) *adj.* Pertaining to the ear or the sense of hearing; auricular. [<L *auris* ear + -AL]
au·ral[2] (ôr′əl) *adj.* Pertaining to an aura.
au·rate[1] (ôr′āt) *adj.* Having ears or earlike expansions. Also **au′rat·ed.** [<L *auris* ear + -ATE[1]]
au·rate[2] (ôr′āt) *n.* A salt of auric acid, containing the trivalent radical AuO_3: ammonium *aurate* (fulminating gold). [<AUR(IC ACID) + -ATE[3]]
au·re·ate (ôr′ē·it) *adj.* Of the color of gold; golden. [<LL *aureatus* <L *aureus* < *aurum* gold]
Au·re·li·a (ô·rē′lē·ə, ô·rēl′yə; *Du., Ger.* ou·rā′·lē·ä; *Ital., Sp.* ou·rā′lyä) A feminine personal name. Also *Fr.* **Au·ré·lie** (ō·rā·lē′). [<L, golden]
Au·re·li·an (ô·rē′lē·ən, ô·rēl′yən), 212?–275, Lucius Domitius Aurelianus, Roman emperor 270–275.
Au·re·li·us (ô·rē′lē·əs, ô·rēl′yəs) A masculine personal name. [<L, golden]
Aurelius, Marcus, 121–180, nephew, son-in-law and adopted son of Antoninus Pius; Roman emperor 161–180, and Stoic philosopher: full name: *Marcus Aurelius Antoninus.*
au·re·o·la (ô·rē′ə·lə) *n.* **1** In art, a radiance enveloping the whole figure or head of Christ or any sanctified being; a glory; halo; aureole. **2** A radiance, or something resembling or likened to it. **3** In the Roman Catholic Church, a reward added to the essential bliss of heaven for spiritual victories achieved on earth. [<L < *aureolus* golden, dim. of *aureus* < *aurum* gold]
au·re·ole (ôr′ē·ōl) *n.* **1** *Astron.* The corona of the sun; a halo surrounding the image of a brilliant body as seen in a telescope. **2** An aureola. [<L *aureolus.* See AUREOLA]
au·re·o·lin (ô·rē′ə·lin) *n.* A bright, permanent yellow pigment made from cobalt and potassium: used in water colors and oil paints. [<L *aureol(us)* golden + -IN]
Au·re·o·my·cin (ôr′ē·ō·mī′sin) *n.* Proprietary name for a brand of chlortetracycline: used as an antibiotic. [<L *aureus* golden (from its color) + Gk. *mykēs* fungus + -IN]
au·re·ous (ôr′ē·əs) *adj.* Of the color of gold; golden. [<L *aureus* golden < *aurum* gold]
au·re·us (ôr′ē·əs) *n. pl.* **au·re·i** (ôr′ē·ī) A gold coin of the Roman Empire, weighing, under Augustus, 1/42 of a libra.
au re·voir (ō rə·vwàr′) *French* Good-by; till we meet again; literally, to the seeing again.
au·ric (ôr′ik) *adj.* Of, pertaining to, or containing gold, especially when combined in its highest or triad valency: *auric* chloride, $AuCl_3$. [<L *aurum* gold]
auric acid **1** Hydrated auric oxide, $Au(HO)_3$, which combines with bases to form aurates. **2** Auric oxide, a dark-brown powder, Au_2O_3, formed by heating auric hydroxide.
au·ri·cle (ôr′i·kəl) *n.* **1** *Anat.* **a** An atrium of the heart. **b** An auricular appendix. **c** The external ear; pinna. **2** An ear or ear-shaped appendage or part. **3** An ear trumpet. [<L *auricula,* dim. of *auris* ear] **— au′ri·cled** *adj.*
au·ric·u·la (ô·rik′yə·lə) *n. pl.* **·lae** (-lē) or **·las** **1** A primrose from the Alps *(Primula auricula)*: also called *bear's-ear.* **2** A small ear-shaped appendage. [<L, dim. of *auris* ear]
au·ric·u·lar (ô·rik′yə·lər) *adj.* **1** Of or pertaining to the ear or the sense of hearing. **2** Intended for or perceived by the ear; audible; confidential. **3** Ear-shaped. **4** Of or pertaining to an auricle. **—** *n. Ornithol.* One of the feathers overlying the ear: usually in the plural.
au·ric·u·late (ô·rik′yə·lit, -lāt) *adj.* **1** Having ear-shaped appendages or projections. **2** *Bot.* Having rounded projections at the base, as a leaf. **3** Like an ear. Also **au·ric′u·lat′ed. — au·ric′u·late·ly** *adv.*
au·rif·er·ous (ô·rif′ər·əs) *adj.* Containing gold. [<L *aurifer* < *aurum* gold + *ferre* bear] **— au·rif′er·ous·ly** *adv.*
au·ri·flamme (ôr′ə·flam) See ORIFLAMME.
au·ri·form (ôr′ə·fôrm) *adj.* Shaped like or resembling an ear; ear-shaped. [<L *auris* ear + -FORM]
Au·ri·ga (ô·rī′gə) A northern constellation, the Charioteer or Wagoner. See CONSTELLATION. [<L, charioteer]
Au·rig·na·cian (ôr′ig·nā′shən) *adj. Anthropol.* Of or pertaining to an Upper Paleolithic culture appearing toward the end of the Pleistocene. It is associated with the rise of Cro-Magnon man in western Europe and is characterized by implements of flint, bone, and horn, delicately modeled ivory figurines, and early examples of cave painting. [from *Aurignac,* town in Haute-Garonne, France, where the relics were discovered]
Au·ri·gny (ō·rē·nyē′) The French name for ALDERNEY.
au·ri·lave (ôr′ə·lāv) *n.* An instrument with which to clean the ears. [<L *auris* ear + *lavare* wash]
Au·riol (ō·ryôl′), **Vincent,** 1884–1966, French lawyer; president of France 1947–54.
au·ris (ôr′is) *n. pl.* **au·res** (ôr′ēz) *Latin* The ear.
au·ri·scope (ôr′ə·skōp) *n.* An instrument for examining the ear. **— au·ris·co·py** (ô·ris′kə·pē) *n.*
au·rist (ôr′ist) *n.* A specialist in diseases of the ear.
au·rochs (ôr′oks) *n.* The extinct European bison; urus. [<G *auerochs* <OHG *ūrohso* < *ūr* the urus + *ohso* ox]
au·ro·ra (ô·rôr′ə, ô·rō′rə) *n.* **1** The dawn. **2** The early stage or development of anything. **3** *Meteorol.* A luminous, sometimes richly colored display of arcs, bands, streamers, etc., occasionally seen in the skies of high northern and southern latitudes: it is caused by electrical disturbances in the atmosphere: also **au·ro′ra po·la·ris** (pə·lâr′is). [<L, dawn]
Au·ro·ra (ô·rôr′ə, ô·rō′rə) In Roman mythology, the goddess of the dawn: identified with the Greek *Eos.*
aurora aus·tra·lis (ôs·trā′lis) *Meteorol.* The aurora as seen in far southern latitudes: also called *southern lights.* [<NL, southern aurora <L *auster* south wind]
aurora bo·re·al·is (bôr′ē·al′is, -ā′lis, bō′rē-) *Meteorol.* The aurora as seen in the high northern latitudes: also called *northern lights.* [<NL, northern aurora <Gk. *boreas* north wind]
au·ro·ral (ô·rôr′əl, ô·rō′rəl) *adj.* **1** Pertaining to or like the dawn; dawning; roseate. **2** Of, like, or caused by an aurora: an *auroral* display. Also **au·ro·re·an** (ô·rôr′ē·ən, ô·rō′rē-), **au·ro′ric. — au·ro′ral·ly** *adv.*
au·rous (ôr′əs) *adj.* Of, pertaining to, or containing gold, especially in its monad valency: *aurous* chloride, AuCl. See AURIC. [<L *aurum* gold]
au·rum (ôr′əm) *n.* Gold. [<L]
aurum po·tab·i·le (pō·tab′ə·lē) *Latin* Literally, potable gold: a medieval cordial containing minute grains of gold.
Au·sa·ble River (ô·sā′bəl) A river 20 miles long in NE New York, flowing through **Ausable Chasm,** a gorge 1 1/2 miles long, to Lake Champlain.
Au·schwitz (ou′shvits) The German name for Oświecim, a city in SW Poland; site of a German extermination camp in which about 4,000,000 victims, mostly Jews, were slaughtered during World War II.
aus·cul·tate (ôs′kəl·tāt) *v.t.* & *v.i.* **·tat·ed, ·tat·ing** *Med.* To examine by auscultation. [<L *auscultatus,* pp. of *auscultare* listen, give ear to] **— aus·cul·ta·tive** (ôs·kul′tə·tiv) *adj.*
aus·cul·ta·tion (ôs′kəl·tā′shən) *n.* **1** *Med.* The act, art, or process of listening, as with a stethoscope, for sounds produced in the chest, abdomen, etc., to determine any abnormal condition. **2** A listening.
aus·cul·ta·tor (ôs′kəl·tā′tər) *n.* **1** One skilled in or practicing auscultation. **2** A stethoscope. **3** One who listens. **— aus·cul·ta·to·ry** (ôs·kul′tə·tôr′ē, -tō′rē) *adj.*
Aus·gleich (ous′glīkh) *n. German* Adjustment; agreement; compromise; specifically, the treaty of 1867 between Austria and Hungary, which formulated the organization of the former dual monarchy into a political union.
aus·pex (ôs′peks) *n. pl.* **aus·pi·ces** (ôs′pə·sēz) An augur, soothsayer, or diviner of ancient Rome; especially, one who observed and interpreted the omens connected with the flight, singing, cries, or feeding, etc., of birds; a bird-viewer. [<L *auspex* < *avis* bird + *specere* look at, observe]
aus·pi·cate (ôs′pi·kāt) *v.t.* To initiate or begin, especially under favorable circumstances, as with a ceremony calculated to insure good luck. [<L *auspicatus,* pp. of *auspicari* take omens, begin < *auspex.* See AUSPEX.]
aus·pice (ôs′pis) *n. pl.* **aus·pi·ces** (ôs′pə·sēz) **1** *Usually pl.* Favoring influence or guidance; patronage. **2** An augury, omen, or sign, especially when taken from meteorological phenomena, the movements of birds, etc. **3** The observation of such omens, etc. [<F <L *auspicium* < *auspex.* See AUSPEX.]
aus·pi·cial (ôs·pish′əl) *adj.* **1** Pertaining to augury. **2** Auspicious.
aus·pi·cious (ôs·pish′əs) *adj.* **1** Of good omen; propitious. **2** Successful; prosperous; fortunate. **— aus·pi′cious·ly** *adv.* **— aus·pi′·cious·ness** *n.*
Synonyms: encouraging, favorable, fortunate, happy, hopeful, lucky, opportune, promising, propitious, prosperous, successful. See PROPITIOUS. *Antonyms*: baleful, discouraging, hopeless, inauspicious, unfavorable, unpromising, unpropitious.
Aus·sig (ou′sikh) The German name for USTI NAD LABEM.
Aus·ten (ôs′tən), **Jane,** 1775–1817, English novelist.
aus·ten·ite (ôs′tən·īt) *n. Metall.* A solid solution of carbon in pure iron, used in the making of steel which is non-magnetic at ordi-

nary temperatures. [after Sir W. C. Roberts-*Austen,* 1843–1902, English metallurgist]—**aus'ten·it'ic** (-it'ik) *adj.*

Aus·ter (ôs'tər) *n. Poetic* **1** The south wind. **2** The south. [<L]

aus·tere (ô·stir') *adj.* **1** Severe, grave, or stern, as in aspect, disposition, judgment, or conduct. **2** Morally strict; abstemious; ascetic. **3** Sour and astringent. **4** Severely simple; unadorned. [<OF<L *austerus* <Gk. *austēros* harsh, bitter <*auein* dry] **—aus·tere'ly** *adv.*

Synonyms: hard, harsh, morose, relentless, rigid, rigorous, severe, stern, strict, unrelenting, unyielding. The *austere* person is severely simple or temperate, *strict* in self-restraint or discipline, and similarly *unrelenting* toward others. We speak of *austere* morality, *rigid* rules, *rigorous* discipline, *stern* commands, *severe* punishment, *harsh* speech or a *harsh* voice, *hard* requirements, *strict* injunctions, and *strict* obedience. *Strict* discipline holds one exactly and unflinchingly to the rule; *rigorous* discipline punishes severely any infraction of it.

aus·ter·i·ty (ô·ster'ə·tē) *n. pl.* **·ties** **1** Gravity or rigor in attitude or conduct toward others. **2** Severe self-restraint. **3** Rigid economy in expenditure. **4** *pl.* Austere acts or practices. Also **aus·tere'ness.**

Aus·ter·litz (ôs'tər·lits, *Ger.* ous'tər·lits) A town in Moravia, Czechoslovakia; site of Napoleon's greatest victory, in 1805, over the Russian and Austrian armies.

Aus·tin (ôs'tən) Var. of AUGUSTINE.

Aus·tin (ôs'tən) A city on the Colorado River; the capital of Texas.

Aus·tin (ôs'tən), **Alfred,** 1835–1913, English poet laureate 1896–1913. **—John,** 1790–1859, English jurist. **—Mary Hunter,** 1868–1934, U.S. writer. **—Stephen Fuller,** 1793–1836, U.S. colonizer in Texas. **—Warren Robinson,** 1877–1963, U.S. lawyer and politician.

Austin Friar An Augustinian Hermit.

aus·tral (ôs'trəl, os'-) *adj.* Southern; torrid. [<L *australis* southern <*auster* south wind]

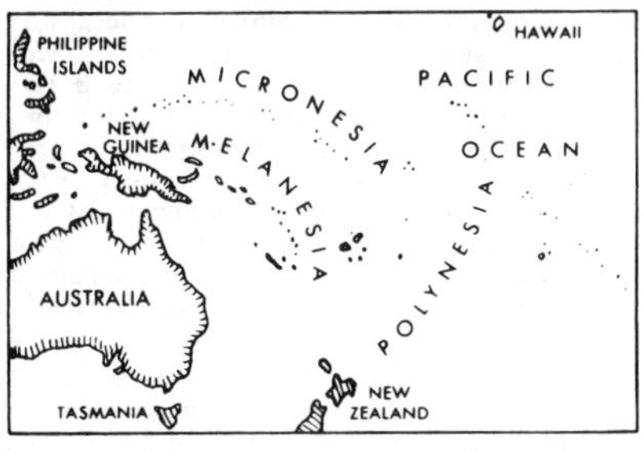

Aus·tral·a·sia (ôs'trəl·ā'zhə, -ā'shə, os'-) The islands of the South Pacific, including Australia, New Zealand, New Guinea, and adjacent islands; sometimes applied to all of Oceania. **—Aus'tral·a'sian** *adj. & n.*

Aus·tral English (ôs'trəl, os'-) Australian English.

Aus·tra·lia (ô·strāl'yə, o-) An island continent SE of Asia, comprising the **Commonwealth of Australia,** a self-governing member of the Commonwealth of Nations, consisting of a union of six states and two territories together with its dependencies; 2,948,366 square miles; capital, Canberra.

Australia Day An Australian holiday, January 26th, commemorating the landing of the British in 1788. Also *Anniversary Day.*

Aus·tra·lian (ô·strāl'yən, o-) *n.* **1** A native or naturalized inhabitant of Australia. **2** One of the Australian aborigines. **3** Any of the aboriginal languages of Australia. *—adj.* Designating a zoogeographical region including Australia, New Guinea and adjacent islands, New Zealand, and Polynesia.

Australian Alps A mountain range in SE New South Wales and eastern Victoria, Australia; highest peak, 7,316 feet.

Australian ballot See under BALLOT.

Australian Capital Territory A region within New South Wales containing Canberra, capital of Australia; 911 square miles: formerly *Federal Territory.*

Australian crawl See under CRAWL.

Australian English The English language as spoken and written in Australia: sometimes called *Austral English.*

Aus·tra·lian·ism (ô·strāl'yən·iz'əm, o-) *n.* **1** A trait, custom, or tradition of Australia or Australians. **2** A word, phrase, or usage characteristic of Australian English. **3** Devotion to Australia, its institutions, etc.

Australian pine Any of several species (genus *Casuarina*) of rapidly growing, dicotyledonous evergreen trees and shrubs having leaves reduced to whorls of pointed scales, native to Australia and established as a nuisance in southern Florida.

Aus·tral Islands (ôs'trəl) See TUBUAI ISLANDS.

Aus·tra·lite (ôs'trə·līt, os'-) *n.* A small, smooth lump of black glass, presumably a meteorite, found in the southern parts of Australia and elsewhere: also called *blackfellow's button.* Compare TEKTITE.

Aus·tra·loid (ôs'trə·loid) *adj.* Pertaining to, designating, or belonging to the ethnic group composed of the aborigines of Australia.

Aus·tra·lo·pi·the·cus (ô·strā'lō·pi·thē'kəs) *n.* A genus of small-brained primates of the Pliocene and early Pleistocene, first identified from a fossil juvenile skull found in 1924 at Taungs, South Africa; subsequent remains confirm its position as a transitional form between ape and man. Also called *Taungs skull.* **—Aus·tra'lo·pi·the'cine** (-thē'sīn, -sin) *adj.* [<NL <L *australis* southern + Gk. *pithēkos* ape]

Aus·tri·a (ôs'trē·ə) A federal republic of central Europe; 32,375 square miles; capital Vienna; German *Österreich.* **—Aus'tri·an** *adj. & n.*

Aus·tri·a-Hun·ga·ry (ôs'trē·ə·hung'gə·rē) A former dual monarchy of central Europe, 1867–1918, comprising the Austrian empire, Hungary, and other crownlands.

Austro- *combining form* **1** Austrian: *Austro-Hungarian.* **2** Australian: *Austro-Malayan.*

Aus·tro-A·si·at·ic (ôs'trō·ā'zhē·at'ik, -ā'shē-) *n.* A family of languages of SE Asia, including the Mon-Khmer and Munda subfamilies. *—adj.* Of or pertaining to this linguistic family.

Aus·tro-Hun·gar·i·an (ôs'trō·hung·gâr'ē·ən) *adj.* Of or pertaining to Austria-Hungary.

Aus·tro-Ma·lay·an (ôs'trō·mə·lā'ən) *adj.* Of or pertaining to the Papuan subregion north of Australia, including islands from San Cristobal to Celebes.

Aus·tro·ne·sia (ôs'trō·nē'zhə, -shə) The islands of Indonesia, Melanesia, Micronesia, and Polynesia.

Aus·tro·ne·sian (ôs'trō·nē'zhən, -shən) *adj.* Of or pertaining to Austronesia, its inhabitants, or their languages. *—n.* A family of languages spoken throughout the Pacific in an area roughly bounded by Madagascar to the west, Easter Island to the east, Formosa to the north, and New Zealand to the south, but excluding Australia, Tasmania, and a large part of New Guinea. The Austronesian family is divided linguistically into three subfamilies: Indonesian or Malayan, Oceanic (including the Melanesian and Micronesian languages), and Polynesian. Also *Malayo-Polynesian.*

aut- Var. of AUTO-[1].

au·ta·coid (ô'tə·koid) *n.* Hormone. [<AUT- + Gk. *akos* remedy + -OID]

au·tar·chy (ô'tär·kē) *n.* **1** Absolute rule or sovereignty or a country under such rule; unrestricted power; autocracy. **2** Self-government. **3** Autarky. [<Gk. *autarchos* absolute ruler <*autos* self + *archein* rule] **—au·tar·chic** (ô·tär'kik) or **·chi·cal** *adj.*

au·tar·ky (ô'tär·kē) *n.* National economic self-sufficiency; a policy of establishing independence of imports from other countries: also *autarchy.* [<Gk. *autarkeia* self-sufficiency <*autos* self + *arkeein* suffice] **—au·tar·ki·cal** (ô·tär'ki·kəl) *adj.*

au·te·col·o·gy (ô'tē·kol'ə·jē) *n.* The ecology of individual organisms: distinguished from *synecology.*

au·teur (ō·tœr') *n.* A film director whose work is the product of personal vision and total production control. [<F, lit., author]

au·then·tic (ô·then'tik) *adj.* **1** According with the facts; authoritative; trustworthy; reliable. **2** Of undisputed origin; genuine. **3** *Law* Duly executed before the proper officer. Also **au·then'ti·cal.** [<OF *autentique* <L *authenticus* <Gk. *authentikos* <*authentēs* the doer of a deed] **—au·then'ti·cal·ly** *adv.*

Synonyms: accepted, accredited, authoritative, authorized, certain, current, genuine, legitimate, original, real, received, sure, true, trustworthy, veritable. *Antonyms*: apocryphal, baseless, counterfeit, disputed, exploded, fabulous, false, fictitious, spurious, unauthorized.

au·then·ti·cate (ô·then'ti·kāt) *v.t.* **·cat·ed, ·cat·ing** **1** To make genuine, credible, or authoritative. **2** To give legal force or validity to. **3** To establish or certify, as a book or painting, to be the work of a certain person. **—au·then'ti·ca'tion** *n.*

au·then·ti·ca·tor (ô·then'ti·kā'tər) *n.* **1** One who or that which authenticates. **2** *Telecom.* A code signal transmitted with a radio message as a proof of genuineness.

au·then·tic·i·ty (ô'thən·tis'ə·tē) *n.* The state or quality of being authentic, authoritative, or genuine. Also **au·then'tic·ness.**

au·thor (ô'thər) *n.* **1** An originator; first cause; creator. **2** The original writer, as of a book; also, one who makes literary compositions his profession. **3** An author's writings collectively. See synonyms under CAUSE. *—v.t. Informal* To be the author of; write. [<OF *autor* <L *auctor* originator, producer <*augere* increase] **— au'thor·ess** *n. fem.* **—au·tho·ri·al** (ô·thôr'ē·əl, ô·thō'rē-) *adj.*

au·thor·i·tar·i·an (ə·thôr'ə·târ'ē·ən, ə·thor'-) *adj.* Encouraging and upholding authority against individual freedom; specifically, relating to a type of government in which the individual and his rights are subordinated to interests of state. *—n.* A defender of the principle of authority or of a type of government organized on an authoritarian basis. **—au·thor'i·tar'i·an·ism** *n.*

au·thor·i·ta·tive (ə·thôr'ə·tā'tiv, ə·thor'-) *adj.* **1** Possessing or proceeding from proper authority; duly sanctioned. **2** Exercising authority; positive; commanding; dictatorial. See synonyms under ABSOLUTE, AUTHENTIC, DOGMATIC, IMPERIOUS. **—au·thor'i·ta'tive·ly** *adv.* **—au·thor'i·ta'tive·ness** *n.*

au·thor·i·ty (ə·thôr'ə·tē, ə·thor'-) *n. pl.* **·ties** **1** The right to command and to enforce obedience; the right to act officially. **2** Personal power that commands influence, respect, or confidence. **3** The person or persons in whom government or command is vested: often in the plural. **4** That which is or may be appealed to in support of action or belief, as an author, volume, etc. **5** An authoritative opinion, decision, or precedent. See synonyms under INFLUENCE, PERMISSION, PRECEDENT. [<F *autorité* <L *auctoritas, -tatis* power, authority <*augere* increase]

au·thor·i·za·tion (ô'thər·ə·zā'shən) *n.* **1** The act of conferring legality. **2** Formal legal power; sanction.

au·thor·ize (ô'thər·īz) *v.t.* **·ized, ·iz·ing** **1** To confer authority upon; empower; commission. **2** To warrant; justify. **3** To sanction; approve. **4** *Obs.* To vouch for. See JUSTIFY. **—au'thor·iz'er** *n.*

au·thor·ized (ô'thər·īzd) *adj.* **1** Endowed with authority; accepted as authoritative. **2** Formally or legally sanctioned.

Authorized Version The King James Bible. See under BIBLE.

au·thor·ship (ô'thər·ship) *n.* **1** The profession or occupation of an author. **2** Origin or source.

au·tism (ô'tiz·əm) *n. Psychol.* A tendency to morbid daydreaming and introspection uninfluenced by objective norms and realities. [<AUT- + -ISM] **—au·tis·tic** (ô·tis'tik) *adj.*

au·to (ô'tō) *U.S. Colloq. n.* An automobile. *—v.i.* To ride in or travel by an automobile.

auto-[1] *combining form* **1** Arising from some process or action within the object; not induced by any stimulus from without; as in:

autoagglutination	**autofecundation**
autocombustible	**autohybridization**
autoelectrolysis	**autoinduction**
autoelectrolytic	**autoinhibitive**
autoexcitation	**autoluminescence**

autoretardation	**autosepticemia**
autorhythmic	**autosymbolic**

2 Acting, acted, or directed upon the self; as in:

autoanalysis	**autoimmunity**
autoanalytic	**autolavage**

Also, before vowels, *aut-*, as in *autism.* [< Gk. *autos* self]

auto-² *combining form* Self-propelled: *auto-boat.* [< *automobile*]

au·to·bahn (ou′tō·bän) *n. pl.* **·bahns** or *German* **·bahn·en** In Germany, a superhighway.

au·to·bi·og·ra·phy (ô′tə·bī·og′rə·fē, -bē·og′-) *n. pl.* **·phies** The story of one's life written by oneself. See synonyms under HISTORY. —**au′to·bi·og′ra·pher** *n.* —**au·to·bi·o·graph·ic** (ô′tə·bī′ə·graf′ik) or **·i·cal** *adj.* —**au′to·bi′o·graph′i·cal·ly** *adv.*

au·to·boat (ô′tō·bōt) *n.* A boat propelled by motor power.

au·to·bus (ô′tō·bus) *n.* An omnibus propelled by motor power.

au·to·ceph·a·li (ô′tō·sef′ə·lī) *n. pl.* In the Greek Church, those churches or bishops rejecting patriarchal jurisdiction and claiming to be self-governing. [< Gk. *autokephalos* < *autos* self + *kephalē* head]

au·to·ceph·a·lous (ô′tō·sef′ə·ləs) *adj.* **1** *Eccl.* Independent of patriarchal or archiepiscopal jurisdiction. **2** Having jurisdiction as an independent head or chief. Also **au·to·ce·phal·ic** (ô′tō·sə·fal′ik).

au·to·chrome (ô′tə·krōm) *n.* A single plate for three-color photography.

au·toch·thon (ô·tok′thən) *n. pl.* **·thons** or **·tho·nes** (-thə·nēz) **1** Originally, one sprung from the earth itself. **2** *pl.* The aboriginal inhabitants. **3** *Ecol.* An indigenous animal or plant. [< Gk. *autochthōn* indigenous < *autos* self + *chthōn* earth, land]

au·toch·thon·ism (ô·tok′thən·iz′əm) *n.* Origin from the soil of a country; origination in or primitive occupation of a region. Also **au·toch·tho·ny** (ô·tok′thə·nē).

au·toch·tho·nous (ô·tok′thə·nəs) *adj.* **1** Sprung from the soil; native to a place; indigenous; aboriginal. **2** *Geol.* Of or pertaining to rocks which, with their constituents, have been formed *in situ,* as rock salt, stalactites, etc. Also **au·toch′tho·nal, au·toch·thon·ic** (ô′·tok·thon′ik). —**au·toch′tho·nous·ly** *adv.*

au·to·clave (ô′tə·klāv) *n.* **1** A strong gastight vessel in which chemical reactions can be effected under pressure. **2** An enclosed chamber for the sterilization of drugs, vaccines, instruments, etc., under specified pressure. **3** A steamtight cooking utensil; a pressure cooker. [< F < *auto-* AUTO-¹ + L *clavis* a key]

au·toc·ra·cy (ô·tok′rə·sē) *n.* **1** Absolute government by an individual; rule or authority of an autocrat. **2** A state ruled by an autocrat. **3** Complete power or dominance over others.

au·to·crat (ô′tə·krat) *n.* **1** A supreme ruler of unrestricted power. **2** One exercising unlimited power over others. **3** An arrogant, dictatorial person. [< F *autocrate* < Gk. *autokratēs* self-ruling, independent < *autos* self + *kratos* power] —**au′to·crat′ic** or **·i·cal** *adj.* —**au′to·crat′i·cal·ly** *adv.*

au·to-da-fé (ô′tō·də·fā′, ou′-) *n. pl.* **au·tos-da-fé** (ô′tōz-, ou′tōz-) The public announcement and execution of the sentence of the Inquisition, with the attendant ceremonies, as the burning of heretics at the stake, etc. Also *Spanish* **au·to de fe** (ou′tō dā fā′). [< Pg., lit., act of the faith]

au·to·de·tec·tor (ô′tō·di·tek′tər) *n. Electr.* An automatic coherer.

au·to·dyne (ô′tə·dīn) *adj. Telecom.* Designating the manner of producing oscillations in a detector tube so as to secure beats. See BEAT, HETERODYNE.

au·toe·cious (ô·tē′shəs) *adj. Bot.* **1** Having male and female reproductive organs on the same plant, as certain mosses. **2** Completing the whole development on a single host, as seen in certain rust fungi and other parasites: opposed to *heteroecious.* [< AUTO-¹ + Gk. *oikos* dwelling]

au·toe·cism (ô·tē′siz·əm) *n.* The condition of being autoecious.

au·to·er·o·tism (ô′tō·er′ə·tiz′əm) *n.* **1** *Psychoanal.* Sexual impulses taking one's own body as their object, without association with or stimulus from another person. **2** Masturbation. Also **au·to·e·rot·i·cism** (ô′tō·i·rot′ə·siz′·əm). [< AUTO-¹ + Gk. *erōs, erotos* love] —**au·to·e·rot·ic** (ô′tō·i·rot′ik) *adj.*

au·tog·a·mous (ô·tog′ə·məs) *adj. Bot.* Self-fertilized; capable of self-fertilization: said of certain flowers.

au·tog·a·my (ô·tog′ə·mē) *n.* **1** *Biol.* Self-fertilization; fecundation of a flower by its own pollen. **2** *Biol.* The union of closely related cells or of nuclei within a cell; karyogamy. [< AUTO-¹ + Gk. *gameein* marry]

au·to·gen·e·sis (ô′tō·jen′ə·sis) *n. Biol.* Spontaneous formation of a tissue or organism.

au·to·ge·net·ic (ô′tō·jə·net′ik) *adj.* **1** Of or pertaining to autogenesis. **2** *Geog.* Of, pertaining to, regulated by, or indicating a self-established system of drainage. —**au′to·ge·net′i·cal·ly** *adv.*

au·tog·e·nous (ô·toj′ə·nəs) *adj.* **1** Self-produced or independent. **2** *Physiol.* Developed within the body, as new tissue or skeletal parts. **3** *Mech.* Designating a process of soldering by means of a hydrogen flame. Also **au·to·gen·ic** (ô′tō·jen′ik). [< Gk. *autogenēs* self-produced]

autogenous vaccine Vaccine made from bacteria obtained from the person to be inoculated.

Au·to·gi·ro (ô′tə·jī′rō) *n. pl.* **·ros** An airplane having horizontal rotary airfoils which act only as a means of lift and support: a trade name. See GYROPLANE. [< AUTO-¹ + Gk. *gyros* a circle]

au·to·graft (ô′tō·graft′, -gräft) *n.* A mass of tissue transplanted from one site to another on the same organism. —*v.t.* To transplant (tissue) in making an autograft.

au·to·graph (ô′tə·graf, -gräf) *n.* **1** One's own handwriting or signature. **2** Something in one's own handwriting; a manuscript in an author's handwriting. —*v.t.* **1** To write one's name in or affix one's signature to. **2** To write in one's own handwriting. —*adj.* Written by one's own hand, as a will. [< L *autographum,* orig. neut. of *autographus* < Gk. *autographos* written with one's own hand < *autos* self + *graphein* write]

au·to·graph·ic (ô′tə·graf′ik) *adj.* **1** Of the nature of or like an autograph. **2** Written in one's own or the author's handwriting. **3** In telegraphy, recording or transmitting in facsimile. Also **au to·graph′i·cal.** —**au′to·graph′·i·cal·ly** *adv.*

au·tog·ra·phy (ô·tog′rə·fē) *n.* **1** The writing of a document in one's own handwriting. **2** Autographs collectively. **3** One's own handwriting. **4** Facsimile reproduction.

au·to·harp (ô′tō·härp) *n.* A musical instrument resembling a zither, but having a piano scale and an arrangement of dampers enabling the player to produce the correct chords easily.

au·to·hyp·no·sis (ô′tō·hip·nō′sis) *n* The state or condition of self-hypnotism.

au·to·im·mune (ô″tō·i·myōōn′) *adj.* Caused by antibodies that operate against the body's own tissues: *autoimmune* diseases. —**au′to·im·mu′ni·ty** *n.*

au·to·in·fec·tion (ô′tō·in·fek′shən) *n. Pathol.* Infection due to agents or toxins generated in the body, as the infection causing peritonitis when perforation of the intestine occurs.

au·to·in·oc·u·la·tion (ô′tō·in·ok′yə·lā′shən) *n.* Inoculation with a virus or other morbid matter already present in one's own body. **2** The spreading of infection from a center to other portions of the same body.

au·to·in·tox·i·ca·tion (ô′tō·in·tok′sə·kā′shən) *n.* Autotoxemia.

au·to·ki·net·ic (ô′tō·ki·net′ik, -kī-) *adj.* Self-moving. [< Gk. *autokinētos* self-moved < *autos* self + *kineein* move]

au·to·load·ing (ô′tō·lō′ding) *adj.* Self-loading: said of firearms.

Au·tol·y·cus (ô·tol′i·kəs) A Greek astronomer and mathematician of the fourth century B.C. —**Autolycus** In Greek mythology, the son of Hermes, famous for his thievery, who could change the form of his plunder or render it invisible.

au·tol·y·sate (ô·tol′ə·sāt) *n.* A substance resulting from the autolysis of organic material.

au·to·ly·sin (ô′tə·lī′sin) *n. Biochem.* A substance which initiates or promotes autolysis.

au·tol·y·sis (ô·tol′ə·sis) *n.* **1** *Biochem.* The disintegration of cells and tissues after death by the action of enzymes already present: distinguished from *heterolysis.* **2** *Physiol.* Self-digestion of organic material. [< NL < AUTO-¹ + Gk. *lysis* dissolution < *lyein* loosen, dissolve] —**au·to·lyt·ic** (ô′tə·lit′ik) *adj.*

au·to·mat (ô′tə·mat) *n.* **1** An automatic device: applied to various articles, as a camera shutter, etc. **2** *U.S.* A restaurant in which food is automatically made available from a receptacle when money is deposited in a slot alongside.

au·to·mat·a·ble (ô′tə·mat′ə·bəl) *adj.* Suitable for or capable of automation: an *automatable* production process.

au·to·mate (ô′tə·māt) *v.* **·mat·ed, ·mat·ing** *v.t.* To adapt, as a machine, factory, or process, for automation. —*v.i.* To install or convert to automation equipment.

au·to·mat·ic (ô′tə·mat′ik) *adj.* **1** Self-moving, self-regulating, or self-acting. **2** Acting mechanically. **3** *Psychol.* Done from force of habit or without volition. **4** *Physiol.* Independent of the will, as a reflex action. **5** *Mech.* Having a self-acting mechanism by which certain operations are performed under predetermined conditions: an *automatic* pilot. Also **au′to·mat′i·cal, au·tom·a·tous** (ô·tom′ə·təs). —*n.* A self-acting machine, device, or weapon. See synonyms under SPONTANEOUS [< Gk. *automatos* acting of oneself. See AUTOMATON.] —**au′to·mat′i·cal·ly** *adv.*

au·tom·a·tic·i·ty (ô·tom′ə·tis′ə·tē) *n.* State or condition of being automatic.

automatic pilot *Aeron.* An automatic-control mechanism operating on the gyroscope principle: designed to keep an aircraft in level flight and on an even course: also called *gyro pilot, robot pilot.*

au·to·ma·tion (ô′tə·mā′shən) *n. Technol.* **1** The automatic transfer of one unit of a complex industrial assembly to a succession of self-acting machines each of which completes a specified stage in the total manufacturing process from crude material to finished product. **2** The application of fully automatic procedures in the efficient performance and control of operations involving a sequence of complex, standardized, or repetitive processes on a large scale. **3** The theory, art, and technique of converting a mechanical process to maximum automatic operation, especially by the use of electronic control mechanisms and electronic computers for the rapid organizing and processing of data in a wide range of technical, industrial, and business information. [< AUTOM(ATIC) + (OPER)ATION]

au·tom·a·tism (ô·tom′ə·tiz′əm) *n.* **1** The state or quality of being automatic; automatic action. **2** *Philos.* The theory that consciousness does not control one's actions but is only a by-product of physiological changes. **3** *Physiol.* The functioning or power of functioning of muscular or other processes in response to external stimuli but independent of conscious control, as winking. **4** *Biol.* Spontaneous activity of cells and tissues, as the beating of a heart freed from its nervous connections. **5** *Psychol.* **a** A condition in which actions are performed without the conscious knowledge or will of the subject. **b** Any such action. **6** Suspension of the conscious mind in order to release for expression the repressed ideas and images of the subconscious, as practiced by surrealist artists and writers. —**au·tom′a·tist** *n.*

au·tom·a·tize (ô·tom′ə·tīz) *v.t.* **·tized, ·tiz·ing** **1** To render automatic. **2** To reduce to an automaton.

au·tom·a·ton (ô·tom′ə·ton, -tən) *n. pl.* **·tons** or **·ta** (-tə) **1** A contrivance or apparatus that appears to function of itself by the action of a concealed mechanism. **2** Any living being whose actions are or appear to be involuntary or mechanical. **3** Anything capable of spontaneous movement or action. [< Gk. *automaton,* neut. of *automatos* acting of oneself, independent]

au·to·mo·bile (ô′tə·mə·bēl′, ô′tə·mə·bēl′, ô′tə·mō′bēl) *n.* A self-propelled vehicle; specifically, one driven by an internal-combustion engine or storage battery and independent of rails or tracks; a motorcar. —*v.i.* **·biled, bil·ing** To ride in or drive an automobile. —*adj.* (ô′tə·mō′bil) **1** Self-propelling. **2** Of or for automobiles. [< F]

au·to·mo·bil·ism (ô′tə·mə·bēl′iz·əm, -mō′bil·iz′əm) *n.* The practice of using motorcars; also, the acts and methods of those who use them. —**au·to·mo·bil·ist** (ô′tə·mə·bēl′ist, -mō′·bil·ist) *n.*

au·to·mo·tive (ô′tə·mō′tiv) *adj.* 1 Self-propelling. 2 Of or for automobiles: *automotive* parts.

au·to·nom·ic (ô′tə·nom′ik) *adj.* 1 Autonomous. 2 *Biol.* Spontaneous: said of functions in plants and animals produced by inherent conditions. Also **au′to·nom′i·cal.** —**au′to·nom′i·cal·ly** *adv.*

autonomic nervous system A plexus of nerve ganglia and fibers originating in the spinal column and acting to innervate and control the efferent functions of all body tissues and organs not subject to voluntary control, as the heart, blood vessels, smooth muscle, glands, stomach, and intestines.

au·ton·o·mous (ô·ton′ə·məs) *adj.* 1 Independent; self-governing. 2 Of or pertaining to an autonomy. 3 *Biol.* Independent of any other organism. 4 *Bot.* Autonomic. [<Gk. *autonomos* independent < *autos* self + *nomos* law, rule] —**au·ton′o·mous·ly** *adv.*

au·ton·o·my (ô·ton′ə·mē) *n. pl.* **·mies** 1 The condition or quality of being autonomous; especially the power or right of self-government. 2 A self-governing community or local group in a particular sphere, as in religion, education, etc. 3 Self-determination, as of the will. [<Gk. *autonomia* independence <*autonomos.* See AUTONOMOUS.] —**au·ton′o·mist** *n.*

au·to·pho·bi·a (ô′tə·fō′bē·ə) *n.* Morbid fear of oneself or of being alone: also called *eremophobia, monophobia.* —**au·to·pho·bic** (ô′tə·fō′bik, -fob′ik) *adj.*

au·to·plas·ty (ô′tə·plas′tē) *n. Surg.* The operation of repairing wounds or diseased parts by means of living tissue from other parts of the same body. —**au′to·plas′tic** *adj.*

au·top·sy (ô′top·sē, ô′təp-) *n. pl.* **·sies** 1 Postmortem examination of a human body, especially to determine the cause of death for medical or legal purposes. Compare BIOPSY.] 2 The act of seeing with one's own eyes. [<NL *autopsia* <Gk. *autopsia* a seeing for oneself < *autos* self + *opsis* a seeing]

au·top·tic (ô·top′tik) *adj.* 1 Seen with one's own eyes. 2 Of or as of an eyewitness. Also **au·top′ti·cal.**

au·to·ra·di·o·graph (ô′tō·rā′dē·ə·graf′, -gräf′) *n. Med.* A photograph taken by autoradiography: also called *radioautograph, radioautogram.*

au·to·ra·di·og·ra·phy (ô′tō·rā′dē·og′rə·fē) *n. Med.* Radiography which utilizes the emanations of radioactive elements or isotopes incorporated for the purpose of study and analysis in test material, as of a tissue: also called *radioautography.*

au·to·some (ô′tə·sōm) *n. Biol.* Any chromosome other than those which determine the sex of an organism. [<AUTO-[1] + (CHROMO)SOME] —**au′to·so′mal** *adj.*

au·to·sta·bil·i·ty (ô′tō·stə·bil′ə·tē) *n.* Stability owing to innate qualities, or to automatic machinery.

au·to·sug·gest·i·bil·i·ty (ô′tō·səg·jes′tə·bil′ə·tē) *n.* 1 The state or quality of being autosuggestive. 2 Ability to hypnotize oneself.

au·to·sug·ges·tion (ô′tō·səg·jes′chən) *n. Psychol.* Suggestion, particularly with a view to producing a condition of autohypnosis, emanating from self only. —**au′to·sug·ges′tive** *adj.*

au·tot·o·my (ô·tot′ə·mē) *n. Zool.* The spontaneous shedding of a part of an organism from the whole, as in starfish, salamanders, and crabs. [<AUTO-[1] + Gk. *tomē* a cutting < *temnein* cut]

au·to·tox·e·mi·a (ô′tō·tok·sē′mē·ə) *n.* The poisoning of self from noxious secretions of one's own body; autointoxication. Also **au′to·tox·ae′mi·a, au·to·tox·i·co·sis** (ô′tō·tok′si·kō′sis).

au·to·tox·in (ô′tō·tok′sin) *n.* Any toxin produced by changes of tissue within an organism.

au·to·tox·is (ô′tō·tok′sis) *n.* Autotoxemia. Also **au·to·tox·i·ca·tion** (ô′tō·tok′si·kā′shən). —**au′·to·tox′ic** *adj.*

au·to·trans·form·er (ô′tō·trans·fôr′mər) *n. Electr.* An automatic compensator used with alternating-current motors, in which the motor is fed from different points in an impedance coil placed across the supply circuits; a compensator.

au·to·troph·ic (ô′tə·trof′ik) *adj. Bot.* Self-nourishing: said of green plants that make their own food by photosynthesis, and of bacteria which can grow without organic carbon and nitrogen. [<AUTO-[1] + Gk. *trophē* food < *trephein* nourish]

au·tot·ro·pism (ô·tot′rə·piz′əm) *n. Bot.* The tendency of the organs of a plant, uninfluenced from without, to grow in straight lines. [<AUTO-[1] + Gk. *tropē* a turning < *trepein* turn] —**au·to·trop·ic** (ô′tə·trop′ik) *adj.*

au·to·truck (ô′tō·truk) *n.* A motor-propelled truck.

au·to·type (ô′tə·tīp) *n.* 1 A photographic process by which pictures are produced in monochrome in a carbon pigment. 2 The print so produced. 3 A facsimile. —**au·to·typ·ic** (ô′tə·tip′ik) *adj.*

au·to·ty·pog·ra·phy (ô′tō·tī·pog′rə·fē) *n.* The art or process of drawing on gelatin, with a special ink, relief designs which are then transferred by pressure to soft metal plates from which copies may be printed.

au·to·ty·py (ô′tə·tī′pē) *n.* Reproduction by the autotype process.

au·tox·i·da·tion (ô·tok′sə·dā′shən) *n. Chem.* 1 Oxidation of a substance or compound on exposure to air. 2 Oxidation occurring only in the presence of a second substance which serves to complete the reaction.

au·tres temps, au·tres moeurs (ō′tr′ täṅ′ ō′tr′ mœrs′) *French* Other times, other customs.

au·tumn (ô′təm) *n.* 1 The third season of the year; in the northern hemisphere, September, October and November: often called *fall.* 2 A time of maturity and incipient decline. —*adj.* Autumnal. [Earlier *autumpne* <OF *autompne* <L *autumnus*; ult. origin uncertain]

au·tum·nal (ô·tum′nəl) *adj.* 1 Of, pertaining to, or like autumn; ripening or harvested in autumn. 2 Past maturity; denoting a later period of life; declining. —**au·tum′nal·ly** *adv.*

autumnal equinox See under EQUINOX.

au·tun·ite (ô′tən·īt) *n. Mineral.* A pearly, light-yellow, hydrous calcium-uranium phosphate, crystallizing in the orthorhombic system. [from *Autun,* a city in France]

Au·vergne (ō·vârn′, ō·vûrn′; *Fr.* ō·vern′y′) A region and former province of south central France.

Auvergne Mountains A range in south central France; highest peak, 6,188 feet.

aux (ō; *before vowel sounds* ōz) *French* To the; at the; according to: used before plurals.

aux·a·nom·e·ter (ôk′sə·nom′ə·tər) *n. Bot.* An instrument for measuring the growth of plants. [<Gk. *auxanein* increase, grow + -METER]

aux armes! (ō zärm′) *French* To arms!

Aux Cayes (ō kā′) See LES CAYES.

Aux·erre (ō·sâr′) A city of north central France.

aux·il·ia·ry (ôg·zil′yər·ē, -zil′ər-) *adj.* 1 Giving or furnishing aid. 2 Subsidiary; accessory. —*n. pl.* **·ries** 1 One who or that which aids or helps; assistant; associate. 2 *Gram.* **a** A verb that helps to express the tense, mood, voice, or aspect of another verb, as *have* in "We *have* gone," *may* in "I *may* leave tomorrow": also called *helping verb.* Also **auxiliary verb. b** A word which functions as a subordinate element in a sentence and is fully meaningful only in association with the main words, as a preposition or conjunction. 3 *pl.* Foreign troops associated with those of a nation at war. 4 An auxiliary vessel. [<L *auxiliarius* < *auxilium* a help < *augere* increase]

Synonyms (noun): accessory, aid, ally, assistant, coadjutor, confederate, helper, mercenary, promoter, subordinate. *Allies* unite as equals; *auxiliaries,* in military usage, are troops of one nation uniting with the armies, and acting under the orders, of another. *Mercenaries* serve only for pay; *auxiliaries* often for reasons of state, policy, or patriotism as well. Compare ACCESSORY, APPENDAGE. *Antonyms*: antagonist, hinderer, opponent.

auxiliary vessel, ship, etc. 1 *Naut.* A vessel, yacht, etc., equipped with an engine and propeller as auxiliaries to its sails as motive power. 2 A naval vessel not designed for or assigned to combat service, as a transport, hospital ship, tug, etc.

aux·i·mone (ôk′si·mōn) *n. Biochem.* One of several plant foods, analogous to vitamins, minute quantities of which are sufficient for plant nutrition. [<Gk. *auximos* assisting growth]

aux·in (ôk′sin) *n. Bot.* Any of a group of plant hormones which in minute quantities act to promote or modify the growth of plants, as in root and bud formation, stem curvature, and leaf drop. [<Gk. *auxein* increase + -IN]

aux·o·chrome (ôk′sə·krōm) *n. Chem.* Any of certain radicals which will convert a chromophore into an acidic or basic dye suitable for use in textile fabrics. [<Gk. *auxein* increase + -CHROME]

aux·o·spore (ôk′sə·spôr, -spōr) *n.* A comparatively large cell in diatoms. [<Gk. *auxein* increase + *sporos* seed]

a·va (ə·vä′) *adv. Scot.* At all; of all.

a·vail (ə·vāl′) *n.* 1 Utility for a purpose; benefit; good. 2 *pl.* Proceeds. See synonyms under PROFIT, UTILITY. —*v.t.* To assist or aid; profit. —*v.i.* To be of value or advantage; suffice. —**to avail oneself of** To take advantage of; utilize. [<OF *a-* to (<L *ad-*) + *valoir* <L *valere* be strong] —**a·vail′ing** *adj.* —**a·vail′ing·ly** *adv.*

a·vail·a·ble (ə·vā′lə·bəl) *adj.* 1 Capable of being used advantageously; usable; profitable; at one's disposal, as funds. 2 Of adequate power for a result; effectual; valid. —**a·vail′a·bil′i·ty, a·vail′a·ble·ness** *n.* —**a·vail′·a·bly** *adv.*

av·a·lanche (av′ə·lanch, -länch) *n.* 1 The fall of a mass of snow or ice down a mountain slope. 2 The mass so falling. 3 Something like an avalanche, as in power, destructiveness, etc. —*v.i.* To fall or slide like an avalanche. —*v.t.* To fall or come down upon like an avalanche. [<F <dial. F (Swiss) *lavenche* (of uncertain origin); infl. by OF *avaler* descend < *a val* to the valley <L *ad vallem*]

Av·a·lon (av′ə·lon) In Arthurian legend, the island tomb of King Arthur: generally identified with Glastonbury.

Av·a·lon Peninsula (av′ə·lon) The SE part of Newfoundland, connected with the mainland by an isthmus four miles wide; 4,000 square miles.

a·vant (ə·vänt′, *Fr.* à·väṅ′) Before; forward: the first element in some compounds from the French. [<F *avant* before <LL *abante* <L *ab* from, + *ante* before]

a·vant-cou·ri·er (ə·vänt′ko͝or′ē·ər) *n.* 1 One who is sent to give notice of the approach of another; a herald. Also *French* **a·vant-cou·reur** (à·väṅ′ko͞o·rœr′). 2 *pl.* The scouts or advance guard of an army.

a·vant-garde (à·väṅ·gàrd′) *n.* Vanguard: applied to the group of those who support or further the most recent trends or ideas in a movement. —*adj.* Of or pertaining to this group. [<F, lit., advance guard]

A·va·rau (ä′vä·rou′) See PALMERSTON.

av·a·rice (av′ə·ris) *n.* Passion for riches; covetousness; greed. [<OF <L *avaritia* < *avarus* greedy < *avere* desire, crave]

av·a·ri·cious (av′ə·rish′əs) *adj.* Greedy of gain; grasping; miserly. —**av′a·ri′cious·ly** *adv.* —**av′a·ri′cious·ness** *n.*

Synonyms: close, covetous, greedy, miserly, niggardly, parsimonious, penurious, rapacious, sordid, stingy. The *avaricious* man desires both to get and to keep, the *covetous* man to get something away from its possessor; *miserly* and *niggardly* persons seek to gain by mean and petty savings; the *miserly* by stinting themselves, the *niggardly* by stinting others. *Parsimonious* and *penurious* may apply to one's outlay either for himself or for others; in the latter use, they are somewhat less harsh and reproachful terms than *niggardly. Greedy* and *stingy* are used not only of money, but often of other things, as food, etc. The *greedy* child tries to get everything for himself; the *stingy* child, to keep others from getting what he has. *Antonyms*: bountiful, free, generous, liberal, munificent, prodigal, wasteful.

a·vast (ə·vast′, ə·väst′) *interj. Naut.* Stop! hold! cease! [<Du. *hou′ vast, houd vast* hold fast]

av·a·tar (av′ə·tär′) *n.* In Hindu mythology, the incarnation of a god. 2 Any concrete manifestation. [<Skt. *avatāra* descent]

a·vaunt (ə·vônt′, ə·vänt′) *interj. Archaic* Begone! away! [<OF *avant* forward <LL *abante* <*ab* from + *ante* before]

a·ve (ā′vē, ä′vā) *interj.* 1 Hail! 2 Farewell! —*n.* The salutation *ave.* [<L, hail or farewell]

A·ve (ā′vē, ä′vā) *n.* 1 A prayer of invocation to the Virgin Mary: also called *Ave Maria.* 2 The time when the Ave Maria is to be said, marked by the ringing of the Ave bell. Compare ANGELUS. 3 The small beads on a rosary, used to number the Aves repeated.

a·vec plai·sir (à·vek′ plā·zēr′) *French* With pleasure.

A·vel·la·ne·da (ä′vā·yä·nā′thä) A city in Argentina, a suburb of Buenos Aires.

A·ve Ma·ri·a (ä′vā mə·rē′ə, ä′vē) A Catholic prayer to the Virgin Mary, consisting of Biblical salutations (*Luke* i 28, 42) and a plea for her intercession. Also **A·ve Mar·y** (ā′vē mâr′ē). [<L, Hail Mary]

av·e·na·ceous (av′ə·nā′shəs) *adj.* Of, pertaining to, or resembling oats or kindred grasses. [<L *avenaceus* <*avena* oats]

a·venge (ə·venj′) *v.t.* **a·venged, a·veng·ing** 1 To take vengeance or exact exemplary punishment for, as in behalf of a person or persons. 2 To inflict revenge upon, as for an act or insult. —*v.i.* 3 To take vengeance. [<OF *avengier* <*a-* to (<L *ad-*) + *vengier* punish <L *vindicare* avenge] — **a·veng′er** *n.* —**a·veng′ing** *adj.* —**a·veng′ing·ly** *adv.*

Synonyms: punish, retaliate, revenge, vindicate, visit. To *avenge* is to *visit* some offense with fitting punishment; to *revenge* is to inflict harm or suffering upon another through personal anger and resentment. See REVENGE. *Antonyms*: see synonyms for PARDON.

av·ens (av′inz) 1 Any plant of the genus *Geum,* of the rose family, as *G. urbanum,* the yellow avens, or *G. rivale,* the purple avens. 2 A similar plant of some other genus, as the mountain avens. [<OF *avence;* of unknown origin]

Av·en·tine (av′ən·tīn, -tin) The Aventine Hill, one of the seven on which Rome was built. *Latin* **Mons Av·en·ti·nus** (monz av′ən·tī′nəs).

a·ven·tu·rine (ə·ven′chər·in) *n.* 1 An opaque, brown glass, flecked with fine metal particles. 2 A variety of quartz or feldspar containing shining particles, usually of mica or hematite: also called *sunstone.* Also **a·ven′tu·rin.** [<F <Ital. *avventurina* <*avventura* chance; def. 1 so called from its accidental discovery]

av·e·nue (av′ə·nyōō, -nōō) *n.* 1 A broad thoroughfare. 2 A way of approach, as to a building, bordered with trees or statues. 3 A mode of access. See synonyms under WAY. [<F *avenue,* orig. fem. pp. of *avenir* approach <L *advenire* <*ad-* toward + *venire* come]

a·ver (ə·vûr′) *v.t.* **a·verred, a·ver·ring** 1 To declare confidently as fact; affirm. 2 *Law* To assert formally; prove or justify (a plea). See synonyms under AFFIRM, ALLEGE, ASSERT, AVOW. [<OF *averer* confirm <L *ad-* to + *verus* true] — **a·ver′ment** *n.* —**a·ver′ra·ble** *adj.*

av·er·age (av′rij, av′ər·ij) *n.* 1 *Math.* **a** The quotient of any sum divided by the number of its terms; the arithmetic mean. **b** A number representing an array of values of which it is a function. 2 The ordinary rank, degree, or amount; general type. 3 In marine law: **a** The loss arising by damage to a ship or cargo. **b** The proportion of such loss falling to a single person in an equitable distribution among those interested. — *adj.* 1 Obtained by calculating the mean of several. 2 Medium; ordinary. —*v.* **·aged, ·ag·ing** *v.t.* 1 To fix or calculate as the mean. 2 To amount to or obtain an average of: He *averages* three dollars profit every hour. 3 To apportion on the average. —*v.i.* 4 To be or amount to an average. [<F *avarie* damage to a ship or its cargo (see *n.* def. 3) <Ital. *avaria;* ult. origin uncertain] — **av′er·age·ly** *adv.*

A·ver·no (ä·ver′nō) A crater lake 10 miles west of Naples, southern Italy; anciently regarded as the entrance to Hades. Ancient **A·ver·nus** (ə·vûr′nəs). [<L *Avernus* <Gk. *aornos* <*a-* without + *ornis* bird; so called because the volcanic vapors from the lake were said to kill birds that flew overhead] —**A·ver·ni·an** (ə·vûr′nē·ən), **A·ver·nal** (ə·vûr′·nəl) *adj.*

A·ver·rho·es (ə·ver′ō·ēz), 1126–98, Arab philosopher, born in Córdoba, Spain. Also **A·ver′ro·es.**

Av·er·rho·ism (av′ə·rō′iz·əm) *n.* The doctrines of Averrhoes and his disciples, chiefly consisting of a form of pantheism based on an interpretation of Aristotle. Also **Av′er·ro′ism.** —**Av′er·rho′ist** *n.* —**Av′er·rho·is′tic** *adj.*

a·verse (ə·vûrs′) *adj.* 1 Opposed; unfavorable; reluctant: with *to.* 2 *Bot.* Turned away from the main axis: opposed to *adverse.* See synonyms under INIMICAL. [<L *aversus,* pp. of *avertere* turn aside. See AVERT] —**a·verse′ly** *adv.* — **a·verse′ness** *n.*

a·ver·sion (ə·vûr′zhən, -shən) *n.* 1 Extreme dislike; opposition; antipathy. 2 That to which one is averse. See synonyms under ABOMINATION, ANTIPATHY, HATRED.

a·vert (ə·vûrt′) *v.t.* 1 To turn or direct away or aside from, as one's regard. 2 To prevent or ward off, as a danger. See synonyms under AVOID. [<OF *avertir* <L *avertere* turn aside <*ab-* away + *vertere* turn] —**a·vert′ed·ly** *adv.* — **a·vert′i·ble, a·vert′a·ble** *adj.*

A·ves (ā′vēz) *n. pl.* A class of the vertebrates which comprises the birds. See BIRD. [<L, pl. of *avis* bird]

A·ves·ta (ə·ves′tə) *n.* The sacred writings of Zoroastrianism. See ZEND-AVESTA.

A·ves·tan (ə·ves′tən) *n.* The ancient, Iranian language in which the Avesta was written. —*adj.* Of the Avesta or its language.

a·vi·an (ā′vē·ən) *adj.* Pertaining to birds. Also **a·vic·u·lar** (ə·vik′yə·lər). —*n.* A bird. [<L *avis* bird]

a·vi·ar·y (ā′vē·er′ē) *n. pl.* **·ar·ies** An enclosure or large cage for live birds. [<L *aviarium* <*avis* bird] —**a·vi·ar·ist** (ā′vē·er′ist, -ər·ist) *n.*

a·vi·ate (ā′vē·āt, av′ē-) *v.i.* **·at·ed, ·at·ing** To operate an aircraft. [Back formation <AVIATION]

a·vi·a·tion (ā′vē·ā′shən, av′ē-) *n.* 1 The act, science, or art of flying heavier-than-air aircraft. 2 The aircraft flown. [<F <L *avis* bird]

aviation medicine A branch of medicine that deals with the diagnosis, prevention, treatment, and cure of disorders caused by or associated with the conditions encountered in aviation; aeromedicine.

a·vi·a·tor (ā′vē·ā′tər, av′ē-) *n.* One who flies airplanes and other heavier-than-air aircraft; a pilot. —**a′vi·a′tress** (-tris) or **a·vi·a·trix** (ā′vē·ā′triks, av′ē-) *n. fem.*

Av·i·cen·na (av′ə·sen′ə), 980–1037, Arab physician and philosopher. Arabic **ibn-Sina** (ib′·ən·sē′nä).

a·vic·u·lar·i·um (ə·vik′yə·lâr′ē·əm) *n. pl.* **·lar·i·a** (-lâr′ē·ə) *Zool.* A prehensile, beaklike organ found in many polyzoans. [<NL <L *avicula,* dim. of *avis* bird]

a·vi·cul·ture (ā′vi·kul′chər, av′i-) *n.* The rearing of birds. [<L *avis* bird + CULTURE]

av·id (av′id) *adj.* Very desirous; eager; greedy. [<L *avidus* <*avere* crave] —**av′id·ly** *adv.*

av·i·din (av′ə·din) *n. Biochem.* A protein found in egg white which inhibits the action of biotin. [<AVID(ITY) + -IN; so called from its affinity for biotin]

a·vid·i·ty (ə·vid′ə·tē) *n.* 1 Extreme eagerness; greediness. 2 *Chem.* Affinity.

a·vi·fau·na (ā′və·fô′nə) *n. Ecol.* The birds of a given region: also called *ornis.* [<L *avis* bird + FAUNA] —**a′vi·fau′nal** *adj.*

av·i·ga·tion (av′ə·gā′shən) *n.* The handling and guidance of aircraft in the air. [<AVI(ATION) + (NAVI)GATION]

A·vi·gnon (à·vē·nyôṅ′) A city in SE France on the Rhone; papal seat, 1309–77.

a·vion (à·vyôṅ′) *n. French* An airplane.

a·vi·on·ics (ā′vē·on′iks, av′ē-) *n.* The study of the applications of electricity and electronics to aviation. [<AVI(ATION ELECTR)ONICS] —**a′·vi·on′ic** *adj.*

a·vi·so (ə·vī′zo) *n. pl.* **·sos** 1 Advice; information. 2 A dispatch boat. [<Sp., information, advice]

a·vi·ta·min·o·sis (ā·vī′tə·min·ō′sis) *n. Pathol.* A condition caused by vitamin deficiency. [<A-[4] without + VITAMIN + -OSIS]

Av·lo·na (äv·lō′nä) A former name for VALONA.

av·o·ca·do (av′ə·kä′dō, ä′və-) *n. pl.* **·dos** 1 A tropical American evergreen tree *(Persea americana)* having leathery leaves and bearing large pear-shaped drupes with a dark leathery rind and bland, buttery flesh. 2 The edible fruit for which this tree is commercially cultivated. Also called *alligator pear.* [<Sp., alter. of AGUACATE <Nahuatl *ahuacatl*]

av·o·ca·tion (av′ə·kā′shən) *n.* 1 A casual or transient occupation; diversion; hobby. 2 One's business or vocation: now rarely used, to avoid confusion with def. 1. 3 *Obs.* A calling away; withdrawal. See synonyms under HOBBY. [<L *avocatio, -onis* a calling away, diversion <*ab-* away + *vocare* call]

a·voc·a·to·ry (ə·vok′ə·tôr′ē, -tō′rē) *adj.* Recalling; calling away or back: Letters *avocatory* are used by a sovereign to recall his citizens from a state with which he is at war.

av·o·cet (av′ə·set) *n.* A long-legged shore bird (genus *Recurvirostra*) having webbed feet and slender up-curved bill. Also **av′o·set.** [<F *avocette* <Ital. *avocetta*]

A·vo·ga·dro (ä′vō·gä′drō), **Amedeo,** 1776–1856, Conte di Quaregna, Italian physicist.

Avogadro number The actual number of molecules in one gram-molecule or the actual number of atoms in one gram-atom of an element or any pure substance. This number is 6.023×10^{23}. Also **Avogadro's constant.**

Avogadro's hypothesis or **rule** The rule that equal volumes of all gases, at the same temperature and pressure, contain the same number of molecules.

a·void (ə·void′) *v.t.* 1 To keep away or at a distance from; shun; evade, as an unpleasant duty. 2 *Law* To make void. 3 *Obs.* To void; empty. See synonyms under ESCAPE. [<AF *avoider,* OF *esvuidier* empty <*es-* out (<L *ex-*) + *vuidier* <L *viduare* empty, deprive] —**a·void′a·ble** *adj.* — **a·void′a·bly** *adv.* —**a·void′er** *n.*

a·void·ance (ə·void′ns) *n.* 1 The act of avoiding. 2 *Law* Annulment; a making void.

av·oir·du·pois (av′ər·də·poiz′) *n.* 1 The ordinary system of weights of the United States and Great Britain in which 16 ounces avoirdupois make a pound. See under WEIGHT. 2 *Colloq.* Weight; corpulence: a facetious use. [<OF *avoir de pois* goods of (i.e., sold by) weight <L *habere* have + *de* of + *pensum* weight]

A·von (ā′vən, av′ən) 1 A river in England, flowing SE 96 miles from Northampton past Stratford to the Severn at Tewksbury. 2 Any of several other rivers in England, Scotland, and Wales.

à vo·tre san·té (à vô′tr′ säṅ·tā′) *French* To your health.

a·vouch (ə·vouch′) *v.t.* 1 To vouch for; guarantee. 2 To affirm positively; proclaim. 3 To acknowledge; avow. See synonyms under ASSERT, AVOW. [<OF *avochier* affirm <L *advocare* call to one's aid, summon <*ad-* to + *vocare* call]

a·vow (ə·vou′) *v.t.* To declare openly, as facts; own or confess frankly; acknowledge: to *avow* oneself a conspirator. [<OF *avouer* <L *advocare* summon (<*ad-* to + *vocare* call) or LL *advotare* bind by oath <*ad-* to + *votare* freq. of *vovere* vow] —**a·vow′a·ble** *adj.* —**a·vow′·a·ble·ness** *n.* —**a·vow′a·bly** *adv.* —**a·vow′er** *n.*

Synonyms: acknowledge, admit, aver, avouch, confess, declare, own, proclaim, profess, protest, testify, witness. To *avow* is to declare boldly and openly, commonly as something one is ready to justify, maintain, or defend against challenge or opposition. A man *acknowledges* another's claim or his own promise; he *admits* an opponent's advantage or his own error; he *declares* either what he has seen or experienced or what he has received from another; he *avers* what he is sure of from his own knowledge or consciousness; he *avows* openly a belief or intention that he has silently held. Compare ACKNOWLEDGE, AFFIRM, ALLEGE, ASSERT, CONFESS, STATE. *Antonyms*: contradict, deny, disavow, disclaim, disown, ignore, repudiate.

a·vow·al (ə·vou′əl) *n.* Open declaration; frank admission or acknowledgment. See synonyms under BELIEF.

a·vowed (ə·voud′) *adj.* Openly acknowledged; plainly declared. See synonyms under OSTENSIBLE. —**a·vow·ed·ly** (ə·vou′id·lē) *adj.* —**a·vow′ed·ness** *n.*

a·vow·ry (ə·vou′rē) *n. pl.* **·ries** *Law* The acknowledgment and justification of the taking of the goods by the defendant in an action of replevin. [<OF *avouerie* <*avouer.* See AVOW.]

A·vranches (à·vräñsh′) A town in Normandy, France, on the Gulf of Saint-Malo; site of a decisive Allied victory of World War II in 1944.

a·vulse (ə·vuls′) *v.t.* To remove forcibly; tear away. [<L *avulsus,* pp. of *aveller* < *ab-* away + *vellere* pull]

a·vul·sion (ə·vul′shən) *n.* **1** A pulling off or tearing away; forcible separation. **2** That which is torn away. **3** *Law* A sudden removal of the soil from the estate of one and its deposit upon or adjunction to the land of another by the violent action of water. The land thus torn away continues to be vested in the original owner. [<L *avulsio, -onis* < *avellere.* See AVULSE.]

a·vun·cu·lar (ə·vung′kyə·lər) *adj.* Of or pertaining to an uncle. [<L *avunculus* maternal uncle, dim. of *avus* grandfather]

a·vun·cu·late (ə·vung′kyə·lit, -lāt) *n. Anthropol.* A form of social relationship characteristic of certain clan societies, in which a close bond exists between male children and their maternal uncles. Compare AMITATE.

a·wa (ə·wô′, ə·wä′) *adv. Scot.* Away.

a·wait (ə·wāt′) *v.t.* **1** To wait for; expect. **2** To be ready or in store for. See synonyms under ABIDE. [<OF *awaitier* watch for < *a-* to (<L *ad-*) + *waitier* watch <OHG *wahtēn* watch]

A·wa·ji (ä·wä·jē) A minor Japanese island between Harima Sea and Osaka Bay, and between Honshu and Shikoku islands; 228 square miles.

a·wake (ə·wāk′) *adj.* Not asleep; alert; vigilant. — *v.* **a·woke** or **a·waked** (ə·wākt′), **a·waked** or **a·woke, a·wak·ing** *v.t.* **1** To arouse from sleep. **2** To stir up; excite. — *v.i.* **3** To cease to sleep; become awake. **4** To become alert or aroused. See note under WAKE[1]. [OE *onwæcnan* rise from sleep < *on-* A-[1] + *wæcnan* rise and *āwacian* arise < *ā-* A-[2] + *wacian* watch]

a·wak·en (ə·wā′kən) *v.t.* & *v.i.* To awake. See note under WAKE[1]. See synonyms under STIR. [OE *onwæcnan* arise < *on-* A[1] + *wæcnan* rise] — **a·wak′en·er** *n.*

a·wak·en·ing (ə·wā′kən·ing) *adj.* Stirring; exciting. — *n.* **1** The act of waking. **2** An arousing of attention or interest; revival.

a·ward (ə·wôrd′) *v.t.* **1** To adjudge as due, as by legal decisions. **2** To bestow as the result of a contest or examination, as a prize. See synonyms under ALLOT. — *n.* **1** A decision, as by a judge, umpire, or arbitrator. **2** The document containing it. **3** That which is awarded. **4** A badge, medal, citation, or the like, given for meritorious service, as to a soldier. [<AF *awarder,* OF *esguarder* observe, examine < *es-* out (<L *ex-*) + *guarder* watch <Gmc.] — **a·ward′a·ble** *adj.* — **a·ward′er** *n.*

a·ware (ə·wâr′) *adj.* Possessing knowledge (of some fact or action); conscious; cognizant. See synonyms under CONSCIOUS, SURE. [OE *gewær* watchful] — **a·ware′ness** *n.*

a·wash (ə·wosh′, ə·wôsh′) *adv.* & *adj.* **1** Level with or just above the surface of the water. **2** Tossed or washed about by waves. **3** Covered or overflowed with water.

A·wash (ä′wäsh) A river in eastern Ethiopia, flowing 500 miles NE to Lake Abbé: formerly *Hawash.*

a·way (ə·wā′) *adv.* **1** From a given place; off. **2** Far; at or to a distance. **3** In another direction; aside. **4** Out of existence; at an end. **5** On and on continuously: to peg *away* at a task. **6** From one's keeping, attention, or possession. **7** At once, without hesitation: Fire *away!* — **to do** (or **make**) **away with** **1** To get rid of. **2** To kill. — *adj.* **1** Absent. **2** At a distance. — *interj.* Begone! [OE *on weg* on (one's) way]

awe[1] (ô) *v.t.* **awed, aw·ing** or **awe·ing** To impress with reverential fear. — *n.* **1** Reverential fear; dread mingled with veneration. **2** *Obs.* Overawing influence. **3** *Obs.* Dread; terror. See synonyms under AMAZEMENT, FEAR, REVERENCE, VENERATION. [<ON *agi* fear]

awe[2] (ô) *v.t. Scot.* To owe.

a·wea·ry (ə·wir′ē) *adj.* Wearied; weary.

a·weath·er (ə·weth′ər) *adv.* & *adj. Naut.* At, to, or toward the windward side.

a·wee (ə·wē′) *adv. Scot.* Awhile.

a·weel (ə·wēl′) *interj.* & *adv. Scot.* Well; well then!

a·weigh (ə·wā′) *adv. Naut.* Hanging with the flukes just clear of the bottom so that the vessel is free to move: said of an anchor.

awe·less (ô′lis) *adj.* Without fear; fearless. Also **aw′less.**

awe·some (ô′səm) *adj.* **1** Inspiring awe. **2** Characterized by or expressing awe; reverential. — **awe′some·ly** *adv.* — **awe′some·ness** *n.*

aw·ful (ô′fəl) *adj.* **1** Inspiring or suited to inspire awe; majestically or solemnly impressive. **2** Inspiring fear; terrible; dreadful. **3** *Colloq.* Exceedingly bad, monotonous, or unpleasant; ugly. **4** *Colloq.* Exceedingly great. **5** Filled with awe; reverential. Also *Scot.* **aw·fu′** (ô′fōō). — **aw′ful·ness** *n.*

Synonyms: alarming, appalling, august, dire, direful, dread, dreadful, fearful, frightful, grand, horrible, imposing, majestic, noble, portentous, shocking, solemn, stately, terrible, terrific. In careful speech *awful* should not be used of things which are merely disagreeable or annoying, nor of all that are *alarming* and *terrible,* but only of such as bring a solemn awe upon the soul, as in the presence of a superior power; as, the *awful* hush before a battle. We speak of an *exalted* station, a *grand* mountain, an *imposing* presence, a *majestic* cathedral, a *noble* mien, a *solemn* litany, a *stately* march, an *august* assembly. See FRIGHTFUL, GRAND. *Antonyms*: base, beggarly, commonplace, contemptible, despicable, humble, inferior, lowly, mean, paltry, undignified, vulgar.

aw·ful·ly (ô′fəl·ē) *adv.* **1** In an awful manner. **2** (ô′flē) *Colloq.* Excessively; very: *awfully* rich.

a·while (ə·hwīl′) *adv.* For a brief time. [OE *āne hwīle* a while]

a·whirl (ə·hwûrl′) *adj.* & *adv.* In a whirl; whirling.

awk·ward (ôk′wərd) *adj.* **1** Ungraceful in bearing. **2** Unskilful in action; bungling. **3** Embarrassing or perplexing. **4** Difficult or dangerous to deal with, as an opponent. **5** Inconvenient for use; uncomfortable. **6** *Obs.* Perverse; untoward. [<ON *afug* turned the wrong way + -WARD] — **awk′ward·ly** *adv.* — **awk′ward·ness** *n.*

Synonyms: boorish, bungling, clownish, clumsy, gawky, maladroit, uncouth, ungainly, unhandy, unskilful. *Awkward* is *offward,* turned the wrong way; it was anciently used of a back-handed blow in battle, of squinting eyes, etc. *Clumsy* originally signified benumbed, stiffened with cold; as, *clumsy* fingers, *clumsy* limbs. Thus, *awkward* primarily refers to action, *clumsy* to condition. See RUSTIC. *Antonyms*: adroit, clever, dexterous, handy, skilful.

awl (ôl) *n.* A pointed steel instrument for making small holes. ◆ Homophone: *all.* [OE *æl, awel*]

awl·wort (ôl′wûrt′) *n.* A small stemless aquatic plant *(Subularia aquatica)* of the mustard family *(Brassicaceae)* having awl-shaped leaves.

aw·mous (ô′məs) *n. Scot.* Charity; alms.

awn (ôn) *n. Bot.* A bristlelike appendage of certain grasses; beard, as of wheat or rye. [<ON *ögn* chaff] — **awned** (ônd) *adj.* — **awn′less** *adj.* — **awn′y,** *Scot.* **awn′ie** *adj.*

awn·ing (ô′ning) *n.* **1** A rooflike cover, as of canvas, for protection from sun or rain. **2** A shelter resembling this. [Origin unknown]

a·woke (ə·wōk′) Past tense of AWAKE.

AWOL (*as an acronym pronounced* ā′wôl) *Mil.* Absent or absence without leave. Also **awol, A.W.O.L., a.w.o.l.**

a·wry (ə·rī′) *adj.* & *adv.* **1** Toward one side; crooked; distorted; obliquely. **2** Out of the right course; erroneously; perversely. [<A-[1] on + WRY]

ax[1] (aks) *n. pl.* **ax·es** **1** A tool with a bladed head mounted on a handle, used for chopping, hewing, etc. **2** An ax-hammer. See also ICE AX. — *v.t.* To cut, shape, trim, or fashion with an ax. — **to have an ax to grind** *Colloq.* To have a private purpose or interest to pursue. Also **axe.** [OE *æx, eax*] — **ax′like′** *adj.*

ax[2] (aks) *v.t.* & *v.i. Scot.* To ask.

Ax·el Hei·berg (ak′səl hī′bûrg) The largest of the Sverdrup Islands in Franklin District of the Northwest Territories, Canada; 13,583 square miles.

ax·es[1] (ak′sēz) *n.* Plural of AXIS.

ax·es[2] (ak′siz) *n.* Plural of AX.

axes of an aircraft *Aeron.* Three fixed lines of reference, usually centroidal and mutually rectangular, called respectively the **longitudinal** *(X)* **axis,** the **vertical** *(Z)* **axis,** and the **lateral** *(Y)* **axis.**

ax-ham·mer (aks′ham′ər) *n.* A stonecutter's tool with cutting edges at either end of the head, or one cutting edge and one hammer face. — **ax′-ham′mered** *adj.*

ax·i·al (ak′sē·əl) *adj.* **1** Of, pertaining to, or constituting an axis. **2** On or along an axis.

axial angle **1** The angle between the optic axes of a biaxial crystal. **2** The angle between any two crystallographic axes.

axial cable *Aeron.* A wire running through the axis of a rigid airship from bow to stern.

ax·il (ak′sil) *n. Bot.* **1** The cavity or angle formed by the junction of the upper side of a leafstalk, branch, etc., with a stem or branch. **2** *Anat.* The axilla. [<L *axilla* armpit]

ax·ile (ak′sil, -sīl) *adj.* Of, pertaining to, or situated in, or in the line of, an axis.

ax·il·la (ak·sil′ə) *n. pl.* **ax·il·lae** (-sil′ē) **1** The armpit. **2** An axil. [<L]

ax·il·lar (ak′sə·lər) *adj.* Axillary. — *n. Ornithol.* One of the relatively long, stiff feathers on the undersurface of the wing of a bird.

ax·il·lar·y (ak′sə·ler′ē) *adj.* **1** *Bot.* Of, pertaining to, or situated in an axil or axilla: *axillary* buds. **2** *Anat.* Attached to a joint. — *n. pl.* **·lar·ies** An axillar.

ax·i·nite (ak′sə·nīt) *n.* An aluminum-calcium borosilicate, with varying amounts of iron and manganese. [Gk. *axinē* ax; from the resemblance of the crystals to an ax head]

ax·i·ol·o·gy (aks′ē·ol′ə·jē) *n. Philos.* The theory or study of values or of the nature of value. [<Gk. *axios* worthy + -LOGY]

ax·i·om (ak′sē·əm) *n.* **1** A self-evident or universally recognized truth. **2** An established principle or rule. **3** *Logic* & *Math.* A proposition assumed to be true without proof. [<F *axiome* <L *axioma* <Gk. *axiōma* a thing thought worthy, a self-evident thing < *axioein* think worthy < *axios* worthy]

Synonym: truism. Both the *axiom* and the *truism* are instantly seen to be true, and need no proof; but in an *axiom* there is progress of thought, while the *truism* simply says what is too manifest to need saying. Hence the *axiom* is valuable and useful, while the *truism* is weak and flat. Compare ADAGE, PROVERB. *Antonyms*: absurdity, contradiction, demonstration, nonsense, paradox, sophism.

ax·i·o·mat·ic (ak′sē·ə·mat′ik) *adj.* **1** Of, pertaining to, or resembling an axiom; self-evident. **2** Full of axioms; aphoristic, as a literary style. Also **ax′i·o·mat′i·cal.** — **ax′i·o·mat′i·cal·ly** *adv.*

Ax·i·os (äk′sē·ôs′) The Greek name for the VARDAR.

ax·is[1] (ak′sis) *n. pl.* **ax·es** (ak′sēz) **1** A line around which a turning body revolves or may be supposed to revolve. **2** *Geom.* **a** One of the principal lines through the center of a plane or solid figure, especially the longest or shortest, or a line as to which the plane figure or solid is symmetrical. **b** A fixed line along which distances are measured or to which positions are referred. **3** An imaginary line through the center of a drawing or sculpture for purposes of measurement or reference. **4** The central line about which parts of a body are symmetrically arranged. **5** *Bot.* The central body, part, line, or longitudinal support on, along, or above which organs or other parts are arranged. **6** *Anat.* **a** A short arterial trunk from which several nearly equal branches radiate. **b** The second cervical vertebra, or the large, blunt, toothlike odontoid process which surmounts it and forms a pivot on which the atlas and head turn. **7** One of the lines of reference meeting at the center of a crystal, and determining to which system it belongs. **8** *Geol.* The dominant central section of a mountain chain, or the line tracing the crest throughout its length. **9** *Aeron.* One of the three axes of an aircraft. **10** An affiliation or coalition of two or more nations to promote and insure mutual interest, cooperation, and solidarity of front in their relations with foreign powers; also, the nations so affiliated. [< L, axis, axle]

ax·is[2] (ak′sis) *n.* A small deer (genus *Axis*) of southern Asia, having the body spotted with white. Also **axis deer.** [< L]

Ax·is (ak′sis) *n.* A coalition which developed from the Rome-Berlin Axis of 1936 and ultimately included Germany, Italy, Japan, Rumania, Bulgaria, Hungary, and others: opposed to the Allied and associated powers in World War II. Also **Axis Powers.**

axis cylinder *Anat.* The central conducting portion of a nerve fiber.

ax·le (ak′səl) *n.* **1** A crossbar supporting a vehicle, and on or with which its wheel or wheels turn: also called **ax′le·tree′**. **2** A shaft or spindle on which a wheel is mounted and on or with which it turns. [ME *axel* in *axeltre* axletree < ON *öxultrē* < *öxull* axle + *trē* tree, bar] — **ax′led** *adj.*

ax·man (aks′mən) *n. pl.* **·men** (-mən) One who wields an ax; a woodman. Also **axe′man.**

Ax·min·ster (aks′min·stər) *n.* **1** A carpet with a long, soft pile; formerly made by hand in **Axminster,** a town of eastern Devonshire, England. **2** A carpet made in imitation of this.

ax·o·lotl (ak′sə·lot′l) *n.* A North American tailed amphibian (genus *Ambystoma*), as *A. mexicanum* of Mexican lakes and marshes, which retains its external gills, and breeds in a larval state. [< Sp. < Nahuatl, lit., servant of water]

MEXICAN AXOLOTL
(From 6–9 inches long)

ax·on (ak′son) *n.* **1** *Zool.* The body axis of a vertebrate. **2** *Anat.* The axis-cylinder process of a nerve cell, usually carrying impulses away from the cells. See DENDRITE, NEURON. Also **ax·one** (ak′sōn). [< NL < Gk. *axōn* axis]

ax·seed (aks′sēd′) *n.* An Old World perennial crownvetch *(Coronilla varia)* with odd-pinnate leaves, and pink or white flowers, cultivated in the United States. [< AX + SEED; from the shape of the pods]

Ax·um (äk·sōōm′) See AKSUM.

ay[1] (ā) *adv. Poetic* Ever; always. Also *aye.* [< ON *ei* always]

ay[2] (ī) See AYE[1].

ay[3] (ā) *interj. Archaic* O! oh! ah!: an expression of sorrow, surprise, etc. [ME *ey, ei*]

A·ya·cu·cho (ä′yä·kōō′chō) A town in south central Peru; site of Sucre's victory over Spain, 1824, that secured Peruvian independence.

a·yah (ä′yə) *n. Anglo-Indian* A native nurse or lady's maid. [< Hind. *āya* < Pg. *aia* nurse]

ay·a·huas·ca (ī′ä·wäs′kä) *n.* A Brazilian plant *(Banisteria caapi)* whose alkaloid principle has powerful hallucinatory effects. See BANISTERINE. [< native Brazilian name]

a·ya·tol·lah (ä′yə·tō′lə) *n.* Title of the highest-ranking teacher of religion in Iran. [< Arabic *ayatollah* sign of God]

Ay·din (ī·din′) A town in western Turkey: also *Aidin.*

aye[1] (ī) *n.* An affirmative vote or voter. —*adv.* Yes; yea. Also *ay.* ◆ Homophone: *eye.*

aye[2] (ā) See AY[1].

aye-aye (ī′ī′) *n.* A nocturnal arboreal lemur (genus *Daubentonia*) of Madagascar, about the size of a cat and having rodentlike teeth. [< F < Malagasy *aiay*; so called from its cry]

A·ye·sha (ä′i·shä) See AISHA.

a·yin (ä′yēn) The sixteenth Hebrew letter. See ALPHABET.

Ayl·mer (āl′mər), **John,** 1521–94, English prelate.

Ay·ma·ra (ī′mä·rä′) *n.* One of a tribe of South American Indians, of highly developed pre-Incan culture, at the Aymaran linguistic stock: formerly occupying nearly all of Bolivia and Peru, and still comprising three-fourths of the population of Bolivia.

Ay·ma·ran (ī′mä·rän′) *adj.* Of or pertaining to a large and important linguistic stock of South American Indians inhabiting Bolivia and Peru.—*n.* The family of languages spoken by the Aymaran tribes: now largely superseded by Quechua.

Ay·mé (e·mā′), **Marcel,** born 1902, French novelist, dramatist, and short-story writer.

a·yont (ə·yont′) *prep. & adv. Scot & Brit. Dial.* Beyond; farther.

Ay·ot Saint Law·rence (ā′ət sānt lôr′əns, lor′əns) A town in Hertford, England; residence of George Bernard Shaw.

Ayr (âr) **1** A county in SW Scotland; 1,132 square miles: also **Ayr·shire** (âr′shir, -shər). **2** Its burgh, a port on the **Ayr River,** which flows 38 miles west to the Firth of Clyde.

Ayr·shire (âr′shir, -shər) *n.* One of a breed of dairy cattle especially adapted for milk production, originating in Ayrshire.

Ayr stone A very fine-grained stone widely employed in polishing sculptured marbles and also in fine metalwork: first found in Ayrshire. Also called *Scotch stone; water of Ayr.*

a·yun·ta·mien·to (ä·yōōn′tä·myen′tō) *n. pl.* **·tos** *SW U.S.* **1** A municipal council or legislative body of a town or city; town council. **2** City hall; municipal building. [< Sp.]

a·yur·ve·dism (ä′yōōr·vā′diz·əm) *n.* Medical treatment by plants and drugs indigenous to India: so called from the **Ayur Veda,** an ancient Hindu medical treatise sometimes regarded as a fifth Veda. [< Skt. *ayus* span of life + *vid* know] —**a′yur·ve′dist** *n.*

A·yut·tha·ya (ä·yōō′tä·yä) A former capital city in SE Thailand; site of early Thai ruins; destroyed, 1767. Also **A·yu′thi·a.**

az- Var. of AZO-.

a·zal·ea (ə·zāl′yə) *n.* A flowering shrub of the heath family (genus *Rhododendron,* formerly *Azalea*), especially the flame azalea *(R. calendulaceum)* with showy scarlet or orange flowers. [< NL < Gk. *azalea,* fem. of *azaleos* dry < *azein* parch, dry up; from its preference for dry soil]

a·zan (ä·zän′) *n. Arabic* In Moslem countries, the muezzin's call to prayer, usually given from the minaret of a mosque five times a day; also, the time spent in these prayers.

A·za·ña (ä·thä′nyä), **Manuel,** 1880–1940, president of the Spanish Republic 1936–39: full name *Azaña y Díez.*

Az·a·ri·ah (az′ə·rī′ə) A masculine personal name etymologically identical with *Eleazar:* 28 persons of this name are mentioned throughout the Old Testament. Also **Az·a·ri·as** (az′ə·rī′əs) [< Hebrew, helped by Jehovah]

az·a·role (az′ə·rōl) *n.* **1** The edible orange-red or yellow pomelike fruit of a Mediterranean shrub or tree *(Crataegus azarolus)* of the rose family. **2** The tree itself. [< F < Arabic *az-zu′rūr*]

A·za·zel (ə·zā′zəl, az′ə·zel) **1** In Mohammedan mythology, the chief among the Eblis who married the daughters of men. **2** In Milton's *Paradise Lost,* the standard-bearer of Satan. **3** The scapegoat sent into the wilderness as a sin atonement. *Lev.* xvi 21–28. [< Hebrew, scapegoat]

Az·ben (az·ben′) See AÏR.

a·zed·a·rach (ə·zed′ə·rak) *n.* **1** A large ornamental Eastern tree *(Melia azedarach)* of Asia and tropical America, with bipinnate leaves and panicles of lilac-colored flowers, succeeded by yellowish drupes: also called *Chinaberry tree, hagbush, pride of China.* **2** The bark from the roots of this tree, used as a cathartic, emetic, or vermifuge. [< F *azédarac,* ult. < Persian *āzād dirakht* noble tree]

a·ze·o·trope (ə·zē′ə·trōp) *n. Chem.* A mixture of substances, as water and hydrochloric acid, which has a constant boiling point at specified concentration. [< Gk. *a-* not + *zein* boil + *tropē* a turning] —**az·e·o·trop·ic** (az′ē·ō·trop′ik) *adj.*—**az·e·ot·ro·pism** (az′ē·ot′rə·piz′əm), **az′e·ot′ro·py** *n.*

A·zer·bai·jan (ä′zər·bī·jän′, az′ər-) **1** A constituent republic of the southern U.S.S.R., west of the Caspian Sea; 33,100 square miles; capital, Baku. Also **A′zer·bai·dzhan′**. Officially **Azerbaijan Soviet Socialist Republic. 2** A former province of NW Iran between Turkey and the Caspian Sea; 41,000 square miles; chief city, Tabriz.

A·zer·bai·ja·ni (ä′zər·bī·jä′nē, az′ər-) *n. pl.* **·ni** or **·nis** (-nēz) **1** A native or inhabitant of Azerbaijan. **2** The Turkic language of these people.

A·zil·ian (ə·zil′yən) *adj. Anthropol.* Designating a subdivision of Mesolithic culture associated with artifacts found in the **Mas d'A·zil** (màs dà·zēl′), a village of southern France.

az·i·muth (az′ə·məth) *n.* **1** *Astron.* The arc of the horizon that a vertical plane passing through a heavenly body makes with the meridian of the place of observation. **2** *Mil.* **a** Direction to right or left of a horizontal plane. **b** That element in the movement of a bomb or guided missile to the right or left of its downward course: distinguished from *range.* [< F *azimut* < Arabic *as-sumūt* the ways, pl. of *samt* way] —**az·i·muth·al** (az′ə·muth′əl) *adj.* — **az′i·muth′al·ly** *adv.*

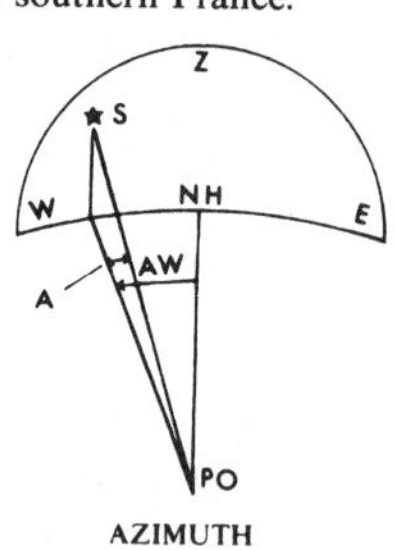

AZIMUTH
PO. Observation point. *A.* Altitude. *AW* Azimuth west. *W.* West. *E.* East. *NH.* North horizon. *Z.* Zenith. *S.* Star.

az·ine (az′ēn, -in) *n. Chem.* One of a class of nitrogenous heterocyclic compounds arranged in a six-membered ring, identified by the number of nitrogen atoms, as *diazine, triazine,* etc. [< AZ- + -INE[2]]

az·o (az′ō, ā′zō) *adj. Chem.* Containing nitrogen: an *azo* compound, *azo* dye. [< AZOTE]

azo- *combining form Chem.* Indicating the presence of nitrogen, especially in those organic compounds in which two atoms of nitrogen are connected with two similar radicals of the benzene series: *azobenzene,* C_6H_5N: NC_6H_5. Also, before vowels, *az-,* as in *azine.* [< AZOTE]

azo dye Any of an important class of coaltar dyes containing the azo radical N:N.

a·zo·ic (ə·zō′ik) *adj. Geol.* Of or pertaining to those periods on earth before life appeared; without organic remains. [< Gk. *azōos* lifeless < *a-* without + *zōē* life]

az·ole (az′ōl, ə·zōl′) *n. Chem.* Pyrrole. [< AZ(O)- + -OLE[1]]

az·on (az′on) *n.* A type of bomb equipped with control surfaces in the tail to permit radio guidance in azimuth only. [< *az(imuth) on(ly)*]

a·zon·ic (ā·zon′ik) *adj.* Not peculiar to any zone or region; not local.

A·zores (ə·zôrz′, ā′zôrz) Three island groups west of Portugal, divided into three Portuguese districts: *Angra do Heroísmo, Horta,* and *Ponta Delgada;* total area, 888 square miles. *Portuguese* **A·ço·res** (ə·sō′rēsh).

az·ote (az′ōt, ə·zōt′) *n.* Nitrogen: former name. [< F < Gk. *a-* not + *zōein* live; so called by Lavoisier from its inability to support life] — **az·ot·ed** (az′ō·tid, ə·zō′tid) *adj.*

az·oth (az′oth) *n.* **1** Mercury: the name given by the alchemists. **2** The universal remedy of Paracelsus. [< Arabic *az-zāūq* the quicksilver]

a·zot·ic (ə·zot′ik) *adj.* Of, pertaining to, or containing azote or nitrogen.

az·o·tize (az′ə·tīz) *v.t.* **·tized, ·tiz·ing** To nitrogenize.

A·zo·to·bac·ter (ə·zō′tō·bak′tər) *n.* A type of bacteria, chiefly *Clostridium pasteurianum,* which live in soil and have the power of fixing nitrogen, and thus contribute to soil fertility. Also **Az·o·bac·ter** (az′ō·bak′tər).

A·zov (ä·zôf′), **Sea of** A northern arm of the Black Sea in southern U.S.S.R.; 14,000 square miles. Also **A·zof′.**

Az·ra·el (az′rē·əl) In the Moslem and ancient Jewish mythology, the angel who separates the soul from the body at death. [< Hebrew, help of God]

Az·tec (az′tek) *n.* **1** One of tribe of Mexican Indians of Nahuatlan stock, founders of the Mexican Empire which was at its height when Cortés invaded the country in 1519. **2** Any of the Uto-Aztecan dialects spoken by the Aztecs; Nahuatl. —*adj.* Of or pertaining to the Aztec Indians, their language, culture, or empire: also **Az·tec·an** (az′tek·ən).

Aztec Ruins National Monument A group of pre-Columbian ruins in NW New Mexico, established as a national monument in 1923.

az·ure (azh′ər, ā′zhər) *adj.* **1** Like the blue of the sky; sky-blue. **2** Like the clear sky; cloudless; spotless. —*n.* **1** A clear sky-blue color or pigment. **2** *Poetic* The sky. **3** *Her.* Blue: represented in engraving by parallel horizontal lines. [<OF *azur* <Arabic *al-lāzward* <Persian *lazhward* lapis lazuli]

az·u·rite (azh′ə·rīt) *n.* A vitreous, monoclinic, azure blue, basic copper carbonate: also called *blue bice.* 2 A gemstone.

a·zy·go·spore (ə·zī′gə·spôr, -spōr) *n. Bot.* A spore parthenogenetically formed in certain fungi, and resembling a zygospore. Also **a·zy′·go·sperm.**

az·y·gous (az′i·gəs) *adj. Biol.* Having no mate; occurring singly; not paired. [<Gk. *azygos* unpaired <*a-* without + *zygon* a yoke]

az·yme (az′īm, -im) *n.* Unleavened bread. Also **az·ym** (az′im). [<Gk. *azymos* unleavened <*a-* without + *zymē* leaven] **—a·zym·ic** (ə·zim′ik), **az·y·mous** (az′ə·məs) *adj.*

az·zi·mi·na (äd′zē·mē′nä) *n. Italian* Elaborate, metallic decoration in damask patterns.

B

b, B (bē) *n. pl.* **b's, B's** or **Bs, bs, bees** (bēz) **1** The second letter of the English alphabet: from Phoenician *beth,* through Greek *beta,* Roman *B.* **2** The sound of the letter *b,* the voiced bilabial stop. See ALPHABET. *—symbol* **1** *Music* **a** One of a series of tones, the seventh in the natural diatonic scale of C. **b** The pitch of this tone or the written note representing it. **c** A scale built upon B. **2** *Chem.* Boron (symbol B).

ba (bä) *n.* In Egyptian mythology, the soul, believed to depart from the body at death and expected to return to it: represented by a bird with a human head. [<Egyptian]

Ba *Chem.* Barium (symbol Ba).

ba' (bä, bô) *n. Scot.* A ball.

baa (bä, ba) *v.i.* **baaed, baa·ing** To bleat, as a sheep. *—n.* The bleat, as of a sheep. [Imit.]

Ba·al (bā′əl, bāl) *n. pl.* **Ba·al·im** (bā′əl·im) **1** Any of several ancient Semitic gods of fertility and flocks; a sun god. **2** An idol or false god. [<Hebrew *Ba'al* lord] **—Ba′al·ish** *adj.*

Baal·bek (bäl′bek) A tourist center in central Lebanon; site of ancient Phoenician temple to Baal: Greek *Heliopolis.*

Ba·al·ist (bā′əl·ist) *n.* **1** A worshiper of Baal. **2** A worshiper of idols. Also **Ba′al·ite** (-īt). **—Ba′al·ism** *n.*

Baan (bän) See PAAN.

Bab (bäb) *n.* The title of the founder of Babism.

Bab (bab) Diminutive of BARBARA.

ba·ba (bä′bä) *n.* A cake made with yeast and steeped in rum. Also *French* **ba·ba au rhum** (bȧ·bȧ′ ō rôm′). [<F, prob. <Polish *baba* grandmother]

Ba·bar (bä′bər) See BABER.

ba·bas·su (bä′bə·so͞o′) *n.* **1** A Brazilian palm tree *(Orbignya martiana)* bearing nuts yielding an oil used in making margarine, soap, etc. **2** The oil from this tree: also called **babassu oil.** [<native Brazilian name]

bab·bitt (bab′it) *v.t.* To line, bush, fill, or face with Babbitt metal. *—n.* Babbitt metal.

Bab·bitt (bab′it) *n.* A type of conventional American businessman, ambitious in his business, but otherwise provincial, mediocre, and smug: from George *Babbitt,* a character in Sinclair Lewis's novel *Babbitt* (1922).

Bab·bitt (bab′it), **Irving,** 1865–1933, U.S. scholar and critic.

Babbitt metal 1 A soft, white, anti-friction alloy of tin, copper, and antimony. **2** Any of a group of similar alloys. [after Isaac *Babbitt,* 1799–1862, U.S. metallurgist]

Bab·bitt·ry (bab′it·rē) *n.* The behavior or attitudes of Babbitts as a class or group.

bab·ble (bab′əl) *n.* **1** A murmuring or rippling sound, as of a stream. **2** Prattle, as of an infant. **3** A confusion of sounds, as of a crowd. **4** *Telecom.* The confused sound of cross-talk from a number of interfering radio channels. *—v.* **bab·bled, bab·bling** *v.t.* **1** To utter unintelligibly. **2** To blurt out; tell thoughtlessly or foolishly. *—v.i.* **3** To utter inarticulate sounds or meaningless noises, as a baby or idiot. **4** To murmur, as a brook. **5** To talk unwisely or foolishly. [ME *babelen*] **—bab′ble·ment** *n.* **—bab′bler** *n.*

Synonyms (verb): blab, blurt, cackle, chat, chatter, gabble, gossip, jabber, murmur, palaver, prate, prattle, tattle, twaddle. Most of these words are onomatopoetic. The *cackle* of a hen, the *gabble* of a goose, the *chatter* of a magpie, the *babble* of a running stream, as applied to human speech, indicate a rapid succession of what are to the listener meaningless sounds. *Blab* and *blurt* refer to the letting out of what the lips can no longer keep in. To *chat* is to talk in an easy, pleasant way, not without sense, but without special purpose; to *prattle* is to talk freely and artlessly, as children. To *prate* is to talk idly, presumptuously, or foolishly, but not necessarily incoherently. To *jabber* is to utter a rapid succession of unintelligible sounds, generally more noisy than *chattering.* To *gossip* is to talk of petty personal matters. To *twaddle* is to talk feeble nonsense. To *murmur* is to utter suppressed or even inarticulate sounds, suggesting the notes of a dove, or the sound of a running stream. Compare SPEAK.

babe (bāb) *n.* **1** An infant; baby. **2** *U.S. Colloq.* An artless person; one lacking experience, sophistication, or guile. **3** *U.S. Slang* A girl. [ME; of uncertain origin]

ba·bel (bā′bəl, bab′əl) *n.* A confusion of many voices or languages; tumult. Also **Ba′bel.**

Ba·bel (bā′bəl, bab′əl) An ancient city in Shinar. **—Tower of Babel 1** A tower built by the descendants of Noah in Babel and intended to reach to heaven: God punished the builders for their presumption by confusing their language, preventing them from understanding each other and from completing the tower *Gen.* xi 9. **2** Any impractical scheme or structure; a visionary project.

Bab-el-Man·deb (bab′el·män′deb) A strait between the Red Sea and the Gulf of Aden; 17 miles wide.

Ba·bel·thu·ap (bä′bəl·to͞o′äp) Largest of the Palau Islands; 143 square miles.

Ba·ber (bä′bər), 1483–1530, founder of the Great Mogul dynasty in India: real name Zahir ed-Din Mohammed: also spelled *Babar, Babur.*

Ba·beuf (bȧ·bœf′), **François Emile,** 1760–97, French socialist.

Ba·bi (bä′bē) *n.* An adherent of Babism.

ba·bies'-breath (bā′bēz·breth) *n.* Baby's-breath.

Bab·ing·ton (bab′ing·tən), **Anthony,** 1561–86, English Roman Catholic conspirator against Queen Elizabeth.

ba·biche (bȧ·bēsh′) *n. Canadian* Rawhide thongs or lacings. [<Can. F]

bab·i·ru·sa (bab′ə·ro͞o′sə, bä′bə-) *n.* A wild hog *(Babirussa babirussa)* of SE Asia and the East Indies. The lower canines of the male pierce the upper lips and curve backwards. Also **bab′i·rous′sa, bab′i·rus′sa.** [<Malay *bābi* hog + *rūsa* deer]

Ba·bism (bä′biz·əm) *n.* The principles and practices of the Babis, a pantheistic Persian sect founded in 1844 by the Bab, Mirza Ali Mohammed ibn Radhik, 1824–50. Its philosophy recognizes the equality of the sexes and forbids polygamy, drinking, and mendicancy. [<Persian *bāb* gate] **—Ba·bite** (bä′bīt), **Ba′·bist** *adj. & n.*

Ba·bol (bä·bôl′) A city in northern Iran near the Caspian Sea: formerly *Barfrush.* Also **Ba·bul** (bä·bo͞ol′).

ba·boon (ba·bo͞on′) *n.* A large, terrestrial monkey (*Papio* and related genera) of Africa and Asia, having front and back legs of nearly equal length, doglike muzzle, large bare callosities on the buttocks, and usually a short tail. [<OF *babuin*] **—ba·boon′ish** *adj.*

BABOON
(About 30 inches high at the shoulder)

ba·boon·er·y (ba·bo͞o′nər·ē) *n.* Baboonish antics or behavior.

Bab·son (bab′sən), **Roger Ward,** 1875–1967, U.S. statistician.

ba·bu (bä′bo͞o) *n.* **1** A Hindu gentleman: a polite form of address, equivalent to *sir* or *Mr.* **2** In India, a native merchant or clerk who can write English. **3** A native of India with a smattering of English education: a derogatory term. Also **ba′boo.** [<Hind. *bābū,* a term of respect] **—ba′bu·ism** *n.*

ba·bul (bä·bo͞ol′) *n.* **1** An acacia *(Acacia arabica)* yielding a hard and heavy wood, and a gum used as a substitute for gum arabic. **2** The bark or gum of this acacia. Also **ba·bool′.** [<Hind., the acacia tree]

Ba·bur (bä′bər) See BABER.

ba·bush·ka (bə·bo͝osh′kə) *n.* A woman's scarf, often made or folded in a triangular shape, worn as a hood with the ends tying under the chin. [<Russian, grandmother]

Ba·bu·yan Channel (bä′bo͞o·yän′) The southernmost part of Luzon Strait, between Luzon and the Babuyan Islands.

Babuyan Islands A Philippine island group north of Luzon; 225 square miles.

ba·by (bā′bē) *n. pl.* **ba·bies 1** A very young child of either sex; an infant. **2** The youngest or smallest member of a family or group. **3** One who has the appearance, behavior, or disposition of a young child, especially one with little courage or fortitude. **4** *Slang* A girl. **5** Any young animal. **6** *Obs.* A doll or puppet. *—adj.* **1** For a baby: *baby* shoes. **2** Childish; infantile: *baby* ways. **3** Small; diminutive; miniature. *—v.t.* **ba·bied, ba·by·ing** To treat as a baby; play tenderly with; pamper. **—ba′by·hood** *n.* **—ba′by·like′** *adj.* [ME *baby,* dim. of *babe* BABE]

ba·by-blue-eyes (bā′bē·blo͞o′īz′) *n.* Any of several annual plants (genus *Nemophila,* especially *N. menzies* of the Pacific Coast) with alternate leaves and showy sky-blue flowers: also called *blueball.* Also **baby blue-eyes.**

baby farm A place where babies may be boarded and cared for.

ba·by·ish (bā′bē·ish) *adj.* Childish; infantile. See synonyms under CHILDISH. **—ba′by·ish·ly** *adv.* **—ba′by·ish·ness** *n.*

Bab·y·lon (bab′ə·lən, -lon) **1** An ancient city of Mesopotamia on the Euphrates, capital of Babylonia from about 2100 B.C.; celebrated as a seat of wealth, luxury, and vice. **2** Any city or place of great wealth, luxury, or vice. **3** Any place of captivity: in allusion to the *Babylonian captivity.* **—Bab′y·lon′ic** (-lon′ik), **Bab′y·lo′nish** (-lō′nish) *adj.*

Bab·y·lo·ni·a (bab′ə·lō′nē·ə) An ancient empire of Mesopotamia; capital, Babylon; surrendered to Persia 538 B.C.

Bab·y·lo·ni·an (bab′ə·lō′nē·ən) *adj.* **1** Of, like, or pertaining to ancient Babylon or Babylonia. **2** Wicked; luxurious. *—n.* **1** A native or inhabitant of Babylonia. **2** The Semitic language of ancient Babylonia, belonging to the Akkadian group.

Babylonian captivity 1 The exile of the Jews deported by Nebuchadnezzar into Babylonia, 597 B.C. **2** The interval of forced residence of the Popes at Avignon, 1309–77. Also **Babylonian exile.**

ba·by's-breath (bā′bēz·breth′) *n.* **1** An Old World perennial *(Gypsophila paniculata)* with numerous clusters of small, white or pink, fragrant flowers. 2 Any of certain other fragrant herbs, as the naturalized wild madder of the eastern United States: also spelled *babies'-breath.* Also **ba'by's-breath'.**

ba·by-sit (bā'bē·sit') *v.*-**sat, -sit·ting** To act as a baby sitter.

baby sitter (bā'bē sit'ər) *n.* A person employed to take care of young children during the hours when the parents are absent.

Ba·car·di (bə·kär'dē) *n.* A kind of Cuban rum. [after *Bacardi,* the original distillers]

bac·ca·lau·re·ate (bak'ə·lôr'ē·it) *n.* **1** The degree of bachelor of arts, bachelor of science, etc. **2** A sermon or address to a graduating class at commencement: also **baccalaureate sermon.** [< Med. L *baccalaureatus* < *baccalaureus,* var. of *baccalarius* a young farmer, ? < LL *bacca* cow; infl. in form by *bacca lauri* laurel berry. See BACHELOR]

bac·ca·rat (bak'ə·rä', bak'ə·rä) *n.* A card game of chance. The winnings are decided by comparison of hands with that of the banker. Also **bac'ca·ra'.** [< F *baccara,* a game of cards]

bac·cate (bak'āt) *adj. Bot.* **1** Like a berry. **2** Bearing berries. Also **bac'cat·ed.** [< L *baccatus* < *bacca* berry]

Bac·chae (bak'ē) **1** In Greek mythology, the female companions of Bacchus or Dionysus in his travels through the East. **2** Women taking part in the Dionysian celebrations. Also **Bac'chæ.**

bac·cha·nal (bak'ə·nəl) *n.* **1** A votary of Bacchus; hence, a drunken reveler. **2** *pl.* Bacchanalia. **3** A drunken revel; orgy. —*adj.* Bacchanalian. [< L *bacchanalis* of Bacchus < *Bacchus* god of wine]

bac·cha·na·li·a (bak'ə·nā'lē·ə, -nāl'yə) *n. pl.* Drunken revelries; orgies.

Bac·cha·na·li·a (bak'ə·nā'lē·ə, -nāl'yə) *n. pl.* An ancient Roman festival in honor of Bacchus.

bac·cha·na·li·an (bak'ə·nā'lē·ən, -nāl'yən) *adj.* Of, pertaining to, or indulging in orgies; carousing; uproariously drunk. —**bac'cha·na'·li·an·ism** *n.*

bac·chant (bak'ənt) *n. pl.* **bac·chants** or **bac·chan·tes** (bə·kan'tēz) A votary of Bacchus; hence, a carouser; bacchanal. —*adj.* Given to drunkenness. [< L *bacchans, -antis* ppr. of *bacchari* celebrate the festival of Bacchus, carouse]

bac·chan·te (bə·kan'tē, bə·kant', bak'ənt) *n.* A female votary of Bacchus.

bac·chic (bak'ik) *adj.* Riotous; orgiastic; drunken. Also **bac'chi·cal.**

Bac·chic (bak'ik) *adj.* Of, pertaining to, or like Bacchus or his rites.

Bac·chus (bak'əs) In Roman mythology, the god of wine and revelry: identified with the Greek *Dionysus.*

bac·cif·er·ous (bak·sif'ər·əs) *adj. Bot.* Bearing or yielding berries. [< L *baccifer* bearing berries < *bacca* berry + *ferre* bear]

bac·ci·form (bak'sə·fôrm) *adj.* Berry-shaped. [< NL *bacciformis* berry-formed < *bacca* berry + -FORM]

Bac·cio del·la Por·ta (bät'chō del'lä pôr'tä) Fra Bartolommeo.

bac·civ·o·rous (bak·siv'ər·əs) *adj. Zool.* Feeding on berries. [< L *bacca* berry + *vorare* eat]

bach (bach) *v.i. Colloq.* To live as a bachelor; keep house alone or for oneself.

Bach (bäkh) A family of German musicians and composers, of whom the best known are **Johann Sebastian,** 1685–1750, and his sons, **Karl Philipp Emanuel,** 1714–88 and **Johann Christian,** 1735–82.

Ba·chan (bä·chän') See BATJAN.

bach·e·lor (bach'ə·lər, bach'lər) *n.* **1** An unmarried man. **2** One who has taken his first university or college degree. **3** A young knight serving under another's banner: also **bach'e·lor-at-arms'.** **4** A fresh-water fish, the crappie. **5** A young male fur seal kept from the breeding grounds by the older males: also called *holluschick.* [< OF *bacheler* < Med. L *baccalaris;* origin and meaning uncertain]—**bach'e·lor·hood'** *n.* —**bach'e·lor·ship'** *n.*

Bachelor of Arts **1** A degree given by a college or university to a person who has completed a four-year course or its equivalent in the humanities. **2** A person who has received this degree. Abbr. *B.A., A.B.*

Bachelor of Science **1** A degree given by a college or university to a person who has completed a four-year course or its equivalent, majoring in science rather than the humanities. **2** A person who has received this degree. Abbr. *B.S., B.Sc.*

bach·e·lor's-but·ton (bach'ə·lərz·but'n, bach'lərz-) *n.* Any of several plants with button-shaped flowers or flower heads, especially certain species of the genus *Centaurea,* as the cornflower *(C. cyanus).*

bac·il·lar·y (bas'ə·ler'ē) *adj.* **1** Rod-shaped: also **ba·cil·li·form** (bə·sil'ə·fôrm). **2** Pertaining to, characterized by, or due to bacilli: also **ba·cil·lar** (bə·sil'ər, bas'ə·lər).

ba·cil·lo·my·cin (bə·sil'ō·mī'sin) *n.* An antibiotic isolated from a soil organism *(Bacillus subtilis);* it has a strong action against fungi, especially those causing athlete's foot. [< BACILLUS + Gk. *mykēs* fungus + -IN]

ba·cil·lus (bə·sil'əs) *n. pl.* **ba·cil·li** (-sil'ī) **1** Any of a large and numerous class of straight, rod-shaped bacteria having both beneficial and pathogenic effects: distinguished from *coccus* and *spirillum* types. **2** Any of a family *(Bacillaceae)* of straight, rod-shaped, aerobic, spore-forming bacteria, occurring singly or in chains. **3** Loosely, a bacterium. For illustration see BACTERIA. [< NL < *bacillum,* dim. of *baculus* a stick]

bac·i·tra·cin (bas'ə·trā'sin) *n.* An antibiotic produced from a bacillus, used in the treatment of some bacterial skin infections.

back¹ (bak) *n.* **1** The part of the body nearest the spine; in man the hinder, in quadrupeds the upper part, extending from the neck to the base of the spine. ◆Collateral adjective: *dorsal, fergal.* **2** The backbone. **3** The rear or posterior part: Sit in the *back* of the car. **4** The farther or other side; the part away from the beholder: the *back* of the door. **5** The part which comes behind or is opposite to the part used in the ordinary movements of a thing: the *back* of a knife, the *back* of the hand. **6** The part of the leaves of a book sewed together into the binding; also, the part of the binding around this part. **7** The lining attached to the unexposed side of a thing, as for reinforcement. **8** In football, a member of the offensive or defensive backfield. **9** The ridge of a hill. **10** *Phonet.* The part of the tongue directly behind the front and below the velum. —**at one's back** Following closely. —**behind one's back** **1** Secretly. **2** Treacherously. —**in back of** *Colloq.* Behind; to the rear of. —**to be (flat) on one's back** To be helplessly ill. —**to get (or put) one's back up** To become (or make) angry or obstinate. —**to put one's back into** To exert all the physical strength of which one is capable. —**to turn one's back on** To show contempt or ill feeling toward by turning away from or ignoring. —**with one's back to the wall** Cornered; having no issue save by fighting one's way out. —*v.t.* **1** To cause to move or go backwards; force to the rear: often with *up.* **2** To form the back of; supply with a back. **3** To strengthen at the back. **4** To support, assist, or uphold; be in favor of: often with *up* . **5** To support financially. **6** To bet on the success or chances of. **7** To mount, sit, or ride on the back of, as a horse. **8** To write on the back of; address or endorse, as a check. —*v.i.* **9** To move or go backward: often with *up.* **10** To shift counterclockwise: said of the wind: opposed to *veer.* —**to back and fill** **1** *Naut.* To keep (a vessel) in mid-channel by alternately filling and spilling the sails, so as to be advanced by the current alone. **2** To be irresolute; vacillate. —**to back down** To withdraw from a position, abandon a claim, etc. —**to back off** To retreat, as from contact. —**to back out** To withdraw from or refuse to carry out an engagement or contest. —**to back water** **1** To retard the progress or reverse the motion of a vessel by reversing the action of the oars or of the propelling machinery. **2** To withdraw from a position; retract, as a claim. —*adj.* **1** In the rear; behind: a *back* room. **2** Distant; remote: the *back* country. **3** Of or for a date earlier than the present: *back* taxes. **4** In arrears; overdue, as a debt. **5** In a backward direction: a *back* thrust. **6** *Phonet.* Describing those vowels produced with the tongue pulled back in the mouth, as (o͞o) in *food.* [OE *bœc* back]

back² (bak) *adv.* **1** At, to, or toward the rear: to move *back.* **2** In, to, or toward a former place: to go *back* home. **3** In, to, or toward a former condition: My cold has come *back.* **4** In time past; ago: years *back.* **5** In return or retort: to talk *back.* **6** In reserve or concealment: to keep something *back.* —**back and forth** First in one direction and then in the opposite. —**back of** Behind. —**to go back on** *Colloq.* **1** To refuse to keep a promise or engagement. **2** To desert or betray (a cause). [< ABACK]

back³ (bak) *n.* A brewer's tub or vat. [< Du. *bak* trough < F *bac* tub, basin]

back·ache (bak'āk') *n.* An ache or pain in one's back.

Back Bay A fashionable residential district of Boston.

back·bite (bak'bīt') *v.t. & v.i.* **·bit, ·bit·ten** or *Colloq.* **·bit, ·bit·ing** To revile or traduce behind one's back; slander. See synonyms under ASPERSE. —**back'bit'er** *n.* —**back'bit'·ing** *n.*

back·blocks (bak'bloks') *n. pl. Australian* Inland farming areas.

back·board (bak'bôrd', -bōrd') *n.* **1** A board forming or supporting the back of something. **2** In basketball, the vertical board behind the basket to which it is attached.

back·bone (bak'bōn') *n.* **1** *Anat.* The spine or vertebral column. **2** Any main support or stiffening part; especially, the highest or most extensive mountain range of a region or a continent. **3** Firmness; resolution; courage. —**back'boned'** *adj.*

back-break·ing (bak'brā'king) *adj.* Physically exhausting; fatiguing.

back·chat (bak'chat') *Colloq.* Back talk.

back country Unpopulated or undeveloped areas adjoining settled areas.

back court **1** In tennis and other games, the rear part of the court. **2** In basketball, the defensive half of the court of each team.

back·cross (bak'krôs', -kros') *v.t. & v.i. Genetics* To cross (a hybrid offspring) with one of its parents. —*n.* The offspring of a hybrid and either of the parents.

back-door (bak'dôr', -dōr') *adj.* **1** Relating or belonging to the back door of a house. **2** Underhand; indirect; secret.

back·drop (bak'drop') *n.* The curtain hung at the rear of a stage, often painted to represent a scene. Also **back cloth.**

backed (bakt) *adj.* **1** Provided with or having a back, background, or backing: often used in composition: low-*backed.* **2** In weaving, having an extra weft, warp, or another ply of cloth woven or knitted on the back.

back·er (bak'ər) *n.* **1** One who or that which backs or furnishes a back to; especially, one who supports with money; a patron. **2** One who bets or gambles on a contestant. See synonyms under ADHERENT.

back·field (bak'fēld') *n.* **1** In American football, the players behind the forward linemen, consisting of the fullback, right and left halfbacks, and quarterback. **2** The area in which these players are regularly stationed.

back·fill (bak'fil') *n.* Soil and other material used to refill an excavation. —*v.t.* To refill (an excavation).

back·fire (bak'fīr') *n.* **1** A fire built to check an advancing forest or prairie fire by creating a barren area in its path. **2** Premature explosion in the cylinder of an internal-combustion engine. **3** An explosion in the back part of a gun. —*v.i.* **·fired, ·fir·ing** **1** To set or use a backfire. **2** To explode in a backfire. **3** To have consequences contrary to those desired: The plan to raise revenue by increasing the sales tax *backfired* when sales dropped off.

back-fo·cus (bak'fō'kəs) *n. Phot.* The distance from the main focus of a lens to its nearest face. —**back'-fo'cused** *adj.*

back formation *Ling.* **1** The creation, by analogy, of one word from another in cases where the original word would seem to be the derivative, as in the derivation of *emote* from *emotion.* **2** A word so formed.

back·gam·mon (bak'gam'ən, bak'gam'ən) *n.* **1** A game played by two persons, on a special board, the moves of the pieces being determined by dice throws: formerly called *tables.* **2** A victory in this game before the defeated player advances all his men beyond the first six points, resulting in a tripled score for the victor. —*v.t.* To win a backgammon from. [ME *back gamen* back game; because sometimes the pieces must go back to the start]

back·ground (bak'ground') *n.* **1** That part in

a picture which is behind the principal objects represented or which forms a setting. **2** Ground in the rear or distance. **3** A subordinate position; obscurity; retirement. **4** The aggregate of one's experiences, training, cultural environment, etc. **5** Music or sound effects employed in accompaniment to a dialog, recital, etc. **6** The events leading up to or causing a situation. **7** Information explaining a situation, person, etc.

back·hand (bak′hand′) *adj.* Backhanded. —*n.* **1** Handwriting that slopes toward the left. **2** The hand turned backward in making a stroke, as with a racket. **3** A stroke made with the hand turned backward, as in tennis. —*adv.* With a backhand stroke.

back·hand·ed (bak′han′did) *adj.* **1** Delivered or made with the back of the hand, or with back of the hand turned forward, as a stroke in tennis. **2** Equivocal; insincere; ironical: a *backhanded* compliment. **3** Sloping to the left, as handwriting. **4** Turned or twisted in a direction opposite to the normal, as a cable. —**back′hand′ed·ly** *adv.* —**back′hand′ed·ness** *n.*

back·house (bak′hous′) *n.* A building in the rear; a privy.

back·ing (bak′ing) *n.* **1** Support or assistance given to a person, cause, etc. **2** Supporters or promoters collectively. **3** Motion backward; the act of moving backward. **4** The back of anything, especially anything added at the back for extra support or strength. **5** The act of supporting or strengthening at or with the back. **6** *Law* Endorsement by a magistrate of a warrant.

back·lash (bak′lash′) *n.* **1** *Mech.* **a** The reaction or tendency to jar or recoil, as machinery subjected to sudden strain. **b** The amount of loose play in a part subject to such tendency or reaction. **2** In angling, a snarl or tangle of the line on a reel, as caused by a faulty cast. **3** A sudden, violent recoil or reaction, as of public opinion.

back·log (bak′lôg′, -log′) *n.* *U.S.* **1** A large log placed at the back of an open fireplace to maintain and concentrate the heat. **2** Any reserve, as of funds, business orders, etc.

back·most (bak′mōst) *adj.* Farthest to the rear; hindmost.

back number **1** An out-of-date issue of a magazine or newspaper. **2** *U.S. Colloq.* An old-fashioned, out-of-date person.

back·pack (bak′pak′) *n.* A pack or knapsack carried on the back, as by campers. —*v.t.* & *v.i.* To carry (equipment) in a backpack. —**back′pack′er** *n.*

back·rest (bak′rest′) *n.* A support for or at the back.

back·rope (bak′rōp′) *n.* *Naut.* A lateral stay from the martingale of a vessel to the bows.

back seat **1** A seat in the rear, as of a vehicle, theater, hall, etc. **2** Status of little or no importance: to take a *back seat.*

back-seat driver (bak′sēt′) A passenger in a vehicle who offers advice and directions for driving.

back·set (bak′set′) *n.* **1** A setback; relapse. **2** An eddy; backwater, as of a stream.

back·sheesh, back·shish (bak′shēsh) See BAKSHEESH.

back·side (bak′sīd′) *n.* The posterior part of a person or an animal; rump.

back·sight (bak′sīt′) *n.* **1** In surveying, a sight laid on a known point in order to determine the position or elevation of an instrument. **2** A sight laid on a previously taken instrument station from a newly located point.

back·slide (bak′slīd′) *v.i.* **·slid, ·slid** or **slid·den, ·slid·ing** To return to wrong or vicious ways or opinions after reformation or conversion; relapse; apostatize. —**back′slid′er** *n.*

back-spin (bak′spin′) *n.* Reverse rotation of a round object that is moving forward, causing it to rebound.

back·stage (bak′stāj′) *adv.* In or toward the portion of a theater behind the stage proper or acting area, including the wings, dressing rooms, etc. —*n.* The back portion of the stage. —*adj.* (bak′stāj′) Placed backstage, so as to be hidden.

back·stairs (bak′stârz′) *adj.* Indirect; underhanded. Also **back′stair′.**

back·stay (bak′stā′) *n.* **1** *Naut.* A stayrope supporting a mast of a vessel on the aft side. **2** A support for various mechanical purposes. **3** The leather band at the back and sides of a shoe above the heel and below the body of the counter.

back·stitch (bak′stich′) *n.* A stitch made by carrying the thread back half the length of the preceding stitch. —*v.t.* & *v.i.* To sew with backstitches.

back·stop (bak′stop′) *n.* A fence or screen to stop the ball from going too far in certain games, as baseball, tennis, etc.

back·strap (bak′strap′) *n.* The harness band extending from crupper to hames or saddle. See illustration under HARNESS.

back·stretch (bak′strech′) *n.* That part of a race course farthest from the spectators: opposite of *homestretch.*

back·stroke (bak′strōk′) *n.* **1** A blow or stroke in return; a backhanded stroke. **2** In swimming, a stroke executed while on one's back. —*v.* **·stroked, ·strok·ing** *v.t.* To strike, as a ball, with a backstroke. —*v.i.* To swim with a backstroke.

back·swept (bak′swept′) *adj.* *Aeron.* Swept-back.

back·sword (bak′sôrd′, -sōrd′) *n.* **1** A sword with one sharp edge; a broadsword. **2** A stick with a basket hilt, used in fencing practice or in single-stick play. **3** One who uses a backsword. —**back′sword′man, back′swords′·man** *n.*

back talk Impudent retort; insolent answering back.

back·track (bak′trak′) *v.i.* *U.S.* **1** To retrace one's steps. **2** To withdraw from a position, undertaking, etc.

back·up (bak′up′) *n.* **1** A support or backing. **2** An accumulation, as of water or waste, caused by a stoppage. **3** A substitute held in readiness for contingent use: often used attributively: a *backup* plan; a *backup* quarterback. Also **back′-up′.**

back·ward (bak′wərd) *adj.* **1** Turned to the back or rear; reversed. **2** Retiring; bashful. **3** Slow in growth or development; retarded. **4** Late; slow; behindhand. **5** Done the reverse way. —*adv.* **1** In the direction of the back; to the rear. **2** Into time past; toward earlier times. **3** With the back foremost. **4** In reverse order. **5** From better to worse. Also **back′wards** *adv.* —**back′ward·ly** *adv.* —**back′·ward·ness** *n.*

back·wash (bak′wosh′, -wôsh′) *n.* **1** The water moved backward, as by a boat, oars, etc. **2** The backward current of air set up by aircraft propellers. **3** Any condition resulting from some previous act, remark, etc.

back·wa·ter (bak′wô′tər, -wot′ər) *n.* **1** Water set, thrown, or held back, as by a dam, a current, etc.; also, the body of water held back. **2** Any place or condition regarded as stagnant, backward, etc.

back·woods (bak′wo͝odz′) *n. pl.* *U.S.* Wild, heavily wooded, or sparsely settled districts. —*adj.* In, from, or like the backwoods: also **back′wood′.** —**back′woods′man** (-mən) *n.*

ba·con (bā′kən) *n.* **1** The salted and dried or smoked flesh of the hog, especially the back and sides. **2** *U.S. Colloq.* Money, profit, or gain from any undertaking: to bring home the *bacon.* [<OF <OHG *bacho, bakho* ham, side of bacon]

Ba·con (bā′kən), **Francis,** 1561–1626, first Baron Verulam, Viscount St. Albans, English philosopher, essayist, and statesman. —**Nathaniel,** 1647–76, American colonial leader of a rebellion (1676) demanding governmental reforms. —**Roger,** 1214?–92?, English scientist and philosopher.

Ba·co·ni·an (bā·kō′nē·ən) *adj.* Of or pertaining to Francis Bacon, his philosophy, or his literary style. —*n.* One who believes in the philosophy of Francis Bacon or in the Baconian theory.

Baconian theory The theory that Francis Bacon wrote the plays attributed to Shakespeare.

ba·con·y (bā′kən·ē) *adj.* Like bacon; fatty.

bac·te·re·mi·a (bak′tə·rē′mē·ə) *n.* *Pathol.* The presence of bacteria in the blood.

bac·te·ri·a (bak·tir′ē·ə) Plural of BACTERIUM.

bac·te·ri·cide (bak·tir′ə·sīd) *n.* An agent destructive of bacteria. —**bac·te′ri·ci′dal** *adj.*

bac·te·rin (bak′tə·rin) *n.* A vaccine prepared from dead pathogenic bacteria. Also **bac′te·rine** (-rēn).

bacterio- *combining form* Of or pertaining to bacteria: *bacterioscopy.* [Gk. *baktērion,* dim. of *baktron* rod, staff]

bac·te·ri·ol·o·gy (bak·tir′ē·ol′ə·jē) *n.* The branch of biology and medicine that deals with bacteria. —**bac·te·ri·o·log·i·cal** (bak·tir′·ē·ə·loj′i·kəl) *adj.* —**bac·te′ri·o·log′i·cal·ly** *adv.* —**bac·te′ri·ol′o·gist** *n.*

bac·te·ri·o·ly·sin (bak·tir′ē·ə·lī′sin) *n.* A specific antibody formed in the blood by the action of bacteria and having the power to disintegrate or dissolve them.

bac·te·ri·ol·y·sis (bak·tir′ē·ol′ə·sis) *n.* **1** Decomposition effected through bacteria without oxygen. **2** Destruction or breaking down of cells. —**bac·te·ri·o·lyt·ic** (bak·tir′ē·ə·lit′ik) *adj.*

bac·te·ri·o·phage (bak·tir′ē·ə·fāj′) *n.* An ultramicroscopic filter-passing agent which has the power of destroying bacteria and of inducing bacterial mutation.

bac·te·ri·os·co·py (bak·tir′ē·os′kə·pē) *n.* Microscopic study or investigation of bacteria. —**bac·te·ri·o·scop·ic** (bak·tir′ē·ə·skop′ik) or **·i·cal** *adj.* —**bac·te′ri·o·scop′i·cal·ly** *adv.* —**bac·te′ri·os′co·pist** *n.*

bac·te·ri·o·stat·ic (bak·tir′ē·ə·stat′ik) *adj.* Arresting the growth or development of bacteria.

bac·te·ri·um (bak·tir′ē·əm) *n.* *pl.* **·te·ri·a** (-tir′·ē·ə) One of numerous widely distributed unicellular micro-organisms of the class *Schizomycetes*; autotrophic, heterotrophic, parasitic or saprophytic, they exhibit both plant and animal characteristics, and in their three varieties of *bacillus, coccus,* and *spirillum* range from the harmless and beneficial to the intensely virulent and lethal. [<NL <Gk. *baktērion,* dim. of *baktron* staff, stick] —**bac·te′ri·al** *adj.* —**bac·te′ri·al·ly** *adv.*

bac·ter·ize (bak′tər·īz) *v.t.* **·ized, iz·ing** To change by the action of bacteria. —**bac′ter·i·za′tion** *n.*

bac·ter·oid (bak′tə·roid) *adj.* Resembling the forms of bacteria. Also **bac′ter·oi′dal, bac·te·ri·oid** (bak·tir′ē·oid). —*n.* A bacterium found in tubercles on the roots of leguminous plants.

Bac·tra (bak′trə) The ancient name for BALKH.

Bac·tri·a (bak′trē·ə) A satrapy of the ancient Persian empire, lying partly in NE Afghanistan and partly in SW Asiatic U.S.S.R. —**Bac′·tri·an** *adj.* & *n.*

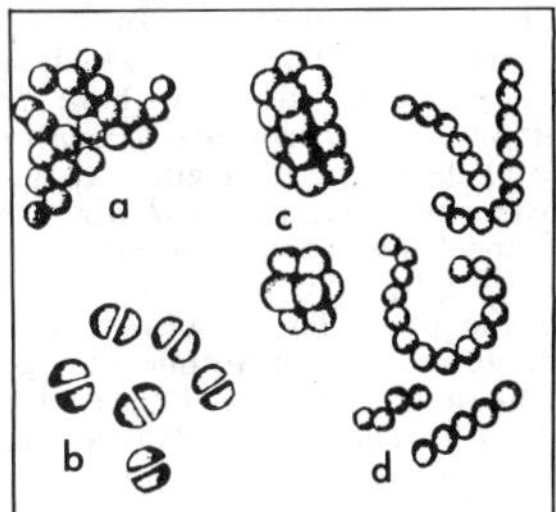

COCCUS FORMS OF BACTERIA
a. Staphylococcus.
b. Diplococcus.
c. Sarcina.
d. Streptococcus.

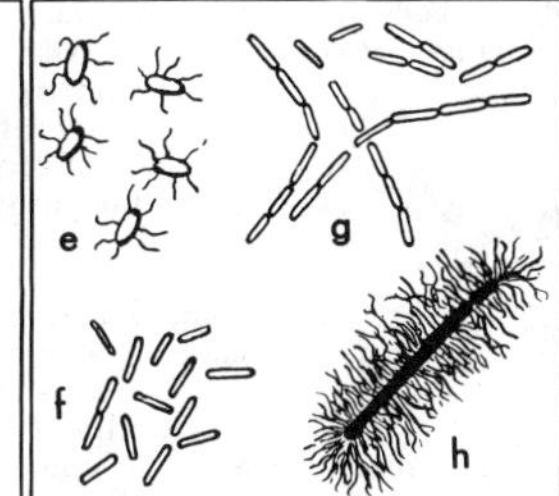

BACILLUS FORMS OF BACTERIA
e. Bacillus typhosus.
f. Bacillus sporagenes.
g. Bacillus subtilis.
h. Bacillus proteus.

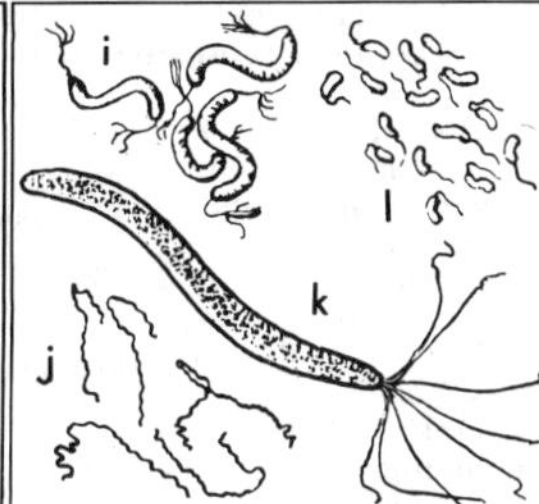

SPIRILLUM FORMS OF BACTERIA
i. Spirillum undulam.
j. Species of spirochaete.
k. Thiospirillum.
l. Vibrio cholerae.

ba·cu·li·form (bə·kyōō′lə·fôrm) *adj.* Shaped like a rod; straight. [<L *baculum* rod + -FORM]

bad[1] (bad) *adj.* **worse, worst 1** Not good in any manner or degree; not up to standard; unsatisfactory; inferior; poor: a *bad* meal; They played a *bad* game and lost. **2** Disagreeable; unpleasant: *bad* weather; *bad* manners. **3** Inadequate; deficient: *bad* wiring. **4** Lacking skill or proficiency: a *bad* musician. **5** Rotten; decaying: *bad* apples. **6** Immoral; corrupt; wicked. **7** Mischievous; naughty; ill-behaved: a *bad* child. **8** Incorrect; erroneous: *bad* grammar. **9** Injurious; harmful: a *bad* habit. **10** Severe: a *bad* sprain. **11** Sick; in poor health. **12** Injured or diseased; not sound: a *bad* knee; a *bad* heart.**13** Sorry; concerned: to feel *bad* about it. **14** Inexpedient; wrong; improper; inauspicious: He spoke at a *bad* time and regretted it later. **15** Invalid; illegal: a *bad* check. **16** In finance, outstanding and not collectable: a *bad* debt.
—**in bad** *Colloq.* **1** In difficulty. **2** In disfavor. —**not bad** Rather good: also **not half bad, not so bad.** —*n.* **1** That which is bad. **2** Those who are bad, taken collectively. **3** A bad state or condition; bad luck; wickedness. —**to go to the bad** *Colloq.* To degenerate; become bad. —*adv. Colloq.* Badly. [ME *bad, baddle,* ? <OE *bæddel* effeminate man] —**bad′ness** *n.*
Synonyms (adj.): abominable, baleful, baneful, base, corrupt, corrupting, decayed, decaying, deceitful, deceptive, defective, deleterious, depraved, detrimental, dishonest, evil, false, foul, fraudulent, hurtful, ill, immoral, imperfect, incompetent, inferior, injurious, mean, mischievous, naughty, noxious, pernicious, poor, putrid, rascally, rotten, sad, saddening, scurvy, serious, severe, shabby, sinful, sorrowful, sorry, unfair, unfortunate, unhappy, unlucky, unprincipled, untrue, untrustworthy, unwelcome, unwholesome, unworthy, vile, villainous, wicked, worthless, wretched. See HARD, IMMORAL, PERNICIOUS. *Antonyms*: see synonyms for GOOD.

bad[2] (bad) Obsolete past tense of BID.

Ba·da·joz (bä·thä·hōth′) A province of western Spain, constituting Lower Estremadura; 8,360 square miles; capital, Badajoz.

Badb (biv) In Old Irish mythology, an evil spirit delighting in carnage, appearing as the crow that feeds on the slain after battle: also spelled *Bodb.*

bad blood Hostility; long-standing enmity; strife.

bad·der-locks (bad′ər·loks) *n.* An edible European seaweed *(Alaria esculenta).*

bade (bad) Past tense of BID.

Ba·den (bäd′n) A former state of SW Germany; after 1945 divided into (1) Baden, in the Federal Republic (1949); 3,842 square miles; capital, Freiburg; and (2) WÜRTTEMBERG-BADEN.

Ba·den-Ba·den (bäd′n·bäd′n) A resort city of southern Baden, Germany.

Ba·den-Pow·ell (bäd′n·pō′əl), **Lord,** 1857–1941, Robert Stephenson Smyth, British general; founder of the Boy Scouts in 1908.

badge (baj) *n.* **1** A token, mark, decoration, or insignia of office, rank or membership. **2** Any distinguishing mark. **3** A ribbon worn on the field uniform to indicate award of a decoration, or a device to indicate branch, organization, rank, rating, or professional attainment. —*v.t.* **badged, badg·ing** To decorate or provide with a badge. [ME *bage, bagge*]

badg·er (baj′ər) *n.* **1** A small, burrowing, nocturnal, carnivorous mammal, with a broad body, short legs, and long-clawed toes. There are several species, including the **American badger** *(Taxidea americana),* the **European badger** *(Meles taxus),* and the balisaur and the ratel of Asia. **2** In Australia, the bandicoot, the rock wallaby, or the wombat. **3** The fur of a badger, or a brush made of its hair. —*v.t.* To worry or persecute persistently; bait; nag. [?<BADGE, with ref. to mark on head]

BADGER
(Body length about 2 feet, 4 inches; tail, 6 inches)

Badger State Nickname of WISCONSIN.

bad·i·nage (bad′ə·näzh′, bad′ə·nij) *n.* Playful raillery; banter. —*v.t.* **·naged, ·nag·ing** To subject to or tease with badinage. See synonyms under BANTER. [<F <*badiner* jest < *badin* silly, jesting <Provencal *bader* <LL *badare* gape]

bad·lands (bad′landz′) *n.* A barren area characterized by numerous ridges, peaks, and mesas cut by erosion.

Bad·lands (bad′landz′) An arid plateau in South Dakota, Nebraska, and North Dakota, eroded into peaks, pinnacles, and valleys. Also **Bad Lands.**

bad·ly (bad′lē) *adv.* **1** Improperly; imperfectly; incorrectly. **2** Unpleasantly. **3** Harmfully. **4** *Colloq.* Very much; greatly: I need to see you *badly.*

bad·man (bad′man′) *n.* A desperado.

bad·min·ton (bad′min·tən) *n.* **1** A game played by batting a shuttlecock back and forth over a high narrow net with a light racket. **2** A drink made with claret, sugar, and soda water. [from *Badminton* in England, the estate of the Duke of Beaufort]

bad-mouth (bad′mouth′) *v.t. U.S. Slang* To voice damaging criticism of; speak ill of.

Ba·do·glio (bä·dō′lyō), **Pietro,** 1871–1956, Italian marshal; premier 1943–44.

bad-tem·pered (bad′tem′pərd) *adj.* Having a bad temper; cross; irritable.

Bae·da (bē′də) See BEDE.

Bae·de·ker (bā′di·kər) *n.* **1** Any of a series of travelers' guidebooks issued by **Karl Baedeker,** 1801–59, German publisher, or his firm. **2** Loosely, any guidebook.

Baeke·land (bāk′lənd), **Leo Hendrik,** 1863–1944, U.S. chemist and inventor, born in Belgium. See BAKELITE.

Bae·yer (bā′yər), **Johann Friedrich Wilhelm Adolf von,** 1835–1917, German chemist.

baff (baf) *Scot. v.t. & v.i.* **1** To beat or strike. **2** In golf, to strike the ground under the ball with the sole of a wooden club so as to send the ball too high in the air. —*n.* **1** A stroke; blow. **2** In golf, a baffed stroke.

Baf·fin (baf′in), **William,** 1584–1622, English navigator.

Baffin Bay An arm of the North Atlantic between Greenland and the Northwest Territories, Canada.

Baffin Island The largest and most easterly island in the Arctic Archipelago, Northwest Territories, Canada; 197,754 square miles. Also **Baffin Land.**

baf·fle (baf′əl) *v.* **baf·fled, baf·fling** *v.t.* **1** To thwart or frustrate; defeat; perplex: Police detectives were completely *baffled* by the absence of a motive. **2** *Naut.* To beat back or hinder: The ship was *baffled* by the storm. —*v.i.* **3** To struggle to no avail: The gull *baffles* with the wind. —*n.* **1** A baffleplate. **2** A partition with a small central hole set in front of a radio loudspeaker to prevent excessive flow of air in either direction. **3** Any movable surface, as a board or blanket, used to control and direct sound effect in filming motion pictures. [Origin uncertain]—**baf′fle·ment** *n.* —**baf′fler** *n.* —**baf′fling** *adj.* —**baf′·fling·ly** *adv.*
Synonyms (verb): balk, circumvent, defeat, foil, frustrate, outgeneral, outmaneuver, outwit, thwart. All the words of this list imply *defeat* by something less than direct resistance. A plan, a scheme, or an opponent may be *baffled* by any artifice sufficient to prevent success. An attempt is *foiled* which is made to miss its mark by some craft or skill of an opponent. An attempt is *frustrated* which is made vain by any means, with or without design; as, the attempt at surprise was *frustrated* by the accidental discharge of a gun. An undertaking, movement, etc., is *balked* which is effectually stopped by some obstacle. To *thwart* is to *defeat* by some force or action coming across the path. To *circumvent* is to gain an advantage by passing around; "to get round" a person or a scheme. Compare CONQUER, HINDER. *Antonyms*: abet, advance, aid, assist, encourage, help, promote, prosper.

baf·fle·plate (baf′əl·plāt) *n.* **1** A partition, as in a furnace, to change the direction of the gases of combustion. **2** A grating placed in a pipe or channel to control eddies and secure a uniform flow of the liquid passing through it. **3** *Electronics* A metal plate serving to reduce the cross-section of electromagnetic waves passing through a guide.

baf·fy (baf′ē) *n. pl.* **·fies** A wooden golf club with a short shaft and deeply pitched face, for lofting the ball. [<BAFF]

Ba·fing (bä′fing) The unnavigable headstream of the Senegal in French West Africa, flowing NE about 350 miles.

bag (bag) *n.* **1** A sack or pouch. **2** A sac or similar structure in various animals, as the udder of a cow. **3** The amount a bag will hold. **4** The amount of game caught or killed. **5** The bulged part of any object, as of a sail. **6** *pl. Colloq.* Clothes, especially ill-fitting ones. **7** *pl. Brit. Colloq.* Men's slacks. **8** A purse. **9** A suitcase. **10** *Slang* One's personal interest or habit. **11** *Slang* A situation, matter, or problem. —**in the bag** *Slang* Virtually certain. —**to be left holding the bag** *U.S. Colloq.* To be left to assume full responsibility. —*v.* **bagged, bag·ging** *v.t.* **1** To put into a bag or bags. **2** To cause to fill out or bulge like a bag. **3** To capture or kill, as game. —*v.i.* **4** To bulge or swell like a bag. **5** To hang loosely. [?<ON *baggi* pack, bundle]

bag and baggage *Colloq.* **1** (With) all one's possessions. **2** Entirely; completely.

ba·gasse (bə·gas′) *n.* **1** The dry refuse of sugarcane after the juice has been expressed. **2** Similar refuse from other sources, as beets and olives: also called *megass, megasse.* Also **ba·gass′.** [<F <Sp. *bagazo* refuse of grapes, olives, etc., after pressing]

bag·a·telle (bag′ə·tel′) *n.* **1** A trifle; something of minor importance. **2** A game similar to billiards. **3** Pinball. **4** A short musical composition, especially for the piano. [<F < Ital. *bagatella,* dim. of *baga* sack]

Bage·hot (baj′ət), **Walter,** 1826–77, English economist and political writer.

ba·gel (bā′gəl) *n.* A doughnut-shaped roll of unsalted yeast simmered in water and baked. [<Yiddish <*beigen* bend, twist]

bag·gage (bag·ij) *n.* **1** The trunks, packages, etc., of a traveler. **2** An army's movable equipment. **3** A lively, pert, or impudent young woman. **4** *Archaic* A prostitute. [<OF *bagage* <*bague* bundle <Med. L *baga* sack]

bag·gage·mas·ter (bag′ij·mas′tər, -mäs′-) *n.* One in charge of receiving and sending baggage, as at a railway station.

bag·gie (bäg′ē, beg′ē) *n. Scot.* The stomach.

bag·ging (bag′ing) *n.* A coarse material for making bags.

bag·gy (bag′ē) *adj.* **bag·gi·er, bag·gi·est** Like a bag; loose; bulging or ill-fitting; puffy: a *baggy* dress. —**bag′gi·ly** *adv.* —**bag′gi·ness** *n.*

Bagh·dad (bag′dad, bäg·däd′) A city on the Tigris, capital of Iraq. Also **Bag′dad.**

Bagh·dad·i (bag·dad′ē, bäg·dä′dē) *n.* A native or inhabitant of Baghdad.

bag·man (bag′mən) *n. pl.* **·men** (-mən) *Brit.* A traveling salesman.

bagn·io (ban′yō, bän′-) *n.* **1** A brothel. **2** A bathhouse; a bath. **3** In the Orient, a prison. [<Ital. *bagno* <L *balneum* <Gk. *balaneion* bath]

bag·pipe (bag′pīp′) *n.* *Often pl.* A reed musical instrument in which the several drone pipes and the melody pipe with its finger stops are supplied with air from a windbag filled by a pipe to the player's mouth: now played chiefly in Scotland and Ireland. —**bag′·pip′er** *n.*

BAGPIPE

Ba·gra·ti·o·novsk (bä·grä·tyē·ô′nôfsk) A city on the Polish border of Russian S.F.S.R.: formerly *Eylau* in East Prussia, site of a battle between Napoleon and Russian and Prussian forces, 1807.

ba·guette (ba·get′) *n.* **1** *Archit.* A small, bead-shaped molding. **2** A gem or crystal cut in long, narrow, rectangular form. **3** This form. Also **ba·guet′.** [<F <Ital. *bacchetta* dim. of *bacchio* <L *baculum* staff, stick]

ba·guio (bä′gyō) *n. Spanish* A tropical cyclone in the Philippines.

Ba·gui·o (bag′ē·ō, bä′gē·ō) A city in northern Luzon, the summer capital of the Philippines.

bag·worm (bag′wûrm′) *n.* The larva of any of certain moths (family *Psychidae*), characterized by its baglike cocoon.

bah (bä, ba) *interj.* An exclamation expressing contempt, scorn, or dismissal.

ba·ha·dur (bə·hä′dŏŏr) *n.* A Hindu title of respect, generally given to European officers in state documents or ceremonies.
Ba·ha·i (bə·hä′ē) *n.* *pl.* **Ba·ha·is** A teacher or follower of Bahaism.
Ba·ha·ism (bə·hä′iz·əm) *n.* One of the two sectarian creeds of Babism, named after the elder brother of Mirza Yahva, Mirza Husayn Ali, who, as *Bahaullah*, proclaimed himself first successor to the Bab in 1863. — **Ba·ha′ist** *n.* & *adj.*
Ba·ha·ma Islands (bə·hä′mə, -hā′-) An island group in the western North Atlantic between Florida and Hispaniola, comprising a British colony; 4,375 square miles; capital, Nassau. Also **Ba·ha′mas.**
Ba·ha·sa Indonesia (bä·hä′sə) The official language of Indonesia, based on Malay.
Ba·ha·ul·lah (bä·hä′ŏŏl·lä′), 1817–92, Mirza Husayn Ali, Persian founder of Bahaism. Also **Ba·ha′ Ul·lah′.**
Ba·ha·wal·pur (bə·hä′wəl·pŏŏr) One of the Punjab states of western Pakistan; 15,918 square miles; capital, Bahawalpur.
Ba·hi·a (bə·ē′ə) **1** A coastal state of eastern Brazil; 217,688 square miles; capital, Salvador: also **Ba·ii′a.** **2** Former name of SALVADOR, Brazil.
Ba·hí·a Blan·ca (bä·ē′ä vläng′kä) A port in southern Buenos Aires province, Argentina.
Bah·rein Islands (bä·rān′) An archipelago in the Persian Gulf near the coast of Saudi Arabia, comprising a sheikdom under British protection; 213 square miles; capital, Manameh. Also **Bah·rain′, Bah·rayn′.**
Bahr-el-Ab·iad (bär′el·ab′yäd), **-el-Az·raq** (-el·az′räk), **-el-Jeb·el** (-el·jeb′el) See under NILE.
Bahr-el-Yem·en (bär′el·yem′ən) The Arabic name for the RED SEA.
Bahr-en-Nil (bär′en·nēl′) See under NILE.
baht (bät) *n.* *pl.* **bahts** or **baht** **1** The silver monetary unit of Thailand, equivalent to about 40 cents in U.S. currency: formerly called *tical.* **2** A tical, a Thai unit of weight. Also spelled *bat.*
Ba·ia (bä′yä) A village in Campania, southern Italy; site of ancient **Bai·ae** or **Bai·æ** (bā′ē), a favorite bathing resort of the Romans.
baik (bāk) *n. Scot.* **1** A biscuit. **2** Beck. —*v.t.* To bake.
Bai·kal The world's deepest freshwater lake, in southern Siberia, Russia: 12,150 square miles; greatest depth, 5,712 feet.
bail[1] (bāl) *n.* A scoop or bucket for dipping out fluids, as from a boat. — *v.t.* & *v.i.* **1** To dip (water) as from a boat, with or as with a bail. **2** To clear (a boat) of water by dipping out. — **to bail out** To jump from an airplane or other aircraft, equipped with parachute, in order to land; to parachute. ◆ Homophone: *bale.* [<OF *baille* <LL *bacula,* dim. of *baca, bacca* shallow trough, tub]
bail[2] (bāl) *n.* **1** A partition between the stalls of a stable. **2** A frame to confine a cow's head while milking. **3** In cricket, one of the crosspieces of the wicket. **4** A crossbar. **5** A bailey. **6** *pl. Obs.* Palisades. ◆ Homophone: *bale.* — **to bail up** *Austral. Slang* **1** To hold up and rob. **2** To corner or accost someone. [<OF *baile* barrier, ? <*bailler* enclose, shut]
bail[3] (bāl) *Law n.* **1** One who becomes surety for the debt or default of another, especially of a person under arrest. **2** The security or guaranty given or agreed upon. **3** Release, or the privilege of release, on bail. See synonyms under SECURITY. — *v.t.* **1** To release (an arrested person) on bail for appearance at a stipulated time: often with *out.* **2** To obtain the release of (an arrested person) on bail: usually with *out.* **3** To deliver, as goods, to another's disposition or care without transference of ownership. — **to go** (or **stand**) **bail for** To provide bail for. ◆ Homophone: *bale.* [<OF, power, custody <*baillier* guard, control <L *bajulare* carry, manage]
bail[4] (bāl) *n.* **1** The semicircular handle of a pail, kettle, etc. **2** An arch-shaped support, as for holding up the cloth of a canopy. — *v.t.* To provide with a bail or handle. ◆ Homophone: *bale.* [<ON *beygla* hook, ring]
bail·a·ble (bā′lə·bəl) *adj. Law* Admitting of, or entitled to, bail.
Bai·lan Pass (bī·län′) See BELEN PASS.
Baile Atha Cli·ath (bal ä klē′ə) The Gaelic name for DUBLIN: literally, the town of the ford of the hurdles.
bail·ee (bā′lē′) *n. Law* One to whom property is bailed.
bail·er[1] (bā′lər) *n.* One who bails.
bail·er[2] (bā′lər) *n.* In cricket, a ball that strikes the bails.
bai·ley (bā′lē) *n.* *pl.* **bai·leys** **1** The outer court of a castle, or any court of a fortress. **2** A court of justice or a prison. Also **bai′lie.**
Bai·ley (bā′lē), **Liberty Hyde,** 1858–1955, U.S. horticulturist and writer. — **Nathan** or **Nathaniel,** died 1742, English lexicographer.
Bailey bridge A portable bridge consisting of a series of interchangeable prefabricated steel panels in the form of lattices, over which a prepared roadway can be laid. [after Donald Colman *Bailey,* born 1901, English engineer]
bai·lie (bā′lē) *n.* **1** *Scot.* A municipal officer corresponding to an alderman in England. **2** *Obs.* A bailiff. [<OF *baillif* bailiff]
Bail·lie (bā′lē), **Joanna,** 1762–1851, Scottish dramatist and poet.
bai·liff (bā′lif) *n.* **1** An officer of court having custody of prisoners under arraignment. **2** A sheriff's deputy for serving processes and warrants of arrest. **3** A custodian of property and its management for the owner; steward; overseer. **4** *Brit.* A subordinate magistrate with jurisdiction limited to a certain district or to certain functions, as to keeping the peace in the hundreds. **5** The first civil officer in each of the Channel Islands. [<OF *baillif* <L *bajalus* porter, manager]
bai·li·wick (bā′lə·wik) *n.* **1** The office, jurisdiction, or district of a bailiff. **2** One's own special place or province. [<BAILI(E) + OE *wic* village]
bail·ment (bāl′mənt) *n. Law* The act of bailing an accused person, goods, etc.
bail·or (bā′lər, bā′lôr′) *n. Law* One who delivers goods, etc., in bailment.
bails·man (bālz′mən) *n.* *pl.* **·men** (-mən) One who provides bail for another.
bail-up (bāl′up′) *n. Austral. Slang* **1** A demand for money or attention. **2** A hold-up by bushrangers.
Bai·ly's beads (bā′lēz) *Astron.* A series of luminous points appearing along the advancing edge of the moon's disk just before totality in a solar eclipse. [after Francis *Baily,* 1774–1844, English astronomer]
Bain (bān), **Alexander,** 1818–1903, Scottish psychologist.
bain·ie (bā′nē) *adj. Scot.* Bony.
bain-ma·rie (bań·mà·rē′) *n.* *pl.* **bains-ma·rie** (bań-) *French* A water bath, especially as used in the preparation of drugs and in cookery.
Bai·ram (bī·räm′) *n.* Either of two Moslem festivals, one of which, the **Lesser Bairam,** is in the beginning of the tenth month, at the end of Ramadan, and lasts from one to three days, while the other, the **Greater Bairam,** of four days, is seventy days later. [<Turkish]
Baird (bârd), **John Logie,** 1888–1946, Scottish inventor.
Baird Mountains (bârd) A range in NW Alaska.
Bai·reuth (bī·roit′) See BAYREUTH.
bairn (bârn) *n. Scot.* A young child; a son or a daughter.
Bairns·fa·ther (bârnz′fä′thər), **Bruce,** 1888–1959, English soldier and cartoonist.
bairn·team (bârn′tēm′) *n. Scot.* Children; progeny; offspring.
bait[1] (bāt) *n.* **1** Food or other enticement placed as a lure in a trap, on a hook, etc. **2** Any allurement or enticement. **3** A halt on a journey for food or refreshment. — *v.t.* **1** To put food or some other lure on or in: to *bait* a trap. **2** To torment, as by setting dogs upon, for sport: to *bait* a bear. **3** To harass; heckle. **4** To lure; entice. **5** *Obs.* To feed (a horse, etc.) while resting. — *v.i.* **6** *Obs.* To stop for rest and refreshment. ◆ Homophone: *bate.* [<ON *beita* cause to bite] — **bait′er**
bait[2] (bāt) *n. Dial.* **1** A quantity; an amount. **2** Enough. ◆ Homophone: *bate.*
bait[3] (bāt) See BATE.[3]
baith (bāth) *adj., pron.,* & *conj. Scot.* Both.
baize (bāz) *n.* **1** A plain, loosely woven cotton or woolen fabric, usually dyed green and napped to imitate felt: used for table covers, etc. **2** An article made of this fabric. [<OF *baies,* fem. pl. of *bai* chestnut-brown <L *badius*]
Ba·ja Ca·li·for·nia (bä′hä kä′lē·fôr′nyä) The Spanish name for LOWER CALIFORNIA.
Baj·er (bī′ər), **Fredrik,** 1837–1922, Danish statesman and writer.
ba·ju (bä′jŏŏ) A short jacket worn by men and women in Malay countries. [<Malay]
bake (bāk) *v.* **baked, bak·ing** *v.t.* **1** To cook by dry and continuous heat, as food in an oven. **2** To harden or vitrify by heat, as bricks or pottery. **3** *Obs.* To cake; harden. — *v.i.* **4** To bake bread, pastry, meat, or other food. **5** To become baked or hardened by heat, as soil. — *n.* **1** A baking or the amount baked. **2** *U.S.* A social gathering at which certain foods are baked and served. **3** *Scot.* A cracker. [OE *bacan*]
bake·house (bāk′hous′) *n.* A bakery.
Ba·ke·lite (bā′kə·līt) *n.* Trade name of a group of thermosetting plastics formed by the chemical reaction of phenol, formaldehyde, and their derivatives, having a wide range of properties and uses. [after L. H. *Baekeland*]
bak·er (bā′kər) *n.* **1** One who bakes and sells bread, cake, etc. **2** A portable oven.
Ba·ker (bā′kər), **Ernest Albert,** born 1869, English librarian and author. — **George Pierce,** 1866–1935, U.S. educator and editor. — **Newton Diehl,** 1871–1937, U.S. lawyer; secretary of war 1916–21. — **Ray Stannard,** 1870–1946, U.S. author: pseudonym *David Grayson.* — **Sir Samuel White,** 1821–93, English explorer in Africa.
Baker, Mount A peak in the Cascade Range, northern Washington; 10,750 feet.
Baker Island A United States possession (1936) in the Pacific Ocean near the equator, used as a refueling point; one square mile.
bakers' dozen Thirteen: from a former custom of giving an excess to make sure of avoiding the heavy penalties exacted for short weight or measure.
bak·er·y (bā′kər·ē, bāk′rē) *n.* *pl.* **·er·ies** **1** A place for baking bread, cake, etc. **2** A shop where bread, cake, pastry, etc., are sold at retail: also **bake′shop′.**
Bakh·mut (bäkh′mŏŏt) The former name of ARTEMOVSK.
bak·ing (bā′king) *n.* **1** The act of baking. **2** The quantity baked.
baking powder A finely powdered mixture of baking soda and an acid salt, giving off carbon dioxide when moist: it is used as a substitute for yeast in baking.
baking soda Sodium bicarbonate.
bak·sheesh (bak′shēsh) *n.* In India, Turkey, Egypt, and other countries, a gratuity or tip. — *v.t.* & *v.i.* To give a tip (to). Also spelled *backsheesh, backshish.* [<Persian *bakhshīsh* <*bakhshīdan* give]
Bakst (bäkst), **Leon Nikolaievich,** 1866?–1924, Russian painter and scenic designer.
Ba·ku The capital of Azerbaijan, pop. 1,700,000; an oil exporting port on the Caspian Sea.
Ba·ku·nin (bä·kŏŏ′nyin), **Mikhail,** 1814–76, Russian anarchist writer.
BAL (bal, *or pronounced as initials*) Proprietary name for a brand of dimercaprol, originally developed in England as an antidote to lewisite. [<B(RITISH) A(NTI-) L(EWISITE)]
Ba·laam (bā′ləm) A prophet, reproached by the ass he rode for cursing the Israelites. *Num.* xxii–xxiv.
Ba·la·ki·rev (bä·lä′ki·ryif), **Mili,** 1837–1910, Russian composer.
Bal·a·kla·va (bal′ə·klä′və) A Crimean port on the Black Sea, near which the Charge of the Light Brigade took place (1854).
bal·a·lai·ka (bal′ə·lī′kə) *n.* A Russian musical instrument having a triangular body, a guitar neck, and three strings. [<Russian]

BALALAIKA

bal·ance (bal′əns) *n.* **1** An instrument for weighing, often a bar pivoted on a central point according to the weight placed in or hung from a matched scale or pan at either end; scales: often used in the plural, either scale being called a *balance,* and the two a *pair of balances.* **2** The imaginary scales of destiny by which deeds and principles are weighed: a symbol of justice: Thou hast been weighed in the *balance* and found wanting. **3** The power to decide fate, value, etc., as by a balance. **4** A state of being in equilibrium; equipoise; equality. **5** Mental or emotional stability; sanity. **6** Harmonious proportion, as in the design or arrangement of parts in a work of art. **7** Something used to produce an equilibrium; counteracting influence; counterpoise. **8** The act of balancing or weighing. **9** Equality between the credit and debit totals of an account. **10** A difference between such totals; the excess on either side. **11** *U.S. Colloq.* Whatever is left over; remainder; surplus. **12** A balance wheel. **13** An instrument for measuring electricity or its effects by opposing some other force, as gravity. **14** A movement in dancing. See synonyms under REMAINDER. **—in the balance** Being judged; not yet settled. **—to strike a balance** To find or take an intermediate position; compromise. *—v.* **·anced, ·anc·ing** *v.t.* **1** To bring into or keep in equilibrium; poise. **2** To weigh in a balance. **3** To compare or weigh in the mind, as alternative courses of action; estimate the importance or consequence of. **4** To offset or counteract. **5** To keep or be in proportion to. **6** To be equal to. **7** To compute the difference between the debit and credit sides of (an account). **8** To reconcile, as by making certain entries, the debit and credit sides of (an account). **9** To adjust (an account) by paying what is owed. *—v.i.* **10** To be or come into equilibrium. **11** To be equal: The accounts *balance.* **12** To hesitate or waver; tilt: to *balance* on the edge of a chasm. **13** To move or lean back and forth as from one foot to another. [<F <L *bilanx, -ancis* having two plates <*bis* two + *lanx, lancis* dish, plate] **—bal′ance·a·ble** *adj.*

Bal·ance (bal′əns) The constellation Libra. See CONSTELLATION.

balanced load *Electr.* A distribution of power, current, and voltage over a polyphase circuit such that each phase of the circuit is balanced with respect to the others.

balanced surface *Aeron.* A control surface, as an aileron or rudder, part of which is forward of its pivot.

balance of payments The difference in payments made and received between a country and other countries, including costs of exports and imports of goods and services and the exchange of gold and capital.

balance of power A distribution of forces among nations such that no single nation or combination of nations will dominate or endanger any other.

balance of trade The difference in value between exports and imports of a country.

bal·anc·er (bal′ən·sər) *n.* **1** One who or that which balances. **2** A tightrope dancer; an acrobat. **3** *Entomol.* One of the paired halteres on each side of the thorax of certain dipterous insects. **4** An apparatus used to increase the precision of a radio direction finder.

balance-reef (bal′əns·rēf′) *Naut. v.t.* To reduce (a fore-and-aft sail) to the last reef. *—n.* A reef band diagonally across a fore-and-aft sail: the last reef on such a sail.

balance sheet A statement in tabular form to show assets and liabilities, profit and loss, etc., of a business at a specified date.

balance wheel The oscillating wheel of a watch or chronometer, which determines its rate of motion.

ba·lan·dran (bə·lan′drən) *n.* A wide wrap worn in the Middle Ages. Also **ba·lan·dra·na** (bə·lan′drə·nə). [<OF <Med. L *balandrana*]

Ba·lan·ga (bä·läng′gä) A town in southern Luzon, capital of Bataan province.

bal·as (bal′əs) *n.* A spinel having a rosy to yellowish color, used as a gemstone. [<OF *balais* <Arabic *balakhsh* <Persian *Badakhshan,* district where the gem is found]

bal·a·ta (bal′ə·tə) *n.* **1** The juice of the bullytree, used industrially as an elastic gum. **2** The tree. [<Sp. <Tupian]

Ba·la·ton (bä′lä·tōn), **Lake** A lake in western Hungary; 231 square miles: German *Plattensee.*

ba·laus·tine (bə·lôs′tin) *n.* The pomegranate, or its dried astringent flowers, bark, or rind. [<L *balaustium* pomegranate flower <Gk. *balaustion*]

Bal·bo (bäl′bō), **Italo,** 1896–1940, Italian general and aviator.

bal·bo·a (bal·bō′ə) *n.* A silver monetary unit of Panama, equivalent to about one U.S. dollar. [after Vasco de *Balboa*]

Bal·bo·a (bal·bō′ə) The port at the Pacific terminus of the Panama Canal, in Canal Zone.

Bal·bo·a (bal·bō′ə, *Sp.* bäl·vō′ä), **Vasco Nuñez de,** 1475?–1517, Spanish explorer; discovered the Pacific Ocean 1513.

Balboa Heights Administrative headquarters of Canal Zone.

bal·brig·gan (bal·brig′ən) *n.* **1** A fine, unbleached, knitted cotton hosiery fabric first made at Balbriggan, Eire. **2** A lightweight cotton fabric made in imitation of this. **3** *pl.* Clothes, especially underwear and hose, made of balbriggan. *—adj.* Made of balbriggan.

Bal·brig·gan (bal·brig′ən) A town on the Irish Sea 20 miles north of Dublin.

bal·bu·ti·es (bal·byōō′shi·ēz) *n.* A speech defect characterized by stuttering; stammering. [<NL <L *balbutire* stammer]

Balch (bôlch), **Emily Greene,** 1867–1961, U.S. economist and sociologist.

bal·co·ny (bal′kə·nē) *n. pl.* **·nies 1** A balustraded platform projecting from a wall of a building, usually before a window. **2** A projecting gallery inside a theater or other public building. [<Ital. *balcone* <*balco* a beam <OHG *balcho*] — **bal′co·nied** *adj.*

BALCONY WITH BALUSTRADE

bald (bôld) *adj.* **1** Without hair on the head. **2** Without natural covering or growth, as a mountain. **3** Unadorned; without embellishments. **4** Without disguise. **5** *Zool.* Having white feathers or fur on the head: the *bald* eagle. [? <Welsh *bāl* white] — **bald′ly** *adv.* **—bald′ness** *n.*

bal·da·chin (bal′də·kin, bôl′-) *n.* **1** A heavy, rich fabric, formerly made of silk and gold: also *baudekin.* **2** A canopy of such fabric, as one carried in religious processions. **3** *Archit.* A canopy of stone or metal, as over an altar or throne. Also **bal′da·quin.** [<F *baldaquin* <Ital. *baldacchino* <*Baldacco* Baghdad, where the cloth was first made]

bald cypress A timber tree (genus *Taxodium*) of the swampy regions of the southern United States, especially *T. distichum* and *T. ascendens.*

bald eagle A species of dark brown eagle *(Heliaeetus leucocephalus),* the adults having white head and tail feathers, formerly found throughout North America but in danger of extinction. Also called *American eagle.*

Bal·der (bôl′dər) In Norse mythology, god of sunlight, spring, and joy; son of Odin and Frigga. He was killed by the treachery of Loki. Also **Bal′dr.**

bal·der·dash (bôl′dər·dash) *n.* A meaningless flow of words; nonsense. [Origin uncertain]

bald·face (bôld′fās′) *n.* **1** The widgeon. **2** A horse having a white face.

bald-faced (bôld′fāst′) *adj.* **1** Having a white face or white markings on the face: said of animals. **2** Brash; undisguised: *bald-faced* lie.

bald·head (bôld′hed′) *n.* **1** One whose head is bald. **2** A breed of pigeons. **3** The widgeon. **4** The bald eagle.

bald-head·ed (bôld′hed′id) *adj.* Having a bald head. *—adv. U.S. Colloq.* Roughly, precipitately: to go at something *bald-headed.*

bald·ing (bôl′ding) *adj. U.S. Colloq.* Beginning to grow bald.

bald·pate (bôld′pāt′) *n.* A bald-headed person. **2** The widgeon. **—bald′-pat′ed** *adj.*

bal·dric (bôl′drik) *n.* A belt worn over one shoulder and across the breast, to support a sword, bugle, etc.: also spelled *bawdric.* Also **bal′drick.** [? <OF *baudrei*]

bald rush An American sedge (genus *Psilocarya*).

Bald·win (bôld′win) *n.* A red variety of winter apple.

Bald·win (bôld′win) A masculine personal name. Also *Dan., Ger.* **Bal·du·in** (bäl′dōō·ən); *Ital.* **Bal·do·vi·no** (bäl′dō·vē′nō); *Lat.* **Bal·du·i·nus** (bal′dōō·ī′nəs). [<Gmc., bold friend] **—Baldwin,** 1058–1118, king of Jerusalem 1100; fought in first crusade.

Bald·win (bôld′win), **James Mark,** 1861–1934, U.S. psychologist. **—Stanley,** 1867–1947, Earl Baldwin of Bewdly, prime minister of Great Britain, 1923–24, 1924–29, 1935–37.

Bald·y (bôl′dē) **1** Old Baldy. **2** A peak in northern New Mexico; 12,623 feet.

bale[1] (bāl) *n.* A large package of bulky goods corded or otherwise prepared for transportation. *—v.t.* **baled, bal·ing** To make into a bale or bales. ◆ Homophone: *bail.* [<OF *bale* round package, ? <OHG *balla* ball]

bale[2] (bāl) *n. Archaic* **1** That which causes ruin or sorrow; evil. **2** Pain; woe. ◆ Homophone: *bail.* [OE *bealu* evil, wickedness]

bale[3] (bāl) *n.* A balefire. ◆ Homophone: *bail.* [OE *bæl* fire, funeral pile]

Bâle (bäl) French name for BASEL.

Bal·e·ar·ic Islands (bal′ē·ar′ik, bə·lir′ik) A Spanish province in the western Mediterranean, comprising a group of four islands (Mallorca, Menorca, Iviza, and Formentera) and 11 islets; 1,936 square miles; capital, Palma, on Mallorca. *Spanish* **Is·las Ba·le·a·res** (ēz′läz vä′lā·ä′rās).

ba·leen (bə·lēn′) *n.* Whalebone. [<F *baleine* <L *balæna* <Gk. *phalaina* whale]

baleen knife A curved double-handled knife for splitting whalebone.

bale·fire (bāl′fīr′) *n.* **1** A signal fire; beacon. **2** A funeral pyre. **3** Any great outdoor fire. [OE *bælfyr* <*bæl* bale[3] + *fyr* fire]

bale·ful (bāl′fəl) *adj.* **1** Hurtful; malignant. **2** *Archaic* Sorrowful; miserable. See synonyms under BAD. **—bale′ful·ly** *adv.* **—bale′ful·ness** *n.*

bale hook A box hook.

bal·er (bā′lər) *n.* **1** One who or that which bales. **2** A baling machine.

Bal·four (bal′fōōr), **Arthur James,** 1848–1930, first Earl of Balfour, prime minister of Great Britain 1902–05.

Balfour Declaration A declaration issued by the British Government, November, 1917, favoring reestablishment of a Jewish "National Home" in Palestine.

Ba·li (bä′lē) One of the Lesser Sunda Islands, east of Java; 2,095 square miles; capital, Singaradja.

Ba·lik·pa·pan (bä′lik·pä′pän) A port and oil center on the eastern coast of the Indonesian part of Borneo.

Ba·li·nese (bä′lə·nēz′, -nēs′) *adj.* Of or pertaining to Bali, its people, or their language. *—n. pl.* **Ba·li·nese 1** A native or inhabitant of Bali. **2** The Indonesian language of Bali.

Ba·lin·tang Channel (bä′lēn·täng′) The central part of Luzon Strait, between the Batan and Babuyan Islands of north Luzon.

Bal·iol (bāl′yəl), **John de,** 1248–1315, king of Scotland. **—Edward,** died 1363, son of John; king of Scotland. Also spelled *Balliol.*

bal·i·saur (bal′ə·sôr) *n.* A long-tailed badger *(Arctonyx collaris)* of India and Siam. [<Hind. *bālusūr* <*bālu* sand + *sūr* hog]

Ba·lize (bə·lēz′) See BELIZE.

balk (bôk) *v.t.* **1** To render unsuccessful; thwart; frustrate. **2** *Obs.* To heap up in ridges or balks; also, to make a balk in (land). *—v.i.* **3** To stop short and refuse to proceed or take action. *—n.* **1** That which balks or hinders; an obstacle; hindrance. **2** An error; miss; blunder. **3** A feint or false motion, as a movement of the pitcher in baseball as if to pitch the ball, or the failure of a jumper to leap after taking his run. **4** A ridge left unplowed between furrows or between plowed strips of land. **5** A squared beam or timber. **6** The space between the balk line and the cushion of a billiard table. **7** One of the stringers or joist-shaped spars placed from boat to boat, upon which the chess or flooring of a pontoon bridge is placed. Also spelled *baulk.* See synonyms under ERROR. [OE *balca* bank, ridge]

Bal·kan (bôl′kən) *adj.* **1** Of or pertaining to the Balkan Peninsula, to the people of this region, their customs, etc. **2** Of or pertaining to the Balkan Mountains.

Balkan frame *Med.* A frame supported on four posts, with pulleys and slats for holding up the legs in the treatment of fractures. [First used in the *Balkan* States]

bal·kan·ize (bôl′kən·īz) *v.t.* **·ized, ·iz·ing** To separate (a country) into small, dissenting political units or states, as the Balkans after World War I. Also **Bal′kan·ize.** —**bal′kan·i·za′tion** *n.*

Balkan Mountains A mountain range in Bulgaria, extending 350 miles westward from the Black Sea to the Yugoslav border; highest point, 7,793 feet.

Balkan Peninsula A peninsula of SE Europe lying south of the lower Danube and bounded by the Black, Aegean, Mediterranean, Ionian, and Adriatic Seas.

Balkan States The countries occupying the Balkan Peninsula: Albania, Bulgaria, Greece, Rumania, Yugoslavia, and the western part of Turkey. Also **the Balkans.**

Balkan Wars See table under WAR.

Balkh (bälkh) A town in northern Afghanistan, capital of ancient Bactria: ancient *Bactra.*

Bal·khash (bäl·khäsh′) A salt lake in SE Kazakh S.S.R., 100 miles west of the Chinese border; 6,680 square miles.

Bal·kis (bal′kis) The Arabic name, used in the Koran, for the QUEEN OF SHEBA.

balk line (bôk) **1** In billiards, a line partitioning off a space in the corner, along the sides, or around the entire edge of the table. **2** In sports, especially track events, a line, progress beyond which counts as a trial.

balk·y (bô′kē) *adj.* **balk·i·er, balk·i·est** Disposed to stop suddenly or refuse to go: also spelled *baulky.* See synonyms under RESTIVE.

ball[1] (bôl) *n.* **1** A spherical or nearly spherical body. **2** Such a body, of any size and made of various substances, used in a number of games. **3** Any of several such games, especially baseball. **4** The mode of throwing or pitching a ball: a foul *ball,* a high or swift *ball.* **5** In baseball, a delivery by the pitcher in which the ball fails to pass over the home plate between the batsman's shoulder and knees and is not struck at by him: distinguished from *strike.* **6** *Mil.* **a** Any spherical or conoid projectile, larger than a small shot. **b** Such projectiles collectively: to load with *ball.* **7** A roundish protuberance or part of something, especially of the human body or of some organ. **8** A planet or star, especially the earth. —**to be on the ball** *Slang* To be competent or efficient —**to have something on the ball** *Slang* To have ability. —**to play ball 1** To begin or resume playing a ball game or some other activity. **2** *Colloq.* To cooperate. —*v.t.* & *v.i.* To form, gather, or wind into a ball: to *ball* worsted. —**to ball up** *Slang* To embarrass; confuse or become confused. ◆ Homophone: *bawl.* [<ON *böllr*]

ball[2] (bôl) *n.* A formal social assembly for dancing. ◆ Homophone: *bawl.* [<F *bal* a dance <*baler* < LL *ballare* dance]

Ball (bôl), **John,** died 1381, English priest; a leader of Wat Tyler's peasants' revolt.

bal·lad (bal′əd) *n.* **1** A narrative poem or song of popular origin in short stanzas, often with a refrain: originally handed down orally, often with changes and additions. **2** A sentimental song of several stanzas, in which the melody is usually repeated for each stanza. [<OF *balade* dancing song]

bal·lade (bə·läd′, ba-) *n.* **1** A verse form consisting of three stanzas of eight or ten lines each and an envoy of four or five lines: the last line of each stanza and of the envoy is the same. **2** A musical composition, usually of romantic or dramatic nature, usually for piano or orchestra. [<OF *balade* dancing song]

bal·lad·eer (bal′ə·dir′) *n.* A ballad singer.

bal·lad·mon·ger (bal′əd·mung′gər, -mong′-) *n.* **1** A seller of popular ballads. **2** A poetaster.

bal·la·drom·ic (bal′ə·drom′ik) *adj.* Pursuing a course heading for the target: said of rockets and guided missiles. [<Gk. *ballein* hurl (a missile) + *dromos* course]

bal·lad·ry (bal′əd·rē) *n.* **1** Ballad poetry. **2** The art of making or singing ballads.

ballad stanza A four-line stanza used in ballads, generally riming the second and fourth lines.

ball and chain 1 A heavy metal ball fastened by a chain to a prisoner to keep him from escaping. **2** *Slang* One's wife or husband.

ball-and-sock·et joint (bôl′ən·sok′it) *Mech.* A joint composed of a sphere working in a bearing permitting a degree of free turning in any direction.

bal·lant (bal′ənt) *n. Scot.* A ballad.

Bal·lan·tyne (bal′ən·tīn), **James,** 1772–1833, Scottish printer.

Bal·la·rat (bal′ə·rat′) A city of central Victoria, Australia. Also **Bal·la·a·rat** (bal′ə·ə·rat′).

bal·last (bal′əst) *n.* **1** Any heavy substance, as sand, stone, etc., laid in the hold of a vessel or in the car of a balloon to steady it. **2** Gravel or broken stone laid down as a stabilizer for a railroad bed. **3** That which gives stability to character, morality, etc. —*v.t.* **1** To provide or fill with ballast. **2** To steady with or as if with ballast; stabilize. **3** *Obs.* To weigh down. [<ODan. *barlast* <*bar* bare, mere + *last* load]

ball bearing *Mech.* **1** A bearing in which the shaft at its points of support rests upon or is surrounded by small metal balls that turn freely as the shaft revolves: used to reduce friction. **2** Any of the metal balls in such a bearing.

ball cartridge *Mil.* Live ammunition as distinguished from blank ammunition.

ball cock *Mech.* A stopcock for regulating the supply of water, in which the valve is opened or shut by the rising or falling of a hollow floating ball.

BALL COCK

bal·le·ri·na (bal′ə·rē′nə) *n.* A female ballet dancer. [<Ital., fem. of *ballerino* dancer]

bal·let (bal′ā, ba·lā′) *n.* **1** An elaborate kind of dramatic group dance using conventionalized movements, often for narrative effects. **2** This style of dancing. **3** Dancers of ballet, expecially a company of such dancers. **4** A danced interlude, as in an opera. **5** A musical composition written as an accompaniment to a ballet performance. [<F, dim. of *bal* a dance. See BALL[2].]

bal·let·o·mane (ba·let′ə·mān) *n.* A ballet enthusiast. [<F <*ballet* + *-(o)mane* <Gk. *mania* enthusiasm.]

ball·flow·er (bôl′flou′ər) *n. Archit.* A ball-like ornament resembling a ball placed in a flower of which the petals form a globe around it.

ball-gov·er·nor (bôl′guv′ər·nər) *n.* Governor (def. 2).

bal·li·bun·tl (bal′i·bun′təl) *n.* **1** A lightweight, glossy straw, woven of buntal. **2** A hat made of this straw. [<*Baliuag* in the Philippine Islands + BUNTAL]

bal·lis·ta (bə·lis′tə) *n. pl.* **·tae** (-tē) An engine used in ancient and medieval warfare for hurling missiles. [<L <Gk. *ballein* throw]

ROMAN BALLISTA

bal·lis·tic (bə·lis′tik) *adj.* Pertaining to projectiles or to ballistics.

ballistic coefficient A number which expresses the power of a projectile to maintain its velocity during flight.

ballistic curve The actual path of a projectile, as affected by wind, etc.

ballistic density A constant air density assumed to have the same effect upon a projectile in flight as the actual varying densities.

bal·lis·tics (bə·lis′tiks) *n.* The science that deals with the motion of projectiles, either while they are still in the bore **(interior ballistics)** or after they leave the muzzle **(exterior ballistics).** —**bal·lis·ti·cian** (bal′ə·stish′ən) *n.*

ballistic table A table showing the character and values of the factors affecting the flight of a projectile, as range, angle of fire, muzzle velocity, time of flight, etc.

ballistic wave The compression of air immediately in front of a projectile in flight, regarded as a wave formation.

bal·lis·tite (bal′is·tīt) *n.* A nearly smokeless gunpowder invented by Alfred Nobel in 1888.

bal·lo·net (bal′ə·net′) *n.* **1** A small balloon. **2** An airtight bag set in the interior of a spherical or nonrigid dirigible balloon to maintain pressure on the outer envelope. [<F *ballonnet,* dim. of *ballon* balloon]

bal·loon (bə·lo͞on′) *n.* **1** A large, airtight bag, inflated with gas lighter than air, designed to rise and float in the atmosphere: larger kinds have a car or basket attached, for carrying passengers, instruments, etc. Compare DIRIGIBLE, BLIMP. **2** A small inflatable rubber bag, used as a toy. **3** *Chem.* A spherical glass vessel. **4** A balloon-shaped outline connected with the mouth of a person, containing the words he is represented as speaking, as in comic strips. —**captive balloon** A balloon restrained from free flight by means of a cable that holds it to the ground. —**kite balloon** An elongated form of captive balloon, fitted with a tail appendage to keep it headed into the wind. —**observation balloon** A captive balloon used as an observation post. —**sounding balloon** A balloon sent up unmanned for obtaining meteorological data recorded on instruments which return to earth after the bursting of the balloon. Compare RADIOSONDE. —*v.i.* **1** To increase quickly in scope or magnitude; expand: The rumor *ballooned* into a scandal. **2** To swell out like a balloon, as a sail. **3** To travel or ascend in a balloon. —*v.t.* **4** To inflate or swell with air: A gust of wind *ballooned* the sail. [<Ital. *ballone* large ball <*balla* ball, sphere <Gmc.] —**bal·loon′ist** *n.*

balloon cloth A closely woven cotton fabric vulcanized with thin sheets of rubber so as to be airtight: used for balloons and dirigibles.

balloon foresail *Naut.* A light foresail set between the foretopmasthead and the jibboom end, used mostly by yachts in light winds. Also **balloon jib.**

balloon sail A spinnaker or a balloon foresail.

balloon tire A pneumatic tire filled with air at low pressure for reducing the shock of bumps.

bal·loon·vine (bə·lo͞on′vīn′) *n.* A tropical American climbing herb *(Cardiospermum halicacabum),* bearing inflated membranaceous three-celled pods; heartseed.

bal·lot (bal′ət) *n.* **1** A written or printed slip or ticket used in voting. **2** A little ball used in voting: the original sense. **3** The act or system of voting secretly by ballots or by voting machines. **4** The whole number of votes cast in an election. —**Australian ballot** A ballot bearing the names of all the candidates of all parties, so arranged as to insure absolute secrecy and liberty in polling votes. —*v.* **bal·lot·ed, bal·lot·ing** *v.i.* **1** To cast a ballot; vote or decide by ballot. **2** To draw lots or determine by lot: to *ballot* for position. —*v.t.* **3** To vote for or decide on by means of a ballot: to *ballot* a question. [<Ital. *ballotta,* dim. of *balla* ball. See BALLOON.]

bal·lotte·ment (bə·lot′mənt) *n. Med.* Impulse given to a body loosely suspended in a sac or cavity by which it rises on impact and returns again; sometimes applied in the diagnosis of pregnancy, floating kidney, etc. [<F <*ballotter* toss <*ballotte* small ball]

ball-peen (bôl′pēn′) *n.* A hemispherical peen on a hammerhead, used especially for riveting. See illustration under HAMMER.

ball·play·er (bôl′plā′ər) *n. U.S.* A baseball player.

ball point pen A fountain pen having for a point a ball bearing that rolls against an ink cartridge and deposits a line on the writing surface.

ball·room (bôl′ro͞om′, -ro͝om′) *n.* A large room for dancing, especially one with a polished floor. [<BALL[2]]

ballroom dancing A kind of social dancing in which two people dance as partners.

ball turret *Aeron.* A ball-shaped projection on the bottom part of certain bombers, power-driven and containing machine-guns which can swing in any direction.

ball valve **1** A ball-shaped valve. **2** A valve controlled by a floating ball.

bal·ly (bal′ē) *adj. & adv. Brit. Slang* A euphemism for BLOODY.

bal·ly·hack (bal′ē·hak) *n. Slang* A smash; wreck. Also **bal′ly·wack** (-wak).

bal·ly·hoo (bal′ē·ho͞o) *n. Colloq.* **1** Noisy patter: the *ballyhoo* of a side-show .announcer. **2** Any immoderate, unrestrained advertising. **3** Conspicuous noisiness of speech, manner, or habit. —*v.t.* & *v.i.* **·hooed, ·hoo·ing** To advocate or promote by means of ballyhoo. [Origin unknown]

balm (bäm) *n.* **1** An aromatic, resinous exudation from various trees or shrubs, used as medicine; balsam. **2** Any oily, fragrant, resinous substance. **3** Any tree or shrub yielding such a substance; especially, any tree of the genus *Commiphora.* **4** Any of various aromatic plants of the genus *Melissa,* especially *M. officinalis.* **5** Any pleasing fragrance. **6** Anything that soothes or heals. [<OF *basme* <L *balsamum* <Gk. *balsamon* ? <Semitic. Doublet of BALSAM.]

bal·ma·caan (bal′mə·kän′) *n.* A loose overcoat with raglan sleeves, made of rough woolen cloth. [from *Balmacaan,* estate in Scotland]

balm of Gilead **1** Any of several Oriental trees of the myrrh family (genus *Commiphora*). **2** The fragrant balsam obtained from them. **3** The balsam fir, or the balm obtained from it. **4** A European shade tree (*Populus candicans*).

Bal·mor·al (bal·môr′əl, -mor′-) *n.* **1** A striped heavy woolen stuff. **2** A petticoat made of such material. **3** A brimless Scottish cap. **4** A laced walking shoe: also **bal·mor′al.** [from *Balmoral* Castle]

Balmoral Castle Royal residence in SW Aberdeenshire, Scotland: built by Queen Victoria in 1854.

Bal·mung (bäl′mo͝ong) In the *Nibelungenlied,* the sword which Siegfried took from the Nibelungs.

balm·y (bä′mē) *adj.* **balm·i·er, balm·i·est** **1** Having the qualities of balm; aromatic. **2** Healing; soothing; mild. **3** *Brit. Slang* Slightly crazy; overly foolish. —**balm′i·ly** *adv.* —**balm′i·ness** *n.*

bal·ne·al (bal′nē·əl) *adj.* Of or pertaining to baths and bathing. [<L *balneum* bath]

bal·ne·ol·o·gy (bal′nē·ol′ə·jē) *n.* The science of treating disease by baths and the waters of mineral springs. [<L *balneum* bath + -LOGY]

ba·lo·ney (bə·lō′nē) *n.* **1** *Slang* Stuff and nonsense; bunkum. **2** *Colloq.* Bologna sausage. Also spelled *boloney, bolony.* [def. 1 <BOLOGNA SAUSAGE]

Bal·or (bal′ôr) In Celtic mythology, a giant king of the Fomorians whose single eye killed whatever it looked at; blinded and slain by his grandson, Lug.

bal·sa (bôl′sə, bäl′-) *n.* **1** A tree (*Ochroma pyramidale*) of tropical America and the West Indies. **2** The very light wood from this tree: called *corkwood.* **3** A raft originally made of light logs fastened together by a platform. **4** A catamaran. [<Sp. *balza*]

bal·sam (bôl′səm) *n.* **1** Any of a group of fragrant oleoresins obtained chiefly from the exudations of various trees. **2** Any such tree. **3** Any fragrant ointment; balm. **4** An aromatic resin containing cinnamic and benzoic acid, or the tree that yields it. **5** A flowering plant of the genus *Impatiens,* especially the common garden annual *I. balsamina.* **6** Any soothing or healing agent or circumstance. **7** The balsam fir. —*v.t.* To anoint with balsam; salve. [<L *balsamum* <Gk. *balsamon* balsam tree, ? <Semitic. Doublet of BALM.] —**bal·sa·ma·ceous** (bôl′sə·mā′shəs) *adj.*

balsam fir A tree (*Abies balsamea*) of the pine family, growing in the northern United States and Canada and yielding the Canada balsam: also called *balm of Gilead.*

bal·sam·ic (bôl·sam′ik, bal-) *adj.* **1** Of, like, or containing balsam. **2** Soothing; balmy.

bal·sam·if·er·ous (bôl′sə·mif′ər·əs, bal′-) *adj.* Yielding balsam or balm.

bal·sa·mi·na·ceous (bôl′sə·mə·nā′shəs, bal′-) *adj.* Belonging to a family of plants (*Balsaminaceae*) composed of the genera *Impatiens* and *Hydrocera.*

balsam of Peru A balsam from a tropical American tree (*Myroxylon pereirae*), used as a perfume in medicine: also called *Peru balsam.*

balsam of To·lu (tə·lo͞o′) An oleoresinous medicinal preparation obtained from a South American evergreen (*Myroxylon balsamum*), containing the volatile oil toluene: used as a basis for many cough mixtures.

balsam poplar The tacamahac (def. 2).

Bal·sas (bäl′säs), **Río de las** A large, unnavigable river in south central Mexico, flowing 450 miles SW to the Pacific.

Balt (bôlt) *n.* A native or inhabitant of the Baltic States.

Bal·tha·sar (bal·thā′zər, -thaz′ər) **1** One of the three Magi. Also **Bal·tha′zar.** **2** The alias of Portia in Shakespeare's *Merchant of Venice.*

Bal·tic (bôl′tik) *adj.* Of or pertaining to the Baltic Sea or the Baltic States. —*n.* A branch of the Balto-Slavic languages, including Lithuanian, Lettish (or Latvian), and Old Prussian (extinct).

Baltic Sea An inlet of the Atlantic enclosed by Sweden, Denmark, East Germany, West Germany, Poland, the U.S.S.R., and Finland; 163,000 square miles.

BALTIC SEA REGION

Baltic States A collective name for Lithuania, Latvia, and Estonia, formed in 1918 as independent republics from Russian provinces and governments; annexed in 1940 by the U.S.S.R.

Bal·ti·more (bôl′tə·môr, -mōr) A port in northern Maryland at the upper end of Chesapeake Bay.

Baltimore, Lord See CALVERT, GEORGE.

Baltimore oriole An American oriole (*Icterus galbula*): so named because the orange and black of the male were the colors of the coat of arms of Lord Baltimore.

Bal·to-Sla·vic (bôl′tō·slä′vik, -slav′ik) *n.* A subfamily of Indo-European languages, consisting of Baltic and Slavic branches.

Ba·lu·chi (bə·lo͞o′chē) *n.* The Indo-Iranian language of Baluchistan.

Ba·lu·chi·stan (bə·lo͞o′chə·stän′, bə·lo͞o′chə·stan) A mountainous region of west Pakistan; 134,139 square miles: divided into Baluchistan proper, a province of Pakistan; 52,900 square miles; capital, Quetta; four princely states; and a small area on the SW coast belonging to Oman.

bal·us·ter (bal′əs·tər) *n.* **1** One of a set of small pillars that support a hand rail and form with the hand rail a balustrade. **2** One of the small columns forming a chair back. [<F *balustre* <Ital. *balaustro* baluster <*balaustra* pomegranate flower; so called from the resemblance in form]

bal·us·trade (bal′ə·strād′) *n.* A hand rail supported by balusters. See illustration under BALCONY.

Bal·zac (bal′zak, bôl′-; *Fr.* bȧl·zȧk′), **Honoré de,** 1799–1850, French novelist and dramatist.

bam (bam) *Slang v.t.* To cheat; bamboozle. —*n.* A cheat, imposition, or deception.

Ba·ma·ko (bä·mä·kō′) A city in west Africa, capital of Mali.

bam·bang (bäm′bäng) *n.* A Javanese musical instrument, similar to the xylophone. [<Malay]

Bam·berg (bäm′berkh) A city in northern Bavaria, Germany.

bam·bi·no (bam·bē′nō) *n. pl.* **·ni** (-nē) **1** A little child; a baby. **2** A figure of the child Jesus. [<Ital., dim. of *bambo* simple, childish]

bam·boo (bam·bo͞o′) *n.* **1** A tall, treelike or shrubby grass of tropical and semi-tropical regions (genus *Bambusa* or related genera). **2** The tough, hollow, jointed stem of this plant, widely used for building, furniture, utensils, etc. [<Malay *bambu*]

bam·boo·zle (bam·bo͞o′zəl) *v.* **·zled, ·zling** *v.t.* **1** To impose upon; mislead; cheat. **2** To perplex. —*v.i.* **3** To practice trickery or deception. [Origin unknown] —**bam·boo′zle·ment** *n.* —**bam·boo′zler** *n.*

bam·bou·la (bam·bo͞o′lə) *n.* **1** A primitive drum made of bamboo. **2** A dance performed by Negroes of Louisiana to the beating of this drum. [<Creole]

bam·bu·co (bam·bo͞o′kō) *n.* A South American dance originating with the Indians of Colombia, and introduced into the United States in the mid-twentieth century. [<Sp. < native name]

ban[1] (ban) *v.t.* **1** To forbid; to proscribe or prohibit. **2** To place under an ecclesiastical ban; excommunicate; anathematize; interdict. **3** *Archaic* To curse; execrate. —*n.* **1** An official proclamation or edict, especially one of prohibition. **2** *pl.* An announcement of intention to marry: often spelled *banns.* **3** Informal disapproval or prohibition, as by public opinion. **4** An ecclesiastical edict of excommunication or interdiction. **5** A sentence of outlawry or banishment. **6** The summoning of vassals to arms by a feudal lord; also, the forces so collected. **7** *Archaic* A curse or denunciation. [*v.* <OHG *bannan* curse, prohibit and Med. L *bannum* proclamation; *n.* < *v.* and OF *ban* <Med. L *bannum* <Gmc.]

ban[2] (ban) *v.t. Obs.* To summon; call forth; call for. [OE *bannan* proclaim]

ban[3] (ban) *n.* A fine muslin made in the East Indies, from the fiber of the banana leafstalk. [<BANANA]

ban[4] (ban) *n. Archaic* **1** The title of the ruler of the southern marches of Hungary. **2** The governor of Croatia and Slavonia. [<Serbo-Croatian *bān* lord, ruler]

ban[5] (bän) *n. pl.* **ba·ni** (bä′nē) A Rumanian copper coin, worth 1/100 of a leu.

ba·nal (bā′nəl, bə·nal′, ban′əl) *adj.* Meaningless from overuse; commonplace; trivial. [<F <OF *ban* feudal summons (to service performed communally for a lord); hence ordinary, common] —**ba·nal·i·ty** (bə·nal′ə·tē) *n.* —**ba′nal·ly** *adv.*

ba·nan·a (bə·nan′ə) *n.* **1** A large, herbaceous plant (*Musa paradisiaca sapientum*) growing 10 to 20 feet high, cultivated in tropical climates for its edible pulpy fruit which grows in long pendent clusters. **2** The fruit of this plant. [<Sp. < native African name]

BANANA PLANT (From 10 to 20 feet high)

banana oil **1** Isoamyl acetate, $C_7H_{14}O_2$, a sweet-smelling, colorless, liquid ester widely used as a solvent and in artificial fruit flavors, cosmetics, etc.: also called *pear oil.* **2** *U.S. Slang* Fulsome flattery; cajolery.

Ba·na·ras (bə·nä′rəs) A sacred city of the Hindus, on the Ganges River in SE Uttar Pradesh, India: formerly *Benares.*

Ba·nat (bä·nät′) A region of SE Hungary formerly governed by a ban; divided (1920) into the **Rumanian Banat;** 6,975 square miles; the **Yugoslav Banat,** a small region of northern Serbia; and the **Hungarian Banat,** a small region near Szeged.

ba·nau·sic (bə·nô′sik) *adj. Rare* Suitable for a mechanic. [<Gk. *banausikos* mechanical < *banausos* artisan, mechanic]

Ban·bur·y (ban′ber′ē, bam′bər·ē) A municipal borough in northern Oxfordshire, England, famous for its cakes.

ban·ca (bäng′kä) *n.* In the Philippines, a form of dug-out canoe. [<Sp. <Tagalog *bangca*]

Ban·ca (bäng′kä) See BANGKA.

Ban·croft (ban′krôft, -kroft), **George,** 1800–1891, U.S. historian.

band[1] (band) *n.* **1** A flat flexible strip of any material used for binding. **2** Any strip of fabric used to finish, strengthen, or trim an article of dress. **3** *pl.* A pair of linen strips hanging from the front of the neck, worn with certain clerical or academical garments: also called **Geneva bands.** **4** Any broad stripe of contrasting color, material, or surface. **5** *Physics* **a** Any of the broad stripes found in typical molecular spectra: seen as distinct lines upon high magnification. **b** A group of states whose energies are so closely spaced as to be unresolvable and which therefore provide a continuous range of energies throughout an interval. **6** *Electronics* A range of sound frequencies or wavelengths within two stated limits: the standard broadcast *band.* **7** *Mech.* A flexible driving belt, communicating motion between wheels by friction. **8** A circular strip or loop of metal; a ring: a golden *band* on one's finger. — *v.t.* **1** To unite or tie with a band; encircle. **2** To mark with a band, as birds; to mark with a stripe. [<F *bande* <OF *bende,* ult. <Gmc. Akin to BIND.]

band[2] (band) *n.* **1** A company of persons associated, organized, or bound together. **2** A company of persons organized to play musical instruments, especially wind and percussion instruments. **3** A group of certain instruments in an orchestra: the string *band.* **4** A drove of animals, nomadic peoples, etc., wandering together. — **to beat the band** *U.S. Colloq.* Inordinately; surpassingly: He shouted *to beat the band.* — *v.t.* To join or unite, as associates in a league or company: often with *together.* — *v.i.* To confederate. [<F *bande.* Akin to BIND.]

band[3] (band) *n.* That which binds, ties, or unites; a bond. [<ON. Akin to BIND.]

band·age (ban′dij) *n.* **1** A strip, usually of soft cloth, used in dressing wounds, etc. **2** Any band. — *v.t.* **·aged, ·ag·ing** To bind or cover with a bandage. [<F < *bande* band]

Band-Aid (band′ād′) *n.* A gauze patch attached to an adhesive strip, used to cover minor wounds: a trade name. Also **band′aid′.**

ban·da·lore (ban′də·lôr, -lōr) *n.* A toy worked by means of a spring which returns it to the hand on a cord when thrown. [Origin unknown]

ban·dan·na (ban·dan′ə) *n.* A large, bright-colored handkerchief with spots or figures. Also **ban·dan′a.** [<Hind. *bāndhnū* mode of dyeing < *bāndh* tie]

Ban·dar Shah·pur (bän·där′ shä·po͝or′) A port of SW Iran at the head of the Persian Gulf.

Ban·da Sea (bän′də, ban′-) A part of the Pacific Ocean bounded by the southern Moluccas, Celebes, and the Lesser Sunda Islands.

band·box (band′boks′) *n.* A light round or oval box, for carrying hats, etc.: originally used for collars (formerly called *bands*).

ban·deau (ban·dō′) *n. pl.* **·deaux** (-dōz′) **1** A narrow band, especially one worn about the hair; fillet. **2** A brassière. [<F <OF *bandel,* dim of *bande* band]

banded ant-eater A small Australian marsupial (*Myrmecobius fasciatus*), rust-red with white bands on the back: also called *numbat.*

band·er (ban′dər) *n.* One who belongs to a band or league.

ban·de·ril·la (bän′dā·rē′lyä) *n. Spanish* In bullfighting, a dart with streamers attached, stuck into the neck and shoulders of the bull.

ban·de·ril·le·ro (bän′dā·rē·lyā′rō) *n. Spanish* In bullfighting, one who places banderillas to infuriate the bull.

ban·de·role (ban′də·rōl) *n.* **1** A small flag, pennant, or streamer, as at the end of a lance, etc., often bearing an inscription. **2** In painting and sculpture, a ribbon or scroll bearing an inscription. **3** A banner over a tomb or carried at a funeral. Also **ban′de·rol:** also *bannerole.* [<F <Ital. *banderuola,* dim. of *bandiera* banner]

ban·di·coot (ban′di·ko͞ot) *n.* **1** A large rat (*Mus* or *Nesokia bandicota*) of India and Ceylon, often over a foot in length. **2** A small insectivorous marsupial (genus *Parameles*) of Australia, Tasmania, etc. [<Telugu *pandikokku* pig-rat]

ban·dit (ban′dit) *n. pl.* **ban·dits** or **ban·dit·ti** (ban·dit′ē) A highwayman; brigand. See synonyms under ROBBER. [<Ital. *bandito,* pp. of *bandire* proscribe, outlaw] — **ban′dit·ry** *n.*

Ban·djer·ma·sin (bän′jər·mä′sin) See BANJERMASIN.

band·mas·ter (band′mas′tər, -mäs′tər) *n.* The conductor of a musical band.

ban·dog (ban′dôg′, -dog′) *n.* **1** A large, fierce dog, commonly kept chained as a watchdog. **2** A bloodhound or a mastiff. [<BAND[3] + DOG]

ban·do·leer (ban′də·lir′) *n.* **1** A broad band, usually of canvas webbing, with loops for holding cartridges, worn over the shoulder. **2** An ammunition box attached to this band. Also **ban′do·lier′.** [<F *bandoulière* <Ital. *bandoliera* shoulder belt, ult. < *banda* band]

ban·do·line (ban′də·lēn, -lin) *n.* A gummy liquid made from tragacanth and quince seeds: used for dressing the hair. [Origin uncertain]

ban·dore (ban·dôr′, -dōr′) *n.* An ancient lute-like musical instrument. [<Sp. *bandurria* <L *pandura* <Gk. *pandoura* lute]

band saw *Mech.* A saw consisting of a toothed endless belt on wheels.

band shell A concave, hemispherical band-stand for concerts.

bands·man (bandz′mən) *n. pl.* **·men** (-mən) A member of a musical band.

band·stand (band′stand′) *n.* An outdoor platform for a band of musicians, often roofed. Also **band stand.**

Ban·dung (bän′do͝ong) A city of western Java. *Dutch* **Ban′doeng.**

band·wag·on (band′wag′ən) *n.* A high, decorated wagon to carry a band in a parade. — **to climb on the bandwagon** To avow adherence publicly to a political principle or candidate evidently destined to win; adopt prevalent opinions and attitudes.

ban·dy (ban′dē) *v.t.* **ban·died, ban·dy·ing** **1** To give and take; exchange, as blows, quips, or words: often with *about.* **2** To pass along; circulate: to *bandy* stories. **3** To pass, throw, or knock back and forth, as a ball. — *adj.* Crooked outward at the knees; curved; bowed. — *n. pl.* **ban·dies** **1** A game resembling hockey; also, a crooked stick used in this game. **2** An ancient form of tennis. [Origin uncertain]

ban·dy-leg·ged (ban′dē·leg′id, -legd′) *adj.* Having crooked legs; bowlegged.

bane (bān) *n.* **1** Anything destructive or ruinous; ruin. **2** A deadly poison: now used only in composition: *henbane.* **3** *Obs.* Death. [OE *bana* murderer, destruction]

bane·ber·ry (bān′ber′ē, -bər·ē) *n. pl.* **·ries** **1** The poisonous berry of any species of *Actaea.* **2** The plant bearing this berry.

bane·ful (bān′fəl) *adj.* Noxious; poisonous; injurious; deadly; ruinous. See synonyms under BAD, PERNICIOUS. — **bane′ful·ly** *adv.* — **bane′ful·ness** *n.*

Banff (bamf) **1** A mountainous county of NE Scotland; 630 square miles; county seat, Banff. Also **Banff·shire** (bamf′shir). **2** A resort town in **Banff National Park,** a scenic park in SW Alberta, Canada; 2,564 square miles.

bang[1] (bang) *n.* **1** A sudden or noisy blow, thump, whack, or explosion. **2** *Colloq.* A sudden spring; dash. **3** *U.S. Slang* Thrill; excitement: to get a *bang* out of flying. [<*v.*] — *adv.* **1** With a violent blow or loud and sudden noise. **2** All at once; abruptly. — *v.t.* **1** To beat or strike resoundingly. **2** To shut noisily, as a door. **3** To give a thrashing to; drub. — *v.i.* **4** To make a heavy, loud sound. **5** To strike noisily: The car *banged* into the wall. [<ON *banga* hammer, beat]

bang[2] (bang) *n.* Front hair cut straight across: usually in the plural. — *v.t.* To cut straight across, as the front hair. [<BANG[1], *adv.*; from the hair being cut off abruptly]

bang[3] (bang) See BHANG.

Ban·ga·lore (bang′gə·lôr′, -lōr′) The administrative capital of Mysore state, India.

ban·ga·lore torpedo (bang′gə·lôr, -lōr) *Mil.* A length of metal piping filled with high explosive and used chiefly to clear a safe path through a mine field or barbed-wire entanglements. [from *Bangalore*]

Bang·gai Archipelago (bäng·gī′) An Indonesian island group east of Celebes; 1,222 square miles.

Bang·ka (bäng′kä) An Indonesian island east of Sumatra; 4,600 square miles: also *Banca, Banka.*

bang·kok (bang′kok) *n.* **1** Smooth, lightweight, dull straw woven of buntal fibers. **2** An article made of this straw. [from *Bangkok*]

Bang·kok (bang′kok) A port on the Chao Phraya, capital of Thailand. *Siamese* **Krung Thep** (kro͝ong tep′).

Ban·gla Desh (bäng′glä desh′) A republic in southern Asia; 54,501 square miles; capital, Dacca.

ban·gle (bang′gəl) *n.* A decorative bracelet or anklet. [<Hind. *bangrī* glass bracelet]

Ban·gor (bang′gôr, -gər) **1** A city on the Penobscot River, central Maine. **2** A municipal borough of northern Caernarvonshire, Wales.

Bang's disease An infectious brucellosis in cattle, caused by a bacterium (*Brucella abortus*), often resulting in abortion. Compare UNDULANT FEVER. [after B. L. F. *Bang,* 1848–1932, Danish veterinarian]

bang·tail (bang′tāl′) *n.* **1** A horse's tail cut horizontally across. **2** *Slang* A horse, especially a race horse. [<BANG[2] + TAIL] — **bang′·tailed′** *adj.*

bang-up (bang′up′) *adj. Slang* Excellent.

Bang·we·u·lu (bang′wē·o͞o′lo͞o) A swampy lake in NE Northern Rhodesia; 3,800 square miles.

ba·ni (bä′nē) Plural of BAN[5].

ban·ian (ban′yən) *n.* **1** A Hindu merchant or trader belonging to a caste refusing to eat meat. **2** A loose shirt, jacket, or gown. **3** Banyan. [<Pg. <Arabic *banyān,* ult. <Skt. *vaṇij* merchant]

ban·ish (ban′ish) *v.t.* **1** To compel to leave a country by political decree; exile. **2** To expel, as from any customary or desired place; drive away; dismiss, as a thought from one's mind. [<OF *baniss-,* stem of *banir* <LL *banire* banish < *bannum* proclamation <Gmc.] — **ban′ish·er** *n.* — **ban′ish·ment** *n.*

Synonyms: ban, discharge, dislodge, dismiss, eject, evict, exile, expatriate, expel, ostracize, oust. From a country, a person may be *banished, exiled,* or *expatriated; banished* from any country where he may happen to be, but *expatriated* or *exiled* only from his own. One may *expatriate* or *exile* himself; he is *banished* by others. *Banish* is a word of wide import; one may *banish* disturbing thoughts; care may *banish* sleep. To *expel* is to drive out with violence, and often with disgrace. See EXTERMINATE.

ban·is·ter (ban′is·tər) *n.* **1** A baluster. **2** *pl.* A balustrade on a staircase. Also *bannister.* [Alter. of BALUSTER]

ban·is·ter·ine (ban·is′tər·ēn, -in) *n.* An alkaloid derivative, $C_{13}H_{12}ON_2$, of a South American plant (*Banisteriopsis caapi*): a hallucinating drug which has been used to treat encephalitis lethargica: also called *harmine.* [after John *Banister,* 17th c. American botanist]

Ba·ni·yas (bä′nē·yäs′) A village in SW Syria: ancient *Caesarea Philippi.*

Ban·jer·ma·sin (bän′jər·mä′sin) A town in SW Indonesian Borneo: also *Bandjermasin.*

ban·jo (ban′jō) *n. pl.* **·jos** A long-necked, stringed musical instrument having a hoop-shaped body covered on top with stretched skin and played by plucking the strings with the fingers or a plectrum. [Alter. of Sp. *bandurria.* See BANDORE.] — **ban′jo·ist** *n.*

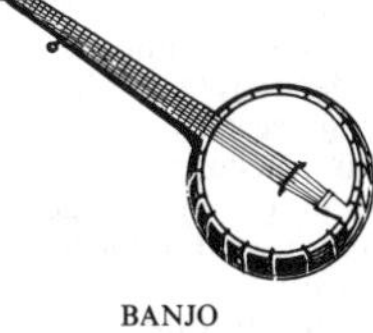

BANJO

banjo clock A 19th century American clock having a banjo-shaped case.

ban·jo·rine (ban′jə·rēn′) *n.* A musical instrument similar to the banjo, but tuned a fourth higher.

bank[1] (bangk) *n.* **1** Any moundlike formation or mass; ridge. **2** A steep acclivity; rising ground. **3** The slope of land at the edge of a watercourse or of any cut or channel: often in the plural. **4** A raised portion of the bed of a river, lake, or ocean: the Newfoundland *banks;* also a shallow; sandbar; shoal. **5** The cushion of a billiard table. **6** *Aeron.* The sidewise inclination of an airplane in making a turn. **7** The ground at the top of the shaft of a mine. — *v.t.* **1** To enclose, cover, or protect by a bank, dike, or border; embank. **2** To heap up into a bank or mound. **3** To give an upward lateral slope to, as the curve of a road. **4** To incline (an airplane) laterally. **5** In billiards and pool, to cause (a ball) to rebound at an angle from a cushion; also, to pocket (a ball) in this manner. — *v.i.* **6** To form or lie in banks. **7** To incline an airplane laterally. **—to bank** (or **bank up) a fire** To cover a fire with ashes or earth so as to keep it alive but burning low. [ME *banke,* ult. <Gmc. Akin to BENCH.]

Synonyms (noun): beach, border, bound, brim, brink, coast, edge, marge, margin, rim, shore, strand. *Bank* is a general term for the land along the edge of a watercourse. A *beach* is a strip or expanse of incoherent wave-worn sand, which is often pebbly or full of boulders. *Strand* is a more poetic term for a wave-washed shore, especially as a place for landing or embarking; as, the keel grates on the *strand.* The whole line of a country or continent that borders the sea is a *coast. Shore* is any land, whether cliff, or sand, or marsh, bordering water. We do not speak of the *coast* of a river, nor of the *banks* of the ocean, though there may be *banks* by or under the sea. *Edge* is the line where land and water meet; as, the water's *edge. Brink* is the place from which one may fall; as, the *brink* of a precipice, the *brink* of ruin.

bank[2] (bangk) *n.* **1** An institution for lending, borrowing, exchanging, issuing , or caring for money. **2** An office or building used for banking purposes. **3** The funds of a gaming establishment or the fund held by the dealer or banker in some gambling games. **4** In some games, reserve piece from which the players are permitted to draw, as in dominoes. **5** A store or reserve supply of anything needed for future use or emergency: a blood *bank.* **6** Any place of storage. **7** *Obs.* A money-changer's table. — *v.t.* **1** To deposit in a bank. **2** To back financially or furnish funds for, as a business enterprise. — *v.i.* **3** To do business as or with a bank or banker. **4** In gambling, to keep the bank at a gambling table. **5** To have faith in; rely or count: with *on.* [<F *banque* <Ital. *banca* money-changer's table, ult. <Gmc.]

bank[3] (bangk) *n.* **1** A set of like articles grouped together in a line. **2** A rowers' bench in a galley; a thwart. **3** A horizontal rank of keys in a piano or organ. **4** In journalism, lines under a headline; deck. **5** *Printing* **a** The heavy sloping table on which type galleys or dead type are held. **b** A pressman's table for holding sheets. **c** The track along which the carriage of a printing press moves. — *v.t.* To bring together in a bank, as transformers. [<OF *banc* <LL *bancus* bench, ult. <Gmc. Akin to BENCH.]

Ban·ka (bäng′kä) See BANGKA.

bank·a·ble (bangk′ə·bə) *adj.* Capable of being banked; receivable by or acceptable to a bank.

bank acceptance A draft endorsed or acknowledged by a bank on which it is drawn. Also **banker's acceptance.**

bank account **1** An account with a bank. **2** A sum of money deposited in a bank to the credit and subject to the withdrawal of a depositor.

bank annuities The legal name for CONSOLS.

bank bill **1** A banknote. **2** A draft drawn on one bank by another: also **banker's bill.**

bank·book (bangk′bo͝ok′) *n.* A book in which a depositor's accounts are entered: held by the depositor and serving as a receipt for deposits: also called *passbook.*

bank discount A deduction beforehand of interest reckoned on the face of a bill or note.

bank·er[1] (bangk′ər) *n.* **1** A person or company that owns or manages a bank. **2** One who acts as dealer and keeps the bank, as in certain gambling games.

bank·er[2] (bangk′ər) *n.* A vessel or person engaged in cod-fishing on the Newfoundland banks.

bank·er[3] (bangk′ər) *n.* A stonemason's or sculptor's workbench.

bank holiday **1** *Brit.* Any of six holidays on which banks are legally closed, usually a general holiday. **2** Sunday or a legal holiday upon which banks are officially closed.

bank·ing (bangk′ing) *n.* The business of a bank or banker.

bank night *Colloq.* An evening when cash prizes are given by lottery to patrons of a motion-picture theater.

bank·note (bangk′nōt′) *n.* A promissory note, issued by a bank, payable on demand, and serving as currency.

Bank of the United States Either of two banking institutions (1791–1816 and 1817–36) that acted as fiscal agents of the U.S. government.

bank·pa·per (bangk′pā′pər) *n.* **1** Banknotes. **2** Negotiable, discountable commercial papers, as securities, bank drafts, bills of exchange, etc.

bank rate The rate of discount determined by banks.

bank·rupt (bangk′rupt) *n.* **1** A person unable to pay his debts or without credit or resources. **2** *Law* One who is unable to make payment of a just debt when due and demanded of him: a bankrupt is judicially declared insolvent and his property is administered for and divided among his creditors, under a bankruptcy law. — *adj.* **1** Unable to pay one's debts; insolvent. **2** Subject to the conditions of bankruptcy law. **3** Lacking in some quality. — *v.t.* To make bankrupt. [<F *banqueroute* <) Ital. *banca rotta* bankruptcy < *banca* bench + *rotta* broken <L *ruptus,* pp. of *rumpere* break]

bank·rupt·cy (bangk′rupt·sē, -rəp·sē) *n. pl.* **·cies** **1** The state of being insolvent; failure or inability to pay just debts. **2** Any complete ruin or failure.

bankrupt worm A threadworm (genus *Trichostrongylus*) which causes gastroenteritis in livestock: so called from the financial damage caused by this parasite.

Banks (bangks), **Sir Joseph,** 1743–1820, English explorer and naturalist.

bank·si·a (bangk′sē·ə) *n.* One of a genus *(Banksia)* of Australian evergreen trees or shrubs with leathery leaves and long, dense heads of yellow flowers. [after Sir Joseph *Banks*]

Bank·side (bangk′sīd) A district on the south bank of the Thames in London: site of Shakespeare's Globe Theater.

Banks Island Westernmost island in the Arctic Archipelago, Northwest Territories, Canada; approximately 26,000 square miles.

ban·ner (ban′ər) *n.* **1** A cloth bearing a device, suspended from a pole by a crossbar. **2** Any flag or standard. **3** *Bot.* The large upper petal of a papilionaceous blossom. **4** In journalism, a headline extending across the full width of a newspaper page. — *v.t.* To furnish with a banner. — *adj.* Leading; foremost; outstanding. [<OF *banere* <LL *bandum* banner, ult. <) Gmc.]

ban·ner·et[1] (ban′ə·ret′) *n.* A small banner. Also **ban′ner·ette′.**

ban·ner·et[2] (ban′ər·it, -et) *n.* **1** One of a grade of knights, next below a baron, entitled to lead vassals under his own banner. **2** The title of such a knight. Also **knight banneret.**

ban·ner·ole (ban′ə·rōl) See BANDEROLE.

ban·net (ban′it) *n. Scot.* A bonnet.

ban·nis·ter (ban′is·tər) See BANISTER.

ban·nock (ban′ək) *n. Scot. Brit. Dial.* A thin cake of meal baked on a griddle. [OE *bannuc* part, piece, bit]

Ban·nock·burn (ban′ək·bûrn) A village in NE Stirlingshire, Scotland; site of a battle, 1314, in which Robert Bruce defeated the English.

banns (banz) See BAN[1] (*n.* def. 2).

ban·quet (bang′kwit) *n.* **1** An elaborate or sumptuous feast. **2** A formal or ceremonial dinner, often followed by speeches. — *v.t. v.i.* To entertain at a banquet; feast sumptuously or formally. [<F, dim. of *banc* table] — **ban′quet·er** *n.*

ban·quette (bang·ket′) *n.* **1** *Mil.* A raised earthen platform or bank behind an earthwork, upon which soldiers stand to deliver their fire. See illustration under BASTION. **2** An upholstered bench, as along a wall in a restaurant. **3** Any bank, ledge, etc., as a shelf on a sideboard. **4** A sidewalk. [<F, dim. of *banc* bench]

Ban·quo (bang′kwō, -kō) In Shakespeare's *Macbeth,* a thane whose ghost appears only to Macbeth, his murderer.

bans (banz) See BAN[1] (*n.* def. 2).

ban·shee (ban′shē, ban·shē′) *n.* In Gaelic folklore, a supernatural being whose wailing outside a house was supposed to foretell a death in the family. [<Irish *bean sīdhe* < *bean* woman + *sīdhe* fairy]

ban·tam (ban′təm) *n.* **1** A breed of domestic fowl characterized by small size and pugnacity. Also **Ban′tam. 2** Hence, a pugnacious person of small size. — *adj.* Like a bantam; small; combative. [from *Bantam,* Java]

Ban·tam (bän·täm′, ban′təm) A ruined town in NW Java, site of the first Dutch settlement in Indonesia.

ban·tam·weight (ban′təm·wā t′) *n.* A boxer or wrestler who weighs 118 pounds or less.

ban·ter (ban′tər) *n.* Good-humored ridicule; raillery; repartee. — *v.t.* To tease or ridicule good-naturedly. — *v.i.* To exchange good-natured repartee. [Origin unknown] **—ban′·ter·er** *n.* **—ban′ter·ing·ly** *adv.*

Synonyms (noun): badinage, chaff, derision, irony, jeering, mockery, raillery, ridicule, sarcasm, satire. *Banter* is the touching upon some unimportant fault or weakness of another in a way half to pique and half to please; *badinage* is delicate, refined *banter. Raillery* has more sharpness, but is usually good-humored and well-meant. *Irony,* the saying one thing that the reverse may be understood, may be either mild or bitter. *Ridicule* makes a person or thing the subject of contemptuous merriment; *derision* seeks to make the object derided seem utterly despicable—to laugh it to scorn. *Jeering* is loud, rude *ridicule,* as of a hostile crowd or mob. *Mockery* may include mimicry and personal violence, as well as scornful speech. A *satire* is a formal composition; a *sarcasm* may be an impromptu sentence. The *satire* shows up follies to keep people from them; the *sarcasm* hits them because they are foolish, without inquiring whether it will do good or harm. See MOCK, RIDICULE.

Ban·ting (ban′ting), **Sir Frederick Grant,** 1891–1941, Canadian physician; discovered insulin treatment for diabetes.

Ban·ting·ism (ban′ting·iz′əm) *n.* A method of reducing corpulence by dietetic treatment. [from William *Banting,* 1797–1878, English dietician.]

bant·ling (bant′ling) *n.* **1** A young child; infant. **2** A bastard. [<G *bänkling* bastard]

Ban·tu (ban′to͞o) *n. pl.* **Ban·tu** or **Ban·tus** (-to͞oz) **1** A family of Niger-Congo languages spoken in central and southern Africa. **2** A member of any of a group of African people who speak Bantu languages. **3** An offensive and vulgar term of contempt for black Africans of the Republic of South Africa.

Ban·ville (bä·vēl′), **Théodore de,** 1823–91, French poet and dramatist.

ban·yan (ban′yən) *n.* An East Indian fig-bearing tree *(Ficus benghalensis)* which sends down from its branches roots that develop into new trunks, thus producing a thick and shady grove: also spelled *banian.* [<BANIAN, from the use of the ground under the tree as a market place]

BANYAN TREE
(From 80 to 100 feet high)

ban·zai (bän′zī′) *interj.* A Japanese greeting, battle cry, or cheer, meaning: (May you live) ten thousand years!

banzai attack A desperate attempt to carry a position by infantry charge: used by the Japanese in World War II. Also **banzai charge.**

ba·o·bab (bā′ō·bab, bä′ō-) *n.* An African tree *(Adansonia digitata)* with a thick trunk, bearing edible, gourdlike fruit; the monkey-bread tree. [<native African name]

bap (bap) *n. Scot.* A loaf or roll of bread.

bap·tism (bap′tiz·əm) *n.* **1** The act of baptizing or of being baptized; specifically, a sacrament in which water is used to initiate the recipient into a Christian church, to symbolize purification, to acknowledge consecration to Christ, etc. 2 Any initiatory or purifying experience. 3 A religious ablution signifying a purification or consecration, as that by which proselytes were Judaized. 4 In Christian Science, purification by Spirit; submergence in Spirit. [<OF *baptesme* <LL *baptismus* <Gk. *baptismos* immersion] — **bap·tis·mal** (bap·tiz′məl) *adj.* — **bap·tis′mal·ly** *adv.*

baptismal name A name given to a person when he is baptized.

baptism of fire 1 In the Bible, baptism with the Holy Spirit; spiritual baptism. 2 Martyrdom. 3 A soldier's first experience under actual combat. 4 Any crucial ordeal or purifying experience or trial.

Bap·tist (bap′tist, *Ger.* bäp′-) A masculine personal name. Also *Fr.* **Bap·tiste** (bà·tēst′); *Lat.* **Bap·tis·ta** (bap·tis′tə). [<Gk., baptizer]

Bap·tist (bap′tist) *n.* 1 A member of various Protestant denominations holding that baptism should be given only to professed adult believers, and, generally, that baptism should be by immersion rather than by sprinkling. 2 One who baptizes. — **the Baptist** John the Baptist.

bap·tis·ter·y (bap′tis·tər·ē, -tis·trē) *n. pl.* **·ter·ies** 1 A font or tank for baptism. 2 A part of a church or other building set apart for baptism. Also **bap′tis·try** (-trē).

bap·tize (bap·tīz′, bap′tīz) *v.t.* **·tized, ·tiz·ing** 1 To immerse in water or pour water on in the Christian sacrament of baptism, symbolizing dedication to Christ, purification, and admission into a specific church. 2 To christen or name at the sacrament of baptism. 3 To cleanse; sanctify. 4 To consecrate or dedicate to special uses by some ceremony resembling baptism. Also *Brit.* **bap·tise′.** [<F *baptiser* <LL *baptizare* <Gk. *baptizein* immerse, wash] — **bap·tiz′er** *n.*

bar[1] (bär) *n.* 1 A piece of solid material, evenly shaped and long in proportion to its width and thickness: often used as a unit of quantity, a fastening, a barrier, etc. 2 Any barrier or obstruction. 3 A bank, as of sand, at the entrance to a river or harbor. 4 The enclosed place in court occupied by counsel; also, the place where a prisoner stands to plead; hence, the court or any place of justice, or anything considered as analogous; a judgment seat. 5 Lawyers collectively; the legal profession. 6 A room or a counter where liquors or refreshments are dispensed. 7 A stripe; a band, as of color or light. 8 *Music* **a** The vertical line that divides a staff into measures. **b** A double bar. **c** The unit of music between two bars; measure. 9 A horizontal timber or other

BARS IN MUSIC *(def. 8)*
a. Single. *b.* Double.

piece connecting two parts of a framework. 10 The solid metal mouthpiece of a horse's bridle; also, the space in front of a horse's upper molar teeth in which the bit is placed; also, that portion of a horse's foot that bends toward the frog. 11 In needlepoint, a transverse thread or group of threads passed from one side or corner of an opening to another: usually twisted or buttonholed and sometimes finished with knots. 12 *Law* The preventing or stopping of an action by showing that the plaintiff has no right of action. 13 *Her.* An ordinary formed by two parallel lines drawn horizontally across a shield, covering one fifth of the field. See synonyms under BARRIER, IMPEDIMENT, LOCK. — **the Bars** The Confederate flag. — *v.t.* **barred, bar·ring** 1 To fasten, lock, or secure with or as with a bar. 2 To confine or shut out with or as with bars. 3 To obstruct or hinder: to *bar* the way. 4 To exclude or except. 5 To mark with bars. See synonyms under HINDER, OBSTRUCT. — *prep.* Barring; excepting: *bar* none. [<OF *barre* <LL *barra* bar]

bar[2] (bär) *n.* The cgs international unit of pressure, equal to 1,000,000 dynes a square centimeter or a pressure of 29.531 inches of mercury at 32° F. and in latitude 45°: sometimes incorrectly called *barye.* [<Gk. *baros* weight]

Ba·rab·bas (bə·rab′əs) A thief released in place of Jesus at the demand of the multitude. *Matt.* xxvii 16–21.

Ba·rac·a (bə·rak′ə) *n.* An interdenominational, world-wide organization of young men's Bible classes. [<Hebrew *berakah* blessing]

Bar·ak (bâr′ak) A warrior who, with Deborah, overcame Sisera and the Canaanites. *Judges* iv 6. [<Hebrew, lightning]

Bar·a·nof Island (bar′ə·nôf) An island in the Alexander Archipelago, SE Alaska; 1,607 square miles.

Ba·ra·nov (bä·rä′nôf), **Aleksandr Andreevich,** 1747–1819, Russian fur trader; first governor of Russian America (now Alaska).

Bá·rá·ny (bä′rä·ny′), **Robert,** 1876–1939, Austrian physician and otologist.

Bar·a·tar·i·a Bay (bar′ə·târ′ē·ə) A lagoon in extreme SE Louisiana, mouth of the Mississippi. Also **Barataria Bayou.**

bar·a·the·a (bar′ə·thē′ə) *n.* A soft fabric of silk combined with cotton or wool. [Origin uncertain]

barb[1] (bärb) *n.* 1 A backward-projecting point on a sharp weapon, as on an arrow, fish hook, or spear, intended to prevent easy extraction. 2 Any similar sharp point: the *barbs* on a barbed-wire fence. 3 *Bot.* A beard, as in certain grains and grasses; awn. 4 *Ornithol.* One of the lateral processes of a bird's feather. See illustration under FEATHER. 5 A band or scarf worn about the neck and covering the breast: the *barb* of a nun. 6 *pl.* Paps or folds of the mucous membrane under the tongue of cattle and horses. 7 *pl.* The disease characterized by their inflammation. 8 *Obs.* A beard. — *v.t.* To provide with a barb or barbs: to *barb* an arrow. [<F *barbe* <L *barba* beard]

barb[2] (bärb) *n.* 1 A horse of the breed introduced by the Moors from Barbary into Spain: noted for speed and endurance. 2 A blackish or dun pigeon with a short stout beak. [<F *barbe* <*Barbarie,* ult. <Arabic *Barbar* native of N. Africa]

Bar·ba·dos (bär·bā′dōz) An island in the West Indies east of the Windward Islands, comprising a British colony; 166 square miles; capital, Bridgetown. — **Bar·ba′di·an** *adj.* & *n.*

Barbados pride Flowerfence.

bar·bal (bär′bəl) *adj.* Of or pertaining to the beard. [<L *barba* beard]

Bar·ba·ra (bär′bə·rə, -brə; *Du., Ger., Ital.* bär′bä·rä) A feminine personal name. Also *Fr.* **Barbe** (bàrb), *Sp.* **Bár·ba·ra** (bär′bä·rä). [<Gk., foreign, strange]

bar·bar·i·an (bär·bâr′ē·ən) *n.* 1 One whose state of culture is between savagery and civilization; a member of an uncivilized tribe or race. 2 Any rude, brutal, or uncultured person. 3 One destitute of, or not caring for, culture. 4 According to ancient Greek and Latin usage, a foreigner or outlander. — *adj.* 1 Uncivilized; cruel; barbarous. 2 Foreign; alien. See synonyms under BARBAROUS. — **bar·bar′i·an·ism** *n.*

bar·bar·ic (bär·bar′ik) *adj.* 1 Of or characteristic of barbarians. 2 Wild; uncivilized; crude. See synonyms under BARBAROUS. [<OF *barbarique* <L *barbaricus* <*barbarus* barbarian. See BARBAROUS.]

bar·ba·rism (bär′bə·riz′əm) *n.* 1 The stage between savagery and civilization. 2 Absence of culture; rudeness in manners, speech, living standards, etc. 3 The usage of words or forms not approved or standard in a language; also, an instance of this. See synonyms under LANGUAGE. 4 A barbarous act.

bar·bar·i·ty (bär·bar′ə·tē) *n. pl.* **·ties** 1 Brutal or barbarous conduct. 2 A barbarous deed. 3 A barbarism of language.

bar·ba·rize (bär′bə·rīz) *v.* **·rized, ·riz·ing** *v.t.* To make barbarous; corrupt, as language, from classical standards. — *v.i.* To become barbarous.

Bar·ba·ros·sa (bär′bə·ros′ə) 1 The name of two brothers, Barbary pirates: **Horuk,** 1473?–1518, and **Khair-ed-Din,** 1466?–1546, rulers of Algiers. 2 The nickname (Latin, red-beard) of Frederick I of Germany.

bar·ba·rous (bär′bər·əs) *adj.* 1 Pertaining to or like a barbarian. 2 Uncultivated; lacking the refinements of advanced civilization; rude. 3 Cruel; brutal; savage. 4 Marked by barbarisms in speech; unpolished. 5 Rude or harsh in sound. 6 In Greek and Roman usage, of or pertaining to foreigners. [<L *barbarus* foreign, barbarian <Gk. *barbaros* non-Hellenic, foreign, rude] — **bar′ba·rous·ly** *adv.* — **bar′ba·rous·ness** *n.*

Synonyms: atrocious, barbarian, barbaric, brutal, cruel, inhuman, merciless, rude, savage, uncivilized, uncouth, untamed. *Barbarous* refers to the worst side of *barbarian* life, and to acts of cruelty. We may, however, say *barbarous* nations, *barbarous* tribes, without implying anything more than want of civilization and culture. *Antonyms*: civilized, courtly, cultured, delicate, elegant, graceful, humane, nice, polite, refined, tender, urbane.

Bar·ba·ry (bär′bər·ē) The Moslem countries of northern Africa west of Egypt, including the former Barbary States.

Barbary ape An easily trained, tailless ape *(Macaca sylvana)* of North Africa and southern Spain: also called *magot.*

Barbary Coast 1 The coastal region of Barbary. 2 A waterfront region of San Francisco before the earthquake of 1906, infamous for its saloons, gambling houses, and brothels.

Barbary States Formerly, Tripolitania, Algeria, Tunisia, and, generally, Morocco; centers of piracy until occupation by the European powers in the 19th century.

bar·bate (bär′bāt) *adj.* 1 Bearded. 2 *Bot.* Tufted with long hairs. [<L *barbatus* bearded <*barba* beard]

bar·be·cue (bär′bə·kyōō) *n.* 1 An outdoor feast at which the whole animal carcass is roasted over an open fire and served. 2 Any meat roasted on a spit over an open fire. — *v.t.* **·cued, ·cu·ing** 1 To roast whole. 2 To roast (usually beef or pork) in large pieces or whole over an open fire or in a trench, often using a highly seasoned sauce. 3 To cook (meat) with a highly seasoned sauce. [<Sp. *barbacoa* <Taino *barbacoa* framework of sticks]

barbed (bärbd) *adj.* 1 Having a barb or barbs. 2 Pointed, piercing, or wounding: a *barbed* remark.

barbed wire Fence wire having barbs at intervals.

bar·bel (bär′bəl) *n.* 1 One of the soft filiform appendages to the jaws, chin, or nostrils of certain fishes: an organ of touch. 2 A carp-like Old World cyprinoid fish (genus *Barbes*). [<OF <LL *barbellus,* dim. of *barbus* barbel <*barba* beard]

bar·bel·late (bär′bə·lāt, bär·bel′it) *adj. Bot.* Having or studded with short, stiff hairs or bristles.

bar·ber (bär′bər) *n.* One who cuts the hair, shaves the beard, etc., as a business. — *v.t.* To cut or dress the hair of; shave or trim the beard of. ◆ Collateral adjective: *tonsorial.* [<OF *barbeor,* ult. <L *barba* beard]

Bar·ber (bär′bər), **Samuel,** born 1910, U.S. composer.

bar·ber·ry (bär′ber′ē, -bər·ē) *n.* 1 A shrub (genus *Berberis*) bearing yellow flowers and bright-red oblong berries. 2 Its fruit. [<Med. L *berberis, barbaris*]

bar·ber·shop (bär′bər·shop′) *n.* The place of business of a barber. — *adj. U.S.* Like, pertaining to, or characterized by close harmony, especially of male voices in sentimental songs.

bar·bet (bär′bit) *n.* 1 A tropical bird (family *Capitonidae*), having a broad bill surrounded by bristles at the base: related to the toucans: also called *scansorial barbet.* 2 A variety of small poodle. [<OF *barbet* <L *barbatus* bearded]

bar·bette (bär·bet′) *n.* 1 *Nav.* An armored cylinder protecting a revolving turret on a warship. 2 *Mil.* A platform from which cannon are fired over a parapet. [<F *barbette,* dim. of *barbe* beard]

bar·bi·can (bär′bi·kən) *n.* An outer fortification or outwork. See synonyms under RAMPART. [<F *barbacane*; ult. origin uncertain]

bar·bi·cel (bär′bə·sel) *n. Ornithol.* One of the very small simple processes fringing the lower edges of the barbule of a feather. [<NL *barbicella,* dim. of *barba* beard]

bar·bi·tal (bär′bə·tôl, -tal) *n.* A slow-acting and long-lasting barbiturate, $C_8H_{12}N_2O_3$, used as a sedative, hypnotic, and anticonvulsant. Also *Brit.* **bar′bi·tone** (-tōn).

bar·bit·u·rate (bär·bich′ər·it, bär′bə·to͞or′it, -tyo͞or′it) *n.* Any of various derivatives of barbituric acid which act as depressants on the central nervous system and are often used as sedatives, hypnotics, and anticonvulsants.

bar·bi·tu·ric acid (bär′bə·to͞or′ik, -tyo͞or′-) A synthetic compound, $C_4H_4O_3N_2$, from which barbiturates are derived. Also called *malonylurea.* [<NL *(Usnea) barbata* bearded (lichen) + -URIC]

Bar·bi·zon school (bär′bə·zon, *Fr.* bȧr·bē·zôṅ′) A group of French landscape painters of the 19th century, including Corot, Daubigny, Millet, and Théodore Rousseau. [from *Barbizon,* a village in NE France where they worked]

Bar·bour (bär′bər), **John,** 1320?–95, Scottish poet.

Bar·bu·da (bär·bo͞o′də) An island dependency of Antigua.

bar·bule (bär′byo͞ol) *n.* **1** A small barb or beard. **2** A process fringing the barb of a feather. [<L *barbula,* dim. of *barba* beard]

Bar·busse (bȧr·büs′), **Henri,** 1873–1935, French novelist.

Bar·ca (bär′kə) An influential Carthaginian family to which Hamilcar, Hannibal, and Hasdrubal belonged.

Bar·ca (bär′kə) **1** Cyrenaica. **2** The ancient name for BARCE.

bar car *U.S.* A railroad passenger car fitted out for serving drinks and short orders.

bar·ca·role (bär′kə·rōl) *n.* **1** A Venetian gondolier's song. **2** A melody in imitation of such a song. Also **bar′ca·rolle.** [<F *barcarolle* <Ital. *barcaruola* boatman's song <*barca* boat.]

Bar·ce (bär′chā) A town in western Cyrenaica, Libya: ancient *Barca.*

Bar·ce·lo·na (bär′sə·lō′nə, *Sp.* bär′thā·lō′nä) **1** A port of NE Spain. **2** A province in Catalonia, Spain; 2,975 square miles; capital, Barcelona. **3** A city of NE Venezuela.

Bar·clay (bär′klē), **Robert,** 1648–90, Scottish Quaker author.

Bar·clay de Tol·ly (bär·klī′ də tô′lyi), **Prince Mikhail,** 1761–1818, Russian field marshal.

bard[1] (bärd) *n.* **1** A Celtic poet and minstrel. **2** *Poetic* A poet. [<Celtic] **—bard′ic** *adj.*

bard[2] (bärd) *n.* Any piece of armor worn by horses. —*v.t.* To arm with bards. Also **barde.** [<F *barde,* ult. <Arabic *al-barda'ah* the pack-saddle]

Bard of Avon William Shakespeare, born in Stratford-on-Avon.

bare[1] (bâr) *adj.* **1** Devoid of covering or dress; naked. **2** Destitute of or poorly provided with what is used or necessary; unfurnished. **3** Unarmed; unsheathed. **4** Not more than just suffices; mere. **5** Threadbare. **6** Exposed to view; made manifest or apparent; undisguised. **7** Lacking in embellishment or in interest or attraction; plain; meager: *bare* description. **8** Bareheaded; also, barefoot. See synonyms under BLANK. —*v.t.* **bared, bar·ing** To make or lay bare; reveal; expose. Homophone: *bear.* [OE *bær*]

bare[2] (bâr) Obsolete past tense of BEAR.

bare·back (bâr′bak′) *adj.* Riding a horse without a saddle. —*adv.* Without a saddle. **—bare′·backed′** *adj.*

bare·faced (bâr′fāst′) *adj.* **1** Having the face bare. **2** Unconcealed; open. **3** Impudent, audacious. **—bare·fac·ed·ly** (bâr′fā′sid·lē, -fāst′lē) *adv.* **—bare′·fac′ed·ness** *n.*

bare·fit (bâr′fit) *adj. Scot.* Barefoot.

bare·foot (bâr′fo͝ot′) *adj. & adv.* With the feet bare. Also **bare′·foot′ed** *adj.*

ba·rege (bə·rezh′) *n.* A thin fabric of silk and worsted or cotton and worsted, used for veils, etc. [from *Barèges,* a French village]

bare·hand·ed (bâr′han′did) *adj.* With the hands uncovered. —*adv.* **1** In the act of committing a crime. **2** With the hands uncovered.

bare·head·ed (bâr′hed′id) *adj. & adv.* With head bare.

Ba·reil·ly (bə·rā′lē) A city in north central Uttar Pradesh, India, capital of Rohilkhand. Also **Ba·re′li.**

bare·leg·ged (bâr′leg′id, -legd′) *adj. & adv.* With the legs bare.

bare·ly (bâr′lē) *adv.* **1** Only just; scarcely. **2** Nakedly. **3** Openly; boldly; plainly. See synonyms under BUT.

Ba·rend (bä′rent) Dutch and German form of BERNARD.

Ba·rents (bä′rənts), **Willem,** died 1597, Dutch explorer.

Bar·ents Sea (bar′ənts, bä′rənts) An arm of the Artic Ocean north of Norway and European U.S.S.R.

bare·sark (bâr′särk) *n.* A berserk. —*adv.* Without armor. [Alter. of BERSERK]

Ba·ret·ti (bä·rāt′tē), **Giuseppi Marc Antonio,** 1719–89, Italian critic.

bar·fly (bär′flī′) *n. pl.* **·flies** *Slang* A habitual frequenter of barrooms.

Bar·frush (bär·fro͞osh′) A former name for BABOL.

bar·gain (bär′gən) *n.* **1** A mutual agreement between persons, especially one to buy or sell goods. **2** That which is agreed upon or the terms of the agreement. **3** The agreement as it affects one of the parties to it: He made a bad *bargain.* **4** An article bought or offered at a price favorable to the buyer. See synonyms under CONTRACT. **—into the bargain** In addition to what was agreed; thrown in for good measure; besides. **—to strike a bargain** To come to an agreement. —*v.i.* **1** To discuss or haggle over terms for selling or buying. **2** To make a bargain; reach an agreement. —*v.t.* **3** To barter, as goods for others of equal value. **—to bargain for** To expect; count on: This is more than I *bargained for.* [<OF *bargaine;* ult. origin uncertain]

barge (bärj) *n.* **1** A flat-bottomed freight boat or lighter for harbors and inland waters, or other large boat, as for pleasure excursions. **2** A large and elegantly furnished boat, for pleasure or for state occasions. **3** *Nav.* A boat for the use of a flag officer. **4** *Obs.* In New England, a long, open vehicle, sometimes boat-shaped, for passengers. **5** A house-boat. —*v.* **barged, barg·ing** *v.t.* **1** To transport by barge. —*v.i.* **2** To move clumsily and slowly. **3** *Colloq.* To collide with: with *into.* **4** *Colloq.* To intrude; enter rudely: with *in* or *into.* [<OF <LL *barga.* Akin to BARK[3].]

barge·board (bärj′·bôrd′, -bōrd′) *n.* A board, often ornate, attached along the barge couples and following the outline of a gable end.

BARGEBOARD
a.a. **Barge course.**
b.b. **Bargeboards.**
c.c. **Rafters.**
d.d. **Barge couples.**

barge couple One of a pair of outside rafters **(barge couples)** that support the projecting end of a gable roof.

barge course **1** The part of a gable roof projecting beyond the bargeboards or end wall. **2** A course of bricks laid edgewise to form the coping of a wall.

barge·man (bärj′mən) *n. pl.* **·men** (-mən) One who has charge of or is employed on a barge; a boatman or oarsman. Also *Brit.* **bar·gee** (bär·jē′).

bar·ghest (bär′gest) *n.* A goblin, often dog-shaped, whose appearance is supposed to forebode death or misfortune. [Cf. G *berggeist* gnome]

Bar·ham (bär′əm), **Richard Harris,** 1788–1845, English churchman and humorist: pen name *Thomas Ingoldsby.*

Bar Harbor A resort and port of entry on Mount Desert Island, Maine.

Ba·ri (bä′rē) A port on the Adriatic in southern Italy. Formerly **Bari del·le Pu·glie** (dāl′·lā po͞o′lyā).

bar·i·a·trics (bar′ē·at′riks) *n.* The branch of medicine concerned with the treatment of the overweight. [<Gk. *baros* weight + -IATRICS]

bar·ic[1] (bar′ik) *adj.* Of or pertaining to weight, especially of air; barometric. [<Gk. *barys* heavy]

bar·ic[2] (bar′ik) *adj.* Of, pertaining to, derived from, or containing barium.

ba·ril·la (bə·ril′ə) *n.* **1** An impure sodium carbonate and sulfate obtained by burning certain land or marine plants; soda ash. **2** Any plant used in making soda ash, especially the saltwort. [<Sp. *barrilla* impure soda]

Bar·ing (bâr′ing), **Alexander** See ASHBURTON. **—Evelyn,** 1841–1917, first Earl of Cromer, English diplomat. **—Maurice,** 1874–1945, English novelist.

Bar·ing-Gould (bâr′ing·go͞old′), **Sabine,** 1834–1924, English clergyman and hymn-writer.

Ba·ri·sal (bu·ri·säl′) A city in SE Bengal, East Pakistan.

bar·ite (bâr′īt) *n.* A heavy, vitreous, usually white, orthorhombic barium sulfate, $BaSO_4$: also called *heavy spar.*

bar·i·tone (bar′ə·tōn) *n.* **1** A male voice of a register higher than bass and lower than tenor. **2** One having such a voice. **3** A brass wind instrument, used chiefly in military bands, having a similar range. —*adj.* **1** Of, like, or pertaining to a baritone. **2** Having the range of a baritone. Also spelled *barytone.* [<Ital. *baritono* <Gk. *barytonos* deep-sounding <*barys* deep + *tonos* tone]

bar·i·um (bâr′ē·əm) *n.* An element (symbol Ba, atomic number 56) of the alkaline-earth group, resembling calcium chemically and forming salts of which the water-soluble ones and the carbonate are poisonous. See PERIODIC TABLE. [<NL <Gk. *barys* heavy]

barium hydroxide A basic compound, $Ba(OH)_2 \cdot 8H_2O$, that crystallizes in tetragonal prisms produced by rendering caustic barium carbonate or by dissolving the monoxide in water.

barium oxide *Chem.* A yellowish-white, poisonous alkaline compound, BaO, used in glassmaking and as a reagent: it forms barium hydroxide on the addition of water: also called *baryta.*

barium sulfate An insoluble compound, $BaSO_4$, produced synthetically as an insoluble white precipitate: used in roentgenology to facilitate X-ray pictures of the stomach and intestines.

barium yellow A pale, sulfur-yellow pigment with a greenish tone, made from barium chromate.

bark[1] (bärk) *n.* **1** The short, abrupt, explosive sound characteristically made by a dog. **2** Any sound like this. —*v.i.* **1** To utter a bark, as a dog, or to make a sound like a bark. **2** *Colloq.* To cough. **3** To speak loudly and sharply. **4** *U.S. Slang* To announce the attractions of a show at its entrance. —*v.t.* **5** To say roughly and curtly: He *barked* an order. **—to bark up the wrong tree** *Colloq.* To be mistaken as to one's object or the means of attaining it. [OE *beorcan*]

bark[2] (bärk) *n.* **1** The tissue covering the stems, branches, and roots of a tree or shrub, extending from the cambium layer to the outer surface. **2** This tissue removed from a particular species for its special medicinal or other properties. —*v.t.* **1** To remove the bark from; scrape; girdle. **2** To rub off or abrade the skin of. **3** To cover with or as with bark. **4** To tan or treat with an infusion of bark [<Scand.]

bark[3] (bärk) *n.* **1** A three-masted vessel square-rigged except for the mizzenmast, which is fore-and-aft rigged. **2** *Poetic* Any vessel or boat. Also spelled *barque.* [<F *barque* <LL *barca* bark]

BARK

bark beetle One of several small burrowing beetles (family *Scolytidae*) which breed between the bark and wood of trees, thus destroying the trees. See illustration under INSECT (injurious).

bar·keep·er (bär′kē′pər) *n.* **1** One who owns or manages a bar where alcoholic liquors are served. **2** A bartender. Also **bar′keep′.**

bar·ken·tine (bär′kən·tēn) *n.* A three-masted vessel square-rigged on the foremast and fore-and-aft rigged on the other two masts: also spelled *barquentine.*

bark·er[1] (bär′kər) *n.* **1** One who or that which barks or clamors. **2** A person stationed at the door of a shop or entrance to a show to attract patrons by loud, animated patter.

bark·er[2] (bär′kər) *n.* One who or that which removes bark from trees or works with bark.

Bar·kis (bär′kis) In Dickens's *David Copperfield,* a bashful carrier who is constantly declaring by deputy that "Barkis is willin' " to marry Clara Peggotty.

bark•it (bär′kit) *adj. Scot.* Barked; tanned.
Bark•la (bär′klə), **Charles Glover,** 1877–1944, English physicist.
bark•less (bärk′lis) *adj.* Unable to bark, as certain breeds of dogs.
Bark•ley (bärk′lē), **Alben William,** 1877–1956, U.S. lawyer, vice president of the United States 1949–53.
bark•y (bär′kē) *adj.* Covered with or resembling bark.
Bar-le-Duc (bär-lə-dük′) *n.* A preserve from seeded gooseberries or currants, originally made at **Bar-le-Duc,** a town of NE France.
Bar•let•ta (bär-let′tä) A port in Apulia, SE Italy, on the Adriatic.
bar•ley[1] (bär′lē) *n.* **1** A hardy, bearded cereal grass *(Hordeum vulgare)* of temperate regions, with long leaves, stout awns, and triple spikelets at the joints which distinguish it from wheat. **2** The grain borne by this grass. [OE *baerlīc*]
bar•ley[2] (bär′lē) *interj. Scot.* Truce!: a cry in children's games: also spelled *barly.*
bar•ley•corn (bär′lē-kô rn) *n.* **1** A grain of barley. **2** A unit of measure, originally the breadth of a barley grain, equal to one third of an inch. **3** A planed groove between moldings. **—John Barleycorn** A humorous personification of malt liquor, or of intoxicating liquors in general.
barley sugar A clear, brittle confection made by boiling sugar with a barley extract.
barley water A drink made by boiling barley in water, for invalids, etc.
Bar•low (bär′lō), **Jane,** 1860–1917, Irish novelist. **—Joel,** 1755–1812, U.S. poet and diplomat.
Barlow's disease Infantile scurvy. [after Sir Thomas *Barlow,* 19th c. English physician]
barm (bärm) *n.* The froth or foam rising on fermented malt liquors. [OE *beorma* yeast]
bar•maid (bär′mād′) *n.* A woman bartender.
Bar•me•cide (bär′mə-sīd) Any member of a former wealthy and princely family of Baghdad; specifically, in the *Arabian Nights,* the member of this family who served an imaginary feast to a beggar, setting only empty dishes before him.
Barmecide feast Any imaginary, illusory, or disappointing hospitality or generosity.
Bar•men (bär′mən) See WUPPERTAL.
bar miz•vah (bär mits′və) In Judaism, a boy commencing his thirteenth year, the age of religious duty and responsibility; also, the ceremony celebrating this: also spelled *bar mitzvah* or *mitzwah.*
barm•y (bär′mē) *adj.* **barm•i•er, barm•i•est 1** Full of barm; frothy. **2** *Brit. Slang* Silly; flighty. Also *Scot.* **barm′ie.**
barn[1] (bärn) *n.* A building for storing hay, stabling livestock, etc. [OE *bern*]
barn[2] (bärn) *n. Physics* A unit of area used in measuring the cross-sections of atomic nuclei: equal to 10^{-24} square centimeter: so called in allusion to the phrase "He can't hit the side of a barn door."
Bar•na•bas (bär′nə-bəs; *Dan., Du., Ger., Lat.* bär′nä-bäs) A masculine personal name. Also **Bar•na•by** (bä r′nə-bē), *Fr.* **Bar•na•bé** (bär-nä-bā′), *Ital.* **Bar•na•ba** (bär′nä-bä) or **Bar•na** (bär′nä), *Pg.* **Bar•na•be** (bä r′nə-bä). [<Hebrew, son of consolation]
Barnabas, Saint (properly *Joses*) First century Christian apostle; reputed author of an apocryphal gospel and epistle.
bar•na•cle[1] (bär′nə-kəl) *n.* **1** A marine shellfish (order *Cirripedia*) that attaches itself to rocks, ship bottoms, etc.; especially, the **rock barnacle** *(Balanus balanoides)* and the **goose barnacle** *(Lepas fascicularis),* the latter so called because the barnacle goose was once supposed to hatch from it. **2** A European wild goose of northern seas *(Branta leucopsis)* : also **barnacle goose. 3** Something or someone that clings tenaciously; a persistent follower; a hanger-on. [ME *bernacle;* origin uncertain] **—bar′na•cled** *adj.*
bar•na•cle[2] (bär′nə-kəl) *n. Usually pl.* An instrument for pinching the nose of an unruly horse. [OF *bernacle,* dim. of *bernac* a bit]
Bar•nard (bär′nərd) See BERNARD.
Bar•nard (bär′nərd), **George Grey,** 1863–1938, U.S. sculptor. **—Henry,** 1811–1900, U.S. educator.**—Christiaan Neethling,** 1922– South African Surgeon.
Bar•na•ul (bär′nä-o͞ol′) A city on the Ob, capital of Altai Territory in SW Siberia.
Barn•burn•er (bärn′bûr′nər) *n.* A member of one of the progressive factions of the Democratic party in New York state in 1842: opposed to the *Hunkers.*
barn dance 1 A dance held in a barn, especially with square dances, rural music, etc. **2** A country dance resembling the schottische.
Bar•ne•gat Bay (bär′nə-gat) An arm of the Atlantic extending about 30 miles along the coast of eastern New Jersey.
Barnes (bärnz), **Harry Elmer,** 1889–) 1968, U.S. sociologist and educator.
Bar•net (bär′nit) A town in southern Hertfordshire, England; site of a battle, 1471, between Yorkists and Lancastrians.
Bar•ne•veldt (bär′nə-velt), **Jan van Olden,** 1549–1619, Dutch patriot.
barn owl A North American owl *(Tyto alba pratincola)* with brownish upper parts and white underparts flecked with black: often found in barns, where it preys on mice.

BARN OWL
(15 to 17 inches tall.)

Barns•ley (bärnz′lē) A county borough of southern Yorkshire, England.
barn•storm (bärn′stôrm′) *v.i.* **1** To tour rural districts, giving plays, making political speeches, etc. **2** To tour rural districts, giving exhibitions of stunt flying, short airplane excursions, etc. **—barn′storm′er** *n.* **—barn′storm′ing** *n.* [<BARN + STORM, *v.*]
barn swallow The common swallow of North America and Europe: it frequently nests in the eaves of barns and other buildings.
Bar•num (bär′nəm), **P(hineas) T(aylor),** 1810–91, U.S. showman and circus proprietor.
barn•yard (bärn′yärd′) *n.* An enclosed space adjoining a barn.
baro- *combining form* Weight; atmospheric pressure: *barodynamics.* [<Gk. *baros* weight]
Ba•roc•chio (bä-rôk′kyō) See BAROZZI, GIACOMO.
bar•o•cy•clo•nom•e•ter (bar′ ō-sī′klə-nom′ə-tər) *n. Meterol.* An instrument for ascertaining the location, direction, distance, and movement of cyclones. [<BARO- + CYCLONE + -METER]
Ba•ro•da (bə-rō′də) A district of northern Bombay State; until 1948 a princely state in northern India; 8,236 square miles; capital, Baroda.
bar•o•dy•nam•ics (bar′ō-dī-nam′iks) *n.* The dynamics of heavy structures, as dams, bridges, etc., especially in relation to pressure and gravitation. **—bar′o•dy•nam′ic** *adj.*
bar•o•gram (bar′ə-gram) *n.* The record of a barograph.
bar•o•graph (bar′ə-graf, -gräf) *n.* An automatically recording barometer. **— bar′o•graph′•ic** *adj.*
Ba•ro•ja (bä-rō′hä), **Pio,** 1872–1956, Spanish novelist.
ba•rom•e•ter (bə-rom′ə-tər) *n.* **1** An instrument for measuring atmospheric pressure: used for forecasting the weather, measuring elevations, etc. **2** Anything that indicates changes. **—bar•o•met•ric** (bar′ ə-met′rik) or **•ri•cal** *adj.* **— bar′o•met′ri•cal•ly** *adv.* **—ba•rom′e•try** *n.*
bar•on (bar′ən) *n.* **1** A member of the lowest order of hereditary nobility in several European countries; also, the dignity or rank itself. The title was used at first in England to designate one who held land by military or other honorable service. **2** *U.S.* One who has great power in a commercial field: a *coal* baron. **3** In the Middle Ages, a feudal tenant of the king; a noble. ◆Homophone: *barren.* [<OF <LL *baro, -onis* man <Gmc.]
bar•on•age (bar′ən-ij) *n.* **1** Barons collectively. **2** The dignity or rank of a baron.
bar•on•ess (bar′ən-is) *n.* **1** The wife or widow of a baron. **2** A woman holding a barony in her own right.
bar•on•et (bar′ən-it, -ə-net) *n.* **1** An inheritable English title, below that of baron. **2** The bearer of the title, who is not a member of the nobility: A baronet is designated by "Sir" before the name and "Baronet" or the abbreviation "Bart." after.
bar•on•et•age (bar′ən-it-ij, -ə-net′-) *n.* **1** Baronets collectively. **2** The dignity or rank of a baronet.
bar•on•et•cy (bar′ən-it-sē, -ə-net′-) *n. pl.* **•cies 1** The title or rank of a baronet. **2** The patent giving such rank.
ba•rong (bä-rông′, -rong′) *n.* In the Philippines, a cutlas cleaverlike weapon used by the Moros.
ba•ro•ni•al (bə-rō′nē -əl) *adj.* Pertaining to or befitting a baron, a barony, or the order of barons.
bar•o•ny (bar′ə-nē) *n.* pl. **•nies** The rank, dignity, or domain of a baron.
ba•roque (bə-rōk′) *adj.* **1** Irregularly shaped: said of pearls. **2** Of, like, or characteristic of a style of art, architecture, and decoration characterized by extravagant and fantastic forms, curved rather than straight lines in ornament, and exaggerated and theatrical effects, as those developed in the 16th and 17th centuries in Europe. — *n.* **1** The baroque style. **2** An object, ornament, or design in this style. [<F <Pg. *barroco* rough or imperfect pearl]

BAROQUE *(def. 2)*
Venice: Church of Santa Maria della, Salute, 1631–56

bar•o•scope (bar′ə-skōp) *n.* **1** An instrument for approximately indicating atmospheric pressure; a weatherglass. **2** A device indicating the loss in weight of objects in air. **— bar′o•scop′ic** (-skop′ik) or **•i•cal** *adj.*
bar•o•switch (bar′ə-swich) *n. Meterol.* That component of a radiosonde apparatus which indicates pressure values during the ascent and, in a definite order, actuates the temperature, humidity, and other recording components.
Ba•rot•se•land (bə-rot′sē-land) A province of western Zambia; 63,000 square miles; capital, Mongu. Also **Western Province.**
ba•rouche (bə-ro͞osh′) *n.* A four-wheeled, low-bodied pleasure-vehicle with folding top, two inside seats facing each other, and an upper outside seat for the driver. [<G *barutsche* <Ital. *baroccio* <L *bis* twice + *rota* wheel]
Ba•roz•zi (bä-rôt′tsē), **Giacomo,** 1507–73, Italian architect: also known as *Giacomo da Vignola.* Also *Barocchio.*
barque (bärk), **bar•quen•tine** (bär′kən-tēn) See BARK[3], BARKENTINE.
Bar•qui•si•me•to (bär′kē -sē-mā′tō) A city in NW Venezuela.
bar•rack[1] (bar′ək) *n.* **1** *Usually pl.* A structure or group of structures for the lodgment of soldiers. **2** *Usually pl.* A temporary or rough shelter for a gang of laborers, etc. **3** A light adjustable roof for sheltering hay, etc. — *v.t. v.i.* To house in barracks. [ltF *baraque* <Ital. *baracca* soldiers' tent]
bar•rack[2] (bar′ək) *v.t. v.i. Austral.* To shout for or against (a group, team, etc.): often with *for* or *against.* [<dial. E]
barracks bag A soldier's cloth bag with a draw cord, for holding clothing and equipment. Also **barrack bag.**
bar•ra•coon (bar′ə-ko͞on′) *n.* A barrack or enclosure for the confinement of slaves or convicts. [<Sp. *barracon,* aug. of *barraca* barrack]
bar•ra•cu•da (bar′ə-ko͞o′də) *n. pl.* **•da** or **•das** A voracious pike-like fish (genus *Sphyraena)* of tropical seas. The **great barracuda** *(S. barracuda),* found off the Florida coast, is often 8 feet long. [<Sp.]
bar•rage[1] (bär′ij) *n.* **1** The act of barring. **2** An artificial bar placed in a watercourse, to increase its depth for irrigating, etc. [<F < *barre* bar]
bar•rage[2] (bə-räzh′) *n.* **1** *Mil.* Concentrated fire on a part of any enemy's lines to prevent the advance of reinforcements. **2** *Mil.* A curtain of fire to close off part of the front

from enemy assault, isolate part of his position, or, by movable curtain, to protect advance of troops. **3** Any overwhelming attack, as of words or blows. **— balloon barrage** A curtain of captive balloons raised above a defense area to entangle enemy aircraft and prevent penetration of the area. **— box barrage** A curtain of artillery fire falling around an area and preventing the escape or reinforcement of troops. [<F *(tir de) barrage* barrage (fire)]

bar·ra·mun·da (bar′ə·mun′də) *n. pl.* **·da** or **·das** A large, edible, dipnoan mudfish *(Neoceratodus forsteri)* of Australia: also called *ceratodus.* Also **bar′ra·mun′di** (-dē). [<native Australian name]

bar·ran·ca (bə·rang′kə) *n. SW U.S.* A deep ravine or gorge. [<Sp.]

Bar·ran·quil·la (bär′räng·kē′yä) A port on the Magdalena, northern Colombia.

bar·ra·tor (bar′ə·tər) *n.* One guilty of barratry. Also **bar′ra·ter.**

bar·ra·try (bar′ə·trē) *n. pl.* **·tries 1** Any wilful and unlawful act committed by the master or mariners of a ship, whereby the owners sustain injury. **2** In Scots law, the acceptance of a bribe by a judge. **3** The buying or selling of ecclesiastical positions. **4** *Law* The offense of exciting lawsuits; the stirring up of quarrels, spreading false rumors, etc. Also spelled *barretry.* [<OF *baraterie* misuse of office < *barat* fraud] **— bar′ra·trous** *adj.*

barred (bärd) *adj.* **1** Fastened with bars. **2** Obstructed by bars. **3** Made of bars. **4** Ornamented with bars; striped. **5** Prohibited; not allowed.

barred owl See under OWL.

bar·rel (bar′əl) *n.* **1** A large, round, wooden vessel, made with staves and hoops, having a flat base and top and slightly bulging sides. **2** As much as a barrel will hold: a varying measure of quantity. The standard U.S. barrel for fruits, vegetables, and other dry commodities contains 7,056 cubic inches. A barrel of petroleum contains 42 U.S. gallons. **3** Something resembling or having the form of a barrel. **4** *Ornithol.* The quill of a feather. **5** *Naut.* The rotating drum of a windlass, capstan, etc., around which the rope winds. **6** The cylindrical box containing the mainspring of a watch, around which the chain is wound. **7** In firearms, the tube through which the projectile is discharged. **8** The piston chamber of a pump. **— *v.*** **bar′reled** or **bar′relled, bar′rel·ing** or **bar′rel·ling** *v.t.* To put or pack in a barrel. **— *v.i. U.S. Slang*** To move at high speed. [<OF *baril*; ult. origin unknown]

barrel catch The mechanism which locks the barrel and cylinder of a revolver in firing position.

barrel chair An upholstered chair having a high, rounded back shaped like the vertical half of a barrel.

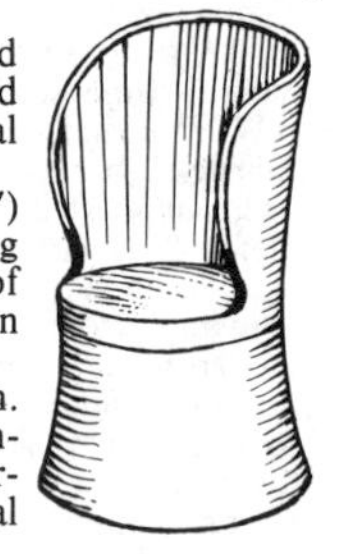

MODERN BARREL CHAIR

bar·rel·house (bar′əl·hous′) *n.* **1** A cheap drinking house. **2** An early style of jazz, originally played in barrelhouses.

barrel organ A hand organ.

barrel roll *Aeron.* A complete rotation of an airplane around its longitudinal axis.

bar·ren (bar′ən) *adj.* **1** Incapable of producing, or not producing, offspring; sterile. **2** Not producing fruit; unfruitful. **3** Unprofitable, as an enterprise. **4** Lacking in interest or attractiveness; dull. **5** Not producing; lacking: *barren* of creative effort. See synonyms under BLANK, MEAGER. **— *n.* 1** A tract of barren land. **2** *Usually pl.* A tract of level land, having a sandy soil without trees and producing only scrubby growth. ◆Homophone *baron.* [<OF *baraigne*] **— bar′ren·ly** *adv.* **— bar′ren·ness** *n.*

Barren Grounds An arctic prairie region of northern Canada, extending west from Hudson Bay. Also **Barren Lands.**

Bar·rès (bå·res′), **Maurice,** 1862–1923, French novelist and essayist.

bar·ret (bar′it) *n.* **1** A biretta. **2** A flat cap formerly worn by soldiers. [<F *barrette* <LL *birettum* cap < *birrus* red cloak]

bar·re·try (bar′ə·trē) See BARRATRY.

bar·rette (bə·ret′) *n.* **1** A small bar or comb with a clasp used for keeping a woman's hair in place. **2** In fencing, the guard of a foil. [<F, dim. of *barre* bar]

bar·ret·ter (bar′it·ər, bə·ret′ər) *n. Electr.* A device for detecting electrical oscillations, consisting of an extremely fine, bulb-enclosed platinum wire loop, the resistance of which is increased by the heating effect of oscillations passing through it. Also **Barretter lamp.** [Origin uncertain]

bar·ri·cade (bar′ə·kād′, bar′ə·kād) *n.* **1** A barrier hastily built for obstruction or for defense. **2** Any obstruction or barrier closing a passage, as a street, a waterway, etc. See synonyms under BARRIER, RAMPART. **— *v.t.* ·cad·ed, ·cad·ing** To enclose, obstruct, or defend with a barricade or barricades. See synonyms under OBSTRUCT. [<F <Sp. *barricada* barrier < *barrica* barrel; the first barricades having been barrels filled with earth, stones, etc.] **— bar′ri·cad′er** *n.*

Bar·rie (bar′ē), **Sir James Matthew,** 1860–1937, Scottish novelist and playwright.

bar·ri·er (bar′ē·ər) *n.* **1** Any line of boundary and separation, natural or artificial, placed or serving as a limitation or obstruction. **2** Something that bars, keeps out, obstructs progress, or prevents encroachment: a *barrier* to ambition; a language *barrier.* **3** A palisade or stockade to defend the entrance to a fortified place. **4** A fortress on a frontier commanding a main passage into a country; a customs gate. **5** A fence or railing to shut out trespassers or strangers. **6** The narrow blank space which separates the frames of a motion-picture film or divides the sound track from the picture track. **7** *pl.* The palisades enclosing the ground for a tournament; the lists. **8** *Geog. Sometimes cap.* The part of the ice cap of Antarctica extending over the ocean beyond the land. [<OF *barriere* < *barre* bar]

Synonyms: bar, barricade, breastwork, bulwark, hindrance, obstacle, obstruction, parapet, prohibition, rampart, restraint, restriction. A *bar* is something that is or may be firmly fixed, ordinarily with intent to prevent entrance or egress; as, the *bars* of a prison cell. A *barrier* obstructs, but is not necessarily impassable. *Barricade* denotes some hastily piled obstruction, commonly an improvised street fortification. A *parapet* is a low or breast-high wall, as about the edge of a roof; in military use, such a wall for the protection of troops; a *rampart* is the embankment surrounding a fort, on which the *parapet* is raised; the word *rampart* is often used as including the *parapet. Bulwark* is a general word for any defensive wall, but in present technical use it signifies the raised side of a ship above the upper deck, topped by the rail. Compare BOUNDARY, IMPEDIMENT, RAMPART. *Antonyms:* admittance, entrance, opening, passage, road, thoroughfare, transit.

barrier berg A level-topped iceberg that has become detached from the Antarctic barrier.

barrier cream See COSMETIC (*n.* def. 3).

barrier reef A long, narrow ridge of rock or coral parallel to the coast and close to or above the surface of the sea.

Barrier Reef See GREAT BARRIER REEF.

bar·ring (bär′ing) *prep.* Excepting; apart from.

bar·ri·o (bär′rē·ō) *n. pl.* **·os 1** In Spanish-speaking countries, a district or ward of a town or city. **2** *U.S.* A section of a city or town populated largely by Spanish-speaking people. [<Sp.]

bar·ris·ter (bar′is·tər) *n.* In English law, an advocate who argues cases in the courts, as distinguished from a *solicitor,* who prepares them. In the United States an attorney combines the two functions. [<BAR[1]]

bar·room (bär′ro͞om′, -ro͝om′) *n.* A room where alcoholic liquors are served across a counter.

Bar·ros (bär′ro͞osh), **João de,** 1496–1570, Portuguese historian.

bar·row[1] (bar′ō) *n.* **1** A frame, tray, or box, with or without a wheel or wheels, having handles or shafts by which it is pushed, pulled, or carried. **2** The load carried on or capacity of a barrow. **3** A wheelbarrow. **4** A pushcart. [OE *bearwe*]

bar·row[2] (bar′ō) *n.* **1** A burial mound; cairn. **2** A hill. [OE *beorg* hill, burial mound]

bar·row[3] (bar′ō) *n.* A castrated pig. [OE *bearg* pig]

Bar·row (bar′ō), **Isaac,** 1630–77, English mathematician and theologian.

Bar·row (bar′ō), **Point** A cape of the northernmost part of Alaska in the Arctic Ocean.

Bar·row-in-Fur·ness (bar′ō·in·fûr′nes) A county borough in NW Lancashire, England.

Bar·ry (bar′ē, *Fr.* bå·rē′), **du** See DU BARRY.

Bar·ry (bar′ē), **Philip,** 1896–1949, U.S. dramatist.

Bar·ry·more (bar′ə·môr, -mōr) A family of U.S. actors: **Maurice** (real name, Herbert Blythe), 1847–1905, father of **Lionel,** 1878–1954, **Ethel,** 1879–1959, **John,** 1882–1942.

bar sinister See BATON SINISTER under BATON.

Bart (bärt, *Fr.* bår), **Jean,** 1651?–1702, French naval hero. Also **Barth.**

bar·tend·er (bär′ten′dər) *n.* One who serves liquors over a bar.

bar·ter (bär′tər) *v.i.* To trade by exchange of goods or services without use of money. **— *v.t.*** To trade (goods or services) for something of equal value. **— *n.*** The exchanging of commodities or a commodity given in exchange. See synonyms under BUSINESS. [<OF *barater* exchange] **— bar′ter·er** *n.*

Barth (bärt), **Heinrich,** 1821–65, German explorer. **— Karl,** 1886–1968, Swiss theologian.

Bar·thol·di (bär·thol′dē, *Fr.* bår·tôl·dē′), **Frédéric Auguste,** 1834–1904, French sculptor of the Statue of Liberty.

Bar·thol·o·mew (bär·thol′ə·myo͞o) A masculine personal name. Also *Lat.* **Bar·thol·o·mae·us** (bär·tol′ə·mē′əs), *Fr.* **Bar·thé·le·my** (bår·tāl·mē′) or **Bar·tho·lo·mé** (bår·tô·lô·mā′), *Ital.* **Bar·to·lo·me·o** (bär·tō′lō·mâ′ō), *Pg.* **Bar·to·lo·meu** (bär·tō′lō·mā′o͞o), *Sp.* **Bar·to·lo·mé** (bär·tō′lō·mā′), *Du.* **Bar·thol·o·me·us** (bär·tôl′ō·mā′o͞os), *Ger.* **Bar·tho·lo·mä·us** (bär·tō′lō·mā′·o͞os) or **Bar·thel** (bär′təl). [<Hebrew, son of furrows]

— Bartholomew, Saint One of the twelve apostles, on whose feast day, August 24, in 1572 a slaughter of Huguenots (the **Massacre of St. Bartholomew**) occurred in France.

Bar·ti·mae·us (bär′tə·mē′əs) A beggar cured of blindness. *Mark* x 46–52. Also **Bar′ti·me′us.**

bar·ti·zan (bär′tə·zən, bär′·tə·zan′) *n.* A turret, with loopholes, jutting out from a wall. [Alter. of *bratticing* <BRATTICE] **— bar·ti·zaned** (bär′tə·zənd, bär′tə·zand′) *adj.*

BARTIZAN ON A TOWER

Bart·lett (bärt′lit) *n.* A variety of large, juicy pear developed in England about 1770 and introduced into America by Enoch Bartlett of Dorchester, Massachusetts. Also **Bartlett pear.**

Bart·lett (bärt′lit), **John,** 1820–1905, U. S. publisher; compiled *Familiar Quotations,* 1855. **— Josiah,** 1729–1795, American physician and Revolutionary leader. **— Robert Abram,** 1875–1946, Canadian Arctic explorer.

Bar·tok (bär′tôk), **Bé·la** (bā′lä), 1881–1945, Hungarian composer.

Bar·to·lom·me·o (bär′tō·lōm·mâ′ō), **Fra,** 1475–1517, Florentine painter: also known as *Baccio della Porta.*

Bar·ton (bär′tən), **Clara,** 1821–1912, founder of the American Red Cross.

Bar·tram (bär′trəm), **John,** 1699–1777, American botanist.

Bar·uch (bâr′ək) **1** The amanuensis of Jeremiah. *Jer.* xxxii–xxxvi. **2** A book in the Old Testament Apocrypha attributed to Baruch. [<Hebrew, blessed]

Ba·ruch (bə·ro͞ok′), **Bernard Mannes,** 1870–1965, U.S. financier and statesman.

Bar·won (bär′won) The upper Darling River, northern New South Wales, Australia.

bar·ye (bar′ē) *n.* In the cgs system, a unit expressing a pressure of one dyne a square centimeter. [<Gk. *barys* heavy]

Ba·rye (bå·rē′), **Antoine Louis,** 1795–1875, French sculptor.

bar·y·on (bar′ē·on) *n. Physics* Any strongly interacting particle whose spin is half an odd integer; a nucleon or hyperon. [<Gk. *barys* heavy + -ON]

bar·y·sphere (bar′i·sfir) *n. Geol.* The centrosphere. [<Gk. *barys* heavy + SPHERE]

ba·ry·ta (bə·rī′tə) *n.* Barium oxide. [<Gk. *barytēs* weight < *barys* heavy]

ba·ry·tes (bə·rī′tēz) *n.* Barite.

bar·y·tone[1] (bar′ə·tōn) *n.* In Greek grammar,

a word having the last syllable unaccented. [<Gk. *barytonos* unaccented]

bar·y·tone[2] (bar′ə·tōn) See BARITONE.

ba·sal (bā′səl) *adj.* **1** Pertaining to, of, or at the base. **2** Basic; fundamental. **3** *Physiol.* Designating a standard of reference or comparison: *basal* metabolism. **4** *Surg.* Serving to prepare for deeper levels of unconsciousness: *basal* anesthesia preliminary to surgical anesthesia. **—ba′sal·ly** *adv.*

basal metabolism *Physiol.* The minimum energy, measured in calories, required by the body at rest in maintaining essential vital activities.

basal age *Psychol.* The highest age level manifested in a completed series of mental tests graded to include items appropriate to each successive age level.

ba·salt (bə·sôlt′, bas′ôlt) *n.* **1** A fine-grained, igneous, volcanic rock of high density and dark color, composed chiefly of plagioclase and pyroxene, usually exhibiting a columnar structure. **2** A black, unglazed pottery resembling basalt, developed by Josiah Wedgwood: also **ba·salt′ware′**. [<L *basaltes* dark marble] **—ba·sal′tic** *adj.*

bas-bleu (bä·blœ′) *n. French* A bluestocking.

Bas·co (bäs′kō) Capital of Batanes province, Philippines.

bas·cule (bas′kyōōl) *n.* A mechanical apparatus

BASCULE BRIDGE
Tower Bridge, London

of which each end counterbalances the other: used in a kind of drawbridge (**bascule bridge**) operated by a counterpoise. [<F, see-saw]

base[1] (bās) *n.* **1** The lowest or supporting part of anything; bottom; foundation. **2** *Ling.* The form of a word used in making derivatives, as by adding prefixes or suffixes; root or stem. **3** A determining ingredient; a common element with which other more distinctive elements unite to form a product; essential or preponderant element or part of anything. **4** *Chem.* **a** A compound which is capable of so uniting with an acid as to neutralize its acid properties and form a salt, as sodium hydroxide, NaOH. **b** A compound that yields hydroxyl ions in solution. **c** Any molecule or radical that takes up protons. **5** A basis of military or naval operations or of supplies. **6** In baseball, any one of the four points of the diamond; also, in certain other games, or in a race, the goal or starting point. **7** Any point, part, line, number, or quantity from which a reckoning, inference, or conclusion proceeds, or on which any other dimension depends; any principle or datum; a basis: the *base* of an argument, the *base* of a triangle. **8** A very accurately measured line on the earth's surface, from whose known length other lines in a survey are determined. **9** A number on which a mathematical system or calculation depends: In the Arabic notation, 10 is the *base* of the decimal system. **10** *Geom.* **a** That side of a rectilineal figure or that face of a solid on which the figure is conceived to be erected. **b** A side or face which has some special mark or character, or to which other parts are referred. **11** *Biol.* The end opposite to the apex; the point of attachment. **12** *Archit.* The lowest member of a structure, as the basement of a building, the plinth (when present) and base moldings of a column, or the lowest course of a wall; a pedestal. **13** The celluloid component of a motion-picture film. **14** *Her.* The lower part of the shield. **—off base 1** In baseball, not on the base one should be on. **2** *Colloq.* Utterly wrong about something. **—** *v.t.* **based, bas·ing 1** To place or ground on a logical basis, as an argument, decision, or theory: with *on* or *upon.* **2** To make or form a base for. **—** *adj.* **1** Serving as a base: a *base* line. **2** Situated at or near the base: a *base* angle. ◆ Homophone: *bass*[2]. [<F <L *basis* <Gk. *basis* step, pedestal < *bainein* go]

base[2] (bās) *adj.* **1** Low in sentiment, morals, or rank. **2** Low in value. **3** Alloyed, debased, or counterfeit, as money; not silver or gold: *base* metals. **4** *Music* Bass. **5** In English law, held by villeinage: opposed to *free*: said of a tenure of an estate. **6** *Obs.* Of humble or ignoble birth; also, illegitimate. **7** Menial; servile. **8** Not classical: said of languages. ◆ Homophone: *bass*[2]. [<OF *bas* <LL *bassus* low] **—base′ly** *adv.* **—base′ness** *n.*

Synonyms: abject, beggarly, cheap, contemptible, cringing, degraded, degrading, despicable, groveling, ignoble, infamous, low, low-minded, mean, mean-spirited, menial, miserable, obsequious, paltry, poor, poor-spirited, scurvy, servile, shabby, slavish, sneaking, sordid, squalid, subservient, vile, worthless, wretched. *Antonyms*: arrogant, conceited, dignified, eminent, esteemed, exalted, haughty, honorable, illustrious, independent, insolent, lofty, noble, pompous, princely, proud, self-assertive, self-conceited, self-reliant, self-respectful, supercilious, superior, supreme, vain, worthy.

base·ball (bās′bôl′) *n.* **1** A game played with a wooden bat and a hard ball by two teams, properly of nine players each, one team being at bat and the other in the field, alternately,

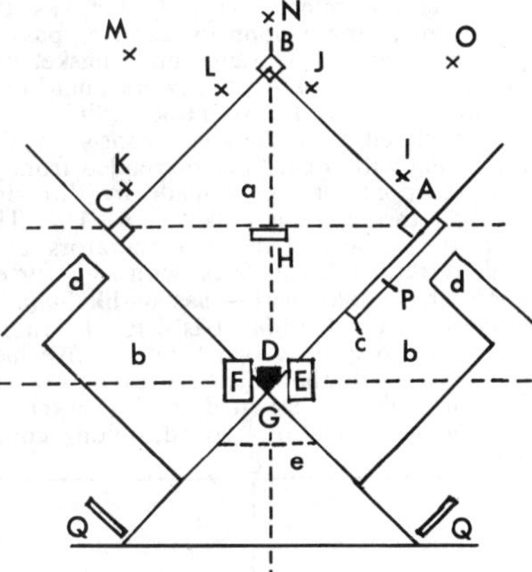

BASEBALL FIELD

a. Diamond (90 feet x 90 feet).
b. Players' line (75 feet x 75 feet).
c. Three-foot line (48 x 3 feet).
d. Coaches' lines.
e. Catcher's lines.
A. First base (15 inches x 15 inches).
B. Second base (15 inches x 15 inches).
C. Third base (15 inches x 15 inches).
D. Home base (17 x 8 1/2 x 12 x 8 1/2 x 12 inches; five-sided).
E., F. Batter's boxes.
G. Catcher.
H. Pitcher's plate (24 inches x 6 inches).
I. First baseman.
J. Second baseman.
K. Third baseman.
L. Shortstop.
M., N., O. Outfielders.
P Space to which base runner must confine himself.
Q. Players' benches.

for a minimum of nine innings: the game is played on a field having four bases marking the course each player must take in scoring a run. **2** The ball used in this game.

base·board (bās′bôrd′, -bōrd′) *n.* **1** A board skirting the interior wall of a room, next to the floor. **2** A board forming the base of anything.

base-born (bās′bôrn′) *adj.* **1** Born out of wedlock. **2** Of low birth; plebeian. **3** Mean.

base·burn·er (bās′bûr′nər) *n.* A coal stove or furnace in which the fuel is fed from above into a central fuel chamber.

base command *Mil.* An area organized for the unified administration of all military operations carried on by the base or bases functioning within it.

Ba·se·dow's disease (bä′zə·dōz) Exophthalmic goiter. [after a 19th c. German physician]

base hit In baseball, a hit by which the batter reaches base without help of an opposing player's error or without forcing out a runner previously on base.

Ba·sel (bä′zəl) A city on the Rhine in northern Switzerland: ancient *Basilia*: also *Basle*: French *Bâle.*

base·less (bās′lis) *adj.* Without foundation in fact; unfounded; groundless. See synonyms under VAIN.

base level The lowest level of erosion possible to a watercourse in any geographical area.

base·man (bās′mən) *n. pl.* **·men** (-mən) A baseball player stationed at first, second, or third base.

base·ment (bās′mənt) *n.* **1** The lowest floor of a building, usually underground and just beneath the principal story. **2** The substructure or the basal portion of any building or other structure or member.

base metal 1 Any metal which oxidizes easily when exposed to or heated in air, as iron, lead, or tin: opposed to *noble metal.* **2** *Chem.* A metal whose hydroxide is soluble in water.

ba·sen·ji (bə·sen′jē) *n.* A small, barkless dog, similar in build to a fox terrier, with a smooth, reddish coat and white-tipped tail and feet. [<Afrikaans, bush thing]

BASENJI

base of operations *Mil.* A region or area from which a military force begins an offensive action and to which it falls back in case of withdrawal.

base runner In baseball, a member of the team at bat who has reached base.

bas·es[1] (bā′siz) Plural of BASE.

ba·ses[2] (bā′sēz) Plural of BASIS.

bash (bash) *v.t.* To strike heavily; smash in. **—** *n.* A smashing blow. [? Akin to Dan. *baske* thwack]

Ba·shan (bā′shən) A region east of the Jordan in ancient Palestine.

ba·shaw (bə·shô′) *n.* **1** A Turkish official. **2** *Colloq.* An important or self-important personage. [<Turkish *bāshā*, var. of *pāshā*, ? < *bāsh* head]

bash·ful (bash′fəl) *adj.* **1** Shrinking from notice; shy; timid; diffident. **2** Characterized by or indicating sensitiveness and timid modesty. [< *bash*, var. of ABASH + -FUL] **—bash′ful·ly** *adv.* **—bash′ful·ness** *n.*

Ba·shi Channel (bä′shē) The northernmost part of Luzon Strait, between the Batan Islands and Taiwan.

bash·i-ba·zouk (bash′ē·bə·zōōk′) *n.* A member of a class of mounted Turkish irregular soldiers, noted for brutality. [<Turkish *bashi* headdress + *bozuq* disorderly]

Bash·kir Autonomous Soviet Socialist Republic (bäsh·kir′) An administrative division of eastern European Russian S.F.S.R.; 55,400 square miles; capital, Ufa.

bash·lyk (bash′lik) *n.* A fitted cloth hood covering the head and ears. Also **bash′lik.** [<Russian]

ba·sic (bā′sik) *adj.* **1** Pertaining to, forming, or like a base or basis. **2** Essential; fundamental. **3** *Chem.* **a** Above normal in base-producing constituents: a *basic* salt. **b** Yielding hydroxyl ions when dissolved in an ionizing solvent. **c** Showing an alkaline reaction. **4** *Geol.* Containing comparatively little silica: said of igneous rocks, as basalt. **5** *Metall.* Designating the basic process of making steel. **—** *n.* In the U.S. Army, an enlisted man who has completed or is pursuing the minimum course of military training.

ba·si·cal·ly (bā′sik·lē) *adv.* Essentially; fundamentally.

Basic English A highly simplified form of English, devised by C. K. Ogden, intended for use as an international auxiliary language. It consists of 600 common nouns, 18 verbs, 150 adjectives, and 82 assorted pronouns, prepositions, conjunctions, and adverbs. The

850 words of the general vocabulary are supplemented by an additional 150 for scientific purposes. Also called **Basic.** [*Basic,* acronym for British, American, Scientific, International, Commercial]

ba·sic·i·ty (bā·sis′ə·tē) *n. Chem.* **1** The state or condition of being a base. **2** The ability of an acid to unite with one or more equivalents of a base, depending upon the number of replaceable hydrogen atoms contained in a molecule of the acid.

basic oxide A metallic oxide which is capable of interacting with an acid to form a salt, as calcium oxide or lime, CaO.

basic process A method of steelmaking which uses a furnace lined with a basic refractory material, as dolomite or magnesite: it yields a **basic slag** rich in lime and phosphorus.

ba·sid·i·o·my·ce·tous (bə·sid′ē·ō·mī·sē′təs) *adj. Bot.* Belonging to a class *(Basidiomycetes)* of fungi having the spores borne on basidia. It includes parasites and saprophytes: mushrooms, smuts, rusts, etc. [<BASIDIUM + Gk. *mykēs, -ētos* fungus]

ba·sid·i·um (bə·sid′ē·əm) *n. pl.* **·sid·i·a** (-sid′·ē·ə) *Bot.* A mother cell in basidiomycetous fungi, on which spores (usually four) are borne at the extremity of slender stalks. [< NL <Gk. *baseidion,* dim. of *basis* base]

ba·si·fy (bā′sə·fī) *v.t.* **·fied, ·fy·ing** To change into a base by chemical means. **—ba′si·fi·ca′tion** *n.* **—ba′si·fi′er** *n.*

bas·il (baz′əl) *n.* **1** Any of certain aromatic plants of the mint family (genus *Ocimum*), especially the European *sweet basil (O. basilicum).* **2** The American mountain mint (genus *Pycnanthemum*) or **wild basil.** [<OF *basile* <L *basilicum* <Gk. *basilikon (phyton)* royal (plant), basil < *basileus* king]

Bas·il (baz′əl, bā′zəl) A masculine personal name. Also *Fr.* **Ba·sile** (bà·zēl′), *Lat.* **Ba·sil·i·us** (bə·sil′ē·əs; *Dan., Du., Ger., Sw.* bä·zē′·lē·o͝os), *Ital., Pg., Sp.* **Ba·si·li·o** (bä·sē′lē·ō). [<Gk., kingly]
— **Basil the Great, Saint,** 329?–379, one of the four Greek doctors of the church; bishop of Caesarea.

Ba·si·lan (bä·sē′län) An island of the Philippines east of Mindanao; 494 square miles.

bas·i·lar (bas′ə·lər) *adj.* Pertaining to or situated at the base; basal. Also **bas·i·lar·y** (bas′·ə·ler′ē).

basilar membrane *Anat.* The membrane separating the two vestibules of the cochlea of the ear and acting as a receptor of the sound vibrations transmitted by the auditory nerve.

Ba·sil·i·a (bə·zil′ē·ə) The ancient name for BASEL.

ba·sil·ic (bə·sil′ik) *adj.* **1** Pertaining to a basilica. **2** Royal. **3** *Anat.* Pertaining to the largest vein of the arm. Also **ba·sil′i·cal.** [< Gk. *basilikos* kingly]

ba·sil·i·ca (bə·sil′i·kə) *n.* **1** Originally, in ancient Athens, a portico used as a court of justice. **2** In ancient Rome, a rectangular building divided into nave and aisles: used as a hall of justice and adopted as the type of the earliest buildings for Christian worship. **3** A church shaped like a Roman basilica. **4** In the Roman Catholic Church, a church accorded certain liturgical privileges. [<L <Gk. *basilikē,* fem. of *basilikos* royal] **—ba·sil′i·can** *adj.*

Ba·sil·i·ca (bə·sil′i·kə) *n.* The Byzantine code of law of Basil I (9th century), chiefly adapted from that of Justinian: a plural used also as a singular. [<Gk. *basilika (nomima)* (laws) of Basil]

Ba·si·li·ca·ta (bä·sē′lē·kä′tä) A region of southern Italy at the instep of the Italian boot: ancient *Lucania.*

bas·i·lisk (bas′ə·lisk) *n.* **1** A fabled reptile of the African desert whose breath and look were fatal. **2** A tropical American lizard (genus *Basiliscus,* family *Iguanidae*) having an erectile crest and a dilatable pouch on the head. [<L *basiliscus* <Gk. *basiliskos,* dim. of *basileus* king]

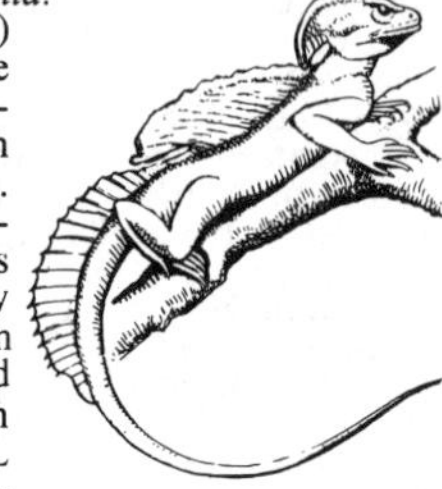
THE HOODED BASILISK

ba·sin (bā′sən) *n.* **1** A round, wide, shallow vessel, often with sloping sides, used especially for holding liquids. **2** The amount that a basin will hold. **3** A sink or wash bowl. **4** A depression in the earth's surface, as a valley, or the region drained by a river. **5** A depressed region in the floor of the ocean. **6** A comparatively circular and shallow area or arm of the sea: the Minas *Basin.* [<OF *bacin* <LL *bachinus* < *bacca* bowl] **—ba′sined** *adj.* **—ba′sin·like′** *adj.*

bas·i·net (bas′ə·nit, -net) *n.* A small, close-fitting helmet. [<OF *bacinet,* dim. of *bacin* basin]

ba·si·on (bā′sē·ən) *n. Anat.* The point where the anterior border of the foramen magnum of the skull cuts the median plane. [<Gk. *basis* base]

ba·sip·e·tal (bā·sip′ə·təl) *adj. Bot.* Growing in the direction of the base.

ba·sis (bā′sis) *n. pl.* **ba·ses** (bā′sēz) **1** That on which anything rests; support; foundation. **2** Fundamental principle. **3** The chief component or ingredient of a thing. [<L <Gk., base, pedestal]

bask (bask, bäsk) *v.i.* **1** To lie in and enjoy a pleasant warmth, as of the sun or a fire. **2** To enjoy or expose oneself to a benign influence, pleasant situation, etc.: to *bask* in the favor of a king. — *v.t.* **3** To expose to warmth. [<ON *badhask* bathe oneself]

Bas·ker·ville (bas′kər·vil), **John,** 1706–75, English printer and type founder; designer of the type face known by his name.

bas·ket (bas′kit, bäs′-) *n.* **1** A container made of interwoven twigs, splints, rushes, strips, etc. **2** Something resembling a basket, as the structure under a balloon for carrying passengers or ballast. **3** The amount a basket will hold; a basketful. **4** An openwork guard over the hilt of a sword: also **basket hilt. 5** In basketball, either of the goals, consisting of a metal ring with a cord net suspended from it; also, the point or points made by throwing the ball through the basket. **6** *Mil.* The platform supporting the two operators of a tank turret, which rotates with the turret. [ME; origin unknown] **—bas′ket·like′** *adj.*

bas·ket·ball (bas′kit·bôl′, bäs′-) *n.* **1** An indoor game played by two teams of five men each, in which the object is to throw the ball through the elevated goal (basket) at the opponent's end of a zoned, oblong court.

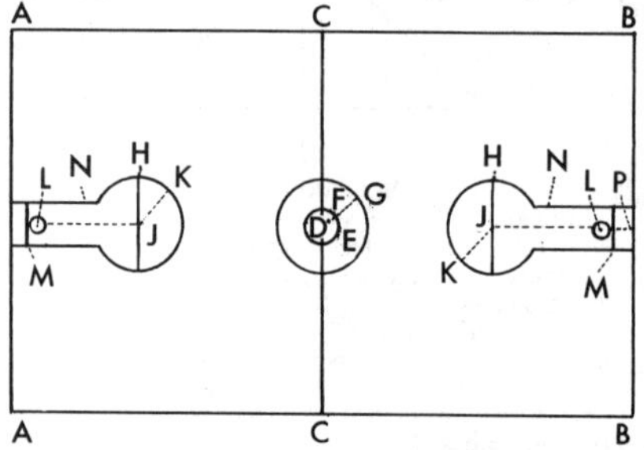

BASKETBALL COURT

C.	Center division line.	*N.*	Foul lines.
E.	Restraining circle.	*DF.*	Radius 2 feet.
H.	Free throw lines.	*DG.*	Radius 6 feet.
J.	Free throw circles.	*JK.*	Radius 6 feet.
L.	Baskets.	*JM.*	15 feet.
M.	Backboards.	*JP.*	19 feet.

AA, BB. End lines, vary from 35 to 50 feet.
AB, AB. Side lines, vary from 84 to 94 feet. The basket is raised 10 feet from playing floor.

On each team the players consist of a center, two forwards, and two guards. **2** The round, inflated leather ball used in this game.

basket dance *Anthropol.* A ceremonial dance centering the action on a basket held in the left hand of a woman dancer, who strews grain or meal from it as a symbol of vegetation fertility: danced in many culture areas of the Old and New World.

bas·ket·fish (bas′kit·fish′, bäs′-) *n.* A starfish (genus *Gorgonocephalus*) having many branched or interlacing arms: common off the New England coast.

Basket Maker One of a class of prehistoric cave-dwelling people of SW North America, of a culture more ancient than the cliff-dwellers or Pueblos, characterized by their basket-making and lack of pottery.

basket meeting *U.S.* A social gathering to which people bring their suppers in a basket.

bas·ket·ry (bas′kit·rē, bäs′-) *n.* **1** Baskets collectively; basketwork. **2** The art or craft of making baskets.

bas·ket·weave (bas′kit·wēv′, bäs′-) *n.* A weave with two or more warp and filling threads woven side by side to resemble a plaited basket.

bas·ket·work (bas′kit·wûrk′, bäs′-) *n.* A fabric or texture of woven or plaited osiers or twigs, or an imitation of it in some other substance; wickerwork.

basking shark A shark *(Cetorhinus maximus)* of the North Atlantic, attaining a length of over 30 feet and valued for its liver oil: named from its habit of basking on the surface of the water.

Basle (bäl) See BASEL.

ba·so·phile (bā′sə·fīl, -fil) *n. Biol.* A tissue or cell having a special affinity for basic staining dyes: also spelled *basiphile.* [<BASIC (dye) + -PHILE] **—ba·so·phil·ic** (bā′sə·fil′ik), **ba·soph·i·lous** (bā·sof′ə·ləs) *adj.*

ba·so·phil·i·a (bā′sə·fil′ē·ə) *n. Pathol.* A condition in which an excessive number of basophiles are present in the blood.

basque (bask) *n.* A woman's closely fitting bodice, separate from the dress skirt: originally from the Basque costume.

Basque (bask) *n.* **1** One of a people living in the western Pyrenees in Spain and France, of unknown racial origin but having such distinctive racial traits that they are believed to be unrelated to any other racial stock. **2** The agglutinative language of the Basque people, unrelated to any other language: possibly a survival of the lost ancient Iberian. — *adj.* Of or pertaining to the Basques or to their language, or to the Basque Provinces.

Basque Provinces Three provinces in northern Spain on the Bay of Biscay; combined area, 2,803 square miles. *Spanish* **Vas·con·ga·das** (väs′kōng·gä′thäs).

Bas·ra (bus′rə) A port of SE Iraq on the Shatt-el-Arab: also *Bassora, Bussora, Busra.* Also **Bas′rah.**

bas-re·lief (bä′ri·lēf′, bas′-) *n.* Sculpture or a piece of sculpture in which the figures project only slightly from the background: also called *basso-rilievo.* See RELIEF. [<F <Ital. *basso* low + *rilievo* relief]

Bas-Rhin (bä·raṅ′) A department of France in Alsace; 1,848 square miles; capital, Strasbourg.

bass[1] (bas) *n.* **1** One of various spiny-finned, marine and fresh-water food fishes, especially the European sea bass *(Dicentrarchus labrax),* the American striped bass *(Roccus lineatus),* and the black basses (genus *Micropterus*). **2** The European perch *(Perca fluviatilis).* **3** The cabrilla (def. 2). [OE *bærs*]

bass[2] (bās) *n. Music* **1** The lowest-pitched male singing voice. **2** A deep, low sound, as of this voice or of certain low-pitched instruments. **3** The notes in the lowest register of the piano, pipe organ, etc. **4** The lowest part in vocal or instrumental music. **5** One who sings or an instrument that plays such a part, especially a bass viol. **6** Such parts collectively. — *adj.* **1** Low in pitch; having a low musical range. **2** Pertaining to, for, or able to play bass. ◆ Homophone: *base.* [<OF *bas* low; infl. in spelling by Ital. *basso*]

bass[3] (bas) *n.* **1** The basswood. **2** Bast. [Alter. of BAST]

Bas·sa·ni·o (bə·sä′nē·ō) In Shakespeare's *Merchant of Venice,* Portia's successful suitor.

bass clef (bās) *Music* **1** The sign on a staff showing that the notes are below middle C. **2** The notes so shown.

bass drum (bās) The largest of the drums, beaten on both heads and having a deep sound: also called *double drum.*

Bas·sein (bä·sēn′, -sān′) A port on one of the mouths of the Irrawaddy, Lower Burma.

bas·set[1] (bas′it) *n.* A hound characterized by a long, low body, long head and nose, and short, heavy, crooked forelegs: used in hunting. Also **bas′set·hound′.** [<OF *basset,* fem. dim. of *bas*·low]

bas·set[2] (bas′it) *Geol. n.* An outcropping. — *v.i.* **·set·ed, ·set·ing** To crop out; appear at the surface, as coal. [Origin uncertain]

Basse·terre (bäs·târ′) A town on St. Kitts, capital of the St. Christopher, Nevis and Anguilla presidency of the Leeward Islands.

Basse–Terre (bäs·târ′) **1** A port on the SW

coast of Basse-Terre island, capital of the French overseas department of Guadeloupe. 2 One of the twin islands comprising Guadeloupe department: also *Guadeloupe*.

bas·set-horn (bas′it·hôrn′) *n.* A tenor clarinet having a compass of three and a half octaves. It has four more low keys than the ordinary clarinet. [<Ital. *corno di bassetto* < *bassetto*, dim. of *basso* low + *corno* horn]

bass horn (bās) A tuba.

bas·si·net (bas′ə·net′) *n.* 1 A basket, usually with a hood over one end, used as a baby's cradle. 2 A small basket for holding the clothing of an infant. 3 A kind of perambulator. [<F, dim. of *bassin* basin]

bas·so (bas′ō, *Ital.* bäs′sō) *n. pl.* **bas·sos** (bas′ōz), *Ital.* **bas·si** (bäs′sē) 1 A bass singer. 2 The bass part. [<Ital., low]

bas·soon (ba·sōōn′, bə-) *n. Music* 1 A large, double-reed woodwind instrument with a long, curved mouthpiece. 2 An organ stop like a bassoon in its low tone. [<F *basson*, aug. of *bas* low]

basso pro·fun·do (prə·fun′dō, *Ital.* prō·fōōn′dō) 1 A singer who sings the deepest bass. 2 The lowest bass voice.

Bas·so·ra (bas′ə·rə) Basra. Also **Bas′so·rah.**

bas·so-re·lie·vo (bas′ō·ri·lē′vō) *n. pl.* **·vos** (-vōz) Bas-relief.

bas·so·ri·lie·vo (bäs′sō·ri·lyâ′vō) *n. pl.* **·ri·lie·vi** (-ri·lyâ′vē) *Italian* Bas-relief.

Bass Strait (bas) The passage between the coasts of the Australian mainland and Tasmania, from the Indian Ocean to the Tasman Sea.

bass viol (bās) *Music* 1 The double-bass. 2 The viola da gamba.

bass·wood (bas′wŏŏd′) *n.* The linden.

bast (bast) *n. Bot.* 1 The fibrous inner bark of trees or a cordage made from it: also called *bass*. 2 A vegetable tissue found especially in the inner bark of dicotyledons, composed of tough, spindle-shaped, thick-walled fibers or cells. 3 Phloem. [OE *bæst*]

bas·tard (bas′tərd) *n.* 1 An illegitimate child. 2 Any hybrid plant, tree, or animal. 3 Any spurious, irregular, inferior, or counterfeit thing. 4 A refuse sugar from previously boiled sirup. —*adj.* 1 Born out of wedlock. 2 False; spurious. 3 Resembling but not typical of the genuine thing: *bastard* mahogany. 4 Unusual in size, shape, or proportion; abnormal; irregular: *bastard* type. [<OF *bastard* < *fils de bast* packsaddle child; with ref. to the use of the saddle as a bed]

bas·tard·ize (bas′tər·dīz) *v.* **·ized, ·iz·ing** *v.t.* 1 To prove to be, or stigmatize as, a bastard. 2 To make degenerate; debase. —*v.i.* 3 To become debased. —**bas′tard·i·za′tion** *n.*

bas·tard·ly (bas′tərd·lē) *adj.* 1 Bastardlike; of illegitimate birth. 2 Debased; counterfeit.

bastard wing *Ornithol.* An alula.

bas·tard·y (bas′tər·dē) *n.* 1 The begetting of a bastard. 2 The state of being a bastard; illegitimacy.

baste[1] (bāst) *v.t.* **bast·ed, bast·ing** To sew loosely together, as with long, temporary stitches. [<OF *bastir* <OHG *bestan* sew with bast]

baste[2] (bāst) *v.t.* **bast·ed, bast·ing** To moisten (meat or fish) with drippings, butter, etc., while cooking. [<OF *basser* soak, moisten]

baste[3] (bāst) *v.t. Colloq.* 1 To cudgel; thrash. 2 To attack verbally; abuse. [prob. <Scand., cf. ON *beysta* beat]

Bas·tia (bäs′tyä) A port on the NE coast of Corsica; chief city and former capital of the island.

Bas·tien-Le·page (bȧs·tyaṅ′lə·pȧzh′), **Jules,** 1848–84, French painter.

bas·tille (bas·tēl′) *n.* 1 A prison; especially, one used as a government prison or operated tyrannically. 2 In ancient warfare, a small fortress. Also **bas·tile′.** [<OF, building]

Bas·tille (bas·tēl′, *Fr.* bȧs·tē′y′) A fortress in Paris, built in 1369 and stormed and destroyed in the French Revolution on July 14, 1789.

Bastille Day The national holiday of republican France, July 14, commemorating the fall and destruction of the Bastille.

bas·ti·na·do (bas′tə·nā′dō) *n. pl.* **·does** 1 A beating with a stick, usually on the soles of the feet: an Oriental punishment. 2 A stick or cudgel. —*v.t.* **·doed, ·do·ing** To beat with a stick, usually on the soles of the feet. See synonyms under BEAT. Also **bas′ti·nade′.** [<Sp. *bastonado* < *bastón* cudgel]

bast·ing (bās′ting) *n.* 1 The act of sewing loosely together. 2 *pl.* Long, loose, temporary stitches. 3 The thread used for this purpose. [<BASTE[1]]

bas·tion (bas′chən, -tē·ən) *n.* 1 In fortifications, a projecting work having two faces and two flanks so constructed that the adjacent curtain may be defended from it. 2 Any fortified or strongly defended place or position. [<F <Ital. *bastione* < *bastire* build] —**bas′tioned** *adj.*

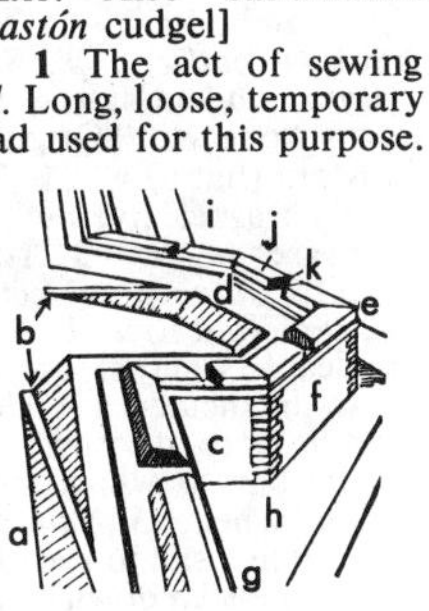

BASTION

a. Boulevard. *b.* Ramps. *c.* Flank. *d.* Banquette. *e.* Salient. *f.* Face of rampart. *g.* Berm. *h.* Moat. *i.* Glacis. *j.* Scarp. *k.* Embrasure in parapet.

The curtains extending from its flanks (*c*) are on both sides of the bastion.

Bas·togne (bas·tōn′, *Fr.* bȧs·tôn′y′) A town in SE Belgium; besieged and nearly destroyed during the German counter-offensive of World War II in December, 1944. *Flemish* **Bas·te·na·ken** (bäs′tə·nä′kən).

Ba·su·to·land (bə·sōō′tō·land′) A former British territory in southern Africa. See LESOTHO.

bat[1] (bat) *n.* 1 Any heavy cudgel or club. 2 Batting. 3 In baseball, cricket, and other games: **a** A stick or club for striking the ball, usually having one end wider or heavier than the other. **b** A turn at bat or the right to such a turn. **c** A racket, as in tennis. **d** The act of batting. **e** The batsman, as in cricket. 4 A fragment or lump of clay. 5 *Colloq.* A blow, as with a stick. 6 *Colloq.* Speed; rate of motion. 7 *Slang* A drunken carousal; a spree. —**at bat** In the act or position of batting. —**to go to bat for** *Colloq.* To defend or advocate the cause of. —*v.* **bat·ted, bat·ting** *v.i.* 1 In baseball, cricket, and other games: **a** To use a bat. **b** To take a turn at bat. 2 *Slang* To go hurriedly. —*v.t.* 3 To strike with or as with a bat. —**to bat around** *Slang* 1 To move or travel about. 2 To discuss, as a proposal or idea. 3 In baseball, to have the whole team bat in one inning. [OE *batt* cudgel]

bat[2] (bat) *n.* Any of numerous nocturnal flying mammals (order *Chiroptera*), having greatly elongated fore limbs and digits that support a thin wing membrane extending to the hind limbs and sometimes to the tail. —**blind as a bat** Altogether blind. —**to have bats in the belfry** *Slang* To be crazy. [ME *bakke*, ? <Scand.] —**bat′like′** *adj.*

bat[3] (bat) *v.t. Colloq.* To wink; flutter. —**not bat an eye** *Colloq.* Not show surprise or other reaction. [Var. of BATE[3]]

bat[4] (bät) See BAHT.

Ba·taan (bə·tän′, -tan′) A province in southern Luzon, Philippines; 517 square miles; capital, Balanga; occupying **Bataan Peninsula,** scene of World War II surrender of United States and Philippine forces to the Japanese, April, 1942.

Ba·tang (bä·täng′) Former name for PAAN.

Ba·tan·gas (bä·täng′gäs) A province in southern Luzon, Philippines; 1,192 square miles; capital, Batangas.

Ba·tan Islands (bä·tän′) An island group in the Philippines, constituting **Ba·ta·nes** (bä·tä′näs) province; total area, 76 square miles; capital, Basco.

Ba·ta·vi (bə·tā′vī) *n. pl.* An ancient Germanic people who inhabited the region about the mouths of the Rhine.

Ba·ta·vi·a (bə·tā′vē·ə, *Du.* bä·tä′vē·ä) A former name for JAKARTA. —**Ba·ta′vi·an** *adj.* & *n.*

batch[1] (bach) *n.* 1 The dough for one baking, or the quantity of bread, etc., baked. 2 The grain for one grinding; grist. 3 Any set of things made, done, dispatched, etc., at one time. 4 The amount of material, quantity of articles, etc., required for one operation. [ME *bacche*. Akin to BAKE.]

batch[2] (bach) *n. Slang* A bachelor.

bate[1] (bāt) *v.* **bat·ed, bat·ing** *v.t.* 1 To lessen the force or intensity of; moderate: to *bate* one's breath. 2 To deduct; take away. 3 *Obs.* To depress; decrease. —*v.i.* 4 To diminish; become reduced. ◆ Homophone: *bait.* [Var. of ABATE]

bate[2] (bāt) *n.* A solution of chemicals or manure containing natural or synthetic enzymes: used to soften skins or hides. —*v.t.* 1 To soak, as hides. 2 To separate and soften, as jute. ◆ Homophone: *bait.* [? <ON *beita* cause to bite. Akin to BAIT and BITE.]

bate[3] (bāt) *v.i.* **bat·ed, bat·ing** In falconry, to beat or flap the wings, as an impatient hawk: also spelled *bait.* ◆ Homophone: *bait.* [<F *battre* beat <L *battuere* strike, beat]

ba·teau (ba·tō′) *n. pl.* **·teaux** (-tōz′) 1 A light, flat-bottomed boat. 2 A pontoon for a floating bridge. [<F <OF *batel*, ult. <Gmc.]

bateau bridge A pontoon bridge.

Bates (bāts), **Katharine Lee,** 1859–1929, U.S. poet and educator.

Bate·son (bāt′sən), **William,** 1861–1926, English biologist.

bat·fish (bat′fish′) *n.* 1 A fish, as *Ogocephalus vespertilio* and other species of the Atlantic coast of the United States, resembling a bat. 2 The Pacific sting ray.

bat·fowl (bat′foul′) *v.i.* To catch birds at night by dazzling them with a light and netting or striking them down. —**bat′fowl′er** *n.* [<BAT[1] + FOWL]

bath[1] (bath, bäth) *n. pl.* **baths** (bat͟hz, bät͟hz; baths, bäths) 1 The act of washing or immersing something, especially the body, in water or other liquid. ◆ Collateral adjective: *balneal.* 2 The liquid substance or element used for this. 3 The container for such a liquid; a bathtub. 4 A bathroom. 5 A set of rooms or a building for bathing: often in the plural. 6 An establishment or resort where bathing is part of a medical treatment: often in the plural. 7 *Chem.* An apparatus for applying steady heat or heat of a given degree. 8 *Phot.* Any solution, or the vessel containing it, in which photographic plates, etc., are immersed for treatment. 9 *Metall.* The molten material in a reverberatory furnace. 10 The condition of being soaked or covered with a liquid. —*v.t.* To place or wash in a bath; immerse. [OE *bæth*]

bath[2] (bath) *n.* An ancient Hebrew liquid measure, one tenth of a homer: equivalent to about 8 1/2 gallons. [<Hebrew]

Bath (bath, bäth) A city in NE Somersetshire, England, famous since Roman times for its hot springs.

Bath brick A fine calcareous and siliceous material, usually pressed into brick shape, used for polishing and cleansing metal objects: originally found near Bath, England.

Bath chair A hooded wheelchair for invalids. Also **bath chair.** [from *Bath*, England, where originally used]

bathe (bāt͟h) *v.* **bathed, bath·ing** *v.t.* 1 To place in liquid; immerse. 2 To wash; wet. 3 To apply liquid to for comfort or healing; lave. 4 To cover or suffuse as with liquid: The hill was *bathed* in rosy light. —*v.i.* 5 To wash oneself; take a bath. 6 To go into or remain in water so as to swim or cool off. 7 To be covered or suffused as if with liquid. —*n. Brit.* The act of bathing, as in the sea. [OE *bathian*] —**bathe′a·ble** *adj.* —**bath′er** *n.*

ba·thet·ic (bə·thet′ik) *adj.* Pertaining to, exhibiting, or of the nature of bathos. [<BATHOS]

bath·house (bath′hous′, bäth′-) *n.* 1 A building with conveniences for taking baths. 2 A small structure at a bathing resort used as a dressing-room.

bath·ing suit (bāt͟h′ing) A garment, sometimes consisting of two pieces, worn for swimming.

batho- *combining form* Depth: *bathometer.* [<Gk. *bathos* depth]

bath·o·lith (bath′ə·lith) *n. Geol.* A large irregular mass of intrusive igneous rock which has melted or forced its way into surrounding strata. Also **bath′o·lite** (-līt). —**bath′o·lith′ic, bath′o·lit′ic** (-lit′ik) *adj.*

ba·thom·e·ter (bə·thom′ə·tər) *n.* An apparatus for determining the depth of water, as by pressure. [<BATHO- + METER]

ba·thoph·i·lous (bə·thof′ə·ləs) *adj.* Of or pertaining to organisms adapted to life at great depths in the ocean. [<BATHO- + -PHILOUS]

bath·o·pho·bi·a (bath′ə·fō′bē·ə) *n. Psychiatry* Morbid fear of depths. Compare ACROPHOBIA. —**bath′o·pho′bic** (-fō′bik, -fob′ik) *adj.*

ba·thos (bā′thos) *n.* **1** A descent from the lofty to the commonplace in discourse; anticlimax. **2** Insincere pathos; sentimentality. [<Gk. *bathos* depth < *bathys* deep]

bath·robe (bath′rōb′, bäth′-) *n.* A long, loose garment for wear before and after bathing.

bath·room (bath′rōōm′, -rŏŏm′, bäth′-) *n.* **1** A room in which to bathe. **2** A toilet (def. 4).

bath salts A perfumed mixture of crystal salts used to soften bath water.

Bath·she·ba (bath·shē′bə, bath′shi·bə) Wife of Uriah and later of David; mother of Solomon. II *Sam.* xi–xii.

bath·tub (bath′tub′, bäth′-) *n.* **1** A vessel in which to bathe. **2** Such a vessel installed as a permanent fixture in a bathroom.

Bath·urst (bath′ərst, bäth′-) **1** A municipality in east central New South Wales, Australia. **2** An Atlantic port, capital of Gambia, British West Africa.

bathy- *combining form* Deep: of the sea or ocean depths: *bathymeter*, *bathysphere*. [<Gk. *bathys* deep]

ba·thym·e·ter (bə·thim′ə·tər) See BATHOMETER.

ba·thym·e·try (bə·thim′ə·trē) *n.* The science or art of deep-sea sounding. **—bath·y·met·ric** (bath′ə·met′rik) *adj.*

bath·y·scaph (bath′ə·skaf) *n.* A bathysphere equipped with ballast for reaching ocean depths of over 12,000 feet and a gasoline-filled float for surfacing. [<BATHY- + Gk. *skaphē* bowl]

bath·y·seism (bath′ə·sī′zəm) *n.* An earthquake occurring at great depths. [<BATHY- + Gk. *seismos* earthquake]

bath·y·sphere (bath′ə·sfir) *n.* A spherical diving bell equipped with fused quartz windows for deep-sea observations.

ba·tik (bə·tēk′, bat′ik) *n.* **1** A process for coloring fabrics, originating in the East Indies, in which parts of a fabric are covered with melted wax so that only the uncovered portions will take the dye, the wax then being dissolved in boiling water. The process is often repeated to obtain multicolored designs. **2** The fabric so colored. Also *battik.* [<Malay]

bat·ing (bā′ting) *prep. Archaic* Making deduction for.

Ba·tis·ta y Zal·dí·var (bä·tēs′tä ē säl·dē′vär), **Fulgencio,** 1901–1973, Cuban soldier and politician; president 1940–44, 1950–58.

ba·tiste (bə·tēst′) *n.* **1** A sheer fabric made of cotton, silk, or spun rayon. The cotton batiste is sometimes mercerized. **2** A fine woolen fabric lighter than challis. **3** Originally, a fine linen cloth. [<F; after Jean *Baptiste*, 13th c. French linen weaver]

Ba·tjan (bä·chän′) An Indonesian island SW of Halmahera; 913 square miles: also *Bachan.*

bat·man (bat′mən, bä′mən) *n. pl.* **·men** (-mən) *Brit.* An officer's servant. [<F *bat* <OF *bast* packsaddle + MAN]

ba·ton (ba·ton′, bat′n; *Fr.* bȧ·tôṅ′) *n.* **1** A short official staff or truncheon borne as a weapon or as an emblem of authority or privilege: a marshal's *baton.* **2** *Music* A slender stick or rod used for beating time. **3** *Her.* A bend borne sinisterwise across the shield as a mark of bastardy: also **baton sinister,** erroneously *bar sinister.* [<F *bâton* <OF *baston* <LL *bastum* stick]

Bat·on Rouge (bat′n rōōzh′) A port on the Mississippi River, capital of Louisiana.

Ba·tra·chi·a (bə·trā′kē·ə) *n. pl.* Former name for AMPHIBIA. [<Gk. *batrachos* frog]

ba·tra·chi·an (bə·trā′kē·ən) *adj.* **1** Of or pertaining to the *Batrachia,* especially to the frogs and toads; amphibian. **2** Froglike. **—***n.* One of the *Batrachia.*

bat·ra·chite (bat′rə·kīt) *n.* **1** A stone that is froglike in color. **2** A fossil batrachian.

bat·ra·choid (bat′rə·koid) *adj.* Froglike.

bats·man (bats′mən) *n. pl.* **·men** (-mən) In baseball or cricket, the batter.

batt (bat) See BATTING.

bat·tai·lous (bat′i·ləs) *adj. Obs.* Bellicose. [<OF *bataillos* < *bataille* battle]

bat·ta·lia (bə·tāl′yə, -täl′-) *n. Obs.* **1** An army. **2** Order of battle.

bat·tal·ion (bə·tal′yən) *n.* **1** *Mil.* **a** A unit, normally part of a regiment, consisting of a headquarters and two or more companies, batteries, or comparable units. **b** A body of troops. **2** *Usually pl.* A large group or number. [<F *battaillon* <Ital. *battaglione* < *battaglia* battle]

Bat·tam·bang (bä′täm·bäng′) A town in western Cambodia.

bat·tels (bat′lz) *n. pl. Brit.* At Oxford University, a student's account with his college for provisions, etc. [Origin uncertain]

bat·ten[1] (bat′n) *v.i.* **1** To grow fat or thrive. **2** To prosper; live well, especially at another's expense. **—***v.t.* **3** To make fat, as cattle. [<ON *batna* grow better, improve]

bat·ten[2] (bat′n) *n.* **1** A narrow strip of wood; a cleat, as across parallel boards in a door. **2** In the theater: **a** A cleat placed on a muslin flat or piece of scenery to stiffen it. **b** A round metal bar to which spotlights or floodlights are attached. **3** *Naut* **a** A thin strip of wood placed in a sail to keep it flat. **b** A similar strip used to fasten down a tarpaulin covering on a hatchway. **—***v.t.* **1** To make, furnish, or strengthen with battens. **2** To fasten with battens. **—to batten down the hatches** *Naut.* To put tarpaulins over a hatchway and secure them by strips of wood. [Var. of BATON] **—bat′ten·er** *n.*

bat·ter[1] (bat′ər) *n.* **1** A heavy blow; also, repeated blows, or the condition resulting from them. **2** In ceramics, a mallet for beating a lump of plastic clay. **3** *Printing* **a** The breakage or marring of type or a plate. **b** The type thus broken. **c** The resulting defect in print. [< *v.*] **—***v.t.* **1** To strike with repeated, violent blows. **2** To damage or injure with or as with such blows. **—***v.i.* **3** To pound or beat with blow after blow; hammer. See synonyms under BEAT. [<F *battre* <L *battuere* beat]

bat·ter[2] (bat′ər) *n.* In baseball and cricket, the player whose turn it is to bat.

bat·ter[3] (bat′ər) *n.* A thick liquid mixture of eggs, flour, and milk, beaten up for use in cookery. [<OF *bature* beating < *battre* beat]

bat·ter[4] (bat′ər) *n.* An inward and upward slope of a wall, giving greater resistance to thrust or firmer base. **—***v.t.* & *v.i.* To slope back from the base, as a wall. [Origin uncertain]

batter bread Spoonbread.

bat·ter·ing-ram (bat′ər·ing·ram′) *n.* A long, stout beam, with heavy head, used in ancient warfare for forcing gates and making breaches in walls, either carried by the assailants, or suspended in a frame.

BATTERING–RAM

Bat·ter·sea (bat′ər·sē) A metropolitan borough of London, on the south side of the Thames.

bat·ter·y (bat′ər·ē) *n. pl.* **·ter·ies** **1** *Mil.* **a** An earthwork or parapet for protecting one or more guns. **b** Two or more pieces of artillery constituting a tactical unit. **c** A unit of an artillery regiment equivalent to an infantry company, or their guns and other equipment. **2** *Nav.* The armament of a war vessel, or a special part of it. **3** *Electr.* **a** An arrangement of two or more primary cells, dynamos, etc., for the purpose of building up a strong electric current: a *battery* of Leyden jars. **b** Any of several types of such cells used to heat the filaments of a vacuum tube, provide current, or supply voltage: an A, B, or C *battery.* **4** *Law* The illegal beating or touching of another person. **5** In baseball, the pitcher and catcher together. **6** *Music* The percussion instruments of an orchestra, collectively. **7** *Optics* The group of prisms in a spectroscope. **8** Any unit, apparatus, or grouping in which a series or set of parts or components are assembled to serve a common end: a *battery* of tests. **9** The act of battering or beating. **10** The instrument for such an act. **—dry battery** *Electr.* A battery composed of cells whose contents are solid or nearly so; a dry pile. **—in battery** *Mil.* In firing position, after recovery from recoil: said of a heavy gun. [<F *batterie* < *battre* beat]

Battery, the A park at the southern extremity of Manhattan: so named from the guns mounted there in colonial and Revolutionary times. Also **Battery Park.**

battery cup A small metal cup which surrounds the cap (primer) of a shell or cartridge.

bat·tik (bə·tēk′, bat′ik) See BATIK.

bat·ting (bat′ing) *n.* **1** Wadded cotton or wool prepared in sheets or rolls: used for interlinings, stuffing mattresses, comforters, etc.: also *bat, batt.* **2** The act of one who bats.

Bat·tis·ta (bät·tēs′tä) Italian form of BAPTIST.

bat·tle (bat′l) *n.* **1** A combat between hostile armies or fleets; a military or naval engagement. **2** Armed combat. **3** Any fighting, conflict, or struggle: to do *battle* for a cause. **4** *Obs.* A battalion. **—***v.* **bat·tled, bat·tling** *v.i.* To contend in or as in battle; struggle; strive. **—***v.t.* To fight. See synonyms under CONTEND, DISPUTE. [<OF *bataille* <LL *battalia* gladiators' exercises < *battuere* beat] **—bat′tler** *n.*

Synonyms (noun): action, affair, bout, combat, conflict, contest, encounter, engagement, fight, skirmish, strife. *Conflict* is a general word which describes opponents, whether individuals or hosts, as dashed together. One continuous *conflict* between entire armies is a *battle.* Another *battle* may be fought upon the same field after a considerable interval; or a new *battle* may follow immediately, the armies meeting upon a new field. An *action* is brief and partial; a *battle* may last for days. *Engagement* is a somewhat formal expression for *battle.* A protracted war, including many *battles,* may be a stubborn *contest. Combat,* originally a hostile *encounter* between individuals, is now used also for extensive *engagements.* A *skirmish* is between small detachments or scattered troops. An *encounter* may be either purposed or accidental, between individuals or armed forces. *Fight* is a word of less dignity than *battle;* we should not ordinarily speak of Waterloo as a *fight,* unless where the word is used in the sense of fighting; as, I was in the thick of the *fight. Antonyms*: armistice, concord, peace, truce.

bat·tle-ax (bat′l·aks′) *n.* **1** A large ax formerly used in battle; a broad-ax. **2** *U.S. Slang* A formidable, disagreeable woman. Also **bat′tle-axe′.**

Battle Creek A city on the Kalamazoo River in SW Michigan.

battle cruiser A war vessel less heavily armored than a battleship, having cruiser speed and battleship armament.

battle cry **1** A shout used by troops in battle. **2** A slogan or identifying phrase used in any conflict or contest.

bat·tled (bat′ld) *adj. Obs.* Provided with battlements.

bat·tle·dore (bat′l·dôr, -dōr) *n.* **1** A flat paddle or bat, either of wood, webbed, or covered with parchment, used to drive a shuttlecock. **2** The game in which a shuttlecock is so batted: also **battledore and shuttlecock.** **—***v.t.* & *v.i.* **·dored, ·doring** To drive or fly back and forth. [? <Provençal *batedor* an implement for beating]

battle fatigue *Psychiatry* A psychoneurotic condition, characterized by anxiety, depression, etc., occurring among soldiers engaged in active warfare: formerly called *shell shock*: also *combat fatigue.*

bat·tle·field (bat′l·fēld′) *n.* The ground on which a battle is fought. Also **bat′tle·ground′.**

bat·tle·ment (bat′l·mənt) *n.* A parapet indented along its upper line. **—bat·tle·ment′ed** (bat′l·men·tid) *adj.* [<OF *ba(s)tillier* fortify]

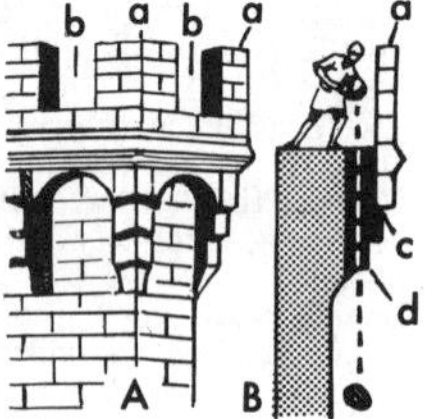

BATTLEMENT
A. Outer view: — *a, a.* Merlons; *b, b.* Embrasures. *B.* Cross-section: — showing use of corbel, *c,* for machicolation, *d.*

bat·tle·plane (bat′l·plān′) *n.* Formerly any airplane for combat use.

battle royal **1** A fight involving numerous combatants. **2** A protracted, rigorous battle.

bat·tle-scarred (bat′l·skärd′) *adj.* **1** Having scars, marks, etc., received in combat. **2** Having received the effects of a long and varied experience; experienced.

bat·tle·ship (bat′l·ship′) *n. Nav.* A vessel having a large displacement and radius of action, maximum armament and powerful batteries.

bat·tle·wag·on (bat′l·wag′ən) *n. Slang* A battleship.

bat·tol·o·gy (bə·tol′ə·jē) *n.* Unnecessary repetition in speaking or writing. [<Gk. *battologia*

stammering] **—bat·to·log·i·cal** (bat′ə·loj′i·kəl) *adj.* **—bat·tol′o·gist** *n.*

batts (bats, bäts) *n. pl. Scot.* Colic.

bat·tue (ba·to͞o′, -tyo͞o′) *n.* **1** The driving of game from cover within reach of sportsmen previously posted. **2** A hunt so conducted. **3** Any wanton slaughter. [< F, fem. pp. of *battre* beat]

bat·ty (bat′ē) *adj.* **·ti·er, ·ti·est 1** Of, pertaining to, or like a bat. **2** *U.S. Slang* Crazy; foolish; odd.

Ba·tum (bə·to͞om′) A port on the Black Sea in Georgian S.S.R. near the Turkish frontier. *Georgian* **Ba·tu·mi** (bä·to͞o′mē).

bau·bee (bô·bē′, bô′bē) See BAWBEE.

bau·ble (bô′bəl) *n.* **1** A worthless, showy trinket; gew-gaw; toy. **2** *Archaic* The wand of a jester. Also spelled *bawble.* See synonyms under GAUD. [< OF *baubel* toy, ? < L *bellus* pretty]

Bau·cis (bô′sis) In Greek mythology, a Phrygian peasant who, with Philemon, her husband, sheltered Zeus and Hermes.

baud (bôd) *n.* A unit of speed in telegraphy, based on the time interval required to transmit a given signal, usually the dot. [after J. M. E. *Baudot,* 1845–1903, French inventor]

bau·de·kin (bô′də·kin) See BALDACHIN (def. 1).

Baude·laire (bōd·lâr′), **Charles Pierre,** 1821–1867, French poet.

Bau·doin (bō·dwan′) French form of BALDWIN. **—Baudoin,** born 1930, king of Belgium 1951–.

baud·rons (bôd′rənz) *n. Scot.* A cat.

Bau·er (bou′ər), **Harold,** 1873–1951, English pianist. **—Marion Eugenia,** 1887–1955, U.S. composer.

Bau·haus (bou′hous′) An institute of art study, design, and research, established by Walter Gropius in Weimar, Germany, in 1919: known for its experiments in associating technology and art.

bauk·ie (bô′kē) *n. Scot.* A bat.

bauld (bôld) *adj. Scot.* Bold; forward.

baulk (bôk) See BALK.

Baum (bôm), **Lyman Frank,** 1856–1919, U.S. children's story writer; author of *The Wizard of Oz.* —(boum) **Vicki,** 1889–1960, U.S. novelist born in Austria.

Bau·mé (bō·mā′) *n.* **1** A hydrometer for the measurement of the densities of liquids. **2** The scale used on this instrument. [after Antoine *Baumé,* 1728–1804, French pharmacist]

Bau·mes Law (bô′məs) A statute introduced in New York State in 1926 to curb crime: it provides for life imprisonment for fourth offenders. [after C. H. *Baumes,* 1863–1937, N.Y. legislator]

bau·son (bô′sən) *n. Archaic* A badger. [< OF *bausant* spotted]

bau·sond (bô′sənd) *adj. Scot.* Marked with white, especially on the face, as a horse. Also **bau′son-faced′.**

Bau·tis·ta (bou·tēs′tä) Spanish form of BAPTIST.

baux·ite (bôk′sīt, bō′zīt) *n.* A whitish to reddish brown material composed of hydrated aluminum oxides along with various siliceous, ferric, and other impurities and forming the principal commercial source of aluminum. [from Les *Baux,* town in southern France]

Ba·var·i·a (bə·vâr′ē·ə) A southeastern state of the Federal Republic of Germany; 27,119 square miles; capital, Munich; formerly a duchy, kingdom, and republic: German *Bayern.*

Ba·var·i·an (bə·vâr′ē·ən) *adj.* Of or pertaining to Bavaria, its people, or their dialect. *—n.* **1** A native or inhabitant of Bavaria. **2** The High German dialect spoken in Bavaria.

baw·bee (bô·bē′, bô′bē) *n. Scot.* **1** A halfpenny. **2** *Archaic* A copper coin of 6*d.* Scots. Also spelled *baubee.*

baw·cock (bô′kok) *n. Archaic* A fine fellow. [< F *beau* beau + *coq* cock]

bawd (bôd) *n.* The keeper of a brothel; a procuress. [ME *bawde;* origin uncertain]

bawd·ry (bôd′rē) *n.* **1** Indecent language or behavior. **2** The occupation of a bawd.

bawd·y (bô′dē) *adj.* **bawd·i·er, bawd·i·est** Of or like a bawd; obscene; indecent. **—bawd′i·ly** *adv.* **—bawd′i·ness** *n.*

bawd·y-house (bô′dē·hous′) *n.* A brothel.

bawl (bôl) *n.* A loud shout or outcry. *—v.t.* **1** To proclaim or call out noisily; bellow. **2** *U.S. Slang* To berate: with *out.* **3** To cry for sale. *—v.i.* **4** To weep or sob noisily. See synonyms under CALL. ◆ Homophone: *ball.* [< ON *baula* low, as a cow] **—bawl′er** *n.*

baw·tie (bô′tē) *n. Scot.* **1** A dog. **2** A hare. Also **baw′ty.**

Bax (baks), **Sir Arnold Edward Trevor,** 1883–1953, English composer.

Bax·ter (bak′stər), **Richard,** 1615–91, English Puritan minister and author.

bay[1] (bā) *n.* **1** A body of water partly enclosed by land; an arm of the sea. **2** A recess of low land between hills. **3** Land partly surrounded by woods. ◆ Homophone: *bey.* [< F *baie* < LL *baia*]

bay[2] (bā) *n.* **1** A space in a barn for storing hay or fodder. **2** *Engin.* A principal compartment or division, as the space between two piers or pontoons of a bridge. **3** *Archit.* **a** A division of a window between adjacent mullions. **b** Part of a vault between transverse ribs or of a ceiling between panel beams. **c** A vertical division of an arcade, as the space between two adjacent pillars. **4** The head of a canal lock. **5** *Naut.* The forward part of a ship between decks on each side: commonly used as a hospital. **6** *Aeron.* **a** A compartment in the body of an aircraft: a bomb *bay.* **b** A portion of the fuselage between adjoining struts, bulkheads, or frame positions. ◆ Homophone: *bey.* [< F *baie* < *bayer* gape, ult. < LL *badare*]

bay[3] (bā) *adj.* Reddish-brown: said especially of horses. *—n.* **1** A horse (or other animal) of this color. **2** This color. ◆ Homophone: *bey.* [< F *bai* < L *badius*]

bay[4] (bā) *n.* **1** A deep bark or cry, as of dogs in hunting. **2** The situation of or as of a hunted creature compelled to turn on its pursuers. **3** The condition of being kept at a standstill or in check by an opponent, quarry, etc. **—at bay 1** Cornered; with no escape. **2** Held off: He kept his attackers *at bay.* **—to bring to bay** To force into a position from which there is no escape; corner and force to fight. *—v.i.* **1** To utter a deep-throated, prolonged bark, as a hound. *—v.t.* **2** To utter as with this bark: to *bay* defiance. **3** To pursue or beset with barking of this kind so as to bring to bay. ◆ Homophone: *bey.* [Var. of *abay* < OF *abai* a barking; ult. origin uncertain; in sense "at bay" appar. < OF *tenir a bay* hold in suspense < LL *badare* gape]

bay[5] (bā) *n.* **1** Laurel (def. 1): also called *baytree.* **2** A laurel wreath, bestowed as a garland of honor, especially on a poet. **3** *pl.* Fame; poetic renown. **4** The bayberry. **5** Any of several plants resembling the laurels. **6** *U.S. Dial.* Low marshy ground abounding in bay and other shrubs: also **bay-gall** (bā′gôl′). ◆ Homophone: *bey.* [< F *baie* < L *baca* berry]

ba·ya·dere (bä′yə·dir′) *n.* **1** A dancing girl, especially one serving in a temple in India. **2** A fabric or pattern with stripes running crosswise. Also **ba′ya·deer′.** [< F *bayadère* < Pg. *bailadera* female dancer]

ba·ya·mo (bä·yä′mō) *n. Meteorol.* A violent wind blowing on the south coast of Cuba. [from *Bayamo,* town in eastern Cuba]

bay·ard (bā′ərd) *n.* **1** A bay horse. **2** Any horse: a humorous use. *—adj.* Bay in color. [< OF]

Bay·ard (bā′ərd) In medieval romance, a magical horse given to Rinaldo by Charlemagne.

Bay·ard (bā′ərd, *Fr.* bȧ·yȧr′), **Chevalier de,** 1475–1524, Pierre du Terrail, heroic French soldier: called the knight "without fear and without reproach"; hence, a man of heroic courage and chivalry.

bay·ber·ry (bā′ber′ē, -bər·ē) *n. pl.* **·ber·ries 1** One of various trees, as the wax myrtle or laurel, or its fruit. **2** A tropical American tree *(Pimenta racemosa)* whose leaves are used in making bay rum. [< BAY[5] + BERRY]

bay·cu·ru root (bī·ko͞o′ro͞o) The root of a tropical American plant *(Limonium brasiliense)* which yields a powerful astringent known as **bay·cu·rine** (bī·ko͞o′rēn, -rin). [< Tupian]

Bay·ern (bī′ərn) German name for BAVARIA.

Ba·yeux tapestry (bā·yo͞o′, *Fr.* bȧ·yœ′) A linen roll, 77 yards long and 20 inches wide, embroidered in colored worsteds, depicting over 70 scenes in the life of William the Conqueror, traditionally ascribed to his queen, Matilda: now preserved at **Bayeux,** a town in Normandy, France.

Bayle (bel), **Pierre,** 1647–1706, French philosopher.

Bay·lor (bā′lər), **Robert Emmet,** 1793?–1873, U.S. jurist and Baptist preacher.

bay lynx The common wildcat of North America.

bay·o·net (bā′ə·nit, -net) *n.* A daggerlike weapon attachable to the muzzle of a musket or rifle, for close fighting. *—v.t.* **·net·ed, ·net·ing** To stab or pierce with a bayonet. [< F *bayonette,* from *Bayonne,* France, where first made]

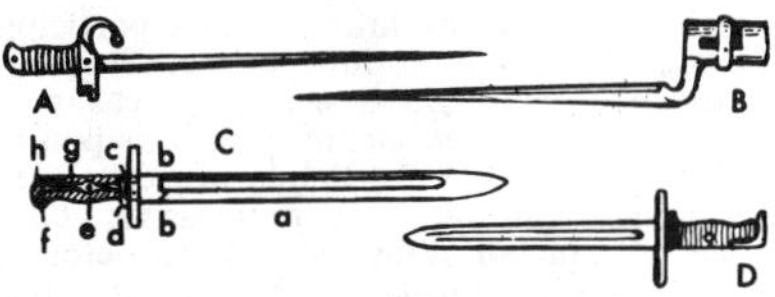

BAYONETS

A. One type of sword bayonet.
B. 18th–19th century bayonet.
C. Sword bayonet.
D. Type of United States Army bayonet.
a. Blade. *b.* Guard. *c.* Bayonet spring. *d.* Scabbard catch. *e.* Tang. *f.* Pommel. *g.* Bayonet catch. *h.* Undercut groove.

Ba·yonne (bā·yōn′) **1** (*Fr.* bȧ·yôn′) A city in SW France near the Bay of Biscay. **2** A city in NE New Jersey.

bay·ou (bī′o͞o) *n.* **1** A marshy inlet or outlet of a lake or bay. **2** A branch of a stream flowing through a delta. [< Choctaw *bayuk* small stream]

Bayou State Nickname of MISSISSIPPI.

Bay·reuth (bī·roit′) A city in NE Bavaria, capital of Upper Franconia: known for its annual Wagner music festivals.

bay rum An aromatic liquid used in medicines and cosmetics, originally obtained by distilling rum with the leaves of the bayberry, now consisting mainly of alcohol, water, and essential oils.

Bay State Nickname of MASSACHUSETTS.

bay·tree (bā′trē) *n.* **1** Bay[5] (def. 1). **2** The magnolia of eastern North America.

bay window 1 A window structure projecting from the wall of a building and forming an extension within. **2** *Slang* A protruding abdomen.

bay·wood (bā′wo͝od′) *n.* A coarse mahogany from Honduras or the region around the Gulf of Campeche.

ba·zaar (bə·zär′) *n.* **1** An Oriental market place or range of shops. **2** A shop or store for the sale of miscellaneous wares. **3** A sale of miscellaneous articles, as for charity. Also **ba·zar′.** [< Persian *bāzār* market]

Ba·zaine (bȧ·zen′), **François Achille,** 1811–88, French marshal.

Ba·zin (bȧ·zaṅ′), **René,** 1853–1932, French novelist.

ba·zoo·ka (bə·zo͞o′kə) *n. Mil.* A long, tubular missile weapon which fires an explosive rocket, and is used for short-range action against tanks and fortifications. [from fancied resemblance to the *bazooka,* a comical musical instrument invented and named by Bob Burns, U.S. comedian]

BB A standard, commercial size of lead shot, 0.18 in. in diameter.

B battery *Electr.* The battery which supplies direct-current voltage to the plate and grid of a vacuum tube.

bdel·li·um (del′ē·əm) *n.* **1** A variety of gum resin resembling myrrh, yielded by various trees (genus *Commiphora*) of India and Africa; also, any of such trees. **2** A substance mentioned in the Old Testament, variously interpreted as crystal, carbuncle, pearl, or amber. [< L < Gk. *bdellion* a plant, and its fragrant gum]

Be *Chem.* Beryllium (symbol Be).

be (bē, *unstressed* bi) *v.i.* **been, be·ing** Present indicative: *sing.* **am, are** (*Archaic* **art**), **is,** *pl.* **are;** past indicative: *sing.* **was, were** (*Archaic* **wast** or **wert**), **was,** *pl.* **were;** present subjunctive: **be;** past subjunctive: *sing.* **were, were** (*Archaic* **wert**), **were,** *pl.* **were** **1** As a substantive the verb **be** is used to mean: **a** To have existence, truth, or actuality: God *is*; There *are* bears in the zoo. **b** To take place; happen: The party *is* next week. **c** To stay or continue: She *was* here for one week. **d** To belong; befall: often with *to* or *unto*: Joy *be* unto you. **2** As a copulative verb *be* forms a link between the subject and predicate nominative or qualifying word or phrase in declarative, interrogative, and imperative sentences; it also forms infinitive and participial phrases: Money *is* nothing to me; The book *is* too expensive; He *is* sick; the pleasure of *being* here. **3** As an auxiliary verb *be* is used: **a** With the present participle of other verbs to express continuous or progressive action: I *am* working. **b** With the past participle of transitive verbs to form the passive voice: He *was* injured. **c** With the past participle of intransitive verbs to form the perfect tense: Christ *is* come; I *am* finished. **d** With the infinitive or present participle to express purpose, duty, possibility, futurity, etc.: We *are* to start on Monday; We *are* leaving Monday.

The verb is defective, and its conjugation is made up of fragments of three independent verbs, furnishing **be, am (are, is), was (were),** respectively. ◆ For usage as to the cases of personal pronouns following impersonal forms of the verb *to be,* see note under ME. [OE *bēon*]

be– *prefix* Used to form transitive verbs from nouns, adjectives, and verbs. [OE *be-, bi-,* var. of *bī* near, by]

Be– may appear as a prefix in hyphemes or solidemes, with the following meanings:

1 (from verbs) Around; all over; throughout; as in:

beclasp	**befreckle**	**beshackle**
beclog	**begirdle**	**beshadow**
beclothe	**bejumble**	**beshroud**
becompass	**bekiss**	**beslobber**
becrimson	**belick**	**besmother**
becrust	**bemingle**	**besmudge**
bedabble	**bemix**	**bespeckle**
bedarken	**berake**	**besprinkle**
bediaper	**bescour**	**betattered**
bedimple	**bescreen**	**bewrap**
befinger	**bescribble**	**bewreath**

2 (from verbs) Completely; thoroughly; as in:

beclamor	**beflatter**	**bescourge**
becrowd	**befluster**	**beshiver**
becudgel	**begall**	**besmear**
becurse	**beknotted**	**besoothe**
bedamn	**bemaddening**	**bethank**
bedeafened	**bemuddle**	**bethump**
bedrabble	**bemuzzle**	**betrample**
bedrench	**besanctify**	**beweary**
bedrug	**bescorch**	**bewidow**

3 (from verbs) Off; away from: *behead, bereave.*

4 (from intransitive verbs) About; at; on; over; against; for; as in:

bechatter	**behowl**	**beshout**
becrawl	**bejuggle**	**besmile**
bedrivel	**beleap**	**beswarm**
begaze	**bemurmur**	**bethunder**
begroan	**beshame**	**beweep**

5 (from adjectives and nouns) To make; cause to be; as in:

beclown	**bedumb**	**begrim**
becoward	**bedunce**	**beknight**
becripple	**bedwarf**	**bemonster**
bedirty	**befoul**	**besmooth**
bedoctor	**beglad**	**bespouse**

6 (from nouns) To provide with; affect by; cover with; as in:

beblister	**beflea**	**beslime**
beblood	**beflower**	**beslipper**
becap	**befringe**	**besmoke**
becarpet	**beglitter**	**besmut**
bechalk	**begloom**	**besnow**
becharm	**begulf**	**bethorn**
becloak	**bejewel**	**bewelcome**
becrime	**beliquor**	**bewhisker**
bedinner	**bemist**	**beworm**

7 (from nouns) To call; name; as in:

bebrother	**belady**	**berascal**
becoward	**bemadam**	**bescoundrel**
behypocrite	**bemonster**	**bevillain**

8 (from nouns) To furnish with, excessively or conspicuously (almost always in participial form); as in:

be–altared	**begarlanded**	**beruffled**
bebelted	**begartered**	**besainted**
bebuttoned	**behusbanded**	**beslaved**
becapped	**bejeweled**	**bespangled**
becarpeted	**belaced**	**bespectacled**
bechained	**bemedaled**	**bestarred**
becupided	**bemitered**	**besteepled**
becurtained	**bemottoed**	**bestrapped**
becushioned	**bepilgrimed**	**beswordeed**
bedaughtered	**berailroaded**	**betaxed**
bedotted	**beribboned**	**betinseled**
befathered	**beringed**	**be–uncled**
befeathered	**beringleted**	**be–uniformed**
beflowered	**berobed**	**bewinged**
befrilled	**berouged**	**bewrathed**

beach (bēch) *n.* **1** The sloping shore of a body of water; strand. **2** Loose pebbles on the shore; shingle. See synonyms under BANK, MARGIN. —*v.t.* & *v.i.* To drive or haul up (a boat or ship) on a beach; strand. ◆ Homophone: *beech.* [Origin unknown]

beach·comb·er (bēch′kō′mər) *n.* **1** A vagrant living on what he can find or beg around the wharves and beaches of ports, especially such a person in the South Sea islands. **2** A long wave rolling upon the beach.

beach flea A small amphipod crustacean (family *Talitridae*) that hops like a flea: found on sea beaches.

beach·grass (bēch′gras′, -gräs′) *n.* A tough, coarse grass (*Ammophila arenaria*) found on lake and ocean beaches: also called *marram.*

beach·head (bēch′hed′) *n. Mil.* **1** A position on a hostile shore established by an advance invasion force to make possible the landing of troops and supplies. **2** A fortified place on a beach.

beach–la–mar (bēch′lə·mär′) See BÊCHE-DE-MER.

beach·y (bē′chē) *adj.* Shingly; pebbly.

Beachy Head A chalk promontory in southern Sussex, England; 565 feet high.

bea·con (bē′kən) *n.* **1** Any prominent object, as a pole, tower, flag, or the like, set on a shore, shoal, buoy, reef, or in a similar position, as a guide or warning to mariners or others. **2** Something that serves as a conspicuous warning or a guide. **3** A lighthouse. **4** *Aeron.* Any of various marker, signal light, or radio devices used to establish and plot flight courses. See RADIO BEACON. —*v.t.* **1** To furnish with a beacon. **2** To light up (darkness, etc.). **3** To guide by a light or beacon. —*v.i.* **4** To shine or serve as a beacon. [OE *bēacen* sign, signal. Related to BECKON.]

Bea·cons·field (bē′kənz·fēld) See DISRAELI.

bead (bēd) *n.* **1** Any small, usually round piece of glass, wood, stone, etc., perforated and intended to be strung with others like it on a thread or attached to a fabric for decoration. **2** *pl.* A string of beads; especially, a rosary. **3** A bubble or bubbles on the surface of a liquid; froth. **4** A liquid drop, as of sweat. **5** A small spherical knob used as the front sight of a gun. **6** *Chem.* A small mass of borax or other flux, placed on a platinum wire to receive a substance for blowpipe testing **7** *Metall.* The spherical piece of refined metal resulting from cupellation. **8** *Archit.* **a** A molding composed of a row of half-oval ornaments resembling a string of beads. **b** A small convex molding. **9** That part of a pneumatic tire which grips the rim of a wheel. —**to draw a bead on** To take careful aim at. —**to tell (count,** or **say) one's beads** To recite prayers with a rosary. —*v.t.* To decorate with or as with beads or beading. —*v.i.* To collect in beads or drops. [OE *gebed* prayer]

bead·house (bēd′hous′) *n.* An almshouse or hospital in which the inmates were required to pray for the founders: also spelled *bedehouse.*

bead·ing (bē′ding) *n.* **1** *Archit.* **a** A bead. **b** Beads collectively. **2** A narrow openwork lace through which a ribbon may be run. **3** Beadwork.

bea·dle (bēd′l) *n.* **1** A minor parish officer in the Church of England whose duties include keeping order during services. **2** *Brit.* An official who leads university processions. **3** A court messenger. **4** The apparitor of a guild. [OF *bedel* messenger]

bea·dle·dom (bēd′l·dəm) *n.* **1** Beadles collectively, or their characteristics. **2** A show of petty and stupid officialism.

bead·roll (bēd′rōl′) *n.* **1** Originally, a list or catalog. **2** In the Roman Catholic Church, a list of persons to be prayed for.

bead–ru·by (bēd′rōō′bē) *n. pl.* **·bies** A small perennial herb (*Maianthemum canadense*) of northern North America with small crimson berries and four-lobed terminal flowers: akin to the Solomonseal.

beads·man (bēdz′mən) *n. pl.* **·men** (-mən) **1** *Brit.* The resident of an almshouse. **2** *Scot.* A privileged or licensed beggar receiving public alms. **3** One who prays for another, especially when hired to do so: also spelled *bedeman.* Also **bead′man.** —**beads′wom′an** *n. fem.*

bead·work (bēd′wûrk′) *n.* **1** Decorative work made with or of beads. **2** *Archit.* Beading.

bead·y (bē′dē) *adj.* **bead·i·er, bead·i·est** **1** Beadlike. **2** Full of or covered with beads. **3** Foamy.

bea·gle (bē′gəl) *n.* A small, short-coated hound with short legs and drooping ears. [ME *begle*; origin uncertain]

BEAGLE
(About 15 inches high at the shoulder)

beak[1] (bēk) *n.* **1** The horny projecting mouth parts of birds; the bill or neb. **2** A beaklike part or organ, as the horny jaws of cephalopods and turtles, the elongated snout of various fishes, etc. **3** *Slang* The nose of a person. **4** *Naut.* That part of ancient warships fastened to the bow and used for piercing or ramming an enemy vessel. **5** *Archit.* A downward-projecting molding on the extreme edge of the lower member of a cornice to prevent the drip from working back under it. **6** Something projecting and pointed like a beak, as the spout of a pitcher. **7** That part of a retort or still which conducts the vapor to the worm or condenser. [<F *bec* <LL *beccus,* ult. <Celtic] —**beaked** (bēkt, bē′kid) *adj.* —**beak′less** *adj.* —**beak′like′** *adj.*

beak[2] (bēk) *n. Brit. Slang* **1** A policeman. **2** A magistrate. **3** At Eton, a master.

beak·er (bē′kər) *n.* **1** A large, wide-mouthed cup or goblet. **2** A cylindrical, flat-bottomed vessel of quartz, porcelain, aluminum, or thin annealed glass, having a flaring top: used in chemical analysis, etc. **3** The contents or capacity of a beaker. [<ON *bikarr*; spelling infl. by BEAK]

be–all (bē′ôl′) *n.* All that is to be; the whole of something.

beam (bēm) *n.* **1** A long, horizontal piece of wood, stone, or metal, forming part of the frame of a building or other structure. **2** The bar of a balance. **3** *Naut.* **a** One of the heavy pieces of timber or iron set transversely across a vessel to support the decks and stay the sides. **b** The greatest width of a vessel. **4** The widest part of anything. **5** A horizontal cylindrical bar, in a loom, upon which warp or woven goods are wound. **6** The pole of a carriage. **7** *Mech.* A horizontal bar that transmits power to the crankshaft through the connecting rod. **8** *Optics* A ray of light, or a group of nearly parallel rays. **9** *Aeron.* A continuous radio signal from a flying field to guide incoming pilots: also **radio beam.** **10** The main stem of a deer's antler. **11** The area of maximum sound clarity in front of a microphone. **12** The horizontal piece in a plow to which the share and the handles are attached. **13** A trough containing lights in the ceiling of a stage. —**off the beam** **1** *Aeron.* Not following the radio beam. **2** *Slang* On the wrong track; wrong. —**on the beam** **1** *Naut.* In a direction at right angles with the keel; abeam. **2** *Aeron.* Following the radio beam. **3** *Slang* In the right direction; just right; correct. —*v.t.* **1** To send out in or as in beams or rays. **2** In radio, to aim or transmit (a signal) in a specific direction: to *beam* a program to France. **3** *Aeron.* To guide (an airplane) to a destination by means of radio beams. —*v.i.* **4** To emit light. **5** To smile or grin radiantly. [OE, tree] —**beamed** *adj.* —**beam′less** *adj.* —**beam′like′** *adj.*

beam compass A drawing compass in which

the points are arranged to slide on a rod, instead of fixed on dividers.

beam-ends (bēm′endz′) *n. pl. Naut.* The ends of a ship's beams. **—on beam-ends** 1 *Naut.* Canted over so far as to be in danger of overturning. 2 In an embarrassing or hopeless predicament.

beam·ing (bē′ming) *adj.* Radiant; bright; cheerful. See synonyms under BRIGHT. **—beam′·ing·ly** *adv.*

beam·ish (bē′mish) *adj.* Radiant; beaming with light. [<BEAM + -ISH; coined by Lewis Carroll in *Jabberwocky*]

beam-shy (bēm′shī′) *adj. Aeron.* Failing, through inexperience or nervousness, to locate the radio beam.

beam·y (bē′mē) *adj.* **beam·i·er, beam·i·est** 1 Sending out beams of light; radiant. 2 Like a beam; massive. 3 *Naut.* Having much breadth of beam: said of vessels. 4 Antlered, as a stag.

bean (bēn) *n.* 1 The oval edible seed of any of various leguminous plants, especially of genus *Phaseolus.* 2 A plant that bears beans. 3 One of several beanlike seeds or plants. 4 *Slang* The head. —*v.t. U.S. Slang* To hit on the head, especially with a thrown object, as a baseball. [OE]

bean·bag (bēn′bag′) *n.* A small cloth bag filled with beans, used as a toy.

bean ball In baseball, a pitch aimed at the head of the batter.

bean beetle See MEXICAN BEAN BEETLE.

bean caper A small tree or shrub (*Zygophyllum fabago*) of the caltrop family, native to eastern Mediterranean regions, having flower buds which are used as capers.

bean·feast (bēn′fēst′) *n. Brit.* A free dinner given by an employer to his employees.

bean·o[1] (bē′nō) *n.* Bingo.

bean·o[2] (bē′nō) *n. Brit. Slang* A spree; a merry party. [<BEANFEAST]

bean·pole (bēn′pōl′) *n.* 1 A tall pole for a bean plant to climb on. 2 *Slang* A tall, thin person.

bean·stalk (bēn′stôk′) *n.* The principal stem of a bean plant.

bean tree 1 One of various trees or shrubs bearing beanlike pods, as the catalpa. 2 The Moreton Bay chestnut *(Castanospermum australe)* of Australia.

bear[1] (bâr) *v.* **bore** (*Archaic* **bare**), **borne** or **born, bear·ing** *v.t.* 1 To support; hold up. 2 To carry; convey. 3 To show visibly; carry: to *bear* a seal or a scar. 4 To conduct or guide. 5 To spread; disseminate: to *bear* tales. 6 To hold in the mind; maintain or entertain: to *bear* a grudge. 7 To suffer or endure; undergo. 8 To accept or acknowledge; assume, as responsibility or expense. 9 To produce; give birth to. 10 To conduct or comport (oneself). 11 To manage or carry (oneself or a part of oneself). 12 To press against or thrust back: The wind *bore* the ship backward. 13 To render; give: to *bear* witness. 14 To be able to withstand; allow: His story will not *bear* investigation. 15 To have or stand (in comparison or relation): with *to*: What relation does this *bear* to the other? 16 To possess as a right or power: to *bear* title. —*v.i.* 17 To carry burdens; convey. 18 To rest heavily; lean; press: His duties *bear* heavily upon him. 19 To endure patiently; suffer: often with *with*: *Bear* with me. 20 To produce fruit or young. 21 To move, point, or lie in a certain direction; take an aim or course: Later, we *bore* west. 22 To be relevant; have reference: with *on* or *upon*: The argument *bears* on the subject. See synonyms under ABIDE, CARRY, ENDURE, LEAN, PRODUCE, SUPPORT. **—to bear company** To accompany. **—to bear down** To force down; overpower or overcome. **—to bear down upon** 1 *Naut.* To approach from the weather side: said of a vessel; hence, to approach. 2 To press hard; put pressure on. **—to bear in mind** To keep in recollection; remember. **—to bear out** To support; confirm; justify. **—to bear up** To keep up strength or spirits. **—to bear upon** To be trained upon, as cannon, so as to bring within the line of fire. [<OE *beran* carry, wear, bear, suffer]

bear[2] (bâr) *n.* 1 A large plantigrade carnivorous or omnivorous mammal (family *Ursidae*) with massive thick-furred body and short tail. ◆ Collateral adjective: *ursine.* 2 One of various other animals like or likened to a bear: the ant-*bear.* 3 The caterpillar of the tiger moth. 4 One of two constellations, the Great Bear or the Little Bear. 5 An ill-mannered or morose person. 6 A speculator who seeks to depress prices or who sells in the belief that there is likely to be a decline in prices. 7 *Mech.* A portable device for punching iron plates. 8 *Naut.* A weighted block of wood faced with sandstone and used for scouring the decks of a ship. **—Great Bear** A large northern constellation *(Ursa Major).* See CONSTELLATION. **—Little Bear** A northern constellation *(Ursa Minor)* including the polestar. See CONSTELLATION, POINTERS. **—the Bear** Russia. —*v.t.* To endeavor to depress the price of (stocks, etc.) by selling or offering to sell. ◆ Homophone: *bare.* [<OE *bera*]

bear[3] (bir) *n. Scot.* Four-rowed barley: also spelled *bere.*

bear·a·ble (bâr′ə·bəl) *adj.* Capable of being borne; endurable. **—bear′a·ble·ness** *n.* **—bear′·a·bly** *adv.*

bear-bait·ing (bâr′bā′ting) *n.* The sport of inciting dogs to attack a chained bear. **—bear′-bait′er** *n.*

bear·ber·ry (bâr′ber′ē, -bər·ē) *n.* 1 A trailing, thick-leaved evergreen plant *(Arctostaphylos uva-ursi)* of the heath family, having small red berries and astringent leaves. 2 The deciduous holly *(Ilex decidua)*: also called *possumhaw.*

bear·cat (bâr′kat′) *n.* The panda (def. 1).

beard (bird) *n.* 1 The hair on a man's face, especially on the chin, usually excluding the mustache. 2 *Zool.* **a** The long hair on the chin of some animals, as the goat. **b** The feathers near the mouth of certain birds, as the turkey; the vibrissae. 3 Any similar growth or appendage. 4 *Bot.* A tuft of hairlike processes; an awn, as of grass. 5 The barb of an arrow, or of any hook. 6 *Ornithol.* The vane or barbs of a feather. 7 *U.S. Slang* In radio broadcasting, an error in performance, usually a misreading of a part. 8 *Printing* That part of a type which divides the face from the shoulder. —*v.t.* 1 To take by the beard; pull the beard of. 2 To defy courageously. 3 To furnish with a beard. [OE] **—beard′ed** *adj.* **—beard′less** *adj.* **—beard′·like′** *adj.*

Beard (bird), **Charles Austin,** 1874–1948, and his wife, **Mary Ritter,** 1876–1958, U.S. historians. **—Daniel Carter,** 1850–1941, founder of the Boy Scouts of America.

bearded eagle The lammergeier.

Beards·ley (birdz′lē), **Aubrey Vincent,** 1872–1898, English artist and illustrator.

beard tongue Penstemon.

bear·er (bâr′ər) *n.* 1 One who or that which bears, carries, or has in possession. 2 A person to whom a note, check, or draft is made payable without naming him; hence, as no endorsement is required, the person who presents such instrument for collection. 3 A tree or vine producing fruit. 4 A carrier or porter. 5 A pallbearer.

bear·gar·den (bâr′gär′dən) *n.* 1 A place where bears are exhibited or kept, especially for bear-baiting. 2 Any place or scene of tumult or strife.

bear·grass (bâr′gras′, -gräs) *n.* 1 Any of various species of *Yucca.* 2 The camas *(Camassia scilloides)* of Oregon. 3 A yucca-like plant *(Dasylirion texanum)* of the lily family of the SW United States.

bear·ing (bâr′ing) *n.* 1 Deportment; manner of conducting or carrying oneself. 2 The act, capacity, or period of producing. 3 That which is produced; crops; yield. 4 The act or capacity of enduring; endurance. 5 *Archit.* The part of an arch or beam that rests upon a support. 6 *Mech.* A part that rests on something, or on which something rests, or in which a pin, journal, etc., turns. 7 *Her.* A device or charge on a field. 8 The point of a compass in which an object is seen. 9 *Often pl.* The situation of an object relative to that of another, or of other points or places. 10 Reference or relation; connection: What *bearing* does his evidence have on the problem? See synonyms under AIR, BEHAVIOR, DIRECTION.

bearing rein A checkrein.

bear·ish (bâr′ish) *adj.* 1 Like a bear; rough; surly. 2 Tending to depress the price of stocks by offering to sell. **—bear′ish·ly** *adv.* **—bear′ish·ness** *n.*

bear-lead·er (bâr′lē′dər) *n.* 1 One who leads about a trained bear. 2 Hence, a young man's private tutor or traveling companion.

bear market In finance, a market in which prices decline.

Bé·arn (bā·år′, -årn′) A region and former province of SW France.

bé·ar·naise sauce (bā·år·nâz′) A variation of hollandaise sauce made with chopped parsley and vinegar.

bear pit A place, usually a pit, where bears are kept, as in a zoological garden.

Bear River A river in Utah, Wyoming, and SE Idaho, flowing 350 miles from NE Utah to Great Salt Lake.

Bear State Nickname of ARKANSAS.

bear's-breech (bârz′brēch′) *n.* Any species of *Acanthus*; especially, the European *Acanthus spinosus,* having spiny leaves.

bear's-ear (bârz′ir′) *n.* The auricula.

bear's-foot (bârz′fo͝ot′) *n.* Helleboraster. Also **bears′foot′.**

bear·skin (bâr′skin′) *n.* 1 The skin of a bear or a coat or robe made of it. 2 A tall, black fur headdress worn as a part of some military uniforms. 3 A coarse, shaggy woolen cloth.

bear·wood (bâr′wo͝od′) *n.* Cascara buckthorn.

Be·as (bē′äs) A river in Punjab, NW India, flowing 285 miles SW to the Sutlej: also *Bias.*

beast (bēst) *n.* 1 Any animal except man. 2 Any large quadruped. 3 Animal characteristics or animal nature. 4 A cruel, rude, or filthy person. See synonyms under ANIMAL. [<OF *beste* <LL *besta* <L *bestia* beast] **—beast′like′** *adj.*

beast·ie (bēs′tē) *n. Scot.* A little beast: a term of endearment.

beast·ly (bēst′lē) *adj.* 1 Resembling a beast; brutish; vile; degraded. 2 *Colloq.* Disagreeable or unpleasant; nasty; abominable. See synonyms under BRUTISH. —*adv. Brit. Slang* Very. **—beast′li·ness** *n.*

beast marriage An incident in folklore in which a human being is married to a beast, in very primitive tales to an actual animal, in later elaborations to a human being doomed to exist in beast form.

beast of burden An animal used for carrying loads.

beat (bēt) *v.* **beat, beat·en** (*Colloq.* **beat**), **beat·ing** *v.t.* 1 To strike repeatedly; pound. 2 To punish by repeated blows; thrash; whip. 3 To dash or strike against, as wind or waves. 4 To make, as one's way, by repeated blows: to *beat* a path to the door. 5 To forge or shape by or as by hammering. 6 To make flat by tramping or treading, as a path. 7 To subdue or defeat; master. 8 To flap; flutter, as wings. 9. *Music* To mark or measure with or as with a baton: to *beat* time. 10 To hunt over; search: to *beat* the countryside. 11 To sound (a signal) as on a drum. 12 To stir; turn (ingredients) over and over so as to make lighter or frothier. 13 *Colloq.* To baffle; perplex: It *beats* me. 14 *Slang* To defraud; swindle. —*v.i.* 15 To strike repeated blows. 16 To strike or smite as with blows: The sound *beats* on our ears. 17 To throb; pulsate. 18 To give forth sound, as when tapped or struck. 19 To sound a signal, as on a drum. 20 *Physics* To alternate in intensity so as to pulsate. 21 To be adaptable to beating: The yolk *beats* well. 22 To hunt through underbrush, etc., as for game. 23 To win a victory or contest. 24 *Naut.* To work against contrary winds or currents by tacking. **—to beat about** To search by one means and then another. **—to beat about the bush** To approach a subject in a round-about way. **—to beat a retreat** To give a signal for retreat, as by beat of drums; hence, to turn back; flee. **—to beat down** To force or persuade (a seller) to accept a lower price. **—to beat it** *Slang* To depart hastily. **—to beat the air** To make futile exertions. **—to beat up** *Colloq.* To thrash thoroughly. —*n.* 1 A stroke or blow, especially one producing sound or serving as a signal. 2 A pulsation or throb, as of the pulse. 3 *Physics* **a** A regularly recurring pulsation or throb heard when two tones not quite in unison are sounded together: caused by the interference of sound waves. **b** A similar property belonging to light waves and other waves. 4 *Naut.* A tack. 5 *Music* **a** The unit of measure for indicating rhythm. **b** The gesture or symbol for this. 6 The stroke or tick of a watch or clock. 7 A round, line, or district regularly traversed, as by a sentry or a policeman. 8 A division of a county. 9 In newspaper slang, a scoop. 10 *U.S. Slang* A deadbeat (def. 1). 11 *Colloq.* A member of the Beat Generation. — *adj.* 1 *U.S. Colloq.* Fatigued; worn out. 2 Pertaining to the Beat Generation. [OE *bēatan*]

Synonyms (verb): bastinado, batter, belabor, bruise, castigate, chastise, conquer, cudgel, cuff, defeat, flog, overcome, pommel, pound, scourge, smite, strike, surpass, thrash, vanquish, whip, worst. *Strike* is the word for a single blow; to *beat* is to *strike* repeatedly. Others of the words above describe the manner of *beating*, as *bastinado*, to *beat* on the soles of the feet; *belabor*, to inflict an exhaustive *beating*; *cudgel*, to *beat* with a stick; *thrash* (originally identical with "thresh"), to *beat* with repeated blows, as wheat was *beaten* out with the old hand flail; to *pound* is to *beat* with a heavy, and *pommel* with a blunt, instrument. To *batter* and to *bruise* refer to the results of *beating*; that is *battered* which is broken or defaced by repeated blows; that is *bruised* which has suffered even one severe blow. To *beat* a combatant is to disable or dishearten him for further fighting. Hence *beat* becomes the synonym for every word which implies getting the advantage of another. Compare CONQUER, SUBDUE. *Antonyms*: fail, fall, surrender.

be·a·tae me·mo·ri·ae (bē·ā′tē me·mō′ri·ē) *Latin* Of blessed memory.

beat·en (bēt′n) *adj.* 1 Shaped by beating; having undergone blows. 2 Worn by use or travel: the *beaten* path. 3 Conquered or subdued; baffled.

beat·er (bē′tər) *n.* 1 One who or that which beats. 2 An implement or device for beating. 3 In hunting, one who arouses game and drives it from cover.

Beat Generation A group of post–World War II artists, writers, and musicians who seek spiritual fulfilment through sensual experience, disclaiming social responsibility to a hostile and thoroughly materialistic society.

be·a·tif·ic (bē′ə·tif′ik) *adj.* Making blessed or blissful. — **be′a·tif′i·cal·ly** *adv.*

be·at·i·fi·ca·tion (bē·at′ə·fi·kā′shən) *n.* 1 The act of blessing, or the state of being blessed or beatified. 2 In the Roman Catholic Church, an act of the Pope declaring a deceased person beatified (*beatus*) and worthy of a certain degree of public honor: usually the last step toward canonization.

be·at·i·fy (bē·at′ə·fī) *v.t.* **·fied, ·fy·ing** 1 To make supremely happy. 2 In the Roman Catholic Church, to declare as blessed and worthy of public honor by an act of the Pope. 3 To exalt above others. [<F *béatifier* <LL *beatificare* bless < *beatus* happy + *facere* make]

beat·ing (bē′ting) *n.* 1 The action of one who or that which beats, or the process involved. 2 Punishment by blows; flogging. 3 Pulsation; throbbing, as of the heart. 4 A defeat.

be·at·i·tude (bē·at′ə·tōōd, -tyōōd) *n.* 1 Supreme blessedness or felicity. 2 A blessing. — **the Beatitudes** Eight declarations of special blessedness pronounced by Jesus in the Sermon on the Mount. *Matt.* v 3–11. [<F *béatitude* <L *beatitudo* blessedness < *beatus* happy]

beat·nik (bēt′nik) *n.* A member of the Beat Generation.

beat–note (bēt′nōt′) *n.* An audible radio frequency caused by the interaction of two frequencies of different value.

Be·a·trice (bē′ə·tris, *Ital.* bā′ä·trē′chā) A feminine personal name. Also **Be·a·trix** (bē′ə·triks; *Dan., Du., Ger., Sw.* bā·ä′triks), *Fr.* **Bé·a·trice** or **Bé·a·trix** (bā·à·três′), *Pg., Sp.* **Be·a·triz** (*Pg.* bā′ä·trēsh′, *Sp.* -trēth′). [<L, she who makes happy]
— **Beatrice** The heroine of Shakespeare's *Much Ado About Nothing*.
— **Beatrice** The idealized and symbolic heroine of Dante's *Divine Comedy*: identified with Beatrice Por·ti·na·ri (pôr′tē·nä′rē), 1266–90, Florentine lady.

Beat·ty (bē′tē), **Lord David,** 1871–1936, first Earl of Brooksby and the North Sea; British admiral of the fleet in World War I. — **James,** 1735–1803, Scottish poet.

beau (bō) *n. pl.* **beaus** or **beaux** (bōz) 1 A dandy; fop. 2 An escort. 3 A lover; swain. ◆ Homophone: *bow*³. [<F <L *bellus* fine, pretty] — **beau′ish** *adj.*

Beau Brum·mell (brum′əl) A dandy or fop. [after George (*"Beau") Brummell,* 1778–1840, English dandy]

Beau·clerc (bō′klâr) See HENRY I.

Beau·fort (bō′fərt), **Henry,** 1370?–1447, English cardinal.

Beau·fort scale (bō′fərt) *Meteorol.* A scale of wind velocities, ranging from 0 (calm) to 12 (hurricane). The wind velocity is measured by its pressure on a disk one square foot in area at a height of 33 feet in the open. See table below for scale as used by the U.S. Weather Bureau. [after Sir Francis *Beaufort,* 1774–1857, British admiral]

BEAUFORT SCALE

Code No.	*Description*	*Pressure lbs. per sq. ft.*	*Speed miles per hour.*
0	Calm	0.	Less than 1
1	Light air	.01	1–3
2	Light breeze	.08	4–7
3	Gentle breeze	.28	8–12
4	Moderate breeze	.67	13–18
5	Fresh breeze	1.31	19–24
6	Strong breeze	2.3	25–31
7	*Moderate gale	3.6	32–38
8	Fresh gale	5.4	39–46
9	Strong gale	7.7	47–54
10	Whole gale	10.5	55–63
11	Storm	14.	64–75
12	Hurricane	Above 17	Above 75

* Intermediate between breeze and gale.

Beaufort Sea That part of the Arctic Ocean between northern Alaska and the Arctic Archipelago.

beau geste (bō zhest′) *pl.* **beaux gestes** (bō zhest′) *French* 1 Literally, a fine gesture; hence, a kindly act. 2 A gesture of kindliness, often made for diplomatic or selfish reasons.

Beau·har·nais (bō·àr·ne′), **Vicomte Alexandre de,** 1760–94, first husband of Empress Josephine. — **Eugène de,** 1781–1824, French general, son of preceding. — **Hortense Eugénie de,** 1783–1837, daughter of Josephine, wife of Louis Bonaparte; queen of Holland, mother of Napoleon III.

beau i·de·al (bō ī·dē′əl) 1 The highest conceivable standard of beauty or excellence. 2 A model of perfection or excellence. [<F *beau idéal* (the) ideal beautiful]

Beau·mar·chais (bō·màr·she′), **Pierre Augustin Caron de,** 1732–99, French dramatist.

beau monde (bō mônd′) *French* The fashionable world.

Beau·mont (bō′mont), **Francis,** 1584–1616, English dramatist who collaborated with John Fletcher. — **William,** 1785–1853, U.S. surgeon.

Beau·re·gard (bō′rə·gärd), **Pierre Gustave Toutant,** 1818–93, Confederate general in the Civil War.

beaut (byōōt) *n. U.S. Slang* Something beautiful: often used ironically: a *beaut* of a black eye.

beau·te·ous (byōō′tē·əs) *adj.* Beautiful. See synonyms under BEAUTIFUL. — **beau′te·ous·ly** *adv.* — **beau′te·ous·ness** *n.*

beau·ti·cian (byōō·tish′ən) *n.* One who works in a beauty parlor, or a person trained in hairdressing, manicuring, massaging, etc.

beau·ti·ful (byōō′tə·fəl) *adj.* Possessing beauty; conforming to esthetic standards, or arousing esthetic pleasure. — *n.* 1 Beauty in the abstract. 2 That which is beautiful. — **beau′ti·ful·ly** *adv.* — **beau′ti·ful·ness** *n.*

Synonyms (adj.): attractive, beauteous, bewitching, bonny, charming, comely, delightful, elegant, exquisite, fair, fine, graceful, handsome, lovely, picturesque, pretty. *Beautiful* implies softness of outline and delicacy of mold; it is opposed to all that is hard and rugged. *Pretty* expresses in a far less degree that which is pleasing to a refined taste. That is *handsome* which is superficially pleasing, and also well and harmoniously proportioned. *Handsome* is a term far inferior to *beautiful*; we may even say a *handsome* villain. *Fair* denotes what is bright, smooth, clear, and without blemish; as, a *fair* face. In a specific sense, *fair* has the sense of blond, as opposed to dark or brunette. One who possesses pleasing qualities may be *attractive* without beauty. *Comely* denotes an aspect that is smooth, genial, and wholesome, with fulness of contour and pleasing symmetry, while falling short of the *beautiful*. That is *picturesque* which would make a picture. See FINE, GRACEFUL, LOVELY. *Antonyms*: awkward, clumsy, deformed, disgusting, frightful, ghastly, grim, grisly, grotesque, hideous, horrid, odious, repulsive, shocking, ugly, unattractive, uncouth, ungainly, unlovely, unpleasant.

beau·ti·fy (byōō′tə·fī) *v.t. & v.i.* **·fied, ·fy·ing** To make or grow beautiful; embellish; adorn. See synonyms under ADORN, GARNISH. — **beau′·ti·fi·ca′tion** *n.* — **beau′ti·fied** *adj.* — **beau′ti·fi′er** *n.*

beau·ty (byōō′tē) *n. pl.* **·ties** 1 Any of those qualities of objects, sounds, emotional or intellectual concepts, behavior, etc., that gratify or arouse admiration to a high degree, especially by the perfection of form resulting from the harmonious combination of diverse elements in unity. 2 A person or thing that is beautiful, especially a woman. 3 A special grace or charm. [<OF *beaute,* ult. <L *bellus* handsome, fine, pretty]

beauty pack A face pack.

beauty parlor *U.S.* An establishment for the hairdressing, manicuring, cosmetic treatment, etc., of women. Also **beauty salon, beauty shop.**

beauty spot 1 A small black patch put on the face to enhance the brilliance of the complexion. 2 A mole or other natural mark resembling this. 3 Any place regarded as especially beautiful.

Beau·vais (bō·ve′) A cathedral city of northern France.

Beau·voir (bō·vwär′), **Simone de,** born 1908, French novelist.

beaux (bōz) Plural of BEAU.

Beaux (bō), **Cecilia,** 1863–1942, U.S. painter.

beaux–arts (bō·zàr′) *n. pl. French* The fine arts, as music, painting, sculpture, etc.

beaux–es·prits (bō·zes·prē′) Plural of BEL-ESPRIT.

beaux yeux (bō zyœ′) *French* Beautiful eyes; hence, a pretty face.

bea·ver¹ (bē′vər) *n.* 1 An amphibious rodent (family *Castoridae*), with a scaly, flat, oval tail and webbed hind feet, noted for skill in damming shallow streams: valued for its fur. 2 The fur of the beaver. 3 A high silk hat, originally made of this fur. 4 A heavy twill–woven woolen cloth with a napped finish, used for outer garments. [OE *beofor*]

BEAVER
(2 1/2 to 4 feet long, including tail)

bea·ver² (bē′vər) *n.* 1 A movable piece of medieval armor covering the lower part of the face, especially when worn with a vizor; later, both chinpiece and vizor. 2 *Slang* A beard. [<OF *bavière* child's bib < *bave* saliva]

bea·ver·board (bē′vər·bôrd′, -bōrd′) *n.* A light, stiff building material made of compressed or laminated wood pulp: used chiefly for walls and partitions.

Bea·ver·brook (bē′vər·brŏŏk), **Baron,** 1879–1964, William Maxwell Aitken, English publisher and statesman, born in Canada.

beaver cutting A place where the trees have been gnawed and leveled by beavers.

beaver dam A dam built by beavers.

beaver lodge A beaver den.

beaver pond A pond made by a beaver dam.

Beaver State Nickname of Oregon.

be·bee·rine (bi·bē′rēn, -rin) *n.* An amorphous alkaloid, $C_{18}H_{19}NO_3$, contained in the bark of the greenheart tree: used in medicine as a tonic and febrifuge. [<BEBEERU + -INE]

be·bee·ru (bi·bē′rōō) *n.* The greenheart tree. [<Sp. *bibiru* <Cariban]

Be·bel (bā′bəl), **Ferdinand August,** 1840–1913, German socialist.

be-bop (bē′bop′) *n.* A variety of jazz characterized by deliberate departures from key and extreme improvisation in rhythmic pattern, and sung with meaningless sounds. Also **be′bop′.**

be·calm (bi·käm′) *v.t.* **1** To make quiet or calm; still. **2** To cause to be motionless for lack of wind, as a ship: used in the passive: The ship was *becalmed* off Africa.

be·came (bi·kām) Past tense of BECOME.

be·cause (bi·kôz′) *conj.* For the reason that; on account of the fact that; since. [ME *bi cause* by cause]

Synonyms: as, for, since. *Because* is the most direct and complete word for giving the reason of a thing. *Since,* originally denoting succession in time, signifies a succession in a chain of reasoning, a natural inference or result. *As* indicates something like, coordinate, parallel. *Since* is weaker than *because; as* is weaker than *since:* either may introduce the reason before the main statement; thus, *since* or *as* you are going, I will accompany you. Often the weaker word is the more courteous, implying less constraint. *Antonyms:* although, however, nevertheless, notwithstanding, yet.

because of On account of; by reason of: He was unable to attend *because of* illness.

bec·ca·fi·co (bek′ə·fē′kō) *n. pl.* **·cos** Any of various small European birds, mostly warblers, supposed to eat figs; especially, the garden warbler *(Sylvia hortensis),* much esteemed as food. [<Ital. < *beccare* peck + *fico* <L *ficus* fig]

bé·cha·mel sauce (bā·shá·mel′) A white sauce made of cream, butter, flour, etc., and flavored with onion and seasonings. [after Louis de *Béchamel,* steward to Louis XIV, who invented it]

be·chance (bi·chans′, -chäns′) *v.t. & v.i.* **be·chanced, be·chanc·ing** To befall; happen by chance.

bêche-de-mer (bâsh·də·mâ r′) *n.* **1** The trepang. **2** A lingua franca of largely English vocabulary, used between Europeans and the natives of the SW Pacific: originally developed through commerce with trepang fishermen: also called *beach-la-mar.* [<F, sea spade]

Bech·u·a·na (bech′o͞o·ä′nə, bek′yo͞o-) *n. pl.* **·na** or **·a·nas 1** One of an important Bantu tribe inhabiting the region between the Orange and Zambesi Rivers, SW Africa. **2** The Bantu language of this tribe.

Bech·u·a·na·land (bech′o͞o·ä′nə·land, bek′yo͞o-) A former British protectorate in southern Africa. Now known as Botswana. See BOTSWANA.

Bechuanaland Protectorate Once a British protectorate in southern Africa, bounded by then Southern Rhodesia, the Union of South Africa, and South-West Africa; about 275,000 square miles; extraterritorial capital, Mafeking, in former Union of South Africa.

beck[1] (bek) *n.* A nod or other gesture of summons. **—at one's beck and call** Subject to one's slightest wish. — *v.t. & v.i.* **1** To beckon. **2** *Scot.* To recognize (a person) by a nod; bow or curtsy. [Var. of BECKON]

beck[2] (bek) *n.* A small brook, or the valley in which it runs. [<ON *bekkr* stream, brook]

beck·et (bek′it) *n.* **1** Naut. A device for holding a ship's spars, ropes, etc., in position, as a cleat, a strap, loop, or rope, or a small grommet. **2** *Slang* A trouser pocket. [Origin unknown]

Beck·et (bek′it,) **Thomas à, Saint,** 1117–70, English archbishop of Canterbury, murdered for his opposition to Henry II.

becket hitch *Naut.* A hitch or bend used when a rope is to be temporarily fastened to another rope or into an eye. Also **becket bend.**

Beck·ford (bek′fərd), **William,** 1759–1844, English writer.

beck·on (bek′ən) *v.t. & v.i.* **1** To signal, direct, or summon by sign or gesture. **2** To entice or lure. — *n.* A summoning gesture; beck. [OE *biecnan, beacnian* make signs <) *bēacen* a sign. Related to BEACON.]

be·cloud (bē·kloud′) *v.t.* **1** To obscure by a cloud or clouds; darken. **2** To confuse, as an issue.

be·come (bi·kum′) *v.* **be·came, be·come, be·com·ing** *v.i.* **1** To undergo development; grow to be: The chick *becomes* the chicken. **2** To come to be: The land *became* dry. — *v.t.* **3** To suit or befit: Your words do not *become* you. **4** To be suitable to; show to advantage: Your dress *becomes* you. **—to become of** To be the fate of: I don't know what *became of* him. [OE *becuman* happen, come about]

be·com·ing (bi·kum′ing) *adj.* **1** Appropriate; suitable. **2** Pleasing; adorning. **—be·com′·ing·ly** *adv.* — **be·com′ing·ness** *n.*

Synonyms: befitting, beseeming, comely, congruous, decent, decorous, fit, fitting, graceful, meet, neat, proper, seemly, suitable, worthy. That is *becoming* in dress which suits the complexion, figure, and other qualities of the wearer, so as to produce a pleasing effect. That is *decent* which does not offend modesty or propriety. That is *suitable* which is adapted to the age, station, situation, and other circumstances of the wearer. In conduct much the same rules apply. The dignity and gravity of a patriarch would not be *becoming* to a child; at a funeral lively, cheery sociability would not be *decorous,* while noisy hilarity would not be *decent. Meet* now expresses chiefly a moral fitness; as, *meet* for heaven. Compare APPROPRIATE. *Antonyms:* awkward, ill-becoming, ill-fitting, improper, indecent, indecorous, unbecoming, unfit, unseemly, unsuitable.

Becque·rel (bek·rel′) Family of French physicists, including **Antoine César,** 1788–1878, **Alexandre Edmond,** 1820–91, son of preceding, and **Antoine Henri,** 1852–1908, son of Alexandre Edmond.

Becquerel rays Rays emitted by radioactive substances. [after Antoine Henri *Becquerel,* who discovered them]

bed (bed) *n.* **1** An article of furniture to rest or sleep in or on: either the stuffed tick or mattress, on which the body rests, the mattress and bedclothes, the bedstead, or all combined; a couch. **2** Any place or thing used for a couch or for sleeping in or on. **3** Something likened to or serving as a bed, foundation, or support: the *bed* of a lake, a rocky *bed.* **4** The marriage bed; marriage. **5** Conjugal cohabitation, or the right to it. **6** A heavy horizontal mass of matter or a collection of closely massed objects, especially used as a foundation or support. **7** Anything resembling or used for a bed. **8** A part or surface that serves as a foundation. **9** The part of a printing press which supports the form, or a part from which work is fed to a machine. **10** A layer of mortar in which stones or bricks are to be laid. **11** A horizontal course of a stone wall. **12** The lower side of a slate, tile, or brick. **13** A plot of ground prepared for planting some particular thing, or the plants, etc., growing in such a plot. **14** A roadbed or a foundation for rails. **15** *Geol.* Any layer in a mass of stratified rock; a seam; a deposit, as of ore, parallel to the stratification. **16** A wagon body. — *v.* **bed·ded, bed·ding** *v.t.* **1** To furnish with a bed. **2** To put to bed. **3** To make a bed for; provide with litter: often with *down:* to *bed* cattle down. **4** To set out or plant in a bed or earth. **5** To have sexual intercourse with. **6** To lay flat or arrange in layers; to *bed* oysters. **7** To place firmly; embed. — *v.i.* **8** To go to bed. **9** To form a closely packed layer; stratify. [OE] **—bed′der** *n.* ◆ *Bed* may appear as a combining form, in hyphemes or solidemes, or as the first element in two-word phrases, which name things used for, in, or about a bed; as in:

bedchair	**bed light**	**bedquilt**
bedcover	**bedmaker**	**bed sock**
bedframe	**bedmaking**	**bedspring**
bedgown	**bedmate**	**bedstand**
bed jacket	**bed pad**	**bedtime**
bed lamp	**bedpost**	**bedwarmer**

be·daub (bi·dôb′) *v.t.* **1** To smear with something oily or sticky; soil. **2** To abuse; vilify. **3** To load with vulgar ornament or flattery.

be·daz·zle (bi·daz′əl) *v.t.* **·zled, ·zling 1** To blind by excess of light. **2** To bewilder; confuse.

bed·bug (bed′bug′) *n.* A bloodsucking hemipterous insect *(Cimex lectularius)* of reddish-brown color, infesting houses and especially beds. See illustration under INSECTS (injurious).

bed·cham·ber (bed′chām′bər) *n.* A sleeping apartment; a bedroom.

bed·clothes (bed′klōz′, -klō thz′) *n. pl.* Covering for a bed, as sheets, blankets, quilts, etc.

bed·ding (bed′ing) *n.* **1** The furnishings for a bedstead. **2** Straw or other litter for animals to sleep on. **3** A putting to bed. **4** That which forms a bed or foundation. **5** *Geol.* Stratification of rocks.

bedding plant Any plant used for placing in a bed, especially one conspicuous in its foliage or flowers and grown in masses with others.

Bed·does (bed′ōz), **Thomas Lovell,** 1803–49, English poet and dramatist.

Bede (bēd), **Saint,** 673–735, English theologian and historian: called "The Venerable Bede." Also *Be·da* (bē′də).

be·deck (bi·dek′) *v.t.* To deck; adorn; ornament. See synonyms under ADORN.

bede·man (bēd′mən) *n.* A beadsman.

be·dev·il (bi·dev′əl) *v.t.* **·iled** or **·illed, ·il·ing** or **·il·ling 1** To torment; worry. **2** To harass with diabolical treatment or abuse. **3** To spoil; corrupt, as by witchcraft. **4** To possess with or as with a devil; bewitch. **5** To make or transform into a devil. **—be·dev′il·ment** *n.*

be·dew (bi·do͞o′, -dyo͞o′) *v.t.* To moisten with or as with dew.

bed·fel·low (bed′fel′ō) *n.* One who shares a bed with another.

Bed·ford (bed′fərd) A county in south central England; 473 square miles; county seat, Bedford. Also **Bed·ford·shire** (bed′fərd·shir, -shə r), shortened form **Beds.**

Bed·ford (bed′fərd), **Duke of,** 1389–1435, John of Lancaster; English statesman; regent of France.

Bedford cord A strong rib-weave fabric having raised, lengthwise cords of wool, silk, cotton or rayon.

be·dight (bi·dīt′) *v.t.* **be·dight, be·dight·ing** *Archaic* To furnish with dress or ornament; adorn; apparel; bedeck.

be·dim (bi·dim′) *v.t.* **be·dimmed, be·dim·ming** To make dim; obscure.

Bed·i·vere (bed′ə·vir) In Arthurian legend, one of the knights of the Round Table.

be·diz·en (bi·diz′ən, -dī′zən) *v.t.* To dress or adorn with tawdry splendor. **—be·diz′en·ment** *n.*

bed·lam (bed′ləm) *n.* **1** An excited crowd. **2** An incoherent uproar. **3** A lunatic asylum; a madhouse. [<BEDLAM]

Bed·lam (bed′ləm) The hospital of St. Mary of Bethlehem in London, used for the insane. [Alter. of BETHLEHEM] **—Bed′lam·ite** (-īt) *n.*

bed·lam·ite (bed′ləm·īt) *n.* A lunatic.

bed linen Sheets, pillow cases, etc., for beds.

Bed·ling·ton terrier (bed′ling·tən) A muscular terrier used in hunting badgers, foxes, etc. See under TERRIER.

BEDLINGTON TERRIER
(About 16 inches high at the shoulder)

Bed·loe's Island (bed′lōz) A former name for LIBERTY ISLAND.

bed·mold·ing (bed′·mōl′ding) *n. Archit.* A molding, or one of a series of moldings, under the corona in a cornice.

Bed·ou·in (bed′o͞o·in, -ēn) *n.* **1** One of the nomadic Arabs of Syria, Arabia, etc. **2** Such nomads collectively. **3** Any nomad or vagabond. — *adj.* **1** Of or pertaining to the Bedouins. **2** Roving; nomadic. Also spelled *Beduin.* [<F <Arabic *badāwīn* desert dweller < *badw* desert]

bed·pan (bed′pan′) *n.* **1** An earthenware or porcelain vessel to be used in bed by a sick person for urination or defecation. **2** A warming pan.

bed·plate (bed′plāt′) *n.* Mech. A plate or frame to which the lighter parts of a machine are bolted.

bed·post (bed′pōst′) *n.* One of the posts supporting a bedstead.

be·drag·gle (bi·drag′əl) *v.t. & v.i.* **·gled, ·gling** To make or become wet or soiled, as by dragging through mire.

bed·rid·den (bed′rid′ən) *adj.* Confined to bed, by sickness or weakness. Also **bed′rid′.** [OE *bedrida* <*bed* bed + *rida* rider]

bed·rock (bed′rok′) *n. Geol.* The solid rock underlying the looser materials of the earth's surface. —**down to bedrock 1** Down to the lowest limit: Prices dropped *down to bedrock.* **2** Down to fundamentals; down to the truth of the matter.

bed·roll (bed′rōl′) *n.* **1** Bedding compactly rolled to facilitate carrying. **2** The cover for a roll of bedding.

bed·room (bed′ro͞om′, -ro͝om′) *n.* A sleeping room.

bed·side (bed′sīd′) *n.* Place by a bed; the side of the bed. —*adj.* Pertaining to or suitable for the bedside: a *bedside* manner.

bed·sore (bed′sôr′, -sōr′) *n.* An ulcer on the body, caused by lying long in one position.

bed·spread (bed′spred′) *n.* A quilt or counterpane.

bed·spring (bed′spring′) *n.* The framework of springs supporting the mattress of a bed.

bed·staff (bed′staf′, -stäf′) *n. pl.* **·staves** (-stāvz′) **1** A stick or staff used in some way about a bed, as to smooth a featherbed or to spread the coverlets. **2** A bar at the side to keep the bedclothes in place.

bed·stead (bed′sted′) *n.* A framework for supporting a mattress, bedding, etc.

bed·straw (bed′strô′) *n.* Any of a genus *(Galium)* of woody herbs of the madder family with whorled sessile leaves and small flowers: so called because formerly used as stuffing in beds.

bed·time (bed′tīm′) *n.* The time for retiring to bed. —*adj.* Of or for this time: *bedtime* stories.

bed·ward (bed′wərd) *adv.* **1** Toward bed. **2** Toward bedtime. Also **bed′wards.**

bed–wet·ting (bed′wet′ing) *n.* Nocturnal enuresis.

Be·dzin (ben·jēn) A city in southern Poland. *German* **Bend·zin** (ben′tsēn), *Russian* **Ben·din** (byän′dyin).

bee[1] (bē) *n.* **1** Any of a large number of hymenopterous insects of the family *Apoidea,* solitary or social in habit, with smooth or hairy bodies, variously colored, and feeding largely upon nectar and pollen. **2** The common hive or honey bee *(Apis mellifera).* **3** A social gathering of neighbors for work or competitive activity: a quilting *bee.* —**to have a bee in one's bonnet** To be excessively concerned about or obsessed with one idea. [OE *beo*]

bee[2] (bē) *n. Naut.* A strip of timber or iron bolted to each side of the bowsprit of a vessel, through which to reeve the foretopmast stays. Also **bee block.** [OE *bēag* ring]

bee balm Any of various aromatic North American herbs (genus *Monarda*) of the mint family, especially the Oswego tea and the wild bergamot.

Bee·be (bē′bē), **Charles William,** 1877–1962, U.S. ichthyologist and ornithologist.

bee beetle A European clerid beetle *(Trichodes apiarius)* parasitic in beehives.

bee·bread (bē′bred′) *n.* A mixture of pollen and certain proteins as stored by bees for food.

beech (bēch) *n.* **1** Any of a family of trees of temperate regions with smooth, ash–gray bark, and bearing an edible nut; especially, the widely cultivated European beech *(Fagus sylvatica)* and the American beech *(F. grandifolia).* **2** One of various trees similar to the beech: the blue *beech (Carpinus caroliniana).* **3** The wood of this tree. ◆ Homophone: *beach.* [OE *bēce*] —**beech′en** *adj.*

Bee·cham (bē′chəm), **Sir Thomas,** 1879–1961, English orchestral conductor.

beech·drops (bēch′drops′) *n.* **1** A low–growing plant (genus *Epifagus*) of the broomrape family, parasitic on the roots of beech trees: also called *pinedrops.* **2** The squawroot.

Beech·er (bē′chər), **Henry Ward,** 1813–87, U.S. pulpit orator and writer. —**Lyman,** 1775–1863, U.S. theologian; father of preceding.

beech·mast (bēch′mast′, -mäst′) *n.* The nuts of the beech.

beech·nut (bēch′nut′) *n.* The edible nut of the beech.

bee–eat·er (bē′ē′tər) *n.* Any of certain bright–plumaged European birds (family *Meropidae*) of insectivorous habits.

beef (bēf) *n. pl.* **beeves** (bēvz) or **beefs** *for def.* **2; beefs** *for def.* **4 1** The flesh of a slaughtered adult bovine animal. **2** Any adult bovine animal, as an ox, cow, steer, bull, etc., fattened for the butcher. **3** *Colloq.* Muscular power; brawn. **4** *U.S. Slang* A complaint. —**bully beef** Canned or pickled beef. —**dried beef** Beef preserved by salting and drying, usually in smoke. —*v.i. U.S. Slang* To complain or grouse. [<OF *boef* <L *bos, bovis* ox]

beef·eat·er (bēf′ē′tər) *n.* **1** An eater of beef; hence, an Englishman (so called by the French), or a well–fed servant. **2** A bluebottle or fleshfly.

Beefeater One of the Yeomen of the Guard who attend the British sovereign on state occasions, or one of the similarly uniformed warders of the Tower of London.

beefed–up (bēft′up′) *adj. Colloq.* Strengthened or reinforced to increase load capacity: said of an aircraft.

beef·ing (bē′fing) *n.* **1** A kind of apple, so named because of its deep–red, beeflike color. **2** *U.S. Slang* Complaining.

bee·fly (bē′flī′) *n. pl.* **·flies** A hairy fly (family *Bombyliidae*) somewhat resembling a bee: the larvae destroy the young of wasps and other insects. For illustration see INSECTS (beneficial).

beef·steak (bēf′stāk′) *n.* A slice of beef suitable for broiling or frying.

beef tea A beverage made by boiling lean beef or from a beef extract.

beef·y (bē′fē) *adj.* **beef·i·er, beef·i·est 1** Like an ox; fat; dull. **2** *Colloq.* Brawny; muscular. —**beef′i·ness** *n.*

bee gum 1 A hollow gum tree in which bees nest. **2** A beehive, especially one made from a hollow gum tree.

bee·hive (bē′hīv′) *n.* **1** A hive for a colony of honey bees. **2** Any place filled with busy workers. **3** A woman's hair style in which the hair is coiled in a conical mound.

Beehive State Nickname of UTAH.

bee·keep·er (bē′kē′pər) *n.* One who keeps bees; an apiarist.

bee–kill·er (bē′kil′ər) *n.* One of several species of large flies (family *Asilidae*) that habitually prey on bees.

bee·line (bē′līn′) *n.* The shortest course from one place to another, as of a bee to its hive.

Be·el·ze·bub (bē·el′zə·bub) **1** The prince of the demons or of false gods; the devil. **2** In Milton's *Paradise Lost,* a chief of the lost angels ranking next to Satan. **3** A Semitic god, worshiped as the lord of flies: the original sense.

bee moth The honeycomb moth.

been (bin, *Brit.* bēn) Past participle of BE.

beep (bēp) *n.* A short, usually high–pitched mechanical or electronic sound used as a signal or warning. —*v.i.* **1** To make such a sound. —*v.t.* **2** To sound (a horn): taxi drivers *beeping* their horns. **3** To transmit (a message) by a beep or beeps. [Imit.]

bee plant Any plant valuable as a honey–producer; specifically, a spiderflower *(Cleome serrulata)* of the western United States, cultivated for bees, or a figwort, especially *Scrophularia fornica.*

beer (bir) *n.* **1** An alcoholic fermented liquor made from malt and hops. **2** A slightly fermented beverage made from the roots, etc., of various plants, as sassafras, ginger, spruce, etc. ◆ Homophone: *bier.* [OE *bēor*]

Beer·bohm (bir′bōm), **Max,** 1872–1956, English critic and caricaturist.

Beer·she·ba (bir·shē′bə, bir′shi·bə) A town in the Negev in southern Israel; in Biblical history it marked the southern limit of Palestine.

beer·y (bir′ē) *adj.* **1** Of, pertaining to, or like beer. **2** Stained or tainted with beer. **3** Addicted to or affected by beer: a *beery* voice. **4** Maudlin.

beest·ings (bēs′tingz) *n.* The first milk from a cow after calving; the colostrum: also spelled *biestings.* [OE *bȳsting*< *beost*]

bees·wax (bēz′waks′) *n.* A white or yellowish plastic substance, secreted by honey bees, from which they make the cells of their comb: widely used in medicine and the arts. —*v.t.* To smear with beeswax; wax.

bees·wing (bēz′wing′) *n.* **1** A filmy crust of scales of tartar on the surface of some old wines, as port. **2** The wine so crusted.

beet[1] (bēt) *n.* **1** The fleshy succulent root of a biennial herb of the goosefoot family (genus *Beta*); especially, the common or red beet *(B. vulgaris),* used as a vegetable, and the sugar beet *(B. saccharifera),* used in making sugar. **2** The plant. ◆ Homophone: *beat.* [OE *bēte* < L *beta*]

beet[2] (bēt) *v.t. Brit. Dial.* **1** To kindle or replenish, as a fire; hence, to rouse; stir. **2** *Obs.* To mend or amend; correct. Also **beete.** ◆ Homophone: *beat.* [OE *bētan* make better, amend]

Bee·tho·ven (bā′tō·vən), **Ludwig van,** 1770–1827, German composer.

bee·tle[1] (bēt′l) *n.* **1** Any coleopterous insect having biting mouth parts and hard, horny elytra that serve as a cover for the membranous posterior wings when at rest. For illustrations see under INSECT. **2** Loosely, any insect resembling a beetle. **3** A short–sighted or intellectually blind person; a blockhead. —*adj.* Shaggy; overhanging: a *beetle* brow: also **bee′tling.** —*v.i.* **·tled, ·tling** To jut out; overhang. [OE *bitula* <*bītan* bite]

bee·tle[2] (bēt′l) *n.* **1** A heavy wooden hammer or mallet; a maul. **2** A pestle or mallet for pounding clothes, or for various other purposes, as mashing potatoes. **3** A beetling machine. —*v.t.* **·tled, ·tling** To beat or stamp with or as with a beetle, mallet, beetling machine, etc. [OE *bīetel* mallet <*bēatan* beat]

bee·tle–browed (bēt′l·broud′) *adj.* Having prominent, overhanging eyebrows.

bee·tle–headed·ed (bēt′l·hed′id) *adj.* Densely stupid or dull.

beetling machine A machine for stamping goods as they are wound over a roller.

bee tree 1 A hollow tree inhabited by bees; a bee gum. **2** The American linden *(Tilia americana),* or other tree with honey–bearing flowers.

beeves (bēvz) A plural of BEEF.

bee·wolf (bē′wo͝olf′) *n.* The larva of the bee beetle.

be·fall (bi·fôl′) *v.* **be·fell, be·fall·en, be·fall·ing** *v.i.* **1** To come about; happen; occur. **2** *Obs.* To fall as one's right or share; belong; be fitting. —*v.t.* **3** To happen to. [OE *bef(e)allan* fall]

be·fit (bi·fit′) *v.t.* **be·fit·ted, be·fit·ting** To be suited to; be appropriate for.

be·fit·ting (bi·fit′ing) *adj.* Becoming; adequate; suitable. See synonyms under APPROPRIATE, BECOMING. —**be·fit′ting·ly** *adv.*

be·fog (bi·fôg′, fog′) *v.t.* **be·fogged, be·fog·ging 1** To envelop in or as in fog. **2** To confuse; obscure.

be·fool (bi·fo͞ol′) *v.t.* **1** To make a dupe or fool of; hoodwink; delude. **2** To call or treat as a fool.

be·fore (bi·fôr′, -fōr′) *adv.* **1** In front; ahead. **2** Preceding in time; previously. **3** Earlier; sooner. —*prep.* **1** In front of; ahead of. **2** Face to face with; in the presence of: The prisoner stood *before* the court. **3** Prior to, in time; earlier or sooner than. **4** In advance of, as in rank, development, or attainment. **5** Demanding the attention of: The bill is *before* the senate. **6** In the cognizance or power of: *Before* God, I swear it. **7** Driven in front of; moved by: The ship sailed *before* the wind. —*conj.* **1** Previous to the time when; sooner than. **2** In preference to; rather than: They will die *before* yielding. [OE *beforan* in front of]

be·fore·hand (bi·fôr′hand′, -fōr′-) *adv. & adj.* In anticipation or advance; ahead of time.

before the mast Forward of the foremast: said of the common sailors, whose quarters are forward.

be·fore·time (bi·fôr′tīm′, -fōr′-) *adv.* In former time; formerly.

be·foul (bi·foul′) *v.t.* To make foul or dirty; sully.

be·friend (bi·frend′) *v.t.* **1** To be a friend to; stand by; help in time of need. **2** To become a friend to; make friends with. See synonyms under AID, HELP.

be·fud·dle (bi·fud′l) *v.t.* **·dled, ·dling** To confuse, as with liquor or glib arguments.

beg[1] (beg) *v.* **begged, beg·ging** *v.t.* **1** To ask for or solicit in charity. **2** To entreat of; beseech. —*v.i.* **3** To ask alms or charity. **4** To entreat humbly. —**to beg off** To free or attempt to free oneself (from a duty, engagement, obligation, etc.) by persuasion, excuse, or pleading. **—to beg the question** To take for granted the matter in dispute. **—to go begging 1** To fail of acceptance, adoption, or use: The office *went begging.* **2** To live the life of a beggar. [? <AF *begger* beg <OF *begard* mendicant friar. See BEGHARD.]

beg² (beg) *n.* A bey.

be·gan (bi·gan′) Past tense of BEGIN.

be·get (bi·get′) *v.t.* **be·got** (*Archaic* **be·gat**), **be·got·ten** or **be·got, be·get·ting 1** To procreate; be the father of. **2** To cause to be; occasion. [OE *begitan*] **—be·get′ter** *n.*

beg·gar (beg′ər) *n.* **1** One who asks alms, especially one who makes his living by begging. **2** A person in poor or impoverished circumstances; a pauper. **3** A fellow; rogue: used contemptuously or humorously: a sulky *beggar*; smart little *beggar.* **—*v.t.* 1** To reduce to want; impoverish. **2** To outdo; exhaust the resources of: It *beggars* analysis. [<OF *begard* mendicant friar] **—beg′gar·dom, beg′gar·hood** *n.* **—beg′gar·er** *n.*

beg·gar·ly (beg′ər·lē) *adj.* **1** Miserably poor; like or characteristic of a beggar. **2** Mean; sordid; contemptible. **—beg′gar·li·ness** *n.*

beg·gar's–lice (beg′ərz·līs′) *n.* Any of various plants bearing prickly fruit which adheres readily to clothes, as bedstraws and stickseeds.

beg·gar·ticks (beg′ər·tiks′) *n.* **1** The bur marigold or its seed vessels. **2** Beggar's–lice. Also **beg′gar's–ticks′.**

beg·gar·weed (beg′ər·wēd′) *n.* **1** Any of several species of plants used for forage and a cover crop in the southern United States, especially the Florida beggarweed or clover (*Desmodium tortuosum*). **2** A low annual plant (*Spergula arvensis*), now cultivated in some regions for forage and fertilizing: also called *corn spurry.*

beg·gar·y (beg′ər·ē) *n.* **1** The state or condition of being a beggar; extreme indigence or deficiency, penury. **2** Beggars as a class. **3** The act or habit of begging. See synonyms under POVERTY.

Beg·hard (beg′ərd, bi·gärd′) *n.* A member of one of the several lay fraternities which arose in Flanders in the 13th century in imitation of the Beguines: in France called *Beguins.* [<Med. L *beghardus,* after Lambert *Begue,* 12th c., founder of the order of Beguines]

be·gin (bi·gin′) *v.* **be·gan, be·gun, be·gin·ning** *v.t.* **1** To commence or enter upon. **2** To give origin to; start. **—*v.i.* 3** To start. **4** To come into being; arise. **5** To have the essentials or the ability: used with a negative: She doesn't *begin* to sing as well as her sister. [OE *beginnan*]

Synonyms: commence, inaugurate, initiate, undertake. See INSTITUTE.

be·gin·ner (bi·gin′ər) *n.* **1** A founder; originator. **2** One beginning to learn a trade or skill, study a new subject, etc.; a novice; tyro.

be·gin·ning (bi·gin′ing) *n.* **1** The starting point in space, time or action; origin. **2** The first stage or part. **3** The source or first cause of anything.

Synonyms: commencement, foundation, fountain, inauguration, inception, initiation, opening, origin, outset, rise, source, spring, start. The Latin *commencement* is more formal than the Anglo–Saxon *beginning*, as the verb *commence* is more formal than *begin. Commencement* is for the most part restricted to some form of action, while *beginning* has no restriction, but may be applied to whatever may be conceived of as having a first part, point, degree, etc. An *origin* is the point from which something starts or sets out, often involving causal connections; as the *origin* of a nation, government, or a family. A *source* is that which furnishes a first and continuous supply; as, the *source* of a river. A *rise* is thought of as in an action; we say that a lake is the *source* of a certain river, or that the river takes its *rise* from the lake. Compare CAUSE. *Antonyms*: see synonyms for END.

be·gird (bi·gûrd′) *v.t.* To gird; encircle; encompass. [OE *begyrdan*]

beg·ohm (beg′ōm′) *n.* One billion ohms, or one thousand megohms: a unit of electrical resistance. [< *beg-* billion (on analogy with *meg-* million) + OHM]

be·gone (bi·gôn′, -gon′) *interj.* Depart! Go away!

be·gon·ia (bi·gōn′yə) *n.* A plant of a large and widely distributed semitropical genus (*Begonia*) with brilliantly colored leaves and showy irregular flowers. [after Michel *Begon,* 1638–1710, French colonial administrator]

be·got (bi·got′) Past tense and past participle of BEGET.

be·got·ten (bi·got′n) A past participle of BEGET.

be·goud (bi·gŏŏd′) *Scot.* Past tense of BEGIN.

be·grime (bi·grīm′) *v.t.* **be·grimed, be·grim·ing** To soil; make dirty with grime.

be·grudge (bi·gruj′) *v.t.* **be·grudged, be·grudg·ing 1** To envy one the possession or enjoyment of (something). **2** To give or grant reluctantly. **—be·grudg′ing·ly** *adv.*

be·guile (bi·gīl′) *v.t.* **be·guiled, be·guil·ing 1** To deceive; mislead by guile. **2** To cheat; defraud: with *of* or *out of.* **3** To while away pleasantly, as time. **4** To charm; divert. See synonyms under DECEIVE, ENTERTAIN. **—be·guile′ment** *n.* **—be·guil′er** *n.*

Beg·uin (beg′in, *Fr.* bā·gaṅ′) *n.* A Beghard.

Beg·uine (beg′ēn, *Fr.* bā·gēn′) *n.* One of a lay Catholic sisterhood, originating in the Netherlands (12th century), devoted to a religious life, but not bound by irrevocable vows.

be·gum (bē′gəm) *n.* A Moslem princess, or woman of rank in India. [<Hind. *begam* <Turkish *bigim* princess]

be·gun (bi·gun′) Past participle of BEGIN.

be·half (bi·haf′, -häf′) *n.* The interest or defense (of anyone): preceded by *in, on,* or *upon.* [OE *be healfe* by the side (of)]

Be·har (bə·här′) See BIHAR.

be·have (bi·hāv′) *v.* **be·haved, be·hav·ing** *v.i.* **1** To comport oneself properly: Will you *behave?* **2** To act; conduct oneself or itself: The car *behaves* well. **3** To react to stimuli or environment. **—*v.t.* 4** To conduct (oneself) properly or suitably. [ME *be-* thoroughly + *have* hold oneself, act]

be·hav·ior (bi·hāv′yər) *n.* **1** Manner of one's conduct; demeanor; deportment. **2** Manner or action of a machine, a chemical, substance, organ, organism, etc. **3** *Psychol.* The form of nervous, muscular, and emotional response of an individual to internal or external stimuli. Also *Brit.* **be·hav′iour.**

Synonyms: action, bearing, breeding, carriage, conduct, demeanor, deportment, manner, manners. *Behavior* is our *action* in the presence of others; *conduct* is a more general term, usually having ethical reference. *Demeanor* is the bodily expression, not only of feelings, but of moral states; as, a devout *demeanor. Breeding*, unless with some adverse limitation, denotes that *manner* and *conduct* which result from good birth and training. *Deportment* is *behavior* as related to a set of rules; as, the pupil's *deportment* was faultless. A person's *manner* may be that of a moment, or toward a single person: his *manners* are his habitual *behavior* toward or before others, especially in matters of etiquette and politeness; as, good *manners* are always pleasing. Compare AIR.

be·hav·ior·ism (bi·hāv′yər·iz′əm) *n.* *Psychol.* The theory that human behavior and activities are the result of individual reaction to definite objective stimuli or situations, and not of subjective factors. **—be·hav′ior·ist** *n.* **—be·hav′ior·is′tic** *adj.*

be·head (bi·hed′) *v.t.* To take the head from; decapitate. **—be·head′al** *n.*

be·held (bi·held′) Past tense and past participle of BEHOLD.

be·he·moth (bi·hē′məth, bē′ə-) *n.* In the Bible, a colossal beast, probably a hippopotamus. [<Hebrew *behēmōth,* pl. of *behēmāh* beast, ? <Egyptian *p-ehe-mah* water–ox]

be·hest (bi·hest′) *n.* An authoritative request; command. [OE *behæs* promise, vow]

be·hind (bi·hīnd′) *adv.* **1** In, toward, or at the rear; backward: looking *behind.* **2** In a previous place, condition, etc.: They left their regrets *behind.* **3** In time gone by: The days of youth are *behind.* **4** In reserve; to be made known: There is no evidence *behind.* **5** In arrears; not according to schedule: to fall *behind* in one's work. **6** Retarded in time, as a train or clock. **—*prep.* 1** At the back or farther side of: The house is *behind* those trees. **2** To or toward the rear: Look *behind* you as you come. **3** Following after: The infantry came *behind* the cavalry. **4** Remaining after: He left a fortune *behind* him. **5** Later than: He stayed *behind* the others that day. **6** Sustaining; supporting: He has wealth *behind* him. **7** Inferior to, as in position, accomplishments, etc.; not so well advanced as: He is *behind* the others in his lessons. **8** Not yet revealed or made known about: something strange *behind* that remark. **—to put behind one** To refuse to accept or consider. **—*n.* *Colloq.*** The buttocks. [OE *behindan*]

be·hind·hand (bi·hīnd′hand′) *adv.* & *adj.* **1** Behind time; late. **2** In arrears. **3** In a backward state; not sufficiently advanced.

behind the times Old–fashioned; antiquated; out–of–date.

be·hint (bi·hint′) *adv.* & *prep.* *Scot.* Behind.

Be·hi·stun (bā′hi·stōōn′) A village in western Iran; near it is a bas–relief with inscriptions in Old Persian, Elamitic, and Assyrian: also *Bisutun.*

be·hold (bi·hōld′) *v.t.* **be·held, be·hold·ing** To look at or upon; observe. **—*interj.*** Look! See! See synonyms under LOOK. [OE *beh(e)aldan* hold] **—be·hold′er** *n.*

be·hold·en (bi·hōl′dən) *adj.* Indebted.

be·hoof (bi·hōōf′) *n.* That which benefits; advantage; use. [OE *behōf* advantage]

be·hoove (bi·hōōv′) *v.* **be·hooved, be·hoov·ing** *v.t.* To be becoming to; be needful or right for: used impersonally: It *behooves* me to leave. **—*v.i.* *Archaic*** To be needful, essential or fit: used impersonally. Also **be·hove** (bi·hōv′). [OE *behōfian*] **—be·hoove′ful** *adj.*

Beh·ring (bā′ring), **Emil Adolf von,** 1854–1917, German physician, discoverer of diphtheria antitoxin.

Behring Sea See BERING SEA.

Behr·man (bâr′mən), **Samuel Nathaniel,** 1893–1973, U.S. playwright.

beige (bāzh) *n.* **1** The color of natural, undyed, unbleached wool. **2** A soft fabric of undyed, unbleached wool. **—*adj.*** Of the color of natural wool. [<F]

beik (bīk) *n.* See BIKE².

Bei·lan Pass (bī·län′) See BELEN PASS.

bein (bēn) *adj.* Bien.

be·ing (bē′ing) Present participle of BE. **—*n.* 1** Any person or thing that exists or is conceived of as existing. **2** Existence, especially, conscious existence. **3** Essential nature of anything: His whole *being* is musical.

Be·ing (bē′ing) *n.* God: used often with qualifying words: the Supreme *Being.*

Bei·ra (bā′rə) **1** A former province of north central Portugal. **2** A port in central Mozambique.

Bei·rut (bā′rōōt, bā·rōōt′) A port on the Mediterranean and the capital of Lebanon: ancient *Berytus*: also *Beyrouth.*

Beith (bēth), **John Hay,** 1876–1952, English author: pen name *Ian Hay.*

Be·káa (bi·kä′) A rich agricultural region, constituting a province of central Lebanon: ancient *Coele–Syria*: also *El Bekáa.*

Bé·kés·csa·ba (bā′kāsh·chä′bä) A city in SE Hungary: also *Csaba.*

bel (bel) *n.* *Physics* A unit representing the ratio of the values of two amounts of power on a logarithmic scale to the base 10. [after A. G. *Bell*]

Bel (bāl) In Babylonian mythology, the god of heaven and earth.

Be·la (bā′lə) The capital of Las Bela, West Pakistan.

be·la·bor (bi·lā′bər) *v.t.* **1** To beat; thrash soundly. **2** To assail verbally. **3** *Obs.* To toil over; work at. See synonyms under BEAT. Also *Brit.* **be·la′bour.**

Be·las·co (bə·las′kō), **David,** 1854–1931, U.S. playwright and producer.

be·lat·ed (bi·lā′tid) *adj.* Delayed past the usual or proper time. **—be·lat′ed·ly** *adv.* **—be·lat′ed·ness** *n.*

be·lay (bi·lā′) *v.* **be·layed, be·lay·ing** *v.t.* **1** *Naut.* To make fast (a rope) by winding on a cleat or pin. **2** In mountain–climbing, to hitch (a rope) over a rock, piton, or other support. **—*v.i.* 3** *Colloq.* To stop or hold; cease: *Belay* there. **—*n.*** A rock or other support, about which a rope may be hitched in order to provide security for a mountain climber; also, the state of being thus secured: He was in *belay*. [OE *belecgan*]

be·lay·ing-pin (bi·lā′ing·pin′) *n. Naut.* A movable pin of wood or metal to which running gear may be made fast.

bel can·to (bel kän′tō) The traditional Italian method of singing, characterized by ease of production and purity of tone. [<Ital., beautiful song]

belch (belch) *v.t.* & *v.i.* **1** To eject, throw out, or to come forth forcibly or violently; vomit. **2** To eject (gas) noisily from the stomach through the mouth; eructate. —*n.* An eructation. [OE *bealcian*] —**belch′er** *n.*

Belch (belch), **Sir Toby** The roistering uncle of Olivia in Shakespeare's *Twelfth Night.*

bel·cher (bel′chər) *n. Brit.* A garish neckcloth, especially a blue one with white spots. [after Jim *Belcher*, English boxer]

Bel·cher (bel′chər), **Jonathan,** 1681–1757, American governor of the colonies of Massachusetts, New Hampshire, and New Jersey.

beld (beld) *adj. Scot.* Bald.

bel·dam (bel′dəm) *n.* A forbidding or malicious old woman; a hag. Also **bel·dame** (bel′·dəm, -dām′). [ME, grandmother <*bel* grand (<OF *bel* fine) + *dam* mother <OF *dame* lady]

be·lea·guer (bi·lē′gər) *v.t.* **1** To surround or shut in with an armed force. **2** To harass or annoy. See synonyms under ATTACK *verb.* [<Du. *belegeren* <*be-* about + *leger* camp] —**be·lea′guered** *adj.*

Be·lém (be·leṅ′) The capital of the state of Pará, northern Brazil: formerly *Pará.*

bel·em·nite (bel′əm·nīt) *n.* **1** *Paleontol.* The pointed cylindrical fossil shell of an extinct cephalopod related to the cuttlefish. **2** A thunderstone. [<NL *belemnites* <Gk. *belemnon* dart]

Be·len Pass (be·len′) A mountain defile in southern Turkey, identified with the Syrian Gates of antiquity: also *Bailan Pass, Beilan Pass.*

bel-es·prit (bel·es·prē′) *n. pl.* **beaux-es·prits** (bō·zes·prē′) *French* A person of culture or wit.

Bel·fast (bel′fast, -fäst) The capital of Northern Ireland; a county borough and port at the head of **Belfast Lough** (lôkh), an inlet between County Antrim and County Down.

Bel·fort (bel·fôr′) A town in eastern France commanding the Belfort Gap.

Bel·fort Gap (bel′fôr gap′) A strategic passageway from the Rhine valley to the Paris Basin: also *Burgundy Gate. French* **Trou·ée de Bel·fort** (trōō·ā′ də bel·fôr′).

bel·fry (bel′frē) *n. pl.* **·fries** **1** A tower in which a bell is hung. **2** The part containing the bell. [<OF *berfrei* tower, ult. <Gmc.] —**bel′fried** *adj.*

bel·ga (bel′gə) *n.* The unit of Belgian currency in foreign exchange, equal to five francs.

Bel·gae (bel′jē) *n. pl.* An ancient people, occupying, in Caesar's time, the region that is now Belgium and northern France.

Bel·gian (bel′jən, -jē·ən) *adj.* Of or pertaining to Belgium. —*n.* A native or citizen of Belgium.

Belgian Congo See ZAIRE REPUBLIC.

Belgian griffon A wire-haired toy dog, a type of Brussels griffon but with a black, or black mixed with brown or tan, coat.

Belgian hare A fancy strain of the common domestic rabbit, originally developed in England from Belgian stock.

Belgian marble Rance.

Bel·gic (bel′jik) *adj.* Of or pertaining to the ancient Belgae, to Belgium, or to the Netherlands.

Bel·gium (bel′jəm, -jē·əm) A constitutional monarchy of NW Europe; 11,779 square miles; capital, Brussels. *Flemish* **Bel·gi·ë** (bel′·gē·ə); *French* **Bel·gique** (bel·zhēk′).

Bel·go·rod-Dnes·trov·ski A city in the Ukraine on the Dniester estuary; ancient Tyras; former Russian and Turkish Akkerman. *Rumanian* **Ce·ta·tea Al·bă** (che·tä′tyä äl′bə).

Bel·grade A port on the Danube, the capital of both Yugoslavia and Serbia; *Serbo-Croatian: Beograd.*

Bel·gra·vi·a (bel·grā′vē·ə) A formerly fashionable residential district of London surrounding Belgrade Square. —**Bel·gra′vi·an** *adj.* & *n.*

Be·li·al (bē′lē·əl, bēl′yəl) **1** The ancient Hebrew personification of lawlessness; the devil. **2** Any fiend: used by Milton in *Paradise Lost* as the name of one of the fallen angels.

be·lie (bi·lī′) *v.t.* **be·lied, be·ly·ing** **1** To misrepresent; disguise: His clothes *belie* his station. **2** To prove false; contradict: Her actions *belied* her words. **3** To disappoint; fail to fulfil: to *belie* hopes. **4** To traduce; slander. [OE *belēogan*] —**be·li′er** *n.*

be·lief (bi·lēf′) *n.* **1** Probable knowledge. **2** Mental conviction; acceptance of something as true or actual. **3** Confidence; trust in another's veracity. **4** That which is believed; creed. **5** Religious faith.

Synonyms: admission, assent, assurance, avowal, confidence, conviction, credence, credit, creed, opinion, reliance, trust. See DOCTRINE, FAITH, FANCY, IDEA. *Antonyms*: denial, disavowal, disbelief, dissent, distrust, doubt, misgiving, rejection, unbelief.

be·lieve (bi·lēv′) *v.* **be·lieved, be·liev·ing** *v.t.* **1** To accept as true or real. **2** To accept the word of (someone); credit with veracity. **3** To think; assume: with a clause as object: I *believe* that I will be there tomorrow. —*v.i.* **4** To accept the truth, existence, worth, etc., of something: with *in*: I *believe* in freedom. **5** To trust someone; have confidence: with *in*: The country *believes* in you. **6** To have religious faith. See synonyms under TRUST. [ME *beleven* <*be-* completely + *leven* <OE *gelēfen* believe] —**be·liev′a·ble** *adj.* —**be·liev′·er** *n.* —**be·liev′ing** *adj.* —**be·liev′ing·ly** *adv.*

be·like (bi·līk′) *adv. Obs.* Perhaps; probably.

Be·lin·da (bi·lin′də) A feminine personal name. [<Gmc., serpent]

Bel·i·sar·i·us (bel′ə·sâr′ē·əs) 505?–565, Byzantine general.

be·lit·tle (bi·lit′l) *v.t.* **·tled, ·tling** To cause to seem small or less; disparage; minimize. See synonyms under DISPARAGE.

Be·li·tung (be·lē′tōōng) An Indonesian island between Borneo and Bangka; 1,866 square miles; chief town, Tanjungpandan: also *Billiton. Dutch* **Be·li·toeng** (be·lē′tōōng).

be·live (bi·līv′) *adv. Scot.* **1** Soon; anon. **2** Quickly; eagerly.

Be·lize (bə·lēz′) **1** The capital of British Honduras. *Spanish* **Be·li·ce** (bā·lē′sā). **2** Former name for BRITISH HONDURAS.

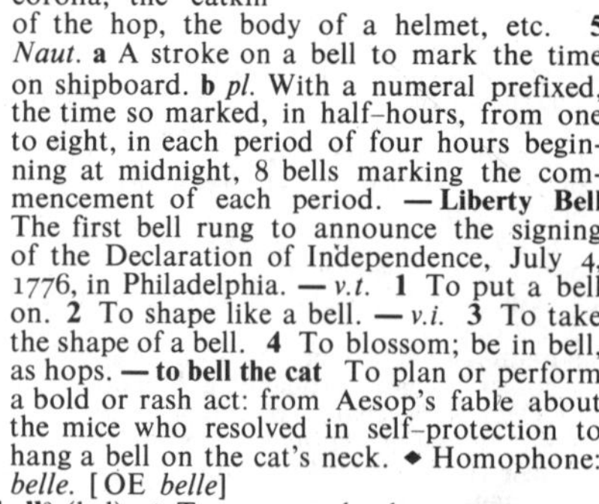
LIBERTY BELL

bell[1] (bel) *n.* **1** A hollow metallic instrument, usually cup-shaped, which gives forth a ringing sound when it is struck. **2** Anything in the shape of or suggesting a bell. **3** The lower termination of a tubular musical instrument. **4** A bell-shaped flower or corolla, the catkin of the hop, the body of a helmet, etc. **5** *Naut.* **a** A stroke on a bell to mark the time on shipboard. **b** *pl.* With a numeral prefixed, the time so marked, in half-hours, from one to eight, in each period of four hours beginning at midnight, 8 bells marking the commencement of each period. —**Liberty Bell** The first bell rung to announce the signing of the Declaration of Independence, July 4, 1776, in Philadelphia. —*v.t.* **1** To put a bell on. **2** To shape like a bell. —*v.i.* **3** To take the shape of a bell. **4** To blossom; be in bell, as hops. —**to bell the cat** To plan or perform a bold or rash act: from Aesop's fable about the mice who resolved in self-protection to hang a bell on the cat's neck. ◆ Homophone: *belle.* [OE *belle*]

bell[2] (bel) *v.i.* To cry, as a buck or stag at rutting time. —*n.* The cry of a deer, bittern, etc.; also, a bellow. ◆ Homophone: *belle.* [OE *bellan* bellow]

Bell (bel), **Alexander Graham,** 1847–1922, U.S. physicist and inventor of the telephone, born in Scotland. —**Sir Charles,** 1774–1842, Scottish anatomist and surgeon.

bel·la·don·na (bel′ə·don′ə) *n.* **1** A perennial herb *(Atropa belladonna)* with purple-red flowers and shining black berries; deadly nightshade: the leaves and roots yield a number of poisonous alkaloids, as atropine, used in medicine. **2** The belladonna lily. [<Ital. *bella donna* beautiful lady]

belladonna lily An ornamental South African plant *(Amaryllis belladonna)*, with large, showy, funnel-shaped flowers of pale rose color penciled with red.

Bel·la·my (bel′ə·mē), **Edward,** 1850–98, U.S. author.

Bel·lay (be·lā′), **Joachim du,** 1522–60, French poet.

bell·bird (bel′bûrd′) *n.* **1** One of various birds having a bell-like note; especially, the South American campanero *(Chasmorhynchus niveus)*, with an erectile horn-shaped crest. **2** Any of various birds of Australia and New Zealand, as the honeyeater.

bell·boy (bel′boi′) *n.* A porter, man or boy, in a hotel. Also **bell·hop** (bel′hop′).

belle (bel) *n.* A beautiful and attractive woman; a reigning social beauty. ◆ Homophone: *bell.* [<F, fem. of *beau* beautiful]

Belle (bel) A feminine personal name.

Bel·leau Wood (bel′ō) A region in northern France, site of a notable American engagement (June, 1918) in World War I. *French* **Bois de Bel·leau** (bwä də be·lō′).

bel·leek (bə·lēk′) *n.* A thin, delicate pottery resembling porcelain, having an iridescent or pearly glaze: made originally at Belleek. Also **belleek ware.**

Bel·leek A town of NW County Fermanagh, Northern Ireland.

Belle Isle An island (20 square miles) at the entrance to the **Strait of Belle Isle,** the northern entrance to the Gulf of Saint Lawrence, lying between Labrador and Newfoundland.

Bel·ler·o·phon (bə·ler′ə·fon) In Greek mythology, a hero who slew the Chimera with the aid of the winged horse, Pegasus, and later perished in an attempt to scale heaven.

BELLEROPHON AND PEGASUS
After a sculpture in the Spada Palace, Rome.

belles-let·tres (bel′·let′rə) *n. pl.* Works of literary art, esthetic rather than informational or didactic; poetry, drama, fiction, etc.; the humanities. See synonyms under HUMANITY, LITERATURE. [<F, fine letters] —**bel·let·rist** (bel′let′rist) *n.* —**bel·le·tris·tic** (bel′le·tris′tik) *adj.*

bell·flow·er (bel′flou′ər) *n.* The campanula.

bel·li·cose (bel′ə·kōs) *adj.* Pugnacious; warlike. [<L *bellicosus* warlike <*bellum* war] —**bel′li·cose′ly** *adv.* —**bel′li·cos′i·ty** (-kos′·ə·tē) *n.*

bel·lig·er·ent (bə·lij′ər·ənt) *adj.* **1** Warlike; bellicose. **2** Engaged in or pertaining to warfare. —*n.* A power or person engaged in legitimate warfare. [Earlier *belligerant* <F *belligérant* <L *belligerans, -antis,* ppr. of *belligare* wage war] —**bel·lig′er·en·cy, bel·lig′er·ence** *n.* —**bel·lig′er·ent·ly** *adv.*

bell·ing (bel′ing) *n. Dial.* A charivari.

Bel·ling·ham (bel′ing·ham) A city in NW Washington on **Bellingham Bay,** an inlet of the Pacific north of Seattle.

Bel·ling·ham (bel′ing·əm, -ham), **Richard,** 1592–1672, English lawyer and colonial governor of Massachusetts.

Bel·lings·hau·sen Sea (bel′ingz·hou′zən) That part of the South Pacific bordering Antarctica.

Bel·li·ni (bel·lē′nē) Name of three Venetian painters, **Jacopo,** 1400?–70?, and his two sons, **Gentile,** 1429?–1507, and **Giovanni,** 1430?–1516.

—**Vincenzo,** 1801–35, Italian composer.

bell jar A glass vessel having the shape of a bell, used to cover articles that may be injured by dust or air currents. Also **bell glass.**

bell·man (bel′mən) *n. pl.* **·men** (-mən) A town crier.

bell metal An alloy of copper and tin, used for the manufacture of bells.

bell-mouthed (bel′mouthd′, -moutht′) *adj.* Having a bell-shaped mouth, as a flask.

Bel·loc (bel′ok), **Hilaire,** 1870–1953, English writer born in France: full name *Joseph Hilaire Pierre Belloc.*

Bel·lo Ho·ri·zon·te (be'lô·rē·zôn'tē) Former name for BELO HORIZONTE.

Bel·lo·na (bə·lō'nə) In Roman mythology, the goddess of war, sister or wife of Mars.

bel·low (bel'ō) *v.i.* **1** To utter a loud, hollow sound; roar, as a bull. **2** To roar; shout: to *bellow* with anger. —*v.t.* **3** To utter with a loud, roaring voice. —*n.* A loud, hollow cry or roar. [ME *belwen,* ? <OE *bylgan*] —**bel'low·er** *n.*

bel·lows (bel'ōz, *earlier* bel'əs) *n.* **1** An instrument with an air chamber and flexible sides, for drawing in air and expelling it under strong pressure through a nozzle or tube.

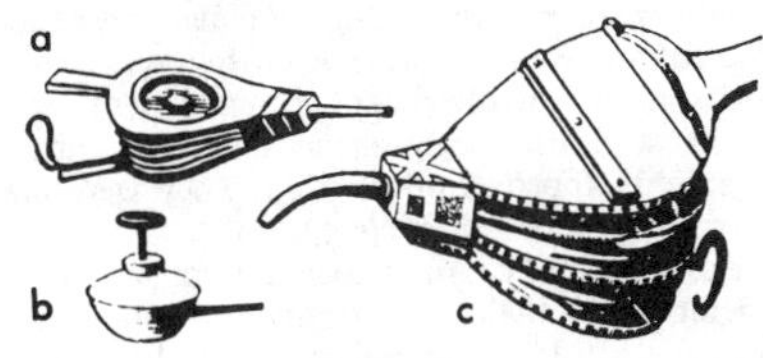

BELLOWS
a. Kitchen. *b.* For insect powders. *c.* Blacksmith's.

2 The expansible portion of a camera. **3** *Colloq.* The lungs. [OE *belg, belig* bag; a later plural from the same source as BELLY]

Bel·lows (bel'ōz), **George Wesley,** 1882–1925, U.S. painter and lithographer.

bell·weth·er (bel'weth'ər) *n.* **1** The wether that wears a bell and leads a flock of sheep. **2** One who leads a group, especially a thoughtless group, in any cause.

bell·wort (bel'wûrt') *n.* **1** A plant of the lily family (genus *Uvularia*) having terminal, solitary, drooping flowers of a yellowish color with bell-shaped perianth. **2** Any plant of the bellflower family (*Campanulaceae*).

bel·ly (bel'ē) *n. pl.* **bel·lies** **1** *Anat.* **a** The anterior part of a vertebrate body, extending from the sternum to the pelvis and containing the organs below the diaphragm. **b** The under part of a quadruped or lower animal. **c** The abdomen. **d** The protuberance of a bulging muscle. **2** The stomach and its associated organs. **3** Appetite. **4** Anything resembling a belly; as, the *belly* of a flask, the *belly* of a wind-filled sail. **5** The sounding box of certain stringed instruments, as the violin, viola, etc. **6** *Obs.* The womb. —*v.t.* & *v.i.* **bel·lied, bel·ly·ing** To swell out or fill, as a sail. [OE *belg, belig* bag]

bel·ly·ache (bel'ē·āk') *n.* Intestinal colic; pain in the bowels. —*v.i.* **·ached, ·ach·ing** *Slang* To complain sullenly.

bel·ly·band (bel'ē·band') *n.* A transverse strap passing beneath a draft animal, to fasten the saddle, harness, etc., or hold the shafts; a girth. See illustration under HARNESS.

bel·ly·but·ton (bel'ē·but'n) *n. Colloq.* The navel.

bel·ly·ful (bel'ē·fo͝ol') *n.* **1** Fullness resulting from much eating. **2** *Colloq.* An excessive fullness or surfeit of anything.

be·long (bi·lông', -long') *v.i.* **1** To be in the possession of someone: with *to.* **2** To be a part of or an appurtenance to something: with *to*: The screw *belongs* to this fan. **3** To have a proper place; be suitable: That lamp *belongs* in this room. **4** To have relation or be a member: with *to*: He *belongs* to the club. [ME *belongen* <*be-* completely + *longen,* OE *langian* go along with]

be·long·ing (bi·lông'ing, -long'-) *n.* **1** That which or one who belongs to a person or thing. **2** *pl.* Possessions; effects, as clothes, furniture, etc.

Be·lo·rus·sia The former name of the **Republic of Belorus.**

Be·lo·rus *Also* **Belarus** A republic in eastern Europe; 80,150 square miles; pop. 10,250,000; capital, Minsk; a member of the Commonwealth of Independent States. Formerly **White Russia,** the **Grand Duchy of Lithuania,** and the **Belorussian S.S.R.**

Be·lo·stok (bye·lə·stôk') Russian name for BIAŁYSTOK.

be·love (bi·luv') *v.t.* **be·loved, be·lov·ing** To love: now only in the passive. [ME *biloven* <*be-* completely + *loven* love]

be·lov·ed (bi·luv'id, -luvd') *adj.* Greatly loved; dear to the heart. —*n.* One greatly loved.

be·low (bi·lō') *adv.* **1** In or to a lower place. **2** To a place under the floor or deck: Get *below!* **3** Farther down on a page or farther on in a list, book, etc. **4** On the earth, as distinguished from heaven. **5** In or to hell or Hades. **6** Lower in rank or authority: His case will be tried in the court *below.* —*prep.* **1** Farther down than: His apartment is *below* theirs. **2** Lower down in direction or course: the town *below* this one on the river. **3** Inferior to in degree, rank, value, etc.: The yield was *below* average. **4** Unworthy of. [<BE- + LOW[1]]

Bel·sen (bel'zən) A village in NW Germany, site of a large Nazi concentration camp and extermination center.

Bel·shaz·zar (bel·shaz'ər) The last Babylonian king, defeated and slain by Cyrus. He gave a banquet, **Belshazzar's Feast,** at which handwriting, foretelling the downfall of Babylonia, appeared on a wall. *Dan.* v.

belt (belt) *n.* **1** A band worn around the waist. **2** *Mech.* **a** A flexible band of leather or other material passing over two or more wheels and serving to transmit power in machinery and to communicate motion from one part to another. **b** A moving assembly line in a factory, intended to convey parts from one operation or worker to another. **3** Any broad, encircling band, region, etc. **4** *Ecol.* A characteristic zone or stretch of country favoring the development of a certain type of animal or plant life; a zone; strip; as, a forest *belt,* a corn *belt.* **5** A strait. **6** *Mil.* **a** A girdle of armor plates protecting a warship along the water line. **b** A strip of webbing designed to hold a weapon or to contain cartridges. **7** *Colloq.* A blow, as with the fist. —**below the belt** **1** In boxing, under the waistband. **2** Hence, unfairly; in violation of accepted codes. —**to tighten one's belt** To practice thrift; retrench; consume less food. —*v.t.* **1** To gird with or as with a belt. **2** To fasten with a belt: to *belt* on a sword. **3** To mark with belts or bands. **4** *Colloq.* To strike with force. [OE *belt* <L *balteus* girdle]

Bel·tane (bel'tān) *n.* **1** The Scottish name for May Day (old style). **2** The ancient Celtic festival celebrating the coming of summer, observed by the kindling of fires on the hills. [<Scotch Gaelic *bealtainn*]

belt·ed (bel'tid) *adj.* **1** Wearing a belt; distinguished by a belt. **2** Having a mark like a belt: the *belted* kingfisher.

Bel·ter (bel'tər) *adj.* Pertaining to or naming a type of furniture, usually of rosewood, carved in elaborate floral designs. [after John H. *Belter,* mid-19th c. New York cabinetmaker]

belt·ing (bel'ting) *n.* Belts collectively, or the material for belts.

belt line A transportation route encircling a city or district.

Bel·trán (bel·trän') Spanish form of BERTRAM.

be·lu·ga (bə·lo͞o'gə) *n. pl.* **·ga** or **·gas** **1** A dolphin (*Delphinapterus leucas*) of arctic and sub-arctic seas; adults are of a white color and from 10 to 12 feet long: also called *white whale.* **2** The great white sturgeon (*Acipenser huso*), found in the Caspian Sea and the Black Sea; its roe is **Beluga caviar.** [<Russian *byelukha* <*byelo* white]

Be·lu·kha (bye·lo͞o'khə) The highest summit in the Altai Mountains, southern Siberia; 15,157 feet.

Be·lus (bē'ləs) **1** A legendary Assyrian king. **2** In Roman mythology, a king of Tyre, father of Dido and Pygmalion.

bel·ve·dere (bel'və·dir') *n.* An elevated point of vantage affording an extensive view; especially, an upper story of an Italian building, open on one or more sides so as to command a view. —**the Belvedere** A part of the Vatican containing many famous works of art. [<Ital., beautiful view] —**bel've·dered'** *adj.*

be·ma (bē'mə) *n. pl.* **be·ma·ta** (bē'mə·tə) The enclosure about the altar; sanctuary; chancel, especially in the Eastern churches. [<Gk. *bema* a step, a platform <*bainein* go, walk]

Bem·bo (bem'bō), **Pietro,** 1470–1547, Italian cardinal and scholar.

be·mean (bi·mēn') *v.t.* To lower or abase (oneself).

be·mire (bi·mīr') *v.t.* **be·mired, be·mir·ing** **1** To soil with or as with mud or mire. **2** To fix or stall in mud.

be·moan (bi·mōn') *v.t.* **1** To express sympathy or pity for. **2** To lament, as a loss. —*v.i.* **3** To mourn or lament. See synonyms under MOURN. [OE *bemænan*] —**be·moan'a·ble** *adj.*

be·muse (bi·myo͞oz') *v.t.* **·mused, ·mus·ing** To muddle or stupefy, as with drink.

be·mused (bi·myo͞ozd') *adj.* **1** Stupefied; dazed. **2** Engrossed.

ben (ben) *n. Brit. Dial.* The inner room of a house. —*adv.* & *adj.* Within; in; inner. —**to be far ben with** To be intimate with. [OE *binnan* <*be-* by + *innan* within]

Ben (ben) Diminutive of BENJAMIN.

be·name (bi·nām') *v.t.* **be·named, be·named** or **be·nempt** or **be·nempted, be·nam·ing** *Obs.* To name. [OE *benemnan*]

Be·na·res (bə·nä'riz) Former spelling of BANARAS.

Be·na·ven·te y Mar·ti·nez (bā'nä·vān'tā ē mär·tē'nāth), **Jacinto,** 1866–1954, Spanish dramatist.

Ben·bow (ben'bō), **John,** 1653–1702, English admiral.

bench (bench) *n.* **1** A long, wooden seat, with or without a back. **2** A stout table for mechanical work. **3** The judges' seat in court; the judge or the judges collectively; the judiciary; also, the court. **4** A row of stalls on platforms or benches for the exhibition of animals, as dogs. **5** *Geog.* A terrace formed in rocks; also, elevated ground along the bank of a lake or river. —*v.t.* **1** To furnish with benches. **2** To seat on a bench. **3** To exhibit, as dogs at a dog show. **4** In sports, to remove (a player) from a game by sending him to a bench on the sidelines. [OE *benc.* Akin to BANK[1], BANK[3].]

bench·er (ben'chər) *n. Brit.* **1** A senior member of the English bar; a governor of one of the Inns of Court. **2** One of the populace; a loafer, as about taverns.

bench hook A clamp, usually of wood, for holding work upon a carpenter's bench.

bench·leg·ged (bench'leg'id, -legd') *adj.* Having the legs wide apart: said of a dog or a horse.

Benchley (bench'lē), **Robert Charles,** 1889–1945, U.S. humorist.

bench·mark (bench'märk') *n.* **1** A permanent reference mark fixed in the ground for use in surveys, tidal observations, etc. **2** A reference point serving as a standard for comparing or judging other things.

bench·root (bench'ro͞ot', -ro͝ot') *n. Bot.* A misshapen condition of roots caused by tenacious seed coats.

bench show An exhibition of animals, especially dogs, in stalls on benches, indoors.

bench warrant A warrant issued by the judge presiding at a session, directing that an offender be brought into court.

bend[1] (bend) *v.* **bent** (*Archaic* **bend·ed**), **bend·ing** *v.t.* **1** To cause to take the form of a curve; crook; bow. **2** To direct or turn, as one's course, in a certain direction; deflect. **3** To subdue; cause to yield, as to one's will. **4** To apply closely; concentrate, as the mind. **5** *Naut.* To tie; make fast, as a rope; place in position, as a sail. **6** *Archaic* To strain; make tense: with *up.* —*v.i.* **7** To assume the form of a bow. **8** To take a certain direction. **9** To bow in submission or respect; yield; conform. **10** To apply one's energies: with *to.* —*n.* **1** A curve or crook. **2** An act of bending or bowing. **3** A loop or knot by which a rope is fastened to any object. **4** A wale or rib. **5** *Scot.* A deep draft. [OE *bendan*]

Synonyms (verb): bias, crook, curve, deflect, deviate, diverge, incline, influence, mold, persuade, stoop, submit, turn, twine, twist, warp, yield. In some cases a thing is spoken of as *bent* where the parts make an angle; but oftener to *bend* is understood to be to draw to or through a curve; as, to *bend* a bow. To *submit* or *yield* is to *bend* or surrender to another's wishes. To *incline* or *influence* is to *bend* another's wishes toward our own; to *persuade* is to draw them quite over. To *warp* is to *bend* slightly through the whole fiber, as a board in the sun. To *crook* is to *bend, turn,* or *twist* irregularly. *Deflect, deviate,* and *diverge* are said of any turning away from a direct line; *deviate* commonly of a slight and gradual movement, *diverge* of a more sharp and decided one. To *bias* is to influence feeling, opinion, or action in the direction of some prevailing (often unconscious) tendency; personal enmity against the accused will *bias* a witness or a juror so as to distort his view of the facts or motives involved in the case. *Mold* is a stronger word than *bend*; we may *bend* by a superior force that which resists the constraint; as, *bend* a bow; we *mold* something plastic entirely and permanently to some desired form. See TWIST.

bend[2] (bend) *n.* **1** *Her.* A band drawn diagonally across the shield from dexter chief to

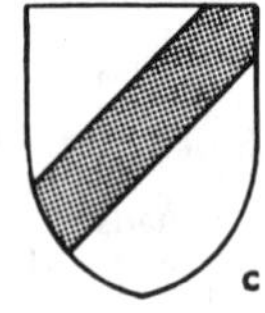

BENDS
a. A bend. *b.* A bend cottised. *c.* A bend sinister.

sinister base. **2** In the leather trade, a butt cut in two. [OE *bend* strap; infl. in meaning by OF *bende* strip, band]

Ben·da (bañ·dá'), **Julien**, 1867–1956, French philosopher.

Ben Da·vis (ben dā'vis) A variety of large, red, winter apple: used chiefly in cooking.

Ben Day (ben' dā') A process or method in photoengraving that produces a pattern of shaded areas of dots, lines, or other markings in an illustration; also, a background produced by this process. Also **ben'day'**. [after *Ben(jamin) Day,* 1838–1916, New York printer]

bend·er (ben'dər) *n.* **1** A person or thing that bends. **2** *Slang* A drinking spree. **3** *Brit. Slang* A sixpence.

Ben·di·go (ben'di·gō) A city in central Victoria, Australia.

Ben·dix (ben'diks), **Vincent**, 1882–1945, U.S. inventor and industrialist.

bends (bendz) *n. pl.* Decompression disease.

bend sinister *Her.* A bend drawn diagonally from sinister chief to dexter base: a mark of bastardy. Compare BATON SINISTER.

ben·dy (ben'dē) *n. Anglo-Indian* Okra.

bene[1] (bēn) *n. Obs.* A prayer. [OE *bēn*]

ben·e[2] (ben'ē) See BENNE.

be·neath (bi·nēth') *adv.* **1** At a lower point; in a lower position. **2** On the underside of; underneath. *—prep.* **1** In a lower place or position than: a rock *beneath* the waves. **2** Pressed or crushed by: The ground gave *beneath* his foot. **3** Subdued or dominated by: *beneath* the yoke of the conqueror. **4** Influenced or controlled by: helpless *beneath* the ban. **5** Inferior to; unworthy of: His assignment was *beneath* his ability. **6** Unsuited to the dignity of; lower in rank than: She married *beneath* her station. [OE *beneathan*]

Synonyms (prep): below, under, underneath. *Under* strictly implies that another object is directly upon or over in a vertical line. *Below* signifies that one object is lower than another, so as to be looked down upon from it, or hidden from view by it; as, *below* (not *under* nor *beneath*) the horizon. *Under* has also the sense of being subject to or subjected to; as, *under* tutors and governors, *under* examination. *Antonyms*: see synonyms for ABOVE.

ben·e·cep·tor (ben'ə·sep'tər) *n. Physiol.* An element of the nervous system, as a receptor or sense organ, specialized in the transmission of pleasurable stimuli: opposed to *nociceptor.* [<NL <L *bene* well + *-ceptor,* as in RECEPTOR]

ben·e·dic·i·te (ben'ə·dis'ə·tē) *n.* A blessing; grace or thanksgiving, especially at table. *—interj.* Bless you! [<LL, bless ye, imperative of *benedicere* bless, commend]

Ben·e·dic·i·te (ben'ə·dis'ə·tē) *n.* The canticle beginning "O all ye works of the Lord, bless ye the Lord"; also, the music of this canticle.

Ben·e·dick (ben'ə·dik) In Shakespeare's *Much Ado About Nothing,* the hero, a bachelor, who eventually marries Beatrice.

ben·e·dict (ben'ə·dikt) *n.* A newly married man. Also **ben'e·dick.** [<BENEDICK]

Ben·e·dict (ben'ə·dikt) A masculine personal name. Also *Lat.* **Ben·e·dic·tus** (ben'ə·dik'təs), *Ital.* **Be·ne·det·to** (bā'nā·det'tō), *Pg., Sp.* **Be·ne·dic·to** (*Pg.* bā'nā·dē'to͞o, *Sp.* bā'nā·dēk'tō), *Ger.* **Be·ne·dikt** (bā'nə·dikt). [<L, blessed]

—Benedict Name of 15 popes; notably: **Benedict XIV,** 1675–1758, real name Prospero Lambertini, pope 1740–58; and **Benedict XV,** 1854–1922, real name Giacomo della Chiesa, pope 1914–22.

—Benedict, Saint, 480–543, Italian monk; founder of the Benedictine Order.

Ben·e·dict (ben'ə·dikt), **Ruth Fulton**, 1887–1948, U.S. anthropologist.

Ben·e·dic·ta (ben'ə·dik'tə, *Pg.* bā'nā·dē'tə) A feminine personal name; feminine of BENEDICT. Also *Ger.* **Be·ne·dik·ta** (bā'nə·dik'tä), *Ital.* **Be·ne·det·ta** (bā'nā·det'tä). [<L, *fem.,* blessed]

ben·e·dic·tine (ben'ə·dik'tēn) *n.* A brandy liqueur formerly made at the Benedictine monastery at Fécamp, France.

Ben·e·dic·tine (ben'ə·dik'tin, -tēn) *adj.* Pertaining to St. Benedict or his order. *—n.* One of the order of monks established by St. Benedict at Subiaco, in Italy, about 530: sometimes called "Black Monks" from the color of their robes.

ben·e·dic·tion (ben'ə·dik'shən) *n.* **1** The act of blessing, as at the close of worship. **2** The invocation of divine favor upon a person. **3** Any of various formal ecclesiastical ceremonies of blessing; a dedication or consecration. **4** Divine grace or favor; the state of blessedness. **5** The giving of thanks before or after meals; grace. [<L *benedictio, -onis* <*benedicere* bless] **—ben'·e·dic'tive, ben·e·dic·to·ry** (ben'ə·dik'tər·ē) *adj.*

Ben·e·dic·tus (ben'ə·dik'təs) *n.* **1** Either of two canticles, *Luke* i 68–71, and *Matt.* xxi 9, each named from the first word, *benedictus,* "blessed," of its Latin version. **2** A musical setting of either canticle mentioned above.

ben·e·fac·tion (ben'ə·fak'shən) *n.* **1** A kindly or generous act; a gift or boon; beneficence. **2** The act of bestowing charity or conferring a benefit. See synonyms under GIFT. [<L *benefactio, -onis* <*benefacere* do well]

ben·e·fac·tor (ben'ə·fak'tər, ben'ə·fak'-) *n.* A friendly helper; a patron. **—ben'e·fac'tress** *n. fem.*

be·nef·ic (bə·nef'ik) *adj.* Beneficent; kindly. [<L *beneficus* generous]

ben·e·fice (ben'ə·fis) *n.* **1** An ecclesiastical living or preferment; a church office endowed with funds or property. **2** The revenue so devoted: generally limited to parsonages, rectories, vicarages, and donatives. **3** A feudal fee or life interest in a landed estate, subject to the will of the donor. *—v.t.* **·ficed, ·fic·ing** To invest with a benefice. [<OF <L *beneficium* favor]

be·nef·i·cence (bə·nef'ə·səns) *n.* **1** The quality of being beneficent; active goodness. **2** A beneficent act or gift. See synonyms under BENEVOLENCE. [<F *bénéficence* <L *beneficentia* <*beneficus* generous]

be·nef·i·cent (bə·nef'ə·sənt) *adj.* **1** Bringing about or doing good. **2** Characterized by charity and kindness. See synonyms under CHARITABLE. **—be·nef'i·cent·ly** *adv.*

ben·e·fi·cial (ben'ə·fish'əl) *adj.* **1** Benefiting or tending to benefit; conferring benefits; advantageous; helpful. **2** *Law* Entitled to receive the income of an estate without its title, custody, or control; as, a *beneficial* interest in land. [<F *bénéficial* <LL *beneficialis* <*beneficium* favor] **—ben'e·fi'cial·ly** *adv.* **—ben'e·fi'cial·ness** *n.*

ben·e·fi·ci·ar·y (ben'ə·fish'ē·er'ē, -fish'ər·ē) *adj.* **1** Pertaining to benefits or benevolence. **2** Of the nature of a charity or donation. **3** Held by feudal tenure or privilege. *—n. pl.* **·ar·ies** **1** One who receives or uses a charitable provision or privilege. **2** The holder of a benefice or church living. **3** *Law* One who is lawfully entitled to the profits and proceeds of an estate or property, the title to which is vested in another, as in a trustee. **4** The person to whom the amount of an insurance policy or annuity is payable. [<L *beneficiarius* <*beneficium* favor]

ben·e·fit (ben'ə·fit) *n.* **1** Profit; advantage; promotion of welfare or prosperity; helpful result. **2** A benefaction or deed of kindness; favor bestowed; privilege. **3** A special theatrical or musical performance, at which the performers usually serve gratuitously, and the proceeds of which are bestowed on some particular person or on some charity. **4** Pecuniary aid extended by a benefit society. See synonyms under FAVOR, PROFIT, UTILITY. *—v.* **·fit·ed, ·fit·ing** *v.t.* To be helpful or useful to. *—v.i.* To profit; gain advantage. See synonyms under SERVE. [<AF *benfet,* OF *bienfait* <L *benefactum* good deed <*benefacere* do well]

benefit of clergy **1** *Law* A privilege accorded to the clergy and afterward extended to all who could read, by which one who had been convicted in a secular court of some felony, less than treason, that involved capital punishment, could claim a hearing before the bishop's court. **2** Churchly approval or sanction: They were married without *benefit of clergy.*

benefit society An association of which the members, by the regular payment of small sums, become entitled to pecuniary aid in old age or in time of sickness; in Great Britain called a *friendly society.* Also **benefit association.**

Ben·e·lux (ben'ə·luks) *n.* The customs union of Belgium, the Netherlands, and Luxembourg. [<BE(LGIUM) + NE(THERLANDS) + LUX(EMBOURG)]

be·nempt (bi·nempt'), **be·nempt·ed** (bi·nemp'·tid) Past participles of BENAME.

Be·neš (be'nesh), **Eduard**, 1884–1948, president of Czechoslovakia, 1935–38, 1946–48.

Be·nét (bi·nā'), **Stephen Vincent**, 1898–1943, U.S. poet. **—William Rose,** 1886–1950, brother of preceding, U. S. poet and critic.

Be·ne·ven·to (bā'nā·ven'tō) A town in Campania, southern Italy: ancient *Maleventum*; later **Be'ne·ven'tum** (-təm).

be·nev·o·lence (bə·nev'ə·ləns) *n.* **1** Desire for the well-being or comfort of others; love for mankind; charitableness. **2** Any act of kindness or well-doing; charity; humanity. **3** An enforced loan sometimes exacted by English sovereigns.

Synonyms: almsgiving, beneficence, benignity, bounty, charity, generosity, humanity, kind-heartedness, kindliness, kindness, liberality, munificence, philanthropy, sympathy. Originally *beneficence* was the doing well, *benevolence* the wishing or willing well to others; but *benevolence* has come to include *beneficence* and to displace it. *Charity* is now almost universally applied to some form of *almsgiving* and is much more limited in meaning than *benevolence. Benignity* suggests some occult power of blessing, such as was formerly ascribed to the stars; we may say a good man has the air of *benignity. Kindness* and *tenderness* are personal; *benevolence* and *charity* are general. *Humanity* is *kindness* and *tenderness* toward man or beast. We speak of the *bounty* of a generous host, the *liberality* or *munificence* of the founder of a college, or of the *liberality* of a person toward holders of conflicting beliefs. *Philanthropy* applies to wide schemes for human welfare, often, but not always, involving large expenditures in *charity* or *benevolence.* Compare MERCY. *Antonyms*: barbarity, brutality, churlishness, greediness, harshness, illiberality, inhumanity, malevolence, malignity, niggardliness, selfishness, self-seeking, stinginess, unkindness.

be·nev·o·lent (bə·nev'ə·lənt) *adj.* **1** Characterized by benevolence. **2** Kindly, charitable, beneficent. See synonyms under CHARITABLE, GOOD, HUMANE. [<OF *benivolent* <L *benevolens, -entis* <*bene* well + *volens,* ppr. of *velle* wish] **—be·nev'o·lent·ly** *adv.*

Ben·gal (ben·gôl', beng-) A former province of NE British India, divided (1947) into: (1) **East Bengal,** formerly a province of Pakistan; since 1972, the country of Bangla Desh; 54,501 square miles; capital, Dacca; (2) **West Bengal,** a constituent state of the republic of India; 29,476 square miles; capital, Calcutta. **—Ben·ga·lese** (ben'·gə·lēz', -lēs', beng'-) *adj. & n.*

Bengal, Bay of A broad arm of the Indian Ocean, between India and the Andaman Sea.

Ben·ga·li (ben·gô'lē, beng-) *adj.* Of or pertaining to Bengal. *—n.* **1** A native of Bengal.

2 The modern vernacular Indic language of Bengal.

ben•ga•line (beng′gə•lēn, beng′gə•lēn′) *n.* A silk, wool, or rayon fabric of fine weave with widthwise cords. [<BENGAL]

Bengal light A colored fire much used in signaling. Also **Bengal fire.**

Ben•ga•si (ben•gä′zē, beng-) A port in NE Libya, co-capital of Libya, on the Gulf of Sidra: ancient *Berenice.* Also **Ben•gha′zi, Ben•ga′zi.**

Ben-Gur•i•on (ben•gŏŏr′ē•ən), **David,** 1886–1973, Russian-born Israeli statesman; prime minister of Israel 1948–53 and 1955–63.

Be•ni (bā′nē) A river of NW Bolivia, flowing north 600 miles to the Madeira river.

be•night•ed (bi•nī′tid) *adj.* 1 Involved in darkness or gloom, whether intellectual or moral; ignorant; unenlightened. 2 Overtaken by night. **—be•night′ed•ness** *n.*

be•nign (bi•nīn′) *adj.* 1 Gracious; generous; kindly. 2 Soft; genial; propitious; mild. 3 *Pathol.* Of a mild type: opposed to *malignant:* a *benign* tumor or disease. See synonyms under BLAND, CHARITABLE, PROPITIOUS. [<OF *benigne* <L *benignus* kindly] **—be•nign′ly** *adv.*

be•nig•nant (bi•nig′nənt) *adj.* 1 Condescending; gentle; gracious. 2 Helpful; salutary. See synonyms under AMIABLE, CHARITABLE, HUMANE, MERCIFUL. [<BENIGN, on analogy with MALIGNANT] **—be•nig′nant•ly** *adv.*

be•nig•ni•ty (bi•nig′nə•tē) *n. pl.* **•ties** 1 Kindliness; beneficence: also **be•nig•nan•cy** (bi•nig′•nən•sē). 2 A gracious action or influence. See synonyms under BENEVOLENCE, MERCY.

Be•ni Has•san (bā′nē hä′sän) A village in Upper Egypt, on the east bank of the Nile; site of ancient rock tombs.

Be•nin (be•nēn′) 1 An independent republic in western Africa; 44,290 square miles; capital, Porto-Novo: formerly *Dahomey.* 2 A river in southern Nigeria, flowing west 60 miles into the **Bight of Benin,** an Atlantic bay of the Gulf of Guinea on the coast of west central Africa. 3 A province in southern Nigeria; 8,627 square miles; capital, Benin City.

ben•i•son (ben′ə•zən, sən) *n.* A benediction; blessing. [<OF *beneison* <LL *benedictio, -onis* benediction]

Be•ni Suef (bā′nē swäf′) A city in Upper Egypt on the west bank of the Nile. Also **Ba′ni Suwayf′.**

Be•ni•ta (bā•nē′tä) Spanish form of BENEDICTA.

ben•ja•min (ben′jə•mən) *n.* Benzoin (def. 1). [Alter. of BENZOIN]

Ben•ja•min (ben′jə•mən; *Dan., Ger.* ben′yə•mēn; *Fr.* ba•zhä•ma′; *Pg.* be•zhə•mē n′) A masculine personal name. Also *Sp.* **Ben•ja•mín** (ben′hä•mēn′), *Ital.* **Ben•ia•mi•no** (ben′•yä•mē′nō). [<Hebrew, son of the right hand]

Benjamin The youngest son of Jacob by Rachel; also, the tribe descended from him. *Gen.* xxxv 18.

Ben•ja•min (ben′jə•mən), **Judah Philip,** 1811–1884, American lawyer and Confederate cabinet member.

benjamin bush The spicebush; feverbush.

Ben•jy (ben′jē) Diminutive of BENJAMIN.

Ben•ku•len (ben•kōō′lən) A port in SE Sumatra. *Indonesian* **Beng•ku•lu** (beng•kōō′l;ov), *Dutch* **Ben•koe′len.**

Ben Lo•mond (ben lō′mənd) 1 A mountain in NW Stirlingshire, Scotland; 3,192 ft. 2 The highest mountain range in Tasmania; highest peak, Legge Tor, 5,160 ft.

ben•ne (ben′ē) *n.* An East Indian plant, the sesame, widely cultivated for its seeds which yield **benne oil:** also spelled *bene.* [<Malay *bijen* seed]

ben•net (ben′it) *n.* 1 The avens; especially, either of two American species *(Geum canadense* and *G. strictum).* 2 Herb-bennet. [<OF *(herbe) beneite* blessed (herb) <L *benedicta*]

Ben•net (ben′it) Variant of BENEDICT.

Ben•nett (ben′it), **(Enoch) Arnold,** 1867–1931, English novelist and playwright. **—James Gordon,** 1795–1872, U.S. journalist born in Scotland; founded New York *Herald* 1835. **—James Gordon,** 1841–1918, U.S. newspaper proprietor and editor; son of the preceding. **—Viscount Richard Bedford,** 1870–1947, Canadian prime minister 1930–35.

Ben Ne•vis (nē′vis, nev′is) A mountain in SW Invernessshire, Scotland; highest peak in Great Britain; 4,406 feet.

Ben•ning•ton (ben′ing•tən) A town in Vermont; near site of battle, 1777, in which American colonial forces defeated the British.

Ben•ny (ben′ē) Diminutive of BENJAMIN.

Be•noîte (bə•nwät′) French form of BENEDICTA.

Ben•o•ni (ben•ō′nī) In the Bible, Benjamin: so called by Rachel. [<Hebrew, son of sorrow]

Be•no•ni (bə•nō′nī) A mining city in Gauteng, Republic of South Africa.

Ben•son (ben′sən), **Arthur Christopher,** 1862–1925, English educator and author. **—Edward Frederick,** 1867–1940, English novelist, brother of the preceding. **—Frank Weston,** 1862–1951, U.S. painter. **—William Shepherd,** 1855–1932, U.S. admiral.

bent[1] (bent) Past tense and past participle of BEND. — *adj.* 1 Deflected from a straight line; crooked. 2 Made fast to a spar or other object: said of a sail, etc. 3 Fixed in a course; set; as, on pleasure *bent.* — *n.* 1 The state of being inclined or the direction in which inclined; also, inclination; penchant; tendency; bias; disposition. 2 The degree of tension; limit of endurance or capacity. 3 *Engin.* A section of a framed building; a portion of a framework or scaffolding of a building, designed to carry both vertical and transverse loads. 4 A cast of the eye. 5 *Obs.* Concentrated force; impetus. See synonyms under INCLINATION.

bent[2] *n.* 1 One of various stiff wiry grasses (genus *Agrostis*): also **bent grass.** 2 The stiff flower stalk of various grasses. 3 *Brit.* The stalk or seeding spike of either of the two common species of plantain *(Plantago major* and *P. lanceolata).* 4 Land unenclosed and covered only with grass or sedge, as opposed to wood, a heath moor, or other waste land. [OE *beonet*]

Ben•tham (ben′thəm), **Jeremy,** 1748–1832, English jurist and philosopher.

Ben•tham•ism (ben′thəm•iz′əm) *n.* The political and ethical philosophy of Jeremy Bentham, who taught that nature has placed mankind under the governance of two sovereign masters, pain and pleasure, and that pleasure is the supreme end of life. **—Ben′tham•ite** (-īt) *n.*

ben•thos (ben′thos) *n. Ecol.* The whole assemblage of plants or animals living on the sea bottom: distinguished from *plankton.* [<Gk., the deep, depth of the sea] **—ben•thic** (ben′thik), **ben•thon•ic** (ben•thon′ik) *adj.*

ben•tho•scope (ben′thə•skōp) *n.* An undersea research apparatus resembling a bathysphere, but designed and built to withstand pressures at a depth of 10,000 feet: intended for the study of submarine life. [<Gk. *benthos* depth + -SCOPE]

Ben•tinck (ben′tingk), **Lord William Cavendish,** 1774–1839, son of William Henry, first governor general of India 1833. **—William Henry Cavendish,** 1738–1809, third duke of Portland; British prime minister 1783, 1807–1809.

Bent•ley (bent′lē), **Richard,** 1662–1742, English classical scholar.

Ben•ton (ben′tən), **Thomas Hart,** 1889–1975, U.S. painter.

Ben•ton•ville (ben′tən•vil) A town in central North Carolina; site of one of the final major engagements in the Civil War.

bent wood Designating a style of furniture constructed of wood sections curved and bent to desired shapes.

Be•nu•e (bā′nōō•ā) A river in Nigeria; flowing about 800 miles to the Niger river: also *Binue.*

be•numb (bi•num′) *v.t.* 1 To make numb; deaden. 2 To render insensible; stupefy. [OE *benumen,* pp. of *beniman* deprive. See NUMB.] **—be•numbed** (bi•numd′) *adj.* **—be•numb′ment** *n.*

ben•zal•de•hyde (ben•zal′də•hīd) *n. Chem.* A colorless, highly refractive liquid, C_7H_6O, having the characteristic odor of essence of almonds. It is used largely in the dye and perfume industries. [<BENZ(OIN) + ALDEHYDE]

Ben•ze•drine (ben′zə•drēn, -drin) *n.* Proprietary name of a brand of amphetamine.

ben•zene (ben′zēn, ben•zēn) *n. Chem.* A colorless, volatile, inflammable, liquid hydrocarbon, C_6H_6, obtained chiefly from coal tar by fractional distillation. It is useful as a solvent, as an illuminant in gas-manufacture, and is important as the starting point in the formation of the compounds of the benzene series. [<BENZOIN]

benzene ring *Chem.* The graphic formula of the aromatic hydrocarbon benzene. The hexagon formula shows six carbon atoms, each associated with a hydrogen atom one or more of which may be replaced to form any of a large class of benzene derivatives. Also **benzene nucleus.**

BENZENE RING

ben•zi•dine (ben′zə•dēn, -din) *n. Chem.* A crystalline hydrocarbon, $C_{12}H_{12}N_2$, synthesized from benzene derivatives: used in the preparation of dyes and as a test for blood. Also **ben′zi•din** (-din). [<BENZOIN]

ben•zine (ben′zēn, ben•zēn) *n.* A colorless inflammable liquid derived from crude petroleum by fractional distillation and consisting of various hydrocarbons. It is used as a solvent for fats, resins, etc., to cleanse clothing, and as a motor fuel: also called *petroleum spirit.* Sometimes confused with *benzene.* Also **ben′zin** (-zin), **ben•zo•line** (ben′zə•lēn).

ben•zo•ate (ben′zō•it, -āt) *n. Chem.* A salt of benzoic acid.

benzoate of soda Sodium benzoate.

ben•zo•ic (ben•zō′ik) *adj.* 1 Pertaining to or derived from benzoin. 2 Pertaining to benzoic acid.

benzoic acid *Chem.* An aromatic compound, $C_7H_6O_2$, contained in resins, as benzoin, and in coal-tar oil, etc., and obtained also by synthesis: used as a food preservative and in medicine.

ben•zo•in (ben′zō•in, -zoin) *n.* 1 A gum resin from various East Indian plants (genus *Styrax*), used in medicine and as a perfume: also called *benjamin.* 2 *Chem.* A crystalline chemical compound, $C_{14}H_{12}O_2$, obtained variously, as from benzaldehyde by the action of an alcoholic solution of potassium cyanide: also called *flowers of benzoin.* 3 Any plant of a small genus *(Lindera)* of North American and Asian shrubs or trees of the laurel family, including the spicebush. [<F *benjoin* <Pg. *beijoin* or Ital. *benzoi* <Arabic *lubān jāwī* incense of Java]

ben•zol (ben′zōl, -zol) *n.* A grade of crude benzene. Also **ben′zole** (-zōl).

ben•zo•phe•none (ben′zō•fē ′nōn) *n. Chem.* A crystalline compound, $C_{13}H_{10}O$, a ketone obtained variously, as from calcium benzoate by dry distillation. [<BENZENE + PHENOL + -ONE]

ben•zo•yl (ben′zō•il) *n. Chem.* The univalent organic radical, C_6H_5CO, derived from benzoic acid.

benzoyl peroxide *Chem.* A white, crystalline derivative of benzoic acid, $C_{12}H_{10}C_2O_4$, used in bleaching oils, waxes, flour, etc.

ben•zyl (ben′zil) *n. Chem.* The univalent radical, $C_6H_5CH_2$, derived from toluene.

Be•o•grad (be•ô′gräd) The Serbo-Croatian name for BELGRADE.

Be•o•wulf (bā′ə•wŏŏlf) A warrior prince in an eighth century Anglo-Saxon epic poem, *Beowulf,* who kills the monsters Grendel and Grendel's mother and dies in old age of a wound received in battle with a dragon.

Bep•pu (bep′ōō) A city on NE Kyushu, Japan.

be•queath (bi•kwēth′, -kwēth′) *v.t.* 1 *Law* To give, as personal property, by will; make a bequest of: compare DEVISE. 2 To hand down to posterity; transmit. 3 *Obs.* To devote. [OE *becwethan*]

be•quest (bi•kwest′) *n.* The act of bequeathing or that which is bequeathed. See synonyms under GIFT. [ME *biqueste*]

Bé•ran•ger (bā•rä•zhā′), **Pierre Jean de,** 1780–1857, French lyric poet.

Be•rar (bā•rär′) The SW division of Madhya Pradesh state, India, on the Deccan Plateau; 17,808 square miles; administrative center, Amraoti.

be·rate (bi·rāt′) *v.t.* **be·rat·ed, be·rat·ing** To chide severely; scold.

Ber·ber (bûr′bər) *n.* **1** A member of a group of Moslem tribes inhabiting northern Africa, especially the Kabyles of Algeria. **2** The Hamitic language of the Berbers, comprising the dialects spoken in Algeria, Tunisia, Morocco, and the Sahara, as Kabyle, Tuareg, etc. *—adj.* Of or pertaining to the Berbers or their language.

Ber·ber (bûr′bər) A town on the eastern bank of the Nile in northern Sudan.

Ber·ber·a (bûr′bər·ə) A port on the Gulf of Aden, former winter capital of British Somaliland.

Ber·ber·i (bûr′bər·ē) *n.* Nuba (def. 3).

ber·ber·i·da·ceous (bûr′bər·i·dā′shəs) *adj.* Pertaining or belonging to the barberry family of herbs and shrubs, as the May apple.

ber·ber·ine (bûr′bər·ēn, -in) *n.* A yellow crystalline bitter alkaloid, $C_{20}H_{19}O_5N$, contained in the bark of the barberry and some other plants: it is used in medicine as a tonic. Also **ber′ber·in** (-in). [<LL *berberis* barberry]

ber·ceuse (bâr·sœz′) *n. pl.* **·ceuses** (-sœz′) *Music* A cradle song. [<F]

Berch·tes·ga·den (berkh′tes·gä′dən) A resort village in Upper Bavaria; noted as the private retreat of Adolf Hitler.

Ber·di·chev (ber·dē′chef) A city in central Ukrainian S.S.R.

bere (bir) *n. Scot.* Barley.

be·reave (bi·rēv′) *v.t.* **be·reaved** or **be·reft** (bi·reft′), **be·reav·ing 1** To deprive, as of hope or happiness. **2** To leave desolate or saddened through loss: with *of*: He was *bereaved* of his father. Commonly in past participle: *bereaved* or *bereft* of a relative, but *bereft* of love or other immaterial object. **3** *Obs.* To despoil; rob. [OE *bereafian*]

be·reave·ment (bi·rēv′mənt) *n.* The act of bereaving, or the state of being bereaved; an afflictive loss, as by death. See synonyms under MISFORTUNE.

be·reft (bi·reft′) Alternative past tense and past participle of BEREAVE. *—adj.* Deprived: *bereft* of all hope.

Ber·e·ni·ce (ber′ə·nī′sē) A feminine personal name. Also spelled *Bernice.* [<Gk., victorious]
—Berenice Daughter of Herod Agrippa I. *Acts* xxv 13.

Ber·e·ni·ce (ber′ə·nī′sē) An ancient name for BENGASI.

Berenice's Locks or **Hair** Coma Berenices.

Ber·en·son (ber′ən·sən), **Bernard,** 1865–1959, U.S. art critic and writer born in Lithuania.

be·ret (bə·rā′, ber′ā) *n.* A soft, flat cap, usually of wool, originating in the Basque regions of France and Spain. [<F, ult. <LL *birettum* cap]

Ber·e·zi·na (ber′ə·zē′nə) A river in Belorussian S.S.R. flowing south 350 miles to the Dnieper; crossed by Napoleon (1812) at the battle of Borisov.

berg (bûrg) *n.* **1** An iceberg. **2** In South Africa, a mountain.

Berg (berkh), **Alban,** 1885–1935, Austrian composer.

Ber·ga·ma (ber′gə·mä) A town of western Turkey north of Smyrna, on the site of ancient Pergamum.

Ber·ga·mo (ber′gä·mō) A city in Lombardy, northern Italy.

ber·ga·mot[1] (bûr′gə·mot) *n.* **1** A tree *(Citrus bergamia)* of the rue family, the bergamot orange. **2** Its fruit, furnishing an oil used as a perfume. **3** Any of several plants of the mint family, as the horsemint in the United States, and *Mentha aquatica* and *Mentha citrata* (also called **bergamot-mint**) in England. **4** Snuff scented with bergamot. [? from *Bergamo,* Italy]

ber·ga·mot[2] (bûr′gə·mot) *n.* A minor variety of pear. [<F. *bergamote* <Ital. *bergamotta* <Turkish *beg-armūdi* prince's pear; spelling infl. by BERGAMOT[1]]

Ber·gen (bûr′gən, *Norw.* ber′gən) A port in SW Norway.

Ber·ge·rac (bâr·zhə·rák′) See CYRANO DE BERGERAC.

Bergh (bûrg), **Henry,** 1820–88, U.S. philanthropist; founded Society for Prevention of Cruelty to Animals, 1866.

Ber·gi·us (ber′gē·ōōs), **Friedrich,** 1884–1949, German chemist.

berg·schrund (bûrg′shrund, *Ger.* berkh′·shrōōnt) *n.* A crevasse or series of crevasses at the head of a glacier, near the base of the cliff against which the snow field lies. [<G]

Berg·son (berg′sən), **Henri Louis,** 1859–1941, French philosopher. **—Berg·so·ni·an** (berg·sō′nē·ən) *adj. & n.*

Berg·son·ism (berg′sən·iz′əm) *n.* The philosophy of Henri Bergson, who held that the world is a continuing process of creative evolution, hence, of inevitable novelty and change, rather than the result of fixed or unaltering laws of nature. Reality is the expression of the creative or vital force *(élan vital)* inherent in all organisms. Knowledge of reality comes through intuition rather than through analytical intellectual processes. Compare VITALISM.

Be·ri·a (be′rē·ə), **La·vren·ti** (lə·vren′tē) **Pavlovich,** 1899–1953, U.S.S.R. politician; executed. Also **Be′ri·ya.**

ber·i·ber·i (ber′ē·ber′ē) *n. Pathol.* An oriental disease of the peripheral nerves, characterized by partial paralysis, swelling of the legs, and general dropsy: due to the absence of vitamins of the B complex in a diet consisting principally of polished rice. [<Singhalese *beri* weakness] **—ber′i·ber′ic** *adj.*

be·rime (bi·rīm′) *v.t.* **·rimed, ·rim·ing 1** To mention or celebrate in rime. **2** To compose in rime. Also spelled *berhyme.*

Ber·ing Sea (bâr′ing, bir′-) An arm of the North Pacific Ocean between Alaska and Siberia, north of the Aleutian Islands: *Russian* **Be·ring·o·vo Mo·re** (be·ring′ə·və mô′re): connected by **Bering Strait** to the Arctic Ocean. Also *Behring Sea.*

Berke·le·ian·ism (bûrk·lē′ən·iz′əm, *Brit.* bärk-) *n.* The idealistic system of philosophy propounded by George Berkeley. **—Berke·le′ian** *adj. & n.*

Berke·ley (bûrk′lē, *Brit.* bärk′-), **George,** 1684–1753, English prelate and philosopher born in Ireland. **—Sir William,** 1606–77, English governor of Virginia.

berke·li·um (bûrk′lē·əm) *n.* A very rare, unstable element (symbol Bk, atomic number 97) of the actinide series, first obtained by bombarding americium with alpha particles, the most stable isotope having mass number 247 and a half-life of 1400 years. See PERIODIC TABLE. [from *Berkeley,* California, location of the University of California, where first produced]

Berk·shire (bûrk′shir, -shər) *n.* One of a breed of black-haired swine from Berkshire, England, of medium size, with short legs, broad, straight backs, square hams and shoulders, and short heads.

Berk·shire (bûrk′shir, -shər; *Brit.* bärk′-) A county in southern England; 725 square miles; county seat, Reading. Shortened form **Berks** (bûrks, *Brit.* bärks).

Berk·shire Hills (bûrk′shir, -shər) A wooded region of western Massachusetts; highest peak, 3,505 feet.

Ber·lich·ing·en (ber′likh·ing′ən), **Götz von** (gœts fôn), 1480–1562, German knight; the hero of Goethe's drama of the same name: called "Götz of the Iron Hand."

ber·lin (bər·lin′, bûr′lin) *n.* **1** An automobile of limousine type but with the driver's seat entirely enclosed: also **ber·line** (bər·lin′, *Fr.* ber·lēn′). **2** A four-wheeled covered carriage with a shelter seat behind. **3** Zephyr or worsted for knitting: also **Berlin wool.** [from *Berlin,* Germany]

Ber·lin (bər·lin′, *Ger.* ber·lēn′) A city of central Prussia and the largest city in Germany, of which it was the capital until 1945; the eastern sector is the capital of the German Democratic Republic.

Ber·lin (bər·lin′), **Irving,** born 1888, U.S. song writer.

Ber·li·oz (ber′lē·ōz, *Fr.* bâr·lyôz′), **Hector,** 1803–69, French composer.

berm (bûrm) *n.* **1** The bank of a canal opposite the towpath. **2** A horizontal ledge part way up a slope; bench. **3** A ledge dug near the top of a trench to support beams and prevent caving in of the sides. **4** A narrow, level ledge at the outside foot of a parapet, to retain material which might otherwise fall from the slope into the moat. **5** The outside or downhill side of a ditch or trench. For illustration see BASTION. Also **berme.** [<F *berme*]

Ber·me·jo (ber·me′hō) A river in northern Argentina, flowing about 650 miles to the Paraguay.

Ber·mu·da (bər·myōō′də) An island group in the western North Atlantic, comprising a British colony; 22 square miles; capital, Hamilton. Also **Ber·mu′das.** **—Ber·mu·di·an** (bər·myōō′dē·ən) *adj. & n.*

Bermuda shorts Shorts which extend to just above the knees.

Bern (bûrn, bern) The capital of Switzerland. Also **Berne.**

Ber·na·be (ber′nä·bā′) Spanish form of BARNABAS.

Ber·na·dette (bûr′nə·det′, *Fr.* ber·ná·det′), **Saint,** 1844–79, Bernadette Soubirous, a French maiden who saw a vision of the Virgin Mary at Lourdes; canonized 1933.

Ber·na·dotte (bûr′nə·dot, *Fr.* ber·ná·dôt′) Family name of royal house of Sweden, founded by **Jean Baptiste Jules Bernadotte,** 1764–1844, French marshal, who became king of Sweden as Charles XIV John, in 1818.

Ber·nard (bûr′nərd, bər·närd′) A masculine personal name. Also *Fr.* **Ber·nard** (ber·nár′) or **Ber·nar·din** (ber·nár·daṅ′), *Ital., Sp.* **Ber·nar·do** (*Ital.* ber·när′dō, *Sp.* -thō), *Lat.* **Ber·nar·dus** (bər·när′dəs). [<OHG, hardy bear]
—Bernard of Clairvaux, Saint, 1091–1153, French Cistercian monk, founder of the monastery of Clairvaux.
—Bernard of Cluny, 1122–56, French Benedictine monk and hymn writer.

Ber·nard (ber·nár′), **Claude,** 1812–78, French physiologist.

Ber·nar·din de Saint-Pierre (ber·nár·daṅ′ də saṅ·pyâr′), **Jacques Henri,** 1737–1814, French novelist and author.

Ber·nar·dine (bûr′nər·din, -dēn) *adj.* Pertaining to St. Bernard of Clairvaux, 1091–1153, or to the Cistercian order founded by him. *—n.* A Cistercian monk.

Bern·burg (bern′bōōrkh) A city in Saxony-Anhalt, East Germany.

Ber·ners (bûr′nərz), **Lord,** 1883–1950, Gerald Hugh Tyrwhitt-Wilson, English composer and painter.

Ber·nese (bûr·nēz′, -nēs′) *adj.* Of or pertaining to Bern, Switzerland. *—n.* **1** A resident of Bern, Switzerland. **2** A Swiss mountain dog, characterized by a short, compact body, straight forelegs, long, soft coat, and usually with white feet and with white blaze on face and chest.

Bernese Alps The northern division of the Swiss Alps; highest peak, 14,026 feet: also *Bernese Oberland.* (See OBERLAND).

Bern·hard (bern′härt) Danish and German form of BERNARD. Also *Du.* **Bern·har·dus** (bern′·här·doos).

Bern·hardt (bûrn′härt, *Fr.* ber·nár′), **Sarah,** 1844–1923, French actress: original name Rosine Bernard.

Ber·nice (bər·nēs′, bûr′nis) See BERENICE.

Ber·ni·ci·a (bər·nish′ē·ə) An Anglian kingdom founded in 547; later included in Northumbria.

ber·ni·cle (bûr′ni·kəl, bär′-) *n.* The barnacle goose.

Ber·ni·na (ber·nē′nä), **Piz** (pēts) Highest peak (13,304 feet) of the **Bernina Alps,** a part of the Rhaetian Alps, Switzerland; traversed by **Bernina Pass,** elevation, 7,645 feet.

Ber·ni·ni (ber·nē′nē), **Giovanni Lorenzo,** 1598–1680, Italian sculptor and architect.

Ber·noul·li (*Fr.* ber·nōō·yē′, *Ger.* ber·nōō′lē), **Jacob** (or **Jacques**), 1654–1705, Swiss mathematician. **—Daniel,** 1700–82, nephew of the preceding, Swiss mathematician.

Bern·stein (bern′stīn), **Henry Léon,** 1876–1953, French dramatist.

Bern·storff (bern′shtôrf), **Count Johann Heinrich von,** 1862–1939, German diplomat.

ber·ret·ta (bə·ret′ə) *n.* A biretta.

ber·ry (ber′ē) *n. pl.* **ber·ries 1** Any small, succulent fruit: the black*berry,* straw*berry,* goose*berry.* **2** *Bot.* A simple fruit with the seeds in a juicy pulp, as the tomato, grape, and currant. ◆ Collateral adjective: *baccate.* **3** A coffee bean; also, the dry kernel of various grains. **4** Something likened to a berry, as an egg of a crustacean. **5** *Slang* A dollar. *—v.i.* **ber·ried, ber·ry·ing 1** To form or bear berries. **2** To gather berries. ◆ Homophone: *bury.* [OE *berie*] **—ber′ried** *adj.*

Ber·ry (be·rē′) A region and former province of central France. Also **Ber·ri′.**

Ber·sa·glie·re (ber′sä·lye′rā) *n. pl.* **·ri** (-rē) *Italian* A marksman; rifleman; specifically, one of a special corps of sharpshooters in the Italian army.

ber·seem (bər·sēm′) *n.* A clover *(Trifolium alexandrinum)* grown as forage in Egypt and the United States. [<Arabic *birshīm* clover]

ber·serk (bûr′sûrk, bər·sûrk′) *n.* **1** In Norse mythology, a furious fighter, who could assume the form of wild beasts, and whom fire and iron could not harm; hence figuratively, one who fights with frenzied fury. **2** A freebooter. Also **ber′serk·er.** —*adj.* Violently or frenziedly destructive. **—to go berserk** To run wild; have a fit of destructive rage. [<ON *berserkr* bear-shirt]

Bert (bûrt) Diminutive of ALBERT, BERTRAM, HERBERT.

berth (bûrth) *n.* **1** A bunk or bed in a vessel or sleeping-car, etc. **2** Any place in which a vessel may lie at anchor or at a dock; sea room. **3** A place or engagement on a vessel. **4** Office or employment in general. **—to give a wide berth to** To avoid; keep out of the way of. —*v.t.* & *v.i.* **1** To provide with or occupy a bed. **2** *Naut.* To provide with or come to an anchorage. ◆ Homophone: *birth.* [Origin unknown]

ber·tha (bûr′thə) *n.* A deep collar falling from the bodice neckline over the shoulders: in imitation of a short shoulder cape formerly so called. [after Charlemagne's mother]

Ber·tha (bûr′thə; *Du., Ger., Sw.* ber′tä) A feminine personal name. Also *Fr.* **Berthe** (bert), *Ital., Sp.* **Ber·ta** (ber′tä). [<Gmc., bright or famous]

Ber·tie (bûr′tē) Diminutive of ALBERT, BERTRAM, HERBERT.

Ber·the·lot (ber·tə·lō′), **Pierre Eugène Marcelin,** 1827–1907, French chemist.

Ber·til·lon system (bûr′tə·lon, *Fr.* ber·tē·yôn′) A system of coded physical measurements, later extended to include personal characteristics, such as the color of the eyes, scars, deformities, and the like (sometimes, also, photographs), used as a means for identification, especially as applied to criminals. [after Alphonse *Bertillon,* 1853–1914, French anthropologist]

Ber·tin (ber·taṅ′), **Exupère Joseph,** 1712–81, French anatomist.

Ber·tram (bûr′trəm) A masculine personal name. Also *Fr.* **Ber·trand** (ber·träṅ′), *Ital.* **Ber·tran·do** (ber·trän′dō), *Pg.* **Ber·trão** (ber·trouṅ′), *Ger.* **Ber·tram** (ber′träm) or **Ber·trand** (ber′tränt). [<Gmc., fair, illustrious]

Ber·wick (ber′ik) A county in SE Scotland; 457 square miles; county seat, Duns. Also **Ber′wick·shire** (-shir, -shər).

Berwick-on-Tweed A municipal borough in northern Northumberland, England. Also **Berwick-upon-Tweed.**

ber·yl (ber′əl) *n.* A vitreous, green or emerald-green, light-blue, yellow, pink, or white silicate of aluminum and beryllium crystallizing in the hexagonal system. The aquamarine and emerald varieties are used as gems. [<OF <L *beryllus* <Gk. *bēryllos* beryl] **—ber·yl·line** (ber′ə·lin, -līn) *adj.*

be·ryl·li·um (bə·ril′ē·əm) *n.* A hard, very light metallic element (symbol Be, atomic number 4), transparent to X rays and highly toxic, whether in compounds or metallic form. See PERIODIC TABLE. [<NL <L *beryllus* beryl]

Be·ry·tus (bə·rī′təs) The ancient name for BEIRUT.

Ber·ze·li·us (bər·zē′lē·əs, *Sw.* ber·sā′lē·o͞os), **Baron Jöns Jacob,** 1779–1848, Swedish chemist.

Bes (bes) In Egyptian mythology, a god presiding over art, the dance, and music, and having power to avert witchcraft.

Be·san·çon (bə·zäṅ·sôṅ′) A city in eastern France: ancient *Vesontio.*

Bes·ant (bez′ənt), **Annie,** 1847–1933, *née* Wood, English theosophist.
—Be·sant (bi·zant′), **Sir Walter,** 1836–1901, English novelist and historian.

be·seech (bi·sēch′) *v.t.* **be·sought, be·seech·ing 1** To entreat earnestly; implore. **2** To beg for earnestly; plead. See synonyms under ASK, PLEAD. [OE *besēcan*] **—be·seech′er** *n.* **—be·seech′ing** *adj.* **—be·seech′ing·ly** *adv.* **—be·seech′ing·ness** *n.*

be·seem (bi·sēm′) *v.i.* To be fitting or appropriate: used impersonally: It ill *beseems* you to speak thus. **—be·seem′ing** *adj.*

be·seen (bi·sēn′) *adj. Obs.* **1** Clad; adorned. **2** Accomplished; versed.

be·set (bi·set′) *v.t.* **be·set, be·set·ting 1** To attack on all sides; harass. **2** To hem in; encircle. **3** To set or stud with, as gems. See synonyms under ATTACK. [OE *besettan*] **—be·set′ment** *n.*

be·set·ting (bi·set′ing) *adj.* Constantly attacking or troubling.

be·show (bi·shō′) *n.* The black candlefish *(Anoplopoma fimbria),* of the Pacific coast of the U.S. [<N. Am. Ind. *bishowk*]

be·shrew (bi·shro͞o′) *v.t. Obs.* To wish ill to; execrate: a mild imprecation.

be·side (bi·sīd′) *prep.* **1** At the side of; in proximity to: a path *beside* the river. **2** In comparison with: My merit is little *beside* yours. **3** Away or apart from: This discussion is *beside* the point. **4** Other than; over and above: I have no treasure *beside* this. **—beside oneself** Out of one's senses, as from anger, fear, etc. —*adv.* In addition to; besides. See synonyms under ADJACENT. [OE *be sidan* by the side (of)]

be·sides (bi·sīdz′) *adv.* **1** In addition; as well: There are, *besides,* some remarkable books here. **2** Moreover; furthermore: He is rich; *besides,* he is virtuous. **3** Not included in that mentioned; otherwise; else: Loving me, her heart is stone to all the world *besides.* —*prep.* **1** In addition to; other than: *Besides* this we have much more. **2** Beyond; apart from: I care for nothing *besides* this.

be·siege (bi·sēj′) *v.t.* **be·sieged, be·sieg·ing 1** To beset or surround; lay siege to, as a castle. **2** To crowd around; block. **3** To harass or overwhelm, as with invitations or prayers. See synonyms under ATTACK. **—be·sieg′er** *n.* **—be·siege′ment** *n.*

Bes·kid Mountains (bes′kid, bes·kēd′) A mountain group of the Carpathians along the Czechoslovak-Polish border; highest point, 5,658 feet. Also **Bes′kids.**

be·smear (bi·smir′) *v.t.* To smear over; sully.

be·smirch (bi·smûrch′) *v.t.* **1** To soil; stain. **2** To sully; dishonor, as a reputation. **—be·smirch′er** *n.* **—be·smirch′ment** *n.*

be·som[1] (bē′zəm) *n.* **1** A bundle of twigs used as a broom; any agency that cleanses or abolishes. **2** The broom *(Cytisus scoparius).* [OE *besma* broom]

be·som[2] (bē′zəm, biz′əm) *n. Scot.* A drab; slattern; street woman.

be·sot (bi·sot′) *v.t.* **be·sot·ted, be·sot·ting 1** To stupefy, as with drink. **2** To make foolish or stupid. **3** To infatuate. **—be·sot′ted** *adj.*

be·sought (bi·sôt′) Past tense and past participle of BESEECH.

be·span·gle (bi·spang′gəl) *v.t.* **·gled, ·gling** To decorate with or as with spangles.

be·spat·ter (bi·spat′ər) *v.t.* **1** To cover or soil by spattering. **2** To spatter about. **3** To besmirch; sully.

be·speak (bi·spēk′) *v.t.* **be·spoke** (*Archaic* **be·spake**), **be·spoke** or **be·spo·ken, be·speak·ing 1** To ask or arrange for in advance; reserve. **2** To give evidence of; indicate: His face *bespeaks* his happy lot. **3** To foretell; foreshadow: The present *bespeaks* a sad future. **4** *Obs.* To speak to. [OE *besprecan*]

be·spec·ta·cled (bi·spek′tə·kəld) *adj.* Wearing glasses.

be·spoke (bi·spōk′) Past tense and alternative past participle of BESPEAK. —*adj. Brit.* Ordered ahead of time; made to order, as a suit of clothing.

be·spread (bi·spred′) *v.t.* **be·spread, be·spread·ing** To cover or spread over thickly.

be·sprent (bi·sprent′) *adj. Obs.* Besprinkled; strewed. [OE, pp. of *besprengan* sprinkle]

be·sprin·kle (bi·spring′kəl) *v.t.* **·kled, ·kling** To scatter or spread over by sprinkling.

Bess (bes) Diminutive of ELIZABETH. Also **Bes·sie** (bes′ē), **Bes′sy.**

Bes·sa·ra·bi·a (bes′ə·rā′bē·ə) A region of SW European U.S.S.R.; about 18,000 square miles; formerly a Rumanian province. *Rumanian* **Ba·sa·ra·bia** (bä′sä·rä′byä). **—Bes′sa·ra′bi·an** *adj.* & *n.*

Bes·sel method (bes′əl) A method of determining one's position by sighting through points on a map correctly oriented to the corresponding features of the terrain. [after Friedrich *Bessel,* 1784–1846, German astronomer]

Bes·se·mer (bes′ə·mər) *n.* Steel prepared by the Bessemer process. [after Sir Henry *Bessemer,* 1813–98, British engineer]

Bessemer converter *Metall.* A large pear-shaped vessel for containing the molten iron to be converted into steel by the Bessemer process.

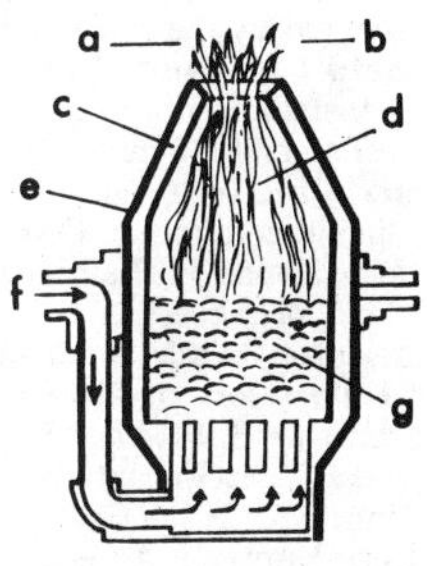

BESSEMER CONVERTER
a. CO_2 *b.* SO_2 *c.* Sand bricks. *d.* Flames. *e.* Steel. *f* Hot compressed air. *g.* Molten iron.

Bessemer process *Metall.* **1** A process for eliminating the carbon and silicon from pig iron by forcing a blast of air through the molten metal preparatory to its conversion into steel or ingot iron. **2** A similar process for eliminating sulfur from copper matte.

best (best) *adj.* [*Superlative of* GOOD] **1** Excelling all others in a given quality. **2** Most advantageous, desirable, or serviceable. **3** Most; largest; as, the *best* part of an hour. —*n.* The most excellent thing, part, etc.; the highest degree or state; the utmost. —*adv.* [*Superlative of* WELL] **1** In the most excellent or suitable manner. **2** With the most favorable result. **3** To the utmost degree. —*v.t.* To defeat; overcome. [OE *betst*]

be·stain (bi·stān) *v.t.* Mark with stains.

be·stead (bi·sted′) *v.t.* **be·stead·ed** or **be·sted, be·stead·ing** To be of service to; help.

bes·tial (bes′chəl, best′yəl) *adj.* **1** Pertaining to or like beasts or a beast; animal. **2** Having the qualities of an animal; brutish; sensual; depraved. **3** Irrational; rude; savage. See synonyms under BRUTISH. [<OF <L *bestialis* <*bestia* beast] **—bes′tial·ly** *adv.*

bes·ti·al·i·ty (bes′chē·al′ə·tē, -tē·al′-) *n.* **1** The quality or state of being bestial. **2** Character or conduct befitting beasts. **3** Human sexual relations with an animal; sodomy.

bes·tial·ize (bes′chəl·īz, best′yəl-) *v.t.* **·ized, ·iz·ing** To brutalize.

bes·ti·ar·y (bes′tē·er′ē) *n. pl.* **·ar·ies** A medieval allegory or moralizing treatise on animals.

be·stir (bi·stûr′) *v.t.* **be·stirred, be·stir·ring** To incite or rouse to activity.

best man The chief groomsman at a wedding.

be·stow (bi·stō′) *v.t.* **1** To present as a gift: with *on* or *upon.* **2** To expend; apply: He *bestowed* his life on science. **3** *Obs.* To give in marriage. **4** *Obs.* To deposit; store; also, to house; lodge. See synonyms under GIVE. [ME *bistowen* <*bi-* to, upon + *stowen* place] **—be·stow′a·ble** *adj.* **—be·stow′al** or **be·stow′ment** *n.*

be·strad·dle (bi·strad′l) *v.t.* **·dled, ·dling** To bestride; straddle.

be·strew (bi·stro͞o′) *v.t.* **be·strewed, be·strewed** or **be·strewn, be·strew·ing 1** To cover or strew (a surface). **2** To scatter about. **3** To lie scattered over. Also **be·strow** (bi·strō′). [OE *bestreowian*]

be·stride (bi·strīd′) *v.t.* **be·strode, be·strid·den, be·strid·ing 1** To mount; sit astride of; ride astride; straddle. **2** To stride over or across.

best-sell·er (best′sel′ər) *n.* A book or phonograph record currently selling in large numbers.

bet (bet) *v.* **bet** or (less commonly) **bet·ted, bet·ting** *v.t.* **1** To stake or pledge (money, etc.) in support of an opinion or on an uncertain outcome, as of a race. **2** To declare as in a bet: I'll *bet* he doesn't come. —*v.i.* **3** To place a wager. **—you bet** *U.S. Slang* Certainly. —*n.* **1** The act of betting; a wager. **2** The stake in any wager. **3** That on which the bet is placed: The black horse is the best *bet.* [Origin uncertain]

be·ta (bā′tə, bē′-) *n.* **1** The second letter of the Greek alphabet (Β, β): corresponding to English *b.* As a numeral it denotes 2. **2** The second object in any order of arrangement or classification, as, in astronomy the second brightest star in a constellation, in chemistry the second of a group of isomeric compounds, in botany the second subspecies, etc. [<Gk.]

be·ta-block·er (bā′tə·blok′ər) *n.* A drug that relieves heart stress by inhibiting absorption of adrenalin by the heart and blood vessels.

Beta Cen·tau·ri (sen·tôr′ē) The star Beta in the constellation of Centaurus; one of the 20 brightest stars, 0.86 magnitude.

be·ta·ine (bē′tə·ēn, -in) *n. Chem.* A crystalline alkaloid compound, $C_5H_{11}O_2N \cdot H_2O$ related to glycine, found in the beet and various other plants. [<L *beta* beet]

be·take (bi·tāk′) *v.t.* **be·took, be·tak·en, be·tak·ing** **1** To resort or have recourse: used reflexively: with *to*: She *betook* herself to prayer. **2** To go; take (oneself): with *to*: He *betook* himself to an inn.

beta particle An electron.

beta rays *Physics* A stream of electrons projected by radioactive substances. They are identical with cathode rays, possess great penetrative power, and are easily deflected by an electric or magnetic field in a direction opposite to that of the alpha rays.

beta rhythm A frequency of 13 to 30 per second in brain waves, characteristic of an alert or aroused state in the normal human adult.

be·ta·tron (bā′tə·tron) *n.* An electromagnetic apparatus for liberating electrons and accelerating them in a quarter-cycle alternating field to the required velocity for discharge against a chosen target. [<BETA (RAY) + (ELEC)TRON]

be·ta·tro·pic (bā′tə·trō′pik, -trop′ik) *adj. Physics* **1** Of or pertaining to a difference of one beta particle in the nucleus of an atom. **2** Designating either of two atoms, one of which has been formed by the ejection of a beta particle from the nucleus, with an increase of 1 in the nuclear charge. [<BETA (PARTICLE) + -TROPIC]

be·tel (bēt′l) *n.* A climbing plant *(Piper betle)* of Asia, the leaves of which are chewed by the natives of Malaya and other Asian countries. See BETELNUT. [<Pg. *betel* <Malay *vettila*]

Be·tel·geuse (bē′təl·jōōz, bet′əl·jœz) A giant red star, Alpha in the constellation of Orion. It is an irregular variable with a magnitude of 1.2. Also **Be′tel·guese, Be′tel·geux.** [<F *Bételgeuse* <Arabic *bat al-jauza,* ? shoulder of the giant]

be·tel·nut (bēt′l·nut′) *n.* The astringent seed of an East Indian palm, the **betel palm** *(Areca catechu),* used for chewing with betel leaves.

bête noire (bāt′ nwär′, *Fr.* bet nwȧr′) Anything real or imaginary that is an object of hate or dread; a bugaboo. [<F, black beast]

beth (beth) The second Hebrew letter. See ALPHABET.

Beth (beth) Diminutive of ELIZABETH.

be·thank·it (bi·thang′kit) *n. Scot.* Grace said at table: elliptical for *God be thanked.*

Beth·a·ny (beth′ə·nē) In the New Testament, a village in Palestine near Jerusalem, mentioned as the home of Lazarus, Martha, and Mary.

beth·el (beth′əl) *n.* **1** A seamen's church or chapel, floating or on shore. **2** *Brit.* A dissenters' chapel. **3** A hallowed place. [<Hebrew *bēth-ēl* house of God]

Beth·el (beth′əl) An ancient town of Palestine, near Jerusalem. *Gen.* xxviii 19.

Be·thes·da (bə·thez′də) *n.* **1** A pool in Jerusalem reputed to have healing properties. *John* v 2. **2** A meeting house; chapel.

be·think (bi·thingk′) *v.* **be·thought, be·think·ing** *v.t.* To remind (oneself); bear in mind; consider: generally used reflexively: *Bethink* yourself of what you are. *—v.i. Archaic* To meditate.

Beth·le·hem (beth′lē·əm, -lə·hem) **1** An ancient town in Judea, SW of Jerusalem; birthplace of Jesus. *Matt.* ii 1. **2** A town in Palestine on the same site. **3** A manufacturing city on the Lehigh River in eastern Pennsylvania **—Beth′le·hem·ite′** *n.*

Beth·mann-Holl·weg (bāt′män·hōl′väkh), **Theobald von,** 1856–1921, German chancellor 1909–17.

Beth·nal Green (beth′nəl) A metropolitan borough of London north of the Thames.

be·thought (bi·thôt′) Past tense and past participle of BETHINK.

Beth·sa·i·da (beth·sā′ə·də) A ruined town on the northern shore of the Sea of Galilee, Palestine. *John* i 44. Also **Bethsaida of Galilee.**

Bé·thune (bā·tün′) A town of northern France.

be·tide (bi·tīd′) *v.t.* & *v.i.* **be·tid·ed, be·tid·ing** To happen (to) or befall. See synonyms under HAPPEN. [ME *betiden*]

be·times (bi·tīmz′) *adv.* In good season or time; also, soon. Also *Obs.* **be·time′.** [ME *betymes* in time, seasonably]

Be·ti·o (bā′tsē·ō, bāt′shē·ō) An islet SW of Tarawa; World War II capital of the Gilbert and Ellice Islands Colony.

bê·tise (be·tēz′) *n. French* **1** A stupid thing; an absurdity. **2** Stupidity; nonsense.

be·to·ken (bi·tō′kən) *v.t.* **1** To be a sign of; portend. **2** To give evidence of; indicate. See synonyms under AUGUR, IMPORT. [ME *bitacnien*] **—be·to′ken·er** *n.*

bé·ton (bā·tôn′) *n. French* A concrete of lime, sand, and cement.

bet·o·ny (bet′ə·nē) *n. pl.* **·nies** **1** A European herb (genus *Stachys,* formerly *Betonica)* of the mint family, once used as an emetic. **2** One of various other plants, as a British species of figwort (the water *betony*), etc. [<F *bétoine* <L *betonica,* var. of *vettonica* < *Vettones,* a people of Portugal]

be·took (bi·tŏŏk′) Past tense of BETAKE.

be·tray (bi·trā′) *v.t.* **1** To deliver up to an enemy; be a traitor to. **2** To prove faithless to; disappoint: to *betray* a trust. **3** To disclose, as secret information. **4** To reveal unwittingly: to *betray* ignorance. **5** To deceive; seduce and desert. **6** To indicate; show: The smoke *betrays* a fire. See synonyms under DECEIVE. [ME *bitraien* <*bi* over, to + OF *trair* <L *tradere* deliver, give up] **—be·tray′al, be·tray′ment** *n.* **—be·tray′er** *n.*

be·troth (bi·trōth′, -trôth′) *v.t.* **1** To engage to marry; affiance. **2** To contract to give in marriage. [ME *bitreuthien* <*bi-* + *treuthe* truth]

be·troth·al (bi·trō′thəl, -trôth′əl) *n.* **1** The act of betrothing, or the state of being betrothed. **2** Engagement or contract to marry. Also **be·troth′·ment.**

be·trothed (bi·trōthd′, -trôtht′) *adj.* Engaged to be married; affianced. *—n.* A person engaged to be married.

Bet·sy (bet′sē) Diminutive of ELIZABETH.

bet·ter[1] (bet′ər) *adj.* [Comparative of GOOD] **1** Superior in excellence, amount, or value; excelling or surpassing. **2** Larger; greater: the *better* half of the cake. **3** Improved in health; convalescent. *—n.* **1** That which is in any way better; also, advantage; superiority. **2** A superior, as in ability, rank, age, etc. *—v.t.* **1** To make better; improve. **2** To surpass; excel. *—v.i.* **3** To grow better. See synonyms under AMEND. *—adv.* [Comparative of WELL] **1** In a superior manner; more thoroughly or correctly; in a higher degree. **2** *Colloq.* More: We've been here *better* than a week. [OE *betera*]

bet·ter[2] (bet′ər) *n.* One who lays wagers. Also **bet′tor.**

bet·ter·ment (bet′ər·mənt) *n.* **1** Improvement. **2** An addition to the value of real property.

Bet·ter·ton (bet′ər·tən), **Thomas,** 1635?–1710, English actor and producer; said to have inaugurated scene-shifting.

Bet·ty (bet′ē) Diminutive of ELIZABETH.

bet·u·la·ceous (bech′ŏŏ·lā′shəs) *adj.* Belonging to a family *(Betulaceae)* of trees and shrubs including the birch, the alder, and the hazel. [<L *betula* birch]

be·tween (bi·twēn′) *adv.* In intervening time, space, position, or relation; at or during intervals: Rest periods were few and far *between.* **—in between** In an intermediate position or state; undecided. *—prep.* **1** In or at some point within the space separating two places or objects: He stepped *between* the combatants. **2** Intermediate in relation to qualities, conditions, periods of time, etc.: a flavor *between* sweet and sour; Come *between* one and two. **3** Involving in or as in joint or reciprocal action or relation: They had only five dollars *between* them. **4** Connecting, as in continuous extent or motion: the plane *between* New York and Paris. **5** One or the other of: How can you choose *between* them? **6** As a result of: *Between* her job and her housework, she had little time for her children. [OE *betweonan* <*be-* by + *tweonan* <*twā* two]

Synonym (prep.): among. In strict usage *between* is used only of two objects; *among* of more than two; divide the money *between* the two, *among* the three. *Between* is, however, used at times of more than two objects, particularly when some reciprocal relation is denoted; as, a treaty *between* the three powers. See AMID.

between the devil and the deep (blue) sea Intermediate between unpleasant alternatives.

between you and me Confidentially.

be·twixt (bi·twikst′) *adv.* & *prep. Archaic* or *Poetic* Between. See synonyms under AMID. [OE *betweohs* twofold <*be* by + *-tweohs* <*twā* two]

betwixt and between In an intermediate state or position; neither the one nor the other.

beuk (byŏŏk) *n. Scot.* Book.

Beu·lah (byŏŏ′lə) A feminine personal name. [<Hebrew *be'ūlāh* married]

Beu·lah (byŏŏ′lə) The land of Israel. *Isa.* lxii 4. **—Land of Beulah** In Bunyan's *Pilgrim's Progress,* the land of rest where pilgrims abide till death.

Bev or **bev** (bev) *n. Physics.* Billion (10^9) electron volts.

bev·a·tron (bev′ə·tron) *n. Physics* An atom-smashing machine resembling the synchrotron in operating principle but capable of accelerating protons to an energy level in excess of one billion electron volts; a proton synchrotron: also called *cosmotron.* [<B(ILLION) E(LECTRON) V(OLTS) + (ELEC)TRON]

bev·el (bev′əl) *n.* **1** An inclination of two surfaces other than 90°, as at the edge of a timber, etc. **2** An adjustable instrument for measuring angles: also **bevel square.** *—adj.* Oblique; slanting; beveled. *—v.* **bev·eled** or **bev·elled, bev·el·ing** or **bev·el·ling** *v.t.* To cut or bring to a bevel. *—v.i.* To slant. [? <OF. Cf. F *beveau.*]

BEVEL SQUARE

bevel gear *Mech.* A gear having beveled teeth, as for transmitting rotary motion at an angle. See illustration under COGWHEEL.

bev·er·age (bev′rij, bev′ər·ij) *n.* Drink; that which is drunk. [<OF *bevrage* <*beivre* drinking <L *bibere* drink]

Bev·er·idge (bev′ər·ij), **Albert Jeremiah,** 1862–1927, U.S. politician and historian. **—Sir William** 1879–1963 English economist.

Beveridge plan A proposal (1942) for the unification of the various types of social insurance in Great Britain: formulated by Sir William Beveridge.

Bev·er·ly Hills (bev′ər·lē) A residential city in California, on the western boundary of Los Angeles.

Bevin (bev′in), **Ernest,** 1884–1951, English labor leader and politician.

bev·y (bev′ē) *n. pl.* **·ies** **1** A small group of persons, usually of girls or women. **2** A flock of birds, especially of quail, grouse, or larks. **3** A small herd, especially of roes. See synonyms under FLOCK. [ME *bevey;* origin uncertain]

be·wail (bi·wāl′) *v.t.* & *v.i.* To mourn; lament. See synonyms under MOURN.

be·ware (bi·wâr′) *v.t.* & *v.i.* **be·wared, be·war·ing** To look out (for); be cautious or wary (of): often with *of, lest, that, not, how.* [OE *wær* cautious; orig. *be ware* be on guard, be cautious]

be·wil·der (bi·wil′dər) *v.t.* **1** To confuse utterly; perplex. **2** *Archaic* To cause to lose the way or course. See synonyms under ABASH. **—be·wil′dered** *adj.* **—be·wil′dered·ly** *adv.* **—be·wil′der·ing** *adj.* **—be·wil′der·ing·ly** *adv.*

be·wil·der·ment (bi·wil′dər·mənt) *n.* **1** A state or condition of being bewildered. **2** A confusion; entanglement. See synonyms under PERPLEXITY.

be·witch (bi·wich′) *v.t.* **1** To gain power over by charms or incantations. **2** To attract irresistibly; charm; fascinate. See synonyms under CHARM. **—be·witch′er** *n.* **—be·witch′·ment, be·witch′er·y** *n.*

be·witch·ing (bi·wich′ing) *adj.* Charming; captivating. See synonyms under BEAUTIFUL. **—be·witch′ing·ly** *adv.*

be·wray (bi·rā′) *v.t. Obs.* To disclose; betray.

[ME *bewreien* < *be-* + *wreien,* OE *wrēgan* accuse]

bey (bā) *n.* **1** The governor of a minor Turkish province or district. **2** A native ruler of Tunis. **3** A Turkish title of respect. Also spelled *beg.* ◆ Homophone: *bay.* [< Turkish *beg* lord] — **bey′i·cal** *adj.*

Beyle (bāl), **Marie Henri.** See STENDHAL.

bey·lik (bā′lik) *n.* **1** The authority of a bey. **2** The district ruled by a bey. Also **bey′lic.**

be·yond (bi·yond′) *prep.* **1** Farther or more distant than; on or to the far side of: the house *beyond* the turn of the road. **2** Extending further than: staying *beyond* his usual hour. **3** Out of the reach or scope of: Algebra is *beyond* me. **4** Surpassing; superior to; exceeding: a woman lovely *beyond* description. —*adv.* Farther on or away; at a distance. **—the (great) beyond** Whatever comes after death. [OE *begeondan* < *be-* near + *geondan* yonder]

Bey·routh (bā′ro͞ot, bā·ro͞ot′) See BEIRUT.

bez·ant (bez′ənt, bə·zant′) *n.* **1** The solidus (def. 1). **2** *Archit.* A flat disk used in ornamentation. Also spelled *byzant.* [< OF *besant* < L *Byzantius* Byzantine]

bez antler (bez, bāz) The second branch of a deer's antler, the one above the brow antler. Also **bez tine.** For illustration see ANTLER. [< OF *bes-* < L *bis* twice]

bez·el (bez′əl) *n.* **1** A bevel on the edge of a cutting tool. **2** That part of a cut gem which is above the girdle, including the table and surrounding facets. **3** A groove and flange made to receive a beveled edge, as of a watch crystal. **4** A flat, engraved gold seal. [? < OF. Cf. F *biseau.*]

Bé·ziers (bā·zyā′) A city in southern France.

be·zique (bə·zēk′) *n.* A game of cards based on the declaring of certain combinations upon taking a trick: also, such a combination in this game. [< F *bésigue*]

be·zoar (bē′zôr, -zōr) *n.* **1** A concretion found in the stomach and intestines of ruminants and some other animals, formerly supposed to have medicinal value. **2** *Obs.* An antidote or panacea. [< NL < Persian *pādzahr* < *pād* expelling + *zahr* poison]

Bha·ga·vad-Gi·ta (bug′ə·vəd·gē′tä) *n.* A sacred Hindu text consisting of philosophical dialog in the *Mahabharata,* expounding the duties of caste and the yoga doctrines of devotion to the Supreme Spirit. [< Skt., Song of the Blessed One (i.e., Krishna)]

Bha·mo (bä′mō) A district of Upper Burma; 4,148 square miles; capital, Bhamo.

bhang (bang) *n.* **1** Indian hemp. **2** The dried leaves and capsules of the Indian hemp: used for their intoxicant and narcotic properties. Also spelled *bang.* [< Hind. < Skt. *bhangā* hemp]

Bha·rat (bu′rut) The ancient name for INDIA.

Bhat·pa·ra (bät·pä′rə) A city in West Bengal, India; an ancient seat of Sanskrit learning.

Bhau·nag·ar (bou·nug′ər) **1** A former princely state on the west coast of India. **2** A port on the Gulf of Cambay; former capital of the state. Also **Bhav·nag′ar** (bou-).

bhees·tee (bēs′tē) *n.* In India, a native water carrier. Also **bhees′tie, bhis′tie.** [< Hind. *bhīstī* < Persian *bihishti,* lit., one from heaven]

Bho·pal (bō·päl′) A chief commissioner's state in central India; 6,921 square miles; capital, Bhopal.

Bhu·ba·nes·war (bo͞o′və·nesh′vər) A town and pilgrimage site in eastern India; capital of Orissa. Also **Bhu′va·nesh′war.**

Bhu·tan (bo͞o·tän′) A semi-independent kingdom between NE India and Tibet; 18,000 square miles; capital Punaka.

Bhu·tan·ese (bo͞o′tən·ēz′, -ēs′) *n. pl.* **·ese 1** A native of Bhutan. **2** The Sino-Tibetan language of Bhutan. —*adj.* Of or pertaining to Bhutan, its people, or their language.

Bi *Chem.* Bismuth (symbol Bi).

bi- *prefix* **1** Twice; doubly; two; especially, occurring twice or having two; as in:

biangulate	**bicephalic**	**biradiate**
bicapitate	**biciliate**	**bispiral**
bicellular	**bicolumnar**	**bistipular**
bicentral	**biflorate**	**bistipulate**

2 *Chem.* **a** Having two equivalents of the substance named: *bichloride.* **b** Indicating the presence of the named component in double the ordinary proportion, or the doubling of a radical, etc., in an organic compound. Also: *bin-* before a vowel, as in *binaural; bis-* before *c, s,* as in *bissextile.* [< L *bi-* < *bis* twice]

bi·a·cu·mi·nate (bī′ə·kyo͞o′mə·nāt) *adj. Bot.* Two-pointed.

Bi·a·fra (bē·ä′frə), **Bight of** A bay of the western Gulf of Guinea, Africa.

Bi·ak (bē·yäk′) The largest of the Schouten Islands; 948 square miles.

Bia·lys·tok (byä·lis′tôk) A city in NE Poland. *Russian* **Be·lo·stok** (byi·lə·stôk′).

Bian·ca (byäng′kä) The Italian form of BLANCH.

Bian·co (byäng′kō), **Mon·te** (môn′tā) Italian name for MONT BLANC.

bi·an·gu·lar (bī·ang′gyə·lər) *adj.* Having two angles.

bi·an·nu·al (bī·an′yo͞o·əl) *adj.* Occurring twice a year; semiannual. **—bi·an′nu·al·ly** *adv.*

bi·an·nu·late (bī·an′yə·lāt, -lit) *adj. Zool.* Having two rings or bands, as of color.

Bi·ar·ritz (bē′ə·rits, *Fr.* byȧ·rēts′) A resort town in SW France on the Bay of Biscay.

bi·as (bī′əs) *n. pl.* **bi·as·es** or **bi·as·ses 1** A line, cut, or seam running obliquely across the threads of a fabric: a dress sewn on the *bias.* **2** A mental predilection or prejudice. See synonyms under INCLINATION, PREJUDICE. **3** *Electronics* A grid bias. **4** In bowling, a lopsided shape of a ball, causing it to swerve; also, the swerving course of such a ball. —*adj.* Cut, running, set, or folded diagonally; slanting. —*adv.* Slantingly; diagonally. —*v.t.* **bi·ased** or **bi·assed, bi·as·ing** or **bi·as·sing 1** To influence or affect unduly or unfairly. **2** *Electronics* To impose a steady negative potential upon (a grid). [< F *biais* oblique]

Bi·as (bē′äs) See BEAS.

bi·au·ric·u·lar (bī′ô·rik′yə·lər) *adj.* **1** Of or pertaining to two auricles. **2** Biauriculate. **3** Having two ears.

bi·au·ric·u·late (bī′ô·rik′yə·lit) *adj. Anat.* Having two auricles, as the heart.

bi·ax·i·al (bī·ak′sē·əl) *adj.* Having two axes, as a crystal. Also **bi·ax·al** (bī·ak′səl). **—bi·ax′i·al·ly** *adv.*

bib (bib) *v.t.* & *v.i.* **bibbed, bib·bing** *Obs.* To drink; tipple. —*n.* **1** A cloth worn under the chin by children at meals to catch drink or food that is dribbled. **2** A waistpiece attached to a woman's apron. **3** A bibcock. [< L *bibere* drink]

bib and tucker *Colloq.* Clothes.

bi·ba·sic (bī·bā′sik) *adj.* Dibasic.

bibb (bib) *n. Naut.* A cleat or bracket bolted to the hounds of a mast of a vessel to support the trestletrees. **2** A bibcock. [< BIB (*n.* def. 1)]

bib·ber (bib′ər) *n.* A tippler.

bib·cock (bib′kok′) *n.* A cock or faucet having the nozzle bent downward.

bibe·lot (bib′lō, *Fr.* bēb·lō′) *n.* A small, decorative, or curious article of virtu or object of art. [< F]

bi·bi·va·lent (bī′bī·vā′lənt, bī·biv′ə-) *adj. Chem.* Pertaining to or designating an electrolyte that breaks down into two bivalent ions.

Bi·ble (bī′bəl) *n.* **1** The writings of the Old and New Testaments, as accepted by the Christian Church as a divine revelation: in certain churches embracing also parts of the Apocrypha. **2** A copy of this. **3** The Old Testament Scriptures in the form accepted by the Jews. **4** Any book, record, or history considered authoritative: in this sense usually not capitalized. **—Douai Bible** An English translation of the Latin Vulgate by members of the English College at Douai, 1582–1610; revised and altered for modern use in the Roman Catholic Church: also **Douay Bible. —King James Bible** A revision of the English Bible proposed by King James I in 1604, the work of 50 revisors, published in 1611; the most widely used Protestant version of the Bible in English-speaking countries: also called *Authorized Version.* Compare REVISED VERSION. [< OF < L *biblia* < Gk., pl. of *biblion* book]

Bible paper See INDIA PAPER.

Bib·li·cal (bib′li·kəl) *adj.* **1** Pertaining to, like, quoted, or derived from the Bible. **2** In harmony with the Bible. Also **bib′li·cal.** — **Bib′li·cal·ly** *adv.*

Bib·li·cist (bib′lə·sist) *n.* **1** A person thoroughly versed in the Bible. **2** One who adheres to the letter of the Bible.

biblio- *combining form* Of or pertaining to a book or books, or to the Bible: *bibliophile, bibliomancy.* [< Gk. *biblion* book]

bib·li·o·film (bib′lē·ə·film′) *n.* A kind of microfilm used especially to reproduce rare or much-used books, etc.

bib·li·og·ra·phy (bib′lē·og′rə·fē) *n. pl.* **·phies 1** The description and history of books including details of authorship, editions, dates, typography, etc.; also a book containing such descriptions. **2** A list of the works of an author, or of the literature bearing on a particular subject. — **bib′li·og′ra·pher, bib′li·o·graph′** *n.* **—bib·li·o·graph·ic** (bib′lē·ə·graf′ik) or **·i·cal** *adj.* [< BIBLIO- + -GRAPHY]

bib·li·ol·a·try (bib′lē·ol′ə·trē) *n.* **1** Extravagant homage paid to the letter of the Bible. **2** Excessive worship of books. [< BIBLIO- + Gk. *latreia* worship] **—bib′li·ol′a·ter** *n.* **—bib′li·ol′a·trous** *adj.*

bib·li·o·man·cy (bib′lē·ō·man′sē) *n.* Divination by means of reference to some passage taken at random from a book, usually the Bible.

bib·li·o·ma·ni·a (bib′lē·ō·mā′nē·ə) *n.* An intense passion for collecting and owning books. — **bib′li·o·ma′ni·ac** (-ak) *n.* & *adj.*

bib·li·op·e·gy (bib′lē·op′ə·jē) *n.* The art or practice of bookbinding. [< *biblio-* + Gk. *pēgnynai* fasten, join]

bib·li·o·phile (bib′lē·ə·fīl′, -fil′) *n.* One who loves books. Also **bib′li·o·phil′** (fil′), **bib·li·oph·i·list** (bib′lē·of′ə·list). **—bib′li·oph′i·lism** *n.* **—bib′li·oph′i·lis′tic** *adj.*

bib·li·o·pole (bib′lē·ə·pōl′) *n.* A dealer in rare books. Also **bib·li·op·o·list** (bib′lē·op′ə·list). [< L *bibliopola* < Gk. *bibliopōlēs* bookseller < *biblion* book + *pōleein* sell] **—bib′li·o·pol′ic** (-pol′ik) or **·i·cal** *adj.* **—bib′li·op′o·lism** *n.*

bib·li·o·ther·a·py (bib′lē·ō·ther′ə·pē) *n. Pathol.* The treatment of certain nervous and mental disorders by the reading of selected books. — **bib′li·o·ther′a·pist** *n.*

Bib·list (bib′list, bī′blist) *n.* A Biblicist.

bib·u·lous (bib′yə·ləs) *adj.* **1** Given to drink; fond of drinking. **2** Taking up moisture readily; absorbent. [< L *bibulus* drinking readily < *bibere* drink] **—bib·u·los′i·ty** (-los′ə·tē) *n.* — **bib′u·lous·ly** *adv.* **—bib′u·lous·ness** *n.*

bi·cam·er·al (bī·kam′ər·əl) *adj.* Consisting of two chambers, houses, or branches, as a legislature.

bi·cap·su·lar (bī·kap′sə·lər, -syə-) *adj. Bot.* **1** Having two capsules. **2** Having a two-celled capsule.

bi·car·bo·nate (bī·kär′bə·nit, -nāt) *n. Chem.* A salt of carbonic acid in which one of the hydrogen atoms is replaced by a metal: sodium *bicarbonate.*

bice (bīs) *n.* **1** A blue or green pigment made from varieties of basic copper carbonate ore. **bice green** is now usually called malachite green and **blue bice,** azurite. **2** The color of any of these pigments. [< OF *bis* dark-colored]

bi·cen·te·nar·y (bī·sen′tə·ner′ē, bī′sen·ten′ər·ē) *adj.* **1** Occurring once in 200 years. **2** Lasting or consisting of 200 years. —*n. pl.* **·nar·ies 1** A period of 200 years. **2** A 200th anniversary. Also **bi·cen·ten·ni·al** (bī′sen·ten′ē·əl).

bi·ceph·a·lous (bī·sef′ə·ləs) *adj. Biol.* Having two heads.

bi·ceps (bī′seps) *n. pl.* **bi·ceps** *Anat.* **1** The large front muscle, or flexor, of the upper arm, the **biceps bra·chi·i** (brā′kē·ī). **2** The large flexor muscle at the back of the thigh, the **biceps cru·ris** (kro͞or′is). **3** Loosely, muscular strength. [< L, two-headed < *bis* twofold + *caput* head]

Bi·chat (bē·shȧ′), **Marie François Xavier,** 1771–1802, French anatomist; founder of histology.

biche (bēch) *n.* A Mexican hairless dog. [< Nahuatl, naked]

bi·chlo·ride (bī·klôr′īd, -id, -klō′rīd, -rid) *n. Chem.* **1** A salt in which there are two atoms of chlorine. **2** Bichloride of mercury, or corrosive sublimate, a dangerous poison used as a disinfectant.

bi·chro·mate (bī·krō′māt, -mit) *n. Chem.* **1** Dichromate. **2** Potassium dichromate.

bi·cip·i·tal (bī·sip′ə·təl) *adj. Anat.* **1** Having

two heads. 2 Pertaining to the biceps. Also **bi·cip′i·tous** (-təs).

bick·er[1] (bik′ər) *v.i.* 1 To dispute petulantly; wrangle. 2 To flow noisily, as a brook; gurgle. 3 To flicker, as a flame; twinkle. —*n.* 1 A petulant or angry dispute; a petty altercation: also **bick·er·ing.** 2 A clattering, babbling noise. 3 A flicker, or a tremulous or unsteady motion. See synonyms under QUARREL. [ME *bikeren;* origin uncertain] —**bick′er·er** *n.*

bick·er[2] (bik′ər) *n. Scot.* A wooden vessel for food or drink. [Var. of BEAKER]

Bi·col (bi·kōl′) *n.* 1 One of a Malayan people, inhabiting SE Luzon and professing Christianity before the Spanish conquest. 2 The Indonesian language of these people. Also spelled *Bikol.*

bi·col·or (bī′kul′ər) *adj.* Having two colors.

bi·con·cave (bī·kon′kāv, -kong′-, bī′kon·kāv′) *adj.* Concave on both sides.

bi·con·vex (bī·kon′veks, bī′kon·veks′) *adj.* Convex on both sides.

bi·corn (bī′kôrn) *n.* 1 A two-cornered, crescent-shaped hat with upturned brim; specifically, the two-cornered hat worn by French gendarmes: also **bi·corne.** 2 A two-horned animal: compare UNICORN. —*adj.* Two-horned; two-pronged; having two hornlike projections: also **bi·cor·nous** (bī·kôr′nəs), **bi·cor·nu·ate** (bī·kôr′nyōō·āt). [< L *bicornis* < *bis* twofold + *cornus* horn]

bi·cor·po·ral (bī·kôr′pər·əl) *adj.* Double-bodied, as certain signs of the zodiac. Also **bi·cor·po·re·al** (bī′kôr·pôr′ē·əl, -pō′rē-).

bi·cron (bī′kron) *n.* The one-billionth part of a meter; micromillimeter.

bi·cul·tur·al·ism (bī·kul′chə·rə·liz′əm) *n.* The policy of union between two separate cultures within one nation.

bi·cus·pid (bī·kus′pid) *adj.* 1 Having two cusps or points. 2 Double-pointed, as a premolar tooth, the valve at the left auricular opening of the heart, or a curve or crescent: also **bi·cus′pi·dal** (-dəl), **bi·cus′pi·date** (-dāt). —*n.* A premolar tooth, of which there are eight in the normal human jaws, two between each cuspid and the first molar tooth. Also **bi·cus′pis.** [< L *bis* twofold + *cuspis, -idis* point]

bi·cy·cle (bī′sik·əl) *n.* A two-wheeled vehicle with the wheels in tandem, a saddle or saddles, a steering handle, and propelled by foot pedals or a motor. —*v.i.* **·cled, ·cling** To ride a bicycle. Also *cycle.* [< L *bis* twofold + Gk. *kyklos* wheel] —**bi′cy·cler, bi′cy·clist** *n.*

bi·cy·clic (bī·sī′klik, -sik′lik) *adj.* 1 Pertaining to bicycles or bicycling. 2 *Bot.* Disposed in two cycles or whorls: also **bi·cy′cli·cal.**

bid (bid) *n.* 1 An offer to pay or accept a price. 2 The amount offered. 3 In card games, the number of tricks or points that a player engages to make; also, a player's turn to bid. 4 An effort to acquire, win, or attain: He made a *bid* for the governorship. 5 *Colloq.* An invitation. —*v.* **bade** (*Archaic* **bad**) *for defs.* **3, 4, 6** or **bid** *for defs.* **1, 2, 5, 7, bid·den** or **bid, bid·ding** *v.t.* 1 To make an offer of (a price), as at an auction or for a contract. 2 In card games, to declare (the number of tricks one will engage to take) and specify (the trump suit or no-trump under which the hand will be played): I *bid* six spades. 3 To command; order. 4 To invite. 5 *U.S. Colloq.* To invite to join: The fraternity will *bid* you. 6 To utter, as a greeting or farewell: I *bid* you good day. —*v.i.* 7 To offer a price. —**to bid fair** To seem probable. —**to bid in** At an auction, to attempt to raise the price (of an object) by competing with spurious bids. —**to bid up** To increase the price by offering higher bids. [Fusion of OE *biddan* ask, demand and *bēodan* proclaim, command]

bi·dar·ka (bī·där′kə) *n.* A skin-covered canoe used by natives of Alaska. [< Russian *baidarka,* dim. of *baidara* canoe]

Bi·dault (bē·dō′), **Georges,** born 1899, French statesman.

bid·da·ble (bid′ə·bəl) *adj.* 1 Of sufficient value to offer a bid on, as a bridge hand. 2 Inclined to do as bidden; obedient; docile.

bid·der (bid′ər) *n.* 1 One who makes a bid. 2 In contract bridge, the player who first names the trump suit, or no-trump, in which a hand is played; the declarer.

bid·ding (bid′ing) *n.* 1 A notification or command. 2 A solicitation or invitation. 3 The making of a bid or bids, as at a sale, in the game of contract bridge, etc.; bids collectively.

Bid·dle (bid′l) A prominent Philadelphia family, including **Nicholas,** 1786–1844, financier; **Francis,** 1886–1968 U.S. attorney general 1941–45; **George,** 1885–1973 brother of Francis, painter. —**John,** 1615–62, founder of Unitarianism in England.

bid·dy[1] (bid′ē) *n. pl.* **·dies** A chicken; especially, a hen. [Origin uncertain]

bid·dy[2] (bid′ē) *n. pl.* **·dies** *U.S. Colloq.* A female domestic; strictly, an Irish servant girl. [< BIDDY]

Bid·dy (bid′ē) Diminutive of BRIDGET.

bide (bīd) *v.* **bid·ed** (*Archaic* **bode**), **bid·ing** *v.t.* 1 To endure; withstand: to *bide* a storm. 2 *Archaic* To tolerate; submit to. —*v.i.* 3 To dwell; abide; stay. —**to bide one's time** To await the most favorable opportunity. See synonyms under ABIDE. [OE *bīdan* wait, stay]

bi·den·tate (bī·den′tāt) *adj.* Having two teeth or toothlike processes. Also **bi·den′tal.**

bi·det (bi·dā′) *n.* A small porcelain commode with running water, used for cleansing the genital and anal areas. [< F]

bi·di·a·lect·al·ism (bī′dī·ə·lek′tə·liz′əm) *n.* The use of two distinct dialects of a single language.

bid·ing (bī′ding) *n.* 1 An awaiting; expectation. 2 Residence; habitation.

bid·ri (bid′rē) *n.* An alloy of copper, lead, and tin used for making **bidri ware,** an Indian ware damascened with silver or gold. Also **bid′ree, bid′der·y.** [from *Bidar,* town in India]

Bie·der·mei·er (bē′dər·mī′ər) *adj.* Of or pertaining to a style of German furniture of the first half of the 19th century, based on French Empire forms. [after Gottlieb *Biedermeier,* character invented by L. Eichrodt, 1827–92, German poet]

Bie·la (bē′lä), **Baron Wilhelm von,** 1782–1856, German astronomer.

bield (bēld) *Scot. v.t.* To protect. —*n.* A shelter. —**bield′y** *adj.*

Bie·le·feld (bē′lə·felt) A city in NW Germany.

Bie·lid (bē′lid) See ANDROMED.

bien (bēn) *adj. Scot.* 1 Well-to-do; comfortably off, as a farmer. 2 Comfortably furnished; cosy, as a house. Also spelled *bein.* [< F *bien* well]

bien en·ten·du (byaṅ näṅ·täṅ·dü′) *French* Of course; lit., well understood.

bi·en·ni·al (bī·en′ē·əl) *adj.* 1 Occurring every second year. 2 Lasting or living for two years. —*n.* 1 *Bot.* A plant that produces leaves and roots the first year and flowers and fruit the second, then dies. 2 An event occurring once in two years. [< L *biennis* < *bis* twofold + *annus* year] —**bi·en′ni·al·ly** *adv.*

bien·ve·nue (byaṅ·və·nü′) *n. French* A welcome.

Bien·ville (byaṅ·vēl′), **Sieur de,** Jean Baptiste Le Moyne, 1680–1768, French governor of Louisiana and founder of New Orleans.

bier[1] (bir) *n.* A framework for carrrying a corpse to the grave; a coffin. ◆ Homophone: *beer.* [OE *bǣr*]

bier[2] (bēr) *n. German* Beer.

Bierce (birs), **Ambrose Gwinnett,** 1842–1914?, U.S. journalist and author.

Bie·rut (bye′rōōt), **Bo·le·slaw** (bô·le′släf), born 1892, president of Poland 1947–52; premier 1952–54.

biest·ings (bēs′tingz) *n.* Beestings.

bi·fa·cial (bī·fā′shəl) *adj.* 1 Having two fronts, as an effigy on a medal. 2 *Bot.* Having the opposite faces unlike, as a leaf. 3 Being alike on the opposite surfaces.

bi·far·i·ous (bī·fâr′ē·əs) *adj.* 1 Two-ranked. 2 *Bot.* Disposed in two vertical rows, as leaves on a branch. [< LL *bifarius* double < *bis* twofold + *fari* speak] —**bi·far′i·ous·ly** *adv.*

biff (bif) *Slang v.t.* To give a blow. —*n.* A whack; blow. [Imit.]

bif·fin (bif′in) *n. Brit.* 1 A cooking apple: a Norfolk *biffin.* 2 A baked apple flattened into a cake. [Var. of BEEFING]

bi·fid (bī′fid) *adj.* Doubly cleft: forked. Also **bif·i·date** (bif′i·dāt), **bif′i·dat′ed.** [< L *bifidus* < *bis* twofold + *findere* split] —**bi·fid·i·ty** (bī·fid′ə·tē) *n.* —**bi′fid·ly** *adv.*

bi·fi·lar (bī·fī′lər) *adj.* Formed of, having, or supported by two threads. —*n.* A bifilar micrometer. [< BI- + L *filum* thread] —**bi·fi′lar·ly** *adv.*

bi·flag·el·late (bī·flaj′ə·lāt) *adj. Zool.* Having two flagella or whiplike processes.

bi·flex (bī′fleks) *adj.* Bent in two places; alternately convex and concave. [< BI- + L *flexus,* pp. of *flectere* bend]

bi·fo·cal (bī·fō′kəl) *adj. Optics* Having two foci: said of a lens ground of both near and far vision. [< BI- + L *focus* hearth, focus of a lens]

bi·fo·cals (bī·fō′kəlz, bī′fō·kəlz) *n. pl.* Eyeglasses with bifocal lenses ground for distant vision in the upper portion of the lenses and for near vision in the lower.

bi·fold (bī′fōld′) *adj.* Twofold.

bi·fo·li·ate (bī·fō′lē·it) *adj. Bot.* Having two leaves.

bi·fo·li·o·late (bī·fō′lē·ə·lāt′) *adj. Bot.* Having two leaflets.

bi·fo·rate (bī·fôr′āt, -fō′rāt) *adj.* Having two perforations. [< BI- + L *foratus,* pp. of *forare* bore]

bi·forked (bī′fôrkt′) *adj.* Bifurcate.

bi·form (bī′fôrm′) *adj.* Having or combining the characteristics of two distinct forms, as the Minotaur. Also **bi′formed′.**

Bif·rost (bēf′rost) In Norse mythology, the bridge of the rainbow between Asgard and Midgard.

bi·fur·cate (bī′fər·kāt, bī·fûr′kāt) *v.t. & v.i.* **·cat·ed, ·cat·ing** To fork; divide into two branches or stems. —*adj.* (bī′fər·kāt, bī·fûr′·kit) Forked: also **bi′fur·cat′ed, bi·fur·cous** (bī·fûr′kəs). [< BI- + L *furca* fork] —**bi′fur·cate·ly** (-kit·lē) *adv.* —**bi′fur·ca′tion** *n.*

big[1] (big) *adj.* **big·ger, big·gest** 1 Of great size, amount, or intensity; large; bulky. 2 Fruitful; pregnant. 3 Full to overflowing; teeming. 4 Puffed up; pompous. 5 Important: a *big* day in his life. 6 Generous; magnanimous. See synonyms under LARGE. —*adj. Colloq.* Pompously; extravagantly: to talk *big.* [ME; origin uncertain] —**big′gish** *adj.* —**big′ly** *adv.* —**big′ness** *n.*

big[2] (big) *v.t. & v.i. Scot.* To build. Also **bigg.**

big·a·mist (big′ə·mist) *n.* One guilty of bigamy.

big·a·mous (big′ə·məs) *adj.* 1 Guilty of or living in bigamy. 2 Involving bigamy. —**big′a·mous·ly** *adv.*

big·a·my (big′ə·mē) *n.* The criminal offense of marrying any other person while having a legal spouse living. [< OF *bigamie* < LL *bigamus* < *bis* twice + Gk. *gamos* wedding]—**bi·gam·ic** (bī·gam′ik) *adj.*

big·ar·reau (big′ə·rō, big′ə·rō′) *n.* A type of sweet, firm-fleshed, heart-shaped cherry. Also **big·a·roon** (big′ə·rōōn′). [< F < *bigarré.* pp. of *bigarrer* variegate]

big bang theory Astronomical theory that the universe began in a single, gigantic explosion of flammable gases.

Big Ben 1 A bell which strikes the hour in the Westminster clock in the tower of the Houses of Parliament, London. 2 The clock itself.

Big Bend National Park A government reservation (1,082 square miles) in westernmost Texas, established in 1944 in **Big Bend,** the wide angle of the Rio Grande forming the Mexican border.

Big Dipper A group of seven stars resembling a dipper in outline in the constellation Ursa Major.

Big-end·i·an (big·en′dē·ən) *n.* A partisan in small matters of dispute: from Swift's *Gulliver's Travels,* in which one religious party (the *Big-endians*) of Lilliput opposed the other (the Little-endians) by maintaining that boiled eggs should be broken at the big end.

bigg (big) *n. Scot.* 1 The four-rowed barley *(Hordeum vulgare),* a hardy species grown in high latitudes. 2 Loosely, barley. Also **big.** [< ON *bygg*]

big game 1 Large wild animals hunted for sport. 2 *Colloq.* The objective of any important or difficult undertaking.

big·gin (big′in) *n.* 1 A head covering; especially, a child's cap. 2 *Brit.* The coif of a sergeant at law. 3 *Brit. Dial.* A nightcap. [< F *beguin* cap, orig. worn by the Beguines]

big·ging (big′in) *n. Scot.* 1 A house; residence. 2 The act of building. Also **big′gin.** [< BIG[2]]

big·gi·ty (big′ə·tē) *adj. U.S. Dial.* Conceited; pompous; uppity.

big·head (big′hed′) *n.* 1 *Colloq.* Inflated conceit; pomposity. 2 A bulging of the skull of an animal, due to osteomalacia. 3 A contagious inflammation of the lungs and intestines of young turkeys.

big-head·ed fly (big′hed′id) A fly (family *Pipunculidae*) with a large hemispherical head almost completely covered by two large compound eyes. The larvae destroy leafhoppers. See illustration under INSECT (beneficial).

big-heart·ed (big′här′tid) *adj.* Generous; charitable.

big·horn (big′hôrn′) *n. pl.* **·horns** or **·horn** The Rocky Mountain sheep *(Ovis canadensis),* remarkable for its large horns: also called *American argali.*

Bighorn Mountains A range of the Rockies in southern Montana and northern Wyoming; highest peak, 13,165 feet.

Bighorn River A river in northern Wyoming and southern Montana, flowing north 461 miles to the Yellowstone River.

bight (bīt) *n.* **1** A slightly receding bay; a small recess in a bay. **2** A bend in a river, or the like. **3** A loop or turn in a rope, as around a post, the two ends being fast. **4** A bending or angle. —*v.t.* To secure (a load, sail, etc.) as with a bight. ◆ Homophone: *bite.* [OE *byht* corner, bay < *būgan* bend]

Big Inch A 24-inch oil pipeline, 1,400 miles from Longview, Texas, to the Atlantic seaboard.

big money *U.S. Colloq.* A large amount of money; huge profits.

big·no·ni·a (big·nō′nē·ə) *n.* Any of a genus *(Bignonia)* of woody climbing plants, mostly of tropical America, with clusters of large, trumpet-shaped flowers. [after A. J. *Bignon,* 1711–72, librarian to Louis XV]

big·no·ni·a·ceous (big·nō′nē·ā′shəs) *adj.* Of or belonging to the *Bignoniaceae,* or bignonia family, a large group of trees, shrubs, and woody vines characterized by trumpet-shaped flowers.

big·ot (big′ət) *n.* An illiberal or intolerant adherent of a religious creed or of any party or opinion. [<F]

big·ot·ed (big′ət·id) *adj.* Stubbornly attached to a creed, party, system, or opinion. —**big′·ot·ed·ly** *adv.*

big·ot·ry (big′ət·rē) *n. pl.* **·ries** Obstinate and intolerant attachment to a cause or creed. See synonyms under FANATICISM.

big shot *Slang* A person of importance.

Big Stone Lake A narrow lake between NE South Dakota and western Minnesota; 25 miles long.

Big Thomp·son River (tomp′sən) A river in northern Colorado, flowing 78 miles east to the South Platte River.

big top *U.S. Colloq.* The main tent of a circus.

big tree The redwood of California.

big wheel *U.S. Slang* A person of importance.

big·wig (big′wig′) *n. Colloq.* A person of importance: in allusion to the big wigs formerly worn by people of consequence in England.

Bi·har (bi·här′) **1** A constituent state of NE India; 70,368 square miles; capital, Patna; formerly **Bihar and Orissa,** a province of British India. **2** A city in north central Bihar.

Bi·ha·ri (bi·hä′rē) *n.* **1** A native of Bihar. **2** The Sanskritic language spoken in NE India, belonging to the Indic branch of the Indo-Iranian languages.

bi-hour·ly (bī·our′lē) *adj.* Occuring once in two hours.

Biisk (bēsk) See BISK.

bi·jou (bē′zhōō, bē·zhōō′) *n. pl.* **bi·joux** (bē′·zhōōz, bē·zhōōz′) A jewel; a trinket. [<F]

bi·jou·te·rie (bē·zhōō′tər·ē) *n.* Jewelry; especially, an article of fine workmanship.

bi·ju·gate (bī′jōō·gāt, bī·jōō′git) *adj. Bot.* Two-paired, as a pinnate leaf with two pairs of leaflets. Also **bi·ju·gous** (bī′jōō·gəs).

Bi·ka·ner (bē′kə·nēr′) A city in northern Rajasthan; former capital of a princely state of the same name now included in Rajasthan.

bike[1] (bīk) *n. Colloq.* A bicycle. [Alter. of BICYCLE]

bike[2] (bīk) *n. Scot.* A nest or swarm of wild bees, wasps, ants, etc.; hence, a swarm; a crowd: also spelled *byke, beik.*

bi·ki·ni (bi·kē′nē) *n.* An extremely abbreviated or scanty bathing suit.

Bi·ki·ni (bi·kē′nē) An atoll in the Marshall islands; 2 square miles; site of U.S. atomic bomb tests, July 1946.

Bi·kol (bi·kōl′) *n.* Bicol.

bi·la·bi·al (bī·lā′bē·əl) *adj.* **1** *Phonet.* Articulated with both lips, as certain consonants. **2** Having two lips. —*n. Phonet.* A speech sound formed with both lips, as (b), (p), (m), and (w).

bi·la·bi·ate (bī·lā′bē·āt, -it) *adj. Bot.* Two-lipped: said of a corolla.

bil·an·der (bil′ən·dər, bī′lən-) *n.* A small two-masted vessel having a lateen mainsail: used principally on the canals in the Low Countries. [<Du. *bylander*]

bi·lat·er·al (bī·lat′ər·əl) *adj.* Pertaining to two sides; two-sided: a *bilateral* agreement. —**bi·lat′er·al·ly** *adv.* —**bi·lat′er·al·ness** *n.*

Bil·ba·o (bil·bä′ō) A port in northern Spain on **Bilbao Bay,** an inlet of the Bay of Biscay.

bil·ber·ry (bil′ber′ē, -bər·ē) *n.* **1** The European whortleberry. **2** Its blue-black fruit. [<Scand. Cf. Dan. *böllebær*]

bil·bo (bil′bō) *n. pl.* **·boes** **1** A finely tempered Spanish sword made at Bilbao. **2** A fetter consisting of two sliding shackles attached to an iron bar. [from BILBAO]

bile (bīl) *n.* **1** *Physiol.* A bitter viscid fluid, yellowish in man and green in herbivores, secreted by the liver. **2** Anger; peevishness. [<L *bilis* bile, anger]

bi·lec·tion (bī·lek′shən) *n.* Bolection.

bile ducts *Physiol.* The excretory ducts of the gall bladder.

bile·stone (bīl′stōn′) *n. Pathol.* A biliary calculus; gallstone.

bilge (bilj) *n.* **1** *Naut.* The rounded part of a ship's bottom; specifically, that part extending from the keel to the point from which the sides rise vertically. **2** The bulge of a barrel. **3** Bilge water. **4** *Slang* Stupid or trivial chatter or writing. —*v.t. & v.i.* **bilged, bilg·ing** **1** To break open the bottom of (a vessel). **2** To bulge or cause to bulge. [Var. of BULGE]

bilge·keel (bilj′kēl′) *n. Naut.* An outside keel set lengthwise on each side of the bilge of a vessel to lessen rolling. Also **bilge′piece′.**

bilge water Foul water that collects in the bilge of a ship.

bilg·y (bil′jē) *adj.* Resembling bilge water, as in smell.

bil·har·zi·a·sis (bil′här·zī′ə·sis) *n.* Schistosomiasis. [after Theodore M. *Bilharz,* 1825–1862, German parasitologist]

bil·i·ar·y (bil′ē·er′ē) *adj.* Pertaining to or conveying bile.

bi·lin·e·ar (bī·lin′ē·ər) *adj.* Formed of or related to two lines.

bi·lin·gual (bī·ling′gwəl) *adj.* **1** Recorded or expressed in two languages. **2** Speaking two languages. —**bi·lin′gual·ly** *adv.* —**bi·lin′gual·ism** *n.*

bil·ious (bil′yəs) *adj.* **1** *Pathol.* Suffering from real or supposed disorder of the liver. **2** Of, pertaining to, containing, or consisting of bile. **3** Ill-natured; cross. [<F *bilieux* <L *biliosus*] —**bil′ious·ly** *adv.* —**bil′ious·ness** *n.*

bi·lit·er·al (bī·lit′ər·əl) *adj.* Composed of two letters. —**bi·lit′er·al·ism** *n.*

-bility *suffix* Forming nouns of quality from adjectives in *-ble*: *probability* from *probable.* [<F *-bilité* <L *-bilitas, -tatis*]

bilk (bilk) *v.t.* **1** To cheat; swindle; evade payment to. **2** To escape; dodge. **3.** To balk. —*n.* **1** A swindler; deadbeat. **2** A trick; a hoax. [Origin unknown] —**bilk′er** *n.*

bill[1] (bil) *n.* **1** A statement of an account or of money due. **2** A banknote or treasury note: a ten-dollar *bill.* **3** A list of items: a *bill* of fare. **4** The draft of a proposed law. **5** *Law* A paper filed in a court calling for some specific action. **6** Some public notice or advertisement; the program of a theatrical performance. **7** *Brit.* A bill of exchange. **8** Loosely, a promissory note. **9** In Scots law, a petition to the court of sessions. **10** *Obs.* Any writing; a billet; petition. See synonyms under MONEY. —*v.t.* **1** To enter in a bill; charge. **2** To present a bill to. **3** To advertise by bills or placards. [<LL *billa,* var. of *bulla.* See BULL[2].]

bill[2] (bil) *n.* A beak, as of a bird. —*v.i.* To join bills, as doves; caress. —**to bill and coo** To caress lovingly; make love in soft murmuring tones. [OE *bile*]

bill[3] (bil) *n.* **1** A hook-shaped instrument used by gardeners in pruning: also **bill′hook′.** **2** An ancient weapon with a hook-shaped blade; a halberd. **3** The point or peak of the fluke of an anchor. [OE *bill* sword, ax]

bill[4] (bil) *n.* **1** A bellow or roar. **2** A boom, as of the bittern. [Var. of BELL[2]]

Bill (bil) Diminutive of WILLIAM.

bill·a·ble (bil′ə·bəl) *adj.* Indictable.

bil·la·bong (bil′ə·bong) *n. Austral.* **1** A blind branch or channel leading from a river; an incomplete anabranch. **2** A pool of stagnant water or the backwaters of a stream. [<native Australian *billa* water + *bong* dead]

bill·board (bil′bôrd′, -bōrd′) *n.* A board, panel, or tablet intended for the display of posters or placards; a bulletin board.

bil·let[1] (bil′it) *n.* **1** A written missive; a note. **2** A requisition on a household to maintain a soldier. **3** The place where soldiers are so lodged. **4** *Brit.* A position; appointment. —*v.t. & v.i.* **1** To lodge (soldiers), or to be quartered or lodged, in a private house. **2** To serve with a missive. [<OF *billete,* dim. of *bille* <L *bulla* seal, document] —**bil′let·er** *n.*

bil·let[2] (bil′it) *n.* **1** A stick, as of firewood. **2** Any short, thick stick. **3** *Archit.* One of a series of short, cylindrical ornaments, forming part of a molding. **4** A harness strap that passes through a buckle; also, the loop or pocket for receiving such a strap after it passes through the buckle. **5** *Metall.* A bloom of iron or steel drawn into a small bar. [<OF *billete,* dim. of *bille* log]

bil·let d'a·mour (bē·ye dà·mōōr′) *French* Love letter; billet-doux.

bil·let-doux (bil′ē·dōō′, *Fr.* bē·ye·dōō′) *n. pl.* **bil·lets-doux** (bil′ē·dōōz′, *Fr.* bē·ye·dōō′) A love letter; lover's note. [<F, lit., sweet note]

bill·fish (bil′fish′) *n. pl.* **·fish** or **·fish·es** One of various fishes having elongated jaws; especially, the saury or skipper, or the spearfish.

bill·fold (bil′fōld′) *n.* A folding case for paper money.

bill·head (bil′hed′) *n.* A heading on paper used for making out bills or itemized statements.

bil·liard (bil′yərd) *n. U.S. Colloq.* A carom. —*adj.* Of or pertaining to billiards: *billiard* cue, *billiard* player.

bil·liards (bil′yərdz) *n.* A game played with hard elastic or ivory balls **(billiard balls)** propelled by cues on an oblong, cloth-covered, cushion-edged table. [<F *billard* <OF *billart* cue < *bille* log] —**bil′liard·ist** *n.*

bill·ing (bil′ing) *n.* **1** The listing of performers or acts on a theater billboard, playbill, etc. **2** The relative eminence given to an actor or an act on such a listing.

Bil·lings (bil′ingz), **Josh** Pen name of Henry Wheeler Shaw, 1818–85, U.S. humorist.

bil·lings·gate (bil′ingz·gāt) *n.* Vulgar and abusive language. [from *Billingsgate* fish market, London]

bil·lion (bil′yən) *n.* **1** A thousand millions (1,000,000,000). **2** *Brit.* A million millions (1,000,000,000,000). [<F] —**bil·lionth** (bil′·yənth) *adj. & n.*

bil·lion·aire (bil′yən·âr′) *n.* One who owns property worth a billion of money.

Bil·li·ton (bi·lē′ton) See BELITUNG.

Bill·jim (bil′jim) *n.* The typical Australian: a nickname.

bill of exchange. See under EXCHANGE.

bill of fare A list of the dishes provided at a meal; a menu.

bill of health An official certificate of the crew's health issued to a ship's master on departure from a port.

bill of lading A written acknowledgment of goods received for transportation.

bill of rights **1** A formal summary and declaration of the fundamental principles of government and of the rights of individuals. **2** *Often cap.* The first ten amendments to the U.S. Constitution. **3** *Often cap.* The declaration of rights setting forth those fundamental principles of the British constitution, the observance of which was to be imposed upon William and Mary upon their acceptance of the crown in 1689.

bill of sale An instrument by which the transfer of title to personal property is declared and established.

bil·lon (bil′ən) *n.* **1** An alloy of gold or silver with some baser metal, generally copper or tin. **2** A low alloy of silver with a large proportion of copper, used in making tokens and medals. [<F <OF *bille* log]

bil·low (bil′ō) *n.* **1** A great wave of the sea; a

storm wave. **2** Any wave, as of sound, etc. **3** *pl.* The sea. — *v.i.* To rise or roll in billows; surge; swell. [<ON *bylgja*] — **bil′low·y** *adj* — **bil′low·i·ness** *n.*

bill·post·er (bil′pōs′tər) *n.* A person whose occupation it is to post bills on walls, fences, etc. Also **bill′stick′er.** — **bill′post′ing, bill′·stick′ing** *n.*

bil·ly[1] (bil′ē) *n. pl.* **bil·lies 1** A short bludgeon; a policeman's club. **2** A slubbing machine, used in the manufacture of textiles. [<*Billy,* a nickname for William]

bil·ly[2] (bil′ē) *n. Scot.* A comrade; crony; chum; also, a young fellow. Also **bil′lie.**

bil·ly[3] (bil′ē) *n. Austral.* A can used for heating water. [<native Australian *billa* water]

bil·ly·cock (bil′ē·kok′) *n. Brit.* A low-crowned felt hat; derby. Also **billycock hat.**

billy goat A male goat.

Billy the Kid Sobriquet of William H. Bonney, 1859–81, notorious Western cattle thief and murderer.

bi·lo·bate (bī·lō′bāt) *adj.* Divided into or having two lobes. Also **bi·lo′bat·ed.**

bi·lo·ca·tion (bī′lō·kā′shən) *n.* The power of being in two places at the same time.

bi·loc·u·lar (bī·lok′yə·lər) *adj. Biol.* Two-celled; divided into two cells.

Bi·lox·i (bi·lok′sē) *n.* One of a tribe of North American Indians of Siouan stock.

Bi·lox·i (bi·lok′sē) A city in SE Mississippi, on a peninsula in **Biloxi Bay,** an arm of Mississippi Sound.

bil·sted (bil′sted) *n. U.S.* The sweetgum.

bil·tong (bil′tong) *n.* Dried and cured meat of the ox, antelope, or buffalo, cut into strips and eaten raw. [<Afrikaans *bil* buttock + *tong* tongue; because it is cut mostly from the rump and resembles smoked tongue]

bim·a·nous (bim′ə·nəs, bī·mā′-) *adj.* Two-handed. [<NL *bimanus* <L *bis* twofold + *manus* hand]

bi·man·u·al (bī·man′yōō·əl) *adj.* Employing both hands. — **bi·man′u·al·ly** *adv.*

bi·men·sal (bī·men′səl) *adj.* Bimonthly.

bi·mes·tri·al (bī·mes′trē·əl) *adj.* Lasting two months. [<L *bimestris*]

bi·met·al·ism (bī·met′əl·iz′əm) *n.* The concurrent use of both gold and silver as the standard of currency and value. Also **bi·met′·al·lism.** — **bi·met′al·ist, bi·met′al·list** *n.*

bi·me·tal·lic (bī′mə·tal′ik) *adj.* **1** Consisting of or relating to two metals. **2** Having a double metallic coin standard. **3** Of or pertaining to bimetalism. [<F *bimétallique*]

Bim·i·ni Islands (bim′ə·nē) An island group in the NW Bahamas; 9 square miles; the legendary fountain of youth sought by Ponce de Leon was said to be here. Also **Bim′i·nis.**

bi·mo·lec·u·lar (bī′mə·lek′yə·lər) *adj. Chem.* Relating to two molecules: a *bimolecular* reaction.

bi·month·ly (bī·munth′lē) *adj.* & *adv.* Occurring once in two months. — *n.* A publication issued once in two months.

bi·mo·tored (bī·mō′tərd) *adj.* Having two motors, as an airplane.

bin (bin) *n.* **1** An enclosed place or large receptacle for holding meal, coal, etc. **2** A compartment in a wine cellar. **3** A basket used by hop pickers. — *v.t.* **binned, bin·ning** To store or deposit in a bin. [OE *binn* basket, crib <Celtic]

bin- Var. of BI-.

bi·nal (bī′nəl) *adj.* Double; twofold. [<L *bini* two]

bi·na·ry (bī′nə·rē) *adj.* **1** Pertaining to, characterized by, or made up of two; double; paired. **2** *Astron.* Denoting a pair of stars revolving about a common center. — *n. pl.* **·ries 1** A combination of two things; a couple; duality. **2** A binary star. [<L *binarius* <*bini* two, double]

binary star See under STAR.

binary system 1 A method of counting which has 2 for its base: still in use among certain primitive tribes of Australia and Africa. **2** *Math.* A system of numeration which can express any number by means of two digits, 0 and 1, in various combinations: applied especially in the operation of digital computers.

bi·nate (bī′nāt) *adj. Bot.* Being or growing in couples or pairs. [<NL *binatus* paired <L *bini* double, two by two] — **bi′nate·ly** *adv.*

bi·na·tion (bī·nā′shən) *n.* In the Roman Catholic Church, celebration of two masses within the same day by the same priest. [<Med. L *binatio, -onis* duplication <*bini* double]

bin·au·ral (bin·ôr′əl) *adj.* **1** Hearing with both ears. **2** Designating an apparatus for communicating faint or distant sounds simultaneously to both ears: a *binaural* stethoscope. **3** Two-eared. **4** Stereophonic.

bind (bīnd) *v.* **bound, bound** (*Archaic* **bound·en**), **bind·ing** *v.t.* **1** To tie together; make fast by tying. **2** To encircle, as with a belt. **3** To bandage; swathe: often with *up.* **4** To cause to cohere; cement. **5** To strengthen or ornament at the edge, as a garment. **6** To fasten together and secure within a cover, as a book. **7** To make irrevocable; seal, as a bargain. **8** To constrain or oblige to do or not to do, as by moral or legal authority: often with *over.* **9** To make constipated or costive. **10** To apprentice: often with *out.* — *v.i.* **11** To tie up anything: to reap and *bind.* **12** To cohere; stick together. **13** To have binding force; be obligatory. **14** To become stiff or hard, as cement; jam, as gears. — **to bind over** *Law* To hold under bond for appearance at a future time. — *n.* **1** That which fastens, ties, or binds. **2** *Music* A curved line, tie, or brace. [OE *bindan*]

Synonyms (verb): compel, engage, fasten, fetter, fix, oblige, restrain, restrict, secure, shackle, tie. *Binding* is primarily by something flexible, as a cord or bandage drawn closely around an object or a group of objects, as when we *bind* up a wounded limb. We *bind* a sheaf of wheat with a cord; we *tie* the cord in a knot; we *fasten* by any means that will make things hold together, as a board by nails or a door by a lock. *Bind* has an extensive figurative use. One is *bound* by conscience or honor; he is *obliged* by some imperious necessity; *engaged* by his own promise; *compelled* by physical force or its moral equivalent. *Antonyms*: free, loose, unbind, unfasten, unloose, untie.

bind·er (bīn′dər) *n.* **1** One who or that which binds. **2** One who binds books. **3** *Agric.* A device on a reaping machine for binding grain. **4** An attachment on a sewing machine to secure an edging. **5** A surety or written pledge for payment or performance of a contract. **6** A folder in which sheets of paper may be fastened, as for a notebook. **7** In painting, a material used to cause the pigment to adhere to a surface, as solutions of gum, glue, or casein, oils and resins, and (in fresco painting) lime. **8** In construction, a beam of steel or wood serving to support the bridging joists in a floor. **9** *Metall.* A substance used to promote the cohesion of crushed ore particles or finely powdered metallic dust before or in the process of sintering. **10** The cord or braiding which binds the edges of a fabric.

bind·er·y (bīn′dər·ē) *n. pl.* **·er·ies** A place where books are bound.

bind·ing (bīn′ding) *adj.* Causing to be bound; obligatory. — *n.* **1** The act of fastening or joining. **2** Anything that binds objects to each other, as the cover of a book. **3** Any thickening substance added to a mixture to cause the various ingredients to adhere; a binder. **4** A strip sewed over an edge for protection. **5** A course of masonry by which adjoining parts are secured. — **bind′ing·ly** *adv.* — **bind′ing·ness** *n.*

binding energy *Physics* The energy associated with the loss of mass occurring when the constituent particles of an atomic nucleus are closely bound together.

bind·weed (bīnd′wēd′) *n.* Any plant of the genus *Convolvulus,* or similar plant of strong twining habit.

bine (bīn) *n.* A flexible shoot or climbing stem of a plant; specifically, a hop vine: used of other climbers, in composition: wood*bine.* [Var. of BIND]

Bi·net-Si·mon (bi·nā′sī′mən, *Fr.* bē·ne′sē·môṅ′) **scale** *Psychol.* A system of rating the intelligence and mental development of children according to their performance in carefully selected and graded tests: used in the determination of mental age. See also STANFORD REVISION. [after Alfred *Binet,* 1857–1911, and Théodore *Simon,* born 1873, French psychologists]

bing[1] (bing) *interj.* A word imitating any sharp metallic sound, as of a rifle shot. — *n.* The sound thus produced. — *v.i.* To make this sound: The guns *binged* away. [Imit.]

bing[2] (bing) *n. Scot.* & *Brit. Dial.* A pile or heap of anything. [<ON *bingr* heap]

binge (binj) *n. Slang* A drunken carousal; spree. [? <dial. E *binge* soak]

Bing·en (bing′ən) A town on the Rhine in Rhineland-Palatinate, Germany.

Bing·ham·ton (bing′əm·tən) A city on the Susquehanna River in south central New York.

bin·go (bing′gō) *n.* A variety of keno: also called *beano.* [Origin unknown]

Binh·dinh (bin′din′) A town in southern Vietnam. Also **Binh Dinh.**

bin·it (bin′it) *n.* Bit[4].

bin·na·cle (bin′ə·kəl) *n. Naut.* A stand or case for a ship's compass: placed usually before the steering wheel. [Var. of *bittacle* <Pg. *bitacola* <LL *habitaculum* little house]

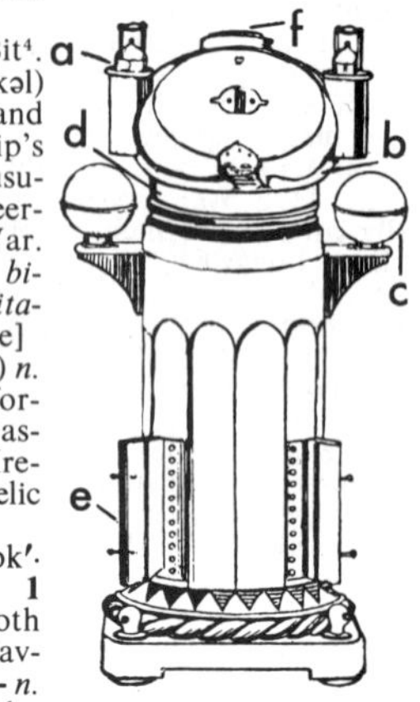

BINNACLE
a. Lamp.
b. Hood.
c. Quadrilateral sphere.
d. Compass chamber.
e. Magnet chamber.
f. Window to admit light to compass chamber.

bin·nogue (bin′ōg) *n.* A headdress formerly worn by peasant women in Ireland. [<Irish Gaelic *beannōg*]

bin·oc·u·lar (bə·nok′·yə·lər, bī-) *adj.* **1** Pertaining to both eyes at once. **2** Having two eyes. — *n. Often pl.* A telescope, opera glass, etc., adapted for use by both eyes at once. Also **bin·o·cle** (bin′ə·kəl). — **bin·oc′u·lar′i·ty** (-lar′·ə·tē) *n.* — **bin·oc′u·lar·ly** *adv.*

bi·no·mi·al (bī·nō′mē·əl) *adj.* Consisting of two names or terms. — *n.* **1** *Math.* An algebraic expression having two terms. **2** In taxonomy, a name consisting of two words, one indicating the genus, the other the species of a plant or animal. [<Med. L *binomius* having two names] — **bi·no′mi·al·ly** *adv.*

binomial system The system which assigns to every plant and animal a Latinized scientific name consisting of two terms, the first indicating the genus and the second the species: *Latrodectus mactans,* the black-widow spider. Also **binomial nomenclature.**

binomial theorem *Math.* The theorem stating the general form of any power of an algebraic binomial.

bi·nom·i·nal (bī·nom′ə·nəl) *adj.* Of, having, or characterized by two names.

bi·nu·cle·ate (bī·nōō′klē·āt, -nyōō′-) *adj.* Having two nuclei, as a cell. Also **bi·nu′cle·ar, bi·nu′cle·at′ed.**

Bin·ue (bin′wā) See BENUE.

Bin·yon (bin′yən), **Laurence,** 1869–1943, English poet and art critic.

bio- *combining form* Life: *biology, biography.* [<Gk. *bios* life]

bi·o-aer·a·tion (bī′ō·âr·ā′shən, -ā′ə·rā′-) *n.* A method of purifying sewage by aerating it in specially designed centrifugal pumps.

bi·o-as·say (bī′ō·as′ā) *n.* The determination of the properties and effects of a drug by testing it under controlled conditions in the bodies of standard laboratory animals.

Bí·o-Bí·o (bē′ō·bē′ō) A river in south central Chile, flowing 240 miles to the Pacific.

bi·o·blast (bī′ə·blast) *n.* Bioplast.

bi·o·cat·a·lyst (bī′ō·kat′ə·list) *n.* An enzyme.

bi·oc·el·late (bī·os′ə·lāt, bī′ō·sel′it) *adj. Biol.* Having two eyelike marks or ocelli. [<BI- + OCELLATE]

bi·o·chem·is·try (bī′ō·kem′is·trē) *n.* That branch of chemistry relating to vital processes, their mode of action, and their products. — **bi′o·chem′ic, bi′o·chem′i·cal** *adj.* — **bi′o·chem′i·cal·ly** *adv.* — **bi′o·chem′ist** *n.*

bi·o·chore (bī′ə·kôr, -kōr) *n. Ecol.* **1** That region of the earth having a climate favorable to life. **2** A climatic boundary for a given plant group. [<Gk. *bios* life + *chōrē* land, country] — **bi′o·chor′ic** *adj.*

bi·o·ci·dal (bī′ə·sīd′l) *adj.* Destructive of life, as certain poisons and antibiotics.
bi·o·coe·no·sis (bī′ō·sē·nō′sis) *n. Ecol.* An association of plants and animals in a given habitat and under similar environmental conditions. Also **bi·o·coe·nose** (bī′ō·sē′nōs). [< BIO- + Gk. *koinōsis* sharing] **—bi′o·coe·not′ic** (-not′·ik) *adj.*
bi·o·de·grad·a·ble (bī′ō·di′grā′də·bəl) *adj. Chem.* Capable of being broken down, as a compound, by bacterial action. [< BIO- + DEGRADABLE]
bi·o·dy·nam·ics (bī′ō·dī·nam′iks) *n.* The branch of biology that treats of the activities of living organisms. **—bi′o·dy·nam′ic** or **·i·cal** *adj.*
bi·o·e·lec·tric·i·ty (bī′ō·i·lek′tris′ə·tē) *n.* Those phenomena of electricity which are associated with and characteristic of living matter. — **bi′o·e·lec′tri·cal** *adj*
bi·o·eth·ics (bī′ō·eth′iks) *n. pl. (construed as sing.)* The study of the ethical implications of medical practice, especially in regard to the preservation of human life. **—bi′o·eth′i·cal** *adj.* — **bi′o·eth′i·cist** (-eth′ə·sist) *n.*
bi·o·feed·back (bī′ō·fēd′bak) *n.* Voluntary control by feedback of involuntary functions, as heart rate.
bi·o·gen (bī′ə·jən) *n. Biochem.* The hypothetical large protein molecular unit assumed to be active in the functioning of body tissues.
bi·o·gen·e·sis (bī′ō·jen′ə·sis) *n.* **1** The doctrine that life is generated from living organisms only. **2** Such generation itself: opposed to *abiogenesis.* Also **bi·og·e·ny** (bī·oj′ə·nē). **—bi·o·ge·net·ic** (bī′ō·jə·net′ik) or **·i·cal** *adj.* **—bi′o·ge·net′i·cal·ly** *adv.*
bi·o·ge·og·ra·phy (bī′ō·jē·og′rə·fē) *n.* The science of the geographical distribution of living organisms. **—bi′o·ge′o·graph′ic** (-jē′ə·graf′ik) or **·i·cal** *adj.* **—bi′o·ge′o·graph′i·cal·ly** *adv.*
bi·og·ra·pher (bī·og′rə·fər, bē-) *n.* One who writes an account of a person's life.
bi·og·ra·phy (bī·og′rə·fē, bē-) *n. pl.* **·phies** **1** A written account of a person's life. **2** That form of literature dealing with the facts and events of individual experience. **3** Biographies collectively. See synonyms under HISTORY. [< LGk. *biographia* < *bios* life + *graphein* write] **—bi·o·graph·ic** (bī′ə·graf′ik) or **·i·cal** *adj.* **—bi′o·graph′i·cal·ly** *adv.*
bi·o·log·i·cal (bī′ə·loj′i·kəl) *adj.* **1** Of or pertaining to biology, or to the science of vital functions, structures, and processes. **2** Used for or produced by biological research or practice. Also **bi′o·log′ic. —bi′o·log′i·cal·ly** *adv.*
biological engineering The artificial selection of different strains of a plant or animal species to improve the structure, function, or yield of an organism, esp. a plant or animal of economic importance.
bi·o·log·i·cals (bī′ə·loj′i·kəlz) *n. pl.* Drugs and medicinal preparations obtained from animal tissues and other organic sources.
bi·ol·o·gism (bī·ol′ə·jiz′əm) *n. Philos.* The doctrine that biological methods are applicable to the entire field of human experience.
bi·ol·o·gist (bī·ol′ə·jist) *n.* One having special knowledge of biology.
bi·ol·o·gy (bī·ol′ə·jē) *n.* The science of life and of the origin, structure, reproduction, growth, and development of living organisms collectively: its two main divisions are botany and zoology. [< BIO- + -LOGY]
bi·o·lu·mi·nes·cence (bī′ō·lōō′mə·nes′əns) *n.* The emission of light by living organisms, as fireflies, certain fungi, and deep-sea fishes. — **bi′o·lu′mi·nes′cent** *adj.*
bi·ol·y·sis (bī·ol′ə·sis) *n.* The dissolution of life. [< BIO- + Gk. *lysis* loosing] **—bi·o·lyt·ic** (bī′ə·lit′ik) *adj.*
bi·o·mass (bī′ō·mas′) *n.* The total amount of plant material in a given area, esp. when considered as an energy source.
bi·o·me·chan·ics (bī′ō·mə·kan′iks) *n.* The study of the mechanics of living organisms, especially under conditions of sudden, violent, or prolonged strain. **—bi′o·me·chan′i·cal** *adj.* — **bi′o·me·chan′i·chal·ly** *adv.*
bi·om·e·try (bī·om′ə·trē) *n.* **1** A measuring or calculating of the probable duration of human life. **2** Biology from a statistical point of view, especially with reference to problems of variation: also **bi·o·met·rics** (bī′ə·met′riks). [< BIO + -METRY] **—bi′o·met′ric** or **·ri·cal** *adj.* — **bi′o·met′ri·cal·ly** *adv.*
bi·on·ics (bī·on′iks) *n.* The science of relating the functioning of biological systems to the development of electronic devices. [< BIO- + (ELECTR)ONICS]
bi·o·nom·ics (bī′ə·nom′iks) *n.* The branch of biology treating of habits and adaptation; ecology. **—bi′o·nom′ic** or **·i·cal** *adj.* **—bi′o·nom′·i·cal·ly** *adv.* **—bi·on·o·mist** (bī·on′ə·mist) *n.*
bi·o·phys·ics (bī′ō·fiz′iks) *n.* The study of biological function, structure, and organization in relation to and by the methods of physics. — **bi′o·phys′i·cal** *adj.*
bi·o·plasm (bī′ō·plaz′əm) *n.* Formative living matter; protoplasm.
bi·op·sy (bī′op·sē) *n. Med.* The clinical and diagnostic examination of tissue and other material excised from the living subject: opposed to *autopsy, necropsy.* [< BIO- + Gk. *opsis* sight] — **bi·op·sic** (bī·op′sik) *adj.*
bi·o·psy·chol·o·gy (bī′ō·sī·kol′ə·jē) *n.* Psychobiology.
bi·o·rhythm (bī′ō·rith′əm) *n.* Any cyclic pattern of activity in an organism. **—bi′o·rhyth′mic** *adj.* **—bi·o·rhyth·mic·i·ty** (bī′ō·rith′mis′ə·tē) *n.*
bi·o·scope (bī′ə·skōp) *n.* **1** A motion-picture projector. **2** An instrument used in bioscopy.
bi·os·co·py (bī·os′kə·pē) *n. Med.* An examination to ascertain whether life exists or has ceased. [< BIO- + -SCOPY] **—bi·o·scop·ic** (bī′ə·skop′ik) *adj.*
-biosis *combining form* Method of living: *aerobiosis, symbiosis.* [< Gk. *biōsis* < *bios* life]
bi·os·o·phy (bī·os′ə·fē) *n.* A system of character development and national and international peace education. [< Gk. *bios* life + *sophia* knowledge]
bi·o·sphere (bī′ə·sfir) *n.* That portion of the earth and its environment within which life in any of its forms is manifested.
bi·o·stat·ics (bī′ō·stat′iks) *n.* The branch of biology that treats of the potentialities of organisms or of structure as related to function: distinguished from *biodynamics.* **—bi′o·stat′ic** or **·i·cal** *adj.*
bi·o·syn·the·sis (bī′ō·sin′thə·sis) *n.* The chemical synthesis of organic materials, especially of a fibrous nature, from elementary living units or cells. **—bi·o·syn·thet·ic** (bī′ō·sin·thet′·ik) *adj.*
bi·o·ta (bī·ō′tə) *n. Ecol.* The combined fauna and flora of any geographical area or geological period. [< Gk. *biotē* life, living < *bios* life]
bi·o·tech·nol·o·gy (bī′ō·tek·nol′jē) *n.* The application of industrial techniques to the exploitation of biological processes.
bi·ot·ic (bī·ot′ik) *adj.* Pertaining to life. Also **bi·ot′i·cal.**
biotic potential **1** *Biol.* The inherent capacity of an organism to survive and reproduce under given or optimum conditions. **2** A measure of the innate vitality of a species confronted by an unfavorable or hostile environment.
bi·ot·ics (bī·ot′iks) *n.* The science of the functions of living organisms.
bi·o·tin (bī′ə·tin) *n. Biochem.* A crystalline acid, $C_{10}H_{16}O_3N_2S$, forming part of the vitamin B complex: it is essential in preventing the death of animals from an excess of egg white in the diet: also called *vitamin H.*
bi·o·tite (bī′ə·tīt) *n.* A common, brown or dark-green magnesium iron mica. [after J. B. *Biot,* 1774–1862, French physicist] **—bi′o·tit′ic** (-tit′ik) *adj.*
bi·o·tope (bī′ə·tōp) *n. Ecol.* An area, usually small and of uniform environmental conditions, characterized by relatively stable biotypes. [< BIO- + Gk. *topos* region]
bi·o·tox·ic (bī′ō·tok′sik) *adj.* Of or pertaining to natural poisons produced by plants and animals.
bi·o·type (bī′ō·tīp) *n. Biol.* **1** A race or strain that breeds true or almost true. **2** A group of individuals all of which have the same genotype. — **bi′o·typ′ic** (-tip′ik) *adj.* **—bi′o·ty·pol′o·gy** (-tī·pol′ə·jē) *n.*
bi·pa·ri·e·tal (bī′pə·rī′ə·təl) *adj. Anat.* Of or pertaining to the two parietal bones.
bip·a·rous (bip′ə·rəs) *adj.* **1** *Bot.* Having two lateral axes, as certain cymes. **2** *Zool.* Bringing forth two at a birth. [< BI- + -PAROUS]
bi·par·ti·san (bī·pär′tə·zən) *adj.* Composed of, pertaining to, or advocated by representatives of two political parties. **—bi·par′ti·san·ship** *n.*
bi·par·tite (bī·pär′tīt) *adj.* **1** Consisting of two corresponding parts. **2** *Bot.* Two-parted almost to the base, as certain leaves. Also **bi·part′ed.** — **bi·par′tite·ly** *adv.* **—bi·par·ti·tion** (bī′pär·tish′ən) *n.*
bi·ped (bī′ped) *n.* An animal having two feet. —*adj.* Two-footed: also **bi·pe·dal** (bī′pə·dəl, bip′ə-). [< L *bipes, bipedis* two-footed]
bi·pet·al·ous (bī·pet′əl·əs) *adj. Bot.* Dipetalous.
bi·phen·yl (bī·fen′əl, -fē′nəl) *n. Chem.* A colorless crystalline hydrocarbon, $C_6H_5{\cdot}C_6H_5$, found in coal tar: used in lacquers and as a preservative of citrus fruit. Also called *diphenyl.*
bi·pin·nate (bī·pin′āt) *adj. Bot.* Twice or doubly pinnate, as a leaf. Also **bi·pin′nat·ed.** — **bi·pin′nate·ly** *adv.*
bi·plane (bī′plān′) *n. Aeron.* A type of airplane having two parallel connected wings arranged one above the other: distinguished from *monoplane* and *triplane.*
bi·pod (bī′pod) *n.* A two-legged rest or stand, as for a rifle or machine-gun. [< BI- + -POD]
bi·po·lar (bī·pō′lər) *adj.* **1** Relating to or possessing two poles. **2** *Biol.* **a** Describing marine organisms found in both polar regions but nowhere else. **b** Having two prolongations of cell matter: said of nerve cells. **—bi·po·lar·i·ty** (bī′pō·lar′ə·tē) *n.*
bi·pro·pel·lant (bī′prə·pel′ənt) *n.* A propellant for rockets consisting of two chemicals, each of which is fed separately into the combustion chamber.
bi·quad·rate (bī·kwod′rāt) *n. Math.* A fourth power or the square of a square.
bi·quad·rat·ic (bī′kwod·rat′ik) *Math. adj.* Containing or referring to a fourth power. —*n.* **1** A fourth power. **2** A biquadratic equation.
bi·ra·di·al (bī·rā′dē·əl) *adj. Biol.* Having the radii set bilaterally and radially, as certain sea anemones.
birch (bûrch) *n.* **1** Any of an important genus *(Betula)* of deciduous trees and shrubs of the northern hemisphere, often having outer bark easily separable in sheets. **2** A rod or twig from a birch tree, used as a whip. **3** The tough, close-grained hardwood of the birch tree. **—v.t.** To whip with a birch rod; flog. —*adj.* Composed or fashioned of birch: also **birch·en.** [OE *birce*]
bird (bûrd) *n.* **1** A warm-blooded, feathered, egg-laying vertebrate (class *Aves*), having the forelimbs modified as wings. ◆Collateral adjective: *avian.* **2** A game bird; in England, a partridge. **3** *Obs.* The young of a fowl; a nestling. **4** *Slang* A peculiar or remarkable person. **5** *U.S. Slang* A hiss, or other call of disapproval, by an audience; usually in the phrases *to give* (one) *the bird, to get the bird.* **6** A clay pigeon; also, the shuttlecock in badminton. **—for the birds** *Slang* Worthless. —*v.t.* To trap or shoot birds. [OE *bridd*]

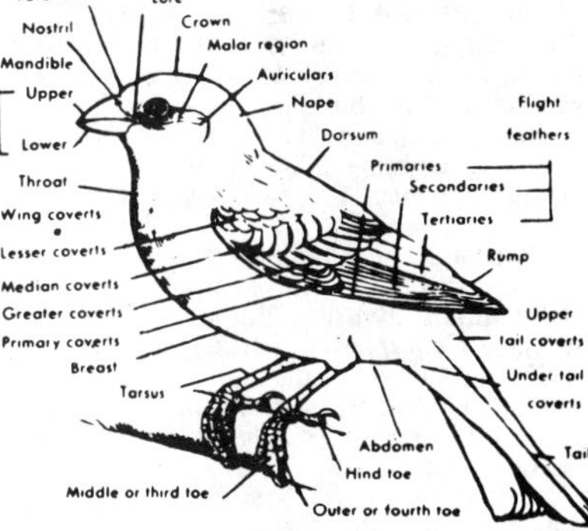

BIRD
Nomenclature for anatomical parts

bird·call (bûrd′kôl′) *n.* **1** An instrument for decoying birds by imitating their notes. **2** A bird's note in calling.
bird dog A dog that is trained to locate birds and retrieve them for hunters; specifically, a setter or pointer.

bird·grass (bûrd′gras′, -gräs′) *n.* **1** A North American grass *(Poa trivialis),* much cultivated for lawns. **2** Knotgrass.

bird·house (bûrd′hous′) *n.* **1** A small house or enclosure for birds; an aviary. **2** A small house, placed in trees, etc., in which birds may nest. Also **bird house.**

bird·ie (bûr′dē) *n.* **1** A small bird. **2** A whistling birdlike chirp, as on a radio transmission line, or in the body of an automobile, etc. **3** In golf, one stroke less than par in playing a hole.

bird·lime (bûrd′līm′) *n.* A sticky substance made from the inner bark of the holly or mistletoe: smeared on twigs to catch small birds. — *v.t.* **·limed, ·lim·ing** To smear or snare with birdlime; trap.

bird·man (bûrd′man′, -mən) *n. pl.* **·men** (-men′, -mən) **1** *Colloq.* An aviator. **2** A fowler. **3** An ornithologist.

bird of Minerva The owl.

bird of paradise A bird of New Guinea *(Paradisea apoda),* noted for the curious form and beauty of the plumage in the male.

bird of passage A bird that migrates with the changing seasons.

bird of prey Any of various raptorial birds, as an eagle, hawk, vulture, falcon, etc.

bird·pep·per (bûrd′pep′ər) *n.* Capsicum (def. 2).

birds·eye (bûrdz′ī′) *adj.* **1** Marked with spots resembling birds' eyes: *birdseye* cotton, *birdseye* maple. **2** Seen at a glance, and from above: a *birdseye* view; also, cursory. — *n.* **1** A plant with small, bright-colored flowers, the birdseye primrose *(Primula farinosa).* **2** The germander speedwell. **3** A textile fabric woven in a pattern of small eyelike indentations. **4** Any of various fabrics having such a pattern. Also **bird's′-eye′.**

bird's-foot (bûrdz′fo͝ot′) *n.* **1** Any plant of the genus *Ornithopus,* of the bean family, bearing curving pods. **2** Any one of various other plants, as a South African spurge *(Euphorbia ornithopus).*

bird's-foot fern A fern *(Pellaea mucronata)* from California, with tufted, deltoid, bipinnatifid fronds, 4 to 6 inches long, on rigid, dark chestnut-brown stipes.

bird's-foot trefoil Any plant of the genus *Lotus;* especially, the common species *(L. corniculatus)* of the Old World, a hardy perennial trailer.

bird's-foot violet A large-flowered pedate violet *(Viola pedata)* with large, pale-blue or purple, beardless flowers. See under VIOLET.

birds·nest (bûrdz′nest′) *n.* **1** The mucus secreted in the salivary glands of certain Asian swifts, used for building nests, and highly esteemed for making soup. **2** One of various plants resembling a bird's nest, as the wild carrot. **3** *Naut.* A crow's-nest. Also **bird's′-nest′.**

bird's nest A nest built by birds in which to lay eggs and hatch the young.

bird·wom·an (bûrd′wo͝om′ən) *n. fem. pl.* **·wom·en** *Colloq.* An aviatrix.

bird·y (bûr′dē) *n.* Birdie.

bi·reme (bī′rēm) *n.* An ancient galley having two banks of oars. [<L *biremis* < *bis* twofold + *remus* oar]

bi·ret·ta (bi·ret′ə) *n.* A stiff, square cap with three or four upright projections on the crown, worn by clerics of the Roman Catholic and other churches: also spelled *berretta.* [<Ital. *berretta* or Sp. *birreta* <LL *birretum* cap, dim. of *birrus* cape, cloak]

BIRETTA FOR PRIESTS

Bir·git·ta (bir·git′ə) Swedish form of BRIDGET.

bi·rit·u·al·ism (bi·rich′o͞o·əl·iz′əm) *n.* In the Roman Catholic Church, the use of a non-Latin rite, permitted a priest in cases of necessity.

birk (bûrk, birk) *n. Scot.* The birch. — **birk′en, birk′in** *adj.*

Birk·beck (bûrk′bek), **George,** 1776–1841, English physician; former of mechanics' institutions.

Bir·ken·head (bûr′kən·hed) A county borough in NW Cheshire, England, on the Mersey River opposite Liverpool.

Bir·ken·head (bûr′kən·hed), **Earl of,** 1872–1930, Frederick Edwin Smith, English jurist and statesman.

birl (bûrl) *v.t.* & *v.i.* **1** To rotate rapidly. **2** To spin with a humming sound. — *n.* A droning noise. ◆Homophone: *burl.* [Blend of BIRR and WHIRL]

birle (bûrl, birl) *v.t.* & *v.i. Brit. Dial.* To ply with drink; carouse: also spelled *byrl.* Also **birl.** [OE *byrelian* pour out drink < *byrele* cupbearer]

birl·ing (bûr′ling) *n.* A game between two lumberjacks in which each stands on an end of a floating log and rotates it with his feet so as to dislodge his opponent. [Origin uncertain]

Bir·ming·ham 1 (bûr′ming·əm) A city located in the West Midlands, England. **2** (bûr′ming·ham) A manufacturing city in north central Alabama.

Bir·ney (bûr′nē), **James G.,** 1792–1857, U.S. abolitionist.

Bi·ro·bi·dzhan (bir′ō·bi·jän′) An administrative division of the U.S.S.R. on the NE border of Manchuria; 13,800 square miles; capital, Birobidzhan: also *Jewish Autonomous Oblast.* Also **Bi′ro·bi·jan′.**

Bi·ron (byē′rən), **Ernst Johann,** 1690–1772, Russian statesman.

birr (bûr) *n. Scot.* **1** Onward rush; momentum; emphatic and rapid utterance. **2** A whirring or buzzing sound. **3** *Obs.* A rushing wind. — *v.i.* To move with or make a whirring noise. ◆Homophones: *bur, burr.* [<ON *byrr* favorable wind]

Bir·rell (bir′əl), **Augustine,** 1850–1933, English author.

birse (bûrs, *Scot.* birs) *Scot.* **1** A bristle; collectively, bristles. **2** Short hair, as of the head or beard. — **to set up one's birse** To make one angry.

birth (bûrth) *n.* **1** The fact or act of being born; nativity. **2** A beginning; an origin. **3** The bringing forth of offspring; parturition. **4** Ancestry or descent; lineage; also, the class into which one is born. **5** Offspring; issue. See synonyms under AFFINITY, KIN. ◆Homophone: *berth.* [<ON *byrth*] — **to give birth** To produce offspring.

birth canal *Anat.* The passage through which a child is delivered at birth, extending from the cervix uteri to the vulva.

birth control The regulation of conception by employing preventive methods or devices.

birth·day (bûrth′dā′) *n.* The day of one's birth or its anniversary: used also adjectively.

birth·mark (bûrth′märk′) *n.* A mark or stain existing on the body from birth; a nevus.

birth·place (bûrth′plās′) *n.* The place of one's birth or of origin in general.

birth rate The number of births per 1,000 inhabitants of a given district in any given period.

birth·right (bûrth′rīt′) *n.* Native right or privilege.

birth·root (bûrth′ro͞ot′, -ro͝ot′) *n.* Any of a genus *(Trillium)* of typically North American perennial herbs of the lily family; especially, *T. erectum,* which has astringent tuberlike rootstocks: sometimes used to hasten parturition.

birth·stone (bûrth′stōn′) *n.* A jewel identified with a particular month of the year: thought to bring good luck when worn by a person whose birthday falls in that month.

birth trauma *Psychoanal.* The deep psychic anxiety assumed to be implanted in a child at the moment of and by the act of birth: sometimes considered the basis for subsequent psychoneurotic disorders.

birth tree In folklore, a tree planted at the birth of a child in the belief that its welfare has some mysterious connection with the welfare of the child all his life.

birth·wort (bûrth′wûrt′) *n.* **1** Any plant of the genus *Aristolochia;* especially, *A. clematitis* of Europe, with stimulant tonic roots used as aromatic bitters. **2** Birthroot.

bis (bis) *adv.* **1** Twice: noting duplication or repetition. **2** Encore: a call for the repetition of a performance. [<L]

bis- Var. of BI-.

Bi·sa·yan (bē·sä′yən) See VISAYAN.

Bisayan Islands The Visayan Islands. Also **Bi·sa·yas** (bē·sä′yəz).

Bis·cay (bis′kā, -kē) One of the Basque provinces of northern Spain; 858 square miles; on the **Bay of Biscay,** a wide inlet of the Atlantic indenting the coast of western Europe from Brittany, France, to NW Spain: Spanish *Vizcaya.*

Bis·cayne Bay (bis′kān, bis·kān′) A shallow arm of the Atlantic south of Miami, Florida.

bis·cuit (bis′kit) *n.* **1** A kind of shortened bread baked in small cakes, raised with baking powder or soda. **2** *Brit.* A sweetened cracker or cookie. **3** Unglazed pottery which has been fired in the oven; bisque. [<OF *bescoit* < *bes* twice (<L *bis*) + *coit,* pp. of *cuire* cook <L *coquere*]

bis·cuit·root (bis′kit·ro͞ot′, -ro͝ot′) *n.* Wild parsley.

bise (bēz) *n.* **1** A cold northerly wind in Switzerland and parts of France, destructive to vegetation. **2** Misfortune; disaster.

bi·sect (bī·sekt′) *v.t.* **1** To cut into two parts; halve. **2** *Geom.* To divide into two parts of equal size. — *v.i.* **3** To fork, as a road. [<BI- + L *sectus,* pp. of *secare* cut] — **bi·sec′tion** *n.* — **bi·sec′tion·al** *adj.* — **bi·sec′tion·al·ly** *adv.*

bi·sec·tor (bī·sek′tər) *n.* **1** That which bisects. **2** *Geom.* A line or plane that bisects an angle or another line.

bi·sec·trix (bī·sek′triks) *n. pl.* **bi·sec·tri·ces** (bī′sek·trī′sēz) **1** The line bisecting the angle formed by the optic axes of a crystal. **2** A bisector.

bi·ser·rate (bī·ser′āt, -it) *adj.* **1** *Bot.* Doubly serrate, as a leaf. **2** *Entomol.* Serrate on both sides, as the antenna of an insect.

bi·sex·u·al (bī·sek′sho͞o·əl) *adj.* **1** *Biol.* Having the organs of both sexes. **2** *Bot.* Hermaphroditic, as a flower with both stamens and pistils. **3** Showing characters derived from both parents, as a hybrid. **4** *Psychol.* Equally attracted by both sexes. — **bi·sex′u·al·ism** *n.* — **bi·sex′u·al·ly** *adv.*

bish·op (bish′əp) *n.* **1** A spiritual overseer in the Christian church; in various churches, a clergyman of the highest order, and head of a diocese. **2** A hot drink made with mulled wine, sugar, oranges, etc. **3** A chessman, often carved to represent a miter, which may be moved diagonally any number of unoccupied squares of the same color. [OE *biscop* <LL *episcopus* bishop <Gk. *episkopos* overseer]

BISHOP (*def. 3*)

bish·op·ric (bish′əp·rik) *n.* The office or the diocese of a bishop.

bish·ops·cap (bish′əps·kap′) *n.* Any species of miterwort; especially, *Mitella diphylla.* Also **bish′op's-cap′.**

Bi·si·tun (bē′sə·to͞on′) See BEHISTUN.

Bisk (bēsk) A city in central Altai Territory, Russian S.F.S.R.: also *Biisk.*

Bis·marck (biz′märk) The capital of North Dakota, a city on the Missouri River.

Bis·marck (biz′märk, *Ger.* bis′-), **Prince Karl Otto Eduard Leopold von,** 1815–98, German statesman; founder of the German Empire.

Bismarck Archipelago An island group in the United Nations Trust Territory of New Guinea, comprising New Britain, New Ireland, Lavongai, and the Admiralty Islands; total, 19,200 square miles.

Bismarck Mountains A range in NE New Guinea; highest peak, 14,107 feet.

Bismarck Sea The SW arm of the Pacific enclosed by the Bismarck Archipelago.

bis·muth (biz′məth) *n.* A heavy, grayish, brittle, metallic element (symbol Bi, atomic number 83) used in alloys and in medicines and cosmetics. See PERIODIC TABLE. [<G] — **bis·muth·al** (biz′məth·əl) *adj.*

bis·mu·thic (biz·myo͞o′thik, -muth′ik) *adj. Chem.* Containing bismuth in its highest valence.

bis·muth·ous (biz′·məth·əs) *adj. Chem.* Containing bismuth in its lowest valence.

bi·son (bī′sən, -zən) *n.* A bovine ruminant, nearly related to the true ox; especially, the North American buffalo *(Bos* or *Bison bison). B. bonasus* is the European bison. [<L *bison* wild ox, ult. <Gmc.]

NORTH AMERICAN BISON (Up to 5¾ feet high at the shoulders)

bisque[1] (bisk) *n.* **1** A thick, rich soup made from meat or fish, especially shellfish. **2** A kind of ice-cream containing crushed macaroons. Also **bisk.** [<F]

bisque[2] (bisk) *n.* **1** In ceramics, biscuit. **2** Any of several shades of pinkish–beige. [< BISCUIT]

bisque[3] (bisk) *n.* An advantage given to an opponent in various games, as lawn tennis, consisting of a point or stroke to be taken at any time. [<F]

Bis·sau (bi·sou′) A port; the capital of Guinea–Bissau, formerly Portuguese Guinea, transferred here in 1941 from Bolama.

bis·sex·tile (bi·seks′təl, -tīl) *adj.* **1** Pertaining to the extra day occurring in leap year. **2** Pertaining to a leap year. —*n.* A leap year. [<L *bisextilis* intercalary <*bis* twice + *sextilis* sixth; so called because the sixth day before March 1 was doubled in leap year in the Julian calendar]

bis·ter (bis′tər) *n.* **1** A non–permanent, yellowish–brown pigment made from beechwood soot: used chiefly as a water–color wash. **2** A dark–brown color. Also **bis′tre.** [<F *bistre* dark brown] —**bis′tered** *adj.*

bis·tort (bis′tôrt) *n.* **1** A perennial herb *(Polygonum bistorta)* of Europe and Asia, with creeping rootstocks having astringent properties: also called *snakeweed.* **2** An allied herb, the Virginia bistort *(Tovara virginiana).* [<F <L *bis* twice + *tortus,* pp. of *torquere* twist]

bis·tou·ry (bis′tŏŏ·rē) *n. pl.* **·ries** *Surg.* A narrow–bladed knife for making minor incisions. [<OF *bistorie* dagger]

bis·tro (bis′trō, *Fr.* bē·strō′) *n. Colloq.* **1** A small night club or bar. **2** A restaurant or tavern where wine is served. [<F]

bi·sul·cate (bī·sul′kāt) *adj.* **1** Cleft in two; cloven–hoofed. **2** Two–grooved. Also **bi·sul′·cat·ed.** [<L *bisulcus* <*bis* twofold + *sulcus* furrow]

bi·sul·fate (bī·sul′fāt) *n. Chem.* An acid sulfate containing the group HSO_4.

bi·sul·fide (bī·sul′fīd) *n.* Disulfide. Also **bi·sul′·phide.**

bi·sul·fite (bī·sul′fīt) *n. Chem.* A salt of sulfurous acid in which the metal has replaced half the hydrogen in the acid: sodium *bisulfite,* $NaHSO_3$. Also **bi·sul′phite.**

Bi·su·tun (bē′sə·tōōn′) See BEHISTUN.

bi·sym·met·ri·cal (bī′si·met′ri·kəl) *adj.* Bilaterally symmetrical. Also **bi′sym·met′ric.** —**bi′·sym·met′ri·cal·ly** *adv.* —**bi·sym·met·ry** (bī·sim′·ə·trē) *n.*

bit[1] (bit) *n.* **1** A small piece, portion, or fragment; a little. **2** The smallest quantity; a whit; jot. **3** A small quantity of food; a morsel; taste; bite. **4** In Great Britain, a small coin, usually of a named value: a threepenny *bit.* **5** In the United States, the Spanish real or its equivalent, 12½ cents. **6** A short time. **7** *Slang* A typical or standard practice, procedure, or way of acting. —**a long bit** *U.S. Dial.* 15 cents. —**a short bit** *U.S. Dial.* 10 cents. —**two bits** *U.S. Colloq.* 25 cents. [OE *bita* <*bītan* bite]

Synonyms: dole, driblet, drop, installment, item, mite, morsel, particle, scrap.

BITS AND BITSTOCK
a. Brace.
b. Screwdriver bit.
c. Drill bit.
d. Ship auger bit.
e. Auger bit.
f. Expanding bit.
g. Cross-section of chuck for holding bits.

bit[2] (bit) *n.* **1** A wood–boring tool adapted to be used with a stock or brace. **2** The metallic mouthpiece of a bridle. **3** Anything that controls or holds in subjection. **4** One of various objects somewhat like a boring bit or a bridle bit. **5** The part of a key that engages the bolt or tumblers of a lock. **6** The cutting blade of a plane. —*v.t.* **bit·ted, bit·ting 1** To put a bit in the mouth of; train, as a horse, to the use of a bit. **2** To curb; restrain. **3** To make a bit on (a key). [OE *bite* a biting <*bītan* bite]

bit[3] (bit) Past tense of BITE.

bit[4] (bit) *n. Telecom.* A single unit of information; specifically, one of the coded digital signals forming part of a complete message in the operation of an electronic computing machine: also called *binit.* [<B(INARY) (DIG)-IT]

bi·tar·trate (bī·tär′trāt) *n. Chem.* A salt containing the univalent tartaric acid radical $C_4H_5O_6$; acid tartrate: potassium *bitartrate.*

bitch (bich) *n.* **1** The female of the dog or other canine animal. **2** *Slang* Wench; hussy: an abusive epithet, often implying lewdness. —*v.i. Slang* To complain. —**to bitch up** *Slang* To botch. [OE *bicce*]

bite (bīt) *v.* **bit, bit·ten** or *Colloq.* **bit, bit·ing** *v.t.* **1** To seize, tear, or wound with the teeth. **2** To cut or tear off with or as with the teeth: usually with *off:* He *bit* off his words. **3** To cut or pierce, as with a sword. **4** To sting, as mosquitoes. **5** To cause to smart, as a cold wind. **6** To eat into; corrode, as acid. **7** To grip; take hold of. **8** To cheat; trick. —*v.i.* **9** To seize or cut into something with the teeth. **10** To sting; have the effect of biting, as mustard. **11** To take firm hold; grip. **12** To take a bait, as fish. **13** To be tricked; accept a deceptive offer. —**to bite off more than one can chew** To attempt something beyond one's capabilities. —**to bite the dust** (or **ground**) To be vanquished or slain. —*n.* **1** The act of biting, or the hurt inflicted by biting; also, a painful sensation; smart. **2** A morsel of food; mouthful. **3** The grip or hold taken by a tool or piece of mechanism. ◆ Homophone: *bight.* [OE *bītan*] —**bit′a·ble, bite′a·ble** *adj.* —**bit′er** *n.*

Bi·thyn·i·a (bi·thin′ē·ə) An ancient country in NW Asia Minor.

bit·ing (bī′ting) *adj.* Keen; pungent; stinging. See synonyms under BITTER. —**bit′ing·ly** *adv.* —**bit′ing·ness** *n.*

Bi·tolj (bē′tôl·y′) A town in southern Yugoslavia. Also **Bi·tol** (bē′tôl). Turkish **Mon·as·tir** (mun·əs·tēr′).

bit part A small role in a play.

bit·stock (bit′stok′) *n.* A brace for a bit. For illustration see BIT.

bitt (bit) *n. Naut.* A post or vertical timber on a ship's deck, to which cables, etc., are made fast: usually in pairs. —*v.t.* To take a turn of (a cable) around a bitt or pair of bitts. [? <ON *biti* beam]

BITTS

bit·ten (bit′n) Past participle of BITE.

bit·ter[1] (bit′ər) *adj.* **1** Having a peculiar acrid taste, as quinine. **2** Producing pain of body or mind; keen; poignant; severe. **3** Feeling or showing hate or resentment. **4** Stinging; sharp; severe: said of words. —*n.* **1** That which is bitter; bitterness. **2** *pl.* A bitter vegetable tonic, usually spirituous. **3** *Brit.* Bitter beer. —*v.t. & v.i.* To make or become bitter. [OE *biter* <*bītan* bite] —**bit′ter·ish** *adj.* —**bit′ter·ly** *adv.* —**bit′ter·ness** *n.*

Synonyms (adj.): acerb, acetous, acid, acidulated, acidulous, acrid, acrimonious, biting, caustic, cutting, harsh, irate, pungent, savage, sharp, sour, stinging, tart, vinegarish, virulent. *Acid, sour,* and *bitter* agree in being contrasted with *sweet,* but *acid* or *sour* applies to the taste of vinegar or lemon juice; *bitter* to that of quassia, quinine, or strychnine. *Acrid* is nearly allied to *bitter. Pungent* suggests the effect of pepper or snuff on the organs of taste or smell; as, a *pungent* odor. *Caustic* indicates the corroding effect of some strong chemical, as nitrate of silver. In a figurative sense we say a *sour* face, *sharp* words, *bitter* complaints, *caustic* wit, *cutting* irony, *biting* sarcasm, a *stinging* taunt, *harsh* judgment, a *tart* reply. *Harsh* carries the idea of intentional and severe unkindness, *bitter* of a severity that arises from real or supposed ill–treatment. *Tart* and *sharp* utterances may proceed merely from a wit recklessly keen; *cutting, stinging,* or *biting* speech indicates more or less of hostile intent. The *caustic* utterance is meant to burn. Compare MALICIOUS, MOROSE. *Antonyms*: dulcet, honeyed, luscious, nectared, saccharine, sweet.

bit·ter[2] (bit′ər) *n. Naut.* A turn of the cable round a mooring bitt. [<BITT]

bitter apple The colocynth.

bitter end 1 *Naut.* The extreme end of a cable or rope, attached to the bitt. **2** The last extremity, as defeat or death.

bit·ter·end·er (bit′ər·en′dər) *n.* One who determines to continue a political, social, or any struggle to the end.

Bitter Lakes Two lakes in NE Egypt, joined and traversed by the Suez Canal.

bit·tern[1] (bit′ərn) *n.* A small, speckled, pale-buff heron *(Botaurus lentiginosus)* of North America, which utters a booming note in the breeding season. —**least bittern** The American dwarf bittern *(Ixobrychus exilis).* [<OF *butor,* ? <L *butio, -onis* a hawk]

bit·tern[2] (bit′ərn) *n.* **1** In salt manufacture, the waste liquor remaining after crystallization from brine. **2** A bitter mixture of quassia.

bitter principle Any of numerous bitter substances found in plants and not yet chemically classified.

bit·ter–root (bit′ər·rōōt′, -rŏŏt′) *n.* **1** An herb *(Lewisia rediviva)* with nutritious roots: State flower of Montana. **2** Any one of certain other North American plants, as the dogbane.

Bit·ter·root Range (bit′ər·rōōt′, -rŏŏt′) A range of the Rockies along the Idaho–Montana border; highest peak, 10,175 feet.

bit·ter·sweet (bit′ər·swēt′) *n.* **1** A coarse trailing plant, the woody nightshade, having oval bright–red berries. Its twigs and root have a taste at first bitter and afterward sweetish. **2** A shrubby or climbing plant *(Celastrus scandens),* with green flowers succeeded by orange pods that display a red aril. —*adj.* Combining bitter and sweet.

bit·ter·weed (bit′ər·wēd′) *n.* **1** A ragweed; especially, *Ambrosia artemisifolia.* **2** Any of various other plants yielding a bitter principle, as the horseweed and sneezeweed.

Bit·u·mas·tic (bich′ŏŏ·mas′tik) *n.* A quick–drying, bituminous paint resistant to heat and chemical fumes: a trade name.

bi·tu·men (bi·tōō′mən, -tyōō′-, bich′ŏŏ·mən) *n.* **1** Any native mixture of solid and semi-solid hydrocarbons, as naphtha or asphalt. **2** A brown paint made by mixing asphalt with a drying oil: used by artists. [<L] —**bi·tu·mi·noid** (bi·tōō′mə·noid, -tyōō′-) *adj.*

bi·tu·mi·nize (bi·tōō′mə·nīz, -tyōō′-) *v.t.* **·ized, ·iz·ing** To render bituminous; treat with bitumen. —**bi·tu′mi·ni·za′tion** *n.*

bi·tu·mi·nous (bi·tōō′mə·nəs, -tyōō′-) *adj.* **1** Of, pertaining to, or containing bitumen. **2** Containing, as coal, many volatile hydrocarbons.

bi·va·lence (bī·vā′ləns, biv′ə-) *n. Chem.* The property of having a valence of two. Also **bi·va′len·cy.**

bi·va·lent (bī·vā′lənt, biv′ə-) *adj.* **1** *Chem.* **a** Having a valence of two, or twice that of a univalent. **b** Having two valences: also *divalent.* **2** *Biol.* Composed of or characterizing chromatin rods representing two chromosomes joined end to end. [<BI- + L *valens, -entis,* ppr. of *valere* have power]

bi·valve (bī′valv′) *n.* **1** *Zool.* An acephalous mollusk having a shell of two lateral valves. **2** *Bot.* A seed vessel that splits into two parts, as a pea pod. —*adj.* Having two valves, as a mollusk or seed vessel: also **bi′valved′, bi·val·vous** (bī·val′vəs), **bi·val·vu·lar** (bī·val′·vyə·lər).

biv·ou·ac (biv′ōō·ak, biv′wak) *n.* A temporary encampment with or without shelter. —*v.i.* **biv·ou·acked, biv·ou·ack·ing** To encamp for the night with or without tents. [<F <G *beiwacht* guard]

Bi·wa (bē·wä), **Lake** The largest lake in Japan, located in southern Honshu; 261 square miles. *Japanese* **Bi·wa–ko** (bē·wä·kō).

bi·week·ly (bī·wēk′lē) *adj.* **1** Occurring or appearing once in two weeks. **2** Semiweekly. —*n.* A publication issued every other week.

bi·year·ly (bī·yir′lē) *adj. & adv.* **1** Occurring twice within one year. **2** Biennial.

bi·zarre (bi·zär′) *adj.* Grotesque; odd; fantastic. See synonyms under ODD. [<F, ? ult.< Basque] —**bi·zarre′ly** *adv.* —**bi·zarre′ness** *n.*

Bi·zen (bē·zen) A former province of SW Honshu, Japan; famous for pottery known as **Biz·en·ware** (biz′ən·wâr′).

Bi·zer·te (bi·zûr′tə, *Fr.* bē·zert′) The northernmost city in Africa, a port in northern Tunisia; ancient *Hippo Zarytus.* Also **Bi·zer′ta.**

Bi·zet (bē·zā′), **Georges,** 1838–75, French composer: original name *Alexandre César Léopold Bizet.*

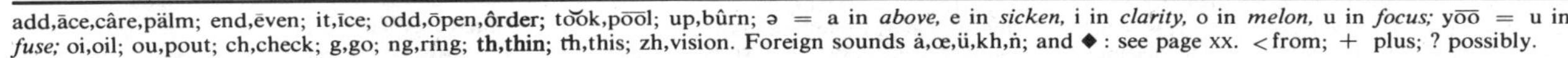

add,āce,câre,pälm; end,ēven; it,īce; odd,ōpen,**ôrder**; tŏŏk,pōōl; up,bûrn; ə = a in *above,* e in *sicken,* i in *clarity,* o in *melon,* u in *focus;* yōō = u in *fuse;* oi,oil; ou,pout; ch,check; g,go; ng,ring; **th,thin**; th,this; zh,vision. Foreign sounds á,œ,ü,kh,ṅ; and ◆ : see page xx. <from; + plus; ? possibly.

bizz (biz) *v.i. Scot.* To buzz.

Björn·son (byœrn′sən), **Björn·stjer·ne** (byœrn′·styâr·nə), 1832–1910, Norwegian poet, novelist, and dramatist.

Björns·son (byœrs′sôn), **Sveinn,** 1881–1952, Icelandic statesman; president of Iceland 1945–52.

Bk *Chem.* Berkelium (symbol Bk).

blab (blab) *v.t. & v.i.* **blabbed, blab·bing 1** To tell or repeat indiscreetly. **2** To prattle. See synonyms under BABBLE. [< *n*] — *n.* **1** One who betrays confidence. **2** Idle chatter. [ME *blabbe* idle talker] — **blab′ber** *n.*

blab·ber·mouth (blab′ər·mouth′) *n.* One who talks too much and can't be trusted to keep secrets.

black (blak) *adj.* **1** Having little or no power to reflect light: of the color of jet: the opposite of *white.* **2** Belonging to a group having dark skin. **3** Of or relating to the African American people or their culture: *black power, black studies, black pride.* **4** Swarthy; somber; dark. **5** Destitute of light; gloomy; dismal; forbidding. **6** Soiled; stained. **7** Evil; malignant; wicked; deadly; slanderous; malicious; threatening: a *black*-hearted wretch. **8** Wearing black garments: *black* monks. See synonyms under DARK. — *n.* **1** The absence of or complete absorption of light; the darkest of all colors. **2** Something that is black; also, mourning apparel or drapery. **3** A stain. **4** A member of the so-called black race. — **in the black** In the credit column of an account: converse of *in the red.* — *v.t. & v.i.* **1** To make or become black. **2** To blacken and polish. — **to black out 1** To extinguish or screen all light. **2** To lose vision or consciousness temporarily. **3** To censor; delete by scoring through. See BLACKOUT. [OE *blæc* dark] — **black′ly** *adv.* — **black′ness** *n.*

Black (blak), **Hugo La Fayette,** 1886–1971, associate justice of the United States Supreme Court 1937–1971.

black-and-blue (blak′ən·blōō′) *adj.* Discolored: said of skin that has been bruised.

Black and Tan Formerly, the auxiliary division of the Royal Irish Constabulary: so called from its uniform and accouterments.

black and white Writing or printing.

black art Necromancy; magic.

black·ball (blak′bôl′) *v.t.* **1** To use one's vote to ban from membership. **2** To exclude or ostracize: *blackballed* from the television industry. — *n.* **1** A single negative vote resulting in the rejection of an application for membership. **2** Any willful exclusion or act of ostracism. [<BLACK + BALL[1] from the use of a black ball to signify a negative vote during balloting] — **black′·ball′er** *n.*

black bass 1 A voracious fresh-water percoid fish (genus *Micropterus*) of the eastern United States and Canada. **2** The black sea bass (family *Serranidae*) of the North Atlantic; the blackwill.

black bear The common American bear *(Euarctos americanus).*

black belt *U.S.* **1** The highest degree of proficiency in judo or karate. **2** A person holding this degree. **3** A section of certain states in the U.S., especially of Alabama and Mississippi, characterized by rich black soil. **4** An area densely populated by blacks.

black·ber·ry (blak′ber′ē, -bər·ē) *n. pl.* **·ber·ries 1** The black, edible fruit of certain shrubs (genus *Rubus*) of the rose family. **2** Any of the plants producing it.

blackberry lily A perennial herb *(Belamcanda chinensis)* of the iris family: so called from its ripened seed vessel, which resembles a blackberry.

black bindweed 1 A twining, perennial vine *(Tamus communis)* of the yam family, with long angular stems and a small red fruit; the European black bryony. **2** An herbaceous twining plant *(Polygonum convolvulus)* growing as a weed in the United States.

black birch A species *(Betula lenta)* of birch of eastern North America with aromatic twigs and dark brown bark that becomes furrowed with age. Also called *sweet birch.*

black·bird (blak′bûrd′) *n.* **1** A common European thrush *(Turdus merula),* the male of which is black, with a yellow bill. **2** One of various black or blackish North American birds (family *Icteridae*), as the **crow blackbird** *(Quiscalus quiscula),* **marsh blackbird** *(Agelaius phoeniceus),* etc.

black·board (blak′bôrd′, -bōrd′) *n.* A blackened surface, for marking upon with chalk.

black body *Physics* **1** An ideal body that completely absorbs all radiant energy incident upon it. **2** The blackened interior of an opaque box or chamber with a very narrow slit.

black book A book or record of misdemeanors kept at some universities. — **to be in one's black book** To be in disfavor.

black·boy (blak′boi′) *n.* The grasstree.

black buck 1 The common Indian antelope *(Antilope cervicapra)* of a prevailing blackish-brown color. **2** The sable antelope *(Hippotragus niger)* of South Africa.

Black·burn (blak′bərn) A county borough in central Lancashire, England.

Blackburn, Mount A peak in southern Alaska; 16,140 feet.

Black Canyon 1 A gorge of the Colorado River, between Arizona and Nevada; site of Hoover Dam. See MEAD, LAKE. **2** A gorge of the Gunnison River in SW Colorado, a 10-mile section of which is included in **Black Canyon of the Gunnison National Monument,** established 1933.

black·cap (blak′kap′) *n.* **1** Any of several birds having a black crown, as the European warbler, chickadee, etc. **2** The black raspberry, or its fruit.

black·cock (blak′kok′) *n.* The male of the heath grouse.

black country A highly industrialized region of England in Staffordshire, Warwickshire, and Worcestershire.

black·damp (blak′damp′) *n.* Chokedamp.

black death A bubonic plague of exceptional virulence and duration prevalent in Asia and Europe in the 14th century.

black diamond 1 Mineral coal: only in plural. **2** Carbonado or bort.

black disease An acute, infectious, generally fatal hepatic disease of sheep, caused by an anaerobic bacterium *(Clostridium novyi)* transmitted by liver flukes.

black·en (blak′ən) *v.* **black·ened, black·en·ing** *v.t.* **1** To make black or dark. **2** To slander; defame. — *v.i.* **3** To become black; darken. — **black′en·er** *n.*

Black English A dialect of English spoken by many American blacks, and distinguished by special pronunciation, vocabulary, and grammatical or syntactic structure.

black eye 1 An eye with a black iris. **2** An eye having the adjacent surface discolored by a blow or bruise. **3** *Colloq.* A bad reputation. — **black′-eyed′** *adj.*

black-eyed Susan 1 One of the coneflowers *(Rudbeckia hirta):* the State flower of Maryland: also known as *yellow daisy.* **2** The bladder ketmia.

black·face (blak′fās′) *n.* **1** Makeup worn by a performer playing a black character, esp. in a minstrel show. **2** A performer wearing such makeup.

Black·feet (blak′fēt′) *n. pl. sing.* **·foot** A confederacy of Algonquian North American Indian tribes, consisting of the Siksika or Blackfeet, the Kainah, and the Piegan, formerly inhabiting the territory between the Saskatchewan and Missouri Rivers, now on reservations in Alberta and Montana.

black·fel·low (blak′fel′ō) *n.* An Australian aborigine.

black·fel·low's button (blak′fel·ōz) *Austral.* An Australite.

black·fish (blak′fish′) *n.* **1** One of various dark-colored cetaceans, as the pilot whale (genus *Globicephala*). **2** One of various fishes, as the tautog, the black sea bass, etc. **3** A food fish *(Dallia pectoralis)* of northern Alaskan and Siberian waters.

black flag See under FLAG.

black·fly (blak′flī′) *n.* **1** Any of certain small, stocky, dark-colored, biting flies (genus *Simulium*) having aquatic larvae, especially common in forested mountainous regions; especially, *S. hirtipes* of North America. **2** The buffalo gnat.

Black·foot (blak′fŏŏt′) *n.* A member of any of the tribes of North American Indians known as Blackfeet. — *adj.* Pertaining or belonging to the Blackfeet tribes: *Blackfoot* tales.

Black Forest A mountainous wooded region in southern Germany; highest peak, 4,898 feet: German *Schwarzwald.*

Black Friar A Dominican: so named from his black cloak.

Black·fri·ars (blak′frī′ərz) An area in the SW angle of old London city, England: named for the large number of Dominican monasteries in the district.

black frost A frost severe enough to turn vegetation black.

black·guard (blag′ərd, -ärd) *n.* A low, vicious fellow; a scoundrel. — *v.t.* To revile; vilify. — *v.i.* To act like a blackguard. — *adj.* Of or like a blackguard; base; vile: also **black′guard·ly.** [< *black guard,* orig., the scullions and low menials of a great house or army; later applied to any base person] — **black′guard·ism** *n.*

black·gum (blak′gum′) *n.* A large tree *(Nyssa sylvatica)* of the dogwood family, with an ovoid, blue-black drupe and close-grained wood hard to split; pepperidge; sour gum.

Black Hand 1 A society of anarchists in Spain, repressed in 1883. **2** A secret organization in the United States, especially of Italians, for the purpose of vengeance or blackmail. See MAFIA.

black·haw (blak′hô′) *n.* **1** The black oval drupe of certain species of *Viburnum.* **2** The sweet viburnum or sheepberry.

Black Hawk, 1767–1838, American Indian chief who fought against the United States in 1831–32.

black·head (blak′hed′) *n.* **1** An American scaup duck. **2** An infectious, often fatal protozoan disease of turkeys and certain wildfowl: it attacks chiefly the liver and intestines. **3** A facial blemish; comedo.

black·heart (blak′härt′) *n.* **1** A variety of early black cherry. **2** A blackening of the internal tissues of various trees and of the potato.

black-heart·ed (blak′här′tid) *adj.* Malign; wicked.

Black Hills A mountainous region in SW South Dakota and NE Wyoming; highest point, 7,242 feet; about 6,000 square miles.

black hole 1 A dark cell or dungeon. **2** A military lock-up: in allusion to the Black Hole in Fort William, at Calcutta, a room 18 feet square, into which 146 British subjects were forced on the night of June 20, 1756, of whom 123 died of asphyxia before morning. **3** A hypothetical hole in space into which stars and other celestial objects that have condensed to a certain radius collapse under the influence of gravity.

black horehound A fetid herb *(Ballota nigra)* of the mint family.

black·ing (blak′ing) *n.* **1** A preparation used to give blackness or luster, or both, to shoes, stoves, etc. **2** *Brit.* Shoe polish.

black·ish (blak′ish) *adj.* Somewhat black; darkened. — **black′ish·ly** *adv.*

black ivory 1 A pigment composed of carbonized ivory. **2** Formerly, blacks as merchandise in the slave trade.

black·jack (blak′jak′) *n.* **1** A small bludgeon with a flexible handle. **2** A black flag; a pirate's ensign. **3** A small oak *(Quercus marilandica)* of the SE United States. **4** Vingt-et-un: a card game. **5** A drinking can, formerly of leather, now of japanned metal. **6** Sphalerite or zincblende. **7** Caramel: used to color soups, wines, etc. — *v.t.* **1** To strike with a blackjack. **2** To coerce by threat.

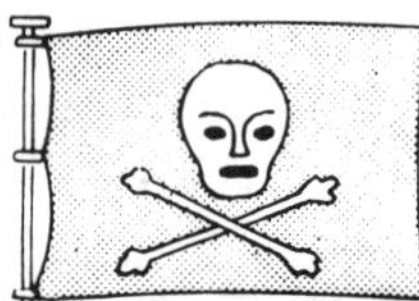
BLACKJACK *(def. 2)*

black-ja·pan (blak′jə·pan′) *n.* Japan black.

black knot 1 A disease of plum and cherry trees, producing black knotlike excrescences on the branches, caused by a fungus *(Sphaeria morbosa).* **2** The fungus.

black lead Graphite.

black·leg (blak′leg′) *n.* **1** An acute, infectious, often fatal disease of young cattle, caused by an anaerobic bacterium *(Clostridium chauvoei)* and characterized by fever and loss of appetite accompanied by swellings or tumors under the skin. **2** An injurious disease of cabbage and other cruciferous plants; also, a bacterial rot of potatoes. **3** A professional swindler or gambler; a cheat; sharper. **4** *Brit. Colloq.* A strikebreaker.

black letter *Printing* The Gothic or Old English letter.

This line is in black letter.

black-let·ter (blak′let′ər) *adj.* **1** Of or pertaining to manuscript printed or written in black letter. **2** Unfortunate or unlucky: a *black-letter* day. Also **black′-let′tered.**

black·light (blak′līt′) *n. Physics* Ultraviolet radiation capable of exciting fluorescence in properly treated materials or objects.

black·list (blak′list′) *n.* A list of persons or organizations under suspicion or censure, or refused approval for any cause. — *v.t.* To place the name of (a person) on or as on a blacklist.

black lung A form of pneumoconiosis that afflicts coal miners.

black·ly (blak′lē) *adv.* In a manner showing blackness or darkness; gloomily; threateningly.

black Magellanic cloud *Astron.* One of several dark spaces in the Milky Way, especially one near the Southern Cross.

black magic See under MAGIC.

black·mail (blak′māl′) *n.* **1** Extortion by threats of public accusation or of exposure. **2** *Scot.* A tax formerly paid to bandits to insure immunity from pillage. — *v.t.* **1** To levy blackmail upon. **2** To force (to do something) as by threats: with *into.* [<BLACK + MAIL³] — **black′mail′er** *n.*

Black Ma·ri·a (mə·rī′ə) *Colloq.* A prison van or police patrol wagon.

black mark A mark or symbol used to record failure or bad conduct.

black market A place or firm where merchandise is offered for sale contrary to legal restrictions, or in quantities or at terms contrary to such restrictions. Also **black bourse.**

black match Strands of twine impregnated with gunpowder, used to ignite fireworks, etc.

black measles *Pathol.* A severe form of measles, marked by very dark eruptions.

black medic An annual herb of the bean family *(Medicago lupulina)* with yellow flowers and curved pods: also called *hop clover.*

Black Mountains The highest range of the Appalachians and a spur of the Blue Ridge Mountains in western North Carolina; highest point, 6,684 feet.

Black Muslim *n.* A member of a chiefly black group that follows Islamic religious beliefs.

black nationalist *n.* A member of a group of militant blacks who advocate separatism from whites and the creation of self-governing black communities.

black nightshade The common nightshade.

black·out (blak′out′) *n.* **1** A defensive or precautionary measure against aerial attack, consisting of the extinguishment or screening of all lights visible from the air. **2** *Physiol.* The partial or complete loss of vision and sometimes of consciousness, experienced by airplane pilots during rapid changes in velocity. **3** In theatrics, a fade-out or cut-out, as of part of a scene, eliminating it from view. **4** An official ban on the publication of news in war time, imposed for security reasons.

Black Panther *n.* A member of a militant black American organization of the same name.

black·poll (blak′pōl′) *n.* A North American wood warbler *(Dendroica striata),* the male of which has glossy black plumage on the top of the head.

Black·pool (blak′po͞ol′) A county borough in west Lancashire, England; a seaside resort.

black·pot (blak′pot′) *n.* In ceramics, a type of coarse, unglazed pottery, manufactured chiefly in England.

black power The power of black Americans to establish their rights by collective action.

Black Prince See under EDWARD.

black racer The blacksnake.

Black River A river in Northern Vietnam, flowing 500 miles SE to the Red River: Annamese *Song Bo.*

Black Rod **1** *Brit.* An officer of the royal household, who acts as messenger from the House of Lords to the House of Commons. **2** An usher in the legislatures of British colonies and dominions.

black rot Leaf spot.

Black Sea A large inland sea between Europe and Asia, connected with the Mediterranean by the Bosporus, the Sea of Marmara, and the Dardanelles; 159,000 square miles: also *Euxine Sea.* Ancient **Pon·tus Eux·i·nus** (pon′təs yo͞ok·sī′nəs).

black sheep **1** One, among a herd of white sheep, that is black. **2** An evil-disposed or disreputable member of an otherwise decent family or society.

Black Shirt **1** A member of the Italian Fascist party, in allusion to the black shirts worn by members. **2** A member of the Nazi Schutzstaffel.

black·smith (blak′smith′) *n.* A workman who works in or welds wrought iron. Compare WHITESMITH.

black·snake (blak′snāk′) *n.* **1** A large, agile, non-venomous snake of the eastern United States *(Coluber constrictor)* with smooth, satiny, black scales; the black racer. **2** A dangerous Australian snake *(Pseudechis porphyriacus)* with blue-black scales and a venom similar to that of the cobra. **3** A heavy pliant whip of braided leather or rawhide.

black spruce A North American evergreen tree *(Picea mariana)* with deep blue-green foliage and firmly attached cones.

Black·stone (blak′stōn′, -stən), **Sir William,** 1723–80, English jurist.

black·thorn (blak′thôrn′) *n.* **1** A thorny European shrub *(Prunus spinosa)* of the rose family: the sloe. **2** A cane made from its wood. **3** An American hawthorn *(Crataegus calpodendron).*

black tie **1** A black bow tie. **2** A tuxedo and its correct accessories. **3** A phrase used on invitations to indicate semiformal dress.

black·top (blak′top′) *n.* Asphalt used for paving. — *v.t.* **-topped, -top·ping** To surface with blacktop.

black tracker *Austral.* An Australian aborigine used by police to track down a lost or wanted person in rough country.

black vomit **1** Yellow fever. **2** The dark bloody matter vomited in its later stages.

black walnut See under WALNUT.

Black Watch A regiment of the British Army, officially known as the Royal Highlanders: so called because of their somber tartan.

black·wa·ter fever (blak′wô′tər, -wot′ər) *Pathol.* A dangerous form of malaria characterized by the excretion of black or dark red urine; malarial hematuria.

black·weed (blak′wēd′) *n.* The ragweed.

Black·well's Island (blak′welz, -wəlz) Former name for WELFARE ISLAND.

black whale The blackfish *(Globicephala melaena):* also called *pilot whale.*

black widow A medium-sized, venomous female spider *(Latrodectus mactans)* common in dark, sheltered places in the United States, having a black body with an hourglass-shaped red mark on the abdomen: so called from its color and its habit of eating its mate.

black·will (blak′wil′) *n.* The black bass.

black·wood (blak′wo͝od′) *n.* The black mangrove of Florida and tropical America *(Rhizophora mangle).*

blad (blad, bläd) *n. Scot.* A fragment or portion.

blad·der (blad′ər) *n.* **1** *Anat.* **a** A distensible membranous sac in the anterior part of the pelvic cavity, for the temporary retention of urine. **b** Some part or organ of analogous structure. ◆Collateral adjective: *vesical.* **2** *Biol.* An air vessel or an air cell in some seaweeds. **3** Anything puffed out, empty, or unsubstantial. **4** A blister or pustule. [OE *blædre*]

bladder campion A perennial herb *(Silene latifolia)* belonging to the pink family, and having the calyx much inflated.

blad·der·fish (blad′ər·fish′) *n.* The globefish.

bladder ket·mi·a (ket′mē·ə) **1** The flower-of-an-hour, a European annual *(Hibiscus trionum)* of the mallow family, naturalized in America, with ephemeral pale yellow flowers and a purple-veined, bladderlike calyx. **2** The black-eyed Susan. Also **bladder ket·mie** (ket′mē).

blad·der·nose (blad′ər·nōz′) *n.* The hooded seal.

blad·der·nut (blad′ər·nut′) *n.* **1** Any plant of the genus *Staphylea* of the soapberry family, with large, inflated, three-lobed pods. **2** A seed pod of one of these plants.

blad·der·worm (blad′ər·wûrm′) *n. Zool.* An encysted larval tapeworm; a scolex; hydatid.

blad·der·wort (blad′ər·wûrt′) *n.* Any aquatic herb of the genus *Urticularia,* usually having little bladders on the leaves, in which minute organisms are trapped for nutriment.

blad·der·wrack (blad′ər·rak′) *n.* Any rock-weed of the genus *Fucus.* See FUCUS.

blad·der·y (blad′ər·ē) *adj.* **1** Like a bladder. **2** Covered with or having bladders or vesicles.

blade (blād) *n.* **1** The flat, cutting part of any edged tool or weapon. **2** The thin, flat part of any instrument or utensil, as of an oar, screw propeller, plow, etc. **3** *Bot.* The leaf of grasses or certain other plants, especially, a leaf of Indian corn. **4** A rakish young man; wild, reckless fellow. **5** A swordsman; also, a sword. **6** *Phonet.* The upper flat part of the tongue immediately behind the tip and directly below the alveolar ridge. **7** The expanded or broad flat part of a leaf, petal, etc.; the lamina. **8** *Anat.* The shoulder blade or scapula. [OE *blæd* blade of a oar or sword] — **blad′ed** *adj.*

blae (blā, blē) *adj. Scot.* Blackish-blue or bluish-gray; livid; also, cloudy; bleak.

Bla·go·vesh·chensk (blä′gō·vyesh′chensk) A city on the Amur, Russian S.F.S.R.

blah (blā) *n. Slang* Excessive hyperbole; fustian; buncombe. — *adj.* Uninteresting; dull: a *blah* story.

blain (blān) *n. Pathol.* A pustular tumor; a blister. [OE *blegen*]

Blaine (blān), **James Gillespie,** 1830–93, U.S. statesman.

Blake (blāk), **Robert,** 1599–1657, English admiral. —**William,** 1757–1827, English painter, poet, and mystic.

blam·a·ble (blā′mə·bəl) *adj.* Deserving blame; culpable; faulty. — **blam′a·ble·ness** *n.* — **blam′a·bly** *adv.*

blame (blām) *v.t.* **blamed, blam·ing** **1** To accuse of fault or error: often with *for.* **2** To find fault with; reproach. **3** To place the responsibility for (an action or error): with *on.* — **to be to blame** To be at fault. — *n.* Faultfinding; censure; also, the fault; culpability. See synonyms under ANIMADVERSION. [<OF *blasmer* <LL *blasphemare* revile, reproach <Gk. *blasphēmein.* Doublet of BLASPHEME.]

Synonyms (verb): censure, chide, condemn, rebuke, reprehend, reproach, reprobate, reprove. We blame a person *for* a fault, or lay the blame *upon* him. See CONDEMN, REPROVE. Compare ARRAIGN. *Antonyms:* acquit, approve, eulogize, exculpate, exonerate, extol, laud, praise.

blamed (blāmd) *adj. U.S. Dial.* Damned: a *blamed* fool: a euphemism. — *adv.* Very; exceedingly: *blamed* hot.

blame·ful (blām′fəl) *adj.* **1** Deserving of blame. **2** Imputing blame. — **blame′ful·ly** *adv.* — **blame′ful·ness** *n.*

blame·less (blām′lis) *adj.* Innocent; guiltless. See synonyms under PERFECT. — **blame′less·ly** *adv.* — **blame′less·ness** *n.*

blame·wor·thy (blām′wûr′thē) *adj.* Deserving of blame. — **blame′wor′thi·ness** *n.*

Bla·mey (blā′mē), **Sir Thomas Albert,** 1884–1951, Australian general.

Blanc (blängk, blangk; *Fr.* blän), **Cape** A cape of Tunisia on the northernmost tip of Africa. *French* **Cap Blanc** (kȧp blän′).

Blanc (blän), **Jean Joseph Charles Louis,** 1811–82, French socialist and historian.

Blanc, Mont See MONT BLANC.

Blan·ca Peak (blang′kə) Highest peak in the Sangre de Cristo Mountains, southern Colorado; 14,363 feet.

blanc fixe (blän fēks′) Fine-grained barium sulfate, used as a base in making certain pigments, and in water colors, where it retains its white color.

blanch[1] (blanch, blänch) *v.t.* **1** To remove the color from; bleach. **2** To cause to turn pale, as from fear or anger. **3** To remove the skin of, as almonds, by scalding. **4** To whiten, as meat, by scalding. **5** *Bot.* To bleach by removing from light, as celery or endives. **6** *Metall.* To whiten or brighten (metals), as with acids or by coating with tin. —*v.i.* **7** To turn or become white or pale. See synonyms under BLEACH. —*adj.* **1** In heraldry, white; argent. **2** In English law, based on a slight payment, often in silver: said of tenures. **3** In Scottish law, designating a merely nominal quit-rent, as a pair of gloves, or the tenure thus held. [<F *blanchir* <*blanc* white] —**blanch′er** *n.*

blanch[2] (blanch, blänch) *v.t.* To turn, as a deer, aside or back. [Var. of BLENCH[1]]

Blanch (blanch, blänch) A feminine personal name. Also **Blanche,** *Fr.* **Blanche** (blänsh), *Ital.* **Bian·ca** (byäng′kä), *Sp.* **Blan·ca** (bläng′·kä). [<Gmc., white, shining]

blanc·mange (blə·mänzh′, -mänzh′) *n.* A whitish, jellylike preparation of milk, eggs, sugar, cornstarch, flavoring, etc.: used for desserts, etc. [<F *blanc-manger* white food]

Blan·co (blang′kō), **Cape** The westernmost point of Oregon.

bland (bland) *adj.* **1** Affable in manner; gentle; suave. **2** Mild; balmy; genial. **3** Not stimulating or irritating. **4** Smooth and mild in flavor; as, a *bland* sauce. [<L *blandus* mild]—**bland′ly** *adv.* —**bland′ness** *n.*

Synonyms: affable, balmy, benign, complaisant, courteous, genial, gentle, gracious, mild, smooth, soft, tender. *Antonyms*: acrid, biting, brusk, curt, harsh, rough, rude.

Blan·ding's turtle (blan′dingz) The emyd. [after William *Blanding,* 19th c. U.S. herpetologist]

blan·dish (blan′dish) *v.t.* To wheedle; flatter; cajole. [<OF *blandiss-*, stem of *blandir* flatter < L *blandiri* <*blandus* mild, gentle] —**blan′·dish·er** *n.*

blan·dish·ment (blan′dish·mənt) *n.* Soothing, caressing, or flattering speech or action; cajolery.

blank (blangk) *adj.* **1** Wholly or partly free from writing or print. **2** Lacking in ornament, variety, interest, or results. **3** Empty; void. **4** Without expression or animation: a *blank* stare. **5** Without rime: *blank* verse. **6** Disconcerted; confused. **7** Utter; downright. **8** Pale or white; colorless. **9** Having no finishing cuts, slots, grooves, teeth, or the like; unfinished: common in such phrases as *blank arcade, arch, file, key, saw, window,* etc. —*n.* **1** A paper containing no written or printed matter. **2** A written or printed paper with blank spaces. **3** A vacant space; void interval. **4** A lottery ticket which has drawn no prize; a disappointing result. **5** A partially prepared piece, as of wood or metal, ready for forming into a finished object, as a coin, key, button, etc. **6** The central white spot of a target; bull's-eye. **7** A blank verse. **8** A blank cartridge. —*v.t.* **1** To delete; invalidate: often with *out.* **2** In games, to prevent (an opponent) from scoring. **3** *Archaic* To disconcert; put out of countenance. [<F *blanc* white, ult. <Gmc.] —**blank′ly** *adv.* —**blank′ness** *n.*

Synonyms (adj.): bare, barren, clear, empty, plain, unfilled, unlimited, unmarked, unsigned. See BLEAK, VACANT.

Blan·ka (bläng′kä) Swedish form of BLANCH.

blank·book (blangk′bŏŏk′) *n.* A book with blank leaves, for accounts, memoranda, etc.

blank cartridge A cartridge loaded only with powder.

blank check *Colloq.* Carte blanche.

blank endorsement The writing of one's name as an indorser across the back of a negotiable instrument, without any words of restriction or contingency, making it payable to bearer.

blan·ket (blang′kit) *n.* **1** A heavy woolen covering, as of a bed. **2** A robe of like material used, by Indians, as a garment, or for horses, etc., as a protection. **3** A sheet of other material, as cotton, of like appearance. **4** Anything that covers, conceals, or protects: a *blanket* of snow; a *blanket* of smoke; a *blanket* of rubber. —*adj.* **1** Designating anything which covers a wide range or large number of interrelated names, conditions, objects, items, or the like; covering every phase of a subject; all-embracing: a *blanket* ballot; *blanket* injunction. **2** Using blankets for garments: a *blanket* Indian. —*v.t.* **1** To cover with or as with a blanket. **2** To cover or apply uniformly: The new law *blankets* the nation. **3** To obscure or suppress; interfere: A strong broadcast *blankets* a weak one. **4** *Naut.* To deprive (a sailboat) of wind by passing close on the windward side. **5** To toss in a blanket as sport or punishment. [<OF *blankete,* dim. of *blanc* white; orig. a white or undyed cloth]

blank verse Verse without rime; specifically, iambic pentameter verse, the principal verse form in English epic and dramatic poetry.

blan·quette (blän·ket′) *n.* A stew of veal, lamb, chicken, or any white meat served in an egg sauce, garnished with mushrooms and onions. [<F <*blanc* white]

blare (blâr) *v.t.* & *v.i.* **blared, blar·ing 1** To sound loudly, as a trumpet. **2** To announce loudly. —*n.* **1** A loud brazen sound. See synonyms under NOISE. **2** Brightness or glare, as of color. [Prob. imit.]

blar·ney (blär′nē) *n.* Wheedling flattery. —*v.t.* & *v.i.* To flatter, cajole, or wheedle. [<BLARNEY STONE]

Blar·ney (blär′nē) A village in central County Cork, Ireland.

Blarney Stone A stone in a 15th century castle in Blarney, Ireland, which, when kissed, reputedly endows one with invincible eloquence.

Blas·co-I·bá·ñez (bläs′kō-ē·vä′nyāth), **Vicente,** 1867–1928, Spanish novelist.

bla·sé (blä·zā′, blä′zā) *adj.* Sated with pleasure; wearied or worn out, as by dissipation; indifferent. [<F, pp. of *blaser* satiate]

blas·pheme (blas·fēm′) *v.* **·phemed, ·phem·ing** —*v.t.* **1** To speak in an impious or irreverent manner of (God or sacred things). **2** To speak ill of; malign. —*v.i.* **3** To utter blasphemy. [<OF *blasfemer* <LL *blasphemare* <Gk. *blasphēmein* revile <*blasphēmos* evil-speaking. Doublet of BLAME.]

blas·phe·mous (blas′fə·məs) *adj.* Impious; irreverent; profane. See synonyms under PROFANE. —**blas′phe·mous·ly** *adv.* —**blas′phe·mous·ness** *n.*

blas·phe·my (blas′fə·mē) *n. pl.* **·mies 1** Evil or profane speaking of God or sacred things; claiming the attributes of God. **2** In the Old Testament, any attempt to lessen reverence for the name of Jehovah. **3** Any irreverent act or utterance. See synonyms under OATH.

blast (blast, bläst) *v.t.* **1** To rend in pieces by or as by explosion. **2** To cause to wither or shrivel; destroy. —*n.* **1** A strong or sudden wind. **2** *Metall.* The strong artificial current of air in a blast furnace. **3** The discharge of an explosive, or its effect. **4** The charge of dynamite or other explosive used in shattering rocks, as for a building foundation, tunnel, etc. **5** A loud, sudden sound, as of a trumpet. **6** A blight or blighting influence. **7** The draft of air near the muzzle of a cannon at its discharge. **8** *Slang* A party. **9** *Slang* An important or surprising event or occasion. **10** *Slang* A drink of hard liquor. See synonyms under RUPTURE. —**in blast** In operation: said of a smelting furnace. —**at full blast** At capacity operation or maximum speed. [OE *blæst* blowing. Akin to BLOW[1].] —**blast′er** *n.*

-blast *combining form Biol.* Growth; sprout: *ameloblast.* [<Gk. *blastos* bud]

blast·ed (blas′tid, bläs′-) *adj.* **1** Blighted; withered or destroyed. **2** *Colloq.* Confounded: a euphemistic oath.

blas·te·ma (blas·tē′mə) *n. pl.* **·ma·ta** (-mə·tə) Embryonic protoplasm; the formative material of an ovum. [<Gk. *blastēma* offspring]

blast furnace *Metall.* A smelting furnace in which the fire is intensified by an air blast.

blast·ing (blas′ting, bläs′-) *n.* **1** The act of rending by charges of explosives. **2** A blighting or withering. **3** *Telecom.* The distortion resulting from the imposing on a microphone or loudspeaker of a greater volume of sound than can be properly transmitted.

blasting gelatin A high explosive, made by dissolving collodion cotton in nine times its weight of nitroglycerin.

blast·ment (blast′mənt, bläst′-) *n. Obs.* A blast; a blight.

blasto– *combining form Biol.* Growth, sprout: *blastoderm.* Also, before vowels, **blast–.** [<Gk. *blastos* a sprout]

blas·to·cele (blas′tə·sēl) *n. Biol.* The cavity of the blastodermic vesicle. Also **blas′to·coele.**

blas·to·cyst (blas′tə·sist) *n.* The blastula.

blas·to·derm (blas′tə·dûrm) *n. Biol.* The germinal disk. [<BLASTO- + Gk. *derma* skin] —**blas′to·der′mic** *adj.*

blas·to·disk (blas′tə·disk) *n. Biol.* A nucleated disk of protoplasm which forms on the surface of the yolk mass in certain eggs. Also **blas′·to·disc.**

blast–off (blast′ôf′) *n.* The launching of a rocket or missile.

blas·to·gen·e·sis (blas′tə·jen′ə·sis) *n. Biol.* **1** Origin from the germ plasm: opposed to *pangenesis.* **2** Reproduction by budding. —**blas′·to·gen′ic** *adj.*

blas·to·mere (blas′tə·mir) *n. Biol.* One of the large number of small cells formed during the cleavage of the fertilized ovum. —**blas′to·mer′·ic** (-mer′ik) *adj.*

blas·to·pore (blas′tə·pôr, -pōr) *n. Biol.* The exterior opening of the primitive intestine. —**blas′to·por′ic** (-pôr′ik, -por′ik) *adj.*

blas·to·sphere (blas′tə·sfir) *n. Biol.* **1** The blastodermic vesicle of the mammalian egg. **2** A blastula.

blas·tu·la (blas′chŏŏ·lə) *n. pl.* **·lae** (-lē) *Biol.* The stage of the embryo just preceding the formation of the gastrula; a hollow sphere of one layer of blastomeres enclosing a blastocele or segmentation cavity. [<NL <Gk. *blastos* sprout] —**blas′tu·lar** *adj.*

blat (blat) *v.* **blat·ted, blat·ting** *v.t. Colloq.* To utter heedlessly; blurt out. —*v.i.* To bleat, as a sheep. [Var. of BLEAT]

bla·tant (blā′tənt) *adj.* **1** Loud or noisy; offensively loud or clamorous. **2** Making a bellowing or bleating noise: said of animals. **3** Tumid; pretentious; obtrusive. [Coined by Edmund Spenser. Cf. L *blatire* babble; ME *blait* bleat.] —**bla′tan·cy** *n.* —**bla′tant·ly** *adv.*

blath·er (blath′ər) *v.t.* & *v.i.* To talk garrulously or foolishly. —*n.* Foolish talk; nonsense. Also spelled *blether.* Also **blat·ter** (blat′ər). [<ON *blathra* talk stupidly <*blathr* nonsense]

blath·er·skite (blath′ər·skīt) *n.* **1** A blustering, noisy fellow; a hoodlum. **2** Blustering talk; balderdash. **3** The ruddy duck. [<BLETHER + SKATE[3]]

blau·bok (blou′bok) *n. pl.* **·bok** or **·boks 1** An extinct South African antelope *(Hippotragus leucophaeus)* with bluish hair. **2** A South African antelope (genus *Cephalopus)* about the size of a rabbit. [<Afrikaans]

Bla·vat·sky (blə·vät′skē), **Helena Petrovna,** 1831–91, Russian theosophist.

blaw (blô) *v.t.* & *v.i. Scot.* To blow.

blawn (blôn) *Scot.* Blown.

blaze[1] (blāz) *v.* **blazed, blaz·ing** *v.i.* **1** To burn brightly. **2** To burn as with emotion: to *blaze* with anger. **3** To shine; be resplendent. —*v.t.* **4** *Rare* To cause to flame or shine brightly. See synonyms under BURN. —**to blaze away** To keep on firing; hence, to go on or proceed with anything. —*n.* **1** A vivid glowing flame; fire. **2** Brightness or brilliance and heat; effulgence; also, glare. **3** Excitement or ardor. See synonyms under FIRE, LIGHT. [OE *blæse* firebrand]

blaze[2] (blāz) *v.t.* **blazed, blaz·ing 1** To mark (a tree) by chipping off a piece of bark. **2** To mark out (a path) in this way. —*n.* **1** A white spot on the face of an animal, as a horse. **2** A mark chipped on a tree, to indicate a path; a path so indicated. [Akin to ON *blesi* white spot on a horse's face]

blaze[3] (blāz) *v.t.* **blazed, blaz·ing 1** To publish abroad or noise about. **2** *Obs.* To blare forth. [ON *blāsa* blow]

blaz·er (blā′zər) *n.* **1** A lightweight jacket of flannel or silk in vivid colors, usually worn in outdoor sports. **2** A dish with a small brazier under it for hot coals. **3** *Colloq.* That which blazes.

blazing star 1 A smooth herb *(Chamaelirium luteum)* of the lily family, with wandlike racemes of white flowers: also called *fairy wand.* **2** One of various perennial herbs of the genus *Liatris,* of the composite family, especially *L. squarrosa.* **3** *Her.* A six-pointed star with the tail of a comet, used as a bearing. **4** *Obs.* A comet. **5** In the western United States, a stampede of animals. **6** A center of interest; cynosure.

bla·zon (blā′zən) *n.* **1** *Her.* A coat of arms or armorial bearing, or a banner bearing such representation; a technical description or a graphic representation of armorial bearings. **2** A proclaiming or publishing abroad. **3** Ostentatious display. — *v.t.* **1** To inscribe or adorn, as with names or symbols. **2** *Her.* To describe technically or paint (coats of arms). **3** To proclaim; publish. See synonyms under PUBLISH. [<F *blason* coat of arms, shield] — **bla′zon·er** *n.* — **bla′zon·ment** *n.*

bla·zon·ry (blā′zən·rē) *n.* **1** The art of describing or depicting heraldic devices. **2** A coat of arms. **3** Decoration; show.

-ble See -ABLE.

bleach (blēch) *v.t.* **1** To deprive of color, as by exposure to the sun or chemicals; whiten. **2** To make pale: Fear *bleached* his face. — *v.i.* **3** To become colorless, pale or white. — *n.* **1** An act or the act of bleaching; also, the result of the act or degree of bleaching obtained. **2** A fluid or powder used as a bleaching agent. [OE *blǣcean*]

Synonyms (verb): blanch, whiten, whitewash. To *whiten* is to make white in general, but commonly it means to overspread with white coloring matter. *Bleach* and *blanch* both signify to *whiten* by depriving of color, the former permanently (as linen), the latter either permanently (as, to *blanch* celery) or temporarily (as, to *blanch* the cheek with fear). To *whitewash* is to *whiten* the surface of, literally with whitewash, or figuratively with false praise or by minimizing a fault. *Antonyms*: blacken, color, darken, dye, soil, stain.

bleach·er (blē′chər) *n.* **1** One who or that which bleaches. **2** *Usually pl.* An outdoor uncovered seat or stand for spectators.

bleach·er·y (blē′chər·ē) *n.* *pl.* **·er·ies** A place where bleaching is done.

bleach·ing (blē′ching) *n.* The process of whitening, as textile fibers and fabrics, by treatment with chemicals or exposure to the sun and weather.

bleaching powder A white or grayish-white powder with a slight odor of hypochlorous acid, formed by treating slaked lime with chlorine, and used for bleaching and as a disinfectant: also called *chloride of lime.*

bleak[1] (blēk) *adj.* **1** Exposed to wind and weather; bare; barren; dreary. **2** Cold, cutting, or penetrating. [<ON *bleikja* pale] — **bleak′ish** *adj.* — **bleak′ly** *adv.* — **bleak′ness** *n.*

Synonyms: blank, cheerless, chill, cold, cutting, desolate, dreary, exposed, piercing, stormy, unsheltered, waste, wild, windy. *Antonyms*: balmy, bright, cheerful, genial, homelike, mild, sheltered, sunny, warm.

bleak[2] (blēk) *n.* *pl.* **bleak** or **bleaks** A small European cyprinoid fish (genus *Alburnus*), whose scales are lined with a silvery pigment used in making artificial pearls. [<ON *bleikja*]

blear (blir) *adj.* **1** Dimmed, as by tears or rheum; dull. **2** Causing dimness of sight; also, dim; obscure; indistinct; hazy. — *v.t.* **1** To dim or inflame (the eyes). **2** To obscure, as the face with tears; blur. **3** To mislead; hoodwink. — *n.* That which renders vision indistinct; also, a blurry condition or look. [ME *blere.* Akin to LG *bleer-oged* blear-eyed.] — **blear′y** *adj.* — **blear′i·ness** *n.*

blear-eyed (blir′īd′) *adj.* **1** Having inflamed or rheumy eyes. **2** Weak-sighted. Also **blear′y-eyed′.**

bleat (blēt) *n.* The cry of the sheep, goat, or calf; also, any sound resembling it. — *v.i.* **1** To cry, as a sheep or goat. **2** To speak with such a sound, as with fear or in complaint. — *v.t.* **3** To utter with the sound of a bleat. **4** To babble foolishly; prate. [OE *blǣtan*] — **bleat′er** *n.* — **bleat′ing** *adj.* — **bleat′ing·ly** *adv.*

bleb (bleb) *n.* A blister, or bladderlike body; a bulla. [ME *bleb*; imit.] — **bleb′by** *adj.*

bled (bled) Past tense and past participle of BLEED.

Bled (bled) A village and resort in NW Slovenia, Yugoslavia, on the shores of **Bled Lake.**

bleed (blēd) *v.* **bled, bleed·ing** *v.t.* **1** To draw blood from; leech. **2** To exude, as sap, blood, or other fluid. **3** To draw sap or other fluid from. **4** To empty of liquid or gaseous matter. **5** To extort money from; overcharge. **6** In bookbinding, to trim (a page) too closely, so as to cut into or mar the printed or engraved matter. — *v.i.* **7** To lose or shed blood. **8** To exude sap or other fluid. **9** To suffer wounds or die, as in battle: He *bled* for his country. **10** To feel grief, sympathy, or anguish. **11** To suffer by extortion; be overcharged. **12** To be cut into, as a printed page. **13** To run, as dyes in wet cloth. — **to bleed (someone) white** To extort money from in very large amounts. — *n.* **1** A page or plate so trimmed as to cut the printing or engraving. **2** The part of a page or plate on which printing or an illustration extends beyond the usual printing edge. [OE *blēdan*]

bleed·er (blē′dər) *n.* **1** One who or that which bleeds. **2** A person who bleeds profusely from slight wounds; a hemophiliac.

bleeding heart **1** Any of various plants having racemes of pink, drooping, heart-shaped flowers; especially, the ornamental garden herb *(Dicentra spectabilis).* **2** *Colloq.* One whose political views are unduly influenced by sympathy for alleged suffering.

BLEEDING HEART (From 1 to 3 feet tall.)

bleek·bok (blēk′bok) *n.* An antelope, the oribi. [<Afrikaans]

blel·lum (blel′əm) *n.* *Scot.* A noisy talker.

blem·ish (blem′ish) *v.t.* To mar the perfection of; sully. — *n.* A disfiguring defect; also, moral reproach or stain. [<OF *blemiss-*, stem of *blemir* make livid <*blême* pale, wan] — **blem′·ish·er** *n.*

Synonyms (noun): blot, blur, brand, crack, daub, defacement, defect, deformity, dent, disfigurement, disgrace, dishonor, fault, flaw, imperfection, injury, reproach, smirch, soil, speck, spot, stain, stigma, taint, tarnish. A *blemish* is superficial; a *flaw* or *taint* is in structure or substance. In the moral sense, a *blemish* comes from one's own ill-doing; a *brand* or *stigma* is inflicted by others; as, the *brand* of infamy; we speak of a *blot* or *stain* upon reputation; a *flaw* or *taint* in character. A *defect* is the want or lack of something; *fault,* primarily a failing, is something that fails of an apparent intent or disappoints a natural expectation. See INJURY.

Blem·my·es (blem′mē·ēz) *n. pl.* A fabled people of ancient Libya who had no heads, but eyes and mouth placed in the breast.

blench[1] (blench) *v.i.* **1** To shrink back; flinch. **2** *Obs.* To turn aside. [OE *blencan* deceive] — **blench′er** *n.*

blench[2] (blench) See BLANCH.

blend (blend) *v.* **blend·ed** or **blent, blend·ing** *v.t.* **1** To mix, as paints or whiskies, so as to obtain a combined product of a desired quality, taste, color, or consistency. **2** To prepare by such process. — *v.i.* **3** To mix; intermingle. **4** To pass or shade imperceptibly into each other, as colors. **5** To harmonize; suit one another. See synonyms under MIX, UNITE. — *n.* **1** The act or result of mixing; a mixture. **2** *Ling.* A word resulting from the combining of parts of two distinct words of generally similar meaning, as *brunch* from *breakfast* and *lunch*: also called *portmanteau word, telescope word.* [Fusion of OE *blendan,* var. of *blandan* mix and ON *blanda* mingle]

blende (blend) *n.* **1** Sphalerite; zinc sulfide. **2** One of a number of rather bright minerals, generally a compound of sulfur with a metallic element. [<G *blendendes erz* deceptive ore] — **blend′ous, blend′y** *adj.*

blend·er (blen′dər) An automatic electrical device that mixes and blends foods, paints, cement, etc.

Blen·heim (blen′əm) See under SPANIEL.

Blen·heim (blen′əm) A village in western Bavaria, Germany; scene of Marlborough's and Eugene of Savoy's victory in an important battle, 1704, in the War of the Spanish Succession: German *Blindheim.*

Blenheim Park An estate and parish in central Oxfordshire, England; site of **Blenheim Palace,** voted by Parliament as a grant to the Duke of Marlborough for his victory at Blenheim and built by Vanbrugh, 1705–16.

Blen·ner·has·set (blen′ər·has′it), **Harman,** 1764–1831, Anglo-American lawyer involved with Aaron Burr in a plot to conquer Texas and Mexico.

blen·ny (blen′ē) *n.* *pl.* **blen·nies** A small percoid marine fish (family *Blennidae*) having the pelvic fins placed close together below the throat. [<L *blennius* <Gk. *blennos* slime] — **blen·ni·oid** (blen′ē·oid) *adj.*

bleph·a·ri·tis (blef′ə·rī′tis) *n.* *Pathol.* Inflammation of the eyelids.

blepharo- *combining form Anat., Pathol.* Eyelid. Also, before vowels, **blephar-,** as in *blepharitis.* [<Gk. *blepharon* eyelid]

Blé·riot (blā·ryō′) , **Louis,** 1872–1936, French aviator and designer.

bles·bok (bles′bok) *n.* *pl.* **·bok** or **·boks** A large South African antelope *(Damaliscus albifrons),* of a prevailing violet color and having a white blaze extending over its face. Also **bles·buck** (-buk). [<Afrikaans]

bless (bles) *v.t.* **blessed** or **blest, bless·ing** **1** To consecrate; make holy by religious rite. **2** To honor and exalt; glorify. **3** To sanctify or protect by making the sign of the cross over. **4** To invoke God's favor upon (a person or thing). **5** To bestow happiness or prosperity upon; make happy. **6** To endow, as with a gift: She was *blessed* with a beautiful face. **7** To guard; protect: used as an exclamation: God *bless* me; *Bless* me! See synonyms under PRAISE. [OE *blēdsian* consecrate (with blood) < *blōd* blood] — **bless′er** *n.*

bless·ed (bles′id, blest) *adj.* **1** Being in enjoyment of felicity in heaven; beatified. **2** Worthy of veneration or of blessing. **3** Joyful; healing. **4** Happy; favored. **5** Confounded, cursed, or the like: a euphemistic, ironical, or merely intensive use: not a *blessed* cent. Also **blest** (blest). See synonyms under HAPPY, HOLY. — **bless′ed·ly** *adv.*

blessed event *Colloq.* The birth of a baby.

bless·ed·ness (bles′id·nis) *n.* The state of one who is blessed; felicity. — **single blessedness** The unmarried state.

Bless·ed Sacrament (bles′id) In the Roman Catholic Church, the consecrated elements in the mass, especially the Host.

bless·ing (bles′ing) *n.* **1** That which makes happy or prosperous; a gift of divine favor. **2** A benediction. **3** Grateful adoration; worship. **4** Cursing or scolding: a euphemism. See synonyms under FAVOR, MERCY.

blest (blest) *adj.* Blessed.

blet (blet) *v.i.* **blet·ted, blet·ting** To decay internally, as a fleshy fruit after ripening. — *n.* Incipient decay in overripe fruit. [<F *blet* overripe]

bleth·er (bleth′ər) *n.* *Scot.* Blather.

blew (bloo͞) Past tense of BLOW.

Bli·da (blē′də) A city in north central Algeria.

Bligh (blī), **William,** 1754–1817, British naval officer.

blight (blīt) *n.* **1** Any of a number of destructive plant diseases, as mildew, rust, smut, etc. **2** Anything that withers hopes or prospects; also, the act of ruining or destroying. **3** A minute insect, usually an aphis, injurious to trees. **4** A deteriorating influence or condition affecting use, development, and value, as of real estate. — *v.t.* **1** To cause to decay; blast. **2** To ruin; frustrate. — *v.i.* **3** To suffer blight. [Origin unknown]

Bligh·ty (blī′tē) *n.* *Brit. Slang* **1** England; hence, home. **2** A wound severe enough to necessitate one's being sent to England for treatment. [Alter. of Hindustani *Bilāyati* foreign country]

blimp (blimp) *n.* *Colloq.* **1** A non-rigid, lighter-than-air, dirigible balloon. **2** The soundproof cover enclosing a motion-picture camera: also called *bungalow.* [<Type *B-Limp,* a kind of British dirigible]

blind (blīnd) *adj.* **1** Without the power of seeing. **2** Lacking in perception or judgment. **3** Acting or proceeding at random. **4** Difficult to understand or trace; illegible; unintelligible. **5** Having no opening or outlet: a *blind* ditch. **6** Having but one opening; open at one end only: a *blind* alley. **7** Difficult to find or follow: a *blind* path. **8** Of or relating to blind persons as a class. **9** Dark; obscure. — **to go it blind** **1** To bet in a poker game before looking at one's hand. **2** Hence, to undertake anything without reasonable inquiry. —*n.* **1** Something that obstructs vision or shuts off light; particularly, a window shade; a screen or shutter. **2** A subterfuge; ruse. **3** One who is, or those who are, blind. **4** A place of ambush; hiding place. **5** A baggage car with no end door: also **blind baggage.** See synonyms under ARTIFICE. —*v.t.* **1** To make blind. **2** To dazzle. **3** To deprive of judgment or discernment. **4** To darken; obscure. **5** To outshine; eclipse. [OE]

blind alley 1 An alley, road, etc., open at one end only. **2** Any search, occupation, or the like, in which progress is blocked.

blind date A date with a person whom one has not previously seen or met, usually arranged by a third person.

blind·er (blīn′dər) *n.* **1** One who or that which blinds. **2** A flap on the side of a horse's bridle, to obstruct his side view: also called *blinker.* For illustration see HARNESS.

blind·fish (blīnd′fish′) *n.* A fish of subterranean streams without functional eyes; especially, the cavefish *(Amblyopsis spelaeus)*, found in the Mammoth Cave of Kentucky.

blind·fold (blīnd′fōld′) *v.t.* **1** To cover or bandage the eyes of. **2** To hoodwink; mislead. —*n.* A bandage, etc., over the eyes. —*adj.* **1** Having the eyes bandaged. **2** Having the mental vision darkened; rash. Also **blind′·fold′ed** *adj.* [ME *blindfellen* < *blind* blind + *fellen* strike; infl. in spelling by FOLD]

blind gut The cecum.

Blind·heim (blint′hīm) German name for BLENHEIM.

blind hinge A shutter hinge constructed so that the shutter or other piece hinged thereby closes itself by its own weight when not held open. For illustration see under HINGE.

blind·ing (blīn′ding) *adj.* Making blind or as if blind, physically or mentally: *blinding* tears; *blinding* passions. —**blind′ing·ly** *adv.*

blind·ly (blīnd′lē) *adv.* Without sight or without foresight; recklessly.

blind·man's–buff (blīnd′manz′buf′) *n.* A game in which one who is blindfolded must catch and identify someone.

blind poker A game of poker in which bets are made before the hands are seen.

blind side The weakest or most vulnerable side.

blind spot 1 *Anat.* A small area on the retina of the eye that is insensible to light because of the entrance of the fibers of the optic nerve. **2** A subject or a phase of thought in which one is unable to be objective or critical.

blind staggers Staggers (def. 1).

blind·sto·ry (blīnd′stôr′ē, -stō′rē) *n. pl.* **·sto·ries** A story without windows; the triforium.

blind tiger *Slang* A place where intoxicants are illegally served and sold. Also **blind pig.**

blind·worm (blīnd′wûrm′) *n.* A small, limbless, snakelike lizard with very small but perfect eyes; especially the slowworm *(Anguis fragilis)* of Europe and Africa.

blink (blingk) *v.i.* **1** To wink rapidly. **2** To look with half-closed eyes, as in sunlight; squint. **3** To twinkle; glimmer; also, to flash on and off. **4** To ignore something: He *blinked* at the law. —*v.t.* **5** To cause to wink. **6** To shut the eyes to; evade: to *blink* matters. **7** To send (a message) by blinker light. —*n.* **1** A glance or glimpse. **2** A shimmer or glimmer. **3** Light reflected from floating ice; iceblink. [<Du. *blinken*]

blink·er (blingk′ər) *n.* **1** One who or that which blinks. **2** A blinker light. **3** *pl.* Goggles. **4** A horse's blinder.

blinker light 1 A light set to blink at regular intervals, usually as a warning. **2** A light used to signal messages.

blin·tze (blin′tsə) *n.* A thin pancake folded about a filling, as of cheese. Also **blintz** (blints). [<Yiddish]

blip (blip) *n.* **1** *Telecom.* A visual display of a radar echo. **2** A short, sharp sound. —*v.i.* **blipped, blip·ping 1** To make blips. —*v.t.* **2** To delete (speech) from a videotape, as in censoring, thus creating a discontinuity: to *blip* swearwords. [Imit.]

bliss (blis) *n.* **1** Superlative happiness; heavenly joy. **2** Gladness; joy. **3** A cause of delight. See synonyms under HAPPINESS, RAPTURE. [OE *bliths* < *blithe* joyous] —**bliss′ful** *adj.* —**bliss′ful·ly** *adv.* —**bliss′ful·ness** *n.*

blis·ter (blis′tər) *n.* **1** A thin vesicle, especially one on the skin, containing watery matter, as from a scald, bruise, etc. **2** A similar vesicle on a plant, on steel, or on a painted surface. **3** Any substance used for blistering. **4** *Nav.* A bulge on the hull of a warship below the waterline to protect it from torpedoes. **5** *Aeron.* A bulge or projection from the fuselage of certain aircraft, containing guns and used for observation. —*v.t.* **1** To produce a blister or blisters upon. **2** To rebuke; lash with words. —*v.i.* **3** To become blistered. [OF *blestre* <ON *blāstr* swelling]

blister beetle 1 A beetle (family *Meloidae*), yielding a vesicating substance; especially, the Spanish fly. **2** A long, slender beetle (genus *Epicauta*), widely distributed in the United States, especially *E. pennsylvanicus*, very destructive of the potato. See illustrations under INSECTS (injurious).

blis·tered (blis′tərd) *adj.* **1** Having blisters. **2** Covered with raised spots resembling blisters. **3** Having slits which reveal material of a different color or a different type of material, especially in 16th century costumes.

blister gas *Mil.* A gaseous vesicant used in warfare.

blister rust A serious disease of pine trees, especially the white-pine blister rust, caused by a fungus (genus *Cronartium*) that raises blisters on the bark.

blis·ter·y (blis′tər·ē) *adj.* Marked by or full of blisters.

blithe (blīth) *adj.* Characterized by gladness or mirth; joyous; gay; merry; sprightly. See synonyms under CHEERFUL, HAPPY, MERRY. [OE] —**blithe′ly** *adv.*

blithe·some (blīth′səm) *adj.* Showing or imparting gladness; cheerful; merry. See synonyms under HAPPY. —**blithe′some·ly** *adv.* —**blithe′some·ness** *n.*

blitz (blits) *v.t. Colloq.* To attack with sudden and overwhelming force. —*n.* Sudden force; lightninglike destruction. —*adj.* Lightning-like. [<G, lightning]

blitz·krieg (blits′krēg) *n.* **1** Lightning war. **2** Sudden overwhelming attack with powerful force. [<G]

bliz·zard (bliz′ərd) *n. Meteorol.* **1** A high, cold wind accompanied by blinding snow. **2** A severe and heavy snowstorm of long duration. [< dial.E *blizzer* sudden blow, flash of lightning]

bloat[1] (blōt) *v.t.* **1** To cause to swell, as with fluid or gas. **2** To puff up; make proud or vain. —*v.i.* **3** To swell; become puffed up. —*n.* **1** One who is bloated; a drunkard. **2** An accumulation of gas in the rumen or intestinal tract of an animal brought on by the fermentation of green forage. —*adj.* Bloated; puffed; swollen. [ME *blout,* ? <ON *blautr* soft, soaked]

bloat[2] (blōt) *v.t.* To cure, as herring, by half-drying in smoke. —*adj.* Smoke-cured: a *bloat* herring. [ME *blote,* ? <ON *blautr* soft, soaked]

bloat·ed (blō′tid) *adj.* **1** Swollen with fluid or gas. **2** Turgid; edematous. **3** Puffed up; conceited.

bloat·er (blō′tər) *n.* **1** A selected smoked herring. **2** A whitefish *(Argyrosomus prognathus)* of the Great Lakes of North America.

blob (blob) *n.* **1** A soft, globular mass; a drop, as of viscous liquid; a blotch or daub. **2** A noise like that made by a fish flopping in water. —*v.* **blobbed, blob·bing** *v.t.* **1** To smear with ink or color; blur. —*v.i.* **2** To rise in bubbles or produce bubbles. **3** To flop, as a fish in water. [Imit.]

bloc (blok) *n.* A group, as of politicians, combined to foster special interests or to obstruct legislative action: originally, a combination of members of different political parties in the French Chamber of Deputies. Compare BLOCK[2]. [<F]

Bloch (blok, *Ger.* blôkh), **Ernest,** 1880–1959, U.S. composer born in Switzerland.

block[1] (blok) *n.* **1** A solid piece of wood, metal, or other material. **2** A wooden log or the like upon which chopping is done. **3** A temporary support; shore. **4** The stand on which slaves were sold at auction. **5** A wooden billet on which condemned persons are beheaded. **6** The form or piece on which the final shape is given to a hat body, or one on which a hat is placed to be ironed. **7** A wooden support for a wig: a barbers' *block.* **8** A continuous portion of land: a 10-acre *block.* **9** A sheave or pulley, or set of pulleys, in a frame or shell. **10** The land and buildings enclosed in a single square, or the like, bounded by streets; the distance along a street from

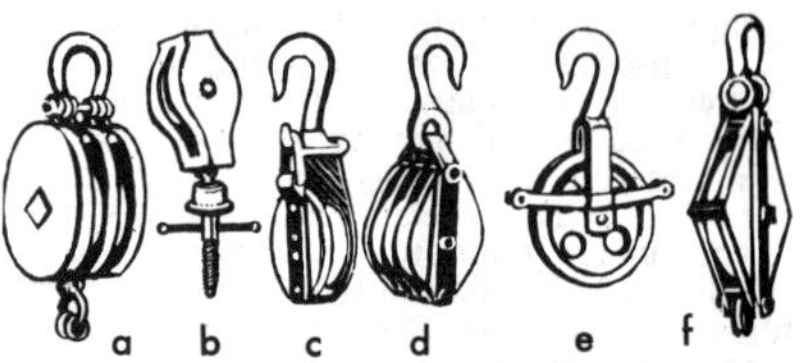

TYPES OF BLOCKS
a. Tackle. *b.* Dock. *c.* Link snatch. *d.* Triple-sheave steel. *e.* Gin. *f.* Square-cheeked.

one cross-street to another. **11** A group acting or considered as a unit: a *block* of theater seats; the Asian *block* of nations. **12** *Austral.* The public promenade of a city; also, one of the sections into which the public lands available for settlement are divided. **13** A section of a railroad controlled by signals. **14** A set, as of tickets, shares of stock, etc., handled as a unit. —*v.t.* **1** To shape into blocks. **2** To shape, mold, or stamp with a block, as a hat. **3** To secure or strengthen with blocks. —**to block out** To plan broadly without details. —**to block up** To raise on blocks. [<F *bloc,* ult. <Gmc.]

block[2] (blok) *n.* **1** That which hinders or obstructs, or the condition of being obstructed; an obstruction. **2** In sports, interference. **3** The blocking of a ball with a bat, as in cricket. **4** *Pathol.* An obstruction, as of a nerve or blood vessel. —*v.t.* **1** To obstruct; stop or impede the progress of. **2** To stop with or as with a block; blockade: often with *up.* **3** In sports, to hinder the movements of (an opposing player), usually by bodily contact; also, to stop (a ball), as with the body. **4** *Physiol.* To stop (a nerve) from functioning, as with an anesthetic. —*v.i.* **5** To act so as to hinder. See synonyms under HINDER. —**to block out** To obscure from view. —**to block up** To fill (an area or space) so as to prevent movement into or through. [<F *bloquer* obstruct < *bloc* block, ult. <Gmc.]

block·ade (blo·kād′) *v.t.* **·ad·ed, ·ad·ing** To close to traffic or communication by military or naval force; obstruct. —*n.* **1** The investing of a coast by a hostile naval force with intent to close it to maritime commerce. **2** A blockading force. **3** Any hindrance or obstruction to action. —**to run the blockade** To elude blockading forces. [<BLOCK[2]]

block·ad·er (blo·kā′dər) *n.* One who or that which blockades, as a warship.

blockade runner 1 A vessel engaged in passing through a blockade. **2** The captain of such a vessel, or a member of the crew.

block·bust·er (blok′bus′tər) *n.* **1** An aerial bomb capable of devastating a large area. **2** *U.S.* One who engages in blockbusting.

block·bust·ing (blok′bust′ing) *n. U.S.* The practice of inducing home owners to sell hastily and often at a loss by arousing the fear that the sale of nearby homes to members of a minority group will lower the values of their houses.

block·er (blok′ər) *n.* **1** One who or that which blocks. **2** In football, a player who obstructs an opposing tackler.

block front In American furniture, a form of front, as in a desk or chest of drawers, characterized by three vertical panels, the center concave, the end panels convex or blocked. —**block′-front′** *adj.*

block·head (blok′hed′) *n.* A stupid person.

block·house (blok′·hous′) *n.* **1** A fortification, formerly of logs and heavy timbers, now of concrete or other very resistant material, having loopholes from which to fire guns. **2** *U.S.* A house made of hewn logs set square.

BLOCKHOUSE

block·ish (blok′ish) *adj.* Like a block; stupid; dull. Also **block′like′.**

Block Island An island resort off the south coast of and belonging to Rhode Island.

block lava Lava in the form of angular blocks with sharp, rough surfaces.

block letter 1 Printing type cut from wood. 2 A style of printing without serifs, resembling letters cut from wood. — **block-let·ter** (blok′·let′·ər) *adj.*

block·line (blok′līn′) *n.* A line passing over one or more blocks and pulleys.

block plane A small carpenter's plane for trimming wood across the grain.

block printing A method of printing from wooden blocks on which designs have been engraved.

block signal A signal functioning as part of a block system.

block system A system of regulating the running of trains on a railway, by automatic signals or otherwise, in which the track is divided into sections called blocks, on any one of which, ordinarily, only one train at a time is allowed.

block tin 1 Tin cast in ingots. 2 Pure tin as distinguished from tin plate.

block·y (blok′ē) *adj.* **·i·er, ·i·est** 1 Unequally shaded, as if printed in blocks. 2 Short and stout; stocky.

Bloem·fon·tein (blōōm′fon·tān) A city, capital of Orange Free State province and judicial capital of the Republic of South Africa.

Blois (blwä) A city on the Loire, north central France.

bloke (blōk) *n. Brit. Slang* A fellow; guy.

Blom·i·don (blom′i·dən), **Cape** A headland on the north coast of Nova Scotia.

blond (blond) *adj.* 1 Having a fair skin with light eyes and hair. 2 Flaxen or golden, as hair. — *n.* 1 A blond person: feminine **blonde** (blond). 2 A variety of silk lace. [<F, yellow-haired <Med.L *blondus,* prob. <Gmc.]

blood (blud) *n.* 1 The chemically complex and usually red fluid that circulates through the vascular system of most vertebrates. Consisting essentially of semi-solid corpuscles suspended in plasma, it delivers oxygen and nutrients to all the cells and tissues, distributes internal secretions, removes waste products, guards against infection, and helps to maintain homeostasis of the organism. ◆Collateral adjective: *hemal.* 2 Kinship by descent; race; especially, noble lineage. Compare FULL BLOOD, HALF BLOOD. 3 Vitality; temperament; mood. 4 Bloodshed; war; murder. 5 A dashing fellow; gallant. 6 One of various red liquids, as the sap of some trees. 7 A blood horse. 8 The life blood of a sacrificial victim, especially as in the atonement of Christ. See synonyms under AFFINITY, KIN. — *v.t.* 1 To draw blood from; bleed. 2 To give (a hunting dog) its first sight or smell of blood; also, to give (troops) their first experience of battle. — *adj.* Blooded; of superior breed: a fine *blood* mare. [OE *blōd*]

blood-and-thun·der (blud′ən·thun′dər) *adj.* Characterized by violence and bloodshed; sensational; melodramatic: said of certain fiction or drama.

blood bank *Med.* A reserve of blood, either in liquid form classified according to blood groups, or in the form of dried plasma, for use in transfusion.

blood bath A massacre; slaughter.

blood-bol·tered (blud′bōl′tərd) *adj.* Daubed or clotted with blood.

blood count *Med.* A measure giving the number and proportion of red and white cells in a given sample of blood: used for clinical and diagnostic purposes.

blood-cur·dling (blud′kurd′ling) *adj.* Terrifying or horrifying enough to curdle or congeal the blood.

blood·ed (blud′id) *adj.* 1 Having blood or temper of a specified character: cold-*blooded.* 2 Having pure blood or lineage; thoroughbred.

blood group *Physiol.* One of four great classes into which all human beings may be divided on the basis of specific genetic differences in the composition and properties of blood: in the classification of Landsteiner, they are designated as AB, A, B, and O. Also **blood type.**

blood·guilt (blud′gilt′) *n.* The crime of unrighteous bloodshed. — **blood′guilt′i·ness** *n.* — **blood′guilt′y** *adj.*

blood heat *Physiol.* The normal temperature of human blood, about 98.6°F. or 37°C.

blood·hound (blud′hound′) *n.* A large hound with an unusual ability to follow a scent: characterized by a powerful body, straight and large-boned forelegs, and loose skin: often used to track fugitives: also called *sleuthhound.*

blood·less (blud′lis) *adj.* 1 Having no blood; without color; pale. 2 Lifeless. 3 Cold-hearted. 4 Without bloodshed. — **blood′less·ly** *adv.* — **blood′less·ness** *n.*

blood·let·ting (blud′let′ing) *n.* Bleeding for a therapeutic purpose. — **blood′let′ter** *n.*

blood·line (blud′līn′) *n.* Strain or pedigree, as of livestock.

blood·mo·bile (blud′mə·bēl) *n.* An automobile or other vehicle equipped to obtain and carry supplies of blood for emergency transfusion.

blood money Money paid to a hired murderer, or, as compensation, to the kin of a murdered man.

blood plasma *Physiol.* The liquid part of the blood, containing all the components of whole blood except hemoglobin.

blood platelet *Physiol.* A thrombocyte; one of the minute circular or oval bodies found in the blood of higher vertebrates, essential to the coagulating process.

blood poisoning Introduction of virulent bacteria into the blood stream, usually from a local infection, such as a boil or wound; septicemia.

blood pressure *Physiol.* The pressure of the blood on the walls of the arteries, varying with the force of the heart action, resilience of the arteries and blood vessels, amount and viscosity of blood, etc.

blood pudding An article of food composed of swine's blood, coagulated by cooking, intermingled with particles of fat and usually stuffed into skins. Also **blood sausage.**

blood-red (blud′red′) *adj.* Colored with or like blood. See synonyms under BLOODY.

blood relation A person of the same stock or parentage; a kinsman by birth.

blood·root (blud′rōōt′, -rŏŏt′) *n.* 1 A low perennial North American herb *(Sanguinaria canadensis),* having pale green leaves, a single white or pink flower, and a thick rhizome with abundant red, acrid juice. Also called *red puccoon.*

blood·shed (blud′shed′) *n.* The shedding of blood; slaughter; carnage. Also **blood′shed′·ding.** — **blood′shed′der** *n.*

blood·shot (blud′shot′) *adj.* Suffused or shot with blood; red and inflamed or irritated: said of the eye.

blood·stain (blud′stān′) *n.* A spot produced by blood. — *v.t.* To stain with blood. — **blood′·stained′** *adj.*

blood·stone (blud′stōn′) *n.* A stone of green chalcedony flecked with particles of red jasper: often cut as a gem.

blood·stream (blud′strēm) *n.* The stream of blood coursing through a living body.

blood·suck·er (blud′suk′ər) *n.* 1 An animal that sucks blood, as a leech. 2 A cruel extortioner. — **blood′suck′ing** *adj.*

blood test *Med.* Any of various procedures for indicating the presence of blood under set conditions, or for determining its specific type or its condition in health or disease.

blood·thirst·y (blud′thûrs′tē) *adj.* Thirsting for blood; murderous; cruel. — **blood′thirst′i·ly** *adv.* — **blood′thirst′i·ness** *n.*

blood transfusion *Med.* The transfer of a quantity of the blood from one person into the vascular system of another.

blood type Blood group.

blood vessel Any tubular canal in which the blood circulates: an artery, vein, or capillary.

blood·wood (blud′wŏŏd′) *n.* 1 Haematoxylon. 2 Any of various other woods characterized by a red or reddish heartwood, especially the Jamaica ironwood *(Laplacea haematoxylon)* valued as timber, and the bloodwood cacique *(Brosimum caloxylon),* used by the Panama Indians as a tribal medicine.

blood·worm (blud′wûrm′) *n.* Any of various annelid worms (genera *Polycirrus* and *Enoplobranchus*), having long, slender bodies and bright-red blood: found in mud and shallow water.

blood·wort (blud′wûrt′) *n.* 1 Any plant of the family *Haemodoraceae.* 2 The salad burnet *(Sanguisorba minor).* 3 The red-veined dock (genus *Rumex*). 4 Bloodroot.

blood·y (blud′ē) *adj.* **blood·i·er, blood·i·est** 1 Covered or stained with blood: also **blood′ied.** 2 Consisting of, containing, or mixed with blood. 3 Characterized by or delighting in bloodshed; saguinary; bloodthirsty. 4 Red like blood; suggesting blood. 5 *Brit. Slang* Damned; accursed; confounded: also used adverbially, meaning very, exceedingly, damnably; as, not *bloody* likely: a low vulgarism. — *v.t.* **blood·ied, blood·y·ing** To smear or stain with blood. — **blood′i·ly** *adv.* — **blood′i·ness** *n.*

Synonyms (adj.): blood-dyed, blood-red, blood-stained, crimson, gory, reeking, sanguinary. *Bloody* is commonly used in the literal, *sanguinary* in the figurative sense. We say a *sanguinary* or *bloody* battle, a *sanguinary* temper, a *bloody* weapon, a *bloody* field. *Crimson* refers to the color of blood; *gory* signifies covered or daubed with gore, or clotted blood, and always keeps the physical signification. *Reeking,* which is capable of other meanings, is often used alone to signify wet with steaming blood; as a *reeking* blade. *Antonyms:* bloodless, calm, conciliatory, gentle, harmless, peaceable, peaceful, tranquil, unwarlike.

bloody shirt The bloodstained shirt of one who has been killed, exhibited to incite or perpetuate vengeance: used especially as the symbol of enmity between the North and South after the Civil War. — **to wave the bloody shirt** To keep alive or incite hostility by displaying the bloodstained shirts of those slain by an enemy: often used figuratively.

bloom[1] (blōōm) *n.* 1 The act of florescence or the state of being in flower. 2 A growing or flourishing condition; freshness; also, flush; glow. 3 A flower; blossom; also, flowers collectively. 4 *Bot.* The powdery, waxy substance on certain fruits, as the plum or grape, and on certain leaves, as those of the cabbage. 5 A clouded appearance on a varnished surface. 6 A yellow appearance on tanned leather. 7 A fluorescence seen in lubricating oils. 8 *Phot.* A moist film on the surface of a lens, film, or glass plate. 9 A fine variety of sundried raisin: also **bloom raisin.** 10 An earthy mineral, usually bright-colored, and ordinarily a decomposition product. — *v.i.* 1 To bear flowers; blossom. 2 To glow with health and beauty; be at one's prime. 3 To glow with a warm color; be rosy. — *v.t.* 4 To bring into bloom; cause to flourish. 5 To invest with a warm color. 6 To cloud, as a varnished surface. [<ON *blōm* flower, blossom. Akin to BLOSSOM.]

bloom[2] (blōōm) *n.* 1 *Metall.* A mass of malleable iron from which the slag has been forced by hammer or roller. 2 A lump of melted glass. [OE *bloma* lump of metal]

bloom·er[1] (blōō′mər) *n.* 1 A costume of loose trousers under a short skirt; also, a woman so dressed. 2 *pl.* Loose, wide knickerbockers gathered at the knees: worn by women. 3 *pl.* Canvas guards attached to turrets of battleships and enclosing the barrels of turret guns to keep out dampness. [after Mrs. Amelia *Bloomer,* U.S. feminist reformer, 1818–94, who first proposed it]

bloom·er[2] (blōō′mər) *n. Slang* A bad mistake; an error. [? <Australian slang *a bloom(ing) er(ror)*]

bloom·er·y (blōō′mər·ē) *n. pl.* **·er·ies** *Metall.* 1 An apparatus or establishment for making malleable iron directly from the ore. 2 A puddling furnace.

Bloom·field (blōōm′fēld), **Leonard,** 1887–1949, U.S. linguist.

bloom·ing (blōō′ming) *adj.* Coming into flower; hence, fresh and beautiful; prosperous. See synonyms under FRESH. — **bloom′ing·ly** *adv.* — **bloom′ing·ness** *n.*

bloom·y (blōō′mē) *adj.* 1 Abounding in blooms; flowery. 2 Covered with bloom, as a fruit.

bloop (blōōp) *n.* In sound reproduction of motion pictures, the dull thud caused by a poorly made patch of material placed over a splice in the sound track. [Imit.]

bloop·er (blōō′pər) *n.* 1 *U.S. Slang* An error

or blunder. **2** In baseball: **a** A weakly hit fly ball reaching just beyond the infield. **b** A high, weakly thrown pitch. [Imit.]

blos·som (blos′əm) *n.* **1** A flower, especially one of a plant yielding edible fruit. **2** The state or period of flowering; bloom. **3** *Geol.* A weathered or decomposed outcrop of a coal bed or mineral bed. — *v.i.* **1** To come into blossom; bloom. **2** To prosper; thrive. See synonyms under FLOURISH. [OE *blostma.* Akin to BLOOM.] — **blos′som·less** *adj.* — **blos′·som·y** *adj.*

blot[1] (blot) *n.* **1** A spot or stain, as of ink. **2** Reproach; blemish; a stain on a reputation. **3** An erasure. See synonyms under BLEMISH, STAIN. — *v.* **blot·ted, blot·ting** *v.t.* **1** To spot, as with ink; stain. **2** To disgrace; sully. **3** To mark over or obliterate, as writing: often with *out.* **4** To dry with blotting paper. **5** To obscure; darken: usually with *out.* **6** To paint roughly; daub. — *v.i.* **7** To spread in a blot or blots, as ink. **8** To become blotted; acquire spots. **9** To absorb: This paper *blots* well. [ME *blotte*; origin uncertain]

blot[2] (blot) *n.* **1** In backgammon, an exposed man liable to be forfeited. **2** Any exposed point; a weak spot. [Origin uncertain]

blotch (bloch) *n.* **1** A spot or blot. **2** An inflamed eruption on the skin. — *v.t.* To mark or cover with blotches. [Blend of BLOT[1] and BOTCH[2]] — **blotch′y** *adj.*

blot·ter (blot′ər) *n.* **1** A sheet, pad, or book of blotting paper. **2** The daily record of arrests and charges in a police station. **3** Anything that blots or defiles.

blotting paper Unsized paper for absorbing excess ink.

Blount (blunt), **Charles,** 1563–1605?, Earl of Devonshire; English statesman; suppressed Irish rebellion, 1603.

blouse (blous, blouz) *n.* **1** A woman's loose waist or bodice of various types, extending from the neck to the waist or below, and worn tucked into the skirt or outside. **2** A loose, knee-length shirt or frock, usually belted at the waist, worn chiefly by French workmen. **3** A U.S. Army service coat. [<F; ult. origin uncertain]

bloused (bloust, blouzd) *adj.* **1** Wearing a blouse. **2** Made loose like a blouse, as a waist.

blow[1] (blō) *v.* **blew, blown, blow·ing** *v.t.* **1** To move by a current of air. **2** To overthrow or extinguish by a current of air. **3** To emit, as air or smoke, from the mouth. **4** To force air upon, as from the mouth: often with *up*: to *blow up* a fire. **5** To empty or clear by forcing air through, as pipes. **6** To cause to sound, as a bugle or horn. **7** To sound (a signal): The bugle *blew* taps. **8** To form or shape, as by inflating: to *blow* glass. **9** To put out of breath, as a horse. **10** To shatter or destroy by or as by explosion: usually with *up, down, out, through,* etc.: to *blow out* a tire; to *blow down* a pole; to *blow* a hole *through* a wall; to *blow up* a house. **11** To melt (a fuse). **12** To lay eggs in, as flies in meat. **13** *Slang* To spend (money) lavishly; also, to treat or entertain: I'll *blow* you to a meal. **14** *Slang* To leave; go out of. **15** *Slang* To damn: a euphemism: Well, I'll be *blowed.* — *v.i.* **16** To be in motion: said of wind or air. **17** To move in a current of air; be carried by the wind. **18** To emit a current or jet of air, water, steam, etc. **19** To sound by being blown: The bugle *blew* at dawn. **20** To fail or become useless, as by melting: The fuse *blew.* **21** To explode: usually with *up, down, to,* etc.: The engine *blew up.* **22** To pant; gasp for breath. **23** *Colloq.* To talk boastfully. **24** *Slang* To leave; go. — **to blow a fuse** *Colloq.* To lose self-control; become enraged. — **to blow hot and cold** *Colloq.* To vacillate; be uncertain. — **to blow off** **1** To let off steam, as from a boiler. **2** *Slang* To speak in anger, as to relieve pent-up emotion. — **to blow out** To subside; become less intense: The storm will *blow* itself *out.* — **to blow over** To pass, as a storm; subside. — **to blow up** **1** To inflate. **2** To enlarge, as a photographic print. **3** *Colloq.* To lose self-control; become enraged. **4** To arise; become increasingly intense, as a storm. — *n.* **1** The act of blowing; a blast; gale. **2** The oviposition of a fly; a flyblow. **3** *Metall.* A single blast of the Bessemer converter, or the quantity of metal acted on at one time. **4** *Mining* The violent inrush of gas from or into a coal seam; also, the collapse of a mine roof. **5** *Slang* Boastfulness: oratorical *blow.* **6** Time to get the breath; the act of getting the breath when winded. [OE *blāwan.* Akin to BLAST.]

blow[2] (blō) *n.* **1** A sudden or violent stroke; thump; thwack. **2** A sudden misfortune. **3** A hostile or combative act: usually in the plural: coming to *blows.* — **at a** (or **one**) **blow** By a single stroke or action; all at one time. — **to come to blows** To start fighting one another. [ME *blaw*]

Synonyms: box, buffet, calamity, concussion, cuff, cut, disaster, hit, knock, lash, misfortune, rap, shock, stripe, stroke, thump. A *blow* is a sudden impact, as of a fist or a club; a *stroke* is a sweeping movement: the *stroke* of a sword, of an oar, of the arm in swimming. A *slap* is given with the open hand, a *lash* with a whip, thong, or the like; we speak also of the *cut* of a whip. A *cuff* is a somewhat sidelong *blow,* generally with the open hand: a *cuff* or *box* on the ear. In the metaphorical sense, *blow* is used for sudden, stunning, staggering *calamity* or sorrow; *stroke* for sweeping *disaster,* and also for sweeping achievement and success. We say a *stroke* of paralysis, or a *stroke* of genius. We speak of the *buffets* of adverse fortune. *Shock* is used of that which is at once sudden, violent, and prostrating; we speak of a *shock* of electricity, the *shock* of an amputation, a *shock* of surprise. Compare BEAT, MISFORTUNE.

blow[3] (blō) *v.* **blew, blown, blow·ing** *v.t.* **1** To cause to bloom, as a plant. **2** To produce, as flowers. — *v.i.* **3** To bloom; blossom. — *n.* **1** The state of flowering. **2** A mass of blossoms; blossoms in general. [OE *blowan* blossom]

blow-back (blō′bak′) *n.* **1** The escape from the rear of a gun of gases formed by discharge of the projectile. **2** A defective cartridge or primer causing this escape.

blow·by (blō′bī′) *n.* **1** The exhaust fumes of a car, truck, etc. **2** A device on the car, etc., to reduce such fumes.

blow·er (blō′ər) *n.* **1** One who or that which blows. **2** A device for forcing a draft of air through a building, furnace, machinery, etc. **3** *Slang* A boaster.

blow·fish (blō′fish′) *n.* *pl.* **·fish** or **·fish·es** **1** The walleyed perch. **2** A swellfish or any like fish which can puff up its body.

blow·fly (blō′flī′) *n.* *pl.* **·flies** Any of several metallic-blue or -green flies (family *Calliphoridae*), whose larvae live in carrion or in the wounds of living animals.

blow·gun (blō′gun′) *n.* A long tube through which a missile, as an arrow, may be blown by the breath.

blow-hard (blō′härd′) *Slang n.* A braggart. — *adj.* Boastful.

blow·hole (blō′hōl′) *n.* **1** *Zool.* The nasal openings in the heads of certain cetaceans. **2** *Geol.* A small crater formed on the surface of a lava flow for the escape of gas, etc. **3** A vent for the release of gas and bad air, as from mines. **4** *Metall.* A defect in a metal casting due to an air bubble caught during solidification. **5** A hole in the ice to which seals, whales, etc., come to breathe.

blow·ing (blō′ing) *n.* **1** The action of emitting or applying a current of air. **2** The act or sound of breathing, especially hard breathing, as of an animal. **3** *Metall.* An inrush of steam or gas through molten metal.

blown[1] (blōn) Past participle of BLOW[1]. — *adj.* **1** Winded from overexertion. **2** Spoiled, as food, by exposure, keeping, or oviposition; tainted. **3** Inflated or swollen with gas. **4** Made with a blowpipe: *blown* glass.

blown[2] (blōn) Past participle of BLOW[3]. — *adj.* In full flower or bloom.

blow·off (blō′ôf′, -of′) *n.* **1** The expelling of water, vapor, etc. **2** An apparatus for blowing off steam, water, etc., as from boilers.

blow·out (blō′out′) *n.* **1** *Electr.* The explosive destruction of a fuse by an overcharge. **2** *Slang* A formal entertainment that becomes disorderly; also, an elaborate social function or, especially, an elaborate meal. **3** A puncture in or bursting of an automobile tire. **4** A flameout.

blow·pipe (blō′pīp′) *n.* **1** A tube by which air or gas is blown through a flame for the purpose of fusing, heating, or melting something. **2** A blowtube (def. 3). **3** A blowgun.

blowse (blouz) *n.* *Obs.* A fat, red-faced woman. [Origin uncertain]

blow·torch (blō′tôrch′) *n.* An apparatus for vaporizing a combustible fluid under pressure and expelling it from a nozzle as a long, intensely hot flame: used for soldering, etc.

BLOWTORCH

blow·tube (blō′tōōb′, -tyōōb′) *n.* **1** A pea-shooter. **2** A blowgun. **3** A tube used for blowing molten glass into the desired shape.

blow-up (blō′up′) *n.* **1** An explosion. **2** *Colloq.* Bankruptcy. **3** *Colloq.* Loss of self-control. **4** An enlargement, as of a photograph, page of print, etc. **5** A rapid increase in the intensity or spread of a fire.

blow·y (blō′ē) *adj.* **blow·i·er, blow·i·est** Windy.

blowz·y (blou′zē) *adj.* **·i·er, ·i·est** **1** Slatternly or unkempt; slovenly. **2** Having a red or flushed face. Also **blows·y** (blou′zē), **blowzed** (blouzd). [<BLOWSE]

blub·ber[1] (blub′ər) *v.t.* **1** To disfigure, wet, or swell with weeping. **2** To utter sobbingly. — *v.i.* **3** Weep and sob noisily. [ME *blubren*] — **blub′ber·er** *n.* — **blub′ber·ing·ly** *adv.*

blub·ber[2] (blub′ər) *n.* **1** *Zool.* The layer of fat beneath the skin of a cetacean, used as a source of oil. **2** The act of blubbering. [ME *bluber*]

blub·ber·y (blub′ər·ē) *adj.* **1** Like blubber; very fat. **2** Swollen, as cheeks; protruding.

blu·cher (blōō′chər, -kər) *n.* **1** A half boot, or high shoe. **2** A shoe in which there is no front seam, the upper meeting above in two projecting flaps. [after BLÜCHER]

Blü·cher (blōō′chər, -kər, *Ger.* blü′khər), **Gebhard Leberecht von,** 1742–1819, German field marshal commanding Prussian army at Waterloo.

blude (blüd) *n.* *Scot.* Blood.

bludg·eon (bluj′ən) *n.* A short club, commonly loaded at one end, used as a weapon. — *v.t.* **1** To strike with or as with a bludgeon. **2** To coerce; bully. [Origin unknown]

blue (blōō) *adj.* **blu·er, blu·est** **1** Having the color of the clear sky. **2** Dismal; dreary; melancholy; despondent; also, depressing; discouraging: Things look *blue.* **3** Severe or Puritanic; strict: *blue* laws. **4** Faithful; genuine; sterling: He is true *blue.* **5** Livid, as from contusion, cold, or fear. **6** Devoted to literature; pedantic: said of women. **7** Denoting venous blood that shows through the skin. **8** Designating a flame, as of a candle, where the red glare is absent: said to be an omen of the presence of evil spirits. — *n.* **1** One of the chief colors of the spectrum, between green and violet; the color of the clear sky; azure. **2** The coloring matter or pigment used for imparting a blue color. **3** A blueprint. **4** One who wears blue clothing or insignia. **5** *pl.* See BLUES. **6** The bluish-gray winter coat of a deer. **7** A small butterfly of the family *Lycaenidae.* **8** A bluestocking. — **out of the blue** At an unexpected time and from an unsuspected source; completely unforeseen. — *v.t.* **blued, blu·ing** **1** To make blue. **2** To treat with bluing. [<OF *bleu,* ult. <Gmc.] — **blue′ly** *adv.* — **blue′ness** *n.*

Blue (blōō) *n.* **1** A soldier of the Federal Army in the American Civil War. Compare GRAY. **2** *Brit.* An athlete wearing the colors of his university in contests between Oxford (dark blue) and Cambridge (light blue). **3** *Brit.* A member of the Royal Horse Guard.

blue-and-white (blōō′ən·hwīt′) *n.* Nanking porcelain.

blue baby An infant born with cyanosis resulting from a congenital heart lesion or from defective expansion of the lung.

blue·ball (blōō′bôl′) *n.* Baby-blue-eyes.

Blue·beard (blōō′bird′) In folklore, a man who married and then murdered his wives one after another.

blue·bell (blōō′bel′) *n.* **1** Any one of various plants that bear blue bell-shaped flowers. **2** The grape hyacinth. **3** The Virginia cowslip. **4** The wood hyacinth. **5** The harebell.

blue·ber·ry (blōō′ber′ē, -bər·ē) *n.* *pl.* **·ries** **1** A many-seeded, edible, blue or black American berry of the genus *Vaccinium.* **2** The plant that bears it. Compare HUCKLEBERRY.

blue·bill (blōō′bil′) *n.* The scaup duck.

blue·bird (blōō′bûrd′) *n.* A small American passerine bird (genus *Sialia*), with a prevailing blue plumage, especially the eastern bluebird (*S. sialis*) common in North America, and the Mexican bluebird (*S. mexicana*).
blue blindness Tritanopia.
blue blood 1 Blood of a supposed finer or purer kind. 2 Aristocratic lineage, character, or bearing. 3 A person of noble or aristocratic family. —**blue′–blood′ed** *adj.*
blue·bon·net (blōō′bon′it) *n.* 1 The cornflower. 2 An annual leguminous herb (*Lupinus subcarnosus*) with blue flowers: the State flower of Texas. 3 A woolen cap worn by the Scots; hence, a Scot.
blue·book (blōō′bŏŏk′) *n.* 1 A register of names of persons employed by the U.S. government. 2 A classified register, as of persons in high society. 3 *Brit.* A governmental publication, issued in blue covers.
blue·bot·tle (blōō′bot′l) *n.* 1 A blowfly (family *Callephoridae*) with a brilliant metallic–blue or –green abdomen. 2 Any of various flowers, wild or cultivated, with tubular florets, blue, violet, etc., each borne on a tall, slender stalk. 3 The cornflower.
blue·cap (blōō′kap′) *n.* 1 The bluebonnet. 2 A bluish titmouse. 3 A Scot.
blue chip 1 In poker, a blue–colored chip of high value. 2 A high–priced common–stock issue of a leading company that pays regular dividends. —**blue′–chip′** *adj.*
blue·coat (blōō′kōt′) *n.* A person wearing a blue uniform, as a policeman; during the Civil War, a Union soldier. —**blue′·coat′ed** *adj.*
blue cohosh See under COHOSH.
blue–col·lar (blōō′kol′ər) *adj.* Of, pertaining to, or designating employees engaged in physical or manual work that requires them to wear rough–textured, dark, or special clothing for protection or as a uniform. Compare WHITE–COLLAR.
Blue Cross 1 *U.S.* A non–profit organization providing hospital insurance. 2 *Brit.* An organization devoted to the humane treatment of animals, especially of horses and dogs.
blue·curls (blōō′kûrlz′) *n.* 1 Any herb of the genus *Trichostema*, of the mint family: from its resemblance to pennyroyal, called *bastard pennyroyal*. 2 The selfheal (def. 1).
blue devils 1 Great depression of spirits; despondency; morbid melancholy. 2 Delirium tremens.
blue–eyed (blōō′īd′) *adj.* Having blue eyes.
blue–eyed grass Delicate grasslike plants (*Sisyrinchium angustifolium*) of the iris family, with blue flowers on slender, winged scapes.
Blue·fields (blōō′fēldz′) A port in SE Nicaragua.
blue·fish (blōō′fish′) *n. pl.* **·fish** or **·fish·es** 1 A voracious food fish (*Pomatomus saltatrix*) common along the Atlantic Coast of the United States. 2 One of various other fishes of a bluish color, as the cunner.
blue flag See under FLAG[2].
blue fox A small fox of Arctic regions (*Alopex lagopus*) whose pelt acquires a bluish color in summer.
blue·gill (blōō′gil′) *n.* An edible American fresh–water sunfish (*Lepomis pallidus*) ranging from the Great Lakes to Florida and Mexico.
blue grass (blōō′gras′, –gräs′) *n.* 1 One of various grasses (genus *Poa*); esp., the Kentucky bluegrass (*P. pratensis*) with many running rootstocks. 2 Traditional country music, esp. of the southern United States.
Bluegrass Country A region of central Kentucky. Also **the Bluegrass.**
Bluegrass State Nickname of KENTUCKY.
blue–green algae (blōō′grēn′) Primitive unicellular and unspecialized algae (class *Cyanophyceae*) in which the chlorophyll is mixed with a blue pigment: they give a scum to the surface of stagnant water.
Blue Grotto A wave–cut cave on the north shore of Capri, famous for the blue reflections of the sea within it.
blue grouse Any of several grouse of western North America (genus *Dendrogapus*), with dusky gray or blackish plumage: also called *dusky grouse, sooty grouse.*
blue·gum (blōō′gum′) *n.* Any of several eucalyptus trees with aromatic bitter astringent leaves.
blue hen's chickens Natives of the State of Delaware.
blue·ing (blōō′ing) See BLUING.
blue·jack (blōō′jak′) *n.* 1 Blue vitriol. 2 A small oak (*Quercus cinerea*) of the southern United States.
blue·jack·et (blōō′jak′it) *n.* An enlisted man in the U.S. Navy.
blue jay A small, crested corvine bird (*Cyanocitta cristata*) of eastern North America.
blue jeans Trousers made of blue denim or a similar fabric.
blue law A law proscribing or dictating private personal behavior in the interests of a narrow moral code; specifically, any such law common in the early American colonies; also, any law regulating the observance of Sunday as a day of rest.
blue·line (blōō′līn′) *n.* Either of two blue lines across a hockey rink between the center of the rink and each goal.
blue mold A destructive rotting disease of apples and citrus fruits, caused respectively by the fungi *Penicillium expansum* and *P. digitatum. P. crustaceum* or *glaucum* is the typical blue–green mold of bread, cheese, etc.: also called *green mold.*
blue Monday Monday conceived as gloomy because of the resumption of work.
blue moon A period of time considered as occurring when the moon is blue; hence, never. —**once in a blue moon** Seldom or hardly ever.
Blue Mountains 1 A wooded range in NE Oregon, highest point, 6,500 feet. 2 An extensive plateau west of Sydney, Australia; highest point, Bird's Rock, 3,871 feet.
blue movie, a pornographic motion picture.
Blue Nile See NILE.
blue·nose (blōō′nōz′) *n.* 1 *Usually cap. Canadian* A Nova Scotian person or vessel. 2 A puritanical person.
blue–pen·cil (blōō′pen′səl) *v.t.* 1 To edit or revise (a manuscript) with or as with a blue pencil. 2 *Colloq.* To veto; disapprove; censor.
blue peter A square, blue flag with a white rectangle in the center. In the International Maritime Code it signifies the letter P. It is also raised to indicate that a ship is sailing within 24 hours. [<*blue (re)peater*]
blue plate 1 A dinner plate divided by ridges into sections for holding apart several kinds of food. 2 A main course, as of meat and vegetables, listed as a single item on a menu.
Blue Point An oyster from off the shore of Blue Point, Great South Bay, Long Island, New York.
blue·print (blōō′print′) *n.* 1 A ferricyanide positive photographic print from a transparent negative original. 2 A plan or drawing made by printing on sensitized paper, the drawing showing in white lines on a blue ground. 3 Any detailed plan. —*v.t.* To make a blueprint of.
blue racer A greenish–gray variety of the American blacksnake.
blue ribbon 1 The badge of the Order of the Garter. 2 A badge indicating the first competitive prize; a prize; an honor. —**blue′–rib′·bon·er, blue′–rib′bon·ist** *n.*
blue–rib·bon (blōō′rib′ən) *adj.* 1 Having high skill or intelligence. 2 Having special qualifications: a *blue–ribbon* jury.
Blue Ridge The SE portion of the Appalachian Mountains extending from Virginia into northern Georgia. Also **Blue Ridge Mountains.**
blues (blōōz) *n. pl.* 1 Downcast or depressed feeling; melancholy. 2 A type of popular song written in minor keys, and characterized by slow jazz rhythms and melancholy words. [Short for BLUE DEVILS]
blue–sky laws (blōō′skī′) Laws enacted to prevent the sale of worthless stocks and bonds by corporations, etc., to the public.
blue·stock·ing (blōō′stok′ing) *adj.* Pertaining to or characteristic of a learned woman, or one affecting literary tastes. —*n.* A learned or literary woman.
blue·stone (blōō′stōn′) *n.* 1 Blue vitriol. 2 A bluish sandstone, used for paving and building. 3 Any stone of a blue–gray color.
blue streak *Colloq.* 1 Speed as swift as lightning. 2 Light caused by swift motion. 3 Rapid and incessant language: to talk a *blue streak.*
blu·et (blōō′it) *n.* 1 One of various plants having blue flowers. 2 A delicate meadow flower of the madder family (*Houstonia caerulea*). 3 In England, a garden flower of the composite family. [<F *bleuet*, dim. of *bleu* blue]
blue vitriol A deep blue, crystalline copper sulfate, $CuSO_4·5H_2O$, used in electric batteries, calico–printing, etc.: also called *bluestone.*
blue·weed (blōō′wēd′) *n.* A rough, bristly herb, viper's–bugloss (*Echium vulgare*) of the borage family, with showy blue flowers, naturalized in the United States from Europe.
blue·wood (blōō′wŏŏd′) *n.* A shrub or small tree (*Condalia obovata*) of the buckthorn family, of the SW United States.
bluff[1] (bluf) *v.t.* 1 To fool or deceive by putting on a bold front. 2 To frighten with empty threats. 3 In poker, to attempt to deceive (an opponent) by betting heavily on a poor hand. —*v.i.* 4 To pretend to knowledge, ability, strength, etc., which one does not have. —**to bluff one's way** To obtain (an object) by bluffing. —*n.* 1 Bold speech or manner intended to overawe, impress, or deceive. 2 Pretense; deceit. 3 A pretender. [? <Du. *bluffen* deceive, mislead] —**bluff′er** *n.*
bluff[2] (bluf) *n.* A bold, steep headland; a steep bank. —*adj.* 1 Blunt, frank, and hearty; rude or abrupt, but kindly. 2 Presenting an upright, broad, flattened front: said of a ship's bows or a water frontage. [? <Du. *blaf* flat, as in *blaf aensicht* broad flatface] —**bluff′ly** *adv.* —**bluff′ness** *n.*
Synonyms (adj.): abrupt, blunt, blustering, bold, brusk, coarse, discourteous, frank, impolite, inconsiderate, open, plain–spoken, rough, rude, uncivil, unmannerly. *Bluff* is a word of good meaning, as are *frank* and *open.* The *bluff* man talks and laughs loudly and freely, with no thought of annoying or giving pain to others. The *blunt* man often says things which he is perfectly aware are disagreeable, either from a defiant indifference to others' feelings, or from the pleasure of tormenting; *blunt*, in this use, is allied in meaning with *impolite, inconsiderate, rough, rude, uncivil,* and *unmannerly.* Compare BLUNT, CANDID. *Antonyms*: bland, courteous, genial, polished, polite, refined, reserved, urbane.
bluid (blüd) *n. Scot.* Blood.
blu·ing (blōō′ing) *n.* 1 The giving of a blue tint to; also, the tint so given. 2 The blue coloring matter used in laundry work to counteract the yellow tinge of linen. Also **blue′ing.**
blu·ish (blōō′ish) *adj.* Somewhat blue. Also **blue′ish.** —**blu′ish·ness** *n.*
Blum (blōōm), **Léon,** 1872–1950, French Socialist leader; premier 1936–37; provisional president 1946.
blume (blüm) *v.i. Scot.* To blossom.
Blu·men·bach (blōō′mən·bäkh), **Johann Friedrich,** 1752–1840, German anthropologist.
blun·der (blun′dər) *n.* A stupid mistake. See synonyms under ERROR. —*v.i.* 1 To proceed carelessly or awkwardly; stumble; bungle. 2 To make a stupid and awkward mistake; err egregiously. —*v.t.* 3 To confuse (two things); jumble. [ME *blondren* mix up, confuse. Akin to BLIND and BLEND.] —**blun′der·er** *n.* —**blun′der·ing·ly** *adv.*
blun·der·buss (blun′dər·bus) *n.* 1 An old–fashioned, short gun with large bore and flaring mouth. 2 A noisy blusterer. [Blend of BLUNDER and Du. *donderbus* thunder box]

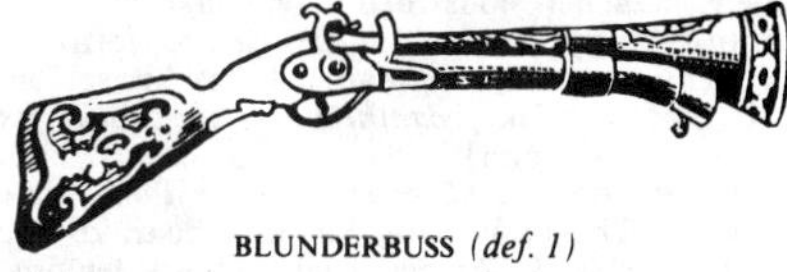

BLUNDERBUSS (*def. 1*)

blung·er (blun′jər) *n.* 1 A wooden implement shaped like a spatula, but much larger, used in mixing clay with water in the manufacture of ceramics. 2 A pug mill. See under PUG[1].
blunt (blunt) *adj.* 1 Having a thick end or edge; not sharp or piercing. 2 Abrupt in manner; plain–spoken; unceremonious; brusk. 3 Slow of wit; dull. —*v.t.* & *v.i.* 1 To make or become blunt or dull. 2 To make or be-

come less keen or poignant. [ME *blunt*; origin unknown]—**blunt'ly** *adv.* —**blunt'ness** *n.*
Synonyms (adj.): dull, edgeless, obtuse, pointless, round, smooth, thick. See BLUFF. *Antonyms*: acute, keen, pointed, sharp.

blunt·ie (blun'tē) *n. Scot.* A blockhead; stupid fellow. Also **blunt'y**.

Bluntsch·li (bln̄ōōnch'lē), **Johann Kaspar,** 1808–81, Swiss legal scholar.

blur (blûr) *n.* **1** A smeared or indistinct marking or figure. **2** A blemish; also, a moral stain. See synonyms under BLEMISH. —*v.* **blurred, blur·ring** *v.t.* **1** To stain; blemish. **2** To make obscure or indistinct in outline. **3** To impair the perceptiveness of; render insensitive. —*v.i.* **4** To become obscure. **5** To smear; make blurs. —**blur'ry** *adj.*

blurb (blûrb) *n.* A publisher's statement concerning an author or a book, containing a description of its chief characteristics, frequently excessively commendatory. [Coined by Gelett Burgess]

blurt (blûrt) *v.t.* To utter abruptly; burst out with as if on impulse. See synonyms under BABBLE. —*n.* An ejaculatory utterance; abrupt exclamation. [? Blend of BLOW and SPURT]

blush (blush) *v.i.* **1** To redden, especially in the face; flush. **2** To become red or rosy, as flowers. **3** To feel shame or regret: usually with *at* or *for.* —*v.t.* **4** To make red. **5** To exhibit or make known by blushing: She *blushed* her pride. —*n.* **1** A reddening of the face from modesty, shame, or confusion. **2** A red or rosy tint; flush. **3** A glance; glimpse; view: obsolete except in the phrase *at* or *on first blush.* —*adj.* Colored like one blushing: a *blush* rose. [OE *blyscan* redden]—**blush'ful** *adj.* —**blush'ing** *adj.*

blush·er (blush'ər) *n.* **1** One who blushes. **2** A cosmetic to give the skin a rosy color.

blus·ter (blus'tər) *n.* **1** Boisterous talk or swagger. **2** A fitful and noisy blowing of the wind; blast. See synonyms under TUMULT. —*v.i.* **1** To blow gustily and with violence and noise, as the wind. **2** To utter loud, empty threats; swagger noisily. —*v.t.* **3** To utter noisily and boisterously. **4** To force or bully by blustering. [Cf. ON *blāstr* blast, blowing] —**blus'ter·er** *n.*

blus·ter·ing (blus'tər·ing) *adj.* **1** Windy; disagreeable. **2** Noisy; swaggering. See synonyms under BLUFF, NOISY. —**blus'ter·ing·ly** *adv.*

blus·ter·y (blus'tər·ē) *adj.* Stormy; rough; violent; given to bluster. Also **blus'ter·ous, blus'·trous.**

B'nai B'rith (bə·nā' brith') A Jewish fraternal organization. [<Hebrew, sons of the covenant]

bo·a (bō'ə) *n. pl.* **bo·as** **1** Any of several non-venomous serpents (family *Boidae*) having vestigial hind legs in the form of stout spurs, including the anaconda and the python. **2** A tropical American snake *(Constrictor constrictor),* distinguished from a python and notable for the crushing power of its coils: also **boa constrictor.** **3** A long feather or fur neckpiece for women. [<L]

Bo·ab·dil (bō'əb·dēl'), died 1533?, last of the Moorish rulers of Granada 1482–92.

Bo·a·di·ce·a (bō'ə·də·sē'ə), died A.D. 62, British queen, suffered defeat by Romans and poisoned herself.

Bo·a·ner·ges (bō'ə·nûr'jēz) **1** Literally, sons of thunder: name given by Jesus to the two sons of Zebedee. *Mark* iii 17. **2** A vehement preacher: construed as singular.

bo·an·thro·py (bō·an'thrə·pē) *n.* A form of dementia in which a man believes himself an ox. [<NL <Gk. *boanthrōpos* <*bous* bull, ox + *anthrōpos* man]

boar (bôr, bōr) *n. pl.* **boars** or **boar** **1** A male hog. **2** The native hog, or **wild boar,** of the Old World. **3** A medieval military engine. ◆ Homophone: *bore.* [OE *bār*] —**boar'ish** *n.*

board (bôrd, bōrd) *n.* **1**A flat piece of wood whose length is much greater than its width. **2** A table, spread for serving food; the food served. **3** Meals regularly furnished for pay. **4** An organized official body: a *board* of directors; also, a table at which the sessions of a council are held. **5** *pl.* The stage of a theater. **6** Pasteboard; a pasteboard bookcover. **7** A thin slab of wood, cardboard, or the like for a specific purpose: a *chessboard.* **8** *Naut.* **a** The deck or side of a vessel: *on board.* **b** The course followed by a vessel while tacking. **9** A wooden rack in the box office of a theater containing tickets: sometimes arranged according to the seating plan. **10** A bulletin board for notices of rehearsals. **11** *Telecom.* The control panel connected with all the microphones on a radio broadcast, and operated by the engineer in the control room. **12** The wooden enclosure of a hockey rink. —**binder's board** Board used by bookbinders; a single-ply pasteboard made from a base stock of kiln- or plate-dried mixed papers and ranging in thickness from .03 to .30 of an inch. —**on board** On or in a vessel; also, on or in a conveyance: He jumped *on board* the train. —**to go by the board** **1** To go over the ship's side: said of a mast broken off short. **2** To go to utter wreck or ruin. —**to tread the boards** To appear as an actor. —*v.t.* **1** To cover or enclose with boards. **2** To furnish with meals or meals and lodging for pay. **3** To place (someone) where meals are provided, as in a boarding school. **4** *Naut.* To come alongside or go on board of (a ship), usually for hostile purposes. **5** To enter, as a ship or train. **6** *Obs.* To approach; accost. —*v.i.* **7** To take meals or meals and lodging. **8** *Naut.* To tack. [OE *bord*]

board·er (bôr'dər, bōr'-) *n.* **1** A person who receives regular meals, or meals and lodging at a fixed place, for pay. **2** One detailed to board an enemy's ship.

board foot *pl.* **board feet** The contents of a board 1 foot square and 1 inch thick; 144 cubic inches, or 2359.8 cubic centimeters: the common unit of measure for logs and lumber in the United States.

board·ing (bôr'ding, bōr'-) *n.* **1** Boards collectively; a structure of boards. **2** The obtaining of food, or food and lodging, regularly for pay. **3** The act of going on board a ship, a train, etc. **4** The operation of softening leather and developing the grain by rubbing the surfaces together. **5** The shaping of hosiery on heated metal boards.

boarding house A house for keeping boarders.

boarding school A school in which pupils are boarded: opposed to *day school.*

board measure A system of cubic measure applied to boards, the unit of which is the board foot.

board of trade **1** An association of merchants, bankers, etc., to promote business interests. **2** In England, a special committee of the privy council on commerce.

board rule A graduated stick for determining the number of board feet in boards of given widths and lengths.

board school In England, an undenominational elementary school having a parliamentary grant andaged by a school board.

board·walk (bôrd'wôk', bōrd'-) *n.* A promenade along a beach.

boar·fish (bôr'fish', bōr'-) *n.* Any one of several marine fishes (order *Zeomorphi*) related to the John Dory, having a hoglike snout.

boar·hound (bôr'hound', bōr'-) *n.* A dog used for hunting boars, usually the Great Dane.

boar·ish (bôr'ish, bōr'ish) *adj.* **1** Pertaining to or characteristic of a boar. **2** Swinish; rough; brutal. —**boar'ish·ly** *adv.* —**boar'ish·ness** *n.*

Bo·as (bō'äz), **Franz,** 1858–1942, U.S. anthropologist born in Germany.

boast[1] (bōst) *v.i.* **1** To vaunt or extol the deeds or abilities of oneself or of another; brag. —*v.t.* **2** To vaunt or extol (deeds or abilities); brag about. **3** To be proud to possess; take pride in: The school *boasts* a new laboratory. See synonyms under FLAUNT. —*n.* **1** A boastful speech. **2** A source of pride. [ME *bosten*; origin unknown]

boast[2] (bōst) *v.t.* **1** In masonry, to pare, as stone, with a broad chisel. **2** In sculpture, to block out, as a statue, before finishing in detail. [Origin uncertain]

boast·er (bōs'tər) *n.* **1** One who exults. **2** A boasting chisel.

boast·ful (bōst'fəl) *adj.* Characterized by or addicted to boasting. —**boast'ful·ly** *adv.* —**boast'ful·ness** *n.*

boast·ing[1] (bōs'ting) *adj.* Exulting; bragging; ostentatious. —**boast'ing·ly** *adv.*

boast·ing[2] (bōs'ting) *n.* The dressing of stone with a boaster.

boat (bōt) *n.* **1** A small, open watercraft propelled by oars, sails, or an engine. **2** *Colloq.* Any watercraft of any size, ranging from a rowboat to an ocean liner. **3** Any article, as a dish, resembling a boat. —**to be in the same boat** To be equally involved; to run the same risks; in the same situation. —*v.i.* **1** To travel by boat. **2** To go boating for pleasure. —*v.t.* **3** To transport or place in a boat: to *boat* oars. [OE *bāt*]

boat·a·ble (bō'tə·bəl) *adj.* **1** Navigable by boats. **2** Transportable by boat.

boat·age (bō'tij) *n.* **1** Carriage by boat, or the charge for such carriage. **2** The carrying capacity of a ship's boats.

boat·bill (bōt'bil') *n.* A tropical American wading bird *(Cochlearius cochlearius)* related to the night herons, with a greatly depressed bill excessively widened laterally.

boat hook A pole having a sharp point and a hook: used in holding a boat to or pushing it off from some object, etc. For illustration see HOOK.

boat·house (bōt'hous') *n.* A building along the water used for storing boats.

boat·ing (bō'ting) *n.* **1** Boats collectively. **2** use of or transportation by boats, etc.; rowing; cruising; sailing.

boat·load (bōt'lōd') *n.* **1** The full amount that a boat can hold. **2** The load carried by a boat.

boat·man (bōt'mən) *n. pl.* **·men** **1** One who manages, rows, or works on a boat. **2** An aquatic insect (family *Corixidae*) of which one pair of legs is long and oarlike: also **boat bug.** **3** An aquatic insect (family *Notonectidae*) that swims on its back. —**boat'man·ship** *n.*

boat·swain (bō'sən, *rarely* bōt'swān') *n.* **1** A subordinate officer of a vessel, who has general charge of the rigging, anchors, etc., and whose business it is to pipe the crew to duty with his whistle, which is his badge. **2** On a fighting ship, a warrant officer, trained in seamanship. Also spelled *bosun.*

boatswain's chair A short board slung by rope, used as a seat by a seaman working aloft, and also by painters on the outside of houses.

BOATSWAIN'S CHAIR

boat·tail (bōt'tāl') *n.* A tapering, streamlined rear end of a shell or bomb, providing greater range and accuracy.

Bo·az (bō'az) A Bethlehemite who married Ruth. *Ruth* iii 10.

bob[1] (bob) *n.* **1** In fishing, a cork or float on a line; a set or gang of fish hooks; a grapple. **2** A large, ball-shaped bait for eels, catfish, etc., made by stringing angleworms, rags, etc. **3** A grub or worm used for bait. **4** A small, pendent object, as on a pendulum. **5** A jerky bow or curtsy; any short, jerky movement. **6** A style of haircut for women or children cut short to fall about the ears. **7** The docked tail of a horse. **8** *sing. & pl. Brit. Colloq.* A shilling. **9** *Scot.* A bunch; cluster; nosegay, **10** A short, stout sleigh-runner; also, a bobsled. **11** The refrain of a song. —*v.* **bobbed, bob·bing** *v.t.* **1** To move up and down: to *bob* the head. **2** To effect by moving up and down: to *bob* a curtsy. **3** To cut short, as hair. —*v.i.* **4** To move up and down with an irregular motion. **5** To curtsy. **6** To fish (for eels) with a bob. —**to bob up** To appear or emerge suddenly. [ME *bobbe* a hanging cluster; origin uncertain] —**bob'ber** *n.*

bob[2] (bob) *v.t.* **bobbed, bob·bing** To strike lightly and quickly; tap. —*n. Obs.* A rap or blow; a shake or jog. [ME *bobben*; origin unknown]

bob[3] (bob) *v.t. Obs.* **1** To mock. **2** To delude; cheat. —*n.* A trick; also, a jeer or taunt; jibe. [OF *bober*]

Bob (bob), **Bob·by** (bob'ē) Diminutives of ROBERT.

Bo·ba·dil·la (bō'vä·thē'lyä), **Francisco de,** died 1502, Spanish viceroy of the Indies; arrested Columbus.

bobbed (bobd) *adj.* **1** Cut short, as the hair of a child or of a woman. **2** Docked, as a horse's tail.

bob·ber·y (bob′ər·ē) *n. Anglo-Indian* A disturbance; tumult.

bob·bin (bob′in) *n.* **1** A slender spool to hold weft or thread in spinning, weaving, or in machine sewing. **2** A small piece of wood attached to the end of a latchstring. **3** A small pin or spool used in making bobbin lace to steady the threads. **4** A cord or braid used in haberdashery. [<F *bobine*]

Bob·bin-and-Joan (bob′in·ən·jōn′) *n.* The cuckoo pint.

bob·bi·net (bob′ə·net′) *n.* An open reticulated fabric; a machine-made lace.

bobbin lace A hand-made lace in which several bobbins are used to form a pattern, as on a pillow. Also *pillow lace.*

bob·ble (bob′əl) *n.* **1** *Brit. Colloq.* A slight swell or sea. **2** *U.S. Slang* A fumble or miss. —*v.t.* **·bled, ·bling** *U.S. Slang* To mishandle; drop: He *bobbled* the ball. [Freq. of BOB[1]]

bob·by (bob′ē) *n. pl.* **·bies** *Brit. Colloq.* A policeman. [after Sir Robert *(Bobby)* Peel]

bobby pin A metal hairpin so shaped as to clasp and hold the hair tightly: used with bobbed hair. Also **bobbie pin.**

bobby socks *Colloq.* Ankle-length socks worn by girls.

bobby sox·er (sok′sər) *U.S. Colloq.* A young girl who is a devotee of the changing fads and fashions current among adolescents.

bob·cat (bob′kat′) *n.* The American lynx.

bob·o·link (bob′ə·lingk) *n.* An American thrushlike singing bird *(Dolichonyx oryzivorus),* the male having in spring black plumage with white or buff markings: also called *ricebird.* [Imit.; from its call]

Bo·bruisk (bə·brōō′isk) A city in central Belorussia. Also **Bo·bruysk′.**

bob·sled (bob′sled′) *n.* **1** Either of two short sleds or pairs of runners connected tandem by a top plank. **2** The entire vehicle so formed. Also *bob.* —*v.i.* To go coasting on a bobsled. Also **bob′sleigh′** (-slā′).

bob·stay (bob′stā′) *n. Naut.* A chain or rope from the end of the bowsprit to the stem, to counteract the strain of the forestays.

bob·tail (bob′tāl′) *n.* **1** A short tail or a tail cut short. **2** An animal with such a tail. **3** The rabble; common herd. **4** Dishonorable discharge from military service. —*adj.* Having the tail docked; inadequate; incomplete. —*v.t.* To cut the tail of; dock. —**bob′tailed′** *adj.*

bob·white (bob′hwīt′) *n.* The North American quail *(Colinus virginianus)*; also, its cry. [Imit.; from its call]

bo·cac·cio (bə·kä′chō) *n.* A rockfish *(Sebastodes paucispinis)* of the California coast. [< Ital. *boccaccio* <*boccaccia* large mouth]

Boc·cac·ci·o (bō·kä′chē·ō, *Ital.* bōk·kät′chō), **Giovanni,** 1313–75, Italian writer and poet, author of the *Decameron.*

Boc·che·ri·ni (bōk′kā·rē′nē), **Luigi,** 1743–1805, Italian composer.

boc·cie (boch′ē) *n.* An Italian variety of lawn bowling, played on a small court. Also **boc·ci** (boch′ē, *Ital.* bōt′chē), **boc·cia** (boch′ə, *Ital.* bōt′chä) [<Ital. *bocce* bowls, pl. of *boccia* ball]

Boche (bosh, *Fr.* bôsh) *n. French Slang* **1** A German: a derogatory term. **2** A bloodthirsty rioter or revolutionist. **3** A blockhead. Also **boche.** [? Alter. of F *caboche* thickhead, hardhead]

Bo·chum (bō′khoom) A city in North Rhine-Westphalia, West Germany.

bock (bok) *v.i. Scot. & Brit. Dial.* To retch; vomit; belch; gush.

bock beer (bok) An extra strong beer brewed in the winter and served in early spring. Also **bock.** [<G *bockbier* <*Eimbockbier,* from *Einbeck,* town in Hanover]

Böck·lin (bœk·lēn′), **Arnold,** 1827–1901, Swiss painter.

Bodb (bōv) See BADB.

bod·dle (bod′l) *n.* Bodle.

bode[1] (bōd) Archaic past tense and past participle of BIDE.

bode[2] (bōd) *v.* **bod·ed, bod·ing** *v.t.* **1** To be a token of; presage, as good, evil, etc. **2** *Obs.* To predict; foretell. —*v.i.* **3** To presage good or ill. See synonyms under AUGUR. [OE *bodian* announce] —**bode′ment** *n.*

bo·de·ga (bō·dē′gə, *Sp.* bō·thā′gä) *n.* A wine shop or warehouse. [<Sp.]

Bo·den·see (bō′dən·zā) German name for CONSTANCE, LAKE.

bo·dhi·satt·va (bō′di·sat′wə) *n.* In Buddhism, a candidate for Buddhaship; one who, by his virtues and meditations, is held to be a future Buddha or savior of the world. [<Skt. < *bodhi* knowledge + *sattva* essence]

bod·ice (bod′is) *n.* **1** The waist of a woman's dress. **2** A woman's ornamental laced waist. **3** *Obs.* A corset laced in front. [Var. of *bodies,* pl. of BODY]

bod·ied (bod′ēd) *adj.* Having a body: usually with an adjective forming a compound word: full-*bodied.*

bod·i·less (bod′i·lis) *adj.* Having no body; without material form; incorporeal.

bod·i·ly (bod′ə·lē) *adj.* **1** Pertaining to the body. **2** Corporeal; material. See synonyms under PHYSICAL. —*adv.* **1** In the body; in person. **2** All together; in one mass; wholly; completely.

bod·ing (bō′ding) *adj.* Portending evil; ominous. —*n.* An omen; presage, especially of evil. —**bod′ing·ly** *adv.*

bod·kin (bod′kin) *n.* **1** An instrument for drawing tape through a hem. **2** A pointed instrument for piercing holes in cloth, etc. **3** A pin for fastening the hair. **4** A pointed instrument for picking type from a form. **5** *Obs.* A stiletto. [ME *boydekin* dagger; origin unknown]

bod·le (bod′l) *n. Scot.* **1** An old Scotch copper coin worth about one third of a cent; the smallest coin. **2** A trifle. Also spelled *boddle.* [? after *Bothwell,* a Scotch mintmaster]

Bod·lei·an (bod·lē′ən, bod′lē·ən) *adj.* Of or pertaining to the library of the University of Oxford, England, restored in the seventeenth century by Sir Thomas Bodley, 1544–1613. Also **Bod·ley′an.**

Bo·do·ni (bō·dō′nē), **Giambattista,** 1740–1813, Italian printer.

Bo·drum (bō·droom′) A Turkish town on the site of ancient Halicarnassus.

bod·y (bod′ē) *n. pl.* **bod·ies 1** The entire physical part of a man or other animal, living or dead. **2** A corpse, cadaver, or carcass. **3** The trunk, or main part, of an animal or person, distinguished from the limbs and head. **4** A person; an individual: *somebody.* **5** The principal part or mass of anything. **6** The main part of a legal document as distinguished from the recitals and other introductory parts. **7** The box of a vehicle. **8** A mass of matter: the celestial *bodies.* **9** *Geom.* A solid. **10** A collection of persons, things, facts, or the like, as one whole. **11** Opacity, density, or consistency; substance: a wine with *body.* **12** That part of a garment that covers the body; waist. **13** Matter, as opposed to spirit. **14** *Printing* The size or depth of type, as distinguished from its face or style. **15** *Naut.* The hull of a ship; also, a section of it when seen from different points: the fore *body.* **16** *Aeron.* The supporting frame of an airplane, where the planes are fixed, and on which are the mechanical apparatus, seats, etc.; fuselage. —*v.t.* **bod·ied, bod·y·ing 1** To furnish with or as with a body. **2** To exhibit in bodily form; represent. [OE *bodig*]

Synonyms (noun): ashes, carcass, clay, corpse, dust, form, frame, remains, system, trunk. *Body* denotes the entire physical structure, considered as a whole, of man or animal; *form* looks upon it as a thing of shape and outline, perhaps of beauty; *frame* regards it as supported by its bony framework; *system* views it as an assemblage of many related and harmonious organs. *Body, form, frame,* and *system* may be either dead or living; *clay* and *dust* are ordinarily used only of the dead. *Corpse* is the plain technical word for a dead body still retaining its unity; *remains* may be used after any lapse of time. *Carcass* applies only to the *body* of an animal, or of a human being regarded with contempt and loathing. Compare COMPANY, MASS. *Antonyms*: intellect, intelligence, mind, soul, spirit.

body corporate An association of persons duly incorporated for a specific purpose or enterprise; a corporation.

bod·y·guard (bod′ē·gärd′) *n.* A guard of the person, as of a king; also, a retinue.

body language The unconscious gestures and postures of the body as a form of communication.

body linen Shirts, underwear, etc., made of linen or cotton.

body politic The state or nation as an organized political body; the people, taken collectively.

bod·y-snatch·er (bod′ē·snach′ər) *n.* One who illegally and surreptitiously removes bodies from the grave; a grave-robber; resurrectionist. —**bod′y-snatch′ing** *n.*

Boece (bois), **Hector,** 1465?–1536, Scottish historian.

Boe·ing (bō′ing), **William Edward,** 1881–1956, U.S. airplane designer and manufacturer.

Boe·o·tia (bē·ō′shə, -shē·ə) A nome of east central Greece; 1,300 square miles; capital, Levadia; comprised an ancient republic. Also **Bœ·o′tia.** *Greek* **Voio·ti·a** (vyô·tē′ä).

Boe·o·tian (bē·ō′shən) *adj.* **1** Of or pertaining to Boeotia, noted for the rusticity of its people. **2** Dull; clownish. —*n.* **1** A native of Boeotia. **2** A dull-witted person.

Boer (bōr, bôr, boor) *n.* A Dutch colonist, or person of Dutch descent in South Africa. [< Du., farmer]

Boer·haa·ve (bōōr′hä·və), **Hermann,** 1668–1738, Dutch physician; professor of botany, medicine, and chemistry.

Boer War See table under WAR.

Bo·e·thi·us (bō·ē′thē·əs), **Anicius,** 475?–525, Roman philosopher. Also **Bo·e·ti·us** (bō·ē′·shē·əs) and, formerly, **Bo·ece** (bō·ēs′).

bog (bog, bôg) *n.* Wet and spongy ground; marsh; morass. —*v.t. & v.i.* **bogged, bog·ging** To sink or stick in a bog: often with *down.* [<Irish, soft] —**bog′gish** *adj.* —**bog′gish·ness** *n.*

bo·gan (bō′gən) *n. Canadian* A backwater or tributary.

bog asphodel Any species of *Narthecium* of the lily family; especially, the American *N. americanum* and *N. californicum,* and the Old World Lancashire asphodel *(N. ossifragum).*

bog·bean (bog′bēn′, bôg′-) *n.* The buckbean.

bo·gey[1] (bō′gē) *n. pl.* **bo·geys** In golf: **1** An estimated standard score. **2** One stroke over par on a hole. Also **bo′gie.** [after Col. *Bogey,* an imaginary partner who plays a faultless game]

bo·gey[2] (bō′gē) *n.* Bogy[1].

bog·gle (bog′əl) *v.* **bog·gled, bog·gling** *v.i.* **1** To hesitate, as from doubt or scruples; shrink back. **2** To start with fright, as a horse. **3** To equivocate; dissemble. **4** To work in a clumsy manner; fumble. —*v.t.* **5** To make a botch of; bungle. —*n.* **1** The act of shying, as of a horse. **2** A scruple; objection; difficulty. **3** *Colloq.* A bungle. [<BOGLE] —**bog′·gler** *n.*

bog·gy (bog′ē, bôg′ē) *adj.* **bog·gi·er, bog·gi·est** Swampy; miry. —**bog′gi·ness** *n.*

bo·gie[1] (bō′gē) *n.* **1** A railway truck mounted on one axle and two wheels or two axles and four wheels. **2** One of the small rollers or wheels that distribute the weight of a tractor or tank along the track. Also **bo′gy.** [<dial. E. (Northern), a kind of truck or cart]

bo·gie[2] (bō′gē) See BOGY[1].

bog iron An impure ferruginous deposit formed in swampy or marshy ground by the oxidizing action of bacteria and algae.

bo·gle (bō′gəl) *n.* A hobgoblin or bogy; bugbear. Also **bog·gle** (bog′əl). [? Akin to BUG[2]]

bog oak Wood of the trunks of oaks, sunk and preserved in the peat bogs.

bog orchid 1 The addermouth. **2** A European orchid *(Malaxis paludosa)* having small green flowers. Also **bog orchis.**

bog ore An iron hydroxide ore, as limonite, from marshy places.

Bo·go·tá (bō′gə·tä′) **1** The capital of Colombia. **2** A river in central Colombia, flowing 120 miles SW to the Magdalena: also *Funza.*

bog·trot·ter (bog′trot′ər, bôg′-) *n.* **1** One who trots over or lives among bogs. **2** Humorously, an Irish peasant.

bo·gus (bō′gəs) *n. U.S.* **1** An apparatus used in making counterfeit coins. **2** Counterfeit money. **3** Any counterfeit article. —*adj.* Counterfeit; spurious; fake. [Origin unknown]

bog·wood (bog′wood′, bôg′-) *n.* Wood of trees buried and preserved in peat bogs; bog oak.

bo·gy[1] (bō′gē) *n. pl.* **bo·gies** A goblin; bugbear. Also **bo′gie, bo′gey.** [? Akin to BUG[2]] **— bo′gey·ism** *n.*

bo·gy[2] (bō′gē) See BOGIE[1].

bo·hea (bō·hē′) *n.* A black tea: once applied to the choicest picking, then to black tea, now to the poorest grade. [from the *Wu-i* Hills (pronounced bo͞o′ē) of China]

Bo·he·mi·a (bō·hē′mē·ə) A historic province of western Czechoslovakia; with Moravia and Silesia comprising one of the two constituent states (Slovakia is the other) of Czechoslovakia; 20,102 square miles; capital Prague; formerly a kingdom: German *Böhmen,* Czech *Cechy.*

Bo·he·mi·an (bō·hē′mē·ən) *adj.* **1** Relating to Bohemia. **2** Leading the life of a Bohemian; unconventional. **—*n.*** **1** An inhabitant of Bohemia. **2** A gipsy. **3** A person, usually of artistic or literary tastes, who lives in a more or less unconventional manner: also **bo·he′mi·an.** **4** A former name for the Czech dialect of Czechoslovakian. **— Bo·he′mi·an·ism** *n.*

Bohemian Brethren A religious association or sect that arose in the 15th century, the original of the Moravian Church.

Bohemian Forest A wooded mountain range along the Czechoslovak-German border.

Böh·me (bœ′mə), **Jacob,** 1575–1624, German mystic. Also **Böhm** (bœm).

Bo·hol (bō·hôl′) One of the Visayan Islands of the south central Philippines; 1,492 square miles.

Bohr (bōr), **Niels,** 1885–1962, Danish physicist.

Bohr theory *Physics* The theory that the spectrum lines of an atom are indicators of the energy changes produced in it by the jumps of electrons from one orbit to another.

bo·hunk (bō′hungk) *n. U.S. Slang* A foreign-born laborer, especially one of central European extraction: also called *hunky*: a prejudicial term. [<BO(HEMIAN) + HUNG(ARIAN)]

Bo·iar·do (bō·yär′dō), **Matteo Maria,** 1434?–1494, Count of Scandiano, Italian poet. Also spelled *Bojardo.*

Bo·i·dae (bō′ə·dē) *n. pl.* A family of nonvenomous snakes extensive in warm regions, including the largest living species, as the python, anaconda, etc. [<NL <L *boa* serpent]

Boiel·dieu (bwål·dyœ′), **François Adrien,** 1775–1834, French composer.

boil[1] (boil) *v.i.* **1** To be agitated, as a liquid, by gaseous bubbles rising to the surface; also said of the container in reference to the contents: The kettle *boils.* **2** To reach the boiling point. **3** To undergo the action of a boiling liquid, as meat. **4** To be agitated; to seethe: The water *boiled* with sharks. **5** To be stirred or agitated, as by violent emotion. **—*v.t.*** **6** To bring to the boiling point. **7** To cook or cleanse by boiling: to *boil* rice; to *boil* shirts. **8** To separate by means of evaporation caused by boiling: to *boil* sugar. **— to boil away** To evaporate in boiling. **— to boil down** **1** To reduce in bulk by boiling. **2** To condense; edit. **— to boil over** **1** To overflow (the container) while boiling. **2** To become enraged. **—*n.*** **1** The act or state of boiling. **2** An immersion in boiling water. [<OF *boillir* <L *bullire* boil]

boil[2] (boil) *n. Pathol.* A purulent and painful nodule of bacterial origin lodged beneath the skin; a furuncle. [OE *byl, byle*]

Boi·leau-Des·pré·aux (bwä·lō′dā·prā·ō′), **Nicolas,** 1636–1711, French poet and critic: called *Boileau.*

boiled shirt *U.S. Colloq.* **1** A man's white or, especially, dress shirt. **2** A pretentious person: also often called *stuffed shirt.*

boil·er (boi′lər) *n.* **1** A utensil in which food or liquid is boiled. **2** A closed vessel, usually cylindrical, used in generating steam, as for motive power. **3** A receptacle for hot-water storage; a hot-water tank. **4** One who boils.

boil·er·plate (boi′lər·plāt′) *n.* **1** Iron plate for making boilers. **2** *U.S.* Material in stereotype or mat form sent out to newspapers; filler.

boiler scale Layers of calcium sulfate and other mineral wastes deposited by the action of water on the inner surfaces of boilers.

boil·ing (boi′ling) *n.* **1** The state or process of ebullition. **2** A thing boiled or to be boiled.

boiling point The temperature at which the vapor pressure in a liquid equals the external pressure; at normal atmospheric pressure the boiling point of water is 212° F.

Bois de Bou·logne (bwä′ də bo͞o·lôn′, *Fr.* bwäd·bo͞o·lôn′y′) A park and fashionable pleasure ground in Paris, France. Also **the Bois.**

Boi·se (boi′zē, -sē) The capital of Idaho, in the SW part of the State.

boise·rie (bwäz′rē) *n.* Woodwork; specifically, carved wall paneling characteristic of 17th and 18th century French interiors. [<F]

Bois-le-Duc (bwä·lə·dük′) The French name for s' HERTOGENBOSCH.

bois·ter·ous (bois′tər·əs) *adj.* **1** Vociferous and rude; tempestuous; unrestrained. **2** *Obs.* Rough; coarse; big; rank. See synonyms under NOISY, TURBULENT. [ME *boistous*; origin unknown] **— bois′ter·ous·ly** *adv.* **— bois′ter·ous·ness** *n.*

Bo·i·to (bō′ē·tō), **Arrigo,** 1842–1918, Italian composer and librettist.

Boj·a·dor (boj′ə·dōr′), **Cape** A headland of Spanish West Africa in the Atlantic.

Bo·jar·do (bō·yär′dō) See BOIARDO.

Boj·er (boi′ər), **Johan,** born 1872, Norwegian author.

Bok (bok), **Edward William,** 1863–1930, U.S. editor born in Holland.

Bo·kha·ra (bō·kä′rə) See BUKHARA.

Bokhara clover See under MELILOT.

bo·la (bō′lə) *n.* A missile weapon, consisting of balls fastened to cords and used in South America in hunting cattle and large game. Also **bo·las** (bō′ləs). [<Sp., a ball]

BOLA

Bo·la·ma (bo͞o·lä′mə) A city in Portuguese Guinea; capital until 1941.

Bo·lan Pass (bō·län′) A narrow gorge in central Baluchistan, West Pakistan; historical gateway to India for invaders and traders.

bo·lar (bō′lər) *adj.* Pertaining to or consisting of bole; clayey. Also **bo·lar·y** (bō′lər·ē).

bold (bōld) *adj.* **1** Possessing, showing, or requiring courage; audacious; fearless; spirited. **2** Presuming; forward; brazen. **3** Regardless of conventions; striking; vigorous; as language. **4** Clear; prominent; in high relief: *bold* sculpture, *bold* outlines. **5** Abrupt; steep, as a cliff. **6** Having a swift, strong current: a *bold* stream. See synonyms under BLUFF, BRAVE, IMMODEST, IMPUDENT. **— to make bold** To take the liberty; venture. [OE *bald*] **— bold′ly** *adv.* **— bold′ness** *n.*

bold·face (bōld′fās′) *n.* **1** An impudent person. **2** *Printing* A type in which the lines have been thickened to give a very black impression, often used for emphasis: also called *blackface.* **— bold′-faced′** *adj.*

bole[1] (bōl) *n.* The trunk of a tree. ◆ Homophone: *bowl.* [<ON *bolr*]

bole[2] (bōl) *n.* A fine, compact, soft clay. ◆ Homophone: *bowl.* [<LL *bolus* <Gk. *bōlos* clod of earth]

bole[3] (bōl) *n. Scot. & Irish* A small rectangular recess in the wall of a room, or an unglazed aperture in a wall; a locker. ◆ Homophone: *bowl.*

bo·lec·tion (bō·lek′shən) *n. Archit.* A molding following the outside edge of a panel and projecting beyond the face of the frame in which the panel is held: also called *bilection.* [Origin unknown]

bo·le·ro (bō·lâr′ō) *n. pl.* **·ros** **1** A short jacket open at the front, worn over a blouse or the like. **2** A Spanish dance, usually accompanied by castanets; also, the music for it. [<Sp.]

bo·le·tus (bō·lē′təs) *n.* One of a genus *(Boletus)* of fleshy, quick-rotting fungi of the family *Polyporaceae,* widely distributed in the United States. [<L *boletus* <Gk. *bōlitēs* mushroom]

Bol·eyn (bo͝ol′in), **Anne,** 1507–36, second wife of Henry VIII of England; beheaded. Also spelled *Bullen.*

bo·lide (bō′līd, -lid) *n.* A brilliant shooting star; a meteor, especially one that explodes. [<F <L *bolis, -idis* meteor <Gk. *bolis* missile < *ballein* hurl]

Bol·ing·broke (bol′ing·brook, bo͝ol′-), 1367–1413, Henry of Lancaster, later Henry IV of England: Shakespeare's *Bolingbroke.*

Bolingbroke, Viscount, 1678–1751, Henry Saint John, English prime minister.

bol·i·var (bol′ə·vər, *Sp.* bō·lē′vär) *n. pl.* **bol·i·vars,** *Sp.* **bo·li·va·res** (bō′lē·vä′rās) The monetary unit of Venezuela. [after Simón *Bolívar*]

Bo·lí·var (bō·lē′vär), **Ciudad** See CIUDAD BOLÍVAR.

Bol·í·var (bol′ə·vər, *Sp.* bō·lē′vär), **Simón,** 1783–1830, Venezuelan patriot: called "the liberator of South America."

bo·liv·i·a (bə·liv′ē·ə) *n.* A soft woolen or worsted pile fabric, with finish resembling velvet or plush. [from *Bolivia*]

Bo·liv·i·a (bə·liv′ē·ə) A republic of South America; 412,777 square miles; constitutional and judiciary capital, Sucre; de facto capital and chief city, La Paz. **— Bo·liv′i·an** *adj. & n.*

bo·li·via·no (bō·lē′vyä′nō) *n. pl.* **·nos** (-nōs) The monetary unit of Bolivia.

boll (bōl) *n.* **1** *Bot.* A round pod or seed capsule, as of flax or cotton. **2** A knob. **—*v.i.*** To form pods. [Var. of BOWL[1]]

Bol·land (bol′ənd), **John,** 1596–1665, Flemish Jesuit writer. Also **Bol·lan·dus** (bə·lan′dəs).

bol·lard (bol′ərd) *n.* **1** *Naut.* A vertical post, as on a wharf, to which to attach a hawser. **2** *Aeron.* A similar post located on the hull or float of a seaplane for mooring purposes. [? <BOLE[1] + -ARD]

bol·lix (bol′iks) *v.t.* **·lixed, ·lix·ing** *Slang* To bungle; botch; make a mess of: usually with *up.* [Alter. of earlier *ballocks* testicles, dim. pl. of BALL]

boll weevil A grayish curculio *(Anthonomus grandis)* that infests and destroys cotton bolls. For illustration see under INSECTS (injurious).

boll·worm (bōl′wûrm′) *n.* **1** The very destructive larva of a pale-brown moth *(Platyedra gossypiella)* that feeds on cotton bolls. **2** The corn-ear worm.

bo·lo (bō′lō) *n. pl.* **·los** (-lōz) A heavy, single-edged, cutlaslike weapon used by natives of the Philippine Islands. [<Sp. <Visayan]

Bo·lo·gna (bō·lō′nyä) A city of north central Italy. **— Bo·lo·gnese** (bō′lə·nēz′, -nēs′) *adj. & n.*

Bo·lo·gna sausage (bə·lō′nə, -lōn′yə, -lō′nē) A highly seasoned sausage of mixed meats. Also *Colloq. baloney.*

Bo·lo·gna stone (bə·lōn′yə) Barium sulfate occurring in round masses and exhibiting phosphorescence after calcination.

bo·lo·graph (bō′lə·graf, -gräf) *Physics* A continuous automatic record of the temperature indications of the bolometer. Compare BOLOMETER. [<Gk. *bolē* ray of light + -GRAPH] **— bo′lo·graph′ic** *adj.* **— bo′lo·graph′i·cal·ly** *adv.* **— bo·log·ra·phy** (bō·log′rə·fē) *n.*

bo·lom·e·ter (bō·lom′ə·tər) *n. Physics* An instrument for the measurement of minute differences of radiant energy by changes in the electric resistance of a blackened conductor exposed to it. [<Gk. *bolē* ray of light + -METER] **— bo·lo·met·ric** (bō′lə·met′rik) *adj.*

bo·lo·ney (bə·lō′nē) See BALONEY. Also **bo·lo′ny.**

Bol·sha·ya (bol·shä′yə) The Russian name for MCKINLEY, MOUNT.

Bol·she·vik (bōl′shə·vik, bol′-) *n. pl.* **Bol·she·viks** or **Bol·she·vi·ki** (bōl′shə·vē′kē, bol′-) **1** A member of the radical and dominant branch of the Russian Social Democratic Party: since 1918, called the *Communist Party.* Compare MENSHEVIK. **2** Loosely, any radical or any communist. Also **bol′she·vik.** [<Russian *bolshe* greater; referring to the majority group in the party]

Bol·she·vism (bōl′shə·viz′əm, bol′-) *n.* **1** The Marxian doctrines and policies of the Bolsheviki. **2** A government based on these policies. Also **bol′she·vism. — Bol′she·vist** *n.* **— Bol′she·vis′tic** *adj.*

bol·son (bōl′sən) *n. SW U.S.* A low, enclosed basin of ground surrounded by hills. [<Sp. *bolsón,* aug. of *bolso* purse]

bol·ster (bōl′stər) *n.* **1** A long, narrow pillow as wide as a bed. **2** A pad used as a support or for protection. **3** Anything shaped like or used as a bolster. **4** *Archit.* **a** The lateral part of the volute of an Ionic capital. **b** A crosspiece of an arch centering, running from rib to rib and bearing the voussoirs. **5** *Mech.* A steel block which supports the die in a punching machine. **—*v.t.*** **1** To support with a pillow. **2** To prop up, as something ready to fall: with *up.* **3** To furnish with padding. [OE] **— bol′ster·er** *n.*

bolt[1] (bōlt) *n.* **1** A sliding bar or piece for fastening a door, etc. **2** A pin or rod used for holding anything in its place. **3** An arrow. **4** A long cylindrical shot for a cannon, or the like. **5** Anything coming suddenly; as, a *thunderbolt.* **6** A refusal to support a party, candidate, or policy. **7** A sudden start, departure, or spring. **8** A roll of cloth containing a certain number of yards, usually 30 or 40; also, a roll of wallpaper. **9** *Obs.* A shackle. **See** synonyms under LOCK. **—a bolt from the blue** A sudden and wholly unexpected event. **—to shoot one's bolt** To do one's utmost; perform at the top of one's ability. —*v.i.* **1** To move, go, or spring suddenly: usually with *out* or *from*: He *bolted* from the room. **2** To start suddenly; break from control and run away. **3** *U.S.* To break away, as from a political party; refuse to support party policy. —*v.t.* **4** To fasten with or as with bolts. **5** *U.S.* To break away from, as a political party. **6** To chew and swallow hurriedly; gulp, as food. **7** To arrange or roll into bolts, as cloth. **8** To blurt out; say impulsively or hastily. —*adv.* Like an arrow; swiftly; straight. [OE *bolt* an arrow for a crossbow, the bolt of a door]

bolt[2] (bōlt) *n.* A rotating cylindrical or prismoidal frame, covered with silk or the like with very regular meshes, for sifting flour. —*v.t.* **1** To sift; pass through a sieve. **2** To examine as by sifting. [<OF *bulter, buleter* sift <*burete,* dim. of *bure* coarse cloth]

bol·tel (bōl'təl) *n. Archit.* **1** A shaft of a clustered pillar; a shaft engaged in a jamb. **2** A convex molding, semicircular or quadrantal in cross–section. [Origin uncertain. Cf. BOLT[1].]

bolt·er[1] (bōl'tər) *n.* **1** One who or that which bolts. **2** A horse given to shying or running away. **3** A person who refuses to support a political nomination.

bolt·er[2] (bōl'tər) *n.* A sifter for meal or flour.

bolt·head (bōlt'hed') *n.***1** *Chem.* A spherical glass vessel with a long, narrow neck: also called *matrass, receiver.* **2** The head of a bolt.

Bol·ton (bōl'tən) A county borough in south central Lancashire, England. Also **Bolton-le-Moors** (-lə·mo͝orz').

bol·to·ni·a (bōl·tō'nē·ə) *n.* Any member of a genus *(Boltonia)* of tall, erect perennials of the composite family native in the eastern United States, Europe, and Asia, with alternate leaves and white to purplish asterlike flowers. [<NL, after James *Bolton,* 18th c. English botanist]

bolt·rope (bōlt'rōp') *n. Naut.* A rope forming the border of a sail.

bolt upright In an erect position.

Boltz·mann (bôlts'män), **Ludwig,** 1844–1906, Austrian physicist.

bo·lus (bō'ləs) *n. pl.* **bo·lus·es** **1** A large pill. **2** Any dose hard to swallow. **3** Any rounded mass. [<L <Gk. *bōlos* clod of earth, lump]

Bol·za·no (bōl·tsä'nō) A province of northern Italy; 3,090 square miles; capital, Bolzano.

Bo·ma (bō'mə) A port at the mouth of the Congo.

bomb (bom) *n.* **1** *Mil.* A hollow projectile containing explosive, incendiary, or chemical material to be discharged by concussion or by a time fuze. **2** Any similar receptacle, of any shape, containing an explosive: a dynamite *bomb.* **3** *Geol.* A roughly shaped spherical or ellipsoidal mass of lava hurled from a volcano during an explosive eruption. **4** An unexpected occurrence. **5** *U.S. Slang* A complete failure; flop; dud; disaster. **6** *Football* A long forward pass. See also GRENADE, MINE, SHELL. **—aerial bomb** Any bomb dropped from an airplane. **—atomic bomb** A bomb of formidable destructive power, utilizing the energy released by the continuing fission of atomic nuclei, especially those of radioactive elements, as uranium: also called **A–bomb, atom bomb. —chemical bomb** A bomb which discharges noxious chemicals, fumes, and the like. **—demolition bomb** A high–explosive bomb used to destroy buildings and installations. **—depth bomb** A drum–shaped bomb which explodes under water at a desired depth: used against underwater mines and submarines: also called *ashcan; depth charge.* **—fragmentation bomb** A shrapnel–like bomb for use against ground troops and personnel. **—hung bomb** A bomb that fails to be released from an aircraft. **—incendiary bomb** A bomb filled with any of various inflammable materials as gasoline, oil, powdered magnesium, etc. **—robot bomb** A high–explosive bomb equipped with a jet–propulsion engine or rocket mechanism permitting it to travel under its own power after being launched on the target: also called *guided missile, pilotless plane.* Also **buzz bomb, flying bomb, rocket bomb.** —*v.t.* **1** To attack or destroy with or as with bombs. —*v.i.* **2** *U.S. Slang* To fail utterly. [<F *bombe* <Ital. *bomba* <L *bombus* loud sound<Gk. *bombos* hollow noise]

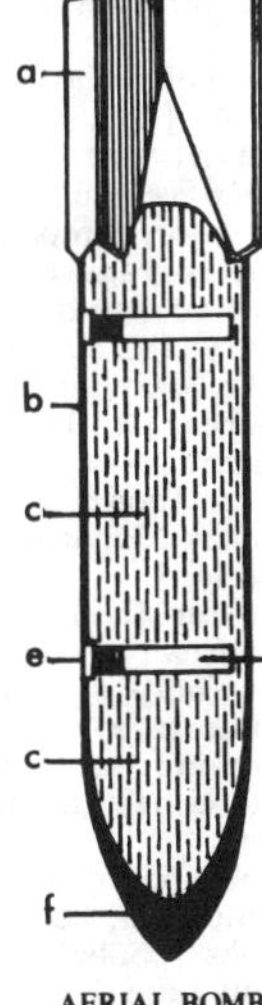

AERIAL BOMB
a. Metal vanes.
b. Steel walls.
c. Bursting charge.
d. Booster charge.
e. Fuze.
f. Steel base.

bom·ba·ca·ceous (bom'bə·kā'shəs) *adj. Bot.* Of or pertaining to a family *(Bombacaceae)* of trees native in the American tropics, with dry or fleshy fruit, some yielding a cottony fiber; the silk–cotton family. [<LL *bombax* cotton. See BOMBAST.]

bom·bard (bom·bärd') *v.t.* **1** To attack with bombs or shells. **2** To attack or press as with bombs: to *bombard* with questions. **3** To expose (substances) to the effect of radiation or to the impact of high–energy atomic particles. —*n.* (bom'·bärd) **1** The earliest form of cannon. **2** A leather liquor jug; blackjack. [<MF *bombarder* < *bombarde* a cannon]**—bom·bard'er** *n.* **—bom·bard'ment** *n.*

BOMBARD (*n. def. 1*)

bom·bar·dier (bom'bər·dir') *n.* **1** *Mil.* **a** The member of the crew of a bomber who operates the bombsight and releases bombs. **b** An artilleryman in charge of mortars, etc. **2** A ground beetle *(Brachinus tscherniki)* which, on irritation, ejects an acrid liquid. [<F]

bom·bar·don (bom'bər·dən, bom·bär'dən) *n.* **1** A wind instrument of the bassoon type, used as a bass for an oboe or hautboy; a bass saxhorn. **2** A pedal reed stop on the organ with 16–foot tone. [<Ital. *bombardone*]

bom·bast (bom'bast) *n.* **1** Grandiloquent language; rant. **2** *Obs.* Stuffing; filling. [<OF *bombace* cotton padding <LL *bombax, -acis,* earlier *bambax* cotton <LGk.*bambax* (infl. by Gk. *bambyx* silk) <Gk. *pambax*<Persian *pambak* cotton]

bom·bas·tic (bom·bas'tik) *adj.* Inflated; grandiloquent. Also **bom·bas'ti·cal. —bom·bas'·ti·cal·ly** *adv.*

Bom·bay (bom·bā') **1** A constituent state of western India; 115,570 square miles; formerly a presidency of British India. **2** Its capital, a port on the Arabian Sea.

Bombay hemp Sunn.

bom·ba·zine (bom'bə·zēn', bom'bə·zēn) *n.* A fine twilled fabric usually with silk or artificial silk warp and worsted filling. Also **bom'ba·sine'.** [<F *bombasin* <LL *bombasinum* < *bombax* cotton. See BOMBAST.]

bomb bay A compartment in military aircraft in which bombs are carried and from which they are dropped.

bomb–bay door (bom'bā') A door at the bottom of a bomber, opened when bombs are to be released. Also **bomb door.**

bombe (bôṅb) *n.* A confection in the form of a ball; especially, a mold containing different kinds of ice–cream. [<F, bomb; so called from its shape]

bombed (bombd) *adj. U.S. Slang* Drunk.

bomb·er (bom'ər) *n.* **1** A soldier who throws bombs. **2** An airplane employed in bombing. **—dive bomber** A fast, bomb–carrying airplane which, with motors running, dives toward its target and drops its bombs at close range. **—medium bomber** An airplane equipped to carry a moderately heavy bomb load over a moderate distance.

bom·bo (bom'bō) *n. Austral. Slang* Cheap wine.

bom·bo·ra (bom·bôr'ə) *n. Austral.* A dangerous area of broken water, as near the base of a cliff with submerged rocks.Also **bom·boor'a** (-bo͝or'ə). [<native Australian]

bomb·proof (bom'pro͞of') *adj.* So constructed as to resist injury from bombs. —*n.* A structure or chamber for refuge from bombs.

bomb rack See under RACK[1].

bomb·shell (bom'shel') *n.* A bomb (def. 1).

bomb·sight (bom'sīt') *n. Mil.* An instrument for aiming aerial bombs.

bomb–throw·er (bom'thrō'ər) *n. Mil.* **1** A gun of the howitzer type used in firing heavy shells. **2** A catapult–like military engine for throwing bombs.

bom·by·cid (bom'bə·sid) *n.* A moth or the larva of any moth belonging to the family *Bombycidae.* [See BOMBYX]

bom·byx (bom'biks) *n.* A silkworm (genus *Bombyx*). [<L <Gk. *bombyx* silkworm] **—bom·bic** (bom'bik) *adj.*

Bo·mu (bō'mo͞o) A river forming the border between Zaïre and Central African Republic, flowing 450 miles west to the Ubangi: also *M'bomu.*

Bon (bōn) A Japanese festival celebrated in July, honoring the ancestral household spirits: sometimes called *Feast of Lanterns.*

Bon (bon, *Fr.* bôṅ), **Cape** A promontory of Tunisia; 50 miles long. *Arabic* **Ras Ad·dar** (räs ad·där').

Bo·na (bō'nə) A former name for BÔNE.

bo·na·ci (bō'nä·sē') *n.* One of various important food fishes of the grouper type found in Floridian and West Indian waters, especially the **bonaci cardinal** *(Mycteroperca venenosa apua).* [<Am.Sp. *bonasí*<native name]

Bo·na De·a (bō'nə dē'ə) In Roman mythology, the goddess of fertility and chastity: often identified with *Maia*: also called *Fauna.* [<L, the good goddess]

bo·na–fide (bō'nə·fīd', -fī'dē) *adj.* **1** Acting or carried out in good faith: *bona–fide* transactions. **2** Legitimate: *bona–fide* owners. [<L *bona fide* in good faith]

Bon·aire (bô·nâr') An island in the western group of the Netherlands West Indies; 95 square miles; chief town, Kralendijk. *Spanish* **Buen Ai·re** (bwān ī'rā).

bon a·mi (bôṅ nà·mē') *French* Good friend; sweetheart. **—bonne a·mie** (bôn à·mē') *fem.*

bo·nan·za (bə·nan'zə) *n.* **1** A rich mine, vein, or find of ore. **2** Any profitable operation. [<Sp., success <L *bonus* good]

Bo·na·parte (bō'nə·pärt) Name of a prominent Corsican French family: **Napoleon,** 1769–1821, French military leader and conqueror 1795–1815, emperor of the French 1804–15, as *Napoleon I*; his brothers, **Joseph,** 1768–1844, king of Naples 1806, of Spain 1808; **Louis,** 1778–1846, king of Holland 1806; **Lucien,** 1775–1840, Prince de Canino; his son **François Charles Joseph,** 1811–32, *Napoleon II,* although he never ascended the throne: often called "l'Aiglon" (the Eaglet); his nephew **Louis Napoleon,** 1808–73, emperor of France 1852–71, as *Napoleon III,* deposed 1871. Also spelled **Buo·na·par·te** (bwô'nä·pär'tā).

Bo·na·part·ist (bō'nə·pär'tist) *adj.* Of or pertaining to the Imperial cause in France. —*n.* An adherent of Napoleon Bonaparte or the Imperial cause. **—Bo'na·part'ism** *n.*

Bon·ar Law (bon'ər lô) See LAW, BONAR.

bo·na·sus (bə·nā'səs) *n.* The European bison; aurochs. [<L <Gk. *bonasos* bison]

Bon·a·ven·tu·ra (bon'ə·ven·to͝or'ə,-tyo͝or'ə), **Saint,** 1221–74, Giovanni di Fidanza, Italian Franciscan monk and theologian. Also **Bon·a·ven·ture** (bon'ə·ven'chər).

bon–bon (bon'bon', *Fr.* bôṅ·bôṅ') *n.* A sugared candy. [<F <*bon* good]

bon·bon·nière (bôṅ·bô·nyâr') *n. French* A decorated box, dish, or small metal box for confections.

bond (bond) *n.* **1** That which binds; a band; tie. **2** *pl.* Fetters; captivity. **3** An obligation or constraint. **4** *Law* An obligation in writing under seal. **5** An interest–bearing debt certificate. **6** In insurance, a policy covering losses suffered through the acts of an employee. **7** The condition of being bonded. See BONDED (def. 2). **8** Bail; a surety. **9** In building, timbers or stones which help to bind together. **10** *Chem.* A unit of combining power between the atoms of a molecule, associated with the energy of electrons. **11** The attachment of an adhesive material at the interface of two surfaces. **12** Bond paper. **—bottled in bond** *U.S.* A straight, 100–proof whiskey at least 4 years old, bottled under government supervision before payment of taxes. **—debenture bond 1** A bond acknowledging loan indebtedness and securing repayment out of some designated fund or income. **2** A certificate issued by customs officials stating that an importer is entitled to a drawback on goods imported and afterward exported. **3** A bond for the payment of money stipulating that government securities or the stock of a corporate company shall be held as security. **—indemnity bond** A release signed by a shipper, relieving a railroad of responsibility. **—*v.t.* 1** To put a certified debt upon; mortgage. **2** To furnish bond for; be surety for (someone). **3** To place, as goods or an employee, under bond (*n.* def. 6); guarantee. **4** In masonry, to place, as bricks, in interlocking patterns, so as to strengthen a wall, etc. **—*v.i.* 5** To interlock or cohere, as bricks. **—*adj.*** Subject to servitude; enslaved. [Var. of BAND[1]]

bond·age (bon′dij) *n.* **1** Compulsory servitude; slavery; imprisonment. **2** Captivity; subjection. **3** In old English law, villenage.

Synonyms: captivity, enthralment, serfdom, servitude, slavery, subjection, subjugation, thraldom. See FETTER.

bond·ed (bon′did) *adj.* **1** Hypothecated for payment of bonds; mortgaged. **2** Held in bond for payment of duties. **3** Secured by bonds, as a debt. **4** Held close together, as by a strong adhesive or by chemical action.

bonded warehouse A warehouse for bonded goods.

bond·er (bon′dər) *n.* **1** One who bonds, puts goods into bond, or owns goods in bond. **2** A stone or a brick extending through a wall and binding it together: also **bond′stone′**.

bond·hold·er (bond′hōl′dər) *n.* One owning or holding bonds. **—bond′hold′ing** *adj.* & *n.*

bond·maid (bond′mād′) *n.* A female slave.

bond·man (bond′mən) *n. pl.* **·men** (-mən) **1** A male slave or serf. **2** A villein. Also **bonds′·man.— bond′wom′an, bonds′wom′an** *n. fem.*

bond paper A stiff, strong, uncalendered paper of superior fiber: used in printing bonds and banknotes, for business letters, etc.

bond·ser·vant (bond′sûr′vənt) *n.* One in servitude without wages; slave. Also **bond′slave′**.

bonds·man (bondz′mən) *n. pl.* **·men** (-mən) **1** One bound as security for another. **2** A bondman.

bon·duc·nut (bon′duk·nut′) *n.* The prickly seed of the nickernut tree. [<F *bonduc* <Arabic *bunduq* hazelnut]

bone (bōn) *n.* **1** *Anat.* **a** A hard, dense, porous structure composed of calcium salts (mainly of phosphate) and organic materials, forming the skeleton of vertebrate animals. **b** A separate piece of the skeleton of a vertebrate animal. ◆Collateral adjective: *osteal.* **2** *pl.* The skeleton as a whole; mortal remains. **3** One of various objects made of bone or similar material; specifically, one of a pair of dice; also, one of a pair of clappers, as used by minstrels; also, whalebone in a waist or corset. **4** *pl. U.S.* The end man on the right in a minstrel show (who plays the bones). **5** A ground of contention. **6** *pl. Slang* Dice. **—to feel in (one's) bones** To be sure of; have an intuition of. **—to have a bone to pick** To have grounds for complaint or dispute. **—to make no bones about** To have no scruples about; find no difficulty with. **—to point** (or **sing**) **a bone at** *Austral.*To invoke death or disaster upon (someone) by an aboriginal ritual. **—*v.* boned, bon·ing.** *v.t.* **1** To remove the bones from. **2** To stiffen with whalebone. **3** To fertilize with bonedust. **—*v.i.* 4** *Slang* To study intensely: often with *up*: to *bone up* for an exam. **5** *Austral.* To bring misfortune to; jinx. [OE *bān*]

Bône (bōn) A port of NE Algeria: ancient *Hippo Regius*: formerly *Bona.*

Bone (bōn), **Sir Muirhead,** 1876–1953, Scottish etcher and painter.

bone ash A white, friable substance, the ash of bones, composed mainly of calcium phosphate: used in cupellation, china–making, and other arts. Also **bone earth.**

bone–black (bōn′blak′) *n.* A black pigment made by calcining finely ground bones in airtight containers; animal charcoal.

bone china Porcelain in which bone ash is used.

bone conduction The transmission of sounds to the inner ear by means of the bones of the skull rather than through the auditory canal.

bone·head (bōn′hed′) *n. Colloq.* A slow–witted, stupid person.

bone house An elevated, covered platform on which certain American Indians stored the bones of their dead to await burial.

bone meal Pulverized bone, used as fertilizer.

bone of contention A cause or subject of disagreement; a reason for argument.

bone oil A viscid oily substance obtained from bones by dry distillation: used in disinfectants and insecticides.

bon·er (bō′nər) *n. Slang* An error; faux pas.

bone·set (bōn′set′) *n.* A bitter tonic and diaphoretic herb of the genus *Eupatorium*: also called *thoroughwort.*

bone·set·ter (bōn′set′ər) *n.* **1** One who sets broken bones, especially one who does so without regular surgical training. **2** *Colloq.* A doctor. **—bone′set′ting** *n.*

bone·yard (bōn′yärd′) *n.* **1** A place where the bones of horses and cattle are collected. **2** The reserve pieces in a game of dominoes. **3** *Slang* A cemetery.

bon·fire (bon′fīr′) *n.* **1** Formerly, a large fire for the burning of bones, as a funeral pile, etc. **2** A large fire in the open air for amusement, burning trash, a beacon, etc. [<BONE + FIRE]

bon·go (bong′gō) *n. pl.* **·gos** A large, reddish, white–striped, forest antelope of the genus *Taurotragus* of equatorial Africa, related to the eland, and having heavy, lyrate horns in both sexes. [<native African name]

bon·go drums (bong′gō) A pair of drums, attached together and played with the hands, originally from Africa. Also **bon′gos.**

Bon·heur (bô·nœr′), **Rosa,** 1822–99, French painter: full name *Marie Rosalie Bonheur.*

bon·ho·mie (bon′ə·mē′, *Fr.* bô·nô·mē′) *n.* Genial nature or manner; good fellowship. Also **bon′hom·mie′.** [<F]

bon·i·face (bon′ə·fās) *n.* An innkeeper; hotel landlord. [after *Boniface,* innkeeper in Farquhar's *Beaux' Stratagem*]

Bon·i·face (bon′ə·fās) Name of nine popes; especially **Boniface VIII,** 1228–1303, real name Benedict Cajetan, pope 1294–1303; emphasized the temporal supremacy of the papacy. **—Boniface, Saint,** 680–755, English monk, apostle to Germany.

Bo·nin Islands (bō′nin) As island group in the North Pacific, SE of Japan; 40 square miles; administered by the United States after World War II; restored to Japan in 1968. Japanese name *Ogasawara Jima.*

bo·ni·to (bə·nē′tō) *n. pl.* **·tos** or **·toes 1** One of various large, mackerel–like marine fishes of the Atlantic and Pacific (genus *Sarda*), as the California bonito (*S. lineolata).* **2** The skipjack. [<Sp.]

BONITO
(Up to 30 inches long)

bon jour (bôn zhōōr′) *French* Good day; good morning.

bon mot (bôn mō′) *pl.* **bons mots** (bôn mōz′, *Fr.* mō′) A clever saying; terse witticism. [<F]

Bonn (bon) A city on the Rhine in North Rhine–Westphalia; capital of the German Federal Republic.

Bon·nard (bô·nȧr′), **Pierre,** 1867–1947, French painter.

bonne (bôn) *n. French* A housemaid or nursemaid.

bonne foi (bôn fwȧ′) *French* Good faith.

bon·net (bon′it) *n.* **1** A covering, or an article of apparel, for the head. **2** An outdoor headdress for women. **3** A brimless cap for men and boys, worn especially in Scotland. **4** An American Indian headdress of feathers. **5** The velvet cap lining a crown or coronet. **6** A gambler's or auctioneer's decoy. **7** The yellow waterlily. **8** One of various constructions or devices having a form or use analogous to that of a bonnet. **9** A cover or plate which can be removed to inspect a valve or other part of machinery in a chamber. **10** Any metal hood, canopy, projection, or cowl. **11** *Naut.* A supplementary sail laced to the foot of a jib of a vessel in light winds. **12** *Brit.* The hood of an automobile. **—*v.t.*** To cover with or as with a bonnet. [<OF *(chapel de), bonet* (cap of) bonet (a fabric) < Med. L *bonetus*]

Bon·net (bô·ne′), **Georges,** 1889–1973, French diplomat.**— Henri,** 1888–1978, French historian and diplomat.

bonnet pepper A shrub *(Capsicum frutescens),* native to tropical America, grown as a source of paprika: also called *cluster red pepper.*

bon·net·piece (bon′it·pēs′) *n.* A coin of James V of Scotland, bearing a figure of the king's head wearing a bonnet.

bon·net rouge (bô·ne rōōzh′) *pl.* **bon·nets rouges** (bô·ne rōōzh′) *French* **1** The red cap of the French revolutionists of 1793. **2** A radical republican, anarchist, or communist.

Bon·ne·ville (bon′ə·vil), **Lake** A large body of water that covered Utah, extending into Nevada and Idaho, in prehistoric times.

Bonneville Dam A dam in the Columbia River between Washington and Oregon; 170 feet high; completed 1937.

bon·ny (bon′ē) *adj.* **bon·ni·er, bon·ni·est 1** Having homelike beauty; sweet and fair. **2** Blithe; merry; cheery. **3** *Scot.* Fine; spacious. **4** *Brit. Dial.* Healthy; robust; plump. Also **bon′nie.** See synonyms under BEAUTIFUL. [< F *bon* good] **—bon′ni·ly** *adv.* **—bon′ni·ness** *n.*

bon·ny·clab·ber (bon′ē·klab′ər) *n.* Milk curdled by natural souring. [<Irish *bainne clabair* <*bainne* milk + *clabair* clabber < *claba* thick]

Bo·no·mi (bō·nō′mē), **Ivanoe,** 1873–1951, Italian Socialist; premier 1921–22, 1944–45.

bon·sai (bon′sī, bōn′-) *n. pl.* **·sai 1** A dwarfed tree or shrub trained, as by pruning, into a pleasing design. **2** The art of creating such trees or shrubs. [<Japanese]

bon soir (bôn swȧr′) *French* Good evening; good night.

bon·spiel (bon′spēl, -spəl) *n. Scot.* A match game; especially,a curling or golf match. Also **bon′spell** (-spəl).

bon·te·bok (bon′tə·bok) *n. pl.* **·bok** or **·boks** A nearly extinct South African antelope of the genus *Damaliscus*; the pied antelope. [< Afrikaans <*bont* pied + *bok* buck, deer]

bon–ton (bôn·tôn′) *n.* **1** The fashionable world. **2** Good style or breeding. [<F, good tone]

bo·nus (bō′nəs) *n. pl.* **bo·nus·es 1** An allowance in addition to what is usual, current, or stipulated: a *bonus* on stocks. **2** Compensation, as for the obtaining of a loan. **3** A grant, as of money, insurance, etc., made by a government to citizens who have rendered military service. **4** A payment out of surplus, made by a life–insurance company to its policy holders. See synonyms under SUBSIDY. [<L, good]

bon vi·vant (bôn vē·vän′) *pl.* **bons vi·vants** (bôn vē·vän′) **1** A high liver; an epicure. **2** A boon companion. [<F]

bon vo·yage (bôn vwȧ·yȧzh′) *French* A pleasant voyage or trip.

bon·y (bō′nē) *adj.* **bon·i·er, bon·i·est 1** Of, like, pertaining to, or consisting of bone or bones. **2** Having prominent bones; thin; gaunt. **—bon′i·ness** *n.*

bonze (bonz) *n.* A Buddhist monk. [<F <Pg. *bonzo*<Japanese <Chinese *fan seng* religious person]

bon·zer (bon′zər) *n. Austral. Slang* Something unusually good;a stroke of good luck.

boo (bōō) *n.* & *interj.* A vocal sound made to indicate contempt or to frighten. **—*v.* booed, boo·ing** *v.i.* To utter *boos.* **—*v.t.*** To shout *boo* at, either to startle or to express contempt for.

boob (bōōb) *n. U.S. Slang* A gullible person; simpleton; booby.

boobs (bōōbz) *n. pl. Slang* The female breasts.

boob tube *Slang* **1** Television. **2** A television set.

boo·by (bōō′bē) *n. pl.* **boo·bies 1** A dull fellow; dunce. **2** In some games, the person who makes the poorest score. **3** A gannet or swimming bird of warm seas related to the pelican, especially *Sula piscator* of the coasts of the tropical and subtropical Americas: named from its apparent stupidity. [<Sp. *bobo* fool <L *balbus* stupid, dull]

booby hatch 1 *Naut.* A small hatch giving access inside a vessel without removing the main hatches. 2 *Slang* An insane asylum.

booby prize A mock award, given in good-natured derision, for the worst score or performance in a contest, game, etc.

booby trap A concealed mechanism designed to operate and cause damage when inadvertently disturbed; specifically, a mine actuated by movements of the enemy.

boo·dle (bo͞od′l) *n.* 1 *U.S. Slang* Money. 2 A bribery fund; corruption money. 3 Public plunder. 4 Caboodle. 5 Counterfeit money. —*v.i.* **·dled, ·dling** To receive money corruptly. [Cf. Du. *boedel* property] —**boo′dler** *n.*

boo·dling (bo͞od′ling) *n.* The use of bribery in politics.

boog·er (bo͝og′ər) *n.* 1 A hobgoblin. 2 *U.S. Slang* A person who is subject to contemptuous derision; also, one held in pitying affection: also *bugger.* [Origin unknown]

boog·ie–woog·ie (bo͝og′ē·wo͝og′ē) *n.* 1 A style of jazz piano–playing characterized by a rhythmic, ostinato bass with melodic inventions rhapsodizing in the treble. 2 A piece of music in this style. —*adj.* Of, in, or pertaining to this style. [Origin uncertain]

boo·hoo (bo͞o·ho͞o′) *v.i.* **·hooed, ·hoo·ing** To weep loudly. —*n. pl.* **·hoos** Noisy sobbing. [Imit.]

book (bo͝ok) *n.* 1 A number of sheets of paper bound or stitched together; especially, a printed and bound volume. 2 A literary composition or treatise of some length. 3 Any one of the writings of which the Bible is made up. 4 A subdivision of a literary composition or treatise. 5 A list of horses entered in a race, with the odds laid for and against them. 6 A booklike pack of gold leaf. 7 The words of a play or opera; a libretto: The music of the new opera is good, but the *book* is poor. 8 In whist and similar games, six tricks taken by one side; in other games, all the cards of one set. 9 A business record or register, as a ledger, etc.: often in the plural: The *books* show a steady loss. 10 A volume prepared for written entries. 11 Anything considered as a record or a setting forth of truth: the *book* of nature. 12 A bundle of tobacco leaves cut in half longitudinally and without the stems. —**by the book** According to rule; unoriginal; also, literal. —**like a book** Thoroughly: He knows the town *like a book.* —**the book** The telephone directory. —**the Book** The Bible. —**by the book** According to the correct form; in the usual manner. —**to throw the book at** *Slang* 1 To sentence a lawbreaker to the maximum penalties for all charges against him. 2 To punish or reprimand severely. —*v.t.* 1 To enter or list in a book. 2 To arrange for beforehand, as accommodations or seats. 3 To engage, as actors or a play, for performance. 4 To make a record of charges against (someone) on a police blotter. [<OE *bōc*]

book·bind·er (bo͝ok′bīn′dər) *n.* One whose trade is the binding of books.

book·bind·er·y (bo͝ok′bīn′dər·ē) *n. pl.* **·er·ies** A place where books are bound.

book·bind·ing (bo͝ok′bīn′ding) *n.* The art or trade of binding books.

book·case (bo͝ok′kās′) *n.* A case containing shelves for holding books.

book–end (bo͝ok′end′) *n.* A support or prop used to hold upright a row of books.

book·ie (bo͝ok′ē) *n. Slang* In gambling, a bookmaker.

book·ing (bo͝ok′ing) *n.* 1 The act or process of registering in a book, rarely of forming into a book. 2 The buying of a passage ticket. 3 The engaging of actors for dramatic productions; also, any part thus contracted for. 4 A contracting to present a play at a theater; the contract or play itself.

book·ish (bo͝ok′ish) *adj.* 1 Fond of books; book–learned. 2 Pedantic; unpractical. —**book′ish·ly** *adv.* —**book′ish·ness** *n.*

book jacket A removable cover to protect the binding of a book, usually designed to aid in displaying and advertising it.

book·keep·er (bo͝ok′kē′pər) *n.* One who keeps accounts; an accountant.

book·keep·ing (bo͝ok′kē′ping) *n.* The art, method, or practice of recording business transactions systematically.

book·land (bo͝ok′land′) *n.* A freehold as held by deed charter.

book–learn·ing (bo͝ok′lûr′ning) *n.* 1 The knowledge of, or obtained from, books. 2 Mere literary culture or attainment as opposed to practical experience.

book·let (bo͝ok′lit) *n.* A small book, often paperbound.

book·lore (bo͝ok′lôr′, -lōr′) *n.* Book–learning.

book louse Any of various small, fragile, winged or wingless insects (order *Corrodentia*) which damage books by eating away the paste and glue of the bindings.

book·mak·er (bo͝ok′mā′kər) *n.* 1 One who compiles, prints, or binds books. 2 A professional betting man, especially as connected with the turf.

book·man (bo͝ok′mən) *n. pl.* **·men** (-mən) 1 One versed in books; a scholar. 2 One who publishes or sells books.

book·mark (bo͝ok′märk′) *n.* Any object, as a ribbon, to be placed between or in the leaves of a book to mark a place for ready reference.

book·mo·bile (bo͝ok′mə·bēl) *n.* A motor truck equipped with shelves for the transport, display, and loan of books forming part of a traveling library. [<BOOK + (AUTO)MOBILE]

book·plate (bo͝ok′plāt′) *n.* 1 An engraved label, often artistic in design, placed on or in a book to indicate ownership or proper place in a library. 2 An electrotype or stereotype of a page of a book.

book·rack (bo͝ok′rak′) *n.* 1 A frame to hold an open book: also **book′rest′.** 2 A framework to hold books, as on a table.

book review An article or essay discussing or critically examining a book.

book scorpion A small, flattened arachnid (order *Chelonethida*), especially the common house scorpion *(Chelifer cancroides)*, found in old books, etc.

book·sell·er (bo͝ok′sel′ər) *n.* One who sells books.

book·shop (bo͝ok′shop′) *n.* A shop where books are sold; bookstore.

book·stack (bo͝ok′stak′) *n.* A tall rack containing shelves for books in a library.

book·stall (bo͝ok′stôl′) *n.* A stall or stand where books are sold.

book·stand (bo͝ok′stand′) *n.* 1 A rack for books. 2 A bookstall.

book·store (bo͝ok′stôr′, -stōr′) *n.* A store for the sale of books.

book·work (bo͝ok′wûrk′) *n.* Work involving reading or writing in books.

book·worm (bo͝ok′wûrm′) *n.* 1 A person exclusively devoted to books and study. 2 Any of various insects destructive to books, especially one of the order *Corrodentia.*

boom[1] (bo͞om) *n.* 1 *Naut.* A spar holding the foot of a fore–and–aft sail, or that attached to a yard or to another boom to extend it. 2 A chain of logs to intercept or retard the advance of a vessel, to confine timbers, sawlogs, etc. 3 A pole set up to mark a navigable channel. 4 A long mobile beam projecting from the foot of a derrick to carry a load raised from its outer end. —**to lower the boom** *Slang* To act decisively to correct abuses; crack down. —*v.t.* 1 To extend (a sail) by means of a boom: with *out.* 2 To shove off or away, as a vessel from a wharf: with *off.* 3 To equip (a river, lake, etc.) with a barrier to stop floating logs. [<Du. *boom* tree, beam. Akin to BEAM.]

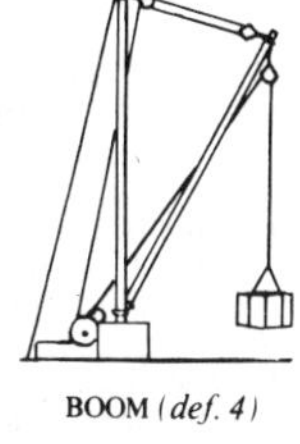
BOOM (*def. 4*)

boom[2] (bo͞om) *v.i.* 1 To emit a deep, resonant sound, as cannon or drums. 2 To hum loudly, as bees. 3 To rush swiftly or in tumult. 4 To grow rapidly; flourish. —*v.t.* 5 To utter or sound in a deep resonant tone: to *boom* the hour. 6 To extol; praise or advertise vigorously. 7 To cause to flourish: Prosperous times *boomed* my business. 8 To rush, as logs, down a river. —*n.* 1 A deep, reverberating sound, as of a supersonic aircraft, waves, etc. 2 Any sudden or rapid growth or popularity. [Imit. Cf. G *bummen* hum, Gk. *bombos* hollow noise.]

boom·e·rang (bo͞o′mə·rang) *n.* 1 A curved, wooden missile weapon originated in Australia, one form of which will return to the thrower. 2 Any proceeding that recoils upon the originator. —*v.i.* To react harmfully on the doer or user. [<native Australian name]

BOOMERANGS

boom town A town that has sprung up quickly, or one that has suddenly increased in population, as from a discovery of gold or oil.

boon[1] (bo͞on) *n.* 1 A good thing bestowed; favor; blessing. 2 *Obs.* A petition. See synonyms under FAVOR. [<ON *bon* petition]

boon[2] (bo͞on) *adj.* 1 Possessing convivial qualities; genial; jovial. 2 Benign; bounteous. [<F *bon* <L *bonus* good]

boon·docks (bo͞on′doks′) *n. pl. U.S. Slang* An uncivilized, out–of–the–way, or backwards area: used with *the.* [<Tagalog *bundok* mountain]

boon·dog·gle (bo͞on′dôg′əl, -dog′əl) *v.i.* **·dog·gled, ·dog·gling** *U.S. Colloq.* To work, especially for the government, on wasteful or unnecessary projects. —*n.* A wasteful or worthless project. [Origin uncertain] —**boon′·dog′gler** *n.* —**boon′dog′gling** *n.*

Boone (bo͞on), **Daniel,** 1735?–1820, American frontiersman in Kentucky and Missouri.

boor (bo͝or) *n.* 1 A coarse rustic. 2 An ill-bred fellow. 3 A peasant, especially a Dutch peasant. [<Du. *boer* farmer, rustic]

boor·ish (bo͝or′ish) *adj.* Rude; clownish. See synonyms under AWKWARD, RUSTIC. —**boor′·ish·ly** *adv.* —**boor′ish** *n.*

boost (bo͞ost) *v.t. U.S.* 1 To raise by or as by pushing from beneath or behind. 2 *Slang* To speak in praise of; help by speaking well of. 3 *Colloq.* To increase: to *boost* prices. —*n.* 1 A lift; help. 2 *Colloq.* An increase. [Origin uncertain]

boost·er (bo͞os′tər) *n.* 1 Any device for increasing the power or thrust of an engine, mechanism, etc. 2 *U.S. Colloq.* One who gives enthusiastic support to a person, organization, community, or cause. 3 The first stage of a multistage rocket, the source of thrust during takeoff. 4 A booster shot. 5 *Slang* A professional shoplifter.

booster shot Another injection, as of a vaccine, to reinforce immunity, administered at an interval after the initial dose.

boot[1] (bo͞ot) *n.* 1 A leather covering for the foot and leg. 2 A high shoe. 3 *Brit.* A compartment in an automobile, coach, etc., for carrying baggage. 4 A medieval instrument of torture, compressing the foot and leg. 5 A ring–shaped appliance put on the leg of a horse to prevent interference. 6 A leather flap fastened to the dashboard of an open carriage, to be drawn up as a shield from rain or mud. 7 A carbine bucket fitted to a military saddle. 8 A box encasing the lower pulley in a grain elevator. 9 The part of a reed pipe containing the reed, as of an organ. 10 *Ornithol.* A tarsal envelope of a bird, as in thrushes. 11 *Bot.* The lowest leaf–bearing segment of a stalk of wheat. 12 *Colloq.* In the U.S. Navy, a new recruit, or one but recently arrived from a training station. —**big in one's boots** Proud. —**the boot is on the other foot** The case is reversed. —**to get the boot on the wrong foot** —To make a mistake in attribution, interpretation, etc. —**to die with one's boots on** 1 To die by violence; die fighting. 2 To die working, *i.e.,* without ever resting. —**to get the boot** *Slang* To be discharged. —*v.t.* 1 To put boots on. 2 To torture with the boot. 3 To kick; also, in football, to punt. 4 *Slang* To dismiss; fire; eject: often with *out.* [<OF *bote*]

boot[2] (bo͞ot) *v.i. Obs.* To be of avail. —*v.t. Obs.* To benefit. —*n.* 1 Something over and above given in barter. 2 Advantage; resource; help. —**to boot** In addition; over and above. [OE *bōt* profit]

boot·black (bo͞ot′blak′) *n.* One who cleans and blacks boots.

boot camp The primary training station for enlisted naval personnel; so called because

of the leggings or *boots* worn by the recruits.
boot·ed (bōō′tid) *adj.* **1** Wearing boots. **2** *Ornithol.* Not divided into scutella except at the extreme lower portion; covered with feathers, as the tarsi of some birds.
boo·tee (bōō·tē′, bōō′tē) *n.* **1** A woman's or child's short, light boot; a half-boot. **2** A knitted woolen boot for a baby.
Bo·ö·tes (bō·ō′tēz) A northern constellation, whose brightest star is Arcturus. See CONSTELLATION.
booth (bōōth, bōōth) *n.* **1** A stall at a fair, market, polls, etc. **2** A temporary shelter. [ME *bothe*, ult. <Scand.]
Booth (bōōth) Family of English reformers and religious leaders, including **William,** 1829–1912, founder of the Salvation Army: known as *General Booth*; **Ballington,** 1859–1940, son of William, founder of the Volunteers of America; **Evangeline Cory,** 1865–1950, daughter of William; **William Bramwell,** 1856–1929, son of William.
— **Edwin Thomas,** 1833–93, U.S. actor.
— **John Wilkes,** 1838–65, U.S. actor, brother of preceding, assassinated Abraham Lincoln.
Boo·thi·a (bōō′thē·ə), **Gulf of** An inlet of the Arctic Ocean between Boothia Peninsula and Baffin Island.
Boothia Peninsula The most northerly part of the North American continent, extending north 190 miles into the Arctic Ocean from Northwest Territories, Canada. Formerly **Boothia Fe·lix** (fē′liks).
boot·jack (bōōt′jak′) *n.* A forked implement by which a boot may be held by the heel while the wearer withdraws his foot.
Boo·tle (bōōt′l) A county borough adjoining Liverpool, England.
boot·leg (bōōt′leg′) *v.t.* & *v.i.* **·legged, ·leg·ging** To make, sell, or carry for sale (liquor, etc.) illegally; smuggle. —*adj.* Unlawful: *bootleg* whisky. —*n.* **1** The part of a boot above the instep. **2** Liquor, or other merchandise, that is unlawfully carried, produced, sold, or offered for sale. Compare BLACK MARKET. [With ref. to the smuggling of liquor in bootlegs] — **boot′leg′ger** *n.*
boot·leg·ging (bōōt′leg′ing) *n.* The act of producing, carrying, selling, or offering for sale liquor or other merchandise in violation of the law.
boot·less (bōōt′lis) *adj.* Profitless; useless; unavailing. — **boot′less·ly** *adv.* — **boot′less·ness** *n.*
boot·lick (bōōt′lik′) *v.t.* & *v.i.* To flatter servilely; to toady. — **boot′lick′er** *n.* — **boot′·lick′ing** *n.* & *adj.*
boots (bōōts) *n. Brit.* A hotel bootblack.
boot–tree (bōōt′trē′) *n.* An apparatus for stretching or shaping boots, or for keeping them in shape.
boo·ty (bōō′tē) *n. pl.* **boo·ties** **1** The spoil of war; plunder. **2** Gain. See synonyms under PLUNDER. [<F *butin* <MLG]
booze (bōōz) *n.* **1** Strong drink; liquor. **2** A drunken spree; carouse. [<*v.*] —*v.i.* **boozed, booz·ing** To drink to excess; tipple. Also **boose, bouse.** [<MDu. *busen* drink, tipple] — **boozed** *adj.* — **booz′er** *n.*
booz·y (bōō′zē) *adj.* Somewhat intoxicated; tipsy. Also **boos′y.** — **booz′i·ly** *adv.* — **booz′i·ness** *n.*
bop[1] (bop) *v.t.* **bopped, bop·ping** *Slang* To hit or strike. [Imit.]
bop[2] (bop) See BE–BOP.
bo–peep (bō–pēp′) *n.* The game of peek–a–boo.
Bo·peep (bō·pēp′), **Little** The little nursery-rime shepherdess who lost her sheep.
bo·ra (bō′rə) *n. Meteorol.* A blustering dry wind from the Julian Alps, blowing over the Adriatic in winter. See BOREAS. [<Ital.]
bo·rac·ic (bə·ras′ik) *adj.* Boric.
bo·ra·cite (bôr′ə·sīt, bō′rə-) A vitreous, white, translucent chloride and borate of magnesium, $Mg_7Cl_2B_{16}O_{30}$, that crystallizes in the isometric system.
bor·age (bûr′ij, bôr′-, bor′-) *n.* An erect, rough European herb *(borago officinalis)* with blue flowers, used medicinally. [<Med. L *borrago* <*borra, burra* rough hair]
bo·rag·i·na·ceous (bə·raj′ə·nā′shəs) *adj. Bot.* Of or pertaining to the borage family *(Boraginaceae)* of herbs, shrubs, or trees, including the forget–me–not, alkanet, and heliotrope.
Bor·ah (bôr′ə, bō′rə), **William Edgar,** 1865–1940, U.S. lawyer; senator from Idaho.
bo·rane (bôr′ān, bō′rān) *n. Chem.* Boron hydride, BH_3, forming part of many boron compounds and their organic derivatives.
Bo·rås (bōō·rōs′) A city in SW Sweden.
bo·rate (bôr′āt, bō′rāt) *n. Chem.* A salt of boric acid. — **bo′rat·ed** *adj.*
bo·rax (bôr′aks, bō′raks) *n.* A white crystalline compound, $Na_2B_4O_7 \cdot 10H_2O$, with a sweetish, alkaline taste, found native as tincal, and used as an antiseptic, in preserving food, in medicine, and as a flux, also of value in glass-manufacture and certain smelting operations. [<OF *boras* <Med. L *borax* <Arabic *bōraq* <Persian *būrah*]
bo·ra·zon (bôr′ə·zon, bō′rə-) *n. Chem.* A crystalline compound of boron and nitrogen, BN, produced under extremely high temperature and pressure: it equals the diamond in hardness but has a much higher melting point. [<BOR(ON) + AZO- + *-n*]
Bor·deaux (bôr·dō′) A port of SW France on the Garonne.
Bor·deaux (bôr·dō′) *n.* A white or red wine produced in the vicinity of Bordeaux, France. Red Bordeaux is often called *claret.*
Bordeaux mixture A fungicide and insecticide prepared by mixing solutions of copper sulfate and lime, or of copper arsenate and phenols.
bor·del (bôr′dəl) *n. Archaic* A brothel. [<OF *bordel*, dim. of *borde* cottage, hut, ult. <Gmc.]
Bor·de·laise (bôr·də·lâz′) *n.* A sauce made of meat stock, white wine, and flavored with onions, carrots, thyme, and garlic. [from *Bordeaux*, France]
bor·del·lo (bôr·del′ō) *n.* A house of prostitution; a brothel. [<Ital. <Med. L *bordellus*, dim. of *borda* cottage]
Bor·den (bôr′dən), **Sir Robert Laird,** 1854–1937, Canadian lawyer and statesman; prime minister 1911–20.
bor·der (bôr′dər) *n.* **1** A margin or edge; outer portion or limit; brink; verge. **2** The frontier line or district of a country or state; hence, a boundary or frontier, especially the western frontier of the United States. **3** A surrounding or enclosing strip of ground in a garden, commonly planted with flowers; also, a decorative edge or margin: a *border* of lace on a cap. **4** A shallow drop curtain hanging at the top of a stage set, to conceal lights, mask the gridiron, etc. See synonyms under BANK, BOUNDARY, MARGIN. — **the Border** or **Borders** The boundary and nearby land between England and Scotland. —*adj.* **1** Of or pertaining to a territorial border. **2** Living on or characteristic of a frontier: *border* costumes. **3** Situated on a frontier: a *border* town. —*v.t.* **1** To put a border or edging on. **2** To lie next to; form a boundary to. —*v.i.* **3** To resemble; have the appearance: with *on* or *upon*: That *borders* on piracy. **4** To touch or abut: with *on* or *upon.* [<OF *bordure* <*bord* edge, ult. <Gmc.] — **bor′der·er** *n.* — **bor′der·ing** *adj.*
bor·dered (bôr′dərd) *adj.* Having a border distinctively marked in structure, coloring, etc.
bor·der·land (bôr′dər·land′) *n.* **1** Land on or near the border of two adjoining countries. **2** Debatable or indeterminate ground: the *borderland* of history.
border light One of a series of overhead stage lights masked by a border.
bor·der·line (bôr′dər·līn′) *n.* A line of demarcation. Also **border line.** —*adj.* Difficult to classify, such as might conceivably fall into one or another category.
border rider A freebooter on the borders of England and Scotland.
border ruffian A pro–slave partisan in Missouri (1854–58) who crossed into Kansas to vote illegally, and by acts of violence kept anti–slavers from voting.
Bor·det (bôr·de′), **Jules,** 1870–1961, Belgian bacteriologist and physiologist.
bor·dure (bôr′jər) *n. Her.* A border around a shield. See SUBORDINARY. [<F]
bore[1] (bôr, bōr) *v.* **bored, bor·ing** *v.t.* **1** To make a hole in or through, as with a drill. **2** To make (a tunnel, hole, well, etc.) by or as by drilling. **3** To advance or force (one's way). **4** To weary by monotony, iteration, etc.; tire. —*v.i.* **5** To make a hole, etc., by or as by drilling. **6** To admit of being drilled: This wood *bores* easily. **7** To force one's way; advance by persistent motion. —*n.* **1** A hole made by or as if by boring. **2** The interior diameter of a firearm or cylinder. **3** Caliber. **4** A tiresome person or thing; an annoyance. See synonyms under HOLE. ◆ Homophone: *boar.* [*v.*, OE *borian* <*bor* auger; *n.* <*v.* + ON *bora* hole]
bore[2] (bôr, bōr) *n.* A high crested wave caused by the rush of flood tide up a river, as in the Amazon or the Bay of Fundy. Compare EAGER[2]. ◆ Homophone: *boar.* [<ON *bāra* billow]
bore[3] (bôr, bōr) Past tense of BEAR.
bo·re·al (bôr′ē·əl, bō′rē-) *adj.* Pertaining to the north or the north wind. [<LL *borealis* <BOREAS]
Bo·re·al (bôr′ē·əl, bō′rē-) *adj.* **1** Pertaining to or designating a climatic period of the Mesolithic Baltic culture, centering around 6,000 B.C. **2** Describing a subdivision of the Holarctic region, including the great belt of coniferous forests extending from New England to Alaska.
Bo·re·as (bôr′ē·əs, bō′rē-) *n.* In Greek mythology, the north wind. [<Gk.]
bore·dom (bôr′dəm, bōr′-) *n.* **1** The condition of being bored; ennui. **2** *Rare* The habit of being a bore. **3** *Rare* Bores as a class.
bor·er (bôr′ər, bō′rər) *n.* **1** One who or that which bores. **2** A beetle, moth, or worm that burrows in plants, wood, etc.; especially, the **metallic wood borer** (family *Buprestidae*), the **palm borer** (family *Bostrichidae*), the **maple borer** (family *Cerambycidae*). For illustration see INSECTS (injurious). **3** The shipworm.
Bor·ge·se (bôr·jā′zā), **Giuseppe Antonio,** 1882–1952, U.S. author, born in Sicily.
Bor·ghe·se (bôr·gā′zā) A noble family in the Republic of Siena and later at Rome, flourishing in the 16th and 17th centuries.
Bor·gia (bôr′jä) Aristocratic Spanish family, a branch of which emigrated to Italy.
— **Alfonso,** 1378–1458; became Pope Calixtus III, 1455–58.
— **Cesare,** 1478–1507, Duc de Valentinois, Italian cardinal, soldier, and adventurer.
— **Francisco de,** 1510–72, Spanish Jesuit, third general of the order; canonized 1671.
— **Lucrezia,** 1480–1519, sister of Cesare, and wife of Alfonso, Duke of Esté; heroine of opera by Donizetti.
— **Rodrigo Lanzol y,** 1431–1503; became Pope Alexander VI, 1492–1503.
Bor·glum (bôr′gləm), **Gut·zon** (gut′sən), 1867–1941, U.S. sculptor; full name *John Gutzon de la Mothe Borglum.*
Bo·ri· (bō′rē), **Lucrezia,** 1888–1960, Spanish operatic soprano.
bo·ric (bôr′ik, bō′rik) *adj. Chem.* Of, pertaining to, or derived from boron: also called *boracic.*
boric acid *Chem.* A white crystalline compound, H_3BO_3, obtained in volcanic lagoons of Tuscany, Italy, and by treating borax with sulfuric acid: used as a preservative, and mild antiseptic. Also **bo·rac′ic acid.**
bo·ride (bôr′īd, bō′rīd) *n.* A combination of boron with another element or radical.
bor·ing (bôr′ing, bō′ring) *n.* **1** The act or process of making a hole with or as with a boring tool. **2** A hole so made; a bore hole. **3** *pl.* Material removed by boring.
Bo·ris (bôr′is, bō′ris) A masculine personal name. [<Russian]
— **Boris III,** 1894–1943, king of Bulgaria 1918–43.
Bo·ri·sov (bo·ryē′sôf) A city on the Berezina in Byelorussia NE of Minsk.
born (bôrn) *adj.* **1** Brought forth or into being, as offspring. **2** Natural; ingrained: a *born* musician. [OE *boren*, pp. of *beran* bear]
borne (bôrn, bōrn) Past participle of BEAR.
Bor·ne·o (bôr′nē·ō, bōr′-) The third largest island in the world, between Sumatra and Celebes; 286,969 square miles; divided into (1) *Sabah*; (2) *Sarawak*; (3) *Brunei*; and (4) Borneo, a part of the Republic of Indonesia; 208,285 square miles; chief town, Banjermasin: formerly *Dutch Borneo. Indonesian* **Ka·li·man·tan** (kä′lē·män′tän).
bor·ne·ol (bôr′nē·ōl, -ol, bōr′-) *n. Chem.* A translucent crystalline solid, $C_{10}H_{18}O$, found in cavities in the trunk of a large tree *(Dryobalanops aromatica)* of Borneo and Sumatra: also called *camphol.* [<BORNE(O) + -OL]
Born·holm (bôrn′hôlm) A Danish island in the Baltic Sea; 228 square miles; chief port, Rönne.
born·ite (bôr′nīt) *n.* A metallic, reddish-brown, copper–iron sulfide showing purple

tarnish: also called *horseflesh ore, peacock copper.* [after Ignaz von *Born,* 1742–91, Austrian metallurgist]

Bor·nu (bôr·no͞o′) A province of NE Nigeria, 900 square miles; capital, Maiduguri; formerly a Moslem native kingdom.

Bo·ro·bu·dur (bō′rō·bo͝o·do͝or′) Site of a huge, ruined Buddhist temple in central Java. Also **Bo′ro·boe·doer′.**

Bor·o·din (bôr′ə·dēn, *Russian* bə·rô·dyēn′), **Alexander Porphyrievich,** 1834–87, Russian composer.

Bor·o·di·no (bôr′ə·dē′nō, *Russian* bə·rə·dyi·nô′) A village near Moscow; site of one of Napoleon's important victories over the Russians, 1812.

bo·ron (bôr′on, bō′ron) *n.* A non-metallic element (symbol B) obtained as an odorless and very infusible powder, **amorphous boron,** from its oxide and in octahedral or prismatic diamondlike crystals, **crystalline** or **adamantine boron,** from amorphous boron heated with aluminum. See ELEMENT. [<BOR(AX) + (CARB)ON]

boron carbide *Chem.* A compound of carbon and boron, B_4C, an extremely hard material, often used in cutting tools.

bo·ro·sil·i·cate (bôr′ə·sil′ə·kit, -kāt, bō′rə-) *n. Chem.* A salt in which both boric and silicic acids are united with a base.

bor·ough (bûr′ō) *n.* **1** An incorporated village or town; a subdivision of a city, having a limited self-government; specifically, one of the five administrative divisions of New York, N.Y. **2** *Brit.* A municipal corporation, not a city, endowed by royal charter with certain privileges, a **municipal borough;** a town, whether corporate or not, entitled to representation in Parliament, a **parliamentary borough.** **3** *Obs.* Any town. ◆ Homophone: *burrow.* [OE *burg, burh* fort, town, ult. <Gmc. Related to BOURG, BURG.]

bor·ough-Eng·lish (bûr′ō·ing′glish) *n.* An old custom in certain parts of England by which the youngest son, or, in default of issue, the youngest brother, inherits the estate.

bor·ough·mon·ger (bûr′ō·mung′gər, -mong′-) *n.* One who trades in borough representation in Parliament.

bor·row (bôr′ō, bor′ō) *v.t.* **1** To take or obtain (something) on a promise to return it or its equivalent. **2** To adopt for one's own use, as words or ideas. **3** *Math.* In subtraction, to add ten to any figure of the minuend, at the same time withdrawing one from the next figure of the process. —*v.i.* **4** To borrow something. —*n.* **1** A place, as a bank of earth, where material is removed to be used as filling elsewhere. **2** *Obs.* A pledge; surety; the act of borrowing. [OE *borgian* give a pledge, borrow < *borg* pledge] —**bor′row·er** *n.*

Bor·row (bôr′ō, bor′ō), **George Henry,** 1803–1881, English writer and authority on Romany language and customs.

borscht (bôrsht) *n.* A Russian beet soup, often served with sour cream and eaten hot or cold. Also **borsch** (bôrsh). [<Russian]

borscht circuit A series of summer resorts, chiefly in the Catskill Mountains, where professional entertainment is provided for the guests: so called from a characteristic item of the cuisine of these resorts.

bort (bôrt) *n.* An impure diamond, used only for cutting and polishing: often called *carbonado.* Also **bortz** (bôrts). [? <OF *bort* bastard] —**bort′y** *adj.*

Bo·rus·sian (bō·rush′ən) *n.* The Old Prussian language. See under PRUSSIAN.

bo·ryl (bôr′əl, bō′rəl) *n. Chem.* The boron radical H_2B. [<BOR(ON) + -YL]

bor·zoi (bôr′zoi) *n.* A breed of Russian hounds, generally resembling the greyhound, but with a long, silky coat, usually white: also called *Russian wolfhound.* [<Russian, swift]

Bo·san·quet (bō′zən·ket), **Bernard,** 1848–1923, English philosopher.

bos·cage (bos′kij) *n.* A mass of shrubbery; a thicket; clump. Also **bos′kage.** [<OF, ult. <Gmc. Akin to BUSH.]

Bosch (bos), **Hieronymus,** 1450?–1516, Dutch painter. Also **Jerom Bos.**

—**Bosch** (bôsh), **Karl,** 1874–1940, German chemist.

bosch·bok (bosh′bok) *n.* A bushbuck. Also **bosh′bok.** [<Du. *bosch* wood + *bok* buck]

bosch·vark (bosh′värk) *n.* A wild hog of South Africa *(Potamochoerus choeropotamus)*; the bush pig. [<Du. *bosch* wood + *vark* pig]

Bose (bōs), **Sir Jagadis Chandra,** 1858–1937, Indian physicist and plant physiologist.

bosh[1] (bosh) *n. Colloq.* Empty words; nonsense. [<Turkish, empty, worthless]

bosh[2] (bosh) *n. Metall.* **1** That part of one of the sloping sides of a blast furnace extending from the belly to the hearth. **2** A trough for cooling ingots, etc. [Cf. G *böschung* slope]

bosk (bosk) *n.* A thicket of bushes; a small wood. [ME, var. of *busk* bush] —**bosk′y** *adj.* —**bosk′i·ness** *n.*

bos·ket (bos′kit) *n.* A cluster of trees in a garden; a thicket. Also **bos′quet.** [<F *bosquet* <Ital. *boschetto,* dim. of *bosco* wood, ult. <Gmc.]

Bos·ni·a and Her·ze·go·vi·na (boz′nē·ə; her′·tsə·gō·vē′nə) A republic founded from Yugoslavia; 19,999 square miles; capital, Sarajevo; formerly under Turkish rule, later annexed to Austria-Hungary: divided into two regions, **Bosnia** in the north and Herzegovina in the south.

Bos·ni·an (boz′nē·ən) *adj.* Of or belonging to Bosnia: — *n.* **1** A native of Bosnia; especialy, one of the Slavic people inhabiting the region around the northern Adriatic. **2** The language spoken by the Bosnians.

bos·om (bo͝oz′əm, bo͞o′zəm) *n.* **1** The breast of a human being, especially that of a woman. **2** The breast with the arms, considered as an enclosure in embracing. **3** That portion of a garment covering the breast, as a shirt front, or the receptacle which it forms. **4** The breast as the seat of affection. **5** Any deep or enclosed place or supporting surface, suggesting, in purpose or function, the human breast: the *bosom* of the earth. —*adj.* **1** Close, as if held to the bosom; confidential; intimate; cherished: a *bosom* friend. **2** Cherished in secret: a *bosom* sin. —*v.t.* **1** To have or cherish in the bosom; embrace. **2** To hide in the bosom; conceal. [OE *bōsm*]

Bos·po·rus (bos′pə·rəs) A strait between the Black Sea and the Sea of Marmara, separating European from Asian Turkey; 17 miles long. Also **Bos·pho·rus** (bos′fə·rəs). *Turkish* **Ka·ra·de·niz Bo·ğa·zi** (kä′rä·deng·ēz′ bō′ä·zi′).

boss[1] (bôs, bos) *n.* **1** *U.S. Colloq.* A superintendent or employer of workmen; manager; foreman. **2** Any employer or any director of the work of others. **3** *U.S.* An organizer or dictator of a political party. See synonyms under MASTER. —*adj.* Being at the head of a working force; superintending; also, expert; master: *boss* shoemaker. —*v.t.* & *v.i.* **1** To have control (of) or supervision (over). **2** To domineer. [<Du. *baas* master]

boss[2] (bôs, bos) *n.* **1** A circular prominence; a knob; stud. **2** *Archit.* An ornament, sometimes a pendant, at the intersection of the ribs of a groined arch, or in any similar position. **3** *Mech.* An enlargement of a shaft to couple with a wheel or another shaft. **4** *Geol.* A domelike mass of igneous rock. —*v.t.* **1** To work with bosses. **2** To ornament with bosses. [<OF *boce* bump, knob]

BOSS *(def. 2)*

boss[3] (bos, bôs) *n.* **1** A calf or a cow. **2** A word used to call a calf or a cow. Also **boss′y.** [Cf. L *bos* cow]

bos·set (bôs′it, bos′-) *n.* A small protuberance, boss, or knob. [<F *bossette,* dim. of *bosse* knob]

boss·ism (bôs′iz·əm, bos′-) *n.* Political party management by bosses; acts, arts, or practices of bosses.

boss rule Domination of voters by political leaders.

Bos·suet (bô·swe′), **Jacques Bénigne,** 1627–1704, French bishop and writer.

boss·y[1] (bôs′ē, bos′ē) *adj. Colloq.* **boss·i·er, boss·i·est** Like a boss; domineering.

boss·y[2] (bôs′ē, bos′ē) *adj.* Decorated with or as with bosses.

bos·ton (bôs′tən, bos′-) *n.* **1** A game of cards, somewhat resembling whist; also, a bid to make five tricks, the lowest in the game. **2** A form of the waltz. [from *Boston,* Mass.]

Bos·ton (bôs′tən, bos′-) **1** A New England port on Boston Bay; capital of Massachusetts. **2** A municipal borough and port in eastern Lincolnshire, England. —**Bos·to·ni·an** (bôs·tō′nē·ən, bos-) *n.* & *adj.*

Boston bag A small handbag opening at the top and having a handle at each side of the opening.

Boston Bay The inner portion of Massachusetts Bay.

Bos·ton·ese (bôs′tən·ēz′, -ēs′) *n.* Speech characteristic of Boston, Massachusetts.

Boston Harbor The northern arm of Boston Bay.

Boston Massacre A riot in Boston, Mass., March 5, 1770, during which several colonials were killed and others wounded by British troops.

Boston Mountains The ruggedest section of the Ozarks, in Oklahoma and Arkansas.

Boston rocker An American 19th century rocking chair having an up-curved wooden seat and a high back with spindles held at the top by a wide rail.

Boston Tea Party An uprising in Boston, Mass., in 1773, against the British customs officials, during which colonists, disguised as Indians, boarded British ships in the harbor and dumped chests of tea overboard.

bo·sun (bō′sən) *n.* Boatswain.

Bos·well (boz′wel, -wəl), **James,** 1740–95, Scottish lawyer and writer; biographer of Samuel Johnson.

Bos·worth Field (boz′wûrth) A region in western Leicestershire, England; scene of the final battle, in 1485, in the Wars of the Roses.

bot (bot) *n.* The larva of a botfly. Also spelled *bott.* [Origin unknown]

bo·ta (bō′tə) *n.* A Portuguese wine cask or butt, holding about 128 gallons. [<Pg.]

bo·tan·i·cal (bə·tan′i·kəl) *adj.* **1** Of or pertaining to botany. **2** Connected with the study or cultivation of plants. Also **bo·tan′ic.** [<F *botanique* <Gk. *botanikos* < *botanē* plant, pasture < *boskein* feed, graze] —**bo·tan′i·cal·ly** *adv.*

bot·a·nist (bot′ə·nist) *n.* A student of or one versed in botany.

bot·a·nize (bot′ə·nīz) *v.* **·nized, ·niz·ing** *v.i.* **1** To study botanical specimens. **2** To gather plants for study. —*v.t.* **3** To explore in search of botanical specimens. —**bot′a·niz′er** *n.*

bot·a·ny (bot′ə·nē) *n. pl.* **·nies 1** That division of biology which treats of plants with reference to their structure, functions, classification, etc. **2** The total plant life of a country, region, zone, etc.: the *botany* of Oceania. **3** The characteristics of a group of plants treated collectively: the *botany* of orchids.

Botany Bay An inlet of the Pacific south of Sydney, Australia; formerly site of a British penal colony.

Botany wool Wool from the Merino sheep: so called from Botany Bay, Australia, the original source of this quality of wool. Also **Botany** or **botany.**

botch[1] (boch) *v.t.* **1** To patch or mend clumsily. **2** To bungle; do or say ineptly. —*n.* A bungled piece of work; a bad job; an ill-finished patch. [ME *bocchen;* origin unknown] —**botch′er** *n.* —**botch′er·y** *n.*

botch[2] (boch) *n. Brit. Dial.* A superficial swelling or ulcer; a boil. [<OF *boche,* var. of *boce* knob, lump]

botch·y (boch′ē) *adj.* Imperfect; botched; poorly done. —**botch′i·ly** *adv.*

bote (bōt) *n. Obs.* **1** In English law, a fine or compensation: *manbote,* a fine paid for killing a man. **2** In English law, a privilege to use things needful for repair or subsistence, etc.: *hedgebote, housebote,* etc. **3** Boot; remedy; relief. ◆ Homophone: *boat.* [OE *bot* benefit]

bot·fly (bot′flī′) *n.* A fly of the family *Gasterophilidae* or *Oestridae,* the larvae of which are parasitic in vertebrates, especially the **horse botfly** *(Gasterophilus intestinalis).* For illustration see under INSECTS (injurious).

both (bōth) *adj.* The two inclusively or together: *Both* girls laughed. —*pron.* The two; the one and the other; the pair: *Both* of the girls were there. —*adv.* & *conj.* Equally; alike;

as well: with *and:* The bill passed *both* the House and the Senate. [<ON *badhir*]

Synonyms: twain, two. As an adjective or pronoun *both* emphasizes the idea of *two* and should not be connected with or refer to more than two objects. But as a conjunction *both* has a more extended meaning than it has as an adjective or a pronoun; thus, it is permissible to say, "He lost all his livestock–*both* horses, cows and sheep." When so used it emphasizes the extent or comprehensiveness of the assertion. *Twain* is a nearly obsolete form of *two. The two,* or *the twain,* is practically equivalent to *both; both,* however, expresses a closer unity. Compare EVERY.

Bo·tha (bō'tə), **Louis,** 1862–1919, South African statesman; premier 1910–19.

both·er (both'ər) *v.t.* **1** To pester; give trouble to. **2** To confuse; fluster. —*v.i.* **3** To trouble or concern oneself. —*n.* A source of annoyance; petty perplexity; vexation. [? dial. E (Irish) var. of POTHER]

both·er·a·tion (both'ə·rā'shən) *n. Colloq.* Annoyance; vexation.

both·er·some (both'ər·səm) *adj.* Causing bother or perplexity.

Both·ni·a (both'nē·ə), **Gulf of** A northern arm of the Baltic Sea between Sweden and Finland.

bot·o·né (bot'ə·nā) *adj. Her.* Having an ornament of three leaf-shaped or button-shaped projections. Also **bot'o·née, bot·o·ny** (bot'ə·nē). [<OF *botonné,* pp. of *botonner* bud, button]

bo tree (bō) *Anglo-Indian* The sacred Buddhist fig tree or pipal *(Ficus religiosa).* [<Skt. *bodhi(-taru)* perfect knowledge (tree)]

bot·ry·oi·dal (bot'rē·oid'l) *adj.* Like a cluster of grapes. Also **bot'ry·oid.** [<Gk. *botryoeidēs* <*botrys* cluster of grapes + *eidos* form, shape] —**bot'ry·oi'dal·ly** *adv.*

bot·ry·ose (bot'rē·ōs) *adj.* **1** *Bot.* Designating an indeterminate form of inflorescence, as the raceme, corymb, umbel, capitulum, etc. **2** Botryoidal.

bots (bots) *n.* A disease of horses, sheep, etc., caused by the botfly.

Bot·swa·na (bot·swä'nä) An independent member of the Commonwealth of Nations in southern Africa; 222,000 sq. mi.; capital, Gaberones; formerly *Bechuanaland Protectorate.*

bott (bot) *n.* A bot.

Bot·ti·cel·li (bot'ə·chel'ē, *Ital.* bōt'tē·chel'lē), **Alessandro,** 1447?–1515, Florentine painter: real name *Filipepi.*

bot·tle (bot'l) *n.* **1** A vessel for holding, carrying, and pouring liquids, having a neck and a narrow mouth that can be stopped. **2** As much as a bottle will hold: also **bot'tle·ful. 3** In the U.S., a unit of capacity for wines or spirits, equal to approximately 26 fluid ounces. **4** The act or habit of drinking intoxicants. —**to hit the bottle** To drink to excess. —*v.t.* **·tled, ·tling 1** To put into a bottle or bottles. **2** To restrain; shut in, as if in a bottle: often with *up* or *in.* [<OF *bouteille, botel* <LL *buticula* flask, dim. of *butis* vat, vessel] —**bot'tler** *n.*

bottle cap A small, round, usually metal lid covering the opening of a bottle.

bottled in bond See under BOND.

bottle glass Green glass.

bottle green A dark, dull green, like the color of bottle glass.

bottle imp 1 A Cartesian devil. **2** An imp or spirit shut up in a bottle. See ALADDIN.

bot·tle·neck (bot'l·nek') *n.* **1** A narrow or congested way. **2** Any condition that retards progress.

bot·tle·nose (bot'l·nōz') *n.* One of various dolphins, especially *Tursiops truncatus* of the North Atlantic, about 10 feet long.

bot·tle·stone (bot'l·stōn') *n.* A mineral, sometimes used as a gemstone, having the characteristics of ordinary bottle glass; chrysolite; moldavite.

bot·tle·tree (bot'l·trē') *n.* A Queensland tree *(Brachychiton rupestre)* the trunk of which is swollen out like a bottle, or the similar *B. populneum* of Victoria.

bot·tom (bot'əm) *n.* **1** The lowest part of anything; undersurface; base; support. **2** The ground beneath a body of water. **3** The real meaning; base; root; the foundation or basis of any state of affairs; idea; plan: to knock the *bottom* out of an argument. **4** Lowland along a river: often in plural. **5** *Naut.* The part of a vessel below the water line; hence, a vessel. **6** The part of the body on which one sits; the posterior; buttocks. **7** Residuum or dregs. **8** Endurance; stamina; grit. **9** All of a shoe below the upper. —*adj.* Lowest; fundamental; basal. —*v.t.* **1** To provide with a bottom. **2** To base or found: with *on* or *upon.* **3** To fathom; comprehend. —*v.i.* **4** To be founded; rest. **5** To touch or rest upon the bottom. [OE *botm*]

bottom dollar *U.S.* One's last and only dollar.

bottom land Lowland along a river.

bot·tom·less (bot'əm·lis) *adj.* **1** Having no bottom. **2** Unfathomable. **3** Baseless; visionary.

bottom line 1 *Colloq.* The line of a business accounting statement showing net profit or loss: with *the.* **2** *U.S. Slang* The condition or status of any enterprise after assets and liabilities have been calculated: with *the.*

bot·tom·ry (bot'əm·rē) *n.* A maritime contract whereby the owner or master of a vessel borrows money, pledging the vessel as security.

bot·u·lin (boch'oo·lin) *n.* A highly active nerve poison formed by an anerobic bacterium *(Clostridium botulines)* and sometimes present in spoiled or imperfectly prepared food; it has the property of resisting the action of gastrointestinal secretions.

bot·u·lism (boch'ŏŏ·liz'əm) *n.* Poisoning caused by eating spoiled food or food improperly prepared or canned, caused by botulin and characterized by acute gastrointestinal and nervous disorders. [<L *botulus* sausage; so called because the bacteria were first isolated from spoiled sausage]

bou·chée (bōō·shā') *n. French* A small cake, tart shell, or puff, filled with cream, marmalade or forcemeat, and sometimes glazed.

Bou·cher (bōō·shā'), **François,** 1703–70, French painter.

Bou·ci·cault (bōō'si·kō), **Dion,** 1822–90, U.S. dramatist and actor born in Ireland.

bou·clé (bōō·klā') *n.* A wool, rayon, cotton, silk, linen, or combination fabric woven or knitted with a looped or knotted surface. [<F, pp. of *boucler* buckle, curl]

bou·doir (bōō'dwär, bōō·dwär') *n.* A lady's private sitting-room. [<F, lit., pouting room <*bouder* pout, sulk] —**bou·doir·esque** (bōō'·dwär·esk') *adj.*

bouf·fant (bōō·fänt') *adj.* Puffed-out; flaring: a *bouffant* skirt. —*n.* A woman's hairstyle in which the hair hangs straight from the top of the head and puffs out over the ears and neck to frame the face. [<F, ppr. of *bouffer* swell]

bouffe (bōōf) *n.* Opera bouffe. [<F *(opéra) bouffe* comic (opera) <Ital. *buffa* joke, jest]

Bou·gain·ville (bōō'gən·vil) The largest of the Solomon Islands, comprising with Buka a part of the United Nations Trust Territory of New Guinea; 3,880 square miles.

Bou·gain·ville (bōō·gaṅ·vēl'), **Louis Antoine de,** 1729–1811, French navigator, 1766–69.

bou·gain·vil·le·a (bōō'gən·vil'ē·ə) *n.* Any of a genus *(Bougainvillea)* of small climbing shrubs: widely cultivated as hothouse plants. [after L. A. de *Bougainville*]

bough (bou) *n.* **1** A limb of a tree. **2** *Obs.* The gallows. ◆ Homophones: *bow*[1] and *bow*[2]. [OE *bog* shoulder, bough. Akin to BOW[1].]

bought (bôt) Past tense and past participle of BUY.

bought·en (bôt'n) *adj. Dial.* Bought at a store or shop: opposed to *home-made.*

bou·gie (bōō'jē, -zhē) *n.* **1** *Med.* **a** A smooth, slender, flexible instrument to be introduced into a canal of the body, for removing obstructions, etc. **b** A suppository. **2** A wax candle. [from *Bougie,* a town in Algeria, where the candles were made]

Bou·gue·reau (bōō·grō'), **Adolphe William,** 1825–1905, French painter.

bouil·la·baisse (bōōl'yə·bās', *Fr.* bōō·yȧ·bes') *n.* A chowder made of several varieties of fish and crustaceans, flavored with wine and saffron. [<F <Provençal *bouiabaisso* <*boui* boil + *abaisso* settle, go down]

bouil·lon (bool'yon, -yən; *Fr.* bōō·yôṅ') *n.* **1** Clear soup from beef, chicken, or other meats. **2** A special preparation used as a culture medium for bacteria. [<F<*bouillir* boil]

Bou·lan·ger (bōō·läṅ·zhā'), **Georges Ernest,** 1837–91, French general.

—**Nadia,** 1887–1979, French musician; professor of harmony and counterpoint.

boul·der (bōl'dər) *n.* A large stone moved by natural agencies from its original bed. Also **bowl'der.** [ME *bulderston* <Scand. Cf. Sw. *bullersten* rumbling stone (in a stream).]

Boul·der (bōl'dər) A university city in northern Colorado.

Boulder Canyon A gorge of the Colorado River above Hoover Dam, now covered by Lake Mead.

Boulder Dam The former name of HOOVER DAM.

bou·le[1] (bōō'lē) *n. Greek* **1** An ancient Greek legislative council. **2** The modern Greek legislative assembly, especially the lower house. Also spelled *bule.*

boule[2] (bōōl) *n.* A small mass of fused alumina, usually pear-shaped, and tinted to resemble the natural ruby, sapphire, etc. [<F, ball]

boul·e·vard (bool'ə·värd, bōō'lə-) *n.* **1** A broad city avenue, often planted with trees. **2** The decorative plot of trees, turf, or shrubbery along such an avenue. **3** Originally, a rampart; hence, a street laid out on the site of former ramparts. [<F <G *bollwerk* fortification. Akin to BULWARK.]

bou·le·ver·se·ment (bōōl·vers·mäṅ') *n. French* An overthrow; confusion; convulsion.

Bou·logne (bōō·lōn', *Fr.* bōō·lôn'y') A port of northern France on the English Channel. Also **Boulogne-sur-Mer** (-sür·mâr').

Bou·logne-Bil·lan·court (bōō·lôn'y'·bē·yäṅ·kōōr') A city on the Seine River, SW of Paris, France.

bounce (bouns) *v.* **bounced, bounc·ing** *v.t.* **1** To cause to bound or rebound. **2** To cause to move noisily; bang; thump. **3** *U.S. Slang* To eject forcibly. **4** *U.S. Slang* To discharge from employment. —*v.i.* **5** To bound or rebound. **6** To move suddenly and violently; jump or spring. **7** To move hurriedly: with *out of* or *into.* **8** *Informal* To be returned because of insufficient funds: said of a check. —*n.* **1** A sudden, or violent spring or leap; a bounding or elastic motion; rebound. **2** *Colloq.* Enthusiasm; vivacity; spirit; verve. **3** *Slang* Dismissal; discharge; expulsion. **4** A heavy blow; a bang. **5** *Brit. Colloq.* An audacious lie; a bouncer; boastful exaggeration; bluster; swagger. [ME *bunsen* <MLG. Cf. Du. *bonzen.*]

bounc·er (boun'sər) *n.* **1** A large or strong person or thing. **2** One who or that which bounces. **3** *U.S. Colloq.* A strong man employed in a theater, saloon, etc., to throw out objectionable customers. **4** An audacious lie; also, a braggart.

bounc·ing (boun'sing) *adj.* **1** Strong and active. **2** Large; strapping; buxom. **3** Exaggerated; boastful.

bouncing Bet The soapwort.

bound[1] (bound) *v.i.* **1** To strike and spring back from a surface, as a ball. **2** To leap; move by a series of leaps. —*v.t.* **3** To cause to rebound. —*n.* **1** A light elastic leap or spring; also, a rebound. **2** The distance passed over in a leap or bound. See synonyms under LEAP. [<F *bondir* leap]

bound[2] (bound) *v.t.* **1** To set limits to; restrict. **2** To form the boundary of. **3** To describe or name the boundaries of. —*v.i.* **4** To adjoin. See synonyms under CIRCUMSCRIBE, LIMIT. [<*n.*] —*n.* **1** That which circumscribes or limits; boundary. **2** *pl.* The district included within a boundary or limits. See synonyms under BANK, BOUNDARY. [<OF *bonne, bonde* <LL *bodina* limit. Related to BOURN[1].]

bound[3] (bound) Past tense and past participle of BIND.—*adj.* **1** Made fast; tied; confined in bonds. **2** Constrained or compelled. **3** Having a cover or binding. **4** Apprenticed. **5** *Colloq.* Determined; resolved. **6** Constipated.

bound[4] (bound) *adj.* Having one's course directed; on the way; destined: with *for* or *to.* [<ON *buinn* <*bua* prepare]

bound·a·ry (boun'də·rē, -drē) *n. pl.* **·ries 1** A limiting or dividing line or mark. **2** Any object serving to indicate a limit or confine.

Synonyms: barrier, border, bound, bourn, bourne, confines, edge, enclosure, frontier, landmark, limit, line, marches, marge, margin, term, termination, verge. The *boundary* was originally the *landmark,* that which marked off one piece of territory from another. The *bound* is the *limit,* marked or unmarked. Now, however, the difference between the two words has come to be simply one of usage. As regards territory, we speak of the *boundaries* of a nation or of an estate; the *bounds* of a college, a ball ground, etc. A *barrier* is something that bars ingress or egress. A *barrier* may be a *boundary,* as was the Great Wall of China for many centuries. *Bourn,* or *bourne,* is a poetical expression for *bound* or *boundary.* A *border* is a strip, as of land, along the *boundary. Edge* is a sharp terminal line, as where river or ocean meets the land. *Limit* is now used almost wholly in the figurative sense; the *limit* of discussion, of time, of jurisdiction. *Line* is a military term: within the *lines,* or through the *lines,* of an army. Compare BARRIER, END, MARGIN.

boundary layer 1 *Aeron.* A tenuous stratum or film of air in contact with the surface of an airfoil. **2** *Physics* Any layer of fluid close to the surface of a body in a moving stream that reduces the pressure of impact.

boundary rider *Austral.* An employe of a sheep or cattle station who patrols boundaries to prevent the straying of stock or to inspect fences.

bound·en (boun′dən) *adj.* **1** Obligatory; necessary, as a duty. **2** *Obs.* Under obligations; obliged. [Var. of BOUND[3]]

bound·er (boun′dər) *n.* **1** One who fixes or marks bounds. **2** *Colloq.* One whose manners, etc., are offensive; a cad.

bound form *Ling.* A morpheme which occurs only as part of a larger form, as the *-s* in *cats* and the *-ing* in *looking:* opposed to *free form.*

bound·less (bound′lis) *adj.* Having no limit; vast; measureless; infinite. See synonyms under INFINITE. **—bound′less·ly** *adv.* **—bound′less·ness** *n.*

bound-out (bound′out′) *adj.* Indentured; apprenticed.

boun·te·ous (boun′tē·əs) *adj.* **1** Giving freely and largely; generous; beneficient. **2** Marked by liberality or bounty; plentiful. **—boun′te·ous·ly** *adv.* **—boun′te·ous·ness** *n.*

boun·ti·ful (boun′tə·fəl) *adj.* **1** Bounteous; generous. **2** Abundant; displaying abundance. See synonyms under AMPLE, GENEROUS. **—boun′ti·ful·ly** *adv.* **—boun′ti·ful·ness** *n.*

boun·ty (boun′tē) *n. pl.* **·ties 1** Liberality in giving or bestowing; munificence. **2** Gifts or favors generously bestowed. **3** A grant or allowance from a government, as for fisheries, manufactures, exports, enlistment, etc. **4** A reward paid by a government to encourage the killing of predatory animals (formerly also of Indians). See synonyms under BENEVOLENCE, GIFT, SUBSIDY. [<OF *bonté* <L *bonitas, -tatis* goodness]

boun·ty-fed (boun′tē·fed′) *adj.* Aided and encouraged by government grants or premiums; subsidized: *bounty-fed* industries.

boun·ty-jump·er (boun′tē·jum′pər) *n.* One who, having enlisted for the bounty, deserts as soon as possible, as in the Civil War.

bounty land Land given as a bounty for military service.

bounty money Money given as a bounty, especially for military service.

bou·quet (bō·kā′, bōō·kā′ *for def. 1;* bōō·kā′ *for def. 2) n.* **1** A bunch of flowers; a nosegay. **2** Delicate odor; particularly, the distinctive aroma of a wine. [<F <OF *boschet,* dim. of *bosc* wood, ult. <Gmc.]

bou·quet gar·ni (bōō·ke′ gȧr·nē′) *French* A bundle of herbs and vegetables used for seasoning.

Bour·bon (bŏŏr′bən) **1** A dynasty which reigned over France, 1589–1792, 1815–48. **2** A member of the deposed royal house of France, or of the Spanish or Neapolitan branches of the same family. **3** One who is stubbornly conservative in politics; one opposed to progressive movement. **—Bour′bon·ism** *n.* **—Bour′bon·ist** *n.*

Bour·bon (bŏŏr′bən, *Fr.* bōōr·bôṅ′), **Charles,** 1490–1527, French general under Charles V: called "Connétable de Bourbon."

Bour·bon Island (bŏŏr′bən) A former name for RÉUNION ISLAND.

Bour·bon whisky (bûr′bən) Whisky distilled from corn and barley, originally in Bourbon County, Ky. Also **bour′bon.**

bourd (bōōrd) *n. Scot.* A jest; anecdote; also, merriment.

bour·don[1] (bŏŏr′dən) *n.* **1** An organ stop, commonly of 16-foot tone. **2** The drone of a bagpipe. **3** A humming, monotonous, or continuous sound. *—v.i.* To drone a melody. [<Med. L *burdo* drone]

bour·don[2] (bŏŏr′dən) *n. Obs.* A pilgrim's staff. [<F]

bourg (boorg) *n.* A fortified medieval town; a Continental market town. [<F <LL *burgus,* ult. <Gmc. Related to BOROUGH.]

bour·geois[1] (bŏŏr′zhwä, bŏŏr·zhwä′) *adj.* Of or pertaining to the commercial or middle class, as distinguished from the nobility or from the working class: used by some writers as signifying uncultivated; ill-bred; common. *—n. pl.* **·geois 1** A citizen; a member of the commercial or middle class; a townsman; tradesman. **2** A 14th century coin. **3** In radical circles, anyone who owns property. [<F <OF *burgeis.* Doublet of BURGESS.]

bour·geois[2] (bər·jois′) *n.* A size of type: about 9-point. [? after a French printer]

Bour·geois (bŏŏr·zhwä′), **Léon Victor,** 1851–1925, French statesman.

bour·geoi·sie (bŏŏr′zhwä·zē′) *n.* **1** The middle class of society, especially in France: used collectively. **2** That class of society having private property. used especially by radical socialists. [<F <*bourgeois* middle class]

bour·geon (bûr′jən) *v.* & *n.* Burgeon.

Bourges (bōōrzh) A city in central France.

Bour·get (bōōr·zhe′), **Paul,** 1852–1935, French novelist, poet, and critic.

Bour·gogne (bōōr·gôn′y′) The French name for BURGUNDY.

Bour·gui·gnonne (bōōr·gē·nyôn′) *adj.* Prepared in a red wine sauce garnished with mushrooms and small onions. [<F, Burgundian]

bourn[1] (bôrn, bōrn, bŏŏrn) *n.* **1** That which limits; bound; goal; end: the *bourn* of man's life. **2** *Obs.* Realm; region; domain. Also **bourne.** See synonyms under BOUNDARY. [<F *borne* <OF *bodne* <LL *bodina* limit. Related to BOUND[2].]

bourn[2] (bôrn, bōrn, bŏŏrn) *n.* A brook or rivulet: used also in combination: *Eastbourne.* Compare BURN[2]. Also **bourne.** [Var. of BURN[2]]

Bourne·mouth (bôrn′məth, bōrn′-) A county borough and seaside resort in SW Hampshire, England.

bourre·let (bŏŏr·lā′) *n.* A ridgelike band between the ogive and body of a shell, fitting closely to the bore of the gun and centering the projectile. [<F]

bourse (bŏŏrs) *n.* An exchange or money market: applied to Continental stock exchanges, and especially to the Paris stock exchange. [<F, purse <LL *bursa* bag]

bour·tree (bŏŏr′trē) *n. Scot.* The European elder tree *(Sambucus nigra).*

bouse[1] (bōōz, bouz) *n.* & *v.i.* Booze.

bouse[2] (bous, bouz) *v.t. Naut.* To lift or haul with blocks and tackle: also spelled *bowse.* [Origin unknown]

bou·stro·phe·don (bŏŏ′strə·fēd′n, bou′-) *n.* The early Greek method of writing, alternately from right to left and from left to right, as in inscriptions. [<Gk. *boustrophēdon* turning like oxen (in plowing) <*bous* ox + *strephein* turn] **—bou·stroph·e·don·ic** (bōō·strof′ə·don′ik, bou-), **bou·stroph·ic** (bōō·strof′ik, bou-) *adj.*

bous·y (bōō′zē, bou′-) *adj.* Boozy.

bout (bout) *n.* **1** A single turn, as in mowing a field. **2** A set-to or contest, as at boxing, etc. **3** A fit of drunkenness, reveling, or illness. **4** A bend or turn, as of a rope; bight. See synonyms under BATTLE. [Var. of ME *bought* bending, turn. Cf. LG *bucht* bend, turn.]

bou·tique (bōō·tēk′) *n. French* A small retail store in which dress accessories are sold.

bou·ton·nière (bōō′tə·nyâr′) *n.* A buttonhole bouquet, or a single flower worn in the buttonhole. [<F]

Bou·vier (bōō·vir′), **John,** 1787–1851, U.S. jurist born in Italy.

bou·vier des Flan·dres (bōō·vyā′ dā flän′dr′) A breed of powerfully built, medium-sized working dog, native to Belgium. [<F, cowherd of Flanders]

bou·zou·ki (bə·zōō′kē) *n.* A mandolinlike stringed instrument having a very long neck. [<New Gk. *mpouzouki*]

Bo·ve·ri (bō·vā′rē), **Theodor,** 1862–1915, German zoologist.

bo·vid (bō′vid) *n. Zool.* One of the *Bovidae.*

Bo·vi·dae (bō′vi·dē) *n. pl.* A family of ruminants, generally embracing those having paired hollow horns ensheathing horn cores, as antelopes, cattle, sheep, goats, etc.: distinguished from the deer family especially by non-deciduous, unbranched horns. [<L *bos, bovis* ox]

bo·vine (bō′vīn, -vin) *adj.* **1** Of or pertaining to the *Bovidae* or the genus *Bos.* **2** Oxlike; slow; patient; dull. *—n.* A bovine animal, as an ox, cow, etc. [<LL *bovinus* <L *bos* ox]

bow[1] (bou) *n.* **1** The forward part of a vessel; also, the front part of an airship. **2** The forward oarsman of a boat. ◆ Homophone: *bough.* [<Dan. *bov* bow of a ship. Akin to BOUGH.]

bow[2] (bou) *v.* **bowed, bow·ing** *v.t.* **1** To bend (the head, knee, etc.), as in reverence, courtesy, or assent. **2** To express with bows: to *bow* agreement. **3** To escort with bows: He *bowed* us into the room. **4** To cause to yield; coerce: He *bowed* her to his will. **5** To weigh down; cause to stoop: Fatigue *bowed* his head. *—v.i.* **6** To bend the head, knee, etc., as in reverence, courtesy, or assent. **7** To express thanks, greeting, agreement, etc., by bowing. **8** To bend or incline downward: The waves *bowed* over and broke. **9** To submit; yield. **—to bow out** To withdraw; resign. *—n.* An inclination of the body or head forward and downward, as in salutation or worship. ◆ Homophone: *bough.* [OE *bugan* bow, bend, flee] **—bow′er** *n.*

bow[3] (bō) *n.* **1** A bend or curve, or something bent or curved. **2** A rainbow. **3** A weapon made from a strip of elastic wood or other pliable material, bent by a cord and projecting an arrow by its recoil when suddenly released; also, an archer. **4** *Music* A rod having parallel hairs strained between raised ends, used with a violin or other stringed instrument by drawing across the strings; also, the movement or mode of moving this. **5** A knot with a loop or loops, as of ribbon, etc. **6** Any one of various bow-shaped objects. **7** A U-shaped wooden piece passing upward through a yoke and retained by pins; oxbow. **8** *Geom.* A polygonal or curved projection from a straight line or wall on the ground plane. **9** Either of the rims of a pair of spectacles or one of the curved supports passing over the ears. *—adj.* Bent; curved; bowed. *—v.t.* & *v.i.* **bow·ed, bow·ing 1** To bend into the shape of a bow. **2** *Music* To play (a stringed instrument) with a bow. ◆ Homophone: *beau.* [OE *boga*] **—bow′er** *n.*

bow arm (bō) In playing a violin, the right arm; in archery, the left.

Bow bells (bō) The bells of St. Mary-le-Bow, in Cheapside, London, within sound of which cockneys were said to be born; hence, the region within London called *cockneydom.*

Bow china (bō) A delicate ware made at Stratford-le-Bow, near London, in the 18th century.

bow compass (bō) *Geom.* A pair of very small compasses, properly having, instead of a joint, a curved metal strip between the legs, for drawing small circles or arcs of small radius.

Bow·ditch (bou′dich), **Nathaniel,** 1773–1838, U.S. mathematician and navigator.

bowd·ler·ize (boud′lər·īz) *v.t.* **·ized, ·iz·ing** To expurgate or edit prudishly. [after Dr. Thomas *Bowdler's* "family" edition of Shakespeare (1818)] **—bowd′ler·i·za′tion** *n.* **—bowd′ler·ism** *n.*

Bow·doin (bōd′n), **James,** 1726–90, American patriot.

bow·el (bou′əl, boul) *n.* **1** An intestine. **2** *pl.* The intestines or entrails collectively. **3** *pl.* The inner part of anything: the *bowels* of the earth. **4** *pl.* The intestinal regions, formerly considered as the seat of the tender emotions; hence, pity; compassion; heart. *—v.t.* **·eled** or **·elled, ·el·ing** or **·el·ling** To remove the bowels from; disembowel. [<OF *boel* <L *botellus,* dim. of *botulus* sausage]

bow·er[1] (bou′ər) *n.* **1** A shady recess; a retired dwelling; a rustic cottage. **2** A private apartment; boudoir. **3** An arbor. *—v.t.* To enclose in or as in a bower; embower. [OE *bur* chamber] **—bow′er·y** *adj.*

bow·er[2] (bou′ər) *n.* Either of the two highest cards (the knave of trumps or **right bower** and the knave of the same color or **left bower**) in the game of euchre, unless the joker is used, which is then usually called the **best bower.** [<G *bauer* peasant, knave in a deck of cards]

bower[3] (bou′ər) *n. Naut.* A large anchor carried on the bow of a vessel. Also **bower anchor.**

bow·er·bird (bou′ər·bûrd′) *n.* An Australian bird that builds a bower or playhouse to attract the female, ornamenting it with shells, feathers, etc.; especially, the **great bowerbird** *(Chlamydera nuchalis).*

bow·er·y (bou′ər·ē) *n. pl.* **·er·ies** A farm or plantation: so called by the Dutch settlers of New York. [<Du. *bouwerij* farm <*bouwer, boer* farmer]

Bow·er·y (bou′ər·ē), **the** A street and section in New York City occupying the site of Governor Stuyvesant's farm or bowery: noted for its saloons, shabby hotels, and cheap shops.

bow·fin (bō′fin′) *n.* A small, predaceous, ganoid fish *(Amia calva),* having a long dorsal fin, being the sole member of the family Amiidae, which inhabits lakes and sluggish fresh water in North America. Also called *amia, mudfish, dogfish.*

bow·head (bō′hed′) *n.* The right whale.

bow·ie knife (bō′ē, bo͞o′ē) A strong hunting knife with two-edged point, hilt, crosspiece, and sheath: its invention is usually attributed to James Bowie, 1799–1836, Texan fighter who died at the Alamo; his brother, Rezin P. Bowie, also claimed to be the inventor.

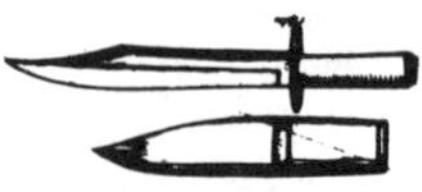
BOWIE KNIFE AND SHEATH

bow-key (bō′kē′) *n.* The wooden pin which fastens the oxbow to the yoke: also called *bowpin.*

bow·knot (bō′not′) *n.* An ornamental slipknot made by doubling ribbon, cord, fabric, etc., into one or more loops, usually tied so as to leave ends free to draw the loops easily through the knot. See illustration under KNOT.

bowl[1] (bōl) *n.* **1** A concave domestic vessel, nearly hemispherical and larger than a cup. **2** The amount it will hold. **3** A drinking-vessel for wine, etc. **4** A large goblet. **5** Anything shaped like a bowl, as a stadium. ◆Homophone: *bole.* [OE *bolla*]

bowl[2] (bōl) *v.t.* **1** To strike or hit with or as with a bowl; knock down. **2** To roll (a ball). **3** To carry or transport on or as on wheels. **4** In cricket, to put out (the batsman): with *out.* —*v.i.* **5** To play at bowls. **6** To throw or roll a bowl or round object. **7** In cricket, to deliver the ball to the batsman. **8** To move smoothly and swiftly: usually with *along:* The ship *bowled* along. **—to bowl over** To cause to be confused or helpless; knock down or out. —*n.* **1** A large wooden ball for playing bowls or tenpins. **2** A turn or inning at a game of bowls. **3** A roller in a knitting machine. ◆Homophone: *bole.* [<F *boule* ball <L *bulla* bubble]

bowl·der (bōl′dər) *n.* Boulder.

bow·leg (bō′leg′) *n.* A leg bent in an outward curve. **—bow′leg′ged** *adj.*

bowl·er (bō′lər) *n.* **1** One who plays bowls. **2** The player who delivers the ball. **3** *Brit.* A low-crowned, stiff felt hat; a derby hat.

Bowles (bōlz), **Samuel,** father 1797–1851, and son 1826–78, U.S. newspaper editors and publishers. **—Chester,** born 1901, U.S. public administrator and diplomat.

bow·line (bō′lin, -līn′) *n.* **1** *Naut.* A rope to keep the weather edge of a vessel's square sail forward when sailing close-hauled. **2** A knot. **—on a bowline** Close-hauled to the wind; said of a vessel.

BOWLINE KNOTS
a. Bowline knot.
b. Running bowline.

bowl·ing (bō′ling) *n.* **1** A game played on a narrow lane along which a ball is rolled in an attempt to knock down ten pins at the far end of the lane. **2** Any of various similar games. **3** The playing of any of these games.

bowling alley 1 A long, narrow, planked space for playing at tenpins. **2** A building containing one or more such alleys. **3** Any enclosure for playing bowls.

bowling ball A hard, heavy ball used in the game of bowling, usually having three finger holes for gripping.

bowling green A smooth lawn for playing at bowls.

Bowling Green 1 A small park at the foot of Broadway, New York City. **2** A city in southern Kentucky.

bowls (bōlz) *n. pl. (construed as sing.)* Any of various bowling games, especially one (also called **lawn bowling**) played outdoors with weighted balls rolled at a stationary ball.

bow·man[1] (bō′mən) *n. pl.* **·men** (-mən) An archer.

bow·man[2] (bou′mən) *n. pl.* **·men** (-mən) The oarsman nearest the bow.

bow pen (bō) *Geom.* A pair of jointless compasses carrying a pen or pencil: used for drawing very small circles.

bow·pin (bō′pin′) *n.* A bow-key.

bowse (bo͞oz, bouz) See BOUSE[2].

bow·shot (bō′shot′) *n.* The distance which an arrow may be sent from the bow.

bow·sprit (bou′sprit′, bō′-) *n. Naut.* A spar projecting forward from the bow of a vessel.

bow·string (bō′string′) *n.* **1** The string of a bow. **2** A string for strangling criminals. **3** Execution by strangling. —*v.t.* To execute by strangling; garrotte.

bowstring hemp A perennial, erect herb of the lily family (genus *Sansevieria*) with narrow white or yellowish-white flowers and hemplike fiber.

bow't (bōt) *adj. Scot.* Bowed; crooked; bent.

bow·tie (bō′tī′) *n.* A necktie worn in a bowknot.

bow window (bō) A projecting window built up from the ground level, properly one of curved ground plan. Compare BAY WINDOW.

bow-wow (bou′wou′) *n.* **1** The bark of a dog, or an imitation of it. **2** A dog: a child's word. **3** *pl. Colloq.* Ruin; damnation: going to the *bow-wows.* —*v.i.* To bark.

bow·yer (bō′yər) *n.* A maker or seller of bows.

box[1] (boks) *n.* **1** A receptacle or case of wood or other material, usually having a lid. **2** Any of various objects or receptacles resembling a box. **3** *Mech.* An axle bearing, casing, or other enclosed cavity. **4** The raised seat of a coach, the body of a wagon, etc. **5** A building, structure, or compartment with some resemblance or analogy to a box, as a compartment in a theater, restaurant, etc. **6** The quantity contained in a box or that a box will hold. **7** Either of the rectangular spaces on a baseball field in which the batsman or pitcher stands. **8** A gift or present packed in a box. **9** A box stall for a horse or bovine animal. **10** A flag house, sentry house, or similar small building for a watchman or the like. **11** A small house in the country; a shooting-box. **12** The place in a courtroom where the jury, a prisoner, or witnesses are railed in. **13** A cavity made in the trunk of a tree to collect its sap, as in extracting turpentine, etc. **14** A difficulty or predicament. —*v.t.* **1** To put into or enclose in a box: often with *up.* **2** To furnish with a bushing or box. **3** To boxhaul. **4** To fit into a mortise, as a tenon. **—to box the compass 1** To recite in order the 32 points of the compass. **2** To make a complete revolution; adopt successively all possible opinions on a question. [OE <Med. L *buxis,* blend of L *buxus* boxwood and *pyxis* box (both <Gk. *pyxos* boxwood). Doublet of PYX.] **—box′er** *n.*

box[2] (boks) *v.t.* **1** To cuff or buffet, especially about the ears and side of the head. **2** To fight (another) in a boxing match. —*v.i.* **3** To fight in a boxing match. **4** To be a prize fighter. —*n.* A slap or cuff with the hand on the ear or the cheek. See synonyms under BLOW [ME; origin uncertain]

box[3] (boks) *n.* A small evergreen tree or shrub (genus *Buxus*) of the Old World, cultivated as a border or hedge; especially, any variety of *B. sempervirens.* [OE <L *buxus* <Gk. *pyxos* boxwood]

box·ber·ry (boks′ber′ē, -bər·ē) *n. pl.* **·ber·ries 1** The checkerberry or wintergreen. **2** The partridgeberry.

box calf Tanned calfskin with square markings on the grain produced by lengthwise and crosswise rolling.

box·car (boks′kär′) *n.* A railway car shaped like a rectangular box, for carrying freight.

box coat 1 A coachman's heavy overcoat. **2** A greatcoat, especially one worn by travelers on the tops of coaches. **3** A loosely fitting overcoat, snug only at the shoulders.

box elder A North American tree of the maple family *(Acer negundo)* having leaves with 3 or 5 compound leaflets.

box·er[1] (bok′sər) *n.* A pugilist.

box·er[2] (bok′sər) *n.* A breed of medium-sized dog, related to the bulldog, characterized by a short, sturdy body, smooth coat, fawn or brindle in color, and a black mask. [Alter. of G *-beisser* in *Bullenbeisser* bulldog]

Box·er (bok′sər) *n.* A member of a Chinese secret society, active in 1900, which aimed to rid China of foreigners by force.

box·haul (boks′hôl′) *v.t. Naut.* To veer (a square-rigged vessel) round instead of tacking: done when tacking is impracticable.

box hook A sickle-shaped hook with a wooden handle, usually T-shaped, used for gripping and moving heavy boxes or bales of merchandise, waste, etc.: also called *bale hook.*

box·ing[1] (bok′sing) *n.* The act or practice of sparring, as with gloves; pugilism.

box·ing[2] (bok′sing) *n.* **1** The act of enclosing in a box. **2** Material from which to make boxes. **3** A casing or niche, as for window shutters.

Boxing Day The first weekday after Christmas, a British legal holiday on which presents (Christmas boxes) are given to employees, letter-carriers, etc.

boxing glove A glove with padded back, for boxing.

boxing match A prize fight or sparring contest.

box iron A smoothing and pressing iron containing a receptacle for a heater: distinguished from *sad-iron.*

box kite A kite having two rectangular, box-shaped, covered frames fitted together.

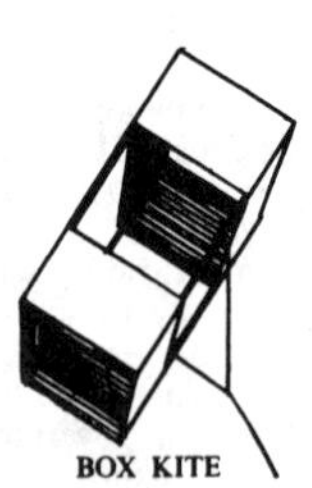
BOX KITE

box office The ticket office of a theater, etc.

box-of·fice (boks′ôf′is, -of′·is) *adj.* Of such a character as to attract large audiences, and, therefore, destined to make large profits.

box pleat Material folded twice and in opposite directions, the edges turned under and meeting. Also **box plait.**

box set A series of wooden frames covered with canvas, assembled to form the three walls of an interior stage setting.

box spring A mattress foundation consisting of an upholstered wood or metal frame set with an arrangement of coil springs to provide resiliency.

box stall A large, boxed-in stall for horses or cattle, in which they do not have to be tied.

box·thorn (boks′thôrn′) *n.* Any of various evergreen or deciduous ornamental plants (genus *Lycium*) of the nightshade family, with long, drooping, flowering branches and usually scarlet berries, especially *L. halimifolium:* also called *matrimony vine.*

box·wood (boks′wo͝od′) *n.* **1** The hard, close-grained, durable wood of the box evergreen shrub (genus *Buxus*). **2** The shrub.

boy (boi) *n.* **1** A male child; lad; youth; son. **2** *pl.* Comrades; fellows. **3** A male servant, especially a personal servant: often used of Orientals or Africans. [ME *boi;* origin unknown]

bo·yar (bō·yär′, boi′ər) *n.* **1** A member of a class of the old Russian aristocracy, abolished in the time of Peter the Great. **2** In Rumania, one of a privileged class. Also **bo·yard** (bō·yärd′, boi′ərd). [<Russian *boyarin* noble]

boy·cott (boi′kot) *v.t.* **1** To combine together in refusing to deal or associate with, so as to punish or coerce. **2** To refuse to use or buy. —*n.* The act, pressure, or an instance of boycotting. [after Capt. C. *Boycott,* 1832–1897, landlord's agent in Ireland, who was first victim, 1880]

boy friend *Colloq.* **1** A girl's or woman's sweetheart, favorite male companion, etc. **2** A male friend. Also **boy·friend** (boi′frend′).

boy·hood (boi′ho͝od) *n.* **1** The state or period of being a boy. **2** Boys collectively.

boy·ish (boi′ish) *adj.* Of, pertaining to, or like boys or boyhood. See synonyms under YOUTHFUL. **—boy′ish·ly** *adv.* **—boy′ish·ness** *n.*

Boyle (boil), **Robert,** 1627–91, English chemist and physicist, born in Ireland.

Boyle's law *Physics* The statement that the volume of a gas kept at constant temperature varies inversely as the pressure. [after Robert *Boyle*]

Boyne (boin) A river in NE Ireland, flowing NE 70 miles to the Irish Sea.

boy scout 1 A member of the **Boy Scouts,** an organization for training boys between the ages of 12 and 19 in self-reliance and good citizenship through a program of constructive, recreational training: initiated in England in 1908 by Lieut. Gen. Sir Robert Baden-Powell. **2** A member of the Boy Scouts of America, incorporated in 1910.

boy·sen·ber·ry (boi′zən·ber′ē) *n. pl.* **·ries 1** A hybrid plant obtained by crossing the blackberry, raspberry, and loganberry. **2** Its edible fruit, resembling the raspberry in taste. [after Rudolph *Boysen,* 20th c. U.S. horticulturist, the originator]

Boz (boz) An early pen name of Charles Dickens.

Boz·ca·a·da (bôz·jä′ä·dä′) The Turkish name for TENEDOS. Also **Boz·ca Island** (bôz′jä).

bo·zo (bō′zō) *n. U.S. Slang* A fellow; guy.

Boz·za·ris (bot′sä·rēs, bō·zar′is), **Marcos,** 1788–1823, Greek patriot.

Br *Chem.* Bromine (symbol Br).

bra (brä) *n.* A brassière.

Bra·ban·çon griffon (brȧ·bäṅ·sôṅ′) A toy dog similar to the Brussels griffon except that its coat is short and smooth, reddish-brown or black mixed with reddish-brown.

Bra·ban·çonne (brȧ·bäṅ·sôn′) The national anthem of the Belgians since 1830. [< F < *Brabant,* province in Belgium]

Bra·bant (brə·bant′, brä′bənt) A former duchy, now divided into North Brabant, Netherlands, and Brabant province in Belgium; 1,268 square miles; capital, Brussels.

brab·ble (brab′əl) *v.i.* **·bled, ·bling** To quarrel noisily about trifles. [? < Du. *brabbelen* jabber] — **brab′ble·ment** *n.*

brac·cate (brak′āt) *adj. Ornithol.* Having the feet feathered down to the claws, as certain birds. [< L *bracatus* wearing breeches < *bracae* breeches]

BRACCATE CLAWS

brace (brās) *v.* **braced, brac·ing** *v.t.* **1** To make firm or steady; strengthen by or as by equipping with braces. **2** To make ready to withstand pressure, impact, assault, etc. **3** To tie or fasten firmly, as with straps. **4** To stimulate; enliven. **5** *Naut.* To turn (the yards) by means of the braces. **6** *Slang* To ask a loan or favor from. —*v.i.* **7** To strain against pressure. **—to brace up** *Colloq.* To rouse one's courage or resolution. —*n.* **1** A support, as of wood or metal, to hold something firmly in place. **2** A cranklike handle, as for a bit. **3** A clasp or clamp used for connecting, fastening, etc. **4** A doubly curved line (⏟), used in writing and printing to connect words, lines, or staves of music. **5** A pair; couple; two: a *brace* of ducks, etc. **6** The state of being braced; tension. **7** *Naut.* A rope fastened to a yardarm and reaching the deck, to swing the yard for the wind and to hold it in place. **8** *pl. Brit.* Suspenders. [< OF *bracier* embrace < *brace, brache* two arms < L *brachia,* pl. of *brachium* arm]

brace·let (brās′lit) *n.* **1** An ornamental band encircling the wrist or arm. **2** *Colloq.* A handcuff. [< OF, dim. of *bracel* < L *brachiale* bracelet < *brachium* arm]

brac·er (brā′sər) *n.* **1** That which braces or steadies; a band; support. **2** A protective covering for the forearm in archery. **3** A tonic; stimulant. **4** A stimulating drink.

bra·ce·ro (brə·sâr′ō) *n. pl.* **·ros** A Mexican laborer brought into the United States under contract for seasonal farm work. [< Sp., day laborer]

brach (brach, brak) *n. Archaic* A hound bitch. Also **brach·et** (brach′it). [< OF *brachet* hunting dog < OHG]

bra·chi·al (brā′kē·əl, brak′ē-) *adj.* **1** Of or pertaining to the arm, especially the upper arm. **2** *Zool.* Of, pertaining to, or designating the armlike appendages or brachia of various invertebrates. **3** Armlike. [< L *brachialis* < *brachium* arm]

bra·chi·ate (brā′kē·it, -āt, brak′ē-) *adj. Bot.* Having branches in pairs, each pair forming a right line with each other, and standing at right angles to the stem, or widely diverging. —*v.i.* (-āt) **·at·ed, ·at·ing** *Zool.* To move by a swinging motion of the arms, as from branch to branch of trees: said especially of certain arboreal apes not fully adapted to the erect posture and bipedal locomotion. [< L *brachiatus* having arms < *brachium* arm] **—bra′chi·a′tion** *n.*

brachio- *combining form* Arm; of the arm: *brachiotomy.* Also, before vowels, **brachi-**. [< Gk. *brachiōn* arm]

bra·chi·ot·o·my (brā′kē·ot′ə·mē, brak′ē-) *n. Surg.* The cutting off or removal of an arm.

bra·chi·o·pod (brā′kē·ə·pod′, brak′ē-) *n. Zool.* One of a phylum or class *(Brachiopoda)* of nearly extinct molluscoid marine animals having a bivalve shell and a pair of brachial appendages rising from the sides of the mouth; a lamp shell. — **bra·chi·op·o·dous** (brā′kē·op′ə·dəs, brak′ē-) *adj.*

bra·chis·to·chrone (brə·kis′tə·krōn) *n. Physics* The line of motion along which a particle acted upon by a constraining force will move from one given point to another in the shortest time: also spelled *brachystochrone.* [< Gk. *brachistos* shortest + *chronos* time]

bra·chi·um (brā′kē·əm, brak′ē-) *n. pl.* **bra·chi·a** (brā′kē·ə, brak′ē-) **1** The upper arm, or its homolog in any animal. **2** Any armlike process or appendage. [< L]

brachy- *combining form* Short: *brachycranic.* [< Gk. *brachys* short]

brach·y·ce·phal·ic (brak′i·sə·fal′ik) *adj.* **1** *Anat.* Having a short skull of excessive breadth; round-headed. **2** In anthropometry, characterized by a skull whose cephalic index is at least 80. Also **brach·y·ceph·a·lous** (brak′·ē·sef′ə·ləs). [< NL *brachycephalicus* < Gk. *brachykephalos* < *brachys* short + *kephalē* head] **—brach′y·ceph′a·ly** *n.*

brach·y·cra·nic (brak′i·krā′nik) *adj.* Brachycephalic. [< BRACHY- + Gk. *kranion* head]

brach·y·dac·tyl·ic (brak′i·dak·til′ik) *adj.* Having abnormally short fingers or toes. [< Gk. *brachydaktylos* < *brachys* short + *daktylos* finger] — **brach′y·dac′tyl·ism** (-dak′təl·iz′əm) *n.*

brach·y·dome (brak′i·dōm) See under DOME (def. 4).

brach·y·dro·mic (brak′i·drō′mik) *adj.* Taking a deflected or slanting path with reference to the target; heading short: said of guided missiles. [< Gk. *brachydromos* < *brachys* short + *dromos* course]

bra·chyl·o·gy (brə·kil′ə·jē) *n.* Brevity and conciseness of speech; an abridged form of expression; especially, omission of a word necessary for correct grammatical expression. [< Gk. *brachylogia* < *brachys* short + *-logia* speech]

bra·chyp·ter·ous (brə·kip′tər·əs) *adj. Ornithol.* Having short wings. [< Gk. *brachypteros* < *brachys* short + *pteron* wing]

brach·y·u·ran (brak′i·yŏŏr′ən) *adj. Zool.* Of or relating to a suborder *(Brachyura)* of decapods, comprising the crabs. Also **brach′y·u′rous** (-yŏŏr′əs). —*n.* A short-tailed crustacean. [< NL *brachyura* < Gk. *brachys* short + *oura* tail]

brac·ing[1] (brā′sing) *adj.* Imparting tone or vigor; invigorating; tonic.

brac·ing[2] (brā′sing) *n.* **1** The act of bracing, or the state of being braced. **2** A system of braces, as in bridge-building.

brack·en (brak′ən) *n.* **1** A brake or other large fern. **2** Brakes collectively. [ME *braken* < Scand. Cf. Sw. *bräken* fern.]

brack·et (brak′it) *n.* **1** A piece projecting from a wall to support a shelf or other weight. **2** A projecting gas fixture or lamp holder, etc. **3** A brace used to strengthen an angle. **4** *Printing* One of two marks [ ], used to enclose any part of the text. **5** A vinculum. **6** A number of persons considered as a group because of some common characteristics: the high-income *bracket.* —*v.t.* **1** To provide or support with a bracket or brackets. **2** To enclose within brackets. **3** To group or categorize together. **4** *Mil.* To fire both over and short of (a target). [< Sp. *bragueta,* dim. of *braga* < L *bracae,* pl., breeches]

brack·et·ing (brak′it·ing) *n.* **1** Wooden skeleton pieces to which the lath and plaster forming the surface of a cornice are fastened, and which give shape to the latter. **2** The act of furnishing with brackets. **3** A series of brackets.

brack·ish (brak′ish) *adj.* **1** Somewhat saline, as a mixture of salt water and fresh; briny. **2** Distasteful. [< Du. *brak* salty] **—brack′ish·ness** *n.*

bract (brakt) *n. Bot.* A modified leaf in a flower cluster or subtending a flower. [< L *bractea* thin metal plate] — **brac·te·al** (brak′tē·əl) *adj.*

brac·te·ate (brak′tē·it, -āt) *adj. Bot.* Having bracts.

brac·te·o·late (brak′tē·ə·lāt′) *adj. Bot.* Having bracteoles.

brac·te·ole (brak′tē·ōl) *n. Bot.* A diminutive bract. Also **bract·let** (brakt′lit).

BRACT
Surrounding a composite flower.

brad (brad) *n.* A small and slender nail, often having, in place of head, a projection on one side. [< ON *broddr* spike]

brad·awl (brad′ôl′) *n.* A short, non-tapering awl, with a cutting edge on the end.

Brad·dock (brad′ək), **Edward,** 1695?–1755, English general in French and Indian War.

Brad·ford (brad′fərd) A county borough in SW Yorkshire, England.

Brad·ford (brad′fərd), **Ga·ma·li·el** (gə·mā′lē·əl), 1863–1932, U.S. biographer. **—Roark** (rôrk, rōrk), 1896–1948, U.S. novelist and short-story writer. **—William,** 1590–1657, Pilgrim governor of Plymouth Colony. **—William,** 1722–91, American printer: called "Patriot Printer of 1776."

Brad·ley (brad′lē), **Francis Herbert,** 1846–1924, English philosopher. **—Henry,** 1845–1923, English lexicographer. **—Omar Nelson,** born 1893, U.S. general.

Brad·street (brad′strēt), **Anne,** 1612–72, *née* Dudley, first woman poet in America. **—Simon,** 1603–97, colonial governor of Massachusetts; husband of Anne.

brady- *combining form* Slow: *bradycardia.* [< Gk. *bradys* slow]

brad·y·car·di·a (brad′i·kär′dē·ə) *n. Pathol.* Slowness of the heartbeat, indicated by a pulse rate of 60 or less. [< NL < BRADY- + Gk. *kardia* heart] **—brad′y·car′dic** *adj.*

brae (brā) *n. Scot.* A bank; hillside; slope. ◆ Homophone: *bray.*

brag (brag) *v.* **bragged, brag·ging** *v.i.* To vaunt oneself or one's deeds or abilities. —*v.t.* To declare or assert boastfully; boast of. —*n.* **1** The act of bragging; boastfulness; boastful language. **2** The thing bragged of; boast. **3** A person who brags. **4** A game of cards resembling poker. — *adj.* **1** To be bragged about: a *brag* crop. **2** *Obs.* Boastful; also, spirited; valiant. [Origin uncertain] **—brag′ger** *n.*

Bra·ga (brä′gə), **Teófilo,** 1843–1924, Portuguese reformer and author.

Bra·gan·ça (brə·gaṅ′sə) A city in northern Portugal, site of the castle of the Braganças, former royal family of Portugal. Also **Bra·gan·za** (brə·gan′zə).

Bragg (brag), **Braxton,** 1817–76, Confederate general. **—Sir William Henry,** 1862–1942, English physicist and chemist. **—William Lawrence,** 1890-1971, English physicist: son of the preceding.

brag·ga·do·ci·o (brag′ə·dō′shē·ō) *n. pl.* **·ci·os 1** Pretentious boasting. **2** One who talks boastfully; a swaggerer. [after *Braggadochio,* a boastful character in Spenser's *Faerie Queene*]

brag·gart (brag′ərt) *n.* A vain boaster. —*adj.* Overboastful. **—brag′gart·ism** *n.*

brag·get (brag′it) *n.* An ancient drink of ale and honey fermented with yeast; later, mulled ale sweetened and spiced. [< Welsh *bragawd*]

Bragg method *Physics* A method for studying and analyzing crystal structure by means of X-rays: originated by Sir W. H. Bragg.

Bra·gi (brä′gē) In Norse mythology, the god of poetry, son of Odin, husband of Ithunn, and one of the original Æsir. Also **Bra·ge** (brä′gə).

Bra·he (brä′ə), **Ty·cho** (tü′kō), 1546–1601, Danish astronomer.

Brah·ma[1] (brä′mə) *n.* 1 In Hindu religion, the absolute primordial essence; the supreme soul of the universe, self-existent, absolute, and eternal, from which all things emanate and to which all return. 2 God, conceived of as comprising the Hindu trinity Brahma, Vishnu, and Siva; also, specifically, the personification of the first of the trinity, as supreme creator. [<Skt. *Brahmā*]
Brah·ma[2] (brä′mə, brā′-) *n.* A large variety of the domestic hen of an Asian breed. [from *Brahmaputra*]
Brah·man (brä′mən) *n. pl.* **·mans** 1 A member of the first of the four Hindu castes of India; the sacerdotal class: also spelled *Brahmin.* 2 A species of cattle originally imported from India and bred in the southern United States. [<Skt. *brāhmana* < *brahman* praise, worship] — **Brah·man·i** (brä′mən·ē) *n. fem.* — **Brah·man·ic** (brä·man′ik) or **·i·cal** *adj.*
Brah·man·ism (brä′mən·iz′əm) *n.* The religious and social system of the Brahmans: also spelled *Brahminism.* — **Brah′man·ist** *n.*
Brah·man·y (brä′mən·ē) *adj.* Held sacred according to Brahmanic rites, or consecrated to the use of Brahmans: said especially of certain animals and trees: *Brahmany* bull, fig tree, etc. Also **Brah′min·y.**
Brahmany bull The white male zebu.
Brah·ma·pu·tra (brä′mə·po͞o′trə) A river of southern Asia, flowing 1,800 miles across Tibet, SW China, Assam, and East Pakistan to the Bay of Bengal.
Brah·min (brä′min) *n.* 1 Brahman (def. 1). 2 An aristocrat; a highly cultured person; specifically, an ultra-intellectual New Englander.
Bra·min·ism (brä′min·iz′əm) *n.* 1 Brahmanism. 2 The attitude, mannerisms, etc., of Brahmins.
Brahms (brämz, *Ger.* bräms), **Johannes,** 1833–97, German composer.
Bra·hu·i (brä·ho͞o′ē) *n.* A Dravidian language spoken in eastern Baluchistan.
braid[1] (brād) *v.t.* 1 To weave together or intertwine several strands of; plait. 2 To bind or ornament (the hair) with ribbons, etc. 3 To form by braiding: to *braid* a mat. 4 To ornament (garments) with braid. — *n.* 1 A narrow, flat tape or strip for binding or ornamenting fabrics. 2 Anything braided or plaited: a *braid* of hair. 3 A string or band used in arranging the hair. [OE *bregdan* brandish, weave, braid] — **braid′er** *n.*
braid[2] (brād) *adj. Scot.* Broad.
braid·ing (brā′ding) *n.* 1 Braids collectively. 2 Embroidery done with braid.
brail (brāl) *n.* 1 *Naut.* One of the ropes for gathering up the foot and leeches of a fore-and-aft sail for furling. 2 A leather fastening for a hawk's wing. — *v.t.* 1 *Naut.* To haul in (a sail) by means of brails: usually with *up.* 2 To fasten with a brail, as a hawk's wing. [<OF *braiel* <L *bracale* a belt for breeches < *bracae* breeches]
Bră·i·la (brə·ē′lä) A city on the Danube in eastern Rumania.
Braille (brāl) *n.* A system of printing or writing

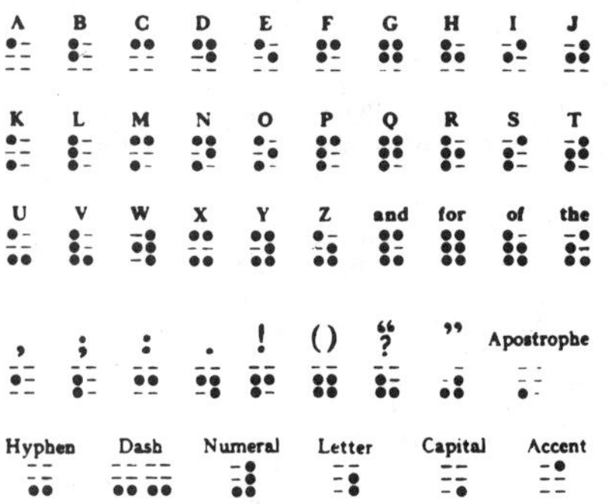

A B C D E F G H I J
K L M N O P Q R S T
U V W X Y Z and for of the
, ; : . ! ( ) “ ? ” Apostrophe
Hyphen Dash Numeral Letter Capital Accent

BRAILLE ALPHABET

for the blind in which the characters consist of raised dots to be read by the fingers; also, the characters themselves. See POINT SYSTEM (def. 2). [after Louis *Braille,* 1809–52, French educator, who invented it]
brain (brān) *n.* 1 *Anat.* The enlarged and greatly modified portion of the central nervous system contained within the cranium of vertebrates: its functions are shared between the two cerebral hemispheres, the cerebellum, and the medulla oblongata, which are of great development in higher mammals and in man. 2 Mind; intellect: often in the plural. 3 *Zool.* The principal regulating ganglion of invertebrates. See synonyms under MIND. — **to have on the brain** To be obsessed by. — *v.t.* To dash out the brains of. [OE *brægen*]
brain·child (brān′chīld′) *n.* An idea, project, or other product of the mind considered as belonging to its creator.
brain·fag (brān′fag′) *n.* Extreme mental fatigue.
brain fever Inflammation of the meninges.
brain·less (brān′lis) *adj.* 1 Without a brain. 2 Destitute of intelligence; senseless. — **brain′·less·ly** *adv.* — **brain′less·ness** *n.*
brain·pan (brān′pan′) *n.* The bony case enclosing the brain; cranium; skull.
brain·sick (brān′sik′) *adj.* Mentally disordered; whimsical. — **brain′sick′ly** *adv.* — **brain′sick′·ness** *n.*
brain·stem (brān′stem′) *n.* All the brain except the cerebellum and the cerebral cortex; that is, the segmental apparatus.
brain storm 1 Cerebral disturbance of a sudden and violent character. 2 *Colloq.* Any momentary confusion of mind. 3 *Colloq.* A burst of inspiration.
brain trust Any group of experts or, derisively, of pretended experts: used in 1933 to designate the group of educators in political science and economy who advised President Franklin D. Roosevelt.
brain·wash (brān′wosh′, -wôsh′) *v.t.* To alter the convictions, beliefs, etc., of by means of brainwashing.
brain·wash·ing (brān′wosh′ing, -wôsh′ing) *n.* 1 Indoctrination. 2 The systematic alteration of personal convictions, beliefs, habits, and attitudes to follow politically acceptable lines.
brain wave 1 *Physiol.* A rhythmical fluctuation of electrical potential between different parts of the brain. 2 *Colloq.* A sudden inspiration.
brain·work (brān′wûrk′) *n.* Work involving primarily the use of the mind, rather than manual or mechanical skills. — **brain′ work′er** *n.*
brain·y (brā′nē) *adj.* **brain·i·er, brain·i·est** Possessed of brains; mentally able; smart. — **brain′i·ly** *adv.* — **brain′i·ness** *n.*
braise (brāz) *v.t.* **braised, brais·ing** To cook (meat) by searing till brown and then simmering in a covered pan. [<F *braiser* < *braise* charcoal]
brais·er (brā′zər) *n.* A covered kettle or pan used in braising.
braize (brāz) *n.* A European sparoid fish (genus *Pagrus*). [Origin uncertain]
brake[1] (brāk) *n.* 1 A device for retarding or arresting the motion of a vehicle, a wheel, etc. 2 A harrow. 3 An instrument for separating the fiber of flax, hemp, etc., by bruising. 4 A lever for working a pump or other machine. 5 A baker's kneading machine. 6 A framework to hold a horse's foot while it is being shod. 7 A machine for extracting juice from fruits and vegetables. 8 An old instrument of torture. — *v.* **braked, brak·ing** *v.t.* 1 To apply a brake to; reduce the speed of. 2 To bruise and crush, as flax. 3 To pulverize (clods) with a harrow. 4 To knead (dough). — *v.i.* 5 To operate a brake or brakes. ◆Homophone: *break.* [MDu. *braeke* brake for flax; infl. in meaning by F *brac,* var. of *bras* arm, and by BREAK]
brake[2] (brāk) *n.* Break (def. 7).
brake[3] (brāk) *n.* 1 A variety of fern; bracken. 2 A canebrake. ◆Homophone: *break.* [ME < *braken* BRACKEN]
brake[4] (brāk) *n.* A thicket. ◆Homophone: *break.* [Cf. MLG *brake* stumps, broken branches]
brake[5] (brāk) Archaic past tense of BREAK.
brake·age (brā′kij) *n.* The action or controlling power of a brake.
brake band A flexible band or strap which encircles a brake drum and grips it when tightened.
brake drum A metal drum attached to the axle or transmission shaft of a vehicle and connecting with the brake mechanism.
brake horsepower The effective horsepower of an engine, as measured by a brake or dynamometer attached to the driving shaft.
brake lining The friction-producing material with which the working parts of a brake are lined.
brake·man (brāk′mən) *n. pl.* **·men** (-mən) One who tends a brake or brakes on a railroad car or in a mine. Also **brakes′man.**
brake shoe A brake lining.
brake wheel A hand wheel on the roof of a railroad car for controlling the brakes.
brake·y (brā′kē) *n. Slang* A brakeman on a train.
Brak·pan (brak′pan) A town in Gauteng, Republic of South Africa.
bra·ky (brā′kē) *adj.* Overgrown with bracken or brushwood.
Bra·man·te (brä·män′tā), **Donato d'Agnolo,** 1444–1514, Italian architect and painter.
bram·ble (bram′bəl) *n.* 1 The European blackberry, or any other species of the genus *Rubus.* 2 Any prickly plant or shrub. [OE *bræmble.* Akin to BROOM.] — **bram′bly** *adj.*
bram·bling (bram′bling) *n.* The European mountain finch *(Fringilla montifringilla).*
bran (bran) *n.* 1 The coarse, outer coat of cereals, as separated from the flour by sifting or bolting. 2 Grain by-products as used for cattle feed. [<OF *bran, bren*]
Bran (bran) 1 A mythical king of Britain. 2 In Celtic mythology, a god of the underworld. 3 In Icelandic saga, the faithful hound of Frithiof.
branch (branch, bränch) *n.* 1 A secondary stem of a tree, shrub, or the like; a limb: distinguished from *twig;* an offshoot. 2 A separate part; side issue; division; department. 3 *Geog.* A tributary stream; in the southern United States, any stream of water smaller than a river. 4 Anything having an analogy to a branch, as one of the subdivisions of a deer's antler, a part of a family, a subhead of a general subject, etc. 5 A local division of a highway, railroad, etc., connecting with a main line. 6 *Archit.* One of the ribs in the Gothic style of vaulting. 7 A division used in classifying the subdivisions of linguistic families and stocks, including more than a group and less than a stock. 8 A subordinate local office, store, etc. 9 *Physics* **a** In a band spectrum, a section of the component lines proceeding in both directions from a common zero line. **b** Any of the subdivisions due to varying transformations of a radioactive series. — *v.t.* 1 To divide into branches. 2 To embroider with a pattern of flowers or foliage. — *v.i.* 3 To put forth branches; divide into branches. 4 To spring off from the main part; come out from the trunk, etc. — **to branch off** 1 To separate into branches; fork, as a road. 2 To diverge; go off on a tangent. — **to branch out** To extend or expand, as one's business or interests. — *adj.* Diverging from or tributary to a trunk, stock, or main part. [<F *branche* <LL *branca* paw]
bran·chi·a (brang′kē·ə) *n. pl.* **·chi·ae** (-ki·ē) 1 *Zool.* A gill. 2 *pl.* Gills or gill-like appendages; respiratory organs of fish, modified for breathing the air contained in water. [<L <Gk. *branchia,* pl., gills] — **bran′chi·al** *adj.*
branchial cleft Gill slit.
bran·chi·ate (brang′kē·it, -āt) *adj.* Having gills.
branchio- *combining form* Gills: *branchiopod.* Also, before vowels, **branchi-.** [<Gk. *branchia,* pl., gills of fishes]
bran·chi·o·pod (brang′kē·ə·pod′) *n.* One of a group *(Branchiopoda)* of aquatic crustaceans having a typically elongated body and many pairs of leaflike thoracic appendages having a respiratory function. [<BRANCHIO- + Gk. *pous, podos* foot]
Bran·cusi (bron′ko͝osh), **Constantin,** 1876–1957, Rumanian sculptor.
brand (brand) *v.t.* 1 To mark with or as with a hot iron. 2 To stigmatize; mark as infamous. [< *n.*] — *n.* 1 A burning stick; firebrand. 2 A mark burned with a hot iron. 3 A name or trademark used to identify a product or group of products of a particular manufacturer. 4 A herd of cattle marked with a certain brand. 5 Quality; kind. 6 A branding iron. 7 *Archaic* A sword. 8 *Bot.* A pustular appearance of plants, caused by a parasitic fungus. See synonyms under BLEMISH, BURN. [OE, torch, sword. Akin to BURN[1].] — **brand′er** *n.*
Bran·deis (bran′dīs), **Louis Dembitz,** 1856–1941, U.S. jurist.
bran·den·burg (bran′dən·bûrg) *n.* 1 One of a series of ornamental loops worn on an outer

garment in the place of buttons; a frog. **2** A facing of embroidery on a military coat: usually in parallel bars. [from *Brandenburg*]

Bran·den·burg (bran′dən·bûrg, *Ger.* brän′dən·bo͝orkh) A state in the German Democratic Republic; 10,416 square miles; capital, Potsdam; formerly a province of Prussia.

brand·er[1] (bran′dər) *n.* **1** One who or that which brands. **2** *Dial.* A support of a grain stack. [<BRAND]

brand·er[2] (bran′dər) *n.* **1** *Scot.* A gridiron. **2** *Dial.* A stand for a kettle; trivet. [ME *brandire* < *branden* burn + *ire* iron]

Bran·des (brän′des), **Georg Morris Cohen,** 1842–1927, Danish literary critic.

brand goose The brant.

bran·died (bran′dēd) *adj.* Mixed, flavored with, or preserved in brandy: *brandied* cherries.

branding iron An iron for burning in a brand. Also **brand iron.**

BRANDING IRON AND CATTLE BRANDS

bran·dish (bran′dish) *v.t.* To wave, shake, or flourish triumphantly, menacingly, or defiantly. See synonyms under SHAKE. —*n.* A flourish, as with a weapon. [<OF *brandiss-*, stem of *brandir* < *brand* sword] —**brand′·ish·er** *n.*

brand·ling (brand′ling) *n. Brit.* A small red earthworm *(Eisenia foetida),* used as bait. [<BRAND, *n.* + -LING]

brand-new (brand′no͞o′, -nyo͞o′) *adj.* Quite new; fresh and bright: also *bran-new.*

bran·dy (bran′dē) *n. pl.* **bran·dies** An alcoholic liquor distilled from wine and also from the fermented juice of fruits other than the grape. —*v.t.* **bran·died, bran·dy·ing** **1** To mix, flavor, strengthen, or preserve with brandy. **2** To serve or refresh with brandy. [<Du. *brandewijn* brandy, lit., distilled wine]

brandy sling A drink made of brandy, water, sugar, and lemon juice.

brandy smash A drink made of brandy, crushed ice, and mint sprigs.

Bran·dy·wine (bran′di·wīn′) A creek in SE Pennsylvania and northern Delaware; site of Washington's defeat by the British, 1777.

Brang·wyn (brang′win), **Sir Frank,** 1867–1956, English painter, etcher, and illustrator.

branle (bräṅl) *n.* A form of dance in vogue in France in the 16th and 17th centuries, still performed by French Canadians. [<F < *branler* shake]

bran-new (bran′no͞o′, -nyo͞o′) *adj.* Brand-new.

bran·ny (bran′ē) *adj.* Made of, containing, or like bran.

brant (brant) *n. pl.* **brants** or **brant** A small, dark-colored wild goose *(Branta bernicla)* of the coasts of Europe and eastern North America, breeding only within the Arctic Circle, coming south in great flocks in autumn. Also **brant goose.** [? <ON *brandgās* sheldrake]

Brant (brant), **Joseph,** 1742–1807, Mohawk chief who fought for the British against the American colonists.

bran·tail (bran′tāl′) *n.* The European redstart.

Bran·ting (brän′ting), **Karl Hjalmar,** 1860–1925, Swedish statesman.

Bran·tôme (bräṅ·tôm′), **Seigneur de,** 1540?–1614, Pierre de Boudeilles, French historian.

Braque (bråk), **Georges,** 1882–1963, French painter.

brash[1] (brash) *adj.* Brittle: said of wood or timber. [Cf. dial. E (Northern) *brassish* brittle]

brash[2] (brash) *adj.* **1** Quick-tempered; irascible; hasty; rash. **2** Saucy; pert. **3** Active; quick. [Cf. G *barsch* harsh and Sw. *barsk* impetuous] —**brash′ly** *adv.* —**brash′ness** *n.*

brash[3] (brash) *n.* **1** A transient attack of sickness, especially one arising from a disordered stomach. **2** A rash or eruption. **3** An attack; bout; brush. **4** *Brit. Dial.* A shower of rain. [? Blend of BREAK and CRASH, DASH, SPLASH, etc.] —**brash′i·ness** *n.* —**brash′y** *adj.*

brash[4] (brash) *n.* **1** A heap of rubbish. **2** Any brittle wood. [Prob. <F *brèche* rubble]

bra·sier (brā′zhər) *n.* Brazier.

Bra·sí·li·a (brə·zē′lē·ə) The capital of Brazil, in a Federal District in the central part.

bras·i·lin (braz′ə·lin) *n. Chem.* Brazilin.

Bra·şov (brä·shôv′) The Rumanian name for STALIN. Also **Bra·shov′.**

brass (bras, bräs) *n.* **1** An alloy essentially of copper and zinc, harder than copper, ductile, and capable of being hammered into thin leaves. **2** Formerly, any alloy of copper, especially one with tin. **3** An ornament or utensil of brass, as a candlestick, doorknob, etc.: chiefly in the plural. **4** The brass wind instruments of an orchestra collectively. **5** *Colloq.* Impudence; effrontery. **6** *Slang* Money. **7** A bearing box or bush, properly of a copper alloy. **8** A monumental tablet of brass. **9** *Colloq.* High-ranking military officers collectively. [OE *bræs*]

bras·sage (bras′ij, bräs′-) *n.* The mintage fee for coining. Compare SEIGNIORAGE. [<F < *brasser* stir (fused metal)]

bras·sard (bras′ärd, brə·särd′) *n.* **1** A cloth band worn on the left arm by military police, umpires at maneuvers, and others, bearing insignia which denote the special duties of the wearer. **2** A piece of armor for the arm. Also **bras·sart** (bras′ərt). [<F < *bras* arm]

brass band A band of musicians using mostly brass instruments.

brass hat *Colloq.* **1** A high-ranking officer in the armed services. **2** Hence, a person in high position in business, government, etc.

bras·si·ca·ceous (bras′i·kā′shəs) *adj. Bot.* Of, pertaining, or belonging to a genus *(Brassica)* of erect, tall, branched herbs of the mustard family, yielding many edible plants, as cabbages, turnips, and radishes. [<L *brassica* cabbage]

bras·sière (brə·zir′) *n.* A woman's undergarment shaped to support the breasts. [<F, shoulder strap < *bras* arm]

brass tacks *Colloq.* Concrete facts; details.

brass winds *Music* The wind instruments of a band or orchestra that are made of metal: distinguished from *woodwinds*; specifically, the trumpet, horn, trombone, and tuba.

brass·y (bras′ē, bräs′ē) *adj.* **brass·i·er, brass·i·est** **1** Covered with, made of, or like brass. **2** Impudent; shameless. **3** Debased; degenerate. —*n. pl.* **brass·ies** A wooden golf club with a brass plate on the sole: also **brass′ie.** —**brass′i·ly** *adv.* —**brass′i·ness** *n.*

brat[1] (brat) *n.* A child: now only contemptuously. [? <BRAT[2] (def. 1)]

brat[2] (brat) *n. Scot.* **1** An apron; bib; rag or clout. **2** The scum on boiled milk, porridge, etc. [OE *bratt,* ult. <Celtic]

Bra·ti·sla·va (brä′ti·slä′və) A city on the Danube in SW Czechoslovakia; capital of Slovakia: Hungarian *Pozsony,* German *Pressburg.*

brat·tice (brat′is) *n.* **1** A plank partition; especially, inside planking in a mine. **2** In old fortifications, a temporary parapet or breastwork. —*v.t.* **brat·ticed, brat·tic·ing** To furnish with a brattice. [<OF *bretesche,* ult. <Gmc.]

brat·tle (brat′l) *v.i.* **·tled, ·tling** **1** To make a rattling or clattering noise. **2** To run with clatter; scamper noisily. —*n.* A rattling or clattering noise. [Imit.]

brat·wurst (brät′wûrst, -vûrst, brat′-) *n.* A small German sausage made mainly of pork or of pork and veal and various seasonings. [<G < *brat* fried + *wurst* sausage]

Braun (broun), **Karl Ferdinand,** 1850–1918, German physicist and inventor in wireless telegraphy.

Braun·schweig (broun′shvīkh) The German name for BRUNSWICK.

bra·va·do (brə·vä′dō) *n. pl.* **·dos** or **·does** Arrogant defiance or menace; affectation of reckless bravery. [<Sp. *bravada* < *bravo* brave]

brave (brāv) *adj.* **brav·er, brav·est** **1** Having or showing courage; intrepid; courageous. **2** Having elegance; showy; splendid. **3** *Obs.* Excellent. —*v.* **braved, brav·ing** *v.t.* **1** To meet or face with courage and fortitude. **2** To defy; challenge. **3** *Obs.* To make splendid. —*v.i.* **4** *Obs.* To boast. —*n.* **1** A man of courage; a soldier. **2** A North American Indian warrior. **3** A bully; bravo. **4** *Obs.* A boast or defiance. [<F <Ital. *bravo,* ? <L *barbarus* wild, fierce] —**brave′ly** *adv.* —**brave′ness** *n.*

Synonyms (adj.): adventurous, bold, chivalric, chivalrous, courageous, daring, dauntless, doughty, fearless, gallant, heroic, intrepid, undaunted, undismayed, valiant, venturesome. The *adventurous* man goes in quest of danger; the *bold* man stands out and faces danger or censure audaciously; the *brave* man combines confidence with firm resolution in presence of danger; the *chivalrous* man puts himself in peril for others' protection. The *daring* step out to defy danger; the *dauntless* will not flinch before anything that may come to them; the *doughty* will give and take limitless hard knocks; the *venturesome* may be simply heedless, reckless, or ignorant. The *fearless* and *intrepid* possess unshaken nerves in any place of danger. *Courageous* is more than *brave,* adding a moral element; the *courageous* man steadily encounters perils to which he may be keenly sensitive, at the call of duty; the *gallant* are *brave* in a dashing, showy, and splendid way; the *valiant* not only dare great dangers, but achieve great results; the *heroic* are nobly *daring* and *dauntless,* truly *chivalrous,* sublimely *courageous.* Compare CALM. *Antonyms*: afraid, cowardly, craven, cringing, faint-hearted, fearful, frightened, pusillanimous, shrinking, timid, timorous.

brav·er·y (brā′vər·ē) *n. pl.* **·er·ies** **1** The quality or state of being brave; valor; gallantry; heroism. **2** Elegance of attire; show; splendor; beauty. **3** *Obs.* Ostentation; bravado. See synonyms under COURAGE.

bra·vis·si·mo (brä·vis′sē·mō) *interj. Italian* Excellent! splendid!

bra·vo[1] (brä′vō) *interj.* Good! well done! —*n. pl.* **·vos** A shout of "bravo!" [<Ital. See BRAVE.]

bra·vo[2] (brä′vō, brā′-) *n. pl.* **·voes** or **·vos** A daring villain; hired assassin; bandit. [<Ital. See BRAVE.]

bra·vu·ra (brə·vyo͝or′ə, *Ital.* brä·vo͞o′rä) *n.* **1** *Music* A passage in a composition that requires dashing and brilliant execution; also, a brilliant style of execution. **2** Any pretentious attempt or display; dashing or daring style. [<Ital., dash, daring < *bravo* BRAVE]

braw (brô, brä) *adj. Scot.* Brave or bravely dressed; splendid; handsome; fine. —**braw′ly,** *Obs.* **braw′lie** *adv.*

brawl[1] (brôl) *n.* **1** A noisy quarrel or wrangle; a row. **2** A roaring stream. See synonyms under ALTERCATION, QUARREL. —*v.i.* **1** To quarrel noisily; fight. **2** To move noisily, as water. [ME *braulen,* ? <LG; cf. Du. *brallen*] —**brawl′er** *n.* —**brawl′ing·ly** *adv.*

brawl[2] (brôl) *n.* A dance in which one or two dancers lead the others; also, the music for it. [<F *branle* < *branler* shake, sway]

brawn (brôn) *n.* **1** Flesh; firm muscle; strength. **2** The flesh of the boar, especially when boiled, pickled, and pressed. **3** The arm, calf of the leg, or buttock. [OF *braon* slice of flesh, ult. <Gmc.]

brawn·y (brô′nē) *adj.* **brawn·i·er, brawn·i·est** Having or characterized by firm muscle; strong. —**brawn′i·ness** *n.*

braws (brôz, bräz) *n. pl. Scot.* Finery; best clothes.

brax·y (brak′sē) *n.* **1** A carbuncular fever of sheep, caused by a bacterium *(Clostridium septicum).* **2** A sheep affected with this disease. —*adj.* Affected with braxy. [Cf. OE *bræc* sickness, rheum]

bray[1] (brā) *v.t.* **1** To utter in a loud, harsh manner. —*v.i.* **2** To give forth a loud, harsh cry, as an ass. **3** To sound harshly, as a trumpet. —*n.* Any loud, harsh sound, as the cry of an ass. ◆ Homophone: *brae.* [<OF *braire* cry out] —**bray′er** *n.*

bray[2] (brā) *v.t.* To bruise, pound, or mix, as in a mortar. ◆ Homophone: *brae.* [<OF *breier,* ult. <Gmc.]

bray·er (brā′ər) *n.* A roller mounted for use by hand, to spread ink evenly over a printing surface. [See BRAY[2]]

bra·ye·ra (brə·yâr′ə) *n.* Cusso. [after A. Brayer, 1775?–1848, French physician]

bra·za (brä′thä, -sä) *n.* A Spanish measure of

length equivalent to 5.48 feet; in Argentina, 5.68 feet. [<Sp.]

braze[1] (brāz) *v.t.* **brazed, braz·ing 1** To make of brass. **2** To make hard like brass. **3** To ornament with or as with brass. **4** *Poetic* To color as with brass. [OE *brasian* <*bræs* brass]

braze[2] (brāz) *v.t.* **brazed, braz·ing** *Metall.* To join the surfaces of similar or dissimilar metals by partial fusion with a layer of a soldering alloy applied under very high temperature. [<F *braser* solder <OF, burn, ult. <Gmc; infl. in meaning by BRAZE[1]] — **braz′er** *n.*

bra·zen (brā′zən) *adj.* **1** Made of, colored like, or resembling brass. **2** Sounding like brass. **3** Impudent; shameless. See synonyms under IMMODEST, IMPUDENT. —*v.t.* **1** To face or treat with effrontery or impudence: with *out.* **2** To make bold or reckless. —**bra′zen·ly** *adv.* —**bra′zen·ness** *n.*

brazen age In classical mythology, a period of war and violence when Neptune reigned: distinguished from *bronze age.*

bra·zen·face (brā′zən·fās′) *n.* A person marked by boldness or impudence.

brazen sea The great bronze laver in Solomon's temple at Jerusalem: also called *molten sea.*

bra·zier[1] (brā′zhər) *n.* A worker in brass: also spelled *brasier.* [ME *brasiere*]

bra·zier[2] (brā′zhər) *n.* An open pan for holding live coals: also spelled *brasier.* [<F *braiser* <*braise* hot coals]

bra·zil (brə·zil′) *n.* **1** The red wood of a Brazilian tree *(Caesalpinia echinata),* or of several related species: used as a dyestuff. **2** A dyewood from several nearly allied genera. **3** The dye obtained from the wood. **4** The Oriental sapanwood *(C. sappan).* Also **bra·zil′wood′.** [<Sp. *brasil,* or Ital. *brasile,* an Oriental dyewood]

Bra·zil (brə·zil′) A republic in South America; 3,287,842 square miles; capital, Brasília: officially **The United States of Brazil.** *Portuguese* **Es·ta·dos U·ni·dos do Bra·sil** (ēsh·tä′thōōz ōō·nē′·thōōz thōō brə·zil′). —**Bra·zil′ian** *adj. & n.*

braz·i·let·to (braz′i·let′ō) *n.* An inferior variety of brazilwood from certain West Indian and South American trees, as *Caesalpinia brasiliensis* and *C. crista,* and several other tropical species. [<Sp. *brasilete,* dim. of *brasil* BRAZIL]

braz·i·lin (braz′ə·lin) *n. Chem.* A crystalline compound, $C_{16}H_{14}O_5$, contained in brazilwood, sapanwood, and other woods of the genus *Caesalpinia,* of which it is the red coloring principle. Also spelled *brasilin.*

Brazil nut One of the triangular edible seeds of a South American tree *(Bertholletia excelsa).*

brazing solder A brass alloy of high tensile strength used to make brazing joints.

brazing tongs Clamping irons used in brazing.

Bra·zos River (brä′zəs, brā′-) A river in central Texas, flowing SE about 800 miles to the Gulf of Mexico.

Braz·za·ville (braz′ə·vil, *Fr.* brà·zà·vēl′) A city on the Congo, capital of the Congo Republic.

breach (brēch) *n.* **1** The act of breaking; infraction; infringement. **2** Violation of duty, right, or legal obligation. **3** A gap or break, as in a wall, dike, etc. **4** A rupture of amicable relations; dissension; quarrel. **5** The breaking of waves or surf; a surge. **6** The leaping of a whale from the water. **7** *Obs.* An injury; wound. —*v.t.* To make a breach in; break through. ◆Homophone: *breech.* [<OE *bryce* breaking; infl. in form by F *brèche* fragment, piece. Akin to BREAK.]

Synonyms (noun): chasm, chink, cleft, crack, cranny, crevice, fissure, flaw, hole, opening, rent, rupture. Compare BREAK, GAP, HOLE, QUARREL, RUPTURE. *Antonyms:* adhesion, connection, contact, contiguity, union, unity.

breach of promise Failure to fulfil a promise, especially a promise to marry.

breach·y (brē′chē) *adj.* **1** Apt to break out of an enclosure: said of livestock. **2** Full of breaches.

bread (bred) *n.* **1** An article of food made with flour or meal: commonly raised with yeast, kneaded, and baked. **2** Food in general; also, the necessaries of life. **3** Beebread. **4** *Slang* Money. —**light bread** Bread made with wheat flour and leavened with yeast. —*v.t.* To dress with bread crumbs before cooking. [OE, bit, crumb]—**bread′ed** *adj.*

bread and butter 1 Bread spread with butter. **2** *Colloq.* Subsistence; maintenance; livelihood.

bread–and–but·ter (bred′ən·but′ər) *adj.* **1** Actuated by personal need; mercenary; *bread–and–butter* candidates. **2** Youthful; immature or unformed: a *bread–and–butter* miss. **3** Prosaic. **4** Expressing gratitude for hospitality: a *bread–and–butter* letter.

bread basket 1 A basket or tray for carrying bread or rolls. **2** *Colloq.* The stomach.

bread·fruit (bred′frōōt′) *n.* **1** The fruit of a moraceous tree of the South Sea Islands *(Artocarpus altilis),* which, when roasted, resembles bread. **2** The tree.

BREADFRUIT (Fruit: 4–8 inches in diameter)

bread·line (bred′līn′) *n.* A line of persons waiting for charitable donations of bread or other food.

bread mold A mold developed on bread by a black fungus *(Rhizopus nigricans).*

bread·nut (bred′nut′) *n.* The edible fruit of a West Indian tree *(Brosimum alicastrum)* of the mulberry family.

bread riot A people's riot caused by extreme hunger.

bread·root (bred′rōōt′, -rŏŏt′) *n.* **1** A leguminous plant *(Psoralea esculenta)* of the plains of the United States. **2** Its starchy, edible root.

bread·stuff (bred′stuf′) *n.* **1** Material for bread; grain, meal, or flour. **2** *pl.* Such materials collectively. **3** Bread.

breadth (bredth, bretth) *n.* **1** Measure or distance from side to side; as distinguished from length and thickness; width. **2** Catholicity; liberality. **3** That which has breadth; especially, a piece of a fabric of the full width. **4** The impression, in art, of largeness and comprehensiveness. [OE *braedu* <*brad* broad; *-th* added on analogy with *length*]

breadth·wise (bredth′wīz′, bretth′-) *adv.* In the direction of the breadth. Also **breadth′ways′** (-wāz′).

bread·win·ner (bred′win′ər) *n.* One who supports himself and others by his earnings; a producer.

break (brāk) *v.* **broke** (*Archaic* **brake**), **bro·ken** (*Archaic* **broke**), **break·ing** *v.t.* **1** To separate into pieces or make a fracture in; divide into fragments; shatter. **2** To part; sever, as a rope or bonds. **3** To disable or render useless by shattering or crushing. **4** To puncture or pierce the surface of (the skin). **5** To part the surface of, as ground or water. **6** To violate: to *break* a contract or a law. **7** To diminish the force of; moderate by interrupting: to *break* a fall. **8** To dispel or interrupt, as darkness or silence. **9** To destroy the order, continuity, or completeness of: to *break* step. **10** To interrupt the course of, as a journey; disconnect, as an electrical circuit. **11** To terminate forcibly; overwhelm: to *break* a strike. **12** To open forcibly (an entrance or way), as into or through a barrier. **13** To escape from: to *break* jail. **14** To surpass; excel, as a record. **15** To subdue or destroy the spirit or health of, as with toil or discipline. **16** To demote; reduce in rank or status. **17** To make bankrupt or short of money. **18** To discontinue (a habit): usually with *off.* **19** To cause (someone) to discontinue a habit: to *break* a child of biting his nails. **20** To tell; announce, as news. **21** *Law* **a** To enter (a shop or house) illegally. **b** To invalidate (a will) by court action. —*v.i.* **22** To become divided into fragments or pieces. **23** To dissolve and disperse; come apart: The clouds *broke.* **24** To become unusable or inoperative: The pencil *broke.* **25** To be grief–stricken, as the heart. **26** To burst away; free oneself: He *broke* free from the crowd. **27** To appear above the surface, as a periscope or arm. **28** To come into being or evidence, as the day. **29** To become bankrupt or short of funds. **30** To change or alter in direction, course, etc.: The horse *broke* from the track. **31** In baseball, to curve near the plate: said of the ball. **32** To crack, as a boy's voice. **33** *Music* To change from one quality of tone to another. —**to break bread** To take or share a meal. —**to break down 1** To become inoperative. **2** To have a physical or nervous collapse. **3** To give way to grief or strong feelings. **4** To overcome, as opposition. **5** To analyze. —**to break in** To cause to obey. —**to break into** (or **in**) **1** To interrupt or intervene. **2** To enter by force. —**to break in on** (or **upon**) To interrupt.—**to break off 1** To stop or cease, as from doing something. **2** To sever (relations); discontinue. **3** To become separate or detached. —**to break out 1** To start; have inception, as a fire or plague. **2** To have an eruption or rash, as the skin. **3** To make an escape, as from prison. —**to break out into** (or **forth in, into,** etc.) To begin to do or perform: The birds *broke* into song. —**to break up 1** To disperse; scatter: The meeting *broke up.* **2** To dismantle; take apart. **3** To put an end to; stop. **4** To distress: The loss *broke up* the old man. **5** To sever or discontinue relations: They decided to *break up.* —**to break with** To sever relations. —*n.* **1** An opening or breach; tear; fracture. **2** A starting or opening out: The *break* of day. **3** That which causes an opening, breach, or interruption. **4** *Electr.* **a** An apparatus for interrupting the flow or reversing the direction of an electric current. **b** The interruption of the current. **5** *Printing* A place where one paragraph ends and another begins. **6** In prosody, a caesura. **7** A high, four–wheeled carriage or wagonette: also brake. **8** A breach of continuity; interruption; especially, an interruption of physical continuity. **9** In writing, address, verse, etc., an interruption in the text or thought, as by an omission, or a space left to be filled out, or by a digression or aposiopesis. **10** A rupture of friendship; a falling out. **11** A sudden decline in prices. **12** *Music* The point where the chest tone changes to the head tone in singing; hence, sometimes, the point where one register or quality of voice changes to another, as alto to soprano; a similar point in the tones of a musical instrument. **13** In pool, the first play; the shot that scatters the balls. **14** In bowling, the act of playing a frame without making a strike or a spare. **15** In baseball or cricket, a deflection of the ball from a straight course when thrown. **16** In billiards, pool, and croquet, an uninterrupted series of successful shots. **17** *Colloq.* An unfortunate remark or ill–considered reaction: He made a bad *break.* **18** *Colloq.* An opportunity; a piece of luck, good or bad. **19** An agitation on the surface of water caused by the rising of a fish. **20** A dash or run; especially, an attempt to escape. **21** A sudden change in the gait of a horse. ◆ Homophone: *brake.* [OE *brecan.* Akin to BREACH.]

Synonyms (verb): bankrupt, burst, cashier, crack, crush, demolish, destroy, fracture, rend, rive, rupture, sever, shatter, shiver, smash, split, sunder, transgress. To *break* is to divide sharply, with severance of particles, as by a blow or strain. To *burst* is ordinarily to *break* by pressure from within, as a bombshell.To *crush* is to *break* by pressure from without, as an egg shell. To *crack* is to *break* without complete severance of parts. *Fracture* has a somewhat similar sense. A *shattered* object is *broken* suddenly and in numerous directions, as a vase is *shattered* by a blow. A *shivered* glass is *broken* into numerous minute, needle-like fragments. To *smash* is to *break* thoroughly to pieces with a crashing sound by some sudden act of violence. To *split* is to part, as wood in the way of the grain, or of other natural cleavage. To *rupture* is to cause to part less violently and completely than by explosion. To *demolish* is to beat down, as a mound, building, fortress, etc.; to *destroy* is to put by any process beyond restoration physically, mentally, or morally. Compare REND, RUPTURE. *Antonyms:* attach, bind, fasten, join, mend, repair, secure, unite, weld.

break·a·ble (brā′kə·bəl) *adj.* Capable of being broken. See synonyms under FRAGILE. —**break′a·ble·ness** *n.*

break·age (brā′kij) *n.* **1** A breaking, or the state of being broken. **2** Articles broken. **3** Compensation for damage or loss due to articles broken in shipment or use.

break–a·way (brāk′ə·wā′) *n.* **1** A motion–

picture set or prop so designed as to break apart quickly. 2 In pugilism, a separation of the antagonists. 3 The start of the contestants in a race.

break·bone (brāk′bōn′) *n. Pathol.* Dengue. Also **breakbone fever.**

break·down (brāk′doun′) *n.* 1 The act of breaking down; a collapse, as of a machine, one's health, etc. 2 A shuffling, stamping dance. 3 *Chem.* Decomposition or analysis of compounds. 4 The arrangement of large groups, as of facts, figures, operations, and processes, into categories permitting more efficient interpretation or management. Also **break′–down′.**

break·er (brā′kər) *n.* 1 One who or that which breaks. 2 A wave of the sea that breaks on a beach, etc. 3 A structure in which large masses of anthracite coal are broken up, sorted in various sizes, and cleaned for the market. 4 A strip of rubberized fabric attached to a pneumatic tire before the tread is put on, serving to distribute the pressure of the tire in contact with the ground. 5 *Naut.* A small barrel or cask containing drinking water for those in a lifeboat.

break·fast (brek′fəst) *n.* 1 The first meal of the day. 2 That with which a fast is broken; a meal. —*v.t.* To give a breakfast to; furnish with a breakfast. —*v.i.* To eat breakfast. —**break′fast·er** *n.*

breakfast food Any of various kinds of cereal eaten at breakfast; especially, a cereal prepared to be eaten without cooking.

break·front (brāk′frunt′) *n.* A cabinet, bookcase, or the like, having a central section which extends forward from those at either side.

break–in (brāk′in′) *n.* The act of breaking into a place, as to commit burglary.

breaking and entering *Law* Burglary; housebreaking.

break·neck (brāk′nek′) *adj.* Likely to break the neck; dangerous to life and limb: at *breakneck* speed.

break·o·ver (brāk′ō′vər) *n.* The front of a forest fire that jumps across a natural barrier or control line set to confine its range of devastation: also called *slopover.*

break·through (brāk′thrōō′) *n.* 1 A decisive or dramatic advance, especially in research, knowledge, understanding, etc. 2 *Mil.* An attack that penetrates an enemy's defensive system into the rear area.

break·up (brāk′up′) *n.* 1 The act of breaking up. 2 *Canadian* The time when the ice breaks up in the northern streams; spring.

break·wa·ter (brāk′wô′tər, -wot′ər) *n.* A mole or wall for protecting a harbor or beach from the force of waves.

bream[1] (brēm) *n. pl.* **breams** or **bream** 1 A European fresh–water fish *(Abramis brama),* with deep, compressed body. 2 Any of various fresh–water sunfishes, especially the blue bream *(Leponis pallidus).* 3 A porgy or sailor's–choice *(Lagodon rhomboides).* [<F *brême* <OF *bresme,* ult. <Gmc.]

bream[2] (brēm) *v.t. Naut.* To clean (a ship's bottom) of barnacles, seaweed, etc., by heating the pitch and then scraping. [Akin to BRAMBLE and BROOM]

breast (brest) *n.* 1 *Anat.* The front of the chest from the neck to the abdomen. 2 One of the mammary glands; a teat. 3 That part of a garment that covers the breast. 4 The seat of the affections, etc.; the mind or heart. 5 Anything likened to the human or animal breast. 6 The front of a plow moldboard. 7 The working face of a mine, from which material is being, or may be, removed. —**to make a clean breast of** To make a complete confession of. —*v.t.* 1 To encounter or oppose with the breast. 2 To meet or oppose boldly; advance against: to *breast* one's problems. [OE *brēost*]

breast·bone (brest′bōn′) *n. Anat.* A bone in the front part of the chest, with which some of the ribs are joined; the sternum.

Breast·ed (bres′tid), **James Henry,** 1865–1935, U.S. Egyptologist.

breast–feed (brest′fēd′) *v.t. & v.i.* **–fed, –feed·ing** To suckle.

breast·it (brēs′tit) *adj. Scot.* Breasted.

breast·pin (brest′pin′) *n.* A pin worn at the breast to close a garment; brooch; scarfpin.

breast·plate (brest′plāt′) *n.* 1 A piece of defensive plate armor for the breast; also, a metalworker's protective plate. 2 A strap crossing a horse's breast. 3 A square piece of linen cloth, embroidered with gold, adorned with twelve precious stones symbolizing the twelve tribes of Israel, worn by the Jewish high priest. 4 The plastron of a turtle.

BREASTPLATE

breast pocket A pocket in a garment situated over the breast, as the inside pocket of a jacket.

breast pump A suction instrument for drawing milk from the breast.

breast–stroke (brest′strōk′) *n.* In swimming, a stroke made while lying face down, the arms being simultaneously thrust forward from the breast under or on the surface, then brought laterally back to the sides, the legs at the same time being moved in a frog kick. —**breast′–strok′er** *n.*

breast·work (brest′wûrk′) *n.* A low, temporary, defensive work, usually breast–high; a parapet. See synonyms under BARRIER, RAMPART.

breath (breth) *n.* 1 Air inhaled or exhaled in respiration. 2 A single act of respiration: He drew a long *breath.* 3 Power to breathe, or to breathe freely; life. 4 The time of a single respiration; an instant. 5 Something resembling breath; a gentle movement of air; an exhalation. 6 Some slight thing, as a word or a rumor. 7 *Phonet.* An exhalation of air without vibration of the vocal cords, as in the production of (p) and (f). 8 The moisture condensed on cold objects or in cold air caused by the act of breathing. 9 Anything caused by breathing, as an utterance. 10 Time to breathe; delay; intermission; respite. —**in the same breath** At the same moment; without a pause or break. —**to take one's breath away** To overawe; produce sudden emotion. —**under one's breath** In a whisper. [OE *brǣth* vapor, odor]

breath·a·lys·er (breth′ə·lī′zər) *n.* A balloonlike device that measures the alcoholic content of blood by analyzing expelled breath, used especially to test motorists for intoxication. [< BREATH+ (AN)ALYSER, Brit. spelling of *analyzer;* the device was originated in Britain]

breathe (brēth) *v.* **breathed (brēthd), breath·ing** *v.t.* 1 To inhale and exhale, as air; respire. 2 To emit by breathing. 3 To utter; whisper. 4 To express; manifest. 5 *Phonet.* To utter with the breath only, without vibration of the vocal cords. 6 To exhaust; put out of breath. 7 To inject or infuse by or as by breathing: to *breathe* new life into a project. —*v.i.* 8 To inhale and exhale air; respire. 9 To be alive; exist. 10 To exhale, as fragrance. 11 To pause for breath. 12 To move gently, as breezes. 13 To allow air to penetrate: said of a fabric or garment. [ME *brethen* <*breth* breath]—**breath′a·ble** *adj.*

breath·er (brē′thər) *n.* 1 One who or that which breathes. 2 *Colloq.* That which exercises or exhausts the breath, as a run. 3 *Colloq.* A brief rest period: to take a *breather* during a workout.

breath·ing (brē′thing) *adj.* Respiring; living. See synonyms under ALIVE. —*n.* 1 The act of respiration; a breath. 2 Time to take breath. 3 Exercise that quickens the breath. 4 *Gram.* An aspiration; aspirate. In Greek the **rough breathing** (ʽ) over an initial vowel indicates the sound equivalent to our letter *h;* the **smooth breathing** (ʼ), its absence.

breath·less (breth′lis) *adj.* 1 Out of breath. 2 Intense or eager, as if holding the breath. 3 Without breath; dead. —**breath′less·ly** *adv.* —**breath′less·ness** *n.*

breath·tak·ing (breth′tā′king) *adj.* Astounding; overawing.

breath·y (breth′ē) *adj.* Characterized by audible breathing; aspirate.

brec·ci·a (brech′ē·ə, bresh′-) *n. Geol.* A rock made up of angular fragments embedded in a matrix which may or may not be of the same nature or origin. [<Ital., gravel] —**brec·ci·at·ed** (brech′ē·ā′tid, bresh′-) *adj.*

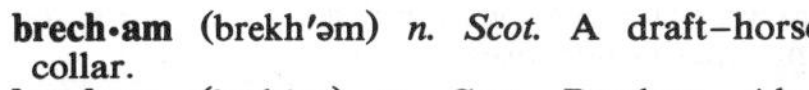

brech·am (brekh′əm) *n. Scot.* A draft–horse collar.

brech·an (brek′ən) *n. Scot.* Bracken. Also **breck′an.**

Brecht (brekht), **Bertolt,** 1898–1956, German playwright and poet.

Breck·in·ridge (brek′in·rij), **John Cabell,** 1821–75, U.S. statesman.

Breck·nock (brek′nok) The county seat of Brecknockshire. Also **Brec·on** (brek′ən).

Breck·nock·shire (brek′nok·shir) A county in SE central Wales; 733 square miles. Also **Breck′nock.**

bred (bred) Past tense and past participle of BREED.

Bre·da (brā·dä′) A town in SW Netherlands.

brede (brēd) *n.* 1 *Obs.* A braid or twist. 2 A piece of braiding or embroidery. [Var. of BRAID[1], *n.*]

bree (brē) *n. Scot.* Broth; brew; moisture: also called *broo:* also spelled *brie.*

breech (brēch) *n.* 1 The posterior and lower part of the body; the buttocks. 2 The rear end of a gun, cannon, etc. —*v.t.* (brēch, brich) 1 To clothe with breeches. 2 To provide with a breech, as a gun. 3 To fasten by a breeching, as a ship's cannon. 4 *Obs.* To flog on the breech. ◆ Homophone: *breach.* [OE *brec,* pl., breeches]

breech·block (brēch′blok′) *n.* The movable piece which closes the breech of a breech–loading firearm, but is withdrawn to insert the cartridge, and replaced before firing.

breech·cloth (brēch′klôth′, -kloth′) *n.* A loincloth. Also **breech′clout′** (-klout′).

breech·es (brich′iz) *n. pl.* 1 A garment for men, covering the waist, hips, and thighs. 2 Trousers. [OE *brec* breeches]

breeches buoy *Naut.* A life–saving apparatus, consisting of canvas breeches, attachable at the waist to a ring–shaped lifebuoy, to be slung and run upon a rope stretched from the shore to a wrecked vessel.

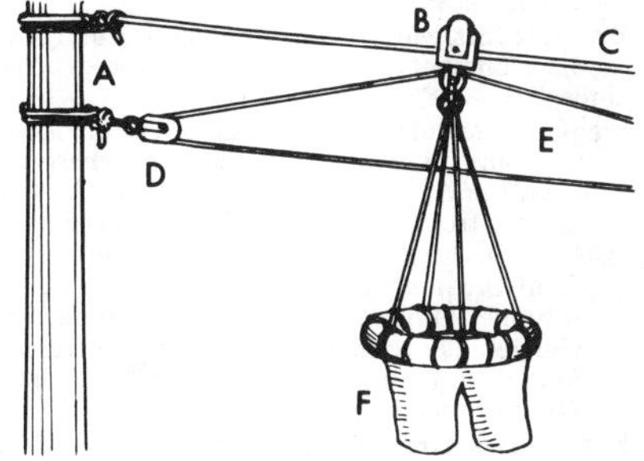

BREECHES BUOY
A. Mast of vessel.
B. Traveling block.
C. Hawser running from mast to shore.
D. Tailblock.
E. Whip, or endless line, by which buoy is hauled to and from shore.
F. Breeches buoy.

breech·ing (brich′ing, brē′ching) *n.* 1 A holdback strap passing behind a horse's haunches. For illustration see HARNESS. 2 The parts composing the breech of a gun. 3 A heavy rope used for securing a ship's cannon. 4 A flogging.

breech·load·er (brēch′lō′dər) *n.* A firearm the load of which is inserted at the breech. —**breech′load′ing** *adj.*

breed (brēd) *v.* **bred, breed·ing** *v.t.* 1 To produce (offspring); give birth to; hatch. 2 To cause; favor the development of: Familiarity *breeds* contempt. 3 To cause to give birth; develop new strains in: He *breeds* horses. 4 To bring up; train, as to a profession. —*v.i.* 5 To produce young; procreate. 6 To originate or be caused: Militarism *breeds* in armies. See synonyms under PRODUCE. —*n.* 1 The progeny of one stock; a race or strain of animals deliberately cultivated by man. 2 A sort or kind. 3 The character or degree of perfection possessed by a wine. [OE *brēdan* <*brod* brood. Related to BROOD.]

breed·er (brē′dər) *n.* 1 One who or that which breeds or produces; author; source. 2 One who manages the breeding of animals. 3 An animal suitable, or intended primarily for, reproductive purposes.

breeder reactor *Physics* An apparatus for the generation of atomic energy in which the fuel is converted into more fissionable material than is consumed. Compare REACTOR (def. 4).

breed·ing (brē′ding) *n.* **1** The generating, bearing, or training of young. **2** Nurture or its effect on character and behavior. **3** Manners, especially good manners. See synonyms under BEHAVIOR, EDUCATION, NUTURE

Breed's Hill (brēdz) A hill near Bunker Hill. See BUNKER HILL.

breeks (brēks) *n. pl. Scot.* Breeches. —**breek′less** *adj.*

breeze[1] (brēz) *n.* **1** A moderate current of air; a gentle wind. See BEAUFORT SCALE. **2** *Brit. Colloq.* A flutter of excitement; agitation; disturbance. **3** A vague rumor; whisper. See synonyms under WIND. **4** *Slang* Ease; facility: The horse won in a *breeze.* —*v.i.* **breezed, breez·ing 1** To blow moderately; begin to blow: It's *breezing* up. **2** *Slang* To go or proceed quickly and blithely. —**to breeze in** *Slang* To enter in an airy, vivacious manner. —**to breeze up** To spring up, as a wind; also, to grow stronger. [< Sp. and Pg. *brisa, briza* northeast wind]

breeze[2] (brēz) *n.* A gadfly or a botfly. [OE *breosa* gadfly]

breeze[3] (brēz) *n. Brit.* Refuse cinders, small coke, or fine coal used in burning bricks in a kiln. [? < F *braise* hot embers]

breeze·way (brēz′wā′) *n.* A roofed, open passageway from house to garage or between two buildings.

breez·ing (brē′zing) *n.* The blurring of a motion picture on the screen caused by distorted focus, uneven shrinkage of film, or unevenly placed track perforations.

breez·y (brē′zē) *adj.* **breez·i·er, breez·i·est 1** Like a breeze; airy; windy. **2** Brisk or animated. **3** Somewhat pert; brash. —**breez′i·ly** *adv.* —**breez′i·ness** *n.*

Bre·genz (brā′gents) A city in western Austria on Lake Constance, capital of Vorarlberg province: Roman *Brigantium.*

breg·ma (breg′mə) *n. pl.* **·ma·ta** (-mə·tə) *n. Anat.* That point on the vault of the skull where the coronal and sagittal sutures meet. [< Gk. *bregma* front of the head] —**breg·mate** (breg′māt), **breg·mat·ic** (breg·mat′ik) *adj.*

bre·hon (brē′hən) *n.* An ancient Irish lawgiver and judge, who made the law and decided controversies. The **brehon laws** prevailed in Ireland through the 16th century. [< Irish *breitheamh* < OIrish *brithem* judge]

Breit (brīt), **Gregory,** born 1899, U.S. nuclear physicist born in Russia.

Brei·ten·feld (brī′tən·felt) A district near Leipzig, in east central Germany; scene of Swedish victory in the Thirty Years' War.

Breiz (brez) The Breton name for BRITTANY.

bre·loque (brə·lôk′) *n. French* A charm, seal, or other ornament for wearing on a watch chain.

Brem·en (brem′ən, brā′mən) A state of northern Germany; 156 square miles; including the cities of Bremerhaven and Bremen, a port on the Weser.

Brem·er·ha·ven (brem′ər·hā′vən, *Ger.* brā′·mər·hä′fən) The ocean port of Bremen.

Bren gun (bren) *Mil.* A fast, accurate machinegun, introduced into the British Army in World War II. [< *Br(no),* Czechoslovakia, where first made, + *En(field),* England, where perfected]

Bren·nan (bren′ən), **William J(oseph),** born 1906, U.S. jurist; associate justice of the Supreme Court 1956.

Bren·ner Pass (bren′ər) Lowest of the main Alpine passes, on the Austrian-Italian border, 4,495 feet. *Italian* **Pas·so Bren·ne·ro** (päs′sō bren·nā′rō).

brent (brent) *adj. Scot.* Smooth; unwrinkled; also, high; prominent: said of the forehead.

Brere·ton (brâr′tən), **Lewis Hyde,** 1890–1967, U.S. general.

Br'er Rabbit (brûr, brer) Brother Rabbit: the principal figure in the animal folktales told by Uncle Remus. See UNCLE REMUS.

Bres (bres) In Old Irish mythology, a handsome Fomorian king who married Brigid, and later instigated the war between the Fomorians and the gods.

Bre·scia (brā′shä) A city in Lombardy, Italy.

Bresh·kov·sky (bresh·kôf′skē), **Catherine,** 1844–1934, Russian revolutionist.

Bres·lau (bres′lou, brez′-) The German name for WROCLAW.

Brest (brest) **1** A port and naval station in NW France. **2** A city on the Bug in Belorussia: Polish *BrześRnad Bugiem;* until 1921 **Brest-Li·tovsk** (-li·tôfsk′); Russo-German peace treaty signed here, 1918.

Bre·tagne (brə·tân′y′) French name for BRITTANY.

breth·ren (breth′rən) *n. pl.* **1** Brothers. **2** Members of a brotherhood. [ME, pl.]

Bret·on (bret′n) *adj.* Of or pertaining to Brittany, its inhabitants, or their language. —*n.* **1** A native of Brittany. **2** The language of the Bretons, belonging to the Brythonic branch of the Celtic languages: also called *Armorican.*

Bre·ton (brə·tôn′), **André,** 1896–1966, French surrealist poet and critic. —**Jules Adolphe,** 1827–1906, French painter and author.

Bret·ton Woods (bret′n) A village in north central New Hampshire; site of an international monetary conference, September, 1944.

Breu·ghel (brœ′gəl) See BRUEGHEL.

breve (brēv) *n.* **1** A mark (˘) placed over a vowel to indicate that it has a short sound, as the *a* in *hat* compare MACRON); or, in prosody, placed over a syllable to show that it is not stressed. **2** A royal or papal commission or mandate; brief. **3** A judicial writ or brief. **4** *Music* A note equivalent to two whole notes, or the sign for it. [< Ital. < L *brevis* short]

bre·vet (brə·vet′, *esp. Brit.* brev′it) *n. Mil.* **1** A commission advancing an officer in honorary rank without advance in pay or in command. **2** A commission or promotion awarded for achievement, usually on the field of battle. —*v.t.* **bre·vet·ted** or **bre·vet·ed, bre·vet·ting** or **bre·vet·ing** To raise in rank by brevet. —*adj.* Held or conferred by brevet; holding rank by brevet; brevetted. [< OF *brevet,* dim. of *bref* letter, document]

bre·vet·cy (brə·vet′sē) *n. pl.* **·cies** Brevet rank.

brevi- *combining form* Short: *brevipennate.* [< L *brevis* short]

bre·vi·ar·y (brē′vē·er′ē, brev′ē-) *n. pl.* **·ar·ies** *Eccl.* A book of daily offices and prayers for the canonical hours. [< L *breviarium* abridgment < *brevis* short]

bre·vier (brə·vir′) *n. Printing* A size of type, about 8-point. [? < G, breviary; with ref. to its use in breviaries]

brev·i·lin·e·al (brev′i·lin′ē·əl) *adj.* Denoting a type of body built along broad, short lines: opposed to *longilineal.* [< BREVI- + L *linea* line]

brev·i·pen·nate (brev′i·pen′āt) *adj. Ornithol.* Short-winged, as the ostrich, cassowary, etc. —*n.* A brevipennate bird, as the auk, guillemot, etc. [< BREVI- + L *penna* wing]

brev·i·ros·trate (brev′i·ros′trāt) *adj. Ornithol.* Having a short bill or beak. Also **brev′i·ros′tral.** [< BREVI- + L *n. rostrum* beak]

brev·i·ty (brev′ə·tə) *n.* pl. **·ties 1** Shortness of duration; brief time. **2** Condensation of language; conciseness. [< L *brevitas, —tatis < brevis* short]

brew (brōō) *v.t.* **1** To make, as beer or ale, by steeping, boiling, and fermentation of malt, hops, etc. **2** To make (any beverage) as by boiling or mixing. **3** To concoct; devise, as mischief. —*v.i.* **4** To make ale, beer, or the like. —**to be brewing** To be imminent; gather, as a storm, trouble, etc. —*n.* That which is brewed; the product of brewing. [OE *breōwan.* Related to BROTH .] —**brew′er** *n.*

brew·age (brōō′ij) *n.* **1** The process of brewing. **2** A drink prepared by brewing or mixing. **3** A concocted plot.

brew·er·y (brōō′ər·ē) *n. pl.* **·er·ies** An establishment for brewing.

brew·ing (brōō′ing) *n.* **1** Brewage. **2** The amount of liquor brewed at one time. **3** A mixture; concoction. **4** A gathering of storm clouds.

brew·is (brōō′is) *n.* **1** Bread or oatmeal soaked in pot liquor, hot milk, or the like. **2** Thickened broth. **3** In New England, porridge made of brown bread, milk, and butter. [ME *browes* < OF *brouet,* dim. of *breu, bro* broth; infl. by BREW]

Brew·ster (brōō′stər), **William,** 1567–1644, one of the Pilgrim Fathers.

Brewster chair An early New England type of chair with heavy turned posts and spindles arranged in tiers in the back and below the seat in front: named for William Brewster.

Brezh·nev (bryezh·nyôf′), **Leonid Ilyich,** 1906–82, Soviet statesman; first secretary of the Communist party 1964–82.

Bri·an (brī′ən) A masculine personal name. Also *Ital.* **Bri·a·no** (brē·ä′nō). [< Celtic, strong]

Bri·an Bo·ru (brī′ən bô·rō′, bô·rōō′) 926–1014, a king of Ireland, killed at battle of Clontarf. Also **Brian Bo·roimhe′.**

Bri·and (brē·äṅ′), **Aristide,** 1862–1932, French statesman.

Bri·ansk (brē·ansk′) See BRYANSK.

bri·ar (brī′ər), **bri·ar·root** (-rōōt′, -rŏŏt′), **bri·ar·wood** (-wŏŏd′) See BRIER, etc.

bri·ard (brē·ärd′) *n.* A breed of French work dog with a large head, pointed muzzle, heavily boned legs, and long, stiff coat. [< F, a native of Brie, France]

Bri·ar·e·us (brī·âr′ē·əs) One of the Hecatoncheires. —**Bri·ar′e·an** *adj.*

bribe (brīb) *n.* **1** Any gift or emolument used corruptly to influence public or official action. **2** Anything that seduces or allures; an allurement. See synonyms under GIFT. —*v.* **bribed, brib·ing** *v.t.* **1** To offer or give a bribe to. **2** To gain or influence by means of bribery. —*v.i.* **3** To give bribes. [< OF, piece of bread given a beggar] —**brib′a·ble** *adj.* —**brib′er** *n.*

brib·er·y (brī′bər·ē) *n. pl.* **·er·ies** The giving, offering, or accepting of a bribe.

bric-à-brac (brik′ə·brak) *n.* Objects of curiosity or decoration; rarities; antiques; knickknacks. [< F]

brick (brik) *n.* **1** A molded block of clay, sun-baked or kiln-burned in various shapes and sizes, but usually about 8 1/2 x 4 x 2 1/2 inches: used for building, paving, etc. **2** Bricks collectively; also, any object shaped like a brick. **3** *Colloq.* An admirable or first-rate fellow. —*v.t.* **1** To build or line with bricks. **2** To cover or wall in with bricks: with *up* or *in.* [< OF *brique* fragment, bit, ult. < Gmc. Cf. OE *bryce* fragment.]

brick·bat (brik′bat′) *n.* A piece of a brick, especially when used as a missile.

brick·kiln (brik′kil′, -kiln′) *n.* A structure in which bricks are burnt.

brick·lay·er (brik′lā′ər) *n.* One who builds with bricks. —**brick′lay′ing** *n.*

brick·le (brik′əl) *adj.* **1** *Dial.* Changeable; fickle: *brickle* weather. **2** *Brit. Dial.* Brittle.

brick red Any of several shades of dull, yellowish- or brownish-red, like the color of the common red clay brick. —**brick-red** (brik′red′) *adj.*

brick·work (brik′wûrk′) *n.* Any construction of bricks laid in courses.

brick·yard (brik′yärd′) *n.* A place where bricks are made.

bri·cole (bri·kōl′, brik′əl) *n.* **1** A harness worn by men for dragging field guns over ground where horses cannot be used. **2** A side stroke against the wall of a tennis court. **3** A cushion shot in billiards. **4** A medieval military engine for throwing stones or darts. [< F]

bri·dal (brīd′l) *adj.* Pertaining to a bride or a wedding; nuptial. —*n.* A marriage festival; wedding. See synonyms under MATRIMONIAL. ◆ Homophone: *bridle.* [OE *brȳldeala* wedding feast]

Bri·dal·veil (brīd′l·vāl′) A cataract in Yosemite National Park, California; 620 feet.

bri·dal·wreath (brīd′l·rēth′) *n.* A spring-flowering shrub *(Spiraea prunifolia)* of the rose family, with umbels of white flowers and ovate-oblong leaves.

bride[1] (brīd) *n.* A newly married woman, or a woman about to be married. [OE *brȳd*]

bride[2] (brīd) *n.* **1** A loop, tie, etc., made in lace or needlework; also, a bonnet string. **2** *Obs.* A bridle. [< F, bridle, string]

Bride (brīd), **Saint** See BRIGID, SAINT.

bride·groom (brīd′grōōm′, -grŏŏm′) *n.* A man newly married or about to be married. [OE *brȳdguma* < *brȳ* bride + *guma* man; infl. in ME by *grome* lad, groom]

brides·maid (brīdz′mād′) *n.* A young, usually unmarried woman who attends a bride at her wedding.

brides·man (brīdz′mən) *n. pl.* **·men** (-mən) A groomsman.

bride·well (brīd′wel, -wəl) *n.* A house of correction; a lock-up. [from St. *Bride's well,* in London, near which a prison was located]

bridge[1] (brij) *n.* **1** A structure erected to afford passage for pedestrians, vehicles, railroad trains, etc., across a waterway, a railroad, a ravine, etc.; a raised support. **2** *Naut.* An observation platform or partial deck built across and above a ship's deck for the use of the officers, the pilot, etc. **3** Something likened to a bridge. **4** The arched or central portion of the nose. **5** The part of a pair of spectacles or eyeglasses crossing over or resting upon this portion of the nose. **6** A block for raising the strings of a musical instrument, as a violin or guitar. **7** *Anat.* The pons Varolii. **8** A low, vertical, crosswise division wall, as in a boiler setting or a metallurgic furnace. **9** A mounting for holding false teeth, attached to adjoining teeth on each side. **10** *Electr.* A device used in measuring electrical resistance. **11** In billiards or pool, the hand or a notched support for a billiard cue, used when a player is about to strike a ball. **12** In the theater, a platform immediately inside the teaser, for suspending lights and providing space for electricians, etc. **—to burn one's bridges** To cut off all possibility of retreat. **—suspension bridge** Any bridge in which the roadway is hung from cables strong-

SUSPENSION BRIDGE
Brooklyn Bridge spanning East River, New York

ly anchored over towers and without support from below. See also under BASCULE, CANTILEVER, DRAWBRIDGE, PONTOON. **—*v.t.* bridged, bridg·ing 1** To construct a bridge or bridges over. **2** To make a passage over or across by a bridge; get over. [OE *brycg*]

bridge[2] (brij) *n.* A card game similar to whist, except that the dealer, or his partner (the dummy), has the right to name the trump. Odd tricks vary in value according to the suit declared. Partners first scoring 30 win the game. Also BRIDGE WHIST. **—auction bridge** A variety of the game of bridge, in which, instead of the dealer or his partner having the declaration, it goes to the player who undertakes to score the highest number of points. **—contract bridge** A variation of bridge in which the declarer, if successful, scores toward game only the tricks named in the bid; the awards are high, and failure is heavily penalized. **—duplicate bridge** The game of bridge, auction bridge, or contract bridge in which a series of hands is played over again, each side holding the cards previously held by its opponent. [Origin uncertain]

bridge·board (brij′bôrd′, -bōrd′) *n.* A notched board to which stair treads and risers are fastened.

bridge·head (brij′hed′) *n.* **1** *Mil.* A position on or near the bank of a river or defile that is established by advance troops of an attacking force to protect and cover the crossing of the main body of troops over the river or defile. **2** Loosely, a beachhead.

Bridge of Sighs 1 A covered bridge in Venice, over which condemned prisoners formerly passed to the place of execution. **2** *U.S.* The covered passageway, now destroyed, between the Tombs prison and the Criminal Courts building, New York City.

Bridge·port (brij′pôrt, -pōrt) A city on Long Island Sound, SW Connecticut.

Bridg·es (brij′iz), **Robert,** 1844–1930, English physician and poet laureate. **—Calvin Blackman,** 1889–1938, U.S. geneticist.

Bridg·et (brij′it) A feminine personal name. **—Bridget, Saint** (of Ireland) See BRIGID. **—Bridget, Saint** (of Sweden), 1303?–73, Roman Catholic nun; founder of the order of St. Saviour, or the Brigittines: also spelled *Birgitta* or *Brigitta.*

Bridge·town (brij′toun) The capital of Barbados, British West Indies.

bridge·work (brij′wûrk′) *n.* **1** *Dent.* A partial denture, variously attached to the natural teeth. **2** The construction of bridges.

bridg·ing (brij′ing) *n.* Wooden struts or braces between joists or other beams to keep them apart and to stiffen the structure.

Bridg·man (brij′mən), **Percy Williams,** 1882–1961, U.S. physicist.

bri·dle (brīd′l) *n.* **1** The head harness of a horse, including bit and reins. **2** Anything that restrains, limits, or guides movement, action, or development; a check; also, a curb. **3** The clevis of a plow. **4** *Anat.* A ligament or frenum attaching two parts or surfaces of an organism to each other. **5** A former instrument of torture, used for scolds. **6** *Aeron.* In the handling of airships and dirigibles, a sling of cordage or wire with ends fixed at two different points, to the bight of which a single line may be attached, movable or fixed, thus distributing the pull of the single line to two points or more in the case of a multiple bridle. **7** A span of mooring cables. **—*v.* bri·dled, bri·dling *v.t.* 1** To put a bridle on. **2** To check or control with or as with a bridle. **—*v.i.* 3** To raise the head and draw in the chin through resentment, pride, etc. See synonyms under REPRESS, RESTRAIN, SUBDUE. ◆ Homophone: *bridal.* [OE *brīdel*] **—bri′dler** *n.*

bridle hand The left hand, in which the reins are usually held.

bri·dle·path (brīd′l·path′, -päth′) *n.* A path intended only for saddle horses or pack-animals.

bri·dle·wise (brīd′l·wīz′) *adj.* Answering the pressure of the bridle rein on the neck, instead of on the bit: said of a horse.

bri·doon (bri·dōōn′) *n.* A snaffle and rein of a military bridle used in connection with, or acting independently of, the curb bit and its rein. [<F *bridon* snaffle, bit < *bride* bridle, check]

brie (brē) *n. Scot.* Bree.

Brie (brē) *n.* A soft, white, creamy cheese, mold- or bacteria-ripened. [from *Brie-Comte-Robert,* town in central France, where first made]

brief (brēf) *adj.* **1** Short in time or space; quickly passing. **2** Of few words; concise; also, curt or abrupt in speech. **3** Curtailed in extent; limited. See synonyms under TERSE, TRANSIENT. **—*n.* 1** Any short or abridged statement; a summary. **2** *Law* A concise statement in writing of the law and authorities relied upon in trying a cause; also, a memorandum of all the material facts of a client's case prepared for the instruction of counsel. **3** In the Roman Catholic Church, a letter from the Pope; less formal than a bull. **4** Briefing. **—in brief** Briefly; in short. **—to hold a brief for** To be on the side of; champion; aid. **—*v.t.* 1** To epitomize; make a summary of. **2** To instruct or advise in advance: He *briefed* his salesmen on the coming campaign. **3** *Brit.* To inform by a legal brief. **4** *Brit.* To retain as counsel. **—*adv. Obs.*** Shortly; briefly. [<OF *bref* <L *brevis* short] **—brief′ly** *adv.* **—brief′ness** *n.*

brief·case (brēf′kās′) *n.* A leather portfolio for carrying briefs, commercial papers, manuscripts, etc.

brief·ing (brē′fing) *n.* Final instructions given to aircraft pilots and crew members before a flight or raid.

brief·less (brēf′lis) *adj.* Having no briefs or clients.

Bri·enz (brē·ents′) A village in central Switzerland, on the **Lake of Brienz** (11 square miles).

bri·er (brī′ər) *n.* **1** A prickly bush or shrub, especially of the rose family, as the sweetbrier. **2** A pipe of brier-root. **3** A thorn or prickle; also, the white or tree heath. Also spelled *briar.* [OE *brēr*] **—bri′er·y** *adj.*

bri·er-root (brī′ər·rōōt′, -rŏŏt′) *n.* The root of the white or tree heath of southern Europe *(Erica arborea),* used in making tobacco pipes. Also spelled *briar-root.*

bri·er·wood (brī′ər·wŏŏd′) *n.* **1** The wood of the brier-root. **2** A pipe made from it. Also spelled *briarwood.*

Bri·eux (brē·œ′), **Eugène,** 1858–1932, French dramatist.

brig[1] (brig) *n. Naut.* A two-masted ship, square-rigged on both masts. [Short for BRIGANTINE]

BRIG

brig[2] (brig) *n. Scot.* A bridge.

brig[3] (brig) *n.* A place of confinement on shipboard. [Origin unknown]

bri·gade (bri·gād′) *n.* **1** *Mil.* A tactical unit intermediate between a regiment and a division, commanded by a brigadier general. **2** Any considerable body of persons more or less organized: a fire *brigade.* **—*v.t.* bri·gad·ed, bri·gad·ing 1** To form into a brigade. **2** To classify or combine. [<MF <Ital. *brigata* company, crew < *brigare* brawl, fight]

brig·a·dier (brig′ə·dir′) *n.* **1** See under GENERAL. **2** In some European armies, a cavalry subaltern whose rank corresponds with that of an infantry corporal.

brig·and (brig′ənd) *n.* A robber; a bandit; especially, one of a band of outlaws and plunderers. See synonyms under ROBBER. [<F <Ital. *brigante* fighter < *brigare* brawl, fight] **—brig′and·age** (-ij) *n.* **—brig′and·ish** *adj.* **—brig′and·ism** *n.*

brig·an·dine (brig′ən·dēn, -dīn) *n.* A medieval coat of mail made of metal plates, scales, or rings, sewn upon linen, leather, or the like. [<MF, armor for fighter < *brigand.* See BRIGAND.]

brig·an·tine (brig′ən·tēn, -tīn) *n. Naut.* A two-masted vessel, square-rigged on the foremast, and fore-and-aft rigged on the mainmast: also called *hermaphrodite brig, jackass brig.* [<MF *brigandin* a fighting vessel <Ital. *brigantino* < *brigare* fight]

Bri·gan·ti·um (bri·gan′shē·əm) The Roman name for BREGENZ.

Briggs (brigz), **Lyman James,** 1874–1963, U.S. physicist.

bright (brīt) *adj.* **1** Emitting or reflecting much light; shining; sparkling. **2** Possessing or showing quick intelligence or sparkling wit; quick-witted. **3** Full of or marked by gladness, prosperity, or hope; cheery; auspicious. **4** Illustrious; glorious. **5** Of brilliant color; clear and transparent. **6** Resplendent with excellence or beauty. **7** Watchful; alert. **—*adv.*** Brightly: The moon shines *bright.* **—*n. Poetic*** Brilliancy; splendor; brightness. [OE *beorht, briht*] **—bright′ly** *adv.*

Synonyms (adj.): beaming, brilliant, burnished, cheerful, cheering, cheery, effulgent, flashing, gleaming, glorious, glowing, luminous, lustrous, radiant, refulgent, resplendent, shining, sparkling, splendid, sunny, sunshiny. See CHEERFUL, CLEVER, FRESH, HAPPY, INTELLIGENT, VIVID. Compare LIGHT. *Antonyms:* See synonyms under DARK.

Bright (brīt), **John,** 1811–89, English Quaker, statesman, and free-trade advocate.

bright·en (brīt′n) *v.t.* & *v.i.* To make or become bright or brighter. **2** To make or become cheerful: The outlook is *brightening.* **—bright′·en·er** *n.*

bright·ness (brīt′nis) *n.* **1** The state, quality, or condition of being bright, in any sense. **2** The luminous intensity of any surface in a given direction, per unit of projected area of the surface as viewed in that direction. **3** That attribute of a color which identifies it as equivalent to some member of the achromatic color series, ranging from black or very dim, to white or very bright. Compare LIGHTNESS, HUE, SATURATION. See COLOR.

Brigh·ton (brīt′n) **1** A county borough and seaside resort in southern Sussex, England. **2** A resort city in southern Victoria, Australia.

Bright's disease *Pathol.* A disease characterized by degeneration of the kidneys and imperfect elimination of uric acid from the system. [after Richard *Bright,* 1789–1858, English physician]

bright·work (brīt′wûrk′) *n.* Those parts of a

machine, building, etc., in which the metal is made bright, as by planing, turning, or polishing.

Brig·id (brij′id, brē′id), **Saint,** 453?–523, patroness of Ireland; identified with **Brigid,** ancient Irish goddess of fire, fertility, and the manual arts: also *Bride, Bridget.*

Bri·git·te (brē·git′ə) German form of BRIDGET. Also *Fr.* **Bri·gitte** (brē·zhēt′).

brill (bril) *n. pl.* **brill** or **brills** A flatfish of Europe *(Bothus* or *Scophthalmus rhombus)* related to the turbot. [Prob. <Cornish *brilli* mackerel]

Bril·lat-Sa·va·rin (brē·yȧ′sȧ·vȧ·raṅ′), **Anthelme,** 1755–1826, French writer and epicure.

bril·liance (bril′yəns) *n.* **1** The quality of being brilliant; brightness; radiance; luster. **2** The presence of many rich overtones and high frequencies in a sound record made under suitable conditions. **3** A high degree of insight or understanding; skill and finish of execution in artistic performance, creative work, etc. **4** In colorimetry, lightness. Also **bril′lian·cy.**

bril·liant (bril′yənt) *adj.* **1** Sparkling or glowing with luster or light; very bright. **2** Showy; accomplished; illustrious; splendid: a *brilliant* mind, *brilliant* record. — *n.* **1** A diamond of the finest cut, or one possessing a single large face surrounded by a bezel of 33 facets and, below the girdle, a pavilion of 25 facets. For illustration see DIAMOND. **2** *Printing* A small type, about 3 1/2-point. [<MF *brillant,* ppr. of *briller* sparkle, ? <L *beryllus* beryl] — **bril′liant·ly** *adv.* — **bril′liant·ness** *n.*

bril·lian·tine (bril′yən·tēn) *n.* **1** A smooth, fine, wiry fabric in plain or twill weave, having a cotton warp and worsted or mohair filling. **2** A mixture of oil and perfume, used to impart a gloss to the hair.

brim (brim) *n.* **1** The rim of a cup. **2** The margin of a river. **3** A projecting rim, as of a hat. See synonyms under BANK, MARGIN. — *v.t.* & *v.i.* **brimmed, brim·ming** To fill or be filled to the brim. — **to brim over** To fill to the brim and overflow. [OE *brim* seashore]

brim·ful (brim′fo͝ol′, brim′fo͝ol′) *adj.* Full to the brim; brimming.

brim·mer (brim′ər) *n.* A vessel full to the brim; a brimming cup.

brim·stone (brim′stōn′) *n.* **1** Sulfur in its solid state or in some form derived from the solid state. **2** A spitfire; scold. [OE *brynstān* < *bryn-* burning (< *brinnen* burn) + *stān* stone] — **brim′ston′y** *adj.*

brin (brin) *n.* One of the radiating sticks of a fan.

brind·ed (brin′did) *adj.* Irregularly streaked; brindled. [Akin to BRAND]

Brin·di·si (brēn′dē·zē) A port of Apulia, SE Italy: ancient *Brundisium.*

brin·dle (brin′dəl) *adj.* Brindled. — *n.* A brindled color, or a brindled animal.

brin·dled (brin′dəld) *adj.* Tawny or grayish with irregular streaks or spots; also, barred; streaked. [Var. of BRINDED]

brine (brīn) *n.* **1** Water saturated or strongly impregnated with salt, as the water of the sea, that of salt wells and springs. **2** Saline water in which meats are preserved. **3** The water of the sea; ocean. **4** Tears. **5** A solution of sodium or calcium chloride used as a refrigerant in the making of ice. — *v.t.* **brined, brin·ing** To treat with brine; steep in brine. [OE *brȳne*] — **brin′ish** *adj.*

Bri·nell hardness (bri·nel′) *Metall.* The hardness of a metal, alloy, or similar material as measured by the area of indentation produced on its surface by a rigid steel ball of given diameter acted upon by a given force. [after J. A. *Brinell,* 1849–1925, Swedish engineer]

brine pit A salt spring, or a well the water of which yields salt on evaporation.

bring (bring) *v.t.* **brought, bring·ing** **1** To convey or cause (a person or thing) to come with oneself to or toward a place: *Bring* your friend to the party. **2** To cause to come about; involve as a consequence: War *brings* destruction. **3** To introduce into the mind; cause to appear: He *brought* her face into his thoughts. **4** To cause (a person) to adopt or admit, as a persuasion, course of action, etc.: He *brought* her to his point of view. **5** To sell for: The house *brought* a good price. **6** *Law* **a** To prefer, as a charge. **b** To institute: to *bring* suit. **c** To set forth, as evidence or an argument. — **to bring about** **1** To accomplish; cause to happen. **2** *Naut.* To reverse; turn, as a ship. — **to bring around** (or **round**) **1** To cause to adopt or admit, as an opinion or persuasion. **2** To revive; restore to consciousness. — **to bring down** **1** To cause to fall. **2** To fell by wounding or killing. — **to bring down the house** To evoke wild applause or acclaim. — **to bring forth** **1** To give birth. **2** To produce (foliage). — **to bring forward** **1** To adduce, as an argument. **2** In bookkeeping, to carry, as a sum, from one page or column to another. — **to bring home** To prove conclusively, so as to be understood. — **to bring home the bacon** *Colloq.* **1** To provide support or livelihood. **2** To gain a desired end or object. — **to bring in** **1** To import. **2** To render or submit (a verdict). **3** To yield or produce, as profits. — **to bring off** To do successfully. — **to bring on** **1** To cause; lead to. **2** To produce; cause to appear: *Bring on* the dancing girls! — **to bring out** **1** To reveal; cause to be evident, as the truth. **2** To publish or produce, as a book or play. **3** To introduce, as a young girl to society. — **to bring to** **1** To revive; restore to consciousness. **2** *Naut.* To cause (a ship) to come up into the wind and lie to. — **to bring to bear** To cause to have reference, application, or influence. — **to bring up** **1** To rear; educate. **2** To suggest or call attention to, as a subject. **3** To cough or vomit up. [OE *bringan*] — **bring′er** *n.*

bring·ing-up (bring′ing·up′) *n.* Care, training, and education of a person in childhood. See also UPBRINGING.

brink (bringk) *n.* **1** The verge of a steep place, or of a dangerous condition, action, event, or time. **2** The margin of any water; bank; shore. See synonyms under BANK, MARGIN. [ME *brenk* <Scand.]

brink·man·ship (bringk′mən·ship) *n.* A willingness to expose oneself to major risk to achieve some end; especially, a national policy embodying such a position. [<BRINK + *-manship,* on analogy with *showmanship,* etc.]

brin·y (brī′nē) *adj.* **brin·i·er, brin·i·est** Of the nature of brine; salty. — *n. Colloq.* The ocean: a dip in the *briny.* — **brin′i·ness** *n.*

bri·o (brē′ō) *n. Music* Spirit; vivacity: usually in the phrase *con brio.* [<Ital.]

bri·oche (brē′ōsh, -osh, *Fr.* brē·ôsh′) *n.* A soft, sweet roll made of butter, eggs, flour, and yeast. [<F]

bri·o·lette (brē′ə·let′) *n.* A gemstone cut with triangular or long facets, generally pear- or drop-shaped. For illustration see DIAMOND. [<F < *brillant* diamond]

bri·quet (bri·ket′) *n.* A block of compressed coal dust, used as fuel. Also **bri·quette′.** [<F *briquette,* dim. of *brique* brick]

bri·sance (brē·zäṅs′) *n.* The shattering effect of a high-explosive shell or of any blasting substance, usually measured in terms of detonating velocity. [<F *brisant,* ppr. of *briser* crush]

Bris·bane (briz′bān, -bən) The capital and principal port of Queensland, Australia.

Bri·se·is (brī·sē′is) In the *Iliad,* Achilles' concubine, whose seizure by Agamemnon led to a quarrel between the two men.

brisk (brisk) *adj.* **1** Moving, acting, or taking place rapidly; quick. **2** Energetic; vivacious; spirited; lively. **3** Sharp or stimulating, as cold air. **4** Sparkling; effervescent: said of liquors. See synonyms under ACTIVE, ALERT, ALIVE, NIMBLE. — *v.t.* & *v.i.* To make or become lively; animate: with *up.* [Cf. F *brusque* abrupt, sudden] — **brisk′ly** *adv.* — **brisk′ness** *n.*

bris·ket (bris′kit) *n.* The breast of a quadruped, especially of one whose flesh is used as food. [OF *bruschet,* ult. <Gmc.]

bris·ling (bris′ling) *n.* The sprat. [<Scand.]

bris·tle (bris′əl) *n.* **1** A coarse, stiff hair, as of swine. **2** *Bot.* A slender, stiff hair; morphologically, a trichome. — *v.* **bris·tled, bris·tling** *v.i.* **1** To erect the bristles, as an animal when aroused: often with *up.* **2** To show anger, irritation, etc., as by stiffening the body: often with *up.* **3** To be thickly set as with bristles: The plain *bristled* with bayonets. — *v.t.* **4** To erect as or like bristles: often with *up*: A cock *bristles* up his crest. **5** To cover or line as with bristles. **6** To agitate; ruffle violently: The storm *bristled* the lake. [ME *bristel,* OE *byrst*] — **bris′tly** *adj.*

bris·tle·tail (bris′əl·tāl′) *n.* The silverfish.

Bris·tol (bris′təl) A county borough and port in SW Gloucestershire, England.

Bristol board A fine quality of calendered cardboard. [from *Bristol*]

Bristol Channel An inlet of the Atlantic between Wales and SW England.

brit (brit) *n. pl.* **brit** A young herring, once thought to be a species. [Origin unknown]

Brit·ain (brit′n) Great Britain. Abbr. *Brit.*; *Br.*

bri·tan·ni·a (bri·tan′ē·ə, -tan′yə) *n. Metall.* A silver-white alloy of tin, copper, and antimony: used for cheap tableware. Also **Britannia metal.** [from *Britannia*]

Bri·tan·ni·a (bri·tan′ē·ə, -tan′yə) **1** The Roman name for Britain. **2** Great Britain, Ireland, and the Dominions. **3** A female figure representing Great Britain or the British Empire.

Bri·tan·nic (bri·tan′ik) *adj.* Of or pertaining to Great Britain; British. [<L *Britannicus*]

Brit·i·cism (brit′ə·siz′əm) *n.* A word, expression, or usage characteristic of Great Britain or the British. Also *Britishism, Britticism.*

Brit·ish (brit′ish) *adj.* **1** Pertaining to Great Britain, the United Kingdom, or the British Empire. **2** Of or pertaining to the ancient Britons, the original Celtic people of Britain. — *n.* **1** *pl.* The people of Great Britain or of the British Empire. **2** The language of the ancient Britons; Brythonic. [OE *Brettisc* <*Bret* a Briton].

British America **1** Canada: also **British North America.** **2** All British possessions in or adjacent to North or South America.

British Bechuanaland See BECHUANALAND.

British Columbia The westernmost province of Canada; 366,255 square miles; capital, Victoria. Abbr. *B.C.*

British Commonwealth of Nations A political association comprising the United Kingdom, Australia, Canada, Ceylon, Cyprus, Gambia, Ghana, India, Jamaica, Malawi, Malaysia, New Zealand, Nigeria, Pakistan, Sierra Leone, Tanzania, Trinidad and Tobago, Uganda, Western Samoa, and Zambia, and including the dependencies of member nations: officially *The Commonwealth.* Also *Commonwealth of Nations.*

British East Africa A former association of territories including Kenya, Tanganyika, Uganda, and Zanzibar. Abbr. *B.E.A.*

British Empire The sovereign states under the British Crown, comprising those in the BRITISH COMMONWEALTH OF NATIONS with their dependencies, colonies, territories, etc.

Brit·ish·er (brit′ish·ər) *n.* A native or subject of Great Britain.

British Guiana A British crown colony on the NE coast of South America; 83,000 square miles; capital, Georgetown.

British Honduras A British crown colony in Central America south of Yucatán peninsula; 8,866 square miles; capital, Belize. Formerly *Belize.*

British India Formerly, the territories in India subject to British law.

British Isles Great Britain, Ireland, Isle of Man, and the Channel Islands.

Brit·ish·ism (brit′ish·iz′əm) See BRITICISM.

British Malaya Formerly, the British possessions and dependencies in Malaya; now substantially the same as the FEDERATION OF MALAYA.

British New Guinea The former name of PAPUA.

British North America Act The act of Parliament that in 1867 created the Government of Canada for the federation of Ontario, Quebec, Nova Scotia, and New Brunswick. Manitoba joined in 1870, British Columbia in 1871, Prince Edward Island in 1873, Alberta and Saskatchewan in 1905, and Newfoundland in 1949.

British North Borneo See NORTH BORNEO.

British Solomon Islands See SOLOMON ISLANDS.

British Somaliland See SOMALILAND.

British thermal unit *Physics* The quantity of heat required to raise the temperature of one pound of water one degree Fahrenheit: at a starting temperature of 60° F. it is equal to 1054.6 joules. Abbr. *B.T.U.*

British Togoland See GHANA.

British Virgin Islands A presidency of the British colony of the Leeward Islands, comprising about 30 islands; 67 square miles; capital, Road Town.

British West Africa An association of territories including Cameroons, Gambia, Gold

Coast, Nigeria, Sierra Leone, and Togoland. Abbr. *B.W.A.*

British West Indies The possessions of Great Britain in the West Indies, including Bahamas, Bermuda, Jamaica, Trinidad, Tobago, and islands in the Lesser Antilles. Abbr. *B.W.I.*

Brit·on (brit'n) *n.* **1** One of any of the tribes inhabiting ancient Britain before the Anglo-Saxon invasion, probably belonging to the Brythonic branch of the Celts. **2** A native or citizen of Great Britain; an Englishman. [< OF *Breton* <L *Britto, -onis* <Celtic]

Brit·ta·ny (brit'ə·nē) A region and former province of western France, occupying the peninsula between the English Channel and the Bay of Biscay: French *Bretagne,* Breton *Breiz.*

Brit·ten (brit'n), **(Edward) Benjamin,** 1913–1976, English composer.

Brit·ti·cism (brit'ə·siz'əm) See BRITICISM.

brit·tle (brit'l) *adj.* Liable to break or snap; frangible;fragile. [ME *britel.* Akin to OE *bryttian* divide.] **—brit'tle·ness** *n.*

Brit·ton (brit'n), **Nathaniel Lord,** 1859–1934, U.S.botanist.

britz·ska (brits'kə) *n.* A light, four-wheeled carriage with calash top. Also **brits'ka, britz'·ka.** [<Polish *bryczka,* dim. of *bryka* freight wagon]

BRITZSKA

Brno (bûr'nô) The second largest city in Czechoslovakia; former capital of Moravia.

broach[1] (brōch) *v.t.* **1** To introduce or mention for the first time, as a subject. **2** To open for the first time, as a cask of wine. **3** To draw off; let out: to *broach* wine. **4** To dress or enlarge with a broach. [<*n.*] **—*n. Mech.*** A pointed, tapering tool for boring or reaming; a reamer; also a spit. [<OF *broche*<Med. L *brocca* spike, spit, ult. <Celtic]

broach[2] (brōch) *v.t. & v.i.* To veer. **—to broach to** *Naut.* To fall off with the wind, especially broadside to the wind and waves, and thus risk capsizing. [? <BROACH[1], *v.*]

broach·er (brō'chər) *n.* One who or that which broaches.

broad (brôd) *adj.* **1** Extended in lateral measurement; of unusual width; wide; expanded; vast. **2** Of wide range, sympathy, etc. **3** Widely diffused; comprehensive: a *broad* education. **4** Catholic; liberal; tolerant: *broad* views. **5** Strongly dialectal; also, rude and vigorous, as speech. **6** Strongly defined; plain; clear: a *broad* hint. **7** Loose; indelicate; bold. **8** Denoting the chief features of a thing; not detailed: a *broad* outline. **9** *Phonet.* Formed with the oral passage wide open and the tongue low and flat, as the *a* in *calm;* open. See synonyms under LARGE. **—*n.*** **1** The broad part of anything. **2** A former English gold coin; a broadpiece. **3** A type of incandescent flood lamp used on motion-picture sets; a broadside. **4** The broadening out of a river over flat land; a fenny lake. **5** *Slang* A woman or girl. **—*adv.*** Completely; fully. [OE *brād*] **—broad'ly** *adv.*

broad arrow **1** A broad-headed arrow. **2** A mark shaped like a barbed arrow placed on British government property, as convicts' uniforms, ordnance stores, etc.

broad-ax (brôd'aks') *n.* An ax with broad edge and short handle. Also **broad'-axe'.**

broad·bean (brôd'·bēn') *n.* The large, usually flat, orbicular or angular, seed of a strong, erect annual vine *(Vicia faba)* of the Old World.

broad·bill (brôd'bil') *n.* **1** The scaup duck. **2** The shoveler duck. **3** The European spoonbill. **4** The swordfish.

BROADBILL *(def. 3)*

broad·brim (brôd'brim') *n.* A hat with a broad brim.

Broad·brim (brôd'brim') *n. Colloq.* A Friend or Quaker.

broad·cast (brôd'kast', -käst') *v.* **·cast** or **·casted, ·cast·ing** *v.t.* **1** To send or transmit (music, newscasts, etc.) by radio or television. **2** To scatter or cast, as seed, over a wide area; sow. **3** To disseminate; make public, as gossip. **—*v.i.*** **4** To speak, sing, etc., for broadcasting purposes. **—*adj.*** **1** Transmitted by radio. **2** Cast or scattered abroad, as seeds. **—*n.*** **1** *Telecom.* **a** The process of transmitting a program by radio. **b** A radio program. **c** The time period of a broadcast. **2** A casting or scattering of seed, etc., over the ground. **—*adv.*** By scattering abroad, or so as to scatter abroad or disseminate.

broad·cast·er (brôd'kas'tər, -käs'-) *n.* **1** One who owns or operates a broadcasting station. **2** One who makes broadcasts.

Broad Church The liberal wing of the Church of England, or, by extension, of any church. **—Broad'-Church'** *adj.* **—Broad'-Church'ism** *n.***—Broad'-Church'man** *n.*

broad·cloth (brôd'klôth', -kloth') *n.* **1** A fine quality of woven wool, napped and calendered, in plain or twill weave: used for suits, skirts, etc. **2** A closely woven fabric of silk, cotton, etc., in plain weave with a light crosswise rib: used for shirts, dresses, etc.

broad·en (brôd'n) *v.t. & v.i.* To make or become broad or broader.

broad-gage (brôd'gāj') *adj.* **1** Having a gage wider than the standard gage of 56½ inches, as a railway. **2** Broad-minde Also **broad'-gauge', broad'-gaged', broad'-gauged'.**

broad hatchet A hatchet with a broad blade. For illustration see HATCHET.

broad·horn (brôd'hôrn') *n.* **1** A large flatboat, used formerly on the Mississippi and Ohio Rivers. **2** A Rocky Mountain sheep. **3** One of a herd of Texas longhorn cattle.

broad·ish (brô'dish) *adj.* Somewhat broad.

broad jump A jump for distance; a long jump.

broad·leaf (brôd'lēf') *n.* **1** A tree *(Terminalia catappa)* of the myrobalan family, of Jamaica, with almondlike fruit. **2** Any variety of tobacco plant suitable for cigarmaking, having especially broad leaves.

broad-minded (brôd'mīn'did) *adj.* Liberal in beliefs and opinions; tolerant; free from bigotry and prejudice. **—broad'-mind'ed'ly** *adv.* **—broad'-mind'ed·ness** *n.*

broad·piece (brôd'pēs') *n.* An English gold coin of James II.

Broads (brôdz), **The** A region of marshy lakes in Norfolk **(the Norfolk Broads)** and Suffolk **(the Suffolk Broads),** England.

broad seal The official seal of a government.

broad·side (brôd'sīd') *n.* **1** All the guns on one side of a man-of-war, or their simultaneous discharge. **2** Any sweeping attack; hence, a volley of abuse or denunciation. **3** *Naut.* A vessel's side above the water line. **4** A large sheet of paper, printed on one side: also **broad'sheet'.** **5** The broad, unbroken surface of anything. **6** The side of an animal between the ham and the shoulder, used as meat; specifically, a side of bacon. **7** A flood lamp: see BROAD (*n.* def. 3). **—*adv.*** With the broadside turned, presented, or exposed.

Broad·stairs (brôd'stârz) A resort town in NE Kent, England.

broad·sword (brôd'sôrd', -sōrd') *n.* A sword with a broad cutting blade and obtuse point.

broad·tail (brôd'tāl') *n.* **1** A family of fat-tailed sheep. **2** The pelt of very young fat-tailed lambs, whose soft, lustrous fur lacks the tight curl characteristic of older lambs and sheep.

Broad·way (brôd'wā) **1** A street running north and south through New York City, famous for its brightly lighted entertainment district. **2** The New York entertainment industry. **—*adj.*** Situated on, characteristic of, or like Broadway in New York.

Brob·ding·nag (brob'ding·nag) The giants' country in Swift's *Gulliver's Travels.* **—Brob'·ding·nag'i·an** (-nag'ē·ən) *adj. & n.*

Bro·ca (brô·kà'), **Paul,** 1824–80, French surgeon.

Broca's area *Anat.* A convolution located on the left frontal lobe of the brain: its function is the coordination of the sensory and motor processes involved in speech. [after Paul *Broca*]

bro·cade (brō·kād') *n.* A rich fabric of satin or twill background interwoven with raised flower or figure design in silken or gold or silver threads. **—*v.t.*** **·cad·ed, ·cad·ing** To weave (a cloth) with a raised design or figure. [<Sp. *brocado* <Med. L *broccata,* fem. pp. of *broccare* embroider] **—bro·cad'ed** *adj.*

broc·a·tel (brok'ə·tel') *n.* A brocaded fabric of silk, wool, cotton, or the like, with a more highly raised pattern than in brocade. Also **broc'a·telle'.** [<F *brocatelle* <Ital. *broccatello,* dim. of *broccato* brocade]

broc·co·li (brok'ə·lē) *n.* A hardy variety of cauliflower which does not head, of which the green sprouts and tender stalks are eaten. [< Ital., pl. of *broccolo* cabbage sprout]

broch (brokh) *n.* A type of corbelled stone tower of the Bronze Age found in Scotland. [<ON *borg* castle]

bro·ché (brō·shā') *adj.* Woven with a raised design; embossed; brocaded; stitched, as a book. [<F *broché,* pp. of *brocher* stitch, brocade]

bro·chette (brō·shet') *n.* A small spit used in roasting; a skewer. [<OF, dim. of *broche* skewer, spit]

bro·chure (brō·shŏŏr') *n.* A pamphlet; anything written or published in pamphlet form. [<F <*brocher* stitch]

brock (brok) *n.* **1** A badger. **2** *Brit. Dial.* A foul, dirty fellow. [OE *broc*]

Brock·en (brok'ən) The highest peak of the Harz Mountains in central Germany; 3,747 feet; famous for its "specter," caused by its shadow cast on clouds. Also **Blocks·berg** (blôks'·berk).

brock·et (brok'it) *n.* **1** A stag in its second year with its first horns as simple spikes. **2** A small deer of tropical America (genus *Mazama*). [<F *brocart* <*broche* tine of antlers]

Brock·ton (brok'tən) A city in eastern Massachusetts.

brod (brod) *n. Scot.* A prod; goad.

Brod·ribb (brod'rib), **John Henry** See IRVING, SIR HENRY.

bro·gan (brō'gən) *n.* A coarse, heavy shoe kept on the foot by side flaps laced or buckled over a short tongue. [<Irish *brōgan,* dim. of *brōg* shoe]

brög·ger·ite (brœg'ər·īt) *n.* A variety of uraninite from which helium has been obtained. [after W. C. *Brögger,* 1851–1940, Norwegian mineralogist]

Bro·glie (brôl'y'), **de** See DE BROGLIE.

brogue[1] (brōg) *n.* A dialectal pronunciation of English, especially that of the Irish people. [<Irish *barrōg* defect of speech]

brogue[2] (brōg) *n.* **1** A heavy oxford with low heels, decorated with stitchings, pinkings, and perforations. **2** A rude shoe of untanned hide with the hair outside, tied with thongs: worn formerly in Ireland and the Scottish Highlands. [<Irish *brōg* brogue (def. 2)]

brogue[3] (brōg) *n. Scot.* A fraud; cheating trick.

broi·der (broi'dər) *v.t. Obs.* To embroider. [< MF *broder* stitch; infl. by ME *broid,* var. of *braid*] **—broi'der·y** *n.*

broil[1] (broil) *v.t.* **1** To cook, as meat, by subjecting to direct heat. **2** To expose to great heat; scorch. **—*v.i.*** **3** To be exposed to great heat; cook. **4** To become impatient; burn with anger. **—*n.*** **1** Something broiled. **2** A broiling heat. [<OF *bruiller*]

broil[2] (broil) *n.* A turmoil; noisy quarrel; brawl. See synonyms under ALTERCATION, QUARREL. **—*v.i.*** To engage in a broil; brawl; quarrel. [<F *brouiller* confuse]

broil·er (broi'lər) *n.* **1** A device for broiling, as a gridiron. **2** A chicken suitable for broiling. **3** *Colloq.* A very hot day.

broil·ing (broi'ling) *adj.* Extremely hot; torrid. **—broil'ing·ly** *adv.*

bro·kage (brō'kij) *n.* Brokerage. [<AF *brocage*]

broke[1] (brōk) *v.i.* **broked, brok·ing** To act as a broker.

broke[2] (brōk) Past tense and archaic past participle of BREAK. **—*adj.*** **1** Ruined; bankrupt. **2** *Colloq.* Without any money. **—go for broke** *Slang* To risk everything on an uncertain course of action.

bro·ken (brō′kən) Past participle of BREAK. —*adj.* **1** Separated forcibly into parts; fractured; shattered; ruptured. **2** Crushed in feeling or spirit; humbled; contrite. **3** Reduced to subjection; trained. **4** Made infirm; weakened. **5** Violated, transgressed, or disobeyed. **6** Reduced or shattered in estate or fortune; ruined; bankrupt. **7** Incomplete or interrupted, as sleep, utterance, etc. **8** Disordered or disarranged, as troops. **9** Rough, rugged, or irregular: *broken* ground; also, plowed or dug up, as land. **10** Faultily spoken: *broken* English. **—bro′ken·ly** *adv.* **—bro′ken·ness** *n.*

bro·ken-down (brō′kən·doun′) *adj.* **1** Broken in health or strength; ruined; wrecked. **2** Having the parts or a part broken; powerless: a *broken-down* engine.

bro·ken·heart·ed (brō′kən·här′tid) *adj.* Overwhelmed or crushed in spirit, as by sorrow or grief.

Broken Hill A city in western New South Wales, Australia.

broken wind Wind-broken respiration; the heaves.

bro·ken-wind·ed (brō′kən·win′did) *adj.* **1** Habitually short of breath. **2** Affected with the heaves, as a horse.

bro·ker (brō′kər) *n.* One who buys and sells for another on commission or who arranges for the negotiation of contracts of various types; especially, a stockbroker. [<AF *brocour* <OF *brochier* tap, broach (a wine cask)]

bro·ker·age (brō′kər·ij) *n.* The business or commission of a broker.

brom- Var. of BROMO-.

bro·ma (brō′mə) *n.* **1** The dry powder of cacao seeds after the oil has been expressed. **2** A beverage prepared therefrom. **3** *Med.* Solid food. [<Gk. *brōma* food]

brom·ac·e·tone (brom·as′ə·tōn) *n. Chem.* A colorless volatile liquid, C_3H_5OBr, of toxic properties: used as a tear gas in World War I.

bro·mal (brō′məl) *n. Chem.* A colorless liquid compound resembling chloral, C_2HBr_3O, with a pungent taste and penetrating odor: obtained by the action of bromine on alcohol and used in medicine as a hypnotic and anodyne. [<BROM- + AL(COHOL)]

bro·mate (brō′māt) *Chem. n.* A salt of bromic acid containing the univalent BrO_3 radical. —*v.t.* **·mat·ed, ·mat·ing** To combine, saturate, or impregnate with bromine.

bro·ma·tol·o·gy (brō′mə·tol′ə·jē) *n.* The study of food and diet. [<Gk. *brōma, -atos* + -LOGY]

bro·mat·o·ther·a·py (brō·mat′ə·ther′ə·pē) *n. Med.* The treatment of disease by means of food. Also **bro′ma·ther′a·py** (brō′mə-). [<Gk. *brōma, -atos* + THERAPY]

Brom·berg (brôm′berkh) The German name for BYDGOSZCZ.

brome·grass (brōm′gras′, -gräs′) *n.* Any grass of the genus *Bromus,* widely cultivated for hay and pasturage. Also **brome.** [<Gk. *bromos* oats]

bro·me·li·a·ceous (brō·mē′lē·ā′shəs) *adj. Bot.* Belonging to a family *(Bromeliaceae)* of tropical or subtropical American monocotyledonous plants, including the Spanish moss and the pineapple. [<NL *Bromeliaceae,* after Olaf *Bromel,* 1639–1705, Swedish botanist]

Brom·field (brom′fēld), **Louis,** 1896–1956, U.S. novelist.

bromic (brō′mik) *adj. Chem.* Of, pertaining to, or containing bromine, especially in its higher valence.

bro·mide[1] (brō′mīd, -mid) *n.* **1** *Chem.* A compound of bromine with an element or an organic radical; a salt of hydrobromic acid: potassium *bromide,* KBr. **2** A photograph printed on paper, etc., that has been subjected to the effects of bromide of silver. Also **bro′·mid** (-mid). [<BROM(INE) + -IDE]

bro·mide[2] (brō′mīd, -mid) *n. Colloq.* **1** One who utters platitudes; a commonplace bore. **2** A platitude; a dull remark. [<BROMIDE[1]; with ref. to the sedative effect of some bromides] **—bro·mid·ic** (brō·mid′ik) *adj.*

bro·mi·nate (brō′mə·nāt) *v.t.* **·nat·ed, ·nat·ing** To bromate.

bro·mine (brō′mēn, -min) *n.* A heavy, reddish-brown non-metallic liquid element (symbol Br, atomic number 35) belonging to the halogen group and having a toxic, suffocating vapor. See PERIODIC TABLE. Also **bro′min** (-min). [<F *brome* (<Gk. *brōmos* stench) + -INE]

bro·mism (brō′miz·əm) *n. Pathol.* Chronic poisoning by bromides.

bro·mize (brō′mīz) *v.t.* **·mized, ·miz·ing** *Chem.* To combine, impregnate, or treat with bromine or a bromide.

bromo- *combining form* Used to indicate the presence of bromine as a principal element in chemical compounds. Also, before vowels, *brom-*. [<BROMINE]

bron·chi (brong′kī) *Anat.* Plural of BRONCHUS.

bron·chi·a (brong′kē·ə) *n. pl. Anat.* The bronchial tubes. [<LL <Gk. *bronchia* bronchial tubes]

bron·chi·al (brong′kē·əl) *adj. Anat.* Of or pertaining to the chief air passages of the lungs.

bronchial tubes *Anat.* The subdivisions of the trachea conveying air into the lungs.

bron·chi·tis (brong·kī′tis) *n. Pathol.* Inflammation of the bronchial tubes, or, loosely, of the bronchi or trachea. [<BRONCH(O)- + -ITIS] **—bron·chit·ic** (brong·kit′ik) *adj.*

broncho- *combining form* Windpipe: *bronchoscope.* Also, before vowels, **bronch-.** [<Gk. *bronchos*]

bron·cho·cele (brong′kə·sēl) *n.* Goiter. [<Gk. *bronchokēlē* tumor in the throat <*bronchos* windpipe + *kēlē* tumor]

bron·cho·pneu·mon·ia (brong′kō·nōō·mōn′yə, -nyōō-) *n. Pathol.* Bronchitis complicated with inflammation of the surrounding substance of the lungs; catarrhal pneumonia.

bron·cho·scope (brong′kə·skōp) *n. Med.* An instrument for inspecting or treating the interior of the bronchi. **—bron·chos·co·py** (brong·kos′kə·pē) *n.*

bron·chot·o·my (brong·kot′ə·mē) *n. Surg.* The operation of making an incision into the windpipe; tracheotomy. [<BRONCHO- + -TOMY]

bron·chus (brong′kəs) *n. pl.* **·chi** (-kī) *Anat.* One of the two forked branches of the trachea. [<Gk. *bronchos* windpipe]

bron·co (brong′kō) *n. pl.* **·cos** A small, wild, or partly broken horse of the western United States. —*adj.* **1** Consisting of, or like broncos. **2** Wild; unruly. Also **bron′cho.** [<Sp. *bronco* rough]

bron·co·bust·er (brong′kō·bus′tər) *n. U.S. Colloq.* One who breaks a bronco to the saddle. Also **bron′cho·bust′er.**

Bronk (brongk), **Detlev W.,** 1897–1975, U.S. neurophysiologist.

Bron·të (bron′tē) Name of three English novelists, sisters: **Anne,** 1820–49; **Charlotte,** 1816–1855; **Emily Jane,** 1818–48. Pseudonyms, respectively, *Acton, Currer,* and *Ellis Bell.*

bron·tides (bron′tīdz) *n. pl. Meteorol.* Brief, thunderlike noises accompanying the activity of faint earthquakes in seismic regions. [<Gk. *brontē* thunder + *-eidēs* like, similar to]

bron·to·sau·rus (bron′tə·sôr′əs) *n. Paleontol.* A huge, herbivorous dinosaur (order *Sauropoda*) of the Jurassic period, found fossil in western North America. [Gk. *brontē* thunder + *sauros* lizard]

BRONTOSAURUS
(Up to 70 feet in length, 20 tons in weight)

Bronx (brongks), **the** A mainland borough of New York City.

Bronx cheer *U.S. Slang* A voiced and forced expulsion of the breath through nearly-closed lips to express contempt or derision.

bronze (bronz) *n.* **1** *Metall.* **a** A reddish-brown alloy essentially of copper and tin, used in making bells and statues. **b** A similar alloy of copper and some other metal, as aluminum or manganese. **2** A pigment of the color of bronze. **3** A statue or bust cast in bronze. —*v.* **bronzed, bronz·ing** *v.t.* To harden or color like bronze; make brown. —*v.i.* To become brown or tan. [<MF <Ital. *bronzo, bronzino,* ? <L *(aes) Brundisinum* (alloy) of Brundisium] **—bronz′y** *adj.*

bronze age A mythological period of time characterized by violence and war, following the silver age of Zeus; often called *brazen age.*

Bronze Age *Archeol.* A period of time following the Stone Age and preceding the Iron Age during which weapons and other implements were made of bronze.

Bronze Star A U.S. military decoration in the form of a bronze star having a much smaller raised star in the center: awarded for heroic or meritorious achievement not involving participation in an aerial flight.

broo (brōō) *n. Scot.* Juice; broth: also *bree.*

brooch (brōch, brōōch) *n.* An ornamental pin for wearing on the breast. [Var. of BROACH[1], *n.*]

brood (brōōd) *n.* **1** All the young birds of a single hatching; also, offspring; progeny. **2** Species; kind; race. See synonyms under FLOCK. —*v.t.* **1** To sit upon or incubate (eggs). **2** To protect (young) by covering with the wings. —*v.i.* **3** To sit on eggs; incubate. **4** To meditate or ponder moodily and deeply: usually with *on* or *upon.* —*adj.* Kept for breeding purposes: a *brood* mare [OE *brod.* Related to BREED.]

brood·er (brōō′dər) *n.* **1** A covered and warmed receptacle, usually with an outside run, for protecting chicks reared without a hen. **2** One who broods over things in thought.

brood mare A mare used for breeding.

brood·y (brōō′dē) *adj.* **brood·i·er, brood·i·est 1** Inclined to brood, or sit on eggs, as a hen. **2** Prolific; capable of breeding. **3** Meditative; moody.

brook[1] (brŏŏk) *n.* A small, natural stream, smaller than a river or creek; a rivulet. See synonyms under STREAM. [OE brōc]

brook[2] (brŏŏk) *v.t.* To put up with; endure; tolerate: usually with the negative: I cannot *brook* such conduct. See synonyms under ENDURE. [OE *brūcan* use, enjoy]

Brooke (brŏŏk), **Sir Alan Francis,** 1883–1963, British chief of staff in World War II. **—Sir Fulke Greville,** 1554–1628, English poet and statesman. **—Rupert,** 1887–1915, English poet.

Brook Farm A farm near West Roxbury, Massachusetts, where a group of American scholars and writers attempted to set up a communistic community, 1841–47.

brook·let (brŏŏk′lit) *n.* A little brook.

(brŏŏk′lin) A borough of New York City on the western end of Long Island.

Brooks (brŏŏks), **Phillips,** 1835–93, U.S. divine and writer. **—Van Wyck,** 1886–1963, U.S. biographer and critic. **—William Robert,** 1844–1921, U.S. astronomer; discovered 23 comets.

Brooks Range The northernmost part of the Rocky Mountains, in northern Alaska, forming a watershed between the Yukon River and the Arctic Ocean; highest point, 9,239 feet.

brook trout 1 The speckled trout *(Salvelinus fontinalis)* of eastern North America. **2** The European brown trout *(Salmo trutta).*

brook·weed (brŏŏk′wēd′) *n.* Either of two water pimpernels, the European *(Samolus valerandi),* or the American *(S. floribundus).*

broom (brōōm, brŏŏm) *n.* **1** A brush attached to a long handle for sweeping: made chiefly of broomcorn. **2** Any of various shrubs (genus *Cytisus*) of the pea family, especially the **Scotch broom** *(C. scoparius),* with yellow flowers and stiff green branches. —*v.t.* To remove with a broom; sweep. [OE *brōm* broom. Akin to BRAMBLE.] **—broom′y** *adj.*

broom·corn (brōōm′kôrn′, brŏŏm′-) *n.* A cane-like grass (genus *Sorghum*) of which brooms are made.

broom·rape (brōōm′rāp′, brŏŏm′-) *n.* Any of various Old World fleshy herbs (genus *Orobanche,* family *Orobanchaceae*), destitute of green foliage and parasitic on the roots of other plants.

broom·stick (brōōm′stik′, brŏŏm′-) *n.* The handle of a broom.

broose (brōōz) *n. Scot.* A race for a prize at a wedding, as practiced in the Highlands.

brose (brōz) *n. Scot.* Porridge hastily made by pouring boiling water, or sometimes milk, beef broth, or the like, on meal, and stirring them together. **—bro′sy** *adj.*

broth (brôth, broth) *n.* **1** A fluid food made by boiling flesh, vegetables, etc., in water; a thin or strained soup. **2** *Irish Colloq.* A manly boy or young man of good character. **—a broth of a boy** A fine fellow. [OE. Related to BREW.]

broth·el (broth′əl, broth′-, brôth′əl, brôth′-) *n.* A house of prostitution. [ME, a worthless person, OE *brothen,* pp. of *breothan* ruin, decay; infl. by BORDEL]

broth·er (bruth'ər) *n. pl.* **broth·ers** or *Archaic* **breth·ren 1** A male person having the same parent as another or others. Sons of the same two parents are **full** or **whole brothers;** those having only one parent in common are *half-brothers.* **2** A person of the same descent, profession, trade, company, etc., with another or others; one having the same racial heritage; a kinsman. **3** A fellow human being. **4** One closely united with another or others by religious, political, or family bond. **5** One of a male religious order; a monk. **6** *U.S. Colloq.* A black man; a fellow black. —*v.t.* To treat or address as a brother. [OE *brōthor*]

broth·er·hood (bruth'ər·hŏŏd) *n.* **1** Fraternal relationship; the state of being brothers. **2** A society, fraternity, guild, etc. **3** A body of persons of the same occupation, profession, etc.

broth·er-in-law (bruth'ər·in·lô') *n. pl.* **broth·ers-in-law** A brother of a husband or wife, a sister's husband, or, loosely, a wife's sister's husband.

Brother Jonathan The people of the United States collectively: said to be from Washington's frequent allusion to Jonathan Trumbull by this name.

broth·er·ly (bruth'ər·lē) *adj.* Pertaining to or like a brother; fraternal; affectionate. See synonyms under FRIENDLY. —*adv.* Like a brother; kindly. —**broth'er·li·ness** *n.*

brougham (brōōm, brōō'əm, brō'əm) *n.* **1** A closed, four-wheeled carriage with front wheels turning short on a pivot, seating two or more persons, and having a high, uncovered driver's seat: drawn by one or two horses. **2** An electric automobile built on these lines, but seating four or five persons. **3** An automobile with a limousine body and the driver's seat outside. [after Lord Henry *Brougham,* 1778–1868, British statesman]

BROUGHAM

brought (brôt) Past tense and past participle of BRING.

brou·ha·ha (brōō'hä·hä) *n.* Hubbub; uproar; hurly-burly. [<F]

brow (brou) *n.* **1** The front upper part of the head; the forehead. **2** The eyebrow. **3** The countenance in general. **4** The upper edge of a cliff or the like. [OE *brū*]

brow antler The branch of an antler nearest the brow. For illustration see ANTLER.

brow·band (brou'band') *n.* **1** A band about the brow. **2** A band, as of a bridle, passing across a horse's forehead. For illustration see HARNESS.

brow·beat (brou'bēt') *v.t.* **·beat, ·beat·en, ·beat·ing** To intimidate by a stern, overbearing manner; bully. See synonyms under FRIGHTEN.

brown (broun) *n.* **1** A dark color, shading toward red, yellow, or black, as the color of faded leaves. **2** A pigment or dye used to produce it; a thing or part that is brown. —*adj.* Of the dusky or tanned color known as brown. **—to do up brown** *Slang* To do thoroughly and perfectly. —*v.t. & v.i.* To make or become brown; tan, as by sunbathing. [OE *brun*] **—brown'ish** *adj.* — **brown'ness** *n.*

Brown (broun), **Charles Brockden,** 1771–1810, American novelist. **—John,** 1800–59, American abolitionist, led raid on arsenal at Harpers Ferry to establish stronghold for escaped slaves; hanged for treason.

brown algae any members of a division of plants (Phaeophyta) consisting of multicellular, mostly marine algae containing a brown pigment that masks the green color of chlorophyll, such as kelp, gulfweed, and rockweed.

brown bagging 1 The practice of carrying in a small paper bag one's own liquor into a restaurant, where its sale is prohibited. **2** The practice of taking one's lunch to work in a brown paper bag.

brown Bess The bronzed flint musket formerly used in the British Army.

brown Betty Baked pudding made of bread crumbs, apple, and milk and sweetened.

brown bread 1 Bread made of unbolted wheat flour; Graham bread. **2** Bread made of rye flour and corn meal.

brown coal Lignite.

Browne (broun), **Charles Far·rar** (far'ər). See ARTEMUS WARD. **—Sir Thomas,** 1605–82, English physician and writer.

Brown·i·an movement (brou'nē·ən) *Physics* The rapid oscillatory movement of small particles when suspended in liquids. Also **Brownian motion.** [after Robert *Brown,* 1773–1858, English botanist, who discovered it]

brown·ie (brou'nē) *n.* **1** A homely, good-natured sprite, supposed to haunt farmhouses and do useful work at night. **2** A small, flat chocolate cake with nuts, usually square.

Brown·ie (brou'nē) *n.* A junior girl scout of the age group seven through nine.

Brown·ing (brou'ning), **Elizabeth Barrett,** 1806–61, English poet; wife of Robert. **—Robert,** 1812–89, English poet.

Browning automatic rifle An air-cooled, gas-operated, self-loading rifle, firing from a magazine: it is both automatic and semi-automatic. [after John Moses *Browning,* 1855–1926, U.S. inventor]

Browning machine-gun A machine-gun used by the U.S. Army, firing .30 or .50 caliber ammunition.

Brown·ist (brou'nist) *n.* A follower of Robert Browne, a Puritan, who separated from the Church of England about 1580. **—Brown'ism** *n.* **—Brown·is'tic** or **·ti·cal** *adj.*

brown lung Byssinosis.

brown-out (broun'out') *n.* **1** A partial diminishing of lights as a defensive measure against aerial attacks. **2** Any diminution of electric power.

brown recluse A small, brown, venomous spider *(Loxosceles reclusa)* with a violin-shaped mark on its back.

brown rice Unpolished rice grains, with the bran layers and most of the grains intact.

brown rot A serious disease of stone fruits caused by a fungus of the *Sclerotinia* genus.

Brown Shirt 1 A member of the Sturmabteilung. **2** A Nazi.

brown·stone (broun'stōn') *n.* A brownish-red sandstone used for building. —*adj.* **1** Made of brownstone. **2** Pertaining to the well-to-do class: the *brownstone* vote.

brownstone front A house having a front of brownstone.

brown study Deep meditation; absent-mindedness.

brown sugar Sugar that is unrefined or partly refined.

Browns·ville (brounz'vil) A port on the Rio Grande in southern Texas.

Brown Swiss A type of hardy dairy cattle originating in Switzerland.

brown·tail (broun'tāl') *n.* A white European moth *(Euproctis chrysorrhoea),* reddish-brown at the posterior end: its larvae defoliate shade trees. Also **brown'-tailed' moth.**

brown thrasher See under THRASHER.

browse (brouz) *v.* **browsed, brows·ing** *v.t.* **1** To crop; nibble at (leaves, grasses, etc.). **2** To graze on. —*v.i.* **3** To feed on grasses, leaves, etc. **4** To dip into books, etc., for casual reading. [<*n.,* or <MF *brouster* browse] —*n.* **1** Growing shoots or twigs used as fodder. **2** The act or process of browsing. [<MF *broust* bud, sprout] **—brows·er** *n.*

Broz (brōz) See TITO.

Bruce (brōōs), **Sir David,** 1855–1931, English physician and bacteriologist. **—Robert the,** 1274–1329, king of Scotland; defeated Edward II at Bannockburn: also known as *Robert I, Robert Bruce.* **—Viscount Stanley Melbourne,** born 1883, Australian statesman; prime minister 1923–29.

bru·cel·lo·sis (brōō'sə·lō'sis) *n.* Undulant fever. [after Sir David *Bruce*]

bru·cine (brōō'sēn, -sin) *n. Chem.* A bitter poisonous crystalline alkaloid, $C_{23}H_{26}O_4N_2 4H_2O$, found, with strychnine, in the seed and bark of the nux vomica, and in other species of the same genus *(Strychnos).* Also **bru'cin** (-sin). [after J. *Bruce,* 1730–94, Scottish explorer in Africa]

bru·cite (brōō'sīt) *n.* A magnesium hydrate, $Mg(OH)_2$. [after Archibald *Bruce,* 1777–1818, U.S. mineralogist]

Bruck·ner (brook'nər), **Anton,** 1824–96, Austrian composer.

Brue·ghel (brœ'gəl) Family of Flemish painters, especially, **Peter,** 1520?–69, known as *the Elder,* and his sons, **Peter,** 1564?–1638?, known as *the Younger,* and **Jan,** 1568–1625. Also spelled *Breughel, Bruegel.*

Bruges (brōōzh, brōō'jiz) A city of NW Belgium, capital of West Flanders province. *Flemish* **Brug·ge** (brœkh'ə).

bru·in (brōō'in) *n.* A bear; especially, a brown bear. [<Du., brown]

bruise (brōōz) *v.* **bruised, bruis·ing** *v.t.* **1** To injure, as by a blow, without breaking the surface of the skin; contuse. **2** To dent or mar the surface of. **3** To hurt or offend slightly, as feelings. **4** To crush; pound small, as with a mortar and pestle. —*v.i.* **5** To become discolored as the result of a blow. —*n.* A surface injury caused by violent contact, usually with discoloration of the skin but without laceration or fracture; contusion. [Fusion of OE *brȳsan* crush and OF *bruisier* break, shatter]

bruis·er (brōō'zər) *n.* **1** One who bruises. **2** A professional pugilist. **3** A pugnacious ruffian; a bully.

bruit (brōōt) *v.t.* To noise abroad; talk about: used mainly in the passive. See synonyms under PUBLISH. [<*n.*]—*n.* **1** *Obs.* A rumor noised abroad. **2** A din; clamor. **3** *Med.* A sound, generally abnormal, heard in auscultation. ◆ Homophone: *brute.* [<F *bruit* noise <*bruire* roar, make a noise, ? <L *rugire* roar, bellow] — **bruit'er** *n.*

Bru·maire (brü·mâr') The second month in the calendar of the first French republic. See CALENDAR (Republican). [<F <*brume* fog, mist]

bru·mal (brōō'məl) *adj.* Wintry. [<L *brumalis* wintry]

brum·by (brum'bē) *Austral.* A wild horse.

brume (brōōm) *n.* Fog; mist. [<F <L *bruma* winter] **—bru·mous** (brōō'məs) *adj.*

brum·ma·gem (brum'ə·jəm) *adj.* Cheap and showy; spurious, bogus. —*n.* An imitation; a sham; especially, cheap, imitation jewelry. [Alter. of *Birmingham,* England, where cheap jewelry was made]

Brum·mell (brum'əl), **George Bryan.** See BEAU BRUMMELL.

brunch (brunch) *n.* A late morning meal combining breakfast and lunch. [Blend of BREAKFAST and LUNCH]

Brun·dis·i·um (brun·diz'ē·əm) An ancient name for BRINDISI.

Bru·nei (broo·nī') A sultanate under British protection in NW Borneo; 2,226 square miles; capital, Brunei.

Bru·nel·les·chi (brōō'nel·les'kē), **Filippo,** 1377–1446, Italian architect and sculptor. Also **Bru'·nel·les'co** (-les'kō).

bru·net (brōō·net') *n.* A man or boy of dark complexion, eyes, and hair. —*adj.* Brunette.

bru·nette (brōō·net') *adj.* Dark-hued; having dark complexion, hair, and eyes. —*n.* A woman or girl of dark complexion, eyes, and hair. [<F, fem. dim. of *brun* brown]

Brun·hild (brōōn'hild, *Ger.* brōōn'hilt) In the *Nibelungenlied,* a queen of Iceland, married to Gunther, for whom she is won by Siegfried: discovering the deceit of her conquest, she persuades Hagen to avenge her by murdering Siegfried. Compare BRÜNNEHILDE, BRYNHILD.

Brü·ning (brü'ning), **Heinrich,** 1885–1970, German statesman, chancellor of Germany 1930–32. Also **Brue'ning.**

Brünn (brün) The German name for BRNO.

Brünne·hil·de (brün·hil'də) In Wagner's *Ring of the Nibelung,* a Valkyrie who incurs the anger of Wotan for assisting Siegmund and is put in a trance in a flame-encircled fastness, but is eventually released by Siegfried. Compare BRUNHILD, BRYNHILD.

Bru·no (brōō'nō) A masculine personal name. [<OHG, brown]

—Bruno, Saint, 1030?–1101, German monk, founder of the Carthusian Order, 1086.

Bru·no (brōō'nō), **Giordano,** 1548?–1600, Italian philosopher; burned as a heretic. **—Bru·nis·tic** (brōō·nis'tik) *adj.*

Bru·no·ni·an (broo·nō'nē·ən) *n.* An adherent of the **Brunonian theory,** now obsolete, that disease is a result of defective stimuli. [after John *Brown,* 1735–88, Scottish physician]

brun·stane (brun'stān) *n. Scot.* Brimstone.

Bruns·wick (brunz'wik) **1** A port in SE Georgia. **2** A former duchy and state of north central Germany; also, its former capital, a city in Lower Saxony: German *Braunschweig.*

Bruns·wick-black (brunz'wik·blak') *n.* Japan (def. 2).

brunt (brunt) *n.* **1** The main force, shock, strain, or stress of a blow, an attack, etc.; the hardest part. **2** *Obs.* A blow; assault; collision. [? <ON *bruna* advance quickly, as a fire]

Bru·sa (broo'sä) A city in NW Turkey in Asia: ancient *Prusa:* also *Bursa.*

brush[1] (brush) *n.* **1** An implement having bristles, hair, feathers, wire, or other flexible fibrous material, fixed in a handle or a back, and used for sweeping, scrubbing, painting, cleansing, smoothing, etc. **2** The act of brushing. **3** A light, grazing touch. **4** A skirmish; a short, brisk fight. **5** Brushwork. **6** Any object resembling a brush, as the bushy tail or bushy part of the tail of various animals, especially the fox. **7** *Elect.* **a** A strip of metal, bundle of wire, or bunch of slit metal plates, bearing on the commutator cylinder of a dynamo, for carrying off the current or for an external current through a motor. **b** A brush discharge. **8** A brushlike appearance in certain phenomena of polarized light. —*v.t.* **1** To use a brush on; sweep, polish, smooth, paint, etc., with or as with a brush. **2** To remove with or as with a brush. **3** To touch lightly in passing; touch upon briefly. —*v.i.* **4** To move lightly and quickly, often with a touch: to *brush* past someone. —**to brush aside** To deny consideration to. —**to brush up 1** To refresh one's knowledge of. **2** To renovate; refurbish. —**to brush up against** To come into slight contact with. [<OF *brosse* butcher-broom, brush, ? <Gmc.]

brush[2] (brush) *n.* **1** A growth of small trees and shrubs; hence, wooded country sparsely settled; backwoods. **2** Lopped-off bushes or branches of trees; brushwood. [<OF *broche,* ? <Gmc.]

brush discharge *Electr.* A discharge of low luminosity which issues in brushlike form from the terminals of an electric circuit. Compare CORONA (def. 6).

brushed wool A knit or woven woolen fabric on which a nap has been raised by a process using circular brushes.

brush fire 1 A fire in the brush. **2** A fire built of brushwood.

brush hook A hook for cutting brush.

brush-off (brush'ôf', -of') *n. U.S. Colloq.* An abrupt refusal or dismissal.

brush-tail possum (brush'tāl') A marsupial (*Trichosurus vulpecula fuliginosis*) of Tasmania, about two feet high and largest of the Australian possums.

brush turkey A jungle fowl of Australia or New Guinea; especially, the Australian *Alectura lathami,* about the size of a turkey but having a bright-yellow wattle.

brush wheel A wheel with bristles, buff leather, etc., on its periphery: used to rotate a similar wheel, or for cleaning, polishing, etc.

brush·wood (brush'wood') *n.* **1** A low thicket; underwood. **2** Cut bushes, or branches.

brush·work (brush'wûrk') *n.* A painter's characteristic style or way of applying paint with a brush.

brush·y (brush'ē) *adj.* **brush·i·er, brush·i·est 1** Covered with brushwood. **2** Resembling a brush; shaggy; rough; bushy.

Bru·si·lov (broo·sē'lôf), **Alexei Alexeivich,** 1853–1926, Russian general in World War I.

brusk (brusk, *esp. Brit.* broosk) *adj.* Rude or curt; abrupt; blunt; rough. See synonyms under BLUFF. Also **brusque.** [<MF *brusque* <Ital. *brusco* rough, rude] —**brusk'ly** *adv.* —**brusk'ness** *n.*

brus·que·rie (brus'kə·rē, *Fr.* brüs·kə·rē') *n.* Bluntness; bruskness; a brusk act or speech.

Brus·sels (brus'əlz) The capital of Belgium and of the province of Brabant. *French* **Brux·elles** (brü·sel', brük·sel'); *Flemish* **Brus·sel** (brœs'əl).

Brussels carpet A machine-made worsted carpet of linen or cotton and linen web.

Brussels griffon A toy dog of European origin, having a flat face and shaggy, reddish-brown hair. See BELGIAN GRIFFON, BRABANÇON GRIFFON.

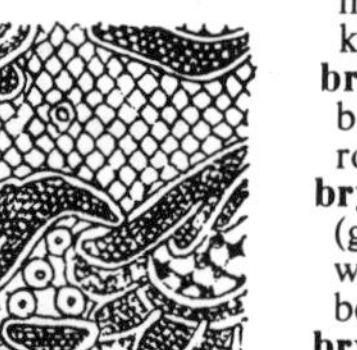
BRUSSELS LACE

Brussels lace Net lace, made by machine, with designs separately made and appliquéd upon it.

Brussels sprouts 1 A cultivated variety of wild cabbage (*Brassica oleracea gemmifera*), with blistered leaves and stems covered with heads like little cabbages. **2** The small edible heads or sprouts of this plant.

brut (brüt) *adj.* Dry: said of wines. [<F, lit., rough, raw <L *brutus* rough, rude]

Brut (broot) Legendary king of Britain; great-grandson of Aeneas and founder of the British race. See LAYAMON. Also **Brute, Bru'tus.**

bru·tal (broot'l) *adj.* **1** Characteristic of or like a brute; cruel; savage. **2** Unfeeling; rude; coarse. See synonyms under BARBAROUS, BRUTISH. [<L *brutus* stupid] —**bru'tal·ly** *adv.*

bru·tal·i·ty (broo·tal'ə·tē) *n. pl.* **·ties 1** The state or quality of being brutal; cruelty. **2** A brutal or cruel act.

bru·tal·ize (broo'təl·īz) *v.t.* & *v.i.* **·ized, ·iz·ing** To make or become brutal. —**bru'tal·i·za'·tion** *n.*

brute (broot) *n.* **1** Any animal other than man, as a horse, dog, etc. **2** A brutal person. See synonyms under ANIMAL. —*adj.* **1** Wanting the rational faculty; merely animal. **2** Unintelligent; also, sensual; brutal. **3** Merely material; inanimate. ◆ Homophone: *bruit.* [<F *brut* <L *brutus* stupid]

bru·ti·fy (broo'tə·fī) *v.t.* & *v.i.* **·fied, ·fy·ing** To brutalize.

brut·ish (broo'tish) *adj.* **1** Pertaining to, characteristic of, or resembling brutes. **2** Stupid; irrational; sensual; gross. —**brut'·ish·ly** *adv.* —**brut'ish·ness, brut'ism** *n.*

Synonyms: animal, base, beastly, bestial, brutal, brute, carnal, coarse, ignorant, imbruted, insensible, lascivious, sensual, sottish, stolid, stupid, swinish, unintellectual, unspiritual, vile. A *brutish* man simply follows his *animal* instincts, without special inclination to do harm; the *brutal* have always a spirit of malice and cruelty. *Brute* or *animal* simply indicates what a brute or an animal might possess; *animal* leans more to the side of sensuality, *brute* to that of force, as appears in the familiar phrase "*brute* force." Hunger is an *animal* appetite; a *brute* impulse may prompt one to strike a blow in anger. *Bestial* implies an intensified and degrading animalism. *Beastly* refers largely to the outward and visible consequences of excess; as, *beastly* drunkenness. Compare ANIMAL. *Antonyms:* elevated, enlightened, exalted, grand, great, humane, intellectual, intelligent, noble, refined, spiritual.

Brut·ti·um (brut'ē·əm) The ancient Roman name for CALABRIA.

Bru·tus (broo'təs), **Marcus Junius,** 85–42 B.C., Roman republican leader, one of Caesar's assassins.

brux·ism (bruk'siz·əm) *n.* A grinding or gnashing of the teeth in sleep or for other than chewing purposes: injurious to dental health. [<Gk. *bruchē* gnashing (of teeth) < *bruchein* gnash]

Bry·an (brī'ən) Variant of BRIAN.

Bry·an (brī'ən), **William Jennings,** 1860–1925, U.S. statesman and orator.

Bry·ansk (brē·ansk') A city in western Russian S.F.S.R.: also *Briansk.*

Bry·ant (brī'ənt), **William Cullen,** 1794–1878, U.S. poet.

Bryce (brīs), **James,** 1838–1922, Viscount Bryce of Dechmont, British diplomat and writer.

Bryce Canyon National Park (brīs) A region of wide canyons and eroded pinnacles in SW Utah; 56 square miles; established 1928.

Bryn·hild (brün'hilt) In the *Volsunga Saga* and in William Morris's *Sigurd the Volsung,* a Valkyrie who is thrown into an enchanted sleep by Odin, from which she is awakened by Sigurd. Compare BRUNHILD, BRÜNNEHILDE.

bry·o·chore (brī'ə·kôr, -kōr) *n. Ecol.* The tundra region characteristic of Siberia and arctic North America. [<Gk. *bryon* moss + *chorē* country, region]

bry·ol·o·gy (brī·ol'ə·jē) *n.* The department of botany that treats of mosses. [<Gk. *bryon* moss + -LOGY] —**bry·o·log·i·cal** (brī'ə·loj'i·kəl) *adj.* —**bry·ol'o·gist** *n.*

bry·o·nin (brī'ə·nin) *n. Chem.* An amorphous bitter glucoside, $C_{48}H_{66}O_{18}$, contained in the root of bryony: used in medicine.

bry·o·ny (brī'ə·nē) *n.* A common English herb (genus *Bryonia*) of the gourd family, with white or yellowish flowers and black or red berries. [<Gk. *bryōnē*]

bry·o·phyte (brī'ə·fīt) *n. Bot.* Any moss or liverwort of the phylum *Bryophyta.* [Gk. *bryon* moss + -PHYTE] —**bry'o·phyt'ic** (-fit'ik) *adj.*

bry·o·zo·an (brī'ə·zō'ən) *n. Zool.* One of a phylum or class (*Bryozoa*) of small aquatic animals which generate by budding, usually found in permanent colonies: of delicately branched or mosslike formation, or else of flat, crustlike growth. [<Gk. *bryon* moss + *zōon* organism]

Bryth·on (brith'ən) *n.* A Briton; specifically, a Welshman or a Celt of the Brythonic group. [<Welsh]

Bry·thon·ic (bri·thon'ik) *adj.* Of or pertaining to the Brythons or to their languages. —*n.* That branch of the Celtic languages which includes Welsh, Breton, and the extinct Cornish; Cymric: distinguished from *Goidelic.*

Brześć nad Bu·giem (bzheshch näd boo'gyem) The Polish name for BREST (def. 2).

bub (bub) *n. Colloq.* A small boy; youngster; young man: used in direct address. [Alter. of BROTHER]

bu·bal (byoo'bəl) *n.* A large antelope (genus *Alcelaphus*), especially the North African **bubal hartebeest** (*A. boselaphus*). Also **bu·bale** (byoo'bəl), **bu·ba·lis** (byoo'bə·lis). [<L *bubalus* <Gk. *boubalos* African antelope. Related to BUFFALO.]

bu·ba·line (byoo'bə·līn, -lin) *adj.* **1** Resembling the bubal. **2** Of, pertaining to, or like a buffalo.

bub·ble (bub'əl) *n.* **1** A vesicle of cohesive liquid, filled with air or other gas. **2** A globule of air or other gas in any confined space, as in a liquid or solid substance. **3** Anything unsubstantial; a delusion; cheat; fraud. **4** The process or sound of bubbling. [< *v.*] —*v.* **·bled, ·bling** *v.t.* **1** To form bubbles in, as a liquid. **2** To emit or utter by or as by bubbling: He *bubbled* the good news. **3** *Archaic* To cheat; swindle. —*v.i.* **4** To form bubbles; rise in bubbles. **5** To move or flow with a gurgling sound. **6** To express emotion, joy, etc., with a gurgling sound: He *bubbled* with glee. [ME *buble*; prob. imit.] —**bub'bly** *adj.*

bubble and squeak *Brit.* Cabbage and meat fried together. Also **bub'ble-and-squeak'** *n.*

bub·bler (bub'lər) *n.* A drinking fountain fitted with a vertical nozzle from which water flows in a small stream.

bubble sextant *Aeron.* A sextant in which an artificial horizon is represented by the position of a bubble in an instrument similar to a carpenter's level.

bu·bo (byoo'bō) *n. pl.* **bu·boes** *Pathol.* An inflammatory swelling of a lymph gland in the groin, especially one due to venereal infection. [<LL <Gk. *boubōn* groin] —**bu·bon·ic** (byoo·bon'ik) *adj.*

bubonic plague *Pathol.* A malignant, contagious, epidemic disease, characterized by fever, vomiting, diarrhea, and buboes: it is caused by a bacterium of the genus *Pasteurella* transmitted to man by fleas which have been infected by rats.

bu·bon·o·cele (byoo·bon'ə·sēl) *n. Pathol.* Inguinal hernia. [<Gk. *boubōnokēlē* < *boubōn* groin + *kēlē* abscess]

Bu·ca·ra·man·ga (boo'kä·rä·mäng'gä) A city in north central Colombia.

buc·cal (buk'əl) *adj. Anat.* **1** Of or pertaining to the cheek: the *buccal* artery. **2** Pertaining to the mouth; oral. [<L *bucca* cheek]

buc·ca·neer (buk'ə·nir') *n.* **1** A pirate or freebooter. **2** One of the piratical rovers of the 17th and 18th centuries who preyed upon the Spaniards, along the Spanish coasts of America. See synonyms under ROBBER. [<F *boucanier,* orig. one of the hunters of wild oxen in Haiti, who later turned to piracy <Tupian *boucan* a frame for the smoking and curing of meat]

buc·ci·na·tor (buk'sə·nā'tər) *n. Anat.* A muscle

of the middle cheek, used in blowing. [<L, trumpeter < *buccina* trumpet]

Bu·cen·taur (byōō·sen′tôr) *n.* **1** The state barge of Venice, used by the Doge on Ascension Day. **2** A mythical monster, half bull and half man. [<Ital. *bucentoro,* ? <Med. Gk. *boukentauros* bucentaur < Gk. *bous* bull + *kentauros* centaur; with ref. to the vessel's figurehead]

BUCENTAUR

Bu·ceph·a·lus (byōō·sef′ə·ləs) The war horse of Alexander the Great. [<L <Gk. *boukephalos* bull-headed < *bous* bull, ox + *kephalē* head]

Bu·cer (bōō′tsər), **Martin,** 1491–1551, German Lutheran reformer: also *Butzer.*

Buch·an (buk′ən), **John,** 1875–1940, first Baron Tweedsmuir, Scottish writer and statesman.

Bu·chan·an (byōō·kan′ən), **James,** 1791–1868, president of the United States 1857–61.

Bu·cha·rest (bōō′kə·rest, byōō′-) The capital of Rumania. *Rumanian* **Bu·cu·resti** (bōō·kōō·resht′)

Buch·en·wald (bŏŏk′ən·wôld, *Ger.* bŏŏkh′ən·vält) Site of a notorious Nazi concentration and extermination camp near Weimar, Germany.

Buch·man·ism (bŏŏk′mən·iz′əm) *n.* A religious movement founded by **Frank Buchman,** 1878–1961, U.S. evangelist: also called *Oxford Group* movement. — **Buch′man·ite** (-īt) *n.*

Buch·ner (bŏŏkh′nər), **Eduard,** 1860–1917, German chemist.

buck[1] (buk) *n.* **1** The male of certain animals, as of antelopes, deer, goats, rabbits, and rats. **2** A dashing fellow; a young blood. **3** An adult male Negro or Indian. — *v.i.* **1** To leap upward suddenly and come down with the legs stiff, as a horse or pack-animal, in an attempt to dislodge rider or burden. **2** *U.S. Colloq.* To resist stubbornly; object. **3** *U.S. Colloq.* To move with jerks and jolts: said of vehicles. **4** To provide resistance against which a rivet may be driven or some other pounding or pushing work done. — *v.t.* **5** To throw (a rider) by bucking. **6** *U.S. Colloq.* To butt with the head. **7** *U.S. Colloq.* To resist stubbornly; oppose. **8** To provide resistance for pounding or pushing (a rivet, etc.). **9** In football, to charge into (the opponent's line) with the ball. — **to buck up** *Colloq.* To encourage or become encouraged. [Fusion of OE *buc* he-goat and *bucca* male deer]

buck[2] (buk) *n.* **1** A sawhorse. **2** A padded frame in the shape of a sawhorse, used by gymnasts. [<Du. *zaagbok* sawbuck]

buck[3] (buk) *n.* **1** A buckskin, formerly taken as a standard of value by North American Indians. **2** *U.S. Slang* A dollar.

buck[4] (buk) *n. Brit.* Suds or lye, for washing clothes; also, the clothes washed. [< *v.*] — *v.t. Dial.* To wash or bleach in lye. [ME *bouken.* Akin to LG *büken* steep in lye]

buck[5] (buk) *n.* **1** In card games, an object placed before a player as a reminder of his turn to deal. **2** In poker, a marker occasionally put into a jackpot, indicating that he who receives the buck must order another jackpot when it is his deal. — **to pass the buck** *U.S. Colloq.* To shift responsibility, blame, etc., from oneself to someone else. [Origin uncertain]

Buck (buk), **Dudley,** 1839–1909, U.S. composer. — **Pearl S.,** 1892–1973, U.S. novelist.

buck-and-wing (buk′ən·wing′) *n.* An intricate, fast tap dance.

buck·a·roo (buk′ə·rōō, buk′ə·rōō′) *n.* A cowboy. Also **buck·ay·ro** (buk·ā′rō). [Alter. of Sp. *vaquero* cowboy]

buck·bean (buk′bēn′) *n.* A perennial herb (*Menyanthes trifoliata*) of the gentian family, having racemed white or reddish flowers: also called *bogbean.*

buck·ber·ry (buk′ber′ē, -bər·ē) *n.* **1** A small, wild, black huckleberry (*Gaylussacia ursina*) native in SE United States. **2** The deerberry (*Vaccineum stamineum*) common in eastern North America.

buck·board (buk′bôrd′, -bōrd′) *n.* A light, four-wheeled, horse-drawn vehicle having a long flexible board in place of body and springs. Also **buck′wag′on.** [<BUCK, *v.* (def. 3) + BOARD]

BUCKBOARD

buck·een (buk·ēn′) *n.* In Ireland, formerly, a young man of the impoverished gentry, or a younger son of the poorer aristocracy who aped the wealthy.

buck·er (buk′ər) *n.* **1** One who or that which bucks. **2** *U.S. Slang* One who bolts from a political party.

buck·et (buk′it) *n.* **1** A deep cylindrical vessel, with a bail, for dipping or carrying liquids; a pail. **2** As much as a bucket will hold: also **buck′et·ful′.** **3** A compartment on a water wheel, or the like. **4** A piston, as in a lifting pump, with a valve opening upward. — *v.t.* & *v.i.* **1** To draw or carry in a bucket. **2** *Colloq.* To ride (a horse) hard. **3** To move along rapidly. — **to kick the bucket** *Slang* To die. [? <OF *buket* kind of tub; infl. by OE *bucc* pitcher]

bucket seat A single, low, often adjustable seat with a rounded back: used in racing and sports cars, airplanes, etc.

buck·et-shop (buk′it·shop′) *n.* An office for gambling in fractional lots of stocks, grain, etc., with no delivery of securities or commodities sold or purchased.

buck·eye (buk′ī′) *n.* **1** The horse chestnut of the United States. **2** The glossy brown seed or nut of this tree. [<BUCK[1] + EYE]

Buck·eye (buk′ī′) *n.* A native or inhabitant of Ohio.

Buckeye State Nickname of OHIO.

buck fever *U.S. Colloq.* The state of excitement felt by an inexperienced hunter when first sighting game.

buck·horn (buk′hôrn′) *n.* The horn of a buck deer: often used to make knife handles, buttons, etc.

buck·hound (buk′hound′) *n.* **1** A large hound formerly used for hunting bucks. **2** The Scottish deerhound: also called *staghound.*

buck·ie (buk′ē) *n. Scot.* **1** A seashell, as that of the whelk. **2** A mischievous fellow.

Buck·ing·ham (buk′ing·əm) A county in southern England; 749 square miles; county seat, Aylesbury. Also **Buck′ing·ham·shire′** (-shir′); shortened form **Bucks.**

Buck·ing·ham (buk′ing·əm), **Duke of,** 1592–1628, George Villiers, English courtier. — **Duke of,** 1628–87, George Villiers, English statesman, son of the preceding.

buck·ish (buk′ish) *adj.* Dapper; foppish.

buck·le[1] (buk′əl) *n.* **1** A metal frame with movable tongue for fastening together two loose ends, as of straps, etc. **2** An ornament for shoes, etc., devised like a buckle. — *v.t.* **1** To fasten or attach with or as with a buckle. **2** To apply (oneself) assiduously. — *v.i.* **3** To apply oneself vigorously: often with *down to* or *to.* **4** To fight; grapple. [<F *boucle* cheek-strap, boss of a shield <L *buccula,* dim. of *bucca* cheek]

buck·le[2] (buk′əl) *v.t.* & *v.i.* **·led, ·ling** To bend under pressure; warp, curl, or crumple. —*n.* A bend; in mechanics, a permanent distortion or bend. [<F *boucler* bulge]

Buck·le (buk′əl), **Henry Thomas,** 1821–62, English historian.

buck·ler (buk′lər) *n.* **1** A shield; especially, a small round shield. **2** One who defends or protects; one who shields. **3** A protective covering on various animals. — *v.t.* To shield, as with a buckler; defend; protect. [OF *boucler* having a boss]

Buck·ley's chance (buk′lēz) *Austral. Slang* No chance at all, or very little chance, of success.

Buck·ner (buk′nər), **Simon Bolivar,** 1823–1914, American Confederate general and politician. — **Simon Bolivar,** 1886–1945, U.S. general, son of the preceding.

buck·o (buk′ō) *n. pl.* **·oes 1** A bully; blusterer.

buck private *U.S. Colloq.* An enlisted man of the lowest rank in the U.S. Army.

buck·ra (buk′rə) *adj.* White, or belonging to a white man; like or characteristic of white people: a term used among the Negroes of Africa, the West Indies, and the southern United States: a *buckra* house, *buckra* manners. — *n.* A white man. [<Efik *mbākara*]

buck·ram (buk′rəm) *n.* **1** A coarse, glue-sized cotton fabric, for stiffening garments, and for bookbinding. **2** Stiffness of manner. **3** Originally, a fine linen or cotton fabric. —*adj.* Of or like buckram; stiff; precise. —*v.t.* To stiffen with or as with buckram. [Cf. OF *boquerant*]

buck·saw (buk′sô′) *n.* A saw set in an adjustable H-shaped frame, used for sawing firewood on a buck.

BUCKSAW

buck·shee (buk′shē) *adj. Brit. Slang* Gratis. [See BAKSHEESH]

buck·shot (buk′shot′) *n.* Shot of a large size, used in hunting deer and other large game.

buck·skin (buk′skin′) *n.* **1** The skin of a buck: also **buck skin.** **2** A soft, strong, grayish-yellow leather, formerly made from deerskins, now chiefly from sheepskins. **3** *pl.* Breeches or a suit made of such skin. **4** A person clad in such skin; especially, one of the American soldiers in the Revolution. **5** A horse of a buckskin color. **6** A cream-colored woolen cloth of close weave: also **buckskin cloth.**

buck·thorn (buk′thôrn′) *n.* A shrub or small tree of the genus *Rhamnus,* having alternate pinnately veined leaves and axillary flowers. — **southern buckthorn** A tree (*Bumelia lycioides*) of the southern United States. [<BUCK[1] + THORN]

buck·tooth (buk′tōōth′) *n. pl.* **·teeth** A projecting tooth. [<BUCK[1] + TOOTH]

buck·toothed (buk′tōōtht′, -tōōthd′) *adj.* Having projecting teeth.

buck·wheat (buk′hwēt′) *n.* A plant of the genus *Fagopyrum,* yielding triangular seeds used as fodder and for flour. **2** Its seeds. **3** The flour. [OE *bōc* beech + WHEAT, from resemblance of seeds to beech seeds]

buck·y diaphragm (buk′ē) In roentgenography, an apparatus for preventing secondary X-rays from affecting the plate, thus ensuring a clearer picture. [after Gustav *Bucky,* 1880–1963, German-American roentgenologist]

bu·col·ic (byōō·kol′ik) *adj.* Pertaining to or like shepherds or herdsmen; pastoral; rustic: also **bu·col′i·cal.** — *n.* **1** A pastoral poem. **2** A rustic; farmer: humorous usage. See synonyms under RUSTIC. [<L *bucolicus* <Gk. *boukolikos* < *boukolos* herdsman < *bous* ox] — **bu·col′i·cal·ly** *adv.*

Bu·co·vi·na (bōō′kə·vē′nə) The Rumanian spelling of BUKOVINA.

bud[1] (bud) *n.* **1** *Bot.* **a** An undeveloped stem, branch, or shoot of a plant, with rudimentary leaves or unexpanded flowers. **b** The act or stage of budding. **2** *Zool.* A budlike projection, as in polyps, etc., developing into a new individual; also, a budlike part. **3** Any immature person or thing. — **to nip in the bud** To stop in the initial stage. — *v.* **bud·ded, bud·ding** *v.t.* **1** To put forth as buds. **2** To graft by inserting a bud of (a tree or plant) into the stock of another type of tree or plant. **3** To cause to bud. — *v.i.* **4** To put forth buds. **5** To begin to grow or develop. [ME *budde*; origin uncertain] — **bud′der** *n.*

bud[2] (bud) *n. U.S. Colloq.* A term of direct address to a man or boy. Also **buddy.** [Alter. of BROTHER]

Bu·da·pest (bōō′də·pest) The capital of Hungary, on the Danube.

Bud·dha (bŏŏd′ə, bōō′də) *n.* Literally, the Enlightened; an incarnation of selflessness, virtue, and wisdom; specifically, Gautama Siddhartha, 563?–483? B.C., the founder of Buddhism, regarded by his followers as the last of a series of deified religious teachers of central and eastern Asia. [<Skt.]

Bud·dhism (bŏŏd′iz·əm, bōō′diz-) *n.* A mystical and ascetic religious faith of eastern Asia, founded in northern India by Buddha in the sixth century B.C., teaching that Nirvana, which is the conquest of self and subsequent freedom from sorrow and mortality, is reached by the Eightfold Path of right belief, right resolution, right speech, right action, right living, right effort, right thinking, and peace of mind through meditation. —**Bud′·dhist** *adj.* & *n.* —**Bud·dhis′tic** or **·ti·cal** *adj.*

bud·ding (bud′ing) *n.* **1** *Zool.* A mode of asexual reproduction, as in various polyps, ascidians, etc., in which a small part of the substance of the parent is protruded as a bud or gemma and develops into a new organism; gemmation. **2** *Bot.* A similar mode of reproduction occurring in some cryptogams.

bud·dle (bud′l) *n. Mining* **1** An inclined shallow trough, used for separating ores by shaking or raking in running water. **2** One of various circular and conical machines, stationary or rotary, working on the same principle. [Origin unknown]

bud·dle·ia (bud·lē′ə, bud′lē·ə) *n.* Any plant of a large genus (*Buddleia*) of shrubs or herbs, with lanceolate, opposite leaves and small yellow or purplish flowers: native in warm regions of America, Asia, and southern Africa: also called *butterfly bush.* [after Adam *Buddle,* died 1715, English botanist]

bud·dy (bud′ē) *n. pl.* **·dies** *Colloq.* **1** Brother. **2** Pal; chum; companion. **3** Little boy: used in direct address. [See BUD²]

Bu·dën·ny (bo͞o·den′ē, *Russian* bo͞o·dyôn′i), **Semyon Mikhailovich,** born 1883?, Russian general in Revolution of 1917 and marshal in World War II.

budge¹ (buj) *v.t.* & *v.i.* **budged, budg·ing** To move or stir slightly: usually with the negative. —*n.* A slight movement. [<F *bouger* stir, move]

budge² (buj) *n.* **1** Lambskin with the wool side out: formerly used for edgings on the gowns of scholastics, etc. **2** A leather bag made with the wool side out. —*adj.* **1** Trimmed with budge, or wearing budge. **2** Hence, pompous; imposing; formal. [Origin uncertain]

budg·et (buj′it) *n.* **1** A statement of probable revenue and expenditure and of financial proposals for the ensuing year as presented to or passed upon by a legislative body. **2** A summary of probable income for a given period, as of a family or an individual, with approximate allowances for certain expenditures over that period. **3** A collection or store, as of news, anecdotes, etc. **4** A small sack or its contents; hence, a loose bundle. —*v.t.* **1** To determine in advance the expenditure of (time, money, etc.) over a period of time. **2** To put on or into a budget: He *budgeted* his trip. [<F *bougette,* dim. of *bouge* <L *bulga* leather bag] —**budg·et·ar·y** (buj′ə·ter′ē) *adj.* —**budg′et·er** *n.*

Bud·weis (bo͞ot′vīs) The German name for ČESKÉ BUDĚJOVICE.

Bu·ell (byo͞o′əl), **Don Carlos,** 1818–98, U.S. general.

Bue·na Vis·ta (bwā′nə vis′tə) A village in SE Coahuila, Mexico; scene of United States victory, 1847, in the Mexican War.

Bue·nos Ai·res (bwā′nəs ī′riz, bō′nəs âr′ēz) **1** A province in eastern Argentina; 116,322 square miles; capital, La Plata. **2** The largest city of Latin America, a federal district and port on the La Plata, capital of Argentina; 77 square miles: a native of the city is known as a *Porteño.*

buff¹ (buf) *n.* **1** A thick, soft, flexible leather, undyed and unglazed, made from the skins of buffalo, elk, oxen, etc: also **buff leather. 2** Its color, a light yellow. **3** A coat made of buff leather. **4** *Colloq.* The bare skin; the nude: in the *buff.* **5** A stick or wheel covered with leather, velvet, etc., and used with emery and other powders in polishing: also **buff′er.** —*adj.* Made of, or of the color of, buff leather; brownish-yellow. —*v.t.* **1** To clean or polish with or as with a buff. **2** In leather-making, to shave, as cowskin, on the grain side until very thin, producing an imitation of calf leather. **3** To make buff in color. [<F *buffle* buffalo]

buff² (buf) *n.* A blow; buffet: only in *blind-man's-buff.* —*v.t.* **1** To deaden the shock of. **2** To strike; buffet. —*v.i.* **3** To act as a buffer. [<OF *buffe* blow]

buff³ (buf) *n.* **1** Originally, a voluntary, unofficial auxiliary of a fire department. **2** One who rushes to attend fires. **3** An enthusiast in any special field, who attends all possible events: a theater *buff.* [? Special use of BUFF¹]

buf·fa·lo (buf′ə·lō) *n. pl.* **·loes** or **·los 1** A large Old World ox, now extensively domesticated, one of which, the African **Cape buffalo** (*Syncerus caffer*), has horns that broaden at the base. ◆ Collateral adjective: *bubaline.* **2** The Indian water buffalo. **3** The North American bison. **4** A buffalo robe. **5** A buffalo fish. **6** *Naut.* One of the bulwarks on each side of the stem of the forecastle deck in the extreme bow. —*v.t. U.S. Slang* To overawe; hoodwink. [<Ital. <L *bufalus,* var. of *bubalus* <Gk. *boubalos* buffalo. Related to BUBAL.]

AFRICAN OR CAPE BUFFALO

Buf·fa·lo (buf′ə·lō) A city in western New York at the eastern end of Lake Erie.

buf·fa·lo·ber·ry (buf′ə·lō·ber′ē) *n.* The edible crimson berry of either of two American shrubs, the thorny silverleaf (*Shepherdia argentea*) or the russet buffaloberry (*S. canadensis*).

Buffalo Bill See CODY, WILLIAM F.

buffalo bug The carpet beetle. Also **buffalo moth.**

buffalo fish A large, carplike, fresh-water fish (genus *Ictiobus*) of the sucker family, native in North America: named from its humped back, resembling that of a buffalo.

buffalo gnat A small, black, winged insect (*Simulium* and related genera) which attacks all warm-blooded animals, usually in swarms: also called *black fly.*

buf·fa·lo·grass (buf′ə·lō·gras′, -gräs′) *n.* **1** A low, creeping grass (*Buchloë dactyloides*) covering large prairies east of the Rocky Mountains, highly esteemed for winter forage. **2** The curly mesquite (*Hilaria belangeri*) of the SW United States and Central America.

Buffalo Indian A Plains Indian.

buffalo robe The skin of the North American bison, dressed with the hair on for use as a lap robe.

buff·er¹ (buf′ər) *n.* One who or that which buffs. [<BUFF¹, *v.*]

buff·er² (buf′ər) *n.* A device for lessening the shock of concussion. [<BUFF², *v.*]

buffer state A small country situated between two larger rival powers regarded as less likely to open hostilities with each other because they have no common boundary.

buf·fet¹ (bo͞o·fā′, *Brit.* buf′it) *n.* **1** A sideboard; also, a cupboard for china, glassware, etc. **2** A counter or bar for serving lunch or refreshments; also, a public lunchroom. [<F]

buf·fet² (buf′it) *v.t.* **1** To strike or cuff, as with the hand. **2** To strike repeatedly; knock about. **3** To force (a way) by pushing or striking, as through a crowd. —*v.i.* **4** To fight; struggle. **5** To force a way. —*n.* A blow; cuff; assault. [<OF *buffet,* dim. of *buffe* blow, slap] —**buf′fet·er** *n.*

buf·fet car (bo͞o·fā′) A parlor car or sleeping car on a train equipped with a small kitchen.

buf·fet supper (bo͞o·fā′) A light meal at which the guests serve themselves. Also **buffet lunch.**

buff·ing wheel (buf′ing) Buff¹ (def. 5).

buf·fle·head (buf′əl·hed′) *n.* A North American duck (*Charitonetta albeola*) having the feathers of the head elongated, and with plumage black above and white below: also called *butterball.* [<F *buffle* buffalo + HEAD]

buf·fo (bo͞o′fō, *Ital.* bo͞of′fō) *n. pl.* **·fi** (-fē) A comic actor in opera; comic singer: usually a bass. [<Ital., foolish, comic]

Buf·fon (bü·fôṅ′), **Comte de,** 1707–88, Georges Louis Leclerc, French naturalist.

buf·foon (bu·fo͞on′) *n.* A clown; one given to jokes, coarse pranks, etc. [<F *buffon* <Ital. *buffone* clown <*buffa* jest] —**buf·foon′er·y** *n.* —**buf·foon′ish** *adj.*

buff·skin (buf′skin′) *n.* Buff¹ (def. 1).

buff·y (buf′ē) *adj.* **1** Of a buff color. **2** Characterized by or resembling buff. **3** Designating or pertaining to a buffy coat.

buffy coat *Physiol.* A yellowish or grayish coat formed on coagulating blood.

Bu·fo (byo͞o′fō) *n.* A genus of toads. [<L *bufo* toad]

bug¹ (bug) *n.* **1** Any of an order (*Hemiptera*) or suborder (*Heteroptera*) of terrestrial or aquatic insects with piercing, sucking mouth parts, wingless or with two pairs of wings, the anterior pair typically horny with an apical membranous part, as the stinkbug, squashbug, bedbug. For illustrations see under INSECT. **2** Loosely, any insect or small arthropod. **3** *Often pl. U.S. Colloq.* Any small but troublesome defect in the design, structure, or operation of an instrument, motor, machine, or the like. **4** *Slang* An enthusiast; a monomaniac. **5** *Colloq.* A pathogenic microorganism. **6** *Colloq.* A miniature electronic microphone, used in wiretapping, etc. —*v.* **bugged, bug·ging** *v.i.* **1** To stare; stick out: said of eyes. —*v.t.* **2** *Colloq.* To fix an electronic eavesdropping device in (a room, etc.) or to a (wire, etc.). **3** *U.S. Slang* To annoy or anger; also, to bewilder or puzzle. —**to bug off** *U.S. Slang* Go away! Get lost! —**to bug out** *U.S. Slang* To quit, especially hastily or ignominiously. [Origin unknown]

bug² (bug) *n. Obs.* A specter; bugbear. [ME *bugge* scarecrow. Cf. Welsh *bwg* ghost.]

Bug (bo͞og) **1** A river in southern Ukrainian S.S.R., flowing 532 miles SE to the Black Sea; also **Southern Bug.** *Russian* **Yuzh·nyy Bug** (yo͞ozh′nē bo͝ok′). **2** A river rising in western Ukrainian S.S.R., flowing about 500 miles NW to form the Poland–U.S.S.R. border: also **Western Bug.** *Russian* **Za·pad·nyy Bug** (zä′pəd·nē bo͝ok′).

bug·a·boo (bug′ə·bo͞o) *n. pl.* **·boos** A bugbear. [<BUG² + BOO]

Bu·gan·da (byo͞o·gan′də) A kingdom under British protection, comprising a province of southern Uganda; 25,631 square miles; capital, Kampala.

bug·bane (bug′bān′) *n.* A perennial herb (genus *Cimicifuga*) of the crowfoot family, as the **European bugbane,** *C. foetida,* used to drive away vermin, or the **American bugbane,** *C. americana.*

bug·bear (bug′bâr′) *n.* An imaginary object of terror; a specter: also called *bugaboo.* [<BUG² + BEAR²]

bug·eye (bug′ī′) *n. Naut.* A centerboard sailing vessel of shallow draft, fore-and-aft rigged on two raked masts: used in dredging oysters in Chesapeake Bay.

bug-eyed (bug′īd′) *adj. Slang* With the eyes bulging out, as from astonishment.

bug·ger (bug′ər) *n.* **1** One guilty of sodomy. **2** A contemptible person. **3** *U.S. Slang* A chap; person; child: used in mild or humorous disparagement. [<OF *boulgre* <Med. L *Bulgarus* a Bulgarian; with ref. to a Bulgarian sect of heretics (11th c.) to whom sodomy was imputed]

bug·ger·y (bug′ər·ē) *n.* Sodomy.

bug·gy¹ (bug′ē) *n. pl.* **·gies 1** A light, four-wheeled, horse-drawn vehicle with a hood. **2** The caboose of a freight train. [Origin uncertain]

bug·gy² (bug′ē) *adj.* **·gi·er, ·gi·est 1** Infested with bugs. **2** *Slang* Crazy. —**bug′gi·ness** *n.*

bug·house (bug′·hous′) *U.S. Slang n.* An asylum for the insane. —*adj.* Crazy; insane.

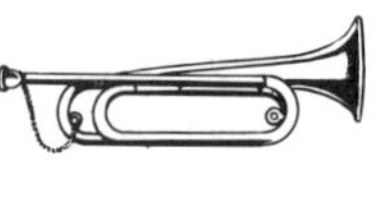
BUGLE

Bu·gin·vil·lae·a (bo͞o′·gən·vil′ē·ə) *n.* Bougainvillea.

bu·gle¹ (byo͞o′gəl) *n.* **1** A brass wind instrument resembling a horn or trumpet, with or without keys or valves. **2** A huntsman's horn. —*v.t.* & *v.i.* **bu·gled, bu·gling 1** To summon with or as with a bugle. **2** To sound a bugle. [<OF <L *buculus,* dim. of *bos* ox; because first made from the horns of oxen] —**bu′gler** *n.*

bu·gle² (byo͞o′gəl) *n.* A tube-shaped glass bead, commonly black, used for ornamenting garments. —*adj.* Of, resembling, or adorned with bugles. [Origin uncertain] —**bu′gled** *adj.*

bu·gle³ (byo͞o′gəl) *n.* A British plant of the mint family (genus *Ajuga*), especially the **carpet bugle** (*A. reptans*). [<F <LL *bugula*]

bu·gle·weed (byo͞o′gəl·wēd′) *n.* Any of several herbs (genus *Lycopus*); especially, **sweet Virginia bugleweed** (*L. virginicus*) used medicinally, and **bitter American bugleweed** (*L. americanus*).

bug·light (bug′līt′) *n.* **1** A small lighthouse. **2** A small flashlight.

bu·gloss (byōō′glos, -glôs) *n.* Any of various genera (as *Anchusa, Lycopsis,* and *Echium*) of coarse, hairy, boraginaceous plants having funnel-shaped, blue flowers. Also called *alkanet, oxtongue.* [<F *buglosse* <L *buglossa* <Gk. *bouglossos* <*bous* bull, ox + *glossa* tongue]

bug·seed (bug′sēd′) *n.* A low, branching annual herb *(Corispermum hyssopifolium)* of the goosefoot family, the flat seeds of which resemble bugs.

bu·hach (byōō′hach) *n.* The powdered flower heads of pyrethrum, used as an insect powder. [Origin uncertain]

buhl (bōōl) *n.* Metal or tortoise shell inlaid in furniture; also, cabinetwork so decorated. Also **buhl′work′.** [after A. C. *Boulle,* 1642–1732, French cabinetmaker]

buhr·stone (bûr′stōn′) *n.* Burrstone.

build (bild) *v.* **built** (*Archaic* **build·ed**), **build·ing** *v.t.* **1** To construct, erect, or make by assembling separate parts or materials. **2** To establish and increase: to *build* a business. **3** To found; make a basis for: We *build* our hopes on peace. **4** In cards, to form sequences or combinations of cards, as by suit or number. —*v.i.* **5** To be in the business of building. **6** To base or form an idea, theory, etc.: with *on* or *upon.* **—to build up 1** To renew; strengthen, as health or physique. **2** To fill, as an area, with houses. See synonyms under CONSTRUCT. —*n.* **1** The manner or style in which anything is built; form; figure. **2** A cumulative increase in power and effectiveness, as of a dramatic performance as the climax is approached. [OE *byldan* <*bold* house]

build·er (bil′dər) *n.* **1** One who or that which builds. **2** One who follows the occupation of building, or who controls or directs the actual work of building. **3** An abrasive or other substance added to soap to increase its cleansing effect.

build·ing (bil′ding) *n.* **1** An edifice for any use; that which is built, as a dwelling house, barn, etc. **2** The occupation, business, or art of constructing. **3** The act or process of erecting or establishing. See synonyms under HOUSE.

building and loan association A society, usually an incorporated joint-stock company, organized to aid some of its members in building homes or other edifices with money lent or subscribed by all the members.

build-up (bild′up′) *n.* **1** A gradual accumulation or increase, as of buildings. **2** *Mil.* The accumulation of troops or materiel in a given area. **3** In forestry, the steady acceleration of a fire under conditions favoring its spread and in spite of attempts at effective control. **4** *Colloq.* An enhancement of reputation, as by praise or favorable publicity.

built-in (bilt′in′) *adj.* Made part of or permanently attached to the structure, as of a house or room.

buird·ly (bürd′lē) *adj. Scot.* Large and well made; stately; burly; stalwart; sturdy; stout.

Buis·son (bwē·sôn′), **Ferdinand,** 1841–1932, French educator.

Bui·ten·zorg (bœi′tən·zôrkh) The Dutch name for BOGOR.

Bu·ka (bōō′kə) One of the Solomon Islands, comprising, with Bougainville, a part of the United Nations Trust Territory of New Guinea; 220 square miles.

Bu·kha·ra (bōō·kä′rə) A division of central Uzbek S.S.R.; 49,600 square miles; capital, Bukhara; also *Bokhara.*

Bu·kha·rin (bōō·khä′rin), **Nicolai Ivanovich,** 1888–1938, U.S.S.R. revolutionist and editor; executed for treason.

Bu·ko·vi·na (bōō′kə·vē′nə) A region of eastern Europe in NE Rumania and western Ukrainian S.S.R.; formerly an Austrian duchy: Rumanian *Bucovina. German* **Bu·ko·wi·na** (bōō′kō·vē′nä).

Bul (bōōl) See HESHWAN.

Bu·la·wa·yo (bōō′lə·wä′yō) A city in SW Zimbabwe also *Buluwayo.*

bulb (bulb) *n.* **1** *Bot.* **a** A leaf bud comprised of a cluster of thickened, scalelike leaves, growing usually underground and sending forth roots from the lower face, as the onion or lily. **b** Any of several underground stems resembling bulbs, as the corm of a crocus or a dahlia tuber. **2** Any protuberance resembling a plant bulb, as the bulb at the root of a hair (see illustration under HAIR), the enlarged end of a thermometer tube, etc. **3** *Electr.* An evacuated glass container holding the filament of an incandescent electric light. **4** A vacuum tube. **5** *Anat.* The medulla oblongata. [<L *bulbus* <Gk. *bolbos* bulbous root] **—bul·ba·ceous** (bul·bā′shəs) *adj.* **—bul′bous** *adj.*

bul·bar (bul′bər) *adj.* Of or pertaining to a bulb, especially the bulb of the medulla oblongata: *bulbar* paralysis.

bul·bif·er·ous (bul·bif′ər·əs) *adj.* Producing bulbs. [<NL *bulbifer* <L *bulbus* bulb + *ferre* bear]

bulb·i·form (bul′bə·fôrm) *adj.* Having the form of a bulb.

bul·bil (bul′bil) *n.* **1** A small bulb. **2** *Bot.* An aerial, deciduous, fleshy leaf bud, capable of developing into a new individual, as in the tiger lily: also **bul′bel** (-bel). [<NL *bulbillus,* dim. of *bulbus* bulb]

bul·bul (bōōl′bōōl) *n.* **1** Any of various thrushlike birds (family *Pycnonotidae*) of the tropics of the Old World, with short legs, rounded wings, and typically dull coloration. **2** The Persian nightingale (genus *Luscinia*). [<Persian <Arabic]

Bul·finch (bōōl′finch), **Charles,** 1763–1844, American architect. **—Thomas,** 1796–1867, compiler of myths; son of the preceding.

Bul·ga·nin (bōōl·gä′nyin), **Nikolai Aleksandrovich,** 1895–1975, U.S.S.R. marshal; premier 1955–58.

Bul·gar (bul′gär, bōōl′-) *n.* **1** A Bulgarian. **2** The Bulgarian language.

Bul·gar·i·a (bul·gâr′ē·ə, bōōl-) A state in SE Europe; 142,471 square miles; capital, Sofia: officially **People's Republic of Bulgaria.** *Bulgarian* **Bl·ga·ri·ya** (bul·gä′rē·yä).

Bul·gar·i·an (bul·gâr′ē·ən, bōōl-) *adj.* Of or pertaining to Bulgaria, the Bulgarians, or to their language. —*n.* **1** A native or citizen of Bulgaria. **2** One of an ancient people considered to be of Mongolian stock, who, in the 7th century, migrated from the region west of the Ural Mountains and north of the Caspian Sea, and settled Bulgaria. **3** The language of the Bulgarians, belonging to the South Slavic group of the Balto-Slavic languages.

bulge (bulj) *v.t.* & *v.i.* **bulged, bulg·ing** To make or be protuberant; swell out. [<*n.*] —*n.* **1** The most convex part, as of a cask. **2** A protuberant part; swelling. **3** *U.S. Colloq.* Advantage; especially, a slight but telling advantage. **—to get the bulge on** *U.S. Colloq.* To gain the advantage over. [<OF *boulge*] **—bulg′y** *adj.* **—bulg′i·ness** *n.*

Bulge (bulj), **Battle of the** The last major German counter-offensive of World War II, repulsed in January, 1945, during which the line of combat formed a deep bulge on the Belgian front.

bulg·er (bul′jər) *n.* **1** In golf, a driver or a brassy having a convex face: also **bulger driver. 2** A stick used in hockey, having a flat-faced, heavy head with a convex back.

bu·lim·i·a (byōō·lim′ē·ə) *n. Pathol.* Insatiable appetite, or the disease of which this is a characteristic. [<Gk. *boulimia* great hunger <*bou-* ox-like, great + *limos* hunger] **—bu·lim′ic** *adj.*

bulk[1] (bulk) *n.* **1** The substance or body of anything material considered with reference to its magnitude, as of a ship, a man, an elephant, etc. **2** A large body; mass; volume; size. **3** Greater or principal part; main body; majority. **4** *Naut.* The whole space in a ship's hold for stowing goods; also, the whole cargo. See synonyms under MAGNITUDE, MASS. **—in bulk** Loose; in mass; not in boxes, bales, sacks, or packages. —*v.i.* **1** To have an appearance of largeness or weight; be of importance: The weather *bulks* large in our plans. **2** *Obs.* To swell; expand: with *up.* —*v.t.* **3** To cause to expand or grow large: with *out.* [Cf. ON *būlki* heap, cargo, and Dan. *bulk* lump]

bulk[2] (bulk) *n.* A projecting part of a building; a framework in front of a shop; stall. [?<ON *bǫlkr* beam]

bulk·age (bul′kij) *n. Physiol.* The non-assimilable accessory of food elements, such as vegetable fiber, that stimulates intestinal activity.

bulk·head (bulk′hed′) *n.* **1** *Naut.* One of various partitions in a vessel, to separate it into rooms or to divide the hold into watertight compartments. **2** A partition of stone or wood to keep back earth, gas, etc., as in a mine. **3** A horizontal or sloping door outside a house, giving entrance to the cellar. **4** A framework or casing to cover a staircase or elevator shaft. **—bulk′head′ed** *adj.*

bulk·y (bul′kē) *adj.* **bulk·i·er, bulk·i·est** Huge; large; massive; unwieldy. **—bulk′i·ly** *adv.* **—bulk′i·ness** *n.*

bull[1] (bōōl) *n.* **1** The male of domestic cattle or of some other animals, as of the elephant, moose, giraffe, whale, seal, etc. ◆ Collateral adjective: *taurine.* **2** A dealer who seeks or expects higher prices, and buys stocks or bonds accordingly. **3** One possessing characteristics suggestive of a bull. **4** *U.S. Slang* A policeman or detective, usually in plain clothes. —*v.t.* **1** To attempt to raise the price of or in. **2** To push or force (a way). —*v.i.* **3** To go up in price: said of stocks, etc. **4** *Slang* To go or push ahead: to *bull* through a crowd. —*adj.* **1** Large; bull-like; male. **2** Going up or advancing: a *bull* market. [ME *bule;* cf. OE *bulluc* bullock]

bull[2] (bōōl) *n.* **1** An official and authoritative document issued by the Pope, usually an edict, decree, or other proclamation, sealed with a bulla. **2** Bulla (def. 1). [<L *bulla* edict, seal]

bull[3] (bōōl) *n.* A ridiculous blunder in speech. [?<F *boule* lie, deceit <L *bulla* bubble]

bull[4] (bōōl) *n. Slang* Nonsense; bluff.

Bull (bōōl) The constellation and astrological sign Taurus. See CONSTELLATION.

Bull (bōōl), **Ole Bornemann,** 1810–80, Norwegian violinist.

bul·la (bōōl′ə, bul′ə) *n. pl.* **bul·lae** (bool′·ē, bul′ē) **1** A seal of lead, used by the Pope, or of gold or other metal used by the Greek and early German emperors and sovereigns. **2** *Pathol.* A small blister or large vesicle filled with watery serum; a bleb. [<L, seal]

bul·lar·i·um (bōōl·âr′ē·əm) *n.* A collection of papal bulls. [<Med. L]

bul·late (bōōl′āt, -it, bul′-) *adj.* **1** *Biol.* Having blisterlike prominences, as a leaf or surface. **2** *Anat.* Swollen; inflated. [<L *bullatus* <*bulla* bubble]

bull-bait·ing (bōōl′bā′ting) *n.* The setting of dogs upon bulls: a former English sport.

bull·bat (bōōl′bat′) *n.* The nighthawk (genus *Chordeiles*): named from the noise it makes while flying.

bull·dog (bōōl′dôg′, -dog′) *n.* **1** A medium-sized, short-haired, powerful dog, originally bred in England for use in bull-baiting: also called *English bulldog.* **2** A pistol; especially, a short-barreled revolver of large caliber: also, formerly, a cannon. —*adj.* Resembling a bulldog; courageous; tenacious. —*v.t. U.S. Colloq.* To throw (a steer) by gripping its horns and twisting its neck.

BULLDOG (About 16 inches high at the shoulders)

bulldog edition The early edition of a morning newspaper, often appearing the evening before, for distribution out of town.

bull·doze (bōōl′dōz′) *v.* **·dozed, ·doz·ing** *v.t.* **1** *U.S. Slang* To intimidate; bully. **2** To clear, dig, scrape, etc., with a bulldozer. —*v.i.* **3** To operate a bulldozer. [?<BULL, *adj.* + DOSE, with ref. to the violent or excessive treatment given to the victim.]

bull·doz·er (bōōl′dō′zər) *n.* **1** A powerful, tractor-driven machine equipped with a heavy steel blade: used for clearing wooded areas and moving soil in road construction. **2** A power-driven machine for stamping heads on wires and small rods. **3** *U.S. Slang* One who bulldozes.

bull dust *Austral.* **1** Dry silt. **2** *Slang* Nonsense; foolish chatter; bluff.

Bul·len (bōōl′ən), **Anne** See BOLEYN.

Bull·ers of Buch·an (bo͝ol′ərz əv bukh′ən) A large, hollow rock formation on the east coast of Scotland into which the sea rushes at high tide; 200 feet deep and 50 feet in diameter.

bul·let (bo͝ol′it) *n.* **1** A small projectile for a firearm. **2** Any small ball. [<F *boulette,* dim. of *boule* ball]

bul·le·tin (bo͝ol′ə·tən) *n.* **1** A brief official summary. **2** A brief news statement, issued in printed form, as in a newspaper, or by word of mouth, as transmitted by radio. **3** A periodical publication, as of the proceedings of a society. —*v.t.* To make public by bulletin. [<F <Ital. *bulletino,* double dim. of *bulla* <L, edict] —**bul′le·tin·ist** *n.*

bul·let·proof (bo͝ol′it·pro͞of′) *adj.* Not penetrable by bullets.

bull·fight (bo͝ol′fīt′) *n.* A combat in an arena between men and a bull or bulls, popular among the Spanish, Portuguese, and Spanish Americans. —**bull′fight′ing** *n.* —**bull′fight′er** *n.*

bull·finch[1] (bo͝ol′finch′) *n.* **1** A European singing bird (genus *Pyrrhula*) having a short, stout bill and red breast. **2** Any of certain American grosbeaks. [<BULL, *adj.* + FINCH]

bull·finch[2] (bo͝ol′finch′) *n. Brit.* A strong high hedge. [Prob. alter. of BULL FENCE]

bull·frog (bo͝ol′frog′, -frôg′) *n.* A large North American frog *(Rana catesbiana)* with a deep bass croak.

bull·head (bo͝ol′hed′) *n.* **1** One of various fishes (genus *Ameiurus*) with a broad head, as the horned pout *(A. nebulosus).* **2** The sculpin. **3** A plover (family *Charadriidae*). **4** The goldeneye duck *(Glaucionetta clangula).* **5** An obstinate, stupid person.

bull–head·ed (bo͝ol′hed′id) *adj.* Stupid and obstinate.

bull·horn (bo͝ol′hôrn′) *n.* An electrical, handheld voice amplifier resembling a megaphone.

bul·lion[1] (bo͝ol′yən) *n.* Gold or silver uncoined or in mass, as in bars, plates, or the like. See synonyms under MONEY. [<AF *bullion,* OF *bouillon* boiling, melting < *bouillir* boil; ? infl. by OF *billon* base metal]

bul·lion[2] (bo͝ol′yən) *n.* A heavy, twisted, cord fringe, especially that of which the cords are covered with fine gold or silver wire. [<OF *bouillon* <L *bulla* bubble]

bull·ish[1] (bo͝ol′ish) *adj.* **1** Of or characteristic of a bull. **2** Characterized by or suggesting a trend toward higher prices, as in the stock market; also, hopeful of such a trend. **3** Confidently optimistic. —**bull′ish·ly** *adv.* —**bull′ish·ness** *n.*

bull·ish[2] (bo͝ol′ish) *adj.* Having the character of a bull or blunder.

Bul·litt (bo͝ol′it), **William Christian,** 1891–1967, U.S. diplomat.

bull moose The male moose.

Bull Moose A member of the Progressive political party formed in 1912 by Theodore Roosevelt.

bull·neck (bo͝ol′nek′) *n.* **1** A short, thick neck like that of a bull. **2** The canvasback. **3** The American scaup duck.

bull nose A form of rhinitis occurring in swine, caused by a micro-organism *(Actinomyces necrophorus)* and characterized by enlargement and necrosis of the nose.

bul·lock (bo͝ol′ək) *n.* **1** A gelded bull; a steer or an ox. **2** Formerly, a bull calf. [OE *bulluc*]

bull·pen (bo͝ol′pen′) *n. U.S.* **1** An enclosure for one or more bulls; also, an enclosure for a bullfight. **2** *Colloq.* A corral for temporary detention of prisoners; hence, a jail. **3** *Colloq.* The living quarters in a lumber camp. **4** A place of practice for baseball pitchers who may be needed in an emergency.

bull·pout (bo͝ol′pout′) *n.* A catfish; bullhead.

bull·ring (bo͝ol′ring′) *n.* A circular enclosure for bullfights.

bull·roar·er (bo͝ol′rôr′ər, -rōr′-) *n.* **1** A toy consisting of a small slat of wood fastened to a thong or string, to be whirled in the air to produce a roaring sound. **2** A larger device of this kind used by Australian aborigines in their religious rites.

Bull Run A creek in NE Virginia; scene of Civil War battles, 1861 and 1862, in which Union forces were defeated. See MANASSAS.

bull's–eye (bo͝olz′ī′) *n.* **1** The center of a target, or a shot that hits it. **2** A circular window or mirror. **3** A thick disk or lens of glass, or a lantern fitted with one. **4** *Naut.* A small wooden block perforated for ropes. **5** A thick, rounded lump of candy, usually flavored with peppermint. **6** An old-fashioned, thick, open-faced watch. **7** A depression or wave in mirror glass which causes a distortion of the image. **8** *Meteorol.* **a** A small area of clear sky marking the center of a cyclone storm; the eye of the storm. **b** A small detached cloud indicating the top of a developing bull's-eye squall.

bull's–eye squall *Meteorol.* A fair-weather squall off the coasts of South Africa: usually identified by the detached cloud marking the peak of its invisible vortex.

bull snake A gopher snake.

bull–strong (bo͝ol′strông′, -strong′) *adj.* Strong enough to hold a bull: said of fences.

bull terrier See under TERRIER.

bull–tongue (bo͝ol′tung′) *n.* In cotton farming, a heavy plow with a nearly vertical moldboard.

bull·weed (bo͝ol′wēd′) *n.* Knapweed.

bull·whip (bo͝ol′hwip′) *n.* A long, tough whip used by teamsters. —*v.t.* **·whipped, ·whip·ping** To strike or beat with a bullwhip.

bul·ly[1] (bo͝ol′ē) *adj.* **bul·li·er, bul·li·est** **1** *Colloq.* Excellent, admirable. **2** Quarrelsome; blustering. **3** Jolly; dashing; gallant. —*n. pl.* **bul·lies** **1** A quarrelsome, swaggering, cowardly fellow; one who terrorizes or threatens those weaker than himself. **2** *Archaic* A hired ruffian. **3** *Obs.* A pimp. **4** *Obs.* Sweetheart; darling: a term formerly applied to both sexes. —*interj.* Well done! —*v.* **bul·lied, bul·ly·ing** *v.t.* To coerce by threats; intimidate. —*v.i.* To be quarrelsome and blustering. [Cf. Du. *boel* friend, lover]

bul·ly[2] (bo͝ol′ē) *n.* Canned or pickled beef. Also **bul′ly·beef′.** [Prob. <F *bouilli,* pp. of *bouillir* boil]

bul·ly·boy (bo͝ol′ē·boi′) *n.* A jovial fellow.

bul·ly·rag (bo͝ol′ē·rag′) *v.t.* **·ragged, ·rag·ging** To bully; intimidate. [? <BULLY, *v.* + RAG[1]]

bul·ly·tree (bo͝ol′ē·trē′) *n.* One of several tropical American trees yielding balata gum, especially *Manilkara bidentata.* Also **bul′let·wood′.**

Bü·low (bü′lō), **Prince Bernhard von,** 1849–1929, German chancellor 1900–09. —**Friedrich Wilhelm von,** 1755–1816, Prussian general at the battle of Waterloo. —**Hans Guido,** 1830–94, German orchestral conductor and composer.

bul·rush (bo͝ol′rush′) *n.* **1** A tall, rushlike plant growing in damp ground or water, as the tall sedge *(Scirpus lacustris),* the common American rush *(Juncus effusus),* and the common English cat-tail *(Typha latifolia).* **2** Papyrus. *Exodus* ii 3. [<BULL[1], *adj.* + RUSH[2]]

bul·wark (bo͝ol′wərk) *n.* **1** A defensive wall or rampart; fortification. **2** Any safeguard or defense. **3** *Naut.* The raised side of a ship, above the upper deck: usually in the plural. See synonyms under BARRIER, DEFENSE, RAMPART. —*v.t.* To surround and fortify with, or as with, a bulwark. [<MHG *bolwerc.* Akin to BOULEVARD.]

Bul·wer (bo͝ol′wər), **William Henry Lytton Earle,** 1801–72, Baron Dalling and Bulwer, English diplomat.

Bul·wer–Lyt·ton (bo͝ol′wər·lit′n) See LYTTON.

bum[1] (bum) *n.* **1** *U.S. Colloq.* A worthless or dissolute loafer; tramp. **2** A spree; debauch. —**on the bum 1** Out of order; broken. **2** Living as a vagrant. —*adj.* Bad; inferior. —*v.* **bum·med, bum·ming** *v.i.* **1** To live by sponging from others. **2** To live idly and in dissipation. —*v.t.* **3** To get by begging: to *bum* a ride. [Short for *bummer,* alter. of G *bummler* loafer, dawdler] —**bum′mer** *n.*

bum[2] (bum) *v.i.* **bummed, bum·ming** *Brit. Dial.* To hum, as a top. [Var. of BOOM[2]]

bum[3] (bum) *n. Brit. Slang* The buttocks. [ME *bom*; origin uncertain]

bum·bai·liff (bum′bā′lif) *n. Brit.* A sheriff's deputy or county-court bailiff whose duties are to levy and attach. Also **bum′bail′ey** (-bā′·lē). [<BUM[3] + BAILIFF; because he follows closely behind a person]

bum·ble (bum′bəl) *v.t.* & *v.i.* **·bled, ·bling** To bungle; confuse, especially in an officious manner. [Imit.] —**bum′bling** *adj.* & *n.*

bum·ble·bee (bum′bəl·bē′) *n.* Any of certain large, hairy, social bees (family *Bombidae*). [<dial. E *bumble,* freq. of BUM[2] + BEE[1]]

bum·ble·foot (bum′bəl·fo͝ot′) *n.* A suppurative swelling of the foot in domestic fowls, arising from a bacterial infection of a cut or bruise.

bum·boat (bum′bōt′) *n.* A boat employed in peddling provisions and small wares among vessels in port or offshore. [<LG *bumboot* broad-beamed boat]

bum·kin (bum′kin) *n. Naut.* A projecting boom on a vessel, placed at each side of the bow to haul the foretack to, or on the quarter, for the standing part of the mainbrace, or over the stern to extend the mizzen sail: also *bumpkin.* [<Du. *boomkin,* dim. of *boom* tree, beam]

bum·ming[1] (bum′ing) *n.* **1** Carousing. **2** Living like a bum.

bum·ming[2] (bum′ing) *adj. Scot.* Humming.

bump (bump) *v.t.* **1** To come into contact with; knock into. **2** To cause to knock into or against. **3** *U.S. Colloq.* To displace, as from a position or seat. —*v.i.* **4** To come into contact; knock together. **5** To move or proceed with jerks and jolts. —**to bump off** *Slang* To kill, especially with a gun. —*n.* **1** A violent impact or collision; a heavy blow. **2** A protuberance like that caused by a blow. **3** The act of bumping. **4** One of the protuberances of the human head said to denote a certain faculty. **5** *Aeron.* A gust of wind striking the surface of an aircraft with the effect of a sharp blow. [Imit.]

bump·er[1] (bum′pər) *n.* **1** Something that either bumps or causes a bump. **2** A buffer, as on a railroad car. **3** A guard on the front or rear of an automobile to attenuate the shock of collision.

bump·er[2] (bum′pər) *n.* A cup or glass filled to the brim. —*adj.* Unusually full or large: a *bumper* crop. —*v.t.* **1** To fill to the brim. **2** To drink toasts to. —*v.i.* **3** To drink from bumpers. [? Alter. of F *bombarde* large cup, infl. in form by BUMP]

bump·i·ness (bum′pē·nis) *n.* **1** The state or condition of being bumpy. **2** *Aeron.* A condition of irregular atmospheric density, as from rising or falling air currents, which results in sudden jolts to aircraft.

bump·kin (bump′kin) *n.* **1** An awkward rustic; a clown; a lout. **2** A bumkin. [? <Du. *boomkin* little tree, block. Cf. BLOCKHEAD.]

bumps (bumps) *n. pl.* In motion pictures, a series of low-frequency sounds caused by irregularities in the sound track.

bump·tious (bump′shəs) *adj.* Aggressively and offensively self-conceited. —**bump′tious·ly** *adv.* —**bump′tious·ness** *n.*

bump·y (bum′pē) *adj.* **bump·i·er, bump·i·est** Having bumps or bumpiness; jolty. —**bump′i·ly** *adv.* —**bump′i·ness** *n.*

bum's rush *Slang* Forced expulsion or ejection, as of an undesirable person.

bun[1] (bun) *n.* **1** A small bread roll, sometimes sweetened or glazed with sugar, containing currants, citron, etc. **2** *Brit.* A small sweet cake. **3** A roll of hair shaped like a bun and worn at the nape of the neck. [ME *bunne*; origin uncertain]

bun[2] (bun) *n. Brit. Dial.* A rabbit's tail; hence, a rabbit or squirrel. [Cf. Irish *bun* stump]

bu·na (bo͞o′nə, byo͞o′-) *n. Chem.* A synthetic rubber made by the polymerization of butadiene with certain other substances, as styrene. Also **Bu′na.** [<BU(TADIENE) + NA(TRIUM)]

bunch (bunch) *n.* **1** A compact collection, usually of objects of the same kind; also, a group; cluster. **2** A hunch; hump; protuberance. —*v.t.* & *v.i.* **1** To make into or form bunches or groups. **2** To gather, as in pleats or folds. [ME *bonche, bunche*; origin unknown]

bunch·ber·ry (bunch′ber′ē, -bər·ē) *n. pl.* **·ries** The dwarf cornel *(Cornus canadensis)* with bright red, closely clustered berries.

Bunche (bunch), **Ralph Johnson,** 1904–1971, U.S. educator and United Nations statesman.

bunch·flow·er (bunch′flou′ər) *n.* A plant *(Melanthium virginicum)* of the lily family of the United States, having linear leaves and a pyramidal panicle of greenish flowers.

bunch grass Any of various grasses growing in clumps or tufts.

bun·co (bung′kō) *n. U.S. Colloq.* A swindling game in which confederates join to rob a stranger. —*v.t.* To swindle or bilk. Also spelled *bunko.* [Prob. <Sp. *banco,* a card game]

bun·combe (bung′kəm) *n.* **1** Bombastic speechmaking or any specious utterance for political effect. **2** Humbug. Also spelled *bunkum.* [from *Buncombe* County, N.C., whose Congressman (1819–21) often insisted on making empty, unimportant speeches "for Buncombe"]

bun·co-steer·er (bung′kō·stir′ər) *n. U.S. Slang* A swindler.

bund[1] (bund) *n.* **1** An embankment or dike. **2** A thoroughfare along a waterfront. —**the Bund,** an esplanade in Shanghai, China. [<Hind. *band*]

bund[2] (bŏŏnd, bund; *Ger.* bŏŏnt) *n.* A confederation; league; a society. [<G]

Bund (bŏŏnt) *n. pl.* **Bün·de** (bün′də) **1** A confederation of German states established in 1867. **2** The German-American Bund, a former pro-Nazi organization in the United States.

Bun·del·khand (bŏŏn′dəl·khund) A region in Vindhya Pradesh and Uttar Pradesh states, central India; formerly a subdivision, **Bundelkhand Agency,** of the Central India Agency, including about 30 native states.

bun·der (bun′dər) *n. Anglo-Indian* In the Orient, a landing place: the Apollo *bunder* at Bombay. [<Hind. *bandar*]

Bun·des·rat (bŏŏn′dəs·rät′) *n.* A federal council, as formerly in Germany or Austria. Also **Bun′des·rath′.** [<G, lit., council of the league]

bun·dle (bun′dəl) *n.* **1** A number of things or a quantity of anything bound together. **2** Anything folded or wrapped and tied up; a package. **3** A group; collection. **4** *Bot.* A cluster of one or more elementary tissues lying across other tissues: also called *vascular bundle.* ◆ Collateral adjective: *fascicular.* —*v.* **·dled, ·dling** *v.t.* **1** To tie, roll or otherwise secure in a bundle. **2** To send away or place in summarily or in haste: with *away, off, out,* or *into.* —*v.i.* **3** To leave or proceed hastily or in a bustling manner: They *bundled* down the stairs. **4** To practice bundling. [<MDu. *bondel,* dim. of *bond* group. Akin to BIND.] —**bun′dler** *n.*

bun·dling (bun′dling) *n.* An old courting custom, prevalent in New England, in which sweethearts lay or slept together in bed without undressing.

bung (bung) *n.* **1** A stopper for the large hole through which a cask is filled. **2** Bunghole. **3** A large sac between the small intestine and the colon of beef viscera. —*v.t.* **1** To close with or as with a bung: often with *up* or *down.* **2** *Slang* To damage; maul: usually with *up.* [<MDu. *bonghe*]

bun·ga·low (bung′gə·lō) *n.* **1** In India, a one-storied house with wide verandas. **2** A small house or cottage, usually with one or one and a half stories. **3** The blimp of a motion-picture camera. [<Hind. *banglā* Bengalese <*Banga* Bengal]

bun·gee (bung·gē′) *n. Aeron.* An apparatus, operated by the pilot of an aircraft, which restricts or controls the action of certain movable parts, as a bomb-bay door. [Origin uncertain]

bung·hole (bung′hōl′) *n.* A hole in a keg or barrel from which liquid is tapped. [<MDu. *bonghe* a stopper, plug + HOLE]

bun·gle (bung′gəl) *v.t.* & *v.i.* **·gled, ·gling** To work, make, or do (something) clumsily; botch. —*n.* An awkward, clumsy, and imperfect job or performance; botch. —**bun′gler** *n.* —**bun′gle·some** (-səm) *adj.* —**bun′gling** *adj.* —**bun′gling·ly** *adv.* [Cf. Sw. *bangla* work ineffectually]

Bun·gu·ran Islands (bŏŏng′ŏŏ·rän′) An Indonesian island group in the South China Sea; total, 816 square miles: also *Natuna Islands. Dutch* **Boen′goe·ran′ Islands.**

Bu·nin (bōō′nyin), **Ivan Alexeyevich,** 1870–1953, Russian novelist and poet.

bun·ion (bun′yən) *n. Pathol.* A painful swelling of the foot, usually at the outer side of the base of the great toe: at first an enlarged bursa, eventually producing a distortion of the bony structure. [Akin to OF *bugne* swelling]

bunk[1] (bungk) *n.* **1** A small compartment, shelf, box, or recess, etc., used as a sleeping place, as in a vessel, lodging house, sleeping car, etc. **2** A piece of timber across a lumberman's sled; also, the sled so arranged. —*v.i.* **1** To sleep in a bunk. **2** To share a bed. [Cf. MDu. *banc* bench, shelf and BANK[3] (def. 2)]

bunk[2] (bungk) *n. Slang* Inflated or empty speech; balderdash. [Short for BUNCOMBE]

bun·ker (bung′kər) *n.* **1** A large bin, as for coal on a ship. **2** A box or chest that serves also for a seat. **3** In golf, a sandy hollow or a mound of earth serving as an obstacle on a course. **4** *Mil.* **a** A steel and concrete fortification, usually underground. **b** A bulwark of earth erected to protect a gun emplacement. —*v.i.* To fill the coal bunkers of a ship. —*v.t.* In golf, to drive (a ball) into a bunker. [Cf. OSw. *bunke* hold of a ship and BANK[3] (def. 2)]

Bun·ker Hill (bung′kər) A hill in Charlestown, Massachusetts, near which (on *Breed's Hill*) occurred the first organized engagement of the Revolutionary War, June 17, 1775.

bunk·house (bungk′hous′) *n.* A structure used as sleeping quarters.

bunk·mate (bungk′māt′) *n.* One who shares a bunk. Also **bunk·ie** (bung′kē), **bunk′y.**

bun·ko (bung′kō), **bun·kum** (bung′kəm) See BUNCO, BUNCOMBE.

bunn (bun) *n.* Bun [1].

Bun·ner (bun′ər), **Henry Cuyler,** 1855–96, U.S. humorist.

bun·ny (bun′ē) *n. pl.* **·nies** A rabbit or squirrel: a pet name. [<BUN[2]]

bun·ny-hug (bun′ē·hug′) *n. U.S.* A dance in ragtime rhythm, popular in about 1910.

Bun·sen (bun′sən, *Ger.* bŏŏn′zən), **Robert William Eberhard,** 1811–99, German chemist and inventor.

Bun·sen burner (bun′sən) A type of gas burner in which a mixture of gas and air is burned at the top of a short metal tube, producing a very hot flame. [after R. W. E. *Bunsen*]

a b c d d e

BUNSEN BURNER
a. Complete combustion. *b.* Incomplete combustion. *c.* Non-burning mixture. *d.* Air. *e.* Gas.

bunt[1] (bunt) *v.t.* & *v.i.* **1** To strike or push as with horns; butt. **2** In baseball, to bat (the ball) lightly to the infield, without swinging the bat. —*n.* **1** A push or shove; a butt. **2** In baseball, a short hit to the infield, made by allowing a pitched ball to bounce off a loosely held bat. [Nasalized var. of BUTT[1]]

bunt[2] (bunt) *n.* **1** *Naut.* The middle or belly-ing portion of a square sail. **2** The middle, sagging part of a fishnet. **3** *Naut.* The middle part of a yard. —*v.t. Naut.* To haul up the middle part of (a square sail) in furling. —*v.i.* To swell out; belly. [Origin unknown]

bunt[3] (bunt) *n.* **1** A parasitic fungus (*Tilletia foetens*), a species of smut, which destroys the grains of wheat by converting the interior into a fetid black powder. **2** The disease caused by it: also called *stinking smut.* [Origin unknown]

bun·tal (bŏŏn·täl′) *n.* A white Philippine fiber obtained from unopened palm-leaf stems, from which a fine straw is woven. [<Tagalog]

bunt·ing[1] (bun′ting) *n.* **1** A light woolen stuff used for flags. **2** A light cotton fabric resembling cheesecloth. **3** Flags, banners, etc., collectively. [? ME *bonten* sift]

bunt·ing[2] (bun′ting) *n.* One of various birds related to the finches and sparrows: the indigo and snow *buntings.* [ME *bountyng*; origin unknown]

bunt·line (bunt′lin, -līn) *n. Naut.* A rope used in hauling a square sail of a vessel up to the yard for furling.

bun·ya-bun·ya (bun′yə·bun′yə) *n.* An evergreen tree of Australia (*Araucaria bidwillii*), of the pine family: its cones contain edible seeds. Also **bun′ya.** [< native name]

Bun·yan (bun′yən), **John,** 1628–88, English preacher and author of *Pilgrim's Progress.* —**Paul** See PAUL BUNYAN.

Bun·yip (bun′yip) *n.* In Australian folklore, a bellowing water monster who lives at the bottom of lakes and water holes, into which he draws his human victims.

Buo·na·par·te (bwô′nä·pär′tā) See BONAPARTE.

Buo·nar·ro·ti (bwô′när·rô′tē) See MICHELANGELO.

buoy (boi, bōō′ē) *n.* **1** *Naut.* A float moored on a dangerous rock or shoal or at the edge of a channel, as a guide to navigators. Many are named according to shape or function: **can buoy** (cylindrical); **nun buoy** (conical); **spar buoy** (a spar anchored at one end); **bell buoy, whistling buoy** (buoys devised to sound with the motion of the waves: used to mark dangerous shoals or harbor entrances, respectively). **2** Any device or object for keeping a person in the water afloat: also called *lifebuoy.* Compare BREECHES BUOY. —*v.t.*

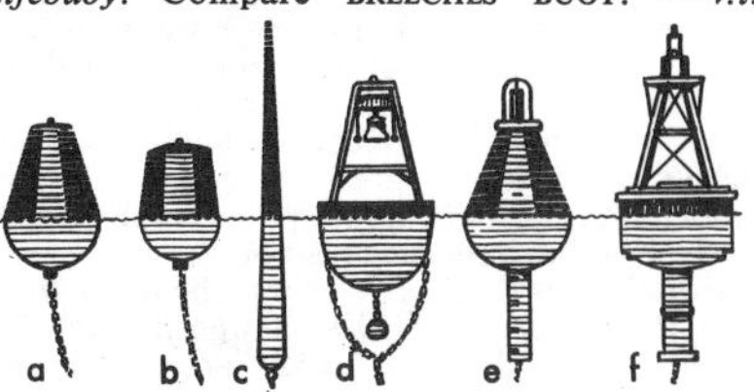

TYPES OF BUOYS
a. Nun buoy. *b.* Can buoy. *c.* Spar buoy. *d.* Bell buoy. *e.* Whistling buoy. *f.* Gas-lighted buoy.

1 To keep from sinking in a liquid; keep afloat. **2** To sustain the courage or heart of; encourage: usually with *up.* **3** *Naut.* To mark, as a channel, with buoys. [<MDu. *boeie*]

buoy·age (boi′ij, bōō′ē·ij) *n.* **1** Buoys collectively. **2** A system of buoys.

buoy·an·cy (boi′ən·sē, bōō′yən·sē) *n.* **1** The property of keeping afloat. **2** Power or tendency of a liquid or gas to keep an object afloat. **3** Resultant upward pressure of fluid on an immersed or floating body. **4** Elasticity of spirits; cheerfulness. Also **buoy′·ance.**

buoy·ant (boi′ənt, bōō′yənt) *adj.* **1** Having buoyancy. **2** Vivacious; cheerful; hopeful. See synonyms under CHEERFUL, HAPPY, SANGUINE. [Prob. <Sp. *boyante* <*boyar* float] —**buoy′ant·ly** *adv.*

bu·pres·tid (byōō·pres′tid) *n.* Any of a family (*Buprestidae*) of brilliantly colored beetles with the first and second vertical segments confluent and membranous-lobed tarsi, and whose larvae are destructive woodborers. [<L *buprestis* <Gk. *bouprēstis* <*bous* ox + *prēthein* swell]

bur[1] (bûr) **1** *Bot.* A rough or prickly flower head, or the like, as of the chestnut and burdock. **2** The burdock or other plant that bears burs. **3** A protuberance; lump; specifically, a knot or excrescence on a tree. **4** An impediment or unwelcome adherent. —*v.t.* **burred, bur·ring** To remove burs from, as wool. Also spelled *burr.* ◆ Homophones: *birr, burr.* [<Scand. Cf. Dan. *borre* bur.]

bur[2] (bûr) See BURR[1].

bu·ran (bōō·rän′) *n. Meteorol.* A violent windstorm of Siberia and the Russian steppes: a hot duststorm in summer and a blizzard in winter. Also **bu·ra** (bōō·rä′). [<Russian]

Bur·bage (bûr′bij), **Richard,** 1567?–1619, English actor; associate of Shakespeare.

Bur·bank (bûr′bangk), **Luther,** 1849–1926, U.S. horticulturist.

bur·ble (bûr′bəl) *v.i.* **·bled, ·bling** **1** To bubble; gurgle. **2** To talk excitedly and confusedly. [ME; imit.]

bur·bling (bûr′bling) *n. Aeron.* A turbulence in the airflow around an airplane, especially such as to increase the drag.

bur·bot (bûr′bət) *n. pl.* **·bots** or **·bot** A fresh-water fish (*Lota lota*) of the northern hemisphere, with barbels on the nose and chin: also called *ling.* [<F *bourbotte,* ult. <L *barbata* bearded; infl. in form by TURBOT]

Burch·field (bûrch′fēld), **Charles Ephraim,** 1893–1967, U.S. painter.

Burck·hardt (bŏŏrk′härt), **Jakob,** 1818–97, Swiss cultural historian. —**Johann Ludwig,** 1784–1817, Swiss traveler.

burd (bûrd) *n. Brit. Dial.* A maiden. Also **burd·ie** (bûr′dē). [ME *burde*; origin uncertain]

bur·den[1] (bûr′dən) *n.* **1** Something heavy that is borne or carried; responsibility; a load. **2** *Naut.* **a** The carrying capacity of a vessel. **b** The weight of the cargo. **3** The employment of carrying loads: beasts of *burden.* —*v.t.* To load or overload; oppress, as with care: *burdened* with responsibilities. See synonyms under LOAD. Also spelled *burthen.* [OE *byrthen* load]

bur·den[2] (bûr′dən) *n.* **1** Something often repeated or dwelt upon; the prevailing idea or tone: The *burden* of the speech was a desire for war. **2** A refrain repeated at the end of every stanza of a song. **3** The drone of a bagpipe. Also spelled *burthen.* [<F *bourdon* bass <LL *burdo* drone]

burden of proof The obligation resting upon one or other of the parties to a controversy, or action at law, to establish by proofs a given proposition before being entitled to receive an answer from the other side.

bur·den·some (bûr′dən·səm) *adj.* Hard or heavy to bear; oppressive. See synonyms under HEAVY, TROUBLESOME. **— bur′den·some·ly** *adv.* **— bur′den·some·ness** *n.*

bur·dock (bûr′dok) *n.* A coarse, biennial weed *(Arctium lappa)* of the composite family, with a globular bur and large roundish leaves. [<BUR + DOCK[4]]

bu·reau (byŏŏr′ō) *n. pl.* **bu·reaus** or **bu·reaux** (byŏŏr′ōz) **1** A chest of drawers for clothing, etc., commonly provided with a mirror. **2** A public department. **3** An organized staff of literary workers, etc.; also, the place where the work is done. **4** A writing desk; escritoire. [<F, cloth-covered desk <OF *burel* coarse woolen cloth]

bu·reauc·ra·cy (byŏŏ·rok′rə·sē) *n. pl.* **·cies** **1** Government by bureaus, especially by rigid and arbitrary routine. **2** Government officials collectively.

bu·reau·crat (byŏŏr′ə·krat) *n.* **1** A member of a bureaucracy. **2** An official who governs by rigid routine. **— bu′reau·crat′ic** or **·i·cal** *adj.* **— bu′reau·crat′i·cal·ly** *adv.*

bu·rette (byŏŏ·ret′) *n.* **1** *Chem.* A finely graduated glass tube from which a small quantity of a solution can be drawn off at a time. **2** A decorated cruet; an altar cruet. Also **bu·ret′.** [<F, dim. of *buire* vase <OF *buise* drink]

burg (bûrg) *n.* **1** *Colloq.* A town; city. **2** *Archaic* A fortified place. [OE *burg.* Related to BOROUGH.]

bur·gage (bûr′gij) *n.* **1** In feudal law, a tenure by which houses and lands in an ancient borough were held of the lord at a certain yearly rent; land so held. **2** A form of tenure by which property in royal burgs is held of the king for the nominal service of watching and warding. [<OF <Med. L *burgagium* < *burgus* town <Gmc.]

Bur·gas (bŏŏr·gäs′) A port on the **Gulf of Burgas,** the westernmost inlet of the Black Sea in eastern Bulgaria.

bur·gee (bûr′jē) *n. Naut.* A triangular or swallow-tailed pennant flown on vessels for identification. [Origin unknown]

Bur·gen·land (bŏŏr′gən·länt) An autonomous province of eastern Austria; 1,526 square miles; capital, Eisenstadt.

bur·geon (bûr′jən) *v.t.* & *v.i.* To put forth (buds or shoots); sprout. [< *n.*] **—** *n.* **1** A bud; sprout. **2** A boss for protecting the binding of a book. Also spelled *bourgeon.* [<OF *burjon*]

Burg·er (bûr′gər), **Warren Earl,** born 1907, U.S. jurist; chief justice of the Supreme Court 1969–.

bur·gess (bûr′jis) *n.* **1** A freeman, citizen, or officer of a borough or burg. **2** In colonial times, a member of the lower house of the legislature, the **House of Burgesses,** of Maryland or Virginia: now called *delegate.* **3** *Brit.* Formerly, a member of Parliament for a borough or university. [<OF *burgeis* < *bourg* town <Gmc. Doublet of BOURGEOIS[1].] **— bur′·gess-ship** *n.*

Bur·gess (bûr′jis), **(Frank) Gelett,** 1866–1951, U.S. humorist and illustrator.

burgh (bûrg, *Scot.* bûr′ō, -ə) *n.* **1** In Scots law, a corporate body erected by charter of the sovereign, consisting of the inhabitants of the district designated in the charter; a borough. **2** *Archaic* A castle or fortification. [Var. of BOROUGH] **— burgh·al** (bûr′gəl) *adj.*

Burgh (bûrg), **Hubert de,** died 1243, English statesman.

burgh·er (bûr′gər) *n.* **1** A citizen of a burgh. **2** An early Dutch inhabitant or citizen of New York. [<Du. *burger* < *burg* town. Akin to BURGESS.]

Burgh·ley (bûr′lē), **Lord** See CECIL. Also **Bur′leigh.**

bur·glar (bûr′glər) *n.* One who commits a burglary. See synonyms under ROBBER. [<Med. L *burglator* ? <OF *bourg* dwelling (<Gmc.) + *laire* robbery (<L *latro* robber)]

burglar alarm A device, usually electric, by which an alarm is given, by bell, gong, flashing light, etc., upon forcible intrusion of a building, safe, etc.

bur·glar·i·ous (bər·glâr′ē·əs) *adj.* Relating to or of the nature of a burglary. **— bur·glar′i·ous·ly** *adv.*

bur·glar·ize (bûr′glə·rīz) *v.t.* **·ized, ·iz·ing** **1** To commit burglary upon. **2** To enter or steal by burglary.

bur·gla·ry (bûr′glər·ē) *n. pl.* **·ries** The breaking and entering of a building (primarily of a dwelling, by night), with felonious intent.

bur·gle (bûr′gəl) *v.t.* & *v.i.* **·gled ·gling** *Colloq.* To commit burglary; burglarize. [Back formation <BURGLAR]

bur·go·mas·ter (bûr′gə·mas′tər, -mäs′-) *n.* **1** A Dutch, Flemish, German, or Austrian municipal magistrate; a mayor. **2** A large arctic gull *(Larus hyperboreus).* [<Du. *burgemeester*]

bur·go·net (bûr′gə·net) *n. Archaic* A light, open helmet. [<OF *bourguignotte* Burgundian <*Bourgogne* Burgundy, where first used]

bur·goo (bûr′gōō, bər·gōō′) *n. pl.* **·goos** **1** A kind of oatmeal porridge or mush formerly served at sea. **2** *U.S. Dial.* A thick, highly seasoned soup or stew of meat; also, the meals at which this is served, especially picnics and barbecues. Also **bur′gout** (-gōō). [Cf. Turkish *burghul* porridge]

Bur·gos (bŏŏr′gōs) A city in northern Spain; capital of the former kingdom of Castile.

Bur·goyne (bər·goin′), **John,** 1723–92, English general, surrendered to Gates at Saratoga, 1777.

bur·grave (bûr′grāv) *n.* The governor or lord of a fortified town or a military fortress. [<G *burg* walled town + *graf* count]

Bur·gun·dy (bûr′gən·dē) A region of east central France; formerly a kingdom, duchy, and province: French *Bourgogne.* **— Bur·gun·di·an** (bər·gun′dē·ən) *adj.* & *n.*

Bur·gun·dy (bûr′gən·dē) *n. pl.* **·dies** A kind of red or white wine originally made in Burgundy.

Burgundy Gate The Belfort Gap. *French* **Porte de Bourgogne** (pôrt də bŏŏr·gôn′y′).

bur·i·al (ber′ē·əl) *n.* The burying of a dead body; sepulture. [OE *byrgels* tomb]

bur·i·er (ber′ē·ər) *n.* One who or that which buries.

bu·rin (byŏŏr′in) *n.* **1** An engraver's tool; graver. **2** The style or manner of execution of an engraver.

BURINS
a. For engraving on wood.
b. For carving copper or stone.
c. For carving steel.
d. For use by mechanics.

burke (bûrk) *v.t.* **burked, burk·ing** **1** To murder by suffocating, so as to leave no marks. **2** To get rid of by quietly suppressing; dispose of. [after William *Burke,* 1792–1829, Irish murderer who sold his victims' bodies for dissection]

Burke (bûrk), **Edmund,** 1729–97, British orator, writer, and statesman born in Ireland.

burl (bûrl) *n.* **1** A knot or lump in wool or cloth. **2** A large, wartlike excrescence, usually a flattened hemisphere, formed on the trunks of trees. **3** A veneer made from it. **—** *v.t.* To dress (cloth) by removing burls, loose thread, etc. ◆ Homophone: *birl.* [<OF *bourle* tuft of wool <L *burra* shaggy hair] **— burled** *adj.* **— burl′er·** *n.*

bur·lap (bûr′lap) *n.* A coarse fabric resembling canvas, made of jute, flax, hemp, or cotton: used for wrapping, bagging, etc. [Origin uncertain]

bur·lesque (bər·lesk′) *n.* **1** Ludicrous imitation or representation; broad caricature; travesty. **2** A product of such imitation, as a literary or dramatic work intended to produce laughter by its caricature or satire. **3** *U.S.* A theatrical entertainment marked by low comedy, strip-tease, etc. See synonyms under CARICATURE. **—** *v.* **·lesqued, ·les·quing** *v.t.* To represent by grotesque parody or ridicule. **—** *v.i.* To use burlesque. **—** *adj.* Marked by ludicrous incongruity or broad caricature. [<F <Ital. *burlesco* < *burla* joke] **— bur·les′quer** *n.*

bur·ley (bûr′lē) *n.* A fine, light tobacco used chiefly in plug form for chewing, and grown principally in Kentucky. Also **Bur′ley.** [? after *Burley,* name of a grower]

Bur·lin·game (bûr′lin·gām, -ling·gām), **Anson,** 1820–70, U.S. diplomat.

Bur·ling·ton (bûr′ling·tən) The largest city in Vermont, on Lake Champlain.

bur·ly[1] (bûr′lē) *adj.* **bur·li·er, bur·li·est** Large of body; bulky; stout; lusty. See synonyms under CORPULENT. [ME *borlich;* origin unknown] **— bur′li·ly** *adv.* **— bur′li·ness** *n.*

bur·ly[2] (bûr′lē) *adj.* Having burls or knots, as a tree.

Bur·ma The former name of Myanmar, a country in SE Asia bordered by India and Bangladesh on the western side and China, Laos, and Thailand on the east; 261,228 square miles; capital, Rangoon (Yangon); pop. 43,000,000; the coastal border is on the Bay of Bengal. Formerly **the Union of Burma,** (1948–1989). Although the borders remained the same after 1989, the name was changed to reflect the non-Burmese population of the country. *adj.* & *n.* **— Burman.**

Bur·mese *n.* **1** *usu. pl.* The ethnic Burmans from Myanmar (Burma), or their language. The other ethnic groups of Myanmar are the Karens, Shans, Kachins, Chins, and Chinese. **2** A native or inhabitant of Burma. **3** The Sino-Tibetan language of Burma, written in the Pali alphabet. **—** *adj.* **-mese** Of or pertaining to the ethnic Burmans, or their language.

burn[1] (bûrn) *v.* **burned** or **burnt, burn·ing** *v.t.* **1** To destroy or consume by fire. **2** To set afire; ignite. **3** To injure or kill by fire; execute by fire. **4** To injure or damage by friction, heat, steam, etc.; scald; wither. **5** To produce by fire, as a hole in a suit. **6** To brand; also, to cauterize. **7** To finish or harden by intense heat; fire. **8** To use; employ, so as to give off light, heat, etc. **9** To cause a feeling of heat in: The pepper *burned* his tongue. **10** To sunburn. **11** *Chem.* To cause to undergo combustion. **12** *Slang* To electrocute. **13** *Slang* To cheat. **—** *v.i.* **14** To be on fire; blaze. **15** To be destroyed or scorched by fire; undergo change by fire. **16** To give off light, heat, etc.; shine. **17** To die by fire. **18** To appear or feel hot: He *burns* with fever. **19** To be eager, excited, or inflamed. **20** *Chem.* To oxidize; undergo combustion. **21** *Slang* To be electrocuted. **— to burn down** To be razed by fire. **— to burn one's fingers** To suffer from taking part in. **— to burn out** **1** To become extinguished through lack of fuel. **2** To destroy or wear out by heat, friction, etc. **3** To burn up the house, store, or property of. **4** To drive out by heat. **— to burn the candle at both ends** To exhaust one's strength by overwork or dissipation. **— to burn up** **1** To consume by fire. **2** *Slang* To make or become irritated or enraged. **—** *n.* **1** An effect or injury from burning; a burnt place. **2** A brand. **3** The process of burning. **4** *Usually pl.* A defective area in window glass caused by overheating in the annealing furnace. **5** A place where vegetation has been burned away, in a forest, on the prairie, etc. [Fusion of OE *beornan* be on fire and OE *bærnan* set afire]

Synonyms (verb): blaze, brand, cauterize, char, consume, cremate, flame, flash, ignite, incinerate, kindle, scorch, singe. To *burn* is to effect either partial change or complete combustion: to *burn* wood in the fire; to *burn* one's hand on a hot stove; the sun *burns* the face. One *brands* with a hot iron, but *cauterizes* with some corrosive substance, as silver nitrate. *Cremate* is now used specifically for *consuming* a dead body by intense heat. To *kindle* is to *ignite,* the scientific word for the same thing. To *scorch* and to *singe* are superficial, and to *char* usually so. Both *kindle* and *burn* have extensive figurative use. Compare LIGHT. *Antonyms:* cool, extinguish, smother, stifle, subdue.

burn[2] (bûrn) *n. Scot.* A brook or rivulet: also spelled *bourn, bourne.*

Burne-Jones (bûrn′jōnz′), **Sir Edward,** 1833–98, English painter.

burn·er (bûr′nər) *n.* **1** One who or that which burns. **2** The light-giving or flame-giving part of a lamp, etc.

bur·net (bûr′nit) *n.* Any of several perennial herbs (genus *Sanguisorba*) of the rose family, with alternate, pinnate leaves and small flowers in a dense head or spike. [Var. of BRUNETTE]

Bur·nett (bər·net′), **Frances Hodgson,** 1849–1924, U.S. novelist.

Bur·ney (bûr′nē), **Fanny,** 1752–1840, Madame d'Arblay, English novelist: original name Frances Burney.

bur·nie (bûr′nē) *n. Scot.* A little burn; brooklet.

burn·ing (bûr′ning) *adj.* Consuming or being consumed by fire; intense; vehement; exciting. See synonyms under ARDENT, EAGER, HOT. —*n.* **1** A state or sensation of inflammation. **2** A destruction or putting to death by fire. **3** The baking, as of brick or pottery. See synonyms under FIRE.

burn·ing·bush (bûr′ning·bŏŏsh′) *n.* **1** The wahoo. **2** The strawberry bush.

burning glass A convex lens for concentrating the sun's rays upon an object so as to heat or ignite it.

bur·nish (bûr′nish) *v.t. & v.i.* To polish by friction; make or become brilliant or shining. —*n.* Polish; luster; brightness. [OF *burniss-*, stem of *burnir* polish] —**bur′nish·ment** *n.*

bur·nish·er (bûr′nish·ər) *n.* **1** One who burnishes. **2** A tool with a smooth, rounded head used for giving a lustrous surface to metal, porcelain, etc. **3** A tool used to soften the hard lines of an engraving.

Burn·ley (bûrn′lē) A county borough in eastern Lancashire, England.

bur·noose (bər·nōōs′, bûr′·nōōs) *n.* A cloak with hood, worn by Arabs and Moors. Also **bur·nous′, bur·nus′.** [<F *burnous* <Arabic *burnus*]

burn·out (bûrn′out′) *n.* **1** *Agric.* A severe parching of the soil in areas subjected to prolonged or excessive solar heat. **2** The point at which one of the parts of a rocket or guided missile drops off the main assembly after having completed its work.

BURNOOSE

Burns (bûrnz), **Robert,** 1759–1796, Scottish poet.

burn·sides (bûrn′sīdz) *n. pl.* Side whiskers and mustache worn with closely shaven chin. [after Ambrose E. *Burnside,* 1824–81, U.S. major general]

burnt (bûrnt) A past tense and past participle of BURN. —*adj.* **1** Affected or consumed by fire; charred. **2** Diseased, as grain.

burnt cork A paste of powdered charred cork mixed with water: formerly used by actors to simulate Negro coloring.

burnt ocher A permanent, brick-red pigment made by heating ocher in a furnace.

burnt offering An animal, food, etc., burnt upon an altar as a sacrifice or offering to a god.

burnt orange A shade of light orange, with a brownish cast.

burnt sienna Raw sienna, calcined or roasted, noted for its dark brown color: used as an artist's pigment.

burnt umber A reddish-brown pigment made by calcining raw umber.

burp (bûrp) *n. Colloq.* A belch. —*v.t. & v.i.* To belch or cause to belch. [Imit.]

burr[1] (bûr) **1** A roughness or rough edge, especially one left on metal in casting or cutting. **2** A tool or device that raises a burr. **3** A dentist's drill with rough knothead: also **burr drill. 4** A millstone made of burrstone: also spelled *buhr.* **5** The lobe of the ear. **6** A metal ring on the staff of a lance or handle of a battle-ax to keep the hand from slipping. **7** A halo around the moon or a star. **8** A blank punched out of a sheet of metal. **9** A washer to be slipped upon the end of a rivet before swaging, as in riveting leather. **10** A partly vitrified brick. **11** A hard lump of ore imbedded in a vein of softer material. **12** Bur[1]. —*v.t.* **1** To form a rough edge on. **2** To remove a rough edge from. —*v.i.* **3** To operate a dentist's drill. Also spelled *bur.* ◆ Homophone: *birr* [Var. of BUR[1]]

burr[2] (bûr) *n.* **1** A rough guttural sound of *r* caused by the vibration of the uvula against the back part of the tongue: common in the north of England, but not to be confused with the Scottish trill. **2** Any rough, dialectal pronunciation: the Scottish *burr.* **3** A whirring sound; a buzz. —*v.t.* **1** To pronounce with a rough or guttural articulation. —*v.i.* **2** To speak with a burr. **3** To whir. Also spelled *bur.* ◆ Homophone: *birr.* [Imit.]

Burr (bûr), **Aaron,** 1756–1836, American lawyer and statesman; vice president of the United States 1801–05.

bur reed An herb (genus *Sparganium*), with ribbon-shaped leaves and spherical burlike fruit.

bur·ro (bûr′ō, bŏŏr′ō) *n. pl.* **·ros** A small donkey, used as a pack animal. [<Sp.]

Bur·roughs (bûr′ōz), **John,** 1837–1921, U.S. naturalist and writer.

bur·row (bûr′ō) *n.* **1** A hole made in and under the ground, as by a rabbit, etc., for habitation. **2** A mound or barrow. —*v.t.* **1** To make by burrowing. **2** To perforate with or as with burrows. —*v.i.* **3** To live or hide in or as in a burrow. **4** To make a burrow or hole. **5** To dig into, under, or through something; bore. ◆ Homophone: *borough.* [ME *borow.* Related to BOROUGH.] —**bur′·row·er** *n.*

burrowing owl Ground owl.

burr·stone (bûr′stōn′) *n.* A cellular, compact siliceous rock used for making millstones: also spelled *buhrstone, burstone.*

bur·ry (bûr′ē) *adj.* Having or resembling burs; rough; prickly.

bur·sa (bûr′sə) *n. pl.* **·sae** (-sē) **1** *Anat.* A pouch or saclike cavity; especially, one containing a viscid fluid and located at points of friction in the bodies of vertebrates. **2** *Pathol.* A cyst or abnormal sac. [<Med. L, sack, pouch]

Bur·sa (bŏŏr′sä) See BRUSA.

bur·sal (bûr′səl) *adj.* **1** Of or pertaining to a bursa. **2** Of or pertaining to the public revenue.

bur·sar (bûr′sər, -sär) *n.* A treasurer, as of a college. [<Med. L *bursarius* treasurer] —**bur·sar·i·al** (bər·sâr′ē·əl) *adj.*

bur·sa·ry (bûr′sər·ē) *n. pl.* **·ries 1** The treasury of a public institution or a religious order. **2** *Scot.* A grant for the maintenance of beneficiary students.

Bur·schen·schaft (bŏŏr′shən·shäft′) *n. pl.* **·schaf·ten** (-shäf′tən) *German* A students' association, especially one operated as a social organization; a fraternity.

burse (bûrs) *n.* **1** A purse. **2** *Eccl.* A lined case used to carry the folded corporal to and from the altar. **3** A scholarship. [<F *bourse* <LL *bursa* wallet <Gk. *byrsa* hide]

bur·seed (bûr′sēd′) *n.* An Old World stickseed (*Lappulla echinata*), naturalized in Canada and the northern United States.

bur·ser·a·ceous (bûr′sə·rā′shəs) *adj. Bot.* Designating or belonging to a small family (*Burseraceae*) of tropical balsamiferous or resinous polypetalous trees or shrubs with alternate compound leaves: the resin, leaves, and roots are used medicinally. [<NL *Burseraceae,* after J. *Burser,* 1603–89, German botanist]

bur·si·form (bûr′sə·fôrm) *adj.* Pouch-shaped; saclike.

bur·si·tis (bər·sī′tis) *n. Pathol.* Inflammation of a bursa.

burst (bûrst) *v.* **burst, burst·ing** *v.i.* **1** To break open or come apart suddenly and violently; explode, as from internal force. **2** To be full to the point of breaking open; bulge. **3** To issue forth or enter suddenly or violently. **4** To appear, begin; become audible or evident, etc.: A sound *burst* upon their ears. **5** To give sudden expression to passion, grief, etc.: to *burst* into tears; also, to be filled with violent emotion: He was *bursting* with rage. —*v.t.* **6** To cause to break open suddenly or violently; force open; puncture. **7** To fill or cause to swell to the point of breaking open. —*n.* **1** A sudden or violent explosion, rending, or disruption. **2** *Mil.* **a** The explosion of a bomb or shell on impact or in the air. **b** The number of bullets fired by one pressure on the trigger of an automatic weapon: a short *burst.* **3** A sudden effort; spurt; rush. **4** A sudden opening to view; prospect. [OE *berstan*]

burst·er (bûr′stər) *n.* **1** One who bursts. **2** *Mil.* An explosive which breaks open and scatters the contents of chemical shells, bombs, or mines.

bur·stone (bûr′stōn′) See BURRSTONE.

bur·then (bûr′thən) See BURDEN.

bur·ton (bûr′tən) *n. Naut.* A light hoisting tackle, usually one kept hooked to the pendant at the topmasthead of a vessel. [Origin uncertain]

Bur·ton (bûr′tən), **Harold Hitz,** born 1888, U.S. jurist; associate justice of the Supreme Court 1945–59. —**Sir Richard Francis,** 1821–1890, English traveler and writer. —**Robert,** 1577–1640, English scholar, author, and clergyman.

Bur·ton-up·on-Trent (bûr′tən·ə·pon′trent′) A county borough in eastern Staffordshire, England. Also **Bur′ton-on′-Trent′.**

Bu·ru (bōō′rōō) An Indonesian island in the Banda Sea west of Ceram; 3,668 square miles. *Dutch* **Boe·roe** (bōō′rōō).

Bu·run·di (bōō·rōōn′dē) A kingdom in central Africa, part of the former UN Trust Territory of Ruanda-Urundi; 10,747 square miles; pop. about 2,000,000; capital, Usumbura.

Bu·ru·shas·ki (bōō′rōō·shas′kē) *n.* An unrelated language spoken in NW India.

bur·weed (bûr′wēd′) *n.* Any of various weeds bearing burlike fruits, as the burdock.

bury[1] (ber′ē) *v.t.* **bur·ied, bur·y·ing 1** To put (a dead body) in a grave, tomb, or the sea; perform burial rites for; inter. **2** To cover, as for concealment. **3** To end; put out of mind: to *bury* a friendship or a difference. **4** To occupy deeply; engross: He *buried* himself in study. ◆ Homophone: *berry.* [OE *byrgan*]

Synonyms: conceal, cover, entomb, hide, inter, overwhelm. Anything which is effectually *covered* and *hidden* under any mass or accumulation is *buried.* Money is *buried* in the ground; a body is *buried* in the sea; a paper is *buried* under other documents. Whatever is *buried* is *hidden* or *concealed;* but there are many ways of *hiding* or *concealing* a thing without *burying* it. So a person may be *covered* with wraps, and not *buried* under them. *Bury* may be used of any object, *entomb* and *inter* only of a dead body. Compare HIDE, IMMERSE. *Antonyms:* disclose, disinter, exhume, expose, raise, restore, reveal, show, uncover.

bur·y[2] (ber′ē) *n. Obs.* A borough; castle; manor: often in composition: *Salisbury.* ◆ Homophone: *berry.* [Var. of BOROUGH]

Bur·y (ber′ē) A county borough in SE Lancashire, England.

Bur·yat-Mon·gol Autonomous S.S.R. (bŏŏr·yät′mong′gəl) An autonomous republic in southern Siberia, Russian S.F.S.R.; 135,700 square miles; capital, Ulan-Ude.

burying beetle Sexton (def. 2).

bur·y·ing-ground (ber′ē·ing·ground′) *n.* A cemetery.

Bur·y St. Ed·munds (ber′ē sānt ed′məndz) A municipal borough in Suffolk, England.

bus (bus) *n. pl.* **bus·es** or **bus·ses 1** A large motor vehicle that carries passengers; an omnibus. **2** *Colloq.* An automobile. —*v.* **bused** or **bussed, bus·ing** or **bus·sing** *v.t.* **1** To transport by bus. —*v.i.* **2** To go by bus. **3** *Colloq.* To do the work of a bus boy. [Short form of OMNIBUS]

bus bar *Electr.* A short bar of copper or aluminum, usually uninsulated, forming a connection between two or more electrical circuits: also called *omnibus bar.*

bus boy An employee in a restaurant whose duty it is to clear tables of soiled dishes, assist the waiters, etc.

bus·by (buz′bē) *n. pl.* **·bies** A tall fur cap worn as part of the full-dress uniform of British hussars, artillerymen, and engineers. [Origin uncertain]

BUSBY

bush[1] (bŏŏsh) *n.* **1** A low, treelike or thickly branching shrub. **2** A scrubby growth, or land covered by scrub; a forest with undergrowth. **3** A bough: used as a sign for a tavern; hence, a tavern. **4** A fox's brush. **5** A bushy growth, as of hair. —**the bush 1** Country covered with thick woods and dense undergrowth. **2** A rural, arid, scrub-

covered region, especially of Australia. —*v.i.* **1** To grow or branch as or like a bush. **2** To be or become bushy. —*v.t.* **3** To protect (plants) with bushes or bushwood set round about; support with bushes. —*adj. U.S. Slang* Bush-league; small-time. [< ON *buskr*]
bush[2] (bo͞osh) *v.t.* To line with a bushing, as an axle bearing, a pivot hole, etc. —*n.* A bushing. [< MDu. *busse* box]
bush baby Any of several species (genera *Galago* and *Euoticus*) of small, agile, gregarious nocturnal primates of African forests, having fluffy fir, long tails, and large eyes. Also **bush-baby.** Also called *galago.*
bush·boy (bo͞osh′boi′) *n.* A bushman.
bush·buck (bo͞osh′buk′) *n.* A small South African forest antelope *(Tragelaphus sylvaticus)*: also *boschbok.* Also **bush′goat′.**
bush clover A North American plant *(Lespedeza capitata)* with an erect, woolly stem.
bush cranberry The cranberry tree.
bushed (bo͞osht) *adj. Colloq.* **1** Exhausted; worn out. **2** *Austral.* Lost; confused.
bush·el[1] (bo͞osh′əl) *n.* **1** A measure of capacity; four pecks, 35.238 liters, or 2150.42 cubic inches. **2** A vessel holding that amount. [< OF *boissel,* dim. of *boiste* box]
bush·el[2] (bo͞osh′əl) *v.t.* & *v.i.* To mend or alter, as men's clothes. [Cf. G *bosseln* do small jobs] —**bush′el·er, bush′el·ler** *n.* —**bush′el·man** (-mən) *n.*
bush·el·ing (bo͞osh′əl·ing) *n.* The repairing of garments.
bush·ham·mer (bo͞osh′ham′ər) *n.* A mason's hammer, used in dressing stone.
bush honeysuckle Any of various small shrubs (genus *Diervilla*) having opposite leaves and sweet-scented, reddish-yellow flowers.
bush hook A long pole with a sharp, hooked blade at the end, for cutting brush or limbs.
bu·shi·do (bo͞o′shē·dō) *n.* The code of the medieval Japanese Samurai, prescribing rigorous military training and practice, severe self-discipline, concern for personal honor, and loyalty to superiors and country. Also **Bu′shi·do.** [< Japanese, way of the warrior]
bush·ing (bo͞osh′ing) *n.* **1** A metallic lining for a hole, as in the hub of a wheel, designed to insulate or to prevent abrasion between parts. **2** A tube for insertion in a pump barrel or a pulley bore to reduce the diameter. **3** *Electr.* A lining inserted in a socket to protect an electric current.
bush jacket A hip-length jacket of strong material with a belt and four pockets.
bush·land (bo͞osh′land′) *n. Canadian* Unsettled northern forest land.
bush league *U.S. Slang* **1** In baseball, a minor league. **2** Anything minor or second-rate. —**bush′-league′** *adj.*
bush-lea·guer (bo͞osh′lē′gər) *n. U.S. Slang* **1** A player in a bush league. **2** Any person working or acting in a petty way.
bush·man (bo͞osh′mən) *n. pl.* **·men** (-mən) *Austral.* A dweller or farmer in the bush.
Bush·man (bo͞osh′mən) *n. pl.* **·men** (-mən) **1** One of a nomadic people of South Africa, considered to be related to the Pygmies. **2** The language of the Bushmen comprising many dialects, characterized by clicks, and forming a subfamily of the Khoisan family of African languages. [< Du. *boschjesman*]
bush·mas·ter (bo͞osh′mas′tər, -mäs′-) *n.* A large and venomous pit viper *(Lachesis mutus)* of Central America and tropical South America, sometimes 12 feet long.
bush pig Boschvark.
bush·rang·er (bo͞osh′rān′jər) *n.* **1** One who lives as a wanderer in the bush. **2** *Austral.* A robber or brigand; originally, an outlaw living in the bush.
bush·whack (bo͞osh′hwak′) *v.i.* **1** To cut bushes or underbrush with a bushwhacker. **2** To ride or range in the bush; fight in the bush, as a guerrilla. [< Du. *boschwachter* forest-keeper; infl. by WHACK]
bush·whack·er (bo͞osh′hwak′ər) *n.* **1** One who ranges or fights in the bush. **2** A Confederate guerrilla. **3** A stout scythe for cutting bushes; also, one who uses it. **4** A backwoodsman. **5** *Austral.* A dweller or worker in the bush.
bush·whack·ing (bo͞osh′hwak′ing) *n.* **1** Pulling a boat against the current by grabbing bushes. **2** Using underhand methods in politics. **3** Marauding; guerrilla fighting.
bush·y (bo͞osh′ē) *adj.* **bush·i·er, bush·i·est** **1** Covered with or full of bushes. **2** Like a bush; shaggy. —**bush′i·ly** *adv.* —**bush′i·ness** *n.*
bus·ied (biz′ēd) Past tense and past participle of BUSY.
bus·i·ly (biz′ə·lē) *adv.* In a busy manner; industriously.
busi·ness (biz′nis) *n.* **1** A pursuit or occupation; trade; profession; calling. **2** Commercial affairs. **3** A matter or affair. **4** Interest; concern; duty. **5** A commercial enterprise or establishment. **6** Those details other than and exclusive of dialog, by which actors portray their parts and interpret a play. **7** (biz′ē·nis) *Obs.* The state of being busy: now *busyness.* —**to mean business** To be serious. [OE *bysignis*] —**busi·ness·like** *adj.*

Synonyms: art, avocation, barter, calling, commerce, concern, craft, duty, employment, handicraft, industry, job, labor, occupation, profession, trade, trading, traffic, vocation, work. A *business* is what one follows regularly and for profit; an *occupation* is what he is engaged in, either continuously or temporarily, for any purpose, whether of profit, or of amusement, learning, philanthropy, etc. *Pursuit* is an *occupation* which one follows with ardor. A *profession* implies scholarship; as, the learned *professions.* A *vocation* or a *calling* is that to which one feels himself called, as by special fitness or sense of duty, often now also used to characterize an occupation or profession; an *avocation* is a secondary interest, including hobbies and other activities whether for pleasure or profit, that interrupt one's *vocation* or *business* or that may parallel and eventually become a vocation. A job is a piece of *business* viewed and paid for as a single undertaking; colloquially, any regular *employment* is often termed a *job. Trade* and *commerce* may be used as equivalents, but *trade* may have a more limited application; as, the *trade* of a village, the *commerce* of a nation; in the special sense, a *trade* is an *occupation* involving manual training and skilled labor. *Barter* is the direct exchange of commodities without use of money. *Work* is any application of energy to secure a result, or the result thus secured; we may speak of the *work* of an artist, or of a janitor. A single branch of productive *work* is called an *industry*; as, the steel *industry. Labor* is ordinarily used, in this connection, for unskilled *work; employment* for *work* done in the service of another. *Art* in the industrial sense is a system of rules and methods for accomplishing some practical result; as, the *art* of printing; collectively, the *arts.* A *craft* is some occupation requiring technical skill or manual dexterity, or the persons, collectively, engaged in its exercise; as, the weaver's *craft.* Compare ACTION, DUTY, TRAFFIC, TRANSACTION, WORK. *Antonyms*: idleness, inaction, inactivity, indolence, leisure, unemployment, vacation.

business card A card printed with one's name, business, and business address.
business English **1** English as used in business procedure. **2** A course in such English, including spelling, composition, etc.
business letter A letter about a business transaction, often following a certain form.
busi·ness·man (biz′nis·man′) *n. pl.* **·men** (-men′) One engaged in commercial or industrial activity. —**busi′ness·wom′an** *n. fem.*
bus·ing (bus′ing) *n.* **1** Transporting by bus. **2** The transportation of pupils by bus to schools other than in their own neighborhoods, in order to have racial balance in those schools.
busk[1] (busk) *n.* **1** A thin, elastic strip of wood, whalebone, or steel, placed in a corset or the like. **2** A corset. [< F *busc* ? < LL *boscum* bush, wood]
busk[2] (busk) *v.t. Scot.* or *Obs.* **1** To dress. **2** To prepare. [< ON *buask* get ready] —**busk′er** *n.*
busk·er (buskər) *n. Brit.* An itinerant musician or entertainer.
bus·kin (bus′kin) *n.* **1** A high shoe or half-boot reaching half-way to the knee, and strapped or laced to the ankle. **2** A laced half-boot, worn by Athenian tragic actors. **3** Tragedy. Compare SOCK[1]. [Origin uncertain]

BUSKIN

bus·kined (bus′kind) *adj.* **1** Having the feet laced in buskins, as on the stage. **2** Of or pertaining to the tragic drama. **3** Tragic, lofty, dignified.
bus·kit (bus′kit) *adj. Scot.* **1** Clothed. **2** Prepared; made ready.
bus·man (bus′mən) *n. pl.* **·men** (-mən) One who operates a bus.
busman's holiday A holiday spent by choice in activity similar to one's regular work.
Bus·ra (bus′rə) Basra. Also **Bus′rah.**
buss[1] (bus) *Colloq. n.* A kiss; smack. —*v.t.* & *v.i.* To kiss heartily. [Imit. Cf. dial. G *bussen,* Sw. *puss,* Sp. *buz* (? < L *basiare*)]
buss[2] (bo͞os, bo͝os) *n. Scot.* A bush.
buss·es (bus′iz) A plural of BUS.
Bus·so·ra (bus′ə·rə) Basra. Also **Bus′so·rah.**
bust[1] (bust) *n.* **1** The human chest or breast. **2** A piece of statuary representing the human head, shoulders, and breast. [< F *buste* < Ital. *busto* trunk of the body]
bust[2] (bust) *Slang v.t.* **1** To burst. **2** To tame; train, as a horse. **3** To make bankrupt or short of funds. **4** To reduce in rank; demote. **5** To hit; strike. —*v.i.* **6** To burst. **7** To become bankrupt or short of funds. —*n.* **1** A bankruptcy. **2** Any failure; flop; dud. **3** A spree of any kind. **4** An arrest. [Alter. of BURST]
bus·tard (bus′tərd) *n.* Any member of a family *(Otididae)* of large Old World game birds related to the plovers and cranes, especially the **great bustard** *(Otis tarda),* the largest European land bird. [< OF *bistarde, oustarde* < L *avis tarda,* lit., slow bird]
bust·er (bus′tər) *n.* **1** *Slang* Something great, large, or remarkable; a person of exceptional ability. **2** *Slang* A spree; a bust. **3** *U.S. Colloq.* Little boy: used in direct address. —**southerly buster** *Austral.* **1** A powerful southerly wind. **2** A mixed alcoholic drink.
bus·tic (bus′tik) *n.* A tree *(Dipholis salicifolia)* of southern Florida, with a very hard, strong, close-grained wood. [Origin unknown]
bus·tle[1] (bus′əl) *n.* Excited activity; noisy stir; fuss. See synonyms under TUMULT. —*v.t.* & *v.i.* **·tled, ·tling** To hurry noisily; make a stir or fuss [? Related to BUSK[2]]
bus·tle[2] (bus′əl) *n.* **1** A frame or pad, formerly worn by women on the back below the waist to distend the skirts. **2** Fullness, as of gathered material, a bow, etc., worn over the back of a skirt below the waist. [? < BUSTLE[1]]
bus·tling (bus′ling) *adj.* Active; agitated. See synonyms under ACTIVE, ALERT, BUSY. —**bus′·tling·ly** *adv.*
bus·y (biz′ē) *adj.* **bus·i·er, bus·i·est** **1** Intensely active; constantly or habitually occupied. **2** Temporarily engaged; not at leisure. **3** Officiously active; prying; meddling. **4** Pertaining to or filled with business. **5** Engaged: said of a telephone line or number. —*v.t.* **bus·ied, bus·y·ing** To make or be busy; occupy (oneself). See synonyms under OCCUPY. [OE *bysig* active]

Synonyms(adj.): active, assiduous, bustling, diligent, employed, engaged, industrious, occupied. *Busy* applies to an activity which may be temporary, *industrious* to a habit of life. *Diligent* indicates also a disposition, which is ordinarily habitual, and suggests more of heartiness and volition than *industrious.* We say one is a *diligent,* rather than an *industrious* reader. The *assiduous* worker gives patient and unremitting devotion to a task until it is done, or until nothing more can be done. Compare ACTIVE, INDUSTRIOUS, INDUSTRY. *Antonyms*: dilatory, dull, idle, inactive, indolent, lazy, listless, negligent, remiss, slack, slothful.

bus·y·bod·y (biz′ē·bod′ē) *n. pl.* **·bodies** One who officiously meddles with the affairs of others.
bus·y·ness (biz′ē·nis) *n.* The state of being busy: distinguished from *business.*
busy signal In a dial telephone, the sharp, recurrent buzzing tone indicating that the number called is already connected on another line. Compare DIAL TONE.
bus·y·work (biz′ē·wûrk′) *n.* Unnecessary work that is done only to keep one busy.
but[1] (but, *unstressed* bət) *conj.* **1** On the other hand; yet: I thought him honest, *but* he was lying. **2** Unless; if not: It never rains *but* it pours. **3** Excepting: Nothing would satisfy him *but* I come along. **4** Other than; otherwise than: I cannot choose *but* hear. **5** That: We don't doubt *but* matters will improve. **6** That . . . not: He is not so strong *but* a little

exercise will do him good. **7** Who . . . not; which . . . not: Few sought his advice *but* were enlightened by it. —*prep.* With the exception of; save: owning nothing *but* his clothes. —*adv.* **1** Only; just: If I had *but* thought. **2** Merely; not otherwise than: She is *but* a child. **—all but** Almost: He is *all but* well. **—but for** Were it not for; without: *But for* me, how would you have succeeded? **—but what 1** But that; but those which: There are no events *but what* have meaning. **2** *Colloq.* But that: I don't know *but what* I will. —*n.* A verbal objection; exception; condition: without any ifs or *buts.* [OE *buten* <*be* by + *ūtan* outside]

Synonyms (conj.): and, barely, besides, except, further, however, just, merely, moreover, nevertheless, notwithstanding, only, provided, save, still, that, though, unless, yet. *But* ranges from the faintest contrast to absolute negation; as, I am willing to go, *but* (on the other hand) content to stay; he is not an honest man, *but* (on the contrary) a villain. *Except* and *excepting* are slightly more emphatic than *but.* Such expressions as "words are *but* breath" (nothing *but*) may be referred to the restrictive use by ellipsis. *But* never becomes a full synonym for *and; and* adds something like, *but* adds something different; "brave *and* tender" implies that tenderness is natural to the brave; "brave *but* tender" implies that bravery and tenderness are rarely combined. The omission or insertion of *but* often reverses the meaning. "I have no fear *that* he will do it" and "I have no fear *but that* he will do it" have contrary senses, the former indicating the feeling of certainty *that he will not do it,* and the latter the feeling of certainty *that he will do it.* Where ambiguity or haziness results from the use of *but that,* it can ordinarily be avoided by recasting the sentence. Compare NOTWITHSTANDING.

but[2] (but) *n. Brit.* Any of various kinds of flatfish, especially the halibut and flounder: also spelled *butt.* [? <Gmc. Cf. Du. *bot* flounder, Sw. *butta* turbot.]

but[3] (but) *v.t. & v.i.* **but·ted, but·ting** To abut.

but[4] (but) *n. Scot.* The kitchen or outer room of a two-roomed house. **—to be but and ben with** To live in close intimacy with.

but[5] (but) See BUTT[4].

bu·ta·di·ene (byōō′tə·dī′ēn, -dī·ēn′) *n. Chem.* A hydrocarbon, C_4H_6, closely related to isoprene, variously prepared from acetylene, petroleum, or alcohol: an important component in the manufacture of synthetic rubber. [<BUTANE + DI-[3] + -ENE]

bu·tane (byōō′tān, byōō·tān′) *n. Chem.* A colorless, inflammable, gaseous compound, C_4H_{10}, of the aliphatic hydrocarbon series, contained in petroleum and formed synthetically by the action of zinc on ethyl iodide. [<L *butyrum* butter]

bu·tane·thi·ol (byōō′tān·thī′ōl, -ol) *n.* Butyl mercaptan. [<BUTANE + THIOL]

bu·ta·no·ic acid (byōō′tə·nō′ik) Butyric acid.

bu·ta·nol (byōō′tə·nôl, -nol) *n.* Butyl alcohol. [<BUTAN(E) + (ALCOH)OL]

bu·ta·none (byōō′tə·nōn) *n. Chem.* An inflammable colorless ketone, C_4H_8O, used in making plastics and as a solvent. [<BUTAN(E) + -ONE]

Bu·ta·ri·ta·ri (bōō·tä′rē·tä′rē) An atoll of the northern Gilbert Islands; 4 square miles: also *Makin.*

butch (bŏŏch) *adj. Slang* Masculine, as in appearance or manner: said of one who adopts a masculine role, especially a female homosexual. —*n.* **1** A closely cropped haircut for boys or men. **2** *Slang* A butch woman, especially a lesbian. [Prob. <*Butch,* a boy's nickname, often applied to young toughs]

butch·er (bŏŏch′ər) *n.* **1** One who slaughters animals or deals in meats for food. **2** A bloody or cruel murderer. **3** A vendor of candy, cigarettes, newspapers, etc., on trains. **4** In journalism, a copyreader. —*v.t.* **1** To slaughter or dress (animals) for market. **2** To kill (people or game) barbarously or brutally. **3** *Slang* To ruin by bungling treatment; botch. See synonyms under KILL. [<OF *bouchier* man who slaughters bucks <*boc* buck, he-goat] **—butch′er·er** *n.*

butch·er·bird (bŏŏch′ər·bûrd′) *n.* A shrike: named from its habit of impaling its prey upon thorns.

butch·er·broom (bŏŏch′ər·brōōm′, -brŏŏm′) *n.* Any plant of the genus *Ruscus* of the lily family; especially, *R. aculeatus,* a low, evergreen shrub with leathery, leaflike branches bearing scarlet berries: also **butch′er's-broom′.**

butch·er·y (bŏŏch′ər·ē) *n. pl.* **·er·ies 1** Wanton or wholesale slaughter. **2** A slaughterhouse. **3** Butcher's trade. **4** The result of butchering. See synonyms under MASSACRE.

bute (byōōt) See BUTTE.

Bute (byōōt) **1** A county in SW Scotland; 218 square miles; capital, Rothesay: also **Bute′shire** (-shir). **2** An island in the Firth of Clyde, Scotland; 47 square miles.

bu·te·o (byōō′tē·ō) *n.* Any of the numerous large, thickset hawks of the genus *Buteo,* having broad wings and rounded tails. Also called *buzzard.*

but·ler (but′lər) *n.* **1** A man servant in charge of the dining-room, wine, plate, etc. **2** Formerly, an official in charge of a royal wine cellar. [<OF *bouteillier* cupbearer <Med. L *buticularius* <*buticula* bottle] **—but′ler·ship** *n.*

Butler (but′lər), **Benjamin Franklin,** 1818–1893, U.S. general. **—Joseph,** 1692–1752, English theologian. **—Nicholas Murray,** 1862–1947, U.S. educator, president of Columbia University, New York, 1902–45. **—Pierce,** 1866–1939, U.S. jurist, associate justice of the Supreme Court 1923–39. **—Samuel,** 1612–1680, English satirical poet. **—Samuel,** 1835–1902, English novelist. **—Smedley Darlington,** 1881–1940, U.S. general.

butler's pantry A room between the kitchen and the dining-room, arranged for storage, serving, etc.

but·ler·y (but′lər·ē) *n. pl.* **·ler·ies** The butler's pantry.

butt[1] (but) *v.t.* **1** To strike with or as with the head or horns; ram. **2** To touch or bump against. **3** To cause to abut. **4** To abut on. **5** To join two things at the end; attach (one thing) to another, as a beam to a wall. —*v.i.* **6** To make a butting motion; move by butting. **7** To project; jut out. **8** To make a butt joint. **9** To be or lie adjacent; abut. —*n.* **1** A stroke, thrust, or push with or as with the head. **2** A thrust in fencing. **—to butt in** *Colloq.* To interrupt; interfere. [<OF *abouter* strike, ult. <Gmc.]

butt[2] (but) *n.* **1** A target, as for a rifle range. **2** *Often pl.* The range itself. **3** The shelter for the score-keeper on a rifle range. **4** The retaining wall placed behind a target to stop the bullets: also *target butt.* **5** A target for ridicule or criticism. **6** A limit; bound. [<OF *but* end, goal, ult. <Gmc.]

butt[3] (but) *n.* **1** The larger or thicker end of anything, as of a log. **2** That end or edge of a piece of timber where it comes squarely against another piece, or the joint thus formed. **3** A hinge. **4** The thick part of a tanned hide of leather. **5** The large end of the loin in beef. **6** *U.S. Colloq.* The buttocks. **7** The unused end of a cigar or cigarette. [Akin to Dan. *but* blunt, Du. *bot* short, stumpy]

butt[4] (but) *n.* **1** A large cask. **2** A measure of wine, 126 U.S. gallons. Also *but.* [<OF *boute*]

butt[5] (but) See BUT[2].

butte (byōōt) *n. Geog.* A conspicuous hill or natural turret, especially one with steep sides and a flattened top: also *bute.* [<F]

Butte (byōōt) A copper mining city in SW Montana.

but·ter[1] (but′ər) *n.* **1** The fatty constituent of milk, separated by churning into a soft, whitish-yellow solid; also, this substance prepared and processed for cooking and table use. **2** A substance having the consistency or other qualities of butter, as the chlorides of some metals, a fruit preserve of a semisolid consistency: apple *butter,* and certain easily fused vegetable oils: peanut *butter.* **—to look as if butter would not melt in one's mouth** To look innocent. —*v.t.* **1** To put butter on. **2** *Colloq.* To flatter: usually with *up.* **—to know which side one's bread is buttered on** To be aware of the true sources of one's fortune or security and to behave accordingly. [OE *butere,* ult. <Gk. *boutyron* <*bous* cow + *tyros* cheese]

butt·er[2] (but′ər) *n.* A person or animal that butts.

but·ter-and-eggs (but′ər·ən·egz′) *n.* Any of various plants having two shades of yellow in the flower, as the toadflax in the United States, and a species of narcissus in England.

but·ter·ball (but′ər·bôl′) *n.* **1** The bufflehead. **2** *Colloq.* A very fat person.

butter bean 1 Wax bean **2** *Southern U.S.* Lima bean.

but·ter·bough (but′ər·bou′) *n.* The inkwood.

but·ter·burr (but′ər·bûr′) *n.* An Old World herb (genus *Petasites*), with round or roundish leaves often a foot wide. Also **but′ter·bur′.**

but·ter·cup (but′ər·kup′) *n.* **1** One of various species of crowfoot (genus *Ranunculus*), as *R. acris* and *R. bulbosus,* with yellow, cup-shaped flowers. **2** The flower. Also **but′ter·flow′er.**

but·ter·fat (but′ər·fat′) *n.* The fatty substance obtained from the milk of mammals, consisting of the glycerides of various fatty acids.

but·ter·fin·gers (but′ər·fing′gərz) *n.* An inept or clumsy person; one who drops things easily. —**but′ter·fin′gered** *adj.*

but·ter·fish (but′ər·fish′) *n. pl.* **·fish** or **·fish·es** One of various marine food fishes of the North Atlantic with an oily skin, as the dollarfish: also called *pumpkinseed.*

but·ter·fly (but′ər·flī′) *n. pl.* **·flies 1** A diurnal lepidopterous insect (division *Rhopalocera*) with large, often brightly colored wings, club-shaped antennae, and slender body. Compare MOTH. **2** A gay idler or trifler. [OE *buttorflēoge*]

butterfly bush Buddleia.

butterfly fish *n.* **1** One of various tropical marine fishes (family *Chaetodontidae*) having brightly colored bodies. **2** A brilliantly colored Chinese fish *(Macropodus viridiauratus).*

butterfly stroke In swimming, a stroke made while lying face down, the arms being brought forward laterally above the water: performed in conjunction with a fishtail kick.

butterfly table A small drop-leaf table, the leaves supported by brackets that resemble a butterfly's wings.

butterfly tie A bow tie.

butterfly valve *Mech.* **1** A valve resembling a double clack valve, composed of two semicircular pieces attached to a cross-rib in the pump bucket. **2** A disk turning on a diametral axis, used as a damper in a pipe.

butterfly weed 1 A bushy species of milkweed *(Asclepias tuberosa),* common in the United States and Canada, and conspicuous in midsummer by its large masses of orange-red flowers: also called *orange* or *vermilion milkweed.* **2** A native North American plant *(Gaura coccinea)* of the primrose family, with small pink, red, or white flowers. **3** Pleurisy root.

BUTTERFLY WEED *(def. 1)*

but·ter·ine (but′ər·ēn, -in) *n.* Artificial butter; oleomargarine.

butter knife A small, blunt-edged knife for cutting or spreading butter.

but·ter·milk (but′ər·milk′) *n.* The sour liquid left after the butterfat has been separated from milk or cream.

but·ter·nut (but′ər·nut′) *n.* **1** The oily, edible nut of the North American white walnut *(Juglans cinerea).* **2** The tree, or its cathartic inner bark. **3** An oily, nutlike seed of a tall tree *(Caryocar nuciferum),* native in British Guiana, having a hard, brown, tubercled shell: also called *souari nut.* **4** The dye obtained from the bark and roots of the butternut tree. **5** A Confederate soldier; also, a Southern sympathizer in the Civil War. **6** Cloth or a garment dyed with butternut.

but·ter·scotch (but′ər·skoch′) *n.* **1** Hard, sticky candy made with brown sugar, butter, and flavoring. **2** A flavoring extract consisting of similar ingredients. —*adj.* Made of or flavored with butterscotch.

but·ter·weed (but′ər·wēd′) *n.* **1** The horseweed. **2** A groundsel *(Senecio lobatus)* of the southern United States. **3** The Indian mallow.

but·ter·wort (but′ər·wûrt′) *n.* Any of several small stemless herbs (genus *Pinguicula*), with broad fleshy leaves that secrete a greasy substance in which insects are captured.

but·ter·y[1] (but′ər·ē) *adj.* **1** Containing, like, or smeared with butter. **2** Grossly flattering; adulating.

but·ter·y[2] (but′ər·ē, but′rē) *n. pl.* **·ter·ies 1** A pantry; a wine cellar. **2** In English universities, a place in each college from which the students are supplied with provisions. [<OF *boterie* <LL *botaria* <*butta* bottle]

butt hinge A hinge composed of two plates or leaves which are screwed to the abutting surfaces of the door and the jamb. For illustration see under HINGE.

but·ting (but′ing) *n.* An abuttal.

butt joint A joint made by placing the component parts end to end and holding them in place either by welding or by side plates riveted thereto.

but·tock (but′ək) *n.* **1** *Naut.* The hinder part of a ship's hull. **2** *Anat.* **a** Either of the two fleshy prominences which form the rump. **b** *pl.* The rump. ◆ Collateral adjective: *gluteal.* [Dim. of BUTT[3]]

but·ton (but′n) *n.* **1** A knob or disk, as of bone or metal, which, when forced through a narrow opening, or buttonhole, fastens one part of a garment to another. **2** Anything resembling a button, as an emblem of membership, usually worn in the lapel, a political emblem on a celluloid disk, etc. **3** A pivoted fastener for a door, window, etc. **4** A knob or protuberance, as for operating an electric bell, at the end of a foil, etc. **5** *pl. Brit. Colloq.* A boy in attendance; a page: so called from the buttons on his uniform. **6** *Metall.* A small globular or disklike mass of metal found in a crucible after fusion. **7** *Bot.* **a** A bud or other like protuberance on a plant. **b** The small round flower head of some composite plants. **c** A small seed vessel. **d** The head of an immature mushroom. **8** *Zool.* **a** The bud that forms at the initial stage of a stag's horns. **b** The small round knob at the end of the rattles of a rattlesnake. **9** *U.S.* A guessing game. **10** *Slang* The point of the jaw. **11** *pl. Slang* Wits: Some of his *buttons* are missing. —*v.t.* **1** To fasten with or as with a button or buttons. **2** To provide with buttons. —*v.i.* **3** To admit of being buttoned. **4** To bud or form heads, as a cauliflower. [<OF *boton* button, bud] —**but′ton·er** *n.* —**but′ton·like′** *adj.*

but·ton·bush (but′n·bŏŏsh′) *n.* A North American shrub *(Cephalanthus occidentalis)*: so called from its spherical white flower heads.

but·ton·hole (but′n·hōl′) *n.* A slit to receive and hold a button. —*v.t.* **·holed, ·hol·ing 1** To work buttonholes in. **2** To sew with a buttonhole stitch. **3** To detain by conversation; importune. —**but′ton·hol′·er** *n.*

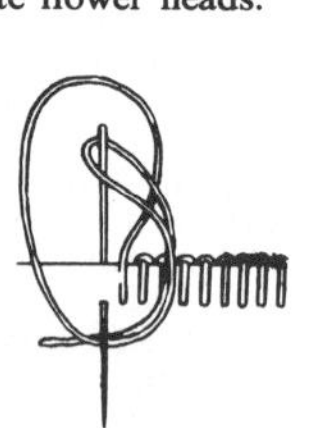

BUTTONHOLE STITCH

buttonhole stitch A perpendicular stitch fastened with a loop at the top, worked in a row or series for making a firm edge as in buttonholes: also called *close stitch.*

but·ton·hook (but′n·hook′) *n.* A hook for buttoning gloves or shoes.

but·ton·mold (but′n·mōld′) *n.* A disk of wood or other material which is made into a button by covering with fabric, leather, etc.

button snakeroot 1 Any of several plants (genus *Liatris*): so called from the small round flower heads. **2** A stout-stemmed plant *(Eryngium aquaticum),* with linear leaves and globose heads of flowers.

button spider The black widow.

but·ton·weed (but′n·wēd′) *n.* **1** The knapweed. **2** The Indian mallow.

but·ton·wood (but′n·wŏŏd′) *n.* **1** The sycamore or plane tree of the United States: also **but′ton·ball′**. **2** A tree or shrub of tropical America and Africa *(Conocarpus erecta)* with heavy, close-grained wood and an astringent bark: also **but′ton·tree′**.

but·ton·y (but′ən·ē) *adj.* Of the nature of, like, or covered with buttons.

butt plate A plate, usually corrugated to prevent slipping on the shoulder, attached to the end of a gunstock.

but·tress (but′ris) *n.* **1** *Archit.* A structure built against a wall to strengthen it. **2** Any support or prop: *buttresses* to faith. **3** Any formation suggesting a buttress. **4** A projecting rock or hillside. **5** A horny growth on a horse's hoof. See synonyms under PROP. —**flying buttress** *Archit.* A rampant arch extending from a wall or pier to a supporting abutment, usually receiving the thrust of another arch on the other side of the wall, which it supports by its upper end. —*v.t.* **1** *Archit.* To support with a buttress. **2** To prop up; sustain; fortify: *buttressed* by her religious convictions. [<OF *bouterez,* nominative sing. of *bouteret* <*bouter* push, thrust]

butt shaft An arrow with a blunt head.

butt·weld (but′weld′) *n.* A weld made between two abutting ends or edges without overlapping.

Bu·tung (bōō′tŏŏng) An Indonesian island just SE of Celebes; 1,759 square miles: also *Buton.*

bu·tyl (byōō′til) *n. Chem.* A univalent hydrocarbon radical, C_4H_9, from butane. [<BUT(YRIC) + -YL]

butyl alcohol *Chem.* Any of three isomeric alcohols derived from butane, and having the formula C_4H_9OH: also *butanol.*

bu·ty·lene (byōō′tə·lēn) *n. Chem.* A gaseous hydrocarbon, C_4H_8, of the olefin series, existing in three isomeric modifications: an ingredient of synthetic rubber.

butyl mercaptan *Chem.* A noxious sulfur compound, C_4H_9SH: used in dilutions to protect stored foods against rats, and as a warning agent in natural-gas service: also *butanethiol.*

bu·ty·ra·ceous (byōō′tə·rā′shəs) *adj.* Having the nature, qualities, or appearance of butter; buttery. Also **bu·ty·rous** (byōō′tər·əs). [<L *butyrum.* See BUTTER[1].]

bu·ty·rate (byōō′tə·rāt) *n. Chem.* A salt or ester of butyric acid.

bu·tyr·ic (byōō·tir′ik) *adj.* Of, pertaining to, or derived from butter. [<L *butyrum.* See BUTTER[1].]

butyric acid *Chem.* Either of two isomeric acids, C_3H_7COOH, especially one found as an ester in butter and certain oils, and free in rancid butter, perspiration, etc.: also *butanoic acid.*

bu·ty·rin (byōō′tər·in) *n. Chem.* Any one of three analogous compounds formed by treating glycerol with butyric acid at a high temperature.

bux·om (buk′səm) *adj.* **1** Characterized by health and vigor; plump; comely: said of women. **2** Having a large bosom. [OE *buhsum* pliant. Akin to OE *bugan* bend, bow.] —**bux′om·ly** *adv.* —**bux′om·ness** *n.*

buy (bī) *v.* **bought, buy·ing** *v.t.* **1** To obtain for a price; purchase. **2** To be a price for. **3** To obtain by an exchange or sacrifice: to *buy* wisdom with experience. **4** To bribe; corrupt. **5** *Slang* To believe or accept, as an excuse. —*v.i.* **6** To make purchases; be a purchaser. —**to buy in 1** To buy from the owner, as at an auction when bids are too low. **2** To buy stock or an interest, as in a company. **3** *Slang* To pay money as a price for joining. —**to buy off** To obtain a promise of nonintervention by bribing. —**to buy out** To purchase the stock, interests, etc., of, as in a business. —*n. Colloq.* **1** Anything bought or about to be bought. **2** A bargain. [OE *bycgan*] —**buy′a·ble** *adj.* —**buy′er** *n.*

buzz[1] (buz) *v.i.* **1** To make a humming, vibrating sound, as a bee or hummingbird. **2** To talk, discuss, or gossip excitedly: The town *buzzed* with the news. **3** To move from place to place; bustle about. —*v.t.* **4** To utter or express in a buzzing manner; gossip. **5** To cause to buzz, as wings. **6** *Colloq.* To fly an airplane low over: He *buzzed* the ship. **7** *Colloq.* To call on the telephone. —*n.* **1** A low murmur, as of bees, talk, or distant sounds. **2** Rumor; gossip. **3** *Colloq.* A telephone call. [Imit.]

buzz[2] (buz) *v.t. Brit.* To drain to the last drop. [Origin unknown]

buzzard (buz′ərd) *n.* **1** One of several large, slow-flying hawks, as the **red-tailed buzzard** *(Buteo borealis),* an American species. **2** An American vulture; the turkey buzzard. [<OF *busart,* prob. <L *buteo* hawk]

buz·zard[2] (buz′ərd) *n. Brit. Dial.* A noisy insect, as a cockchafer, dor beetle, etc. [<BUZZ[1] + -ARD]

buzzard dollar The silver dollar of 412½ grains coined under the Bland bill, 1878: in allusion to the design of the eagle on the reverse.

Buzzards Bay An inlet of the Atlantic in southern Massachusetts.

buzz bomb See under BOMB.

buzz·er (buz′ər) *n.* **1** One who or that which buzzes. **2** An electric signal making a buzzing sound, as on a telephone switchboard.

buzz saw A circular saw: so called from the sound it emits.

buzz·wig (buz′wig′) *n.* **1** A large, thick wig. **2** A person who wears such a wig. **3** A person of importance.

Bwa·na (bwä′nä) *n.* Master; sir. [<Swahili< Arabic *Abuna* our father]

by (bī) *prep.* **1** Next to; near: the house *by* the road. **2** Along the course of: the railroad tracks *by* the river. **3** Past or beyond: The train flashed *by* us. **4** In the course of; during: birds flying *by* night. **5** Not later than: Be here *by* four tomorrow. **6** For the period of; according to: They work *by* the day. **7** As a result of the effort, means, or action of: a play written *by* Shakespeare; a house struck *by* lightning. **8** With the perception of: a loss felt *by* all. **9** By means of: leading a child *by* the hand. **10** In consequence of: a case won *by* default. **11** As a means of conveyance; via: Mail your letters *by* air. **12** To the extent or amount of: insects *by* the thousands. **13** On the basis of: a road four miles long *by* actual measurement. **14** Considered according to: advancing step *by* step; reading word *by* word. **15** With reference to: to do well *by* one's friends. **16** Multiplied by: a room ten *by* twelve. **17** In the name of: swearing *by* all that is sacred. —*adv.* **1** In the presence or vicinity; at hand; near; as, to keep one's sword *by.* **2** Up to and beyond something; past: the train roared *by.* **3** Apart; aside, as discarded or saved for future use: to lay something *by.* **4** At or into a person's house, store, etc.: to stop *by.* —*adj. & n.* Bye. [OE *bī* near, about]

Synonyms (prep.): through, with. *By* refers to the agent; *through,* to the means, cause, or condition; *with,* to the instrument. *By* commonly refers to persons; *with,* to things; *through* may refer to either. The road having become impassable *through* long disuse, a way was opened *by* pioneers *with* axes. *By,* however, may be applied to any object which is viewed as partaking of action and agency; as, the metal was corroded *by* the acid; skill is gained *by* practice. "His friends were displeased *by* the selection of another chairman" means that the action displeased them; "His friends were displeased *with* the selection," etc., means that the man selected was not their choice. *Through* implies a more distant connection than *by* or *with,* and more intervening elements. Material objects are perceived *by* the mind *through* the senses. *By* is in frequent use after call, judge, know, measure, perceive, see, seem, take, understand, etc., to indicate the determining object; as, to call *by* name; I judge *by* his dress that he is poor; I saw *by* his glance that he was a rogue. *Accompanied* and *attended* take *by* of persons, *with* (commonly) of things; we say, *surrounded by.*

by– *combining form* **1** Secondary; inferior; incidental: *by-product.* **2** Near; close: *bystander.* **3** Aside; out of the way: *byway.*

By (bī), **John,** 1781–1836, Canadian military engineer; founder of Ottawa.

by all means Certainly; on every account.

by and by 1 At some time in the future; soon; before long. **2** *Obs.* At once; immediately.

by–and–by (bī′ən·bī′) *n.* Future time; hereafter.

by and large 1 Generally speaking; on the whole. **2** *Naut.* Alternatively well up to and off from the wind: This boat sails well *by and large.*

by–bid·der (bī′bid′ər) *n.* A person who runs up prices at an auction for the seller or owner. —**by′–bid′ding** *n.*

by–blow (bī′blō′) *n.* **1** A side or chance blow; one that falls short of its aim. **2** An illegitimate child.

Byd·goszcz (bid′gôshch) A city in north central Poland: German *Bromberg.*

bye (bī) *n.* **1** Something of minor or secondary importance; a side issue. **2** In cricket, a run made on a ball missed by the batsman and which has passed by the wicket-keeper. **3** The position of a person who is assigned no opponent and automatically advances to the next round, as in the preliminary pairings of a tennis tournament. **4** In golf, any hole or holes remaining unplayed when the match ends. —*adj.* Not principal or main; secondary. Also *by.* [Var. of BY]

bye-bye (bī′bī′) *interj.* A child's word for good-bye. Also **bye.**

Bye·lā·ya A river in Bashkortostan, flowing 882 miles to the Kama river; also **Belaya.**

by-e·lec·tion (bī′i·lek′shən) *n. Brit.* A parliamentary election between general elections, held to fill a vacancy.

Bye·lo·rus·sia See **Belorus.**

bye-low (bī′lō′) *adv.* & *interj.* Hush!: a child's word, used in lullabies.

by·gone (bī′gôn′, -gon′) *adj.* Gone by; former; past; out-of-date. —*n.* Something past; that which has gone by: usually in the plural.

byke (bīk) See BIKE².

by-lane (bī′lān′) *n.* **1** A byway. **2** A side passage in a mine.

by·law (bī′lô′) *n.* **1** A rule or law adopted by an association, a corporation, or the like, which is subordinate to a constitution or charter. **2** *Obs.* An accessory law. [ME *bilawe* < *by, bi* village (< ON *bȳr*) + *lawe* law; infl. by BY].

by-line (bī′līn′) *n.* The line at the head of an article in a newspaper, etc., giving the name of the writer.

by-name (bī′nām′) *n.* **1** A secondary name; surname; sobriquet. **2** A nickname; epithet.

Byng (bing), **George,** 1663–1733, British admiral. —**Julian Hedworth George,** 1862–1935, Viscount Byng of Vimy, British field marshal.

by-pass (bī′pas′, -päs′) *n.* **1** Any road, path, or route connecting two points in a course other than that normally used; a detour. **2** A device to lead a flow of gas or liquid around a pipe, fixed connection, or obstacle. **3** An electric switch. —*v.t.* **1** To go around (an obstacle). **2** To provide with a by-pass.

by·past (bī′past′, -päst′) *adj.* Bygone.

by-path (bī′path′, -päth′) *n.* A side, secluded, or secondary path.

by-play (bī′plā′) *n.* **1** Action on the stage conducted through asides or dumb show as an accompaniment to the main action. **2** Any diversion from the main action.

by-prod·uct (bī′prod′əkt) *n.* Any material or product contingent upon or incidental to a manufacturing process: Bagasse is a *by-product* in the making of cane sugar.

Byrd (bûrd), **Harry Flood,** 1887–1966, U.S. politician. —**Richard Evelyn,** 1888–1957, U.S. rear admiral, aviator, polar explorer, and writer: brother of the preceding. —**William,** 1674–1744, Virginia planter and author. —**William,** 1543?–1623, English composer.

byre (bīr) *n.* A cow stable. [OE, stall, shed]

byrl (bûrl, birl) See BIRLE.

Byrnes (bûrnz), **James Francis,** 1879–1972, U.S. statesman; secretary of state 1945–47.

byr·nie (bûr′nē) *n. Archaic* A coat of mail. [Var. of ME *brynie*]

by·road (bī′rōd′) *n.* **1** A back road or crossroad; a private way. **2** Secret means.

By·ron (bī′rən), **Lord,** 1788–1824, George Gordon Noel Byron, sixth baron, English poet.

By·ron·ic (bī·ron′ik) *adj.* Of or pertaining to Lord Byron or his writings. **2** Like or characteristic of Byron or his style: proud, romantic, passionate, etc. Also **By·ro·ni·an** (bī·rō′·nē·ən), **By·ron′i·cal.**

bys·si·no·sis (bis′ə·nō′sis) *n.* A pulmonary disease caused by the inhalation of cotton dust in mills. [< Latin *byssinum* linen + -OSIS]

bys·sus (bis′əs) *n. pl.* **bys·sus·es** or **bys·si** (bis′ī) **1** Formerly, any costly white stuff of cotton, silk, or linen. **2** *Zool.* A bunch of silky thread secreted by the foot of certain stationary bivalve mollusks, as mussels, and serving as a means of attachment to an anchorage. **3** *Bot.* A filamentous fungus of the obsolete group *Byssi.* [< L < Gk. *byssos* fine linen]

by·stand·er (bī′stan′dər) *n.* One who stands by; a looker-on. See synonyms under SPECTATOR.

by-street (bī′strēt′) *n.* A side street; a byway.

by-talk (bī′tôk′) *n.* Incidental talk; small talk.

byte (bīt) *n.* A group of eight bits in a computer memory that form a character, a symbol, or a keyboard function. [< B(INAR)Y (DIGI)T E(IGHT)]

by the bye Incidentally; by the way. Also **by the by.**

by the way Incidentally; by the bye.

By·tom (bī′tôm) Polish name for BEUTHEN.

by·wa·ter (bī′wô′tər, -wot′ər) *n.* A diamond that is slightly yellowish or off color. [< BY, *adv.* (def. 3) + WATER (def. 5)]

By·wa·ter (bī′wô·tər), **Ingram,** 1840–1914, English classical scholar.

by·way (bī′wā′) *n.* A branch or side road.

by·word (bī′wûrd′) *n.* **1** A phrase, person, institution, etc., that has become an object of derision or mockery. **2** A nickname. **3** A trite saying; proverbial phrase. See synonyms under ADAGE. [OE *biword* proverb]

by·work (bī′wûrk′) *n.* Work for odd hours during leisure time.

byz·ant (biz′ənt) See BEZANT.

Byz·an·tine (biz′ən·tēn, -tīn, bi·zan′tin) *adj.* **1** Of or pertaining to Byzantium. **2** Pertaining to a style of architecture developed in the Byzantine Empire during the fourth century, characterized by the round arch springing from four columns or piers, and in which the dome rests on pendentives, with centralized plans, colorful mosaics, and rich decoration. For illustration see under CAPITAL. —*n.* A native or inhabitant of Byzantium. Also **By·zan·ti·an** (bi·zan′·shē·ən, -shən). [< L *Byzantinus* < *Byzantium*]

BYZANTINE ARCHITECTURE
Santa Sophia, Constantinople, A.D. 538.

Byzantine Empire The eastern part of the later Roman Empire (395–1453): Arabic *Rum:* also *Byzantium, Eastern Empire, Eastern Roman Empire.*

Byzantine rite Religious ceremonies as performed by the Greek Orthodox Church.

By·zan·ti·um (bi·zan′shē·əm, -tē·əm) **1** A former name for ISTANBUL. **2** The Byzantine Empire.

Bzu·ra (bzōō′rä) A river in central Poland, flowing 85 miles NE to the Vistula.

C

c, C (sē) *n. pl.* **c's** or **cs, C's Cs, cees** (sēz) **1** The third letter of the English alphabet: from Phoenician *gimel,* through Hebrew *gimel,* Greek *gamma,* Roman *C* or *G.* **2** The sound of the letter *c.* See ALPHABET. —*symbol* **1** In Roman notation, the numeral 100. See under NUMERAL. **2** *Chem.* Carbon (symbol C). **3** *Music* **a** The tonic note of the natural musical scale, *do.* **b** The pitch of this tone or the written note representing it. **c** The scale built upon C. **d** Common or 4–4 time.

Ca *Chem.* Calcium (symbol Ca).

ca' (kô) *v.t. Scot.* **1** To call. **2** To drive, as cattle. Also spelled *caw.*

Caa·ba (kä′bə, kä′ə·bə) See KAABA.

cab ¹ (kab) *n.* **1** A one-horse public carriage. **2** A taxicab. **3** The covered part of a locomotive or motortruck. [Short form of CABRIOLET]

cab² (kab) *n.* A Hebrew measure equivalent to about two quarts: also spelled *kab.*

ca·bal (kə·bal′) *n.* **1** A number of persons secretly united for some private purpose. **2** Intrigue; conspiracy. —*v.i.* **ca·balled, ca·bal·ling** To form a cabal; plot. [< MF *cabale* < Med. L *cabbala* < Hebrew *qabbālāh* tradition]
Synonyms (noun): combination, conclave, confederacy, conspiracy, crew, faction, gang, junto. See CONSPIRACY.

cab·a·la (kab′ə·lə, kə·bä′lə) *n.* **1** The mystic theosophy of the Hebrews. **2** Any secret, occult, or mystic system. Often spelled *cabbala, kabala, kabbala.* [< Hebrew *qabbālāh* tradition < *qābal* receive] —**ca·bal′ic** *adj.* —**cab·a·lism** (kab′ə·liz′əm) *n.*

cab·a·list (kab′ə·list) *n.* **1** A student of the cabala. **2** A mystic; occultist.

cab·a·lis·tic (kab′ə·lis′tik) *adj.* **1** Pertaining to the cabala. **2** Having a mystic sense; mysterious. Also **cab′a·lis′ti·cal.** See synonyms under MYSTERIOUS. —**cab′a·lis′ti·cal·ly** *adv.*

ca·bal·la·da (kä′bəl·yä′də) *SW U.S.* A herd of horses or mules.

cab·al·le·ro (kab′əl·yâr′ō) *n. pl.* **·ros** **1** A Spanish gentleman; cavalier: used with as broad a signification as the English word *gentleman.* **2** *SW U.S.* **a** A lady's escort. **b** A horseman.

cab·al·line (kab′ə·līn, -lin) *adj.* Of, pertaining to, or suited to horses: *caballine* aloes. [< L *caballinus* < *caballus* horse]

caballine fountain The fountain Hippocrene; hence, a fountain of inspiration. Also **caballine spring.**

ca·ba·na (kə·bä′nə, -ban′ə; *Sp.* kä·bä′nyä) *n.* **1** A small cabin. **2** A bathhouse on a beach. Also **ca·ba′ña.** [< Sp.]

Ca·ba·na·tuan (kə·bä′nə·twän′) A town in central Luzon; site of a Japanese prisoner of war camp in World War II.

ca·bane (kə·ban′) *n. Aeron.* **1** A framework to support the wings of an airplane at the fuselage. **2** The system of trusses supporting the overhang of a wing. [< F, Cabin]

cab·a·ret (kab′ə·rā′) *n.* **1** A restaurant or café which provides singing, dancing, etc., as entertainment for its patrons. **2** Entertainment of this type. **3** A tavern or wine shop. **4** A tea or coffee set, including tray and dishes. [< F]

cab·as (kab′ə, kə·bä′) *n.* **1** A rush basket. **2** A woman's workbag or basket. [< F]

cab·as·set (kab′ə·set) *n.* An open helmet with a rounded top and narrow brim. [< F, dim. of *cabas* basket]

cab·bage¹ (kab′ij) *n.* **1** The close-leaved head formed by certain brassicaceous plants. **2** The plant *(Brassica oleracea)* producing it. **3** The large terminal leaf bud of the cabbage palm used as a vegetable. —*v.i.* **·baged, ·bag·ing** To form a head, as cabbage; to grow into a head. [< OF *caboche* < L *caput* head]

cab·bage[2] (kab′ij) *v.t. & v.i.* **·baged, ·bag·ing** To pilfer; take dishonestly; purloin: said originally of a tailor who appropriated a part of his customers' cloth. —*n.* Cloth appropriated by a tailor in cutting out garments; hence, anything purloined. [Origin uncertain]

cabbage bug The harlequin bug.

cabbage butterfly Any of several butterflies (genus *Pieris*) whose larvae feed on plants of the mustard family; especially *P. rapae*, the green larvae of which destroy cabbage. For illustration see under INSECT (injurious).

cabbage green The soft, grayish blue-green color of cabbage leaves.

cabbage palm 1 A palm with a terminal leaf bud used as a vegetable, as the cabbage palm *(Sabal palmetto)* of Florida. **2** The feather palm *(Ptychosperma elegans)* of Australia. **3** The fan palm.

cab·ba·la (kab′ə·lə, kə·bä′lə), etc. See CABALA.

cab·by (kab′ē) *n. pl.* **·bies** *Colloq.* A cabman.

Cab·ell (kab′əl), **James Branch,** 1879–1958, U.S. novelist.

ca·ber (kā′bər) *n. Scot.* A mastlike pole, generally the stem of a tree, used in the Highland athletic game **tossing the caber:** also spelled *kabar, kebar.*

Ca·be·za de Va·ca (kä·vā′thä thā vä′kä), **Alvar Núñez,** 1490?–1559?, Spanish explorer of North and South America.

cab·in (kab′in) *n.* **1** A small, rude house; hut. **2** A compartment in a vessel for officers or passengers. **3** *Aeron.* The enclosed space in an airplane for passengers, pilot, etc.; the cockpit. see synonyms under, HOUSE, HUT. —*v.t. & v.i.* To shut up or dwell in or as in a cabin; crib; hamper. [< F *cabane* < LL *capanna* cabin]

cabin boy A boy who waits on the officers and passengers of a vessel.

cabin class A class of accommodations for steamship passengers, higher than tourist class, lower than first class.

Ca·bin·da (kə·bin′də) An exclave of Angola north of the Congo on the Gulf of Guinea; about 3,000 square miles.

cab·i·net (kab′ə·nit) *n.* **1** The body of official advisers of a king, president, or chief of state. **2** A council, or the chamber in which it meets. **3** A room for works of art, etc.; also, the articles collected. **4** A piece of furniture fitted with shelves and drawers. **5** *Obs.* A little cabin. **6** A small private room; a study or closet. —*adj.* **1** Pertaining to or suitable for a cabinet in any sense. **2** Secret; confidential. [< F < Ital. *gabinetto* closet, chest of drawers; in def. 4, dim. of CABIN]

cab·i·net·mak·er (kab′ə·nit·mā′kər) *n.* One who does fine woodworking, as for cabinets, furniture, etc.

cab·i·net·work (kab′ə·nit·wûrk′) *n.* The work of a cabinetmaker; expert woodwork.

ca·ble (kā′bəl) *n.* **1** *Naut.* **a** A heavy rope or chain, as for mooring vessels, etc. **b** A cable's length. **2** *Electr.* An insulated electrical conductor or group of conductors, protected by a waterproof coat, as for a submarine telegraph. **3** A cablegram. —*v.t.* **ca·bled, ca·bling 1** To fasten, as by a cable; tie fast. **2** To equip with cable or cables. **3** To send, as a message, by submarine telegraph. —*v.i.* **4** To communicate by submarine telegraph. [Akin to F *câble,* Sp. *cable* < LL *capulum, caplum* rope < *capere* take, grasp]

Ca·ble (kā′bəl), **George Washington,** 1844–1925, U.S. writer.

cable car A car or cage, pulled by an overhead or underground cable.

ca·ble·gram (kā′bəl·gram) *n.* A telegraphic dispatch sent by cable.

ca·ble-laid (kā′bəl·lād′) *adj.* Made up of three three-stranded ropes twisted together left-handed: a ropemaking term.

cable railroad A railroad in which the cars are attached to an endless moving cable by means of an adjustable grip usually passing through a slot in the roadway.

cable's length A unit of nautical measure: in the United States 720 feet, in England 608 feet.

ca·blet (kā′blit) *n.* A cable rope less than 10 inches in circumference: a hawser. [Dim. of CABLE]

cable TV or **cable television** A system for transmitting television programs by coaxial cable to individual subscribers. Abbr. CATV

cab·man (kab′mən) *n. pl.* **·men** (-mən) The driver of a cab.

ca·bob (kə·bob′) See KABAB.

ca·boched (kə·bosht′) *adj. Her.* Full-faced: said of the head of a stag, bull, or other beast. Also **ca·boshed′.** [< OF *caboché,* pp. of *cabocher* cut off the head < L *caput* head]

cab·o·chon (kab′ə·shon, *Fr.* kȧ·bô·shôn′) *adj.* Cut convex and highly polished but not faceted. —*n.* Any gem so cut. **—en cabochon** Cut and polished but not faceted: said of gems. [< F, aug. of *caboche* head]

Ca·bo Ju·bi (kä′vō hōō′vē) A headland of Spanish West Africa opposite the Canary Islands; site of Villa Bens. *English* **Cape Ju·by** (jōō′bē).

ca·boo·dle (kə·bōōd′l) *n. Colloq.* Aggregate or collection; lot; usually with an intensive, as **the whole caboodle, the whole kit and caboodle.** [Prob. intens. form of BOODLE]

ca·boose (kə·bōōs′) *n.* **1** *U.S.* A car on a freight train or work train equipped with stove and bunks for the use of the train crew or work crew. **2** *Brit.* The cook's galley on a ship. Also spelled *camboose.* [< MDu. *cabuse* cook's galley]

Cab·ot (kab′ət), **John,** 1451?–98, Venetian navigator in English service; discovered American continent (Labrador) 1497. **—Sebastian,** 1474–1557, English navigator: son of preceding.

cab·o·tage (kab′ə·tij) *n.* **1** Coastwise navigation; coast pilotage; coasting trade. **2** Air transport passengers and goods within the same national territory. [< F]

Ca·bral (kə·vräl′), **Pedro Álvarez,** 1460?–1526?, Portuguese navigator; claimed Brazil for Portugal.

ca·bres·ta (kä·bres′tä), **ca·bres·to** (-tō) See CABESTRO.

ca·bril·la (kə·bril′ə, *Sp.* kä·brē′yä) *n.* **1** One of various serranoid food fishes; specifically, one of the groupers (genus *Epinephelus*) common on the West Indian and Florida coasts. **2** A fish of the genus *Paralabrax,* as the California rock bass *(P. clathratus).* ob < Sp.]

Ca·bri·ni (kä·brē′nē), **Saint Frances Xavier,** 1850–1917, first U.S. citizen canonized, 1946: known as *Mother Cabrini.*

cab·ri·ole (kab′rē·ōl) *n.* A curved, tapering leg, often with a decorative foot: characteristic of Chippendale and Queen Anne furniture. [< MF. See CABRIOLET.]

cab·ri·o·let (kab′rē·ə·lā′, -let′) *n.* **1** A one-horse covered carriage with two seats; a cab. **2** An automobile of the coupé type, having a collapsible top. [< F, dim. of MF *cabriole* leap < Ital. *capriola* < L *capreolus* wild goat]

cab·stand (kab′stand′) *n.* A specified place where cabs are stationed for hire.

ca' can·ny (kä kan′ē, kô) **1** *Brit.* A deliberate slowing down of production on the part of workers. **2** *Scot.* Go warily.

ca·ca·o (kə·kā′ō, -kä′ō) *n. pl.* **·ca·os 1** The large, nutritive seeds of a small evergreen tropical American tree *(Theobroma cacao)*: also called *chocolate nuts.* **2** the sweet-scented, yellowish oil of this tree, widely used in medicine and cosmetics, and in making cocoa and chocolate. **3** The tree producing these nuts or seeds: also called *chocolate tree.* [< Sp. < Nahuatl *cacauatl* cacao]

cacao butter A hard, yellowish, fatty substance obtained from cacao beans, consisting chiefly of glycerides of stearic, palmitic, and lauric acid: used for soap, cosmetics, etc.: also called *cocoa butter.*

cac·cia·to·re (käch′ə·tôr′ē, -tō′rē) *adj.* Stewed in tomatoes and wine: chicken *cacciatore.* [< Italian]

Cá·ce·res (kä′thā·räs) A province of western Spain, constituting Upper Estremadura; 7,699 square miles; capital, Cáceres.

cach·a·lot (kash′ə·lot, -lō) *n.* The sperm whale. [< F, prob. < dial. F *cachalut* toothed]

cache (kash) *v.t.* **cached, cach·ing** To conceal or store, as in the earth; hide in a secret place. —*n.* A place for hiding or storing provisions, equipment, etc.; also, the things stored or hidden. [< F < *cacher* hide]

ca·chec·tic (kə·kek′tik) *adj.* Of, pertaining to, or affected with cachexia. Also **ca·chec′ti·cal.** [< MF *cachectique* < L *cachecticus* < Gk. *kachektikos*]

cache·pot (kash′pot, *Fr.* kȧsh·pō′) *n.* A jardinière or an ornamental pot or a casing concealing an ordinary flowerpot. [< F]

ca·chet (ka·shā′, kash′ā) *n.* **1** A seal. **2** A distinctive mark; stamp of individuality. **3** A hollow wafer used for enclosing nauseous medicine. **4** A stamped or printed mark, picture, etc., put on mail as a slogan, commemoration mark, etc. See LETTRE DE CACHET. [< F < *cacher* hide]

ca·chex·i·a (kə·kek′sē·ə) *n. Pathol.* Malnutrition and general bad health, characterized by a waxy or sallow complexion, as in cancer, tuberculosis, etc. Also **ca·chex·y** (kə·kek′sē). [< LL *cachexia* < Gk. *kachexia* poor condition or state < *kakos* bad + *-hexia* < *echein* hold oneself, be]

cach·in·nate (kak′ə·nāt) *v.i.* **·nat·ed, ·nat·ing** To laugh immoderately or noisily. [< L *cachinnatus,* pp. of *cachinnare* laugh loudly] **—cach′in·na′tion** *n.*

cach·o·long (kash′ə·long) *n.* An opaque white, yellowish, or reddish variety of opal. [< Kalmuck *kaschschilon* beautiful stone]

ca·chou (kə·shōō′, ka-) *n.* **1** An aromatic pill or pastille, used to perfume the breath. **2** Catechu. [< F < Malay *kāchū* catechu]

ca·chu·cha (kä·chōō′chä) *n. Spanish* An Andalusian dance or dance tune in 3–4 time, resembling the bolero.

ca·cique (kə·sēk′) *n.* **1** A prince or chief among the Indians of the West Indies, Mexico, Peru, etc. **2** An oriole of the warmer parts of America. Also spelled *cazique.* [< Sp. < native Haitian word for "chief"]

cack·le (kak′əl) *v.* **·led, ·ling** *v.i.* **1** To make a shrill cry, as a hen that has laid an egg. **2** To laugh or talk with a sound resembling this cry. —*v.t.* **3** To utter in a cackling manner. —*n.* **1** The shrill, broken cry made by a hen after laying an egg; the gabbling of a goose. **2** Idle talk; chattering or chuckling. See synonyms under BABBLE. [Imit.] **—cack′ler** *n.*

caco- *combining form* Bad; diseased; vile: *cacography.* [< Gk. *kakos* bad, evil]

cac·o·de·mon (kak′ə·dē′mən) *n.* **1** A devil, or evil spirit. **2** One supposedly possessed by an evil spirit. Also **cac′o·dae′mon.** [< Gk. *kakodaimōn* evil genius]

cac·o·dyl (kak′ə·dil, -dēl,) *n.* **1** *Chem.* The univalent arsenic radical, C_2H_6As, which unites with oxygen, sulfur, chlorine, etc., to form stinking, poisonous compounds. **2** A colorless, poisonous, stinking liquid, some of whose derivatives are used as accelerators in making rubber. [< Gk. *kakōdia* (< *kakos* bad + *ozein* smell) + -YL] **—cac′o·dyl′ic** (-dil′ik) *adj.*

cac·o·e·thes (kak′ō·ē′thēz) *n.* **1** A bad propensity or habit; a mania. **2** *Pathol.* A malignant ulcer. [< L < Gk. *kakoēthēs* < *kakos* bad + *ēthos* habit, disposition]

cacoethes lo·quen·di (lō·kwen′dī) *Latin* A passion for talking.

cac·o·gen·ics (kak′ə·jen′iks) *n.* The scientific study of race degeneration; also, race degeneration, as from inbreeding or inferior mating. [< CACO- + (EU)GENICS] **—cac′o·gen′ic** *adj.*

ca·cog·ra·phy (kə·kog′rə·fē) *n.* Bad handwriting or spelling. **—ca·cog′ra·pher** *n.* **—cac·o·graph·ic** (kak′ə·graf′ik) or **·i·cal** *adj.*

ca·col·o·gy (kə·kol′ə·jē) *n.* Mischoice or misuse of words; bad pronunciation or speech. [< Gk. *kakologia* bad style, abuse]

cac·o·mis·tle (kak′ə·mis′əl) *n.* A long-tailed, raccoonlike carnivore (genus *Bassariscus*); especially, *B. astutus* of Mexico and adjacent parts of the United States. Also **cac′o·mis′cle, cac′o·mix′l** (-mis′əl, -mik′səl), **cac′o·mix′le.** [< Sp. < Nahuatl *tlacomiztli*]

ca·coph·o·nous (kə·kof′ə·nəs) *adj.* **1** Having a harsh, discordant, disagreeable sound: opposed to *euphonious.* **2** *Music* Discordant; dissonant: opposed to *harmonious. Also* **cac·o·phon·ic** (kak′ə·fon′ik) or **·i·cal** **—ca·coph′o·nous·ly, cac′o·phon′i·cal·ly** *adv.*

ca·coph·o·ny (kə·kof′ə·nē) *n.* **1** Discord; a disagreeable sound. **2** The use of harsh combinations of sounds, words, etc., in speech. **3** *Music* Dissonance; also, the frequent use of dissonance. [< F *cacaphonie* < Gk. *kakophlōnia* < *kakos* bad + *phōneein* sound]

cac·ta·ceous (kak·tā′shəs) *adj. Bot.* Of or belonging to the cactus family *(Cactaceae).*

cac·tus (kak′təs) *n. pl.* **·tus·es** or **·ti** (-tī) Any one of various polypetalous, green, fleshy, mostly leafless and spiny plants of the family *Cactaceae,* native in arid regions of America, often having showy flowers. [< L < Gk. *kaktos* a prickly plant]

ca·cu·men (kə·kyōō′mən) *n.* The apex or top. [< L]

ca·cu·mi·nal (kə·kyōō′mə·nəl) *adj.* **1** Pertaining to the top, as of a plant. **2** *Phonet.* Describing those consonants pronounced with the tip of the tongue turned up and back toward the hard palate, as *ṭ* and *ḍ* in the Indic and Dravidian languages; cerebral; retroflex. —*n.* *Phonet.* A consonant so formed.

Ca·cus (kā′kəs) In Roman mythology, a giant, son of Vulcan, who stole the cattle of Hercules and was killed by him.

cad (kad) *n.* **1** A vulgar, ill-bred, obtrusive person; one not behaving as a gentleman. **2** *Obs.* In England, one who caters to the sports of public-school boys or university students; at Oxford, a townsman. **3** *Obs.* The conductor of an omnibus. [Short form of CADET] **—cad′dish** *adj.* **—cad′dish·ly** *adv.* **—cad′dish·ness** *n.*

ca·das·ter (kə·das′tər) *n.* A register, survey, or map of the extent, ownership, value, etc., of the lands of a country, as a basis of taxation. Also **ca·das′tre.** [< F *cadastre* < LL *capitastrum* tax register < *caput* head] **—ca·das′tral** *adj.* **—cad·as·tra·tion** (kad′əs·trā′·shən) *n.*

ca·dav·er (kə·dav′ər, -dā′vər) *n.* A dead body; especially, that of a human being intended for dissection; a corpse. [< L]

ca·dav·er·ine (kə·dav′ər·in, -ēn) *n.* *Biochem.* A thick, colorless, liquid ptomaine, $C_5H_{14}N_2$, of noxious odor, formed by putrefying animal tissue.

ca·dav·er·ous (kə·dav′ər·əs) *adj.* Like a corpse; pale; ghastly; gaunt. Also **ca·dav′er·ic. —ca·dav′er·ous·ly** *adv.* **—ca·dav′er·ous·ness** *n.*

cad·die (kad′ē) *n.* A messenger or errand boy, especially one paid to carry clubs for golf players. —*v.i.* **·died, ·dy·ing** To act as a caddie. Also spelled *caddy.* [< CADET]

cad·dis (kad′is) *n.* **1** A coarse, sergelike fabric. **2** A narrow, tapelike worsted fabric for bindings, etc. **3** Worsted yarn; crewel. Also **cad′dice.** [< MF *cadis,* a woolen fabric]

cad·dis fly (kad′is) Any of certain four-winged insects (order *Trichoptera*): their aquatic larvae, known as **caddis worms,** construct, inhabit, and carry cylindrical, silklined cases covered with sand, gravel, etc. [Origin uncertain]

Cad·do (kad′ō) *n. pl.* **·do** or **·does** A member of a North American Indian confederacy belonging to the southern group of the Caddoan linguistic stock, formerly living along the Red River in Louisiana, Arkansas, and eastern Texas: now in Oklahoma.

Cad·do·an (kad′ō·ən) *n.* A North American Indian linguistic stock formerly numerous west of the Mississippi, and including the Arikaras of the Dakotas, the tribes of the Pawnee confederacy of Nebraska and Kansas, the Caddo of Oklahoma, Arkansas, Louisiana, and Texas, and the Wichita of Oklahoma and Texas.

cad·dy[1] (kad′ē) *n. pl.* **·dies 1** A receptacle for tea. **2** A small box or case. [< Malay *kati,* a measure of weight, equal to 1 1/4 lbs.]

cad·dy[2] (kad′ē) See CADDIE.

cade[1] (kād) *adj.* **1** Brought up by hand: a *cade* colt. **2** Coddled. [Origin unknown]

cade[2] (kād) *n.* A large, bushy shrub *(Juniperus oxycedrus)* of Mediterranean regions: its wood yields a brown, thick liquid having a tarry odor, known as **cade oil,** used in soaps and medicinally. [< F]

cade[3] (kād) *n. Obs.* A barrel or keg, especially for herring. [< F < L *cadus* < Gk. *kados* jar]

Cade (kād), **John,** died 1450, English rebel: known as *Jack Cade.*

ca·delle (kə·del′) *n.* A small, black beetle *(Tenebrioides mauritanicus)* which in both larval and adult stages feeds upon stored grain. [< F]

ca·dence (kād′ns) *n.* **1** Rhythmic or measured flow or movement, as in poetry, music, oratory. **2** *Mil.* Uniform pace and time in marching expressed in so many steps to the minute; measure; beat. **3** Modulation, as of the voice or of elemental sounds; also, a fall of the voice, as at a period. **4** Intonation or inflection of the speaking voice as distinctive of a language or locality. **5** *Music* **a** A succession of chords naturally closing a musical phrase or period: the **perfect, complete,** or **whole cadence,** proper at the end of a movement; the **imperfect** or **half cadence,** often a reversal of the dominant perfect. **b** A cadenza. See synonyms under TUNE. [< F < Ital. *cadenza* < LL *cadentia* a falling < *cadere* fall. Doublet of CHANCE, CADENZA.] **—ca′denced** *adj.*

ca·den·cy (kād′n·sē) *n. pl.* **·cies 1** Cadence; rhythm. **2** *Her.* The relative position of the younger members of the same family or branches of the same house.

ca·dent (kād′nt) *adj.* **1** Having cadence or rhythm. **2** *Obs.* Falling.

ca·den·za (kə·den′zə, *Ital.* kä·dent′sä) *n.* *Music* An embellishment or flourish, prepared or improvised, for a solo voice or an instrument, before the close of a movement or between divisions of a movement, especially in the first movement of a concerto. [< Ital. Doublet of CADENCE, CHANCE.]

ca·det (kə·det′) *n.* **1** A student at a military or naval school. **2** A student in training at the United States Military or Coast Guard Academy for commissioning as an officer: at the United States Air Force Academy the official designation is **Air Force cadet. 3** A younger son or brother in a noble family. **4** *Archaic.* A gentleman who entered the army without a commission so as to gain military experience and thus earn a commission. **5** *Colloq.* A pander or pimp; whoremonger. [< F, ult. < dim. of L *caput* head, chief]

Ca·det (kə·det′) *n.* A member of the Constitutional Democratic party of Russia, formed about 1905. [< Russian *Kadet* < *K(onstitutsionalnyie) + D(emokrati)*]

ca·det·ship (kə·det′ship) *n.* **1** The state or condition of being a cadet. **2** Appointment as cadet. Also **ca·det′cy.**

ca·dette (kȧ·det′) *n. fem.* **1** *French* A younger daughter or sister in a noble family. **2** In New Zealand, a young woman who has passed a competitive test and been appointed to the civil service.

cadet teacher A college student who does practice teaching in public schools.

cadge (kaj) *v.* **cadged, cadg·ing** *v.i. Brit. Dial.* To go about as a peddler or beggar. —*v.t. Colloq.* To beg; sponge. [? Var. of CATCH]

cadg·y (kaj′ē) *adj.* **1** Cheerful; frolicsome. **2** Wanton; amorous. [Origin uncertain]

ca·di (kä′dē,kā′-) *n. pl.* **·dis** In Moslem communities, a chief judge or magistrate whose decisions are based on Moslem law: also spelled *kadi.* [< Arabic *qāḍī*]

Cad·il·lac (kad′ə·lak, *Fr.* kȧ·dē·yȧk′), **Antoine de la Mothe,** 1657?–1730, French explorer; founded Detroit.

Cá·diz (kə·diz′, kā′diz, *Sp.* kä′thēth) **1** A province of SW Spain; 2,827 square miles. **2** Its capital, a port on the Atlantic coast of Andalusia.

Cádiz, Gulf of A wide Atlantic inlet of the SW Iberian Peninsula.

Cad·man (kad′mən), **Charles Wakefield,** 1884–1946, U.S. composer.

Cad·me·an (kad·mē′ən) *adj.* Of or pertaining to Cadmus.

Cadmean victory A victory that is ruinous to the victor.

cad·mi·um (kad′mē·əm) *n.* A soft, bluish-white, toxic metallic element (symbol Cd, atomic number 48) occurring in zinc ores and used in the manufacture of fusible alloys, in electroplating, and in controlling fission in nuclear reactors. See PERIODIC TABLE. [< NL < L *cadmia* zinc ore < Gk. *kadmeia(gē)*]

cadmium sulfide A pigment, CdS, varying in hue from lemon to orange: also **cadmium yellow** or **cadmium orange.**

Cad·mus (kad′məs) In Greek mythology, a Phoenician prince who killed a dragon sacred to Ares and sowed its teeth on the site of Thebes: from these teeth sprang up armed men who fought and destroyed each other except for five who helped him found the city. Cadmus introduced the Phoenician alphabet into Greece.

Ca·dor·na (kä·dōr′nä), **Count Luigi,** 1850–1928, Italian general: commander in chief in World War I.

cad·re (kad′rē, *Fr.* kä′dr′) *n.* **1** The officers and men necessary to establish and train a military unit. **2** Trained personnel essential in the conduct and management of an organization, enterprise, etc. **3** A nucleus; skeleton; framework. [F, frame of a picture < Ital. *quadro* < L *quadrum* square]

ca·du·ce·us (kə·dōō′sē·əs, -dyōō′-) *n. pl.* **·ce·i** (-sē·ī) **1** The wand or staff of Mercury, the messenger of the gods. **2** A similar wand used in the armed services as the emblem of the medical corps or department; also often used as the symbol of the medical profession. [< L < Gk. (Doric) *karykion* herald's staff] **—ca·du′ce·an** *adj.*

CADUCEUS

ca·du·ci·ty (kə·dōō′sə·tē, -dyōō′-) *n.* **1** The state or quality of being caducous. **2** Old age; senility.

ca·du·cous (kə·dōō′kəs, -dyōō′-) *adj.* **1** *Biol.* Dropping or falling off, especially at an early stage of development, as the sepals of a poppy or the gills of salamanders, etc. **2** Having a tendency to fall or perish; perishable. [< L *caducus* falling < *cadere* fall]

Cad·wal·la·der (kad·wol′ə·dər) A masculine personal name. Also **Cad·wal′a·der.** [Welsh, battle arranger]

cae- For words not found here, see under CE-.

cae·cil·i·an (si·sil′ē·ən) *n.* One of a family *(Caecilidae)* of tropical, burrowing, legless amphibians, resembling worms or small snakes. [< L *caecilia,* a kind of lizard]

Cae·cil·i·us (si·sil′ē·əs) Latin form of CECIL.

cae·cum (sē′kəm), etc. See CECUM, etc.

Cæd·mon (kad′mən) Seventh century English poet, the first to write in the vernacular.

Cae·li·an (sē′lē·ən) One of the seven hills of Rome. Also **Cæ′li·an.**

Caen (käṅ) A port in Normandy, NW France.

cae·o·ma (sē·ō′mə) *n. Bot.* An aecium of a fungus (genus *Caeoma)* of the *Uredinales.* [< NL < Gk. *kaiein* burn; with ref. to its color]

caer·i·mo·ni·a·ri·us (ser′i·mō′nē·ā′rē·əs) *n. pl.* **·ri·i** (-rē·ī) A director of ceremonies in solemn offices, as in Roman Catholic cathedral services. [< L *caerimonia* ceremony]

Caer·le·on (kär·lē′ən) An urban district in Monmouth, England, on the Usk; identified with Camelot.

Caer·nar·von (kär·när′vən) A county of NW Wales; 569 square miles; county town, Caernarvon: also *Carnarvon.* Also **Caer·nar′von·shire** (-shir).

caes·al·pin·i·a·ceous (sez′al·pin′ē·ā′shəs, ses′-) *adj. Bot.* Belonging to a genus *(Caesalpinia)* of tropical trees, shrubs, or herbs of the bean family. [< after A. *Caesalpinus,* 1519–1603, Italian botanist]

Cae·sar (sē′zər) **1** A masculine personal name: also spelled *Cesar.* **2** The title of any one of the Roman emperors from Augustus to Hadrian. **3** Any powerful emperor or despot.

—Caesar, Gaius Julius, 100–44 B. C., Roman general, statesman, and historian.

Caes·a·re·a (ses′ə·rē′ə, sez′-) An ancient port in Palestine, site of the Sdot Yam settlement. Also **Caesarea Palestine; Caesarea Maritime.** Also **Cæs′a·re′a.**

Caesarea Maz·a·ca (maz′ə·kə) The ancient name for KAYSERI.

Cae·sar·e·an (si·zâr′ē·ən) *adj.* Pertaining to Caesar. —*n.* A Caesarean operation. Also spelled *Cesarean, Cesarian.* Also **Cae·sar′i·an.**

Caesarean operation *Surg.* The delivery of a child by section of the abdominal walls and the womb of the mother when ordinary delivery is apparently impossible: reported to have been performed at the birth of Julius Caesar: also spelled *Cesarean.* Also **Caesarean section.**

Caesarea Phi·lip·pi (fi·lip′ī, fil′i·pī) The ancient name for BANIYAS.

Cae·sar·ism (sē′zər·iz′əm) *n.* Government like that of the Caesars; imperialism; military despotism. **—Cae′sar·ist** *n.*

cae·si·um (sē′zē·əm) See CESIUM.

caes·tus (ses′təs) See CESTUS.

cae·su·ra (si·zhŏŏr′ə, -zyŏŏr′ə) *n. pl.* **·su·ras** or **·su·rae** (-zhŏŏr′ē, -zyŏŏr′ē) **1** In prosody, a break or pause in the middle of a foot, usually near the middle of a verse. **2** A break or interruption. **3** *Music* A rest or pause indicating a rhythmic division point in an air or melody; also, the stressed note preceding. Also spelled *cesura.* [<L, cutting, caesura <*caedere* cut] — **cae·su′ral** *adj.*

Cae·ti·té (kī·tē·tā′) A city in central Bahia, eastern Brazil.

ca·fé (kə·fā′, ka-) *n.* **1** A coffee house; restaurant. **2** A barroom. **3** Coffee. [<F]

ca·fé au lait (kȧ·fā′ ō lā′) *French* **1** Coffee made with scalded milk. **2** A light brown.

ca·fé noir (kȧ·fā′ nwȧr′) *French* Black coffee.

café society The set customarily frequenting cafés or night clubs, especially in New York City.

caf·e·te·ri·a (kaf′ə·tir′ē·ə) *n.* A restaurant where the patrons wait upon themselves. [<Am. Sp., coffee store]

caf·fe·ic (ka·fē′ik) *adj.* Of, pertaining to, or derived from coffee. [<F *caféique* <*café* coffee]

caf·feine (kaf′ēn, *in technical usage* kaf′ē·in) *n. Chem.* A crystallizable, slightly bitter alkaloid, $C_8H_{10}N_4O_2 \cdot H_2O$, found in the leaves and berries of coffee, and chemically identical with theine: used as a stimulant and diuretic. [<F *caféine* <*café* coffee]

Caf·fer (kaf′ər) See KAFFIR. Also **Caf′fre.**

Caf·fer·y (kaf′rē, kaf′ər·ē), **Jefferson,** 1886–1974, U.S. diplomat.

caf·fe·tan·nic (kaf′ē·tan′ik) *adj. Chem.* Of, pertaining to, or derived from caffeine and tannin together. Also **caf′fe·o·tan′nic** (kaf′ē·ō·tan′ik). [<CAFFE(INE) + TANNIC]

caf·tan (kaf′tən, käf·tän′) *n.* An undercoat having long sleeves and a sash, worn in Mediterranean countries: also spelled *kaftan.* [<F *cafetan* <Turkish *qaftān*]

Ca·ga·yan (kä′gä·yän′) **1** A province of northern Luzon, Philippines; 3,470 square miles. **2** An island in the Sulu Sea, belonging to Palawan province, Philippines. **3** The largest river of the Philippines, flowing about 220 miles north across Luzon to Babuyan Channel. *Spanish* **Ri·o Gran·de de Ca·ga·yan** (rē′ō grän′dā thā kä′gä·yän′).

Cagayan Sulu Island An island in the Sulu Sea NE of Borneo, belonging to Sulu province, Philippines; 26 square miles.

cage (kāj) *n.* **1** A structure, with openwork of wire or bars, as for confining birds or beasts. **2** A room or place enclosed by a grating, for confining prisoners. **3** Any lockup, prison, or place of confinement, or anything that confines or imprisons. **4** Any cagelike structure, framework, or grating, as a timber framework lining a shaft. **5** A platform, elevator car, or the like, protected by gratings. **6** A wire mask worn by the catcher in baseball. **7** The iron or steel skeleton frame of a high building. **8** A table from which quick-firing guns are discharged. **9** An enclosure in a gymnasium for interior baseball practice. —*v.t.* **caged, cag·ing** To shut up in or as in a cage; confine; imprison. [<OF <L *cavea* <*cavus* empty, hollow]

cage·ling (kāj′ling) *n.* A caged bird.

ca·gey (kā′jē) *adj. Colloq.* **ca·gi·er, ca·gi·est** Shrewd; wary of being duped. Also **ca′gy.** — **ca′gi·ly** *adv.* —**ca′gi·ness** *n.*

Ca·glia·ri (kä′lyä·rē) The capital of Sardinia, a port on the **Gulf of Cagliari,** an inlet of the Mediterranean in southern Sardinia.

Ca·glia·ri (kä′lyä·rē), **Paolo** See VERONESE.

Ca·glio·stro (kä·lyôs′trō), **Count Alessandro di,** 1743–95: Sicilian adventurer and supposed magician: real name *Giuseppe Balsamo.*

Ca·gou·lard (kȧ·gōō·lȧr′) *n.* A member of a secret French organization whose conspiracy to overthrow the government and eventually restore the monarchy in France was exposed in 1937. [<F *cagoule* monk's hood <L *cuculla* hood]

ca·hier (kä·yā′) *n.* **1** A memorial, report of proceedings, or the like. **2** A quarter of a quire of writing paper. **3** A few leaves, as of printed matter, loosely stitched together; a number of a book issued in parts. [<F <OF *quaier* <L *quaterni* by fours <*quattuor* four]

ca·hoots (kə·hōōts′) *n. pl. U.S. Slang* Partnership; close cooperation; collusion: to be in *cahoots.* [? <F *cahute* cabin]

Cai·a·phas (kā′ə·fəs, kī′-) A Jewish high priest: presided at the council which condemned Jesus. *Matt.* xxvi 57–68.

Cai·cos (kī′kōs) See TURKS AND CAICOS ISLANDS.

Cail·laux (kȧ·yō′), **Joseph Marie,** 1863–1944, French politician.

cai·man (kā′mən) *n. pl.* **·mans** A tropical American crocodilian (genus *Caiman*) closely related to the alligator, as the **spectacled caiman** *(C. sclerops),* having prominent ridges above the upper eyelid. Also spelled *cayman.* [<Sp., probably <a Carib word]

cain (kān) See KAIN.

Cain (kān) **1** The eldest son of Adam, who slew his brother Abel. *Gen.* iv 1–10. **2** Hence, a fratricide or murderer. —**to raise Cain** *Slang* To raise a rumpus; make a noisy disturbance.

ca·in·ca root (kə·ing′kə) The root of the tropical American snowberry: the bark of this root yields a glycoside used as a purgative. Also **ca·hin·ca root** (kə·hing′kə).

Caine (kān), **(Sir Thomas Henry) Hall,** 1853–1931, English novelist.

Cain·ite (kā′nīt) *n.* A member of a heretical sect of the second century which professed reverence for Cain, Esau, and other wicked Old Testament characters. —**Cain′ism** *n.* —**Cain·it·ic** (kā·nit′ik) *adj.*

Cai·no·zo·ic (kī′nə·zō′ik) See CENOZOIC.

ca·ique (kä·ēk′) *n.* **1** A long, narrow, pointed skiff with from two to ten oars, used on the Bosporus. **2** A small Levantine sailing vessel. [<F <Ital. *caicco* <Turkish *qāyiq*]

ça i·ra (sȧ′ ē·rȧ′) *French* Literally, it will go, meaning it will succeed: the refrain of a popular song of the French Revolution.

caird (kârd) *n. Scot.* A tinker; gipsy.

Caird (kârd), **Edward,** 1835–1908, Scottish philosopher.

Caird Coast (kârd) The part of Antarctica on the SE coast of the Weddell Sea.

Cai·rene (kī′rēn, kī·rēn′) *n.* One born or living in Cairo. —*adj.* Pertaining to Cairo.

cairn (kârn) *n.* A mound or heap of stones for a memorial or a marker. [<Scottish Gaelic *carn* heap of stones] —**cairned** *adj.*

cairn·gorm (kârn′gôrm) *n.* A smoky, yellow to brown variety of quartz; smoky quartz. [from *Cairngorm* Mountains]

Cairn·gorm Mountains (kârn′gôrm) A range in Inverness and Banffshire, Scotland; highest peak, 4,296 feet.

Cairn terrier (kârn) See under TERRIER.

Cai·ro (kī′rō) **1** The capital of Egypt and the largest city of Africa, on the east bank of the Nile at the head of its delta: an inhabitant of the city known as a **Cai·rene** (kī·rēn′). **2** (kâr′ō) A city in Illinois at the confluence of the Mississippi and Ohio Rivers.

cais·son (kā′sən, -son) *n.* **1** An ammunition chest or wagon. **2** A two-wheeled vehicle carrying such a chest to serve a gun in firing position with its immediate needs in ammunition. **3** A large watertight chamber within which work is done under water, as on a bridge pier. **4** A watertight box, or other apparatus, to be placed beneath a sunken vessel and inflated in order to raise it. **5** A gate for closing the entrance to a drydock. [<F, aug. of *caisse* box, chest]

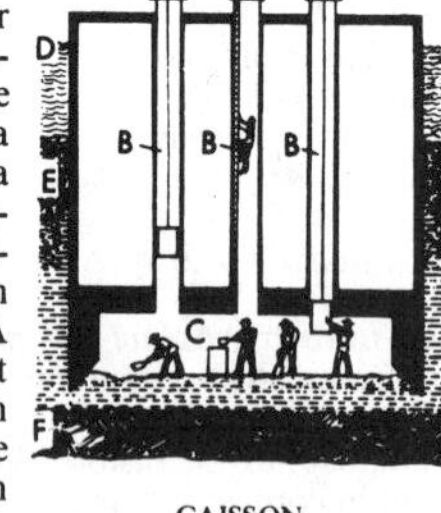

CAISSON
A. Airlocks. *B.* Shafts for entrance of men and materials. *C.* Work chamber. *D.* Water level. *E.* River bottom. *F.* Bedrock.

caisson disease Decompression sickness.

Caith·ness (kāth′nes, kāth·nes′) A county of NE Scotland; 686 square miles; capital, Wick. Also **Caith′ness·shire** (-shir).

cai·tiff (kā′tif) *n.* A base wretch. —*adj.* Vile; basely wicked. [<AF *caitif* weak, wretched <L *captivus.* Doublet of CAPTIVE.]

Cai·us (kā′əs, kī′-) See GAIUS.

Caius (kēz), **John,** 1510–72, English physician and educator.

Ca·jal (kä·häl′) See RAMÓN Y CAJAL.

Ca·ja·mar·ca (kä′hä·mär′kä) A city in NW Peru.

caj·e·put (kaj′ə·pət) *n.* **1** The California laurel *(Umbellularia californica).* **2** The cajuput. [<Malay *kāyupūtih* <*kāyu* tree + *pūtih* white]

ca·jole (kə·jōl′) *v.* **ca·joled, ca·jol·ing** *v.t.* To persuade or coax with flattery or delusive promises. —*v.i.* To wheedle; to practice cajolery. See synonyms under ALLURE. [<F *cajoler*] — **ca·jole′ment** *n.* —**ca·jol′er** *n.* —**ca·jol′ing·ly** *adv.*

ca·jol·er·y (kə·jō′lər·ē) *n. pl.* **·er·ies** The act of cajoling; the art or practice of wheedling by flattery.

ca·jon (kä·hōn′) *n. pl.* **ca·jo·nes** (kä·hō′nās) *SW U.S.* A canyon or narrow gorge with steep sides. [<Sp.]

Ca·jun (kā′jən) *n.* A reputed descendant of the Acadian French in Louisiana. [Alter. of ACADIAN]

caj·u·put (kaj′ə·pət) *n.* **1** A small tree *(Melaleuca leucadendron)* of the myrtle family, native in the Moluccas. **2** A greenish-yellow, odorous oil distilled from the fresh leaves and twigs of this tree: used chiefly in the treatment of skin diseases. Also **caj′a·put.** Sometimes spelled *cajeput, kajeput.* [See CAJEPUT]

cake (kāk) *n.* **1** A baked mixture of flour, eggs, milk, etc.: distinguished from bread or pudding. **2** A small or thin mass of dough, etc., baked or fried: *pancake.* **3** A hardened mass of any material: a *cake* of soap, etc. **4** *Pathol.* A morbid hardening or coagulation in the body. —**to take the cake** *Colloq.* To take the prize; be the best of or at something. —*v.t.* & *v.i.* **caked, cak·ing** To form into a hardened mass. [<ON *kaka*]

cakes and ale A carefree way of life; soft, easy living.

cake urchin A sea urchin (family *Clypeastridae*) having a disklike body with a raised central surface and a mass of velvety spines.

cake·walk (kāk′wôk′) *n.* **1** Originally, a promenade or march of American Negro origin in which a cake is awarded as prize for the most original steps. **2** A dance based on this or the music for such a dance. —*v.i.* To do a cakewalk; strut. —**cake′walk′er** *n.*

cal·a·bar (kal′ə·bär) *n.* **1** The pelt of the gray Siberian squirrel. **2** The squirrel. Also **cal′a·ber** (-bər). [<F *Calabre* Calabria]

Cal·a·bar (kal′ə·bär′, kal′ə·bär) A port in SE Nigeria, formerly **Old Calabar,** on the **Calabar River,** flowing 70 miles SW to the Gulf of Guinea.

Calabar bean The highly poisonous seed of an African twining climber *(Physostigma venenosum)* of the bean family, the source of physostigmine: also called, from its use as a native test for crime or witchcraft, *ordeal bean.*

cal·a·bash (kal′ə·bash) *n.* **1** The calabash tree. **2** Any vessel, pipe, or utensil made from the calabash gourd. [<F *calebasse* <Sp. *calabaza* pumpkin <Persian *kharbuz* melon]

calabash gourd The common gourd from the calabash tree, used for making pipes, etc.

calabash tree **1** A tropical American tree *(Lagenaria siceraria)* of the trumpet-flower family, bearing a gourdlike fruit or calabash. **2** A tropical American tree *(Crescentia cujete)* of the bignonia family, with a hard-shelled, gourdlike fruit. **3** The African baobab.

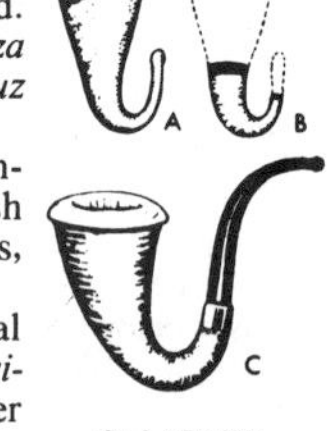

CALABASH
A. Gourd.
B. Portion used in making pipe.
C. Finished pipe with meerschaum bowl.

cal·a·ba·zil·la (kal′ə·bə·sēl′yə) *n.* A squash *(Cucurbita foetidissima),* the macerated root of which is used as a remedy for hemorrhoids and the pulp of its green fruit as soap. [<Sp., dim. of *calabaza* gourd]

cal·a·boose (kal′ə·bōōs) *n. U.S. Colloq.* A jail; lockup. [<Sp. *calaboza*]

Ca·la·bri·a (kə·lā′brē·ə, *Ital.* kä·lä′bryä) A region of southern Italy; 5,828 square miles, occupying the toe of the Italian boot: ancient *Bruttium.* — **Ca·la′bri·an** *adj* & *n.*

ca·la·di·um (kə·lā′dē·əm) *n.* One of a genus *(Caladium)* of tuberous tropical American herbs of the arum family with large, variegated sagittate leaves. [<NL <Malay *kělādy*]

Ca·lah (kā′lə) The biblical name for KALAKH.

Cal·ais (kal′ā, ka·lā′, kal′is; *Fr.* kȧ·le′) A French port on the English Channel, facing Dover.

cal·a·man·co (kal′ə·mang′kō) *n.* **1** A glossy, woolen, Flemish fabric, or a garment made from it. **2** A glazed linen stuff. Also spelled *calimanco.* [<Sp.]

cal·a·man·der (kal′ə·man′dər) *n.* The wood of various trees of the ebony family, especially the rare *Diospyros quaesita* of Ceylon, finely veined, hard, and valued for cabinetwork. [Alter. of *Coromandel* (Coast)]

cal·a·mar·y (kal′ə·mâr′ē, -mər·ē) *n. pl.* **·mar·ies** A squid. [<L *calamarius* <*calamus* pen <Gk. *kalamos* reed]

Ca·la·mian Islands (kä′lä·myän′) A Philippine island group between Mindoro and Palawan; 600 square miles. *Spanish* **Is·las Ca·la·mi·a·nes** (ēs′läs kä′lä·myä′näs).

cal·am·bak (cal·am·bak′) *n.* A wood used in fine inlay work; also called *aloes wood.*

cal·a·mif·er·ous (kal′ə·mif′ər·əs) *adj.* Bearing reeds [<CALAMUS + L *ferre* bear]

ca·lam·i·form (kə·lam′ə·fôrm) *adj.* Shaped like a reed.

cal·a·mine (kal′ə·mīn, -min) *n.* **1** Hemimorphite. **2** Smithsonite. **3** A native zinc carbonate, a pink powder much used in the form of a zinc and ferric oxide as a lotion or ointment for the treatment of skin ailments.—*v.t.* **·mined, ·min·ing** To apply calamine to. [<F <LL *calamina* <L *cadmia.* See CADMIUM.]

cal·a·mint (kal′ə·mint) *n.* A menthaceous plant (genus *Satureia*) of the north temperate zone, especially *S. calamintha.* Also **calamint balm.** [<MF *calament* <Med. L *calamentum* <L *calaminthe* <Gk. *kalaminthē*]

cal·a·mite (kal′ə·mīt) *n.* A fossil plant (genus *Calamites,* division *Pteridophyta*) of the later Paleozoic era, resembling the modern horsetails in general appearance but growing to a height of 100 feet and more. [<NL *calamites* <L *calamus* reed]

ca·lam·i·tous (kə·lam′ə·təs) *adj.* Disastrous; causing or resulting in a calamity. **—ca·lam′i·tous·ly** *adv.*

ca·lam·i·ty (kə·lam′ə·tē) *n. pl.* **·ties 1** A misfortune or disaster. **2** A state or time of affliction, adversity, or disaster. See synonyms under ACCIDENT, ADVERSITY, BLOW, CATASTROPHE, MISFORTUNE. [<F *calamité* <L *calamitas*]

Ca·lam·i·ty Jane (kə·lam′ə·tē jān′), 1852?–1903, U.S. frontier marksman: real name *Martha Jane Burke, née* Canary.

cal·a·mus (kal′ə·məs) *n. pl.* **·mi** (-mī) **1** The sweetflag. **2** The quill of a feather. [<L <Gk. *kalamos* reed]

Cal·a·mus (kal′ə·məs) *n.* A genus of oriental climbing palms; the climbing rattans. [See CALAMUS]

ca·lan·do (kä·län′dō) *adj.* & *adv. Music* Diminishing in strength of tone and in rapidity. [<Ital.]

ca·lash (kə·lash′) *n.* **1** A low-wheeled light carriage with folding top. **2** A folding carriage top or hood. **3** A woman's hood supported by hoops, to be pulled over the head or folded back, fashionable in the 18th century. Also spelled *calèche.* [<F *calèche,* ult. <Slavic]

CALASH (*def. 3*)

cal·a·thus (kal′ə·thəs) *n. pl.* (-thī) In ancient Greece, a vase-shaped basket for fruit: regarded as a symbol of fruitfulness, as on statues of Demeter, etc. [<L <Gk. *kalathos* basket]

cal·a·ver·ite (kal′ə·vâr′īt) *n.* A telluride of gold and silver, usually granular in structure, with a silvery-white metallic luster: an important ore of gold. [from *Calaveras* County, Calif.]

Ca·la·yan (kä′lä·yän′) The largest of the Babuyan Islands, Philippines; 73 square miles.

cal·ca·ne·um (kal·kā′nē·əm) *n. pl.* **·ne·a** (-nē·ə) *Anat.* The heel bone. See illustration under FOOT. Also **cal·ca′ne·us.** [<L <*calx* heel]

cal·car[1] (kal′kär) *n.* **1** A calcining oven. **2** An annealing oven. [<L *calcaria* limekiln]

cal·car[2] (kal′kär) *n. pl.* **cal·car·i·a** (kal·kâr′ē·ə) *Biol.* A spur, or spurlike projection, as at the base of a petal or on the leg or wing of a bird. [<L, spur <*calx* heel]

cal·ca·rate (kal′kə·rāt, -rit) *adj. Biol.* Having a calcar, or spur; spurred. Also **cal′ca·rat′ed.**

cal·car·e·ous (kal·kâr′ē·əs) *adj.* **1** Composed of, containing, or of the nature of limestone or calcium carbonate. **2** Containing calcium. [<L *calcarius* of lime <*calx* lime]

cal·ca·rif·er·ous (kal′kə·rif′ər·əs) *adj. Biol.* Bearing spurs.

cal·ce·ate (kal′sē·āt, -it) *adj.* Wearing shoes; shod: said of certain religious orders. [<L *calceatus,* pp. of *calceare* shoe]

cal·ced·o·ny (kal·sed′ə·nē) See CHALCEDONY.

cal·ce·i·form (kal′sē·ə·fôrm′) *adj. Bot.* Calceolate.

cal·ce·o·lar·i·a (kal′sē·ə·lâr′ē·ə) *n.* A member of a large genus *(Calceolaria)* of herbs and shrubs of the figwort family, with opposite leaves and small axillary or racemose flowers having the lowest petal the longest: also called *slipperwort.* [<L *calceolus,* dim. of *calceus* shoe]

cal·ce·o·late (kal′sē·ə·lāt) *adj. Bot.* Slipper-shaped. **—cal′ce·o·late′ly** *adv.*

cal·ces (kal′sēz) A plural of CALX.

Cal·chas (kal′kəs) In the *Iliad,* a priest of Apollo who accompanied the Greeks to Troy.

calci- *combining form* Lime: *calciferous.* [<L *calx, calcis* lime]

cal·cic (kal′sik) *adj.* Of, pertaining to, or containing calcium or lime. [<L *calx* lime]

cal·cic·o·lous (kal·sik′ə·ləs) *adj. Ecol.* Growing upon limestone: said of certain plants. [<CALCI- + L *colere* cultivate, dwell]

cal·ci·co·sis (kal′si·kō′sis) *n. Pathol.* A disease of the lungs occurring among workers in limestone dust. [<L *calx* lime + -OSIS]

cal·cif·er·ol (kal·sif′ər·ōl, -ol) *n. Biochem.* The anti-rachitic vitamin D_2, a white, crystalline, fat-soluble, accessory food factor, $C_{28}H_{44}O$, formed by the ultraviolet irradiation of ergosterol: found in fish oils, milk, eggs, etc. [<CALCIFER(OUS) + (ERGOSTER)OL]

cal·cif·er·ous (kal·sif′ər·əs) *adj.* Yielding or containing calcium carbonate, as rocks. Also **cal·cif·ic** (kal·sif′ik).

cal·ci·fi·ca·tion (kal′sə·fi·kā′shən) *n.* **1** Conversion into chalk, or into stony or bony substance, by the deposition of lime salts, as in petrifaction and ossification. **2** Such a lime formation. **3** *Pathol.* A petrifactive retrogression observed in tissue which has degenerated. **4** The accumulation by a surface soil of sufficient calcium to bring soil colloids close to saturation, as in Chernozem soils.

cal·ci·form[1] (kal′sə·fôrm) *adj.* **1** *Obs.* Having the form of lime or chalk. **2** Pebble-shaped.

cal·ci·form[2] (kal′sə·fôrm) *adj.* Having a projection like a heel. [<L *calx* heel + -FORM]

cal·cif·u·gous (kal·sif′yə·gəs) *adj. Ecol.* Not growing on limestone: said of certain saxicolous lichens. Also **cal·cif′u·gal.** [<CALCI- + L *fugere* flee]

cal·ci·fy (kal′sə·fī) *v.t.* & *v.i.* **·fied, ·fy·ing** To make or become stony by the deposit of lime salts.

cal·ci·mine (kal′sə·mīn, -min) *n.* A white or tinted wash consisting of whiting, or zinc white, with glue and water, for ceilings, walls, etc. —*v.t.* **·mined, ·min·ing** To apply calcimine to. Also spelled *kalsomine.* [<L *calx* lime]

cal·cin·a·to·ry (kal·sin′ə·tôr′ē, -tō′rē) *adj.* For calcining. —*n. pl.* **·ries** An apparatus for calcining, as a calcining furnace. [<LL *calcinatorium* <*calcinare* calcine]

cal·cine (kal′sīn, -sin) *v.* **·cined, ·cin·ing** *v.t.* **1** To expel volatile matter (as carbon dioxide or water) from (a substance) by heat, for the purpose of rendering it friable: to *calcine* limestone. **2** To reduce to a calx, as copper ore, by subjecting to heat; roast. —*v.i.* **3** To become changed by the action of dry heat into a friable powder. Also **cal′cin·ize.** [<F *calciner* <Med. L *calcinare* <L *calx* lime] **—cal′cined** *adj.* **—cal·ci·na·tion** (kal′sə·nā′shən) *n.*

cal·ciph·i·lous (kal·sif′ə·ləs) *adj. Ecol.* Thriving on chalk; lime-loving: said of plants that grow best in soils containing lime. [<CALCI- + Gk. *philos* loving <*phileein* love]

cal·ciph·o·bous (kal·sif′ə·bəs) *adj. Ecol.* Not thriving on soils rich in lime. [<CALCI- + Gk. *-phobos* fearing <*phobeein* fear]

cal·cite (kal′sīt) *n.* A widely diffused calcium carbonate, $CaCO_3$, usually colorless or whitish in hexagonal crystals: massive varieties include chalk, limestone, and marble. See ICELAND SPAR. **—cal·cit·ic** (kal·sit′ik) *adj.*

cal·ci·tra·tion (kal′sə·trā′shən) *n.* Kicking. See RECALCITRATE. [<L *calcitrare* kick]

cal·ci·um (kal′sē·əm) *n.* An abundant, silvery-white metallic element (symbol Ca, atomic number 20) belonging to the alkaline-earth group and forming an essential constituent of living organisms. See PERIODIC TABLE. [<L *calx* lime]

calcium carbide *Chem.* A compound, CaC_2, made from quicklime and carbon in an electric furnace: treated with water it yields acetylene. Also **calcium acetylide.**

calcium carbonate *Chem.* A fine white amorphous powder, $CaCO_3$: used in toothpowders and dental cements.

calcium chloride *Chem.* A white, very deliquescent, hygroscopic salt, $CaCl_2$: used as a drying agent, preservative, refrigerant, and to prevent dust.

calcium cyanamide *Chem.* A compound, $CaCN_2$, produced in the electric furnace from the nitrogen of the air; an artificial fertilizer.

calcium fluoride *Chem.* A white powder, CaF_2, which becomes luminous on the application of heat: used for etching glass and in the manufacture of enamels.

calcium hydroxide *Chem.* Slaked lime, $Ca(OH)_2$: also used in solution; limewater.

calcium light A powerful light produced by the incandescence of lime in an oxyhydrogen flame; the Drummond light: limelight.

calcium phosphate *Chem.* Any of a class of earthy phosphates formed in various animal tissues and otherwise; especially, tribasic calcium phosphate or bone ash, $Ca_3(PO_4)_2$, used as an antacid, polishing agent, etc.

calcium sulfate *Chem.* A white compound, $CaSO_4$, occurring in nature as anhydrite and as gypsum.

cal·cog·ra·phy (kal·kog′rə·fē) *n.* The art of drawing with colored chalks or pastels. [<L *calx, calcis* chalk, lime + -GRAPHY] **—cal·co·graph·ic** (kal′kə·graf′ik) *adj.*

calc·sin·ter (kalk′sin′tər) *n.* A loose deposit of massive calcite in caverns or river beds; travertine. [<G *kalksinter* <*kalk* chalk (<L *calx* lime) + *sinter* slag]

calc·spar (kalk′spär′) *n.* Crystallized carbonate of lime. [<CALC(AREOUS) + SPAR[3]]

calc·tuff (kalk′tuf′) *n. Geol.* A porous deposit of carbonate of lime found in calcareous springs. Also **calc·tu·fa** (kalk′tōō′fə, -tyōō′-). [<CALC(AREOUS) + TUFA]

cal·cu·la·ble (kal′kyə·lə·bəl) *adj.* Capable of being calculated, estimated, or forecast; reliable. **—cal′cu·la·bly** *adv.*

cal·cu·late (kal′kyə·lāt) *v.* **·lat·ed, ·lat·ing** *v.t.* **1** To determine by computation; arrive at by arithmetical means. **2** To predict or ascertain beforehand, as by computation: to *calculate* an eclipse. **3** To adapt or fit, as to a purpose or function: used chiefly in the passive: a truck *calculated* to carry a two-ton load. **4** To estimate or determine after deliberation; reckon: He *calculated* his chances. —*v.i.* **5** To perform a mathematical process; compute. **6** *U.S. Dial.* & *Colloq.* To suppose or believe; think. **—to calculate on** *Colloq.* To depend or rely on. [<LL *calculatus,* pp. of *calculare* reckon <*calculus* pebble <*calx* lime; with ref. to the use of pebbles in counting]

Synonyms: account, compute, consider, count, deem, enumerate, estimate, number, rate, reckon. *Number* is the generic term. To *count* is to *number* one by one. To *calculate* is to use more complicated processes, as multiplication, division, etc. *Compute* allows more of the element of probability, which is still more strongly expressed by *estimate*; as, to *estimate* the cost of a proposed building. To *enumerate* is to mention item by item; as to *enumerate* one's grievances. To *rate* is to *estimate* by comparison, as if the object were one of a series. We *count* upon a desired future; we do not *count* upon the undesired. As applied to the present we *reckon* or *count* a thing precious or worthless. Compare ESTEEM.

cal·cu·lat·ing (kal′kyə·lā′ting) *adj.* **1** Inclined to reckon or estimate, especially for one's own chances or interests; planning; scheming: a *calculating* politician. **2** Designed for computation: a *calculating* machine.

calculating machine A keyboard machine that automatically adds, subtracts, multiplies, and divides a series of numbers recorded by the operator.

cal·cu·la·tion (kal′kyə·lā′shən) *n.* **1** The act or art of computing. **2** A computation; reckoning. **3** An estimate of probability; a forecast or deduction; the result of calculating. **4** Shrewd caution; prudence.

cal·cu·la·tive (kal′kyə·lā′tiv) *adj.* Of or pertaining to calculation; given to calculation.

cal·cu·la·tor (kal′kyə·lā′tər) *n.* **1** One who calculates. **2** A calculating machine or set of tables.

cal·cu·lous (kal′kyə·ləs) *adj.* **1** Stony; gritty. **2** Pertaining to, like, or affected with calculus. [<L *calculosus* gritty, pebbly]

cal·cu·lus (kal′kyə·ləs) *n. pl.* **·li** (-lī) or **·lus·es** **1** *Pathol.* A stonelike concretion, as in the bladder. **2** *Math.* A method of calculating by the use of a highly specialized system of algebraic symbols. **— differential calculus** That branch of analysis which investigates the infinitesimal changes of constantly varying quantities when the relations between the quantities are given. **— integral calculus** That branch of analysis which, from the relations among the infinitesimal changes or variations of quantities, deduces relations among the quantities themselves, as in finding the area enclosed by a given curve. [<L, a pebble (used in counting)]

Cal·cut·ta (kal·kut′ə) A port on the Hooghly; the largest city in India, and the capital of West Bengal.

cal·dar·i·um (kal·dâr′ē·əm) *n. pl.* **·dar·i·a** (-dâr′ē·ə) In ancient Rome, a room for the hot bath. [<L < *calidus* hot]

Cal·de·cott (kôl′də·kət), **Randolph,** 1846–86, English artist and illustrator.

cal·de·ra (kal·dē′rə, *Sp.* käl·dā′rä) *n.* **1** *Geol.* A large, roughly circular depression, in many cases with a partially broken-down rim, formed by the explosive disruption of a volcanic cone, or by the collapse of a crater floor. **2** A large caldron. [<Sp.]

Cal·de·rón de la Bar·ca (käl′dā·rōn′ thā lä vär′kä), **Pedro,** 1600–81, Spanish dramatist.

cal·dron (kôl′drən) *n.* A large kettle or boiler: also spelled *cauldron.* [<AF *caudron* <L *caldaria* kettle < *calidus* hot]

Cald·well (kôld′wel, -wəl), **Erskine,** born 1903, U.S. writer.

Ca·leb (kā′ləb) A masculine personal name. [<Hebrew, dog]

— Caleb The associate of Joshua in spying on the land of Canaan. *Num.* xiii 30.

ca·lèche (kå·lesh′) See CALASH.

Cal·e·do·ni·a (kal′ə·dō′nē·ə, -dōn′yə) The Roman name for the part of England north of the Firths of Clyde and Forth; now used poetically to mean all of Scotland. **— Cal′e·do′ni·an** *adj.* & *n.*

Caledonian Canal A waterway from Moray Firth to Loch Linnhe, Argyllshire, Scotland; 60 1/2 miles.

cal·e·fa·cient (kal′ə·fā′shənt) *adj.* Causing heat or warmth. **—** *n. Med.* Something that produces heat or warmth, as a mustard plaster. [<L *calefaciens, -entis,* ppr. of *calefacere* < *calere* be warm + *facere* make, cause] **— cal′e·fac′tion** (-fak′shən) *n.* **— cal′e·fac′tive** *adj.*

cal·e·fac·to·ry (kal′ə·fak′tər·ē) *adj.* Adapted or used for heating or warming; communicating warmth. **—** *n.* An artificially warmed room in a monastery.

ca·len·dal (kə·len′dəl) *adj.* Of or pertaining to the Roman calends or the first day of any month. [<L *calendae* first day of the month]

cal·en·dar (kal′ən·dər) *n.* **1** A systematic arrangement of subdivisions of time, as years, months, days, weeks, etc. **2** An almanac. **3** A schedule or list of things or events classified or chronologically arranged: a *calendar* of causes for trial in court. **4** *Obs.* A guide; example; model. **—** *v.t.* To register in a calendar or list; place in the calendar of saints; digest and index, as documents. ◆ Homophone: *calender.* [<L *calendarium* account book < *calendae* calends]

— Chinese calendar An ancient calendar, no longer in official use, with days and years reckoned in cycles of sixty. Each year consists of twelve lunar months, with adjustment to the solar year by periodic intercalation.

— ecclesiastical calendar A lunisolar calendar reckoning the year from the first Sunday in Advent: used for regulating the dates of church feasts.

— Gregorian calendar The calendar now in general use in most parts of the world; first prescribed in 1582 by Pope Gregory XIII to correct the Julian year to the solar year; adopted in England Sept. 3/14, 1752, the first being the *Old Style (O.S.)* date and the last being the *New Style (N.S.).* (Thus, although George Washington's birthday is commemorated on February 22, he was born on February 11, 1732, by the Old Style calendar.)

— Hebrew calendar The present-day calendar of the Jews, based on a lunar month, and adjusted to the solar year by intercalating the month Veadar between Adar and Nisan 7 times in a 19-year cycle. The months, having alternately 30 and 29 days, are Tishri, Heshwan, Kislew, Tebet, Shebat, Adar, Nisan, Iyyar, Siwan, Tammuz, Ab, and Elul; Heshwan and Kislew, however, may add or lose a day respectively as needed. The year now begins on Tishri 1, though anciently it began in Nisan. The Hebrew calendar reckons the creation at 3760 years 3 months B.C., as compared with Archbishop Ussher's 4004 B.C.

— Hindu calendar A solar calendar, reckoned in 12 months, each beginning when the sun enters a new sign of the zodiac.

— Julian calendar The calendar prescribed by Julius Caesar, which, though using the bissextile year, was in error one day in 128 years. The months, after some changes by Augustus, had the length now in use in Europe and America.

— Mohammedan calendar A lunar calendar of 12 months dating from A.D. 622 (July 15), the year of the Hegira. There is no seasonal intercalation, the seasons retrogressing in a period of 32 1/2 years. The names of the months, alternately 29 and 30 days, are Muharram (30 days), Saphar, Rabia 1, Rabia 2, Jomada 1, Jomada 2, Rajab, Shaaban, Ramadan, Shawwal, Dulkaada, and Dulheggia.

— perpetual calendar A calendar by which the day of the week for any given date may be ascertained during a widely extended period of time.

— Republican or **Revolutionary calendar** The calendar instituted on Oct. 5, 1793, by the first French Republic, and abolished Dec. 31, 1805. Its scheme divided the year into 12 months of 30 days each, with five (in leap years, six) supplementary days *(sansculottides)* at the end of the last month. The first year (Year I) began Sept. 22, 1792. The months were: Vendémiaire, Brumaire, Frimaire, Nivose, Pluviose, Ventose, Germinal, Floréal, Prairial, Messidor, Thermidor (or Fervidor), and Fructidor.

— Roman calendar A lunar calendar, attributed to Numa. The day of the new moon was the *calends,* and the day of the full moon the *ides* (the 13th or 15th of the month). Days were reckoned backward from these dates and from the *nones,* ninth day before the ides by inclusive reckoning.

— world calendar A proposed reformed calendar designed to equalize the lengths of the quarters of the year, each to have one month of 31 and two of 30 days. It provides for extra days to conform to solar time.

cal·en·der[1] (kal′ən·dər) *n.* A machine for giving a gloss to cloth, paper, etc., by pressing between rollers. **—** *v.t.* To press in a calender. ◆ Homophone: *calendar.* [<F *calendre* <L *cylindrus* <Gk. *kylindros* roller] **— cal′en·dered** *adj.* **— cal′en·der·er** *n.*

cal·en·der[2] (kal′ən·dər) *n.* A mendicant dervish of Persia or Turkey. ◆ Homophone: *calendar.* [<Persian *qalandar*]

cal·ends (kal′əndz) *n. pl.* The first day of the Roman month: also spelled *kalends.* **— at** (or **on) the Greek calends** At a date that will never come, the Greeks having had no calends. [<L *calendae* calends]

ca·len·du·la (kə·len′jŏŏ·lə) *n.* **1** Any of a small genus *(Calendula)* of annual or perennial herbs of the composite family, the pot marigolds, having alternate entire leaves, and heads of yellow or orange flowers. **2** The dried florets of this plant, containing a bitter principle used to promote the healing of wounds. [<NL, dim. of *calendae* calends; because it blooms almost every month]

cal·en·ture (kal′ən·chŏŏr) *n. Pathol.* **1** A tropical remittent fever caused by extreme heat and accompanied by delirium and hallucinations. **2** Sunstroke. [<F <Sp. *calentura* fever <L *calere* be warm]

ca·le·sa (kä·lā′sä) *n. Spanish* A small, two-wheeled carriage; Spanish chaise; cab.

ca·les·cence (kə·les′əns) *n.* The condition of growing warm; increasing warmth. [<L *calescens, -entis,* ppr. of *calescere,* inceptive of *calere* be warm] **— ca·les′cent** *adj.*

calf[1] (kaf, käf) *n. pl.* **calves** (kavz, kävz) **1** The young of the cow or various other bovine animals. ◆ Collateral adjective: *vituline.* **2** The young of various large mammals, as the elephant, whale, hippopotamus, etc. **3** The skin of the calf, or leather made from it: also *calfskin.* **4** *Colloq.* A raw, gawky, witless young person; a blockhead; dolt. **5** A floating fragment of ice near an iceberg. **— the golden calf** **1** The molten image made by Aaron and worshiped by the Israelites. *Ex.* xxxii. **2** Riches, as unduly prized; mammon. [OE *cealf*]

calf[2] (kaf, käf) *n. pl.* **calves** (kavz, kävz) The muscular hinder part of the human leg below the knee. ◆ Collateral adjective: *sural.* [<ON *kālfi*]

calf love *Colloq.* Adolescent or immature love felt by a boy for a girl or a girl for a boy.

calf's-foot jelly (kafs′fŏŏt′, käfs′-) A gelatinous deposit sometimes found between the bones of calves' feet and processed by boiling: also spelled *calvesfoot jelly.*

calf's-head (kafs·hed) *n.* The pitcherplant.

calf·skin (kaf′skin′, käf′-) *n.* **1** The skin or hide of a calf. **2** A kind of fine leather made from the skin of a calf. Also *calf.*

Cal·ga·ry (kal′gər·ē) A city in southern Alberta, Canada.

Cal·houn (kal·hōōn′), **John Caldwell,** 1782–1850, U.S. statesman.

Ca·li (kä′lē) A city in western Colombia.

Cal·i·ban (kal′ə·ban) In Shakespeare's *The Tempest,* a deformed savage slave of Prospero.

cal·i·ber (kal′ə·bər) *n.* **1** The internal diameter of a tube. **2** *Mil.* **a** The internal diameter of the barrel of a gun, cannon, etc., expressed in decimals of an inch for small arms, millimeters for rifles, centimeters for cannon. **b** The diameter of a bullet, shell, etc. **c** The ratio of the length of a gun's bore to its diameter: a unit of length. **3** Degree of individual capacity or intellectual power; personal ability, quality, or worth. Also **cal′i·bre.** [<F *calibre,* ? <Arabic *qālib* mold, form]

cal·i·brate (kal′ə·brāt) *v.t.* **·brat·ed, ·brat·ing** **1** To graduate the tube of (a measuring instrument) into appropriate units. **2** To determine the reading of (such an instrument). **3** To ascertain the caliber of. [Cf. F *calibrer*] **— cal′i·bra′tion** *n.* **— cal′i·bra′tor** *n.*

Cal·i·burn (kal′ə·bûrn), **Cal·i·bur·no** (kal′ə·bûr′nō) See EXCALIBUR.

cal·i·ces (kal′ə·sēz) Plural of CALIX.

ca·li·che (kä·lē′chā) *n.* **1** The native, impure sodium nitrate of Chile, $NaNO_3$; Chile saltpeter. **2** A calcareous sediment typical of soils in warm, semiarid, or desert regions. [<Am. Sp.]

cal·i·cle (kal′i·kəl) *n. Zool.* A small, cup-shaped part or organ, as a polyp cell in corals or a hydrotheca in hydrozoans; a calycle. [<L *caliculus,* dim. of *calix* cup]

cal·i·co (kal′i·kō) *n. pl.* **·coes** or **·cos** **1** Any cheap cotton cloth printed in bright colors. **2** *Brit.* White cotton cloth. **—** *adj.* **1** Made of calico: a *calico* dress. **2** Resembling printed calico; dappled or streaked; variegated: a *calico* cat. [from *Calicut*]

cal·i·co·back (kal′i·kō·bak′) *n.* **1** The turnstone. **2** The harlequin bug. **3** The calico bass.

calico bass A varicolored food fish *(Pomoxys sparoides)* of the Mississippi Valley, etc.: also called *strawberry bass.*

cal·i·co·bush (kal′i·kō·bo͝osh′) *n.* The mountain laurel. Also **cal′i·co·tree′.**

ca·lic·u·la (kə·lik′yə·lə) See CALYCLE.

Cal·i·cut (kal′ə·kut) A port in SW Madras, India.

ca·lif (kā′lif, kal′if), **cal·i·fate** (kal′ə·fāt, -fit), etc. See CALIPH, etc.

Cal·i·for·nia (kal′ə·fôrn′yə, -fôr′nē·ə) A Pacific State of the United States; 156,803 square miles; capital, Sacramento; entered the Union Sept. 9, 1850: nickname *Golden State.* Abbr. CA

California, Gulf of An arm of the Pacific, between Mexico and Lower California.

California, Lower See LOWER CALIFORNIA.

California condor A large, rare vulturine bird *(Gymnogyps californianus),* native within a restricted range of the mountains of southern California.

California fuchsia A perennial herbaceous shrub *(Zauschneria californica),* with large scarlet flowers.

Cal·i·for·nian (kal′ə·fôrn′yən, -fôr′nē·ən) *adj.* Of or pertaining to California. —*n.* **1** A native or inhabitant of California. **2** An aboriginal of California. **3** One of the original Spanish settlers of California.

California poppy Any of several plants of the poppy family; specifically, the yellow-flowered *Eschscholtzia californica,* State flower of California; the creamcups and the mission poppy.

cal·i·for·nite (kal′ə·fôr′nīt) *n.* A compact variety of vesuvianite, resembling jade, found in California.

cal·i·for·ni·um (kal′ə·fôr′nē·əm) *n.* A synthetic radioactive element (symbol Cf, atomic number 98), having isotopic mass numbers from 242 to 253 and half-lives ranging from 3.7 minutes to approximately 800 years. See PERIODIC TABLE. [<from the University of *California,* where first produced]

ca·lig·i·nous (kə·lij′ə·nəs) *adj.* Obscure; dark; dim. [<L *caliginosus* misty, dark <*caligo* fog, darkness] —**ca·lig′i·nous·ly** *adv.* —**ca·lig′·i·nous·ness, ca·lig′i·nos′i·ty** (-nos′ə·tē) *n.*

ca·lig·ra·phy (kə·lig′rə·fē) See CALLIGRAPHY

Ca·lig·u·la (kə·lig′yə·lə), 12–41, Roman emperor 37–41; assassinated: real name *Gaius Caesar.*

cal·i·man·co (kal′ə·mang′kō) See CALAMANCO.

cal·i·pash (kal′ə·pash, kal′ə·pash′) *n.* The part of a turtle next to the upper shell, a greenish gelatinous substance esteemed as a table delicacy: also spelled *callipash.* [? Alter. of Sp. *carapacho* carapace]

cal·i·pee (kal′ə·pē, kal′ə·pē′) *n.* The part of a turtle next the lower shell, a yellowish gelatinous edible substance: also spelled *callipee.* [Cf. CALIPASH.]

cal·i·per (kal′ə·pər) *n.* **1** An instrument like a pair of compasses, usually with curved legs, for measuring diameters: usually in the plural: also **caliper compass. 2** A caliper rule. —*v.t. & v.i.* To measure by using calipers. Also spelled *calliper.* [Var. of CALIBER]

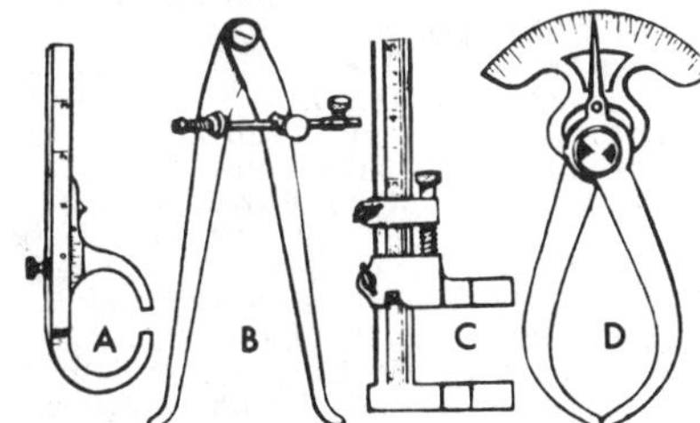

TYPES OF CALIPERS
A. Graduating. *B.* Inside.
C. Square or beam. *D.* Outside-adjusting.

caliper rule 1 A caliper for determining the weight of a ball from its diameter, and vice versa. **2** A scaled rule with sliding jaw.

ca·liph (kā′lif, kal′if) *n.* The spiritual and civil head of a Moslem state: title taken by the sultans of Turkey, abolished in 1924: also spelled *calif, kalif, khalif.* [<F *caliphe.* <Arabic *khalīfah* successor (to Mohammed)] —**cal·i·phate** (kal′ə·fāt, -fit) *n.*

cal·i·sa·ya (kal′ə·sā′ə) *n.* Cinchona; specifically, the species rich in quinine, *Cinchona calisaya*: also called *yellowbark.* [<Sp. <Quechua]

cal·is·then·ics (kal′is·then′iks) *n. pl.* **1** Light gymnastics to promote grace and health: construed as plural. **2** The science of such exercises: construed as singular. Also spelled *callisthenics.* [<Gk. *kalli-* <*kalos* beautiful + *sthenos* strength] —**cal′is·then′ic** *adj.*

ca·lix (kā′liks kal′iks) *n. pl.* **cal·i·ces** (kāl′ə·sēz) **1** A cup; hence, any cup-shaped organ or part. **2** *Eccl.* A chalice. Compare CALYX. [<L, cup]

Ca·lix·tine (kə·lik′stin) *n.* One of a Hussite sect in Bohemia in the 15th century, who demanded the cup in the Eucharist for the laity and also a limitation of the exclusive rights of the clergy. [<L *calix* cup]

Ca·lix·tus (kə·lik′stəs), **Georg,** 1586–1656, German Lutheran theologian, advocate of a united Protestant church: original name *Georg Callisen.*

calk[1] (kôk) *v.t.* **1** *Naut.* To make tight, as a boat's seams, by plugging with soft material, as oakum or hemp fiber. **2** To hammer or fasten together, as the edges of the plates of a boiler. **3** To plug up the crevices of, as a window frame. Also spelled *caulk.* [<OF *cauquer* <L *calcare* tread] —**calk′ing** *n.*

calk[2] (kôk) *n.* **1** A spur on a horse's shoe to prevent slipping. **2** A plate with sharp points worn on the sole of a person's boot or shoe to prevent slipping. Also **calk′er, calk′in.** —*v.t.* **1** furnish with calks. **2** To wound with a calk. [Prob. <L *calx* heel]

calk·er (kô′kər) *n.* **1** One who calks the seams of a vessel or a boiler. **2** A tool used for calking.

call (kôl) *v.t.* **1** To appeal to by word of mouth. **2** To utter or read aloud. **3** To summon in any way; convoke, as Congress; convene; invoke solemnly: to *call* God to witness. **4** To designate or characterize in any way; name; style; suppose; assume to be so much. **5** To read aloud from a list of names: *Call* the roll. **6** To arouse, as from sleep. **7** To designate for a special work: to *call* to the ministry. **8** To lure (birds or animals) by imitating their cry with a whistle, call, or other imitative means. **9** To insist upon payment of, as by written notice. **10** To communicate by telephone. **11** To fix the time for; bring to action: to *call* a case to court. **12** *Colloq.* In the game of pool, to designate (a shot), before making the play. **13** In baseball, to stop or suspend (a game) because of rain, darkness, etc. —*v.i.* **14** To lift up the voice in address, command, or entreaty; send out a cry of summons; appeal; sound a signal. **15** To communicate by telephone: I will *call* tomorrow. **16** To make a brief visit, stop or stay: followed by *at, on,* or *upon*: The steamer *calls* at Southampton. **17** In poker, to demand a show of hands, upon staking an amount equal to the bet of each previous player. **18** In whist and other card games, to make a demand or give a signal, as for trumps or for a particular card. **19** To ask for a showdown on anything. —**to call back 1** To summon back; recall; revoke; retract. **2** To call in return, as by telephone. —**to call one's bluff** To take a challenge; ask for a showdown. —**to call down 1** To pray heaven to send or cause to descend: to *call down* the wrath of the gods. **2** To rebuke; reprimand. —**to call off 1** To count; announce. **2** To cancel. —**to call out 1** To shout. **2** To bring an actor or actress out before the curtains by applause. **3** To summon workers to go out on strike. —**to call up 1** To bring before the memory or mind's eye. **2** To bring up for action or discussion, as a legislative measure. **3** To demand payment of, as amounts due on shares. **4** To notify to appear before some tribunal, as a court; cite. **5** To notify to appear for induction into the armed forces; also, to summon (troops) for active service. **6** To summon to stand up and speak. **7** To communicate with by telephone. —*n.* **1** A shout or cry to attract attention or response. **2** A lifting up of the voice in speech or other utterance; specifically, a thing called or indicated. **3** A summons or invitation; also, a roll call, a bugle call, or telephone call. **4** A requirement; claim; right; obligation: the *call* of duty. **5** A brief visit. **6** An assessment or demand; specifically, a contract requiring, in consideration of money paid, the delivery of some article named, as stocks, at a certain price. Compare PUT *n.* (def. 2). **7** A request by a government or corporation that holders of its redeemable bonds present them for payment. **8** An assessment on the members of a corporation or joint-stock company for the payment of subscription instalments, or for cash to meet losses. **9** A blast on a hunting horn to encourage the hounds. **10** The characteristic cry of an animal or a bird. **11** *Law* A visible natural object or an established point mentioned in the descriptive part of a deed for tracing a line of vision or boundary: a *call* of the deed. **12** An inward urge to a certain line of work; a vocation. **13** *Colloq.* Right or occasion for: You've no *call* to do that. **14** In poker, a demand for a show of hands: made only after equaling preceding bets. **15** A notice of rehearsals, instructions to actors, etc., posted on the callboard. —**at (or on) call** Payable on demand, or without previous notice, as a loan or deposit. —**to have the call** To have the advantage; also, to be the leader in popular favor. —**within call** Readily accessible or within hearing; also, subject to call. ◆Homophone: *caul.* [<ON *kalla*]

Synonyms (verb): bawl, bellow, clamor, cry, ejaculate, exclaim, roar, scream, shout, shriek, vociferate, yell. To *call* is to send out the voice in order to attract another's attention, either by word or by inarticulate utterance. Animals *call* their mates, or their young; a man *calls* his dog, his horse, etc. The sense is extended to include summons by bell or other audible signal. To *shout* is to *call* or *exclaim* with the fullest volume of sustained voice; to *scream* or *shriek* is to utter a shriller cry. We *shout* words; in *screaming, shrieking,* or *yelling* there is often no attempt at articulation. To *bawl* is to utter senseless, noisy cries, like a child in pain or anger. *Bellow* and *roar* are applied to the utterances of animals, and only figuratively to those of persons. To *clamor* is to utter with noisy iteration; it applies also to the confused cries of a multitude. To *vociferate* is commonly applied to loud, excited speech. One may *exclaim,* or *ejaculate* with no thought of others' presence; when he *calls,* it is to attract another's attention. See CONVOKE, EXCLAIM. *Antonyms,* harken, hush, list, listen.

cal·la (kal′ə) *n.* **1** A South African plant *(Zantedeschia aethiopica)* of the arum family, with a large, milk-white spathe that resembles a flower: also called *lily-of-the-Nile.* **2** A marsh plant of North America and Europe *(Calla palustris)* bearing red berries in dense clusters. Also **calla lily.** [<L *calla,* a plant name]

cal·lant (kä′lənt) *n. Scot.* A lad; youth. Also **cal·lan** (kä′lən).

Cal·la·o (kä·yä′ō) A port on **Callao Bay,** an inlet of the Pacific in western Peru.

call-back (kôl′bak′) *n.* The recall of a product by its manufacturer in order to correct previously undetected defects.

call·board (kôl′bōrd′, -bōrd′) *n.* A theater bulletin board for posting notices of rehearsals, instructions, etc.

call·boy (kôl′boi′) *n.* **1** A boy who answers calls, in a hotel or on board ship; a bellboy. **2** A boy who calls actors to go on stage.

call-down (kôl′doun′) *n.* A rebuke or scolding.

call·er[1] (kô′lər) *n.* **1** One who or that which calls. **2** One making a brief, formal visit. **3** A head waiter. **4** In square dancing, one who calls the successive steps of a set.

cal·ler[2] (kal′ər, kä′lər) *Scot. v.t.* To freshen; cool. —*adj.* **1** Cool or refreshing. **2** Fresh.

Cal·les (kä′yās), **Plutarco Elias,** 1877–1945, Mexican general; president 1924–28.

call girl *Colloq.* A prostitute who goes to assignations in response to telephone calls.

calli- For words not found here, see under CALI-.

cal·li·graph (kal′ə·graf, -gräf) *n.* A specimen of beautiful or ornamental penmanship.

cal·lig·ra·phy (kə·lig′rə·fē) *n.* **1** Beautiful penmanship. 2 Handwriting in general. [<Gk. *kalligraphia* < *kalos* beautiful + *graphein* write] —**cal·lig'ra·pher, cal·lig'ra·phist** *n.* —**cal·li·graph·ic** (kal'ə·graf'ik) *adj.* —**cal'li·graph'·i·cal·ly** *adv.*

Cal·lim·a·chus (kə·lim'ə·kəs) Fifth century B.C. Greek sculptor.

call·ing (kô'ling) *n.* 1 A speaking, crying, or shouting to command attention. 2 A convocation or summoning. 3 A solemn appointment or summons. 4 Habitual occupation; profession; vocation; business. 5 Social condition or status; rank.

calling card A small card, printed or engraved with one's name: used to announce a visit or call.

cal·li·o·pe (kə·lī'ə·pē, kal'ē·ōp) *n.* A musical instrument consisting of a series of steam whistles played by means of a keyboard; a steam organ. [after *Calliope*]

Cal·li·o·pe (kə·lī'ə·pē) The Muse of eloquence and epic poetry. [<L <Gk. *Kalliopē* the beautiful-voiced < *kalos* beautiful + *ops* voice]

cal·li·op·sis (kal'ē·op'sis) See COREOPSIS.

cal·li·per (kal'ə·pər) See CALIPER.

cal·li·pyg·i·an (kal'ə·pij'ē·ən) *adj.* Having beautiful buttocks. Also **cal'li·py'gous** (-pī'·gəs). [<Gk. *kallipygos* < *kalos* beautiful + *pygē* buttocks]

Cal·lis·the·nes (kə·lis'thə·nēz), 360?–328? B.C., Greek philosopher and historian.

cal·lis·then·ics (kal'is·then'iks) See CALISTHENICS.

Cal·lis·to (kə·lis'tō) 1 In Greek and Roman mythology, a nymph loved by Zeus and transformed into a bear by Artemis or Hera: set as Ursa Major among the stars by Zeus. 2 *Astron.* The fifth satellite of Jupiter: the largest satellite in the solar system.

Cal·lis·tra·tus (kə·lis'trə·təs), died 355 B.C., Athenian orator and general.

cal·li·type (kal'ə·tīp') *v.t.* **·typed, ·typ·ing** To make a copy of (reading matter) on printing plates by photoengraving typewritten sheets. [< *calli-* beautiful (<Gk. *kalos*) + -TYPE] —**cal'li·typ'y** *n.*

call letters The code letters identifying a radio or television transmitting station.

call loan A loan of money to be repaid on demand, or call, at any time.

call money See under MONEY.

call number A classifying number employed by libraries to indicate the subject and author of a book and its place on the shelves.

cal·lose (kal'ōs) *n. Biochem.* A hard, thick, insoluble carbohydrate assumed to develop in the cell walls of certain plants. [<L *callosus* hard-skinned]

cal·los·i·ty (kə·los'ə·tē) *n. pl.* **·ties** 1 *Physiol.* A thickened, hardened portion of the skin, produced by or as by pressure or friction. 2 *Biol.* A hard or thickened part, as on the legs of horses, on or in a plant, etc.; a callus. 3 Hardness; insensibility.

cal·lous (kal'əs) *adj.* 1 Thickened and hardened, as the skin by friction or pressure. 2 Hardened in feeling; insensible; unfeeling. See synonyms under HARD. ◆ Homophone: *callus.* [<L *callosus* < *callus* hard skin] —**cal·loused** (kal'əst) *adj.* —**cal'lous·ly** *adv.* —**cal'·lous·ness** *n.*

cal·low (kal'ō) *adj.* 1 Unfledged; not yet feathered, as a bird. 2 Inexperienced; youthful. 3 Of or pertaining to an unfledged bird or a youth. [OE *calu* bare, bald]

call rate The interest rate on call loans.

call slip A printed form on which a library patron writes his request for a desired book.

cal·lus (kal'əs) *n. pl.* **·lus·es** 1 A callosity or thickening. 2 *Physiol.* The new bony tissue between and around the fractured ends of a broken bone in the process of reuniting. 3 *Bot.* The parenchymatous tissue which forms over a cut on a stem and protects the exposed wood. —*v.i.* To form a callosity or callus. ◆ Homophone: *callous.* [<L, hard skin]

calm (käm) *adj.* Free from disturbance or agitation; without motion; in repose; also, unmoved by passion or emotion; serene. —*n.* 1 Stillness; serenity. 2 Lack of wind or motion. See synonyms under REST. —*v.t.* To bring into repose; still; soothe. —*v.i.* To become quiet or placid. See synonyms under ALLAY, SETTLE. [<MF *calme* <Ital. *calma* <LL *cauma* heat of the day <Gk. *kauma* heat; with ref. to the rest or siesta at midday] —**calm'ly** *adv.* —**calm'ness** *n.*

Synonyms (adj.): collected, composed, cool, dispassionate, imperturbable, peaceful, placid, quiet, sedate, self-controlled, self-possessed, serene, smooth, still, tranquil, undisturbed, unruffled. That is *calm* which is free from disturbance or agitation; in the physical sense, free from violent motion or action; in the mental or spiritual sense, free from excited or disturbing emotion or passion. We speak of a *calm* sea, a *placid* lake, a *serene* sky, a *still* night, a *quiet* day, a *quiet* home. We speak, also, of *still* waters, *smooth* sailing, which are different modes of expressing freedom from manifest agitation. *Cool,* in this connection, always suggests the recognition of some form of danger or risk. One may be *calm* by assured superiority to danger, by ignorance of its existence or of its magnitude, or by indifference to the result, or by the apathy of hopelessness, as we speak of the *calmness* of despair; one is *cool* who, while intensely alive to danger or need, has all his faculties concentrated on the means of meeting or overcoming it; a *calm* boxer would probably be an easy victim, while a *cool* boxer would be a dangerous antagonist. *Cool* is stronger than *composed* or *collected.* One is *composed* who has subdued excited feeling; he is *collected* when he has every thought, feeling, or perception awake and at command. *Tranquil* refers to a present state, *placid* to a prevailing tendency. We speak of a *tranquil* mind, a *placid* disposition. The *serene* spirit dwells as if in the clear upper air, above all storm or agitation. See PACIFIC, SOBER. *Antonyms*: agitated, boisterous, disturbed, excited, fierce, frantic, frenzied, furious, heated, passionate, raging, roused, ruffled, stormy, turbulent, violent, wild, wrathful.

cal·ma·tive (kal'mə·tiv, kä'mə-) *adj.* Having a soothing effect; sedative. —*n.* A sedative; tranquilizer.

calm·y (kä'mē) *adj. Obs.* Calm.

cal·o·mel (kal'ə·mel, -məl) *n. Med.* Mercurous chloride, HgCl, a heavy, white, tasteless compound: used as a purgative. [<F <Gk. *kalos* beautiful + *melas* black]

cal·o·mon·din (kal'ə·mon'din) *n.* A hardy orange (*Citrus mitis*) with a small, acid, orange-red fruit.

Ca·lo·o·can (kä'lô·ô'kän) A municipality of southern Luzon, Philippines.

Ca·loo·sa·hatch·ee River (kə·lōō'sə·hach'ē) A river in southern Florida, flowing 75 miles SW to the Gulf of Mexico.

cal·o·res·cence (kal'ə·res'əns) *n. Physics* The generation of visible light from invisible heat radiation, as by directing a stream of infrared rays upon a thin platinum plate. [<L *calor* heat + -ESCENCE]

ca·lor·ic (kə·lôr'ik, -lor'-) *adj.* Of or pertaining to heat. —*n.* 1 Heat. 2 Formerly, a supposed principle of heat. [<F *calorique* <L *calor* heat]

cal·o·ric·i·ty (kal'ə·ris'ə·tē) *n.* The power of developing heat, possessed by animals.

cal·o·rie (kal'ə·rē) *n.* 1 One of two recognized units of heat used especially to express the heat- or energy-producing content of foods. The **great, greater, large,** or **kilogram calorie** is the amount of heat required to raise the temperature of one kilogram of water 1° C. The **lesser, small,** or **gram calorie** is the amount of heat required to raise one gram of water 1° C. 2 *Physiol.* The large calorie, used as a measure of the energy value of foods or the heat output of organisms. Also **cal'o·ry.** [<F *calorie* <L *calor* heat]

cal·o·rif·ic (kal'ə·rif'ik) *adj.* 1 Able to produce heat; heating. 2 Carrying or conducting heat; thermal. Also **cal'o·rif'i·cal.** [<F *calorifique* <L *calorificus*]

ca·lor·i·fi·ca·tion (kə·lôr'ə·fi·kā'shən, -lor'-) *n.* The production of heat.

calorific power The heat resulting from complete combustion of a gram of fuel. Also **calorific value.**

cal·o·rif·ics (kal'ə·rif'iks) *n.* 1 The science of heating. 2 The branch of physics that treats of heat.

cal·o·rim·e·ter (kal'ə·rim'ə·tər) *n.* Any apparatus for measuring the quantity of heat generated by friction, combustion, or chemical change. —**bomb calorimeter** A calorimeter in the form of a steel-walled container in which measured quantities of fuel or other substances may be burned to determine their calorific value. [<L *calor* heat + -METER] —**ca·lor·i·met·ric** (kə·lôr'ə·met'rik, -lor'-) or **·met'ri·cal** *adj.* —**cal'o·rim'e·try** *n.*

ca·lotte (kə·lot') *n.* 1 A skullcap worn by the Roman Catholic clergy. 2 Any small, close-fitting cap. [<F <Ital. *calotta,* prob. <Gk. *kalyptra* veil, hood < *kalyptein* cover]

cal·o·yer (kal'ə·yər, kə·loi'ər) *n.* A monk of the Eastern Church, especially one of the order of St. Basil. [<F <Ital. *caloiero* venerable <LGk. *kalogēros* < *kalos* fair + *gerōn* old]

cal·pac (kal'pak) *n.* A black sheepskin or felt cap worn by Armenians, Turks, etc.: also spelled *kalpac.* Also **cal'pack.** [<Turkish *qālpāq*]

Cal·ta·nis·set·ta (käl'tä·nēs·sāt'tä) A city in central Sicily.

cal·trop (kal'trəp) *n.* 1 *Mil.* A small iron instrument shaped like a ball from which four sharp-pointed curved spikes project and are so mounted that one is always upright: formerly used to impede cavalry or infantry. 2 One of various plants with spiny heads or fruit that entangle the feet, as the **hairy caltrop** (*Kalestroemia hirsutissima*), the puncturevine, the star thistle, and the water chestnut. Also **cal'trap** (-trəp). [OE *coltetraeppe* <L *calx* heel + LL *trappa* trap]

cal·u·met (kal'yə·met, kal'yə·met') *n.* A tobacco pipe with a long, ornamented reed stem, and, usually, a red clay bowl: used by American Indians in religious and magic ceremonies, to ratify war and peace treaties, etc.: often called *peace pipe.* [<F, pipe stem <L *calamellus,* dim. of *calamus* reed]

CALUMET

ca·lum·ni·ate (kə·lum'nē·āt) *v.t.* & *v.i.* **·at·ed, ·at·ing** To accuse falsely; defame; slander. See synonyms under ASPERSE, REVILE. [<L *calumniatus,* pp. of *calumniari* slander < *calumnia* slander] —**ca·lum'ni·a'tion** *n.* —**ca·lum'ni·a'tor** *n.* —**ca·lum·ni·a·to·ry** (kə·lum'·nē·ə·tôr'ē, -tō'rē).

ca·lum·ni·ous (kə·lum'nē·əs) *adj.* Slanderous; defamatory. —**ca·lum'ni·ous·ly** *adv.*

cal·um·ny (kal'əm·nē) *n. pl.* **·nies** A false, malicious, and injurious accusation or report; defamation; slander. See synonyms under SCANDAL. [<MF *calomnie* <L *calumnia* slander. Doublet of CHALLENGE.]

cal·u·tron (kal'yə·tron) *n.* An electromagnetic device for the separation of isotopes, especially in the study and production of atomic energy. [<CAL(IFORNIA) U(NIVERSITY) (CYCLO)TRON]

Cal·va·dos (kål·vä·dōs') *n.* A French brandy made from cider. [from *Calvados,* a department in NW France]

cal·var·i·a (kal·vâr'ē·ə) *n. Anat.* The vaulted upper portion of the cranium. Also **cal·var'·i·um** (-ē·əm). [<L, skull]

cal·va·ry (kal'vər·ē) *n. pl.* **·ries** A sculptured representation of the Crucifixion, usually erected in the open air.

Cal·va·ry (kal'vər·ē) The place where Christ was crucified; Golgotha. *Luke* xxiii 33. [<L *calvaria* skull, trans. of Aramaic *gogolthā*]

Calvary cross See under CROSS.

calve (kav, käv) *v.t.* & *v.i.* **calved, calv·ing** 1 To bring forth (a calf). 2 To throw off (a berg), as a glacier. [OE *cealfian* < *cealf* calf]

Cal·vé (kål·vā'), **Emma,** 1858–1942, *née* de Roquer, French operatic soprano.

Cal·vert (kal'vərt), **Sir George,** 1580?–1632, first Baron Baltimore, English statesman; founder of Maryland. —**Leonard,** 1606?–1647, English statesman; first governor of Maryland, son of the preceding.

calves (kavz, kävz) Plural of CALF.

Cal·vin (kal'vin, *Fr.* kål·vaṅ') A masculine personal name. Also *Lat.* **Cal·vi·nus** (kal·vī'nəs), *Sp.* **Cal·vo** (käl'vō).

Cal·vin (kal'vin), **John,** 1509–64, French Protestant reformer.

Cal·vin·ism (kal'vin·iz'əm) *n.* 1 *Theol.* **a** The system or doctrines of John Calvin, emphasizing the depravity and helplessness of man, the sovereignty of God, and predestination, and characterized by an austere moral code. **b** Any later system based upon the teachings of Calvin. 2 Belief in or support for such a system. —**Cal'vin·ist** *n.*

Cal·vin·is·tic (cal'vin·is'tik) *adj.* 1 Pertaining

to Calvinism or Calvinists. 2 Austere: strict; severe. —**Cal'vin·is'ti·cal** *adj.* —**Cal'vin·is'ti·cal·ly** *adv.*

cal·vi·ti·es (kal·vish'i·ēz) *n.* Baldness, especially on the top or back of the head. [< L < *calvus* bald]

calx (kalks) *n. pl.* **calx·es** or **cal·ces** (kal'sēz) **1** The residue from the calcination of minerals. **2** Lime or chalk. [< L]

cal·y·ces (kal'ə·sēz, kā'lə-) A plural of CALYX.

cal·y·cine (kal'ə·sin, -sīn) *adj.* **1** Of or pertaining to a calyx. **2** Of the nature of, situated on, or like a calyx. Also **ca·lyc·i·nal** (kə·lis'ə·nəl). [< L *calyx.* See CALYX.]

cal·y·cle (kal'i·kəl) *n. Bot.* An accessory calyx outside of the true calyx: also called *calicula.* [< L *caliculus,* dim. of *calyx*]

ca·lyc·u·lar (kə·lik'yə·lər) *adj.* Having calycles. Also **ca·lyc'u·late** (-lāt, -lit).

ca·lyc·u·lus (kə·lik'yə·ləs) See CALYCLE.

Cal·y·don (kal'ə·don) An ancient city in Aetolia, west central Greece, on the **Gulf of Calydon,** modern Gulf of Patras. —**Cal·y·do·ni·an** (kal'·ə·dō'nē·ən, -dōn'yən) *adj.* & *n.*

Calydonian boar In Greek mythology, a great boar sent by Artemis to ravage Calydon. See MELEAGER, OENEUS.

ca·lyp·so[1] (kə·lip'sō) *n.* Any orchid of the genus *Cytherea,* having only one species *(C. bulbosa),* growing in boggy regions of northern Europe and North America. [after *Calypso*]

ca·lyp·so[2] (kə·lip'sō) *n.* A type of song, originally improvised and sung by natives of Trinidad, dealing with topical, sexual, or humorous themes and achieving its effect by only approximate rime, flexible syllabic emphasis, and colloquial language. [Origin uncertain]

Ca·lyp·so (kə·lip'sō) In the *Odyssey,* a nymph who kept Odysseus for seven years on the island of Ogygia where he had been shipwrecked.

ca·lyp·tra (kə·lip'trə) *n.* **1** A hood or lid. **2** *Bot.* **a** In mosses, the hood or covering of the capsule. **b** In flowering plants, any similar hood-shaped organ. Also **ca·lyp'ter** (-tər). [< NL < Gk. *kalyptra* veil < *kalyptein* cover]

ca·lyp·trate (kə·lip'trāt) *adj.* Covered with, having, or like a calyptra.

ca·lyx (kā'liks, kal'iks) *n. pl.* **ca·lyx·es** or **cal·y·ces** (kal'ə·sēz, kā'lə-) **1** The outermost series of leaf-like parts of a flower, individually called sepals: usually green and more or less leaf-shaped, but frequently colored and petaloid. Compare COROLLA. **2** *Zool.* A cup-shaped part or organ. Compare CALIX. [< L < Gk. *kalyx* husk, pod]

cam[1] (kam) *n. Mech.* A rotating piece of irregular shape, as on a wheel in a machine: used to change the direction of the motion of another part moving against it, as rotary into reciprocating or variable motion. [< Du. *cam* tooth, cog of a wheel]

cam[2] (käm) *Scot.* Past tense of COME.

Cam (kam) A river in Cambridgeshire, England, flowing north 40 miles to the Ouse: also *Granta.*

Ca·ma·cho (kä·mä'chō), **(Manuel) 'Avila,** 1897–1955, president of Mexico 1940–46.

Ca·ma·güey (kä'mä·gwā') A city in eastern Cuba.

ca·ma·ieu (kà·mà·yœ') *n. French* **1** A cameo. **2** Painting in one color or in different shades of one color. —**en camaieu** In monochrome.

ca·mail (kə·māl') *n.* A piece of chain mail depending from a basinet and protecting the neck and shoulders; also, a hood of mail. [< F] —**ca·mailed'** *adj.*

ca·ma·ra·de·rie (kä'mə·rä'dər·ē) *n.* Comradeship; loyalty; fellowship. Also **com'rade·ry.** [< F]

cam·a·ril·la (kam'ə·ril'ə, *Sp.* kä'mä·rē'lyä) *n.* **1** A group of unofficial advisers, as of a king; a clique of persons exercising political powers secretly and unofficially; a cabal. **2** A little chamber; es pecially, the audience chamber of a king. [< Sp., dim. of *camara* chamber]

cam·as (kam'əs) *n.* **1** Any of several North American bulbous herbs of the lily family (genus *Camassia*); especially, *C. quamash,* having an edible bulb. **2** The death camas. Sometimes spelled *cammas, quamash.* Also **cam'ass.** [< Chinook jargon]

Cam·bay (kam·bā') A town of northern Bombay state, India; capital of the former princely state of Cambay, on the **Gulf of Cambay,** an inlet of the Arabian Sea between Bombay and Kathiawar peninsula.

cam·ber (kam'bər) *v.t.* To cut or bend to a slight upward convex form. —*v.i.* To have or assume a slight upward convex curve, as a ship's, deck. —*n.* A slight upward bend or convexity, as of a timber or an airfoil; a slight central rise. [< MF *cambrer* arch < L *camerare* < *camera* curved roof, vault]

Cam·ber·well (kam'bər·wel) A metropolitan borough in SE London.

Camberwell beauty A mourning cloak butterfly.

cam·bist (kam'bist) *n.* **1** A manual giving the moneys, weights, and measures of different countries, and their equivalents. **2** One versed in exchange values. [< F *cambiste* < Ital. *cambista b* < LL *cambiare* exchange]

cam·bi·um (kam'bē·əm) *n. Bot.* A zone of cells which generate new phloem and xylem in the stems and roots of many vascular plants. For illustration see EXOGEN. [< LL, exchange] **cam·bi·al** (kam'bē·əl) *adj.*

Cam·bo·di·a (kam·bō'dē·ə) See KHMER REPUBLIC.

Cam·bo·di·an (kam·bō'dē·ən) *adj.* Pertaining to Khmer Republic (Cambodia), its people, or their language. —*n.* A native or inhabitant of Khmer Republic.

cam·boose (kam·bo͞os') See CABOOSE.

Cam·brai (kän·bre') A city of northern France.

Cam·bri·a (kam'brē·ə) The ancient Roman name for WALES.

Cam·bri·an (kam'brē·ən) *adj.* **1** Of or pertaining to Cambria or Wales; Welsh. **2** *Geol.* Of or pertaining to the earliest of the periods of the Paleozoic era. See chart under GEOLOGY. —*n.* **1** The Cambrian strata or period. **2** A Welshman.

Cambrian Mountains A mountain range throughout Wales.

cam·bric (kām'brik) *n.* **1** A fine white linen fabric or a similar fabric of cotton. **2** A coarse cotton fabric used for linings. [< Flemish *Kameryk* Cambrai]

cambric tea *n.* A drink made of sweetened hot water and milk, sometimes flavored with a little tea.

Cam·bridge (kām'brij) **1** A county of SE England; with Ely 867 square miles; county seat, Cambridge, site of Cambridge University. Also **Cam'bridge·shire** (-shir). **2** A city in eastern Massachusetts, site of Harvard University. A native of either the county or the city, or a student at or graduate of either university, is known as a *Cantabrigian.*

Cam·by·ses (kam·bī'sēz), died 521? B.C., king of Persia 529?–522 B.C., son of Cyrus the Great.

cam·cord·er (kam'kôr'dər) *n.* A portable TV camera and videotape recorder combination.

Cam·den (kam'dən) **1** A port of entry on the Delaware River in SW New Jersey. **2** A town in central South Carolina; scene of Revolutionary War battles, 1780–81.

Cam·den (kam'dən), **William,** 1551–1623, English antiquary and historian.

came[1] (kām) Past tense of COME.

came[2] (kām) *n. Brit.* A leaden sash bar or grooved strip for fastening together panes in latticed or stained glass windows. [Prob. var. of CAM[1]]

cam·el (kam'əl) *n.* **1** A large Asian or African ruminant (genus *Camelus*) with a humped back, capable of subsisting for extended periods of time without water: used as a beast of burden. There are two species, the **Arabian camel** or **dromedary,** having one hump, and the **Bactrian camel** *(C. bactrianus),* having two. **2** A buoyant, watertight contrivance for lifting wrecks, etc. [OE < L *camelus* < Gk. *kamēlos* < Semitic] —**cam'el·ish** *adj.*

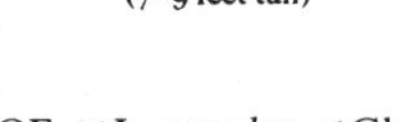

CAMELS
A. Arabian. *B.* Bactrian. (7–9 feet tall)

cam·el·eer (kam'əl·ir') *n.* A camel driver or a soldier mounted on a camel.

ca·mel·lia (kə·mēl'yə, mel'ē·ə) *n.* A tropical Asian tree or shrub *(Camellia* or *Thea japonica)* with glossy leaves and white, pink, red, or variegated flowers: also called *Japan rose.* [after George Joseph *Kamel,* 1661–1706, Jesuit traveler]

ca·mel·o·pard (kə·mel'ə·pärd) *n. Archaic* The giraffe. [< L *camelopardus* < Gk. *kamēlopardalis* < *kamēlos* camel + *pardalis* leopard]

Ca·mel·o·par·da·lis (kə·mel'ə·pär'də·lis) A northern constellation, the Giraffe, between Ursa Major and Cassiopeia. See CONSTELLATION. Also **Ca·mel'o·pard, Ca·mel'o·par'dus** (-dəs).

Cam·e·lot (kam'ə·lot) In Arthurian legend, the seat of King Arthur's court: identified with Caerleon and Winchester.

cam·el's-hair (kam'əlz·hâr') *n.* A heavy, warm, tan cloth made of camel's hair, sometimes mixed with wool or other fibers. —*adj.* Made of, like, or the color of camel's-hair. Also **cam'el·hair'.**

Cam·em·bert (kam'əm·bâr, *Fr.* kà·män·bâr') *n.* A rich, creamy, soft cheese. [from *Camembert,* town in NW France]

Ca·me·nae (kə·mē'nē) *n. pl.* In Roman mythology, prophetic nymphs of springs or fountains: later identified with the Greek *Muses.*

cam·e·o (kam'ē·ō) *n.* **1** A striated stone (as onyx or agate) or shell, carved in relief so as to show the design on differently colored layers. **2** The art of so carving. Compare INTAGLIO. **3** A brief appearance by an actor or actress in a film or play. —*adj.* Miniature; on a small scale. [< Ital. *cammeo;* ult. origin unknown]

cameo glass *n.* Glass fused in layers of different colors and cut in relief like a cameo: also called **onyx glass.**

cam·er·a (kam'ər·ə, kam'rə) *n. pl.* **·er·as** *for defs.* 1 *and* 2, **·er·ae** *for defs.* 3, 4, 5, 6. **1** A lightproof chamber or box in which the image of an exterior object is projected upon a sensitized plate or film through a shuttered opening usually equipped with a lens or lenses. **2** An enclosed unit containing the special light-sensitive vacuum tube which converts optical images into electrical impulses for television transmission. **3** A chamber, as of the heart. **4** In Italy, a legislative chamber; also, the financial department of the papal curia. **5** *Law* A judge's chamber or private room. **6** A camera obscura. —**in camera** *Law* Not in public court; privately; secretly. [< L, vaulted room < Gk. *kamara.* Doublet of CHAMBER.]

camera gun A camera mounted on a machine-gun frame in an airplane, and used in gunnery practice to record each shot.

cam·er·al (kam'ər·əl) *adj.* Pertaining to a camera, chamber, public office, or treasury.

cam·er·al·is·tics (kam'ər·əl·is'tiks) *n.* The science of state finances. —**cam'er·al·ist** *n.* —**cam'er·al·is'tic** *adj.*

camera lu·ci·da (lo͞o'si·də) A device by which the image of a body seems to be projected on a sheet of paper or other surface, so that it may be traced.

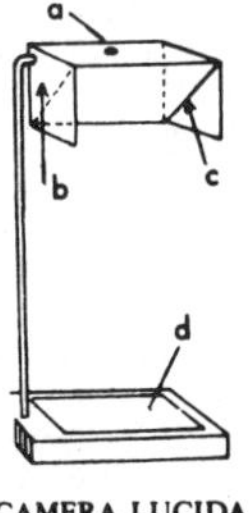

CAMERA LUCIDA
a. Eyepiece.
b. Mirror.
c. Glass slide.
d. Image here.

cam·er·a·man (kam'ər·ə·man', kam'rə-) *n. pl.* **·men** (-men') The operator of a camera, especially a motion-picture camera.

camera ob·scu·ra (ob·skyo͝or'ə) A darkened box in which the real image of an object, received through a small aperture, is projected upon a plane surface, for viewing, tracing, or photographing.

cam·er·lin·go (kam'ər·ling'gō) *n.* In the Roman Catholic Church, the cardinal who administers the finances and secular interests of the Pope. Also **cam'er·len'go** (-leng'gō). [< Ital. *camerlingo* chamberlain < L *camera* chamber]

Cam·er·o·ni·an (kam'ə·rō'nē·ən) *n.* A follower of **Richard Cameron,** died 1680, Scottish Presbyterian preacher and Covenanter.

Cam·er·on of Loch·iel (kam'ər·ən əv lokh·ēl'), **Sir Ewen,** 1629–1719, Scottish chieftain.

— **Donald,** 1695?–1748, Scottish chieftain and soldier; grandson of the preceding.

Cam·e·roon (kam′ə·rōōn′) **1** A volcanic mountain group in south Cameroons; the highest in western Africa; highest point 13,350 feet. **2** An estuarial inlet of the Gulf of Guinea in the Cameroons coast.

Cameroons, British A former United Nations Trust Territory. See CAMEROUN, NIGERIA.

Cameroons, French See CAMEROUN.

Cam·e·roun (kam′ə·rōōn, kam′rōōn) An independent republic in western Africa, including the southern part of the former British Cameroons; 184,252 square miles; capital, Yaoundé; formerly French Cameroons, a United Nations Trust Territory.

Ca·mi·guin (kä′mē·gēn′) **1** One of the Babuyan Islands, northern Philippines; 63 square miles; site of **Mount Camiguin,** an active volcano; 2,372 feet. **2** An island in the southern Philippines; 96 square miles; site of Hibokhibok.

Ca·mil·la (kə·mil′ə, *Ital.* kä·mēl′lä) A feminine personal name. Also *Fr.* **Ca·mille** (kȧ·mēl′), *Sp.* **Ca·mi·la** (kä·mē′lä). [<L, fem., attendant at a sacrifice]

— **Camilla** In Roman legend, the virgin queen of the Volscians who aided Turnus against Aeneas.

cam·i·on (kam′ē·ən, *Fr.* kȧ·myôṅ′) *n.* A military motor truck. [<F]

ca·mi·sa (kä·mē′sä) *n. SW U.S.* A chemise; shirt; specifically, a thin waist worn by women. [<Sp.]

cam·i·sa·do (kam′i·sā′dō) *n. Obs.* A night attack by soldiers wearing shirts over their armor for mutual recognition; also, a shirt so worn. Also **cam′i·sade′** (-sād′). [<Sp. *camisada* < *camisa* shirt]

Cam·i·sard (kam′i·zärd) *n.* One of the French Calvinists who fought for civil and religious liberties after the revocation of the Edict of Nantes in 1685. [<F, lit., a smockwearer]

ca·mise (kə·mēs′) *n.* A loose shirt; a light, loose gown. Compare CHEMISE. Also **ca·mis·i·a** (kə·mis′ē·ə). [<Arabic *qamīs* <LL *camisa* shirt]

cam·i·sole (kam′ə·sōl) *n.* **1** Formerly, a woman's wrapper. **2** A woman's fancy underwaist or corset cover. **3** A straitjacket having long sleeves that can be tied behind the patient's back. **4** Formerly, a man's jacket or jersey with sleeves. [<F <Sp. *camisola,* dim. of *camisa* shirt]

Cam·lan (kam′lən) In Arthurian legend, the battlefield where King Arthur was killed.

cam·let (kam′lit) *n.* **1** A stiff, closely woven fabric of camel's-hair, or an imitation of it. **2** A garment made from this fabric. [<MF *camelot* <OF *chamelot,* ? <Arabic *khamlat* nap, pile on cloth]

Cam·maerts (käm′ärts), **Émile,** 1878–1953, Belgian poet.

cam·mas (kam′as) See CAMAS.

Cam·o·ëns (kam′ō·ens), **Luis de,** 1524–80, Portuguese poet. Also *Pg.* **Ca·mões** (kə·moiṅsh′).

cam·o·mile (kam′ə·mīl) *n.* **1** A strongly scented bitter herb of the genus *Anthemis*; especially, the European perennial *(A. nobilis)* whose bitter, aromatic flowers and leaves are used in medicine. **2** Any plant of a genus *(Matricaria)* of widely distributed herbs of the composite family. Also spelled *chamomile.* — **wild** (or **stinking) camomile** Mayweed. [<F *camomille* <L *chamomilla* <Gk. *chamaimēlon* < *chamai* on the ground + *mēlon* apple]

Ca·mor·ra (kə·môr′ə, -mor′ə; *Ital.* kä·môr′·rä) *n.* A secret society of Naples, Italy, practicing violence and extortion. See MAFIA. — **Ca·mor′rism** *n.* — **Ca·mor′rist** *n.*

cam·ou·flage (kam′ə·fläzh) *n.* **1** *Mil.* Disguise by masking, as artillery, with an arbor of leaves built around a gun; also, artificial scenery, etc., painted on canvas to conceal military installations and movements. **2** *Nav.* Disguise by painting, as ships, as protection from attack by submarines, etc. **3** Any disguise or pretense. — *v.t.* & *v.i.* **·flaged, ·flag·ing** To hide or obscure, as with disguises. [<F < *camoufler* disguise] — **cam′ou·flag′er** *n.*

ca·mou·flet (kȧ·mōō·fle′) *n. Mil.* A small underground cavity caused by the explosion of a deeply buried mine or bomb which shows little or no surface effect; also, an explosive that will make such a cavity. [<F]

cam·ou·fleur (kam′ə·flər, *Fr.* kȧ·mōō·flœr′) *n. Mil.* One who constructs or paints camouflage. [<F]

camp[1] (kamp) *n.* **1** A group of tents or other shelters, as for soldiers or hunters, or the place so occupied; also, a single tent, cabin, etc. **2** An army encamped; hence, military life or the field of battle. **3** A chapter or lodge of various fraternal organizations. **4** A new community or town hastily gathered around the mines: so called because the people originally lived in tents. **5** A group of buildings for temporary (usually summer) habitation, built on a lake, or seashore, or in the mountains. **6** A stage of a journey. **7** A place where open-air religious or political meetings are held. **8** A body of persons who support or defend a policy, theory, or doctrine: Avarice dominates the *camp* of the profiteers. **9** A mass of facts or arguments arrayed in support or defense of a policy, theory, or doctrine. — *v.t.* **1** To shelter or station, as troops, in a camp. — *v.i.* **2** To form an encampment. **3** To live temporarily in a camp. **4** To hold stubbornly to a position: Strikers *camped* in front of the factory. — **to camp down** To settle down. — **to camp on the trail of** To follow closely; dog. — **to camp out** To sleep in a tent; live in the open. [<MF <Ital. *campo* field <L *campus* level plain]

camp[2] (kamp) *n.* **1** A comical style or quality typically perceived in banal, flamboyant, or patently artificial gestures, appearances, literary works, etc., that intentionally or unwittingly seem to parody themselves. **2** A person, thing, aspect, etc., marked by this style or quality. — *adj.* Of or characterized by camp, or by a ready appreciation of camp: the *camp* sensibility; in the *camp* tradition of Hollywood's gangster films. — *v.i. Slang* **1** To behave, dress, etc., in a theatrical or bizarre way to get attention. — *v.t.* **2** To invest with a camp quality: to *camp* the play up with weird effects. [? < dial. E *camp* or *kemp* bold, impetuous fellow]

Cam·pa·gna (käm·pä′nyə) A lowland surrounding Rome; about 800 square miles. Also **Campagna di Ro·ma** (dē rō′mä).

cam·paign (kam·pān′) *n.* **1** A series of connected military actions or maneuvers conducted for a particular objective, in a particular area, etc. **2** A series of connected political, commercial, or other activities designed to bring about a result: a welfare *campaign.* — *v.i.* To serve, operate in, or conduct a campaign. [<F *campagne* open country, field <Med. L *compania* <L *campus*]

cam·paign·er (kam·pā′nər) *n.* **1** One who campaigns. **2** A person of long experience in campaigns; a veteran.

cam·pa·ne·ro (käm′pä·nā′rō) *n.* The bellbird of South America. [<Sp., bellman <LL *campana* bell]

Cam·pa·nia (kam·pā′nē·ə, *Ital.* käm·pä′nyä) A region of southern Italy; 5,249 square miles; capital, Naples. — **Cam·pa′ni·an** *adj.* & *n.*

cam·pan·i·form (kam·pan′ə·fôrm) *adj.* Bell-shaped; campanulate. [<LL *campana* bell + -FORM]

cam·pa·ni·le (kam′pə·nē′lē, *Ital.* -nē′lā) *n. pl.* **·ni·les** or **·ni·li** (-nē′lē) A bell tower, especially a detached one. [<Ital. <LL *campana* bell]

cam·pa·nol·o·gy (kam′pə·nol′ə·jē) *n.* The science and art of casting and ringing bells. [<LL *campana* bell + -LOGY] — **cam′pa·nol′o·gist** *n.*

cam·pan·u·la (kam·pan′yə·lə) *n.* **1** A member of a very large genus of plants *(Campanula),* the bellflowers, as the bluebell of Scotland, Canterbury bell, etc. **2** *Zool.* A bell-shaped structure. [<NL, dim. of LL *campana* bell]

campanula blue The bluish-mauve color of various campanulas or bellflowers.

cam·pan·u·la·ceous (kam·pan′yə·lā′shəs) *adj. Bot.* Belonging to the bellflower family *(Campanulaceae)* of herbs, shrubs, and trees.

cam·pan·u·late (kam·pan′yə·lit, -lāt) *adj.* Bell-shaped, as a corolla.

Camp·bell (kam′bəl, kam′əl), **Alexander,** 1788–1866, U.S. theologian born in Ireland; founder of the Disciples of Christ. **Thomas,** 1777–1844, Scottish poet. — **Thomas,** 1763–1854, U.S. theologian born in Ireland; cofounder, with his son Alexander, of the Disciples of Christ.

Camp·bell-Ban·ner·man (kam′bəl·ban′ər·mən, kam′əl-), **Sir Henry,** 1836–1908, British statesman; prime minister 1905–08.

Camp·bel·lite (kam′əl·īt, kam′bəl-) *n.* A member of the Disciples of Christ, founded by Thomas and Alexander Campbell. The name *Campbellite* is rejected by the denomination.

camp chair A light, folding chair.

Cam·pe·a·dor (käm·pā′ä·thōr′), **El** See CID.

Cam·pe·che (kam·pē′chē, *Sp.* käm·pā′chā) A state in SE Mexico; 19,672 square miles; capital, Campeche.

Campeche, Gulf of The SW part of the Gulf of Mexico.

camp·er (kamp′ər) *n.* **1** One who camps out or lives in a camp. **2** A member of a camp, as a summer camp for children. **3** A vehicle affording shelter and usually sleeping accommodations for travelers and campers: also **camper wagon.**

cam·pes·tral (kam·pes′trəl) *adj.* Growing in or pertaining to the fields or open country. [<L *campestris* < *campus* field]

camp·fire (kamp′fīr′) *n.* **1** A fire in an outdoor camp, for cooking, warmth, etc. **2** A fire in a camp used as the center of social evening gatherings. **3** A meeting or social gathering; especially, a reunion. Also **camp fire.**

campfire girl A girl between 12 and 20 years of age, belonging to the **Camp Fire Girls of America,** an organization incorporated in 1914 for promoting the health and welfare of young women by encouraging outdoor life, etc.

camp follower **1** A civilian who follows an army about, usually a merchant or prostitute. **2** One who supports a movement, etc., without formally belonging to it; hanger-on.

camp·ground (kamp′ground′) *n.* An area used for a camp or a camp meeting.

cam·phene (kam′fēn, kam·fēn′) *n. Chem.* One of a series, $C_{10}H_{16}$, of solid hydrocarbons similar to camphor, isomeric with oil of turpentine: used as a camphor substitute. [<CAMPHOR]

cam·pho·gen (kam′fə·jen) *n. Chem.* Cymene.

cam·phol (kam′fōl, -fol) *n. Chem.* Borneol.

cam·phor (kam′fər) *n.* A white, volatile, translucent crystalline compound, $C_{10}H_{16}O$, with a penetrating, fragrant odor and pungent taste, distilled from the wood and bark of the camphor tree and also obtained by organic synthesis: used in medicine as a sedative, as an antispasmodic, in liniments, etc., and in the chemical and plastics industries. [<F *camphre* <Arabic *kāfūr* <Malay *kāpūr*] — **cam·phor·ic** (kam·fôr′ik, -for′-) *adj.*

cam·phor·ate (kam′fə·rāt) *v.t.* **·at·ed, ·at·ing** To treat or saturate with camphor.

camphor ball A moth ball.

camphor ice A mixture of camphor, white wax, spermaceti, and castor oil: used for chapped skin, etc.

camphor tree **1** A large evergreen tree of eastern Asia *(Cinnamomum camphora)* yielding the camphor of commerce. **2** A tree of Borneo, Sumatra, and Malaya *(Dryobalanops aromatica)* yielding borneol.

Cam·pi·na Gran·de (kaṅm·pē′nə graṅn′di) A city in NE Brazil.

Cam·pi·nas (kaṅm·pē′nəs) A city in SE Brazil.

camp·ing (kamp′ing) *n.* The act or practice of living outdoors, as in tents or without any shelter, especially for recreation.

cam·pi·on (kam′pē·ən) *n.* One of various herbs of the pink family, as the **rose campion.** [Origin uncertain]

Cam·pi·on (kam′pē·ən), **Thomas,** 1567–1619, English poet.

camp meeting A prolonged series of religious meetings held in a grove or field, usually in a tent.

cam·po[1] (kam′pō, käm′-) *n. pl.* **·pi** (-pē) In Italy, an open space in a town. [<Ital.]

cam·po[2] (kam′pō, käm′-) *n. pl.* **·pos** In South American countries, an open, level plain, with scattered shrubbery and trees. [<Sp.]

Cam·po·bel·lo (kam′pō·bel′ō) An island in SW New Brunswick, eastern Canada, in the Bay of Fundy.

Cam·po·for·mi·do (käm′pō·fôr′mē·dō) A town in NE Italy. Also **Cam′po·for′mio** (-fôr′myō).

Cam·pos (kaṅm′pōōs) A city in SE Brazil.

cam·po san·to (käm′pō sän′tō) *Italian* A cemetery; literally, holy field.

Campo Santo The cathedral cemetery at Pisa, Italy, to which earth from Mount Calvary was brought.

camp stool A light, folding stool or seat.

cam·pus (kam′pəs) *n.* **1** *U.S.* The grounds of a school or college or the court enclosed by the buildings. 2 In ancient Rome, an open field where military drills, games, etc., were held. [<L, field]

cam·py·lot·ro·pal (kam′pi·lot′rə·pəl) *adj. Bot.* Bent on itself so as to bring the true apex or micropyle down to the base or hilum: said of an ovule. Also **cam′py·lot′ro·pous** (-pəs). [< NL <Gk. *kampylos* bent + *tropos* direction <*trepein* turn]

cam shaft The shaft to which a cam is attached.

Ca·mus (kȧ·mü′), **Albert,** 1913–1960, French writer.

cam·wood (kam′wŏŏd′) *n.* The red wood of a tree *(Baphia nitida)* of western Africa, used in dyeing. [? <native African name]

can[1] (kan, *unstressed* kən) *v.* Present: *sing.* **can, can** (*Archaic* **canst**), **can,** *pl.* **can**; past: **could** A defective verb now used only in the present and past tenses as an auxiliary followed by the infinitive without *to,* or elliptically with the infinitive unexpressed, in the following senses: **1** To be able to. **2** To know how to. **3** To have the right to. **4** *Colloq.* To be permitted to; may. [OE *cunnan* know, be able]

◆ **can, may** In informal speech and writing, *can* is now acceptable in the sense of *may,* to express permission, especially in questions or negative statements: *Can* I leave now? You *cannot.* At the formal level, the distinction between *can* and *may* is still observed: *can,* to express ability to perform, either mentally or physically; *may,* to denote permission.

can[2] (kan) *n.* **1** A vessel for holding or carrying liquids. **2** A vessel of tin-plated iron or other metal, in which fruit, meat, tobacco, or the like is sealed, often hermetically: called *tin* in Great Britain. **3** A drinking mug or cup; a tankard. **4** A radio headphone. **5** *Slang* Jail; prison. **6** *Slang* Toilet; bathroom. **7** *Slang* Buttocks; backside. —**in the can** Ready for distribution or exhibition: said of a motion picture.— *v.t.* **canned, can·ning 1** To put up or preserve in cans, glass jars, or the like. **2** *Slang* To dismiss; discharge; also, to expel from school. **3** To preserve for reproduction, as on a phonograph record: *canned* music. **4** *Slang* To suppress; jail; imprison. [OE *canne* cup] —**can′ner** *n.*

Ca·na (kā′nə) A Biblical locality in northern Palestine; scene of Christ's first miracle. *John* ii 1. Also **Cana of Galilee.**

Ca·naan (kā′nən) The fourth son of Ham.

Ca·naan (kā′nən) The Israelite name of the part of Palestine between the Jordan and the Mediterranean; the Promised Land.

Ca·naan·ite (kā′nən·īt) *n.* **1** A dweller in the land of Canaan prior to the Israelite conquest. **2** A descendant of Canaan, son of Ham. **Ca′naan·it′ish** (-ī′tish), **Ca′naan·it′ic** (-it′ik) *adj.*

ca·ña·da (kä·nyä′də) *n. SW U.S.* A narrow canyon. [<Sp.]

Can·a·da (kan′ə·də) A self-governing member of the Commonwealth of Nations, comprising ten provinces and two territories in North America; 3,851,809 square miles; capital, Ottawa: also *British North America.*

Canada balsam A yellowish turpentine derived from the balsam fir.

Canada bluegrass Wiregrass.

Canada goose See under GOOSE.

Canada jay A non-migratory, sooty-gray bird of the crow family *(Perisoreus canadensis),* native in Canada and the NE United States: also called *venison bird.*

Canada lily An American lily *(Lilium canadense)* with drooping orange or yellow flowers, sometimes spotted with brown: also called *meadow lily.*

Canada thistle See under THISTLE.

Ca·na·di·an (kə·nā′dē·ən) *adj.* Of or pertaining to Canada or its inhabitants, their industries, products, etc.— *n.* A native of Canada or a legally constituted citizen of Canada.

Canadian English The English language as spoken and written in Canada.

Canadian French The French language as spoken and written by French Canadians.

Ca·na·di·a·nism (kə·nā′dē·ən·iz′əm) *n.* **1** A trait, custom, or tradition characteristic of the people of Canada or some of them. **2** A word, phrase, or usage especially characteristic of Canadian English or French. **3** Devotion to Canada, its institutions, etc.

Canadian River A river in the SW United States, flowing 906 miles east to the Arkansas River.

Canadian Shield The shield-shaped region of Archean rock in central Canada and Greenland on which the later strata rest; approximately 2,000,000 square miles: also *Laurentian Plateau.*

ca·naille (kə·nāl′, *Fr.* kȧ·nä′y′) *n.* The rabble; mob. [<F <Ital. *canaglia* pack of dogs <L *canis* dog]

ca·nal (kə·nal′) *n.* **1** An artificial inland waterway connecting two navigable bodies of water. **2** An artificial channel for irrigating tracts of land. **3** Any channel, groove, passage, or duct: the auditory *canal.* **4** *Zool.* A groove, as for the siphon in the shells of gastropods, or a pore, as in sponges, etc. **5** *Astron.* One of the peculiar markings visible on the face of the planet Mars. —**central canal** The ventricle of the spinal cord. — *v.t.* **ca·nalled** or **ca·naled, ca·nal·ling** or **ca·nal·ing** To build a canal or canals across or through; canalize. [<MF <L *canalis* groove. Doublet of CHANNEL.]

ca·nal·age (kə·nal′ij) *n.* **1** The construction of canals. **2** Canals collectively. **3** A charge for transportation through a canal.

canal boat A long barge, principally used on canals and drawn either by electric power or by horses or mules on a towpath.

Ca·nal du Nord (kȧ·nȧl′ dü nôr′) See SAINT-QUENTIN CANAL.

ca·nal·er (kə·nal′ər) *n.* **1** One who works on a canal boat. **2** A canal boat. Also **ca·nal′·ler.**

Ca·na·let·to (kä′nä·let′tō), **Antonio,** 1697–1768, Venetian painter. Also **Ca·na·le** (kä·nä′lā).

can·a·lic·u·late (kan′ə·lik′yə·lit, -lāt) *adj.* Channeled or grooved. Also **can′a·lic′u·lar** (-lər), **can′a·lic′u·lat′ed.**

can·a·lic·u·lus (kan′ə·lik′yə·ləs) *n. pl.* **·li** (-lī) *Anat.* A small tube or canal, as in a bone. [< L *canaliculus,* dim. of *canalis* pipe, groove]

ca·nal·ize (kə·nal′īz, kan′əl·īz) *v.t.* **·ized, ·iz·ing 1** To convert into a canal, as a stream or chain of lakes. **2** To furnish with a canal, or a system of canals, or waterways. **3** To furnish with an outlet. —**ca·nal·i·za·tion** (kə·nal′ə·zā′shən, kan′ə·lə-) *n.*

canal rays *Physics* A stream of positively charged ions emitted from the anode of a vacuum tube and emerging through openings in the cathode: also called *positive rays.*

Canal Zone A strip of territory leased in perpetuity to the United States by the Republic of Panama, extending five miles on each side of the Panamȧ Canal, across the Isthmus of Panama; 648 square miles; administrative headquarters, Balboa Heights.

Can·an·dai·gua Lake (kan′ən·dā′gwə) One of the Finger Lakes in western New York.

Ca·nan·ga oil (kə·nang′gə) A volatile oil used in perfume, obtained from the ylang-ylang.

can·a·pé (kan′ə·pē, -pā; *Fr.* kȧ·nȧ·pā′) *n.* Bread, fried or toasted, on which relishes are served. [<F, sofa, couch]

Ca·na·ra (kä′nə·rə, kə·nä′rə) A former spelling of KANARA.

ca·nard (kə·närd′, *Fr.* kȧ·när′) *n.* **1** A fabricated, sensational story; newspaper hoax. **2** *Aeron.* An airplane which has the controlling surfaces, etc., in front of the wings. [<F]

Ca·na·rese (kä′nə·rēz′, -rēs′) See KANARESE.

ca·nar·y (kə·nâr′ē) *n. pl.* **·nar·ies 1** A small finch *(Serinus canarius)* originally native in the Canary Islands, having generally yellow plumage: popular as a cage bird for its song. **2** A bright yellow color: also **canary yellow. 3** A sweet, white wine from the Canary Islands. **4** An old French dance in rapid time. — *v.i.* To dance the canary.[<F *canarie* <Sp. *canario* < L *Canaria (Insula)* Dog (Island) <*canis* dog; so called from a breed of dogs found there]

ca·nar·y·grass (kə·nâr′ē·gras′, -gräs′) *n.* A grass *(Phalaris canariensis)* native in the Canary Islands and cultivated for its seeds, which are used as food for cage birds.

Canary Islands An island group off the NW coast of Africa, comprising two Spanish provinces; 2,894 square miles. Also **Canaries.** *Spanish* **Is·las Ca·na·rias** (ēz′läs kä·nä′ryäs).

canary seed Seed used as food for canaries and other cage birds.

ca·nas·ta (kə·nas′tə) *n.* A card game based on the principles of rummy, for two to six players, using a double deck of cards.[<Sp., basket]

ca·nas·ter (kə·nas′tər) *n.* A coarse-grained tobacco formerly packed in rush baskets. [< Sp. *canastro* <Gk.*kanastron* rush basket]

Ca·nav·er·al (kə·nav′ər·əl), **Cape** See KENNEDY, CAPE.

Can·ber·ra (kan′bər·ə) The capital of the Commonwealth of Australia, in Australian Capital Territory: formerly *Yass-Canberra.*

can but Have no other course than to. See CANNOT BUT.

Can·by (kan′bē), **Henry Seidel,** 1878–1961, U.S. editor and writer.

can·can (kan′kan′, *Fr.* kän·kän′)*n.* A Parisian dance, introduced about 1830, in which the figures of the quadrille are diversified by high kicking and other wild or suggestive movements. [<F, gossip] —**can′can′ing** *adj.*

can·cel (kan′səl) *v.t.* **can·celed** or **·celled, can·cel·ing** or **·cel·ling 1** To mark out or off, as by drawing or stamping lines across written matter to signify that it is to be omitted; blot or strike out; obliterate. **2** To remove, as by cutting out; suppress, as pages of a book. **3** To render null and void; annul, revoke, or set aside. **4** To make up for; compensate; neutralize; countervail. **5** To mark or ink (a postage stamp) to show that it has been used. **6** *Math.* To eliminate (a common factor, as a figure or quantity) from the numerator and denominator of a fraction, or from both sides of an equation. —*n.* In printing and bookbinding, the striking or cutting out, omission, or suppression of a leaf, leaves, or any part of any printed matter or work; also, any printed matter thus suppressed, or the matter substituted for that stricken out. [<MF *canceller* <L *cancellare* cross out<*cancelli,* dim. pl. of *cancer* lattice]

Synonyms (verb): abolish, abrogate, annul, discharge, efface, erase, expunge, nullify, obliterate, quash, remove, repeal, rescind, revoke, vacate. *Cancel, efface, erase, expunge,* and *obliterate* have as their first meaning the removal of written characters or other forms of record. To *cancel* is, literally, to make a lattice by cross lines, exactly our English *cross out*; to *efface* is to rub off, smooth away the face of, as of an inscription; to *expunge* is to punch out with some sharp instrument, so as to show that the words are no longer part of the writing; to *obliterate* is to cover over or remove, as a letter, as was done by reversing the Roman stylus, and rubbing out with the rounded end what had been written with the point on the waxen tablet. What has been *canceled, erased, expunged,* may perhaps still be traced; what is *obliterated* is gone forever, as if it had never been. The figurative use of the words keeps close to the primary sense. Compare ABOLISH, ANNUL. *Antonyms*: approve, confirm, enact, enforce, establish, maintain, perpetuate, record, reenact, sustain, uphold.

can·cel·a·ble (kan′səl·ə·bəl) *adj.* That can be canceled. Also **can′cel·la·ble.**

can·cel·er (kan′səl·ər) *n.* **1** A person or thing that cancels. **2** A device for canceling. Also **can′cel·ler.**

can·cel·late (kan′sə·lāt) *adj.* **1** *Anat.* Latticelike in structure; also, having reticulations, as certain bones, or parts of bones. **2** Chambered; cell-like. Also **can′cel·lat′ed, can′cel·lous** (-ləs).

can·cel·la·tion (kan′sə·lā′shən) *n.* **1** That which is canceled. **2** The mark which cancels. **3** A network formed by small interlacing bars; a reticulation.

can·cel·li (kan·sel′ī) *n. pl.* **1** Bars of latticework, as in a latticed window or in the screen separating the choir from the nave of a church. **2** Bars in the railing of a court. **3** Reticulations; especially, the latticework of bony spicules that forms the spongy or interior portion of a bone.

can·cer (kan′sər) *n.* **1** *Pathol.* A malignant neoplasm or tumor, characterized by a morbid proliferation of epithelial cells in various parts of the body, spreading into adjacent tissue, with consequent progressive degeneration which often ends fatally: also called *carci-*

noma, sarcoma. 2 Any inveterate and spreading evil. —**colloid cancer** A variety of cancer which chiefly attacks the alimentary canal, uterus, or peritoneum. —*v.t.* To eat or penetrate like a cancer. [<L, crab]

Can·cer (kan′sər) The Crab, the fourth sign of the zodiac, which the sun enters at the summer solstice. See CONSTELLATION. —**Tropic of Cancer** See under TROPIC.

can·cer·ate (kan′sə·rāt) *v.i.* **·at·ed, ·at·ing** *Pathol.* To become cancerous; develop into a cancer. —**can′cer·a′tion** *n.*

can·cer·ous (kan′sər·əs) *adj.* 1 *Pathol.* Pertaining to, of the nature of, or affected with a cancer. 2 Virulent; incurable.

can·cer·root (kan′sər·ro͞ot′, -ro͝ot′) *n.* Beechdrops: so called from its supposed value in the external treatment of cancerous ulcer.

can·croid (kang′kroid) *adj.* 1 Like a crab. 2 Resembling a cancer. —*n. Pathol.* An epithelioma of the skin.

can·del·a (kan·del′ə) *n. Physics* A unit of luminous intensity equal to that of 1/60 square centimeter of a black body operating at the temperature of solidification of platinum: also called *candle, standard candle.* Abbr. *cd*

can·de·la·brum (kan′də·lä′brəm, -lā′-) *n. pl.* **·bra** or **·brums** A large, branched candlestick. Also **can′de·la′bra** *pl.* **·bras.** [<L <*candela* candle]

can·dent (kan′dənt) *adj.* Glowing with heat; incandescent. [<L *candens, -entis,* ppr. of *candere* glow]

can·des·cence (kan·des′əns) *n.* Incandescence. —**can·des′cent** *adj.*

Can·di·a (kan′dē·ə) 1 The largest city in Crete, a port on the **Gulf of Candia,** a bay of the Aegean in northern Crete: Greek *Hērakleion.* 2 A former name for CRETE.

can·did (kan′did) *adj.* 1 Sincere; ingenuous; frank. 2 Impartial; fair. 3 *Obs.* White; also, pure. [<MF *candide* pure, honest <L *candidus* <*candere* gleam, shine] —**can′did·ly** *adv.* —**can′did·ness** *n.*

Synonyms: aboveboard, artless, fair, frank, guileless, honest, impartial, ingenuous, innocent, naive, open, simple, sincere, straightforward, transparent, truthful, unbiased, unprejudiced, unreserved, unsophisticated. A *candid* statement is meant to be true to the real facts and just to all parties; a *fair* statement is really so. *Fair* is applied to the conduct but *candid* is not; as, *fair* treatment, a *fair* field and no favor. One who is *frank* has a fearless and unconstrained truthfulness. *Honest* and *ingenuous* unite in expressing total lack of deceit. On the other hand, *artless, guileless, naive, simple,* and *unsophisticated* express the goodness which comes from want of the knowledge or thought of evil. *Sincere* applies to the feelings as being all that one's words would imply. See HONEST. *Antonyms*: adroit, artful, crafty, cunning, deceitful, designing, diplomatic, foxy, insincere, intriguing, knowing, maneuvering, sharp, shrewd, sly, subtle, tricky, wily.

can·di·date (kan′də·dāt, -dit) *n.* A nominee or aspirant for any position or honor. [<L *candidatus* wearing white <*candidus* white; because office-seekers in Rome wore white togas] —**can·di·da·cy** (kan′də·də·sē), **can′di·date′ship, can·di·da·ture** (kan′də·də·chər, -dā′·chər) *n.*

candid camera A small camera with a fast lens, used for taking informal pictures of unposed subjects.

Can·dide (käṅ·dēd′) Hero of Voltaire's romance *Candide* (1759), which satirizes the optimistic theory that this is "the best of all possible worlds."

can·died (kan′dēd) *adj.* 1 Converted into candy; preserved in sugar. 2 Coated with something resembling sugar; frosted. 3 Flattering; honeyed; sugared.

Can·di·ot (kan′dē·ot) *adj.* Cretan; of or pertaining to Candia. —*n.* A Cretan. Also **Can′·di·ote** (-ōt).

can·dle (kan′dəl) *n.* 1 A cylinder of tallow, wax, or other solid fat, containing a wick, to give light when burning. 2 Anything like a candle in shape or purpose. 3 *Mil.* A cylindrical container which, when ignited, emits a cloud of smoke or gas. 4 *Physics* A candela. —**to hold a candle to** To compare with favorably: used in the negative. —*v.t.* **·dled, ·dling** 1 To test (eggs) by holding between the eye and a light, translucency indicating soundness. 2 To test (bottled wines) for clarity. [OE *candel* <L *candela* <*candere* shine, gleam] —**can′dler** *n.*

can·dle·ber·ry (kan′dəl·ber′ē) *n. pl.* **·ries** 1 The wax myrtle or bayberry. 2 Its fruit. 3 An East Indian and Polynesian tree *(Aleurites moluccana);* the candlenut.

candleberry cactus The ocotillo.

can·dle·fish (kan′dəl·fish′) *n.* An edible, oily smeltlike marine fish *(Thaleichthys pacificus)* of the northern Pacific, which, when dried, may be burned as a candle.

can·dle–foot (kan′dəl·fo͝ot′) *n.* Foot-candle.

can·dle·light (kan′dəl·līt′) *n.* 1 Light given by a candle. 2 The time of day when candles are first needed; early evening. Also **candle light, can′dle·light′ing.**

Can·dle·mas (kan′dəl·məs) *n.* The feast of the Purification, or of the Presentation of Christ in the temple, held on Feb. 2; also, the day itself. Also **Candlemas Day.** [OE *candelmæsse* <*candel* candle + *mæsse* mass]

can·dle·mold (kan′dəl·mōld′) *n.* A tin mold with multiple tubular compartments in which to insert wicks and pour melted tallow or wax for making candles.

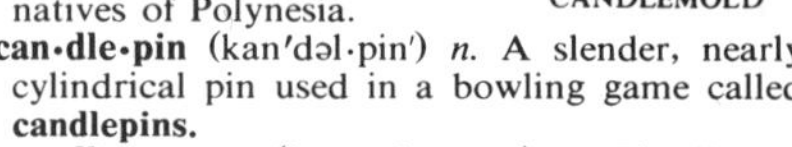
CANDLEMOLD

can·dle·nut (kan′dəl·nut′) *n.* 1 The candleberry (def. 3). 2 The fruit of this tree, burned as candles by the natives of Polynesia.

can·dle·pin (kan′dəl·pin′) *n.* A slender, nearly cylindrical pin used in a bowling game called **candlepins.**

can·dle·pow·er (kan′dəl·pou′ər) *n.* The illuminating power of a standard candle: used as a measure of other illuminants.

can·dle·stand (kan′dəl·stand′) *n.* A small table fitted with candle holders, or on which to set a candlestick.

can·dle·stick (kan′dəl·stik′) *n.* A support for a candle or candles. [OE *candelsticca* <*candel* candle + *sticca* stick]

can·dle·wick (kan′dəl·wik′) *n.* The wick of a candle, or the soft, twisted fibers from which wicks are made; candlewicking. [OE *candelweoca* <*candel* candle + *weoca* wick]

can·dle·wick·ing (kan′dəl·wik′ing) *n.* 1 Thick, soft, cotton thread used to make wicks for candles. 2 Tuftings of such threads worked into a fabric, usually in the form of a design, to give a napped surface.

can·dle·wood (kan′dəl·wo͝od′) *n.* 1 Any of several trees or shrubs, as the ocotillo *(Fouquiera splendens).* 2 Any resinous wood finely split so as to give light when burned on the hearth.

Can·dolle (käṅ·dôl′), **Augustin Pyrame de,** 1778–1841, Swiss botanist.

can·dor (kan′dər) *n.* 1 Freedom from mental reservation or prejudice. 2 Openness; frankness; impartiality; fairness. 3 *Obs.* Brightness; fairness. Also *Brit.* **can′dour.** See synonyms under VERACITY. [<L, sincerity, purity < *candere* gleam, shine]

c–and–w or **C–and–W** Country-and western music.

can·dy (kan′dē) *n. pl.* **·dies** 1 Sugar or molasses crystallized by evaporation; also, a confection of sugar or molasses crystals. 2 Any of numerous confections in various colors, flavors, and forms, and consisting chiefly of cane or beet or other sugar to which has been added chocolate, milk products, fruits, fruit extracts, nuts, or the like; also, such confections collectively: usually called *sweets* in Great Britain. —*v.* **·died, ·dy·ing** *v.t.* 1 To cause to form into crystals of sugar. 2 To preserve by boiling or coating with sugar, as orange peels. 3 To render pleasant; sweeten. 4 To overlay with any crystalline substance, as ice or sugar. —*v.i.* 5 To become crystallized into or covered with sugar. [Short for *sugar candy* <F *(sucre) candi* <Arabic *qandī* made of sugar <*qand* sugar, ult. <Skt.]

Can·dy (kan′dē) A former spelling of KANDY.

can·dy–pull (kan′dē·po͝ol′) *n.* A party at which pulling taffy candy is the chief entertainment.

can·dy·tuft (kan′dē·tuft′) *n.* A plant of the mustard family (genus *Iberis*) with white, pink, or purple flowers.

cane (kān) *n.* 1 A walking stick. 2 A stem of cane grass. 3 The stem of a raspberry or allied plant. 4 Any rod, especially one used for flogging. —*v.t.* **caned, can·ing** 1 To strike or beat with a cane. 2 To bottom or back with cane, as a chair. [<OF <L *canna* <Gk. *kanna* reed <Semitic] —**can′er** *n.*

Ca·ne·a (kä·nē′ä) The capital of Crete, a port on the **Gulf of Canea,** a bay of the Aegean in western Crete: ancient *Cydonia*: Greek *Khania.*

cane blade A blade or stalk of cane grass.

cane·brake (kān′brāk′) *n.* Land overgrown with canes.

cane grass Any of various plants with slender, flexible stems, usually jointed, as the rattan or sugarcane.

ca·nel·la (kə·nel′ə) *n.* The pale, orange-yellow, aromatic inner bark of a tropical American tree *(Canella winterana)*: used as a tonic and condiment. Also **canella bark.** [<Med. L, dim. of *canna* reed]

cane patch A small field of cane grass.

ca·neph·o·rus (kə·nef′ə·rəs) *n. pl.* **·ri** (-rī) The basket-bearer: an Athenian maiden selected to carry the baskets of sacred utensils in the processions of Demeter, Bacchus, and Athena: a frequent subject in Greek art. Also **ca·neph′·o·ros** (-ros), **ca·neph′o·ra** (-rə). [<L *canephora* <Gk. *kanēphoros* <*kaneon* basket + *pherein* carry]

ca·nes·cence (kə·nes′əns) *n.* A whitish color; hoariness.

ca·nes·cent (kə·nes′ənt) *adj.* Becoming, or tending to become, white or hoary. [<L *canescens, -entis,* ppr. of *canescere,* inceptive of *canere* be white]

cane sugar Sucrose obtained from the sugarcane.

Ca·nes Ve·nat·i·ci (kā′nēz vi·nat′ə·sī) A northern constellation, the Hunting Dogs, near Boötes. See CONSTELLATION.

Ca·ney (kä·nā′), **El** See EL CANEY.

Can·field (kan′fēld), **Dorothy,** 1879–1958, U.S. author: married name *Fisher.*

cangue (kang) *n.* A heavy wooden collar or yoke, formerly worn around the neck by convicts in China as a punishment. [<F <Pg. *cango*]

Ca·nic·u·la (kə·nik′yə·lə) The star Sirius; the Dog Star.

ca·nic·u·lar (kə·nik′yə·lər) *adj.* 1 Relating to the Dog Star or to dog days. 2 Relating to a dog: used humorously. [<L *canicularis* < *caniculus,* dim. of *canis* dog]

can·i·kin (kan′ə·kin) See CANNIKIN.

ca·nine (kā′nīn) *adj.* 1 Of, pertaining to, or like a dog. 2 *Zool.* Of or pertaining to the dog family *(Canidae).* 3 Of or pertaining to a canine tooth. —*n.* 1 A dog or other canine animal. 2 A canine tooth. [<L *caninus* <*canis* dog]

canine tooth *Anat.* A tooth growing directly behind the intermaxillary suture in the upper jaw, or the opposite one of the lower jaw; an eyetooth of the upper jaw, or stomach tooth of the lower jaw.

can·ions (kan′yənz) *n. pl.* Sausagelike rolls worn in the 16th and 17th centuries as ornaments around the bottoms of breeches' legs. [<Sp. *cañon,* aug. of *caña* tube,]

Ca·nis (kā′nis) *n. Zool.* The genus including the dog (wild and domestic), the wolf, the fox, and the jackal. [<L, dog]

Ca·nis Ma·jor (kā′nis mā′jər) A northern constellation, the Greater Dog: contains the bright star, Sirius. See CONSTELLATION.

Canis Mi·nor (mī′nər) A northern constellation, the Lesser Dog, including the star Procyon, used by navigators. See CONSTELLATION.

can·is·ter (kan′is·tər) *n.* 1 A metal case, as for tea, coffee, or spices. 2 Shot or bullets packed in a metallic cylinder, to be fired from a cannon; case shot; shrapnel. [<L *canistrum* basket <Gk. *kanastron* <*kanna* reed]

ca·ni·ti·es (kə·nish′i·ēz) *n.* The turning gray of the hair. [<L <*canus* white]

can·ji·ar (kan′jē·är) *n.* A poniard: also spelled *khanjar.* Also **can·jar** (kan′jär). [<Arabic *khanjar*]

can·ker (kang′kər) *n.* 1 *Pathol.* Any ulcer with a tendency to gangrene; a group of small ulcers in the mouth. 2 A disease of fruit trees. 3 Any secret or spreading evil. 4 A disease affecting the feet of horses, characterized by the discharge of an evil-smelling exudate. 5 An inflammation of the external ear in cats and dogs. 6 The cankerworm. 7 *Obs.* The dog rose; also **canker blossom.** —*v.t.* 1 To infect with canker. 2 To eat away or into like a canker; corrode; corrupt. —*v.t.* 3 To

fester with or be attacked by a canker. [<AF *cancre* <L *cancer* crab, ulcer]
can·kered (kang′kərd) *adj.* 1 Affected by or as by canker. 2 Corrupted; malignant; venomous.
can·ker·ous (kang′kər·əs) *adj.* 1 Of the nature of a canker; gangrenous. 2 Causing canker. 3 Corroding; corrupting.
canker rash Scarlet fever.
can·ker·root (kang′kər·ro͞ot′, -ro͝ot′) *n.* One of several plants with astringent roots, as the marsh rosemary.
can·ker·worm (kang′kər·wûrm′) *n.* Any of several insect larvae which destroy fruit and shade trees; especially, the measuring worms of the family *Geometridae.*
can·ker·y (kang′kər·ē) *adj.* 1 Affected with canker. 2 *Scot.* Crabbed; cross; vexatious.
can·na[1] (kan′ə) *n.* Any of a genus (*Canna*) of erect, mostly tropical American plants with red or yellow irregular flowers. [<L <Gk. *kanna* reed] —**can·na·ceous** (kə·nā′shəs) *adj.*
can·na[2] (kän′nə) *Scot.* Cannot.
can·na·bin (kan′ə·bin) *n.* A white, poisonous crystalline resin in Indian hemp, of which it is believed to be the active narcotic principle.
can·nab·in·ol (kə·nab′ə·nōl, -nol) *n. Chem.* The principal resinous ingredient of *Cannabis sativa*, $C_{21}H_{30}O_2$, a thick, reddish-yellow oil, subject to deterioration on exposure to air.
Can·na·bis (kan′ə·bis) *n.* 1 A genus of plants of the mulberry family having only one known species, Indian hemp, from the flowering tops of which are derived the resinous alkaloids noted for their narcotic properties. 2 Hashish. [<L <Gk. *kannabis* hemp]
Can·nae (kan′ē) An ancient town of southern Italy; scene of Hannibal's victory over the Romans, 216 B.C. Also **Can′næ.**
canned (kand) *adj.* 1 Preserved in a can or jar. 2 *Slang* Recorded: *canned* music.
can·nel (kan′əl) *n.* A bituminous coal, rich in gas, with low heating power: also called *kennel.* Also **cannel coal.** [Alter. of *candle coal*]
can·ne·lon (kȧn·lôṅ′) *n. French* 1 A hollow roll of puff paste. 2 A roll of richly seasoned chopped meat, either fried or baked.
can·ne·lure (kan′ə·lo͝or) *n.* A groove or a fluting, especially around the rim of a bullet or the head of a rimless cartridge case. [<F] —**can′ne·lured** *adj.*
can·ner·y (kan′ər·ē) *n. pl.* **·ner·ies** A factory or other establishment where foods are canned.
Cannes (kan, kanz; *Fr.* kȧn) A port and resort city on the Riviera, SE France.
can·ni·bal (kan′ə·bəl) *n.* 1 A human being who eats human flesh. 2 An animal that devours members of its own species. —*adj.* Of or like cannibals or their feasts. [<Sp. *Canibales,* var. of *Caribes* Caribs] —**can′ni·bal·ism** *n.* —**can·ni·bal·ic** (kan′ə·bal′ik), **can′ni·bal·is′tic** *adj.* —**can′ni·bal·is′ti·cal·ly** *adv.*
can·ni·bal·ize (kan′ə·bəl·īz′) *v.t.* **·ized, ·iz·ing** *Mil.* To take parts from (tanks, airplanes, etc.) in order to repair other damaged equipment and vehicles. —**can′ni·bal·i·za′tion** *n.*
can·nie (kan′ē) *Scot.* See CANNY.
can·ni·kin (kan′ə·kin) *n.* 1 A small can or drinking cup. 2 A small wooden pail. Also spelled *canikin.* [Dim. of CAN[2]]
can·ning (kan′ing) *n.* The act, process, or business of preserving fruits, vegetables, meats, etc., in hermetically sealed tin cans, glass jars, etc.
Can·ning (kan′ing), **George,** 1770–1827, English statesman. —**Charles John,** 1812–62, first viceroy of India; son of the preceding. —**Stratford,** 1786–1880, Viscount Stratford de Redcliffe, British diplomat.
can·non (kan′ən) *n. pl.* **·nons** or **·non** 1 *Mil.* **a** A large tubular weapon for discharging a heavy projectile; especially, one mounted on a carriage, movable or fixed. **b** A big artillery gun. **c** Artillery collectively. 2 The great bone between the fetlock and knee or hock of the horse and allied animals: also **cannon bone.** 3 A carom. 4 *Mech.* A loose metallic sleeve on a shaft. 5 A smooth round bit for a horse: also **cannon bit.** 6 The ear of a bell; one of the parts by which it is hung. —*v.t.* 1 To attack with cannon shot. 2 In billiards, to cause to carom. 3 To cause to rebound from one object to another. —*v.i.* 4 To fire cannon repeatedly. 5 In billiards, to make a carom. 6 To rebound from one object to another. ◆ Homophone: *canon.* [<OF *canon* <Ital. *cannone,* aug. of *canna* tube, pipe]
Can·non (kan′ən), **Annie Jump,** 1863–1941, U.S. astronomer. —**Joseph Gurney,** 1836–1926, U.S. politician, member of the House of Representatives 1873–91, 1893–1913, 1915–1923.
can·non·ade (kan′ən·ād′) *v.* **·ad·ed, ·ad·ing** *v.t.* To attack with cannon shot. —*v.i.* To fire cannon repeatedly. —*n.* A continued attack with or discharge of cannon.
cannon ball Any missile to be shot from a cannon; originally, a spherical solid shot.
can·non·eer (kan′ən·ir′) *n.* 1 An artilleryman belonging to a gun squad. 2 A soldier who serves as gunner. Also **can′non·ier′.**
cannon fodder Soldiers, as considered expendable in wartime.
can·non·ry (kan′ən·rē) *n.* Artillery; also, its discharge.
cannon shot 1 A shot or projectile for a cannon; a cannon ball. 2 The distance which the shot of a cannon may achieve.
can·not (ka′not) *v.i.* Am, is, or are not able to.
cannot but Have no alternative except to: objected to by some as a double negative, but long established in formal literary usage.
can·nu·la (kan′yə·lə) *n. Med.* A tube to be inserted by means of a trocar into a cavity, through which pus, etc., may escape or medicine be introduced: also spelled *canula.* [<L, dim. of *canna* reed, tube] —**can′nu·lar** *adj.*
can·nu·late (kan′yə·lāt) *v.t.* **·lat·ed, ·lat·ing** To make hollow or tubular. —*adj.* (kan′yə·lit, -lāt) Tubular. Also spelled *canulate.*
cannulated needle *Surg.* A ligating needle having a bore through which the wire or thread may pass.
can·ny (kan′ē) *adj.* **can·ni·er, can·ni·est** 1 Careful in determining or acting; prudent; knowing; thrifty; shrewd. 2 Skilful; clever. 3 Lucky; safe. 4 Quiet; sly; dry: said of humor as characteristically Scottish. 5 Comfortable; cozy; snug. Also spelled *cannie.* [<CAN (def. 3)] —**can′ni·ly** *adv.* —**can′ni·ness** *n.*
Ca·no (kä′nō), **Alonso,** 1601–67, Spanish painter, sculptor, and architect.
ca·noe (kə·no͞o′) *n.* 1 A small, long, narrow boat, pointed at both ends, made from a hollowed log, bark, light wood, or animal skins, and propelled by paddles: used by primitive peoples. 2 A modern adaptation of this, made of canvas, light wood, or aluminum. Compare illustration under CATAMARAN. —*v.t.* 1 To convey by canoe. —*v.i.* 2 To paddle, sail, or travel in a canoe. 3 To operate a canoe. [<Sp. <Taino *canoa* boat] —**ca·noe′ing** *n.* —**ca·noe′ist** *n.*

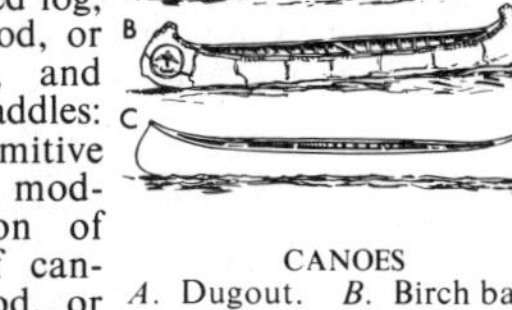

CANOES
A. Dugout. *B.* Birch bark. *C.* Modern.

ca·noe·wood (kə·no͞o′wo͝od′) *n.* Tulipwood.
can·on[1] (kan′ən) *n.* 1 A rule or law; standard; criterion. 2 The books of the Bible that are recognized by the Church as inspired. 3 The list of an author's works which are accepted as genuine: the Shakespearian *canon.* 4 *Eccl.* An official list or catalog, as of the saints recognized by a church, or of the members of a cathedral chapter. 5 *Eccl.* A rule of faith or discipline, especially one enacted by a church council and (in the Roman Catholic Church) ratified by the Pope. 6 *Often cap.* The portion of the mass between the Sanctus and the Lord's Prayer. 7 *Printing* A size of type nearly four times as large as pica; 48-point type. See PICA. 8 *Music* A composition having voices or parts wherein each voice or part in turn takes up the same melody (called the subject), and all combine to make harmony: the strictest form of musical imitation. 9 One of the metal loops at the top of a bell, by which it is hung. See synonyms under LAW, RULE. ◆ Homophone: *cannon.* [OE <L <Gk. *kanōn* rule, straight rod]
can·on[2] (kan′ən) *n.* A member of the chapter of a cathedral or collegiate church. ◆ Homophone: *cannon.* [OE *canonic* <LL *canonicus* cleric < *canon* rule. See CANON[1].]
cañ·on (kan′yən, *Sp.* kä·nyōn′) See CANYON.
ca·non·i·cal (kə·non′i·kəl) *adj.* 1 Belonging to or characteristic of the canon of Scripture. 2 Regular; lawful; accepted or approved. Also **ca·non′ic.** [<Med. L *canonicalis* <LL *canonicus* <L *canon.* See CANON[1].] —**ca·non′i·cal·ly** *adv.*
canonical age The age required by canon law for ordination or for the performance of any particular act.
canonical hours 1 *Eccl.* The seven stated daily periods, fixed by canon, for prayer and devotion. They are named respectively matins (including nocturns and lauds), prime, tierce, sext, nones, vespers, and compline. 2 *Brit.* The hours (from 8 a.m. to 3 p.m.) during which marriage may be legally performed in parish churches.
ca·non·i·cals (kə·non′i·kəlz) *n. pl.* The habits or robes prescribed by canon to be worn by the clergy when they officiate.
ca·non·i·cate (kə·non′i·kāt, -kit) *n.* The office of a canon.
can·on·ic·i·ty (kan′ən·is′ə·tē) *n.* 1 The quality of being canonical. 2 Conformity to the canon; orthodoxy.
can·on·ist (kan′ən·ist) *n.* One skilled in canon law. —**can′on·is′tic** or **·ti·cal** *adj.*
can·on·i·za·tion (kan′ən·ə·zā′shən, -ī·zā′-) *n.* 1 The formal enrolling of a deceased and beatified person in the Roman Catholic canon, or calendar of saints. 2 The act of canonizing or regarding as a saint; the state of being canonized.
can·on·ize (kan′ən·īz) *v.t.* **·ized, ·iz·ing** 1 To place (a deceased person) in the canon, or catalog of saints; declare to be or regard as a saint. 2 To recognize as part of the canon of Scripture. 3 To sanction as being conformable to the canons of the Church. 4 To give or ascribe glory to; glorify.
canon law The body of ecclesiastical law by which a church is governed.
can·on·ry (kan′ən·rē) *n. pl.* **·ries** 1 The office or dignity of a canon; the benefice of a canon. 2 Canons collectively. Also **can′on·ship.**
can–o·pen·er (kan′ō′pən·ər) *n.* A device for opening cans, especially those containing food.
Ca·no·pic (kə·nō′pik) *adj.* Of or pertaining to Canopus.
Canopic vase or **jar** A vase with a top in the form of a human head: used in ancient Egypt to hold the viscera of embalmed bodies: also called **Canopic urn.**
Ca·no·pus (kə·nō′pəs) One of the 20 brightest stars, –0.86 magnitude; Alpha in the constellation Carina. See STAR. [<L]
Ca·no·pus (kə·nō′pəs) A port in ancient Egypt NE of Alexandria.
can·o·py (kan′ə·pē) *n. pl.* **·pies** 1 A covering suspended over a throne, bed, shrine, or the like, or held over a person in a procession. 2 Any covering overhead, as the arch of the sky. 3 An ornamental feature covering a niche, or an altar or tomb, or placed over a statue. 4 *Aeron.* **a** The main lifting surface of a parachute, whose unfolding reduces the velocity of descent. **b** The semicircular sliding panel enclosing the cockpit cowling of an airplane. —*v.t.* **·pied, ·py·ing** To cover with or as with a canopy. [<F *canapé* sofa <L *canopeum* mosquito net <Gk. *kōnōpeion* bed with mosquito net < *kōnōps* mosquito]
ca·no·rous (kə·nôr′əs, -nō′rəs) *adj.* Having a singing quality; tuneful; melodious; musical. [<L *canorus* < *canor* song < *canere* sing] —**ca·no′rous·ly** *adv.*
Ca·nos·sa (kə·nos′ə, *Ital.* kä·nôs′sä) A ruined castle in north central Italy; scene of Henry IV's penance before Gregory VII in 1077. —**to go to Canossa** To do penance; be reconciled.
Ca·no·va (kä·nō′vä), **Antonio,** 1757–1822, Italian sculptor.
Cá·no·vas del Cas·til·lo (kä′nō·väs thel käs·tē′lyō), **Antonio,** 1828–97, Spanish statesman and writer.
can·so (kan·sō′) *n. pl.* **·sos** A lyric poem in Provençal troubadour literature, characterized by great formal elaboration and generally concerning themes of mundane gallantry (*canso d'amor*): also spelled *canzo.* [<Provençal <L *cantio* < *canere* sing]
Can·so (kan′sō), **Cape** The easternmost point

of the Nova Scotia peninsula. **— Strait of Canso** The strait between Cape Breton Island and the mainland of Nova Scotia. Also **Canso Strait.**

canst (kanst) Can: obsolescent or poetic second person singular, present tense of CAN: used with *thou.*

cant[1] (kant) *n.* **1** An inclination or tipping; a slope or set to one side. **2** A motion that produces a slant or an overturn. **3** A salient angle, as of a bolthead. **4** A slant surface, as one produced by cutting off a corner or edge. *— v.t.* **1** To set slantingly; tip up; tilt. **2** To give a bevel to. **3** To throw out or off; also, to jerk; toss. *— v.i.* **4** To tilt; slant. *— adj.* **1** Oblique; slanting. **2** Having canted sides or corners. [Prob. <OF <Med. L *cantus* corner, side]

cant[2] (kant) *n.* **1** Hypocritical or ostentatious religious talk. **2** Any technical or professional jargon: legal *cant.* **3** The secret language of thieves, gipsies, beggars, etc.; argot. **4** Any jargon employed for secrecy. **5** Hackneyed phraseology assumed as a fashion or for effect. **6** Whining speech, especially of beggars. See synonyms under HYPOCRISY, SLANG.*— v.t.* **1** To say with affected religiousness or in a hypocritical way. *— v.i.* **2** To chant; whine, as a beggar. **3** To talk with hypocritical or exaggerated unction, especially about religion. *— adj.* Like cant; insincere; hypocritical. [< AF, singing <L *cantus* song < *canere* sing] **— cant'er** *n.*

cant[3] (känt) *adj. Scot. & Brit. Dial.* Bold; brisk; lively.

can't (kant, känt) Cannot: a contraction.

can·ta·bi·le (kän·tä'bē·lā) *Music adj.* Melodious; flowing. *— n.* Music characterized by flowing melody. [<Ital.]

Can·ta·bri·an Mountains (kan·tā'brē·ən) A range in northern Spain; highest peak, 8,687 feet. *Spanish* **Cor·dil·le·ra Can·tá·bri·ca** (kôr'·thē·lyā'rä kän·tä'vrē·kä).

Can·ta·brig·i·an (kan'tə·brij'ē·ən) *adj.* **1** Of or pertaining to Cambridge, England, or its university. **2** Of or pertaining to Cambridge, Massachusetts, or to Harvard University. *— n.* **1** A resident of Cambridge, England; also, a student or graduate of Cambridge University. **2** A student or graduate of Harvard University, or a resident of Cambridge, Massachusetts. [<LL *Cantabrigia* Cambridge]

can·ta·lev·er (kan'tə·lev'ər, -lē'vər) See CANTILEVER.

can·ta·loupe (kan'tə·lōp) *n.* A variety of muskmelon *(Cucumis melo cantalupensis).* Also **can'ta·loup.** [<F from *Cantalupo,* Italian castle where first grown in Europe]

can·tank·er·ous (kan·tang'kər·əs) *adj.* Quarrelsome; ill-natured; perverse. [ME *contak* strife] **— can·tank'er·ous·ly** *adv.* **— can·tank'·er·ous·ness** *n.*

can·tar (kan'tär) *n.* A unit of weight in Moslem countries, commonly between 100 and 130 pounds: also spelled *kantar.* [<Sp. *cantaro* <Arabic *qintar* hundredweight, ult. <L *centenarius* hundredfold]

can·ta·ta (kən·tä'tə) *n. Music* A choral composition in the style of an oratorio or drama, sung but not acted. [<Ital.]

Can·ta·te (kan·tā'tē) The 98th Psalm (97th in the Douai version), used as an alternative canticle in the Book of Common Prayer at Evening Prayer: so called from the first words in Latin, *Cantate Domino* (Sing unto the Lord).

Cantate Sunday The fourth Sunday after Easter, the introit for which is the first verse of the Cantate.

can·ta·tri·ce (kän'tä·trē'chā) *n. pl.* **·tri·ci** (-trē'chē) *Ital.* A female professional singer.

cant·dog (kant'dôg', -dog') *n.* A cant-hook.

can·teen (kan·tēn') *n.* **1** A small, metal flask for water, coffee, etc. **2** A refreshment and liquor shop; formerly, a shop at a military camp where soldiers might buy provisions. See POST EXCHANGE. **3** An entertainment center or club operated by civilians for enlisted personnel of Army, Navy, Air Force, Marine, and other military units. [<F *cantine* <Ital. *cantina* cellar]

can·ter (kan'tər) *n.* A moderate, easy gallop. *— v.t. & v.i.* To ride or go at an easy gallop. [Short for *Canterbury gallop*; with ref. to the pace of pilgrims riding to Canterbury] **— can'·ter·er** *n.*

Can·ter·bur·y (kan'tər·ber'ē) **1** A county borough and archbishopric in Kent, England; seat of the primate of the English Church. **2** A provincial district of eastern South Island, New Zealand; 13,940 square miles.

Canterbury bell One of various cultivated bellflowers, especially *Campanula medium.*

Canterbury gallop A canter: the original term. Also **Canterbury pace, rack,** or **trot.**

Canterbury Tales An uncompleted work (1387–1400) by Chaucer, consisting of a series of tales, largely in verse, told by a group of pilgrims to each other on their way to Canterbury.

can·thar·i·des (kan·thar'ə·dēz) *n.* The dried powder obtained by crushing the Spanish fly or blister beetle: used externally as a rubefacient and vesicant and internally as a diuretic and aphrodisiac. [See CANTHARIS]

can·thar·i·din (kan·thar'ə·din) *n. Chem.* The bitter crystalline anhydride principle, $C_{10}H_{12}O_4$, contained in cantharides: a powerful blistering agent. Also **can·thar'i·dine** (-din, -dēn).

can·tha·ris (kan'thə·ris) *n. pl.* **can·thar·i·des** (kan·thar'ə·dēz) The Spanish fly. [<L <Gk. *kantharis*]

cant-hook (kant'·hŏŏk') *n.* A lever equipped with a hook for handling logs.

CANT–HOOK

can·thus (kan'thəs) *n. pl.* **·thi** (-thī) *Anat.* The angle at the outer or inner junction of the eyelids. [<L <Gk. *kanthos*]

can·ti·cle (kan'ti·kəl) *n.* A non-metrical hymn, as one with words taken directly from the Bible text, to be chanted, as in certain church services. [<L *canticulum,* dim. of *canticum* song]

Can·ti·cles (kan'ti·kəlz) The Song of Solomon.

Can·ti·gny (käṅ·tē·nyē') A village in northern France; scene of the first engagement of U.S. troops in World War I, May 27–28, 1918.

can·ti·lev·er (kan'tə·lev'ər) *n.* **1** *Engin.* One of two long structural members, as a truss, beam, or slab, lying across a support, with the two projecting arms in balance, as in a **cantilever bridge. 2** *Archit.* A heavy bracket supporting

CANTILEVER BRIDGE

a balcony, or the like. **3** *Aeron.* A form of airfoil without external bracing. *— v.t. & v.i.* To project (a building member) outward and in balance beyond the base. Sometimes spelled *cantalever.* Also **can'ti·liv'er** (-liv'ər). [Origin uncertain]

can·til·late (kan'tə·lāt) *v.t. & v.i.* **·lat·ed, ·lat·ing** To recite by intoning or chanting: said especially of the manner of rendering the service in Jewish or other rituals. [<L *cantillatus,* pp. of *cantillare* sing low, hum < *cantare* sing] **— can'til·la'tion** *n.*

can·ti·na (kan·tē'nə) *n. SW U.S.* A place where liquor is sold; a bar or saloon. [<Sp.]

can·tle (kan'təl) *n.* **1** A piece cut or broken off; a segment; corner. **2** The hind bow of a saddle. [<AF *cantel* <LL *cantellus,* dim. of *cantus* corner]

can·to (kan'tō) *n. pl.* **·tos 1** A division of an extended poem. **2** *Archaic* The part of a musical score to which the melody is assigned; the air. [<Ital. <L *cantus* song]

can·ton (kan'tən, -ton, kan·ton') *n.* **1** A district of the Swiss confederation. **2** A subdivision of an arrondissement in France. **3** The rectangular part of a flag next the staff. **4** *Her.* The diminutive of the quarter, occupying one third of the chief, usually on the dexter side of the shield. **5** An assemblage of village communities. *— v.t.* **1** To divide into cantons. **2** To sever; separate. **3** To assign to quarters, as military troops. [<OF <Ital. *cantone,* aug. of *canto* corner <L *cantus*] **— can·ton·al** (kan'tən·əl) *adj.*

Can·ton 1 (kan·ton') A port on the Canton River, the capital of Kwangtung province, southern China: Chinese *Kwangchow.* **2** (kan'·tən) A city in NE Ohio.

Can·ton crêpe (kan'tən) A soft silk crêpe, having more body than crêpe de Chine. [from *Canton,* China]

can·toned (kan'tənd) *adj.* **1** *Her.* Placed in the midst of four bearings or groups of bearings on a shield, as a cross, or having a single canton, as a shield. **2** *Mil.* Assigned to quarters, as soldiers.

Can·ton·ese (kan'tən·ēz', -ēs') *n. pl.* **·ese 1** A native of Canton, China. **2** The Chinese language spoken in Kwangtung province and other parts of southern China.

can·ton flannel (kan'tən) A heavy cotton fabric having a long nap, usually on one side only: used for undergarments, infants' nightwear, etc. [from *Canton,* China]

Can·ton Island (kan'tən) The largest and northernmost of the Phoenix Islands, comprising a condominium (1939) of the United States and Great Britain; 3 1/2 square miles.

can·ton·ment (kan·ton'mənt, -tōn'-, kan'tən·mənt; *Brit.* kan·tōōn'mənt) *n.* **1** A group of wooden buildings for housing troops; a military station **2** The act of cantoning troops. [<F *cantonnement* < *cantonner* quarter]

Can·ton River (kan·ton') A river in southern Kwangtung province, China, flowing 110 miles to the South China Sea: also *Pearl River*: Chinese *Chu Kiang.*

can·tor (kan'tər, -tôr) *n.* **1** A precentor; a chief singer. **2** A liturgical singer in a synagog. [<L]

can·trip (kan'trip) *n. Scot.* **1** An incantation; charm; piece of witchcraft. **2** A mischievous trick or mad prank.

cant timber *Naut.* One of the heavy timbers forming part of a ship's hull at either end and supported by the deadwood.

can·tus (kan'təs) *n. pl.* **can·tus 1** A style of church song. **2** The principal voice of a polyphonic work. [<L, song, singing]

cantus fir·mus (fûr'məs) **1** The plain song or chant. **2** *Music* The fixed, simple melody to which other parts are added to make a polyphonic work.

can·ty (kän'tē) *adj. Scot.* Brisk; glad; lively. Also **can'tie.**

Ca·nuck (kə·nuk') *Slang adj.* Canadian. *— n.* **1** A Canadian. **2** A French Canadian. Also **Ca·nuck'er.**

can·u·la (kan'yə·lə) See CANNULA.

can·u·late (kan'yə·lāt) See CANNULATE.

Ca·nute (kə·nōōt', -nyōōt'), 994?–1035, king of England 1016?–35 and of Denmark 1018–1035: also spelled *Cnut, Knut.*

can·vas (kan'vəs) *n.* **1** A heavy, strong cloth of various grades, used for sails, tents, etc. **2** A piece of such cloth; a sail. **3** A strong, closely woven cloth stretched on a frame and prepared for the reception of colors, as in paintings. **4** A painting. **5** A square-meshed fabric of linen, silk, or the like, on which embroidery or tapestry is worked with a needle. **6** A tent; especially, a circus tent. **— under canvas 1** With sails set. **2** In tents. ◆ Homophone: *canvass.* [<AF *canevas* <L *cannabis* hemp]

can·vas·back (kan'vəs·bak') *n.* A North American sea duck *(Nyroca valisineria)* with a grayish white back, highly esteemed for its flesh.

can·vass (kan'vəs) *n.* **1** The going about to solicit orders, interest, or votes. **2** A political campaign. **3** A survey taken to ascertain sentiment. **4** A detailed examination; especially, a sifting of votes in an election; a recount. *— v.t.* **1** To go about an area to solicit, as votes. **2** To scrutinize; examine; sift. *— v.i.* **3** To go about seeking votes, orders or the like: to *canvass* for votes. See synonyms under EXAMINE. ◆ Homophone: *canvas.* [<CANVAS; with ref. to the earlier use of canvas for sifting] **— can'vass·er** n.

can·y (kā'nē) *adj.* Full of canes; made of cane.

can·yon (kan'yən) *n.* A deep gorge or ravine, with steep or precipitous sides: also spelled *cañon.* See synonyms under VALLEY. [<Sp. *cañón*]

Canyon de Chelly National Monument

(də shā′) A region of cliff-dweller ruins in NE Arizona; established as a national park in 1931.

can·zo (kan·sō′) See CANSO.

can·zo·ne (kän·tsō′nā) *n. pl.* **·ni** (-nē) **1** A Provençal or Italian ballad or song. **2** The music for such a song. [<Ital. <L *cantio* song]

can·zo·net (kanzə·net′) *n.* A short song; light air. [<Ital. *canzonetta,* dim of *canzone* song]

caout·chouc (kōō′chōōk, kou·chōōk′) *n.* Rubber; especially, crude rubber. [<F <Tupian *caú-uchú*]

cap[1] (kap) *n.* **1** A covering to be worn on the head; specifically, a brimless head covering, often with a shade or vizor in front. **2** A head covering for a woman or an infant made of lace or some soft fabric. **3** Any headgear of unique design to distinguish some order, office, dignity, or characteristic of the wearer. **4** Anything resembling or used as a cap: a bottle *cap.* **5** The primer of a cartridge or shell case. **6** *Bot.* The pileus of a mushroom. **7** The top of an oil well. **8** Any of various large sizes of writing paper. See FOOLSCAP, LEGAL CAP. **9** *Archit.* The upper member of a column or pilaster; a capital. **—test cap** A protective covering for the exposed end of a cable, excluding dirt, moisture, etc. **—to set one's cap for** To try to win as a suitor or husband. — *v.t.* **capped, cap·ping 1** To put a cap on, as the head. **2** To fit the top or summit of with a cover: Bees *cap* their cells. **3** To serve as a cap to; lie on top of; crown: The cloud *capped* the mountain. **4** To add the final touch to; complete. **5** To excel; top. **—to cap the climax** To surpass the climax; exceed the limit. [OE *cæppe* <LL *cappa* hooded cloak, cap, prob. < *caput* head]

cap[2] (kap) *n. Colloq.* A capital letter.

ca·pa·bil·i·ty (kāpə·bil′ə·tē) *n.* pl. **·ties 1** The state or quality of being capable; capacity; ability. **2** Susceptibility to some particular form of use, treatment, or development. **3** *Usually pl.* A feature or condition that may be improved or developed. See synonyms under ABILITY.

Ca·pa·blan·ca (käpä·vläng′kä), **José Raoul,** 1882–1942, Cuban world chess champion: full name *Capablanca y Granperra.*

ca·pa·ble (kā′pə·bəl) *adj.* **1** Having adequate ability or capacity to do or to receive; efficient; able; qualified; competent. **2** *Obs.* Comprehensive. **3** Adaptable; susceptible: with *of.* See synonyms under CLEVER, COMPETENT. [<F <LL *capabilis* <L *capere* take, receive] **—ca′·pa·ble·ness** *n.* **—ca′pa·bly** *adv.*

ca·pa·cious (kə·pā′shəs) *adj.* Able to contain or receive much; spacious; roomy. See synonyms under LARGE. [<L *capax, -acis* able to hold, roomy < *capere* take] **—ca·pa′cious·ly** *adv.* **—ca·pa′cious·ness** *n.*

ca·pac·i·tance (kə·pas′ə·təns) *n.* Electr. **1** In a conductor or system of conductors, the ratio of electrical charge to a resulting potential. **2** That property of a body expressed by the amount of electricity required to give it a potential greater than its surroundings. [<CAPACI(TY) + (REAC)TANCE]

ca·pac·i·tate (kə·pas′ə·tāt) *v.t.* **·tat·ed, ·tat·ing 1** To render capable. **2** To qualify according to law.

ca·pac·i·tive (kə·pas′ə·tiv) *adj.* Electr. Of or relating to capacitance.

ca·pac·i·tor (kə·pas′ə·tər) *n.* A device for accumulating and holding a charge of electricity, consisting of two conductors separated by a dielectric and having equal, opposite charges.

ca·pac·i·ty (kə·pas′ə·tē) *n.* pl. **·ties 1** Ability to receive or contain; cubic extent; carrying power or space. **2** Adequate mental power to receive, understand, etc.; also, ability; talent; capability. **3** Specific position, character, or office. **4** Legal qualification. **5** *Electr.* **a** Capacitance. **b** The output of an electric generator. See synonyms under ABILITY, POWER. [<F *capacité* <L *capacitas, -tatis* < *capax.* See CAPACIOUS .]

cap and bells A cap ornamented with little bells, worn by a fool or court jester.

cap and gown The apparel worn at some academic ceremonies, consisting of a flat cap *(mortarboard)* and a long, dark gown: often used figuratively for the academic life.

Cap·a·neus (kap′ə·nōōs, -nyōōs, kə·pā′nē·əs) See SEVEN AGAINSTTHEBES.

cap-a-pie (kapə·pē′) *adv.* From head to foot. Also **cap-à-pie′.** [<OF]

ca·par·i·son (kə·par′ə·sən) *n.* **1** Decorative trappings for a horse. **2** Showy or sumptuous apparel. — *v.t.* To put ornamental trappings on; clothe richly. [<OF *caparasson* <Sp. *caparazón* <LL *cappa* cape]

Synonyms (noun): accouterments, harness, housings, trappings. *Harness* was formerly used of the armor of a knight as well as of a horse; it is now used almost exclusively of the equipment of a horse when attached to a vehicle. We speak of the *accouterments* of a soldier. *Caparison* and *trappings* denote the ornamental outfit of a horse, or, in a humorous sense, showy human apparel. Compare ARMS, DRESS.

cape[1] (kāp) *n.* A point of land extending into the sea or a lake. **—the Cape 1** The Cape of Good Hope. **2** *U.S.* Cape Cod. [<F *cap* <L *caput* head]

cape[2] (kāp) *n.* A circular, sleeveless upper garment; a short cloak. [<F <LL *cappa*] **—caped** (kāpt) *adj.*

Cape Bret·on Island (brit′n, bret′n) An island off the NE end of Nova Scotia; 3,975 square miles.

Cape Coast A port on the Gulf of Guinea, former capital of Gold Coast Colony. Formerly **Cape Coast Castle.**

Cape Cod 1 See COD, CAPE. **2** A style of cottage developed chiefly on Cape Cod in the 18th and early 19th centuries, typically a one-story wooden cottage with a gable roof.

Cape Cod Canal A canal, 13 miles long, across Cape Cod from Buzzards Bay Cape Cod Bay.

Cape Colony A former administrative division of the Republic of South Africa. See CAPE OF GOOD HOPE PROVINCE.

Cape Dutch Afrikaans.

Cape Fear River See FEAR, CAPE.

Cape-Horn·er (kāp·hôr′nər) *n.* A vessel whose run is around Cape Horn. See HORN, CAPE.

Ča·pek (chä′pek), **Karel,** 1890–1938, Czech playwright and novelist.

cap·e·lin (kap′ə·lin) *n.* pl. **·lin** or **·lins** A small, edible fish *(Mallotus villosus)* of the smelt family, with many-rayed pectoral fins, found in northern seas: much used as cod bait: also spelled *caplin.* [<F *caplan, capelan*]

Ca·pel·la (kə·pel′ə) One of the 20 brightest stars, 0.21 magnitude and of a yellow color; Alpha in the constellation Auriga. See STAR. [<L, she-goat]

Cape of Good Hope See GOODHOPE, CAPE OF.

Cape of Good Hope Province A former province of the Republic of South Africa roughly corresponding to the Eastern, Western, and Northern Cape provinces; formerly *Cape Colony.*

ca·per[1] (kā′pər) *n.* **1** A leaping or frisking; a skip or jump; prank; antic. **2** Any wild or fantastic action activity. **—to cut a caper** (or **capers**) To caper; frolic. — *v.i.* To leap playfully; frisk. See synonyms under FROLIC. [Short for CAPRIOLE] **—cap′per·er** .

ca·per[2] (kā′pər) *n.* **1** The flower bud of a low shrub of Mediterranean countries, used as a condiment. **2** The shrub *(Capparis spinosa)* producing it. [<L *capparis* <Gk. *kapparis*]

cap·er·cail·lie (kapər·kāl′yē) *n.* A large, black European grouse *(Tetrao urogallus).* Also **cap·er·cail′zie** (-yē, -zē). [<Scottish Gaelic *capullcoille* horse of the wood]

Ca·per·na·um (kə·pûr′nē·əm) A Biblical locality in NE Palestine by the Sea of Galilee. *Matt.* iv 13.

Cape Sable 1 See SABLE, CAPE. **2** See under SABLE ISLAND.

cape·skin (kāp′skin) *n.* A kind of leather made from lamb or sheep skins, originally from the Cape of Good Hope: used especially for gloves.

Ca·pet (kā′pit, kap′it) See HUGH CAPET.

Ca·pe·tian (kə·pē′shən) *adj.* **1** Pertaining to or descended from Hugh Capet, or pertaining to the dynasty founded by him which ruled France until 1328, or to the collateral branches of that dynasty which ruled until 1792. See HUGHCAPET. **—***n.* A descendant, direct or indirect, of Hugh Capet.

Cape Town A port on Table Bay, capital of West Cape Province, Republic of South Africa. Also **Cape′town.**

Cape Verde See VERDE, CAPE.

Cape Verde Islands A Portuguese overseas province west of Cape Verde, comprising two groups of islands; 1,557 square miles; capital, Praia, on São Tiago. *Portuguese* **I·lhas do Ca·bo Ver·de** (ē′lyəz hthōō kä′vōō vär′di).

Cape York Peninsula The NE part of Queensland, Australia.

Cap Hai·tien (kāp hā′shən) A port in northern Haiti. Also **Le Cap** (lə kä′). *French* **Cap Ha·ï·tien** (kȧ·pȧ ·ē·syȧ′).

ca·pi·as (kā′pē·əs, kap′ē·əs) *n. pl.* **·as·es** *Law* A judicial writ issued to an officer, commanding him to take and hold in custody the person named therein subject to the order of the court; a writ of arrest. [<L, you may take]

cap·il·la·ceous (kapə·lā′shəs) *adj.* Hairlike; capillary. [<L *capillaceus* < *capillus* hair]

cap·il·lar·i·ty (kapə·lar′ə·tē) *n.* **1** The state or quality of being capillary. **2** *Physics* The interaction between the molecules of a liquid and those of a solid: a form of surface tension. When the adhesive force is stronger the liquid will tend to rise above mean level at the points of contact with the solid, as water in clean glass; when cohesion dominates, the liquid will tend to fall below this level, as mercury. [<F *capillarité*]

cap·il·lar·y (kap′ə·lerē) *adj.* **1** Of, pertaining to, or like hair; fine; slender. **2** Having a hairlike bore, as a tube or vessel; also, pertaining to such a tube. **—***n.* pl. **·lar·ies 1** *Anat.* A minute vessel, as those connecting the arteries and veins. **2** Any tube with a fine bore. [<L *capillaris* < *capillus* hair]

capillary attraction and repulsion Capillarity.

cap·il·li·ti·um (kapə·lish′ē·əm) *n.* pl. **·li·ti·a** (-lish′ē·ə) *Bot.* The sterile, branching or anastomosing, threadlike tubes or filaments mixed with the spores in a sporangium, or fruit body, as in myxomycetes. [<L < *capillus* hair]

Ca·pis·tra·no (käpi·strä′nō) *n.* A native or inhabitant of Capri.

cap·i·ta (kap′ə·tə) Plural of CAPUT.

cap·i·tal[1] (kap′ə·təl) *adj.* **1** Standing at the head or beginning; chief; principal. **2** Excellent; admirable. **3** Of or pertaining to the death penalty; punishable with death. **4** Of or pertaining to funds or capital. See synonyms under EXCELLENT, GOOD. **—***n.* **1** The chief city or town of a country, state, province, etc., usually the seat of government. **2** A capital letter. **3** Wealth employed in or available for producing more wealth. **4** Property used in the business of a firm or corporation at a valuation on which profits and dividends are calculated. **5** The aggregate of the products of industry directly available for the support of human existence or for promoting additional production. **6** Possessors of wealth, as a class. **7** Any resource or circumstance that can be utilized for an ambitious objective. ◆Homophone: *capitol.* [<F <L *capitalis* < *caput* head]

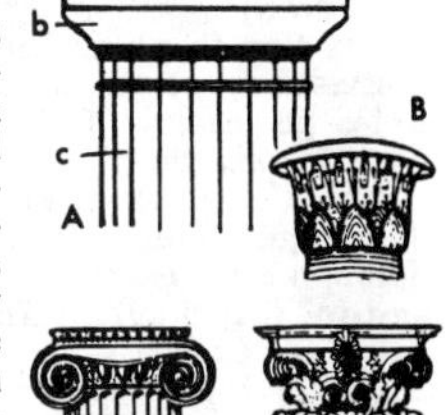

CAPITALS
A. Doric.
a. Abacus. *b.* Echinus.
c. Channeled shaft.
B. Egyptian.
C. Ionic.
D. Corinthian.
E. Byzantine.
F. Romanesque.

cap·i·tal[2] (kap′ə·təl) *n. Archit.* The upper member of a column or pillar. ◆Homophone: *capitol.* [<L *capitellum,* double dim. of *caput* head]

capital account A statement of the amount and value of a business at a given time, consisting of two columns representing assets and liabilities balanced by profit and loss, indicating a surplus or a deficit.

capital expenditure Expenditure for permanent additions or improvements to property, as opposed to money spent for repairs.

capital gain Profit from the sale of capital investments, such as stocks, real estate, etc.

capital goods Materials used in industry in the production of consumers' goods.

cap·i·tal·ism (kap′ə·təl·iz′əm) *n.* **1** An economic system in which the means of production and distribution are for the most part privately owned and operated for private profit. **2** The possession and concentration of private capital and its resulting power and influence.

cap·i·tal·ist (kap′ə·təl·ist) *n.* **1** One who shares in or adheres to capitalism. **2** An owner of capital; especially, one who has large means employed in productive enterprise. **3** Loosely, any person of apparent wealth. —**cap′i·tal·is′tic** *adj.* —**cap′i·tal·is′ti·cal·ly** *adv.*

cap·i·tal·i·za·tion (kap′ə·təl·ə·zā′shən, -ī·zā′-) *n.* **1** The act or process of capitalizing. **2** The value of the entire property of a business, usually represented by the stock or shares issued as permanent liabilities of the business.

cap·i·tal·ize (kap′ə·təl·īz) *v.t.* **·ized, ·iz·ing 1** To begin with capital letters, or write or print in capital letters. **2** To convert into capital or cash. **3** To convert (a periodical payment) into a sum in hand; compute the value of in a single payment or capital sum. **4** To invest for profit; provide capital. **5** To organize on a basis of capital. **6** To profit by: with *on:* He *capitalized* on his enemy's errors.

capital letter In writing and printing, the form of the alphabetic letter used at the beginning of a sentence, with proper names, etc.: in printing called *cap* or *upper case letter* as distinguished from *lower case letter.* Compare CASE[2] (def. 3). —**small capital** A letter used in printing having the same form as but of smaller size than the CAPITAL of the same font: also called *small cap.* In this dictionary cross–references are in SMALL CAPITALS.

capital levy A tax on capital; a property tax: distinguished from *income tax.*

cap·i·tal·ly (kap′ə·təl·ē) *adv.* **1** Firstly; chiefly. **2** Excellently. **3** So as to deserve death.

capital punishment The death penalty for a crime.

capital ship A warship of large size (including aircraft carriers) carrying guns of over 8–inch caliber; battleship or battle cruiser.

capital stock The amount of property owned by an individual or a corporation: distinguished from *income.*

cap·i·tate (kap′ə·tāt) *adj.* **1** *Bot.* Head–shaped; headed: a *capitate* flower. **2** *Zool.* Enlarged terminally, or knobbed at the end, as tentacles. [<L *capitatus* having a head < *caput* head]

cap·i·ta·tion (kap′ə·tā′shən) *n.* **1** An individual assessment or tax; a poll tax. **2** Any count or fee per capita. [<LL *capitatio, -onis* poll tax <L *caput* head]

cap·i·tol (kap′ə·təl) *n.* The building in which a State legislature convenes; a statehouse. ◆ Homophone: *capital.*

Cap·i·tol (kap′ə·təl) **1** The official building of the U.S. Congress in Washington. **2** The temple of Jupiter Maximus in ancient Rome, or the Capitoline Hill on which it stood. [< L *Capitolium* the Capitoline <*caput* head]

Capitol Hill 1 The site of the Capitol in Washington, D.C. **2** The U.S. Congress.

Cap·i·to·line (kap′ə·tə·līn′) *adj.* Pertaining to the Roman Capitol, to its presiding god, Jupiter Capitolinus, or to the Capitoline Hill. —*n.* One of the seven hills of Rome: site of the Temple of Jupiter and of the Tarpeian rock.

ca·pit·u·lar (kə·pich′o͝o·lər) *adj.* **1** Of or belonging to a cathedral chapter; capitulary. **2** *Bot.* Of, pertaining to, or growing in a capitulum. —*n.* **1** Any of the collections of laws issued by Charlemagne and his successors. **2** A member of a cathedral chapter. [<L *capitularis* <*capitulum* chapter, dim. f *caput* head]

ca·pit·u·lar·y (kə·pich′o͝o·ler′ē) *adj.* Relating to an ecclesiastical hapter. —*n. pl.* **·lar·ies** A capitular.

ca·pit·u·late (kə·pich′o͝o·lāt) *v.* **·lat·ed, ·lat·ing** *v.t.* To surrender, as a fort or army, to an enemy on stipulated conditions. —*v.i.* To surrender on stipulated terms; make terms. —*adj.* (kə·pich′o͝o·lit, -lāt) *Bot.* Headed; having a capitulum. [<L *capitulatus,* pp. of *capitulare* draw up in chapters, arrange terms] —**ca·pit′u·la′tor** *n.* —**ca·pit·u·la·to·ry** (kə·pich′o͝o·lə·tôr′ē, tō′rē) *adj.*

ca·pit·u·la·tion (kə·pich′o͝o·lā′shən) *n.* **1** A conditional surrender, or the instrument embodying it; a charter or treaty. **2** A statement, summary, or enumeration.

ca·pit·u·lum (kə·pich′o͝o·ləm) *n. pl.* **·la** (-lə) **1** *Bot.* In phanerogams, a close, head–shaped cluster of sessile flowers, as in the button daisy. See illustration under INFLORESCENCE. **2** *Anat.* A small rounded body, as at the head of a rib. **3** *Zool.* The headlike part of ticks and mites. **4** *Entomol.* The enlarged tip of the antenna or mouth of certain insects. [< L, dim. of *caput* head]

ca·po (kä′po) *n. Slang* The head of one of the units or branches of the Mafia.

ca·po das·tro (kä′pō däs′trō) A clamp or nut attached to the finger board of a guitar to raise uniformly the pitch of the strings. Also **capo tas·to** (täs′tō). [<Ital. *capo di tastro* cap for the keys]

ca·pon (kā′pon, -pən) *n.* A rooster gelded to improve the flesh for eating. [OE *capun* <L *capo, -onis*]

cap·o·ral[1] (kap′ə·ral′) *n.* A form of cut tobacco. [<F *(tabac du) caporal* corporal's tobacco]

ca·po·ral[2] (kä′pō·räl′) *n. SW U.S.* One who supervises laborers; a boss. [<Sp.]

Cap·o·ret·to (kap′ə·ret′ō, *Ital.* kä′pō·ret′tō) A town in NW Slovenia, Yugoslavia; in Italy until 1947; scene of Italian defeat (1917) of World War I. *Serbo–Croatian* **Ko·ba·rid** (kō′·bä·rēd).

ca·pot (kə·pot′) *n.* The winning of all the tricks in the game of piquet. —*v.t.* **ca·pot·ted, ca·pot·ting** To win all the tricks from. [<F]

ca·pote (kə·pōt′) *n.* **1** A hooded coat or cloak. **2** The adjustable top of a vehicle, as a buggy; hood. **3** A bonnet. [<F, dim. of *cape* cape, hood]

Ca·po·te (kə·pō′tē), **Truman,** born 1924, U.S. author.

ca·pouch (kə·po͞osh′, -po͞och′) See CAPUCHE.

Cap·pa·do·ci·a (kap′ə·dō′shē·ə, -shə) An ancient region of Asia Minor. —**Cap′pa·do′·ci·an** *adj. & n.*

cap·pa·ri·da·ceous (kap′ə·ri·dā′shəs) *adj. Bot.* Belonging to a family *(Capparidaceae)* of herbs and shrubs, the caper family. [<L *capparis* caper]

cap·per (kap′ər) *n.* **1** One who or that which caps. **2** A maker or seller of caps. **3** *U.S. Slang* A person employed by gamblers as a decoy; also, a professional or hired "bidder–up" at an auction.

cap pistol A toy pistol with a hammer for firing caps.

Cap·ra (kap′rə), **Frank,** born 1897, U.S. motion–picture director born in Sicily.

cap·re·o·late (kap′rē·ə·lāt, kə·prē′-) *adj. Bot.* Like or bearing a tendril. [<L *capreolus* tendril]

Ca·pri (kä′prē, kə·prē′) A resort island at the SE entrance of the Bay of Naples; 4 square miles: a native of the island is known as a *Capistrano.*

Ca·pri blue A vivid turquoise blue: so called from the tones of the Blue Grotto of Capri.

cap·ric (kap′rik) *adj.* Of, pertaining to, derived from, or like a goat. [<L *caper, capri* goat]

capric acid *Chem.* A colorless crystalline compound, $C_{10}H_{20}O_2$ of goatlike odor, found in butter, coconut oil, etc.: used in perfumery.

ca·pric·ci·o (kə·prē′chē·ō, *Ital.* kä·prēt′chō) *n. pl.* **·ci·os** or *Ital.* **ca·pric·ci** (kä·prēt′chē) **1** *Music* A composition of lively and spirited mood and fancifully irregular in form. **2** A prank. [<Ital. <*capro* goat <L *caper*]

ca·pric·ci·o·so (kə·prē′chē·ō′sō, *Ital.* kä′prēt·chō′sō) *adj. Music* Fanciful; lively; irregular; fantastic. [<Ital.]

ca·price (kə·prēs′) *n.* **1** A sudden unreasonable change of mood or opinion; a whim. **2** Any sudden, arbitrary act or fanciful idea. **3** The mood or state of mind that causes sudden changes or fancies. **4** A capriccio. See synonyms under FANCY, WHIM. [<F <Ital. *capriccio.* See CAPRICCIO.]

ca·pri·cious (kə·prish′əs, kə·prē′shəs) *adj.* Characterized by or resulting from caprice; fickle; whimsical; inconstant; unpredictable; also, fanciful. See synonyms under IRRESOLUTE. [<F *capricieux*] —**ca·pri′cious·ly** *adv.* —**ca·pri′cious·ness** *n.*

Cap·ri·corn (kap′rə·kôrn) **1** The tenth sign of the zodiac, entered by the sun at the winter solstice. **2** A zodiacal constellation; the Goat. See CONSTELLATION. Also **Cap′ri·cor′nus** (-kôr′ nəs). [<L *capricornus* <*caper* goat + *cornu* horn]

cap·ri·fi·ca·tion (kap′rə·fi·kā′shən) *n.* **1** The process and effect of exposing the cultivated fig, at the time when the flowers are within the growing fruit, to the attack of a chalcid insect that infests the wild fig, so as to hasten the ripening and improve the quality of the fruit. **2** Artificial fertilization of the fig or date by this method. [<L *caprificatio, -onis* <*caprificare* ripen figs<*caprificus* wild fig]

cap·ri·fo·li·a·ceous (kap′ri·fō′lē·ā′shəs) *adj. Bot.* Belonging to the honeysuckle family *(Caprifoliaceae)* of herbs, woody shrubs, and vines. [<Med. L *caprifolium* honeysuckle <L *caper* goat + *folium* leaf]

cap·ri·form (kap′rə·fôrm) *adj.* Having the form or appearance of a goat. [<L *caper, capri* goat +-FORM]

cap·ri·ole (kap′rē·ōl) *n.* An upward leap made by a trained horse while standing. —*v.i.* **·oled, ·ol·ing** To perform a capriole; leap upward. [<F <Ital. *capriola,* dim. of *capra* she–goat <L *capra*]

Capri pants Tight–fitting women's trousers, worn informally. Also **Capris.**

ca·pro·ic (kə·prō′ik) *adj.* Of or pertaining to a goat.

caproic acid *Chem.* A colorless, inflammable fatty acid, $C_6H_{12}O_2$, derived from butter and other sources: used in organic synthesis.

cap·sa·i·cin (kap·sā′ə·sin) *n. Chem.* A white crystalline compound, $C_{18}H_{27}O_3N$, extracted from cayenne pepper: used in medicine as a rubefacient. [<NL *capsicum*]

cap screw A screw bolt with a long thread and, generally, a square head: used to secure cylinder covers, etc.

Cap·si·an (kap′sē·ən) *adj. Anthropol.* Denoting an Upper Paleolithic culture roughly contemporaneous with the Magdalenian.

cap·si·cum (kap′si·kəm) *n.* **1** An herb or shrub of the nightshade family (genus *Capsicum*), including the common red and other peppers producing many–seeded pods prepared as condiments or gastric stimulants. **2** The fruit of these plants. [<L *capsa* box (from the shape of the fruit)]

cap·size (kap·sīz′, kap′sīz) *v.t. & v.i.* **·sized, ·siz·ing** To upset or overturn. [? <Sp. *capuzar* sink a ship by the head <*cabo* head]

cap·stan (kap′stən) *n. Naut.* A drum-like apparatus for hoisting anchors or other weights by exerting traction upon a cable. [<F *cabestan* <L *capistrum* halter < *capere* hold]

CAPSTAN
a. Drumhead. *b.* Bar–hole. *c.* Capstan bar. *d.* Barrel. *e.* Pawls. *f.* Pawl–rim.

capstan bar A lever used in turning a capstan.

cap·stone (kap′stōn′) *n.* Copestone.

cap·su·late (kap′sə·lāt, -syo͝o-) *adj.* **1** Enclosed in a capsule. **2** Having or formed into a capsule or capsules. Also **cap′su·lat′ed.** [<NL *capsulatus* <L *capsula,* dim. of *capsa* box] —**cap′su·la′·tion** *n.*

cap·sule (kap′səl, -syo͝ol) *n.* **1** *Bot.* **a** A dry dehiscent seed vessel made up of more than one carpel, as of a pink or a lily. **b** The spore case of a moss or other cryptogam. **2** *Med.* A small gelatinous case for containing a dose of a drug. **3** *Biol.* A capsulelike organ, membrane, or structure: the suprarenal *capsule.* **4** The cargo or passenger container of a space rocket. **5** A metallic shell, cap, or seal, as of a cartridge or percussion cap. —*v.t.* **1** To furnish with or enclose in or as in a capsule. **2** To summarize. —*adj.* Small and compact; condensed; brief. [<F<L *capsula,* dim. of *capsa* box] —**cap·su·lar** (kap′sə·lər, -syo͝o-) *adj.*

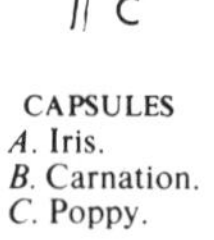

CAPSULES
A. Iris.
B. Carnation.
C. Poppy.

cap·tain (kap′tən, -tin) *n.* **1** One at the head of or in command of others; a chief; leader; commander. **2** The master or commander of a vessel, regardless of rank. **3** In the U.S. Army, Air Force, or Marine Corps, a commissioned officer ranking next above a first lieutenant and next below a major. **4** In the U.S. Navy and Coast Guard, a commissioned officer ranking next above a commander and next below a rear admiral: equal in rank to a colonel in the Army, Air Force, or Marine Corps. See table under GRADE. See synonyms under CHIEF, MASTER. —*v.t.* To be captain over; act as captain to; command; manage; lead. [<OF *capitaine* <LL *capitaneus* <L *caput* head. Doublet of CHIEFTAIN.] —**cap′tain·cy, cap′tain·ship** *n.*

Captain Lynch Lynch law.

cap·tion (kap′shən) *n.* **1** The title or introductory part of a legal document, showing time, place, circumstances, authority, etc., or a notary's affidavit, endorsed or affixed. **2** A heading of a chapter, section, document, etc. **3** The title of an illustration. **4** The subtitle in a motion picture. **5** *Obs.* Any seizure or capture. —*v.t.* To provide a caption for. [<L *captio, -onis* seizure, deception, sophism < *capere* take; in senses 1–4 infl. in meaning by L *caput* head]

cap·tious (kap′shəs) *adj.* **1** Apt to find fault; hypercritical. **2** Perplexing; sophistical. [<L *captiosus* fallacious < *captio* sophism < *capere* take] —**cap′tious·ly** *adv.* —**cap′tious·ness** *n.*
Synonyms: carping, caviling, censorious, critical, cross, cynical, faultfinding, hypercritical. *Antonyms*: appreciative, approving, commendatory, eulogistic, flattering, laudatory.

cap·ti·vate (kap′tə·vāt) *v.t.* **·vat·ed, ·vat·ing** **1** To charm; win; fascinate. **2** *Obs.* To capture; subdue. See synonyms under ALLURE, CHARM. [<LL *captivatus,* pp. of *captivare* capture < *captivus* CAPTIVE] —**cap′ti·va′tion** *n.* —**cap′ti·va′tor** *n.*

cap·tive (kap′tiv) *n.* **1** One captured and held in confinement or restraint; a prisoner. **2** One who is held captive in will and feeling. —*adj.* **1** Taken prisoner, as in war; held in confinement or bondage. **2** Charmed or subdued in will or feeling. [<F *captif* <L *captivus* < *capere* take. Doublet of CAITIFF.]

captive audience Any audience which has little or no choice but to watch or listen to something, as a radio broadcast on a public vehicle.

captive balloon See under BALLOON.

cap·tiv·i·ty (kap·tiv′ə·tē) *n.* The state of being held captive; thraldom. See synonyms under BONDAGE.

cap·tor (kap′tər) *n.* One who takes or holds captive.

cap·ture (kap′chər) *v.t.* **·tured, ·tur·ing** **1** To take captive; seize and hold or carry off, as in war. **2** To take possession of; catch; gain; win. See synonyms under ARREST, CATCH. —*n.* **1** A capturing, or being captured. **2** The person or thing captured. [<MF <L *captura* < *capere* take]

Cap·u·a (kap′yōō·ə, *Ital.* kä′pwä) A town in southern Italy. —**Cap′u·an** *adj.* & *n.*

ca·puche (kə·pōōsh′, -pōōch′) *n.* A hood or cowl; especially, that worn by a Capuchin friar: also spelled *capouch.* [<F <Ital. *cappuccio,* aug. of *cappa* hood]

cap·u·chin (kap′yōō·chin, -shin) *n.* **1** A woman's hooded cloak, or hood. **2** A long-tailed South American ceboid monkey (genus *Cebus*) whose head is covered with a cowl-like growth of hair. [<Ital. *cappuccino* < *cappuccio*]

Cap·u·chin (kap′yōō·chin, -shin) *n.* A member of a branch of the Franciscan order, wearing a habit with a distinctive capuche. [<F <*capuche* CAPUCHE]

Cap·u·let (kap′yə·let, -lit) The family of Juliet, in Shakespeare's *Romeo and Juliet.*

ca·put (kā′pət, kap′ət) *n.* *pl.* **cap·i·ta** (kap′ə·tə) **1** The head; also, any rounded extremity of an organ; top. **2** *Law* The person; a citizen; one holding civil rights; the status of a citizen before the law. **3** The former governing council of Cambridge University in England. [<L, head]

caput mor·tu·um (môr′chōō·əm) *Archaic* Colcothar. [<L, dead head]

cap·y·ba·ra (kap′i·bä′rə) *n.* A South American rodent (*Hydrochoerus capybara*) about 4 feet long, with coarse, dark brown fur, webbed feet, and a stumpy tail: it frequents the borders of lakes and rivers. [<Sp. *capibara* <Tupian *kapigwara*]

Ca·que·ta (kä′kā·tä′) See JAPURÁ.

car (kär) *n.* **1** A vehicle for use on tracks. **2** Any wheeled vehicle, as an automobile. **3** *Poetic* A chariot. **4** The contents of a car; carload. **5** The cage of an elevator. **6** The basket of a balloon or the like. **7** A floating box for live fish. [<AF *carre* <LL *carra,* var. of *carrus* wagon, ult. <Celtic]

Car (kär) A group of stars in Ursa Major: also called *The Northern Car.*

ca·ra·ba·o (kä′rə·bä′ō) *n.* *pl.* **·ba·os** or **·ba·o** In the Philippines, a water buffalo. [< Sp. <Malay *karbau*]

CARABAO
(5 to 5 1/2 feet high at the shoulder)

car·a·bid (kar′ə·bid) *n.* Any of an extensive family (*Carabidae*) of predatory ground beetles, variously colored and usually nocturnal, including the caterpillar hunters. [< NL <L *carabus* small crab <Gk. *karabos* crayfish]

car·a·bin (kar′ə·bin), **car·a·bine** (-bīn) See CARBINE.

car·a·bin·eer, car·a·bin·ier (kar′ə·bin·ir′) See CARBINEER.

ca·ra·bi·nie·re (kä·rä·bē·nyā′rā) *n.* *pl.* **·nie·ri** (-nyā′rē) A member of the Italian military police, recruited from the regular army for a term of five years. [<Ital.]

car·a·cal (kar′ə·kal) *n.* **1** The Persian lynx (*Felis* or *Lynx caracal*) of SW Asia and the greater part of Africa, somewhat larger than a fox, reddish-brown with black-tipped ears. **2** Its pelt or fur. [<F <Turkish *qarah qulaq* < *qarah* black + *qulaq* ear]

Car·a·cal·la (kar′ə·kal′ə), 188–217, Marcus Aurelius Antoninus, Roman emperor 212–217.

ca·ra·ca·ra (kä′rə·kä′rə) *n.* A large, vulturelike hawk of South America: **Audubon's caracara** (*Polyborus cheriway*) sometimes reaches as far north as the southern borders of the United States. [<Sp. *caracará* <Tupian]

Ca·ra·cas (kə·rä′kəs, -rak′əs; *Sp.* kä·rä′käs) The largest city and capital of Venezuela.

car·ack (kar′ək) *n.* A large Portuguese or Spanish merchant vessel, frequently armed, in use from the 15th to the 17th century: also spelled *carrack.* [<OF *carraque* <Med. L *carraca,* ? <Arabic *qaraqīr,* pl. of *qorqūr* merchant ship]

car·a·cole (kar′ə·kōl) *n.* A sudden half turn to the right or left made by a horseman in riding; curvet. —*v.* **·coled, ·col·ing** *v.t. Rare* To cause to curvet or half-wheel: He was fond of *caracoling* his horse. —*v.i.* To make or cause one's horse to make caracoles; prance; wheel in line of files, as cavalry. Also **car′a·col** (-kol). [<F <Ital. *caracollo*]

Ca·rac·ta·cus (kə·rak′tə·kəs) British chieftain of about A.D. 50. Also *Welsh* **Ca·rad·oc** (kə·rad′ək).

car·a·cul (kar′ə·kəl) See KARAKUL.

ca·rafe (kə·raf′, -räf′) *n.* A glass water bottle; decanter. [<F, ? <Arabic *gharafa* draw water]

car·a·geen, car·a·gheen (kar′ə·gēn), etc. See CARRAGEEN, etc.

car·a·mel (kar′ə·məl, -mel, kär′məl) *n.* **1** A confection, variously colored and flavored, composed of sugar, butter, and other ingredients. **2** Burnt sugar; the brown or black, soluble material obtained by heating sugar or molasses, or from starch by converting it into glucose: used to color soups, liquids, gravies, and the like. **3** A reddish tan, the color of burnt sugar. [<F, alter. of OF *calemele* <Med. L *calamellus,* alter. of *canna mellis* sugarcane, under the infl. of L *calamus* reed]

car·a·mel·ize (kar′ə·məl·īz′, kär′məl-) *v.t.* **·ized, ·iz·ing** To heat (sugar) slowly until melted and brown. —**car′a·mel·i·za′tion** *n.*

ca·ran·goid (kə·rang′goid) *adj.* Belonging to a family (*Carangidae*) of fishes having a rudimentary dorsal fin, and usually two anal spines forming a detached portion, as in cavallies, pompanos, etc. —*n.* Any member of this family. [<NL *caranx, -angis* <Sp. *carangue* flatfish]

car·a·pace (kar′ə·pās) *n.* **1** *Zool.* The hard bony or chitinous outer case on the back of various animals, as of a turtle or a lobster. **2** Any protective, umbrellalike covering. Also **car′a·pax** (-paks). [<F <Sp. *carapacho*] —**car′a·pa′cic** (-pā′sik) *adj.*

ca·ras·sow (kə·ras′ō) See CURASSOW.

car·at (kar′ət) *n.* **1** A unit of weight for gems: one metric carat is 200 milligrams, or 3.086 grains. **2** Loosely, a karat. ◆ Homophone: *carrot.* [<F <Ital. *carato* <Arabic *qīrāt* weight of 4 grains <Gk. *keration* seed, small weight]

ca·ra·te (kä·rä′tā) *n.* Pinta.

Ca·ra·vag·gio (kä′rä·väd′jō), **Michelangelo Amerighi da,** 1569–1609, Italian painter.

car·a·van (kar′ə·van) *n.* **1** An Oriental armed company of traders, pilgrims, etc. **2** A traveling company or menagerie. **3** A van; a house on wheels. **4** A company of people traveling together with wagons, pack horses, etc. **5** A train of wagons or pack horses, or of motor vehicles. [<F *caravane* <Persian *kārwān* caravan]

car·a·van·sa·ry (kar′ə·van′sə·rē) *n.* *pl.* **·ries** **1** A large square building enclosing a court for the shelter of caravans in Oriental countries. **2** A hostelry or inn. Also **car′a·van′se·rai** (-rī, -rā), **car′a·van′se·ry.** [<F *caravansérai* <Persian *kārwānsarāī* < *kārwān* caravan + *sarāī* inn]

car·a·vel (kar′ə·vel) *n.* A fleet vessel of Spain and Portugal in the 15th century: sometimes spelled *carvel.* Also **car′a·velle.** [<MF *caravelle* <Sp. *carabela,* dim. of *caraba* boat <L *carabus* <Gk. *korabus*]

CARAVELS
A. The *Santa Maria* of Columbus.
B. A caravel, showing the set of the sails.

car·a·way (kar′ə·wā) *n.* A European biennial herb (*Carum carvi*) of the parsley family: its fruits, called **caraway seeds,** are small, spicy, aromatic seeds used for flavoring food. [<Sp. *alcarahueya* <Arabic *al* the + *karwīyā* caraway <Gk. *karon*]

carb– Var. of CARBO–.

car·ba·mate (kär′bə·māt, kär·bam′āt) *n.* *Chem.* A salt or ester of carbamic acid containing the univalent NH_2COO radical.

car·bam·ic (kär·bam′ik) *adj.* *Chem.* Of, pertaining to, or derived from the amide of carbonic acid and the amide radical NH_2.

carbamic acid *Chem.* A theoretical compound, NH_2COOH, known only by its salts and esters.

car·bam·ide (kär·bam′īd, -id, kär′bə·mīd) *n.* *Chem.* Urea or one of its isomers. Also **car·bam′id** (-id). [<CARB- + AMIDE]

car barn A building or shed for street or railroad cars.

car·ba·zole (kär′bə·zōl) *n.* *Chem.* A white crystalline compound, $C_{12}H_9N$, derived from coal tar: used in dyes and as a stabilizer in making explosives. [<CARB- + AZOLE]

car·bide (kär′bīd, -bid) *n.* *Chem.* A compound of carbon with a more positive element: calcium *carbide,* CaC_2.

car·bine (kär′bīn, -bēn) *n.* *Mil.* A light, short-barreled rifle originally devised for mounted troops. A magazine-fed, gas-operated carbine weighing about five pounds was adopted in the United States in World War II for certain ranks previously armed with pistols. Also spelled *carabin, carabine.* [<F *carabine*]

car·bi·neer (kär′bə·nir′) *n.* A soldier armed with a carbine: also spelled *carabineer, carabinier.*

car·bi·nol (kär′bə·nōl, -nol) *n. Chem.* Methanol. [<G; name given to wood alcohol by Adolf Kolbe, German chemist, 1818–84]
carbo- *combining form* Carbon: *carbohydrate.* Also, before vowels, *carb-.* [<L *carbo* coal]
car·bo·hy·drate (kär′bō·hī′drāt) *n. Biochem.* Any one of a group of compounds containing carbon combined with hydrogen and oxygen in the form of an aldose or a ketose, essential in the metabolism of plants and animals. The carbohydrates include sugars, starches, and cellulose.
car·bo·late (kär′bə·lāt) *n. Chem.* An ester of carbolic acid.
car·bo·lat·ed (kär′bə·lā′tid) *adj.* Carbolized.
car·bol·ic (kär·bol′ik) *adj. Chem.* **1** Of, pertaining to, or derived from carbon and oil. **2** Of or pertaining to coal-tar oil. [<CARB- + L *oleum* oil]
carbolic acid Phenol (def. 2).
car·bo·lize (kär′bə·līz) *v.t.* **·lized, ·liz·ing** *Chem.* To treat or impregnate with carbolic acid.
Car·bo·loy (kär′bə·loi) *n.* A cemented tungsten carbide, just under the diamond in hardness: used for high-speed machine tools: a trade name.
car·bon (kär′bən) *n.* **1** A nonmetallic element (symbol C, atomic number 6) found free as diamond, graphite, and amorphous carbon, and having the property of forming stable rings and long chains which are the basis of millions of organic compounds. See PERIODIC TABLE. **2** *Electr.* A rod of carbon, used as an electrode in an arc light. **3** A piece of carbon paper. **4** A carbon copy. —*adj.* **1** Of, pertaining to, or like carbon. **2** Treated with carbon: *carbon* paper. [<F *carbone* <L *carbo, -onis* coal]
carbon 13 *Physics* A heavy carbon isotope of mass 13, used as a tracer element in the study of physiological processes.
carbon 14 *Physics* Radiocarbon.
car·bo·na·ceous (kär′bə·nā′shəs) *adj.* Of, pertaining to, or yielding carbon.
car·bo·na·do[1] (kär′bə·nā′dō) *n. pl.* **·does** or **·dos** A bird, fish, or piece of meat scored and broiled. —*v.t.* **·doed, ·do·ing** *Obs.* **1** To hack or slash. **2** To score and broil. [<Sp. *carbonada* <*carbón* coal <L *carbo*]
car·bo·na·do[2] (kär′bə·nā′dō) *n. pl.* **·does** Bort. [<Pg., carbonated]
Car·bo·na·ri (kär′bō·nä′rē) *n. pl. of* **Car·bo·na·ro** (-rō) Members of a Neapolitan anti-French secret society of the 19th century. [<Ital. <L *carbonarius* charcoal burner <*carbo* coal] — **Car′bo·na′rism** (-nä′riz·əm) *n.*
car·bon·ate (kär′bə·nāt) *Chem. v.t.* **·at·ed, ·at·ing** **1** To charge with carbonic acid. **2** To carbonize. —*n.* (kär′bə·nāt, -nit) A salt or ester of carbonic acid.
carbon bisulfide Carbon disulfide.
carbon black A deep, smooth, permanent black pigment made of pure carbon: also called *lampblack, ivory black.*
carbon copy **1** A copy of a typewritten letter, etc., made by means of carbon paper. **2** An exact replica; duplicate.
carbon cycle **1** *Physics* A 6-stage thermonuclear process taking place in the interior of stars, by which hydrogen is transformed into helium through the catalytic action of carbon and nitrogen. Compare PROTON-PROTON REACTION. **2** *Biol.* The biological elaboration and destruction in the biosphere of carbon compounds derived from atmospheric carbon dioxide by photosynthesis.
Car·bon·dale (kär′bən·dāl) A city in NE Pennsylvania.
carbon dioxide A heavy, colorless, non-flammable gas, CO_2, formed by the oxidation of carbon, by the interaction of carbonates and acids, and in the respiration of plants and animals. It is irrespirable, extinguishes fire, and is moderately soluble in water.
carbon disulfide *Chem.* A colorless, limpid, volatile, and highly inflammable liquid, CS_2, with a disagreeable odor: used as a solvent for oils, resins, etc., and for the extermination of vermin.
car·bon·ic (kär·bon′ik) *adj.* Of, pertaining to, or obtained from carbon.
carbonic acid *Chem.* A weak, unstable dibasic acid, H_2CO_3, existing only in solution and readily dissociating into water and carbon dioxide.
car·bon·ic-ac·id gas (kär·bon′ik·as′id) Carbon dioxide.
car·bon·if·er·ous (kär′bə·nif′ər·əs) *adj.* Of, pertaining to, containing, or yielding carbon or coal.
Car·bon·if·er·ous (kär′bə·nif′ər·əs) *adj. Geol.* Of or pertaining to a period of the Upper Paleozoic era succeeding the Devonian, characterized by the formation of extensive coal beds. In North America the Carboniferous system of strata is divided into the Mississippian, Pennsylvanian, and Permian series. See chart under GEOLOGY.
car·bon·i·za·tion (kär′bən·ə·zā′shən, -ī·zā′-) *n.* The conversion of organic matter, as wood, into coal or charcoal.
car·bon·ize (kär′bən·īz) *v.t.* **·ized, ·iz·ing** **1** To reduce to carbon; char. **2** To coat with carbon, as paper. **3** To charge with carbon.
carbonized cloth Cloth charred in a vacuum: used for high electrical resistance.
car·bon·iz·er (kär′bən·ī′zər) *n.* Carburetor (def. 1).
carbon monoxide *Chem.* A colorless, odorless gas, CO, formed by the incomplete oxidation of carbon. It burns with a blue flame to form carbon dioxide, and is highly poisonous when inhaled, since it combines with the hemoglobin of the blood to the exclusion of oxygen.
carbon paper Tissue paper so prepared with carbon or other material that it will reproduce on paper underneath a copy of anything impressed upon it, as by pencil or typewriter. Also **carbon tissue.**
carbon process A photographic printing process employing a tissue or film of gelatin colored with a permanent and insoluble pigment. Also **carbon printing.**
carbon tetrachloride *Chem.* A colorless, nonflammable liquid, CCl_4, produced by the action of chlorine on carbon disulfide: used as a solvent, local anesthetic, fire extinguisher, cleaning fluid.
car·bon·yl (kär′bən·il) *n. Chem.* **1** A bivalent organic radical, CO, known only in combination. **2** A compound of a metal and carbon monoxide: nickel *carbonyl.* —**car′bon·yl′ic** *adj.*
carbonyl chloride *Chem.* Phosgene.
car·bo·ra (kär·bôr′ə, -bō′rə) *n.* An Australian worm that bores into timber, as of piers, exposed at low tide. [<native Australian]
Car·bo·run·dum (kär′bə·run′dəm) *n.* An abrasive of silicon carbide: a trade name.
car·box·yl (kär·bok′sil) *n. Chem.* A univalent acid radical, COOH, characteristic of nearly all organic acids. [<CARB(ON) + OX(YGEN) + -YL] —**car·box·yl·ic** (kär′bok·sil′ik) *adj.*
car·box·y·lase (kär·bok′sə·lās) *n. Biochem.* An enzyme found in yeast which splits carbon dioxide from the carboxyl group of amino acids. [<CARBOXYL + -ASE]
car·boy (kär′boi) *n.* A large glass bottle enclosed in a box or in wickerwork: used as a container for corrosive acids, etc. [<Persian *qarāba* demijohn]
car·bun·cle (kär′bung·kəl) *n.* **1** *Pathol.* An inflammation of the subcutaneous tissue, resembling a boil but larger and more painful. **2** A red garnet cut without facets and concave below, to show the color. **3** Any deep red gem. [<AF <L *carbunculus,* dim. of *carbo* coal] —**car·bun·cu·lar** (kär·bung′kyə·lar) *adj.*
car·bu·ret (kär′bə·rāt, -byə·ret) *v.t.* **·ret·ed** or **·ret·ted, ·ret·ing** or **·ret·ting** To carburize; combine chemically with carbon. [<NL *carburetum* carbide] —**car·bu·re·tion** (kär′bə·rā′shən, -byə·resh′ən) *n.*
car·bu·re·tor (kär′bə·rā′tər, -byə·ret′ər) *n.* **1** An apparatus used to charge air or gas with volatilized hydrocarbons to give it illuminating power: also called *carbonizer.* **2** A device for carrying a current of air through or over a liquid fuel, so that the air may take up the vapor to form the explosive mixture, as in internal-combustion engines. **3** A hydrocarbon so used. Also **car·bu·ret·tor** (kär′byə·ret′·ər), **car′bu·ret′ter.**
car·bu·rize (kär′bə·rīz, -byə-) *v.t.* **·rized, ·riz·ing** **1** To combine or impregnate with carbon, as gas to increase its illuminating power. **2** *Metall.* To impregnate the surface layer of (low-carbon steel) with carbon: a stage in casehardening. Also *Brit.* **car′bu·rise.** [<F *carbure* carbide + -IZE] —**car′bu·ri·za′tion** *n.* —**car′bu·riz′er** *n.*
car·byl·a·mine (kär′bil·ə·mēn′, -am′in) *n. Chem.* An organic compound containing the radical -NC.
car·ca·jou (kär′kə·jōō, -zhōō) *n.* The wolverine. [<dial. F (Canadian) <native Algonquian name]
car·ca·net (kär′kə·net) *n.* **1** An ornamental collar or necklace of gold set with jewels. **2** A jeweled circlet formerly worn in the hair. [<F, dim. of *carcan* iron collar worn by prisoners <Med. L *carcanum* <Gmc.] —**car′ca·net′ed** or **car′ca·net′ted** *adj.*
car·cass (kär′kəs) *n.* **1** The dead body of an animal. **2** The human body: a contemptuous or humorous use. **3** Something from which the vital principle, importance, or value has departed; lifeless or worthless remains. **4** A framework or skeleton, as of a construction. Also **car′case.** See synonyms under BODY. [<AF *carcas* <Med. L *carcasium* infl. in form by MF *carcasse* a corpse <Ital. *carcassa*]
Car·cas·sonne (kȧr·kȧ·sôn′) A city in southern France.
car·cel (kär′səl) *n.* The light of a Carcel lamp burning 42 grams of colza oil an hour with a flame 40 millimeters high: a photometric standard, equal to 9.6 international candles. [after B. G. *Carcel,* 1750–1812, French inventor]
Carcel lamp A lamp in which colza oil is constantly pumped up to the wick: used in lighthouses and as a photometric standard.
Car·cha·ri·as (kär·kā′rē·əs) *n.* The typical genus of a family of sharks *(Carcharinidae).* [<NL <Gk. *karcharias* a saw-toothed shark]
Car·che·mish (kär′kə·mish, kär·kē′-) An ancient city of the Hittites in southern Turkey.
car·cin·o·gen (kär′sin′ə·jen) *n.* A cancer-producing substance. —**car·cin·o·gen·ic** (kär′sən·ə·jen′ik) *adj.*
car·ci·no·ma (kär′sə·nō′mə) *n. pl.* **·mas** or **·ma·ta** (-mə·tə) A cancer; a malignant tumor that arises from epithelial cells and spreads by metastasis. [<L <Gk. *karkinoma* <*karkinos* cancer] —**car′ci·nom′a·tous** (-nom′ə·təs, -nō′mə-) *adj.*
card[1] (kärd) *n.* **1** A piece of cardboard bearing, or intended to bear, written or printed words, symbols, etc.: used for social and business purposes. **2** A piece of cardboard imprinted with symbols, for use in certain games of chance and skill: in such use specifically called a **playing card.** **3** *pl.* Any or all games played with playing cards. **4** A small advertisement or published statement printed on a card. **5** A chart giving a table of information, etc. **6** A program or a menu; hence, an authorized announcement of a coming event. **7** *Naut.* The dial of a compass. **8** *Colloq.* A person manifesting some peculiarity: He is a queer *card.* **9** Cardboard. —**on the cards** **1** Listed on the program; scheduled to occur. **2** Possible; likely to happen. —**to put one's cards on the table** To reveal one's intentions or resources with complete frankness. —*v.t.* **1** To fasten or write upon a card or cards. **2** To provide with a card. [<F *carte* <Ital. *carta* card, sheet of paper <L *charta* paper <Gk. *chartēs.* Doublet of CHART.]
card[2] (kärd) *n.* **1** A wire-toothed brush for combining and cleansing wool and other fiber. **2** A similar instrument for currying cattle and horses. —*v.t.* To comb, dress, or cleanse with a card. [<MF *carde* <Ital. *carda* <Med. L <*cardus* <L *carduus* thistle] —**card′er** *n.*
car·da·mom (kär′də·məm) *n.* **1** The fruit of an East Indian or Chinese plant of the ginger family *(Elettaria cardamomum)* having aromatic seeds, used as a condiment. **2** One of the plants yielding this fruit. Also **car′da·mon** (-mən), **car′da·mum.** [<L *cardamomum* <Gk. *kardamōmon* <*kardamon* cress + *amōmon* spice]
card·board (kärd′bôrd′, -bōrd′) *n.* A thin, stiff pasteboard used for making cards, boxes, etc. —*adj.* **1** Made of cardboard. **2** Flimsy; insubstantial.
card·case (kärd′kās′) *n.* **1** A case to hold playing or other cards; specifically, a pocket case for calling cards. **2** In library use, a case of drawers for card catalogs, etc.
card catalog A catalog made out on cards, especially for library books.
Cár·de·nas (kär′thā·näs) A port in western Cuba.
Cár·de·nas (kär′thā·näs), **Lá·za·ro** (lä′sä·rō), 1895–1970, president of Mexico 1934–40.
card file A systematic arrangement of cards containing records or other data.
cardi- -Var. of CARDIO-.

car·di·a (kär′dē·ə) *n. Anat.* The upper orifice of the stomach, where the esophagus discharges. [<Gk. *kardia* heart]

car·di·ac (kär′dē·ak) *Med. adj.* **1** Pertaining to, situated near, or affecting the heart or the cardia. **2** Of, pertaining to, or designating the upper esophageal orifice of the stomach. Also **car·di·a·cal** (kär·dī′ə·kəl). —*n.* **1** One suffering from a heart disease. **2** A cardiac remedy or stimulant; a cordial.

cardiac neurosis *Psychiatry* Abnormal heart action due primarily to nervous disorder or emotional disturbance, without pathological change.

car·di·al·gi·a (kär′dē·al′jē·ə) *n. Pathol.* A burning sensation of the stomach, caused by indigestion; gastric neuralgia; heartburn: once thought to be an affliction of the heart. Also **car′di·al′gy.** [<NL <Gk. *kardialgia* <*kardia* heart + *algos* pain] **—car′di·al′gic** *adj.*

Car·diff (kär′dif) A county borough and port in SE Wales, capital of Glamorganshire.

Cardiff giant A rude statue of gypsum dug up in 1869 near Cardiff, in central New York, exhibited as a prehistoric human fossil, and later proved a hoax.

car·di·gan (kär′də·gən) *n.* A jacket of knitted wool; a sweater opening down the front. Also **cardigan jacket** or **sweater.** [after the seventh Earl of *Cardigan* (1797–1868)]

Car·di·gan (kär′də·gən) A county in western Wales; 693 square miles; capital, Cardigan. Also **Car′di·gan·shire′** (-shir′).

car·di·nal (kär′də·nəl) *adj.* **1** Of prime importance; chief; fundamental; principal. **2** Of a deep scarlet color. **3** Of or relating to a cardinal or cardinals. —*n.* **1** One of the ecclesiastical body of the Roman Catholic Church known as the sacred college, an electoral college by which the Pope is elected and which constitutes his chief advisory council; a prince and senator of the Church. **2** A cardinal bird. **3** A short, hooded cloak worn by women in the 18th century. **4** A deep scarlet, the color of a cardinal's cassock. **5** A dyestuff, derived from magenta, for dyeing cardinal-red. **6** A cardinal number. [<F <L *cardinalis* important <*cardo* hinge] — **car′di·nal·ly** *adv.*

car·di·nal·ate (kär′də·nəl·āt′) *n.* The rank, dignity, or term of office of a cardinal. Also **car′di·nal·ship′.**

cardinal bird A North American bright-red, crested finch (genus *Richmondena*); especially, the common redbird of the eastern United States. Also **cardinal grosbeak.**

cardinal flower A perennial North American herb *(Lobelia cardinalis)* having large red flowers: also called *red lobelia.*

car·di·nal·i·ty (kär′də·nal′ə·tē) *n. Math.* The property of being expressible by a cardinal number, as any finite or restricted series of numbers.

cardinal number See under NUMBER.

cardinal point Any one of the four principal points of the compass.

cardinal sins See SEVEN DEADLY SINS.

cardinal virtues Virtues of the first importance or rank, as the "natural virtues" of ancient philosophy: justice, prudence, temperance, and fortitude; with the "theological virtues," faith, hope, and charity, these form the seven cardinal virtues of medieval and modern writers.

card index An index made out on cards filed in alphabetical order.

card·ing (kär′ding) *n.* **1** The preparing of wool, flax, or cotton fibers before drawing or spinning. **2** Material as it comes from the carding machine.

carding machine A machine for carding cotton, wool, flax, etc., by the action of wire-toothed cylinders. Also **carding engine.**

cardio- *combining form* Heart: *cardiogram.* Also, before vowels, *cardi-.* [<Gk. *kardia* heart]

car·di·o·gram (kär′dē·ə·gram′) *n.* The graphic record of heart movements produced by the cardiograph.

car·di·o·graph (kär′dē·ə·graf′, -gräf′) *n.* An instrument for tracing and recording the force of the movements of the heart. **—car′di·o·graph′ic** *adj.* **—car·di·og·ra·phy** (kär′dē·og′rə·fē) *n.*

car·di·oid (kär′dē·oid) *Math.* A heart-shaped curve generated by a point in the circumference of a circle which rolls on another fixed circle of the same size.

car·di·ol·o·gy (kär′dē·ol′ə·jē) *n.* The science of the heart and its physiology and pathology.

car·di·o·pul·mo·nar·y (kär′dē·ō·pōōl′mə·ner′ē) *adj.* Pertaining to or affecting the heart and lungs: *cardiopulmonary* resuscitation. Also *cardiorespiratory.*

cardiopulmonary resuscitation (kär′dē·ō·pōōl′mə·ner·ē, -pul′-) A first-aid method of restoring the heartbeat and breathing by alternately compressing the chest and applying mouth-to-mouth insufflation. Also *CPR.*

car·di·o·res·pi·ra·to·ry (kär′dē·ō·res′pər·ə·tôr·ē, -ri·spīr·ə-) *adj.* Cardiopulmonary.

car·di·ot·o·my (kär′dē·ot′ə·mē) *n. Surg.* Incision of the heart or of the cardiac end of the esophagus.

car·di·o·vas·cu·lar (kär′dē·ō·vas′kyə·lər) *adj.* Pertaining to or affecting the heart and the blood vessels: *cardiovascular* disease.

car·di·tis (kär·dī′tis) *n. Pathol.* Inflammation of the muscular substance of the heart.

car·doon (kär·dōōn′) *n.* A perennial plant of the Mediterranean region *(Cynara cardunculus),* allied to the artichoke and eaten as a vegetable. [<MF *cardon* <Ital. *cardone,* aug. of *cardo* thistle <L *carduus*]

Car·do·zo (kär·dō′zō), **Benjamin Nathan,** 1870–1938, U.S. jurist and author; associate justice, U.S. Supreme Court 1932–38.

cards (kärdz) *n. pl.* **1** Any game played with playing cards. **2** The playing of such a game.

card·sharp (kärd′shärp′) *n.* One who cheats at cards, especially as a profession. Also **card′·sharp′er.** **—card′sharp′ing** *n.*

car·du·a·ceous (kär′jōō·ā′shəs) *adj. Bot.* Of or belonging to the thistle group (formerly the *Carduaceae*) of the composite family, having heavy-headed radiate flowers. [<NL <L *carduus* thistle]

care (kâr) *v.i.* **cared, car·ing 1** To have or show regard, interest or concern as respecting some person, thing, or event. **2** To be wishful or inclined: Do you *care* to read this book? **3** To mind or be concerned; harbor an objection: used chiefly in negative or conditional expressions: I don't *care* if it rains. **—to care for 1** To protect or provide for; guard; watch over. **2** To be interested in or concerned for some person or thing; also, to feel affection for; hold in high regard or esteem. —*n.* **1** A state of oppressive anxiety or concern; solicitude. **2** Responsible charge or oversight. **3** Watchful regard or attention; heed. **4** Any object of solicitude or guardianship. **5** Affliction; distress. [OE *carian*] **—car′er** *n.*

Synonyms (noun): anxiety, attention, caution, charge, circumspection, concern, direction, forethought, heed, management, oversight, perplexity, precaution, prudence, solicitude, trouble, vigilance, wariness, watchfulness, worry. *Care* inclines to the positive, *caution* to the negative; *care* is shown in doing, *caution* largely in not doing. *Precaution* is allied with *care, prudence* with *caution*; a man rides a dangerous horse with *care*; caution may keep him from mounting the horse; *precaution* looks to the saddle girths, bit, and bridle, and all that may make the rider secure. *Circumspection* is watchful observation and calculation, but without the timidity implied in *caution. Concern* denotes a serious interest, milder than *anxiety*; as, *concern* for the safety of a ship at sea. *Heed* implies *attention* without disquiet; it is now largely displaced by *attention* and *care. Solicitude* involves especially the element of personal concern for another not expressed in *anxiety,* and of hopefulness not implied in *care. Watchfulness* recognizes the possibility of danger, *wariness* the probability. A man who is not influenced by *caution* to keep out of danger may display great *wariness* in the midst of it. *Care* has also the sense of responsibility, with possible control, as expressed in *charge, management, oversight*; as, these children are under my *care*; send the money to me in *care* of the firm. Compare ALARM, ANXIETY, OVERSIGHT, PRUDENCE. *Antonyms*: carelessness, disregard, heedlessness, inattention, indifference, neglect, negligence, omission, oversight, recklessness, remissness, slight.

CARE (kâr) A non-profit organization begun after World War II to send food and clothing parcels overseas to the needy. [<C(OOPERATIVE FOR) A(MERICAN) R(EMITTANCES) E(VERYWHERE)]

ca·reen (kə·rēn′) *v.t.* **1** To cause to turn over to one side; heel over, as for repairing or cleaning the bottom of: to *careen* a ship. **2** To clean, repair, or calk (a careened ship.) —*v.i.* **3** To heel over, as a vessel in the wind. **4** To clean, repair, or calk a ship when turned on one side. **5** To lurch or twist from side to side: The car *careened* down the slope. —*n.* **1** The act of inclining a ship to one side. **2** The cleaning or repairing of a ship that is turned over. **3** A careening. [<F *cariner, caréner* <*carène* keel of a ship <L *carina*] — **ca·reen′er** *n.*

ca·reen·age (kə·rē′nij) *n.* **1** The charge for careening. **2** A place where a ship is careened for repairs.

ca·reer (kə·rir′) *n.* **1** A free and swift course; a swift run or charge. **2** A complete course or progress extending through the life or a portion of it, especially when abounding in remarkable actions or incidents: His was a remarkable *career.* **3** A course of business, activity, or enterprise; especially, a course of professional life or employment. **4** A short, rapid gallop or encounter, as in a tournament; a charge; an assault. **5** *Obs.* Originally, a racecourse. —*v.i.* To move with a swift, free, and headlong motion. [<F *carrière* racecourse <LL *carraria (via)* road for carriages <*carrus* wagon] **—ca·reer′er** *n.*

Synonyms (noun): achievement, charge, course, flight, passage, race, rush. Compare BUSINESS.

ca·reer·ist (kə·rir′ist) *n.* A person chiefly or exclusively concerned with advancing himself professionally. **—ca·reer′ism** *n.*

career woman A woman devoted to a business or professional career.

care·free (kâr′frē′) *adj.* Free of troubles; without responsibilities; light-hearted.

care·ful (kâr′fəl) *adj.* **1** Exercising, marked by, or done with care. **2** Attentive and prudent; circumspect. See synonyms under PRECISE, THOUGHTFUL. **—care′ful·ly** *adv.* **—care′ful·ness** *n.*

care·less (kâr′lis) *adj.* **1** Neglectful; indifferent; heedless. **2** Free from solicitude or anxiety; light-hearted. **3** Negligent; unconcerned. **4** Not studied or constrained; easy: a *careless* attitude. See synonyms under CURSORY, IMPROVIDENT, IMPRUDENT, INATTENTIVE, SECURE. **—care′less·ly** *adv.* **—care′less·ness** *n.*

ca·ress (kə·res′) *n.* A gentle, affectionate movement; an expression of affection or attachment by touching, as by patting, embracing, or stroking. —*v.t.* To touch or handle lovingly; fondle; embrace; pet. [<F *caresse* <Ital. *carezza* <L *carus* dear] **—ca·ress′er** *n.* **—ca·ress′ing** *adj.* — **ca·ress′ive** *adj.*

Synonyms (verb): coddle, embrace, flatter, fondle, kiss, pamper, pet. To *caress* is less than to *embrace. Fondling* is always by touch; *caressing* may be also by words, or other tender and pleasing attentions. See PAMPER.

car·et (kar′ət) *n.* A sign (^) placed below a line to denote an omission. [<L, it is missing]

care·tak·er (kâr′tā′kər) *n.* **1** One who takes care of a place, thing, or person. **2** One employed to watch over property or keep it in order, as a house in the absence of its owner, or the property of an insolvent, to see that nothing is removed.

care-worn (kâr′wôrn′) *adj.* Harassed with troubles or worries.

car·fare (kär′fâr′) *n.* The charge for a ride on a bus, streetcar, etc.

car·ga·dor (kär′gə·dôr) *n.* **1** *SW U.S.* A loader and driver of pack animals. **2** In the U.S. Army, the member of a pack train who supervises packers in their duties. [<Sp.]

car·go (kär′gō) *n. pl.* **·goes** or **·gos 1** Goods and merchandise taken on board a vessel; lading. **2** Load. [<Sp. <LL *carricum* load <*carricare* load <*carrus* wagon]

cargo vessel 1 A vessel of the merchant marine, carrying goods or merchandise exclusive of passengers or animals. **2** A naval vessel for transporting goods.

car·hop (kär′hop′) *n. Colloq.* A waiter or waitress at a drive-in restaurant.

Car·i·a (kâr′ē·ə) An ancient region of SW Asia Minor.

Car·ib (kar′ib) *n.* One of a Cariban tribe of Indians formerly found in Brazil, Guiana, Venezuela, and the Lesser Antilles; now surviving in small numbers on the coasts of Guiana, Venezuela, Dominica, Honduras, Guatemala, and Nicaragua. [<Sp. *Caribe* Carib, cannibal <Cariban *caribe* brave]

Car·ib·an (kar′ə·bən) *adj.* Of or pertaining to a linguistic family of South American and Caribbean coastal Indians. —*n.* This family of languages.

Car·ib·be·an (kar′ə·bē′ən, kə·rib′ē·ən) *n.* A Carib Indian. —*adj.* **1** Of or pertaining to the Caribbean Sea. **2** Of the Carib Indians, their language, culture, etc.

Caribbean Sea An arm of the Atlantic between the West Indies and Central and South America.

car·i·be (kar′ə·bē, *Sp.* kä·rē′bā) *n.* A carnivorous, fresh-water characin fish of tropical South America (genus *Serrasalmo*), with massive jaws and sharp trenchant teeth. They are attracted by blood, and, in schools, will attack man or the larger animals: also called *piranha, piraya.* [<Sp., cannibal]

Car·i·bees (kar′ə·bēz) The Lesser Antilles.

Car·i·boo Mountains (kar′ə·bo͞o) A range of the Rockies in British Columbia, Canada; highest peak, 11,750 feet.

car·i·bou (kar′ə·bo͞o) *n.* The North American reindeer. The **woodland caribou** (*Rangifer caribou*) is found from Maine to Lake Superior and northward, and the smaller and lighter colored (sometimes white) **Barren Grounds caribou** (*R. arcticus*) in the treeless arctic regions. [<Canadian F <Algonquian *khalibu* pawer, scratcher]

CARIBOU
(About 4 feet high at the shoulder)

car·i·ca·ture (kar′i·kə·cho͝or, -chər) *n.* **1** A picture or description deliberately making use of ridiculous exaggeration or distortion; burlesque. **2** The act or art of caricaturing. **3** A poor, inept, or badly distorted likeness or imitation. —*v.t.* **·tured, ·tur·ing** To represent so as to make ridiculous; travesty; burlesque. [<F <Ital. *caricatura,* lit., an overloading <*caricare* load, exaggerate] —**car′·i·ca·tur′al** *adj.* —**car′i·ca·tur′ist** *n.*

Synonyms (noun): burlesque, exaggeration, extravaganza, imitation, mimicry, parody, take-off, travesty.

car·ies (kâr′ēz, -i·ēz) *n. Pathol.* Ulceration and decay of a bone or of a tooth. [<L]

car·il·lon (kar′ə·lon, kə·ril′yən) *n.* **1** A set of bells so hung and arranged as to be capable of being played upon, either by hand or by machinery, as a musical instrument. **2** A small instrument provided with bells, played upon by means of a pianoforte keyboard. **3** An air arranged for a chime of bells, or any rapid ringing of changes on a chime. —*v.i.* **·lonned, ·lon·ning** To play a carillon. [<F <Med. L *quadrilio, -onis* set of four bells]

car·il·lon·neur (kar′ə·lə·nûr′) *n.* One who plays a carillon. [<F]

ca·ri·na (kə·rī′nə) *n. pl.* **·nae** (-nē) *Biol.* In certain plants and animals, a keel or keel-shaped formation. [<L, keel] —**ca·ri′nal** *adj.*

Ca·ri·na (kə·rī′nə) A southern constellation, formerly part of the larger one, Argo Navis: Canopus is its principal star. See CONSTELLATION.

car·i·nate (kar′ə·nāt) *adj. Biol.* Having a carina; keeled; keel-shaped: said especially of birds having a breastbone. Compare RATITE. Also **car′i·nat′ed.** [<L *carinatus,* pp. of *carinare* supply with a keel]

Ca·rin·thi·a (kə·rin′thē·ə) A province of southern Austria; formerly a duchy; 3,681 square miles; capital, Klagenfurt: German *Kärnten.* —**Ca·rin′thi·an** *adj.* & *n.*

car·i·o·ca (kar′ē·ō′kə) *n.* A South American dance. [See CARIOCAN]

Car·i·o·can (kar′ē·ō′kən) *n.* A resident of Rio de Janeiro, Brazil. Also **Car′i·o′ca.** [from Serra de *Carioca,* a mountain range near the city]

car·i·ole (kar′ē·ōl) *n.* A small carriage: also spelled *carriole.* [<F <Ital. *carriuola,* dim. of *carra* cart, wagon]

car·i·op·sis (kar′ē·op′sis) See CARYOPSIS.

car·i·ous (kâr′ē·əs) *adj.* Affected with caries; decayed. Also **car·ied** (kâr′ēd). See synonyms under ROTTEN. —**car′i·os′i·ty** (-os′ə·tē), **car′·i·ous·ness** *n.*

cark (kärk) *Archaic v.t.* & *v.i.* To fill or be filled with anxiety: *carked* with care. —*n.* A burden of care. [<AF *carkier,* ult. <L *carricare.* See CHARGE.] —**cark′ing** *adj.*

carl (kärl) *n. Archaic* **1** A rustic. **2** *Scot.* A boor; churl. **3** A feudal serf. Also **carle.** [<ON *karl* man, freeman. Akin to CHURL.]

Carl (kärl) A masculine personal name. [<OHG *karl* freeman]

Carle·ton (kärl′tən), **Guy,** 1724–1808, Baron Dorchester, British general and administrator in America.

carl hemp *Bot.* The seed-bearing or female hemp plant: so named because formerly supposed to be the male. Also **carl.**

car·lie (kär′lē) *n. Scot.* A little man; a precocious boy.

car·lin (kär′lin) *n. Scot.* An old woman.

car·line[1] (kär′lin) *adj.* Of or pertaining to a genus (*Carlina*) of thistles. —*n.* A plant of the genus *Carlina.* [? after *Charlemagne,* whose soldiers were supposedly cured of a plague with it]

car·line[2] (kär′lin) *n.* **1** *Naut.* A short fore-and-aft timber connecting the beams on which the deck of a vessel is laid. **2** One of the cross-pieces supporting the roof boards of a railway car; rafter. Also **car′ling** (-ling). [Cf. F *carlingue*]

Car·lisle (kär·līl′) A city in NW England, county town of Cumberland.

Carl·ist (kär′list) *n.* **1** In France, a supporter of Charles X and his line. **2** In Spain, a supporter of the pretender, Don Carlos de Borbón, 1788–1855, and of his representatives. —**Carl′ism** *n.*

Car·lo (kär′lō) Italian form of CHARLES.

car·load (kär′lōd′) *n.* A minimum load carried by a railroad freight car at a lesser rate (**carload rate**) than for a smaller shipment: a unit of measure of varying tonnage.

carload lot A freight shipment meeting the official minimum weight for a carload amount.

Car·los (kär′lōs), **Don,** 1788–1855, pretender to the Spanish throne: full name *Carlos María Isidro de Borbón.*

Car·los (kär′lōs) Spanish form of CHARLES.

car·lot (kär′lət) *n. Obs.* A carl or churl; peasant. [<CARL]

Car·lo·ta (kär·lō′tä), 1840–1927, Marie Charlotte Amélie, wife of Maximilian, Archduke of Austria; empress of Mexico 1864–67.

Car·lot·ta (kär·lôt′tä) Italian form of CHARLOTTE. Also *Sp.* **Car·lo·ta** (kär·lō′tä).

Car·lo·vin·gi·an (kär′lə·vin′jē·ən) *adj.* Of or pertaining to the dynasty or family of Charlemagne. —*n.* A member of the royal house of Charlemagne or a sovereign in that line. Also called *Caroline, Carolingian.*

Car·low (kär′lō) A county of Leinster province, SE Ireland; 346 square miles; county seat, Carlow.

Carls·bad (kärlz′bad, *Ger.* kärls′bät) See KARLSBAD.

Carls·bad Caverns National Park (kärlz′bad) A series of immense, subterranean limestone caves in SE New Mexico; 77 square miles; established 1930.

Carl·son (kärl′sən), **Anton Julius,** 1875–1956, U.S. physiologist born in Sweden. —**Evans Fordyce,** 1896–1947, U.S. general.

Carls·ruh·e (kärls′ro͞o′ə) See KARLSRUHE.

Car·lyle (kär·līl′), **Thomas,** 1795–1881, Scottish essayist and historian.

Car·ma·gnole (kär′mən·yōl′, *Fr.* kȧr·mȧ·nyôl′) *n.* **1** A wild dance and song of the French revolutionists of 1789. **2** The coat and general costume worn by them. **3** A soldier of the French Revolution. [<F, from *Carmagnola,* a town in Piedmont occupied by the revolutionists]

car·man (kär′mən) *n. pl.* **·men** (-mən) **1** One who drives a car. **2** One who drives a cart.

Car·man (kär′mən), **(William) Bliss,** 1861–1929, Canadian poet.

Car·ma·ni·a (kär·mā′nē·ə) The ancient name for KERMAN.

Car·mar·then (kär·mär′thən) A county in southern Wales; 920 square miles; county seat, Carmarthen: also **Car·mar′then·shire** (-shir), **Caer·mar′then.**

Car·mel (kär′məl), **Mount** A mountain in NW Israel; 1,791 feet.

car·mel·ite (kär′məl·īt) *n.* **1** A fine, usually beige or gray, woolen stuff. **2** A variety of pear. [<CARMELITE]

Car·mel·ite (kär′məl·īt) *n.* **1** An inhabitant of Carmel. I *Sam.* xxx 5. **2** A member of the mendicant order of Our Lady of Mt. Carmel (*White Friars*) founded in Syria in 1156. **3** A nun of this order. —*adj.* Of or relating to the Carmelites. —**Car·mel·it·ess** (kär′məl·īt′is) *n. fem.*

car·min·a·tive (kär·min′ə·tiv, kär′mə·nā′tiv) *Med. adj.* Tending to relieve flatulence; warming. —*n.* A remedy for flatulence. [<L *carminatus,* pp. of *carminare* cleanse]

car·mine (kär′min, -mīn) *n.* **1** A rich purplish-red color. **2** An impermanent lake pigment prepared from cochineal; rouge. [<F *carmin* <Med. L *carminus,* contraction of *carmesinus* <OSp. *carmesin.* Doublet of CRIMSON.] —**car·min·ic** (kär·min′ik) *adj.*

Car·mo·na (kär·mō′nə), **Antonio Oscar,** 1869–1951, Portuguese general; president of Portugal 1926–51.

car·nage (kär′nij) *n.* **1** Extensive and bloody slaughter; massacre. **2** *Obs.* The bodies of the slain. See synonyms under MASSACRE. [<MF <Ital. *carnaggio* <LL *carnaticum* <L *caro, carnis* flesh, meat]

car·nal (kär′nəl) *adj.* **1** Pertaining to the fleshly nature or to bodily appetites. **2** Sensual; sexual. **3** Pertaining to the flesh or to the body; not spiritual; hence, worldly. See synonyms under BRUTISH. [<LL *carnalis* fleshly <*caro, carnis* flesh] —**car′nal·ist** *n.* —**car·nal·i·ty** (kär·nal′ə·tē) *n.* —**car′nal·ly** *adv.*

car·nal·lite (kär′nəl·īt) *n.* A massive, milk-white, hydrous chloride of magnesium and potassium: an important source of potassium. [after R. von *Carnall,* 1804–74, German mineralogist]

Car·nar·von (kär·när′vən) See CAERNARVON.

car·nas·si·al (kär·nas′ē·əl) *adj.* Adapted for tearing flesh; sectorial: specifically said of the last upper premolar and the first lower molar in carnivores. —*n.* A carnassial tooth. [<F *carnassier* carnivorous <Provençal *carnacier* <*carnaza* flesh <L *caro, carnis* flesh]

Car·nat·ic (kär·nat′ik) A region of SE Madras, India. Also **Kar·nat′ic.**

car·na·tion (kär·nā′shən) *n.* **1** The perennial, herbaceous, fragrant flower of any of the many cultivated varieties of the pink family (genus *Dianthus*), especially the clove pink or scarlet carnation (*D. caryophyllus*): State flower of Ohio. **2** A light pink, bright rose, or scarlet color. **3** *Obs.* In painting, the flesh tints in the human face and figure. [<F, flesh pink <L *carnatio, -onis* fleshiness <*caro, carnis* flesh]

car·nau·ba (kär·nou′bə) *n.* **1** The Brazilian wax palm (*Copernicia cerifera*). **2** The greenish or yellow wax from its leaves, used as a polish and for making phonograph records. [<Pg. <Tupian]

Car·ne·gie (kär·nā′gē, -neg′ē, kär′nə·gē), **Andrew,** 1837–1919, U.S. industrialist and philanthropist born in Scotland.

Carnegie Institution An institution for investigation, research, and discovery, founded at Washington, D.C., 1902, by Andrew Carnegie.

car·nel·ian (kär·nēl′yən) *n.* A clear red chalcedony, often cut as a gem: also spelled *cornelian.* [Earlier *cornelian* <MF *corneline* <Med. L *corneolus, cornelius* chalcedony]

Car·nic Alps (kär′nik) A range of the eastern

Alps along the Austro-Italian border; highest peak, 9,219 feet.

car·ni·fy (kär′nə·fī) *v.t.* & *v.i.* **·fied, ·fy·ing** **1** To change to a fleshlike consistency. **2** To form into flesh; grow fleshy. [<L *carnificare* < *caro, carnis* flesh + *facere* make] — **car′·ni·fi·ca′tion** *n.*

Car·ni·o·la (kär′nē·ō′lə) A former duchy of Austria; 3,845 square miles; since 1947 included in Yugoslavia.

car·ni·val (kär′nə·vəl) *n.* **1** A period of festival and gaiety immediately preceding Lent, observed in Roman Catholic countries and in some cities in the United States, especially by the Latin peoples. It commonly lasts from three days to a week, Shrove Tuesday being the conclusion, and is marked by street revelry, masking, pageants, and the like. **2** Any gay festival, wild revel, or masquerade. **3** Riotous sport and confusion. **4** A traveling amusement show, with merry-go-round, ferris wheel, side shows, etc. [<Ital. *carnivale* < Med. L *carnelevarium* <L *caro, carnis* flesh + *levare* remove]

Car·niv·o·ra (kär·niv′ə·rə) *n. pl.* An order of flesh-eating mammals.

car·ni·vore (kär′nə·vôr, -vōr) *n.* **1** One of the *Carnivora.* **2** An insectivorous plant.

car·niv·o·rous (kär·niv′ə·rəs) *adj.* **1** Eating or living on flesh. **2** Of or pertaining to the *Carnivora.* [<L *carnivorus* < *caro, carnis* flesh + *vorare* eat, devour] — **car·niv′o·rous·ly** *adv.* — **car·niv′o·rous·ness** *n.*

car·nos·i·ty (kär·nos′ə·tē) *n. pl.* **·ties** *Pathol.* An abnormal fleshy growth or excrescence upon any bodily organ. [<OF *carnosité* < Med. L *carnositas, -tatis* < *carnosus* fleshy]

Car·not cycle (kär·nō′) *Physics.* A thermodynamic cycle consisting of four reversible changes in the operation of an ideal heat engine working at maximum efficiency. [after N. L. S. *Carnot,* 1796–1832, French physicist]

car·no·tite (kär′nə·tīt) *n.* A yellow, earthy vanadate containing potassium, uranium, and slight traces of radium, found in western Colorado: one of the sources of uranium [after M. A. *Carnot,* Inspector General of Mines in France]

car·ob (kar′əb) *n.* **1** An evergreen tree of the Mediterranean region *(Ceratonia siliqua).* **2** Its long, sickle-shaped, fleshy pods, used for fodder: sometimes called *St. John's bread*: also **carob bean.** [<F *caroube* <Arabic *kharrūbah* bean pods]

ca·roche (kə·rōch′, -rōsh′) *n.* **1** A carriage of the 16th and 17th centuries. Also **ca·roach′, ca·roch′**: sometimes spelled *carroch.* **2** A carroccio. [<MF *carroche* <Ital. *carroccio,* aug. of *carro* chariot <L *carrus* wagon]

car·ol (kar′əl) *v.* **·oled** or **·olled, ·ol·ing** or **·ol·ing** *v.t.* **1** To utter in song, as a bird; sing. **2** To celebrate or praise in song. — *v.i.* **3** To sing in a cheerful or joyous strain; warble. **4** To sing. — *n.* **1** A song of joy or praise; especially, a Christmas song. **2** The warbling of birds. **3** *Obs.* A dance performed in a circle; also, the song accompanying it. See synonyms under SING. [<OF *carole,* prob. <L *choraules* a flutist <Gk. *choraulēs* < *choros* a dance + *aulein* play the flute < *aulos* a flute] — **car′o·ler, car′ol·ler** *n.*

Car·ol (kar′əl) A masculine or feminine personal name. [<Med. L *Carolus*]
— **Carol II,** 1893–1953, king of Rumania 1930–40; abdicated.

Car·o·le·an (kar′ə·lē′ən) *adj.* Of, or pertaining to the furniture and decoration of the period of Charles II of England. [<Med. L *Carolus* Charles]

Car·o·let·ta (kar′ə·let′ə) Latin form of CHARLOTTE.

Car·o·li·na (kar′ə·lī′nə) An English colonial settlement, divided in 1729 into what is now North and South Carolina. — *adj.* Of, pertaining to, or from North or South Carolina.

Carolina dove The mourning dove.

Carolina parrot An extinct American parakeet *(Conuropsis carolinensis),* native to the Carolinas.

Carolina pink The pinkroot.

Carolina potato The common sweet potato.

Car·o·li·nas (kar′ə·lī′nəz), **the** **1** North and South Carolina. **2** The Caroline Islands.

Car·o·line (kar′ə·līn, -lin; *Fr.* kà·rō·lēn′; *Dan., Ger.* kä′rō·lē′nə) A feminine personal name. Also **Car′o·lyn,** *Ital., Sp.* **Ca·ro·li·na** (kä′rō·lē′nä). [<F]
— **Caroline Amelia Elizabeth,** 1768–1821, British queen; wife of George IV.
— **Caroline Wilhelmina,** 1683–1737, British queen; wife of George II.

Car·o·line (kar′ə·līn, -lin) *adj.* **1** Pertaining to Charles I and II of England and their times, or to Charles I of Spain. **2** Carlovingian. [<Med. L *Carolinus* < *Carolus* Charles]

Caroline Island A British possession in the Line Islands. Formerly **Thorn·ton Island** (thôrn′tən).

Caroline Islands An island group east of the Philippines, comprising part of the United Nations Trust Territory of the Pacific Islands; 510 square miles; Japanese mandate, 1919–1944; formerly **New Philippines:** administered as the **Western Carolinas,** capitals, Palau and Yap; and the **Eastern Carolinas,** capitals, Ponape and Truk: also *the Carolinas.* Also **the Car′o·lines.**

Car·o·lin·gi·an (kar′ə·lin′jē·ən) See CARLOVINGIAN.

Car·o·lin·i·an (kar′ə·lin′ē·ən) *adj.* **1** Of or pertaining to North Carolina or South Carolina. **2** Carlovingian. — *n.* A native or naturalized citizen of North or South Carolina.

car·o·lus (kar′ə·ləs) *n. pl.* **·lus·es** or **·li** (-lī) An ancient English gold coin of the value of about twenty shillings. [<Med. L, Charles]

Car·o·lus (kar′ə·ləs) Latin form of CHARLES.

car·om (kar′əm) *v.t.* To cause to make a glancing movement: He *caromed* one ball off the other. — *v.i.* To make a glancing movement: The car *caromed* off the wall. — *n.* **1** In billiards, the impact of one ball against two others in succession, or the stroke producing it. **2** In other games, the glancing of one object from another: in England, this word has been altered to *cannon.* Also spelled *carrom.* [<F *carambole*]

Ca·ro·ní (kä′rō·nē′) A river of SE Venezuela, flowing 430 miles NW to the Orinoco.

car·o·tene (kar′ə·tēn) *n. Biochem.* A deep-yellow or red crystalline hydrocarbon, $C_{40}H_{56}$, which acts as a plant pigment: it occurs also in various animal tissues, and is changed in the body to vitamin A. Also **car′o·tin** (-tin): sometimes spelled *carrotin.* [<L *carota* carrot]

ca·rot·e·noid (kə·rot′ə·noid) *n. Biochem.* One of a large variety of nitrogen-free, light-yellow to deep-red lipochrome pigments found in plant and animal tissues. Also **ca·rot′i·noid.**

ca·rot·id (kə·rot′id) *adj. Anat.* Of, pertaining to, or near one of the two major arteries on each side of the neck. Also **ca·rot′i·dal.** [<Gk. *karōtides,* pl. < *karoein* stupefy; so called from the belief that pressure on them would cause unconsciousness]

ca·rotte (ka·rot′) *n.* A roll of tobacco; especially, the perique tobacco of Louisiana. [<F, carrot]

ca·rou·sal (kə·rou′zəl) *n.* A jovial feast or banquet; boisterous or drunken revelry. See synonyms under FROLIC.

ca·rouse (kə·rouz′) *v.i.* **ca·roused, ca·rous·ing** To drink deeply, freely, and jovially; engage in a carousal. — *n.* **1** A carousal. **2** *Obs.* The draining of a full bumper of liquor. See synonyms under FROLIC. [<G *gar aus (trinken)* (drink) all out] — **ca·rous′er** *n.*

car·ou·sel (kar′ə·sel′, -zel′) *n.* **1** A merry-go-round. **2** A tournament, tilting match, or military pageant. Also spelled *carrousel.* [<F *carrousel* <Ital. *carosello* tournament]

carp[1] (kärp) *v.i.* To find fault unreasonably; complain; cavil. [<ON *karpa* boast] — **carp′·er** *n.*

carp[2] (kärp) *n. pl.* **carp** or **carps** **1** A fresh-water food fish *(Cyprinus carpio),* originally of China but now widely distributed in Europe and America. **2** Any of various other cyprinoid fishes, as dace, minnows, and goldfish. [<OF *carpe* <LL *carpa*]

-carp *combining form* Fruit; fruit (or seed) vessel: *pericarp.* [Gk. *karpos* fruit]

car·pal (kär′pəl) *adj. Anat.* Of, pertaining to, or near the wrist. — *n.* A carpal bone. [<NL *carpalis* <L *carpus* wrist <Gk. *karpos*]

car·pa·le (kär·pā′lē) *n. pl.* **·li·a** (-lē·ə) *Anat.* A bone of the carpus or wrist; especially, one articulating with the metacarpal bones. [<NL, neut. of *carpalis* CARPAL]

Car·pa·thi·an Mountains (kär·pā′thē·ən) A range of central and eastern Europe, enclosing the Great Hungarian Plain; highest peak, 8,737 feet. Also **the Car·pa′thi·ans.**

Car·pa·tho-U·kraine (kär·pā′thō·yōō·krān′) See RUTHENIA.

car·pe di·em (kär′pē dī′em) *Latin* Enjoy the present; seize today's opportunities; literally, seize the day.

car·pel (kär′pəl) *n. Bot.* A simple pistil or seed vessel. See illustration under FRUIT. Also **car·pel·lum** (kär·pel′əm). [<NL *carpellum* <Gk. *karpos* fruit] — **car·pel·lar·y** (kär′pə·ler′ē) *adj.*

car·pel·late (kär′pə·lāt) *adj. Bot.* Possessing, or like, carpels.

Car·pen·tar·i·a (kär′pən·târ′ē·ə), **Gulf of** An arm of the Arafura Sea indenting the NE coast of Australia.

car·pen·ter (kär′pən·tər) *n.* An artificer who builds with timber or wood, as in the construction of houses, ships, and other wooden structures. — *v.t.* To make by carpentry. — *v.i.* To work with wood. [<AF *carpentier* <LL *carpentarius* carpenter, wagon-maker <L *carpentum* two-wheeled carriage] — **car′pen·ter·ing** *n.* — **car′pen·try** *n.*

Car·pen·ter (kär′pən·tər), **John Alden,** 1876–1951, U.S. composer.

carpenter bee A large, hairy, solitary bee (genus *Xylocopa*) that bores tunnels in wood for its nest, as *X. violacea* of Europe or *X. virginica* of the United States.

carpenter moth A large, light-brown moth *(Prionoxystus robiniae),* with two blue horizontal bars on its wings, whose larvae, called **carpenter worms,** bore beneath the bark of certain trees.

car·pet (kär′pit) *n.* **1** A heavy ornamental floor covering; also, the fabric used for it. **2** Any smooth surface upon which one may walk. — **on the carpet** *Colloq.* Subjected to reproof or reprimand. — *v.t.* To cover with or as with a carpet. [<OF *carpite* <LL *carpita* thick woolen covering < *carpere* pluck]

car·pet·bag (kär′pit·bag′) *n.* A handbag for travelers; especially, one made of carpeting.

car·pet·bag·ger (kär′pit·bag′ər) *n.* A person traveling with all his possessions in a carpetbag: said originally of unscrupulous itinerant bankers of the West; later, of political or profit-seeking adventurers who infested the South after the Civil War. Compare SCALAWAG. — **car′pet·bag′ger·y, car′pet·bag′gism** *n.*

carpet beetle A beetle *(Attagenus piceus)* whose reddish-brown larvae are destructive of carpets, woolen fabrics, and animal products. Also called *buffalo bug.* See illustration under INSECTS (injurious). Also **carpet bug.**

car·pet·ing (kär′pit·ing) *n.* **1** Material or fabric used for carpets; carpets collectively. **2** The act of covering with, or as with, a carpet.

carpet knight One knighted for other than military achievements; a stay-at-home soldier: used contemptuously.

car·pet-sweep·er (kär′pit·swē′pər) *n.* A hand-operated apparatus for sweeping carpets: when pushed over the floor a revolving brush sweeps the dirt into a dustpan.

carpet weed A procumbent North American herbaceous annual *(Mollugo verticillata),* the leaves of which, clustered in whorls, form mats on the ground.

car·phol·o·gy (kär·fol′ə·jē) *n. Pathol.* A delirious, automatic picking at the bedclothes in forms of low fever. [<Gk. *karphologia* < *karphos* straw + *legein* pick, collect]

-carpic *combining form* See -CARPOUS.

carp·ing (kär′ping) *adj.* Censorious; fault-finding. — **carp′ing·ly** *adv.*

carpo- *combining form* Fruit: *carpology.* [<Gk. *karpos* fruit]

car·pog·e·nous (kär·poj′ə·nəs) *adj. Bot.* Fruit-producing: said of the cell or groups of cells from which the spores are formed in certain algae. [<CARPO- + -GENOUS]

car·po·go·ni·um (kär′pə·gō′nē·əm) *n. pl.* **·ni·a** (-nē·ə) *Bot.* The female organ of certain algae; especially, in the red algae, the carpogenous

cell or cells of the procarp which, after fertilization, develop a sporocarp. [<CARPO- + -GONIUM] —**car'po·go'ni·al** *adj.*
car·pol·o·gy (kär·pol'ə·jē) *n.* That department of botany which treats of fruits in general. [<CARPO- + -LOGY] —**car·po·log·i·cal** (kär'·pə·loj'i·kəl) *adj.* —**car·pol'o·gist** *n.*
car·poph·a·gous (kär·pof'ə·gəs) *adj.* Frugivorous; fruit-eating. [<CARPO- + -PHAGOUS]
car·po·phore (kär'pə·fôr, -fōr) *n. Bot.* **1** In flowering plants, a portion of the receptacle prolonged between the carpels, as in the geraniums and many umbelliferous plants. **2** In fungi, any fruit-bearing structure or organ.
car·port (kär'pôrt', -pōrt') *n.* A roof projecting from the side of a building, used as a shelter for motor vehicles.
-carpous *combining form* Having a certain kind or number of fruits: *acrocarpous.* Also *-carpic.* [<Gk. *karpos* fruit]
car·pus (kär'pəs) *n. pl.* **·pi** (-pī) **1** *Anat.* The wrist. **2** *Zool.* A part analogous to or like a wrist. [<NL <Gk. *karpos* wrist]
Car·rac·ci (kär·rät'chē) A family of Italian painters: **Agostino,** 1557–1602; **Annibale,** 1560–1609; **Ludovico,** 1555–1619.
car·rack (kar'ək) See CARACK.
car·ra·geen (kar'ə·gēn) *n.* A small, purplish, edible marine alga *(Chondrus crispus),* the Irish moss of commerce: used in medicine as a demulcent. Often spelled *carageen, carageen, carrigeen.* Also **car'ra·gheen.** [from *Carragheen,* near Waterford, Ireland]
Car·ran·za (kär·rän'sä), **Ve·nus·tia·no** (vā'·nōō·styä'nō), 1859–1920, president of Mexico 1915–20; assassinated.
Car·ra·ra (kə·rä'rə, *Ital.* kär·rä'rä) A city in central Italy; famous for the white marble quarried nearby.
Car·rel (kə·rel', kar'əl), **Alexis,** 1873–1944, French surgeon and physiologist, active in the United States.
car·rell (kar'əl) *n.* A small space, as among the stacks in a library, for solitary study. Also **car'rel.** [Var. of CAROL]
Car·rère (kə·râr'), **John Merven,** 1858–1911, U.S. architect.
car·re·ta (kä·rā'tə) *n. SW U.S.* A long, narrow cart. [<Sp.]
car·riage (kar'ij) *n.* **1** A wheeled vehicle for carrying persons. **2** That which carries something, as in a machine. **3** Transportation; the charge for, or cost of, carrying. **4** Deportment; bearing. **5** The carrying of a besieged place. **6** The act of carrying. **7** Execution; management; control. **8** *Obs.* That which is carried. **9** *Obs.* Import; meaning. Compare BEHAVIOR. See synonyms under AIR, MANNER. [<AF *cariage* < *carier* CARRY]
carriage dog A Dalmatian.
carriage trade The wealthy patrons of a restaurant, theater, etc.: so called because of the former association of wealth with private carriages.
car·rick bend (kar'ik) *Naut.* A knot used for joining two hawsers, etc.
carrick bitt *Naut.* One of the two vertical posts on a ship's deck that support the ends of a windlass.
Car·rick·fer·gus (kar'ik·fûr'gəs) A port and municipal borough of County Antrim in eastern Northern Ireland.
Car·rick-on-Shan·non (kar'ik·on·shan'ən) The county town of County Leitrim, Ireland.
Car·rie (kar'ē) Diminutive of CAROLINE, CATHERINE.
car·ried (kar'ēd) Past tense and past participle of CARRY.
car·ri·er (kar'ē·ər) *n.* **1** One who or that which carries; hence, a person or company that undertakes to carry persons or goods for hire, as a railroad company, etc.; also, one who carries or delivers messages, letters, etc. **2** A carrier pigeon. **3** A conduit. **4** *Chem.* A material used as an intermediary or vehicle, as a catalytic agent acting to transfer an element between compounds. **5** *Mech.* A device or attachment that conveys, drives, moves, or supports something. **6** A ship for carrying aircraft. **7** *Bacteriol.* One who is immune to a disease but transmits it to others by carrying the bacteria in his body. **8** A carrier wave. —**common carrier** A person or company that undertakes to carry persons or goods for pay when called to do so, whether by land, air, or water, and that is liable for all loss or damage during transportation except such losses as arise from natural causes.
carrier pigeon A homing pigeon.
carrier wave *Telecom.* The current, wave frequency, or voltage transmitted in various forms of electrical communication; especially, in radio, the wave which is subjected to amplitude or frequency modulation.
car·ri·ole (kar'ē·ōl) See CARIOLE.
car·ri·on (kar'ē·ən) *n.* Dead and putrefying flesh; a carcass. —*adj.* **1** Feeding on carrion. **2** Like or pertaining to carrion; putrefying. [<AF *caroigne,* ult. <L *caro, carnis* flesh]
carrion crow **1** The common crow *(Corvus corone)* of Europe. **2** The black vulture *(Coragyps atratus)* of the southern United States, Mexico, and Central America.
car·ritch (kar'ich) *n. Scot.* A catechism; catechizing. [Alter. of CATECHISM]
car·roc·cio (kär·rôt'chō) *n. pl.* **·ci** (-chē) *n. Italian* The great car or chariot on which the standard of any of the medieval Italian republics was borne in battle: also *caroche.*
car·roch (kə·rōch', -rōsh') See CAROCHE.
Car·roll (kar'əl), **Charles,** 1737–1832, American patriot; signed the Declaration of Independence. —**Lewis** See DODGSON. —**Paul Vincent,** 1900–1968, Irish playwright.
car·rom (kar'əm) See CAROM.
car·ro·ma·ta (kär'rō·mä'tä) *n.* In the Philippines, a light, narrow, two-wheeled, covered vehicle, usually pulled by a single horse. [<Sp. *carromato* < *carro* cart]
car·ro·nade (kar'ə·nād') *n.* Formerly, a short, chambered ordnance piece of large caliber and short range. [from the *Carron* ironworks, Scotland]
car·ron oil (kar'ən) A mixture of limewater and linseed oil: used for treating burns. [from the *Carron* ironworks, Scotland]
car·rot[1] (kar'ət) *n.* **1** The long, reddish-yellow, edible root of an umbelliferous plant *(Daucus carota).* **2** The plant itself. ◆ Homophone: *carat.* [<F *carotte* <L *carota* <Gk. *karōton*]
car·rot[2] (kar'ət) *v.t.* To brush (furs) with a mercury and nitric acid solution, in order to prepare the fibers for the operations of matting and felting: so called from the yellowish color of the furs when dried. ◆ Homophone: *carat.* [<CARROT[1]] —**car'rot·ing** *n.*
car·ro·tin (kar'ə·tin) See CAROTENE.
car·rot·y (kar'ət·ē) *adj.* **1** Like a carrot. **2** Having red hair.
car·rou·sel (kar'ə·sel', -zel') See CAROUSEL.
car·ry (kar'ē) *v.* **·ried, ·ry·ing** *v.t.* **1** To bear from one place to another; transport; convey. **2** To have or bear upon or about one's person or in one's mind. **3** To serve as a means of conveyance or transportation: The wind *carries* sounds. **4** To lead; urge; move; influence: Love for art *carried* him abroad. **5** To win; capture. **6** To bear up; sustain; hold in position: The ship *carries* sail well. **7** To conduct (oneself) or demean (oneself); behave. **8** To transfer, as a number or figure, to another column, or, as in bookkeeping, from one account book to another. **9** To have or keep on hand: We *carry* a full stock. **10** To win, as an election; win the support of. **11** To be pregnant with. **12** To bear, as crops, or sustain, as cattle. **13** To give support to, as evidence; corroborate; confirm. **14** To extend; continue: He *carries* this farce too far. **15** In golf, to cover or pass, as a distance or object, in one stroke. **16** In hunting, to follow or trail by scent. **17** *U.S. Dial.* To conduct; escort. —*v.i.* **18** To act as bearer or carrier: fetch and *carry.* **19** To have or exert impelling or propelling power: The rifle *carries* nearly a mile. **20** To hold the head and neck habitually in a given manner: The horse *carries* well. **21** In falconry, to fly off with the game. —**to carry all before one** To meet with unimpeded and uniform success. —**to carry arms** **1** To belong to the army. **2** To bear weapons. **3** To hold a weapon in a prescribed position against the shoulder. —**to carry away** **1** To move the feelings greatly; enchant, as with passion or rapture. **2** To break off, as from a ship; lose by breaking off in a collision or gale. —**to carry forward** **1** To progress or proceed with. **2** In bookkeeping, to transfer, as an item, to the next column or page. —**to carry off** **1** To cause to die. **2** To win, as a prize or honor. **3** To face consequences boldly; brazen out. **4** To abduct. —**to carry on** **1** To keep up; keep going; continue. **2** To behave in a free, frolicsome manner. **3** To perpetuate; continue, as a tradition. —**to carry out** To accomplish; bring to completion. —**to carry over** **1** In bookkeeping, to repeat, as an item, on another page or in another column. **2** To influence to join the opposed party. —**to carry through** **1** To carry to completion or success. **2** To sustain or support to the end. —*n. pl.* **·ries** **1** A portage, as between navigable streams; also, the act of carrying, as a canoe, luggage, etc. **2** The range of a gun or a projectile; also, the distance covered by a projectile, as a golf ball. **3** *Mil.* The position of carry arms, or carry swords, etc. [<AF *carier* <LL *carricare* L *carrus* cart. Doublet of CHARGE.]

Synonyms (verb): bear, bring, convey, lift, move, remove, sustain, take, transmit, transport. A person may *bear* a load when either in motion or at rest; he *carries* it only when in motion. The stooping Atlas *bears* the world on his shoulders; swiftly moving Time *carries* the hourglass and scythe; a person may be said either to *bear* or to *carry* a scar, since it is upon him whether in motion or at rest. If an object is to be *moved* from the place we occupy, we say *carry;* if to the place we occupy, we say *bring.* A messenger *carries* a letter to a correspondent, and *brings* an answer. *Take* is often used in this sense in place of *carry;* as, *take* that letter to the office. *Carry* often signifies to *transport* by personal strength, without reference to the direction; as, that is more than he can *carry;* yet even so, it would not be admissible to say *carry* it to me, or *carry* it here; in such case we must say *bring.* To *lift* is simply to raise an object from its support, if only for an instant, with no reference to holding or moving; one may be able to *lift* what he cannot *carry.* The figurative uses of *carry* are very numerous; as, to *carry* an election, *carry* the country, *carry* (in the sense of *capture*) a fort, *carry* an audience, *carry* a stock of goods, etc. Compare CONVEY, KEEP, SUPPORT. *Antonym*: drop.
car·ry-all (kar'ē·ôl') *n.* **1** A one-horse, four-wheeled covered vehicle. **2** A closed automobile having two seats arranged lengthwise and facing each other. [Alter. of CARIOLE]
carrying charge In instalment buying, the interest charged on the unpaid balance.
car·ry-o·ver (kar'ē·ō'vər) *n.* **1** The item or entry in bookkeeping repeated from the bottom of one page to the top of the next. **2** The remainder of a crop, supply of stock, etc., to be disposed of along with the next crop or lot.
carse (kärs, kers) *n. Scot.* A stretch of intervale along a river; alluvial land.
car-sick (kär'sik') *adj.* Nauseated from riding in a car or train.
Car·so (kär'sō) A limestone plateau in NW Yugoslavia and Trieste: German *Karst.* *Serbo-Croatian* **Kras** (kräs).
Car·son (kär'sən), **Christopher,** 1809–68, U.S. frontiersman: known as *Kit Carson.* —**Edward Henry,** 1854–1935, Baron Carson of Duncairn, English jurist and statesman.
Car·son City (kär'sən) The capital of Nevada.
Car·stensz (kär'stənz), **Mount** The highest peak in New Guinea and the highest island peak in the world, in west central New Guinea; about 16,400 feet.
cart (kärt) *n.* **1** A heavy two-wheeled vehicle, for carrying loads. **2** A light two-wheeled pleasure vehicle with springs. **3** Loosely, any two- or four-wheeled vehicle. —*v.t.* To convey or carry in or as in a cart. —*v.i.* To drive or use a cart. [OE *cræt*] —**cart'er** *n.*
cart·age (kär'tij) *n.* The act of or price charged for carting.
Car·ta·ge·na (kär'tə·jē'nə, *Sp.* kär'tä·hā'nä) **1** A port in SE Spain. **2** A port in northern Colombia on the **Bay of Cartagena,** an arm of the Caribbean.
carte[1] (kärt) *n.* **1** A card or paper. **2** *Scot.* A playing card. **3** A bill of fare. [<F, card]
carte[2] (kärt) See QUARTE.
Carte (kärt), **Richard D'Oy·ly** (doi'lē), 1844–1901, English theatrical impresario.
carte blanche (kärt' blänsh', *Fr.* kȧrt bläṅsh') *n. pl.* **cartes blanches** (kärts' blänsh', *Fr.* kȧrt bläṅsh') **1** An authorization signed in blank to be filled in at discretion. **2** Unrestricted authority. [<F, white card]
carte de vi·site (kärt' də vē·zēt') *pl.* **cartes**

de visite (kȧrt) 1 A visiting card. 2 A small photograph on a card formerly used as a visiting card. [<F]

car·tel (kär·tel′, kär′təl) *n.* 1 A written official agreement between governments, especially when at war, as for the exchange of prisoners. 2 A written challenge to single combat. 3 An international combination of independent enterprises in the same branch of production, aiming at a monopolistic control of the market by means of weakening or eliminating competition. Compare MONOPOLY, SYNDICATE, TRUST. 4 An agreement among states to maintain mutually beneficial customs rates or otherwise act as a unit for a common purpose. See ANSCHLUSS. [<F <Ital. *cartello,* dim. of *carta* paper]

Car·ter (kär′tər), **Howard,** 1873–1939, English archeologist. **—Jimmy (James Earl),** born 1924, 39th president of the United States, 1977–81.

Car·ter·et (kär′tər·it), **John,** 1690–1763, first Earl Granville, English statesman.

Car·te·sian (kär·tē′zhən) *adj.* Of or pertaining to René Descartes, a French philosopher and geometer of the 17th century, or to his doctrines and methods. *—n.* A follower of Descartes, or believer in his doctrines. [<NL *Cartesianus* <*Cartesius,* Latinized form of *Descartes*] — **Car·te′sian·ism** *n.*

Cartesian coordinate system *Geom.* 1 A plane system for indicating the curve of an equation graphically by means of two axes, graduated in both directions from the origin: when intersecting at right angles, the coordinates are called *rectangular,* when intersecting at any angle other than 90°, the coordinates are called *oblique.* 2 A three-dimensional system for indicating the shape of a solid by means of three planes intersecting at right angles to each other at a point called the origin: from the three points of reference required, any point in space with coordinates *x, y,* and *z* can be located. See illustration under OCTANT. Also called *rectangular coordinate system.*

Cartesian devil A hollow figure partly filled with air, and immersed in water in a glass jar, the jar being provided with an elastic cover, by pressure upon which the immersed figure is made to sink, rising again when the pressure is removed: sometimes called *bottle imp.* Also **Cartesian diver, Cartesian imp.**

Car·thage (kär′thij) An ancient city-state in North Africa near modern Tunis; destroyed by the Romans in 146 B.C. Ancient **Car·tha·go** (kär·thā′gō, -tä′-).

Car·tha·gin·i·an (kär′thə·jin′ē·ən) *adj.* Of or pertaining to Carthage. *—n.* A native or inhabitant of Carthage.

Carthaginian peace A peace on drastically severe terms: so called in allusion to the Roman destruction of Carthage (146 B.C.).

Carthaginian Wars See PUNIC WARS in table under WAR.

Car·thu·sian (kär·thōō′zhən) *n.* A monk or nun of the order founded in 1086 in Chartreuse in the French Alps. *—adj.* Of or pertaining to the order of Carthusians. [<Med. L *Cartusianus* <*Carturissium* Chartreuse]

Car·tier (kȧr·tyā′), **Sir George Etienne,** 1814–1873, Canadian statesman. **—Jacques,** 1491–1557, French navigator; discoverer of the St. Lawrence River 1535.

car·ti·lage (kär′tə·lij) *n Biol.* 1 A tough, elastic supporting tissue in animals, composed of cells embedded in an opalescent matrix, either homogeneous or fibrous; gristle. 2 A structure or part consisting of cartilage. [<MF <L *cartilago* gristle]

car·ti·lag·i·nous (kär′tə·laj′ə·nəs) *adj.* 1 Of or like cartilage; gristly. 2 Having a gristly skeleton, as sharks.

Car·tist (kär′tist) *n.* A supporter of the Constitution in Spain or Portugal. [<Sp. *carta* charter]

cart·load (kärt′lōd′) *n.* 1 As much as a cart will hold. 2 The contents of a cart.

car·to·gram (kär′tə·gram) *n.* A map giving statistical information by means of comparative diagrams. [<F *cartogramme*]

car·tog·ra·phy (kär·tog′rə·fē) *n.* The science, technology, or art of drawing or compiling, maps or charts. [<*carto-* map (<L *charta*) + -GRAPHY] **—car·to·graph** (kär′tə·graf, -gräf) *n.* **—car·tog′ra·pher** *n.* **—car′to·graph′ic** or **·i·cal** *adj.*

car·ton (kär′tən) *n.* 1 A pasteboard box. 2 Pasteboard. 3 A white disk within the bull's-eye of a target or a shot striking it. [<F. See CARTOON.]

car·toon (kär·tōōn′) *n.* 1 A drawing or caricature as in a newspaper or periodical; especially, one intended to affect public opinion as to some matter or person. 2 A sketch for a fresco or mosaic. 3 A comic strip. 4 A motion-picture film, called an **animated cartoon,** made by photographing a series of carefully prepared black-and-white or colored drawings, each representing a further stage in the action of the film, which is usually synchronized for sound effects and music. See synonyms under PICTURE. *—v.t.* To make a caricature or cartoon of; satirize pictorially. *—v.i.* To make cartoons. [<F *carton* <Ital. *cartone* pasteboard, aug. of *carta* card <L *charta* paper] — **car·toon′ist** *n.*

car·toph·i·ly (kär·tof′ə·lē) *n. U.S.* The collecting of illustrative cards, as those enclosed in packages of retail goods: a humorous term. [<*carto-* card (<F *carte*) + Gk. *philia* <*phileein* love] — **car·toph′i·list** *n.*

car·touche (kär·tōōsh′) *n.* 1 An oblong or oval figure containing the name of a king, queen, or deity, as on ancient Egyptian monuments and papyri. 2 *Archit.* An ornamental tablet or scroll with inscription or emblem; a scroll-shaped bracket, etc. 3 A cartridge; a cartridge box; an ammunition bag. 4 The case containing the inflammable materials in some fireworks. 5 *Astron.* A curve exhibiting the varying visibility of an object, as of a canal on Mars. Also **car·touch′.** [<F <Ital. *cartoccio,* aug. of *carta* card <L *charta* paper]

car·tridge (kär′trij) *n.* 1 An explosive charge for a pistol, rifle, machine gun, or other small arm, consisting of primer, gunpowder, cardboard or metal case, and projectile or projectiles. 2 *Phot.* A roll of protected sensitized films. — **blank cartridge** A cartridge containing powder but no projectile. [Alter. of CARTOUCHE]

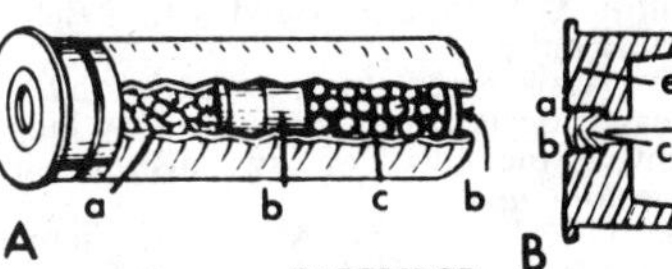

CARTRIDGE
A. Shotgun shell.
a. Powder. *b., b.* Wads. *c.* Shot.
B. Section of center-fire metallic rifle or pistol cartridge case.
a. Primer-cup. *b.* Percussion composition. *c.* Anvil. *d.* Vent. *e.* Base of case.

cartridge belt A belt having loops or pockets for cartridges or cartridge clips.

cartridge clip Clip[1] (def. 6).

car·tu·lar·y (kär′chōō·ler′ē) *n. pl.* **·lar·ies** 1 A collection or a register of charters, etc., as of a monastery. 2 An officer in charge of such records. Also spelled *chartulary.* [<LL *cartularium*]

cart·wheel (kärt′hwēl′) *n.* 1 *U.S. Colloq.* A silver dollar. 2 *Aeron.* A flight maneuver which causes an airplane to rotate about its long axis while describing an inverted U in the air: a variation of the half-roll. 3 A lateral handspring.

Cart·wright (kärt′rīt), **Edmond,** 1743–1823, English clergyman and inventor of the power loom, etc. **—Thomas,** 1535–1603, English Puritan clergyman.

ca·ru·ca (ka·rōō′kə) *n.* 1 A plow. 2 A plow team of four oxen or horses yoked abreast. [<Med. L *carruca* a plow]

car·u·cage (kar′ə·kij) *n.* In old English law, a tax imposed on every plow or on every carucate.

car·u·cate (kar′ə·kāt) *n.* A Norman measure of land: the amount of land that could be plowed in a year and a day by one caruca, usually about 120 acres.

car·un·cle (kar′ung·kəl, kə·rung′-) *n.* 1 *Zool.* A fleshy excrescence, as a cock's comb. 2 *Bot.* A protuberant growth of the seed coat at or near the hilum. Also **ca·run·cu·la** (kə·rung′kyə·lə). [<MF <L *caruncula,* dim. of *caro, carnis* flesh] **—ca·run·cu·lar** (kə·rung′kyə·lər) or **·late** (-lit, -lāt) or **·lous** (-ləs) *adj.*

Ca·ru·so (kə·rōō′sō, *Ital.* kä·rōō′zō), **Enrico,** 1873–1921, Italian operatic tenor.

car·va·crol (kär′və·krōl, -krol) *n. Chem.* A colorless, oily, aromatic liquid, $C_{10}H_{14}O$, obtained from origan, camphor, thyme, and other plants of the mint family: used in perfumery and in medicine as an antiseptic. [<F *carvi* caraway + L *acer, acris* biting + -OL]

carve (kärv) *v.* **carved, carv·ing** *v.t.* 1 To cut figures or designs upon. 2 To make by cutting or chiseling. 3 To cut up, as cooked meat; divide. *—v.i.* 4 To make carved work or figures. 5 To cut up cooked meat served at table. See synonyms under CUT. *—n.* A cut or stroke in carving. [OE *ceorfan*] **—carv′er** *n.*

car·vel (kär′vəl) *n.* A caravel. [See CARAVEL]

car·vel-built (kär′vəl·bilt′) *adj. Naut.* Built with carvel joints: distinguished from *clinker-built.* See illustration under CLINKER-BUILT.

carvel joint *Naut.* A flush joint, as of two planks or plates in a vessel's side.

carv·en (kär′vən) *adj. Poetic* or *Archaic* Wrought by carving or graving; carved.

Car·ver (kär′vər), **George Washington,** 1864?–1943, U.S. Negro scientist. **—John,** 1575–1621, English Pilgrim father; first governor of Plymouth Colony.

Carver chair A type of early American chair with turned posts and spindles, and usually having a rush seat: named for one owned by John Carver.

carv·ing (kär′ving) *n.* 1 The act of one who carves. 2 That which is carved; sculpture.

Car·y (kâr′ē), **Alice,** 1820–71, U.S. poet and novelist. **—Henry Francis,** 1772–1844, English clergyman and poet. **—Phoebe,** 1824–71, U.S. poet, sister of Alice. **—Joyce,** 1889–1957, English novelist.

car·y·at·id (kar′ē·at′·id) *n. pl.* **·ids** or **·i·des** (-ə·dēz) *Archit.* A supporting column in the form of a sculptured female figure. [<L *Caryatis, -ides* <Gk. *Karyiatis* a priestess of Artemis at Karyai, town of Laconia, Greece] — **car·y·at·i·dal** (kar′ē·at′ə·dəl), **car·y·at·i·de·an** (kar′ē·at′ə·dē′·ən), **car·y·a·tid·ic** (kar′ē·ə·tid′ik) *adj.*

CARYATIDS

caryo- See KARYO-.

car·y·o·ki·ne·sis (kar′·ē·ō·ki·nē′sis) See KARYOKINESIS

car·y·o·phyl·la·ceous (kar′ē·ō·fi·lā′shəs) *adj. Bot.* 1 Pertaining or belonging to a family *(Caryophyllaceae)* of herbs, the pink family, characterized by stems enlarged at the nodes, opposite entire leaves, and perfect or rarely dioecious flowers: also called *silenaceous.* 2 Having a tubular calyx with five long-clawed petals. [<NL <Gk. *karyophyllon* <*karyon* nut + *phyllon* leaf]

car·y·op·sis (kar′ē·op′sis) *n. pl.* **·op·ses** (-op′sēz) or **·op·si·des** (-op′sə·dēz) *Bot.* A seedlike fruit, as the grains of wheat and rye: also spelled *cariopsis.* [<Gk. *karyon* nut + Gk. *opsis* appearance]

car·y·o·tin (kar′ē·ō′tin) See KARYOTIN.

Ca·sa·ba (kə·sä′bə) *n.* A winter variety of muskmelon with sweet white flesh and yellow rind: also spelled *Cassaba.* Also **Casaba melon.** [from *Kasaba,* a town in western Turkey]

Cas·a·blan·ca (kas′ə·blang′kə, kä′sə·bläng′kə) A port and the largest city of Morocco: Arabic *Dar-el-beida.*

Cas·a Gran·de National Monument (kas′ə·gran′dē) A region of prehistoric ruins in southern Arizona, including **Casa Grande,** an adobe watchtower built in 1350; established as a national park in 1918.

Ca·sals (kä·säls′), **Pablo,** 1876–1973, Spanish violoncellist, conductor, and composer.

Cas·a·no·va (kas′ə·nō′və, kaz′-; *Ital.* kä′sä·nô′vä), **Giovanni Giacomo,** 1725–98, Italian adventurer, known for his *Memoirs*: full surname *Casanova de Seingalt.*

Ca·sau·bon (kə·sô′bən, *Fr.* kȧ·zō·bôṅ′), **Isaac,**

1559–1614, French scholar and theologian.

ca·sa·va (kə·sä′və) See CASSAVA.

Cas·bah (käz′bä) The native quarter of Algiers or of other cities with a large Arab population. Also spelled *Kasbah.*

cas·ca·bel (kas′kə·bel) *n.* **1** A knob or breeching loop behind the breech of a cannon, to facilitate handling. **2** A rattlesnake or its rattle. Also **cas′ca·ble** (-bəl). [<Sp.]

cas·cade (kas·kād′) *n.* **1** A fall of water over steeply slanting rocks, or one of a series of such falls. **2** Anything resembling a waterfall, as the lace trimming of a dress. **3** *Chem.* A connection in series of two or more electrolytic cells or tanks so arranged as to produce a flow of the electrolyte from higher to lower levels. **4** *Physics* A successive operation, as cooling a gas by utilizing the effect of a previously expanded gas. — *v.i.* **·cad·ed, ·cad·ing** To fall in the form of a waterfall; form cascades. [<F <Ital. *cascata* <*cascare* fall <L *cadere*]

cascade amplification *Electronics* An amplifying system in which two or more vacuum tube units are connected to form a number of stages, each stage deriving its input from the output of the one preceding.

cascade control *Electr.* A method of turning street lights on and off in sections, each section being controlled by the energizing and de-energizing of preceding sections.

Cascade Range A range of mountains in Oregon, Washington, and British Columbia; highest peak, 14,408 feet.

cas·car·a buckthorn (kas·kâr′ə) A buckthorn *(Rhamnus purshiana)* of the NW United States: its bark yields **cascara sa·gra·da** (sə·grā′də), used as a laxative: also called *bearwood.* Also **cas·car′a.** [<Sp. *cáscara* bark]

cas·ca·ril·la (kas′kə·ril′ə) *n.* **1** The aromatic bark of a West Indian shrub *(Croton eluteria)* of the spurge family, sometimes used as a tonic. **2** The shrub. Also **cascarilla bark.** [<Sp., dim. of *cáscara* bark]

cas·ca·ron (kas′kə·rōn′) *n.* An eggshell filled with confetti, thrown by revelers at balls, carnivals, etc. [<Sp. *cascarón* eggshell]

Cas·co Bay (kas′kō) An inlet of the Atlantic in SW Maine, including Portland Harbor.

case[1] (kās) *n.* **1** The state of things in a given instance; a special condition of affairs; juncture: What shall be done in this *case*?; also, the actual circumstance; the fact or facts: Such is not the *case.* **2** An event; contingency: in *case* of fire. **3** A particular instance or example: a *case* of pneumonia; a *case* of fraud. **4** *Law* A cause of action; a suit; an action. **5** State; physical condition or situation; plight. **6** *Gram.* **a** The syntactical relationship of a noun, pronoun, or adjective to other words in a sentence, as indicated, generally, in inflected languages, by declensional endings or, in non-inflected languages, by prepositions and word order. **b** The form of a word indicating this relationship. **c** These relationships or forms as a group. Evidence would indicate that primitive Indo-European had eight cases — nominative, genitive, dative, accusative, ablative, instrumental, locative, and vocative. See SUBJECTIVE, POSSESSIVE, and OBJECTIVE for the cases surviving in Modern English. **7** *Colloq.* A peculiar or exceptional person. See synonyms under EVENT, PRECEDENT, SAMPLE. — **in any case** No matter what; regardless. — **in case** In the event that; if. [<F *cas* <L *casus* event <*cadere* fall; the grammatical cases (def. 6) were thought of as "falling" from the nominative]

case[2] (kās) *n.* **1** A box, sheath, bag, or other covering in which something is or may be kept. **2** A box and the quantity or number contained in it; a set. **3** *Printing* A tray, with compartments for holding type. Cases are commonly made in pairs, called **upper** or **cap case,** for capital letters, and **lower case,** for small letters, respectively. **4** The frame or casing for a door, window, etc., or a hollow box beside a casing, as for sash weights. **5** *Archit.* An outer facing of a building, as of stone over brick. **6** The cavity in the upper anterior part of the head of a sperm whale containing the spermaceti. **7** In bookbinding, a binding or cover made separately. **8** *Her.* The skin of an animal. **9** *Obs.* The clothes of a person; also, the exterior, in any sense. **10** *Obs.* A brace or pair, as of pistols. — *v.t.* **cased, cas·ing** **1** To cover with a case; incase. **2** *Slang* To look over; inspect. **3** *Obs.* To flay. [<AF *casse* <L *capsa* box <*capere* take, hold]

ca·se·ase (kā′sē·ās) *n. Biochem.* A tryptic enzyme of bacterial origin which dissolves casein and hastens ripening in cheese. [<CASE(IN) + -ASE]

ca·se·ate (kā′sē·āt) *v.i.* **·at·ed, ·at·ing** To become cheesy; undergo caseation. [<L *caseatus* mixed with cheese <*caseus* cheese]

ca·se·a·tion (kā′sē·ā′shən) *n.* **1** Conversion into cheese or curd; coagulation. **2** *Pathol.* Caseous degeneration, as of the tissues.

ca·se·fy (kā′sə·fī) *v.t.* & *v.i.* **·fied, ·fy·ing** To make or become like cheese. [<L *caseus* cheese]

case·hard·en (kās′här′dən) *v.t.* **1** *Metall.* To harden by carburizing the surface of (iron), followed by quenching. **2** To make callous or insensible to influences, especially good influences.

case history The record of an individual, as made and filed by hospitals, social agencies, insurance companies, etc., giving the salient facts on health, family, financial condition, economic and social status.

ca·se·in (kā′sē·in, -sēn) *n. Biochem.* A phosphoprotein found especially in milk, constituting the principal ingredient in cheese: a white friable substance of acid character, used in preparing cotton cloth for calico printing, as an adhesive in certain varieties of cement, and as an important ingredient in plastics and synthetic resins. [<L *caseus* cheese] — **ca·se·ic** (kā′sē·ik) *adj.*

ca·se·in·o·gen (kā′sē·in′ə·jen, kā·sē′nə-) *n.* The casein-bearing protein of milk. [<CASEIN + -GEN]

case knife **1** A knife provided with a sheath. **2** A table knife.

case law Law based upon or settled by decided cases; decisions handed down by judges and having the effect of law: distinguished from *statute law.*

case·mate (kās′māt) *n.* **1** A vaulted chamber in a fortification. **2** A bombproof shelter from which guns fire through openings, or an armored bulkhead on shipboard, with openings for guns. [<F <Ital. *casamatta,* ? <Gk. *chasmata,* pl. of *chasma* opening] — **case′·mat′ed** *adj.*

case·ment (kās′mənt) *n.* **1** The sash of a window when arranged to open on hinges at the side, or a window arranged with such sashes. **2** A case; covering; incasement. [<OF *encassement*] — **case′ment·ed** *adj.*

Case·ment (kās′mənt), **Sir Roger,** 1864–1916, Irish patriot, hanged by the British for treason.

ca·se·ose (kā′sē·ōs) *n. Biochem.* An intermediary product in the hydration of caseins, either artificial or in the digestive process: one of the proteoses. [<L *caseus* cheese]

ca·se·ous (kā′sē·əs) *adj.* Of, pertaining to, or like cheese; cheesy.

ca·sern (kə·zûrn′) *n.* A barrack of soldiers in a garrison town. Also **ca·serne′.** [<F *caserne* <Sp. *caserna* small hut <L *quaterna* four each]

Ca·ser·ta (kä·zer′tä) A town in Campania, southern Italy.

case shot An assortment of small shot, as shrapnel or canister, enclosed in a metal case.

case system A system of teaching law in which selected cases form the basis for study, supplemented by textbooks.

case·work (kās′wûrk′) *n.* The investigation and guidance by a social worker of the cases of maladjusted individuals and families. — **case′·work′er** *n.*

case·worm (kās′wûrm′) *n.* A caddis worm.

Ca·sey Jones (kā′sē jōnz′), 1864–1900, John Luther Jones, U.S. railroad hero who died in a train wreck.

cash[1] (kash) *n.* **1** Current money in hand or readily available. **2** Money paid down; immediate payment: five percent discount for *cash.* See synonyms under MONEY. — *v.t.* To convert into ready money, as a check; give or receive money for. — **to cash in** **1** In gambling, to turn in one's chips and receive cash. **2** *U.S. Slang* To die. — **to cash in on** To turn to advantage; make a profit from. [<F *caisse* cash box, cash <Ital. *cassa* <L *capsa* box] — **cash′a·ble** *adj.*

cash[2] (kash) *n. pl.* **cash** Any of various little coins used as small change in parts of the East Indies and China; especially, a Chinese coin made of copper and lead, with a square hole in the middle. [<Pg. *caixa* <Tamil *kāsu* small coin]

cash·a (kash′ə) *n.* A soft woolen fabric similar to flannel, with an admixture of Cashmere goat's hair. [Prob. <CASHMERE]

cash-and-car·ry (kash′ən·kar′ē) *adj.* Operated on a system of cash purchase and no delivery.

ca·shaw (kə·shô′) *n.* **1** The honey mesquite. **2** The cushaw. [Var. of CUSHAW]

cash basis A system of bookkeeping that includes only cash receipts as income and only cash payments as expense: opposed to *accrual basis.*

cash·book (kash′bŏŏk′) *n.* A book devoted to a cash account.

cash discount A discount from the purchase price allowed the purchaser provided he pays within a stipulated period.

cash·ew (kash′ōō, kə·shōō′) *n.* **1** A tropical American tree (genus *Anacardium)* now naturalized in Africa and Asia. **2** Its small, kidney-shaped, edible fruit, the **cashew nut.** [<F *acajou* <Tupian *acajoba*]

cash·ier[1] (ka·shir′) *n.* **1** A custodian of money; especially, one who has charge of the receipts, disbursements, cash on hand, etc., of a banking or mercantile house. **2** A paymaster. [<F *caissier* <*caisse.* See CASH[1].]

cash·ier[2] (ka·shir′) *v.t.* **1** To dismiss in disgrace, as a military officer. **2** To discard. See synonyms under BREAK. [<Du. *casseren* <F *casser* <LL *cassare* annul and L *quassare* destroy]

cashier's check A check drawn by a bank's cashier upon its own funds.

cash·mere (kash′mir) *n.* **1** A fine wool obtained from Cashmere goats. **2** A soft fabric made from this or similar wool. **3** A dress, shawl, etc., made of cashmere. [from *Kashmir,* India]

Cash·mere (kash·mir′, kash′mir) See KASHMIR.

Cashmere goat A variety of goat originally native in Kashmir.

cash on delivery Immediate cash payment to the bearer on delivery of goods: abbr. *C.O.D.*

ca·shoo (kə·shōō′) See CATECHU.

cash register An automatic mechanical device with keyboard, for recording, adding, and displaying the amount of cash placed in its money drawer.

cas·i·mere, cas·i·mire (kas′ə·mir) See CASSIMERE.

cas·ing (kā′sing) *n.* **1** That with which a thing or place is incased or lined, as a wall of firebrick on the door of a kiln. **2** The framework around a door or window. **3** The outer covering or shoe of an automobile tire. **4** *pl.* The intestines of cattle, hogs, etc., cleaned and salted for use as sausage containers. [<CASE[2]]

ca·si·no (kə·sē′nō) *n.* **1** A room or building for public amusement, dancing, gambling, etc. **2** In Italy, a summerhouse, or the like; also, a house built in imitation of the Italian casino. **3** A game of cards for from two to four players: also spelled *cassino.* [<Ital., dim. of *casa* house]

Ca·si·quia·re (kä′sē·kyä′rā) A river in southern Venezuela, flowing 140 miles SW, linking the Orinoco and Amazon basins.

cask (kask, käsk) *n.* **1** A barrel-shaped wooden vessel or receptacle, made of staves, hoops, and flat heads. A cask for liquor or liquids may be larger or smaller than a barrel, and is usually of heavier material. **2** The quantity a cask will hold. **3** *Obs.* A casket. ◆ Homophone: *casque.* [<Sp. *casco* skull, potsherd, cask, ? ult. <L *quassare* break. Related to *casque.*]

cas·ket (kas′kit, käs′-) *n.* **1** A small box or chest, as for jewels or other valuables. **2** A coffin. — *v.t.* To enclose in or as in a casket. [<F *cassette* <*casse* chest; form infl. by CASK]

Cas·lon (kaz′lən) *n.* A style of type created by the English type founder **William Caslon,** 1692–1766.

Cas·par Milque·toast (kas′pər milk′tōst′) A creation by H. T. Webster, U.S. cartoonist, of a painfully timid man; hence, any apologetic or non-assertive person; a milksop.

Cas·per (kas′pər) A masculine personal name. Also **Cas′par.** [? <Persian, master of the treasure]

Cas·per (kas′pər) A city in central Wyoming.

Cas·pi·an Sea (kas′pē·ən) The largest salt-water lake and inland sea in the world, between SE Europe and SW Asia in the U.S.S.R. and Iran; 163,800 square miles.
casque (kask) *n.* **1** Any piece of armor to cover the head. **2** A helmet. **3** A helmet-like protuberance, as the bony crest of a cassowary or the horny process of a hornbill. ◆ Homophone: *cask.* [<F, ult. <L *quassare.* Related to CASK.] —**casqued** (kaskt) *adj.*

CASQUE
Surmounted by a crest.

cas·quette (kas·ket′) *n.* A woman's brimless hat. [<F, dim. of *casque* helmet]
Cass (kas), **Lewis,** 1782–1866, U.S. statesman.
Cas·sa·ba (kə·sä′bə) See CASABA.
Cas·san·dra (kə·san′drə) In Greek mythology, a daughter of Priam whose prophecies were fated by Apollo always to be true but never to be believed; hence, anyone who utters unheeded prophecies of disaster.
cas·sa·reep (kas′ə·rēp) *n.* A condiment made from the juice of the cassava plant. [<F *cassiry* <Tupian *cachiri*]
cas·sa·tion (ka·sā′shən) *n.* **1** The act of making null or abrogating, as a judgment or decree. **2** *Music* A composition in several movements, similar to a suite. [<F <LL *cassatio, -onis* < *cassare* annul <L *cassus* empty]
Cas·satt (kə·sat′), **Mary,** 1855–1926, U.S. painter.
cas·sa·va (kə·sä′və) *n.* **1** One of several tropical American shrubs or herbs (genus *Manihot*), cultivated for their edible roots; especially, the sweet cassava *(M. dulcis)* and the bitter cassava *(M. exculens)*; manioc. **2** A starch made from the roots of these plants, valued as the source of tapioca. Also spelled *casava.* [<F *cassave* <Taino *casavi*]
casse (kas) *n.* A darkening in the color of wines due to the chemical action of excess iron or copper. [<F, a breaking]
Cas·se·grain·i·an (kas′ə·grā′nē·ən) *adj. Astron.* Describing a type of reflecting telescope which employs a hyperbolic mirror inside the prime focus to form an image which passes through an aperture in the primary mirror at the bottom of the tube. [after N. *Cassegrain,* 17th c. French physician, who invented it in 1672]
Cas·sel (kas′əl, *Ger.* käs′əl) See KASSEL.
cas·se·role (kas′ə·rōl) *n.* **1** A saucepan. **2** A baking dish of earthenware, glass, etc., in which food may be baked and served: food so served is said to be **en casserole. 3** A dish with a handle used by chemists. [<F]
cas·sette (kə·set′, ka-) *n.* **1** *Photog.* A light-proof magazine for holding a sensitized plate or film in a camera or X-ray device. **2** *Electronics* A cartridge containing magnetic tape for the storage of audio or video material, as for use in a tape recorder or television receiver. [<F, lit., small box]
cas·sia (kash′ə) *n.* **1** A coarse variety of cinnamon, especially that obtained from the bark of *Cinnamomum cassia*: also **cassia bark. 2** The tree yielding it. **3** Any of a large genus *(Cassia)* of shrubs or herbs of the senna family. **4** A medicinal product of a plant of the genus *Cassia*; especially, the laxative pulp obtained from the pods of *C. fistula* of the East Indies. Compare SENNA. [<L <Gk. *kasia* <Hebrew *qetsi′ah* < *qātsa′* strip off bark]
cas·si·mere (kas′ə·mir) *n.* A woolen cloth for men's wear: also called *kerseymere*: also spelled *casimere, casimire.* [<F *casimir* cashmere]
cas·si·no (kə·sē′no) See CASINO (def. 3).
Cas·si·no (kə·sē′nō, *Ital.* käs·sē′nō) A town in central Italy; site of Benedictine **Monte Cassino Abbey** and scene of German resistance to the Allied advance on Rome in World War II, 1943–44.
cas·si·o·ber·ry (kas′ē·ō·ber′ē) *n. pl.* **·ries 1** The shining black edible drupe of a North American shrub *(Viburnum obovatum).* **2** The yaupon or its fruit. [<N. Am. Ind.]
Cas·si·o·do·rus (kas′ē·ō·dō′rəs), **Flavius Magnus Aurelius,** died 575? A.D., Roman statesman and historian.
Cas·si·o·pe·ia (kas′ē·ə·pē′ə) **1** In Greek mythology, the wife of Cepheus and mother of Andromeda. **2** A constellation near the north pole: from the arrangement of its five brightest stars in the form of an irregular W, also called **Cassiopeia's Chair.** See CONSTELLATION.
cas·sis (kä·sēs′) *n.* **1** The black currant of Europe. **2** A cordial made from black currants. [<F]
cas·sit·e·rite (kə·sit′ə·rīt) *n.* A tetragonal, brown to black tin dioxide, SnO_2: the most important ore of tin. [<Gk. *kassiteros* tin]
Cas·sius Lon·gi·nus (kash′əs lon·jī′nəs), **Gaius,** died 42 B.C. Roman general, conspirator against Caesar.
cas·sock (kas′ək) *n.* **1** A close-fitting garment, reaching to the feet, worn by the Roman Catholic and many of the Protestant clergy. **2** A short garment or loose jacket worn under the Geneva gown by Presbyterian ministers. **3** A clergyman or the clerical office. **4** *Obs.* Any long coat or gown; especially, a military cloak. [<MF *casaque* <Ital. *casacca* greatcoat] —**cas·socked** (kas′əkt) *adj.*
cas·so·ne (käs·sô′nā) *n. Italian* A large chest, usually with painted, carved, or inlaid decoration.
cas·so·war·y (kas′ə·wer′ē) *n. pl.* **·war·ies** A large, three-toed, ratite bird of Australia and New Guinea (genus *Casuarius*), related to the emu. [<Malay *kasuārī*]
cast (kast, käst) *v.* **cast, cast·ing** *v.t.* **1** To throw with force; drive by force, as from the hand or from an engine; fling; hurl. **2** To place as if by throwing; put with violence or force, as by the sea or wind: The waves *cast* us on the beach. **3** To throw up, as with a shovel: to *cast* a mound of earth. **4** To throw down; defeat; especially with the feet upward: He *cast* his enemy to the ground. **5** To deposit; give: He *cast* his vote. **6** To draw by chance; throw, as dice. **7** To cause to fall upon or over; throw in a particular direction; emit: *cast* a shadow. **8** To throw out or forth; get rid of. **9** To let down; put out; let drop: to *cast* anchor. **10** To abandon or shed, as in the process of growth; molt. **11** To give birth to, especially prematurely; drop: The mare *cast* her foal. **12** *Metall.* To shape in a mold; make a cast of; found. **13** To stereotype or electroplate. **14** To assign roles, as in a play; to assign to a part. **15** To add; total, as a column of figures. **16** To calculate mathematically: He *cast* his horoscope. **17** *Law* To defeat in a suit. **18** To winnow, as grain, by throwing in the air. **19** To reject; discard; disqualify: to *cast* horses for bad temper. **20** In falconry, to place upon the perch. **21** *Naut.* To turn, as a ship, to another course. —*v.i.* **22** To revolve something in the mind; scheme; consider: to *cast* about for a solution. **23** To anticipate; forecast; conjecture. **24** *Metall.* To take shape in a mold, as metal. **25** To add up a column of figures; make a computation: with *up.* **26** To throw a fish line. **27** *Naut.* To turn from the wind; fall off, as in getting under way; to tack; put about. **28** To warp, as timber. **29** In hunting, to make a detour or run, as a dog, in search of a lost scent or trail. **30** To swarm, as bees. —**to cast about 1** To consider ways and means; scheme. **2** To warp; tack. —**to cast away** To discard; reject. —**to cast down 1** To overthrow; destroy. **2** To cause to feel dejection; discourage; depress. —**to cast off 1** To reject or discard. **2** To let go, as a ship from a dock. —*n.* **1** The act of throwing or casting: a *cast* of a fly in angling. **2** A throw of dice; also, the number or total thrown. **3** The distance to which a thing may be thrown: a stone's *cast.* **4** Anything that is thrown out or off, as an insect's skin, the dung of an earthworm, the undigested matter ejected from the stomach of an owl or hawk. **5** In angling, a leader, sometimes including the flies. **6** An object founded or run in or as in a mold, as of metal, plaster, wax, etc. **7** *Pathol.* A morbid substance molded as in one of the urinary tubules: a renal *cast.* **8** A stereotype or electrotype plate. **9** A reverse copy, in plaster of Paris or similar material, of a mold: usually distinguished from a *casting,* which is of iron or other metal or alloy. **10** The material run into molds at one operation. **11** An impression as of a harder in a softer body: a *cast* of a man's face. **12** An impressed form of the inner surface of an animal or plant, either of the bony outline or particularly of the organs of an animal: distinguished from *mold.* **13** A characteristic formation or inclination; also, stamp; type; kind; sort. **14** Shade; dash; tinge: white, with a bluish *cast.* **15** A twist or perversion; warp; squint. **16** The distribution of parts to performers in a play; also, the performers collectively. **17** In hunting, a detour in search of the scent. **18** A stroke or turn: a *cast* of one's skill. **19** A pair of hawks or other birds. **20** A course or change in a course. **21** A forecast or conjecture. **22** A contrivance; scheme. **23** A look; turning of a glance in a certain direction. ◆ Homophone: *caste.* [<ON *kasta* throw]
Cas·ta·li·a (kas·tā′lē·ə) A fountain on Mount Parnassus, near Delphi, sacred to Apollo and the Muses, and supposed to give inspiration to those who drank of it. Also **Cas·ta·ly** (kas′tə·lē). —**Cas·ta′li·an** *adj.*
cas·ta·net (kas′tə·net′) *n.* One of a pair of small concave disks of wood or ivory, clapped together with the fingers, as an accompaniment to song or dance. [<Sp. *castañeta,* dim. of *castaña* <L *castanea* chestnut]

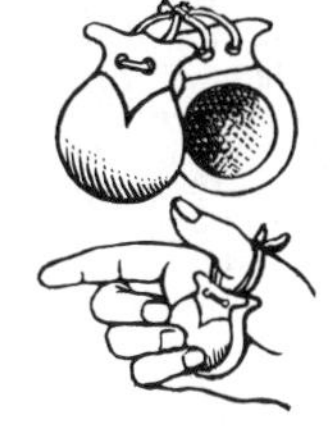
CASTANETS

cast·a·way (kast′ə·wā′, käst′-) *adj.* **1** Adrift; shipwrecked. **2** Thrown away; discarded. —*n.* One who is wrecked, adrift, or abandoned; an outcast.
caste (kast, käst) *n.* **1** One of the hereditary classes into which Hindu society is divided in India. **2** The principle or practice of such division or the position it confers. **3** The division of society on artificial grounds; a social class. **4** Reputation; standing. See synonyms under CLASS. —**to lose caste** To lose one's former or rightful position in a community; lose standing. ◆ Homophone: *cast.* [<Pg. *casta* unmixed breed <L *castus* pure]
cas·tel·lan (kas′tə·lən) *n.* The keeper or commander of a castle; a chatelain. [<AF *castelain* <L *castellanus* < *castellum* castle]
cas·tel·lat·ed (kas′tə·lā′tid) *adj.* **1** Having battlements; built like a castle; fortified. **2** Having a castle or castles. [<Med. L *castellatus,* pp. of *castellare* build a castle <L *castellum* castle] —**cas′tel·la′tion** *n.*
Cas·tel·lón de la Pla·na (käs′tā·lyōn′ dā lä plä′nä) A port in eastern Spain.
Cas·tel·ros·so (käs·tel′rōs′sō) See KASTELLORIZO.
cas·tel·ry (kas′əl·rē, käs′-) *n. pl.* **·ries 1** The government, tenure, or jurisdiction of a castle. **2** The territory subject to the lord of the castle. Also spelled *castlery.*
Cas·tel·ve·tro (käs·tel′vā′trō), **Lodovico,** 1505–71, Italian critic.
cast·er (kas′tər, käs′-) *n.* **1** One who or that which casts. **2** A cruet for condiments. **3** A swiveling roller fastened under an article of furniture, or a similar mounting for wheels, etc. **4** An axle offset on a motor vehicle. Also *castor* for defs. 2 and 3.
cas·ti·gate (kas′tə·gāt) *v.t.* **·gat·ed, ·gat·ing** To punish with or as with the rod; chastise. See synonyms under BEAT, CHASTEN. [<L *castigatus,* pp. of *castigare* chasten, ult. < *castus* pure] —**cas′ti·ga′tion** *n.* —**cas′ti·ga′tor** *n.* —**cas·ti·ga·to·ry** (kas′ti·gə·tôr′ē, -tō′rē) *adj.*
Cas·ti·glio·ne (käs′tē·lyô′nā), **Count Bal·das·sa·re** (bäl′däs·sä′rā), 1478–1529, Italian diplomat; author of *The Courtier.*
Cas·tile (kas·tēl′) A region and former kingdom in northern and central Spain. *Spanish* **Cas·til·la** (käs·tē′lyä).
Cas·tile soap (kas′tēl, kas·tēl′) A hard, white, odorless soap made with olive oil.
Cas·til·ian (kas·til′yən) *n.* **1** A citizen of Castile. **2** The official and literary form of Spanish as used in Spain; originally, the dialect of Castile. —*adj.* Pertaining to Castile: in Spanish, **cas·tel·la·no** (käs′tā·lyä′nō).
cast·ing (kas′ting, käs′-) *n.* **1** The act of cast-

ing. 2 That which is cast. 3 Any substance, as metal or plastics, cast in a mold.

casting vote See under VOTE.

cast iron *Metall.* Commercial iron produced in a blast furnace and containing a large proportion of carbon. It may be hard and brittle or soft and strong.

cast–i·ron (kast′ī′ərn, käst′-) *adj.* 1 Made of cast iron. 2 Like cast iron; rigid; unyielding.

cas·tle (kas′əl, käs′-) *n.* 1 A strong fortress. 2 Any massive or imposing building; hence, any place of defense and security. 3 A castle-shaped chessman; a rook. 4 A close helmet; casque. 5 A wooden tower on the back of an elephant. See synonyms under FORTIFICATION. —*v.* **·tled, ·tling** *v.t.* 1 To place in or as in a castle; fortify. 2 In chess, to move the king two squares to the right or left, at the same time bringing the castle (rook) from that side of the board toward which the king is moved to the square over which the king has passed. —*v.i.* 3 In chess, to move the castle and king in this manner. [Fusion of OE *castel* village and AF *castel* castle, both <L *castellum,* dim. of *castrum* camp, fort]

cas·tled (kas′əld, käs′-) *adj.* 1 Having or furnished with a castle or castles. 2 Castellated; fortified.

castle in the air A fanciful, impractical scheme: also called **castle in Spain.**

Cas·tle·reagh (kas′əl·rā, käs′-), **Viscount,** 1769–1822, Robert Stewart, second Marquis of Londonderry, English statesman.

cas·tle·ry (kas′əl·rē, käs′-) See CASTELRY.

cast–off (kast′ôf′, -of′, käst′-) *adj.* Thrown or laid aside; discarded: *cast–off* garments. —*n.* 1 *Printing* A computation of the space required by any matter to be printed. 2 A person or thing no longer wanted or used.

cas·tor[1] (kas′tər, käs′-) *n.* 1 A beaver, or its fur. 2 A hat of beaver or other fur; also, a silk hat. 3 An oily odorous secretion of beavers: used in medicine and perfumery: also **cas·to·re·um** (kas·tôr′ē·əm, -tō′rē·əm). [<L <Gk. *kastōr* beaver]

cas·tor[2] (kas′tər, käs′-) See CASTER (defs. 2 and 3).

Cas·tor and Pol·lux (kas′tər, käs′-; pol′əks) 1 In Greek mythology, the Dioscuri, twin sons of Leda and brothers of Helen and Clytemnestra, set by Zeus among the stars. 2 *Astron.* The two brightest stars in the constellation Gemini.

castor bean 1 The seed of the castor-oil plant. 2 The plant.

castor oil A viscous fixed oil, colorless or pale yellow, extracted from the seeds of the castor–oil plant: used as a cathartic and lubricant.

cas·tor–oil plant (kas′tər·oil′, käs′-) A herbaceous plant *(Ricinus communis)* of the spurge family, native in India but widely naturalized in warm climates, yielding the castor bean: also called *palma–Christi.*

cas·tra·me·ta·tion (kas′trə·mə·tā′shən) *n.* The art or act of, or plan for, laying out a camp, especially an army camp. [<F *castramétation* <L *castrum* camp + *metari* measure, lay out]

cas·trate (kas′trāt) *v.t.* **·trat·ed, ·trat·ing** 1 To remove the testicles from; emasculate; geld. 2 To remove the ovaries from; spay. 3 To expurgate, as a book; mutilate. [<L *castratus,* pp. of *castrare* castrate] —**cas·tra′tion** *n.*

Cas·tries (kàs·trē′, käs′trēs) The capital of St. Lucia, Windward Islands: also *Port Castries.*

Cas·tri·o·ta (kas′trē·ō′tə), **George.** See SCANDERBEG.

Cas·tro (käs′trō, kas′-), **Fidel,** born 1926, Cuban revolutionary leader; premier 1959–

Cas·tro·ism (kas′trō·iz·əm) *n.* The revolutionary doctrines and practices associated with Fidel Castro.

Ca·strop–Rau·xel (käs′trəp·rouk′səl) A city in the Ruhr valley, North Rhine–Westphalia, Germany.

cast steel *Metall.* Steel cast in molds to provide special machine parts or other articles.

cas·u·al (kazh′o͞o·əl) *adj.* 1 Occurring by chance; accidental; unusual. 2 Occurring at irregular intervals; occasional. 3 *Brit.* Of or pertaining to laborers, vagrants, or paupers who receive temporary aid or shelter. 4 Nonchalant; careless. 5 Unmethodical; haphazard. 6 Of, pertaining to, or caused by accident; a *casual* patient. 7 Informal: *casual* clothes. 8 *Obs.* Precarious. See synonyms under INCIDENTAL. —*n.* 1 A casual laborer, patient, or pauper. 2 A chance visitor. 3 *Mil.* A soldier subject to individual regulation because of his physical separation from an organization or lack of assignment or attachment to one. [<F *casuel* <L *casualis* < *casus* accident < *cadere* fall] —**cas′u·al·ly** *adv.* —**cas′u·al·ness** *n.*

cas·u·al·ism (kazh′o͞o·əl·iz′əm) *n.* The doctrine that chance prevails in all things. —**cas′u·al·ist** *n.*

cas·u·al·ty (kazh′o͞o·əl·tē) *n. pl.* **·ties** 1 A fatal or serious accident. 2 A chance occurrence. 3 *Mil.* **a** A soldier missing in action or removed from active duty by death, wounds, or capture. **b** *pl.* Losses arising from death, wounds, illness, capture, or desertion. See synonyms under ACCIDENT, HAZARD.

casual water Water which has temporarily accumulated on a golf course, but is not treated as a hazard except where it lodges in a bunker.

cas·u·ist (kazh′o͞o·ist) *n.* A theologian, philosopher, etc., who studies or resolves ethical problems or cases of conscience involving a seeming conflict of right and wrong: often used derogatorily. [<F *casuiste* <L *casus* event, case]

cas·u·is·tic (kazh′o͞o·is′tik) *adj.* 1 Pertaining to a casuist or casuistry. 2 Sophistical; equivocal. Also **cas′u·is′ti·cal.** —**cas′u·is′ti·cal·ly** *adv.*

cas·u·ist·ry (kazh′o͞o·is·trē) *n. pl.* **·ries** 1 The science or doctrine of resolving doubtful cases of conscience or questions of right and wrong according to the injunctions of sacred books or of individual authority or social conventions: often used derogatorily. 2 Sophistical or equivocal reasoning.

ca·sus (kā′səs) *n. Law.* 1 That which happens; an occurrence. 2 An accident or calamity. 3 An occasion; case. [<L]

ca·sus bel·li (kā′səs bel′ī) *Latin* An occurrence held to warrant hostilities; a cause for war.

cat (kat) *n.* 1 A domesticated carnivorous mammal *(Felis domestica)* with retractile claws: it kills mice and rats and is of world-wide distribution in various breeds. ◆ Collateral adjective: *feline.* 2 Any animal of the cat family *(Felidae),* as a lion, tiger, lynx, ocelot, etc. 3 *Naut.* A purchase for hoisting an anchor. 4 A whip with nine lashes; a cat-o′–nine–tails. 5 A catboat. 6 A double-pointed piece of wood used in the game of tipcat; also, the game. 7 A game of ball, called from the number of batters *one old* (or *o′*) *cat, two old cat,* etc. 8 *Colloq.* A spiteful woman given to gossip and scandal. 9 *Colloq.* A prostitute. 10 *U.S. Colloq.* A Caterpillar tractor. 11 *U.S. Slang* A musician in a jazz band. —**to let the cat out of the bag** To divulge a secret. —**see which way the cat jumps** See how things turn out. —*v.t.* **cat·ted, cat·ting** To hoist or raise to and fasten at the cathead, as an anchor. 2 To flog with a cat-o′–nine–tails. [OE *cat, catte*]

cata– *prefix* 1 Down; against; upon: *cataclysm.* 2 Back; over: *cataphonic.* 3 With a pejorative or intensive sense: *cataphyllon.* Also, before vowels, **cat–;** before *h,* **cath–.** [<Gk. *kata-* < *kata* down, against, back]

ca·tab·a·sis (kə·tab′ə·sis) *n. pl.* **·ses** (-sēz) 1 A going downward; descent: opposed to *anabasis.* 2 *Pathol.* The decreasing of a disease. [<Gk. *katabasis* < *kata-* down + *bainein* go] —**cat·a·bat·ic** (kat′ə·bat′ik) *adj.*

ca·tab·o·lism (kə·tab′ə·liz′əm) *n. Biol.* The series of changes by which living matter or protoplasm breaks down into less complex and more stable substances within a cell or organism; destructive metabolism: opposed to *anabolism.* Also spelled *katabolism.* [<Gk. *katabolē* destruction < *kata-* down + *ballein* throw] —**cat·a·bol·ic** (kat′ə·bol′ik) *adj.* —**cat′a·bol′i·cal·ly** *adv.*

ca·tab·o·lite (kə·tab′ə·līt) *n.* Any product resulting from catabolism.

cat·a·caus·tic (kat′ə·kôs′tik) *adj. Optics* Denoting a caustic curve formed by reflected rays of light: opposed to *diacaustic.* —*n.* A catacaustic curve. [<CATA- + CAUSTIC (def. 3)]

cat·a·chre·sis (kat′ə·krē′sis) *n.* 1 The misuse of a word; application of a meaning to a word not its own, as *asset* used in the sense of *advantage*; also, a mixed or strained metaphor. 2 The use of a wrong form of a word, through a misunderstanding of its etymology. [<L <Gk. *katachrēsis* < *kata-* against + *chraesthai* use] —**cat·a·chres·tic** (kat′ə·kres′tik) or **·ti·cal** *adj.* —**cat′a·chres′ti·cal·ly** *adv.*

cat·a·cli·nal (kat′ə·klī′nəl) *adj. Geol.* Running in the direction of the dip: said of a valley: distinguished from *anaclinal.* [<Gk. *kataklinēs* sloping < *kata-* down + *klinein* bend]

cat·a·clysm (kat′ə·kliz′əm) *n.* 1 An overwhelming flood. 2 *Geol.* Any violent and extensive subversion of the ordinary phenomena of nature on the earth's surface. 3 Any sudden overwhelming change or political or social upheaval. See synonyms under CATASTROPHE. [<Gk. *kataklysmos* flood < *kata-* down + *klyzein* wash] —**cat·a·clys·mal** (kat′ə·kliz′məl), **cat′a·clys′mic, cat′a·clys·mat′ic** (-kliz·mat′ik) *adj.*

cat·a·comb (kat′ə·kōm) *n. Usually pl.* A long underground gallery with excavations in its sides for tombs or in which human bones are stacked or piled. [<F *catacombe* <LL *catacumbas*]

ca·tad·ro·mous (kə·tad′rə·məs) *adj. Zool.* Running down: said of fishes that go down rivers to the sea to spawn: opposed to *anadromous.* [<CATA- + -DROMOUS]

cat·a·falque (kat′ə·falk) *n.* 1 A temporary raised structure or staging that supports the coffin, usually draped, of a deceased personage lying in state. 2 The drapery on or the hangings over it. 3 A stately funeral car. [<F <Ital. *catafalco*]

Cat·a·lan (kat′ə·lan, -lən) *adj.* Of or pertaining to Catalonia, a former province of Spain, its people, or their language. —*n.* 1 One of Catalonian descent or blood. 2 The Romance language of Catalonia and Valencia, closely related to Provençal.

cat·a·lase (kat′ə·lās) *n. Biochem.* An animal and vegetable enzyme which decomposes hydrogen peroxide into water and oxygen. [<CATAL(YSIS) + -ASE]

Ça·tal·ca (chä′täl·jä′) A town near Istanbul, Turkey: also *Chatalja.*

cat·a·lec·tic (kat′ə·lek′tik) *adj.* In prosody, describing a line of verse which terminates in an incomplete foot. [<Gk. *katalēktikos* < *kata-* wholly + *lēgein* stop]

cat·a·lep·sy (kat′ə·lep′sē) *n. Psychiatry* Inordinate maintenance of physical postures; muscular rigidity: common in certain nervous diseases, especially hysteria and schizophrenia. [<Med. L *catalepsia* <Gk. *katalēpsis* < *kata-* upon + *lēpsis* seizure < *lambanein* grasp] —**cat′a·lep′tic** (-lep′tik) *adj.* & *n.*

Cat·a·li·na Island (kat′ə·lē′nə) See SANTA CATALINA.

cat·a·lo (kat′ə·lō) *n. pl.* **·loes** or **·los** A fertile hybrid between the bison and the domestic cow: also spelled *cattalo.* [<CAT(TLE) + (BUFF)ALO]

cat·a·log (kat′ə·lôg, -log) *n.* 1 A list or enumeration of names, persons or things, usually in alphabetical order, sometimes with accompanying description. 2 A publication listing wares for sale by a commercial establishment: a mail-order *catalog.* See synonyms under RECORD. —*v.* **·loged, ·log·ing** *v.t.* To make an alphabetical list of; insert in a catalog. —*v.i.* To work upon or make such a list. [<F <LL *catalogus* <Gk. *katalogos* list < *kata-* down + *legein* select, choose] —**cat′a·log′er, cat′a·log′ist** *n.*

cat·a·logue (kat′ə·lôg, -log) *n., v.t.* & *v.i.* **·logued, ·logu·ing** Catalog. —**cat′a·logu′er, cat′a·logu′ist** *n.*

ca·ta·logue rai·son·né (kà·tà·lôg′ re·zô·nā′) *French* A catalog or list classified by subjects, often with explanatory notes.

Cat·a·lo·ni·a (kat′ə·lō′nē·ə) A region of NE Spain; 12,332 square miles. *Spanish* **Ca·ta·lu·ña** (kä′tä·lo͞o′nyä). —**Cat′a·lo′ni·an** *adj.* & *n.*

ca·tal·pa (kə·tal′pə) *n.* A tree (genus *Catalpa*) of the bignonia family of China, Japan, and North America, having large, ovate leaves, large, fragrant bell–shaped flowers, and long slender pods. [<N. Am. Ind.]

ca·tal·y·sis (kə·tal′ə·sis) *n. pl.* **·ses** (-sēz) *Chem.* An alteration in the speed of a chemical reaction effected by the presence of an agent or substance that itself remains stable. [<Gk. *katalysis* dissolution < *kata-* wholly, completely + *lyein* loosen] —**cat·a·lyt·ic** (kat′ə·lit′ik) *adj.* & *n.*

cat·a·lyst (kat′ə·list) *n. Chem.* Any substance or agent that causes catalysis. A **positive cata-**

lyst accelerates the speed of the reaction; a **negative catalyst** retards it.

CATAMARAN
Twin-hulled
Tahitian
war canoe.

cat·a·lyze (kat′ə·līz) *v.t.* **·lyzed, ·lyz·ing** To submit to or decompose by catalysis. —**cat′a·lyz′er** *n.*

cat·a·ma·ran (kat′ə·mə·ran′) *n. Naut.* **1** A long, narrow raft of logs, often with an outrigger. **2** A life raft of two pointed metal cylinders connected by a platform. **3** A boat having twin hulls. [<Tamil *kaṭṭa-maram* tied wood]

Ca·ta·mar·ca (kä′tä·mär′kä) A province of NW Argentina; 45,829 square miles; capital, Catamarca.

cat·a·me·ni·a (kat′ə·mē′nē·ə) *n. pl. Physiol.* The menses. [<Gk. *katamēnia,* neut. pl. of *katamēnios* monthly < *kata-* by + *mēn* month] —**cat′a·me′ni·al** *adj.*

cat·a·mite (kat′ə·mīt) *n.* A boy used in pederasty. [<L *Catamitus,* alter. of Gk. *Ganymēdēs,* the cupbearer of Zeus]

cat·am·ne·sis (kat′əm·nē′sis) *n. Med.* The history of a patient subsequent to his illness and recovery: distinguished from *anamnesis.* [<NL <Gk. *kata-* down + *-mnēsis* recollection < *mimnēskein* remember] —**cat′am·nes′·tic** (-nes′tik) *adj.*

cat·a·mount (kat′ə·mount) *n.* **1** A wildcat. **2** A cougar or lynx. **3** A catamountain. [Short form of CATAMOUNTAIN]

cat·a·moun·tain (kat′ə·moun′tən) *n.* **1** A catamount. **2** One of various wildcats, as a leopard or panther. [Short form of *cat of the mountain*]

Ca·ta·nia (kä·tä′nyä) The second largest city in Sicily, a port on the **Gulf of Catania,** an inlet of the Ionian Sea in eastern Sicily.

Ca·tan·za·ro (kä′tän·dzä′rō) A port in SE Calabria, Italy.

cat·a·phon·ic (kat′ə·fon′ik) *adj. Physics* Relating to or produced by the reflection of sound. [CATA- + Gk. *phōnē* sound]

cat·a·phon·ics (kat′ə·fon′iks) *n. Physics* The study of the reflection of sound.

cat·a·pho·re·sis (kat′ə·fə·rē′sis) *n.* **1** The movement of medicinal substances in or through living tissue under the influence of an electric field. **2** Electrophoresis. [<NL <Gk. *kata-* down + *phorēsis* carrying < *pherein* bear, carry] —**cat′a·pho·ret′ic** (-ret′ik) *adj.*

cat·a·phyll (kat′ə·fil) *n. Bot.* A rudimentary or scalelike leaf which forms the covering of a bud. [<CATA- + Gk. *phyllon* leaf]

cat·a·pla·si·a (kat′ə·plā′zhē·ə, -zē·ə) *n. Pathol.* A reversion of cells or tissues to a more primitive or embryonic form. Also **ca·tap·la·sis** (kə·tap′lə·sis). [<NL <Gk. *kata-* back + *-plasia* a molding < *plassein* form, mold]

cat·a·plasm (kat′ə·plaz′əm) *n.* A soothing poultice, often medicated. [<Gk. *kataplasma*]

cat·a·plex·y (kat′ə·plek′sē) *n. Psychiatry* A temporary paroxysmic rigidity of the muscles often caused by sudden emotional shock. [<Gk. *kataplēxis* amazement < *kataplēssein* astound < *kata-* down + *plēssein* strike] —**cat′a·plec′tic** (-plek′tik) *adj.*

cat·a·pult (kat′ə·pult) *n.* **1** An engine of ancient warfare for throwing bombs, grenades, stones, spears, or arrows. **2** A toy consisting of an elastic band attached to the prongs of a forked stick: used by boys for throwing missiles. **3** *Aeron.* A device for launching an airplane at flight speed, as from the deck of a ship not having a flight deck. —*v.t.* To hurl from or as from a catapult. —*v.i.* To hurtle through the air as if from a catapult. [<L *catapulta* <Gk. *katapeltēs* < *kata-* down + *pallein* brandish, hurl]

CATAPULT
For ship-borne airplanes.

cat·a·ract (kat′ə·rakt) *n.* **1** A waterfall of great size. **2** *Pathol.* Opacity of the crystalline lens of the eye. **3** A heavy downpour or flood of water; a deluge. [<F *cataracte* <L *cataracta* <Gk. *kataraktēs* < *kata-* down + *arassein* fall headlong]

ca·tarrh (kə·tär′) *n. Pathol.* Excessive secretion from an inflamed mucous membrane, especially of the air passages of the throat and head. [<F *catarrhe* <L *catarrhus* <Gk. *katarrhoos* < *kata-* down + *rheein* flow] —**ca·tarrh′al** *adj.* —**ca·tarrh′ous** *adj.*

ca·tas·ta·sis (kə·tas′tə·sis) *n. pl.* **·ses** (-sēz) **1** In the ancient drama, the heightened part of the action that prepares for the catastrophe. **2** In oratory, the exordium of a speech, especially the part designed to conciliate the audience. [<Gk. *katastasis* settled condition < *kata-* down + *stasis* a settling < *histanai* stand]

ca·tas·tro·phe (kə·tas′trə·fē) *n.* **1** Any final event; a fatal conclusion; great and sudden misfortune. **2** In a drama, the conclusion or unraveling of the plot; the dénouement. **3** A sudden, violent change, especially of the earth's surface; cataclysm. [<Gk. *katastrophē* < *kata-* over, down + *strephein* turn] —**cat·a·stroph·ic** (kat′ə·strof′ik) *adj.*

Synonyms: calamity, cataclysm, dénouement, disaster, mischance, misfortune, mishap, sequel. A *cataclysm* or *catastrophe* is some great convulsion or momentous event that may or may not be a cause of misery to man. In *calamity,* or *disaster,* the thought of human suffering is always present. It has been held by many geologists that numerous *catastrophes* or *cataclysms* antedated the existence of man. In literature the final event of a drama is the *catastrophe,* or *dénouement. Misfortune* ordinarily suggests less of suddenness and violence than *calamity* or *disaster,* and is especially applied to that which is lingering or enduring in its effects. Pestilence is a *calamity*; a defeat in battle, a shipwreck, a failure in business are *disasters*; sickness, loss of property are *misfortunes*; failure to meet a friend is a *mischance*; the breaking of a teacup is a *mishap.* Compare ACCIDENT, MISFORTUNE. *Antonyms*: benefit, blessing, boon, comfort, favor, help, pleasure, privilege, prosperity, success.

ca·tas·tro·phism (kə·tas′trə·fiz′əm) *n. Geol.* The theory or doctrine which attributes the principal stratigraphic and paleontological changes of the earth to sudden and violent physical upheavals. —**ca·tas′tro·phist** *n.*

cat·a·to·ni·a (kat′ə·tō′nē·ə) *n. Psychiatry* A complex of symptoms typical of schizophrenia, characterized by stupor, muscular rigidity, and occasional mental agitation. [<NL < *kata-* down + *tonos* tension, tone < *teinein* stretch] —**cat′a·ton′ic** (-ton′ik) *adj.*

cat·a·wam·pus (kat′ə·wom′pəs) *U.S. Colloq. adj.* **1** Malicious; resentful. **2** Askew; catercornered. —*n.* **1** A malicious person. **2** A hobgoblin or bogy. Also spelled *cattywampus.* [Origin unknown]

Ca·taw·ba (kə·tô′bə) *n.* **1** One of a tribe of North American Indians, the most important eastern tribe of Siouan linguistic stock, formerly occupying the region along the Catawba River, South Carolina. **2** An American red grape. **3** A dry white wine made from it.

Catawba River A river rising in North Carolina and flowing 295 miles south to South Carolina, where it is called the Wateree.

cat·bird (kat′bûrd′) *n.* A small slate-colored North American songbird *(Dumetella carolinensis),* related to the mockingbird: named from its catlike cry.

catbird seat *U.S. Colloq.* The most advantageous and powerful position.

cat·block (kat′blok′) *n. Naut.* A heavy hoisting block used in catting an anchor.

cat·boat (kat′bōt′) *n. Naut.* A small one-masted sailboat, usually equipped with a centerboard and having its mast stepped well forward and carrying a single fore-and-aft sail with boom and gaff.

cat·bri·er (kat′brī′ər) *n.* Any of certain woody vines of the genus *Smilax,* especially the greenbrier.

cat·call (kat′kôl′) *n.* A shrill, discordant call or whistle, in token of impatience or derision. —*v.t.* To deride or express disapproval of with catcalls. —*v.i.* To utter catcalls.

catch (kach) *v.* **caught, catch·ing** *v.t.* **1** To take, seize, or come upon, as something departing or fleeing; take captive; capture. **2** To entrap; ensnare. **3** To captivate, gain, or hold. **4** To apprehend or perceive clearly. **5** To surprise; detect, as in a misdeed. **6** To contract; incur, as a disease. **7** To arrive at or take, as a train or boat, just before its departure. **8** To arrest the motion of; entangle. **9** To grasp and retain. **10** To perceive, as something fleeting, with momentary distinction: to *catch* sight of. **11** To reach, as a person, with a blow: She *caught* him a box on the ear. —*v.i.* **12** To make a movement of grasping or seizing: He *caught* at the idea. **13** In baseball, to act as catcher. **14** To become entangled or fastened. **15** To be communicated or communicable, as a disease or enthusiasm. **16** To take fire; kindle; ignite. **17** *Naut.* To catch the wind: an elliptical expression. —**to catch it** *Colloq.* To receive a reprimand, scolding, drubbing, or the like. —**to catch (one) napping** To take off guard; outwit. —**to catch on** *Colloq.* **1** To understand. **2** To become popular or fashionable. —**to catch out 1** In baseball, to put a batter out by catching the ball. **2** To discover (someone) in error. —**to catch up 1** To overtake. **2** To regain by or as if by overtaking: to *catch up* on one's lessons. —**to catch up with** (or **up to**) To overtake. —*n.* **1** The act of catching; the act of grasping or seizing; specifically, the act of catching a batted or thrown ball before it reaches the ground, as in baseball, cricket, etc.; also a catcher. **2** A hold or grip, as in wrestling. **3** That which catches or fastens; a fastening. **4** That which is or may be caught or gained, such as a person or thing worth obtaining, as in marriage. **5** The amount of fish or the like caught at one time or in a given period. **6** The state in which or the extent to which a crop germinates. **7** An artful trick or question. **8** An impediment; a break, as in the voice or breathing. **9** *Music* A round; also, a scrap of song. —*adj.* Attracting or meant to attract notice; catchy; a *catch* phrase. [<AF *cachier* <LL *captiare,* freq. of *capere* take, hold. Doublet of CHASE.]

Synonyms (verb): apprehend, capture, clasp, clutch, comprehend, discover, ensnare, entrap, grasp, grip, gripe, overtake, secure, seize, snatch, take. To *catch* is to come up with or take possession of something departing, fugitive, or illusive. We *catch* a runaway horse, a flying ball, a mouse in a trap. To "catch at" is to attempt to *catch,* often unsuccessfully. We *clutch* with a swift, tenacious movement of the fingers; we *grasp* with a firm closure of the whole hand; we *grip* or *gripe* with the strongest muscular closure of the whole hand possible to exert. We *clasp* in the arms. We *snatch* with a quick, sudden, and usually a surprising motion. In the figurative sense, *catch* is used of any act that brings a person or thing into our power or possession; as, to *catch* a criminal in the act; to *catch* an idea, in the sense of *apprehend* or *comprehend.* Compare ARREST, GRASP. *Antonyms*: lose, miss, release, restore.

catch-all (kach′ôl′) *n.* A bag or the like to hold odds and ends.

catch basin A filter at the entrance to a drain or sewer to stop matter which might clog the pipes.

catch crop *Agric.* A quick-growing crop raised between two main crops, when the ground would otherwise be idle.

catch·er (kach′ər) *n.* **1** One who or that which catches. **2** In baseball, the player stationed behind home plate to catch balls that pass the batter.

catch·fly (kach′flī) *n.* Any one of several weeds (genus *Silene*) of the pink family, the stem and calyx of which exude a viscid fluid which holds small insects alighting on it.

catch·ing (kach′ing) *adj.* **1** Infectious. **2** Captivating

catch·ment (kach′mənt) *n.* **1** Drainage. **2** The collection of water over a natural drainage area. **3** The water so collected.

catchment basin *Geog.* The area drained by a river or river system. Also **catchment area.**

catch·pen·ny (kach′pen′ē) *adj.* Cheap, poor, and showy. —*n. pl.* **·nies** An inferior article, made to attract buyers.

catch·pole (kach′pōl) *n.* **1** A medieval weapon for catching a person out of arm's reach. **2** One who arrests for debt; a bailiff; taxgatherer: also **catch′poll.** [< Med. L *cacepollus* chaser of fowl]

catch·up (kach′əp, kech′-) See KETCHUP.

catch·weed (kach′wēd′) *n.* Cleavers.

catch·weight (kach′wāt′) *n.* In certain sports, the weight of a contestant as determined by his own discretion, rather than by rule or agreement.

catch·word (kach′wûrd′) *n.* **1** A word or phrase to catch the popular fancy or attention, especially, a word or phrase used as a slogan in a political campaign. **2** In the theater, a cue. **3** A word so placed as to catch the attention. **4** An isolated word at the bottom of a page in old books, inserted to connect the text with the beginning of the next page. **5** A word at the head of a page or column, as of a dictionary, encyclopedia, etc.

catch·y (kach′ē) *adj.* **·i·er, ·i·est 1** Attractive; taking. **2** Entangling; deceptive, puzzling. **3** Broken; fitful.

cate (kāt) *n. Archaic* Delicate or luxurious food: usually in plural. [Earlier *acate* < AF *acat* provision, purchase < *acater* buy]

cat·e·che·sis (kat′ə·kē′sis) *n. pl.* **·ses** (-sēz) **1** Oral instruction in the elements of Christianity, as given to a catechumen; catechizing. **2** A catechetic discourse or writing. [< Gk. *katēchēsis* instruction]

cat·e·chet·ic (kat′ə·ket′ik) *adj.* **1** Of or pertaining to oral instruction: consisting of question and answer. **2** Of or pertaining to instruction in the elementary doctrines of Christianity. Also **cat′e·chet′i·cal.**

cat·e·chin (kat′ə·chin, -kin) *n. Chem.* An amorphous yellow powder, $C_{15}H_{14}O_6·4H_2O$, contained in catechu: used in dyeing.

cat·e·chism (kat′ə·kiz′əm) *n.* **1** A short treatise giving in catechetic form an outline of the fundamental principles of a religious creed. **2** Any brief manual of instruction by questions and answers; an examination of candidates by interrogatories. **3** Catechetic instruction, especially in religious doctrine. [< Med. L *catechismus* < Gk. *katēchizein* instruct]

cat·e·chist (kat′ə·kist) *n.* One who teaches by question and answer; especially, an instructor of catechumens or new converts. Also **cat′e·chiz′er, cat′e·chis′er.** —**cat′e·chis′tic** or **·ti·cal** *adj.*

cat·e·chize (kat′ə·kīz) *v.t.* **·chized, ·chiz·ing 1** To interrogate seriously as to conduct or belief. **2** To question in a searching manner, especially with a view to judgment or reproof. **3** To give systematic oral instruction to; instruct in elementary truths of religion; teach by means of a catechism. **4** To teach the catechism to, as in preparation for confirmation. Also **cat′e·chise.** [< L *catechizare* instruct < Gk. *katēchizein*] —**cat′e·chi·za′tion** *n.*

cat·e·chol (kat′ə·chōl, -kōl) *n. Chem.* Pyrocatechol. [< CATECHU]

cat·e·chol·a·mine (kat′ə·chōl′ə·mēn, -kōl′-) *n.* Any of various amines chemically related to pyrocatechol and having a hormonal effect on the sympathetic nervous system, including epinephrine, norepinephrine, and dopamine.

cat·e·chu (kat′ə·chōō) *n.* A resinous astringent and tanning extract prepared from the wood of various Asian and East Indian plants, especially *Acacia catechu.* Also called *cashoo, cutch.* [< NL < Malay *kachu*] —**cat′e·chu′ic** *adj.*

cat·e·chu·men (kat′ə·kyōō′mən) *n.* **1** One who is under instruction in the elements of Christianity; especially, a new or a young convert in the ancient church; a beginner. **2** One undergoing initiation in any science, art, set of opinions, etc. [< L *catechumenus* < Gk. *katēchoumenos,* ppr. passive of *katēchēein* instruct] —**cat′e·chu′me·nal, cat·e·chu·men·i·cal** (kat′ə·kyōō·men′i·kəl) *adj.*

cat·e·gor·e·mat·ic (kat′ə·gôr′ə·mat′ik, -gor′-) *adj. Logic* Capable of being used alone as the complete subject or predicate of a proposition: opposed to *syncategorematic.* [< Gk. *katēgorēma* logical predicate]

cat·e·gor·i·cal (kat′ə·gôr′i·kəl, -gor′-) *adj.* **1** Without qualification; absolute; unequivocal. **2** or pertaining to a category; in the form of a category. —**cat′e·gor′i·cal·ly** *adv.* —**cat′e·gor′i·cal·ness** *n.*

categorical imperative *Philos.* The principle established by Immanuel Kant, which states, "Act in such a way that the maxim of your will can simultaneously apply as the basis for a universal law."

cat·e·go·rize (kat′ə·gə·rīz′) *v.t.* **·rized, ·riz·ing 1** To put into categories. **2** To treat categorically.

cat·e·go·ry (kat′ə·gôr′ē, -gō′rē) *n. pl.* **·ries 1** Any comprehensive class or description of things. **2** A class, condition, or predicament. **3** One of the several forms of conception or knowledge that together embrace everything predicable or existent. [< L *categoria* < Gk. *katēgoria* < *katēgoreein* allege, predicate < *kata-* against + *agora* public assembly]

cat·e·lec·trot·o·nus (kat′ə·lek·trot′ō·nəs) *Physiol.* A state of increased tension produced in a nerve fiber or muscle at the negative pole of an electric current passing through it. [< CAT(HODE) + ELECTROTONUS]

ca·te·na (kə·tē′nə) *n. pl.* **·nae** (-nē) A chain or closely connected series, usually with reference to succession in time; specifically, a series of excerpts from the works of the fathers of the Church to clear up some point, as of Scriptural exegesis. [< L, chain]

cat·e·nar·y (kat′ə·ner′ē, kə·tē′nə·rē) *n. pl.* **·ies** *Math.* The curve formed by a perfectly flexible, inextensible, infinitely slender cord suspended from two points not in the same vertical line; especially, the common catenary, represented by a chain freely suspended from two fixed points. —*adj.* Relating to or like a catenary or a chain: also **cat·e·nar·i·an** (kat′·ə·nâr′ē·ən). [< L *catenarius* < *catena* chain]

cat·e·nate (kat′ə·nāt) *v.t.* **·nat·ed, ·nat·ing** To connect like the links of a chain; form into a chain; link together. —**cat′e·na′tion** *n.*

cat·e·noid (kat′ə·noid) *n. Math.* The surface formed by the rotation of a catenary about its axis.

ca·ten·u·late (kə·ten′yə·lāt, -lit) *adj.* Consisting of little links; made up of parts united end to end in a chainlike series. [< L *catenula,* dim. of *catena* chain]

ca·ter (kā′tər) *v.t.* **1** To furnish food or entertainment. **2** To provide for the gratification of any need or taste. See synonyms under PROVIDE. [< AF *acater* buy < LL *acceptare* < *ad-* toward + *captare* grasp, seize] —**ca′ter·er** *n.*

cat·er-cor·nered (kat′ər·kôr′nərd) *adj.* Placed cornerwise or diagonally; diagonal: also *catty-cornered, kitty-cornered.* Also **cat′er-cor′ner.** [< *cater* diagonally < F *quatre* four < L *quattuor* + CORNERED]

ca·ter-cous·in (kā′tər·kuz′ən) *n. Obs.* **1** A fourth cousin; remote relative. **2** An intimate friend. [Origin uncertain]

cat·er·pil·lar (kat′ər·pil′ər) *n.* **1** The larva of a butterfly or moth (order *Lepidoptera*), or of certain other insects, as the sawfly. **2** Something resembling a caterpillar or its system of locomotion, as a car fitted with supplementary wheels or a device on the principle of the endless chain. [< AF *catepelose* hairy cat < L *catta* cat + *pilosus* < *pilum* hair]

CATERPILLAR
a. Swallowtail butterfly. *b.* Mourning cloak butterfly. *c.* Emperor moth. *d.* Puss moth. *e.* Eyed hawk moth. *f.* Great peacock moth. *g.* Pale tussock moth.

Cat·er·pil·lar (kat′ər·pil′ər) *n.* A tractor whose driving wheels gear with self-laid, wide metal belts whereby its weight is distributed over a large area, permitting the tractor to move over soft or rough terrain: a trade name.

caterpillar hunter Any of a genus *(Calosoma)* of carabid beetles which prey on caterpillars, especially *C. scrutator,* having dark green elytra. For illustration see INSECTS (beneficial).

cat·er·waul (kat′ər·wôl) *v.i.* **1** To utter the discordant cry peculiar to cats at rutting time. **2** To make any discordant screeching. **3** To argue or dispute noisily. —*n.* The cry of cats at rutting time; also, any similar cry. [ME *caterwawen* < *cater* cat (cf. G *kater* tomcat) + *wawen* wail, howl] —**cat′er·waul′ing** *n.*

Cates (kāts), **Clifton Bledsoe,** born 1893, U.S. Marine Corps general.

Cates·by (kāts′bē), **Mark,** 1679?–1749, English naturalist.

cat-eye (kat′ī′) *n.* A small knot in wood, usually one less than one fourth of an inch in diameter: also called *pin knot.*

cat·face (kat′fās′) *n.* A lesion on the surface of a tree caused by an injury or wound that has not completely healed.

cat·fall (kat′fôl′) *n. Naut.* The tackle for raising an anchor to the cathead.

cat·fish (kat′fish′) *n. pl.* **·fish** or **·fish·es 1** One of numerous silurid fishes, usually carnivorous and of fresh-water habitat, having sensitive barbels around the mouth to enable them to find their prey in muddy waters. **2** Any of many other teleost fishes, as the bullhead.

cat-foot·ed (kat′foot′id) *adj.* **1** Having digitigrade feet with retractile claws like a cat's. **2** Soft; stealthy.

cat·gut (kat′gut′) *n.* **1** A very tough cord, made from the intestines of certain animals, as sheep, and used for stringing musical instruments, making surgical ligatures, etc. **2** A violin or fiddle; hence, stringed instruments generally: a humorous use. **3** A leguminous perennial *(Tephrosia virginiana),* native in the eastern half of the United States.

cath- Var. of CATA-.

Cath·a·ri (kath′ə·rī) *n. pl.* Various Christian sects aiming at or claiming peculiar purity of life or doctrine, as the *Novatians* (3rd century), the *Albigenses* (12th century), and various others. [< Med.L < Gk. *katharos* pure] —**Cath′a·rist** (-rist) *n.* —**Cath′a·rism** *n.*

Cath·a·ri·na (kath′ə·rī′nə, *Pg.* kä′tə·rē′nə) See CATHERINE. Also **Cath·a·rine** (kath′ə·rin, kath′rin).

ca·thar·sis (kə·thär′sis) *n.* **1** *Med.* Purgation or cleansing of any passage of the body, especially of the alimentary canal. **2** A word used by Aristotle to express the effect of tragic drama in purifying and relieving the emotions. **3** *Psychoanal.* Abreaction. Also spelled *katharsis.* [< Gk. *katharsis* cleansing < *katharos* pure]

ca·thar·tic (kə·thär′tik) *adj.* Purgative; purifying: also **ca·thar′ti·cal.** —*n.* A purgative medicine. [< Gk. *kathartikos* < *katharos* pure] —**ca·thar′ti·cal·ly** *adv.*

Ca·thay (ka·thā′) *Poetic* or *Archaic* China.

cat·head (kat′hed′) *n. Naut.* A beam of wood or iron, projecting over the bow, by which the anchor is supported clear of the ship.

ca·the·dra (kə·thē′drə, kath′ə-) *n.* **1** A bishop's seat or throne in the cathedral or chief church of his diocese; hence, the see or dignity of a bishop. **2** A professor's chair. —**ex cathedra** *Latin* **1** Literally, from the seat: applied to a pronouncement on faith or morals by the Pope as head of the Roman Catholic Church. **2** With authority: also used attributively, meaning "officially spoken": an *ex cathedra* pronouncement. [< L < Gk. *kathedra* < *kata* down + *hedra* seat. Doublet of CHAIR.]

ca·the·dral (kə·thē′drəl) *n.* **1** The church containing the cathedra or official chair of the bishop; the mother church of a diocese. **2** Any large or important church. —*adj.* **1** Pertaining to or containing a bishop's chair or see. **2** Of or pertaining to any chair of authority; authoritative; dogmatic. **3** Of, pertaining to, belonging to, or resembling a cathedral: a *cathedral* choir.

cathedral schools Elementary schools founded by the bishops of the Middle Ages and erected close to their cathedrals.

Cath·er (kath′ər), **Willa Sibert,** 1876–1947, U.S. author.

Cath·e·rine (kath′ə·rin, kath′rin, *Fr.* kȧ·trēn′) A feminine personal name. [<Gk.; meaning uncertain]

—**Catherine, Saint** A virgin of Alexandria who, in the fourth century, professed Christianity and died by torture on the wheel.

—**Catherine I,** 1680?–1727, empress of Russia; wife of Peter the Great.

—**Catherine II,** 1729–96; empress of Russia 1762–96: known as **Catherine the Great.**

—**Catherine de Medici** See MEDICI.

—**Catherine of Aragon,** 1485–1536, first wife of Henry VIII of England; divorced 1533.

—**Catherine of Braganza,** 1638–1705, queen of Charles II of England.

Catherine, Mount See KATHERINA, GEBEL.

catherine wheel 1 A rotating firework; a pinwheel, especially a large, showy one. **2** *Her.* The figure of a wheel with the tire armed with hooks, to represent the legendary instrument of St. Catherine's martyrdom.

cath·e·ter (kath′ə·tər) *n. Med.* A slender, tubular, surgical instrument for introduction into canals or passages. [<L <Gk. *katheter* < *kata-* down + *hienai* send, let go]

cath·e·ter·ize (kath′ə·tər·īz′) *v.t.* **·ized, ·iz·ing** To introduce a catheter into.

ca·thex·is (kə·thek′sis) *n. Psychoanal.* **1** Concentration of psychic energy upon the self, another person, a phantasy, idea, or object. **2** The investment or charging of an idea or emotion with significance. [<Gk. *kathexis* holding <*kata-* thoroughly + *echein* hold, have; trans. of G *besetzung*]

cath·ode (kath′ōd) *n. Electr.* The electrode through which negative ions leave a non–metallic conductor and toward which positive ions flow from the anode. It is negative for a battery, electrolytic bath, or a vacuum tube, but positive for a voltaic cell: also spelled *kathode.* [< Gk. *kathodos* a way down <*kata-* down + *hodos* road, way] —**ca·thod·ic** (kə·thod′ik) or **·i·cal** *adj.*

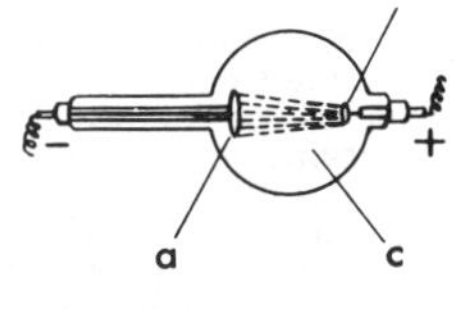

CATHODE–RAY TUBE
a. Cathode.
b. Anode.
c. Vacuum.

cathode rays *Physics* A stream of electrons that pass from a cathode to the opposite wall of a vacuum discharge tube when it is excited by a current of electricity, or by a series of spark discharges.

cathode–ray tube *Electronics* A special type of electron tube in which a beam of electrons is focused by an electric or magnetic field and deflected so as to impinge upon a sensitized screen, forming an image, as on a television receiver.

cath·o·lic (kath′ə·lik, kath′lik) *adj.* **1** Broadminded, as in belief, tastes, or views; liberal; comprehensive; large. **2** Universal in reach; general. [<L *catholicus* <Gk. *katholikos* universal <*kata-* thoroughly + *holos* whole] —**ca·thol·i·cal·ly** (kə·thol′ik·lē) *adv.* —**cath·o·lic·i·ty** (kath′ə·lis′ə·tē) *n.*

Cath·o·lic (kath′ə·lik, kath′lik) *adj.* **1** Universal; of, pertaining to, belonging or addressed to all Christians: a *Catholic* epistle; the *Catholic* faith. **2** Describing the ancient, undivided Christian Church; in accordance with the decrees of the seven ecumenical councils; not heretical or schismatic: the *Catholic* fathers; a *Catholic* creed. **3** Designating the western or Latin Church as opposed to the eastern or Greek Church after their final separation in 1472; not Orthodox. **4** Describing those churches which, after the Reformation and in modern times, claim to have the apostolic doctrine, discipline, orders, and sacraments of the ancient undivided church, and including the Anglican, Eastern Orthodox, Old Catholic, and Roman Churches. —*n.* **1** A member of the Catholic Church, in any of the above senses. **2** Specifically, a Roman Catholic. —**Cath·o·lic·i·ty** (kath′ə·lis′ə·tē) *n.*

Catholic Church The Roman Catholic Church.

Catholic Emancipation Act An act of the English Parliament, passed in 1829, removing certain civil disabilities from Roman Catholics in Great Britain and Ireland.

Ca·thol·i·cism (kə·thol′ə·siz′əm) *n.* **1** The doctrine, system, and practice of the Church universal. **2** The system, doctrine, and practice of the Roman Catholic Church.

ca·thol·i·cize (kə·thol′ə·sīz) *v.t. & v.i.* **·cized, ·ciz·ing** To make or become catholic or Catholic.

ca·thol·i·con (kə·thol′ə·kən) *n.* A supposed universal remedy; a panacea. [<LL <Gk. *katholikos* universal]

cath·o·lyte (kath′ə·līt) *n. Chem.* The liquid formed near the cathode during electrolysis. [<CATHO(DE)+ (ELECTRO)LYTE]

cat·house (kat′hous′) *n. Slang* A house of prostitution; brothel.

Cat·i·line (kat′ə·līn), 108?–62 B.C., Roman conspirator, denounced by Cicero: full name *Lucius Sergius Catilina.*

cat·i·on (kat′ī′ən) *n. Chem.* **1** A positively charged particle which in electrolysis moves toward the cathode or is deposited there. **2** A positive ion, molecule, or radical. Also spelled *kation.* [<Gk. *kation,* ppr. neut. of *katienai*<*kata-* down + *ienai* go]

cat·kin (kat′kin) *n. Bot.* A deciduous scaly spike of flowers, as in the willow; an ament. [<MDu. *katteken,* dim. of *katte* cat]

cat·like (kat′līk′) *adj.* **1** Like a cat; feline. **2** Noiseless; stealthy.

cat·ling (kat′ling) *n.* **1** Catgut. **2** *pl.* Stringed instruments. **3** A kitten.

cat·nap (kat′nap′) *n.* A short doze, usually taken sitting up.

cat·nip (kat′nip) *n.* An aromatic herb *(Nepeta cataria)* of the mint family, of which cats are fond. Also **cat′mint′.**

Ca·to (kā′tō), **Marcus Porcius** Name of two Roman statesmen: **Cato the Elder,** 234–149 B.C., advocate of the destruction of Carthage, known as *Cato the Censor;* and his great–grandson **Cato the Younger,** 95–46 B.C., Stoic philosopher, supporter of Pompey against Caesar.

cat–o′–moun·tain (kat′ə·moun′tən) See CATAMOUNT.

cat–o′–nine–tails (kat′ə·nīn′tālz′) *n.* A whip with nine lashes.

ca·top·trics (kə·top′triks) *n.* That branch of optics which treats of the reflection of light and the formation of images by mirrors. [< Gk. *katoptrikos* <*katoptron* mirror]—**ca·top′·tric** or **·tri·cal** *adj.*

cat owl The great horned owl.

cat rig The rig of a catboat, consisting of one mast far forward and one sail with a long boom and a gaff. —**cat′–rigged′** *adj.*

cat's cradle A game played with a loop of string stretched over the fingers and transferred from one player's hands to another's, so as to produce intricate geometrical arrangements.

cat's–eye (kats′ī′) *n.* A gemstone, usually chrysoberyl or quartz, which shows a line of light across the dome when cut en cabochon.

Cats·kill Mountains (kats′kil) A range of the Appalachians in SE New York; highest peak, 4,205 feet. Also **the Catskills.**

cat's–paw (kats′pô′) *n.* **1** A person used as a tool or dupe. **2** A light wind which barely ruffles the water. **3** *Naut.* A twisting hitch in the bight of a rope. Also **cats′paw′.**

cat·sup (kat′səp, kech′əp) See KETCHUP.

Catt (kat), **Carrie Chapman,** 1859–1947, *née* Lane, U.S. suffragist.

cat–tail (kat′tāl′) *n.* **1** A perennial aquatic plant (genus *Typha*), with long leaves, flowers in cylindrical terminal spikes, and downy fruit: used in making mats, chair seats, etc. **2** *Brit.* Timothy grass. **3** A catkin or ament. **4** A cirrus cloud.

CAT–TAIL
(From 3 to 6 feet tall)

cat·ta·lo (kat′ə·lō) See CATALO.

Cat·ta·ro (kät′tä·rō) The Italian name for KOTOR.

catted chimney A chimney built of sticks and clay.

Cat·te·gat (kat′ə·gat) See KATTEGAT.

Cat·tell (kə·tel′), **James McKeen** 1860–1944, U.S. psychologist and editor.

cat·tle (kat′l) *n.* **1** Domesticated bovine animals. **2** Formerly, all livestock, as horses, sheep, goats, etc. **3** Human beings: a contemptuous term. **4** *Obs.* Vermin, birds, etc. [<AF *catel* <LL *captale* <L *capitale* capital, wealth. Doublet of CHATTEL.]

cat·tle·man (kat′l·mən) *n. pl.* **·men** (-mən) One who raises cattle.

cat·tle·ya (kat′lē·ə) *n.* Any of a genus *(Cattleya)* of tropical American orchids, widely cultivated in many horticultural varieties and esteemed for their showy, variously colored flowers. [<NL, after William *Cattley,* English botanist]

cat·ty[1] (kat′ē) *n. pl.* **·ties** An Oriental and Asiatic weight varying in different countries but equivalent to about 1 1/3 pounds avoirdupois: also called *chang.* Also **cat′tie.** [<Malay *kātī*]

cat·ty[2] (kat′ē) *adj.* **·ti·er, ·ti·est 1** Pertaining to cats. **2** *Colloq.* Malicious; spiteful; backbiting. —**cat′ti·ly** *adv.* —**cat′ti·ness** *n.*

cat·ty–cor·nered (kat′ē·kôr′nərd) See CATER–CORNERED.

Ca·tul·lus (kə·tul′əs), **Gaius Valerius,** 84–54? B.C., Roman poet.

cat·walk (kat′wôk′) *n.* **1** Any narrow walking space, as at the side of a bridge, in an aircraft, near the ceiling of the stage in a theater, etc.

cat–whisk·er (kat′hwis′kər) *n. Electronics* A fine, sharp–pointed wire used to make contact with a sensitive point on the surface of a crystal detector.

Cau·ca (kou′kä) A river in Colombia, flowing 600 miles north to the Magdalena.

Cau·ca·sian (kô·kā′zhən, -shən, -kash′ən) *n.* **1** A member of the white–skinned division of the human race: so called from a skull found in the Caucasus, which was taken as establishing the type. **2** A member of the native peoples of the Caucasus region. **3** A family of languages spoken in the Caucasus region, including Georgian and Circassian: unrelated to the Indo–European, Semitic, Hamitic, Uralic, or Altaic families. —*adj.* **1** Belonging to the region of the Caucasus mountains, its inhabitants, or their languages. **2** Caucasoid. Also **Cau·cas·ic** (kô·kas′ik).

Cau·ca·soid (kô′kə·soid) *adj. Anthropol.* Of or pertaining to the so–called white race, characterized by a skin color ranging from very white to dark brown: variable in stature, body build, eye color, head hair, and cephalic index, with moderate to profuse body hair and generally narrow to medium–broad, high–bridged nose. —*n.* A member of this ethnic group; a Caucasian.

Cau·ca·sus 1 A mountain range between the Black and Caspian Seas; highest peak, 16,512 feet. 2 A region in southern Russia between the Black and Caspian Seas; divided by the Caucasus mountains into Northern Caucasus and Transcaucasia. Also **Cau·ca·sia.** (kô·kā′zhə, -shə, -kash′ə).

Caucasus In·di·cus (in′di·kəs) The ancient name for the HINDU KUSH.

cau·cus (kô′kəs) *n.* **1** A private or preliminary meeting of members of a political party to select candidates or plan a campaign; a primary. **2** *Brit.* A political committee or other body in charge of shaping political policies, or of a local canvass or election. —*v.i.* **cau·cused** or **·cussed, ·cus·ing** or **·cus·sing**To meet in or hold a caucus. [from the *Caucus* Club, Boston, Mass., prob. <Algonquian *caucawasu* advisor]

cau·da (kô′də) *n. pl.* **·dae** (-dē) A tail, or tail–like appendage. [<L, tail]

cau·dad (kô′dad) *adv. Zool.* Toward the tail: opposed to *cephalad.*

cau·dal (kôd′l) *adj. Zool.* **1** Of, pertaining to, or near the tail or posterior part of the body. **2** Having the nature or form of a tail. —**cau′dal·ly** *adv.*

Cau·da·ta (kô·dā′tə) *n. pl.* An order of amphibians with naked skin, limbs, and a tail, including salamanders and newts: formerly called *Urodela.*

cau·date (kô′dāt) *adj. Zool.* Having a tail or tail–like appendage or extremity. Also **cau′·dat·ed.** [<L *caudatus* <*cauda* tail]

cau·dex (kô′deks) *n. pl.* **·di·ces** (-də·sēz) or **·dex·es** *Bot.* **1** The woody axis or trunk of a tree. **2** The woody base of a perennial plant. [<L, var. of *codex* trunk of a tree]

cau·dil·lo (kou·thē′lyō, -thē′yō) *n. Spanish* A chief; leader. — **el Caudillo** The head of the Spanish state: title applied to Francisco Franco (1939–).

Cau·dine Forks (kô′dīn) Two narrow passes in the Apennines, southern Italy.

cau·dle (kôd′l) *n.* A warm drink of gruel with wine, eggs, etc., for invalids. [<AF *caudel* <Med. L *caldellum,* dim. of *caldum, calidum* warm, hot]

cau·dron (kô′drən) *n. Scot.* A caldron.

cauf (kôf) *n. Scot.* A calf: also spelled *cawf.*

caught (kôt) Past tense and past participle of CATCH.

cauk (kôk) *n. Scot.* Chalk; limestone: also spelled *cawk.*

cauk an′ keel (kôk′ ən kēl′) *Scot.* Chalk and red clay used to mark sheep.

caul (kôl) *n. Anat.* **1** That part of the amniotic sac which sometimes envelops the head of a newly born child. **2** The great omentum. ◆ Homophone: *call.* [<OF *cale* cap]

Cau·lain·court (kō·laṅ·ko͝or′), **Marquis Armand Augustine Louis de,** 1772–1827, French general and diplomat.

cauld (kôld, käld, kôd) *adj. & n. Scot.* Cold.

caul·dron (kôl′drən) See CALDRON.

cau·les·cent (kô·les′ənt) *adj. Bot.* Having a clearly defined stem. [<L *caulis* stem + -ESCENT]

cau·li·cle (kô′li·kəl) *n. Bot.* A little stem; specifically, the rudimentary stem in the embryo of a seed. [<L *cauliculus,* dim. of *caulis* CAULIS]

cau·li·flo·rous (kô′lə·flôr′əs, -flō′rəs) *adj. Bot.* Characterized by a growth of flowers; borne on the main stem, as flowers and fruits. [<L *caulis* stem + *florus* flowering]

cau·li·flow·er (kô′lə·flou′ər, kol′i-) *n.* **1** The fleshy, edible head formed by the young flowers of a variety of cabbage (*Brassica oleracea botrytis*). **2** The plant bearing this. [<NL *cauliflora* flowering cabbage; infl. in form by FLOWER]

cau·li·form (kô′lə·fôrm) *adj. Bot.* Shaped like a stem.

cau·line (kô′lin, -līn) *adj. Bot.* Of, pertaining to, or growing on a stem. [<NL *caulinus* <L *caulis* CAULIS]

cau·lis (kô′lis) *n. pl.* **·les** (-lēz) *Bot.* The stem of a plant. [<L <Gk. *kaulos* stem of a plant]

caulk (kôk) See CALK[1].

cau·lome (kô′lōm) *n. Bot.* The axial portion or stem of a plant as distinguished from phyllome, trichome, and root. [<Gk. *kaulos* stalk + -OME] — **cau·lom·ic** (kô·lom′ik) *adj.*

caup (kôp) *n. Scot.* A bowl; cup.

caus·al (kô′zəl) *adj.* Pertaining to, constituting, involving, or expressing a cause. — *n.* A word expressive of cause or reason. [<L *causalis* of a cause <*causa* cause] — **caus′al·ly** *adv.*

cau·sal·gi·a (kô·zal′jē·ə) *n. Pathol.* A burning pain, such as often follows injuries of the nerves; neuralgia with severe local pain. [<NL <Gk. *kausos* heat <*kaiein* burn + *-algia* pain <*algeein* hurt]

cau·sal·i·ty (kô·zal′ə·tē) *n. pl.* **·ties** **1** The relation of cause and effect. **2** Causal action or agency. See synonyms under CAUSE.

cau·sa si·ne qua non (kô′zə sī′nē kwā non′) *Latin* A condition which is indispensable; a prerequisite; literally, cause without which not.

cau·sa·tion (kô·zā′shən) *n.* **1** The act, process, or agency of causing. **2** The relation of cause and effect. **3** The active force of the principle of causality. **4** Causative power or agency. See synonyms under CAUSE. [<L *causatio, -onis* <*causari* bring about <*causa* cause]

caus·a·tive (kô′zə·tiv) *adj.* **1** Effective as a cause. **2** *Gram.* Expressing cause or agency; indicating that the subject causes the action: *en-* in *enfeeble* is a *causative* prefix; *lay* (cause to lie) is a *causative* verb. — *n. Gram.* A form that expresses or suggests causation. [<F *causatif* <L *causativus* <*causa* cause] — **caus′a·tive·ly** *adv.* — **caus′a·tive·ness** *n.*

cause (kôz) *n.* **1** The power or efficient agent producing any thing or event. **2** Any occasion or condition upon the occurrence of which an event takes place. **3** Any rational ground for choice or action; reason. **4** A great enterprise, movement, principle, or aim. **5** *Law* An action or suit; also, a ground of action. **6** *Obs.* Behalf; interest. **7** *Philos.* The object or end for which anything is done or made; purpose; aim. — *v.t.* **caused, caus·ing** To be the cause of; produce; effect; induce; compel. [<F <L *causa* cause, legal case] — **caus′a·ble** *adj.* — **cause′less** *adj.* — **caus′er** *n.*

Synonyms (noun): actor, agent, antecedent, author, causality, causation, condition, creator, designer, former, fountain, motive, occasion, origin, originator, power, precedent, reason, source, spring. The efficient *cause,* that which makes anything to be or be done, is the common meaning of the word, as in the saying "There is no effect without a *cause.*" Every man instinctively recognizes himself acting through will as the *cause* of his own actions. The *Creator* is the Great First *Cause* of all things. A *condition* is something that necessarily precedes a result, but does not produce it. An *antecedent* simply precedes a result, with or without any agency in producing it; as, Monday is the invariable *antecedent* of Tuesday, but not the *cause* of it. The direct antonym of *cause* is *effect,* while that of *antecedent* is *consequent.* An *occasion* is some event which brings a *cause* into action at a particular moment; gravitation and heat are the *causes* of an avalanche; the steep incline of the mountain side is a necessary *condition.* *Causality* is the doctrine or principle of causes, *causation* the action or working of causes. *Motive* is an impulse of an intelligent being which incites to action, and, if unchecked, is a *cause* of action. Compare DESIGN, REASON. *Antonyms*: consequence, creation, development, effect, end, event, fruit, issue, outcome, outgrowth, product, result.

cause cé·lè·bre (kōz sā·leb′r′) *French* **1** A famous legal case. **2** Any well-known controversial issue.

cau·se·rie (kō′zə·rē′, *Fr.* kōz·rē′) *n.* **1** Light conversation; informal discussion. **2** A free, unconventional treatment or criticism of a subject; conversational criticism. [<F]

cause·way (kôz′wā′) *n.* **1** A raised road or way, as over marshy ground. **2** A sidewalk above the street level. **3** A highway. — *v.t.* **1** To make a causeway for or through, as a marshy tract. **2** To pave, as a road. [<AF *caucie* <LL *calciata,* pp. of *calciare* tread, stamp down <L *calx, calcis* heel + WAY]

cau·sey (kô′zē) *n. pl.* **·seys** *Scot. & Brit. Dial.* A paved way, street, or highway.

caus·tic (kôs′tik) *adj.* **1** Capable of corroding or eating away tissues; burning; corrosive. **2** Causing to smart; stinging; biting; sarcastic and severe. **3** *Optics* **a** Designating a surface to which all rays emitted from one point and reflected or refracted from a curved surface are tangents: so called because along such a surface the heating effect is at the maximum. **b** Designating a curve formed by such a surface. — *n.* **1** A caustic substance. **2** *Optics* A caustic curve or surface. Also **caus′ti·cal.** See synonyms under BITTER. [<L *causticus* <Gk. *kaustikos* <*kausos* burning <*kaiein* burn] — **caus′ti·cal·ly** *adv.*

caus·tic·i·ty (kôs·tis′ə·tē) *n.* **1** The quality or state of being caustic. **2** Severity of language. See synonyms under ACRIMONY.

caustic potash Potassium hydroxide.

caustic soda Sodium hydroxide.

cau·ter·ant (kô′tər·ənt) *adj.* Of or pertaining to cautery or a caustic. — *n.* A cauterizing substance.

cau·ter·ize (kô′tər·īz) *v.t.* **·ized, ·iz·ing** **1** To sear with a caustic drug or a heated iron. **2** To make callous or insensible. Also *Brit.* **cau′ter·ise.** See synonyms under BURN. [<LL *cauterizare* <L *cauterium.* See CAUTERY.] — **cau′ter·i·za′tion, cau′ter·ism** *n.*

cau·ter·y (kô′tər·ē) *n. pl.* **·ter·ies** **1** *Med.* The application of a caustic, especially for the purpose of destroying tissue. **2** A cauterizing agent or a searing iron. [<L *cauterium* branding iron <Gk. *kautērion* <*kaiein* burn]

cau·tion (kô′shən) *n.* **1** Care to avoid injury or misfortune; prudence; wariness. **2** An admonition or warning. **3** *Colloq.* A person or thing that alarms, astonishes, or provokes great admiration. — *v.t.* To advise to be prudent; warn. See synonyms under ADMONISH. [<OF <L *cautio, -onis* <*cavere* beware, take heed]

cau·tion·ar·y (kô′shən·er′ē) *adj.* Constituting or conveying a warning; admonitory.

cau·tious (kô′shəs) *adj.* Exercising or manifesting caution; wary; prudent. — **cau′tious·ly** *adv.* — **cau′tious·ness** *n.*

Cau·ver·y (kô′vər·ē) See KAVERI.

Cau·vin (kō·vaṅ′) French form of CALVIN

ca·val (kā′vəl) *adj.* **1** Of or pertaining to a cavity. **2** Large and hollow. [<L *cavus* hollow]

cav·al·cade (kav′əl·kād′, kav′əl·kād) *n.* A company of riders; a parade. See synonyms under PROCESSION. [<MF <Ital. *cavalcata* <*cavalcare* ride on horseback <LL *caballicare* <L *caballus* horse, nag]

cav·a·lier (kav′ə·lir′) *n.* **1** A horseman; knight. **2** A lover; escort; gallant. — *adj.* **1** Free and easy; offhand. **2** Haughty; supercilious. — *v.t.* To escort or play the gallant to, as a lady. — *v.i.* To behave in a cavalier fashion; show arrogance. Also *Obs.* **cav·a·le·ro** (kav′ə·lā′rō), **cav′a·lie′ro** (-lyā′rō). [<MF <Ital. *cavaliere* <LL *caballarius* <*caballus* horse, nag. Doublet of CHEVALIER.]

Cav·a·lier (kav′ə·lir′) *n.* A supporter or member of the court party during the reign of Charles I of England; a royalist: opposed to *Roundhead.* — *adj.* Pertaining to the Cavaliers. — **cav′a·lier′ism** *n.*

cav·a·lier·ly (kav′ə·lir′lē) *adj.* Like or characteristic of a cavalier; gallant; also, haughty. — *adv.* After the manner of a cavalier; disdainfully; haughtily.

Cavalier poets A group of English lyric poets, mainly at the court of Charles I, including Herrick, Carew, Lovelace, and Suckling.

ca·val·ly (kə·val′ē) *n. pl.* **·lies** **1** A carangoid fish (genus *Caranx*); especially, a food fish (*C. hippos*) of the Atlantic. **2** The cero. Also **ca·val·la** (kə·val′ə). [<Sp. *caballa* horse mackerel <L *caballus* horse]

cav·al·ry (kav′əl·rē) *n. pl.* **·ries** **1** Mobile ground troops, organized in mounted, mechanized, or motorized units. **2** One of the principal arms or branches of the U.S. Army and of other armies. **3** Organized, mounted combat troops. **4** Riders, horsemen, etc., collectively. [<MF *cavallerie* <Ital. *cavalleria* <LL *caballarius* horseman <*caballus* horse. Doublet of CHIVALRY.] — **cav′al·ry·man** (-mən) *n.*

ca·van (kä·vän′) *n.* A measure used in the Philippines: approximately equal to 75 liters or 2 1/2 bushels. [<Sp. *cabán*]

Cav·an (kav′ən) A county of southern Ulster province, Ireland; 730 square miles; county seat, Cavan.

cav·a·ti·na (kav′ə·tē′nə, *Ital.* kä′vä·tē′nä) *n. Music* A short and simple kind of aria; especially, a song without a second part. [<Ital.]

cave (kāv) *n.* **1** A natural cavity beneath the earth's surface or in a mountain; a cavern; den. ◆ Collateral adjective: *spelean.* **2** In English politics, a member of a party which seceded from the Liberals in 1866: so called from the application by John Bright of the expression **Cave of Adullam** (I *Sam.* xxii 1, 2) in referring to this party; hence, a seceder or a seceding group. See synonyms under HOLE. — *v.* **caved, cav·ing** *v.t.* **1** To hollow out. **2** To cause to fall down or in, or to become hollow by a partial falling away. **3** To place in or as in a cave. — *v.i.* **4** To fall in or down; give way, as ground when undermined. — **to cave in** **1** To fall in or down, as when undermined; cause to fall in, as by undermining. **2** *Colloq.* To yield utterly; give in, as to argument, hardship, or strain. [<OF <L *cava* <*cavus* hollow]

ca·ve·at (kā′vē·at) *n.* **1** *Law* A formal notification to a court or officer not to take a certain step till the notifier is heard. **2** A description of an invention that is not fully perfected, formerly filed in the U.S. Patent Office, which entitled the person filing it to three months' notice before the issuing of a patent for a like invention to another. **3** A caution. [<L, let him beware]

ca·ve·at emp·tor (kā′vē·at emp′tôr) *Latin* Let the purchaser beware: implying that the purchase is made at his own risk.

ca·ve·a·tor (kā′vē·ā′tər) *n.* One who enters a caveat.

ca·ve ca·nem (kā′vē kā′nəm) *Latin* Beware of the dog.

cave·fish (kāv′fish′) *n. pl.* **·fish** or **·fish·es** Blindfish.

cave–in (kāv′in′) *n.* A collapse or falling in, as

of a mine or tunnel; also, the site of such a collapse.

Cav·ell (kav′əl), **Edith,** 1865–1915, English nurse executed by the Germans in World War I for helping Allied soldiers to escape from occupied Belgium.

cave man **1** A Paleolithic man; a cave dweller. **2** *Colloq.* A man who is rough and brutal, especially in his approach to women.

cav·en·dish (kav′ən·dish) *n.* A brand of American plug tobacco. [after *Cavendish,* proper name]

Cav·en·dish (kav′ən·dish), **Henry,** 1731?–1810, English chemist and physicist. **—William,** 1640–1707, first Duke of Devonshire, English statesman.

cav·ern (kav′ərn) *n.* A large cave; a den; cavity. *—v.t.* **1** To make like a cavern; hollow out. **2** To enclose, shut up, or place in or as in a cavern. [< F *caverne* < L *caverna* < *cavus* hollow]

cav·er·nic·o·lous (kav′ər·nik′ə·ləs) *adj.* Living in caves: *cavernicolous* fish. [< L *caverna* cavern + *colere* dwell + -OUS]

cav·ern·ous (kav′ər·nəs) *adj.* **1** Consisting of or containing caverns; like a cavern; hollow. **2** Hollow-sounding. **3** Pertaining to rocks having cavities or various sizes and shapes. **—cav′ern·ous·ly** *adv.*

cav·es·son (kav′ə·sən) *n.* A headstall furnished with a noseband having rings attached for a rein or cord by which a trainer on foot directs a horse in circles about him. [< F *caveçon* < Ital. *cavezzone,* aug. of *cavezza* halter]

ca·vet·to (kə·vet′ō, *Ital.* kä·vet′tō) *n. pl.* **·ti** (-tē) or **·tos** *Archit.* A molding having a concave profile of not more than 90° curvature, terminating in a vertical fillet, with a projection usually about equal to its altitude. [< Ital., dim. of *cavo* hollow < L *cavus*]

cav·i·ar (kav′ē·är, kä′vē-) *n.* A relish consisting of the roe of sturgeon or other fish, either in the natural state and salted, or pressed and salted, especially as prepared in Russia: considered a delicacy. **—caviar to the general** Something too esoteric to appeal to the popular taste. Also **cav′i·are.** [< F < Turkish *khavyar*]

cav·i·corn (kav′ə·kôrn) *adj. Zool.* Having hollow horns. *—n.* Any one of the hollow-horned ruminants. [< L *cavus* hollow + *cornu* horn]

ca·vie (kā′vē) *n. Scot.* A hencoop; chicken house.

cav·il (kav′əl) *v.* **cav·iled** or **·illed, cav·il·ing** or **·il·ling** *v.t.* To find fault with. *—v.i.* To pick flaws or raise trivial objections; argue or object captiously: with *at* or *about.* *—n.* A captious objection; caviling. [< MF *caviller* < L *cavillari* < *cavilla* a jeering, a scoffing] **—cav′il·er, cav′il·ler** *n.* **—cav′il·ing, cav′il·ling** *adj.* **—cav′il·ing·ly, cav′il·ling·ly** *adv.*

cav·i·ta·tion (kav′ə·tā′shən) *n. Physics* The formation of vapor cavities in the water flowing around the blades of a propeller, due to excessive speed of rotation, and resulting in structural damage or a loss of efficiency. [< CAVITY]

Ca·vi·te (kä·vē′tā) A province in southern Luzon, Philippines; 498 square miles; capital, Cavite.

cav·i·ty (kav′ə·tē) *n. pl.* **·ties** **1** A hollow or sunken space; hole. **2** A natural hollow in the body. **3** A hollow place in a tooth, especially one caused by decay. [< MF *cavité* < LL *cavitas, -tatis* a hollow < *cavus* hollow, empty]

ca·vort (kə·vôrt′) *v.i.* **1** To act up; cut up. **2** To prance and show off, as a horse; curvet. **3** To run and prance without control. [Origin unknown]

Ca·vour (kä·vōōr′), **Count Camillo Benso di,** 1810–61, Italian statesman.

ca·vy (kā′vē) *n. pl.* **·vies** A small South American burrowing rodent with the tail absent or rudimentary, as the guinea pig *(Cavia cobaya),* the **restless cavy** *(C. porcellus),* the **southern cavy** *(C. australis),* common on the Patagonian coast, and the harelike **Patagonian cavy** *(Dolichotis patagonica).* **—giant cavy** The capybara. [< NL *Cavia* < Cariban]

caw[1] (kô) *v.i.* To cry or call: said of crows, rooks, etc.; cry like a crow. *—n.* The cry of a crow, raven, rook, etc. [Imit.]

caw[2] (kô) See CA′.

cawk (kôk) *n. Scot.* Chalk.

Cawn·pore (kôn·pôr′, -pōr′) A former name for KANPUR. Also **Cawn·pur** (kôn·pōōr′).

Ca·xi·as (kə·shē′əs) See DUQUE DE CAXIAS.

Cax·ton (kak′stən) *n.* **1** Any book printed by **William Caxton,** 1422–91, scholar and translator, who introduced printing into England. **2** *Printing* A style of type imitating that of Caxton.

cay (kā, kē) *n.* A coastal reef or sandy islet, as in the Gulf of Mexico. See KEY[2]. [< Sp. *cayo* shoal]

Cay·enne (kī·en′, kā-) The capital of French Guiana.

cayenne pepper A pungent red powder made from the fruit of various capsicums; red pepper. Also **cay·enne′.**

Cayes (kā) See LES CAYES.

cay·man (kā′mən) *n. pl.* **·mans** See CAIMAN.

Cay·mans (kā′mənz, kī·mänz′) A West Indies island group, comprising a dependency of Jamaica; 92 square miles. Also **Cayman Islands.**

cay·ote (kī′ōt) See COYOTE.

Ca·yu·ga (kā·yōō′gə, kī-) *n. pl.* **·ga** or **·gas** A member of a tribe of North American Indians of Iroquoian linguistic stock formerly dwelling around Lake Cayuga, N.Y., the smallest tribe of the confederation known as the Five Nations: now mostly on reservations in Ontario.

Ca·yu·ga Lake (kā·yōō′gə, kī-) One of the Finger Lakes in west central New York.

cay·use (kī·yōōs′) *n.* **1** An Indian pony. **2** A horse of little value: a humorous or derogatory term. [after the *Cayuse* Indians]

Cay·use (kī·yōōs′) *n.* A member of a tribe of North American Indians formerly inhabiting Oregon: now almost extinct.

ca·zique (kə·zēk′) See CACIQUE.

C-bi·as (sē′bī′əs) See GRID BIAS.

Cd *Chem.* Cadmium (symbol Cd).

Ce *Chem.* Cerium (symbol Ce).

Ce·a (sē′ə) See CEOS.

Ce·a·rá (sā′ä·rä′) A state in NE Brazil; 59,168 square miles; capital, Fortaleza.

Ceará rubber The coagulated latex of a tropical American tree *(Manihot glaziovi).*

cease (sēs) *v.* **ceased, ceas·ing** *v.t.* To leave off or discontinue, as one's own actions. *—v.i.* To come to an end; stop; desist. *—n.* End; stopping: obsolete except after *without.* [< F *cesser* < L *cessare* stop < *cedere* withdraw, yield] **—cease′less** *adj.* **—cease′less·ly** *adv.* **—cease′less·ness** *n.*

Synonyms (verb): abstain, conclude, desist, discontinue, end, finish, intermit, pause, quit, refrain, stop, terminate. Strains of music may gradually or suddenly *cease.* A man *quits* work on the instant; he may *discontinue* a practice gradually; he *quits* suddenly and completely; he *stops* short in what he may or may not resume; he *pauses* in what he will probably resume. What *intermits* or is *intermitted* returns again, as a fever that *intermits.* Compare ABANDON, DIE, END, REST. *Antonyms*: begin, commence, inaugurate, initiate, institute, originate, start.

ceb·a·dil·la (seb′ə·dil′ə) See SABADILLA.

ce·boid (sē′boid) *adj. Zool.* Pertaining to or describing any member of a superfamily or group *(Ceboidea)* of monkeys believed to have evolved from the prosimians isolated in South America, and including the marmosets, capuchins, tamarins, sapajous, and spider monkeys. *—n.* A member of this superfamily or group: also **ce·bid** (sē′bid, seb′id). [< NL < Gk. *kēbos,* a long-tailed monkey]

Ce·bu (sā·bōō′) One of the Visayan Islands, Philippines; 1,703 square miles; chief port and principal city, Cebu.

Čech·y (chekh′ē) The Czech name for BOHEMIA.

Ce·cil (sē′səl, ses′əl) A masculine personal name. [< L, poor-sighted]

Cec·il (ses′əl, sis′-), **(Edgar Algernon) Robert,** born 1864, Viscount Cecil of Chelwood, English statesman. **—Lord David,** born 1902, English biographer. **—Robert,** 1563?–1612, Earl of Salisbury and Viscount Cranborne, English statesman. **—Robert Arthur Gascoyne** See SALISBURY. **—William,** 1520–98, Baron Burghley, English statesman.

Ce·cil·i·a (si·sil′ē·ə, -sil′yə; *Ital.* chā·chēl′yä; *Pg.* sā·sēl′yə; *Sp.* thā·thēl′yä) A feminine personal name. Also **Cec·i·ly** (ses′ə·lē), *Fr.* **Cé·cile** (sā·sēl′). [< L. See CECIL.]

—Cecilia, Saint, died 230?, a Roman virgin who professed Christianity and suffered martyrdom in Sicily; patroness of music; her day is Nov. 22.

ce·cro·pi·a moth (si·krō′pē·ə) A large, strikingly marked moth *(Samia cecropia)* common in the eastern United States. [< NL *Cecropia,* genus of an American mulberry tree, named after *Cecrops*]

Ce·crops (sē′krops) In Greek legend, the first king of Attica and founder of Athens, represented as half man, half dragon.

ce·cum sē′kəm) *n. pl.* **ce·ca** (sē′kə) *Anat.* A blind pouch, or cavity, open at one end, especially that situated between the large and small intestines; the blind gut. Also spelled *caecum.* [< L < *caecus* blind] **—ce′cal** *adj.*

ce·dar (sē′dər) *n.* **1** A large tree of the pine family (genus *Cedrus*) having evergreen leaves and fragrant wood. There are several varieties, as the **cedar of Lebanon** *(C. libani),* **deodar cedar** *(C. deodara),* etc. **2** The American red cedar. **3** The arbor vitae. **4** Spanish cedar *(Cedrela odorata),* a deciduous tree of the mahogany family, whose wood is used for cigar boxes. **5** The wood of these and related trees. *—adj.* Pertaining to or made of cedar. [< OF *cedre* < L *cedrus* < Gk. *kedros*]

ce·dar·bird (sē′dər·bûrd′) *n.* The common American waxwing. Also **cedar waxwing.**

Cedar Breaks National Monument (brāks) A region of SW Utah; 10 square miles; established 1933.

cedar brown A warm, light brown, the color of cedar wood.

cedar chest A storage chest for woolens, made of cedar wood, for protection from moths.

ce·darn (sē′dərn) *adj.* **1** Of, pertaining to, or made of cedar. **2** Lined or bordered with cedars. Also **ce′dared.**

Cedar Rapids A city in eastern Iowa.

ce·dar·wood (sē′dər·wōōd′) *n.* The wood from any species of cedar.

cedarwood oil A colorless to pale- or greenish-yellow essential oil obtained by the distillation of cedarwood: used in medicine and in perfumes and insecticides.

cede (sēd) *v.t.* **ced·ed, ced·ing** **1** To yield or give up. **2** To surrender title to; transfer: said especially of territory. See synonyms under ABANDON, GIVE. ◆Homophone: *seed.* [< MF *céder* < L *cedere* withdraw, yield]

ce·dil·la (si·dil′ə) *n.* A mark put under the letter *c* (ç) in some French words to indicate that it is to be sounded as (s). [< Sp., dim. of *zeda,* the letter *z* < Gk. *zēta*; orig., a small *z* placed next to a *c* to indicate its sound]

Ced·ric (sed′rik, sē′drik) A masculine personal name. [< Celtic, war chief]

ced·u·la (sej′ōō·lə, *Sp.* thā′thōō·lä) *n.* **1** An obligation of the government in certain Spanish-American countries. **2** In the Philippines, a personal registration tax certificate; also, the tax itself. [< Sp. *cédula* note, bill]

cee (sē) *n.* The letter *c.*

ce·i·ba (sā′i·bä, sī′bə) *n.* A West Indian and Mexican tree *(Ceiba pentandra),* yielding kapok. [< Sp. < Arawakan]

ceil (sēl) *v.t.* **1** To furnish with a ceiling; line the roof of. **2** To sheathe internally; line, as an apartment. ◆Homophone: *seal.* [< F *ciel* roof, canopy < L *caelum* heaven, sky]

ceil·ing (sē′ling) *n.* **1** The overhead covering of a room. **2** Internal sheathing, as of a vessel. **3** The act of one who ceils. **4** *Aeron.* **a** The maximum height to which a given aircraft can be driven. **b** The upward limit of visibility for flying; the distance, expressed in hundreds of feet, between the ground and the base of an overcast or broken cloud formation. **5** The top limit of anything; specifically, the highest price that can be charged for a given thing. **—absolute ceiling** *Aeron.* The greatest altitude above sea level at which an airplane can sustain horizontal flight under standard air conditions. **—service ceiling** *Aeron.* The maximum height beyond which an airplane under normal conditions may not climb faster than 100 feet a minute.

ceil·om·e·ter (sē·lom′ə·tər) *n. Meteorol.* A photoelectric device used with a mercury-vapor lamp to determine the ceiling height of clouds under all weather conditions.

ce·ja (sā′hä) *n. SW U.S.* The cliff edge or margin of a mesa. [< Sp.]

cel·a·don (sel′ə·don) *n.* **1** A Chinese porcelain famous for its gray-green glaze. **2** A delicate grayish-green color. [< F *céladon*]

Ce·lae·no (se·lē′nō) **1** In Greek mythology, one of the Harpies. **2** One of the Pleiades.

cel·an·dine (sel′ən·dīn) *n.* **1** A European perennial *(Chelidonium majus)* of the poppy family, with yellow flowers. **2** The pilewort. [< OF *celidoine* < L *chelidonia* < Gk. *chelidonion* < *chelidōn* a swallow]

ce·la·tion (sə·lā′shən) *n. Med.* The concealing of pregnancy, or of the birth of a child. [< L *celatio, -onis* < *celare* conceal]

-cele[1] *combining form* Tumor or hernia: *gastrocele.* [< Gk. *kēlē* tumor]

-cele[2] *combining form* Cavity; hollow space: *blastocele.* Also spelled *-coele.* [< Gk. *koilos* hollow]

Cel·e·bes (sel′ə·bēz, sə·lē′bēz) An Indonesian island east of Borneo; 69,277 square miles; chief city, Makassar. *Indonesian* **Su·la·we·si** (sōō′lä·wā′sē).

Celebes Sea A part of the Pacific bounded by Celebes, Borneo, and Mindanao.

cel·e·brant (sel′ə·brənt) *n.* **1** One who celebrates. **2** The officiating priest at a mass.

cel·e·brate (sel′ə·brāt) *v.* **·brat·ed, ·brat·ing** *v.t.* **1** To observe, as a festival or occasion, with demonstrations of respect or rejoicing. **2** To make known or famous; extol, as in song or poem: to *celebrate* a hero. **3** To perform a ceremony publicly and as ordained, as with solemn rites. *—v.i.* **4** To observe or commemorate a day or event. **5** To observe the Eucharist. [< L *celebratus,* pp. of *celebrare* celebrate, honor < *celeber* famous] **—cel′e·brat′er** or **·bra′tor** *n.*

Synonyms (verb): commemorate, keep, observe, solemnize. To *celebrate* any event or occasion is to make some demonstration of respect or rejoicing because of or in memory of it, or to perform such public rites or ceremonies as it properly demands. We *celebrate* the birth, *commemorate* the death of one beloved or honored. We *celebrate* a national anniversary with music, song, firing of guns and ringing of bells; we *commemorate* by any solemn and thoughtful service, or by a monument or other enduring memorial. We *keep* the Sabbath, *solemnize* a marriage, *observe* an anniversary; we *celebrate* or *observe* the Lord's Supper in which believers *commemorate* the sufferings and death of Christ. See KEEP, PRAISE. *Antonyms*: contemn, despise, dishonor, disregard, forget, ignore, neglect, overlook, profane, violate.

cel·e·brat·ed (sel′ə·brā′tid) *adj.* **1** Famous; renowned. **2** Performed or observed with customary rites.

Synonyms: distinguished, eminent, exalted, famed, famous, glorious, illustrious, noted, renowned. See ILLUSTRIOUS. *Antonyms*: degraded, disgraced mean, obscure, unknown.

cel·e·bra·tion (sel′ə·brā′shən) *n.* **1** The act of celebrating. **2** Things done in commemoration of any event.

ce·leb·ri·ty (sə·leb′rə·tē) *n. pl.* **·ties 1** The state or quality of being celebrated; fame. **2** A famous or much publicized person. See synonyms under FAME.

ce·ler·i·ty (sə·ler′ə·tē) *n.* Quickness of motion; speed; rapidity. [< F *célérité* < L *celeritas, -tatis* < *celer* swift]

cel·er·y (sel′ər·ē, sel′rē) *n.* A biennial herb *(Apium graveolens),* whose blanched stems are used as a vegetable or salad. [< F *céleri* < Ital. *sellari,* pl. of *sellaro* < L *selinon* parsley < Gk.]

ce·les·ta (sə·les′tə) *n.* A musical instrument, with keyboard of five octaves and hammers that strike steel plates. [< F *célesta*]

Ce·leste (sə·lest′) A feminine personal name. Also **Ce·les·tine** (se·les′tēn, -tin, sel′is·tīn), *Fr.* **Cé·les·tine** (sā·les·tēn′). [< F < L, heavenly]

ce·les·tial (sə·les′chəl) *adj.* **1** Of or pertaining to the sky or heavens. **2** Heavenly; divine. *—n.* A heavenly being. [< OF < L *caelestis* heavenly < *caelum* sky, heaven] **—ce·les′tial·ly** *adv.*

Ce·les·tial (sə·les′chəl) *adj.* Chinese. *—n.* A Chinese.

celestial body A star, planet, comet, etc.

Celestial Empire The former Chinese Empire: translation of *Tien Chao,* Heavenly Dynasty.

celestial equator *Astron.* The great circle in which the plane of the earth's equator cuts the celestial sphere: also called *equinoctial circle* or *line.*

celestial globe A globe whose surface depicts the geography of the heavens, fixed stars, constellations, etc.; a spherical representation of the heavens.

celestial navigation. Celonavigation.

celestial pole Either of the two points where the earth's axis of rotation pierces the celestial sphere.

celestial sphere The spherical surface on which the heavenly bodies seem to lie: conceived by astronomers as of infinite diameter and enclosing the universe.

Cel·es·tine (sel′is·tīn, sə·les′tīn, -tin) Name of five popes; notably, **Celestine V,** 1214?–96, real name Pietro di Murrhone, elected pope 1294; abdicated after five months.

Cel·es·tine (sel′is·tīn, sə·les′tīn, -tin) *n.* A member of a Benedictine order of hermits founded in 1264 by Celestine V, before his papacy. Also **Cel·es·tin·i·an** (sel′is·tin′ē·ən).

cel·es·tite (sel′is·tīt) *n.* A vitreous, white, often bluish orthorhombic strontium sulfate, $SrSo_4$. Also **cel′es·tine** (-tin, -tīn). [< L *caelestis* heavenly; from its blue color]

Cel·ia (sēl′yə, sē′lē·ə; *Ital.* chā′lyä) A feminine personal name. Also *Fr.* **Cé·lie** (sā·lē′). [< CECILIA]

ce·li·ac (sē′lē·ak) *adj.* Of or pertaining to the abdomen: also spelled *coeliac.* [< L *coeliacus* < Gk. *koiliakos* < *koilia* belly, abdomen < *koilos* hollow]

cel·i·ba·cy (sel′ə·bə·sē) *n.* The state of being unmarried; specifically, abstinence from marriage in accordance with religious vows. [< L *caelebs* unmarried]

cel·i·bate (sel′ə·bit, -bāt) *adj.* **1** Unmarried. **2** Vowed to remain single. *—n.* An unmarried person.

cell (sel) *n.* **1** A small, close room, especially one for a prisoner. **2** *Entomol.* **a** A small space or cavity bounded by the veins or nerves on the surface of an insect's wing. **b** A single compartment of a honeycomb. **3** *Biol.* **a** One of the cases or cuplike cavities containing an individual zoospore. **b** A small, often microscopic mass of protoplasm, variously differentiated in composition, structure, and function, usually containing a central nucleus and enclosed within a semipermeable wall (plant) or membrane (animal). It is the

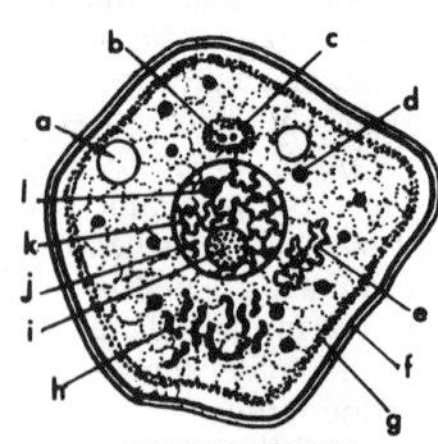

TYPICAL CELL

a.	Vacuole.	*g.*	Plasma membrane.
b.	Centriole.	*h.*	Chondriosome.
c.	Centrosphere.	*i.*	Nucleolus.
d.	Metaplasm.	*j.*	Nuclear sap.
e.	Golgi body.	*k.*	Chromatin.
f.	Cell wall.	*l.*	Karyosome.

fundamental unit of all organisms and the physicochemical basis both of individual development and of organic evolution from the simplest protozoa to the most complex forms of plant and animal life. **4** *Bot.* **a** The cavity of an anther, containing pollen. **b** The seed-bearing cavity of an ovary or pericarp. **5** *Electr.* The unit of a battery, consisting of electrodes in contact with an electrolyte and in which an electric potential is developed by means of chemical action: a voltaic *cell.* **6** *Crystall.* The fundamental structural element of a crystalline lattice: also called *unit cell.* **7** *Aeron.* **a** The full assembly of parts on either side of the fuselage of a biplane. **b** The gas compartment of a balloon or dirigible. **8** A body of persons forming a single unit in an organization of similar groups. **9** A small monastery or nunnery dependent on a larger one. **10** The room occupied by a monk or a nun. ◆ Homophone: *sell.* [< OF *celle* < L cella]

cel·la (sel′ə) *n. pl.* **cel·lae** (sel′ē) The enclosed interior of a temple. [< L, small room]

cel·lar (sel′ər) *n.* **1** An underground room usually under a building: used for storage. **2** A room for storing wines; hence, the wines. *—v.t.* To put or keep in or as in a cellar. [< OF *celier* < L *cellarium* pantry < *cella* cell, small room]

cel·lar·age (sel′ər·ij) *n.* **1** A cellar or cellars. **2** Storage in a cellar or the charge for it.

cel·lar·er (sel′ər·ər) *n.* **1** The keeper of a cellar, as in a monastery. **2** A butler. **3** A wine merchant.

cel·lar·et (sel′ə·ret′) *n.* A case or small cabinet for bottles or decanters, glasses, etc. Also **cel′lar·ette′.**

cell-block (sel′blok′) *n.* In prisons, a group of cells considered as and divided off into a unit.

Cel·le (tsel′ə) A city in Lower Saxony, NW Germany.

cell fusion *Biol.* The artificial creation of a cell containing replicating genetic elements from disparate sources.

Cel·li·ni (chə·lē′nē, *Ital.* chel·lē′nē), **Benvenuto,** 1500–71, Italian sculptor and goldsmith, known for his autobiography.

cel·lo (chel′ō) *n. pl.* **·los** A violoncello. Also **'cel′lo.** [Short for VIOLONCELLO] **—cel′list** *n.*

cel·loi·din (sə·loi′din) *n.* A substance composed of pyroxylin, used for embedding microscopic specimens so that they may be cut in thin sections. [< CELL(ULOSE) + -OID + -IN]

cel·lo·phane (sel′ə·fān) *n.* A specially treated regenerated cellulose which has been processed in thin, transparent, and impermeable strips or sheets, variously colored. [< CELL(ULOSE) + -PHANE]

cel·lu·lar (sel′yə·lər) *adj.* **1** Of, pertaining to, or like a cell or cells. **2** Consisting of or containing cells. [< NL *cellularis* < L *cellula.* See CELLULE.]

cel·lule (sel′yōōl) *n.* **1** *Biol.* A small cell, as on a leaf or the wings of an insect. **2** *Aeron.* A boxlike rectangular area in a biplane or triplane formed by the planes or the struts between. [< L *cellula,* dim, of *cella* cell, small room]

cel·lu·li·tis (sel′yə·lī′tis) *n. Pathol.* Inflammation of the cellular tissue.

Cel·lu·loid (sel′yə·loid) *n.* A hard, elastic, inflammable plastic compound, made by subjecting gun cotton (pyroxylin) mixed with camphor and other substances to hydraulic pressure: a trade name.

cel·lu·lose (sel′yə·lōs) *n. Biochem.* An amorphous white carbohydrate, $(C_6H_{10}O_5)x$, isomeric with starch, insoluble in all ordinary solvents, and forming the fundamental material of the structure of plants. *—adj.* Containing cells. [< L *cellula.* See CELLULE.]

cellulose acetate *Chem.* **1** An acetic acid ester of cellulose: when coagulated or solidified it is used in making artificial leather and synthetic textile yarns and fabrics. **2** Acetate rayon.

cellulose nitrate *Chem.* A nitric acid ester of cellulose, its properties depending upon the nitrogen content: used in the manufacture of explosives and lacquers: also called *nitrocellulose.*

cel·lu·lous (sel′yə·ləs) *adj.* Consisting or full of cells.

ce·lom (sē′ləm) See COELOM.

cel·o·nav·i·ga·tion (sel′ō·nav′ə·gā′shən) *n.* That part of navigation in which position is determined by observation of celestial bodies; nautical astronomy: also called *astronavigation.* [< L *caelum* sky + NAVIGATION]

Cel·o·tex (sel′ə·teks) *n.* A sound-absorbing and heat-insulating board made by compressing bagasse into sheets: a trade name.

Cel·si·us scale (sel′sē·əs) A temperature scale in which the freezing point of water is 0° and the boiling point 100°: term now preferred to *centigrade scale.* [after Anders *Celsius,* 1701–44, Swedish astronomer]

Cel·sus (sel′səs) Epicurean philosopher of the

second century. — **Aurelius Cornelius,** Roman medical writer of the first century.

celt (selt) *n. Archeol.* A prehistoric or primitive implement or weapon of stone or bronze. [<LL *celtis* stone chisel]

CELT
Side. Front.

Celt (selt, kelt) *n.* **1** A person of Celtic linguistic stock, now represented by the Irish, Welsh, Highland Scots, Manx, Cornish, and Bretons, formerly by the ancient Gauls and Britons. **2** One of an ancient people of central and western Europe, known to the Greeks as *Keltoi* and to the Romans as *Celtae,* described as being fair and of great stature. Also spelled *Kelt.*

Celt·ic (sel′tik, kel′-) *n.* A subfamily of the Indo-European family of languages, including ancient Gaulish, the Brythonic or Cymric branch (Cornish, Welsh, Breton), and the Goidelic or Gaelic branch (Irish, Scottish Highland Gaelic, Manx). — *adj.* Of or pertaining to the Celtic peoples, their languages, or culture. Also spelled *Keltic.*

Celtic cross See under CROSS.

Celt·i·cism (sel′tə·siz′əm, kel′-) *n.* **1** A custom, idiom, or peculiarity of the Celts. **2** Devotion to Celtic customs.

Celt·i·cist (sel′tə·sist, kel′-) *n.* An authority on or scholar in the Celtic languages and literature.

Celtic renaissance 1 The resurgence of Irish national spirit, interest in Old Irish literature, and the creation of new, which began in the 1890's, led by Lady Augusta Gregory, Æ, Douglas Hyde, W. B. Yeats, John M. Synge, etc. **2** The revival of Irish Gaelic as the national language in the schools and business of the Irish Free State.

Celt·ism (sel′tiz·əm, kel′-) *n.* The Celtic temperament or spirit.

Celt·ist (sel′tist, kel′-) *n.* An authority on the Celts.

ce·ment (si·ment′) *n.* **1** Any substance, as a preparation of glue, red lead, or lime, the hardening of which causes objects between which it is applied to adhere firmly. **2** Any compound or substance applied in the form of a mortar and used for producing a hard and stony, smooth, waterproof surface, coating, filling, or lining, as for a floor or cistern. Ordinary cement is made by heating limestone and clay, or a natural rock containing both materials in right proportions. When it will harden under water, it is called **hydraulic cement. 3** That which serves to bind together persons or interests; bond of union. **4** *Metall.* **a** A finely divided metal obtained by precipitation: *cement* silver. **b** The substance in which iron is packed in the process of cementation. **5** Auriferous gravel held together by a clayey or silicic bond; also, the binding substance. **6** The glassy base of an igneous rock. **7** Cementum. — **Portland cement** A hydraulic cement made by calcining limestone with clayey matter, such as chalk and river mud. — *v.t.* **1** To unite or join with or as with cement. **2** To cover or coat with cement, as a cistern. — *v.i.* **3** To become united by means of cement; cohere. [<OF *ciment* <L *caementum* rough stone, stone chip < *caedere* cut] — **ce·ment′er** *n.*

ce·men·ta·tion (sē′mən·tā′shən, sem′ən-) *n.* **1** The act of cementing; result of cementing. **2** *Metall.* **a** A process of making steel by heating wrought iron in charcoal until it is carburized, or in making so-called malleable iron by heating cast iron in a bed of red hematite until it is partly decarburized. **b** The method of precipitating a metal from its solution, as the precipitation of metallic copper from a copper sulfate solution by means of metallic iron.

ce·ment·ite (si·men′tīt) *n. Metall.* Iron combined with carbon as it exists in steel before hardening; carbide of iron, Fe_3C.

ce·ment·um (si·men′təm) *n. Anat.* The layer of bony tissue developed over the roots of the teeth about the fifth month after birth: also called *cement.* [<L]

cem·e·ter·y (sem′ə·ter′ē) *n. pl.* **·ter·ies** A place for the burial of the dead; formerly, a churchyard or a catacomb; now, usually, a large parklike enclosure, laid out and kept for purposes of interment. [<L *cemeterium* <Gk. *koimētērion* < *koimaein* put to sleep]

cen·a·cle (sen′ə·kəl) *n.* **1** A small supper room, usually on an upper story. **2** The room in which the Last Supper of Jesus and His disciples was held. [<F *cénacle* <L *cenaculum* < *cena* dinner]

Cen·ci (chen′chē), **Beatrice,** 1577–99, Roman lady, executed as an accessory to her father's murder.

ce·nes·the·sia (sē′nis·thē′zhə, -zhē·ə, sen′is-) *n. Psychol.* The diffuse internal awareness of bodily existence, caused by the interaction of numerous unlocalized sensations whose aggregate expression may be of any degree of pain or pleasure. Also **ce′nes·the′sis.** Sometimes spelled *coenesthesia, coenesthesis.* [<CEN(O)- + Gk. *aisthēsis* feeling] — **ce′nes·thet′ic** (-thet′ik) *adj.*

Ce·nis (sə·nē′), **Mont** (môṅ) An Alpine pass in SE France on the Italian frontier; site of the **Mont Cenis tunnel** between France and Italy; 8 1/2 miles. *Italian* **Mon·te Ce·ni·sio** (mōn′tā chā·nē′zyō).

ceno- *combining form* Common: *cenobite.* Also spelled *coeno-.* Also, before vowels, **cen-.** [<Gk. *koinos* common]

cen·o·bite (sen′ə·bīt, sē′nə-) *n.* A monk; a member of a religious community (convent or monastery), as distinguished from a religious recluse, or *anchorite*: also spelled *coenobite.* [<LL *coenobita* < *coenobium* CENOBIUM] — **cen′o·bit′ic** (-bit′ik) or **·i·cal** *adj.* — **cen·o·bit·ism** (sen′ə·bit·iz′əm, sē′nə-) *n.*

ce·no·bi·um (si·nō′bē·əm) *n. pl.* **·bi·a** (-bē·ə) The abode of a society that has all things in common; especially, a monastery or other such religious community. Also **cen·o·by** (sen′ə·bē, sē′nə-). [<LL *coenobium* <Gk. *koinobion* < *koinos* common + *bios* life]

cen·o·gen·e·sis (sen′ə·jen′ə·sis, sē′nə-) *n. Biol.* A form of development in which the characters of an individual organism are not typical of the group to which it belongs: opposed to *palingenesis.* Also spelled *coenogenesis, kenogenesis.* [<CENO- + Gk. *genesis* origin] — **cen·o·ge·net·ic** (sen′ə·jə·net′ik, sē′nə-) *adj.*

ce·nog·o·nal (si·nog′ə·nəl) *adj.* **1** Having one or more angles in common. **2** *Mineral.* Pertaining to or describing different crystals some of whose angles have identical values. [<Gk. *koinos* common + *gōnia* angle]

cen·o·taph (sen′ə·taf, -täf) *n.* **1** An empty tomb. **2** A monument erected to the dead but not containing the remains. [<MF *cénotaphe* <L *cenotaphium* <Gk. *kenotaphion* < *kenos* empty + *taphos* tomb] — **cen′o·taph′ic** *adj.*

Ce·no·zo·ic (sē′nə·zō′ik, sen′ə-) *adj. Geol.* Of or pertaining to the fourth and latest of the eras of geologic time, following the Mesozoic, and extending to and including the present. The Cenozoic rocks are customarily divided into the Tertiary and Quaternary (or Pleistocene) systems. See chart under GEOLOGY. — *n.* The Cenozoic period: called also the *age of mammals.* Also spelled *Caenozoic, Cainozoic.* [<Gk. *kainos* new + *zōē* life]

cense (sens) *v.t.* **censed, cens·ing 1** To perfume with incense. **2** To offer burning incense to. [<INCENSE²]

cen·ser (sen′sər) *n.* A vessel for burning incense, especially in religious ceremonies; thurible. ◆ Homophone: *censor.* [<OF *censier,* short for *encensier* <Med. L *incensarium* < *incensum* incense]

cen·sor (sen′sər) *n.* **1** An official examiner of manuscripts and plays empowered to prohibit their publication or performance if offensive to the government or subversive of good morals. **2** An official who examines despatches, letters, etc., and, if necessary, prohibits forwarding or publication, especially in time of war. **3** Anyone who censures or arraigns; a critic. **4** In ancient Rome, one of two magistrates who kept the public register of citizens and of their property, and were entrusted with the supervision of public manners and morals. **5** *Psychoanal.* The subconscious mental force that disguises painful or unwanted memories and complexes or prevents them from rising to conscious recognition. — *v.t* To act as censor of; delete. ◆ Homophone: *censer.* [<L < *censere* judge] — **cen·so·ri·al** (sen·sôr′ē·əl, -sō′rē-) *adj.*

cen·so·ri·ous (sen·sôr′ē·əs, -sō′rē-) *adj.* **1** Given to censure; judging severely; faultfinding. **2** Containing or involving censure, as remarks. See synonyms under CAPTIOUS. — **cen·so′ri·ous·ly** *adv.* — **cen·so′ri·ous·ness** *n.*

cen·sor·ship (sen′sər·ship) *n.* **1** The office, term, power, system, or act of a censor or critic. **2** *Psychoanal.* The aggregate of selective agencies, both unconscious and deliberate, which are responsible for the suppression of unpleasant memories and thoughts, for the inhibition of impulses and behavior deemed improper, and for the exercise of discipline over the tendencies of the primitive ego or id.

cen·sur·a·ble (sen′shər·ə·bəl) *adj.* Deserving censure; culpable; blameworthy. — **cen′sur·a·ble·ness** *n.* — **cen′sur·a·bly** *adv.*

cen·sure (sen′shər) *n.* **1** Disapproval; condemnation or blame; adverse criticism. **2** Reprimand or discipline by ecclesiastical or political authority. **3** Critical recension of a literary work; revision. **4** *Obs.* A formal judgment or judicial sentence; opinion. — *v.t.* **·sured, ·sur·ing 1** To express disapproval of; condemn; blame. **2** To punish by a public reprimand, with or without some other penalty. **3** *Obs.* To pass judgment upon. [<F <L *censura* < *censere* judge] — **cen′sur·er** *n.*

cen·sus (sen′səs) *n. pl.* **cen·sus·es 1** An official numbering of the people of a country or district, embracing statistics of nativity, age, sex, employment, possessions, etc.; also, the printed record of it. **2** In ancient Rome, a similar enumeration of the people, but with special reference to their property, in order to determine taxation. [<L <*censere* assess] — **cen·su·al** (sen′shōō·əl) *adj.*

cent (sent) *n.* **1** The hundredth part of a dollar. In the United States it is legal tender for all sums not exceeding twenty-five cents. **2** Centum or cento, hundred: used only in per *cent,* etc. **3** The hundredth part of a standard unit in other money systems, as of the florin of the Netherlands. Equivalent forms are the centavo, centesimo, and centime. **4** *Music* A unit of pitch equal to one one-hundredth of the interval between any two successive semi-tones of the equally tempered scale: An octave contains 1200 *cents.* ◆ Homophone: *scent.* [<F <L *centum* hundred]

cen·tal (sen′təl) *adj.* **1** Of or pertaining to a hundred. **2** Counting by the hundred. — *n. Rare* A hundredweight. [<L *centum* hundred]

cen·tare (sen′târ, *Fr.* säṅ·tàr′) *n.* A measure of land area, equal to one square meter: also spelled *centiare.* See METRIC SYSTEM. [<F *centi-* hundredth (<L *centum* hundred) + *are* ARE²]

cen·taur (sen′tôr) **1** In Greek mythology, one of a race of monsters, having the head, arms, and torso of a man united to the body and legs of a horse. **2** An expert horseman. [<L *Centaurus* <Gk. *Kentauros*]

CENTAUR

Cen·tau·rus (sen·tôr′əs) A constellation of the southern sky which contains **Alpha Centauri,** the third brightest star known. See CONSTELLATION. Also **Cen′taur.**

cen·tau·ry (sen′tô·rē) *n. pl.* **·ries 1** One of certain small, mostly annual herbs (genera *Centaurium* and *Sabatia*) of the gentian family, with opposite leaves and clusters of rose, purple, or pink flowers, especially the Old World *C. umbellatum,* reputed to have medicinal properties. **2** A milkwort *(Polygala polygama).* [< L *centaureum* < Gk. *kentaureion*]

cen·ta·vo (sen·tä′vō) *n. pl.* **·vos** (-vōz, *Sp.* -vōs) **1** A small nickel or copper coin of the Philippines, Mexico, and other countries of Latin America, usually equal to the hundredth part of a peso. **2** A similar coin of Portugal and Brazil, equal to the hundredth part of an escudo. [< Sp.]

cen·te·nar·i·an (sen′tə·nâr′ē·ən) *n.* One who has reached the age of one hundred years. —*adj.* Of or pertaining to a hundred years, or to a hundredth anniversary.

cen·te·nar·y (sen′tə·ner′ē, sen·ten′ə·rē) *adj.* **1** Of or pertaining to a hundred or a century. **2** Completing a century. —*n. pl.* **·nar·ies 1** A hundredth anniversary. **2** A period of a hundred years. [< L *centenarius* hundredfold < *centum* hundred]

cen·ten·ni·al (sen·ten′ē·əl) *adj.* **1** Of or pertaining to a hundredth anniversary. **2** A hundred years old or more. —*n.* **1** A hundredth anniversary; also, its celebration. **2** A period of a hundred years; centennium. [< L *centum* hundred + *annus* a year] —**cen·ten′ni·al·ly** *adv.*

Centennial State Nickname of COLORADO.

cen·ten·ni·um (sen·ten′ē·əm) *n.* A century.

cen·ter (sen′tər) *n.* **1** *Geom.* **a** The point within a circle or sphere equally distant from any point on the circumference or surface. **b** The point within a regular polygon equidistant from the vertices. **2** The middle: the *center* of the town. **3** The point, object, or place about which things cluster or to which they converge. **4** A fixed point or line about which a thing or things revolve; point of attraction or convergence; focal point: the *center* of interest. **5** The point of divergence, emanation, or radiation; nucleus; origin. **6** The earth considered as the center of the universe; the center of the earth. **7** The part of a target nearest the bull's-eye, or a shot striking this part. **8** The middle part of an army in order of battle, occupying the front between the wings. **9** *Mech.* **a** One of two conical points, as in a lathe, between which an object is held and rotated on an axial line. The one at the end from which the object is rotated is the **live center,** the other the **dead center. b** The depression in a piece of revolving work, as a shaft, into which the conical point enters to support it. **10** The person who takes the middle position of the forward line in many athletic games, as football, basketball, etc. **11** Any place considered the hub of a specific activity: a manufacturing *center.* —*v.t.* **1** To place in the center. **2** To supply with a center. **3** To draw or converge in one place; concentrate. **4** In football, to pass the ball from the line to a backfield player. **5** To determine the center of; shape a lens so as to have it thickest in the center. —*v.i.* **6** To be in or at the center; have a focal point: The riots *centered* in the industrial section of the city. **7** To gather or converge, as toward a center: The crowds *centered* in the square. —*adj.* Central; middle. Also spelled *centre.* [< L *centrum* < Gk. *kentron* point (i.e., around which a circle is described)]

Synonyms (noun): middle, midst. We speak of the *center* of a circle, the *middle* of a room or the street. The *center* is equally distant from every point of the circumference of a circle, or from the opposite boundaries on each axis of a parallelogram, etc.; *middle* is more general and less definite. The *center* is a point; the *middle* may be a line or a space. We say *at* the *center*; *in* the *middle. Midst* commonly implies a group or multitude of surrounding objects. Compare synonyms for AMID. *Antonyms*: bound, boundary, circumference, perimeter, rim.

Cen·ter (sen′tər) *n.* In some European legislatures, the members sitting on the middle benches, a position generally assigned to those of moderate views: also spelled *Centre.*

cen·ter·bit (sen′tər·bit′) *n.* A bit with a cutting edge that revolves about a central point.

cen·ter·board (sen′tər·bôrd′, -bōrd′) *n. Naut.* **1** In certain fore-and-aft vessels, a movable device which can be lowered through a watertight slot so as to prevent leeway. **2** A boat furnished with this device.

cen·ter·ing (sen′tər·ing) *n.* **1** The act or operation of bringing an object within the focus of a microscope, telescope, etc. **2** A temporary support of an arch or other part of a building. Also **cen′tring.**

center of mass *Physics* **1** That point in a body at which all its mass can be concentrated without altering the effect of gravitation upon it. **2** The point in which a body near the earth's surface, acted upon by gravity or other parallel forces, is balanced in all positions: commonly known as **center of gravity.**

cen·ter·piece (sen′tər·pēs′) *n.* An ornament in the center of a table, ceiling, etc., or between other ornaments: also spelled *centrepiece.*

center table A medium-sized table of almost any shape, finished on all sides to stand in the center of a room.

cen·tes·i·mal (sen·tes′ə·məl) *adj.* **1** Hundredth; of or divided into hundredths. **2** Pertaining to progression by hundreds. [< L *centesimus* hundredth] —**cen·tes′i·mal·ly** *adv.*

cen·tes·i·mo (sen·tes′ə·mō; *Ital.* chen·tes′ē·mō, & *Sp.* sen·tes′ē·mō) **1** *pl.* **·mi** (-mē) An Italian coin, equal to the hundredth part of a lira. **2** *pl.* **·mos** (-mōz, *Sp.* -mōs) A small Uruguayan coin, equal to the hundredth part of a peso.

centi- *combining form* **1** Hundred: *centipede.* **2** In the metric system, hundredth: *centiliter.* [< L *centum* hundred]

cen·ti·are (sen′tē·âr) See CENTARE.

cen·ti·grade (sen′tə·grād) *adj.* Graduated to a scale of a hundred. On the **centigrade scale** (now called the *Celsius scale*) the freezing point of water at normal atmospheric pressure is 0° and its boiling point 100°. The distance between those two points in the Fahrenheit and Réaumur is 180° and 80° respectively. See TEMPERATURE. [< F < L *centum* hundred + *gradus* step, degree]

cen·ti·gram (sen′tə·gram) *n.* The hundredth part of a gram. See METRIC SYSTEM. Also **cen′ti·gramme.** [< F *centigramme*]

cen·tile (sen′til, -tīl) See PERCENTILE.

cen·ti·li·ter (sen′tə·lē′tər) *n.* The hundredth part of a liter. See METRIC SYSTEM. Also **cen′ti·li′tre** [< F *centilitre*]

Cen·ti·man·us (sen′tə·man′əs) In Roman mythology, a hundred-handed giant: identified with the Greek *Hecatoncheires.*

cen·time (sän′tēm, *Fr.* sän·tēm′) *n.* In France, Belgium, and Switzerland, a hundredth of a franc; also, a coin of this value. [< F < OF *centisme* < L *centesimus* hundredth]

cen·ti·me·ter (sen′tə·mē′tər) *n.* The hundredth part of a meter. See METRIC SYSTEM. Also **cen′ti·me′tre.** [< F *centimètre*]

cen·ti·me·ter-gram-sec·ond (sen′tə·mē′tər·gram′sek′ənd) See CGS.

cen·ti·mo (sen′tə·mō) *n. pl.* **·mos** The hundredth part of a Spanish peseta.

cen·ti·pede (sen′tə·pēd) *n.* Any of a class (Chilopoda) of carnivorous, predatory arthropods having elongate, segmented bodies bearing a pair of legs on each segment, the front pair being modified into poison claws. Also called *chilopod.* [< F < L *centipeda* < *centum* hundred + *pes, pedis* foot]

cen·ti·poise (sen′tə·poiz) *n.* The hundredth part of a poise. [< CENTI- + POISE[2]]

cen·ti·stere (sen′tə·stir) *n.* A hundredth of a stere. See METRIC SYSTEM. [< F *centistère*]

cent·ner (sent′nər) *n.* **1** The hundredweight of various European countries, or 110.23 pounds, equal to 50 kilograms. **2** *Metall.* A hundred pounds. **3** In assaying, one dram. —**metric centner** Quintal. [< G *centner, zentner* hundredweight < L *centenarius* of a hundred]

cen·to (sen′tō) *n. pl.* **·tos 1** A writing composed of selections from various authors or from different works of the same author. **2** *Obs.* Patchwork. [< L, patchwork cloak]

cen·tral (sen′trəl) *adj.* **1** Of or pertaining to, equidistant or acting from, the center. **2** Being a dominant or controlling factor, element, etc.; chief. **3** Constituting the principal point; a *central* event in history. **4** *Phonet.* Formed with a tongue position intermediate between front and back: said of vowels. —*n.* **1** *Colloq.* A telephone exchange; also, the operator in charge of it. **2** In Latin America, a sugar mill grinding for a number of plantations. [< L *centralis* < *centrum* center] —**cen′tral·ly** *adv.* —**cen′tral·ness** *n.*

Central African Republic An independent republic of the French Community; 238,244 square miles; capital, Bangui; formerly *Ubangi-Shari,* a French overseas territory.

Central America A narrow, winding strip of land between North America proper and

the South American continent, generally understood to include Guatemala, British Honduras, Honduras, El Salvador, Nicaragua, Costa Rica, and Panama.

central angle See under ANGLE.

Central Asia See SOVIET CENTRAL ASIA.

central heating A system of heating a building by piping hot steam, water, or air from a central source to heat distributors located in separate rooms, apartments, etc.

Central India A former political agency in India, including a large number of princely states; 51,946 square miles.

cen·tral·ism (sen′trəl·iz′əm) *n.* Concentration of control in a central authority, especially of government control. —**cen′tral·ist** *n.* & *adj.* —**cen′tral·is′tic** *adj.*

cen·tral·i·ty (sen·tral′ə·tē) *n.* **1** The state of being central. **2** Tendency toward or situation at a center.

cen·tral·ize (sen′trəl·īz) *v.* **·ized, ·iz·ing** *v.t.* **1** To make central; bring to a center; concentrate. **2** To concentrate (power or control) in one authority. —*v.i.* **3** To come to a center; concentrate. —**cen′tral·i·za′tion** *n.* —**cen′tral·iz′er** *n.*

Central Kar·roo (kə·rōō′) See GREAT KARROO.

Central Powers The countries opposed to the Allied Nations in World War I: Germany, Austria-Hungary, Bulgaria, and Turkey.

Central Provinces and Berar The former name for MADHYA PRADESH.

central spindle *Biol.* The fibrous portions of protoplasm lying between the asters in a karyokinetic division of a cell, and about which the chromosomes are grouped.

central staging See ARENA THEATER.

Central Standard Time See STANDARD TIME. Abbr. *C.S.T.*

Central Valley The great longitudinal trough in California between the Coast Ranges and the Sierra Nevada: also *Great Valley.*

Central Vietnam Former Annam, now a constituent part of Vietnam.

cen·tre (sen′tər) *n., v.t. & v.i.* **·tred, ·tring** Center.

Cen·tre (sen′tər) See CENTER.

Centre, the *Austral.* The central region of Australia, from 1926–31 a separate administrative area.

centri- *combining form* Center: equivalent of CENTRO-: used in words of Latin origin, as in *centrifugal.* [< L *centrum* center]

cen·tric (sen′trik) *adj.* **1** Central; centrally situated. **2** Belonging to or described around a center. **3** *Physiol.* Related to or connected with a nerve center. Also **cen′tri·cal.** —**cen·tri·cal·i·ty** (sen′tri·kal′ə·tē), **cen·tric·i·ty** (sen·tris′ə·tē) *n.* —**cen′tri·cal·ly** *adv.*

cen·trif·u·gal (sen·trif′yə·gəl, -ə·gəl) *adj.* **1** Directed or tending away from a center; radiating: opposed to *centripetal.* **2** Employing centrifugal force: a *centrifugal* pump. **3** *Bot.* **a** Developing from the center or apex outward, or toward the base; determinate. **b** Turned from the center toward the side of a fruit, as a radicle. **4** *Physiol.* Leading away from the central nervous system; efferent. —*n.* **1** The drum-

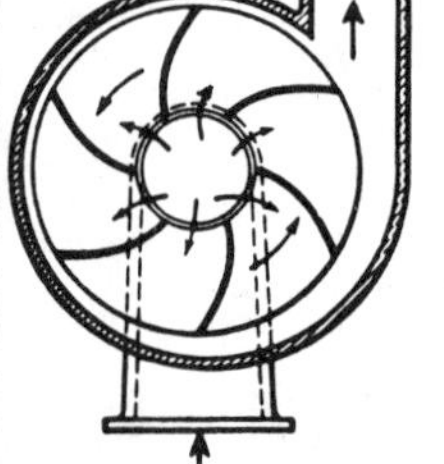
CENTRIFUGAL (*n. def. 1*)

like rotary part of a centrifuge or other centrifugal machine. 2 *pl.* Sugars from which the molasses has been removed by a centrifugal machine: also **centrifugal sugar.** [< NL *centrifugus* < L *centrum* center + *fugere* flee] **—cen·trif′u·gal·ly** *adv.*

centrifugal force *Physics* The inertial reaction of a body against a force constraining it to move in a curved path.

cen·tri·fuge (sen′trə·fyōōj) *n.* A rotary machine, with accessory containers, tubes, etc., for the separation by controlled centrifugal force of substances having different densities. —*v.t.* **·fuged, ·fug·ing** To subject to the action of a centrifuge. **—cen·trif·u·ga·tion** (sen·trif′yə·gā′shən, -ə·gā′-) *n.*

cen·tri·ole (sen′trē·ōl) *n. Biol.* A minute structure, frequently double, enclosed within the centrosome which forms the center of the aster in cell division, and with which it makes up the central body. For illustration see under CELL. [< CENTRI- + -OLE[2]]

cen·trip·e·tal (sen·trip′ə·təl) *adj.* **1** Directed, tending, or drawing toward a center: *centripetal* force. **2** Acting by drawing toward a center: a *centripetal* pump. **3** *Bot.* **a** Developing from without toward the center or in the direction of the apex. **b** Turned toward the axis of the fruit, as a radicle. **4** *Physiol.* Conducting toward the central nervous system; afferent. [< NL *centripetus* < *centrum* center + *petere* seek]

centripetal force *Physics* A force attracting a body toward a center around which it revolves.

cen·trist (sen′trist) *n.* One who takes the middle position in politics, especially in France.

centro- *combining form* Center: used in words of Greek origin, as in *centrosphere.* Also, before vowels, **centr-.** [< Gk. *kentron* center]

cen·tro·bar·ic (sen′trə·bar′ik) *adj. Physics* Relating to the center of gravity of a body. [< CENTRO- + Gk. *baros* weight]

cen·troid (sen′troid) *n.* **1** *Physics* Center of mass. **2** *Mech.* The point at which the area of a body may be concentrated without altering the moment of any line in its plane, as the center of a square or the intersections of the median lines of a triangle.

cen·tro·some (sen′trə·sōm) *n. Biol.* The small area of protoplasm at the center of each aster in cell division: it contains the centrioles. [< CENTRO- + Gk. *sōma* body] **—cen′tro·som′ic** (-som′ik) *adj.*

cen·tro·sphere (sen′trə·sfir′) *n.* **1** *Geol.* The central portion of the terrestrial globe. Compare HYDROSPHERE, LITHOSPHERE. **2** *Biol.* In living cells, the sphere from which the astral rays diverge, and which surrounds the centrosome, if any. For illustration see under CELL.

cen·trum (sen′trəm) *n. pl.* **·trums** or **·tra** (-trə) **1** A center or central mass. **2** *Zool.* The body of a vertebra. [< L]

cen·tum (ken′təm) *n.* One of the two main divisions of the Indo-European languages; namely, the western division, including the Hellenic, Italic, Celtic, and Germanic languages and dialects, in which the proto-Indo-European palatalized velar stop (k) is retained as a velar, as in the Latin word *centum* "hundred." Compare SATEM. See INDO-EUROPEAN.

cen·tum·vir (sen·tum′vər) *n. pl.* **·virs** or **·vi·ri** (-və·rī) In ancient Rome, one of the judges (105 to 180 in number) appointed yearly to try common causes. [< L < *centum* hundred + *vir* man] **—cen·tum′vi·ral** *adj.*

cen·tum·vi·rate (sen·tum′və·rāt) *n.* **1** The office or term of a centumvir. **2** The centumviri as a body. **3** Any body of 100 men.

cen·tu·ple (sen′tə·pəl, sen·tōō′pəl, -tyōō′-) *v.t.* **·pled, ·pling** To increase a hundredfold. —*adj.* Increased a hundredfold. [< F < L *centuplus* hundredfold]

cen·tu·pli·cate (sen·tōō′plə·kāt, -tyōō′-) *v.t.* **·cat·ed, ·cat·ing** To multiply by a hundred; centuple. —*adj.* & *n.* (-kit) Hundredfold. [< LL *centuplicatus,* pp. of *centuplicare* increase a hundredfold < *centuplex* hundredfold]

cen·tu·ri·al (sen·tōōr′ē·əl, -tyōōr′-) *adj.* **1** Of or pertaining to a century of the Roman army or people. **2** Of or pertaining to a hundred years.

cen·tu·ried (sen′chə·rēd) *adj.* **1** Continued or maintained for one or more than one century. **2** Having endured for hundreds of years.

cen·tu·ri·on (sen·tōōr′ē·ən, -tyōōr′-) *n.* A captain of a century in the ancient Roman army. [< L *centurio, -onis*]

cen·tu·ry (sen′chə·rē) *n. pl.* **·ries 1** One hundred consecutive years, reckoning from a specific date. **2** A period of 100 years in any system of chronology, especially in reckoning from the first year of the Christian era: the twentieth *century,* A.D. 1901–2000. **3** A body of Roman foot soldiers (at one time 100 men); one sixtieth of a legion; also, one of the 193 divisions into which the Roman people were divided according to their incomes. **4** A hundred; hundred things of the same kind collectively. [< L *centuria* < *centum* hundred]

century plant An agave *(Agave americana)* which flowers once in twenty or thirty years and then dies. Also called *American aloe.*

ceorl (cheôrl, kyûrl) *n.* In ancient England, a freeman of the lowest rank; a churl. [OE] **—ceorl′ish** *adj.*

Ce·os (sē′os) The ancient name for KEOS: also *Cea.*

ce·pha·e·line (si·fā′ə·lēn, -lin) *n. Chem.* A white, crystalline alkaloid, $C_{28}H_{38}O_4N_2$, from ipecac: regarded as more powerful than emetine. [< NL *cephaelis,* genus name of ipecac]

ceph·a·lad (sef′ə·lad) *adv. Zool.* Toward the head of an animal body: opposed to *caudad.* [< Gk. *kephalē* head]

ceph·a·lal·gia (sef′ə·lal′jē·ə) *n.* A headache. [< Gk. *kephalē* head + *algos* pain]

ce·phal·ic (sə·fal′ik) *adj.* **1** Of, pertaining to, on, in, or near the head. **2** Performing the functions of a head. **3** Relatively nearer the head or the end of the body where the head is situated: the *cephalic* end of the sternum. [< Gk. *kephalē* head]

-cephalic *combining form* Head; skull: *brachycephalic.* [< Gk. *kephalē* head]

cephalic index *Anat.* The figure that expresses the ratio of the greatest breadth of the human skull to the greatest length, the former being multiplied by 100. Skulls are usually designated as *brachycephalic, mesocephalic,* and *dolichocephalic:* also called *cranial index.*

ceph·a·lin (sef′ə·lin) *n. Biochem.* A yellowish amorphous phospholipid obtained from the brain substance or spinal cord of mammals, which acts as a blood coagulant: also spelled *kephalin.*

ceph·a·li·za·tion (sef′ə·lə·zā′shən, -lī·zā′-) *n. Zool.* Concentration or localization of functions, powers, or parts in or toward the head: the *cephalization* of the vertebrate nervous system.

cephalo- *combining form* Head: *cephalometer.* Also, before vowels, **cephal-.** [< Gk. *kephalē* head]

ceph·a·lo·cau·dal (sef′ə·lō·kô′dəl) *adj. Anat.* Of or pertaining to the head or tail, or to the long axis of the body. Also **ceph′a·lo·cer′cal** (-sûr′kəl). [< CEPHALO- + L *cauda* tail]

ceph·a·lo·chor·date (sef′ə·lō·kôr′dāt) *adj. Zool.* Having the notochord continued into the head: said especially of the lancelets. Also **ceph′·a·lo·chor′dal.** —*n.* An animal having such a notochord.

ceph·a·lom·e·ter (sef′ə·lom′ə·tər) *n.* An instrument for measuring the head or skull, as for ascertaining the size of a fetal head (in parturition); craniometer. [< CEPHALO- + Gk. *metron* measure] **—ceph′a·lom′e·try** *n.*

Ceph·a·lo·ni·a (sef′ə·lō′nē·ə, -lōn′yə) One of the Ionian Islands, western Greece; 289 square miles; capital, Argostoli: Greek *Kephallenia.*

ceph·a·lo·pod (sef′ə·lə·pod′) *n.* Any of a class (Cephalopoda) of predaceous marine mollusks, including squids, octopuses, cuttlefish, and nautiluses, having a clearly defined head and eyes and tentacles surrounding the mouth. —*adj.* Of or pertaining to the class Cephalopoda. **— ceph·a·lop·o·dan** (sef′ə·lop′ə·dən) *adj.* & *n.* **— ceph·a·lop·o·dous** (sef′ə·lop′ə·dəs) *adj.*

ceph·a·lo·tho·rax (sef′ə·lō·thôr′aks, -thō′raks) *n. Zool.* The anterior portion of certain arthropods, as crustaceans and arachnids, consisting of the united head and thorax. **—ceph′a·lo·tho·rac′ic** (-thə·ras′ik) *adj.*

ceph·a·lous (sef′ə·ləs) *adj.* Having a head.

-cephalous *combining form* Headed: *hydrocephalous.* [< Gk. *kephalē* head]

Ce·phas (sē′fəs) A masculine personal name. *John* i 42. [< Aramaic, a stone]

Ceph·e·id variable (sef′ē·id) *Astron.* Any of a class of variable stars characterized by a uniform, relatively short-term cycle of brightness associated with corresponding internal changes: so called from the star Delta in the constellation of Cepheus.

Ce·pheus (sē′fyōōs, -fē·əs) **1** In Greek legend, a king of Ethiopia, husband of Cassiopeia and father of Andromeda. **2** A northern constellation near Draco and Cassiopeia. See CONSTELLATION.

ce·ra·ceous (si·rā′shəs) *adj.* Of the nature of or like wax; waxy. [< L *cera* wax]

Ce·ram (si·ram′; *Du.* sā′ram, *Pg.* sə·räṅ′) An Indonesian island in the Banda Sea west of New Guinea; 6,622 square miles.

ce·ram·al (sə·ram′əl) *n. Metall.* A combination of metals, as iron and cobalt, with ceramic materials such as boron or titanium carbide, developed to provide alloys resistant to very high temperatures, as on the blades of turbine airplane engines. [< CERAM(IC) AL(LOY)]

ce·ram·ic (sə·ram′ik) *adj.* Pertaining to pottery and to articles made of clay that have been fired and baked. Also spelled *keramic.* [< Gk. *keramikos* < *keramos* potters' clay]

ce·ram·ics (sə·ram′iks) *n.* **1** The art of molding, modeling, and baking in clay: construed as singular. **2** Objects made of fired and baked clay: construed as plural. **—cer·a·mist** (ser′ə·mist) *n.*

Ceram Sea An arm of the Pacific north of Ceram, extending from Obi to New Guinea.

ce·rar·gy·rite (sə·rär′jə·rīt) *n.* An isometric, brown, easily sectile silver chloride, AgCl; horn silver. [< Gk. *keras* horn + *argyros* silver]

ce·ras·tes (sə·ras′tēz) *n.* A horned viper of North Africa and the Near East *(Cerastes cornutus).* [< L < Gk. *kerastēs* < *keras* horn]

ce·rate (sir′āt) *n.* A medicated ointment of oil or lard mixed with resin, wax, etc. Cerates are intermediate in consistency between ointments and plasters. [< L *ceratus,* pp. of *cerare* smear with wax < *cera* wax]

ce·rat·ed (sir′ā·tid) *adj.* Covered with wax.

cerato- *combining form* Horn; of or like horn: *ceratodus.* Also, before vowels, **cerat-.** [< Gk. *keras, -atos* horn]

ce·rat·o·dus (sə·rat′ə·dəs, ser′ə·tō′dəs) *n.* The barramunda. [< NL < Gk. *keras* horn + *odous* tooth]

cer·a·toid (ser′ə·toid) *adj.* **1** Horny; horn-shaped. **2** Of or pertaining to a superfamily *(Ceratoidea)* of mostly small deep-sea fishes having luminescent organs.

Cer·ber·us (sûr′bər·əs) In Greek and Roman mythology, the three-headed dog guarding the portals of Hades. **—Cer·be·re·an** (sər·bir′ē·ən) *adj.*

CERBERUS

cer·car·i·a (sər·kâr′ē·ə) *n. pl.* **·car·i·ae** (-kâr′i·ē) *Zool.* A larval, parasitic form of a trematode worm, originating as a bud from a birth stage and having a tail that is lost in the adult. [< NL < Gk. *kerkos* tail] **—cer·car′i·al** *adj.* **—cer·car′i·an** *adj.* & *n.*

cer·co·pi·the·coid (sûr′kō·pi·thē′koid) *adj. Zool.* Relating to or describing any of a superfamily or group *(Cercopithecoidea)* of Old World monkeys evolved from prosimian stock by adaptive radiation and including macaques, mandrills, baboons, langurs, and Barbary apes. —*n.* A member of this group. [< NL < L *cercopithecus* < Gk. *kerkopithēkos* < *kerkos* tail + *pithēkos* ape]

cer·cus (sûr′kəs) *n. pl.* **·ci** (-sī) *Entomol.* One of a pair of anal appendages found in many insects, as in the cockroach. [< NL < Gk. *kerkos* tail]

cere[1] (sir) *v.t.* **cered, cer·ing 1** *Obs.* To cover with or as with wax; to wax. **2** To wrap in cerecloth; wrap (a dead body). ◆ Homophones: *sear, sere.* [< F *cirer* < L *cerare* smear with wax < *cera* wax]

cere[2] (sir) *n. Ornithol.* A waxlike, fleshy area about the bill, in parrots and birds of prey, containing the nostrils. ◆ Homophones: *sear, sere.* [< F *cire* < L *cera* wax]

ce·re·al (sir′ē·əl) *n.* **1** An edible starchy grain yielded by certain plants of the grass family, as rice, wheat, rye, oats, etc. **2** Any of the plants yielding such grains. **3** A breakfast food made from a cereal grain. —*adj.* Pertaining to edible grain. ◆ Homophone: *serial.* [< L *cerealis* of grain < *Ceres,* goddess of grain]

cer·e·bel·lum (ser′ə·bel′əm) *n. pl.* **·bel·lums** or **·bel·la** (-bel′ə) The massive, dorsally located organ of the central nervous system forming that part of the brain below and behind the cerebrum. It consists of a central lobe and two lateral lobes and acts as the coordination center of voluntary movements, posture, and equilibrium. [< L, dim. of *cerebrum* brain] —**cer′e·bel′lar** *adj.*

cer·e·bral (ser′ə·brəl, sə·rē′-) *adj.* **1** Of or pertaining to the cerebrum or the brain. **2** Appealing to the intellect; requiring mental activity; intellectual. **3** *Phonet.* Cacuminal. —*n. Phonet.* A cerebral consonant, as *ṭ* and *ḍ* in the Indic languages. [< F *cérébral* < L *cerebrum* brain]

cerebral hemisphere *Anat.* One of the two halves into which the brain is divided.

cerebral palsy *Pathol.* Any paralysis affecting the ability to control movement and caused by brain lesions resulting from prenatal defect or birth injury.

cer·e·brate (ser′ə·brāt) *v.* **·brat·ed, ·brat·ing** *v.t.* **1** To perform by brain action. —*v.i.* **2** To have or manifest brain action. **3** To think. [< L *cerebrum* brain]

cer·e·bra·tion (ser′ə·brā′shən) *n.* **1** The functional activity of the cerebrum. **2** The act of thinking; thought.

cer·e·brin (ser′ə·brin) *n.* A cerebroside found in brain substance and isolated as a yellowish-white powder, $C_{17}H_{33}NO_3$.

cer·e·bri·tis (ser′ə·brī′tis) *n. Pathol.* Inflammation of the cerebrum.

cerebro- *combining form* Brain; pertaining to the brain: *cerebrospinal.* Also, before vowels, **cerebr-** [< L *cerebrum* brain]

cer·e·bro·side (ser′ə·brō·sīd′) *n. Biochem.* A nitrogenous fatty substance found in brain and nerve tissue, containing galactose and forming a series of complex fatty acids, as phrenosin: also called *galactolipin.* [< CEREBR(O)- + -OSE + -IDE]

cer·e·bro·spi·nal (ser′ə·brō·spī′nəl) *adj.* Of or pertaining to the brain and spinal cord.

cerebrospinal fever Meningitis.

cer·e·brum (ser′ə·brəm) *n. pl.* **·bra** (-brə) or **·brums** The enlarged upper and anterior part of the brain in vertebrates, consisting of two lateral hemispheres. [< L] —**cer·e·bric** (ser′ə·brik, sə·rē′-) *adj.*

cere·cloth (sir′klôth′, -kloth′) *n.* A cloth coated or saturated with wax or some gummy substance, used as a waterproof covering, a medicinal application, or a winding sheet. [orig. *cered cloth* < CERE[1]]

cered (sird) *adj.* **1** Having a cere. **2** Smeared or saturated with wax.

cere·ment (sir′mənt) *n.* A cerecloth; a garment or wrapping for the dead; usually in the plural. [< F *cirement* a waxing < *cirer* CERE[1]]

cer·e·mo·ni·al (ser′ə·mō′nē·əl) *adj.* Of or pertaining to ceremony; ritual; formal. —*n.* **1** A system of rules of ceremony; ritual; also, social etiquette. **2** A ceremony. See synonyms under FORM. —**cer′e·mo′ni·al·ism** *n.* —**cer′e·mo′ni·al·ist** *n.* —**cer′e·mo′ni·al·ly** *adv.*

cer·e·mo·ni·ous (ser′ə·mō′nē·əs) *adj.* **1** Observant of or conducted with ceremony; formal. **2** Conventional; studiously polite. **3** Ceremonial. —**cer′e·mo′ni·ous·ly** *adv.* —**cer′e·mo′ni·ous·ness** *n.*

cer·e·mo·ny (ser′ə·mō′nē) *n. pl.* **·nies** **1** A formal or symbolical act or observance, or a series of them, as on religious and state occasions. **2** The doing of some formal act in the manner prescribed by authority or usage: the *ceremonies* at an ordination, inauguration, or coronation. **3** Mere outward form. **4** Observance of etiquette or conventional forms in social matters; formal civility; adherence to the prescribed forms of amenity. —**to stand on ceremony** **1** To observe conventions. **2** To be formal, stiff, or uncordial. See synonyms under FORM, SACRAMENT. [< OF *cerymonie* < L *caerimonia* awe, veneration]

Ce·ren·kov effect (se·ren′kôf) *Physics* The emission of light by a charged particle passing through a medium with a velocity greater than the velocity of light in that medium. Also **Cerenkov radiation.** [after P. A. *Cerenkov,* U.S.S.R. physicist]

Ce·res (sir′ēz) **1** In Roman mythology, the goddess of grain and harvests: identified with the Greek *Demeter.* **2** *Astron.* The first of the asteroids to be discovered.

cer·e·sin (ser′ə·sin) *n.* Ozocerite. [< L *cera* wax]

ce·re·us (sir′ē·əs) *n.* Any of a genus of cactuses *(Cereus)* having large lateral tubular flowers, often nocturnal, whence several have the name of *night-blooming cereus.* [< L *cereus* waxy < *cera* wax]

ce·ri·a (sir′ē·ə) *n. Chem.* An infusible compound, CeO_2, used in the manufacture of incandescent mantles; cerium dioxide.

ce·rif·er·ous (sə·rif′ər·əs) *adj.* Yielding or producing wax. [< L *cera* wax + *ferre* bear]

Ce·ri·go (chā′rē·gō) The Italian name for KYTHERA.

cer·iph (ser′if) See SERIF.

ce·rise (sə·rēz′, -rēs′) *adj.* Of a vivid red. —*n.* A vivid red color. [< F, cherry]

ce·rite (sir′īt) *n.* A resinous, brown, orthorhombic hydrous cerium silicate. [< CERIUM]

ce·ri·um (sir′ē·əm) *n.* A silvery-white, ductile, highly reactive and electropositive metallic element (symbol Ce, atomic number 58), being the most abundant of the lanthanide series. See PERIODIC TABLE. [after the asteroid *Ceres*]

cerium metals A subgroup of the lanthanide series of elements, including lanthanum, cerium, praseodymium, neodymium, illinium, samarium, europium, and gadolinium.

cer·met (sûr′met) *n.* An alloy of a heat-resistant compound and a metal, used for strength and to withstand high temperatures. [< CER(AMIC) + MET(AL)]

Cer·nă·u·ţi (cher′nə·ōōts′) The Rumanian name for CHERNOVTSY.

cer·nu·ous (sûr′nyōō·əs) *adj. Bot.* Drooping or nodding, as a flower. [< L *cernuus* stooping]

ce·ro (sir′ō) *n. pl.* **·ros** A scombroid fish *(Scomberomorus regalis,* or *S. cavalla)* closely related to, but larger than, the Spanish mackerel. The **common cero** *(S. regalis)* weighs as much as 20 pounds, and the **spotted** or **king cero** *(S. cavalla)* up to 100 pounds. See PINTADO. [< Sp. *sierra* < L *serra* saw]

cero- *combining form* Wax: *cerotype.* Also, before vowels, **cer-.** [< L *cera* or Gk. *kēros* wax]

ce·rog·ra·phy (si·rog′rə·fē) *n.* **1** The art of engraving or writing on wax. **2** Painting by the encaustic method. **3** The wax process of printing. [< Gk. *kērographia* < *kēros* wax + *graphein* write] —**ce·ro·graph** (sir′ə·graf, -gräf) *n.* —**ce′ro·graph′ic** *adj.* —**ce·rog′ra·phist** *n.*

ce·roon (sə·rōōn′) See SEROON.

ce·ro·plas·tic (sir′ə·plas′tik) *adj.* **1** Pertaining to or of the nature of wax modeling. **2** Modeled in wax. [< Gk. *kēroplastikos* < *kēros* wax + *plassein* mold]

ce·rot·ic (si·rot′ik) *adj.* Of, pertaining to, or derived from beeswax, as **cerotic acid,** $C_{26}H_{53}COOH$. [< Gk. *kērōtos* waxed < *kēros* wax]

cer·o·type (sir′ə·tīp′, ser′-) *n.* **1** A process of engraving in which a metal plate is coated with wax, which is cut away according to some design, and a cast made therefrom in plaster. **2** A printing plate so produced.

ce·rous[1] (sir′əs) *adj. Chem.* Of, pertaining to, or containing cerium in its lower valence.

ce·rous[2] (sir′əs) *adj.* Of the nature of a cere.

Cer·ro de Pas·co (ser′rō thā päs′kō) **1** A town in central Peru. **2** A peak of the Peruvian Andes in this vicinity; 15,100 feet.

Cer·ro Gor·do (ser′ō gôr′dō) A mountain pass NE of Mexico City.

cer·tain (sûr′tən) *adj.* **1** Established as fact or truth so as to be absolutely known, accepted as true, and depended upon; beyond doubt or question; demonstrable; true. **2** Absolutely confident as to truth or reality; sure; convinced. **3** Definitely settled so as not to be variable or fluctuating; fixed; determined; stated. **4** That may be absolutely predicted; sure to come; inevitable: Death is *certain.* **5** Sure in its workings or results; reliable; effectual. **6** Determinate, but not particularized or named; indefinite, but assumed to be determinable: a *certain* man. See synonyms under AUTHENTIC, CONSCIOUS, INCONTESTABLE, SECURE, SURE. [< OF < L *certus* < *cernere* determine]

cer·tain·ly (sûr′tən·lē) *adv.* With certainty; surely.

cer·tain·ty (sûr′tən·tē) *n. pl.* **·ties** **1** The quality or fact of being certain. **2** A known truth. **3** Precision; accuracy.

Synonyms: assurance, certitude, confidence, conviction, demonstration, evidence, infallibility, positiveness, proof, surety. See DEMONSTRATION. Compare ASSURANCE. *Antonyms*: conjecture, doubt, dubiousness, hesitation, indecision, misgiving, precariousness, uncertainty.

cer·tes (sûr′tēz) *adv. Archaic* Truly; certainly; verily. [< OF < *a certes* < L *certus.* See CERTAIN.]

cer·tif·i·cate (sər·tif′ə·kit) *n.* **1** A written declaration or testimonial. **2** A writing signed and legally authenticated. **3** A writing or statement certifying that the one named therein has satisfactorily completed a certain educational course. —**gold** (or **silver**) **certificates** Certificates issued by the U.S. government, and used as currency, on the basis of gold (or silver) bullion of equal amounts deposited with the government for their redemption. —*v.t.* (-kāt) **·cat·ed, ·cat·ing** To furnish with or attest by a certificate. [< Med. L *certificatus,* pp. of *certificare.* See CERTIFY.] —**cer·tif·i·ca·to·ry** (sər·tif′ə·kə·tôr′ē, -tō′rē) *adj.*

certificate of deposit A statement issued by a bank certifying that a person has a specified sum on deposit.

cer·ti·fi·ca·tion (sûr′tə·fi·kā′shən) *n.* **1** The act of certifying; the guaranteeing of the truth or validity of; attestation. **2** A certified statement; a certificate.

certified check A check marked or stamped, as by a bank official, to certify that it is genuine and that it represents an account having sufficient funds for the bank to guarantee its payment.

certified milk Milk produced and bottled under sanitary conditions, in compliance with all State and municipal regulations.

certified public accountant See under ACCOUNTANT.

cer·ti·fy (sûr′tə·fī) *v.* **·fied, ·fy·ing** *v.t.* **1** To give certain knowledge of; attest. **2** To assert as a matter of fact; assure. **3** To give a certificate of, as insanity. —*v.i.* **4** To make attestation as to truth or excellence. [< F *certifier* < Med.L *certificare* attest < L *certus* certain + *facere* make] —**cer′ti·fi′a·ble** *adj.* —**cer′ti·fi′er** *n.*

cer·ti·o·ra·ri (sûr′shē·ə·râr′ē, -râr′ī) *n. Law* A writ from a superior to an inferior court, directing a certified record of its proceedings in a designated case to be sent up for review. [< LL, to be certified]

cer·ti·tude (sûr′tə·tōōd, -tyōōd) *n.* **1** Perfect assurance; confidence. **2** Assured fact or reality; sureness and precision. See synonyms under CERTAINTY. [< Med.L *certitudo* < L *certus.* See CERTAIN.]

ce·ru·le·an (sə·rōō′lē·ən) *adj.* & *n.* Sky blue. [< L *caeruleus* dark blue]

cerulean blue A light-blue pigment made from the combined oxides of cobalt and tin.

ce·ru·men (sə·rōō′mən) *n.* Earwax. [< NL < L *cera* wax] —**ce·ru′mi·nous** *adj.*

ce·ruse (sir′ōōs, sə·rōōs′) *n.* **1** White lead. **2** A cosmetic made from it. [< F *céruse* < L *cerussa*]

ce·rus·site (sir′ə·sīt) *n.* An orthorhombic, white to grayish-black lead carbonate, $PbCO_3$. Also **ce′ru·site.**

Cer·van·tes (sər·van′tēz, *Sp.* ther·vän′tās), **Miguel de,** 1547–1616, Spanish novelist and dramatist; author of *Don Quixote*: full surname *Cervantes Saavedra.*

cer·vi·cal (sûr′vi·kəl) *adj. Anat.* Of, pertaining to, or situated in or near the neck or cervix: *cervical* vertebrae. [< L *cervix, -icis* neck]

cervico- *combining form* Neck: *cervicofacial.* Also, before vowels, **cervic-.** [< L *cervix, -icis* neck]

cer·vi·co·fa·cial (sûr′vi·kō·fā′shəl) *adj. Anat.* Pertaining to the neck and the face.

Cer·vin (ser·vaṅ′), **Mont** (môṅ) See MATTERHORN.

cer·vine (sûr′vīn, -vin) *adj.* **1** Of or pertaining

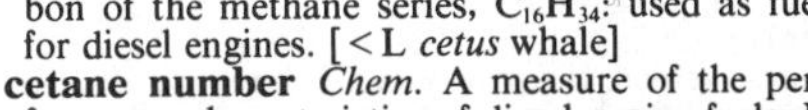

to deer. **2** Designating the subfamily *(Cervinae)* of deer representing the typical deer. [< L *cervinus* < *cervus* deer]

cer·vix (sûr′viks) *n. pl.* **cer·vix·es** or **cer·vi·ces** (sər·vī′sēz, sûr′və·sēz) **1** The neck. **2** The cervix uteri. **3** A necklike part. [< L]

cer·vix u·ter·i (sûr′viks yo͞o′tər·ī) *Anat.* The constricted neck of the uterus which distends during parturition.

cer·void (sûr′void) *adj.* Resembling a deer. [< L *cervus* deer + —OID].

Cer·y·ne·ia (ser′ə·nē′ə) A city in ancient Achaea.

Ce·sar (sē′zər) See CAESAR. Also *Fr.* **Cé·sar** (sā·zȧr′), *Ital.* **Ce·sa·re** (chā′zä·rā), *Pg.* **Ce·sar** (sā′zär), *Sp.* **Cé·sar** (thā′sär).

Ce·sar·e·an (si·zâr′ē·ən) See CAESAREAN. Also **Ce·sar′i·an.**

Ce·sar·e·vitch (si·zär′ə·vich) See CZAREVITCH.

Ce·se·na (chā·zā′nä) A town in north central Italy.

ce·si·ous (sē′zē·əs) *adj.* Pale greenish-blue: also spelled *caesious.* [< L *caesius* bluish-gray]

ce·si·um (sē′zē·əm) *n.* A steel-gray, ductile metallic element (symbol Cs, atomic number 55) that is the most electropositive of the alkali metals. See PERIODIC TABLE. [< L *caesius* bluish-gray]

Čes·ké Bu·dě·jo·vi·ce (ches′ke bo͞o′dye·yô′vi·tse) A city in southern Bohemia, Czechoslovakia: German *Budweis.*

ces·pi·tose (ses′pə·tōs) *adj. Bot.* Growing in tufts or clumps, as a plant; matted; turfy: also spelled *caespitose.* [< L *caespes, caespitis* turf] — **ces′pi·tose·ly** *adv.*

ces·pi·tous (ses′pə təs) *adj.* Cespitose.

cess[1] (ses) *n. Brit. Dial.* A public rate; tax; assessment. —*v.t.* To tax; assess; rate. [Short for ASSESS]

cess[2] (ses) *n. Irish* Luck; success: used in the phrase **bad cess to** Bad luck to. [? Short for SUCCESS]

ces·sa·tion (se·sā′shən) *n.* A ceasing; stop; pause. See synonyms under END, REST. [< L *cessatio, -onis* < *cessare* stop]

ces·sion (sesh′ən) *n.* **1** The act of ceding; surrender. **2** An assignment of property or rights to another or others. **3** The ceding of territory by a nation or state; also, the territory ceded. ◆ Homophone: *session.* [< L *cessio, -onis* surrender < *cessus* pp. of *cedere* yield]

ces·sion·ar·y (sesh′ən·er′ē) *adj.* Giving up; surrendering. —*n.* An assignee or grantee.

cess·pool (ses′po͞ol′) *n.* **1** A covered well or pit for the drainage from sinks, etc. **2** Any repository of filth. Also spelled *sesspool.* Also **cess′pit′.** [Origin uncertain]

ces·ta (ses′tə, *Sp.* thās′tä) *n.* In jai alai, a curved wicker racket attached to the hand. [< Sp.]

c'est-à-dire (se·tȧ·dēr′) *French* That is to say.

c'est la guerre (se lȧ gâr′) *French* It is war; hence, it cannot be helped.

c'est la vie (se lȧ vē′) *French* That is life.

ces·tode (ses′tōd) *n.* A tapeworm. [< Gk. *kestos* girdle] —**ces·toid** (ses′toid) *adj.*

c'est se·lon (se sə·lôṅ′) *French* That depends (on the circumstances).

c'est une au·tre chose (se tün ō′tr′ shōz) *French* That is another thing, or a different matter.

ces·tus[1] (ses′təs) *n. pl.* **ces·tus** An ancient Roman device of thongs, often weighted, wound about the hands by boxers: also spelled *caestus.* [< L *caestus* < *caedere* kill]

CESTUS

ces·tus[2] (ses′təs) *n. pl.* **·ti** (-tī) **1** A belt or girdle. **2** In classical mythology, the girdle of Aphrodite, which could awaken love in whoever beheld it. [< L < Gk. *kestos*]

ce·su·ra (si·zho͞or′ə, -zyo͞or′ə) See CAESURA.

Ce·ta·cea (si·tā′shə) *n. pl.* An order of aquatic mammals, especially those of a fishlike form with teeth conic or absent: the whales, dolphins, and porpoises. [< L *cetus* < Gk. *kētos* whale] — **ce·ta′cean** *adj. & n.* —**ce·ta′ceous** *adj.*

ce·tane (sē′tān) *n. Chem.* A saturated hydrocarbon of the methane series, $C_{16}H_{34}$: used as fuel for diesel engines. [< L *cetus* whale]

cetane number *Chem.* A measure of the performance characteristics of diesel engine fuels. It is the percentage of cetane (value = 100) in a mixture of cetane and *alpha*-methylnaphthalene (value = 0) which gives the same ignition performance as the fuel being tested. Compare OCTANE NUMBER.

Ce·ta·tea Al·ba (che·tä′tyä äl′bə) See BELGOROD DNESTROVSKI.

ce·te·ris pa·ri·bus (set′ər·is par′i·bəs) *Latin* Other things being equal.

Ce·tin·je (tse′tin·ye) The former capital of Montenegro, now in Yugoslavia.

ce·tol·o·gy (si·tol′ə·jē) *n.* The branch of zoology dealing with whales. [< Gk. *kētos* + -LOGY] — **ce·to·log·i·cal** (sē′tə·loj′i·kəl) *adj.* —**ce·tol′o·gist** *n.*

Cette (set) See SÈTE.

Ce·tus (sē′təs) A southern constellation, the Sea Monster. See CONSTELLATION. [< L, the whale]

Ceu·ta (syo͞o′tə, so͞o′-; *Sp.* thā′o͞o·tä) A port and an enclave in Morocco opposite Gibraltar; 7 1/2 square miles.

cev·a·dil·la (sev′ə·dil′ə) See SABADILLA.

Cé·vennes (sā·ven′) A mountain range west of the Rhone in southern France; highest peak, 5,755 feet.

Cey·lon (si·lon′) See SRI LANKA. —**Cey·lon·ese** (sē′lən·ēz′, -ēs′) *adj. & n.*

Ceylon moss A red seaweed of the East Indies *(Gracilaria lichenoides),* a principal source of agar-agar.

Ce·yx (sē′iks) In Greek mythology, the husband of Alcyone.

Cé·zanne (sā·zȧn′), **Paul,** 1839–1906, French painter.

Cf *Chem.* Californium (symbol Cf).

cgs The centimeter-gram-second system of measurement in which the unit of length is the centimeter, the unit of mass the gram, and the unit of time one second. Thus, the cgs unit of force is the dyne, of work the erg, etc. Also **c.g.s., C.G.S.**

chab·a·zite (kab′ə·zīt) *n.* A rhombohedral, white or flesh-colored hydrous silicate of calcium and aluminum. Also **chab′a·site** (-sīt). [< F *chabazie,* alter. of Gk. *chalazios,* a precious stone < *chalaza* hail]

cha·blis (shȧ·blē′) *n.* A dry, white, Burgundy wine made in the region of **Chablis,** a town in north central France.

cha·bouk (chä′bo͝ok) *n.* A horsewhip; specifically, a long whip used in the Orient for corporal punishment. Also **cha′buk.** [< Persian *chābuk* horsewhip]

chace (chās) See CHASE[1] *n.*

chac·ma (chak′mə) *n.* A large, black and gray South African baboon *(Papio porcarius).* [< Hottentot]

Cha·co (chä′kō) An interior province of northern Argentina; 38,041 square miles; capital, Resistencia.

Cha·co Canyon National Monument (chä′kō) A region of NW New Mexico containing cliff-dweller ruins; 33 square miles; established as a national park in 1907.

cha·conne (shȧ·kôn′) *n.* A slow dance of the 18th century; also, the music for it. [< F < Sp. *chacona*]

cha·cun à son goût (shȧ·kœṅ nȧ sôṅ go͞o′) *French* Each to his own taste.

Chad (chad) An independent republic of the French Community in north central Africa; 501,000 square miles; capital, Fort-Lamy; formerly a French overseas territory.

Chad (chad), **Lake** A lake in NW central Africa; 4,000 square miles in dry, 8,000 in rainy season.

Chad·i·an (chad′ē ən) *adj.* Pertaining to Chad. —*n.* A native or citizen of Chad.

Chad·wick (chad′wik), **George Whitefield,** 1854–1931, U.S. composer and conductor. —**Sir James,** 1891–1974, English physicist.

Chaer·o·ne·a (ker′ə·nē′ə) An ancient Boeotian city of central Greece; scene of victories of Philip of Macedon over Athens and Thebes, 338 B.C., and of Sulla over Mithridates, 86 B.C. Also **Chær′o·ne′a.**

chae·ta (kē′tə) *n. pl.* **·tae** (-tē) *Zool.* A bristle or seta. [< NL < Gk. *chaitē* hair]

chaeto- *combining form* Hair: *chaetopod.* Also, before vowels, **chaet-.** [< Gk. *chaitē* hair, bristle]

chae·to·don (kē′tə·don) *n.* One of a family *(Chaetodontidae)* of fishes having the dorsal fins stiff and spiny, including certain angelfishes of West Indies and Florida waters. [< NL < Gk. *chaitē* bristle + *odous, odontos* tooth]

chae·tog·nath (kē′tog·nath) *n. Zool.* Any of a phylum *(Chaetognatha)* of small, active, widely distributed marine animals having characteristic bristles around the mouth and elongate, arrow-shaped, almost transparent bodies adapted for swift motion through the water. [< NL < Gk. *chaitē* hair + *gnathos* jaw.]

chae·to·pod (kē′tə·pod) *n. Zool.* Any of a class *(Chaetopoda)* of annelid worms having conspicuous segments provided with locomotor organs and setae, including clamworms and earthworms. [< NL < Gk. *chaitē* + *pous, podos* foot]

chafe (chāf) *v.* **chafed, chaf·ing** *v.t.* **1** To abrade or make sore by rubbing; gall. **2** To make warm by rubbing. **3** To fret; irritate; annoy. —*v.i.* **4** To be irritated; fret; fume. —*n.* **1** Soreness or wear from friction; friction. **2** Irritation or vexation; restlessness. [< OF *chaufer* warm < L *calefacere* < *calere* be warm + *facere* make] —**chaf′er** *n.*

chaf·er (chā′fər) *n.* The cockchafer or other scarabaeid beetle. Also **chaf·fer** (chaf′ər). [OE *ceafor*]

chaff[1] (chaf, chäf) *n.* **1** The external envelopes or husks of grain. **2** Straw or hay cut fine. **3** Refuse; trifles collectively. See synonyms under WASTE. [OE *ceaf*]

chaff[2] (chaf, chäf) *v.t.* To poke fun at; ridicule. —*n.* Good-natured raillery; banter. See synonyms under BANTER, RIDICULE, MOCK. [Origin uncertain] —**chaff′er** *n.*

Chaf·fee (chaf′ē), **Adna Romanza,** 1884–1941, U.S. major general; organized the first mechanized brigade.

chaf·fer (chaf′ər) *v.t.* **1** *Obs.* To buy or sell; barter. **2** To say idly; bandy. —*v.i.* **3** To haggle about price; bargain. **4** To talk idly. [< *n.*] —*n.* **1** A disputatious bargaining. **2** *Obs.* Trade; traffic. [ME *chapfare,* OE *cēap* bargain + *faru* going] — **chaf′fer·er** *n.*

chaf·finch (chaf′inch) *n.* A European song finch *(Fringilla caelebs),* popular as a cage bird. [< CHAFF[1] + FINCH]

chaff·y (chaf′ē, chä′fē) *adj.* **1** Of, pertaining to, or like chaff. **2** *Bot.* Paleaceous. **3** Light as chaff; unsubstantial; empty.

chaf·ing dish (chā′fing) A vessel with a heating apparatus beneath it, to cook or keep hot its contents at the table.

chaft (chaft, chäft) *n. Scot. & Brit. Dial.* **1** A jaw. **2** *pl.* The jaw bones; chops.

Cha·gall (shə·gäl′), **Marc,** born 1887, Russian painter, active in France.

Cha·gas disease (chä′gäs) *Pathol.* A form of trypanosomiasis prevalent in South and Central America, communicated by the bite of the assassin bug. [after C. *Chagas,* 1879–1934, Brazilian physician]

Cha·gres (chä′gres) A river in the Panama Canal Zone, largely utilized by the Panama Canal.

Chagres fever *Pathol.* A malignant malaria endemic along the Chagres.

cha·grin (shə·grin′) *n.* Distress or vexation caused by disappointment, failure, or wounded pride; mortification. —*v.t.* To humiliate; mortify: used in the passive. [< F. See SHAGREEN.]

Synonyms (noun): confusion, disappointment, discomposure, dismay, humiliation, mortification, shame, vexation. *Chagrin* unites *disappointment* with some degree of *humiliation.* A rainy day may bring *disappointment;* needless failure in some enterprise brings *chagrin. Shame* involves the consciousness of fault, guilt, or impropriety; *chagrin* of failure of judgment, or harm to reputation. A consciousness that one has displayed his own ignorance will cause him *mortification;* if there was a design to deceive, the exposure will cover him with *shame.* Compare ABASH.

Antonyms: delight, exultation, glory, rejoicing, triumph.

Cha·har (chä′här) A province of northern China, 45,000 square miles; capital, Kalgan.

chain (chān) *n.* **1** A series of connected rings or links, serving to bind, drag, hold, or ornament. **2** Shackles; bonds; enthralment: usually in the plural. **3** Any connected series; a succession. **4** A range of mountains. **5** A measuring line or tape of 100 links; the **engineer's** (or **Ramden's**) **chain** is 100 feet long; the **surveyor's** (or **Gunter's**) **chain** is 66 feet long. **6** The warp threads of a fabric; also, the pattern chain of a loom. **7** *pl. Naut.* The flat iron bars on the side of a ship that receive the strain of the shrouds; a chain plate or channel plate. **8** *Chem.* A series of atoms of the same or different kinds, linked together and acting as a unit. See CLOSED CHAIN, OPEN CHAIN, SIDE CHAIN. **9** A series of associated stores, banks, etc. — *v.t.* **1** To fasten, as with a chain; also, to bring into or hold in subjection; enthrall. **2** In surveying, to measure with a chain. [<OF *chaeine* <L *catena*] — **chain′less** *adj.*

Chain (chān), **Ernest Boris,** born 1906, German pathologist, active in England.

chain gang A gang of convicts chained together while doing hard labor.

chain letter **1** A letter written to a group of people and sent from one to another in rotation, each recipient adding to it before forwarding it to the next. **2** A letter, duplicates of which are sent by one person to two or more others, each of whom forwards it to two or more others.

chain lightning **1** Forked or zigzag lightning. **2** *U.S. Slang* Cheap whisky.

chain mail See under MAIL[2].

chain·man (chān′mən) *n.* *pl.* **·men** (-mən) In surveying, a man who carries one end of the measuring chain. Also **chain′bear′er.**

chain pump A pump that raises water by means of buckets or disks on an endless chain passing under water and up over a wheel.

chain reaction *Physics* **1** A series of reactions each of which develops from the energy released by the previous reaction within the system. **2** The spontaneous explosive fission of atomic nuclei through the repeated capture of free neutrons, as in an atomic bomb or in the controlled generation of atomic energy.

chain shot Cannon balls or half-balls chained together: formerly used in warfare.

CHAIN
a. Chain shot.
b. Chain stitch.

chain-smok·er (chān′smō′kər) *n.* One who smokes cigars or cigarettes in unending succession.

chain stitch **1** In sewing, a loop stitch. **2** A chainlike stitch used in crocheting, embroidery, etc. Also **chain′work′.**

chain store A retail store selling the same type of goods, food, etc., as a number of other like stores, all of which are under the same management or ownership.

chain·wale (chān′wāl, chä′nəl) See CHANNEL[2].

chair (châr) *n.* **1** A movable or stationary seat, usually with four legs and a back and for one person. **2** A seat of office, as of a professor or moderator. **3** An office or officer; a chairman. **4** An iron block for holding railroad tracks in place. **5** The seat with long projecting arms on which the glassblower rolls his blowpipe; also, the set of men working with him. **6** *Obs.* A sedan. — *v.t.* **1** To put into a chair; install in office. **2** To preside over (a meeting). **3** In England, to carry in a chair in public; bear in triumph in a chair. [<F *chaiere* <L *cathedra.* Doublet of CATHEDRA.]

chair car A railroad passenger car equipped with comfortable single armchairs instead of the usual double seats; a parlor car.

chair·man (châr′mən) *n.* *pl.* **·men** (-mən) **1** One who presides over an assembly, committee, etc. **2** *Obs.* One of the carriers of a sedan chair. — *v.t.* To take the chair at (a meeting); preside over.

chair rail A wooden molding running around the walls of a room to protect them against damage from the backs of chairs.

chair-ta·ble (châr′tā′bəl) See TABLE-CHAIR.

chair·wom·an (châr′wo͝om′ən) *n.* *pl.* **·wom·en** (-wim′ən) A woman who presides over an assembly, committee, etc.

chaise (shāz) *n.* **1** A two-wheeled, one-horse vehicle for two persons, having a calash top, and the body usually hung on long leather straps. **2** A light, four-wheeled carriage, usually open. *Chay,* or *shay,* was formerly a common colloquial variant, from the notion that *chaise* was a plural form. [<F, var. of *chair* chair]

chaise-longue (shāz′lông′, *Fr.* shez lôṅg′) *n.* A couchlike chair having a backrest at one end and the seat prolonged to support the sitter's outstretched legs. [<F, lit., long chair]

cha·la·za (kə·lā′zə) *n.* *pl.* **·zas** or **·zae** (-zē) **1** *Biol.* One of the two spirally twisted albuminous threads that are attached to each end of the lining membrane of an egg and keep the yolk in position with the germinating spot uppermost. See illustration under EGG. **2** *Bot.* The part of an ovule where the coats are united to each other and to the nucellus. [<NL <Gk., hailstone, small lump]

Chal·ce·don (kal′sə·don, kal·sē′dən) An ancient Greek port in Asia Minor on the Bosporus; site of modern Turkish *Kadikoy.*

chal·ced·o·ny (kal·sed′ə·nē, kal′sə·dō′nē) *n.* *pl.* **·nies** A waxy, translucent, crypto-crystalline variety of quartz: also spelled *calcedony.* [from *Chalcedon*]

chal·ced·o·nyx (kal·sed′ə·niks, kal′sə·don′iks) *n.* A variety of agate in which white and gray layers alternate. [<CHALCED(ONY) + ONYX]

chal·cid (kal′sid) *n.* A tiny hymenopterous fly (family *Chalcididae*) whose larvae are parasitic on the larvae of other insects. Also **chalcid fly.** [<NL <Gk. *chalkos* copper; with ref. to its color]

Chal·cid·i·ce (kal·sid′ə·sē) A peninsula of NE Greece extending into the Aegean. *Modern Greek* **Khal·ki·di·ki** (khäl′kē·thē·kē′).

Chal·cis (kal′sis, Gk. khäl·kēs′) A city on Euboea, eastern Greece: Greek *Khalkis.* Also **Chal·kis** (kal′kis).

chalco- *combining form* Copper; brass: *chalcography.* [<Gk. *chalkos* copper]

chal·co·cite (kal′kə·sīt) *n.* An orthorhombic, metallic, blackish-gray copper sulfide, Cu_2S: also called *copper glance.*

chal·cog·ra·phy (kal·kog′rə·fē) *n.* The art of engraving on plates of copper or steel; line engraving. [<CHALCO- + -GRAPHY] — **chal·co·graph** (kal′kə·graf, -gräf) *n.* — **chal·cog′ra·pher** *n.* — **chal′co·graph′ic** *adj.* — **chal·cog′ra·phist** *n.*

chal·co·py·rite (kal′kə·pī′rīt, -pir′it) *n.* A tetragonal, metallic, brass-yellow copper-iron sulfide, $CuFeS_2$; copper pyrites.

Chal·de·a (kal·dē′ə) In Biblical geography, the southernmost part of the valley of the Tigris and the Euphrates: sometimes extended to include Babylonia. Also **Chal·dae′a.**

Chal·de·an (kal·dē′ən) *n.* **1 a** A native of Chaldea. **b** One of an ancient Semitic people of the Tigris and Euphrates Valley, who conquered and ruled Babylon. **c** A Babylonian. **2** One versed in the occult learning of the Chaldeans; an astrologer; hence, a magician. **3** The ancient Semitic language of the Chaldeans. — *adj.* Of or pertaining to Chaldea, the Chaldeans, or their language or culture: also **Chal·da·ic** (kal·dā′ik). Also **Chal·dae′an.**

Chal·dee (kal·dē′, kal′dē) *n.* **1** A Chaldean. **2** Biblical Aramaic: erroneous use. — *adj.* Chaldean: also **Chal·da·ic** (kal·dā′ik).

chal·der (chôl′dər) *n. Scot.* A former measure of 32 to 96 bushels. [<OF *chaldere* <L *caldaria* pot for boiling <*calidus* warm, hot]

chal·dron (chôl′drən) *n.* A weight or measure for coal and coke: in England 32 to 36 bushels; in the United States 36 bushels or 1.268 cubic meters. [Var. of CALDRON]

cha·let (sha·lā′, shal′ā) *n.* **1** A small building made of planks or of squared timbers, having a gently sloping and projecting roof, built by herdsmen in the Alpine regions of central Europe, especially in Switzerland. **2** A Swiss cottage with a projecting roof. **3** Any house built in this style. [<F]

CHALET

Cha·leur Bay (shə lo͝or′, -lûr′) An inlet of the Gulf of Saint Lawrence between the Gaspé Peninsula and New Brunswick.

Cha·lia·pin (shä·lyä′pin), **Feodor Ivanovich,** 1873–1938, Russian basso.

chal·ice (chal′is) *n.* **1** A consecrated cup used in the celebration or administration of the Lord's Supper. **2** Any drinking cup, goblet, or bowl. **3** *Bot.* A cup-shaped flower. [<OF <L *calix, calicis* cup]

chal·iced (chal′ist) *adj. Bot.* Having a cup-shaped flower.

chal·i·co·there (kal′i·kō·thir′) *n.* *Paleontol.* One of a family (*Chalicotheridae*) of extinct ungulates resembling both the horse and rhinoceros and having legs ending in three-clawed hoofs. [<NL <Gk. *chalix* gravel + *thēr* wild beast]

chalk (chôk) *n.* **1** A soft, grayish-white or yellowish compact limestone, largely composed of the shells of foraminifers. **2** A piece of chalk or chalklike material, either natural or artificial and frequently colored, used for marking or drawing. **3** A score in a game, because often recorded with chalk. **4** A debit, formerly often marked with chalk upon the wall or door, as of an ale house. — *v.t.* **1** To put chalk on or in; also, to mark with chalk; to bleach. **2** To record, as charges or debits; score. **3** To put an official mark on. — **to chalk up** **1** To raise the price of. **2** To score. **3** To give credit. — *adj.* Made with chalk. [OE *cealc* <L *calx* limestone] — **chalk′i·ness** *n.* — **chalk′y** *adj.*

chalk·board (chôk′bôrd′, -bōrd′) *n.* A flat surface of hard material for marking upon with chalk, used for classroom instruction.

chal·ki·tis (kal·kī′tis) *n.* *Pathol.* An inflammation of the eyes caused by rubbing the eyes with hands that have been working on or with brass. [<NL <Gk. *chalkos* brass]

chalk·stone (chôk′stōn′) *n.* **1** *Pathol.* A gouty concretion in the joints. **2** A piece of chalk.

chal·lenge (chal′ənj) *v.* **·lenged, ·leng·ing** *v.t.* **1** To dare to a contest or trial of superiority. **2** To invite to personal combat: to *challenge* to a duel. **3** To invite or defy, as scrutiny or proof: to *challenge* criticism. **4** To claim as due, as attention or respect. **5** To call in question; dispute; object to, as a choice of jurors. **6** *Mil.* To stop and demand a countersign of, as a sentry does. — *v.i.* **7** To utter or make a challenge. **8** In hunting, to open and cry, as hounds on picking up the scent. — *n.* **1** A call or defiance to personal contest; a dare or summons to fight, especially to a duel. **2** A formal objection or exception to a person or thing. **3** *Mil.* A sentry's call, requiring one to halt and give the countersign. **4** *Telecom.* An electromagnetic signal requesting identification, as in radar communication. [<OF *chalenger* <LL *calumniare* accuse falsely <*calumnia* slander. Doublet of CALUMNY.] — **chal′lenge·a·ble** *adj.* — **chal′leng·er** *n.*

chal·lis (shal′ē) *n.* A light dress fabric, usually printed. Also **chal′lie.** [Origin uncertain]

Chal·mers (chä′mərz), **Alexander,** 1759–1834, Scottish biographer and editor. — **Thomas,** 1780–1847, Scottish divine and writer.

Chal·na Anchorage (chäl′nə) See PORT JINNAH.

chal·one (kal′ōn) See COLYONE.

Châ·lons-sur-Marne (shä·lôṅ′sür·márn′) A city in NE France; scene of the defeat of Attila, 451 A.D.

Cha·lon-sur-Saône (shä·lôṅ′sür·sōn′) A town in eastern France.

chal·u·meau (shal′yə·mō′, *Fr.* shà·lü·mō′) *n.* **1** The lowest register of the clarinet. **2** An old, single-reed wind instrument from which the clarinet developed. [<F <OF *chalemel* <L *calamellus,* dim. of *calamus* reed]

cha·lutz (khä·lo͞ots′) See HALUTZ.

Chal·y·be·an (kal′ə·bē′ən, kə·lib′ē·ən) *adj.* Of or pertaining to the ancient **Chal·y·bes** (kal′ə·bēz), a people of Asia Minor, famous for their work in iron and steel. [<L *chalybeius* <Gk. *chalybēis* <*chalyps, chalybos* steel]

cha·lyb·e·ate (kə·lib′ē·āt, -it) *adj.* **1** Impregnated with compounds of iron: said of mineral waters. **2** Resembling iron in taste or action. — *n.* A medicine or water containing iron in solution. [<NL *chalybeatus* <L *chalybeius.* See CHALYBEAN.]

chal·y·bite (kal′ə·bīt) *n.* Siderite.

cham (kam) *n. Archaic* A Tatar or Mogul ruler; a khan. [<F <Turkish *khān* ruler]

cha·made (shə·mäd′) *n. Mil.* A signal, made with drum or trumpet, for a parley. [<F <Pg. *chamada* < *chamar* <L *clamare* cry out, shout]

Cham·bal (chum′bəl) A river in west central India, flowing 550 miles NE to the Jumna.

cham·ber (chām′bər) *n.* **1** A room in a dwelling house; especially, a bedroom. **2** *pl.* A suite of rooms or offices for the use of one person; specifically, a lawyer's or judge's office or apartment. **3** Lodgings. **4** A hall where an assembly or council meets; also, the assembly itself: the *chamber* of commerce. **5** The popular branch of a legislature. **6** An enclosed space at the breech of a gun containing the explosive charge; also, one of the cavities in the cartridge cylinder of a revolver. **7** A room in which a monarch or other great personage gives audience. **8** *Anat.* A space enclosing the aqueous humor of the eye, separated by the iris into an anterior and a posterior chamber. **9** A chamber pot. **10** A lock on a canal. — **cloud chamber** *Physics* An enclosed receptacle containing air or gas saturated with water vapor whose sudden cooling indicates the presence of ions as condensation nuclei of water droplets. The movements of these nuclei are revealed by the cloud tracks marked out by the droplets. Also **expansion chamber, fog chamber.** — **lower chamber** The lower house of a bicameral legislature. — **upper chamber** The upper house of a bicameral legislature. — *v.t.* **1** To make chambers in, as a gun. **2** To fit into a chamber; also, to fit compactly, as shot in a cartridge. [<F *chambre* <L *camera* vaulted room <Gk. *kamara.* Doublet of CAMERA.] — **cham′·bered** *adj.*

chamber concert A concert of chamber music.

cham·ber·lain (chām′bər·lin) *n.* **1** A high European court official. **2** A steward or treasurer of a corporation or municipality. **3** *Obs.* The chamber attendant of a monarch or lord. [<OF *chamberlenc* <OHG *chamarlinc* < *chamara* room <L *camera.* See CHAMBER.] — **cham′ber·lain·ship′** *n.*

Cham·ber·lain (chām′bər·lin), **Joseph,** 1836–1914, English statesman. — **Sir (Joseph) Austen,** 1863–1937, son of the preceding, English statesman. — **(Arthur) Neville,** 1869–1940, brother of Austen, English statesman; prime minister 1937–40.

Cham·ber·lin (chām′bər·lin), **Thomas Chrowder,** 1843–1928, U.S. geologist.

cham·ber·maid (chām′bər·mād′) *n.* A woman whose work is taking care of the bedrooms in a hotel.

chamber music Music written for a small number of instruments (less than ten), suitable for performance in a small room or hall.

chamber of commerce An association of merchants and businessmen for the protection and regulation of commerce.

chamber pot A portable receptacle used in a bedchamber as a toilet.

Cham·bers (chām′bərz), **Robert,** 1802–71, Scottish publisher and editor.

Cham·bord (shäṅ·bôr′) A village in north central France; site of a celebrated chateau built by Francis I.

cham·bray (sham′brā) *n.* A strong cotton fabric woven with colored warp and white filling that gives a changeable colored surface. [from *Cambrai,* France]

cha·me·le·on (kə·mē′lē·ən, -mēl′yən) *n.* **1** A tropical tree lizard (genus *Chamaeleon*) with a long protrusible tongue, prehensile limbs and tail, and the power of changing its color. **2** A person of changeable character or habits like a chameleon. [<L *chamaeleon* <Gk. *chamaileōn* < *chamai* on the ground + *leōn* lion] — **cha·me·le·on·ic** (kə·mē′lē·on′ik) *adj.*

Cha·me·le·on (kə·mē′lē·ən, -mēl′yən) A southern constellation. Also **Cha·mae′le·on.** See CONSTELLATION.

cham·fer (cham′fər) *v.t.* **1** To cut a channel in. **2** To bevel. [< *n.*] — *n.* A groove or channel; a bevel. [<F *chanfrein* <OF *chanfraindre* cut off an edge]

cham·frain (cham′frin) *n.* Armor for the front of a war horse's head. Also **cham·fron** (cham′frən). [<OF *chanfrain*]

Cha·mi·nade (shà·mē·nàd′), **Cécile Louise Stéphanie,** 1861–1944, French composer.

Cha·mis·so (shä·mē′sō), **Adalbert von,** 1781–1838, German poet, born in France.

cham·ois (sham′ē, *Fr.* shà·mwä′) *n. pl.* **·ois 1** A mountain antelope of Europe, the Caucasus, and western Asia (*Rupicapra rupicapra*). **2** A soft leather originally prepared from the skin of the chamois, now from sheep, goats, deer, etc.: also spelled *shammy, shamois.* Also **cham′my. 3** The color of this leather, a yellowish-beige. — *v.t.* **1** To dress (leather or skin) like chamois. **2** To clean or dry with a chamois skin, as an automobile. [<F]

CHAMOIS
(About 2 1/2 feet at the shoulder)

cham·o·mile (kam′ə·mīl) See CAMOMILE.

Cha·mo·nix (sham′ə·nē, *Fr.* shà·mô·nē′) The valley of the Arve north of Mont Blanc, France; site of **Chamonix-Mont-Blanc,** a resort town. Also **Cha·mou·ni** (sham′o͞o·nē, *Fr.* shà·mo͞o·nē′).

Cha·mor·ro Var·gas (chä·môr′rō vär′gäs), **Emiliano,** 1871–1966, Nicaraguan general; president of Nicaragua 1917–20, 1926.

champ[1] (champ) *v.t.* **1** To crush and chew noisily; munch. **2** To bite upon restlessly. **3** *Scot.* To mash, as potatoes; trample underfoot. — *v.i.* **4** To make a biting or chewing movement with the jaws. — *n.* The action of chewing or biting. [Prob. imit.]

champ[2] (champ) *n. Slang* Champion.

cham·pa·col (cham′pə·kōl, -kol) *n. Chem.* A white, crystalline, camphorlike substance, $C_{15}H_{26}O$, extracted from the wood of the champak tree. [<CHAMPAK + -OL[1]]

cham·pagne (sham·pān′) *n.* **1** A sparkling white wine made from grapes grown in the area of the former province of Champagne. **2** A still, white wine from this region. **3** Any light, effervescent wine made in imitation of French champagne. **4** The color of champagne, a pale, tawny or greenish yellow.

Cham·pagne (sham·pān′, *Fr.* shäṅ·pàn′y′) A region and former province of NE France.

cham·paign (sham·pān′) *n.* **1** Flat and open ground; clear, level country; a plain. **2** Figuratively, field of observation; expanse. **3** *Obs.* An area of unenclosed or common land. **4** *Archaic* The field of military operation. — *adj.* Of or pertaining to level ground or open country. [<OF *champaigne* <Med. L *campania.* See CAMPAIGN.]

cham·pak (cham′pak, chum′puk) *n.* An Indian tree (*Michelia champaca*) of the magnolia family, bearing golden-yellow fragrant flowers, and whose wood yields champacol. Also **cham′pac.** [<Skt. *campaka*]

cham·per·ty (cham′pər·tē) *n. pl.* **·ties** *Law* A bargain made by one not a party to the suit to bear expenses of litigation in consideration of a share of the matter sued for. [<F *champart* <OF <L *campi pars* share of the field] — **cham′per·tous** *adj.*

cham·pi·gnon (sham·pin′yən, *Fr.* shäṅ·pē·nyôṅ′) *n.* **1** The fairy-ring mushroom (*Marasmius oreades*). **2** In France, a mushroom or fungus. [<F, ult. <L *campania* < *campus* field]

cham·pi·on (cham′pē·ən) *n.* **1** Originally, one who fights in behalf of another; one who defends a person, principle, etc. **2** The victor in an open contest. **3** Something of highest excellence; anything which has been given first prize. — *adj.* Acknowledged superior to all competitors; holding the first prize, or having first excellence. — *v.t.* To defend; advocate; stand up for the rights of. [<OF <LL *campio, -onis* fighter <L *campus* field] — **cham′pi·on·ess** *n. fem.*

cham·pi·on·ship (cham′pē·ən·ship′) *n.* **1** The state of being a champion; supremacy. **2** The position or honor of a champion. **3** The act of championing; advocacy; defense.

Cham·plain (sham·plān′), **Lake** A lake between New York and Vermont; 435 square miles; 107 miles long.

Cham·plain (sham·plān′, *Fr.* shäṅ·plaṅ′), **Samuel de,** 1570–1635, French explorer; founder of Quebec.

champ·le·vé (shamp′lə·vā′) *n.* **1** An enamelware produced by cutting depressions in a metal plate, leaving a ridge between them which forms the outline of a design, the hollows then being filled with enamel powder or paste and fired. **2** The process of making this ware, or an article so made. [<F, pp. of *champlever* engrave < *champ* surface + *lever* raise]

Cham·pol·lion (shäṅ·pô·lyôṅ′), **Jean François,** 1790–1832, French Egyptologist; deciphered hieroglyphic system.
— **Champollion-Fi·geac** (-fē·zhȧk′), **Jean Jacques,** 1778–1867, French archeologist, brother of the preceding.

Champs É·ly·sées (shäṅ zā·lē·zā′) *French* A fashionable avenue in Paris, France; literally, the Elysian Fields.

chance (chans, chäns) *n.* **1** The unknown or the undefined cause of events not subject to calculation; luck; fortune. **2** An unknown agency, assumed to account for unusual or unexplained events. **3** The operation of this agency: often personified or, in antiquity, deified. **4** A fortuitous event; an accident. **5** A favorable conjuncture of circumstances; opportunity. **6** Undetermined probability in general; contingency. See synonyms under ACCIDENT, HAZARD, PROBABILITY. — *v.* **chanced, chanc·ing** *v.i.* **1** To occur accidentally; happen. — *v.t.* **2** To take the chance of; hazard: I'll *chance* it. **3** *Archaic* To befall; happen to. — **to chance upon** To find unexpectedly or undesignedly; come upon; stumble over. — *adj.* Occurring by chance; casual; accidental. [<OF *cheance* <LL *cadentia.* Doublet of CADENCE, CADENZA.]

chance·ful (chans′fəl, chäns′-) *adj.* **1** Full of chance or chances; eventful. **2** *Obs.* Dependent on chance.

chan·cel (chan′səl, chän′-) *n.* The space in a church reserved for the officiating clergy and the choir, often separated from the rest of the building by a screen or railing. [<OF <LL *cancellus* < *cancelli,* pl., lattice, railing; because it is so enclosed]

chan·cel·ler·y (chan′sə·lər·ē, chän′-, chans′·lər·ē, chäns′-) *n. pl.* **·ries 1** The office or dignity of a chancellor. **2** The building or room in which a chancellor has his office. **3** A court and its officials. **4** The office of an embassy or legation. Also **chan·cel·ry** (chan′·səl·rē, chän′-).

chan·cel·lor (chan′sə·lər, chän′-, chans′lər, chäns′-) *n.* **1** A high officer of state or of a university. **2** A judicial officer sitting in a court of chancery or equity. **3** In Germany, formerly, the president of the Federal Council. **4** In France, formerly, the keeper of the great seal and president of the Councils. **5** A chief secretary, as of an embassy. **6** A keeper of the great seal under the Eastern Empire, the Holy Roman Empire, etc. Also **chan′cel·or.** — **lord high chancellor** In Great Britain, the highest judicial officer of the crown. Also **lord chancellor.** [<OF *chancelier* <LL *cancellarius* one who stands at the bar in a court < *cancelli.* See CHANCEL.] — **chan′cel·lor·ship′** *n.*

chancellor of the Exchequer The minister of finance in the British cabinet.

Chan·cel·lors·ville (chan′sə·lərz·vil′, chän′-) A village in NE Virginia; scene of a Union defeat in a Civil War battle of 1863.

chance-med·ley (chans′med′lē, chäns′-) *n.* **1** *Law* Unpremeditated wounding or killing in self-defense in a casual affray; homicide upon sudden encounter. **2** A haphazard combination or mixture; any inadvertent act. [<OF *chance medlée* mixed case or event < *chance* CHANCE + *medlée,* pp. of *medler* mix]

chan·cer·y (chan′sər·ē, chän′-) *n. pl.* **·cer·ies 1** In the United States, a court of equity, as distinguished from a common-law court. **2** *Brit.* Previously to 1873, the court presided over by the Lord High Chancellor of England, the highest court next to the House of Lords; since the Judicature Act of 1873, one of the five divisions of the High Court of Justice.

3 A court of records; archives. 4 A chancellery. 5 The business and legal offices of a Roman Catholic diocese or archdiocese. 6 A wrestling hold. — **in chancery 1** Pending in a court of chancery; also, under the supervision of the Lord Chancellor. 2 In a hopeless predicament. 3 In boxing, said of the head caught and held under the arm of an opponent. [<OF *chancellerie* < *chancelier.* See CHANCELLOR.]

chan·ci·fy (chan′sə·fī, chän′-) *v.* **·fied, ·fy·ing** *v.t.* 1 To make fully random, as by the thorough mixing of an array of lottery tickets. — *v.i.* 2 To become fully random. 3 In the theory of games, to provide for the equiprobability of any in a series of results or events by deliberately altering the number, range, or effect of chance factors. [<CHANCE + -FY]

chan·cre (shang′kər) *n. Pathol.* A primary syphilitic lesion resembling a sore with a hard base. [<F <L *cancer* crab, ulcer] — **chan·crous** (shang′krəs) *adj.*

chan·croid (shang′kroid) *n. Pathol.* A venereal sore resembling chancre, but not infecting the system; soft chancre.

chanc·y (chan′sē, chän′-) *adj.* **·i·er, ·i·est 1** *Colloq.* Subject to chance; risky. 2 *Scot.* Favored by chance; auspicious; favorable.

chan·de·lier (shan′də·lir′) *n.* A branched support for lights, as a gas or electric fixture, suspended from a ceiling. [<F <Med. L *candelarius* <L *candela* candle]

chan·delle (shan·del′) *n. Aeron.* An abrupt climbing turn of an airplane, utilizing momentum to gain altitude while the direction of flight is changed. [<F]

Chan·der·na·gore (chun′dər·nə·gôr′) A free city and former French settlement on the Hooghly in West Bengal, India. *French* **Chan·der·na·gor** (shän·der·nà·gôr′).

chan·dler (chan′dlər, chän′-) *n.* 1 A trader; dealer: ship *chandler.* 2 In England, a retailer of common groceries, provisions, and the like; a petty shopkeeper. 3 One who makes or sells candles: tallow *chandler.* [<F *chandelier* chandler, candlestick. See CHANDELIER.]

chan·dler·y (chan′dlər·ē, chän′-) *n. pl.* **·dler·ies 1** The goods sold by a chandler: often in the plural. 2 A chandler's shop. 3 A place for keeping candles.

Chan·dra·gup·ta (chun′drə·gŏŏp′tə) **I,** fourth century B.C., Indian ruler of the Maurya kingdom: also *Sandrocottus.* — **II,** 383?–413, Indian ruler of the Gupta dynasty.

chang (chang) See CATTY[1].

Chang·chow (chäng′jō′) 1 A former name for LUNGKI. 2 A city in southern Kiangsu province, China.

Chang·chun (chäng′chŏŏn′) A city in western Kirin province of Manchuria: formerly *Hsinking.*

change (chānj) *v.* **changed, chang·ing** *v.t.* 1 To make different; alter; transmute. 2 To exchange; interchange: to *change* places. 3 To give or cause another to give the equivalent of, as money, in smaller units or foreign currency. 4 To put other garments, coverings, etc., on: to *change* the bed. — *v.i.* 5 To become different; vary. 6 To enter upon a new phase: the moon has *changed.* 7 To make a change or exchange. 8 To transfer from one train to another. 9 To put on other garments. — **to change color** To blush or turn pale. — **to change front 1** In a military sense, to face a different way; alter the direction of a line of attack. 2 To adopt a new line of argument. 3 To alter one's attitude or principles. — **to change hands** To pass from one possessor to another. — *n.* 1 The act or fact of changing; alteration; substitution or something used in substitution. 2 A place for general transaction of business; an exchange. 3 The money returned to a purchaser who has given a bill or coin of greater value than his purchase. 4 Money of smaller denomination given in exchange for larger; small coins collectively. 5 A passage from one phase to another: the *change* of the moon. 6 *Music* **a** A modulation or variation of key. **b** Any order, other than that of the diatonic scale, in which a peal of bells is struck: usually in the plural. 7 *Obs.* Want of constancy; caprice. 8 Religious conversion. — **to ring the changes 1** To operate a chime of bells so as to produce a variety of tuneful combinations. 2 To repeat something with every possible variation of language and illustration. [<OF *changer* <LL *cambiare* exchange] — **chang′er** *n.*

Synonyms (verb): alter, commute, convert, exchange, metamorphose, modify, qualify, shift, substitute, transfigure, transform, transmute, turn, vary, veer. To *change* is to make a thing other than it has been; to *exchange,* to put or take something else in its place; to *alter* is ordinarily to *change* partially. To *exchange* is often to transfer ownership; as, to *exchange* city for country property. *Change* is often used in the sense of *exchange*; as, to *change* horses. To *transmute* is to *change* the qualities while the substance remains the same; as, to *transmute* baser metals into gold. To *transform* is to *change* form or appearance, with or without deeper and more essential change. *Transfigure* is, as in its Scriptural use, to *change* in an exalted and glorious spiritual way. To *metamorphose* is to make some remarkable change, as of a caterpillar into a butterfly, or of the crystalline structure of rocks, hence called "metamorphic rocks." To *vary* is to *change* from time to time, often capriciously. To *commute* is to put something easier, lighter, milder, etc., in place of that which is *commuted*; as, to *commute* daily fares on a railway to a monthy payment. To *convert* is primarily to *turn* about, and signifies to *change* in form, character, use, etc.; iron is *converted* into steel, joy into grief, etc. *Turn* is a popular word for *change* in any sense short of the meaning of *exchange,* being often equivalent to *alter, convert, transform, transmute,* etc. We *modify* a statement by some limitation, *qualify* it by some addition. See CONVEY. *Antonyms*: abide, bide, continue, endure, hold, keep, persist, remain, retain, stay.

Synonyms (noun): alteration, conversion, diversity, innovation, mutation, novelty, regeneration, renewal, renewing, revolution, transformation, transition, transmutation, variation, variety, vicissitude. *Mutation* is a more formal word for *change,* often suggesting repeated or continual *change*; as, the *mutations* of fortune. *Revolution* is specifically and most commonly a *change* of government. *Variation* is a partial *change* in form, qualities, position, or action; as, the *variation* of the magnetic needle or of the pulse. *Vicissitude* is sharp. sudden, or violent *change*; as, the *vicissitudes* of politics. *Transition* is change by passing from one place or state to another, especially in a natural, regular, or orderly way; as, the *transition* from spring to summer. An *innovation* is a *change* that breaks in upon an established order or custom. See MOTION. *Antonyms*: constancy, continuance, firmness, fixedness, fixity, identity, invariability, permanence, persistence, steadiness, unchangeableness, uniformity.

change·a·ble (chān′jə·bəl) *adj.* 1 Capable of being changed; alterable. 2 Likely to change or vary; inconstant. 3 Reflecting light so as to appear of different color from different points of view. See synonyms under FICKLE, MOBILE. — **change·a·bil·i·ty** (chān′jə·bil′ə·tē), **change′a·ble·ness** *n.* — **change′a·bly** *adv.*

change·ful (chānj′fəl) *adj.* Full of or given to change; variable. See synonyms under FICKLE. — **change′ful·ly** *adv.* — **change′ful·ness** *n.*

change·less (chānj′lis) *adj.* 1 Without change; monotonous. 2 Constant; enduring; unchanging. — **change′less·ly** *adv.* — **change′less·ness** *n.*

change·ling (chānj′ling) *n.* 1 An ill-favored or stupid child believed to have been substituted, especially by supernatural or demonic agency, for a normal or beautiful child. 2 A fickle person: used also adjectivally. 3 *Obs.* A silly or weak-minded person; simpleton; imbecile.

change of life The menopause.

change–ring·ing (chānj′ring′ing) *n.* The art or science of producing every possible variation in the ringing of a set of bells, starting from the time the bells leave the position of rounds to the time they return to it.

Chang·hua (chäng′hwä′) A city in west central Taiwan.

Chang·jin (chäng·jin) A river in northern Korea, flowing 160 miles NE; **Changjin reservoir** in its upper course was the site of fierce fighting in the Korean war, 1950. *Japanese* **Cho·sin** (chō·shin).

Chang·sha (chäng′shä′) A port of eastern China, capital of Hunan province.

Chang·teh (chäng′du′) A city in NW Hunan province, central China.

Chang Tso-lin (jäng′ tsō′lin′), 1873–1928, Chinese general.

Chan·kiang (chän′jyäng′) A municipality of SW Kwangtung province, China; leased to France, 1898–1945: French *Kwangchowan.*

chan·nel[1] (chan′əl) *n.* 1 The bed of a stream. 2 A wide strait: the English *Channel.* 3 Any groove or passage. 4 *Naut.* The deep part of a river, harbor, strait, or estuary, where the current or tide is strongest; especially, a navigable passage between the shoal parts. 5 That through which anything flows or passes: a news *channel.* 6 *Telecom.* **a** A path for the transmission of telegraph, telephone, and radio communications. **b** A wave band of specified frequency over which radio and television messages or programs are transmitted. 7 A flanged iron beam having a bracket-shaped section: also **channel bar.** 8 In motion pictures, a complete assemblage of all the necessary recording equipment. — *v.t.* **chan·neled** or **·nelled, chan·nel·ing** or **·nel·ling 1** To cut or wear channels in. 2 To convey through or as through a channel. [<OF *chanel* <L *canalis* groove. Doublet of CANAL.]

chan·nel[2] (chan′əl) *n. Naut.* A flat piece of wood or iron attached to the side of a vessel, to spread the shrouds and keep them clear of the bulwarks: originally called *chainwale.* [Alter. of *chainwale* <CHAIN (def. 7) + WALE (def. 2)]

Channel Islands A group of British islands in the English Channel off the coast of Normandy, including Jersey, Guernsey, Alderney, and Sark; 75 square miles. *French* **Iles Nor·mandes** (ēl nôr·mänd′).

Chan·ning (chan′ing), **William Ellery,** 1780–1842, U.S. Unitarian divine and writer.

chan·son (shan′sən, *Fr.* shäṅ·sôṅ′) *n.* A song. [<F <L *cantio, -onis* song <*canere* sing]

chan·son de geste (shäṅ·sôṅ′ də zhest′) An Old French epic tale in verse, generally written in assonant verse of ten syllables a line, arranged in irregular stanzas, and dealing with ancient French history and legend. The most celebrated one is the *Chanson de Roland.* [<F, song of noble deeds]

chant (chant, chänt) *n.* 1 A melody adapted to words without strict rhythm, or containing both recitative and rhythm: the most ancient and simple form of choral music. 2 A psalm or canticle so recited. 3 A song; melody. 4 Any measured monotonous singing or reciting of words. 5 A singing intonation in speech; twang. [<*v.*] — *v.t.* 1 To sing to a chant; intone, as in public worship. 2 To celebrate in song: to *chant* the praises of. 3 To say repetitiously and monotonously; harp upon. — *v.i.* 4 To sing chants. 5 To make melody; sing. 6 To talk monotonously and continuously. Also spelled *chaunt.* [<OF *chanter* <L *cantare,* freq. of *canere* sing]

chant·age (chan′tij, chän′-; *Fr.* shäṅ·tàzh′) *n.* The extortion of money by threats of exposure; blackmailing. [<F]

chant·er (chan′tər, chän′-) *n.* 1 A singer; especially, a singer in a chantry; a chorister; precentor. 2 The fingerpipe of a bagpipe: distinguished from *drone.* 3 The hedge sparrow. Also **chan′tor.**

chan·te·relle[1] (shäṅ·trel′) *n. Music* The highest string of certain stringed instruments, as a violin. [<F]

chan·te·relle[2] (shan′tə·rel′, chan′-) *n.* An edible yellow mushroom (*Cantharellus cibrius*), with a short stem. [<F <NL *cantharellus,* dim. of *cantharus* drinking cup <Gk. *kantharos*]

chan·teuse (shäṅ·tœz′) *n. French* A woman singer.

chant·ey (shan′tē, chan′-) *n. pl.* **·eys** A rhythmical working song of sailors: also spelled *shanty.* [Alter. of F *chantez,* imperative of *chanter* sing]

chan·ti·cleer (chan′tə·klir) *n.* A cock: used as a proper name. [<OF *chantecler* (name of the cock in the medieval "Reynard the Fox") <*chanter* sing, crow + *cler* aloud]

Chan·til·ly (shan·til′ē, *Fr.* shäṅ·tē·yē′) A town in northern France.

Chantilly lace A fine variety of lace formerly produced in Chantilly, France.

chant ro·yal (shäṅ rwä·yàl′) A lyric poem, related to the ballade, consisting of five 11–

line stanzas with an 8-line envoy, the stanzas and the envoy having the last line identical. [< F]

chan·try (chan′trē, chän′-) *n. pl.* **·tries 1** A chapel in or attached to a church or monastery, endowed for maintaining daily masses for the soul of the founder or of others nominated by him (the chapel usually containing the tomb of the founder). **2** Formerly, the endowment itself. **3** A chapel for subsidiary church services. [< OF *chanterie* < *chanter.* See CHANT.]

Cha·nu·ca (khä′noo·kä) See HANUKKAH.

Chao·an (chou′än′) A city in SE China on the Han. Formerly **Chao·chow** (chou′jō′).

Chao K'uang-yin (jou′kwäng′yin′), died 976, Chinese emperor; founder of Sung dynasty.

Chao Phra·ya (chou′ prä·yä′) The chief river of Thailand, flowing 140 miles south to the Gulf of Siam: also *Mae Nam, Menam.*

cha·os (kā′os) *n.* **1** A condition of utter disorder and confusion, as the unformed primal state of the universe. **2** Any thing or condition of which the elements or parts are in utter disorder and confusion. **3** *Obs.* Any vast gulf or chasm; an unfathomable abyss. [< L < Gk., abyss < *chainein* gape, yawn]

cha·ot·ic (kā·ot′ik) *adj.* **1** Of, pertaining to, or like chaos. **2** Unformed; completely disordered. Also **cha·ot′i·cal. —cha·ot′i·cal·ly** *adv.*

chap[1] (chap) *n.* **1** *Colloq.* A fellow; lad. **2** *Obs.* A chapman; a dealer; buyer. [Short for CHAPMAN]

chap[2] (chap) *v.* **chapped** or **chapt, chap·ping** *v.t.* **1** To cause to split, crack, or become rough. **2** *Scot.* To strike with a hammer; pound on. *—v.i.* **3** To split, crack, or redden. **4** *Scot.* To beat or knock, as on a door; to strike, as a clock. **—to chap out** *Scot.* To summon by a tap, as on the window. *—n.* **1** A crack or roughened place in the skin. **2** *Scot.* A rap on the door; a knock of any sort. [ME *chappen.* Related to CHIP, CHOP.]

chap[3] (chap, chop) *n.* **1** A jaw. **2** *pl.* The mouth and cheeks. **3** The jaw of a vise. Also spelled *chop.* [Cf. ME *chaftjaw*]

cha·pa·re·jos (chä′pä·rā′hōs) *n. pl. SW U.S.* Chaps. Also **cha·pa·ra·jos** (chä′pä·rä′·hōs), **cha·par·re·ras** (chä′·pär·rā′räs). [< Sp.]

chap·ar·ral (chap′ə·ral′) *n.* A thicket of dwarf oak, low thorny shrubs, etc. [< Sp. < *chaparra* evergreen oak]

chaparral cock The roadrunner.

chaparral pea A thorny shrub of California *(Pickeringia montana)* of the pea family, growing densely over chaparrals.

chap·book (chap′book′) *n.* One of a former class of cheap popular books sold by chapmen.

CHAPS

chape (chāp) *n.* **1** A metal tip, as of a scabbard, or an outer case, as of a mold. **2** The backpiece by which a buckle is fastened to a strap or the like; any attaching loop of metal or leather. [< F < LL *capa, cappa* cap]

cha·peau (sha·pō′, *Fr.* shå·pō′) *n. pl.* **·peaux** (-pōz′, *Fr.* -pō′) or **peaus** (-pōz′) A hat.

chapeau bras (brä) A soft, three-cornered dress hat that can be folded and carried under the arm: worn commonly in the 18th century and still with court and diplomatic dress. [< F < *chapeau* hat + *bras* arm]

chap·el (chap′əl) *n.* **1** A place of worship other than a large and regular church. **2** A compartment or recess of a church, where independent services may be held. **3** Any place of worship not connected with the state or established church. **4** In England, any dissenting church. **5** A building or large room in a university, college, or school, for religious services; also, the services. **6** An official choir or orchestra, as of a court or nobleman's establishment. **7** The body of journeymen printers in a given office usually organized under a chairman, known in Great Britain as the *father of the chapel.* **8** *Archaic* A printing house. [< OF *chapele* < Med. L *capella,* dim. of *cappa* cloak; orig., a sanctuary where the cloak of St. Martin was kept as a relic]

chap·el·mas·ter (chap′əl·mas′tər, -mäs′-) See KAPELLMEISTER.

chap·er·on (shap′ə·rōn) *n.* **1** A woman who acts as attendant or protector of a young unmarried woman in public. **2** An older person who attends a social function to maintain its decorum and propriety. *—v.t.* To attend (a young unmarried woman) in mixed company; act as chaperon to. Also **chap′er·one.** [< F, hood < *chape* cape; because she protects her charges from harm] **— chap·er·on·age** (shap′ə·rō′nij) *n.*

chap·fall·en (chap′fô′lən, chop′-) *adj.* **1** Having the chap or jaw drooping. **2** Dejected; crestfallen. Also spelled *chop-fallen.*

chap·i·ter (chap′i·tər) *n. Archit.* The capital of a pillar. See CAPITAL[2]. [< F *chapitre.* See CHAPTER.]

chap·lain (chap′lin) *n.* **1** A clergyman with special functions, such as conducting religious services in a legislative assembly, in a regiment, or on board a ship. **2** A clergyman attached to a chapel for permanent or occasional duty. [< OF *chapelain* < Med. L *cappellanus* < *cappella* CHAPEL] **—chap′lain·cy, chap′lain·ship** *n.*

chap·let (chap′lit) *n.* **1** A wreath or garland for the head. **2** A necklace. **3** A rosary, or, more strictly, the third part of a rosary, or fifty-five beads. **4** A string of beads, or anything resembling it, as an astragal molding, or a rope of frog or toad spawn. [< OF *chapelet,* double dim. of *chape* hood < LL *cappa* hooded cape]

Chap·lin (chap′lən), **Charles Spencer,** 1889–1977, English motion-picture actor and producer, active in the United States.

chap·man (chap′mən) *n. pl.* **·men** (-mən) **1** peddler. **2** *Obs.* A buyer; dealer; merchant. [OE *ceapman* < *ceap* business + *man* man]

Chap·man (chap′mən), **Frank Michler,** 1864–1945, U.S. ornithologist. **—George,** 1557–1634, English poet, dramatist, and translator of Homer. **—John** See APPLESEED, JOHNNY.

chaps (shaps, chaps) *n. pl. U.S.* Leather overalls without a seat, worn over trousers by cowboys to protect the legs: also called *chaparejos.* [Short for CHAPAREJOS]

chap·ter (chap′tər) *n.* **1** A division of a book or treatise, usually marked by a number and heading. **2** The body of clergy connected with a cathedral or other collegiate church; also, a council of such body, or their place of assembly. **3** *Eccl.* The meeting of any order. **4** In certain church services, a short Scriptural passage read immediately after the psalms. **5** A branch of a club, brotherhood, or other association, especially of a college fraternity or sorority. **—cathedral chapter** The personnel of canons attached to a cathedral. **—conventual chapter** The assembly of the clergy of one house or of an entire order for the purpose of regulating domestic affairs. *—v.t.* To divide into chapters, as a book. [< F *chapitre* < OF *chapitle* < L *capitulum,* dim. of *caput* head, capital, chapter]

chapter house A house of assembly for a chapter or a fraternity; especially, such a structure connected with a cathedral.

Cha·pul·te·pec (chə·pool′tə·pek) A fortified hill SW of Mexico City; captured (1847) by U.S. forces in the Mexican War.

cha·que·ta (chä·kā′tä) *n. SW U.S.* A jacket, usually of leather, worn by cowboys, especially when riding in a bushy region. [< Sp.]

char[1] (chär) *n. Brit.* A chore; an odd job; also, work done by the day. *—v.i.* **charred, char·ring** To perform arduous work, as cleaning and scrubbing; serve as a charwoman. Also spelled *chare.* [OE *cerr* turn of work]

char[2] (chär) *v.* **charred, char·ring** *v.t.* **1** To burn or scorch the surface of, as timber. **2** To convert into charcoal by incomplete combustion. *—v.i.* **3** To become charred. See synonyms under BURN. *—n.* Charcoal. [? < CHARCOAL]

char[3] (chär) *n. pl.* **chars** or **char** Any fish (genus *Salvelinus*) characterized by small scales and having red spots, as the brook trout: also spelled *charr.* [< Scottish Gaelic *ceara* blood-red]

char·a·banc (shar′ə·bangk, -bang) *n. pl.* **char·a·bancs** A long open vehicle with transverse seats. [< F *char à bancs* car with benches]

char·a·cin (kar′ə·sin) *n. Zool.* Any of a large and diversified family of fishes *(Characinidae)* native to South America and Africa, including the voracious caribe and many popular aquarium species. [< NL *Characinidae* < Gk. *charax* a sea fish < *charassein* sharpen, whet]

char·ac·ter (kar′ik·tər) *n.* **1** The combination of qualities distinguishing any person or class of persons; any distinctive mark or trait, or such marks or traits collectively, belonging to any person, class, or race; the individuality which is the product of nature, habits, and environment. **2** High qualities; moral force. **3** Reputation. **4** A representation; assumed part; role. **5** One assuming a certain role. **6** Position; status. **7** The person holding or represented as holding a certain position or rank. **8** A figure engraved, written, or printed; mark; sign; letter. **9** A style of handwriting or printing. **10** A form of secret writing; a cipher. **11** Fidelity and vigor in artistic representation of characteristic features. **12** An individual considered as possessing a combination of distinctive features; a personage; also, popularly, a humorous or eccentric person. **13** A representation or characterization, as of one's qualities or abilities; especially, a written testimonial given by an employer to an employee to aid in obtaining employment. **14** That by which a thing is especially known or distinguished; a quality; property: Ductility is a *character* of gold. **15** *Genetics* Any structural or functional trait in an organism regarded as the expression of a gene or genes. [< F *caractère* < L *character* < Gk. *charaktēr* stamp, mark < *charassein* carve, sharpen, engrave]

character actor An actor who plays the part of a character markedly different from himself in age, temperament, manner, etc.

char·ac·ter·is·tic (kar′ik·tə·ris′tik) *adj.* **1** Distinguishing or contributing to distinguish; marking; characterizing; showing the character, traits, and disposition of; typical. **2** Constituting or pertaining to the character. See synonyms under PARTICULAR. *—n.* **1** A distinctive feature; peculiarity. **2** The integral part of a logarithm; index. **—char′ac·ter·is′ti·cal** *adj.* **— char′ac·ter·is′ti·cal·ly** *adv.*

Synonyms (noun): attribute, character, distinction, feature, indication, mark, peculiarity, property, quality, sign, singularity, trace, trait. Compare ATTRIBUTE, CHARACTER, MARK.

char·ac·ter·ize (kar′ik·tə·rīz′) *v.t.* **·ized, iz·ing 1** To describe by qualities or peculiarities; designate. **2** To be a mark or peculiarity of; distinguish. **3** To supply character to. **— char′ac·ter·i·za′tion** *n.* **—char′ac·ter·iz′er** *n.*

char·ac·ter·o·log·i·cal (kar′ik·tər·ə·loj′ə·kəl) *adj.* Pertaining to the study of character or personality: *characterological* features. **—char′ac·ter·ol′o·gy** *n.*

character sketch 1 A literary profile of a person or a type of personality. **2** In the theater, a short impersonation.

char·ac·ter·y (kar′ik·tər·ē, -trē) *n. pl.* **·ter·ies** A system of characters or signs; mode; representation.

char·ac·to·nym (ka·rak′tə·nim) *n.* A word or name indicating the principal charateristic, occupation, or other distinguishing mark of a person; an epithet. [< CHARACTER + Gk. *onoma* name]

cha·rade (shə·rād′) *n.* A guessing game in which each syllable of a word, and finally the whole word, is acted in pantomime or represented in tableau. [< F < Provençal *charrado* chatter < *charra* chatter, prattle]

char·bon (shär′bən) *n. Pathol.* Anthrax. [< F < L *carbo, -onis* coal]

char·coal (chär′kōl′) *n.* **1** A black, porous, odorless carbonaceous substance, burning with little or no flame, obtained by the imperfect combustion of organic matter, as of wood: it is used as a fuel, an adsorbent, a filter, etc. **2** A drawing pencil or crayon made of charcoal dust. **3** A drawing made in charcoal. *—v.t.* **1** To write, draw, mark, or blacken with or as with charcoal. **2** To subject to or suffocate with charcoal fumes. [ME *charcole;* origin unknown]

Char·cot (shär·kō′), **Jean Martin,** 1825–93, French physician and specialist in nervous diseases.

chard (chärd) *n.* **1** The blanched leaves, leafstalks, or midribs of certain plants, as of the artichoke: used as a vegetable. **2** A variety of white beet *(Beta vulgaris cicla)* cultivated for its large leaves and leafstalks, which are used for salad and as a vegetable: also called *Swiss chard, leaf beet.* [<F *carde* <L *carduus* thistle]

Char·din (shär·dan′), **Jean Baptiste Simeon,** 1699–1779, French painter.

chare (châr) See CHAR[1].

Cha·rente (shä·ränt′) A river in western France, flowing 220 miles west to the Bay of Biscay.

charge (chärj) *v.* **charged, charg·ing** *v.t.* **1** To lay or impose a load upon; to burden. **2** To put something into or upon; fill. **3** To exhort or instruct solemnly or authoritatively: to *charge* a jury. **4** *Electr.* To replenish, as a storage battery. **5** To accuse: with *with*: They *charged* him with reckless driving. **6** To make an onset against or attack upon, as a fort. **7** To emblazon, as with heraldic emblems. **8** To set or state, as a price. **9** To set down or record, as a debt to be paid or accounted for. **10** To load, as a weapon. — *v.i.* **11** To demand or fix a price: Do you *charge* for your services? **12** To debit. **13** To make an onset: *Charge*! **14** To crouch or lie down, as hunting dogs. **—to charge off** To regard or write off as a loss. **— to be in charge of 1** To have the responsibility or control of. **2** To be under the supervision or control of. See synonyms under ARRAIGN, ATTACK, ATTRIBUTE, LOAD. — *n.* **1** The quantity of gunpowder, fuel, etc., put or to be put into a firearm, a furnace, etc. **2** The quantity of static electricity present in a saturated storage battery. **3** *Physics* The energy, measured in electrostatic units, present in an atomic particle, as the proton, electron, meson, etc. **4** Care and custody of that which is under one's care. **5** A price. **6** An entry of indebtedness. **7** A tax; expense; cost. **8** An address of instruction or admonition: the *charge* to a jury. **9** An accusation. **10** An impetuous attack or onslaught; also, the signal for it. **11** *Her.* A figure or device; a bearing. **12** *Obs.* A burden; load. See synonyms under CARE, CAREER, LOAD, OVERSIGHT, PRICE. [<OF *chargier* <LL *carricare* carry < *carrus* cart. Doublet of CARRY.]

char·gé (shär·zhā′) *n.* A chargé d'affaires. [<F]

charge·a·ble (chär′jə·bəl) *adj.* **1** Capable of being or rightfully to be charged, as an obligation, expense, accusation, etc. **2** Liable to be charged or rendered subject to some duty, expense, etc.; responsible or indictable. **3** *Obs.* Burdensome; also, important.

charge account An account against which the purchase of merchandise in a store is charged.

char·gé d'af·faires (shär·zhā′ də·fâr′, *Fr.* shär·zhā′ dä·fâr′) *pl.* **char·gés d'af·faires** (shär·zhāz′ də·fâr′, *Fr.* shär·zhā′ dä·fâr′) **1** A person who temporarily assumes the command of a diplomatic mission in the absence of the regularly appointed chief: in full *chargé d'affaires ad interim.* **2** A diplomatic representative of the fourth rank accredited by one foreign minister to another, and not to the chief of state. Compare MINISTER RESIDENT, DIPLOMATIC AGENT.

char·gé des af·faires (shär·zhā′ dā·zä·fâr′) A person who has custody of the archives or other property of a mission in a country with which formal diplomatic relations are not maintained. He has no diplomatic status or immunity, and his relations with the foreign government are purely informal.

Charge of the Light Brigade Tennyson's poem commemorating the heroic British charge at Balaklava during the Crimean War.

charg·er (chär′jər) *n.* **1** One who or that which charges; especially, a war horse. **2** An apparatus for charging electric storage batteries. **3** A large shallow dish for meat.

Cha·ri (shä·rē′) The French name for the SHARI.

char·i·ly (châr′ə·lē) *adv.* In a chary manner; warily.

char·i·ness (châr′ē·nis) *n.* **1** The quality of being chary. **2** Integrity; scrupulousness.

Char·ing Cross (châr′ing) A district at the west end of the Strand in London, England.

char·i·ot (char′ē·ət) *n.* **1** An ancient two-wheeled vehicle used in war and in racing. **2** An ornate four-wheeled carriage. — *v.t.* & *v.i.* To convey, ride, or drive in or as in a chariot. [<OF, aug. of *char* car <L *carrus* cart, wagon]

ETRUSCAN WAR CHARIOT OF BRONZE

char·i·o·teer (char′ē·ə·tir′) *n.* One who drives a chariot. — *v.t.* To act as driver of (a vehicle) or for (a person).

Char·i·o·teer (char′ē·ə·tir′) The constellation Auriga.

cha·ris·ma (kə·riz′mə) *n.* **1** *Theol.* A gift or power bestowed by the Holy Spirit for use in the propagation of the truth or the edification of the church and its adherents. **2** The aggregate of those special gifts of mind and character which are the source of the personal power of exceptional individuals and upon which they depend for their capacity to secure the allegiance of, and exercise decisive authority over, large masses of people. Also **char·ism** (kar′iz·əm). [<Gk., grace, favor] — **char·is·mat·ic** (kar′iz·mat′ik) *adj.*

char·i·ta·ble (char′ə·tə·bəl) *adj.* **1** Of, pertaining to, or characterized by charity. **2** Generous in gifts to the poor; liberal. **3** Characterized by love and good will; tolerant; benevolent; kindly; lenient. — **char′i·ta·ble·ness** *n.* — **char′i·ta·bly** *adv.*

Synonyms: beneficent, benevolent, benign, benignant, compassionate, considerate, forgiving, indulgent, kind, lenient, liberal, loving, merciful, mild, patient, placable. *Antonyms*: implacable, relentless, revengeful, unforgiving.

char·i·ty (char′ə·tē) *n. pl.* **·ties 1** Liberality to the poor. **2** Almsgiving; alms. **3** An institution for the help of the needy. **4** Readiness to overlook faults; tolerance; leniency. **5** Spiritual benevolence; Christian love. **6** *Law* A gift of real or personal property for the public benefit. See synonyms under BENEVOLENCE, LOVE. [<OF *charité* <L *caritas, -tatis* love < *carus* dear]

cha·riv·a·ri (shə·riv′ə·rē′, shiv′ə·rē′, shä′rē·vä′rē) *n.* A noisy and discordant burlesque serenade, as to a newly married couple or an unpopular personage, performed with tin pans, horns, kettles, etc.: also spelled *shivaree.* [<F]

chark (chärk) See CHAR[2]. [Back formation from CHARCOAL]

char·kha (chûr′kə, chär′-) *n.* The spinning wheel of India. Also **char′ka.** [<Hind. *carkhā*]

char·la·tan (shär′lə·tən) *n.* A pretender to knowledge or skill, especially to medical knowledge; quack. — **char′la·tan′ic** (-tan′ik) *adj.* — **char′la·tan·ry, char′la·tan·ism** *n.* [<F <Ital. *ciarlatano* babbler < *ciarlare* babble < *ciarla* chat, idle talk]

Char·le·magne (shär′lə·mān), 742–814, king of the Franks 768–814; emperor of the West, 800–814: known as *Charles the Great.*

Char·le·roi (shär·lə·rwä′) A town in SW Belgium; site of the first battle of World War I (1914). Also **Char·le·roy** (shär·lə·rwä′).

Charles (chärlz, *Fr.* shärl) A masculine personal name. See CARLO, CARLOS, KARL. [<F <L *Carolus* <Gmc., a freeman]

— **Charles I,** 1600–49, Charles Stuart, king of England 1625–49; beheaded.

— **Charles I of Anjou,** 1226–85, king of Sicily 1265–82; of Naples 1266–85.

— **Charles II,** 1630–85, king of England 1660–85.

— **Charles V,** 1337–80, king of France 1364–80: known as *Charles the Wise.*

— **Charles V,** 1500–58, emperor of Germany 1519–56, and, as **Charles I,** king of Spain 1516–56; abdicated.

— **Charles VII,** 1403–61, king of France 1422–61.

— **Charles IX,** 1550–74, king of France 1560–74.

— **Charles X,** 1757–1836, king of France 1824–30.

— **Charles XII,** 1682–1718, king of Sweden 1697–1718.

— **Charles Edward Stuart** See STUART, CHARLES EDWARD.

— **Charles Mar·tel** (mär·tel′), 688–741, Frankish ruler; grandfather of Charlemagne: called "The Hammer."

— **Charles the Great** See CHARLEMAGNE.

Charles, Cape The northern point at the entrance of Chesapeake Bay, Virginia.

Charles (shärl), **Jacques Alexandre César,** 1746–1823, French aeronaut and physicist.

Charles River A river in eastern Massachusetts, flowing 60 miles to Boston Harbor.

Charles's law (chärl′ziz) *Physics* The statement that the volume of a gas kept at constant pressure varies directly with the absolute temperature: exact only for perfect gases: also called *Gay-Lussac law.* [after J. A. C. *Charles*]

Charles's Wain See under WAIN.

Charles·ton (chärlz′tən) **1** A port in SE South Carolina. **2** The capital of West Virginia.

Charles·ton (chärlz′tən) *n.* A fast dance in four-four time; also, the music for it. [from *Charleston,* S.C.]

Charles·town (chärlz′toun) Formerly a city, now part of Boston, Massachusetts; site of Bunker Hill.

Char·le·voix (shär′lə·voi) A resort city in NW Michigan.

Char·le·voix (shär·lə·vwä′), **Pierre F. X. de,** 1682–1761, French Jesuit missionary in Canada.

Char·ley (chär′lē) Diminutive of CHARLES. Also **Char′lie.**

char·ley–horse (chär′lē·hôrs′) *n. U.S. Colloq.* A rupture or severe strain in the muscles of the leg or arm, caused by excessive exertion. [Origin unknown]

char·lock (chär′lək) *n.* Wild mustard *(Brassica arvensis)*: often a troublesome weed. [OE *cerlic*]

char·lotte (shär′lət) *n.* A dessert made of fruits, whipped cream, custard, etc., in a mold of cake, bread, or crumbs. [<F, from the fem. name]

Char·lotte (shär′lət; *Fr.* shär·lôt′; *Ger.* shär·lot′ə) A feminine personal name. Also *Dan., Sw.* **Char·lot·ta** (shär·lot′ä). [<F]

Char·lotte (shär′lət) A city in southern North Carolina.

Char·lot·te A·ma·li·e (shär·lot′ə ə·mä′lē·ə) A port on Saint Thomas Island, capital of the Virgin Islands of the United States: formerly *Saint Thomas.*

Char·lot·ten·burg (shär·lot′ən·bûrg, *Ger.* shär·lôt′ən·bŏŏrkh) The chief residential district of Berlin.

charlotte russe (rōōs) A dessert made of whipped cream or custard in a mold of sponge cake. [<F, Russian charlotte]

Char·lottes·ville (shär′ləts·vil) A city in central Virginia.

Char·lotte·town (shär′lət·toun) A port, capital of Prince Edward Island province, Canada.

charm[1] (chärm) *v.t.* **1** To attract irresistibly; bewitch; enchant. **2** To influence as by magic power; soothe; assuage. **3** To influence the senses or mind of by some quality or attraction, as beauty; delight. **4** To protect as by a spell: a *charmed* life. — *v.i.* **5** To be pleasing or fascinating. **6** To act as a charm; work as a spell. **7** To use spells or incantations. [<*n.*] — *n.* **1** The power of alluring or delighting; fascination. **2** That which charms; beauty; appeal. **3** A magical spell. **4** A small ornament worn on a watchguard, bracelet, etc., for decoration, to avert evil, or to insure good fortune. **5** Originally, the chanting of a verse supposed to possess magical power; an incantation. See synonyms under TALISMAN. [<F *charme* <L *carmen* song, incantation] — **charm′er** *n.*

Synonyms (verb): bewitch, captivate, delight, enchant, enrapture, entice, entrance, fascinate. See RAVISH. *Antonyms*: annoy, disenchant, disgust, distress, disturb, irritate, repel.

charm[2] (chärm) *n. Obs.* Singing, especially of birds; hence, song or melody. [ME *cherme,* var. of *chirm* CHIRM]

char·meuse (shär·mœz′) *n.* A soft, light fabric with satin weave, having a dull back and semilustrous surface. [<F]

charm·ing (chär′ming) *adj.* **1** Having power to charm. **2** Enchanting; fascinating; bewitching. — **charm′ing·ly** *adv.* — **charm′ing·ness** *n.*

Synonyms: bewitching, captivating, delightful, enchanting, enrapturing, entrancing, fascinating, winning. That is *charming* or *bewitching* which is adapted to win others as if by a magic spell. *Enchanting, enrapturing, entrancing* represent the influence as not only supernatural, but irresistible and *delightful*. That which is *fascinating* may win without delighting, as a serpent its prey; we can speak of horrible *fascination*. *Charming* applies only to what is external to oneself; *delightful* may apply to personal experiences or emotions as well; we speak of a *charming* manner, a *charming* dress, but of *delightful* anticipations. Compare AMIABLE, BEAUTIFUL, LOVELY.

char·nel (chär′nəl) *n.* A burying place; cemetery; mortuary; also, a sepulcher. — *adj.* Fitted or used for the reception of dead bodies. [<OF <LL *carnalis* fleshly < *caro, carnis* flesh]

charnel house A room or vault, sometimes in a church, for or filled with dead bodies or with bones.

Charn·wood (chärn′wo͝od), **Baron,** 1864–1945, Godfrey Rathbone Benson, English biographer.

Char·on (kâr′ən) **1** In Greek mythology, the ferryman who carried the dead over the river Styx to Hades. **2** A ferryman: a humorous use.

Char·pen·tier (shȧr·pän·tyā′), **Gustave,** 1860–1956, French composer.

char·poy (chär′poi′) *n.* The typical bedstead or cot of India, usually having a bamboo frame interlaced with twine. Also **char·pai** (chär′pī′). [<Hind. *chārpāī* < *chār* four + *pāī* foot]

char·qued (chär′kid) *adj.* Dried or jerked: said of meat. See JERK[2]. [<Sp. *charqué,* var. of *charquí* dried beef]

char·qui (chär′kē) *n.* Thin strips of sun-dried meat; jerked beef: also called *jerky.* Also **char′qué.** [<Sp. *charquí* <Quechua *echarqui* dried beef]

charr (chär) See CHAR[3].

char·ry (chär′ē) *adj.* **·ri·er, ·ri·est** Pertaining to or like charcoal.

chart (chärt) *n.* **1** A map on which selected features or characteristics are clearly indicated; especially, one for the use of navigators, aviators, and meteorologists. **2** A sheet showing facts graphically or in tabular form. **3** An outline or diagram having some geographical or physical application. **4** A graph showing changes and variation of temperature, population, circulation of publications, death rate, etc. — *v.t.* To map out; lay out on a chart. [<OF *charte* <L *charta* <Gk. *chartē* leaf of paper. Doublet of CARD.]

char·ta (kär′tə) *n.* *pl.* **·tae** (-tē) A sheet of paper impregnated with medicines, applied externally. [<L *charta* paper]

char·ter (chär′tər) *n.* **1** An act of incorporation of a municipality, company, institution, or the like. **2** A writing permitting the establishment of a branch or chapter of a society. **3** A document granting special rights or privileges. **4** A lease, as of a vessel, or the contract by which it is leased: also **char′ter·par′ty.** **5** Written evidence of agreement or contract, as a deed. — *v.t.* **1** To hire by charter. **2** To hire by contract, as a train or car. **3** To establish by charter; give a charter to, as a bank, railroad, colony, etc. [<OF *chartre* <L *chartula,* dim. of *charta* paper] — **char′ter·er** *n.*

char·ter·age (chär′tər·ij) *n.* The act or business of chartering vessels; shipbrokerage; also, a shipbroker's fee.

charter colony In American history, a colony established under a royal charter, which freed it from direct parliamentary control, as Massachusetts.

chartered accountant See under ACCOUNTANT.

Char·ter·house (chär′tər·hous′) A school and asylum established in London in 1611 in a suppressed Carthusian monastery.

charter member An original member of a corporation, or of an order or society.

Charter of the United Nations The charter adopted by the United Nations Conference on International Organization at San Francisco, April–June, 1945, making the United Nations a permanent organization, and establishing the General Assembly, the Security Council, the Economic and Social Council, the Trusteeship Council, the International Court of Justice, and the Secretariat as its component parts. See UNITED NATIONS, INTERNATIONAL COURT OF JUSTICE under COURT.

Char·ters Towers (chär′tərz) A town in Queensland, Australia.

Chart·ism (chär′tiz·əm) *n.* **1** A movement for democratic social and political reform in England, based on principles embodied in the *People's Charter* (1838). **2** The principles of this movement. — **Chart′ist** *n.*

chart·less (chärt′lis) *adj.* **1** Not laid down in a chart. **2** Without a chart. **3** Unguided.

char·tog·ra·pher (kär·tog′rə·fər) See CARTOGRAPHER.

Chartres (shȧr′tr′) A city in NW France; noted for its 11th–13th century Gothic cathedral.

char·treuse (shȧr·trœz′) *n.* **1** A yellow, pale green, or white liqueur made by the Carthusian monks. **2** (*also* shär·tro͞oz′) A pale yellowish-green color. — *adj.* Of this color. [from CHARTREUSE]

Char·treuse (shȧr·trœz′) A Carthusian monastery, especially **La Grande Chartreuse,** the original house of the Carthusian order, near Grenoble, France.

Char·treux (shȧr·trœ′) *n. Obs.* A Carthusian monk. [<F]

char·tu·lar·y (kär′cho͞o·ler′ē) See CARTULARY.

char·wom·an (chär′wo͝om′ən) *n.* *pl.* **·wom·en** A woman employed to do cleaning, scrubbing, etc., as in office buildings. [<CHAR[1] + WOMAN]

char·y (châr′ē) *adj.* **char·i·er, char·i·est** **1** Cautious; wary. **2** Careful; prudent; sparing; hence, stingy. [OE *cearig* sorrowful, sad < *cearu* care]

Cha·ryb·dis (kə·rib′dis) In Greek mythology, a monster dwelling in a whirlpool on the Sicilian coast opposite the rock Scylla. See SCYLLA.

chase[1] (chās) *v.* **chased, chas·ing** *v.t.* **1** To pursue with intent to catch, capture, or molest. **2** To drive away; dispel: often with *away, out* or *off.* **3** To hunt, as deer. **4** To drive by pursuing: He *chased* the hens into the coop. — *v.i.* **5** To follow in pursuit. **6** *Colloq.* To rush; go hurriedly. — *n.* **1** Earnest pursuit; also, that which is pursued; the prey or quarry. **2** The practice of hunting. **3** *Archaic* The right to hunt on a certain tract. **4** Hunters collectively; the hunt. **5** *Brit.* A private game preserve. **6** In court tennis, a scoring stroke, as when the ball bounces a second time in certain parts of the court. Also spelled *chace.* [<OF *chacier* <LL *captiare,* freq. of *capere* take, hold. Doublet of CATCH.] — **chas′ing** *n.*

chase[2] (chās) *n.* **1** *Printing* A strong rectangular metal frame into which pages of type are fastened for printing. **2** The part of a cannon between the trunnions and the swell of the muzzle. **3** A groove or slot: the *chase* of a water wheel. **4** A longitudinal groove for a tenon or tongue; a form of rabbet. **5** The circular trough of a cider mill, where the apples are crushed by the runner. — *v.t.* **chased, chas·ing** To ornament by indenting; also, to form by embossing, indenting, etc.: to *chase* silverware. [<F *châsse, chas* <OF *chasse* <L *capsa* box] — **chas′er** *n.*

CHASE[2] (*n. def. 1*)

Chase (chās), **Mary Ellen,** born 1887, U.S. educator and author. — **Salmon Portland,** 1808–73, U.S. lawyer; chief justice of the United States 1864–73.

chas·er (chā′sər) *n.* **1** One who chases or pursues; a hunter. **2** A steeplechaser. **3** A pursuing or following airplane or vessel. **4** A gun at the bow or stern of such a vessel for use in pursuit of or by another vessel: a bow *chaser* and a stern *chaser.* **5** *U.S. Colloq.* A drink of water or of some mild beverage taken after or with whisky, rum, etc. **6** A small quantity of alcoholic liquor taken at the end of a meal; a chasse.

chasm (kaz′əm) *n.* **1** A yawning hollow; deep gorge. **2** An abrupt interruption of continuity; a gap or void. See synonyms under BREACH, HOLE. [<Gk. *chasma* < *chainein* gape, open wide] — **chas·mal** (kaz′məl) *adj.*

chasse[1] (shȧs) *n.* A small glass of alcoholic liquor served at the end of a meal. Also *French* **chasse-ca·fé** (-kȧ·fā′). [Short for *chasse-café* < *chasser* chase + *café* (the taste of) coffee]

chasse[2] (shäs) *n.* A casket for the relics of a saint. [<F *châsse* <L *capsa* box]

chas·sé (sha·sā′) *n.* In dancing, a movement across or to right and left. — *v.i.* **chas·séd, chas·sé·ing** To perform a chassé. Also popularly called *sashay.* [<F, pp. of *chasser* chase]

chasse·pot (shȧs·pō′) *n.* A French breechloading rifled needle gun. [after A. A. *Chassepot,* 1833–1905, French inventor]

chas·seur (sha·sûr′) *n.* **1** A light-armed soldier of cavalry or infantry. **2** A semimilitary household servitor among the European nobility. **3** A huntsman. **4** A hotel servant. [<F, hunter < *chasser* <OF *chacier* CHASE[1]]

Chas·si·dim (khä·sē′dim) *n.* *pl.* of **Chas·sid** (khä′sid) A sect of Jewish mystics: also spelled *Hasidim.* [<Hebrew, pious] — **Chas·si·dic** (khä·sē′dik) *adj.*

chas·sis (shas′ē, chas′ē) *n.* *pl.* **chas·sis** (shas′ēz, chas′-) **1** The frame and springs of a motor vehicle; also, all other mechanical parts of the car, including the wheels and motor. **2** *Aeron.* The landing gear of an aircraft; the wheels, floats, or other structures which support the main weight of an airplane. **3** In radio: **a** The metal framework to which the tubes and other components of a receiver, amplifier, etc., are attached. **b** The assembled framework and components. **4** In coast artillery, a movable railway for running the top carriage of a gun into and out of firing position. [<F *châssis* < *chas.* See CHASE[2].]

chaste (chāst) *adj.* **1** Free from sexual impurity; virtuous. **2** Pure in thought. **3** Pure in style; free from literary or artistic extravagances. **4** *Obs.* Unmarried; single. See synonyms under MODEST, PURE. [<OF *chaste* <L *castus* pure] — **chaste′ly** *adv.* — **chaste′ness** *n.*

chast·en (chā′sən) *v.t.* **1** To discipline by punishment or affliction; chastise. **2** To moderate; soften; temper. **3** To refine; purify. — **chast′en·er** *n.* — **chast′en·ing** *n.*

Synonyms: afflict, castigate, chastise, correct, discipline, humble, punish, purify, refine, soften, subdue, try. *Castigate* and *chastise* refer strictly to corporal punishment, although both are somewhat archaic. *Punish* is distinctly retributive in sense; *chasten,* wholly corrective and merciful in intent and result. See REPRESS, REPROVE. [<OF *chastier* <L *castigare* correct. See CASTIGATE.]

chas·tise (chas·tīz′) *v.t.* **·tised, ·tis·ing** **1** To punish, especially with the rod; whip. **2** To refine or subdue; chasten. See synonyms under BEAT, CHASTEN. [ME *chastisen*] — **chas·tis′a·ble** *adj.* — **chas·tise·ment** (chas′tiz·mənt, chas·tīz′-) *n.* — **chas·tis′er** *n.*

chas·ti·ty (chas′tə·tē) *n.* **1** The state or quality of being chaste; purity. **2** Virginity or celibacy. See synonyms under VIRTUE. [<OF *chasteté* <L *castitas, -tatis* purity < *castus* pure]

chastity belt A fettered girdle worn by women in the Middle Ages to prohibit sexual intercourse during the absence of their husbands.

chas·u·ble (chaz′yə·bəl, chas′-) *n.* The outer vestment worn by a priest in celebrating the mass or Eucharist: a sleeveless mantle falling low in front and behind, and having a cross on the back. [<F <Med. L *casubula,* var. of *casula* cloak <L, dim. of *casa* house]

chat[1] (chat) *v.i.* **chat·ted, chat·ting** To converse in an easy or gossipy manner; talk familiarly. — *n.* **1** Easy and familiar speech; informal conversation. **2** Any of several singing birds: so called from their notes. See synonyms under CONVERSATION. [Short for CHATTER]

chat[2] (chat) *n. Bot.* The inflorescence, catkin, or seed of various plants, as the ament of the pine, the samara of the maple, etc. [<F, cat; so called from its appearance]

Cha·tal·ja (chä′täl·jä′) See ÇATALCA.

cha·teau (sha·tō′, *Fr.* shä·tō′) *n.* *pl.* **·teaux** (-tōz′, *Fr.* -tō′) **1** A French castle or manor house. **2** A house on a country estate, particularly a large house resembling a French manor. Also *French* **châ·teau′.** [<F <OF *chastel* <L *castellum* CASTLE]

Châ·teau·bri·and (shȧ·tō·brē·äṅ′), **François**

René, 1768–1848, Vicomte de Chateaubriand, French writer and diplomat.

Châ·teau·roux (shä·tō·ro͞o′) A town in central France.

Châ·teau–Thier·ry (shä·tō′tye·rē′) A town in northern France; scene of heavy fighting (1918) in World War I.

château wine Any wine made, named for, and usually bottled on, the estate of a château in France where the grapes are grown, particularly those near Bordeaux.

chat·e·lain (shat′ə·lān) See CASTELLAN.

chat·e·laine (shat′ə·lān) *n.* **1** A chain, hanging from a woman's belt to hold small articles; also, a clasp to hold a watch or purse. **2** The mistress of a chateau or castle. [<F *châtelaine,* fem. of *châtelain* CASTELLAN]

Cha·tel·per·ro·ni·an (sha·tel′pə·rō′nē·ən) *adj. Anthropol.* Describing a culture stage of the Upper Paleolithic closely related to and merging with the Aurignacian: also called *Lower Perigordian.* [from *Chatelperron* town in southern France where artifacts were found]

Chat·ham (chat′əm) A municipal borough and port in Kent, England.

Chat·ham (chat′əm), **Earl of.** See PITT.

Chat·ham Island (chat′əm) See SAN CRISTÓBAL ISLAND.

Chatham Islands Two New Zealand Islands, **Chatham** and **Pitt,** east of South Island; total, 372 square miles.

Chatham Strait A navigable channel of SE Alaska through the Alexander Archipelago.

Châ·til·lon (shä·tē·yôn′) A town of north central France. Also **Châtillon–sous–Bag·neux** (-so͞o·bä·nyœ′)

cha·toy·ant (shə·toi′ənt, *Fr.* shà·twà·yäṅ) *adj.* **1** Possessing a changeable luster, like that of a cat's eye in the dark. **2** Exhibiting a narrow band of light, as certain gemstones when cut and polished. —*n.* A stone having such a luster; cat's–eye. [<F, ppr. of *chatoyer* change, as a cat's eye] —**cha·toy′an·cy** *n.*

Cha·tri·an (shà·trē·äṅ′), **Alexandre** See ERCKMANN–CHATRIAN.

Chat·ta·hoo·chee River (chat′ə·ho͞o′chē) A river forming the boundary between southern Georgia and Alabama, flowing 235 miles SW to the Apalachicola.

Chat·ta·noo·ga (chat′ə·no͞o′gə) A city in SE Tennessee; scene of decisive Union victories (1863) in the Civil War.

chat·tel (chat′l) *n. Law* **1** An article of personal property; a movable. **2** Any interest or right in land less than a freehold; a leasehold estate in lands for a determinate period: called a **chattel real.** As distinguished from freeholds, chattels real are regarded as personal property; but, as being interests in real property, they are so designated to distinguish them from other chattels, which are called **chattels personal. 3** *Archaic* A bondman; serf. See synonyms under PROPERTY. [<OF *chatel* <L *capitale* property <*caput* head. Doublet of CATTLE.]

chattel mortgage A conditional transfer of rights in movable property as security for a debt or obligation, insuring the debtor reversion of ownership upon payment of the obligation.

chat·ter (chat′ər) *v.i.* **1** To click together rapidly, as the teeth in shivering. **2** To talk rapidly and trivially; blather. **3** To make rapid and indistinct sounds, as a monkey or squirrel. **4** To clatter or vibrate while operating improperly, as a power tool. —*v.t.* **5** To utter in a trivial or chattering manner. See synonyms under BABBLE. —*n.* **1** Idle prattle. **2** Jabbering, as of a monkey. **3** A rattling of the teeth. **4** The jar or vibration of a chattering tool. [Imit.]

chat·ter·box (chat′ər·boks′) *n.* A voluble talker.

chat·ter·er (chat′ər·ər) *n.* **1** One who or that which chatters. **2** A passerine bird, as a waxwing, especially the Bohemian waxwing.

Chat·ter·ji (chä′tər·jē), **Bankim Chandra,** 1838–94, Indian novelist.

chatter marks 1 *Mech.* Irregular, very fine tool markings caused by vibration of a tool. **2** *Geol.* Transverse crescent–shaped marks in a continuous series, sometimes occurring in deeply gouged glacial striae as the result of vibration.

Chat·ter·ton (chat′ər·tən), **Thomas,** 1752–1770, English poet.

chat·ty[1] (chat′ē) *adj.* **·ti·er, ·ti·est** Given to chat; loquacious. —**chat′ti·ly** *adv.* —**chat′ti·ness** *n.*

chat·ty[2] (chat′ē) *n. pl.* **·ties** An East Indian porous water jar. [<Hind. *chāṭī*]

Chau·cer (chô′sər), **Geoffrey,** 1340?–1400, English poet.

Chau·ce·ri·an (chô·sir′ē·ən) *adj.* Of, related to, or characteristic of Chaucer or his writings. —*n.* A student or admirer of Chaucer.

chauf·fer (chô′fər, shô′-) *n.* A small chemical furnace. Also **chau′fer.** [Var. of CHAFER]

chauf·feur (shō′fər, shō·fûr′) *n.* One who drives or operates an automobile; especially, one whose work is to drive an automobile for someone else. [<F, stoker <*chauffer* warm]

chaul·moo·gra (chôl·mo͞o′grə) *n.* An East Indian and Malayan tree *(Taraktogenos kurzii,* family *Flacourtiaceae),* from whose seeds is extracted the yellowish **chaulmoogra oil,** used in the treatment of leprosy and other skin diseases. Also **chaul·mu′gra.** [<Bengali *cāulmugrā*]

Chau·mont (shō·môn′) A city in NE France, capital of Haute–Mar department.

Chaun·cey (chôn′sē, chän′-) A masculine personal name. [<OF, chancellor]

chaunt (chônt, chänt) See CHANT.

Chau·pa·ya (chou·pä′yä) See MENAM.

chausses (shōs) *n. Archaic.* **1** Medieval leg harness or hose of mail. **2** Tight pantaloons covering the hips, legs, and feet. [<OF *chauces*<L *calceus* boot <*calx, calcis* heel]

Chaus·son (shō·sôn′), **Ernest,** 1855–99, French composer.

chaus·sure (shō·sür′) *n.* Foot covering. [<F < L *calceare* shoe <*calceus.* See CHAUSSES.]

chau·tau·qua (shə·tô′kwə) *n. U.S.* Any educational association, especially one of a number holding sessions in a circuit of communities. [from *Chautauqua*]

Chau·tau·qua (shə·tô′kwə) A summer resort, seat of an educational association, **Chautauqua Institution,** on **Lake Chautauqua,** 18 miles long, in western New York.

chau·vin·ist (shō′vən·ist) *n.* **1** Anyone absurdly jealous of his country's honor or puffed up with an exaggerated sense of national glory; an extravagant glorifier of his country. **2** One who is belligerently attached to his own race, group, etc.: white *chauvinist.* [after Nicolas *Chauvin,* an extremely devoted soldier and overzealous supporter of Napoleon Bonaparte] —**chau′vin·ism** *n.* —**chau′vin·is′tic** *adj.* —**chau′vin·is′ti·cal·ly** *adv.*

Cha·vannes (shà·vàn′) See PUVIS DE CHAVANNES.

Chá·vez (chä′väs), **Carlos,** 1899–1978, Mexican composer and conductor.

chaw (chô) *v.t. & n. Dial.* Chew. [Var. of CHEW]

chay (shā) *n. Dial.* A chaise: also spelled *shay.* [Alter. of F *chaise* chair]

cha·zan (khä′zən) See HAZZAN.

cheap (chēp) *adj.* **1** Bearing or bringing a low price in the market; that may be bought at low price; inexpensive. **2** Obtainable at a low rate. **3** Depreciated: said of money. **4** Being of little value; hence, poor; of inferior quality. **5** Not esteemed. **6** Low: a *cheap* person. **7** Embarrassed; sheepish. See synonyms under BASE, COMMON. —*n. Obs.* **1** A market; still used in combination in some place names: *Cheap*side and East*cheap* in London. **2** A bargain. —*adv.* In a cheap manner [Earlier *good cheap* a bargain <OE *ceap* business, trade] —**cheap′ly** *adv.* —**cheap′·ness** *n.*

cheap·en (chē′pən) *v.t.* **1** To make cheap or cheaper. **2** *Obs.* To chaffer or bargain for. **3** To bring into contempt, belittle, or disparage. —*v.i.* **4** To become cheap. —**cheap′en·er** *n.*

Cheap·side (chēp′sīd) A district of London, a market center in the Middle Ages and the site of the Mermaid Tavern.

cheap·skate (chēp′skāt′) *n. U.S. Slang* An unpleasant, miserly person.

cheat (chēt) *v.t.* **1** To deceive or defraud. **2** To impose upon; delude; trick. **3** To elude or escape; foil: to *cheat* the hangman. —*v.i.* **4** To practice fraud or act dishonestly. —**to cheat on** *Slang* To be sexually unfaithful to. —*n.* **1** An act of cheating; fraud; imposture. **2** *Law* The obtaining of property by imposture: indictable at common law when the act injures the public welfare. **3** A systematic cheater; swindler. **4** Any of several types of bromegrass: so called because they resemble the grain among which they grow. See CHESS[2]. **5** An article or object of fictitious value; a sham. See synonyms under ARTIFICE, FRAUD, HYPOCRITE. [ME *chete,* short for *achete* escheat] —**cheat′ing** *adj.* —**cheat′ing·ly** *adv.*

cheat·er (chē′tər) *n.* **1** One who cheats; swindler; defrauder. **2** *pl. U.S. Slang* Spectacles; eyeglasses.

che·bec (chi·bek′) *n.* The least flycatcher. [Imit.]

Che·bok·sa·ry (chi·bok·sä′rē) A port on the Volga, capital of Chuvash Autonomous S.S.R.

che·cha·ko (chē·chä′kō) See CHEECHAKO.

check (chek) *n.* **1** A sudden stopping or arrest; rebuff; reverse; delay. **2** Any person or thing that controls or restrains. **3** A checkrein. **4** A written order for money, drawn upon a bank or banker: also *Brit. cheque.* **5** A numbered tag, etc., used in duplicate to identify the owner of article. **6** Any examination, test, or comparison for verification; also, a mark for verification or identification. **7** A square in a checkered surface; also, any checkered pattern or fabric having a checkered pattern. **8** In chess, an attack upon or menace to the king. **9** In mining, a slight fault. **10** A chip used in games. **11** A crack, as in timber, caused by uneven seasoning, or, in steel, caused by uneven tempering. **12** A notch or rabbet in a piece of wood or stone into which another piece fits. **13** A curb on administrative power, as a constitutional right: the *checks* and balances of republican government. **14** A bill in a restaurant. **15** *Obs.* Rebuke; reproof. See synonyms under ANIMADVERSION, REPROOF. —*v.t.* **1** To stop or restrain forcibly or suddenly. **2** To curb; hold in restraint, as with a checkrein. **3** To ascertain correctness of, as by comparison; investigate. **4** To mark with a check or checks. **5** To mark with a pattern of criss–crosses, as cloth. **6** To cause to crack; to make checks or chinks in. **7** To rebuke; rebuff; repulse: They *checked* the attack. **8** In chess, to put an opponent's king in check. **9** To deposit temporarily for safekeeping: to *check* one's luggage. **10** *Agric.* To plant so as to form checkrows. —*v.i.* **11** pause or make a stop. **12** To crack, as paint. **13** To agree item for item: My figures *check* with yours. **14** In chess, to give check to a king. **15** *U.S.* To draw on a checking account. **16** In hunting, to pause, as hounds, to locate a lost scent. **17** In falconry, to forsake proper quarry for baser game: with *at.* —**to check in** *U.S.* To register as a guest at a hotel. —**to check out** *U.S.* **1** To pay one's bill and leave, as from a hotel; also, to depart; die. **2** To investigate or confirm. **3** To be true or as expected, upon investigation. **4** To count and charge for (merchandise). **5** test the performance of. —**to check up 1** To test; examine: often with *on.* **2** To put a checkrein on. —*interj.* **1** An exclamation proclaiming that the opponent's king is in check. **2** Correct; that is right. —*adj.* **1** Checkered. **2** Serving to verify or confirm: a *check* test. [<OF *eschek* defeat, check <Arabic *shāh* king <Persian; orig. from chess, indicating the king was in danger]

check·book (chek′book′) *n.* A book of bank checks in blank, usually with marginal stubs for date, amount, and name of payee.

checked (chekt) *adj.* **1** Marked with squares: *checked* gingham. **2** Made of a fabric marked or woven in squares: a *checked* suit. **3** Restrained; stopped; kept in check.

check·er (chek′ər) *n.* **1** A piece in the game of checkers, usually a small disk. **2** One of the squares in a checkered surface. **3** *pl.* A game for two persons played with 24 pieces upon a checkerboard; draughts. **4** One who checks; especially, one who inspects, counts, or supervises the disposal of merchandise, as in a market. **5** The cultivated service tree. **6** The wild European service tree *(S. torminalis):* also called **checkertree. 7** The fruit of either tree. —*v.t.* **1** To mark with squares or crossed lines. **2** To mark with vicissitudes; diversify. Also *Brit. chequer.* [<OF *eschequier* chessboard <Med. L *scaccarium* < *scacci* chess <Arabic *shāq.* See CHECK.]

check·er·ber·ry (chek′ər·ber′ē) *n. pl.* **·ries 1** The wintergreen. **2** Its red berry. **3** Loosely, the partridgeberry.

check·er·board (chek′ər·bôrd′, -bōrd′) *n.* A

board divided into 64 squares, used in playing checkers or chess.

check·ered (chek′ərd) *adj.* 1 Divided into squares of different colors; checked, as with black and white. 2 Showing any alternating spaces of color or of light and darkness. 3 Marked by vicissitudes; alternating, as between good and evil fortune.

checking account A bank account against which a depositor may draw checks.

check list 1 A list by which something may be confirmed or verified; specifically, a roll or list of voters used at the polls on election days for checking off the names of those who vote. 2 A list of plants, animals, minerals, fossils, etc., usually limited to one natural division, for students and collectors, to check when recognized or acquired.

check·mate (chek′māt′) *v.t.* **·mat·ed, mat·ing** 1 In chess, to put (an opponent's king) in check from which no escape is possible, thus winning the game: commonly shortened to *mate.* 2 Hence, to defeat by a skilful maneuver. See synonyms under CONQUER. — *n.* 1 The act or position of checkmating. 2 Complete defeat. [<OF *eschec mat* <Arabic *al-shāh māt* the king is dead <Persian]

check·off (chek′ôf′, -of′) *n.* The collection of trade-union dues by deduction at source from the pay of each employee, the employer's accounting office serving as collecting agent. Also **check′-off′.**

check·out (chek′out′) *n.* 1 The series of actions by which the condition or performance of someone or something is tested. 2 The operation or act of examining and charging for purchases, as in a market.

check·rein (chek′rān′) *n.* 1 A rein from the bit of the bridle to the saddle of a harness to keep a horse's head up. 2 The branch rein connecting a driving rein of one horse to the bit of his mate in a double team. Also **check′line′.**

check·room (chek′ro͞om′, -ro͝om′) *n.* A room in a railway station, restaurant, theater, etc., where small packages, coats, hats, luggage, etc., may be left temporarily.

check·row (chek′rō′) *n.* One of the standing rows, as of trees, in a farm or orchard that partition it into squares. — *v.t.* To plant in this fashion.

checks and balances Complementary or balanced powers among the branches of a government, as among the legislative, executive, and judiciary branches.

check-up (chek′up′) *n.* A thorough examination or testing of a living organism, the operation of a mechanism or machine, the progress of work or the finished work of a person or group, etc., to ascertain health, accuracy, value, etc.

check valve *Mech.* A one-way valve, as in a boiler, which closes automatically to prevent return of fluid passing through it. See illustration under HYDRAULIC RAM.

Ched·dar (ched′ər) *n.* Any of several types of white to yellow, hard, smooth cheese. Also **Cheddar cheese.** [from *Cheddar,* Somersetshire, England]

ched·dite (ched′īt, shed′-) *n.* An explosive used in blasting, consisting essentially of nitrated naphthalene containing a chlorate or perchlorate mixed with an oily substance, as castor oil. [from *Chedde,* France]

chee·cha·ko (chē·chä′kō) *n. U.S. Dial.* In Alaska and the NW United States, a newly arrived miner; a newcomer; tenderfoot: also spelled *chechako.* Also **chee·cha′co.** [<Chinook *t'shi* new + *chakho* come]

cheek (chēk) *n.* 1 Either side of the face below the eye and above the mouth. ◆ Collateral adjective: *buccal.* 2 A side or part analogous to the side of a face: the *cheek* of a vise. 3 *Naut.* One of two corresponding projections on either side of a mast, supporting the trestletrees. 4 *Colloq.* Assurance; impudence. — *v.t. Brit. Colloq.* To confront or address impudently. [OE *cēce, cēace*]

cheek by jowl 1 With cheek close to cheek. 2 Closely juxtaposed. 3 Confidential; intimate. Also *Scot.* **cheek for chow.**

cheek·y (chē′kē) *adj.* **cheek·i·er, cheek·i·est** Impudent; brazen. — **cheek′i·ly** *adv.* — **cheek′·i·ness** *n.*

chee·la (chē′lä) See CHELA[1].

cheep (chēp) *v.t.* & *v.i.* To utter in a faint, shrill tone; chirp; peep. — *n.* A weak chirp or squeak, as of a young bird. [Imit.] — **cheep·er** *n.*

cheer (chir) *n.* 1 A shout of applause or encouragement. 2 State of mind: Be of good *cheer.* 3 Cheerfulness. 4 Something that promotes cheerfulness. 5 Provisions for a feast. 6 *Obs.* Expression of countenance; look. See synonyms under APPLAUSE, ENTERTAINMENT, HAPPINESS. — *v.t.* 1 To make cheerful; fill with joy; comfort: often with *up.* 2 To applaud or salute with cheers. 3 To urge with words or cries; encourage; incite: often with *on.* 4 To act on like cheer; invigorate: The cup that *cheers.* — *v.i.* 5 To be or become cheerful, happy or glad: with *up.* 6 To utter cheers. 7 *Obs.* To be affected; feel; fare. See synonyms under ENCOURAGE, ENTERTAIN, REJOICE. [<OF *chiere, chere* face, countenance <LL *cara*] — **cheer′er** *n.* — **cheer′ing** *adj.*

cheer·ful (chir′fəl) *adj.* 1 In good spirits; joyous; lively. 2 Willing. — **cheer′ful·ly** *adv.* — **cheer′ful·ness** *n.*

Synonyms: blithe, bright, buoyant, cheering, cheery, gay, genial, happy, jocund, joyous, lively, merry, mirthful, smiling, sprightly, sunny. See BRIGHT, COMFORTABLE, GOOD, HAPPY.

cheer·i·o (chir′ē·ō) *interj.* & *n. Brit.* 1 Hello! 2 Goodbye! Also **cheer′o.**

cheer·less (chir′lis) *adj.* Destitute of cheer; gloomy. See synonyms under BLEAK. — **cheer′·less·ly** *adv.* — **cheer′less·ness** *n.*

cheer·ly (chir′lē) *adv. Archaic* Cheerfully; heartily; cheerily.

cheer·y (chir′ē) *adj.* **cheer·i·er, cheer·i·est** 1 Abounding in cheerfulness. 2 Fitted to cheer; cheering. See synonyms under BRIGHT, CHEERFUL, COMFORTABLE, HAPPY. — **cheer′i·ly** *adv.* — **cheer′i·ness** *n.*

cheese[1] (chēz) *n.* 1 The pressed curd of milk, variously prepared and flavored; also, a cake or mass of this substance. 2 Any of various substances ground and compacted like cheese, as headcheese. [OE *cēse* <L *caseus* cheese]

cheese[2] (chēz) *v.t. Slang* To stop; quit: leave off: especially in the imperative: *Cheese* it! Run away! [Alter. of CEASE]

cheese[3] (chēz) *n. Slang* The correct or most important thing or person. [Prob. <Persian *chīz* thing]

cheese·cake (chēz′kāk′) *n.* 1 A cake containing sweetened curds, eggs, milk, etc.: also **cheese cake.** 2 *Slang* The display of a girl's legs, as in photographs.

cheese·cloth (chēz′klôth′, -kloth′) *n.* A thin cotton fabric, originally used for wrapping a cheese after pressing.

cheese mite A minute acarid infesting cheese, flour, and milk.

cheese-par·ing (chēz′pâr′ing) *adj.* Miserly; parsimonious. — *n.* 1 A paring of cheese. 2 Something of no value. 3 Any mean or stingy practice or disposition.

chees·y (chē′zē) *adj.* **·i·er, ·i·est** 1 Made of or similar to cheese. 2 *Slang* Of inferior grade; second-rate.

chee·tah (chē′tə) *n.* An animal *(Acinonyx jubatus)* of the cat family, resembling the leopard, native to SW Asia and northern Africa: often tamed and trained to hunt antelope. Also spelled *chetah.* [<Hind. *chītā* leopard]

chef (shef) *n.* 1 A head cook. 2 Any cook. 3 A chief or director. [<F]

chef de cui·sine (də kwē·zēn′) *French* Chief cook; head chef.

chef-d'oeu·vre (she·dœ′vr′) *n. pl.* **chefs-d'oeu·vre** (she-) *French* A masterpiece; the most important work of an artist, writer, etc.

Che·foo (chē′fo͞o′) Yentai. Also **Chih′fu′.**

cheg·oe (cheg′ō) See CHIGOE.

cheilo-, etc. See CHILO-, etc.

cheiro-, etc. See CHIRO-, etc.

Chei·ron (kī′ron) See CHIRON.

Che·ju (chā′jo͞o′) A Korean island in the East China Sea; 713 square miles: formerly *Quelpart.*

Che·ka (chā′kä) *n.* A Soviet extraordinary commission working as secret police against counter-revolution: superseded by the OGPU in 1922. [<Russian *Che* C + *Ka* K, initials of *Chrezvychainaya Komissya* extraordinary commission]

Che·khov (chek′ôf), **Anton Pavlovich,** 1860–1904, Russian dramatist and short-story writer. Also **Che′kov, Che′koff.**

Che·kiang (che′kyang′, *Chinese* ju′jyäng′) A province in eastern China; 40,000 square miles; capital, Hangchow. Also **Che′chiang′.**

che·la[1] (chā′lä) *n. Anglo-Indian* A disciple or novice; especially, the disciple of a holy man. Also spelled *cheela.* [<Hind. *chelā* disciple <Skt. *cheṭaka* servant, slave]

che·la[2] (kē′lə) *n. pl.* **·lae** (-lē) *Zool* A terminal pincerlike claw in crustaceans and arachnids, as in lobsters and scorpions. [<NL <Gk. *chēlē* claw]

che·late (kē′lāt) *adj. Zool.* Having a chela or pincerlike claw; cheliform. — *n. Chem.* A compound which has been subjected to chelation.

che·la·tion (kē·lā′shən) *n. Chem.* The inactivation of metallic ions in a solution by an organic reagent with whose molecules they are strongly bound in a ring structure giving maximum stability for specified uses. [<Gk. *chēlē* claw]

che·li·form (kē′lə·fôrm, kel′ə-) *adj. Zool.* Having the form of a chela of a lobster; pincerlike.

Chel·le·an (shel′ē·ən) *adj. Anthropol.* Describing a culture stage of the Paleolithic Age, now more frequently assigned to the Abbevillian, Clactonian, and the earlier portion of the Acheulean. [from *Chelles,* France, where artifacts were first found]

Chelm (khelm) A city in eastern Poland: Russian *Kholm.*

Chelms·ford (chelms′fərd, chelmz′-, chemz′-) A municipal borough, county seat of Essex, England.

che·loid (kē′loid) See KELOID.

Che·lo·ni·a (ki·lō′nē·ə) *n.* An order of reptiles with external skeletons and toothless jaws, including tortoises and turtles. [<NL <Gk. *chelonē* tortoise] — **che·lo′ni·an** *adj.* & *n.*

Chel·sea (chel′sē) A metropolitan borough of SW London.

Chelsea china A fine, decorated china produced at Chelsea, England, from about 1745 to 1770.

Chel·ten·ham (chelt′nəm) A municipal borough in north central Gloucestershire, England.

Che·lya·binsk (chi·lyä′byinsk) A city in west central Russian S.F.S.R., in Asia.

Che·lyus·kin (chi·lyo͞os′kin), **Cape** The northernmost point of Asia, on the Taimur Peninsula.

chem·i·cal (kem′i·kəl) *adj.* 1 Of or pertaining to chemistry or its phenomena, laws, operations, or results: *chemical* analysis. 2 Obtained by or used in chemistry. Also *Obs.* **chem′ic.** — *n.* A substance obtained by or used in a chemical process. — **chem′i·cal·ly** *adv.*

chemical agent 1 Any of numerous chemical compounds used to effect a given purpose. 2 *Mil.* A poison gas, incendiary substance, or screening smoke.

chemical bomb See under BOMB.

chemical bond The force, usually exerted by shared electrons, which holds atoms together in a molecule.

chemical engineering That branch of engineering which studies, develops, and supervises the applications of chemistry to industrial processes.

chemical warfare The technique of using chemical agents, such as burning or poisonous gases, incendiary materials, etc., in defensive or offensive warfare.

chem·i·cide (kem′ə·sīd) *n.* Any of various preparations intended to kill pests or vermin by chemical action.

chem·i·cul·ti·va·tion (kem′i·kul′tə·vā′shən) *n.* The treatment of crops with special chemicals in order to destroy injurious weeds and insect pests.

chem·i·lu·mi·nes·cence (kem′i·lo͞o′mə·nes′əns) *n.* The emission of light from a substance undergoing a chemical reaction. — **chem′i·lu′mi·nes′cent** *adj.*

che·min de fer (shə·maṅ′ də fâr′) *French* 1 Literally, road of iron; a railroad. 2 A form of baccarat.

che·mise (shə·mēz′) *n.* 1 A woman's undergarment. 2 A muslin surgical dressing used mainly in rectal or bladder operations. 3 A dress style. [<F <LL *camisia* shirt]

chem·i·sette (shem′i·zet′) *n.* An ornamental neckpiece or dickey usually made of muslin or lace, worn by women to fill in the open neck of a dress. [<F, dim. of *chemise* CHEMISE]

chem·ism (kem′iz·əm) *n.* Chemical affinity or attraction; chemical properties or activities collectively.

chem·i·sorb (kem′i·sôrb, -zôrb) *v.t.* To adsorb or take up by chemical means. —*v.i.* To be adsorbed in this manner, especially in the presence of a catalyst. —**chem′i·sorp′tion** *n.*

chem·ist (kem′ist) *n.* **1** One versed in chemistry. **2** *Brit.* A druggist. **3** *Obs.* An alchemist. [<ALCHEMIST]

chem·is·try (kem′is·trē) *n.* **1** That science which treats of the structure, composition, and properties of substances and of the transformations which they undergo. **2** Chemical composition or processes.

Chem·nitz (kem′nits) A city in east central Germany.

chemo– *combining form* Chemical; of or with chemicals or chemical reactions: *chemotherapy.* Also, before vowels, **chem–; chemi–**, as in *chemicide.* [<CHEMICAL]

chem·o·cep·tor (kem′ō·sep′tər) *n.* **1** *Physiol.* An organ or nerve element of the body specialized to receive and transmit chemical stimuli, as those of smell and taste. **2** *Biol.* Those receptors within a cell which are supposed to have the power of fixing chemicals. Also **chem′o·re·cep′tor.** [<CHEMO- + (RE)CEPTOR]

chem·o·sphere (kem′ə·sfir′) A region of the atmosphere ranging from 26 to 70 miles above the earth and marked by predominant photochemical activity.

chem·o·sur·ger·y (kem′ō·sûr′jər·ē) *n.* A medical technique which utilizes chemistry, surgery, and microscopic analysis, especially in the treatment of skin cancers.

chem·o·syn·the·sis (kem′ō·sin′thə·sis) *n.* The formation of organic compounds from inorganic constituents by the energy derived from chemical changes. —**chem·o·syn·thet·ic** (kem·ō·sin·thet′ik) *adj.*

chem·o·tax·is (kem′ō·tak′sis) *n.* *Biol.* The property which certain motile living cells possess of approaching (**positive chemotaxis**) or moving away from (**negative chemotaxis**) chemical substances: also called *chemotropism.* [<CHEMO- + Gk. *taxis* order <*tattein* arrange] —**chem′o·tac′tic** (-tak′tik) *adj.*—**chem′o·tac′ti·cal·ly** *adv.*

chem·o·ther·a·peu·tant (kem′ō·ther′ə·pyōō′·tant) *n.* Any substance used in the prevention, treatment, and cure of diseases by chemotherapy.

chem·o·ther·a·py (kem′ō·ther′ə·pē) *n.* *Med.* The treatment of diseases by the chemical disinfection of affected organs and tissues, especially through the use of synthetic drugs whose action is specific against certain pathogenic micro–organisms but non–toxic to the patient. Also **chem′o·ther′a·peu′tics.** —**chem′o·ther′a·peu′tic** *adj.* —**chem′o·ther′a·pist** *n.*

che·mot·ro·pism (ki·mot′rə·piz′əm) *n.* **1** *Biol.* The response of a plant or animal organism to a chemical reaction, as by unequal growth or directed movements. **2** Chemotaxis. [<CHEMO- + TROPISM] —**chem·o·trop·ic** (kem·ō·trop′ik) adj.

Che·mul·po (che·mōōl·pō) See INCHON. Also **Che·mul·pho** (-pō).

chem·ur·gy (kem′ər·jē) *n.* The chemical exploitation of organic raw materials, especially agricultural products, in the industrial development of new products. [<CHEM(O)- + -URGY] —**chem·ur·gic** (kem·ûr′jik) *adj.* —**chem·ur′gi·cal** *adj.*

Che·nab (chi·nab′) A river of NW India, flowing 675 miles west to the Sutlej.

Cheng·teh (chung′du′) A city in Manchuria, capital of Jehol province.

Cheng·tu (chung′dōō′) The capital of Szechwan province, southern China.

Ché·nier (shā·nyā′), **André Marie de,** 1762–1794, French poet, born at Constantinople.

che·nille (shə·nēl′) *n.* **1** A soft, fluffy cord or yarn of silk, rayon, cotton, wool, etc., having a fuzzy pile on all sides: used for embroidery, fringes, tassels, etc. **2** Any fabric made with such yarns, used for rugs, etc. [<F, caterpillar <L *canicula,* dim. of *canis* dog; from its fuzzy appearance]

Chen·nault (shə·nôlt′), **Claire Lee,** 1890–1958, U.S. aviator; major general in World War II.

che·no·pod (kē′nə·pod, ken′ə-) *n.* Any plant of the goosefoot family, including American wormseed *(Chenopodium anthelminticum),* used as a remedy for intestinal worms. [<NL *chenopodium* <Gk. *chēn, chēnos* goose + *pous, podos* foot] —**che·no·po·di·a·ceous** (kē′·nə·pō′dē·ā′shəs, ken′ə-) *adj.*

Che·ops (kē′ops) Egyptian king of the fourth dynasty; builder of the Great Pyramid at Gizeh: also *Khufu.*

cheque (chek) See CHECK (*n.* def. 4).

cheq·uer, etc. (chek′ər) See CHECKER, etc.

Cher (shâr) A river in central France, flowing 200 miles NW to the Loire.

cher a·mi (shâr á·mē′) *French* Dear friend. —**chère a·mie** (shâr á·mē′) *fem.*

Cher·bourg (sher′boorg, *Fr.* sher·bōōr′) A port on the English Channel in northern France.

Cherbourg Peninsula See COTENTIN PENINSULA.

cher·chez la femme (sher·shā′ lá fám′) *French* Seek the woman: implying that a woman is the motive for a specified action.

Cher·i·bon (cher′i·bon′) See TJIREBON.

cher·ish (cher′ish) *v.t.* **1** To care for kindly; hold dear; treat with tenderness; foster. **2** To entertain fondly, as a hope or an idea; hold closely to. [<F *chériss-,* stem of *chérir* hold dear <*cher* dear <L *carus*] —**cher′ish·er** *n.*

Synonyms: cheer, comfort, encourage, entertain, foster, harbor, nourish, nurse, nurture, protect, shelter, treasure, value. To *cherish* is both to hold dear and to treat as dear. To *nurse* is to tend the helpless or feeble. To *nourish* is strictly to sustain and build up by food; to *nurture* includes mental and spiritual training with love and tenderness; to *foster* is simply to maintain and care for.

Cher·kas·sy (chir·kä′sē) A city on the Dnieper in central Ukrainian S.S.R.

Cher·kess Autonomous Region (cher·kes′) A district of SE European S.F.S.R.; 1,500 square miles; capital, Cherkessk.

Cher·kessk (cher·kesk′) The capital of Cherkess Autonomous Region, on the Kuban.

Cher·ni·gov (chir·nyē′gôf) A city on the Desna in northern Ukrainian S.S.R. Also **Cher·ni′·gof.**

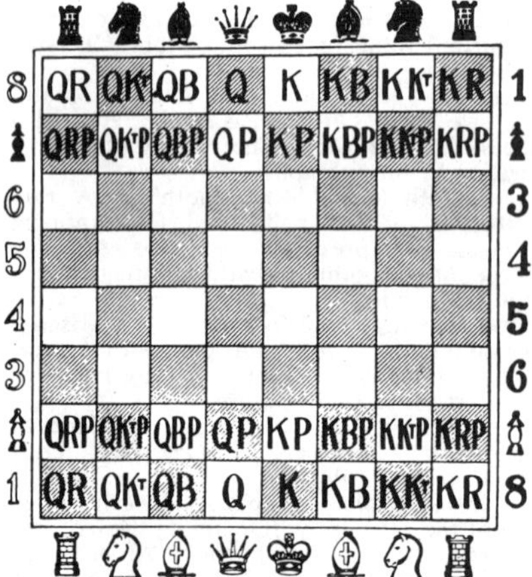

CHESSBOARD
As at the beginning of a game.
B—Bishop Kt (or N)—Knight Q—Queen
K—King P—Pawn R—Rook

In chess notation the ranks (horizontal rows of squares) are numbered 1–8 reading away from each player, and each file (vertical row) is named for the piece standing at its head. The symbol for each piece is opposite the square it occupies at the beginning of the game, excepting the pawns, which are indicated at each end of the pawn rows. Bishops, knights, and rooks are named for the king or queen, according to their positions at the start. Pawns are named for the pieces they stand in front of.

Cher·nov·sy (cher·nôf′tsē) A city on the Prut in western Ukrainian S.S.R.: Rumanian *Cernauți,* German *Czernowitz.*

cher·no·zem (cher′nə·zem) *n.* A soil typical of temperate subhumid grasslands, consisting of a very dark to black surface layer rich in organic materials overlying a layer of accumulated lime. [<Russian *chernozemu* black soil]

Cher·o·kee (cher′ə·kē, cher′ə·kē′) *n. pl.* **·kee** or **·kees 1** One of a great tribe of Iroquoian Indians formerly occupying northern Georgia and North Carolina, now dwelling in Oklahoma: the most advanced in culture of the North American Indians. **2** The Iroquoian language of this tribe.

Cherokee rose A Chinese rose *(Rosa laevigata)* of trailing habit and having large, solitary white flowers, naturalized in the southern United States and the West Indies: the State flower of Georgia.

che·root (shə·rōōt′) *n.* A cigar cut square at both ends, generally of Manila or East Indian make: also spelled *sheroot.* [<F *cheroute* <Tamil *shuruṭṭu* roll, cigar]

cher·ry (cher′ē) *n. pl.* **·ries 1** Any of various trees (genus *Prunus*) of the rose family, related to the plum and the peach and bearing small, round, or heart–shaped drupes enclosing a smooth pit; especially, the sweet cherry *(P. avium),* the sour cherry *(P. cerasus),* and the wild black cherry *(P. serotina).* **2** The wood or fruit of a cherry tree. **3** A bright–red color resembling that of certain cherries: also **cherry red.** —*adj.* **1** Like a cherry; red. **2** Made of cherry wood. [ME *chery,* back formation from AF *cherise* (mistaken for a plural) <L *cerasus* cherry tree <Gk. *kerasos*]

cher·ry·bird (cher′ē·bûrd′) *n.* The waxwing.

cherry bomb A red, round, highly explosive firecracker.

cherry bounce Brandy and sugar, in which cherries have been steeped.

cherry picker Any of several types of crane with a large bucket at the end of an articulated arm and mounted on a truck.

cherry stone 1 The pit of a cherry. **2** A small quahaug.

cher·so·nese (kûr′sə·nēz, -nēs) *n.* A peninsula. [<L *chersonesus* <Gk. *chersonēsos* <*chersos* dry + *nēsos* island]

chert (chûrt) *n.* A dull–colored, impure cryptocrystalline quartz or chalcedony: also called *hornstone.* [Origin uncertain]

cher·ub (cher′əb) *n. pl.* **cher·ubs** *for defs.* **1** *and* **2, cher·u·bim** (cher′ə·bim, -yə·bim) *for defs.* **3** *and* **4. 1** In art, the representation of a beautiful winged child, or the winged head of a child, the accepted type of the angelic cherub. **2** Hence, a beautiful child or infant. **3** One of an order of angelic beings ranking second to the seraphim in the celestial hierarchy. **4** In Scripture, an angelic being, especially as represented on the ark of the covenant, typifying the presence and power of the Deity. See *Ps.* xviii 10; *Ezek.* x; *Heb.* ix 5. [<LL <Hebrew *kerūbh,* an angelic being] —**che·ru·bic** (chə·rōō′bik) or **·bi·cal** *adj.* —**che·ru′bi·cal·ly** *adv.*

Che·ru·bi·ni (kā′rōō·bē′nē), **Maria Luigi,** 1760–1842, Italian composer.

cher·vil (chûr′vəl) *n.* **1** Either of two European garden herbs *(Anthriscus cerefolium* or *Chaerophyllum bulbosum)* of the parsley family, the young leaves of which are used for soups, salads, etc. **2** Any one of several other plants of the same family: the great or sweet chervil *(Myrrhis odorata).* [OE *cerfille* <L *caerefolium* <Gk. *chairephyllon*]

cher·vo·nets (cher·vô′nets) *n. pl.* **·vont·si** (-vônt′sē) A gold monetary unit of the U.S.S.R., equivalent to ten rubles: no longer used. [<Russian]

Ches·a·peake Bay (ches′ə·pēk) A large arm of the Atlantic, running northward into Maryland.

Chesh·ire (chesh′ər, -ir) A county in western England, 1,019 square miles; county seat, Chester.

Cheshire *n.* A kind of crumbly Cheddar: also **Cheshire cheese.** [from *Cheshire,* England]

Cheshire cat In Lewis Carroll's *Alice's Adventures in Wonderland,* a grinning cat that disappeared by gradually fading away until only its grin remained.

chess[1] (ches) *n.* A game of skill played by two persons on a checkered board (a **chess′board′**) divided into 64 squares, with 16 pieces on each side. The aim of each player, proceeding by alternate moves, is to checkmate his opponent's king. [<OF *eschès,* pl. of *eschec.* See CHECK]

chess[2] (ches) *n.* **1** Any of several kinds of brome grass, especially *Bromus secalinus,* a pernicious weed in grain fields in America and Europe: also called *cheat.* **2** The darnel. [Origin uncertain]

chess[3] (ches) *n.* The deck planks of a pontoon bridge. [Origin uncertain]

chest (chest) *n.* **1** A box of wood, metal, or other material, usually large, and having a hinged lid: used for valuables, tools, personal possessions, etc. **2** A receptacle for gases, liquids, etc.: a steam *chest.* **3** The part of the body enclosed by the ribs; the thorax. ◆ Collateral adjective: *pectoral.* **4** A case for packing certain commodities: a *chest* for indigo. **5** The quantity ordinarily carried in certain chests: a *chest* of tea. **6** A public treasury or fund; coffer; also, the funds contained there: the community *chest.* **—to get off one's chest** *Colloq.* To experience the relief of expressing openly (an emotion, opinion, etc.) that one has previously been at pains to withhold. [OE *cest* <L *cista* <Gk. *kistē* basket, box]

Ches·ter (ches'tər) A masculine personal name. [<L, dweller in camp, i.e., soldier]

Ches·ter (ches'tər) **1** The county seat of Cheshire, England. Ancient **De·va·na Cas·tra** (di·vā'nə kas'trə). **2** A city on the Delaware River in eastern Pennsylvania.

ches·ter·field (ches'tər·fēld) *n.* **1** A single-breasted topcoat of knee length, generally with concealed buttons and a velvet collar. **2** A type of overstuffed sofa. [after an Earl of *Chesterfield* of the 19th c.]

Ches·ter·field (ches'tər·fēld), **Lord,** 1694–1773, Philip Dormer Stanhope, fourth Earl of Chesterfield, English statesman and author.

Ches·ter·field·i·an (ches'tər·fēl'dē·ən) *adj.* **1** Of or pertaining to Lord Chesterfield. **2** Suave; polished; elegant.

Ches·ter·ton (ches'tər·tən), **Gilbert Keith,** 1874–1936, English author.

Chester white One of a breed of pigs first developed in Chester County, Pa.

chest·nut (ches'nut', -nət) *n.* **1** An edible nut, growing in a prickly bur. **2** Any of various trees (genus *Castanea*) of the beech family that bear this nut. **3** One of certain other trees: the horse *chestnut.* **4** A reddish-brown color; also, a horse of such a color. **5** *Colloq.* A worn-out joke; hence, anything trite. **6** A small, horny, wartlike callosity on the inner surface of the leg, as of a horse. *—adj.* **1** Reddish-brown. **2** Made of the wood of the chestnut tree. Also **ches'nut'.** [ME *chesten,* var. of *chesteine* <OF *chastaine* <L *castanea* <Gk. *kastanea* + NUT]

chest of drawers A piece of furniture consisting of a frame containing a set of drawers for storing linens, wearing apparel, etc.

chest on chest A chest of drawers in two sections, one placed upon the other which is usually wider and has feet.

chest register The lower or chest tones of the human voice.

chest·y (ches'tē) *adj. Colloq.* **chest·i·er, chest·i·est 1** Having a large chest, lung capacity, etc. **2** Proud; self-important.

che·tah (chē'tə) See CHEETAH.

cheth (kheth) See HETH.

Chet·nik (chet'nik) *n. pl.* **Chet·ni·ci** (chet'nē·tsē) or **Chet·niks** A Serbian nationalist guerrilla in World War II. [<Serbo-Croatian]

che·val-de-frise (shə·val'də·frēz') *n. pl.* **che·vaux-de-frise** (shə·vō'-) **1** A portable obstacle of barbed wire supported on a sawhorse construction. **2** Formerly, an obstacle or obstruction of projecting spikes, used to hinder the progress of cavalry. [<F, lit., horse of Friesland; because first used by the Frisians]

che·va·let (shə·və·lā') *n.* The bridge of a stringed instrument. [<F, dim. of *cheval* horse]

che·val glass (shə·val') A full-length mirror mounted on horizontal pivots in a frame.

chev·a·lier (shev'ə·lir') *n.* **1** A knight or cavalier; especially, a French knight or nobleman. **2** *Obs.* A gallant gentleman; chivalrous man. **3** A member of the French Legion of Honor or other order of knighthood. **4** A cadet of the old French nobility who went into the army. **5** *Her.* An armed knight mounted. [<F <LL *caballarius.* Doublet of CAVALIER.]

che·vals (shə·valz') *n. pl.* Riding breeches.

che·ve·lure (shəv·lür') *n. French* A head of hair.

chev·i·ot (shev'ē·ət) *n.* A type of rough woolen cloth of twill weave, used for suits, overcoats, etc., originally made from the wool of the Cheviot sheep.

Chev·i·ot (chev'ē·ət, chē'vē-) *n.* One of a breed of large mountain sheep, originating in the Cheviot Hills, much esteemed for their wool.

Chev·i·ot Hills (chev'ē·ət, chē'vē-) A range on the boundary between Scotland and England; highest peak, 2,676 feet.

chev·on (shev'ən) *n.* Goat flesh used as food. [<F *chèv(re)* goat, she-goat + *(mout)on* sheep]

chev·ron (shev'rən) *n.* **1** A V-shaped insigne, made of cloth and worn on the sleeve to indicate rank, rating, wounds, or length of service: used in the U.S. Army, the police force, etc. In the U.S. service, the rank of corporal is indicated by two chevrons, sergeant by three. **2** Any V-shaped mark or zigzag pattern, especially as used in Romanesque architecture: also **chevron molding.** **3** *Her.* An honorable ordinary. [<OF <Med. L *capro, -onis* rafter <L *caper* goat]

CHEVRONS
Sergeant—Army
a. United States.
b. Great Britain.
c. France.

chev·ro·tain (shev'rə·tān, -tin) *n.* A small, deerlike, hornless ruminant (family *Tragulidae*) of Africa and Asia; the mouse deer. [<F <OF *chevrot,* dim. of *chèvre* she-goat<L *capra,* fem. of *caper* goat]

chev·y[1] (chev'ē) *n. pl.* **chev·ies** *Brit.* **1** A hunt; chase. **2** The game of prisoner's base. **3** A cry or shout in hunting. *—v.* **chev·ied, chev·y·ing.** *—v.i.* To chase about; race; scamper. *—v.t.* To worry; harass; torment. Also **chev'ey:** sometimes spelled *chivy, chivvy.* [Prob. <*Chevy* Chase]

chev·y[2] (chev'ē) See SHIV.

Chev·y Chase (chev'ē) An old English ballad dealing with the battle of Otterburn.

chew (cho͞o) *v.t.* **1** To cut or grind with the teeth. **2** To meditate upon; consider carefully. *—v.i.* **3** To perform the act of cutting or grinding with the teeth: with *on* or *upon.* **4** To meditate: with *on* or *upon.* **5** *Colloq.* To use chewing tobacco continually. **—chew out** *Slang* To scold or reprimand severely. **—chew the fat** or **rag** *Slang* To chat; gossip *—n.* The act of chewing, or that which is chewed; a quid; cud: a *chew* of tobacco. [OE *cēowan*] **—chew'er** *n.*

chewing gum See under GUM.

che·wink (chi·wingk') *n.* One of several finches or buntings; especially, the towhee of the eastern United states. [Imit.]

chew·y (cho͞o'ē) *adj.* **chew·i·er, chew·i·est** Relatively soft and requiring chewing: Caramels are *chewy.* [<CHEW + -Y]

Chey·enne (shī·en') *n. pl.* **·enne** or **·ennes** One of an Algonquian tribe of North American Indians formerly inhabiting territory which is now Wyoming, Nebraska, and the western Dakotas: now on reservations in Montana and Oklahoma.

Chey·enne (shī·en') The capital of Wyoming.

Cheyenne River A river in Wyoming and South Dakota, flowing 527 miles NE to the Missouri.

Chey·ne (chā'nē), **Thomas Kelly,** 1841–1915, English Bible scholar and editor.

chez (shā) *prep. French* At; at the home of; by.

Chhat·tis·garh (chut'is·gär) A former native states agency in NE India.

chi (kī) The twenty-second letter in the Greek alphabet (see ALPHABET), transliterated into Latin, English, and German by *ch.*

chi·a (chē'ə) *n. SW U.S.* A Californian and Mexican herb *(Salvia columbariae)* of the mint family, whose seeds yield a beverage and an oil, **chia oil.** [<Sp. Nahuatl]

Chia·mus·su (jyä'mo͞o'so͞o') See KIAMUSZE.

Chi·an (kī'ə) *adj.* Of, pertaining to, or produced in Chios: *Chian* wine. *—n.* A native of Chios.

Chiang Kai-shek (chäng' kī'shek', chang'; *Chinese* jyäng'), 1887–1975, Chinese generalissimo and statesman; head of the Nationalist government of the Republic of China: real name *Chiang Chung-cheng.*

—Madame Chiang Kai-shek See under SOONG.

Chiang·mai (chyäng'mī') A city in northern Thailand: also *Chiengmai.*

chian·ti (kyän'tē) *n.* A red or white table wine from the Monti Chianti region; also, any similar wine.

Chian·ti (kyän'tē), **Mon·ti** (môn'tē) A small range of the Apennines in Tuscany, Italy; highest peak, 2,930 feet.

Chi·a·pas (chē·ä'päs) A state in southern Mexico; 28,732 square miles; capital, Tuxtla.

chi·a·ro·scu·ro (kē·är'ə·skyo͝or'ō) *n. pl.* **·ros 1** The distribution and treatment of lights and shades in a picture. **2** A kind of painting or drawing using only light and shade to achieve its effects of depth, design, etc. **3** The characteristic use or mastery of light and shade by an artist. Also called *clair-obscure.* Also **chi·a·ro·o·scu·ro** (kē·är'ə·ō·skyo͝or'ō). [<Ital. < *chiaro* clear (<L *clarus*) +*oscuro* dim, obscure <L *obscurus*]**—chi·a'ro·scu'rist** *n.*

chi·asm (kī'az·əm) *n.* **1** *Anat.* An intersecting or X-like commissure which unites the optic nerves at the base of the brain. **2** *Genetics* The point of intersection of two chromosomes. Also **chi·as·ma** (kī·az'mə). [<NL *chiasma* <Gk. <*chiazein* mark with a chi] **—chi·as'mal, chi·as'mic** *adj.*

chi·as·ma·ty·py (kī·az'mə·tī'pē) *n. Genetics* The intertwining of two homologous chromosomes during side-by-side conjugation of the chromosome threads in meiosis, resulting in blending and possible crossing over at points of contact. [<Gk. *chiasma* crossing + *typos* impression]**—chi·as'ma·type'** *adj. & n.*

chi·as·mus (kī·az'məs) *n.* In rhetoric, a contrast by parallelism in reverse order, as in Pope's "they fall successive, and successive rise." [<Gk. *chiasmos* <*chiazein* mark crosswise]

chi·as·to·lite (kī·as'tə·līt) *n. Mineral.* An andalusite in which the crystals in transverse section appear crossed or checkered: also called *macle.* [<Gk. *chiastos* crossed]

chiaus (chous, choush) *n.* A Turkish official messenger or sergeantat arms: also *choush.* [< Turkish *chāush*]

Chia·yi (jyä'yē') A city in west central Taiwan: also *Kiayi. Japanese* **Ka·gi** (kä·gē).

Chi·ba (chē·bä) A city on central Honshu island, Japan.

Chib·cha (chib'chə) *n.* An Indian belonging to an important linguistic stock, the **Chibchan,** of South and Central American Indians, formerly occupying territory from Honduras southward and eastward through Nicaragua, Costa Rica, Panama, and Colombia; specifically, an Indian of the Chibchan tribes of Colombia: next highest in culture to the Incas at the time of the Spanish conquest. **—Chib'chan** *adj. & n.*

chi·bouk (chi·bo͝ok', -bo͝ok') *n.* A Turkish pipe having a long straight stem, and a bowl of red clay. Also **chi·bouque', chi·buk'.** [<F *chiboque* <Turkish *chibūk*]

chic (shēk, shik) *adj.* Smart; stylish; elegant. — *n.* Originality, elegance, and taste, as in dress; smartness. [<F]

Chi·ca·go (shə·kä'gō, -kô'-) A city in NE Illinois on Lake Michigan.

chi·ca·lo·te (chē'kä·lō'tā) *n.*A prickly poppy *(Argemone platyceras)* of the SW United States. [<Sp. <Nahuatl *chicalotl*]

chi·cane (shi·kān') *v.* **·caned, ·can·ing** *v.t.* **1** To overreach by trickery. **2** To quibble about. *—v.i.* **3** To resort to quibbles, shifts, or tricks. *—n.* **1** Mean, petty trickery, with pretense of fairness. **2** A bridge or whist hand containing no trumps. [<F *chicaner*]

chi·can·er·y (shi·kā'nər·ē) *n. pl.* **·er·ies 1** The use of mean or paltry artifices, subterfuges, or shifts; especially, legal trickery or underhandedness. **2** A trick or dodge.

Chi·ca·no (chi·kä'nō) *n. pl.* **·nos** *U.S.* A Mexican-American.

Chich·a·gof Island (chich'ə·gôf) An island in

the Alexander Archipelago, SE Alaska; 2,104 square miles.

Chi·chén–It·zá (chē·chen'ēt·sä') A ruined Maya city of Yucatán, Mexico.

Chich·es·ter (chich'is·tər) The county town of West Sussex, England.

chick (chik) *n.* **1** A young chicken. **2** A child. **3** *Slang* A young woman. [Short for CHICKEN]

chick·a·dee (chik'ə·dē) *n.* An American titmouse (genus *Penthestes*) without a crest and with the top of the head and the throat black or dark–colored; especially, the **black–capped chickadee** (*P. atricapillus*) of eastern North America. [Imit. of its cry]

CHICKADEE

Chick·a·hom·i·ny River (chik'ə·hom'ə·nē) A river in eastern Virginia, flowing SE 90 miles to the James River.

Chick·a·mau·ga (chik'ə·mô'gə) A city in NW Georgia on **Chickamauga Creek**; scene of Civil War battle, 1863.

chick·a·ree (chik'ə·rē) *n.* The American red squirrel (*Sciurus hudsonicus*), smallest of the tree–climbing diurnal squirrels. [Imit. of its cry]

Chick·a·saw (chik'ə·sô) *n. pl.* **·saw** or **·saws** One of a tribe of Muskhogean North American Indians formerly occupying the country along the Mississippi River and eastward: now dwelling in Oklahoma.

chick·en (chik'ən) *n.* **1** The young of the common domestic fowl. **2** Loosely, a fowl of any age; also, its flesh used as food. **3** *Colloq.* A child; an inexperienced person. — *adj.* **1** Containing, made from, or flavored with chicken. **2** *Slang* Cowardly. —**to chicken out** *Slang* To refrain from doing something because of fear or cowardice. [< OE *cȳcen*]

chick·en–breast (chik'ən·brest') *n. Pathol.* A malformed, prominent sternum or breastbone, with lateral flattening of the chest; pigeon breast. —**chick'en–breast'ed** *adj.*

chicken feed *Slang* A petty sum of money.

chicken hawk One of various hawks that prey on poultry; especially, the eastern goshawk (*Astur atricapillus*), Cooper's hawk, and the red–tailed hawk of the eastern United States.

chick·en–heart·ed (chik'ən·här'tid) *adj.* Faint–hearted or cowardly.

chick·en–liv·ered (chik'ən·liv'ərd) *adj.* Cowardly or timorous.

chicken louse One of a species of wingless insects (order *Mallophaga*, the bird lice) that live on chickens, where they feed on feathers and the epidermis. For illustration see INSECTS (injurious).

chicken pox *Pathol.* A contagious disease, principally of children, caused by a virus and characterized by eruptions, a slight fever, and a typically brief course; varicella.

chick·pea (chik'pē') *n.* **1** A plant (*Cicer arietenum*) of Mediterranean regions and central Asia. **2** Its edible seed, enclosed in short, hairy pods: widely used as a food in Asia and Latin America; Egyptian pea. [Alter. of ME *chich–pease* <F *pois chiche* <*pois* pease + *chiche* <L *cicer*, a small pea]

chick·weed (chik'wēd') *n.* A spreading, white–flowered, Old World starwort (*Stellaria media*), used for feeding caged birds.

chic·le (chik'əl) *n.* **1** The milky juice of the sapodilla: used as the basic principle of chewing gum. **2** A gum prepared from it. Also **chicle gum.** [<Sp. <Nahuatl *chictli*]

chi·co (chē'kō) *n. pl.* **·cos** The western American greasewood (*Sarcobatus vermiculatus*). [< Sp. *chicalote*]

chic·o·ry (chik'ə·rē) *n. pl.* **·ries 1** A perennial herb of the composite family (*Cichorium intybus*) with pink, white, or azure flowers: naturalized in the United States. **2** Its dried, roasted, and ground roots, used for mixing with coffee or as a coffee substitute. Also spelled *chiccory.* [<F *cichorée*<L *cicorium* < Gk. *kichora*]

chi·co·te (chē·kō'tā) *n. SW U.S.*A whip with a short wooden handle, used by cowboys. Also **chi·co·ta**(chē·kō'tä). [<Sp.]

chide (chīd) *v.t. & v.i.* **chid·ed** or **chid** (chid), **chid·ed** or **chid** or **chid·den** (chid'n), **chid·ing** To scold; utter words of reproof or reprimand. See synonyms under BLAME, REPROVE. [OE *cīdan*] —**chid'er** *n.*

chief (chēf) *n.* **1** A ruler, leader, head, principal actor or agent, or principal part of anything, as of a tribe, party, army, fleet, police force, government bureau, or establishment of any kind. **2** An official superior to another or others in office or authority; one having authority. **3** One who or that which is specially eminent, esteemed, efficient, or active. **4** *Her.* The upper part of a shield. See illustration under ESCUTCHEON. —*adj.* **1** Highest in rank or authority. **2** Principal, most important, or most eminent, in any respect. **3** Most distinguished, influential, valuable, or active. **4** Main; foremost; leading; greatest. See synonyms under FIRST, PARAMOUNT, PREDOMINANT. —**in chief 1** At the head; in or having the highest place or authority: used in titles: commander *in chief.* **2** Chiefly. [<OF *chef, chief* <L *caput* head]

Synonyms (*noun*): captain, chieftain, commander, head, leader, master, principal, ruler, sachem. A *chief* is either the *ruler* of a tribe or the *head* of some department of established government; as, the *chief* of police. The word is colloquially applied to one holding some analogous position in literary or mercantile life, etc. *Chieftain* is now mainly employed in poetic and literary use; it has special historic application to the *head* of a Scottish clan. A *leader* is one who is voluntarily followed because of ability to overcome and control, or as the choice of a party. A *master* is one who can enforce obedience. The highest officer of any considerable military force is called the *commander*; of all the forces of a nation, the *commander in chief.* See MASTER. *Antonyms*: adherent, attendant, follower, minion, retainer, satellite, subaltern, subordinate, vassal.

chief justice The presiding judge of a court composed of several justices.

Chief Justice The official head of the U.S. Supreme urt.

chief·ly (chēf'lē) *adv.* **1** Most of all or above all; preeminently; especially; particularly. **2** Generally; usually.

chief magistrate The highest administrative official of civil affairs in a community; also, loosely, the president of the United States.

Chief of Staff 1 The senior officer or head of a staff. **2** *U.S.* The principal staff officer in assistance to a command officer in higher military echelons. Compare EXECUTIVE OFFICER. **3** The ranking officer in the U.S. Army or in the U.S. Air Force, immediately under the secretary of his department.

chief·tain (chēf'tən) *n.* **1** The head of a Highland clan. **2** Any chief; leader. See synonyms under CHIEF. [<OF *chevetain* <LL *capitaneus* <L *caput* head. Doublet of CAPTAIN.] —**chief'tain·cy, chief'tain·ship** *n.*

chiel (chēl) *n. Scot.* A lad; a fellow; a child. Also **chield** (chēld).

Chieng·mai (chyeng'mī') See CHIANGMAI.

Ch'ien–lung (chyen'loong') Imperial title of Hung–li, 1711–99, fourth Ch'ing emperor, 1736–96: also *Kien Lung.*

chiff·chaff (chif'chaf', -chäf') *n.* A small, brownish–white, Old World warbler (*Phylloscopus rufus*), known for its peculiar cry. [Imit.]

chif·fon (shi·fon') *n.* **1** A sheer silk or rayon fabric. **2** *Obs.* Any decorative object worn by women, as a ribbon or sash. [<F, dim. of *chiffe* rag]

chif·fo·nier (shif'ə·nir') *n.* **1** An ornamental cabinet. **2** A high chest of drawers. Also **chif'fon·nier'.** [<F <*chiffon* CHIFFON]

chif·fo·robe (shif'ə·rōb) *n.* An article of furniture having a wardrobe compartment alongside a chest of drawers. [<CHIFFO(NIER) + (WARD)ROBE]

Chif·ley (chif'lē), **Joseph Benedict,** 1885–1951, Australian politician; prime minister of Australia 1945–49.

chig·e·tai (chig'ə·tī) See DZIGGETAI.

chig·ger (chig'ər) *n.* **1** Any of certain mites of the southern United States whose larvae burrow under the skin: also spelled *jigger.* **2** The chigoe. [Alter. of CHIGOE]

chi·gnon (shēn'yon, *Fr.* shē·nyôn') *n.* A knot or roll of hair worn at the back of the head by women. [<F]

chig·oe (chig'ō) *n.* **1** A flea (*Tunga penetrans*) of the West Indies and South America. The female burrows under the skin, especially of the feet, causing sores: also called *chigger* or *jigger.* **2** The chigger. Also spelled *chegoe.* [<F *chique* <Cariban]

Chih·li (chē'lē', *Chinese* ju'lē') A former name for HOPEH, China.

Chihli, Gulf of An arm of the Yellow Sea in NE China; connected with the Yellow Sea by the **Strait of Chihli.**

Chi·hua·hua (chi·wä'wä) A state in northern Mexico; 94,831 square miles; capital, Chihuahua.

Chi·hua·hua (chi·wä'wä) *n.* One of an ancient breed of very small, smooth–coated dog with large, pointed ears, originally native to Mexico. [from *Chihuahua*, Mexico]

chil·blain (chil'blān) *n. Pathol.* An inflammation of the hands or feet, caused by exposure to cold; erythema. [<CHILL+ BLAIN] —**chil'blained** *adj.*

child (chīld) *n. pl.* **chil·dren 1** An offspring of either sex of human parents; a son or daughter. **2** A young person of either sex at any age less than maturity, but most commonly one between infancy and youth. **3** A descendant in any degree: the *Children* of Israel. **4** A childish person; one immature in judgment or discretion. **5** A person or thing considered as an offspring or product: Poems are the *children* of fancy. **6** A follower or disciple. **7** *Law* A legitimate son or daughter. In some States, as in Louisiana, the term includes all descendants in the direct line. —**with child** Pregnant; enceinte. [OE *cild*] —**child'less** *adj.*

Child (chīld), **Francis James,** 1825–96, American scholar; authority on the English and Scottish ballad.

child·bear·ing (chīld'bâr'ing) *n.* Producing or giving birth to children.

child·bed (chīld'bed') *n.* The state of a woman who is in labor or confined to bed as the result of it.

child·birth (chīld'bûrth') *n.* Parturition. Also **child'bear'ing.**

childe (chīld) *n. Archaic* A youth of noble or gentle birth, especially one training to be a knight. [Var. of CHILD]

Chil·der·mas (chil'dər·məs) Holy Innocents' Day (December 28th), commemorating Herod's slaughter of the children of Bethlehem. *Matt.* ii 16. Also **Childermas Day.** [OE *cildra*, genitive pl. of *cild* child+ *mæsse* mass]

child·hood (chīld'hood) *n.* The state or time of being a child. —**second childhood** A time or state in which the physical and mental powers are enfeebled or impaired by old age; dotage.

child·ing (chīl'ding) *adj.* **1** Child–bearing; pregnant; hence, fruitful; productive. **2** *Bot.* Having young blossoms clustered around an older blossom.

child·ish (chīl'dish) *adj.* **1** Of, pertaining to, or characteristic of a child. **2** Puerile; petty; mentally or physically weak. —**child'ish·ly** *adv.* —**child'ish·ness** *n.*

Synonyms: babyish, childlike, foolish, imbecile, infantile, paltry, petty, puerile, silly, trifling, trivial. *Childlike* refers to the lovable qualities, *childish* to the less desirable traits of childhood. See YOUTHFUL. *Antonyms*: bold, manly, masculine, mature, resolute, strong, vigorous, virile.

child labor 1 Work done by children. **2** The employment of minors under 14 or 16 in industry.

child·like (chīld'līk') *adj.* **1** Like a child. **2** Artless; confiding. **3** Docile; submissive. Also **child'ly.** See synonyms under CHILDISH, YOUTHFUL.—**child'like'ness** *n.*

child·ness (chīld'nis) *n.* Childish nature, humor, character, or manners.

chil·dren (chil'drən) Plural of CHILD.

Children of Israel The descendants of Jacob; Israelites; the Jews.

Children's Crusade An ill–fated expedition (1212) of some 70,000 German and French children to recover Jerusalem from the Saracens.

child's play Any easy or simple activity.

chil·e (chil'ē) *n.* The acrid red pod or fruit of certain peppers, especially *Capsicum frutescens*, the source of red or cayenne pepper: also spelled *chilli, chilly.* Also **chil'i.** [<Sp. <Nahuatl *chilli*]

Chil·e (chil'ē, *Sp.* chē'lā) A republic on the SW

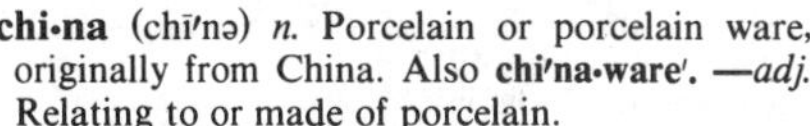

coast of South America; 286,396 square miles; capital, Santiago. **—Chil′e·an** *adj. & n.*

chil·e con car·ne (chil′ē kon kär′nē) A Mexican dish of red peppers minced and mixed with meat, beans, spices, etc. [< Sp., chile with meat]

Chile saltpeter See under SALTPETER.

chile sauce A spiced condiment sauce made with tomatoes, red peppers, etc.

chil·i·ad (kil′ē·ad) *n.* **1** A thousand. **2** A period of a thousand years; a millennium. [< L *chilias* < Gk. *chilias, -ados* < *chilioi* thousand]

chil·i·arch (kil′ē·ärk) *n.* In Greek antiquity, a commander of a thousand men. [< Gk. *chiliarchos* < *chilioi* thousand + *archos* leader]

chil·i·asm (kil′ē·az′əm) *n.* The doctrine that Christ will reign upon earth a thousand years; the millennium. [< Gk. *chiliasmos* < *chilias.* See CHILIAD.] **—chil′i·ast** *n.* **—chil′i·as′tic** *adj.*

Chil·koot Pass (chil′kōōt) A mountain pass from SE Alaska to the Yukon valley; elevation, 3,502 feet.

chill (chil) *n.* **1** A sensation of cold, as that which precedes a fever, often with shivering or shaking. **2** A disagreeable feeling of coldness. **3** A check to ardor, joy, or the like. **4** *Metall.* A metal mold so constructed as to cool suddenly the surface of iron cast therein: also called *coquille.* *—v.t.* **1** To reduce to a low temperature. **2** To make chilly; seize with a chill. **3** To discourage; dispirit; check, as ardor. **4** To harden (metal) by sudden cooling. *—v.i.* **5** To become cold. **6** To be stricken with a chill. **7** To harden by sudden cooling, as metal. *—adj.* **1** Moderately, unpleasantly, or injuriously cold; chilly. **2** Somewhat affected by cold; feeling cold. **3** Cold in manner or disposition; distant; formal. **4** Dispiriting; discouraging. See synonyms under BLEAK. [OE *ciele, cyle*] **—chill′ing·ly** *adv.* **—chill′ness** *n.*

Chil·lán (chē·yän′) A city in south central Chile.

chill·er (chil′ər) *n.* **1** One who or that which chills. **2** *Metall.* One who sprays hot molds with water in steelworking. **3** *Slang* A horror story or moving picture.

chil·li (chil′ē) See CHILE.

Chil·ling·worth (chil′ing·wûrth), **William,** 1602–44, English theologian.

Chil·lon (shi·lon′, *Fr.* shē·yôṅ′) A castle on the eastern shore of Lake Geneva; prison of François de Bonnivard, 1496–1570, hero of Byron's poem *The Prisoner of Chillon.*

chill·y[1] (chil′ē) *adj.* **chill·i·er, chill·i·est 1** Producing or feeling cold. **2** Disheartening; depressing. **3** Not genial or cordial; unfriendly. **—chil′i·ly** *adv.* **—chill′i·ness** *n.*

chill·y[2] (chil′ē) See CHILE.

chilo- *combining form* Lip: *Chilopoda.* Also, before vowels, **chil-.** [< Gk. *cheilos* lip]

chi·lo·pod (kī′lə·pod) *n.* Centipede. **—chi·lop·o·dan** (kī·lop′ə·dən) *adj. & n.*

chi·lo·pod·ol·o·gy (kī′lə·pə·dol′ə·gē) *n.* The branch of zoology concerned with centipedes. **—chi′lo·po·dol′o·gist** *n.*

Chil·tern Hundreds (chil′tərn) *Brit.* **1** An ancient, now purely nominal sinecure under the British crown, for which, by a legal fiction, a member of Parliament applies when he wishes to retire. **2** The hundreds of Burnham, Desborough, and Stoke in Buckinghamshire, England. See HUNDRED (*n.* def. 2).

Chi·lung (jē′lōōng′) See KEELUNG.

Chil·wa (chil′wä) A shallow lake between Mozambique and SE Nyasaland, length 30 miles: also *Shirwa.*

Chi·mae·ra (kə·mir′ə, kī-) *n.* **1** A genus of fishes related to the sharks and rays, having a smooth skin, jaws equipped with solid dental plates, and a short anterior dorsal fin with a spine in front. **2** Chimera. [Var. of CHIMERA] **—chi·mae′rid** *n.*

Chim·bo·ra·zo (chim′bō·rä′zō) An inactive volcano in central Ecuador; 20,577 feet.

chime[1] (chīm) *v.* **chimed, chim·ing** *v.t.* **1** To cause to ring musically; play tunefully with or upon, as by striking. **2** To announce, as the hour, by the sound of bells. **3** To summon, welcome, or send by chiming. **4** To recite in unison or cadence. *—v.i.* **5** To ring out in harmony or unison, as bells. **6** To extract melodious sound, as by striking a bell or set of bells. **7** To harmonize; agree: with *with*: Her remarks *chimed* with his intentions. **8** To recite or intone in cadence. **—to chime in 1** To be in accord with; agree. **2** To take part in or interrupt, as a conversation. *—n.* **1** A set of bells tuned to a scale. **2** The mechanism for ringing the changes on bells; also, the music from such bells. **3** Accord; harmony. [ME *chimbe, chime,* alter. of OE *cimbal* < L *cymbalum* cymbal] **—chim′er** *n.*

chime[2] (chīm) *n.* **1** The edge or brim of a cask, barrel, or tub: also *chine.* **2** A channel in a vessel's deck. *—v.t.* To make a chime in (a stave, etc.). Also **chimb** (chīm). [OE *cimb-* edge, as in *cimbing* a joint]

chi·me·ra (kə·mir′ə, kī-) *n.* **1** An absurd creation of the imagination; a groundless or impracticable conception or fancy; any horrible fancy. **2** *Bot.* A novel or unusual plant growth caused by the grafting of tissue from two or more plants; a graft hybrid of mixed characteristics. **3** *Biol.* An organism incorporating cells of more than one genotype. Also **chi·mae′ra.** [See CHIMERA]

Chi·me·ra (kə·mir′ə, kī-) In Greek mythology, a fire-breathing monster, part lion, part goat, and part serpent, which was killed by Bellerophon: also spelled *Chimaera.* [< L *chimaera* < Gk. *chimaira* she-goat]

chi·mere (chi·mir′, shi-) *n.* **1** The sleeveless upper robe of a bishop. **2** *Obs.* A loose upper robe. Also **chim·ar** (chim′ər, shim′-), **chim′er.** [< OF *chamarre*]

chi·mer·i·cal (kə·mer′i·kəl, kī-) *adj.* **1** Like a chimera; imaginary; fanciful. **2** Impracticable; visionary. See synonyms under FANCIFUL, IMAGINARY, ROMANTIC. Also **chi·mer′ic. —chi·mer′i·cal·ly** *adv.*

Chim·kent (chim·kent′) A city in southern Kazakh S.S.R.

chim·la (chim′lə) *n. Scot.* A chimney. Also **chim·ley** (chim′lē).

chim·ney (chim′nē) *n.* **1** A flue for the smoke or gases from a fire. **2** A structure containing it, or something resembling such a structure. **3** A tube for enclosing a flame, as of a lamp. **4** *Obs.* A fireplace, hearth, or forge. **5** *Geol.* **a** A formation of rock shaped like a chimney; specifically, a cleft in a steep mountain cliff or rock wall, wide enough to admit a climber's body and which can be ascended by pressure against the opposite sides. **b** A long spur of ore extending downward through the main vein; a pipe. [< OF *cheminée* < LL *caminata* < L *caminus* furnace, oven < Gk. *kaminos*]

chimney corner 1 The space between the jamb or side of a large, old-fashioned fireplace and the fire, where one might sit. **2** The fireside.

chimney money See HEARTH MONEY.

chim·ney·piece (chim′nē·pēs′) *n.* **1** A mantelpiece. **2** *Obs.* An ornament, as a picture, placed over a fireplace.

chimney pot A pipe on the top of a chimney, to improve the draft.

chimney swallow 1 The chimney swift. **2** The European swallow.

chim·ney·sweep (chim′nē·swēp′) *n.* One who cleans chimneys, especially by the old method of ascending the flue. Also **chim′ney·sweep′er.**

chimney swift An American swift that nests in chimneys. See under SWIFT.

chim·pan·zee (chim′·pan·zē′, chim·pan′·zē) *n.* A West African arboreal anthropoid ape *(Pan troglodytes),* about 5 feet in height, with very large ears, dark-brown hair, smaller, less erect, and more intelligent than the gorilla. [< native West African name]

CHIMPANZEE
(About 4 1/2 feet standing erect)

chin (chin) *n.* **1** *Anat.* The central and anterior part of the lower jaw. ◆ Collateral adjectives: *genial*[2], *mental.* **2** *Entomol.* The second sclerite of the labium of an insect. **3** *Zool.* A small ciliated muscular process below the mouth, as in certain rotifers (genus *Pedalion*). *—v.* **chinned, chin·ning** *v.t.* To lift (oneself) by the hands until the chin is level with the hands. *—v.i. U.S. Colloq.* To talk idly. [OE *cin*]

chi·na (chī′nə) *n.* Porcelain or porcelain ware, originally from China. Also **chi′na·ware′.** *—adj.* Relating to or made of porcelain.

Chi·na (chī′nə) A country of eastern Asia, the most populous and second largest in the world; 3,800,000 square miles; divided (1949) into the **People's Republic of China;** capital, Peking; and the **Republic of China;** temporary capital, Taipei, on Taiwan. Abbr. *Chin., Ch.*

China aster An erect hairy plant *(Callistephus chinensis)* of the composite family, with terminal heads and rayed flowers: cultivated in many varieties.

china bark 1 Cinchona bark. **2** Quillai.

chi·na·ber·ry (chī′nə·ber′ē) *n. pl.* **·ries** The baccate fruit of the chinaberry tree (def. 2).

chinaberry tree 1 The azedarach. **2** Either of two trees *(Sapindus saponaria* and *S. marginatus)* of the soapberry family: found in Mexico and the SW United States, where each is known as the **China tree.**

china closet A closet, cupboard, or cabinet, often with glass front and sides, for household china.

Chi·na·man (chī′nə·mən) *n. pl.* **·men** (-mən) One of the Chinese: an offensive term.

Chinaman's chance *Colloq.* The merest chance.

Chi·nan (jē′nän′) See TSINAN.

China Sea The part of the Pacific bordering on China, divided by Taiwan into the *East China Sea* and the *South China Sea.*

China squash See CUSHAW.

Chi·na·town (chī′nə·toun′) The Chinese quarter of any city outside China, especially of San Francisco and of New York City.

chin·ca·pin (ching′kə·pin) See CHINKAPIN.

chinch (chinch) *n.* **1** A small, brown and black hemipterous insect *(Blissus leucopterus)* destructive to grain: also **chinch bug. 2** The bedbug. [< Sp. *chinche* < L *cimex* bug]

chin·chil·la (chin·chil′ə) *n.* **1** A small rodent *(Chinchilla laniger)* native in the Andes, about the size of a squirrel, having a soft pearl-gray fur. **2** The valuable fur of this rodent. **3** A heavy, woolen, twilled fabric used for coating, having a napped surface that is rolled into little tufts or nubs: originally woven to resemble chinchilla fur. [< Sp., ? alter. of Quechua *sinchi* strong]

Chin·chow (jin′jō′) A city in SW Manchuria, capital of Liaosi province: also *Kinchow.*

chin·cough (chin′kôf′, -kof′) *n.* Whooping cough.

Chin·dwin (chin′dwin′) A river in upper Burma, flowing over 500 miles south to the Irrawaddy.

chine[1] (chīn) *n.* **1** The spine, backbone, or back. **2** A piece of meat from the back. **3** A ridge. *—v.t.* **chined, chin·ing 1** To cut through the backbone of; cut into chines. **2** To cut up. [< OF *eschine* backbone < Gmc.]

chine[2] (chīn) See CHIME[2].

chine[3] (chīn) *n. Geog.* A deep or narrow ravine or fissure. [OE *cinu*]

Chi·nee (chī·nē′) *n. Slang* A Chinese: an illiterate or humorous usage.

Chi·nese (chī·nēz′, -nēs′) *adj.* Of or pertaining to the Chinese Republic or China, its people, or their languages. *—n. pl.* **·nese 1** A native or naturalized inhabitant of China. **2** The standard language of China, based on the language spoken in Peking; Mandarin. **3** A subfamily of the Sino-Tibetan family of languages, including the many languages and dialects spoken in China, as those of Peking, Canton, Amoy, Foochow, etc. **4** Any of these languages or dialects, some of which are mutually unintelligible.

Chinese blue Prussian blue.

Chinese carved lacquer Lacquer built up in layers, frequently colored vermilion with ground cinnabar, and carved: also called *cinnabar lacquer, Peking lacquer.*

Chinese Chippendale See under CHIPPENDALE.

Chinese Empire China as ruled by various

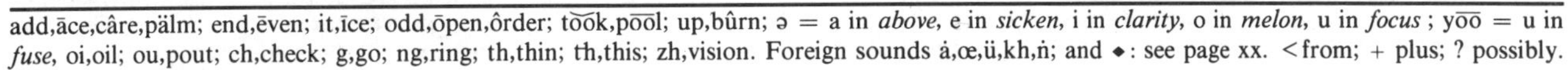

imperial dynasties until the founding of the Chinese Republic, 1912.

Chinese ink India ink.

Chinese lantern A collapsible lantern made of thin, brightly colored paper.

Chinese puzzle 1 An intricate puzzle originally made by the Chinese. **2** Any problem difficult to solve.

Chinese red 1 Chrome red. **2** Vermilion. Also **Chinese vermilion.**

Chinese Republic See CHINA.

Chinese Revolution See under REVOLUTION.

Chinese Turkestan See under TURKESTAN.

Chinese Wall See GREAT WALL OF CHINA.

Chinese wax The yellowish-white, tasteless, waxy secretion of an insect *(Ceroplastes ceriferus)* deposited on the branches and twigs of a certain Chinese ash tree: used in candles, as a furniture polish, and as a sizing material: also called *insect wax.*

Chinese white 1 A pigment composed of barium sulfate. **2** Very thick zinc oxide used as a pigment.

Chinese windlass See under WINDLASS.

Chinese wood oil Oil from the tung tree.

Ching·hai (ching′hī′) See TSINGHAI.

Chin Hills (chin) A mountain range of Upper Burma; highest point, 10,018 feet.

chink[1] (chingk) A small, narrow cleft; crevice. —*v.t.* **1** To make cracks or fissures in. **2** To fill the cracks of, as a wall; plug up. —*v.i.* **3** To open in clefts or cracks; crack. [ME *chynke*] **—chink′y** *adj.*

chink[2] (chingk) *n.* **1** A short, sharp, metallic sound. **2** *Slang* Coin; ready money; cash. —*v.t. & v.i.* To make or cause to make a short, sharp, clinking sound by striking together, as coins. [Imit.]

Chink (chingk) *n. Slang* A Chinese: a contemptuous usage.

chin·ka·pin (ching′kə·pin) *n.* **1** Any of several trees (genus *Castanea*) of the United States; especially, the dwarf chestnut *(C. pumila)* and the giant chinkapin *(Castanopsis chrysophylla)* of the Pacific coast. **2** The edible nut of any of these trees. Also **chin′qua·pin**: sometimes spelled *chincapin.* [<N. Am. Ind.]

Chin·kiang (chin′kyang′) A port of eastern China, on the Yangtze.

Chin·ne·reth (kin′ə·reth), **Sea of** The Old Testament name for the SEA OF GALILIEE.

chi·no (chē′nō) *n.* **1** A strong, mercerized cotton fabric with a twilled weave. **2** *pl.* Trousers or slacks made of this material. [<Sp., toasted; with ref. to the original tan color]

Chino- *combining form* Belonging to or connected with China (the country): *Chino-Japanese.* See SINO-.

chi·noi·se·rie (shē·nwàz·rē′) *n. French* **1** A Chinese mannerism or characteristic. **2** An object of Chinese origin or Chinese art or decoration, especially as imitated in the occidental decorative arts.

chi·nook (chi·no͞ok′, -no͞ok′) *n. Meteorol.* **1** A warm wind of the Oregon and Washington coasts; first named because it came from the direction of Chinook territory. **2** A warm, dry wind that descends the eastern slopes of the Rocky Mountains in the NW United States and western Canada. **3** Any warm wind occurring during the cold season in the western United States: often called *snow-eater.*

Chi·nook (chi·no͞ok′, -no͞ok′) *n. pl.* **·nook** or **·nooks 1** One of a tribe of North American Indians of the Chinook linguistic stock, formerly occupying the region of the Columbia River, Oregon. **2** A family of American Indian languages spoken by the Chinook. **3** Chinook jargon. — **Chi·nook′an** *adj.*

Chinook jargon A lingua franca comprised of words from Chinook and other Indian languages, mixed with English and French: formerly used as a commercial language by traders and Indians from Oregon to Alaska.

Chinook salmon The quinnat.

chintz (chints) *n.* A cotton fabric printed in various colors and usually glazed. Also **chints.** [<Hind. *chīnt* <Skt. *chitra* variegated]

chintz·y (chints′ē) *adj.* **chintz·i·er, chintz·i·est 1** Decorated with chintz. **2** *Colloq.* Cheap; sleazy. **3** *Slang* Stingy.

Chi·os (kī′os) A Greek island in the Aegean off the western coast of Asia Minor; 320 square miles: Greek *Khios. Italian* **Sci·o** (shē′ō), *Turkish* **Sa·kis·A·da·si** (sä·kiz′ä·dä·sï′)

chip[1] (chip) *n.* **1** A small piece cut or broken off. **2** A small disk or counter used in games, as in poker. **3** One of the dried droppings of animals available as fuel: usually in the plural: buffalo *chips.* **4** Anything insipid, vain, or worthless. **5** An overdone piece of meat, etc. **6** A small, crisp morsel: potato *chips.* **7** A crack produced by chipping. **8** A very small piece of silicon on which integrated circuits can be printed. **—a chip off the old block** *Colloq.* A child that resembles either of its parents. —*v.* **chipped, chip·ping** *v.t.* **1** To break or scale off a part of, as a piece of china. **2** To chop or cut, as with an ax or chisel. **3** To hew or shape by cutting off pieces. **4** *Obs.* To pare, as a crust of bread. —*v.i.* **5** To scale off in small pieces. **6** In golf, to hit a chip shot. **—to chip in 1** *Colloq.* To contribute, as help or money. **2** In poker, to put chips in as one's ante or bet. [ME *chippe.* Related to CHAP, CHOP.] — **chip′per** *n.*

chip[2] (chip) *v.i.* To cheep. —*n.* A squeak or weak chirp, as of a bird or mouse. [Imit.]

chip[3] (chip) *n.* In wrestling, a leg movement to trip one's opponent. [Cf. ON *kippa* a pull, sudden motion]

chip·munk (chip′mungk) *n.* Any of various striped North American rodents of the squirrel family of terrestrial or burrowing habits; especially, the common *Tamias striatus* of the eastern United States and Canada, and the genus *Eutamias* of the West, having many subspecies: also called *ground squirrel, striped squirrel.* Also **chip·muck** (chip′muk), **chipping squirrel.** [<N. Am. Ind.]

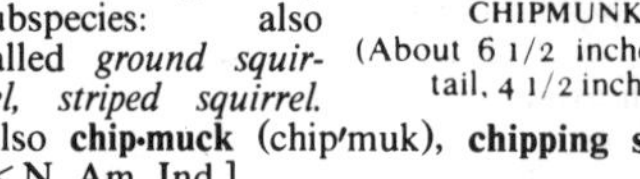

CHIPMUNK
(About 6 1/2 inches long: tail, 4 1/2 inches)

chipped (chipt) *adj.* Smoked and sliced thin, as beef.

Chip·pen·dale (chip′ən·dāl) *adj.* Pertaining to or naming a graceful, rococo style of furniture. — **Chinese Chippendale** Chippendale furniture characterized by the adaptations of Chinese forms and motifs. [after Thomas *Chippendale,* 1718–79, English cabinetmaker]

chip·per (chip′ər) *v.i.* **1** To chirp, as a bird; twitter; babble, as a brook. **2** To talk quickly, in a heated way; be rude. —*adj.* **1** Brisk; hearty; cheerful. **2** Neat; spruce; smart. [<CHIP[2]]

Chip·pe·wa (chip′ə·wä, -wā, -wə) *n. pl.* **·wa** or **·was** Ojibwa. Also **Chip·pe·way** (chip′ə·wā).

Chippewa River A river in west central Wisconsin, flowing 200 miles SW to the Mississippi.

chipping sparrow A small common sparrow *(Spizella passerina)* of eastern North America, with a reddish-brown cap.

chip·py (chip′ē) *n. pl.* **·pies 1** The chipping sparrow. **2** A squirrel or chipmunk. **3** *Slang* **a** A promiscuous girl or woman. **b** A prostitute.

chip shot In golf, a short, lofted shot made in approaching the green.

chi·ral·i·ty (kī·ral′ə·tē) *n. Chem., Physics.* The property by which a form is distinguishable from its mirror image; handedness. [<Gk. *cheir* hand] **—chi·ral** (kī′rəl) *adj.*

Chi·ri·co (kē′rē·kō), **Giorgio di,** 1888–1978, Italian painter.

chir·i·men (chir′i·men) *n.* A Japanese silk crêpe fabric. [<Japanese]

chirk (chûrk) *v.i.* **1** *Scot.* To make a screeching or gritting noise; creak; shriek. **2** *Colloq.* To be or become cheerful: with *up.* [OE *cearcian* creak]

chirm (chûrm) *n.* Twittering; warbling, as of many birds or insects. —*v.i.* To make a twittering sound. [OE *cirm* <*cirman* cry out]

chiro- *combining form* Hand; of or with the hand: *chirograph.* Also, before vowels, **chir-**: also spelled *cheiro-.* [<Gk. *cheir, cheiros* hand]

chi·rog·no·my (kī·rog′nə·mē) *n.* The study of the hand as a means of interpreting character and personality. [<CHIRO- + -GNOMY]

chi·rog·nos·tic (kī′rog·nos′tik) *adj.* Having the ability to distinguish between the right and left sides of the body. [<CHIRO- + Gk. *gignōskein* know]

chi·ro·graph (kī′rə·graf, -gräf) *n. Law* A legal paper, as an acknowledgment of a debt written in the handwriting of the borrower.

chi·rog·ra·phy (kī·rog′rə·fē) *n.* The art, style, or character of handwriting. **—chi·rog′ra·pher** *n.* — **chi·ro·graph·ic** (kī′rə·graf′ik) or **·i·cal** *adj.*

chi·ro·man·cy (kī′rə·man′sē) *n.* Palmistry. — **chi′ro·man′cer, chi′ro·mant** *n.*

Chi·ron (kī′ron) In Greek mythology, the wisest of the centaurs, tutor of Achilles and Asclepius: also *Cheiron.*

chi·ron·ja (che·ron′hä) *n.* A citrus fruit produced by crossing the grapefruit with the orange. [<Am. Sp. *china* orange + *toronja* grapefruit]

chi·ro·plas·ty (kī′rə·plas′tē) *n.* Plastic surgery of the hand.

chi·rop·o·dy (kə·rop′ə·dē, kī-) *n.* The treatment of ailments of the foot, as bunions, corns, etc. See PODIATRY. [<CHIRO- + Gk. *pous, podos* foot] **—chi·rop′o·dist** *n.*

chi·ro·prac·tic (kī′rə·prak′tik) *n.* A method of therapy based on the theory that disease is mainly due to a malfunction of the nerves which may be corrected by manipulation of bodily structures, especially the spinal column. [<CHIRO- + Gk. *praktikos* effective <*prattein* do, act] **—chi·ro·prac·tor** (kī′rə·prak′tər) *n.*

chi·rop·ter (kī·rop′tər) *n.* A bat; any member of the order Chiroptera. [<CHIRO- + Gk. *pteron* wing] **—chi·rop′ter·an** *adj. & n.*

chirp (chûrp) *v.i.* **1** To give a short, acute cry, as a sparrow, locust, or cricket; to cheep, as a young bird. **2** To make a similar sound, as in urging a horse. **3** To talk in a quick and cheerful manner. —*v.t.* **4** To utter with a quick, sharp sound. —*n.* A short, sharp sound, as made by some birds and insects. [ME *chirpen,* var. of *chirken* CHIRK] **—chirp′er,** *n.* **—chirp′ing·ly** *adv.*

chirr (chûr) *v.i.* To make a sharp trilling sound, as that of the grasshopper, cicada, and some birds: chirp. —*n.* The trilling sound made by crickets, locusts, cicadas, etc. Also **chirre.** [Imit.]

chir·rup (chir′əp) *v.i.* **1** To chirp continuously or repeatedly, as a bird. **2** To chirp with the lips, as in urging or calling a horse. —*v.t.* **3** To utter with chirps. —*n.* A chirp; a cheery sound. [<CHIRP] **—chir′rup·y** *adj.*

chi·rur·geon (ki·rûr′jən) *n. Archaic* A surgeon. [<OF *cirurgien* <LL *chirurgicus* <L *chirurgus* <Gk. *cheirourgos* <*cheir* hand + *ergon* work] **—chi·rur′ger·y** *n.* **—chi·rur′gic** or **·gi·cal** *adj.*

chis·el (chiz′əl) *n.* A cutting tool with a beveled edge, used for cutting, engraving, or mortising metal, stone, or wood. —*v.* **chis·eled** or **·elled, chis·el·ing** or **·el·ling** *v.t.* **1** To cut, engrave, or carve, as with a chisel. **2** *Colloq.* To cheat; swindle. **3** *Colloq.* To obtain by dishonest or unfair methods. —*v.i.* **4** To use a chisel. **5** *Colloq.* To use dishonest or unfair methods. [<AF, ult. <L *caedere* cut] **—chis′el·er** or **chis′el·ler** *n.*

chis·eled (chiz′əld) *adj.* Distinctly outlined; finely molded with, or as with, a chisel; clearcut. Also **chis′elled.**

Chi·shi·ma Ret·to (chē·shē·mä ret·tō) The Japanese name for the KURILE ISLANDS.

Chis·holm Trail (chiz′əm) An old cattle trail from San Antonio, Texas, to Abilene, Kansas.

Chi·şi·nău (kē′shē·nu′o͞o) The Rumanian name for KISHINEV.

Chis·le·hurst and Sid·cup (chiz′əl·hûrst; sid′kup) A residential district of NW Kent, England.

Chis·leu (kis′lef) See KISLEW.

chit[1] (chit) *n.* **1** *Brit.* A note; letter; memorandum. **2** A voucher of a small sum owed, as for food or drink; restaurant check. Also **chit′ty.** [<Hind. *chiṭṭhī* note]

chit[2] (chit) *n. Brit. Dial.* A budding shoot. —*v.i.* **chit·ted, chit·ting** To sprout, as a seed or plant. [OE *cith* sprig]

chit[3] (chit) *n.* A pert child, girl, or young woman. [ME *chitt.* ? Related to CAT.]

Chi·ta (chē·tä′) A city near the Mongolian border of Russian S.F.S.R.

chit-chat (chit′chat′) *n.* **1** Informal or familiar talk. **2** Gossip.

chi·tin (kī′tin) *n. Biochem.* A colorless, horny, amorphous polysaccharide, intermediate between proteins and carbohydrates, forming the principal constituent of the hard covering of insects and crustaceans. [<F *chitine* <Gk. *chitōn* tunic] **—chi′ti·nous** *adj.*

chi·ton (kī′tən) *n.* **1** A gown or tunic worn by men and women in ancient Greece. **2** Any of a family *(Chitonidae)* of gastropods, found mostly on rocks. [<Gk.]

Chi·tral (chi·träl′) A princely state in West Pakistan; 4,000 square miles; capital, Chitral.

Chit·ta·gong (chit′ə·gong) The main port of Bangladesh.

chit·ter (chit′ər) *v.i.* **1** *Obs.* To twitter. **2** *Scot.* To shiver, as with cold. [Var. of CHATTER]

chit·ter·ling (chit′ər·ling) *n.* **1** *pl.* The small intestine of pigs or calves, especially as prepared as food: also **chit′ling. 2** *pl.* Shreds: torn to *chitterlings.* **3** *Archaic* A short frill having wrinkled folds. [Cf. G *kutteln* entrails]

Chiu·si (kyōō′sē) A town in Tuscany, central Italy: ancient *Clusium.*

chiv (chiv) See SHIV.

chiv·al·rous (shiv′əl·rəs) *adj.* **1** Having the qualities of the ideal knight: gallant, courteous, generous, brave, etc. **2** Pertaining to the feudal system of chivalry. See synonyms under BRAVE. — **chiv′al·rous·ly** *adv.* —**chiv′al·rous·ness** *n.*

chiv·al·ry (shiv′əl·rē) *n.* **1** The feudal system of knighthood; knight-errantry; also, the spirit and customs of medieval knight-errantry. **2** Disinterested courtesy; bravery; magnanimity. **3** A body of knights, warriors, or gallant gentlemen. **4** *Obs.* Mounted and armed fighting men. [<OF *chevalerie* <LL *caballarius* cavalier. Doublet of CAVALRY.] —**chiv·al·ric** (shiv′əl·rik, shi·val′rik) *adj.*

chiv·a·ree (shiv′ə·rē′) See CHARIVARI.

chive (chīv) *n.* A perennial herb *(Allium schoenoprasum)* allied to the leek and onion: used as a flavoring in cooking. Also **chive garlic.** [<AF <L *cepa* onion]

chiv·y (chiv′ē) *v.t.* & *v.i.* To chevy. Also **chiv′vy.**

chlam·y·date (klam′ə·dāt) *adj. Zool.* Having a mantle, as certain mollusks. [<L *chlamydatus* cloaked <Gk. *chlamys, -ydos* cloak]

chla·myd·e·ous (klə·mid′ē·əs) *adj. Bot.* Pertaining to the floral envelope of a plant. [<Gk. *chlamys, -ydos* cloak]

chlam·y·do·spore (klam′i·dō·spôr′, -spōr′) *n.* **1** *Bot.* A non-sexual accessory spore in certain fungi, possessing a very thick membrane. **2** *Zool.* A spore with protective envelope, as formed by fission from an encysted protozoan. [<Gk. *chlamys, -ydos* cloak + -SPORE]

chla·mys (klā′mis, klam′is) *n. pl.* **chla·mys·es** or **chlam·y·des** (klam′ə·dēz) A short cloak caught up on the shoulder, worn by hunters, soldiers, and horsemen in ancient Greece. [<Gk.]

CHLAMYS

chlo·an·thite (klō·an′thīt) *n.* A tin-white arsenide of nickel, $NiAs_2$. [<Gk. *chloanthēs* budding < *chloē* bud, sprout]

Chlod·wig (klōt′vikh) See CLOVIS.

Chlo·e (klō′ē) A feminine personal name. See DAPHNIS AND CHLOE. [<Gk., bud, sprout]

chlor- Var. of CHLORO-.

chlor·a·cet·o·phe·none (klôr′ə·set′ə·fi·nōn′, klōr′-) *n. Chem.* A colorless, crystalline compound, C_8H_7ClO, with an odor of apple blossoms: it is used as a lacrimator and harassing agent in chemical warfare. Symbol, CN. [<CHLOR- + ACETO- + PHEN(YL) + -ONE]

chlor·ac·ne (klôr·ak′nē, klōr-) *n.* A severe skin disorder resembling acne and caused by exposure to chlorinated organic compounds, especially dioxin.

chlo·ral (klôr′əl, klō′rəl) *n. Chem.* **1** A colorless, oily, liquid compound, $CCl_3{\cdot}CHO$, with a penetrating odor, obtained variously, as by the action of chlorine on alcohol. **2** A white crystalline pungent compound, $CCl_3CHO{\cdot}H_2O$, used medicinally as a hypnotic, etc., which in large doses acts as a poison, paralyzing the heart: also **chloral hydrate.** [<CHLOR(INE) + AL(COHOL)]

chlo·ra·mine-T (klôr′ə·mēn·tē′, klō′rə-) *n. Chem.* A white crystalline compound, $C_7H_7SO_2NClNa$, used as a surgical antiseptic and decontaminating agent for mustard gas. [<CHLOR- + -AMINE]

chlo·ram·phen·i·col (klôr′am·fen′i·kōl, -kol, klō′ram-) *n. Chem.* A crystalline nitrogenous compound, $C_{11}H_{12}Cl_2O_5N_2$, obtained from a soil bacillus *(Streptomyces venezuelae)* and also made synthetically: used as an antibiotic in the treatment of certain viral, bacterial, and rickettsial diseases. [<CHLOR- + AM(IDE) + PHE(NOL) + NI(TROGEN) + (GLY)COL]

chlo·ran·thy (klə·ran′thē) *n. Bot.* The transformation into leaflike organs of the parts of a flower. [<CHLOR- + Gk. *anthos* flower]

chlo·rate (klôr′āt, klō′rāt) *n. Chem.* A salt of chloric acid containing the univalent ClO_3 radical.

chlor·dane (klôr′dān, klōr′-) *n.* An oily, chlorinated hydrocarbon, $C_{10}H_6Cl_8$, used as an insecticide and very toxic to humans, being absorbable through the skin. Also **chlor·dan.**

chlo·ren·chy·ma (klə·reng′kə·mə) *n. Bot.* Stem tissue of a plant containing chlorophyll. [<CHLOR(OPHYLL) + (PAR)ENCHYMA]

chlo·ric (klôr′ik, klō′rik) *adj. Chem.* Of, pertaining to, or combined with chlorine: said specifically of chlorine compounds containing relatively more oxygen than the chlorous compounds.

chloric acid *Chem.* A monobasic, pungent acid, $HClO_3$, like nitric acid in oxidizing properties, but much less stable.

chlo·ride (klôr′īd, -id, klō′rīd, -rid) *n. Chem.* A compound of chlorine with a more positive element or radical, as hydrogen *chloride* (muriatic acid) or sodium *chloride* (common salt). — **chlo·rid·ic** (klə·rid′ik) *adj.*

chloride of lime *Chem.* A disinfecting and bleaching agent made by the action of chlorine gas on slaked lime; bleaching powder.

chlo·rin·ate (klôr′ə·nāt, klō′rə-) *v.t.* **·at·ed, ·at·ing** *Chem.* To treat, impregnate, or cause to combine with chlorine, as in whitening fabrics or separating gold from ore. —*n.* A soluble bleaching compound made by subjecting potassium or sodium hydroxide to the action of chlorine. — **chlo′rin·a′tion** *n.* —**chlo′rin·a′tor** *n.*

chlo·rine (klôr′ēn, -in, klō′rēn, -rin) *n.* A greenish-yellow, poisonous, readily liquefiable gaseous element (symbol Cl, atomic number 17), a very chemically active member of the halogens and an essential constituent of living organisms. See PERIODIC TABLE. [<Gk. *chlōros* green]

chlo·rin·i·ty (klə·rin′ə·tē) *n.* A measure of the total amount of chlorine per kilogram of sea water: it bears a constant relation to salinity according to the formula $S = 0.03 \times 1.805 \times C$.

chlo·rite (klôr′īt, klō′rīt) *n.* **1** Any one of several green hydrous silicates, closely related to the micas. **2** One of the salts of chlorous acid. [<Gk. *chlōritis* greenstone]

chloro- *combining form* **1** Light-green: *chlorophyll.* **2** Chlorine: *chlorohydrin.* Also, before vowels, *chlor-*. [<Gk. *chlōros* green]

chlo·ro·a·ce·tic acid (klôr′ō·ə·sē′tik, -ə·set′ik, klō′rō-) *Chem.* A colorless, corrosive compound, $CH_2ClCOOH$, derived from acetic acid in the form of deliquescent crystals: used chiefly in the synthesis of dyestuffs and in medicine as a caustic.

chlo·ro·form (klôr′ə·fôrm, klō′rə-) *n. Chem.* A colorless, volatile, sweetish liquid compound, $CHCl_3$, used as an anesthetic and anodyne and as a solvent of wax, resin, plastics, etc. —*v.t.* **1** To administer chloroform to. **2** To anesthetize or kill with chloroform. [<CHLORO- + FORM(YL)]

chlo·ro·hy·drin (klôr′ə·hī′drin, klō′rə-) *n. Chem.* Any of a group of organic compounds containing the hydroxyl radical and chlorine.

chlor·o·meth·ane (klôr′ə·meth′ān, klōr′-) *n.* Methyl chloride.

Chlo·ro·my·ce·tin (klôr′ə·mī·sē′tən, klō′rə-) *n.* Proprietary name for a brand of chloramphenicol, used as an antibiotic.

chlo·ro·phane (klôr′ə·fān, klō′rə-) *n.* A variety of fluorite emitting a green phosphorescence when heated. [<CHLORO- + Gk. *phainein* appear]

chlo·ro·phyll (klôr′ə·fil, klō′rə-) *n. Biochem.* The green nitrogenous coloring matter contained in the chloroplasts of plants and essential to their growth by photosynthesis of carbohydrates. It occurs in two forms: the bluish-green **chlorophyll-A,** $C_{55}H_{72}O_5N_4Mg$, the most abundant form; and the yellowish-green **chlorophyll-B,** $C_{55}H_{70}O_6N_4Mg$: some derivatives are used as dyes, in cosmetics, and in medicine as vulneraries. Also **chlo′ro·phyl.** [<CHLORO- + Gk. *phyllon* leaf] —**chlo·ro·phyl·la·ceous** (klôr′ə·fi·lā′shəs, klō′rə-), **chlo′ro·phyl′lose** (-fil′ōs), **chlo′ro·phyl′lous** (-fil′əs) *adj.*

chlo·ro·plast (klôr′ə·plast, klō′rə-) *n. Bot.* One of the flattened bodies or plastids containing chlorophyll found in the cell cytoplasm of plants. Also **chlo′ro·plas′tid.** [<CHLORO- + PLAST(ID)]

chlo·ro·prene (klôr′ə·prēn, klō′rə-) *n. Chem.* A colorless liquid, C_4H_5Cl, synthesized from acetylene and chlorine: in its polymerized forms it yields a number of compounds essential in the making of synthetic rubber. [<CHLORO- + (ISO)PRENE]

chlo·ro·sis (klə·rō′sis) *n.* **1** *Pathol.* An anemic disease affecting young women, characterized by a greenish pallor, hysteria, etc.; greensickness. **2** *Bot.* The blanching or etiolation of plants, usually caused by lack of iron and other mineral salts. [<NL <Gk. *chlōros* green] —**chlo·rot·ic** (klə·rot′ik) *adj.*

chlo·rous (klôr′əs, klō′rəs) *adj. Chem.* Of, pertaining to, or combined with chlorine: *chlorous* acid.

chlor·pic·rin (klôr·pik′rin, klōr-) *n. Chem.* A colorless, oily liquid, CCl_3NO_2, obtained by distilling chloride of lime with picric acid; nitrochloroform: its nauseous vapor is called *vomiting gas.* Symbol, PS. Also **chlo′ro·pic′rin.**

chlor·pro·ma·zine (klôr·prō′mə·zēn, -zin, klōr-) *n. Med.* A synthetic ataractic drug used in the control of severe excitement in psychiatric cases, particularly of the manic-depressive type. [A composite word from di*methyl* amino*propyl* *chloro*phenothi*azine* hydrochloride]

chlor·sul·fon·ic acid (klôr′sul·fon′ik, klōr′-) *Chem.* A colorless, fuming liquid. $HClSO_3$, used as a smoke-producer in chemical warfare. Symbol, FS.

chlor·tet·ra·cy·cline (klôr′tet·rə·sī′klin, klōr′-) *n. Chem.* An organic compound chemically related to tetracycline, obtained from the soil bacillus *Streptomyces aureofaciens*: used as an antibiotic, chiefly in the form known as Aureomycin.

cho·an·o·cyte (kō·an′ə·sīt) *n.* Collar cell. [<Gk. *choanē* funnel + -CYTE]

chock (chok) *n.* **1** A block or wedge, so placed as to prevent or limit motion. **2** *Naut.* A heavy piece of metal or wood fastened to a deck, or the like, and having jaws through which a rope or cable may pass. —*v.t.* To fit or wedge in tightly, as a boat, barrel, or wheel. —*adv.* **1** Completely: He stood *chock* still. **2** All the way: *chock* to the edge. [<AF *choque* log]

CHOCK

chock-a-block (chok′ə·blok′) *adj.* **1** Drawn to the limit, with blocks touching: said of a tackle. **2** Close together; crowded. —*adv.* Close; very near.

chock-full (chok′fōōl′) *adj.* **1** Completely full; full to crowding or choking. **2** Deeply moved with emotion. Also *choke-full.* [ME *chokke-fulle*]

chock·stone (chok′stōn′) *n. Geol.* A block or mass of loose rock wedged in a mountain chimney.

choc·o·late (chôk′lit, chôk′ə·lit, chok′-) *n.* **1** Cacao nuts roasted and ground without removing the fat, usually sweetened and flavored. **2** A beverage or confection made from this preparation. **3** Dark-brown color. —*adj.* Flavored, made with, or colored like chocolate. [<Sp. <Nahuatl *chocólatl*]

Choc·taw (chok′tô) *n. pl.* **·taw** or **·taws 1** One of a tribe of North American Indians of Muskhogean linguistic stock, formerly living between the Mobile and Mississippi Rivers: now in Oklahoma. **2** The language of this tribe.

choice (chois) *n.* **1** The act, fact, power, or privilege of choosing; selection. **2** One who or that which is chosen or to be chosen; preference. 3 A number or a variety from which to choose; also, an alternative. 4 The power to prefer or select. 5 The right or privilege to choose; option. 6 The best part. See synonyms, under ALTERNATIVE. —*adj.* **choic·er, choic·est** 1 Meriting, preference; select; elegant; excellent; also, precious. 2 Dainty; fastidious. 3 *Dial.* Careful of; fond of. [< OF *choisir* choose] **—choice′ly** *adv.* **—choice′ness** *n.*

Synonyms (adj.): cherished, chosen, costly, dainty, elegant, excellent, exquisite, nice, picked, precious, rare, select. See EXCELLENT. *Antonyms*: cheap, common, inferior, mean, ordinary, poor, valueless, worthless.

choir (kwīr) *n.* 1 A body of trained singers or that part of a church occupied by them; chancel. 2 Originally, any band or organized company, especially of dancers or singers. 3 One of the nine orders in the angelic hierarchy. —*v.i.* To sing, as in a choir. —*v.t.* To sing or utter in chorus. Also spelled *quire.* ◆Homophone: *quire.* [< OF *cuer* < L *chorus*; infl. in form by F *choeur.* Doublet of CHORUS.]

choir boy A young boy who sings in a choir.

choir loft A gallery in a church set aside for the choir.

choir·mas·ter (kwīr′mas′tər, -mäs′-) *n.* One who directs or trains a choir.

Choi·seul (shwä·zœl′) Northeasternmost of the British Solomon Islands; about 1,500 square miles.

Choi·seul (shwä·zœl′), **Duc Étienne de,** 1719–1785, French statesman.

choke (chōk) *v.* **choked, chok·ing** *v.t.* 1 To stop the breathing of by obstructing or constricting the windpipe; strangle. 2 To keep back; suppress. 3 To fill completely. 4 To obstruct or close up by filling. 5 To retard the progress, growth, or action of. 6 To make a chokebore. 7 To lessen the air intake of the carburetor in order to enrich the fuel mixture of (a gasoline engine). —*v.i.* 8 To become suffocated or stifled. 9 To become clogged, fouled, or obstructed. —*n.* 1 The act of choking. 2 The narrowest part of a chokebored gun. 3 A device to control the supply of oxygen to a gasoline engine. 4 A choke coil. [OE *acēocian*]

choke·ber·ry (chōk′ber′ē, -bər·ē) *n. pl.* **·ries** 1 A North American shrub (genus *Aronia*) of the rose family. 2 The small, red or purple astringent fruit of this shrub.

choke·bore (chōk′bôr′, -bōr) *n.* 1 The bore of a shotgun narrowed at the muzzle. 2 A gun so bored.

choke·cher·ry (chōk′cher′ē) *n. pl.* **·ries** A North American wild cherry *(Prunus virginiana).*

choke coil *Electr.* A low-resistance coil of sufficient inductance to limit or suppress any fluctuating current without impeding the flow of a steady current.

choke·damp (chōk′damp′) *n.* A nonexplosive, asphyxiating atmosphere deficient in oxygen, found in mines, wells, etc. Also called *blackdamp.*

choke-full (chōk′fool′) See CHOCK-FULL.

chok·er (chō′kər) 1 One who or that which chokes. 2 *Colloq.* A wide white tie or neck cloth worn high around the throat. 3 A person who wears such a tie; especially, a minister. 4 A small fur neckpiece, closely fitting the neck. 5 A closely fitting necklace.

chok·ing (chō′king) *adj.* 1 Causing strangling; stifling. 2 Strained with emotion: said of the voice. **—chok′ing·ly** *adv.*

chok·y (chō′kē) *adj.* **chok·i·er, chok·i·est** 1 Suffocating; causing suffocation; stifling. 2 Somewhat choked: a *choky* voice. Also **chok′ey.**

chol·a·gog (kol′ə·gôg, -gog) *n. Med.* A purgative causing evacuations of bile. [< Gk. *cholagogos* < *cholē* bile + *agein* lead] **—chol·a·gog·ic** (kol′ə·goj′ik) *adj. & n.*

cho·lan·gi·ot·o·my (kə·lan′jē·ot′ə·mē) *n. Surg.* The opening of a bile duct through the substance of the liver, to remove gallstones. [< CHOLE- + ANGIO- + -TOMY]

chol·an·gi·tis (kol′an·jī′tis) *n. Pathol.* Inflammation of the biliary ducts. Also **chol′an·gei′tis.** [< CHOL- + ANGI(O)- + -ITIS]

chole- *combining form* Bile; gall: *cholesterol.* Also, before vowels, **chol-:** also **cholo-.** [< Gk. *cholē bile*]

chol·e·cyst (kol′ə·sist) *n. Anat.* The gall bladder. [< NL *cholecystis* < Gk. *cholē* gall + *kystis* bladder]

cho·led·o·cho·plas·ty (kə·led′ə·kō·plas′tē) *n.* Plastic surgery on the bile duct. [< NL *choledochus* bile duct (< Gk. *cholē* bile + *dechesthai* contain) + -PLASTY] **—cho·led′o·cho·plas′tic** *adj.*

cho·le·mi·a (kə·lē′mē·ə) *n. Pathol.* The presence of bile in the blood; jaundice. Also **cho·lae′·mi·a.** [< CHOLE- + -EMIA]

chol·er (kol′ər) *n.* 1 Anger or hastiness of temper: formerly believed to be caused by disturbance of the liver or gall bladder. 2 *Obs.* Bile; also, biliousness. See synonyms under ANGER. [< OF *colère* < L *cholera* CHOLERA]

chol·er·a (kol′ər·ə) *n. Pathol.* An acute, infectious, chiefly epidemic disease, occurring in many forms and characterized principally by serious intestinal disorders: it is caused by a bacterium *(Vibrio comma)* and in its more malignant forms, as Asiatic cholera, is usually fatal. [< L < Gk., cholera morbus (in Hippocrates)]

cholera in·fan·tum (in·fan′təm) *Pathol.* A warm-weather, non-contagious, often fatal diarrhea of children, possibly caused by the bacterium *Vibrio proteus.* [< L, cholera of infants]

cholera mor·bus (môr′bəs) *Pathol.* Acute gastroenteritis, a warm-weather complaint. Also **cholera nos·tras** (nos′tras). [< L, cholera disease]

chol·er·ic (kol′ər·ik, kə·ler′ik) *adj.* 1 Of a bilious temperament; in a bilious condition. 2 Easily provoked; irascible. 3 Of the nature of anger. See synonyms under HOT.

cho·les·ter·ol (kə·les′tə·rōl) *n. Biochem.* A fatty monatomic crystalline alcohol. $C_{27}H_{45}OH$, derived principally from bile and present in most gallstones: it is found also in the blood, brain and nerve tissue, kidneys, liver, etc. Also **cho·les′ter·in.** [< CHOLE- + Gk. *stereos* solid + -OL[2]]

cho·lic acid (kō′lik, kol′ik) *Biochem.* A white, bitter crystalline acid; $C_{24}H_{40}O_5$, found in bile acids and in animal excrements.

cho·line (kō′lēn, kol′ēn, -in) *n.* An alkaline compound, $C_5H_{15}NO_2$, forming a part of the vitamin B complex and used in the biosynthesis of acetylcholine.

chol·la (chōl′yä) *n.* A variety of the prickly-pear cactus *(Cylindropuntia)* having spiny cylindrical stems: it is a frequent pest on stock ranges in the SW United States. [< Sp.]

chon·dri·fy (kon′drə·fī) *v.t. & v.i.* **·fied, ·fy·ing** To convert into or become cartilage. **—chon′·dri·fi·ca′tion** *n.*

chon·dri·o·some (kon′drē·ə·sōm) *n. Biol.* A small granular body found, alone or in clusters, in the cytoplasm of a cell and subject to rapid changes both in shape and position: also called *mitochondria.* See illustration under CELL. [< Gk. *chondrion,* dim. of *chondros* cartilage + *sōma* body]

chon·drite (kon′drīt) *n.* A stony meteorite containing chondrules. **—chon·drit·ic** (kon·drit′ik) *adj.*

chondro- *combining form* 1 Cartilage: chondrotomy. 2 Grain: *chondr*ule. Also, before vowels, **chondr-.** [< Gk. *chondros* cartilage]

chon·droid (kon′droid) *adj.* Resembling cartilage.

chon·dro·ma (kon·drō′mə) *n. pl.* **·mas** or **·ma·ta** (-mə·tə) *Pathol.* A cartilaginous tumor.

Chon·dros·te·i (kon·dros′tē·ī) *n. pl.* An order of fishes with cartilaginous skeletons, as the paddle fishes and sturgeons. [< NL < Gk. *chondros* cartilage + *osteon* bone] **—chon·dros′te·an** *adj. & n.*

chon·drot·o·my (kon·drot′ə·mē) *n. Surg.* The cutting of cartilages. [< CHONDRO- + -TOMY]

chon·drule (kon′drōōl) *n.* Any of the small, rounded beads of various mineral composition found embedded in chondrites.

Chong·jin (chông·jin) A port of North Korea. *Japanese* **Sei·shin** (sā·shen).

Chong·ju (chông·jōō) A city of South Korea. *Japanese* **Sei·shu** (sā·shōō).

choose (chōōz) *v.* **chose, cho·sen, choos·ing** *v.t.* 1 To select as most desirable; take by preference; elect. 2 To desire or have a preference for. 3 To please or think proper (to do something): with infinitive as object. —*v.i.* 4 To make selection or decision. 5 To have an alternate. **—cannot choose but** Has no alternative choice. **—to pick and choose** To select with great deliberation. [OE *cēosan*] **—choos′er** *n.*

Synonyms: cull, elect, pick, prefer, select. *Prefer* indicates a state of desire and approval; *choose,* an act of will. Prudence or generosity may lead one to *choose* what he does not *prefer. Select* implies a careful consideration of the reasons for preference and choice. Among objects so nearly alike that we have no reason to *prefer* any one to another, we may simply *choose* the nearest, but we could not be said to *select* it. Aside from theology, *elect* is popularly confined to the political sense; as, a free people *elect* their own rulers. *Cull* means to collect, as well as to *select.* In a garden we *cull* the choicest flowers. To *pick* is to *choose* for special fitness; as, a guard of *picked* men; *chosen,* in this sense, is somewhat archaic. *Antonyms*: decline, disclaim, dismiss, leave, refuse, reject.

choos·y (chōō′ze) *adj.* **choos·i·er, choos·i·est** *Colloq.* Disposed to be particular or fussy in one's choices.

chop[1] (chop) *v.* **chopped, chop·ping** *v.t.* 1 To cut or make by strokes of a sharp tool; hew. 2 To cut up in small pieces; mince. 3 To utter jerkily; cut short. 4 To make a cutting, downward stroke at (the ball), as in tennis. —*v.i.* 5 To make cutting strokes, as with an ax. 6 To interrupt abruptly, as in conversation: with *in*: to *chop in* with a remark. 7 To go, come, or move with sudden or violent motion. —*n.* 1 A cut of meat, chopped off, usually containing a rib. 2 A cleft or fissure; a crack, especially in the lip. 3 The act of chopping. 4 A tool for chopping. 5 A sudden bite or snap. 6 A sudden motion of waves; also, a choppy sea. 7 In boxing, a short, sharp, downward punch. 8 In tennis or cricket, a sharp, cutting, downward stroke. [ME *choppen.* Related to CHAP, CHIP.]

chop[2] (chop) *v.t.* 1 *Obs.* To barter; exchange. —*v.i.* 2 To veer suddenly; shift, as the wind; vacillate. 3 *Obs.* To bargain; barter. [ME *choppen.* Related to CHEAP.]

chop[3] (chop) *n.* 1 A jaw. 2 *pl.* The jaws and the parts about the mouth. 3 *pl.* The entrance or mouth of a harbor, channel, valley, etc.; especially, the entrance of the English Channel from the Atlantic. —*v.t.* 1 To seize with the jaws; snap. 2 To utter quickly and sharply. Also spelled *chap.* [Var. of CHAP[3]]

chop[4] (chop) *n.* 1 An official stamp or seal in India, China, etc.; hence, a clearance, passport, or permit. 2 *Anglo-Indian* Brand or quality. **—first chop** *Slang* Superior brand or quality. [< Hind. *chhāp* stamp]

chop chop! (chop′ chop′) In Pidgin English, quickly! in a hurry!

chop-fal·len (chop′fô′lən) See CHAP-FALLEN

chop house An eating house specializing in serving chops and steaks.

chop·house (chop′hous′) *n.* A Chinese custom house.

Cho·pin (shō′pan, *Fr.* shō·pan′), **Frédéric François,** 1810–49, Polish composer and pianist, active in France.

cho·pine (chō·pēn′, chop′in) *n.* A high clog worn under a shoe. Also **chop·in** (chop′·in). [< Sp. *chapin* < *chapa* metal plate]

CHOPINE
Sixteenth century.

chop·log·ic (chop′loj′ik) *n.* 1 Hair-splitting argument. 2 *Obs.* A contentious, argumentative person.

chop·per (chop′ər) *n.* 1 One who or that which chops. 2 *Telecom.* A device, usually one that rotates, used to interrupt a continuous-wave radio signal in a transmitter or receiver. 3 *pl. Slang* Teeth. 4 *Slang* A helicopter.

chop·ping (chop′ing) *adj.* 1 Shifting suddenly, as a wind. 2 Full of short, broken waves.

chop·py[1] (chop′ē) *adj.* **·pi·er, ·pi·est** Full of cracks, chops, or fissures.

chop·py[2] (chop′ē) *adj.* 1 Full of short, rough waves. 2 Variable; shifting, as wind.

chop shop A place where stolen cars are disassembled so that their parts can be sold.

chop·sticks (chop′stiks′) *n. pl.* Slender rods of ivory or wood, used in pairs, in China, Japan, etc., to convey food to the mouth. [< Pidgin English *chop* quick + STICK; trans. of Chinese name]

chop-su·ey (chop′sōō′ē) *n.* A Chinese-American dish consisting of fried or stewed meat or chicken, bean sprouts, onions, celery, mushrooms, etc., cooked in their own juices and served with rice. [<Chinese *tsa-sui,* lit., mixed pieces]

cho•ra•gus (kō·rā′gəs) *n. pl.* **•gi** (-jī) **1** In ancient Greece, the leader of a chorus, as at the performance of a play. **2** Any leader of a chorus or band. Also **cho•re•gus** (kō·rē′gəs). [<L <Gk. *chorēgos* <*choros* chorus + *agein* lead] **—cho•rag•ic** (kō·raj′ik) *adj.*

cho•ral[1] (kə·ral′) *n.* A hymn characterized by a simple melody and firm rhythm, and often sung in unison. Also **cho•rale′.** [<G *choral*]

cho•ral[2] (kôr′əl, kō′rəl) *adj.* **1** Pertaining to a chorus or choir. **2** Written for or sung by a chorus. [<Med. L *choralis* <L *chorus* CHORUS] **—cho′ral•ly** *adv.*

Cho•ras•mi•a (kə·raz′mē·ə) A province of ancient Persia, extending from the Oxus to the Caspian Sea.

chord[1] (kôrd) *n. Music* A combination of three or more tones sounded together according to the laws of harmony. The most important chords are the **common chord,** consisting of a fundamental tone with its major or minor third and its perfect fifth, and the **chord of the seventh,** called the dominant seventh. **—***v.i.* To be in harmony or accord. ◆ Homophone: *cord.* [Earlier *cord,* short for ACCORD; form infl. by CHORD[2]]

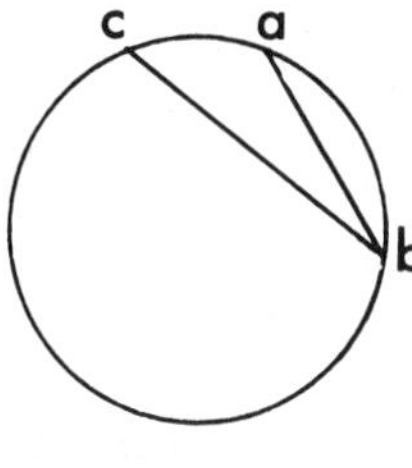

CHORD
cb and *ab* are chords.

chord[2] (kôrd) *n.* **1** A string or cord of a musical instrument; hence, emotional response or reaction. **2** *Geom.* A straight line connecting the extremities of an arc; a secant; the portion of a straight line contained by its intersections with a curve. **3** *Eng.* One of the principal members of a bridge truss, horizontal or inclined. **4** *Anat.* A tendon, a connective ligament. **5** *Aeron.* The length of an airplane. ◆ Homophone: *cord.* [<L *chorda* <Gk. *chordē* string of a musical instrument. Doublet of CORD.] **—chord′al** *adj.*

Chor•da•ta (kôr·dā′tə) *n. pl.* A phylum of the animal kingdom which includes the vertebrates and whose members are characterized by an internal skeleton (which in primitive forms is a slender, axial rod, the *notochord*), a dorsally located central nervous system, and gill slits, present in the embryos of terrestrial forms. [<NL <*chorda* CHORD[2]] **—chor•date** (kôr′dāt) *adj. & n.*

chore (chôr, chōr) *n.* **1** A small job. **2** *pl.* The routine duties of a household or farm. **3** An unpleasant or hard task. [Var. of CHAR[1]]

-chore *combining form Bot.* Denoting a plant that is distributed in a specified manner: *anemochore.* [<Gk. *chōrein* spread]

cho•re•a (kô·rē′ə, kō-) *n. Pathol.* A nervous disease characterized by involuntary muscular twitching; St. Vitus's dance. [<NL <Gk. *choreia* dance] **—cho•re′al** *adj.*

cho•re•o•graph (kôr′ē·ə·graf, kō′rē-) *v.t.* To provide the choreography for.

cho•re•og•ra•phy (kôr′ē·og′rə·fē, kō′rē-) *n.* **1** The art of devising ballets and incidental dances. **2** The written representation of figures and steps of dancing. **3** The art of dancing; ballet. Also **cho•reg•ra•phy** (kə·reg′rə·fē). [<Gk. *choreia* dance + -GRAPHY] **—cho′re•og′ra•pher** *n.* **—cho′re•o•graph′ic** *adj.*

cho•re•ol•o•gy (kôr′ē·ol′ə·jē, kō′rē-) *n.* The systematic study and analysis of choreographic notation or dance–scores.

cho•re•o•ma•ni•a (kôr′ē·ə·mā′nē·ə, -mān′yə, kō′·rē-) *n.* A morbid craving to dance, often communal and epidemic and characterized by hysterical religious exaltation; dancing mania. [< Gk. *choreia* dance + -MANIA] **—cho′re•o•man′ic** *adj.*

cho•ri•amb (kôr′ē·amb, kō′rē-) *n.* In prosody, a metrical foot of four syllables, the second and third short and the others long (¯ ˘ ˘ ¯). Also **cho•ri•am•bus** (kôr′ē·am′bəs, kō′rē-). [< L *choriambus* <Gk. *choriambos* <*choreios* trochee + *iambos* iambus] **—cho′ri•am′bic** *adj. & n.*

cho•ric (kôr′ik, kō′rik) *adj.* Relating to or like a chorus.

cho•rine (kôr′ēn, kō′rēn) *n. Colloq.* A chorus girl.

cho•ri•on (kôr′ē·on, kō′rē-) *n.* **1** *Anat.* The external protective and nutritive membrane that invests the fetus of the higher vertebrates and attaches it to the uterus. **2** *Entomol.* The outer case of an insect egg. [<Gk. *chorion*]

cho•ri•pet•al•ous (kôr′ē·pet′əl·əs, kō′rē-) *adj. Bot.* Having free, unconnected petals; polypetalous. [<Gk. *chōris* apart + *petalon* leaf]

cho•rist (kôr′ist, kō′rist) *n.* A member of a chorus. **—cho•ris•tic** (kə·ris′tik) *adj.*

chor•is•ter (kôr′is·tər, kor′-) *n.* **1** A member of a choir; specifically, a male singer in a church choir. **2** A leader of a choir or of congregational singing; a precentor. **3** Any singer, as a bird.

cho•rog•ra•phy (kô·rog′rə·fē, kō-) *n. pl.* **•phies** **1** The delineation or mapping of regions. **2** A map or chart of any particular region. [< Gk. *chōros* region + -GRAPHY] **—cho•rog′ra•pher** *n.* **—cho•ro•graph•ic** (kôr′ə·graf′ik, kō′rə) or **•i•cal** *adj.* **—cho′ro•graph′i•cal•ly** *adv.*

cho•roid (kôr′oid, kō′roid) *adj. Anat.* Resembling the chorion: said of highly vascular membranes. **—***n.* The choroid coat, the middle or vascular tunic of the eyeball. See illustration under EYE. Also **cho•ri•oid** (kôr′ē·oid, kō′rē-).

cho•rol•o•gy (kô·rol′ə·jē, kō-) *n. Ecol.* The study of the migrations of plants and animals, especially in relation to areas of distribution. [<Gk. *chōros* region + -LOGY]

cho•ro•script (kôr′ə·skript, kō′rə-) *n.* A system of choreographic notation devised for the correct teaching and permanent recording of the steps and figures of a dance: also called *dance script.* [<Gk. *choros* dance + SCRIPT]

chor•tle (chôr′təl) *v.i.* **•tled •tling** To chuckle or make a loud noise expressive of joy. **—***n.* A chuckle; joyful vocal sound. [Blend of CHUCKLE and SNORT; coined by Lewis Carroll in *Through the Looking–Glass*]

cho•rus (kôr′əs, kō′rəs) *n.* **1** A musical composition, usually in parts, for performance by a large group of singers. **2** A body of singers, or singers and dancers, who perform together in concerts, opera, ballet, musical comedy, etc. **3** Any group of individuals singing or speaking something together simultaneously; also, that which is thus uttered. **4** The part of a work written for or performed by a chorus; the burden or refrain of a song, which others join a soloist in singing. **5** In ancient Greece, a ceremonial dance, accompanied by the singing of odes, and performed in honor of Dionysus. **6** In Greek drama, a body of actors who through song, dance, and dialog commented upon and sometimes took part in the main action of a play; also, the parts of a play so performed. **7** In later drama, especially the Elizabethan, a single actor who recites the prolog and epilog and comments upon the plot. **—***v.t. & v.i.* **cho•rused** or **•russed, cho•rus•ing** or **•rus•sing** To sing or speak in concert. [<L <Gk. *choros* dance. Doublet of CHOIR.]

chorus girl A woman performing in the chorus of a musical comedy, cabaret, etc.

Cho•rzów (khô′zhōōf) A city in southern Poland: formerly *Królewska Huta.*

chose[1] (chōz) Past tense of CHOOSE.

chose[2] (shōz) *n. Law* Anything that is personal property. [<F, thing <L *causa* matter, cause]

chose ju•gée (shōz zhü·zhā′) *French* An adjudicated case; hence, any matter which has been decided.

cho•sen (chō′zən) Past participle of CHOOSE.**—** *adj.* **1** Made an object of choice; selected. **2** Worthy of special preference; select; choice. **3** *Theol.* Elect.

Cho•sen (chō·sen) The Japanese name for KOREA.

chosen people The Israelites. *Deut.* xiv 2.

Cho•ta Nag•pur (chō′tə näg′pōōr) A plateau region mainly in Madhya Pradesh and Bihar states, India.

chou (shōō) *n. pl.* **choux** (shōō) *French* A cabbage.

Chou (jō) An early Chinese imperial dynasty (1122?–249 B.C.)

Chou En–lai (jō′ en′lī′), 1898–1976, Chinese premier and foreign minister of the People's Republic of China 1949–76.

chough (chuf) *n.* A bird of the crow family, especially the red–legged or Cornish chough *(Pyrrhocorax pyrrhocorax)* with black plumage and red beak and feet. ◆ Homophone: *chuff.* [ME *choghe.*]

chouse (chous) *v.t.* **choused, chous•ing** *Colloq.* To cheat; swindle. [<*n.*] **—***n.* **1** *Obs.* A sharper; swindler. **2** *Obs.* A dupe. [<Turkish *chaush* messenger; ? with ref. to a dishonest 17th c. Turkish agent in London]

choush (choush) See CHIAUS.

chow[1] (chou) *n.* **1** A medium–sized, heavy–coated, muscular dog native to China, having a thick coat of brown or black, a massive head, and characteristically blue–black tongue: also *chow–chow.* **2** *Slang* Food. [Short for CHOW–CHOW]

CHOW
(20 inches high at its shoulder)

chow[2] (chou) *n.* A Chinese subordinate district or its chief city: used frequently in combination in place names: *Foochow.*

chow[3] (chou) *n. Scot.* The jowl.

chow–chow (chou′chou′) *n.* **1** A relish consisting of a mixture of chopped–up vegetables pickled in mustard. **2** A chow dog. **—***adj.* Miscellaneous; mingled. [<Pidgin English]

chow•der (chou′dər) *n.* **1** A dish, usually of clams or fish stewed with vegetables, often in milk. **2** A picnic, usually on the seashore, where chowder is served. [<F *chaudière* kettle <L *caldaria.* See CALDRON.]

chow–mein (chou′mān′) *n.* A Chinese–American dish consisting of a stew of shredded chicken or meat, onions, mushrooms, celery, bean sprouts, etc., served with fried noodles. [<Chinese *ch'ao* fry + *mien* flour]

chow•ry (chou′rē) *n. pl.* **•ries** *Anglo–Indian* A fly flapper originally made from the bushy tail of a yak: formerly a symbol of royalty in eastern Asia. [<Hind. *chaunrī*]

chre•ma•tis•tic (krē′mə·tis′tik) *adj.* Of or pertaining to the accumulation of wealth; money–making. [<Gk. *chrēmatistikos* <*chrēmatizein* deal with, transact <*chrēma* money]

chre•ma•tis•tics (krē′mə·tis′tiks) *n.* The branch of economics that treats of the accumulation of wealth; also, political economy as a whole.

chres•ard (kres′ərd) *n. Ecol.* The available water of the soil: opposed to *echard.* [<Gk. *chrēsthai* use + *ardeia* irrigation]

Chres•tien de Troyes (krā·tyań′ də trwä′), 1140?–91, French poet; the first author to relate original versions of the Arthurian legends. Also **Chré•tien′ de Troyes′.**

chres•tom•a•thy (kres·tom′ə·thē) *n. pl.* **•thies** A collection of choice extracts; especially, one compiled for instruction in a language. [<Gk. *chrēstos* useful + *manthanein* learn]

Chré•tien (krā·tyań′) French form of CHRISTIAN, personal name. Also **Chres•tien** (krā·tyań′).

Chris (kris) Diminutive of CHRISTIAN or of CHRISTOPHER.

chrism (kriz′əm) *n.* **1** An unguent of oil and balm used for anointing at baptism, confirmation, unction, etc., in the Greek Orthodox and Roman Catholic Churches. **2** Loosely, any unguent. Also spelled *chrisom.* [OE *crisma* < LL *chrisma* <Gk. <*chriein* anoint. Doublet of CREAM.] **—chris•mal (kriz′məl)** *adj.*

chris•ma•to•ry (kriz′mə·tôr′ē, -tō′rē) *n. pl.* **•ries** A vessel or container for chrism. [<Med. L *chrismatorium* <*chrisma* chrism]

chris•om (kriz′əm) *n.* **1** A baptismal or christening robe. **2** Chrism. [Var. of CHRISM]

chrisom child **1** An innocent baby; a newborn child. **2** A child who dies within a month after baptism: formerly buried in its baptismal robe.

Chris•sie (kris′ē) Diminutive of CHRISTIANA.

Christ (krīst) *n.* **1** The Anointed; the Messiah: the deliverer of Israel whose coming was foretold by the Hebrew prophets. **2** Specifically, a title of Jesus of Nazareth, regarded as fulfilling this prophecy: at first used as a title *(Jesus the Christ)* but later a proper name *(Jesus Christ).* **3** In Christian Science, the divine manifestation of God, which comes to the flesh to destroy incarnate error. [OE *Crist* < L *Christus* < Gk. *Christos* (< *chriein* anoint); trans. of Hebrew *māshīach* anointed] **—Christ′li·ness** *n.* **—Christ′ly** *adj.*

Chris·ta·bel (kris′tə·bel) A feminine personal name. [< *Christ* + L *bella* beautiful]

Christ·church (krīst′chûrch) A city on the eastern coast of South Island, New ealand.

christ-cross (kris′krôs′, -kros′) *n.* **1** The mark of the cross (+), formerly placed before the alphabet in hornbooks, before and after treatises, inscriptions, etc. **2** *Brit. Dial.* A mark or cross made by a person who cannot sign his name. **3** *Obs.* The alphabet; christ-cross-row. See CRISS-CROSS. [< *Christ's cross*]

christ-cross-row (kris′krôs′rō′, -kros′-) *n. Obs.* The alphabet: so called because once printed with a cross at the beginning. Also **criss′-cross′-row′.**

chris·ten (kris′ən) *v.t.* **1** To name in baptism: He was *christened* John. **2** To administer the rite of Christian baptism to. **3** To give a name to in baptism, or in some ceremony considered as analogous; dedicate; hence, in general, to name: The ship was *christened.* **4** To use for the first time. [OE *cristnian* < *cristen* CHRISTIAN]

Chris·ten·dom (kris′ən·dəm) *n.* **1** Christian lands, or Christians collectively; the Christian world. **2** *Obs.* Christianity.

chris·ten·ing (kris′ən·ing) *n.* **1** Any Christian baptismal ceremony. **2** Specifically, the baptizing and naming of an infant.

Christ·hood (krīst′hŏŏd) *n.* The condition of being the Christ; the Messiahship.

Chris·tian (kris′chən) *adj.* **1** Professing or following the religion of Christ. **2** Relating to or derived from Christ or his doctrine. **3** Manifesting the spirit of Christ or of his teachings. **4** Characteristic of Christianity or Christendom. **5** *Colloq.* Human; civilized; decent. *—n.* **1** One who believes in or professes belief in Jesus as the Christ; a member of the Christian church. **2** A disciple of Jesus of Nazareth; one whose profession and life conform to the example and teaching of Jesus. **3** *Colloq.* Any human being as distinguished from a brute: That dog knows as much as a *Christian.* **4** *Colloq.* A civilized, decent, or respectable person. **5** *U.S.* A Campbellite; a member of the Disciples of Christ. [OE *cristen* < LL *christianus* < *Christus* CHRIST] **— Chris′tian·ly** *adv.*

Chris·tian (kris′chən; *Dan., Ger.* kris′tē·än) A masculine personal name. [< L]

—Christian The central character in Bunyan's *Pilgrim's Progress.*

—Christian X, 1870–1947, king of Denmark 1912–47.

Chris·ti·an·a (kris′tē·an′ə) A feminine personal name. Also *Ger.* **Chris·ti·a·ne** (kris′tē·ä′nə). [< L]

Christian Brothers A Roman Catholic lay order devoted to education; also called *Brothers of the Christian Schools.*

Christian era The period beginning January 1, 754 A.U.C., or nine months and seven days after March 25, 753 A.U.C., calculated by Dionysius Exiguus in A.D. 527 as the date of Christ's incarnation, now placed four to six years earlier.

Chris·ti·a·ni·a (kris′tē·ä′nē·ə) *n.* In skiing, a turn effected by shifting the weight to one advanced ski and turning its tip outward: also called *Christy.*

Chris·tia·ni·a (kris·tyä′nē·ä) A former name for OSLO.

Chris·tian·ism (kris′chən·iz′əm) *n.* Christianity.

Chris·ti·an·i·ty (kris′chē·an′ə·tē) *n.* **1** The Christian religion. **2** Christians collectively. **3** The state of being a Christian.

Chris·tian·ize (kris′chən·īz) *v.* **·ized, ·iz·ing** *v.t.* **1** To convert to Christianity. **2** To imbue with Christian ideas, principles, and faith. *—v.i.* **3** *Rare* To adopt Christianity; become Christian. **—Chris′tian·i·za′tion** *n.* **—Chris′tian·iz′er** *n.*

Christian name A baptismal name; first or given name: distinguished from *family name* or *surname.*

Christians See DISCIPLES OF CHRIST.

Christian Science A religious system embodying metaphysical healing, founded in 1866 by Mary Baker Eddy and based on her exposition of the Scriptures: officially called the **Church of Christ, Scientist.**

Chris·tians·haab (krēs′tyäns·hôp) A settlement on the west coast of Greenland; founded 1743.

Chris·tian·sted (kris′chən·sted) The capital of St. Croix in the Virgin Islands; former capital of the Danish West Indies.

Chris·ti·na (kris·tē′nə, *Pg.* krēs·tē′nə) A feminine personal name. Also **Chris·tine** (kris·tēn′; *Fr.* krēs·tēn′; *Ger.* kris·tē′nə). [Var. of CHRISTIANA]

—Christina, 1626–89, queen of Sweden, 1632–54.

Christ·less (krīst′lis) *adj.* **1** Without Christ or his spirit. **2** Without faith in Christ; unchristian. **—Christ′less·ness** *n.*

Christ·like (krīst′līk′) *adj.* **1** Resembling Christ or like that of Christ. **2** Having the spirit of Christ. **—Christ′like′ness** *n.*

Christ·mas (kris′məs) *n.* **1** The 25th of December, held as the anniversary of the birth of Jesus Christ: widely observed as a holy day or a holiday. Also **Christmas Day.** **2** A church festival observed annually at this date in memory of the birth of Jesus Christ; the Feast of the Nativity; especially, the anniversary day, the 25th of December. The season of Christmas extends from Christmas Eve (Dec. 24) to Epiphany (Jan. 6), and is known as **Christmastide.** [< CHRIST + MASS[2]]

Christmas box **1** A box of Christmas gifts sent to an absent person. **2** *Brit.* A gratuity given at Christmas.

Christmas Eve The evening of December 24, before Christmas Day.

Christmas Island **1** An island SW of Java, comprising part of the British crown colony of Singapore; 60 square miles. **2** The largest atoll in the Line Islands district of the Gilbert and Ellice Islands Colony; 220 square miles.

Christmas rose The white-flowering hellebore: so called because its single roselike flowers bloom from December to February.

Christmas tree An evergreen tree decorated with ornaments and lights at Christmas.

Chris·tol·o·gy (kris·tol′ə·jē) *n.* The branch of theology that treats of the person and attributes of Christ. **2** Loosely, any theory or doctrine concerning Christ. [< CHRIST + -LOGY] **— Chris·to·log·i·cal** (kris′tə·loj′i·kəl) *adj.*

Chris·tophe (krēs·tôf′), **Henri,** 1767–1820, Negro king of Haiti 1811–20.

Chris·to·pher (kris′tə·fər) A masculine personal name. Also *Lat.* **Chris·toph·o·rus** (kris·tof′ə·rəs), *Fr.* **Chris·tophe** (krēs·tôf′), *Pg.* **Chris·to·vão** (krēs′tō·vouṅ′), *Ger.* **Chris·to·pho·rus** (kris′tō·fôr′əs) or **Chris·toph** (kris′tōf). [< Gk., bearer of Christ]

—Christopher, Saint A Christian martyr of the third century.

Christ's-thorn (krīsts′thôrn′) *n.* **1** A Palestinian shrub of the buckthorn family *(Paliurus spina-cristi),* with long sharp thorns: so called from a belief that Christ's crown of thorns was made of it: also called *Jew's-thorn.* **2** The jujube.

Chris·ty (kris′tē) Dim. of CHRISTIAN, personal name.

Chris·ty (kris′tē) See CHRISTIANIA (ski turn).

Chris·ty (kris′tē), **Howard Chandler,** 1873–1952, U.S. illustrator and painter.

chrom- Var. of CHROMO-.

chro·ma (krō′mə) *n.* Color intensity; the degree of hue and saturation in a color other than white, black, or gray. [< Gk. *chrōma* color]

chro·maf·fin (krō·maf′in) *adj. Biol.* Having the property of staining when treated with dichromate.

chro·mate (krō′māt) *n. Chem.* A salt of chromic acid.

chro·mat·ic (krō·mat′ik) *adj.* **1** Pertaining to color or colors. **2** *Music* Using or proceeding by semitones. Also **chro·mat′i·cal.**

chromatic aberration See under ABERRATION.

chro·ma·tic·i·ty (krō′mə·tis′ə·tē) *n. Physics* That quality of a color which is defined by its dominant or complementary wavelength taken together with its purity.

chro·mat·ics (krō·mat′iks) *n.* The science of colors.

chromatic scale *Music* The diatonic scale proceeding by semitones.

chro·ma·tid (krō′mə·tid) *n. Biol.* One of the four members of a tetrad formed by the longitudinal splitting of a chromosome during meiosis.

chro·ma·tin (krō′mə·tin) *n. Biol.* The deeply staining filamentous material in the protoplasm of the cell nucleus: during mitosis chromatin develops into chromosomes: also called *chromoplasm.* See illustration under CELL. [< Gk. *chrōma, -atos* color]

chro·ma·tism (krō′mə·tiz′əm) *n.* **1** *Optics* Chromatic aberration. **2** *Bot.* The assumption by normally green plant organs, as leaves, of a color approximating that of the petals. Also **chro·mism** (krō′miz·əm).

chromato- *combining form* Color; coloring or pigmentation: *chromatoscope.* Also, before vowels, **chromat-.** [< Gk. *chrōma, -atos* color]

chro·mat·o·gram (krō·mat′ə·gram) *n. Chem.* The complete array of distinctively colored bands produced by chromatography.

chro·ma·tog·ra·phy (krō′mə·tog′rə·fē) *n. Chem.* A method for the separation and analysis of small quantities of substances by passing a solution through a column of finely divided powder which selectively adsorbs the constituents in one or more sharply defined, often colored bands. [< CHROMATO- + -GRAPHY] **—chro·mat·o·graph·ic** (krō·mat′ə·graf′ik) *adj.*

chro·ma·tol·o·gy (krō′mə·tol′ə·jē) *n. pl.* **·gies** **1** The science of color. **2** A treatise on colors. [< CHROMATO- + -LOGY]

chro·ma·tol·y·sis (krō′mə·tol′ə·sis) *n. Biol.* The solution and disappearance of chromatin from a neuron or other cell. [< CHROMATO- + -LYSIS]

chro·ma·to·phore (krō′mə·tə·fôr′, -fōr′) *n.* **1** *Zool.* One of the pigment-bearing sacs with contractile walls by which changes of color are effected in various animals, as in chameleons; a pigment cell. **2** *Bot.* A pigment-bearing plastid found in diatoms and other plants. — **chro·ma·to·phor·ic** (krō′mə·tə·fôr′ik, -for′-), **chro·ma·toph·o·rous** (krō′mə·tof′ə·rəs) *adj.*

chrome (krōm) *n.* **1** Chrome yellow. **2** Chromium. *—v.t.* **chromed, chrom·ing** To subject to the action of a solution of potassium dichromate. [< F < Gk. *chrōma* color]

-chrome *combining form* **1** Color; colored: *polychrome.* **2** *Chem.* Chromium: *ferrochrome.* [Gk. *chrōma* color]

chrome alum *Chem.* Any double sulfate of chromium with potassium, sodium, or ammonium: *chrome alum ammonium,* $Cr(NH_4)(SO_4)_2 \cdot 12H_2O$, a dark, violet-red compound used as a mordant in dyeing.

chrome green **1** A green pigment derived from chromic oxide, Cr_2O_3. **2** The color of this, a dull, dark green.

chrome red A pigment made from basic lead chromate.

chrome steel *Metall.* A very hard steel alloyed with chromium: when the chrome is 12 percent or more, the resulting alloy is known as *stainless steel.* Also **chromium steel.**

chrome yellow **1** *Chem.* A yellow pigment consisting of natural lead chromate, $PbCrO_4$. **2** Any of several shades of yellow ranging from lemon to deep orange.

chro·mic (krō′mik) *adj.* **1** *Chem.* Of, from, or pertaining to chromium. **2** Pertaining to compounds in which chromium is present in its higher valency.

chromic acid *Chem.* A hypothetical acid, H_2CrO_4, known only in solution and forming chromates.

chromic oxide *Chem.* A green compound, Cr_2O_3; chromium sesquioxide: used as a pigment.

chro·mi·nance (krō′mə·nəns) *n. Physics* The colorimetric difference between a given color and a reference color of equal brightness and specified chromaticity.

chro·mite (krō′mīt) *n.* Chromic iron ore, $FeCr_2O_4$, a valuable source of chromium.

chro·mi·um (krō′mē·əm) *n.* A grayish-white, very hard metallic element (symbol Cr): used in making alloys, pigments, as a mordant, etc. See ELEMENT. [< Gk. *chrōma* color; so called from its many brightly colored, poisonous compounds]

chromium trioxide *Chem.* A red crystalline

substance, CrO_3; chromic anhydride: a powerful oxidizing agent.

chro•mo (krō′mō) *n. pl.* **•mos** A picture printed in colors; a chromolithograph. [Short for CHROMOLITHOGRAPH]

chromo– *combining form* **1** Color; in or with color: *chromophotography.* **2** *Chem.* Chromium: *chromotype.* Also, before vowels, *chrom–* [Gk. *chrōma* color]

chro•mo•gen (krō′mə·jen) *n.* **1** *Chem.* **a** Any organic coloring matter or substance capable of yielding a dye. **b** Any dye derived from naphthalene which develops a brown color on wool by oxidation. **2** *Biol.* Any substance in an animal or plant which under certain conditions becomes colored or deepens its hue. **— chro′mo·gen′ic** *adj.*

chro•mo•gen•e•sis (krō′mə·jen′ə·sis) *n.* The origin or development of color.

chro•mo•lith•o•graph (krō′mō·lith′ə·graf, -gräf) *n.* A print in colors obtained by chromolithography. **— chro·mo·li·thog·ra·pher** (krō′·mō·li·thog′rə·fər) *n.* **— chro′mo·lith′o·graph′ic** *adj.*

chro•mo•li•thog•ra•phy (krō′mō·li·thog′rə·fē) *n.* The process of reproducing a colored original from a set of stones by lithography.

chro•mo•mere (krō′mə·mir) *n. Biol.* One of the granules of chromatin forming the chromosome.

chro•mo•phore (krō′mə·fôr, -fōr) *n. Chem.* A group of atoms so arranged as to produce the colors of dyestuffs when combined under proper conditions with hydrocarbon radicals. **— chro·mo·phor·ic** (krō′mə·fôr′ik, -for′-), **chro·moph·o·rous** (krō·mof′ə·rəs) *adj.*

chro•mo•pho•to•graph (krō′mō·fō′tə·graf, -gräf) *n.* A photograph in colors.

chro•mo•pho•tog•ra•phy (krō′mō·fə·tog′rə·fē) *n.* Photography in colors.

chro•mo•plasm (krō′mə·plaz′əm) *n.* Chromatin.

chro•mo•plast (krō′mə·plast) *n. Bot.* A colored protoplasmic granule of a color other than green.

chro•mo•some (krō′mə·sōm) *n. Biol.* One of the deeply staining, rod– or loop–shaped bodies into which the chromatin of the cell nucleus divides during mitosis, generally of a fixed number for any given species: regarded as a carrier of the genes or units of heredity. See HAPLOID, POLYPLOID. **— accessory chromosome** A chromosome of which the shape, size, and purpose differ from those of other chromosomes of the same cell. [<CHROMO- + -SOME[2]]

chro•mo•sphere (krō′mə·sfir′) *n. Astron.* An envelope of incandescent red gas surrounding the sun beyond the photosphere: it is composed chiefly of hydrogen and helium. **— chro·mo·spher·ic** (krō′mə·sfer′ik) *adj.*

chro•mo•type (krō′mə·tīp′) *n.* **1** A photographic process in which some salt of chromium is the sensitive agent. **2** A chromolithograph. **3** A photograph in colors. Also **chro′ma·type′.**

chro•mous (krō′məs) *adj. Chem.* Of or pertaining to chromium in its lower valence.

chro•nax•y (krō′nak·sē) *n. Physiol.* The time that a current of twice the rheobase requires to excite a muscle, nerve fiber, etc. Also **chro′·nax·ie, chro·nax·i·a** (krō·nak′sē·ə). [<CHRON(O)- + Gk. *axia* value]

chron•ic (kron′ik) *adj.* **1** Continuing for a long period. **2** Inveterate; habitual: a *chronic* complainer. **3** Prolonged; lingering: said of a disease: opposed to *acute.* Also **chron′i·cal.** [<F *chronique* <L *chronicus* <Gk. *chronikos* of time < *chronos* time] **— chron′i·cal·ly** *adv.*

chron•i•cle (kron′i·kəl) *n.* A register of events in the order of time; a historical record chronologically arranged. See synonyms under HISTORY, RECORDS. **—** *v.t.* **·cled, ·cling** To record. [<AF *cronicle* <L *chronica,* neut. pl. of *chronicus.* See CHRONIC.] **— chron′i·cler** *n.*

Chron•i•cles (kron′i·kəlz) The two books of the Old Testament following *Kings.*

chrono– *combining form* Time: *chronograph.* Also, before vowels, **chron–.** [<Gk. *chronos* time]

chron•o•gram (kron′ə·gram) *n.* **1** A record of a chronograph. **2** A writing or an inscription recording a date in numeral letters.

chron•o•graph (kron′ə·graf, -gräf) *n.* An instrument for recording graphically the moment or duration of an event, measuring intervals of time, etc.

chron•o•log•i•cal (kron′ə·loj′i·kəl) *adj.* **1** Occurring or recorded in temporal sequence, as a series of events. **2** Pertaining to or occupied with the science of time. Also **chron′o·log′ic. — chron′o·log′i·cal·ly** *adv.*

chro•nol•o•gy (krə·nol′ə·jē) *n. pl.* **·gies 1** The science that treats of the measurement of time, or the order of events. **2** Any particular chronological system. **3** Any tabulated arrangement of events of historical or scientific import, in the order of the time of their occurrence. [<CHRONO- + -LOGY] **— chro·nol′o·ger, chro·nol′o·gist** *n.*

chro•nom•e•ter (krə·nom′ə·tər) *n.* A portable timekeeping instrument of high precision and accuracy for use in navigation and scientific work. [<CHRONO- + -METER] **— chron·o·met·ric** (kron′ə·met′rik) or **·ri·cal** *adj.* **— chron′o·met′ri·cal·ly** *adv.*

chro•nom•e•try (krə·nom′ə·trē) *n.* **1** The measurement of time. **2** The science or method of measuring time.

chron•o•scope (kron′ə·skōp) *n.* A chronograph or the like for measuring a minute interval of time. **— chron·o·scop·ic** (kron′ə·skop′ik) *adj.*

-chroous *combining form* Having (a certain) color: *isochroous.* [<Gk. *chrōs, chroos* color]

chrys– Var. of CHRYSO–.

chrys•a•lid (kris′ə·lid) *n.* A chrysalis; especially, the intermediate or pupal stage in butterflies. **—** *adj.* Of, pertaining to, or like a chrysalis: also **chry·sal·i·dal** (kri·sal′ə·dəl).

chrys•a•lis (kris′ə·lis) *n. pl.* **chrys·a·lis·es** or **chry·sal·i·des** (kri·sal′ə·dēz) *Entomol.* **1** The pupa of an insect, especially of a butterfly; the capsule–enclosed stage between caterpillar and butterfly during which the individual develops and from which the winged adult emerges. See illustration under PUPA. **2** Anything in an undeveloped or transitory stage. [<L <Gk. *chrysallis* golden sheath of a butterfly < *chrysos* gold]

chrys•an•i•line (kris·an′ə·lin, -līn) *n. Chem.* A coal–tar dyestuff, $C_{19}H_{15}N_3$, obtained from rosaniline, that gives a golden–yellow color.

chrys•an•the•mum (kri·san′thə·məm) *n.* **1** Any of a genus of perennials (*Chrysanthemum*) of the composite family, some cultivated varieties of which have large heads of showy flowers of various colors. **2** The flower. [<L <Gk. *chrysanthemon* marigold, lit., golden flower]

chrys•a•ro•bin (kris′ə·rō′bin) *n. Chem.* An orange–yellow compound, $C_{15}H_{12}O_3$, which forms the essential principle of Goa powder. Also **chrys·a·ro·bi·num** (kris′ə·rō′bi·nəm). [<CHRYS- + Tupian *araroba* bark]

Chry•se•is (krī·sē′is) In the *Iliad,* the daughter of a priest of Apollo, given as a slave to Agamemnon: she was returned after Apollo sent a plague upon the Greeks.

chrys•el•e•phan•tine (kris′el·ə·fan′tin) *adj.* Made or covered with gold and ivory, as certain ancient Greek statues. [<Gk. *chryselephantinos* of gold and ivory < *chrysos* gold + *elephas* ivory]

chrys•ene (kris·ēn′) *n. Chem.* A reddish–violet, fluorescent crystalline compound, $C_{18}H_{12}$, contained in coal tar and other substances.

chryso– *combining form* Gold; of a golden color: *chrysolite.* Also, before vowels, *chrys–.* [<Gk. *chrysos* gold]

chrys•o•ber•yl (kris′ə·ber′əl) *n.* A vitreous, yellowish or greenish, transparent to translucent beryllium aluminate: used as a gem. [<L *chrysoberyllus* <Gk. *chrysoberyllos* < *chrysos* gold + *beryllos* beryl]

chrys•o•lite (kris′ə·līt) *n.* A vitreous, orthorhombic, olive–green, transparent to translucent magnesium iron silicate, $(Mg,Fe)_2SiO_4$: used as a gem: also called *olivine.* [<OF *crisolite* <Med. L *crisolitus* <L *chrysolithus* <Gk. *chrysolithos* < *chrysos* gold] **— chrys·o·lit·ic** (kris′ə·lit′ik) *adj.*

chrys•o•prase (kris′ə·prāz) *n.* A semiprecious, apple–green variety of chalcedony, colored by nickel oxide: used as a gem. [<OF *crisopace* <L *chrysoprasus* <Gk. *chrysoprasos* < *chrysos* gold + *prason* leek]

Chrys•os•tom (kris′əs·təm, kris·os′təm), **Saint John,** 345?–407, Greek Church father; patriarch of Constantinople 398–404.

Chrys•o•tham•nus (kris′ə·tham′nəs) *n.* A genus of low, flowering shrubs related to the aster group of the *Compositae* and native in western North America. Certain species, especially *C. nauseosus,* yield a rubber latex. [<CHRYSO- + Gk. *thamnos* bush]

chrys•o•tile (kris′ə·til) *n.* A fibrous, silky variety of serpentine. [<CHRYSO- + Gk. *tilos* hair, fiber]

chtho•ni•an (thō′nē·ən) *adj.* **1** Of, pertaining to, or being in the nether world; underground; subterranean. **2** Specifically, pertaining to the Greek underworld gods as distinguished from those of Olympus. Also **chthon·ic** (thon′·ik). [<Gk. *chthōn* the earth]

Chu (chōō) A river in Kirghiz and Kazakh S.S.R., flowing 700 miles NW.

chub (chub) *n. pl.* **chubs** or **chub 1** A European carplike fish of the cyprinoid order (genus *Leuciscus*). **2** One of various other fishes, as the fallfish, tautog, etc. [ME *chubbe*; origin unknown]

chu•bas•co (chōō·bäs′kō) *n. Meteorol.* A violent thunder squall along the west coast of Central America. [<Sp.]

chub•by (chub′ē) *adj.* **·bi·er, ·bi·est** Plump; rounded. [<CHUB] **— chub′bi·ness** *n.*

Chu•but (chōō·vōōt′) A national territory of southern Argentina; 65,669 square miles; capital, Rawson; drained by the **Chubut River,** flowing 500 miles SE to the Atlantic.

chuck[1] (chuk) *n.* **1** A chick; hen. **2** A short clucking sound; a cluck. **3** *Archaic* An endearing sound or word. **—** *v.i.* To cluck, as a fowl does, or as in calling fowls. [Imit.]

chuck[2] (chuk) *v.t.* **1** To pat or tap affectionately or playfully, as under the chin. **2** To throw or pitch: to *chuck* a baseball. **3** *Colloq.* To throw away; discard. **4** *Colloq.* To throw out forcibly; eject: with *out.* **5** *Brit. Slang* To quit: He *chucked* his job. **—** *n.* **1** A playful pat, throw, or toss. **2** *Brit.* A game of pitch–and–toss, played with coins or pebbles: also called **chuck′–far′thing.** [Cf. F *choquer* shake, jolt]

chuck[3] (chuk) *n.* **1** *Mech.* A clamp, chock, or wedge to hold a tool, as a drill. See illustration under BIT. **2** The part of a beef extending from the neck to the shoulder blade. **3** *Colloq.* **a** Food. **b** A meal. **c** Mealtime. **—** *v.t.* To place or fix in or by means of a chuck; do with a chuck. [Var. of CHOCK]

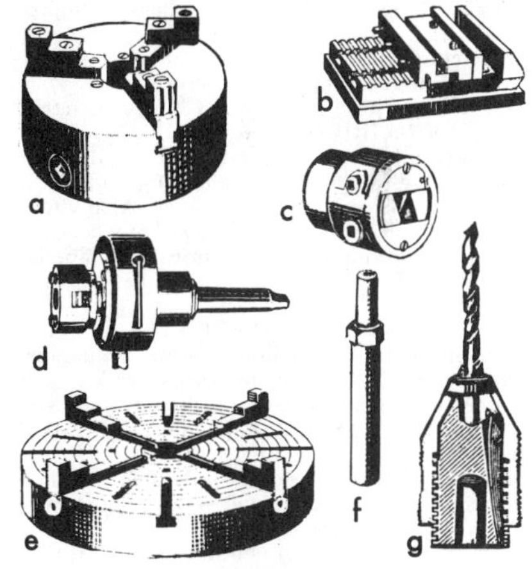

CHUCKS
a. Geared scroll chuck.
b. Planer chuck.
c. Drill chuck.
d. Tapping chuck.
e. Independent reversible–jaw lathe chuck.
f. Beach drill chuck.
g. Sectional view of drill chuck.

chuck–a–luck (chuk′ə·luk′) *n.* A gambling game employing three dice. Also **chuck′–luck′.**

chuck–full (chuk′fōōl′) *adj.* Chock–full.

chuck•hole (chuk′hōl′) *n. U.S. Dial.* A mudhole in a road.

chuck·ie (chuk'ē) *n. Scot.* **1** A chuckiestone; jackstone. **2** The game of chuck. Also **chuck'y.**

chuck·ie·stone (chuk'ē·stōn') *n. Scot.* **1** A pebble suitable for use in the game of chuck. **2** *pl.* A game played with such stones. Also **chuck'stone'.**

chuck·le[1] (chuk'əl) *v.i.* **·led, ·ling 1** To laugh quietly, especially to oneself. **2** To cluck, as a hen. —*n.* A low, suppressed, or broken laugh. [Freq. of CHUCK[1]] —**chuck'ler** *n.*

chuck·le[2] (chuk'əl) *adj.* Thick or clumsy. [? < CHUCK[3] (def. 1)]

chuck·le·head (chuk'əl·hed') *n. Colloq.* A stupid fellow; blockhead. —**chuck'le·head'ed** *adj.*

chuck wagon *U.S.* A food wagon that carries provisions and cooking equipment around to cowboys, harvest hands, etc.

chuck·wal·la (chuk'wol'ə) *n.* A large, herbivorous lizard *(Sauromalus ater)* of the deserts of the SW United States. Also **chuck·a·wal·la** (chuk'ə·wol'ə). [<N. Am. Ind.]

chuck–will's–wid·ow (chuk'wilz'wid'ō) *n.* A large goatsucker *(Caprimulgus carolinensis)* of the southern United States: so called from its note.

chuck·y (chuk'ē) *n. Scot.* **1** A chicken; fowl. **2** A little chick.

chud·der (chud'ər) *n. Anglo–Indian* A large, square shawl of fine wool, made in India. Also **chud'dar.** [<Hind. *chadar* square piece of cloth]

Chud·sko·e (chōōt'skə·yə) The Russian name for PEIPUS.

chu·fa (chōō'fə) *n.* **1** A sedge *(Cyperus esculentus)* whose tuberous roots are eaten in southern Europe. **2** One of the tubers. [< Sp.]

chuff (chuf) *n. Brit. Dial.* **1** A rustic. **2** A boor. **3** A coarse, churlish fellow. **4** A miser. —*adj.* Gruff; crusty: also **chuf'fy.** ◆ Homophone: *chough.* [Origin unknown]

chuf·fy (chuf'ē) *adj.* Chubby; plump. Also **chuf'fie.** —**chuf'fi·ly** *adv.* —**chuf'fi·ness** *n.*

chug (chug) *n.* An explosive sound, as of the exhaust of an engine.—*v.i.* **chugged, chug·ging** To work or go with a series of small explosions: The old car *chugged* along. [Imit.]

Chu·gach Mountains (chōō'gak) A part of the Coast Ranges in southern Alaska; highest peak, 13,250 feet.

Chuk·chi Peninsula (chŏŏk'chē) The NE extremity of Asia and Siberia.

Chu–Kiang (jōō'jyäng') The Chinese name for the CANTON RIVER.

chuk·ker (chuk'ər) *n.* In polo, one of the periods during which the ball is continuously in play: a chukker lasts 7½ minutes. Also **chuk'·kar.** [<Hind. *chakkar* <Skt. *chakra* wheel]

Chu·lym (chōō·lim') A river in central Siberian Russian S.F.S.R., flowing 1,000 miles north to the Ob.

chum[1] (chum) *n.* **1** Originally, a roommate. **2** An intimate companion. —*v.i.* **chummed, chum·ming** To share the same room with someone; hence, to be very intimate. See synonyms under ASSOCIATE [? Short for CHAMBER FELLOW]

chum[2] (chum) *n.* Pieces of oily fish, used as fish bait, or pressed for oil. —*v.i.* To fish with chum. [Origin uncertain]

chum·my (chum'ē) *adj.* **·mi·er, ·mi·est** *Colloq.* Friendly; intimate. —**chum'mi·ly** *adv.*

chump[1] (chump) *n.* **1** A chunk of wood. **2** The thick end, as of a loin of mutton. **3** The head: a humorous use. **4** *Colloq.* A stupid or unskilful person. —**off his chump** *Brit. Slang* Out of his senses; silly. [? Var. of CHUNK]

chump[2] (chump) *v.t.* To chew; munch. [< CHAMP[1]

Chun·chon (chōōn·chôn) A city in northern South Korea. *Japanese* **Shun·sen** (shoon·sen).

Chung·king (chōōng'king') A port on the Yangtze, capital of China in World War II.

chunk (chungk) *n.* **1** A short, stout thing, person, or animal; especially, a short, thick piece of wood. **2** A lump or large piece of anything. —*v.t.* **1** To throw clods of earth, stones, etc., at. **2** To throw, as clods of earth, stones, etc. **3** To put (chunks of wood) on a fire. [Var. of CHUCK]

chunk·er (chung'kər) *n.* A coal boat on a canal.

chunk·y (chung'kē) *adj.* **chunk·i·er, chunk·i·est 1** Short and thick–set; stocky. **2** In a chunk or chunks.

Chur (kōōr) A town in eastern Switzerland, capital of Grisons canton. *French* **Coire** (kwår).

church (chûrch) *n.* **1** A building for Christian worship. **2** Regular religious services; public worship. **3** A local congregation of Christians. **4** *Usually cap.* A distinct body of Christians having a common faith and discipline; a denomination: the Episcopal *Church.* **5** All Christian believers collectively. **6** Ecclesiastical organization and authority, as distinguished from secular authority: the separation of *church* and state. **7** The clerical profession; holy orders. **8** Any religious body or society. —*v.t.* **1** To call to account before the congregation; to reprimand or punish publicly according to church discipline. **2** To conduct a religious service for (a person, especially a woman after childbirth). [OE *circe,* ult. <Gk. *kyriakon (dōma)* the Lord's (house) <*kyrios* Lord]

church–go·er (chûrch'gō'ər) *n.* One who goes regularly to church. —**church'–go'ing** *adj.* & *n.*

Church·ill (chûrch'il, -əl) A port at the mouth of **Churchill River,** flowing 1,000 miles NE to Hudson Bay in northern Manitoba, Canada.

Church·ill (chûrch'il, -əl), **John** See MARLBOROUGH. —**Lord Randolph (Henry Spencer),** 1849–95, British statesman. —**Winston,** 1871–1947, U.S. novelist. —**Sir Winston (Leonard Spencer),** 1874–1965, British statesman; prime minister, 1940–45; 1951–55.

church·ing (chûr'ching) *n.* **1** A woman's appearance in church, to return thanks after confinement; also, the service for this occasion. **2** The process of subjecting to church discipline.

church·ly (chûrch'lē) *adj.* **1** Of, pertaining to, or suitable to a church. **2** Devoted to church polity and ritual. **3** Not secular. —**church'·li·ness** *n.*

church·man (chûrch'mən) *n. pl.* **·men** (-mən) **1** A devoted supporter or member of a church, especially of an established church. **2** *Obs.* A clergyman; ecclesiastic. —**church'·man·ly** *adj.* —**church'man·ship** *n.* —**church'·wom'an** *n. fem.*

Church of Christ, Scientist See CHRISTIAN SCIENCE.

Church of England The church established and endowed by law as the national church of England: also called *Anglican Church.*

Church of God Any of various small religious groups in the United States, for the most part unrelated.

Church of God, Adventist See under ADVENTIST.

Church Slavonic See under SLAVONIC.

church text *Printing* Old English type.

church·war·den (chûrch'wôr'dən) *n.* **1** In tne Church of England, an elected lay officer who assists in the administration of a parish, and acts as its legal representative. **2** In the Protestant Episcopal Church, one of two elected lay officers of a vestry who, with the other vestrymen, administer the property and temporal affairs of the parish, and represent the congregation on certain occasions. **3** A long–stemmed clay pipe. Also **church warden.**

church·yard (chûrch'yärd') *n.* The yard or graveyard of a church; a cemetery.

churl (chûrl) *n.* **1** A low–bred, surly fellow. **2** A miserly or niggardly person. **3** A peasant. **4** In England of Saxon times, a freeman of low degree. [OE *ceorl.* Akin to CARL.]

churl·ish (chûr'lish) *adj.* **1** Of or like a churl; rude; boorish. **2** Hard to work or manage; intractable. See synonyms under HAUGHTY, MOROSE. —**churl'ish·ly** *adv.* —**churl'ish·ness** *n.*

churn (chûrn) *n.* **1** A vessel in which milk or cream is agitated to separate the oily globules and gather them as butter. **2** Any vessel or receptacle similar in shape to a milk churn. —*v.t.* **1** To stir or agitate (cream or milk), as in a churn, to make butter. **2** To make by agitation, as butter. **3** To agitate violently: The oars *churned* the water. —*v.i.* **4** To stir or agitate cream or milk in making butter. **5** To produce or be in violent agitation; seethe. [OE *cyrin*] —**churn'er** *n.*

churn·ing (chûr'ning) *n.* **1** The process of churning. **2** The butter churned at one time. **3** *Med.* A splashing sound from the chest sometimes heard in pleural effusion and resembling the sound made by a churn.

churr (chûr) *n.* The whirring sound made by certain birds, as the partridge or nightjar, or insects, as the cockchafer. —*v.t.* To utter with a churr. —*v.i.* To utter a low trill or similar vibrant sound, as a partridge. [Imit.]

Chur·ri·guer·esque (chōō·rē'gər·esk') *adj.* **1** Pertaining to or in the style of **José Chur·ri·gue·ra** (chōōr'rē·gā'rä), 1650–1723, Spanish architect. **2** Highly ornate; rococo.

Chu·ru·bus·co (chōō'rōō·bōōs'kō) A suburb SE of Mexico City; site of a battle of the Mexican War, 1847.

chute (shōōt) *n.* **1** A narrow, rocky rapid in a river. **2** A sluice through a dam for logs. **3** A passageway for fish through a dam. **4** An inclined trough or slide for grain, ore, coal, mail, baggage, etc. **5** A narrow pen for branding or shipping cattle. **6** A precipitous slide in an amusement park. **7** A toboggan slide. **8** *Colloq.* A parachute. —*v.t.* & *v.i.* **chut·ed, chut·ing** To descend or cause to descend (on) a chute. ◆ Homophone: *shoot.* [< F, fall]

Chu Teh (jōō' du'), 1886–1976, Chinese Communist military leader.

chut·ney (chut'nē) *n.* A piquant relish of fruit, spices, etc. Also **chut'nee.** [<Hind. *chatni*]

chutz·pah (hōōts'pə, khōōts'-) *n. U.S. Slang* Brazen effrontery; gall. [<Yiddish <Hebrew]

Chu·vash (chōō'väsh) *n. pl.* **Chu·vash·es** or **Chu·vash 1** One of a Bulgarian people living chiefly in the Chuvash Autonomous S.S.R. **2** The Turkic language of these people.

Chuvash Autonomous S.S.R. An administrative division of central European Russian S.F.S.R.; 7,100 square miles; capital, Cheboksary.

Chu Yüan–chang (jōō' yōō·än'jäng') Imperial title of Hung Wu, 1328–98, Chinese emperor 1368–98; founder of the Ming dynasty.

Chu·zen·ji (chōō·zen·jē) A lake in central Honshu island, Japan; altitude, 4,000 feet: also *Tyuzenzi.*

chyle (kīl) *n. Physiol.* The milky emulsion of lymph and fat taken up from the intestines during digestion and passed from the thoracic duct into the veins, where it mixes with the blood. [<F <L *chylus* <Gk. *chylos* juice < *cheein* pour]—**chy·la·ceous** (kī·lā'shəs), **chy·lous** (kī'ləs) *adj.*

chyme (kīm) *n. Physiol.* The partly digested food in liquid form as it passes from the stomach into the small intestines. [<L *chymus*<Gk. *chymos* juice <*cheein* pour] —**chy·mous** (kī'məs) *adj.*

chym·ic (kim'ik), **chym·ist** (kim'ist), etc. Archaic spellings for CHEMIC, CHEMIST,

chy·mif·er·ous (kī·mif'ər·əs) *adj.* Conveying or containing chyme. [<CHYME + -(I)FEROUS]

chy·mo·sin (kī'mə·sin) *n.* Rennin. [<CHYME + (PEP)SIN]

Cia·no (chä'nō), **Count Ga·le·az·zo** (gä'lā·ät'·tsō), 1903–44, son–in–law of Mussolini; Fascist foreign minister of Italy 1936–43; executed.

Cib·ber (sib'ər), **Colley,** 1671–1757, English dramatist and poet laureate.

cib·ol (sib'əl) *n.* **1** The Welsh onion *(Allium fistulosum)* having hollow stems and a very small bulb: also spelled *sybo.* **2** The shallot. Also **cib'oule.** [<L *ciboule* <LL *cepulla* bed of onions <L *cepa* onion]

Ci·bo·la (sē'bō·lä), **Seven Cities of** See SEVEN CITIES OF CIBOLA.

ci·bo·ri·um (si·bôr'ē·əm, -bō'rē-) *n. pl.* **·bo·ri·a** (-bôr'ē·ə, -bō'rē·ə) **1** An arched canopy over an altar; especially, a baldachin supported on four pillars. **2** A receptacle for the wafers of the Eucharist. [<Med. L <Gk. *kibōrion* cup]

ci·ca·da (si·kā'də, -kä'-) *n. pl.* **·das** or **·dae** (-dē) A large homopterous insect (family *Cicadidae*), the male being equipped at the base of the abdomen with vibrating membranes and sound chambers that produce a loud, shrill sound. The larvae develop underground. Often called *locust.* [<L]

CICADA

cicada killer A digger wasp *(Sphecius speciosus)* that preys upon the cicada. For illustration see under INSECTS (beneficial).

ci·ca·la (si·kä'lə) *n.* A cicada.[<Ital.]

cic·a·tric·le (sik'ə·trik'əl), *n.* **1** *Biol.* The

germinating point in the yolk of an egg or in the embryo of a seed; the tread of an egg: also **cic·a·tri·cule** (sik′ə·tri·kyo͞ol′). **2** *Bot.* A small scar, as that left by the stem of a detached leaf. [< L *cicatricula,* dim. of *cicatrix* scar]

cic·a·trix (sik′ə·triks) *n. pl.* **cic·a·tri·ces** (sik′·ə·trī′sēz) **1** *Med.* A scar or seam consisting of new tissue formed in the healing of wounded or ulcerous parts and remaining after their cure: also **cic·a·trice** (sik′ə·tris). **2** *Biol.* A scar or scar-like marking, as that left on the interior of a bivalve shell by the attachment of the adductors, or that left by the fall of a leaf or other organ. [< L] **—cic·a·tri·cial** (sik′ə·trish′əl), **ci·cat·ri·cose** (si·kat′ri·kōs) *adj.*

cic·a·trize (sik′ə·trīz) *v.t.* & *v.i.* **·trized, ·triz·ing** To heal or become healed by the formation of a scar. **—cic′a·tri·za′tion** *n.*

cic·e·ly (sis′ə′lē) *n. pl.* **·lies** A fragrant perennial herb *(Myrrhis odorata)* of the parsley family. — **fool's-cicely** Fool's-parsley. [< L *seselis* < Gk.; infl. in form by *Cecily,* a feminine name]

cic·e·ro (sis′ə·rō) *n. Printing* A unit of typographical measurement in Europe, similar to the pica but slightly larger: from the type size used in an edition of Cicero printed in 1458.

Cic·e·ro (sis′ə·rō), **Marcus Tullius,** 106–43 B.C., Roman orator, author, and politician: sometimes called *Tully.*

cic·e·ro·ne (sis′ə·rō′nē, *Ital.* chē′chā·rô′nā) *n. pl.* **·nes,** *Ital.* **·ni** (-nē) A guide who explains to tourists and sightseers the curiosities and antiquities of a place; a local guide. [< Ital., Cicero; with ref. to the usual talkativeness of a guide]

Cic·e·ro·ni·an (sis′ə·rō′nē·ən) *adj.* Of or pertaining to Cicero or to his rhetorical style; polished; eloquent.

cich·lid (sik′lid) *n.* One of a family *(Cichlidae)* of spiny-finned, fresh-water fishes with a compressed oblong body, interrupted lateral line, and single nostril. [< NL *Cichlidae* < Gk. *kichlē,* a sea fish]

ci·cho·ri·a·ceous (si·kō′rē·ā′shəs) *adj. Bot.* Of or pertaining to the chicory family *(Cichoriaceae)* of herbs and shrubs, yielding a milky juice, which, in some species, has narcotic properties. [< NL *Cichoriaceae* < L *cichorium* chicory < Gk. *kichōrion*]

ci·cis·be·o (si·sis′bē·ō, *Ital.* chē′chēz·bā′ō) *n. pl.* **·be·i** (-bi·ē, *Ital.* -bā′ē) The acknowledged gallant of a married woman. [< Ital.]

Cid (sid, *Sp.* thēth), **the,** 1044?–99, Rodrigo Díaz, Count of Bivar, a Christian champion in the wars with the Moors in Spain; hero of a 12th century epic: also called *El Cid Campeador.*

-cidal *combining form* Killing; able to kill: *homicidal.* [< L *caedere* kill]

-cide *combining form* **1** Killer or destroyer of: *regicide.* **2** Murder or killing of: *parricide.* [def. 1 < L *-cida* killer < *caedere* kill; def. 2 < L *-cidium* slaughter < *caedere*]

ci·der (sī′dər) *n.* The expressed juice of apples used to make vinegar, and as a beverage before fermentation **(sweet cider)** or after fermentation **(hard cider)**. [< OF *sidre* < LL *sicera* strong drink < Hebrew *shēkār*]

ci-de·vant (sē·də·väṅ′) *adj. French* Former.

Cien·fue·gos (syen·fwā′gōs) A port in south central Cuba.

ci·gar (si·gär′) *n.* A small roll of tobacco leaves prepared and shaped for smoking. [< Sp. *cigarro*]

cig·a·rette (sig′ə·ret′, sig′ə·ret) *n.* **1** A small roll of finely cut tobacco in thin paper or, rarely, in tobacco leaf. **2** A similar roll with medicinal filling. Also **cig′a·ret′.** [< F, dim. of *cigare* cigar]

cigar fish A carangoid food fish *(Decapterus punctatus)* found in the West Indies and along the Atlantic Coast of the United States: also called *round robin.*

cil·i·a (sil′ē·ə) Plural of CILIUM.

cil·i·ar·y (sil′ē·er′ē) *adj.* **1** Of, pertaining to, or like cilia. **2** *Anat.* **a** Pertaining to or situated near the eyelashes. **b** Pertaining to the set of muscle fibers which are attached to ligaments supporting the lens of the eye. [< L *cilium* eyelid]

cil·i·ate (sil′ē·it, -āt) *adj. Biol.* Having cilia or motile hairlike processes: *ciliate* leaves. Also **cil′i·at′ed.** *—n. Zool.* One of a class *(Ciliata)* of infusorians possessing cilia in both young and adult stages.

cil·ice (sil′is) *n.* **1** A coarse cloth, originally made of goats' hair. **2** A shirt made of this; a hair shirt, formerly worn by monks and others in doing penance. [< F < L *cilicium* < Gk. *Kilikia* Cilicia, where the cloth was woven] **—ci·li·cious** (si·lish′əs) *adj.*

Ci·li·cia (si·lish′ə) An ancient country in SE Asia Minor: also *Little Armenia.*

Ci·li·cian (si·lish′ən) *adj.* Belonging to Cilicia. — *n.* An inhabitant or a native of Cilicia.

Cilician Gates The ancient name for GÜLEK BOGHAZ. *Latin* **Ci·li·ci·ae Py·lae** (si·lish′i·ē pī′lē).

cil·i·o·late (sil′ē·ə·lit, -lāt) *adj.* Fringed with small cilia.

cil·i·um (sil′ē·əm) *n. pl.* **cil·i·a** (sil′ē·ə) **1** *Biol.* A vibratile, microscopic, hairlike process on the surface of a cell, organ, plant, etc. **2** An eyelash. [< L, eyelid]

Ci·ma·bu·e (chē′mä·bo͞o′ā), **Giovanni,** 1240–1302, Florentine painter.

Cim·ar·ron River (sim′ə·ron′, sim′ə·rōn, -ron) A river rising in NE New Mexico and flowing 692 miles east to the Arkansas River.

Cim·bri·an Cher·so·nese (sim′brē·ən kûr′sə·nēz′) Jutland. Also **Cim·bric Chersonese** (sim′brik).

ci·mex (sī′meks) *n. pl.* **cim·i·ces** (sim′ə·sēz) An insect of the genus *Cimex;* a bedbug. [< L, bug]

cim·i·tar or **cim·i·ter** (sim′ə·tər) See SCIMITAR.

Cim·me·ri·an (si·mir′ē·ən) *adj.* Densely dark; shrouded in gloom: with reference to the **Cim·me·ri·i** (si·mir′ē·ī), a mythical people mentioned by Homer as living in perpetual darkness. *—n.* **1** One of the mythical Cimmerii. **2** A member of a nomadic tribe of the Crimea which overran Asia Minor in the seventh century B.C.

Ci·mon (sī′mən), 507?–449 B.C., Athenian general and statesman.

cinch[1] (sinch) *n. U.S.* **1** A saddle girth, as of horsehair. **2** *Colloq.* A tight grip. **3** *Slang* A sure thing; a certainty. **4** *Slang* An easy thing to do. *—v.t.* **1** To fasten a saddle girth around. **2** *Slang* To get a tight hold upon; make sure of. *—v.i.* **3** To tighten a saddle girth: often with *up.* [< Sp. *cincha* girth < L *cingula* girdle < *cingere* bind]

cinch[2] (sinch) *n.* A game of cards in which the five of trumps is the most important card. [Prob. < Sp. *cinco* five]

cin·cho·na (sin·kō′nə) *n.* **1** Any of various Peruvian trees and shrubs (genus *Cinchona*) of the madder family, now widely cultivated in India and Java as a source of quinine and related alkaloids. **2** The bark of any of these trees. [after the Countess of *Cinchón,* 1576–1639, wife of the viceroy of Peru] **—cin·chon·ic** (sin·kon′ik) *adj.*

cin·chon·i·dine (sin·kon′ə·dēn, -din) *n. Chem.* A crystalline, bitter alkaloid, $C_{19}H_{22}N_2O$, derived from cinchona, isomeric with cinchonine, but less powerful: used medicinally.

cin·cho·nine (sin′kə·nēn, -nin) *n. Chem.* A crystalline alkaloid, $C_{19}H_{22}N_2O$, derived from cinchona, similar to cinchonidine, of which it is an isomer.

cin·cho·nism (sin′kə·niz′əm) *n. Pathol.* An abnormal condition caused by overdoses of cinchona, characterized by buzzing in the head, giddiness, deafness, and temporary loss of sight.

cin·cho·nize (sin′kə·nīz) *v.t.* **·nized, ·niz·ing** To bring under the influence of cinchona or quinine. **—cin′cho·ni·za′tion** *n.*

Cin·cin·nat·i (sin′sə·nat′ē, -nat′ə) A city on the Ohio River in SW Ohio.

Cin·cin·na·tus (sin′sə·nā′təs), **Lucius Quinctius,** 519?–439 B.C., Roman patriot.

cinc·ture (singk′chər) *n.* **1** Something bound about the waist; a belt or girdle. **2** Any covering about the loins: The savages wore a *cincture* of leaves. **3** Anything that encircles or encloses; also, the act of cincturing. *—v.t.* **·tured, ·tur·ing** To surround with or as with a cincture; gird. [< L *cinctura* < *cingere* gird]

cin·der (sin′dər) *n.* **1** Any partly burned combustible substance, before it has been reduced to ashes, especially when combustion has entirely ceased. **2** A thoroughly charred bit of wood, coal, or the like; an ember. **3** *pl.* Ashes. **4** A scale of iron oxide thrown off in forging; also, light slag. **5** *pl. Geol.* Fragments of scoriaceous lava explosively ejected from a volcano during an eruption; scoria. *—v.t.* To burn or reduce to a cinder. [OE *sinder;* infl. in form by L *cinis, cineris* ash] **—cin′der·ry** *adj.*

Cin·der·el·la (sin′dər·el′ə) **1** Heroine of a fairy tale, who, though treated as a servant by her stepmother and stepsisters, is aided by her fairy godmother to attend a court ball and finally marries a prince. **2** Any girl whose beauty or merit becomes known only after a period of neglect.

cin·e·ma (sin′ə·mə) *n.* **1** A motion-picture theater. **2** A motion picture or motion pictures collectively. **3** The art or business of making or exhibiting motion pictures. [Short for CINEMATOGRAPH]

Cin·e·ma·Scope (sin′ə·mə·skōp′) *n.* A motion-picture process employing a special type of lens to project a panoramic, three-dimensional image upon a wide, curved screen: a trade name.

cin·e·mat·ic (sin′ə·mat′ik) *adj.* Of, pertaining to, or suitable for motion-picture presentation. — **cin′e·mat′i·cal·ly** *adv.*

cin·e·mat·o·graph (sin′ə·mat′ə·graf, -gräf) *n.* A camera for producing motion pictures, so constructed that a large number of separate exposures or frames are made in very rapid succession: also called *kinetograph.* — *v.t.* & *v.i.* To take photographs of (something) with a motion-picture camera: also **cin·e·ma·tize** (sin′ə·mə·tīz′). [< Gk. *kinēma, -atos* movement + -GRAPH]

cin·e·ma·tog·ra·phy (sin′ə·mə·tog′rə·fē) *n.* The art and process of making motion pictures. **—cin′e·ma·tog′ra·pher** *n.* **—cin·e·mat·o·graph·ic** (sin′ə·mat′ə·graf′ik) *adj.* **—cin′e·mat′o·graph′·i·cal·ly** *adv.*

cin·e·ma·tome (sin′ə·mə·tōm′) *n.* An apparatus by means of which very thin sections of rock or other solid material may be sliced and then photographed on motion-picture film.

ci·ne·ma ve·ri·té (sin′ə·mə ver·ə·tā′) A kind of motion-picture technique that emphasizes realism and spontaneity. [< French *cinéma-vérité* truth cinema]

cin·e·o·graph (sin′ē·ə·graf, -gräf) *n.* A motion picture; kineograph. [< Gk. *kineein* move + -GRAPH]

cin·e·ol (sin′ē·ōl, -ol) *n.* Eucalyptol. Also **cin′e·ole** (-ōl) [Transposition of NL *ole(um) cin(ae)* oil of wormwood]

Cin·e·ram·a (sin′ə·ram′ə, -rä′mə) *n.* A motion picture having a very wide angle of projection to give the effect of panoramic vision: a trade name. [< CINE(MA PANO)RAMA]

cin·e·rar·i·a (sin′ə·râr′ē·ə) *n.* A cultivated, ornamental plant *(Senecio cruentus)* of the composite family, originally from the Canary Islands, having heart-shaped leaves and showy white, red, or purple flowers. [< NL < L, fem. of *cinerarius* ashy < *cinis, cineris* ash]

cin·e·rar·i·um (sin′ə·râr′ē·əm) *n. pl.* **·rar·i·a** (-râr′ē·ə) A niche in a tomb or other place for an urn containing the ashes of a cremated body. [< L] **—cin·er·ar·y** (sin′ə·rer′ē) *adj.*

cin·er·a·tor (sin′ə·rā′tər) *n.* Incinerator.

cin·e·ri·tious (sin′ə·rish′əs) *adj.* Of the nature of ashes; ashen: said of ash-colored brain- or nerve-substance. Also **ci·ne·re·ous** (si·nir′ē·əs). [< L *cineritius* ashen]

cin·gu·lum (sing′gyə·ləm) *n. pl.* **·la** (-lə) *Zool.* A band, zone, or girdle, as of the carapace of an armadillo, of a tooth near the gum, the clitellum of an earthworm, or a raised spiral line on certain univalves. [< L < *cingere* gird] **—cin·gu·late** (sing′gyə·lit, -lāt) or **cin′·gu·lat′ed** *adj.*

cin·na·bar (sin′ə·bär) *n.* **1** A crystallized red mercuric sulfide, HgS, the chief ore of mercury. **2** A mixture formed by subliming mercury and sulfur, known as **artificial cinnabar:** used as a pigment, called *vermilion.* [< L *cinnabaris* < Gk. *kinnabari,* ult. < Persian *zinifrah*]

cinnabar lacquer Chinese carved lacquer.

cin·nam·ic (si·nam′ik, sin′ə·mik) *adj.* Of, pertaining to, or derived from cinnamon. Also **cin·na·mon·ic** (sin′ə·mon′ik).

cinnamic acid *Chem.* A colorless, crystalline, volatile compound, $C_9H_8O_2$, contained in cinnamon and various balsams, and made synthetically.

cin·na·mon (sin′ə·mən) *n.* **1** The aromatic inner bark of any of several tropical trees of the laurel family, used as a spice. **2** Any tree that yields cinnamon; especially, *Cinnamomum zeylanicum,* cultivated in Ceylon, Java, etc. **3** Cassia. **4** A shade of light reddish-brown. [<L *cinnamomum* <Gk. *kinnamōmon* <Hebrew *qinnāmōn*]

cinnamon bear A cinnamon-colored variety of the American black bear.

cinnamon stone A cinnamon-colored garnet; essonite.

cin·na·myl (sin′ə·mil) *n. Chem.* The univalent radical, C_9H_9, an important constituent of many compounds used in making soap, perfumes, drugs, etc. [<CINNAM(ON) + -YL]

cin·quain (sing·kān′) *n.* A stanza of five lines. [<F]

cinque (singk) *n.* The number five, in cards or dice; also, the throw in dice that turns up five. [<F *cinq* <L *quinque* five]

cin·que·cen·tist (ching′kwə·chen′tist) *n.* **1** An Italian artist or writer of the 16th century. **2** An imitator or student of 16th century art or style. [<Ital. *cinquecentista* <*cinquecento* five hundred, short for *mil cinque cento* fifteen hundred, i.e., the 16th century]

cin·que·cen·to (ching′kwə·chen′tō) *n.* The 16th century, especially with reference to Italy, or its art and literature; the Renaissance. [<Ital. <*(mil)cinquecento* (one thousand) five hundred]

cinque·foil (singk′foil) *n.* **1** *Archit.* A five-cusped ornament or window; a five-leaved rosette. **2** *Bot.* Any one of several species of a genus *(Potentilla)* of plants of the rose family, with five-lobed leaves. [<F <L *quinque* five + *folium* leaf]

CINQUEFOIL

cinque·pace (singk′pās) *n.* An old French dance with a five-step movement.

Cinque Ports (singk) An association of maritime towns in southern England, including Dover, Hastings, Hythe, Romney, and Sandwich, which formerly furnished men and ships for the king's service in return for special privileges. [<OF *cinq porz* five ports]

Cin·tra (sēn′trə) A town and royal residence of central Portugal: also *Sintra.*

ci·on (sī′ən) *n. Bot.* A piece cut from a plant or tree; a twig or shoot used for grafting. See SCION. [Var. of SCION]

-cion Var. of -TION.

Ci·pan·go (si·pang′gō) *Poetic* Japan: a name used by Marco Polo.

ci·pher (sī′fər) *n.* **1** The character 0, the symbol of the absence of quantity, in numerical notation; zero. **2** A person or thing of no value or importance. **3** A cryptogram made by rearranging the individual characters of a plain text or by substituting others in their place. **4** The method of making such a cryptogram; also, the key for deciphering it. **5** A monogram; a character consisting of two or more interwoven or interlaced letters. **6** Any numerical character; a number. Also spelled *cypher.* — *v.t.* **1** To calculate arithmetically. **2** To write in characters of hidden meaning; encipher. **3** To add a cipher to. — *v.i.* **4** To work out arithmetical examples. [<OF *cyfre* <Arabic *ṣifr.* Doublet of ZERO.]

cip·o·lin (sip′ə·lin) *n.* An Italian marble having layers of alternating white and green. [<F <Ital. *cipollino,* dim. of *cipolla* onion; with ref. to its layered structure]

cir·ca (sûr′kə) *prep. Latin* About; around: used to indicate approximate dates.

cir·ca·di·an (sər·kā′dē·ən) *adj. Biol.* Pertaining to or designating those vital processes in plants and animals that tend to recur in cycles of approximately 24 hours. [<L *circa* around + *dies* day]

Cir·cas·sia (sər·kash′ə, -kash′ē·ə) A region of the NW Caucasus, Russian S.F.S.R.

Cir·cas·sian (sər·kash′ən, -kash′ē·ən) *n.* **1** A person belonging to one of a group of tribes of the Caucasus region. **2** The agglutinative language of these tribes, belonging to the Northwest Caucasian group of the Caucasian languages. —*adj.* Of or pertaining to Circassia, the Circassians, or their language: also **Cir·cas·sic** (sər·kas′ik).

Circassian walnut See under WALNUT.

Cir·ce (sûr′sē) In the *Odyssey,* an enchantress who transformed the companions of Odysseus into swine by a magic drink.

Cir·ce·an (sər·sē′ən) *adj.* **1** Of, pertaining to, or characteristic of Circe. **2** Bewitching and degrading.

cir·ci·nate (sûr′sə·nāt) *adj.* **1** Ringed; ring-shaped. **2** *Bot.* Rolled inward from the apex into a coil. [<L *circinatus,* pp. of *circinare* make round <*circinus* circle] —**cir′ci·nate′ly** *adv.*

cir·cle (sûr′kəl) *n.* **1** A plane figure bounded by a curved line everywhere equally distant from the center; also, the circumference of such a figure. **2** A circular object or arrangement of objects, or whatever is included within it; an enclosure; ring; halo: a *circle* around the moon. **3** Loosely, a round or spherical body. **4** An association of persons having the same interests or pursuits; a set; class; coterie. **5** A series ending at the starting point; a repeated succession; hence, a completed series or system: the *circle* of the months. **6** A circular path or course; circuit. **7** An indirect statement; circumlocution. **8** *Logic* A form of argument in which the conclusion is virtually assumed to prove the premise and vice versa: also called *argument in a circle.* **9** In some European countries, an administrative governmental district. **10** An astronomical or other instrument whose important parts are graduated circles. **11** A circus ring. **12** A tier of seats or gallery in a theater: the dress *circle.* **13** A crown; diadem. **14** *Astron.* The orbit of a heavenly body; formerly, the supposed sphere of a planet or other body. **15** The domain of a special influence. — *v.* **·cled, ·cling** *v.t.* **1** To enclose with or as with a circle; encompass; surround. **2** To move around, as in a circle: The dog *circles* the field. — *v.i.* **3** To move in a circle; revolve. [<L *circulus,* dim. of *circus* ring] —**cir′cler** *n.*

cir·clet (sûr′klit) *n.* A small ring or ring-shaped object, especially as used as a personal ornament. [<F *cerclet,* dim. of *cercle* ring; infl. in form by CIRCLE]

cir·cuit (sûr′kit) *n.* **1** A passing or traveling round; a revolution. **2** A journey from place to place, as by a judge or clergyman, in the discharge of duties. **3** A district or route within certain limits or boundaries; especially, a division assigned to a peripatetic judge for the holding of courts at stated intervals. **4** The persons undertaking these peripatetic journeys, as the judges. **5** In the Methodist Church, and in the Evangelical Association, a district in charge of an itinerant minister. **6** Distance around; compass; circumference. **7** *Electr.* **a** The entire course traversed by an electric current. When it is complete, so that the current will flow, it is a **made** or **closed circuit;** when interrupted, so that the current stops, it is a **broken** or **open circuit. b** The complete assembly of generators, conductors, vacuum tubes, switches, etc., by which an electric current is transmitted. **8** A circuit court. See under COURT. **9** A radio transmission and reception system. —**to ride the circuit** To travel an assigned route in the capacity of minister, lawyer, judge, etc. — *v.t.* & *v.i.* To go or move in a circuit. [<F <L *circuitus* <*circumire* <*circum-* around + *ire* go]

circuit binding A style of bookbinding in which the sides of a book are made to overlap the edge of the pages to protect them from injury.

circuit breaker *Electr.* A switch or relay for breaking a circuit under specified or abnormal conditions of current flow.

circuit judge A judge of a circuit court.

cir·cu·i·tous (sər·kyōō′ə·təs) *adj.* Of the nature of a circuit; indirect; round-about. —**cir·cu′·i·tous·ly** *adv.* —**cir·cu′i·tous·ness** *n.*

circuit rider A minister who preaches at churches on a circuit or district route.

cir·cuit·ry (sûr′kit·rē) *n.* The design and arrangement of circuits in any device, instrument, or system carrying an electric current: radio *circuitry.*

cir·cu·i·ty (sər·kyōō′ə·tē) *n. pl.* **·ties 1** Movement in a circuit; circular form or movement. **2** Indirectness; round-about procedure or speech.

cir·cu·lar (sûr′kyə·lər) *adj.* **1** Forming, or bounded by, a circle; round. **2** Moving or occurring in a circle or round. **3** Ending at the point of beginning. **4** Constantly repeated in the same or similar order: *circular* motion. **5** Intended for public circulation. **6** Circuitous; devious; indirect. —*n.* A communication for general circulation; a circular letter or announcement, such as a printed advertisement. See synonyms under ROUND. [<L *circularis* <*circulus* CIRCLE] —**cir·cu·lar·i·ty** (sûr′kyə·lar′ə·tē), **cir′cu·lar·ness** *n.* —**cir′cu·lar·ly** *adv.*

cir·cu·lar·ize (sûr′kyə·lə·rīz′) *v.t.* **·ized, ·iz·ing 1** To make circular. **2** To ply with circulars. —**cir′cu·lar·i·za′tion** *n.* —**cir′cu·lar·iz′er** *n.*

circular measure A system of measurement for circles:

60 seconds of an arc (60″)	=	1 minute of an arc (1′)
60 minutes of an arc	=	1 degree (1°)
90 degrees	=	1 quadrant
4 quadrants (360°)	=	1 circle

circular mil A unit of measurement for the cross-sectional area of wires, equal to the area of a circle having a diameter of 1 mil.

circular sailing *Naut.* Sailing by the arc of a great circle: also called *great-circle sailing.*

circular saw A disk-shaped saw having a toothed edge, rotated at high speed by a motor.

circular triangle *Geom.* A triangle whose sides are formed by the arcs of a circle.

cir·cu·late (sûr′kyə·lāt) *v.* **·lat·ed, ·lat·ing** *v.t.* **1** To spread about; disseminate, as news. —*v.i.* **2** To move by a circuitous course back to the starting point, as the blood through the body. **3** To spread abroad, or become diffused. **4** *Colloq.* To travel about. **5** To repeat indefinitely a number or set of numbers in a decimal quantity. See synonyms under SPREAD. [<L *circulatus,* pp. of *circulari* form a circle <*circulus* CIRCLE] —**cir′cu·la′tor** *n.*

circulating decimal A decimal number in which one or more digits are repeated indefinitely, as 0.444 . . . , 0.16353535 . . . , 0.82437437 . . . : also called *recurring decimal, repeating decimal.*

circulating medium Currency used in exchange.

cir·cu·la·tion (sûr′kyə·lā′shən) *n.* **1** The act of circulating or state of being circulated. **2** Motion around or through something back to the starting point: the *circulation* of the blood. **3** Transmission; diffusion; dissemination. **4** The extent or amount of distribution; number of copies issued, as of a paper or periodical, etc. **5** A current medium of exchange, as coin, etc. [<L *circulatio, -onis* <*circulari.* See CIRCULATE.] —**cir′cu·la′tive** *adj.* —**cir·cu·la·to·ry** (sûr′kyə·lə·tôr′ē, -tō′rē) *adj.*

circum- *prefix*
1 About; around; on all sides; surrounding:

circumagitate	**circummigration**
circumanal	**circumnatant**
circumbasal	**circumnuclear**
circumcircle	**circumocular**
circumesophagal	**circumoral**
circumfulgent	**circumscrive**
circumgenital	**circumspheral**
circumhorizontal	**circumtropical**
circummedullary	**circumundulate**

2 Revolving around:

circumlunar	**circumsolar**

[<L *circum-* around, about <*circus* circle]

cir·cum·am·bi·ent (sûr′kəm·am′bē·ənt) *adj.* Extending or going around; encompassing. —**cir′cum·am′bi·ence, cir′cum·am′bi·en·cy** *n.*

cir·cum·am·bu·late (sûr′kəm·am′byə·lāt) *v.t.* & *v.i.* **·lat·ed, ·lat·ing** To walk around. [<L *circumambulatus,* pp. of *circumambulare* <*circum-* around + *ambulare* walk] —**cir′cum·am′bu·la′tion** *n.* —**cir′cum·am′bu·la′tor** *n.*

cir·cum·ben·di·bus (sûr′kəm·ben′di·bəs) *n.* A round-about course or method; circumlocution: a humorous usage. [Coined from L *circum* + BEND + L *-ibus*]

cir·cum·cise (sûr′kəm·sīz) *v.t.* **·cised, ·cis·ing 1** To cut off the prepuce or, in females, the inner labia of, especially as a religious rite. **2** In the Bible, to purify from sin; to cleanse spiritually. [<OF *circonciser* <L *circumcisus,*

pp. of *circumcidere* < *circum-* around + *caedere* cut] — **cir′cum·cis′er** *n.*

cir·cum·ci·sion (sûr′kəm·sizh′ən) *n.* **1** The act of circumcising; the initiatory rite of Judaism, also practiced by Moslems. **2** Figuratively, spiritual purification. **3** Those purified under this rite; the Jewish people. — **Feast of the Circumcision** The festival of the circumcision of Jesus, observed on Jan. 1.

cir·cum·fer·ence (sər·kum′fər·əns) *n.* **1** The boundary line of a circle. **2** Distance around; circuit; compass. [<L *circumferentia* < *circum-* around + *ferre* bear] — **cir·cum·fer·en·tial** (sər·kum′fər·en′shəl) *adj.* — **cir·cum′·fer·en′tial·ly** *adv.*

cir·cum·flex (sûr′kəm·fleks) *n.* A mark (ˆ ˜ ˆ) used over a letter to indicate the combination of a rising with a falling tone or to mark a long vowel, contraction, etc., or used as a diacritical mark in phonetics. In the pronunciations in this dictionary, the circumflex is used over *a* to indicate the vowel sound in *care* (kâr), over *o* for the vowel in *fall* (fôl), and over *u* for the vowel in *earn* (ûrn). — *adj.* **1** Pronounced or marked with the circumflex accent. **2** Bent in a curvilinear manner, as certain vessels and nerves. — *v.t.* **1** To utter with a circumflex intonation or accent; mark with a circumflex. **2** To wind around; bend about. [<L *circumflexus,* pp. of *circumflectere* < *circum-* around + *flectere* bend] — **cir·cum·flex·ion** (sûr′kəm·flek′shən) *n.*

cir·cum·flu·ent (sər·kum′flo͞o·ənt) *adj.* **1** Flowing around; surrounding. **2** Surrounded by, or as by, water. Also **cir·cum′flu·ous.** [<L *circumfluens, -entis,* ppr. of *circumfluere*< *circum-* around + *fluere* flow]

cir·cum·fuse (sûr′kəm·fyo͞oz′) *v.t.* **·fused, ·fus·ing** **1** To pour, scatter, or spread about. **2** To surround, as with a liquid. [<L *circumfusus,* pp. of *circumfundere* < *circum-* around + *fundere* pour] — **cir·cum·fu·sion** (sûr′kəm·(fyo͞o′zhən) *n.*

cir·cum·gy·rate (sûr′kəm·jī′rāt) *v.t.* & *v.i.* **·rat·ed, ·rat·ing** To turn or roll about. [< CIRCUM- + L *gyratus,* pp. of *gyrare* spin]

cir·cum·gy·ra·tion (sûr′kəm·jī·rā′shən) *n.* The act of turning around; rotation; motion in a circular course. — **cir·cum·gy·ra·to·ry** (sûr′·kəm·jī′rə·tôr′ē, -tō′rē) *adj.*

cir·cum·ja·cent (sûr′kəm·jā′sənt) *adj.* Bordering on all sides; surrounding. [<L *circumjacens, -entis,* ppr. of *circumjacere* < *circum-* around + *jacere* lie] — **cir′cum·ja′cence, cir′·cum·ja′cen·cy** *n.*

cir·cum·lo·cu·tion (sûr′kəm·lō·kyo͞o′shən) *n.* Indirect or round-about expression; the use of superfluous words. [<L *circumlocutio, -onis* < *circum-* around + *locutio* speaking < *loqui* speak] — **cir·cum·loc·u·tory** (sûr′kəm·lok′yə·tôr′ē, -tō′rē) *adj.*

Synonyms (noun): diffuseness, periphrasis, pleonasm, prolixity, redundance, redundancy, surplusage, tautology, tediousness, verbiage, verbosity, wordiness. *Circumlocution* is the more common, *periphrasis* the more technical word. *Diffuseness* is a scattering both of words and thought; *redundance* or *redundancy* is an overflow. *Prolixity* goes into endless petty details, without selection or perspective. *Pleonasm* may be an emphatic, *tautology* is a useless repetition of a word or words. "I saw it with my eyes" is a *pleonasm*; "all the members agreed unanimously" is *tautology*. *Verbiage* is the use of mere words without thought. *Verbosity* and *wordiness* denote an excess of words in proportion to the thought. *Antonyms*: brevity, compactness, conciseness, condensation, directness, succinctness, terseness.

cir·cum·mure (sûr′kəm·myo͝or′) *v.t.* **·mured, mur·ing** To wall around. [<CIRCUM- + LL *murare* build a wall <L *murus* wall]

cir·cum·nav·i·gate (sûr′kəm·nav′ə·gāt) *v.t.* **·gat·ed, ·gat·ing** To sail around. [<L *circumnavigatus,* pp. of *circumnavigare* < *circum-* around + *navigare* sail] — **cir·cum·nav·i·ga·ble** (sûr′kəm·nav′ə·gə·bəl) *adj.* — **cir′cum·nav′i·ga′tion** *n.* — **cir′cum·nav′i·ga′tor** *n.*

cir·cum·nu·ta·tion (sûr′kəm·nyo͞o·tā′shən) *n.* *Bot.* A nodding or turning successively in all directions, as observed in the tips of young and growing plant organs, such as tendrils, stems, or roots. [<CIRCUM- + L *nutatio, -onis* a nodding < *nutare* nod]

cir·cum·po·lar (sûr′kəm·pō′lər) *adj.* Near or surrounding one of the terrestrial or celestial poles: applied specifically to stars revolving about the pole without setting.

cir·cum·pose (sûr′kəm·pōz′) *v.t.* **·posed, ·pos·ing** To place around. — **cir·cum·po·si·tion** (sûr′kəm·pə·zish′ən) *n.*

cir·cum·ro·tate (sûr′kəm·rō′tāt) *v.i.* **·tat·ed, ·tat·ing** To turn in the manner of a wheel; revolve. — **cir·cum·ro·ta·to·ry** (sûr′kəm·rō′·tə·tôr′ē, -tō′rē), **cir′cum·ro′ta·ry** (-rō′tə·rē) *adj.* — **cir′cum·ro·ta′tion** *n.*

cir·cum·scis·sile (sûr′kəm·sis′il) *adj.* *Bot.* Dehiscent, as a capsule, in a transverse circular line, so that the top separates like a lid, as in the common purslane. [<L *circumscissus,* pp. of *circumscindere* < *circum-* around + *scindere* cut]

cir·cum·scribe (sûr′kəm·skrīb′) *v.t.* **·scribed, scrib·ing** **1** To draw a line or figure around; encircle. **2** To mark out the limits of; define. **3** To confine within bounds; restrict. **4** *Geom.* **a** To surround with or as with a figure that touches at every possible point: to *circumscribe* a triangle with a circle. **b** To cause to surround a figure thus: to *circumscribe* a circle about a triangle. [<L *circumscribere* < *circum-* around + *scribere* write] — **cir′·cum·scrib′a·ble** *adj.* — **cir′cum·scrib′er** *n.*

Synonyms: bound, confine, define, delineate, describe, designate, enclose, fence, limit, restrict. See RESTRAIN. *Antonyms*: dilate, distend, enlarge, expand, open.

cir·cum·scrip·tion (sûr′kəm·skrip′shən) *n.* **1** The act of circumscribing. **2** The state of being limited or bounded; limitation; restriction. **3** The line marking the external boundary of an object; surrounding margin or edge; periphery. **4** The space or district circumscribed. **5** *Obs.* Definition; description. **6** *Obs.* Something written around, as an inscription surrounding a coin. [<L *circumscriptio, -onis* < *circumscribere.* See CIRCUMSCRIBE.] — **cir′cum·scrip′tive** *adj.*

cir·cum·so·lar (sûr′kəm·sō′lər) *adj.* Near, revolving about, or surrounding, the sun.

cir·cum·spect (sûr′kəm·spekt) *adj.* Attentive to everything; watchful in all directions, as against danger or error; cautious; wary. See synonyms under THOUGHTFUL. [<L *circumspectus,* pp. of *circumspicere* < *circum-* around + *specere* look] — **cir′cum·spect′ly** *adv.* — **cir′cum·spect′ness** *n.*

cir·cum·spec·tion (sûr′kəm·spek′shən) *n.* Cautious and careful observation with a view to wise conduct. See synonyms under CARE, PRUDENCE.

cir·cum·spec·tive (sûr′kəm·spek′tiv) *adj.* Cautious; watchful.

cir·cum·stance (sûr′kəm·stans) *n.* **1** Something existing or occurring incidentally to some other fact or event; a related or concomitant act or thing; an accessory detail. **2** An event, happening, or fact, especially if incidental or subordinate: a *circumstance* in English history. **3** *pl.* The surrounding facts, means, influences, etc., especially as related to one's support and way of living. **4** Environment: He is the victim of *circumstance*; also, environment with reference to state or condition resulting from adventitious surroundings. **5** That which is unessential or of no account; detail; circumstantiality. **6** *Archaic* Formal show or display; ceremony; pomp. — **under no circumstances** Never; under no conditions. — **under the circumstances** Since such is the case; things being as they are or were. — *v.t.* **·stanced, ·stanc·ing** **1** To place in or under limiting circumstances or conditions: chiefly in past participle. **2** *Obs.* To set forth circumstantially; relate with details. [<OF <L *circumstantia* < *circumstare* < *circum-* around + *stare* stand]

Synonyms (noun): accompaniment, concomitant, detail, event, fact, feature, incident, item, occurrence, particular, point, position, situation. A *circumstance* is something existing or occurring in connection with or relation to some other fact or event, modifying or throwing light upon the principal matter without affecting its essential character; an *accompaniment* is something that unites with the principal matter, but is not necessary to it; as, the piano *accompaniment* to a song; a *concomitant* goes with a thing in natural connection, but in a subordinate capacity, or perhaps in contrast. A *circumstance* is not strictly, nor usually, an occasion, condition, effect, or result. Nor is the *circumstance* properly an *incident.* All the *circumstances* make up the *situation.* Compare ACCIDENT, CAUSE, EVENT.

cir·cum·stanced (sûr′kəm·stanst) *adj.* **1** Being in or under certain conditions. **2** Supported by conditions, facts, details, etc., as an argument.

cir·cum·stan·tial (sûr′kəm·stan′shəl) *adj.* **1** Consisting of details; minute; particular. **2** Pertaining to or dependent on circumstances; indirect; presumptive. **3** Having to do with one's circumstances: *circumstantial* prosperity. **4** Incidental or casual; not essential. **5** *Archaic* Full of circumstance or display; ceremonial. See synonyms under MINUTE, PARTICULAR.

circumstantial evidence See under EVIDENCE.

cir·cum·stan·ti·al·i·ty (sûr′kəm·stan′shē·al′·ə·tē) *n.* *pl.* **·ties** **1** The quality or characteristic of being particular, detailed, or minute. **2** A particular matter; a detail.

cir·cum·stan·tial·ly (sûr′kəm·stan′shəl·ē) *adv.* At length; minutely.

cir·cum·stan·ti·ate (sûr′kəm·stan′shē·āt) *v.t.* **·at·ed, ·at·ing** To set forth or establish by circumstances or in detail.

cir·cum·val·late (sûr′kəm·val′āt) *v.t.* **·lat·ed, ·lat·ing** To surround with a rampart or a trench. — *adj.* Enclosed by or as by a wall or rampart: *circumvallate* papillae. [<L *circumvallatus,* pp. of *circumvallare* < *circum-* around + *vallare* fortify < *vallum* rampart] — **cir′cum·val·la′tion** *n.*

cir·cum·vent (sûr′kəm·vent′) *v.t.* **1** To get around; get the better of, as by craft, artifice, or fraud; outwit. **2** To surround or entrap, as an enemy, by craft or strategem. **3** To pass around: to *circumvent* a town. **4** To forestall (an occurrence or happening). See synonyms under BAFFLE, DECEIVE. [<L *circumventus,* pp. of *circumvenire* < *circum-* around + *venire* come] — **cir′cum·ven′tive** *adj.* — **cir′·cum·ven′tion** *n.*

cir·cum·ven·tor (sûr′kəm·ven′tər) *n.* **1** One who circumvents. **2** A surveying instrument having at the top a compass box, used for laying out horizontal angles. Also **cir′cum·vent′er.**

cir·cum·vo·lu·tion (sûr′kəm·və·lo͞o′shən) *n.* **1** The act of winding. **2** A single fold or turn of something wound. **3** A turning round an axis or center; rotation; revolution. **4** Convolution; sinuosity. [<L *circumvolutus,* pp. of *circumvolvere* < *circum-* around + *volvere* turn, spin]

cir·cum·volve (sûr′kəm·volv′) *v.t.* & *v.i.* **·volved, ·volv·ing** To revolve.

cir·cus (sûr′kəs) *n.* **1** A traveling show in which feats of horsemanship, tumbling, and strength, as well as clowns, wild animals, etc., are exhibited; also, a performance of such a show. **2** The circular, tented enclosure in which such a show is commonly held. **3** The troupe of performers in such a show. **4** In ancient Rome, a large oval or oblong enclosure with tiers of seats around it, used for races, games, etc. **5** *Brit.* A circle formed by bow-shaped rows of houses. **6** *Colloq.* Any person or thing regarded as uproariously entertaining. [<L, a ring, racecourse <Gk. *kirkos.* Doublet of CIRQUE.]

Cir·cus Max·i·mus (sûr′kəs mak′si·məs) A large arena built around 330 B.C. in ancient Rome, used for chariot races, gladiatorial contests, etc.

Ci·re·na·i·ca (chē′rā·nä′ē·kä) The Italian name for CYRENAICA.

Ci·ren·ces·ter (sis′i·tər, sī′rən·ses′tər) An urban district of SE Gloucestershire, England; site of Roman ruins.

Ci·re·ne (chē·rā′nā) Italian name for CYRENE.

Ci·ri·lo (thē·rē′lō) Spanish form of CYRIL. Also *Ital.* **Ci·ril·lo** (chē·rēl′lō).

cirque (sûrk) *n.* **1** A circular enclosure; circus. **2** *Geol.* A circular valley with precipitous walls, usually formed by the action of glaciers. **3** A circlet; ring: a poetical usage. [<F <L *circus.* Doublet of CIRCUS.]

cir·rate (sir′āt) *adj.* Having curls or cirri. [<L *cirratus* <*cirrus* curl]

cir·rho·sis (si·rō′sis) *n. Pathol.* An abnormal formation of connective tissue, with wasting of the proper tissue of the liver or other organ. [<NL <Gk. *kirrhos* tawny; with ref. to the color of the cirrhotic liver] —**cir·rhot·ic** (si·rot′ik) *adj.*

cir·ri (sir′ī) Plural of CIRRUS.

cir·ri·ped (sir′ə·ped) *n.* One of an order *(Cirripedia)* of crustaceans which become attached or parasitic in the adult stage, as the barnacles. —*adj.* Of or pertaining to this order.

cirro– *combining form* Cirrus: *cirrostratus.* Also **cirri–.** [<L *cirrus* curl]

cir·ro·cu·mu·lus (sir′ō·kyōō′myə·ləs) *n. Meteorol.* A mass of fleecy, globular cloudlets in contact with one another, with an average height of 5 miles; mackerel sky. —**cir′ro·cu′mu·lar** or **cir′ro·cu′mu·lous** or **cir·ro·cu·mu·la·tive** (sir′ō·kyōō′myə·lā′tiv, -lə·tiv) *adj.*

cir·ro·stra·tus (sir′ō·strā′təs) *n. Meteorol.* A fine, whitish veil of cloud with an average height of 6 miles. —**cir′ro·stra′tive** *adj.*

cir·rous (sir′əs) *adj.* **1** Having or like cirri. **2** Of or pertaining to a cirrus cloud. Also **cir·rose** (sir′ōs).

cir·rus (sir′əs) *n. pl.* **cir·ri** (sir′ī) **1** *Meteorol.* A type of white, wispy cloud, usually consisting of ice crystals and having an average height of 7 miles, seen in tufts or feathery–shaped bands across the sky. **2** *Bot.* A tendril. **3** *Zool.* A threadlike appendage serving as an organ of touch. [<L, ringlet]

cir·soid (sûr′soid) *adj.* Resembling a varix; varicose. [<Gk. *kirsos* a dilated vein]

cir·sot·o·my (sər·sot′ə·mē) *n. Surg.* The incision of varicose veins. [<Gk. *kirsos* dilated vein + -TOMY]

Cis (sis) Diminutive of CECILIA. Also **Cis′sie.**

cis– *prefix* **1** On this side of: opposed to TRANS– or ULTRA–: *cisatlantic.* **2** Since; following: opposed to PRE–: *cis–Elizabethan.* [<L *cis* on this side]

cis·al·pine (sis·al′pīn, -pin) *adj.* On the Roman side of the Alps. [<L *cisalpinus* <*cis* on this side + *Alpes* the Alps]

Cisalpine Gaul An ancient name for northern Italy.

cis·at·lan·tic (sis′ət·lan′tik) *adj.* On this side of the Atlantic: opposed to *transatlantic.*

Cis·cau·ca·sia (sis′kô·kā′zhə, -shə) See NORTHERN CAUCASUS.

cis·co (sis′kō) *n. pl.* **·coes** or **·cos** A whitefish (genus *Leucichthys)* of North America; especially, the lake herring *(L. artedi)* of Lakes Michigan and Ontario. [? <N. Am. Ind.]

cis·lu·nar (sis·lōō′nər) *adj.* On this side of the moon.

cis·mon·tane (sis·mon′tān) *adj.* **1** On this side of the mountains. **2** Cisalpine. Opposed to *ultramontane.* [<L *cismontanus* <*cis* on this side + *mons, montis* a mountain]

cis·soid (sis′oid) *Math. n.* A curve *GAP* intersecting a circle at the two extremities of a diameter and having a cusp the apex of which is at the point on the circumference where the perpendicular bisector of the diameter falls: the curve traces the locus of a point moving so that a straight line *BC* drawn through the apex of the cusp at *A* through the curve at any point *P* intersects the tangent *DEF* (with *E* on the circumference diametrically opposite to *A*) at point *M*, so that *AP* = *NM*. —*adj.* Contained within two curves that intersect each other, as an angle: opposed to *sistroid*: The angle interior to both curves is a *cissoid* angle; the exterior and opposite a *sistroid.* [<Gk. *kissoeidēs* like ivy <*kissos* ivy + *eidos* form]

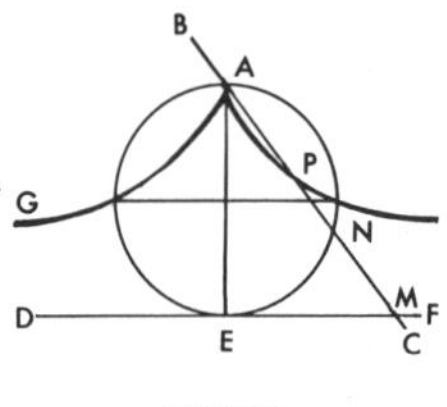

CISSOID

cist[1] (sist) *n.* A casket; box. [<L *cista* CHEST]

cist[2] (sist, kist) *n.* A small sepulchral chamber, or chest, made of flat stones; a kistvaen. [<Welsh, chest <L *cista* chest]

cis·ta·ceous (sis·tā′shəs) *adj. Bot.* Designating the rockrose family *(Cistaceae)* of shrubby or herbaceous plants, with regular, perfect, often showy flowers. [<NL *Cistaceae* <Gk. *kistos* rockrose]

Cis·ter·cian (sis·tûr′shən) *n.* A monk of an order founded in 1098 at Cistercium (modern *Cîteaux*), France, as an offshoot of the Benedictines. —*adj.* Of or pertaining to this order.

cis·tern (sis′tərn) *n.* **1** A reservoir, usually of masonry, wood, or metal, for storing water or other liquids; also, any natural reservoir. **2** Any analogous receptacle in which fluid is stored. **3** *Anat.* A large lymph space; a sac. [<OF *cisterne* <L *cisterna* <*cista* chest]

cis·tus (sis′təs) *n.* A plant of a genus *(Cistus)* of European evergreen shrubs of the rockrose family: gum ladanum is produced by several species. [<Gk. *kistos* rockrose]

cist·vaen (kist′vīn) See KISTVAEN.

cit (sit) *n. Archaic* A resident of a city; citizen.

cit·a·del (sit′ə·dəl, -del) *n.* **1** A fortress commanding a city. **2** Any strong fortress. **3** The heavily plated central casemate containing the guns in a war vessel. See synonyms under FORTIFICATION. [<F *citadelle* <Ital. *cittadella,* dim. of *città* city]

ci·ta·tion (sī·tā′shən) *n.* **1** The act of citing, or a passage quoted. **2** A public commendation for exceptional military conduct or achievement. **3** *Law* A judicial summons. **4** Recounting; enumeration. [<F <L *citatio, -onis* <*citare* CITE] —**ci·ta·to·ry** (sī′tə·tôr′ē, -tō′rē) *adj.*

cite (sīt) *v.t.* **cit·ed, cit·ing 1** To quote or refer to as an authority, illustration, or exemplification for proof or support. **2** To refer to specifically, as in a military report. **3** *Law* To summon to appear, as before a tribunal. See synonyms under ALLEGE, ARRAIGN, QUOTE. ◆ Homophones: *sight, site.* [<F *citer* <L *citare,* freq. of *cire* call] —**cit′a·ble, cite′a·ble** *adj.*

Ci·thae·ron (si·thē′ron) A mountain of east central Greece, regarded as sacred to Dionysus; 4,623 feet: Greek *Kithairon.* Formerly **El·a·ti·as** (el′ə·tī′əs).

cith·a·ra (sith′ə·rə) *n.* **1** An ancient Greek stringed instrument with a wooden case, the strings extending to the base from a crosspiece connecting the straight hollow arms: the instrument of professional musicians. **2** Loosely, any of the stringed instruments of ancient Greece. Also spelled *kithara.* [<L <Gk. *kithara.* Doublet of GUITAR and ZITHER.]

CITHARA

cith·er (sith′ər) *n.* **1** A zither. **2** A cithern. **3** A cithara.

cith·ern (sith′ərn) *n.* A medieval lute or guitar having wire strings plucked with a plectrum: the original of the zither: also spelled *cittern, zittern.* [Blend of CITHER and GITTERN]

cit·i·fied (sit′i·fīd) *adj.* Having the ways and means of city life; following city fashions: also spelled *cityfied.*

cit·i·zen (sit′ə·zən) *n.* **1** A native or naturalized person owing allegiance to, and entitled to protection from, a government: opposed to *alien.* **2** A resident of a city or town. **3** A private person; one who is not a public officer nor a soldier; a civilian. [<AF *citezein,* var. of OF *citeain* <*cité* CITY] —**cit′i·zen·ess** *n. fem.*

cit·i·zen·ry (sit′ə·zən·rē) *n.* Citizens collectively.

cit·i·zen·ship (sit′ə·zən·ship′) *n.* The status of a citizen, with its rights and duties; state of being a citizen.

Cit·lal·té·petl (sēt′läl·tā′pet·l) See ORIZABA, PICO DE.

citra– *prefix* On this side; cis–. [<L]

cit·ral (sit′rəl) *n. Chem.* An oily liquid aldehyde, $C_{10}H_{16}O$, contained in geranium, lemon, and other oils: used as a flavoring extract and in perfumery; geranial. [<CITR(US) + AL(DEHYDE)]

cit·rate (sit′rāt, -rit, sī′trāt) *n. Chem.* A salt of citric acid.

cit·re·ous (sit′rē·əs) *adj.* Having the yellow color of a citron or lemon; citrine. [<L *citreus* <*citrus* citron tree]

cit·ric (sit′rik) *adj.* Derived from lemons, oranges, or similar fruits.

citric acid *Chem.* A white, crystalline, sharply sour compound, $C_6H_8O_7$, contained in various fruits, and obtained from lemons, limes, and sour oranges, etc., and also made synthetically.

cit·ri·cul·ture (sit′ri·kul′chər) *n.* The cultivation of oranges, lemons, grapefruit, and other citrus fruits. —**cit′ri·cul′tur·ist** *n.*

cit·rin (sit′rin) *n. Biochem.* A constituent of vitamin P, consisting of a mixture of glycosides and occurring in citrus fruits.

cit·rine (sit′rin) *adj.* **1** Having the yellow color of a citron or lemon. **2** Pertaining to the citron, lemon, and allied trees. —*n.* **1** Citron color. **2** A light–yellow, vitreous variety of quartz so fused as to resemble topaz. [<F *citrin*]

cit·ron (sit′rən) *n.* **1** A fruit like a lemon, but larger and less acid. **2** The tree *(Citrus medica)* producing this fruit. **3** A watermelon *(Citrullus vulgaris citroides),* with a small, hard–fleshed fruit. **4** The rind of either of these fruits, preserved and used in confections. [<F <Ital. *citrone* <L *citrus* citrus tree]

cit·ron·el·la (sit′rə·nel′ə) *n.* A grass *(Cymbopogon nardus)* cultivated in Ceylon, yielding **citronella oil,** which is used in perfumery, in cooking for flavoring, and as protection against mosquitos. Also **citronella grass.** [<NL <CITRON; so called from its odor]

cit·ron·el·lal (sit′rə·nel′al) *n. Chem.* An unsaturated aldehyde, $C_9H_{17}CHO$, found in citronella oil and other essential oils: used in making soaps and perfumes.

citron wood 1 The wood of the sandarac tree, used in cabinetwork. **2** The wood of the citron tree.

cit·rus (sit′rəs) *adj.* Of or pertaining to a genus *(Citrus)* of trees or shrubs of the rue family, cultivated for their fruits. Also **cit′rous.** [<L, citron tree]

citrus fruits Fruits of the genus *Citrus*: the orange, lemon, lime, citron, grapefruit, etc.

Cit·tà del Va·ti·ca·no (chēt·tä′ del vä′tē·kä′nō) The Italian name for VATICAN CITY.

Cit·tà Vec·chia (chēt·tä′ vek′kyä) The Maltese name of MDINA. Also **Città No·ta·bi·le** (nō·tä′bē·lā).

cit·tern (sit′ərn) See CITHERN.

cit·y (sit′ē) *n. pl.* **cit·ies 1** A place inhabited by a large, permanent, organized community. **2** In the United States and Canada, a municipality of the first class, governed by a mayor and aldermen and created by charter. **3** Any one of the ancient Greek city–states. **4** The people of a city, collectively. **5** In ancient times, a citadel or central walled section used by the dwellers in a district as a market, a place of worship or festivity, and a refuge in time of invasion. —**The City** That part of London which is governed by the Lord Mayor and corporation; also, the financial center of this district. [<F *cité* <L *civitas* <*civis* citizen]

city block 1 A division of a city bounded by four streets. **2** A unit of measure as long as this. **3** The distance along one side of it.

cit·y–bred (sit′ē·bred′) *adj.* Brought up in a city.

city editor On a newspaper, the editor having charge of the city news and the reportorial staff.

city father One who directs the public affairs of a city; a mayor, councilman, etc.

cit·y·fied (sit′i·fīd) See CITIFIED.

city hall 1 An administrative building of a city in which the chief government offices are situated. **2** The city government presently in office. **3** Bureaucratic procedures or officials characterized as obstinately unresponsive: Go fight *city hall.*

city manager An administrator not publicly elected but appointed by a city council to act as manager of the city.

City of God Heaven.

City of Seven Hills Rome.

city planning Public control of the physical development of a city, as by regulation of the size and use of buildings and streets, location of parks and public facilities, etc.

cit·y·scape (sit′ē·skāp′) *n.* A view of a city, as in a painting.

cit·y–state (sit′ē·stāt′) *n.* A state consisting of an independent city, having sovereignty over contiguous territories, as in ancient Greece.

cit·y·ward (sit′ē·wərd) *adj.* Directed toward the city. —*adv.* In the direction of the city.

Ciu·dad Bo·lí·var (syōō·thäth′ bō·lē′vär) A port on the Orinoco, SE Venezuela.

Ciudad Juá·rez (hwä′rās) A city in northern Mexico, on the Rio Grande; formerly *El Paso del Norte.* Also **Juárez.**

Ciudad Tru·jil·lo (trōō·hē′yō) The name of

the capital of the Dominican Republic from 1936–61, when its original name of Santo Domingo was restored.

Ciudad Vic·to·ria (vēk·tō′ryä) The capital of Tamaulipas state, Mexico.

civ·et (siv′it) *n.* **1** A substance of musklike odor, secreted by certain glands of the civet cat: used as a perfume. **2** A foxlike carnivore of Africa (genus *Viverra*), dark grey in color and banded and spotted with black, that secretes this substance: also **civet cat.** **3** The fur of this animal. See ZIBET. [< MF *civette* < Arabic *zabād*]

civ·ic (siv′ik)*adj.* Of or pertaining to a city, a citizen, or citizenship; civil. [< L *civicus* < *civis* citizen]

civ·ics (siv′iks) *n.* The science of government.

civ·il (siv′əl) *adj.* **1** Observing the social proprieties; decently polite; not rude. **2** Of or pertaining to civil or everyday life: distinguished from *ecclesiastical, naval, military.* **3** Pertaining to citizens or to the state, or to relations between the citizen and the state or between citizens, as regulated by law; belonging to private legal rights; established by law: distinguished from *criminal, political,* or *natural*: civil rights. **4** Occurring within the state or between citizens; intestine: *civil* war. **5** In accordance with the requirements of civilization; civilized. **6** Of or pertaining to civil law. See CIVIL LAW. See synonyms under POLITE. [< F < L *civilis* < *civis* citizen] **—civ′il·ly** *adv.*

civil day See CIVIL TIME under TIME

civil death The total deprivation of civil rights and standing, as by life imprisonment, etc.

civil defense A program of action by civilians for the protection of the population and the maintenance of essential services in the event of overt enemy action, as nuclear bombardment.

civil disobedience Passive resistance.

civil engineer A professional engineer trained to design and build roads, bridges, tunnels, harbors, canals, docks, irrigation systems, and other public works.

ci·vil·ian (sə·vil′yən) *n.* **1** One who follows the pursuits of civil life, as distinguished from military, naval, or clerical. **2** *Obs.* One learned in the Roman or civil law. *—adj.* Of or pertaining to a civilian or civil life. [< OF *civilien* < L *civilis.* See CIVIL.]

ci·vil·i·ty (sə·vil′ə·tē) *n. pl.* **·ties 1** The quality of being civil; courtesy; cold or formal politeness. **2** A civil act or speech. **3** *pl.* The amenities of social life. See synonyms under FAVOR.

civ·i·li·za·tion (siv′ə·lə·zā′shən, -lī·zā′-) *n.* **1** The state of human society regarded as having reached a high level of intellectual, social, and cultural development. **2** The countries and peoples considered to have reached this stage. **3** A stage in the cultural development of any specific people, country, or geographical region: Greek *civilization;* a primitive *civilization.* See CULTURE.

civ·i·lize (siv′ə·līz) *v.t.* **·lized, ·liz·ing** To bring into a state of civilization; educate from savagery; refine. Also *Brit.* **civ′i·lise. —civ′i·lized** *adj.* **—civ′i·liz′er** *n.*

civil law See under LAW[1].

civil liberty Freedom of the individual citizen from government control or restraint of, or interference with, his property, opinions, or affairs, except as the public good may require.

civil list 1 That part of the revenue annually appropriated in the United States for the salaries and expenses of civil officers and the government. **2** The body of such officers. **3** In Great Britain and elsewhere, the amount voted by the legislature for the personal and household expenses of the sovereign.

civil marriage A marriage solemnized as a civil contract, as distinguished from an ecclesiastical marriage considered as a sacrament.

civil rights Private, non-political privileges; specifically, exemption from involuntary servitude, as established by the 13th and 14th amendments to the U.S. Constitution and by certain acts of Congress.

civil servant One employed in the civil service.

civil service 1 The branches of governmental service that are neither military, naval, legislative, or judicial. **2** The body of persons employed in these branches.

civil time See under TIME.

civil war War between parties of the same government, between states within a nation, between fellow citizens, etc.

Civil War See table under WAR.

civ·ism (siv′iz·əm) *n.* Devotion to the public weal; good citizenship.

Ci·vi·ta·vec·chia (chē·vē·tä·vek′kyä) A city on the Tyrrhenian Sea, the chief port for Rome.

Cl *Chem.* Chlorine (symbol Cl).

clab·ber[1] (klab′ər) *n.* Milk curdled by souring. *—v.t. & v.i.* To curdle, as milk. [Short for BONNYCLABBER]

clab·ber[2] (klab′ər) *n.* Mire; mud. [< Irish *clabar*]

clach·an (klakh′ən) *n. Scot.* A Highland hamlet; also, a village inn or a village church. Also **clach** (klakh).

clack (klak) *v.t.* **1** To strike together so as to make a cracking sound; clap; rattle. **2** To utter heedlessly; babble. *—v.i.* **3** To make a rattling, clapping, or cracking sound. **4** To talk hastily or continually; chatter. **5** To cluck or cackle, as a hen. *—n.* **1** A sharp, short, clapping sound, or something producing it. **2** Continual and confused talk; chatter. **3** *Slang* The tongue: Hold your *clack*; hence, a gossip. [Imit.] **—clack′er** *n.*

Clack·man·nan (klak·man′ən) A country in east central Scotland; 54.6 square miles; county seat, Clackmannan. Also **Clack·man′nan·shire** (-shir).

clack valve *Mech.* A valve hinged at one edge, permitting flow of fluid in one direction only. See illustration under HYDRAULIC.

Clac·to·ni·an (klak·tō′nē·ən) *adj. Anthropol.* Pertaining to a culture stage of the Lower Paleolithic, roughly contemporaneous with the Abbevillian but characterized by stone tools of a more advanced flake type. [from *Clacton,* England, where artifacts were found]

clad (klad) Past tense of CLOTHE. *—adj.* Clothed.

cla·dis·tics (klə·dis′tiks) *n.* A branch of biology dealing with the evolutionary interrelationships of organisms. [< Gk. *klados* sprout + (STAT)ISTICS]

clad·o·phyll (klad′ə·fil) *n. Bot.* A leaflike branch stemming from the axil of a leaf. Also **clad·ode** (klad′ōd). [< Gk. *klados* branch + *phyllos* leaf]

claim (klām) *v.t.* **1** To demand on the ground or right; affirm to be one's due; assert ownership or title to. **2** To hold to be true against implied denial or doubt. **3** To require or deserve: The problem *claims* our attention. *—v.i.* **4** To derive a right; make a claim, especially by descent: He *claims* from royal lineage. See synonyms under ALLEGE, ASSERT, ASSUME, DEMAND. *—n.* **1** The demand for something as due or on the ground of right; the assertion of a right; a right or title. **2** An assertion, as of a fact. **3** A tract of government land, petitioned for, marked out, and claimed by a settler. **4** A piece of public land staked out by a miner to be worked by him. See synonyms under RIGHT. **—Court of Claims** See under COURT. [< OF *clamer* call, claim < L *clamare* declare] **—claim′a·ble** *adj.* **—claim′er** *n.*

claim·ant (klā′mənt) *n.* One who makes a legal claim or asserts a right, title, etc.

claiming race A horse race in which any horse entered is subject to the claim of right to buy for a given price by any registrant starting a horse in that meeting

claim-jum·per (klām′jum′pər) *n.* One who seizes another's claim.

clair de lune (klâr′ də lün′) **1** In ceramics, a faint, grayish-blue glaze applied to certain varieties of Chinese porcelain. **2** The color of this glaze. [< F, moonlight] **—clair′-de-lune′** *adj.*

Claire (klâr) French form of CLARA.

clair-ob·scure (klâr′əb·skyoor′) See CHIAROSCURO.

clair·schach (klär′shäkh) *n.* An ancient Irish harp; especially, a festival harp having from 29 to 58 strings. [< Irish *clairseach* harp]

clair·voy·ance (klâr·voi′əns) *n.* **1** The ability to see things not visible to the normal human eye; second sight. **2** Intuitive sagacity or perception; mind-reading. [< F] **—clair·voy′ant** *adj. & n.*

claise (klāz) *n. Scot.* Clothes. Also **claithes** (klāz).

claith (klāth) *n. Scot.* Cloth.

clam[1] (klam) *n.* **1** Any of various bivalve mollusks; especially, the edible quahog of North Atlantic American coasts, and the **long** or **soft clam** *(Mya arenaria)* of the southern Atlantic coasts. **2** *U.S. Colloq.* An uncommunicative person. **—giant clam** A huge bivalve mollusk *(Tridacna gigas)* of the Indian and Pacific Oceans: the shell may exceed 3 feet in length and weigh more than 500 pounds. *—v.i.* **clammed, clam·ming** to hunt for or dig clams. **—to clam up** *U.S. Slang* To maintain silence, as a criminal under interrogation. [Short for *clamshell* < *clam* a clamp, OE *clamm* + SHELL]

GIANT CLAM

clam[2] (klam) *Brit. Dial. v.t.* To smear with a sticky substance; glue or stick: to *clam* paper to the wall. *—v.i.* To be sticky or clammy; be damp or cold. *—adj.* Sticky. *—n.* **1** Clamminess; cold dampness. **2** A sticky substance. [Cf. OE *clæman* smear, Du. *klam* sticky]

clam[3] (klam) *n.* A clamp, as of bricks. [OE *clamm* grip, grasp]

clam[4] (klam) *Brit. n.* The simultaneous ringing of all the bells in a chime; hence, clangor; clamor. *—v.i.* **1** To ring all the bells of a chime together. **2** To muffle or jangle a bell. [Imit.]

cla·mant (klā′mənt) *adj.* **1** Calling for help or remedy; crying; insistent. **2** Clamorous; resounding: a poetic usage. [< L *clamans, -antis,* ppr. of *clamare* cry out]

clam·a·to·ri·al (klam′ə·tôr′ē·əl, -tō′rē) *adj. Ornithol.* Relating to a suborder *(Clamatores)* of raucous-voiced passerine birds, as the kingbirds. [< NL *Clamatores* < L *clamare* cry out]

clam·bake (klam′bāk′) *n.* **1** A picnic where roasted clams are the principal dish: especially common at the seashore in New England, where the clams, often with other articles of food, are usually cooked on hot stones, sometimes in a hole covered with seaweed. **2** The meal served at such a picnic. **3** *U.S. Slang* A radio broadcast that breaks down because of bad handling and mistakes; any poor broadcast. **4** *U.S. Slang* An informal gathering of jazz musicians to improvise music for their own enjoyment.

clam·ber (klam′bər) *v.t. & v.i.* To climb up, down, or along by using hands and feet; also, to climb by attaching tendrils, as certain vines. [Akin to CLIMB] **—clam′ber·er** *n.*

clam·jam·fer·y (klam·jam′fər·ē) *n. Scot.* **1** Rubbish; trumpery. **2** Worthless people. Also **clam·jam·phrie** (klam·jam′frē).

clam·my (klam′ē) *adj.* **·mi·er, ·mi·est 1** Damp and cold. **2** Soft and sticky. [< CLAM[2] *adj.*] **—clam′mi·ly** *adv.* **—clam′mi·ness** *n.*

clam·or[1] (klam′ər) *n.* **1** Any loud, repeated outcry, din, or noise; vociferation; noisy confusion of voices. **2** A continuous, vehement objecting or demanding; public outcry. See synonyms under NOISE. *—v.t.* **1** To utter with loud outcry. **2** To move or drive by clamor. *—v.i.* **3** To make loud outcries, demands, or complaints; vociferate. Also *Brit.* **clam′our.** [< OF < L < *clamare* cry out] **—clam′or·er** *n.*

clam·or[2] (klam′ər) *v.t. & v.i. Obs.* To stop the noise of; silence: often with *down.* Also *Brit.* **clam′our.** [< CLAM[4]]

clam·or·ous (klam′ər·əs) *adj.* Making or made with clamor; noisy. See synonyms under NOISY. **—clam′or·ous·ly** *adv.* **—clam′or·ous·ness** *n.*

clamp[1] (klamp) *n.* A device for compressing, holding in position, or binding together two or more parts. *—v.t.* To join or bind with or as with a clamp. [< M Du. *klampe*]

clamp[2] (klamp) *v.i.* To walk heavily; tramp. — *n.* A heavy tread; tramp. [Imit.]
clamp[3] (klamp) *n.* **1** *Brit.* A kiln with impervious walls. **2** A pile or heap, as of ore. [<Du. *klamp* heap]
clamp·er (klam′pər) *n.* An attachment for fastening to shoes to prevent the wearer from slipping on ice; a creeper.
clamp·ers (klam′pərz) *n. pl. Scot.* Pliers.
clam·shell (klam′shel′) *n.* **1** The shell or half-shell of a clam. **2** A dredging box or bucket shaped and hinged like the shell of a clam.
clam·worm (klam′wûrm′) *n.* Nereis.
clan (klan) *n.* **1** A united group of relatives, or families, having a common ancestor, one hereditary chieftain, and the same surname, especially in the Scottish Highlands. **2** In certain primitive societies, a body of kindred related in only one line, the members of which do not intermarry, having its own council, property, religion, etc.; an exogamous subdivision of a tribe: also called *sib.* **3** A clique, or set of persons; a fraternity; club. See synonyms under CLASS. [<Scottish Gaelic *clānn*]
clan·des·tine (klan·des′tin) *adj.* Kept secret for a purpose; concealed; surreptitious; furtive; underhand. See synonyms under SECRET. [<L *clandestinus* < *clam* in secret] —**clan·des′tine·ly** *adv.* —**clan·des′tine·ness** *n.*
clang (klang) *v.t.* **1** To cause to send forth a loud, ringing metallic sound. —*v.i.* **2** To send forth such a sound: The bells *clanged.* **3** To strike together with such a sound: The shields *clanged* together. —*n.* **1** A ringing sound, as of metal struck. **2** In acoustics, a tone with its overtones; acoustic color; timbre. **3** The ringing call of cranes or geese. [Prob. imit. Cf. L *clangere.*]
clan·gor (klang′gər, klang′ər) *n.* Repeated clanging; a clanging or noisy ringing; clamor. —*v.i.* To ring noisily; clang. Also *Brit.* **clan′gour.** [<L < *clangere* clang] —**clan′gor·ous** *adj.* —**clan′gor·ous·ly** *adv.*
clank (klangk) *n.* An abrupt, short, harsh, metallic sound. — *v.t.* & *v.i.* To emit, or cause to emit, a clank. [Blend of CLANG and CLINK]
clan·nish (klan′ish) *adj.* **1** Like a clan; disposed to cling together. **2** Bound by family tradition, class, or clan prejudice, etc.; narrow. —**clan′nish·ly** *adv.* —**clan′nish·ness** *n.*
clan·ship (klan′ship) *n.* Union under a chief.
clans·man (klanz′mən) *n. pl.* **·men** (-mən) A member of a clan or of the same clan.
clap[1] (klap) *v.* **clapped** or **clapt, clap·ping** *v.t.* **1** To strike together with a sharp, explosive sound. **2** To applaud by clapping the hands. **3** To strike suddenly, as in greeting. **4** To place quickly or suddenly. **5** To make or build hastily: often with *together* or *up.* **6** To flap, as wings. **7** *Obs.* To shut, as a door or window. —*v.i.* **8** To come together with a sharp, explosive sound, as flat surfaces. **9** To applaud by striking the hands together. **10** *Archaic* To close with a clapping sound. —**to clap eyes on** To see. —*n.* **1** A sharp sudden noise, as of two hard flat objects coming together. **2** The act of striking sharply together flatwise: a *clap* of the hands. **3** A sudden, but slight blow with the flat of the hand; a slap. **4** *Obs.* A sudden stroke or event. [OE *clæppan*]
clap[2] (klap) *n.* Gonorrhea: usually with *the*: a vulgarism. [<OF *clapoir* a venereal sore]
clap·board (klab′ərd, klap′bôrd′, -bōrd′) *n.* **1** A lapping weatherboard, usually with one edge thicker than the other. **2** A rived roofing board larger than a shingle. —*v.t.* To cover with clapboards. [Partial trans. of MDu. *klapholt* barrel stave]
clap·per (klap′ər) *n.* **1** One who or that which claps, as the tongue of a bell, or either of a pair of sticks, bones, or the like, held between the fingers and struck together, as an accompaniment to music. **2** *Slang* The tongue; also, the mouth.
clap·per·claw (klap′ər·klô′) *v.t.* & *v.i.* **1** *Obs.* To slap, scratch, and claw; attack with tooth and nail. **2** To scold vehemently.
clap·trap (klap′trap) *n.* **1** Any device, language, or conduct designed to evoke applause. **2** Cheap, sensational, or unworthy artifice.
claque (klak) *n.* Hired applauders in a theater. **2** Any set of persons concerting to praise or applaud from interested motives. [<F < *claquer* clap]
Clar·a (klar′ə, klâr′ə; *Du., Ger., Pg., Sp.* klä′rä) A feminine personal name. [<L, famous]
clar·a·bel·la (klar′ə·bel′ə) *n.* An organ stop with open wooden pipes, giving a soft, sweet tone. [<L *clarus* clear + *bellus* pretty]
clar·ain (klâr·ān′) *n. Geol.* A type of bituminous coal having a finely banded structure of translucent materials which impart a bright, silky luster. [<L *clarus* clear + (FUS)AIN]
Clare (klâr) Diminutive of CLARA or CLARISSA. —**Clare of Assisi, Saint** Italian founder of the Order of Poor Clares in 1212, under the rule given to her by Saint Francis.
Clare (klâr) A county in Munster province, western Ireland; 1,231 square miles; county seat, Ennis.
Clar·ence (klar′əns) A masculine personal name. [after the Duke of *Clarence*]
—**Clarence, Duke of,** 1449–78, George Plantagenet, brother of Edward IV and Richard III of England; murdered.
clar·ence (klar′əns) *n.* A four-wheeled, closed carriage, having seats for four persons inside and, usually, a glass front. [after the Duke of *Clarence,* later William IV of England]
clar·en·don (klar′ən·dən) *n. Printing* A style of type having a somewhat heavy and condensed face. [from the *Clarendon* Press, Oxford, England]
Clar·en·don (klar′ən·dən), **Earl of,** 1609–74, Edward Hyde, English royalist statesman, historian, premier, and lord chancellor.
clar·et (klar′ət) *n.* **1** Any red table wine; especially, one from the region around Bordeaux. **2** A loose color term for various shades ranging from ruby to a deep purplish-red. [<OF *(vin)claret* clear (wine) < *cler* <L *clarus* bright]
Clar·i·bel (klar′ə·bel) A feminine personal name. [<L, brightly fair]
Clar·ice (klar′is, klə·rēs′) See CLARISSA.
clar·i·fy (klar′ə·fī) *v.* **·fied, ·fy·ing** *v.t.* **1** To make clear or understandable. **2** To free from impurities, as wines or fats. —*v.i.* **3** To become clear or transparent. **4** To become understandable or clear: The situation *clarified.* See synonyms under PURIFY. [<OF *clarifier* <LL *clarificare* < *clarus* clear + *facere* make] —**clar′i·fi·ca′tion** *n.* —**clar′i·fi′er** *n.*
clar·i·net (klar′ə·net′) *n.* **1** A cylindrical wood-wind instrument with bell mouth, having a single reed mouthpiece, finger holes, and keys. Clarinets are made in various keys and sizes: those in B♭ and A are used in both orchestras and jazz bands; those in C and E♭ are used in jazz bands only. **2** An organ stop having a sound similar to that of a clarinet. Also **clar·i·o·net** (klar′ē·ə·net′). —**bass clarinet** A large clarinet pitched an octave lower than the common B♭ clarinet. [<F *clarinette,* dim. of *clarine* bell] —**clar′i·net′ist** or **clar′i·net′·tist** *n.*

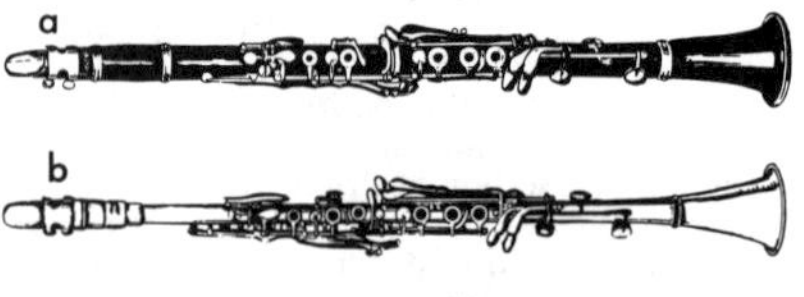

CLARINETS
a. Wood.
b. Metal.

clar·i·on (klar′ē·ən) *n.* **1** A small trumpet. **2** The sound of a trumpet, or any sound resembling it. —*v.t.* & *v.i.* To proclaim with or as with a clarion; blow a clarion. —*adj.* Shrill; clear. [<OF *claron, clairon* <L *clarus* clear]
Cla·ris·sa (klə·ris′ə; *Ger.* klä·ris′ä, *Ital.* klä·rēs′sä) A feminine personal name. Also *Clarice.* [<L, famous]
clar·i·ty (klar′ə·tē) *n.* Clearness as of sight, language, understanding, etc.
Clark (klärk), **Champ,** 1850–1921, James Beauchamp Clark, U.S. politician. —**George Rogers,** 1752–1818, American soldier and pioneer. —**Mark Wayne,** born 1896, U.S. general. —**Thomas Campbell,** born 1899, U.S. jurist; associate justice of the Supreme Court. —**William,** 1770–1838, brother of George Rogers; with Meriwether Lewis, led expedition to Columbia River, 1804–06.
Clark Fork River A river in Montana and Idaho, flowing 360 miles NW in the Columbia River system.
cla·ro (klä′rō) *adj.* Light in color and mild: said of cigars. [<Sp.]
clart·y (klär′tē) *adj.* **clart·i·er, clart·i·est** *Brit. Dial.* Dirty; sticky. [Origin unknown]
clar·y (klâr′ē) *n. pl.* **clar·ies** Any of several species of sage; especially, the common clary (*Salvia sclarea*), native in Italy, Syria, etc.; and the wild English or vervain clary (*S. verbenaca*). [<F *sclarée* <Med. L *sclarea*]
clash (klash) *v.t.* **1** To strike or dash together or against with a confused, harsh, metallic sound. —*v.i.* **2** To collide with loud and confused noise; to collide. **3** To conflict; be in opposition. —*n.* A confused, resounding, metallic noise, as of striking or colliding; collision; conflict, opposition. See synonyms under COLLISION [Imit. Cf. CLAP, DASH.]
clasp (klasp, kläsp) *n.* **1** A fastening by which things are bound together. **2** A firm grasp or embrace. **3** A small bar affixed to the ribbon of a military decoration: a **battle clasp** designates the campaign in which the wearer has taken part, a **service clasp** the country in which he has served. See synonyms under LOCK. —*v.t.* **1** To take hold of with an encircling grasp; embrace. **2** To fasten with or as with a clasp. **3** To grasp firmly in or with the hand. See synonyms under CATCH, EMBRACE, GRASP. [ME *claspe*; origin unknown]
clasp·er (klas′pər, kläs′-) *n.* **1** One who or that which clasps. **2** *Zool.* **a** One of the paired organs accessory to copulation in various animals, as the external genital organs in male insects, etc. **b** One of the grooved cartilaginous appendages to the ventral fins of sharks, rays, etc.
clasp knife A knife with a blade that folds into the handle; a pocket knife.
class (klas, kläs) *n.* **1** A number or body of persons with common characteristics: the educated *class.* **2** Social rank; caste. **3** A group of students under one teacher, or pursuing a study together; a group of students in a school or college having the same standing and graduating together. **4** *Biol.* A group of plants or animals standing below a phylum and above an order. **5** A number of objects, facts, or events having common accidental or essential properties; a set; kind. **6** A grading according to quality, value, or rank: first-*class* mail; to travel second-*class.* **7** *Slang* Superiority; elegance. —**the classes** The wealthier, more educated, or higher social classes. —*v.t.* To arrange or group according to characteristics or properties; assign to a class; classify. —*v.i. Rare* To be placed or ranked, as in a class. [<F *classe* <L *classis* group, class]
Synonyms (noun): association, caste, circle, clan, clique, club, company, coterie, grade, order, rank, set. A *caste* is hereditary; a *class* may be independent of lineage or descent; membership in a *caste* is normally for life, and hereditary; membership in a *class* may be very transient; a religious and ceremonial sacredness attaches to the *caste,* but not to the *class. Grade* implies some regular scale of valuation; as, the coarser and finer *grades* of wool. A *coterie* is a small company of persons of similar tastes. A *clique* is always fractional, implying some greater gathering of which it it is a part; the *association* breaks up into *cliques.* A *set,* while exclusive, is more intensive than a *clique,* and chiefly of persons who are united by common social station, etc. *Circle* is similar in meaning to *set,* but of wider application; we speak of scientific as well as of social *circles.*
class-con·scious·ness (klas′kon′shəs·nis, kläs′-) *n.* Awareness among a social group of its own nature, interests, and unity. —**class′-con′·scious** *adj.*
class day A day set apart, during school or college commencements, for exercises and ceremonies relating to and conducted by the graduating class.
clas·sic (klas′ik) *adj.* **1** Belonging to the first class or rank in literature or art. **2** Pertaining to standard and authoritative principles and forms in literature, art, music, etc. **3** Connected with or made famous by the ancient Greek or Latin authors. Compare ROMANTIC. **4** Balanced; formal; finished; regular; simple; austere: a term variously interpreted, and often opposed to *romantic.* **5** Having literary or historical traditions: *classic* lands. See synonyms under PURE. —*n.* **1** A work of literature or art, generally recognized

as excellent; especially, one of Greek or Roman workmanship or authorship. 2 *Rare* One who is familiar with classical literature. 3 Any author whose work is generally accepted as being a standard of excellence. — **the classics** Greek and Roman literature and authors. [<L *classicus* of the first rank < *classis* order, class]

clas·si·cal (klas′i·kəl) *adj.* 1 Of, pertaining to, or characteristic of ancient Greek and Roman art and literature. 2 Learned in, or based on Greek and Latin: a *classical* education. 3 Formal; finished; polished; modeled after Greek and Roman forms: often opposed to *romantic.* 4 Being of or modeled after the best in art, music, or literature. 5 *Music* **a** Following strict and established form, as a fugue or sonata. **b** Composed by the great masters. 6 *Physics* Pertaining to or describing those physical theories based upon or derived from Newtonian mechanics, especially as distinguished from relativity theory and quantum mechanics. — **clas′si·cal·ly** *adv.*

clas·si·cal·ism (klas′i·kəl·iz′əm) *n.* 1 Adherence to, imitation or knowledge of Greek or Roman art, literature, or antiquities. 2 Classicism.

clas·si·cal·i·ty (klas′ə·kal′ə·tē) *n.* 1 The quality of being classical. 2 An instance, exemplification, or piece of classicality; a classical characteristic. 3 Classicism. Also **clas′si·cal·ness.**

clas·si·cism (klas′ə·siz′əm) *n.* 1 Classic principles and style. 2 Any idiom found in the classics. 3 Adherence to or imitation of the classic style in literature or art. 4 Classical scholarship.

clas·si·cist (klas′ə·sist) *n.* 1 One versed in the classics. 2 An adherent or imitator of classic style.

clas·si·cize (klas′ə·sīz) *v.* **·cized, ·ciz·ing** *v.t.* To make classic. — *v.i.* To affect the classic style.

clas·si·fi·ca·tion (klas′ə·fə·kā′shən) *n.* 1 The act, process, or result of classifying. 2 Taxonomy. 3 Systematics. 4 The systematic arrangement of books, documents, archives, and other printed material in accordance with categories, as of subject, author, time, etc.

clas·si·fi·ca·to·ry (klas′ə·fə·kā′tər·ē, klə·sif′ə·kə·tôr′ē, -tō′rē) *adj.* Of or pertaining to classification; taxonomical.

clas·si·fy (klas′ə·fī) *v.t.* **·fied, ·fy·ing** 1 To arrange or put in a class or classes on the basis of resemblance or differences. 2 To declare or designate as of aid to an enemy and restrict as to circulation or use, as a document, weapon, or item of information. [<L *classis* class + -FY] — **clas′si·fi′a·ble** *adj.* — **clas′si·fi′er** *n.*

clas·sis (klas′is) *n. pl.* **clas·ses** (klas′ēz) 1 A court in the Dutch and German Reformed churches, composed of ministers and ruling elders. 2 The district it represents. [<L]

class·mate (klas′māt′, kläs′-) *n.* A member of the same class in school or college.

class·room (klas′rōōm′, -rōōm′, kläs′-) *n.* 1 A room allotted to a certain class in a school. 2 A room in a school or college in which recitations and lectures are held.

class struggle The conflict between classes in society; particularly, the economic struggle for power between employers, as a general class or group, and employees.

class·y (klas′ē) *adj. Slang* **class·i·er, class·i·est** Grand; elegant.

clas·tic (klas′tik) *adj.* 1 *Biol.* Breaking, separating, or dividing into parts: a *clastic* cell. 2 Something that may be taken apart and reassembled: a *clastic* anatomical model. 3 *Geol.* Composed of fragments, especially of preexisting rocks: distinguished from *crystalline.* [<Gk. *klastos* broken]

clath·rate (klath′rāt) *n. Chem.* Any of a class of organic compounds whose molecules are so interlocked through hydrogen bonds as to form 3-dimensional lattices exhibiting trigonal symmetry. — *adj.* 1 Designating such a compound. 2 Having a latticelike appearance. [<L *clathri* lattice]

clat·ter (klat′ər) *v.i.* 1 To make a rattling noise or racket; give out short, sharp noises rapidly or repeatedly. 2 To advance, go, or proceed with a rattling noise. 3 To chatter; tattle. — *v.t.* 4 To cause to make a rattling noise. — *n.* 1 A rattling noise. 2 Noisy talk; chatter. See synonyms under NOISE. [OE *clatrung* a clattering noise] — **clat′ter·er** *n.*

Claude (klôd, *Fr.* klōd) A masculine personal name. See CLAUDIUS.

Claude Lor·rain (klōd lô·raṅ′) See LORRAIN, CLAUDE.

Clau·del (klō·del′), **Paul,** 1868–1955, French diplomat, poet, and dramatist.

Clau·di·a (klô′dē·ə; *Du., Ger., Ital., Sw.* klou′·dē·ä; *Sp.* klou′thē·ä) A feminine personal name: feminine of CLAUDIUS.

Clau·di·an (klô′dē·ən) *adj.* Of or pertaining to the Roman emperors of the Claudius family (Tiberius, Caligula, Claudius, and Nero, A.D. 14–68).

Clau·di·an (klô′dē·ən), 365–408, Latin epic poet. Also *Latin* **Clau·di·us Clau·di·a·nus** (klô′·dē·əs klô′dē·ā′nəs).

clau·di·cant (klô′di·kənt) *adj. Obs.* Limping; lame. [<L *claudicans, -antis,* ppr. of *claudicare* limp < *claudus* lame]

clau·di·ca·tion (klô′di·kā′shən) *n.* A limp or the act of limping.

Clau·dine (klō·dēn′) French form of CLAUDIA.

Clau·di·us (klô′dē·əs; *Dan., Du., Ger., Sw.* klou′·dē·ōōs) A masculine personal name. Also *Ital., Sp.* **Clau·di·o** (*Ital.* klou′dē·ō, *Sp.* -thē·ō). [<L, lame]

— **Claudius** In Shakespeare's *Hamlet,* king of Denmark, Hamlet's stepfather and uncle.

— **Claudius, Appius,** Roman decemvir. See APPIUS.

— **Claudius I,** 10 B.C.–A.D. 54, Tiberius Claudius Drusus, Roman emperor 41–54; successor to Caligula.

— **Claudius II,** 214–270, Marcus Aurelius Claudius, Roman emperor 268–270.

Clau·di·us (klou′dē·ōōs), **Matthias,** 1740–1815, German poet.

claught (klôkht) *Scot. v.t.* To seize; clutch. — *n.* 1 A grasp; clutch. 2 A handful.

clause (klôz) *n.* 1 *Gram.* A group of words containing a subject and predicate, but forming a subordinate part of a compound or complex sentence: distinguished from *phrase.* 2 A distinct part of a composition, as a paragraph or article. 3 A separate statement or proviso in a legal or state document. — **principal clause** *Gram.* The clause which contains the main predication of a sentence. — **relative clause** *Gram.* A subordinate clause introduced by a relative pronoun. — **subordinate** (or **dependent**) **clause** *Gram.* A clause which has the effect of a noun, adjective, or adverb in the structure of a sentence. [<OF <Med. L *clausa* <L *clausus,* pp. of *claudere* close] — **claus′al** *adj.*

Clau·se·witz (klou′zə·vits), **Karl von,** 1780–1831, Prussian general and writer.

Clau·si·us (klou′zē·əs), **Rudolf Julius Emanuel,** 1822–88, German physicist.

claus·tral (klôs′trəl) *adj.* Cloistral.

claus·tro·pho·bi·a (klôs′trə·fō′bē·ə) *n. Psychiatry* Morbid fear of enclosed or confined places. [<L *claustrum* a closed place + -PHOBIA] — **claus′tro·pho′bic** *adj.*

clau·su·ra (klô′zhōō·rə) *n.* In the Roman Catholic Church, the rule which separates part of a monastery or convent from outsiders. [<L, a barrier < *claudere* close]

claut (klôt) *Scot. n.* 1 A rake, hoe, etc. 2 A grasping clutch. 3 A handful. 4 A lump or piece. — *v.t.* To scratch; scrape; rake.

cla·vate (klā′vāt) *adj. Biol.* Denoting an organ or part having a thickened or bulbous end; club-shaped. Also **cla′vat·ed.** [<L *clavatus,* pp. of *clavare* stud with nails; infl. in meaning by L *clava* club] — **cla′vate·ly** *adv.*

clave (klāv) Archaic past tense of CLEAVE[1] and CLEAVE[2].

clav·e·cin (klav′ə·sin) *n.* A harpsichord. [<F] — **clav′e·cin·ist** *n.*

cla·ver (klā′vər, klav′ər) *v.t. Scot.* To talk idly; gossip. — *n.* Foolish or empty talk; gossip.

clav·i·chord (klav′ə·kôrd) *n.* A keyboard musical instrument whose tones are produced by the blow of brass pins on horizontal strings: a forerunner of the piano. [<Med. L *clavichordium* <L *clavis* key + *chorda* string]

clav·i·cle (klav′ə·kəl) *n. Anat.* The bone connecting the shoulder blade and breastbone; collar bone. [<L *clavicula,* dim. of *clavis* key] — **cla·vic·u·lar** (klə·vik′yə·lər) *adj.*

clav·i·corn (klav′ə·kôrn) *adj. Entomol.* Of, pertaining to, or belonging to a superfamily of beetles (*Staphylinoidea,* formerly *Clavicornia*) having club-shaped antennae. [<NL *Clavicornia* <L *clava* club + *cornu* horn] — **clav·i·cor·nate** (klav′ə·kôr′nāt) *adj.*

clav·i·er (klav′ē·ər, klə·vir′ *for defs. 1 and 3;* klə·vir′ *for def. 2*) *n.* 1 A keyboard. 2 Any keyboard stringed instrument, as a clavichord, etc.; especially, a piano. 3 A dummy keyboard: used for the perfection of technique. [<F, keyboard <L *clavis* key]

clav·i·form (klav′ə·fôrm) *adj.* Club-shaped; clavate. [<L *clava* club + -FORM]

claw (klô) *n.* 1 *Zool.* **a** A sharp, usually curved, horny nail on the toe of a bird, mammal, or reptile. **b** A limb terminating in a claw or pincers, as in certain insects and crustaceans. 2 Anything sharp and hooked. 3 A stroke, clutch, or scratch from or as with claws. — *v.t.* & *v.i.* To tear, scratch, dig, pull, etc., as with claws. [OE *clawu*]

claw hammer 1 A hammer with one end of its head forked and curved like a claw for drawing nails. See illustration under HAMMER. 2 *Colloq.* A swallowtail coat or dress coat: from its shape.

claw hatchet A hatchet having the head forked at one end. See illustration under HATCHET.

clax·on (klak′sən) See KLAXON.

clay (klā) *n.* 1 A common earth of various colors and fine texture, compact and brittle when dry, but plastic and tenacious when wet. It is a hydrous aluminum silicate, generally mixed with powdered feldspar, quartz, sand, iron oxides, and various other minerals. 2 Earth in general. 3 Earth as a symbol of the human body; also, the body itself. See synonyms under BODY. — *v.t.* To cover, mix, or treat with clay. [OE *clæg*] — **clay′ish** *adj.*

Clay (klā), **Henry,** 1777–1852, U.S. statesman and orator.

clay·bank (klā′bangk′) *n.* 1 A bank of clay: also **clay′bluff′.** 2 A yellowish-brown color. 3 A horse of this color.

clay-eat·er (klā′ē′tər) *n.* 1 A person who eats clay. Compare GEOPHAGY. 2 *U.S. Slang* A poor white of North or South Carolina: a contemptuous use.

clay·ey (klā′ē) *adj.* **clay·i·er, clay·i·est** Of, like, abounding in, mixed or covered with clay.

clay·more (klā′môr, -mōr) *n.* A double-edged broadsword of the Scottish Highlanders. [<Scottish Gaelic *claidheamh* sword + *mor* great]

clay pigeon In trapshooting, a saucer-shaped disk of some brittle material, as baked clay, projected from a trap as a flying target.

clay stone 1 One of the concretionary nodules found in alluvial clay. 2 A dull-colored igneous rock containing feldspar and clay in a compact mass.

Clay·ton (klā′tən), **John Middleton,** 1796–1856, U.S. lawyer and statesman.

clay·to·ni·a (klā·tō′nē·ə) *n.* One of a genus (*Claytonia*) of low herbs of the purslane family: also called *springbeauty.* [after John *Clayton,* 1693–1773, botanist, of Virginia]

-cle *suffix of nouns* Small; minute: *particle; corpuscle.* [<F <L *-culus,* dim. suffix]

clean (klēn) *adj.* 1 Free from dirt, soil, impurity, or defilement; unblemished; pure. 2 Ginned: *clean* cotton. 3 Free from bungling; dexterous; complete: He's a *clean* shot. 4 Well-proportioned; symmetrical. 5 Ceremonially pure; conforming to the ceremonial law. 6 Completely cleared or rid of something. 7 Having no imperfection; perfect; whole. 8 Clear: a *clean* title to land. 9 In baseball, without error. — *v.t.* 1 To purify or cleanse; to free from dirt or impurities. 2 To draw and prepare (fowl, game, etc.) for cooking. — *v.i.* 3 To undergo or perform the act of cleaning. — **to clean out** 1 To clear of trash or rubbish. 2 To force out; overcome: to *clean* the gangsters *out* of town. 3 To empty (a place) of contents or occupants: The crowd *cleaned out* the store. 4 *Colloq.* To leave without money: The depression *cleaned* him *out.* — **to clean up** 1 To remove dirt; put in order: Today we *clean up.* 2 *Colloq.* To win a large amount or make large profits. 3 *Colloq.* To defeat: to *clean up* the enemy.

4 To remove undesirable persons or scandalous activities from: to *clean up* politics. —*adv.* In a clean manner; unqualifiedly, wholly. [OE *clæne* clear, pure] —**clean′a·ble** *adj.* —**clean′ness** *n.*

clean-cut (klēn′kut′) *adj.* **1** Cut with smooth edge or surface; made with skill and neatness. **2** Sharply defined. **3** Clear. **4** Neat in appearance; trim: a *clean-cut* young man.

clean·er (klē′nər) *n.* **1** One who or that which cleans. **2** Any substance or mechanical device which removes dirt.

clean·ly (klen′lē) *adj.* **1** Habitually and carefully clean; neat; tidy; clean. **2** Cleansing. —*adv.* (klēn′lē) In a clean manner. —**clean·li·ness** (klen′lē·nis) *n.*

cleanse (klenz) *v.t.* **cleansed, cleans·ing** To free from dirt or defilement; clean; purge. [OE *clænsian* < *clæne* clean] —**cleans′er** *n.*
Synonyms: brush, clean, disinfect, dust, mop, purify, rinse, scour, scrub, sponge, sweep, wash, wipe. *Cleanse* implies a worse condition to start from, and more to do, than *clean*; as, Hercules *cleansed* the Augean stables. *Cleanse* and *purify* are used extensively in a moral sense; *wash* in that sense is archaic. See AMEND, PURIFY. *Antonyms*: befoul, besmear, besmirch, bespatter, contaminate, corrupt, debase, defile, deprave, pollute, soil, spoil, stain, sully, taint, vitiate.

Cle·an·thes (klē·an′thēz) Greek Stoic philosopher of the third century B.C.

clean-up (klēn′up′) *n.* **1** *U.S. Colloq.* A big financial success. **2** In mining, the periodic collecting of gold or other mineral from the gravel in the sluices.

clear (klir) *adj.* **1** Free from anything that dims or darkens; light. **2** Unclouded; distinct; intelligible. **3** Able to see, discern, or discriminate: a *clear* mind. **4** Free from obstruction or hindrance. **5** Free from encumbrance, responsibility, or guilt. **6** Free from adulteration, defect, or blemish. **7** Without deduction; net. **8** Undisturbed; serene. **9** Plain; evident. **10** Free from uncertainty. **11** Without trees or underbrush, as land. **12** Without knots or imperfections, as lumber or shingles. —*v.t.* **1** To make clear; brighten. **2** To free from foreign matter, impurities, blemishes, or muddiness. **3** To remove, as obstructions, in making clear: to *clear* dishes from the table. **4** To disentangle: to *clear* a rope. **5** To free from imputations or accusations of guilt; acquit. **6** To free from doubt or ambiguity; make plain. **7** To free from debt by payment. **8** To pass or get by or over without touching: to *clear* a fence. **9** To obtain or give clearance, as for a ship or cargo. **10** To net or gain over and above expenses. **11** To pass through a clearing-house, as a check. —*v.i.* **12** To become free from fog, cloud, or obscurity; grow bright; become fair. **13** To pass away, as mist or fog. **14** To settle accounts by exchange of bills and checks, as in a clearing-house. —**to clear for action** To prepare for battle by clearing the decks. —**to clear in** (or **inward**) *Naut.* To discharge cargo. —**to clear out** **1** To leave port, as a ship. **2** To empty. **3** *Colloq.* To leave; depart. —**to clear the air** To dispel emotional tensions or disagreements. —**to clear the land** *Naut.* To get beyond danger of land and shoals into sea room. —**to clear up** **1** To grow fair, as the weather. **2** To free from confusion or mystery. **3** To free from obligation. —*adv.* Wholly; completely; quite; clearly; plainly. —*n.* **1** Unbroken or unobstructed distance or space; clearance. **2** Inside measurements, from boundary to boundary. —**in the clear** **1** In plain language; not written in code or cipher: said of military messages. **2** Innocent; not liable. **3** Free from limitations or obstructions. [<OF *cler* <L *clarus* clear, bright] —**clear′a·ble** *adj.* —**clear′ly** *adv.*
Synonyms (adj.): apparent, diaphanous, distinct, evident, explicit, intelligible, limpid, lucid, manifest, obvious, pellucid, perspicuous, plain, straightforward, translucent, transparent, unadorned, unambiguous, unequivocal, unmistakable. A substance is said to be *clear* that offers no impediment to vision, is not dim, dark, or obscure; *transparent*, when objects are readily seen through it; we speak of a stream as *clear* when we think of the water itself, as *transparent* with reference to the ease with which we see the pebbles at the bottom. *Clear* is said of that which comes to the senses without dimness, dulness, obstruction, or obscurity; hence, the word is used for that which is free from any kind of obstruction; as, a *clear* field. *Lucid* and *pellucid* refer to a shining clearness, as of crystal. *Translucent* is less than *transparent*; a *translucent* body allows light to pass through, but may not permit forms and colors to be distinguished. *Limpid* refers to a liquid clearness, or that which suggests it; as, *limpid* streams. That which is *distinct* is well-defined, as in outline. That is *plain* which is level to the thought, so that one goes straight on without difficulty or hindrance; as, *plain* language; a *plain* statement. *Perspicuous* is often equivalent to *plain*, but *plain* never wholly loses the meaning of *unadorned*, so that we can say the style is *perspicuous* even if highly ornate, when we could not call it at once ornate and *plain*. Compare APPARENT, BLANK, EVIDENT, FINE, FREE, INNOCENT, MANIFEST, PLAIN, PURE, SURE, VIVID. *Antonyms*: ambiguous, cloudy, dim, dubious, foggy, indistinct, mysterious, obscure, opaque, turbid, unintelligible, vague.

Clear, Cape The southernmost point of Ireland, in County Cork.

clear·ance (klir′əns) *n.* **1** The act or process of clearing. **2** A certificate permitting a vessel to sail; also, the obtaining or granting of such permission. **3** The space by which a moving vehicle, machine, or part clears something. **4** The passage of checks, bank drafts, etc., through the clearing-house.

Cle·ar·chus (klē·är′kəs) Spartan general of the fifth century B.C., treacherously killed by Persians in 401 B.C.

clear-cut (klir′kut′) *adj.* **1** Distinctly and sharply outlined. **2** Concise; plainly put.

clear-eyed (klir′īd′) *adj.* **1** Having bright, clear eyes; keen-sighted. **2** Acute; wise.

clear-head·ed (klir′hed′id) *adj.* Not mentally confused or befogged; clear in understanding; sensible. —**clear′-head′ed·ness** *n.*

clear·ing (klir′ing) *n.* **1** A making or becoming clear. **2** That which is clear or cleared; a tract of land cleared of trees, underbrush, etc. **3** The settlement of balances between banks arising from the interchange of checks, drafts, etc., carried on at a clearing-house. **4** *pl.* The total of checks, drafts, etc., presented daily at a clearing-house.

clear·ing-house (klir′ing·hous′) *n.* An office where bankers exchange drafts and checks and adjust balances.

clear·ness (klir′nis) *n.* **1** The state or quality of being clear; distinctness to sight or understanding. **2** Transparence. **3** In rhetoric, that property of style by means of which thought is so presented as to be immediately understood, depending on precision and simplicity of diction and sentence structure.

clear-sight·ed (klir′sī′tid) *adj.* Of keen vision; having accurate perception and good judgment; discerning. —**clear′-sight′ed·ly** *adv.* —**clear′-sight′ed·ness** *n.*

clear·starch (klir′stärch′) *v.t.* To stiffen with clear or pure starch. —**clear′starch′er** *n.*

clear·sto·ry (klir′stôr′ē, -stō′rē) See CLERESTORY.

clear text Plain text.

clear·way (klir′wā′) *n. Aeron.* An unobstructed area beyond the stopway of an airport to permit safe landing of an aircraft that fails to attain a proper altitude.

clear·weed (klir′wēd′) *n.* Richweed.

clear·wing (klir′wing′) *n.* A moth of the families *Aegeriidae* or *Sphingidae*, having nearly transparent wings.

cleat (klēt) *n.* **1** A strip of wood or iron fastened across a surface, or nailed against a wall, to strengthen, support, or prevent slipping. **2** *Naut.* **a** A piece of metal or wood with arms, usually fastened in place by a bolt, on which to belay a rope. **b** A wedgelike piece of wood fastened to a spar to keep rigging from slipping up or down. **3** A piece of metal or leather fastened to the underside of a shoe to prevent slipping: used by athletes. **4** A spurlike attachment used to grip a pole or tree in climbing. —*v.t.* **1** To furnish or strengthen with a cleat or cleats. **2** *Naut.* To fasten (rope, etc.) to or with a cleat. [ME *clete*. Akin to CLOT.]

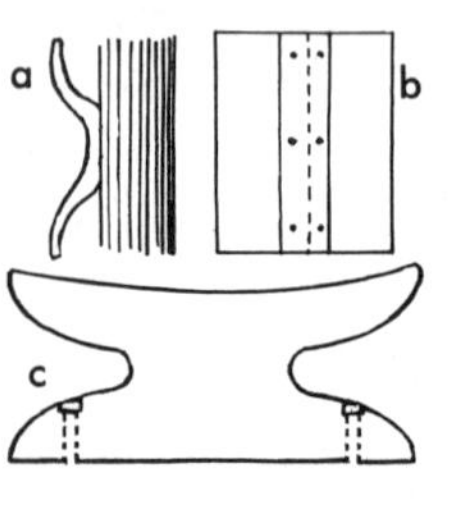

TYPES OF CLEATS
a. Pole. *b.* Surface. *c.* Deck.

cleav·age (klē′vij) *n.* **1** A cleaving or being cleft; a split; cleft; division or the manner in which a thing divides. **2** *Mineral.* A tendency in certain rocks or crystals to divide or split in certain directions. **3** *Biol.* The process of division of a fertilized ovum by which the original single cell becomes a mass of smaller cells.

cleave[1] (klēv) *v.* **cleft** or **cleaved** or **clove** (*Archaic* **clave**), **cleft** or **cleaved** or **clo·ven** (*Archaic* **clove**), **cleav·ing** *v.t.* **1** To sunder, as with an ax or wedge; split, especially along structural lines or with the grain. **2** To make or achieve by cutting. **3** To pass through; penetrate. —*v.i.* **4** To split or divide by natural lines of cleavage. **5** To pass; make one's way: with *through*. [OE *clēofan*] —**cleav′a·ble** *adj.*

cleave[2] (klēv) *v.i.* **cleaved** (*Archaic* **clave**), **cleaved, cleav·ing** **1** To stick fast; adhere. **2** To be faithful: with *to*. [OE *cleofian, clifian*]

cleav·er (klē′vər) *n.* **1** One who or that which cleaves. **2** A butcher's chopper.

cleav·ers (klē′vərz) *n. pl.* A species of bedstraw (*Galium aparine*), so called because of the hooked prickles on stem and fruit: also called *catchweed*.

cleck (klek) *v.t.* & *v.i. Scot.* To hatch; litter.

cleck·in (klek′in) *n. Scot.* A brood; litter.

cle·don·ism (klē′də·niz′əm) *n.* Avoidance of the use of words considered ominous or unlucky; the practice of using euphemisms. [<Gk. *klēdōn* omen]

cleed (klēd) *Scot. v.t.* To shelter; clothe. —*n.* A garment; dress.

cleek (klēk) *v.t.* & *v.i. Scot.* **1** To clutch; hook. **2** To marry. —*n.* **1** A large hook; a crooked staff. **2** A golf club with an iron head.

clef (klef) *n.* In musical notation, a symbol placed upon the staff to determine the pitch: namely, **treble** or **G clef, bass** or **F clef**, and the **tenor** or **C clef** of ancient music. [<F <L *clavis* key]

CLEFS
Showing position of Middle C on each:
1. Treble or G clef. *2.* Bass or F clef.
3., 4., 5., C clefs (Soprano, Alto, Tenor).

cleft (kleft) *v.* A past tense and past participle of CLEAVE[1]. —*adj.* **1** Divided partially or completely. **2** *Bot.* Divided about half-way down: said of leaves. —*n.* **1** An opening made by cleaving; a fissure in a rock; crevice; rift. **2** A chap or crack in the human skin. **3** The space between the two parts of a horse's foot. See synonyms under BREACH. [ME *clift*. Related to CLEAVE[1].]

cleft palate A congenital longitudinal fissure in the roof of the mouth.

Cleis·the·nes (klīs′thə·nēz) Athenian statesman of the sixth century B.C.: also spelled *Clisthenes*.

cleisto- *combining form* Closed: *cleistogamous*. Also, before vowels, **cleist-**. [<Gk. *kleistos* closed < *kleiein* close]

cleis·tog·a·mous (klīs·tog′ə·məs) *adj. Bot.* Closed or non-expanding and self-fertilizing: said of certain closed flowers, as some violets: also spelled *clistogamous*. Also **cleis·to·gam·ic** (klīs′tə·gam′ik). [<CLEISTO- + -GAMOUS]

cleis·tog·a·my (klīs·tog′ə·mē) *n. Bot.* Self-fertilization; self-pollination.

clem·a·tis (klem′ə·tis) *n.* **1** A plant of a large genus (*Clematis*) of perennial shrubs or vines of the crowfoot family. **2** Any vine of a related genus (*Atragene*). [<Gk. *klēmatis*, dim. of *klēma* vine]

Cle·men·ceau (klem′ən·sō′, *Fr.* kle·män·sō′) **Georges Eugène**, 1841–1929, French statesman; premier 1906–09; 1917–20.

clem·en·cy (klem′ən·sē) *n. pl.* **·cies** **1** Mildness of temper, especially toward offenders; leniency; mercy. **2** Mildness of climate, weather, etc. See synonyms under MERCY. [<L *clementia* <*clemens* mild]

Clem·ens (klem′ənz), **Samuel Langhorne** See MARK TWAIN.

clem·ent (klem′ənt) *adj.* **1** Lenient; merciful. **2** Mild or pleasant: said of weather. See synonyms under HUMANE. [<L *clemens, -entis* mild, merciful] — **clem′ent·ly** *adv.*

Clem·ent (klem′ənt) A masculine personal name. Also *Fr.* **Clé·ment** (klā·mäṅ′); *Ital., Sp.* **Cle·men·te** (klā·men′tā); *Ger.* **Cle·mens** (klā′·mens). [<L, merciful]
— **Clement** The name of 17 popes.
— **Clement I** Third bishop of Rome; pope 90?–99?: called "Clement of Rome."
— **Clement V,** 1264–1314, real name Bertrand d'Agoust, pope 1305–14; removed the papal seat to Avignon, 1309.
— **Clement VII,** 1478?–1534, real name Giulio de' Medici, pope 1523–34; by a bull against Henry VIII caused the severance of the English church from Rome.
— **Clement XIV,** 1705–74, real name Giovanni Ganganelli, pope 1769–74; decreed the suppression of the Jesuits, 1773.
— **Clement of Alexandria,** 150?–220?, Greek Christian theologian.

Clem·en·ti·na (klem′ən·tē′nə, *Ital.* klā′men·tē′nä) A feminine personal name. Also **Clem·en·tine** (klem′ən·tēn, -tīn; *Ger.* klem′ən·tē′nə), *Fr.* **Clé·men·tine** (klā·mäṅ·tēn′). [<L, merciful]

Clem·en·tine (klem′ən·tin, -tīn) *adj.* Of or pertaining to any of several popes and theologians named Clement.

clench (klench) *v.t.* **1** To grasp or grip firmly; clamp: to *clench* something in a vise. **2** To close tightly or lock, as the fist or teeth. **3** To clinch, as a nail. **4** *Naut.* To fasten by making a clinch. — *n.* A clenching; clinch. [OE *-clenc(e)an* in *beclencan* hold fast]

Cle·o·bu·lus (klē′ō·byōō′ləs) Greek lyric poet of the sixth century B.C.

cle·o·me (klē·ō′mē) *n.* Any of a large genus (*Cleome*) of woody or herbaceous plants of the caper family, with solitary or racemose, often showy, white, yellow, or purple flowers: also called *spiderflower.* [<LL, a plant]

Cle·om·e·nes (klē·om′ə·nēz) Name of three kings of Sparta; especially **Cleomenes III,** reigned 235–219? B.C.

Cle·on (klē′on) Athenian demagog of the fifth century B.C.

Cle·o·pat·ra (klē′ə·pat′rə, -pā′trə, -pä′trə), 69–30 B.C., queen of Egypt; loved by Julius Caesar and Mark Antony.

Cleopatra's Needle The popular name for either of two Egyptian obelisks, one in Central Park in New York City, the other in London, England.

Cle·os·tra·tus (klē·os′trə·təs), died 432 B.C., Greek astronomer.

clepe (klēp) *v.t.* **cleped** or **clept, clep·ing** *Archaic* To name; call: in the past participle also spelled *ycleped, yclept.* [OE *cleopian*]

clep·sy·dra (klep′sə·drə) *n. pl.* **·dras** or **·drae** (-drē) An ancient instrument for measuring time by the regulated flow of water; a water clock. [<L <Gk. *klepsydra* <*kleptein* steal + *hydōr* water]

clep·to·ma·ni·a (klep′tə·mā′nē·ə) See KLEPTOMANIA.

clere·sto·ry (klir′stôr′ē, -stō′rē) *n. Archit.* **1** The highest story of the nave and choir of a church, with windows opening above the aisle roofs, etc. **2** A similar story or elevated part in the roofs of other structures. Also **clere′sto′rey:** sometimes spelled *clearstory.* [<earlier *clere* clear + STORY]

cler·gy (klûr′jē) *n. pl.* **·gies** **1** The group of people ordained for service in a Christian church: distinguished from *laity.* **2** *Brit.* The ministers of the Established Church. — **regular clergy** The body of ecclesiastics of the Roman Catholic Church bound by monastic rules: distinguished from **secular clergy,** those not bound by such rules. [<OF *clergie* <*clerc* clerk, cleric <LL *clericus*]

cler·gy·man (klûr′jē·mən) *n. pl.* **·men** (-mən) One of the clergy; an ordained minister.

cler·ic (kler′ik) *adj.* Clerical. — *n.* **1** A member of the clergy. **2** A member of a clerical party. [<LL *clericus*]

cler·i·cal (kler′i·kəl) *adj.* **1** Of, belonging to, or characterizing the clergy. **2** Of or pertaining to a clerk or penmanship; composed of clerks: a *clerical* staff. — *n.* **1** A cleric. **2** One of a party seeking to preserve or extend the authority of the church in social or political matters. — **cler′i·cal·ly** *adv.*

cler·i·cal·ism (kler′i·kəl·iz′əm) *n.* The principle or policy of clerical control over education, marriage laws, etc. — **cler′i·cal·ist** *adj.* & *n.*

cler·id (kler′id) *n.* Any of a family (*Cleridae*) of small, slender, soft-bodied, variously colored coleopterous insects. [<NL *Cleridae* <Gk. *klēros,* a type of beetle]

cler·i·hew (kler′ə·hyōō) *n.* A satiric or comic poem in two couplets concerning some well-known personage whose name furnishes one of the rimes. [after Edmund *Clerihew* Bentley, 1875–1956, English writer, the originator]

cler·i·sy (kler′ə·sē) *n.* The literate, or well-educated class. [<Med. L *clericia*]

clerk (klûrk, *Brit.* klärk) *n.* **1** An officer or employee of a court, legislative body, corporation, society, commercial establishment, or the like, charged with the care of its records, correspondence, and accounts; a secretary. **2** A salesman or saleswoman in a store. **3** A hotel employee who assigns guests to their rooms. **4** In the Anglican Church, one who leads in the responses. **5** *Obs.* A clergyman or cleric; anciently, any person who could read or write. — *v.i.* To work or act as clerk. [OE *clerc* <LL *clericus* <Gk. *klērikos* <*klēros* lot, portion] — **clerk′li·ness** *n.* — **clerk′ly** *adj.* & *adv.* — **clerk′ship** *n.*

Cler·mont-Fer·rand (kler·môṅ′fe·räṅ′) A city of central France.

cleve·ite (klēv′īt) *n.* A radioactive variety of uraninite that is rich in uranium oxide and contains yttrium earths and helium. [after Per *Cleve,* 1840–1905, Swedish chemist]

Cleve·land (klēv′lənd), **(Stephen) Grover,** 1837–1908, U.S. statesman, president of the United States 1885–89, 1893–97.

Cleve·land (klēv′lənd) A city in NE Ohio on Lake Erie.

clev·er (klev′ər) *adj.* **1** Ready and adroit with hand or brain; dexterous; capable; quick-witted; talented. **2** *U.S. Dial.* Good-natured; obliging. **3** *U.S. Dial.* Finely built; well-trained, as a horse. **4** *Dial.* Honest. **5** *Obs.* Handy; convenient; agreeable. [Cf. ME *cliver* adroit] — **clev′er·ly** *adv.* — **clev′er·ness** *n.*

Synonyms: able, adroit, apt, bright, capable, dexterous, expert, gifted, happy, ingenious, intellectual, intelligent, keen, knowing, quick, quick-witted, sharp, skilful, smart, talented. *Clever,* as used in England, implies an aptitude for study or learning, and for excellent while not preeminent mental achievement. The early New England usage as implying simple and weak good nature has largely affected the use of the word throughout the United States. *Smart,* indicating dashing ability, is now coming to have a suggestion of unscrupulousness, similar to that of the word *sharp.* The discriminating use of such words as *able, gifted, talented,* etc., is preferable to an excessive use of the word *clever.* Compare ABILITY, ACUMEN, BRIGHT, INTELLIGENT, KNOWING. *Antonyms*: awkward, bungling, clumsy, dull, foolish, idiotic, ignorant, senseless, slow, stupid, thick-headed, witless.

Cleves (klēvz) A city in North Rhine-Westphalia, Germany; seat of a former duchy: German *Kleve.*

clev·is (klev′is) *n.* A U-shaped or stirrup-shaped piece of iron for attaching the draft chain to the end of a plow beam, wagon tongue, whiffletree, etc. [Akin to CLEAVE[1]]

clew (klōō) *n.* **1** A thread that guides through a maze. **2** Something that leads to the solution of a mystery: in this sense now spelled *clue.* **3** *Naut.* A lower corner of a square sail or the lower aft corner of a fore-and-aft sail; also, a loop at the corner. **4** *pl.* The small cords by which the two ends of a hammock are slung. **5** A ball of yarn, thread, or the like. — *v.t.* **1** To move or fasten by or as by a clew or clew line. **2** To coil into a ball; roll up into a bunch. [OE *cleowan*]

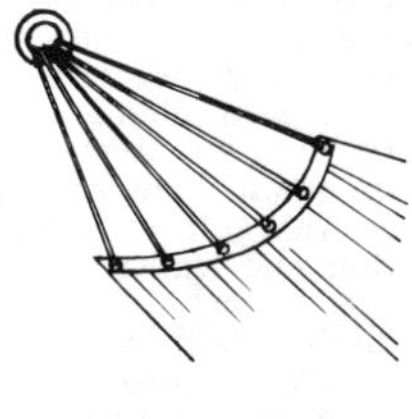

HAMMOCK CLEWS

clew line *Naut.* A rope by which the clew of a sail is run up to the yards.

cli·ché (klē·shā′) *n.* **1** A fixed or stereotyped expression which has lost its significance through frequent repetition. **2** *Printing* **a** An electrotype or stereotype plate. **b** A printing block made by the half-tone or similar process. — *adj.* Being a cliché; hackneyed. [<F, pp. of *clicher* stereotype]

Cli·chy (klē·shē′) A suburb of Paris, France. Also **Cli·chy-la-Ga·renne** (-là·gà·ren′).

click (klik) *n.* **1** A short, sharp, or dull metallic sound, as that made by the latch of a door. **2** A detent or stop; a pawl. **3** *Phonet.* An articulation occurring in the Hottentot and Bushman languages, produced by the sudden withdrawal of the tip or side of the tongue from the teeth or palate. **4** The trip, in wrestling, in which an opponent's foot is knocked from under him. — *v.t.* **1** To cause to make a click or clicks. — *v.i.* **2** To produce a click or succession of clicks. **3** *Slang* To succeed: The show *clicked.* **4** *Slang* To suit exactly; agree. [Imit.] — **click′er** *n.*

click beetle An elaterid; a snapping beetle. For illustration see INSECT (injurious).

cli·ent (klī′ənt) *n.* **1** One in whose interest a lawyer acts. **2** Hence, one who engages the services of any professional adviser. **3** Loosely, a customer or patron. **4** A dependent or follower, as of an ancient Roman patrician. [<L *cliens, -entis,* var. of *cluens,* ppr. of *cluere* hear, listen] — **cli′en·cy** *n.* — **cli·en·tal** (klī·en′təl, klī′ən·təl) *adj.*

cli·en·tele (klī′ən·tel′) *n.* A body of clients, dependents, customers, or adherents; a following. Also **cli·ent·age** (klī′ən·tij). [<F]

cliff (klif) *n.* A high steep face of rock, as on the seashore; a precipice. [OE *clif*]

cliff-dwell·er (klif′dwel′ər) *n.* **1** One of certain aboriginal North American Indian tribes of the SW United States and NW Mexico who built their dwellings in natural or excavated recesses in the sides of cliffs and canyons: antecedents of the tribes now known as Pueblo Indians. **2** *U.S. Colloq.* A person who lives in a city apartment house. — **cliff′-dwell′ing** *n.*

cliff·hang·er (klif′hang′ər) *n.* **1** A situation marked by suspense or uncertainty of outcome. **2** A serialized drama marked by suspense at the end of each episode. Also **cliff′-hang′er.** — **cliff′hang′ing** *adj.* & *n.*

Clif·ford (klif′ərd) A masculine personal name. [from a surname]

cliff swallow A North American swallow (*Petrochelidon albifrons*) which builds mud nests under the eaves of buildings or against cliffs.

cliff·y (klif′ē) *adj.* Abounding in or resembling cliffs; craggy.

Clif·ton (klif′tən) A masculine personal name. [from a surname]

cli·mac·ter·ic (klī·mak′tər·ik, klī′mak·ter′ik) *n.* **1** A critical year or period, or one of marked change, as in human life. **2** The menopause. — **grand climacteric** One's sixty-third year. — *adj.* **1** Of or pertaining to a climax; climactic. **2** Pertaining to or designating a critical year or period; marking, or marked by, a crisis. Also **cli·mac·ter·i·cal** (klī′mak·ter′i·kəl). [<L *climactericus* <Gk. *klimakterikos* <*klimaktēr* rung of a ladder]

cli·ma·gram (klī′mə·gram) *n. Meteorol.* Any graphic diagram representing one or more climatic elements of a region.

cli·mate (klī′mit) *n.* **1** The temperature, humidity, precipitation, winds, radiation, and other meteorological conditions characteristic of a locality or region over an extended period of time. **2** A region characterized by a certain average temperature, rainfall, dryness, etc. **3** Any region. **4** A prevailing or dominant trend in social affairs: *climate* of opinion. [<OF *climat* <LL *clima* <Gk. *klima, -atos* region, zone <*klinein* slope] — **cli·mat·ic** (klī·mat′ik) or **·i·cal** *adj.*

climato- *combining form* Climate; pertaining to climate or climatic conditions: *climatology.*

Also, before vowels, **climat-**. [<Gk. *klima, -atos* region]

cli·ma·tol·o·gy (klī′mə·tol′ə·jē) *n.* The science of climate. — **cli·ma·to·log·ic** (klī′mə·tə·loj′ik) or **·i·cal** *adj.* — **cli′ma·tol′o·gist** *n.*

cli·ma·to·ther·a·py (klī′mə·tō·ther′ə·pē) *n.* The treatment of diseases by subjecting patients to appropriate climate.

cli·max (klī′maks) *n.* **1** A progressive increase in force throughout a rhetorical or musical passage, culminating at the close. **2** *Ecol.* A relatively stable community of plants and animals dominant in a given locality. **3** Loosely, the culmination; acme. — *v.t.* & *v.i.* To reach or bring to a climax; culminate. [<L <Gk. *klimax* ladder] — **cli·mac·tic** (klī·mak′tik) or **·ti·cal** *adj.*

climb (klīm) *v.* **climbed** (*Archaic* **clomb**), **climb·ing** *v.t.* **1** To ascend or descend, especially by means of the hands and feet; go up or down by holding or getting a foothold; mount. — *v.i.* **2** To mount, rise, or go up, especially by using the hands and feet. **3** To rise by effort, as in position or dignity. **4** To incline or slope upward. **5** To rise during growth, as certain vines, by entwining a support or clinging by means of tendrils. — *n.* **1** The act or process of climbing. ◆ Collateral adjective: *scansorial.* **2** A place that can be ascended only by climbing. ◆ Homophone: *clime.* [OE *climban*] — **climb′a·ble** *adj.*

climb·er (klī′mər) *n.* **1** One who or that which climbs. **2** *Bot.* A plant that supports its growth by its tendrils, rootlets, or the like. **3** *Colloq.* A social climber.

climbing fish See ANABAS.

climbing irons Iron bars bearing spur points, for strapping to the boots or legs, to aid in climbing telegraph poles, trees, glaciers, etc. See CLEAT *n.* Also **climb·ers** (klī′mərz).

clime (klīm) *n. Poetic* A country; region; climate. ◆ Homophone: *climb.* [<L *clima* CLIMATE]

cli·nan·dri·um (kli·nan′drē·əm) *n. pl.* **·dri·a** (-drē·ə) *Bot.* A depression in the summit of the column in certain orchids, in which the anther is lodged. [<NL <Gk. *klinē* bed + *anēr, andros* man]

cli·nan·thi·um (kli·nan′thē·əm) *n. pl.* **·thi·a** (-thē·ə) *Bot.* The receptacle in the heads of composite plants. [<NL <Gk. *klinē* bed + *anthos* flower]

clinch (klinch) *v.t.* **1** To secure firmly, as a nail or staple, by bending down the protruding point. **2** To fasten together by this means. **3** To grapple with. **4** To confirm, as a bargain or agreement. **5** *Naut.* To fasten by making a clinch. — *v.i.* **6** To take a strong, close hold; grapple, as combatants, with one another. **7** *Slang* To embrace or hug. — *n.* **1** A clinching, or that which clinches; especially, a clinched nail or bolt; a clamp. **2** A decisive or conclusive argument. **3** *Naut.* A rope knot made by a half-hitch and seizings: called an **inside** or an **outside clinch.** **4** A grip or struggle at close quarters, as in boxing. **5** *Slang* A close embrace. Also called *clench.* [Var. of CLENCH]

Clinch River (klinch) A river in Virginia and Tennessee, flowing 300 miles SW through the Great Appalachian Valley into Norris Reservoir.

clinch·er (klin′chər) *n.* **1** One who or that which clinches. **2** A person or device that clinches nails; a clencher. **3** A nail made for clinching. **4** *Colloq.* The final unanswerable proof in or as in an argument.

clinch·er-built (klin′chər·bilt′) *adj.* Clinker-built.

clincher rim A rim of an automobile wheel with turned-in edges, to grip and hold a clincher tire.

clincher tire A tire with flanges on each side of the inner circumference fitting into turned-over edges of the wheel rim.

cline (klīn) *n. Ecol.* A graded series of changes in a biotype, induced by corresponding gradual alterations in the environmental factors operating within a large area. [<Gk. *klinein* slope, bend]

cling (kling) *v.i.* **clung, cling·ing** **1** To hold on to something firmly, as by grasping, embracing, or winding round. **2** To remain in contact; resist separation: with *together.* **3** To stick to or continue tenaciously, as in the memory; be loyal. **4** To adhere closely; stick. [OE *clingan*] — **cling′er** *n.* — **cling′y** *adj.*

cling·fish (kling′fish′) *n. pl.* **·fish** or **·fish·es** Any of a group of small marine fishes (family *Gobiesocidae*) having a large central suction disk by which they cling to rocks, shells, etc.

cling·ing (kling′ing) *adj.* Adhering closely, as a garment. — **cling′ing·ly** *adv.*

clinging vine A woman who displays extreme dependence on a man in an attempt to gain his sympathy, attentions, protection, etc.

Cling·mans Dome (kling′mənz) One of the Great Smoky Mountains between Tennessee and North Carolina; 6,642 feet.

cling·stone (kling′stōn′) *n.* A variety of peach in which the pulp adheres to the stone.

clin·ic (klin′ik) *n.* **1** The teaching of medicine and surgery by treatment of or operation upon the patients in the presence of a class in a hospital or dispensary. **2** A class receiving such instruction. **3** An infirmary or dispensary connected with a hospital or medical college, for the treatment of nonresident patients. [<F *clinique* <L *clinicus* <Gk. *klinikos* < *klinē* bed < *klinein* recline]

clin·i·cal (klin′i·kəl) *adj.* **1** Of or pertaining to a sickbed or a clinic. **2** Pertaining to the practical, experimental method of medical education by the observation and treatment of patients in clinics. **3** Administered to one on a deathbed or sickbed: *clinical* baptism. — **clin′i·cal·ly** *adv.*

clinical thermometer See under THERMOMETER.

cli·ni·cian (kli·nish′ən) *n.* An active practitioner of medicine: distinguished from a teacher or from one who is consulted only at his office.

clink[1] (klingk) *v.t.* **1** To cause to make a short, slight, ringing sound. **2** *Scot.* & *Brit. Dial.* To clinch; rivet. — *v.i.* **3** To make a short, slight, ringing sound. **4** To rime or jingle. — *n.* **1** A tinkle, as of glass or small metallic bodies in collision. **2** *Scot.* Money; chink. **3** The shrill note of certain birds, as the whinchat. **4** A rime or jingle. [Imit. Cf. MDu. *klinken.*]

clink[2] (klingk) *n. Slang* A prison. [? after *Clink* prison in London]

clink·er (kling′kər) *n.* **1** A thing that clinks, especially the earthy residue left by coal in burning. **2** A large, irregular porous fragment of lava. **3** A brick impregnated with niter and burned very hard. **4** A vitrified or overburned brick; a mass of fused bricks. **5** A clincher. **6** *U.S. Slang* **a** A bad verbal mistake in a radio or television broadcast. **b** A wrong note in a musical performance. **c** A failure; flop. — *v.t.* & *v.i.* To form or cause to form a clinker; become clogged with clinker. [<Du. *klinckaerd,* kind of brick]

A B

CLINKER–BUILT
In shipbuilding:
A. Clinker-built.
B. Carvel-built.

clink·er-built (kling′kər·bilt′) *adj.* Built with overlapping and riveted planks or plates, as a ship: also *clincher-built.*

clink·stone (klingk′stōn′) *n.* A compact, grayish rock that clinks like metal when struck; phonolite.

clino- *combining form* Bend; slope; incline: *clinometer.* [<Gk. *klinein* bend]

cli·nom·e·ter (klī·nom′ə·tər, kli-) *n.* An instrument for determining angular inclination, as of guns, slopes, etc.: also *anglemeter.* [<CLINO- + -METER]

cli·no·met·ric (klī′nə·met′rik) *adj.* **1** Pertaining to or measured by the clinometer. **2** Pertaining to oblique crystalline forms or to their measurement. Also **cli′no·met′ri·cal.**

clin·quant (kling′kənt) *adj.* Glittering with or as with gold or silver; tinseled. — *n.* Imitation gold leaf: tinsel. [<F, ppr. of *clinquer* ring, glitter]

Clin·ton (klin′tən) A family prominent in American history, including **James,** 1736–1812, general in American Revolution; **George,** 1739–1812, brother of James, governor of New York, and vice president of the United States; **De Witt,** 1769–1828, son of James, lawer and statesman. — **Sir Henry,** 1738–95, British commander in chief in the American Revolution, 1778–1782.

clin·to·ni·a (klin·tō′nē·ə) *n.* A plant of a small genus (*Clintonia*) of perennial herbs of the lily family, having broadly lanceolate, radical leaves, and a naked scape, bearing usually an umbel of flowers succeeded by berries. [after De Witt *Clinton*]

Cli·o (klī′ō) The Muse of history. [<Gk. *kleein* celebrate, make famous]

cli·o·met·rics (klī′ō·met′riks) *n.pl.* (*construed as sing.*) The systematic application of statistical methods to the study of history, as in the collection and analysis of quantitative data. [< CLIO + METRICS] — **cli′o·met′ric** *adj.* — **cli·o·me·tri·cian** (klī′ō·mə·trish′ən) *n.*

clip[1] (klip) *n.* **1** Any appliance that clasps, grips, or holds fast. **2** *Med.* An appliance for stopping the bleeding of arteries, etc. **3** A flange on a horseshoe, projecting upward above the calk. **4** A spring clasp for holding letters, papers, etc.: also **paper clip.** **5** A pinching device for stopping the flow of a fluid in a flexible tube. **6** A metal container holding cartridges for a rapid-fire gun, as an automatic rifle: also **cartridge clip.** — *v.t.* **clipped, clip·ping** **1** *Archaic* To clasp; embrace. **2** To encircle; hold tightly. [OE *clyppan* clasp]

clip[2] (klip) *v.t.* **clipped, clip·ping** **1** To cut or trim with shears or scissors, as hair or fleece. **2** To snip a part from, as a coin. **3** To cut short; curtail: to *clip* the ends of words. **4** *Colloq.* To strike with a sharp blow. **5** In football, to hurl oneself illegally across the backs of the legs of (an opponent who is not carrying the ball.) **6** *Slang* To cheat or defraud. — *v.i.* **7** To cut or trim. **8** *Colloq.* To run or move swiftly. — **to clip the wings of** To check the aspirations or ambitions of. — *n.* **1** The act of clipping, or that which is clipped off. **2** The wool yielded at one shearing or season. **3** *Colloq.* A blow with the hand or fist; a swinging or glancing hit. **4** *Colloq.* A quick pace: going at a good *clip.* **5** *pl.* Shears; snuffers. **6** *Colloq.* An effort or attempt. [<ON *klippa*]

clip·board (klip′bôrd′, bōrd′) *n.* A small board for writing and having a spring clip for holding paper in place.

clipped form A shortened form of a polysyllabic word, as *bus* for *omnibus, gym* for *gymnasium,* or *exam* for *examination.* Also **clipped word.**

clip·per (klip′ər) *n.* **1** One who or that which clips. **2** One who clips coins. **3** An instrument for clipping hair. **4** *pl.* Shears; especially, pruning shears or sheep shears. **5** *Naut.* A certain type of sailing vessel built for speed, with tall, aft-raked masts: also **clipper ship.** **6** *Colloq.* One who or that which moves swiftly, as a swift horse, a sled, or smart person.

Clip·per·ton Island (klip′ər·tən) A Pacific Island SW of Mexico, awarded to France in 1931; .6 square mile.

clip·ping (klip′ing) *adj.* **1** That cuts or clips. **2** That moves rapidly. — *n.* **1** The act of one who or that which clips. **2** That which is cut off or cut by clipping: a newspaper *clipping.*

clique (klēk, klik) *n.* An exclusive or clannish set; coterie. — *v.i.* **cliqued, cli·quing** To unite in a clique; act clannishly. See synonyms under CLASS. [<F < *cliquer* click, clap]

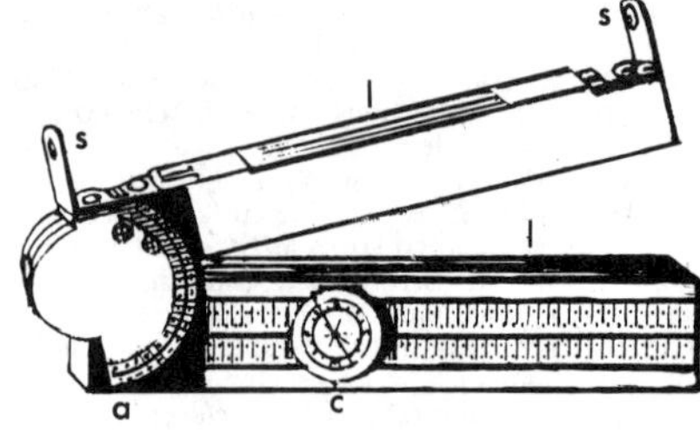

CLINOMETER
s.,s. Sights. *l.,l.* Levels. *a.* Sliding scale.
c. Compass for taking bearings of objects.

cli·quish (klē′kish, klik′ish) *adj.* Inclined to form cliques; exclusive. Also **cli′quey, cli′quy.** — **cli′quish·ly** *adv.* — **cli′quish·ness** *n.*

cli·sere (klī′sir) *n. Ecol.* A series of climax formations or zones which follow each other in a particular region as a consequence of a distinct change of climate. [< CLI(MATE) + SERE[2]]

clish·ma·clav·er (klish′mə·klav′ər) *n. Scot.* Foolish talk; gossip.

clis·tase (klīs′tās) *n. Ecol.* The state or condition of vegetation in a given layer of fossil plant deposits, indicating a climatic change. [< CLI(MAX), def. 2 + STASE

Clis·the·nes (klis′thə·nēz) See CLEISTHENES.

clis·tog·a·mous (klīs·tog′ə·məs) See CLEISTOGAMOUS.

cli·tel·lum (kli·tel′əm) *n.* The swollen, glandular portion of the skin in some earthworms. [< NL < L *clitellae* packsaddle]

clith·ro·pho·bi·a (klith′rə·fō′bē·ə) *n.* Claustrophobia. [< Gk. *kleithron* bar + -PHOBIA]

cli·to·ris (klī′tə·ris, klit′ə-) *n. Anat.* An erectile organ of the female of most vertebrates, at the anterior part of the vulva: the homolog of the penis. [NL < Gk. *kleitoris* < *kleiein* close, confine]

Clive (klīv), **Robert,** 1725–74, Baron Clive of Plassey, English general and statesman, founded the empire of British India.

cli·vers (klī′vərz) See CLEAVERS.

clo·a·ca (klō·ā′kə) *n. pl.* **·cae** (-sē) **1** *Zool.* The common cavity into which the various ducts of the body open in certain fishes, reptiles, insects, etc. **2** A sewer; sink; privy; a general receptacle for or repository of filth. [< L, a drain] —**clo·a′cal** *adj.*

cloak (klōk) *n.* **1** A loose outer garment. **2** Something that covers or hides; a pretext; disguise; mask. See synonyms under PRETENSE. —*v.t.* To cover with a cloak; disguise; conceal. See synonyms under HIDE, MASK, PALLIATE. [< OF *cloque, cloke* < Med. L *cloca* bell, cape; so called from its bell-like shape. Doublet of CLOCK.]

cloak·room (klōk′ro͞om′, -ro͝om′) *n.* A room where hats, coats, luggage, etc., are cared for temporarily.

clob·ber (klob′ər) *v.t. Slang* To beat or trounce; strike (someone) severely. [? Freq. of CLUB[1], *v.*]

cloche (klōsh, *Fr.* klôsh) *n.* **1** A woman's close-fitting, bell-shaped hat. **2** A portable translucent cover for the protection and forcing of young plants. [< F, bell]

clock[1] (klok) *n.* **1** An instrument for measuring and indicating time by mechanical movements; a timepiece. **2** Any clocklike, mechanical, registering device for recording distance, output, etc. —**what o'clock, six o'clock,** etc. See O'CLOCK. —*v.t.* To determine the rate of speed of an automobile or of any racing event by means of a stopwatch. [< MDu. *clocke* < OF *cloque, cloche* bell < Med. L *cloca.* Doublet of CLOAK.]

clock[2] (klok) *n.* An embroidered ornament on the side of a stocking or sock at the ankle. —*v.t.* To ornament with clocks. [Origin uncertain]

clock·mak·er (klok′mā′kər) *n.* One who makes or repairs clocks.

clock·wise (klok′wīz′) *adj. & adv.* Moving in the direction traveled by the hands of a clock.

clock·work (klok′wûrk′) *n.* The machinery of a clock, or any similar mechanism. —**like clockwork** With regularity and precision.

clod (klod) *n.* **1** A lump of earth, clay, etc.; hence, the soil. **2** Anything earthy, as the body of man compared with his soul. **3** The cut of beef on the back part of the foreshoulder above the shank. **4** A dull, stupid fellow, —*v.t.* **clod·ded, clod·ding 1** To throw clods or stones at. —*v.i.* **2** To turn into clods; clot; coagulate. [Var. of CLOT] —**clod′dish** *adj.* —**clod′dish·ness** *n.* —**clod′dy** *adj.*

clod·hop·per (klod′hop′ər) *n.* **1** A plowman; rustic; lout. **2** *pl.* Large, heavy shoes, such as those worn by plowmen, farm workers, etc.

Clo·do·ve·o (klō′tho·vā′ō) Spanish form of CLOVIS.

clod·pate (klod′pāt′) *n.* A blockhead; a stupid person. Also **clod·poll** (klod′pōl′), **clod′pole′.**

clog (klog) *n.* **1** Anything that impedes motion, as a block attached to an animal or a vehicle. **2** An encumbrance; a hindrance. **3** A wooden-soled shoe. **4** A clog dance. See synonyms under IMPEDIMENT, LOAD. —*v.* **clogged, clog·ging** —*v.t.* **1** To choke up or obstruct. **2** To place impediments in the way of; hinder. **3** To fasten a clog to; hamper the movements of by a clog; hobble. —*v.i.* **4** To become choked up. **5** To be retarded or hindered. **6** To adhere in a mass; coagulate. **7** To perform a clog dance. See synonyms under HINDER, OBSTRUCT. [ME *clogge* block of wood] —**clog′gy** *adj.* —**clog′gi·ness** *n.*

clog almanac An early form of calendar made by cutting notches on the edges of a square block of wood, brass, or horn, and engraving devices upon it: also called *runic staff.*

clog dance A dance performed with clogs or other shoes, the clatter of which emphasizes the rhythm of the music.

cloi·son·né (kloi′zə·nā′) *n.* **1** A method of producing designs in enamel by laying out the pattern with strips of flat wire and filling the interstices with enamel paste, which is then fused in place. **2** The ware so produced. —*adj.* Of, pertaining to, or made by this method. [< F < *cloison* a partition]

clois·ter (klois′tər) *n.* **1** A covered walk, generally following the walls of buildings enclosing a quadrangle, as in a monastery or college. **2** A building devoted to the secluded life; a monastery; convent. **3** Monastic life. —*v.t.* **1** To seclude; confine, as in a cloister. **2** To provide with cloisters. [OF *cloistre* < L *claustrum* enclosed place] —**clois′ter·er** *n.* —**clois′tral** *adj.*

Synonyms (noun): abbey, convent, friary, hermitage, monastery, nunnery, priory. *Cloister, abbey, convent,* and *priory* are for either sex; a *friary* is always for men, a *nunnery* for women, a *monastery* commonly for men. A *priory* (governed by a prior or prioress) is inferior to an *abbey* (governed by an abbot or abbess). The word *monastery* lays stress upon the loneliness; *convent* emphasizes the association of its inmates. A *hermitage* was originally for a single recluse, but the word came to be applied to collections of hermits' cells.

clois·tered (klois′tərd) *adj.* **1** Built with cloisters. **2** Living in cloisters: *cloistered* nuns. **3** Concealed or withdrawn from the world.

clois·tress (klois′tris) *n.* A nun.

clomb (klōm) Archaic past tense and past participle of CLIMB.

clone (klōn) *n.* **1** A group of organisms derived from a single individual by asexual means. **2** An exact genetic replica of an organism. **3** A duplicate. Also **clon** (klōn, klon). —*v.t.* **cloned, clon·ing 1** To produce in the form of a clone. **2** To produce a clone. [< Gk. *klōn* sprout, twig] —**clon′al** *adj.*

clon·ing (klōn′ing) *n.* The production of progeny that is genetically identical with a single progenitor.

clo·nus (klō′nəs) *n. Pathol.* A form of muscular convulsion, characterized by violent contraction and relaxation. [< Gk. *klonos* motion] —**clon·ic** (klon′ik) *adj.* —**clo·nic·i·ty** (klə·nis′ə·tē) *n.*

cloot (klo͞ot) *n. Scot.* A cloven hoof, or one of its parts.

Cloot (klo͞ot) *Scot.* The devil. Also **Cloo·tie** (klo͞o′tē).

Clootz (klōts), **Baron Jean Baptiste,** 1755–94, French revolutionary leader, born in Prussia: called *Anacharsis Clootz.*

close (klōs) *adj.* **clos·er, clos·est 1** Enclosed or partly enclosed; shut in or about; confined; encompassed by limits, walls, or bounds; hence, kept in confinement: a *close* prisoner. **2** Closed so as to confine, restrict, or keep out something; fast shut: a *close* box. **3** Near or near together, in space, time, etc.: The two houses were *close* to each other. **4** Divided by small intervals: a *close* sequence of events. **5** Marked by nearness in space, order, or arrangement: marching in *close* order. **6** Dense; compact: a *close* fabric. **7** Affectionately associated; trusty; intimate: a *close* friend. **8** Exactly or literally executed; near in thought or performance to some aim, purpose, or standard: a *close* copy. That shot was *close.* **9** Narrowly confined or attentive to some object; watchful; strict; searching: a *close* search. **10** Nearly even or equal, without much difference in favor of either side: a *close* election. **11** Concealing one's thoughts and feelings; secretive; reticent. **12** Not liberal; stingy. **13** Ill-ventilated; heavy; stifling; dense: *close* weather. **14** *Colloq.* Difficult to obtain; tight: said of money or the money market. **15** Shut or restricted by law; not open or free: a *close* season for fishing; a *close* corporation. **16** Fitting tightly or snugly: a *close* cap. **17** Near to the surface: a *close* shave. **18** *Phonet.* Describing those vowels pronounced with a part of the tongue relatively close to the palate, as the (ē) in *seat*; high: opposed to *open.* See synonyms under ADJACENT, AVARICIOUS, FIRM, IMMEDIATE, IMPENETRABLE, TACITURN. —*v.* (klōz) **closed, clos·ing** *v.t.* **1** To shut, as a door. **2** To fill or obstruct, as an opening or passage. **3** To bring the parts of together, as a knife or book. **4** To bring into contact; join, as parts of an electric circuit. **5** To bring to an end; terminate. **6** To shut in; enclose. —*v.i.* **7** To become shut or closed. **8** To come to an end. **9** To grapple; come to close quarters. **10** To join; coalesce; unite. **11** To come to an agreement. **12** To be worth at the end of a business day: Stocks *closed* at an average three points higher. —**to close down 1** To come upon; enfold: Night *closed down.* **2** To suppress: The law *closed down* on gambling. **3** To discontinue a business or venture. —**to close in** To advance and surround. —**to close out** *U.S.* To sell all of, as goods, usually at a reduced price. —**to close up** To make all final arrangements: to *close up* one's affairs. —*n.* (klōz) **1** The end; conclusion. **2** A grapple. **3** A junction; meeting. **4** (klōs) Any place shut in or enclosed, as by a fence; specifically, the precinct of a cathedral or abbey. **5** (klōs) *Law* Land adjoining a house. **6** (klōs) An interest in the soil entitling the holders to damages in event of trespass. —**to break close** To trespass. —*adv.* (klōs) Closely. [< OF *clos,* pp. of *clore* close < L *claudere* close] —**close·ly** (klōs′lē) *adv.* —**close·ness** (klōs′nis) *n.* —**clos·er** (klō′zər) *n.*

close-bod·ied (klōs′bod′ēd) *adj.* **1** Fitting closely, as the body of a coat. **2** Close-grained.

close call (klōs) *U.S.* A narrow escape.

closed chain (klōzd) *Chem.* Atoms of a molecule arranged in a cyclical form and represented by the symbol of a ring, as in benzene and aromatic compounds.

closed corporation A business enterprise in which the stock ownership is vested in a few persons. Also **close corporation** (klōs).

closed season That part of the year during which it is unlawful to catch or kill certain varieties of fish or game.

closed shop An establishment in which all the employees are union members.

closed syllable See under SYLLABLE.

close·fist·ed (klōs′fis′tid) *adj.* Stingy; miserly. —**close′fist′ed·ness** *n.*

close-fit·ting (klōs′fit′ing) *adj.* Fitting so tightly as to show the contours of the body.

close-grained (klōs′grānd′) *adj.* Compact in growth or structure; solid: said of wood, crystals, etc.

close-hauled (klōs′hôld′) *adj. & adv. Naut.* With the sails set for sailing as close to the wind as possible.

close-mouthed (klōs′mouthd′, -moutht′) *adj.* Not given to imparting formation; taciturn; uncommunicative.

close-or·der drill (klōs′ôr′dər) *Mil.* A systematic exercise in information marching and in the formal handling of arms.

close quarters 1 In fighting, an encounter at close range or hand-to-hand. **2** A small, confined space or lodgment.

close shave *Colloq.* A narrow escape; close call.

close stitch The buttonhole stitch.

close-stool (klōs′sto͞ol′) *n.* A covered box containing a commode.

clos·et (kloz′it) *n.* **1** A small chamber, side room, or recess for storage of clothes, linen, etc., or for privacy. **2** The private chamber of a ruler, used as a council chamber, or as a chapel for devotion. **3** A watercloset; privy. —*v.t.* **clos·et·ed, clos·et·ing** To shut up or conceal in or as in a closet, especially for privacy: usually used with a reflexive pronoun. —*adj.* **1** Private; confidential. **2** Based on theory rather than practice: *closet* strategy. [< OF, dim. of *clos.* See CLOSE.]

closet drama A play or dramatic poem writ-

ten solely, or chiefly, for reading rather than performance.
close-up (klōs′up′) *n.* **1** In motion pictures and television, a picture of a character or a scene taken with the camera at close range. **2** A close look or view.
clos·trid·i·um (klos·trid′ē·əm) *n. pl.* **·trid·i·a** (-trid′ē·ə) *n. Bacteriol.* Any of a genus *(Clostridium)* of rod-shaped, spore-bearing, anaerobic bacteria, including pathogenic forms causing botulism, gas gangrene, and tetanus. [<NL <Gk. *klōstēr* spindle]
clo·sure (klō′zhər) *n.* **1** A proceeding to stop debate in a deliberative body in order to secure a prompt vote: also *cloture.* Compare PREVIOUS QUESTION. **2** A closing or shutting up: the *closure* of a shop. **3** *Obs.* That which closes or encloses; enclosure. — *v.t.* **clo·sured, clo·sur·ing** To apply closure to (a debate, etc.). [<OF <L *clausura* a closing < *claudere* close]
clot (klot) *n.* **1** A coagulated mass. **2** A thick, viscid, or coagulated mass of blood. — *v.t.* & *v.i.* **clot·ted, clot·ting** To form into clots; coagulate; mat, fill, or cover with clots. [OE *clott* lump, mass] — **clot′ty, clot′ted** *adj.*
cloth (klôth, kloth) *n. pl.* **cloths** (klôthz, klothz, klôths, kloths) **1** A woven fabric of wool, cotton, rayon, etc.; a piece of such fabric. **2** A piece of cloth for a special use, as a tablecloth. **3** *Naut.* A sail, or a breadth of the canvas that goes to make up a sail. **4** *Obs.* Raiment; clothes. — **the cloth** Clerical attire; hence, the clerical office; the clergy. [OE *clath*]
clothe (klōth) *v.t.* **clothed** or **clad, cloth·ing** **1** To cover or provide with clothes; dress. **2** To cover as if with clothing; invest. [OE *clathian*]
clothes (klōz, klōthz) *n. pl* **1** The articles of raiment worn by human beings; garments collectively; raiment; clothing. **2** Covering for a bed; bedclothes. See synonyms under DRESS. [OE *clathas,* pl. of *clath* cloth]
clothes hanger A metal, plastic, or wooden device on which a garment may be hung.
clothes·horse (klōz′hôrs′, klōthz′-) *n.* **1** A frame on which to hang or dry clothes. **2** *Slang* A person regarded as excessively concerned with dress or as having little ability except for dressing well.
clothes·line (klōz′līn′, klōthz′-) *n.* A cord, rope, or wire on which to hang clothes to dry.
clothes moth Any of various moths, especially of the family *Tineidae,* whose larvae are destructive of wool, fur, and other animal products. For illustration see under INSECT (injurious).
clothes·pin (klōz′pin′, klōthz′-) *n.* A peg or clamp with which to fasten clothes on a line.
clothes·press (klōz′pres′, klōthz′-) *n.* A closet or chest for clothes; wardrobe.
clothes·tree (klōz′trē′, klōthz′-) *n.* A stand having arms or hooks on which to hang hats, coats, etc.
cloth·ier (klōth′yər) *n.* One who makes or sells cloths or clothing.
cloth·ing (klō′thing) *n.* **1** Dress collectively; apparel. **2** A covering.
Clo·tho (klō′thō) One of the three Fates. [<Gk. *klōthein* spin]
cloth-yard (klôth′yärd′, kloth′-) *n.* A rod used for measuring cloth, formerly 27 inches, now equal in length to the standard yard of 36 inches.
cloth-yard shaft An early English arrow for the longbow, a cloth-yard in length.
clo·ture (klō′chər) See CLOSURE (def. 1).
cloud (kloud) *n.* **1** *Meteorol.* A mass of visible vapor or an aggregation of watery or icy particles, floating in the atmosphere at various heights and exhibiting a large variety of shapes, which partly aid in the determination of weather conditions. In the International Code, clouds have been classified, according to height and typical formation, into four families and ten genera. See table below. **2** Something that darkens, obscures, dims, confuses, or threatens. **3** A dimmed appearance; a spot. **4** *Law* A defect; blemish: a *cloud* on a title. **5** A great multitude; a cloudlike mass: a *cloud* of arrows. — **in the clouds 1** Imaginary; fanciful. **2** Impractical. — *v.t.* **1** To cover with or as with clouds; dim; obscure. **2** To render gloomy or troubled. **3** To cover with obloquy or disgrace. **4** To variegate, as marble. — *v.i.* **5** To be overcast with or as with clouds. [OE *clūd* rocky mass, hill] — **cloud′less** *adj.* — **cloud′less·ly** *adv.*

CLOUD TABLE—INTERNATIONAL CODE

Families: A: high clouds, from 20,000 feet up; B: middle clouds, 6,500–20,000 feet; C: low clouds, near surface to 6,500 feet; D: vertical displacement clouds, 1,600–20,000 feet.

Type	*Symbol*	*Family*	*Av. ht. miles*
Altocumulus	Ac	B	2 1/2
Altostratus	As	B	3 1/2
Cirrocumulus	Cc	A	5
Cirrostratus	Cs	A	6
Cirrus	Ci	A	7
Cumulonimbus	Cb	D	4
Cumulus	Cu	D	2
Nimbostratus	Ns	C	1/4
Stratocumulus	Sc	C	1
Stratus	St	C	1/4

The following variations of the International Code are also accepted in the U.S. Weather Bureau procedure: *altocumulus castellatus* (Acc), *cumulonimbus mammatus* (Cm), *fractocumulus* (Fc), and *fractostratus* (Fs).
cloud attack In chemical warfare, a gas attack made with aircraft or by igniting chemical candles.
cloud band In Chinese art, a wavy ribbonlike conventionalization of a cloud.
cloud·ber·ry (kloud′ber′ē) *n. pl.* **·ries** An arctic or alpine species of raspberry *(Rubus chamaemorus)* producing an amber-colored fruit.
cloud·burst (kloud′bûrst′) *n.* A sudden flood of rain, as if a whole cloud had been discharged at once.
cloud-capped (kloud′kapt′) *adj.* Having clouds encircling the top.
cloud chamber See under CHAMBER.
cloud-drift (kloud′drift′) *n.* A mass of broken and flying clouds. Also **cloud′rack′.**
cloud·land (kloud′land′) *n.* The realm of fancy and dreams or of theory and speculation.
cloud·let (kloud′lit) *n.* A little cloud.
cloud·y (klou′dē) *adj.* **cloud·i·er, cloud·i·est** **1** Overspread with clouds. **2** Of or like a cloud or clouds. **3** Obscure; vague; confused. **4** Gloomy; sullen. **5** Not limpid or clear. **6** Marked with cloudlike spots. — **cloud′i·ly** *adv.* — **cloud′i·ness** *n.*
Clou·et (klōō·e′), **François,** 1516?–72, son of Jean, court painter to King Francis I. — **Jean,** 1485–1541, French painter.
clough (kluf, klou) *n.* A gorge or ravine. [ME *clough, cloghe,* OE (assumed) *cloh*]
Clough (kluf), **Arthur Hugh,** 1819–61, English poet.
clour (klōōr) *v.t. Scot.* To knock; thump; dent. — *n.* A blow, bump, or bash on the head.
clout[1] (klout) *n.* **1** A piece of cloth or leather; patch; rag. **2** *Often pl.* A swaddling cloth. **3** The center of a target. **4** An iron plate. **5** A short, stout nail for boot or shoe soles; a flat-headed nail for fastening iron plates: also called **clout nail. 6** *Colloq.* A heavy blow or cuff with the hand. **7** In baseball, a long hit to the outfield. **8** *U.S. Slang* Influence or power; especially, political weight; pull. — *v.t.* **1** *Colloq.* To hit or strike, as with the hand; cuff. **2** To patch or bandage crudely. **3** To protect with an iron plate. **4** To stud with iron nails. [OE *clut*]
clout[2] (klout) *n. Brit. Dial.* A stupid, loutish person; clod. [<Du. *kluit* clod]
clout·ed (klou′tid) *adj.* Clotted: said of cream.
clout·er·ly (klou′tər·lē) *adj. Brit. Dial.* Unhandy; clumsy.
clove[1] (klōv) *n.* A dried flower bud of a tropical evergreen tree *(Syzygium aromaticum),* the **clovetree** of the myrtle family: used as a spice. [<OF *clou (de girofle)* nail (of clove) <L *clavus* nail; so called from its shape]
clove[2] (klōv) A past tense and archaic past participle of CLEAVE[1].
clove[3] (klōv) *n. Bot.* One of the small bulbs formed in the axis of the scale of a mother bulb, as in garlic. [OE *clufu*]
clove-hitch (klōv′hich′) *n. Naut.* A knot consisting of two half-hitches, with the ends of the rope going in opposite directions: used for fastening a rope around a spar. See illustration under HITCH.
clo·ven (klō′vən) *adj.* Parted; split. See CLEAVE[1].
clo·ven-hoofed (klō′vən·hōōft′, -hōōft′) *adj.* **1** Having the foot cleft or divided, as cattle: also **clo′ven-foot′ed. 2** Satanic; bearing the mark of the evil one.
clove pink Any of several varieties of *Dianthus caryophyllus* having a sweet clovelike odor. Also **clove gilliflower.**
clo·ver (klō′vər) *n.* **1** Any of several species of plants (genus *Trifolium*) of the legume family, having dense flower heads and the leaves divided into three leaflets; especially, the common **red clover** *(T. pratense)* used for forage and adopted as the State flower of Vermont. **2** Any of certain other plants of the legume family, as melilot. — **in clover 1** Originally, in good pasture, as cattle in a clover field. **2** Prosperous; having an abundance. [OE *clāfre* trefoil]
clo·ver·leaf (klō′vər·lēf′) *n.* **1** An open automobile of early style, seating three or four persons, with entrance only through doors in front of forward seats. **2** A highway intersection designed so as to route traffic with-

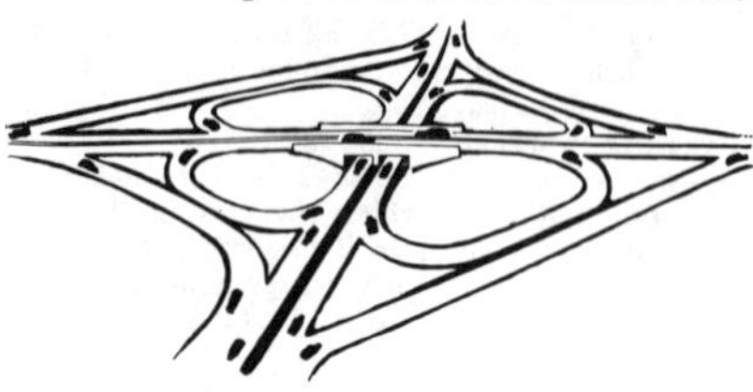

CLOVERLEAF

out interference, by means of a system of curving ramps from one level to another, in the form of a four-leaf clover. **3** *Aeron.* A testing maneuver in which an airplane flies in a course or pattern like a double figure-8 or a highway cloverleaf.
Clo·vis (klō′vis), 466–511, king of the Franks 481–511; traditional founder of the French kingdom: also called *Chlodwig.*
clown (kloun) *n.* **1** A professional buffoon in a play or circus, who entertains by antics, jokes, tricks, etc.; a zany; a jester. **2** A coarse or vulgar fellow; boor. **3** A countryman. — *v.i.* To behave like a clown. [Earlier *cloune* <MLG. Cf. Du. *kloen,* dial. Frisian *klönne*] — **clown′er·y** *n.*
clown·ish (klou′nish) *adj.* Of or like a clown; rude; ill-bred. See synonyms under AWKWARD. — **clown′ish·ly** *adv.* — **clown′ish·ness** *n.*
clown·ism (klou′niz·əm) *n.* Clownish gait and behavior, especially in certain psychiatric disorders.
cloy (kloi) *v.t.* To satiate, as with sweetness; surfeit. See synonyms under SATISFY. [Var. of earlier *accloy* <OF *encloyer* nail up, block, overload <LL *inclavare* nail < *clavus* a nail] — **cloy′ing·ly** *adv.* — **cloy′ing·ness** *n.*
club[1] (klub) *n.* **1** A stout stick or staff; cudgel; truncheon. **2** A staff with curved head of metal or wood used in golf, hockey, etc. **3 a** A three-lobed spot on a playing card. **b** A card so marked. **c** *pl.* The suit so marked. **4** *Naut.* A small spar by means of which a good set is given to a gaff topsail or a staysail; also, a similar spar on a staysail or jib to which the sheet is made fast. **5** *Entomol.* A clavate organ or part. — **Indian clubs** Bottle-shaped wooden clubs used in gymnastics. — *v.* **clubbed, club·bing** *v.t.* **1** To beat, as with a stick or club. **2** *Archaic* To gather into a clublike mass, as hair. — *v.i.* **3** *Archaic* To gather in a mass. — **to club a rifle** or **musket** or **gun** To turn a firearm so that the stock is uppermost and may be used as a club. [<ON *klubba.* Akin to CLUMP.]
club[2] (klub) *n.* **1** An organization of persons for social intercourse or other common object. **2** A house or room reserved for the meetings of such an organization. — *v.* **clubbed, club·bing** *v.t.* To contribute for a common purpose; make common stock of: to *club* resources. — *v.i.* To combine with a common object; form a club: often with *together.* — *adj.* Of, pertaining to, or belonging to a club; *club* grounds. [Special meaning of CLUB[1]]
club·ba·ble (klub′ə·bəl) *adj. Colloq.* Having tastes or qualities suited to club life; sociable. Also **club′a·ble.**
club car A railroad passenger car furnished with easy chairs, card tables, a buffet or bar, etc.
club·foot (klub′fōōt′) *n. pl.* **·feet 1** Congenital

distortion of the foot; talipes. 2 A foot so affected. **—club′foot′ed** *adj.*

club·grass (klub′gras′, -gräs′) *n.* The cat-tail.

club·hand (klub′hand′) *n.* 1 A deformity of the hand, analogous to clubfoot; talipomanus. 2 A hand so deformed.

club·haul (klub′hôl′) *v.t. Naut.* To put (a vessel) about when in danger of drifting on a lee shore, by letting go the lee anchor, hauling to windward by the hawser, when the vessel's head has come into the wind, and cutting the hawser when the sails are trimmed on the new tack.

club·house (klub′hous′) *n.* The building occupied by a club.

club·man (klub′mən, -man′) *n. pl.* **·men** (-mən, -men′) A man who is a member of a club or clubs, especially one who frequents fashionable places of entertainment.

club·moss (klub′môs′, -mos′) *n.* A widely distributed evergreen herb (genus *Lycopodium*).

club sandwich A sandwich containing three or more layers of bread filled with meat, lettuce, tomatoes, mayonnaise, etc.

club steak A small beefsteak cut from the loin.

club topsail *Naut.* A sail, as a gaff topsail, extended on the foot by a club.

club·wom·an (klub′wŏŏm′ən) *n. pl.* **·wom·en** (-wim′ən) A woman who is a member of a club or clubs, especially one who devotes much time to club social affairs.

cluck (kluk) *v.t.* 1 To call by clucking, as chickens. 2 To utter with a like sound: to *cluck* disapproval. *—v.i.* 3 To make the noise of a hen calling her chicks or brooding. 4 To make a sound of suction in the side of the mouth, as in urging a horse; make any sound similar to a cluck. *—n.* 1 A sound like that made by a brooding hen to call her chicks. 2 A hen. 3 *Slang* A person resembling a hen in stupidity. [Imit.]

clue (klōō) *n.* A guiding fact or idea which leads to the solution of a problem or mystery. See CLEW. [Var. of CLEW]

Cluj (klōōzh) A city in west central Rumania; former capital of Transylvania: German *Klausenburg*, Hungarian *Kolozsvár*.

Clum·ber spaniel (klum′bər) See under SPANIEL.

clump (klump) *n.* 1 A thick cluster; tuft; lump. 2 A dull sound, as of heavy tramping. 3 An irregular, clumsy, thick piece or mass. 4 *Bacteriol.* A mass of bacteria in a state of rest, as by the agency of agglutinins. *—v.t.* 1 To place or plant in a cluster or group. 2 To put an extra sole on (a shoe). 3 *Bacteriol.* To cluster together, as bacteria. *—v.i.* 4 To walk clumsily and noisily. 5 To form clumps. [<LG. Cf. Du. *klomp*. Akin to CLUB.] **—clump′y, clump′ish** *adj.*

clum·sy (klum′zē) *adj.* **·si·er, ·si·est** 1 Lacking dexterity, ease, or grace; awkward. 2 Rudely constructed; ill-contrived, so as to be unwieldy; ungainly. See synonyms under AWKWARD. [ME *clumsed*, pp. of *clumsen* be numb (with cold) <Scand. Cf. dial. Sw. *klumsen* benumbed.] **—clum′si·ly** *adv.* **—clum′si·ness** *n.*

clung (klung) Past tense and past participle of CLING.

Clu·ny (klü·nē′) A town in east central France; site of remains of a medieval Benedictine abbey.

clu·pe·id (klōō′pē·id) *n.* 1 Any one of a family of teleost fishes *(Clupeidae)* having compressed bodies, including the herrings, shads, etc. *—adj.* Pertaining to the *Clupeidae.* [<NL *Clupeidae* <L *clupea*, a kind of small fish]

clu·pe·oid (klōō′pē·oid) *adj.* Herringlike. *—n.* A fish of the herring family.

Clu·si·um (klōō′zhē·əm, -zē·əm) The ancient name for CHIUSI.

clus·ter (klus′tər) *n.* 1 A group or bunch, as of grapes. 2 A group of bombs dropped simultaneously. 3 An assembly; congregation. 4 In pyrotechnic illumination, a group of stars burning at the same time. *—v.t.* 1 To bring forth in or collect into clusters. 2 To provide with clusters. *—v.i.* 3 To grow in clusters, as grapes. 4 To gather in a cluster or clusters. [OE *clyster*] **—clus′tered** *adj.* **—clus′ter·y** *adj.*

cluster redpepper Bonnet pepper.

clutch[1] (kluch) *v.t.* 1 To seize eagerly; snatch, as with hands or talons. 2 To grasp and hold firmly. *—v.i.* 3 To attempt to seize, snatch, or reach: with *at*: to *clutch at* shadows. *—n.* 1 A tight, powerful grasp. 2 *pl.* Cruel, powerful claws or hands; hence, rapacious or cruel power: to fall into the *clutches* of an enemy. 3 A talon, paw, claw, or hand. 4 *Mech.* Any of variously constructed and operated devices for coupling two working parts; also, any appliance suitable for seizing and holding. See synonyms under CATCH. [ME *clucchen*, var. of *clicche*, OE *clyccan* grasp]

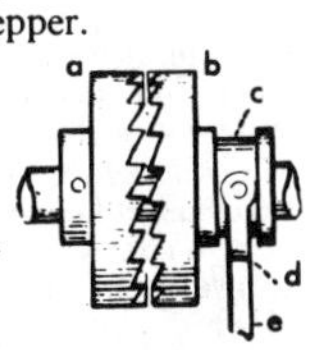

CLUTCH
a. Fixed member.
b. Slidable and splined member.
c. Collar.
d. Fork.
e. Lever.
The fork is controlled by the lever which slides *b* into connection with *a*.

clutch[2] (kluch) *n.* A sitting of eggs; a brood of chickens. *—v.t.* To hatch [<ON *klekja* hatch]

Clu·tha (klōō′thə) The largest river of South Island, New Zealand, flowing 210 miles SE to the Pacific.

clut·ter (klut′ər) *n.* 1 A disordered state or collection; litter. 2 A clattering, confused noise; chattering. *—v.t.* 1 To litter, heap, or pile in a confused manner: often with *up.* *—v.i.* 2 To be littered or strewn with objects in a disorderly manner. 3 To run or move with bustle or confusion; clatter. 4 To speak hurriedly and inexactly. [Var. of earlier *clotter*, freq. of CLOT]

Clyde (klīd), **Baron** See CAMPBELL, SIR COLIN.

Clyde (klīd) A river in SW Scotland, flowing 106 miles NW to the **Firth of Clyde,** its delta on the North Channel.

Clydes·dale (klīdz′dāl) *n.* A breed of draft horses originating in the valley of the Clyde, Scotland.

Cly·mer (klī′mər), **George,** 1739–1813, American patriot; legislator; signer, from Pennsylvania, of the Declaration of Independence.

clyp·e·ate (klip′ē·āt) *adj.* 1 Shield-shaped: also **clyp·e·i·form** (klip′ē·ə·fôrm′). 2 Having a clypeus. Also **clyp′e·at′ed.**

clyp·e·us (klip′ē·əs) *n. pl.* **clyp·e·i** (klip′ē·ī) 1 *Entomol.* A shieldlike plate on the front part of the head of an insect. 2 *Bot.* A band encircling the perithecium of certain fungi. [<L, shield]

clys·ter (klis′tər) *n. Med.* An intestinal injection; enema. [<F *clystère* <Gk. *klystēr* <*klyzein* wash out, rinse]

Cly·tem·nes·tra (klī′təm·nes′trə) In Greek legend the wife of Agamemnon who, with her lover Aegisthus, killed her husband on his return from the Trojan War and was herself killed by her son Orestes. Also **Cly′taem·nes′tra.**

Cm *Chem.* Curium (symbol Cm).

Cni·dus (nī′dəs) An ancient Greek city in SW Asia Minor. Also **Cni′dos.**

Cnos·sus (nos′əs) An ancient city of Crete, its capital during the Minoan period: also *Knossos.* Also **Cnos′sos.**

Cnut (knōōt) See CANUTE.

Co *Chem.* Cobalt (symbol Co).

co-[1] *prefix* With; together; joint or jointly: used with verbs, nouns, adjectives, and adverbs. See the foot of the page for a list of self-explanatory words containing the prefix *co-.* [<L *co-*, var. of *com-* before *gn, h,* and vowels <*cum* with]

co-[2] *prefix* 1 *Math.* Of the complement: *cosine.* 2 *Astron.* Complement of: *codeclination.* [<L *complementum* complement]

co·a·cer·vate (kō′ə·sûr′vāt, kō·as′ər-) *n. Chem.* The material precipitated in coacervation. [<L *coacervatus*, pp. of *coacervare* pile up <*co-* together + *acervus* heap]

co·ac·er·va·tion (kō·as′ər·vā′shən) *n. Chem.* The precipitation of minute liquid droplets from a mixture of two hydrophilic colloids having opposite electric charges.

coach (kōch) *n.* 1 A large four-wheeled closed carriage. 2 A two-door, two-seated, closed automobile. 3 A stagecoach. 4 A passenger bus. 5 A railway passenger car, usually providing the lowest-priced accommodations on a train. 6 A private tutor. 7 A trainer and director in athletics. 7 In baseball, a member of the team at bat stationed near first or third base to advise the base runners. *—v.t.* 1 To tutor or train; prepare by training or drilling. 2 To place or carry in a coach. 3 In baseball, to direct base runners in their movements, as from first or third base. *—v.i.* 4 To study with or be trained by a coach or trainer. 5 To act as coach or trainer. 6 To ride or drive in a coach. [<MF *coche* <Magyar *kocsi* of Kocs, a Hungarian village where first used]

coach-and-four (kōch′ən·fôr′, -fōr′) *n.* A coach drawn by four horses.

coach dog A Dalmatian.

coach·er (kō′chər) *n.* 1 One who coaches. 2 In baseball, a coach. 3 A coach horse. 4 *Obs.* A coachman.

coach horse A horse suitable for drawing a coach.

coach·man (kōch′mən) *n. pl.* **·men** (-mən) 1 One who drives a coach or a carriage. 2 In angling, a variety of artificial fly.

co-act (kō·akt′) *v.i.* To act or work together. **—co·ac′tion** *n.* **—co·ac′tive** *adj.*

co·act (kō·akt′) *v.t.* To force; compel; coerce. [<L *coactus*, pp. of *cogere* compel <*co-* together + *agere* do, drive]

co·ac·tion (kō·ak′shən) *n.* The exertion of force in compulsion or restraint.

co·ac·tive (kō·ak′tiv) *adj.* Having power to compel or constrain; compulsory.

co·ad·ju·tant (kō·aj′ə·tənt) *adj.* Cooperating. *—n.* An assistant; colleague. [<CO- + L *adjutans, -antis*, ppr. of *adjutare* help]

co·ad·ju·tor (kō·aj′ə·tər, kō′ə·jōō′tər) *n.* An associate in action; a co-worker or colleague, especially one appointed to assist in official duties, as the assistant of a bishop. See synonyms under ACCESSORY, ASSOCIATE, AUXILIARY. **—co·ad′ju·tress, co·ad′ju·trix** *n. fem.*

co·ad·u·nate (kō·aj′ə·nāt) *v.t.* To join together. *adj.* (kō·aj′ə·nit, -nāt) *Biol.* Closely joined, especially during the growth of an organ or part. [<L *coadunatus*, pp. of *coadunare* unite <*co-* together + *ad* to + *unus* one] **—co·ad′u·na′tion** *n.* **—co·ad′u·na′tive** *adj.*

co·ae·val (kō·ē′vəl) See COEVAL.

co·ag·u·lant (kō·ag′yə·lənt) *n.* A coagulation agent, as rennet. [<L *coagulans, -antis*, ppr. of *coagulare* curdle]

co·ag·u·late (kō·ag′yə·lāt) *v.t. & v.i.* **·lat·ed, ·lat·ing** To change from a liquid state into a clot or jelly, as blood. [<L *coagulatus*, pp. of *coagulare* curdle] **—co·ag′u·la·bil′i·ty** *n.* **—co·ag·u·la·ble** (kō·ag′yə·lə·bəl) *adj.* **—co·ag′u·la′tion** *n.* **—co·ag′u·la′tive** *adj.* **—co·ag′u·la′tor** *n.*

co·ag·u·lum (kō·ag′yə·ləm) *n. pl.* **·la** (-lə) Any coagulated mass, as a gel, curd, or clot. [<L, that which binds together]

Co·a·hui·la (kō′ä·wē′lä) A state in northern Mexico; 58,067 square miles; capital, Saltillo.

coak (kōk) See COKE[1].

coal (kōl) *n.* 1 A black, brittle, compact, amorphous substance of variable physical and chemical composition, produced by the carbonization of prehistoric vegetation: found in beds or veins in the earth and used as fuel; the principal varieties are bituminous coal, anthracite, and lignite. 2 A piece of coal as broken for use; such pieces collectively: in Great Britain commonly used in the plural. 3 A fragment of burned wood; charcoal. 4 An ember. **—to haul, rake,** etc., **over the coals** To criticize; reprimand. *—v.t.* 1 To supply with coal. 2 To reduce to coal, as wood, by burning. *—v.i.* 3 To take in coal. ◆ Homophone: *cole.* [OE *col*]

Coal may appear as a combining form in

coadequate	**coadmire**	**coagitate**	**coambassador**	**coapparition**	**coapprover**	**coassessor**
coadminister	**coadmit**	**coagitation**	**coanimate**	**coappear**	**coarbiter**	**coassignee**
coadministration	**coadventure**	**coagitator**	**coannex**	**coappearance**	**coarrange**	**coassist**
coadministrator	**coagency**	**coagriculturist**	**coannihilate**	**coappriser**	**coarrangement**	**coassistance**
coadmiration	**coagent**	**co-allied**	**coapostate**	**coapprove**	**coassession**	**coassistant**

hyphemes or in solidemes, or in two-word phrases, as in:

coal ashes	**coal-dark**	**coal-heaver**
coal barge	**coal-dealer**	**coal-laden**
coalbin	**coal-dealing**	**coal mine**
coal-black	**coal deposit**	**coal-miner**
coal-blue	**coal-digger**	**coal-mining**
coalbox	**coal-digging**	**coalmonger**
coal bunker	**coal district**	**coal-producing**
coal-burner	**coal dust**	**coal-rationing**
coal-burning	**coal-eyed**	**coal-rich**
coal chute	**coalfield**	**coalshed**
coal-consumer	**coal-fired**	**coal strata**
coal-consuming	**coal furnace**	**coalyard**

coal bank A vein of coal at the surface.
coal bed A receptacle or place for coals, as in a forge. See illustration under FORGE.
coal car A railroad car designed to carry coal, as from a mine.
coal·er (kō′lər) *n.* One who or that which supplies or transports coal; a collier.
co·a·lesce (kō′ə·les′) *v.i.* **·lesced, ·lesc·ing** To grow or come together into one; fuse; blend. See synonyms under UNITE. [< L *coalescere* unite < *co-* together + *alescere,* inceptive of *alere* grow up] **—co′a·les′cence** *n.* **—co′a·les′cent** *adj.*
coal·fish (kōl′fish′) *n. pl.* **·fish** or **·fish·es** 1 A dark-colored food fish *(Pollachius virens)* of the cod family; the common pollack of the Atlantic. 2 The sablefish.
coal gas 1 The poisonous gas produced by the combustion of coal. 2 A gas used for illuminating and heating: produced by the distillation of bituminous coal and consisting chiefly of methane, carbon monoxide, and hydrogen.
coal·hole (kōl′hōl′) *n.* 1 A place for storing coal. 2 A covered hole in a sidewalk, through which coal is chuted to a bin or cellar.
coal·ing (kō′ling) *n.* 1 The burning of wood into charcoal; also, the place where this is done. 2 Loading with coal.
coaling station A place where boats or trains stop to take on coal.
co·a·li·tion (kō′ə·lish′ən) *n.* 1 An alliance of persons, parties, or states. 2 Coalescence. See synonyms under ALLIANCE, UNION. [< L *coalitio, -onis* < *coalescere.* See COALESCE.] **—co′a·li′·tion·ist** *n.*
Coal Measures A division of the Carboniferous series containing workable beds of coal.
coal oil Kerosene.
coal·pit (kōl′pit′) *n.* 1 A pit from which coal is obtained. 2 A pit for making charcoal.
coal·sack (kōl′sak′) *n.* 1 A sack for coal. 2 *Astron.* One of several dark spaces in the Milky Way, especially **the Coalsack,** a large space near the Large and Small Magellanic clouds in the constellation of the Southern Cross.
coal scuttle A bucketlike container with a lip and a handle, used for containing and carrying coal.
coal tar The black viscid pitch distilled from bituminous coal, and yielding a large variety of organic compounds used in the making of dyestuffs, explosives, flavoring extracts, drugs, plastics, etc. **—coal′-tar′** *adj.*
coam·ing (kō′ming) *n. Naut.* 1 A raised curb about a hatchway, well, or skylight, to keep water from entering: also spelled *combing.* 2 One of the pieces in such a curb. [Origin unknown]
co·arc·tate (kō·ärk′tāt) *adj.* 1 *Bot.* Crowded together, as a panicle of flowers; compressed. 2 *Entomol.* Constricted at the base, as the abdomen of an insect. [< L *coarctatus,* pp. of *coarctare,* var. of *coartare* confine, constrain < *co-* together + *artus* crowded]
co·arc·ta·tion (kō′ärk·tā′shən) *n.* Stricture or contraction, as of a cavity or orifice.
coarse (kôrs, kōrs) *adj.* 1 Composed of large or rough parts or particles; not fine or delicate. 2 Inferior in quality; common. 3 Low; vulgar; indelicate. See synonyms under BLUFF, BRUTISH, COMMON, IMMODEST, LARGE, ROUGH, RUSTIC, VULGAR. ◆ Homophone: *course.* [Adjectival use of COURSE in sense "customary sequence" (as in *of course*); hence, usual, ordinary] **—coarse′ly** *adv.* **—coarse′ness** *n.*
coarse-grained (kôrs′grānd′, kōrs′-) *adj.* 1 Having a coarse grain or texture. 2 Crude; indelicate; low.
coars·en (kôr′sən, kōr′-) *v.t.* & *v.i.* To make or become coarse.
coast (kōst) *n.* 1 The land next to the sea; the seashore. 2 *Obs.* A region; boundary: used chiefly in the plural. 3 A slope suitable for sliding, as on a sled; also, a slide down it. **—the Coast** *U.S.* That part of the United States bordering on the Pacific Ocean. **—the coast is clear** There is no danger or difficulty now. *—v.t.* 1 To sail or travel along, as a coast or border. *—v.i.* 2 To sail or travel along a coast or littoral, keeping in sight of land; to travel from port to port along a coast. 3 To slide or ride down a slope by force of gravity alone, as on a sled or bicycle. 4 To continue moving on momentum after the source of power has been stopped. 5 To move or behave aimlessly. [< OF *coste* < L *costa* rib, flank]
coast·al (kōs′təl) *adj.* 1 Of or pertaining to the coast. 2 Bordering or skirting a coastline.
coast artillery Units of heavy artillery, fixed or movable, for defense against hostile ships.
coast·er (kōs′tər) *n.* 1 One who or that which coasts, as a person or vessel engaged in the coasting trade. 2 A sled or toboggan. 3 Formerly, a tray used in passing a decanter around a dining table. 4 A small disk of glass or other material on which to set a drinking glass to protect the surface underneath from moisture or heat.
coaster brake A free-wheel clutch brake on a bicycle, operated by reversing the pressure on the pedals.
coast guard 1 Naval or military coast police. 2 A member of this police. **—United States Coast Guard** A police or military force stationed along the coasts to enforce customs, immigration, and navigation laws and maintain an ice patrol. It operates in wartime within the U.S. Navy and at other times under the Department of the Treasury.
coast·ing (kōs′ting) *n.* 1 The act of sliding down a snow-covered hill or track on a sled. 2 The act of going down grade by force of gravity, as on a bicycle or in a car. 3 Trade up and down the same coast from port to port: also **coasting trade.**
Coast Mountains A range in western British Columbia and southern Alaska; highest point, 13,260 feet.
Coast Province A region of SE Kenya on the Indian Ocean; 26,651 square miles; capital, Mombasa.
Coast Ranges A mountain belt of western North America, extending along the Pacific coast from Alaska into Lower California; highest peak, 19,850 feet.
coast·ward (kōst′wərd) *adj.* Directed or facing toward the coast. *—adv.* Toward the coast: also **coast′wards.**
coast·wise (kōst′wīz′) *adj.* Following or along the coast. *—adv.* By way of or along the coast: also **coast′ways′.**
coat (kōt) *n.* 1 A sleeved outer garment opening down the front, of varying length: worn as part of an outfit or as an out-of-door covering over one's usual clothing. 2 Any outer covering, as the fur of an animal, a layer of ice or paint, etc. 3 A coat of arms. 4 *Dial.* A skirt; petticoat. 5 *Obs.* The distinctive vesture of an order of men; cloth. *—v.t.* To cover with or as with a coat, as of paint. [< OF *cote* < Med. L *cota* garment] **—coat′·less** *adj.*
coat·ed (kō′tid) *adj.* 1 Having a covering, layer, or coat. 2 In papermaking, having a calendered surface of mineral matter, as sizing or china clay.
coat·ee (kō·tē′) *n.* A short coat.
Coates (kōts), **Albert,** 1882–1954, English conductor born in Russia. **—Joseph Gordon,** 1878–1943, New Zealand statesman.
co·a·ti (kō·ä′tē) *n. pl.* **·tis** A carnivorous, raccoonlike mammal (genus *Nasua*) of tropical America, with mobile snout, plantigrade feet, elongated body, and a long, ringed tail. Also **co·a′ti-mon′di, co·a′ti-mun′di** (-mun′dē). [< Tupian]
coat·ing (kō′ting) *n.* 1 A covering layer; coat. 2 Cloth for coats.
coat of arms The armorial bearings of a person or family.
coat of mail See under **mail**[2].
coat·tail (kōt′tāl′) *n.* 1 The loose hinder part of a coat below the waist. 2 *Usually pl.* The pendent, tapering, rear part of a man's dress coat.
Co·at·za·co·al·cos (kō·ät′sä·kō·äl′kōs) A city on the Gulf of Campeche in Veracruz state, SE Mexico: formerly *Puerto Mexico.*
coax (kōks) *v.t.* 1 To persuade or seek to persuade by gentleness and tact; wheedle. 2 To obtain by coaxing or cajolery. *—v.i.* 3 To use persuasion or cajolery. See synonyms under ALLURE, PERSUADE. *—n.* One who coaxes. **—coax′er** *n.* **—coax′ing·ly** *adv.* [< Earlier *cokes* a fool, dupe; origin unknown]
co·ax·i·al (kō·ak′sē·əl) *adj.* Having a common axis or coincident axes: also **co·ax·al** (kō·ak′səl).
coaxial cable A conducting wire for the transmission of radio or television signals or of multiple telegraph or telephone messages; held in the center of a metal tube by a series of closely-spaced disks, every element of the assembly being well insulated.
cob[1] (kob) *n.* 1 A roundish mass, heap, or lump, as a piece of coal or stone. 2 The woody spike of an ear of corn around which the kernels grow; a corncob. 3 A strong, thick-set, short-legged horse. 4 The male of the swan. 5 *Brit. Dial.* A leading man; a leader. [ME *cobbe*; origin uncertain]
cob[2] (kob) *n. Brit.* A gull, especially the great black-backed gull *(Larus marinus).* Also **cobb.** [Cf. Du. *kobbe* gull]
co·balt (kō′bôlt) *n.* A hard, brittle, magnetic metallic element (symbol Co, atomic number 27) usually found in iron and nickel ores, used in alloys, and biologically essential for the activity of several enzymes. See PERIODIC TABLE. [< G *kobalt,* var. of *kobold* goblin; so called by early miners who thought it a worthless, injurious ore]
cobalt bloom Erythrite.
cobalt blue 1 A permanent deep-blue pigment resembling ultramarine, made from the oxides of cobalt and aluminum. 2 An intense, pure blue.
co·bal·tic (kō·bôl′tik) *adj. Chem.* Designating a compound containing cobalt in its higher valence.
co·bal·tite (kō·bôl′tīt, kō′bôl·tīt) *n.* A metallic, silver-white, brittle cobalt sulfarsenide, CoAsS. Also **co·balt·ine** (kō′bôl·tēn, -tin).
co·bal·tous (kō·bôl′təs) *adj. Chem.* Designating a compound containing cobalt in its lower valence.
Cobb (kob), **Irvin Shrewsbury,** 1876–1944, U.S. humorist.
cob·ber (kob′ər) *Austral. Slang* A friend; companion; workfellow.
Cob·bett (kob′it), **William,** 1762–1835, English political economist.
cob·ble[1] (kob′əl) *n.* 1 A cobblestone. 2 A lump of coal as big as a cobblestone. *—v.t.* To pave with cobblestones. [Akin to COB[1]]
cob·ble[2] (kob′əl) *v.* **·bled, ·bling** *v.t.* 1 To make, patch, or repair, as boots or shoes. 2 To put together roughly. *—v.i.* 3 To work as a shoemaker. [Origin uncertain]
cob·ble[3] (kob′əl) See COBLE.
cob·bler[1] (kob′lər) *n.* 1 A shoemaker. 2 A clumsy workman. [< COBBLE[2]]
cob·bler[2] (kob′lər) *n.* 1 An iced drink made of wine, sugar, fruit juices, etc. 2 A deep-dish fruit pie with no bottom crust. [Origin unknown]
cob·ble·stone (kob′əl·stōn′) *n.* A rounded stone formerly much used for paving. [See COBBLE[1]]
cob coal A large round piece of coal; also, coal in such pieces or lumps.
Cob·den·ism (kob′dən·iz′əm) *n.* The policies of free trade, international peace, and aloof-

coassume	**co-attribution**	**co-believer**	**co-constituent**	**cocreditor**	**co-derive**	**coeffect**
co-attend	**co-auditor**	**coclause**	**co-contractor**	**cocurator**	**co-descendant**	**co-embody**
co-attest	**co-author**	**co-connection**	**co-covenanter**	**co-debtor**	**co-dominion**	**coembrace**
co-attestation	**co-authority**	**co-conscious**	**cocreate**	**co-defendant**	**co-edify**	**coeminency**
co-attribute	**co-authorship**	**co-conspirator**	**cocreator**	**co-delinquent**	**co-editor**	**coemperor**

ness from the European struggle for supremacy, advanced by **Richard Cobden,** 1804–1865, English statesman and political economist.

co•bel•lig•er•ent (kō′bə•lij′ər•ənt) *n.* A country fighting on the same side with another, or others, against a common enemy: distinguished from an *ally* in international usage in that it is not bound by an alliance.

Cóbh (kōv) A port in SW Ireland: formerly *Queenstown.*

Cob•ham (kob′əm), **Lord,** 1360?–1417, John Oldcastle, English Lollard leader.

cob•le (kob′əl) *n.* **1** *Brit.* A flat-bottomed fishing boat. **2** *Scot.* A flat-bottomed rowboat. Also spelled *cobble.* [OE (Northumbrian) *cuopl*]

Co•blenz (kō′blents) A city at the junction of the Rhine and Moselle in western Germany: also *Koblenz.*

cob•nut (kob′nut′) *n.* **1** A large nut from a cultivated variety of hazel tree *(Corylus avellana grandis).* **2** The tree producing it. **3** A children's game played with such nuts. [? < COB[1] (def. 1) + NUT]

co•bra[1] (kō′brə) *n.* Any of a genus *(Naja)* of very venomous snakes of Asia and Africa that when excited can dilate their necks into a broad hood; especially, the **spectacled cobra** *(N. naja)* of India, and the **king cobra** *(Ophiophagus hannah),* the largest known of all venomous snakes. [< Pg. < L *colubra* snake]

COBRA
a. Indian or spectacled cobra.
b. Back of head, showing markings or "spectacles."
(Up to 6 feet in length)

co•bra[2] (kob′rə) See COPRA.

co•bra-de-ca•pel•lo (kō•brə•dē•kə•pel′ō) *n. pl.* **co•bras-de-ca•pel•lo** The spectacled cobra. [< Pg., snake with a hood]

Co•burg (kō′bûrg, *Ger.* kō′bŏŏrkh) A city in Upper Franconia, central Germany: also *Koburg.*

cob•web (kob′web′) *n.* **1** The network of fine thread spun by a spider; also, a single thread of this. **2** A snare, or anything fine-spun or flimsy. —*v.t.* **cob•webbed, cob•web•bing** To cover with or as with cobwebs. [ME *coppeweb* < *coppe* spider + WEB] **—cob′web′ber•y** *n.*

cob•work (kob′wûrk′) *n.* A structure of logs laid crosswise, with ends secured by dovetailing.

co•ca (kō′kə) *n.* **1** The dried leaves of a South American shrub (genus *Erythroxylon*), yielding cocaine and other alkaloids and sometimes chewed for their stimulant properties. **2** Either of the two species of this shrub which yield these alkaloids. [< Sp. < Quechua]

co•caine (kō•kān′, kō′kān; *in technical usage* kō′kə•ēn) *n.* A white, bitter, crystalline alkaloid, $C_{17}H_{21}NO_4$, contained in coca leaves: used in medicine as a local anesthetic and as a narcotic. Also **co•cain′.** [< COCA]

co•cain•ism (kō•kā′niz•əm, kō′kə•niz′əm) *n. Pathol.* A morbid condition produced by the excessive use of cocaine; cocaine poisoning.

co•cain•ize (kō•kā′nīz, kō′kə•nīz) *v.t.* **•ized, •iz•ing** To bring under the specific effect of cocaine. **—co•cain′i•za′tion** *n.*

co•car•box•yl•ase (kō′kär•bok′səl•ās) *n.* A coenzyme necessary in the production and activity of carboxylase.

co•car•cin•o•gen (kō′kär′sin′ə•jən) *n.* Any noncarcinogenic agent that enhances the action of a carcinogen.

coc•cid (kok′sid) *n. Entomol.* Any member of a superfamily *(Coccoidae)* of hemipterous insects, including mealybugs and scale insects. [< NL *Coccoidae* < Gk. *kokkos* berry]

coc•cid•i•oi•dal granuloma (kok•sid′ē•oid′l) A disease caused by a fungus (genus *Coccidioides*) superficially resembling tuberculosis, which affects the lymph nodes of some animals and of man. [< NL *Coccidioides* < Gk. *kokkos* a berry + *eidos* form]

coc•cid•i•o•sis (kok•sid′ē•ō′sis) *n.* One of a group of specific infectious diseases caused by protozoan parasites (order *Coccidia*) which attack the epithelial tissue of animals, birds, and, rarely, man. [< NL *Coccidia* (< Gk. *kokkos* a berry) + -OSIS]

coc•cif•er•ous (kok•sif′ər•əs) *adj. Bot.* Bearing or producing berries. [< Gk. *kokkos* berry + -(I)FEROUS]

coc•coid (kok′oid) *adj. Bacteriol.* Like a coccus: applied to certain forms of bacteria which tend to be round in form.

coc•co•lith (kok′ə•lith) *n. Geol.* A minute oval or rounded body often abundant in deep-sea mud. [< Gk. *kokkos* berry + -LITH]

coc•cu•lus in•di•cus (kok′yə•ləs in′də•kəs) The fishberry.

coc•cus (kok′əs) *n. pl.* **coc•ci** (kok′sī) **1** *Bot.* **a** One of the dry, one-seeded portions into which a schizocarp splits. **b** A spore mother cell in which the spores are contained for a time after their maturity. **2** *Bacteriol.* One of the principal forms of bacteria, characterized by an ovoid or spherical shape: often used in combination: *streptococcus.* See illustration under BACTERIUM. **3** *Entomol.* One of a genus *(Coccus)* of scale insects. [< NL < Gk. *kokkos* berry]

coc•cyx (kok′siks) *n. pl.* **coc•cy•ges** (kok•sī′jēz) *Anat.* The caudal end of the spine. [< L < Gk. *kokkyx* cuckoo; from a fancied resemblance to a cuckoo's bill] **—coc•cyg•e•al** (kok•sij′ē•əl) *adj.*

Co•cha•bam•ba (kō′chä•bäm′bä) A city in central Bolivia.

Co•chin (kō′chin′) An administrative division of northern Travancore-Cochin, southern India; 1,493 square miles; capital, Ernakulam.

Co•chin (kō′chin, koch′in) *n.* A variety of large domestic fowl, of Asiatic origin, having heavily feathered legs. Also **Co′chin•chi′na.**

Cochin China A former name of SOUTH VIETNAM.

coch•i•neal (koch′ə•nēl′, koch′ə•nēl) *n.* A coloring matter yielding a brilliant scarlet dye, consisting of the dried bodies of the female *Dactylopius coccus,* a scale insect of tropical America and of Java. [< F *cochenille* < Sp. *cochinilla* < L *coccineus* scarlet < *coccus* a berry, grain of kermes < Gk. *kokkos*]

coch•le•a (kok′lē•ə) *n. pl.* **•le•ae** (-li•ē) *Anat.* A winding cavity in the internal ear, containing the essential organs of hearing. See illustration under EAR. [< L *cochlea* snail] **—coch′le•ar** *adj.*

coch•le•ate (kok′lē•āt) *adj.* Spirally twisted like a snail shell. Also **coch′le•at′ed.**

co•ci•na (kō•sē′nä) *n. SW U.S.* A kitchen. [< Sp.]

co•ci•ne•ra (kō′sē•nā′rä) *n. SW U.S.* A cook. [< Sp.]

cock[1] (kok) *n.* **1** A full-grown male of the domestic fowl. **2** Any male bird. **3** A leader; champion. **4** A weathercock. **5** A faucet, often with the nozzle bent downward. **6** In a firearm, the hammer; also, the position at which the hammer rests when raised. **7** A significant jaunty tip or upward turn; a bending or pricking up, as of a hat brim, the ears, eyes, etc. —*v.t.* **1** To raise the cock or hammer of (a firearm) preparatory to firing. **2** To turn up or to one side alertly, jauntily, or inquiringly, as the head, eye, ears, etc. —*v.i.* **3** To raise the hammer of a firearm. **4** To stick up; be prominent. —*adj.* Male: a *cock* lobster. [OE *cocc*]

cock[2] (kok) *n.* A small conical pile of straw or hay. —*v.t.* To arrange in piles or cocks, as hay. [< ON *kökkr* lump, heap]

cock[3] (kok) *n.* A ship's small boat; cockboat. [< F *coque*]

cock•ade (kok•ād′) *n.* A rosette, knot of ribbon, or the like, worn on the hat. [< MF *coquarde* < *coq* cock] **—cock•ad′ed** *adj.*

Cockade State Nickname of MARYLAND.

cock-a-doo•dle-doo (kok′ə•dōōd′l•dōō′) *n.* The characteristic crow of a cock; hence, a rooster.

cock-a-hoop (kok′ə•hōōp′, -hŏŏp′) *adj.* **1** Elated; exultant. **2** Boastful. —*adv.* Triumphantly. [Origin uncertain]

Cock•aigne (kok•ān′) *n.* **1** An imaginary region of luxury and ease. **2** Cockneydom. Also **Cock•agne′.** [< OF *cocaigne*; ult. origin uncertain]

cock•a•lo•rum (kok′ə•lôr′əm, -lō′rəm) *n.* A self-important little man. [Cf. Du. *kockeloeren* crow]

cock-and-bull (kok′ən•bŏŏl′) *adj.* Highly improbable; incredible: a *cock-and-bull* story.

cock•a•tiel (kok′ə•tēl′) *n.* An Australian cockatoo of the genus *Leptolophus,* especially *L. hollandicus.* Also **cock′a•teel′.** [< Du. *kaketielje*]

cock•a•too (kok′ə•tōō′, kok′ə•tōō) *n. pl.* **•toos** Any of various, bright-colored, crested parrots of the East Indies or Australia, especially one of the genus *Kakatoë.* [< Du. *kaketoe* < Malay *kākatūa*; infl. in form by COCK]

COCKATOO
(About 12 inches tall)

cock•a•trice (kok′ə•tris) *n.* **1** A fabulous serpent, said to be hatched from a cock's egg, deadly to those who felt its breath or met its glance. Compare **basilisk. 2** In the Bible, an unidentified species of deadly serpent. [< OF *cocatris,* infl. by *coq* cock, < Med. L *calcatrix* (< L *calcare* tread, walk), used to translate Gk. *ichneumōn* ICHNEUMON]

cock•boat (kok′bōt′) *n.* A small rowboat: also called *cock.* [< COCK[3] + BOAT]

cock•chaf•er (kok′chā′fər) *n.* Any of a widely distributed family *(Melolonthidae)* of scarabaeoid beetles, especially *Melolontha melolontha,* a large, European variety destructive to vegetation. [< COCK[1] (def. 3) + CHAFER]

cock•crow (kok′krō′) *n.* The early morning. Also **cock′crow′ing.**

cocked hat (kokt) **1** A hat with the brim turned up, especially one turned up in three places; a three-cornered hat. **2** A game of bowls played with three pins. **—to knock into a cocked hat** To demolish; ruin.

cock•er[1] (kok′ər) *n.* **1** A cocker spaniel. See under SPANIEL. **2** A cockfighter.

cock•er[2] (kok′ər) *v.t.* To spoil by indulgence; coddle. [Prob. < Scand. Cf. Norw. *kokla* crow, fuss over, pamper.]

cock•er•el (kok′ər•əl) *n.* A young cock. [Dim. of COCK[1]]

Cock•er•mouth (kok′ər•muth) A town in Cumberland County, England; birthplace of Wordsworth.

cock-eye (kok′ī′) *n.* A squinting eye.

cock-eye bob (kok′ī′) *Austral. Slang* A willy willy (def. 1).

cock-eyed (kok′īd′) *adj.* **1** Cross-eyed. **2** *Slang* Off center; askew. **3** Absurd; crazy. **4** Drunk; intoxicated.

cock•fight (kok′fīt′) *n.* A battle between cocks, especially between gamecocks. Also **cock′-match′. —cock′fight′er** *n.* **—cock′fight′ing** *adj.* & *n.*

cock•horse (kok′hôrs′) *n.* A child's rocking-horse, hobbyhorse, or the like.

cock•i•ness (kok′ē•nis) *n.* Jauntiness; also, conceit.

cock•ing (kok′ing) *n.* **1** Cockfighting. **2** The shooting of woodcocks.

cock•ish (kok′ish) *adj.* **1** Cocklike; cocky. **2** Strutting; self-assertive. **—cock′ish•ly** *adv.* **—cock′ish•ness** *n.*

cock•le[1] (kok′əl) *n.* **1** An edible European bivalve mollusk *(Cardium edule).* **2** The cockleshell. **3** A confection made with sugar

---

coemploy	**coendure**	**coerect**	**coestate**	**coexecutant**	**cofeoffeer**	**coheritor**
coenact	**coepiscopacy**	**coerectant**	**coeternal**	**coexecutor**	**coheir**	**co-incline**
coenactor	**coequate**	**coessential**	**coeternally**	**coexert**	**coheiress**	**co-include**
coenamor	**coequated**	**coestablish**	**coexchange**	**coexertion**	**coheirship**	**co-incorporate**
coenamorment	**coequation**	**coestablishment**	**coexchangeable**	**coextend**	**coheritage**	**co-idemnify**

and flour. **4** The fire chamber or dome of a hot-air furnace. **5** A shallow boat. **— cockles of one's heart** The depths or bottom of one's heart, or feelings. — *v.t.* & *v.i.* **cock·led, cock·ling** To wrinkle; pucker. [<F *coquille* <L *conchylium* shell <Gk. *conchylion,* dim. of *conchylē* shell, mussel]

cock·le[2] (kok′əl) *n.* A grass that grows among grain; the darnel. [OE *coccel*]

cock·le·boat (kok′əl·bōt′) *n.* A cockboat or cockle.

cock·le·bur (kok′əl·bûr′) *n.* **1** A low-branching, rank weed (genus *Xanthium*) of the composite family, with hard ovoid or oblong two-celled burs about an inch long. **2** *Brit.* The burdock.

cock·le·shell (kok′əl·shel′) *n.* **1** The shell of a cockle; especially, one valve of a scallop's shell worn in a pilgrim's hat. **2** A scallop shell. **3** A frail, light boat.

cock·loft (kok′lôft′, -loft′) *n.* A loft or attic under a roof. [Origin uncertain]

cock·ney (kok′nē) *n.* **1** One born in the East End of London, traditionally within the sound of the bells of St. Mary-le-Bow Church, in Cheapside, and speaking a characteristic dialect. **2** One having the traits or dialect of such a person; especially, an uneducated yet pretentious city person. **4** The characteristic dialect or accent of East End Londoners. **5** *Obs.* A petted child; an effeminate youth. — *adj.* Of or like cockneys or their speech. [ME *cokeney,* lit., cock's egg < *coken* cock's + OE *æg* egg; later, a pampered child, a soft or effeminate person, a city man] **— cock′ney·ish** *adj.* **— cock′ney·ism** *n.*

cock·ney·dom (kok′nē·dəm) *n.* The sphere or realm of cockneys; London and its suburbs.

cock·ney·ese (kok′nē·ēz′, -ēs′) *n.* Cockney dialect.

cock·ney·fy (kok′ni·fī) *v.t.* **·fied, ·fy·ing** Cause to resemble a cockney in speech or manners.

cock of the plains A large grouse (*Centrocercus urophasianus*): also called *sage cock, prairie cock.*

cock of the walk One who has overcome all opposition; leader or chief in any group. Also **cock of the loft.**

cock·pit (kok′pit′) *n.* **1** A pit or ring for cockfighting; hence, any place where many battles have taken place. **2** An apartment for the wounded in a warship. **3** *Naut.* In small yachts, a space lower than the rest of the deck. **4** *Aeron.* In some airplanes, an enclosed space for the pilot and co-pilot or a passenger. **5** *Obs.* The pit of a theater.

cock·roach (kok′rōch′) *n.* Any of a large group of swift-running, chiefly nocturnal insects (families *Blattidae* and *Phyllodromidae*) of world-wide distribution, having flat, oval, variously colored bodies, biting mouth parts, and a typically offensive odor, including such household pests as the Croton bug, the dark-brown Oriental cockroach (*Blatta orientalis*) and the large, winged American cockroach (*Periplaneta americana*). For illustration see INSECTS (injurious). [<Sp. *cucaracha*]

cocks·comb (koks′kōm′) *n.* **1** A plant (genus *Celosia*) with red flowers, suggesting the comb of a cock. **2** A coxcomb (def. 1). **3** A scarlet ridge on a jester's cap; also, the cap. Also spelled *coxcomb.*

cocks·head (koks′hed′) *n.* An annual shrubby herb (*Onobrychis caputgalli*) of the Mediterranean region, with purple flowers and small, crested, spine-bearing pods.

cock·shut (kok′shut′) *n. Obs.* Twilight.

cock·shy (kok′shī′) *n. pl.* **·shies** *Brit. Colloq.* **1** A mark to be shied or thrown at, as at fairs. **2** A throw, as at a mark.

cock·spur (kok′spûr′) *n.* **1** A spur on the leg of a cock. **2** A kind of hawthorn (*Crataegus crusgalli*) with long thorns: also **cockspur thorn.**

cock·sure (kok′shŏŏr′) *adj.* **1** Absolutely sure. **2** Self-confident; presumptuously sure. **3** *Obs.* Perfectly safe. **— cock′sure′ness** *n.*

cock·swain (kok′sən, -swān′) See COXSWAIN.

cock·tail[1] (kok′tāl′) *n.* **1** A short, mixed, alcoholic drink, variously flavored and prepared. **2** An appetizer, as chilled, diced fruits, fruit juices, or sea food seasoned with a highly spiced sauce. [? Alter. of F *coquetel,* a mixed drink popular in the 18th c.]

cock·tail[2] (kok′tāl′) *n.* **1** A horse with a docked tail. **2** An underbred horse. **3** A person of low breeding. [<COCK[1] (def. 1) + TAIL; with ref. to the appearance of a horse's docked tail]

cock-up (kok′up′) *n.* **1** A turned-up or cocked part or point of anything. **2** A cocked hat.

cock·y[1] (kok′ē) *adj.* **cock·i·er, cock·i·est** *Colloq.* Pert or forward; confident or overconfident; conceited; snobbish. **— cock′i·ly** *adv.*

cock·y[2] (kok′ē) *n. Austral.* A small farmer: cow *cocky*; cane *cocky*; bee *cocky.*

co·co (kō′kō) *n. pl.* **·cos** A widely distributed tropical palm tree (*Cocos nucifera*) that produces coconuts. Also **coco palm, coconut palm.** — *adj.* Made of coco fiber. [<Pg., grinning face; with ref. to the eyes of a coconut]

co·coa (kō′kō) *n.* **1** A powder made from the roasted, husked seed kernels of the cacao; chocolate. **2** A beverage made from it. **3** The light reddish-brown color of cocoa powder. [Alter. of CACAO]

cocoa butter Cacao butter.

co·co·bo·lo (kō′kō·bō′lō) *n.* Granadillo. [<Sp.]

co·co·grass (kō′kō·gras′, -gräs′) *n.* The nut-grass.

co·con·scious·ness (kō·kon′shəs·nis) *n. Psychol.* A latent or accompanying consciousness, on the fringe of awareness. **— co·con′scious** *adj.* **— co·con′scious·ly** *adv.*

co·co·nut (kō′kə·nut′, -nət) *n.* **1** The fruit of the coco palm, a white-meated seed enclosed in a hard shell, and containing a milky liquid **2** *Slang* The head or skull. Also **co′coa·nut′.**

coconut palm The coco or coco palm.

co·coon (kə·kōōn′) *n.* **1** The envelope spun by the larvae of certain insects, as silkworms, in which they are enclosed in the pupal or chrysalis state. **2** Any analogous structure, as the egg-bearing case of spiders, earthworms, etc. **3** *Mil.* The weatherproof covering of cellophane or quick-drying synthetic resin in which military or other heavy equipment may be sealed during transport or when not in use. — *v.t.* To envelop or place in a cocoon. [<F *cocon* < *coque* shell]

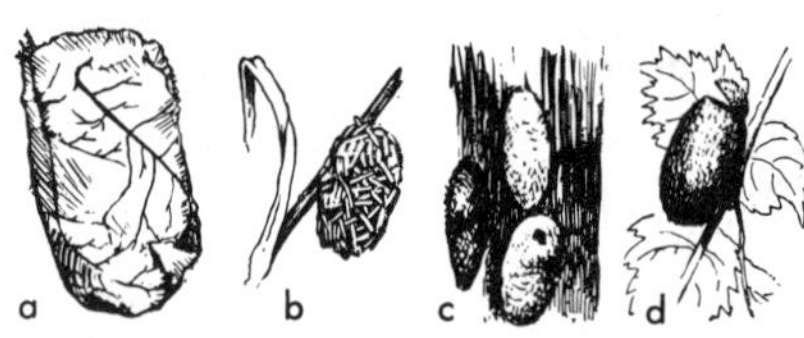

COCOONS
a. American silkworm. *b.* Caddis fly. *c.* Weevil under bark. *d.* Sawfly.

Co·cos Islands (kō′kōs) An island group SW of Java, comprising a dependency of Australia; 1.5 square miles: also *Keeling Islands.* Also **Co′cos-Kee′ling.**

co·cotte (kō·kot′, kə-) *n.* A young woman of dubious character or loose morals. [<F]

Coc·teau (kok·tō′), **Jean,** 1891–1963, French dramatist, novelist, critic, and poet.

coc·tion (kok′shən) *n.* The act or process of boiling. [<L *coctio, -onis* <*coquere* cook]

co·cur·ric·u·lum (kō′kə·rik′yə·ləm) *n.* The extra-curricular activities of students in the modern secondary school, such as athletics, student councils, clubs, fraternities, etc. **— co′cur·ric′u·lar** *adj.*

Co·cy·tus (kō·sī′təs) In Greek mythology, the river of wailing, one of the five rivers surrounding Hades.

cod[1] (kod) *n.* **1** An important gadoid food fish (*Gadus callarias*) of the North Atlantic, found especially from Newfoundland to Norway. **2** Any other gadoid fish. [Origin unknown]

cod[2] (kod) *n.* **1** A pod or husk. **2** A bag or envelope. **3** *Scot.* A pillow or cushion. [OE *codd* bag]

Cod (kod), **Cape** A peninsula of SE Massachusetts projecting 65 miles into the Atlantic and enclosing **Cape Cod Bay.**

co·da (kō′də) *n.* An independent musical passage, introduced at the conclusion of a movement, forming a more decided and usually somewhat elaborate termination; the finale of a sonata movement or of a fugue. [<Ital. <L *cauda* tail]

cod·der (kod′ər) *n.* A person or vessel occupied in codfishing.

cod·dle (kod′l) *v.t.* **·dled, ·dling** **1** To seethe or simmer in water; cook gently. **2** To treat as a baby or an invalid; pamper. See synonyms under CARESS, PAMPER. [? Akin to CAUDLE] **— cod′dler** *n.*

code (kōd) *n.* **1** A systematized body of law. **2** A system of signals, characters, or symbols with arbitrary, conventionalized meanings, used in communication: Language is a form of *code.* **3** A set of prearranged symbols, usually letters, used for purposes of secrecy or brevity in transmitting messages: the meanings of the symbols are given in a code book. Compare CIPHER. **4** A system of rules and regulations for the purpose of ensuring adequate standards of practice and uniformity in workmanship. See synonyms under LAW, LEGISLATION. **— civil code** A code regulating the civil relations of citizens. **— criminal** or **penal code** A code defining crimes and prescribing the method and degree of punishment. **— telegraphic code** A code convenient for use in telegraphing; specifically, the Morse or the International code, consisting of dots and dashes. — *v.t.* **cod·ed, cod·ing** **1** To systematize as laws; make a digest of. **2** To put into the symbols of a code. [<F <L *codex* writing tablet]

code beacon *Aeron.* A beacon which assists aviators in maintaining their flight course by flashing signals in code.

co·dec·li·na·tion (kō′dek·lə·nā′shən) *n. Astron.* The complement of the angle of declination: also called *polar distance.* [<CO-[2] + DECLINATION]

co·deine (kō′dēn, kō′di·ēn) *n. Chem.* A white crystalline alkaloid, $C_{18}H_{21}NO_3$, derived from morphine and widely used in medicine as a mild narcotic. Also **co·de·in** (kō′dē·in, kō′·dēn), **co·de·ia** (kō·dē′ə). [<Gk. *kōdeia* head of a poppy]

Code Na·po·lé·on (kôd nà·pô·lā·ôN′) The body of French civil law, put in force by Napoleon I between 1804–07.

co·dex (kō′deks) *n. pl.* **co·di·ces** (kō′də·sēz, kod′ə-) **1** A medieval manuscript in leaf form: distinguished from *scroll.* **2** A collection of canons or of formulas. **3** A code of laws. [<L, writing tablet]

Co·dex Ju·ris Ca·non·i·ci (kō′deks jŏŏr′is kə·non′ə·sī) A compilation of legislation of the Roman Catholic Church: in effect since 1918.

codg·er (koj′ər) *n. Colloq.* **1** A chap; a fellow. **2** A testy or eccentric old man. [Prob. var. of *cadger.* See CADGE.]

co·di·ces (kō′də·sēz, kod′ə-) Plural of CODEX.

cod·i·cil (kod′ə·səl) *n.* A supplement to a will. [<L *codicillus,* dim. of *codex* writing tablet] **— cod·i·cil·la·ry** (kod′ə·sil′ə·rē) *adj.*

cod·i·fy (kod′ə·fī, kō′də-) *v.t.* **·fied, ·fy·ing** To systematize, as laws. **— cod′i·fi·ca′tion** *n.* **— cod′i·fi′er** *n.*

cod·ling[1] (kod′ling) *n.* **1** A young cod. **2** A gadoid fish (genus *Phycis*) with filamentous ventral fins of two or three rays; a hake. [Dim. of COD[1]]

cod·ling[2] (kod′ling) *n.* **1** One of a group of varieties of cooking apple, elongated and tapering. **2** Formerly, any hard apple for stewing. Also **cod·lin** (kod′lin). [ME *querdling*; origin uncertain]

codling moth A moth (*Carpocapsa pomonella*) whose larvae, the apple worms, feed on the interior of apples, pears, quinces, and several other fruits. For illustration see under INSECT (injurious). Also **codlin moth.**

cod-liv·er oil (kod′liv′ər) Oil from the livers of cod, especially rich in vitamins A and D: used in cases of malnutrition.

---

co-indicate
co-infer
co-inhabit
co-inhabitant
co-inhabitor
co-inhere
co-inheritance
co-inheritor
co-inmate
co-inspire
co-inter
co-interest
co-intersect
co-inventor
co-involve
co-laborer
co-latitudinal
co-legatee
co-legislator
colunar
co-meddle
comortgagee
comourner
co-oblige
co-occupy
co-organize
co-original
co-originality
co-owner
co-ownership
co-parent
co-partner
co-passionate
co-pastor
co-patentee

cod·piece (kod′pēs′) *n.* An ornamented bag or flap attached to the front of the tight breeches worn by men of the 15th and 16th centuries. [ME *cod* scrotum + PIECE]

co·dress (kō′dres) *n.* A radiotelegraph message in which the address is given in the same code system as the body of the message. Compare PLAINDRESS. [<CO(DE) + (AD)DRESS]

Co·dy (kō′dē), **William Frederick,** 1846–1917, U.S. plainsman, army scout, and showman: called "Buffalo Bill."

co–ed (kō′ed′) *n. Colloq.* A young woman being educated at the same institution with young men. —*adj. Colloq.* Co–educational. Also **co′ed′.**

co–ed·u·ca·tion (kō′ej·o͝o·kā′shən) *n.* The education of both sexes together in the same classes or institution. —**co′–ed·u·ca′tion·al** *adj.*

co·ee–bird (kō′ē·bûrd′) *n.* The koel.

co·ef·fi·cient (kō′ə·fish′ənt) *n.* **1** A cooperating agent. **2** *Math.* A number or letter put before an algebraic expression and multiplying it. **3** *Physics* A number indicating the degree of magnitude, or the kind and amount of change under given conditions. —*adj.* Jointly efficient; acting together to a common end. —**co′ef·fi′cien·cy** *n.*

coefficient of friction *Physics* A number expressing the ratio between the force required to move one surface along another and the force, normal to the surfaces, pressing them together.

coe·la·canth (sē′lə·kanth) *n. Zool.* A large–bodied, hollow–spined crossopterygian fish, one species of which *(Latimeria chalumnae)* still survives. [<COEL(O)- + Gk. *akantha* spine]

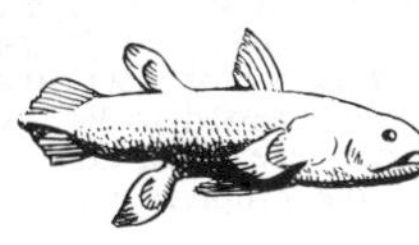
COELACANTH
(From 4 to 5 1/2 feet in length)

-coele See -CELE[2].

coe·len·ter·ate (si·len′tə·rāt) *n.* Any of a phylum of invertebrate animals *(Coelenterata)* having an enteric cavity occupying the entire interior of the body and functioning as a vascular as well as a digestive system: the phylum includes sea anemones, corals, jellyfish, and hydras. —*adj.* Belonging or pertaining to the *Coelenterata.* [<COEL(O)- + Gk. *enteron* intestine] —**coe·len·ter·ic** (sē′len·ter′ik) *adj.*

coe·len·ter·on (si·len′tə·ron) *n. pl.* **·ter·a** (-tər·ə) *Zool.* The primitive intestinal cavity of coelenterates; the archenteron.

Coe·le–Syr·i·a (sē′lē·sir′ē·ə) An ancient name for BEKÁA.

coe·li·ac (sē′lē·ak) See CELIAC.

coelo- *combining form* Cavity; cavity of the body, or of an organ. Also, before vowels, **coel-.** [<Gk. *koilos* hollow]

coe·lom (sē′ləm) *n. Zool.* The body cavity of a metazoan; the space between the viscera and the body wall. Also **coe·lome** (sē′lōm). [<Gk. *koilōma* cavity <*koilos* hollow]

coe·lo·stat (sē′lə·stat) *n. Astron.* An instrument consisting of a mirror driven by clockwork and mounted in such a way as to keep the same celestial image reflected continuously to the eyepiece or camera attachment of a fixed telescope. [<L *caelum* heavens +*status* a standing <*stare* stand]

coe·nes·the·sia (sē′nis·thē′zhə, -zhē·ə, sen′is-) See CENESTHESIA.

coeno- See CENO-.

coe·no·cyte (sē′nə·sīt, sen′ə-) *n. Bot.* An aggregation of protoplasmic units enclosed within a common wall: exemplified in the lower algae and fungi.

coe·nure (sē′nyo͝or) *n.* The many–headed bladderworm or larval stage of a dog tapeworm *(Taenia coenurus),* attacking the brain of sheep and producing gid or staggers. Also **coe·nu·rus** (si·nyo͝or′əs). [<COEN(O)- + Gk. *oura* tail]

co·en·zyme (kō·en′zīm, -zim) *n. Biochem.* Any substance present in a fermenting mixture that increases the activity of the enzyme.

co·e·qual (kō·ē′kwəl) *adj.* Of the same value, age, size, or importance; equal and conjoined. —*n.* The equal of another or others. —**co·e·qual·i·ty** (kō′i·kwol′ə·tē) *n.* —**co·e′qual·ly** *adv.*

co·erce (kō·ûrs′) *v.* **co·erced, co·erc·ing** *v.t.* **1** To constrain by force, law, authority, or fear; compel. **2** To bring into subjection or under control by superior force; repress. **3** To bring about by coercion: to *coerce* obedience. —*v.i.* **4** To use coercive measures, as in government. See synonyms under COMPEL. [<L *coercere* <*co-* together + *arcere* shut up, restrain] —**co·er′ci·ble** *adj.*

co·er·cion (kō·ûr′shən) *n.* **1** Forcible constraint or restraint, moral or physical; compulsion. **2** Government by force. —**co·er·cion·ar·y** (kō·ûr′shən·er′ē) *adj.* —**co·er′cion·ist** *n.*

co·er·cive (kō·ûr′siv) *adj.* Serving or tending to coerce. —**co·er′cive·ly** *adv.* —**co·er′cive·ness** *n.*

coercive force See under FORCE.

co·e·ta·ne·ous (kō′i·tā′nē·əs) *adj.* Originating at the same time; of equal age; contemporary. [<LL *coetaneus* <*co-* together + *aetas* age] —**co′e·ta′ne·ous·ly** *adv.* —**co′e·ta′ne·ous·ness** *n.*

Coeur de Li·on (kûr′ də lē′ən) "Lion–heart": epithet applied to Richard I of England. [<F]

co·e·val (kō·ē′vəl) *adj.* Of or belonging to the same age: usually implying remote time or long duration. —*n.* One of the same age; a contemporary. Also spelled *coaeval.* [<LL *coaevus* <*co-* together + *aevus* age] —**co·e′·val·ly** *adv.*

co·ex·ist (kō′ig·zist′) *v.i.* To exist together, in the same place or at the same time. —**co′ex·ist′ent** *adj.*

co·ex·ist·ence (kō′ig·zis′təns) *n.* **1** The state of coexisting. **2** The simultaneous existence of two (or more) societies, nations, etc., which differ in ideology but which agree, often tacitly, to non–interference in each other's political affairs.

coff (kof) *v.t.* **coft, coff·ing** *Scot.* To buy.

cof·fee (kôf′ē, kof′ē) *n.* **1** The seeds or beans enclosed in the dark berrylike fruit of a tropical evergreen shrub (genus *Coffea*), native in Asia and Africa and widely grown in Brazil. **2** A beverage made from the roasted and ground beans of this plant. **3** The shrub or tree itself. **4** The brown color of coffee, especially of coffee when containing milk or cream. —**black coffee** Coffee taken without milk or cream. [<Ital. *caffè* <Turkish *qahveh* <Arabic *qahwah*]

coffee break A recess from work for the purpose of taking coffee or other refreshments.

cof·fee–cake (kôf′ē·kāk′, kof′ē-) *n.* Any of several kinds of cake often containing raisins or nuts, topped with melted sugar, cinnamon, or butter crumbs, and eaten with coffee.

coffee house A house where coffee and other refreshments are served; a café.

coffee mill A hand mill for grinding roasted coffee beans; a coffee grinder.

coffee nut The Kentucky coffee tree or its fruit.

coffee pot A covered vessel in which coffee is prepared or served.

coffee shop A public restaurant or room in a hotel or a restaurant where coffee and food are served. Also **coffee room.**

coffee table Any low table, generally placed in front of a sofa, for serving refreshments.

coffee tree **1** The cascara buckthorn. **2** The Kentucky coffee tree.

coffee weed Chicory.

cof·fer (kôf′ər, kof′ər) *n.* **1** A chest or box; strongbox; safe. **2** *pl.* A treasury; financial resources. **3** A decorative, sunk panel in a dome or vault. **4** A canal–lock chamber; a caisson. —*v.t.* **1** To place in a coffer. **2** To adorn with coffers, or form in coffers, as a ceiling. [<F *coffre* <L *cophinus.* See COFFIN.]

cof·fer·dam (kôf′ər·dam′, kof′-) *n.* **1** A temporary enclosing dam built in the water and pumped dry, to protect workmen. **2** A watertight structure attached to a ship's side when repairs are made below the water line.

cof·fin (kôf′in, kof′-) *n.* **1** The case in which a corpse is buried. **2** The part of a horse's hoof below the coronet. —*v.t.* To put into or as into a coffin. [<OF *cofin* <L *cophinus* <Gk. *kophinos* basket]

Cof·fin (kôf′in, kof′-), **Robert Peter Tristram,** 1892–1955, U.S. poet and author.

coffin bone The bone of a horse's foot that is enclosed within the hoof.

cof·fle (kof′əl) *n.* A gang of animals or slaves, chained together for marching or sale. —*v.t.* **·fled, ·fling** To form into a coffle. [<Arabic *qāfilah* caravan]

coft (koft) Past tense of COFF.

cog[1] (kog) *n.* **1** *Mech.* A tooth or one of a series of teeth projecting from the surface of a wheel or gear to impart or receive motion. **2** A tenon on a joist or beam to fit a mortise on another. **3** A person regarded as making a minor or insignificant contribution to the working of a large organization or process. [<Scand. Cf. Sw. *kugge* cog.]

cog[2] (kog) *v.* **cogged, cog·ging** *v.t.* **1** To load or mishandle, as dice, in order to cheat. **2** *Obs.* To mislead or deceive. —*v.i.* **3** To cheat, as with loaded dice. —*n.* A trick; imposition; a lie. [Origin unknown]

cog[3] (kog, kōg) *n.* **1** A small rowboat or fishing vessel; cockboat. **2** Formerly, a broadly built transport or other vessel: also spelled *cogue.* [<OF *cogue*]

co·gent (kō′jənt) *adj.* Compelling belief, assent, or action; forcible; convincing. See synonyms under POWERFUL. [<L *cogens, -entis,* ppr. of *cogere* compel. See COACT.]

cog·ger (kog′ər) *n. Brit.* **1** A sharper. **2** A flatterer. [< COG[2]]

cog·gie (kog′ē) *n. Brit. Dial.* A small wooden bowl.

cog·ging (kog′ing) *n. Metall.* The operation of reducing a metal ingot to a billet by application of a forging press or hammer.

cog·i·tate (koj′ə·tāt) *v.* **·tat·ed, ·tat·ing** *v.t.* To think over; ponder; meditate. —*v.t.* To think about or upon; devise. See synonyms under MUSE. [<L *cogitatus,* pp. of *cogitare* think <*co-* together + *agitare* consider] —**cog·i·ta·ble** (koj′ə·tə·bəl) *adj.* —**cog′i·ta′tor** *n.*

cog·i·ta·tion (koj′ə·tā′shən) *n.* Consideration; reflection; thought. [<OF *cogitaciun* <L *cogitatio, -onis* <*cogitare.* See COGITATE.]

cog·i·ta·tive (koj′ə·tā′tiv) *adj.* Capable of cogitation; reflective; contemplative. —**cog′i·ta′tive·ly** *adv.* —**cog′i·ta′tive·ness** *n.*

co·gi·to er·go sum (koj′i·tō ûr′gō sum′) *Latin* I think, therefore I exist: the basic proposition of Descartes' philosophy.

co·gnac (kōn′yak, kon′-) *n.* **1** Brandy distilled from wine produced in the Cognac region of western France. **2** Any brandy.

cog·nate (kog′nāt) *adj.* **1** Allied by blood; kindred; especially, related through females only. **2** Allied by derivation from the same source; belonging to the same stock or root: English *cold* and Latin *gelidus* are *cognate* words. **3** Allied in radical characteristics; having the same nature or quality. —*n.* One who or that which is closely related to other persons or things. [<L *cognatus* <*co-* together + *(g)natus,* pp. of *(g)nasci* be born]

cog·na·tion (kog·nā′shən) *n.* Relationship by blood or derivation.

cog·ni·tion (kog·nish′ən) *n.* **1** The act, power, or faculty of apprehending, knowing, or perceiving. **2** Knowledge; a conception, perception, or notion. [<L *cognitio, -onis* knowledge <*cognoscere* know <*co-* together + *(g)noscere* know] —**cog·ni′tion·al** *adj.* —**cog·ni·tive** (kog′nə·tiv) *adj.*

cog·ni·za·ble (kog′nə·zə·bəl, kon′ə-) *adj.* Capable of being known or of being judicially tried or examined. —**cog′ni·za·bly** *adv.*

cog·ni·zance (kog′nə·zəns, kon′ə-) *n.* **1** Apprehension or perception; knowledge; recog-

co–patron	**co–please**	**coraise**	**co–reign**	**co–resonant**	**cosheathe**	**co–tenant**
co–patroness	**co–plot**	**co–rector**	**co–rejoice**	**co–revel**	**cosigner**	**co–traitor**
co–petitioner	**co–project**	**co–redeem**	**co–religionist**	**co–revolve**	**cosound**	**co–translate**
co–plaintiff	**co–promote**	**co–regency**	**co–renounce**	**coriparian**	**cosovereign**	**co–trustee**
co–plant	**co–proprietor**	**co–regnant**	**co–residence**	**cosettle**	**cospecies**	**co–worker**

nition; also, the range or sphere of what can be known by observation. 2 *Law* Knowledge on which a judge acts without requiring proof; judicial notice, as of statutes or public events. 3 Jurisdiction. 4 *Law* Acknowledgment of a fine of land and tenements; a confession. [<OF *conoisance* <*conistre* know <L *cognoscere.* See COGNITION.]

cog·ni·zant (kog′nə·zənt, kon′ə-) *adj.* Having knowledge; aware: with *of.* See synonyms under CONSCIOUS.

cog·nize (kog′nīz) *v.t.* **·nized, ·niz·ing** To know, perceive, or recognize. See synonyms under KNOW. Also *Brit.* **cog′nise.** [<L *cognoscere* know. See COGNITION.]

cog·no·men (kog·nō′mən) *n. pl.* **·no·mens** or **·nom·i·na** (-nom′ə·nə) 1 In ancient Rome, the last of three names; a surname used to denote some physical or mental characteristic: Publius Ovidius *Naso.* 2 A surname. 3 Loosely, any name, nickname, or appellation. See synonyms under NAME. [<L <*co-* together + *(g)nomen* name] **—cog·nom·i·nal** (kog·nom′ə·nəl) *adj.*

co·gno·scen·te (kō′nyō·shen′tā) *n. pl.* **·ti** (-tē) A connoisseur: also spelled *conoscente.* [<Ital.]

cog·nos·ci·ble (kog·nos′ə·bəl) *adj.* Capable of being known, recognized, or ascertained; knowable. [<L *cognoscere.* See COGNITION.] **— cog·nos′ci·bil′i·ty** *n.*

cog·no·vit (kog·nō′vit) *n. Law* A written acknowledgment, by a defendant, that the plaintiff's demand is just. [<L *cognovit (actionem)* he has acknowledged (the action)]

co·gon (kə·gōn′) *n.* A tall, rank grass *(Imperata cylindrica)* of the Philippines: used for fodder and in thatching. [<Sp. *cogón* < Tagalog]

cog rail *n.* A cogged center rail with a cogwheel that permits a locomotive to make steep ascents. Also **cog′-rail′way.**

cogue (kog, kōg) See COG[3].

cog·way (kog′wā′) *n.* A rack railway.

cog·wheel (kog′hwēl′) *n.* A wheel with cogs; a gearwheel.

COGWHEELS
A. Spur-gears.
B. Spur and crown gears.
C. Bevel-gears.
D. Square gears.
E. Annular gears.
F. Elliptical gears.

co·hab·it (kō·hab′it) *v.i.* 1 To live together, usually illegally, as husband and wife. 2 *Obs.* To inhabit together the same place or country. [<LL *cohabitare* <*co-* together + *habitare* live] **—co·hab′i·tant, co·hab′it·er** *n.* **—co·hab′i·ta′tion** *n.*

Co·han (kō·han′), **George M(ichael),** 1878–1942, U.S. playwright and actor.

Co·hee (kō′hē) *n. U.S.* Formerly, a settler in western Virginia and western Pennsylvania. [? <dial. E (Scottish) *quo' he* quoth he; with ref. to a characteristic phrase in their speech]

Co·hen (kō′ən), **Morris,** 1880–1947, U.S. philosopher and logician of science, born in Russia.

co·here (kō·hir′) *v.i.* **co·hered, co·her·ing** 1 To stick or hold firmly together. 2 To be logically consistent or connected. 3 To be coherent, as the parts of an address. 4 *Obs.* To agree. See synonyms under UNITE. [<L *cohaerere* <*co-* together + *haerere* stick]

co·her·ence (kō·hir′əns) *n.* 1 A sticking to or a sticking together; union; conjunction. See COHESION (def. 2). 2 Logical consistency; agreement: also **co·her′en·cy.** 3 *Physics* That relation of coincidence between two sets of waves, as light or sound waves, which will produce interference phenomena.· [<MF *cohérence* <L *cohaerentia* <*cohaerere* COHERE]

co·her·ent (kō·hir′ənt) *adj.* 1 Cleaving or sticking together. 2 Logically consistent. **— co·her′ent·ly** *adv.*

co·her·er (kō·hir′ər) *n.* A device formerly employed to detect radio waves, in which loosely touching metallic particles in a glass tube are made to cohere closely under the action of the wave, thus momentarily completing a local electric signaling circuit.

co·he·sion (kō·hē′zhən) *n.* 1 The act or state of cohering; union; consistency. 2 *Physics* That force by which molecules of the same kind or of the same body are held together so that the substance or body resists separation: distinguished from *adhesion.* 3 *Bot.* The joining of one part with another. [<F *cohésion* <L *cohaerere* COHERE]

co·he·sive (kō·hē′siv) *adj.* Belonging to, having, or exerting the property of cohesion; causing to cleave. **— co·he′sive·ly** *adv.* **— co·he′sive·ness** *n.*

Cohn (kōn), **Ferdinand Julius,** 1828–98, German botanist: called "the founder of bacteriology."

co·ho·bate (kō′hō·bāt) *v.t.* **·bat·ed, ·bat·ing** To redistil by restoring the distillate to the retort, to mingle again with the matter there. [<Med. L *cohobatus,* pp. of *cohobare,* ? <Arabic *ka'aba* repeat]

co·hoes (kō·ās′) *n. U.S. Dial.* Land originally overgrown with pine. Also **co·hos′.** [<Du. <Algonquian *koowa,* a small pine tree]

co·hog (kō′hôg, -hog) See QUAHAUG.

co·honk (kə·hôngk′, -hongk′) *n.* 1 The Canada goose. 2 *Obs.* The season, beginning in October, when this wild goose makes its appearance. [Imit. of its call]

co·hort (kō′hôrt) *n.* 1 The tenth of an ancient Roman military legion, 400 to 600 men. 2 A band of soldiers. 3 Any group of associates. 4 A companion or follower. [<L *cohors, cohortis.* Doublet of COURT.]

co·hosh (kō′hosh, kō·hosh′) *n.* 1 Either of two North American herbs, sometimes used medicinally; especially, the **blue cohosh** *(Caulophyllum thalictroides),* often called *squawroot,* and the black snakeroot or **black cohosh** *(Cimicifuga racemosa).* 2 The baneberry. [<N. Am. Ind.]

co·hune (kō·hōōn′) *n.* A feather-leaved palm *(Orbignya cohune)* of Central and South America, from which a fatty oil is obtained. Also **cohune palm.** [< native Honduran name]

Coi (koi), **Song** (sông) The Annamese name for the RED RIVER, Vietnam.

coif (koif) *n.* 1 Any close-fitting cap, hood, or headdress; especially, a close-fitting hood or skull cap for either sex, tied under the chin. 2 In England, an inner skull cap of lawn, formerly worn by sergeants at law; hence, the office or rank of a sergeant at law. 3 A soldier's thick skull cap of steel or leather, worn under the helmet. **—** *v.t.* To put a coif on; invest with or as with a coif. [<OF *coife* <LL *cofia* <Gmc.]

coif·feur (kwä·fœr′) *n. French* A male hairdresser. **— coif·feuse** (kwä·fœz′) *n. fem.*

coif·fure (kwä·fyōōr′, *Fr.* kwä·für′) *n.* 1 An arrangement or dressing of the hair. 2 A headdress. [<F <OF *coife* COIF.]

coign (koin) *n.* A projecting angle or stone; a corner. Also **coigne.** [Var. of QUOIN]

coign of vantage An advantageous position.

coil[1] (koil) *n.* 1 A ring or spiral formed by winding. 2 An involvement; a perplexity. 3 A spiral pipe, or a series of pipes, forming a continuous conduit which reverses two or more times. 4 An induction coil. **— Ruhmkorff coil** An induction coil with circuit breaker for use with direct and constant current. [< *v.*] **—** *v.t.* 1 To wind spirally or in rings; wind round and round. 2 To enwrap with coils, as a lasso or the folds of a boa constrictor. **—** *v.i.* 3 To form rings or coils. 4 To move in spirals, as a hawk. [<OF *coillir* <L *colligere.* See COLLECT.] **— coil′er** *n.*

coil[2] (koil) *n. Archaic* Confusion or tumult; turmoil. [Origin unknown]

Coim·ba·tore (koim′bə·tōr′) A city in SW Madras state, India.

Co·im·bra (kō·im′brə) A city in north central Portugal; former capital of Portugal and site of the **University of Coimbra** (founded at Lisbon in 1290, established here in 1537).

coin (koin) *n.* 1 A piece of metal stamped by government authority, for use as money. 2 Metal currency, collectively. 3 Kind or means of recompense. 4 A corner; quoin. See synonyms under MONEY. **—** *v.t.* 1 To stamp or mint (coins) from metal. 2 To make into coins, as metal. 3 To originate or invent, as a word or phrase. 4 *Colloq.* To make or gain rapidly: to *coin* money. **—** *v.i.* 5 *Brit. Colloq.* To counterfeit money. [<F, wedge, die <L *cuneus* wedge] **— coin′a·ble** *adj.* **— coin′er** *n.*

coin·age (koi′nij) *n.* 1 The making of coins, or the coins made; the system of coins of a country. 2 The cost or charge for coining money. 3 The act of fabricating, or the thing fabricated. 4 *Ling.* An artificially created word, as *blurb.*

co·in·cide (kō′in·sīd′) *v.i.* **·cid·ed, ·cid·ing** 1 To correspond because of identity in parts, elements, space occupied, or position. 2 To agree exactly; be of one opinion, idea, or interest. 3 To occur at the same time; endure an equal span of time. See synonyms under AGREE, ASSENT. [<MF *coincider* <Med. L *coincidere* <L *co-* together + *incidere* < *in-* upon + *cadere* fall]

co·in·ci·dence (kō·in′sə·dəns) *n.* 1 The fact or condition of coinciding; correspondence. 2 A remarkable occurrence of events, ideas, etc., at the same time or in the same way, apparently by mere accident. 3 *Geom.* Exact correspondence in space or in time. See synonyms under ANALOGY.

co·in·ci·dent (kō·in′sə·dənt) *adj.* 1 Agreeing or coinciding as in position, extent, time, etc.; concurring. 2 Exactly corresponding; identical. **— co·in′ci·dent·ly** *adv.*

co·in·ci·den·tal (kō·in′sə·den′təl) *adj.* Characterized by or involving coincidence. **— co·in′ci·den′tal·ly** *adv.*

co·in·sur·ance (kō′in·shōōr′əns) *n.* Joint insurance with another; specifically, a form of insurance in which the person who insures his property for less than its entire value is understood to be his own insurer for the difference which exists between the true value of the property and the amount of the insurance.

co·in·sure (kō′in·shōōr′) *v.t.* & *v.i.* **·sured, ·sur·ing** 1 To insure with another or others. 2 To insure according to the specific terms of coinsurance.

Coin·treau (kwaṅ·trō′) An orange-flavored liqueur with a curaçao base: a trade name.

coir (koir) *n.* Coconut-husk fiber, used in making cables, ropes, matting, etc.: also called *kyar.* [<Malay *kāyar* rope]

coi·stril (koi′strəl) *n. Archaic* 1 A groom; lackey. 2 A low fellow. Also **coi′strel.** [? <OF *coustillier* soldier]

co·i·tion (kō·ish′ən) *n.* Sexual intercourse; copulation. Also **co·i·tus** (kō′i·təs). [<L *coitio, -onis*: *co-* together + *ire* go]

coke[1] (kōk) *n.* A solid, carbonaceous fuel obtained by distilling the volatile constituents from coal by heating in ovens or retorts. **—** *v.t.* & *v.i.* **coked, cok·ing** To change or be changed into coke. Also spelled *coak.* [? ME *colke*; origin uncertain]

coke[2] (kōk) *n. Slang* Cocaine.

coke[3] (kōk) *n. Colloq.* A carbonated soft drink. [<*Coke,* short for *Coca-Cola,* a trade name]

Coke (kōōk, kōk), **Sir Edward,** 1552–1634, lord chief justice of England. **— Thomas,** 1747–1814, English preacher; first bishop of Methodist Episcopal Church in America.

col (kol) *n.* 1 *Geog.* A depression between two mountains; a gap in a ridge, serving as a pass from one valley to another: also called *saddle.* 2 *Meteorol.* A necklike area of low pressure between two anticyclones. [<F <L *collum* neck]

col-[1] Assimilated var. of COM-.

col-[2] Var. of COLO-.

co·la (kō′lə) *n.* 1 A small African tree *(Cola acuminata),* naturalized in the West Indies: also **co′la·nut′ tree.** 2 The seed of this tree or the extract of it, yielding caffeine and other substances, said to have tonic and antiseptic qualities: used in the manufacture of beverages: also **co′la·nut′.** Also spelled *kola.* [NL <native African name]

col·an·der (kul′ən·dər, kol′-) *n.* A perforated vessel for straining liquids, etc.: also spelled *cullender.* [Cf. Sp. *colador* <L *colare* strain]

co·lat·i·tude (kō·lat′ə·tōōd, -tyōōd) *n.* In navigation, the complement of the latitude; distance in degrees from the nearest pole. [<CO-[2] + LATITUDE]

Col·bert (kôl·bâr′), **Jean Baptiste,** 1619–83, French statesman and financier.

Col·by (kōl′bē), **Bainbridge,** 1869–1950, U.S. lawyer and statesman.

col·can·non (kəl·kan′ən, kôl′kan·ən) *n.* An Irish dish of potatoes and greens cooked together. [< Irish *cāl ceannain* white-headed cabbage]

Col·ches·ter (kōl′ches′tər, -chis·tər) A municipal borough of NE Essex, England.

col·chi·cine (kol′chə·sēn, kol′kə-) *n.* A pale-yellow, bitter, poisonous alkaloid, $C_{22}H_{25}O_6N$, obtained from the roots of the colchicum: used in medicine.

col·chi·cum (kol′chə·kəm, kol′kə-) *n.* **1** A plant of a genus *(Colchicum)* of Old World bulbous plants of the lily family. **2** The corm or the seed of *C. autumnale,* the autumn crocus or meadow saffron, which yields colchicine. **3** A medical preparation made from this. [< L < Gk. *kolchikon* < *Kolchis* Colchis, home of the legendary sorceress Medea]

Col·chis (kol′kis) A lowland region of western Georgian S.S.R.; identified with a legendary kingdom east of the Black Sea, the land of the Golden Fleece.

col·co·thar (kol′kə·thər) *n.* A dark-red ferric oxide formed by heating ferrous sulfate: used as a polish and as the pigment Indian red. [< Med. L < Arabic *qolqotār*]

cold (kōld) *adj.* **1** Of a relatively low temperature as compared with a normal or standard temperature, or with the normal temperature of the human body. **2** Having no perceptible heat; gelid; frigid. **3** Dead. **4** Having the sensation due to too rapid loss of heat from the body. **5** Feeling no warmth or not sufficient warmth; chilled; chilly. **6** Having little or no liveliness, ardor, or enthusiasm; displaying no feeling or passion; unmoved; stolid; indifferent. **7** Lacking signs of life; unconscious: to be knocked *cold.* **8** Chilling or depressing to the spirits; awakening no enthusiasm; not cordial; disappointing; frigid; discouraging. **9** Weak to the taste; wanting sharpness or pungency. **10** Lacking odor or freshness: a *cold* trail. **11** Distant from the object sought; wide of the mark: said of a seeker in a game, or a guesser. **12** Bluish in tone or effect; not suggestive of warmth. —*n.* **1** A low temperature. **2** Lack of heat, or the sensation caused by it. **3** A catarrhal affection of the respiratory tract, often following exposure to cold, dampness, or draft. **4** Temperature below the freezing point. **5** The sensation characterized by lack of enthusiasm, or by fear or dejection. [OE *cald*] —**cold′ly** *adv.* —**cold′ness** *n.*

cold blood 1 Blood not warmed by exercise or emotion. **2** Heartlessness or deliberate cruelty. —**in cold blood** Without feeling; pitilessly; not prompted by impulse or excitement.

cold-blood·ed (kōld′blud′id) *adj.* **1** Lacking body heat; frigid; sensitive to cold. **2** *Zool.* Having a variable temperature dependent on the temperature of the surrounding medium, as a fish or reptile; ectothermic. **3** Unfeeling; heartless; deliberately cruel. —**cold′-blood′ed·ly** *adv.* —**cold′-blood′ed·ness** *n.*

cold chisel A chisel of tempered steel for cutting cold metal.

cold cream A cleansing and soothing ointment for the skin.

cold deck A deck of cards prearranged to the advantage of a certain player.

cold-drawn (kōld′drôn′) *adj.* Stretched or drawn while cold: *cold-drawn* steel wire.

cold feet *Colloq.* Loss of courage; timidity. —**to get cold feet** *Colloq.* To lose courage.

cold·frame (kōld′frām′) *n.* A wooden frame set into the ground and having a glass top: used to protect plants against cold.

cold front *Meteorol.* The irregular, forward edge of a cold air mass advancing beneath and against a warmer mass.

cold-ham·mer (kōld′ham′ər) *v.t.* To hammer when cold, as metals.

Cold Harbor A village in eastern Virginia; scene of Civil War battles, 1862, 1864.

cold light Light which is not produced by incandescence or combustion, as phosphorescent light.

cold pack 1 *Med.* A wrapping of cold, wet blankets or sheets about a patient as a means of therapy. **2** A canning process in which raw food is packed in cans or jars, which are then heated for sealing and cooking.

cold rubber A synthetic rubber, chemically related to buna, which has been polymerized at low temperatures of 41° F. or less to impart better wearing qualities and greater resistance to abrasion.

cold shoulder *Colloq.* A deliberate slight or show of indifference.

cold snap A sudden, short interval of very cold weather.

cold sore An eruption about the mouth or nostrils, often accompanying a cold or fever: a form of herpes.

cold storage The storage of perishable food, furs, etc. in a refrigerated chamber.

cold turkey *U.S. Slang* **1** The abrupt and total deprivation of a substance, as a narcotic drug or cigarettes, from one addicted to its use. **2** Blunt, candid talk, often unwelcome to the listener.

cold war Intense rivalry between nations in diplomacy, economic strategy, and military preparedness, falling just short of armed conflict.

cold wave *Meteorol.* An unusual drop in temperature; a spell of very cold weather, usually traveling along a specified course.

cole (kōl) *n.* A plant of the same genus as the cabbage, especially rape *(Brassica napus).* Also **cole·wort** (kōl′wûrt′). ◆ Homophone: *coal.* [OE *cawl* < L *caulis* cabbage]

Cole (kōl), **G(eorge) D(ouglas) H(oward),** 1889–1959, English historian, sociologist, and economist.
—**Thomas,** 1801–48, U.S. painter born in England.

co·lec·to·my (kə·lek′tə·mē) *n. Surg.* The excision of all or part of the colon.

cole·man·ite (kōl′mən·īt) *n.* A colorless, transparent, hydrous calcium borate, $Ca_2B_6O_{11}\cdot 5H_2O$, occurring massive or in monoclinic crystals: used in the manufacture of borax. [after W.T. *Coleman,* 1824–93, of California]

Co·le·op·ter·a (kō′lē·op′tər·ə, kol′ē-) *n. pl.* A large, cosmopolitan order of insects, including the beetles and weevils, having horny front wings that fit as cases over the hind wings. [< NL < Gk. *koleos* sheath + *pteron* wing] —**co′le·op′ter, co′le·op′ter·an** *n.* —**co′le·op′ter·ous, co′le·op′ter·al** *adj.*

co·le·op·tile (kō′lē·op′til, kol′ē-) *n. Bot.* The first leaf appearing above the ground in grass seedlings. [< NL < Gk. *koleos* sheath + *ptilon* feather]

co·le·o·rhi·za (kō′lē·ə·rī′zə, kol′ē-) *n. pl.* **·zae** (-zē) *Bot.* The root sheath in certain plants, through which the radicle bursts in germination. [< NL < Gk. *koleos* sheath + *rhiza* root]

Cole·ridge (kōl′rij), **Samuel Taylor,** 1772–1834, English poet, critic, and philosopher.

Coles (kōlz), **Elisha,** 1640?–80, English teacher and encyclopedist.

cole·seed (kōl′sēd′) *n.* Colza.

cole·slaw (kōl′slô′) *n.* A salad made of finely shredded, raw cabbage. [< Du. *kool sla* cabbage salad]

co·les·see (kō′les·ē′) *n.* A joint lessee; cotenant.

co·les·sor (kō′les′ôr, kō′les·ôr′) *n.* One of the makers of a lease.

Cö·les·ti·ne (tsœ′les·tē′nə) German form of CELESTINE.

Col·et (kol′it), **John,** 1467?–1519, English humanist.

Co·lette (kō·let′) Pseudonym of Sidonie Gabrielle Claudine, 1873–1954, French writer and novelist.

co·le·us (kō′lē·əs) *n.* A plant of a large genus *(Coleus)* of tropical African and East Indian herbs or shrubs of the mint family, cultivated for their showy foliage. [< NL < Gk. *koleos* sheath]

cole·wort (kōl′wûrt′) *n.* A plant of the cabbage genus; rape or kale.

Col·fax (kōl′faks), **Schuyler,** 1823–85, vice president of the United States 1869–73.

col·ic (kol′ik) *n.* Acute spasmodic pain in the bowels. —*adj.* **1** Pertaining to, near, or affecting the bowels. **2** Pertaining to or like colic. [< F *colique* < L *colicus* sick with colic < Gk. *kōlikos* < *kolon* colon] —**col′ick·y** *adj.*

colic root 1 The intensely bitter tonic and stomachic root of a North American herb *(Aletris farinosa)* of the lily family. **2** The root of the wild yam or of the blazing star.

colic weed One of several plants, as dutchman's-breeches, the squirrel corn, or the pale corydalis *(Corydalis sempervirens).*

Co·li·gny (kô·lē·nyē′), **Gaspard de,** 1519–72, French admiral and Huguenot leader. Also **Co·li·gni′.**

Co·li·ma (kō·lē′mä) A state in western Mexico; 2,010 square miles; capital, Colima; site of the **Vol·cán de Colima** (vōl·kän′), a smoking volcano; 12,631 feet.

col·in (kol′in) *n.* An American quail (genus *Colinus*), especially the bobwhite. [< Am. Sp. *colín* < Nahuatl]

—coline See -COLOUS.

Col·i·se·um (kol′ə·sē′əm) See COLOSSEUM.

col·i·se·um (kol′ə·sē′əm) *n.* A large stadium or amphitheater.

co·li·tis (kə·lī′tis) *n. Pathol.* Inflammation of the colon: also called *colonitis.* [< COL(O)- + -ITIS]

col·lab·o·rate (kə·lab′ə·rāt) *v.i.* **·rat·ed, ·rat·ing 1** To labor or cooperate with another, especially in literary or scientific pursuits. **2** To cooperate willingly and traitorously with the enemy; be a collaborationist. [< LL *collaboratus,* pp. of *collaborare* < L *com-* with + *laborare* work] —**col·lab′o·ra′tion** *n.* —**col·lab′o·ra′tive** *adj.* —**col·lab′o·ra′tor** *n.*

col·lab·o·ra·tion·ist (kə·lab′ə·rā′shən·ist) *n.* A citizen of a country invaded or occupied by foreign troops who cooperates with the enemy.

col·lage (kə·läzh′) *n.* **1** A composition of flat objects, as newspaper, cloth, cardboard, etc., pasted together on a surface and often combined with related lines and color for artistic effect. **2** The clarifying or fining of a wine by means of an albuminous substance. [< F, pasting < *colle* glue < L *colla* < Gk. *kolla*]

col·la·gen (kol′ə·jen) *n. Biochem.* A protein forming the chief constituent of the connective tissues of the body, as cartilage, skin, bone, hair, etc. [< Gk. *kolla* glue + -GEN]

col·lapse (kə·laps′) *v.* **·lapsed, ·laps·ing** *v.i.* **1** To give way; cave in. **2** To fail utterly; come to ruin. **3** To assume a more compact form by the folding in of parts, as of camp chairs. **4** To lose health or strength completely, as from exhaustion or disease; become suddenly and completely prostrated. **5** To lose courage or boldness; sink suddenly from notice. —*v.t.* **6** To cause to collapse. —*n.* **1** A falling or sinking together. **2** Extreme prostration. **3** Utter failure; ruin. [< L *collapsus,* pp. of *collabi* < *com-* together + *labi* fall] —**col·laps′i·ble** or **·a·ble** *adj.* —**col·laps′i·bil′i·ty** *n.*

col·lar (kol′ər) *n.* **1** An article worn about the neck, as a band or circlet of some fabric, worn as an article of dress; the neckpiece of a garment. **2** A band of leather or metal for the neck of an animal. **3** *Biol.* **a** A ring or band on or about anything, as in certain plants and insects. **b** A growth of fur or ring of color about the neck of an animal. **4** *Mech.* Any of various cylindrical or ring-shaped devices used to limit or control the action of machine parts, secure stability, etc. —*v.t.* **1** To grasp by or provide with a collar. **2** To take possession of; capture. [< AF *coler* < L *collare* < *collum* neck]

collar bone The clavicle.

collar cell *Zool.* A flagellate cell having the base of the flagellum surrounded by a collar-like expansion, as in certain infusorians and sponges: also called *choanocyte.*

col·lard (kol′ərd) *n.* A variety of cabbage that does not gather its edible leaves into a head. [Alter. of *colewort.* See COLE.]

col·lar·et (kol′ər·et′) *n.* A small collar; also, a narrow fichu of lace or the like. Also **col′lar·ette′.** [< F *collerette,* dim. of *collier* collar]

col·la·sir·i (kol′ə·sir′ē, *Sp.* kô′lyä·sē′rē) *n. pl.* Among the modern Aymara Indians, specialized magicians and medicine men who are bonesetters, who diagnose disease by divination from the viscera of animals brought into contact with the patient, and claim to effect cures by magical transference of the disease to the animal or object. [< Aymaran]

col·late (kə·lāt′, kol′āt) *v.t.* **·lat·ed, ·lat·ing 1** To compare critically, as writings or facts. **2** In bookbinding, to examine (the gathered sheets to be bound) in order to verify and correct their arrangement. **3** In bibliography, to examine (the pages of a book) to see that none are missing or out of order. **4** To appoint or admit (a cleric) to a benefice. See synonyms under COMPARE. [<L *collatus*, pp. to *conferre* < *com-* together + *ferre* bear, carry]

col·lat·er·al (kə·lat'ər·əl) *adj.* **1** Subordinately connected; attendant or secondary; incidental. **2** Corroborative; confirmatory. **3** Being or lying alongside; parallel; bordering. **4** Descended from the same ancestor in a different line: distinguished from *lineal*. **5** Pertaining to property, as stocks or bonds, deposited as security additional to one's personal obligation: a *collateral* note. See synonyms under INCIDENTAL. —*n.* **1** Collateral security, which in case of default, is subject to immediate forfeiture, without recourse to legal proceedings. See COLLATERAL SECURITY. **2** A kinsman or kinswoman descended from the same ancestor in a different line. **3** An accompanying or subordinate fact, condition, or part. **4** *Anat.* A part connected with or derived from a main branch: the *collaterals* of a nerve fiber. See synonyms under SECURITY. [<Med. L *collateralis* < *com-* together + *lateralis* lateral < *latus, -eris* side] —**col·lat'er·al·ly** *adv.*

collateral security Property, money, etc., hypothecated as security additional to one's personal obligation.

col·la·tion (kə·lā'shən) *n.* **1** A collating; comparison. **2** The collection and critical comparison of writings or the published result of such a comparison. **3** In bookbinding, the examination of the collected sheets of a book before binding, to detect errors in arrangement. **4** A lunch or light repast: originally confined to the light evening refection of monks; also, the light supper permitted in seasons of fast, such as Lent. **5** The presentation of a clergyman to a church living. **6** In civil law, the return to an estate of property advanced to an heir, with a view to a common distribution of the whole. [<OF *collacion* <L *collatio, -onis* < *conferre*. See COLLATE.]

col·la·tive (kə·lā'tiv) *adj.* **1** Collating. **2** Bestowed, bestowable, or held by collation: said especially of a church living of which the bishop is patron.

col·la·tor (kə·lā'tər) *n.* An extensible, compartmentalized device used in offices to facilitate gathering the pages of duplicated material in proper order.

col·league (kol'ēg) *n.* A fellow member of an official body; an associate in office. See synonyms under ACCESSORY, ASSOCIATE. [<F *collègue* <L *collega* < *com-* together + *legere* choose] —**col'league·ship** *n.*

col·lect[1] (kə·lekt') *v.t.* **1** To gather or come together; assemble. **2** To bring together as for a hobby, as stamps or books. **3** To gather or obtain payments of money. **4** To regain control of; bring or call back: to *collect* one's wits. —*v.i.* **5** To assemble or congregate, as people; accumulate, as sand. **6** To gather payments or donations. See synonyms under AMASS, CONVOKE. —*adj.* To be paid for on delivery: a telegram sent *collect*. [<F *collecter* <L *colligere* < *com-* together + *legere* choose] —**col·lect'a·ble** or **·i·ble** *adj.*

col·lect[2] (kol'ekt) *n.* A formal, condensed prayer used in several western liturgies, usually containing a single petition and varying with the season or occasion. [<F *collecte* <L *collecta* a gathering together < *colligere*. See COLLECT[1].]

col·lec·ta·ne·a (kol'ek·tā'nē·ə) *n. pl.* Passages selected from different authors; a miscellany. [<L, (things) gathered together]

col·lect·ed (kə·lek'tid) *adj.* **1** Assembled; gathered. **2** Composed; self-possessed. See synonyms under CALM, SOBER. —**col·lect'ed·ly** *adv.* —**col·lect'ed·ness** *n.*

col·lec·tion (kə·lek'shən) *n.* **1** A collecting; a group of collected objects or individuals. **2** An aggregation; accumulation. **3** A sum of money solicited and contributed, as for church expenses, missions, charity, or the like. **4** The act of receiving or enforcing payment, or the amount of such payment. **5** The act of collecting one's thoughts, feelings, etc., or the resultant state; composure. See synonyms under AGGREGATE, ASSEMBLY, COMPANY. [<L *collectio, -onis* < *colligere* COLLECT]

col·lec·tive (kə·lek'tiv) *adj.* **1** Relating to, consisting of, or denoting an aggregate or group: opposed to *individual*. **2** Having the power or quality of bringing together. **3** *Gram.* Denoting in the singular number a collection or aggregate of individuals: The word "army" is a *collective* noun. —*n.* **1** *Gram.* A singular noun naming a collection or group. It takes either a singular or a plural verb, according as it refers to the objects composing it as one aggregate (**collective singular**) or as separate individuals (**collective plural**): The audience *was* large; The audience *were* divided in opinion. **2** A collection or gathering. **3** Any collective enterprise. —**col·lec'tive·ly** *adv.* —**col·lec'tive·ness** *n.*

collective bargaining Negotiation between organized workers and their employer or employers for reaching an agreement on working conditions, wages, hours, etc.

collective farm A farm worked and managed by cooperative labor, and in which the machinery and buildings are communally or state-owned.

collective fruit *Bot.* A fruit which is the product of a number of distinct flowers growing in a compact mass, as a mulberry or a pineapple: also called *multiple fruit*.

collective security Maintenance of world peace by the concerted action of all countries toward an aggressor or potential aggressor, as by the imposition of sanctions or the formation of alliances.

col·lec·tiv·ism (kə·lek'tiv·iz'əm) *n.* The doctrine that the people as a whole should own or control the material and means of production, or the spirit which determines production by the masses rather than by individuals. Compare SOCIALISM. —**col·lec'·tiv·ist** *adj.* & *n.* —**col·lec'tiv·is'tic** *adj.*

col·lec·tiv·i·ty (kol'ek·tiv'ə·tē) *n.* **1** The whole taken together; the quality or state of being collective. **2** The people as a body. **3** Collectivism.

col·lec·tiv·ize (kə·lek'tiv·īz) *v.t.* **·ized, ·iz·ing** To organize (an agricultural settlement, industry, economy, etc.) on a collectivist basis, so that management and labor function cooperatively, the material and means of production being owned communally. —**col·lec'tiv·i·za'tion** *n.*

col·lec·tor (kə·lek'tər) *n.* **1** One who or that which collects. **2** One who receives taxes, duties, etc., or collects debts. —**col·lec'tor·ship** *n.*

col·leen (kol'ēn, kə·lēn') *n.* A girl. [<Irish *cailīn*, dim. of *caile* countrywoman]

col·lege (kol'ij) *n.* **1** An incorporated school for instruction in the liberal arts or professional studies; a school of higher learning that grants degrees at the completion of courses of study; one of the educational institutions of a university; especially one that offers a general, four-year course toward the bachelor's degree: distinguished from graduate and professional schools. **2** A building, or collection of buildings, owned and used by a college. **3** A body of associates or colleagues. **4** A course of lectures or studies. **5** *Brit. Slang* A prison. **6** Any assemblage or gathering: a *college* of bees. [<OF *collège* <L *collegium* body of associates < *collega* COLLEAGUE[1]]

College of Cardinals The body of cardinal-bishops, cardinal-priests, and cardinal-deacons, varying in number up to 70, who constitute the papal council and electorate: also called *Sacred College*.

col·leg·er (kol'ij·ər) *n.* **1** A member of a college. **2** A pupil at Eton College, England, supported by endowment of the college.

college widow A woman who has been popular with several college generations of male students.

col·le·gi·al (kə·lē'jē·əl) *adj.* Collegiate.

col·le·gian (kə·lē'jən, -jē·ən) *n.* **1** A member or attendant of a college; a college student. **2** *Brit. Slang* A prisoner or jailbird.

col·le·giate (kə·lē'jit, -jē·it) *adj.* Pertaining to, like or conducted like, or connected with a college or colleges. —*n.* A collegian. —**col·le'giate·ly** *adv.*

collegiate church **1** An association of churches having pastors in common: the *Collegiate* Dutch Church. **2** A Roman Catholic or an Anglican church, not a cathedral, which has a chapter of canons. **3** A Scottish church served by two or more joint incumbents.

Col·lem·bo·la (kə·lem'bə·lə) *n. pl.* An order of small, primitive, wingless insects with chewing mouth parts, adhesive ventral tubes, and a tail-like organ used in jumping; the springtails. [<NL <Gk. *kolla* glue + *embolon* wedge, peg]

col·len·chy·ma (kə·leng'kə·mə) *n. Bot.* A form of thick-walled, elastic plant tissue, composed of elongated cells strongly thickened at the angles with colloidal material. [<NL <Gk. *kolla* glue + *enchyma* infusion]

Col·le·o·ni (kôl'lā·ō'nē), **Bartolommeo,** 1400–1474, Venetian commander born in Bergamo, Italy; subject of notable equestrian statue by Verrocchio.

col·let (kol'it) *n.* **1** *Mech.* A collar, clutch, or clamping-piece, as for a rod. **2** The ring or rim in which a gem is set. **3** The circular flange which supports the inner terminal of the balance spring in a watch. **4** Culet. —*v.t.* **·let·ed, ·let·ing** To place in or furnish with a collet. [<F, dim. of *col* neck <L *collum*]

col·lide (kə·līd') *v.i.* **·lid·ed, ·lid·ing** **1** To come together with violent impact; crash. **2** To come into conflict; clash. [<L *collidere* < *com-* together + *laedere* strike]

col·lie (kol'ē) *n.* A breed of large shepherd dogs which originated in Scotland, characterized by a long, narrow head and tapering nose and an abundant long-haired coat. [Prob. <Scottish Gaelic *cuilean* puppy]

col·lied (kol'ēd) *adj. Obs.* Blackened, as with soot; coal-black.

col·lier (kol'yər) *n.* **1** A coal-miner. **2** A vessel employed in carrying coal; also, one of the crew. **3** Formerly, a dealer in coal. [ME *colier* <OE *col* coal + -IER]

Col·lier (kol'yər), **Jeremy,** 1650–1726, English clergyman. —**Peter Fenelon,** 1849–1909, U.S. publisher; founded *Collier's Weekly*, 1896.

col·lier·y (kol'yər·ē) *n. pl.* **·lier·ies** **1** A coal mine. **2** The coal trade.

col·lie·shang·ie (kol'ē·shang'ē) *n. Scot.* A wrangle; brawl; hubbub.

col·li·gate (kol'ə·gāt) *v.t.* **·gat·ed, ·gat·ing** **1** To tie, group, or fasten together. **2** *Logic* To bind together (facts) by means of some suitable conception or explanation: Certain material phenomena are *colligated* by the law of gravity. [<L *colligatus*, pp. of *colligare* < *com-* together + *ligare* bind] —**col'li·ga'tion** *n.* —**col'li·ga'tive** *adj.*

col·li·mate (kol'ə·māt) *v.t.* **·mat·ed, ·mat·ing** **1** To bring into line. **2** To adjust the line of sight of, as of a telescope or other optical instrument. **3** To make parallel, as refracted rays of light or a gunsight with the axis of the gun's barrel. [<L *collimatus*, alter. of *collineatus*, pp. of *collineare* < *com-* together + *lineare* align] —**col'li·ma'tion** *n.*

col·li·ma·tor (kol'ə·mā'tər) *n. Optics* A device used to obtain parallel rays of light, as a fixed telescope or the convex lens and slit used in a spectroscope.

col·lin·e·ar (kə·lin'ē·ər) *adj.* Being in the same straight line: said of three or more points. —**col·lin'e·ar·ly** *adv.*

Col·ling·wood (kol'ing·wo͝od) A city in SE Australia near Melbourne.

Col·lins (kol'inz), **Michael,** 1890–1922, Irish patriot. —**Michael,** born 1930, U.S. astronaut; member of first space flight to land men on the moon, July 16–24, 1969. —**William,** 1721–59, English poet. —**Wilkie,** 1824–89, English novelist: full name *William Wilkie Collins*.

col·lin·si·a (kə·lin'sē·ə, -zē·ə) *n.* **1** An annual or biennial plant (genus *Collinsia*) of the figwort family with whorled leaves. **2** Any of the variously colored flowers of this plant. [after Z. *Collins*, 1764–1831, U.S. botanist]

col·li·sion (kə·lizh'ən) *n.* **1** The act of colliding. **2** Violent contact; clashing; antagonism. [<LL *collisio, -onis* < *collidere* COLLIDE]

Synonyms: clash, clashing, concussion, conflict, contact, encounter, impact, meeting, opposition, shock. *Collision* is the result of motion or action and is sudden and momentary; *contact* may be a condition of rest and be continuous and permanent. *Impact* is the blow given by the striking body. *Concussion* is often by transmitted force rather than by direct *impact*; an explosion of dynamite shatters neighboring windows by *concussion*. *Shock* is the result of *collision*. *Opposition* is used chiefly of persons, less frequently of opinions or interests; *conflict* is used indifferently of all. See ENCOUNTER. *Antonyms*:

agreement, amity, coincidence, concert, concord, concurrence, conformity, harmony, unison, unity.

col·lo·cate (kol′ō·kāt) *v.t.* **·cat·ed, ·cat·ing** To put in certain order; arrange together. [< L *collocatus,* pp. of *collocare* < *com-* together + *locare* place] **—col′lo·ca′tion** *n.*

col·lo·di·on (kə·lō′dē·ən) *n.* A solution of guncotton or pyroxylin in ether and alcohol, deposited as a film on the evaporation of the ether, and used as a coating for wounds and for photographic plates. Also **col·lo·di·um** (kə·lō′·dē·əm). [< Gk. *kollōdēs* gluelike]

col·logue (kə·lōg′) *v.i.* **·logued, ·lo·guing** *Brit. Dial.* **1** To confer secretly; plot. **2** *Obs.* To use flattery and deceit; cajole; wheedle. [Prob. < F *colloque* conference < L *colloquium*]

col·loid (kol′oid) *n.* **1** Any gluelike or jellylike substance, as gelatin, starch, raw egg white, etc., which diffuses not at all or very slowly through vegetable and animal membranes, and whose components do not separate as in a true solution or simple mixture: distinguished from *crystalloid.* **2** *Chem.* A state of matter in which very finely divided particles of one substance (the *disperse phase*) are suspended in another (the *dispersion medium*) in such manner and degree that the electrical and surface properties acquire special importance. **3** *Med.* A translucent, gelatinous substance resulting from certain forms of tissue degeneration. *—adj.* Of or pertaining to a colloid or the colloid state: also **col·loi·dal** (kə·loid′l). [< Gk. *kollōdēs* gluelike] **—col·loi·dal·i·ty** (kol′oi·dal′ə·tē) *n.*

colloid system *Chem.* Any aggregate of substances exhibiting the properties of a colloid, as sols, gels, emulsions, etc. Eight of these systems are known, occurring in solid, liquid, and gaseous forms, each identified in terms of the relationship existing between the disperse phase and the dispersion medium. See table below.

COLLOID SYSTEMS

Components	*Term*	*Example*
Solid in solid	solid sol	alloys, paper
Solid in liquid	suspension	paints
Solid in gas	smoke	iodine vapor
Liquid in solid	gel	celluloid, glue, gelatin
Liquid in liquid	emulsion	milk, blood
Liquid in gas	fog	clouds, steam
Gas in solid	solid foam	pumice, rubber
Gas in liquid	foam	lather, froth
Gas in gas		(No example known)

col·lop (kol′əp) *n.* **1** A slice or morsel of meat for stewing. **2** A small portion or piece of anything. [Cf. Sw. *kalops* slices of stewed beef]

col·lo·qui·al (kə·lō′kwē·əl) *adj.* **1** Characteristic of or suitable to the informal language of ordinary conversation or familiar writing, but inappropriate for use on the formal level. Colloquial language is widely used by the educated in informal discourse and is not to be confused with substandard speech. **2** Conversational. Abbr. *colloq.* **—col·lo′qui·al·ly** *adv.* **—col·lo′qui·al·ness** *n.*

col·lo·qui·al·ism (kə·lō′kwē·əl·iz′əm) *n.* **1** An expression or form of speech of the type used in informal conversation. **2** Informal, conversational style.

col·lo·quy (kol′ə·kwē) *n. pl.* **·quies 1** An informal conference; conversation. **2** A literary work written in conversational or dialog form. [< L *colloquium* conversation < *com-* together + *loqui* speak] **—col′lo·quist** *n.*

col·lo·type (kol′ə·tīp) *n.* **1** A photomechanical printing process in which the negative is printed on a plate covered with a light-sensitive gelatin coat which is then rendered selectively ink-repellent by treatment with glycerin and salt water. **2** A print or plate made by this process. *—v.t.* **·typed, ·typ·ing** To make a collotype of. [< Gk. *kolla* glue + -TYPE] **—col·lo·typ·ic** (kol′ə·tip′ik) *adj.* **—col·lo·typ·y** (kol′ə·tī′pē) *n.*

col·lude (kə·lōōd′) *v.i.* **·lud·ed, ·lud·ing** To cooperate secretly; conspire; connive. [< L *colludere* < *com-* together + *ludere* play, trick] **—col·lud′er** *n.*

col·lu·sion (kə·lōō′zhən) *n.* Cooperation in fraud. [< L *collusio, -onis* < *colludere* COLLUDE]

col·lu·sive (kə·lōō′siv) *adj.* Fraudulently concerted or devised. **—col·lu′sive·ly** *adv.* **—col·lu′sive·ness** *n.*

col·ly (kol′ē) *Brit. Dial. n.* Coal dust; soot. *—v.t.* **·lied, ·ly·ing** To blacken as with coal smut or soot; begrime. [ME *colie,* OE *col* coal]

col·lyr·i·um (kə·lir′ē·əm) *n.* A medicated eyewash or eye salve. [< L < Gk. *kollyrion* poultice, dim. of *kollyra* bread]

Col·mar (kōl′mär, *Fr.* kôl·mȧr′) A city of eastern France, capital of Haut-Rhin department. *German* **Kol·mar** (kōl′mär).

colo- *combining form* Colon: *colotomy.* Also, before vowels, *col-.* [< Gk. *kolon* colon]

Co·lô·a·ne (kōō·lō′ə·nə) See under MACAO.

col·o·cynth (kol′ə·sinth) *n.* **1** A Mediterranean vine *(Citrullus colocynthis)* of the gourd family. **2** Its small gourdlike fruit from which is obtained a cathartic drug: also called *bitter apple, coloquintida.* [< L *colocynthis* < Gk. *kolokynthē* gourd]

co·logne (kə·lōn′) *n.* A toilet water consisting of alcohol scented with aromatic oils: often called *eau de Cologne.* Also **Cologne water.** [from *Cologne*]

Co·logne (kə·lōn′) A city in North Rhine-Westphalia, Germany, on the Rhine: German *Köln.*

Co·lombes (kô·lôṅb′) A NW suburb of Paris, France.

Co·lom·bi·a (kə·lum′bē·ə, *Sp.* kō·lōm′byä) A republic in NW South America; 439,828 square miles; capital, Bogotá. **—Co·lom′bi·an** *adj.* & *n.*

Co·lom·bo (kə·lum′bō) The capital of Sri Lanka; a port on the west coast.

co·lon[1] (kō′lən) *n. pl.* **co·lons** *for def.* **1,** cola (kō′lə) *for def.* **2 1** A punctuation mark (:) indicating a pause greater than a semicolon, but less than a period: used as a sign of apposition or equality to connect one clause with another that explains it, as in introducing an enumeration or catalog; also used after a word introducing a speech, quotation, etc., in expressing clock time, in citations, and in mathematical proportions. **2** In ancient prosody, a member or section of a rhythmical period. [< Gk. *kōlon* member, limb, clause]

co·lon[2] (kō′lən) *n. pl.* **co·lons** or **co·la** (kō′lə) *Anat.* The portion of the large intestine between the cecum and the rectum. [< Gk. *kolon*] **—co·lon·ic** (kə·lon′ik) *adj.*

co·lon[3] (kō·lōn′) *n. pl.* **co·lons** (kō·lōnz′), *Sp.* **co·lo·nes** (kō·lō′näs) The monetary unit of Costa Rica and El Salvador.

Co·lón (kō·lōn′) A port of Panama at the Atlantic entrance to the Panama Canal: formerly *Aspinwall.*

Co·lón (kō·lōn′), **Cristóbal** See COLUMBUS, CHRISTOPHER.

Co·lón Archipelago (kō·lōn′) The official name for the GALAPAGOS ISLANDS.

colo·nel (kûr′nəl) *n.* A commissioned officer of the sixth rank in the U.S. Army, U.S. Air Force, or U.S. Marine Corps, ranking next above a lieutenant colonel and next below a brigadier general. **—lieutenant colonel** A commissioned officer of the fifth rank in the U.S. Army, U.S. Air Force, or U.S. Marine Corps, ranking next above a major and next below a colonel. ◆ Homophone: *kernel.* [Earlier *coronel* < F *coronnel* < Ital. *colonnello* < *colonna* column of soldiers] **—colo′nel·cy, colo′nel·ship** *n.*

co·lo·ni·al (kə·lō′nē·əl) *adj.* **1** Of, pertaining to, produced in or living in, like, or forming a colony or colonies, especially one of the thirteen British Colonies that became the United States. **2** Characteristic of colonial times; antique. *—n.* A citizen or inhabitant of a colony. **—co·lo′ni·al·ly** *adv.*

co·lo·ni·al·ism (kə·lō′nē·əl·iz′əm) *n.* The policy of a nation seeking to acquire, extend, or retain overseas dependencies; imperialism.

col·o·nist (kol′ə·nist) *n.* **1** A member or inhabitant of a colony. **2** A settler or founder of a colony.

col·o·ni·tis (kol′ə·nī′tis) See COLITIS.

col·o·ni·za·tion·ist (kol′ə·nə·zā′shən·ist, -nī·zā′-) *n.* An advocate of colonization; specifically, one of the American anti-slavery reformers who favored colonizing emancipated Negroes in Liberia.

col·o·nize (kol′ə·nīz) *v.* **·nized, ·niz·ing** *v.t.* **1** To settle a colony or colonies in. **2** To establish or place as colonists. *—v.i.* **3** To establish or unite in a colony or colonies. **4** To settle in colonies. Also *Brit.* **col′o·nise. —col′o·ni·za′tion** *n.* **—col′o·niz′er** *n.*

col·on·nade (kol′ə·nād′) *n. Archit.* A range of columns connected by an entablature. [< F < *colonne* column] **—col′on·nad′ed** *adj.*

col·on·nette (kol′ə·net′) *n.* **1** *Archaic* A small column. **2** *Anat.* A small column of bone. [< F, dim. of *colonne* column]

col·o·ny (kol′ə·nē) *n. pl.* **·nies 1** A body of emigrants or their descendants in a remote region under the control of a parent country. In Great Britain the term *colony* designates a region that has a responsible government, whether or not it has an elective legislature. **2** Any aggregation of individuals in a common group, as of alien residents in a country, or of bees, beavers, etc. **3** The territory occupied by early settlers or their descendants. **4** *Biol.* A group of organisms of the same species, usually from the same parent cell, functioning in close association and with varying degrees of independence, as certain bacteria, protozoans, and algae. **5** *Ecol.* **a** Two or more species of plants developing in a locality as a result of invasion. **b** A group of plants isolated from others of the same species, but growing in the same locality. [< L *colonia* < *colonus* farmer]

col·o·phon (kol′ə·fon, -fən) *n.* An inscription or device, often ornamental, as the publisher's distinctive emblem, at the beginning or end of books. [< LL < Gk. *kolophon* summit]

Col·o·phon (kol′ə·fon) An ancient city NW of Ephesus, Asia Minor.

col·o·pho·ny (kol′ə·fō′nē, kə·lof′ə·nē) *n.* Rosin. [< L *colophonia (resina)* (rosin) from Colophon] **—col·o·phon·ic** (kol′ə·fon′ik) *adj.*

col·o·quin·ti·da (kol′ə·kwin′ti·də) See COLOCYNTH.

col·or (kul′ər) *n.* **1** A visual attribute of bodies or substances distinct from their spatial characteristics and depending upon the spectral composition of the wavelengths of radiant energy capable of stimulating the retina and its associated neural mechanisms. **Achromatic colors** include black and white and the entire series of intermediate grays, varying only in *lightness* and *brightness.* **Chromatic colors** may also vary in *hue,* as red, green, blue, and purple; and in *saturation.* **2** A paint, dyestuff, or pigment, as used in industry and the arts. **3** An appearance; semblance; pretense; disguise. **4** *pl.* An ensign or flag of a nation, also of a military or naval unit, as a regiment, warship, etc. **5** *pl.* In the U.S. Navy, the salute made to the national flag when it is hoisted in the morning and lowered in the evening. **6** The hue of the human skin; complexion: equal rights regardless of race, creed, or *color.* **7** In art, coloring. **8** *Music* Timbre; clang; also, the tone, or characteristic effect, of a composition, as produced by specific harmonic, rhythmic, or melodic means. **9** *Law* An apparent or prima-facie right, authority, etc. **10** A small particle or trace of gold in auriferous sand or gravel. **11** Liveliness or animation, vividness, especially in literary work. **—complementary color 1** Either of a pair of spectrum colors which when combined give a white or nearly white light. **2** One of two pigments whose mixture produces a third color, as blue and yellow blended to produce green. **—primary colors 1** The principal colors in which white light is separated by a prism; the colors of the rainbow. **2** The colors red, yellow, green, and blue, by mixing which any desired color or hue may be obtained; to these white and black may be added. *—v.t.* **1** To apply or give color, as by painting, staining, or dyeing. **2** To misrepresent by distortion or exaggeration. **3** To modify in nature or character. *—v.i.* **4** To take on or change color, as ripening fruit. **5** To blush or flush. Also *Brit.* **col′our** [< OF *colour* < L *color*] **—col′or·a·ble** *adj.* **—col′or·a·bly** *adv.* **—col′or·er** *n.*

Col·o·ra·dan (kol′ə·rä′dən, -rad′ən) *n.* A native or citizen of Colorado. —*adj.* Of or pertaining to Colorado.

col·o·ra·do (kol′ə·rä′dō) *adj.* **1** Denoting medium strength and color: said of cigars. **2** Red; reddish: used in geographic names. [<Sp., colored, red]

Col·o·ra·do (kol′ə·rä′dō, -rad′ō) A western State of the United States; 103,967 square miles; capital, Denver; entered the Union Aug. 1, 1876: nicknamed *Centennial State* : abbr. CO

Colorado beetle The potato beetle.

Colorado Desert An arid region in SE California and northern Lower California.

Colorado River **1** A river of the SW United States, flowing 1,400 miles SW to the northern tip of the Gulf of California. **2** A river in Texas, flowing 900 miles SE to the Gulf of Mexico: also **Eastern Colorado River.**

col·or·a·tion (kul′ə·rā′shən) *n.* Particular marking or arrangement of colors, as in an animal or plant; coloring.

col·or·a·tu·ra (kul′ər·ə·to͝or′ə,-tyo͝or′ə) *n.* The effect of giving color to vocal music, by means of grace notes, runs, trills, or other florid decoration. **2** The runs, etc., themselves. —*adj.* Characterized by or suitable for coloratura. Also **col·or·a·ture** (kul′ər·ə·choor). [<Ital. *coloratura* ration]

coloratura soprano **1** A clear, high voice of flexible range. **2** A singer with such a voice.

col·or·blind (kul′ər·blīnd′) *adj.* Totally or partially unable to discriminate between hues as distinguished from light or shade.

col·or·blind·ness (kul′ər·blīnd′nis) *n.* Achromatopsia.

col·or·cast (kul′ər·kast′, -käst′) *n.* A television broadcast in color.

color corrector An electronic device used in the preparation of precision color negatives in photoengraving.

color diagram A graphic chart or table which illustrates the interrelations of colors in respect of hue, lightness, saturation, etc. When in three dimensions, such a diagram is called a **color solid** or **color pyramid.**

col·ored (kul′ərd) *adj.* **1** Having color. **2** Embellished or exaggerated; prejudiced; specious. **3** Of a race other than the white, especially black; taken to be offensive. **4** Of mixed race; taken to be offensive.

col·or·fast (kul′ər·fast′, -fäst′) *adj.* Retaining color of dye or paint substantially unfaded when fabric or surface is subjected to the action of water, cleaning fluid, or a reasonable amount of light; resistant to fading: *colorfast* fabrics; a *colorfast* paint job.

color filter A layer of substance, in solid, liquid, or gaseous form, which will absorb a certain wavelength of light: used in photography to change the relative intensities of impinging light waves. Also called **color screen.**

col·or·ful (kul′ər·fəl) *adj.* **1** Full of colors, especially contrasting colors; bright: a *colorful* scene. **2** In literature, vivid; animated: a *colorful* plot. — **col′or·ful·ly** *adv.* — **col′or·ful·ness** *n.*

color guard In the U.S. Army, Navy, and Air Force, the flagbearers and guards who conduct the colors in a ceremony.

col·or·if·ic (kul′ə·rif′ik) *adj.* Pertaining to the production or imparting of color. [<F *colorifique*]

col·or·im·e·ter (kul′ə·rim′ ə·tər) *n.* An apparatus for determining the hue, purity, and brightness of a color, especially as compared with a specified standard: used in chemical analysis and in medicine. [<COLOR + -(I) METER] — **col·or·i· met·ric** (kul′ər·ə·met′rik) or **·ri·cal** *adj.* — **col′or· i·met′ri·cal·ly** *adv.*

col·or·im·e·try (kul′ə·rim′ə·trē) *n.* The measurement and analysis of color by comparison with a standard or in terms of physical and spectral characteristics.

color index **1** *Astron.* The difference between the photographic and visual magnitude of a star. **2** *Med.* A number expressing the amount of hemoglobin in the red blood cells. **3** *Mineral.* A number indicating the percentage of light to dark and heavy minerals in igneous rock: also called **color ratio.**

col·or·ing (kul′ər·ing) *n.* **1** The imparting of color, or that which imparts color. **2** The general color of anything; coloration; style of applying colors. **3** Peculiar style or air. **4** Appearance; especially, false appearance.

col·or·ist (kul′ər·ist) *n.* **1** One who uses color. **2** An artist skilled in the use of color.

col·or·ize (kul′ər·īz) *v.t.* **·ized, ·iz·ing** To add color to originally black-and-white movies by means of computer-enhanced techniques. — **col′or·i· za′tion** *n.*

col·or·less (kul′ər·lis) *adj.* **1** Without color. **2** Dull; uninteresting. See synonyms under PALE.

color scheme An arrangement of colors according to a planned design, as in a room.

color sergeant See under SERGEANT.

color temperature *Physics* The temperature of a blackbody when its color exactly matches that of a given source of radiation.

color wheel A wheel designed to exhibit the proportion of primary colors in any shade of color.

Co·los·sae (kə·los′ē) An ancient city of SW Phrygia, Asia Minor.

co·los·sal (kə·los′əl) *adj.* Enormous; huge; tremendous. See synonyms under IMMENSE. — **co·los′sal·ly** *adv.*

Col·os·se·um (kol′ə·sē′əm) The Flavian amphitheater in Rome, built by Vespasian and Titus in A.D. 75–80: also spelled *Coliseum.*

Co·los·sian (kə·losh′ən) *adj.* Pertaining to Colossae, in ancient Phrygia. —*n.* **1** A native or inhabitant of Colossae. **2** *pl.* Saint Paul's epistle to the Colossians, a book of the New Testament.

co·los·sus (kə·los′əs) *n.* pl. **co·los·si** (kə·los′ī) or **co·los·sus·es** **1** A gigantic statue. **2** Any strikingly huge or great person or object. [<L <Gk. *kolossos* gigantic statue]

Colossus of Rhodes A 100-foot bronze statue of Helios set at the entrance to the harbor of ancient Rhodes in 285 B.C. See SEVEN WONDERS OF THE WORLD.

co·los·to·my (kə·los′tə·mē) *n. pl.* **·mies** *Surg.* The formation of an artificial opening into the colon. [<COLO- + -STOMY]

co·los·trum (kə·los′trəm) *n.* The first milk of a mammal after parturition; beestings. [<L]

col·our (kul′ər) See COLOR.

–colous *combining form* Dwelling in or inhabiting: *arenicolous.* [<L *colere* dwell, inhabit]

col·pi·tis (kol·pī′tis) *n.* Inflammation of the vagina; vaginitis. [<Gk. *kolpos* womb + -ITIS]

col·por·tage (kol′pôr·tij) *n.* A colporteur's work.

col·por·teur (kol′pôr·tər) *n.* **1** A peddler, especially one who hawks books, almanacs, etc., in country districts. **2** A traveling agent of a religious society, who sells or gives away Bibles, tracts, etc. [<F < *colporter* peddle < *col* neck + *porter* carry]

colt (kōlt) *n.* **1** A young horse, ass, etc.; specifically, a young male horse. **2** A frisky person. [OE] — **colt′ish** *adj.*

Colt (kōlt) *n.* A kind of pistol or revolver: a trade name. [after Samuel *Colt,* 1814–) 62, U.S. inventor]

col·ter (kōl′tər) *n.* A blade or disk on the beam of a plow, to cut the sod: also spelled *coulter.* [OE *culter* <L *culter* knife]

colts·foot (kōlts′foot′) *n. pl.* **·foots** A low, perennial, Old World herb of the composite family *(Tussilago farfara),* bearing yellow flowers: formerly used in medicine.

col·u·brine (kol′yə·brīn, -brin) *adj.* **1** Of, pertaining to, or like a snake. **2** Of or pertaining to a widely distributed family of snakes *(Colubridae);* especially to the subfamily *Colubrinae,* which includes the typically nonvenomous snakes, as the garter snake, blacksnake, etc. [<L *colubrinus* < *coluber* snake]

co·lu·go (kə·lo͞o′gō) *n.* pl. **·gos** The flying lemur.

Col·um (kol′əm), **Padraic,** 1881–1972, Irish poet and playwright.

Co·lum·ba (kə·lum′bə) A southern constellation, the Dove. See CONSTELLATION.

Co·lum·ba (kə·lum′bə), **Saint,** 521–597, Irish monk and missionary in Caledonia.

Co·lum·bae (kə·lum′bē) *n. pl.* An extensive suborder of birds of the order *Columbiformes,* including pigeons and doves. [<L *columba* dove]

Co·lum·ban (kə·lum′bən), **Saint,** 543?–615, Irish monk and missionary in France, Switzerland, and Italy.

col·um·bar·i·um (kol′ əm·bâr′ē·əm) *n. pl.* **·bar·i·a** (-bâr′ē·ə) **1** A dovecot; also, a pigeonhole in a dovecot: also **col·um·bar·y** (kol′· əm·ber′ē). **2** In ancient Rome, a sepulcher with niches for cinerary urns. [<L < *columba* dove]

COLUMBARIUM

Co·lum·bi·a (kə·lum′· bē·ə) *n. Poetic* The personification of the United States of America. [after Christopher *Columbus*]

Co·lum·bi·a (kə·lum′bē·ə) The capital of South Carolina.

Columbia, Cape A promontory of Ellesmere Island in the Arctic Ocean, the northernmost point of Canada.

Columbia, District of See DISTRICT OF COLUMBIA.

co·lum·bi·ad (kə·lum′bē·ad) *n.* A heavy smooth-bore cannon first used in the War of 1812: now obsolete. [from *Columbia,* the United States]

Co·lum·bi·ad (kə·lum′bē·ad) *n.* An epic of America; especially, *The Columbiad* in 12 books, by Joel Barlow, 1807.

Co·lum·bi·an (kə·lum′bē·ən) *adj.* **1** Of or pertaining to Columbia (the United States). **2** Pertaining to Christopher Columbus.

Co·lum·bi·an (kə·lum′bē·ən) *n. Printing* A style and size of type, 16-point.

Columbia River A river in SW Canada and NW United States, flowing 1,200 miles to the Pacific Ocean.

col·um·bine (kol′əm·bīn) *n.* A herbaceous plant (genus *Aquilegia*) of the crowfoot family with variously colored flowers of five petals; especially the **Colorado columbine** *(A. coerulea),* State flower of Colorado. — *adj.* Dovelike. [<F <Med. L *columbinus* dovelike < *columba* dove; from the resemblance of its flowers to a flock of doves]

Col·um·bine (kol′əm·bīn) A stock character in pantomimes: the daughter of Pantaloon and the sweetheart of Harlequin.

COLUMBINE

co·lum·bite (kə·lum′bīt) *n.* A black, brittle mineral, containing variable proportions of niobium and tantalum, associated with iron and manganese.

co·lum·bi·um (kə·lum′bē·əm) *n.* Former name for the element niobium. [<NL < *Columbia,* the United States]

Co·lum·bus (kə·lum′bəs) The capital of Ohio.

Co·lum·bus (kə·lum′bəs), **Christopher,** 1446–1506, Italian navigator; discovered America for Spain, Oct. 12, 1492. Spanish *Cristóbal Colón.*

Columbus Day October 12, a holiday observed in most States of the United States in commemoration of the discovery of America by Christopher Columbus in 1492: also called *Discovery Day.*

col·u·mel·la (kol′yə·mel′ə) *n. pl.* **·mel·lae** (-mel′·ē) *Biol.* A little rod, pillar, or central axis, as the central rod of the cochlea, the axial pillar of a spiral shell, etc. Also **col·u·mel**

(kol′yə·mel). [<L, dim. of *columna* column] **—col′u·mel′lar** *adj.* **—col·u·mel·li·form** (kol′·yə·mel′ə·fôrm) *adj.*

col·umn (kol′əm) *n.* **1** *Archit.* A vertical shaft or pillar, usually having a base and a capital, and primarily for the support of superincumbent weight. **2** Any object or structure resembling a column in form position, or use: th spinal *column*; a *column* of vapor. **3** *Printing* A vertical series of lines, separated from adjoining columns by a rule or a blank space. **4** *Mil.* A unit of troops in single file, or formed several lines abreast. **5** *Naut.* A fleet of ships in single file. **6** A department of a newspaper in which a special writer presents a daily article of contemporary comment. See synonyms under PROCESSION. [<L *columna*] **—col·umned** (kol′·əmd) *adj.*

ROMAN COLUMN WITH ENTABLATURE (*a.–c.*)
a. Cornice.
b. Frieze.
c. Architrave.
d. Capital (in Corinthian style)
e. Astragal.
f. Shaft.
g. Base.
From the Pantheon, Rome

co·lum·nar (kə·lum′·nər) *adj.* **1** Of, pertaining to, or having the form of a column or columns; like the shaft of a column. **2** *Geol.* Describing the six-sided structural formation characteristic of basaltic rock.

co·lum·ni·a·tion (kə·lum′nē·ā′shən) *n.* Grouping of columns; columns collectively.

col·um·nist (kol′əm·nist, -əm·ist) *n.* A journalist who writes or conducts a special column on a daily newspaper.

co·lure (kə·lyŏŏr′, kō′lyŏŏr) *n. Astron.* One of the two great circles of the celestial sphere at right angles to each other, intersecting at the poles and passing through the equinoxes and the solstices respectively. [<L *colurus* <Gk. *kolouros* < *kolos* docked + *oura* tail; because their lower parts are cut off by the horizon]

Col·ville River (kōl′vil) A river of northern Alaska, flowing 375 miles NE to the Beaufort Sea.

Col·vin (kol′vin), **Sir Sidney,** 1845–1927, English author.

co·ly (kō′lē) *n. pl.* **co·lies** The long-tailed African mousebird, one of a genus (*Colius*) having four toes and a strong, slightly curved beak. [<NL *colius* <Gk. *kolios,* a green woodpecker]

co·ly·one (kō′lē·ōn) *n. Biochem.* A secretion which has the property of inhibiting the action of some organ, tissue, or part of the body: distinguished from *hormone*: also called *chalone.* [<Gk. *kōlyōn,* ppr. of *kōlyein* hinder]

col·za (kol′zə) *n.* The summer rape or coleseed whose seeds produce rape oil. [<F <Du. *koolzaad* < *kool* cabbage + *zaad* a seed]

colza oil Rape oil.

com– *prefix* With; together: *combine, compare.* Also: *co–* before *gn, h,* and vowels; *col–* before *l,* as in *collide*; *con–* before *c, d, f, g, j, n, q, s, t, v,* as in *concur, confluence, connect, conspire; cor–* before *r,* as in *correspond.* [<L *com–* < *cum* with]

co·ma[1] (kō′mə) *n. pl.* **co·mas 1** A state of unconsciousness with slow, heavy breathing: sometimes called by the names of the conditions or diseases that cause them: **diabetic coma** (occurring in diabetes), **uremic coma** (from excess of urea), etc. **2** Stupor; lethargy. [<NL <Gk. *kōma* deep sleep]

co·ma[2] (kō′mə) *n. pl.* **co·mae** (kō′mē) **1** *Astron.* The nebulosity around the nucleus of a comet. **2** *Bot.* A tuft of silky hairs, as at the end of certain seeds. **3** *Optics* The hazy border surrounding an object viewed through an imperfect lens. [<L, hair <Gk. *komē*] **—co′mal** *adj.*

Co·ma Ber·e·ni·ces (kō′mə ber′ə·nī′sēz) A northern constellation, Berenice's Hair, near Boötes. See CONSTELLATION.

Co·man·che (kō·man′chē) *n. pl.* **·ches 1** One of a tribe of North American Indians of Shoshonean stock; plains Indians: formerly roaming territory between Kansas and northern Mexico, now in Oklahoma. **2** The Uto-Aztecan language of this tribe.

Co·man·che·an (kō·man′chē·ən) *adj. Geol.* Of or pertaining to the Comanche series and to the epoch during which the series was deposited; Shastan. **—*n.* 1** *Geol.* **a** An epoch of the Mesozoic between the Jurassic and the Cretaceous. **b** The Comanche series of rocks. Also called *Shastan.*

Comanche series *Geol.* The Lower Cretaceous series of rocks in the region of the Gulf of Mexico. [from *Comanche,* a town and county in central Texas]

co·mate[1] (kō′māt) *adj.* **1** *Bot.* Having a coma. **2** *Entomol.* Hairy, as the heads of certain insects.

co·mate[2] (kō·māt′, kō′māt′) *n.* A mate; companion.

co·ma·tose (kō′mə·tōs, kom′ə-) *adj.* **1** Relating to or affected with coma. **2** Lethargic; torpid; abnormally sleepy. Also **co·ma·tous** (kō′mə·təs, kom′ə-). **—co′ma·tose′ly** *adv.* **—co′ma·tose′ness** *n.*

co·mat·u·la (kō·mat′·yə·lə) *n. Zool.* One of a genus (*Comatula*) of free-swimming crinoids, with plumelike arms: also called *feather star.* Also **co·mat′u·lid.** [<NL <L *comatulus,* dim. of *comatus* having hair < *coma* hair]

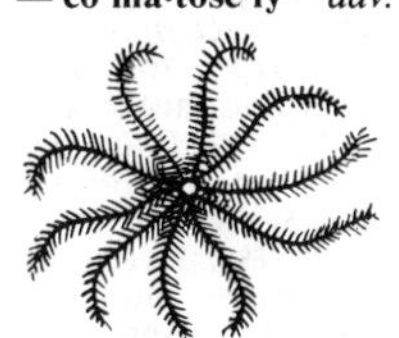

COMATULA
(Mostly microscopic: some up to 2/3 of an inch)

comb[1] (kōm) *n.* **1** A thin piece of horn, metal, ivory, or the like, with teeth, for cleansing, dressing, or fastening the hair. **2** Something resembling such a comb in appearance or use, as a currycomb or a card for dressing wool or flax. **3** The fleshy crest on the head of a fowl. **4** The crest of a hill or wave. **5** Honeycomb. **6** That part of a gunstock in which the cheek rests. **7** The ridge of a roof. **—*v.t.* 1** To dress, disentangle, or smoothe out with or as with a comb, as hair; clear or cleanse with a comb. **2** To card, as wool or flax. **3** In painting, to grain with a comb. **4** To search carefully and exhaustively. **—*v.i.* 5** To crest and break: said of waves. [OE *camb*]

comb[2] (kōōm, kōm) See COOMB.

com·bat (kom′bat, kum′-) *n.* A battle or fight; struggle; contest; duel. **—close combat** Hand-to-hand fighting. **—single combat** A fight between two persons; a duel. **—*v.*** (kəm·bat′) **·bat·ed** or **·bat·ted, ·bat·ing** or **·bat·ting** *v.t.* **1** To fight or contend with; oppose in battle. **2** To resist. **—*v.i.* 3** To do battle; struggle: with *with* or *against.* See synonyms under ATTACK, BATTLE, CONTEND, DISPUTE, OPPOSE. [<F < *combattre* <L *com–* with + *batuere* fight, beat] **—com·bat·a·ble** (kəm·bat′ə·bəl, kom′bat·ə·bəl, kum′-) *adj.* **—com·bat·er** (kom′·bat·ər, kum′-, kəm·bat′ər) *n.*

com·bat·ant (kəm·bat′ənt, kom′bə·tənt, kum′-) *n.* One engaged in or prepared for combat or hostilities. **—*adj.*** Fighting; battling; ready or disposed to combat. [<OF *combatant,* ppr. of *combattre* COMBAT]

combat fatigue Battle fatigue.

com·bat·ive (kəm·bat′iv, kom′bə·tiv, kum′-) *adj.* Inclined or eager to fight; pugnacious. **—com·bat′ive·ly** *adv.* **—com·bat′ive·ness** *n.*

comb·er (kō′mər) *n.* **1** One who or that which combs wool, flax, etc. **2** A long crested wave; a breaker.

com·bi·na·tion (kom′bə·nā′shən) *n.* **1** A joining together; union; alliance. **2** A compound or group. **3** *pl.* Underwear made in one piece. **4** The series of numbers or letters forming the key symbol to a keyless lock or **combination lock;** also, the mechanism operated by such a sequence. **5** *Math.* A group of several things or symbols in which the order of arrangement is immaterial. **6** *Chem.* The union of elements in certain fixed proportions, or the compound thus resulting. **7** An alliance of politicians, or merchants, etc., to protect or further a common interest, activity, or advantage. **8** An alliance of corporations; a combine or monopoly. **9** A railroad car divided into a baggage and a passenger section. See synonyms under CABAL, UNION. [<MF <LL *combinatio, -onis* a joining by twos < *combinare.* See COMBINE.] **—com′bi·na′tion·al** *adj.*

com·bi·na·tive (kom′bə·nā′tiv, kəm·bī′nə-) *adj.* **1** Relating to or effecting combination; tending to combine. **2** Designating those branches of algebra which depend on the theory of combinations. Also **com·bi·na·to·ri·al** (kəm·bī′nə·tôr′ē·əl, -tō′rē-).

com·bine (kəm·bīn′) *v.t.* & *v.i.* **·bined, ·bin·ing 1** To bring or come into a close union; blend; compound; unite. **2** To unite by affinity. **3** To enter into chemical combination: Oxygen and hydrogen *combine* to form water. See synonyms under MIX, UNITE. **—*n.*** (kom′bīn) **1** *Colloq.* An association of persons to raise prices or obstruct the course of trade, or to gain or keep political control, often by unfair or dishonest means; a trust; ring; cabal. **2** A farm machine which combines the processes of heading, threshing, and cleaning grain while harvesting it in the field. [<LL *combinare* < *com–* together + *bini* two by two] **—com·bin′a·ble** *adj.* **—com·bin′er** *n.*

comb·ing (kō′ming) *n.* **1** The act of combing, or what is removed by or from a comb. **2** A coaming.

combining form The stem of a word, usually of Greek or Latin origin (*tele–* and *–phone* in *telephone*), or in an English word unchanged (*over* in *overeat*), used in combination with other forms to create compounds.

comb jelly A ctenophore.

com·bust (kəm·bust′) *adj.* In astrology, obscured by proximity to the sun, as a planet or star. [<OF <L *combustus,* pp. of *comburere* burn up]

com·bus·ti·ble (kəm·bus′tə·bəl) *adj.* **1** Susceptible of combustion; inflammable. **2** Excitable; fiery. **—*n.*** Any substance that will readily burn, as pitch or coal. **—com·bus′·ti·ble·ness, com·bus′ti·bil′i·ty** *n.*

com·bus·tion (kəm·bus′chən) *n.* **1** The action or operation of burning; the state of being on fire. **2** *Chem.* The combination of a substance with oxygen, accompanied by the generation of heat and sometimes light. **3** *Physiol.* Oxidation, as of fuel, or of food in the body. **4** Disturbance; tumult. See synonyms under FIRE. [<LL *combustio, -onis* < *comburere* burn up] **—com·bus′tive** *adj.*

com·bus·tor (kəm·bus′tər) *n.* The chamber of a jet-propulsion engine in which combustion occurs.

comb·y (kō′mē) *adj.* Resembling a comb or honeycomb.

come (kum) *v.* **came, come, com·ing** *v.i.* **1** To move to or toward a position or place from a point further away: opposed to *go.* **2** To move to or toward the speaker: *Come* here. **3** In the imperative, to move mentally where the speaker wills: almost an interjectional sense: *Come,* let us make a visit. **4** To arrive as the result of motion or progress: They *came* to land. **5** To attain to an end or completion: Thy kingdom *come.* **6** To arrive at some state or condition; develop. **7** To advance or move into view; become perceptible: Her color *comes* and goes. **8** To draw near in time; be present; arrive: When Christmas *comes.* **9** To arrive in due course or in orderly progression. **10** To proceed or emanate as from a source. **11** To exist as an effect or result: This *comes* of trifling. **12** To happen or befall: *Come* what may, I'll do it. **13** To get or prove to be; become: The sign *came* true. **14** To reach or extend: with *to.* **15** To be offered, obtainable, or produced: The car *comes* in many colors. **16** To be favorably inclined; yield. **—*v.t.* 17** *Slang* To play the part of; act; also, to perpetrate: He *comes* a joke on us. **18** *Naut.* To loosen: with *up*:

to *come up* the standing rigging. 19 *Brit. Dial.* To fit or suit; become. **— to come about** 1 To take place; happen. 2 *Naut.* To turn in order to proceed on the opposite tack. **— to come by** 1 To pass near. 2 To get, acquire, or obtain. **— to come in** 1 To give birth to a calf. 2 To join a group in some special activity. **— to come it over** *Colloq.* To outwit or humble (someone). **— to come out** 1 To speak frankly; declare one's views. 2 To pass through a contest or competition: to *come out* first. 3 To make one's début in society. **— to come through** 1 To produce (the expected thing); achieve; win. 2 To experience. **— to come to** 1 To recover consciousness; revive; be resuscitated; also, return to, as one's senses. 2 *Naut.* **a** To anchor. **b** To bring a ship close to the wind. 3 To turn sharply to the left: said of a team of oxen or horses. 4 To amount to: The bill *came to* five dollars. [OE *cuman*]

come-at-a·ble (kum·at'ə·bəl) *adj. Colloq.* Easily accessible, as a person; readily acquired or procured, as an object; attainable.

come-back (kum'bak') *n.* 1 *Colloq.* Recovery of health or supremacy, after illness, failure, or deposition. 2 *Slang* A smart retort. 3 *Slang* Grounds for complaint; recourse: The customer has no *come-back.*

co·me·di·an (kə·mē'dē·ən) *n.* 1 A comic actor; one who plays comic parts or in comedies. 2 An entertainer who tells jokes, sings comic songs, etc. 3 One who writes comedies. 4 One who is or tries to be amusing. **— co·me·di·enne** (kə·mē'dē·en') *n. fem.*

com·e·do (kom'ə·dō) *n. pl.* **com·e·dos** or **com·e·do·nes** (kom'ə·dō'nēz) A condition of the sebaceous glands, in which the secretion is retained in the follicle; a blackhead. [< L, glutton < *comedere* eat up < *com-* + *edere* eat]

come-down (kum'doun') *n.* A descent to a lower condition or position; downfall.

com·e·dy (kom'ə·dē) *n. pl.* **·dies** 1 A drama or other literary work with a happy ending. 2 A play or other work of literature, motion pictures, television, radio, etc., characterized by a humorous treatment of characters, situation, etc., and having a happy ending; an entertaining drama: distinguished from the problematic, tragic, or serious. 2 The art of writing, producing, or acting in such plays, motion pictures, etc. 3 Comedies collectively, especially as a branch of the drama. 4 Any comic or ludicrous incident or series of incidents. [< MF *comédie* < L *comoedia* < Gk. *kōmōdia* < *kōmos* revel + *aeidein* sing]

come-hith·er (kum'hith'ər) *U.S. Slang adj.* Alluring; able to attract: a *come-hither* look. — *n.* Lure; attraction.

come·ly (kum'lē) *adj.* **·li·er, ·li·est** 1 Pleasing in person; handsome; graceful. 2 *Obs.* Suitable; becoming; decorous. See synonyms under BEAUTIFUL, BECOMING. [OE *cȳmlic*] **— come'li·ly** *adv.* **— come'li·ness** *n.*

Co·me·ni·us (kō·mē'nē·əs), **John Amos,** 1592–1670, Moravian educational reformer and bishop: also called *Komensky.*

come-on (kum'on', -ôn') *n. Slang* 1 Someone or something that lures or inveigles. 2 A beckoning look or gesture.

com·er (kum'ər) *n.* 1 One who comes or arrives. 2 *Colloq.* A person, animal, or thing capable of further growth or development; someone or something showing great promise. **— all comers** All applicants, contestants, etc.: to maintain a position against *all comers.*

co·mes·ti·ble (kə·mes'tə·bəl) *adj.* Edible; pertaining to food. — *n.* An eatable: usually in the plural. [< F < LL *comestibilis* < *comedere.* See COMEDO.]

com·et (kom'it) *n. Astron.* A celestial body drawn within the sun's gravitational field and occasionally close enough to the earth or bright enough to be observed by the naked eye. It consists of a nucleus of more or less condensed material, accompanied by a tenuous coma which always points in a direction away from the sun. A number of periodic comets are now known: among them are **Biela's comet,** with a period of 7 years; **Encke's comet,** period 3 years; **Halley's comet,** period 76 years. [OE *cometa* < L < Gk. *komētēs* long-haired < *komē* hair] **— com·et·ar·y** (kom'ə·ter'ē), **co·met·ic** (kə·met'ik) *adj.*

co·meth·er (kə·meth'ər) *n. Colloq.* 1 An affair; a subject for discussion or feeling. 2 Friendly relations; fellowship. **— to put the** (or **one's**) **comether on** To persuade by flattery; cajole. [Alter. of *come hither*]

com·et-seek·er (kom'it·sē'kər) *n. Astron.* A small telescope usually with an aperture of 3 to 5 inches, of short focal length, mounted to search for comets. Also **com'et-find'er.**

come-up·pance (kum'up'əns) *n. Colloq.* Deserved punishment; retribution.

com·fit (kum'fit, kom'-) *n.* A sweetmeat; confection. Also **com·fi·ture** (kum'fi·chŏŏr, kom'-). [< F *confit* < L *confectus.* Related to CONFECT.]

com·fort (kum'fərt) *n.* 1 Freedom or relief from pain, annoyance, or want; also, anything that contributes to such relief. 2 Relief from sorrow or distress; consolation; also, one who or that which comforts or consoles. 3 A thick, quilted bedcover; a comforter. [< *v.*] — *v.t.* 1 To give cheer or encouragement to; encourage; console; solace. 2 *Law* To countenance; abet. See synonyms under CHERISH, CONSOLE. [< OF *conforter* < LL *confortare* strengthen < *com-* with + *fortis* strong] **— com'fort·ing** *adj.* **— com'fort·ing·ly** *adv.* **— com'fort·less** *adj.*

Synonyms (noun): abundance, amusement, cheer, contentment, ease, enjoyment, happiness, opulence, pleasure, plenty, satisfaction, sufficiency. *Comfort* may be used of simple freedom from pain, annoyance, or privation, with no implication of any previous trouble, sorrow, or want. Thus, we may say one has lived in *comfort* all his life. In this sense, *comfort* is more solid than *amusement,* more quiet and stable than *pleasure,* less positive and vivid than *happiness. Comfort* is also any relief of suffering, want, or sorrow, which makes the distress easier to be borne. See HAPPINESS, SATISFACTION. *Antonyms*: dearth, dreariness, gloom, misery, need, poverty, suffering, want, wretchedness.

com·fort·a·ble (kum'fər·tə·bəl, kumf'tə·bəl) *adj.* 1 Having or imparting comfort. 2 Out of pain; free from suffering. 3 *Colloq.* Moderate; enough: a *comfortable* income. 4 *Obs.* Comforting. — *n.* A wadded bedquilt or comforter. **— com'fort·a·ble·ness** *n.* **— com'fort·a·bly** *adv.*

Synonyms (adj.): agreeable, cheerful, cheery, commodious, contented, convenient, genial, pleasant, satisfactory, satisfied, snug. A person is *comfortable* in mind when *contented* and measurably *satisfied.* A little additional brightness makes him *cheerful.* He is *comfortable* in body when free from pain; quiet, at ease, at rest. He is *comfortable* in circumstances, or in *comfortable* circumstances, when things about him are generally *agreeable* and *satisfactory,* usually with the suggestion of sufficient means to secure that result. *Antonyms*: cheerless, disagreeable, discontented, dissatisfied, distressed, dreary, forlorn, miserable, suffering, uncomfortable, wretched.

com·fort·er (kum'fər·tər) *n.* 1 One who comforts; a consoler. 2 A thick, quilted bedcover. 3 A long woolen scarf. See JOB'S COMFORTER.

Com·fort·er (kum'fər·tər) The Holy Spirit.

comfort station A public rest-room.

com·frey (kum'frē) *n. pl.* **·freys** 1 A rough, hairy herb (genus *Symphytum*) of the borage family. 2 Its root, containing tannin: used in medicine. [< OF *confirie*]

com·ic (kom'ik) *adj.* 1 Pertaining to, like, or connected with comedy. 2 Provoking or meant to provoke mirth; funny; ludicrous. 3 Acting in or composing comedy. See synonyms under HUMOROUS. — *n.* 1 A comical person or thing; especially, a comic actor. 2 A book or motion picture made up of comic strips. 3 *pl. Colloq.* The comic strips of a newspaper. 4 The comic side of art, life, etc. [< L *comicus* < Gk. *kōmikos* < *kōmos* revelry]

com·i·cal (kom'i·kəl) *adj.* 1 Causing amusement; ludicrous; diverting. 2 *Obs.* Of or pertaining to comedy. See synonyms under HUMOROUS, ODD, RIDICULOUS. **— com'i·cal·ly** *adv.* **— com·i·cal·i·ty** (kom'ə·kal'ə·tē), **com'i·cal·ness** *n.*

comic book A magazine of comic strips, usually containing one or more complete stories.

comic strip A strip of cartoons printed in newspapers, magazines, etc., and picturing a serial sequence of comic, dramatic, or historical incidents.

Co·mines (kô·mēn'), **Philippe de,** 1445?–1509, French historian. Also **Com·mines'.**

Com·in·form (kom'in·fôrm) *n.* The Communist Information Bureau, established in September, 1947, for the purpose of coordinating the policies and activities of the various national Communist parties. The original nine members were the Communist parties of Yugoslavia, Bulgaria, Hungary, Czechoslovakia, Poland, Italy, France, Rumania, and the U.S.S.R.: dissolved in April, 1956. [< COM(MUNIST) INFORM(ATION)]

com·ing (kum'ing) *adj.* 1 Approaching, especially in time: the *coming* year. 2 On the way to fame or note: He is the *coming* man. 3 Growing; increasing: a *coming* appetite. — *n.* The act of approaching; arrival; advent.

com·ing-out (kum'ing·out') *n. Colloq.* Entrance into society; debut.

Com·in·tern (kom'in·tûrn) *n.* The Third International, formed at Moscow in 1919, and dissolved in 1943: also spelled *Komintern.* [< COM(MUNIST) INTERN(ATIONAL)]

com·i·ta·tus (kom'ə·tā'təs) *n.* 1 In Roman and medieval history, the retinue of a prince or chieftain, acting as companions and protectors in exchange for maintenance. 2 In old English law, a county or shire; also, an earldom. [< L, a company]

co·mi·ti·a (kə·mish'ē·ə) *n.* In ancient Rome, one of three assemblies for election or legislation. [< L, pl. of *comitium* a place of assembly < *com-* together + *ire* go] **— co·mi·tial** (kə·mish'əl) *adj.*

co·mi·ti·um (kə·mish'ē·əm) *n. pl.* **co·mi·ti·a** (kə·mish'ē·ə) The place of meeting for the comitia of ancient Rome in the Forum adjoining the Sacred Way at the foot of the Capitol. [< L]

com·i·ty (kom'ə·tē) *n.* 1 Kindly consideration for others; friendliness; good will; courtesy. 2 The recognition which one jurisdiction accords within its territory to the laws of another. See synonyms under FRIENDSHIP. [< L *comitas, -tatis* courtesy < *comis* kind]

com·ma (kom'ə) *n.* 1 A punctuation mark (,) indicating separation in ideas or construction within a sentence. 2 A clause, or short group of words, cut off by itself. 3 Any pause or separation. [< L < Gk. *komma* short phrase < *koptein* cut]

comma bacillus *Bacteriol.* A comma-shaped bacillus (*Vibrio comma* or *cholerae*), the causative agent of Asiatic cholera. See illustration under BACTERIUM.

com·mand (kə·mand', -mänd') *v.t.* 1 To order, require or enjoin with authority. 2 To control or direct authoritatively; rule; have at one's disposal or use. 3 To overlook, as from a height; guard. 4 To exact as being due or proper. — *v.i.* 5 To be in authority; rule. 6 To overlook something from a superior position. See synonyms under DICTATE, GOVERN, INFLUENCE. — *n.* 1 The right to command; the authority exercised by an individual over others through his rank or ability; also, the act of commanding. 2 An order; commandment. 3 The troops or district under the command of one person. 4 Dominating power; hence, range of view; control; mastery. 5 In the U.S. Air Force, a unit, usually a wing or more, directed by an officer; also, its base of operations. 6 The distance between the bore of a gun and the adjacent ground. [< OF *comander* < LL *commandare* < *com-* thoroughly + *mandare* order, charge. Related to COMMEND.]

com·man·dant (kom'ən·dant', -dänt') *n.* A commanding officer, as of a service school, military district, etc.

command car A fast, maneuverable automobile of the convertible type, used in the field by a commander and his staff.

com·man·deer (kom'ən·dir') *v.t.* 1 To force into military service. 2 To take possession of or requisition by force for public use, especially under military necessity; sequester; confiscate. 3 To take over by force or by threat of force. [< Afrikaans *kommandeeren* command]

com·mand·er (kə·man'dər, -män'-) *n.* 1 One in command; a military leader. 2 In the U.S. Army, the commanding officer of a post or unit. 3 In the U.S. Navy, an officer ranking next above a lieutenant commander and next below a captain: equivalent in rank to a lieutenant colonel in the U.S. Army. — **lieutenant commander** In the U.S. Navy, an officer ranking next above a lieutenant and next below a commander: equivalent in rank to a major in the U.S. Army.

Com·mand·er (kə·man′dər, -män′-) *n.* **1** The chief officer of various orders, as Knights Templar, Grand Army posts, etc. **2** A member of a higher class in certain orders, as of knighthood.

commander in chief **1** An officer commanding all the armed forces in a certain theater of war. **2** Formerly, the officer commanding the armed forces of an American Colony: often the governor.

Commander in Chief **1** The President of the United States. **2** The highest officer of the American Revolutionary armies: George Washington.

Commander Islands See KOMANDORSKI ISLANDS.

com·mand·er·y (kə·man′dər·ē, -män′-) *n. pl.* **·der·ies** **1** *U.S.* A lodge of various orders, as of the Knights Templar, etc.; also, a division of a military officers' veterans' organization. **2** The rank of commander in an order of knighthood. **3** A district or estate under the authority of a commander; especially, a district or estate in charge of a member of a medieval order of knights; also, the house or priory of such an order: a *commandery* of the Knights of Malta.

com·mand·ing (kə·man′ding, -män′-) *adj.* **1** Fitted to command; impressive; authoritative; dignified. **2** Having a wide, overlooking view or advantageous position. See synonyms under IMPERIOUS, POWERFUL, PREDOMINANT. — **com·mand′ing·ly** *adv.*

com·mand·ment (kə·mand′mənt, -mänd′-) *n.* An authoritative mandate; edict; order; law; especially, a command of God, and specifically one of the divisions of the decalog or moral law. See synonyms under LAW. — **the Ten Commandments** The ten precepts given by God to Moses on Mount Sinai as recorded in *Exodus* XX 1–17; the decalog.

command module *Aerospace* A part of a space vehicle that houses the crew and navigational systems and is equipped for reentry.

com·man·do (kə·man′dō, -män′-) *n. pl.* **·dos** or **·does** **1** A special fighting force trained for quick, destructive raids into enemy territory. **2** A member of such a unit. **3** In South Africa, a militia force; also, a raid. [<Afrikaans <Pg., a group commanded <*commandar* command <LL *commandare.* See COMMAND.]

command performance A theatrical or musical performance presented at royal request.

com·meas·ure (kə·mezh′ər) *v.t.* To be coextensive with or equal to. — **com·meas′ur·a·ble** *adj.*

com·me·dia dell' ar·te (kôm·me′dyä del är′te) A dramatic genre originating in 16th century Italy, characterized by improvisation of dialog, conventional plots, and standard characters such as Pantaloon, Harlequin, Pulcinella, Columbine, etc.

comme il faut (kô mēl fō′) *French* As it should be; correct; in good form.

com·mem·o·rate (kə·mem′ə·rāt) *v.t.* **·rat·ed, ·rat·ing** To celebrate or signalize the memory of; keep in remembrance. Also **com·mem′o·rize.** See synonyms under CELEBRATE. [<L *commemoratus,* pp. of *commemorare* recall <*com-* together + *memorare* remember] — **com·mem·o·ra·ble** (kə·mem′ə·rə·bəl) *adj.* — **com·mem′o·ra′tive, com·mem·o·ra·to·ry** (kə·mem′ə·rə·tôr′ē, -tō′rē) *adj.* — **com·mem′o·ra′·tor** *n.*

com·mem·o·ra·tion (kə·mem′ə·rā′shən) *n.* The act of commemorating, or that which commemorates; a commemorative observance, celebration, recital, or action of any kind; a memorial. — **com·mem′o·ra′tion·al** *adj.*

com·mence (kə·mens′) *v.t.* & *v.i.* **·menced, ·menc·ing** To give origin to; begin; initiate; have or make a beginning; originate; start. See synonyms under INSTITUTE. [<OF *comencer* <L *com-* together + *initiare* begin <*in-* in + *ire* go] — **com·menc′er** *n.*

com·mence·ment (kə·mens′mənt) *n.* **1** A beginning; origin. **2** A celebration of the completion of a school or college course, when degrees are conferred; also, the day so observed. See synonyms under BEGINNING.

com·mend (kə·mend′) *v.t.* **1** To express a favorable opinion of; approve; praise. **2** To recommend; accredit. **3** To present the regards of. **4** To commit with confidence; entrust. **5** To place under the protection of a feudal lord. **6** To bestow *in commendam.* See synonyms under PRAISE. [<L *commendare* <*com-* thoroughly + *mandare* order, charge. Related to COMMAND.] — **com·mend′a·ble** *adj.* — **com·mend′a·ble·ness** *n.* — **com·mend′a·bly** *adv.*

com·men·dam (kə·men′dam) *n.* **1** The right to enjoy the revenues of a religious house or institution in the absence of a superior or during a vacancy (**in commendam**): abolished in England by act of Parliament in 1836. See COMMENDATOR. **2** The benefice so held. [<Med. L *(dare in) commendam* (give in) trust <*commendare.* See COMMEND.]

com·men·da·tion (kom′ən·dā′shən) *n.* **1** The act of commending; approbation. **2** Something that commends. **3** *Obs.* A message of good will; a greeting. See synonyms under EULOGY. [<L *commendatio, -onis* <*commendare.* See COMMEND.]

com·men·da·tor (kom′ən·dā′tər) *n.* One who held a benefice in commendam.

com·mend·a·to·ry (kə·men′də·tôr′ē, -tō′rē) *adj.* **1** Expressing commendation; serving to commend. **2** Holding a benefice as a commendator.

com·men·sal (kə·men′səl) *adj.* **1** Eating at the same table. **2** *Biol.* Associated or living with another in close but non–parasitic relationship, as a sea anemone attached to the shell of a hermit crab. — *n.* **1** A table companion. **2** A commensal organism. [<Med. L *commensalis* <*com-* together + *mensa* table] — **com·men′sal·ism** *n.* — **com·men·sal·i·ty** (kom′en·sal′ə·tē) *n.* — **com·men′sal·ly** *adv.*

com·men·su·ra·ble (kə·men′shər·ə·bəl, -sər·ə-) *adj.* **1** Measurable by a common unit. **2** Proportionate. [<LL *commensurabilis* <*com-* together + *mensurabilis* measurable] — **com·men′su·ra·bil′i·ty, com·men′su·ra·ble·ness** *n.* — **com·men′su·ra·bly** *adv.*

com·men·su·rate (kə·men′shə·rit, -sə·rit) *adj.* **1** Commensurable. **2** In proper proportion; proportionate. **3** Sufficient for the purpose or occasion. **4** Adequate; of equal extent. See synonyms under ADEQUATE. [<LL *commensuratus,* pp. of *commensurare* <*com-* together + *mensurare* measure] — **com·men′·su·rate·ly** *adv.* — **com·men′su·rate·ness** *n.*

com·men·su·ra·tion (kə·men′shə·rā′shən, -sə·rā′-) *n.* **1** The act of proportioning, or the state of being proportioned. **2** Measurement by comparison.

com·ment (kom′ent) *v.i.* To make expository or critical notes or remarks; make reflections or observations. — *v.t.* To make comments or remarks upon; explain or annotate. [<*n.*] — *n.* **1** A note in explanation or criticism. **2** A remark made in observation or criticism. **3** Talk; conversation; gossip. See synonyms under ANIMADVERSION, REMARK. [<OF <L *commentum* invention <*comminisci* contrive] — **com′ment·er** *n.*

com·men·tar·y (kom′ən·ter′ē) *n. pl.* **·tar·ies** **1** A treatise in annotation or explanation, as of the Scriptures; a series or body of comments; exposition. **2** Anything explanatory or illustrative; systematic exposition. **3** A historical narrative or chronological record of events; journal of official acts: the Royal *Commentaries* of Peru. See synonyms under DEFINITION. [<L *commentarius* notebook <*commentari,* freq. of *comminisci* contrive, devise] — **com·men·tar·i·al** (kom′ən·târ′ē·əl) *adj.*

com·men·ta·tor (kom′ən·tā′tər) *n.* **1** A writer of commentaries; an annotator; expounder. **2** One who discusses current events, especially over the radio at regular periods. **3** An actor who serves as a link between audience and players by appropriate commentaries on the action of the play. [<L, author, contriver <*commentari.* See COMMENTARY.]

com·merce (kom′ərs) *n.* **1** Exchange of goods, products, or property, as between states or nations; extended trade. **2** Familiar or social intercourse. **3** A card game in which the hands are varied by exchanging cards. **4** Sexual intercourse. See synonyms under BUSINESS, INTERCOURSE. — **Department of Commerce** An executive department of the U.S. government established in 1913 (from 1903 to 1913 part of the Department of Commerce and Labor), headed by the Secretary of Commerce, which fosters, promotes, and develops foreign and domestic commerce, the mining, manufacturing, shipping, and fishing industries, and transportation facilities. — *v.i.* (kə·mûrs′) **·merced, ·merc·ing** To have intercourse; associate; commune. [<F <L *commercium* <*com-* together + *merx, mercis* wares] — **com·merc′er** *n.*

com·mer·cial (kə·mûr′shəl) *adj.* **1** Of or belonging to trade or commerce; mercantile. **2** Made or put up for the market: *commercial* sulfur. **3** Having financial gain as an object: a *commercial* novel. — *n.* In radio and television, an advertisement. — **com·mer′cial·ly** *adv.*

commercial college A business college.

commercial high school A high school specializing in business subjects.

com·mer·cial·ism (kə·mûr′shəl·iz′əm) *n.* The spirit, methods, or principles of trade; the domination of life by such practices or aims. — **com·mer′cial·ist** *n.* — **com·mer′cial·is′tic** *adj.*

com·mer·cial·ize (kə·mûr′shəl·īz) *v.t.* **·ized, ·iz·ing** To make a matter of trade; put on a commercial basis. — **com·mer′cial·i·za′·tion** *n.*

commercial paper Mercantile paper.

commercial traveler A traveling salesman.

com·merge (kə·mûrj′) *v.t.* & *v.i.* **·merged, ·merg·ing** To merge together; commingle. — **com·mer′gence** *n.*

com·mi·na·tion (kom′ə·nā′shən) *n.* A denunciation or threatening. [<L *comminatio, -onis* <*comminari* <*com-* thoroughly + *minari* threaten]

com·min·a·to·ry (kə·min′ə·tôr′ē, -tō′rē, kom′·in·ə-) *adj.* Threatening punishment or vengeance.

com·min·gle (kə·ming′gəl) *v.t.* & *v.i.* **·gled, ·gling** To mix together; mingle. See synonyms under MIX.

com·mi·nute (kom′ə·no͞ot, -nyo͞ot) *v.t.* **·nut·ed, ·nut·ing** To reduce to minute particles; pulverize; triturate. [<L *comminutus,* pp. of *comminuere* <*com-* thoroughly + *minuere* lessen]

com·mi·nu·tion (kom′ə·no͞o′shən, -nyo͞o′-) *n.* **1** Trituration; pulverization; diminution by a gradual wearing or reduction, as by slicing, rasping, etc. **2** *Surg.* A fracture in which the bones are badly crushed or splintered.

com·mis·er·a·ble (kə·miz′ər·ə·bəl) *adj.* Worthy of commiseration; pitiable.

com·mis·er·ate (kə·miz′ə·rāt) *v.* **·at·ed, ·at·ing** *v.t.* To feel or manifest pity for; sympathize. — *v.i.* To condole: with *with.* [<L *commiseratus,* pp. of *commiserari* <*com-* with + *miserari* feel pity] — **com·mis′er·a′tive** *adj.* — **com·mis′er·a′tive·ly** *adv.* — **com·mis′er·a′·tor** *n.*

com·mis·er·a·tion (kə·miz′ə·rā′shən) *n.* **1** The act of commiserating. **2** A feeling or expression of sympathy, pity, sorrow, or regret; compassion. See synonyms under PITY.

com·mis·sar (kom′ə·sär, kom′ə·sär′) *n.* Formerly, a cabinet minister or an official in charge of a commissariat of the Soviet government. [<F *commissaire* <Med. L *commissarius* <L *committere.* See COMMIT.]

com·mis·sar·i·at (kom′ə·sar′ē·ət) *n.* **1** *Mil.* An army department supplying food and other necessaries. **2** The supply department of a club, household, or the like. **3** The officers and employees of the commissary department collectively. **4** The supplies furnished, as food, equipage, etc.; food supply. **5** Formerly, a major department of the government of the U.S.S.R.: now called *Ministry.* [<F <Med. L *commissarius.* See COMMISSAR.]

com·mis·sar·y (kom′ə·ser′ē) *n. pl.* **·sar·ies** **1** A commissioner. **2** An army officer in charge of subsistence, etc. **3** A church officer appointed by a bishop to exercise spiritual jurisdiction or hold an ecclesiastical court in distant parts of a diocese. **4** A store selling food and general provisions, as at a lumber camp.

5 An administrative division or territory, especially one in Colombia. 6 A wagon carrying food and provisions. —*adj.* Pertaining to, of, housing, or from a commissary. [<Med. L *commissarius.* See COMMISSAR.] **—com·mis·sar·i·al** (kom′ə·sâr′ē·əl) *adj.* **—com′·mis·sar′y·ship** *n.*

com·mis·sion (kə·mish′ən) *n.* 1 The act of committing, doing, or perpetrating; positive doing: contrasted with *omission.* 2 The act of entrusting; the matter entrusted; a trust; charge. 3 A certificate which confers a particular authority; specifically, a document issued by the president of the United States conferring rank and authority as an officer in the armed forces. 4 The rank or authority so conferred. 5 A body of persons acting under public authority. 6 The transaction of business for another under his authority; agency; also, an item of business so transacted. 7 The compensation of an agent. **—to put in** (or **into**) **commission** 1 To put in direct command of a designated officer, as a ship of war, for active service. 2 *Brit.* To entrust temporarily to a commission, as the great seal or the functions of a high office. **—to put out of commission** 1 To render unfit for use; to best or defeat thoroughly. 2 To retire the officers and crew of a naval vessel from active service, either permanently or temporarily. —*v.t.* 1 To give rank or authority to, as an officer. 2 To put into active service, as a ship of war. 3 To appoint; empower; delegate. [<OF <L *commissio, -onis* <*committere* COMMIT] **—com·mis′sion·al, com·mis·sion·ar·y** (kə·mish′ən·er′ē) *adj.*

commissioned officer See under OFFICER.

com·mis·sion·er (kə·mish′ən·ər) *n.* 1 A person who holds a commission to perform certain acts. 2 A member of a commission. 3 A public official appointed as head of an executive department, usually on a state or municipal level. **—com·mis′sion·er·ship′** *n.*

commission house A business house that buys and sells goods as an agent for others for a fee.

commission merchant One who buys and sells goods, either as an agent for a commission, or as a trader or merchant for his own account.

com·mis·sion·naire (kə·mish′ən·âr′) *n. Brit.* 1 The head doorman of a hotel. 2 Formerly, one of a body of disabled and pensioned soldiers, organized in London in 1859, employed as trusty porters, doorkeepers, etc.

commission plan A form of municipal government in which legislative, executive, and administrative powers are in a small elected commission or council, each municipal department being in charge of one commissioner: often called *Galveston plan.*

com·mis·sure (kom′ə·shŏŏr) *n.* 1 The point of union of two bodies, parts, or organs, as at the angle of the lips, etc. 2 A junction; seam; closure. 3 *Anat.* A tract or band of nerve fibers uniting corresponding right and left parts of the brain and spinal column. 4 *Bot.* The face or edge by which two carpels adhere. [<F <L *commissura* a joining <*committere* COMMIT] **—com·mis·su·ral** (kə·mish′yə·rəl, kom′·ə·sŏŏr′əl) *adj.*

com·mit (kə·mit′) *v.t.* **·mit·ted, ·mit·ting** 1 To do; perpetrate. 2 To place in trust or custody; consign; entrust; especially, to consign to an institution or prison. 3 To consign to any person, place, or use. 4 To devote; pledge; hence, to involve, compromise, or bind (oneself). 5 To consign for future reference, preservation, or disposal: to *commit* a speech to memory or to writing; *Commit* these bones to the earth. 6 To refer, as to a committee for consideration or report: a parliamentary term. [<L *committere* join, entrust <*com-* together + *mittere* send] **—com·mit′ta·ble** *adj.*

Synonyms: assign, confide, consign, entrust, relegate, trust. *Commit* is to give in charge, put into care or keeping; to *confide* or *entrust* is to *commit* especially to one's fidelity, *confide* being used chiefly of mental or spiritual, *entrust* also of material things; we *assign* a duty, *confide* a secret, *entrust* a treasure; we *commit* thoughts to writing; *commit* a paper to the flames. *Consign* is a formal word in mercantile use; as, to *consign* goods to an agent. See LEARN, TRUST. *Antonyms*: get, obtain, receive, secure, take.

com·mit·ment (kə·mit′mənt) *n.* 1 The act or process of entrusting or consigning for safekeeping. 2 An act of engagement or pledging. 3 The act of doing; perpetration. 4 *Law* A warrant (*mittimus*) for imprisonment; also, the state of being committed or act of committing to prison. 5 The act of referring a bill to a legislative body. 6 Liability incurred through buying or selling stocks, bonds, etc., or by agreeing to buy or sell. Also **com·mit′tal.**

com·mit·tee (kə·mit′ē) *n.* 1 A person or persons appointed by a larger number to act upon some matter. 2 One or more members of a legislative body appointed to investigate and report on a matter under discussion. 3 *Law* A person or persons appointed by a court to care for the person or property of another.

com·mit·tee·man (kə·mit′ē·mən) *n.* *pl.* **·men** (-mən) A member of a committee. **—com·mit′tee·wom′an** *n. fem.*

committee of the whole A committee consisting of all the members, as of a legislative body, sitting in deliberation on a given matter, but without legislative action, presided over by some member not the regular presiding officer.

com·mix (kə·miks′) *v.t.* & *v.i.* **·mixed** or **·mixt, ·mix·ing** To mingle or mix; intermix; blend. [Back formation <*commixt* <L *commixtus,* pp. of *commiscere* <*com-* together + *miscere* mix]

com·mix·ture (kə·miks′chər) *n.* 1 A mixture. 2 The act or process of mixing. 3 The state of being mingled.

com·mode (kə·mōd′) *n.* 1 A low chest of drawers; a cabinet. 2 A covered washstand. 3 A low chair or cabinet enclosing a chamber pot; a night-chair. 4 A woman's high headdress, worn about 1700. [<F]

COMMODE (*def. 4*)

com·mo·di·ous (kə·mō′dē·əs) *adj* Well adapted to serve the purpose for supplying needs; especially, affording ample accommodation; convenient; spacious. See synonyms under COMFORTABLE, CONVENIENT, LARGE. [<Med. L *commodiosus* <L *commodus* convenient] **—com·mo′di·ous·ly** *adv.* **—com·mo′di·ous·ness** *n.*

com·mod·i·ty (kə·mod′ə·tē) *n.* *pl.* **·ties** 1 A movable article of trade or convenience; an element of economic wealth. 2 Something bought and sold. 3 *Obs.* Convenience; suitability; conveniency; profit. [<MF *commodité* <L *commoditas, -tatis* convenience]

commodity money The currency of a suggested financial system, the unit of which, the **commodity dollar,** has a gold value determined at regular intervals by an index number based on the market prices of certain commodities.

com·mo·dore (kom′ə·dôr, -dōr) *n.* 1 In the U.S. Navy, an officer next above a captain and next below a rear admiral: a rank no longer in use since World War II. 2 In the British Navy, the commander of a squadron or division of a fleet, often having the temporary rank and pay of a rear admiral. 3 A title given to the senior captain of a naval squadron or of a fleet of merchantmen; also to the presiding officer of a yacht club. [Earlier *commandore*? <Du. *kommandeur*]

Com·mo·dus (kom′ə·dəs), **Lucius Aelius Aurelius,** 161–192, Roman emperor 180–192.

com·mon (kom′ən) *adj.* 1 Often occurring, met, or seen; frequent or usual; not distinguished or separated from the ordinary; customary; regular: a *common* occurrence. 2 Pertaining to, connected with, or participated in by two or more persons or things; joint. 3 Belonging to the public: the *common* schools. 4 The most prevalent or familiar: the *common* crow. 5 Commonplace; not excellent or distinguished in tone or quality; banal; coarse; vulgar; low. 6 *Gram.* **a** Of either gender. **b** Applicable to any individual of a class. See COMMON NOUN under NOUN.

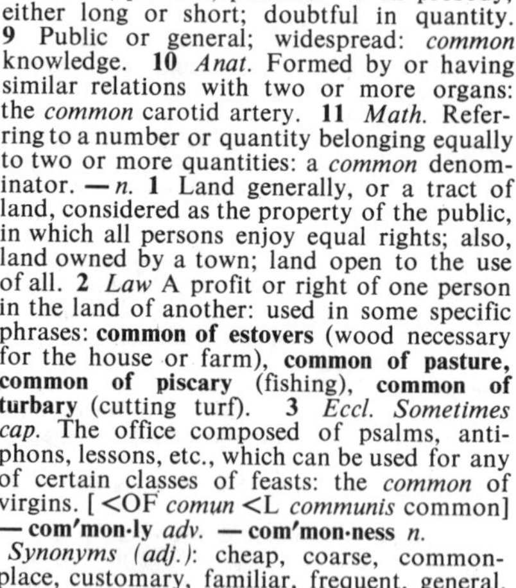

7 Secular; profane; polluted. 8 In prosody, either long or short; doubtful in quantity. 9 Public or general; widespread: *common* knowledge. 10 *Anat.* Formed by or having similar relations with two or more organs: the *common* carotid artery. 11 *Math.* Referring to a number or quantity belonging equally to two or more quantities: a *common* denominator. —*n.* 1 Land generally, or a tract of land, considered as the property of the public, in which all persons enjoy equal rights; also, land owned by a town; land open to the use of all. 2 *Law* A profit or right of one person in the land of another: used in some specific phrases: **common of estovers** (wood necessary for the house or farm), **common of pasture, common of piscary** (fishing), **common of turbary** (cutting turf). 3 *Eccl. Sometimes cap.* The office composed of psalms, antiphons, lessons, etc., which can be used for any of certain classes of feasts: the *common* of virgins. [<OF *comun* <L *communis* common] **—com′mon·ly** *adv.* **—com′mon·ness** *n.*

Synonyms (adj.): cheap, coarse, commonplace, customary, familiar, frequent, general, habitual, low, mean, normal, ordinary, popular, public, threadbare, trite, universal, usual, vile, vulgar. See FREQUENT, GENERAL, HABITUAL, MUTUAL, NORMAL, TRITE, USUAL. *Antonyms*: exceptional, infrequent, odd, peculiar, rare, singular, unusual.

For the following terms, see under the second element:

common council	common multiple
common denominator	common noun
common divisor	common school

com·mon·a·ble (kom′ən·ə·bəl) *adj.* 1 *Law* Entitled to common as of right: applied to beasts essential to the plowing or manuring of land, as horses, oxen, cows, and sheep. 2 Held in common: said of land.

com·mon·age (kom′ən·ij) *n.* 1 A common right to the use of lands; a tenancy of several persons in common to the same property. 2 Land held in common. 3 The common people; the untitled.

com·mon·al·ty (kom′ən·əl·tē) *n.* *pl.* **·ties** 1 The common people; the lower classes as opposed to persons of title or rank; the commons. 2 A body corporate; corporation: the mayor, *commonalty,* and citizens of London.

common carrier An individual or company which, for a fee, provides public transport.

com·mon·er (kom′ən·ər) *n.* 1 One of the commonalty; any subject not a peer. 2 In certain English universities, a student not dependent on the university foundation. 3 One who has a joint right in common ground. 4 Formerly, a member of the House of Commons.

common fraction See under FRACTION.

com·mon–law marriage (kom′ən·lô′) A marriage, or an agreement of marriage, substantiated by writings or conduct, instead of by church or civil ceremony.

Common Market Any of several customs unions, especially the European Economic Community.

common measure 1 In prosody, a four-line stanza in which iambic lines of four stresses and three stresses alternate, usually rhyming the first with the third and the second with the fourth lines: also called *hymnal stanza.* 2 *Music* Common time.

common meter In prosody, common measure.

com·mon·place (kom′ən·plās′) *adj.* Not remarkable or interesting; ordinary; trite. See synonyms under COMMON, GENERAL, TRITE. —*n.* 1 A trite remark; familiar truth; platitude; truism. 2 A note jotted down for reference; a memorandum. 3 Formerly, a book containing a methodical collection of notes, passages, etc.: also called **commonplace book** 4 Commonplace quality; ordinariness. [Trans. of L *locus communis* <Gk. *koinos topos* a general theme or argument].

Common Prayer, Book of The book of ritual used in public worship in the Anglican Churches. See under PRAYER.

com·mons (kom′ənz) *n. pl.* 1 The common people; commonalty. 2 A company eating at a common table, as in a college; the provisions so furnished; hence, allowance of food; rations; fare. 3 The dining hall in a college.

Com·mons (kom′ənz) *n. pl.* The legislators of the lower house, the House of Commons, of the British Parliament.

common sense 1 Practical understanding; capacity to see and take things in their right light; sound judgment. 2 Ordinary mental capacity. —**com'mon-sense'** *adj.*

common time See under TIME. Also **common measure.**

com·mon·weal (kom'ən·wēl') *n.* 1 The general welfare. 2 *Obs.* A commonwealth.

com·mon·wealth (kom'ən·welth') *n.* 1 The people of a state; the state. 2 A state in which the people rule; a republic; the official title of four States of the United States: the *Commonwealth* of Kentucky, of Massachusetts, of Pennsylvania, and of Virginia; also, the official title of Puerto Rico. 3 A body of persons united by some common interest and viewed as equals in authority. See synonyms under PEOPLE.

Commonwealth Day May 24, the anniversary of Queen Victoria's birthday: observed throughout the British Commonwealth of Nations: formerly called *Empire Day.*

Commonwealth of Australia See AUSTRALIA.

Commonwealth of England The republic established in England after the execution of Charles I in 1649 and continued till 1653, when Cromwell assumed the protectorate.

Commonwealth of Nations See BRITISH COMMONWEALTH OF NATIONS.

com·mo·tion (kə·mō'shən) *n.* 1 A violent agitation; excitement. 2 Popular tumult; social disorder; riot. See synonyms under TUMULT. [<L *commotio, -onis* <*commovere* <*com-* thoroughly + *movere* move]

com·move (kə·mo͞ov') *v.t.* **·moved, ·mov·ing** To put in motion or commotion.

com·mu·nal (kom'yə·nəl, kə·myo͞o'nəl) *adj.* 1 Of or pertaining to a commune. 2 Common; public; belonging to a community. —**com·mu'nal·ly** *adv.*

com·mu·nal·ism (kom'yə·nəl·iz'əm, kə·myo͞o'·nəl-) *n.* 1 In France, the theory that each commune should be self-governing and the state a mere federation of communes; hence, local self-government. 2 Communal ownership of goods and property. —**com'mu·nal·ist** *n.* —**com'mu·nal·is'tic** *adj.*

com·mu·nal·i·ty (kom'yə·nal'ə·tē) *n.* The state of being a member of a community.

com·mu·nal·ize (kom'yə·nəl·īz, kə·myo͞o'·nəl·īz) *v.t.* **·ized, ·iz·ing** To render communal; make municipal property of. —**com'mu·nal·i·za'tion** *n.* —**com'mu·nal·iz'er** *n.*

Com·mu·nard (kom'yə·närd) *n.* An adherent of the Paris Commune of 1871. [<F]

com·mune[1] (kə·myo͞on') *v.i.* **·muned, ·mun·ing** 1 To converse or confer intimately. 2 To partake of the Eucharist. —*n.* (kom'yo͞on) Intimate intercourse; communion. [<OF *comuner* share <*comun* COMMON]

com·mune[2] (kom'yo͞on) *n.* 1 A political division of France, governed by a mayor and a council; the people and the government of such a district; also, a similar division elsewhere, as in Italy and Spain. 2 A self-governing community; also, the people of such a community. 3 The commonalty. [<F <L *communis* common]

Com·mune (kom'yo͞on) *n.* 1 The revolutionary committee, elected by the communes, which ruled Paris in 1789–93. 2 The Communards who ruled Paris after the departure of the Germans, 1871. Also **Commune of Paris.**

com·mu·ni·ca·ble (kə·myo͞o'nə·kə·bəl) *adj.* 1 Capable of being communicated or imparted. 2 *Obs.* Ready to communicate; communicative. —**com·mu'ni·ca·bil'i·ty, com·mu'ni·ca·ble·ness** *n.* —**com·mu'ni·ca·bly** *adv.*

com·mu·ni·cant (kə·myo͞o'nə·kənt) *n.* 1 One who communicates or imparts, as information. 2 One who partakes or has a right to partake of the Lord's Supper. —*adj.* Communicating. [<L *communicans, -antis,* ppr. of *communicare.* See COMMUNICATE.]

com·mu·ni·cate (kə·myo͞o'nə·kāt) *v.* **·cat·ed, ·cat·ing** *v.t.* 1 To make another or others partakers of; impart; transmit, as news, a disease, or an idea. 2 To administer the communion to. —*v.i.* 3 To make or hold communication. 4 To be connected, as rooms. 5 To partake of communion. See synonyms under ANNOUNCE, GIVE, INFORM, PUBLISH. [<L *communicatus,* pp. of *communicare* share < *communis* common] —**com·mu'ni·ca'tor** *n.* —**com·mu·ni·ca·to·ry** (kə·myo͞o'·nə·kə·-tô'rē) *adj.*

com·mu·ni·ca·tion (kə·myo͞o'nə·kā'shən) *n.* 1 The act of communicating; intercourse; exchange of ideas, conveyance of information, etc.; correspondence. 2 That which is communicated; a letter or message. 3 Means of communicating, as a highway or passage; also, a telephone, telegraph, or radio system, etc. 4 Eucharistic communion. See synonyms under CONVERSATION, INTERCOURSE.

communication satellite An artificial satellite, as the Telstar or Relay, put into orbit to serve as a relay station for radio or television transmissions.

communications gap A failure of understanding, usually because of a lack of information, esp. between different age groups, economic classes, political factions, or the like.

communication theory Information theory.

com·mu·ni·ca·tive (kə·myo͞o'nə·kā'tiv, -kə·tiv) *adj.* 1 Ready to communicate; frank; talkative. 2 Of or pertaining to communication. —**com·mu'ni·ca'tive·ly** *adv.*—**com·mu'ni·ca'·tive·ness** *n.*

com·mun·ion (kə·myo͞on'yən) *n.* 1 The act of communing or sharing. 2 Sympathetic intercourse; fellowship. 3 The religious fellowship existing between man and God, between Christians, between a Christian and the church, or between autonomous churches. 4 A body or denomination of Christians having a common faith and discipline. 5 *Usually cap.* The Eucharist, or the act of celebrating or partaking of it: often called *Holy Communion.* 6 An antiphon said or chanted after the distribution of the Sacrament. See synonyms under CONVERSATION, INTERCOURSE, SACRAMENT, SECT. [<OF<L *communio, -onis* <*communis* common]

com·mun·ion·ist (kə·myo͞on'yən·ist) *n.* 1 One who has a theory as to the conditions on which a person should be admitted to church communion. 2 A member of a communion. 3 A communicant.

com·mu·ni·qué (kə·myo͞o'nə·kā') *n.* An official message, announcement, etc. [<F]

com·mu·nism (kom'yə·niz'əm) *n.* 1 A social system in which there is community of goods. 2 A theory of social change conceived by Karl Marx, directed to the ideal of a classless society. As developed by Lenin and others, it advocates seizure of power by a conspiratorial political party, maintenance of power during an interim period by stern suppression of internal opposition, centralized public ownership of almost all productive property and the sharing of the products of labor, and mmitment to the ultimate goal of a world-wide communist state. 3 Any social theory that calls for the abolition of private property and control by the community over economic affairs. 4 *Often cap.* **a** The system in force in any state based on this theory. **b** The doctrines and practices of the Communist party of any state; specifically, of the Communist party of the U.S.S.R. —**com'mu·nist** *n.*

Com·mu·nist (kom'yə·nist) *n.* 1 A member of the Communist party, especially in the U.S.S.R. 2 In other countries, a person who endorses, supports, or advocates communism or who belongs to any party or group that advocates the establishment of some type of communism: also **communist.** 3 A Communard.

com·mu·nis·tic (kom'yə·nis'tik) *adj.* 1 Pertaining to or like communism. 2 Tending to, favoring, or in accordance with communism. 3 Shared in common. 4 Occupying the same nest in common, as in certain birds. Also **com'mu·nis'ti·cal.** —**com'mu·nis'ti·cal·ly** *adv.*

Communist Manifesto A pamphlet written in 1848 by Karl Marx and Friedrich Engels, regarded as the first statement of the principles of modern communism.

Communist party 1 The dominant party in Russia since 1917, originally the majority left wing of the Social Democratic party and previously called the Bolshevik party. 2 Any political party advocating communism. See THIRD INTERNATIONAL under INTERNATIONAL.

com·mu·ni·ty (kə·myo͞o'nə·tē) *n. pl.* **·ties** 1 The people who reside in one locality and are subject to the same laws, have the same interests, etc. 2 A body politic. 3 The public; society at large. 4 A group of plants or animals living in a common dwelling under common conditions; also, the region in which they live. 5 A sharing or participation. 6 Identity or likeness: *community* of interest. 7 Common ownership, possession, or enjoyment of property. See synonyms under ASSOCIATION, PEOPLE. [<L *communitas, -tatis* fellowship <*communis* common]

community antenna television A television reception service in which a signal received at a master antenna is distributed to subscribers by cable. Abbr. *CATV*

community center The building or grounds used by a community for its social and recreational activities.

community chest A general fund for charity and public welfare to which individual contributions are made, and which is drawn upon by different organizations.

community church *U.S.* A non-denominational or interdenominational church for the use of a whole community.

com·mu·nize (kom'yə·nīz) *v.t.* **·nized, ·niz·ing** 1 To make common; make public property. 2 To make or cause to become communistic. —**com'mu·ni·za'tion** *n.*

com·mu·tate (kom'yə·tāt) *v.t.* **·tat·ed, ·tat·ing** *Electr.* To alter or reverse the direction of (a current).

com·mu·ta·tion (kom'yə·tā'shən) *n.* 1 A substitution of one kind of payment or service for another; also, the payment or service substituted. 2 *Law* A reduction or change of penalty. 3 *Electr.* The action of a commutator. 4 Daily or periodic travel on a commutation ticket. [<L *commutatio, -onis* < *commutare* change, alter <*com-* thoroughly + *mutare* change]

commutation ticket A railway or other ticket issued at a reduced rate for a specified number of trips within a certain period of time.

com·mu·ta·tive (kə·myo͞o'tə·tiv, kom'yə·tā'tiv) *adj.* Of or characterized by commutation.

com·mu·ta·tor (kom'yə·tā'tər) *n.* *Electr.* 1 Any contrivance for reversing the direction of the current in an electric circuit. 2 An assembly of individually insulated segments connected with the armature of a dynamo or generator and serving to collect and transmit the induced current.

com·mute (kə·myo͞ot') *v.* **·mut·ed, ·mut·ing** *v.t.* 1 To exchange reciprocally for something else. 2 To exchange for something less severe: to *commute* a sentence, debt, or payment. 3 To pay in gross at a reduced rate, as an annuity or railroad fare, instead of in successive payments. 4 *Electr.* To commutate. —*v.i.* 5 *Archaic* To serve as or be a substitute. 6 To pay a railroad fare, etc., in gross at a reduced rate. 7 To use a commutation ticket; specifically, to make daily or regular trips to and from work. See synonyms under CHANGE. —*n.* *U.S. Colloq.* A commuter's trip, or its duration or distance: a two-hour *commute.* [<L *commutare.* See COMMUTATION.] —**com·mut'a·ble** *adj.* —**com·mut'a·ble·ness, com·mut'a·bil'i·ty** *n.*

com·mut·er (kə·myo͞o'tər) *n.* One whose home and place of work are in different communities and who regularly travels between them, as a suburbanite who works in the city.

com·mu·tu·al (kə·myo͞o'cho͞o·əl) *adj.* Reciprocal; mutual.

Co·mo (kō'mō) A province in Lombardy, Italy; 798 square miles; capital, Como.

Como, Lake A lake in Como province, Lombardy; 30 miles long: famous for its beauty. *Italian* **La·go di Co·mo** (lä'gō dē kō'mō).

Com·o·rin (kom'ə·rin), **Cape** The southernmost point of India.

Com·o·ro Islands (kom'ə·rō) A volcanic archipelago NW of Madagascar, formerly a French overseas territory but since 1975 an independent republic; 838 sq. mi.; capital, Moroni.

co·mose (kō'mōs) *adj. Bot.* Having hairs; hairy; tufted; comate. Also **co·mous** (kō'məs). [<L *comosus* <*coma* hair]

com·pact[1] (kəm·pakt', kom'pakt) *adj.* 1 Closely and firmly united; pressed together; solid; dense; also, fine-grained. 2 Condensed; brief; terse. 3 Packed into a small space.

4 Compound; made up: with *of.* See synonyms under FIRM, HARD, STRONG, TERSE. —*v.t.* (kəm·pakt′) To pack or press closely; compress; unite closely; condense. —*n.* (kom′pakt) A small, hinged box for face powder and sometimes rouge, carried in a woman's purse. [<L *compactus,* pp. of *compangere* <*com-* together + *pangere* fasten]—**com·pact′ly** *adv.* —**com·pact′ness** *n.*

com·pact² (kom′pakt) *n.* A covenant, agreement, or contract. See synonyms under ALLIANCE, CONTRACT. [<L *compactum* <*compacisci* <*com-* together + *pacisci* agree]

compact disc A small digital disc on which sound has been recorded, to be replayed on an electronic device utilizing a beam of laser light that reads and reproduces the original sound with a very high level of quality.

com·pa·dre (kom·pä′drā) *n. SW U.S.* A close male companion: used also as a term of address. [<Sp.]

com·pan·ion¹ (kəm·pan′yən) *n.* **1** One who or that which accompanies; a comrade; associate. **2** A person, usually a woman, employed for company and assistance not of a menial nature. **3** A mate; one of a pair. See synonyms under ACCESSORY, ASSOCIATE. —*v.t.* To be a companion to; accompany; associate with. [<OF *compagnon* <LL *companio, -onis* <L *com-* together + *panis* bread]

com·pan·ion² (kəm·pan′yən) *n. Naut.* A companionway; also, the wooden hood over a companionway. [<Du. *kampanje* quarter-deck]

com·pan·ion·a·ble (kəm·pan′yən·ə·bəl) *adj.* Fitted for companionship; inclined to be friendly; sociable. —**com·pan′ion·a·bil′i·ty** *n.* —**com·pan′ion·a·bly** *adv.*

com·pan·ion·ate (kəm·pan′yən·it) *adj.* Of or pertaining to companionship or association; hence, agreed upon; shared.

companionate marriage A proposed form of marriage in which a couple agree not to have children until they are sure they wish to stay married, and which permits divorce by mutual consent.

com·pan·ion·ship (kəm·pan′yən·ship) *n.* The state of being a companion; fellowship; association. See synonyms under ACQUAINTANCE, ASSOCIATION.

com·pan·ion·way (kəm·pan′yən·wā′) *n. Naut.* A staircase leading from the deck of a ship to a cabin.

com·pa·ny (kum′pə·nē) *n. pl.* **·nies 1** The society or presence of another or others; fellowship; association. **2** One or more guests or visitors; persons met for social purposes; society. **3** An assemblage or corporation. **4** A partner or partners not named. **5** A number of persons forming a corporation, guild, or partnership, or associated for some common purpose. **6** The person or persons with whom one has companionship: keeping bad *company.* **7** *Mil.* A body of men commanded by a captain, larger than a platoon and smaller than a battalion: the basic military unit, equivalent to a battery or troop. **8** *Naut.* The whole crew of a ship: a ship's *company.* **9** The entire body of actors and actresses in a play or a theater; cast; a troupe. **10** *Obs.* Friendship —**to keep company (with)** To be sweethearts (with); court. —**to part company (with)** To end friendship or association (with). —*v.t. & v.i.* **·nied, ·ny·ing** *Archaic* To keep or be in company (with); accompany; associate (with). [OF *compagnie* <*compagnon* COMPANION]

Synonyms (noun): assemblage, assembly, body, collection, conclave, concourse, conference, congregation, convention, convocation, crowd, gathering, group, host, meeting, multitude, throng. *Company* is used to include any association of those united permanently or temporarily, for business, pleasure, festivity, travel, etc., or by sorrow, misfortune, or wrong; *company* implies more unity of feeling and purpose than *crowd,* and is a less formal and more familiar word than *assemblage* or *assembly.* An *assemblage* may be of persons or of objects; an *assembly* is usually of persons. *Collection, crowd, gathering, group,* and *multitude* have the unorganized and promiscuous character of the *assemblage;* the other terms come under the general idea of *assembly. Body* is used of a number of persons so organized and unified that they can be thought of as one whole. *Congregation* is now almost exclusively religious. *Gathering* refers to a coming together, commonly of numbers from far and near, as, the *gathering* of the Scottish clans. See ASSEMBLY, ASSOCIATION, CLASS, FLOCK. *Antonyms*: dispersion, loneliness, privacy, retirement, seclusion, solitude.

company union A union of workers formed within an industrial establishment, having no affiliation with any other recognized trade union, and usually considered to be dominated by the employer of its members.

com·pa·ra·ble (kom′pər·ə·bəl) *adj.* **1** Capable of comparison. **2** Worthy of comparison. —**com′pa·ra·ble·ness, com′pa·ra·bil′i·ty** *n.* —**com′pa·ra·bly** *adv.*

com·par·a·tive (kəm·par′ə·tiv) *adj.* **1** Pertaining to, resulting from or using comparison. **2** Estimated by comparison; relative. **3** Almost but not quite. **4** *Gram.* Expressing a degree of an adjective or adverb higher than the positive and lower than the superlative. —*n. Gram.* The comparative degree, or a word or form by which it is expressed: "Better" is the *comparative* of "good." Abbr. *comp.* [<L *comparativus* <*comparare* COMPARE] —**com·par′a·tive·ly** *adv.*

comparative linguistics See under LINGUISTICS.

com·pa·ra·tor (kom′pə·rā′tər) *n.* An instrument for automatically comparing data of length, distance, colors, etc.

com·pare (kəm·pâr′) *v.* **·pared, ·par·ing** *v.t.* **1** To represent or speak of as similar, analogous, or equal: with *to.* **2** To examine so as to perceive similarity or dissimilarity; state the resemblance or difference of: with *with.* **3** *Gram.* To state the degrees of comparison of (an adjective or adverb). —*v.i.* **4** To be worthy of comparison: with *with.* **5** To vie or compete. —*n. Archaic* or *Poetic* Comparison: usually in the phrase *beyond compare.* [<F *comparer* <L *comparare* <*com-* together + *par* equal]

Synonyms (verb): assimilate, collate, liken, parallel. See CONTRAST. To compare one thing *to* another is to liken or suggest as being similar; to compare one thing *with* another is to make a detailed analysis of points of similarity or difference.

com·par·i·son (kəm·par′ə·sən) *n.* **1** A comparing; an estimate or statement of relative likeness or unlikeness. **2** *Gram.* That inflection of adjectives or adverbs which indicates differences of degree. There are three **degrees of comparison,** the positive, comparative, and superlative, the last two being regularly expressed by adding *-er* or *-est* to the positive (except in words of three syllables or more), or by using *more* or *most, less* or *least,* before it. **3** That which in its relation to something else serves as an illustration or example; a parallel: an act without *comparison.* **4** Any rhetorical figure that sets forth the points of similarity or contrast between one person or thing and another, such as a simile or metaphor. See synonyms under ANALOGY, SIMILE. [<OF *comparaison* <L *comparatio, -onis* <*comparare* COMPARE]

com·part (kəm·pärt′) *v.t.* To divide into compartments; partition. [<OF *compartir* <L *compartiri* <*com-* together + *pars, partis* part]

com·part·ment (kəm·pärt′mənt) *n.* **1** One of the parts into which an enclosed space is subdivided by lines or partitions. **2** Any separate section or chamber: watertight *compartments.* **3** In railway passenger cars, a small, private division with sleeping accommodations. [<F *compartiment* <Ital. *compartimento* <L *compartiri.* See COMPART.]

com·part·men·tal·ize (kom′pärt·men′təl·īz) *v.t.* **·ized, ·iz·ing** To divide into compartments.

com·pass (kum′pəs, kom′-) *n.* **1** Extent within limits; area; reach; scope. **2** A boundary, circumference, or circuit. **3** The range of a voice or instrument. **4** An instrument for determining directions by the pointing to magnetic north of a magnetic needle free to turn in a horizontal plane, and carrying a marked card, as in the **mariner's compass. 5** A radio compass. Compare illustrations under BINNACLE, CLINOMETER. **6** *Obs.* A circular course or journey; round; circuit. **7** Compasses. —*v.t.* **1** To go around; make a circuit of. **2** To surround; encompass. **3** To grasp mentally; comprehend. **4** To plot or scheme. **5** To attain or accomplish; achieve. **6** *Obs.* To cause to curve; bend into circular form. [<OF *compas,* ult. <L *com-* together + *passus* step]—**com′pass·a·ble** *adj.*

compass card The circular card or dial resting on the pivot of a mariner's compass, on which the 32 points and 360 degrees of the circle are marked. Also **compass dial.**

COMPASS CARD
The letters are abbreviations of the compass points; to the right of north (at top of card and not lettered) they are read: (N) *north,* (N by E) *north by east,* (NNE) *north-northeast,* (NE by N) *northeast by north,* etc.

com·pass·es (kum′pəs·iz, kom′-) *n. pl.* An instrument having two branches or legs, usually pointed, and hinged at the top by a pivoted joint, used for taking or marking measurements, describing circles, etc. Also **pair of compasses.**

compass heading *Aeron.* A specified flight course which the pilot follows by compass indications.

com·pas·sion (kəm·pash′ən) *n.* Pity for suffering, with desire to help or to spare; commiseration; sympathy. See synonyms under MERCY, PITY. [<MF <LL *compassio, -onis* <L *com-* together + *pati* feel, suffer]

com·pas·sion·ate (kəm·pash′ən·it) *adj.* **1** Feeling compassion or pity; merciful; sympathetic. **2** *Obs.* Pitiable; piteous. See synonyms under CHARITABLE, HUMANE, MERCIFUL. —*v.t.* (kəm·pash′ən·āt) **·at·ed, ·at·ing** To have compassion for; to pity. —**com·pas′sion·ate·ly** *adv.* —**com·pas′sion·ate·ness** *n.*

compass plant 1 A tall, rough, bristly herb *(Silphium laciniatum)* of North American prairies, belonging to the composite family and having large leaves lying in a vertical position with their edges turned north and south. **2** The prickly lettuce *(Lactuca serriola).*

com·pat·i·ble (kəm·pat′ə·bəl) *adj.* **1** Capable of existing together; congruous; congenial. **2** Describing a television set adapted to produce images in color or in black and white. [<F <Med. L *compatibilis* <L *com-* together + *pati* suffer] —**com·pat′i·bil′i·ty, com·pat′·i·ble·ness** *n.* —**com·pat′i·bly** *adv.*

com·pa·tri·ot (kəm·pā′trē·ət, -pat′rē·ət) *n.* **1** A fellow countryman. **2** *Colloq.* A colleague. —*adj.* Having the same country. [<F *compatriote* <LL *compatriota* <L *com-* together + *patria* native land]—**com·pa′tri·ot·ism** *n.*

com·peer (kəm·pir′, kom′pir) *n.* **1** One of equal rank; a peer. **2** A comrade; associate. —*v.t. Obs.* To be the compeer of; equal; rival; match. [<OF *comper* <L *compar* equal <*com-* with + *par* equal]

com·pel (kəm·pel′) *v.t.* **·pelled, ·pel·ling 1** To drive or urge irresistibly; constrain. **2** To force to yield; subdue. **3** To obtain by force; exact. **4** *Obs.* To seize; overpower; extort. **5** To drive together; gather in a company; herd; drive. [<L *compellere* <*com-* together + *pellere* drive]—**com·pel′la·ble** *adj.* —**com·pel′la·bly** *adv.* —**com·pel′ler** *n.*

Synonyms: coerce, constrain, drive, force, make, necessitate, oblige. See ACTUATE, BIND, MAKE. Compare DRIVE, INFLUENCE. *Antonyms*: see synonyms under HINDER.

com·pel·la·tion (kom′pə·lā′shən) *n.* **1** Form of address; appellation. **2** The act of addressing or accosting; an address. [< L *compellatio, -onis* < *compellare* accost]

com·pend (kom′pend) *n.* A compendium. See synonyms under ABRIDGMENT.

com·pen·di·ous (kəm·pen′dē·əs) *adj.* Briefly stated; succinct; concise; containing the substance in narrow compass. See synonyms under TERSE. [< L *compendiosus* brief < *compendium* COMPENDIUM] **—com·pen′di·ous·ly** *adv.* **—com·pen′di·ous·ness** *n.*

com·pen·di·um (kəm·pen′dē·əm) *n. pl.* **·di·ums** or **·di·a** (-dē·ə) An abridgment; abstract; a brief, comprehensive summary. See synonyms under ABBREVIATION, ABRIDGMENT. [< L < *compendere* < *com-* together + *pendere* weigh]

com·pen·sa·ble (kəm·pen′sə·bəl) *adj.* Entitled to be or capable of being compensated.

com·pen·sate (kom′pən·sāt) *v.* **·sat·ed, ·sat·ing** *v.t.* **1** To make suitable amends to or for; requite; remunerate. **2** To counterbalance or make up for; offset. **3** To stabilize the purchasing power of (a monetary unit) by varying gold content to counteract price fluctuations. **4** *Mech.* To provide with a counterbalancing or neutralizing device, as for a variation. *—v.i.* **5** To make returns or amends; serve as an equivalent or substitute. See synonyms under PAY, REQUITE. [< L *compensatus,* pp. of *compensare* < *com-* together + *pensare,* freq. of *pendere* weigh] **—com·pen·sa·tive** (kəm·pen′sə·tiv), **com·pen·sa·to·ry** (kəm·pen′sə·tôr′ē, -tō′rē) *adj.*

com·pen·sa·tion (kom′pən·sā′shən) *n.* **1** The act of compensating, or that which compensates; payment; amends. **2** *Mech.* A means of counteracting variations, as of temperature; neutralizing opposing forces, as of magnetic attraction; or maintaining equilibrium. **3** *Psychol.* A form of behavior whereby an individual disguises or conceals an unpleasant sensation, feeling, or trait by giving prominence to one having desirable results. **4** *Biol.* The correction, by biological processes or medical means, of serious defects in the structure and functions of an organism or a human body. **—workmen's compensation 1** Damages recoverable from an employer by an employee in case of accident. **2** Government insurance against illness, accident, or unemployment. **—com′pen·sa′tion·al** *adj.*

com·pen·sa·tor (kom′pən·sā′tər) *n.* **1** One who or that which compensates. **2** A device for neutralizing the influence of local attraction upon a compass needle. **3** An automatic apparatus for equalizing the pressure of gas in retorts or mains. **4** *Electronics* A device which automatically compensates for errors in a direction finder. **5** *Physics* A device for measuring the components of polarized light.

com·pete (kəm·pēt′) *v.i.* **·pet·ed, ·pet·ing** To contend with another or others for a prize; engage in a contest or competition; vie. See synonyms under CONTEND. [< L *competere* strive < *com-* together + *petere* seek]

com·pe·tence (kom′pə·təns) *n.* **1** The state of being competent; ability. **2** Sufficient means for comfortable living; a moderate income. **3** *Law* Qualification or admissibility; legal capacity, authority, or jurisdiction: the *competence* of a tribunal. Also **com′pe·ten·cy.** See synonyms under ABILITY.

com·pe·tent (kom′pə·tənt) *adj.* **1** Having sufficient ability or authority. **2** Possessing the requisite natural or legal qualifications; qualified. **3** Sufficient; adequate. [< MF *competent* < L *competens, -entis,* ppr. of *competere* be fit, be proper < *com-* together + *petere* go, seek] **—com′pe·tent·ly** *adv.* **—com′pe·tent·ness** *n.*

Synonyms: able, adapted, adequate, capable, fit, qualified. One is *competent* who has all the natural powers, physical or mental, to meet the demands of a situation or work; the word is widely used of ability to meet all requirements, natural, legal, or other; as, a *competent* knowledge of a subject; a court of *competent* jurisdiction. *Qualified* refers to acquired abilities; a *qualified* teacher may be no longer *competent,* by reason of ill health. *Able* and *capable* suggest general ability and reserved power, *able* being the higher word of the two. An *able* man will do something well in any position. A *capable* man will come up to any ordinary demand. Compare ADEQUATE, GOOD. *Antonyms*: disqualified, inadequate, incompetent, unequal, unfit, unqualified.

com·pe·ti·tion (kom′pə·tish′ən) *n.* **1** Contention of two or more for the same object or for superiority; rivalry. **2** The independent endeavor of two or more persons to obtain the business patronage of a third by offering more advantageous terms; also, the conditions which this endeavor produces.

Synonyms: contest, emulation, opposition, rivalry. *Competition* is the striving for something that is sought by another at the same time. *Emulation* regards the abstract, *competition* the concrete; *rivalry* is the same in essential meaning with *competition,* but differs in the nature of the objects contested for. We speak of *competition* in business, *emulation* in scholarship, *rivalry* in love, politics, etc. *Competition* may be friendly, *rivalry* is commonly hostile. Compare AMBITION, EMULATION. *Antonyms*: agreement, association, alliance, combination, confederacy, harmony, monopoly, union. In business and commercial use, the chief antonym of *competition* is *monopoly,* which by bringing all engaged in an industry under a single control forbids them to compete. [< L *competitio, -onis* < *competere* COMPETE]

com·pet·i·tive (kəm·pet′ə·tiv) *adj.* Pertaining to or characterized by competition. **—com·pet′i·tive·ly** *adv.* **—com·pet′i·tive·ness** *n.*

com·pet·i·tor (kəm·pet′ə·tər) *n.* **1** One who or that which competes; especially, one striving for the same thing as another, in business, athletics, etc. **2** *Obs.* An associate; confederate. See synonyms under ENEMY. **—com·pet′i·tor·ship′** *n.* **—com·pet·i·to·ry** (kəm·pet′ə·tôr′ē, -tō′rē) *adj.*

Com·piègne (kôn·pyen′y′) A town in northern France, near the **Forest of Compiègne,** scene of the signing of armistices between the Allies and Germany, 1918, and Germany and France, 1940.

com·pi·la·tion (kom′pə·lā′shən) *n.* **1** The act or process of collecting materials for making a book, statistical table, etc. **2** That which is compiled, as a book made up of material gathered from other books: *compilations* of verse. [< F < L *compilatio, -onis* < *compilare.* See COMPILE.]

com·pile (kəm·pīl′) *v.t.* **·piled, ·pil·ing 1** To compose (a literary work, etc.) from other works. **2** To gather (materials borrowed or transcribed) into a volume or into orderly form. [< L *compilare* < *com-* thoroughly + *pilare* strip, plunder; prob. infl. in meaning by PILE] **—com·pi·la·to·ry** (kəm·pī′lə·tôr′ē, -tō′rē) *adj.* **—com·pil′er** *n.*

com·pla·cen·cy (kəm·plā′sən·sē) *n. pl.* **·cies 1** Satisfaction; self-approval. **2** Equanimity. Also **com·pla′cence.** See synonyms under SATISFACTION.

com·pla·cent (kəm·plā′sənt) *adj.* **1** Feeling or showing complacency or satisfaction; especially, pleased or satisfied with oneself; smug. **2** *Obs.* Disposed to please; complaisant. [< L *complacens, -entis,* ppr. of *complacere* < *com-* thoroughly + *placere* please. Doublet of COMPLAISANT.] **—com·pla′cent·ly** *adv.*

com·plain (kəm·plān′) *v.i.* **1** To express a sense of ill-treatment or of pain, grief, etc.; murmur; find fault; present a grievance. **2** To make a formal accusation; present a charge or complaint. [< F *complaindre* < LL *complangere* < *com-* thoroughly + *plangere* beat (the beast in grief)] **—com·plain′er** *n.*

Synonyms: croak, deplore, growl, grumble, grunt, murmur, remonstrate, repine. To *complain* is to give utterance to dissatisfaction or objection, express a sense of wrong or ill-treatment. One *complains* of a real or assumed grievance; he may *murmur* through mere peevishness or ill temper; he *repines,* with vain distress, at the inevitable. *Complaining* is by speech or writing; *murmuring* is commonly said of half-repressed utterance; *repining* of the mental act alone. One may *complain* of an offense to the offender or to others; he *remonstrates* with the offender only. *Complain* has a legal meaning, which the other words have not, signifying to make a formal accusation, present a specific charge; the same is true of the noun *complaint. Antonyms*: applaud, approve, commend, eulogize, laud, praise.

com·plain·ant (kəm·plā′nənt) *n.* One who complains; especially, one who enters a formal complaint before a magistrate or other authority; a plaintiff or petitioner. [< F *complaignant* a plaintiff, orig. ppr. of *complaindre* COMPLAIN]

com·plaint (kəm·plānt′) *n.* **1** A statement of wrong, grievance, or injury. **2** *Law* The first paper setting forth the plaintiff's cause of action. **3** The act of complaining. **4** A grievance. **5** A physical ailment; disease. See synonyms under DISEASE, ILLNESS. [< F *complainte* < *complaindre* COMPLAIN]

com·plai·sant (kəm·plā′zənt, kom′plə·zant) *adj.* Showing a desire or endeavor to please; yielding; compliant. See synonyms under BLAND, FRIENDLY, POLITE. [< F, ppr. of *complaire* please < L *complacere.* Doublet of COMPLACENT.] **—com·plai′sance** *n.* **—com·plai′sant·ly** *adv.* **—com·plai′sant·ness** *n.*

com·pla·nate (kom′plə·nāt) *adj.* **1** Leveled; flattened. **2** *Bot.* Lying in the same plane, as certain leaves. [< L *complanatus,* pp. of *complanare* < *com-* together + *planare* make level] **—com′pla·na′tion** *n.*

com·plect (kəm·plekt′) *v.t.* To join by weaving; interweave. [< L *complecti* < *com-* together + *plecti* twine, weave]

com·plect·ed (kəm·plek′tid) *adj. U.S. Dial.* Complexioned: used only in compounds: light-*complected.*

com·ple·ment (kom′plə·mənt) *n.* **1** That which fills up or completes; that which must be added to complete a symmetrical whole. **2** Full number: The vessel has her *complement* of men. **3** An addition or appendage; an accessory. **4** *Geom.* The amount by which an angle falls short of 90 degrees. **5** *Gram.* A word or phrase used after a verb of incomplete predication to complete the meaning of the sentence. A **subjective complement** describes or identifies the subject, as the noun *president* in *He is president* or in *He was elected president* or as the adjective *happy* in *She is happy* or in *She was made happy.* An **objective complement** describes or identifies the direct object, as the noun *president* in *They elected him president* or the adjective *happy* in *It made her happy.* **6** *Music* A musical interval which, with the interval already given, will complete an octave. **7** *Immunology* A complex system of unstable, heat-sensitive proteins normally present in human and other serums where it reacts with specific antibodies to destroy related antigens. Also called *alexin.* *—v.t.* To add or form a complement to; supplement; make complete; supply a lack in. ◆ Homophone: *compliment.* [< L *complementum* < *complere* COMPLETE] **—com·ple·men·tal** (kom′plə·men′təl) *adj.* **—com′ple·ment′er** *n.*

com·ple·men·ta·ry (kom′plə·men′tər·ē, -trē) *adj.* **1** Serving as a complement; helping to constitute a whole or to supply a lack; completing complemental. **2** Mutually providing each other's needs. **3** *Geom.* Furnishing the complement of another: see COMPLEMENTARY ANGLE under ANGLE.

complementary cell *Bot.* One of the cellular components of the lenticel in plants.

complementary color See under COLOR.

a d b c

COMPLEMENTARY ANGLES
abd and *dbc* are complementary

com·plete (kəm·plēt′) *adj.* **1** Having all needed or normal parts, elements, or details; lacking nothing; entire; perfect; full. **2** Thoroughly wrought; finished. See synonyms under AMPLE, IMPLICIT, RADICAL, RIPE. *—v.t.* **·plet·ed, ·plet·ing** To make complete; accomplish; finish; fulfil. See synonyms under ACCOMPLISH, EFFECT, END. [< L *completus,* pp. of *complere* < *com-* thoroughly + *plere* fill] **—com·plete′ly** *adv.* **—com·plete′ness** *n.* **—com·ple′tive** *adj.*

com·ple·tion (kəm·plē′shən) *n.* **1** The act of completing, or the state of being completed.

2 Accomplishment; fulfilment. See synonyms under END.

com·plex (kəm·pleks′, kom′pleks) *adj.* **1** Consisting of various parts or elements; composite. **2** Complicated; involved; intricate. —*n.* (kom′·pleks) **1** Something composite or complicated; a complication; collection. **2** *Psychoanal.* A group or cluster of interrelated and usually repressed ideas with strong emotional content which compels the individual to adopt abnormal patterns of thought and behavior. [< L *complexus,* pp. of *complectere* < *com-* together + *plectere* twist] —**com·plex′ly** *adv.* —**com·plex′ness** *n.*

Synonyms (adj.): abstruse, complicated, composite, compound, confused, conglomerate, entangled, heterogeneous, intricate, involved, manifold, mingled, mixed, multiform, tangled. That is *complex* which is made up of a number of connected parts. That is *compound* in which the parts are not merely connected, but combined into a single substance. In a *composite* object the different parts have less of unity than in that which is *complex* or *compound,* and maintain their distinct individuality. In a *heterogeneous* body, mass, or collection, unlike parts or particles are intermingled, often without apparent order or plan. *Conglomerate* (literally, globed together) is said of a *confused* mingling of masses or lumps of various substances. Things are *involved* which are rolled together so as not to be easily separated, either in thought or in fact; threads which are *tangled* or *entangled* hold and draw upon one another in a confusing and obstructive way; a knot is *intricate* when the strands are difficult to follow. An *abstruse* statement or conception is remote from the usual course of thought. *Antonyms:* clear, direct, homogeneous, obvious, plain, simple, uncombined, uncompounded, uniform, unraveled.

complex fraction See under FRACTION.

com·plex·ion (kəm·plek′shən) *n.* **1** The color and appearance of the skin, especially of the face. **2** General aspect; character; quality; hence, temperament; cast of mind or thought. **3** *Archaic* The combination of certain assumed qualities in a definite proportion supposed to control the nature of plants, bodies, etc.; also, the habit ascribed to such combination. [< F < L *complexio, -onis* the constitution of a body < *complectere.* See COMPLEX.] —**com·plex′ion·al** *adj.* —**com·plex′ioned** *adj.*

com·plex·i·ty (kəm·plek′sə·tē) *n. pl.* **·ties 1** The state of being complex. **2** Something complex.

complex sentence See under SENTENCE.

com·plex·us (kəm·plek′səs) *n.* **1** A complicated system; complex. **2** *Anat.* A large muscle of the back, which passes from the spine to the head. [< L < *complectere.* See COMPLEX.]

com·pli·a·ble (kəm·plī′ə·bəl) *adj.* Compliant. —**com·pli′a·ble·ness** *n.* —**com·pli′a·bly** *adv.*

com·pli·ance (kəm·plī′əns) *n.* **1** The act of complying, yielding, or acting in accord. **2** Complaisance. Also **com·pli′an·cy.**

com·pli·ant (kəm·plī′ənt) *adj.* Complying; yielding. See synonyms under DOCILE, OBSEQUIOUS, SUPPLE. [< COMPLY] —**com·pli′ant·ly** *adv.*

com·pli·ca·cy (kom′plə·kə·sē) *n. pl.* **·cies 1** The state of being complicated. **2** That which is complicated; complication.

com·pli·cate (kom′plə·kāt) *v.* **·cat·ed, ·cat·ing** *v.t.* **1** To make complex, difficult, or perplexing. **2** To twist or wind around; intertwine. —*v.i.* **3** To become complex or difficult. See synonyms under INVOLVE, PERPLEX. —*adj.* (kom′plə·kit) **1** Complicated; complex. **2** *Bot.* Folded lengthwise upon itself; conduplicate. **3** *Zool.* Folded longitudinally, as the wings of certain insects. [< L *complicatus,* pp. of *complicare* < *com-* together + *plicare* fold] —**com′pli·ca′tive** *adj.*

com·pli·cat·ed (kom′plə·kā′tid) *adj.* Containing or consisting of a combination of parts or elements difficult to separate, analyze, or understand; intricate. —**com′pli·cat′ed·ly** *adv.* —**com′pli·cat′ed·ness** *n.*

com·pli·ca·tion (kom′plə·kā′shən) *n.* **1** The act of complicating, or the state of being complicated; complexity. **2** Anything that complicates, as a disease coexisting with another disease.

com·plice (kom′plis) *n. Obs.* An accomplice or close associate. [< MF < LL *complex* closely connected]

com·plic·i·ty (kəm·plis′ə·tē) *n. pl.* **·ties 1** The act or state of being an accomplice. **2** Complexity.

com·pli·er (kəm·plī′ər) *n.* One who readily yields or complies.

com·pli·ment (kom′plə·mənt) *n.* **1** An expression of admiration, praise, congratulation, etc. **2** A formal greeting or remembrance: usually in the plural. **3** *Archaic* A gratuity; gift; favor. —*v.t.* (kom′plə·ment) **1** To pay a compliment to. **2** To show regard for, as by a gift or other favor. ◆ Homophone: *complement.* [< MF < Ital. *complimento* < Sp. *cumplimiento,* lit., completion of courtesy < L *complementum.* See COMPLEMENT.] —**com·pli·men·ta·ry** (kom′plə·men′tər·ē, -trē) *adj.* —**com′pli·men′ta·ri·ly** *adv.*

complimentary ticket A free ticket.

com·plin (kom′plin) *n.* The last of the canonical hours; also, the last service of common prayer for the day, generally just after vespers, held at this hour. Also **com·pline** (kom′plin, -plīn), **com′plines, com′plins.** [< OF *complie* < L *completa (hora)* finished (hour) < *complere* COMPLETE]

com·plot (kəm·plot′) *Archaic v.t.* & *v.i.* **·plot·ted, ·plot·ting** To combine in plotting; conspire. —*n.* (kom′plot) A concerted plot; conspiracy. [< F *complote*r; ult. origin uncertain] —**com·plot′·ter** *n.*

com·plu·vi·um (kom·plōō′vē·əm) *n. pl.* **·vi·a** (-vē·ə) A large opening for light and air in the roof of an ancient Roman house, through which rain water ran into the impluvium. [< L < *compluere* flow together (said of rain)]

com·ply (kəm·plī′) *v.i.* **·plied, ·ply·ing 1** To act in conformity; consent; obey: with *with.* **2** *Obs.* To be complaisant or courteous; observe civilities. See synonyms under AGREE, OBEY. [< Ital. *complire* < Sp. *cumplir* complete an act of courtesy < L *complere.* See COMPLETE.]

com·po (kom′pō) *n. pl.* **·pos 1** A compound or mixed substance of any kind, such as mortar, plaster, etc. **2** *Naut.* An instalment of wages paid to a ship's crew. [Short for COMPOSITION]

com·po·nent (kəm·pō′nənt) *n.* **1** A constituent part. **2** *Chem.* One of the ingredients of a mixture, in which it may exist in varying proportions and without loss of its own chemical properties, as salt in water: distinguished from *constituent.* **3** *Physics* **a** The smallest number of independently variable factors needed to establish equilibrium in a given system. Compare PHASE RULE. **b** One of two or more forces which, acting in fixed directions, are the equivalent of a given force. —*adj.* Forming a part or ingredient. [< L *componens, -entis,* ppr. of *componere.* See COMPOSE.]

com·po·ny (kəm·pō′nē) *adj. Her.* Composed of two tinctures, generally metal and color, in alternate squares in one row: said of an ordinary. Also **com·po′né.** [OF *componé,* prob. < L *componere.* See COMPOSE.]

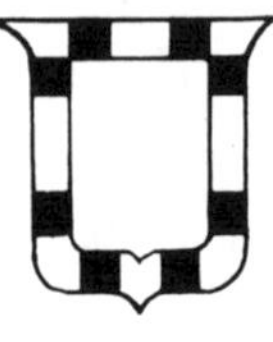

COMPONY

com·port (kəm·pôrt′, -pōrt′) *v.t.* To conduct (oneself). —*v.i.* To be compatible; agree. [< F *comporter* bear, behave < L *comportare* < *com-* together + *portare* carry]

com·port·ment (kəm·pôrt′mənt, -pōrt′-) *n.* Behavior; deportment.

com·pose (kəm·pōz′) *v.* **·posed, ·pos·ing** *v.t.* **1** To be the constituent elements or parts of; constitute; form. **2** *Obs.* To make up of elements or parts; construct. **3** To tranquilize; calm. **4** To reconcile, arrange, or settle, as differences. **5** To create artistically, as a literary or musical work. **6** To arrange (type) in lines; set. —*v.i.* **7** To engage in composition, as of a literary or musical work. **8** To set type. See synonyms under ALLAY, CONSTRUCT, MAKE, SETTLE. [< F *composer* < *com-* together + *poser.* See POSE[1].]

com·posed (kəm·pōzd′) *adj.* **1** Free from agitation; calm. **2** *Obs.* Artfully or well constructed. See synonyms under CALM. —**com·pos·ed·ly** (kəm·pō′zid·lē) *adv.* —**com·pos′ed·ness** *n.*

com·pos·er (kəm·pō′zər) *n.* **1** One who composes. **2** A writer of music.

com·pos·ing (kəm·pō′zing) *n.* **1** The act of one who composes. **2** Typesetting.

composing machine A machine that sets type for printing.

com·pos·ing-room (kəm·pō′zing·rōōm′, -rŏŏm′) *n.* A room where type is set.

com·pos·ing-stick (kəm·pō′zing·stik′) *n. Printing* A tray or receptacle, usually of metal, capable of adjustment so as to vary the length of a line as required, which the compositor holds in his hand, and in which he arranges in words and lines the type that he takes from the cases.

com·pos·ite (kəm·poz′it) *adj.* **1** Made up of separate parts or elements; combined or compounded. **2** *Bot.* Pertaining or belonging to a very large, cosmopolitan family (Compositae) of plants characterized by involucrate flower heads superficially resembling single flowers but typically composed of a central mass of disk florets surrounded by a fringe of ray florets. —*n.* **1** That which is composed or made up of parts; a compound. **2** *Bot.* A composite plant or flower, as a sunflower, daisy, etc. [< L *compositus,* pp. of *componere* < *com-* together + *ponere* put. Doublet of COMPOST.] —**com·pos′ite·ly** *adv.* —**com·pos′ite·ness** *n.*

composite number See under NUMBER.

Composite order *Archit.* A variant of the Corinthian order, having four volutes, like those of the Ionic order, above the acanthus leaves: used in Roman and in Renaissance architecture.

composite photograph A photograph formed by combining several photographs, either on the same plate, or on the same print from various negatives. Also **composite portrait.**

com·po·si·tion (kom′pə·zish′ən) *n.* **1** The act of composing, or the state or manner of being composed; specifically, the act, process, or art of inventing and producing a literary, musical, or artistic work or any part thereof. **2** The general structural arrangement or style of a work of art or a literary or musical production. **3** A literary, artistic, or musical production. **4** A compound or combination. **5** Typesetting. **6** An agreement or settlement; compromise. **7** The state or manner of being put together; also, that which is put together, or the components of which anything is made. **8** *Chem.* The structure of a compound as regards its different elements and the proportions in which they enter into the formation of the compound. See synonyms under PRODUCTION. [< F < L *compositio, -onis* < *componere.* See COMPOSITE.]

com·po·si·tion·al (kom′pə·zish′ə·nəl) *adj.* Of or pertaining to composition.

composition face The face or plane by which the parts of a twin crystal are united. Also **composition plane.**

composition of forces *Physics* The joining of two or more forces, exerted in the same or different directions, into one equivalent force, called the *resultant.*

com·pos·i·tive (kəm·poz′ə·tiv) *adj.* Having the power of compounding; synthetic.

com·pos·i·tor (kəm·poz′ə·tər) *n.* **1** A typesetter. **2** One who composes or sets in order.

com·pos men·tis (kom′pəs men′tis) *Law Latin* Of sound mind; mentally competent: opposed to *non compos mentis.*

com·post (kom′pōst) *n.* **1** A fertilizing mixture of decomposed vegetable matter. **2** A composition for plastering. **3** A mixture; compound. —*v.t.* To make into or cover with compost. [< OF < L *compositum,* var. of *compositum* < *componere.* Doublet of COMPOSITE.]

Com·po·ste·la (kōm′pō·stā′lä) See SANTIAGO DE COMPOSTELA.

com·po·sure (kəm·pō′zhər) *n.* **1** Tranquillity, as of manner or appearance; calmness; serenity. **2** Composition. See synonyms under APATHY, PATIENCE.

com·po·ta·tion (kom′pō·tā′shən) *n. Obs.* A drinking or tippling in company; carouse. [< L *compotatio, -onis* < *com-* together + *potare* drink]

com·pote (kom′pōt, *Fr.* kôṅ·pôt′) *n.* **1** Fruit stewed or preserved in sirup. **2** A dish for holding fruits, etc. [< F < OF *composte.* See COMPOST.]

com·pound[1] (kom′pound) *n.* **1** A combination of two or more elements, ingredients, or parts. **2** A compound engine. **3** A compound word. **4** *Chem.* A definite substance resulting from the combination of specific elements or radicals in fixed proportions: distinguished from *mixture.* —*v.* (kom·pound′, kəm-) *v.t.* **1** To make by the combination of various elements or ingredients. **2** To mix elements or parts to form a compound substance; combine: to *compound* drugs. **3** To compromise; settle for less than the sum due: to *compound* a debt. **4** To cover up or condone (a crime) for a consideration: to *compound* a felony. **5** To compute, as interest, by geometric progression. **6** *Electr.* To place duplex windings on the field magnets of (a dynamo), one serving as a shunt and the other being in series with the main circuit, making the machine self–regulating. **7** *Obs.* To compose; form. —*v.i.* **8** To come to terms; take a compromise settlement. —*adj.* (kom′pound, kom·pound′) Composed of, or produced by the union of, two or more elements, ingredients, or parts; composite. See synonyms under COMPLEX. [<OF *compondre* <L *componere.* See COMPOSITE.] —**com·pound′a·ble** *adj.* —**com·pound′er** *n.*

com·pound[2] (kom′pound) *n.* In the Orient, the walled or fenced enclosure of a residence, cantonment, or factory; also, any similar enclosed place. [<Malay *kampong*]

compound E Cortisone.

compound engine A steam engine in which the exhaust steam from one or more cylinders enters and does work in one or more other cylinders.

compound flower *Bot.* The anthodium or head of the flower of a composite plant.

compound fraction See under FRACTION.

compound fracture See under FRACTURE.

compound interest Interest computed not only on the original principal but also on interest earned in succeeding periods.

compound leaf *Bot.* A leaf having several distinct blades on a common leafstalk. See illustrations under LEAF.

compound number See under NUMBER.

compound sentence See under SENTENCE.

compound triple time See under TIME.

compound word A word composed of two or more words united either with a hyphen (hypheme) or without (solideme), and usually distinguished from a phrase by a reduction of stress on one of the elements and a shortening of the pause between the words, as *green′ house* and *a green′ house′*.

com·pra·dor (kom′prə·dôr′) *n.* In China and other Eastern countries, a native agent in a foreign business house, consulate, etc. Also **com′pra·dore′.** [<Pg., buyer]

com·preg (kom′preg) *n.* Resin–impregnated sheets of wood, bonded together by pressure and heat to impart special properties of strength, density, toughness, and finish. [< COM(PRESSED) +(IM)PREG(NATED)]

com·pre·hend (kom′pri·hend′) *v.t.* **1** To grasp mentally; understand fully. **2** To include, take in, or comprise. —*v.i.* **3** To understand. See synonyms under APPREHEND, CATCH, EMBRACE, KNOW, PERCEIVE. [<L *comprehendere* <*com-* together + *prehendere* seize] —**com′·pre·hend′i·ble** *adj.*

com·pre·hen·si·ble (kom′pri·hen′sə·bəl) *adj.* **1** Capable of being comprehended or grasped by the mind; understandable; conceivable. **2** Capable of being comprised or included. —**com′·pre·hen′si·bil′i·ty, com′pre·hen′si·ble·ness** *n.* —**com′pre·hen′si·bly** *adv.*

com·pre·hen·sion (kom′pri·hen′shən) *n.* **1** The mental grasping of ideas, facts, etc., or the power of doing so; understanding. **2** The act or state of including, containing, or taking in; inclusion; comprehensiveness. **3** *Logic* The complete conception of a term, involving all the elements of its meaning and its correlations. See synonyms under KNOWLEDGE. [< L *comprehensio, -onis* <*comprehendere* COMPREHEND]

com·pre·hen·sive (kom′pri·hen′siv) *adj.* **1** Large in scope or content; including much; broad. **2** Having the power of fully understanding or comprehending. —**com′pre·hen′·sive·ly** *adv.* —**com′pre·hen′sive·ness** *n.*

com·press (kəm·pres′) *v.t.* To press together or into smaller space; condense; compact; concentrate. —*n.* (kom′pres) **1** A device for compressing. **2** *Med.* A soft pad for making local pressure on affected parts of the body. **3** An apparatus for compressing bales of cotton, etc. [<OF *compresser* <LL *compressare,* freq. of *comprimere* <*com-* together +*premere* press] —**com·press′i·bil′i·ty, com·press′i·ble·ness** *n.* —**com·press′i·ble** *adj.* —**com·press′ive** *adj.* —**com·press′ive·ly** *adv.*

com·pressed (kəm·prest′) *adj.* **1** Flattened laterally. **2** *Biol.* Reduced in breadth, as the bodies of certain fishes or the leafstalks of some plants. **3** Pressed together or into smaller compass; made compact.

com·pres·sion (kəm·presh′ən) *n.* **1** The act of compressing or the state of being compressed. **2** The process by which a confined gas is reduced in volume through the application of pressure, as in the cylinder of an internal–combustion engine. Also **com·pres·sure**(kəm·presh′ər). [<L *compressio, -onis* <*comprimere* COMPRESS]

com·pres·sor (kəm·pres′ər) *n.* **1** One who or that which compresses. **2** *Anat.* A muscle that compresses a part of the body: the *compressor narium* of the nostrils. **3** *Surg.* An instrument for compressing a part of the body. **4** *Mech.* A power–driven machine for compressing a gas in order to utilize its expansion, as for refrigeration.

com·prise (kəm·prīz′) *v.t.* **·prised, ·pris·ing** To include and contain; consist of; embrace. [<F *compris,* pp. of *comprendre* <L *comprehendere* COMPREHEND] —**com·pri′sal** *n.*

com·pro·mis (kôṅ·prô·mē′) *n. French* The special agreement for an international arbitration, defining the subject of the dispute and establishing the procedure to be followed: derived from the French Civil Law relating to private arbitration. Also **compromis d′ar·bi·trage** (dȧr·bē·träzh′).

com·pro·mise (kom′prə·mīz) *n.* **1** An adjustment for settlement by arbitration and mutual concession, usually involving a partial surrender of purposes or principles. **2** *Law* An adjustment of a controversy by mutual consent in order to prevent or settle a lawsuit. **3** Anything that is the result of concessions; a medium between two conflicting courses; also, the habit or spirit of concession. **4** An imperiling or surrender, as of character or reputation. — *v.* **·mised, ·mis·ing** *v.t.* **1** To adjust by concessions. **2** To expose, as to suspicion, danger, or disrepute. **3** *Obs.* To bind or pledge mutually. —*v.i.* **4** To make a settlement by concessions. [<F *compromis* <L *compromissum* a mutual agreement to accept arbitration <*com-* together + *promittere* promise] —**com′pro·mis′er** *n.*

compt (kount) *n. Obs.* Account; reckoning. [<F *compte* account]

compte ren·du (kôṅt räṅ·dü′) *French* An official report; literally, account rendered.

compt·i·ble (koun′tə·bəl) *adj. Obs.* Accountable; tractable; sensitive.

Comp·tom·e·ter (komp·tom′ə·tər) *n.* A high–speed adding or calculating machine: a trade name.

Comp·ton (komp′tən), **Arthur Holly,** 1892–1962, U.S. physicist. —**Karl Taylor,** 1887–1954, U.S. physicist; brother of Arthur.

Compton effect *Physics* The phenomenon of the scattering of X–rays when subjected to bombardment by electrons of the lighter elements: the resulting radiation somewhat resembles fluorescence. [after A. H. *Compton*]

Compton shift *Physics* The shift in wavelength produced by the Compton effect.

comp·trol·ler (kən·trō′lər) *n.* A controller: the spelling sometimes employed to designate a city, State, or Federal officer in control of funds. [<Var. of CONTROLLER; infl. by COMPT] —**comp·trol′ler·ship** *n.*

com·pul·sion (kəm·pul′shən) *n.* **1** The act of compelling; coercion. **2** The state of being compelled. **3** *Psychol.* **a** The performance of an act contrary to the conscious will of the subject. **b** An act so performed. See synonyms under NECESSITY. [<MF <L *compulsio, -onis* < *compellere* COMPEL]

com·pul·sive (kəm·pul′siv) *adj.* **1** Compelling or tending to compel; compulsory. **2** *Psychol.* Pertaining to or describing acts or behavior independent of volition. —**com·pul′·sive·ly** *adv.* —**com·pul′sive·ness** *n.*

com·pul·so·ry (kəm·pul′sər·ē) *adj.* **1** Employing compulsion; compelling; coercive. **2** Required by law or other rule; enforced: *compulsory* education. See synonyms under NECESSARY. —**com·pul′so·ri·ly** *adv.* —**com·pul′·so·ri·ness** *n.*

com·punc·tion (kəm·pungk′shən) *n.* **1** Self–reproach for wrong–doing; a sense of guilt, remorseful feeling. **2** A feeling of slight regret. See synonyms under REPENTANCE. [<LL *compunctio, -onis* <*com-* greatly + *pungere* prick, sting] —**com·punc′tious** *adj.* —**com·punc′tious·ly** *adv.*

com·pur·ga·tion (kom′pər·gā′shən) *n.* The ancient practice of clearing an accused person by the oaths of several others, usually twelve, who swore to their belief in his innocence. [< LL *compurgatio, -onis* <*com-* thoroughly + *purgare* cleanse]

com·pur·ga·tor (kom′pər·gā′tər) *n.* One who testifies in favor of or vouches for another; especially, one of the twelve men called in cases of compurgation. [<Med. L <*com-* together +*purgare* cleanse]

com·pu·ta·tion (kom′pyə·tā′shən) *n.* **1** The act of computing; calculation. **2** A computed amount or number.

com·pute (kəm·pyōōt′) *v.t.* **·put·ed, ·put·ing** To estimate numerically; calculate; reckon. —*n.* Computation. [<L *computare* <*com-* together + *putare* reckon. Doublet of COUNT[1].] —**com·put′a·bil′i·ty** *n.* —**com·put′a·ble** *adj.* —**com·put′ist** *n.*

com·put·er (kəm·pyōō′tər) *n.* **1** One who or that which computes. **2** A power–driven machine equipped with keyboards, electronic circuits, storage compartments, and recording devices for the high–speed performance of mathematical operations.

com·rade (kom′rad, -rid) *n.* **1** A friend or intimate companion. **2** A partner, associate, or fellow member, as of a political party: used as a form of address, as in the Communist party. See synonyms under ASSOCIATE. [<MF *camarade* <Sp. *camarada* roommate <L *camera* room] —**com′rade·ship** *n.*

com·rade·ry (kom′rad·rē, -rid-) See CAMARADERIE.

COMSAT (kom′sat′) *adj. trademark/service mark* The services and apparatus utilized in satellite and microwave telecommunications, which are produced by COMSAT Corporation. [COM(MUNICATIONS) + SAT(ELLITE)]

Com·stock·er·y (kum′stok′ər·ē, kom′-) *n.* **1** Exaggerated censorship of immorality in literature, pictures, etc. **2** Prudishness.

Com·stock Lode (kum′stok, kom′-) A rich vein of silver and gold discovered in 1859 at Virginia City, Nevada. [after Henry *Comstock,* 1820–70, U.S. prospector]

comte (kôṅt) *n. French* A count[2].

Comte (kôṅt), **Auguste,** 1798–1857, French philosopher; founder of positivism. —**Com·ti·an** (kom′tē·ən, kôṅ′-) *adj.*

Com·tism (kom′tiz·əm, kôṅ′-) *n.* The philosophy of Comte; positivism. —**Com′tist** *adj.* & *n.*

Co·mus (kō′məs) **1** In Greek and Roman mythology, the young god of revelry, a companion of Dionysos. **2** A mask (1634) by John Milton.

con[1] (kon) *v.t.* **conned, con·ning** To study; peruse carefully; learn. [Var. of CAN[1]] —**con′·ner** *n.*

con[2] (kon) *v.t.* **conned, con·ning** *Naut.* To direct the steering of (a vessel). Also *conn.* [Earlier *cond*<F *conduire* <L *conducere* CONDUCT]

con[3] (kon) *Slang adj.* Shortened form of *confidence*: used in phrases: *con* man; *con* game. —*v.t.* **conned, con·ning** To defraud; dupe; swindle. —*n.* A confidence man.

con[4] (kon) *n.* The contrary; the opposite side; the opponent, etc. —*adv.* Against. See PRO. [<L *contra* against]

con[5] (kon) *n. Slang* A convict.

con- Assimilated var. of COM-.

Co·na·kry (kô·nȧ·krē′) A port in west Africa, the capital of Guinea: also *Konakri.*

con a·mo·re (kōn ä·mō′rā) **1** *Italian* With love. **2** *Music* Lovingly; with enthusiasm or tenderness: a direction to the performer.

Co·nant (kō′nənt), **James Bryant,** 1893–1978, U.S. chemist and educator.

co·na·tion (kō·nā′shən) *n. Psychol.* The element of conscious striving and activity contained in every desire, impulse, aversion, etc. [< L *conatio, -onis* an attempt < *conari* try]

co·na·tive (kon′ə·tiv, kō′nə-) *adj.* **1** *Psychol.* Of or pertaining to conation. **2** *Gram.* Expressing endeavor: said of an aspect of certain Semitic verbs.

co·na·tus (kō·nā′təs) *n. pl.* **co·na·tus 1** An attempt or endeavor; effort. **2** *Biol.* An inherent tendency in plants and animals resembling effort in human beings. [< L < *conari* try]

con bri·o (kōn brē′ō) *Music* With spirit. [< Ital.]

con·cat·e·nate (kon·kat′ə·nāt) *v.t.* **·nat·ed, ·nat·ing** To join or link together; connect in a series. —*adj.* Joined together; connected in a series. [< L *concatenatus,* pp. of *concatenare* < *com-* together + *catena* chain]

con·cat·e·na·tion (kon·kat′ə·nā′shən) *n.* **1** The act of concatenating; union in a chainlike series. **2** A chainlike series, as of associated nerve cells or physiological reflexes. **3** *Mech.* A method of variable speed-control without undue loss of working energy: used on locomotives and motors.

con·cave (kon·kāv′, kon′kāv, kong′-) *adj.* **1** Hollow and rounded, as the interior of a sphere or circle; incurved: opposed to *convex.* **2** Hollow. —*n.* (kon′kāv, kong′-) A concave surface; vault. [< MF < L *concavus* < *com-* thoroughly + *cavus* hollow] —**con·cave′ly** *adv.* —**con·cave′ness** *n.*

con·cav·i·ty (kon·kav′ə·tē) *n. pl.* **·ties 1** The state of being concave. **2** A concave surface; hollow. See synonyms under HOLE.

con·ca·vo-con·cave (kon·kā′vō·kon·kāv′) *adj.* *Optics* Concave on both sides; doubly concave. See illustration under LENS.

con·ca·vo-con·vex (kon·kā′vō·kon·veks′) *adj.* **1** Concave on one side and convex on the other. **2** *Optics* Describing a lens in which the curvature of the concave side is greater than that of the convex; distinguished from *convexo-concave.* See illustration under LENS.

con·ceal (kən·sēl′) *v.t.* To hide; secrete; keep from sight, discovery, or knowledge. See synonyms under BURY, HIDE, MASK, PALLIATE. [< OF *conceler* < L *concelare* < *com-* thoroughly + *celare* hide] —**con·ceal′a·ble** *adj.*

con·ceal·ment (kən·sēl′mənt) *n.* **1** The act of concealing, or state of being concealed. **2** A hiding place.

con·cede (kən·sēd′) *v.* **·ced·ed, ·ced·ing** *v.t.* **1** To grant or yield, as a right or privilege. **2** To acknowledge as true, correct, or proper; admit. —*v.i.* **3** To make a concession. See synonyms under ACKNOWLEDGE, ALLOW, CONFESS. [< L *concedere* < *com-* thoroughly + *cedere* yield, go away] —**con·ced′er** *n.*

con·ceit (kən·sēt′) *n.* **1** Overweening self-esteem. **2 a** A fanciful idea; a quaint or humorous fancy; clever thought or expression. **b** An extended, flowery, strained metaphor. **3** Imagination. **4** A fancy or ingenious article or design. **5** Apprehension; understanding. **6** A conception or thought. See synonyms under EGOTISM, FANCY, IDEA, PRIDE. —**out of conceit with** Displeased with. —*v.t.* **1** *Obs.* To imagine or suppose; think. **2** *Dial.* To take a fancy to; regard favorably. **3** *Obs.* To form a conception or idea; conceive. [< CONCEIVE]

con·ceit·ed (kən·sē′tid) *adj.* **1** Having an excessively fine opinion of oneself; vain. **2** *Brit. Dial.* Fanciful; notional. **3** *Obs.* Intelligent; witty. —**con·ceit′ed·ly** *adv.* —**con·ceit′ed·ness** *n.*

con·ceive (kən·sēv′) *v.* **·ceived, ·ceiv·ing** *v.t.* **1** To procreate; beget or become pregnant with, as young. **2** To form an idea in the mind; think of; fancy. **3** To construct in the mind; formulate, as plans. **4** To believe or suppose; form an opinion. **5** To become possessed with: to *conceive* a hatred. **6** *Obs.* To understand. —*v.i.* **7** To form a mental image; think: with *of.* **8** To become pregnant. See synonyms under APPREHEND. [< OF *conceveir* < L *concipere* < *com-* thoroughly + *capere* take] —**con·ceiv′a·ble** *adj.* —**con·ceiv′a·bil′i·ty, con·ceiv′a·ble·ness** *n.* —**con·ceiv′a·bly** *adv.* —**con·ceiv′er** *n.*

con·cent (kən·sent′) *n. Obs.* Concord or harmony. [< L *concentus* < *concinere* < *com-* together + *canere* sing]

con·cen·ter (kon·sen′tər) *v.t.* To direct or bring to a common point or center; focus. —*v.i.* To come together at a common center; combine. Also **con·cen′tre.** [< F *concentrer* < L *com-* together + *centrum* center]

con·cen·trate (kon′sən·trāt) *v.* **·trat·ed, ·trat·ing** *v.t.* **1** To draw to a common center; concenter; focus. **2** To intensify in strength or to purify by the removal of certain constituents; condense. —*v.i.* **3** To converge toward a center; become compacted or intensified. —*n.* **1** A product of concentration. **2** *Usually pl. Metall.* The product of concentration processes whereby a mass of high metal content has been obtained from the ore or other raw materials. —*adj.* Concentrated. [< CONCENTER + -ATE[1]] —**con·cen·tra·tive** (kon′sən·trā′tiv, kən·sen′trə·tiv) *adj.* —**con′cen·tra′tive·ly** *adv.* —**con′cen·tra′tive·ness** *n.* —**con′cen·tra′tor** *n.*

con·cen·tra·tion (kon′sən·trā′shən) *n.* **1** The act of concentrating: said especially of focusing the attention upon a single object, problem, task, etc. **2** That which is concentrated. **3** A medicine strengthened by evaporation of inactive ingredients. **4** *Chem.* The amount of a substance per unit volume: in a solution it is the amount of the substance dissolved by a given quantity of the solvent.

concentration camp 1 A place of detention for prisoners of war, political prisoners, aliens, etc. **2** *Mil.* A place where troops are marshalled for redistribution.

con·cen·tric (kən·sen′trik) *adj.* Having a common center, as circles: opposed to *eccentric.* Also **con·cen′tri·cal.** —**con·cen′tri·cal·ly** *adv.* —**con·cen·tric·i·ty** (kon′sen·tris′ə·tē) *n.*

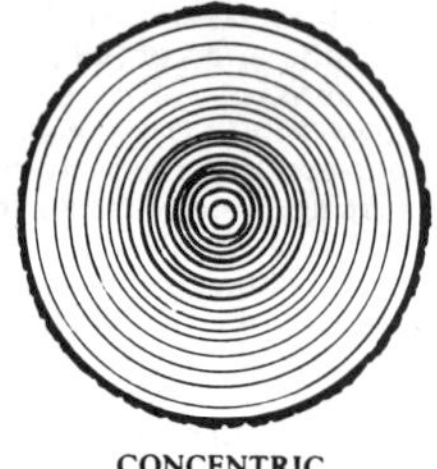

CONCENTRIC TREE RINGS

Con·cep·ción (kōn′·sep·syōn′) A city in south central Chile.

con·cept (kon′sept) *n.* **1** An abstract notion or idea. **2** Any notion combining elements into the idea of one object. **3** A thought or opinion. See synonyms under IDEA. [< L *conceptus* a conceiving < *concipere* CONCEIVE]

con·cep·ta·cle (kən·sep′tə·kəl) *n. Bot.* A special cavity developed on the surface of many algae and fungi, for holding or enclosing reproductive organs. [< L *conceptaculum* a receptacle < *concipere.* See CONCEIVE.]

con·cep·tion (kən·sep′shən) *n.* **1** The act of conceiving or the state of being conceived. **2** The act, faculty, or power of conceiving or forming ideas or notions. **3** *Biol.* The impregnation of an ovum; act of becoming pregnant; also, an embryo; fetus. **4** A commencement; beginning; inception. **5** Anything that is conceived; a plan or invention of the mind; a product of the inventive or constructive faculty. See synonyms under FANCY, IDEA, IMAGE, THOUGHT. —**con·cep′tion·al** *adj.*

con·cep·tive (kən·sep′tiv) *adj.* Capable of conception.

con·cep·tu·al (kən·sep′cho͞o·əl) *adj.* Of or pertaining to conception or a concept. —**con·cep′tu·al·ly** *adv.*

con·cep·tu·al·ism (kən·sep′cho͞o·əl·iz′əm) *n.* The doctrine that general ideas, or universals, exist in the mind only, and that the mind is capable of forming abstract ideas independently of concrete existences: a theory devised as intermediate between the extremes of nominalism and realism. —**con·cep′tu·al·ist** *n.* —**con·cep′tu·al·is′tic** *adj.*

con·cern (kən·sûrn′) *v.t.* **1** To relate or belong to; be of interest or importance to. **2** To occupy, engage, or interest. **3** To affect with solicitude; trouble: usually in the passive. —*v.i.* **4** *Obs.* To be of importance. —*n.* **1** That which concerns one; something affecting one's interest or welfare; affair; business. **2** Solicitude; interest. **3** Relation; reference. **4** A business establishment. **5** *Colloq.* Any object or contrivance. See synonyms under ANXIETY, BUSINESS, CARE. [< MF *concerner* < Med. L *concernere* regard < *com-* thoroughly + *cernere* see, discern]

con·cerned (kən·sûrnd′) *adj.* **1** Having interest or involvement; involved. **2** Having anxiety or uneasiness.

con·cern·ing (kən·sûr′ning) *prep.* In relation to; regarding; about.

con·cern·ment (kən·sûrn′mənt) *n.* **1** The fact or condition of concerning; relation; bearing; importance. **2** Anxiety; solicitude. **3** Connection; participation. **4** Anything that relates to one; affair; concern; business.

con·cert (kon′sûrt) *n.* **1** A musical performance by a number of voices or instruments, or both; also, the combination of voices or instruments to produce harmony. **2** Harmony; agreement; accordance; unity. —*adj.* Of or for concerts. —*v.* (kən·sûrt′) *v.t.* **1** To arrange or contrive by mutual agreement. **2** To plan; contrive. —*v.i.* **3** To act or plan together. [< MF < Ital. *concerto* < *concertare* agree, be in accord]

con·cert·ed (kən·sûr′tid) *adj.* Arranged or agreed upon in concert or for a common purpose; especially, in music, arranged in parts: a *concerted* piece. —**con·cert′ed·ly** *adv.*

concert grand (piano) See under PIANO.

con·cer·ti·na (kon′sər·tē′nə) *n.* **1** A small musical instrument of the accordion type, with bellows and a keyboard at either end. **2** *Mil.* A portable, distensible barbed-wire entanglement, used to hinder the movements of enemy motorized equipment. [< Ital. < *concerto.* See CONCERT.]

con·cer·ti·no (kōn′cher·tē′nō) *n. pl.* **·ni** (-nē) *Music* A short or abridged concerto. [< Ital., dim. of *concerto.* See CONCERT.]

con·cert·mas·ter (kon′sərt·mas′tər, -mäs′-) *n.* The leader of the first violin section of an orchestra, who acts as assistant to the conductor. Also **con·cert·meis·ter** (kon′sərt·mīs′·tər, *Ger.* kôn·tsert′mīs′tər).

con·cer·to (kən·cher′tō) *n. pl.* **·tos,** *Ital.* **·ti** (-tē) *Music* A composition (usually of three movements) for performance by a solo instrument or instruments accompanied by an orchestra. [< Ital. See CONCERT.]

Concert of Europe 1 A tacit agreement of the great European powers, in the years following the Congress of Vienna (1815), to act together in matters concerning the peace of Europe. **2** Any agreement among the European powers. Also **Concert of Powers.**

concerto gros·so (grō′sō) An early form of concerto for a small group of solo instruments and a full orchestra. [< Ital., lit., big concerto]

con·ces·sion (kən·sesh′ən) *n.* **1** The act of conceding, or that which is conceded. **2** A subsidiary business, conducted by lease or by purchase of privilege, in office buildings, railroad stations, etc.: a coatroom *concession.* **3** A strip of land, as one adjoining a port, canal, etc., conceded to an alien government for its economic use, and in which self-government and extraterritorial rights are exercised. See synonyms under FAVOR. [< MF < L *concessio, -onis* < *concedere* CONCEDE]

con·ces·sion·ar·y (kən·sesh′ən·er′ē) *adj.* Bestowed by concession; of or pertaining to a concession. —*n. pl.* **·ar·ies** A concessioner.

con·ces·sion·er (kən·sesh′ən·ər) *n.* One who holds or seeks to secure a concession. Also **con·ces·sion·aire** (kən·sesh′ən·âr′), **con·ces′·sion·naire′.**

concession road *Canadian* In Ontario and Quebec, a road following a survey line.

con·ces·sive (kən·ses′iv) *adj.* **1** Like or tending to concession. **2** *Gram.* Involving concession: said of the conjunctions *though, although,* etc., and of the subordinate adverbial clauses introduced by them.

conch (kongk, konch) *n. pl.* **conchs** (kongks) or **conch·es** (kon′chiz) **1** Any of various large marine gastropod mollusks (family Strombidae) having heavy, colorful, spiral shells. **2** The shell of such a mollusk, used to make cameos and other objects and as a crude trumpet. **3** In Roman mythology, such a shell blown as a horn by the Tritons. **4** *Archit.* A semidome, or the plain concave surface of a dome or vault. **5** *U.S. Dial.* One of a group of people native to the Florida Keys or the Bahamas. [< L *concha* < Gk. *konchē* shell]

CONCH SHELL

con·cha (kong′kə) *n. pl.* **con·chae** (kong′kē) **1** *Anat.* A structure of shell-like appearance, as the external ear, or one of the turbinate bones. **2** *Archit.* A conch (def. 3). [< L See CONCH]

con·chif·er·ous (kong·kif′ər·əs) *adj.* **1** Having or producing a shell; testaceous. **2** Of or pertaining to a former division of mollusks

(Conchifera). [<L *concha* shell + -FEROUS]

con·choid (kong′koid) *n. Math.* A curve traced by the locus of a point at the end of a straight line segment of fixed length rotating about the polar axis in such a way that the length of a perpendicular from the curve to a fixed straight line (its asymptote) is in constant proportion to the length of the segment, and so that the segment of the line intercepted by the curve and its asymptote is of constant length.

CONCHOID

con·choi·dal (kong·koid′l) *adj.* Having shell-shaped depressions and elevations. Also **con′·choid.**

con·chol·o·gy (kong·kol′ə·jē) *n.* The study of shells and mollusks. [<L *concha* shell + -LOGY] —**con·cho·log·i·cal** (kong′kə·loj′i·kəl) *adj.* —**con′cho·log′i·cal·ly** *adv.* —**con·chol′·o·gist** *n.*

con·cho·scope (kong′kə·skōp) *n. Med.* A speculum used in examining the anterior and middle parts of the nasal passages. [<Gk. *konchē* shell + -SCOPE]

con·chy (kon′chē) *n. pl.* **·chies** *Slang* A conscientious objector.

con·ci·erge (kon′sē·ûrzh′, *Fr.* kôn·syârzh′) *n.* **1** A doorkeeper or porter. **2** A janitor. [<F]

con·cil·i·ate (kən·sil′ē·āt) *v.t.* **·at·ed, ·at·ing 1** To overcome the enmity or hostility of; obtain the friendship of; placate; mollify: to *conciliate* an enemy. **2** To secure or attract by reconciling measures; gain; win. [<L *conciliatus,* pp. of *conciliare* <*concilium* council] —**con·cil·i·a·ble** (kən·sil′ē·ə·bəl) *adj.* —**con·cil′i·a′tor** *n.* —**con·cil·i·a·to·ry** (kən·sil′ē·ə·tôr′ē, -tō′rē), **con·cil′i·a′tive** *adj.* —**con·cil′i·a·to′ri·ly** *adv.* —**con·cil′i·a·to′ri·ness** *n.*

con·cil·i·a·tion (kən·sil′ē·ā′shən) *n.* **1** The act of bringing into agreement. **2** The settlement or attempt to settle a labor dispute by the proposal of measures acceptable to the disputants. See ARBITRATION, MEDIATION.

con·cin·ni·ty (kən·sin′ə·tē) *n. pl.* **·ties** Fitness; harmony; elegance, as of rhetorical style. [<L *concinnitas, -tatis* <*concinnus* well adjusted]

con·cise (kən·sīs′) *adj.* Expressing much in brief form; compact; terse. See synonyms under TERSE. [<L *concisus,* pp. of *concidere* < *con-* thoroughly + *caedere* cut] —**con·cise′ly** *adv.* —**con·cise′ness** *n.*

con·ci·sion (kən·sizh′ən) *n.* **1** A cutting off or asunder; schism. **2** The quality or character of being concise. **3** *Obs.* Circumcision. [<L *concisio, -onis* <*concidere.* See CONCISE.]

con·cla·mant (kən·klā′mənt) *adj.* Calling out together, as in lamentation. [<L *conclamans, -antis,* ppr. of *conclamare* <*con-* together + *clamare* cry out]

con·cla·ma·tion (kon′klə·mā′shən) *n.* A calling out together; outcry of several voices.

con·clave (kon′klāv, kong′-) *n.* **1** A secret council or meeting. **2** In the Roman Catholic Church, the apartments in the Vatican in which the college of cardinals meets to choose a pope, and which is kept locked until the election is over; also, the assembly or meeting of the cardinals. See synonyms under ASSEMBLY, CABAL, COMPANY. [<F<L, a place which can be locked up <*com-* together + *clavis* key]

con·clav·ist (kon′klā·vist, kong′-) *n.* An ecclesiastic attendant upon a cardinal at an electoral conclave.

con·clude (kən·klo͞od′) *v.* **·clud·ed, ·clud·ing** *v.t.* **1** To come to a decision about; decide or determine. **2** To infer or deduce as a result or effect. **3** To arrange or settle finally. **4** To terminate; bring to an end. **5** *Obs.* To shut in; enclose. —*v.i.* **6** To come to an end. **7** To infer or deduce a conclusion. See synonyms under CEASE, EFFECT, END. [<L *concludere* <*com-* thoroughly + *claudere* close, shut off] —**con·clud′er** *n.*

con·clu·sion (kən·klo͞o′zhən) *n.* **1** The act of concluding; termination; end. **2** A conviction reached in consequence of investigation, reasoning, inference, etc. **3** A practical determination; decision. **4** The closing part, as of a discourse. **5** *Logic* A proposition the truth of which is inferred from a premise or premises; especially, the third proposition of an Aristotelian syllogism. **6** *Law* An estoppel; a bar; also, the ending of a pleading or deed. See synonyms under DEMONSTRATION, END, INFERENCE, THOUGHT. [<F <L *conclusio, -onis* < *concludere* CONCLUDE]

con·clu·sive (kən·klo͞o′siv) *adj.* **1** Decisive; putting an end to doubt. **2** Leading to a conclusion; final. —**con·clu′s** *adv.* —**con·clu′·sive·ness** *n.*

con·coct (kon·kokt′, kən-) *v.t.* **1** To make by mixing ingredients, as a drink or soup. **2** To contrive; devise. [<L *concoctus,* pp. of *concoquere* <*com-* together + *coquere* cook, boil] —**con·coct′er, con·coc′tor** *n.* —**con·coc′·tive** *adj.*

con·coc·tion (kon·kok′shən, kən-) *n.* The act of concocting, or the thing concocted; contrivance; mixture.

con·col·or·ous (kon·kul′ər·əs) *adj.* Uniform in color; of one color. Also *Brit.* **con·col′our·ous.** [<L *concolor* <*com-* together + *color* color]

con·com·i·tant (kon·kom′ə·tənt, kən-) *adj.* Existing or occurring together; attendant. See synonyms under INCIDENTAL. —*n.* An attendant circumstance. See synonyms under APPENDAGE, CIRCUMSTANCE. [<L *concomitans, -antis,* ppr. of *concomitari* <*com-* with + *comitari* accompany <*comes* companion] —**con·com′i·tance, con·com′i·tan·cy** *n.* —**con·com′i·tant·ly** *adv.*

con·cord (kon′kôrd, kong′-) **1** Unity of feeling or interest; agreement; accord. **2** *Music* Consonance. **3** *Gram.* Agreement of words, as in gender, number, case, or person. See synonyms under HARMONY. [<F *concorde* <L *concordia* <*concors* agreeing <*com-* together + *cor, cordis* heart]

Con·cord (kong′kərd, kon′kôrd) *n.* A dark-blue to black, round American grape, grown extensively for market in New England and the NE United States: also **Concord grape.**

Con·cord (kong′kərd, kon′kôrd) **1** A town in NE Massachusetts; scene of a Revolutionary War battle, April 19, 1775. **2** The capital of New Hampshire.

con·cor·dance (kon·kôr′dəns, kən-) *n.* **1** An alphabetical index of words or topics in a book in their exact context; especially, such an index of the Bible. **2** Concord; agreement.

con·cor·dant (kon·kôr′dənt, kən-) *adj.* Existing in concord; consonant. [<L *concordans, -antis,* ppr. of *concordare* agree <*concors.* See CONCORD.] —**con·cor′dant·ly** *adv.*

con·cor·dan·tial (kon′kər·dan′shəl) *adj.* Of or pertaining to a Biblical concordance.

con·cor·dat (kon·kôr′dat) *n.* **1** In papal history, an agreement between the papal see and a secular power for the settlement and regulation of ecclesiastical affairs. **2** Any public act of agreement. [<Med. L *concordatum* thing agreed upon<*concordare.* See CONCORDANT.]

Con·corde (kon′kôrd, kong′-) *n.* A supersonic commercial aircraft, produced jointly by Great Britain and France.

Con·cor·di·a (kon·kôr′dē·ə) In Roman mythology, the goddess of concord or peace.

con·cor·po·rate (kon·kôr′pə·rāt) *v.t. & v.i.* **·rat·ed, ·rat·ing** *Obs.* To unite in one body or substance. [<L *concorporatus,* pp. of *concorporare* <*com-* together + *corpus* body]

con·cours (kôṅ·ko͞or′) *n. French* **1** Concourse; meeting. **2** Competition; competitive examination.

con·course (kon′kôrs, -kōrs, kong′-)*n.* **1** An assembling or moving together; confluence. **2** An assembly; throng. **3** A large place, open or enclosed, for the passage of crowds; specifically, a boulevard or a long passageway in a railroad station, subway, etc. See synonyms under ASSEMBLY, COMPANY, THRONG. [<F *concours* <L *concursus*<*concurrere.* See CONCUR.]

con·cre·ma·tion (kon′krə·mā′shən) *n.* Cremation together or at the same time, as in the suttee ceremony in India. [<CON- + CREMATION]

con·cres·cence (kon·kres′əns) *n.* **1** *Anat.* A growing together of separate parts, as the roots of adjoining teeth. **2** *Biol.* A fusing together of the cells of an embryo during gastrulation. **3** Increase by addition of parts or particles; growth. [<L *concrescentia* < *concrescere.* See CONCRETE.]

con·crete (kon′krēt, kon·krēt′) *adj.* **1** Joined in or constituting a mass. **2** Embodied in actual existence: opposed to *abstract.* **3** Applied or relating to a particular case; individual; particular. **4** Made of concrete. —*n.* **1** A hardened mass; especially, one of sand and gravel or broken stone united by hydraulic cement. **2** A specific object or the conception of it. **3** Any mass of particles united and solidified. —*v.* (kon·krēt′ *for defs. 1, 2, 4;* kon′·krēt, kon·krēt′ *for def. 3*) **·cret·ed,·cret·ing** *v.t.* **1** To bring or unite together in one mass or body; cause to coalesce. **2** To bring into concrete or specific form; concretize. **3** To treat or cover with concrete. —*v.i.* **4** To coalesce; solidify. [<L *concretus,* pp. of *concrescere* < *com-* together + *crescere* grow] —**con·crete′ly** *adv.* —**con·crete′ness** *n.*

concrete number See under NUMBER.

con·cre·tion (kon·krē′shən) *n.* **1** The act of concreting; a concrete mass. **2** *Geol.* An aggregate of rounded masses found in sedimentary rocks and usually formed around a central core, which may be a fossil. **3** *Med.* **a** A calculus. **b** The abnormal joining of adjacent parts. —**con·cre·tion·ar·y** (kon·krē′shən·er′ē) *adj.* —**con·cre′tive** *adj.* —**con·cre′tive·ly** *adv.*

con·cre·tize (kon′kri·tīz, kong′-) *v.t.* **·tized, ·tiz·ing** To present in concrete terms; to render vivid or specific.

con·cre·tor (kon′krə·tər, kon·krē′tər) *n.* An apparatus for evaporating sugarcane juice and bringing it to a solid mass.

con·cu·bi·nage (kon·kyo͞o′bə·nij) *n.* **1** The state of being a concubine or of having concubines. **2** Habitual cohabitation without marriage.

con·cu·bine (kong′kyə·bīn, kon′-) *n.* **1** A woman who cohabits with a man without a marriage bond. **2** In certain polygamous societies, a secondary wife. **3** *Obs.* A paramour. [<F <L *concubina,* fem. of *concubinus* < *concumbere* <*com-* with + *cumbere* lie] —**con·cu·bi·nal** (kon·kyo͞o′bə·nəl), **con·cu′bi·nar′y** (-ner′ē) *adj.*

con·cu·bi·tant (kən·kyo͞o′bə·tənt) *n. Anthropol.* One whose status at birth carries with it marriage ability with another according to a degree of consanguinity. [<L *concubit-,* stem of *concumbere* lie together + -ANT]

con·cu·pis·cence (kon·kyo͞o′pə·səns) *n.* **1** Undue or illicit sexual desire; lust. **2** Any inordinate appetite or desire. See synonyms under DESIRE.

con·cu·pis·cent (kon·kyo͞o′pə·sənt) *adj.* Lustful; carnal; sensual. Also **con·cu·pis·ci·ble** (kon·kyo͞o′pi·sə·bəl). [<L *concupiscens, -entis,* ppr. of *concupiscere,* inceptive of *concupere* < *com-* thoroughly + *cupere* desire]

con·cur (kən·kûr′) *v.i.* **·curred, ·cur·ring 1** To agree, as in opinion or action; cooperate or combine. **2** To happen at the same time; coincide. **3** To converge to a point, as lines. See synonyms under AGREE, ASSENT. [<L *concurrere* <*com-* together + *currere* run]

con·cur·rence (kən·kûr′əns) *n.* **1** Combination or cooperation. **2** Agreement; approval. **3** A simultaneous occurrence; coincidence. **4** *Geom.* The point where three or more lines meet. **5** Competition; rivalry. **6** *Law* A power jointly held or a claim jointly shared. Also **con·cur′ren·cy.** See synonyms under HARMONY.

con·cur·rent (kən·kûr′ənt) *adj.* **1** Occurring or acting together; meeting in the same point. **2** United in action or application; coordinate; concomitant: *concurrent* remedies or jurisdiction. —*n.* **1** A person or thing that concurs. **2** One proceeding toward the same end or purpose. **3** A rival; competitor. See synonyms under INCIDENTAL. [<L *concurrens, -entis,* pp. of *concurrere.* See CONCUR.] —**con·cur′rent·ly** *adv.*

con·cuss (kən·kus′) *v.t.* **1** To affect or injure (the brain) by concussion. **2** *Scot.* To force or intimidate into action. **3** To agitate; shake. [<L *concussus,* pp. of *concutere* < *com-* together + *quatere* strike, beat]

con·cus·sion (kən·kush′ən) *n.* **1** A violent

add,āce,câre,pälm; end,ēven; it,īce; odd,ōpen,ôrder; to͝ok,po͞ol; up,bûrn; ə = a in *above,* e in *sicken,* i in *clarity,* o in *melon,* u in *focus;* yo͞o = u in *fuse;* oi,oil; ou,pout; ch,check; g,go; ng,ring; th,thin; th,this; zh,vision. Foreign sounds à,œ,ü,kh,ṅ; and ◆: see page xx. <from; + plus; ? possibly.

shaking; shock; jar. 2 *Pathol.* A violent shock to some organ by a fall or sudden blow; also, the condition resulting from it. See synonyms under BLOW, COLLISION. [<L *concussio, -onis* <*concutere.* See CONCUSS.] **—con·cus′sion·al** *adj.* **—con·cus·sive** (kən·kus′iv) *adj.*

Con·dé (kôn·dā′), **Prince de,** 1621–86, Louis II de Bourbon, Prince d'Enghien, French general: called "the Great Condé."

con·demn (kən·dem′) *v.t.* **1** To express opinion against; hold or prove to be wrong; censure. **2** To pronounce judicial sentence against. **3** To forbid the use of, commonly by official order, as something unfit. **4** *U.S. Law* To appropriate for public use by judicial decree; declare forfeited. **5** To pronounce hopeless; give up as incurable. **6** To close up, or to withdraw from public use, as a door, gate, or road. **7** *Obs.* To convict. [<L *condemnare* <*com-* thoroughly + *damnare* condemn] **—con·dem·na·ble** (kən·dem′nə·bəl) *adj.* **—con·dem·na·to·ry** (kən·dem′nə·tôr′ē,-tō′rē) *adj.* **—con·demn·er** (kən·dem′ər) *n.*

Synonyms: blame, censure, convict, denounce, doom, reprobate, reprove, sentence. To *condemn* is to pass judicial sentence or render judgment or decision against. *Condemn* is more final than *blame* or *censure*; a *condemned* criminal has had his trial. A person is *convicted* when his guilt is made clearly manifest; in legal usage one is said to be *convicted* only by the verdict of a jury. To *denounce* is to make public or official declaration against, especially in a violent and threatening manner. Compare ARRAIGN, BLAME, REPROVE. *Antonyms*: absolve, acquit, applaud, approve, exonerate, justify, pardon.

con·dem·na·tion (kon′dem·nā′shən) *n.* **1** The act of condemning, or the state of being condemned. **2** The cause or occasion of condemnation. See synonyms under REPROOF. [<L *condemnatio, -onis* <*condemnare* CONDEMN]

con·den·sate (kən·den′sāt) *adj.* Condensed. *—n.* **1** A product of condensation. **2** *Physics* The liquid obtained by condensing the vapor in which it is suspended. [<L *condensatus,* pp. of *condensare.* See CONDENSE.]

con·den·sa·tion (kon′den·sā′shən) *n.* **1** The act of making dense or denser, or the state of being condensed. **2** Any product of condensing. **3** *Physics* The reduction of a vapor or gas to a liquid or a solid, or of a liquid to a solid or semisolid. **4** *Chem.* The rearrangement of atoms to form a molecule of greater weight, density, or complexity. **5** *Psychol.* A fusion of events, thoughts, elements of speech, individuals, pictures, etc., as in dreams. Compare CONDENSE. See synonyms under ABBREVIATION. **—con·dens′a·tive** *adj.*

con·den·sa·tor (kon′den·sā′tər) *n.* A condenser.

con·dense (kən·dens′) *v.* **·densed, ·dens·ing** *v.t.* **1** To compress or make dense; consolidate. **2** To abridge or make concise; epitomize, as an essay. **3** To change from the gaseous or vaporous to the liquid or solid state, as by cooling or compression. *—v.i.* **4** To become condensed. See synonyms under ABBREVIATE, REDUCE. [<L *condensare* <*condensus* thick <*com-* together + *densus* crowded, close] **—con·dens′a·bil′i·ty** *n.* **—con·dens′a·ble** or **con·dens′i·ble** *adj.*

condensed milk Cow's milk, sweetened, and thickened by evaporation of its water content.

con·dens·er (kən·den′sər) *n.* **1** One who or that which condenses. **2** Any device for reducing a vapor to liquid by removing from the vapor its heat of evaporation, as in a steam-power plant. **3** *Electr.* An arrangement of insulated conductors and dielectrics for the accumulation of an electric charge: used to block the flow of a direct current and to modify the capacity of an electric circuit. **4** *Optics* A combination of lenses for the effective condensation of light rays.

con·de·scend (kon′di·send′) *v.i.* **1** To stoop from a position of rank or dignity; come down to equal terms with an inferior. **2** To behave as if conscious of this stooping; patronize. **3** To lower or degrade oneself. **4** *Rare* To be gracious or affable. [<F *condescendre* <LL *condescendere* <*com-* together + *descendere* stoop. See DESCEND.]

con·de·scen·dence (kon′di·sen′dəns) *n.* **1** In Scots law, a plaintiff's statement of facts. **2** Condescension.

con·de·scend·ing (kon′di·sen′ding) *adj.* Showing condescension; especially, patronizing.

con·de·scen·sion (kon′di·sen′shən) *n.* **1** An act or instance of condescending. **2** Patronizing courtesy toward inferiors. See synonyms under FAVOR. [<LL *condescensio, -onis* <*condescendere.* See CONDESCEND.]

con·dign (kən·dīn′) *adj.* **1** Well-deserved; merited; deserved: said of punishment. **2** *Obs.* Deserving. [<F *condigne* <L *condignus* <*com-* thoroughly + *dignus* worthy] **—con·dign′ly** *adv.* **—con·dign′ness** *n.*

con·di·ment (kon′də·mənt) *n.* A sauce, relish, spice, etc. [<L *condimentum*]

con·di·tion (kən·dish′ən) *n.* **1** The state or mode in which a person or thing exists. **2** State of health; especially, a favorable or sound state of health. **3** A modifying circumstance. **4** An event, fact, or the like that is necessary to the occurrence of some other, though not its cause; a prerequisite. **5** Something required as prerequisite to a promise or to its fulfilment. **6** A grade or rank; especially, high social position. **7** *Gram.* That clause of a conditional sentence usually introduced by *if, unless,* etc. **8** A conditional proposition upon which another proposition depends as consequent. **9** *U.S.* **a** A requirement that a student who has not done satisfactory work in a college or university course do additional work to avoid failing the course. **b** A grade, often indicated by E, signifying this requirement. *—v.t.* **1** To place a stipulation or stipulations upon; prescribe. **2** To be the stipulation of or prerequisite to. **3** To specify as a stipulation or requirement. **4** To render fit. **5** *Psychol.* To train to a behavior pattern or conditioned response. **6** *U.S.* To subject (a student) to a condition. *—v.i.* **7** To stipulate. [<L *condicio, -onis* agreement <*condicere* <*com-* together + *dicere* say] **—con·di′tion·er** *n.*

con·di·tion·al (kən·dish′ən·əl) *adj.* **1** Expressing or imposing conditions: not absolute. **2** *Gram.* Expressing or implying a condition; a *conditional* clause. *—n. Gram.* A word, tense, clause, or mood expressive of a condition. **—con·di·tion·al·i·ty** (kən·dish′ən·al′ə·tē) *n.* **—con·di′·tion·al·ly** *adv.*

con·di·tioned (kən·dish′ənd) *adj.* **1** Limited by or subjected to conditions or stipulations. **2** Circumstanced; placed. **3** *Psychol.* **a** Trained to give an identical response to a given stimulus. **b** Responsive to related stimuli. **4** Accustomed (to). **5** So treated or trained as to be in good condition for some task or contest.

conditioned response *Psychol.* A type of learned response elicited by a stimulus which, though originally ineffective, has fully replaced the normal or natural stimulus after a period of close and repeated juxtaposition with it. Also **conditioned reflex.**

con·di·ti·o si·ne qua non (kən·dish′ē·ō sī′nē kwā non′) *Latin* An indispensable condition.

con·do (kon′dō) *n. U.S. Colloq.* Condominium (def.3).

con·dole (kən·dōl′) *v.* **·doled, ·dol·ing** *v.i.* To grieve or express sympathy with one in affliction: with *with.* *—v.t. Rare* To grieve over with another; bewail. [<LL *condolere* <*com-* together + *dolere* grieve] **—con·do·la·to·ry** (kən·dō′lə·tôr′ē, -tō′rē) *adj.* **—con·dol′er** *n.*

con·do·lence (kən·dō′ləns) *n.* **1** Expression of sympathy with a person in pain, sorrow, or misfortune. **2** *Obs.* Lamentation. Also **con·dole′·ment.**

con do·lo·re (kōn dō·lō′rā) *Music* With sorrow; sadly. [Ital.]

con·dom (kon′dəm, kun′-) *n.* A membranous penile sheath of rubber or similar material, having an anti-venereal or contraceptive function: also spelled *cundum.* [? Alter. of *Conton,* an 18th c. English physician said to have invented it.]

con·do·min·i·um (kon′də·min′ē·əm) *n.* **1** Joint government; joint sovereignty, as over property. **2** *Law* A territory jointly governed by several states under international law. **3** *U.S.* An apartment house in which the units are owned separately by individuals and not by a corporation or cooperative; also, an apartment in such a building. [<NL <L *com-* together + *dominium* rule]

Con·don (kon′dən), **Edward U(hler),** 1902–74, U.S. physicist.

con·done (kən·dōn′) *v.t.* **·doned, ·don·ing** To treat (an offense) as overlooked or forgiven; forgive, See synonyms under PARDON. [<L *condonare* <*com-* thoroughly + *donare* give] **—con·do·na·tion** (kon′dō·nā′shən), **con·done′·ment** *n.* **—con·don′er** *n.*

con·dor (kon′dər) *n.* **1** A vulture of the high Andes *(Vultur gryphus),* characterized by a fleshy comb and a white downy neck ruff: it is one of the largest birds with the power of flight. **2** The California vulture *(Gymnogyps californianus).* [<Sp. <Quechua *cuntur*]

CONDOR (Wing spread 8 1/2 to 10 1/2 feet)

Con·dor·cet (kôn·dôr·se′), **Marquis de,** 1743–94, Marie Jean Caritat, French mathematician and philosopher.

con·dot·tie·re (kōn′dōt·tyâ′·rā) *n. pl.* **·ri** (-rē) **1** A hireling military chief of the14th and 15th centuries. **2** A freelance; adventurer. [<Ital. <*condotto* a mercenary <L *conductus* hired. See CONDUCT.]

con·duce (kən·dōōs′ -dyōōs′) *v.i.* **·duced, ·duc·ing** To help or tend toward a result; contribute. [<L *conducere* bring together. See CONDUCT.] **—con·duc′er** *n.* **—con·du′ci·ble** *adj.* **—con·du′ci·bil′i·ty, con·du′ci·ble·ness** *n.* **—con·du′ci·bly** *adv.*

con·du·cive (kən·dōō′siv, -dyōō′-) *adj.* Contributing; leading; helping: with *to.* Also **con·du·cent** (kən·dōō′sənt, -dyōō′-). **—con·du′cive·ly** *adv.* **—con·du′cive·ness** *n.*

con·duct (kən·dukt′) *v.t.* **1** To accompany and show the way; guide; escort. **2** To manage or control. **3** To direct and lead the performance of. **4** To serve as a medium of transmission for; convey; transmit, as electricity. **5** To act or behave: reflexive *—v.i.* **6** To serve as a conductor. **7** To direct or lead. *—n.* (kon′dukt) **1** One's course of action; behavior. **2** The act of managing; direction; control; skilful management. **3** The action of leading; escort; convoy. [<L *conductus,* pp. of *conducere* <*com-* together + *ducere* lead] **—con·duct′i·bil′i·ty** *n.* **—con·duct′i·ble** *adj.*

con·duc·tance (kən·duk′təns) *n. Electr.* A measure of the ability of a circuit or circuit element to carry current that is effective in producing power, equal to the ratio of the resistance to the square of the magnitude of the impedance: expressed in mhos. Symbol *g, G*

con·duc·tion (kən·duk′shən) *n.* **1** *Physics* The transmission of heat, sound, or electricity through matter without bulk motion of the matter: distinguished from *convection.* **2** *Physiol.* The transference of a stimulus along the nerve fibers from the point of irritation to the nerve center. **3** Transmission or conveyance in general.

con·duc·ti·tious (kon′duk·tish′əs) *adj.* Employed for wages; kept for hire.

con·duc·tive (kən·duk′tiv) *adj.* **1** Having the power of conducting. **2** Proceeding by or resulting from conduction.

con·duc·tiv·i·ty (kon′duk·tiv′ə·tē) *n.* **1** *Physics* The capacity of a substance or body to transmit light, heat, or electricity. **2** *Electr.* The conductance between opposite parallel faces of a given material of unit length and cross-section. **3** *Physiol.* The property of nerve fibers by which they conduct stimuli.

con·duc·tor (kən·duk′tər) *n.* **1** One who or that which leads or shows the way; an escort; guide. **2** An officer of a railroad who has charge of a train or car and collects tickets and fares. **3** Any manager or director of a movement or operation; especially, the director of an orchestra or chorus. **4** Any conducting medium, material, or device; a conduit. **5** Any body or medium having sensible conductivity for electricity or heat. **6** A lightning rod. **—con·duc′tor·ship** *n.***—con·duc′tress** *n. fem.*

con·duit (kon′dit, -dōō·it) *n.* **1** A means for conducting something, as a tube or pipe for a fluid; an aqueduct. **2** A passage or subway for electric wires, underground cables, gas and water pipes, or the like. **3** A fountain or a reservoir. [<F <*conduire* <L *conducere.* See CONDUCT.]

con·du·pli·cate (kon·dōō′plə·kit, -dyōō′-) *adj. Bot.* Doubled together: said of leaves and coty-

con·dyle (kon′dil) *n. Anat.* 1 An enlarged, rounded prominence on the end of a bone, usually associated with a joint. 2 Any process by which an appendage is articulated in a depression or cavity, as the head to the base of the mandible. [<F <L *condylus* knuckle <Gk. *kondylos*] —**con·dy·lar** (kon′də·lər) *adj.*

con·dy·loid (kon′də·loid) *adj.* Resembling or connected with a condyle.

con·dy·lo·ma (kon′də·lō′mə) *n. pl.* **·ma·ta** (-mə·tə) *Pathol.* An indolent wartlike growth, sometimes syphilitic, usually near the anus and external genitals of either sex. —**con·dy·lom·a·tous** (kon′·də·lom′ə·təs, -lō′mə·təs) *adj.*

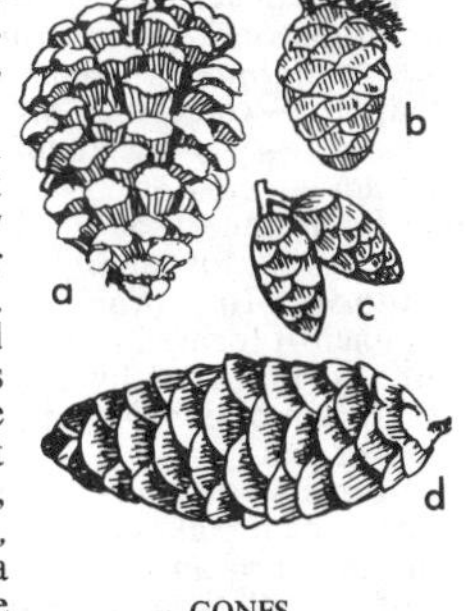

CONES
a. Stone pine.
b. California big tree.
c. Eastern hemlock.
d. Red spruce.

cone (kōn) *n.* 1 A solid figure that tapers uniformly from a circular base to a point. 2 *Geom.* A solid whose surface is generated by the turning of a straight line on a fixed point, called the *vertex,* and intersecting a closed plane curve at all points on the circumference. 3 *Bot.* A dry multiple fruit, as of the pine, composed of scales arranged symmetrically around an axis and enclosing seeds. 4 *Mech.* Any of several conical instruments or parts as either of the two taper drums in the head stock of a spinning mule. 5 *Physiol.* One of the specialized, photosensitive cells in the retina of the eye concerned with the perception of color and with daylight vision. 6 A cone-shaped pastry shell used to hold a ball of ice-cream. —*v.t.* & *v.i.* **coned, con·ing** To shape or be shaped conically. [<L *conus* <Gk. *kōnos*]

cone·flow·er (kōn′flou′ər) *n.* 1 Any of several hardy annual and perennial plants of the composite family, having a broadly conical disk of dark-brown chaff and flowers. 2 A rudbeckia.

con·el·rad (kon′əl·rad) *n. Aeron.* A technique for deliberately scrambling radio signals from separate stations so as to prevent enemy aircraft from using the signals of any one station as a navigation aid or for information: used in civil defense. [< *con(trol of) el(ectromagnetic) rad(iation)*]

cone-nose (kōn′nōz′) *n.* 1 A large hemipterous insect (genus *Triatoma*): the bloodsucking *cone-nose* (*T. sanguisuga*) of the United States. 2 An assassin bug.

cone of dispersion *Mil.* The conical pattern formed by the trajectories of several shots fired from one gun with the same sight setting: differences in the paths of flight are caused by gun vibration, discrepancies in ammunition, shifts in the wind, etc. Also **cone of fire.**

cone of silence *Telecom.* A small area resembling an inverted cone extending upward from a radio transmitting station, within the limits of which signals from that station are inaudible or blurred: also called *null.*

co·ne·pa·te (kō′nä·pä′tā) *n.* A white-backed, tropical American skunk (genus *Conepatus*); specifically, the hog-nosed skunk (*C. mesoleucus*) of South and Central America. Also **co·ne·pa·tl** (kō′nä·pät′l). [<Nahuatl *conepatl* <*conetl* small + *epatl* fox]

Con·es·to·ga wagon (kon′is·tō′gə) A covered wagon with broad wheels, used by American pioneers for prairie traveling. [from *Conestoga,* Pa., where first made]

co·ney (kō′nē, kun′ē) See CONY.

Co·ney Island (kō′nē) A seaside resort and amusement center in Brooklyn borough of New York City.

con·fab·u·late (kən·fab′yə·lāt) *v.i.* **·lat·ed, ·lat·ing** 1 To chat; gossip, converse. 2 *Psychol.* To compensate for loss or impairment of memory by fabrication or invention of details. Also **con·fab** (kon′fab). [<L *confabulatus,* pp. of *confabulari* <*com-* together + *fabulari* chat <*fabula* story] —**con·fab′u·la′tion, con′fab** *n.* —**con·fab·u·la·to·ry** (kən·fab′·yə·lə·tôr′ē, -tō′rē) *adj.*

con·far·re·a·tion (kon·far′ē·ā′shən) *n.* In ancient Rome, the patrician religious form of marriage, in which a cake of spelt was offered to Jupiter before the pontifex maximus and the flamens of Jupiter. [<L *confarreatio, -onis* <*confarreare* marry solemnly <*com-* together + *farreum* cake of spelt <*far* grain, wheat]

con·fect (kən·fekt′) *v.t.* 1 To make into a confection; preserve; prepare. 2 To construct or put together. —*n.* (kon′fekt) *Obs.* A confection. [<L *confectus,* pp. of *conficere* < *com-* together + *facere* make. Related to COMFIT.]

con·fec·tion (kən·fek′shən) *n.* 1 Any mixing or compounding; also, the article produced by either process. 2 An article of confectionery; a sweetmeat. 3 Any medicated conserve or sweetmeat; an electuary; also, any compound of drugs or spices. 4 An attractive, stylish article of dress for women. —*v.t.* To make up into a confection. [<F <L *confectio, -onis* <*conficere.* See CONFECT.]

con·fec·tion·ar·y (kən·fek′shən·er′ē) *adj.* Of, pertaining to, or like confections or confectionery. —*n. pl.* **·ar·ies** 1 A confectioner. 2 A sweetmeat. 3 *Obs.* A room or shop where confections are prepared; a confectionery.

con·fec·tion·er (kən·fek′shən·ər) *n.* One who makes or deals in confectionery.

con·fec·tion·er·y (kən·fek′shən·er′ē) *n. pl.* **·er·ies** 1 Candies, sweetmeats, etc., collectively. 2 A confectioner's shop or the business or trade of a confectioner.

con·fed·er·a·cy (kən·fed′ər·ə·sē) *n. pl.* **·cies** 1 A number of states or persons in league with each other; league; confederation: the *Confederacy* of the Southern States. 2 *Law* An unlawful combination; conspiracy. See synonyms under ALLIANCE, ASSOCIATION, CABAL. —**Southern Confederacy** The Confederate States of America: also **the Confederacy.** [<AF *confederacie* <L *confoederatio* <*confoederare.* See CONFEDERATE.]

con·fed·er·ate (kən·fed′ər·it) *n.* One who is united with another or others in a league or plot; an associate; accomplice. See synonyms under ACCESSORY, AUXILIARY. —*adj.* Associated in a confederacy; united or allied by treaty. —*v.t.* & *v.i.* (kən·fed′ə·rāt) **·at·ed, ·at·ing** To form together or join with in a league, confederacy, or conspiracy. [<LL *confoederatus,* pp. of *confoederare* join in a league <*com-* together + *foedus* league] —**con·fed′er·a′tive** *adj.*

Con·fed·er·ate (kən·fed′ər·it) *adj.* Pertaining to the **Confederate States of America,** a league of eleven southern States of the American Union that seceded from the United

THE CONFEDERATE STATES OF AMERICA
VA. N. C. TENN. ARK. S. C. MISS. ALA. GA. TEXAS LA. ATLANTIC OCEAN FLA. GULF OF MEXICO MEXICO

States in 1860–61. They were South Carolina, Mississippi, Florida, Alabama, Georgia, Louisiana, Texas, Virginia, Arkansas, Tennessee, and North Carolina. —*n.* An adherent, soldier, or sailor of the Confederate States of America.

con·fed·er·a·tion (kən·fed′ə·rā′shən) *n.* 1 The act of confederating. 2 A confederacy. See synonyms under ALLIANCE, ASSOCIATION. —**the Confederation** The union of the American colonies, 1781–89, under the Articles of Confederation.

con·fer (kən·fûr′) *v.* **·ferred, ·fer·ring** *v.t.* 1 To grant as a gift or benefit; bestow. 2 *Obs.* To collate; compare. —*v.i.* 3 To hold conference; consult. See synonyms under CONSULT, DELIBERATE, GIVE. [<L *conferre* <*com-* together + *ferre* bring, carry] —**con·fer′ment** *n.* —**con·fer′ra·ble** *adj.* —**con·fer′rer** *n.*

con·fer·ee (kon′fə·rē′) *n.* 1 A person with whom another confers. 2 A person upon whom some honor, degree, etc., is conferred.

con·fer·ence (kon′fər·əns, -frəns) *n.* 1 A formal meeting for counsel or discussion; an official council, as of two branches of a legislature. 2 Conversation; discourse. 3 *U.S.* One of several orders of assemblies of preachers and laymen of the Methodist Episcopal Church: the Annual *Conference;* the General *Conference;* the District *Conference.* 4 A local organization representing the Congregational churches of a district. 5 The act of bestowing; conferment. 6 A league or association, as of athletic teams. See synonyms under ASSEMBLY, COMPANY, CONVERSATION. [<MF *conférence* <Med. L *conferentia* <L *conferre.* See CONFER.] —**con·fer·en·tial** (kon′fə·ren′shəl) *adj.*

con·fer·va (kən·fûr′və) *n. pl.* **·vae** (-vē) or **·vas** *Bot.* Any member of a genus (*Tribonema*) of greenish, threadlike, fresh-water algae [<L] —**con·fer′val, con·fer′void, con·fer′vous** *adj.*

con·fer·vite (kən·fûr′vīt) *n. Bot.* A fossil plant allied to the aquatic confervae and found chiefly in the formations of the Cretaceous period.

con·fess (kən·fes′) *v.t.* 1 To acknowledge or admit, as a fault, guilt, or debt. 2 To acknowledge belief or faith in. 3 *Eccl.* **a** To admit or make known (one's sins), especially to a priest, to obtain absolution. **b** To hear the confession of: said of a priest. 4 To concede or admit to be true. 5 *Poetic* To demonstrate or make manifest. —*v.i.* 6 To make acknowledgment of, as a fault, crime, or error. 7 To make confession to a priest. [<F *confesser* <L *confessus,* pp. of *confiteri* <*com-* thoroughly + *fateri* own, declare]

Synonyms: accept, acknowledge, admit, allow, avow, certify, concede, disclose, endorse, grant, own, recognize. We *accept* another's statement; *admit* any point made against us; *acknowledge* what we have said or done, good or bad; *avow* our individual beliefs or feelings; *certify* to facts within our knowledge; *confess* our own faults; *endorse* a friend's note or statement; *grant* a request; *own* our faults or obligations; *recognize* lawful authority; *concede* a claim, demand, etc. The chief present use of *confess* is in the sense of making known to others one's own error or wrong-doing; as, to *confess* a crime. *Acknowledge* may be used as a milder word in this sense, but is more freely used of matters not involving error or fault: I *acknowledge* my signature, the receipt of a letter, a check, etc. *Own* commonly indicates a somewhat reluctant acknowledgment. *Admit* and *concede* have a similar suggestion of reluctance or of possible objection. See ACKNOWLEDGE, AVOW. Compare APOLOGY. *Antonyms*: cloak, conceal, cover, deny, disavow, disguise, disown, dissemble, dissimulate, hide, mask, repudiate, screen, secrete, veil.

con·fess·ed·ly (kən·fes′id·lē) *adv.* By admission or confession; indisputably.

con·fes·sion (kən·fesh′ən) *n.* 1 The act of confessing; the avowal or acknowledgment of an action, especially of one that is inculpatory or sinful; admission: a *confession* of crime. 2 An acknowledgment of belief (in another); recognition of a relation (to another): *confession* of Christ. 3 *Law* A voluntary declaration or acknowledgment by a party against whom some misdeed or default is alleged in respect of such allegation. 4 A formulary of faith: also called **confession of faith.** 5 A formulary of public worship embodying a general admission of common sinfulness, used in the Roman Catholic, Anglican, and other liturgies. 6 The contrite acknowledgment to a priest of any sins committed: a part of the sacrament of penance and a condition of absolution: called in full **sacramental** or **auricular confession.** 7 An organization, as a church or communion, using a confession of faith. 8 The tomb of a martyred Christian; also, an altar over such a tomb or the basilica in which the altar stood; an altar-tomb confessionary. See synonyms under APOLOGY.

con·fes·sion·al (kən·fesh′ən·əl) *adj.* Pertaining to a confession. — *n.* **1** A cabinet in a church where a priest hears confessions. **2** The act, performance, or practice of confession before a priest.

con·fes·sion·ar·y (kən·fesh′ən·er′ē) *adj.* & *n. pl.* **·ar·ies** Confessional.

con·fes·sor (kən·fes′ər) *n.* **1** A priest who hears confessions; a spiritual adviser, as of a sovereign. **2** One who confesses or admits anything, as a crime. **3** One who confesses his faith in Christianity, especially in the face of persecution. Also **con·fess′er.** — **con·fes′·sor·ship** *n.*

con·fet·ti (kən·fet′ē) *n. pl.* **1** Small pieces of brightly colored paper thrown about at carnivals, weddings, etc. **2** Bonbons. [<Ital., pl. of *confetto* confection]

con·fi·dant (kon′fə·dant′, kon′fə·dant) *n.* A person to whom secrets are entrusted. [<F *confident* <Ital. *confidente* <L *confidens.* See CONFIDE.] — **con′fi·dante′** *n. fem.*

con·fide (kən·fīd′) *v.* **·fid·ed, ·fid·ing** *v.t.* **1** To reveal in trust or confidence. **2** To put into one's trust or keeping. — *v.i.* **3** To have faith or trust: often with *in.* See synonyms under COMMIT, TRUST. [<L *confidere* <*com-* thoroughly + *fidere* trust] — **con·fid′er** *n.*

con·fi·dence (kon′fə·dəns) *n.* **1** Trust in or reliance upon something or someone; belief in a person or thing. **2** Assurance; presumption. **3** Self-reliance; hence, courage or boldness. **4** Private conversation or communication; a secret. **5** *Obs.* That in which one confides. See synonyms under ASSURANCE, BELIEF, CERTAINTY, FAITH.

confidence game A swindle in which the swindler first wins the confidence of his victim and then defrauds him. Also **confidence trick,** *Colloq.* **con game.**

confidence man One who practices or promotes a confidence game.

con·fi·dent (kon′fə·dənt) *adj.* **1** Having confidence; assured; self-reliant. **2** *Obs.* Forward; impudent. See synonyms under SANGUINE, SECURE, SURE. — *n.* A confidant. [<L *confidens, -entis,* ppr. of *confidere.* See CONFIDE.] — **con′fi·dent·ly** *adv.*

con·fi·den·tial (kon′fə·den′shəl) *adj.* **1** Having secret or private relations; trusted; intimate: a *confidential* clerk. **2** Imparted in confidence; secret: *confidential* information. **3** Disposed to confide in another. **4** *U.S.* Denoting defense information classified next above "for official use only": the next lowest classification. Compare TOP-SECRET, SECRET (*adj.* def. 5). — **con·fi·den·ti·al·i·ty** (kon′fə·den′shē·al′ə·tē), **con′fi·den′tial·ness** *n.*

con·fi·den·tial·ly (kon′fə·den′shəl·ē) *adv.* **1** In a confidential manner: He spoke *confidentially.* **2** Regarding (the following or preceding statement) as a confidence: in function like an adverbial clause modifying a whole sentence: *Confidentially,* he's always late.

con·fid·ing (kən·fī′ding) *adj.* Unsuspicious; trustful. — **con·fid′ing·ly** *adv.* — **con·fid′ing·ness** *n.*

con·fig·u·rate (kən·fig′yə·rāt) *v.* **·rat·ed, ·rat·ing** *v.t.* To give shape or fashion to. — *v.i.* To be congruous. [<LL *configuratus,* pp. of *configurare.* See CONFIGURE.]

con·fig·u·ra·tion (kən·fig′yə·rā′shən) *n.* **1** Structural arrangement; conformation; contour. **2** *Psychol.* In the Gestalt theory, a static or dynamic aggregate of sensations, feelings, reflexes, and ideas so organized as to function as a unit in individual behavior. **3** *Physics* The spatial arrangement of atoms in a molecule or of nucleons and electrons in an atom. — **con·fig′u·ra′tion·ism** *n.*

con·fine (kən·fīn′) *v.* **·fined, ·fin·ing** *v.t.* **1** To shut within an enclosure; imprison. **2** To restrain or oblige to stay within doors. **3** To hold or keep within limits; restrict: to *confine* remarks. — *v.i.* **4** *Obs.* To border; abut. See synonyms under CIRCUMSCRIBE, LIMIT, RESTRAIN. — *n.* **1** *Usually pl.* A boundary; limit; border; frontier. **2** *Obs.* A prison. **3** *Obs.* Region, territory, or district. See synonyms under BOUNDARY, MARGIN. [<F *confiner* <Ital. *confinare* <L *confinis* bordering <*com-* together + *finis* border] — **con·fin′a·ble** *adj.* — **con·fin′er** *n.*

con·fined (kən·fīnd′) *adj.* **1** Limited; restricted. **2** In childbed.

con·fine·ment (kən·fīn′mənt) *n.* **1** The state of being confined; restriction; imprisonment. **2** Accouchement; the state of being in childbed.

con·firm (kən·fûrm′) *v.t.* **1** To assure by added proof; corroborate; verify; make certain. **2** To add firmness to; strengthen. **3** *Law* To ratify; sanction. **4** To establish in office. **5** To receive into the church by confirmation. [<OF *confermer* <L *confirmare* strengthen <*com-* thoroughly + *firmus* strong] — **con·firm′a·ble, con·firm′a·tive, con·firm·a·to·ry** (kən·fûr′mə·tôr′ē, -tō′rē) *adj.* — **con·firm′er** *n.*

Synonyms: assure, corroborate, establish, fix, prove, ratify, sanction, settle, strengthen, substantiate, sustain, uphold. *Confirm* means to add firmness or give stability to. Both *confirm* and *corroborate* presuppose something already existing to which the confirmation or corroboration is added. Testimony is *corroborated* by concurrent testimony or by circumstances; *confirmed* by *established* facts. That which is thoroughly *proved* is said to be *established*; so is that which is official and has adequate power behind it; as, the *established* government. The continents are *fixed.* A treaty is *ratified*; an appointment *confirmed.* An act is *sanctioned* by any person or authority that passes upon it approvingly. A statement is *substantiated*; a report *confirmed*; a controversy *settled*; the decision of a lower court *sustained* by a higher. Just government should be *upheld.* See RATIFY. *Antonyms*: abrogate, annul, cancel, destroy, overthrow, shake, shatter, unsettle, upset.

con·fir·ma·tion (kon′fər·mā′shən) *n.* **1** The act of confirming. **2** That which confirms; proof. **3** *Eccl.* A sacramental rite administered to baptized persons, confirming or strengthening their faith, and admitting them to all the privileges of the church. **4** *Law* An instrument that supplies some defect or omission in a former conveyance. See synonyms under PROOF.

con·firmed (kən·fûrmd′) *adj.* Fixed; firmly established; inveterate: a *confirmed* drunkard.

con·fir·mee (kon′fər·mē′) *n.* **1** *Law* One to whom anything is confirmed. **2** One who is confirmed.

con·fir·mor (kon′fər·môr′, kən·fûr′mər) *n. Law* The person who confirms anything, as a title, to a confirmee.

con·fis·cate (kon′fis·kāt) *v.t.* **·cat·ed, ·cat·ing** **1** To appropriate as forfeited to the public use or treasury, usually as a penalty. **2** To appropriate by or as by authority. — *adj.* Appropriated or forfeited. [<L *confiscatus,* pp. of *confiscare* <*com-* together + *fiscus* chest, treasury] — **con·fis·ca·ble** (kən·fis′kə·bəl), **con′fis·cat′a·ble** *adj.* — **con′fis·ca′tion** *n.* — **con′fis·ca′tor** *n.* — **con·fis·ca·to·ry** (kən·fis′kə·tôr′ē, -tō′rē) *adj.*

Con·fit·e·or (kən·fit′ē·ôr) *n.* The general confession said by the celebrant and servers at the beginning of the Roman Catholic mass. [<L, I confess: the first word]

con·fi·ture (kon′fi·cho͝or) *n.* A confection; a sweet conserve. [<F]

con·fla·grant (kən·flā′grənt) *adj.* Burning fiercely. [<L *conflagrans, -antis,* ppr. of *conflagrare* <*com-* thoroughly + *flagrare* burn]

con·fla·gra·tion (kon′flə·grā′shən) *n.* A great or disastrous fire; destruction by burning. [<L *conflagratio, -onis* <*conflagrare.* See CONFLAGRANT.]

con·flate (kən·flāt′) *v.t.* **·flat·ed, ·flat·ing** **1** To combine from variant readings into a composite reading. **2** To blow together; bring together from diverse sources. — *adj.* **1** Composed of a variety of elements. **2** Blown together. [<L *conflatus,* pp. of *conflare* <*com-* together + *flare* blow] — **con·fla′tion** *n.*

con·flict (kon′flikt) *n.* **1** A struggle to resist or overcome; contest of opposing forces or powers; strife; battle. **2** A state or condition of opposition; antagonism; discord: the *conflict* of testimony. **3** Active antagonism; clash; collision. **4** *Psychoanal.* Painful tension set up by a clash between opposed and contradictory impulses in an individual; specifically, the antagonism existing between primitive desires and instincts and moral, religious, or ethical ideals. — *v.i.* (kən·flikt′) **1** To come into collision; be in mutual opposition; clash. **2** To engage in battle; struggle. [<L *conflictus,* pp. of *confligere* <*com-* together + *fligere* strike] — **con·flic′tion** *n.* — **con·flic′·tive** *adj.*

con·flu·ence (kon′flo͞o·əns) *n.* **1** *Geog.* A junction of streams; the place where streams flow together. **2** A gathering and mingling. **3** A flocking together; concourse. Also **con·flux** (kon′fluks).

con·flu·ent (kon′flo͞o·ənt) *adj.* Flowing together so as to form one; blended into one. — *n. Geog.* A stream that unites with another; a branch of a river. [<L *confluens, -entis,* ppr. of *confluere* <*com-* together + *fluere* flow]

con·fo·cal (kon·fō′kəl) *adj.* Having a common focus or common foci.

con·form (kən·fôrm′) *v.t.* **1** To make like or similar in form or character: with *to.* — *v.i.* **2** To act in accord; correspond; comply. **3** To be or become a conformist. [<F *conformer* <L *conformare* <*com-* together + *formare* shape] — **con·form′a·bil′i·ty, con·form′a·ble·ness** *n.* — **con·form′a·ble** *adj.* — **con·form′a·bly** *adv.* — **con·form′er** *n.*

con·form·ance (kən·fôr′məns) *n.* The act or state of conforming.

con·for·ma·tion (kon′fôr·mā′shən) *n.* **1** The manner of formation of a body; general structure, form, or outline; arrangement of parts. **2** The act of conforming, or the state of being conformed.

con·for·ma·tor (kon′fôr·mā′tər) *n.* An instrument which makes a graphic record of the size and shape of an object, as the head or bust.

con·form·ist (kən·fôr′mist) *n.* **1** One who conforms or complies. **2** In English history, one who adheres to the usages of the Established Church: opposed to *dissenter, nonconformist.*

con·form·i·ty (kən·fôr′mə·tē) *n. pl.* **·ties** **1** Correspondence in form, manner, or use; agreement; harmony; congruity. **2** The act or habit of conforming oneself; acquiescence. **3** In English history, adherence to the Church of England. See synonyms under HARMONY.

con·found (kon·found′, kən-) *v.t.* **1** To strike with confusion or amazement; perplex; overwhelm; abash. **2** To confuse with something else; mix. **3** To confuse or mingle (elements, things, or ideas) indistinguishably. **4** (kon′·found′) To imprecate ill upon: used as a mild oath. **5** *Obs.* To waste. **6** *Archaic* To defeat; overthrow; ruin, as an army or nation. See synonyms under ABASH, PERPLEX, REFUTE. [<OF *confondre* <L *confundere.* See CONFUSE.] — **con·found′er** *n.*

con·found·ed (kon·foun′did, kən-) *adj.* **1** Execrable; damned; outrageous: a mild oath. **2** Perplexed; discomfited; confused. — **con·found′ed·ly** *adv.*

con·fra·ter·ni·ty (kon′frə·tûr′nə·tē) *n. pl.* **·ties** **1** An association, brotherhood, or society of men united for a common object or purpose, especially in some profession; any body or class of men. **2** Specifically, a religious association in the Roman Catholic Church, usually of laymen, for some devotional, charitable, or educational object: called *archconfraternity* when composed of affiliated bodies. [<Med. L *confraternitas, -tatis* <LL *com-* with + *fraternitas* brotherhood]

con·frere (kon′frâr) *n.* A colleague; a fellow member of an association, or of a profession or calling. Also *French* **con·frère** (kôn·frâr′). [<MF <L *com-* with + *frater* brother]

con·front (kən·frunt′) *v.t.* **1** To stand face to face with; face defiantly. **2** To put face to face: with *with*: to *confront* the accused with the witnesses against him. **3** To compare. See synonyms under OPPOSE. [<F *confronter* <L *com-* together + *frons, frontis* face, forehead] — **con·front′er** *n.* — **con·front′ment** *n.*

con·fron·ta·tion (kon′frən·tā′shən) *n.* **1** The act of confronting, or the state of being confronted. **2** A direct challenge to the power of an opposing group or state, as by affirmation of policy, acts of protest, or acts or threats of violence. **3** A crisis or conflict between opposing political groups or states: events leading to a *confrontation* with China.

Con·fu·cian (kən·fyo͞o′shən) *adj.* Of or pertaining to Confucius, his teachings, or his followers. — *n.* An adherent of Confucius or his teachings. — **Con·fu′cian·ism** *n.* — **Con·fu′cian·ist** *n.*

Con·fu·cius (kən·fyo͞o′shəs), 551–478 B.C., Chinese philosopher and teacher, founder of an ethical system based on ancestor worship, devotion to family and friends, and the maintenance of justice and peace: *Chinese* K'ung Fu-tse.

con·fuse (kən·fyo͞oz′) *v.t.* **·fused, ·fus·ing 1** To perplex or perturb; confound; bewilder. **2** To throw into disorder; mix indiscriminately; derange: to *confuse* the colors of a picture. **3** To mix in such a way as to make distinction difficult or impossible: He *confused* the dates of the events. **4** *Obs.* To undo; ruin. See synonyms under ABASH, DISPLACE, EMBARRASS, MIX, PERPLEX. [<L *confusus,* pp. of *confundere* < *com-* together + *fundere* pour. Related to CONFOUND.] —**con·fus·ed·ly** (kən·fyo͞o′zid·lē) *adv.* —**con·fus′ed·ness** *n.* —**con·fus′ing·ly** *adv.*

con·fu·sion (kən·fyo͞o′zhən) *n.* **1** The act of confusing, or the state of being confused; perplexity; distraction. **2** Embarrassment; shame; intellectual discomfiture. **3** *Obs.* Destruction; ruin; overthrow. See synonyms under CHAGRIN, DISORDER, PERPLEXITY, TUMULT. —**con·fu′sion·al** *adj.*

con·fu·ta·tion (kon′fyo͝o·tā′shən) *n.* **1** The act of confuting; the process of showing to be false or illogical; disproof. **2** That which shows an argument, etc., to be false or invalid.

con·fute (kən·fyo͞ot′) *v.t.* **·fut·ed, ·fut·ing 1** To prove to be false or invalid; refute successfully. **2** To prove (a person) to be in the wrong. **3** To confound. See synonyms under REFUTE. [<L *confutare* check, restrain] —**con·fut′er** *n.*

con·ga (kong′gə) *n.* **1** A ballroom dance of Latin-American origin in which the dancers form a winding line. **2** The music for this dance, in fast 4/4 time, with a strongly accented fourth beat. [<Am. Sp.]

Con·ga·ree River (kong′gə·rē′) A river in central South Carolina, flowing SE 50 miles to the Santee River.

con·gé (kon′zhā, *Fr.* kôṅ·zhā) *n.* **1** Leave-taking; parting; especially, a formal leave-taking; also, permission to depart. **2** Dismissal. **3** *Obs.* A polite or formal bow. Also called *congee.* [OF *congié* <L *commeatus* leave of absence < *commeare* come and go < *com-* thoroughly + *ire* go]

con·geal (kən·jēl′) *v.t.* **1** To convert from a fluid to a solid condition, as by freezing or curdling. **2** To clot or coagulate, as blood. —*v.i.* **3** To become hard, stiff, or viscid. [<MF *congeler* <L *congelare* < *com-* together + *gelare* freeze < *gelum* frost] —**con·geal′a·ble** *adj.* —**con·geal′er** *n.* —**con·geal′ment** *n.*

con·gee[1] (kon′jē) *n. Anglo-Indian* Rice water; rice gruel or any similar gruel; rice starch.

con·gee[2] (kon·jē′) *n. Rare* Congé. —*v.i.* **·geed, ·gee·ing** To take formal leave; especially, to bow in leaving.

con·ge·la·tion (kon′jə·lā′shən) *n.* **1** A congealing. **2** A congealed state; clot; concretion. [<L *congelatio, -onis* < *congelare.* See CONGEAL.]

con·ge·ner (kon′jə·nər) *n.* A fellow member of the same genus, class, family, or kind. [<L, of the same race < *com-* together + *genus, generis* race, kind]

con·ge·ner·ic (kon′jə·ner′ik) *adj.* Of the same kind, class, or stock; generically allied. Also **con′ge·ner′i·cal, con·gen·er·ous** (kən·jen′ər·əs).

con·ge·net·ic (kon′jə·net′ik) *adj.* Alike in origin.

con·gen·ial (kən·jēn′yəl) *adj.* **1** Having similar character or tastes; sympathetic. **2** Suited to one's disposition; agreeable. See synonyms under DELIGHTFUL. [<CON- + GENIAL] —**con·ge·ni·al·i·ty** (kən·jē′nē·al′ə·tē) *n.* —**con·gen′·ial·ly** *adv.*

con·gen·i·tal (kən·jen′ə·təl) *adj.* **1** Born with a person; existing at or from birth. **2** Acquired by an individual organism in the course of uterine development subsequent to action by the genes but prior to delivery from the womb: distinguished from *hereditary.* See synonyms under INHERENT. [<L *congenitus* < *com-* together + *genitus,* pp. of *gignere* bear, produce] —**con·gen′i·tal·ly** *adv.*

con·ger (kong′gər) *n.* A marine eel (*Conger conger*) from 4 to 10 feet long, used as a food fish. Also **conger eel.** [<OF *congre* <L *conger* <Gk. *gongros*]

con·ge·ries (kon′jə·rēz, kon·jir′ēz) *n. pl.* **·ge·ries** A collection or aggregation of things; an assemblage of bodies; mass; heap. [<L < *congerere.* See CONGEST.]

con·gest (kən·jest′) *v.t.* **1** To collect or crowd together; overcrowd. **2** *Pathol.* To surcharge an organ or member with blood. **3** *Obs.* To collect; accumulate. —*v.i.* **4** To become congested. [<L *congestum,* pp. of *congerere* < *com-* together + *gerere* bear, carry] —**con·ges′tive** *adj.*

con·ges·tion (kən·jes′chən) *n.* **1** *Pathol.* An excessive accumulation, as of blood in the blood vessels. **2** An overcrowded condition.

con·gi·us (kon′jē·əs) *n. pl.* **con·gi·i** (kon′jē·ī) An ancient Roman liquid measure, containing 6 sextarii or about 0.75 U.S. gallon. [<L]

con·glo·bate (kon·glō′bāt, kong′glō·bāt) *v.t.* & *v.i.* **·bat·ed, ·bat·ing** To gather or form into a globe: also **con·globe** (kon·glōb′). —*adj.* Globular. [<L *conglobatus,* pp. of *conglobare* < *com-* together + *globare* make a ball < *globus* ball]

con·glo·ba·tion (kong′glō·bā′shən) *n.* **1** The act of conglobating. **2** A spherical body or formation.

con·glom·er·ate (kən·glom′ər·it) *adj.* **1** Massed or clustered. **2** *Geol.* Consisting of loosely cemented heterogeneous material: *conglomerate* clay. See synonyms under COMPLEX, HETEROGENEOUS. —*n.* **1** A heterogeneous collection. **2** A large corporation formed by merging a number of separate companies, often in unrelated fields. **3** *Geol.* A rock composed of pebbles or fragments of rock loosely cemented together. —*v.t.* & *v.i.* (kən·glom′ə·rāt) **·at·ed, ·at·ing** To gather into a cohering mass. [<L *conglomeratus,* pp. of *conglomerare* < *com-* together + *glomus, glomeris* ball] —**con·glom·er·at·ic** (kən·glom′ə·rat′ik) or **con·glom′er·it′ic** (-ə·rit′ik) *adj.*

con·glom·er·a·tion (kən·glom′ə·rā′shən) *n.* **1** A conglomerated mass. **2** The act of conglomerating.

con·glu·ti·nant (kən·glo͞o′tə·nənt) *adj.* **1** Causing to stick together. **2** *Med.* Healing by adhesion, as the edges of a wound. —*n. Med.* An application for wounds.

con·glu·ti·nate (kən·glo͞o′tə·nāt) *v.t.* & *v.i.* **·nat·ed, ·nat·ing 1** To glue or stick together; adhere. **2** *Med.* To reunite by adhesion, as wounds or fractures. —*adj.* **1** Glued together; united by adhesion. **2** *Bot.* United as if glued together, but not organically. [<L *conglutinatus,* pp. of *conglutinare* < *com-* together + *glutinare* stick < *gluten* glue] —**con·glu′ti·na′tion** *n.* —**con·glu′ti·na′tive** *adj.*

con·glu·ti·nous (kən·glo͞o′tə·nəs) *adj.* Causing adhesion; gluelike. —**con·glu′ti·nous·ly** *adv.*

con·go (kong′gō) *n.* **1** The congo snake. **2** The mud eel.

Con·go (kong′gō) *n.* A member of any of numerous Negro and Negroid tribes, mostly of Bantu linguistic stock, inhabiting equatorial and southern Africa. Also **Con·go·lese** (kong′gō·lēz′, -lēs′).

Con·go (kong′gō) One of the world's largest rivers, rising in SE Zaire Republic and flowing 2,900 miles to the South Atlantic.

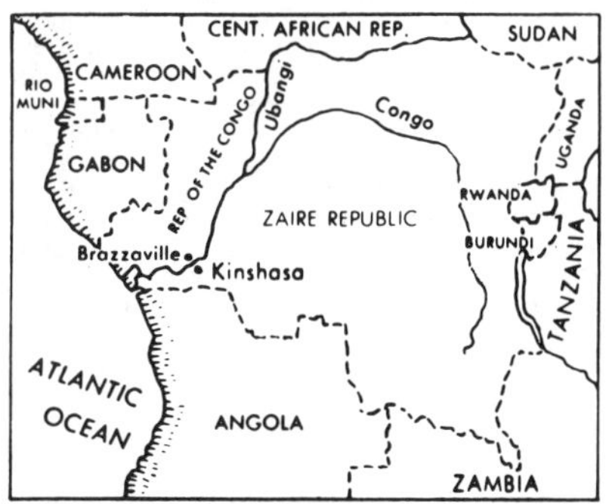

Congo, Democratic Republic of the See ZAIRE REPUBLIC.

Congo Free State A former name for REPUBLIC OF THE CONGO.

Congo group *Chem.* A class of direct dyes from benzidine or tolidine, mostly azo derivatives.

Con·go·lese (kong′gō·lēz′, -lēs′) *adj.* Pertaining to the region of the Congo or to the people inhabiting it. —*n.* A native or inhabitant of the Congo region.

Congo red *Chem.* A dye of the Congo group, used in dyeing cotton and wool, and in the making of **Congo paper,** which, used as an indicator, shows red in neutral or alkaline solutions and blue with acids.

Congo Republic An independent republic of the French Community in western equatorial Africa; 139,000 square miles; capital, Brazzaville: formerly *Middle Congo,* a French overseas territory. —**Con′go·lese′** *adj.* & *n.*

congo snake A tailed aquatic salamander (*Amphiuma means*) of the SE United States, of elongate eel-like form with rudimentary limbs. Also **congo eel.**

con·gou (kong′go͞o) *n.* A grade of black tea from China, the third picking. Also **con·go** (kong′gō), **con′gu.** [<Chinese *kung-fu(ch'a)* labor (tea); tea on which labor has been spent]

con·grat·u·late (kən·grach′o͝o·lāt) *v.t.* **·lat·ed, ·lat·ing 1** To express sympathetic pleasure in the joy, success, or good fortune of (another); felicitate. **2** *Obs.* To salute approvingly; welcome; hail. [<L *congratulatus,* pp. of *congratulari* < *com-* together + *gratulari* rejoice] —**con·grat′u·lant** *adj.* —**con·grat′u·la′tor** *n.* —**con·grat·u·la·to·ry** (kən·grach′o͝o·lə·tôr′ē, -tō′rē) *adj.*

con·grat·u·la·tion (kən·grach′o͝o·lā′shən) *n.* **1** The act of congratulating. **2** *pl.* Expressions of pleasure and good wishes on another's fortune or success; congratulatory speech or writing.

con·gre·gant (kong′grə·gənt) *n.* A member of a congregation; one who joins with others anywhere.

con·gre·gate (kong′grə·gāt) *v.t.* & *v.i.* **·gat·ed, ·gat·ing** To bring or come together into a crowd; assemble. —*adj.* (kong′grə·git) **1** Relating to a congregation. **2** Gathered together; collected. [<L *congregatus,* pp. of *congregare* < *com-* together + *gregare* crowd, collect < *grex, gregis* flock] —**con′gre·ga′tive** *adj.* —**con′gre·ga′tive·ly** *adv.* —**con′gre·ga′·tive·ness** *n.* —**con′gre·ga′tor** *n.*

con·gre·ga·tion (kong′grə·gā′shən) *n.* **1** The act of congregating; the collecting into one mass, body, or assembly; aggregation. **2** An assemblage of people or of things. **3** A group of people met together for worship; also, the body of persons who worship in a local church; a parish. **4** In the Old Testament, the whole body of Israel. **5** *Eccl.* A religious community or order bound by a common rule. **6** Any of several committees of cardinals who administer the departments of the papal government and assist the Pope. **7** In colonial New England, a town or settlement, considered as a religious community. See synonyms under ASSEMBLY, COMPANY. —**con′gre·ga′tion·al** *adj.*

Con·gre·ga·tion·al (kong′grə·gā′shən·əl) *adj.* Belonging or pertaining to the **Congregational Christian Churches,** an evangelical Protestant denomination, forming, since 1957, part of the *United Church of Christ.* See INDEPENDENT. —**Con′gre·ga′tion·al·ist** *n.*

con·gre·ga·tion·al·ism (kong′grə·gā′shən·əl·iz′·əm) *n.* A form of church polity in which each local congregation is autonomous in all ecclesiastical matters.

Congregation of the Holy Office In the Roman Catholic Church, a department of the Curia which defends the faith and supervises morals. See INQUISITION.

con·gress (kong′gris) *n.* **1** An assembly or conference; a gathering. **2** A coming together; intercourse. **3** Sexual union. —*v.i.* (kən·gres′) To assemble; meet together. [<L *congressus* a coming together < *congredi* < *com-* together + *gredi* go, move] —**con·gres·sive** (kən·gres′iv) *adj.*

Con·gress (kong′gris) *n.* **1** The national legislative body of the United States, consisting of the Senate and the House of Representatives. **2** The legislative body of any of several Central and South American republics, usually consisting of a Senate and a Chamber of Deputies.

congress boot A half-shoe or gaiter, with elastic material in the sides. Also **congress gaiter.**

con·gres·sion·al (kən·gresh′ən·əl) *adj.* Pertaining to a congress, especially, *cap.,* the United States Congress.

Congressional district That section of a State, determined by population figures, entitled to one representative in Congress.

con·gres·sion·al·ist (kən·gresh′ən·əl·ist) *n.* A supporter or adherent of a congress. Also **con·gres′sion·ist.**

Congressional Medal of Honor See MEDAL OF HONOR.

Congressional Record The printed debates and proceedings of Congress: the official government publication since 1873, replacing the former **Congressional Globe.**

Con·gress·man (kong′gris·mən) *n. pl.* **·men** (-mən) A member of the U.S. Congress, particularly of the House of Representatives. — **Con′gress·wom′an** *n. fem.*

Congress of Confederation Continental Congress.

Congress of Industrial Organizations A former affiliation of trade unions founded in 1938: it was originally an offshoot of the American Federation of Labor, and, in 1955, merged with it to form the *AFL–CIO.*

Congress of Vienna A conference of European powers, 1814–15, held after the first exile of Napoleon, and aiming, under Metternich's leadership, at territorial readjustment and restoration of monarchical governments.

Con·greve (kon′grēv, kong′-) *n.* **1** A variety of friction match: short for **Congreve match. 2** A military rocket invented in 1808: short for **Congreve rocket.** [after Sir William *Congreve,* who invented both]

Con·greve (kon′grēv, kong′-), **William,** 1670–1729, English dramatist. — **Sir William,** 1772–1828, English engineer.

con·gru·ence (kong′gro͞o·əns) *n.* Harmony, conformity; agreement. Also **con′gru·en·cy.**

con·gru·ent (kong′gro͞o·ənt) *adj.* **1** Having mutual agreement or conformity; correspondent; appropriate. **2** *Math.* Describing two geometric figures which may be exactly superposed on each other, or two numbers which will give the same remainders when divided by a given quantity called the *modulus.* [<L *congruens, -entis,* ppr. of *congruere* agree] — **con′gru·ent·ly** *adv.*

congruent forms In crystallography, two forms which may be derived from each other by the rotation of the crystal.

con·gru·i·ty (kən·gro͞o′ə·tē) *n. pl.* **·ties 1** Agreement; harmoniousness; appropriateness. **2** An example or case of harmoniousness. **3** Geometrical agreement.

con·gru·ous (kong′gro͞o·əs) *adj.* **1** Harmoniously related or combined. **2** Appropriate; consistent. **3** *Math.* Having congruence. [<L *congruus* < *congruere* agree] — **con′gru·ous·ly** *adv.* — **con′gru·ous·ness** *n.*

con·ic (kon′ik) *adj.* **1** Cone-shaped. **2** Relating to or formed by or upon a cone. Also **con′i·cal.** — *n.* A conic section. [<Gk. *kōnikos* < *kōnos* cone] — **con′i·cal·ly** *adv.*

conic projection A type of map in which the terrain is plotted on a cone, the projection then being flattened out to a plane surface.

conic section *Math.* A curve formed by the intersection of a plane with a right circular cone: an ellipse, parabola, or hyperbola, according to the inclination of the cutting plane to the axis.

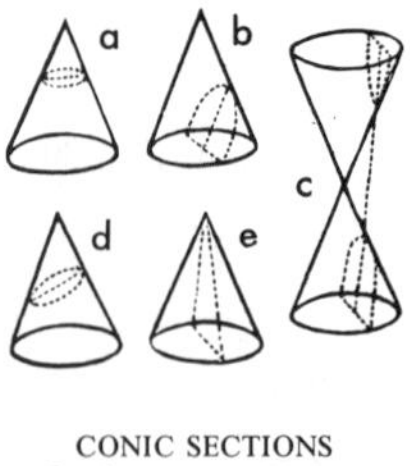

CONIC SECTIONS
a. Circle. *b.* Parabola. *c.* Hyperbola. *d.* Ellipse. *e.* Right line.

conic sections That branch of mathematics which treats of the ellipse, parabola, and hyperbola. Also **con′ics.**

co·nid·i·if·er·ous (kō·nid′ē·if′ər·əs) *adj. Bot.* Bearing conidia. Also **co·nid′i·oph′o·rous** (-of′ər·əs). [<CONIDIUM + -FEROUS]

co·nid·i·o·phore (kō·nid′ē·ə·fôr′, -fōr′) *n. Bot.* A branch of the hypha in the mycelium of fungi which bears the conidia.

co·nid·i·um (kō·nid′ē·əm) *n. pl.* **co·nid·i·a** (kō·nid′ē·ə) *Bot.* A non-sexually produced propagative cell or spore borne upon special branches of the thallus in many species of fungi. Also **co·nid·i·o·spore** (kō·nid′ē·ə·spôr′, -spōr′). [<NL <Gk. *konis* dust] — **co·nid′i·al** *adj.*

con·i·fer (kon′ə·fər, kō′nə-) *n.* Any of an order of evergreen shrubs and trees *(Coniferales)* belonging to the Gymnosperm subdivision of plants, characterized by needle-shaped leaves, strobili or cones, and a resinous wood: includes the pines, spruces, firs, and junipers. [<L < *conus* cone + *ferre* bear]

co·nif·er·in (kō·nif′ər·in) *n. Chem.* A crystalline compound, $C_{16}H_{22}O_8 \cdot 2H_2O$, found in the sap of coniferous trees: used in the preparation of vanillin.

co·nif·er·ous (kō·nif′ər·əs) *adj.* **1** Cone-bearing. **2** Containing or composed of conifers: *coniferous* forests.

co·ni·ine (kō′ni·ēn, -nē·in) *n. Chem.* A yellowish, oily, volatile alkaloid, $C_8H_{17}N$, contained in poison hemlock *(Conium maculatum)*: a narcotic, sometimes used locally to relieve pain. Also **co·nin** (kō′nin), **co·nine** (kō′nēn). [<CONIUM]

co·ni·ol·o·gy (kō′nē·ol′ə·jē) *n.* The scientific study of dust, especially with reference to its effects upon plant and animal life: also spelled *koniology.* [<Gk. *konis* dust + -LOGY]

co·ni·ros·tral (kō′ni·ros′trəl) *adj. Ornithol.* Having a conical beak. [<L *conus* cone + *rostrum* beak]

co·ni·um (kō′nē·əm) *n.* Any of a genus *(Conium)* of tall, highly poisonous, biennial herbs of the parsley family; especially, *C. maculatum,* the poison hemlock. [<L <Gk. *kōneion* hemlock]

con·jec·tur·al (kən·jek′chər·əl) *adj.* **1** Of the nature of or dependent upon conjecture. **2** Given to conjecturing. — **con·jec′tur·al·ly** *adv.*

con·jec·ture (kən·jek′chər) *v.t.* **·tured, ·tur·ing** To conclude or suppose from incomplete evidence; guess; infer. — *v.i.* To make a conjecture. See synonyms under GUESS, SUPPOSE. — *n.* **1** An indecisive opinion; a guess; surmise. **2** The act of conjecturing. **3** *Obs.* Divination; prediction. See synonyms under GUESS, HYPOTHESIS. [<L *conjectura* < *conjicere* < *com-* together + *jacere* throw] — **con·jec′tur·a·ble** *adj.* — **con·jec′tur·a·bly** *adv.* — **con·jec′tur·er** *n.*

con·join (kən·join′) *v.t. & v.i.* To join together; associate; connect; unite. See synonyms under UNITE. [<F *conjoindre* <L *conjungere* < *com-* together + *jungere* join]

con·joint (kən·joint′) *adj.* **1** Associated; conjoined. **2** Joint. [<F, pp. of *conjoindre.* See CONJOIN.] — **con·joint′ly** *adv.*

con·ju·gal (kon′jo͝o·gəl) *adj.* Pertaining to marriage; connubial; matrimonial. [<F <L *conjugalis* < *conjunx, conjugis* spouse < *conjungere* join in marriage] — **con·ju·gal·i·ty** (kon′jo͝o·gal′ə·tē) *n.* — **con′ju·gal·ly** *adv.*

con·ju·gate (kon′jo͝o·gāt) *v.* **·gat·ed, ·gat·ing** *v.t.* **1** *Gram.* To give the inflections of: said of verbs. **2** *Rare* To unite or join together; couple, especially in marriage. — *v.i.* **3** *Biol.* To unite in conjugation. **4** *Rare* To unite in sexual intercourse. — *adj.* (kon′jo͝o·git, -gāt) **1** Joined in pairs; coupled; paired. **2** *Math.* Reciprocally related; interchangeable. **3** *Chem.* Containing two or more radicals acting as one. **4** *Bot.* Composed of two leaflets: said of a pinnate leaf. **5** Kindred in origin and, usually, meaning: said of words; paronymous. Also **con′ju·gat′ed.** — *n.* (kon′jo͝o·git, -gāt) **1** A word closely related to, and usually of kindred meaning with, another or others. **2** A member of a conjugate pair. Also **con′·ju·gant.** [<L *conjugatus,* pp. of *conjugare* < *com-* together + *jugare* < *jugum* yoke] — **con′ju·ga′tive** *adj.* — **con′ju·ga′tor** *n.*

conjugate angle See under ANGLE.

con·ju·ga·tion (kon′jo͝o·gā′shən) *n.* **1** Conjunction; union. **2** *Gram.* The inflection of a verb, or the expression of such inflection; also, a class of verbs similarly inflected, or the mode of inflection. **3** *Biol.* The temporary fusion of two similar protozoans during which exchange of nuclear material takes place.

con·ju·ga·tion·al (kon′jo͝o·gā′shən·əl) *adj.* **1** Of or pertaining to conjugation. **2** *Anat.* Situated at the junction of two bones. — **con′·ju·ga′tion·al·ly** *adv.*

con·junct (kən·jungkt′, kon′jungkt) *adj.* Joined together; conjoined. [<L *conjunctus,* pp. of *conjungere.* See CONJOIN.] — **con·junct′ly** *adv.*

con·junc·tion (kən·jungk′shən) *n.* **1** The state of being joined together, or the things so joined; combination; league. **2** *Astron.* The position of an inferior planet when it is on a direct line with the earth and the sun, or of a superior planet when the sun is on the direct line between it and the earth. **3** Simultaneous occurrence of events. **4** *Gram.* A word used to connect words, phrases, clauses, or sentences: one of the eight traditional parts of speech. See synonyms under ASSOCIATION, UNION. — **coordinate conjunction** A conjunction, as *and, but, or,* which joins words or groups of words of equal rank. — **subordinate conjunction** A conjunction, as *as, because, if, that, though,* which joins clauses of minor rank to principal clauses. — **con·junc′tion·al** *adj.* — **con·junc′tion·al·ly** *adv.*

con·junc·ti·va (kon′jungk·tī′və) *n. pl.* **·vas** or **·vae** (-vē) *Anat.* The mucous membrane lining the eyelids and covering the anterior part of the eyeball. See illustration under EYE. [<NL *(membrana) conjunctiva* connective (membrane)]

con·junc·ti·val (kon′jungk·tī′vəl) *adj.* **1** Serving to join or connect. **2** Of or pertaining to the conjunctiva.

con·junc·tive (kən·jungk′tiv) *adj.* **1** Joining; connective: *conjunctive* tissue. **2** Joined together. **3** *Gram.* **a** Serving to unite words, clauses, etc.; used as a conjunction: a *conjunctive* adverb. **b** Serving to unite both meaning and construction, as the conjunction *and.* — *n. Gram.* A conjunctive word. [<L *conjunctivus* < *conjungere.* See CONJOIN.] — **con·junc′tive·ly** *adv.*

con·junc·ti·vi·tis (kən·jungk′tə·vī′tis) *n. Pathol.* Inflammation of the conjunctiva; ophthalmia.

con·junc·ture (kən·jungk′chər) *n.* **1** A combination of circumstances; juncture; also, a crisis. **2** The act of joining; union.

con·ju·ra·tion (kon′jo͝o·rā′shən) *n.* **1** An enchantment; incantation; spell. **2** Magic or a magical expression used in an appeal for supernatural aid. **3** A solemn invocation; adjuration.

con·jure (kən·jo͝or′ *for v. defs. 1 and 6*; kon′jər, kun′- *for v. defs. 2–5*) *v.* **·jured, ·jur·ing** *v.t.* **1** To call on or appeal to solemnly; adjure. **2** To summon, bring, or drive away by incantation or spell, as a devil or spirit. **3** To accomplish or effect by or as by magic. — *v.i.* **4** To practice magic or legerdemain. **5** To summon a devil or spirit by incantation. **6** *Obs.* To conspire. — *adj.* (kon′jər, kun′-) *U.S. Dial.* Given to practicing magic or curing by magic: a *conjure* man. [<OF *conjurer* <L *conjurare* < *com-* together + *jurare* swear]

con·jur·er (kon′jər·ər, kun′- *for defs. 1 and 2,* kən·jo͝or′ər *for defs. 3 and 4*) *n.* **1** One who practices legerdemain; a juggler. **2** One who practices magic or works through supernatural powers; specifically, an Indian or Negro medicine man. **3** One who appeals or invokes solemnly. **4** *Obs.* A conspirator.

con·ju·ry (kon′jər·ē, kun′-) *n. pl.* **·ries** The practice of magic.

conk (kongk) *n. Slang* **1** The head. **2** *Brit.* The nose. — *v.t.* To hit on the head. — **to conk out** To stall or fail: said of a motor or engine. [? <CONCH]

con man (kon) *Slang* A confidence man.

conn (kon) See CON².

Con·nacht (kon′əkht, kon′ət) A province of western Ireland; 6,611 square miles. Also **Con·naught** (kon′ôt).

con·nate (kon′āt) *adj.* **1** Born in and with one; innate; congenital. **2** Born or existing together or with another; cognate. **3** *Biol.* Congenitally or firmly united, as the parts of an organism. [<L *connatus,* pp. of *connasci,* var. of *cognasci.* See COGNATE.] — **con′·nate·ly** *adv.* — **con′nate·ness** *n.*

con·na·tion (kə·nā′shən) *n.* The state of being connate; congenital union.

con·nat·u·ral (kə·nach′ər·əl) *adj.* **1** Innate; congenital; inborn. **2** Allied; cognate. Also spelled *conatural.* [<Med. L *connaturalis* < *com-* together + *naturalis* NATURAL] — **con·nat′u·ral·ly** *adv.*

con·naught (kon′ôt) A cotton cloth used as a foundation for embroidery. [from *Connaught,* var. of *Connacht*]

con·nect (kə·nekt′) *v.t.* **1** To join together as by links or fastenings; unite or combine. **2** To bring into correlation; associate. **3** To think of as being similar or related; associate mentally. **4** To close or complete, as an electric circuit or telephone connection. — *v.i.* **5** To unite or join; be in close relation; be associated. **6** To meet as scheduled, as buses or trains, for transference of passengers. 7 *U.S. Colloq.* In some sports, to hit the ball or mark. [<L *connectere*, var. of *conectere* <*com-* together + *nectere* bind]

Con·nect·i·cut (kə·net′ə·kət) A State of the NE United States: 5,009 square miles; capital, Hartford; entered the Union Jan. 9, 1788, one of the original thirteen States: nickname, *Nutmeg State.* Abbr. CT

Connecticut River The largest river of New England, flowing 345 miles between Vermont and New Hampshire, and through Massachusetts and Connecticut to Long Island Sound.

connecting rod *Mech.* A rod or bar in an engine, joining two or more moving parts.

con·nec·tion (kə·nek′shən) *n.* **1** The act or means of connecting or the state of being connected; union; combination. **2 a** Family relationship, especially by marriage. **b** A distant relative. **3** A company; denomination; a body of persons connected, or with whom one is connected, by relationship, belief, dealings, etc. **4** A direct transfer from one route to another, as in railway service. **5** Logical coherence or consistency, as the parts of an address. **6** That which connects or serves as a bond of union: There is no *connection* between the two. **7** A mechanism or apparatus which serves to form a union of parts; specifically, a connecting rod or a connecting passageway in a series of flues. Also *Brit.* **con·nex′ion.** See synonyms under ASSOCIATION, KINSMAN. —**con·nec′tion·al** *adj.*

con·nec·tive (kə·nek′tiv) *adj.* Capable of connecting, or serving to connect; causing or involving connection. —*n.* **1** That which connects. **2** *Gram.* A connecting word or particle, as a conjunction. **3** *Bot.* The portion of the filament of a stamen that unites the lobes of an anther. —**con·nec′tive·ly** *adv.*

connective tissue *Anat.* The fibrous tissue that pervades the whole body and serves to unite and support the various parts, as cartilage, bone, or tendon.

con·nec·tiv·i·ty (kon′ek·tiv′ə·tē) *n.* The property of being connective; order of connection.

con·nec·tor (kə·nek′tər) *n.* A person or thing that connects. Also **con·nect′er.**

Con·nel·ly (kon′əl·ē), **Marc,** born 1890, U.S. playwright: full name *Marcus Cook Connelly.*

con·ner[1] (kon′ər) *n.* **1** *Archaic* An inspector; a tester. **2** One who studies and peruses. [OE *cunnere* <*cunnian* test]

con·ner[2] (kon′ər) *n. Naut.* One who directs the steering of a ship from some point of observation. [<CON[2]]

con·ning–tow·er (kon′ing·tou′ər) *n.* **1** The armored pilothouse on the deck of a warship. **2** In submarines, an observation tower serving also as an entrance.

con·nip·tion (kə·nip′shən) *n. U.S. Colloq.* A fit of hysteria, rage, etc. Also **conniption fit.** [Cf. dial. E (Northern) *canapshus* ill–tempered]

con·ni·vance (kə·nī′vəns) *n.* **1** The act or fact of conniving. **2** Silent or indirect assent, especially to wrongdoing. **3** *Law* A guilty assent to or knowledge of a wrongful or criminal act during its occurrence. Also **con·ni′van·cy.**

con·nive (kə·nīv′) *v.i.* **·nived, ·niv·ing 1** To encourage or assent to a wrong by silence or feigned ignorance: with *at.* **2** To be in collusion: with *with.* [<L *connivere*, var. of *conivere* wink, shut the eyes] —**con·niv′er** *n.*

con·ni·vent (kə·nī′vənt) *adj. Biol.* Converging, as stamens or wings. [<L *connivens, -entis*, pp. of *connivere.* See CONNIVE.]

con·nois·seur (kon′ə·sûr′) *n.* A competent critical judge of anything, especially in matters of art and taste. [<F]

Con·nol·ly (kon′əl·ē), **James,** 1870–1916, Irish socialist; executed.

con·no·ta·tion (kon′ə·tā′shən) *n.* **1** The suggestive emotional content or significance of a word, additional to its explicit literal meaning; implication. **2** The act of connoting or connotating, and the quality or qualities connoted. [<Med. L *connotatio, -onis* < *connotare.* See CONNOTE.]

con·no·ta·tive (kon′ə·tā′tiv, kə·nō′tə·tiv) *adj.* **1** Having the quality of connoting. **2** Implying a correlative. —**con′no·ta′tive·ly** *adv.*

con·note (kə·nōt′) *v.t.* **·not·ed, ·not·ing** To indicate or imply along with the literal meaning; mention by implication. Also **con·no·tate** (kon′ə·tāt). [<Med. L *connotare* <*com-* together + *notare* mark]

con·nu·bi·al (kə·nōō′bē·əl, -nyōō′-) *adj.* Pertaining to matrimony; relating to husband or wife; matrimonial; conjugal; nuptial. [<L *connubialis* <*connubium* <*com-* together + *nubere* marry] —**con·nu·bi·al·i·ty** (kə·nōō′·bē·al′ə·tē, -nyōō′-) *n.* —**con·nu′bi·al·ly** *adv.*

cono– *combining form* Cone; conical. Also, before vowels, **con–.** [<Gk. *kōnos* cone]

co·no·dont (kō′nə·dont, kon′ə-) *n. Paleontol.* A small toothlike fossil, found in Paleozoic rocks. [<CON(O)- + Gk. *odous, odontos* tooth]

co·noid (kō′noid) *adj.* Cone–shaped; conical. —*n.* Something having the form of a cone. [< Gk. *kōnoeidēs* conical] —**co·noi·dal** (kō·noid′l), **co·noi′dic** *adj.*

co·no·scen·te (kō′nō·shen′tā) See COGNOSCENTE.

co·no·scope (kō′nə·skōp, kon′ə-) *n.* A polariscope for examining crystals under converging light rays. [<CONO- + -SCOPE]

con·quer (kong′kər) *v.t.* **1** To overcome or subdue by force, as in war; vanquish. **2** To acquire or gain control of by or as by force of arms. **3** To overcome by mental or moral force; surmount. —*v.i.* **4** To be victorious. [<OF *conquerre* <L *conquirere* <*com-* thoroughly + *quaerere* seek] —**con′quer·a·ble** *adj.*

Synonyms: beat, checkmate, crush, defeat, discomfit, down, humble, master, overcome, overmaster, overmatch, overpower, overthrow, reduce, rout, subdue, subject, subjugate, surmount, triumph, vanquish, win, worst. A country is *conquered* when its armies are totally defeated and its territory is occupied by the enemy; it may be *subjected* to indemnity or to various disabilities; it is *subjugated* when it is held helplessly under military control; it is *subdued* when all resistance has died out. Any army is *defeated* when forcibly driven back; it is *routed* when it is converted into a mob of fugitives. Compare BAFFLE, BEAT, GAIN, HINDER, SUBDUE. *Antonyms*: capitulate, cede, fail, fall, fly, forfeit, lose, resign, retreat, submit, succumb, surrender, yield.

con·quer·ing (kong′kər·ing) *adj.* Overcoming; victorious. —**con′quer·ing·ly** *adv.*

con·quer·or (kong′kər·ər) *n.* One who conquers, subdues, or overcomes. —**the Conqueror** William, Duke of Normandy, who became William I of England when he won the battle of Hastings in 1066.

con·quest (kon′kwest, kong′-) *n.* **1** The act of conquering. **2** The thing conquered; that which is captured and taken forcibly, as territory, a person, or the favor of a person. See synonyms under VICTORY. —**the Conquest** The Norman Conquest. [<OF, pp. of *conquerre.* See CONQUER.]

con·qui·an (kong′kē·ən) *n.* A two–handed card game resembling rummy, requiring 40 cards: also spelled *cooncan.* [<Sp. *con quien* with whom]

con·quis·ta·dor (kon·kwis′tə·dôr, *Sp.* kōng·kēs′·tä·thōr′) *n. pl.* **·dors,** *Sp.* **·do·res** (-thō′räs) A conqueror; specifically, any of the Spanish conquerors of Mexico and Peru in the 16th century. [<Sp. <*conquistar* conquer]

Con·rad (kon′rad) A masculine personal name. Also *Fr.* **Con·rade** (kôn·råd′), *Lat.* **Con·ra·dus** (kon·rā′dəs), *Sp.* **Con·ra·do** (kōn·rä′thō). [< Gmc., bold counsel]

Con·rad (kon′rad), **Joseph,** 1857–1924, English author born in Poland: real name *Teodor Jozef Korzeniowski.*

con·san·guin·e·ous (kon′sang·gwin′ē·əs) *adj.* **1** Descended from the same parent or ancestor; akin. **2** Of or pertaining to consanguinity. Also **con·san·guine** (kon·sang′gwin), **con′san·guin′e·al.** [<L *consanguineus* <*com-* together + *sanguis* blood] —**con′san·guin′e·ous·ly** *adv.*

con·san·guin·i·ty (kon′sang·gwin′ə·tē) *n.* **1** The relationship that proceeds from a common ancestry; blood relationship. **2** Any near affinity or relationship. See synonyms under AFFINITY, KIN.

con·science (kon′shəns) *n.* **1** Moral consciousness in general; the activity or faculty by which distinctions are made between right and wrong in one's own conduct and character; the act or power of moral discrimination; ethical judgment or sensibility. **2** Conformity in conduct to one's conceptions of right and wrong. **3** *Obs.* Consciousness. —**in (all) conscience 1** In truth; in reason and honesty. **2** Certainly; assuredly. [<F <L *conscientia* <*com-* together + *scire* know] —**con′science·less** *adj.*

conscience clause A clause in a law which specially relieves persons who have conscientious scruples from performing acts enjoined therein: referring generally to laws relating to religious matters.

conscience money Money secretly paid to atone for some concealed act of dishonesty.

con·sci·en·tious (kon′shē·en′shəs) *adj.* Governed or dictated by conscience; scrupulous. —**con′sci·en′tious·ly** *adv.* —**con′sci·en′·tious·ness** *n.*

conscientious objector One who, on grounds of religious or moral convictions, objects to warfare and refuses to perform military service.

con·scion·a·ble (kon′shən·ə·bəl) *adj.* Conformable to conscience or right. —**con′scion·a·bly** *adv.*

con·scious (kon′shəs) *adj.* **1** Immediately aware of; mentally recognizing, to some degree and extent, one's own inner feeling and thought, or their objective reference. **2** Unjustifiably embarrassed by the sense of one's own individuality; self–conscious. **3** Mentally alert; well aware of some object, impression, or truth. **4** Present in the mind; recognized as belonging to oneself: *conscious* superiority. **5** Cognizant of guilt or fault. **6** Deliberate: a *conscious* lie. **7** Pertaining to consciousness. **8** Having the faculty and psychical attributes of consciousness. **9** *Obs.* Possessing knowledge in common with another; mutually informed. —*n. Psychoanal.* That part of mental life of which an individual is aware.[< L *conscius* <*com-* together + *scire* know] —**con′scious·ly** *adv.*

Synonyms (adj.): aware, cognizant, sensible. One is *aware* of that which exists without him; he is *conscious* of the inner workings of his own mind. *Sensible* may be used in the exact sense of *conscious*, or it may partake of both the senses mentioned above. One may be *sensible* of his own or another's error; he is *conscious* only of his own. A person may feel *assured* or *sure* of something false or non–existent; what he is *aware* of, still more what he is *conscious* of, must be fact. *Sensible* has often a reference to the emotions, where *conscious* might apply only to the intellect; to say a culprit is *sensible* of his degradation is more forcible than to say he is *conscious* of it. *Antonyms*: dead, deaf, ignorant, insensible, unaware, unconscious.

con·scious·ness (kon′shəs·nis) *n.* **1** The state of being conscious; sensation; knowledge. **2** The power of self–knowledge; internal perception. **3** The aggregate of the conscious states in an individual or a group of persons. **4** The awareness of some particular object, state, agency, or influence; an intuition. **5** Any form of intellectual activity or its product in direct and convincing knowledge, whether of external or internal objects. See synonyms under FEELING, MIND.

con·script (kon′skript) *adj.* **1** Registered; enrolled. **2** Compulsorily enlisted, as a soldier or an armed force. —*n.* One who is compulsorily enrolled for military service; a draftee. —*v.t.* (kən·skript′) To force into military service; draft. [<L *conscriptus*, pp. of *conscribere* enrol <*com-* together + *scribere* write]

conscript fathers 1 The senators of ancient Rome; also, the senators of medieval Venice. **2** The members of any legislative body.

con·scrip·tion (kən·skrip′shən) *n.* A compulsory enrolment of men for military service; draft.

con·se·crate (kon′sə·krāt) *v.t.* **·crat·ed, ·crat·ing 1** To set apart as sacred; dedicate to sacred uses with appointed ceremonies; to *consecrate* a church, a bishop, or the elements of the Eucharist. **2** To dedicate solemnly, as from emotions of gratitude or convictions of duty; devote: He *consecrated* his life to the cause. **3** To apotheosize; canonize. **4** To make reverend or venerable; hallow: *consecrated* by time. —*adj.* Hallowed; consecrated. [<L *consecratus,* pp. of *consecrare* <*com-* thoroughly + *sacer* holy] —**con′se·cra′tor** *n.* —**con·se·cra·to·ry** (kon′sə·krə·tôr′ē, -tō′rē) *adj.*

con·se·cra·tion (kon′sə·krā′shən) *n.* **1** The act or ceremony of separating from a common to a sacred use; the state of being consecrated. **2** Canonization, as of a saint; apotheosis, as of a god.

con·se·cu·tion (kon′sə·kyōō′shən) *n.* **1** Actual, logical, or grammatical sequence. **2** *Music* A succession of similar intervals in harmony. **3** Any succession or series. [<L *consecutio, -onis* <*consequi.* See CONSEQUENT.]

con·sec·u·tive (kən·sek′yə·tiv) *adj.* **1** Following in uninterrupted succession; successive. **2** Characterized by logical sequence. **3** Following as a consequence or result; consequent. **4** *Gram.* Denoting result or consequence. [<L *consecutus,* pp. of *consequi.* See CONSEQUENT.] —**con·sec′u·tive·ly** *adv.* —**con·sec′u·tive·ness** *n.*

consecutive fifths *Music* Progressions of perfect fifths or octaves, permissible for intentional emphasis. Also **consecutive octaves, con·sec′u·tives.**

con·sen·su·al (kən·sen′shōō·əl) *adj.* **1** *Law* Existing merely by virtue of acquiescence. **2** *Physiol.* **a** Excited by sympathetic or reflex action. **b** Denoting instinctive and reflex actions and movements which are stimulated by conscious sensations. —**con·sen′su·al·ly** *adv.*

con·sen·sus (kən·sen′səs) *n.* A collective opinion; general agreement. [<L <*consentire* <*com-* together + *sentire* feel, think]

con·sent (kən·sent′) *v.i.* **1** To yield or accede, as to a proposal or request, when one has the right, power, or wish not to do so. **2** To give assent, as to a contract; agree. **3** *Obs.* To agree together; accord. See synonyms under AGREE, ASSENT. —*n.* **1** A voluntary yielding of the will, judgment, or inclination to what is proposed or desired by another; acquiescence; compliance. **2** Harmony in opinion or sentiment; agreement; concord. **3** *Law* A rational and voluntary concurrence in an act or contract. **4** *Obs.* Harmonious correspondence or operation. See synonyms under HARMONY, PERMISSION. [<OF *consentir* <L *consentire.* See CONSENSUS.] —**con·sent′er** *n.*

con·sen·ta·ne·ous (kon′sen·tā′nē·əs) *adj.* **1** Mutually consenting or agreeing; acquiescent. **2** Simultaneous. [<L *consentaneus* agreeing] —**con·sen·ta·ne·i·ty** (kən·sen′tə·nē′ə·tē), **con′sen·ta′ne·ous·ness** *n.* —**con′sen·ta′ne·ous·ly** *adv.*

con·sent·i·ble (kən·sen′tə·bəl) *adj.* Capable of being established or fixed by consent of those interested.

con·sen·tience (kən·sen′shəns) *n.* **1** The state or quality of being in agreement or accord. **2** *Psychol.* The sensuous analog, in automatic or reflex action, of consciousness in conscious action. —**con·sen′tient** *adj.*

con·se·quence (kon′sə·kwens, -kwəns) *n.* **1** That which naturally follows from a preceding action or condition; the effect of a cause; result. **2** The conclusion of a syllogism; inference; deduction. **3** The relation between an antecedent and a consequent; causal or logical consecution; sequence. **4** Distinction; note: said of persons: a man of *consequence*; also, significance; moment: said of things: an event of no *consequence.* **5** Self-importance; consequentiality: used of persons.

Synonyms: consequent, effect, end, event, issue, outcome, outgrowth, result, sequel, upshot. Compare ACCIDENT, CAUSE, CIRCUMSTANCE, DEMONSTRATION, END, EVENT, INFERENCE.

con·se·quent (kon′sə·kwent, -kwənt) *adj.* **1** Following as a natural result or as a logical conclusion. **2** Characterized by correctness of reasoning; logical. —*n.* **1** The conclusion of an inference or syllogism; consequence. **2** That which follows something else, as in time, order, or relation, without causal connection: opposed to *antecedent.* **3** *Math.* **a** The second term of a ratio. **b** In a series of four proportionals, the second and fourth terms. **4** Having a course or direction depending on or resulting from the original slope of the surface. See synonyms under CONSEQUENCE. [<L *consequens, -entis,* ppr. of *consequi* < *com-* together + *sequi* follow]

con·se·quen·tial (kon′sə·kwen′shəl) *adj.* **1** Having or showing importance; self-important. **2** Following logically; consequent. —**con·se·quen·ti·al·i·ty** (kon′sə·kwen′shē·al′ə·tē), **con′se·quen′tial·ness** *n.* —**con′se·quen′tial·ly** *adv.*

con·se·quent·ly (kon′sə·kwent′lē, -kwənt·lē) *adv.* As a result; therefore. See synonyms under THEREFORE.

con·ser·van·cy (kən·sûr′vən·sē) *n. pl.* **·cies** **1** The act of conserving. **2** A board or commission to conserve fisheries, waterways, etc. —**con·ser′vant** *adj.*

con·ser·va·tion (kon′sər·vā′shən) *n.* **1** The act of keeping or protecting from loss or injury: the *conservation* of health, or of social order. **2** The preservation of natural resources for economical use; specifically, the preservation of forests, fisheries, harbors, etc. [<L *conservatio, -onis* <*conservare.* See CONSERVE.] —**con′ser·va′tion·al** *adj.* —**con′ser·va′tion·al·ly** *adv.* —**con′ser·va′tion·ist** *n.*

conservation of energy *Physics* The principle that in any closed material system the total amount of energy remains constant, though it may assume different forms successively.

conservation of mass *Physics* The principle that the total mass of any material system remains constant through all changes taking place within the system.

con·ser·va·tism (kən·sûr′və·tiz′əm) *n.* Conservative principles and practices, as in criticism, theology, politics, etc.; disposition or tendency to be conservative.

con·ser·va·tive (kən·sûr′və·tiv) *adj.* **1** Adhering to and tending to preserve the existing order of things; opposed to change or progress. **2** Conserving; preservative. **3** Moderate; cautious; within a safe margin: a *conservative* estimate or statement. —*n.* A conservative person. —**con·ser′va·tive·ly** *adv.* —**con·ser′va·tive·ness** *n.*

Con·ser·va·tive (kən·sûr′və·tiv) *adj.* In Great Britain or the British Commonwealth, of or pertaining to the Conservative party. —*n.* A member of this party.

Conservative Judaism Judaism as practiced especially in the U.S. by those who hold that both the Scriptures and the oral laws are divinely authoritative but that traditional rituals may be selectively observed or modified to accord with contemporary cultural conditions. Compare ORTHODOX JUDAISM, REFORM JUDAISM.

Conservative Party **1** In Great Britain, the name of the right-wing party since about 1832, opposed by the Labour party. See TORY. **2** In many dominions of the British Commonwealth, the political party of the right wing.

con·ser·va·tize (kən·sûr′və·tīz) *v.t.* & *v.i.* **·tized, ·tiz·ing** To convert to or adopt conservatism. Also *Brit.* **con·ser′va·tise.**

con·ser·va·tor (kon′sər·vā′tər, kən·sûr′və·tər) *n.* A protector; guardian; keeper.

con·ser·va·to·ry (kən·sûr′və·tôr′ē, -tō′rē) *n. pl.* **·ries** **1** A small greenhouse or glass-enclosed room in which plants are grown and displayed. **2** A school of art, especially of music. **3** *Obs.* A place for the preservation or protection of anything: also **con·ser·va·toire** (kən·sûr′və·twär′). —*adj.* Adapted to preserve.

con·serve (kən·sûrv′) *v.t.* **·served, ·serv·ing** **1** To keep from loss, decay, or depletion; supervise and protect. **2** To preserve with sugar. —*n.* (kon′sûrv, kən·sûrv′) **1** A kind of jam made of several fruits stewed together in sugar, often with nuts, raisins, etc. **2** A medicated confection of fresh vegetable substances and sugar. See synonyms under PRESERVE. [<F *conserver* <L *conservare* <*com-* thoroughly + *servare* keep, save] —**con·serv′a·ble** *adj.* —**con·serv′er** *n.*

con·sid·er (kən·sid′ər) *v.t.* **1** To think about or deliberate upon; examine mentally. **2** To look upon or regard as; think to be. **3** To hold as an opinion: with a clause as object. **4** To make allowance for; keep in mind. **5** To take into account; have a regard for: to *consider* the feelings of others. **6** *Archaic* To observe closely. **7** *Obs.* To fee; remunerate. —*v.i.* **8** To think closely; cogitate. [<F *considérer* <L *considerare,* ? <*com-* thoroughly + *sidus, sideris* star; with ref. to astrology]

Synonyms: contemplate, deliberate, examine, meditate, ponder, reflect, study, think, weigh. See CALCULATE, DELIBERATE, ESTEEM, EXAMINE, MUSE. *Antonyms*: disregard, forget, ignore, neglect, overlook, slight, trifle.

con·sid·er·a·ble (kən·sid′ər·ə·bəl) *adj.* **1** Somewhat large in amount, extent, etc. **2** Worthy of consideration by reason of size or quantity; a good deal of; a large part or portion of: He gave his friends *considerable* trouble; *Considerable* fruit has been spoiled. See synonyms under GOOD, LARGE. —*n.* A good deal; much; a pretty large amount. —**con·sid′er·a·bly** *adv.*

con·sid·er·ate (kən·sid′ər·it) *adj.* **1** Exhibiting or given to consideration. **2** Thoughtful; kind; prudent. See synonyms under CHARITABLE, THOUGHTFUL. —**con·sid′er·ate·ly** *adv.* —**con·sid′er·ate·ness** *n.*

con·sid·er·a·tion (kən·sid′ə·rā′shən) *n.* **1** The act of considering. **2** Thoughtful and kindly feeling or treatment. **3** A circumstance to be taken into account. **4** Something given in return for a service; remuneration. **5** Importance; consequence; standing. **6** *Law* The thing given or done, or to be given, done, or abstained from, by one party to a contract, in exchange for the act or promise of the other. Also *Obs.* **con·sid′er·ance.** See synonyms under FRIENDSHIP, PRUDENCE, REASON, REFLECTION, THOUGHT. [<F *considération* <L *consideratio, -onis* <*considerare.* See CONSIDER.]

con·sid·ered (kən·sid′ərd) *adj.* Premeditated; deliberated.

con·sid·er·ing (kən·sid′ər·ing) *prep.* In view of; taking into account the fact of: *Considering* his deafness, he takes a large part in the conversation. —*adv. Colloq.* Taking all the facts into account: He came out quite well, *considering.* —*conj.* In view of: *Considering* how I feel, you're lucky to see me at all.

con·sign (kən·sīn′) *v.t.* **1** To entrust or commit to the care of another. **2** To make over or relegate: They *consigned* his memory to oblivion. **3** To forward or deliver, as merchandise, for sale or disposal. **4** To set apart or devote, as for a specific purpose or use. **5** *Obs.* To impress, as with a seal; sign. —*v.i.* **6** *Obs.* To yield oneself; consent. See synonyms under COMMIT. [<F *consigner* <L *consignare* <*com-* with + *signum* a seal] —**con·sign′a·ble** *adj.* —**con·sign·or** (kən·sī′nər, kon′·sī·nôr′), **con·sign′er** *n.*

con·sig·na·tion (kon′sig·nā′shən) *n.* The act of consigning; consignment. [<LL *consignatio, -onis* <*consignare.* See CONSIGN.]

con·sig·na·to·ry (kən·sig′nə·tôr′ē, -tō′rē) *n. pl.* **·ries** One who signs jointly with another or others.

con·sign·ee (kon′sī·nē′) *n.* A person to whom property has been consigned; a factor.

con·sign·ment (kən·sīn′mənt) *n.* **1** The sending of property to a person for keeping, sale, or shipment. **2** The property consigned. **3** A written instrument by which something is consigned. **4** A method of wholesale or jobber selling whereby the retailer pays for goods only after he has sold them: usually in the phrase **on consignment.**

con·sist (kən·sist′) *v.i.* **1** To be made up or constituted: with *of.* **2** To have as substance, quality, or nature: with *in*: Her beauty *consists* in her virtue. **3** To be compatible; harmonize; exist in agreement: with *with*: His story *consists* with the evidence. [<L *consistere* <*com-* together + *sistere* stand]

con·sis·ten·cy (kən·sis′tən·sē) *n. pl.* **·cies** **1** Compatibility or harmony between things, acts, or statements; logical connection; agreement; also, agreement with what has been previously done, expressed, or agreed on. **2** The condition of holding together; firmness, nearness, or density. **3** Degree of firmness, thickness, or density. Also **con·sis′tence.** See synonyms under HARMONY.

con·sis·tent (kən·sis′tənt) *adj.* **1** Characterized by consistency; agreeing with itself; not self-contradictory. **2** Congruous; compatible. **3** Firmly united; solid. [<L *consistens, -entis* <*consistere.* See CONSIST.] —**con·sis′tent·ly** *adv.*

con·sis·to·ry (kən·sis′tər·ē) *n. pl.* **·ries** **1** *Eccl.* **a** The highest council of the Roman Catholic Church, composed of all the cardinals, and usually presided over by the Pope. **b** In many Reformed Churches, a local governing body consisting of the ministers and elders of a congregation. **c** A court of the Lutheran state churches, appointed by the government to oversee ecclesiastical affairs. **d** A diocesan court of the Church of England, presided over by the chancelor or commissary of the diocese. **2** The place where an ecclesiastical court is held; a council house or hall of justice. 3 A council of dignitaries, as of Freemasons of the 32nd degree. [<LL *consistorium*] **—con·sis·to·ri·al** (kon′sis·tôr′ē·əl, -tō′·rē-), **con′sis·to′ri·an** *adj.*

con·so·ci·ate (kən·sō′shē·āt) *v.t.* & *v.i.* **·at·ed, ·at·ing** To bring or come into association; unite: said especially of pastors and organizations of Congregational churches. —*adj.* (kən·sō′shē·it, -āt) Associated with; united. —*n.* (kən·sō′shē·it) An associate; partner. [<L *consociatus,* pp. of *consociare* <*com-* together + *socius* ally, friend]

con·so·ci·a·tion (kən·sō′sē·ā′shən, -shē-) *n.* 1 The act of consociating. 2 An ecclesiastical court.

con·so·cies (kən·sō′shēz) *n. Ecol.* A plant or animal community marked by the dominance of one species belonging to the life forms typical of the given environment. [<NL <L *com-* together + *socius* ally]

con·sol (kon′sol, kən·sol′) Singular of CONSOLS.

con·so·la·tion (kon′sə·lā′shən) *n.* 1 The act of consoling, or the state of being consoled; solace. 2 A comforting thought, person, or fact. [<F <L *consolatio, -onis* <*consolari.* See CONSOLE.]

con·sol·a·to·ry (kən·sol′ə·tôr′ē, -tō′rē) *adj.* Providing comfort or solace.

con·sole[1] (kən·sōl′) *v.t.* **·soled, ·sol·ing** To comfort (a person) in grief or sorrow; solace; cheer. [<F *consoler* <L *consolari* <*com-* together + *solari* solace] **—con·sol′a·ble** *adj.*

Synonyms: comfort, condole, encourage, sympathize. One *condoles* with another by the expression of kindly sympathy in his trouble; he *consoles* him by considerations adapted to soothe and sustain the spirit; he *encourages* him by the hope of some relief or deliverance; he *comforts* him by whatever act or word tends to bring mind or body to a state of rest and cheer. We *sympathize* with others, not only in sorrow, but in joy. Compare ALLEVIATE, PITY. *Antonyms*: annoy, distress, disturb, grieve, hurt, sadden, trouble, wound.

CONSOLE (*def. 1*)

con·sole[2] (kon′sōl) *n.* 1 A bracket of any kind, especially one used to support cornices or ornamental fixtures; a corbel. 2 A console table. 3 The portion of an organ containing the manuals and stops. 4 A cabinet for a radio, phonograph, or television set, designed to rest on the floor. [<F, a bracket; ult. origin uncertain]

console table A table supported wholly or in part by consoles, or whose legs have the appearance of consoles; a pier table.

con·sol·i·dant (kən·sol′ə·dənt) *adj.* 1 Having the power of consolidating. 2 Tending to heal wounds. —*n.* A medicine for wounds. [<F, ppr. of *consolider* <L *consolidare.* See CONSOLIDATE.]

con·sol·i·date (kən·sol′ə·dāt) *v.* **·dat·ed, ·dat·ing** *v.t.* 1 To make solid, firm, or coherent; strengthen. 2 *Mil.* To secure and strengthen, as a newly captured position. 3 To combine in one body or system; form a union of. —*v.i.* 4 To become united, solid, or firm. See synonyms under UNITE. [<L *consolidatus,* pp. of *consolidare* <*com-* together + *solidus* solid] **—con·sol′i·da′tor** *n.*

con·sol·i·dat·ed (kən·sol′ə·dā′tid) *adj.* Merged with one or more like concerns: a *consolidated* railroad.

Consolidated Fund A British public fund into which the main part of the revenue is paid, and out of which are paid interest on the national debt and other charges.

consolidated school See under SCHOOL.

con·sol·i·da·tion (kən·sol′ə·dā′shən) *n.* 1 The act of consolidating, or the state of being consolidated. 2 Combination; centralization.

con·sols (kon′solz, kən·solz′) *n. pl.* A British governmental security. [Short for *consolidated annuities*]

con·so·lute temperature (kon′sə·lo͞ot) Critical solution temperature.

con·som·mé (kon′sə·mā′, *Fr.* kôn·sô·mā′) *n.* A clear soup made of meat and sometimes vegetables boiled in water. [<F, pp. of *consommer* <L *consummare.* See CONSUMMATE.]

con·so·nance (kon′sə·nəns) *n.* 1 Agreement; accord; harmony. 2 *Physics* The induced vibration of one sonorous body acting in sympathy with another, as of one piano string with another; resonance. 3 *Music* A combination of tones regarded as pleasing and not requiring resolution. Also **con′so·nan·cy.** See synonyms under HARMONY.

con·so·nant (kon′sə·nənt) *adj.* 1 Being in agreement or harmony; consistent. 2 Consonantal. 3 *Music* Having the quality of consonance. Also **con′so·nous.** —*n.* 1 *Phonet.* A sound produced by a contact or constriction of the speech organs which results in complete or partial blockage of the breath stream. Distinguished from *vowels,* which are characterized primarily by the shape of the resonance cavity, consonants are described by their place of articulation (bilabial, alveolar, etc.), vibration or non-vibration of the vocal cords (voiced or voiceless), presence or absence of nasality, and manner of formation (stop, fricative, etc.). 2 A letter representing such a sound. [<MF <L *consonans, -antis,* ppr. of *consonare* <*com-* together + *sonare* sound] **—con′so·nant·ly** *adv.* **—con′so·nant·ness** *n.*

con·so·nan·tal (kon′sə·nan′təl) *adj.* 1 Of the nature of a consonant. 2 Having a consonant or consonants.

con·sort (kon′sôrt) *n.* 1 A companion or associate. 2 A husband or wife; mate. 3 An accompanying vessel. 4 Companionship; company. —*v.t.* (kən·sôrt′) 1 To join; associate. 2 *Obs.* To accompany; escort. —*v.i.* 3 To keep company; associate. 4 To be in agreement; harmonize. [<F <L *consors, consortis* <*com-* together + *sors* share, lot]

con·sor·ti·um (kən·sôr′shē·əm) *n. pl.* **·ti·a** (-shē·ə) 1 *Law* The right of a husband to the society and conjugal affection of his wife. 2 *Law* Coalition; union, as of incorporated companies. 3 *Bot.* The close association of certain algae and lichens. [<L, fellowship] **—con·sor·tial** (kən·sôr′shəl) *adj.*

con·spec·tus (kən·spek′təs) *n. pl.* **·tus·es** 1 A general view of a subject. 2 A digest or summary. See synonyms under ABRIDGMENT. [<L <*conspicere.* See CONSPICUOUS.]

con·sperse (kən·spûrs′) *adj.* 1 Sprinkled. 2 *Ornithol.* Irregularly dotted, as certain birds' eggs. [<L *conspersus,* pp. of *conspergere* sprinkle *com-* + *spargere* scatter]

con·spic·u·ous (kən·spik′yo͞o·əs) *adj.* 1 Clearly visible; prominent and distinct; obvious. 2 Readily attracting attention; unusual; striking. See synonyms under EMINENT, EVIDENT, MANIFEST. [<L *conspicuus* <*conspicere* <*com-* together + *specere* look at] **—con·spic′u·ous·ly** *adv.* **—con·spic′u·ous·ness** *n.*

con·spir·a·cy (kən·spir′ə·sē) *n. pl.* **·cies** 1 An agreement between two or more persons to do an evil act in concert; a plot; secret combination of men for an evil purpose. 2 *Law* A combination of two or more persons to commit any act punishable by law. 3 Any striking concurrence of persons, classes, or agencies. **—con·spir·a·tor** (kən·spir′ə·tər) *n.* **—con·spir·a·to·ri·al** (kən·spir′ə·tôr′ē·əl, -tō′rē-) *adj.* **—con·spir′a·tress** *n. fem.*

Synonyms: cabal, combination, conclave, crew, faction, gang. A *conspiracy* is a combination of persons for an evil purpose, or the act of so combining. A *faction* is more extensive than a *conspiracy,* less formal in organization, less definite in plan. *Faction* and its adjective, *factious,* have always an unfavorable sense. *Cabal* commonly denotes a *conspiracy* of leaders. A *gang* is a company of workmen all doing the same work under one leader; the word is used figuratively only of *combinations* which it is meant to stigmatize as rude and mercenary; *crew* is used in a closely similar sense. A *conclave* is secret, but of larger numbers, ordinarily, than a *cabal,* and may have honorable use; as, the *conclave* of cardinals. See CABAL.

con·spire (kən·spīr′) *v.* **·spired, ·spir·ing** *v.t.* 1 To plot; scheme for. —*v.i.* 2 To form a plot, especially secretly, for evil or unlawful purposes. 3 To concur in action or endeavor, as circumstances. [<F *conspirer* <L *conspirare* <*com-* together + *spirare* breathe] **—con·spir·ant** (kən·spī′rənt) *adj.* & *n.* **—con·spir′er** *n.*

con spi·ri·to (kōn spē′rē·tō) *Music* With spirit and vigor. [<Ital.]

con·sta·ble (kon′stə·bəl, kun′-) *n.* 1 An officer of the peace; a policeman. 2 A high military officer in medieval monarchies. 3 The keeper or governor of a castle. **—Lord High Constable of England** A former military and judicial officer of high rank. [<OF *conestable* <LL *comes stabuli* count of the stable, chief groom] **—con′sta·ble·ship′** *n.*

Con·sta·ble (kun′stə·bəl), **John,** 1776–1837, English landscape painter.

con·stab·u·lar·y (kən·stab′yə·ler′ē) *adj.* Pertaining to or consisting of constables. Also **con·stab′u·lar** (-lər). —*n. pl.* **·lar·ies** 1 Constables collectively. 2 A military police force.

Con·stance (kon′stəns, *Fr.* kôn·stäns′) A feminine personal name. Also *Lat.* **Con·stan·ti·a** (kon·stan′shē·ə, -shə), *Pg.* **Con·stan·ci·a** (kôn·stän′sē·ə), *Sp.* **Con·stan·za** (kōn·stän′thä). [<L, constant, firm]

Con·stance (kon′stəns) A city in southern Baden, Germany, on the Lake of Constance at the efflux of the Rhine: German *Konstanz.*

Constance, Lake of A lake between NE Switzerland, Austria, and southern Germany; 207 square miles: German *Bodensee.*

con·stan·cy (kon′stən·sē) *n.* 1 Steadiness in purpose or action; faithfulness in service or affection. 2 Stability. See synonyms under FIDELITY, INDUSTRY, PERSEVERANCE.

con·stant (kon′stənt) *adj.* 1 Steady in purpose; resolute; persevering; faithful. 2 Steady in movement. 3 Long-continuing, or continually recurring. 4 Invariable. 5 *Obs.* Firm; positive; consistent. —*n.* 1 That which is permanent or invariable. 2 *Math.* A quantity which retains a fixed value throughout a given discussion. 3 In the sciences, any characteristic of a substance, event, or phenomenon, numerically determined, that remains always the same under specified conditions, as gravitation, the velocity of light, the melting or freezing point, etc. See synonyms under CONTINUAL, PERPETUAL. [<L *constans, -antis,* ppr. of *constare* <*com-* thoroughly + *stare* stand] **—con′stant·ly** *adv.*

Con·stant (kon′stənt, *Fr.* kôn·stäń′) A masculine personal name. Also *Lat.* **Con·stans** (kon′stənz), *Pg., Sp.* **Con·stan·ci·o** (*Pg.* kôn·stäń′sē·ō, *Sp.* kōn·stän′thē·ō). [<L, constant, firm]

Con·stant (kôn·stäń′), **Jean Joseph Benjamin,** 1845–1902, French portrait painter. **—Constant de Re·becque** (də rə·bek′), **Benjamin,** 1767–1830, French writer and statesman.

Con·stan·ța (kôn·stän′tsä) A city in SE Rumania on the Black Sea. Also **Con·stan′tsa.**

con·stant·an (kon′stən·tan) *n.* A ductile, non-corrosive alloy of nickel and copper with high thermal and electrical resistance: used in rheostats and thermocouples. [Arbitrary coinage <CONSTANT]

Con·stan·tine (kon′stən·tēn, *Fr.* kôn·stäń·tēn′) A city in NE Algeria.

Con·stan·tine (kon′stən·tēn, -tīn) A masculine personal name. Also *Du.* **Con·stan·tijn** (kōn′·stän·tīn), *Fr.* **Con·stan·tin** (kôn·stäń·tań′), *Lat.* **Con·stan·ti·nus** (kon′stən·tī′nəs), *Pg., Sp.* **Con·stan·ti·no** (*Pg.* kôn′stäń·tē′no͞o, *Sp.* kōn′stän·tē′nō). [<L, constant, firm]

—Constantine The appellation of a number of early Christian emperors.

—Constantine I, Flavius Valerius Aurelius, 272–337, first Christian emperor of Rome: called "The Great."

—Constantine VII, 905–959, emperor of the East; as an author known as *Porphyrogenitus.*

—Constantine XI (erroneously **XIII**), 1394–1453, surnamed Palaeologus; last emperor of the East: known as *Dracoses.*

Con·stan·ti·no·ple (kon′stan·tə·nō′pəl) A former name for ISTANBUL.

Con·stan·tius II (kən·stan′shəs), 317–361, Roman emperor 337–361.

con·stel·late (kon′stə·lāt) *v.t.* & *v.i.* **·lat·ed, ·lat·ing** To group in constellations. —*adj.* Adorned or studded with constellations. [<LL *constellatus* studded with stars <*com-* together + *stella* star]

Table of Constellations

Explanation: Group N includes all constellations within 45 degrees of the north pole. Group E includes all constellations within 45 degrees of each side of the equator. Group S includes all constellations within 45 degrees of the south pole.

Name	Group	On the Meridian at 9 P. M.	Name	Group	On the Meridian at 9 P. M.	Name	Group	On the Meridian at 9 P. M.
Andromeda	E	Nov.	Delphinus	E	Sept.	Pegasus	E	Oct.
Antlia	E	April	Dorado	S	Jan.	Perseus	N	Dec.
Apus	S	July	Draco	N	June	Phœnix	S	Nov.
Aquarius	E	Oct.	Equuleus	E	Sept.	Pictor	S	Jan.
Aquila	E	Aug.	Eridanus	E	Dec.	Pisces	E	Nov.
Ara	S	July	Fornax	E	Dec.	Piscis Austrinus	E	Oct.
Aries	E	Dec.	Gemini	E	Feb.	Puppis	E	Feb.
Auriga	E	Feb.	Grus	S	Oct.	Pyxis	E	March
Boötes	E	June	Hercules	E	July	Reticulum	S	Jan.
Cælum	E	Jan.	Horologium	S	Dec.	Sagitta	E	Aug.
Camelopardalis	N	March	Hydra	E	April	Sagittarius	E	Aug.
Cancer	E	March	Hydrus	S	Dec.	Scorpius	E	July
Canes Venatici	E	May	Indus	S	Oct.	Sculptor	E	Nov.
Canis Major	E	Feb.	Lacerta	N	Oct.	Scutum	E	Aug.
Canis Minor	E	March	Leo	E	April	Serpens	E	July
Capricornus	E	Sept.	Leo Minor	E	April	Sextans	E	April
Carina	S	March	Lepus	E	Jan.	Taurus	E	Jan.
Cassiopeia	N	Nov.	Libra	E	June	Telescopium	S	Aug.
Centaurus	E	May	Lupus	E	June	Triangulum	E	Dec.
Cepheus	N	Nov.	Lynx	N	Feb.	Triangulum Australe	S	July
Cetus	E	Dec.	Lyra	E	Aug.	Tucana	S	Oct.
Chameleon	S	April	Mensa	S	Jan.	Ursa Major	N	April
Columba	E	Feb.	Microscopium	E	Sept.	Ursa Minor	N	....
Coma Berenices	E	May	Monoceros	E	March	Vela	E	March
Corona Australis	E	Aug.	Musca	S	May	Virgo	E	June
Corona Borealis	E	July	Norma	S	July	Volans	S	March
Corvus	E	May	Octans	S	....	Vulpecula	E	Sept.
Crater	E	April	Ophiuchus	E	July			
Crux	S	May	Orion	E	Jan.			
Cygnus	E	Sept.	Pavo	S	Aug.			

The four constellations Carina, Puppis, Pyxis, and Vela were formerly considered as a single one, called Argo Navis.

con·stel·la·tion (kon′stə·lā′shən) *n.* **1** *Astron.* An apparent group or cluster of stars, fortuitously associated on mythological or pictorial grounds. See table above. **2** An assemblage of brilliant things or persons. **3** In astrology, the aspect of the planets at the time of one's birth; hence, disposition or character as influenced by one's horoscope. **4** *Psychol.* A group of associated emotions, ideas, tendencies, etc., centering around a dominant element. **—con·stel·la·to·ry** (kən·stel′ə·tôr′ē, -tō′rē) *adj.*

con·ster·nate (kon′stər·nāt) *v.t.* **·nat·ed, ·nat·ing** *Rare* To overwhelm with terror and confusion; dismay. [<L *consternatus,* pp. of *consternare,* var. of *consternere* < *com-* thoroughly + *sternere* prostrate]

con·ster·na·tion (kon′stər·nā′shən) *n.* **1** Complete confusion; bafflement. **2** Sudden overwhelming fear; terror with confusion; dismay. See synonyms under ALARM, AMAZEMENT, FEAR.

con·sti·pate (kon′stə·pāt) *v.t.* **·pat·ed, ·pat·ing** To cause constipation in. [<L *constipatus,* pp. of *constipare* < *com-* together + *stipare* crowd] **—con′sti·pat′ed** *adj.*

con·sti·pa·tion (kon′stə·pā′shən) *n.* A morbid inactivity of the bowels; difficult evacuation.

con·stit·u·en·cy (kən·stich′o͞o·ən·sē) *n. pl.* **·cies 1** A body of constituents. **2** The district from which a representative is elected to a legislative body.

con·stit·u·ent (kən·stich′o͞o·ənt) *adj.* **1** Serving to form or compose as a necessary part; constituting: Chlorine and sodium are the *constituent* elements of salt. **2** Entitled to vote for a public officer or representative. **3** Having the power to frame or modify a constitution. **—***n.* **1** One represented politically or in business; a voter; client. **2** A necessary part of a chemical compound: distinguished from *component.* See synonyms under PART. [<L *constituens, -entis,* ppr. of *constituere.* See CONSTITUTE.]

con·sti·tute (kon′stə·to͞ot, -tyo͞ot) *v.t.* **·tut·ed, ·tut·ing 1** To form or be the substance of; compose; make up. **2** To impart a given character to. **3** To make or form, as of materials or elements; construct. **4** To establish or found, as a school. **5** To set up or enact, as a law. **6** To depute or appoint, as to an office or function. **7** To give legal or official form to, as a court or assembly. **8** *Obs.* To place or put in position. See synonyms under MAKE. [<L *constitutus,* pp. of *constituere* < *com-* together + *statuere* place, station] **—con′sti·tut′er** *n.* **—con′sti·tu′tive** *adj.* **—con′sti·tu′tive·ly** *adv.* **—con′sti·tu′tive·ness** *n.*

con·sti·tu·tion (kon′stə·to͞o′shən, -tyo͞o′-) *n.* **1** The act of constituting. **2** A system of related parts; composition; specifically, bodily frame or temperament. **3** The fundamental laws and practices that normally govern the operation of a state or association; especially, **the Constitution** of the United States of America, which was framed and adopted by a convention called for that purpose (1787), subsequently ratified by each State separately, and went into operation Mar. 4, 1789. **4** *Archaic* An imperial ordinance or rescript. See synonyms under CHARACTER. **—rigid constitution** A constitution, like that of the United States, which can be amended only by special process of law. **—unitary constitution** A constitution that vests all or most of the power in the central organs of government.

Con·sti·tu·tion (kon′stə·to͞o′shən, -tyo͞o′-) An American frigate active in the War of 1812: called *Old Ironsides.*

con·sti·tu·tion·al (kon′stə·to͞o′shən·əl, -tyo͞o′-) *adj.* **1** Pertaining to, inherent in, or affecting the constitution of a person or of a state; consistent with the constitution of a state; lawful. **2** Acting under and controlled by a constitution: a *constitutional* monarchy. **3** Loyal to the constitution. **4** Framing or amending a constitution. See synonyms under RADICAL. **—***n.* A walk taken for one's health. **—con·sti·tu·tion·al·i·ty** (kon′stə·to͞o′shən·al′ə·tē, -tyo͞o′-) *n.* **—con′sti·tu′tion·al·ly** *adv.*

Constitutional amendment A legal alteration of or addition to the Constitution of the United States, ratified by three fourths of the States.

constitutional clergy In French history, that part of the clergy which accepted the civil constitution of the church established by the National Assembly at Paris in 1790.

con·sti·tu·tion·al·ism (kon′stə·to͞o′shən·əl·iz′·əm, -tyo͞o-) *n.* **1** The theory or principle of constitutional government. **2** Adherence to this theory. **3** A constitutional form of government.

con·sti·tu·tion·al·ist (kon′stə·to͞o′shən·əl·ist, -tyo͞o′-) *n.* **1** One who adheres to the constitution of the country. **2** One who advocates constitutionalism in opposition to absolutism, etc. **3** A student of constitutionalism.

con·strain (kən·strān′) *v.t.* **1** To compel by physical or moral means; oblige. **2** To confine, as by bonds. **3** To restrain; compel to inaction. **4** *Obs.* To violate; force. See synonyms under COMPEL, MAKE, RESTRAIN. [<OF *constreindre* <L *constringere* < *com-* together + *stringere* bind tight. Doublet of CONSTRINGE.] **—con·strain′a·ble** *adj.* **—con·strain′·er** *n.*

con·strained (kən·strānd′) *adj.* Subjected to or resulting from constraint; compulsory; repressed. **—con·strain·ed·ly** (kən·strā′nid·lē) *adv.*

con·straint (kən·strānt′) *n.* **1** The act of constraining, or the state of being constrained; compulsion. **2** Repression or embarrassment. **3** Anything that constrains. See synonyms under MODESTY, RESERVE. [<OF *constreinte* < *constreindre.* See CONSTRAIN.]

con·strict (kən·strikt′) *v.t.* To compress or draw together at some point; bind; cramp. [<L *constrictus,* pp. of *constringere.* See CONSTRAIN.] **—con·stric′tive** *adj.*

con·stric·tion (kən·strik′shən) *n.* **1** A constricting, or a constricted part. **2** That which constricts or is constricted.

con·stric·tor (kən·strik′tər) *n.* **1** That which constricts. **2** *Anat.* A muscle which contracts a part or organ of the body. **3** A serpent that crushes its prey by coiling around it and squeezing.

con·stringe (kən·strinj′) *v.t.* **·stringed, ·string·ing** To cause contraction in; shrink; compress. [<L *constringere.* Doublet of CONSTRAIN.]

con·strin·gent (kən·strin′jənt) *adj.* **1** Tending to constrict. **2** Causing constriction. [<L *constringens, -entis,* ppr. of *constringere.* See CONSTRAIN.] **—con·strin′gen·cy** *n.*

con·struct (kən·strukt′) *v.t.* **1** To put together and set up; build; arrange. **2** To devise. **—***n.* (kon′strukt) **1** Anything systematically constructed or composed. **2** *Psychol.* A complex of mental images and impressions, deliberately synthesized in a form to aid the imagination in further speculation. [<L *constructus,* pp. of *construere.* See CONSTRUE.] **—con·struct′er, con·struc′tor** *n.*

con·struc·tion (kən·struk′shən) *n.* **1** The act of constructing; also, that which is constructed. **2** Style of building or composing. **3** The act of construing, or the interpretation thereby arrived at. **4** *Gram.* **a** The putting together of forms syntactically, as in sentences, or morphologically, as in words; also, an example of this. **b** The syntactical relationship of words, clauses, and sentences to each other. **—con·struc′tion·al** *adj.*

con·struc·tion·ist (kən·struk′shən·ist) *n.* **1** One who construes laws, etc., or one who advocates a particular construction. **2** One who interprets literally a law or body of writings, especially the U.S. Constitution or the Bible.

con·struc·tive (kən·struk′tiv) *adj.* **1** Involving the act or possessing the power of constructing. **2** *Law* Assumed or inferred as being included within the intent or application of a law or a legal document. **3** Tending toward or resulting in positive conclusions; affirmative. **—con·struc′tive·ly** *adv.* **—con·struc′tive·ness** *n.*

con·strue (kən·stro͞o′) *v.* **·strued, ·stru·ing** *v.t.* **1** To analyze the grammatical structure of (a clause or sentence) so as to determine the use, interrelations, and function of each word; parse. **2** To translate orally. **3** To deduce by inference; interpret. **4** *Gram.* To combine (words, etc.) according to syntax: The noun *aerodynamics* is *construed* as a singular. **—***v.i.* **5** To determine grammatical structure. **6** To infer; deduce. **7** To admit of grammatical analysis. **—***n.* **1** A construction or act of construing. **2** A translation according to a given construction. [<L *construere* < *com-* together + *struere* build up] **—con·stru′a·ble** *adj.* **—con·stru′er** *n.*

con·sub·stan·tial (kon′səb·stan′shəl) *adj.* Having the same substance: The Son is *consubstantial* with the Father. See TRINITY.

— **con·sub·stan′tial·ly** *adv.* — **con·sub·stan·ti·al·i·ty** (kon′səb·stan′shē·al′ə·tē) *n.*

con·sub·stan·ti·ate (kon′səb·stan′shē·āt) *v.* **·at·ed, ·at·ing** *v.t.* 1 To unite in one common substance. 2 To regard as being so united. — *v.i.* 3 To become one in substance. 4 To believe in the doctrine of consubstantiation. [<Med. L *consubstantiatus,* pp. of *consubstantiare* < *com-* together + *substantia* SUBSTANCE]

con·sub·stan·ti·a·tion (kon′səb·stan′shē·ā′shən) *n. Theol.* The theory of the substantial presence of Christ in the consecrated eucharistic elements, together with the unchanged substance of bread and wine.

con·sue·tude (kon′swi·to͞od, -tyo͞od) *n.* Custom; association. [<OF <L *consuetudo* CUSTOM] — **con·sue·tu·di·nar·y** (kon′swi·to͞o′də·ner′ē, -tyo͞o′-), **con′sue·tu′di·nal** *adj.*

con·sul (kon′səl) *n.* 1 An officer appointed to reside in a foreign port or city, chiefly as the representative of his country's commercial interests. 2 Either of two chief magistrates ruling conjointly in the Roman republic. 3 Any of the three chief magistrates of the French republic, 1799–1804. [<L] — **con·su·lar** (kon′sə·lər) *adj.*

con·su·late (kon′sə·lit) *n.* 1 The office or term of office of a consul: also **con′sul·ship.** 2 Government by consuls. 3 The official place of business of a consul. [<L *consulatus* < *consul* consul]

consul general A consular officer of the highest rank stationed in an important foreign commercial city, who supervises the other consuls in his district.

con·sult (kən·sult′) *v.t.* 1 To ask advice or information of. 2 To have regard to, as interest or duty; consider. 3 *Obs.* To contrive or devise. — *v.i.* 4 To ask advice. 5 To compare views; take counsel: with *with.* [<L *consultare,* freq. of *consulere* seek advice] — **con·sult′er, con·sul′tor** *n.*

Synonyms: confer, deliberate. *Confer* suggests the interchange of counsel, advice, or information; *consult* indicates almost exclusively the receiving of it. A man *confers* with his associates, *consults* a physician or a dictionary. See DELIBERATE.

con·sult·ant (kən·sul′tənt) *n.* 1 A person referred to for expert or professional advice. 2 One who consults.

con·sul·ta·tion (kon′səl·tā′shən) *n.* 1 The act of consulting. 2 A meeting, as of physicians, for conference.

con·sult·a·to·ry (kən·sul′tə·tôr′ē, -tō′rē) *adj.* Proceeding from consultation; advisory.

con·sult·ing (kən·sul′ting) *adj.* Giving professional advice on consultation: a *consulting* physician.

con·sult·ive (kən·sul′tiv) *adj.* Involving consultation; deliberative. Also **con·sult·a·tive** (kən·sul′tə·tiv).

con·sume (kən·so͞om′) *v.* **·sumed, ·sum·ing** *v.t.* 1 To destroy, as by burning. 2 To eat or drink up. 3 To expend wastefully; squander; use up, as money or time. 4 To hold the interest of; engross. — *v.i.* 5 To be wasted or destroyed. See synonyms under ABSORB, BURN. [<L *consumere* < *com-* thoroughly + *sumere* take up, use] — **con·sum′·a·ble** *adj.*

con·sum·ed·ly (kən·so͞o′mid·lē) *adv.* Excessively; unrestrainedly.

con·sum·er (kən·so͞o′mər) *n.* 1 One who or that which consumes. 2 One who uses up an article of exchangeable value; one of the buying public.

con·sum·er·ism (kən·so͞o′mər·iz′əm) *n.* The policy or program of protecting the interests of the consumer. [< CONSUMER + -ISM, on analogy with *capitalism,* etc.]

consumers' goods *Econ.* Products for satisfying people's needs rather than for producing other goods or services; goods sold for use: opposed to *producers' goods.*

con·sum·mate (kon′sə·māt) *v.t.* **·mat·ed, ·mat·ing** 1 To bring to completion or perfection; achieve. 2 To fulfil, as a marriage by cohabitation. See synonyms under ACCOMPLISH, EFFECT. — *adj.* (kən·sum′it) Of the highest degree; perfect; complete. [<L *consummatus,* pp. of *consummare* < *com-* together + *summa* sum, total] — **con·sum′mate·ly** *adv.* — **con′·sum·ma′tion** *n.* — **con′sum·ma′tive, con·sum·ma·to·ry** (kən·sum′ə·tôr′ē, -tō′rē) *adj.* — **con′·sum·ma′tor** *n.*

con·sump·ti·ble (kən·sump′tə·bəl) *adj.* Consumable, as by use. — *n.* Anything that can be consumed or used.

con·sump·tion (kən·sump′shən) *n.* 1 The act or process of consuming; gradual destruction, as by burning, etc. 2 *Pathol.* A wasting disease; specifically, pulmonary tuberculosis. 3 *Econ.* The use and consequent destruction of goods in the satisfying of people's needs. [<L *consumptio, -onis* < *consumere.* See CONSUME.]

con·sump·tive (kən·sump′tiv) *adj.* 1 Tending to, causing, or designed for consumption. 2 Connected with or affected by pulmonary tuberculosis. — *n.* A person affected with pulmonary tuberculosis. — **con·sump′tive·ly** *adv.* — **con·sump′tive·ness** *n.*

con·ta·bes·cence (kon′tə·bes′əns) *n. Bot.* A condition in which the stamens and pollen are abortive: often in hybridized plants. [<L *contabescens, -entis,* ppr. of *contabescere* < *com-* thoroughly + *tabes* a wasting away, dwindling] — **con′ta·bes′cent** *adj.*

con·tact (kon′takt) *n.* 1 The coming together, meeting, or touching of two bodies. 2 *Electr.* The touching or joining of points or surfaces of conductors, permitting the passage or flow of a current. 3 Immediate proximity or association. 4 Helpful vocational or social acquaintance. See synonyms under COLLISION. — *v.t.* 1 To bring or place in contact; touch. 2 *Colloq.* To get or be in touch with (a person); communicate with: I will *contact* you tomorrow. — *v.i.* 3 To be or come in contact; touch: with *with.* [<L *contactus,* pp. of *contingere* < *com-* together + *tangere* touch] — **con·tac·tu·al** (kən·tak′cho͞o·əl) *adj.*

contact flight *Aeron.* Control of the course of an aircraft by observing landmarks.

contact lens A thin corrective lens of hard or soft plastic that fits against the eyeball.

con·tac·tor (kon′tak·tər) *n. Electr.* A device for repeatedly opening and closing an electric circuit other than by hand.

contact print *Phot.* A positive print obtained by exposure of a photosensitive surface in direct contact with the negative.

contact process Catalysis.

contact twin A twin crystal, the two parts of which are united by some common crystal plane.

con·ta·gion (kən·tā′jən) *n.* 1 The communication of disease by contact, direct or indirect, or, figuratively, of mental states by suggestion or association. 2 Pestilential influence; pestilence; plague. 3 The medium of transmission of disease; contagium. [<F <L *contagio, -onis* < *contingere.* See CONTACT.]

Synonym: infection. The best usage limits *contagion* to diseases that are transmitted by contact with the diseased person, either directly by touch or indirectly by use of the same articles, by breath, effluvia, etc. *Infection* is applied to diseases produced chiefly by common climatic, malarious, or other wide-spread conditions believed to be chiefly instrumental.

con·ta·gious (kən·tā′jəs) *adj.* 1 Transmissible by contact, as a disease, or by sympathy, as emotions. 2 Catching; spreading. 3 Transmitting disease; pestilential. — **con·ta′gious·ly** *adv.* — **con·ta′gious·ness** *n.*

con·ta·gi·um (kən·tā′jē·əm) *n. pl.* **·gi·a** (-jē·ə) 1 The specific matter by which contagious disease is communicated: syphilitic *contagium.* 2 Contagion. [<L, var. of *contagio.* See CONTAGION.]

con·tain (kən·tān′) *v.t.* 1 To hold or enclose. 2 To include or comprise. 3 To be capable of containing; be able to hold. 4 To keep within bounds; restrain, as oneself or one's feelings. 5 *Math.* To be exactly divisible. 6 *Mil.* To hold, as an enemy, to a position or area, as by actual or feigned attacks. See synonyms under EMBRACE. [<OF *contenir* <L *continere* < *com-* together + *tenere* hold] — **con·tain′a·ble** *adj.* — **con·tain′er** *n.*

con·tain·er·i·za·tion (kən·tān′ər·i·zā′shən) *n.* The packing and shipping of freight in very large, sealed containers, thus facilitating loading and unloading. — **con·tain′er·ized** *adj.*

con·tain·er·ship (kən·tān′ər·ship′) *n.* A ship equipped to handle containerized cargo. Also **container ship.**

con·tain·ment (kən·tān′mənt) *n.* 1 *Mil.* The engagement of the enemy so that he is unable to extricate forces for use elsewhere. 2 In international politics, the forestalling or offsetting, by political and economic policy, of territorial or ideological extension by an inimical power.

con·tam·i·nate (kən·tam′ə·nāt) *v.t.* **·nat·ed, ·nat·ing** To make impure by contact or admixture; taint; defile; pollute. — *adj. Obs.* Contaminated. [<L *contaminatus,* pp. of *contaminare* < *contamen, contagmen* < *com-* together + *tag-,* root of *tangere* touch] — **con·tam′i·nant** *n.* — **con·tam′i·na′tive** *adj.* — **con·tam′i·na′tor** *n.*

con·tam·i·na·tion (kən·tam′ə·nā′shən) *n.* 1 The act of contaminating, or the state of being contaminated or polluted. 2 That which contaminates; defilement; taint.

con·tan·go (kən·tang′gō) *n. pl.* **·goes** *Brit.* 1 The putting off of payment due for stock till next settling day, on payment of a premium. 2 The premium or interest so paid. [? Alter. of CONTINGENT]

conte (kônt) *n. French* A short story, particularly one involving events of a humorous or startling nature.

con·temn (kən·tem′) *v.t.* To despise; scorn. [<OF *contemner* <L *contemnere* < *com-* thoroughly + *temnere* slight, scorn] — **con·temn·er** (kən·tem′ər, -tem′nər), **con·tem·nor** (kən·tem′nər) *n.*

con·tem·plate (kon′təm·plāt) *v.* **·plat·ed, ·plat·ing** *v.t.* 1 To look at attentively; gaze at. 2 To consider thoughtfully; ponder. 3 To intend or plan. 4 To treat of as contingent or possible: Secession was not *contemplated* in the Constitution. — *v.i.* 5 To meditate; muse. [<L *contemplatus,* pp. of *contemplari* < *com-* together + *templum* temple; with ref. to the art of divination] — **con·tem·pla·ble** (kən·tem′plə·bəl) *adj.* — **con′tem·pla′tor** *n.*

con·tem·pla·tion (kon′təm·plā′shən) *n.* 1 The act of keeping the eye or the mind fixed upon some object or subject. 2 Continued thought or abstraction in general; musing: *contemplation* of the heavens; absorbed in *contemplation.* 3 Expectation or intention of doing, or deliberation on something to be done, as of taking a journey. 4 Holy meditation; a life of prayer and meditation as practiced by certain Roman Catholic orders. See synonyms under REFLECTION, THOUGHT.

con·tem·pla·tive (kon′təm·plā′tiv, kən·tem′·plə-) *adj.* Of or given to contemplation; meditative. — **con′tem·pla′tive·ly** *adv.* — **con′·tem·pla′tive·ness** *n.*

con·tem·po·ra·ne·ous (kən·tem′pə·rā′nē·əs) *adj.* Living or occurring at the same time: also spelled *cotemporaneous.* [<L *contemporaneus* < *com-* together + *tempus, temporis* time] — **con·tem·po·ra·ne·i·ty** (kən·tem′pə·rə·nē′ə·tē), **con·tem′po·ra′ne·ous·ness** *n.* — **con·tem′po·ra′·ne·ous·ly** *adv.*

Synonym: contemporary. *Contemporaneous* is used chiefly of facts and events, *contemporary* of persons: *contemporary* writers; *contemporaneous* writings.

con·tem·po·rar·y (kən·tem′pə·rer′ē) *adj.* 1 Contemporaneous; living or existing at the same time. 2 Having the same age; coeval. — *n. pl.* **·rar·ies** A person or thing that is contemporary. Also spelled *cotemporary.* See synonym under CONTEMPORANEOUS.

con·tem·po·rize (kən·tem′pə·rīz) *v.t.* & *v.i.* **·rized, ·riz·ing** To make or be equal in respect of time; synchronize.

con·tempt (kən·tempt′) *n.* 1 The act of despising; disdain; scorn. 2 *Law* Wilful disregard of authority, as of a court. 3 The state of being despised; disgrace; shame. 4 An action implying contempt. See synonyms under SCORN. [<L *contemptus* < *contemnere* despise, disdain. See CONTEMN.]

con·tempt·i·ble (kən·temp′tə·bəl) *adj.* 1 Deserving of contempt; despicable; vile. 2 *Obs.* Contemptuous. See synonyms under BASE, LITTLE, PITIFUL. — **con·tempt′i·bil′i·ty, con·tempt′i·ble·ness** *n.* — **con·tempt′i·bly** *adv.*

con·temp·tu·ous (kən·temp′cho͞o·əs) *adj.* Disdainful. See synonyms under HAUGHTY.

—con·temp′tu·ous·ly *adv.* **—con·temp′tu·ous·ness** *n.*

con·tend (kən·tend′) *v.t.* **1** To maintain or assert in argument: with an objective clause. *—v.i.* **2** To debate earnestly; dispute. **3** To strive in competition or rivalry; vie: to *contend* for a prize. **4** To struggle or fight in opposition or combat. [<L *contendere* <*com-* together + *tendere* strive, strain] **—con·tend′er** *n.*

Synonyms: antagonize, argue, battle, combat, compete, contest, cope, dispute, fight, grapple, oppose, strive, vie, wrangle. See ARGUE, OPPOSE. *Antonyms*: see synonyms for AGREE, ALLOW.

con·tent[1] (kon′tent) *n.* **1** *Usually pl.* All that a thing contains. **2** The constituent elements of a conception, or meaning and relations involved; hence, significance or basic meaning. **3** Holding capacity; size. **4** Included area or space; extent. **5** The quantity of a specified part: the silver *content* of a ton of ore. **—latent content** *Psychoanal.* The underlying thoughts or repressed desires that motivate a dream. **—manifest content** *Psychoanal.* The incidents of a dream that are remembered and related by the dreamer. [<L *contentum*, pp. neut. of *continere.* See CONTAIN.]

con·tent[2] (kən·tent′) *n.* **1** Rest of mind; satisfaction; freedom from worry. **2** The means of contentment. *—adj.* Satisfied; not inclined to complain or desire something more or different than what one has. *—v.t.* To fulfil the hopes or expectations of; satisfy. See synonyms under INDULGE, SATISFY. [<L *contentus*, pp. of *continere.* See CONTAIN.]

con·tent·ed (kən·ten′tid) *adj.* Satisfied with things as they are; content; willing. See synonyms under COMFORTABLE. **—con·tent′ed·ly** *adv.* **—con·tent′ed·ness** *n.*

con·ten·tion (kən·ten′shən) *n.* **1** The act of contending; strife; conflict; struggle; dispute. **2** An object or point in debate or controversy. **3** A statement in support of an argument; also, the argument itself. See synonyms under ALTERCATION, FEUD, QUARREL. [<F <L *contentio, -onis* < *contendere.* See CONTEND.]

con·ten·tious (kən·ten′shəs) *adj.* Of, pertaining to, or fond of contention or strife; disputatious; quarrelsome: a *contentious* person. **—con·ten′tious·ly** *adv.* **—con·ten′tious·ness** *n.*

con·tent·ment (kən·tent′mənt) *n.* **1** The condition or fact of being content; satisfaction. **2** *Archaic* The act of satisfying or making content.

con·ter·mi·nous (kən·tûr′mə·nəs) *adj.* Having a common boundary line; coextensive: also *coterminous.* Also **con·ter′mi·nal.** See synonyms under ADJACENT. [<L *conterminus* <*com-* together + *terminus* limit] **—con·ter′mi·nous·ly** *adv.*

con·test (kon′test) *n.* **1** A struggle; competition; conflict. **2** Verbal conflict; controversy. See synonyms under BATTLE, COMPETITION, FEUD, QUARREL. [<*v.*] *—v.t.* (kən·test′) **1** To fight about; contend for; strive to take, keep, or control. **2** To strive to win, as a battle. **3** To argue about, especially in opposition; challenge; litigate: to *contest* an election. *—v.i.* **4** To contend, struggle, or vie: with *with* or *against.* [<F *contester* <L *contestari* bring legal action against <*com-* together + *testari* bear witness <*testis* witness] **—con·test′a·ble** *adj.* **—con·tes·ta·tion** (kon′tes·tā′shən) *n.* **—con·test′er** *n.*

con·test·ant (kən·tes′tənt) *n.* **1** One who enters a contest; a competitor. **2** A defeated political candidate who challenges election returns. [<F <L *contestans, -antis*, ppr. of *contestari.* See CONTEST.]

con·text (kon′tekst) *n.* The portions of a discourse, treatise, etc., that immediately precede and follow and are connected with a passage quoted or considered. [<L *contextus*, pp. of *contexere* <*com-* together + *texere* weave] **—con·tex·tu·al** (kən·teks′chōō·əl) *adj.* **—con·tex′tu·al·ly** *adv.*

con·tex·ture (kən·teks′chər, kon-) *n.* **1** A weaving together. **2** Something interwoven. **3** Style or manner of interweaving; texture. **—con·tex′tur·al** *adj.*

Con·ti (kōn′tē), **Niccolò de′**, 15th century Venetian traveler and writer.

con·ti·gu·i·ty (kon′tə·gyōō′ə·tē) *n.* **1** Nearness; proximity. **2** Uninterrupted connection; continuity. **3** An unbroken or continuous mass or series.

con·tig·u·ous (kən·tig′yōō·əs) *adj.* Touching or joining at the edge or boundary; adjacent. See synonyms under ADJACENT, IMMEDIATE. [<L *contiguus* < *contingere.* See CONTACT.] **—con·tig′u·ous·ly** *adv.* **—con·tig′u·ous·ness** *n.*

con·ti·nence (kon′tə·nəns) *n.* Self-restraint; moderation; especially, self-restraint in sexual passion; chastity. Also **con′ti·nen·cy.** See synonyms under ABSTINENCE.

con·ti·nent (kon′tə·nənt) *n.* **1** One of the great bodies of land on the globe, generally regarded as six in number: Africa, Asia, Australia, Europe, North America, and South America: Antarctica is sometimes regarded as the seventh continent. **2** *Obs.* That which contains; a boundary: also, that which is contained. **—the Continent** Europe, exclusive of the British Isles. *—adj.* **1** Self-restrained; abstinent; chaste. **2** *Obs.* Restraining; limiting. [<OF <L *continens, -entis*, ppr. of *continere.* See CONTAIN.] **—con·ti·nen·tal** (kon′tə·nen′təl) *adj.* **—con′ti·nent·ly** *adv.*

Con·ti·nen·tal (kon′tə·nen′təl) *adj.* **1** European; pertaining to the continent of Europe. **2** Pertaining to the United States during the Revolutionary War, or to the continental portion of the United States. *—n.* **1** A native or resident of the continent of Europe; European. **2** A soldier of the regular forces under the control of Congress in the Revolutionary War. **3** A note of the rapidly depreciated paper money issued by Congress during the Revolution. **—not worth a Continental** Practically valueless.

Continental Congress The legislative and governing body (1774–89) of the Revolutionary American colonies, at first merely *de facto* but later *de jure* under the Articles of Confederation, when it was also known as the *Congress of the Confederation.*

Continental Divide The great ridge of the Rocky Mountain summits separating west-flowing streams from east-flowing streams in North America: also *Great Divide.*

continental drift *Geol.* The theory that the continental land masses are subject to slow movement through the action of underlying magmatic material.

Continental Guinea See RÍO MUNI.

continental Morse code International Morse code.

continental shelf *Geog.* The submerged border of a continent, of varying width and degree of slope, which separates the land mass from the ocean depths.

con·tin·gen·cy (kən·tin′jən·sē) *n.* *pl.* **·cies** **1** Possibility of occurrence. **2** A fortuitous event; accident; casualty. **3** Something that is incidental. Also **con·tin′gence.** See synonyms under ACCIDENT, EVENT, HAZARD.

con·tin·gent (kən·tin′jənt) *adj.* **1** Likely to occur. **2** Fortuitous; possible. **3** *Law* Dependent upon an uncertain future event. *—n.* **1** A contingency. **2** A proportionate share; representation: the American *contingent* at the conference. **3** *Mil.* A quota of troops. See synonyms under INCIDENTAL. [<L *contingens, -entis*, ppr. of *contingere.* See CONTACT.] **—con·tin′gent·ly** *adv.*

con·tin·u·al (kən·tin′yōō·əl) *adj.* **1** Renewed in regular succession; often repeated. **2** Continuous (in time); uninterrupted. ◆ While *continual* is limited to continuity in time, and *continuous* refers to either space or time, usage now tends further to limit *continual* to the sense of "continuing after interruptions," in which sense it is not interchangeable with *continuous.* **—con·tin′u·al·ly** *adv.*

Synonyms: ceaseless, constant, continuous, incessant, invariable, perpetual, regular, unbroken, unceasing, uninterrupted, unremitting, unvarying. *Continuous* describes that which is absolutely without pause or break; *continual*, that which often intermits, but as regularly begins again. A similar distinction is made between *incessant* and *ceaseless*, but *ceaseless* may have the further meaning of unending, perpetual. *Constant* is sometimes used in the sense of *continual*; but its chief reference is to steadiness, as of purpose, sentiment, or movement; as, *constant* devotion; *constant* advance. See PERPETUAL.

con·tin·u·ance (kən·tin′yōō·əns) *n.* **1** The state of continuing; duration. **2** Uninterrupted succession; survival. **3** *Law* Postponement. **4** A continuation or sequel, as of a novel.

con·tin·u·ant (kən·tin′yōō·ənt) *n.* *Phonet.* A consonant whose sound may be prolonged on a single breath without a change in quality, as the fricatives (f) and (s): opposed to *stop.* [<L *continuans, -antis*, ppr. of *continuare.* See CONTINUE.]

con·tin·u·ate (kən·tin′yōō·āt) *adj.* **1** Closely joined together. **2** Unbroken; uninterrupted. [<L *continuatus*, pp. of *continuare.* See CONTINUE.]

con·tin·u·a·tion (kən·tin′yōō·ā′shən) *n.* **1** The act or state of continuing. **2** Something added which protracts, extends, or carries on; a sequel: the *continuation* of a novel. **—con·tin′u·a′tor** *n.*

con·tin·u·a·tive (kən·tin′yōō·ā′tiv) *adj.* Denoting or causing continuance or duration. *—n.* **1** That which causes continuation. **2** *Gram.* A conjunction which prolongs a sentence by introducing a subordinate clause at the end. **—con·tin′u·a′tive·ly** *adv.* **—con·tin′u·a′tive·ness** *n.*

con·tin·ue (kən·tin′yōō) *v.* **·tin·ued, ·tin·u·ing** *v.t.* **1** To extend or prolong in space or time. **2** To persist in or carry forward. **3** To cause to last or remain, as in a position or office. **4** To take up again, as a course of action or a narrative, after an interruption. **5** *Law* To postpone, as a judicial proceeding; grant a continuance of. *—v.i.* **6** To be durable; last; endure. **7** To keep on or persist. **8** To remain, as in a place or position; abide. **9** To resume after an interruption. See synonyms under ABIDE, LIVE, PERSEVERE, PERSIST, PROTRACT, STAND. [<L *continuare* <*continuus* <*continere.* See CONTAIN.] **—con·tin′u·a·ble** *adj.* **—con·tin′u·er** *n.*

con·tin·ued (kən·tin′yōōd) *adj.* **1** Extended in space or time; uninterrupted. **2** Continual.

continued fraction See under FRACTION.

continued proportion *Math.* A series of three or more quantities in which the ratio is the same between each two adjacent terms; as, 2, 4, 8, 16, where 2 : 4 :: 4 : 8 :: 8 : 16.

con·ti·nu·i·ty (kon′tə·nōō′ə·tē, -nyōō′-) *n.* **1** The state or quality of being continuous. **2** That which has or gives an orderly sequence, as a scenario for motion pictures or a radio script. **3** The close coordination of all details necessary to ensure smooth performance of a dramatic production, radio or television broadcast, etc.

con·tin·u·ous (kən·tin′yōō·əs) *adj.* **1** Connected, extended, or prolonged without a break; unbroken; uninterrupted. **2** Repeating, as a performance, without intermission: said of motion-picture showings, etc. See synonyms under CONTINUAL, GRADUAL, PERPETUAL. [<L *continuus* <*continere.* See CONTAIN.] **—con·tin′u·ous·ly** *adv.* **—con·tin′u·ous·ness** *n.*

con·tin·u·um (kən·tin′yōō·əm) *n.* *pl.* **·tin·u·a** (-tin′yōō·ə) **1** A total that is continuous and uninterrupted. **2** That which has perfect continuity: the *continuum* of space. **3** A basic, common character underlying a series or aggregation of indefinite variations. **4** *Math.* A set of numbers or points such that between any two of them a third may be interpolated. [<L, neut. of *continuus* CONTINUOUS]

con·to (kon′tō) *n.* *pl.* **·tos** A Portuguese money of account, formerly equal to 1,000,000 reis, now equal to 1,000 escudos in Portugal or 1,000 cruzeiros in Brazil.

con·tort (kən·tôrt′) *v.t.* To twist violently; wrench out of shape or place. See synonyms under TWIST. [<L *contortus*, pp. of *contorquere* <*com-* together + *torquere* twist] **—con·tor′tive** *adj.*

con·tor·tion (kən·tôr′shən) *n.* **1** The act of contorting. **2** Unnatural spasmodic writhing or wryness, as of the limbs.

con·tor·tion·ist (kən·tôr′shən·ist) *n.* An acrobat trained to distort his limbs.

con·tour (kon′tŏŏr) *n.* The line bounding a figure or body; outline. *—v.t.* **1** To make or draw in outline or contour; make contour lines on or determine the contour lines of. **2** To carry, as a road, around the contour of a ridge or hill. [<F <Ital. *contorno* <*contornare* <LL *com-* together + *tornare* round off, make round]

contour feathers The outer feathers that determine the outline of a bird; pennae.

contour line **1** The line, or one of the lines, constituting the boundary of a plane. **2** In maps, the line connecting points on the earth which are at the same elevation above sea level.

contour map A map constructed to show the comparative elevation of topographic features by a series of contour lines, each separated from the next by a definite difference in height, called a **contour interval.**

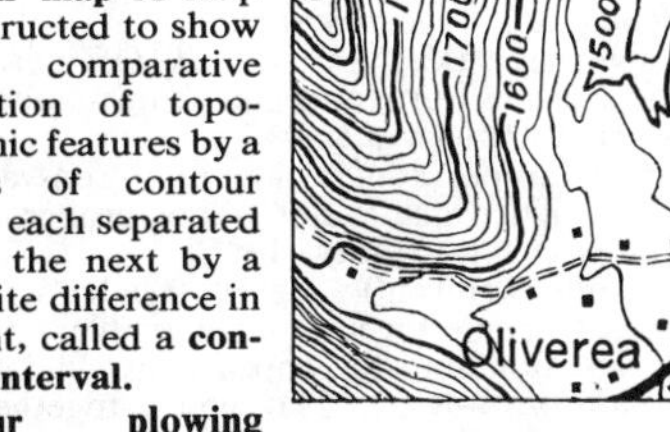

CONTOUR MAP WITH INTERVALS

contour plowing *Agric.* A method of cultivation in which the furrows follow the contours of uneven land in such a way as to minimize the destructive action of wind and erosion.

contra- *prefix* Against; opposite; contrary: *contradict.* [< L < *contra* against]

con·tra (kon′trə) *n.* A rebel soldier in Central America, especially one in revolt during the 1980s against the Sandinistas in Nicaragua. [< Spanish, short for *contra-revolucionario* a counterrevolutionary]

con·tra·band (kon′trə·band) *adj.* Prohibited or excluded, as by military law; forbidden. —*n.* **1** Contraband goods or trade. **2** Any fugitive slave who took refuge within the Union lines during the Civil War. **3** Contraband of war. [< Sp. *contrabanda* a smuggling < Ital. *contrabando* < *contra* against + *bando* < LL *bannum* law, proclamation] —**con′tra·band′ist** *n.*

contraband of war Anything furnished by a neutral to a belligerent that is by the laws of war subject to seizure. Arms and military supplies are classed as **absolute contraband**; grain, horses, etc., as **occasional contraband**; goods consigned to a neutral country which may be transferred to a belligerent or to a belligerent country which may be used by the army or navy are **conditional contraband.**

con·tra·bass (kon′trə·bās) *n.* A double bass. —*adj.* Having its pitch an octave lower than another instrument of the same class; of deep range: a *contrabass* horn. [< Ital. *contrabasso*]

con·tra·bass·ist (kon′trə·bā′sist) *n.* One who performs on the contrabass.

con·tra·bas·soon (kon′trə·bə·sōōn′) *n.* The double-bassoon.

con·tra·cep·tion (kon′trə·sep′shən) *n.* The prevention of conception or fecundation. [< CONTRA- + (CON)CEPTION]

con·tra·cep·tive (kon′trə·sep′tiv) *adj.* **1** Serving or acting to prevent conception or impregnation. **2** Pertaining to contraception. —*n.* Any device or substance that inhibits conception.

con·tract (kən·trakt′ *for v. defs. 1, 2, 4–8;* kon′trakt, kən·trakt′ *for v. def. 3*) *v.t.* **1** To reduce in size; abridge in compass or duration; shrink; narrow. **2** To wrinkle; draw together, as the brow. **3** To arrange or settle by agreement; enter upon with reciprocal obligations. **4** To acquire or become affected with, as a disease or habit. **5** *Gram.* To shorten, as a word, by omitting or combining medial letters or sounds. **6** To betroth. —*v.i.* **7** To shrink; become reduced in size. **8** To make a contract. —*n.* (kon′trakt) **1** *Law* A formal agreement, or the writing containing it. **2** A betrothal or marriage. **3** The department of law dealing with contracts. **4** Contract bridge: see under BRIDGE². —**yellow dog contract** A contract whereby an employee agrees not to join a union. [< L *contractus,* pp. of *contrahere* < *com-* together + *trahere* pull, draw]

Synonyms (noun): agreement, arrangement, bargain, cartel, compact, convenant, engagement, promise, stipulation. An *agreement* or a *contract* may be oral or written, but a consideration or compensation is essential to a *contract.* A *covenant,* in law, is a written *contract* under seal. *Convenant* is frequent in religious usage, as *contract* is in law and business. *Compact* is essentially the same as *contract,* but is applied to international *agreements,* treaties, etc. A *bargain* is a mutual *agreement* for an exchange of values, without the formality of a *contract.* A *stipulation* is a single item in an *agreement* or *contract.* Compare SALE.

con·tract·ed (kən·trak′tid) *adj.* **1** Having undergone contraction; shrunken. **2** Not broad or liberal; narrow; mean; scanty. —**con·tract′ed·ly** *adv.* —**con·tract′ed·ness** *n.*

con·trac·tile (kən·trak′təl) *adj.* Having the power to contract or to induce a contraction. Also **con·tract′i·ble** or **con·tract′a·ble, con·trac′tive.** —**con·tract′i·bil′i·ty, con·tract′i·ble·ness, con·trac·til·i·ty** (kon′trak·til′ə·tē) *n.*

contractile tissue *Physiol.* Body tissue composed of smooth or striated muscle cells whose contraction aids in the production of movement.

con·trac·tion (kən·trak′shən) *n.* **1** The act of contracting or the state of being contracted. **2** That which is contracted, as a word by the omission of one or more medial letters or sounds. See synonyms under ABBREVIATION.

contract labor Laborers brought into a country under contract.

con·trac·tor (kon′trak·tər, kən·trak′tər *for defs. 1 and 2;* kən·trak′tər *for def. 3*) *n.* **1** One of the parties to a contract. **2** One who executes plans under contract; especially, one who agrees to supply labor or materials, or both, on a large scale. **3** *Anat.* A muscle that serves to contract.

con·trac·tu·al (kən·trak′chōō·əl) *adj.* Connected with or implying a contract.

con·trac·ture (kən·trak′chər) *n.* **1** *Med.* A permanent contraction and rigidity of muscles. **2** *Archit.* The narrowing of the higher part of a column.

con·tra·dance (kon′trə·dans′, -däns′) See CONTREDANSE. Also **con′tra·danse′.**

con·tra·dict (kon′trə·dikt′) *v.t. & v.i.* **1** To maintain the opposite of (a statement); refute or gainsay; deny. **2** To be inconsistent with or opposed to. See synonyms under OPPOSE. [< L *contradictus,* pp. of *contradicere* < *contra-* against + *dicere* say, speak] —**con′tra·dict′a·ble** *adj.* —**con′tra·dict′er** or **con′tra·dic′·tor** *n.* —**con′tra·dic′tion** *n.* —**con′tra·dic′tive** *adj.* —**con′tra·dic′·tive·ness** *n.*

con·tra·dic·to·ry (kon′trə·dik′tər·ē) *adj.* **1** Involving or of the nature of a contradiction; inconsistent; contrary. **2** Given or inclined to contradiction. See synonyms under ALIEN, CONTRARY, INCONGRUOUS, INIMICAL. —*n. pl.* **·ries** *Logic* A proposition by means of which another proposition is absolutely denied. —**con′tra·dic′to·ri·ly** *adv.* —**con′tra·dic′to·ri·ness** *n.*

con·tra·dis·tinct (kon′trə·dis·tingkt′) *adj.* Distinguished by contrary qualities or by contrast. —**con′tra·dis·tinct′ly** *adv.*

con·tra·dis·tinc·tion (kon′trə·dis·tingk′shən) *n.* Distinction by contrast or by contrasting qualities: a large corporation in *contradistinction* to a small business. —**con′tra·dis·tinc′·tive** *adj.* —**con′tra·dis·tinc′tive·ly** *adv.*

con·tra·dis·tin·guish (kon′trə·dis·ting′gwish) *v.t.* To discriminate by contrasting opposite qualities.

con·tra·fa·got·to (kon′trə·fə·got′ō) *n.* **1** A double-bassoon, an octave lower than the bassoon. **2** An organ stop made to imitate a contrafagotto. [< Ital.]

con·trail (kon′trāl) *n. Aeron.* The vapor trail which sometimes streams out in the wake of an airplane flying at high altitudes, caused by the condensation of moisture from exhaust gases of the engine. [< *con(densation) trail*]

con·tra·in·di·cate (kon′trə·in′də·kāt) *v.t. Med.* To indicate the danger or undesirability of (a given drug or method of treatment). —**con′·tra·in′di·cant** *adj. & n.* —**con′tra·in′di·ca′·tion** *n.*

con·tral·to (kən·tral′tō) *n. pl.* **·tos** or **·ti** (-tē) **1** The lowest female voice, intermediate between soprano and tenor: also called *alto.* **2** *Music* A part written for such a voice. **3** A singer with such a voice. [< Ital.]

con·tra·po·si·tion (kon′trə·pə·zish′ən) *n.* **1** *Logic* Conversion by negation, or by changing the quality of the judgment while the quantity remains unchanged; transposition. **2** A placing opposite.

con·trap·tion (kən·trap′shən) *n. Colloq.* A contrivance or gadget. [? < CONTRIVE] —**con·trap′tious** *adj.*

con·tra·pun·tal (kon′trə·pun′təl) *adj. Music* **1** Of or pertaining to counterpoint. **2** Characterized by the use of counterpoint; con-structed according to the principles of counterpoint. [< Ital. *contrapunto* counterpoint] —**con′tra·pun′tal·ly** *adv.* —**con′tra·pun′tal·ist, con′tra·pun′tist** *n.*

con·tra·ri·e·ty (kon′trə·rī′ə·tē) *n. pl.* **·ties** **1** The quality or state of being contrary. **2** A quality or a proposition contrary to another; an inconsistency; a contrary.

con·trar·i·ous (kən·trâr′ē·əs) *adj.* **1** Showing refractory opposition. **2** Harmful; vexatious: said of things. —**con·trar′i·ous·ly** *adv.* —**con·trar′i·ous·ness** *n.*

con·trar·i·wise (kon′trer·ē·wīz′; *for def. 3, also* kən·trâr′ē·wīz′) *adv.* **1** On the contrary; on the other hand. **2** In the reverse order; conversely. **3** Captiously; perversely.

con·trar·y (kon′trer·ē; *for adj. def. 4, also* kən·trâr′ē) *adj.* **1** Opposed in situation, direction, aim, purpose, or operation; antagonistic. **2** Adverse: *contrary* winds. **3** Opposite; opposing. **4** Characterized or swayed by perversity; inclined to opposition or contradiction; captious. —*n. pl.* **·trar·ies** **1** One of two opposing things. **2** The opposite. **3** *Logic* A statement whose truth is undetermined by the falsity of another, but which cannot be true if the latter is true: "The man is a perjurer" is the *contrary* of "The man is honest." —**by contraries** By way of opposition to anticipated procedure. —**on the contrary** Contrariwise; on the other hand. —**to the contrary** To the opposite effect. —*adv.* In a contrary manner; contrariwise. [< AF *contrarie* < L *contrarius* < *contra* against] —**con′trar·i·ly** *adv.* —**con′trar·i·ness** *n.*

Synonyms (adj.): antagonistic, conflicting, contradictory, contrasted, different, discordant, dissimilar, incompatible, incongruous, inconsistent, opposed, opposite, unlike. Things are *contradictory* which mutually exclude each other, so that both cannot exist in the same object at the same time, as life and death. Things are *contrary* when the highest degree of both cannot exist in the same object at the same time, but where a middle term is possible, partaking of the qualities of both, as wisdom and folly, or heat and cold. See ALIEN, INCONGRUOUS, INIMICAL, PERVERSE.

con·trast (kən·trast′) *v.t.* **1** To place or set in opposition so as to show dissimilarities. **2** To set off; afford a contrast to. —*v.i.* **3** To manifest dissimilarities when placed or set in opposition. —*n.* (kon′trast) **1** The unlikeness between two or more things or persons, as revealed by comparison. **2** A person or thing that shows unlikeness to another. [< OF *contraster* < Ital. *contrastare* < LL < L *contra-* against + *stare* stand] —**con·trast′a·ble** *adj.*

Synonyms (verb): compare, differentiate, discriminate, oppose. To *compare* is to place together in order to show likeness or unlikeness; to *contrast* is to set in opposition in order to show unlikeness. We *contrast* objects that have been already *compared.* We must *compare* them, at least momentarily, even to know that they are different. We *contrast* them when we observe their unlikeness in a general way; we *differentiate* them when we note the difference exactly and point by point. See DIFFERENCE.

con·tra·ter·rene (kon′trə·te·rēn′) *adj.* **1** Opposed to or destructive of the earth. **2** *Physics* Pertaining to or having the characteristics of antimatter. —*n.* Antiworld.

con·tra·val·la·tion (kon′trə·və·lā′shən) *n.* A chain of fortifications raised by besiegers round an invested place, to protect themselves from sallies of the garrison. [< F *contrevallation* < LL *contra-* against + *vallatio, -onis* rampart < *vallum* wall]

con·tra·vene (kon′trə·vēn′) *v.t.* **·vened, ·ven·ing** **1** To transgress; violate or infringe upon, as a law. **2** To deny or run counter to; oppose or be inconsistent with in principle. See synonyms under OPPOSE. [< F *contrevenir* < LL *contravenire* < L *contra-* against + *venire* come] —**con′tra·ven′er** *n.* —**con·tra·ven·tion** (kon′·trə·ven′shən) *n.*

con·tra·yer·va (kon′trə·yûr′və) *n.* **1** The stimulant and tonic root of a tropical American plant (*Dorstenia contrajerva*) of the mulberry family. **2** The plant. [< Sp. *contrayerba* antidote < *contra* against + *yerba* herb < L *herba*]

contre– *prefix* Counter; against; in opposition to. [<F <L *contra.* See CONTRA-.]

con·trec·ta·tion (kon′trek·tā′shən) *n.* The impulse to caress or fondle a person of the opposite sex. [<L *contrectatio, -onis* <*contrectare* <*com-* thoroughly + *tractare* touch, fondle]

con·tre·danse (kôn·trə·däṅs′) *n.* **1** A country dance. **2** One of the figures composing a quadrille. Also **con·tre·dance** (kon′trə·dans′, -däns′): also spelled *contradance, contradanse.* [<F, alter. of COUNTRY DANCE]

Con·tre·ras (kôn·trā′räs) A town in central Mexico; site of a battle of the Mexican War, 1847.

con·tre·temps (kôṅ·trə·täṅ′) *n.* *pl.* **·temps** (-täṅz′, *Fr.* -täṅ′) An embarrassing occurrence; awkward incident. [<F]

con·trib·ute (kən·trib′yo͞ot) *v.* **·ut·ed, ·ut·ing** *v.t.* **1** To give or furnish in common with others; give for a common purpose. **2** To submit, sell, or furnish, as an article or story, to a magazine or other publication. —*v.i.* **3** To share in effecting a result: These causes *contributed* to the king's downfall. **4** To make or give a contribution. [<L *contributus,* pp. of *contribuere* <*com-* together + *tribuere* grant, allot] —**con·trib′ut·a·ble** *adj.* —**con·trib′u·tive** *adj.* —**con·trib′u·tive·ly** *adv.* —**con·trib′u·tive·ness** *n.* —**con·trib′u·tor** *n.*

con·tri·bu·tion (kon′trə·byo͞o′shən) *n.* **1** The act of contributing, or that which is contributed. **2** A piece of writing furnished to a magazine, etc. **3** An impost; tax; levy. —**con′tri·bu′tion·al** *adj.*

con·trib·u·to·ry (kən·trib′yə·tôr′ē, -tō′rē) *adj.* **1** Contributing. **2** *Law* Casually sharing in some act. **3** Liable to an impost. —*n.* *pl.* **·ries** One who or that which contributes.

con·trite (kən·trīt′, kon′trīt) *adj.* **1** Broken in spirit because of a sense of sin; penitent; sorry. **2** Resulting from contrition. [<OF *contrit* <L *contritus,* pp. of *conterere* <*com-* together + *terere* rub] —**con·trite′ly** *adv.*

con·tri·tion (kən·trish′ən) *n.* **1** Deep and sincere sorrow for wrongdoing. **2** *Theol.* A feeling of repentance for sin, with an intention to amend, arising from love of God and consideration of His goodness (**perfect contrition**), or from inferior motives, as fear of punishment (**imperfect contrition**). Compare ATTRITION (def. 3). Also **con·trite′ness.** See synonyms under PENITENCE, REPENTANCE.

con·tri·vance (kən·trī′vəns) *n.* **1** The act of contriving or adapting something to a special purpose. **2** A device, tool, or implement. **3** A strategem, plan, or scheme. See synonyms under ARTIFICE.

con·trive (kən·trīv′) *v.* **·trived, ·triv·ing** *v.t.* **1** To scheme or plan; devise. **2** To plot or conspire. **3** To make ingeniously; improvise; invent: He *contrived* an extra sail. **4** To manage or carry through, as by some device or scheme. —*v.i.* **5** To form designs; plot. [<OF *controver* find, invent, ? <L *com-* together + *turbare* stir up, disclose, find] —**con·triv′a·ble** *adj.* —**con·triv′er** *n.*

con·trol (kən·trōl′) *v.t.* **·trolled, ·trol·ling 1** To exercise a directing, restraining, or governing influence over. **2** To regulate or verify, as an experiment, by comparison with a parallel experiment or other relevant standard. **3** To check, as an account, by means of a duplicate register; verify or rectify. —*n.* **1** The act of controlling; restraining or directing influence; regulation; check; government. **2** One who or that which controls. **3** *Mech.* Any of variously designed and operated devices for the control of airplanes, motorcars, ships, machines, and the like. **4** *Meteorol.* An element, as atmospheric pressure, physical features, altitude, etc., serving as a determinant of climate. **5** A standard of comparison against which to check the results of an experiment, especially in the biological and medical sciences. **6** In spiritualism, a spirit presumed to act upon and through a medium in seances. [<MF *contrôler,* earlier *contreroller* keep a check list <Med. L *contrarotulus* a check list <L *contra-* against + *rotulus* list] —**con·trol′la·bil′i·ty, con·trol′la·ble·ness** *n.* —**con·trol′la·ble** *adj.* —**con·trol′ling** *adj.* —**con·trol′ment** *n.*

control chart *Stat.* A chart on which the numerical values of a series of observations are plotted in the order of their occurrence and checked to determine the extent of variation from designated standards of quality, quantity, performance, etc.

control day Any of various days whose weather is popularly believed to control the weather of a group of following days, as St. Swithin's Day.

control experiment An experiment designed to check the data in a series of related experiments by altering one of a group of specified factors and comparing the results with a view to exposing differences that might have causal significance.

con·trol·ler (kən·trō′lər) *n.* **1** One who or that which controls. **2** A magnet used in automatic regulation of an electric current. **3** An officer to examine and verify accounts: also spelled *comptroller.* —**con·trol′ler·ship** *n.*

control stick *Aeron.* The lever which operates the longitudinal and lateral control surfaces of an airplane: also called *joy-stick.*

control surface *Aeron.* Any movable device, as an airfoil, aileron, rudder, etc., operated to guide or control an aircraft, rocket, guided missile, etc.

con·tro·ver·sial (kon′trə·vûr′shəl) *adj.* **1** Debatable; open to argument; causing controversy; disputable. **2** Given to controversy; disputatious. —**con′tro·ver′sial·ist** *n.* —**con′tro·ver′sial·ly** *adv.*

con·tro·ver·sy (kon′trə·vûr′sē) *n.* *pl.* **·sies 1** Debate or disputation; discussion as to schemes or opinions. **2** A quarrel or dispute. See synonyms under ALTERCATION, FEUD, QUARREL. [<L *controversia* <*controversus* <*contra-* against + *versus,* pp. of *vertere* turn]

con·tro·vert (kon′trə·vûrt, kon′trə·vûrt′) *v.t.* To endeavor to disprove; oppose in debate. See synonyms under DISPUTE. [<L *controversus,* on analogy with *convert, revert,* etc. See CONTROVERSY.] —**con′tro·vert′er** *n.* —**con′tro·vert′i·ble** *adj.* —**con′tro·vert′i·bly** *adv.*

con·tu·ma·cy (kon′to͞o·mə·sē, -tyo͞o-) *n.* *pl.* **·cies** Contemptuous disregard of the requirements of rightful authority; insolent and stubborn perverseness; incorrigible obstinacy. Also **con·tu·mac·i·ty** (kon′to͞o·mas′ə·tē, -tyo͞o-). [<L *contumacia* <*contumax* stubborn] —**con·tu·ma·cious** (kon′to͞o·mā′shəs, -tyo͞o-) *adj.* —**con′tu·ma′cious·ly** *adv.* —**con′tu·ma′cious·ness** *n.*

con·tu·me·ly (kon′to͞o·mə·lē, -tyo͞o-, -mē′lē; kən·to͞o′mə·lē, -tyo͞o′-) *n.* *pl.* **·lies 1** Insulting rudeness in speech or manner; scornful insolence. **2** An act or statement exhibiting haughtiness and contempt. See synonyms under SCORN. [<OF *contumelie* <L *contumelia* reproach] —**con·tu·me·li·ous** (kon′to͞o·mē′lē·əs, -tyo͞o-) *adj.* —**con′tu·me′li·ous·ly** *adv.* —**con′tu·me′li·ous·ness** *n.*

con·tuse (kən·to͞oz′, -tyo͞oz′) *v.t.* **·tused, ·tus·ing** To bruise by a blow. [<L *contusus,* pp. of *contundere* <*com-* together + *tundere* beat] —**con·tu·sive** (kən·to͞o′siv, -tyo͞o′-) *adj.*

con·tu·sion (kən·to͞o′zhən, -tyo͞o′-) *n.* **1** The act of bruising, or the state of being bruised. **2** A bruise.

co·nun·drum (kə·nun′drəm) *n.* **1** A riddle, often depending on a pun. **2** Any perplexing question or thing. [Origin unknown]

con·ur·ba·tion (kon′ûr·bā′shən) *n.* A complex of towns, villages, and small cities closely associated with the needs and activities of a central metropolis. [<CON- + *urbs* city]

con·va·lesce (kon′və·les′) *v.i.* **·lesced ·lesc·ing** To recover from a sickness. [<L *convalescere* <*com-* thoroughly + *valescere,* inceptive of *valere* be strong]

con·va·les·cence (kon′və·les′əns) *n.* **1** Gradual recovery from illness. **2** The period of such recovery. Also **con′va·les′cen·cy.**

con·va·les·cent (kon′və·les′ənt) *adj.* Recovering health after sickness. —*n.* One who is convalescing. [<L *convalescens, -entis,* ppr. of *convalescere.* See CONVALESCE.]

Con·val·lar·i·a (kon′və·lâr′ē·ə) *n. pl.* A genus of monocotyledonous herbs of the lily family, with regular and perfect flowers and berrylike fruits. The only known species is the lily-of-the-valley.

con·vec·tion (kən·vek′shən) *n.* **1** The act of conveying. **2** *Physics* The diffusion of heat through a liquid or gas by motion of its parts: distinguished from *conduction.* **3** *Meteorol.* A thermal process whereby atmospheric circulation is maintained through the upward or downward transfer of air masses of different temperature. [<L *convectus,* pp. of *convehere* <*com-* together + *vehere* carry] —**con·vec′tion·al** *adj.* —**con·vec′tor** *n.*

con·vec·tive (kən·vek′tiv) *adj.* Of, pertaining to, causing, or resulting from convection. —**con·vec′tive·ly** *adv.*

con·ve·nance (kon′və·näns, *Fr.* kôṅ·və·näṅs′) *n.* **1** That which is suitable or proper. **2** *pl.* The conventionalities. [<F]

con·vene (kən·vēn′) *v.* **·vened, ·ven·ing** *v.t.* **1** To cause to come together or assemble; convoke. **2** To summon to appear, as by judicial authority. —*v.i.* **3** To come together; assemble. See synonyms under CONVOKE. [<L *convenire* <*com-* together + *venire* come] —**con·ven′a·ble** *adj.* —**con·ven′er** *n.*

con·ven·ience (kən·vēn′yəns) *n.* **1** The state, time, or quality of being convenient; suitableness; fitness. **2** Freedom from difficulty or discomfort; ease. **3** That which is convenient; that which gives ease or comfort; anything handy or labor-saving. **4** A convenient occasion. Also **con·ven′ien·cy.** See synonyms under OPPORTUNITY.

con·ven·ient (kən·vēn′yənt) *adj.* **1** Conducive to comfort or ease; serviceable; suitable; commodious; favorable; timely. **2** Near at hand; handy. **3** *Obs.* Of a fit character or quality. [<L *conveniens, -entis,* ppr. of *convenire.* See CONVENE.] —**con·ven′ient·ly** *adv.*

Synonyms: adapted, commodious, favorable, fit, fitted, handy, helpful, opportune, proper, seasonable, suitable, suited, useful. See COMFORTABLE, EXPEDIENT, GOOD. *Antonyms*: awkward, clumsy, inconvenient, superfluous, unhandy, unmanageable, unseasonable, useless.

con·vent (kon′vent, -vənt) *n.* **1** A religious community or association; a body of monks or nuns, especially the latter. **2** The building or buildings occupied by such a body. See synonyms under CLOISTER. [<L *conventus* meeting, assembly <*convenire.* See CONVENE.]

con·ven·ti·cle (kən·ven′ti·kəl) *n.* **1** A religious meeting, especially a secret one of Scottish Covenanters. **2** The building in which such meetings are held. **3** *Obs.* An assembly. [<L *conventiculum,* dim. of *conventus.* See CONVENT.] —**con·ven′ti·cler** *n.*

con·ven·tion (kən·ven′shən) *n.* **1** A formal or stated meeting of delegates or representatives, especially for legislative, political, religious, or professional purposes. **2** The act of coming together. **3** General consent, or something established by it; precedent; custom; specifically, a rule, principle, form, or technique in conduct or art; a conventionality. **4** A formal agreement or compact between two or more states relating usually to one specific subject: often used interchangeably with *treaty.* **5** *Law* An agreement or mutual engagement between persons. See synonyms under ASSEMBLY, COMPANY.

con·ven·tion·al (kən·ven′shən·əl) *adj.* **1** Established by convention or custom; agreed; stipulated; customary; formal. **2** Or or pertaining to a convention of delegates. **3** Represented according to artistic convention or rule, rather than to nature or fact. —**con·ven′tion·al·ism** *n.* —**con·ven′tion·al·ist** *n.* —**con·ven′tion·al·ly** *adv.*

con·ven·tion·al·i·ty (kən·ven′shən·al′ə·tē) *n.* *pl.* **·ties 1** Adherence to established forms, customs, or usages; conformity to the accepted and traditional. **2** The state or quality of being in accord with convention. **3** A conventional act or utterance. —**the conventionalities** The accepted procedures and customs of social intercourse; the proprieties.

con·ven·tion·al·ize (kən·ven′shən·əl·īz) *v.t.* **·ized, ·iz·ing 1** To make conventional. **2** *Art* To draw, design, or represent in a conventional manner. —**con·ven′tion·al·i·za′tion** *n.*

con·ven·tu·al (kən·ven′cho͞o·əl) *adj.* Belonging to a convent. —*n.* One who belongs to a convent. [<Med. L *conventualis* <*conventus.* See CONVENT.]

Con·ven·tu·al (kən·ven′cho͞o·əl) *n.* A member of a branch of the Franciscan order which follows a modified rule permitting the ownership of property in common.

con·verge (kən·vûrj′) *v.* **·verged, ·verg·ing** *v.t.* **1** To cause to tend toward one point. —*v.i.* To move toward one point; come together by gradual approach. **3** To tend toward the same conclusion or result. [<LL *convergere* <*com-* together + *vergere* bend]

con·ver·gence (kən·vûr′jəns) *n.* **1** The act or

process of converging. **2** State or quality of being convergent. **3** Degree or point of convergence. **4** *Meteorol.* The net horizontal inflow of air into a given layer of the atmosphere. **5** *Math.* The gradual approach of a series of values to a fixed limit as new values are added. **6** *Physiol.* The focusing of both eyes upon a near point. **7** *Biol.* The tendency of organisms of different types to develop similar functional and structural forms in response to the same environmental conditions. Also **con·ver′gen·cy** for defs. 1–3. **—con·ver′·gent** *adj.*

con·ver·sance (kon′vər·səns, kən·vûr′səns) *n.* The state or quality of being conversant; familiarity; acquaintanceship. Also **con′ver·san·cy.**

con·ver·sant (kon′vər·sənt, kən·vûr′sənt) *adj.* **1** Familiar, as a result of study, application, etc.: with *with* or, rarely, *in*: *Conversant* with the principles of a subject. **2** *Rare* Intimately acquainted, as with a person. [<OF, ppr. of *converser* <L *conversari.* See CONVERSE.] **— con′ver·sant·ly** *adv.*

con·ver·sa·tion (kon′vər·sā′shən) *n.* **1** The speaking together of two or more persons; informal exchange of ideas, information, etc.; colloquy. **2** Intimate association or intercourse. **3** *pl.* Diplomatic intercourse; specifically, an informal international conference on matters to be treated more officially later. **4** *Obs.* Deportment. **5** *Obs.* The act or condition of being or living anywhere, as in intimacy. **—criminal conversation** *Law* Unlawful sexual intercourse with a married person; adultery. [<OF <L *conversatio, -onis* < *conversari.* See CONVERSE[1].] **—con′·ver·sa′tion·al** *adj.* **—con′ver·sa′tion·al·ly** *adv.*

Synonyms: chat, colloquy, communication, communion, confabulation, conference, converse, dialog, discourse, intercourse, parley, talk. *Conversation* is, etymologically, an interchange of ideas with some other person or persons. *Talk* may be wholly one-sided. There may be *intercourse* without *conversation,* as by looks, signs, etc.; *communion* is of hearts, with or without words; *communication* is often by writing, and may be uninvited and unreciprocated. *Talk* may denote the mere utterance of words with little thought; thus, we say idle *talk,* empty *talk,* rather than idle or empty *conversation. Discourse* is applied chiefly to public addresses. A *conference* is more formal than a *conversation.* A *dialog* may be real and informal, but the word denotes ordinarily an artificial or imaginary *conversation,* strictly of two persons, but sometimes of more. A *colloquy* is indefinite as to number, and generally somewhat informal. See INTERCOURSE. Compare BEHAVIOR.

con·ver·sa·tion·al·ist (kon′vər·sā′shən·əl·ist) *n.* **1** One who converses. **2** An interesting talker. Also **con′ver·sa′tion·ist.**

conversation piece A type of genre painting popular in the 18th century, showing a group of people, usually of the upper classes, engaged in conversation; hence, any article of furniture, decoration, etc., that arouses comment, discussion, etc.

con·ver·sa·zi·o·ne (kon′vər·sat′sē·ō′nē, *Ital.* kōn′ver·sä·tsyō′nā) *n. pl.* **·nes** (-nēz), *Ital.* **·ni** (-nē) *Italian* A meeting for conversation, particularly on some special topic, as literature or art.

con·verse[1] (kən·vûrs′) *v.i.* **·versed, ·vers·ing** **1** To speak together informally and alternately; engage in familiar conversation or colloquy. **2** *Obs.* To associate; have intercourse; commune. **—** *n.* (kon′vûrs) **1** Conversation; interchange of thoughts. **2** Close intercourse; communion; fellowship. [<OF *converser* <L *conversari,* freq. of *convertere* < *com-* together + *vertere* turn] **—con·vers′·a·ble** *adj.* **—con·vers′a·bly** *adv.* **—con·vers′·er** *n.*

con·verse[2] (kən·vûrs′, kon′vûrs) *adj.* Turned about so that two parts are interchanged; transposed; reversed. **—** *n.* (kon′vûrs) **1** That which exists in a converse relation; opposite. **2** *Logic* A proposition that is the result of conversion. See CONVERSION BY LIMITATION. [<L *conversus,* pp. of *convertere* < *com-* thoroughly + *vertere* turn] **—con·verse·ly** (kən·vûrs′lē, kon′vûrs·lē) *adv.*

con·ver·sion (kən·vûr′zhən, -shən) *n.* **1** The act of converting, or the state of being converted, in any sense. **2** The act of turning or of being turned to religious belief. **3** *Law* **a** Wrongful appropriation to one's own use of the goods of another. **b** The exchange of real to personal property or the reverse, which is considered to have taken place where no actual exchange has been effected, as in settling the affairs of an estate. **4** *Logic* A form of immediate inference in which the subject and predicate or antecedent and consequent terms of a judgment change places in such a way that the converse or transposed form is a legitimate inference from the original judgment. **5** *Math.* The formation of a new proportion from four proportional terms by substituting for the second the difference between the first and second and for the fourth the difference between the third and fourth. **6** *Psychoanal.* The process by which a psychic conflict finds expression in motor or sensory disturbances associated with and partially satisfying the repressed emotion or desire: also **conversion hysteria;** see REPRESSION. See synonyms under CHANGE. **—con·ver′sion·al, con·ver·sion·ar·y** (kan·vûr′zhən·er′ē, -shən-) *adj.*

conversion by limitation *Logic* Conversion in which the quantity is changed from universal to particular while the quality remains unchanged.

con·vert (kən·vûrt′) *v.t.* **1** To change into another state, form, or substance; transform. **2** To apply or adapt to a new or different purpose or use. **3** To change from one belief, doctrine, creed, opinion, or course of action to another. **4** To turn from a sinful to a righteous life. **5** To exchange for an equivalent value, as goods for money. **6** To exchange for value of another form, as preferred for common stock. **7** *Chem.* To change chemically. **8** *Logic* To transpose the subject and predicate of (a proposition) by conversion. **9** *Law* To assume possession of illegally. **—** *v.i.* **10** To become changed in character. **11** In football, to score the extra point after touchdown, as by kicking a field goal. **—** *n.* (kon′vûrt) A person who has been converted, as from a sinful to a pious life, or from one opinion, creed, etc., to another. [<OF *convertir* <L *convertere.* See CONVERSE[2].]

Synonyms (noun): disciple, neophyte, proselyte. The name *disciple* is given to the follower of a certain faith, without reference to any previous belief or allegiance; a *convert* is a person who has come to one faith from a different belief or unbelief. A *proselyte* is one who has been led to accept a religious system, whether with or without true faith; a *convert* is always understood to be a believer. A *neophyte* is a new *convert,* not yet fully indoctrinated, or not admitted to full privileges. The antonyms *apostate, pervert,* and *renegade* are condemnatory names applied to the *convert* by those whose faith he forsakes.

con·vert·er (kən·vûr′tər) *n.* **1** One who or that which converts. **2** A vessel in which materials are changed from one condition into another. **3** A Bessemer converter. **4** *Electr.* An apparatus for converting direct into alternating current and vice versa. **5** One who converts raw textiles into finished products. Also **con·ver′tor.**

con·vert·i·ble (kən·vûr′tə·bəl) *adj.* Capable of being converted. **—** *n.* **1** A convertible thing. **2** An automobile with a retractable top. **—con·vert′i·bil′i·ty, con·vert′i·ble·ness** *n.* **—con·vert′i·bly** *adv.*

con·vert·i·plane (kən·vûr′tə·plān′) *n.* An aircraft combining the advantages of a helicopter with the ability to attain high speed in normal flight: also called *planicopter.* [< *converti(ble) (air)plane*]

con·vert·ite (kon′vər·tīt) *n. Archaic* A convert.

con·vex (kon·veks′, kon′veks) *adj.* Curving outward like a segment of a globe or of a circle viewed from outside; bulging out: opposed to *concave.* Compare illustration under LENS. **—** *n.* (kon′veks) A convex surface or body; convexity. [<L *convexus* vaulted, curved < *convehere* < *com-* together + *vehere* bring, carry] **—con·vex′ed·ly, con·vex′ly** *adv.*

con·vex·i·ty (kon·vek′sə·tē) *n. pl.* **·ties** **1** The state of being convex. **2** A convex surface. Also **con·vex′ed·ness, con·vex′ness.**

con·vex·o-con·cave (kon·vek′sō·kon·kāv′) *adj.* **1** Convex on one side and concave on the other. **2** *Optics* Describing a lens of which the convex surface has a greater curvature than the opposite concave surface: distinguished from *concavo-convex.* See illustration under LENS.

con·vex·o-con·vex (kon·vek′sō·kon·veks′) *adj.* Convex on both sides.

con·vex·o-plane (kon·vek′sō·plān′) *adj.* Plano-convex.

con·vey (kən·vā′) *v.t.* **1** To carry from one place to another; transport. **2** To serve as a medium or path for; transmit. **3** To make known or impart; communicate. **4** To transfer ownership of, as real estate. **5** *Obs.* To accompany; guide. [<AF *conveier* travel with <L *com-* together + *via* road, way. Doublet of CONVOY, *v.*] **—con·vey′a·ble** *adj.* **—con·vey′er, con·vey′or** *n.*

Synonyms: carry, change, give, move, remove, sell, shift, transfer, transmit, transport. *Convey, transmit,* and *transport* all imply delivery at a destination; *carry* does not necessarily imply delivery, and often does not admit of it. A man *carries* an appearance, *conveys* an impression, the appearance remaining his own, the impression being given to another; I will *transmit* the letter; *transport* the goods. *Transfer* may or may not imply delivery to another person; as, items may be *transferred* from one account to another or a word *transferred* to the following line. In law, real estate, which cannot be moved, is *conveyed* by simply *transferring* title and possession. *Transport* usually refers to material objects; *transfer, transmit,* and *convey* may refer to immaterial objects; we *transfer* possession, *transmit* intelligence; we *convey* ideas, but do not *transport* them. In the case of *convey* the figurative sense now predominates. Compare CARRY, LEAD. *Antonyms*: hold, keep, possess, preserve, retain.

con·vey·ance (kən·vā′əns) *n.* **1** The act of conveying. **2** That by which anything is conveyed. **3** A vehicle. **4** *Law* A document transferring title to property. **5** *Obs.* A device; artifice.

con·vey·anc·ing (kən·vā′ən·sing) *n. Law* The business of preparing conveyances of property, especially real estate, including the investigation of titles. **—con·vey′anc·er** *n.*

con·vict (kən·vikt′) *v.t.* **1** To prove guilty; find guilty after a judicial trial. **2** To awaken to a sense of sin. See synonyms under CONDEMN. **—** *adj. Obs.* Proved guilty. **—** *n.* (kon′vikt) One found guilty of or undergoing punishment for crime; a criminal. [<L *convictus,* pp. of *convincere.* See CONVINCE.] **—con·vic′tive** *adj.*

con·vic·tion (kən·vik′shən) *n.* **1** The act of convicting. **2** The fact or state of being convicted. **3** The state or condition of being convinced or fully awakened to awareness: under *conviction* of sin. **4** A doctrine or proposition which one firmly believes. **5** Fixed belief: He spoke with *conviction.* See synonyms under FAITH. **—con·vic′tion·al** *adj.*

con·vict·ism (kon′vik·tiz′əm) *n.* Convicts as a class.

con·vince (kən·vins′) *v.t.* **·vinced, ·vinc·ing** **1** To satisfy by evidence; persuade by argument. **2** *Obs.* To convict. [<L *convincere* < *com-* thoroughly + *vincere* overcome, conquer] **—con·vince′ment** *n.* **—con·vinc′er** *n.* **—con·vinc′i·ble** *adj.* **—con·vinc′ing** *adj.* **—con·vinc′ing·ly** *adv.* **—con·vinc′ing·ness** *n.*

Synonym: persuade. One is *convinced* by argument or evidence addressed to the intellect; he is *persuaded* by appeals addressed to the affections and the will. See PERSUADE.

con·viv·i·al (kən·viv′ē·əl) *adj.* Pertaining to a feast, especially a drinking feast; festive; jovial. [<L *convivialis* < *convivium* a feast, banquet < *convivere* < *com-* together + *vivere* live] **—con·viv′i·al·ist** *n.* **—con·viv·i·al·i·ty** (kən·viv′ē·al′ə·tē) *n.* **—con·viv′i·al·ly** *adv.*

con·vo·ca·tion (kon′vō·kā′shən) *n.* **1** The act of summoning together an assembly. **2** The assembly thus summoned. See synonyms under ASSEMBLY, COMPANY. [<L *convocatio,*

-onis < *convocare.* See CONVOKE.] **—con'vo·ca'tion·al** *adj.* **—con·voc·a·tive** (kən·vok'ə·tiv) *adj.* **—con'vo·ca'tor** *n.*

Con·vo·ca·tion (kon'vo·kā'shən) *n.* **1** An ecclesiastical body of the Church of England, similar to a synod, but meeting only at the call of some authority: the *Convocation* of Canterbury. **2** A voluntary convention of Protestant Episcopal clergy and laymen from a division of a diocese, meeting unofficially to discuss and promote church measures; also, the district thus organized.

con·voke (kən·vōk') *v.t.* **·voked, ·vok·ing** To call together; summon. [< F *convoquer* < L *convocare* < *com-* together + *vocare* call, summon] **—con·vok'er** *n.*

Synonyms: assemble, call, collect, convene, gather, muster, summon. A convention is *called* by some officer or officers, as by its president, its executive committee, or some eminent leaders; the delegates are *assembled* or *convened* in a certain place, at a certain hour. *Convoke* implies an organized body and a superior authority; *assemble* and *convene* express more independent action; Parliament is *convoked*; Congress *assembles.* Troops are *mustered*; witnesses and jurymen are *summoned. Antonyms*: adjourn, disband, discharge, dismiss, disperse, dissolve, prorogue, scatter, separate.

con·vo·lute (kon'və·lo͞ot) *adj.* **1** Rolled one part on another or inward from one side. **2** *Bot.* Coiled longitudinally, as the petals of the wallflower. Also **con'vo·lut'ed, con'vo·lu'tive** [< L *convolutus,* pp. of *convolvere.* See CONVOLVE.] **—con'vo·lute'ly** *adv.*

con·vo·lu·tion (kon'və·lo͞o'shən) *n.* **1** The act of convolving. **2** The state of being convolved. **3** turn; fold. **4** *Anat.* One of the folds of the surface of the brain.

con·volve (kən·volv') *v.* **·volved, ·volv·ing** *v.t.* To roll together; wind around something; twist; turn. *—v.i.* To turn or wind upon itself. [< L *convolvere* < *com-* together + *volvere* spin, twist]

con·vol·vu·la·ceous (kən·vol'vyə·lā'shəs) *adj. Bot.* Designating a family *(Convolvulaceae)* of gamopetalous, chiefly climbing herbs, shrubs, or trees with alternate leaves and showy flowers; the morning-glory family.

con·vol·vu·lar (kən·vol'vyə·lər) *adj.* **1** Winding in upon itself. **2** Twisted; wound together.

con·vol·vu·lus (kən·vol'vyə·ləs) *n.* Any of a genus *(Convolvulus)* of twining herbs with large, showy, trumpet-shaped flowers. [< L, bindweed]

con·voy (kon'voi) *n.* **1** A protecting force accompanying property in course of transportation, as a ship at sea or a military party by land. **2** The property so accompanied, as a ship or fleet at sea or a baggage train onland. **3** The act of convoying; the state of being convoyed, or the agency used in transportation or conveyance. [< MF *convoi* < *convoyer*] *—v.t.* (kən·voi', kon'-) To escort and protect; guide; act as convoy to. < L *com-* together + *via* road. Doublet of CONVEY.]

con·vulse (kən·vuls') *v.t.* **·vulsed, ·vuls·ing 1** To affect with violent movements; agitate violently. **2** To cause to laugh violently. [< L *convulsus,* pp. of *convellere* < *com-* together + *vellere* pull] **—con·vul·sive** (kən·vul'·siv) *adj.* **—con·vul'·sive·ly** *adv.* **—con·vul'sive·ness** *n.*

con·vul·sion (kən·vul'shən) *n.* **1** A violent and abnormal muscular contraction of the body; spasm; fit. **2** Any violent commotion or disturbance. **—con·vul·sion·ar·y** (kən·vul'·shən·er'ē) *adj.* & *n.*

Con·vul·sion·ar·y (kən·vul'shən·er'ē) *n. pl.* **·ar·ies** One of a group of religious fanatics of the 18th century. *—adj.* Of or pertaining to these fanatics. Also **Con·vul'sion·ist.**

co·ny (kō'nē, kun'ē) *n. pl.* **co·nies 1** A rabbit, especially the European rabbit. **2** Rabbit fur. **3** In the Bible, the hyrax or daman. **4** The pika. **5** *Archaic* A dupe; one who is cheated. Also *coney.* [< OF *cony* < L *cuniculus* rabbit]

coo (ko͞o) *v.* **cooed, coo·ing** *v.t.* **1** To utter with the soft murmuring sound of a dove or pigeon. *—v.i.* **2** To utter the coo of a dove, or a similar sound. **3** To make love in low, murmuring tones: to bill and *coo.* *—n.* A murmuring note, as of a dove. [Imit.] **—coo'er** *n.* **—coo'ing·ly** *adv.*

Co·o (kô'ō) The Italian name for KOS.

Cooch Be·har (ko͞och' bi·här') A district of NE West Bengal, India; 1,318 square miles; capital, Cooch Behar: formerly *Kooch Behar.*

coo·ee (ko͞o'ē) *n.* A long, shrill cry of the Australian aborigines. Also **coo'ey. —within cooee** Within calling distance; close at hand. *—v.i.* **coo·eed, coo·ee·ing** To make this cry. [Imit.]

coof (ko͝of) *n. Scot.* A lout; blockhead; coward.

cook (ko͝ok) *v.t.* **1** To prepare for consumption by the action of heat, as by roasting or boiling. **2** *Colloq.* To tamper with surreptitiously; garble; falsify. *—v.i.* **3** To do the work of a cook; act as a cook. **4** To undergo cooking. **—to cook (someone's) goose** To kill or ruin one; frustrate one's schemes or plans. **—to cook up** *Colloq.* To concoct or invent, as a plot. [< *n.*] *—n.* One who prepares food for eating. [OE *coc* < L *coquus*] **—cook'er** *n.*

Cook (ko͝ok), **James,** 1728–1779, English explorer: known as *Captain Cook.*

Cook, Mount 1 A mountain on the Yukon-Alaska border in the St. Elias range; 13,760 feet. **2** The highest peak in New Zealand, on South Island; 12,349 feet: also *Aorangi.*

cook·book (ko͝ok'bo͝ok') *n.* A book containing recipes and instructions for cooking.

Cooke (ko͝ok), **Jay,** 1821–1905., U.S. financier and railroad magnate.

cook·er·y (ko͝ok'ər·ē) *n. pl.* **·er·ies 1** The art or practice of cooking. **2** A place for cooking.

Cook Inlet An inlet of the Gulf of Alaska in southern Alaska.

Cook Islands An archipelago comprising a New Zealand dependency SW of Samoa; total, 90 square miles; capital, Raratonga.

cook·out (ko͝ok'out') *n. U.S. Colloq.* A picnic at which the meal is cooked out-of-doors.

Cook Strait The passage between North Island and South Island, New Zealand; narrowest point, 16 miles.

cook·y (ko͝ok'ē) *n. pl.* **cook·ies 1** A small, sweet cake. **2** *Slang.* A person; also, a young woman or girl; sweetheart. Also **cook·ey, cook·ie.** [< Du. *koekje,* dim. of *koek* cake]

cool (ko͞ol) *adj.* **1** Moderate in temperature; not warm; some what cold. **2** Serving to produce or giving the effect of coolness. **3** Self-controlled; self-possessed. **4** Indifferent; chilling; slighting. **5** Audacious; impudent. **6** *Colloq.* Actual; absolute; not exaggerated: a *cool* million dollars. **7** *Art* Suggesting a sense of coolness: said of the colors blue, green, and violet. **8** *Slang* Very good; well done. See synonyms under CALM, FRESH. *—v.t.* **1** To lower the temperature of; make cooler or less hot. **2** To render less excited or excitable: allay, as passion; calm; moderate. *—v.i.* **3** To become cool or less hot. **4** To lose the heat of excitement or passion; become less ardent, angry, zealous, or affectionate. **—to cool it** *Slang* To calm down; take it easy. **—to cool one's heels** To wait long and wearily in attendance. *—n.* **1** A moderate temperature approaching cold: the *cool* of the day. **2** That which is cool. **3** *Slang* Calm detachment; composure. **—to blow one's cool** *Slang* To get excited; become emotional. [OE *col*] **—cool'ish** *adj.* **—cool'ly** *adv.* **—cool·ness** *n.*

cool·ant (ko͞o'lənt) *n.* Any substance of low freezing point used as a cooling medium, as for an internal combustion engine.

cool·er (ko͞o'lər) *n.* **1** That which cools, as a vessel to cool liquids. **2** A refreshing beverage. **3** *Slang* A jail.

Coo·ley's anemia (ko͞o'lez) A severe form of thalassemia developing in infants or young children who are homozygous for the causative genetic error. [after Thomas B. *Cooley,* 1871–1945, U.S. physician]

Coo·lidge (ko͞o'lij), **Calvin,** 1872–1933, thirtieth president of the United States 1923–1929. **—Julian Lowell,** 1873–1954. U.S. mathematician.

Coo·lidge tube An X-ray tube the temperature of whose spiral cathode can be closely controlled. [after W. D. *Coolidge,* 1873–1975. U.S. physicist]

coo·lie (ko͞o'lē) *n.* **1** In the Orient, an unskilled laborer or menial. **2** Any such person doing heavy work, especially for low wages. Also **coo'ly.** [Prob. < *Kuli,* an aboriginal Gujarat tribe; infl. by Tamil *kuli* hire, wages]

coomb (ko͞om) *n. Brit.* A bowl-shaped valley or hollow. Also spelled *comb, combe.* Also **coombe.** [OE *cumb.* ? < Celtic]

coon (ko͞on) *n.* **1** The raccoon. **2** *Slang* A Negro: a derogatory use. [Short for RACCOON]

coon·can (ko͞on'kan') See CONQUIAN.

coon dog A dog used for hunting raccoons.

coon's age *U.S. Slang* A very long time.

coon·tie (ko͞on'tē) *n.* A tropical American plant (genus *Zamia*) of the cycad family, whose stems and roots yield a starch. [< N. Am. Ind.]

coop (ko͞op, ko͝op) *n.* **1** An enclosure for small animals, as fowls or rabbits. **2** *Slang* A jail; prison. **—to fly the coop** *Slang* To decamp; quit. *—v.t.* To put into a coop; confine. [ME *cupe* < MLG. Cf. MDu. *kupe* cask]

co-op (kō'op, kō·op') *n. Colloq.* A cooperative enterprise, as a store or market.

coop·er (ko͞o'pər, ko͝op'ər) *n.* One whose business it is to make casks, barrels, etc. *—v.t.* & *v.i.* To make or mend (casks, barrels, etc.) [ME *couper* < LG. Cf. MDu. *kuper* < *kupe* a cask]

Coop·er (ko͞o'pər, ko͝op'ər), **Hugh Lincoln,** 1865–1937, U.S. engineer. **—James Fenimore,** 1789–1851, U.S. novelist. **—Peter,** 1791–1883, U.S. manufacturer and philanthropist.

coop·er·age (ko͞o'pər·ij, ko͝op'ər-) *n.* **1** The work of the cooper or the cost of such work. **2** A cooper's workshop.

co·op·er·ate (kō·op'ə·rāt) *v.i.* **·at·ed, ·at·ing 1** To operate together for a common object: with *with.* **2** To practice economic cooperation. See synonyms under AID, HELP. [< L *cooperatus.* pp. of *cooperari* < *co-* together + *operari* < *opus* work] **—co·op'er·a'tor** *n.*

co·op·er·a·tion (kō·op'ə·rā'shən) *n.* **1** Joint action; profit-sharing. **2** A union of laborers or small capitalists for the purpose of advantageously manufacturing, buying, or selling goods, or of pursuing other modes of mutual benefit. **—co·op'er·a'tion·ist** *n.*

co·op·er·a·tive (kō·op'rə·tiv, -ə·rā'tiv) *n.* **1** An organization carrying on any of various economic activities for the mutual benefit of its members. **A consumers' cooperative,** buying and selling at market prices, distributes the savings over cost of operation to its members in proportion to their patronage. A **producers' cooperative** conducts marketing operations for the pooled output of primary producers, usually farmers. **2** An apartment house owned by an organization of tenants, with each tenant's share determined by the value of his own apartment; also, an apartment in such building. *—adj.* **1** Pertaining to or organized for economic cooperation: a *cooperative* store. **2** Working together for a common purpose. **—co·op'er·a·tive·ly** *adv.*

Cooperative Commonwealth Federation Former name of the NEW DEMOCRATIC PARTY.

coop·er·y (ko͞o'pər·ē, ko͝op'ər·ē) *n. pl.* **·ies 1** The trade or workshop of a cooper; cooperage. **2** A cooper's wares, collectively.

co·opt (kō·opt') *v.t.* **1** To choose by joint action; specifically, to elect to fill a vacant membership, as of a committee, board, etc. **2** To make ineffectual as an instrument for radical change by incorporating within the established order. Also **co·op'tate.** [< L *cooptare* < *co-* together + *optare* choose] **—co·op·ta·tive** (kō·op'tə·tiv) *adj.* **—co·op'tion, co'op·ta'tion** *n.*

co·or·di·nal (kō·ôr'də·nəl) *adj.* **1** *Biol.* Belonging to the same order, as in botany or zoology. **2** Having or defined by (a certain number of) coordinates.

co·or·di·nate (kō·ôr'də·nit, -nāt) *adj.* **1** Of the same order or rank; existing together in similar relation. **2** *Math.* Of or pertaining to coordinates. **3** Having separate colleges for men and women: a *coordinate* university. *—n.* **1** One who or that which is of the same order, rank, power, etc. **2** *Math.* Any of a set of magnitudes by means of which the position of a point, line, or angle is determined with reference to fixed elements. *—v.* (kō·ôr'·də·nāt) **·nat ·ed, ·nat·ing** *v.t.* **1** To put in the same rank, class, or order. **2** To harmonize or adjust; bring into harmonious relation or action. *—v.i.* **3** To be of the same order or rank. **4** To act in harmonious or reciprocal relation; come into adjustment. [< Med. L *coordinatus,* pp. of *coordinare* arrange < *co-* together + *ordinare* set in order < *ordo, -inis* rank] **—co·or'di·nate·ly** *adv.* **—co·or'di·nate·ness** *n.* **—co·or'di·na'tive** *adj.* **—co·or'di·na'tor** *n.*

co·or·di·na·tion (kō·ôr'də·nā'shən) *n.* **1** The act of coordinating. **2** The state of being coordinate. 3 The harmonious, integrated action of the various parts and processes of a machine, organization, organism, etc.

Coorg (ko͞org) A chief commissioner's state in SW India; 1,593 square miles; capital, Mercara: sometimes *Kurg.*

Coo·sa River (ko͞o'sə) A river in NW Georgia and eastern Alabama, flowing 286 miles to the Alabama River.

coost (ko͞ost) *Scot.* Past tense of CAST.

coot (ko͞ot) *n.* 1 An aquatic bird of the genus *Fulica,* resembling the rails. 2 A sea duck, especially any of the North American scoters. 3 *Slang* A common or stupid fellow. [ME *cote* <LG. Cf. Du. *koet.*]

coot·er (ko͞o'tər) *n.* 1 The Carolina box turtle *(Terrapene carolina).* 2 A turtle or tortoise of Florida *(Pseudemys floridana).* [Origin uncertain]

coot·ie[1] (ko͞o'tē) *Slang* A body louse. [? <Indonesian *kutu,* a parasitic insect; orig. nautical slang]

coot·ie[2] (ko͞o'tē) *n. Scot.* A small wooden basin or bowl for use in the kitchen.

co-own·er (kō·ō'nər) *n.* A joint owner. — **co-own'er·ship** *n.*

cop[1] (kop) *n.* 1 The top, as of a hill or the head of a thing. 2 The conical roll of thread formed on the spindle of a spinning machine; also, the tube on which this thread or yarn is wound. [OE *copp* summit]

cop[2] (kop) *Slang v.t.* **copped, cop·ping** 1 To take; steal; appropriate. 2 To win: to *cop* a prize. 3 To catch or seize. **—to cop out** *U.S. Slang* To back down or turn away, as from one's responsibilities or ideals; renege. *—n.* A policeman: short for *copper*[2]. [? Var. of *cap* catch, take <OF *caper* <L *capere*]

co·pai·ba (kō·pā'bə, -pī'-) *n.* A viscous, aromatic South American balsam from some species of *Copaifera,* used in affections of the mucous membrane and in varnishes. Also **co·pai'va** (-və). [<Sp. <Tupian *cupauba*]

co·pal (kō'pəl) *n.* A hard, transparent resin exuded by various tropical trees, used for varnishes. [<Sp. <Nahuatl *copalli* incense]

co·palm (kō'päm) *n.* 1 The sweetgum tree. 2 The balsam obtained from it. [Origin uncertain]

Co·pán (kō·pän') A city of western Honduras; site of Mayan ruins.

co·par·ce·nar·y (kō·pär'sə·ner'ē) *n. pl.* **·nar·ies** 1 *Law* An estate in lands inherited by coparceners. 2 Partnership. Also **co·par·ce·ny** (kō·pär'sə·nē).

co·par·ce·ner (kō·pär'sə·nər) *n. Law* One of two or more coheirs. [<CO-[1] + PARCENER]

co-part·ner (kō·pärt'nər) *n.* One who shares with another; specifically, an equal partner in a business. **—co-part'ner·ship** *n.*

co·pa·set·ic (kō'pə·set'ik) See COPESETIC.

cope[1] (kōp) *v.* **coped, cop·ing** *v.i.* 1 To contend or strive on equal terms; oppose successfully: often with *with.* 2 *Archaic* To meet or encounter: with *with.* 3 *Brit. Colloq.* To deal with a situation successfully. *—v.t.* 4 *Obs.* To deal with; meet in combat. 5 *Obs.* To requite. See synonyms under CONTEND. [<OF *couper* strike <*coup, colp* a blow <L *colaphus*]

cope[2] (kōp) *n.* 1 Anything that arches overhead: the *cope* of heaven. 2 A coping, as of a roof or over a window. 3 A semicircular mantle worn by priests or bishops on solemn or ceremonial occasions; also, a coronation, state, processional, or choral vestment often worn by laymen. *—v.t.* **coped, cop·ing** 1 To dress in a cope or cloak. 2 To furnish with or form a coping, as a wall; bend or arch. 3 To form (a joint in a molding) without mitering, as in a sash frame. [<Med. L *cāpa* cape, cope, var. of LL *cappa.* See CAP.]

co·peck (kō'pek) See KOPECK.

Co·pen·ha·gen (kō'pən·hā'gən, -hä'-) A port on the east coast of Zealand Island, largest city and capital of Denmark: Danish *København.*

copenhagen blue A dusty, light blue.

co·pe·pod (kō'pə·pod) *n.* One of an order *(Copepoda)* of small, free-swimming, fresh-water and marine crustaceans. *—adj.* 1 Of, pertaining to, or belonging to this order. 2 Oar-footed, as a crustacean. Also **co·pep·o·dan** (kō·pep'ə·dən). [<NL <Gk. *kōpē* oar + *pous, podos* foot] — **co·pep'o·dous** *adj.*

Co·per·ni·cus (kō·pûr'nə·kəs), **Nicholas,** 1473–1543, Polish astronomer who in 1543 declared that the planets revolve around the sun and that the earth rotates on its axis. **—Co·per'ni·can** *adj.*

co·pe·set·ic (kō'pə·set'ik) *adj. Slang.* Tip-top; first-rate; fine: also spelled *copasetic.* Also **co'pe·set'tic.** [U.S. coinage, c. 1930]

cope·stone (kōp'stōn') *n.* 1 The top stone of a wall. 2 One of the stones of a coping. 3 The final or crowning stroke; culmination.

cop·i·er (kop'ē·ər) *n.* 1 A copyist. 2 One who imitates closely the style of another.

co-pi·lot (kō'pī'lət) *n.* The assistant or relief pilot of an aircraft.

cop·ing (kō'ping) *n.* The top course of a wall, usually sloping to shed water.

coping saw A narrow-bladed saw set in a recessed frame and used for cutting small curved pieces from sections of wood.

cop·i·o·pi·a (kop'ē·ō'pē·ə) *n.* Eyestrain; asthenopia. [<Gk. *kopos* suffering + -OPIA]

co·pi·ous (kō'pē·əs) *adj.* 1 Possessing or showing abundance. 2 Ample; plenteous: large in quantity: *copious* notes. See synonyms under AMPLE. [<L *copiosus* <*copia* abundance] **—co'pi·ous·ly** *adv.* **—co'pi·ous·ness** *n.*

co·pla·nar (kō·plā'nər) *adj. Math.* In the same plane: said of figures.

Cop·land (kōp'lənd), **Aaron,** born 1900, U.S. composer.

Cop·ley (kop'lē), **John Singleton,** 1738–1815, U.S. portrait painter.

co·pol·y·mer (kō·pol'ə·mər) *n. Chem.* A compound formed by the polymerization of two or more unlike substances and having properties different from those of either component taken singly.

co·pol·y·mer·i·za·tion (kō·pol'ə·mər·ə·zā'shən) *n. Chem.* A process similar to polymerization, but involving the union of two or more distinct molecular species, each of which is capable of being polymerized alone, and yielding a copolymer.

co·pol·y·mer·ize (kō·pol'ə·mə·rīz') *v.t. & v.i.* **·ized, ·iz·ing** To subject to or undergo copolymerization.

cop-out (kop'out') *n. U.S. Slang* 1 A way of avoiding responsibility; especially, an easy or cowardly resolution of a problem; evasion. 2 One who cops out. [<criminal slang *cop out, cop a plea* to plead guilty]

copped (kopt) *adj.* Conical; pointed.

Cop·pée (kô·pā'), **François,** 1842–1908, French poet and novelist.

cop·per[1] (kop'ər) *n.* 1 A reddish, ductile, metallic element (symbol Cu, atomic number 29) occurring native and in combination, and a very good conductor of heat and electricity. See PERIODIC TABLE. 2 An article made of this metal; specifically, a vessel in which clothes are boiled. 3 A coin made of copper. 4 Any of several shades of rich, lustrous, reddish-brown, similar to the color of polished copper. *—v.t.* 1 To cover or coat with copper. 2 *Slang* To bet against. [OE *coper* <LL *cuprum* <L *(aes) cyprium* Cyprian (metal) <Gk. *kyprios* <*Kypros* Cyprus] — **cop'per·y** *adj.*

cop·per[2] (kop'ər) *n. Slang* A policeman; detective; cop. [<COP[2]]

cop·per·as (kop'ər·əs) *n.* A green, crystalline, astringent ferrous sulfate, $FeSO_4 \cdot 7H_2O$, used in dyeing, inkmaking, photography, etc.: also called *green vitriol.* [<MF *couperose* <Med. L *cuperosa, cuprosa* <*(aqua) cuprosa* copper (water) <LL *cuprum.* See COPPER.]

copper barilla A native copper mixed with sandstone, found in Bolivia.

copper glance Chalcocite.

cop·per·head (kop'·ər·hed') *n.* A venomous North American crotaline snake *(Agkistrodon mokasen)* having red-dish-brown markings on a buff-colored body: one of the pit vipers.

COPPERHEAD
(2 feet in length; rarely up to 3 feet)

Cop·per·head (kop'·ər·hed') *n.* During the Civil War, a Northerner who sympathized with the Confederate States.

Cop·per·mine River (kop'ər·mīn') A river in Northwest Territories, Canada, flowing 525 miles NW to the Beaufort Sea.

copper nickel Niccolite.

cop·per·plate (kop'ər·plāt') *n.* An engraved plate of copper or an engraving or impression printed from it: often used adjectivally.

copper pyrites See PYRITES.

cop·per·smith (kop'ər·smith') *n.* 1 One who makes utensils of copper. 2 The crimson-breasted barbet *(Xantholaena haematocephala),* common in India, Ceylon, Burma, and the Philippines.

copper sulfate Blue vitriol.

cop·pice (kop'is) *n. & v.* Copse.

cop·ple-crown (kop'əl·kroun') *n.* 1 A bird's crest. 2 A hen with a crest or topknot. [<dim. of COP[1] + CROWN] **—cop'ple-crowned'** *adj.*

co·pra (kop'rə) *n.* The dried and broken kernel of the coconut, yielding coconut oil: also spelled *cobra.* Also **cop·per·ah** (kop'ər·ə), **cop'rah.** [<Pg. <Malayalam *koppara*]

cop·re·mi·a (kop·rē'mē·ə) *n. Pathol.* A poisoning of the blood from retained fecal matter in cases of obstruction of the bowels. Also **cop·rae'mi·a.** [<COPR(O)- + Gk. *haima* blood]**—cop·re'mic** *adj.*

copro- *combining form* Dung; feces; filth: *coprolite.* Also, before vowels, **copr-.** [<Gk. *kopros* dung]

cop·ro·la·li·a (kop·rō·lā'lē·ə) *n. Psychiatry* Abnormal indecency of speech, regarded as a sign of mental disorder. [<COPRO- + Gk. *lalein* speak]

cop·ro·lite (kop'rə·līt) *n.* The petrified dung of extinct vertebrates, in some localities forming, in part, a phosphatic rock which is mined for a fertilizer. **—cop'ro·lit'ic** (-lit'ik) *adj.*

cop·rol·o·gy (kop·rol'ə·jē) *n.* 1 A collection of filth. 2 Indecency or filth in art or literature; also, the study of this. [<COPRO- + -LOGY]

cop·roph·a·gous (kop·rof'ə·gəs) *adj.* Feeding upon dung, as scarabaeid beetles. [<NL <Gk. *koprophagos* <*kopros* dung + *phagein* eat]

cop·ro·phil·i·a (kop'rə·fil'ē·ə) *n. Psychiatry* Gratification derived from the contemplation or handling of filth. [<COPRO- + Gk. *philia* love] — **cop'ro·phil'ic** *adj.*

cop·roph·i·lous (kop·rof'ə·ləs) *adj.* 1 Growing readily on dung, as certain fungi. 2 Coprophagous. [<COPRO- + -PHILOUS]

cop·ro·phyte (kop'rə·fīt) *n.* A saprophyte found in dungheaps.

copse (kops) *n.* 1 A low-growing thicket. 2 Wood gathered from a copse; undergrowth. Also **copse'wood'.** *—v.t.* **copsed, cops·ing** 1 To clip or turn down, as brushwood. 2 To plant or keep in growth, as underwood. *—v.i.* 3 To form a copse; grow up as a copse. [Earlier COPPICE <OF *copeiz* <*coper* cut]

Copt (kopt) *n.* 1 A native Egyptian descended from ancient Egyptian stock. 2 A member of the Coptic Church. [<Med. L *Coptus, Cophtus* <Arabic *quft* <Coptic *gyptios, kyptaios* <Gk. *Aigyptios* Egyptian]

Cop·tic (kop'tik) *adj.* Of or pertaining to the Copts, or to their language. *—n.* The Hamitic language of the Copts, the latest form of the ancient Egyptian: a dead language since 1500 but still the liturgical language of the Coptic Church.

Coptic Church The principal Christian sect of Egypt, which became a separate body in 451, adhering to the Monophysitic doctrine after this was rejected by the Council of Chalcedon. See MONOPHYSITE.

cop·u·la (kop'yə·lə) *n. pl.* **·las** or **·lae** (-lē) *Gram.* A verb that merely connects the subject and the predicate of a sentence without asserting action, particularly the verbs *be, appear, become, feel, look, seem, smell, sound,* and *taste*; a link verb. [<L, a link, band] **—cop'u·lar** *adj.*

cop·u·late (kop'yə·lāt) *v.i.* **·lat·ed, ·lat·ing** To unite in sexual intercourse. [<L *copulatus,* pp. of *copulare* fasten, link <*copula* a link] — **cop'u·la'tive** *adj. & n.* **—cop'u·la'tive·ly** *adv.* — **cop·u·la·to·ry** (kop'yə·lə·tôr'ē, -tō'rē) *adj.*

cop·u·la·tion (kop'yə·lā'shən) *n.* 1 The act

of coupling; also, the state of being coupled together. 2 Sexual intercourse.

copulative conjunction *Gram.* A coordinate conjunction, as *and.*

cop·y (kop′ē) *n. pl.* **cop·ies** 1 A reproduction or imitation; duplicate. 2 A single printed pamphlet, book, etc., of an edition or issue. 3 A pattern given for imitation. 4 Manuscript or other matter to be reproduced in type. 5 In journalism, someone or something that is newsworthy: He is good *copy.* — **certified copy** A copy attested by an officer having charge of the original. — *v.* **cop·ied, cop·y·ing** *v.t.* 1 To make a copy of; transcribe; reproduce; make in imitation, as in writing or painting. 2 To follow as a model; imitate, as in actions or opinions. — *v.i.* 3 To make a copy or reproduction. 4 To admit of being copied: That page *copies* well. 5 To do in imitation. [<F *copie* <Med. L *copia* transcript <L, supply, abundance]

cop·y·book (kop′ē·bo͝ok′) *n.* A book containing copies to be imitated in penmanship; a writing book.

cop·y–boy (kop′ē·boi′) *n.* An errand boy in a newspaper office who delivers copy to the editor, composing room, etc.

cop·y·cat (kop′ē·kat′) *n. Colloq.* An imitator: a child's term of derision.

cop·y–desk (kop′ē·desk′) *n.* A desk in a newspaper office where copy is edited and prepared for the typesetters.

cop·y·graph (kop′ē·graf, -gräf) *n.* A hectograph.

cop·y·hold[1] (kop′ē·hōld′) *n. Law* A tenure of lands evidenced by a copy of the court roll.

cop·y·hold[2] (kop′ē·hōld′) *v.i. Colloq.* To act as copyholder.

cop·y·hold·er (kop′ē·hōl′dər) *n.* 1 One who or that which holds copy; specifically, one who holds and reads copy so that a proofreader may detect errors in printed matter. 2 In English law, one who holds land by tenure of copyhold.

copying ink An ink containing sugar, glycerin, or some similarly acting substance, for use in any writing or printing to be reproduced in the copying press.

copying paper An unsized paper used in the copying press.

copying press A press for duplicating writing or printing done with copying ink.

cop·y·ist (kop′ē·ist) *n.* 1 One whose business it is to copy. 2 An imitator.

cop·y·read·er (kop′ē·rē′dər) *n.* A person in an editorial office, or by assignment elsewhere, who edits work intended for publication.

cop·y·right (kop′ē·rīt′) *n.* The exclusive statutory right of authors, composers, playwrights, artists, publishers, or distributors to publish and dispose of their works for a limited time; in the United States, for 28 years, with privilege of one renewal for an additional 28 years. The common–law property rights in unpublished works continue in effect until publication with or without copyright. — *v.t.* To secure copyright for, as a book or work of art. — **cop′y·right′a·ble** *adj.* — **cop′y·right′er** *n.*

cop·y–writ·er (kop′ē·rī′tər) *n.* One who writes copy for advertisements, including radio and television commercials.

coque·li·co (kōk′li·kō) *n.* 1 The English wild poppy *(Papaver rhoeas).* 2 The reddish–orange color of this flower. [<F]

Coque·lin (kôk·laṅ′), **Benoît Constant,** 1841–1909, French actor.

co·quet (kō·ket′) *v.* **co·quet·ted, co·quet·ting** *v.i.* 1 To flirt; play the coquette; trifle in love: said of women. 2 To act in a trifling, undecided manner; dally. — *v.t.* 3 *Obs.* To flirt with. [<F *coqueter* <*coquet,* dim. of *coq* a cock; with ref. to its strutting]

co·quet·ry (kō′kə·trē, kō·ket′rē) *n. pl.* **·ries** 1 Trifling in love, as a coquette; flirting. 2 The quality of being coquettish.

co·quette (kō·ket′) *n.* A woman or girl who endeavors to attract men's attention and admiration merely for the gratification of vanity; flirt. Also **co·quet′.** [<F, fem. dim. of *coq* a cock. See COQUET.] — **co·quet′tish** *adj.* — **co·quet′tish·ly** *adv.* — **co·quet′tish·ness** *n.*

co·quil·lage (kō·kē·yázh′) *n.* A design made of or imitating shells, prevalent in the decorative arts of the rococo period. [<F <*coquille* shell]

co·quil·la nut (kō·kēl′yə, -kē′yə) The hard-shelled, oval nut of the Brazilian palm *Attalea funifera.* [<Sp. *coquillo,* dim. of *coco* coconut]

co·quille (kō·kēl′) *n.* 1 Any of various dishes, usually of sea food, baked in a shell. 2 Chill (*n.* def. 4). [<F, shell]

co·qui·na (kō·kē′nə) *n.* A soft, highly porous, limestone rock composed of fragments of marine shells: used as building material. [<Sp.]

co·qui·to (kō·kē′tō) *n. pl.* **·tos** 1 A tall, massive feather palm of Chile *(Jubaea spectabilis),* bearing a dense crown of foliage. 2 Its small, edible nut. [<Sp., dim. of *coco* coconut]

cor– Assimilated var. of COM–.

Co·ra (kôr′ə, kō′rə) A feminine personal name. [<Gk., maiden]

cor·a·ci·i·form (kôr′ə·sī′ə·fôrm) *adj.* Designating an order of non–passerine birds *(Coraciiformes),* including the rollers, kingfishers, hornbills, etc. [<NL <Gk. *korax, korakis* raven + -FORM]

cor·a·cle (kôr′ə·kəl, kor′-) *n.* A small fishing boat of hide or oilcloth on a wicker frame. [<Welsh *corwgl* <*corwg* boat]

FRENCH CORACLE

cor·a·coid (kôr′ə·koid, kor′-) *adj.* 1 *Zool.* Designating the posterior inferior process of the shoulder girdle, a separate bone in many animals, as birds, reptiles, and monotremes, that unites with the scapula to form the glenoid cavity. 2 Shaped like a raven's beak. — *n.* 1 The coracoid process. 2 The chief bone of the shoulder girdle of a teleost fish. [<Gk. *korakoeidēs* <*korax, korakis* raven + *eidos* form]

cor·al (kôr′əl, kor′-) *n.* 1 The calcareous skeleton secreted in or by the tissues of various, usually compound marine coelenterates and deposited in various forms and colors. 2 These skeletons collectively. 3 An animal of this type. 4 A yellowish–red color. 5 An object, as a toy or a jewel, made of coral. 6 Lobster or crab roe: so called from its appearance when cooked. — *adj.* 1 Consisting of or like coral. 2 Colored like coral. [<OF <L *coralium* <Gk. *korallion*]

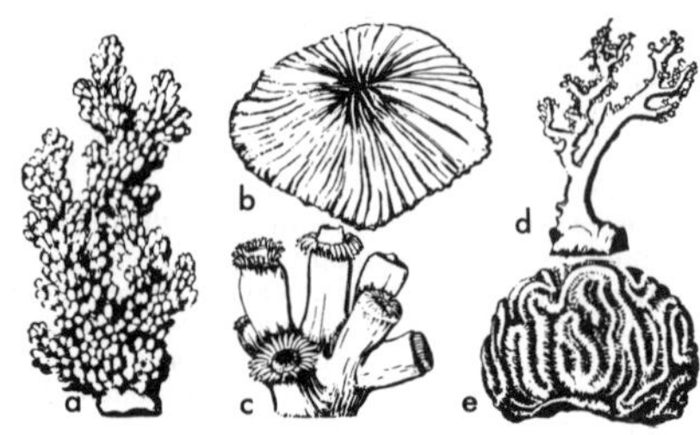

TYPES OF CORAL
a. Reef coral. *b.* Mushroom coral. *c.* Bud coral. *d.* Red coral. *e.* Brain coral.

cor·al·ber·ry (kôr′əl·ber′ē, kor′-) *n. pl.* **·ries** A bushy American shrub *(Symphoricarpos orbiculatus)* with dark berries somewhat resembling currants.

coralli– *combining form* Coral: *coralliferous.* Also, before vowels, **corall–.** [<Gk. *korallion* coral]

cor·al·lif·er·ous (kôr′ə·lif′ər·əs, kor′-) *adj.* Producing or containing coral. [<CORALLI- + -FEROUS]

cor·al·line (kôr′ə·lin, -līn, kor′-) *adj.* 1 Of, pertaining to, producing, or like coral. 2 Pinkish–red. — *n.* 1 A calcareous, coral–like seaweed. 2 A coral or coral–like animal.

cor·al·lite (kôr′ə·līt, kor′-) *n.* 1 An individual skeleton of coral polyp; a cup coral. 2 Fossil coral. — **cor′al·lit′ic** (-lit′ik) *adj.*

cor·al·loid (kôr′ə·loid, kor′-) *adj.* Coral–shaped; especially, branching like coral: also **cor′al·loi′dal.** — *n.* A polyzoan.

co·ral·lum (kə·ral′əm) *n. pl.* **co·ral·la** (kə·ral′ə) Coral, either as a compound mass or as the skeleton of a polyp. [<LL, var. of *coralium* CORAL]

coral reef A reef, often of great extent, formed by the gradual deposit of innumerable coral skeletons, found chiefly in tropical waters.

cor·al·root (kôr′əl·ro͞ot′, -ro͝ot′, kor′-) *n.* Any one of a small genus *(Corallorhiza)* of brownish, leafless orchids with much–branched coral–like rootstocks.

Coral Sea A SW area of the Pacific Ocean east of Australia and New Guinea; scene of Japanese naval defeat by U.S. forces in World War II, 1942.

coral snake Any of a genus *(Micrurus)* of venomous snakes of tropical America and the southern United States, noted for their brilliant red, black, and yellow rings; especially, *M. lemniscus* of South America and the harlequin snake *(M. fulvius)* of Mexico and the southern United States.

co·ram pop·u·lo (kō′ram pop′yə·lō) *Latin* In the presence of the people; publicly.

cor an·glais (kôr äṅ·gle′) *French* 1 The English horn. 2 A reed organ stop resembling the oboe in sound.

co·rant (kə·rant′), **co·ran·to** (kə·ran′tō, -rän′-) See COURANT.

Cor·an·tyn (kôr′ən·tīn, kor′-) See CORENTYN.

cor·ban (kôr′bən, kôr·bän′) *n.* An offering to God, as in fulfilment of a vow. *Mark* vii 11. [<Hebrew *qorbān*]

cor·beil (kôr′bəl) *n.* 1 *Obs.* A gabion. 2 *Archit.* A sculptured basket of fruit or flowers. [<F *corbeille* <L *corbicula,* dim. of *corbis* basket]

cor·bel[1] (kôr′bəl, -bel) *n. Archit.* **a** A projection from the face of a wall to support an overhanging weight; corbeling. **b** A short timber placed lengthwise upon a wall, etc., under a girder to increase its bearing. — *v.t.* **cor·beled** or **·belled, cor·bel·ing** or **·bel·ling** 1 To support by corbels. 2 To make in the form of corbels. [<OF <LL *corvellum,* dim. of *corvus* crow; from its shape]

cor·bel[2] (kôr′bəl, -bel) *n. Archit.* A piece serving as a cushion for a capital, as in a Corinthian column, that rests on the astragal. [<OF <L *corbis* basket]

cor·bel·ing (kôr′bəl·ing) *n. Archit.* An arrangement of stones or bricks in building a wall, in which successive courses project beyond those below them. Also **cor′bel·ling.**

cor·bel–steps (kôr′bəl·steps′) See CORBIE–STEPS.

cor·bie (kôr′bē) *n. Scot.* A crow; raven. Also **cor′by.**

corbie crow *Scot.* The carrion crow.

cor·bie–steps (kôr′bē·steps′) *n. pl. Scot.* Steps in the top of a gable wall, from the eaves to the apex of the roof, such as only a crow or cat could use: often called *crowsteps.*

Cor·co·va·do (*Pg.* kôr′kə·vä′tho͞o, *Sp.* kôr′kō·vä′thō) 1 A peak overlooking Río de Janeiro, Brazil; 2,310 feet. 2 A volcano in southern Chile; 7,550 feet.

Cor·cy·ra (kôr·sī′rə) Ancient name of CORFU.

cord (kôrd) *n.* 1 A string of several strands. 2 A measure for wood; in the United States a pile 4 x 4 x 8 feet, equal to 128 cubic feet, or 3.62 cubic meters. 3 A wale or rib in a fabric giving a raised effect. 4 A corded fabric. 5 *Pl. U.S.* Corduroy trousers. 6 *Anat.* A cordlike structure: the spinal *cord.* 7 *Often pl.* Any feeling that draws or restrains. 6 The rope used by a hangman. — *v.t.* 1 To bind or secure with cord; furnish with cords. 2 To pile (firewood) by the cord. ◆ Homophone: *chord.* [<F *corde* <L *chorda* <Gk. *chordē* string of a musical instrument. Doublet of CHORD.] — **cord′er** *n.*

cord·age (kôr′dij) *n.* 1 Ropes and cords collectively; especially, ropes in the rigging of a ship. 2 The amount in cords, as of wood, on a given area of land.

cor·date (kôr′dāt) *adj.* Heart–shaped, as a leaf. [<L *cordatus* <*cor* heart] — **cor′date·ly** *adv.*

Cor·day (kôr·dā′), **Charlotte,** 1768–93, French patriot; assassinated Marat: full name *Marie Anne Charlotte Corday d'Armont.*

cord·ed (kôr′did) *adj.* 1 Bound or fastened with cord or rope. 2 Striped or ribbed as if with cords: a *corded* fabric. 3 Piled in cord measure: *corded* firewood. 4 With the hair twisted or felted into strings or curls: said of dogs. 5 *Obs.* Made of cord or rope.

Cord·ed (kôr′did) *adj. Anthropol.* Designating a style of pottery decoration produced by the application of cords to the wet surface of the clay.

Corded people A Neolithic people of north central Europe who were named after corded pottery artifacts.

Cor·del·ia (kôr·dēl′yə, -dē′lē·ə; *Ger.* kôr·dā′·lē·ä) A feminine personal name. Also *Fr.* **Cor·dé·lie** (kôr·dā·lē′). [<Celtic, jewel of the sea]
— **Cordelia** The youngest of King Lear's three daughters, and the only one to remain faithful to him. See LEAR.

cor·de·lier (kôr′də·lir′) *n.* An early type of ropemaking machine. [<F]

Cor·de·lier (kôr′də·lir′) *n.* **1** A Franciscan friar who observes a very strict rule. **2** *pl.* A political club of the time of the French Revolution, whose meetings were held in an old Cordelier convent. [<F < *cordelle*, dim. of *corde* a cord; with ref. to the knotted cord worn by these friars]

cor·dial (kôr′jəl) *adj.* **1** Proceeding from the heart; exhibiting or expressing kindliness; imparting vigor or joy; cheering. See synonyms under AMICABLE. —*n.* **1** That which invigorates or exhilarates. **2** A sweet, aromatic alcoholic spirit; a liqueur. [<Med. L *cordialis* <L *cor, cordis* heart] —**cor·dial·i·ty** (kôr·jal′ə·tē, -jē·al′-, -dē·al′-), **cor′dial·ness** *n.* —**cor′dial·ly** *adv.*

cor·di·er·ite (kôr′dē·ə·rīt′) *n. Mineral.* A bluish silicate of magnesium, aluminum, and iron, crystallizing in the orthorhombic system: used as a gemstone: also called *iolite.* [after P. *Cordier*, 1777–1861, French geologist]

cor·di·form (kôr′də·fôrm) *adj.* Heart-shaped; cordate. [<L *cor, cordis* heart + -FORM]

cor·dil·le·ra (kôr′dil·yâr′ə, kôr·dil′ər·ə) *n. Geog.* The entire system of mountain ranges that borders a continent or occurs in the same general region. [<Sp. <OSp. *cordilla*, dim. of *cuerda* rope <L *chorda.* See CORD.] —**cor′·dil·le′ran** *adj.*

Cor·dil·le·ras (kôr′dil·yâr′əz, kôr·dil′ər·əz; *Sp.* kôr′thē·yä′räs) The Andes range in South America and its continuation in the Rocky Mountain system of North America.

cord·ite (kôr′dīt) *n.* A variety of smokeless powder consisting of cellulose nitrate or guncotton, nitroglycerin, and a mineral jelly, used chiefly as a propellant. [<CORD; with ref. to its appearance]

cor·do·ba (kôr′də·bə, *Sp.* kôr′thō·vä) *n.* The monetary unit of Nicaragua. [after Francisco de *Córdoba*, 16th c. Spanish explorer]

Cór·do·ba (kôr′thō·vä) **1** A province in Andalusia in southern Spain; 5,299 square miles; capital, Córdoba. **2** A province of central Argentina; 64,894 square miles; capital, Córdoba. Also **Cor·do·va** (kôr′də·və).

cor·don (kôr′dən) *n.* **1** An extended line, as of men, ships, forts, etc. **2** An ornamental lace, cord, or ribbon worn to secure something in place, as a badge of identification, or for adornment. **3** *Archit.* **a** A stringcourse. **b** A coping projecting from a scarp wall. [<F < *corde* cord]

cor·don bleu (kôr·dôṅ blœ′) *French* **1** The blue ribbon formerly worn by members of the order of the Holy Ghost, the highest order of the Bourbon monarchy. **2** Any high distinction. **3** One entitled to wear the cordon bleu. **4** Any person of distinction in his field.

cor·don·net (kôr′də·net′, *Fr.* kôr·dô·ne′) *n.* **1** The slightly raised edge of a point-lace pattern. **2** Edging made from piping. Also **cor′do·nette′.** [<F, dim. of *cordon.* See CORDON.]

cor·don sa·ni·taire (kôr·dôn′ sà·nē·târ′) *French* **1** A guarded line quarantining an infected area: also *sanitary cordon.* **2** A continuous line of countries cooperating to isolate another country in order to prevent the spread of its influence.

cor·do·van (kôr′də·vən) *n.* **1** Cordwain. **2** Fine horsehide leather.

Cor·do·van (kôr′də·vən) *adj.* Pertaining or belonging to Córdoba. —*n.* A native or resident of Córdoba.

cor·du·roy (kôr′də·roi, kôr′də·roi′) *n.* **1** A thick, corded or ribbed, durable fabric, usually of cotton. **2** *pl.* Trousers made of corduroy. **3** A corduroy road, or the materials used in construction. —*adj.* **1** Made of corduroy, as trousers. **2** Formed from logs laid transversely; a *corduroy* road. —*v.t.* To make into a corduroy road. [<F *corde du roi* fabric of the king]

corduroy road A road, as over miry ground, constructed with small logs laid together transversely.

cord·wain (kôrd′wān) *n. Archaic* Spanish leather: also *cordovan.* [<OF *cordoan* <OSp. *cordovan* of Córdoba]

cord·wood (kôrd′wo͝od′) *n.* Firewood sold by the cord.

cord·y (kôr′dē) *adj.* **1** In glassmaking, having stringlike imperfections due to impurities. **2** Full of cords; cordlike; having cordlike fibers or parts.

Cor·dy·ceps (kôr′di·seps) *n.* A genus of fungi parasitic on the larvae of insects or on certain subterranean fungi. [<NL <Gk. *kordylē* club + L *-ceps* < *caput* head]

core (kôr, kōr) *n.* **1** The central or innermost part of a thing. **2** The heart, as of an apple or pear, containing the seeds. **3** The most important part of anything; the pith of a subject. **4** A solid form placed in a mold, about which metal is poured, so as to be cast hollow. **5** *Electr.* **a** The insulated conducting wires of an electric cable. **b** The iron mass or bundle of iron rods, etc., around which the wire is coiled in an electromagnet or armature. **6** *Engin.* In submarine and geological investigations, a cylindrical mass of test material brought to the surface by a special hollow drill. **7** In fingerprint identification, the inner terminus or focal point which constitutes the approximate center of a pattern and is essential to its correct interpretation. **8** *Anthropol.* A type of Paleolithic stone implement consisting of a central mass of a rock, shaped for use in one of several standard forms, chiefly hand-axes. —*v.t.* **cored, cor·ing** To remove the core of. ◆ Homophone: *corps.* [Origin uncertain] —**core′less** *adj.* —**cor′er** *n.*

Cor·e·go·nus (kôr′i·gō′nəs, kor′-) *n.* A genus of salmonid fishes with small mouths and toothless jaws, including the whitefishes, many species of which inhabit inland waters in the northern hemisphere, and are among the most important of food fishes. [<NL < *korē* pupil of the eye + *gōnia* angle]

co·re·la·tion (kō′ri·lā′shən) See CORRELATION.

co–re·la·tion (kō′ri·lā′shən) *n.* **1** Joint or mutual relation. **2** Correlation.

co·re·lig·ion·ist (kō′ri·lij′ən·ist) *n.* An adherent of the same religion, church, or sect as another.

Co·rel·li (kō·rel′lē), **Arcangelo,** 1653–1713, Italian composer.

Co·rel·li (kə·rel′ē), **Marie,** 1864–1924, English novelist.

co·re·mi·um (kə·rē′mē·əm) *n. pl.* **·mi·a** (-mē·ə) *Bot.* A special form of non-sexual fruit body in the fungi in which spore-bearing hyphae are arranged in parallel order, side by side, to form an erect fascicle. [<Gk. *korema* broom]

Cor·en·tyn (kôr′ən·tīn, kor′-) A river forming the boundary between British Guiana and Dutch Guiana, flowing 450 miles north to the Atlantic: also *Corantyn, Courantyne.* Also **Cor′en·tyne.**

co·re·op·sis (kôr′ē·op′sis, kō′rē-) *n.* A plant of a large genus (*Coreopsis*) of mainly North American herbs of the composite family, with heads of showy yellow or rose-colored flowers: also called *calliopsis.* [<NL <Gk. *koris* bug + *opsis* appearance; with ref. to the shape of the seed]

cor·e·plas·ty (kôr′ə·plas′tē, kor′-) *n. Surg.* Any plastic operation upon the iris. [<Gk. *korē* pupil of the eye + -PLASTY] —**cor′e·plas′tic** *adj.*

cor·er (kôr′ər, kō′rər) *n.* A utensil for removing the cores of apples and other fruit.

co·re·spon·dent (kō′ri·spon′dənt) *n. Law* A joint defendant; especially, in a suit for divorce, one charged with having committed adultery with the husband or wife from whom divorce is being sought. —**co′re·spon′den·cy** *n.*

corf (kôrf) *n. pl.* **corves** (kôrvz) **1** *Brit.* A small freight wagon, formerly a wicker basket, in which coal is carried from the working place to the shaft. **2** *Brit. Dial.* A floating receptacle for holding fish, etc. [ME <LG. Cf. MDu. *korf* basket.]

Cor·fi·ote (kôr′fē·ōt) *n.* A native or inhabitant of Corfu. Also **Cor·fute** (kôr′fyo͞ot).

Cor·fu (kôr·fo͞o′, kôr′fyo͞o) A Greek island in the Ionian group; 229 square miles; capital, Corfu: ancient *Corcyra*: Greek *Kerkyra.*

cor·gi (kôr′gē) *n.* A Welsh working dog. See WELSH CORGI.

CARDIGAN WELSH CORGI (12 inches high at the shoulder)

Co·ri (kô′rē), **Carl Ferdinand,** born 1896, and his wife **Gerty T.,** 1896–1957, *née* Radnitz, U.S. biochemists born in Czechoslovakia.

co·ri·a·ceous (kôr′·ē·ā′shəs, kō′rē-) *adj.* Of a rough leathery texture; like leather. [<L *corium* leather]

co·ri·an·der (kôr′ē·an′dər, kō′rē-) *n.* A plant of the parsley family (genus *Coriandrum*), bearing aromatic seeds used for seasoning and in medicine as a carminative. [<F *coriandre* <L *coriandrum* <Gk. *koriannon*]

Co·rin·na (kə·rin′ə) Diminutive of Cora. Also *Fr.* **Co·rinne** (kô·rin′).
— **Corinna** A Greek lyric poetess, about 490 B.C.

Cor·inth (kôr′inth, kor′-) **1** An ancient city in Argolis, Greece. **2** A modern city, three miles from the site of ancient Corinth, on the **Gulf of Corinth,** an arm of the Ionian Sea between the Peloponnesus and northern Greece: Italian *Gulf of Lepanto.* —**Isthmus of Corinth** An isthmus connecting the Peloponnesus with northern Greece; traversed by the **Corinth Canal,** connecting the Gulf of Corinth and the Saronic Gulf; 4 miles long; 72 feet wide.

Co·rinth (kō·rint′), **Lovis,** 1858–1925, German painter.

Co·rin·thi·an (kə·rin′thē·ən) *adj.* **1** Pertaining to Corinth. **2** *Archit.* Denoting an order marked by slender fluted columns with ornate, bell-shaped capitals decorated with a design of acanthus leaves. For illustration see CAPITAL. **3** Luxurious; licentious, as the people of Corinth were reputed to be. —*n.* **1** A native or inhabitant of Corinth. **2** A dissolute or profligate person. **3** *U.S.* A gentleman sportsman who sails his own yacht. — **Epistle to the Corinthians** Either of two letters addressed by the apostle Paul to the Christians at Corinth, each forming a book of the New Testament.

Cor·i·o·la·nus (kôr′ē·ə·lā′nəs, kor′-) Roman patrician of the fifth century B.C. who led the Volscians against Rome; hero of Shakespeare's tragedy of the same name.

Cor·i·o·lis force (kôr′ē·ō′lis) *Meteorol.* The deflecting effect of the earth's rotation whereby freely moving air masses are deflected to the right in the northern hemisphere and to the left in the southern hemisphere (relatively, to an observer on the earth's surface). [after Gaspard Gustave de *Coriolis,* 1792–1843, French mathematician]

Co·ris·co (kō·ris′kō) An island of Spanish Guinea in the Bight of Biafra, Africa; 5 1/2 square miles.

co·ri·um (kôr′ē·əm, kō′rē-) *n. pl.* **·ri·a** (-ə) **1** *Anat.* The sentient and vascular portion of the skin beneath the epidermis. **2** *Entomol.* In certain insects (order *Heteroptera*), the elongated middle section or harder portion of the forewing. [<L, skin, hide]

cork[1] (kôrk) *n.* **1** A tough, elastic, light, and porous outer bark of an evergreen tree (*Quercus suber*), the cork oak, indigenous to southern Europe: it improves in quality with the age of the tree, and has many uses in industry and the arts. **2** A piece of this bark used as a bottle stopper. **3** Any stopper of other material: a rubber *cork.* **4** *Bot.* A protective tissue that forms in the stems beneath the epidermis of dicotyledons and replaces it. —*v.t.* **1** To stop with a cork, as a bottle. **2** To restrain or confine; check. **3** *U.S.* To blacken with burnt cork. —**to cork up** *U.S. Colloq.* To silence suddenly. [<OSp. *alcorque* a cork slipper <Arabic, ? <L *quercus* oak]

cork[2] (kôrk) See CALK: erroneous usage.

Cork (kôrk) The largest county in Ireland, in southern Munster province; 2,880 square miles; county seat, Cork.

cork·age (kôr′kij) *n.* A charge for serving

wine at a hotel, especially when the wine is the property of the guest.

cork belt A belt or jacket made of pieces of cork enclosed in canvas, to support a person in the water; a life belt. Also **cork jacket.**

cork·board (kôrk′bôrd′, -bōrd′) *n.* A building material formed from compressed and bonded granulated cork.

cork cambium *Bot.* The phellogen, or inner active layers of bark-producing tissue. Also **cork meristem.**

corked (kôrkt) *adj.* **1** Stopped with cork, as a bottle. **2** Having acquired the taste of cork: *corked* wine. **3** *Slang* Very drunk.

cork·er (kôr′kər) *n.* **1** One who or that which corks. **2** *Slang* An argument that puts a stop to discussion; anything that stops competition. **3** *Slang* Any unusual person or thing.

cork·ing (kôr′king) *Slang adj.* Fine; excellent; also, amazing. — *adv.* Fine; excellently.

cork oak An oak tree *(Quercus suber)* of southern Europe and North Africa, whose thick bark yields cork.

cork·screw (kôrk′skrōō′) *n.* **1** A spiral instrument for drawing corks from bottles. **2** A ringlet; curl. — *v.t.* & *v.i.* **1** To move or cause to move like a corkscrew; to twist. **2** *Aeron.* To fly in a spiral course in order to avoid enemy anti-aircraft fire. — *adj.* Shaped like a corkscrew; twisted; spiral.

cork·wood (kôrk′wŏŏd′) *n.* **1** The light, porous wood of several West Indian trees: specifically, of the custard-apple family (genus *Annona*), or of the balsa family, especially *Ochroma pyramidale.* **2** In the SE United States, a small tree *(Leitneria floridana)* with deciduous glossy leaves and a drupaceous fruit.

cork·y (kôr′kē) *adj.* **·i·er, ·i·est** **1** Like cork; especially, shrunken; dried up. **2** Having the flavor or odor of cork: said especially of wines. **3** Of cork. — **cork′i·ness** *n.*

Cor Le·o·nis (kôr lē·ō′nis) See REGULUS.

Cor·liss (kôr′lis), **George Henry,** 1817–88, U.S. inventor and manufacturer.

corm (kôrm) *n. Bot.* A bulblike, solid, fleshy enlargement, usually of the underground stem in plants. [<Gk. *kormos* tree-trunk]

Cor·moph·y·ta (kôr·mof′i·tə) *n. pl.* A former primary division of the vegetable kingdom, embracing plants that possess a stem (axis) with leaves: distinguished from *Thallophyta.* [<NL <*kormos* trunk + *phyton* plant] — **cor·mo·phyte** (kôr′mə·fīt) *n.* — **cor′mo·phyt′ic** (-fit′ik) *adj.*

cor·mo·rant (kôr′·mər·ənt) *n.* **1** A large, web-footed, voracious aquatic bird (genus *Phalacrocorax*) of wide distribution and gregarious habits, having a strongly hooked bill and large throat gular pouch. **2** Hence, a glutton or avaricious person. — *adj.* Like a cormorant; greedy; rapacious. [<F *cormoran* <L *corvus marinus* sea crow]

CORMORANT (Body size varies from 1 1/2 to 3 feet)

corn[1] (kôrn) *n.* **1** The edible seeds of cereal plants: in England, wheat, barley, rye, and oats collectively; in America, maize, or Indian corn. **2** The plants that produce corn when growing in the field; the stalks and ears, or the stalks, ears, and seeds, after harvesting. **3** *Slang* Anything regarded as trite, banal, sentimental, etc., especially popular music. **4** *Colloq.* Whisky distilled from corn. — *v.t.* **1** To preserve in salt or in brine: to *corn* beef. **2** *U.S.* To feed with corn. **3** *Scot.* To feed with oats. **4** To granulate. [OE]

Corn may appear as a combining form in hyphemes or solidemes, or as the first element in two-word phrases:

cornbin	**corn crop**	**corn-growing**
corn brandy	**corn-eating**	**cornland**
corncake	**corn flour**	**cornloft**
corn-colored	**corn-grower**	**cornmill**

corn[2] (kôrn) *n.* **1** A horny thickening of the cuticle, common on the feet. **2** A morbid condition of the forehoofs of horses caused by injuries to the tissue of the sole, producing inflammation of the horn. [<OF <L *cornu.* Akin to HORN.]

cor·na·ceous (kôr·nā′shəs) *adj.* Designating a family *(Cornaceae)* of polypetalous shrubs or trees; the dogwood or cornel family.

corn borer The larva of certain insects which feeds on the ears and stalks of corn, especially the European corn borer *(Pyrausta nubilalis).*

corn·bread (kôrn′bred′) *n.* Bread made from the meal of maize or Indian corn. Also **corn bread.**

corn·cob (kôrn′kob′) *n.* The spike of maize round which the kernels grow. Also **corn cob.**

corncob pipe A pipe whose bowl is cut from a corncob.

corn·cock·le (kôrn′kok′əl) *n.* A tall purple-flowered weed of the pink family, especially *Agrostemma githago*: also called *corn rose.*

corn crake A European crake *(Crex crex)* frequenting cornfields: also called *dakerhen.*

corn·crib (kôrn′krib′) *n.* A building for storage of corn, usually raised on posts, with walls made of slats for ventilation.

corn·dodg·er (kôrn′doj′ər) *n.* A cake of cornmeal baked or fried hard.

cor·ne·a (kôr′nē·ə) *n. Anat.* The transparent anterior part of the outer coat of the eyeball, continuous with the sclera. See illustration under EYE. Also **cornea lens.** [<Med. L *cornea* horny <L *cornu* horn] — **cor′ne·al** *adj.*

corn·ear worm (kôrn′ir′) The bollworm.

corned (kôrnd) *adj.* **1** Preserved in coarse salt or in brine: *corned* beef. **2** *U.S. Slang* Drunk.

Cor·neille (kôr·nā′, *Fr.* kôr·nā′y′), **Pierre,** 1606–84, French dramatist and poet.

cor·nel (kôr′nəl) *n.* Any of a genus *(Cornus)* of shrubs and small trees with hard, compact wood, as the dogwood: also called *cornus.* [<G *kornel(baum)* <Med. L *cornolius* <MF *cornoille,* ult. <L *cornus* cornel tree] — **cor·nel·ian** (kôr·nēl′yən) *adj.*

Cor·nel·ia (kôr·nēl′yə, *Ger.* kôr·nā′lē·ä, *Ital.* kôr·nā′lyä) A feminine personal name. Also *Fr.* **Cor·né·lie** (kôr·nā·lē′). [<L, fem. of *Cornelius*]

— **Cornelia** Roman matron of the second century B.C.; mother of the Gracchi.

— **Cornelia** Wife of Julius Caesar; died 67? B.C.

cor·nel·ian (kôr·nēl′yən) See CARNELIAN.

Cor·nel·ius (kôr·nēl′yəs, *Ger.* kôr·nā′lē·ōōs) A masculine personal name. Also *Fr.* **Cor·né·li·us** (kôr·nā·lē·üs′); *Ital., Sp.* **Cor·ne·lio** (kôr·nā′lyō). [<L, ? war horn]

Cor·ne·li·us (kôr·nā′lē·ōōs), **Peter von,** 1783–1867, German painter.

Cor·nell (kôr·nel′), **Ezra,** 1807–74, U.S. philanthropist; founded Cornell University, 1865. — **Katharine,** born 1898, U.S. actress.

cor·ne·ous (kôr′nē·əs) *adj.* Consisting of horn; of a hornlike texture; horny. [<L *corneus* horny]

cor·ner (kôr′nər) *n.* **1** The point formed by the intersection of two or more lines or surfaces, or the edge formed by the intersection of two surfaces; an angle. **2** The space or surface comprised between two converging walls or lines near their meeting. **3** A retired spot; nook: the chimney *corner.* **4** A position of embarrassment or difficulty, or one from which extrication is difficult. **5** A condition of a financial market when a commodity or security has been largely bought up with a view to forcing a higher price: a *corner* in cotton or stocks. **6** A part or spot, especially a remote or obscure part, of a particular place; also, any of the four directions: the four *corners* of the earth. **7** A tool used in decorating the corners of books: sometimes called **cornerpiece.** **8** A metallic or other guard for the corner of a book, box, or other article. — **to trim one's corners** To take risks. — *v.t.* **1** To force or drive into a corner. **2** To place in a corner. **3** *U.S.* To place in a position of difficulty or embarrassment: to *corner* a witness. **4** To furnish with corners. **5** To acquire control of, as a commodity or stock, so as to demand a high price. — *v.i.* **6** *U.S.* To come together in a corner; be situated on a corner. **7** *Colloq.* To go round a corner, as in racing: The car *corners* beautifully. **8** To form a corner in a commodity or stock. — *adj.* **1** Located at a corner. **2** Designed for a corner. [<OF *cornier* <L *cornu* horn, point]

corner chair A small armchair having the back curved or placed at an angle around two sides of the seat, one leg supporting the front corner of the seat: also called *round-about chair.*

corner cupboard A cupboard, usually for household china, with curved or diagonal front, designed to fit into a corner.

cor·nered (kôr′nərd) *adj.* **1** Having corners. **2** Forced into a position of embarrassment or difficulty.

cor·ner·stone (kôr′nər·stōn′) *n.* **1** A stone uniting two walls at the corner of a building. **2** Such a stone, often inscribed and made into a repository, laid into the foundation of an edifice. **3** Something fundamental or of primary importance.

cor·ner·wise (kôr′nər·wīz′) *adv.* With the corner in front; diagonally.

cor·net[1] (kôr·net′ *for def. 1*; kôr′nit *for defs. 2 and 3*) **1** A small wind instrument of the trumpet class, in which the notes are determined by valves or pistons that open communication into auxiliary bands of tubing, thus varying the length of the vibrating air column. **2** A cone-shaped paper wrapper. **3** A portion of a woman's headdress, of varying shape, from the 14th to the 17th century; also, the headdress itself; also, the tall white headdress of the Sisters of Charity. [<OF, dim. of corn <L *cornu* a horn] — **cor·net′tist** or **cor·net′ist** *n.*

CORNET *(def. 3)*

cor·net[2] (kôr′nit) *n.* **1** Formerly, the lowest commissioned cavalry officer in the British army, or a pennant carried by him. **2** A flag or standard; specifically, a signaling flag. [<F, dim. of *corne* <L *cornu* horn]

cor·net-à-pis·tons (kôr·net′ə·pis′tənz, *Fr.* kôr·ne′á·pē·stôṅ′) *n.* *pl.* **cor·nets-à-pis·tons** (kôr·nets′-, *Fr.* kôr·ne′zá·pē·stôṅ′) Cornet[1] (def. 1).

cor·net·cy (kôr′nit·sē) *n.* *pl.* **·cies** The rank or commission of a cornet.

corn·fac·tor (kôrn′fak′tər) *n. Brit.* A wholesale dealer in grain.

corn-fed (kôrn′fed′) *adj. U.S.* **1** Nourished on corn. **2** *Slang* Strong and healthy, as if fed on an ample diet of corn, but rustic and unsophisticated.

corn·field (kôrn′fēld′) *n.* An area in which corn is grown: also **corn field.** — *adj.* **1** Of, from, or growing in a cornfield. **2** Rustic: *cornfield* philosophy.

corn·flow·er (kôrn′flou′ər) *n.* Any flower growing in grainfields; especially, the bluebottle or bachelor's-button.

corn·husk (kôrn′husk′) *n.* A corn shuck.

corn·husk·ing (kôrn′hus′king) *n. U.S.* **1** The husking of corn. **2** A social gathering used for the purpose of husking corn, usually followed by refreshments, dancing, etc.; a husking bee. — **corn′husk′er** *n.*

cor·nice (kôr′nis) *n.* **1** *Archit.* **a** The horizontal molded projection at the top of a building or of a component part of a building, usually under the eaves. **b** The uppermost member of an entablature. See illustration under ENTABLATURE. **2** An ornamental molding around the walls of a room close to the ceiling; also, a light wooden molding around the walls of a room, gallery, etc., at a convenient height for the support of pictures by hooks. **3** A frame, upholstered or of molding, fastened to a wall or window frame so as to cover the rods and hooks used for hanging curtains, etc. **4** A mass of snow projecting from a mountain ridge. — *v.t.* **·niced, ·nic·ing** To provide or adorn with a cornice. [<Ital. <L *coronis* <Gk. *korōnis* wreath, garland] — **cor′niced** *adj.*

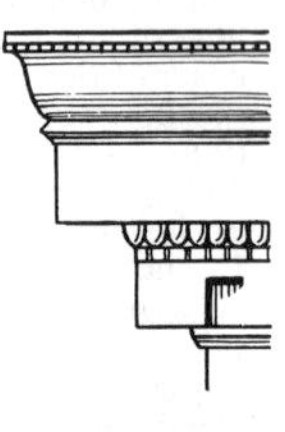

CORNICE

cor·nic·u·late (kôr·nik′yə·lāt, -lit) *adj.* Having horns or hornlike processes. [<L *corniculatus* < *corniculum,* dim. of *cornu* horn]

Cor·ning (kôr′ning) A city in southern New York.

Cor·nish (kôr′nish) *adj.* Pertaining to Cornwall, in England, or its people. — *n.* The former language of Cornwall, belonging to the Brythonic branch of the Celtic languages: extinct since the early nineteenth century and replaced by a dialect of English.

Cor·nish·man (kôr′nish·mən) *n. pl.* **·men** (-mən) A native or inhabitant of Cornwall.

Corn Laws In English history, certain laws, the first dating from 1361, placing restrictions on the grain trade and especially the importation of grain: repealed in 1846.

corn lily 1 Either of two species of convolvulus, the greater or lesser bindweed. 2 Any bulbous plant of the genus *Ixia* of South Africa.

corn mayweed 1 The scentless wild camomile (*Matricaria inodora*): naturalized in parts of the United States. 2 The field camomile (*Anthemis arvensis*) of the eastern United States.

corn·meal (kôrn′mēl′) *n.* 1 Meal made from corn; Indian meal. 2 *Scot.* Oatmeal. Also **corn meal.**

Cor·no (kôr′nō), **Mon·te** (môn′tā) The highest peak of the Apennines, in south central Italy; 9,560 feet. Also **Corno Gran·de** (grän′dā).

corn picker A machine for removing and husking ears of standing corn.

corn pit A section of a produce exchange devoted to business in corn.

corn pith The pith of Indian corn, used in the manufacture of paper, etc.

corn pone Bread made of cornmeal, water, and salt, usually without milk and eggs.

corn–pop·per (kôrn′pop′ər) *n.* A wire box or cylinder used for popping corn over a fire.

corn poppy A weed (*Papaver rhoeas*) growing in grain fields: also called *corn rose.*

corn rose See CORNCOCKLE, CORN POPPY.

corn salad Lamb lettuce (*Valerianella olitoria*), a European plant whose leaves are used for salad.

corn shock A conical bundle of stalks of Indian corn, often tied together at the top.

corn shuck The shuck or husk of an ear of maize: also *cornhusk.*

corn shucks scrub A scrubbing brush made out of corn shucks.

corn smut A widespread disease of corn, due to infection by the smut fungus, *Ustilago zeae,* and characterized by spore–containing tumor masses attached to the ears and other aerial parts of the plant.

corn snow In skiing, fallen snow which has melted slightly and refrozen, forming a coarse, granular surface which enables the skis to slide more easily.

corn spurry Beggarweed.

corn·stalk (kôrn′stôk′) *n.* A stalk of Indian corn. Also **corn stalk.**

corn·starch (kôrn′stärch′) *n.* 1 Starch made from corn. 2 A purified starchy meal used in making puddings.

corn sugar Glucose obtained from corn.

corn't (kôrnt) *adj. Scot.* Fed on oats.

cor·nu (kôr′nyōō) *n. pl.* **·nu·a** (-nyōō·ə) A horn, or anything shaped like a horn: applied to various anatomical structures: the superior and inferior *cornua* of the larynx. [<L, horn]

cor·nu·co·pi·a (kôr′nə·kō′pē·ə) *n.* 1 The horn of plenty, represented as overflowing with fruits and symbolizing peace and prosperity. See AMALTHEA. 2 A paper or cardboard horn for holding candies. 3 A superabundance. [<LL *cornucopia* <L *cornu copiae* horn of plenty] — **cor′nu·co′pi·an** *adj.*

cor·nus (kôr′nəs) See CORNEL.

cor·nute (kôr·nōōt′, -nyōōt′) *adj.* 1 Having horns or a hornlike process or appendage. 2 Shaped like a horn. Also **cor·nut′ed.** [<L *cornutus* < *cornu* horn]

cor·nu·to (kôr·nōō′tō, -nyōō′-) *n. pl.* **·tos** *Obs.* A cuckold. [<Ital.]

Corn·wall (kôrn′wôl, *Brit.* -wəl) A county of SW England; 1,357 square miles; county seat, Bodmin: a native of the country is known as a *Cornishman.*

Corn·wal·lis (kôrn·wôl′is, -wol′-), **Charles,** 1738–1805, first Marquis Cornwallis, English general and statesman.

Corn·wal·lis Island (kôrn·wôl′is, -wol′-) An island in the Northwest Territories, Canada; 2,592 square miles.

corn whisky Whisky distilled from corn.

corn·worm (kôrn′wûrm′) *n.* The bollworm.

corn·y (kôr′nē) *adj.* **corn·i·er, corn·i·est** 1 Of, abounding in, or producing corn. 2 *Slang* Trite, banal, sentimental, or unsophisticated.

cor·o·dy (kôr′ə·dē, kor′-) *n. pl.* **·dies** In old English law, a right pertaining to the king to send one of his chaplains to be maintained by a bishop; also, an allowance, as for food, granted for services: also spelled *corrody.* [<Med. L *corrodium,* var. of *corredium* provision]

co·rol·la (kə·rol′ə) *n. Bot.* The second series or inner circle of flower leaves, usually colored, forming the inner floral envelope or inner perianth, and serving mainly to attract insects; the petals of a flower collectively. Also **cor·ol** (kor′əl). [<L, dim. of *corona* crown] — **cor·ol·late** (kôr′ə·lāt, kor′-), **cor′ol·lat′ed** *adj.*

cor·ol·lar·y (kôr′ə·ler′ē, kor′-; *Brit.* kə·rol′ər·ē) *n. pl.* **·lar·ies** 1 A proposition following so obviously from another that it requires little or no demonstration. 2 An inference; deduction. — *adj.* Like a corollary; deduced; resultant. [<L *corollarium* gift, orig. money paid for a garland < *corolla* garland]

Cor·o·man·del (kôr′ə·man′dəl, kor′-) The coast of SE India from the Kistna to Palk Strait.

Coromandel lacquer A type of Chinese lacquerwork in which the design is cut in intaglio and completed with varied colors and gold: so called because objects thus decorated were imported into western Europe by East India merchants with headquarters on the Coromandel Coast.

CORONA (*def. 4b*)

co·ro·na (kə·rō′nə) *n. pl.* **·nas** or **·nae** (-nē) 1 A garland or wreath given by the ancient Greeks and Romans as a reward for distinguished achievements. 2 *Archit.* The projecting brow of a cornice. 3 A crownlike part, structure, or process, as the crown of the head or the shell of a sea–urchin. 4 *Astron.* **a** A luminous circle around one of the heavenly bodies. **b** The luminous envelope of ionized gases surrounding the chromosphere of the sun and visible during a total eclipse. 5 Loosely, any halo. 6 *Electr.* The luminous discharge at the surface of an electrical conductor under very high voltage. 7 *Bot.* A crownlike process at the top of the tube of the corolla, as in jonquils. 8 *Geol.* A zone of minerals surrounding another mineral or at the junction of two minerals. [<L, crown]

Corona Aus·tra·lis (ôs·trā′lis) The Southern Crown, a constellation south of Sagittarius: also called the *Wreath.* See CONSTELLATION.

Corona Bo·re·al·is (bôr′ē·al′is, -ā′lis, bō′rē-) The Northern Crown, a constellation between Hercules and Boötes. See CONSTELLATION.

cor·o·nach (kôr′ə·nəkh, kor′-) *n.* 1 *Scot.* A dirge, as for a chieftain. 2 In Ireland, a keening or wailing lament for the dead. [<Irish *coranach*]

Co·ro·na·do (kôr′ə·nä′dō, *Sp.* kō′rō·nä′thō), **Francisco Vasquez de,** 1510?–54, Spanish explorer.

co·ro·nal (kə·rō′nəl, kôr′ə·nəl, kor′-) *adj.* 1 Of or pertaining to a corona or halo, or to the crown of the head. 2 *Anat.* Having the direction of the coronal suture: a *coronal* plane. — **cor·o·nal** (kôr′ə·nəl, kor′-) *n.* A crown or garland.

coronal suture *Anat.* The suture between the frontal and the two parietal bones of the skull.

cor·o·nar·y (kôr′ə·ner′ē, kor′-) *adj.* 1 Pertaining to a crown or wreath. 2 *Anat.* Encircling, crowning: the *coronary* ligament of the liver; the two *coronary* arteries rising from the aorta. See illustration under HEART. — *n.* Coronary thrombosis. [<L *coronarius* < *corona* crown]

coronary thrombosis *Pathol.* The formation of a thrombus, or blood clot, in one of the coronary arteries, resulting in interruption of blood supply from the heart.

cor·o·na·tion (kôr′ə·nā′shən, kor′-) *n.* 1 The act or ceremony of crowning a monarch. 2 Accomplishment; fulfilment. [<OF *coronacion* <L *coronatus,* pp. of *coronare* crown]

Co·ro·nel (kō′rō·nel′) A port of south central Chile; scene of a World War I German naval victory, 1914.

cor·o·ner (kôr′ə·nər, kor′-) *n.* A public officer who inquires into the cause of deaths not clearly due to natural causes. [<AF *coruner* officer of the crown < *corune* crown <L *corona*] — **cor′o·ner·ship′** *n.*

coroner's jury See under JURY.

cor·o·net (kôr′ə·net, -nit, kor′-) *n.* 1 A small or inferior crown, denoting noble rank less than sovereign. 2 Any chaplet or wreath for the head; especially, a semicircular band worn by women above the brow as a headdress. 3 The upper margin of a horse's hoof. [<OF *coronete,* dim. of *corone* crown <L *corona*]

BRITISH CORONETS
a. H.R.H. Prince of Wales. *b.* Younger son and brother of the Blood Royal. *c.* Nephew, etc., of the Blood Royal. *d.* Duke. *e.* Marquis. *f.* Earl. *g.* Viscount. *h.* Baron.

co·ro·ni·form (kə·rō′nə·fôrm) *adj.* Having the form of a crown. [<L *corona* crown + -FORM]

Co·rot (kô·rō′), **Jean Baptiste Camille,** 1796–1875, French painter.

cor·po·ra (kôr′pər·ə) Plural of CORPUS.

cor·po·ral[1] (kôr′pər·əl) *adj.* 1 Belonging or relating to the body as opposed to the mind: *corporal* punishment. 2 Personal: *corporal* possession. 3 *Obs.* Having substance; corporeal; not spiritual. See synonyms under PHYSICAL. — *n.* The linen cloth on which the elements are placed during the celebration of the Eucharist: also **cor·po·ra·le** (kôr′pə·rā′lē) or **corporal cloth.** [<L *corporalis* < *corpus* body] — **cor·po·ral·i·ty** (kôr′pə·ral′ə·tē) *n.* — **cor′po·ral·ly** *adv.*

cor·po·ral[2] (kôr′pər·əl) *n.* 1 In the U.S. Army and Marine Corps, an enlisted man ranking next above a private first class and next below a sergeant. 2 In the British Navy; an assistant to the master at arms. 3 *U.S.* The fallfish (*Semotilus corporalis*). —**lance corporal** A private acting as corporal. [<MF *coporal,* var. of *caporal* <Ital. *caporale* < *capo* head <L *caput*]

corporal's guard *Mil.* The squad of men detailed for guard or other duty under a corporal; hence, any small number of persons, especially of attendants or adherents.

cor·po·rate (kôr′pər·it) *adj.* 1 Associated by legal enactment for the transaction of business; incorporated: a body politic and *corporate.* 2 Belonging to a corporation: *corporate* property. 3 Combined as a whole; considered as one; collective. 4 Having a visible body or form; corporeal; not spiritual. [<L *corporatus,* pp. of *corporare* assume a body < *corpus* body] — **cor′po·rate·ly** *adv.*

cor·po·ra·tion (kôr′pə·rā′shən) *n.* 1 An artificial person created by law, consisting of one or more natural persons united in one body under such grants as secure a succession of members without changing the identity of the body, and empowered to act in a certain capacity or to transact business of some designated form or nature like a natural person. 2 *Colloq.* A protuberant abdomen; paunch.

cor·po·ra·tive (kôr′pə·rā′tiv, -pər·ə·tiv′) *adj.* 1 Of or pertaining to a corporation. 2 In political systems, regimenting the operation of the whole social and economic life through one or more corporate bodies selected from employers and employees of principal corporations and controlled by the government. — **cor′po·ra′tive·ly** *adv.*

cor·po·ra·tor (kôr′pə·rā′tər) *n.* A member of a corporation; especially, an original incorporator.

cor·po·re·al (kôr·pôr′ē·əl, -pō′rē·əl) *adj.* 1 Having a body; of a material nature; physical: distinguished from *immaterial, mental,* or *spiritual.* 2 *Law* Perceivable by the bodily senses; substantial and permanent; opposed to *incorporeal: corporeal* hereditaments. See synonyms under PHYSICAL. [<L *corporeus* < *corpus* body] —**cor·po·re·al·i·ty** (kôr·pôr′ē·al′ə·tē, -pō′rē-), **cor·po′re·al·ness, cor·po·re·i·ty** (kôr′pə·rē′ə·tē) *n.* —**cor·po′re·al·ly** *adv.*

cor·po·sant (kôr′pə·zant) *n.* A luminous discharge of atmospheric electricity from sharp points near the earth's surface, as from steeples, treetops, the masts of ships, etc.: also called *St. Elmo's fire.* [<Pg. *corpo santo* <L *corpus sanctus* holy body]

corps (kôr, kōr) *n. pl.* **corps** (kôrz, kōrz) 1 *Mil.* **a** A tactical unit, intermediate between a division and an army, and consisting of two or more divisions. **b** A special department or subdivision: the Quartermaster *Corps.* 2 A number of persons acting together. ◆ Homophone: *core.* [<F, var. of OF *cors.* See CORPSE.]

corps de bal·let (kôr′ də ba·lā′, *Fr.* bȧ·le′) The ballet dancers who perform as a group in a performance and have no solo parts. [<F]

corps de garde (kôr də gȧrd′) *French* 1 The sentry. 2 The guardroom.

corpse (kôrps) *n.* A dead body, usually of a human being. See synonyms under BODY. [ME *corps,* var. of *cors* <OF <L *corpus* body]

corpse fat Adipocere.

corps·man (kôr′mən, kōr′-) *n. pl.* **·men** (-mən) A member of a military corps. In the U.S. Navy, an enlisted man working as a pharmacist; in the U.S. Army, an enlisted man in the Medical Corps assigned to a combat area.

cor·pu·lent (kôr′pyə·lənt) *adj.* Having a great excess of fat; very fleshy. [<F <L *corpulentus* fleshy < *corpus* body] —**cor′pu·lence, cor′pu·len·cy, cor′pu·lent·ness** *n.*

Synonyms: adipose, burly, fat, fleshy, gross, obese, plethoric, portly, pursy, stout. *Antonyms:* bony, emaciated, gaunt, lean, poor, skinny, slight, spare, thin.

cor·pus (kôr′pəs) *n. pl.* **·po·ra** (-pər·ə) 1 A body of a man or animal. 2 The main body or substance of anything. 3 *Law* **a** A material object; especially, a corporeal property. **b** The elements or facts of a case considered collectively. 4 *Anat.* The main part or mass of an organ. [<L]

corpus cal·lo·sum (kə·lō′səm) *Anat.* A large band of commissural fibers connecting the two halves of the cerebral hemispheres. [< NL, hard body]

Cor·pus Chris·ti (kôr′pəs kris′tē, -tī) In the Roman Catholic Church, a festival held in honor of the Eucharist on the first Thursday following Trinity Sunday. [<L, body of Christ]

Cor·pus Chris·ti (kôr′pəs kris′tē) A port in Texas on **Corpus Christi Bay,** an arm of the Gulf of Mexico in southern Texas.

cor·pus·cle (kôr′pəs·əl, -pus·əl) *n.* 1 A minute particle of matter; molecule; atom; electron. 2 *Biol.* **a** Any protoplasmic granule of distinct shape or characteristic function. **b** One of the particles forming part of the blood of vertebrates, either a **red corpuscle** containing hemoglobin for oxygen transport, or a **white corpuscle,** known as a leukocyte. Also **cor·pus·cule** (kôr·pus′kyōōl). [<L *corpusculum,* dim. of *corpus* body] —**cor·pus·cu·lar** (kôr·pus′kyə·lər) *adj.*

corpus de·lic·ti (də·lik′tī) *Law Latin* The existence of the essential fact or facts which prove the commission of a crime, as the finding of stolen goods on the person of an alleged thief. [<L, the body of the offense]

corpus ju·ris (jŏŏr′is) *Latin* The body of law.

Corpus Juris Ca·non·i·ci (kə·non′ə·sī) *Latin* The collective title of the decrees and canons of the Roman Catholic Church, constituting the standard of canon law prior to 1918.

Corpus Juris Ci·vil·is (si·vil′is) *Latin* The collective title of the body of Roman law, comprising the Institutes, the Pandects or Digest, the Code, and the Novels or new laws, of Justinian: promulgated 528–534.

corpus lu·te·um (lōō′tē·əm) *pl.* **cor·po·ra lu·te·a** (-tē·ə) *Anat.* A yellow body formed by a Graafian follicle in the ovary, and appearing during menstruation and pregnancy: it secretes progesterone. [<L, yellow body]

corpus stri·a·tum (strī·ā′təm) *pl.* **cor·po·ra stri·a·ta** (-tə) *Anat.* One of two masses of ganglionic cells situated in front of the thalamus and at the base of either hemisphere of the brain. [<L, striped body]

cor·rach (kûr′əkh, kûr′ə) See CURRACH.

cor·rade (kə·rād′) *v.t.* **·rad·ed, ·rad·ing** *Geol.* To disintegrate, as rocks, either by solution or by solution combined with mechanical wear: said of rivers. [<L *corradere* < *com-* together + *radere* scrape, rub]

cor·ra·di·ate (kə·rā′dē·āt) *v.i.* **·at·ed, ·at·ing** To converge to a focus, as rays of light. [<COR- + RADIATE]

Cor·ra·do (kôr·rä′dō) Italian form of CONRAD.

cor·ral (kə·ral′) *n.* 1 An enclosed space or pen for livestock. 2 A space enclosed by wagons for protection against attack. —*v.t.* **·ralled, ·ral·ling** 1 To drive into and enclose in a corral; pen up. 2 To arrange in the form of a corral: to *corral* wagons. 3 *U.S. Colloq.* To seize or capture; secure. [<Sp., a yard, an enclosed space]

cor·ra·sion (kə·rā′zhən) *n. Geol.* The process of erosion by corrading; specifically, the vertical or lateral cutting performed by a river. Compare EROSION. [<L *corrasus,* pp. of *corradere.* See CORRADE.]

cor·rect (kə·rekt′) *v.t.* 1 To rectify or remove error from; make right. 2 To point out the errors of; set right. 3 To rebuke or chastise. 4 To remedy or counteract, as a malfunction. 5 To make conformable to a standard: to *correct* a lens. See synonyms under AMEND, CHASTEN, RECLAIM. —*adj.* 1 Free from fault or mistake. 2 True, right, or proper; accurate; exact. [<L *correctus,* pp. of *corrigere* < *com-* together + *regere* make straight] —**cor·rect′a·ble** or **·i·ble** *adj.* —**cor·rec′tive** *adj.* & *n.* —**cor·rec′tive·ly** *adv.* —**cor·rect′ly** *adv.* —**cor·rect′ness** *n.* —**cor·rec′tor** *n.*

Synonyms (adj.): accurate, decorous, exact, faultless, perfect, precise, proper, right, true. See EXACT, PERFECT, PRECISE, RIGHT. *Antonyms:* erroneous, false, faulty, inaccurate, incorrect, wrong.

cor·rec·tion (kə·rek′shən) *n.* 1 The act of correcting or setting right; rectification; emendation. 2 That which is offered as an improvement. 3 The act or process of disciplining or chastening. 4 The act or process of neutralizing an undesired quality or condition. —**cor·rec′tion·al** *adj.*

cor·rec·ti·tude (kə·rek′tə·tōōd, -tyōōd) *n.* Freedom from impropriety; correctness.

Cor·reg·gio (kôr·red′jō), **Antonio Allegri da,** 1494–1534, Italian painter.

cor·reg·i·dor (kə·reg′ə·dôr, *Sp.* kôr·rā′hē·thôr′) *n.* 1 The chief magistrate of a Spanish-American town. 2 A similar magistrate whose jurisdiction extends over part of a province. [<Sp. < *corregir* <L *corrigere.* See CORRECT.]

Cor·reg·i·dor (kə·reg′ə·dôr) An island in Manila Bay; 2 square miles; site of the surrender of the Philippines by United States forces to Japan, May, 1942, in World War II.

cor·re·late (kôr′ə·lāt, kor′-) *v.* **·lat·ed, ·lat·ing** *v.t.* 1 To place or put in reciprocal relation; establish a mutual relation between. 2 To show the mutual relation between. —*v.i.* 3 To have a correlation; be mutually or reciprocally related. —*adj.* Having mutual or reciprocal relations. —*n.* A correlative. [< COR- + RELATE]

cor·re·la·tion (kôr′ə·lā′shən, kor′-) *n.* 1 Mutual or reciprocal relation. 2 The act of bringing under relations of union or interaction. 3 *Physiol.* The combination of nervous impulses in sensory centers resulting in adaptive reactions. 4 *Math.* A statement of the kind and degree of relationship between two or more variables. Also spelled *corelation.* —**cor′re·la′tion·al** *adj.*

correlation coefficient *Stat.* A numerical measure of the degree of correlation between two variables.

cor·rel·a·tive (kə·rel′ə·tiv) *adj.* 1 Having correlation; especially, mutually involving or implying one another: *correlative* structures. 2 Mutually related to grammatical or logical significance; referring to each other: *either* and *or* are *correlative* conjunctions. —*n.* 1 One of two or more persons or things united by reason of some natural relation or correspondence. 2 Either of two correlative terms. —**cor·rel′a·tive·ly** *adv.* —**cor·rel′a·tive·ness, cor·rel·a·tiv′i·ty** *n.*

cor·rep·tion (kə·rep′shən) *n.* In classical prosody, the treating of a metrically long syllable as short. Compare PROTRACTION. [<L *correptio, -onis* < *corripere* < *com-* thoroughly + *rapere* seize]

cor·re·spond (kôr′ə·spond′, kor′-) *v.i.* 1 To agree or be conformable in respect to fitness; be proportional. 2 To be similar or analogous in character or in function. 3 To communicate by letters. [<Med. L *correspondere* < *com-* together + *respondere* answer] —**cor·re·spon·sive** (kôr′ə·spon′siv, kor′-) *adj.*

cor·re·spon·dence (kôr′ə·spon′dəns, kor′-) *n.* 1 The act, condition, or state of corresponding. 2 Mutual adaptation; congruity; agreement. 3 Communication by letters; also, the letters themselves. Also **cor′re·spon′den·cy.** See synonyms under INTERCOURSE.

correspondence principle *Physics* The relation assumed to exist between the observed radiation characteristics of an electron orbit and those calculated by classical mechanics.

correspondence school A school which gives its courses of instruction in a series of written lessons and assignments exchanged by mail between teachers and students.

cor·re·spon·dent (kôr′ə·spon′dənt, kor′-) *n.* 1 One who communicates by means of letters; specifically, a newspaper or magazine employee who dispatches news and special reports from a seat of war or other place of public interest. 2 A person, partnership, firm, or corporation that carries on business transactions with another at a distance through letters or telegrams. 3 Anything that corresponds; a correlative. —*adj.* 1 Having correspondence; correlated in nature; adapted: with *to.* 2 *Obs.* Obedient.

cor·re·spond·ing (kôr′ə·spon′ding, kor′-) *adj.* 1 Correspondent; being similar and similarly placed: with *to.* 2 Carrying on a correspondence: with *with.* See synonyms under SYNONYMOUS. —**cor′re·spond′ing·ly** *adv.*

cor·ri·dor (kôr′ə·dər, -dôr, kor′-) *n.* 1 A gallery or passage in a building, usually having various rooms opening upon it. 2 A strip of land across a foreign country by which a landlocked nation has access to the sea. 3 A strip of territory including two or more major cities, typically heavily traveled and as a region densely populated: the Northeast *Corridor* of the United States. [<F <Ital. *corridore* < *correre* run <L *currere*]

cor·rie (kôr′ē, kor′ē) *n. Scot.* A hollow in the side of a hill or at the head of a valley.

Cor·ri·en·tes (kôr′rē·än′tās) A province of NE Argentina; 33,544 square miles; capital, Corrientes.

cor·ri·gen·dum (kôr′ə·jen′dəm, kor′-) *n. pl.* **·da** (-də) 1 Something to be corrected: said of a printer's error. 2 *pl.* A list of corrected errors, as in a printed book. [<L, gerundive of *corrigere.* See CORRECT.]

cor·ri·gi·ble (kôr′ə·jə·bəl, kor′-) *adj.* Capable of being corrected or reformed. [<F <L *corrigere.* See CORRECT.] —**cor′ri·gi·bil′i·ty, cor′ri·gi·ble·ness** *n.* —**cor′ri·gi·bly** *adv.*

cor·rob·o·rant (kə·rob′ər·ənt) *adj.* Having the power to impart strength; invigorating. —*n.* Something that imparts strength or corroborates. [<L *corroborans, -antis,* ppr. of *corroborare.* See CORROBORATE.]

cor·rob·o·rate (kə·rob′ə·rāt) *v.t.* **·rat·ed, ·rat·ing** To strengthen, as conviction; confirm. See synonyms under CONFIRM, RATIFY. [<L *corroboratus,* pp. of *corroborare* < *com-* together + *robur* strength] —**cor·rob′o·rat′er, cor·rob′o·ra′tor** *n.* —**cor·rob′o·ra′tion** *n.* —**cor·rob·o·ra·tive** (kə·rob′ə·rā′tiv, -rob′ər·ə·tiv), **cor·rob·o·ra·to·ry** (kə·rob′ər·ə·tôr′ē, -tō′rē) *adj.* —**cor·rob′o·ra′tive·ly** *adv.*

cor·rob·o·ree (kə·rob′ər·ē) *n.* 1 A native Australian festival to celebrate tribal victories. 2 A noisy celebration. 3 A frog *(Pseudophryne corroboree)* of Australia, having brilliant orange and black stripes.

cor·rode (kə·rōd′) *v.* **·rod·ed, ·rod·ing** *v.t.* To eat away gradually; rust; ruin or destroy little by little. —*v.i.* To be eaten or worn away. [<L *corrodere* < *com-* thoroughly + *rodere* gnaw] —**cor·ro′dent** *adj.* & *n.* —**cor·rod′i·ble, cor·ro·si·ble** (kə·rō′sə·bəl) *adj.*

Cor·ro·den·tia (kôr′ə·den′shə, kor′-) *n. pl.* An order of minute insects, including the book lice: also called *Psocoptera.*

cor·ro·dy (kôr′ə·dē, kor′-) See CORODY.

cor·ro·sion (kə·rō′zhən) *n.* 1 An eating or wearing away; gradual decay. 2 The destructive breaking down of metals into their oxides or metallic salts. 3 The product of corrosive action. [< OF < LL *corrosio, -onis* < *corrodere.* See CORRODE.]

cor·ro·sive (kə·rō′siv) *adj.* Having the power of corroding: often used figuratively. —*n.* That which corrodes; a corroding agent. —**cor·ro′sive·ly** *adv.* —**cor·ro′sive·ness** *n.*

corrosive sublimate *Chem.* Mercuric chloride, a white, crystalline, poisonous compound, $HgCl_2$, formed by subliming a mixture of salt and mercuric sulfate: a strong disinfectant.

cor·ru·gant (kôr′ə·gant, -yə-, kor′-) *adj.* Having the power of corrugating. —*n.* A styptic or astringent. [< L *corrugans, -antis,* ppr. of *corrugare.* See CORRUGATE.]

cor·ru·gate (kôr′ə·gat, -yə-, kor′-) *v.t. & v.i.* **·gat·ed, ·gat·ing** To contract into alternate ridges and furrows; wrinkle. —*adj.* Contracted into ridges or folds; wrinkled: also **cor′ru·gat′ed.** [< L *corrugatus,* pp. of *corrugare* < *com-* together + *ruga* a wrinkle] —**cor′ru·ga′tion** *n.*

corrugated iron Sheets of iron or steel, usually galvanized, having a series of parallel, equally spaced curved ridges and hollows.

cor·rupt (kə·rupt′) *adj.* **1** In a state of decomposition; tainted; putrid. **2** Of a perverted character; depraved. **3** Dishonest; given to bribery. See synonyms under BAD, IMMORAL, ROTTEN. —*v.t.* **1** To cause to become putrescent or putrid; spoil. **2** To render impure; taint; contaminate. **3** To destroy the fidelity or integrity of; bribe: to *corrupt* a voter. **4** To destroy morally; pervert; ruin. **5** To debase or lower the quality or purity of by changes or errors: to *corrupt* a manuscript. **6** *Archaic* To waste; consume; corrode. —*v.i.* **7** To become rotten or corrupt; degenerate. [< OF < L *corruptus,* pp. of *corrumpere* < *com-* thoroughly + *rumpere* break] —**cor·rupt′er, cor·rup′tor** *n.* —**cor·rupt′i·bil′i·ty, cor·rupt′i·ble·ness** *n.* —**cor·rupt′i·ble** *adj.* —**cor·rupt′i·bly** *adv.* —**cor·rupt′ly** *adv.* —**cor·rupt′ness** *n.*

Synonyms (verb): contaminate, debase, defile, deprave, deteriorate, pollute, putrefy, spoil, vitiate. See DECAY, DEFILE, PERVERT, POLLUTE, PUTREFY.

cor·rup·tion (kə·rup′shən) *n.* **1** The act of corrupting, or the state of being corrupted. **2** A corrupting influence, as bribery. **3** A linguistic or orthographic change in a text, word, etc., to an incorrect form; also, an example of such a change: Porpentine is a *corruption* of porcupine.

cor·rup·tion·ist (kə·rup′shən·ist) *n.* **1** A bribe-giver or bribe-taker. **2** One who defends corruption. **3** One who is guilty of corrupt practices while holding public office.

corruption of blood *Law* An immediate consequence of a judgment of attainder of treason or felony whereby the guilty person was deprived of the right to receive or transmit property by inheritance: abolished in 1870.

cor·rup·tive (kə·rup′tiv) *adj.* Of a corrupting character.

cor·sac (kôr′sak) *n.* A small, yellowish Asiatic fox *(Vulpes corsac)*: also called *dog fox.* [< Turkic]

cor·sage (kôr·säzh′) *n.* **1** The bodice or waist of a woman's dress. **2** A small bouquet of fresh flowers for a woman to wear, as at the waist or bodice, [< OF < *cors* body < L *corpus*]

cor·sair (kôr′sâr) *n.* **1** A pirate; also, his vessel. **2** Specifically, a privateer, formerly authorized by the Turkish and Saracen governments to harry the coasts of Christian countries: Barbary *corsairs.* [< F *corsaire* < Med. L *cursarius* < *cursus* inroad, raid < L, a running < *currere* run. Doublet of HUSSAR.]

corse (kôrs) *n.* **1** *Archaic* A ribbon used for vestments. **2** *Poetic* A corpse. [< OF *cors.* See CORPSE.]

corse·let (kôrs′lit *for defs. 1, 2;* kôrs′sə·let′ *for def. 3)* **1** The complete armor of a soldier; also a breastplate. **2** *Zool.* The thorax of an arthropod. **3** A light corset, usually without stays, worn by women. Also **cors′let.** [< MF, double dim. of *cors* body. See CORPSE.]

cor·set (kôr′sit) *n.* **1** A close-fitting undergarment, usually tightened with laces and reinforced by stays, worn to give support or a desired shape to the body. **2** A medieval garment fitting closely to the body. —*v.t.* To enclose or dress in a corset. [< OF, dim. of *cors* body. See CORPSE.]

cor·se·tier (kôr·sə·tya′) *n. French* A maker or fitter of corsets. —**cor·se·tière** (kôr·sə·tyâr′) *n. fem.*

Cor·si·ca (kôr′si·kə) An island in the Mediterranean, comprising a department of Metropolitan France; 3,367 square miles; capital, Ajaccio. *French* **Corse** (kôrs).

Cor·si·can (kôr′si·kən) *adj.* Of or pertaining to Corsica or to its inhabitants. —*n.* **1** A native of Corsica. **2** The Italian dialect spoken in Corsica. —**The Corsican** Napoleon Bonaparte.

cor·tège (kôr·tezh′, -tāzh′) *n.* **1** A train of attendants. **2** A ceremonial procession. See synonyms under PROCESSION. [< F < Ital. *corteggio* < *corte* court]

Cor·tes (kôr′tiz, *Sp.* kôr·tās′) *n.* The national legislature of Spain or of Portugal. [< Sp. < *corte* court]

Cor·tes (kôr·tez′, *Sp.* kôr·tās′), **Hernando,** 1485–1547, Spanish conqueror of Mexico. Also **Cor·tez′.**

cor·tex (kôr′teks) *n. pl.* **·ti·ces** (-tə·sēz) **1** *Bot.* The outer portion of the stem, thalli, or root in plants; specifically, the bark of trees or the rind of fruits. **2** *Zool.* In animals, the outer or investing layer of various organs. **3** *Anat.* **a** The external layer of gray matter of the cerebrum and cerebellum. **b** The external portion of the adrenal glands, enclosing the medullae and indispensable to proper glandular functioning. [< L, bark]

Cor·ti (kôr′tē), **Alfonso,** 1822–76, Italian anatomist.

cor·ti·cal (kôr′ti·kəl) *adj.* **1** Of, pertaining to, or consisting of a cortex, bark, or rind; hence, external. **2** *Physiol.* Designating a process, function, or condition caused by or associated with the cerebral cortex: *cortical* sensibility. [< NL *corticalis* < L *cortex* bark] —**cor′ti·cal·ly** *adv.*

cor·ti·cate (kôr′ti·kit, -kāt) *adj.* Sheathed in bark or in a cortex. Also **cor′ti·cat′ed.** [< L *corticatus* < *cortex* bark]

cor·ti·cose (kôr′ti·kōs) *adj.* Like or of the nature of bark. Also **cor′ti·cous** (-kəs). [< L *corticosus* with a thick bark < *cortex* bark]

cor·ti·cos·ter·one (kôr′ti·kos′tə·rōn) *n. Biochem.* One of a group of steroids, $C_{21}H_{30}O_4$, occurring in, and closely associated with the proper functioning of, the adrenal cortex. [< *cortico-* (< L *cortex, -icis*) + STER(OID) + (HORM)ONE]

cor·ti·co·tro·pin (kor′ti·kō·trō′pin) *n.* A hormonal preparation having adrenocorticotropic activity, obtained from the anterior lobe of the pituitary gland of hogs and other domestic animals. [< *cortico-* (< L *cortex, -icis*) + TROP(IC) + -IN]—**cor′ti·co·tro′pic** *adj.*

cor·tin (kôr′tin) *n. Biochem.* A substance containing various hormones of the adrenal cortex: used in the treatment of certain disorders, as Addison's disease. [< CORT(EX) + -IN]

cor·ti·sone (kôr′tə·sōn, -zōn) *n.* A powerful hormone extracted from the outer part (cortex) of the adrenal gland and also made synthetically: in therapeutic doses it has a palliative effect upon some forms of rheumatoid arthritis and rheumatic fever. Formerly called *compound E.* [Short for CORTICOSTERONE]

Co·ru·ña (kō·rōō′nyä), **La** A province of NW Spain; 3,051 square miles; capital, La Coruña. Also **Co·run·na** (kō·run′ə).

co·run·dum (kə·run′dəm) *n.* A very hard native alumina, Al_2O_3, used in abrasives and represented in colored varieties by gemstones, as rubies, sapphires, etc. [< Tamil *kurundam* < Skt. *kuruvinda* ruby]

cor·us·cate (kôr′ə·skāt, kor′-) *v.i.* **·cat·ed, ·cat·ing** To give out sparkles of light. [< L *coruscatus,* pp. of *coruscare* glitter] —**cor′us·ca′tion** *n.*

cor·vée (kôr·vā′) *n.* **1** Formerly, an obligation to perform feudal service. **2** Any system of forced labor, particularly in repairing roads. [< F < OF *corovée* < L *corrogata (opera)* required (work), pp. of *corrogare* < *com-* together + *rogare* ask]

cor·vette (kôr·vet′) *n.* **1** A small, swift ship armed with depth charges and guns, and used chiefly as an anti-submarine escort vessel. **2** Formerly, a warship equipped with sails and a single tier of guns, and ranking next below a frigate. Also **cor·vet** (kôr·vet′, kôr′vet). [< F < Pg. *corveta* < L *corbita (navis)* cargo (ship) < *corbis* basket]

cor·vi·na (kôr·vi′nə) *n.* **1** A sciaenid food fish *(Micropogon undulatus)* found in Atlantic waters from Cape Cod to Texas. **2** A croaker (*Cynoscion parvipinnis*) of southern California, highly esteemed as a food fish. [< Sp.]

cor·vine (kôr′vin, -vin) *adj.* Of or pertaining to a crow; crowlike. [< L *corvinus* < *corvus* crow]

Cor·vus (kôr′vəs) **1** A southern constellation, the Crow or Raven. See CONSTELLATION. **2** A widely distributed genus of black- or dark-plumaged birds typical of the *Corvidae* family; the crows. [< L, raven]

Cor·y·bant (kôr′ə·bant, kor′-) *n. pl.* **Cor·y·bants** or **Cor·y·ban·tes** (kôr′ə·ban′tēz, kor′-) **1** A priest or attendant of the ancient Phrygian goddess Cybele, whose rites were celebrated with wild dances and revelry. **2** A reveler. [< F *Corybante* < L *Corybas, -antis* < Gk. *Korybas*] —**Cor·y·ban·tian** (kôr′ə·ban′shən, kor′-) or **·ban′tic** (-ban′tik) *adj.*

Co·ryd·a·lis (kə·rid′ə·lis) *n.* A large genus of erect or climbing herbs of the fumitory family, with divided leaves, fibrous or tuberous roots, and racemes of rose, white, or yellow flowers. [< NL < Gk. *korydallis, korydalos* a crested lark]

Co·ryd·a·lus (kə·rid′ə·ləs) *n.* An American genus of large insects (order *Megaloptera*), including the dobsonfly or hellgrammite. [< NL < L < Gk. *korydalos* a crested lark]

Cor·y·don (kôr′ə·dən, kor′ə·don) In pastoral poetry, a name for a shepherd or a rustic swain.

cor·ymb (kôr′imb, -im, kor′-) *n. Bot.* A flat-topped or convex open flower cluster of indeterminate inflorescence. [< L *corymbus* < Gk. *korymbos* flower cluster] —**co·rym·bose** (kə·rim′bōs), **co·rym·bous** (kə·rim′bəs) *adj.* —**co·rym′bose·ly** *adv.*

cor·y·phée (kôr′ə·fā′, kor′-) *n.* A ballet dancer who leads a movement of the corps de ballet.

cor·y·phe·us (kôr′ə·fē′əs, kor′-) *n. pl.* **·phe·i** (-fē′ī) **1** In ancient Greek drama, the leader of the chorus. **2** Any leader, as of a chorus, set, etc. Also **cor′y·phae′us.** [< L < Gk. *koryphaios* leader of the chorus < *koryphē* head, top < *korys* helmet]

co·ry·za (kə·rī′zə) *n.* **1** *Pathol.* Inflammation of the mucous membrane of the nose and connecting sinuses; nasal catarrh; cold in the head. **2** A contagious bacterial disease of the upper air passages of poultry, characterized by morbid secretions in the mouth, throat, and nasal cavities. [< L < Gk. *koryza* catarrh]

cos (kôs, kos) *n.* A kind of lettuce with a cylindrical head of erect, oblong leaves. [from island of *Kos,* where first grown]

Cos (kôs) See KOS.

Co·sa Nos tra (kō′zə nōs′trə) A secret criminal organization in the U.S., associated with the Mafia. [Ital., our thing]

co·se·cant (kō·sē′kənt) *n. Trig.* The secant of the complement of an angle or an arc. [< CO-[2] + SECANT]

COSECANT

co·seis·mal (kō·siz′məl, -sis′-) *adj.* **1** Experiencing an earthquake shock simultaneously at all points: a *coseismal* line or zone. **2** Indicating the progress of an earthquake by a series of connected lines. Also **co·seis′mic,** —*n.* A line on a map, usually forming a rough oval, and connecting the points at which simultaneous earthquake shocks are felt: often called *isoseismal.* [< CO-[1] + SEISMAL]

Co·sen·za (kō·zen′tsä) A town in Calabria, southern Italy.

co·sey (kō′zē) See COZY.

Cos·grave (koz′grāv), **William Thomas,** 1880–1965, Irish patriot.

cosh (kosh) *Brit. Slang n.* A small, loaded bludgeon; a blackjack. —*v.t.* To strike with or as with a cosh.

cosh·er[1] (kosh′ər) *v.t.* To pamper; treat fondly; coddle; pet. [? < dial. E (Northern) *cosh* snug, comfortable]

cosh·er[2] (kosh′ər) *v.i. Irish* To live or be entertained at another's expense. [< Irish *coisir* feast] **—cosh′er·er** *n.* **—cosh′er·ing** *n.*

co·si·ly (kō′zə·lē) See COZILY.

cos·in·age (kuz′ən·ij) *n.* Collateral relationship or kindred by blood; consanguinity: also spelled *cousinage.* [< OF *cousinage*]

co·sine (kō′sīn) *n. Trig.* The sine of the complement of a given angle or arc. [< CO-[2] + SINE]

COSINE
Of the angle ACB, the ratio of EC to BC is the cosine; or, CD being unity, the line BN is the cosine.

cos·me·col·o·gy (koz′mə·kol′ə·jē) *n.* The investigation and study of the effects of cosmic phenomena on life. [< COSM(IC) + ECOLOGY]

cos·met·ic (koz·met′ik) *adj.* Pertaining to or used for beautifying, cleansing, or protecting, especially the skin, hair, nails, or other part of the human body, or of certain animals on exhibition. Also **cos·met′i·cal.** —*n.* **1** Any preparation intended to be applied to any part of the human body for cleansing, beautifying, promoting attractiveness, or altering its appearance, including bath salts, face and hand creams, etc., but excluding soaps other than shampoos and shaving soaps. **2** Any cologne or perfume. **3** A vanishing cream used as a protective barrier for the skin to prevent or correct skin irritations acquired in certain paint and chemical industries: also called *barrier cream.* [< Gk. *kosmetikos* < *kosmos* order, ornament] **—cos·met′i·cal·ly** *adv.*

cos·me·ti·cian (koz′mə·tish′ən) *n.* One who manufactures, sells, or applies cosmetics.

cos·me·tol·o·gy (koz′mə·tol′ə·jē) *n.* The study or art of cosmetics and their application. [< Gk. *kosmetikos* cosmetic + -OLOGY] **—cos′·me·tol′·o·gist** *n.*

cos·mic (koz′mik) *adj.* **1** Pertaining to the universe at large as a harmonious system. **2** Harmonious; orderly: opposed to *chaotic.* **3** Belonging to the material universe, especially that portion outside the solar system: *cosmic* changes. **4** Of a magnitude or extent in space or time suggesting those of the universe; of vast extent or duration. **5** Relating to cosmism. Also **cos′mi·cal.** [< Gk. *kosmikos* < *kosmos* the universe] **—cos′mi·cal·ly** *adv.*

cosmic dust Fine particles of extraterrestrial matter dispersed in space.

cosmic rays *Physics* Radiation of intense penetrating power and high frequency, impinging upon the earth from outer space and subdivided into high-energy *primary rays,* consisting almost entirely of positively charged particles, and *secondary rays,* formed from many types of atomic particles, positive and negative in charge.

cos·mism (koz′miz·əm) *n.* A doctrine of cosmic evolution. **—cos′mist** *n.*

cos·mi·um (koz′mē·əm) *n.* The hypothetical radioactive element of atomic number 137. [< NL < Gk. *kosmos* universe]

cosmo- *combining form* The universe: *cosmogony.* Also, before vowels, **cosm-.** [< Gk. *kosmos* the universe]

cos·mog·o·ny (koz·mog′ə·nē) *n. pl.* **·nies** A theory of creation, as of the world or of the universe. [< COSMO- + -GONY] **—cos·mo·gon·ic** (koz′mə·gon′ik) or **·i·cal, cos·mog′o·nal** *adj.* **—cos·mog′o·nist** *n.*

cos·mog·ra·phy (koz·mog′rə·fē) *n.* The science that describes the universe, including astronomy, geology, and geography. [< COSMO- + -GRAPHY] **—cos·mog′ra·pher, cos·mog′ra·phist** *n.* **—cos·mo·graph·ic** (koz′mə·graf′ik) or **·i·cal** *adj.*

Cos·mo·line (koz′mə·lēn) *n.* A heavy grade of petroleum or paraffin jelly, used as a rust preventive: a trade name.

cos·mol·o·gy (koz·mol′ə·jē) *n. pl.* **·gies** The general science or philosophy of the universe. [< COSMO- + -LOGY] **—cos·mo·log·ic** (koz′mə·loj′ik) or **·i·cal** *adj.* **—cos·mol′o·gist** *n.*

cos·mon (koz′mon) *n. Physics* The hypothetical particle from which the known universe developed, carrying a positive nucleonic charge in opposition to the negative charge attributed to the anticosmon. [< Gk. *kosmos* the universe]

cos·mo·naut (koz′mə·nôt) *n.* A traveler in outer space.

cos·mo·plas·tic (koz′mə·plas′tik) *adj.* Pertaining to the formation of the universe; cosmogonic.

cos·mop·o·lis (koz·mop′ə·lis) *n.* A city with a cosmopolitan population, where many cultures meet. [< COSMO- + Gk. *polis* city]

cos·mo·pol·i·tan (koz′mə·pol′ə·tən) *adj.* **1** Common to all the world; not local or limited. **2** At home in all parts of the world. **3** *Biol.* Widely distributed, as a plant or animal. —*n.* A citizen of the world. **—cos′mo·pol′i·tan·ism, cos′mo·pol′i·tism** *n.*

cos·mo·pol·i·tan·ize (koz′mə·pol′ə·tən·īz′) *v.t.* **·ized, ·iz·ing** To render cosmopolitan. **—cos′·mo·pol′i·tan·i·za′tion** *n.*

cos·mop·o·lite (koz·mop′ə·līt) *n.* **1** One at home everywhere; a person of world-wide experience and travel. **2** One free from local prejudice or affection. **3** *Biol.* A plant or animal widely distributed over the world. —*adj.* World-wide in extent or existence; cosmopolitan. [< Gk. *kosmopolitēs* < *kosmos* world + *politēs* citizen < *polis* city] **—cos·mo·po·lit·i·cal** (koz′mō·pə·lit′i·kəl), **cos·mo·pol·i·tic** (koz′mō·pol′ə·tik) *adj.*

cos·mo·ra·ma (koz′mə·rä′mə, -ram′ə) *n.* An exhibition of scenes from different parts of the world. [< COSMO- + Gk. *horama* sight] **—cos′mo·ram′ic** *adj.*

cos·mos (koz′məs, -mos) *n.* **1** The world or universe considered as a system, perfect in order and arrangement: opposed to *chaos.* **2** Any harmonious and complete system evolved out of complex details. **3** Order; harmony. **4** *Bot.* Any member of a small genus *(Cosmos)* of the composite family of plants, related to the dahlia. [< Gk. *kosmos* order]

cos·mo·scope (koz′mə·skōp) *n.* An orrery.

cos·mo·tron (koz′mə·tron) *n.* A bevatron. [< *cosmo-* (< COSMIC RAYS) + (ELEC)TRON]

coss (kôs) *n.* In India, a unit of land measure, varying from one to three miles. [< Hind. *kos* < Skt. *krośa*]

Cos·sack (kos′ak, -ək) *n.* One of a people of the southern U.S.S.R. in Europe and adjoining regions of Asia, famous as cavalrymen. [< Russ. *kazak* < Turkic *quzzāq* guerrilla, freebooter]

cos·set (kos′it) *v.t.* To fondle; pet. [< *n.*] —*n.* **1** A pet lamb. **2** Any pet. [? OE *cot-sæta* a dweller in a cottage]

Cos·sy·ra (kə·sī′rə) The ancient name of PANTELLERIA.

cost (kôst, kost) *v.* **cost** (*for def. 3, also* **cost·ed**), **cost·ing** *v.i.* **1** To be priced at; require as the price of possession, use, or accomplishment. **2** To cause sacrifice, loss, or suffering: It *cost* him his fortune. —*v.t.* **3** To estimate the cost of production of. —*n.* **1** The price paid for anything; outlay; expense; charge. **2** Loss; suffering; detriment. **3** *pl. Law* **a** The charges fixed by law or allowed by the court in a lawsuit; specifically, the charges payable to an attorney for the opposite side by an unsuccessful litigant. **b** *U.S.* The charges payable by a client to his attorney. See synonyms under EXPENSE, PRICE. [< OF *coster* < L *constare* < *com-* together + *stare* stand]

cos·ta (kos′tə) *n. pl.* **·tae** (-tē) **1** A rib or a riblike structure, vein, part, or marking. **2** *Entomol.* A longitudinal vein along the anterior part of an insect's wing. [< L, rib] **—cos′tal** *adj.*

cost-ac·count·ant (kôst′ə·koun′tənt, kost′-) *n.* An accountant who keeps track of the costs of labor, materials, and overhead incurred in production and distribution. **—cost′-ac·count′ing** *n.*

Co·stan·za (kō·stän′tsä) Italian form of CONSTANCE.

Co·stan·zo (kō·stän′tsō) Italian form of CONSTANT. Also **Co·stan·te** (kō·stän′tā).

co-star (kō′stär′) *n.* An actor or actress given equal prominence with another or other players in a motion picture, play, etc. —*v.i.* & *v.t.* (kō′stär′) **co-starred, co-star·ring** To be or cause to be a co-star.

cos·tard (kos′tərd, kôs′-) *n.* **1** A variety of apple. **2** *Archaic* The head: a humorous usage. [< F *coste* rib]

Cos·ta Ri·ca (kos′tə rē′kə, kôs′tə) A republic of Central America; 19,650 square miles; capital, San José. **—Cos′ta Ri′can** *adj.* & *n.*

cos·tate (kos′tāt) *adj.* Having or bearing ribs. Also **cos′tat·ed.** [< L *costatus* < *costa* rib]

Cos·tel·lo (kos′tə·lō), **John Aloysius,** born 1891, prime minister of Ireland 1948–51, 1954–57.

Co·sten·za (kō·sten′thä) A Spanish form of CONSTANCE.

Cos·ter (kus′tər), **Laurens Janszoon,** 1370?–1450, Dutch inventor; reputed earliest inventor of movable types: also spelled *Koster.*

cos·ter·mon·ger (kos′tər·mung′gər, -mong′-, kôs′-) *n. Brit.* A street hawker of vegetables, etc., especially in the East End of London. Also **cos′tard·mon′ger, cos′ter.** [Earlier *costardmonger* < COSTARD + MONGER]

cos·tive (kos′tiv, kôs′-) *adj.* **1** Constipated. **2** Producing constipation. [< OF *costevé* < L *constipatus.* See CONSTIPATE.] **—cos′tive·ly** *adv.* **—cos′tive·ness** *n.*

cost·ly (kôst′lē, kost′-) *adj.* **·li·er, ·li·est** **1** Of great cost; expensive. **2** Splendid; gorgeous. **3** *Obs.* Free-handed; lavish. See synonyms under CHOICE. **—cost′li·ness** *n.*

cost·mar·y (kost′mâr′ē, kôst′-) *n.* A fragrant southern European herb *(Chrysanthemum majus)*: used in salads. [< L *costum* an Eastern plant + *Maria* Mary]

costo- *combining form* Rib: used in anatomical, surgical, and zoological terms. Also, before vowels, **cost-.** [< L *costa* rib]

cost of living The average cost, as to an individual or family, of the necessities of life: food, clothing, shelter, etc.

cos·tot·o·my (kos·tot′ə·mē, kôs-) *n. Surg.* The operation of cutting or dividing a rib. [< COSTO- + -TOMY]

cost-plus (kôst′plus′, kost′-) *n.* The cost of production plus a percentage of that cost for profit: a term often used in contracts.

cos·tume (kos′to͞om, -tyo͞om) *n.* **1** Dress or apparel, including all the garments worn at one time; external dress, especially that of a woman; hence, dress in general. **2** The dress belonging to a given country, time, class, calling, or the like. **3** Fancy dress: a *costume* ball. **4** Local color in art or literature; congruity and accuracy in the depicting of a given place or period in respect to details of dress, action, accessories, etc. —*v.t.* (kos·to͞om′, -tyo͞om′) **·tumed, ·tum·ing** To furnish with costumes. See synonyms under DRESS. [< F < Ital. *costuma* fashion, guise < L *consuetudo* custom. Doublet of CUSTOM.]

cos·tum·er (kos·to͞o′mər, -tyo͞o′-) *n.* **1** One who makes or furnishes costumes for stage wear or fancy dress. **2** A rack for clothing. Also **cos·tum·ier** (kos·to͞om′yər, -tyo͞om′-; *Fr.* kôs·tü·myā′).

co·sy (kō′zē) See COZY.

cot[1] (kot) *n.* **1** A cottage. **2** A finger stall. See synonyms under HOUSE, HUT. [OE]

cot[2] (kot) *n.* A light, portable bedstead. [< Hind. *khāt* < Skt. *khaṭvā*]

co·tan·gent (kō·tan′jənt) *n. Trig.* The tangent of the complement of an angle. [< CO-[2] + TANGENT]

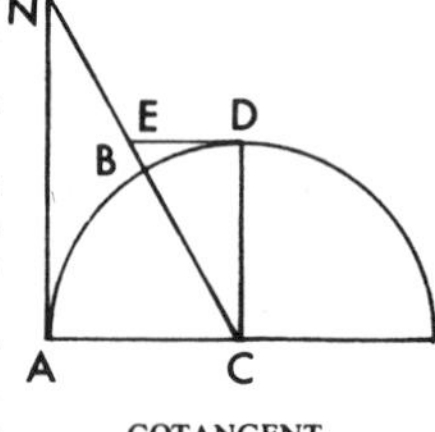

COTANGENT
Of the angle ACB, the ratio of DE to DC is the cotangent; or, DC being unity, the line DE is the cotangent.

co·tan·gen·tial (kō′tan·jen′shəl) *adj.* **1** Of or pertaining to a cotangent. **2** With the same tangent.

cote[1] (kōt) *n.* **1** A small place of shelter for sheep, birds, or chickens, used chiefly in compounds: *dovecote.* **2** *Dial.* A little house; hut. [OE]

cote[2] (kōt) *v.t.* **cot·ed, cot·ing** To go around by the side of; pass by. [? < F *côtoyer* < L *costa* rib, side]

co·teau (kō·tō′) *n. pl.* **co·teaux** (-tōz′, *Fr.* -tō′) **1** A hill or ridge. **2** A high plateau. [< F]

Côte d'A·zur (kōt dà·zür′) The eastern Mediterranean coast of France. See RIVIERA.

Côte d'I·voire (kōt dē·vwär′) The French name for IVORY COAST.

Côte d'Or (kōt dôr′) A department in east

central France; 3,391 square miles; capital, Dijon.

cô·te·lette (kō·tə·let′) *n. French* A cutlet

co·tem·po·ra·ne·ous (kō·tem′pə·rā′nē·əs), **co·tem·po·rar·y** (kō·tem′pə·rer′ē), etc. See CONTEMPORANEOUS, etc.

co·ten·ant (kō·ten′ənt) *n. Law* One of several holding the same property under the same title. — **co·ten′an·cy, co·ten·ure** (kō·ten′yər) *n.*

Co·ten·tin (kô·tän·taṅ′) A peninsula of lower Normandy, France, extending into the English Channel; scene of first landing (June 6, 1944) of Allied invasion troops in World War II: also *Cherbourg Peninsula.*

co·te·rie (kō′tə·rē) *n.* A set of persons who meet habitually; a clique. See synonyms under CLASS. [<F, earlier, an organization of tenants holding land from the same lord < *cotier* cotter < *cote* hut]

co·ter·mi·nous (kō·tûr′mə·nəs) See CONTERMINOUS.

co·thur·nus (kō·thûr′nəs) *n. pl.* **·ni** (-nī) A buskin, or high laced shoe, worn by actors in ancient Greek or Roman tragedies: regarded as a symbol of tragedy. Also **co·thurn** (kō′·thûrn, kō·thûrn′). [<L <Gk. *kothornos*] — **co·thur′nal** *adj.*

co·ti·dal (kō·tīd′l) *adj.* Indicating simultaneity in tides.

cotidal lines Lines on a chart, atlas, or sphere indicating the places at which high tide occurs simultaneously.

co·til·lion (kō·til′yən, kə-) *n.* **1** A square dance; quadrille. **2** The music for such a dance. **3** A series of round dances; the german. Also **co·til·lon** (kō·til′yən, kə-; *Fr.* kô·tē·yôṅ′). [<F *cotillon* petticoat, dim of *cotte* coat]

Co·to·pax·i (kō′tō·pak′sē, *Sp.* kō′tō·pä′hē) A volcano in north central Ecuador; 19,344 feet: probably the world's highest active volcano.

cot·quean (kot′kwēn) *n. Archaic* **1** A low, vulgar woman. **2** A man who meddles with affairs regarded as belonging to women. [<COT[1] + QUEAN]

Cots·wold (kots′wōld, -wəld) *n.* A breed of sheep with long wool, originally bred in the Cotswold Hills.

Cotswold Hills A range of low hills in SW central England. Also **Cots′wolds.**

cot·ta (kot′ə) *n. pl.* **cot·tas** or **cot·tae** (kot′ē) **1** A short surplice, with short sleeves or none. **2** A very coarse blanket. [<Med. L *cota* a coat]

cot·ta·bus (kot′ə·bəs) *n.* A game of the ancient Greeks which consisted of throwing wine from a cup into a basin. [<L <Gk. *kottabos*]

cot·tage (kot′ij) *n.* **1** A humble dwelling. **2** A small house in the suburbs or the country. **3** *U.S.* A temporary vacation residence at a resort. See synonyms under HOUSE, HUT. [<COT[1]]

cottage cheese A soft, white cheese made of strained milk curds, usually seasoned with salt: also called *pot cheese.*

cottage pudding Cake without icing, served with a sweet sauce, whipped cream, etc.

cot·ter[1] (kot′ər) *n.* **1** *Scot.* A tenant occupying a plot of ground and a cottage under a system resembling cottier tenure. **2** *Irish* A cottier. **3** A cottager; farm tenant. Also **cot′tar.** [<Med. L *cotarius* < *cota* a cottage <Gmc.]

cot·ter[2] (kot′ər) *n.* A key or wedge, used to fasten parts of machinery together, as a wheel on its shaft. Also **cot·ter·el** (kot′ər·əl). [Origin uncertain]

cot·ter-pin (kot′ər·pin′) *n. Mech.* A split metal pin for insertion in a nut, bolt, etc., to hold it in place.

Cot·ti·an Alps (kot′ē·ən) A division of the western Alps on the French–Italian border.

cot·ti·er (kot′ē·ər) *n.* **1** Formerly, in Ireland, a tenant of a house and a plot of land at a rental fixed by public competition. **2** A peasant with a small farm. [<OF *cotier* <Med. L *cotarius* COTTER]

cot·tise (kot′is) *n. Her.* A small bend. [<MF *cotisse*] — **cot′tised** *adj.*

cot·ton (kot′n) *n.* **1** The soft, fibrous, white or yellowish material, of high cellulose content, appendant to the seeds of the cotton plant. It is graded chiefly in accordance with the length of the fibers (long–staple and short–staple) and is widely used as a textile, in industry, chemistry, medicine, and the arts. **2** The cotton plant itself; also, cotton plants collectively. **3** Cotton cloth or thread. — *adj.* Woven or composed of cotton cloth or thread. — *v.t.* To wrap up in cotton; hence, to pet or coddle. — **to cotton to** *Colloq.* To become friendly with; take a liking to. — **to cotton up to** *Colloq.* To attempt to please or placate by friendly overtures or flattery. [<F *coton* <OSp. <Arabic *quṭun*]

Cot·ton (kot′n), **Charles,** 1630–87, English author and translator. — **John,** 1584–1642, English clergyman in America; grandfather of Cotton Mather.

cotton belt That region of the southern United States in which cotton is the chief crop.

cotton boll The seed capsule of the cotton plant.

cotton flannel Soft, warm cotton fabric, napped on one or both sides.

cotton gin A machine used to separate the seeds from the fiber of cotton. See GIN[3].

cot·ton·grass (kot′n·gras′, -gräs′) *n.* One of various rushlike plants (genus *Eriophorum*) of the sedge family, growing in swampy places and bearing cottony spikes.

cot·ton-leaf worm (kot′n·lēf′) The larva of a lepidopterous insect (*Alabama argillacea*), injurious to the cotton plant. Also **cotton worm.**

cotton linters See LINTERS.

cot·ton·mouth (kot′n·mouth′) *n.* A venomous pit viper (*Agkistrodon piscivorus*) living along lakes and streams or in swamps of the southern United States; the water moccasin.

cotton picker A machine, usually driven by tractor, designed to remove the ripe cotton from the standing cotton plants.

cotton plant Any of various tropical shrubs or woody herbs (genus *Gossypium*) of the mallow family, widely cultivated for the cotton they produce; especially, in the United States, upland cotton (*G. hirsutum*) and Sea Island cotton (*G. barbadense*).

cot·ton·seed (kot′n·sēd′) *n.* The seed of the cotton plant. Also **cotton seed.**

cottonseed meal Cottonseed ground after the oil has been expressed: used in feeding cattle and as a fertilizer.

cottonseed oil A pale-yellow, viscid oil pressed from cottonseeds: used in cooking, paints, and as a lubricant.

cotton stainer Any of a genus (*Dysdercus*) of bugs that punctures the developing seeds of the cotton boll and stains them with its indelible yellow or red juices.

Cotton State Nickname of ALABAMA.

cot·ton·tail (kot′n·tāl′) *n.* The common American gray rabbit (genus *Sylvilagus*).

cotton tree **1** The cottonwood. **2** An East Indian tree (*Gossypium arboreum*) which produces the silk cotton used in cushions, etc.

cotton waste The refuse of cotton manufacture: used to clean machinery, as packing, etc.

cot·ton·weed (kot′n·wēd′) *n.* **1** A perennial herb (*Diotis candidissima*) of the composite family, grown in rock gardens. **2** The cudweed. **3** The everlasting. Also **cot′ton·rose′.**

cot·ton·wood (kot′n·wŏŏd′) *n.* **1** Any of several American species of poplar trees whose seeds discharge a cottony substance, especially *Populus deltoides.* **2** Its wood.

cotton wool Raw cotton.

cot·ton·y (kot′ən·ē) *adj.* **1** Made or consisting of cotton. **2** Like cotton; fluffy; soft.

Cot·tus (kot′əs) One of the Hecatoncheires.

cot·y·le·don (kot′ə·lēd′n) *n.* **1** *Bot.* A seed leaf, or one of a pair or whorl of the first leaves from a sprouting seed. **2** A genus (*Cotyledon*) of succulent, ornamental herbs native to the Old World. **3** *Anat.* A subdivision of the uterine surface of the placenta. [<L, navelwort <Gk. *kotylēdōn* socket < *kotyle* a hollow, cavity] — **cot′y·le′do·nous, cot′y·le′do·nal** *adj.*

cot·y·loid (kot′ə·loid) *adj.* **1** Cup-shaped. **2** *Anat.* Of or pertaining to a cotyloid cavity: the *cotyloid* ligament. Also **cot′y·loi′dal.** [<Gk. *kotyloeidēs* cup-shaped, hollow]

cotyloid cavity *Anat.* The acetabulum of the hip bone.

couch (kouch) *n.* **1** A structure on which to rest or sleep, as a bed or other support. **2** A long seat or lounge. **3** Any place for repose, as the lair of a wild animal, etc. [<*v.*] — *v.t.* **1** To lay or cause to recline, as on a bed or cot. **2** To place upon a surface; deposit. **3** To embroider, as gold thread, laid flat on a surface. **4** To lower or depress, as a spear for attack: to *couch* a lance. **5** To phrase; put into words; also, to imply subtly: He *couched* a threat in his words. **6** *Surg.* To remove, as a cataract, by pushing down the opaque lens of the eye with a needle, until it lies below the line of vision. **7** In brewing, to spread out, as steeped barley, to germinate. — *v.i.* **8** To lie down; recline. **9** To lie in ambush; hide. **10** To lie in a heap or pile, as leaves. [<F *coucher* put to bed <OF *culcher* <L *collocare* set, place. See COLLOCATE.] — **couch′er** *n.*

couch·ant (kou′chənt) *adj.* **1** Lying down. **2** *Her.* Reclining with head uplifted. [<F, ppr. of *coucher.* See COUCH.]

cou·ché (kōō·shā′) *n. French* A late evening reception, as by a sovereign. Compare LEVEE[2]. Also **cou·chée′.**

couch·grass (kouch′gras′, -gräs′) *n.* A perennial grass (*Agropyron repens*), multiplying injuriously in cultivated grounds by its long rootstocks: also called *cutch, quackgrass, quatchgrass, quickgrass.*

couch·ing (kou′ching) *n.* **1** *Surg.* The operation of removing a cataract. **2** Embroidery made by securing laid gold threads with minute stitches.

Cou·é (kōō·ā′), **Émile,** 1857–1926, French psychologist.

Cou·é·ism (kōō·ā′iz·əm) *n.* The principle of self-mastery by autosuggestion advocated by Émile Coué.

cou·gar (kōō′gər) *n.* The puma. [<F <Tupian]

cough (kôf, kof) *v.i.* **1** To expel air from the lungs in a noisy or spasmodic manner. — *v.t.* **2** To expel by a cough. **3** To utter or express by coughing. — **to cough down** To silence a speaker by continued coughing. — **to cough up** **1** To expel (phlegm, etc.) by a cough or coughs. **2** *Slang* To surrender; hand over, as money. — *n.* **1** A sudden, harsh expulsion of breath. **2** A disease productive of coughing. [ME *coghen, coughen.* Related to OE *cohhetan* cough.] — **cough′er** *n.*

cough·drop (kôf′drop′, kof′-) *n.* A small, medicated lozenge to ease a sore throat and relieve coughing.

could (kŏŏd) Past tense of CAN[1]. [ME *coude,* OE *cuthe* knew how; *l* inserted on analogy with *should* and *would*]

could·na (kŏŏd′nə) *Scot.* Could not.

cou·lee (kōō′lē) *n.* **1** *Geol.* A sheet of solidified lava. **2** *U.S. Colloq.* A deep, usually dry gulch, distinguished by its inclined sides from a canyon. **3** A steep, trenchlike valley, as in the path of former glaciers. Also **cou·lée** (kōō·lā′). [<F < *couler* flow]

cou·leur de rose (kōō·lœr′ də rōz′) *French* Color of rose; idiomatically, in English, in an overly favorable light: to see the world *couleur de rose.*

cou·lisse (kōō·lēs′) *n.* **1** A grooved timber, as one in which the wings of a stage setting slide. **2** A side scene in a theater or one of the spaces between the side scenes. [<F, groove < *couler* slide]

cou·loir (kōō·lwär′) *n.* **1** A deep gorge or gully, especially in rock, ice, or snow. **2** A dredging machine that employs iron buckets on an endless chain. [<F < *couler* flow]

cou·lomb (kōō·lom′) *n.* The practical unit of quantity in measuring electricity: the amount conveyed by one ampere in one second, equal to 6.3 x 10^{18} electrons. — **absolute coulomb** One tenth of an abcoulomb. — **international coulomb** The quantity of electricity passing any section of a circuit in one second when the current is one international ampere. [after C. A. de *Coulomb,* 1736–1806, French physicist]

cou·lom·e·ter (kōō·lom′ə·tər) *n.* An electrolytic cell for measuring the quantity of electricity by the chemical action produced: also called *voltameter.* Also **coulomb meter.**

coul·ter (kōl′tər) See COLTER.

Coul·ter (kōl′tər), **John Merle,** 1851–1928, U.S. botanist.

add,āce,câre,pälm; end,ēven; it,īce; odd,ōpen,ôrder; tŏŏk,pōōl; up,bûrn; ə = a in *above,* e in *sicken,* i in *clarity,* o in *melon,* u in *focus*; yōō = u in *fuse*; oi,oil; ou,pout; ch,check; g,go; ng,ring; th,thin; th,this; zh,vision. Foreign sounds à,œ,ü,kh,ṅ; and ◆: see page xx. < from; + plus; ? possibly.

cou·mar·ic (ko͞o·mar′ik) *adj.* Of or pertaining to coumarin.

cou·ma·rin (ko͞o′mə·rin) *n. Chem.* A fragrant crystalline compound, $C_9H_6O_2$, contained in Tonka beans, sweet clover, and other plants, and also made synthetically: used as a flavor extract and in perfumery: also spelled *cumarin.* [<F *coumarine* <*coumarou* Tonka bean]

cou·ma·rou (ko͞o′mə·ro͞o) *n.* The Tonka bean or its seed. [<Tupian]

coun·cil (koun′səl) *n.* **1** An assembly of persons convened for consultation or deliberation: a *council* of physicians. **2** A body of men elected or appointed to assist in the administration of government, as of a city, or to legislate and advise, as in a territory or colony. **3** The deliberation or consultation that takes place in a council chamber: summoned from *council.* **4** A gathering of Roman Catholic ecclesiastical dignitaries and scholars, for the purpose of discussing and regulating matters of church doctrine and discipline: distinguished as **diocesan** (led by the bishop), **provincial** (led by the archbishop), **national** (led by the primate or patriarch), **general** (led by the Pope or papal legate), and **ecumenical** (world-wide) **councils. 5** The Sanhedrin. —**common council** A municipal, legislative body; also, a coordinate branch of such a body, called a **city council.** —**general council 1** A council made up of delegates representative of the whole of a certain territory or organization, as the British Parliament. **2** The deliberative body of a Scottish university. **3** The administrative board of Oxford University, properly known as the **Hebdomadal Council.** ◆ Homophone: *counsel.* [<OF *cuncile* <L *concilium* <*com-* together + *calare* call]

Council Bluffs A city in SW Iowa.

coun·cil·man (koun′səl·mən) *n. pl.* **·men** (-mən) A member of a council, especially the governing council of a city.

Council of Ten A secret legislative body of ten, later of seventeen, members which governed Venice from 1310 until 1797.

coun·cil·or (koun′səl·ər, -slər) *n.* A member of a council. Also **coun′cil·lor.** —**coun′cil·or·ship** *n.*

coun·sel (koun′səl) *n.* **1** Mutual consultation or deliberation. **2** Opinion; advice. **3** Deliberate purpose. **4** Good judgment; prudence. **5** A lawyer or lawyers engaged in a cause in court; an advocate. —**to keep one's own counsel** To be reticent about one's opinions or affairs. —*v.* **·seled** or **·selled, ·sel·ing** or **·sel·ling** *v.t.* **1** To advise; give advice to. **2** To advise in favor of; recommend. — *v.i.* **3** To take counsel; deliberate. ◆ Homophone: *council.* [<OF *cunseil* <L *consilium* < *consulere* deliberate]

Synonyms (noun): admonition, advice, caution, dissuasion, hortation, persuasion, recommendation, suggestion, warning. *Advice* is an opinion suggesting or urging some course of action, on the ground of real or assumed superior knowledge. *Counsel* implies mutual conference. *Advice* may be unsought and even unwelcome; *counsel* is supposed to be desired. Yet the two words so far approach each other that one is said to seek *advice* from a lawyer, while a lawyer who is engaged to give *advice* or to act as an advocate in a legal proceeding is called the *counsel* of the person so employing him.

counsel of perfection An advisory declaration made by Christ or one of the Apostles as a guide to the highest morality.

coun·sel·or (koun′səl·ər, -slər) *n.* **1** One who gives counsel; an adviser. **2** An attorney at law; advocate. Also **coun′sel·lor.**

count[1] (kount) *v.t.* **1** To list or call off the units of (a group or collection) one by one to ascertain the total; number; enumerate: to *count* a flock. **2** To list numerals in a progressive sequence up to: to *count* ten. **3** To believe or consider to be; judge; think. **4** To determine by computation; reckon. **5** To take note of; include in a reckoning. **6** *Obs.* To place to the account of; ascribe. —*v.i.* **7** To list numbers in sequence. **8** To rely: with *on* or *upon.* **9** To be of (much, little, no) value: His testimony *counts* for naught. **10** *Mus.* To keep time by counting or beating. —**to count in 1** To include: *Count* me *in* **2** To elect by fraud. —**to count out 1** In boxing, to reach a count of ten over (a downed boxer), thus declaring him defeated. **2** To prevent a fraudulently elected candidate from taking office; also, to ignore, as certain votes. **3** To exclude or excuse: *Count* me *out* on the picnic. —**to count the cost** To determine the risk beforehand. —*n.* **1** The act of counting; number. **2** Attention; heed; estimation. **3** An accounting, as of a stewardship or for an action. **4** *Law* A separate charge, as in an indictment. **5** In boxing, the counting from one to ten seconds, during which time the contestant who is down must get up or lose the fight. [<OF *conter* <L *computare.* Doublet of COMPUTE.]—**count′a·ble** *adj.*

count[2] (kount) *n.* In some European countries, a nobleman having a rank corresponding to that of an earl in England. [<AF *counte* <L *comes* an associate]

count–down (kount′doun′) *n.* A specified interval of time measured in a descending order of units, usually seconds, to zero, at which an intended action is to occur.

coun·te·nance (koun′tə·nəns) *n.* **1** The face or features. **2** Expression; appearance. **3** An encouraging aspect; hence, approval; support. See synonyms under FAVOR. —**out of countenance** Disconcerted; without ease or composure; abashed. —*v.t.* **·nanced, ·nanc·ing** To approve; encourage; abet. See synonyms under ABET, ENCOURAGE. [<OF *contenance* <L *continentia* behavior <*continere.* See CONTINENT.] —**coun′te·nanc·er** *n.*

count·er[1] (koun′tər) *n.* One who or that which counts, especially a machine for counting.

coun·ter[2] (koun′tər) *n.* **1** An opposite or that which is opposite; especially, a parry; counterblow; also, the act of delivering such a blow. **2** A piece of material encircling the heel of a shoe to stiffen and support the outer leather. **3** *Naut.* The portion of a ship between the water line and the knuckle of the stern. **4** A horse's breast. —*v.t.* **1** To return, as a blow, by another blow. **2** To oppose; contradict; controvert. **3** To put a new counter on, as a shoe. —*v.i.* **4** In boxing, to give a blow while receiving or parrying one. **5** In chess, to make a countermove. —*adj.* **1** Opposing; opposite; contrary. **2** Duplicate: a *counter* list. —*adv.* Contrary; in an opposite manner or direction: *counter* to etiquette. [<F *contre* against <L *contra*]

coun·ter[3] (koun′tər) *n.* **1** A piece of wood, ivory, etc., used in counting. **2** An imitation coin of inferior metal; counterfeit. **3** A table, board, etc., on which to count money or expose goods for sale. [<AF *counteour* <Med. L *computatorium* <L *computare* compute]

counter– *combining form* **1** Opposing; contrary; acting in opposition or response to the action of the main element (sometimes with the idea of outdoing or checking that action); as in:

counteraddress	**counterinfluence**
counteraffirmation	**counterlegislation**
counteragent	**countermeasure**
counteragitation	**counterorder**
counteralliance	**counterplan**
counterambush	**counterpoison**
counterappeal	**counterproject**
counterargue	**counterpropaganda**
counterargument	**counterproposal**
counterattraction	**counterreform**
counterbid	**counterreligion**
counterblow	**counterremonstrant**
counterconquest	**countersay**
countercry	**countersiege**
counterdeclaration	**counterstatement**
counterdemand	**countersuggestion**
counterdemonstration	**countertendency**
countereffort	**countertheory**
counterexercise	**counterthreat**
counterforce	**counterthrust**
countergambit	**counterview**
counterhypothesis	**countervote**
counterideal	**counterworking**

2 Done or acting in reciprocation or exchange; as in:

counterassurance	**counterquestion**
counterobligation	**countersignal**
counteroffer	**countertoken**

3 Complementing or corresponding; denoting the duplicate or parallel (often with the idea of balancing or sustaining); as in:

counterfugue	**counterstain**
counterseal	**countertally**
countersecure	**countertype**

4 Opposite in direction or position; as in:

counterapse	**counteropening**
counterarch	**counterposition**
countercurrent	**counterpressure**
counterflight	**counterpull**
counterflow	**counterstand**
countermigration	**counterstep**
countermovement	**counterturn**

coun·ter·act (koun′tər·akt′) *v.t.* To act contrary or in opposition to; check; frustrate; hinder. —**coun′ter·ac′tion** *n.* —**coun′ter·ac′·tive** *adj.* —**coun′ter·ac′tive·** *adv.*

coun·ter·at·tack (koun′tər·ə·tak′) *n.* An attack designed to counteract a previous hostile advance. —*v.t. & v.i.* (*usually* koun′tər·ə·tak′) To attack in order to frustrate or offset an enemy's previous attack.

coun·ter·bal·ance (koun′tər·bal′əns) *v.t.* **·anced, ·anc·ing** To oppose with an equal force; offset. —*n.* (koun′tər·bal′əns) **1** Any power equally opposing another. **2** A weight that balances another; counterpoise.

coun·ter·bar·rage (koun′tər·bə·räzh′) *n.* An artillery barrage answering or opposing an enemy barrage.

coun·ter·blast (koun′tər·blast′, -bläst′) *n.* **1** An opposing blast. **2** An answering argument; a denunciation.

coun·ter·bore (koun′tər·bôr′, -bōr′) *n. Mech.* **1** A cylindrical enlargement of the end of a cylinder bore or of a borehole. **2** A form of drill used for enlarging one end of a hole. —*v.t.* **·bored, ·bor·ing** To form a counterbore in; also, to enlarge.

coun·ter·change (koun′tər·chānj′) *v.t. & v.i.* **·changed, ·chang·ing 1** To exchange; interchange. **2** To diversify.

coun·ter·charge (koun′tər·chärj′) *n.* An opposing charge or accusation. —*v.t. & v.i.* (koun′·tər·chärj′) **·charged, ·charg·ing** To make rebuttal, as an opposing charge or accusation.

coun·ter·charm (koun′tər·chärm′) *v.t.* To counteract the effect of a charm upon; win by opposing charms. —*n.* (koun′tər·chärm′) An opposing charm.

coun·ter·check (koun′tər·chek′) *n.* **1** Something which checks or opposes a course of action. **2** Something which checks or thwarts another check. —*v.t.* (*usually* koun′tər·chek′) To check or thwart by counteraction.

coun·ter·claim (koun′tər·klām′) *n. Law* An opposing claim alleged by a defendant in his favor against the plaintiff. —*v.t. & v.i.* (*usually* koun′tər·klām′) To request or demand as a counterclaim; plead a counterclaim. —**coun′ter·claim′ant** *n.*

coun·ter·clock·wise (koun′tər·klok′wīz′) *adj. & adv.* Contrary to the direction taken by the hands of a clock around the dial; from right to left.

coun·ter·cul·ture (koun′tər·kul′chər) *n.* The special culture made up of those, chiefly of the younger generation, who reject the standards and values of established society.

coun·ter·cur·rent (koun′tər·kûr′ənt) *n.* An opposing current; a current opposed to another.

coun·ter·draw (koun′tər·drô′) *v.t.* **·drew, ·drawn, ·draw·ing** To trace in transparent material.

coun·ter·es·pi·o·nage (koun′tər·es′pē·ə·näzh′) *n.* Operations and measures intended to disrupt or counteract the effects of enemy spying.

coun·ter·ev·i·dence (koun′tər·ev′ə·dəns) *n.* Rebutting evidence.

coun·ter·feit (koun′tər·fit) *v.t.* **1** To make a copy of; imitate; hence, to feign; dissemble. **2** To make a spurious semblance of, as money or stamps, with the intent to deceive and defraud. —*v.i.* **3** To practice deception; feign. **4** To make counterfeits. [<*adj.*] See synonyms under IMITATE, PRETEND. —*adj.* Resembling or made to resemble some genuine thing, with intent to defraud; imitated; spurious. —*n.* **1** Something, as a coin, made fraudulently to resemble the genuine. **2** Any imitation, as a portrait or copy. **3** An impostor. [<OF *contrefet,* pp. of *contrefaire* <L *contra-* against + *facere* make] —**coun′ter·feit′er** *n.*

coun·ter·foil (koun′tər·foil′) *n.* A coupon containing a memorandum, as of a check or draft, to be retained by the drawer; stub.

coun·ter·fort (koun′tər·fôrt′, -fōrt′) *n.* **1** A pier or buttress. **2** A spur of a mountain.

coun·ter·glow (koun′tər·glō′) *n. Meteorol.* The gegenschein.

coun·ter·guard (koun′tər·gärd′) *n.* A small rampart in front of and parallel with the faces of a bastion.

coun·ter·in·sur·gen·cy (koun′tər·in·sûr′jən·sē) *n.* Measures, usually of a military nature, designed to combat guerrilla warfare or to suppress revolutionary activities.

coun·ter·ir·ri·tant (koun′tər·ir′ə·tənt) *n. Med.* An agent employed to excite irritation in one place so as to counteract irritation or inflammation existing elsewhere.

coun·ter–jump·er (koun′tər·jum′pər) *n. Slang* A salesman or clerk at a store counter: a derogatory term.

coun·ter·mand (koun′tər·mand′, -mänd′, koun′·tər·mänd) *v.t.* **1** To recall or revoke, as an order. **2** To contradict; oppose. —*n.* (koun′·tər·mand, -mänd) An order contrary to or revoking one previously issued. [<OF *contremander* <L *contra-* against + *mandare* order]

coun·ter·march (koun′tər·märch′, koun′tər·märch′) *v.t. & v.i.* To march back. —*n.* (koun′·tər·märch′) **1** A return march. **2** *Mil.* A reversal of front. **3** Any reversal of conduct or method.

coun·ter·mark (koun′tər·märk′) *n.* An added mark. —*v.t.* (*usually* koun′tər·märk′) To put an added mark on.

coun·ter·mine (koun′tər·mīn′) *v.t. & v.i.* **·mined, ·min·ing 1** To mine counter to (an enemy); hence, to baffle or obstruct by secret means. **2** To sow (an area) with mines in order to detonate enemy mines. —*n.* (koun′·tər·mīn′) **1** A mine or system of galleries run out to meet and destroy similar works of an enemy. **2** Hence, any stratagem to foil the designs of an opponent. **3** An underwater mine intended to detonate enemy mines.

coun·ter·move (koun′tər·mo͞ov′) *v.t.* **·moved, ·mov·ing** To move in a contrary direction. —*n.* (koun′tər·mo͞ov′) A move in the opposite direction.

coun·ter·mure (koun′tər·myo͝or) *n.* A wall raised before (and sometimes behind) a fortification wall to strengthen it. —*v.t.* (koun′tər·myo͝or′) **·mured, ·mur·ing** To strengthen with a countermure. [<MF *contremur* <*contre* against + *mur* wall]

coun·ter–of·fen·sive (koun′tər·ə·fen′siv, koun′·tər·ə·fen′siv) *n.* A large–scale military action designed to stop the offensive of the enemy and to seize the initiative.

coun·ter·pane (koun′tər·pān′) *n.* A coverlet or quilt for a bed. [Alter. of COUNTERPOINT[2], after F *pan* quilt <L *pannus* rag, cloth]

coun·ter·part (koun′tər·pärt′) *n.* **1** A person precisely like another. **2** Anything closely resembling something else. **3** Something corresponding reversely, as the impression to the seal, or the right hand to the left; a complement; supplement; opposite. See synonyms under DUPLICATE.

coun·ter·plea (koun′tər·plē′) *n. Law* A replication; answering plea.

coun·ter·plot (koun′tər·plot′) *n.* One plot opposing another. —*v.t. & v.i.* (koun′tər·plot′) **·plot·ted, ·plot·ting** To oppose (a plot) by another plot.

coun·ter·point[1] (koun′tər·point′) *n.* **1** *Music* **a** The art of adding to a melody a part or parts that shall be related to but independent of it, according to the fixed rules of harmony. **b** The part or parts so arranged. **2** A point or position opposed to another. [<MF *contrepoint* <Med. L *(cantus) contrapunctus* (a melody) with contrasting notes <L *contra* against + *punctus* point, note]

coun·ter·point[2] (koun′tər·point′) *n. Obs.* A counterpane. [<MF *contrepoint,* alter. of OF *cuilte–pointe* <L *culcita puncta* a quilted coverlet]

coun·ter·poise (koun′tər·poiz′) *v.t.* **·poised, ·pois·ing 1** To bring to a poise by opposing with an equal weight; counterbalance. **2** To offset or frustrate. —*n.* (koun′tər·poiz) **1** A counterbalancing weight. **2** A counterbalancing force, power, or influence. **3** A state of equilibrium. [<OF *contrepeser* <L *contra* against + *pensare* weigh]

coun·ter·pro·duc·tive (koun′tər·prə·duk′tiv) *adj.* Producing an effect opposite from that intended; harmful to a purpose: The slurs on his opponent proved *counterproductive.*

coun·ter–re·coil (koun′tər·ri·koil′) *n.* The return of a gun to firing position after its recoil.

coun·ter–re·con·nais·sance (koun′tər·ri·kon′ə·səns, -säns) The act of screening military operations from observation by the enemy.

coun·ter–ref·or·ma·tion (koun′tər·ref′ər·mā′·shən) *n.* A reformation aimed at counteracting and opposing a previous one.

Counter Reformation The movement within the Roman Catholic Church in the 16th century in reaction to the Protestant Reformation.

coun·ter–rev·o·lu·tion (koun′tər·rev′ə·lo͞o′shən) *n.* A revolution which aims at undoing the work of a previous revolution. —**coun′ter–rev′·o·lu′tion·ar′y** *adj. & n.* —**coun′ter–rev′o·lu′·tion·ist** *n.*

coun·ter·scarp (koun′tər·skärp′) *n.* The exterior slope of a ditch opposite the parapet of a fortification.

coun·ter·shaft (koun′tər·shaft′, -shäft′) *n. Mech.* An intermediate shaft driven by the main shaft and transmitting motion.

coun·ter·sign (koun′tər·sīn′, koun′tər·sīn′) *v.t.* To sign alongside of or in addition to (the signature of another); authenticate by an additional signature. —*n.* (koun′tər·sīn′) **1** A secret word or phrase to be given, as to a sentry; a watchword; password. **2** A countersignature.

coun·ter·sig·na·ture (koun′tər·sig′nə·chər) *n.* An additional, validating signature.

coun·ter·sink (koun′tər·singk′, koun′tər·singk′) *v.t.* **·sank** or **·sunk, ·sunk** (*Obs.* **·sunk·en**), **·sink·ing 1** To cut or shape (a depression), as for the head of a screw. **2** To sink, as a bolt or screw, into a corresponding depression. —*n.* (koun′tər·singk′) **1** A tool for countersinking. **2** A depression for a screwhead, bolt, etc.

coun·ter·stroke (koun′tər·strōk′) *n.* A return stroke.

coun·ter·ten·or (koun′tər·ten′ər) *n.* **1** A vocal part for a male voice higher than the tenor and lower than the treble. **2** A male voice of this kind. **3** A singer with such a voice.

coun·ter·vail (koun′tər·vāl′, koun′tər·vāl) *v.t.* To oppose with equal power; counteract; offset. [<AF *countervaloir* <L *contra valere* avail against]

coun·ter·view (koun′tər·vyo͞o′) *n.* An opposing or opposite view.

coun·ter·weigh (koun′tər·wā′) *v.t. & v.i.* To weigh equivalently with; counterbalance.

coun·ter·weight (koun′tər·wāt′) *n.* Any counterbalancing weight, force, or influence. —**coun′ter·weight′ed** *adj.*

counter word A word widely used as a general term, without regard to its exact meaning, as *definitely, heavenly.*

coun·ter·work (koun′tər·wûrk′) *v.t. & v.i.* To work or act in opposition to (a person or thing). —*n.* (koun′tər·wûrk′) The act or effect of counterworking; a work in opposition; antagonism.

count·ess (koun′tis) *n.* **1** The wife or widow of a count, or, in Great Britain, of an earl. **2** A woman whose rank is equal to that of a count or earl. [<OF *contesse,* fem. of *conte.* See COUNT[2].]

count·ing–house (koun′ting·hous′) *n. Brit.* An office or building where the bookkeeping is done in a mercantile or other establishment. Also **coun′ting–room′.**

counting tube See GEIGER COUNTER.

count·less (kount′lis) *adj.* That cannot be counted; innumerable. See synonyms under INFINITE.

count palatine 1 Originally, a palsgrave, or count of the palace of the Holy Roman Empire, whose duties had to do with the royal tribunal, and who was selected from the emperor's comitatus; later, a provincial palsgrave who managed the royal lands, etc. **2** One of those who formerly exercised a king's prerogatives in various counties of England: also *county palatine.*

coun·tra (kun′trə) *Scot.* Country.

coun·tri·fied (kun′tri·fīd) *adj.* Rural or rustic, as the manners of or attributed to country people, etc.

coun·try (kun′trē) *n. pl.* **·tries 1** A land under a particular sovereignty or government, inhabited by a certain people, or within definite geographical limits. **2** A particular nation, or the institutions peculiar to it; the land of one's nativity or allegiance. **3** A tract of land of indefinite extent; a region. **4** A rural region, or farming district, as opposed to the city: with *the:* a summer in the *country.* **5** The general public; the inhabitants of any region, collectively: with *the:* The whole *country* hated him. **6** *Law* A jury. Originally, a jury was summoned from the hundred in which the facts at issue were supposed to have occurred and the question was then said to be tried by the *country.* Litigants were said to put themselves **upon the country. 7** In cricket, that part of the field which is remote from the wicket. See synonyms under LAND. —*adj.* **1** Of or pertaining to, for, from, occurring in, or situated in the rural parts, as distinct from the city; rural; rustic. **2** Wanting in refinement or culture; rude; boorish; unpolished: *country* manners. **3** *Dial.* Relating to one's own country; national. [<OF *contrée* <LL *contrata* <L *contra* on the opposite side]

coun·try–and–west·ern (kun′trē·ənd·west′ərn) *n.* A stylized form of popular music, based on the folk music of the rural southern and western U.S. Abbr. *c–and–w* or *C–and–W.*

country club A club in the outskirts of a town or city, with a clubhouse, grounds, and facilities for outdoor sports.

country cousin A relative from the country, to whom city life is new or confusing.

country dance 1 A kind of quadrille in which the partners are ranged in opposite lines. **2** The music for this. See CONTREDANSE.

coun·try·folk (kun′trē·fōk′) *n. pl.* **1** People who live in the country, especially in a certain district. **2** Compatriots; fellow countrymen.

country gentleman A landed proprietor who lives on his estate.

coun·try·man (kun′trē·mən) *n. pl.* **·men** (-mən) **1** One living in the country; a rustic. **2** An inhabitant of a particular country; one of the same country with another.

coun·try·seat (kun′trē·sēt′) *n.* A dwelling or mansion in the country.

coun·try·side (kun′trē·sīd′) *n.* A section of country, or its inhabitants.

coun·try·wom·an (kun′trē·wo͝om′ən) *n. pl.* **·wom·en** (-wim′ən) **1** A woman of a certain country, or of the same country with another. **2** A woman inhabiting a rural district.

count·ship (kount′ship) *n.* The dignity or position of a count.

coun·ty (koun′tē) *n. pl.* **·ties 1** A civil division of a state or kingdom, created for political, judicial, and administrative purposes. In the United States, it is the division next below a State with the exception of Louisiana, where it is called a *parish.* In England a county is sometimes called a *shire.* In some of the British Colonies a county is a division for administrative purposes. **2** The inhabitants of a county: Your *county* is noted for its intelligence. **3** *Obs.* The domain of an earl or count. **4** *Obs.* An earl or count. [<AF *counté* <L *comitatus* <*comes* count, companion]

county palatine See COUNT PALATINE.

county seat The seat of government of a county.

county town *Brit.* A county seat: also called *shire town.*

coup (ko͞o) *n. pl.* **coups** (ko͞oz, *Fr.* ko͞o) **1** A sudden, telling blow; a master stroke; stratagem. **2** Among North American Indians, the first wound or cut inflicted by hand on an enemy. **3** A coup d'état. —*v.t.* (koup) *Scot.* To turn upside down; upset. Also *cowp.* [<F, ult. <L *colaphus* a blow with the fist <Gk. *kolaphos*]

coup de grâce (ko͞o′ də gräs′) *French* The finishing or mortal stroke, as delivered to a sick or wounded animal; literally, stroke of mercy.

coup de main (ko͞o′ də maṅ′) *French* A sudden, vigorous stroke; surprise; literally, stroke of hand.

coup d'es·sai (ko͞o′ des·se′) *French* A first attempt; a trial.

coup d'é·tat (kōō' dā·tà') *French* An unexpected stroke of policy; a bold seizure of government, executed suddenly and often accompanied by violence; literally, stroke of state.

coup de thé·â·tre (kōō' də tā·ä'tr') *French* **1** A theatrical hit. **2** A theatrical or sensational trick.

coup d'oeil (kōō' dœ'y') *French* A quick, comprehensive glance; literally, stroke of eye.

coupe (kōōp) *n. French* A cup of fresh fruit steeped in liqueur.

cou·pé[1] (kōō·pā'; *for def. 1, also* kōōp) *n.* **1** A closed automobile shorter than a sedan, with a rumble seat or trunk compartment and a capacity of two or more persons. **2** A low, four-wheeled, two-seated closed carriage which seats from two to four persons. **3** The forward compartment of a French diligence, or a half-compartment of a Continental railway carriage. [<F, pp. of *couper* cut]

cou·pé[2] (kōō·pā') *n. French* A wine diluted with water.

cou·pee (kōō·pā') *n.* In dancing, a salute to a partner, made while resting on one foot and swinging the other backward or forward. —*v.i.* **·peed, ·pee·ing** To make such a salute. Also **cou·pé'.** [<F *coupé,* orig. pp. of *couper* cut]

Coupe·rin (kōō·pran'), **François,** 1668–1733, French composer.

Cou·pe·rus (kōō·pā'rəs), **Louis,** 1863–1923, Dutch novelist.

coup·le (kup'əl) *n.* **1** Two of a kind; a pair. **2** Two persons of opposite sex, wedded or otherwise paired; partners in a dance. **3** A coupler; bond; leash. **4** *Mech.* A pair of equal forces acting in opposite and parallel lines, thus tending to turn a body around without moving it from its place. **5** *Electr.* Two dissimilar metals joined to form a voltaic element in a battery; a voltaic couple. —*v.* **coup·led, coup·ling** *v.t.* **1** To join, as one thing to another; link; unite in pairs. **2** To join in wedlock; marry. **3** *Electr.* To connect (two electric currents or circuits) magnetically or directly. —*v.i.* **4** To copulate. **5** To form a pair or pairs. [<OF *cople* <L *copula* a band, a bond]

coup·ler (kup'lər) *n.* **1** One who or that which couples. **2** A mechanical device by which objects are connected. **3** *Telecom.* A device for transferring signals from one circuit to another, or through a condenser or transformer. —**automatic coupler** A contrivance for coupling railroad cars by means of interlocking jaws.

coup·let (kup'lit) *n.* **1** Two similar things taken or considered together. **2** Two lines of verse in immediate sequence, especially of the same length and riming together. [<F, dim. of *couple* a pair]

coup·ling (kup'ling) *n.* **1** The act of joining together; specifically, the act of joining in marriage or copulation. **2** A coupler, or that which couples: a car or carriage *coupling.* **3** The length between the tops of the shoulder blades and the tops of the hip joints in a dog. **4** The part of the body joining the hindquarters of a quadruped to the front part, as in a dog or a horse. See illustrations under DOG, HORSE. **5** *Mech.* A friction or jaw clutch to connect moving parts or break the connection. **6** *Electr.* A connection between two circuits permitting transfer of power from one to the other.

cou·pon (kōō'pon, kyōō'-) *n.* **1** One of a number of dated certificates attached, as to a bond, representing interest accrued and payable at stated periods. **2** A section or detachable portion of a ticket or form, serving as a certificate that the holder is entitled to something, as transportation for a certain number of miles, etc. [<F <*couper* cut]

coupon bond A bond to which are attached coupons representing interest due at fixed periods.

cour·age (kûr'ij) *n.* **1** That quality of mind which meets danger or opposition with intrepidity, calmness, and firmness; the quality of being fearless; bravery. **2** *Obs.* Heart; desire; disposition; condition. [<OF *corage* <L *cor* heart]

Synonyms: boldness, bravery, daring, fearlessness, fortitude, gallantry, hardihood, intrepidity, mettle, pluck, resolution, spirit, valor. See FORTITUDE, PROWESS. Compare BRAVE. *Antonyms*: cowardice, fear, fright, timidity, timorousness.

cou·ra·geous (kə·rā'jəs) *adj.* Possessing or characterized by courage; brave; daring: a *courageous* man; *courageous* words. —**cou·ra'geous·ly** *adv.* —**cou·ra'geous·ness** *n.*

cou·rant (kōō·ränt') *n.* **1** A newspaper; gazette: now used only in titles: the Hartford *Courant.* **2** An old, lively dance in triple measure. **3** The music for such a dance. Also spelled *corant.* Also **cou·rante** (kōō·ränt'), **cou·ran·to** (kōō·rän'tō). [<F, a runner <*courer* run]

Cour·an·tyne (kûr'ən·tīn) See CORENTYN.

Cour·bet (kōōr·be'), **Gustave,** 1819–77, French painter.

Cour·be·voie (kōōr·bə·vwà') A NW suburb of Paris, France.

cou·reur de bois (kōō·rœr' də bwä') *pl.* **cou·reurs des bois** (kōō·rœr' de bwä') *French* Formerly, a French or Canadian hunter or trader who traversed the American forests.

cou·ri·er (kōōr'ē·ər, kûr'-) *n.* **1** A messenger. **2** A traveling attendant. See synonyms under HERALD. [<MF <Ital. *corriere* <*corre* run <L *currere*]

cour·lan (kōōr'lən) *n.* A rail-like, tropical or subtropical American bird (genus *Aramus*) with stiff tail feathers: also called *limpkin.* [<F <native name]

Cour·land (kōōr'land) A region of western and southern Latvia on the **Courland Lagoon,** a Baltic coastal lagoon: also *Kurland.*

course (kôrs, kōrs) *n.* **1** The act of moving onward; career. **2** The way passed over, or the direction taken. **3** A series of connected motions, acts, or events; customary sequence. **4** Line of conduct; manner of procedure; behavior. **5** The portion of a meal served at one time. **6** A row or layer. **7** *pl.* The menses. **8** *Naut.* **a** A sail bent to the lower yard of any square-rigged mast. **b** A point of the compass. **9** A charge or bout in a tournament. **10** A continuous horizontal range, as of stones in a wall. **11** *Mining* **a** An influx of water from one direction. **b** The direction of a lode or adit. **c** A corridor; passageway; the direction in which a mine is being worked. **12** *Music* A series of strings of uniform tone; also, a bell's chime. **13** A definite period of instruction and study in a certain subject: a *course* in French. **14** A series of studies undertaken to earn a degree: a college *course.* **15** In golf, links. **16** Racecourse. See synonyms under CAREER, DIRECTION, WAY. —**of course** As one might expect; naturally. —*v.* **coursed, cours·ing** *v.t.* **1** To hunt or pursue with hounds, as hares; chase. **2** To chase after; pursue. **3** To cause to run; urge to speed: to *course* horses. **4** To run through or over; traverse swiftly. —*v.i.* **5** To move swiftly; race. **6** To take a direction; follow a course. **7** To pursue game with hounds. **8** *Obs.* To engage in a hunt or joust. ◆ Homophone: *coarse.* [<OF *cours* <L *cursus* a running <*currere* run]

cours·er (kôr'sər, kōr'-) *n.* **1** A fleet and spirited horse. **2** One given to the chase. **3** A swift-footed plover (genus *Cursorius*) of arid regions in Asia, Africa, and occasionally Europe, as *C. cursor.* **4** The pratincole.

cours·ing (kôr'sing, kōr'-) *n.* The sport of chasing the hare or similar game with greyhounds, who follow by sight instead of by scent.

court (kôrt, kōrt) *n.* **1** A yard or space surrounded wholly by buildings or walls; a courtyard. **2** A building or group of buildings in a courtyard. **3** An imposing residence. **4** A space enclosed on three sides; a short street; a blind alley. **5** The actual residence of a sovereign, especially as the central seat of government and princely state; a palace. **6** The royal council, family, and retinue of a sovereign. **7** A sovereign and his retinue, considered as a body: the French *court.* **8** A formal assembly or reception held by a sovereign. **9** A place where justice is judicially administered. **10** A tribunal possessing civil, military, or ecclesiastical jurisdiction and duly constituted to administer justice. **11** A level space laid out for playing tennis, basketball, squash, or similar games; also, a subdivision of the ground so marked. **12** *Brit.* An official meeting of a corporation. **13** A local branch of certain fraternal orders; a lodge. **14** Flattery or homage paid to another to win favor. **15** Attention bestowed upon a woman to win her affection or love; wooing; courtship. —**Court of St. James's** The court of the monarch of Great Britain: so called from St. James's Palace. —*v.t.* **1** To make love to; woo. **2** To try to get in the good graces of; seek the favor of. **3** To solicit; attempt to gain: to *court* applause. **4** To lure; invite; entice into. —*v.i.* **5** To make love; act the courtier. —*adj.* Of or pertaining to a court: *court* customs. [<OF *cort* <L *cohors, cohortis* yard, troop of soldiers. Doublet of COHORT.]

—**admiralty court** See ADMIRALTY (def. 2).

—**Appeals, Circuit Court of** The highest U.S. court of appellate jurisdiction below the Supreme Court.

—**Appeals, Court of** A high court of justice to which cases from lower courts are taken for rehearing.

—**Arbitration, Permanent Court of** A tribunal established at The Hague in 1899 for the arbitration of disputes between nations, submission being voluntary: also called *Hague Tribunal.*

—**Assistants, Court of** A New England colonial court of supreme jurisdiction.

—**Assizes, Court of** A court held periodically in each English county. See ASSIZE.

—**chancery, court of** See CHANCERY.

—**circuit court** **1** A Federal court of the United States superior to a district court: abolished, 1911. **2** A State court presided over by a circuit judge.

—**Claims, Court of** A court at Washington, D.C., having jurisdiction over questions relating to claims against the government.

—**Common Pleas, Court of** **1** A common-law court of record, having original jurisdiction over civil and criminal matters. **2** Formerly, an English court with exclusive jurisdiction in various classes of civil cases.

—**district court** A U.S. court serving a Federal judicial district; also, a State court serving a State judicial district.

—**ecclesiastical court** In the United States, one of the courts established by the various churches for legislation and discipline, holding jurisdiction only within their own respective organizations; in England, a court instituted by the sovereign, having jurisdiction over matters pertaining to the established church.

—**equity, court of** See EQUITY (def. 3).

—**Exchequer, Court of** See EXCHEQUER.

—**hustings, court of** See HUSTING.

—**inquiry, court of** A tribunal for investigating matters pertaining to the military or naval service, with no power of trial or adjudication.

—**International Justice, Permanent Court of** An international tribunal established under the Covenant of the League of Nations (1921), empowered to interpret treaties and to give advisory opinions. Its functions, in general, were taken over (1945) by the International Court of Justice. Also called *World Court.*

—**Justice, International Court of** The principal judicial organ of the United Nations, functioning under a statute based on the Statute of the Permanent Court of International Justice as incorporated in the UN charter. All members of the UN are parties *ipso facto*; others join on recommendation of the Security Council.

—**juvenile court** A special court that deals with delinquents, neglected children, etc., under a fixed age.

—**King's** (or **Queen's**) **Bench, Court of** In England, the supreme court of common-law jurisdiction, consisting of a chief justice and four puisne or associate justices: now one of the divisions of the high courts of justice. Also *King's* (or *Queen's*) *Bench.*

—**last resort, court of** A tribunal from which there is no appeal.

—**municipal court** A local, city court having limited jurisdiction.

—**probate court** A court having jurisdiction of the proof of wills, of guardianships, and of the settlement of estates.

—**record, court of** A court keeping a record of its proceedings and having a clerk or prothonotary, a seal, and the power to fine and imprison.

—**Star Chamber, Court of** **1** Formerly, in England, a court held, without the assistance of a jury, by members of the Privy Council, with the addition of two judges of the courts

of common law: abolished, because of abuses, 1641. **2** Any court engaging in arbitrary or illegal procedure.
— **superior court** In some States of the United States, a court between the inferior courts and those of last resort; in England, one of the principal courts at Westminster: King's Bench, Common Pleas, Exchequer.
— **Supreme Court** In the United States and in various States, a court of appellate jurisdiction and, in most cases, of last resort.

court-bar·on (kôrt′bar′ən, kōrt′-) *n.* Formerly, a court held by the steward of a manor for settling controversies between tenants, punishing misdemeanors, etc.

court bouillon A fish stock used primarily for poaching or boiling fish.

court card A king, queen, or jack in a deck of playing cards; a face card. [Alter. of *coat card*]

court cupboard A buffet of the 16th and 17th centuries, usually in two sections, the upper closed with a door or doors, the lower open or closed with doors or drawers.

courte é·chelle (ko͞or′ tā·shel′) *French* In mountaineering, the act of climbing over another climber, in order to reach an otherwise inaccessible spot.

cour·te·ous (kûr′tē·əs) *adj.* Showing courtesy; polite; affable. See synonyms under BLAND, POLITE. [<OF *curteis*] — **cour′te·ous·ly** *adv.* — **cour′te·ous·ness** *n.*

cour·te·san (kôr′tə·zən, kōr′-, kûr′-) *n.* A prostitute or woman of loose morals. Also **cour′te·zan.** [<F *courtisan* <Ital. *cortigiano* courtier < *corte* court]

cour·te·sy (kûr′tə·sē) *n. pl.* **·sies 1** Polite behavior; habitual politeness; courtliness. **2** A courteous favor or act. **3** A curtsy. [<OF *curteisie*]

courtesy of England See CURTESY OF ENGLAND.

courtesy title A title of address of no legal validity, given by social custom to the children of peers.

court hand The Gothic or Saxon handwriting formerly used in English public records. Compare ITALIAN HAND.

court·house (kôrt′hous′, kōrt′-) *n.* **1** A public building occupied by the judicial courts. **2** *U.S. Dial.* A county seat.

court·i·er (kôr′tē·ər, -tyər, kōr′-) *n.* **1** A member of the court circle. **2** One who seeks favor by flattery and complaisance. [<OF *cortoyer* be at court]

court·leet (kôrt·lēt′, kōrt-) See LEET.

court·like (kôrt′līk′, kōrt′-) *adj.* Polite; courtly.

court·ly (kôrt′lē, kōrt′-) *adj.* **·li·er, ·li·est 1** Pertaining to or befitting a court. **2** Elegant in manners. — *adv.* In a polite, stately, and refined manner. See synonyms under POLITE. — **court′li·ness** *n.*

court martial *pl.* **courts martial 1** A military court convened to try persons subject to military law. **2** A trial by such a court.
— **drumhead court martial** A court martial called for summary trial of a military offense committed on the line of march or in action: so called because a drumhead was sometimes used as a table on such occasions.
— **general court martial** The highest military court, consisting of five or more officers and enlisted men, convened to try the gravest offenses and empowered to deliver a death sentence, a dishonorable discharge, or any other punishment not barred by law.
— **special court martial** A court martial, consisting of three or more officers and enlisted men, which tries offenses not warranting a general court martial and delivers sentences of limited imprisonment, forfeiture of pay, or a bad conduct discharge.
— **summary court martial** The least formal court martial, presided over by one officer, which tries enlisted men for minor offenses and imposes limited penalties.

court-mar·tial (kôrt′mär′shəl, kōrt′-) *v.t.* **-mar·tialed** or **·tialled, -mar·tial·ing** or **·tial·ling** To try by court martial.

court plaster Sticking plaster; silk or other fabric coated with an adhesive material, used for covering slight cuts, etc.

Cour·trai (ko͞or·trā′) A town in NW Belgium. *Flemish* **Kort·rijk** (kôrt′rīk).

court·room (kôrt′ro͞om′, -ro͝om′, kōrt′-) *n.* A room in which judicial proceedings are held.

court·ship (kôrt′ship, kōrt′-) *n.* **1** The act or period of courting or wooing. **2** *Obs.* Courtly behavior.

court tennis See TENNIS.

court·yard (kôrt′yärd′, kōrt′-) *n.* An enclosed yard adjoining a building or surrounded by buildings to which it gives access; a court.

cous·in (kuz′ən) *n.* **1** One collaterally related by descent from a common ancestor, but not a brother or sister. Children of brothers and sisters are *first cousins*; children of first cousins are *second cousins* to each other. A *first cousin once removed* is the child of one's first cousin; a *first cousin twice removed* is the grandchild of one's first cousin, etc. *A second cousin once removed* is the child of one's second cousin, etc. **2** A noble of the king's council, or a fellow sovereign: a style of address used by a king. **3** One of a kindred race: our English *cousins.* **4** *Obs.* Any collateral relative more distant than a brother or sister. — *v.t.* To claim as a cousin or relative. [<OF *cosin* <L *consobrinus* child of a maternal aunt] — **cous′in·ly** *adj.* & *adv.*

Cou·sin (ko͞o·zaṅ′), **Victor,** 1792–1867, French philosopher.

cous·in·age (kuz′ən·ij) See COSINAGE.

cousin german A first or full cousin.

cous·in·hood (kuz′ən·ho͝od) *n.* **1** The state, condition, or relationship of cousins. **2** Cousins or kindred collectively. Also **cous′in·ship.**

cous·in·ry (kuz′ən·rē) *n. pl.* **·ries** Cousins collectively.

cou·teau (ko͞o·tō′) *n. pl.* **·teaux** (-tōz′, *Fr.* -tō′) *Obs.* A knife; especially, a long, straight, double-edged knife of the Middle Ages. Also **cou·tel** (ko͞o·tel′). [<F <OF *coutel, coltel* <L *culter* knife]

couteau de chasse (də shȧs′) *French* A hunting knife.

cou·thie (ko͞o′thē) *adj. Scot.* Snug; familiar; kind; agreeable. Also **couth** (ko͞oth).

cou·til (ko͞o′til, *Fr.* ko͞o·tē′) *n.* A linen or cotton canvas for mattresses and corsets. Also **cou·tille** (ko͞o·til′, *Fr.* ko͞o·tē′y′), **cou·telle** (ko͞o·tel′). [<F]

cou·tu·rier (ko͞o·tü·ryā′) *n. masc.* A dressmaker. [<F <*couture* sewing] — **cou·tu·rière** (ko͞o·tü·ryâr′) *n. fem.*

cou·vade (ko͞o·väd′) *n.* Among some primitive peoples, the practice of putting the father to bed as if in childbed while the mother is having the baby. [<F <*couver* brood <L *cubare* lie down]

co·va·lence (kō′vā′ləns) *n. Chem.* **1** A bond formed by the mutual sharing of electrons between the atoms of a compound. **2** The number of pairs of electrons which can be shared between the atoms of different elements. — **co′va′lent** *adj.*

Co·var·ru·bias (kō′vär·ro͞o′byäs), **Miguel,** 1902–57, Mexican artist and illustrator.

cove[1] (kōv) *n.* **1** A small bay or baylike recess. **2** A recess in a mountain. **3** A strip of grassland on the prairies, leading into a wood. **4** *Archit.* A concavity; the concave curved portion interposed in some ceilings between the flat ceiling proper and the wall. — *v.t.* & *v.i.* **coved, cov·ing** To arch over. [OE *cofa* chamber, cave]

cove[2] (kōv) *n. Brit. Slang* A boy or man; fellow. [<Romany *covo* that man]

co·vel·line (kō·vel′īn) *n.* A massive, submetallic, indigo-blue copper sulfide, CuS, crystallizing in the hexagonal system. Also **co·vel·lite** (kō·vel′īt). [after N. *Covelli,* 1790–1829, Italian chemist]

cov·en (kuv′ən) *n. Scot.* An assembly; meeting; especially, a gathering of witches.

cov·e·nant (kuv′ə·nənt) *n.* **1** An agreement entered into by two or more persons or parties; a compact. **2** God's promise of blessing to be fulfilled on the performance of a condition, as of obedience. **3** The solemn pledge by which members of a church bind themselves to maintain its faith, ordinances, etc. **4** *Law* A written agreement between parties under seal; a modifying agreement contained within a contract or deed; also, a form of action to recover damages for breach of contract. — **National Covenant** An agreement extensively signed by all classes of Presbyterians in Scotland, in 1638, to resist by force the introduction of episcopacy by Charles I. — **Solemn League and Covenant** An agreement between the English and the Scottish Parliaments, undertaken in 1643, to support Protestantism. — *v.t.* & *v.i.* To promise by or in covenant. [<OF <*covenir* agree <L *convenire* meet together, agree]

cov·e·nant·al (kuv′ə·nan′təl) *adj.* Of or pertaining to a covenant.

cov·e·nant·ee (kuv′ə·nən·tē′) *n.* The party to a covenant in which obligations are made to him.

cov·e·nant·er (kuv′ə·nən·tər) *n.* The party to a covenant assuming its obligations. Also **cov′e·nan·tor.**

Cov·e·nant·er (kuv′ə·nən·tər) *n.* One of the Scottish Presbyterians who adhered to the National Covenant.

cov·ent (kuv′ənt) *n. Obs.* A convent. [Var. of CONVENT]

Cov·ent Garden (kuv′ənt) A small district in central London; site of the city's chief markets, a theater, and the Royal Opera House.

Cov·en·try (kuv′ən·trē) A city in central Warwickshire, England. — **to send to** (or **put in**) **Coventry** To banish from society or social intercourse; ostracize.

Coventry blue A blue embroidery thread made at Coventry.

cov·er (kuv′ər) *v.t.* **1** To place something over or upon so as to protect or conceal. **2** To provide with a cover or covering; clothe; enwrap. **3** To hide or keep from view; conceal, as actions, facts, or crimes: often with *up.* **4** To provide shelter or protection for, as from evil or danger. **5** To occupy the surface of; overlay; serve as a cover or covering for. **6** To allow for or have provision for; treat of; include. **7** To be sufficient to pay, defray, or offset, as a debt, expense, or loss. **8** To incubate or sit on, as eggs. **9** To copulate with (a female): said of animals. **10** To travel over; traverse. **11** To aim directly at, as with a firearm. **12** *Mil.* **a** To have under command or protection. **b** To provide protective fire for (another person, unit, etc.). **c** To march in a position behind or in front of (another man). **13** In journalism, to report the details of, as an event or meeting. **14** In sports, to hinder the activity of (an opponent); also, to protect an area or position, as one temporarily left or vacated by another player: The shortstop *covered* second base. **15** To provide the equivalent of; equal, as the wager of an opponent. **16** In card games, to play a higher card than (the one previously played). **17** *Archaic* To pardon; put out of remembrance: in Biblical use. **18** *Rare* To don, or replace, as a hat, cap, or the like. — *v.i.* **19** To spread over so as to overlay or conceal something. **20** To put on a hat, cap, or the like. **21** In card games, to play a higher card than the one led. — *n.* **1** That which is spread or fitted over or which encloses anything. **2** A veil or disguise; pretext. **3** A shelter or defense; protection. **4** A thicket or underbrush, etc., sheltering game. **5** A setting of a cloth and articles for eating a meal for one person. **6** An envelope that has been marked at such time or place as to be of interest to philatelists. **7** A cover charge. — **to break cover** To come out from a hiding place. — **under cover** Secret; concealed; secretly. [<OF *covrir* <L *cooperire* <*co-* thoroughly + *operire* hide] — **cov′er·er** *n.* — **cov′er·ing** *n.*

cov·er·age (kuv′ər·ij) *n.* **1** The protection against risks extended by an insurance policy. **2** The amount of gold held in a national treasury as a basis for the issuance of paper currency. **3** In journalism, the extent to which a news story is covered.

cov·er·all (kuv′ər·ôl) *n.* One-piece overalls with sleeves, worn to protect the clothing. Also **cov′er·alls.**

cover charge A fixed charge added to the charge for food and drink at cabarets, hotels, etc., for the entertainment or service provided.

cover crop *Agric.* A crop sown to protect the ground through the winter and to enrich it when plowed under in the spring.

Cov·er·dale (kuv′ər·dāl), **Miles,** 1483?–1569,

English Augustinian monk; translated the Bible into English.

COVERED WAGON

covered wagon A large, canvas-covered wagon; especially, one used by the American pioneers: also called *prairie schooner, Conestoga wagon.*

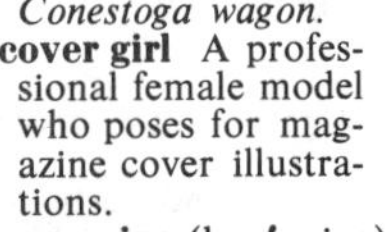

cover girl A professional female model who poses for magazine cover illustrations.

cov·er·ing (kuv′ər·ing) *n.* Anything that serves to cover, protect, conceal, etc.

cov·er·let (kuv′ər·lit) *n.* The outer covering of a bed; a quilt. Also **cov′er·lid.**

Cov·er·ley (kuv′ər·lē), **Sir Roger de** The principal character in a series of sketches in *The Spectator* by Addison and Steele, represented as the typical country gentleman of the early 18th century.

co·versed sine (kō′vûrst) *Trig.* The versed sine of the complement of an angle or arc.

cov·ert (kuv′ərt) *adj.* **1** Concealed; secret. **2** Sheltered. **3** *Law* Under protection or authority, as a married woman. See synonyms under SECRET. — *n.* **1** Something that shelters, defends, or conceals. **2** A shady place or thicket. **3** *pl. Ornithol.* Feathers overlying the bases of the quills of a bird's wings and tail. See illustration under BIRD, FOWL. See synonyms under REFUGE. [<OF, pp. of *covrir* COVER] — **cov′ert·ly** *adv.*

co·vert cloth (kō′vərt, kuv′ərt) A fine, closely woven woolen cloth of double-twisted yarn both in warp and filling, used for suits, overcoats, etc.

covert coat A short riding or shooting coat made of covert cloth.

cov·er·ture (kuv′ər·chər) *n.* **1** *Law* Marriage; the legal state of a married woman. **2** A place, means, or condition of concealment; a covering; hiding; disguise. [<OF]

cov·er–up (kuv′ər·up′) *n.* **1** An act or effort designed to prevent the facts or truth, as of an embarrassing or illegal activity, from becoming known. **2** A means of covering up or concealing something.

cov·et (kuv′it) *v.t.* & *v.i.* To have an inordinate desire for, especially for something belonging to another. [<OF *cuveiter* <L *cupiditas* eager desire < *cupere* desire] — **cov′et·a·ble** *adj.* — **cov′et·er** *n.*

cov·et·ous (kuv′ə·təs) *adj.* Inordinately desirous (of something); avaricious; greedy. See synonyms under AVARICIOUS. — **cov′et·ous·ly** *adv.* — **cov′et·ous·ness** *n.*

cov·ey (kuv′ē) *n. pl.* **·eys 1** A flock of quails or partridges. **2** A company; set; bevy. See synonyms under FLOCK. [<OF *covée,* pp. of *cover* brood <L *cubare* lie down]

cov·ing (kō′ving) *n. Archit.* The projection of the upper stories over the lower. [<COVE[1]]

Cov·ing·ton (kuv′ing·tən) A city in northern Kentucky on the Ohio River.

cow[1] (kou) *n. pl.* **cows** (*Archaic* **kine**) **1** The female of domestic cattle and of some other animals, as the elephant. **2** *Austral. Slang* An unpleasant person or event: also *fair cow.* [OE *cū*]

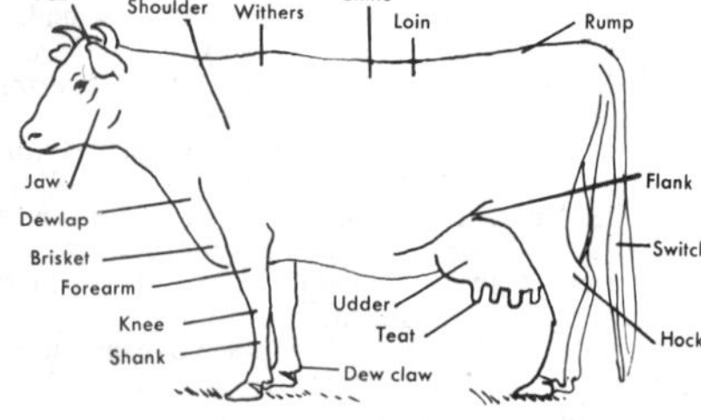

DAIRY COW
NOMENCLATURE OF ANATOMICAL PARTS

cow[2] (kou) *v.t.* To overawe; intimidate; daunt. See synonyms under FRIGHTEN. [<ON *kūga* tyrannize over]

cow[3] (kou, kō) *v.t. Scot.* To remove the head or top of; clip; shear.

cow·age (kou′ij) See COWHAGE.

cow·ard (kou′ərd) *n.* One lacking in courage; a craven; poltroon. — *adj.* Of or pertaining to a coward or cowardice; cowardly. [<OF *couard* < *coue* tail <L *cauda*; with ref. to a dog with its tail between its legs] — **cow′ard·ly** *adj.* & *adv.* — **cow′ard·li·ness** *n.*

Cow·ard (kou′ərd), **Noel,** 1899–1973, English playwright, actor, and composer.

cow·ard·ice (kou′ər·dis) *n.* Unworthy timidity; lack of courage; state of being easily frightened; pusillanimity.

cow·bane (kou′bān′) *n.* **1** The water hemlock. **2** An erect swamp plant (*Oxypolis rigidior*) of the eastern U.S., poisonous to cattle.

cow·bell (kou′bel′) *n.* **1** A wedge-shaped bell, usually of harsh and penetrating sound, hung by a strap around the neck of a cow. **2** The bladder campion.

cow·ber·ry (kou′ber′ē, -bər·ē) *n. pl.* **·ries** Any of a species (*Vaccinium vitis-idaea*) of trailing evergreen shrubs of the heath family, bearing acid red berries: also called *foxberry.*

cow·bind (kou′bīnd′) *n.* The white-berried bryony.

cow·bird (kou′bûrd′) *n.* An American blackbird (*Molothrus ater*), often found with cattle. Also **cow blackbird.**

cow·boy (kou′boi′) *n.* In the western United States, a man, usually working on horseback, who herds and tends cattle on a ranch: also *cowhand.*

cow bunting A cowbird.

cow camp The headquarters of the cowboys engaged in a roundup; also, any place where cowboys have gathered for working a herd.

cow·catch·er (kou′kach′ər) *n.* An iron frame on the front of a locomotive to throw obstructions from the track; pilot.

cow·er (kou′ər) *v.i.* **1** To crouch tremblingly. **2** To tremble; quail. [ME *couren,* prob. <Scand.]

Cowes (kouz) A port and resort center of the Isle of Wight, off Southampton.

cow·fish (kou′fish′) *n. pl.* **·fish** or **·fish·es 1** One of various cetaceans, as a grampus, dolphin, etc. **2** A trunkfish. **3** A sirenian.

cow·hage (kou′ij) *n.* **1** The stinging hairs on the pods of a tropical climbing plant of the bean family (genus *Stizolobium* or *Mucuna*). **2** The pods themselves. **3** The plant. Also *cowage.* [Alter. of Hind. *kawāch,* short for *kawānch*]

cow·hand (kou′hand′) *n.* A cowboy.

cow·herb (kou′ûrb′, -hûrb′) *n.* A smooth-leaved Old World annual (*Saponaria vaccaria*): also *cow soapwort.*

cow·herd (kou′hûrd′) *n.* One who herds cattle.

cow·hide (kou′hīd′) *n.* **1** The skin of a cow, either before or after tanning. **2** A heavy, flexible whip made of braided leather and tapering from stock to lash. — *v.t.* **·hid·ed, ·hid·ing** To whip with or as with a cowhide.

cow killer A large antlike wasp (*Dasymutilla occidentalis*) found in the SW United States.

cowl[1] (koul) *n.* **1** A monk's hood; also, any hooded garment. **2** A hood-shaped top for a chimney. **3** *Aeron.* A cowling. **4** That part of the body of an automobile to which the windshield, instrument board, and the rear end of the hood are attached. **5** *Scot.* A nightcap. — *v.t.* **1** To cloak with a cowl; make like or into a monk. **2** To cover with or as with a cowl. [OE *cugle, cuhle* < *cucullus* hood]

cowl[2] (koul) *n. Brit.* A large vessel for carrying water. [<OF *cuvel* <L *cupella,* dim. of *cupa* cask, vat]

cowled (kould) *adj.* **1** Wearing a cowl; hooded. **2** Shaped like a cowl.

Cow·ley (kou′lē, kōō′-), **Abraham,** 1618–67, English poet.

cow·lick (kou′lik′) *n.* A tuft of hair turned up over the forehead as if licked by a cow.

cowl·ing (kou′ling) *n. Aeron.* **1** A metal covering for an airplane engine and sometimes for part of the fuselage or a nacelle. See illustration under AIRPLANE. **2** The covering of an airplane cockpit.

cowl·staff (koul′staf′, -stäf′) *n. Brit.* A pole by which two persons carry a large water bucket or cowl.

cow·man (kou′mən) *n. pl.* **·men** (-mən) **1** One who owns cows; a rancher. **2** A cowboy.

co–work·er (kō′wûr′kər) *n.* **1** One engaged in the same work as another. **2** One who cooperates in an organization.

cowp (koup) See COUP.

cow–pars·nip (kou′pärs′nip) *n.* Any of a genus (*Heracleum*) of tall, stout, perennial herbs of the parsley family. Also **cow parsnip.**

cow·pea (kou′pē′) *n.* **1** A twining herb of the bean family (*Vigna sinensis*), cultivated in the southern United States. **2** The edible pea of this herb.

Cow·per (kōō′pər, kŏŏp′ər, kou′pər), **William,** 1731–1800, English poet.

Cow·per's glands (kou′pərz, kōō′-) *Anat.* Two small glands near the base of the bladder that discharge into the male urethra. [after William *Cowper,* 1666–1709, English anatomist]

cow·pi·lot (kou′pī′lət) *n.* The pintano: so called from its supposed habit of accompanying the cowfish.

cow pony A small horse or pony used in herding cattle.

cow·pox (kou′poks′) *n.* An acute contagious disease of cows, forming pustules containing a virus which is the source of vaccine for smallpox.

cow·punch·er (kou′pun′chər) *n. U.S. Colloq.* A cowboy.

cow·rin (kōō′rin) *adj. Scot.* Cowering.

cow·ry (kou′rē) *n. pl.* **·ries** A shell with a high gloss, a small variety of which is used as money in Africa and southern Asia. Also **cow′rie.** [<Hind. *kaurī*]

cow shark A large shark (*Hexanchus griseus*) with six gill openings on each side, inhabiting European and West Indian waters.

cow·shed (kou′shed′) *n.* A shelter for cows.

cow·skin (kou′skin′) *n.* The hide of a cow.

cow·slip (kou′slip′) *n.* **1** An English wildflower (*Primula veris*) of the primrose family. **2** The marsh marigold of the United States. [OE *cūslyppe* < *cū* cow + *slyppe* dung; because it commonly grows in pastures]

cow soapwort Cowherb.

cow·tree (kou′trē′) *n.* **1** One of several trees yielding a milky juice which can be used as a food, especially the South American tree *Brosimum utile* of the mulberry family. **2** The bullytree. **3** Any of various other trees, as *Tabernaemontana utilis,* of the dogbane family, and certain members of the fig family.

cox (koks) *n. Colloq.* Coxswain. — *v.t.* & *v.i.* To serve or act as coxswain to (a boat).

cox·a (kok′sə) *n. pl.* **·cox·ae** (kok′sē) **1** *Entomol.* The first joint or body joint of the leg in arthropods. **2** *Anat.* The hip or hip joint. [<L, hip] — **cox′al** *adj.*

cox·al·gi·a (kok·sal′jē·ə) *n. Pathol.* Pain in the hip. Also **cox′al·gy.** [<NL <L *coxa* hip + Gk. *algos* pain] — **cox·al′gic** *adj.*

cox·comb (koks′kōm′) *n.* **1** A pretentious and conceited fop: also spelled *cockscomb.* **2** Cockscomb (def. 1). **3** A piece of red cloth notched like a cock's comb, formerly worn in a jester's cap; also, the cap itself. **4** *Obs.* The top of the head, or the head itself. [Var. of *cockscomb*] — **cox·comb·i·cal, cox·com·i·cal** (koks·kom′i·kəl, -kō′mi-) *adj.* — **cox·comb′i·cal·ly** *adv.*

cox·comb·ry (koks′kōm′rē) *n.* **1** Coxcombs collectively. **2** Foppishness.

Cox·ey's Army (kok′sēz) A large group of unemployed people, led by "General" Jacob S. Coxey (1854–1951), U.S. political reformer, which marched on Washington to petition Federal aid during the depression of 1893.

cox·swain (kok′sən, kok′swān′) *n.* One who steers or has charge of a small boat or a racing shell: often spelled *cockswain.* [<COCK[3] + SWAIN]

coy[1] (koi) *adj.* **1** Shrinking from notice, diffident; shy: said chiefly of women. **2** Simulating diffidence; coquettish. **3** *Obs.* Disdainful. [<F *coi* <OF *quei* <L *quietus.* Doublet of QUIET.] — **coy′ish** *adj.* — **coy′ly** *adv.* — **coy′·ness** *n.*

coy[2] (koi) *n. Dial.* A decoy. [<Du. *kooi* berth, trap]

coy·o·te (kī·ō′tē, kī′ōt) *n.* The prairie wolf (*Canis latrans*) of the western United States. Also spelled *cayote.* [<Am. Sp. <Nahuatl]

Coyote State Nickname of SOUTH DAKOTA.

co·yo·til·lo (kō′yō·tēl′yō, kī′ō-) *n. pl.* **·los** A small shrub (*Karwinskia humboldtiana*) of the buckthorn family, producing poisonous fruit, native in northern Mexico and the SW United States. [<Am. Sp., dim. of *coyote* COYOTE]

coy·pu (koi′pōō) *n. pl.* **·pus** or **·pu** A South American aquatic, beaverlike rodent (*Myocastor coypus*), about 2 feet long, with webbed hind feet and round tail: it yields the fur known as nutria. Also **coy′pou.** [< Am. Sp. < native name]

coz (kuz) *n. Colloq.* A cousin. [Short for COUSIN]

coz·en (kuz′ən) *v.t.* & *v.i.* To cheat in a petty way. [< F *cousiner* deceive by claiming kinship < *cousin* COUSIN] **—coz·en·age** (kuz′ən·ij) *n.* **—coz′en·er** *n.*

co·zy (kō′zē) *adj.* **co·zi·er, co·zi·est 1** Snugly and easily comfortable; contented. **2** Sociable. *—n.* A padded cap or cover for a teapot to prevent the heat from escaping after the tea is infused: also called *tea cozy.* Also spelled *cosy, cosey.* Also **co′zey.** [< dial. E (Scottish) *cosie,* prob. < Scand. Cf. Norw. *kose* comfortable.] **—co′zi·ly** *adv.* **—co′zi·ness** *n.*

CPR Cardiopulmonary resuscitation.

Cr *Chem.* Chromium (symbol Cr).

craal (kräl) See KRAAL.

crab[1] (krab) *n.* **1** Any of various species of ten-footed crustaceans of the suborder *Brachyura* in the order *Decapoda,* characterized by a small abdomen folded under the body, a flattened carapace, and short antennae. They can walk in any direction without turning, but usually move sideways. **2** The hermit crab. **3** The horseshoe crab. **4** A crab louse, *Phthirus pubis.* **5** *Aeron.* The lateral slant in an airplane needed to maintain a flight line in a cross-wind. **6** A form of windlass. **7** *pl.* The lowest throw of a pair of dice. **—to catch a crab.** In rowing, to sink an oar blade too deeply; also, to miss the water entirely or skim the surface in making a stroke, and thus fall backward. *—v.* **crabbed, crab·bing** *v.i.* **1** To take or fish for crabs. **2** *U.S. Colloq.* To back out: to *crab* out of an agreement. **3** *Naut.* To drift sideways, as a ship. *—v.t.* **4** *Aeron.* To head (an airplane) across a contrary wind so as to compensate for drift. [OE *crabba.* Akin to CRAB[3].]

crab[2] (krab) *n.* **1** A crab apple. **2** A crab-apple tree. **3** An ill-tempered, surly, or querulous person. *—v.* **crabbed, crab·bing** *v.t.* **1** *Colloq.* To disparage; belittle; complain about. **2** *Colloq.* To ruin or spoil: He *crabbed* the entire act. **3** *Obs.* To make surly or sour; irritate. **4** *Brit. Dial.* To cudgel or beat, as with a crabstick. *—v.i.* **5** To be ill-tempered. [? < Scand. Cf. dial. Sw. *scrabba* wild apple.]

crab[3] (krab) *v.i.* **crabbed, crab·bing** To seize each other fiercely, as hawks when fighting; claw. [< MDu. *crabben* scratch. Akin to CRAB[1].]

Crab A constellation and sign of the Zodiac; Cancer.

crab angle The angle between the direction of movement of an airplane, rocket or guided missile and the direction in which the nose points, resembling the sideways motion of a crab.

crab apple A kind of small, sour apple: also called *crab.*

crab-ap·ple tree (krab′ap′əl) A tree (genus *Malus*) bearing crab apples: also called *crab, crab tree.*

Crabbe (krab), **George,** 1754–1832, English poet.

crab·bed (krab′id) *adj.* **1** Sour-tempered. **2** Harsh; sour. **3** Hard to understand; abstruse. **4** Irregular in form; cramped. See synonyms under MOROSE. [< CRAB[1], *n.* (def. 1)] **—crab′bed·ly** *adv.* **—crab′bed·ness** *n.*

crab·ber (krab′ər) *n.* **1** One who fishes for or catches crabs. **2** A type of boat used by those who fish for crabs.

crab·bit (krab′it) *adj. Scot.* Crabbed.

crab·by (krab′ē) *adj.* **·bi·er, ·bi·est 1** Cross-grained; ill-tempered. **2** Like or pertaining to a crab.

crab·grass (krab′gras′, -gräs′) *n.* A low-growing or procumbent grass (genus *Digitaria*) with freely rooting stems, especially *D. sanguinalis*; a lawn pest.

crab·stick (krab′stik′) *n.* **1** A cudgel made of crab-tree wood; hence, any cudgel. **2** An ill-tempered person.

crab tree 1 A tree having a bitter bark, as the dogbane, that is used medicinally. **2** The crab-apple tree.

crack (krak) *v.t.* **1** To produce fissures or seams in; break open partially or completely. **2** To cause to give forth a short, sharp sound: to *crack* a whip. **3** To break with such a sound. **4** *Slang* To open in order to drink: to *crack* a bottle. **5** *Colloq.* To break into, as a safe or building, in order to rob. **6** To solve, as a puzzle, crime, or code. **7** *Slang* To tell (a joke). **8** To break or crush mentally, as with sorrow or torture: He *cracked* the man's spirit. **9** To cause (the voice) to become cracked or hoarse. **10** *Colloq.* To strike sharply or with a sharp sound: He *cracked* him on the jaw. **11** To reduce by distillation, as petroleum. **12** *Obs.* To make a boast. *—v.i.* **13** To split or break, especially with suddenness. **14** To make a sharp snapping sound, as a whip or pistol; break with such a sound. **15** Of the voice, to become hoarse or change tone. **16** To become impaired or broken, as the spirit or will. **17** *Slang* To fall back or behind; fail: said of racehorses. **18** *Archaic* To talk boastfully. **—cracked up to be** *Colloq.* Reputed or believed to be. **—to crack a book** *U.S. Slang* To open, as a textbook, and read or study. **—to crack a smile** *Slang* To smile. **—to crack down** *Colloq.* To take severe repressive measures: with *on* or *upon* **—to crack hardy** *Austral. Slang* To put on a bold front in the face of trouble. **—to crack on 1** *Naut.* To crowd on sail. **2** To travel at high speed. **—to crack up** *Colloq.* **1** To smash or destroy, as an airplane or automobile; also, to be in an automobile or airplane accident. **2** To have a breakdown, nervous or physical. **—to crack wise** *U.S. Slang* To wisecrack. *—n.* **1** An incomplete separation into two or more parts with or without a noticeable space between; a fissure; split; chink. **2** The narrow space between two boards, especially in a floor. **3** A sudden sharp or loud sound; report, as of a pistol or rifle. **4** A blow that resounds: He hit him a *crack.* **5** A mental or physical defect or imperfection; flaw. **6** *Colloq.* One of high skill or excellence in a certain line; the best: All the *cracks* were entered for that race. **7** A peculiar sound or tone of the voice, as when changing at puberty or weakened by age. **8** *Colloq.* A witty or sarcastic remark; a pun. **9** *Slang* A burglar; also, a burglary. **10** A moment; an exact instant; the duration of a crack: the *crack* of dawn. **11** *Scot.* A familiar chat. *—adj. Colloq.* Of superior excellence; first-class. [OE *cracian*]

crack·brain (krak′brān′) *n.* A weak-minded person. *—adj.* Weak-minded; crazy; odd: also **crack′-brained′.**

crack-down (krak′doun′) *n. U.S. Colloq.* Summary disciplinary or corrective action.

cracked (krakt) *adj.* **1** Having a crack or cracks; rent; split or broken into small pieces: *cracked* corn or ice. **2** Damaged or blemished. **3** *Colloq.* Crazy; mentally unsound.

crack·er (krak′ər) *n.* **1** A person or thing that cracks. **2** A firecracker. **3** A device consisting of two strips of paper with fulminating powder between them which explodes by friction when the strips are pulled apart, sometimes ornamented and combined with a motto, bonbon, paper cap, etc. **4** The snapper of a whip. **5** A thin brittle biscuit: an oyster *cracker.* **6** An impoverished white inhabitant of parts of the SE United States: a contemptuous term.

crack·er-bar·rel (krak′ər·bar′əl) *adj.* Denoting or characteristic of the informal, rambling discussions of those habitually gathered in a country store: *cracker-barrel* philosophy.

crack·er·jack (krak′ər·jak′) *Slang adj.* Of or pertaining to a person or thing of worth, merit, or the like. *—n.* A person or thing of exceptional value: Among salesman he is a *crackerjack.* Also **crack′a·jack′.**

Cracker State Nickname of GEORGIA.

crack·ing (krak′ing) *n. Chem.* A process by which the molecular structure of petroleum or other complex hydrocarbons is changed under pressure by heat or distillation so that fractions of high boiling point are broken down to those of low boiling point: important in the production of high-octane gasoline.

crack·le (krak′əl) *v.* **·led, ·ling** *v.i.* **1** To crack or snap repeatedly with light, sharp noises. *—v.t.* **2** To crush or crumple, as paper with such sounds. **3** To cover, as china, with a delicate network of cracks. *—n.* **1** A succession of light, cracking sounds; crepitation. **2** The appearance or condition produced in china, porcelain, glass, and the like, by the cracking of the glaze in all directions so as to form a fine network of cracks: also **crack′le·ware′.** [Freq. of CRACK, *v.*] **—crack′ly** *adj.*

crack·ling (krak′ling) *n.* **1** The action or process of giving out small sharp sounds in rapid succession. **2** The crisp browned skin of roasted pork. **3** *pl.* The crisp refuse of fat, as of the hog, after the removal of the lard or tallow. **4** *Brit.* A cake of beef scraps used as dogs' food.

crack·nel (krak′nəl) *n.* **1** A hard, brittle biscuit. **2** *pl.* Bits of crisply fried fat pork. [Alter. of F *craquelin*]

crack of doom 1 The signal announcing the dawn of Judgment Day. **2** Doomsday; the end of the world.

crack·pot (krak′pot′) *n. Slang* A weak-minded or eccentric person; a harmless fanatic; crank. *—adj.* Eccentric; foolish; insane.

crack shot *Colloq.* An excellent marksman.

cracks·man (kraks′mən) *n. pl.* **·men** (-mən) *Slang* A burglar; safe-robber.

crack-up (krak′up′) *n.* **1** *Aeron.* The partial or total destruction of an aircraft due to circumstances beyond the pilot's control. **2** Any sudden, unforseen breakdown.

crack·y (krak′ē) *interj.* An exclamation of surprise, astonishment, or delight. Also **by cracky.**

cra·co·vienne (krȧ·kō·vyen′) *n. French* A lively Polish dance or the music for it: also *krakowiak.*

Crac·ow (krak′ou, krā′kō) A city on the Vistula; a former capital of Poland: Polish *Kraków.*

-cracy *combining form* Government or authority: *democracy.* [< Gk. *-krateia* power < *krateein* rule]

Crad·dock (krad′ək), **Charles Egbert** Pseudonym of Mary Noailles Murfree, 1850–1922, U.S. novelist.

cra·dle (krād′l) *n.* **1** A rocking or swinging bed for an infant. **2** A place of birth; origin. **3** A scythe with fingers that catch the grain when cut. **4** An arch of thin wood or wire, to keep bedclothes from pressing on a tender part of the body; also a light case in which an injured limb can be swung. **5** *Engin.* **a** A frame, usually of heavy timber, for sustaining some heavy object or structure, as a ship on a marine railway or in drydock. **b** A scaffolding suspended by ropes. **6** A support for the frame or keel or an airship or dirigible under construction. **7** *Mining* A box on rockers, for washing auriferous dirt; a rocker; cradle-rocker. **8** *Brit.* A cage swung on gimbals in which miners ascend and descend a shaft. **9** A coarse ribbing on a vaulted surface that is to be plastered. **10** A currycomb-shaped tool for making mezzotint grounds on a metal plate; a rocker. **11** A life car or basket running on a line, to bring persons from a wreck to the shore. **12** *Mil.* The frame in a gun carriage in which the gun moves during a recoil. **13** The double-pronged, electrically connected holder for the operating unit of a handset telephone. *—v.* **·dled, ·dling** *v.t.* **1** To put into or rock in or as in a cradle; soothe. **2** To nurse in infancy; nurture. **3** To cut or reap, as grain, with a cradle. **4** To draw onto or transport in a cradle, as a ship. **5** *Mining* To wash, as gold-bearing gravel, in a cradle. *—v.i.* **6** To lie or rest in or as in a cradle. **7** To cut or reap. **—to rob the cradle** *Colloq.* To marry or take as a sweetheart one much younger than oneself. [OE *cradol*]

cra·dle-snatch·er (krād′l·snach′ər) *n. Slang* One who consorts with or marries a much younger person.

cra·dle·song (krād′l·sông′, -song′) *n.* A lullaby.

craft (kraft, kräft) *n.* **1** Cunning or skill, especially as used with ignoble motives; guile; artifice. **2** Skill or ingenuity in any calling, especially in a manual employment. **3** Occupation or employment; a trade. **4** The membership of a particular trade or organized society; a guild. **5** A vessel; ship; airplane: also used collectively. See synonyms under ARTIFICE, BUSINESS, DECEPTION. [OE *cræft* skill, art, strength, courage]

-craft *combining form* Skill; trade; art of: *woodcraft.* [< CRAFT]

crafts·man (krafts′mən, kräfts′-) *n. pl.* **·men** (-mən) 1 A member of a craft. 2 A skilled mechanic. —**crafts′man·ship** *n.*

craft union A labor union in which membership is limited to workers in a single trade. Compare INDUSTRIAL UNION.

craft·y (kraf′tē, kräf′-) *adj.* **craft·i·er, craft·i·est** Skilful in deceiving; cunning. See synonyms under ASTUTE, INSIDIOUS, POLITIC. —**craft′i·ly** *adv.* —**craft′i·ness** *n.*

crag (krag) *n.* A rough, steep, or broken rock rising or jutting out prominently. [ME *cragg* <Celtic. Cf. Irish *creag,* Welsh *craig.*]

crag·ged (krag′id) *adj.* Having numerous crags. Also **crag′gy.** —**crag′ged·ness, crag′gi·ness** *n.*

crags·man (kragz′mən) *n. pl.* **·men** (-mən) One who climbs or is skilled in climbing crags or cliffs.

craig[1] (krāg) *n. Scot.* The neck or throat. Also **craig′ie.**

craig[2] (krāg) *n. Scot.* Crag.

Crai·gie (krā′gē), **Sir William Alexander,** 1867–1957, British lexicographer.

Craik (krāk), **Dinah Maria,** 1826–87, *née* Mulock, English novelist.

Cra·io·va (krä·yō′vä) A city in southern Rumania.

crake (krāk) *n.* A small, short-billed bird of the rail family, with a harsh cry; especially, the corn crake and the spotted crake. [<ON *kraka* crow]

cram (kram) *v.* **crammed, cram·ming** *v.t.* 1 To press tightly; pack together; crowd. 2 To feed to satiety. 3 To force, as a mass of knowledge or facts, into the mind, as in hurried preparation for an examination. —*v.i.* 4 To eat greedily; stuff oneself with food. 5 To force knowledge into the mind by hurried study. —*n.* 1 The act or process of cramming. 2 One who crams. 3 Hastily acquired knowledge gained by cramming. [OE *crammian* stuff]

Cram (kram), **Ralph Adams,** 1863–1942, U.S. architect.

cram·bo (kram′bō) *n.* 1 A word-riming game. 2 A word that rimes with another. [Alter. of L *crambe* cabbage (<Gk. *krambē*) in phrase *crambe repetita* an unpleasant repetition; lit., cabbage served over]

cram·mer (kram′ər) *n.* 1 One who prepares himself or others for examination by cramming. 2 A mechanical device for cramming poultry. 3 *Brit. Slang* A lie.

cram·oi·sy (kram′oi·zē, -ə·zē) *Obs. adj.* Crimson. —*n.* Crimson cloth. Also **cram′oi·sie.** [<OF *crameisi, cramoisi* <Ital. *cremesi* <Arabic *qirmazī* < *qirmiz* kermes]

cramp[1] (kramp) *n.* 1 A frame with one or more screws, in which pieces may be clamped or forced together, as in joinery; a clamp. 2 An adjustable device of wood or metal upon which vamps are stretched in shoe manufacturing. 3 A bench hook. 4 A narrow place in which it is necessary to deflect sharply the wheels of a vehicle in order to turn. 5 A cramp iron (def. 1).—*v.t.* 1 To restrain or confine the action of, as with a cramp; hamper; hinder. 2 To make fast; hold tightly, as with a cramp iron. 3 To shape over a cramp, as the upper of a boot. 4 To deflect, as the wheel of a vehicle, to one side in making a turn; also, to jam (a wheel) by turning too short. —**to cramp one's style** *Slang* To hamper one's customary skill or self-confidence.—*adj.* 1 Narrowed; straitened. 2 Contracted and irregular in form or action; cramped, as handwriting. [<MDu. *krampe* hook. Related to CRAMP[2].]

cramp[2] (kramp) *n.* 1 An involuntary, sudden, painful muscular contraction, occuring most frequently in the legs and often attacking swimmers; a tonic spasm, caused usually by strain or sudden chill. 2 A paralytic affection of local muscles caused by continued overexertion: writer's *cramp.* 3 Partial paralysis of the hindquarters, sometimes observed in animals during pregnancy. 4 *pl.* Acute abdominal pains. —*v.t.* 1 To affect with cramps. [<OF *crampe* <LG. Related to CRAMP[1].]

cramp·fish (kramp′fish′) *n. pl.* **·fish** or **·fish·es** The electric ray.

cramp iron 1 An iron with bent ends, serving to bind two pieces together more firmly, as in stonework: also called *cramp.* 2 A strip of metal on the side of a vehicle to prevent damage from scraping when the wheel is cramped.

cram·pon (kram′pən) *n.* 1 *Bot.* An aerial root for climbing, as in the ivy. 2 A pair of hooked pieces of iron for raising heavy stones, etc. 3 An iron attached to the shoe for walking on ice or to aid in climbing. Also **cram·poon** (kram·po͞on′). [<F <*crampe* CRAMP[2]]

CRAMPON *(def. 3)*

Cra·nach (krä·näkh′), **Lucas,** 1472–1553, German painter and engraver: also spelled *Kranach.* —**Lucas,** 1515–86, German portrait painter; son of preceding: called "the younger."

cran·ber·ry (kran′ber′ē, -bər·ē) *n. pl.* **·ries** 1 The edible, scarlet, acid berry of a plant *(Vaccinium macrocarpum)* growing in marshy land. 2 The plant itself. —**small cranberry** The common Old World cranberry *(V. oxycoccus).* [<Du. *kranebere*]

cranberry tree The guelder-rose. Also **cranberry bush.**

Cran·borne (kran′bôrn), **Viscount** See CECIL, ROBERT.

cran·dall (kran′dəl) *n.* A stonecutter's hammer for dressing ashlar. [Prob. <*Crandall,* a surname]

crane (krān) *n.* 1 One of a family *(Gruidae)* of large, long-necked, long-legged, heronlike birds allied to the rails; especially, the sandhill crane *(G. americana).* 2 A heron or cormorant. 3 A hoisting machine having the added capacity of moving a load in a horizontal or lateral direction. 4 An iron arm, swinging horizontally, attached to the back or side of a fireplace: used for suspending pots or kettles over a fire. —*v.t.* & *v.i.* **craned, cran·ing** 1 To stretch out, as a crane stretches its neck; elongate or be elongated. 2 To halt and lean forward, as a horse hesitating at a leap; hence, to hesitate at anything. 3 To elevate or lift by or as if by a crane. [OE *cran*]

Crane (krān) The constellation Grus. See CONSTELLATION.

Crane (krān), **Bruce,** 1857–1937, U.S. painter. —**Hart,** 1899–1932, U.S. poet. —**Stephen,** 1871–1900, U.S. poet, novelist, and short-story writer. —**Walter,** 1845–1915, English painter and illustrator.

crane·fly (krān′flī) *n. pl.* **·flies** A fly with very long, slender legs resembling a large mosquito (family *Tipulidae*): in England often called *daddy-long-legs.*

cranes·bill (krānz′bil′) *n.* Geranium (def. 1). Also **crane's-bill.**

cra·ni·al index (krā′nē·əl) Cephalic index.

cra·ni·ate (krā′nē·it, -āt) *adj.* Possessing a cranium. —*n.* Any of a primary division *(Craniata)* of the phylum *Chordata,* which includes all vertebrates having a skull, as fishes, reptiles, birds, and mammals. [<NL *craniata* <Med. L *cranium* CRANIUM]

cranio- *combining form* Cranium; cranial: *craniograph.* Also, before vowels, **crani-.** [<Med. L *cranium* skull <Gk. *kranion*]

cra·ni·og·no·my (krā′nē·og′nə·mē) *n.* The doctrine that regards the form and proportions of the skull as an index of the mental qualities or temperament. [<CRANIO- + -GNOMY]

cra·ni·o·graph (krā′nē·ə·graf′, -gräf′) *n.* An instrument for making a topographical chart of the skull. —**cra·ni·og·ra·phy** (krā′nē·og′rə·fē) *n.*

cra·ni·ol·o·gy (krā′nē·ol′ə·jē) *n.* The branch of anatomy and medicine that treats of the structure and characteristics of skulls. [<CRANIO- + -LOGY] —**cra·ni·o·log·i·cal** (krā′nē·ə·loj′i·kəl) *adj.* —**cra′ni·ol′o·gist** *n.*

cra·ni·om·e·ter (krā′nē·om′ə·tər) *n.* An instrument for measuring skulls. [<CRANIO- + -METER] —**cra·ni·o·met·ric** (krā′nē·ə·met′rik) or **·ri·cal** *adj.* —**cra′ni·o·met′ri·cal·ly** *adv.* —**cra′ni·om′e·try** *n.*

cra·ni·o·sa·cral (krā′nē·ō·sā′krəl) *adj.* Parasympathetic.

cra·ni·os·co·py (krā′nē·os′kə·pē) *n.* 1 Scientific examination of the configuration of the skull. 2 Formerly, phrenology. [<CRANIO- + -SCOPY] —**cra·ni·o·scop·ic** (krā′nē·ə·skop′ik) *adj.* —**cra′ni·os′co·pist** *n.*

cra·ni·ot·o·my (krā′nē·ot′ə·mē) *n. Surg.* 1 Any operation on the cranium. 2 An operation in which the fetal skull is perforated and the cranium compressed to facilitate delivery in difficult parturition. [<CRANIO- + -TOMY]

cra·ni·um (krā′nē·əm) *n. pl.* **·ni·ums** or **·ni·a** (-nē·ə) That part of the skull enclosing the brain; brainpan. [<Med. L <Gk. *kranion* skull] —**cra′ni·al** *adj.*

crank[1] (krangk) *n.* 1 A device for transmitting motion, as by the hand, or for converting rotary into reciprocating motion, as a handle attached at right angles to a shaft. 2 *Colloq.* One who lacks mental balance; a person given to caprices, crotchets, or vagaries. 3 A fantastic turn of speech; quip; conceit; also, a twist or perversion of judgment; whim. 4 An eccentric notion or action. 5 *Colloq.* A grouchy, ill-tempered person. 6 *Obs.* A bend. —*v.t.* 1 To bend into the shape of a crank. 2 To furnish with a crank. 3 To operate or start by a crank. —*v.i.* 4 To turn a crank, as in starting an internal-combustion engine. 5 *Obs.* To bend; twist. [OE *cranc,* as in *crancstæf* a weaving comb]

crank[2] (krangk) *adj.* 1 Ill-balanced; easily capsized: said of a boat. 2 Hence, shaky. Also *cranky.* [Earlier *crank-sided* <Du. *krengd* heeled over <*krengan* push]

crank[3] (krangk) *adj.* Spirited; lively. [Origin uncertain]

crank·case (krangk′kās′) *n. Mech.* The case enclosing an engine crankshaft, as of an automobile or the like.

cran·kle (krang′kəl) *n.* A bend; crinkle. —*v.t.* & *v.i.* **·kled, ·kling** To bend; crinkle. [Dim. of CRANK]

crank·ous (krang′kəs) *adj. Scot.* Irritable; cranky.

crank·pin (krangk′pin′) *n. Mech.* The round pin which joins reciprocating members of a connecting rod.

crank·shaft (krangk′shaft′, -shäft′) *n. Mech.* A shaft that bears one or more cranks.

crank·y[1] (krang′kē) *adj.* **crank·i·er, crank·i·est** 1 Full of whims; irritable; easily exasperated; peevish. 2 Crooked; bent. 3 Loose and rickety. —**crank′i·ly** *adv.* —**crank′i·ness** *n.*

crank·y[2] (krang′kē) See CRANK[2]

Cran·mer (kran′mər), **Thomas,** 1489–1556, first Anglican archbishop of Canterbury; burnt at the stake by Mary Tudor.

cran·nog (kran′əg) *n.* In Scotland and Ireland, an ancient lake dwelling or village built on shallows or on palisaded islands. [<Irish <*crann* tree, timber]

cran·ny (kran′ē) *n. pl.* **·nies** A narrow opening; fissure. —*v.i.* **·nied, ·ny·ing** 1 To become full of fissures or crevices. 2 To enter by crannies, as the wind. See synonyms under BREACH. [<OF *cran, cren* notch] —**cran′nied** *adj.*

crants (krants) *n. Obs.* A garland; wreath. [<G *kranz*]

crap (krap) *n. Scot.* 1 The top; summit. 2 A fowl's crop. 3 Scrap[1] (def. 3).

crape (krāp) *n.* 1 A sheer worsted fabric, usually black, used for funeral hangings and draperies. 2 A piece of this fabric, especially an armband or crêpe veil, worn or hung as a sign of mourning. —*v.t.* **craped, crap·ing** 1 To produce crimps or a crinkled surface in; frizz. 2 To drape with crape; place crape upon as a sign of mourning. [Var. of CRÊPE]

crape·fish (krāp′fish′) *n. pl.* **·fish** or **·fish·es** Codfish salted and pressed.

crape·hang·er (krāp′hang′ər) *n. Slang* A gloomy or pessimistic person: so called in allusion to the hanging of black crape at funerals.

crap·pie (krap′ē) *n. pl.* **·pies** or **·pie** An edible fresh-water fish *(Pomoxis annularis)* of the central United States. [Cf. F *crape* crabfish]

craps (kraps) *n. U.S.* A game of chance, played with two dice. Also **crap game, crap′shoot′ing.** [<F *crabs, craps* <E *crabs,* the lowest throw (two aces) in hazard]

crap·shoot·er (krap′sho͞o′tər) *n. U.S.* One who plays the game of craps.

crap·u·lence (krap′yo͞o·ləns) *n.* 1 Sickness caused by intemperance in eating or drinking; surfeit. 2 Gross intemperance, as in drinking.

crap·u·lent (krap′yo͞o·lənt) *adj.* 1 Grossly

intemperate; drunken; gluttonous. 2 Sick from intemperance in drinking. Also **crap′u·lous.** [<LL *crapulentus* <*crapula* drunkenness <Gk. *kraipalē* drunken headache]

crap·y (krā′pē) *adj.* Crapelike; crimped; wavy, as hair.

crash[1] (krash) *v.t.* **1** To break or dash in pieces noisily and with violence. **2** To force or drive noisily and with violence: He *crashed* his way through the jungle. **3** *U.S. Colloq.* To intrude upon or enter uninvited or without paying admission: to *crash* a party or dance. **4** To cause, as an airplane, truck, or train, to fall to the earth or strike an obstacle. —*v.i.* **5** To break or fall in pieces with a violent, broken sound. **6** To make a noise of clashing or breaking. **7** To move with such a noise: The boulder *crashed* down the hillside. **8** To fall to the earth or strike an obstacle, as an airplane or automobile. **9** To fail or collapse; come to ruin: The stock market *crashed* suddenly. —*n.* **1** A loud noise, as of thunder. **2** Destruction; bankruptcy. **3** A destructive accident caused by collision: an airplane *crash.* [Imit.]

crash[2] (krash) *n.* A coarse fabric woven of thick, uneven yarns: used for towels, curtains, etc. [? <Russian *krashenina*]

Crash·aw (krash′ô), **Richard,** 1613?–49, English religious poet.

crash boat A speedy motorboat for rescuing personnel from forced landings or crashes of aircraft in the water.

crash dive *Nav.* The quick submergence of a submarine, usually to escape detection or attack.

crash helmet A heavy, padded helmet worn by the crew members of tanks and military aircraft.

crash pad Thick padding covering projections in tanks and military aircraft as protection for crew members.

crash program *U.S. Colloq.* An intensive emergency undertaking in government, science, etc., having priority over all others.

cra·sis (krā′sis) *n.* **1** The coalescence of two vowels into one long vowel or diphthong (as the final and initial vowels of two successive words); syneresis. **2** *Med.* A characteristic mixture of constituent elements, as of the blood. **3** Constitutional temperament [<Gk. *krasis* mixture]

cras·pe·do·mor·phol·o·gy (kras′pə·dō·môr·fol′ə·jē) *n.* That branch of photography which deals with the sharpness of images, clarity of detail, and the resolving power of camera lenses. [<Gk. *kraspedon* border, margin + MORPHOLOGY]

crass (kras) *adj.* Coarse in manner or feeling; insensitive; indelicate: *crass* indifference to human suffering. [<L *crassus* thick] —**crass′ly** *adv.* —**crass′ness** *n.*

cras·sa·men·tum (kras′ə·men′təm) *n. Med.* A coagulum or clot, as the semisolid portion of blood. [<L, dregs, sediment]

cras·su·la·ceous (kras′yōō·lā′shəs) *adj. Bot.* Of or pertaining to a family *(Crassulaceae)* of polypetalous, usually succulent herbs or shrubs, including the sedums and houseleeks. [<NL *Crassulaceae* <L *crassus* thick]

Cras·sus (kras′əs), **Marcus Licinius,** 115–53 B.C., Roman general and statesman; triumvir with Caesar and Pompey.

-crat *combining form* A supporter or member of a social class or of a type of government: *democrat, aristocrat.* See -CRACY. [<F *-crate* <Gk. *-kratēs* <*krateein* rule, govern]

crate (krāt) *n.* **1** A large wickerwork hamper or framework of slats, for protection in transporting various articles: also, its contents. **2** A packing box. **3** *Slang* An old or decrepit vehicle or airplane. —*v.t.* **crat·ed, crat·ing** To put in a crate; send or transport in a crate. [<L *cratis* wickerwork. Doublet of GRATE.] —**crat′er** *n.*

cra·ter (krā′tər) *n.* **1** The bowl-shaped depression forming the outlet of a volcano or of a hot spring. **2** Any large bowl or cavity. **3** In ancient Greece and Rome, a large bowl or vase in which wine was mixed with water before being served to guests. **4** The pit resulting from the explosion of a mine, bomb, or shell. [<L <Gk. *kratēr* bowl]

Cra·ter (krā′tər) A constellation of the southern hemisphere; the Cup. See CONSTELLATION.

Crater Lake National Park An area in SW Oregon; 251 square miles; established 1902; contains **Crater Lake,** a circular lake (20 square miles) in the crater of an extinct volcano.

crat·o·ma·ni·a (krat′ə·mā′nē·ə) *n. Psychiatry* A morbid desire for power and preeminence. [<Gk. *kratos* power + -MANIA]

cra·vat (krə·vat′) *n.* A neckcloth or scarf; a necktie. [<F *cravate* <*Cravate* a Croatian <G *Krabate* <Croatian *Hrvat*; with ref. to the neckcloths worn by 17th c. Croatian soldiers]

crave (krāv) *v.* **craved, crav·ing** *v.t.* **1** To beg for humbly and earnestly. **2** To long for; desire greatly. **3** To be in need of; require: His body *craves* nourishment. —*v.i.* **4** To desire or long: with *for* or *after.* [OE *crafian*] —**crav′er** *n.*

cra·ven (krā′vən) *adj.* Lacking in courage; cowardly. —*n.* A base coward. [<OF *cravant* <L *crepans,* ppr. of *crepare* break] —**cra′ven·ly** *adv.* —**cra′ven·ness** *n.*

crav·ing (krā′ving) *n.* A yearning or appetite; intense longing. See synonyms under APPETITE, DESIRE, PETITION. —**crav′ing·ly** *adv.* —**crav′·ing·ness** *n.*

craw[1] (krô) *n.* **1** The first stomach or crop of a bird. **2** The stomach of any animal. [ME *crawe.* Akin to Du. *kraag* neck.]

craw[2] (krô) *n. Scot.* A rook or crow.

craw·dad (krô′dad′) *n. Dial.* A crayfish.

craw·fish (krô′fish′) *n. pl.* **·fish** or **·fish·es** A crayfish. —*v.i. U.S. Colloq.* To back out or retreat, as from a position or a promise. [Var. of CRAYFISH]

Craw·ford (krô′fərd), **Francis Marion,** 1854–1909, U.S. novelist. —**Thomas,** 1813?–57, U.S. sculptor.

crawl[1] (krôl) *v.i.* **1** To move by thrusting one part of the body forward upon a surface and drawing the other part after, as a worm; creep. **2** To move slowly, feebly, or cautiously: A sick person *crawls* about. **3** To move or make progress meanly and insinuatingly; seek influence by servility. **4** To have a sensation as of crawling things upon the body. **5** To progress or grow by extending branches, etc., as a vine or creeping plant. **6** To be filled with things that crawl, as a dead body. **7** *Colloq.* To back down from a declared position. —*n.* **1** The act of crawling; a creeping motion. **2** In swimming, a stroke made while lying face down, the arms being alternately thrust forward above the water. —**American crawl** A crawl stroke which combines a six-beat flutter kick with each stroke. —**Australian crawl** A crawl stroke which combines an eight-beat flutter kick with each stroke, the strokes being shorter than in the American crawl. [<ON *krafla* paw with the hands] —**crawl′er** *n.* —**crawl′ing·ly** *adv.*

crawl[2] (krôl) *n.* A pen or enclosure in the water for containing fish, turtles, etc. [Alter. of Du. *kraal.* See KRAAL.]

crawl space A shallow space beneath a floor, often to provide access to a building's ducts, electrical and plumbing fixtures, etc. Also **crawl·way** (crôl′wā′).

crawl·y (krô′lē) *adj.* **crawl·i·er, crawl·i·est** *Colloq.* **1** Covered or filled with crawling things; crawling. **2** Having a sensation as of things crawling over the flesh.

cray·fish (krā′fish′) *n. pl.* **·fish** or **·fish·es** **1** A spiny lobster. **2** A small, fresh-water crustacean (family *Astacidae*) resembling the lobster, especially the common American crayfish *(Cambarus affinis).* [Earlier *crevice* <OF <OHG *krebiz*; infl. in form by *fish*]

cray·on (krā′ən, -on) *n.* **1** A small cylinder of charcoal, prepared chalk, or other waxy material, as gypsum, and flour or pipe clay, especially colored, as with graphite, red ocher, etc., for drawing on paper. **2** An oily pencil, used in lithography. **3** A carbon point in an arc light. **4** A drawing made with crayons. **5** A piece of prepared chalk used for marking on blackboards. —*v.t.* To sketch or draw with a crayon or crayons. [<F, pencil <*craie* chalk <L *creta*] —**cray′on·ist** *n.*

craze (krāz) *v.* **crazed, craz·ing** *v.t.* **1** To cause to become insane or mentally ill. **2** To make full of minute intersecting cracks, as the glaze of pottery. **3** *Obs.* To impair or weaken; break down. —*v.i.* **4** To become insane. **5** To become full of minute cracks. —*n.* **1** Mental disorder. **2** A transient freak of fashion; a caprice or prejudice. **3** A flaw in the glaze of pottery. [ME *crasen* <Scand. Cf. Sw. *krasa* break.]

crazed (krāzd) *adj.* **1** Insane. **2** Cracked, as glaze.

cra·zy (krā′zē) *adj.* **cra·zi·er, cra·zi·est** **1** Insane; originating in or characterized by insanity. **2** Of or fit for an insane person. **3** Dilapidated; rickety. **4** *Colloq.* Inordinately eager; foolishly desirous. **5** *Colloq.* Inexplicable; odd or unconventional: a *crazy* driver. See synonyms under INSANE. —**cra′zi·ly** *adv.* —**cra′zi·ness** *n.*

crazy bone The funny bone.

crazy quilt A patchwork bed quilt made of pieces of various sizes, shapes, and colors.

cra·zy·weed (krā′zē·wēd′) *n.* Loco or locoweed.

creak (krēk) *v.t.* & *v.i.* To make, or cause to make, a creak. —*n.* A sharp, squeaking sound, as from friction. [Imit.] —**creak′i·ly** *adv.* —**creak′i·ness** *n.* —**creak′y** *adj.*

cream (krēm) *n.* **1** A thick, oily, light-yellow substance composed chiefly of fatty globules that rise and gather on the surface of milk and combine into butter when churned. **2** Any substance formed in a similar manner. **3** A delicacy for the table resembling cream, or made in part from it; also, a candy containing a creamlike substance. **4** The part of something regarded as the choicest or most highly to be appreciated: the *cream* of fashion. **5** A soft, oily cosmetic for cleansing or protecting the skin. See COSMETIC. **6** A rich, sirupy cordial or liqueur. See CRÈME. **7** The lighter part of liquor which rises and gathers on the top. **8** The color of cream: a light-yellow color. —*v.t.* **1** To skim cream from. **2** To take the best part from. **3** To add cream to, as coffee. **4** To permit (milk) to form cream. **5** To beat, as milk and sugar, to a creamy consistency. **6** To cook or prepare (food) with cream or cream sauce. —*v.i.* **7** To be covered with cream; froth. **8** To form cream. [<F *crème* <OF *cresme* <LL *chrisma.* Doublet of CHRISM.] —**cream′i·ness** *n.* —**cream′y** *adj.*

cream cheese Soft, unripened cheese made of cream or a mixture of cream and milk.

cream-col·ored (krēm′kul′ərd) *adj.* Having the yellowish-white color of cream.

cream·cups (krēm′kups′) *n.* An ornamental annual *(Platystemon californicus)* of the poppy family, with cream-colored flowers.

cream·er (krē′mər) *n.* **1** A cooler or other container in which milk is placed and the cream allowed to rise. **2** Any dish or machine in which cream is separated. **3** A cream pitcher.

cream·er·y (krē′mər·ē) *n. pl.* **·er·ies** **1** A place for collecting, keeping, or selling cream. **2** A place where butter and cheese are made, milk and cream are pasteurized, separated, bottled, etc.

cream-faced (krēm′fāst′) *adj.* White; pale.

cream of tartar Potassium bitartrate, $HKC_4H_4O_6$, a white crystalline compound with an acidulous taste, made by purifying argol: an ingredient of baking powder.

cream puff **1** A shell of pastry filled with whipped cream or custard. **2** *Slang* A sissy; weakling.

crease[1] (krēs) *n.* **1** The mark of a wrinkle, fold, or the like. **2** In cricket, any of the lines limiting the position of the bowler or batsman. —*v.* **creased, creas·ing** *v.t.* **1** To make a crease, line, or fold in; wrinkle. **2** To stun or wound by a shot that grazes the flesh. —*v.i.* **3** To become wrinkled or fall into creases. [ME *creaste,* ? var. of *creste* a crest, ridge] —**creas′er** *n.* —**creas′y** *adj.*

crease[2] (krēs) See KRIS.

cre·ate (krē·āt′) *v.* **·at·ed, ·at·ing** *v.t.* **1** To cause to come into existence; originate. **2** To be the cause of; occasion: The speech *created* much interest. **3** To produce, as a painting or poem, from thought and imagination. **4** To be the first to portray, as a character or part. **5** To invest with, as rank or office; appoint. —*v.i.* **6** *Brit. Slang* To make a fuss;

complain noisily. See synonyms under MAKE, PRODUCE. [<L *creatus*, pp. of *creare* produce, create]

cre·a·tine (krē′ə·tēn, -tin) *n. Biochem.* A nitrogenous compound, $C_4H_9N_3O_2$, found in the muscle tissue, brain, and blood of all vertebrate animals. It has been isolated in the form of white crystals, and is also made synthetically. Also **cre′a·tin** (-tin). [<Gk. *kreas, -atos* flesh + -INE[2]]

cre·at·i·nine (krē·at′ə·nēn, -nin) *n. Biochem.* The anhydride of creatine, $C_4H_7ON_3$, occurring normally in blood and urine: isolated as white or yellowish prismatic crystals. [<CREATINE + -INE[1]]

cre·a·tion (krē·ā′shən) *n.* **1** The act of creating; especially, in a theological sense, the original act of God in bringing the world or universe into existence. **2** The universe. **3** An act of construction; the combining or organizing of existing materials into new form: the *creation* of an empire. **4** That which is created; any product of the power of scientific, artistic, or practical construction: the *creations* of genius. **5** The act of investing with a new rank or character or of placing in a new office: the *creation* of two additional judges. —**all creation** Everybody; everything in the world. —**cre·a′tion·al** *adj.* —**cre·a′tion·al·ly** *adv.*

cre·a·tion·ism (krē·ā′shən·iz′əm) *n.* **1** The doctrine that the universe was originally brought into existence without preexistent material by the word of God, and also that new species or forms of being have been successively produced by the direct formative exercise of the Divine wisdom and power. **2** The doctrine that God creates a new soul whenever a human being begins to live: distinguished from *traducianism.* Also **cre·a′tion·al·ism.** —**cre·a′tion·ist** *n.* —**cre·a′tion·is′tic, cre·a′tion·al·is′tic** *adj.*

cre·a·tive (krē·ā′tiv) *adj.* **1** Having the power to create. **2** Productive; constructive. —**cre·a′tive·ly** *adv.* —**cre·a′tive·ness** *n.*

cre·a·tiv·i·ty (krē′ā·tiv′ə·tē) *n.* The quality of being able to produce original work or ideas in any field; creativeness.

cre·a·tor (krē·ā′tər) *n.* **1** One who creates or brings into being. **2** That which produces or causes; creative instrumentality. See synonyms under CAUSE. —**the Creator** God, as the maker of the universe. —**cre·a′tor·ship** *n.*

crea·ture (krē′chər) **1** That which has been created; a creation; a human being. **2** A domestic animal. **3** A person or thing considered as arising from, governed by, or conditioned upon something else: *creatures* of habit. **4** A person dependent upon the power or influence of another; dependent; tool. —**the creature** Strong drink; liquor: a drop of *the creature*: a humorous usage. —**crea′tur·al, crea′ture·ly** *adj.*

creature comforts Things that comfort or refresh the body: applied especially to food and drink.

Cré·bil·lon (krā·bē·yôn′), **Prosper Jolyot de,** 1674–1762, French dramatist. —**Claude Prosper Jolyot de,** 1707–77, French novelist; son of the preceding: known as *Crébillon fils.*

crèche (krāsh, kresh) *n.* **1** A public day-nursery. **2** A foundling asylum. **3** A modeled group representing the Nativity. [<F, crib, cradle]

Cré·cy (krā·sē′) A village in northern France; scene of an English victory over French forces, August, 1346: also *Cressy.* Also **Cré·cy–en–Pon·thieu** (krā·sē′äṅ·pôṅ·tyœ′).

cre·dence (krēd′ns) *n.* **1** Confidence based upon external evidence; belief. **2** That which serves to accredit; credentials. **3** *Eccl.* A small table or shelf near the altar to hold the eucharistic elements before they are consecrated. **4** A sideboard or serving table of medieval and Renaissance Europe. See synonyms under BELIEF, FAITH. [<F *crédence* <Med. L *credentia* < *credere* believe]

cre·den·dum (kri·den′dəm) *n. pl.* **·da** (-də) An article of faith; that which is to be believed: distinguished from *agendum.* [<L, gerundive of *credere* believe]

cre·dent (krēd′nt) *adj. Obs.* **1** Credible; to be believed. **2** Credulous.

cre·den·tial (kri·den′shəl) *n.* **1** That which certifies one's authority or claim to confidence. **2** *pl.* Certificate showing that a person is invested with certain authority or claim to confidence or consideration. —*adj.* Giving a title or claim to credit and confidence; accrediting.

cred·i·bil·i·ty (kred′ə·bil′ə·tē) *n.* **1** The capacity of being believed. **2** The capacity, as of a government or a public official, of maintaining the public's confidence that its report of the conduct of its affairs is worthy of belief.

credibility gap **1** A lessening or loss of credibility, as in a government or public official. **2** The extent or degree of a decline in credibility: The official statement only widened the *credibility gap.*

cred·i·ble (kred′ə·bəl) *adj.* Capable of being believed; worthy of credit, confidence, or acceptance. See synonyms under LIKELY, PROBABLE. [<L *credibilis* < *credere* believe] —**cred′i·ble·ness** *n.* —**cred′i·bly** *adv.*

cred·it (kred′it) *n.* **1** Belief in the truth of a statement or in the sincerity of a person; trust. **2** Reputation for trustworthiness; character; repute. **3** One who or that which adds honor or reputation: a student who is a *credit* to his class. **4** Influence derived from the good opinion or confidence of others: He has *credit* at court. **5** In bookkeeping, the entry in account of any amount paid by a debtor on account of his debt; the amount so entered; also, the right–hand side of an account, upon which are recorded values received: opposed to *debit.* **6** Transfer of property on promise of future payment. **7** Reputation for solvency and probity. **8** The amount to which a person, corporation, or business house may be financially trusted in a given case. **9** In an account, the balance in one's favor. **10** The time extended for the payment of a liability. **11** An amount placed by a bank at a customer's disposal against which he may draw. **12** In education, official certification that a course of study has been finished; also, a recognized unit of school or college work. **13** *Usually pl.* Acknowledgment of work done, as in the making of a motion picture. See synonyms under BELIEF, FAITH, FAME. —*v.t.* **1** To give credit for; accept as true. **2** To ascribe, as intelligence or honor, to: with *with.* **3** *Archaic* To reflect credit upon; bring into good repute. **4** In bookkeeping, to give credit for or enter as credit to. **5** In education, to give educational credits to (a student). [<F *crédit* <L *creditum* a loan < *credere* believe, trust] —**cred′it·a·bil′i·ty, cred′it·a·ble·ness** *n.* —**cred′it·a·ble** *adj.* —**cred′it·a·bly** *adv.*

cred·i·tor (kred′i·tər) *n.* **1** One to whom another is pecuniarily indebted. **2** In bookkeeping, that side of an account upon which are recorded values received or receivable.

credit standing Reputation for meeting financial obligations, paying bills, etc.

credit union A cooperative group for making loans to its members at low rates of interest.

cre·do (krē′dō, krā′-) *n. pl.* **·dos** **1** A creed, as the Apostles' or the Nicene Creed. **2** A musical setting for the creed. [<L, I believe; the opening word of the creed]

cre·du·li·ty (krə·dōō′lə·tē, -dyōō′-) *n.* **1** The state or quality of being credulous. **2** A proneness to believe the improbable or the marvelous. [<L *credulitas, -tatis* < *credulus* CREDULOUS]

cred·u·lous (krej′ōō·ləs) *adj.* **1** Apt or disposed to believe on slight evidence; easily deceived. **2** Arising from credulity. [<L *credulus* < *credere* believe] —**cred′u·lous·ly** *adv.* —**cred′u·lous·ness** *n.*

Cree (krē) *n. pl.* **Cree** or **Crees** **1** One of a tribe of the Algonquian stock of North American Indians formerly dwelling in Manitoba and Assiniboia between the Red River and the Saskatchewan. **2** The language of this tribe. —*adj.* Of or pertaining to this tribe or its language.

creed (krēd) *n.* **1** A formal summary of religious belief; an authoritative statement of doctrine; a confession of faith. **2** That which is believed; doctrine. See synonyms under BELIEF, FAITH. —**the Creed** The Apostles' Creed. [OE *creda* <L *credo* I believe. See CREDO.]

creek (krēk, krik) *n.* **1** A tidal or valley stream between a brook and a river in size: often written *crick.* **2** A small inlet, bay, or cove; a recess in the shore of the sea or of a river. **3** *Brit.* A small seaboard town. See synonyms under STREAM. —**up the creek** *U.S. Colloq.* **1** In a state of uncertainty or bewilderment. **2** Out of luck. [ME *creke, crike* <Scand. Cf. Sw. *krik* cove, inlet.]

Creek (krēk) *n.* **1** A confederacy of the Muskhogean tribes of North American Indians, once occupying a great portion of Georgia, Alabama, and northern Florida. **2** An Indian of any of the tribes in this confederacy. **3** Their Muskhogean language.

creel (krēl) *n.* **1** An angler's willow basket for carrying fish. **2** A cage of wickerwork for catching lobsters. **3** A frame in a spinning machine. —*v.t.* To put in a creel. [<OF *creil* <L *craticula,* dim. of *cratis* wickerwork. Doublet of GRILLE.]

creep (krēp) *v.i.* **crept, creep·ing** **1** To move like a serpent; crawl. **2** To move imperceptibly, slowly, secretly, or stealthily. **3** To exhibit servility; cringe. **4** To have a sensation as of contact with creeping things. **5** To grow along a surface or support: *creeping* plants. **6** To slip out of place: A sleeve *creeps* up the arm. **7** To move slightly along the line of length: said of railroad tracks. —*n.* **1** The act of creeping. **2** *pl.* A nervous sensation as of insects creeping under the flesh; hence, uneasy apprehensiveness. **3** *Metall.* A phenomenon associated with metals subjected to critical temperature and stresses, and characterized by a slow slipping or flow of the material. **4** *Geol.* The gradual movement of rock waste and soil down a slope from which it has been loosened by weathering. [OE *crēopan*]

creep·ie (krē′pē, krip′ē) *n. Scot.* A low stool. Also **creepie chair.**

creep·ie–peep·ie (krē′pē·pē′pē) *n.* A portable, one–man television camera transmitting pictures by wireless: analogous to a walkie–talkie.

creeping myrtle Periwinkle.

creep·y (krē′pē) *adj.* **creep·i·er, creep·i·est** **1** Feeling as if something were creeping over the skin; shivering; especially, chilled with fright. **2** Characterized by creeping. —**creep′i·ly** *adv.* —**creep′i·ness** *n.*

creese (krēs) See KRIS.

creesh (krēsh) *n. Scot.* Grease. —*v.t.* To grease. Also **creish.** —**creesh′y** *adj.*

cre·mate (krē′māt, kri·māt′) *v.t.* **·mat·ed, ·mat·ing** To burn up; reduce, especially a dead body, to ashes. See synonyms under BURN. [<L *crematus,* pp. of *cremare* burn to ashes] —**cre′ma·tor** *n.*

cre·ma·tion (kri·mā′shən) *n.* The act or practice of burning, especially of burning the dead.

cre·ma·to·ry (krē′mə·tôr′ē, -tō′rē, krem′-) *adj.* Related to or connected with cremation. —*n. pl.* **·ries** A place for cremating dead bodies. Also **cre′ma·to′ri·um** (-tôr′ē·əm, -tō′rē-).

crème (krem) *n. French* Cream: used in names of sauces or liqueurs: *crème* de menthe.

crème de ca·ca·o (də kə·kā′ō, -kä′ō) *n.* A sweet, chocolate–flavored liqueur.

crème de la crème (də lȧ krem′) *French* Literally, cream of the cream; the very best; most choice.

crème de menthe (də mäṅt) *French* A sweet, green or white cordial with a strong flavor of mint.

Crem·nitz white (krem′nits) A high–grade pigment made from litharge, or corroded white lead. Also *Kremnitz white.*

crem·o·carp (krem′ə·kärp, krē′mə-) *n. Bot.* The fruit of any plant of the parsley family, consisting of two one–seeded carpels, separating when ripe and hanging from the summit of the slender axis. Also **crem′o·car′pi·um** (-kär′pē·əm). [<Gk. *kremaein* hang + *karpos* fruit]

Cre·mo·na (kri·mō′nə, *Ital.* krā·mō′nä) *n.* Any violin made at Cremona, Italy, from the 16th to the 18th century, by the Amati family, by Antonio Stradivari, or by Josef Guarnerius.

Cre·mo·na (kri·mō′nə, *Ital.* krā·mō′nä) A province in Lombardy, northern Italy; 678 square miles; capital, Cremona.

cre·nate (krē′nāt) *adj. Bot.* Scalloped or toothed with even, rounded notches, as a leaf or margin. Also **cre′nat·ed.** [<NL *crenatus* < *crena* a notch]

cren·a·ture (kren′ə·chōōr, krē′nə-) *n.* **1** The rounded tooth of a crenate organ. **2** The state of being crenate. Also **cre·na·tion** (kri·nā′shən).

cren·el (kren′əl) *n.* **1** An embrasure of a battlement; an indentation. **2** A crenature. — *v.t.* **cren·el·ed** or **·el·led, cren·el·ing** or **·el·ling** To crenelate. Also **cre·nelle** (kri·nel′). [<OF, dim. of *cren* notch]

cren·e·late (kren′ə·lāt) *v.t.* **·lat·ed, ·lat·ing** To fortify or decorate with battlements. — *adj.* Crenulate. Also **cren′el·late.** — **cren′e·la′tion, cren′el·la′tion** *n.*

cren·u·late (kren′yə·lit, -lāt) *adj.* Finely notched or crenate. Also **cren′u·lat′ed.** [<NL *crenulatus* <*crenula,* dim. of *crena* notch]

cren·u·la·tion (kren′yə·lā′shən) *n.* **1** The state of being crenulate. **2** A small crenature.

cre·o·dont (krē′ə·dont) *n. Paleontol.* One of a suborder (*Creodonta*) of primitive Tertiary carnivora, having incisors with closed roots, distinct fibula, and developed otic bulla. [<NL *Creodonta* <Gk. *kreas* flesh + *odous, odontos* tooth]

Cre·ole (krē′ōl) *n.* **1** A native of Spanish America or the West Indies, of European parentage. **2** A descendant of French, Spanish, or Portuguese settlers of Louisiana and the Gulf States who retains his special speech or culture. **3** A Negro born in the Americas, as distinguished from one brought from Africa: also known as a **Creole Negro. 4** The French patois of Louisiana: distinguished from *Cajun.* **5** Any person having both Creole and Negro blood and speaking the Creole patois. — *adj.* Relating or peculiar to the Creoles. [<F *créole* <Sp. *criollo* a native <*criar* produce, bring forth <L *creare* create]

cre·ole (krē′ōl) *n.* A creolized language. — *adj.* Cooked with a savory sauce including peppers, tomatoes, onions, etc.

Creole State Nickname of LOUISIANA.

Cre·o·lin (krē′ə·lin) *n.* Saponified creosote, a thick, black coal-tar liquid, used as an antiseptic, germicide, and deodorant: a trade name.

cre·o·lized language (krē′ə·lizd) An amalgamated language, such as Gullah, resulting from close and prolonged contact between two groups speaking dissimilar languages: it usually incorporates a simplified vocabulary from the dominant language with the grammatical system of the native language, and becomes the only language of the subject group. Compare PIDGIN.

Cre·on (krē′on) In Greek legend, the brother of Jocasta and successor to Oedipus on the throne of Thebes: he sentenced Antigone to death for burying her brother Polynices.

cre·o·sol (krē′ə·sōl, -sol) *n. Chem.* A colorless, aromatic, oily liquid compound, $C_8H_{10}O_2$, derived from beech tar or guaiac by distillation. [<CREOS(OTE) + -OL[2]]

cre·o·sote (krē′ə·sōt) *n. Chem.* **1** An oily liquid consisting principally of cresol and other phenols, obtained by the destructive distillation of wood and having a smoky odor and burning taste: it is an antiseptic, but a poor germicide, and is used to preserve timber, meat, etc. **2** A similar liquid distilled from coal tar: also **coal-tar creosote.** — *v.t.* **·sot·ed, ·sot·ing** To treat or impregnate with creosote, as shingles, etc. [<Gk. *kreas* flesh + *sōtēr* preserver <*sōzein* save]

creosote bush A shrub (*Larrea tridentata*) of the bean caltrop family of Mexico and the Colorado desert, having a resinous foliage that smells like creosote.

crêpe (krāp) *n.* A thin, light fabric, made of silk, cotton, wool, or synthetic fibers, generally with a crinkled, pebbled, or puckered surface: also spelled *crape.* Also **crepe.** [<F (*tissu*) *crêpe* crinkled cloth <L *crispus* curled]

crêpe de Chine (də shēn′) A soft, thin silk dress fabric, with a pebbly surface.

crêpe hair Artificial hair, used in theatrical make-up for beards and moustaches.

crêpe paper A tissue paper resembling crêpe, used for decorative purposes.

crêpe rubber Rubber prepared in crinkled texture for the soles of shoes.

crêpes su·zette (krāp′ sōō·zet′) Thin egg pancakes, rolled in a hot, orange-flavored sauce: usually served aflame in cognac or curaçao.

Cré·pin (krā·paṅ′) French form of CRISPIN.

crep·i·tate (krep′ə·tāt) *v.i.* **·tat·ed, ·tat·ing** To make a succession of quick snapping sounds; crackle; rattle. [<L *crepitatus,* pp. of *crepitare,* freq. of *crepare* creak] — **crep′i·tant** *adj.* — **crep′i·ta′tion** *n.*

crept (krept) Past tense of CREEP.

cre·pus·cu·lar (kri·pus′kyə·lər) *adj.* **1** Pertaining to twilight; like twilight; obscure. **2** Appearing or flying in the morning or evening twilight, as certain birds and insects. Also **cre·pus′cu·lous.**

cre·pus·cule (kri·pus′kyōōl) *n.* Twilight. Also **cre·pus·cle** (kri·pus′əl). [<L *crepusculum* < *creper* dark, dusky]

cre·scen·do (krə·shen′dō, -sen′-) *n. pl.* **·dos** *Music* **1** A gradual increase in the force of sound: expressed by the sign ——< or the abbreviation *cres.* **2** A passage so performed. — *adj.* Slowly increasing in loudness or power. [<Ital. <*crescere* increase]

cres·cent (kres′ənt) *n.* **1** The visible part of the moon in its first quarter, having one concave edge and one convex edge; the new moon. **2** Something crescent-shaped, as the device on the Turkish standard; hence **The Crescent,** the Turkish or Mohammedan power. — *adj.* **1** Increasing: said of the moon in its first quarter. **2** Shaped like the moon in its first quarter. [<L *crescens, -entis,* ppr. of *crescere* increase] — **cres·cen·tic** (kre·sen′·tik) *adj.*

cres·cive (kres′iv) *adj. Obs.* Growing; increasing. [<L *crescere* increase + -IVE]

cre·sol (krē′sōl, -sol) *n. Chem.* Any one of three isomeric liquid or crystalline compounds, C_7H_8O, obtained by the destructive distillation of coal, beechwood, or pinewood: used as an antiseptic. [Var. of CREOSOL]

cress (kres) *n.* One of various plants of the mustard family having a pungent taste and used in salads. [OE *cressa*] — **cress′y** *adj.*

cres·set (kres′it) *n.* An incombustible frame or vessel mounted to hold a torch, a beacon, or fuel for this. [<OF *craicet, craisset*]

Cres·si·da (kres′i·də) In medieval legend, in Chaucer's *Troilus and Criseyde,* and in Shakespeare's *Troilus and Cressida,* a Trojan girl unfaithful to her lover Troilus: also spelled *Criseyde.* Also **Cres′sid.** See PANDARUS.

Cres·sy (kres′ē) See CRÉCY.

crest (krest) *n.* **1** A comb or tuft on the head of an animal or bird. **2** The projection on the top of a helmet; a plume; tuft. **3** The ridge of a wave or of a mountain; the top of anything. **4** A heraldic device placed above the shield in a coat of arms. **5** *Archaic* Loftiness; pride; courage. **6** The ridge of the neck of a horse or a dog. **7** *Archit.* **a** The ridge of a roof. **b** Carved work or any continuous ornament on the ridge or other elevated parts of an edifice; a cresting. — *v.t.* **1** To serve as a crest for; cap. **2** To furnish with or as with a crest. **3** To reach the crest of. **4** To adorn with crestlike streaks or lines. — *v.i.* **5** To come to a crest, as a wave prior to breaking. [<OF *creste* <L *crista* tuft] — **crest′ed** *adj.*

COAT OF ARMS WITH CREST

crested auklet A small, brownish-black diving bird (*Aethia cristatella*), abundant in Alaska and the North Pacific.

crested flycatcher Any flycatcher having a conspicuous crest, especially the great crested flycatcher (*Myiarchus crinitus*) of eastern North America.

crest·fall·en (krest′fô′lən) *adj.* **1** Having the crest or head lowered. **2** Dispirited; dejected.

crest·ing (kres′ting) *n. Archit.* An ornamental ridge surmounting a roof, wall, etc.

crest·less (krest′lis) *adj.* Having no crest.

cres·yl (kres′əl, krē′səl) *n. Chem* Tolyl. [< CRES(OL) + -YL]

cres·y·late (kres′ə·lāt) *n. Chem.* An ester derived from cresol.

cre·syl·ic (kri·sil′ik) *adj. Chem.* Of or derived from cresyl, cresol, or creosote.

cre·ta·ceous (kri·tā′shəs) *adj.* Consisting of or related to chalk; chalky. [<L *cretaceus* <*creta* chalk <*Creta* Cretan, of Crete (where large deposits of chalk occurred)]

Cre·ta·ceous (kri·tā′shəs) *n. Geol.* The third and last of the geologic periods of the Mesozoic era, preceded by the Jurassic and followed by the Tertiary period of the Cenozoic era. See chart under GEOLOGY. — *adj.* Pertaining to or characteristic of this period.

Crete (krēt) A Greek island 160 miles long in the Mediterranean SE of Greece; 3,207 square miles. *Greek* **Kre·te** (krē′tē). — **Cre′tan** *adj.* & *n.* — **Cre′tic** *adj.*

Cre·tic (krē′tik) *n.* In prosody, an amphimacer. [<Gk. *Krētikos* Cretan, a Cretic foot]

cre·tin (krē′tin) *n.* A person afflicted with cretinism. [<F *crétin,* var. of *chrétien* Christian, human being, i.e., not an animal] — **cre′tin·ous** *adj.*

cre·tin·ism (krē′tən·iz′əm) *n. Pathol.* A disease associated with prenatal thyroid deficiency and subsequent thyroid inactivity, marked by physical deformities, arrested development, goiter, and various forms of mental retardation, including imbecility: also called *hypothyroidism.*

cre·tonne (kri·ton′, krē′ton) *n.* A heavy, unglazed cotton, linen, or rayon fabric printed in colored patterns: used especially for draperies, chair coverings, etc. [from *Creton,* a village in Normandy]

Cre·u·sa (krē·ōō′sə) **1** In Greek legend, daughter of Creon and bride of Jason, killed by the jealous Medea. **2** In the *Aeneid,* wife of Aeneas, lost in the escape from Troy.

Creuse (krœz) A river of central France, flowing NW 160 miles to the Loire.

Creu·sot (krœ·zō′), **Le** See LE CREUSOT.

cre·vasse (krə·vas′) *n.* **1** A deep fissure, as in a glacier. **2** A breach in a levee. — *v.t.* **·vassed, ·vass·ing** To split with crevasses. [<F] — **cre·vassed′** *adj.*

Crève·coeur (krev·kœr′), **Michel-Guillaume Jean de,** 1735–1813, French author in America: pseudonym *J. Hector St. John.*

crev·ice (krev′is) *n.* A small fissure or crack. See synonyms under BREACH. [<OF *crevace* <LL *crepatia* <L *crepare* crack, creak] — **crev′iced** *adj.*

crew[1] (krōō) *n.* **1** *Naut.* **a** The company of seamen belonging to one ship or boat: sometimes including officers, and legally including both master and officers unless specifically excepted. **b** The gang of a boatswain, gunner, carpenter, or other petty officer. **2** A body of men organized or detailed for a particular work, as to run a train. **3** A group of students trained to handle a racing shell, consisting of oarsmen and coxswain. **4** A company of people in general; crowd: a motley *crew* of ne'er-do-wells and loafers. **5** Any band or troop of armed men. See synonyms under CABAL. [<OF *creue* an increase <*croistre* grow <L *crescere* increase]

crew[2] (krōō) Past tense of CROW.

crew cut A closely cropped haircut.

Crewe (krōō) A municipal borough in south central Cheshire, England.

crew·el (krōō′əl) *n.* A slackly twisted worsted yarn, used in fancywork. ◆ Homophone: *cruel.* [Origin uncertain]

crewel needle Any large-eyed needle, especially one used for crewel.

crew·el·work (krōō′əl·wûrk′) *n.* Embroidery with crewel.

crib (krib) *n.* **1** A rack or manger. **2** A stall for cattle. **3** A child's bedstead, with side railings. **4** A box, bin, or small building for grain, having slat or openwork sides. **5** A small raft. **6** A frame of wood or timber, used to retain a bank of earth. **7** *Colloq.* A petty theft, or the thing taken; plagiarism. **8** A translation or other unauthorized aid in study. **9** A house, cottage, lodging, etc. **10** In cribbage, the four discarded cards counted by the dealer. See CRIBBAGE. **11** A wickerwork basket. — *v.* **cribbed, crib·bing** *v.t.* **1** To enclose in or as in a crib; confine closely. **2** To line or bolster, as the walls of a pit, with timbers or planking. **3** *Colloq.* To take and pass off as one's own, as an answer or a piece of writing; copy; plagiarize. **4** *Colloq.* To steal; purloin. **5** In logging, to form (logs) into a raft, as for towing.

6 *Colloq.* To translate with the aid of a crib. —*v.i.* 7 *Colloq.* To use a crib in translating. 8 To crib-bite. [OE *cribb*] —**crib′ber** *n.*

crib·bage (krib′ij) *n.* A game of cards for two, three, or four players, in which the score is kept on a small board with rows of holes into which pegs are inserted. [<CRIB, *n.* (def 10)]

crib-bite (krib′bīt′) *v.i.* **-bit, -bit·ten** or **-bit, -bit·ing** To bite a crib or manger, at the same time drawing in the breath with a peculiar sound: said of horses. —**crib′-bit′er** *n.* —**crib′-bit′ing** *n.*

crib·ble (krib′əl) *n.* 1 A coarse sieve. 2 Coarse flour or meal. —*v.t.* **·bled, ·bling** To separate with a coarse sieve or riddle; sift. Also **crib′le.** [<F *crible* <LL *cribellum,* dim. of L *cribrum* sieve]

crib·bled (krib′əld) *adj.* Covered with small punctures or dots, as in engraving or the decoration of wood or metal. [<F *criblé* <*crible* a sieve]

crib·ri·form (krib′rə·fôrm) *adj.* Having the form of a sieve; sievelike.

crib·work (krib′wûrk′) *n.* 1 A frame of logs filled in with stones: used to support wharves or to prevent water from washing out ground. 2 A crib, or anything constructed with cribs.

Crich·ton (krī′tən), **James,** 1560–82?, Scottish scholar and soldier: called "The Admirable Crichton."

crick[1] (krik) *n.* A spasmodic affection of the muscles, as of the neck; a cramp. —*v.t.* To turn or twist so as to produce a crick. [Origin uncertain]

crick[2] (krik) See CREEK (def. 1).

crick·et[1] (krik′it) *n.* A leaping orthopterous insect (family *Gryllidae*), with long antennae and three segments in each tarsus, the male of which makes a chirping sound by friction of the forewings. For illustration see under INSECT (injurious). [<OF *criquet* <LG]

crick·et[2] (krik′it) *n.* 1 An outdoor game played with bats, a ball, and wickets, between two opposing sides numbering eleven each: one of the most popular sports of England. 2 *Colloq.* Fair, gentlemanly behavior; sportsmanship. [<F *criquet* bat, stick <MDu. *cricke*] —**crick′et·er** *n.*

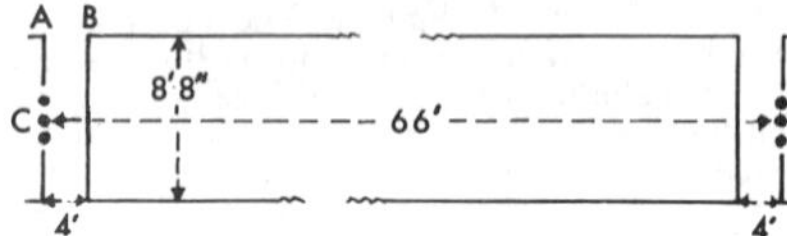

CRICKET FIELD

A. Bowling crease. *B.* Popping crease.
C. The wicket with its 3 stumps 8 inches apart.
The playing field is usually 150 x 100 yards.

crick·et[3] (krik′it) *n. Archit.* A small, sloping roof structure placed, for the purpose of diverting drainage, at the juncture of larger surfaces that meet at an angle. [Origin unknown]

crick·et[4] (krik′it) *n.* A footstool. [Origin unknown]

cri·coid (krī′koid) *Anat. adj.* Ringlike: designating a cartilage at the lowest part of the larynx. —*n.* The topmost cartilaginous ring of the trachea, whose posterior portion serves as a base for the arytenoids. [<Gk. *krikoeidēs* <*krikos* ring + *eidos* shape, form]

cri·co·thy·roid (krī′kō·thī′roid) *adj. Anat.* Of or pertaining to the cricoid and thyroid cartilages. See illustration under LARYNX.

cried (krīd) Past participle and past tense of CRY.

cri·er (krī′ər) *n.* One who publicly cries sales, lost articles, etc.

Crile (krīl), **George Washington,** 1864–1943, U.S. surgeon and scientist.

crime (krīm) *n.* 1 *Law* An act that subjects the doer to legal punishment; the commission or omission of an act specifically forbidden or enjoined by public law. 2 Any grave offense against morality or social order; wickedness; iniquity. See synonyms under ABOMINATION, OFFENSE, SIN. [<F <L *crimen* accusation, charge]

Cri·me·a A peninsula and autonomous republic of the Ukraine on the northern coast of the Black Sea; 10,400 square miles; capital, Simferopol; pop. 2,500,000. *Russian* **Krym (krim).** —*adj.* & *n* **Cri·me′an.**

Crimean War See table under WAR.

cri·men fal·si (krī′mən fal′sē) *Latin* The crime of perjury.

crim·i·nal (krim′ə·nəl) *adj.* 1 *Law* Relating to crime, or pertaining to the administration of penal as opposed to civil law. 2 Implying crime or heinous wickedness. 3 Guilty of crime: the *criminal* classes. —*n.* One who has committed an offense punishable by law. [<F *criminel* <L *criminalis*] —**crim·i·nal·i·ty** (krim′ə·nal′ə·tē), **crim′i·nal·ness** *n.* —**crim′·i·nal·ly** *adv.*

Synonyms (adj.): abominable, culpable, felonious, flagitious, guilty, illegal, immoral, iniquitous, nefarious, sinful, unlawful, vicious, vile, wicked, wrong. Every *criminal* act is *illegal* or *unlawful,* but *illegal* or *unlawful* acts may not be always *criminal.* Offenses against public law are *criminal,* offenses against private rights are *illegal* or *unlawful.* All acts punishable by fine or imprisonment or both are *criminal* in view of the law. It is *illegal* for a man to trespass on another's land, but it is not *criminal*; the trespasser is liable to civil suit for damages, but not to indictment, fine, or imprisonment. A *felonious* act is a *criminal* act punishable by imprisonment in the penitentiary or by death. A *flagitious* crime is one that brings public odium. *Vicious* refers to the indulgence of evil appetites, habits, or passions; *vicious* acts are not necessarily *criminal,* or even *illegal*; we speak of a *vicious* horse. That which is *iniquitous,* that is, contrary to equity, may sometimes be done under the forms of law. See IMMORAL. *Antonyms*: innocent, just, lawful, legal, meritorious, moral, right, virtuous.

criminal conversation See under CONVERSATION.

crim·i·nal·is·tics (krim′ə·nəl·is′tiks) *n.* That branch of criminology which deals especially with the scientific methods of crime detection.

crim·i·nate (krim′ə·nāt) *v.t.* **·nat·ed, ·nat·ing** To accuse of or implicate in crime; incriminate. [<L *criminatus,* pp. of *criminari* accuse of crime] —**crim′i·na′tion** *n.* —**crim′i·na′tive** *adj.* —**crim′i·na′tor** *n.*

crim·i·nol·o·gy (krim′ə·nol′ə·jē) *n.* The scientific study and investigation of crime and criminals. [<L *crimen, criminis* + -LOGY] —**crim·i·no·log·i·cal** (krim′ə·nə·loj′i·kəl) *adj.* —**crim′i·nol′o·gist** *n.*

crimp[1] (krimp) *v.t.* 1 To bend or press into ridges or folds; corrugate; flute. 2 To indent and close, as a cartridge case; crease. 3 To bend into shape, as the uppers of boots. 4 To gash the flesh of with a knife, as fish before cooking, in order to make it firmer and crisper. 5 To curl or wave: to *crimp* the hair. —*n.* 1 Anything crimped; especially, in the plural, waved or curled hair. 2 A crimping machine; crimper. 3 An offset in a piece of structural steel, used to fit one piece over another. 4 A collapse or breakdown of wood fibers, due to inherent weakness or a too rapid drying of timber. —*adj.* 1 Brittle and crisp; friable. 2 Inconsistent or contradictory. 3 Stiff, as if starched. [<MDu. *crimpen* wrinkle, draw together] —**crimp′age** *n.* —**crimp′er** *n.* —**crimp′y** *adj.*

crimp[2] (krimp) *n.* One who procures the impressment of sailors, soldiers, etc., by decoying or entrapping them. —*v.t.* To decoy or entrap into forced military or naval service. [Origin uncertain]

crim·son (krim′zən) *n.* A deep-red color having a tinge of blue, but lighter than purple. 1 Of a deep-red color. 2 Bloody. —*v.t.* & *v.i.* To make or become crimson; redden; blush. [<Sp. *cremesin,* var. of OSp. *carmesin, carmesi* <Arabic *qirmazi* <*qirmiz* kermes (insect used in making a red dye). Doublet of CARMINE.]

cringe (krinj) *v.i.* **cringed, cring·ing** 1 To bow in servility or cowardice; crouch. 2 To wince as with pain or fear. 3 To fawn. —*n.* A servile crouching. [ME *cringen, crengen*; related to OE *cringan* yield, fall] —**cring′er** *n.*

crin·gle (kring′gəl) *n. Naut.* An eye, loop, or grommet in a sail, on the side of a rope, etc. [<Du. *kringel* little ring]

cri·nite[1] (krī′nīt) *adj.* 1 *Bot.* Having hair or bearded with long weak hairs. 2 Resembling a tuft of hair. [<L *crinitus,* pp. of *crinire* cover with hair <*crinis* hair]

cri·nite[2] (krī′nīt, krin′īt) *n.* An encrinite. [<Gk. *krinon* lily]

crin·kle (kring′kəl) *v.t.* & *v.i.* **·kled, ·kling** 1 To form or cause to form, mold, or move with bends, turns, twists, or wrinkles. 2 To wind in and out; wave; corrugate. 3 To crackle metallically. —*n.* A wrinkle; ripple; twist; sinuosity. [ME *crenklen,* freq. of OE *crincan,* var. of *cringan* yield, fall] —**crin′kly** *adj.*

crin·kle·root (kring′kəl·rōōt′, -rŏŏt′) *n.* A toothwort (genus *Dentaria*) of the mustard family, especially *D. diphylla,* with small white or lilac flowers and a white-toothed rootstock with a pungent, aromatic taste: also called *pepperroot.*

crin·kum-cran·kum (kring′kəm·krang′kəm) *n.* 1 An odd, crooked figure or fanciful ornamentation; a zigzag. 2 A whimsy. [Varied reduplication of dial. *crink* a twisting]

cri·noid (krī′noid, krin′oid) *adj.* 1 Of or pertaining to the *Crinoidea.* 2 Containing crinoids: also **cri·noi·dal** (kri·noid′l). —*n.* One of the *Crinoidea.*

Cri·noi·de·a (krī·noi′dē·ə, kri-) *n. pl. Zool.* A class of echinoderms having jointed stems, attached by stalks to the sea bottom, and radial arms; the sea lilies. [NL <Gk. *krinoeidēs* <*krinon* lily + *eidos* form] —**cri·noi′·de·an** *n.* & *adj.*

crin·o·line (krin′ə·lin, -lēn) *n.* 1 A highly sized, stiff fabric, used in puffed sleeves, hems, interlinings, etc.: originally made of horsehair and linen. 2 A skirt stiffened with such fabric. 3 A hoop skirt. —*adj.* Resembling crinoline, or serving an analogous purpose. [<F <L *crinis* hair + *linum* flax, thread]

cri·num (krī′nəm) *n.* Any of a genus (*Crinum*) of frequently cultivated tropical herbs of the amaryllis family, with tunicate bulbs and a solid scape bearing numerous long, narrow leaves and showy, fragrant flowers. [<NL <Gk. *krinon* lily]

cri·o·sphinx (krī′ə·sfingks′) *n.* A sphinx with a ram's head. See SPHINX. [<Gk. *krios* ram + SPHINX]

crip·ple (krip′əl) *n.* 1 A maimed or lamed person or animal; one lacking the natural use of a limb or the body. 2 *U.S. Dial.* A piece of low, marshy land, partly covered by the tide and partly overgrown with trees and brush. 3 A staging used in cleaning windows. —*v.t.* **·pled, ·pling** To lame; impair or disable. [OE *crypel.* Akin to CREEP.]

Cripple Creek A city of central Colorado; center of one of the world's richest gold-producing areas in former years.

crip·pler (krip′lər) *n.* 1 A crimping board or graining board for leather. 2 One who or that which cripples.

Cripps (krips), **Sir (Richard) Stafford,** 1889–1952, English statesman and diplomat.

cris (krēs) See KRIS.

Cri·sey·de (kri·sā′də) See CRESSIDA.

cri·sis (krī′sis) *n. pl.* **cri·ses** (-sēz) 1 A turning point in the progress of an affair or of a series of events; a critical moment. 2 *Pathol.* Any sudden or decisive change in the course of a disease, favorable or unfavorable. [<L <Gk. *krisis* <*krinein* decide]

crisp (krisp) *adj.* 1 Firm and brittle; also, crumbling readily, as pastry. 2 Terse or pithy; curt. 3 Fresh; bracing. 4 Having curls or waves; crinkled; crisped. —*v.t.* & *v.i.* To make or become crisp. [OE <L *crispus* curled] —**crisp′er** *n.* —**crisp′ly** *adv.* —**crisp′ness** *n.* —**crisp′y** *adj.*

cris·pate (kris′pāt) *adj.* Having a crisped or curled appearance. Also **cris′pat·ed.** [<L *crispatus,* pp. of *crispare* curl <*crispus* curled]

cris·pa·tion (kris·pā′shən) *n.* 1 A slight contraction or spasmodic constriction. 2 A minute ripple of a liquid's surface, caused by vibration. Also **crisp·a·ture** (kris′pə·chŏŏr).

Cris·pi (krēs′pē), **Francesco,** 1819–1901, Italian statesman.

Cris·pin (kris′pin) A masculine personal name. Also *Ger.* **Cris·pus** (kris′pŏŏs), *Ital.* **Cris·pi·no** (krēs·pē′nō), **Cris·po** (krēs′pō), *Lat.* **Cris·pi·nus** (kris·pī′nəs), **Cris·pus** (kris′pəs), *Sp.* **Cris·po** (krēs′pō). [<L, curly]

—**Crispin, Saint** A Roman Christian martyr of the late third century; patron saint of shoemakers; hence, **Crispin,** a shoemaker.

cris·sal (kris′əl) *adj.* 1 Of or pertaining to the crissum. 2 Having a bright-colored crissum.

criss-cross (kris′krôs′, -kros′) *v.t.* To cross with interlacing lines. —*v.i.* To move in criss-crosses. —*adj.* Crossing one another in different directions; said of lines or the like. —*n.* 1 The cross of one who cannot write. 2 A congeries of intersecting lines. 3 A game played by children. —*adv.* In different cross-directions; crosswise. [Alter. of CHRIST-CROSS]

criss-cross-row (kris′krôs′rō′, -kros′-) See CHRIST-CROSS-ROW.

cris·sum (kris′əm) *n. Ornithol.* The undertail coverts of a bird; the region or feathers about the anus. [<NL <L *crissare* move the haunches]

cris·tate (kris′tāt) *adj.* 1 Crested. 2 Carinate. Also **cris′tat·ed.** [<L *cristatus* < *crista* crest]

Cris·tia·no (krēs·tyä′nō) Italian and Spanish form of CHRISTIAN, personal name.

Cris·ti·na (krēs·tē′nä) Italian and Spanish form of CHRISTINA.

Cris·tó·bal (krēs·tō′väl) Spanish form of CHRISTOPHER.

Cris·tó·bal (kris·tō′bəl, *Sp.* krēs·tō′väl) A port in Panama at the Atlantic entrance to the Panama Canal.

Cris·to·fo·ro (krēs·tô′fō·rō) Italian form of CHRISTOPHER.

cri·te·ri·on (krī·tir′ē·ən) *n. pl.* **·te·ri·a** (-tir′ē·ə) or **·te·ri·ons** 1 A standard by which a correct judgment can be made; a model or example. 2 A test, rule, or measure for distinguishing between the true or false, perfect or imperfect, etc. [<Gk. *kritērion* < *kritēs* a judge < *krinein* decide]

crit·ic (krit′ik) *n.* 1 One who judges anything by some standard or criterion, particularly one who so judges literary or artistic productions. 2 One who judges severely; a caviler. 3 *Obs.* A critique or review. —*adj.* Pertaining to criticism; critical. [<L *criticus* <Gk. *kritikos* < *kritēs* a judge. See CRITERION.]

crit·i·cal (krit′i·kəl) *adj.* 1 Of, pertaining to, or characteristic of a critic or criticism. 2 Disposed to judge or discriminate with care and precision. 3 Given to severe judgment; faultfinding; carping. 4 Based upon principles or methods of criticism; analytical. 5 Of doubtful result; risky; perilous. 6 Contributing to a decisive judgment: *critical* evidence. 7 *Pathol.* Pertaining to a crisis in the course of a disease. 8 *Math.* Relating to the coalescence of different values. 9 *Physics* Designating a constant value or point indicating a decisive change in a specified condition, as temperature, pressure, speed, etc. 10 Necessary for the prosecution of a war: said of any material for which there is no substitute and of which there is an insufficient supply. See synonyms under CAPTIOUS, MINUTE. —**crit′i·cal·ly** *adv.* —**crit′i·cal·ness** *n.*

critical angle See under ANGLE.

critical point *Physics* The point at which the densities and other physical properties of the liquid and gaseous states of a substance are indistinguishable from each other.

critical solution temperature *Physics* The temperature above which any substance is soluble in any proportion in its solvent: also called *consolute temperature.*

critical speed *Physics* The speed at which a rotating shaft becomes dynamically unstable, and which, if maintained, will result in serious vibration and resonance effects.

critical temperature *Physics* A temperature which is characterized by a change or transition; specifically, the temperature above which a substance can exist only in the gaseous state, no matter what pressure may be applied.

crit·ic·as·ter (krit′ik·as′tər) *n.* A petty critic: a term of contempt. [<CRITIC + -ASTER] —**crit′ic·as′try** *n.*

crit·i·cism (krit′ə·siz′əm) *n.* 1 The act or art of criticizing. 2 A discriminating judgment; an evaluation. 3 A severe or unfavorable judgment. 4 The principles or rules for judging anything, especially works of literature or art. 5 A review, article, etc., expressing a critical judgment. See synonyms under ANIMADVERSION.

crit·i·cize (krit′ə·sīz) *v.t.* & *v.i.* **·cized, ·ciz·ing** 1 To examine and judge as a critic. 2 To judge severely; censure. Also *Brit.* **crit′i·cise.** —**crit′i·ciz′a·ble** *adj.* —**crit′i·ciz′er** *n.*

cri·tique (kri·tēk′) *n.* 1 A criticism; critical review. 2 The art of criticism. [<F]

Crit·ten·den (krit′ən·dən), **Eugene Casson,** born 1880, U.S. physicist; assistant director of the National Bureau of Standards.

crit·ter (krit′ər) *n. U.S. Dial.* 1 A domestic animal. 2 Any living creature. [Var. of CREATURE]

crizz·ling (kriz′ling) *n.* The fine cracks which appear in or on the surface of glass as a result of local chilling in the process of manufacture. [? <CRAZE, *v.* (def. 5)]

croak (krōk) *v.i.* 1 To utter a hoarse, low-pitched cry, as a frog or raven. 2 To speak in a low, hoarse voice. 3 To talk in a doleful tone; forbode evil; grumble. 4 *Slang* To die. —*v.t.* 5 To utter with a croak. 6 *Slang* To kill. —*n.* A hoarse vocal sound, as of a frog or raven. [Imit. Cf. OE *cracethan* croak.] —**croak′y** *adj.*

croak·er (krō′kər) *n.* 1 Any of various animals that croak; especially, one of a class of marine fishes, the grunts. 2 One who speaks dismally or forebodes evil; an alarmist.

Cro·at (krō′at, -ət) *n.* 1 A Slavic native of Croatia. 2 The Croatian language.

Croa·tan Sound (krō′tan) A strait between eastern North Carolina and Roanoke Island.

Cro·a·tia A republic founded from Yugoslavia; 21,611 square miles; capital, Zagreb; formerly an independent kingdom; *Serbo-Croatian: Hr·vat·ska.*

Cro·a·tian *adj.* Pertaining to Croatia or the Croats. —*n.* 1 A Croat. 2 The South Slavic language of the Croats.

Croatoan The word found in 1591 carved on a tree on Roanoke Island, the only clue to the vanished colonists, including Virginia Dare, settled there in 1587 by Sir Walter Raleigh.

Cro·ce (krō′chā), **Benedetto,** 1866–1952, Italian philosopher, critic, historian, and statesman.

cro·ce·in (krō′sē·in) *n. Chem.* One of many artificially produced yellow and bright-red dyes, generally formed of diazo and sulfonic-acid derivatives of benzene and naphthol. [<L *croceus* yellow + -IN]

cro·chet (krō·shā′) *v.t.* & *v.i.* **·cheted** (-shād′), **·chet·ing** (-shā′ing) To form or ornament (a fabric) by interlacing thread with a hooked needle. [< *n.*] —*n.* A kind of fancywork produced by crocheting: now chiefly attributive, as in *crochet hook.* [<F, dim. of *croche* a hook]

cro·cid·o·lite (krə·sid′ə·līt) *n.* 1 A fibrous, silky, blue or green hydrous silicate; blue asbestos. 2 A yellow alteration product of this silicate used as a gemstone; tiger's-eye. [<Gk. *krokis, -idos* nap of cloth + -LITE]

cro·cin (krō′sin) *n.* A vivid red powder, $C_{44}H_{66}O_{28}$, obtained from saffron and from the fruit of a Chinese gardenia (*Gardenia jasminoides*): used as a dye. [<L *crocus* saffron (<Gk. *krokos*) + -IN]

cro·cine (krō′sin, -sēn) *adj.* Of or pertaining to the crocus.

crock[1] (krok) *n.* 1 An earthenware pot or jar. 2 A fragment of earthenware. —*v.t.* To store in a crock, as butter. [OE *crocca*]

crock[2] (krok) *n.* 1 The black product of combustion; soot. 2 The coloring matter that rubs off from cloth; smut. —*v.t.* To stain; soil. [Origin uncertain]

crock[3] (krok) *n. Brit. Dial.* 1 An old ewe. 2 A broken-down horse. 3 *Slang* A worthless, decrepit, or disabled person. 4 *Slang* One who is not expert at a game or sport; a duffer. —*v.i.* To become weak or sick. [ME *crocke* <Scand. Cf. Sw. *krake* a decrepit horse.]

Crock·er (krok′ər), **Charles,** 1822–88, U.S. financier.

crock·er·y (krok′ər·ē) *n.* Earthenware; earthen vessels collectively.

crock·et (krok′it) *n.* 1 A projecting ornament usually terminating in a curve or roll of foliage and flowers: used to decorate pastoral staffs and the angles of pinnacles, spires, gables, and cornices. 2 A terminal tine of a deer's antler. [<AF *croquet,* OF *crocket,* dim. of *croche* hook]

Crock·ett (krok′it), **David,** 1786–1836, U.S. frontiersman and congressman, killed defending the Alamo: called *Davy Crockett.* —**Samuel Rutherford,** 1860–1914, Scottish clergyman and novelist.

croc·o·dile (krok′ə·dīl) *n.* 1 A large, lizardlike, amphibious reptile (order *Crocodilia*) widely distributed in tropical regions, with long jaws, armored skin, and webbed feet; especially, the Nile crocodile (*Crocodylus niloticus*), and the American crocodile (*C. americanus*). The head is longer and narrower than that of an alligator, and the lower molars shut into marginal notches instead of pits. 2 A gavial. [Earlier *cocodrille* <OF <Med. L *cocodrillus,* alter. of L *crocodilus* <Gk. *krokodilos* lizard, crocodile.]

CROCODILE
(Nile: to 18 feet long; American: to 14 feet)

Croc·o·dile (krok′ə·dīl) See LIMPOPO.

crocodile bird A small black-headed plover (*Pluvianus aegyptius*) of northern Africa, that often perches on crocodiles and devours their insect parasites.

crocodile tears Simulated or pretended weeping; hypocritical grief: from the ancient tale that the crocodile weeps over those he devours.

croc·o·dil·i·an (krok′ə·dil′ē·ən) *adj.* 1 Of, pertaining to, or like a crocodile. 2 Of an order (*Crocodilia*) of crocodiles, alligators, and similar reptiles. —*n.* One of the *Crocodilia.* Also **croc′o·dil′e·an.**

cro·co·ite (krō′kō·īt) *n.* An adamantine to vitreous, hyacinth-red, translucent lead chromate, $PbCrO_4$, crystallizing in the monoclinic system: often called *red-lead ore.* Also **cro·co·i·site** (krō·kō′ə·sīt). [<Gk. *krokoeis* saffron-colored]

cro·cus (krō′kəs) *n. pl.* **cro·cus·es** or **cro·ci** (krō′sī) 1 Any of a genus (*Crocus*) of plants of the iris family, with long grasslike leaves and large flowers. 2 The flower of this plant. 3 A red or yellow polishing powder of iron oxide. [<L <Gk. *krokos* saffron]

Croe·sus (krē′səs) A wealthy, sixth century B.C. king of Lydia; hence, any very wealthy man.

croft (krôft, kroft) *n.* A small field near a house. —*v.t.* To bleach (fabrics or clothes) on the grass in the sun. [OE, a field]

croft·er (krôf′tər, krof′-) *n.* A tenant cultivating a croft.

crois·sant (krwä·säṅ′) *n. French* A small, crescent-shaped yeast dough roll.

Croix de Guerre (krwä də gâr′) A French decoration for bravery, awarded to officers, non-commissioned officers, and enlisted men; literally, cross of war.

cro·jik (krō′jik) *n.* A crossjack: altered form.

Cro·ker (krō′kər), **John Wilson,** 1780–1857, English essayist and politician. —**Richard,** 1841–1922, U.S. politician: known as *Boss Croker.*

Cro-Mag·non (krō·mag′non, *Fr.* krō·mȧ·nyôṅ′) A member of a prehistoric race of tall, erect men: so called from the name of a cave in the Dordogne department, France, where their remains have been found. The Cro-Magnons are associated with Aurignacian culture, and are considered to belong to the same species (*Homo sapiens*) as modern man. —*adj.* Pertaining or relating to the Cro-Magnon race.

Cro·mer (krō′mər), **Earl of,** 1841–1917, Evelyn Baring, British colonial administrator and diplomat.

crom·lech (krom′lek) *n.* 1 An ancient sepulchral structure consisting of a large flat stone resting on upright unhewn stones. 2 An ancient monument of standing stones arranged in a circle. [<Welsh < *crom* bent + *llech* flat stone]

cro·mor·na (krə·môr′nə) *n.* A clarinetlike reed-stop in an organ. [<F *cromorne,* alter. of G *krummhorn* crooked horn]

Cromp·ton (kromp′tən), **Samuel,** 1753–1827, English inventor of the spinning mule.

Crom·well (krom′wel, -wəl, krum′-), **Oliver,** 1599–1658, English general and statesman; lord protector of England 1653–58. —**Richard,** 1626–1712, son of the preceding; lord protector of England 1658–59. —**Thomas,** 1485?–1540, English statesman.

Cromwell Current A long, swift Pacific equatorial current running eastward just beneath the surface and terminating at the Galapagos Islands. [after Townsend *Cromwell,* 1922–58, U. S. oceanographer]

Crom·wel·li·an (krom·wel′ē·ən, krum-) *adj.* **1** Of or pertaining to Oliver Cromwell or his times. **2** Pertaining to or naming a severe, angular style of furniture prevalent in England under the Protectorate.

crone (krōn) *n.* **1** A withered old woman. **2** *Rare* A senile man. —*v.i.* **croned, cron·ing** To talk like a crone. [<Du. *kronye* an old ewe <OF *carogne* carcass]

Cron·je (krōn′yə), **Piet Arnoldus,** 1840?–1911, Boer general.

Cro·nus (krō′nəs) See KRONOS.

cro·ny (krō′nē) *n. pl.* **·nies** A familiar friend. [<Gk. *chronios* contemporary; orig. university slang]

croo (kro͞o) *v.i. Brit. Dial.* To coo. Also **crood** (kro͞od). [Imit.]

croo·dle (kro͞od′l) *v.i. Scot.* To coo; coax.

crook (kro͝ok) *n.* **1** A bend or curve; also, something bent or crooked. **2** The curved or bent part of a thing: the *crook* of a branch. **3** A genuflection. **4** A device; scheme; artifice. **5** An implement with a crook in it: a shepherd's *crook.* **6** *Scot.* A pothook. **7** *Colloq.* A criminal; swindler; cheat. **8** *Austral. Slang* Ill; out of sorts; also, angry; annoyed. —**to go crook at** *Austral. Slang* To be angry at. —*v.t.* To bend; make crooked. —*v.i.* To grow crooked. See synonyms under BEND, TWIST. [<ON *krōkr*]

crook·back (kro͝ok′bak′) *n.* A person with a crooked back; a hunchback: also *crouchback.* —**crook′-backed′** *adj.*

crook·ed (kro͝ok′id) *adj.* **1** Not straight; having angles or curves. **2** Not straightforward in conduct. **3** Tricky; dishonest. —**to be** (or **go**) **crooked on** *Austral. Slang* To be ill-disposed toward. See synonyms under IRREGULAR. —**crook′ed·ly** *adv.* —**crook′ed·ness** *n.*

Crookes (kro͝oks), **Sir William,** 1832–1919, English physicist and chemist.

Crookes' space *Physics* A non-luminous region in a vacuum tube containing a gas at low pressure, through which an electric discharge is passing. [after Sir William *Crookes*]

Crookes' tube *Physics* A vacuum tube in which the gases are exhausted to a high degree, permitting the free movement of molecules.

crook·neck (kro͝ok′nek′) *n.* One of several varieties of squash with a long, curved neck.

crool (kro͞ol) *v.i.* To gurgle. [Imit.]

croon (kro͞on) *v.t.* & *v.i.* **1** To sing or hum in a low, monotonous manner; specifically, to sing (popular songs) with exaggerated sentiment or pathos. **2** *Rare* To bellow in a muffled tone. —*n.* **1** A low, mournful humming or singing; the sound made in crooning. **2** A crooning song. [<MDu. *kronen* sing softly, lament] —**croon′er** *n.*

croon song A song of exaggerated sentiment and pathos, adapted for crooning or humming.

crop (krop) *n.* **1** Cultivated plants or grains collectively. **2** The soil product of a particular kind, place, or season. **3** The yield or seasonal product of things other than plants or grains: a *crop* of lambs or calves; the entire yield of anything. **4** The act of cutting; also, the result of cutting; specifically, a short haircut. **5** The first stomach of a bird: a large, pouch-like reservoir at the base of the distensible gullet, serving for preliminary maceration of food; a craw. **6** A growth of hair or beard, especially when short and stiff. **7** A hunting or riding whip with a leather loop for a lash. **8** A collection of things produced: a *crop* of lies. **9** An earmark. **10** The hollow behind a cow's shoulders. **11** An entire hide prepared for sole leather. —*v.* **cropped, crop·ping** *v.t.* **1** To cut or eat off the stems or ends of, as grass or vegetables. **2** To pluck or reap. **3** To cut off closely, as hair; trim, as a dog's ears or tail; formerly, to trim (the ears) of a criminal for punishment. **4** To raise a crop or crops on; cause to bear crops. —*v.i.* **5** To appear above the surface; sprout: with *up* or *out.* **6** To develop or come up unexpectedly: with *up* or *out.* **7** To bear or yield a crop or crops. [OE *cropp*]

crop-eared (krop′ird′) *adj.* **1** Having the ears cropped. **2** With the hair cut short above the ears: said of the Roundheads.

crop·per[1] (krop′ər) *n.* **1** One who raises crops on shares. **2** A tool or machine that crops. **3** A plant that produces a crop: generally with *good, bad, heavy,* etc.: Corn is a heavy *cropper* in Kansas.

crop·per[2] (krop′ər) *n.* A fall, as from a horse when one is thrown over the horse's head. —**to come a cropper** **1** To fall headlong, as from a horse. **2** To fail disastrously in an undertaking. [? <*neck and crop* completely, thoroughly]

crop rotation A method of conserving soil productivity by planting dissimilar crops in successive seasons, thereby in one season replenishing the soil nutrients expended in a previous season, checking a disease cycle, etc.

cro·quet (krō·kā′) *n.* **1** An outdoor game played by knocking wooden balls through a series of wire arches by means of mallets. **2** The act of croqueting. —*v.i.* **cro·queted** (krō·kād′), **cro·quet·ing** (krō·kā′ing) In croquet, to drive one's opponent's ball away from its objective by placing one's own ball in contact with it and striking the latter sharply, keeping it in position with the foot. [<AF *croquet,* var. of *crochet.* See CROCHET.]

cro·quette (krō·ket′) *n.* A ball or cake of previously cooked, minced food, fried in deep fat or baked. [<F <*croquer* crunch]

cro·qui·gnole (krō′kə·nōl, -kin·yōl) *n.* A kind of permanent wave in which the hair is wound from the ends toward the scalp, after which it is treated with chemical heat. Also **croquignole wave.** [<F, a fillip <dial. F *croquer* <*crocher* hook <*croc* a hook]

cro·quis (krō·kē′) *n. French* A rough likeness or quick sketch, especially of a fashion design.

crore (krôr, krōr) *n.* In India, ten millions or one hundred lakhs: a *crore* of rupees. [<Hind. *karōr*]

cro·sier (krō′zhər) *n.* **1** A staff surmounted by a crook or cross, borne by or before a bishop or archbishop on occasions of ceremony. **2** *Bot.* A circinate or coiled young fern frond. Also spelled *crozier.* [<OF *crocier* staff-bearer <Med. L *crociarius* <*crocia* bishop's crook]

Cro·sier (krō′zhər) The Southern Cross constellation; Crux. See CONSTELLATION.

cross (krôs, kros) *n.* **1** A sacred or mystic symbol in many ancient religions, consisting of two intersecting lines, supposed to have been originally emblematic of the union of the active and passive elements in nature. **2** That which resembles a cross: to mark a ballot with a *cross.* **3** An ancient instrument of torture in the form of a cross, on which criminals were fastened and exposed until they died from exhaustion. **4** Any suffering borne patiently for Christ's sake; a trial; tribulation. **5** A structure in the form of or surmounted by a cross, erected in some public place for devotional or memorial purposes. **6** *Biol.* **a** A mixing of varieties or breeds of plants or animals. **b** The product of any intermingling of strains; a hybrid or mongrel. **7** Anything that resembles or is intermediate between two other things: a *cross* between prose and poetry. **8** An old English coin stamped with a cross. **9** *Her.* A figure used as a bearing. **10** An ornament, in some form of the cross, worn as a distinction by knights of various orders and by persons honored for exceptional merit or bravery. **11** *Electr.* The accidental contact of two wires so that a portion of the current from one flows to the other. **12** The geometric mean of two formulas: used in index numbers. —**to take the cross** To turn crusader. —*v.t.* **1** To pass, move or extend from side to side of; traverse; span. **2** To cancel, as by marking with crossed lines: with *off* or *out.* **3** To lay or place over or across: to *cross* the legs. **4** To intersect, as streets or lines. **5** To draw a line across. **6** To meet and pass: Your letter *crossed* mine. **7** To transport across: He *crossed* his army yesterday. **8** To make the sign of the cross upon or over. **9** To obstruct or hinder; thwart. **10** To cause, as plants or animals, to interbreed; hybridize; crossbreed. **11** *Naut.* To put (a yard) in place across a mast. —*v.i.* **12** To intersect; lie athwart. **13** To pass, move, or extend from side to side; traverse; span. **14** To meet and pass. **15** To breed together; interbreed. —**to cross one's mind** To occur to one. —**to cross one's palm** **1** To pay a fortune-teller by marking crosses on his or her palm with a coin and then laying the coin in the fortune-teller's hand. **2** To pay someone money; make a bribe. —**to cross swords** To fight with swords; hence, to contest with. —**to cross up** *Colloq.* To play the traitor to; betray: He *crossed* me *up.* —*adj.* **1** Resulting from or expressive of peevishness or ill-humor; out of humor; disagreeable; peevish. **2** Transverse; crossing; intersecting. **3** Hybrid. **4** Contrary. See synonyms under CAPTIOUS, FRETFUL. —*adv.* **1** Across; crosswise; transversely. **2** Adversely; contrarily; counter. [OE *cros* <ON *kross* <L *crux*] —**cross′ly** *adv.* —**cross′ness** *n.*

—**ansate cross** The tau cross with a loop at the top: also called *crux ansata.* Also **ansated cross.** See ANKH.

—**Calvary cross** *Her.* A Latin cross set on three graduated steps.

—**Celtic cross** An upright cross having a circle behind the crossbeam.

—**cross crosslet** A cross having a small cross near the end of each arm.

—**cross fleu·ry** (flo͞o′rē) A cross whose arms end in fleurs-de-lis.

—**cross for·mée** (fôr·mā′) A cross having arms that gradually expand from the central crossing and nearly form a square. The Maltese cross is a modification of this.

—**cross four·chée** (fo͞or·shā′) A cross proportioned like the Greek cross but having each extremity forked.

—**fiery cross** A cross of light wood whose ends were set on fire, formerly used as a call to arms in Scotland.

—**Geneva cross** A red St. George's or Greek cross on a white ground, worn by members of the Red Cross Society as a badge of neutrality.

—**Greek cross** A cross formed by an upright crossing the middle of a beam of equal length. See also *gammadion.*

—**Iron Cross** A Maltese cross awarded by Germany for conspicuous military service: instituted by Prussia in 1813.

—**Jerusalem cross** A cross having four arms, each ending in a crossbar: also **cross potent.**

—**Latin cross** A cross in which the upright is longer than the beam which crosses it near the top: the cross used by the ancient Romans for crucifixions: also called *crux immissa.*

—**Lorraine cross** A cross having two horizontal arms, the lower one longer than the other: also **cross of Lorraine.**

—**Maltese cross** An eight-pointed cross formed by four arrowheads joining at their points: the badge of the Knights of Malta, worn as an order of chivalry: also **Cross of Malta.**

—**Papal cross** A cross having three crossbars or transoms, the top one the shortest and the bottom one the longest.

—**Patriarchal cross** A cross having two horizontal arms like those of the Lorraine cross but placed nearer together.

TYPES OF CROSSES

a. Latin cross. *b.* Cross of Lorraine. *c.* Tau cross. *d.* Ansate cross. *e.* Celtic cross. *f.* Papal cross. *g.* Maltese cross. *h.* St. Andrew's cross. *i.* Greek cross or cross of St. George. *j.* Cross fourchée. *k.* Jerusalem cross. *l.* Cross fleury. *m.* Cross crosslet.

— **St. Andrew's cross** An oblique cross in the form of the letter X: also called *crux decussata.* See SALTIRE.
— **St. George's cross** The cross of St. George, the patron saint of England: same shape as the Greek cross.
— **St. Patrick's cross** A cross like the diagonal St. Andrew's cross.
— **tau cross** A cross in the form of a T: also called *crux commissa.* Also **St. Anthony's cross.** See TAU.
— **Victoria Cross** A Maltese cross awarded for conspicuous bravery to members of the British army or navy and the Royal Air Force: instituted in 1856.
Cross (krôs, kros) *n.* **1** The emblem of Christianity, a symbolical representation of the instrument of punishment on which Christ died. **2** The crucifixion of Christ; the atonement. **3** The Christian religion; Christianity.
Cross (krôs, kros) A river in SE Nigeria, flowing 300 miles west to the Gulf of Guinea.
Cross (krôs, kros), **Wilbur Lucius,** 1862–1948, U.S. educator and politician.
cross·band (krôs'band', kros'-) *v.t.* To arrange (plywood) so that the grain in each layer is at right angles to the grain of the adjoining layers. — **cross'band'ing** *n.*
cross·bar (krôs'bär', kros'-) *n.* A transverse bar or line used in any structure. — *v.t.* To secure or mark with transverse bars. — **cross'·barred'** *adj.*
cross-bed·ded (krôs'bed'id, kros'-) *adj. Geol.* Characterized by subsidiary beds or layers of rock cutting across the main stratification.
cross·bill (krôs'bil', kros'-) *n.* A finchlike bird (genus *Loxia*), the points of whose mandibles cross each other when the beak is closed.
cross·birth (krôs'bûrth', kros'-) *n. Med.* Any abnormal presentation of a fetus before delivery which requires a manual turning in the womb.
cross·bones (krôs'bōnz', kros'-) *n.* A representation of two bones crossing each other, usually surmounted by a skull, as a symbol of death.
cross·bow (krôs'bō', kros'-) *n.* A medieval missile weapon consisting of a bow fixed transversely on a grooved stock. — **cross'·bow'man** *n.*
cross·breed (krôs'brēd', kros'-) *v.t.* & *v.i.* **·bred, ·breed·ing** *Biol.* To produce a strain or animal by interbreeding or blending two varieties; mix together; hybridize. — *n.* A strain or animal produced by crossbreeding; a hybrid; mongrel. — **cross'bred'** *adj.*
cross bun A hot cross bun.
cross·but·tock (krôs'but'ək, kros'-) *n.* **1** A throw in wrestling in which the wrestler, having his back to his opponent, throws him over his hip. **2** Any unexpected setback.
cross-coun·try (krôs'kun'trē, kros'-) *adj.* Of or pertaining to a route across the country fields and lots, regardless of roads.
cross-cut (krôs'kut', kros'-) *v.t.* **-cut, -cut·ting** To cut crosswise or through; run across; intersect. — *adj.* Used or made for the purpose of cutting something across: a *cross-cut* saw. — *n.* A cut across or a shortcut.
crosse (krôs, kros) *n.* A lacrosse stick.
cross-ex·am·ine (krôs'ig·zam'in, kros'-) *v.t.* **·ined, ·in·ing** **1** To question anew (a witness called by the opposing party) for the purpose of testing the reliability of his previous testimony. **2** To cross-question generally. — **cross'-ex·am'i·na'tion** *n.* — **cross'-ex·am'·in·er** *n.*
cross-eye (krôs'ī', kros'-) *n.* Strabismus. — **cross'-eyed'** *adj.*
cross-fer·ti·li·za·tion (krôs'fûr'tə·lə·zā'shən, kros'-) *n.* **1** *Biol.* The fertilization of an organism by the union of sexually differentiated reproductive cells or gametes, one from the ovum and one from the sperm. **2** *Bot.* The fertilization of one plant or flower by the pollen from another.
cross-fer·ti·lize (krôs'fûr'tə·līz, kros'-) *v.t.* **·lized, ·liz·ing** To fertilize (a plant or animal) by cross-fertilization.
cross-fig·ure (krôs'fig'yər, kros'-) *n.* A style of pattern in veneer consisting of a roll or dip of the grain approximately at right angles to the long axis of the tree.
cross·fire (krôs'fīr', kros'-) *n.* **1** *Mil.* The intersection of two lines of fire; a shooting from two different points so that the lines of fire cross. **2** Any like situation: a *crossfire* of congratulations. **3** *Electr.* The interference in a telegraph or telephone circuit of impulse currents from another communication channel. — *v.i.* **·fired, ·fir·ing** To shoot from different points so that the lines of fire intersect.
Cross-Florida Waterway A system of linked canals, rivers, and lakes extending 155 miles across the Florida peninsula: also *Okeechobee Waterway.*
cross·foot (krôs'fŏŏt', kros'-) *n.* A form of clubfoot which compels walking on the outer border of the foot, with the sole turned inward.
cross-grained (krôs'grānd', kros'-) *adj.* **1** Having the grain gnarled and hard to cut: a *cross-grained* board. **2** Hard to please or persuade; stubborn; perverse: a *cross-grained* man.
cross-hair (krôs'hâr', kros'-) *n.* One of two fine threads or strands, as of a spider's web, crossed in the center of the focal plane of an optical instrument, to define the exact point to which the readings of the circle or micrometer refer: also called *cross-wire.*
cross-hatch (krôs'hach', kros'-) *v.t.* To shade, as a picture, by crossed lines, either diagonal or rectangular. — **cross'-hatch'ing** *n.*
cross-head (krôs'hed', kros'-) *n. Mech.* **1** A beam across the top of something; specifically, a block sliding upon one guide bar, or between two or more bars, to move a piston in a straight line, axial with the cylinder. **2** The connection between the piston and the connecting rods of a reciprocating engine.
cross-in·dex (krôs'in'deks, kros'-) *v.t.* & *v.i.* To insert cross-references in (an index, etc.).
cross·ing (krôs'ing, kros'-) *n.* **1** The place where something, as a roadway or waterway, may be crossed; a ford. **2** Intersection, as of threads or roads. **3** The act of crossing.
cross·jack (krôs'jak', kros'-) *n. Naut.* The sail carried on the lower yard on the mizzenmast of a full-rigged ship: commonly altered to *crojik.*
cross·let (krôs'lit, kros'-) *n. Her.* A small cross. [<AF *croiselette,* dim. of OF *crois* cross]
cross·light (krôs'līt', kros'-) *n.* A light whose rays cross other rays, lighting up what these left dark.
cros·sop·te·ryg·i·an (kro·sop'tə·rij'ē·ən) *n. Zool.* Any of a group (*Crossopterygii*) of bony fishes abundant in the Devonian period, having paddle-shaped, lobate fins: they are regarded as the direct ancestors of amphibians. [<NL *Crossopterygii* <Gk. *krossoi* fringe + *pterygia* fins of a fish, pl. dim. of *pteryx* wing]
cross-o·ver (krôs'ō'vər, kros'-) *n.* **1** A place at which one traverses a road, river, etc.; intersection; passageway. **2** The intersection of two electric lines. **3** A part of a woman's coat, dress, or wrap which crosses from one side to the other. **4** *Genetics* An interchange of parts between two homologous chromosomes in meiosis: known also as *recombination.*
cross·patch (krôs'pach', kros'-) *n.* A cranky, ill-tempered person.
cross-peen (krôs'pēn', kros'-) *n.* A chisel-like peen on a hammer head, with a blunted edge parallel to the shaft.
cross·piece (krôs'pēs', kros'-) *n.* A piece of material of any kind crossing another.
cross-pol·li·nate (krôs'pol'ə·nāt, kros'-) *v.t.* **·nat·ed, ·nat·ing** To cross-fertilize.
cross-pol·li·na·tion (krôs'pol'ə·nā'shən, kros'-) *n. Bot.* **1** Cross-fertilization of flowering plants. **2** Hybridization.
cross-pur·pose (krôs'pûr'pəs, kros'-) *n.* **1** A purpose which antagonizes another; a conflicting aim. **2** *pl.* A conversational game in which questions and answers having no natural connection are brought together.
cross-ques·tion (krôs'kwes'chən, kros'-) *v.t.* To question minutely or in different ways, especially to elicit facts. — *n.* A question asked in a cross-examination. — **cross'-ques'·tion·ing** *n.*
cross-re·fer (krôs'ri·fûr', kros'-) *v.* **·ferred, ·fer·ring** *v.t.* To refer to another passage or part. — *v.i.* To make a cross-reference.
cross-ref·er·ence (krôs'ref'rəns, kros'-) *n.* **1** A reference from one passage in a book or treatise to another passage in the same work. **2** In a library catalog, and in research and documentation, reference from one subject to another.
cross·road (krôs'rōd', kros'-) *n.* A road that crosses another, or that crosses from one main road to another. Also **cross'way'.**
cross·roads (krôs'rōdz', kros'-) *n.* A place where roads cross.
cross·ruff (krôs'ruf', kros'-) *n.* In card games, a condition in which each of two partners alternately trumps the other's lead: also called *see-saw.*
cross-sec·tion (krôs'sek'shən, kros'-) *n.* **1** A plane section of any object cut at right angles to the longitudinal axis. **2** Any specimen, figure, or diagram presenting a representation typical of the whole.
cross-stitch (krôs'stich', kros'-) *n.* **1** A double stitch in the form of a cross. **2** Needlework made with this stitch. — *v.t.* To make or mark with a cross-stitch.
cross-talk (krôs'tôk', kros'-) *n.* The garbled sounds heard in a telephone receiver or on the radio as a result of interfering currents from another channel.
cross-thread (krôs'thred', kros'-) *n.* In hemstitching, one of those threads remaining in a fabric across the space from which a number of parallel threads have been drawn, and which are divided and fastened into clusters in the process of hemstitching. See illustration under HEMSTITCH.
cross-tie (krôs'tī', kros'-) *n.* A tie or sleeper connecting and supporting the parallel rails of a railroad track. — **cross'-tied'** *adj.*
cross-town (krôs'toun', kros'-) *adj.* Going across a town or city: a *cross-town* bus. — *adv.* Across a town or city: They headed *cross-town.*
cross·tree (krôs'trē', kros'-) *n. Naut. Usually pl.* One of the pieces of wood or iron set crosswise at the head of a mast to extend the shrouds.
cross·walk (krôs'wôk', kros'-) *n.* Any lane marked off, usually by white lines, to be used by pedestrians in crossing a street.
cross-wind (krôs'wind', kros'-) *n.* **1** A wind blowing across the take-off or flight path of an aircraft or the course of a ship. **2** Any wind at right angles to a given course or direction.
cross-wire (krôs'wīr', kros'-) *n.* **1** One wire crossing another. **2** Cross-hair.
cross·wise (krôs'wīz', kros'-) *adv.* **1** Across. **2** In the form of a cross. **3** Contrarily; at cross-purposes. Also **cross'ways'.**
cross-word puzzle (krôs'wûrd', kros'-) See under PUZZLE.
crot·a·lus (krot'ə·ləs, krō'tə-) *n. pl.* **·li** (-lī) Any snake of a genus (*Crotalus*) typical of the rattlesnake family (*Crotalidae*). [<NL <Gk. *krotalon* rattle] — **crot'a·line** (-lin, -līn) *adj.*
crotch (kroch) *n.* **1** A point of division or divergence; a separation into two parts or branches; bifurcation; fork: the *crotch* of a tree. **2** A forked support for a swinging boom when not in use. **3** The region of the human body where the legs separate from the pelvis. [Prob. <AF *croche* crook]
crotched (krocht) *adj.* **1** Having a crotch; forked. **2** Ill-tempered; cross; peevish; crotchety.
crotch·et (kroch'it) *n.* **1** A whimsical notion; a conceit; an eccentricity. **2** *Music* A quarter note. **3** A small hook. See synonyms under WHIM. [<F *crochet.* See CROCHET.]
crotch·et·y (kroch'ə·tē) *adj.* **1** Whimsical; eccentric. **2** Like a crotchet. See synonyms under FICKLE, QUEER. — **crotch'et·i·ness** *n.*
crotch·wood (kroch'wŏŏd') *n.* An elaborately patterned veneer obtained from the portion of a tree where two limbs join.
cro·ton (krōt'n) *n.* **1** Any member of a genus (*Croton*) of widely dispersed trees and shrubs of the spurge family. **2** An ornamental tropical shrub (*Codiaeum variegatum*) grown for its foliage. [<NL <Gk. *krotōn* a tick; so called from the appearance of the seeds]
Croton bug A small, light-colored, winged,

cosmopolitan cockroach *(Blattella germanica)*: also called *German cockroach, water bug.* For illustration see INSECT (injurious). [from *Croton* Aqueduct; so called because the first serious infestation in New York City occurred shortly after Croton aqueduct was opened in 1842]

cro·ton·ic acid (krō·ton′ik, -tō′nik) *Chem.* A compound, $C_4H_6O_2$, obtained from croton oil: used in organic synthesis and as a stabilizer in volatile organic solvents.

Cro·ton Lake (krōt′n) An artificial lake formed by damming the **Croton River,** flowing through SE New York: a source of water supply for New York City.

croton oil A pale-yellow or brownish-yellow viscid oil obtained from the seeds of a small East Indian tree *(Croton tiglium)*: used as a purgative and rubefacient.

crouch (krouch) *v.i.* **1** To stoop or bend low with the limbs pressed to the body, as a person in fear or an animal ready to spring. **2** To cringe; abase oneself; cower. —*v.t.* **3** To bend low. —*n.* A crouching or the position taken in crouching. [<OF *crochir* be bent <*croc* a hook]

crouch·back (krouch′bak′) See CROOKBACK.

crouch·ie (kro͞o′chē) *adj. Scot.* Round-shouldered; hunch-backed.

croup[1] (kro͞op) *n. Pathol.* **1** A disease of the throat characterized by hoarse coughing, laryngeal spasm, and the formation of a false membrane. **2** Loosely, inflammation of the larynx. [Imit.] **—croup′ous, croup′y** *adj.*

croup[2] (kro͞op) *n.* The rump; portion of a horse's back behind the saddle. Also **croupe.** [<F *croupe*]

crou·pi·er (kro͞o′pē·ər, *Fr.* kro͞o·pyā′) *n.* **1** A clerk in charge of a gaming table, collecting winnings and paying losses. **2** The assistant chairman at a public dinner. [<F, lit., one who rides on the croup, an assistant]

crouse (kro͞os) *adj. Scot.* Contented and jolly; frisky; saucy. **—crouse′ly** *adv.*

crou·stade (kro͞o·städ′) *n. French.* A small pastry shell filled with custard, mince, oysters, etc.

crou·ton (kro͞o′ton, kro͞o·ton′; *Fr.* kro͞o·tôṅ′) *n.* One of the small crusts or bits of bread fried in butter or oil, often served in soups, etc. [<F *croûton* <*croûte* crust]

crow (krō) *n.* **1** Any of various omnivorous, raucous, oscine birds of the genus *Corvus,* with glossy black plumage; specifically, *C. corone,* the European carrion crow; also, the rook, the raven, and the American species, *C. brachyrhynchos.* ◆ Collateral adjective: *corvine.* **2** A crowbar. **3** The cry of a cock, or any like sound. **—as the crow flies** In a straight line. **—to eat crow** *Colloq.* To recant a statement; back down; to humiliate oneself. —*v.i.* **1** To utter the cry of a cock. **2** To exult; boast. **3** To utter sounds expressive of delight, as an infant. —*v.t.* **4** To announce by crowing. [OE *crāwe*]

Crow (krō) *n.* **1** A North American Indian of a Siouan tribe which formerly inhabited the region between the Platte and the Yellowstone. **2** The language of this tribe.

Crow (krō) The constellation Corvus. See CONSTELLATION.

crow·bar (krō′bär′) *n.* A straight iron or steel bar, with the point flattened and sometimes set at an angle: used as a lever.

crow·ber·ry (krō′ber′ē, -bər·ē) *n. pl.* **·ries** **1** The black berrylike drupe of a low shrubby evergreen *(Empetrum nigrum)* of the family *Emperaceae*: usually called **black crowberry. 2** This plant. **3** The bearberry. [Prob. trans. of G *krähenbeeri*]

crow blackbird A large crowlike bird; especially, the purple grackle.

crowd[1] (kroud) *n.* **1** A numerous collection of persons gathered closely together; multitude; throng. **2** A collection of things. **3** The populace mob. **4** *Colloq.* A particular set of people; a clique. See synonyms under ASSEMBLY, COMPANY, MOB, THRONG. [<*v.*] —*v.t.* **1** To shove or push. **2** To fill to overflowing, as with a crowd; fill to excess. **3** To cram together; force into a confined space. **4** *Colloq.* To put moral pressure upon; press annoyingly. —*v.i.* **5** To gather in large numbers; throng together. **6** To push forward force one's way. **7** To shove or push. See synonyms under HUSTLE, JAM. **—to crowd off** *Naut.* To work a vessel off from the shore under heavy press of sail. **—to crowd out** To drive out or exclude by pushing or pressing, morally or physically; eliminate by pressure: The press of business has *crowded out* this matter. **—to crowd on sail** *Naut.* To spread a very great amount of sail in proportion to the strength of the wind. [OE *crūdan*] **—crowd′er** *n.*

crowd[2] (kroud) *n.* An ancient violinlike instrument, used in Ireland and Wales: also spelled *cruth, crwth.* Also **croud, crowth.** [<Welsh *crwth* violin]

crow·die (kro͞o′dē, kro͝od′ē) *n. Scot.* **1** Porridge. **2** Pressed curds prepared with butter. Also **crow′dy.**

crow·foot (krō′fo͝ot′) *n. pl.* **·foots** *for def. 1,* **·feet** *for defs. 2–6.* **1** Any plant of the genus *Ranunculus* (family *Ranunculaceae*); especially, the common meadow or bulb crowfoot *(R. bulbosus)* of the eastern United States. **2** *Naut.* A number of lines or small divergent cords rove through a euphroe to support an awning. **3** Caltrop (def. 1). **4** An arbitrary mark on drawings as for indicating limits of measurement. **5** *Electr.* A form of battery zinc used in a gravity cell. **6** *Aeron.* Crow's-foot.

crow·hop (krō′hop′) *n.* **1** A short hop. **2** *U.S.* The bucking of a horse with its back arched and legs stiffened.

crown (kroun) *n.* **1** A decorative circlet or covering for the head, especially as a mark of sovereign power. **2** A sovereign ruler: with *the.* **3** Sovereignty. **4** A wreath or garland for the head. **5** A reward; prize. **6** A complete or perfect state or type; acme. **7** The top or summit; crest; the *crown* of a hill. **8** The top of the head: a bald *crown.* **9** The head itself: Jack fell down and broke his *crown.* **10** The upper portion of a hat. **11** *Dent.* **a** The part of a tooth exposed beyond the gum; especially, the grinding surface of a molar. **b** An artificial substitute for a crown. **12** A clerical tonsure. **13** A coin stamped with a crown or crowned head; in England, a five-shilling piece. **14** A knot made with the strands at the end of a rope. **15** *Naut.* The outer point of junction of the two arms of an anchor. **16** *Archit.* **a** The upper projecting part of a cornice; the corona. **b** A lantern or spire formed by converging flying buttresses. **17** A halo. **18** A circlet for candles. **19** A crown lens. See under LENS. **20** The upper part of a tree, including the living branches with their foliage. **21** *Bot.* The point where stem and root unite in a seed plant. **22** *Her.* A bearing representing a crown. **23** The part of a cut gemstone above the girdle. See also CORONA. —*v.t.* **1** To place a crown or garland on the head of. **2** To enthrone; make a monarch of. **3** To surmount; be the topmost part of. **4** To form the ultimate ornament to or aspect of. **5** To endow with honor or dignity. **6** To finish or bring to completion; consummate. **7** To cause to round upward; make convex, as a road. **8** *Colloq.* To hit, as a person, on the head. **9** In checkers, to make into a king. [<AF *coroune* <L *corona*] **—crown′er** *n.* **—crown′less** *adj.*

HISTORIC CROWNS
a. Imperial crown of all the Russias.
b. Crown of the German Empire.
c. Iron Crown of Lombardy.
d. Imperial crown of Charlemagne.

crown colony A colonial dependency of Great Britain in which the crown retains control of legislation: usually administered by a governor, with executive and legislative councils.

crown·er (krou′nər) *n. Brit. Dial.* A coroner.

crown·et (krou′nit) *n. Obs.* A coronet.

crown glass See under GLASS.

crown gold Gold 3.9166 fineness, especially as used in British coinage. Compare STERLING.

crown-im·pe·ri·al (kroun′im·pir′ē·əl) *n.* An ornamental plant *(Fritillaria imperialis)* of the lily family, from Persia, bearing a cluster of large, bell-shaped flowers beneath a crown of leaves.

crown land The real estate belonging hereditarily to the English sovereign: now nearly all surrendered for a fixed annual allowance. Also **crown′lands** (kroun′landz′) *n.*

crown lens See under LENS.

crown′let (kroun′lit) *n.* A small crown.

crown·piece (kroun′pēs′) *n.* **1** A piece forming the top or crown of anything. **2** The strap in a bridle that goes over the horse's head and is buckled with the cheek straps. See illustration under HARNESS.

Crown Point A village in NE New York; site of two colonial forts, strategic in the French and Indian War and captured from the British in the Revolutionary War.

crown prince The heir apparent to a crown, a monarch's oldest living son.

crown princess **1** The wife of a crown prince. **2** The female heir apparent to a sovereign throne.

crown saw A ring-shaped saw with teeth at right angles to its plane, mounted on a cylinder, and operated with a rotary motion.

crown·vetch (kroun′vech′) *n.* Axseed.

crown wheel *Mech.* A wheel with cogs at right angles to its plane, as the wheel that drives the balance in a watch.

crown·work (kroun′wûrk′) *n.* **1** A fortification running into the field, designed to cover some advantageous position and to protect other works. **2** *Dent.* The placing of artificial crowns upon teeth; also, the work so done.

crow·quill (krō′kwil′) *n.* **1** The quill of a crow. **2** A pen made from a crow's quill: used formerly for the finest kind of writing. **3** A fine metallic pen adapted for similar work.

crow's-foot (krōz′fo͝ot′) *n. pl.* **-feet** **1** One of the wrinkles diverging from the outer corner of the eye. **2** A three-pointed embroidery stitch. **3** *Aeron.* An arrangement of short ropes diverging from a main rope: used to distribute strain in the handling of lighter-than-air craft; also *crowfoot.*

crow's-nest (krōz′nest′) *n.* **1** *Naut.* A small sheltered platform at a ship's masthead, used by the lookout. **2** Any similar lookout station, as one ashore.

Croy·don (kroid′n) A county borough of NE Surrey, a residential suburb of London and site of a major airport.

croze (krōz) *n.* **1** The groove in the staves of a cask in which the edge of the head is set. **2** A crozer. [? <OF *croz* groove]

croz·er (krō′zər) *n.* A coopers' tool for making a croze.

cro·zier (krō′zhər) See CROSIER.

croz·zle (kroz′əl) *Brit. Dial. v.i.* To burn to coal; char. —*n.* A partially charred coal, as coke.

cru·ces (kro͞o′sēz) A plural of CRUX.

cru·cial (kro͞o′shəl) *adj.* **1** Determining absolutely the truth or falsity of a view or theory; decisive; searching. **2** Having the form of a cross. **3** Severe; excruciating. [<F <L *crux, crucis* cross, torture] **—cru′cial·ly** *adv.* **—cru·ci·al·i·ty** (kro͞o′shē·al′ə·tē) *n.*

cru·ci·ate (kro͞o′shē·it, -āt) *adj.* **1** Cross-shaped. **2** *Entomol.* Having the wings crossing. **3** *Bot.* Having the parts arranged in the form of a cross with equal arms. [<L *cruciatus,* pp. of *cruciare* crucify <*crux* cross]

cru·ci·ble (kro͞o′sə·bəl) *n.* **1** A pot or vessel made of a substance that will stand extreme heat, as clay, sand, graphite, platinum, etc., for melting metals or minerals. **2** The hollow place in the bottom of a furnace. **3** A trying and purifying test. [<Med. L *crucibulum* earthen pot]

crucible steel *Metall.* A high-grade steel made by reheating small batches of wrought iron with charcoal, ferromanganese, or other special steels in crucibles placed in specially designed furnaces.

cru·ci·fer (kro͞o′sə·fər) *n.* **1** Any plant of a large family (Cruciferae) of annual and perennial herbs characterized by pungent, watery juice and regular flowers with four petals in the form of a cross, as mustard, cress, etc. **2** One who bears a cross in a religious procession. [<LL <L *crux* cross + *ferre* bear] **—cru·cif·er·ous** (kro͞o·sif′ər·əs) *adj.*

cross. 2 *Bot.* Having cruciate flowers; pertaining to or resembling the *Cruciferae.*

cru·ci·fix (kro͞o'sə·fiks) *n.* 1 A cross bearing an effigy of Christ crucified. 2 The cross as a Christian emblem. [< OF *crucefix* < L *cruci fixus* one hanged on a cross < *crux* cross + *figere* fasten]

CRUCIFIX (*def. 1*)

cru·ci·fix·ion (kro͞o'sə·fik'·shən) *n.* 1 The act of putting to death by nailing or binding to a cross. 2 Death upon the cross; especially, **the Crucifixion** of Christ on Mount Calvary. 3 Any pictorial representation of Christ's death.

cru·ci·form (kro͞o'sə·fôrm) *adj.* Cross-shaped; cruciate. [< L *crux* cross + -FORM]

cru·ci·fy (kro͞o'sə·fī) *v.t.* **·fied, ·fy·ing** 1 To put to death by fastening to a cross. 2 Figuratively, to mortify; subdue, as impulses or desires: to *crucify* the lusts of the flesh. 3 To torture; torment. [< OF *crucifier,* ult. < L *cruci figere* fasten to a cross] **—cru'ci·fi'er** *n.*

crud (krud) *n.* 1 *Brit. Dial.* Curd. 2 *Slang* Worthless rubbish. [ME *crud* curd; origin uncertain]

crude (kro͞od) *adj.* **crud·er, crud·est** 1 In a state needing preparation for use; not refined; raw; uncooked. 2 Not having reached its complete or mature form; unripe; immature. 3 Lacking in completeness of form or arrangement; exhibiting roughness; incomplete. 4 Characterized by lack of knowledge or skill; imperfect; superficial: a *crude* effort. 5 Not disguised; bare: *crude* statements. 6 Lacking in tact or good taste; uncultured: a *crude* joke. *—n.* Petroleum as it comes from the well; unrefined petroleum and hydrocarbons. [< L *crudus* immature. Akin to CRUEL.] **—crude'ly** *adv.* **—crude'ness** *n.*

Cru·den (kro͞o'dən), **Alexander,** 1701–70, Scottish compiler of a Biblical concordance.

cru·di·ty (kro͞o'də·tē) *n. pl.* **·ties** 1 The state or quality of being crude. 2 A crude act, remark, etc.

cru·el (kro͞o'əl) *adj.* 1 Disposed to inflict suffering; indifferent to others' suffering; pitiless. 2 Unreasonably severe; harsh; distressing. See synonyms under BARBAROUS, HARD, IMPLACABLE. ◆ Homophone: *crewel.* [< F < L *crudelis* severe. Akin to CRUDE.] **—cru'el·ly** *adv.*

cru·el·ty (kro͞o'əl·tē) *n. pl.* **·ties** 1 The disposition to inflict pain. 2 Indifference to the suffering of other beings; inhumanity. 3 The act of inflicting suffering. 4 An inhuman or brutal act.

cru·et (kro͞o'it) *n.* 1 A small glass bottle, as for vinegar. 2 *Brit.* A caster. [< AF, dim. of OF *crue* pot]

Cruik·shank (kro͝ok'shangk), **George,** 1792–1878, English artist and caricaturist.

cruise (kro͞oz) *v.* **cruised, cruis·ing** *v.i.* 1 To sail about on the ocean with no set destination, as for pleasure or in search of plunder. 2 *Colloq.* To wander about; roam. 3 To move or proceed at a moderate speed, or at the optimum speed for sustained travel: This car *cruises* at 50 miles per hour. *—v.t.* 4 To sail over or about. 5 To proceed aimlessly through or across; wander. *—n.* 1 A voyage at sea; a sailing to and fro or from place to place. 2 A cruse. [< Du. *kruisen* < *kruis* cross < L *crux* cross]

cruise missile A guided missile that flies like an airplane at low altitudes.

cruis·er (kro͞o'zər) *n.* 1 A person, vehicle, or ship that cruises. 2 A fast, maneuverable warship, having long cruising radius, with medium tonnage and armament. 3 A small power vessel equipped with complete living arrangements: also called **cabin cruiser.**

cruising radius The longest round trip a ship or airplane can make without refueling.

crul·ler (krul'ər) *n.* A small, twisted cake of sweetened dough, fried brown in deep fat: also spelled *kruller.* [< Du. < *krullen* curl]

crumb (krum) *n.* 1 A small bit, as of crumbled bread. 2 A morsel. 3 The soft inner part of a loaf, as distinguished from the crust. *—v.t.* 1 To break into small pieces with the fingers; crumble. 2 In cooking, to dress or cover with bread crumbs. 3 *Colloq.* To brush crumbs from. Also **crum.** [OE *cruma; b* added on analogy with *dumb, lamb,* etc.]

crum·ble (krum'bəl) *v.t. & v.i.* **·bled, ·bling** To fall or cause to fall to small pieces; disintegrate; decay. *—n.* 1 A crumb. 2 Any crumbly material. [Freq. of CRUMB, *v.*] **—crum'bly** *adj.*

crumb·y (krum'ē) *adj.* **crumb·i·er, crumb·i·est** 1 Having crumbs. 2 Soft, like the crumb of bread. 3 *U.S. Slang* Inferior; shoddy; lousy. Also **crum'my.**

crum·mie (krum'ē, kro͝om'ē) *Scot. adj.* Crooked; bent. *—n.* A cow with crooked horns: often used as a name for any cow.

crum·mock (krum'ək, kro͝om'ək) *n. Scot.* A staff with a crooked head or stem. Also **crum'muk.**

crump (krump, kro͝omp) *adj. Scot. & Brit. Dial.* Crisp; crusty; brittle.

crum·pet (krum'pit) *n.* A thin, leavened batter cake baked on a gridiron and usually toasted and buttered. [Short for *crumpet cake,* ME *crompid cake,* pp. of *crompen* curl up]

crum·ple (krum'pəl) *v.t. & v.i.* **·pled, ·pling** 1 To become or cause to become wrinkled; rumple. 2 *Colloq.* To collapse. *—n.* A wrinkle, as in cloth or the earth; anything crumpled. [Freq. of obs. *crump,* var. of CRIMP] **—crum'pled** *adj.*

crunch (krunch) *v.t.* 1 To chew with a brittle, crushing sound; crush with the teeth. 2 To crush or grind noisily. *—v.i.* 3 To chew noisily. 4 To move or advance with a crushing sound. *—n.* 1 The act or sound of crunching. 2 *U.S. Slang* A critical time, as the moment of decision. [Imit.]

cru·node (kro͞o'nōd) *n. Math.* A point at which a curve crosses itself and therefore has two tangents. [< L *crux* cross + NODE] **—cru·no'dal** *adj.*

cru·or (kro͞o'ôr) *n.* Clotted blood; gore. [< L, gore]

crup·per (krup'ər) *n.* 1 The looped strap that goes under a horse's tail. 2 The rump of a horse; croup. [< F *croupière* < *croupe* CROUP[2]]

cru·ra (kro͝or'ə) Plural of CRUS.

cru·ral (kro͝or'əl) *adj.* Of or pertaining to the leg or the thigh. [< L *cruralis* < *crus* leg]

crus (krus) *n. pl.* **cru·ra** (kro͝or'ə) 1 *Anat.* a That part of the leg between the knee and the ankle. b *Usually pl.* A stalk or peduncle: applied to compact masses of fibers which connect different parts of the brains. 2 Any part resembling or likened to a leg. [< L, leg]

cru·sade (kro͞o·sād') *n.* 1 Any of the military expeditions undertaken by European Christians from the 11th through the 13th century to recover the Holy Land from the Moslems. 2 Any expedition under papal sanction against heathens or heretics. 3 Any vigorous concerted movement or cause, especially against public evil. *—v.i.* **·sad·ed, ·sad·ing** To go on or engage in a crusade. [< Sp. *cruzada* < Med. L *cruciata* a crossing < *cruciare* mark with a cross < L *crux* a cross; infl. in form by related F *croisade*] **—cru·sad'er** *n.*

cru·sa·do (kro͞o·sā'dō) *n. pl.* **·does** or **·dos** A former Portuguese gold coin: also spelled *cruzado.* [< Pg., lit., marked with a cross]

cruse (kro͞oz, kro͞os) *n.* A small bottle, flask, or jug; cruet: also spelled *cruise.* [? < ON *krūs* jar, pot]

cru·set kro͞o'sit) *n.* A goldsmith's melting pot. [< F *creuset*]

crush (krush) *v.t.* 1 To press or squeeze out of shape; mash. 2 To smash or grind into fine fragments or particles. 3 To obtain or extract by pressure. 4 To press upon; crowd. 5 To rumple or press out of shape. 6 To put down; subdue; conquer. 7 *Archaic* To burden or oppress. 8 *Rare* To drink. *—v.i.* 9 To become broken or misshapen by pressure. See synonyms under BREAK, CONQUER, JAM, REPRESS, SUBDUE. *—n.* 1 A violent colliding; breaking, bruising, or deforming by violent pressure. 2 A pressing or crowding together; a crowd; jam. 3 *Colloq.* A sudden romantic attachment; infatuation. [< OF *croissir* break < Gmc.] **—crush'er** *n.*

crush hat 1 A soft felt hat that can be folded without injury. 2 A collapsible high hat; opera hat.

Cru·soe (kro͞o'sō), **Robinson** See ROBINSON CRUSOE.

crust (krust) *n.* 1 A hard, thin coating, usually over something softer. 2 The outer part of bread; a bit of bread, especially if stale and hard. 3 The pastry envelope of a pie or the like. 4 An incrustation, especially from wine, on the interior of bottles. 5 A coating, as of coagulated blood or other solidified exudate of the body. 6 The cold, exterior portion or zone of the earth. 7 The part of a horse's hoof on which the shoe is nailed. 8 A crisp firm surface upon snow. 9 *Slang* Insolence; impertinence. *—v.t. & v.i.* To cover with or acquire a crust. [< L *crusta* crust] **—crust'al** *adj.* **—crust'ed** *adj.*

crus·ta·cean (krus·tā'shən) *n.* One of a class of arthropods *(Crustacea)* having crustlike shells, and generally aquatic, including lobsters, crabs, barnacles, sow-bugs, etc. *—adj.* Of or pertaining to the *Crustacea.* [< NL *Crustacea* < L *crusta* crust; with ref. to the shell]

crus·ta·ceous (krus·tā'shəs) *adj.* 1 Having, or pertaining to, a crustlike shell. 2 Crustacean.

crust·er (krus'tər) *n. U.S.* One who hunts game, especially deer or moose, in deep snow when the ice crust will hold the weight of a man but not the quarry: a term of contempt. Also **crust'-hunt'er.**

crus·tose (krus'tōs) *adj.* Crustlike: crustaceous.

crust·y (krus'tē) *adj.* **crust·i·er, crust·i·est** 1 Crustlike. 2 Having or hard as a crust. 3 Morosely curt in manner or speech; surly. See synonyms under MOROSE. **—crust'i·ly** *adv.* **—crust'i·ness** *n.*

crutch (kruch) *n.* 1 A staff with a crosspiece fitting under the armpit, used as a support in walking. 2 Any one of various mechanical devices involving the principle or use of such a support. 3 *Naut.* A forked support for a swinging boom when not in use. 4 The horn on a woman's saddle. 5 A rack. 6 A hooked rod used to immerse sheep while washing. 7 The crotch of a human body. *—v.t.* To prop up, as on crutches. [OE *crycc*]

crutched (krucht) *adj.* Bearing the sign of the cross: The *Crutched* Friars. [Earlier *crouched,* pp. of obs. *crouch* mark with a cross]

cruth, crwth (kro͞oth) See CROWD[2].

crux (kruks) *n. pl.* **crux·es** or **cru·ces** (kro͞o'sēz) 1 A pivotal, fundamental, or vital point. 2 A cross. 3 A tormenting or baffling problem; a perplexing difficulty. [< L, a cross]

Crux (kruks) The Southern Cross. See CONSTELLATION.

crux an·sa·ta (an·sā'tə) See ANSATE CROSS under CROSS.

crux com·mis·sa (kə·mis'ə) See TAU CROSS under CROSS.

crux de·cus·sa·ta (dē'kə·sā'tə) See ST. ANDREW'S CROSS under CROSS.

crux im·mis·sa (i·mis'ə) See LATIN CROSS under CROSS.

cru·za·do (kro͞o·sā'dō) *n.* A crusado. [Var. of CRUSADO]

Cru·zan (kro͞o'zən) *n.* A native or inhabitant of St. Croix. *—adj.* Relating to St. Croix.

cru·zei·ro (kro͞o·zā'rō, *Pg.* -ro͞o) *n.* The gold monetary unit of Brazil, equivalent to 100 centavos. [< Pg. < *cruz* cross < L *crux*]

cry (krī) *v.* **cried, cry·ing** *v.t.* 1 To utter loudly or shout out; exclaim. 2 To proclaim loudly and publicly; advertise loudly, as goods or services. 3 *Archaic* To beg or implore: I *cry* you mercy. 4 To affect (one) in some specified way by weeping: to *cry* oneself to sleep. *—v.i.* 5 To speak, call, or appeal loudly; shout; yell. 6 To utter sounds of grief and lamentation; weep; sob. 7 To weep or shed tears inaudibly. 8 To make characteristic calls: said of animals. See synonyms under CALL, ROAR. **—to cry down** 1 To disparage. 2 To silence or put down by cries. **—to cry quits** To declare to be even, or that neither has the advantage. *—n. pl.* **cries** 1 A loud or passionate utterance; a call; shout; yell. 2 The act of weeping. 3 An earnest appeal; entreaty. 4 Advertisement by outcry; proclamation: the hawker's *cry.* 5 General report or rumor; common saying; public opinion. 6 A pack of dogs; hence, in contempt, a company of persons; party. **7** A subject or topic made temporarily important for political purposes; watchword; party phrase. **8** A word or phrase to rally men in battle; war cry. **9** Demand; requisition: a *cry* for clean streets. **10** The characteristic call of a bird or an animal. —**a far cry** The farthest distance over which a cry can be heard; hence, a long way. —**in full cry** In full pursuit, as hunting dogs when baying in chorus. [<F *crier* <L *quiritare* call out]

cry•ba•by (krī′bā′bē) *n. pl.* **•bies** A person, especially a child, given to crying or complaining over his circumstances.

cry•ing (krī′ing) *adj.* Calling for immediate action or redress; self–proclaiming; notorious: a *crying* shame.

cryo– *combining form* Cold; frost: *cryogenic.* [<Gk. *kryos* frost]

cry•o•bi•ol•o•gy (krī′ō·bī·ol′ə·j) *n.* The study of the effects of freezing and low temperatures on living organisms.

cry•o•gen (krī′ə·jən) *n.* A freezing mixture.

cry•o•gen•ic (krī′ə·jen′ik) *adj.* Pertaining to the study of, or experiments in, low temperatures.

cry•o•gen•ics (krī′ə·jen′iks) *n.* The branch of physics dealing with the phenomena of extreme cold.

cry•o•hy•drate (krī′ə·hī′drāt) *n.* A crystalline eutectic mixture of constant composition and melting point, as of salt with water, which forms below the freezing point of water.

cry•o•lite (krī′ə·līt) *n.* A vitreous, snow–white, translucent fluoride of sodium and aluminum, occurring in Greenland: used in the production of aluminum, soda, and glass, to which it gives a milky hue. Also spelled *kryolite, kryolith.*

cry•om•e•ter (krī·om′ə·tər) *n.* An instrument for measuring a lower temperature than the ordinary mercury thermometer will indicate, as an alcohol thermometer. [<CRYO- + -METER]

cry•oph•o•rus (kri·of′ər·əs) *n.* An instrument for showing the decrease of temperature in water through evaporation: socalled because such decrease may freeze the water. [<CRYO- + -PHOROUS]

cry•o•scope (krī′ə·skōp) *n.* An instrument used for determining the freezing point of liquids and other substances.

cry•os•co•py (krī·os′kə·pē) *n.* The study of the freezing points of solutions, especially in relation to the lowered freezing point of the solute.

cry•o•stat (krī′ə·stat) *n.* A receptacle, constructed on the principle of the Dewar flask, for containing substances studied in low–temperature research; a heat regulator for low temperatures.

cry•o•ther•a•py (krī′ə·ther′ə·pē) *n. Med.* The use of low or freezing temperatures as a therapeutic measure.

cry•o•tron (krī′ə·tron) *n. Electronics* A device for utilizing the superconductivity of certain metals at temperatures approaching that of liquid helium. [<CRYO- + (ELEC)TRON]

crypt (kript) *n.* **1** A secret recess or vault; especially, one used, as in the catacombs, for interment. **2** A vault under some churches, used as a chapel, cemetery, etc. **3** *Physiol.* A minute follicle or secreting cavity of the skin or mucous membrane. [<L *crypta* <Gk. *kryptē* <*kryptos* hidden. Doublet of GROTTO.]

cryp•ta•nal•y•sis (krip′tə·nal′ə·sis) *n. pl.* **•ses** (-sēz) The scientific study and conversion into plain text of cryptograms, ciphers, codes, and other forms of secret communication to which the key is not known. [<CRYPTO- + ANALYSIS] —**cryp•tan•a•lyst** (krip·tan′ə·list) *n.* —**cryp′•tan•a•lyt′ic** *adj.*

cryp•tes•the•sia (krip′təs·thē′zhə, -zhē·ə) *n. Psychol.* Any of various modes of supernormal sensibility, as clairvoyance, telepathy, extrasensory perception, etc. [<CRYPTO- + ESTHESIA]

cryptic (krip′tik) *adj.* **1** Secret; occult; arcane. **2** Tending to concealment; puzzling; mysterious. Also **cryp′ti•cal.** [<LL *crypticus* <Gk. *kryptikos* <*kryptos* hidden]

crypto– *combining form* Hidden; secret: *cryptogram.* Also, before vowels, **crypt–.** [<Gk. *kryptos* hidden]

cryp•to•clas•tic (krip′tō·klas′tik) *adj. Geol.* Composed of microscopic fragmental grains, derived from preexisting rocks, as shale. [< CRYPTO- + CLASTIC]

cryp•to•cli•mate (krip′tō·klī′mit) *n.* The range of climatic conditions found within a house, building, or other enclosed structure, especially as compared with the *microclimate* of the local area and the *macroclimate* of the entire region.

cryp•to•crys•tal•line (krip′tō·kris′tə·lin, -lēn) *adj. Mineral.* Possessing a crystalline structure which cannot be resolved into distinct individuals even under the microscope: opposed to *phanerocrystalline.*

cryp•to•gam (krip′tə·gam) *n. Bot.* **1** Any of a former division of plants *(Cryptogamia)* that have no true flowers, but propagate by spores, as algae, fungi, lichens, and mosses. **2** A plant lacking true seeds: opposed to *phanerogam.* Also **cryp′to•phyte** (-fīt). [<CRYPTO- + Gk. *gamos* marriage] —**cryp′to•gam′ic** *adj.*— **cryp•tog•a•mous** (krip·tog′ə·məs) *adj.*

cryp•tog•a•my (krip·tog′ə·mē) *n. Bot.* The state or condition of being cryptogamic or having concealed fructification. [<CRYPTO- + -GAMY]

cryp•tog•e•nous (krip·toj′ə·nəs) *adj.* Of obscure origin. Also **cryp•to•ge•net•ic** (krip′tō·jə·net′ik), **cryp•to•gen•ic** (krip′tə·jen′ik). [<CRYPTO- + -GENOUS]

cryp•to•gram (krip′tə·gram) *n.* A written communication in the form of symbols chosen arbitrarily but according to a system permitting reconversion to the original plain text, as a cipher or code.

cryp•to•graph (krip′tə·graf, -gräf) *n.* **1** A cryptogram. **2** A system of cipher–writing; a cipher. —**cryp•tog•ra•pher** (krip·tog′rə·fər), **cryp•tog′ra•phist** *n.* —**cryp′to•graph′ic** *adj.*

cryp•tog•ra•phy (krip·tog′rə·fē) *n.* **1** The art and process of writing in cipher. **2** Any system of writing in secret characters.

cryp•tol•o•gy (krip·tol′ə·jē) *n.* Enigmatic language; cryptography. [CRYPTO- + -LOGY]

cryp•tom•ne•sia (krip′təm·nē′zhə, -zhē·ə) *n. Psychol.* A form of memory which causes experiences to appear to the subject as new, without conscious recognition of or identification with their original source. [<CRYPTO- + Gk. *mnasthai* remember]

cryp•to•nym (krip′tə·nim) *n.* A secret name. [< CRYPTO- + Gk. *onoma, onyma* name] —**cryp•ton•y•mous** (krip·ton′ə·məs) *adj.*

cryp•to•psy•chics (krip′tə·sī′kiks) *n.* Metapsychics.

cryp•to•zo•ic (krip′tə·zō′ik) *adj. Zool.* Of, pertaining to, or designating animals which live in dark and hidden places.

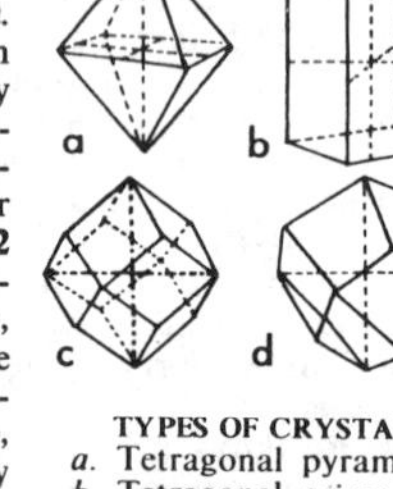

TYPES OF CRYSTALS
a. Tetragonal pyramid.
b. Tetragonal prism.
c. Dodecahedron.
d. Deltahedron.

crys•tal (kris′təl) *n.* **1** The solid form assumed by many minerals; specifically, colorless transparent quartz, or rock crystal. **2** *Physics* A homogeneous solid body, exhibiting a definite and symmetrical internal structure, with geometrically arranged cleavage planes and external faces that assume any of a group of patterns associated with peculiarities of atomic structure. **3** Flint glass, or any fine glass, especially as made into high–grade tableware and decorative pieces. **4** A watchglass. **5** A clear, white diamond. **6** A specially shaped and ground piece of quartz or similar material, used to improve radio reception. —*adj.* Composed of or like crystal; extremely clear; limpid. [<OF *cristal* <L *crystallum* clear ice <Gk. *krystallos* < *krystainein* freeze<*kryos* frost] —**crys•tal•lic** (kris·tal′ik) *adj.*

crystal analysis *Physics* The study of the molecular, atomic, and ionic configuration in crystals, aided by X–ray methods.

crystal ball A ball of crystal or glass used in crystal–gazing.

crystal control *Telecom.* The maintenance of prescribed frequency operation of a radio station by the use of a quartz crystal.

crystal detector *Telecom.* A device consisting of metal electrodes in contact with suitable crystal materials: used to rectify incoming radio signals in a crystal set.

crys•tal–gaz•ing (kris′təl·gā′zing) *n.* The act of looking into a ball of crystal and pretending to see pictures within it or to exercise divination by it; crystallomancy: also **crystal vision.**

crystal grating *Physics* A very fine diffraction grating consisting of a suitably prepared and mounted crystal: used in X–ray work.

crys•tal•lif•er•ous (kris′tə·lif′ər·əs) *adj.* Bearing or containing crystals. [<L *crystallum* clear ice, crystal + -(I)FEROUS]

crys•tal•lig•er•ous (kris′tə·lij′ər·əs) *adj.* Containing crystals. [<L *crystallum* clear ice, crystal + -(I)GEROUS]

crys•tal•line (kris′tə·lin, -lēn) *adj.* **1** Of, pertaining to, or like crystal or crystals: distinguished from *clastic.* **2** Transparent; pure; pellucid: the *crystalline* lens of the eye. —*n.* A crystallized or partly crystallized substance. [<F *cristallin* <L *crystallinus* <Gk. *krystallinos* <*krystallos.* See CRYSTAL.]

crystalline boron See under BORON.

crystalline lens *Anat.* A transparent, biconvex, lentiform body situated between the iris and the vitreous body of the eye, serving to focus an image upon the retina. Also **crystalline humor.**

crys•tal•lite (kris′tə·līt) *n. Mineral.* One of certain minute, spherical, rod–shaped or hairlike bodies without the true properties of a crystal, but resulting from a crystallizing tendency, observable in thin sections of igneous rock and in slags. [<L *crystallum* clear ice, crystal + -ITE[1]] —**crys•tal•lit•ic** (kris′tə·lit′ik) *adj.*

crys•tal•li•tis (kris′tə·lī′təs) *n. Pathol.* Inflammation of the crystalline lens. [<NL <Gk. *krystallos* crystal + -ITIS]

crys•tal•lize (kris′tə·līz) *v.* **•lized, •liz•ing** *v.t.* **1** To cause to form crystals or become crystalline. **2** To bring to definite and permanent form. —*v.i.* **3** To assume the form of crystals. **4** To assume definite and permanent form. —**crys′tal•liz′a•ble** *adj.* —**crys′•tal•li•za′tion** *n.*

crystallo– *combining form* Crystal: *crystallography.* Also, before vowels, **crystall–.** [<Gk. *krystallos* crystal]

crys•tal•lo•graph•ic (kris′tə·lə·graf′ik) *adj.* Of or pertaining to crystallography. Also **crys′•tal•lo•graph′i•cal.** —**crys′tal•lo•graph′i•cal•ly** *adv.*

crystallographic axes Imaginary lines within a crystal, to which its faces can be referred.

crystallographic indices A series of numbers indicating the relative intercepts of a crystal face upon the crystal axes.

crys•tal•log•ra•phy (kris′tə·log′rə·fē) *n.* The science of crystals, including the study of their geometrical, physical, and chemical structure.

crys•tal•loid (kris′tə·loid) *adj.* Like a crystal; of or pertaining to the crystal state of matter. —*n.* **1** *Chem.* One of a class of substances, usually crystallizable, whose solutions are readily diffusible: distinguished from *colloid.* **2** *Bot.* A crystal–like protein body found in plant cells: a protein crystal. [<Gk. *krystalloeidēs* like crystal] —**crys′tal•loi′dal** *adj.*

crys•tal•lo•man•cy (kris′tə·lə·man′sē) *n.* Divination by gazing into a crystal globe. [< CRYSTALLO- + -MANCY]

crys•tal•lon (kris′tə·lon) *n.* A crystal fragment dropped into a saturated solution to provide a nucleus around which the solution may crystallize: also called *seed crystal.* [<Gk., neut. of *krystallos* of crystal]

crys•tal•lose (kris′tə·lōs) *n.* Soluble saccharin: a sweetening compound. [<CRYSTALL(O)- + -OSE]

crystal set A radio receiving set operating with a crystal detector but without vacuum tubes.

crystal system Any of the variously named and classified fundamental patterns by which all crystals may be identified: determined on the basis of the imaginary axes drawn from each face or edge through the center of the crystal. Six major systems are generally recognized. See following table.

CRYSTAL SYSTEMS

	Name	*No. of axes*	*Type example*
I	Isometric	3	fluorite, garnet
II	Tetragonal	3	cassiterite, zircon
III	Hexagonal	4	calcite, quartz
IV	Orthorhombic	3	sulfur, topaz
V	Monoclinic	3	gypsum, augite
VI	Triclinic	3	rhodonite

crystal violet A derivative of rosaniline,

used as an indicator in medicine and bacteriology.

Cs *Chem.* Cesium (symbol Cs).

Csa·ba (chô′bo) See BÉKÉSCSABA.

cte·nid·i·um (tə·nid′ē·əm) *n. pl.* **·nid·i·a** (-nid′ē·ə) *Zool.* **1** One of the respiratory organs of mollusks, resembling a comb. **2** One of the comblike structures situated on the toes of some birds. [<NL <Gk. *ktenidion,* dim. of *kteis* comb]

cteno- *combining form* Comb: *ctenophore.* Also, before vowels, **cten-.** [<Gk. *kteis, ktenos* comb]

cten·oid (ten′oid, tē′noid) *adj. Biol.* Having a comblike margin, as certain plants, and the scales in ctenophores. [<Gk. *ktenoeidēs* like a comb]

cten·o·phore (ten′ə·fôr, -fōr, tē′nə-) *n.* One of the *Ctenophora,* a subphylum or phylum of coelenterates which includes the marine comb jellies. [<NL *Ctenophora* <Gk. *kteis, ktenos* comb + *pherein* bear]

Ctes·i·phon (tes′ə·fon) A ruined ancient city on the Tigris in central Iraq; capital of the Sassanides.

Cu *Chem.* Copper (symbol Cu). [L *cuprum*]

Cuan·za (kwän′zə) A river in central Angola, SW Africa, flowing 600 miles to the Atlantic.

cua·ren·ta (kwä·ren′tä) *n.* A silver coin of Cuba, equal in value to forty centavos. [<Sp., forty]

cub (kub) *n.* **1** The young of the bear, fox, wolf, and certain other carnivores; a whelp. **2** A rough, awkward, uncouth, or ill-mannered youth. **3** A beginner or learner; an apprentice. —*adj.* Young; inexperienced: a *cub* reporter; *cub* pilot. [Origin uncertain] **—cub′bish** *adj.* **—cub′bish·ly** *adv.*

Cu·ba (kyoo′bə) The largest island of the West Indies, comprising a republic; 44,164 square miles; capital, Havana. **—Cu′ban** *adj. & n.*

Cuba li·bre (lē′brə) An alcoholic drink made of rum, lemon juice, and a cola beverage. [<Sp., free Cuba]

Cuban eight *Aeron.* An airplane flight maneuver made up of a 3/4-normal loop, a half-roll, another 3/4-normal loop, and ending with another half-roll.

Cu·ban·go (koo·vang′goo) The Portuguese name for the OKOVANGGO.

cu·ba·ture (kyoo′bə·choor) *n.* **1** The process of determining the cubical contents of a solid. **2** Cubical contents. Also **cu·bage** (kyoo′bij). [<L *cubus* cube]

cub·by·hole (kub′ē·hōl′) *n.* A small, enclosed, space. [<*cubby,* dim. of dial. E *cub* shed + HOLE]

cube[1] (kyoob) *n.* **1** *Geom.* A solid bounded by six equal squares and having all its angles right angles. **2** *Math.* The third power of a quantity; the product of three equal factors. —*v.t.* **cubed, cub·ing 1** To raise (a number or quantity) to the third power. **2** To find the cubic capacity of. **3** To form or cut into cubes or cubelike shapes; dice: to *cube* potatoes. [<MF <LL *cubus* <Gk. *kybos* cube, die[2]]

cu·be[2] (koo′bā) *n.* A substance extracted from the roots of *Lonchocarpus nicou,* a leguminous plant native in Peru: it contains rotenone and tephrosin and is used as a fish poison. [<Sp. *quibey* <native name]

cu·beb (kyoo′beb) *n.* A berry of an East Indian shrub *(Piper cubeba)* of the pepper family: used in treating urinary and bronchial diseases and often smoked in the form of cigarettes. [<MF *cubèbe* <Med.L *cubeba* <Arabic *kabābah*]

cube root The number which, taken three times as a factor, produces a given number called its cube: 4 is the *cube root* of 64.

cu·bic (kyoo′bik) *adj.* **1** Formed like a cube. **2** Being, or equal to, a cube whose edge is a given unit: a *cubic* foot. **3** *Math.* Of the third power or degree. Also **cu′bi·cal.** [<F *cubique* <L *cubicus* <Gk. *kybikos* <*kybos* cube]. **—cu′bi·cal·ly** *adv.* **—cu′bi·cal·ness** *n.*

cu·bi·cle (kyoo′bi·kəl) *n.* **1** A bedroom. **2** A partially enclosed section of a dormitory. **3** Hence, any small room. [<L *cubiculum* bedroom <*cubare* lie down]

cubic measure A unit or system of units for measuring volume, or the amount of space occupied in three dimensions. The principal customary units are given in the table below. See also METRIC SYSTEM.

144 cubic inches (cu. in.)	=	1 board foot (bd. ft.)
1728 cubic inches	=	1 cubic foot (cu. ft.; ft.^{3})
27 cubic feet	=	1 cubic yard (cu. yd.; yd.^{3})
128 cubic feet	=	1 cord (cd.)

cu·bic·u·lar (kyoo·bik′yə·lər) *adj.* Of or pertaining to a bedchamber; private. Also **cu·bic′·u·lar′y** (-ler′ē). [<L *cubicularis* <*cubiculum.* See CUBICLE.]

cu·bic·u·lum (kyoo·bik′yə·ləm) *n. pl.* **·la** (-lə) **1** A small bedchamber; cubicle. **2** A burial chamber with recesses in the walls for dead bodies, as in the Roman catacombs. Also *Obs.* **cu·bic′u·lo** (-lō). [<L]

cu·bi·form (kyoo′bə·fôrm) *adj.* Shaped like a cube.

cu·bism (kyoo′biz·əm) *n.* A school of modern art concerned with the analysis of form by means of abstract and geometric representation, rather than with a realistic interpretation of nature. **—cu′bist** *adj. & n.*

cu·bit (kyoo′bit) *n.* An ancient measure of length, originally represented by the length of the forearm: about 18 to 20 inches. [<L *cubitum* elbow]

cu·bi·tal (kyoo′bə·təl) *adj.* **1** Of or pertaining to the ulna or to the forearm. **2** Of the measure of a cubit.

cu·bi·tus (kyoo′bə·təs) *n. pl.* **·ti** (-tī) **1** A cubit. **2** *Entomol.* **a** The fifth longitudinal vein of an insect's wing. **b** The tibia of the anterior leg. **c** The radial or stigmal vein in the Hemiptera. **3** *Anat.* The forearm. [<L, var. of *cubitum.* See CUBIT.]

cu·boid (kyoo′boid) *n.* **1** *Anat.* The outer distal bone of the tarsus or ankle. **2** *Geom.* A rectangular parallelepiped. —*adj.* Shaped like a cube: also **cu·boi′dal.** [<Gk. *kyboeidēs* like a cube]

cub scout A member of a subdivision of the Boy Scouts, comprising boys eight to eleven years of age.

Cu·chu·lain (koo·khoo′lən) A legendary Irish hero, supposed to have defended his country single-handed against invaders.

cuck·ing stool (kuk′ing) A chair in which disorderly women, scolds, and dishonest tradesmen were tied, left to public derision, and sometimes ducked. [<obs. *cuck* defecate]

cuck·old (kuk′əld) *n.* The husband of an unfaithful wife. —*v.t.* To make a cuckold of. [<OF *cucuault* <*cucu* cuckoo; with ref. to the cuckoo's habit of laying its eggs in another bird's nest.] **—cuck′old·ly, cuck′old·y** *adj.*

cuck·old·ry (kuk′əl·drē) *n.* The cuckolding of a husband.

cuck·oo (kook′oo) *n.* **1** A bird belonging to a large family *(Cuculidae),* many species of which, as the common European cuckoo *(Cuculus canorus),* deposit their eggs in the nests of other birds to be hatched and cared for. **2** Any of various birds similar to the English cuckoo, as the Australasian small owl, or the American yellow-billed cuckoo *(Coccyzus americanus)* and the black-billed cuckoo *(C. erythrophthalmus).* **3** One who repeats the saying of another or follows slavishly, as in politics; a fool; ninny. **4** A cuckoo's cry. **5** One who commits adultery. —*v.* **·ooed, ·oo·ing** *v.t.* To repeat without cessation. —*v.i.* To utter or imitate the cry of the cuckoo. —*adj.* (*also* koo′koo) *Slang* Slightly deranged mentally; crazy; silly. [<OF *cucu, coucou;* imit.]

cuckoo bud A buttercup or kingcup.

cuckoo clock A clock in which a mechanical cuckoo announces the hours.

cuckoo flower 1 A species of bittercress *(Cardamine pratensis)* with showy flowers: also called *lady-smock.* **2** Ragged robin.

cuckoo pint A tuberous herb *(Arum maculatum)* of the arum family, with long leaves and erect, purple-spotted spathes: also called *Bob-bin-and-Joan, lords-and-ladies, wake robin.*

cuckoo spit 1 A frothy secretion exuded upon plants by the larvae of certain insects, as froghoppers: also called *frog spit.* **2** An insect that secretes froth; a froghopper.

cu·cu·ba·no (koo′kə·bä′nō) *n.* The West Indian fire beetle. [<Sp.]

cu·cu·li·form (kyoo·kyoo′lə·fôrm) *adj. Ornithol.* Of or pertaining to an order of birds *(Cuculiformes)* including the cuckoos and roadrunners. [<NL *Cuculiformis* <L *cuculus* cuckoo]

cu·cul·late (kyoo′kə·lāt, kyoo·kul′āt) *adj.* **1** Hood-shaped. **2** *Bot.* Having a hoodlike part, as certain leaves. Also **cu·cul·lat·ed** (kyoo′kə·lā′tid, kyoo·kul′ā·tid). [<LL *cucullatus* <L *cucullus* hood]

cu·cul·li·form (kyoo·kul′ə·fôrm) *adj.* Having the form of a hood; cucullate. [<L *cucullus* hood + -FORM]

cu·cum·ber (kyoo′kum·bər) *n.* **1** The oblong, hard-rinded fruit of a creeping plant of the gourd family *(Cucumis sativus),* cultivated as a vegetable. **2** The plant. [<OF *cocombre* <L *cucumis, -eris*]

cucumber tree 1 A straight, tall tree *(Magnolia acuminata)* of the eastern United States, bearing a fruit resembling a small cucumber. **2** An East Indian tree *(Averrhoa bilimbi)* cultivated for its edible acid berries and its flowers.

cu·cu·mi·form (kyoo·kyoo′mə·fôrm) *adj.* Having the form of a cucumber. [<L *cucumis* cucumber + -FORM]

cu·cur·bit (kyoo·kûr′bit) *n.* **1** The body of an alembic, originally gourd-shaped. **2** Any similar vessel, as the cucurbitula. **3** Any plant of the gourd family. [<F *cucurbite* <L *cucurbita* gourd] **—cu·cur·bi·ta·ceous** (kyoo·kûr′bə·tā′shəs) *adj.*

cu·cur·bit·u·la (kyoo′kər·bit′yoo·lə) *n.* A cupping glass. [<L, dim. of *cucurbita* gourd, cupping glass]

cud (kud) *n.* **1** Food forced up into the mouth from the first stomach of a ruminant and chewed over again. **2** The rumen. [OE *cudu, cwida* cud]

Cud·a·hy (kud′ə·hē), **Michael,** 1841–1910, U.S. meat packer.

cud·bear (kud′bâr) *n.* **1** A purplish-red dyestuff, similar to archil, made from lichens and used as a coloring for foods and drugs. **2** The lichen (genus *Lecanora)* that furnishes the dye. [Coined from his first name by Dr. *Cuthbert* Gordon, who first made it]

cud·die (kud′ē, kood′ē) *n. Scot.* A donkey.

cud·dle (kud′l) *v.* **·dled, ·dling** *v.t.* To protect and caress fondly within a close embrace; hug. —*v.i.* To lie close; hug one another; nestle together. —*n.* An embrace; caress. [? <dial. E (Northern) *couth* snug, cozy] **—cud′dle·some** *adj.* **—cud′dly** *adj.*

cud·dy (kud′ē) *n. pl.* **·dies 1** *Naut.* A small cabin; a cook's galley. **2** Any small cupboard or pantry. [Origin unknown]

cudg·el (kuj′əl) *n.* A short, thick stick used as a club. **—to take up the cudgels** To enter into a contest or controversy. —*v.t.* **·eled** or **·elled, ·el·ing** or **·el·ling** To beat with a cudgel. See synonyms under BEAT. **—to cudgel one's brains** To think hard; puzzle. [OE *cycgel*] **—cudg′el·er** or **cudg′el·ler** *n.*

cudg·el-play (kuj′əl·plā′) *n.* The art of using quarterstaves, singlesticks, or similar weapons, or a contest in which they are used.

cud·weed (kud′wēd′) *n.* Any one of various plants of the composite family (genus *Gnaphalium* or *Helichrysum*), as the everlasting. [<CUD + WEED; because given to cattle]

Cud·worth (kud′wûrth, -wərth), **Ralph,** 1617–1688, English philosopher.

cue[1] (kyoo) *n.* **1** A long, tapering rod, used in billiards, pool, etc., to strike the cue ball. **2** A queue of hair. **3** A queue or line of persons. —*v.t.* **cued, cu·ing 1** To twist, braid, or tie into a cue: to *cue* the hair. **2** In billiards, etc., to hit with a cue. [<F *queue* tail]

cue[2] (kyoo) *n.* **1** The closing words in an actor's speech, serving as a signal for his successor; hence, a catchword; hint; suggestion. **2** A part to be performed by an actor. **3** State of mind; humor. —*v.t.* **cued, cu·ing** To call a cue to (an actor); prompt. [Earlier *Q, qu,* said to have been an abbreviation of L *quando* when, written in actors' copies of plays to mark their entrances.]

cue[3] (kyoo) *n.* The letter Q.

cue ball A white or whitish-yellow ball struck by the cue in billiards or pool.

cue drawing One of the master drawings prepared as a basis for the succession of action drawings to be filmed as an animated cartoon.

Cuen·ca (kweng′kä) **1** A province in east central Spain; 6,588 square miles; capital, Cuenca. **2** A city in south central Ecuador.

Cuer·na·va·ca (kwâr′nä·vä′kä) A resort city in central Mexico.

cue sheet An instruction sheet for stage technicians giving exact details on the character and timing of all changes in lighting, sound effects, etc., during a performance.

cues·ta (kwes′tə) *n. SW U.S.* A ridge or hill that has a steep descent on one side and a gentle slope on the other. [< Sp.]

cuff[1] (kuf) *n.* **1** A band about the wrist. **2** The lower part of a sleeve. **3** The portion of a long glove or gauntlet covering the wrist. **4** The turned-up hem on a trouser leg. **5** A handcuff. —**on the cuff** *U.S. Slang* On credit; with payment postponed. [ME *cuffe, coffe;* origin unknown]

cuff[2] (kuf) *v.t.* To strike, as with the open hand; buffet. —*v.i.* To scuffle or fight; box. —*n.* A blow, especially with the open hand. [? < Scand. Cf. Sw. *kuffa* push.]

cuff links A pair of linked buttons, etc., used to fasten shirt cuffs.

Cu·fic (kyōō′fik) See KUFIC.

Cu·i (kü·ē′), **César Antonovich,** 1835–1918, Russian composer.

Cu·ia·bá (kōō′yä·bä′) A city in western Brazil, capital of Mato Grosso. Formerly **Cu′ya·bá′.**

cui bo·no (kwē′ bō′nō, kī′) *Latin* For whose benefit? Also, inaccurately, for what purpose?

cui·rass (kwi·ras′) *n.* **1** A piece of defensive armor covering the entire upper part of the trunk, and consisting of a breastplate and backplate; also, the breastplate alone. **2** A cuirasslike covering, as the bony plates of a mailed fish, the armor of a ship, etc. —*v.t.* To cover, as with a cuirass. [< F *cuirasse*]

cui·ras·sier (kwi′rə·sir′) *n.* A mounted soldier wearing a cuirass.

cuir-bouil·li (kwēr′bōō·yē′) *n.* Leather made extremely hard by boiling or soaking in hot water and drying, usually shaping in a mold. Also **cuir′-bouil·ly′.** [< F, boiled leather]

cuish (kwish) *n.* Armor, especially plate armor, for the thigh: sometimes written *quish.* Also **cuisse** (kwis). [< OF *cuissel* < *cuisse* thigh < L *coxa* hip]

cui·sine (kwi·zēn′) *n.* **1** Style or quality of cooking. **2** The food prepared. [< F]

culch (kulch) *n.* Refuse; stuff; rubbish: also spelled *cultch.* [? < OF *culche* bed, layer]

Cul·dee (kul′dē) *n.* One of an order of ecclesiastics, with monasteries in Scotland and Ireland, existing from the 9th to the 14th century. [< Irish *cēle dē* < *cēle* servant + *dē* of God] —**Cul·de′an** *adj.*

cul-de-sac (kul′də·sak′, kōōl′-; *Fr.* kü′də·sák′) *n. pl.* **cul·de·sacs,** *Fr.* **culs·de·sac** (kü′-) **1** A passage open only at one end; blind alley; trap. **2** *Anat. & Zool.* A saclike cavity or part open only at one end. **3** *Mil.* The position of a force surrounded by hostile lines. [< F, bottom of the bag]

-cule *suffix of nouns* Small; little: *animalcule.* [< F < L *-culus,* dim. suffix]

Cu·le·bra Cut (kōō·lā′brə) A former name for the GAILLARD CUT.

cu·let (kyōō′lit) *n. pl.* **·lets** or **·lettes** **1** The small lower terminus of a brilliant-cut gem, parallel to the table: also called *collet.* **2** One of the plates of armor for the lower part of the back: often used in the plural. [< OF, dim. of *cul* bottom < L *culus* a buttock]

cu·lex (kyōō′leks) *n.* Any of a large, cosmopolitan genus *(Culex)* of mosquitoes including the common pests of North America and Europe as well as some species that transmit viral diseases of birds, horses, and humans. —**cu·li·cine** (kyōō′·lə·sēn) *adj. & n.*

cul·gee (kul·gē′) *n. Anglo-Indian* **1** A jeweled aigret or plume, as worn on turbans in India. **2** A figured silk fabric of Indian origin. [< Hind. *kalghī* < Persian *kalagī, kalakī* of a festive company]

Cu·lia·cán (kōō′lyä·kän′) A city in western Mexico, capital of Sinaloa state.

cu·li·cid (kyōō·lis′id) *n.* A member of any genus (family Culicidae).

cu·li·cide (kyōō′lə·sīd) *n.* Any agent that destroys mosquitoes. —**cu′li·cid′al** *adj.*

cu·li·nar·y (kyōō′lə·ner′ē) *adj.* Of or pertaining to cooking or the kitchen. [< L *culinarius* < *culina* kitchen]

cull (kul) *v.t.* **culled, cull·ing** **1** To pick or sort out; collect apart. **2** To select and gather: to *cull* a bouquet. See synonyms under CHOOSE. —*n.* Something picked or sorted out; hence, something rejected. [< OF *cuillir* < L *colligere* collect] —**cull′er** *n.*

cul·lay (kə·lī′) See QUILLAI.

Cul·len (kul′ən), **Coun·tée** (koun·tā′), 1903–1946, U.S. Negro poet.

cul·len·der (kul′ən·dər) See COLANDER.

cul·let (kul′it) *n.* Glass waste, variously used as a powder or in melted state. [< F *collet,* dim. of *col* neck < L *collum*; with ref. to the neck of glass left on the pipe after blowing.]

cul·lion (kul′yən) *n.* **1** A bulblike root; an orchid. **2** A poltroon. [< F *couillon* testicle] —**cul′lion·ly** *adj.*

cul·lis (kul′is) *n.* **1** *Archit.* A gutter in a roof. **2** A groove, as for a theatrical side scene. [< F *coulisse*]

Cul·lo·den Moor (kə·lō′dən) A tract in Inverness, Scotland; scene of decisive defeat of Scottish Highlanders by British forces, 1746. Also **Colloden Muir.**

cul·ly (kul′ē) *n. pl.* **·lies** **1** *Colloq.* One who is tricked; a dupe. **2** *Brit. Slang* Fellow; pal. —*v.t.* **·lied, ·ly·ing** *Obs.* To impose upon; gull. [? < *cullion* def. 2)]

culm[1] (kulm) *n. Bot.* The jointed, usually hollow, stem or straw of grasses. —*v.i.* To form a culm. [< L *culmus* stalk] —**cul·mif·er·ous** (kul·mif′·ər·əs) *adj.*

culm[2] (kulm) *n.* **1** Anthracite refuse, or carbonaceous shale. **2** An inferior anthracite coal. [Var. of dial. *coom* soot] —**cul·mif·er·ous** (kul·mif′ər·əs) *adj.*

cul·men (kul′mən) *n.* **1** A summit or eminence. **2** *Ornithol.* The ridge or central longitudinal line of the upper mandible of bird's bill. **3** *Anat.* A small eminence on the upper surface of the cerebellum: also **culmen mon·tic·u·li** (mon·tik′yə·lī). [< L]

cul·mi·nate (kul′mə·nāt) *v.i.* **·nat·ed, ·nat·ing** **1** To attain the highest point or degree. **2** *Astron.* To reach the meridian, or the point of greatest or least altitude. **3** To come to a complete result; reach a final effect. [< LL *culminatus,* pp. of *culminare* mature < *culmen* top, highest point] —**cul′mi·nal** *adj.*

cul·mi·na·tion (kul′mə·nā′shən) *n.* **1** The highest point, condition, or degree. **2** *Astron.* The passage of a heavenly body over the meridian.

culm measures *Geol.* A rock formation belonging to the Lower Carboniferous era, alterloting marine-fossil beds with plant-fossil beds.

cu·lottes (kyōō·lots′, kōō-) *n. pl.* A woman's sportswear garment having knee-length trouser legs cut full to resemble a skirt. [< F]

cul·pa (kul′pə) *n. Law* A fault, especially of negligence. [< L]

cul·pa·ble (kul′pə·bəl) *adj.* Deserving of blame or censure. See synonyms under CRIMINAL. [< OF < L *culpabilis* < *culpa* fault] —**cul′pa·bil′i·ty, cul′pa·ble·ness** *n.* —**cul′pa·bly** *adv.*

Cul·pep·er (kul′pep′ər), **Lord Thomas,** 1635–1689, English colonial governor of Virginia 1680–83.

cul·prit (kul′prit) *n.* **1** A guilty person; criminal. **2** In old English law, one charged with crime, but not yet convicted. [< AF *cul prit,* short for *culpable* guilty (< L *culpabilis*) + *prit* ready for trial < OF *prist, prest* < L *praesto* at hand; orig., prosecutor's reply to plea of "not guilty"]

cult (kult) *n.* **1** Worship or religious devotion; especially, a form of religion. **2** A system of religious observances. **3** Extravagant devotion to a person, cause, or thing; also, the object of such devotion. [< F *culte* < L *cultus* < *colere* worship]

cultch (kulch) *n.* **1** Culch. **2** Gravel, empty shells, etc., used to form a bed to which the spawn of oysters may adhere. **3** Oyster spawn: also spelled *cutch.* [Var. of CULCH]

cul·ti·gen (kul′tə·jən) *n. Bot.* A domesticated plant species of unknown or obscure origin, distinct in its characteristics from known natural species: distinguished from *indigen.* [< CULTI(VATE) + -GEN]

cul·ti·va·ble (kul′tə·və·bəl) *adj.* Capable of cultivation. Also **cul′ti·vat′a·ble.** [< F < *cultiver* cultivate] —**cul′ti·va·bil′i·ty, cul′ti·vat′a·bil′i·ty** *n.*

cul·ti·var (kul′tə·vär) *n. Bot.* A specially cultivated horticultural or garden variety of plant, flower, etc. [< CULTI(VATED) + VAR(IETY)]

cul·ti·vate (kul′tə·vāt) *v.t.* **·vat·ed, ·vat·ing** **1** To work by stirring, fertilizing, sowing, and reaping; raise crops from. **2** To bestow labor and care upon for the purpose of aiding and improving growth. **3** To loosen the soil about (growing plants) with a cultivator, hoe, etc.: to *cultivate* potatoes twice. **4** To improve or develop by study, exercise, or training; refine; civilize. **5** To study carefully; pay special attention to; endeavor to acquire, improve, or develop by study and effort; cherish: to *cultivate* philosophy. **6** To cherish carefully the friendship or society of: to *cultivate* one's relatives. **7** To prepare a culture of bacteria. [< Med. L *cultivatus,* pp. of *cultivare* < *cultivus* tilled < L *cultus,* pp. of *cultivare* < *cultivus* tilled < L *cultus,* pp. of *colere* care for, worship] —**cul′ti·vat′ed** *adj.*

cul·ti·va·tion (kul′tə·vā′shən) *n.* **1** The act of cultivating. **2** Improvement; development; culture. See synonyms under AGRICULTURE, EDUCATION, REFINEMENT.

cul·ti·va·tor (kul′tə·vā′tər) *n.* **1** One who cultivates. **2** *Agric.* A machine for cultivating, commonly having several shares which loosen the ground and destroy weeds.

cul·trate (kul′trāt) *adj.* **1** *Bot.* Sharp-edged and pointed, as a leaf. **2** Shaped like a pruning knife, as the beak of a bird. Also **cul′trat·ed.** [< L *cultratus* < *culter* knife]

cul·tur·al (kul′chər·əl) *adj.* **1** Of, pertaining to, or developing culture: *cultural* books. **2** Resulting from breeding or artificial cultivation, as certain varieties of fruits or plants. —**cul′tur·al·ly** *adv.*

cultural lag *Sociol.* A marked retardation in the rate of development of certain features of a culture as compared with others.

cul·ture (kul′chər) *n.* **1** Cultivation of plants or animals, especially with a view to improvement. **2** The training, improvement, and refinement of mind, morals, or taste. **3** Tillage of the soil. **4** *Bacteriol.* **a** The development of micro-organisms, as in gelatin, beef tea, etc. **b** The organisms so developed. **5** Enlightenment or civilization: Greek *culture.* **6** *Anthropol.* The sum total of the attainments and activities of any specific period, race, or people, including their implements, handicrafts, agriculture, economics, music, art, religious beliefs, traditions, language, and story. **7** Those physical features of a terrain which are of human origin or construction, as roads, trails, canals, buildings, boundary lines; also, their symbolic representation on a map. —*v.t.* **·tured, ·tur·ing** **1** To cultivate (plants or animals). **2** *Bacteriol.* **a** To develop or grow (micro-organisms) in a gelatin or other medium. **b** To inoculate with a prepared culture. **3** *Obs.* To educate or refine. [< F < L *cultura* < *colere* care for] **cul′tur·ist** *n.*

culture area *Sociol.* A region characterized by similar cultural patterns among the different social and ethnic groups inhabiting it.

culture center *Sociol.* The focal district of a culture area, inhabited by communities regarded as being most typical in respect to the cultural features prevailing in the area.

culture complex *Sociol.* An aggregate of culture traits functionally integrated with some dominant community activity, such as that based on the use of horses among the North American Plains Indians.

cul·tured (kul′chərd) *adj.* **1** Possessing manifest education and refinement. **2** Cultivated. **3** Artificially propagated, as a culture of bacteria. **4** Describing a variety of pearl artificially cultivated by inserting a suitable core within the shell or mantle of a mollusk, promoting the growth of nacre around it. See synonyms under POLITE.

culture medium See under MEDIUM.

culture trait *Sociol.* Any socially transmitted element or feature within a culture.

cul·tus (kul′təs) *n.* **1** A cult. **2** State of religious, ethical, or esthetic development. [< L. See CULT.]

cul·ver (kul′vər) *n.* A pigeon or dove. [OE *culfer*]

cul·ver·in (kul′vər·in) *n.* A long cannon used in the 16th century. [< F *coulevrin* < *couleuvre* serpent]

Cul·ver's-phys·ic (kul′vərz·fiz′ik) *n.* A weed (*Veronicastrum virginicum*) from three to eight feet high, with from one to five long terminal racemes of flowers: used as an aperient and tonic. Also **Cul'ver's-root'.**

cul·vert (kul'vərt) *n.* An artificial, covered channel for water, as under a road. [Origin uncertain]

Cu·mae (kyōō'mē) An ancient city on the coast of Campania, Italy; the earliest Greek colony in Italy. Also **Cu'mæ.**

Cu·mae·an (kyōō·mē'ən) *adj.* Of or pertaining to Cumae: the *Cumaean* sibyl.

Cu·ma·ná (kōō'mä·nä') A city in NE Venezuela.

cu·ma·rin (kōō'mə·rin) See COUMARIN.

cum·ber (kum'bər) *v.t.* **1** To hinder by or as by a weight or burden; obstruct. **2** To weigh down; oppress; perplex. **3** *Obs.* To overwhelm; prostrate; destroy. See synonyms under LOAD. — *n. Obs.* **1** Perplexity; distress. **2** An encumbrance. [Cf. OF *encombrer* hinder]

Cum·ber·land (kum'bər·lənd) **1** A county in NW England on the Scottish border; 1,520 square miles; county seat, Carlisle. **2** A city on the Potomac River in western Maryland.

Cum·ber·land (kum'bər·lənd), **Duke of,** 1721–1765, William Augustus, English general; third son of George II.

Cumberland Gap A natural passage through the Cumberland Mountains between Virginia and Tennessee.

Cumberland Mountains The SW division of the Appalachian Mountains, extending from SW West Virginia to NW Alabama. Also **Cumberland Plateau.**

Cumberland River A river in Kentucky and Tennessee, flowing 693 miles west to the Ohio River.

Cumberland Road A national highway, first constructed in the early 19th century from Cumberland, Maryland, westward to the Ohio River: also *National Road.*

cum·ber·some (kum'bər·səm) *adj.* **1** Moving or working heavily or with difficulty; unwieldy. **2** Vexatious; burdensome. — **cum'ber·some·ly** *adv.* — **cum'ber·some·ness** *n.*

cum·brance (kum'brəns) *n.* **1** An encumbrance. **2** A burdened condition; trouble.

Cum·bre (kōōm'brā), **La** See USPALLATA.

cum·brous (kum'brəs) *adj.* Cumbersome. See synonyms under HEAVY. — **cum'brous·ly** *adv.* — **cum'brous·ness** *n.*

cum gra·no sa·lis (kum grā'nō sā'lis) *Latin* With a grain of salt; with some reservation; not literally.

cum·in (kum'in) *n.* **1** An annual (*Cuminum cyminum*) of the carrot family, with fennel-like leaves. **2** Its seeds, used in Eastern countries as a condiment. Also **cum'min.** [OE *cymen* <L *cuminum* <Gk. *kyminon* <Semitic]

cum lau·de (kum lô'dē, kōōm lou'de) *Latin* With praise: used on diplomas to denote the special merit of the recipient's work. — **magna cum laude** With high praise. — **summa cum laude** With highest praise.

cum·mer·bund (kum'ər·bund) *n.* A shawl or broad sash worn as a waistband; also, a girdle; a belt: sometimes spelled *kummerbund.* [<Persian *kamar-band* < *kamar* loin + *band* band]

Cum·mings (kum'ingz), **Edward Estlin,** 1894–1962, U.S. poet, author, and artist: usually written by him as **e. e. cummings.**

cum·quat (kum'kwot) See KUMQUAT.

cum·shaw (kum'shô) *n.* Something given as a present; a tip; baksheesh. — *v.t.* To give baksheesh to; to tip. [<Chinese *kan hsieh* grateful thanks]

cu·mu·late (kyōō'myə·lāt) *v.i.* **·lat·ed, ·lat·ing** To collect into a heap; accumulate. — *adj.* (*also* kyōō'myə·lit) Massed; heaped; accumulated. [<L *cumulatus,* pp. of *cumulare* heap up < *cumulus* a heap] — **cu'mu·la'tion** *n.*

cu·mu·la·tive (kyōō'myə·lā'tiv) *adj.* **1** Gathering volume, strength, or value by addition or repetition; steadily increasing. **2** Consisting of portions gathered or collected one after another. **3** Increasing or accruing, as unpaid interest or dividends, to be paid in the future. **4** *Law* Reinforcing or proving previous evidence. — **cu'mu·la'tive·ly** *adv.*

cu·mu·li·form (kyōō'myə·lə·fôrm') *adj. Meteorol.* Denoting clouds with dome-shaped upper surfaces and generally horizontal under surfaces, usually separated by clear spaces. [<L *cumulus* heap + -FORM[1]]

cumulo- *combining form* Cumulus: *cumulonimbus.*

cu·mu·lo·cir·rus (kyōō'myə·lō·sir'əs) See ALTOCUMULUS.

cu·mu·lo·nim·bus (kyōō'myə·lō·nim'bəs) *n. Meteorol.* Heavy, massive clouds rising vertically in the shape of mountains, turrets, or anvils, with accompanying sheets of fibrous appearance; thunder and shower clouds. See table under CLOUD.

cumulonimbus mam·ma·tus (mə·mā'təs) *Meteorol.* A variation of cumulonimbus having pouchlike protuberances on the lower surface.

cu·mu·lo·stra·tus (kyōō'myə·lō·strā'təs) See STRATOCUMULUS.

cu·mu·lo–vol·ca·no (kyōō'myə·lō·vol·kā'nō) *n.* A volcano characterized by the formation of steep, cumulous masses of lava near the crater.

cu·mu·lus (kyōō'myə·ləs) *n. pl.* **·li** (-lī) **1** A mass; pile; top of a heap; summit. **2** *Meteorol.* Dense clouds with dome-shaped upper surfaces and horizontal bases, seen in fair weather. See table under CLOUD. [<L] — **cu'·mu·lous** *adj.*

Cu·nax·a (kyōō·nak'sə) A town in Babylonia near the Euphrates; scene of a battle between Cyrus the Younger and Artaxerxes II, 401 B.C.

cunc·ta·tion (kungk·tā'shən) *n.* Delay; cautious slowness. [<L *cunctatio, -onis* < *cunctari* delay] — **cunc·ta·tive** (kungk'tə·tiv) *adj.*

cunc·ta·tor (kungk·tā'tər) *n.* One who delays or procrastinates.

cun·dum (kun'dəm) See CONDOM.

cu·ne·al (kyōō'nē·əl) *adj.* Of or pertaining to a wedge-shaped part; cuneiform. [<Med. L *cunealis* <L *cuneus* wedge]

cu·ne·ate (kyōō'nē·it, -āt) *adj.* Wedge-shaped. Also **cu'ne·at'ed, cu·ne·at·ic** (kyōō'nē·at'ik). [<L *cuneatus,* pp. of *cuneare* make wedge-shaped < *cuneus* wedge] — **cu'ne·ate·ly** *adv.*

cuneate lobule *Anat.* A wedge-shaped portion of the median surface of the occipital lobe of the brain. Also **cu·ne·us** (kyōō'nē·əs).

cu·ne·i·form (kyōō·nē'ə·fôrm, kyōō'nē·ə·fôrm') *adj.* **1** Of a wedge shape, as noted in the characters in some ancient Assyrian, Babylonian and Persian inscriptions. **2** *Anat.* Designating a wedge-shaped bone in the wrist, or one of three in the human foot. See illustration under FOOT. —*n.* Cuneiform writing. Also **cu·ni·form** (kyōō'nə·fôrm). [<L *cuneus* wedge + -FORM]

CUNEIFORM (*n.*)

Cu·ne·ne (kōō·nā'nə) A river in west central Angola, SW Africa, flowing about 650 miles SW to the Atlantic: also *Kunene.*

Cun·ha (kōō'nyə), **Tristão da,** 1460?–1540, Portuguese navigator and explorer.

cu·nic·u·lus (kyōō·nik'yə·ləs) *n. pl.* **·li** (-lī) **1** A small underground passage or drain. **2** The track or burrow of a skin parasite. [<L, rabbit, burrow]

cun·ner (kun'ər) *n.* A small, edible fish (*Tautogolabrus adspersus*), abundant along the North Atlantic shores of America. [Origin uncertain]

cun·ning (kun'ing) *n.* **1** Skill in deception; guile; artifice. **2** Knowledge combined with skill; dexterity. See synonyms under ARTIFICE, DECEPTION. — *adj.* **1** Crafty or shrewd; artful; guileful. **2** Attractive; bright; amusing; cute. **3** Ingenious; dexterous; made with skill: a *cunning* design. **4** *Obs.* Learned; knowing. See synonyms under ACUTE, ASTUTE, INSIDIOUS, KNOWING, POLITIC. [OE *cunnung* knowledge < *cunnan.* Related to CAN[1].] — **cun'ning·ly** *adv.* — **cun'ning·ness** *n.*

Cun·ning·ham (kun'ing·ham, -əm), **Sir Andrew Browne,** 1883–1963, British admiral.

cup (kup) *n.* **1** A small open vessel of glass, porcelain, wood, waxed paper, metal, etc., used chiefly for drinking. **2** A cupful; a measure of capacity equal to 8 fluid ounces or 16 tablespoons. **3** The ornamental vessel used in administering the sacramental wine; also, the wine itself. **4** Figuratively, one's lot in life; portion. **5** Intoxicating drink, or the habit of drinking: pleasures of the *cup.* **6** A prize, usually a vase, or a cup-shaped vessel, contended for in races: the Ascot *cup.* **7** *Med.* A cupping glass or vessel for drawing blood. **8** A small hole or cuplike depression in a course; also, a hole especially made in the putting green into which the golf ball is played. **9** Any cup-shaped object: the *cup* of a flower, an oil *cup,* etc. **10** The concave part of any drinking vessel having a base and stem. **11** A beverage made of wine, generally iced, with herbs, fruits, and vegetables: claret *cup.* **12** That curvature of a board or other flat piece of lumber which runs transversely against the rain. — **in one's cups** Intoxicated; also, in the act of drinking. — *v.t.* **cupped, cup·ping 1** To bleed, as by scarification and bringing the blood to the surface under an exhausted cup. **2** To shape like or place in a cup. [OE *cuppe* <LL *cuppa* cup, var. of L *cupa* tub]

Cu·par (kōō'pär, -pər) County town of Fifeshire, Scotland.

cup·bear·er (kup'bâr'ər) *n.* One who serves wine and other drinks to guests.

cup·board (kub'ərd) *n.* **1** A closet or cabinet with shelves, as for tableware. **2** Any small cabinet or closet.

cup·cake (kup'kāk') *n.* A cake baked in cup-shaped receptacles: formerly, most of the ingredients were measured by cupfuls.

cu·pel (kyōō'pəl, kyōō·pel') *v.t.* **·peled** or **·pelled, ·pel·ing** or **·pel·ling** To separate from base metals by cupellation. [< *n.*] — *n.* A shallow, absorbent vessel, generally of bone ash: used in assaying gold and silver ores. [<MF *coupelle* <Med. L *cupella,* dim. of *cuppa* cup]

cu·pel·la·tion (kyōō'pə·lā'shən) *n.* The process of refining gold or silver by the use of a cupel, or in a muffle furnace. [<F]

cup·ful (kup'fōōl) *n. pl.* **·fuls** The quantity held or measured by a cup; half a pint.

Cu·pid (kyōō'pid) **1** In Roman mythology, the god of love: identified with the Greek *Eros.* **2** A representation of the god of love as a naked, winged boy with a bow and arrow. [<L *Cupido* < *cupido* passion, desire]

cu·pid·i·ty (kyōō·pid'ə·tē) *n.* An inordinate wish for possession, especially of wealth; avarice. [<L *cupiditas, -tatis* < *cupidus* desirous]

cup of tea *Brit. Colloq.* That which suits one; a favorite or preferred object, activity, etc.

cu·po·la (kyōō'pə·lə) *n.* **1** A dome; hemispherical roof. **2** *Archit.* Any small structure above the roof of a building. **3** A turret on an armored ship. **4** The small hatch in the turret of certain military tanks. **5** *Metall.* A shaft furnace used for melting iron, especially that for foundry use. **6** *Geol.* The domelike protuberance on the roof of a batholith, a possible reservoir for magma. — *v.t.* **·laed, ·la·ing** To provide with a cupola. [<Ital. <L *cupula,* dim. of *cupa* tub, cask]

cupped (kupt) *adj.* Cup-shaped; concave.

cup·per (kup'ər) *n.* One who carries out the operation of cupping.

cup·ping (kup'ing) *n. Med.* The process of drawing blood to another part by creating a vacuum at that point, as by means of a cupping glass, with or without scarification.

cupping glass *Med.* A cup, generally of glass, applied to the skin in the operation of cupping. also called *cucurbitula.*

cup plant A stout herb (*Silphium perfoliatum*) of the composite family, from 4 to 8 feet high, of the western and southern United States: named from the cup formed around the stem by the upper pair of perfoliate leaves.

cup·py (kup'ē) *adj.* **1** Cup-shaped; having hollows like cups. **2** Marred, as timber, by cupshakes.

cu·pram (kyōō'prəm) *n.* A fungicide formed of ammoniacal copper carbonate. [Short for CUPRAMMONIA]

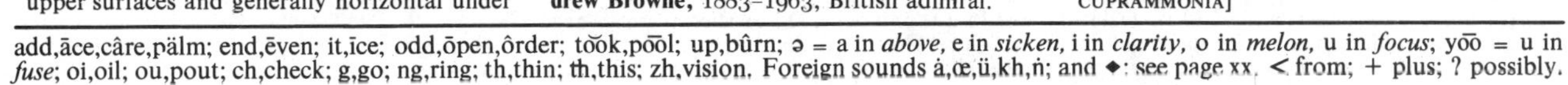

cu·pram·mo·nia (kyōō′prə·mōn′yə, -mō′nē·ə) *n.* *Chem.* Schweitzer's reagent. [< CUPR(O)- + AMMONIA]

cu·pram·mo·ni·um process (kyōō′prə·mō′·nē·əm) *Chem.* A process for making rayon by treating cellulose with Schweitzer's reagent.

cu·pre·ous (kyōō′prē·əs) *adj.* Of, pertaining to, containing, or like copper. [< LL *cupreus* < *cuprum* copper]

cu·pric (kyōō′prick) *adj.* *Chem.* Of or pertaining to copper, especially copper in its highest valence: *cupric* oxide.

cupric acetate *Chem.* Verdigris.

cupric oxide A compound, CuO, occurring in nature as the mineral tenorite and prepared by heating copper in oxygen and also by heating certain copper compounds.

cupric sulfate A white compound, $CuSO_4$, which forms blue vitriol or bluestone.

cu·prif·er·ous (kyōō·prif′ər·əs) *adj.* Yielding or containing copper. [< CUPR(O)- + -(I)FEROUS]

cu·prite (kyōō′prīt) *n.* A red, translucent cuprous oxide found in isometric crystals, and also massive, granular, or earthy: an important ore of copper.

cupro- *combining form* Copper: *cupronickel.* Also, before vowels, **cupr-.** [< L *cuprum* copper]

cu·pro·nick·el (kyōō′prō·nik′əl) *n.* Any of several alloys of copper and nickel, sometimes combined with other elements, as manganese and iron.

cu·prous (kyōō′prəs) *adj.* *Chem.* Of or derived from copper, especially copper in its lowest valence: *cuprous* oxide, Cu_2O.

cu·prum (kyōō′prəm) *n.* Copper. [< L]

cup·shake (kup′shāk) *n.* A division or shrinkage between the annual rings of timber: also called *ringshake.* [< CUP (def. 12) + SHAKE (def. 5)]

cu·pule (kyōō′pyōōl) *n.* **1** A concave or cup-shaped depression. **2** *Bot.* **a** A cup-shaped part, as the involucre of the fruit of the oak, chestnut, beech, etc. **b** The receptacle of certain fungi, mosses, and liverworts. [< LL *cupula.* See CUPOLA.]

Cu·que·nán (kōō′kə·nän′) See KUKENAAM.

cur (kûr) *n.* **1** A mongrel dog. **2** A mean or malicious person. [Short for earlier *kur-dogge.* Cf. dial. Sw. *kurre* dog.] —**cur′rish** *adj.* —**cur′rish·ly** *adv.* —**cur′rish·ness** *n.*

cur·a·ble (kyōōr′ə·bəl) *adj.* Capable of being cured. —**cur′a·bil′i·ty, cur′a·ble·ness** *n.* —**cur′·a·bly** *adv.*

cu·ra·çao (kyōōr′ə·sō′) *n.* A liqueur made by distilling spirits with macerated bitter orange peel. [from *Curaçao*]

Cu·ra·çao (kyōōr′ə·sō′, kōō′rä·sou′) The largest island in the western group of the Netherlands West Indies; 173 square miles; capital, Willemstad.

cu·ra·cy (kyōōr′ə·sē) *n. pl.* **·cies** The position, duties, or term of office of a curate.

cu·ra·re (kyōō·rä′rē) *n.* **1** A blackish, brittle, resinous extract of certain South American trees of the genus *Strychnos,* especially *S. toxifera,* used as an arrow poison, in pharmacological research, and as an adjunct in general anesthesia. **2** The plant from which this extract is abstracted: sometimes written *woorali* or *urare.* Also **cu·ra·ra** (kyōō·rä′rə), **cu·ra′ri.** [< Sp. *curaré* < Tupian]

cu·ra·rine (kyōō·rä′rēn, -rin) *n.* *Chem.* A poisonous alkaloid, $C_{19}H_{26}ON_2$, obtained from curare. [< CURARE + -INE[2]]

cu·ra·rize (kyōōr′ə·rīz, kyōō·rä′rīz) *v.t.* **·rized, ·riz·ing 1** To poison by the use of curare. **2** To administer curare to, as for paralyzing the motor nerves in vivisection. —**cu′ra·ri·za′tion** *n.*

cu·ras·sow (kyōōr′ə·sō, kyōō·ras′ō) *n.* A large turkeylike South American bird (family *Cracidae*) with naked cere and tarsi: also spelled *carassow.* [from *Curaçao*]

cu·rate (kyōōr′it) *n.* A clergyman assisting a parish priest, rector, or vicar. [< Med. L *curatus* < *cura* care, a cure] —**cu′rate·ship** *n.*

cur·a·tive (kyōōr′ə·tiv) *adj.* **1** Possessing power or tendency to cure. **2** Relating to the cure of diseases. —*n.* A remedy. —**cur′a·tive·ly** *adv.* —**cur′a·tive·ness** *n.*

cu·ra·tor (kyōō·rā′tər) *n.* **1** A person having charge, as of a museum or library; a superintendent. **2** *Law* A guardian appointed to take charge of the property of a person not legally qualified to act for himself. **3** In some European universities, a member of a board of managers. [< L < *curare* care for < *cura* care] —**cu·ra·to·ri·al** (kyōōr′ə·tôr′ē·əl, -tō′rē-) *adj.*

cu·ra·tor·ship (kyōō·rā′tər·ship) *n.* **1** A curator's office or position. **2** A body of curators collectively.

curb (kûrb) *n.* **1** A chain or strap to brace a bit against a horse's lower jaw: used to check the horse when the reins are pulled; also, a bit so arranged. **2** Anything that restrains or controls. **3** A curbstone. **4** The framework at the top of a well. **5** Originally, the street as a market for selling securities out of hours or securities not listed on the regular stock exchanges: also *curb exchange.* **6** A hard swelling on a horse's hind leg, especially back of the hock and below its point. —*v.t.* **1** To hold in subjection; control, as with reins and curb. **2** To protect with a curb. **3** To shorten and sharpen (telegraphic signals) in order to obtain more rapid transmission. Also *Brit. kerb.* See synonyms under GOVERN, REPRESS, RESTRAIN. [< F *courbe,* orig. adj., curved < L *curvus*]

curb broker A broker who buys and sells securities traded on the curb exchange.

curb exchange 1 An organization for the sale of securities not listed on the stock exchange, wheat exchange, etc. **2** The building in which this market operates.

curb·ing (kûr′bing) *n.* **1** Curbstones collectively. **2** Material for making a curb. **3** A curb or a part of a curb.

curb roof *Archit.* A roof having two sets of rafters, of which the upper slopes less than the lower.

curb·stone (kûrb′stōn′) *n.* A stone, or a row of stones, on the outer edge of a sidewalk: also *Brit. kerbstone.*

curch (kûrch) *n.* *Scot.* A woman's headkerchief or cap.

cur·chie (kûr′chē) *n.* *Scot.* A curtsy; courtesy.

cur·cu·li·o (kûr·kyōō′lē·ō) *n. pl.* **·os** One of a family *(Curculionidae)* of beetles, characterized by a prolongation of the head into a beak: many species are injurious to fruits and nuts: also called *snout beetle, weevil.* For illustration see under INSECT (injurious). [< L, weevil]

cur·cu·ma (kûr′kyōō·mə) *n.* Any of several plants (genus *Curcuma*) of the ginger family: the perennial rootstocks of *C. longa* yield turmeric, and those of *C. angustifolia* the East Indian arrowroot. [< NL < Arabic *kurkum* saffron]

curcuma paper See TURMERIC PAPER.

cur·cu·min (kûr′kyōō·mən) *n.* **1** The yellow compound, $C_{21}H_{20}O_6$, contained in the turmeric or curcuma root, of which it is the coloring substance. **2** An artificial acid dye. Also **cur′cu·mine** (-mīn). [< CURCUMA + -IN]

curd (kûrd) *n.* The coagulated portion of milk, of which cheese is made, as distinct from the watery portion or whey. —*v.t.* & *v.i.* To form into or become curd; curdle. [Metathetic var. of CRUD] —**curd′i·ness** *n.* —**curd′ly, curd′y** *adj.*

cur·dle (kûrd′l) *v.t.* & *v.i.* **·dled, ·dling 1** To change or turn to curd; coagulate; congeal. **2** To thicken. Also *Dial. cruddle.* [Freq. of CURD, *v.*]

cure (kyōōr) *n.* **1** A restoration or return to a sound or healthy condition. **2** That which restores health or abolishes an evil. **3** Spiritual care; a curacy: the *cure* of souls. **4** A mode or manner of curing anything, as hams, fish, etc. —*v.* **cured, cur·ing** *v.t.* **1** To restore to a healthy or sound condition. **2** To remedy or eradicate, as a disease or bad habit. **3** To preserve, as by salting or smoking. **4** To vulcanize, as rubber. —*v.i.* **5** To bring about recovery. **6** To be preserved, as meat, by salting or drying. [< OF < L *cura* care] —**cure′less** *adj.*

cu·ré (kyōō·rā′) *n.* In France, a parish priest. [< F, curate]

cure-all (kyōōr′ôl′) *n.* That which is asserted to cure all diseases or evils; a panacea.

cure of souls The care for the spiritual needs of the faithful, which devolves upon the clergy of the Anglican and Roman Catholic Churches.

cu·ret·tage (kyōō·ret′ij, kyōōr′ə·täzh′) *n.* The use or application of the curette.

cu·rette (kyōō·ret′) *n.* *Med.* A small instrument, usually resembling a spoon or scoop, used for removing morbid matter by scraping from a cavity, as the ear or throat. —*v.t.* **·ret·ted, ·ret·ting** To apply a curette to. [< F < *curer* cure, restore]

cur·few (kûr′fyōō) *n.* **1** An ancient police regulation requiring fires and lights to be put out at the tolling of a bell. **2** The bell itself. **3** The hour of ringing such a bell. **4** The ringing of a bell at a certain hour in the evening, still prevailing locally, as in parts of the United States and France. **5** A police or military regulation that civilians keep off the streets after a designated hour; also, a municipal order of the same tenor applying to children only. [< AF *coeverfu,* OF *cuevrefu* < *couvrir* cover + *feu* fire]

cu·ri·a (kyōōr′ē·ə) *n. pl.* **·ae** (-ē) **1** A court of justice. **2** The collective body of officials of the papal government; also **Curia Romana. 3** The court or family residence of a medieval monarch or feudal lord. **4** A tribal division made by Romulus, or its meeting place. **5** The Roman senate house or the senate of any Italian city. [< L] —**cu′ri·al** *adj.*

cu·ri·al·ism (kyōō′ē·əl·iz′əm) *n.* The political principles and policy of the papal see, especially in their exclusive tendencies; ultramontanism. —**cu′ri·al·ist** *n.* —**cu′ri·al·is′tic** *adj.*

Cu·ri·a·ti·i (kyōōr′ē·ā′shē·ī) See HORATII.

cu·rie (kyōōr′ē, kyōō·rē′) *n.* *Physics* **1** The unit of radioactivity, equal to 3.70×10^{10} disintegrations per second, of any radioactive nuclide. **2** The quantity of radon emanation in equilibrium with one gram of radium: also called **cu′rie·gram.** [after Marie *Curie*]

Cu·rie (kyōōr′ē, kyōō·rē′; *Fr.* kü·rē′), **Eve,** born 1904, French journalist; daughter of Marie and Pierre. —**Irène** See JOLIOT-CURIE. —**Marie,** 1867–1934, French physicist and chemist, born in Poland; discoverer, with her husband, of radium. —**Pierre,** 1859–1906, French scientist; husband of Marie.

Curie point *Physics* The temperature at which the transformation of ferromagnetism into paramagnetism takes place.

Curie's law *Physics* The statement that paramagnetic substances are magnetically susceptible in inverse proportion to the absolute temperature.

cur·ing (kyōōr′ing) *n.* **1** Any method of treating for preservation: said of meats, vegetables, etc. **2** A method of treating raw hides and skins so as to prevent deterioration during transport or in storage. **3** The transition of a heat-molded plastic from the liquid to the solid state without lowering the temperature.

cu·ri·o (kyōōr′ē·ō) *n. pl.* **·os** A curiosity; a rare or curious article of virtu. [Short for CURIOSITY]

cu·ri·o·log·ic (kyōōr′ē·ə·loj′ik) *adj.* Relating to pictorial hieroglyphics: also spelled *kyriologic.* Also **cu′ri·o·log′i·cal.** [< Gk. *kyriologikos* < *kyrios* literal + *logos* word] —**cu′ri·o·log′i·cal·ly** *adv.*

cu·ri·o·sa (kyōōr′ē·ō′sə) *n. pl.* Books, papers, etc., on unusual, especially pornographic, subjects. [< L, neut. pl. of *curiosus* curious, prying]

cu·ri·os·i·ty (kyōōr′ē·os′ə·tē) *n. pl.* **·ties 1** Desire for knowledge of something. **2** Inquisitive interest in the private affairs of others. **3** An interesting or strange quality. **4** Any object adapted to excite interest or inquiry. **5** *Obs.* Fastidiousness; nicety. [< L *curiositas, -tatis* < *curiosus* CURIOUS]

cu·ri·ous (kyōōr′ē·əs) *adj.* **1** Eager for information; inquisitive; prying. **2** Adapted to attract attention or excite interest; novel; odd; strange; mysterious. **3** Involving ingenuity or skill. **4** *Obs.* Fastidious; delicate; scrupulous. See synonyms under INQUISITIVE, QUEER, RARE[1]. [< OF *curios, curius* < L *curiosus* < *cura* care] —**cu′ri·ous·ly** *adv.* —**cu′ri·ous·ness** *n.*

Cu·ri·ti·ba (kōō′rē·tē′və) A city in southern Brazil, capital of Paraná state.

cu·ri·um (kyōō′rē·əm) *n.* An artificially created, intensely radioactive metallic element (symbol Cm, atomic number 96) produced by bombardment of plutonium in nuclear reactors. See PERIODIC TABLE. [after Marie and Pierre *Curie*]

curl (kûrl) *v.t.* **1** To twist into ringlets or curves, as the hair. **2** To form into a curved or spiralshape. **3** *Obs.* To adorn with curls. —*v.i.* **4** To become curved; take a spiral shape. **5** To play at the game of curling. —*n.* **1** Anything coiled or spiral, as a ringlet. **2**

Sinuosity. **3** A circling or wavelike marking. **4** *Bot.* A disease of plants, especially of peach trees. **5** *Physics* A vector differential operator used in studying phenomena of spin or rotation. [Metathetic var. of ME *crollid, crulled* curled < *crull* curly < MLG] **—curl'i·ness** *n.* **—curl'y** *adj.*

curled toe A disease of growing chicks caused by a vitamin deficiency and characterized by a twisted or flexed condition of the toes.

curl·er (kûr'lər) *n.* **1** A person or thing that curls. **2** One who plays the game of curling.

cur·lew (kûr'lyōō) *n.* **1** A shore bird (family *Scolopacidae*), with long bill and legs, as the European curlew *(Numenius arquatus)* and the Hudsonian curlew *(Phaeopus hudsonicus).* **2** Any bird superficially resembling the curlew. [< OF *corlieu, courlieus*; orig. imit., infl. in form by OF *courlieu* messenger]

curl·i·cue (kûr'li·kyōō) *n.* **1** Anything oddly curled or twisted, as in flourishes with a pen: *curlicues* made in skating. **2** A frolicsome trick; caper. Also **curl'y·cue.** [< CURLY + CUE[1]]

curl·ing (kûr'ling) *n.* A game in which the opposing players slide large, smooth, circular stones along the ice toward a goal or tee at either end.

curling iron An implement of metal, used when heated for curling or waving the hair. Also **curling tongs.**

curling stone One of the heavy stones, provided with a handle, with which the game of curling is played.

SCOTTISH CURLING STONE

cur·mudg·eon (kər·muj'ən) *n.* A miserly or churlish person. [Origin unknown] **—cur·mudg'eon·ly** *adj.*

cur·mur·ring (kər·mûr'ing) *n. Scot.* A low murmuring or grumbling sound.

cur·ple (kûr'pəl) *n. Scot.* Buttocks; crupper.

curr (kûr) *v.i. Scot. & Brit. Dial.* To coo, purr, or hoot like an owl. [< ON *kurra* murmur]

cur·rach (kûr'əkh, kûr'ə) *n. Scot. & Irish* A coracle: sometimes spelled *corrach.* Also **cur'ragh.**

Cur·ragh (kûr'ə) A plain in central County Kildare, Ireland; 8 square miles.

cur·ra·jong (kûr'ə·jong) See KURRAJONG.

cur·rant (kûr'ənt) *n.* **1** A small, round, acid berry, used for making jelly. **2** The bush (genus *Ribes*) producing it; especially, the red or white currant *(R. sativum)* and the black currant *(R. nigrum).* **3** A small seedless raisin from the Levant. ◆ Homophone: *current.* [Back formation < *Corauntz* taken as pl. in AF *(raisins de) Corauntz* (raisins from) Corinth]

cur·ren·cy (kûr'ən·sē) *n. pl.* **·cies 1** The current medium of exchange; coin or bank notes. **2** The state of being current. **3** Current value or estimation; general esteem or standing: to gain *currency* without desert. See synonyms under MONEY. **—blocked currency** Currency subject to abnormal administrative restrictions, usually in the interests of controlling foreign exchange. **—flexible currency** Currency which is regulated by existing business requirements, and increased or decreased with their demands. **—managed currency** A theoretical financial arrangement intended to stabilize currency by regulation of the standard monetary unit.

cur·rent (kûr'ənt) *adj.* **1** Circulating freely. **2** Generally accepted. **3** In actual progress, or belonging to the immediate present. **4** *Math.* Differing from point to point. **5** *Rare* Moving; running; flowing. See synonyms under AUTHENTIC. **—***n.* **1** A continuous onward movement, as of a stream; also, a fluid thus flowing. **2** That part of any body of water which has a more or less steady flow in a definite direction: an ocean *current.* See list of OCEAN CURRENTS below. **3** *Electr.* **a** A movement or flow of electricity passing through a conductor. **b** The rate at which it flows. **4** Any connected onward movement; course. **—alternating current** *Electr.* A current which periodically reverses its direction of flow, each complete cycle having the same value. **—direct current** *Electr.* A current flowing in one direction continuously, with negligible or zero changes in value. **—eddy current** *Electr.* A current produced in a solid conductor, such as the armature or polepiece of a dynamo or motor, which is wasted by conversion into heat: also called **Foucault current.** ◆Homophone: *currant.* [< OF *curant,* ppr. of *corre* < L *currere* run; infl. in form by L *currens, -entis,* ppr. of *currere*] **—cur'rent·ly** *adv.* **—cur'rent·ness** *n.*

OCEAN CURRENTS

—Agulhas current A southern branch of the Equatorial Current, which skirts the east coast of South Africa.

—Australia Current A southern branch of the Equatorial Current, which flows south and east after passing along the eastern coast of Australia.

—Brazil Current A southern branch of the Equatorial Current, flowing southward along the coast of Brazil.

—California Current A broad, cold ocean current flowing southward along the Pacific coast of North America from about 50° N. to the mouth of the Gulf of California.

—Equatorial Current A great drift of ocean waters north and south of the Equator, set in motion by the trade winds and having a general westerly direction except when diverted by coastal features.

—Guinea Current An ocean current moving eastward along the upper coast of Guinea toward the Equatorial Current of the Atlantic.

—Japan Current A warm ocean current flowing northeastwards across the Pacific from Japan to the southern coast of Alaska: also called *Japan Stream, Kuroshiwo.* Also **Black Current.**

—Kamchatka Current The northern branch of the Japan Current, which flows northeast in the direction of the Aleutian Islands.

—Labrador Current An ocean current originating in Davis Strait and flowing southward along the coasts of Labrador and Newfoundland. Also called **Arctic Current.**

—Peruvian Current A cold ocean current flowing north and east along the shores of Chile and Peru. Also called **Chilean Current, Humboldt Current.**

current density See under DENSITY.

Cur·rer Bell (kûr'ər) The pen name of *Charlotte Brontë.*

cur·ri·cle (kûr'i·kəl) *n.* A two-wheeled, two-horse carriage with a pole. [< L *curriculum* race < *currere* run]

cur·ric·u·lum (kə·rik'yə·ləm) *n. pl.* **·lums** or **·la** (-lə) **1** A regular or particular course of study, as in a college. **2** All such courses of study, collectively. [< L, a race < *currere* run] **—cur·ric'u·lar** *adj.*

cur·ric·u·lum vi·tae (kə·rik'yə·ləm vī'tē) *Latin* **1** Course of life; career. **2** A short biographical statement giving information such as one's date of birth, schooling, marital status, record of employment, etc.

cur·ri·er (kûr'ē·ər) *n.* **1** One who curries leather. **2** One who curries horses.

Cur·ri·er and Ives (kûr'ē·ər; īvz) **1** A U.S. firm of lithographers, founded in 1835 by Nathanael Currier, 1813–88, later joined by James Merritt Ives, 1824–95. **2** Any print issued by the firm, the subjects of which were scenes of American life, manners, and history.

cur·ri·er·y (kûr'ē·ər·ē) *n. pl.* **·er·ies** The trade or occupation of a currier, or a currier's shop.

cur·rish (kûr'ish) *adj.* Like a cur; snarling; mean; nasty. **—cur'rish·ly** *adv.* **—cur'rish·ness** *n.*

cur·ry[1] (kûr'ē) *v.t.* **·ried, ·ry·ing 1** To clean with a currycomb; groom (a horse, dog, etc.). **2** To dress (tanned hides) for use. **3** To beat or pummel. **—to curry favor** To seek favor by adulation and subserviency. [< OF *carreier, conreder* make ready, prepare]

cur·ry[2] (kûr'ē) *n. pl.* **·ries 1** A cooked dish consisting of meats, fish, rice, etc., seasoned with curry powder or curry sauce. **2** A pungent sauce of Indian origin, made of vegetables, spices, and strong condiments: also **curry sauce. 3** Curry powder. **—***v.t.* **·ried, ·ry·ing** To flavor with curry. [< Tamil *kari* sauce]

cur·ry·comb (kûr'ē·kōm') *n.* A comb consisting of a series of upright serrated ridges, for grooming horses. **—** *v.t.* To comb with a currycomb.

curry powder A powdered condiment, prepared from the dried leaves of an Indian plant *(Murraya koenigi),* together with other pungent spices, turmeric, etc.: used in making curry sauce and curried dishes.

curse (kûrs) *v.* **cursed** or **curst, curs·ing** *v.t.* **1** To invoke evil or injury upon; anathematize; damn. **2** To swear at; execrate. **3** To cause evil or injury to. **—***v.i.* **4** To utter imprecations; swear; blaspheme. **—***n.* **1** An imprecation of evil; any profane oath. **2** Calamity invoked or threatened. **3** A source of calamity or evil; also, the evil which comes as a result of invocation or as punishment. **4** An object of execration. See synonyms under ABOMINATION, IMPRECATION, OATH. [OE *cursian* < OIrish *cursagim* blame]

curs·ed (kûr'sid, kûrst) *adj.* **1** Under a curse. **2** Deserving a curse; execrable; detestable. **—curs·ed·ly** (kûr'sid·lē) *adv.*

cur·sive (kûr'siv) *adj.* Running; flowing: said of writing in which the letters are joined. **—***n.* A letter or character used in cursive writing. [< Med. L *cursivus* < L *cursus* < *currere* run] **—cur'sive·ly** *adv.*

cur·sor (kûr'sər) *n.* A pointer on a computer screen that shows the position where an operation is taking place.

cur·so·ri·al (kûr·sôr'ē·əl, -sō'rē-) *adj.* **1** Fitted for running or walking, as distinguished from other modes of progression. **2** Having, or executed by means of, limbs of such a character.

cur·so·ry (kûr'sər·ē) *adj.* Rapid and superficial; hasty. Also *Obs.* **cur·so·rar·y** (kûr'sə·rer'ē). [< LL *cursorius* pertaining to running < *cursor* a runner < *currere* run] **—cur'so·ri·ly** *adv.* **—cur'so·ri·ness** *n.*

Synonyms: careless, desultory, hasty, slight, superficial. *Antonyms*: careful, critical, elaborate, exhaustive, minute, painstaking, thorough.

curst (kûrst) A past tense and past participle of CURSE. **—***adj.* Of a hateful disposition; vicious.

curt (kûrt) *adj.* **1** Concise and abrupt in act or expression. **2** Short and sharp in manner; brusk. [< L *curtus* shortened] **—curt'ly** *adv.* **—curt'ness** *n.*

cur·tail (kər·tāl') *v.t.* To cut off or cut short; abbreviate; lessen; reduce. See synonyms under ABBREVIATE, RETRENCH. **—***n.* The scroll-shaped end of an architectural member. [< CURTAL; infl. in form by TAIL] **—cur·tail'er** *n.* **—cur·tail'ment** *n.*

cur·tain (kûr'tən) *n.* **1** A piece of fabric, often adjustable, hung for decoration, concealment, or to shut out light, as before a wall, window, doorway, etc. **2** Something that conceals, covers or separates like a curtain. **3** Part of a rampart that connects the flanks of two bastions or towers. **4** *Archit.* That portion of a wall between two towers. **5** In the theater: **a** The drapery hanging at the front of a stage, drawn up or aside to reveal the stage. **b** The speech or situation in a play occurring immediately before the fall of the curtain. **—***v.t.* **1** To supply or adorn with or as with a curtain or curtains. **2** To conceal or shut off as with a curtain; cover. [< OF *curtine* < LL *cortina*]

curtain call The prolonged applause which a performer acknowledges by appearing on the stage after the end of a play, scene, etc.

curtain lecture A private chiding or faultfinding, as administered by a wife to her husband: supposedly given in an old-fashioned curtained bed.

cur·tain-rais·er (kûr'tən·rā'zər) *n.* A short play or sketch presented before a longer or more important play.

curtain speech In the theater, a speech, as made by one of the actors, from in front of the curtain at the end of a performance.

curtain wall *Archit.* An outside wall that encloses but gives no structural support.

cur·tal (kûr'təl) *Obs. adj.* Cut off; short; curt;

brief. —*n.* An animal with a docked tail. [<OF *curtald*]

cur·tal-ax (kûr′təl·aks′) *n. Obs.* A cutlass. [Alter. of CUTLASS]

curtal friar *Obs.* A short-frocked friar attendant at the gate of a monastery court.

cur·tate (kûr′tāt) *adj.* Shortened. [<L *curtatus*, pp. of *curtare* shorten < *curtus* shortened]

cur·te·sy (kûr′tə·sē) *n. pl.* **·sies** Courtesy.

curtesy of England In English law, the tenure by which a man holds for life the estates of his deceased wife inheritable by their children.

cur·ti·lage (kûr′tə·lij) *n. Law* The ground adjacent to a dwelling house, and used in connection with it. [<AF, var. of OF *cortillage* < *cortil*, dim. of *cortis, cort* COURT]

Cur·tin (kûr′tin), **Jeremiah**, 1838–1906, U.S. ethnologist. —**John**, 1885–1945, Australian politician; premier 1941–45.

Cur·tis (kûr′tis), **Charles**, 1860–1936, U.S. statesman, vice president of the United States 1929–33. —**Cyrus Hermann**, 1850–1933, U.S. publisher.

Cur·tiss (kûr′tis), **Glenn Hammond**, 1878–1930, U.S. pioneer aviator and inventor.

Cur·ti·us (ko͝or′tsē·o͞os), **Ernst**, 1814–96, German archeologist and educator.

curt·sy (kûrt′sē) *n. pl.* **·sies** A gesture of civility or respect, consisting of a slight bending of the knees, and performed chiefly by women: sometimes spelled *courtesy*. —*v.i.* **·sied, ·sy·ing** To bend the knees and lower the body slightly, as a gesture of civility, reverence, or respect. Also **curt′sey.** [Var. of COURTESY]

cu·rule (kyo͝or′o͞ol) *adj.* **1** Of or pertaining to an ancient Roman magisterial chair reserved for state dignitaries. **2** Privileged to sit in the curule chair; hence, magisterial; official. [<L *curulis* < *currus* chariot]

curule chair The official seat of Roman magistrates of the highest rank: also **curule seat.**

curule dignity The right to sit in the curule chair.

cur·va·ceous (kûr·vā′shəs) *adj. Colloq.* Having voluptuous curves; shapely in form: said of a woman.

cur·vate (kûr′vāt) *adj.* Evenly bent; curved. Also **cur′vat·ed.** [<L *curvatus*, pp. of *curvare* bend] —**cur·va′tion** *n.*

cur·va·ture (kûr′və·chər) *n.* **1** The act of bending, or the state of being curved; amount or rate of bending. **2** Any deviation from a normal or expected rectilinear course: a lateral *curvature* of the spine. [<L *curvatura* < *curvare* bend]

curve (kûrv) *n.* **1** A line continuously bent so that no portion of it is straight, as the arc of a circle. **2** A bending, or something bent. **3** An instrument for drawing curves: used by draftsmen. **4** *Math.* The locus of a point moving in such a way that its course can be defined by an equation. **5** *Physics* A line representing variations in force, quantity, temperature, etc. **6** In baseball, the course given to a ball by the pitcher, causing it to curve to one side or the other before crossing the plate. —*v.* **curved, curv·ing** *v.t.* **1** To cause to assume the form of a curve. —*v.i.* **2** To assume the form of a curve. **3** To move in a curve, as a projectile or ball; bend. —*adj.* Curved. [<L *curvum* < *curvus* bent]

curved (kûrvd) *adj.* Having a different direction at every point; bent. —**curv·ed·ly** (kûr′·vid·lē) *adv.* —**curv′ed·ness** *n.*

cur·vet (kər·vet′, kûr′vit) *v.t.* & *v.i.* **·vet·ted** or **·vet·ed, ·vet·ting** or **·vet·ing 1** To prance or cause to prance. **2** To frisk about. —*n.* (kûr′vit) A light, low leap of a horse, made so that at one movement all four legs are off the ground. [<Ital. *corvettare* < *corvetta*, dim. of *corva* bent <L *curvus*]

curvi- *combining form* Curved. [<L *curvus* curved]

cur·vi·fo·li·ate (kûr′və·fō′lē·it, -āt) *adj. Bot.* Having curved leaves.

cur·vi·lin·e·ar (kûr′və·lin′ē·ər) *adj.* Formed by curved lines. Also **cur′vi·lin′e·al.** See synonyms under ROUND.

cur·vi·ty (kûr′və·tē) *n.* The state of being curved; curvature.

Cur·zon (kûr′zən), **George Nathaniel**, 1859–1925, First Marquess Curzon of Kedleston, English statesman; viceroy of India 1899–1905.

Curzon Line The demarcation line between Poland and the U.S.S.R., anchored in its center on the Western Bug: first proposed by George Nathaniel *Curzon* in 1919, altered in 1945 and again in 1951.

Cus·co (ko͞os′kō) See CUZCO.

cus·cus (ko͞os′ko͞os) *n.* Any of various arboreal phalangers (genus *Phalanger*) of Australia and New Zealand, as the **brown cuscus** (*P. orientalis*) or the **spotted cuscus** (*P. maculatus*), having long prehensile tails.

cu·sec (kyo͞o′sek) *n.* A cubic foot per second: a unit for measuring the rate of flow of a liquid. [<CU(BIC) + SEC(OND)]

Cush (kush) A son of Ham. *Gen.* x 6.

Cush (kush) A region referred to in the Bible as settled by the descendants of Cush, identified as Ethiopia: also *Kush*.

cush·at (kush′ət, ko͝osh′-) *n.* The European ring dove (*Columba palumbus*), having the neck partly encircled with a cream-colored mark. [OE *cūscote*]

cu·shaw (kə·shô′) *n.* A variety of the crookneck squash: also called *cashaw, China squash.* [<N. Am. Ind.]

Cush·ing (ko͝osh′ing), **Caleb**, 1800–79, U.S. jurist and diplomat. —**Harvey Williams**, 1869–1939, U.S. surgeon.

cush·ion (ko͝osh′ən) *n.* **1** A flexible bag or casing filled with some soft or elastic material, as feathers, air, etc. **2** Anything resembling a cushion in appearance, construction, or application; especially, any device to deaden the jar or impact of parts, as padding or inserted rubber. **3** The elastic rim of a billiard table. **4** A pincushion. **5** A pillow used in making lace. **6** The motive fluid remaining in the cylinder of a reciprocating engine after the closing of the exhaust port. **7** The fleshy part of the hind quarter of a hog, horse, etc. —*v.t.* **1** To place, seat, or arrange on or as on a cushion; prop up. **2** To provide with a cushion. **3** To cover or hide as with a cushion. **4** To pad, as with a cushion; absorb the shock or effect of. **5** *Mech.* To compress, as exhaust steam or other motive fluid, by closing the exhaust outlet of a cylinder. —*v.i.* **6** In billiards, to cause the cue ball to strike the cushion before contact with the second object ball, either before or after striking the first. [<F *coussin*, ? var. of OF *coissin*, ult. <L *coxa* hip, thigh] —**cush′ion·y** *adj.*

Cush·it·ic (ko͝osh·it′ik) *n.* A group of Hamitic languages spoken in Ethiopia and Somaliland. —*adj.* Pertaining to this group of languages. Also spelled *Kushitic.*

Cush·man (ko͝osh′mən), **Charlotte**, 1816–76, U.S. actress.

cush·y (ko͝osh′ē) *adj. Slang* **cush·i·er, cush·i·est** Comfortable; agreeable. [< CUSHION; orig. Brit. slang]

cusk (kusk) *n. pl.* **cusks** or **cusk 1** An edible codlike fish (*Brosmius brosme*) of northern seas. **2** The burbot. [Origin unknown]

cusp (kusp) *n.* **1** A point or pointed end. **2** *Astron.* Either point of a crescent moon. **3** *Geom.* A point at which two branches of a curve meet and end, with a common tangent. **4** *Archit.* A projecting point between small arcs, as in medieval tracery. **5** *Anat.* **a** A prominence or point, as on the crown of a tooth. **b** The pointed fold forming a segment of the cardiac valves. **6** *Bot.* A sharp, stiff point, as of a leaf. **7** In astrology, the first entrance of a house in the determination of nativities. **8** *Geol.* An angular, projecting beach or portion of a beach, formed by the interaction of conflicting currents. [<L *cuspis, -idis* a point]

cus·pate (kus′pāt) *adj.* **1** Having a cusp or cusps. **2** Cusp-shaped. Also **cus′pat·ed, cusped** (kuspt).

cus·pid (kus′pid) *n.* A canine tooth. —*adj.* Cuspidate.

cus·pi·date (kus′pə·dāt) *adj.* **1** Having a cusp or cusps. **2** *Bot.* Ending in a cusp, as a leaf. Also **cus′pi·dat′ed, cus·pi·dal** (kus′pə·dəl).

cus·pi·da·tion (kus′pə·dā′shən) *n. Archit.* Decoration with cusps.

cus·pi·dor (kus′pə·dôr) *n.* A spittoon. Also **cus′pi·dore.** [<Pg., spitter < *cuspir* spit <L *conspuere* < *com-* thoroughly + *spuere* spit]

cus·pis (kus′pis) *n. pl.* **·pi·des** (-pə·dēz) *Latin* A cusp.

cuss (kus) *U.S. Colloq. v.t.* & *v.i.* To curse. —*n.* **1** A curse. **2** A worthless or disagreeable person: a humorous or contemptuous term. [Var. of CURSE]

cuss·ed (kus′id) *adj. U.S. Colloq.* **1** Cursed. **2** Mean; perverse. —**cuss′ed·ly** *adv.* —**cuss′·ed·ness** *n.*

cus·so (kus′ō) *n.* **1** An Abyssinian tree (*Hagenia abyssinica*) of the rose family. **2** The flowers of this tree, used by natives as a vermifuge; brayera: also spelled *kousso, kusso.* [< native name]

cus·ta·lo·rum (kus′tə·lôr′əm, -lō′rəm) *n. Obs.* Custos rotulorum: a corruption.

cus·tard (kus′tərd) *n.* A mixture of milk, eggs, sugar, and flavoring, either boiled or baked. [Alter. of earlier *crustarde, crustade* <F *croustade*, a type of pie <L *crusta* crust]

custard apple 1 The papaw: also called **custard tree. 2** A tropical American tree (*Annona reticulata*). **3** Its soft, edible fruit.

Cus·ter (kus′tər), **George Armstrong**, 1839–1876, U.S. general and Indian fighter, killed in a battle with Indians at Little Bighorn.

cus·tock (kus′tək) *n. Scot.* The core of a cabbage; a cabbage stalk.

cus·to·di·an (kus·tō′dē·ən) *n.* A guardian; caretaker. —**cus·to′di·an·ship′** *n.*

cus·to·dy (kus′tə·dē) *n. pl.* **·dies 1** A keeping; guardianship. **2** The state of being held in keeping or under guard; restraint of liberty; imprisonment. See synonyms under FETTER. —**to take into custody** To arrest. [<L *custodia* guard < *custos* guardian] —**cus·to·di·al** (kus·tō′dē·əl) *adj.*

cus·tom (kus′təm) *n.* **1** An ordinary or usual manner of doing or acting. **2** The habitual practice of a community or people; common usage. **3** *Law* An old and general usage that has obtained the force of law. **4** Customary frequenting, as of a hotel, or habitual purchase, as of goods, staple commodities, etc., at a particular place; business support; patronage. **5** A tariff or duty assessed by law, levied upon goods imported or exported; hence, any regular toll or tax: in the first of these senses always plural. **6** *pl.* The former ritual sacrifice of human victims in Ashanti and Dahomey, on the death of a chief or king. **7** Customary rent, tribute, or service due from a feudal tenant to his lord. —*adj.* **1** Made to order: also **cus′tom-built′, cus′·tom-made. 2** Specializing in made-to-order goods: a *custom* tailor. **3** From or for customers: *custom* ore; a *custom* smelter. [<OF *custume* <L *consuetudo* < *com-* thoroughly + *suescere* become used to. Doublet of COSTUME.]

Synonyms (noun): fashion, habit, manner, practice, style, use. See HABIT, TAX.

cus·tom·a·ble (kus′təm·ə·bəl) *adj.* Liable or subject to duty or customs; dutiable.

cus·tom·ar·y (kus′tə·mer′ē) *adj.* **1** Conforming to or established by custom. **2** In English law, holding, or held by custom, as a tenant or his tenancy. See synonyms under COMMON, GENERAL, HABITUAL, USUAL. —*n. pl.* **·ar·ies** A written or printed statement of laws and customs. —**cus·tom·ar·i·ly** (kus′tə·mer′ə·lē, kus′tə·mer′ə·lē) *adv.* —**cus′tom·ar′i·ness** *n.*

cus·tom·er (kus′təm·ər) *n.* **1** One who gives his custom or trade; a purchaser. **2** *Colloq.* A person to be dealt with; a fellow: a queer *customer*; an ugly *customer*.

cus·tom·house (kus′təm·hous′) *n.* The place where entries of imports are made, vessels cleared, and duties collected; the department of customs.

customs union An association of nations that remove tariff restrictions among themselves and conduct a common tariff policy toward other nations.

cus·tos (kus′tos) *n. pl.* **cus·to·des** (kus·tō′dēz) **1** A custodian; keeper. **2** *Music* A direct. **3** The superior in certain religious houses. [<L, guardian]

custos mo·rum (môr′əm, mō′rəm) *Latin* Guardian of morals.

custos ro·tu·lo·rum (rō′tə·lôr′əm, -lō′rəm) A principal justice of an English county, who keeps the rolls or records of the sessions of the justices' court. [<L, keeper of the records]

cus·tu·mal (kus′cho͞o·məl, -tyo͞o-) *adj.* Belonging to the customs of a city. —*n.* A written collection of the customs of a city.

cut (kut) *v.* **cut, cut·ting** *v.t.* **1** To pierce, gash, or pass through with or as with a sharp edge. **2** To strike sharply, as with a whip. **3** To affect deeply; hurt the feelings of. **4** To divide, sever, or carve into parts or segments. **5** To fell, hew, or chop down, as a tree or timber: often with *down.* **6** To mow or reap, as grain. **7** To shape, prepare, or make, as gems or carvings. **8** To hollow out, excavate. **9** To trim, shear, or pare. **10** To excise; edit out. **11** To reduce or lessen: to *cut* prices. **12** To dilute or weaken: to *cut* whisky. **13** To dissolve or break down, as fat globules: to *cut* grease. **14** To cross or intersect. **15** To castrate; geld. **16** *Colloq.* **a** To ignore socially, snub. **b** To stay away from wilfully, as work or classes. **17** To divide, as a pack of cards before dealing. **18** In racket sports, to chop (the ball) so it will spin and bound sharply and irregularly. **19** To turn the wheels of, as an automobile, so as to make the vehicle turn sharply. **20** To perform; present: to *cut* a caper. **21** To grow or acquire: to *cut* a tooth. — *v.i.* **22** To cut, cleave, or make an incision; do the work of a sharp edge. **23** To admit of being severed or cut. **24** To use an instrument for cutting. **25** To grow out through the gums: said of teeth. **26** To divide a card pack before dealing. **27** In sports, to chop the ball; also, to veer sharply while running. **28** To move or proceed by the shortest or most direct route: The boys *cut* across the field. —**to cut a figure** **1** To make a fine appearance. **2** To be of importance. **3** To make an impression: to *cut a* poor *figure* in scholarship. —**to cut a melon** To divide, as large profits or gains, with one's associates. —**to cut and run** Formerly, to cut the moorings of a vessel and set sail hastily; hence, to dash off without notice. —**to cut back** **1** To shorten by removing the end. **2** To curtail or cancel, as a contract, before fulfilment. **3** In sports, to run or dash erratically; change direction suddenly. —**to cut corners** To eliminate all but the most necessary items, as clothing for a trip, expenses, etc. —**to cut down** **1** To reduce the length or amount of; shorten; curtail. **2** To kill, as with a sword. —**to cut no ice** *Colloq.* To make no impression; have no significance. —**to cut in** **1** To interrupt a dancing couple in order to take the place of one partner. **2** To interrupt, as a conversation. **3** To move into (a line or queue) out of turn. —**to cut it fine** To arrange or estimate to the narrowest degree of tolerance: He *cut it fine* when he passed that car. —**to cut loose** **1** To release. **2** To speak or behave without restraint. —**to cut off** **1** To put an end to; destroy. **2** To interrupt. **3** To intercept. —**to cut out** **1** *Colloq.* To start away with haste. **2** To displace (another); supplant, as a rival. **3** To quit or renounce, as smoking. **4** To separate from the herd, as a horse or steer. **5** *Austral. Colloq.* To complete wool shearing; to complete any task. —**to cut up** **1** To slice or cut into pieces. **2** *Slang* To behave in an unruly manner. —*n.* **1** The opening, cleft, or wound made by an edged instrument; a gash; slit. **2** A cutting motion or stroke. **3** The part cut off. **4** That which cuts or hurts the feelings. **5** A cutting; excavated passage; groove; a road made through rock or a mountain for a railroad, canal, etc. **6** A direct way, as across an angle. **7** Fashion, form, style; also, number of arrangements of facets: the *cut* of a diamond. **8** An engraved block, or an impression from it. **9** A reduction, as in rates or of written matter; also, the part thus removed. **10** A refusal to recognize an acquaintance. **11** *Colloq.* An intentional failure in attendance, as at classes in college. **12** One of the bits of material used in drawing lots: to draw *cuts.* **13** The act of cutting in card playing. **14** A stroke imparting spin to a ball, in lawn tennis and cricket; also, the spin so imparted. **15** A fancy dancing step. **16** In a strip of motion-picture film, the narrow band separating one frame or exposure from the next. **17** *Chem.* **a** The quantity of resin added to each gallon of solvent. **b** A fraction of petroleum. **18** The output or seasonal yield of anything to be cut, as grain, timber, etc. **19** A group of animals, as cows or steers, separated from a herd to be driven elsewhere. **20** *U.S. Colloq.* A share. —*adj.* **1** Formed or affected by cutting; wounded; severed. **2** Dressed or finished by a tool, as stone or glass. **3** Castrated. **4** Reduced. **5** *Bot.* Incised or cleft. **6** Diluted. [ME *cutten, kytten* <Scand.]

Synonyms (verb): carve, chop, cleave, dissect, gash, hack, hew, sever, shear, slice, sunder, whittle. See RETRENCH.

cut-and-dried (kut′ən·drīd′) *adj.* **1** Prepared and arranged beforehand. **2** Lacking suspense; uninteresting; routine.

cut-and-thrust (kut′ən·thrust′) *adj.* Intended for cutting and thrusting: said of a sword.

cu·ta·ne·ous (kyōō·tā′nē·əs) *adj.* Consisting of, pertaining to, affecting, or of the nature of skin: a *cutaneous* covering; a *cutaneous* disease. [<Med. L *cutaneus* < *cutis* skin]

cut·a·way (kut′ə·wā′) *n.* A man's coat with the front corners cut slopingly away from the waist down to the back: also **cutaway coat.**

cut·back (kut′bak′) *n.* A sharp cut in the scheduled production of raw materials or manufactured goods, due to a sudden or unforeseen lessening of demand.

cutch[1] (kuch) *n.* Couchgrass.

cutch[2] (kuch) *n. Anglo-Indian* Catechu.

Cutch (kuch) A chief commissioner's state in western India; 8,461 square miles; capital, Bhuj; on the NE border lies the **Rann of Cutch,** a vast salt waste. Also *Kutch.*

cut·cher·ry (kə·cher′ē) *n. Anglo-Indian* A hall of justice; also, any public administrative office. Also **cutch·er·y** (kuch′ər·ē).

cute (kyōōt) *adj.* **1** *U.S. Colloq.* Pretty or dainty; attractive. **2** *Dial.* Clever or sharp, especially in looking out for one's own advantage in petty ways. [Var. of ACUTE] —**cute′·ly** *adv.* —**cute′ness** *n.*

cut glass See under GLASS.

cut·grass (kut′gras′, -gräs′) *n.* A swamp grass *(Leersia oryzoides)* with flat, rough-edged leaves that cut the flesh when drawn against it.

Cuth·bert (kuth′bərt), **Saint,** died 687, English monk.

cu·ti·cle (kyōō′ti·kəl) *n.* **1** The outer layer of cells that protect the true skin; epidermis; scarfskin. **2** Any superficial covering. **3** *Zool.* A thick lining membrane, as the cell integument of protozoa. **4** The crescent of toughened skin around the base of a fingernail or toenail. **5** *Bot.* A continuous hyaline film covering the surface of a plant, derived from the layers of epidermal cells. Also **cu·tic·u·la** (kyōō·tik′yə·lə). [<L *cuticula,* dim. of *cutis* skin] —**cu·tic′u·lar** *adj.*

cu·tie (kyōō′tē) *n. U.S. Slang* A pretty young woman. Also **cu′tey.** [<CUTE]

cu·ti·fy (kyōō′ti·fī) *v.i.* To form new skin [<L *cutis* skin + -FY]

cu·tin (kyōō′tin) *n.* **1** *Bot.* A variety of fatty or waxy protective cuticle of leaves, stems, etc., of plants. **2** *Med.* A substitute for catgut or silk used in suturing wounds: it is prepared from the gut of an ox. [<L *cutis* skin + -IN]

cut-in (kut′in′) *n.* **1** The coordination of an automatic train-control system with the moving train so as to ensure application of the brakes. **2** *Printing* An insert in the text matter of a page.

cu·tin·i·za·tion (kyōō′tən·ə·zā′shən, -ī·zā′-) *n. Bot.* The modification of cell walls by the presence of cutin, making them waterproof.

cu·tin·ize (kyōō′tən·īz) *v.t.* & *v.i.* **·ized, ·iz·ing** To make or become cuticular.

cu·tis (kyōō′tis) *n.* The derma or true skin; also, the corium. Also **cutis ve·ra** (vir′ə). [<L]

cut·las (kut′ləs) *n.* A short, swordlike weapon, often curved, formerly used chiefly by sailors in hand-to-hand fighting. Also **cut′lass.** [<F *coutelas,* aug. of *couteau* knife <L *culter*]

CUTLASES
a. British, 10th century.
b. German, 15th century.
c. Mariner's, 17th century.

cutlas fish Scabbard fish.

cut·ler (kut′lər) *n.* One who manufactures or deals in cutlery. [<F *coutelier* <Med. L *cultellarius* maker of knives <L *cultellus,* dim. of *culter* knife]

cut·ler·y (kut′lər·ē) *n.* **1** Cutting instruments collectively; especially, those for use at the dinner table. **2** The occupation of a cutler. [<OF *coutelerie* < *coutelier* CUTLER]

cut·let (kut′lit) *n.* **1** A thin piece of meat from the ribs or leg, for broiling or frying. **2** A flat croquette of chopped meat, fish, etc. [<F *côtelette,* double dim. of *côte* side <L *costa* rib; infl. in form by *cut*]

cut-line (kut′līn′) *n.* The title of an illustration.

cut money Money made by cutting gold and silver coins into pieces: used in the early Spanish colonies.

cut-off (kut′ôf′, -of′) *n.* **1** A short cut. **2** A mechanism that cuts off the flow of a fuel or fluid, as of steam to a boiler. **3** The point at which flow is thus cut off; the act of so doing. **4** A channel, natural or artificial, that diverts the course of a stream.

cut-out (kut′out′) *n.* **1** *Electr.* A switchlike arrangement, as for cutting a light out from a circuit. **2** A device to let the exhaust gases from an internal-combustion engine pass direct to the air without passing through the muffler. **3** The severing of the automatic train-control system from a moving train so as to prevent application of brakes.

cut-o·ver (kut′ō′vər) *adj.* Having the timber cut off: *cut-over* land.

cut-price (kut′prīs′) *adj.* Sharply reduced in price; below the usual rate.

cut·purse (kut′pûrs′) *n.* A pickpocket.

cut rate A reduced price.

cut-rate (kut′rāt′) *adj.* Sold for, or selling goods for, reduced prices: a *cut-rate* ticket, a *cut-rate* store.

Cut·tack (ku·tak′) A city in NE India; former capital of Orissa.

cut·ter (kut′ər) *n.* **1** One who cuts, shapes, or fits anything by cutting. **2** That which cuts, as a tool or a machine. **3** *Naut.* **a** A sloop-rigged, fast-sailing vessel of narrow beam and deep draft, with bow and stern lines of the hull almost perpendicular. **b** A small, swift, armed, engined vessel, as in the revenue marine service. **c** A medium-sized boat used by a man-of-war. **4** A small sleigh usually drawn by one horse.

CUTTER (*def. 4*)

cut-throat (kut′thrōt′) *adj.* **1** Ruffianly; bloodthirsty. **2** Played by three single players: said of poker and other card games. **3** Profitless: *cut-throat* stock. **4** Ruinous; merciless: *cut-throat* competition. —*n.* **1** A bloodthirsty ruffian. **2** A cut-throat card game.

cut·tie (kut′ē) *n.* An auk: also called *black guillemot.*

cut·ting (kut′ing) *adj.* **1** Adapted to cut; edged. **2** Disagreeably penetrating; sharp; chilling. **3** Tending to wound the feelings; sarcastic; bitter. See synonyms under BITTER[1], BLEAK[1]. —*n.* **1** The act of severing. **2** Something obtained or made by cutting; a piece cut off or out. **3** *Bot.* A young plant shoot cut off for rooting or vegetative propagation. **4** An excavation, as for a railroad track. **5** *Chem.* In the making of soap, the separation of the final product from glycerol and aqueous products.

cut·tle (kut′l) *n.* **1** A cuttlefish. **2** Cuttlebone. [OE *cudele*]

cut·tle·bone (kut′l·bōn′) *n.* The internal calcareous plate of a cuttlefish: used as a dietary supplement for birds and, when powdered, as a polishing agent.

cut·tle·fish (kut′l·fish′) *n. pl.* **·fish** or **·fish·es** A carnivorous marine cephalopod (genus *Sepia*), with lateral fins, ten sucker-bearing arms, and an internal calcareous skeleton: it conceals itself by ejecting an inky fluid.

cut·ty (kut′ē, kŏŏt′ē) *Scot. adj.* Short; hasty; quick. —*n. pl.* **·ties** **1** Anything cut short, as a spoon or tobacco pipe. **2** A hare. **3** A thick-set girl. **4** A slattern.

cutty sark (särk) *Scot.* A short chemise.

cutty stool *Scot.* **1** A little stool. **2** A seat in church where offenders sat to receive public rebuke.

cut-up (kut′up′) *n. Colloq.* A person who tries to seem funny to others; a practical joker.

cut·wa·ter (kut′wô′tər, -wot′ər) *n.* **1** The forward part of the prow of a vessel. **2** The sharp edge on the up-stream side of a bridge pier.

cut·worm (kut′wûrm′) *n.* The larva of a moth (family *Noctuidae*) that cuts off young plants, usually at or near the surface of the ground. For illustration see under INSECT (injurious).

cu·vée (kü·vā′) *n. French* **1** The contents of a wine vat or cask; also, a vintage. **2** A blend of wines used in making champagne.

Cu·vi·er (ko͞o′vē·ā, kyo͞o′-; *Fr.* kü·vyā′), **Baron Georges,** 1769–1832, French naturalist.

Cux·ha·ven (ko͞oks′hä·fən) A port at the mouth of the Elbe in NW Germany: also *Kuxhaven.*

Cu·yu·ni (ko͞o·yo͞o′nē) A river in British Guiana and Venezuela, flowing 150 miles NE to the Mazaruni.

Cuz·co (ko͞os′kō) A department of southern Peru; 55,731 square miles; capital, Cuzco, formerly capital of the Inca Empire: also *Cusco.*

Cwm·ry (ko͞om′rē) See CYMRY.

-cy *suffix* Forming nouns: **1** *(from adjectives)* Quality, state, or condition of: *secrecy, bankruptcy.* **2** *(from nouns)* Rank, order, or condition of: *chaplaincy, baronetcy.* [< F *-cie, -tie* < L *-cia, -tia* < Gk. *-kia, -keia, -tia, -teia*; or directly < L or < Gk.]

cyan- Var. of CYANO-.

cy·an·a·mide (sī·an′ə·mīd, -mid, sī′ə·nam′īd, -id) *n. Chem.* A white crystalline compound, CH_2N_2, formed from calcium cyanamide or by the action of cyanogen chloride on ammonia. Also **cy·an·a·mid** (sī·an′ə·mid, sī′ə·nam′id). [< CYAN- + AMIDE]

cyanamide process *Chem.* A method for the fixation of atmospheric nitrogen by passing a current of the gas over superheated calcium carbide and treating with high-pressure steam to yield ammonia.

cy·a·nate (sī′ə·nāt) *n. Chem.* A salt or ester of cyanic acid. [< CYAN- + -ATE[3]]

cy·an·ic (sī·an′ik) *adj.* **1** Of, pertaining to, or containing cyanogen. **2** Of or pertaining to blue.

cyanic acid *Chem.* A volatile liquid compound, HCNO, with a penetrating pungent odor and caustic properties, that is stable at low temperatures only. It is prepared by heating anhydrous cyanuric acid in carbonic acid gas.

cy·a·nide (sī′ə·nīd) *n. Chem.* A compound of cyanogen with a metallic element or radical: potassium *cyanide.* —*v.t.* **·nid·ed, ·nid·ing** *Metall.* To subject to the action of cyanide: to extract gold by *cyaniding* the ore. [< CYAN- + -IDE] —**cy′a·ni·da′tion** *n.*

cyanide process *Metall.* A process of extracting metal (chiefly gold) from ores by means of a dilute potassium-cyanide or sodium-cyanide solution which, assisted by the action of oxygen, dissolves the metal.

cy·a·nin (sī·ə·nin) *n. Biochem.* Any of a group of blue pigments obtained from certain flowers, as the iris, violet, and cornflower: also called *anthocyanin.* [< CYAN- + -IN]

cy·a·nine (sī′ə·nēn, -nin) *n. Chem.* A bluish-green, crystalline derivative, $C_{29}H_{35}N_2I$, of quinoline, used in photography as a sensitizer and indicator. [< CYAN- + -INE[1]]

cy·a·nite (sī′ə·nīt) *n.* A blue, gray, or black aluminum silicate, occurring in long, bladelike, triclinic crystals, and also found columnar to fibrous in structure: often spelled *kyanite.* [< CYAN- + -ITE[1]]

cyano- *combining form* **1** *Chem.* Cyanogen: *cyanogenesis.* **2** *Med.* Characterized by bluish coloring: *cyanosis.* **3** Dark-blue; blue: *cyanometer.* Also, before vowels, **cyan-.** [< Gk. *kyanos* dark-blue]

cy·an·o·gen (sī·an′ə·jən) *n. Chem.* **1** A colorless, intensely poisonous, liquefiable gas, C_2N_2, having an almondlike odor and burning with a purple flame. **2** The univalent radical, CN.

cy·a·no·gen·e·sis (sī′ə·nō·jen′ə·sis) *n. Chem.* **1** The making of hydrocyanic acid. **2** The process by which a glucoside through hydrolysis yields hydrocyanic (prussic) acid as one of its products.

cy·a·nom·e·ter (sī′ə·nom′ə·tər) *n. Meteorol.* An instrument for measuring the intensity of blue, as in the sky. [< CYANO- + -METER] —**cy·a·no·met·ric** (sī′ə·nō·met′rik) *adj.* —**cy′a·nom′e·try** *n.*

cy·a·nop·a·thy (sī′ə·nop′ə·thē) *n.* Cyanosis. [< CYANO- + -PATHY] —**cy·a·no·path·ic** (sī′ə·nō·path′ik) *adj.*

cy·a·noph·i·lous (sī′ə·nof′ə·ləs) *adj.* Stainable with blue dyes. [< CYANO- + -PHILOUS]

cy·a·no·pi·a (sī′ə·nō′pē·ə) *n. Pathol.* A diseased condition in which all things seen appear blue or bluish. Also **cy·a·nop·si·a** (sī′ə·nop′sē·ə). [< CYAN- + -OPIA].

cy·a·no·sis (sī′ə·nō′sis) *n. Pathol.* A disordered condition of the circulation due to inadequate airing of the blood and causing a livid bluish color of the skin. Also **cy·a·no·chroi·a** (sī′ə·nō·kroi′ə), **cy′a·no·der′ma** (-dûr′mə). [< CYAN- + -OSIS] —**cy·a·not·ic** (sī′ə·not′ik) *adj.*

cy·an·o·type (sī·an′ə·tīp′) *n.* A photographic picture, as a blueprint, made with the use of a cyanide.

cy·a·nu·ric (sī′ə·nyo͞or′ik) *adj. Chem.* **1** Of or pertaining to cyanogen and urea. **2** Designating a crystalline acid, $C_3H_3O_3N_3$, obtained variously, as by the dry distillation of uric acid. [< CYAN- + URIC]

Cyb·e·le (sib′ə·lē) In Phrygian mythology, the goddess of nature: identified with the Greek *Rhea*: also called *Great Mother.*

cy·ber·net·ics (sī′bər·net′iks) *n.* The science which treats of the principles underlying the common elements in the functioning of automatic machines and of the human nervous system; the theory of control and communication in machines and organisms. [< Gk. *kybernētēs* steersman + -ICS]

cy·bo·tax·is (sī′bə·tak′sis) *n. Physics* The arrangement of molecules in a liquid in such a manner as to suggest crystal structure, but without permanence or stability at any point. [< Gk. *kybos* cube + *taxis* arrangement] —**cy′bo·tac′tic** (-tak′tik) *adj.*

cy·cad (sī′kad) *n.* Any of a small family *(Cycadaceae)* of primitive, seed-bearing, mostly tropical plants of fernlike or palmlike appearance. [< NL *Cycas, -adis* < Gk. *kykas,* a copyist's error for *koïkas,* accusative pl. of *koïx* a palm tree] —**cyc·a·da·ceous** (sik′ə·dā′shəs) *adj.*

Cyc·la·des (sik′lə·dēz) A Greek island group in the southern Aegean; total, 1,023 square miles. *Greek* **Ki·kla·dhes** (kē·klä′thes).

cyc·la·men (sik′lə·mən, -men) *n.* An Old World bulbous flowering herb (genus *Cyclamen*) of the primrose family, with white, pink, or crimson flowers: also called *sowbread.* [< NL < L *cyclaminos* < Gk. *kyklaminos, kyklamis,* ? < *kyklos* a circle; with ref. to the shape of the root]

cyc·las (sik′ləs, sī′kləs) *n. pl.* **cyc·la·des** (sik′lə·dēz) A close-fitting, often sleeveless tunic or surcoat worn during the Middle Ages. [< L < Gk. *kyklas,* a woman's garment]

cy·cle (sī′kəl) *n.* **1** *Astron.* **a** A period of time, at the end of which certain aspects or motions of the heavenly bodies repeat themselves. **b** An orbit or circle in the heavens. **2** A round of years or of ages; a vast period; eon. **3** *Bot.* An entire turn or circle, as of a spiral leaf-structure. **4** A body of legends, poems, or romances relating to one period, person, etc.; also, a series of miracle plays: the Chester *cycle.* **5** A bicycle, tricycle, etc. **6** *Math.* A closed path in a diagram; loop. **7** A series that repeats itself. **8** *Physics* A recurring series of operations, as in gas or other internal-combustion engines, in which heat is imparted to or taken from a substance, which by expansion or contraction gives out or stores up energy and is finally returned to its original condition. **9** *Electr.* A full period of an alternating current; also, a completed series of variations in electromagnetic waves of a given frequency, as in radio transmission. —*v.i.* **cy·cled, cy·cling 1** To pass through cycles. **2** To ride a bicycle, tricycle, or the like. [< F < LL *cyclus* < Gk. *kyklos* circle]

cycle car A light automobile with three or four wheels, tires, and engine of similar type and size to those of a motorcycle.

cy·clic (sī′klik, sik′lik) *adj.* **1** Pertaining to or characterized by cycles; recurring in cycles. **2** *Chem.* Of, pertaining to, or characterized by a closed chain or ring formation, as benzene, naphthalene, anthracene, etc. **3** *Bot.* Having parts arranged in whorls, as a flower. Also **cy′cli·cal.**

cyclic AMP A cyclic isomer of adenosine monophosphate.

cy·cling (sī′kling) *n.* The sport of riding the bicycle, tricycle, etc.; the art or skill of a cyclist.

cy·clist (sī′klist) *n.* One who rides a bicycle, tricycle, etc. Also **cy′cler.**

cyclo- *combining form* **1** Circular: *cyclograph.* **2** *Chem.* A saturated cyclic hydrocarbon compound: *cyclopropane.* Also, before vowels, **cycl-.** [< Gk. *kyklos* circle]

cy·clo·gen·e·sis (sī′klō·jen′ə·sis) *n. Meteorol.* The conditions which create a new cyclone or intensify the actions of a preexisting one. [< CYCLO(NE) + GENESIS]

cy·clo·gi·ro (sī′klō·jī′rō) *n. Aeron.* An aircraft equipped with airfoils designed to give support by rotating about an axis perpendicular to the longitudinal axis of the plane. Also **cy′clo·gy′ro.** [< CYCLO- + (AUTO)GIRO]

cy·clo·graph (sī′klə·graf, -gräf) *n.* **1** An instrument for drawing arcs of circles by means of two wheels of different diameters. **2** An arcograph. **3** A camera with which a panoramic view of an object may be taken.

cy·clo·hex·ane (sī′klō·hek′sān) *n. Chem.* A saturated hydrocarbon, C_6H_{12}, made by the hydrogenation of benzene and occurring in petroleum: it is composed of six methylene radicals arranged in cyclic form.

cy·cloid (sī′kloid) *adj.* **1** Resembling a circle or somewhat circular: specifically said of fish scales with concentric rings and smooth edges. **2** *Psychiatry* Of or pertaining to a personality type exhibiting marked alternations of mood. —*n. Geom.* The curve described by a point on the circumference of a circle that rolls, without slipping, along a straight line in a single plane. [< Gk. *kykloeidēs* circular] —**cy·cloi′dal** *adj.* —**cy′cloid·ism** *n.*

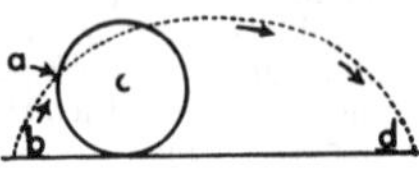

CYCLOID
As the circle *c* rolls along the straight line *bd,* point *a* on its circumference traces the cycloid *bad.*

cy·clom·e·ter (sī·klom′ə·tər) *n.* **1** An instrument for recording the rotations of a wheel to show speed and distance traveled; a speedometer. **2** A device for measuring circular arcs. [< CYCLO- + -METER]

cy·clom·e·try (sī·klom′ə·trē) *n.* The art of measuring circles. —**cy·clo·met·ric** (sī′klō·met′rik) *adj.*

cy·clone (sī′klōn) *n.* **1** *Meteorol.* A system of winds circulating about a center of relatively low barometric pressure, and, at the earth's surface, advancing with clockwise rotation in the southern hemisphere, counterclockwise in the northern. **2** Loosely, any violent and destructive whirling windstorm. [< Gk. *kyklōn,* ppr. of *kykloein* move in a circle < *kyklos*] —**cy·clo·nal** (sī·klō′nəl), **cy·clon·ic** (sī·klon′ik) or **·i·cal** *adj.* —**cy·clon′i·cal·ly** *adv.*

cyclone cellar An underground shelter adapted for use during cyclones and tornadoes. Also **storm cellar.**

cy·clon·o·scope (sī·klon′ə·skōp) *n. Meteorol.* An apparatus for detecting the approach of a cyclone or tornado. [< *cyclono-* (< CYCLONE) + -SCOPE]

Cy·clo·pe·an (sī′klə·pē′ən) *adj.* Of or pertaining to the Cyclopes or their work; gigantic; colossal.

cy·clo·pe·di·a (sī′klə·pē′dē·ə) *n.* **1** A work giving a summary of some branch of knowledge. **2** An encyclopedia. Also **cy′clo·pae′di·a.** [Short for ENCYCLOPEDIA]

cy·clo·pe·dic (sī′klə·pē′dik) *adj.* **1** Of or pertaining to a cyclopedia. **2** Like a cyclopedia; embracing a wide range of knowledge. Also **cy′clo·pae′dic, cy′clo·pe′di·cal, cy′clo·pae′di·cal.** —**cy′clo·pe′di·cal·ly** *adv.*

cy·clo·pe·dist (sī′klə·pē′dist) *n.* One who makes or contributes to a cyclopedia. Also **cy′clo·pae′dist.**

cy·clo·pen·tane (sī′klə·pen′tān) *n. Chem.* A relatively inert liquid compound, C_5H_{10}, obtained from some American and Caucasian mineral oils.

cy·clo·phon (sī′klə·fon) *n. Electronics* A type of vacuum tube in which a beam of electrons serves as a switching or commutating element. [< CYCLO- + Gk. *phōnē* a sound]

cy·clo·ple·gi·a (sī′klə·plē′jē·ə) *n. Pathol.* Paralysis of the ciliary muscle of the eye. —**cy′clo·ple′gic** *adj.*

cy·clo·pro·pane (sī'klə·prō'pān) *n. Chem.* A colorless, pungent, inflammable gas, C_3H_6, used as an inhalation anesthetic.

Cy·clops (sī'klops) *n. pl.* **Cy·clo·pes** (sī·klō'·pēz) **1** In Homeric legend, any of a race of one-eyed giants in Sicily, of whom Polyphemus was chief. **2** In Hesiodic legend, any of the three Titans who forged Zeus's thunderbolts.

cy·clo·ram·a (sī'klə·ram'ə, -rä'mə) *n.* **1** A panorama on the interior of a cylindrical surface, appearing as in natural perspective, the spectator standing in the center. **2** A backdrop curtain, often concave, used on theater stages to give the illusion of perspective; a concave plaster structure, sometimes merely a dome, used in the same way. [< CYCLO- + Gk. *horama* a view] —**cy·clo·ram·ic** (sī'klə·ram'ik) *adj.*

cy·clo·sis (sī·klō'sis) *n. Biol.* The streaming cyclical movement of protoplasm within a cell. [< Gk. *kyklōsis* a going around]

cy·clo·spor·ine (sī'klō·spôr'ēn) *n.* A drug of fungal origin, valuable for its suppressive influence on the body's natural inclination to reject organ transplants.

cy·clo·stome (sī'klə·stōm, sik'lə-) *n.* Any of a class *(Cyclostomata)* of primitive, carnivorous, aquatic vertebrates, having round, suctorial mouths devoid of jaws, and a single nostril; the lampreys and hagfishes. —*adj.* Having a round mouth; also, pertaining to the cyclostomes: also **cy·clos·to·mate** (sī·klos'tə·māt), **cy·clo·stom·a·tous** (sī'klə·stom'ə·təs).

cy·clo·stroph·ic (sī'klə·strof'ik, -strō'fik, sik'·lə-) *adj. Meteorol.* Designating the centrifugal tendency of an air mass or wind current due to the curvature of its path over the earth's surface. Compare GEOSTROPHIC. [< CYCLO- + Gk. *strophē* a turning, a twisting]

cy·clo·style (sī'klə·stīl, sik'lə-) *n.* An apparatus for manifolding manuscript. [< Gk. *kyklos* circle, wheel + STYLE (def. 7)]

cy·clo·thy·mi·a (sī'klə·thī'mē·ə) *n. Psychiatry* Manic-depressive psychosis, especially as characterized by fluctuations of mood from gaiety to depression at frequent intervals. [< CYCLO- + -THYMIA] —**cy'clo·thy'mic** *adj.*

cy·clo·tron (sī'klə·tron) *n. Physics* An apparatus which obtains high-energy deuterons by whirling a stream of electrons or ions at immense speeds in a strong magnetic field alternating in synchronism with their accelerated motion; an atom smasher. [< CYCLO- + (ELEC)TRON]

Cyd·nus (sid'nəs) The ancient name for the TARSUS.

Cy·do·ni·a (sī·dō'nē·ə) The ancient name for CANEA, Crete.

cy·e·sis (sī·ē'sis) *n.* Pregnancy. [< Gk. *kyēsis* < *kyeein conceive, be pregnant]*

cyg·net (sig'nit) *n.* A young swan. ◆ Homophone: *signet.* [< F *cygne* < L *cycnus* < Gk. *kyknos* + -ET]

Cyg·nus (sig'nəs) The Swan, a northern constellation. See CONSTELLATION.

cyl·in·der (sil'in·dər) *n.* **1** *Geom.* **a** A solid described by the circumference of a circle as its center moves along a straight line: the ends of the solid are parallel, equal circles. It is called a *right cylinder* when the line along which the center moves is at right angles to the plane of the circle, and *oblique cylinder* when the line is not at right angles. **b** Any curved surface generated by the motion of a straight line remaining parallel to itself and constantly intersecting a curve. **2** Any cylindrical portion of a machine, especially if hollow, and proportioned so that the length exceeds the diameter. **3** *Mech.* A cylindrical member of a motor in which a piston moves and receives direct impact from the steam or other motive fluid. **4** A rotating cylindrical portion of a printing press. **5** The rotating chamber that holds the cartridges of a revolver. **6** A cylindrical stone bearing an inscription; especially, an inscribed clay tablet, found buried under the corners of edifices in Babylonia and Assyria. —*v.t.* To press or fit with a cylinder. [< L *cylindrus* < Gk. *kylindros* < *kylindein* roll]

cylinder head The detachable end cover of an internal-combustion engine, comprising a portion of the combustion chamber.

cyl·in·der-stop (sil'in·dər·stop') *n.* The mechanism that locks each chamber in the cylinder of a revolver in alinement with the barrel. See illustration under REVOLVER.

cy·lin·dri·cal (si·lin'dri·kəl) *adj.* **1** Of or pertaining to a cylinder. **2** Having the form or shape of a cylinder. Also **cy·lin'dric.** —**cy·lin'·dri·cal·ly** *adv.* —**cy·lin·dri·cal·i·ty** (si·lin'dri·kal'ə·tē) *n.*

cyl·in·droid (sil'in·droid) *n.* A solid body resembling a cylinder but having elliptical bases equal and parallel. [< Gk. *kylindroeidēs*]

cy·lix (sī'liks, sil'iks) See KYLIX.

Cyl·le·ne (si·lē'nē), **Mount** A mountain group in northern Peloponnesus, Greece; highest point, 7,792 feet; traditionally regarded as Hermes' birthplace.

Cyl·le·ni·an (si·lē'nē·ən) *adj.* Of or pertaining to Hermes, who was said to have been born on Mount Cyllene; hence, relating to any of the arts or practices of which he was the patron. —**the Cyllenian art** Thievery.

cy·ma (sī'mə) *n. pl.* **·mae** (-mē) **1** *Archit.* A curved molding with a reversed curve as its profile: frequently placed above a cornice in Greek and Greco-Roman art. **2** *Bot.* A cyme. [< NL < Gk. *kyma* a wave]

cyma rec·ta (rek'tə) *Archit.* A cyma with the convex part nearest the wall.

cyma re·ver·sa (ri·vûr'sə) *Archit.* A cyma with the concave part nearest the wall.

cy·ma·ti·um (si·mā'shē·əm) *n. pl.* **·ti·a** (-shē·ə) *Archit.* A cyma; hence, any molding that caps a division of an entablature, separating it from the next. [< L < Gk. *kymation,* dim of *kyma* a wave]

cym·bal (sim'bəl) *n.* One of a pair of platelike metallic musical instruments played by being clashed together. ◆ Homophone: *symbol.* [OE and < OF *cymbale,* both < L *cymbalum* < Gk. *kymbalon* < *kymbē* cup, hollow of a vessel] —**cym'bal·ist, cym'bal·er** *n.*

Cym·be·line (sim'bə·lēn) Title of a drama by Shakespeare (1609).

cyme (sīm) *n. Bot.* A flat-topped flower cluster in which the central flowers bloom first. [< F < L *cyma* a wave, a sprout < Gk. *kyma*]

cy·mene (sī'mēn) *n. Chem.* One of three isomeric liquid compounds, $C_{10}H_{14}$, with lemonlike odor, contained in several volatile oils, as cumin, wild thyme, etc., and obtained by distilling camphor with phosphoric anhydride: sometimes called *camphogen.* Also **cy·mol** (sī'mōl, -mol). [< Gk. *kyminon* + -ENE]

cym·lin (sim'lin) *n.* A kind of squash: sometimes spelled *simlin.* Also **cym'bling, cym'ling.** [Var. of *simlin,* an alter. of SIMNEL]

cymo- *combining form* Wave: *cymometer.* [< Gk. *kymos* wave]

cy·mo·gene (sī'mə·jēn) *n. Chem.* A volatile, inflammable distillate of petroleum, consisting of hydrocarbons with a high butane content. [< Gk. *kyminon* cumin + -GENE]

cy·mo·graph (sī'mə·graf, -gräf) *n.* **1** An instrument for tracing in profile the outlines of architectural moldings. **2** Kymograph. —**cy'mo·graph'ic** *adj.*

cy·moid (sī'moid) *adj.* Of the form of a cyme.

cy·mom·e·ter (sī·mom'ə·tər) *n.* An instrument for the measurement of wavelengths and of small electrical capacities. [< CYMO- + -METER]

cy·mo·phane (sī'mə·fān) *n.* A variety of chrysoberyl with a changeable luster; the Oriental cat's-eye.

cy·mo·scope (sī'mə·skōp) *n.* An instrument for detecting the presence of electromagnetic waves.

cy·mose (sī'mōs, sī·mōs') *adj. Bot.* Bearing, pertaining to, or like a cyme. Also **cy·mous** (sī'məs). —**cy'mose·ly** *adv.*

Cym·ric (kim'rik, sim'-) *adj.* Relating to the Cymry; Brythonic. —*n.* **1** The Welsh language. **2** The Brythonic branch of the Celtic languages. Also spelled *Kymric.*

Cym·ry (kim'rē, sim'-) *n.* A collective name for the Welsh and their Cornish and Breton kin: also spelled *Cwmry, Kymry.* Also **Cym'ri.** [< Welsh *Cymry* the Welsh, pl. of *Cymro* a Welshman]

Cyn·e·wulf (kin'ə·wo͝olf) Anglo-Saxon poet of the eighth century: also *Kynewulf.*

cyn·ic (sin'ik) *n.* A sneering, captious person; a misanthrope; pessimist. —*adj.* **1** Pertaining to Sirius, the Dog Star. **2** *Rare* Of or like a dog. **3** Cynical. [< Gk. *kynikos* doglike]

Cyn·ic (sin'ik) *n.* One of a sect of Greek philosophers of the fifth and fourth centuries B.C., who held that virtue, rather than intellectual or sensual pleasure, was the ultimate goal of life: their doctrine gradually came to symbolize insolent self-righteousness. —*adj.* Belonging to or like the Cynics: also **Cyn'i·cal.**

cyn·i·cal (sin'i·kəl) *adj.* **1** Given to distrusting evidences of virtue and disinterested motives; inclined to moral skepticism; pessimistic. **2** Currish; sneering. See synonyms under CAPTIOUS. —**cyn'i·cal·ly** *adv.*

cyn·i·cism (sin'ə·siz'əm) *n.* The state or quality of being cynical; contempt for the virtues or generous sentiments of others. Also **cyn'·i·cal·ness.**

cy·no·pho·bi·a (sī'nə·fō'bē·ə, sin'ə-) *n.* An abnormal fear of dogs. [< Gk. *kyōn, kynos* dog + -PHOBIA] —**cy'no·phobe** *n.*

cy·no·sure (sī'nə·sho͝or, sin'ə-) *n.* An object of general interest or attention. [< MF < L *cynosura* < Gk. *kynosoura* the constellation Ursa Minor < *kyōn, kynos* dog + *oura* tail]

Cy·no·sure (sī'nə·sho͝or, sin'ə-) **1** The constellation of the Little Bear, which contains the North Star. **2** The North Star itself.

Cyn·thi·a (sin'thē·ə) A feminine personal name. [< L, fem. of *Cynthius* < Gk. *Kynthios* from Mt. Cynthus, birthplace of Artemis and Apollo]
—**Cynthia** Artemis or Diana; hence, the moon.

Cyn·thus (sin'thəs), **Mount** In ancient geography, a mountain in Delos, Greece, regarded as sacred to Artemis and Apollo.

cy·per·a·ceous (sī'pə·rā'shəs, sip'ə-) *adj. Bot.* Designating a family *(Cyperaceae)* of glasslike or rushlike monocotyledonous herbs, the sedge family, with solid stems and closed sheaths. [< NL *Cyperaceae,* the sedge family < Gk. *kypeiros* sedge]

cy·pher (sī'fər) See CIPHER.

cy pres (sē'prā') *Law* **1** As nearly as possible: applied in interpreting the principle whereby a gift legal in form which cannot be administered just as the testator directed, or which is not specified in a definite manner, may be applied as nearly as possible according to the donor's intentions. [< OF *si pres* as near as]

cy·press[1] (sī'prəs) *n.* **1** An evergreen tree (family *Cupressaceae*) of southern Europe and western Asia, having durable timber; especially, *C. funebris,* having pendulous branches like a weeping willow. **2** Any of various other trees of kindred genera, as the evergreen American cypress or white cedar (genus *Chamaecyparis*), and the bald cypress *(Taxodium distichum)* of the southern United States. **3** The wood of these trees. [< OF *cypres* < LL *cypressus* < Gk. *kyparissos* cypress]

cy·press[2] (sī'prəs) *n. Obs.* A transparent, black lawn fabric: also spelled *cyprus.* [< OF *Cipre, Cypres* Cyprus, whence the cloth was first imported into Europe]

cypress knee A hollow, knee-shaped growth which aerates the roots of the bald cypress.

cypress vine An annual, twining plant *(Quamoclit pennata)* with leaves pinnately parted into linear, parallel lobes, and bearing narrow, funnel-shaped, scarlet, and sometimes white flowers.

Cyp·ri·an (sip'rē·ən) *adj.* **1** Of or pertaining to Cyprus. **2** Of or pertaining to Aphrodite; hence, lewd. —*n.* **1** Cypriote. **2** A prostitute; courtesan. [< L *Cyprius* < Gk. *Kyprios* < *Kypros* Cyprus]

Cyp·ri·an (sip'rē·ən), **Saint,** 200–258, Latin church father, bishop of Carthage; martyred under Valerian.

cy·pri·nid (si·prī'nid, sip'rə·nid) *n.* A cyprinoid fish. —*adj.* Of, like, or pertaining to cyprinoids. [< NL *Cyprinidae,* the carp genus]

cyprino- *combining form* Carp: *cyprinodont.* Also, before vowels, **cyprin-.** [< Gk. *kyprinos* carp]

cy·prin·o·dont (si·prin'ə·dont, si·prī'nə-) *n.* Any of a family *(Cyprinidae)* of fishes with flattish, scaly heads; killifishes, guppies, minnows, etc. [< CYPRIN(O)- + Gk. *odous, odontos* tooth]

cyp·ri·noid (sip'rə·noid, si·prī'-) *adj.* Carplike. — *n.* A fish of the carp family, including barbels, breams, goldfishes, and many of the fresh-water minnows. [<Gk. *kyprinos* carp]

Cyp·ri·ote (sip′rē·ōt) *n.* **1** A native or inhabitant of Cyprus. **2** The ancient or modern Greek dialect of Cyprus. — *adj.* Of or pertaining to Cyprus. Also **Cyp·ri·ot** (sip′rē·ət).

cyp·ri·pe·di·um (sip′rə·pē′dē·əm) *n.* Any of a genus (*Cypripedium*) of orchids, mainly terrestrial, with fibrous roots, plaited leaves, and large flowers with pouchlike lip: called *ladyslipper* and *moccasin flower.* [<NL <Gk. *Kypris* Aphrodite + *podion* a slipper, dim. of *pous, podos* a foot]

cy·prus (sī′prəs) See CYPRESS².

Cy·prus (sī′prəs) An island in the Mediterranean, south of Asia Minor, comprising an independent republic; 3,572 square miles; capital, Nicosia: a native of Cyprus is known as a *Cypriote.*

cyp·se·la (sip′sə·lə) *n. pl.* **·lae** (-lē) *Bot.* An achenium in plants of the sunflower family. [<NL <Gk. *kypselē* hollow vessel]

Cyr·a·no de Ber·ge·rac (sir′ə·nō) də bûr′zhə·rak), **Savinien de,** 1619–55, French poet and soldier, celebrated for his large nose.

Cyr·e·na·ic (sir′ə·nā′ik, sī′rə-) *adj.* **1** Of or relating to Cyrene. **2** Belonging to or characteristic of the Cyrenaics. — *n.* **1** A disciple of the hedonistic school of post-Socratic philosophy founded by Aristippus of Cyrene. **2** A native or inhabitant of Cyrenaica. Also **Cy·re·ni·an** (sī·rē′nē·ən).

Cyr·e·na·i·ca (sir′ə·nā′i·kə, sī′rə-) The eastern division of Libya on the Mediterranean; 300,000 square miles; capital, Benghazi: also *Barca*: Italian *Cirenaica.*

Cy·re·ne (sī·rē′nē) A town in western Cyrenaica; formerly a Greek colony and capital of Cyrenaica: Italian *Cirene.*

Cyr·il (sir′əl) A masculine personal name. Also *Fr.* **Cy·rille** (sē·rēl′), *Ger.* **Cyrill** (tsü·ril′), *Lat.* **Cy·ril·lus** (si·ril·əs). [<Gk., lordly]
— **Cyril, Saint,** 376?–444, Latin church father, archbishop of Alexandria.
— **Cyril, Saint,** 827–869: called "Apostle of the Slavs."

Cy·ril·lic (si·ril′ik) *adj.* Of or pertaining to Saint Cyril.

Cyrillic alphabet An old Slavic alphabet, based mainly on that of the Greeks, said to have been devised by Saint Cyril, the "Apostle of the Slavs," in the ninth century: in its modern forms, used in Bulgaria, Serbia, and the Soviet Union. See Table of Foreign Alphabets, page 42.

Cy·rus (sī′rəs; *Fr.* sē·rü′, *Ger.* tsē′ro͞os) A masculine personal name. [<Persian, the sun]
— **Cyrus the Great,** died 529 B.C., founder of the Persian Empire.
— **Cyrus the Younger,** 424?–401 B.C., second son of Darius Notus, king of Persia, who led 10,000 Greeks against his brother, Artaxerxes II. See ANABASIS.

Cy·rus (sī′rəs) The ancient name for KURA.

cyst¹ (sist) *n.* **1** Any membranous sac or vesicle containing liquid or semisolid material: the biliary *cyst,* the urinary *cyst.* **2** *Pathol.* Any abnormal sac or vesicle in which morbid matter may be collected and retained. **3** *Zool.* A bladderlike sac, as that with which an embryonic tapeworm surrounds itself; also, a bladderworm. **4** *Bot.* **a** A receptacle for oil in the rind of the orange and like fruits. **b** A cell or cavity containing reproductive bodies in certain cryptogams. **c** The spore case of a seaweed. [<Gk. *kystis* bladder <*kyein* contain]

cyst² (sist) *n.* A chest; cist. [Var. of CIST]

cys·tec·to·my (sis·tek′tə·mē) *n. pl.* **·mies** *Surg.* **1** An operation to remove a cyst. **2** Removal of the gall bladder. [<Gk. *kystis* bladder + *ektemnein* excise]

cys·te·ine (sis′ti·ēn, -in) *n.* An amino acid, $H_7C_3SO_2$, derived from cystine. Also **cys′te·in** (-in). [<CYSTINE]

cysti- Var. of CYSTO-.

cys·tic (sis′tik) *adj.* **1** Encysted. **2** Having cysts. **3** Of or pertaining to a cyst or to the bladder. **4** Cystlike. Also **cys′tous.**

cys·ti·cer·cus (sis′tə·sûr′kəs) *n. pl.* **·ci** (-sī) *Zool.* A hydatid cyst which develops from the larva of a tapeworm and gives rise to the head and neck (scolex) of the future tapeworm: formerly regarded as a distinct genus. [<CYSTI- + Gk. *kerkos* tail] — **cys′ti·cer′coid** *adj.*

cys·tid·i·um (sis·tid′ē·əm) *n. pl.* **·tid·i·a** (-tid′ē·ə) *Bot.* A sterile, spherical cell projecting among the basidia in fleshy fungi. [<NL < Gk. *kystis* cyst + *-idion,* dim. suffix]

cys·tine (sis′tēn, -tin) *n. Biochem.* One of the amino acids, $C_6H_{12}O_4N_2S_2$, produced by the digestion or hydrolysis of proteins in the body, and isolated from the urine in the form of white hexagonal crystals. It is an important factor in nutrition. [<CYST(O) + -INE]

cys·ti·tis (sis·tī′tis) *n. Pathol.* Inflammation of the bladder. [<CYST(O)- + -ITIS¹]

cys·ti·tome (sis′tə·tōm) *n. Surg.* An instrument used in opening the capsule of the crystalline lens.

cysto- *combining form* Bladder, cyst: *cystoscope.* Also, before vowels, **cyst-.** [<Gk. *kystis* bladder]

cys·to·carp (sis′tə·kärp) *n. Bot.* The fructification from an archicarp or procarp in fungi and red algae; a sporocarp. — **cys′to·car′pic** *adj.*

cys·to·cele (sis′tə·sēl) *n. Pathol.* A hernia or rupture involving the protrusion of the urinary bladder.

cys·toid (sis′toid) *adj.* Shaped like a cyst; encysted. — *n.* A cystoid growth.

cys·to·lith (sis′tə·lith) *n. Bot.* A mineral and usually somewhat crystalline concretion in the epidermal or subjacent cells of the leaf in some plants, especially of the nettle family.

cys·to·scope (sis′tə·skōp) *n. Med.* A catheter with a device for introducing light into the bladder to permit of ocular examination. — **cys·to·scop·ic** (sis′tə·skop′ik) *adj.* — **cys·tos·co·py** (sis·tos′kə·pē) *n.*

cys·tos·to·my (sis·tos′tə·mē) *n. pl.* **·mies** *Surg.* The making of an artificial outlet from the bladder. [<CYSTO- + Gk. *stoma* mouth]

cys·tot·o·my (sis·tot′ə·mē) *n. pl.* **·mies** *Surg.* A cutting into the bladder; also, the operation of puncturing an encysted tumor. [< CYSTO- + -TOMY]

cy·tase (sī′tās) *n. Biochem.* A digestive enzyme found in the seeds of certain plants and aiding in the formation of mannose and galactose sugars. [<CYT(O) + -ASE]

cy·tas·ter (sī·tas′tər, sī′tas′-) *n. Biol.* A star-like form assumed by the nucleus of a cell undergoing division; specifically, an aster not associated with the chromosomes. [CYT(O)- + Gk. *astēr* star]

-cyte *combining form* Cell: *phagocyte.* [<Gk. *kytos* hollow vessel]

Cy·the·ra (si·thir′ə) The Latin name for KYTHERA.

Cyth·e·re·a (sith′ə·rē′ə) Aphrodite; Venus: so called from the island of Kythera, near which she is fabled to have risen from the sea. Also **Cy·the·ra** (si·thir′ə).

cyto- *combining form* Cell: *cytochrome.* Also, before vowels, **cyt-.** [<Gk. *kytos* hollow vessel < *kyein* contain, be pregnant with]

cy·to·chrome (sī′tə·krōm) *n. Biochem.* A pigment found in the respiratory cells of plants and animals, as chlorophyll, hemoglobin, and also in certain aerobic bacteria.

cy·to·di·ag·no·sis (sī′tō·dī′əg·nō′sis) *n. Med.* A diagnosis from the examination of cells in body fluids.

cy·to·gen·e·sis (sī′tō·jen′ə·sis) *n. Biol.* The formation of cells. Also **cys·to·gen·e·sis** (sis′tō·jen′ə·sis), **cy·tog·e·ny** (sī·toj′ə·nē). — **cy·to·ge·net·ic** (sī′tō·jə·net′ik), **cy·to·gen·ic** (sī′tō·jen′ik) *adj.*

cy·to·ge·net·ics (sī′tō·jə·net′iks) *n.* The scientific investigation of the role of cells in the phenomena of heredity and evolution.

cy·to·ki·ne·sis (sī′tō·ki·nē′sis, -kī-) *n. Biol.* The changes which take place in the cytoplasm of the cell during mitosis, meiosis, and fertilization. [<CYTO- + Gk. *kinēsis* motion]

cy·tol·o·gy (sī·tol′ə·jē) *n.* The scientific study of the structure, organization, and function of cells. [<CYTO- + -LOGY] — **cy·to·log·ic** (sī′tə·loj′ik) or **·i·cal** *adj.* — **cy′to·log′i·cal·ly** *adv.* — **cy·tol′o·gist** *n.*

cy·tol·y·sis (sī·tol′ə·sis) *n. Biol.* The dissolution or breaking up of cells. [<CYTO- + Gk. *lysis* a loosing] — **cy′to·lyt′ic** (-lit′ik) *adj.*

cy·tom·e·ter (sī·tom′ə·tər) *n.* A device for measuring and counting organic cells. [< CYTO- + -METER]

cy·to·mi·cro·some (sī′tō·mī′krə·sōm) *n. Biol.* A cytoplasmic microsome, as differentiated from a nuclear one.

cy·to·mi·tome (sī′tō·mī′tōm, sī·tom′ə·tōm) *n. Biol.* The cytoplasmic threads as opposed to those of the nuclear threadwork. [<CYTO- + Gk. *mitos* thread + -OME]

cy·toph·a·gy (sī·tof′ə·jē) *n. Biol.* The destruction of cells by other cells; phagocytosis. [<CYTO- + -PHAGY]

cy·to·phar·ynx (sī′tō·far′ingks) *n. Zool.* The esophageal tube of a protozoan.

cy·to·plasm (sī′tə·plaz′əm) *n. Biol.* All the protoplasm of a cell except that in the nucleus. — **cy′to·plas′mic** *adj.*

cy·to·plast (sī′tə·plast) *n.* Cytoplasm. — **cy′to·plas′tic** *adj.*

Cyz·i·cus (siz′i·kəs) **1** An ancient city at the southern end of Kapidaği Peninsula, Turkey. **2** The ancient name for the KAPIDAĞI PENINSULA.

czar (zär) *n.* **1** An emperor or absolute monarch; especially, one of the former emperors of Russia: often spelled *tsar.* **2** An absolute ruler; despot. [<Russian *tsare,* ult. <L *Caesar* Caesar, a family name later used as a title of the imperial heirs]

czar·das (chär′däsh) *n.* A Hungarian dance consisting of a slow, melancholy section followed by a quick, fiery one. [<Hungarian *csárdás*]

czar·dom (zär′dəm) *n.* **1** The territory ruled by a czar. **2** The position or power of a czar: also spelled *tsardom.*

czar·e·vitch (zär′ə·vich) *n.* The eldest son of a czar of Russia: also written *cesarevitch, tsarevitch.* [<Russian *tsarevich*]

cza·rev·na (zä·rev′nə) *n.* **1** The wife of the czarevitch. **2** Formerly the title of any daughter of the czar. Also spelled *tsarevna.* [<Russian *tsarevna*]

cza·ri·na (zä·rē′nə) *n.* The wife of a czar of Russia. Also **cza·rit·za** (zä·rit′sə). [<Russian <G *czarin*]

Czech *n.* **1** A member of the Czech Republic, descended from the people of Bohemia, Moravia, and northern Silesia. **2** The language of the Czech: formerly called Bohemian. *adj.* — **Czech′ic, Czech′ish.**

Czech Republic A republic of east Central Europe; 30,449 square miles, pop. 10,300,000; capital Prague. The Czech Republic separated from the Slovak Republic in 1993, dividing Czechoslovakia into the Czech and Slovac Republics. Formerly known as **Bohemia, Czechoslovakia** (1918–1993).

Czech·o·slo·va·ki·a A former republic of east central Europe (1918–1993): in 1918, the Austro-Hungarian Empire separated into Austria, Hungary, and Czechoslovakia: Czechoslovakia divided January 1, 1993, into two separate republics, the Czech Republic and the Slovak Republic.

Czech·o·slo·va·ki·an *n.* **1** a resident of the former Czechoslovakia. **2** The West Slavic language of the Czechoslovaks, including the Czech, Moravian, and Slovak dialects. —*adj.* Of or pertaining to the former Czechoslovakia, its inhabitants, or their language.

Cze·sto·cho·wa (chaṅ′stô·hô′vä) A city in southern Poland.

D

d, D (dē) *n. pl.* **d's, D's** or **Ds, ds, dees** (dēz) **1** The fourth letter of the English alphabet, from Phoenician *daleth,* through the Hebrew *daleth,* Greek *delta,* Roman *D.* **2** The sound of the letter *d,* usually a voiced alveolar stop. See ALPHABET. — *symbol* **1** In Roman notation, the numeral 500. See under NUMERAL. **2** *Music* **a** The second note in the natural scale of C; re. **b** The pitch of this tone, or the written note representing it. **c** The scale built upon D. **3** Differentiation or, in algebra, a known quantity. **4** Anything shaped like a D or a half circle, as the iron loop on a saddle to which articles are attached. **5** Pence (*d.,* from Latin *denarii*) in English money. **6** *Chem.* Deuterium.

dab[1] (dab) *n.* **1** One of various flounders, especially the American **sand dab** *(Limanda ferruginea)* of the Atlantic and Pacific coasts. **2** Any flatfish. [Origin uncertain]

dab[2] (dab) *Brit. Colloq.* A skilful person; an adept. [Origin uncertain]

dab[3] (dab) *n.* **1** A gentle blow; a pat. **2** A quick stroke or thrust; a peck. **3** A small lump or patch of soft substance, as butter or paint; hence, a little bit. — *v.t.* & *v.i.* **dabbed, dab·bing** **1** To strike softly; tap. **2** To peck. **3** To pat with something soft and damp. **4** To apply (paint, etc.) with light strokes. [ME *dabben.* Cf. G *tappe* footprint, MDu. *dabben* fumble, dabble.]

dab·ber (dab′ər) *n.* **1** One who or that which dabs. **2** A printers' inking ball; an engravers' pad, etc.; a dauber.

dab·bing (dab′ing) *n.* The process of indenting, as with a sharp hammer, the surface of a stone.

dab·ble (dab′əl) *v.* **·bled, ·bling** *v.i.* **1** To play, as with the hands, in a liquid; splash gently. **2** To engage in superficially or without serious involvement: to *dabble* in art. — *v.t.* **3** To wet slightly; bespatter, as with water or mud. [Freq. of DAB[3], *v.*] — **dab′bler** *n.*

dab·chick (dab′chik) *n.* **1** A fledgling; hence, an immature or delicate person. **2** A small grebe of Europe *(Podiceps ruficollis)* or the pied-billed grebe of North America *(Podilymbus podiceps)*: often called *helldiver.* [<DAB[3] + CHICK]

dab·ster (dab′stər) *n.* **1** *Brit. Dial.* A handy person; an adept. **2** *Colloq.* A dabbler or bungler.

da ca·po (dä kä′pō) *Music* From the beginning: a direction to repeat a passage or return to the beginning of a movement. [<Ital.]

Dac·ca (dä′kä) The capital of Bangla Desh.

d'ac·cord (dȧ·kôr′) *French* Agreed; in accord.

dace (dās) *n. pl.* **dac·es** or **dace** **1** A small cyprinoid fresh-water fish of Europe *(Leuciscus leuciscus).* **2** A fresh-water fish of North America *(Semotilus atromaculatus).* [<OF *darz, dars,* nominative sing. of *dart,* a small fish]

Da·chau (dä′khou) A town in Upper Bavaria, Germany; site of a Nazi concentration camp.

dachs·hund (däks′ho͝ont′, daks′ho͝ond′, dash′-) *n.* A breed of dog native to Germany, of medium size, with long, compact body and short legs, short coat, usually of red or tan or black and tan. [<G <*dachs* badger + *hund* dog]

DACHSHUND
(From 7 to 9 inches in height at the shoulder)

Da·cia (dā′shə) A region of SE Europe, corresponding roughly to modern Rumania, comprising a province of the ancient Roman empire. — **Da′cian** *adj.* & *n.*

da·cite (dā′sīt) *n.* An igneous rock, usually volcanic, composed of plagioclase and quartz, commonly mixed with hornblende, biotite, or both. [from *Dacia*]

dack·er (dak′ər) *Scot.* & *Brit. Dial. v.i.* **1** To waver. **2** To saunter. — *n.* **1** A saunter. **2** A contest. Also spelled *daiker.*

da·coit (də·koit′) *n.* A member of a robber band in India or Burma: also spelled *dakoit.* [<Hind. *ḍakait* <*ḍākā* robbery by a gang]

da·coit·y (də·koi′tē) *n.* Robbery by dacoits.

Da·cron (dā′kron, dak′ron) *n.* A synthetic polyester fiber of high tensile strength, having great resistance to stretching and wrinkling when woven into fabrics: a trade name.

dac·ry·o·gen·ic (dak′rē·ō·jen′ik) *adj. Med.* Capable of producing tears. [<Gk. *dakryon* a tear + -GENIC]

dac·ry·on (dak′rē·on) *n. pl.* **·ry·a** (-rē·ə) *Anat.* The point near the root of the nose indicating the junction of the frontal, lacrimal, and superior maxillary bones. [<Gk. *dakryon* a tear]

dac·tyl (dak′təl) *n.* **1** In prosody, a three-syllable measure consisting of one long or accented syllable followed by two short or unaccented ones (-˘˘). **2** A finger or toe; digit. [<Gk. *daktylos* finger, dactyl]

dac·ty·late (dak′tə·lāt) *adj.* Having fingerlike organs or processes.

dac·tyl·ic (dak·til′ik) *adj.* Of or pertaining to dactyls. — *n.* A dactylic verse.

dac·tyl·i·og·ra·phy (dak·til′ē·og′rə·fē) *n.* The engraving of gems for rings. [<Gk. *daktylios* finger ring + -GRAPHY]

dac·tyl·i·on (dak·til′ē·on) *n. pl.* **·tyl·i·a** (-til′·ē·ə) **1** The extreme tip or end of the middle finger when the hand is fully extended: a measuring point in anthropometry. **2** The joining or webbing together of fingers; syndactylism. Also **dac·tyl′i·um** (-əm). [<NL <Gk. *daktylos* finger]

dactylo- *combining form* Finger; toe: *dactylology.* Also, before vowels, **dactyl-.** [<Gk. *daktylos* finger]

dac·tyl·o·gram (dak·til′ə·gram) *n.* A fingerprint.

dac·ty·log·ra·phy (dak′tə·log′rə·fē) *n.* The scientific study of fingerprints. [<DACTYLO- + -GRAPHY] — **dac·ty·lo·graph·ic** (dak′tə·lə·graf′ik) *adj.*

dac·ty·lol·o·gy (dak′tə·lol′ə·jē) *n.* The use of the fingers in communicating ideas, as in the deaf-and-dumb alphabet. [<DACTYLO- + -LOGY]

dac·ty·los·co·py (dak′tə·los′kə·pē) *n.* The examination of fingerprints as a means of identification. [<DACTYLO- + -SCOPY] — **dac·ty·lo·scop·ic** (dak′tə·lə·skop′ik) *adj.*

dad (dad) *n. Colloq.* Father: used familiarly, as by children. Also **dad′dy.**

Da·da (dä′dä, -də) *n.* A movement in art and literature, about 1916–20, that declared a program of protest against civilization, rejecting all previous art by means of violent satire and incongruous humor: several of its chief exponents were later associated with surrealism. Also **Da′da·ism.** [<F *dada,* a nonsense word] — **Da′da·ist** *n.*

dad·dle (dad′l) See DIDDLE[1].

dad·dy-long-legs (dad′ē·lông′legz′, -long′-) *n.* **1** A long-legged, insect-eating arachnid of the order *Phalangida,* resembling a spider; the harvestman. **2** *Brit.* The cranefly. **3** A very long-legged person.

da·do (dā′dō) *n. pl.* **da·does** *Archit.* **1** A plain, flat surface at the base of a wall, as of a room: often decorated. **2** One of the faces of a pedestal. [<Ital., a die, a cube <L *datum.* See DIE[2].]

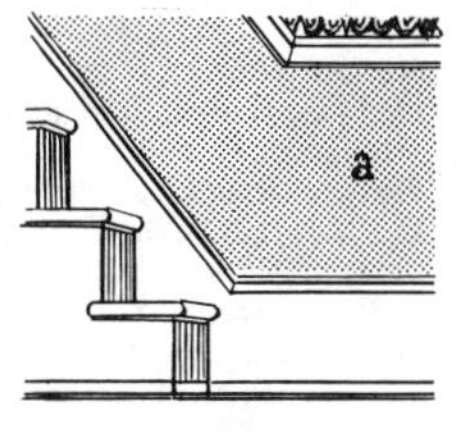

DADO
Area *(a)* between baseboard and wall decoration.

dae·dal (dē′dəl) *adj.* **1** Cunning; ingenious: a *daedal* mind. **2** Skilfully contrived; intricate: a *daedal* plan. Also spelled *dedal.* [<L *daedalus* <Gk. *daidalos* skilful, cunning]

Daed·a·lus (ded′ə·ləs, *Brit.* dē′də-) In Greek mythology, an Athenian architect and inventor who devised the Cretan Labyrinth in which he was later imprisoned with his son Icarus and from which they escaped by means of artificial wings. Also **Dæd′a·lus.** — **Dae·da·li·an, Dae·da·le·an** (di·dā′lē·ən, -dāl′yən) *adj.*

dae·mon (dē′mən), **dae·mon·ic** (dē·mon′ik), etc. See DEMON, etc.

daff[1] (daf, däf) *v.t. Obs.* **1** To toss away; thrust aside; discard. **2** To doff; take off. [Var. of DOFF]

daff[2] (daf, däf) *Scot. v.i.* To play the fool; talk foolishly. — *n. Obs.* A blockhead; idiot. [? Var. of DAFT]

daff·ing (daf′ing, däf′-) *n. Scot.* Foolery; play. Also **daff′in.**

daf·fo·dil (daf′ə·dil) *n.* A plant *(Narcissus pseudo-narcissus)* of the amaryllis family, with solitary yellow flowers. Also **daf′fa·dil′ly, daf′fa·down·dil′ly, daf′fy·down·dil′ly.** [Var. of ME *affodille* <Med. L *affodillus* <L *asphodelus.* Doublet of ASPHODEL.]

daf·fy (daf′ē) *adj.* **·fi·er, ·fi·est** *Colloq.* Crazy; daft. [<DAFF[2]]

daft (daft, däft) *adj.* **1** Silly; imbecile; insane. **2** Frolicsome. [OE *gedæfte* mild, meek] — **daft′ly** *adv.* — **daft′ness** *n.*

daft days *Scot.* The festive holidays at Christmas and the New Year.

dag[1] (dag) *n.* A loose-hanging point, lock, or shred. [ME *dagge*; origin uncertain]

dag[2] (dag) *v.i. Brit. Dial.* To drizzle.

Da·gan (dä′gän) The Babylonian god of the earth.

Dag·da (däg′thə) The chief god of ancient Irish mythology.

Dag·en·ham (dag′nəm) A municipal borough of SW Essex, England, 12 miles NE of London.

dag·ger (dag′ər) *n.* **1** A short, edged, and pointed weapon, for stabbing. **2** *Printing* A reference mark (†): the second in a series. — **double dagger** A mark of reference (‡) used in printing; a diesis: the third in a series. — *v.t.* **1** To pierce with a dagger; stab. **2** *Printing* To mark with a dagger. [ME *dag* pierce, stab. Cf. F *dague* dagger]

TYPES OF DAGGERS

dag·gle (dag′əl) *v.t.* & *v.i.* **·gled, ·gling** To trail or draggle in the mud or wet. [Freq. of dial. *dag* dampen, bemire]

Da·ghe·stan (dä′gə·stän′) An autonomous Soviet Socialist Republic in southeastern U.S.S.R.; 14,750 square miles; capital, Makhachkala. Also **Da′ge·stan′.**

dag·lock (dag′lok′) *n.* A dirty or tangled lock, as of wool on a sheep: also called *taglock.* [<dial. *dag* bemire + LOCK[2]]

da·go (dā′gō) *n. pl.* **·gos** or **·goes** *U.S. Slang* An Italian, or, less commonly, a Spaniard or Portuguese: a contemptuous usage. [Alter. of Sp. *Diego,* a personal name]

da·go·ba (dä′gə·bə) *n.* A dome-shaped Buddhist monument or shrine, built on a mound, and containing sacred relics. [<Singhalese *dāgaba*]

Da·gon (dā′gon) A national god of the Philistines and later of the Phoenicians, represented as half man and half fish.

da·guer·re·an (də·ger′ē·ən) *adj.* Pertaining to the daguerreotype. Also **da·guer′ri·an.**

da·guerre·o·type (də·ger′ə·tīp′, -ē·ə·tīp′) *n.* **1** An early photographic process using silver-coated, light-sensitive metallic plates developed by mercury vapor. **2** A picture made by this process. [after Louis Jacques Mandé *Daguerre,* 1789–1851, French inventor, +

TYPE] —**da·guerre′o·typ′er, da·guerre′o·typ′·ist** *n.* —**da·guerre′o·typ′y** *n.*

da·ha·be·ah (dä′hə·bē′ə) *n.* A passenger boat of the Nile, having a sharp prow and a broad stern, originally equipped with lateen sails, and now generally propelled by engines. Also **da′ha·bi′eh, da′ha·biy′eh.** [< Arabic *dhahabīyah* golden < *dhahab* gold; with ref. to the gilded royal Egyptian barges]

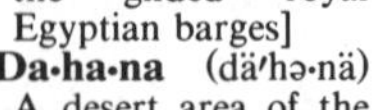

DAHABEAH

Da·ha·na (dä′hə·nä) A desert area of the Arabian Peninsula, comprising a region of east central Arabia. Also **Dah′na.**

Dahl·gren (dal′grən), **John A.,** 1809–70, U.S. rear admiral; inventor of a smooth-bored gun used by the Union navy in the Civil War.

dahl·ia (dal′yə, däl′-, dāl′-) *n.* **1** A tender perennial herb (genus *Dahlia*) of the composite family, having tuberous roots and showy red, purple, yellow, or white flowers. **2** The flower or root of this herb. [after Anders *Dahl,* 18th c. Swedish botanist]

Da·ho·mey (də·hō′mē) See BENIN.

da·hoon (də·ho͞on′) *n.* A small evergreen tree *(Ilex cassine)* of the holly family, found in the southern United States. [Origin uncertain]

dail (dāl) *n. Scot.* Deal[1].

Dail Ei·reann (dôl âr′ən) The lower house of the legislature of Ireland.

dai·ly (dā′lē) *adj.* Occurring, appearing, or pertaining to every day; diurnal. —*n. pl.* **·lies** A daily publication. —*adv.* Day after day; on every day. [OE *dæglic* < *dæg* day]

Synonym (adj.): diurnal. *Daily* is the native English and popular term, *diurnal* the Latin and scientific term. In strict usage, *daily* is the antonym of *nightly* as *diurnal* is of *nocturnal. Daily* is not, however, held strictly to this use; a physician makes *daily* visits if he calls at some time within each period of twenty-four hours. *Diurnal* is more exact in all its uses; a *diurnal* flower opens or blooms only in daylight; a *diurnal* bird or animal flies or ranges only by day: in contradistinction to *nocturnal* flowers, birds, etc. A *diurnal* motion exactly fills an astronomical day or the time of one rotation of a planet on its axis, while a *daily* motion is much less definite. *Antonyms*: nightly, nocturnal.

daily double In horse racing, a single bet, the winning of which depends upon choosing the winner in two specified races.

dai·men (dā′min) *adj. Scot.* Occasional; scattered.

dai·mio (dī′myō) *n.* **1** The former class of hereditary feudal barons in Japan. **2** A member of this class. Also **dai′myo.** [< Japanese < Chinese *dai* great + *mio, myo* name] —**dai·mi·ate** (dī′mē·āt) *n.*

dai·mon (dī′mōn), **dai·mon·ic** (dī·mon′ik), etc. See DEMON, etc.

Dai Nip·pon (dī nēp·pōn) A Japanese name for JAPAN.

dain·ty (dān′tē) *adj.* **·ti·er, ·ti·est 1** Refined or delicate in taste. **2** Delicious; agreeable to the taste. **3** Charming in appearance; pretty. **4** Overly nice; fastidious. [< *n.*] —*n. pl.* **·ties** Something choice, delicate, or delicious. See synonyms under CHOICE, DELICIOUS, ELEGANT, FINE, SQUEAMISH. [< OF *daintié* < L *dignitas, -tatis.* Doublet of DIGNITY.] —**dain′ti·ly** *adv.* —**dain′ti·ness** *n.*

dai·qui·ri (dī′kər·ē, dak′ər·ē) *n.* A cocktail made of rum, lime or lemon juice, and sugar, mixed and chilled. [from *Daiquirí,* Cuba, where the rum originally used for the drink was made]

Dai·ren (dī′ren′) A port at the southern tip of Liaotung Peninsula, Southern Manchuria: Russian *Dalny,* Chinese *Talien.*

dair·y (dâr′ē) *n. pl.* **dair·ies 1** A place where milk and cream are kept and made into butter and cheese. **2** A place for the sale of milk products. **3** A dairy farm. **4** A herd of milk cattle. **5** The business of dealing in such products. [ME *deierie* < *deie* dairymaid < OE *dæge*]

dairy cattle Cows of a breed specially adapted for milk production. Also **dairy cows.**

dairy farm A farm devoted to producing dairy products.

dair·y·ing (dâr′ē·ing) *n.* The business of conducting a dairy farm or a dairy.

dair·y·maid (dâr′ē·mād′) *n.* A woman or girl who works in a dairy.

dair·y·man (dâr′ē·mən) *n. pl.* **·men** (-mən) A man who works in, or for, or keeps a dairy.

da·is (dā′is, dās) *n.* **1** A raised platform in a room. **2** A seat on a dais or against a wall. [< OF *deis* < LL *discus.* Doublet of DESK, DISH, DISK.]

dai·sy (dā′zē) *n. pl.* **dai·sies 1** A low European herb *(Bellis perennis)* of the composite family, having a yellow disk with white or rose-colored rays; the English daisy. **2** A common American field flower, the oxeye daisy *(Chrysanthemum leucanthemum)*: also called *whiteweed.* **3** *Slang* Any very fine, excellent person or thing. [OE *dæges ēage* day's eye] —**dai′sied** *adj.*

Dai·sy (dā′zē) A feminine personal name.

Daisy Millerism Unconventional behavior on the part of women. [after *Daisy Miller,* the unconventional heroine and title character of a novel (1879) by Henry James]

dak (dôk, däk) *n. Anglo-Indian* The East Indian post or inland mail: a relay of palanquin-bearers, running footmen, or horses for the service of travelers: also spelled *dawk.* [< Hind. *dāk*]

Da·kar (dä·kär′, də-) The capital of the Republic of Senegal; a port on Cape Verde.

da·ker·hen (dā′kər·hen′) *n.* The corn crake.

dakh·ma (däk′mə) See TOWER OF SILENCE.

Da·kin's solution (dā′kinz) *Med.* An antiseptic of sodium carbonate dissolved in water, to which chlorinated lime and boric acid are added, forming a neutral sodium hypochlorite solution. [after Henry Drysdale *Dakin,* 1880–1952, U.S. chemist]

da·koit (də·koit′) See DACOIT.

Da·ko·ta (də·kō′tə) A former territory of the United States, comprising what is now North and South Dakota.

Da·ko·ta (də·kō′tə) *n.* **1** A member of the largest division of the Siouan linguistic stock of North American Indians; a Sioux; one of the Plains Indians: now on reservations in North and South Dakota, Minnesota, and Montana. **2** The Siouan language of the Dakotas. —**Da·ko′tan** *adj.* & *n.*

Dakota River See JAMES RIVER (def. 2).

Da·la·dier (dȧ·lȧ·dyā′), **Edouard,** 1884–1970, French politician and statesman, premier 1938–40.

Da·lai La·ma (dä·lī′ lä′mə) The principal one of the two major lamas of Tibet and Mongolia, the other being known as the *Tesho Lama*: often called *Grand Lama.* Also **da·lai′.**

dale (dāl) *n.* A small valley. [OE *dæl.* Akin to DELL.]

Dale (dāl), **Sir Henry Hallett,** 1875–1968, English physiologist. —**Sir Thomas,** died 1619, English governor of Virginia.

Da·lén (dä·lān′), **Nils Gustaf,** 1869–1937, Swedish engineer.

dales·man (dālz′mən) *n. pl.* **·men** (-mən) One living in a dale, especially in the north of England.

da·leth (dä′ləth) The fourth Hebrew letter. See ALPHABET.

Dal·hou·sie (dal·ho͞o′zē), **Earl of,** 1770–1838, George Ramsay, Scottish general; colonial governor of Canada 1819–28. —**Marquis of,** 1812–60, James Andrew Ramsay, British governor general of India 1848–56; son of the preceding.

Da·li (dä′lē), **Salvador,** born 1904, Spanish surrealist painter.

Dal·la·pi·co·la (däl′ä·pē′kō·lä), **Luigi,** 1904–75, Italian pianist and composer.

Dal·las (dal′əs) A city in northern Texas.

Dal·las (dal′əs), **George Mifflin,** 1792–1864, vice president of the United States 1845–49.

dalles (dalz) *n. pl.* In the western United States, rapids running between steep rock walls; also, steep rock walls on either side of a ravine. [< F *dalle* trough, gutter]

dal·li·ance (dal′ē·əns) *n.* The act of dallying; frivolous or flirtatious action.

dal·ly (dal′ē) *v.* **dal·lied, dal·ly·ing** *v.i.* **1** To make love sportively; frolic. **2** To toy with; trifle; flirt: to *dally* with death. **3** To waste time. —*v.t.* **4** To waste (time): with *away.* [< OF *dalier* converse, chat] —**dal′li·er** *n.*

Dal·ma·tia (dal·mā′shə) A region of Croatia, between the Adriatic Sea and Bosnia and Herzegovina; formerly a titular kingdom under Austrian control. *Serbo-Croatian* **Dal·ma·ci·ja** (däl·mä′tsē·yä). —**Dal·ma′tian** *adj.* & *n.*

Dal·ma·tian (dal·mā′shən) *n.* A large, short-haired dog, white with black spots: also called *carriage dog, coach dog, English coach dog.*

dal·mat·ic (dal·mat′ik) *n.* **1** A wide-sleeved tunic, worn over the alb and cassock by the deacon at high mass. **2** A medieval state robe. [< OF *dalmatique* < L *dalmatica (vestis)* Dalmatian (robe) < *Dalmatia* Dalmatia]

Dal·ny (däl′y·nyi) The Russian name for DAIREN.

Dal·rym·ple (dal·rim′pəl, dal′rim′pəl), **James,** 1619–95, Viscount Stair, Scottish jurist and historian. —**John,** 1673–1747, second Earl of Stair, English general and diplomat.

dal se·gno (däl sā′nyō) *Music* From the sign: a direction to return and repeat to the end from the sign :S:. Abbr. *D.S.* [< Ital., from the sign]

dal·ton (dôl′tən) *n. Physics* The unit of atomic mass, equal to 1/12 of the mass of an atom of carbon of mass number 12, or approximately 1.6604×10^{-24} gram. [after John *Dalton*]

Dal·ton (dôl′tən), **John,** 1766–1844, English chemist and physicist; discoverer of colorblindness; originator of the modern atomic theory.

Dal·to·ni·an (dôl·tō′nē·ən) *adj.* Of or pertaining to John Dalton or his atomic theory.

dal·ton·ism (dôl′tən·iz′əm) *n.* Colorblindness, especially to the colors red and green. [after John *Dalton*]

Dalton plan In elementary and secondary education, a system of individual instruction in which a student organizes his own assignments and advances as fast as his ability allows. [from *Dalton,* Mass., where it was first used]

Dalton's law 1 *Chem.* The statement that the elements forming more than one compound unite in amounts which bear a simple multiple relationship to each other. **2** *Physics* The statement that the total pressure of a mixture of gases equals the sum of the partial pressures of each constituent regarded as occupying alone the same volume at the same temperature.

Da·ly (dā′lē), **John Augustin,** 1838–99, U.S. playwright and theatrical manager.

dam[1] (dam) *n.* **1** A barrier to check the flow of a stream. **2** The water held up by a dam. **3** Any barrier for preventing the passage of water, air, or gas. **4** Figuratively, any obstruction. —*v.t.* **dammed, dam·ming 1** To erect a dam in; stop or obstruct by a dam. **2** To keep back; restrain: with *up* or *in.* [< MDu. *damm*]

dam[2] (dam) *n.* A female parent: said of animals. [Var. of *dame*]

Dam (däm), **(Carl Peter) Henrik,** 1895–1976, Danish biochemist.

dam·age (dam′ij) *n.* **1** Destruction or impairment of value; injury; harm. **2** *pl. Law* Money recoverable for a wrong or an injury. See synonyms under INJURY, LOSS. —*v.* **dam·aged, dam·ag·ing** *v.t.* To cause damage to; impair the usefulness or value of. —*v.i.* To be susceptible to damage. See synonyms under ABUSE, HURT. [< OF *dam* loss < L *damnum*] —**dam′age·a·ble** *adj.*

dam·an (dam′ən) *n.* A small, hyracoidean, hoofed mammal (genus *Procavia*) with rhinoceros-like molar teeth, especially *P. syriaca* of Asia Minor. [< Arabic *damān isrāīl* sheep of Israel]

Da·man·hur (dä′män·ho͞or′) A town in Lower Egypt.

Da·mão (də·mouń′) A district of Portuguese India, comprising the region of Damão on the NW coast of India, with the dependent territories of **Da·drá** (də·drä′) and **Na·gar-A·ve·li** (nu·gûr′·ä·vä′lē); total 176 square miles; capital, Damão. Also **Da·man** (də·män′).

Da·ma·ra (dä·mä′rə, də-) *n.* A native of Damaraland.

Da·ma·ra·land (dä·mä′rə·land′, də-) A region in central South-West Africa.

dam·as·cene (dam′ə·sēn, dam′ə·sēn′) *v.t.* **·cened, ·cen·ing** To ornament (metal, iron, steel, etc.) with wavy or variegated patterns. Also **dam·as·keen** (dam′ə·skēn, dam′ə·skēn′). —*adj.* Relating to damascening. —*n.* Work ornamented by damascening.

Dam·a·sce·nus (dam′ə·sē′nəs), **Johannes** See JOHN OF DAMASCUS.

Da·mas·cus (də·mas′kəs) An ancient city, capital of Syria. *Arabic* **Es Sham** (ash sham′), *French* **Da·mas** (dȧ·mäs′). —**Dam·as·cene** (dam′ə·sēn, dam′ə·sēn′) *adj.* & *n.*

Damascus blade A sword or dagger blade made in Damascus, or like those once made there, celebrated for the excellence of its steel, and distinguished by wavy and variegated ornamentation.

Damascus steel The steel formerly used in making swords at Damascus; also, any steel having damascene markings.

dam·ask (dam′əsk) *n.* 1 A rich silk, linen, or wool fabric woven in elaborate patterns. 2 A fine table linen, so woven that two sets of parallel threads on the surface give the pattern different aspects from different points of view. 3 Damascus steel or Damascus work. 4 A deep pink or rose color. —*adj.* 1 Of, pertaining to, or from Damascus. 2 Made of damask steel or fabric. 3 Of the color of damask. —*v.t.* 1 To damascene. 2 To weave or ornament with rich patterns. 3 To make deep pink or rose in color. [from *Damascus*]

damask rose A large pink rose (*Rosa damascena*) of the Near East, noted for its fragrance.

dam·bo·nite (dam′bə·nīt) *n.* A white crystalline compound, $C_8H_{16}O_6$, contained in certain forms of caoutchouc. Also **dam·bon·i·tol** (dam·bon′ə·tōl, -tôl). [< native African *n'dambo,* the tree which produces it + -ITE[1]]

dame (dām) *n.* 1 A woman of high social position; a lady. 2 A married or mature woman; matron. 3 *Archaic* A schoolmistress. 4 A title of address for the lady recipients of the Grand Cross (suffix, G.B.E.), or for the Dames Commanders (suffix, D.B.E.) of the Order of the British Empire, created in 1917. See under ORDER (*n.* def. 9). 5 A female parent or ancestress. 6 *Slang* Any woman. [<OF <L *domina* lady, fem. of *dominus* master. Doublet of DUENNA.]

dame·wort (dām′wûrt′) *n.* A coarse herb of the mustard family (*Hesperis matronalis*), with lanceolate, toothed leaves and fragrant lilac to deep-mauve flowers: also called *dame violet, dame rocket.*

dam·i·an·a (dam′ē·an′ə, -ē·ā′nə) *n.* The leaves of a Mexican plant (*Turnera diffusa*), used as a nerve tonic. [<NL <Sp. <native Mexican name]

Da·mien de Veus·ter (dȧ·myaṅ′ də vœs·târ′), **Joseph,** 1840–89, Belgian Roman Catholic missionary to the lepers in Molokai: known as *Father Damien* (dā′mē·ən).

Dam·i·et·ta (dam′ē·et′ə) A city in NE Egypt, in the Nile Delta: Arabic *Dumyat.*

dam·mar (dam′ər) *n.* 1 An oleoresinous gum yielded by various evergreen trees (genus *Agathis*) of Australia, India, and Asia: used as a colorless varnish in photography, etc. 2 A similar resin from other plant sources, as *Vateria indica, Shorea wiesneri,* etc. Also **dam′ar, dam′mer.** [<Malay *damar*]

damn (dam) *v.t.* 1 To pronounce worthless, unfit, bad, a failure, etc.: to *damn* the opposition or a play. 2 To curse or swear at. 3 *Theol.* To condemn to eternal punishment. 4 To pronounce guilty; bring ruin upon: His words *damned* him. 5 *Obs.* To adjudge guilty; doom. —*v.i.* 6 To swear; curse. —**to damn with faint praise** To praise so reluctantly as to imply adverse criticism. —*n.* 1 A curse; an oath. 2 Anything as valueless as an oath. [<OF *damner* <L *damnare* condemn to punishment]

dam·na·ble (dam′nə·bəl) *adj.* Meriting or causing damnation; detestable; outrageous. [<OF <L *damnabilis* <*damnare* condemn] —**dam′·na·ble·ness** *n.* —**dam′na·bly** *adv.*

dam·na·tion (dam·nā′shən) *n.* 1 Condemnation to future punishment or perdition. 2 The act of damning or the state of the damned. 3 Ruinous adverse criticism or public disapproval, as of a book or play. 4 Cause or occasion of eternal punishment; a mortal sin. 5 *Obs.* Condemnation. [<F <L *damnatio, -onis* <*damnare* condemn]

dam·na·to·ry (dam′nə·tôr′ē, -tō′rē) *adj.* Tending to convict or condemn; consigning to damnation.

damned (damd, *poetic or rhetorical* dam′nid) *adj.* 1 Judicially reprobated and condemned; sentenced to eternal punishment. 2 Damnable; execrably bad; detestable. —*adv. Colloq.* Very; extremely: *damned* funny; *damned* irritating.

damned·est (dam′dist) *Colloq. adj.* Utmost: superlative of *damned.* —*n.* The utmost.

damned Yankee See DAMYANKEE.

dam·ni·fy (dam′nə·fī) *v.t.* **·fied, ·fy·ing** *Law* To cause injury, hurt, or damage to, in person or estate. [<OF *damnifier* <L *damnificare* injure]

damn·ing (dam′ing, dam′ning) *adj.* That damns or condemns; inculpating: *damning* evidence. —**damn′ing·ly** *adv.*

Dam·o·cles (dam′ə·klēz) In Greek legend, a courtier who, having overpraised the happiness of the tyrant Dionysius the Elder, was placed by him at a banquet, with a sword suspended over his head by a single hair to show him the perilous nature of that happiness. —**sword of Damocles** The sword hung over Damocles' head; hence, any impending danger or calamity. —**Dam·o·cle·an** (dam′ə·klē′ən) *adj.*

Da·mo·dar (dä′mə·där) A river in NE India, flowing 340 miles SE to the Hooghly.

Da·mon and Pyth·i·as (dā′mən; pith′ē·əs) In Roman legend, two Syracusan philosophers celebrated for their friendship. When Pythias was sentenced to death by Dionysius the Elder and wished to visit his home before dying, Damon volunteered to remain as hostage; Pythias returned and the loyalty of the two friends moved Dionysius to pardon the offender.

dam·o·sel (dam′ə·zel) *n. Archaic* A damsel. Also **dam·oi·selle** (dam′ə·zel′), **dam′o·sel′la** (-zel′ə), **dam′oy·sele, dam′o·zel.** [Var. of DAMSEL]

damp (damp) *n.* 1 A moderate degree of moisture; dampness; fog; mist. 2 Foul air; poisonous gas, occurring especially in coal mines. 3 Depression of spirits, or that which produces it. —*adj.* 1 Somewhat wet; moist. 2 Dejected. —*v.t.* 1 To moisten; make damp. 2 To check or discourage (energy, ardor, etc.). 3 *Music* To check the vibrations of (a string, etc.); deaden. 4 To bank, as a fire. 5 *Physics* To reduce the amplitude of (a series of waves). [<MDu., vapor, steam] —**damp′ly** *adv.* —**damp′ness** *n.*

damp·en (dam′pən) *v.t.* 1 To make or become damp; moisten. 2 To check; depress, as ardor or spirits. —*v.i.* 3 To become damp. —**damp′en·er** *n.*

damp·er (dam′pər) *n.* 1 One who or that which damps or checks. 2 A device to check the draft, as of a stove, or to stop vibration, as in a piano. 3 *Electr.* A device to check oscillation of a magnetic needle, or to control movement in an electrical mechanism. 4 *Eng.* A shock absorber.

Damp·ier (damp′yər, dam′pē·ər, -pir), **William,** 1652–1715, English privateer, explorer, and author.

damp·ish (dam′pish) *adj.* Slightly damp.

Dam·rosch (dam′rosh), **Walter Johannes,** 1862–1950, U.S. musician and conductor born in Germany.

dam·sel (dam′zəl) *n. Archaic* A young unmarried woman; maiden. [<OF *dameisele* gentlewoman, ult. <L *domina.* See DAME.]

damsel fly A slender-bodied dragonfly (order *Odonata*) with four similar elongate wings that are folded together over the back when at rest. For illustration see under INSECT (beneficial).

dam·son (dam′zən) *n.* 1 An oval purple plum of Syrian origin (*Prunus insititia*). 2 The tree producing it. Also **damson plum.** [ME *damascene* <L (*Prunum*) *Damascenum* plum from Damascus]

dam·yan·kee (dam′yang′kē, dam′-) *n. U.S. Colloq.* A Northerner: a contemptuous term used by Southerners since the Civil War: now chiefly jocular. Also *damned Yankee.*

dan (dan) *n. Obs.* Don; sir: a title of honor.

Dan (dan) A masculine personal name. [< Hebrew, judge]

—**Dan** One of the twelve tribes of Israel; descended from **Dan,** fifth son of Jacob and first of Bilhah. *Gen.* xxx 6.

Dan (dan) A city at the northern extremity of Palestine. Compare BEERSHEBA. —**from Dan to Beersheba** From end to end; throughout: Dan and Beersheba being respectively the extreme northern and southern cities of Palestine.

Da·na (dā′nə), **Charles Anderson,** 1819–97, U.S. editor. —**Edward Salisbury,** 1849–1935, U.S. mineralogist. —**James Dwight,** 1813–1895, U.S. geologist. —**Richard Henry,** 1815–82, U.S. lawyer and writer.

Dan·a·e (dan′i·ē) In Greek mythology, a maiden loved by Zeus in the form of a shower of gold: their son was Perseus.

Dan·a·id (dan′ē·id) *n.* One of the Danaides.

Da·na·i·des (də·nā′ə·dēz) In Greek mythology, the fifty daughters of Danaus who, with the exception of Hypermnestra, murdered their husbands, the sons of Aegyptus, on their bridal night at their father's command: these forty-nine were punished in Hades by having to draw water in a sieve forever. —**Dan·a·id·e·an** (dan′ē·id′ē·ən) *adj.*

Dan·a·us (dan′ē·əs) In Greek mythology, a king of Argos, father of the Danaides.

Dan·bur·y (dan′ber·ē, dan′bər·ē) A city in SW Connecticut.

dance (dans, däns) *v.* **danced, danc·ing** *v.i.* 1 To move the body and feet rhythmically, especially to music. 2 To move or skip excitedly; quiver, as from excitement or emotion. 3 To bob up and down; move about lightly and quickly. —*v.t.* 4 To perform or take part in the steps or figures of (a dance). 5 To effect or bring about by dancing: to *dance* the night away. 6 To cause to dance. 7 To dandle. See synonyms under FRISK, LEAP. —*n.* 1 A series of rhythmic concerted movements and steps timed to music. 2 A dancing party; ball. 3 A tune to dance by. 4 The intricate gyrations of swarming insects. [<OF *danser*] —**danc′er** *n.*

dance fly A small or medium-sized, slender, predacious fly (genus *Empis,* family *Empididae*) which mates in dancing swarms over the surface of land and water. For illustration see under INSECT (beneficial).

dance of death An allegory, often found in medieval art, representing Death as a skeleton leading men of all estates and conditions to the grave: also *danse macabre.*

dance·script (dans′skript′, däns′-) *n.* Choroscript.

dan·de·li·on (dan′də·lī′ən) *n.* A wide-spread plant of the composite family (*Taraxacum officinale*), having yellow flower heads and deeply toothed, edible leaves. [<F *dent de lion* lion's tooth; with ref. to the shape of the leaves]

dan·der[1] (dan′dər) *U.S. Colloq.* Ruffled temper; anger. —**to get one's dander up** *Colloq.* To become angry. [? Var. of Scottish *dunder* ferment]

dan·der[2] (dan′dər) *v.i. Scot.* To saunter about: also spelled *daunder.*

Dan·die Din·mont (dan′dē din′mont) A short-legged, long-bodied, grayish or mustard-colored terrier with drooping ears. Also **Dandie Dinmont terrier.** [after a Scottish farmer who claimed to have started the breed, portrayed in Scott's *Guy Mannering*]

dan·di·fy (dan′də·fī) *v.t.* **·fied, ·fy·ing** To cause to resemble a dandy. —**dan′di·fi·ca′tion** *n.*

dan·di·prat (dan′dē·prat) *n. Obs.* 1 A little fellow. 2 A silver coin issued by Henry VII. Also **dan′dy·prat.** [Origin unknown]

dan·dle (dan′dəl) *v.t.* **·dled, ·dling** 1 To move up and down lightly on the knees or in the arms, as an infant or child. 2 To fondle; caress. [Cf. Ital. *dandolare*] —**dan′dler** *n.*

dan·druff (dan′drəf) *n.* A fine scurf forming on the scalp. Also **dan·driff** (dan′drif). [Origin unknown]

dan·dy[1] (dan′dē) *n. pl.* **·dies** 1 A man excessively and ostentatiously refined in dress and affected in manner; a fop; coxcomb. 2 *Colloq.* A particularly fine specimen of its kind. 3 A dandy roll. 4 A two-wheeled hand cart used about furnaces and mills for carrying fuel, etc. 5 A yawl. — *adj.* 1 Like a dandy. 2 *U.S. Colloq.* Excellent; very fine. [Alter. of *Andy* < *Andrew*, a personal name. Cf. MERRY-ANDREW.]

dan·dy[2] (dan′dē) *n.* *pl.* **·dies** *Anglo-Indian* 1 A Ganges boatman. 2 A cloth hammock slung on a bamboo staff to be carried by bearers. 3 A Sivaistic ascetic who carries a small wand. Also **dan′dee, dan′di.** [<Hind. *ḍānḍī* < *ḍānḍ* a staff, oar]

dan·dy[3] (dan′dē) *n.* In the West Indies, dengue. Also **dandy fever.** [Alter. of DENGUE]

dan·dy·ish (dan′dē·ish) *adj.* Having the appearance or disposition of a dandy; foppish. — **dan′dy·ism** *n.*

dandy roll A cylinder of wire gauze by which a web of paper pulp is given a watermark. Also **dan′dy.**

Dane (dān) *n.* A native or citizen of Denmark. [<ON *Danir* the Danes]

dane·flow·er (dān′flou′ər) See PASQUEFLOWER.

Dane·geld (dān′geld′) *n.* An annual tax imposed about the end of the tenth century in Britain, originally to pay for protection against the Danes, but later continued by the Normans as a land tax. Also **Dane′gelt′** (-gelt′). [<Scand. Cf. ODan. *Danegjeld.*]

Dane·law (dān′lô′) *n.* A code of laws established by the Danes in England; also, the territory ruled under it. Also **Dane′lagh′** (-lô′). [OE *Dena-lagu* Danes' law]

dane·wort (dān′wûrt′) *n.* The European dwarf elder *(Sambucus ebulus)*: also called **Dane's′-blood′, dane′weed′.**

dang (dang) *v.t.* Damn: a euphemism.

dan·ger (dān′jər) *n.* 1 Exposure to chance of evil, injury, or loss; peril; risk; also, a cause of peril or risk. 2 *Obs.* Power; control; ability to injure. [<OF, power of a lord, power to harm <L *dominium* lordship < *dominus* lord]

Synonyms: hazard, insecurity, jeopardy, peril, risk. *Danger* is exposure to injury or evil; *peril* is exposure to imminent, threatening injury or evil. *Jeopardy* involves, like *risk*, more of the element of chance or uncertainty; a man tried upon a capital charge is said to be put in *jeopardy* of life. *Insecurity* is a feeble word, but exceedingly broad, applying to the placing of a dish, or the possibilities of a life, a fortune, or a government. Compare HAZARD. *Antonyms*: defense, immunity, protection, safeguard, safety, security, shelter.

dan·ger·ous (dān′jər·əs) *adj.* Attended with danger; hazardous; perilous; unsafe. See synonyms under FORMIDABLE, SERIOUS. — **dan′ger·ous·ly** *adv.* — **dan′ger·ous·ness** *n.*

dan·gle (dang′gəl) *v.* **·gled, ·gling** *v.i.* 1 To hang loosely; swing to-and-fro. 2 To follow or hover near someone as a suitor or hanger-on. 3 To be hanged. — *v.t.* 4 To hold so as to swing loosely to-and-fro. 5 To hang (someone). — *n.* 1 Manner or act of dangling. 2 Something which dangles. [<Scand. Cf. Dan. *dangle.*] — **dan′gler** *n.*

dan·gle·ber·ry (dang′gəl·ber′ē) See TANGLEBERRY.

Dan·iel (dan′yəl; *Fr.* dà·nyel′; *Ger.* dä′nē·el) A masculine personal name. Also *Ital.* **Da·niel·le** (dä·nyel′lā). [<Hebrew, God is my judge]

— **Daniel** One of the greater Hebrew prophets, captive in Babylon in the sixth century B.C.; also, the book of the Old Testament attributed to him.

Dan·iel (dan′yəl), **Samuel,** 1562–1619, English poet; poet laureate 1599–1619.

Dan·iels (dan′yəlz), **Farrington,** born 1889, U.S. electro-chemist. — **Josephus,** 1862–1948, U.S. journalist and statesman.

Dan·ish (dā′nish) *adj.* Of or pertaining to Denmark, the Danes, or their language. — *n.* The North Germanic language of the Danes. Abbr. *Dan.* [OE *Denisc*]

Danish pastry A rich, flaky pastry made with raised dough, often filled with cheese or jam.

Danish West Indies A former name for the VIRGIN ISLANDS OF THE UNITED STATES.

Dan·ite (dan′īt) *adj.* Of or pertaining to the tribe of Dan. — *n.* 1 A descendant of Dan. 2 One of a reputed Mormon band or secret brotherhood (called also *Destroying Angels*): said to have been organized in the early history of the Mormons to support their cause at any cost.

dank (dangk) *adj.* Unpleasantly damp; moist; wet. — *n.* Disagreeable humidity; wetness. [ME *danke* <Scand. Cf. Sw. *dank* marshy ground.] — **dank′ish** *adj.* — **dank′ish·ness** *n.* — **dank′ly** *adv.*

Dan·ne·brog (dan′ə·brôg) *n.* 1 The Danish national flag. 2 A Danish order of knighthood. [<Dan. <*Dane-* Danish + *brog* cloth]

D'An·nun·zio (dän·no͞on′tsyō), **Gabriele,** 1863–1938, Italian author and soldier.

Da·no-Nor·we·gian (dā′nō·nôr·wē′jən) *n.* Riksmål.

danse ma·ca·bre (däns mà·kä′br′) *French* Dance of death.

dan·seuse (dän·sœz′) *n.* *pl.* **·seus·es** (-sœ′ziz, *Fr.* -sœz′) A female ballet dancer; a ballerina. [<F]

Dan·te A·li·ghie·ri (dän′tā ä′lē·gyâ′rē, dan′tē) 1265–1321, Italian poet; author of the *Divine Comedy*. Also *Durante Alighieri.*

Dan·tesque (dan·tesk′) *adj.* Pertaining to, resembling, or in the style of Dante Alighieri; especially, characterized by solemn and impassioned sublimity. Also **Dan·te·an** (dan′tē·ən, dan·tē′ən). [<Ital. *dantesco* <*Dante*]

Dan·tist (dan′tist) *n.* One versed in the works of Dante.

Dan·ton (dän·tôn′), **Georges Jacques,** 1759–1794, French Revolutionary leader; guillotined.

Dan·u (thän′o͞o) In ancient Irish mythology, the goddess of death and mother of all the gods.

Dan·ube (dan′yo͞ob) A river in central and SE Europe, flowing 1,750 miles eastward from Baden, Germany, to the Black Sea: German *Donau*, Hungarian *Duna*, Rumanian *Dunărea.*

Da·nu·bi·an (dan·yo͞o′bē·ən, də·no͞o′-) *adj.* Pertaining to the Danube or the regions and peoples near it.

Dan·zig (dan′sig, *Ger.* dän′tsikh) A port of northern Poland on the **Gulf of Danzig,** an inlet of the Baltic Sea between Poland and the U.S.S.R.; former capital of the territory of the **Free City of Danzig** (731 square miles) as constituted by the Treaty of Versailles (1919). Polish *Gdańsk.*

dap (dap) *v.i.* **dapped, dap·ping** 1 To dip lightly or suddenly into water, as a bird. 2 To fish by dropping a baited hook gently on the water. 3 To bounce or skip. [Prob. var. of DAB[3]]

daph·ne (daf′nē) *n.* 1 The laurel *(Laurus nobilis)* of southern Europe. 2 Any of a genus *(Daphne)* of shrubs, some deciduous, some evergreen, with fragrant flowers. [<NL <Gk. *daphnē*]

Daph·ne (daf′nē) In Greek mythology, a nymph who became a laurel tree in order to escape from Apollo.

Daph·nis (daf′nis) In Greek mythology, a Sicilian shepherd, son of Hermes and inventor of bucolic poetry.

Daphnis and Chloe A pair of lovers in a Greek pastoral romance attributed to Longus.

dap·per (dap′ər) *adj.* 1 Trim; neat; natty; smartly dressed. 2 Small and active. [<MDu., strong, energetic]

dap·ple (dap′əl) *v.t.* **·pled, ·pling** To make spotted or variegated in color. — *adj.* Spotted; variegated: also **dap′pled.** — *n.* 1 A spot or dot, as on the skin of a horse. 2 An animal marked with spots. [Origin uncertain]

Dap·sang (dup′sung) See K2.

Dar·bhan·ga (dûr·bung′gə) A city in Bihar, India.

dar·bies (där′bēz) *n. pl. Brit. Slang* Handcuffs. [? <*Darby*, a surname]

d'Ar·blay (där′blā, *Fr.* dàr·blā′) See BURNEY, FANNY.

Dar·by and Joan (där′bē; jōn) John Darby and his wife Joan, popularized in an English ballad, about 1735; hence, types of conjugal felicity.

Dar·dan (där′dən) *adj.* & *n.* Trojan. Also **Dar·da·ni·an** (där·dā′nē·ən).

Dar·da·nelles (där′də·nelz′) A narrow strait in NW Turkey connecting the Sea of Marmara with the Aegean; length, 37 miles: ancient *Hellespont. Turkish* **Ça·nak·ka·le Bo·ğa·zi** (chä′näk·kä·le′ bō′ä·zi′).

Dar·da·nus (där′də·nəs) In Greek mythology, a son of Zeus and ancestor of the Trojans.

dare[1] (dâr) *v.* **dared** (*Archaic* **durst**), **dar·ing** *v.t.* 1 To have the courage or boldness to undertake; venture on. 2 To challenge to attempt something as proof of courage, etc. 3 To defy; oppose and challenge. — *v.i.* 4 To have the courage or boldness to do or attempt something; venture. — **I dare say** I am reasonably certain. — *n.* 1 The act of daring; a challenge: to do something on a *dare.* 2 Daring; bravery. [OE *durran*] — **dar′er** *n.*

dare[2] (dâr) *v.* **dared, dar·ing** *Obs. v.t.* 1 To daunt; scare. 2 To dazzle; paralyze. — *v.i.* 3 To be in fear. [OE *darian* lurk]

Dare (dâr), **Virginia,** born 1587, first child of English parents born in America, on Roanoke Island.

dare·dev·il (dâr′dev′əl) *n.* One who is recklessly bold. — *adj.* Venturesome; reckless. — **dare′dev′il·try** *n.*

dare·ful (dâr′fəl) *adj.* Defiant; full of daring.

Dar-el-Bei·da (där′el·bī·dä′, -bā·dä′) The Arabic name for CASABLANCA.

Dar-es-Sa·laam (där′es·sə·läm′) A port on the Indian Ocean, capital of Tanganyika.

Dar·fur (där·fo͝or′) A province of western Sudan; 138,150 square miles; capital, El Fasher.

dar·ic (dar′ik) *n.* An ancient Persian gold coin; also, a silver coin of the same design, worth one twentieth of the gold daric. [<Gk. *Dareikos* coin of Darius]

Dar·i·en (dâr′ē·en′, dâr′ē·en′; *Sp.* dä·ryān′) The eastern part of Panama between the Gulf of San Miguel and the **Gulf of Darien,** a bight of the Caribbean Sea in the east coast of Panama. — **Isthmus of Darien** A former name of the ISTHMUS OF PANAMA.

dar·ing (dâr′ing) *adj.* 1 Possessing courage; bold; brave; venturesome. 2 Audacious; presuming. See synonyms under BRAVE. — *n.* Heroic courage; bravery. See synonyms under COURAGE. — **dar′ing·ly** *adv.* — **dar′ing·ness** *n.*

Da·rí·o (dä·rē′ō), **Rubén,** pen name of Félix Rubén García-Sarmiento, 1867–1916, Nicaraguan poet.

Da·ri·us (də·rī′əs) A masculine personal name.

— **Darius I, Hys·tas·pes** (his·tas′pēz), 558?–485 B.C.; king of Persia 521–485 B.C.; invaded Scythia and Greece, defeated at Marathon: called "Darius the Great."

— **Darius III, Co·do·man·nus** (kō·dō·man′əs), king of Persia 336–330 B.C., conquered by Alexander the Great.

Dar·jee·ling (där·jē′ling) A resort town in northern West Bengal.

dark (därk) *adj.* 1 Lacking light. 2 Of a deep shade; black, or approaching black. 3 Obscure; mysterious; not understandable. 4 Gloomy; disheartening. 5 Unenlightened. 6 Atrocious; dastardly; wicked. 7 Of brunette complexion. 8 Blind; unknowing. 9 Secretive; reticent. — *n.* 1 Lack of light. 2 A place, position, or state where there is little or no light. 3 Night. 4 Obscurity; secrecy. 5 Ignorance: especially in the phrase *in the dark.* 6 A heavy shade or shadow in a drawing or painting. — *v.t.* & *v.i. Obs.* To make or become dark; darken. [OE *deorc*]

Synonyms (adj.): black, dim, dismal, dusky, gloomy, murky, mysterious, obscure, opaque, sable, shadowy, shady, somber, swart, swarthy. Strictly, that which is *black* is absolutely destitute of color; that which is *dark* is absolutely destitute of light. In common speech, however, a coat is *black,* though not optically colorless; the night is *dark,* though the stars shine. That is *obscure, shadowy,* or *shady* from which the light is more or less cut off. *Dusky* is applied to objects which appear as if viewed in fading light; the word is often used, as are *swart* and *swarthy*, of the human skin when quite *dark*, or even verging on *black. Dim* refers to imperfection of outline, from distance, darkness, mist, etc., or from some defect of vision. *Opaque* objects are impervious to light. *Murky* is said of that which is at once *dark, obscure,* and *gloomy*; as, a *murky* den; a *murky* sky. Figuratively, *dark* is emblematic of sadness, agreeing with *somber, dismal, gloomy,* also of moral evil:

as, a *dark* deed. Of intellectual matters, *dark* is now rarely used in the old sense of a *dark* saying, etc. See MYSTERIOUS, OBSCURE. *Antonyms*: bright, brilliant, clear, crystalline, dazzling, gleaming, glowing, illumined, light, lucid, luminous, radiant, shining, transparent, white. Compare synonyms for LIGHT.

Dark Ages 1 The period in European history between the fall of the Western Roman Empire (A.D. 476) and the Italian Renaissance. 2 The early part of the Middle Ages, to the end of the tenth century: so called because the period was considered to be characterized by a waning of Roman civilization and a retardation in social, political, and intellectual development.

Dark and Bloody Ground Kentucky: so called because of the numerous Indian wars in the territory now included within the State.

dark conduction *Electr.* Conductive of residual electricity in a photosensitive substance when not illuminated.

Dark Continent Africa: so called because it was little known until the 19th century.

dark current *Electr.* The current set up in a photoelectric cell when the light beam is interrupted.

dark·en (där′kən) *v.t.* 1 To make dark or darker; deprive of light. 2 To make dark in color; make black. 3 To fill with gloom; sadden. 4 To blind. 5 To obscure; confuse. —*v.i.* 6 To grow dark or darker. 7 To become sad or gloomy; grow dark or flushed, as the face with anger or hatred. 8 To become blind. —**dark′en·er** *n.*

dark-field illumination (därk′fēld′) *Optics* The lighting of the field of a microscope from the side instead of from below, so as to reveal the specimen against a dark background.

dark horse 1 An unknown or little talked-of horse that unexpectedly wins a race. 2 A little-known political candidate unexpectedly nominated.

dark·ish (där′kish) *adj.* Somewhat dark.

dark lantern A lantern having a case with one transparent side, which can be covered by a shield to hide the light.

dar·kle (där′kəl) *v.i.* **·kled, ·kling** 1 To appear darkly or indistinctly; be in darkness. 2 To grow gloomy or dark; darken. [Back formation <DARKLING, *adv.*]

dar·kling (därk′ling) *adj. Poetic* Dim; obscure; occurring or being in the dark. —*adv.* In the dark; blindly; mysteriously.

dark·ly (därk′lē) *adv.* 1 In a dark manner. 2 Obscurely; mysteriously.

dark·ness (därk′nis) *n.* 1 Total or partial absence of light; gloom. 2 Physical, mental, or moral blindness. 3 Want of clearness; obscurity; secrecy. 4 The quality of being dark in color or shade.

dark·room (därk′ro͞om′, -ro͝om′) *n. Phot.* A room equipped to exclude actinic rays, for treating plates, films, etc.

dark·some (därk′səm) *adj. Poetic* Dark; darkish.

dark star See under STAR.

dark·y (där′kē) *n. pl.* **dark·ies** *Colloq.* A Negro: a contemptuous term. Also **dark′ey, dark′ie.**

Dar·lan (dȧr·läṅ′), **Jean François,** 1881–1942, French admiral and politician; assassinated.

dar·ling (där′ling) *n.* One tenderly beloved: often a term of direct address. —*adj.* Tenderly beloved; very dear. [OE *dēorling*, dim. of *dēor* dear]

Darling Range A mountain system of Western Australia; highest peak, 1,910 feet.

Dar·ling River (där′ling) A river in SE Australia, flowing SW 1,910 miles to the Murray River.

Dar·ling·ton (där′ling·tən) A county borough in south Durham, England.

Dar·ling·ton (där′ling·tən), **Cyril Dean,** born 1903, English geneticist.

Darm·stadt (därm′shtät) A city in southern Hesse, Germany.

darn[1] (därn) *v.t. & v.i.* To repair (a garment or a hole or rent) by filling the gap with interlacing stitches. —*n.* A place mended by darning; also, the act of darning. [Earlier *dern*, prob. <OE *dernan* conceal <*derne* hidden]

darn[2] (därn) *v.t., adj., n., & interj. Colloq.* Damn: a euphemism.

darn·dest (därn′dist) *n. & adj. Colloq.* Damnedest: a euphemism.

dar·nel (där′nəl) *n.* A grass (*Lolium temulentum*); ryegrass; an annual weed often found in grain fields. [<dial. F *darnelle*]

DARNEL
A. Spikelet.

darn·er (där′nər) *n.* 1 One who or that which darns. 2 A darning needle.

darning needle 1 A large-eyed needle used in darning. 2 A dragonfly: also devil's-darning-needle. 3 The Venus's-comb.

Darn·ley (därn′lē), **Lord,** 1546–67, Henry Stuart, second husband of Mary Queen of Scots; murdered.

Dar·row (dar′ō), **Clarence Seward,** 1857–1938, U.S. lawyer.

d'Ar·son·val (dȧr·sôṅ·vȧl′), **Jacques Arsène,** 1851–1940, French physicist.

dart (därt) *n.* 1 A pointed missile weapon, as a javelin; also, something like an arrow or having the effect of one. 2 A sudden and rapid motion. 3 A tapering tuck made in a garment by stitching or cutting so as to fit it to the figure. 4 An insect's sting. —*v.t. & v.i.* 1 To emit swiftly or suddenly; shoot out. 2 To move swiftly and suddenly. See synonyms under THROW. [<OF <Gmc.]

dart·er (där′tər) *n.* 1 A small American perch-like fish (subfamily *Estheostomatinae*). 2 The American snakebird.

dar·tle (där′təl) *v.t. & v.i.* **·tled, ·tling** To dart or shoot out repeatedly.

Dart·moor (därt′mo͝or) 1 A wild upland in south Devonshire, England; 350 square miles. 2 A famous prison in this region.

darts (därts) *n.* A game of skill in which small darts are thrown at a bull's-eye target.

Dar·win (där′win) A port, capital of Northern Territory, Australia: formerly *Palmerston.*

Dar·win (där′win), **Charles Robert,** 1809–82, English naturalist; formulated the theory of evolution by natural selection. —**Erasmus,** 1731–1802, English physician and poet; grandfather of the preceding.

Dar·win·i·an (där·win′ē·ən) *adj.* Pertaining to Charles Darwin, or to Darwinism. —*n.* An advocate of Darwinism.

Dar·win·ism (där′win·iz′əm) *n.* 1 The biological doctrine of descent by natural selection with variation, advocated by Charles Darwin. 2 The evolutionary theory of Charles Darwin: also **Darwinian theory.** —**Dar′win·ist** *n. & adj.* —**Dar′win·is′tic** *adj.* —**Dar′win·ite** (-īt) *n.*

Dar·yal Gorge (dûr·yal′, där-) A defile in the central Caucasus north of Tiflis; 5,900 feet deep.

dash[1] (dash) *v.t.* 1 To strike with violence, especially so as to break or shatter. 2 To throw, thrust, or knock suddenly and violently: usually with *away, out, down*, etc. 3 To splash; bespatter. 4 To do, write, etc., hastily: with *off* or *down.* 5 To frustrate; confound: to *dash* hopes. 6 To daunt or discourage. 7 To put to shame; abash. 8 To adulterate; mix: with *with.* 9 *Brit.* To damn: a euphemism. —*v.i.* 10 To strike; hit: The waves *dashed* against the shore. 11 To rush or move impetuously. See synonyms under THROW. —*n.* 1 A sudden advance or onset; short, spirited rush or race. 2 Impetuosity; spirit; vigor. 3 Ostentatious display, especially in the phrase *to cut a dash.* 4 A check or hindrance; discomfiture. 5 A slight admixture; a tinge; a small addition of some other ingredient. 6 A collision or concussion; also, its sound. 7 A horizontal line (—), as a mark of punctuation, etc. 8 The long sound in the Morse code, used in combination with dots to represent letters. 9 A dashboard. 10 The dasher of a churn. [ME *daschen* <Scand. Cf. Dan. *daske* a slap.]

dash[2] (dash) *v.t.* In West Africa, to bribe; also, offer as a bribe. —*n.* A bribe. [Earlier *dashee*, alter. of Pg. *Que das me?* What do you give me?]

dash·board (dash′bôrd′, -bōrd′) *n.* 1 An upright screen on the front of a vehicle to intercept mud, etc., thrown up by a horse. 2 A sprayboard at

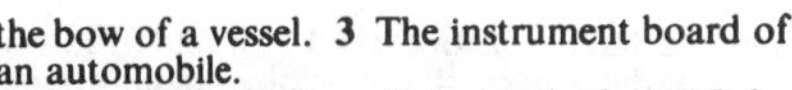

the bow of a vessel. 3 The instrument board of an automobile.

da·sheen (da·shēn′) *n.* A tropical plant (*Colocasia esculenta*) related to the taro, the root of which is a staple food of the tropics. [<F *de Chine* of China]

dash·er (dash′ər) *n.* 1 One who or that which dashes, plunges, or cuts a dash. 2 The plunger of a churn. 3 A dashboard.

da·shi·ki (dä·shē′kē) *n. pl.* **·kis** A loose-fitting, sleeved garment of varying length, often with a print design or embroidery, worn by men and women in West Africa and elsewhere. [<Yoruba]

dash·ing (dash′ing) *adj.* 1 Spirited; bold; impetuous. 2 Ostentatiously showy or gay. —**dash′ing·ly** *adv.*

Dasht-i-Ka·vir (däsht′ē·kä·vēr′) A salt desert of the central Iranian plateau; 200 miles wide.

Dasht-i-Lut (däsht′ē·lo͞ot′) A desert of eastern Iran; 200 miles long, 100 miles wide.

dash·y (dash′ē) *adj.* **dash·i·er, dash·i·est** Stylish.

das·tard (das′tərd) *n.* A base coward; a sneak. —*adj.* Dastardly. [? ME *dased, dast*, pp. of *dasen* daze, stupefy + -ARD]

das·tard·ly (das′tərd·lē) *adj.* Base; cowardly. —**das′tard·li·ness, das′tard·y** *n.*

das·y·ure (das′ē·o͝or) *n.* 1 An arboreal marsupial; especially, a small, spotted, civetlike marsupial, as the **spotted dasyure** (*Dasyurus maculatus*) of Tasmania and southern Australia. 2 The Tasmanian devil. [<Gk. *dasys* hairy + *oura* tail]

DASYURE
(Body length: 1 to 1 1/2 feet)

da·ta (dā′tə, dat′ə, dä′tə) *n. pl.* of DATUM Facts or figures from which conclusions may be drawn: often construed as a singular. [<L, neut. pl. of *datus*, pp. of *dare* give]

data bank An extensive body of information organized and stored in a computer's memory for the quick retrieval of data in response to particular queries.

data processing The operation of digital or analog computers.

da·ta·ry (dā′tə·rē) *n. pl.* **·ries** 1 A papal official, usually a bishop, having charge of grants and dispensations and the dating and registration of all important documents. 2 The office or employment of this official. [<Med. L *datarius* <L *dare* give, grant]

date[1] (dāt) *n.* 1 That part of a writing, inscription, coin, etc., which tells when, or when and where, it was written, published, etc. 2 The time of some event; a point of time. 3 Duration; age. 4 *U.S. Colloq.* An engagement; appointment. —**down to date** Covering the current day. —**out of date** Obsolete. —**up to date** Having modern knowledge, style, etc. —*v.* **dat·ed, dat·ing** *v.t.* 1 To furnish or mark with a date. 2 To ascertain the time or era of; assign a date to. 3 *U.S. Colloq.* To make an appointment with, as a member of the opposite sex. —*v.i.* 4 To have origin in or be in existence since an era or time: usually with *from*: This coin *dates* from the Renaissance. 5 To reckon time. [<F <L *data*, fem. sing. of *datus*, pp. of *dare* give; from first word of Latin formula giving a letter's date and place of writing] —**dat′er** *n.*

date[2] (dāt) *n.* 1 An oblong, sweet, fleshy fruit of the date palm, enclosing a single hard seed. 2 A lofty palm bearing this fruit (*Phoenix dactylifera* and varieties): also called **date palm.** [<OF <L *dactylus* <Gk. *daktylos* finger; with ref. to its shape]

dat·ed (dā′tid) *adj.* 1 Marked with a date. 2 Antiquated; old-fashioned.

date·less (dāt′lis) *adj.* 1 Bearing no date. 2 Without end or limit. 3 Immemorial; of permanent interest.

date line 1 The line containing the date of publication of a periodical or of any contribution, dispatch, etc., printed in it. 2 An imaginary line approximately congruent with 180° longitude from Greenwich, internationally agreed upon as determining those points on the earth's surface where a day is dropped on crossing it from west to east and added on crossing from east to west: also called **International Date Line.**

da·tive (dā′tiv) *n. Gram.* **1** In inflected Indo-European languages, that case of a noun, pronoun, or adjective denoting the remoter, or indirect object: expressed in English by *to* or *for* with the objective or by word order, as in *I told the story to him, I told him the story.* **2** A word in this case. —*adj.* **1** *Gram.* Pertaining to or designating the dative case or a word in this case. **2** *Law* That may be disposed of at will; also, that may be removed; removable as opposed to perpetual: a *dative* officer. [<L *dativus,* trans. of Gk. *(ptōsis) dotikē* (the case of) giving <*didonai* give] **—da′tive·ly** *adv.*

dat·o·lite (dat′ō·līt) *n.* A vitreous, translucent, brittle calcium borosilicate occurring in massive monoclinic crystals. [<Gk. *dateesthai* divide + -LITE]

dat·to (dä′tō) *n. pl.* **·tos 1** In the Philippines, a chief of a Moslem Moro tribe. **2** The headman of a barrio or Malay tribe. Also **da′to.** [<Malay *datōq*]

da·tum (dā′təm, dat′əm, dä′təm) *n. pl.* **da·ta 1** A known, assumed, or conceded fact from which an inference is made. **2** The point from which any reckoning or scale starts. [<L, neut. sing. of *datus.* See DATA.]

datum plane *Engin.* The horizontal plane from which heights and depths are measured: also **datum level.**

da·tu·ra (də·to͞or′ə, -tyo͞or′ə) *n.* One of a genus *(Datura)* of rank-smelling, poisonous plants of the nightshade family, with large funnel-shaped flowers and a prickly capsule, of which the jimsonweed is the best-known species. [<NL <Hind. *dhātūrā,* a plant]

DATURA
a. Fruit.
b. Grain.

daub (dôb) *v.t.* & *v.i.* **1** To smear or coat (something), as with plaster, grease, mud, etc. **2** To paint without skill or taste. —*n.* **1** Mud, plaster, clay, etc.; any sticky application. **2** A smear or spot. **3** A poor, coarse painting. **4** An instance or act of daubing. See synonyms under BLEMISH. [<OF *dauber* <L *dealbare* whitewash]

daub·er (dô′bər) *n.* **1** One who or that which daubs. **2** One who paints coarsely or cheaply. **3** A brush to put blacking on shoes; a dabber. **4** *Obs.* A flatterer. **—daub′er·y, daub′ry** *n.* **—daub′ing** *n.*

Dau·bi·gny (dō·bē·nyē′), **Charles François,** 1817–78, French painter.

daub·y (dô′bē) *adj.* **1** Pertaining to or like daub; sticky. **2** Unskilfully done, as a painting; also, smeary.

daud (dôd, däd) *v.t. & v.i. Scot.* To thump; beat.

Dau·det (dō·de′), **Alphonse,** 1840–97, French novelist. **—Léon,** 1867–1942, French journalist and novelist; son of the preceding.

Dau·ga·va (dou′gä·vä) The Latvian name for the WESTERN DVINA.

daugh·ter (dô′tər) *n.* **1** A female child or descendant. **2** Any person or thing in a relation analogous to that of a female child, regarded with reference to her, or its, origin. **3** *Obs.* A maiden. [OE *dohtor*] **—daugh′ter·ly** *adj.*

daughter cell *Biol.* Either of the two cells resulting from a mitotic division of a cell.

daugh·ter-in-law (dô′tər·in·lô′) *n. pl.* **daugh·ters-in-law** The wife of one's son.

Daughters of the American Revolution A patriotic society of women who are lineal descendants of patriots in the American Revolution, organized in Washington, D.C., in 1890.

Dau·mier (dō·myā′), **Honoré,** 1808–79, French painter and caricaturist.

daun·der (dôn′dər, dän′-) See DANDER[2].

daunt (dônt, dänt) *v.t.* **1** To dishearten or intimidate; cow. **2** To pack into a barrel with a daunt. See synonyms under ABASH, FRIGHTEN. —*n.* **1** A fright. **2** A wooden disk with which to press salted fish, especially herring, into barrels. [<OF *danter, donter* <L *domitare,* freq. of *domare* tame]

daunt·less (dônt′lis, dänt-) *adj.* Fearless; intrepid. See synonyms under BRAVE. **—daunt′less·ly** *adv.* **—daunt′less·ness** *n.*

dau·phin (dô′fin, *Fr.* dō·fan′) *n.* The eldest son of a king of France: a title used from 1349 to 1830. [<F, a dolphin; used as a personal name and title]

Dau·phi·né (dō·fē·nā′) A region and former province of SE France.

dau·phin·ess (dô′fin·is) *n.* The wife of a dauphin. Also **dau′phine** (-fēn).

daur (dôr) *v.t. Scot.* To dare.

daur·na (dôr′nə) *Scot.* Dare not.

daut (dôt, dät) *v.t. Scot.* To fondle: also spelled *dawt.*

daut·ie (dô′tē) *n. Scot.* A little pet: also spelled *dawtie.*

Da·vaine (də·vān′), **Casimir Joseph,** 1812–82, French physician and bacteriologist.

Da·vao (dä′vou) A port on **Davao Gulf,** an inlet on the SE coast of Mindanao, Philippines.

Dav·e·nant (dav′ə·nənt), **Sir William,** 1606–1668, English poet and dramatist; poet laureate 1638–68. Also **D'Av′e·nant.**

dav·en·port (dav′ən·pôrt, -pōrt) *n.* **1** A large, upholstered sofa, often one that can be used as a bed. **2** A small writing desk. [Prob. after the name of the first manufacturer]

Dav·en·port (dav′ən·pôrt, -pōrt) A city on the Mississippi in eastern Iowa.

Dav·en·port (dav′ən·pôrt, -pōrt), **Charles Benedict,** 1866–1944, U.S. zoologist. **—John,** 1597–1670, English clergyman; one of the founders of New Haven.

Da·vid (dā′vid, *Ger.* dä′vēt) A masculine personal name; familiarly **Dave, Da′vie, Da′vy.** Also *Fr.* **Da·vide** (dà·vēd′), *Ital.* **Da·vid** (dä·vēd′), **Da·vi·de** (dä·vē′dā). [<Hebrew, beloved]
—David, 1000?–960? B.C., second king of Israel; reputed writer of *Psalms.*
—David I, 1084–1153, king of Scotland 1124–1153.
—David, Saint, died 601?, patron of Wales.

Da·vid (dà·vēd′), **Gerard,** 1450?–1523, Flemish painter. **—Jacques Louis,** 1748–1825, French painter. **—Pierre Jean,** 1788–1856, French sculptor: also called **"David d'An·gers"** (däṅ·zhā′).

David, Star of See MOGEN DAVID.

Da·vid·son (dā′vid·sən), **Jo,** 1883–1952, U.S. sculptor.

da Vin·ci (dä vēn′chē), **Leonardo** See LEONARDO DA VINCI.

Da·vis (dā′vis), **Jefferson,** 1808–89, U.S. statesman; president of the Confederacy 1862–1865. **—John,** 1550?–1605, English navigator. **—Norman Hezekiah,** 1878–1944, U.S. financier and diplomat. **—Owen,** 1874–1956, U.S. dramatist. **—Richard Harding,** 1864–1916, U.S. journalist and novelist. **—Stuart,** born 1894, U.S. painter. **—William Stearns,** 1877–1930, U.S. educator and historian.

Davis Cup A trophy cup presented to that nation whose team wins the International Lawn Tennis Championship, commonly called the Davis Cup matches. [after Dwight F. *Davis,* 1879–1945, who instituted the tournament in 1900]

Da·vis·son (dā′vis·ən), **Clinton Joseph,** 1881–1958, U.S. physicist.

Davis Strait An arm of the Atlantic between Baffin Island and SW Greenland.

dav·it (dav′it, dā′vit) *n. Naut.* **1** One of a pair of small cranes on a ship's side for hoisting its boats, stores, etc. **2** A curved piece of timber or iron for hoisting the flukes of an anchor. [from *David,* proper name]

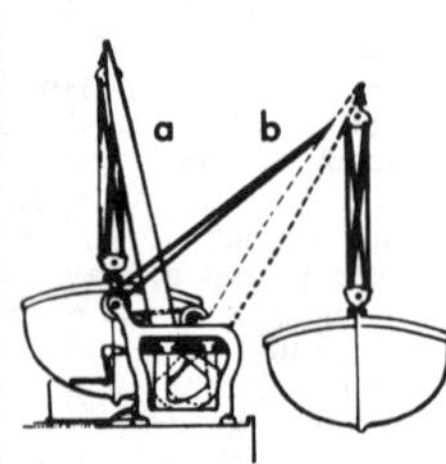

DAVIT
a. Position on deck.
b. Position when lowering lifeboat.

Da·vos (dä·vōs′) A resort town in eastern Switzerland.

Da·vout (dà·vo͞o′), **Louis Nicolas,** 1770–1823, duke of Auerstadt and prince of Eckmühl; French marshal.

da·vy (dā′vē) *n. pl.* **·vies** A safety lamp.

Da·vy (dā′vē), **Sir Humphry,** 1778–1829, English chemist; inventor of the safety lamp, the electrolytic method of preparing potassium, etc.

Da·vy Jones (dā′vē jōnz′) Sailors' name for the spirit of the sea.

Davy Jones's locker The bottom of the ocean, especially as the grave of the drowned.

daw[1] (dô) *n.* **1** A jackdaw. **2** A simpleton. [ME *dawe*]

daw[2] (dô) *n.* & *v.i. Scot.* Dawn.

daw·dle (dôd′l) *v.t.* & *v.i.* **·dled, ·dling** To waste (time) in slow trifling; loiter: often with *away.* See synonyms under LINGER. [Prob. var. of DADDLE] **—daw′dler** *n.*

Dawes (dôz), **Charles Gates,** 1865–1951, U.S. financier and statesman; vice president of the United States 1925–29.

dawk (dôk, däk) See DAK.

dawn (dôn) *v.i.* **1** To begin to grow light. **2** To begin to be understood: with *on* or *upon.* **3** To begin to expand or develop. —*n.* **1** The first appearance of light in the morning; daybreak. ◆ Collateral adjective: *auroral.* **2** An awakening; beginning or unfolding. [Back formation < *dawning,* earlier *dawenyng* daybreak <Scand. Cf. Sw. *dagning.*]

Dawn man Eoanthropus.

Daw·son (dô′sən) A city in western Yukon, Canada; formerly the capital of the territory.

Daw·son (dô′sən), **Sir John William,** 1820–99, Canadian geologist.

Dawson Creek A village in eastern British Columbia; the southern terminal of the Alaska Highway.

dawt (dôt, dät) See DAUT.

Dax (dáks) A resort town of SW France.

day (dā) *n.* **1** The period from dawn to dark; hence, daylight or sunlight. **2** The interval represented by one revolution of the earth upon its axis; twenty-four hours; also, this period as a unit in computing time. ◆ Collateral adjective: *diurnal.* See under TIME. **3** The hours appointed for labor. **4** A day's journey. **5** The period of rotation about its axis of any heavenly body. **6** A time or period; an age. **7** A contest or battle, or its result: The liberals won the *day.* **8** A specified epoch: in Caesar's *day.* **9** A specified date: Independence *Day.* **—day after day** Every day. **—day by day** Each day. **—day in, day out** Every day. **—(from) day to day** From one day to the next; not long-range. **—the day** *Scot.* Today: How are ye *the day?* [OE *dæg*]

Day (dā), **Edmund Ezra,** 1883–1951, U.S. educator; president of Cornell University 1937–49. **—Thomas,** 1748–89, English author. **—William Rufus,** 1849–1923, U.S. statesman and jurist.

Day·ak (dī′ak) See DYAK.

day-bed (dā′bed′) *n.* A lounge or couch, usually with back and sides, that can be converted into a bed at night.

day blindness Hemeralopia.

day·book (dā′bo͝ok′) *n.* **1** In bookkeeping, the book in which transactions are recorded in the order of their occurrence. **2** A diary.

day·break (dā′brāk′) *n.* Dawn; the time when the sun rises.

day camp A camp where children spend the day in supervised activities, returning home each evening.

day-care center (dā′kâr′) A place for the care of young children during the day, especially while their mothers are at work: also called *day nursery.*

day coach A railroad car equipped for daytime travel only, as opposed to a sleeping-car, dining-car, etc.

day·dream (dā′drēm′) *n.* **1** An exercise of the fancy or imagination; a reverie. **2** A delusion of happiness. —*v.i.* To indulge the mind idly in wishful thinking. **—day′dream′er** *n.*

day flower Any species of the genus *Commelina* whose flowers last only a day.

day·fly (dā′flī′) *n.* A mayfly or ephemerid insect.

day labor Labor hired and paid for by the day.

day laborer One who works for pay by the day, as at unskilled manual tasks.

day letter A lettergram sent during the day.

day·light (dā′līt′) *n.* **1** The light received from the sun; the light of day. **2** The period of light during the day. **3** Insight into or understanding of something formerly puzzling. **4** Exposure to view; publicity.

day·lights (dā′līts′) *n. Slang.* **1** Vital organs; life itself: The mule worked his *daylights* out. **2** Consciousness; wits: to shake the *daylights* out of one.

day·light-sav·ing time (dā′līt′sā′ving) Time in which more daylight for the working day is obtained by setting clocks one or more hours ahead of standard time, especially during the summer months.

day·lil·y (dā'lil'ē) *n. pl.* **·lil·ies** 1 Any of several lilyworts (genus *Hemerocallis*), with lanceolate leaves, and large flowers on a round thick scape, usually lasting one day. Two species, *H. fulva*, tawny red, and *H. flava*, bright yellow, are commonly cultivated. 2 A common cultivated lilywort (genus *Hosta*) of Asian origin, with large, broad, ovate or oblong leaves, and generally white flowers.

day·long (dā'lông', -long') *adj.* & *adv.* All day; lasting through the entire day.

day nursery A day-care center.

Day of Atonement Yom Kippur.

Day of Judgment The day of the Last Judgment; the last day of the world.

day school 1 A school that holds classes during the daytime: distinguished from *night school.* 2 A private school attended by pupils living outside the school: distinguished from *boarding school.*

days of grace Days (usually three) allowed for the payment of a note or bill of exchange after the date of payment expressed in the instrument itself.

day·spring (dā'spring') *n. Poetic* The early dawn.

day·star (dā'stär') *n.* 1 The morning star. 2 *Poetic* The sun.

day·time (dā'tīm') *n.* The time of daylight; the time between sunrise and sunset.

Day·ton (dā'tən) A city on the Miami River in SW Ohio.

Day·to·na Beach (dā·tō'nə) A resort city on the NE coast of Florida.

daze (dāz) *v.t.* **dazed, daz·ing** To stupefy or bewilder, as by a glare of light or by a physical or mental shock; stun. —*n.* The state of being dazed. [ME *dasen.* Related to ON *dasask* become weary.] —**daz·ed·ly** (dā'zid·lē) *adv.*

daz·zle (daz'əl) *v.* **·zled, ·zling** *v.t.* 1 To blind or dim the vision of by excess of light. 2 To bewilder or charm, as with brilliant display. —*v.i.* 3 To be blinded by lights or glare. 4 To excite admiration. —*n.* 1 The act of dazzling; dazzled condition. 2 Something that dazzles; brightness. [Freq. of DAZE] —**daz'zling·ly** *adv.*

D-day (dē'dā') *n.* In military operations, the day or date of the launching of an attack: used especially in the planning of operations before a specific date is set or is disclosed.

DDT A powerful insecticide effective on contact. [<D(ICHLORO-)D(IPHENYL-)T(RICHLORO-ETHANE)]

de (də) *prep. French* Of; from: used in names and phrases, as in Cyrano *de* Bergerac; coup *de* main. *De* combines with the masculine singular article *le* to form *du*, and with the plural article *les* to form *des*; before vowels and silent *h* the *e* is elided, as in coup *d'état.*

de- *prefix* 1 Away; off: *deflect, decapitate.* 2 Down: *decline, descend.* 3 Completely; utterly: *derelict, denude.* 4 The undoing, reversing, or ridding of (the action or condition expressed by the main element): *decoding, decentralization, decarbonization.* [<L *de* from, away, down; also <F *dé-* <L *de-*, or <OF *des-* <L *dis-* (see DIS-)]

De- may appear as a prefix in hyphemes or solidemes, with the sense of definition 4; as in:

de-anglicize	**deconsecrate**
de-arm	**decrustation**
de-armed	**decrystallization**
de-arming	**de-emphasis**
debarbarize	**de-emphasize**
debrutalize	**de-energize**
decanonize	**deflocculate**
decapitalize	**dehydrogenize**
decarbonize	**dehypnotize**
decharm	**de-idealize**
de-Christianize	**de-ionize**
decivilize	**depeople**
declass	**depersonalize**
declassed	**depolish**
declassify	**depopularize**
deconcentrate	**desilver**

dea·con (dē'kən) *n.* 1 A lay church officer or subordinate minister. 2 In the Anglican, Greek, and Roman Catholic Churches, a clergyman ranking next below a priest. 3 Any cleric, as a bishop or priest, acting as chief assistant at a high mass; a gospeler. —*v.t. U.S. Colloq.* 1 To read aloud a line or two of (a hymn) at a time, as an aid to congregational singing: an office of the deacon when hymn books were scarce. 2 To arrange (garden or orchard produce) for sale with only the best showing. 3 To do dishonestly; alter; adulterate. [OE <L *diaconus* <Gk. *diakonos* servant, minister] —**dea'con·ry, dea'con·ship** *n.*

dea·con·ess (dē'kən·is) *n.* A woman appointed or chosen as a lay church worker or officer.

de·ac·ti·vate (dē·ak'tə·vāt) *v.t.* **·vat·ed, ·vat·ing** *Mil.* To release (a military unit, ship, etc.) from active duty; demobilize. —**de·ac'ti·va'·tion** *n.*

dead (ded) *adj.* 1 Having ceased to live; lifeless. 2 In a state or condition resembling death; temporarily disabled; lacking in vitality; numb; motionless. 3 Inanimate; inorganic. 4 Complete; utter; absolute; exact: a *dead* stop, a *dead* level. 5 Unfailing; certain; sure; complete or perfect: a *dead* shot. 6 Not productively employed; also, dull or slow: *dead* capital; also, ineffective; inoperative. 7 Without break or variation; flat; unvaried; a *dead* wall. 8 Dull; uninteresting; lusterless; unburnished. 9 Without elasticity or resilience; non-resonant: a *dead* floor. 10 Extinct; obsolete: a *dead* language. 11 *Colloq.* Exhausted; worn-out. 12 Deprived of civil life, as a life-prisoner. 13 Not fresh or invigorating; lifeless; unresponsive, insensible: usually with *to.* 14 In games, not to be counted: a *dead* ball. 15 Giving no light or heat: *dead* cinders. 16 Not imparting motion; spent; also, unsupported, unrelieved, as of strains or weights. 17 Muffled, as a sound. 18 Not transmitting an electric current. 19 Bringing death; deadly. 20 Past the active point of ferment; also, tasteless, as a beverage. 21 Not required for further use, as composed type, etc. 22 Lying so near the hole that the putt is a certainty: said of a golf ball. —*n.* 1 The most lifeless or inactive period: the *dead* of night. 2 Dead persons collectively: with *the.* —*adv.* To the last degree; wholly; absolutely; exactly: *dead* right, *dead* straight. [OE *dēad*] —**dead'ness** *n.*

Synonyms (adj.): deceased, defunct, departed, inanimate, lifeless. See LIFELESS. *Antonyms*: alive, animate, living.

dead air *Telecom.* A silent interval due to a failure in transmission or a breakdown in the scheduled broadcast.

dead·beat[1] (ded'bēt') *adj.* 1 Beating without recoil, as a watch escapement. 2 *Mech.* Coming to rest without oscillation. —*n.* A movement without recoil; a deadbeat escapement.

dead·beat[2] (ded'bēt') *n.* 1 *U.S. Colloq.* One who is notorious for not paying his bills. 2 *Slang* A sponger.

dead beat *Colloq.* Utterly exhausted: I was *dead beat.* ◆ In attributive use, **dead'-beat'**: a *dead-beat* horse.

dead center *Mech.* That position of a crank or crank motion in which the crank axle, crank pin, and connecting rod centers are all in alinement; the point where a connecting rod has no power to turn a crank. It occurs at each end of the stroke. Also *dead point.* —**dead'-cen'ter** *adj.*

dead drunk So intoxicated as to be close to unconsciousness. ◆ In attributive use, **dead'-drunk'.**

dead duck *Slang* A person or thing whose career, power, influence, etc., is ruined or spent.

dead·en (ded'n) *v.t.* 1 To diminish the sensitivity, force, or intensity of. 2 To lessen or impede the velocity of; retard. 3 To render soundproof. 4 To make dull or less brilliant in color. —*v.i.* 5 To become dead. —**dead'·en·er** *n.*

dead-end (ded'end') *n.* An end of a passage, street, road, etc., having no outlet; a blind alley.

dead·en·ing (ded'n·ing) *n.* 1 The act or agent by which something is deadened. 2 Any material used for dulling or shutting out sound, as in walls. 3 The act of killing trees by girdling. 4 A clearing made by girdling trees.

dead·eye (ded'ī') *n. Naut.* A sheaveless block having scores to receive the lanyard: used to set up shrouds, stays, etc., in rigging a vessel.

dead·fall (ded'fôl') *n.* 1 A trap operated by a weight that, when its support is removed, falls upon and kills or holds an animal. 2 Fallen trees and rubbish matted together.

dead·hand (ded'hand') See under MORTMAIN.

dead·head (ded'hed') *n.* 1 One who receives gratis any service or accommodation for which the general public is expected to pay. 2 A wooden buoy. 3 A sunken or partly sunken log. —*v.t.* & *v.i.* 1 To treat or act as a deadhead. 2 In railroading, to travel with empty cars or with no cars at all: said of locomotives.

dead heat A race in which two or more competitors finish together and there is no one winner.

dead horse *U.S. Colloq.* A debt for something already used up or worn out: so called from the old expression *to pay for a dead horse.*

dead·house (ded'hous') *n.* A morgue.

dead letter 1 A letter which, after lying undelivered for a certain length of time, has been sent to the **dead-letter office,** the department of the general post office where unclaimed letters are examined and returned to their writers or destroyed. 2 Something, as a law, that exists in verbal form, but is not enforced or active.

dead lift 1 A lift made without help, leverage, pulleys, etc. 2 A task or effort accomplished under thankless and discouraging conditions.

dead·light (ded'līt') *n.* 1 *Naut.* **a** A strong shutter, usually of iron, to protect a cabin window or porthole in stormy weather. **b** Round thick glass windows in the side or deck of a ship. 2 A skylight that does not open. 3 *Scot.* A will-o'-the-wisp; ignis fatuus.

dead·line (ded'līn') *n.* 1 A bounding line, as within the limits of a military prison, the crossing of which by a prisoner incurs the penalty of being fired upon by the guard. 2 The time limit before or by which one must complete news copy or other work.

dead load The fixed and permanent load of a structure, as the weight of a building or bridge.

dead·lock (ded'lok') *n.* 1 A lock worked from the outside by a key and from the inside by a handle or the like. 2 A lock in which the bolt has to be turned in each direction by a key: opposed to *springlock.* 3 A block or stoppage of business, as in a legislative or other body, caused by the refusal of opposing parties to cooperate. —*v.t.* & *v.i.* To cause or come to a deadlock.

dead·ly (ded'lē) *adj.* **·li·er, ·li·est** 1 Liable or certain to cause death; fatal. 2 Aiming or tending to kill; mortal; implacable. 3 Resembling death; deathly. See synonyms under NOISOME, PERNICIOUS. —*adv. Obs.* So as to cause death. —**dead'li·ly** *adv.* —**dead'li·ness** *n.*

deadly nightshade Belladonna.

deadly sins See SEVEN DEADLY SINS. Compare VENIAL SIN.

dead·man (ded'man) *n. pl.* **·men** (-men) *Naut.* A log, concrete block, or other heavy mass, usually buried and serving as anchorage for a guy line.

deadman's handle The control mechanism or brake valve of a traction motor equipped with a safety device automatically to cut off the current or apply the brake should the operator's hand relax its pressure for any reason. Also **deadman control.**

dead·march (ded'märch') *n.* A piece of solemn music played at a funeral, especially a military one; music written for a funeral procession.

dead·net·tle (ded'net'l) *n.* Any of several herbs of the mint family (genus *Lamium*) having stingless, nettlelike leaves.

dead pan *U.S. Slang* A completely expressionless face. —**dead'-pan'** *adj.* & *adv.*

dead point See DEAD CENTER.

dead reckoning *Naut.* 1 The computation of a vessel's place at sea by log and compass without astronomical observations. 2 The position of a ship so computed.

Dead Sea A salt lake on the border of Jordan and Israel; 49 miles long; 405 square miles; 1,292 feet below sea level.

Dead Sea fruit Apple of Sodom.
Dead Sea Scrolls A number of scrolls of leather or copper, dating from about 100 B.C. to A.D. 100, containing Hebrew and Aramaic texts of Biblical works and liturgical and communal writings earlier than any such manuscripts extant, found in clay jars in Wadi Qumrân caves, 1947, and later at other sites near the Dead Sea.
dead set *Colloq.* Determined: with *on* or *against.*
dead shot 1 A true shot, one that exactly hits the mark. **2** A person who never misses.
dead soldier *Slang* **1** An empty bottle; especially, an empty liquor bottle: also **dead man. 2** An old cigar or cigarette stub: also called *old soldier.* **3** A dull companion; a bore.
dead storage Storage of vehicles, equipment, etc., for an indefinite period.
dead time *Physics* An interval during which a Geiger counter or similar instrument gives no indication of radioactivity.
dead water 1 Still water. **2** The water that eddies about the stern of a moving vessel.
dead•weight (ded′wāt′) *n.* **1** A burden borne without aid; an oppressive weight or load. **2** In shipping, freight charged for by weight instead of by bulk. **3** In railway transportation, weight of rolling stock as distinguished from its load.
dead•wood (ded′wo͝od′) *n. Naut.* **1** A mass of timber built up above the keel of a vessel at either end to support the cant timbers. **2** Worthless material; a profitless or burdensome person or thing. **3** Wood dead upon the tree. **4** In bowling, a fallen pin lying in front of the standing pins, and giving, if not removed, the next ball a great advantage. **—to have the deadwood on** *U.S. Colloq.* To have superiority or power ver.
deaf (def) *adj.* **1** Lacking or deficient in the sense of hearing. **2** Determined not to hear or be persuaded. **3** *Cap* The community of deaf people who use American Sign Language to communicate. [OE *dēaf*] **—deaf′ly** *adv.* **—deaf′ness** *n.*
deaf•en (def′ən) *v.t.* **1** To make deaf. **2** To confuse, stupefy, or overwhelm, as with noise: The noise of the jets taking off was *deafening.* **3** To drown (a sound) by a louder sound. **4** To make soundproof.
deaf-mute (def′myo͞ot′) *n.* A deaf-and-dumb person. Taken to be offensive. Also **deaf mute.**
De•ák (dā·äk′), **Fe•rencz** (fe′rents), 1803–76, Hungarian statesman.
deal[1] (dēl) *n.* A board or plank, or the wood, either fir or pine, of which it is made. [<MDu. *dele* board, plank]
deal[2] (dēl) *v.* **dealt** (delt), **deal•ing** *v.t.* **1** To distribute among a number of persons; meteout, as playing cards. **2** To apportion to (one person) as his or her share. **3** To deliver or inflict, as a blow. *—v.i.* **4** To conduct oneself; behave towards: with *with*: to *deal* effectively with a matter. **5** To be concerned or occupied: with *in* or *with*: I *deal* in facts. **6** To consider, discuss, or administer; take action: with *with*: The court will *deal* with him. **7** To trade; do business: with *in, with,* or *at.* **8** In card games, to act as dealer. See synonyms under APPORTION. *—n.* **1** Distribution; apportionment. **2** The act of distributing; especially, the distribution of, or right to distribute cards; a single round of play; also, the hand dealt. **3** *Colloq.* A secret bargain in politics or commerce. **4** A transaction or bargain. **5** Treatment given or received: a square *deal.* **6** An indefinite quantity, degree, or extent: a great *deal* of trouble. [OE *dælan.* Related to DOLE[1].]
Deal (dēl) A port and resort town in eastern Kent, England.
deal•er (dē′lər) *n.* **1** A trader. **2** The player who distributes the cards.
deal•fish (dēl′fish′) *n. pl.* **•fish** or **•fish•es** A ribbonfish *(Trachypterus arcticus)* of northern seas.
deal•ing (dē′ling) *n.* **1** *Usually pl.* Any transaction with others. **2** The act of one who deals. **3** The method or manner of treatment: honest *dealing.*
de•am•i•na•tion (dē·am′ə·nā′shən) *n. Biochem.* The splitting off of the amino radical, NH_2, from the amino acid molecule in the body, as a stage in the formation of fatty acids from proteins. Also **de•am′i•ni•za′tion.**
dean (dēn) *n.* **1** The chief ecclesiastical officer of a cathedral or of a collegiate church. **2** *Chiefly Brit.* An ecclesiastical officer, often acting as a deputy of a bishop or archdeacon in the administration of part of a diocese: also called *rural dean.* **3** An executive officer of a college or university, having jurisdiction over a particular class or group of students, or acting as head of a faculty: *dean* of men, *dean* of the law school. **4** The senior member, in length of service, of an association or body of men: the *dean* of American composers. [<OF *deien* <LL *decanus* head of ten men <L *decem* ten]
Dean (dēn), **Forest of** A wooded district of western Gloucester, England.
Deane (dēn), **Silas,** 1737–89, American Revolutionary patriot and diplomat.
dean•er•y (dē′nər·ē) *n. pl.* **•er•ies** The office, revenue, jurisdiction, or place of residence of a dean.
dean•ship (dēn′ship) *n.* The office, rank, or title of a dean.
dear[1] (dir) *adj.* **1** Beloved; precious. **2** Highly esteemed: used in letter salutations: *Dear* Sir. **3** Held at a high price, or rate; costly. **4** Characterized by high prices. **5** Intense; earnest: our *dearest* wish. **6** *Obs.* Noble; glorious. *—n.* One who is much beloved; a darling. *— adv.* Dearly. *—interj.* An exclamation of regret, surprise, etc. ◆Homophone: *deer.* [OE *dēore*] **—dear′ness** *n.*
dear[2] (dir) *adj. Obs.* Severe; dire; difficult. Also **dere.** ◆Homophone: *deer.* [OE *dēor* wild]
Dear•born (dir′bôrn′, -bərn) A city in SE Michigan near Detroit.
dear•ly (dir′lē) *adv.* **1** With much affection; fondly; tenderly. **2** At a high price or rate; at great cost. **3** Earnestly; deeply.
dearth (dûrth) *n.* **1** Scarcity; lack; famine. **2** *Obs.* Dearness; costliness. See synonyms under WANT. [ME *derthe*]
death (deth) *n.* **1** Cessation of physical life. **2** Extinction of anything; destruction. **3** Something likely to produce death; a cause or occasion of death. **4** Something considered as terrible as death. **5** The cessation, absence, or opposite of spiritual life; spiritual and eternal ruin. **6** A fatal plague. **7** A personification, type, or representation of mortality, generally a skeleton holding a scythe. **8** Slaughter; bloodshed. **9** The condition of being dead. ◆Collateral adjectives: *lethal, mortal.* **— at death's door** Almost dead. **—to be death on** *Colloq.* **1** To dislike intensely enough to kill. **2** To have a special talent for; be very fond of. **—to death** Very much: He frightened me *to death.* **—to put to death** To kill; execute. [OE *dēath*]
death•bed (deth′bed′) *n.* The bed on which one dies; the last hours of life: also used attributively.
death bell 1 A bell announcing death; a passing bell. **2** A ringing in the ears like a tolling bell: thought by some to presage the news of a death.
death•blow (deth′blō′) *n.* A fatal blow or shock.
death camas Any of several herbaceous plants of the lily family (genus *Zygadenus*) common in the western United States and poisonous to men and animals: often confused with the edible camas.
death camp A concentration camp established for the purpose of eliminating part of the population of a country or minority group by systematic mass executions: also called *extermination camp.*
death chair The electric chair.
death•cup (deth′kup′) *n.* A common, poisonous mushroom *(Amanita phalloides)* having bright-red caps dotted with white.
death duty Inheritance taxes; a tax on property inherited.
death•ful (deth′fəl) *adj.* **1** Deadly; murderous; full of slaughter. **2** Mortal; liable to die. **3** Having the appearance of death. **—death′•ful•ness** *n.*
death house That part of a prison, as a block of cells, in which prisoners condemned to death are confined.
death•less (deth′lis) *adj.* Not liable to die; undying; unending; perpetual. See synonyms under ETERNAL, IMMORTAL. **— death′less•ly** *adv.* **—death′less•ness** *n.*
death•ly (deth′lē) *adj.* **1** Having the semblance or suggestion of death: also **death′like′. 2** Pertaining to death. **3** Deadly. See synonyms under GHASTLY. **—** *adv.* So as to be as one dead or dying. **— death′li•ness** *n.*
death mask A cast of the face taken just after death.
death point *Bacteriol.* The critical upper and lower temperatures beyond which microorganisms cannot live.
death rate The number of persons per thousand of population dying in a given unit of time.
death rattle The rattling sound caused by the breath passing through mucus in the throat of one dying.
death's-head (deths′hed′) *n.* A human skull or a representation of it, as a symbol of death.
death's-head moth A large, Old World sphinx moth (genus *Acherontia*), with markings like a death's-head on the upper surface of the thorax.

DEATH'S-HEAD MOTH

deaths•man (deths′mən) *n. pl.* **•men** (-mən) *Archaic* The hangman.
death•trap (deth′trap′) *n.* A building or structure where the risk of death, particularly from fire, is great.
Death Valley A deep and desert basin in SE California; site of **Death Valley National Monument**; 2,906 square miles; established 1933.
death warrant 1 *Law* An official order for the execution of a person. **2** That which insures destruction or puts an end to hope.
death•watch (deth′woch′, -wôch′) *n.* **1** The last vigil with the dying or with the body of one dead. **2** A guard set over a condemned man before his execution. **3** A small, European, wood-boring beetle. *(Xestobium rufovillosum)* that makes a ticking noise, superstitiously thought to presage death.
death whisper Sound waves of such high frequency as to be inaudible to human ears, and having the power to kill small animals, as fish in water, under certain conditions.
death•y (deth′ē) *adj. adv. Rare* Deathly.
Deau•ville (dō′vil, *Fr.* dō·vēl′)A resort town of NW France on the English Channel.
deave (dēv) *v.t.* Scot. *Brit. Dial.* To deafen or bewilder with noise. [OE *dē afian* in *adēafian* grow deaf]
de•ba•cle (dā·bä′kəl, -bak′əl, di-) *n.* **1** A sudden and disastrous breakdown, overthrow, or collapse, as of a government; ruin; rout. **2** The breaking up of ice in a river, etc. **3** A violent flood carrying great masses of rock and other debris. [<F *débâ cle* <*débâcler* unbar, set free]
de•bar (di·bär′) *v.t.* **• barred, •bar•ring 1** To bar or shut out; exclude: usually with *from.* **2** To prohibit; hinder. See synonyms under PROHIBIT, SUSPEND. [<F *débarrer* <*dé-* away (<L *dis-*) + *barrer* bar]

de·bark (di·bärk′) *v.t.* To put ashore or unload from a ship. —*v.i.* To go ashore; disembark. Compare DISEMBARK. [<F *débarquer* <*dé-* away, from + *barque* a ship] —**de·bar·ka·tion** (dē′bär·kā′shən) *n.*

de·bar·ment (di·bär′mənt) *n.* The act of debarring; exclusion; obstruction.

de·base (di·bās′) *v.t.* **de·based, de·bas·ing** To lower in character, purity, or value; degrade. See synonyms under ABASE, CORRUPT, IMPAIR. [<DE- + obs. *base*, var. of ABASE] —**de·base′·ment** *n.* —**de·bas′er** *n.*

de·bate (di·bāt′) *v.* **de·bat·ed, de·bat·ing** *v.t.* **1** To discuss or argue about, as in a public meeting. **2** To discuss in formal argument. **3** To consider; deliberate upon in the mind, as alternatives. **4** *Obs.* To fight or contend for or over. —*v.i.* **5** To argue; discuss. **6** To engage in formal argument. **7** To deliberate mentally; consider. See synonyms under DELIBERATE, DISPUTE. —*n.* **1** The discussing of any question; argumentation; dispute; controversy. **2** A formal argument conducted systematically to test the reasoning skill of two persons or teams taking opposing sides of a specific question (the resolution). **3** *Obs.* Combat; strife. See synonyms under ALTERCATION, REASONING. [<OF *debatre* <*de-* down (<L *de-*) + *batre* <L *batuere* strike] —**de·bat′a·ble** *adj.* —**de·bat′er** *n.*

de·bauch (di·bôch′) *v.t.* **1** To corrupt in morals; seduce; deprave. **2** *Obs.* To cause to forsake allegiance; disaffect. —*v.i.* **3** To indulge in lechery, gluttony, or drunkenness; dissipate. See synonyms under POLLUTE, VIOLATE. —*n.* **1** An act or occasion of debauchery; a carouse. **2** Excess; intemperance; lewdness. [<F *débaucher* lure from work <OF *desbaucher*]

de·bauched (di·bôcht′) *adj.* **1** Corrupted. **2** Characterized by debauchery. —**de·bauch·ed·ly** (di·bô′chid·lē) *adv.* —**de·bauch′ed·ness** *n.*

deb·au·chee (deb′ô·chē′, -shē′) *n.* One habitually profligate, drunken, or lewd; a libertine.

de·bauch·er (di·bô′chər) *n.* One who debauches; a seducer.

de·bauch·er·y (di·bô′chər·ē) *n. pl.* **·er·ies** **1** Licentiousness; drunkenness. **2** Seduction from virtue, purity, or fidelity. Also **de·bauch′ment.**

Deb·by (deb′ē) Diminutive of DEBORAH.

de Beau·voir (də bō·vwär′) See BEAUVOIR, SIMONE DE.

de·ben·ture (di·ben′chər) *n.* **1** An instrument in the nature of a bond, given as an acknowledgment of debt, and providing for repayment out of some specified fund or source of income: as, a mortgage *debenture*, one secured by a mortgage. **2** A customhouse certificate providing for a drawback. **3** A government pay order. See under BOND, STOCK. [<L *debentur* there are owing <*debere* owe]

debenture bond See under BOND.

De·bierne (də·byârn′), **André Louis,** 1874–1949, French chemist.

de·bil·i·tate (di·bil′ə·tāt) *v.t.* **·tat·ed, ·tat·ing** To make feeble or languid; weaken. [<L *debilitatus*, pp. of *debilitare* <*debilis* weak] —**de·bil′i·tant** *adj.* & *n.* —**de·bil′i·tat′ed** *adj.* —**de·bil′i·ta′tion** *n.* —**de·bil′i·ta′tive** *adj.*

de·bil·i·ty (di·bil′ə·tē) *n. pl.* **·ties** Abnormal weakness; languor; feebleness. [<F *débilité* <L *debilitas, -tatis* <*debilis* weak]

deb·it (deb′it) *v.t.* **1** To enter on the debit side of an account. **2** To charge (a customer) for goods. —*n.* The debit side of an account; a debt or debts recorded; something owed. Compare CREDIT. [<L *debitum*, pp. of *debere* owe. Doublet of DEBT.]

deb·o·nair (deb′ə·nâr′) *adj.* Gentle or courteous; affable; complaisant; gay. Also **deb′·o·naire′, deb′on·naire′.** [<F *debonnaire* <OF *de bon aire* of good mien] —**deb′o·nair′ly** *adv.* —**deb′o·nair′ness** *n.*

de bo·nis non (ad·min·i·stra·tis) (dē bō′nis non ad·min′ə·strā′tis) *Law Latin* Of the goods not (administered): said of unadministered property transferred from an administrator to his successor.

de bonne grâce (də bôn gräs′) *French* With good grace; cheerfully.

Deb·o·rah (deb′ər·ə, deb′rə) A feminine personal name. Also *Fr.* **Dé·bo·ra** (dā·bô·rá′), *Ital.* **De·bo·ra** (dā′bō·rä). [<Hebrew, a bee] —**Deborah** A prophetess of Mount Ephraim, who judged Israel, and who, with Barak, defeated Sisera about 1285 B.C. *Judges* iv 4.

de·bouch (di·bōōsh′) *v.i.* **1** *Mil.* To come forth or issue from a defile or a wood into the open. **2** To come forth; emerge. —*v.t.* **3** To cause to emerge. —*n.* **1** An opening, especially in military works, for the passage of troops. **2** An outlet for commerce; market. Also *French* **dé·bou·ché** (dā·bōō·shā′) *n.* [<F *déboucher* <*dé-* from (<L *dis-*) + *bouche* a mouth]

de·bouch·ment (di·bōōsh′mənt) *n.* **1** *Geog.* The opening out of a valley, stream, etc. **2** The act of debouching. Also *French* **dé·bou·chure** (dā·bōō·shür′).

De·bre·cen (de′bre·tsen) A city in eastern Hungary. Formerly **De′bre·czen.**

dé·bride·ment (dā·brēd·mäṅ′, di·brēd′mənt) *n. Surg.* The excision of tissues and dead matter from the interior of wounds, to prevent septic infection. [<F *débrider* unbridle]

de·brief (dē·brēf′) *v.t. Mil.* To question or instruct (a pilot, agent, etc.) at the end of a mission or period of service.

de·bris (də·brē′, dā′brē; *Brit.* deb′rē) *n.* **1** Accumulated fragments; ruins; rubbish. **2** *Geol.* An aggregation of detached fragments of rocks. Also **dé·bris′.** See synonyms under WASTE. [<F *débris* <OF *débriser* <*des-* away (<L *dis-*) + *brisier* break]

de Bro·glie (də·brœ′y′) A family, originally of Piedmont, distinguished in French history: especially **Duc Achille Charles Léonce Victor,** 1785–1870, statesman; **Maurice,** 1875–1960, and **Louis Victor,** born 1892, physicists.

de Broglie wave *Physics* A wave or group of waves thought to be associated with elementary particles, as electrons, protons, etc. [after Louis Victor *de Broglie*]

Debs (debz), **Eugene Victor,** 1855–1926, U.S. labor leader; Socialist candidate for president 1900–12, 1920.

debt (det) *n.* **1** That which one owes. **2** An obligation. **3** The state of being indebted. **4** *Theol.* A sin; trespass. [<OF *dette* <L *debitum*. Doublet of DEBIT.]

debt·or (det′ər) *n.* **1** One who is in debt; one who is under obligation to another, as for money or goods, or for service, benefit, or help. **2** The left-hand or debit side of an account in bookkeeping. [<OF *dettor* <L *debitor* <*debere* owe]

de·bunk (di·bungk′) *v.t. Colloq.* To reveal the sham, false pretensions, etc., of. [<BUNK[2]]

De·bus·sy (də·byōō′sē, *Fr.* də·bü·sē′), **Claude Achille,** 1862–1918, French composer.

de·but (di·byōō′, dā-, dā′byōō) *n.* A first appearance, as in society or on the stage; first attempt; beginning. Also **dé·but′.** [<F *début* <*débuter* begin, lead off]

deb·u·tante (deb′yōō·tänt′, deb′yōō·tant) *n. fem.* A young girl or woman who makes a debut, especially into society. Also **dé′bu·tante′.** [<F *débutante*, fem. ppr. of *débuter* begin] —**deb′u·tant′** *n. masc.*

deca– *combining form* **1** Ten: *decapod.* **2** In the metric system, deka–. Also, before vowels, dec–.

dec·ade (dek′ād, de·kād′) *n.* **1** A period of ten years. **2** A group or set of ten. [<MF <L *decas, decadis* a group of ten <Gk. *dekas* <*deka* ten]

de·ca·dence (di·kād′ns, dek′ə·dəns) *n.* A process of deterioration; decay; a condition or period of decline, as in literature, art, morals, etc. [<F *décadence* <Med. L *decadentia* <L *decadere* <*de-* down + *cadere* fall]

de·ca·dent (di·kād′nt, dek′ə·dənt) *adj.* Falling into ruin or decay. —*n.* **1** One who has fallen from a high social position. **2** One in a state or process of mental or moral decay; a decadent person. **3** Specifically, a member of a school of French writers of the late 19th century characterized by their cultivation of subtle, refined, artificial qualities in subject and treatment. —**de·ca′dent·ly** *adv.*

DECAGON

dec·a·gon (dek′ə·gon) *n.* A plane figure with ten sides and ten angles. [<Gk. *dekagōnon* <*deka* ten + *gōnia* angle] —**de·cag·o·nal** (di·kag′ə·nəl) *adj.* —**de·cag′o·nal·ly** *adv.*

dec·a·gram (dek′ə·gram) See DEKAGRAM.

dec·a·he·dron (dek′ə·hē′drən) *n.* A solid bounded by ten plane faces. [<DECA- + Gk. *hedra* seat] —**dec′a·he′dral** *adj.*

DECAHEDRON

dé·ca·lage (dā·kä·läzh′) *n. Aeron.* The variance in angle of incidence between two sustaining surfaces of an airplane. [<F <*décaler* shift, set at an angle]

de·cal·ci·fi·ca·tion (dē·kal′sə·fə·kā′shən) *n.* **1** The action of decalcifying. **2** *Dent.* The removal of calcareous matter from the teeth.

de·cal·ci·fy (dē·kal′sə·fī) *v.t.* **·fied, ·fy·ing** To deprive of lime.

de·cal·co·ma·ni·a (di·kal′kə·mā′nē·ə, -mān′yə) *n.* **1** A process of transferring decorative pictures or designs from paper to glass, porcelain, etc. **2** Such a print to be transferred. **3** The decoration of glassware by gumming pictures upon it. Also **de·cal′.** [<F *décalcomanie* <*décalquer* transfer a tracing + *-manie* -MANIA]

de·ca·les·cence (dē′kə·les′əns) *n. Physics* The sudden absorption of heat by metals when the temperature passes a certain critical point, indicating internal structural changes: opposed to *recalescence.* —**de′ca·les′cent** *adj.* [<L *decalescens, -entis*, ppr. of *decalescere* <*de-* not + *calescere* grow hot]

dec·a·li·ter (dek′ə·lē′tər) See DEKALITER.

Dec·a·log (dek′ə·lôg, -log) *n.* The Ten Commandments. *Exod.* xx 2–17. Also **Dec′a·logue.** [<Gk. *dekalogos* <*deka* ten + *logos* word]

De·cam·er·on (di·kam′ər·ən) A collection of 100 stories by Boccaccio (published 1353), told by ten Florentines who secluded themselves for ten days from their plague-striken city. [<Ital. *decamerone* <Gk. *deka* ten + *hēmera* day]

dec·a·me·ter (dek′ə·mē′tər) *n.* **1** A dekameter. **2** Verse consisting of ten rhythmical feet. Also **dec′a·me′tre.** [<F *décamètre* <Gk. *dekametron* <*deka* ten + *metron* measure]

de·camp (di·kamp′) *v.i.* **1** To break camp or leave camp. **2** To leave suddenly or secretly; run away. See synonyms under ESCAPE. —**de·camp′ment** *n.*

De·camps (də·käṅ′), **Alexandre Gabriel,** 1803–60, French painter.

dec·a·nal (dek′ə·nəl, di·kā′nəl) *adj.* Of or pertaining to a dean or deanery. [<LL *decanus*. See DEAN.] —**dec′a·nal·ly** *adv.*

de·can·drous (di·kan′drəs) *adj. Bot.* Having ten stamens. [<DEC(A)- + Gk. *anēr, andros* man]

dec·ane (dek′ān) *n. Chem.* Any of several isomeric hydrocarbons, $C_{10}H_{22}$, of the methane series, variously derived, from coal tar, etc. [<DEC(A)- + -ANE[2]]

de·cant (di·kant′) *v.t.* **1** To pour off gently so as not to disturb the sediment. **2** To pour from one container into another. [<F *décanter* <Med. L *decanthare* <*de-* from + *canthus* lip of a jug <Gk. *kanthos*] —**de·can·ta·tion** (dē′kan·tā′shən) *n.*

de·cant·er (di·kan′tər) *n.* An ornamental bottle for wine, etc.

DECANTER

de·cap·i·tate (di·kap′ə·tāt) *v.t.* **·tat·ed, ·tat·ing** To behead. [<Med. L *decapitare* <*de-* down + *caput* head] —**de·cap′i·ta′tion** *n.* —**de·cap′i·ta′tor** *n.*

dec·a·pod (dek′ə·pod) *adj.* **1** Ten-footed or ten-armed. **2** *Zool.* Of or pertaining to the *Decapoda*, an order of crustaceans with five pairs of legs, including the crabs, lobsters, shrimps, etc. —*n.* A ten-legged crustacean; also, a ten-armed cephalopod, as a cuttlefish or squid. [<Gk. *dekapous, -podos* <*deka* ten + *pous* foot] —**de·cap·o·dal** (di·kap′ə·dəl), **de·cap′o·dous** *adj.*

dec·a·pod·i·form (dek′ə·pod′ə·fôrm) *adj.* Shaped like a decapod.

De·cap·o·lis (di·kap′ə·lis) A region in the north of ancient Palestine containing a confederacy of ten cities. *Matt.* iv 25.

de·cap·su·la·tion (di·kap′sə·lā′shən) *n. Surg.*

The removal of the enveloping membrane of an organ, especially the capsule of the kidney.

de·car·bon·ate (di·kär′bə·nāt) *v.t.* **·at·ed, ·at·ing** To free from carbon dioxide. **—de·car′bon·a′tor** *n.*

de·car·bon·ize (di·kär′bə·nīz) *v.t.* **·ized, ·iz·ing** To decarburize. **—de·car′bon·i·za′tion** *n.* **—de·car′bon·iz′er** *n.*

de·car·box·y·la·tion (dē′kär·bok′sə·lā′shən) *n. Chem.* The elimination of one or more carboxyl radicals from an organic acid, with the release of carbon dioxide. [<DE- + CARBOXYL]

de·car·bu·rize (dē·kär′byə·rīz) *v.t.* **·rized, ·riz·ing 1** To deprive wholly or in part of carbon. **2** To remove carbon from (molten steel or the cylinders of an internal-combustion engine). **—de·car′bu·ri·za′tion** *n.*

dec·are (dek′âr, dek·âr′) See DEKARE.

dec·a·stere (dek′ə·stir) See DEKASTERE.

dec·a·syl·la·ble (dek′ə·sil′ə·bəl) *n.* A line of verse having ten syllables. **—dec·a·syl·lab·ic** (dek′ə·si·lab′ik) *adj.*

de·cath·lon (di·kath′lon) *n.* An athletic contest consisting of ten different track and field events in which each contestant participates. [<DEC(A)- + Gk. *athlon* a contest]

dec·at·ing (dek′āt·ing) *n.* A method for the application of heat, moisture, and pressure to fabrics in order to set the nap, add luster, and control shrinkage. Also **dec·a·tiz·ing** (dek′ə·tī′zing). [<F *dicatir* sponge (a fabric) to set the gloss]

De·ca·tur (di·kā′tər) A city in central Illinois.

De·ca·tur (di·kā′tər), **Stephen,** 1779–1820, U.S. naval officer.

de·cay (di·kā′) *v.i.* **1** To fail slowly in health, beauty, quality, or any form of excellence. **2** To rot; decompose. —*v.t.* **3** To cause to decay. —*n.* **1** A passing into a feeble or reduced condition tending toward dissolution. **2** A gradual decline in health, size or quality; deterioration. **3** Decomposition; corruption; rottenness. **4** *Physics* The disintegration of a radioactive element. See synonyms under RUIN. [<OF *decair,* var. of *decaoir* <L *decidere* <*de-* down + *cadere* fall] **—de·cay′a·ble** *adj.* **—de·cay·ed·ness** (di·kā′id·nis) *n.*

Synonyms (verb): corrupt, decompose, molder, putrefy, rot, spoil. *Rot* is a strong and direct word. To say that a thing is *decayed* may denote only a partial result, but to say it is *decomposed* ordinarily implies that the change is complete or nearly so. *Putrefy* and the adjectives *putrid* and *putrescent,* and the nouns *putridity* and *putrescence,* are used almost exclusively of animal matter in a state of decomposition, the more general word *decay* being used of either animal or vegetable substances. *Decay* may also be extended to any process of decline or breaking down, physical, mental, social, etc. See PUTREFY.

Dec·can Plateau (dek′ən) A triangular tableland covering most of peninsular India.

Deccan States A group of former princely states within south and central Bombay state, India.

de·cease (di·sēs′) *v.i.* **de·ceased, de·ceas·ing** To die. [<*n.*] —*n.* Departure from life; death. [<OF *déces* <L *decessus* <*decedere* <*de-* away + *cedere* go]

de·ceased (di·sēst′) *adj.* Dead. **—the deceased 1** The dead person. **2** Dead persons. See synonyms under LIFELESS.

de·ce·dent (di·sēd′nt) *n.* A person deceased. [<L *decedens, -entis,* ppr. of *decedere.* See DECEASE.]

de·ceit (di·sēt′) *n.* The act of deceiving; deception; lying. **2** A lie or other dishonest action; trick. **3** Deceptiveness. See synonyms under DECEPTION, FRAUD, LIE. [<OF *deceite* < *deceveir* DECEIVE]

de·ceit·ful (di·sēt′fəl) *adj.* Characterized by deception; false; tricky; fraudulent. See synonyms under BAD, DECEPTIVE, INSIDIOUS, PERFIDIOUS, ROTTEN, VAIN. **—de·ceit′ful·ly** *adv.* **—de·ceit′ful·ness** *n.*

de·ceiv·a·ble (di·sē′və·bəl) *adj.* Capable of being deceived; liable to imposition. **—de·ceiv′a·ble·ness** *n.* **—de·ceiv′a·bly** *adv.*

de·ceive (di·sēv′) *v.* **de·ceived, de·ceiv·ing** *v.t.* **1** To mislead by or as by falsehood; impose upon; delude. **2** *Obs.* To while away (time). —*v.i.* **3** To practice deceit. [<OF *deceveir* <L *decipere* <*de-* away, down + *capere* take] **—de·ceiv′ing·ly** *adv.*

Synonyms: beguile, betray, cheat, circumvent, defraud, delude, dupe, ensnare, entrap, mislead, outwit, overreach, trick. See MISLEAD. Compare DECEPTION.

de·ceiv·er (di·sē′vər) *n.* One who deceives. See synonyms under HYPOCRITE.

de·cel·er·ate (dē·sel′ə·rāt) *v.t.* & *v.i.* **·at·ed, ·at·ing** To diminish in velocity. [<DE- + L *celeratus,* pp. of *celerare* hasten <*celer* quick] **—de·cel′er·a′tor** *n.*

de·cel·er·a·tion (dē·sel′ə·rā′shən) *n.* Negative acceleration. See under ACCELERATION (def. 2).

De·cem·ber (di·sem′bər) The twelfth month of the year, having 31 days. [<L <*decem* ten; because December was the tenth month in the old Roman calendar]

De·cem·brist (di·sem′brist) *n.* One of those who conspired against Czar Nicholas I, on his accession, Dec., 1825.

de·cem·vir (di·sem′vər) *n. pl.* **·virs** or **·vi·ri** (-və·rī) A member of any body of ten magistrates; specifically, one commissioned to codify the laws of Rome in 451 B.C. [<L <*decem* ten + *vir* man] **—de·cem′vi·ral** *adj.*

de·cem·vi·rate (di·sem′və·rit, -rāt) *n.* **1** A body of ten men in authority. **2** The office of such a body.

de·cen·cy (dē′sən·sē) *n. pl.* **·cies 1** Propriety in conduct, speech, or dress; modesty. **2** That which is decent, proper, or seemly. **3** *pl.* Things required for a proper or comfortable manner of life. [<L *decentia* <*decens.* See DECENT.]

de·cen·na·ry (di·sen′ər·ē) *adj.* Consisting of or pertaining to ten; pertaining to ten years or to a tithing: also **de·cen′a·ry.** —*n. pl.* **·ries 1** In old English law, a tithing or group of ten freeholders and their families. **2** A period of ten years. [<L *decennis* <*decem* ten + *annus* year]

de·cen·ni·al (di·sen′ē·əl) *adj.* Continuing for or consisting of ten years; occurring every ten years. —*n.* An anniversary observed at periods of ten years. **—de·cen′ni·al·ly** *adv.*

de·cen·ni·um (di·sen′ē·əm) *n. pl.* **·cen·ni·ums** or **·cen·ni·a** (-sen′ē·ə) A period of ten years; decade. [<L <*decem* ten + *annus* year]

de·cent (dē′sənt) *adj.* **1** Characterized by propriety of conduct, speech, manners, or dress; proper; decorous; respectable. **2** Free from indelicacy; modest; chaste. **3** Sufficient; passable; moderate. **4** *Obs.* Appropriate; also, symmetrical; comely. See synonyms under BECOMING, MODEST. [<L *decens, -entis,* ppr. of *decere* be fitting, be proper] **—de′cent·ly** *adv.* **—de′cent·ness** *n.*

de·cen·ter (dē·sen′tər) *v.t.* **1** To put out of center; make eccentric. **2** *Optics* To cut, as a lens for an eyeglass, so that the physical center and the optical center of the lens surfaces do not coincide. Also **de·cen′tre.**

de·cen·tral·ize (dē·sen′trəl·īz) *v.t.* **·ized, ·iz·ing 1** To remove from a center; distribute: used especially of government or other authority. **2** *Econ.* To reorganize (a large enterprise, industry, or corporation) into smaller and more dispersed units in order to permit more efficient management and control. **—de·cen′tral·i·za′tion** *n.*

de·cep·tion (di·sep′shən) *n.* **1** The act of deceiving. **2** The state of being deceived. **3** Anything that deceives or is meant to deceive; a delusion. [<L *deceptio, -onis* <*decipere.* See DECEIVE.]

Synonyms: craft, cunning, deceit, deceitfulness, delusion, dissimulation, double-dealing, duplicity, fabrication, falsehood, finesse, fraud, guile, hypocrisy, imposition, lie, lying, prevarication, trickery, untruth. *Deceit* is especially applied to the habit, *deception* to the act; *guile* applies to the disposition out of which *deceit* and *deception* grow, and also to their actual practice. A *lie, lying,* or *falsehood* is the uttering of what one knows to be false with intent to deceive. *Untruth* is more than lack of accuracy, implying always lack of veracity; but it is a somewhat milder and more dignified word than *lie. Falsehood* and *lying* are in utterance; *deceit* and *deception* may be merely in act or implication. *Deception* may be innocent, and even unintentional, as in the case of an optical illusion; *deceit* always involves injurious intent. *Craft* and *cunning* have not necessarily any moral quality; they are common traits of animals, but stand rather low in the human scale. *Duplicity* is the habitual speaking or acting with intent to appear to mean what one does not. *Dissimulation* is rather a concealing of what is than a pretense of what is not. *Finesse* is simply an adroit and delicate management of a matter for one's own side, not necessarily involving *deceit.* Compare FRAUD, LIE. *Antonyms*: candor, frankness, guilelessness, honesty, openness, simplicity, sincerity, truth, veracity.

de·cep·tive (di·sep′tiv) *adj.* Having power or tendency to deceive. **—de·cep′tive·ly** *adv.* **—de·cep′tive·ness** *n.*

Synonyms: deceitful, delusive, illusive, illusory. Persons are *deceitful*: things are *deceptive.* We speak of a *deceitful,* but not of a *deceptive* man. We speak, however, of *deceitful* promises, as involving personal intent to deceive. It is more accurate to say *deceptive* than *deceitful* appearances. See BAD, COUNTERFEIT. *Antonyms*: fair, frank, genuine, honest.

de·cer·e·brate (dē·ser′ə·brāt) *v.t.* **·brat·ed, ·brat·ing** To remove the brain from, as in certain operations and laboratory experiments. —*adj.* (-brit) Having the brain removed. [<DE- + L *cerebrum* brain] **—de·cer′e·bra′tion** *n.*

de·cer·e·brize (dē·ser′ə·brīz) *v.t.* **·brized, ·briz·ing** To remove the cerebrum or brain from, as in vivisection.

de·cern (di·sûrn′) *v.t.* **1** In Scots law, to decree. **2** To discern. [<F *décerner* <L *decernere* decide <*de-* down + *cernere* decide]

deci- *combining form* A tenth. See METRIC SYSTEM. [<L *decimus* tenth <*decem* ten]

dec·i·are (des′ē·âr) *n.* One tenth of an are. See METRIC SYSTEM. [<F *déciare*]

dec·i·bel (des′ə·bel) *n. Physics* One tenth of a bel: the common unit of measure of loudness of sounds.

de·cide (di·sīd′) *v.* **·cid·ed, ·cid·ing** *v.t.* **1** To determine; settle, as a controversy, dispute, contest, etc.; arbitrate: to *decide* who is right. **2** To cause the outcome of; settle: The charge *decided* the battle. **3** To bring (someone) to a decision. —*v.i.* **4** To give a decision. **5** To make a decision. See synonyms under SETTLE. [<MF *décider* <L *decidere* <*de-* down, away + *caedere* cut] **—de·cid′a·ble** *adj.*

de·cid·ed (di·sī′did) *adj.* **1** Free from uncertainty; unquestionable; unmistakable. **2** Determined; resolute; emphatic. See synonyms under FIRM. **—de·cid′ed·ly** *adv.* **—de·cid′ed·ness** *n.*

de·cid·u·a (di·sij′o͞o·ə) *n. Physiol.* The thickened mucous membrane of the uterus cast off and expelled either during menstruation (*decidua menstrualis*) or at parturition (*decidua graviditatis*). [<NL (*membrana*) *decidua* (membrane) that is cast off <*deciduus.* See DECIDUOUS.] **—de·cid′u·al** *adj.*

de·cid·u·ous (di·sij′o͞o·əs) *adj.* **1** *Bot.* Falling off or shed at maturity or at specific seasons, as petals, fruit, or leaves; also, characterized by such a falling off; not evergreen. **2** *Zool.* Liable to be shed at periodical times, as antlers, hair, teeth, wings of insects, etc. **3** Not enduring; evanescent; short-lived. Compare PERSISTENT. [<L *deciduus* <*decidere* <*de-* down, away + *cadere* fall] **—de·cid′u·ous·ly** *adv.* **—de·cid′u·ous·ness** *n.*

dec·i·gram (des′ə·gram) *n.* The tenth part of a gram. See METRIC SYSTEM. Also **dec′i·gramme.**

dec·ile (des′il) *n. Stat.* One of the parts or intervals of a frequency distribution, each of which contains one tenth of the observations or cases in the complete series. [<F *décile* <L *decem* ten]

dec·i·li·ter (des′ə·lē′tər) *n.* The tenth part of a liter. See METRIC SYSTEM. Also **dec′i·li′tre.**

de·cil·lion (de·sil′yən) *n.* The numeral 1 followed by thirty-three ciphers according to American and French notation, or by sixty ciphers in English notation. [<DEC(A)- + (M)ILLION] **—de·cil′lionth** *adj.*

dec·i·mal (des′ə·məl) *adj.* **1** Pertaining to or founded on the number 10. **2** Proceeding by powers of 10 or of one tenth. —*n.* A decimal fraction or one of its digits. [<Med. L *decimalis* of tenths <*decimus* tenth <*decem* ten]

decimal fraction See under FRACTION.

dec·i·mal·i·za·tion (des′ə·məl·i·zā′shən) *n.* The process or program of adopting the decimal system, as in currency.

dec·i·mal·ize (des′ə·məl·īz′) *v.t.* **·ized, ·iz·ing** To reduce to a decimal system.

decimal point A dot or period used before a decimal fraction.

decimal system A system of reckoning by tens or tenths.

dec·i·mate (des′ə·māt) *v.t.* **·mat·ed, ·mat·ing 1** To destroy or kill a large proportion of. **2** To select by lot and kill one out of every ten of. **3** *Obs.* To exact a tithe from; take a tenth part of. [< L *decimatus,* pp. of *decimare* take a tenth part from < *decem* ten] **—dec′i·ma′tion** *n.* **—dec′i·ma′tor** *n.*

dec·i·me·ter (des′ə·mē′tər) *n.* The tenth part of a meter. See METRIC SYSTEM. Also **dec′i·me′tre.**

de·ci·pher (di·sī′fər) *v.t.* **1** To determine the meaning of, as hieroglyphics or illegible writing. **2** To translate from cipher into ordinary characters. **3** To determine the meaning of (anything obscure). See synonyms under INTERPRET. **—de·ci′pher·a·ble** *adj.* **—de·ci′pher·er** *n.* **—de·ci′pher·ment** *n.*

de·ci·sion (di·sizh′ən) *n.* **1** The act of deciding or making up one's mind. **2** Decisive result; settlement; judgment, as of a court. **3** The quality of being positive and firm; determination. See synonyms under DETERMINATION, WILL. [< F *décision* < L *decisio, -onis* < *decidere.* See DECIDE]

de·ci·sion-making (di·sizh′ən·mā′king) *n.* **1** The process by which decisions are made, especially important decisions affecting others and made by virtue of one's office or position. **2** The power or ability to make decisions of consequence. —*adj.* Of, relating to, or requiring decision-making. **—de·ci′sion-mak′er** *n.*

de·ci·sive (di·sī′siv) *adj.* **1** Putting an end to uncertainty, debate, or question; conclusive. **2** Prompt; positive; decided. **—de·ci′sive·ly** *adv.* **—de·ci′sive·ness** *n.*

dec·i·stere (des′ə·stir) *n.* A cubic decimeter, or the tenth part of a stere. See METRIC SYSTEM.

De·cius (dē′shəs, desh′əs), **Gaius Messius,** 201–51, Roman emperor 249–51.

deck (dek) *n.* **1** *Naut.* **a** A platform covering or extending horizontally across a vessel. **b** The space between two such platforms. **2** Any similar flat surface. **3** A car roof. **4** A covering or shelter. **5** A pack of cards. **6** In journalism, lines under a headline; bank. **—to hit the deck 1** *Slang* To rise from bed quickly; get up. **2** *Slang* To prepare or start to work. **3** *Slang* To drop to a prone position. **—on deck 1** Present; alive and able-bodied. **2** Next at bat in a baseball game. —*v.t.* **1** To array; dress elegantly; adorn; decorate. **2** *Naut.* To put a deck on. **3** *Obs.* To cover, clothe. See synonyms under GARNISH. [< MDu. *dek* roof, covering]

deck·er (dek′ər) *n.* **1** One who decks. **2** A vessel, car, etc., with one or more decks: a *double-decker.*

deck hand A sailor employed about the deck.

deck·house (dek′hous′) *n.* A compartment built on an upper deck of a ship.

deck·le (dek′əl) *n.* **1** In papermaking by hand, a rectangular frame laid upon a wire mold to confine the paper pulp to a definite area, thus limiting the size of the sheet. **2** A raw or ragged edge of paper: also **deckle edge.** [< G *deckel,* dim. of *decke* cover]

deck·le-edged (dek′əl·ejd′) *adj.* Uncut; rough-edged.

de·claim (di·klām′) *v.i.* **1** To speak loudly and in a rhetorical manner. **2** To give a recitation. **3** To condemn or attack verbally and vehemently: with *against.* —*v.t.* **4** To utter aloud in a rhetorical manner. See synonyms under SPEAK. [< L *declamare* < *de-* completely + *clamare* shout] **—de·claim′er** *n.*

dec·la·ma·tion (dek′lə·mā′shən) *n.* **1** The act of declaiming. **2** A speech or selection recited or to be recited from memory.

de·clam·a·to·ry (di·klam′ə·tôr′ē, -tō′rē) *adj.* **1** Using, characterized by, or pertaining to declamation. **2** In a noisy, empty rhetorical style. **—de·clam′a·to′ri·ly** *adv.*

dec·la·ra·tion (dek′lə·rā′shən) *n.* **1** A formal or explicit statement; the act of declaring, or that which is declared. **2** In common-law pleading, the paper filed by the plaintiff in which he alleges the facts constituting his cause of action and demands judgment; also, a solemn declaration made by a witness under the penalties of perjury, equivalent to an oath. **3** In bridge, the naming of the trump suit and the tricks, above six, to be taken: also called *make.*

Declaration of Independence 1 The resolution of the Continental Congress, adopted June 7, 1776, declaring that "these United Colonies are, and of right ought to be, free and independent States." **2** The manifesto of the Continental Congress adopted July 4, 1776, and entitled "A Declaration by the Representatives of the United States of America" (popularly known as the Declaration of Independence), giving the reasons why the colonies had declared their independence.

de·clar·a·tive (di·klar′ə·tiv) *adj.* Making a declaration or statement; affirmative: a *declarative* sentence. Also **de·clar·a·to·ry** (di·klar′ə·tôr′ē, -tō′rē).

de·clare (di·klâr′) *v.* **·clared, ·clar·ing** *v.t.* **1** To assert positively; aver. **2** To announce or state formally and solemnly: to *declare* war or a dividend. **3** To manifest; make known: His actions *declare* him a saint. **4** To make full statement of, as goods liable to duty or tax. **5** In card games, to name (a suit) trumps. —*v.i.* **6** To make a declaration. **7** To proclaim a choice or decision. See synonyms under AFFIRM, ALLEGE, ANNOUNCE, ASSERT, AVOW, PUBLISH, SPEAK. [< L *declarare* < *de-* completely + *clarare* make clear < *clarus* clear] **—de·clar·ed·ly** (di·klâr′id·lē) *adv.* **—de·clar′ed·ness** *n.* **—de·clar′er** *n.*

dé·clas·sé (dā·klà·sā′) *adj. French* Fallen in social status; lowered in class, rank, etc.

de·clen·sion (di·klen′shən) *n.* **1** *Gram.* **a** The inflection of nouns, pronouns, and adjectives to indicate case, number, and gender. **b** A class of words similarly inflected: *Stella* and *nauta* are Latin nouns of the first *declension.* **2** Decline: deterioration. **3** The act of declining. **4** A slope; incline. [< L *declinatio, -onis* < *declinare.* See DECLINE.] **—de·clen′sion·al** *adj.*

dec·li·na·tion (dek′lə·nā′shən) *n.* **1** The act of declining; inclination; descent; slope. **2** Deterioration; decay. **3** Refusal; non-acceptance. **4** Deviation. **5** *Astron.* The angular distance of a heavenly body north or south from the celestial equator; celestial latitude. **6** The angle between the direction in which the magnetic needle points and the true meridian: often called **magnetic declination. 7** *Obs.* Grammatical declension; inflection.

de·cline (di·klīn′) *v.* **·clined, ·clin·ing** *v.i.* **1** To refuse to accept, comply with, or do something, especially politely. **2** To lessen or fail, as in value, health, or force; wane. **3** To bend or incline downward or aside. **4** *Poetic* To fall off morally. —*v.t.* **5** To refuse to accept, comply with, or do, especially politely. **6** To cause to bend or incline downward or aside. **7** *Gram.* To give the inflected forms of (a noun, pronoun, or adjective). See synonyms under ABATE, DIE, FALL. —*n.* **1** The act or result of declining; deterioration; decay. **2** The period of such decay. **3** That stage of a disease during which the symptoms decrease in violence. **4** Any enfeebling disease, as tabes. **5** A declivity; a slope. [< OF *decliner* < L *declinare* lean down] **—de·clin′a·ble** *adj.* **—de·clin′er** *n.*

dec·li·nom·e·ter (dek′lə·nom′ə·tər) *n.* An instrument, often self-registering, for measuring or recording the declination of the magnetic needle. [< DECLINE + -(O)METER]

de·cliv·i·tous (di·kliv′ə·təs) *adj.* Sloping downward; somewhat steep. Also **de·cli·vous** (di·klī′vəs).

de·cliv·i·ty (di·kliv′ə·tē) *n. pl.* **·ties** A downward slope; descending surface of a hill or mountain: opposed to *acclivity.* [< L *declivitas, -tatis* < *declivis* < *de-* down + *clivus* hill, slope]

de·coct (di·kokt′) *v.t.* To extract by boiling; boil down; condense. [< L *decoctus,* pp. of *decoquere* < *de-* down + *coquere* cook]

de·coc·tion (di·kok′shən) *n.* **1** The act of boiling anything, especially in water, to extract its soluble properties: distinguished from *infusion.* **2** An aqueous preparation made by boiling an animal or vegetable substance; an essence or extract.

de·code (dē·kōd′) *v.t.* **·cod·ed, ·cod·ing** To convert (a coded message) into plain language. **—de·cod′er** *n.*

de·co·here (dē′kō·hir′) *v.t.* & *v.i.* **·hered, ·her·ing** To cease or cause to cease cohering. **—de′co·her′ence** *n.*

de·co·her·er (dē′kō·hir′ər) *n.* An electromagnetic device for restoring a coherer to its normal condition after the passing of an electric wave: also called *anticoherer.* See COHERER.

de·co·he·sion (dē′kō·hē′zhən) *n.* The act or state of decohering.

de·col·late (di·kol′āt) *v.t.* **·lat·ed, ·lat·ing** To behead. [< L *decollatus,* pp. of *decollare* < *de-* down, from + *collum* neck] **—de·col′la·tor** *n.*

dé·colle·tage (dā·kôl·täzh′) *n. French* **1** The outline of the bodice of a dress cut low in the neck and shoulders. **2** A dress so cut.

dé·colle·té (dā′kol·tā′, *Fr.* dā·kôl·tā′) *adj.* **1** Cut low in the neck, as a gown. **2** Having the neck and shoulders bare; wearing a low-necked gown. [< F, pp. of *décolleter* bare the neck < *dé-* from (< L *de-*) + *collet,* dim. of *col* neck, shoulder < L *collum*]

de·col·or (dē·kul′ər) *v.t.* To deprive of color; bleach. Also *Brit.* **de·col′our. —de·col′or·a′tion** *n.*

de·col·or·ant (dē·kul′ər·ənt) *adj.* Bleaching. —*n.* A bleaching substance.

de·col·or·ize (dē·kul′ə·rīz) *v.t.* **·ized, ·iz·ing** To decolor. Also *Brit.* **de·col′our·ise. —de·col′or·i·za′tion** *n.* **—de·col′or·iz′er** *n.*

de·com·mis·sion (dē′kə·mish′ən) *v.t.* To take out of active service, as a ship.

de·com·pose (dē′kəm·pōz′) *v.t.* & *v.i.* **·posed, ·pos·ing 1** To separate into constituent parts or elements. **2** To decay; putrefy. **—de′com·pos′a·ble** *adj.* **—de′com·pos′er** *n.*

de·com·pos·ite (dē′kəm·poz′it) *adj.* **1** Compounded of compounds, as a word. **2** *Bot.* Decompound, as a leaf.

de·com·po·si·tion (dē′kom·pə·zish′ən) *n.* The act, process, or result of decomposing by chemical action or by natural decay. **—double decomposition** *Chem.* The formation of two compounds by the union of the radicals formed by the decomposition of two other compounds; metathesis.

de·com·pound (dē·kom′pound′, dē′kəm·pound′) *adj. Bot.* Several times divided or compounded, as a leaf. [< DE- (def. 3) + COMPOUND]

de·com·press (dē′kəm·pres′) *v.t.* **1** To free of pressure. **2** To remove the pressure on (caisson workers, etc.), as in an airlock.

de·com·pres·sion (dē′kəm·presh′ən) *n.* The reduction or removal of pressure, especially in connection with work in caissons or under high atmospheric pressure.

decompression chamber An enclosed chamber equipped for the decompression of bodies subjected to high pressure, or for reducing normal pressure in simulation of or preparatory to high altitude flying.

decompression sickness A painful and potentially fatal syndrome due to the release of bubbles of nitrogen from solution in the blood and tissues following a too-rapid transition from high pressure to atmospheric pressure, such as may occur in high-altitude flying, underwater diving, and tunnel construction. Also called *aeroembolism, the bends, caisson disease, tunnel disease.*

de·con·tam·i·nate (dē′kən·tam′ə·nāt) *v.t.* **·nat·ed, ·nat·ing 1** To rid of contamination. **2** To prepare (a contaminated object or area) for normal use by destroying or neutralizing noxious chemicals or radioactivity.

de·con·trol (dē′kən·trōl′) *v.t.* **·trolled, ·trol·ling** To remove from control, specifically, from government controls. —*n.* The removal of controls.

dé·cor (dā′kôr, dā·kôr′) *n.* **1** The plan or arrangement of furnishings and colors in an interior space, as a home or office. **2** In the theater, scenery. [< F < *décorer* decorate]

dec·o·rate (dek′ə·rāt) *v.t.* **·rat·ed, ·rat·ing 1** To adorn; ornament. **2** To confer a decoration or medal upon. See synonyms under ADORN, GARNISH. [< L *decoratus,* pp. of *decorare* < *decus, decoris* grace, embellishment]

decorated architecture A style of English Gothic architecture prevailing from the end of the 13th to the last part of the 14th century.

dec·o·ra·tion (dek′ə·rā′shən) *n.* **1** The act, process, or art of decorating. **2** Ornamentation; an ornament. **3** A badge or emblem conferred as a mark of honor; a medal.

Decoration Day A day first set apart for decorating the graves of those who fell in the Civil War, now for the dead of any American war: observed as a legal holiday on May 30 in most States: also called *Memorial Day.*

dec·o·ra·tive (dek′rə·tiv, dek′ə·rā′tiv) *adj.* Of, pertaining to, or suitable for decoration; ornamental. —**dec′o·ra·tive·ly** *adv.* —**dec′o·ra·tive·ness** *n.*

dec·o·ra·tor (dek′ə·rā′tər) *n.* One who decorates; especially, an interior decorator.

dec·o·rous (dek′ər·əs, di·kôr′əs, -kō′rəs) *adj.* Proper; becoming; suitable. See synonyms under BECOMING, CORRECT, MODEST. [<L *decorus* <*decus, decoris* grace] —**dec′o·rous·ly** *adv.* —**dec′o·rous·ness** *n.*

de·cor·ti·cate (di·kôr′tə·kāt) *v.t.* **·cat·ed, ·cat·ing 1** To strip off the bark or outer coat of; peel; husk; hull. **2** To strip off a portion of the cortical substance of (the brain, kidney, etc.). [<L *decorticatus,* pp. of *decorticare* <*de-* down + *cortex, corticis* bark] —**de·cor′·ti·ca′tion** *n.* —**de·cor′ti·ca′tor** *n.*

de·co·rum (di·kôr′əm, -kō′rəm) *n. pl.* **·co·rums** or **·co·ra** (-kôr′ə, -kō′rə) **1** Propriety, as in manner, conduct, etc.; politeness. **2** An act demanded by social custom. [<L, neut. of *decorus* DECOROUS]

de·cou·page (dā′kōō·päzh′) *n.* **1** The art of using pieces cut from paper, etc., to decorate an entire surface. **2** A work produced by such means. Also **dé′cou·page′.** [<F]

de·coy (di·koi′, dē′·koi) *n.* **1** One who or that which allures or is intended to allure into danger or temptation. **2** A swindler's accomplice. **3** A lure; a bird or animal, or the likeness of one, used to lure game into a snare or net or within gunshot.

DECOY

4 An enclosed place into which game may be lured for capture. **5** *Mil.* A dummy military installation designed to distract enemy fire from a real position or installation, or to delude the foe as to the point of one's own attack. —*v.t.* & *v.i.* (dē′koi) To lure or be lured into danger, a snare, etc. [Earlier *coy* <Du. *kooi* a cage <L *cavea* <*cavus* hollow] —**de·coy′er** *n.*

de·crease (di·krēs′) *v.t.* & *v.i.* **·creased, ·creas·ing** To grow, or cause to grow, less or smaller; diminish, especially by a gradual process; abate; reduce. —*n.* (*usually* dē′krēs) **1** The act, process, or state of decreasing. **2** The amount or degree of loss; diminution. See synonyms under ABATE, IMPAIR, RETRENCH. [<OF *decreiss-,* stem of *decreistre* <L *decrescere* <*de-* down + *crescere* grow] —**de·creas′ing·ly** *adv.*

de·cree (di·krē′) *n.* **1** A formal order determining what is to be done or not to be done in a particular matter; a law or ordinance of either a civil or an ecclesiastical ruler, council, or legislative body. **2** *Theol.* A foreordaining, eternal purpose of God. See synonyms under LAW. —*v.t.* To order, adjudge, ordain, or appoint by law or edict. —*v.i.* To issue an edict or decree. See synonyms under DICTATE. [<OF *decre, decret* <L *decretum,* neut. pp. of *decernere.* See DECERN.]

dec·re·ment (dek′rə·mənt) *n.* **1** A decreasing; waning. **2** Amount of loss by decrease or waste. **3** *Math.* A decrease in value of a variable quantity; negative increment. [<L *decrementum* <*decrescere.* See DECREASE.]

dec·re·me·ter (dek′rə·mē′tər, di·krim′ə·tər) *n.* *Electr.* An instrument used for measuring the proportional reduction of an electrical oscillation. [<DECRE(MENT) + -METER]

de·crep·it (di·krep′it) *adj.* Enfeebled by old age; broken down. [<L *decrepitus* <*de-* completely + *crepare* creak] —**de·crep′it·ly** *adv.*

de·crep·i·tate (di·krep′ə·tāt) *v.* **·tat·ed, ·tat·ing** *v.t.* To heat (salt, minerals, etc.) so as to cause to crepitate or crackle. —*v.i.* To crackle when heated, as salt. [<NL *decrepitatus,* pp. of *decrepitare* <*de-* completely + *crepitare,* freq. of *crepare* creak]

de·crep·i·ta·tion (di·krep′ə·tā′shən) *n.* **1** The act of decrepitating. **2** The crackling sound produced by certain salts when heated.

de·crep·i·tude (di·krep′ə·tōōd, -tyōōd) *n.* Enfeeblement through infirmity or old age.

de·cre·scen·do (dē′krə·shen′dō) See DIMINUENDO.

de·cres·cent (di·kres′ənt) *adj.* Decreasing; waning. [<L *decrescens, -entis,* ppr. of *decrescere.* See DECREASE.] —**de·cres′cence** *n.*

de·cre·tal (di·krēt′l) *n.* **1** An authoritative decree, or a letter containing such a decree; especially, a letter or rescript of the Pope determining some point in ecclesiastical law. **2** A book or compilation of decrees, orders, or laws. [<F *décrétale* <Med. L *decretale* <L *decretum.* See DECREE.]

De·cre·tals (di·krēt′lz) *n. pl.* The collection of papal laws and decisions published by authority of Gregory IX in 1234, forming part of the canonical laws of the Church.

de·cre·tist (di·krē′tist) *n.* One versed in the Decretals.

de·cre·tive (di·krē′tiv) *adj.* Pertaining to or having the force or nature of a decree. —**de·cre′tive·ly** *adv.*

dec·re·to·ry (dek′rə·tôr′ē, -tō′rē) *adj.* **1** Pertaining to, resulting from, or announcing a decree; judicial. **2** Definitive.

de·crim·i·nal·ize (dē·krim′ə·nəl·īz) *v.t.* **·ized, ·iz·ing** To abstain from applying criminal penalties to; regard as non-punishable. —**de·crim′i·nal·i·za′tion** *n.*

de·cru·des·cence (dē′krōō·des′əns) *n. Med.* A lessening in the intensity of the symptoms of a disease. [<DE- (def. 4) + L *crudescens, -entis,* ppr. of *crudescere* grow harsh <*crudus* harsh] —**de′cru·des′cent** *adj.*

de·cry (di·krī′) *v.t.* **·cried, ·cry·ing 1** To condemn or disparage openly; traduce. **2** To depreciate or condemn officially, as foreign or obsolete coins. See synonyms under ASPERSE, DISPARAGE. [<F *décrier* <*dé-* down (<L *de-*) + *crier* cry] —**de·cri′al** *n.* —**de·cri′er** *n.*

de·cryp·to·graph (dē·krip′tə·graf, -gräf) *v.t.* To convert a cryptogram into plain text by decoding or deciphering or by the use of a combined cipher-code key. Also **de·crypt′.**

dec·u·ba·tion (dek′yōō·bā′shən) *n. Med.* The period of convalescence from an infectious disease, ending with the disappearance of the micro-organisms from the body. [<DE- (def. 4) + L *cubatio, -onis* a lying down <*cubare* recline]

dec·u·man (dek′yōō·mən) *adj.* **1** Principal; chief; large. **2** Of or pertaining to the tenth or hypothetically largest recurrent ocean wave. —*n.* A great wave. [<L *decumanus,* var. of *decimanus* of the tenth part, large <*decimus* tenth]

de·cum·bence (di·kum′bəns) *n.* A decumbent or prostrate state or position. Also **de·cum′·ben·cy.**

de·cum·bent (di·kum′bənt) *adj.* **1** Lying down; recumbent. **2** *Bot.* Prostrate: said of stems, shoots, etc., growing along the ground. [<L *decumbens, -entis,* ppr. of *decumbere* <*de-* down + *cumbere* lie, recline]

dec·u·ple (dek′yōō·pəl) *v.t.* **·pled, ·pling** To increase tenfold. —*adj.* Tenfold. —*n.* A number or quantity ten times as large as another or ten times repeated. [<F *décuple* <L *decuplus* <*decem* ten]

dec·u·pli·cate (dek·yōō′plə·kit) *adj.* **1** Tenfold. **2** Raised to the tenth power. —*v.t.* (-kāt) **·cat·ed, ·cat·ing** To decuple. —*n.* One of ten like things. [<DECUPLE, on analogy with *duplicate, triplicate,* etc.] —**dec·u′·pli·cate·ly** *adv.* —**dec·u′pli·ca′tion** *n.*

de·cu·ri·on (di·kyŏŏr′ē·ən) *n.* **1** An officer who commanded ten soldiers: the lowest military officer of ancient Rome; also, a member of the Roman Senate in a colony or municipal town. **2** Any person having command over or responsibility for ten others. [<L *decurio, -onis* <*decem* ten]

de·cur·rent (di·kûr′ənt) *adj. Bot.* Extending or running downward into another structure, as leaves along a plant stem. [<L *decurrens, -entis,* ppr. of *decurrere* <*de-* down + *currere* run] —**de·cur′rent·ly** *adv.*

de·cur·sive (di·kûr′siv) *adj.* Decurrent. [<L *decursus,* pp. of *decurrere.* See DECURRENT.] —**de·cur′sive·ly** *adv.*

de·curve (di·kûrv′) *v.t.* & *v.i.* **·curved, ·curv·ing** To curve downward.

dec·u·ry (dek′yōō·rē) *n. pl.* **·ries 1** A body of ten men. **2** In ancient Rome, the ten soldiers commanded by a decurion; also, a division of the curiae, of the hundred senators, and of the judges and corporations. [<L *decuria* <*decem* ten]

de·cus·sate (di·kus′āt, dek′ə·sāt) *v.i.* **·sat·ed, ·sat·ing** To intersect; cross in the form of the letter X; interlace. —*adj.* (di·kus′āt, -it) **1** Crossed; intersected. **2** *Bot.* Having each pair of leaves at right angles with the pair next below or above: also **de·cus′sat·ed.** [<L *decussatus,* pp. of *decussare* mark with an X <*decussis* the number ten, X] —**de·cus′·sate·ly** *adv.*

dec·us·sa·tion (dek′ə·sā′shən) *n.* **1** The act or state of decussating; that which decussates. **2** *Anat.* A crossing over of symmetrical parts, as nerve fibers intersecting the median plane of the central nervous system to connect centers on either side.

de·dal (dēd′l) See DAEDAL.

ded·a·lous (ded′ə·ləs) *adj.* Pertaining to or like a labyrinth; involved; intricately and skilfully made. [<L *daedalus* skilfully made <Gk. *daidalos*]

de·dans (dē′dəns) *n.* **1** In court tennis, the gallery, screened off for spectators. **2** The spectators. [<F <*dedans* inside]

De·de·a·gach (de·de′ä·gäch′) A former name for ALEXANDROUPOLIS.

ded·i·cate (ded′ə·kāt) *v.t.* **·cat·ed, ·cat·ing 1** To set apart for sacred uses; consecrate. **2** To set apart for or devote to any special use, duty, or purpose. **3** To preface with a dedication, as a work of literature. See synonyms under INSCRIBE. —*adj.* Dedicated; devoted. [<L *dedicatus,* pp. of *dedicare* <*de-* down + *dicare* proclaim] —**ded′i·ca′tive** *adj.* —**ded′·i·ca′tor** *n.* —**ded′i·ca·to′ry** (-kə·tôr′ē, -tō′rē) *adj.* —**ded′i·ca·to′ri·ly** *adv.*

ded·i·ca·tion (ded′ə·kā′shən) *n.* **1** A dedicating or being dedicated. **2** An inscription in a book, etc., as to a friend or cause.

de·duce (di·dōōs′, -dyōōs′) *v.t.* **·duced, ·duc·ing 1** To derive as a conclusion; infer; conclude. **2** To trace, as derivation or origin. [<L *deducere* <*de-* down + *ducere* lead] —**de·duce′ment** *n.* —**de·duc′i·ble** *adj.*

de·duct (di·dukt′) *v.t.* To subtract; take away. [<L *deductus,* pp. of *deducere.* See DEDUCE.] —**de·duct′i·ble** *adj.*

de·duc·tion (di·duk′shən) *n.* **1** The act of deducing. **2** *Logic* Reasoning from stated premises to the formally valid conclusion; reasoning from the general to the particular. **3** An inference; conclusion. **4** The act of deducting. **5** A subtraction; abatement. See synonyms under DEMONSTRATION, INFERENCE. Compare INDUCTION.

de·duc·tive (di·duk′tiv) *adj.* **1** Of or proceeding by deduction. **2** Inferential; deducible. —**de·duc′tive·ly** *adv.*

dee[1] (dē) *n.* **1** The sound or the shape of the letter D. **2** A metal loop for connecting parts of harness. **3** One of a pair of D-shaped half-hollow cylinder units of a cyclotron in which the stream of entering electrons is continuously accelerated in an electromagnetic field.

dee[2] (dē) *v.i. Scot.* To die.

Dee (dē) **1** A river in NE Scotland, flowing east 87 miles to the North Sea at Aberdeen. **2** A river and lake in SW Scotland. **3** A river in northern Wales and England, flowing NE 70 miles to the Irish Sea.

deed (dēd) *n.* **1** Anything done; an act. **2** An exploit, a notable achievement. **3** Fact; truth; reality. **4** Action performed, as opposed to words. **5** *Law* A written instrument containing a grant signed and sealed by the grantor; an instrument of conveyance under seal: a *deed* for land. Any instrument in writing under seal, whether a bond, agreement, or contract of any kind, is a *deed,* but the word is more frequently used in regard to the conveyance of real estate. See synonyms under ACT, TRANSACTION, WORK. —**in deed** In fact; actually. —*v.t.* To convey or transfer by deed. [OE *dǣd*] —**deed′ful** *adj.* —**deed′·less** *adj.*

deed·ed (dē′did) *adj. Law* Conveyed by a deed.

deem (dēm) *v.t.* & *v.i.* To judge; think; regard; believe. See synonyms under CALCULATE, ESTEEM, SUPPOSE. [OE *dēman,* judge]

de-em·pha·size (dē·em′fə·sīz) *v.t.* **·sized, ·siz·ing** To place less emphasis on. —**de·em′pha·sis** (-sis) *n.*

deem·ster (dēm′stər) *n.* **1** One who deems or dooms; a judge. **2** Either of the two highest judicial officers in the Isle of Man. [ME *demestre*] —**deem′ster·ship** *n.*

deep (dēp) *adj.* **1** Extending or situated far, or comparatively far, below the surface. **2** Extending or entering far back, in, or away from the spectator's point of view. **3** Having a depth, thickness, dimension, or quantity measured from above downward, from before backward, or from without inward. 4 Profound in nature, reach, or degree. 5 Hard to understand or fathom because abstruse, complex, or well concealed. 6 Of great and well-trained or far-reaching intellectual powers; sagacious; penetrating. 7 Of great intensity; great in degree; extreme; hence, heartfelt and earnest. 8 Artful in the concealment of plans or schemes; insidious; scheming; designing. 9 Of low, sonorous, or heavy tone; grave. 10 Of intense or dark hue. 11 Immersed; absorbed: *deep* in a book. — *n.* 1 A place or thing that has great depth; deep water; an abyss; especially, the sea or ocean. 2 Something too profound, vast, or abstruse to be easily comprehended; a mystery. 3 The most profound part; culmination: the *deep* of night. 4 *Naut.* The interval between two successive marked fathoms on a lead line or sounding line of a vessel. — *adv.* 1 Deeply. 2 Far on, in reference to time. [OE *dēop.* Akin to DIP.] — **deep′ness** *n.*

deep-dish pie (dēp′dish′) A pie baked in a deep dish and having only a top crust.

deep-dyed (dēp′dīd′) *adj.* Thoroughgoing; absolute: a *deep-dyed* villain.

deep•en (dē′pən) *v.t.* & *v.i.* To make or become deep or deeper.

deep-freeze (dēp′frēz′) *n.* A refrigerator in which foods may be kept for long periods of time at temperatures approximating 0° F. — *v.t.* -froze or -**freezed,** -**fro•zen** or -**freezed,** -**freez•ing** To place or store in such a refrigerator.

deep-fry (dēp′frī′) *v.t.* **•fried, •fry•ing** To fry in deep fat or oil.

deep-laid (dēp′lād′) *adj.* Made with extreme care and cleverness, usually in secret: *deep-laid* plans.

deep•ly (dēp′lē) *adv.* 1 At or to a great depth. 2 To a great extent or degree; intensely; profoundly; thoroughly. 3 At a low pitch or tone. 4 With deep color. 5 Artfully; intricately.

deep reflex *Physiol.* Any reflex affecting a deep-lying muscle or other internal structure, as produced by tapping an adjacent tendon or bone.

deep-root•ed (dēp′rōō′tid, -rŏŏt′id) *adj.* 1 Having roots that reach far below the surface. 2 Firmly held: said of beliefs, prejudices, etc.

deep-sea (dēp′sē′) *adj.* Of, in, or pertaining to the depths of the sea.

deep-seat•ed (dēp′sē′tid) *adj.* So far in as to be ineradicable or almost ineradicable: said of emotions, diseases, etc.

Deep South The southernmost parts of Alabama, Georgia, Louisiana, and Mississippi, conventionally regarded as typifying Southern culture and traditions.

deer (dir) *n. pl.* **deer** 1 A ruminant (family *Cervidae*) having deciduous antlers, usually in the male only, as the moose, elk, and reindeer. Popularly, *deer* is used mainly of the smaller species. ◆ Collateral adjective: *cervine.* See FALLOW DEER, VENISON. 2 A deerlike animal. 3 Formerly, any quadruped; a wild animal. ◆ Homophone: *dear.* [OE *dēor* beast]

deer•ber•ry (dir′ber′ē) *n. pl.* **•ries** 1 The buckberry (def. 2). 2 The wintergreen. 3 The partridgeberry.

deer•fly (dir′flī′) *n. pl.* **•flies** A bloodsucking fly (genus *Chrysops*), similar to a horsefly but smaller and with banded wings. For illustration see INSECT (injurious).

deer•grass (dir′gras′, -gräs′) *n.* 1 Meadowbeauty. 2 A forage grass (*Muhlenbergia rigens*) of Mexico and the SW United States.

deer•hound (dir′hound′) *n.* A breed of sporting dog, having a long, flat head, pointed muzzle, and a shaggy, dark-gray, or brindle coat: also called *staghound.* Also **Scottish deerhound.**

DEERHOUND (28 to 32 inches high at the shoulder)

deer•let (dir′lət) *n.* A pigmy deer.

deer-lick (dir′lik′) *n.* A place, naturally or artificially salted, where deer come to lick the saline earth.

deer mouse A small, long-tailed, furry mouse (*Peromyscus maniculatus*), many varieties of which are widely distributed in North America; the white-footed mouse.

deer•skin (dir′skin′) *n.* A deer's hide, or leather made from it; buckskin.

deer•stalk•er (dir′stô′kər) *n.* 1 One who hunts deer by stalking. 2 A helmet-shaped cloth cap, usually red, commonly worn by deer hunters.

deer•weed (dir′wēd′) *n.* A branching, leguminous herb (*Lotus scoparius*) found in parts of Arizona and southern California: sometimes utilized for cattle food. Also **deer′vetch′.**

de-es•ca•late (dē-es′kə·lāt) *v.t.* & *v.i.* **•lat•ed, •lat•ing** To decrease or be decreased gradually, as in scope, effect, or intensity: to *de-escalate* a war. — **de-es′ca•la′tion** *n.*

dee•wan (di·wän′) See DEWAN.

de•face (di·fās′) *v.t.* **•faced, •fac•ing** 1 To mar or disfigure the face or surface of. 2 To obliterate wholly or partially, as an inscription; efface. [<obs. F *defacer* <OF *desfacier* <*des-* down, away + *face* face <L *facies*] — **de•face′a•ble** *adj.* — **de•fac′er** *n.* — **de•fac′ing** *adj.* — **de•fac′ing•ly** *adv.*

de•face•ment (di·fās′mənt) *n.* 1 The act of defacing. 2 Anything that disfigures.

de fac•to (dē fak′tō) Actually or really existing, with or without legal sanction, as a government: distinguished from *de jure.* [<L]

de•fal•cate (di·fal′kāt) *v.i.* **•cat•ed, •cat•ing** To commit defalcation; embezzle money. [< Med. L *defalcatus,* pp. of *defalcare* lop off <*de-* down, away + *falx, falcis* scythe] — **de•fal′ca•tor** *n.*

de•fal•ca•tion (dē′fal·kā′shən) *n.* 1 A fraudulent appropriation of money held in trust; embezzlement; also, the amount embezzled. 2 A deducting; an abatement. 3 The amount deducted.

def•a•ma•tion (def′ə·mā′shən) *n.* The act of defaming; aspersion; calumny. See synonyms under SCANDAL. [<L *diffamatio, -onis* a speaking against <*diffamare.* See DEFAME.]

de•fam•a•to•ry (di·fam′ə·tôr′ē, -tō′rē) *adj.* Slanderous.

de•fame (di·fām′) *v.t.* **•famed, •fam•ing** 1 To attack the good name or reputation of; slander; libel. 2 *Obs.* To indict; accuse. See synonyms under ABUSE, ASPERSE, REVILE. [<L *diffamare* <*dis-* away, from + *fama* a report, reputation]

de•fam•er (di·fā′mər) *n.* One who slanders or dishonors another.

de•fault (di·fôlt′) *n.* 1 A failure in or neglect of an obligation or duty; failure to appear or plead in a suit; failure to pay a sum due. 2 Want or deficiency; absence; lack: in *default* of evidence. 3 *Obs.* A fault; transgression. 4 The failure to appear for an athletic contest, race, etc.; failure to finish a contest. See synonyms under NEGLECT, WANT. — **in default of** Owing to lack or failure of. — **judgment by default** A judgment in a civil action rendered for failure to prosecute or defend. — *v.i.* 1 To fail or neglect to fulfil or do a duty, obligation, etc. 2 To fail to meet financial obligations. 3 *Law* To fail to appear in court; also, to lose by default. 4 In sports, to fail to compete or complete a game, etc.; also, to lose or forfeit a game, etc., by default. — *v.t.* 5 To fail to perform or pay. 6 To declare in default, especially legally. 7 In sports, to fail to compete in, as a game; also, to forfeit by default. [<OF *defaut* < *defaillir* < *de-* down + *fallere* deceive]

de•fault•er (di·fôl′tər) *n.* 1 One who defaults; especially, one who fails to appear in court. 2 One who fails to account for trust money; a delinquent; embezzler; also, one who fails to pay debts. 3 *Brit.* A soldier who has committed an offense against military law.

de•fea•sance (di·fē′zəns) *n.* 1 A making null or void; an annulment. 2 *Law* A condition in a deed or collateral instrument by the performance of which the principal deed is rendered void. [<OF *defesance* an undoing <*defaire.* See DEFEAT.]

de•fea•si•ble (di·fē′zə·bəl) *adj.* Capable of being rendered void. — **de•fea′si•ble•ness, de•fea′•si•bil′i•ty** *n.*

de•feat (di·fēt′) *v.t.* 1 To overcome in any contest; vanquish. 2 To baffle; circumvent, as plans; frustrate. 3 *Law* To make void; annul. 4 *Obs.* To destroy; ruin. See synonyms under BAFFLE, BEAT, CONQUER. — *n.* 1 The act or result of defeating; an overthrow; a failure to win or succeed. 2 Prevention; frustration. 3 *Law* An annulment. 4 *Obs.* Destruction. See synonyms under LOSS, RUIN. [<OF *defeit,* pp. of *defaire* <*de-* not (<L *dis-*) + *faire* do <L *facere*]

de•feat•ism (di·fē′tiz·əm) *n.* 1 Acknowledgment or acceptance of defeat, usually on grounds of the futility of resistance. 2 The conduct, state of mind, or propaganda that makes for this. — **de•feat′ist** *n.* & *adj.*

de•fea•ture (di·fē′chər) *n. Obs.* 1 Defeat. 2 A defect or injury.

def•e•cate (def′ə·kāt) *v.* **•cat•ed, •cat•ing** *v.t.* 1 To clear of dregs or impurities, refine; purify. — *v.i.* 2 To become free of dregs. 3 To discharge excrement. — *adj.* Clarified; refined. [<L *defaecatus,* pp. of *defaecare* <*de-* down, away + *faex* dregs] — **def′e•ca′•tion** *n.*

def•e•ca•tor (def′ə·kā′tər) *n.* 1 One who or that which clarifies or purifies. 2 In sugar-making, an apparatus for clearing sirups, juices, etc., of impurities.

de•fect (di·fekt′, dē′fekt) *n.* 1 Lack or absence of something essential; imperfection. 2 A blemish; failing; fault. See synonyms under BLEMISH, FOIBLE, WANT. — *v.i.* (di·fekt′) To desert; go over to the enemy or opposition. [<L *defectus,* pp. of *deficere* fail <*de-* not + *facere* do]

de•fec•tion (di·fek′shən) *n.* 1 Abandonment of allegiance or duty; failure. 2 Apostasy; desertion.

de•fec•tive (di·fek′tiv) *adj.* 1 Incomplete or imperfect; faulty. 2 *Gram.* Lacking one or more of the declensional or conjugational forms normal for its class: Can is a *defective* verb. 3 *Psychol.* Having less than normal intelligence. — *n.* One who or that which is incomplete or imperfect; specifically, a mentally defective person. — **de•fec′tive•ly** *adv.* — **de•fec′tive•ness** *n.*

defective number See under NUMBER.

de•fec•tor (di·fek′tər) *n.* One who deserts an allegiance, army, etc.

de•fence (di·fens′), **de•fence•less** (di·fens′lis), etc. See DEFENSE, etc.

de•fend (di·fend′) *v.t.* 1 To shield from attack or injury; protect. 2 To justify or vindicate; support. 3 *Law* **a** To act in behalf of (an accused). **b** To contest, as a claim, charge, or suit. 4 *Obs.* To forbid. — *v.i.* 5 To make a defense. See synonyms under JUSTIFY, KEEP, PRESERVE, SHELTER. [<L *defendere* <*de-* down, away + *fendere* strike] — **de•fend′a•ble** *adj.*

de•fen•dant (di·fen′dənt) *adj.* 1 Sustaining defense. 2 *Obs.* Defensive. — *n.* 1 *Law* A person against whom an action is brought. 2 One who defends; a defender. [<F *défendant,* ppr. of *défendre* defend]

de•fend•er (di·fen′dər) *n.* One who defends or protects; a champion.

Defender of the Faith A hereditary title given in 1521 by Pope Leo X to Henry VIII of England for writing in defense of the seven sacraments against Luther: revoked later, but restored by Parliament and still used by English sovereigns.

de•fen•es•tra•tion (dē·fen′ə·strā′shən) *n.* The act of throwing out of a window, or the result of or subjection to such an act: used specifically with reference to a mode of executing popular vengeance practiced in Bohemia in the later Middle Ages. [<L *de* out of, down + *fenestra* window]

de•fense (di·fens′) *n.* 1 The act of defending; protection; the state of being defended. 2 Anything that defends. 3 A plea in justification; excuse; apology. 4 *Law* An opposing or denying of the truth, validity, or sufficiency of a plaintiff's complaint; also, whatever is alleged, pleaded, or offered in evidence as sufficient to defeat an action either wholly or in part. 5 The art or science of defending by force of arms; skilfulness in defending oneself, as in fencing or boxing. 6 *Obs.* A prohibitory decree. Also *defence.* — **Department of Defense** An executive department of the U.S.

government (established in 1947), headed by the Secretary of Defense and composed of the Department of the Army, the Department of the Navy, the Department of the Air Force, and various military agencies and staffs: from 1947 to 1949 called the National Military Establishment. [<OF <L *defensus*, pp. of *defendere*. See DEFEND.]

Synonyms: apology, bulwark, exculpation, fortress, guard, justification, protection, rampart, resistance, safeguard, shelter, shield, vindication. The weak may speak or act in *defense* of the strong; none but the powerful can assure others of *protection*. A *defense* is ordinarily against actual attack; *protection* is against possible as well as actual dangers. We speak of *defense* against an assault, *protection* from the cold. *Vindication* is a triumphant *defense* of character and conduct against charges of error or wrong. Compare APOLOGY, RAMPART. *Antonyms*: abandonment, betrayal, capitulation, desertion, flight, surrender.

de·fense·less (di·fens′lis) *adj.* Having no defense or means of defense; unprotected. — **de·fense′less·ly** *adv.* — **de·fense′less·ness** *n.*

defense mechanism 1 *Psychoanal.* An unconscious adjustment of behavior or mental attitude directed toward protection of the personality against unpleasant emotions or realities: also called **defense dynamism, defense reaction.** 2 *Physiol.* Any self-protective reaction, as the resistance of an organism to bacteria.

de·fen·si·ble (di·fen′sə·bəl) *adj.* Capable of being defended, maintained, or justified. — **de·fen′si·bil′i·ty, de·fen′si·ble·ness** *n.* — **de·fen′si·bly** *adv.*

de·fen·sive (di·fen′siv) *adj.* 1 Intended or suitable for defense. 2 Carried on in defense: distinguished from *offensive*. 3 Making defense. — *n.* An attitude or condition of defense: means of defense; safeguard. — **de·fen′sive·ly** *adv.*

de·fen·sor (di·fen′sər) *n.* *Latin* 1 One who defends; a defender. 2 *Law* One who appears for and defends another in an action in court.

de·fer[1] (di·fûr′) *v.t.* & *v.i.* **·ferred, ·fer·ring** To delay or put off to some other time; postpone. See synonyms under PROCRASTINATE, SUSPEND. [<OF *différer* <L *differre*. Doublet of DIFFER.] — **de·fer′ra·ble** *adj.* — **de·fer′·ment** *n.*

de·fer[2] (di·fûr′) *v.i.* **·ferred, ·fer·ring** To yield to the opinions or decisions of another: with *to*. [<MF *déférer* <L *deferre* < *de-* down + *ferre* bear, carry] — **de·fer′rer** *n.*

Synonyms: respect, revere, submit, venerate, yield. We *defer* to recognized superiors in position, ability, or attainments; we *respect* power and worth wherever found. A military officer must *defer* to the views or authority of a superior whom he may not personally *respect*; a discoverer sure of his facts may not *defer to* the incredulity of those whom on other grounds he *respects* most highly. See OBEY. *Antonyms*: defy, despise, disregard, scorn, slight.

def·er·ence (def′ər·əns) *n.* Respectful yielding; respect; regard.

def·er·ent (def′ər·ənt) *adj.* 1 Carrying off; bearing away; adapted to carry or convey. 2 *Anat.* Pertaining to certain ducts, as the vas deferens: opposed to *afferent*. 3 Characterized by deference; deferential. — *n.* In the Ptolemaic astronomy, the circle around the earth, as a center, on the circumference of which the center of the epicycle was supposed to move. See under EPICYCLE. [<L *deferens, -entis*, ppr. of *deferre*. See DEFER[2].]

def·er·en·tial (def′ə·ren′shəl) *adj.* Marked by deference; respectful; courteous. See synonyms under OBSEQUIOUS. — **def′er·en′tial·ly** *adv.*

de·ferred (di·fûrd′) *adj.* 1 Postponed. 2 With benefits or payments held back until a later date.

def·er·ves·cence (def′ər·ves′əns) *n.* 1 The cessation of boiling. 2 *Med.* The fall of temperature, indicating the disappearance of fever. [<L *defervescens, -entis*, ppr. of *defervescere* cool down] — **def′er·ves′cent** *adj.*

Def·fand (de·fäṅ′), **Marquise du,** 1698–1780, *née* Marie de Vichy-Chamrond, a leader in French literary circles.

de·fi·ance (di·fī′əns) *n.* 1 The act of defying; a challenge. 2 Bold opposition; disposition to oppose or resist; contemptuous disregard of authority or opposition.

de·fi·ant (di·fī′ənt) *adj.* Showing or characterized by defiance. [<OF ppr. of *defier*. See DEFY.] — **de·fi′ant·ly** *adv.*

de·fib·ril·late (dē·fib′rə·lāt, dē·fī′brə-) *v.i.* **·lat·ed, ·lat·ing** *Pathol.* To stop fibrillation of (the heart muscle), as by jolting with an electric current. — **de·fib′ril·la′tion, de·fib′ril·la′tor** *n.*

de·fi·bri·na·tion (dē·fī′brə·nā′shən) *n.* The removal of fibrin from the blood or lymph in order to prevent coagulation and facilitate study of the blood cells in liquid form.

de·fi·cien·cy (di·fish′ən·sē) *n.* *pl.* **·cies** 1 The state of being deficient. 2 That which is deficient; lack; insufficiency; defect. Also **de·fi′cience.** See synonyms under WANT.

deficiency disease *Pathol.* 1 A disease, such as pellagra, rickets, scurvy, etc., caused by insufficiency or lack of some necessary element in the body. 2 Avitaminosis.

deficiency judgment *Law* A judgment in favor of a creditor for that amount of a debt, secured by a mortgage, not satisfied by foreclosure and sale.

de·fi·cient (di·fish′ənt) *adj.* 1 Lacking an adequate or proper supply; insufficient. 2 Lackin some essential; incomplete; imperfect; defective. See synonyms under SCANTY. [<L *deficiens, -entis*, ppr. of *deficere*. See DEFECT.] — **de·fi′cient·ly** *adv.*

def·i·cit (def′ə·sit) *n.* A deficiency, or falling short in amount; shortage, especially of revenue. [<L, it is lacking]

de fi·de (dē fī′dē) *Latin* Of the faith; specifically, in the Roman Catholic Church, denoting a truth revealed to and taught by the Church.

de·fi·er (di·fī′ər) *n.* One who defies.

def·i·lade (def′ə·lād′) *v.t.* **·lad·ed, lad·ing** To plan or construct so as to protect from enfilading and from reverse fire: said of a fortification. [< *n.*] — *n.* 1 The act of defilading. 2 The protection afforded by natural cover or object, or other shield against enemy fire or observation: also **de·file′ment.** [<F *défilade* < *défiler* unthread < *dé-* away (<L *dis-*) + *fil* thread <L *filum*]

de·file[1] (di·fīl′) *v.t.* **·filed, ·fil·ing** 1 To make foul or dirty; pollute. 2 To tarnish or sully the brightness of; corrupt the purity of. 3 To sully; profane (a name, reputation, etc.). 4 To render ceremonially unclean. 5 To corrupt the chastity of. [<OF *defouler* < *de-* down (<L *de-*) + *fouler* trample; infl. in form by ME *filen* soil, OE *fȳlan* < *fūl* foul] — **de·file′ment** *n.* — **de·fil′er** *n.*

Synonyms: befoul, contaminate, corrupt, infect, pollute, soil, spoil, stain, sully, taint, tarnish, vitiate. The hand may be *defiled* by a touch of pitch; swine that have been wallowing in the mud are *befouled. Contaminate* and *infect* refer to something evil that deeply pervades and permeates, as the human body or mind. *Pollute* is used chiefly of liquids; as, water *polluted* with sewage. *Tainted* meat is repulsive; *infected* meat contains germs of disease. A *soiled* garment may be cleansed by washing; a *spoiled* garment is beyond cleansing or repair. Bright metal is *tarnished* by exposure; a fair sheet is *sullied* by a dirty hand. We speak of a *vitiated* taste or style; fraud *vitiates* a title or a contract. See ABUSE, CORRUPT, POLLUTE, VIOLATE. *Antonyms:* clean, cleanse, disinfect, hallow, purify, sanctify.

de·file[2] (di·fīl′, dē′fīl) *v.i.* **·filed, ·fil·ing** To march in a line or by files; file off. — *n.* 1 A long narrow pass; a gorge between mountains. 2 A marching in file. [<MF *défiler* < *dé-* down (<L *de-*) + *file* FILE[1] (def. 3)]

de·fine (di·fīn′) *v.t.* **·fined, ·fin·ing** 1 To state the meaning of (a word or phrase). 2 To determine the limits of and specify exactly. 3 To determine and fix the boundaries of. 4 To show or bring out the form or outline of. 5 To constitute the definition of. See synonyms under INTERPRET. [<OF *definer* <L *definire* < *de-* down + *finire* finish < *finis* end] — **de·fin′a·ble** *adj.* — **de·fin′er** *n.*

def·i·nite (def′ə·nit) *adj.* 1 Having precise limits; known with exactness; determined; clear; precise. 2 *Gram.* Limiting; particularizing: The *definite* article in English is *the*. See synonyms under PARTICULAR, PRECISE. [<L *definitus*, pp. of *definire*. See DEFINE.] — **def′·i·nite·ly** *adv.* — **def′i·nite·ness** *n.*

def·i·ni·tion (def′ə·nish′ən) *n.* 1 A description or explanation of a word or thing, by its attributes, properties, or relations, that distinguishes it from all other things. 2 The act of stating or showing what a word means, what a thing is, or what the content of a conception is; the act of defining. 3 The state of being definite; fixed shape; definitiveness. 4 The determining of the outline or limits of anything. 5 The state of being clearly outlined or determined. 6 *Optics* The power of a lens to give a distinct image at whatever magnification. 7 In television, the clarity of detail in a transmitted image, reckoned in terms of the number of picture elements or scanning lines in each image or frame. 8 In radio, the clearness of sounds received.

Synonyms: comment, commentary, description, explanation, exposition, interpretation, rendering, translation. A *definition* is formal and exact, an *explanation* general; a *description* pictorial. A *definition* must include all that belongs to the object defined, and exclude all that does not; a *description* may include only some general features: an *explanation* may simply throw light upon some point of special difficulty. An *exposition* explains a subject in detail. *Interpretation* may translate from other languages, or give the plain meaning of difficult passages, or render the thought and emotion of worthy literature by adequate written or oral expression. *Definition, explanation, exposition,* and *interpretation* are ordinarily blended in a *commentary*, which may also include *description*. A *comment* is upon a single passage; a *commentary* may be the same, but is usually understood to be a volume of *comments*.

de·fin·i·tive (di·fin′ə·tiv) *adj.* 1 Sharply defining or limiting; determinate; explicit; positive. 2 Bringing to an end; conclusive and unalterable. 3 *Biol.* Completely formed; fully developed. 4 Most nearly accurate, complete, etc. — *n.* A word that defines or limits. — **de·fin′i·tive·ly** *adv.* — **de·fin′i·tive·ness** *n.*

def·la·grate (def′lə·grāt) *v.t.* & *v.i.* **·grat·ed, ·grat·ing** To burn quickly and with dazzling light. [<L *deflagratus*, pp. of *deflagrare* < *de-* completely + *flagrare* burn] — **def·la·gra·ble** (def′lə·grə·bəl) *adj.*

def·la·gra·tion (def′lə·grā′shən) *n.* A quick and violent combustion, with or without explosion: distinguished from the instantaneous decomposition of an entire compound in a *detonation*.

def·la·gra·tor (def′lə·grā′tər) *n.* That which induces or produces very rapid combustion.

de·flate (di·flāt′) *v.t.* & *v.i.* **·flat·ed, ·flat·ing** 1 To collapse or cause to collapse by the removal of contained air or gas. 2 To take the conceit, confidence, or self-esteem out of. 3 To devaluate; lessen (currency or prices). [<L *deflatus*, pp. of *deflare* < *de-* down + *flare* blow] — **de·fla′tor** *n.*

de·fla·tion (di·flā′shən) *n.* 1 The act or condition of being deflated or reduced in volume. 2 A decrease in the amount of currency in a country. — **de·fla·tion·ar·y** (di·flā′shən·er′ē) *adj.* — **de·fla′tion·ist** *n.* & *adj.*

de·flect (di·flekt′) *v.t.* & *v.i.* To turn aside; swerve or cause to swerve from a course. See synonyms under BEND. [<L *deflectere* < *de-* down + *flectere* bend] — **de·flec′tive** *adj.* — **de·flec′tor** *n.*

de·flec·tion (di·flek′shən) *n.* 1 A turning aside; deviation. 2 A bending of light rays; see DIFFRACTION. 3 The deviation of a galvanometer or magnetic needle from its normal position or from zero. Also *Brit.* **de·flex′ion.**

de·flex (di·fleks′) *v.t.* To bend downward. [<L *deflexus*, pp. of *deflectere*. See DEFLECT.] — **de·flex·ure** (di·flek′shər) *n.*

de·flo·rate (di·flôr′āt, -it, -flō′rāt) *adj.* *Bot.* 1 Past flowering. 2 Having cast its pollen. [<LL *defloratus*, pp. of *deflorare* DEFLOWER]

def·lo·ra·tion (def′lə·rā′shən) *n.* 1 The act of deflowering. 2 A culling of the choicest part.

de·flow·er (di·flou′ər) *v.t.* 1 To despoil of flowers. 2 To deprive (a woman) of virginity; seduce. 3 To violate; rob of beauty. [<OF *desflorer, desflouer* <LL *deflorare* < *de-* down, away + *flos, floris* flower; infl. in form by flower]

de·flux·ion (di·fluk′shən) *n.* *Pathol.* The flowing off of fluids, as in catarrh. [<LL *defluxio, -onis* < *defluere* < *de-* down + *fluere* flow]

De·foe (di·fō′), **Daniel,** 1661?–1731, English novelist and essayist.

de·fo·li·ate (dē·fō′lē·āt) *v.* **·at·ed, ·at·ing** *v.t.* To deprive or strip of leaves. —*v.i.* To lose leaves. [<Med. L *defoliatus,* pp. of *defoliare* <*de-* down + *folium* leaf] —**de·fo′li·a′tion** *n.* —**de·fo′li·a′tor** *n.*

de·force (di·fôrs′, -fōrs′) *v.t.* **·forced, ·forc·ing** *Law* **1** To withhold, as an estate, from lawful possession. **2** To keep (someone) from lawful possession by force. [<AF *deforcer,* var. of OF *deforcier* <*de-* down, away (<L *de-*) + *forcier* FORCE] —**de·force′ment** *n.*

de·for·ciant (di·fôr′shənt, -fōr′-) *n.* A person chargeable with deforcement.

de·for·est (dē·fôr′ist, -for′-) *v.t.* To clear of forests or trees. —**de·for′es·ta′tion** *n.* —**de·for′est·er** *n.*

De For·est (di fôr′ist, -for′-), **Lee,** 1873–1961, U.S. inventor: called "the father of radio."

de·form (di·fôrm′) *v.t.* **1** To mar or distort the form of; disfigure. **2** To spoil the beauty of; make ugly or dishonorable. **3** *Mech.* To change in form. —*v.i.* **4** To become deformed or disfigured. [<L *deformare* <*de-* away, down + *forma* figure, form] —**de·form′a·bil′i·ty** *n.* —**de·form′a·ble** *adj.* —**de·form′er** *n.*

def·or·ma·tion (def′ər·mā′shən) *n.* **1** The act of deforming; state of being deformed; misshapenness. **2** Change in form for the worse. **3** *Mech.* An alteration in the form of a body subjected to sudden or prolonged stress. **4** An altered form or shape.

de·formed (di·fôrmd′) *adj.* Misshapen. —**de·form·ed·ly** (di·fôr′mid·lē) *adv.* —**de·form′ed·ness** *n.*

de·form·i·ty (di·fôr′mə·tē) *n. pl.* **·ties 1** *Pathol.* **a** A deformed or misshapen condition. **b** A deformed part; that which causes disfigurement. **2** Unsightliness; lack of symmetry. **3** Moral depravity. **4** One who or that which is deformed. See synonyms under BLEMISH. [<OF *deformité* <L *deformitas, -tatis* <*deformis* <*de-* down + *forma* form]

de·foul (di·foul′) *v.t. Obs.* To make foul; defile. [<OF *defouler.* See DEFILE.]

de·fraud (di·frôd′) *v.t.* To take or withhold property, etc., from by fraud; cheat; swindle. See synonyms under DECEIVE. [<OF *defrauder* <L *defraudare* <*de-* completely + *fraus, fraudis* a cheat] —**de·fraud·a·tion** (dē′frô·dā′shən) *n.* —**de·fraud′er** *n.*

de·fray (di·frā′) *v.t.* **1** To pay for; bear the expense of. **2** *Obs.* To disburse; spend. [<F *défrayer* <OF *defraier* <*de-* away (<L *de-*) + *fraier* spend <*frai* cost, charge] —**de·fray′a·ble** *adj.* —**de·fray′al, de·fray′ment** *n.* —**de·fray′er** *n.*

de·frock (dē·frok′) *v.t.* To unfrock.

de·frost (dē·frôst′, -frost′) *v.t.* To remove ice or frost from.

de·frost·er (dē·frôs′tər, -fros′-) *n.* A device for removing the formation of ice or frost, as from an exposed surface.

deft (deft) *adj.* Neat and skilful in action; handy; apt; dexterous; clever. [OE *gedæfte* meek, gentle. Related to DAFT.] —**deft′ly** *adv.* —**deft′ness** *n.*

de·funct (di·fungkt′) *adj.* Dead; deceased; extinct. —*n.* A dead person: with *the.* See synonyms under DEAD, LIFELESS. [<L *defunctus,* pp. of *defungi* <*de-* not + *fungi* perform]

de·fy (di·fī′) *v.t.* **·fied, ·fy·ing 1** To resist or disregard openly or boldly. **2** To challenge: I *defy* you to cross this li· ɛ. **3** To resist successfully; baffle; obstruc.: to *defy* definition. **4** *Archaic* To invite to combat. See synonyms under OPPOSE. —*n. pl.* **·fies** *U.S. Slang* A challenge. [<OF *defier* <Med. L *diffidare* <*dis-* not + *fidare* be faithful <*fidus* loyal]

dé·ga·gé (dā·gà·zhā′) *adj. French* Free in manner; unconstrained.

de·ga·me (də·gä′mə) *n.* Lemonwood. [<Sp. *dagame* <native name]

de·gas (dē·gas′) *v.t.* **·gassed, ·gas·sing 1** To remove noxious and poisonous gases from (contaminated areas or affected persons). **2** To exhaust the gases from (vacuum tubes or thermionic valves).

De·gas (də·gä′), **Edgar Hilaire Germain,** 1834–1917, French painter.

De Gas·pe·ri (dā gäs′pe·rē), **Alcide,** 1881–1954, Italian statesman.

de Gaulle (də·gôl′, *Fr.* də·gōl′), **Charles André Joseph Marie,** 1890–1970, French general and statesman; president 1944–45, 1959–69.

de·gauss (di·gous′) *v.t.* To make (a ship) safe against the action of magnetic mines, especially by the use of a **degaussing cable,** fitted around the hull to neutralize the magnetic field set up by the ship. [<DE- + GAUSS]

de·gen·er·ate (di·jen′ə·rāt) *v.i.* **·at·ed, ·at·ing 1** To become worse or inferior. **2** *Biol.* To revert to a lower type; decline; deteriorate. —*adj.* (di·jen′ər·it) **1** Having become worse or inferior; deteriorated; degraded. **2** *Physics* Having a common value of energy but differing in other dynamical properties. —*n.* (-it) **1** A deteriorated or degraded individual, animal or human. **2** A morally degraded person. [<L *degeneratus,* pp. of *degenerare* <*de-* down, away + *generare* create] —**de·gen′er·ate·ly** *adv.* —**de·gen′er·a′tive** *adj.* —**de·gen′er·ate·ness** *n.*

de·gen·er·a·tion (di·jen′ə·rā′shən) *n.* **1** The process of degenerating; also, a degenerate condition. **2** *Biol.* Progressive deterioration of an organ, tissue, or part, especially as caused by chemical and metabolic changes in the body. **3** *Electronics* A reduction of radio signal strength by feedback.

de·glu·ti·nate (dē·glōō′tə·nāt) *v.t.* **·nat·ed, ·nat·ing** To remove the gluten from, as from wheat. —**de·glu′ti·na′tion** *n.*

de·glu·ti·tion (dē′glōō·tish′ən) *n. Physiol.* The act, process, or power of swallowing. [<F *déglutition* <L *deglutitio, -onis* <*de-* down + *glutire* swallow]

de·grad·a·ble (di·grā′də·bəl) *adj. Chem.* Capable of being degraded, as a compound.

deg·ra·da·tion (deg′rə·dā′shən) *n.* **1** The act of degrading. **2** The state of being reduced in rank or disgraced. **3** *Geol.* Disintegration, especially of rocks by erosion and wind. **4** The degeneration of the physiological body or an organ. —**deg′ra·da′tion·al** *adj.*

de·grade (di·grād′) *v.* **·grad·ed, ·grad·ing** *v.t.* **1** To reduce in rank; remove from office, dignity, etc.; disgrace. **2** To debase or lower in character, morals, etc. **3** To bring into contempt; dishonor. **4** To reduce in quality, intensity, etc. **5** *Biol.* To reduce from a higher to a lower type. **6** *Geol.* To reduce the height of by erosion. **7** *Chem.* To break down (a compound) into less complex parts; decompose. —*v.i.* **8.** To degenerate; become of a lower type. See synonyms under ABASE. [<OF *degrader* <LL *degradi* <*de-* down + *gradi* step]

de·grad·ed (di·grā′did) *adj.* Deteriorated; debased. —**de·grad′ed·ly** *adv.* —**de·grad′ed·ness** *n.*

de·grad·ing (di·grā′ding) *adj.* Debasing; humiliating. —**de·grad′ing·ly** *adv.*

dé·gras (də·grä′, deg′rəs) *n.* **1** A by-product of the tannage of chamois leather with fish oils, consisting of a mixture of fish oil and nitric acid: also called *moellon.* **2** Wool grease obtained by washing sheep's wool; sod oil: used to dress leather, beltings, etc., and to produce lanolin. [<F *dégras* <*dégraisser* remove grease <*dé-* away (<L *de*) + *graisser* <*graisse* grease]

de·gree (di·grē′) *n.* **1** One of a succession of steps, grades, or stages. **2** Relative rank in life; attainment; station. **3** Relative extent, amount, or intensity. **4** *Gram.* One of the three forms in which an adjective or adverb is compared: the positive, comparative, and superlative *degrees.* **5** An academic rank or title conferred by an institution of learning. **6** One remove in the chain of relationship between persons in the line of descent. **7** A subdivision or unit, as in a thermometric scale. **8** The 360th part of a circle, as of longitude or latitude; the 90th part of a right angle; the unit divisions marked accordingly on various instruments. **9** *Math.* The power to which an algebraic quantity, equation, or number is raised. **10** In notation, a group of three figures in a number; a period. **11** *Music* A line or space of a staff. **12** A grade of seriousness: said of crimes: murder in the first *degree.* —**by degrees** Little by little; gradually. —**to a degree** **1** *Brit.* Extremely. **2** Somewhat. [<OF *degre* <*de-* down (<L *de-*) + *gre* <L *gradus* a step]

de·gree-day (di·grē′dā′) *n.* A unit for estimating the fuel requirements of buildings during the heating season: equivalent to a declination in the mean outside temperature for one day of one degree from a standard temperature of (about) 65° F. A decline of 20° in one day would be 20 degree-days.

degree of freedom *Chem.* The particular state of a substance, compound, or body with respect to the arrangement of its parts and the number of variables, as pressure, temperature, volume, etc., required to define the system.

de·gres·sion (di·gresh′ən) *n.* **1** Decrease by steps; descent. **2** Stated decrease in tax rates on sums below a certain amount. [<LL *degressio, -onis* <*degradi.* See DEGRADE.] —**de·gres·sive** (di·gres′iv) *adj.* —**de·gres′sive·ly** *adv.*

de·gum (dē·gum′) *v.t.* **·gummed, ·gum·ming** To remove excess of gum filling from: said of silk.

de·gust (di·gust′) *v.t.* & *v.i. Rare* To taste, especially with care. Also **de·gus′tate.** [<L *degustare* <*de-* completely + *gustare* taste] —**de′gus·ta′tion** *n.*

de gus·ti·bus non est dis·pu·tan·dum (dē gus′ti·bəs non est dis′pyōō·tan′dəm) *Latin* There is no disputing about tastes.

de·hisce (di·his′) *v.i.* **·hisced, ·hisc·ing** *Biol.* To burst open, as the cocoon of a larva or the capsule of a plant. [<L *dehiscere* <*de-* down + *hiscere,* inceptive of *hiare* gape, yawn] —**de·his′cent** *adj.*

de·his·cence (di·his′əns) *n.* **1** A gape or gaping. **2** *Biol.* The opening or manner of opening, as of the cocoon of a larva or of a capsule when discharging seeds.

de·horn (dē·hôrn′) *v.t.* To remove the horns of (cattle).

de·hort (di·hôrt′) *v.t. Obs.* To try to divert by persuasion; deter. [<L *dehortari* <*de-* away + *hortari* entreat, urge] —**de·hort′er** *n.*

de·hor·ta·tion (dē′hôr·tā′shən) *n. Rare* Advice against or dissuasion from anything. —**de·hor·ta·to·ry** (dē·hôr′tə·tôr′ē, -tō′rē), **de·hor′ta·tive** *adj.*

de·hu·man·ize (dē·hyōō′mən·īz) *v.t.* **·ized, ·iz·ing** To divest or deprive of human qualities or attributes. —**de·hu′man·i·za′tion** *n.*

de·hu·mid·i·fi·er (dē′hyōō·mid′ə·fī′ər) *n.* An apparatus for removing moisture from the air.

de·hu·mid·i·fy (dē′hyōō·mid′ə·fī) *v.t.* **·fied, ·fy·ing** To render less humid; remove moisture from. —**de′hu·mid′i·fi·ca′tion** *n.*

de·hy·drate (dē·hī′drāt) *v.* **·drat·ed, ·drat·ing** *v.t.* **1** To deprive of water; anhydrate: to *dehydrate* alcohol. **2** To remove water from, as vegetables, so as to preserve. —*v.i.* **3** To suffer loss of water.

de·hy·dra·tion (dē′hī·drā′shən) *n.* **1** The process of removing water from a substance or body, as by heat, distillation, or chemicals. **2** The artificial drying of food products to reduce weight and preserve them for future use.

de·hy·dro·gen·ize (dē·hī′drə·jən·īz′) *v.t.* **·ized, ·iz·ing** *Chem.* To free from hydrogen; remove hydrogen from (a compound).

de·hyp·no·tize (dē·hip′nə·tīz) *v.t.* **·tized, ·tiz·ing** To awaken (a person) from the hypnotic state.

De·ia·ni·ra (dē′yə·nī′rə) In Greek mythology, the wife of Hercules, who killed herself because she caused his death. See NESSUS. Also **De′ja·ni′ra.**

de-ice (dē·īs′) *v.t.* & *v.i.* **–iced, –ic·ing** To remove (ice) by means of a de-icer.

de-ic·er (dē·ī′sər) *n.* A mechanical or thermal device which breaks up formations of ice, as on an airplane wing.

de·i·cide (dē′ə·sīd) *n.* **1** The killing of a god; especially, the crucifixion of Christ. **2** The slayer of a god. [<L *deus* god + -CIDE]

deic·tic (dīk′tik) *adj.* **1** *Logic* Proving by direct argument; direct: distinguished from *elenchic, refutative,* or *indirect.* **2** *Gram.* Demonstrative: a *deictic* pronoun. [<Gk. *deiktikos* able to show <*deiknynai* show, prove] —**deic′ti·cal·ly** *adv.*

de·if·ic (dē·if′ik) *adj.* **1** Making, or tending to make, divine. **2** Divine. Also **de·if′i·cal.**

de·i·form (dē′ə·fôrm) *adj.* In the form of a god; like a god. [<Med. L *deiformis* <L *deus* god + *forma* form]

de·i·fy (dē′ə·fī) *v.t.* **·fied, ·fy·ing** **1** To make a god of; rank as a deity. 2 To regard or worship as a god. [<F *déifier* <LL *deificare* <L *deus* god + *facere* make] **—de'i·fi·ca'tion** *n.* **—de'i·fi'er** *n.*

deign (dān) *v.t.* 1 To stoop so far as to grant or allow; condescend. 2 *Obs.* To deem worthy of notice or acceptance. *—v.i* 3 To think it befitting oneself (to do something). [<OF *deignier* <L *dignari* <*dignus* worthy]

De·i gra·ti·a (dē'ī grā'shē·ə, dā'ē grä'tē·ä) *Latin* By the grace of God.

deil (dēl) *n. Scot.* 1 The devil. 2 A mischievous fellow.

de·in·sti·tu·tion·al·ize (dē'in·sti·to͞o'shə·nə·līz, -tyo͞o'-) *v.t.* **·ized, ·iz·ing** 1 To remove the institutional character from. 2 *U.S. Colloq.* To remove (someone) from an institution (def. 2).

De·iph·o·bus (dē·if'ə·bəs) In greek mythology, the son of Priam, who married Helen after Paris was killed; slain by Menelaus.

deip·nos·o·phist (dīp·nos'ə·fist) *n.* One who talks learnedly at the table. [<Gk. *deipnosophistēs* <*deipnon* dinner + *sophistēs* a wise man <*sophia* wisdom] **—deip·nos'o·phism** *n.* **—dep·nos'o·phis'tic** *adj.*

de·ip·o·tent (dē·ip'ə·tənt) *adj.* Having divine power. [<L *deus* god + *potens* powerful]

De·i·ra (dē'i·rə) An Anglian kingdom of the sixth century between the Humber and the Tyne; later, a part of Northumbria.

de·ism (dēiz·əm) *n.* 1 The belief in the existence of a personal God, based solely on the testimony of reason and rejecting any supernatural revelation; natural religion. 2 The belief that God created the world and set it in motion, subject to natural laws, but take no interest in it. 3 The belief in a first cause which is not intrinsically perfect or complete, and therefore not a proper object for worship. [<L *deus* a god + -ISM] **—de·is'tic** or **·ti·cal** *adj.* **—de·is'ti·cal·ly** *adv.*

de·ist (dē'ist) *n.* One who subscribes to or profeses deism.

de·i·ty (dē'ə·tē) *n. pl.* **·ties** 1 A god, goddess, or divine person. 2 Divine nature or status; godhead; divinity. **—the Deity** God. [<F *déité* <LL *deitas, -tatis* <L *deus* a god]

dē·jà vu (dā·zha vü') *Psychol.* A distortion of memory in which a new situation or experience is regarded as having happened before: a form of paramnesia. [<F, lit., already seen]

de·ject (di·jekt') *v.t.* 1 To depress or cast down in spirit. 2 *Obs.* To throw down. *—adj.* Dejected: cast down. [<L, *dejectus,* pp. of *dejicere* <*de*-down + *jacere* throw]

de·jec·ta (di·jek'tə) *n. pl.* Excrements. [<L, neut. pl. of *dejectus.* See DEJECT.]

de·ject·ed (di·jek'tid) *adj.* Having low or depressed spirits; disheartened. **—de·ject'ed·ly** *adv.* **—de·ject'ed·ness** *n.*

de·ject·tion (di·jek'shən) *n.* 1 A state or condition of being dejected; depression. 2 *Med.* **a** Evacuation of the bowels. **b** Excrement.

dé·jeu·ner (dé·zhœ·nā') *n.* 1 A late breakfast. 2 Luncheon. [<F, breakfast <*dé-* away (<L *de-*) - *jeun* fasting <L *jejunus*]

de ju·re (dē jo͝or'ē) *Latin* By right; rightfully or legally: distinguished from *de facto.*

deka- *combining form* Ten: used in the metric system, as a *dekagram, dekaliter.* Also, before vowels, **dek-.** [Gk. *deka* ten]

dek·a·gram (dek'ə·gram) *n.* A measure of weight equal to 10 grams. See METRIC SYSTEM. Also **dek'a·gramme.**

De Kalb (di kalb'), **Baron Johann,** 1721–80, German major general under Washington in the American Revolution.

dek·a·li·ter (dek'ə·lē'tər) *n.* A measure of capacity equal to 10 liters: also spelled *decaliter.* See METRIC SYSTEM. Also **dek'a·li'tre.**

dek·a·me·ter (dek'ə·mē'tər) *n.* A measure of length equal to 10 meters. See METRIC SYSTEM. Also **dek'a·me'tre.**

dek·are (dek'âr) *n.* In the metric system, 1,000 square meters or 10 ares: also spelled *decare.* See METRIC SYSTEM.

dek·a·stere (dek'ə·stir) *n.* A measure of volume equal to 10 steres. See METRIC SYSTEM.

Dek·ker (dek'ər), **Thomas,** 1572?–1632? English 1572?–1632? English dramatist: also spelled *Decker.*

de Klerk (də·klark') **Frederik Wilhelm,** 1936–, president of Republic of South Africa (1989–1994).

De·la·croix (də·lȧ·krwä'), **Ferdinand Victor Eugène,** 1799–1863, French painter.

Del·a·go·a Bay (del'ə·gô'ə) An inlet of the Indian Ocean in the south cost of Mozambique.

de·laine (də·lān') *n.* A light, untwilled wool, or cotton and wool, dress material. [<F *(mousse-line) de laine* (muslin) of wool]

De la Mare (də lə mâr', del'ə·mâr), **Walter,** 1973–1956, English poet and novelist.

de·lam·i·nate (dē·lam'ə·nāt) *v.t.* & *v.i.* **·nat·ed, ·nat·ing** To split into thin layers.

de·lam·i·na·tion (dē·lam'ə·nā'shən) *n.* A splitting into layers: said especially of the cells of plant or animal tissue.

De·land (də·land'), **Margaret,** 1857–1945, *née* Margaretta Campbell, U.S. novelist.

de la Roche (də lä rôsh'), **Mazo,** 1885–1961, Canadian novelist.

de·late (di·lāt') *v.t.* **·lat·ed, ·lat·ing** 1 *Scot.* To bring a charge against; accuse; denounce. 2 To publish or spread abroad. [<L *delatus,* pp. to *deferre* bring down, denounce. See DEFER[2].] **—de·la'tion** *n.*

de·la·tor (di·lā'tər) *n.* An informer; accuser; spy.

De·la·vigne (də·lȧ·vēn'y'), **Jean François Casimir,** 1793–1843, French poet and dramatist.

Del·a·ware (del'ə·wâr) *n.* A confederacy of Algonquian tribes of North American Indians; the Lenapes: formerly occupying the whole Delaware River valley, now in Oklahoma. **—Del'a·war'e·an** *adj.*

Del·a·ware (del'ə·wâr) *n.* A small, sweet, reddish, hybrid grape. [from *Delaware*]

Del·a·ware (del'ə·wâr) *n.* A Middle Atlantic State of the United States: 1,978 square miles; capital, Dover; entered the Union Dec. 7, 1787, on of the original thirteen States: nickname *Diamond State:* abbr. *Del.*

Delaware Bay An inlet of the Atlantic Ocean between Delaware and New Jersey.

Delaware River A river separating Pennsylvania and Delaware from New York and New Jersey, flowing SE 350 miles to Delaware Bay.

Delaware Water Gap A resort borough in eastern Pennsylvania, in a narrow cut of the same name through the Kittatinny Mountains, through which the Delaware River flows.

De La Warr (del'ə·wâr, *Brit.* ·wər) **Lord,** 1577–1618, Thomas West, English administrator; first colonial governor of Virginia. Also **Del'a·ware.**

de·lay (di·lā') *v.t.* 1 To put off to a future time; postpone; defer. 2 To cause to be late; detain. *—v.i.* 3 to linger; procrastinate. See synonyms under HINDER, PROCRASTINATE, PROTRACT SUSPEND. *—n.* 1 A putting off; postponement; procrastination. 2 A temporary stoppage or stay; also, a loitering or lingering. See synonyms under RESPITE [<OF *delaier*] **—de·lay'er** *n.*

de·layed-ac·tion di·lād'ak'shən *adj.* Designating a kind of bomb, fuze, or mine designed to explode at a set time after it has been armed or put into action

Del·cas·sé (del·kȧ·sā'), **Théophile,** 1852–1923, French statesman.

de·le (dē'lē) *v.t.* **de·led, de·le·ing** *Printing* To take out; delete: usually an imperative represented by a sign. ( ) Compare STET. [<L, imperative of *delere* erase]

del·e·ble (del'ə·bəl) *adj.* Capable of being erased. Also **del'i·ble.**

de·lec·ta·ble (di·lek'tə·bəl) *adj.* Giving pleasure; delightful; charming. see synonyms under LOVELY. [<OF <L *delectabilis* <*delectare.* See DELIGHT.] **—de·lec'ta·ble·ness** *n.* **—de·lec'·ta·bly** *adv.*

Delectable Mountains In Bunyan's *Pilgrim's Progress,* the mountains from which the Celestial City is seen.

de·lec·tate (di·lek'tāt) *v.t.* **·tat·ed, ·tat·ing** To charm; delight. [<L *delectatus,* pp. of *delectare.* See DELIGHT.]

de·lec·ta·tion (dē'lek·tā'shən) *n.* 1 Delight; enjoyment. 2 Amusement; entertainment.

De·led·da (dā·led'dä), **Grazia,** 1879–1936, Italian novelist.

de·leer·it (də·lir'it) *adj. Scot.* Delirious; demented. Also **de·lier'et.**

del·e·ga·cy (del'ə·gə·sē) *n. pl.* **·cies** 1 The action or system of delegating; authority given to act as a delegate. 2 A body of delegates. 3 The condition of being delegated.

del·e·gant (del'ə·gənt) *n.* 1 One that delegates. 2 One that assigns a debt due him to a creditor.

del·e·gate (del'ə·gāt, ·git) *n.* 1 A person appointed and sent by another, with power to transact business as his representative; deputy; representative, commissioner. 2 *U.S.* A person elected or appointed to represent a Territory in the House of Representatives where he has the right to participate in debates, but not to vote. 3 A member of the House of Delegates. Compare BURGESS. 4 A person sent as a representative to a convention of any kind, take part in the transaction of business. **—walking delegate** A member of a trade union, commissioned to visit other labor organizations and to secure the united action of employees in the advancement of common interests. *—v.t.* (-gāt) **·gat·ed, ·gat·ing** 1 To send as a representative, with authority to act; depute. 2 To commit or entrust (powers, authority, etc.) to another as an agent or representative. 3 To assign (a debtor) to one's creditor to satisfy a claim. *—adj.* (-gāt, -git) Sent as a deputy. [<L *delegatus,* pp. of *delegare* <*de-* down + *legare* send]

Synonyms (noun): deputy, legate, proxy, representative, substitute. These words agree in designating one who acts in the place of some other or others. The *legate* is an ecclesiastical officer representing the pope. In strict usage the *deputy* or *delegate* is more limited in functions and more closely bound by instructions than a *representative.* A single officer may have a *deputy:* many persons combine to choose a *delegate* or *representative.* In the United States informal assemblies send *delegates* to nominating conventions with no legislative authority; *representatives* are legally elected to Congress and the various lawmaking assemblies.

del·e·ga·tion (del'ə·gā'shən) *n.* 1 the act of delegating: a *delegation* of powers or authority. 2 A person or persons appointed to act for another or others; delegates collectively.

del·len·da est Car·tha·go (di·len'də est kär·thā'gō) *Latin* Carthage must be destroyed: a saying ascribed to Cato the Elder.

de·lete (di·lēt') *v.t.* **·let·ed, ·let·ing** To blot out; erase, cancel; dele. [L *deletus,* pp. of *delere* erase, destroy]

del·e·te·ri·ous (del'ə·tir'ē·əs) *adj.* Causing moral or physical injury; hurtful; pernicious. See synonyms under BAD, NOISOME. [<NL *deleterius* <GK. *dēlētērios* harmful <*deleesthai* hurt] **—del'e·te'ri·ous·ly** *adv.* **—del'e·te'ri·our·ness** *n.*

de·le·tion (di·lē'shən) *n.* The act of deleting; erasure; also, matter erased or canceled.

delft (delft) *n.* 1 A colored glazed earthenware. made first a Delft about 1310. 2 Any tableware resembling this. Also **delf** (delf), delft' ware'. [from DELFT]

Delft (delft) A town in western Netherlands.

Del·ga·do (del·gä'dō), **Cape** A headland of northernmost Mozambique.

Del·hi (del'ē) 1 A Union Territory of NE central India containing New Delhi; 578 square miles. 2 Its capital: formerly capital of India (1912–31): also **Old Delhi.** See NEW DELHI.

del·i (del'ē) *n. pl.* **del·is** *U.S. Colloq.* A delicatessen.

Del·ia (dēl'yə) A feminine personal name. [Gk. *Dēlia,* fem. of *Dēlios* of Delos] **—Delia** A name of Artemis.

De·li·an (dē'lē·ən) *adj.* Of or pertaining to Delos. *—n.* A native or inhabitant of Delos.

de·lib·er·ate (di·lib'ə·rāt) *v.* **·t·ed, ·at·ing** *v.i.* 1 To think or consider carefully and at length. 2 To consider reasons or arguments for and against something so as to reach a conclusion or decision. 3 To pause to think. *—v.t.* 4 To think about or consider carefully; weigh. *—adj.* (di·lib'ər·it) 1 Acting with deliberation; carefully thought out; not hasty. 2 Done after deliberation; intentional. [<L *deliberatus,* pp. of *deliberare* <*de-* completely + *librare* weigh <*libra* a scale] **—de·lib'er·ate·ly** *adv.* **—de·lib'er·ate·ness** *n.*

Synonyms (verb): confer, consider, consult, debate, meditate, ponder, reflect, weigh. An individual *considers, meditates, ponders, reflects* by himself. *Consult* and *confer* always imply two or more persons, as does *debate,* except in rare reflexive use. *Deliberate,* which can be applied to a single individual, is also the word for a great number, while *consult* is ordinarily limited to a few; a committee *consults*; an assembly *deliberates. Deliberating* always carries the idea of slowness; a *consultation* may be hasty. We *consider* or *deliberate* with a view to action; *meditation* may be purposeless. See CONSIDER, CONSULT, MUSE.

de·lib·er·a·tion (di·lib′ə·rā′shən) *n.* **1** The act of deliberating. **2** Thoughtfulness and care in deciding or acting. **3** Forethought or intention. See synonyms under REFLECTION, THOUGHT[1].

de·lib·er·a·tive (di·lib′ə·rā′tiv) *adj.* **1** Pertaining to or of the nature of deliberation. **2** Characterized by or existing for deliberation. **—de·lib′er·a′tive·ly** *adv.* **—de·lib′er·a′·tive·ness** *n.*

De·libes (də·lēb′), **Léo,** 1836–91, French composer.

del·i·ca·cy (del′ə·kə·sē) *n. pl.* **·cies 1** The quality or state of being delicate; fineness; daintiness. **2** Sensitiveness of touch or perception. **3** Fragility; frailty. **4** A luxury; dainty. **5** Need of careful treatment; subtlety; nicety. **6** Refinement of feeling; fastidiousness; consideration for others. **7** *Obs.* Voluptuousness; luxuriousness.

del·i·cate (del′ə·kit) *adj.* **1** Fine and light, as in texture or color. **2** Daintily pleasing; delightful. **3** Nicely constructed or adjusted; accurate; sensitive, as an instrument. **4** Easily injured; tender; frail; fragile. **5** Requiring cautious or subtle treatment. **6** Refined and considerate. **7** Pure; chaste. **8** Fastidious; dainty. **9** Nice in discrimination; sensitive. **10** *Obs.* Voluptuous; luxurious. See synonyms under FINE, FRAGILE. **—***n. Obs.* **1** A delicacy; luxury. **2** An effeminate or luxurious person. [<L *delicatus* pleasing] **—del′i·cate·ly** *adv.* **—del′i·cate·ness** *n.*

del·i·ca·tes·sen (del′ə·kə·tes′ən) *n. pl.* **1** Cooked or preserved foods; cooked meats, canned goods, salads, cheeses, pickles, etc.: often construed as singular. **2** A store that sells such foods. [<G, pl. of *delicatesse* dainty food]

de·li·cious (di·lish′əs) *adj.* Extremely pleasant or enjoyable; affording great pleasure, especially to the taste. [<OF <LL *deliciosus* <*delicia* a delight] **—de·li′cious·ly** *adv.* **—de·li′cious·ness** *n.*

Synonyms: dainty, delightful, exquisite, luscious, savory. That is *delicious* which affords a gratification at once vivid and delicate to the senses, especially to those of taste and smell; as, *delicious* fruit; a *delicious* odor; *luscious* has a kindred but more fulsome meaning, inclining toward a cloying excess of sweetness or richness. *Savory* is applied chiefly to cooked food made palatable by spices and condiments. *Delightful* may be applied to the higher gratifications of sense, as *delightful* music, but is chiefly used for that which is mental and spiritual. *Delicious* has a limited use in this way; as, a *delicious* bit of poetry; the word is sometimes used ironically for some pleasing absurdity; as, this is *delicious.* Compare DELIGHTFUL. *Antonyms*: acrid, bitter, nauseous, unpalatable, unsavory.

De·li·cious (di·lish′əs) *n.* A cultivated North American variety of red apple, esteemed for its sweet flavor.

de·lict (di·likt′) *n.* In civil and Scots law, an offense; a misdemeanor: corresponds to *tort* in English and French law. [<L *delictum* <*delinquere.* See DELINQUENT.]

del·i·ga·tion (del′ə·gā′shən) *n.* **1** The act of binding or bandaging. **2** The application of ligatures. [<L *deligatus,* pp. of *deligare* <*de-* completely + *ligare* bind]

de·light (di·līt′) *n.* **1** Great pleasure; gratification; joyful satisfaction. **2** That which affords extreme enjoyment. **3** The quality of delighting; charm. See synonyms under ENTERTAINMENT, HAPPINESS. **—***v.i.* **1** To take great pleasure; rejoice: with *in* or the infinitive. **2** To give great enjoyment. **—***v.t.* **3** To please or gratify highly. See synonyms under CHARM, ENTERTAIN, RAPTURE, RAVISH, REJOICE. [<OF *delit* <*deliter* <L *delectare,* freq. of *delicere* <*de-* away + *lacere* entice]

de·light·ed (di·lī′tid) *adj.* **1** Highly pleased; joyfully gratified. **2** *Obs.* Affording delight; charming. See synonyms under HAPPY. **—de·light′ed·ly** *adv.*

de·light·ful (di·līt′fəl) *adj.* Affording delight; extremely gratifying; charming. **—de·light′·ful·ly** *adv.* **—de·light′ful·ness** *n.*

Synonyms: acceptable, agreeable, congenial, delicious, grateful, gratifying, pleasant, pleasing, pleasurable, refreshing, satisfying, welcome. *Agreeable* refers to whatever gives a mild degree of pleasure; as, an *agreeable* perfume. *Acceptable* indicates a thing worthy of acceptance; as, an *acceptable* offer. *Grateful* is stronger than *agreeable* or *gratifying,* indicating whatever awakens a feeling akin to gratitude. A *pleasant* face and *pleasing* manners arouse *pleasurable* sensations, and make the possessor an *agreeable* companion; if possessed of intelligence, vivacity, and goodness, such a person's society will be *delightful* and *congenial. Satisfying* denotes anything that is received with acquiescence, as substantial food, or established truth. That is *welcome* which is received with heartiness; as, *welcome* tidings. See BEAUTIFUL, CHARMING, DELICIOUS, GRATEFUL, HAPPY, LOVELY. *Antonyms*: depressing, disappointing, distressing, hateful, horrible, melancholy, miserable, mournful, painful, saddening, woeful, wretched.

de·light·some (di·līt′səm) *adj.* Delightful. **—de·light′some·ly** *adv.* **—de·light′some·ness** *n.*

De·li·lah (di·lī′lə) **1** A Philistine woman, the mistress of Samson, who betrayed him to the Philistines by cutting off his hair while he was asleep, thus depriving him of his strength. *Judges* xvi 4–20. **2** A temptress.

de·lim·it (di·lim′it) *v.t.* To prescribe the limits of; bound. Also **de·lim′i·tate.** [<F *délimiter* <L *delimitare* <*de-* completely + *limitare* bound <*limes* a boundary] **—de·lim′i·ta′tion** *n.* **—de·lim′i·ta′tive** *adj.*

de·lin·e·ate (di·lin′ē·āt) *v.t.* **·at·ed, ·at·ing 1** To draw in outline; trace out. **2** To portray pictorially. **3** To describe verbally. See synonyms under CIRCUMSCRIBE. [<L *delineatus,* pp. of *delineare* <*de-* completely + *lineare* draw a line <*linea* a line] **—de·lin′·e·a′tive** *adj.*

de·lin·e·a·tion (di·lin′ē·ā′shən) *n.* **1** The act or art of delineating. **2** A representation either by word or pictorial image. Also **de·lin·e·a ment** (di·lin′ē·ə·mənt), **de·lin′e·a·ture** (-chŏŏr). See synonyms under PICTURE, SKETCH.

de·lin·e·a·tor (di·lin′ē·ā′tər) *n.* **1** One who sketches or delineates. **2** A tailor's expansible pattern for cutting garments of various sizes.

de·lin·quen·cy (di·ling′kwən·sē) *n. pl.* **·cies 1** Neglect of duty; failure to do what is required. **2** A fault; offense; misdemeanor. See synonyms under OFFENSE, SIN.

de·lin·quent (di·ling′kwənt) *adj.* **1** Neglectful of or failing in duty or obligation; faulty. **2** Due and unpaid, as taxes. **—***n.* One who fails to perform a duty or who commits a fault. [<L *delinquens, -entis,* pp. of *delinquere* <*de-* down, away + *linquere* leave] **—de·lin′quent·ly** *adv.*

del·i·quesce (del′ə·kwes′) *v.i.* **·quesced, ·quesc·ing 1** To become liquid by absorption of moisture from the air, as certain salts. **2** To melt or pass away gradually. **3** *Bot.* **a** To become lost by repeated branching, as stems. **b** To become fluid, as a ripe agaric. [<L *deliquescere* <*de-* completely + *liquescere* melt]

del·i·ques·cence (del′ə·kwes′əns) *n.* **1** The act or process of deliquescing. **2** The condition of being deliquescent; also, the resultant liquid.

del·i·ques·cent (del′ə·kwes′ənt) *adj.* **1** Liquefying in the air. **2** *Bot.* **a** Dividing; ramifying; forming many small branches, as an elm tree. **b** Becoming liquid at maturity, as certain mushrooms.

de·liq·ui·um (di·lik′wē·əm) *n.* **1** *Rare* A fainting spell. **2** A softened, impaired, and weakened condition of mind. [<L <*delinquere.* See DELINQUENT.]

del·i·ra·tion (del′ə·rā′shən) *n.* Delirium; irrationality.

de·lir·i·ant (di·lir′ē·ənt) *n.* **1** A poison that induces delirium, as cannabis or hyoscyamine. **2** A delirious person. [<L *delirium* madness + -ANT]

de·lir·i·ous (di·lir′ē·əs) *adj.* Suffering from delirium; light-headed; raving. See synonyms under INSANE. **—de·lir′i·ous·ly** *adv.* **—de·lir′·i·ous·ness** *n.*

de·lir·i·um (di·lir′ē·əm) *n.* **1** A sporadic or temporary mental disturbance associated with fever, intoxication, shock, or injury and marked by restlessness, excitement, hallucinations, and general incoherence. **2** Intense excitement; frenzy; rapture. See synonyms under INSANITY. [<L <*delirare* <*de-* down, away + *lira* a furrow, track]

delirium tre·mens (trē′mənz) A violent form of delirium caused especially by excessive use of alcoholic liquors and narcotic drugs, and characterized by tremblings, acute mental distress, and delusions of the senses. [<NL, trembling delirium]

del·i·tes·cence (del′ə·tes′əns) *n.* **1** *Med.* **a** A sudden subsidence of the symptoms of a disease. **b** The latent period of an infection or a poison. **2** The state of being concealed; retirement; seclusion. Also **del′i·tes′cen·cy.** [<L *delitescens, -entis,* ppr. of *delitescere* <*de-* away + *litescere,* inceptive of *latere* lie hidden] **—del′i·tes′cent** *adj.*

De·li·us (dē′lē·əs, dēl′yəs), **Frederick,** 1863?–1934, English composer.

de·liv·er (di·liv′ər) *v.t.* **1** To hand over; surrender; transfer possession of. **2** To carry and distribute. **3** To utter; give forth in words. **4** To relieve of a child in childbirth; also, to assist in the birth of (a child). **5** To free from restraint, evil, danger, etc.; set free; rescue. **6** To send forth; discharge, as a broadside. **7** To give; strike, as a blow. **8** To throw or pitch, as a ball. **—***adj. Obs.* Nimble; active. [<F *délivrer* <LL *deliberare* <*de-* down, away + *liberare* set free <*liber* free] **—de·liv′er·a·ble** *adj.* **—de·liv′er·er** *n.*

Synonyms (verb): discharge, emancipate, free, liberate, ransom, redeem, rescue, save. See GIVE, RELEASE. *Antonyms*: betray, capture, confine, enslave, imprison, incarcerate.

de·liv·er·ance (di·liv′ər·əns) *n.* **1** The act of delivering or state of being delivered; rescue; release. **2** An expression of opinion; utterance. **3** *Obs.* Parturition.

de·liv·er·y (di·liv′ər·ē) *n. pl.* **·er·ies 1** The act of delivering; liberation; release; transference; surrender. **2** Parturition. **3** Mode of utterance, as in public speaking or singing. **4** Mode of projecting or discharging. **5** That which is or has been delivered: a mail *delivery.*

de·liv·er·y·man (di·liv′ər·ē·mən) *n. pl.* **·men** (-mən) A man who delivers parcels, bulky articles, or the like.

dell (del) *n.* A small, secluded valley; glen; dale. [OE. Akin to DALE.]

Del·la-Crus·can (del′ə·krus′kən) *adj.* Relating to or resembling the Accademia della Crusca (literally, the Academy of Chaff, from its object of sifting or purifying the Italian language) established at Florence in 1582. **—***n.* **1** A member of the Accademia della Crusca. **2** Any of the Della-Cruscan school of 18th century English poets living in Florence, whose affected style and extravagant praises of each other exposed them to public ridicule.

dells (delz) See DALLES.

Del·mar·va Peninsula (del·mär′və) A peninsula between Chesapeake and Delaware Bays, including Delaware and parts of Maryland and Virginia.

de·lo·cal·ize (dē·lō′kəl·īz) *v.t.* **·ized, ·iz·ing** To remove from place or free from local relations; enlarge the scope of; broaden. **—de·lo′·cal·i·za′tion** *n.*

De Long (də lông), **George Washington,** 1844–81, U.S. arctic explorer.

De·lorme (də·lôrm′), **Marion,** 1612?–50, French courtesan: also spelled **de Lorme.** **—Philibert,** 1518?–70, French architect: also spelled **de l'Orme.**

De·los (dē′los) The smallest island of the Cyclades, Greece; traditionally regarded as the birthplace of Apollo and Artemis. *Modern Greek* **Dhí·los** (thē′lôs). **—De′li·an** *adj.* & *n.*

de·louse (dē·lous′) *v.t.* **·loused, ·lous·ing** To remove lice or other insect vermin from.

Del•phi (del′fī) An ancient city in Phocis, Greece; famous for its oracle of Apollo. Also **Del′fi.** **—Del•phi•an** (del′fē•ən) *adj.* & *n.*

Del•phic (del′fik) *adj.* **1** Relating to Delphi or to Apollo's oracle there. **2** Oracular; ambiguous.

Delphic oracle The oracle of Apollo at Delphi: the sayings of its priestess, the Pythia, were enigmatic and ambiguous.

del•phin (del′fin) *adj.* Of or pertaining to a dolphin or to a family of cetaceans *(Delphinidae)*, including dolphins, porpoises, etc. *—n.* **1** *Obs.* A dolphin. **2** A neutral fat contained in the oil of certain dolphins. [< L *delphinus* < Gk. *delphis, delphinos* dolphin]

Del•phin (del′fin) *adj.* Pertaining to the Dauphins of France: The *Delphin* classics were prepared for the use of the son of Louis XIV.

del•phin•ic (del•fin′ik) *adj.* **1** Of, pertaining to, or derived from a dolphin. **2** Of, pertaining to, or derived from the larkspur *(Delphinium)*.

del•phi•nine (del′fə•nēn, -nin) *n.* A poisonous crystalline alkaloid, $C_{34}H_{47}NO_9$, found in the seeds of stavesacre: used in medicine. Also **del′phi•nin** (-nin). [< DELPHIN(IUM) + -INE[2]]

del•phin•i•um (del•fin′ē•əm) *n.* Any of a genus *(Delphinium)* of perennial plants of the crowfoot family, having large, spurred flowers, usually blue; the larkspur. [< NL < Gk. *delphinion* larkspur, dim. of *delphis* dolphin; so called from the shape of the nectary]

Del•phi•nus (del•fī′nəs) The Dolphin: a northern constellation. See CONSTELLATION.

Del•sarte system (del•särt′) A system of exercises for the development of bodily grace, voice, and dramatic expression. [after François Alexandre *Delsarte*, 1811–71, French singer and elocutionist]

del•ta (del′tə) *n.* **1** The fourth letter in the Greek alphabet (Δ, δ): corresponding to English *d.* As a numeral it denotes 4. **2** *Geog.* An alluvial, typically triangular-shaped, silt deposit at or in the mouth of a river. **3** Anything triangular. — **del•ta•ic** (del•tā′ik) *adj.*

delta rays *Physics* The fringe of secondary ionization along tracks formed by the impact of primary cosmic rays upon heavy atomic nuclei.

delta wing A triangular, swept-back aircraft wing that provides speed and lift.

del•ti•ol•o•gy (del′tē•ol′ə•jē) *n.* The collecting of postcards as a hobby. [< Gk. *deltion,* dim. of *deltos* writing tablet + -LOGY]

del•toid (del′toid) *n.* **1** *Anat.* A triangular muscle of the shoulder and upper arm. **2** *Geom.* A quadrilateral formed by two unequal isosceles triangles set base to base. *—adj.* **1** Shaped like a delta; triangular. **2** Of or pertaining to the deltoid. [< Gk. *deltoeidēs* triangular < *delta* the letter Δ + *eidos* form]

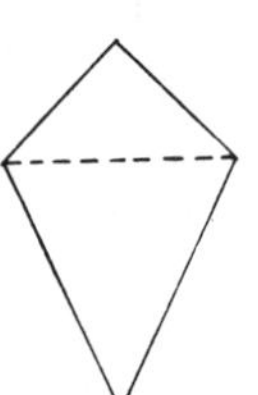
DELTOID

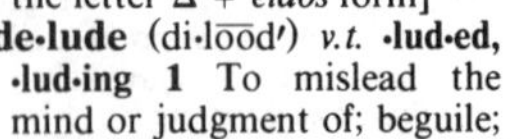

de•lude (di•lo͞od′) *v.t.* **•lud•ed, •lud•ing** **1** To mislead the mind or judgment of; beguile; deceive. **2** *Obs.* To evade; elude. **3** *Obs.* To frustrate. See synonyms under DECEIVE. [< L *deludere* < *de-* down, away + *ludere* play] **—de•lud′er** *n.* **—de•lud′ing•ly** *adv.*

del•uge (del′yo͞oj) *v.t.* **•uged, •ug•ing** To flood with water; inundate; submerge. **2** To overwhelm; destroy. [< *n.*] *—n.* **1** A great flood; inundation. **2** Anything that comes like a flood. — **the Deluge** The flood in the time of Noah. *Gen.* vii. [< F *déluge* < L *diluvium* < *diluere* wash away < *dis-* away + *luere* wash]

de•lu•sion (di•lo͞o′zhən) *n.* **1** The state of being deluded; a false belief, especially when persistent. **2** The act of deluding; deception. **3** The error thus conveyed or believed. **4** *Psychiatry* False belief about the self, often present in paranoia and dementia precox. [< L *delusio, -onis* < *deludere.* See DELUDE.]

Synonyms: error, fallacy, fantasm, hallucination, illusion. A *delusion* is a mistaken conviction, an *illusion* a mistaken perception or inference. An *illusion* may be wholly of the senses; a *delusion* always involves some mental error. We speak of the *illusions* of fancy or of hope, but of the *delusions* of the insane. A *hallucination* is a false image or belief which has nothing, outside of the disordered mind, to suggest it; as, the *hallucinations* of delirium tremens. Compare DECEPTION. *Antonyms*: actuality, certainty, fact, reality, truth, verity.

de•lu•sion•al (di•lo͞o′zhən•əl) *adj.* Consisting of, marked by, or subject to, delusions.

de•lu•sive (di•lo͞o′siv) *adj.* Tending to delude; misleading; deceptive. Also **de•lu•so•ry** (di•lo͞o′sər•ē). See synonyms under DECEPTIVE, VAIN. — **de•lu′sive•ly** *adv.* **—de•lu′sive•ness** *n.*

de•lus•ter•ing (dē•lus′tər•ing) *n.* The treatment of synthetic yarns and fabrics by special pigments or other chemicals in order to reduce their natural luster.

de luxe (di lo͝oks′, di luks′; *Fr.* də lüks′) Elaborate and expensive; of superfine quality. [< F, of luxury]

delve (delv) *v.* **delved, delv•ing** *v.i.* **1** To make careful investigation for facts, knowledge, etc.: to *delve* into a crime. **2** To slope down; descend, as a road or hill. **3** *Archaic* & *Dial.* To engage in digging. *—v.t.* **4** *Archaic* & *Dial.* To turn over or dig (ground). *—n.* An excavation; pit; depression in a surface. [OE *delfan*] **—delv′er** *n.*

de•mag•net•ize (dē•mag′nə•tīz) *v.t.* **•ized, •iz•ing** To deprive (a substance) of magnetism. — **de•mag′net•i•za′tion** *n.* **—de•mag′net•iz′er** *n.*

dem•a•gog (dem′ə•gôg, -gog) *n.* **1** One who leads the populace by pandering to their prejudices and passions; an unprincipled politician. **2** Anciently, any popular leader or orator. Also **dem′a•gogue.** [< Gk. *dēmagōgos* < *dēmos* people + *agein* lead] **—dem′a•gog′ic** (-goj′ik) or **•i•cal** *adj.* **—dem′a•gog′ism** (-gog′iz•əm) or **dem′a•gogu′ism, dem′a•gogu′er•y** (-gog′ər•ē), **dem•a•go•gy** (dem′ə•gō′jē, -gô′gē, -gog′ē) *n.*

de mal en pis (də mȧl äṅ pē′) *French* From bad to worse.

de•mand (di•mand′, -mänd′) *v.t.* **1** To ask for boldly or peremptorily; insist upon. **2** To claim as due; ask for authoritatively. **3** To ask to know; inquire formally. **4** To have need for; require. **5** *Law* **a** To summon to court. **b** To make formal claim to (property). *—v.i.* **6** To make a demand. *—n.* **1** The act of demanding, or that which is demanded; requirement; claim; need. **2** A desire to obtain; call. **3** An actionable legal claim; also, that act of requesting payment or performance of what is due. **4** The desire to possess combined with the ability to purchase; also, the totality of such effectual desire in a given market with reference to a given commodity at a certain price. **5** An inquiry. See synonyms under TAX. **—in demand** Desired; sought after. **—on demand** On presentation: a note payable *on demand.* [< F *demander* < L *demandare* < *de-* down, away + *mandare* command; order] **—de•mand′a•ble** *adj.* **—de•mand′er** *n.*

Synonyms (verb): ask, challenge, claim, exact, request, require. *Demand* is a determined and often an arrogant word; one may rightfully *demand* what is his own or his due, when it is withheld or denied; or he may wrongfully *demand* that to which he has no claim but power. *Require* is less arrogant and obtrusive than *demand,* but is exceedingly strenuous; as, the court *requires* the attendance of witnesses. *Request* is milder than *demand* or *require*: a creditor may *demand* or *require* payment; a friend *requests* a favor. We may speak of a humble *request,* but not of a humble *demand.* Compare ASK. *Antonyms*: decline, deny, refuse, reject, repudiate.

de•man•dant (di•man′dənt, -män′-) *n.* *Law* The plaintiff in a real action; any plaintiff.

demand bill A bill or draft payable on demand.

demand deposit A deposit available to the depositor without advance notice.

demand loan A loan that can be paid, or demanded to be paid, at any time.

demand note A note payable on demand.

de•man•toid (di•man′toid) *n.* An emerald-green garnet. [< G *demant* diamond + -OID]

de•mar•cate (di•mär′kāt, dē′mär•kāt) *v.t.* **•cat•ed, •cat•ing** **1** To mark the bounds or limits of; delimit. **2** To distinguish; discriminate; separate. [Back formation < DEMARCATION]

de•mar•ca•tion (dē′mär•kā′shən) *n.* **1** The fixing of boundaries or limits. **2** Limitation; discrimination. **3** The limit or line fixed. Also **de′mar•ka′tion.** **—Line of Demarcation** The line established, chiefly in modern Brazil, by Pope Alexander VI in 1493 to prevent disputes between Spain and Portugal in regard to their discoveries in the New World. [< Sp. *demarcación* < *demarcar* < *de-* down (< L *de-*) + *marcar* mark a boundary < Gmc.]

De•mar•çay (də•mȧr•sā′), **Eugène,** 1852–1903, French chemist.

de•march (dē′märk) *n.* **1** The chief executive head of an Attic deme. **2** The mayor of a modern Greek town. [< Gk. *dēmarchos* < *dēmos,* district, people + *archein* rule]

dé•marche (dā•mȧrsh′) *n.* *French* **1** A manner of approach or mode of procedure. **2** In diplomacy, a change in plan of action.

de•ma•te•ri•al•ize (dē′mə•tir′ē•əl•īz′) *v.t.* & *v.i.* **•ized, •iz•ing** To lose or cause to lose material attributes. **—de′ma•te′ri•al•i•za′tion** *n.*

Dem•a•vend (dem′ə•vend′) A peak, the highest in Iran, of the Elburz Mountains, 18,603 feet.

deme (dēm) *n.* **1** One of the districts into which the ten tribes of Attica were divided by Cleisthenes. **2** A commune. **3** A local group of organisms whose members freely interbreed only within the group. [< Gk. *dēmos*]

de•mean[1] (di•mēn′) *v.t.* **1** To behave; conduct: always used reflexively. **2** *Obs.* To direct; control. *—n.* *Obs.* Behavior; conduct; bearing. [< OF *demener* < *de-* down (< L *de-*) + *mener* lead < LL *minare* threaten, drive]

de•mean[2] (di•mēn′) *v.t.* To degrade; debase in dignity or reputation. [< DE- + MEAN[2]]

de•mean•or (di•mē′nər) *n.* Behavior; bearing; deportment; mien. Also *Brit.* **de•mean′our.** See synonyms under AIR[1], BEHAVIOR, MANNER.

de•ment (di•ment′) *v.t.* To deprive of mental powers; make insane. [< L *dementare* < *de-* away + *mens, mentis* mind]

de•ment•ed (di•men′tid) *adj.* Deprived of reason; insane. **—de•ment′ed•ly** *adv.* **—de•ment′ed•ness** *n.*

de•men•tia (di•men′shə, -shē•ə) *n.* *Psychiatry* Unsoundness of mind resulting from organic or functional disorders, and leading to total loss or serious impairment of the faculty of coherent thought. See synonyms under INSANITY. [< L, madness]

dementia praecox (prē′koks) *Obs.* Schizophrenia.

dementia se•ni•lis (si•nī′lis) Senile dementia.

Dem•e•rar•a (dem′ə•rȧr′ə, -rä′rə) A river in British Guiana, flowing north 200 miles to the Atlantic Ocean.

de•mer•it (di•mer′it) *n.* **1** In schools, a mark for failure or misconduct. **2** Censurable conduct. [< Med. L *demeritum* a fault < L, pp. of *demerere* < *de-* down, away + *merere* deserve]

Dem•e•rol (dem′ə•rōl, -rôl) *n.* Proprietary name for a brand of meperidine hydrochloride.

de•mer•sal (di•mûr′səl) *adj.* *Ecol.* Found in deep water or on the bottom of streams, pools, or the ocean: said especially of certain fish eggs.

de•mersed (di•mûrst′) *adj.* *Bot.* Situated or growing under water, as leaves of aquatic plants; submersed. [< obs. *demerse* plunge down < L *demersus,* pp. of *demergere* < *de-* down + *mergere* plunge]

de•mes•mer•ize (dē•mes′mə•rīz, -mez′-) *v.t.* **•ized, •iz•ing** To release from mesmeric influence; dehypnotize.

de•mesne (di•mān′, -mēn′) *n.* **1** In feudal law, lands held in one's own power, as distinguished from feudal lands which were held (by permission) of a superior. **2** A manor house and the adjoining lands in the immediate use and occupation of the owner of an estate. **3** The grounds appertaining to any residence, or any landed estate. **4** Any region over which sovereignty is exercised; domain. Also **de•main, de•maine** (di•mān′). [< AF *demeyne,* OF *demeine, demaine.* Doublet of DOMAIN.]

De•me•ter (di•mē′tər) In Greek mythology, the goddess of agriculture, marriage, and fertility: identified with the Roman *Ceres.*

De•me•tri•us (di•mē′trē•əs) A masculine personal name. Also *Ital.* **De•me•tri•o** (dā•mā′trē•ō), *Ger.* **De•me•tri•us** (dā•mā′trē•o͝os), *Fr.* **Dé•mé•tri•us** (dā•mā•trē•üs′), *Russ.* **Dmi•tri** (dmē′trē). [< Gk., of Demeter]

demi- *prefix* **1** Half; intermediate: *demitint, demilune.* **2** Inferior or less in size, quality, etc.; partial: *demigod.* [< F *demi* < L *dimidius* half < *dis-* from, apart + *medius* middle]

dem·i·god (dem′ē·god′) *n.* **1** An inferior or lesser deity; a hero, supposed to be the offspring of a god and a mortal. **2** A man with the attributes of a god. —**dem′i·god′dess** *n. fem.*

dem·i·john (dem′ē·jon′) *n.* A large, juglike glass or crockery vessel enclosed in wickerwork. [<F *dame-jeanne,* lit., Lady Jane]

de·mil·i·ta·rize (dē·mil′ə·tə·rīz′) *v.t.* **·rized, ·riz·ing 1** To remove the military form of; free from militarism. **2** To transfer from military to civilian control. **3** To remove military equipment and troops from and declare neutral, as an area or zone. —**de·mil′·i·ta·ri·za′tion** *n.*

De Mille (də mil′), **Cecil B(lount),** 1881–1959, U.S. motion-picture producer.

dem·i·lune (dem′ē·lo͞on′) *n.* **1** The moon in its first or last quarter. **2** A crescent. **3** A crescent-shaped outwork, having two faces and two small flanks, covering the shoulders and curtain of the bastion. [<F *demi* half + *lune* moon]

dem·i·mon·daine (dem′ē·mon·dān′) *n.* A woman of the demimonde. [<F]

dem·i·monde (dem′ē·mond, dem′ē·mond′) *n.* The class of women who have lost social position and repute as a result of equivocal or scandalous behavior. [<F <*demi-* half, partial + *monde* world; coined by A. Dumas *fils*]

dem·i·pique (dem′ē·pēk) *n. Obs.* A saddle with a pommel half the height of a military saddle. [<DEMI- + PEAK; infl. in form by F *pique* pike]

dem·i·qua·ver (dem′ē·kwā′vər) *n. Music* A sixteenth note; semiquaver.

dem·i–re·lief (dem′ē·ri·lēf′) *n.* Mezzo-relievo. *Italian* **de·mi–ri·lie·vo** (dām·ē·rē·lyā′vō).

dem·i·rep (dem′ē·rep) *n.* A woman of questionable chastity. [<DEMI- + REP(UTATION)]

de·mise (di·mīz′) *n.* **1** Death; decease. **2** *Law* **a** Decease involving as a result the transfer of an estate. **b** A transfer or conveyance of rights or estate. **3** The immediate transfer of a sovereign's rights at his death or abdication to his successor. —*v.* **·mised, ·mis·ing** *v.t.* **1** To bestow by will; bequeath: said especially of sovereignty on the death or abdication of a king, etc. **2** *Law* To lease (an estate) for life or for a term of years. —*v.i.* **3** To pass by will or inheritance. [<OF, fem. of *demis,* pp. of *demettre* send away <L *demittere.* See DEMIT.] —**de·mis′a·ble** *adj.*

dem·i–sem·i (dem′ē·sem′ē) *adj.* Half-half; quarter.

dem·i·sem·i·qua·ver (dem′ē·sem′ē·kwā′vər) *n. Music* A note of the value of 1/4 of a quaver; a thirty-second note.

de·mis·sion (di·mish′ən) *n.* A giving up or relinquishment, as of an office; resignation. [<L *demissio, -onis* <*demittere.* See DEMIT.]

de·mit (di·mit′) *v.* **·mit·ted, ·mit·ting** *v.t.* **1** To resign (an office or dignity). **2** *Obs.* To release; dismiss. —*v.i.* **3** To resign. —*n.* A letter of dismissal or one attesting honorable resignation; a recommendation. [<L *demittere* <*de-* down, away + *mittere* send]

dem·i·tasse (dem′ē·tas′, -täs′) *n.* **1** A small cup in which after-dinner coffee is served; literally, a half cup. **2** The coffee served in such a cup. [<F]

dem·i–tint (dem′ē·tint′) *n.* **1** A half-tint; a tint intermediate between the extremes of dark and light coloring in a painting. **2** Broken tints or tertiary shades of color. **3** The portion of a work of art so tinted.

dem·i·urge (dem′ē·ûrj) *n.* **1** In Plato's philosophy, the creator of the material universe. **2** In the Gnostic systems, Jehovah as an emanation of the Supreme Being; creator of the material world: sometimes also regarded as the creator of evil. **3** One of a class of public officers or magistrates in several ancient Peloponnesian states. Also **dem′i·ur′·gus** (-ûr′gəs), **dem′i·ur′gos.** [<Gk. *demiourgos* skilled or public worker <*dēmos* people + *ergein* work] —**dem′i·ur′geous** (-jəs), **dem′i·ur′gic, dem′i·ur′gi·cal** *adj.*

dem·i·volt (dem′ē·vōlt′) *n.* In horseback riding, a movement of the horse, consisting of a half turn with the forelegs raised. Also **dem′i·volte′.** [<F *demi-volte* <*demi-* half + *volte* a leap]

dem·i·wolf (dem′ē·wo͝olf′) *n.* A mongrel, half wolf and half dog.

de·mob (dē·mob′) *v.t.* **·mobbed, ·mob·bing** *Brit. Slang* To demobilize.

de·mo·bil·ize (dē·mō′bəl·īz) *v.t.* **·ized, ·iz·ing 1** To disband, as troops that have been mobilized. **2** To change, as an army, from a war to a peacetime basis. —**de·mo′bil·i·za′tion** *n.*

de·moc·ra·cy (di·mok′rə·sē) *n. pl.* **·cies 1** A theory of government which, in its purest form, holds that the state should be controlled by all the people, each sharing equally in privileges, duties, and responsibilities and each participating in person in the government, as in the city-states of ancient Greece. In practice, control is vested in elective officers as representatives who may be upheld or removed by the people. **2** A government so conducted; a state so governed; the mass of the people. **3** Political, legal, or social equality. [<F *démocratie* <Med. L *democratia* <Gk. *dēmokratia* <*dēmos* people + *krateein* rule]

De·moc·ra·cy (di·mok′rə·sē) *n.* The principles of the Democratic party; also, the party, or its members collectively.

dem·o·crat (dem′ə·krat) *n.* **1** One who favors a democracy. **2** One who believes in political and social equality.

Dem·o·crat (dem′ə·krat) *n.* A member of the Democratic party in the United States.

dem·o·crat·ic (dem′ə·krat′ik) *adj.* **1** Of or pertaining to democracy or a democracy; characterized by the fact, spirit, or principles of popular government. **2** Pertaining to or characteristic of any democratic party. **3** Tending to level social distinctions; practicing social equality; not snobbish. —**dem′o·crat′·i·cal·ly** *adv.*

Democratic party One of the two major political parties in the United States, dating from 1828.

de·moc·ra·tize (di·mok′rə·tīz) *v.t.* & *v.i.* **·tized, ·tiz·ing** To make or become democratic. —**de·moc′ra·ti·za′tion** *n.*

De·moc·ri·tus (di·mok′rə·təs) 460?–352? B.C., Greek philosopher; propounded the theory that all substance is composed of moving atoms. —**De·moc·ri·te·an** (di·mok′rə·tē′ən), **Dem·o·crit·i·cal** (dem′ə·krit′i·kəl) *adj.*

dé·mo·dé (dā·mô·dā′) *adj. French* Old-fashioned; outmoded; out of style.

de·mod·ed (dē·mō′did) *adj.* Out of fashion.

de·mod·u·late (dē·moj′o͞o·lāt) *v.t.* **·lat·ed, ·lat·ing** *Electronics* To detect. —**de·mod′u·la′·tion** *n.*

De·mo·gor·gon (dē′mə·gôr′gən, dem′ə-) The genius of the earth or underworld: regarded by later classical and medieval writers as a mysterious and dreaded infernal deity or magician.

de·mog·ra·phy (di·mog′rə·fē) *n.* The study of vital and social statistics in their application to ethnology, anthropology, and public health. [<Gk. *dēmos* people + -GRAPHY] —**de·mog′ra·pher, de·mog′ra·phist** *n.* —**dem·o·graph·ic** (dem′ə·graf′ik) or **·i·cal** *adj.* —**dem′o·graph′i·cal·ly** *adv.*

dem·oi·selle (dem′·wä·zel′) *n.* **1** An unmarried woman; a damsel. **2** An Old World crane (Numidian crane, family *Gruidae*) of graceful form and carriage. **3** A dragonfly (family *Agriidae*). [<F, var. of *damoiselle* <OF *dameisele.* See DAMSEL.]

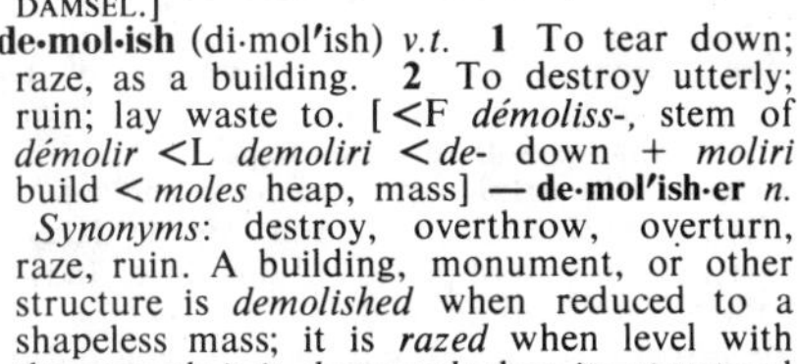
DEMOISELLE
(About 4 feet erect)

de·mol·ish (di·mol′ish) *v.t.* **1** To tear down; raze, as a building. **2** To destroy utterly; ruin; lay waste to. [<F *démoliss-,* stem of *démolir* <L *demoliri* <*de-* down + *moliri* build <*moles* heap, mass] —**de·mol′ish·er** *n.*

Synonyms: destroy, overthrow, overturn, raze, ruin. A building, monument, or other structure is *demolished* when reduced to a shapeless mass; it is *razed* when level with the ground; it is *destroyed* when its structural unity is gone, whether or not its component parts remain. An edifice is *destroyed* by fire or earthquake; it is *demolished* by bombardment; it is *ruined* when, by violence or neglect, it has become unfit for human habitation. Compare ABOLISH, BREAK. *Antonyms*: build, construct, create, make, repair, restore.

dem·o·li·tion (dem′ə·lish′ən) *n.* The act or result of demolishing; destruction. Also **de·mol′ish·ment.** —**dem′o·li′tion·ist** *n.*

demolition bomb See under BOMB.

de·mon (dē′mən) *n.* **1** An evil spirit; devil. **2** A wicked or cruel person. **3** In ancient Greek religion, a supernatural intelligence; a guardian spirit; genius. **4** A person of great energy, skill, etc. —*adj.* Being or possessed of a demon. Also spelled *daemon, daimon.* [<L *daemon* evil spirit (orig., spirit, god) <Gk. *daimōn*] —**de·mon·i·an** (di·mō′nē·ən), **de·mon·ic** (di·mon′ik) *adj.*

de·mon·a·chize (dē·mon′ə·kīz) *v.t.* **·chized, ·chiz·ing** To remove monks from. [<DE- + L *monachus* monk]

de·mon·e·ti·za·tion (dē·mon′ə·tə·zā′shən) *n.* The act of demonetizing, or the condition of being demonetized.

de·mon·e·tize (dē·mon′ə·tīz) *v.t.* **·tized, ·tiz·ing 1** To deprive (currency) of standard value. **2** To withdraw from use as currency.

de·mo·ni·ac (di·mō′nē·ak) *adj.* **1** Of, like, or befitting a demon or evil spirit; devilish. **2** Influenced or produced by or as by demons; mad; violent; frenzied. Also **de·mo·ni·a·cal** (dē′mə·nī′ə·kəl) —*n.* One possessed of a demon or evil spirit; a lunatic. —**de′mo·ni′·a·cal·ly** *adv.*

de·mon·ism (dē′mən·iz′əm) *n.* Belief in the existence and power of demons. —**de′mon·ist** *n.*

de·mon·ize (dē′mən·īz) *v.t.* **·ized, ·iz·ing 1** To make a demon of. **2** To bring under demonic influence.

demono– *combining form* Demon: *demonology.* Also, before vowels, **demon–.** [<Gk. *daimōn* spirit, god]

de·mon·ol·a·try (dē′mən·ol′ə·trē) *n.* The worship of demons. [<DEMONO- + Gk. *latreia* worship] —**de′mon·ol′a·ter** *n.*

de·mon·ol·o·gy (dē′mən·ol′ə·jē) *n.* The study of or belief in demons or demonism. [<DEMONO- + -LOGY] —**de′mon·ol′o·gist** *n.*

de·mon·stra·ble (di·mon′strə·bəl, dem′ən-) *adj.* Capable of being proved. —**de·mon′stra·ble·ness, de·mon′stra·bil′i·ty** *n.* —**de·mon′·stra·bly** *adv.*

de·mon·strance (di·mon′strəns) *n.* Demonstration.

de·mon·strant (di·mon′strənt) *n.* One who makes, furthers, or takes part in a public demonstration.

dem·on·strate (dem′ən·strāt) *v.* **·strat·ed, ·strat·ing** *v.t.* **1** To explain or describe by use of experiments, examples, etc. **2** To explain the operation or use of. **3** To prove or show to be by logic; make evident. **4** To exhibit; make clear, as emotions. —*v.i.* **5** To take part in a public demonstration. **6** To make a show of military force. [<L *demonstratus,* pp. of *demonstrare* <*de-* completely + *monstrare* show, point out]

dem·on·stra·tion (dem′ən·strā′shən) *n.* **1** A pointing out; the act of making known. **2** An exhibition or expression; manifestation. **3** Proof by such evidence of facts, principles, and arguments as precludes denial or reasonable doubt. **4** The exhibition and description of examples in teaching an art or science. **5** A public exhibition of welcome, approval, or condemnation, as by a mass meeting or procession. **6** *Logic* A system of reasoning showing how, from given premises, such as definitions, axioms, postulates, a certain result must follow. **7** A show of military force or of aggressive movement, especially when intended as a feint, or in time of peace as a menace. **8** An exhibition and explanation of the fine points and workability of an article or commodity to be sold.

Synonyms: certainty, conclusion, consequence, deduction, evidence, induction, inference, proof. *Demonstration,* in the strict and proper sense, is the highest form of *proof* and gives the most absolute *certainty,* but cannot be applied outside of pure mathematics or other strictly deductive reasoning;

there can be *proof* and *certainty,* however, in matters that do not admit of *demonstration.* A *conclusion* is the absolute and necessary result of the admission of certain premises; an *inference* is a probable *conclusion* toward which known facts, statements, or admissions point, but which they do not absolutely establish; sound premises, together with their necessary *conclusion,* constitute a *demonstration. Evidence* is that which tends to show a thing to be true. *Proof* in the strict sense is complete, irresistible *evidence*; as, there was much *evidence* against the accused, but not amounting to *proof* of guilt. Moral *certainty* is a conviction resting on such *evidence* as puts a matter beyond reasonable doubt, while not so irresistible as *demonstration.* Compare CERTAINTY, INDUCTION, INFERENCE, PROOF.

de·mon·stra·tive (di·mon′strə·tiv) *adj.* **1** Having the power of demonstrating or pointing out; convincing and conclusive. **2** Inclined to strong expression of feeling or opinions. **3** *Gram.* Serving to indicate the person or object referred to or intended. —*n.* A demonstrative pronoun. **—de·mon′stra·tive·ly** *adv.* **—de·mon′stra·tive·ness** *n.*

demonstrative pronoun See under PRONOUN.

dem·on·stra·tor (dem′ən·strā′tər) *n.* **1** One who demonstrates. **2** One who exhibits and explains, as in an anatomy class. **3** A salesman who demonstrates the desirability and workability of some article or product to the public. **4** The article used for demonstration, as a vacuum cleaner or automobile. Also **dem′on·strat′er.**

dem·o·pho·bi·a (dem′ə·fō′bē·ə) *n. Psychol.* Morbid fear of crowds; also called *ochlophobia.* [< Gk. *dēmos* people + -PHOBIA] **—dem′o·pho′bic** *adj.*

de·mor·al·ize (di·môr′əl·īz, -mor′-) *v.t.* **·ized, ·iz·ing 1** To corrupt or deprave. **2** To dishearten; undermine discipline among, as troops. **3** To throw into disorder. **—de·mor′al·i·za′tion** *n.* **—de·mor′al·iz′er** *n.*

de mor·tu·is nil ni·si bo·num (dē môr′choo͞·is nil nī′sī bō′nəm) *Latin* Of the dead (say) nothing but good.

de·mos (dē′mos) *n.* **1** The people of an ancient Greek state. **2** The common people; the masses. [< Gk. *dēmos*]

De·mos·the·nes (di·mos′thə·nēz), 384?–322 B.C., Athenian orator and patriot.

de·mote (di·mōt′) *v.t.* **·mot·ed, ·mot·ing** To reduce to a lower grade or rank: opposed to promote. [< DE- + (PRO)MOTE] **—de·mo′tion** *n.*

de·mot·ic (di·mot′ik) *adj.* **1** Of or pertaining to the people or to the population of a region, country, locality, etc.; popular. **2** Pertaining to the simplified form of the hieratic alphabet of ancient Egypt. [< Gk. *dēmotikos* < *dēmos* people]

de·mot·ics (di·mot′iks) *n.* Sociology in its most inclusive sense.

de·mount (dē·mount′) *v.t.* To remove, as a motor, from its mounting, setting, or place of support.

de·mount·a·ble (dē·moun′tə·bəl) *adj.* That may be easily taken apart, or removed from its position, as an automobile wheel.

demp·ster (demp′stər) *n.* **1** A deemster. **2** In old Scots law, a doomster. Also **dem′ster.** [Var. of DEEMSTER]

de·mul·cent (di·mul′sənt) *adj.* Soothing. —*n. Med.* A soothing application, especially one to relieve irritated mucous membranes. [< L *demulcens, -entis,* ppr. of *demulcere* < *de-* down + *mulcere* soothe]

de·mur (di·mûr′) *v.i.* **murred, ·mur·ring 1** To offer objections; take exception. **2** To delay; hesitate. **3** *Law* To interpose a demurrer. —*n.* **1** A suspension of decision or action; a delay. **2** An objection. **3** *Obs.* A demurrer. [< OF *demeurer* < L *demorari* < *de-* completely + *morari* delay < *mora* a delay] **—de·mur′ra·ble** *adj.*

de·mure (di·myoo͝r′) *adj.* **1** Having a sedate or modest demeanor. **2** Affecting modesty; prim; coy. See synonyms under SERIOUS. [ME *mure* < OF *meur* < L *maturus* mature, discreet] **—de·mure′ly** *adv.* **—de·mure′ness** *n.*

de·mur·rage (di·mûr′ij) *n.* **1** The detention of a vessel or conveyance by a consigner or consignee beyond the specified time. **2** Compensation for such delay. [< OF *demourage* < *demourer* < L *demorare.* See DEMUR.]

de·mur·ral (di·mûr′əl) *n.* Hesitation; delay; demur.

de·mur·rer (di·mûr′ər) *n.* **1** *Law* A pleading that admits the facts stated in the pleading to which it replies, but denies that they are sufficient to constitute a good cause of action or defense in law. **2** Any objection or exception taken. **3** One who demurs.

de·my (di·mī′) *n. pl.* **de·mies 1** A size of paper, in the United States about 16 × 21 inches. **2** A foundation scholar of Magdalen College, Oxford. [< DEMI-]

de·myth·ol·o·gize (dē′mi·thol′ə·jīz) *v.t.* **-gized, -giz·ing** To divest of mythological elements.

den (den) *n.* **1** A cavern occupied by animals; a lair. **2** A low haunt. **3** A room for privacy; sanctum. See synonyms under HOLE. —*v.i.* **denned, den·ning** To dwell in, or as in, a den. [OE *denn*]

de·nar·i·us (di·nâr′ē·əs) *n. pl.* **·nar·i·i** (-nâr′ē·ī) **1** The most important coin of ancient Rome, made of silver and weighing, under Augustus, 1/84 of a pound; the penny of the New Testament. **2** Later, a small copper coin. **3** A gold coin, the **denarius aureus,** worth 25 silver denarii. *Denarius* was the Latin name of the English penny, the initial of which (*d.*) is preserved in monetary notation. [< L *denarius* (*nummus*) denary (coin); because it was worth ten asses]

ROMAN DENARIUS

den·a·ry (den′ə·rē, dē′nə-) *adj.* Containing ten; decimal. —*n. pl.* **·ries 1** The number 10. **2** A tithing. [< L *denarius* < *deni* by tens < *decem* ten]

de·na·tion·al·ize (dē·nash′ən·əl·īz′) *v.t.* **·ized, ·iz·ing 1** To deprive of national character, status, or rights. **2** To change the nationality of. **—de·na′tion·al·i·za′tion** *n.*

de·nat·u·ral·ize (dē·nach′ər·əl·īz′) *v.t.* **·ized, ·iz·ing 1** To render unnatural. **2** To deprive of naturalization or citizenship; denationalize. **—de·nat′u·ral·i·za′tion** *n.*

de·na·ture (dē·nā′chər) *v.t.* **·tured, ·tur·ing 1** To alter the natural properties of (a substance) by adding an adulterant. **2** *Biochem.* To modify the molecular structure of (a protein or nucleic acid) by physical or chemical means. Also **de·na′tur·ize. —de·na′tur·ant** *n.* **—de·na′tur·a′tion** *n.*

denatured alcohol Ethyl alcohol made unfit for drinking purposes by the addition of a toxic or distasteful substance.

de·na·zi·fy (dē·nät′sə·fī, -nat′-) *v.t.* **·fied, ·fy·ing** To rid of Nazi influences or of Nazism. **—de·na′zi·fi·ca′tion** *n.*

Den·bigh (den′bē) A county in NE Wales; 669 square miles; capital, Denbigh. Also **Den′bigh·shire** (-shir).

den·dri·form (den′drə·fôrm) *adj.* Like a tree in structure; tree-shaped.

den·drite (den′drīt) *n.* **1** *Mineral.* Any mineral crystallizing in a branching, treelike form; a rock or mineral with treelike markings. **2** *Physiol.* A filamentous, arborescent process of a nerve cell which conducts impulses toward the cell body. [< Gk. *dendritēs* of a tree]

den·drit·ic (den·drit′ik) *adj.* **1** Resembling a tree; dendriform. **2** Of or pertaining to a dendrite. Also **den·drit′i·cal. —den·drit′i·cal·ly** *adv.*

dendro- *combining form* Tree: *dendrochore.* Also, before vowels, **dendr-.** Also **dendri-.** [< Gk. *dendron* tree]

den·dro·chore (den′drə·kôr, -kōr) *n. Ecol.* The region of trees and forests: a major division of the biochore. **—den′dro·chor′ic** *adj.*

den·dro·chro·nol·o·gy (den′drə·krə·nol′ə·jē) *n.* The determination of the approximate dates of past events and of periods of time by a study of the growth rings on trees.

den·droid (den′droid) *adj.* Like a tree; dendritic. Also **den·droi′dal.** [< Gk. *dendroeidēs*]

den·dro·lite (den′drə·līt) *n. Bot.* A petrified or fossil shrub, plant, or part of a plant.

den·drol·o·gy (den·drol′ə·jē) *n.* That branch of botany and forestry that deals with trees. [< DENDRO- + -LOGY] **—den·drol′o·gist** *n.*

den·dron (den′dron) *n. Physiol.* A nerve dendrite. [< Gk., tree]

-dendron *combining form* Tree: *philodendron.* [< Gk. *dendron* tree]

dene (dēn) *n. Brit.* A sandy stretch of land or a low, sandy hill near the sea. [Origin uncertain]

Den·eb (den′eb) A star of the first magnitude; Alpha in the constellation Cygnus.

De·neb·o·la (di·neb′ə·lə) The star Beta in the constellation Leo; magnitude, 2.2.

den·e·gate (den′ə·gāt) *v.t.* **·gat·ed, ·gat·ing** *Obs.* To deny; refuse. [< DE- + NEGATE]

den·e·ga·tion (den′ə·gā′shən) *n.* A denial or refusal.

dene·hole (dēn′hōl′) *n. Archeol.* One of a class of ancient excavations found in the chalk formation of southern England.

den·gue (deng′gē, -gā) *n. Pathol.* An acute, tropical, frequently epidemic virus disease transmitted by the bite of the mosquito *Aëdes aegypti* and characterized by fever, eruptions, and severe pains in the joints: also known as *breakbone fever.* [< Sp., ult. < Swahili]

de·ni·a·ble (di·nī′ə·bəl) *adj.* That can be denied. **—de·ni′a·bly** *adv.*

de·ni·al (di·nī′əl) *n.* **1** The act of denying; declaration that a statement made is untrue; contradiction: opposed to *affirmation.* **2** Refusal to acknowledge or admit; a disowning or disavowal; rejection. **3** Refusal to grant, indulge, or agree; non-compliance, as with something urged.

de·nic·o·tin·ize (dē·nik′ə·tin·īz′) *v.t.* **·ized, ·iz·ing** To remove nicotine from.

de·ni·er[1] (di·nī′ər) *n.* One who makes denial.

den·ier[2] (den′yər, də·nir′ *for def. 1,* də·nir′ *for def. 2; Fr.* də·nyā′) *n.* **1** A unit of rayon or silk yarn size, based on a standard weight of five centigrams per 450 meters of silk. **2** A silver coin, introduced by Pepin the Short in 755, which was for centuries the chief silver coin in Europe. [< F < L *denarius* DENARIUS.]

den·i·grate (den′ə·grāt) *v.t.* **·grat·ed, ·grat·ing 1** To make black; blacken. **2** To slander. [< L *denigratus,* pp. of *denigrare* < *de-* completely + *nigrare* blacken < *niger* black] **—den′i·gra′tion** *n.* **—den′i·gra′tor** *n.* **—den·i·gra·to·ry** (den′ə·grə·tôr′ē, -tō′rē) *adj.*

De·ni·ker (dā·nē·kâr′), **Joseph,** 1852–1918, French anthropologist and ethnographer.

den·im (den′əm) *n.* A twilled cotton used for overalls, uniforms, etc. [< F *(serge) de Nîmes* (serge) of Nîmes, where first made]

Den·is (den′is) A masculine personal name. See DIONYSIUS, its original, uncontracted form. Also **Den′nis,** *Fr.* **De·nis** or **De·nys** (də·nē′).

—Denis, Saint, died 280? patron saint of France and first bishop of Paris: also spelled *Denys.*

de·ni·trate (dē·nī′trāt) *v.t.* **·trat·ed, ·trat·ing** *Chem.* To remove nitrogen, nitric or nitrous acid, nitrates, or nitrogen oxide from. **—de′ni·tra′tion** *n.*

de·ni·tri·fy (dē·nī′trə·fī) *v.t.* **·fied, ·fy·ing 1** *Chem.* To remove nitrogen or its compounds from. **2** *Bacteriol.* To reduce (nitrates) to nitrites, nitrogen, or ammonia, as by certain bacteria. Also **de·ni′trize. —de·ni′tri·fi·ca′tion** *n.*

den·i·zen (den′ə·zən) *n.* **1** One who lives in a place; a citizen; inhabitant. **2** *Brit.* An alien who has been admitted to residence and to certain privileges of citizenship. **3** A person, animal, or thing at home in any region, although not a native. —*v.t. Brit.* **1** To admit to the rights of citizenship. **2** To populate with denizens. [< AF *deinzein* < *deinz* inside < L *de intus* from within] **—den′i·zen·a′tion** *n.*

Den·mark (den′märk) A kingdom in NW Europe; 16,575 square miles; capital, Copenhagen. *Danish* **Dan·mark** (dän′märk).

Denmark Strait A channel between Greenland and Iceland, connecting the Atlantic with the Greenland Sea.

de·nom·i·nate (di·nom′ə·nāt) *v.t.* **·nat·ed, ·nat·ing** To give a name to; call: to *denominate* him a thief. —*adj.* (-nit) Made up of units of a designated kind: opposed to *abstract.* [< L *denominatus,* pp. of *denominare* < *de-* down + *nomen* name] **—de·nom′i·na·ble** (-ə·nə·bəl) *adj.*

denominate number See under NUMBER.

de·nom·i·na·tion (di·nom′ə·nā′shən) *n.* **1** The act of naming. **2** A class designation; name; epithet; appellation. **3** A body of Christians having a distinguishing name; sect. **4** A class of arithmetical units of one kind and name. **5** A unit of value: said of money: bills of all *denominations* from $1.00 to $500.00. See synonyms under NAME, SECT. —**de·nom′i·na′·tion·al** *adj.* —**de·nom′i·na′tion·al·ism** *n.* —**de·nom′i·na′tion·al·ist** *n.* —**de·nom′i·na′tion·al·ly** *adv.*

de·nom·i·na·tive (di·nom′ə·nā′tiv, -nə·tiv) *adj.* **1** That gives or constitutes a name; appellative. **2** *Gram.* Derived from a noun or adjective. —*n.* **1** That which describes or denominates. **2** *Gram.* A word, especially a verb, derived from a noun or adjective, as the verb *to garden.* —**de·nom′i·na′tive·ly** *adv.*

de·nom·i·na·tor (di·nom′ə·nā′tər) *n.* **1** One who or that which names. **2** *Math.* That term of a fraction below or to the right of the line which expresses the number of equal parts into which the unit is divided; divisor. —**common denominator** Any common multiple of the denominators of a series of fractions.

de·no·ta·tion (dē′nō·tā′shən) *n.* **1** The act of denoting or distinguishing by name; a marking off; designation or separation. **2** The object or objects denoted by a word, as distinguished from the marks or qualities which it suggests: contrasted with *connotation.* **3** That which indicates; a sign. **4** That which is signified; meaning.

de·no·ta·tive (di·nō′tə·tiv, dē′nō·tā′tiv) *adj.* Having power to denote; significant. —**de·no′ta·tive·ly** *adv.*

de·note (di·nōt′) *v.t.* **·not·ed, ·not·ing** **1** To mark; point out or make known. **2** To serve as a symbol for; signify; indicate. **3** To designate; mean: said of words, symbols, etc. See synonyms under IMPORT. [<L *denotare* <*de-* down + *notare* mark] —**de·not′a·ble** *adj.*

dé·noue·ment (dā·nōō·mäṅ′) *n.* **1** The final unraveling or solution of the plot of a play, novel, or short story; issue; outcome. **2** The point in the plot where this occurs. **3** Any final issue or solution. See synonyms under CATASTROPHE. [<F <*dénouer* <*dé-* away (<L *dis-*) + *nouer* knot <L *nodare* <*nodus* a knot]

de·nounce (di·nouns′) *v.t.* **·nounced, ·nounc·ing** **1** To attack or condemn openly and vehemently; inveigh against. **2** To inform against; accuse. **3** To threaten, as evil or vengeance; menace. **4** To give formal notice of, specifically, of the termination of a treaty or convention. **5** *Obs.* To announce; foretell. See synonyms under CONDEMN. [<OF *denoncer* <L *denuntiare* <*de-* down + *nuntiare* proclaim, announce] —**de·nounce′ment** *n.* —**de·nounc′er** *n.*

de no·vo (dē nō′vō) *Latin* From the beginning; anew.

dense (dens) *adj.* **dens·er, dens·est** **1** Having its parts crowded closely together; compact in structure; thick; close. **2** Hard to penetrate; obtuse; stupid; dull. **3** *Phot.* Opaque when developed, and consequently strongly contrasted in lights and shades; intense: said of a negative. See synonyms under HARD, IMPENETRABLE. [<L *densus*] —**dense′ly** *adv.* —**dense′ness** *n.*

den·sim·e·ter (den·sim′ə·tər) *n.* A hydrometer. [<L *densus* thick + -METER]

den·si·tom·e·ter (den′sə·tom′ə·tər) *n.* *Phot.* An apparatus for determining the density of silver deposits on a plate or film. [<DENSITY + -METER]

den·si·ty (den′sə·tē) *n.* *pl.* **·ties** **1** Compactness; the closeness of any space distribution. **2** *Physics* The mass of a substance per unit of its volume. In the metric system the unit of density is the mass of a cubic centimeter of water at 4°C. **3** *Sociol.* The number of specified units, as persons, families, or dwellings, per acre or square mile. **4** *Electr.* The quantity of current flowing through a given cross-section of a conductor: usually expressed in terms of amperes per square centimeter or square inch: also **current density.** **5** *Ecol.* The relative thickness of the vegetative cover in forests, on prairies, etc., scaled in 10ths with 1 as the maximum growth. [<MF *densité* <L *densitas, -tatis* <*densus* thick]

dent[1] (dent) *n.* A small depression made by striking or pressing; indentation. See synonyms under BLEMISH, HOLE. —*v.t.* To make a dent in. —*v.i.* To become dented. [Var. of DINT]

dent[2] (dent) *n.* **1** The space between two wires in the reed of a loom. **2** A tooth, as of a comb, gear wheel, etc. [<F <L *dens, dentis* tooth]

den·tal (den′təl) *adj.* **1** Of or pertaining to the teeth. **2** Of or pertaining to dentistry. **3** *Phonet.* Describing a consonant produced with the tip of the tongue against or near the upper front teeth, as French *t* and *d.* The English alveolars (t) and (d) are sometimes, inaccurately, called dentals. —*n.* *Phonet.* A dental consonant. [<NL *dentalis* <L *dens, dentis* a tooth]

dental floss A strong, silky filament for cleaning between the teeth.

dental plate A denture.

den·tate (den′tāt) *adj.* **1** Having teeth or toothlike processes; toothed. **2** *Bot.* Having a notched edge resembling teeth, as certain leaves. [<L *dentatus* having teeth] —**den′·tate·ly** *adv.*

den·ta·tion (den·tā′shən) *n.* **1** A toothed formation or condition. **2** The state or quality of being dentate.

denti- *combining form* Tooth: *dentiform.* Also, before vowels, **dent-.** [<L *dens, dentis* tooth]

den·ti·cle (den′ti·kəl) *n.* **1** A small tooth or toothlike projection. **2** *Dent.* A small, calcified mass in the pulp cavity of a tooth. **3** *Archit.* Dentil. [<L *denticulus,* dim. of *dens, dentis* tooth]

den·tic·u·late (den·tik′yə·lit, -lāt) *adj.* **1** Finely dentate or toothed. **2** *Archit.* Formed into dentils. Also **den·tic′u·lat′ed.** —**den·tic′u·late·ly** *adv.* —**den·tic′u·la′tion** *n.*

den·ti·fi·ca·tion (den′tə·fə·kā′shən) *n.* The formation of teeth. [<DENTI- + L *facere* make]

den·ti·form (den′tə·fôrm) *adj.* Tooth-shaped.

den·ti·frice (den′tə·fris) *n.* A preparation for cleaning the teeth. [<MF <L *dentifricium* <*dens, dentis* tooth + *fricare* rub]

den·til (den′til) *n.* *Archit.* A small, square projecting block in a cornice: also *denticle.* **2** *Her.* An indentation or notch. Also **den′tel.** [<MF *dentille,* dim. of *dent* a tooth]

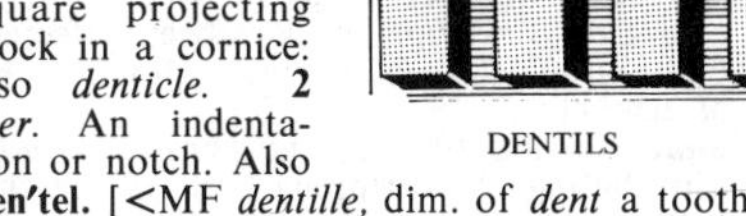
DENTILS

den·ti·la·bi·al (den′ti·lā′bē·əl) *adj.* & *n.* *Phonet.* Labiodental.

den·ti·lin·gual (den′ti·ling′gwəl) *adj.* & *n.* *Phonet.* Interdental.

den·tine (den′tēn, -tin) *n.* The hard calcified substance forming the body of a tooth just beneath the enamel and cementum. Also **den′tin** (-tin). —**den′tin·al** *adj.*

den·ti·phone (den′tə·fōn) *n.* An instrument for hearing sounds by means of vibrations transmitted through the teeth to the auditory nerve. Also **den′ta·phone.**

den·tist (den′tist) *n.* One who practices dentistry. [<F *dentiste* <*dent* a tooth]

den·tist·ry (den′tis·trē) *n.* **1** The branch of medicine which is concerned with the diagnosis, prevention, and treatment of diseases affecting the teeth and their associated structures, including the extraction, filling, and crowning of teeth, the construction of bridges and dentures, and general oral prophylaxis. **2** The work of a dentist.

den·ti·tion (den·tish′ən) *n.* **1** The process or period of cutting teeth; teething. **2** *Biol.* The kind and number of teeth characteristic of an animal, and the manner in which they are arranged in the jaws. [<L *dentitio, -onis* teething <*dentire* cut teeth <*dens, dentis* teeth]

dento- *combining form* Dental. [<L *dens, dentis* tooth]

den·toid (den′toid) *adj.* Like a tooth. [<DENT(I)- + -OID]

D'En·tre·cas·teaux Islands (däṅ·trə·kȧs·tō′) A Papuan island group SE of New Guinea; total, 1,200 square miles.

den·ture (den′chər) *n.* **1** The teeth of an animal collectively. **2** A block or set of teeth. **3** *Dent.* A frame of plastic or other material adapted to fit the upper or lower jaw and containing a partial or complete set of artificial teeth. [<F *dent* tooth] —**den′tur·al** *adj.*

den·ty (den′tē) *adj.* *Scot.* Dainty: also spelled *dentie.*

de·nu·date (di·nōō′dāt, -nyōō′-, den′yōō·dāt) *adj.* Naked; stripped of foliage or other covering. —**den·u·date** (den′yōō·dāt, di·nōō′·dāt, -nyōō′-) *v.t.* **·dat·ed, ·dat·ing** To denude; lay bare. [<L *denudatus,* pp. of *denudare.* See DENUDE.]

den·u·da·tion (den′yōō·dā′shən, dē′nōō-, -nyōō-) *n.* **1** The act of denuding or state of being stripped bare. **2** *Geol.* **a** The laying bare of land, especially by erosion. **b** The slow disintegration of rock surfaces by weathering; a wearing down of hills and mountains.

de·nude (di·nōōd′, -nyōōd′) *v.t.* **·nud·ed, ·nud·ing** **1** To strip the covering from; make naked. **2** *Geol.* To wear away or remove overlying matter from, and so expose to view. [<L *denudare* <*de-* down, completely + *nudare* strip <*nudus* bare, naked]

de·nu·mer·a·ble (di·nōō′mər·ə·bəl, -nyōō′-) *adj.* *Math.* Capable of being put in a one-to-one correspondence with positive integers, as a set of rational numbers. —**de·nu′mer·a·bly** *adv.*

de·nun·ci·ate (di·nun′sē·āt, -shē-) *v.t.* & *v.i.* **·at·ed, ·at·ing** To denounce. [<L *denuntiatus,* pp. of *denuntiare.* See DENOUNCE.] —**de·nun′·ci·a′tor** *n.*

de·nun·ci·a·tion (di·nun′sē·ā′shən, -shē-) *n.* **1** The act of declaring an action or person worthy of reprobation or punishment; arraignment. **2** The declaration of a threatening purpose; the proclamation of impending and deserved evil; a menace. **3** The denouncing of a treaty. **4** *Obs.* A formal announcement; proclamation. See synonyms under OATH, REPROOF. —**de·nun′ci·a′tive** *adj.* —**de·nun′ci·a′tive·ly** *adv.*

de·nun·ci·a·to·ry (di·nun′sē·ə·tôr′ē, -tō′rē, -shē-) *adj.* Containing or bearing denunciation; threatening.

Den·ver (den′vər) The capital of Colorado.

de·ny (di·nī′) *v.t.* **·nied, ·ny·ing** **1** To declare to be untrue; contradict. **2** To reject as false; declare to be unfounded or not real, as a doctrine. **3** To refuse to give; withhold. **4** To refuse (someone) a request. **5** To refuse to acknowledge; disown; repudiate. **6** To refuse access to. **7** *Obs.* To decline; refuse to accept. See synonyms under RENOUNCE. —**to deny oneself** To refuse oneself a gratification. [<OF *denier* <L *denegare* <*de-* completely + *negare* say no, refuse]

de·ob·stru·ent (dē·ob′strōō·ənt) *adj.* Having the power to remove obstructions. —*n.* A medicine for removing obstructions; an aperient. [<NL *deobstruens, -entis* <L *de-* away + *obstruens, -entis,* ppr. of *obstruere.* See OBSTRUCT.]

de·o·dand (dē′ə·dand) *n.* **1** A thing given or forfeited to God. **2** In early English law, any personal chattel that had been immediately instrumental in causing the death of a person, and was therefore forfeited to the crown for pious uses: abolished in 1846. [<LL *deodandum* <L *deus* god + *dandum,* gerundive of *dare* give]

de·o·dar (dē′ə·där) *n.* **1** The East Indian cedar (*Cedrus deodara*), prized for its light-red wood. **2** This wood. [<Hind. <Skt. *devadāru* divine tree]

de·o·dor·ant (dē·ō′dər·ənt) *adj.* Destroying, absorbing, or disguising bad odors. —*n.* A deodorizer; specifically, any cosmetic cream, spray, or powder used to absorb or counteract body odors. [<DE- (def. 4) + L *odorans, -antis,* ppr. of *odorare* have an odor]

de·o·dor·ize (dē·ō′dər·īz) *v.t.* **·ized, ·iz·ing** To modify, destroy, or disguise the odor of. —**de·o′dor·i·za′tion** *n.* —**de·o′dor·iz′er** *n.*

De·o fa·ven·te (dē′ō fə·ven′tē) *Latin* With God's favor.

De·o gra·ti·as (dē′ō grā′shē·əs) *Latin* Thanks to God.

De·o ju·van·te (dē′ō jōō·van′tē) *Latin* With God's help.

de·on·tol·o·gy (dē′on·tol′ə·jē) *n.* The science of moral obligation or duty; ethics. [<Gk. *deon, deontos* necessary, orig. ppr. neut. of *deein* lack, need + -LOGY] —**de·on·to·log·i·cal** (dē·on′tə·loj′i·kəl) *adj.* —**de′on·tol′o·gist** *n.*

De·o vo·len·te (dē′ō vō·len′tē) *Latin* God willing; by God's will.

de·ox·i·dize (dē·ok′sə·dīz) *v.t.* **·dized, ·diz·ing** 1 To remove oxygen from. 2 To reduce from the state of an oxide. Also **de·ox′i·date.** —**de·ox′i·di·za′tion, de·ox′i·da′tion** *n.* —**de·ox′i·diz′er** *n.*

de·ox·y·gen·ate (dē·ok′sə·jə·nāt′) *v.t.* **·at·ed, ·at·ing** To remove oxygen from. Also **de·ox′·y·gen·ize′.** —**de·ox′y·gen·a′tion** *n.*

de·ox·y·ri·bo·nu·cle·ic acid (dē·ok′sē·rī·bō·nōō·klē′ik, -nyōō-) *Biochem.* A nucleic acid of complex molecular structure forming a principal constituent of the genes and known to play an important role in the genetic action of the chromosomes. Abbr. **DNA.**

de·part (di·pärt′) *v.i.* 1 To go away; leave: opposed to *arrive.* 2 To deviate; differ; vary: with *from.* 3 To die. —*v.t.* 4 *Rare* To leave: to *depart* this life. See synonyms under DIE[1], ESCAPE. —*n. Obs.* Departure; death. [<OF *departir* <*de-* away (<L *dis-*) + *partir* divide <L *partire* <*pars, partis* a part]

de·part·ment (di·pärt′mənt) *n.* 1 A distinct part; a division or subdivision of an organization, business, etc. 2 A division in a secondary school, college, or university devoted to teaching courses in a certain subject: French *department, department* of sociology. 3 A subdivision of a U.S. Territory for military purposes: also **territorial department.** 4 A subdivision of a governmental organization: the State *Department, Department* of Labor, etc. 5 In France, a government administrative district. [<OF <*departir.* See DEPART.]

de·part·men·tal (dē′pärt·men′təl) *adj.* 1 Pertaining to a department or to departments. 2 Organized on a system of departments. —**de′part·men′tal·ism** *n.*

de·part·men·tal·ize (dē′pärt·men′təl·īz) *v.t. & v.i.* **·ized, ·iz·ing** To divide into departments.

department store See under STORE.

de·par·ture (di·pär′chər) *n.* 1 The act of departing. 2 The act of deviating from a method, course of action, set of ideas, etc.; divergence. 3 The act of leaving this world; death. 4 *Naut.* **a** Distance east or west of a given meridian. **b** The position of a ship taken at the commencement of a voyage as a basis for calculations by dead reckoning.

de·pas·ture (dē·pas′chər, -päs′-) *v.* **·tured, ·tur·ing** *v.t.* 1 To denude (land) of herbage by grazing. 2 To pasture (cattle). —*v.i.* 3 To graze.

de·pau·per·ate (dē·pô′pə·rāt) *v.t.* **·at·ed, ·at·ing** To deprive of fertility or richness; impoverish; exhaust. —*adj.* (-rit) 1 *Bot.* Diminutive or imperfectly developed, as if starved: said of plants grown in poor soil. 2 *Obs.* Impoverished. [<Med. L *depauperatus,* pp. of *depauperare* <L *de-* down + *pauperare* make poor <*pauper* poor]

de·pe·gram (dē′pi·gram) *n. Meteorol.* A graphic curve relating the dew point to pressure changes at a given atmospheric level. [< DE(W)P(OINT) + E(NTROPY) + -GRAM]

de·pend (di·pend′) *v.i.* 1 To trust; have full reliance: with *on* or *upon.* 2 To be conditioned or determined; be contingent: with *on* or *upon.* 3 To rely for maintenance, support, etc.: with *on* or *upon.* 4 To hang down: with *from.* 5 To be pending, undecided, or in suspension. See synonyms under LEAN[1]. [<OF *dependre* <L *dependere* <*de-* down + *pendere* hang]

de·pend·a·ble (di·pen′də·bəl) *adj.* That can be depended upon; trustworthy. —**de·pend′a·bil′·i·ty, de·pend′a·ble·ness** *n.* —**de·pend′a·bly** *adv.*

de·pen·dence (di·pen′dəns) *n.* 1 The act or relation of depending, or the state of being dependent on or determined by some one or something else. 2 Reliance; trust. 3 Reciprocal reliance. 4 Subordination; subjection; that which is subordinate to or contingent on something else. 5 That on which one relies. Also **de·pen′dance.**

de·pen·den·cy (di·pen′dən·sē) *n. pl.* **·cies** 1 That which is dependent. 2 A subject or tributary state. 3 Dependence. Also **de·pen′dan·cy.**

de·pen·dent (di·pen′dənt) *adj.* 1 Depending upon something exterior; subordinate; contingent: often with *on* or *upon.* 2 Needing support or aid; needy. 3 Hanging down; pendent: often with *from.* 4 *Gram.* Subordinate. See SUBORDINATE CLAUSE under CLAUSE. See synonyms under SUBJECT. —*n.* 1 One who looks to another for support or favor; a retainer. 2 A consequence; corollary. Also **de·pen′dant.** —**de·pen′dent·ly** *adv.*

De·pew (də·pyōō′), **Chauncey Mitchell,** 1834–1928, U.S. senator and orator.

de·phleg·ma·tor (dē·fleg′mā·tər) *n. Chem.* A fractionating column. [<NL <L *dephlegmare* <*de-* away + *phlegma* phlegm <Gk.]

de·pict (di·pikt′) *v.t.* 1 To portray or represent by drawing, sculpturing, painting, etc. 2 To describe verbally. [<L *depictus,* pp. of *depingere* <*de-* down + *pingere* paint] —**de·pic′tion** *n.*

dep·i·late (dep′ə·lāt) *v.t.* **·lat·ed, ·lat·ing** To remove hair from. [<L *depilatus,* pp. of *depilare* <*de-* away + *pilus* hair] —**dep′i·la′·tion** *n.* —**dep′i·la′tor** *n.*

de·pil·a·to·ry (di·pil′ə·tôr′ē, -tō′rē) *adj.* Having the power to remove hair. —*n.* A preparation for removing hair from the human skin.

de·plane (di·plān′) *v.i.* **·planed, ·plan·ing** To disembark from an aircraft.

de·plete (di·plēt′) *v.t.* **·plet·ed, ·plet·ing** 1 To reduce or lessen, as by use, exhaustion, or waste. 2 To empty, or partially empty: to *deplete* the treasury. 3 *Med.* To lessen or remove the contents of (an overcharged organ or vessel), as by purging or bloodletting. [<L *depletus,* pp. of *deplere* <*de-* not + *plere* fill]

de·ple·tion (di·plē′shən) *n.* 1 The act of depleting. 2 The state of being depleted. 3 Reduction of capital. —**de·ple′tive, de·ple·to·ry** (di·plē′tər·ē) *adj.* & *n.*

de·plor·a·ble (di·plôr′ə·bəl, -plō′rə-) *adj.* Lamentable; pitiable; sad. —**de·plor′a·bil′·i·ty** *n.* —**de·plor′a·bly** *adv.*

de·plore (di·plôr′, -plōr′) *v.t.* **·plored, ·plor·ing** To feel or express deep regret or concern for; lament. See synonyms under MOURN. [<L *deplorare* <*de-* completely + *plorare* bewail]

de·ploy (di·ploi′) *v.t. & v.i.* To spread out in line of battle, as troops. [<F *déployer* <OF *desployer, despleier* <LL *displicare* <*dis-* from + *plicare* fold. Doublet of DISPLAY.]

de·ploy·ment (di·ploi′mənt) *n. Mil.* Extension of a battle front from close order to battle formation in lines of skirmishers, foragers, etc., after development has been effected.

de·plu·mate (di·plōō′mit) *adj. Ornithol.* Bare of feathers.

de·plu·ma·tion (dē′plōō·mā′shən) *n. Ornithol.* The falling or stripping off of feathers; molting.

de·plume (dē·plōōm′) *v.t.* **·plumed, ·plum·ing** 1 To strip the plumage or feathers from. 2 To strip; despoil, as of honors or wealth. [<F *déplumer* <*dé-* away (<L *dis-*) + *plume* feather <L *pluma*]

de·po·lar·ize (dē·pō′lə·rīz) *v.t.* **·ized, ·iz·ing** 1 *Electr.* To break up or remove the polarization of, as by separating the electrodes of an electric cell. 2 To deprive of polarity. —**de·po′lar·i·za′tion** *n.* —**de·po′lar·iz′er** *n.*

de·pone (di·pōn′) *v.t. & v.i.* **·poned, ·pon·ing** 1 To testify, especially under oath; depose. 2 *Obs.* To deposit, as a pledge or wager. [<L *deponere* <*de-* down + *ponere* place]

de·po·nent (di·pō′nənt) *adj.* In Latin and Greek grammar, denoting a verb that has the form of the passive or middle voice but is active in meaning. —*n.* 1 A deponent verb. 2 *Law* One who gives sworn testimony, especially in writing.

de·pop·u·late (dē·pop′yə·lāt) *v.t.* **·lat·ed, ·lat·ing** To remove the inhabitants from, by massacre, famine, epidemics, etc. —*adj.* (-lit, -lāt) *Obs.* Depopulated. [<L *depopulatus,* pp. of *depopulari* <*de-* down + *populari* lay waste <*populus* people] —**de·pop′u·la′·tor** *n.*

de·pop·u·la·tion (dē·pop′yə·lā′shən) *n.* 1 The act of depopulating, or the state of being depopulated. 2 That condition of a country in which the birth rate does not compensate for losses by the death rate.

de·port (di·pôrt′, -pōrt′) *v.t.* 1 To transport forcibly; banish. 2 To behave or conduct (oneself). [<OF *deporter* <L *deportare* <*de-* away + *portare* carry]

de·por·ta·tion (dē′pôr·tā′shən, -pōr-) *n.* 1 The act of deporting; the state of being deported; exile. 2 The sending back of an undesirable alien to the country from which he came.

de·por·tee (dē′pôr·tē′, -pōr-) *n.* A person banished from a country as undesirable or as having entered illegally. [<F *déporté* a banished person; orig., pp. of *déporter* banish]

de·port·ment (di·pôrt′mənt, -pōrt′-) *n.* Conduct or behavior; demeanor; bearing. See synonyms under BEHAVIOR, MANNER.

de·pos·al (di·pō′zəl) *n.* The act of deposing, especially removal from office or sovereignty.

de·pose (di·pōz′) *v.* **·posed, ·pos·ing** *v.t.* 1 To deprive of official rank or office; oust, as a king. 2 To state on oath; give testimony of. 3 To take the deposition of. —*v.i.* 4 To bear witness. See synonyms under AFFIRM. [<OF *deposer* <*de-* down (<L *de-*) + *poser.* See POSE[1].] —**de·pos′a·ble** *adj.*

de·pos·it (di·poz′it) *v.t.* 1 To give in trust or for safekeeping. 2 To give as part payment or as security. 3 To put or lay on or in some place or receptacle. 4 To cause, as sediment, to form a layer or deposit. —*n.* 1 That which is or has been deposited or precipitated; especially, sediment; precipitate. 2 Money or property deposited, as in a bank for safekeeping, or as security. 3 The act of depositing, or the state of being deposited. 4 A place where anything is deposited. 5 The condition of being placed to one's order, as in a bank, in trust, or for safekeeping: on *deposit.* 6 *Geol.* An accumulated mass of iron, oil, salt, etc. 7 A layer of metal deposited by electrolytic action. [<L *depositus,* pp. of *deponere.* See DEPONE.]

de·pos·i·tar·y (di·poz′ə·ter′ē) *n. pl.* **·tar·ies** 1 A person entrusted with anything for safekeeping; a trustee. 2 A depository.

dep·o·si·tion (dep′ə·zish′ən, dē′pə-) *n.* 1 The act of depositing. 2 That which is deposited; especially, an accumulation or sediment. 3 The written testimony of a sworn witness; hence, allegation; evidence. 4 The act of deposing, as from office. —**the Deposition** The taking down of Christ's body from the Cross; also, in art, a representation of this. See synonyms under TESTIMONY.

de·pos·i·tor (di·poz′ə·tər) *n.* One who makes a deposit.

de·pos·i·to·ry (di·poz′ə·tôr′ē, -tō′rē) *n. pl.* **·ries** 1 A place where anything is deposited. 2 A person or body of persons to whom something is entrusted for safekeeping.

de·pot (dē′pō, *Mil. & Brit.* dep′ō) *n.* 1 A warehouse or storehouse. 2 *U.S.* A railroad station. 3 *Mil.* A storehouse or collecting station for personnel or materiel. [<F *dépôt* <OF *depost* <L *depositum* a pledge <*deponere.* See DEPONE.]

dep·ra·va·tion (dep′rə·vā′shən) *n.* 1 The act of depraving, or the state of being depraved or deteriorated. 2 A corrupt tendency; a depravity.

de·prave (di·prāv′) *v.t.* **·praved, ·prav·ing** 1 To render bad or worse, especially in morals; corrupt; pervert. 2 *Obs.* To vilify; slander. See synonyms under CORRUPT, POLLUTE. [<L *depravare* <*de-* completely + *pravus* corrupt, wicked] —**de·prav′er** *n.*

de·praved (di·prāvd′) *adj.* Having a corrupt or vicious character.

de·prav·i·ty (di·prav′ə·tē) *n. pl.* **·ties** 1 The state of being depraved; wickedness. 2 A depraved act or habit. See synonyms under SIN[1].

dep·re·cate (dep′rə·kāt) *v.t.* **·cat·ed, ·cat·ing** 1 To express disapproval of or regret for; plead earnestly against. 2 To disparage or belittle; depreciate. 3 *Archaic* To desire or pray for deliverance from, as threatened evil. [<L *deprecatus,* pp. of *deprecari* <*de-* away + *precari* pray] —**dep·re·ca·ble** (dep′rə·kə·bəl) *adj.* —**dep′re·cat′ing·ly** *adv.* —**dep′re·ca′·tion** *n.* —**dep′re·ca′tive** *adj.* —**dep′re·ca′tive·ly** *adv.* —**dep′re·ca′tor** *n.*

dep·re·ca·to·ry (dep′rə·kə·tôr′ē, -tō′rē) *adj.* Apologetic; disparaging.

de·pre·ci·ate (di·prē′shē·āt) *v.* **·at·ed, ·at·ing** *v.t.* 1 To lessen the worth of; lower the price or rate of. 2 To disparage; belittle. —*v.i.* 3 To become less in value, etc. See synonyms under ASPERSE, DISPARAGE. [<L *depretiatus,* pp. of *depretiare* <*de-* down + *pretium* price] —**de·pre′ci·a′tor** *n.*

de·pre·ci·a·tion (di·prē′shē·ā′shən) *n.* 1 The act of depreciating, or the state of being depreciated. 2 The wear and tear of equipment, machinery, plant, etc. 3 A diminished value; also, the amount estimated or written off to offset such loss of value.

de·pre·ci·a·to·ry (di·prē′shē·ə·tôr′ē, -tō′rē) *adj.* Tending to depreciate. Also **de·pre′ci·a′tive.**

dep·re·date (dep′rə·dāt) *v.t.* & *v.i.* **—dat·ed, ·dat·ing** To prey upon; pillage; plunder. [< LL *depraedatus,* pp. of *depraedari* < *de-* completely + *praeda* booty, prey] **—dep′re·da′tor** *n.* **— dep·re·da·to·ry** (dep′rə·dā′tər·ē) *adj.*

dep·re·da·tion (dep′rə·dā′shən) *n.* A plundering; robbery.

de·press (di·pres′) *v.t.* 1 To lower the spirits of; make gloomy; sadden. 2 To lessen in vigor, force, or energy; weaken; make dull. 3 To lessen the price or value of. 4 To press or push down; lower. 5 *Music* To lower the pitch of. 6 *Obs.* To subjugate; suppress. See synonyms under ABASE. [< OF *depresser* < L *depressus,* pp. of *deprimere* < *de-* down + *primere* press]

de·pres·sant (di·pres′ənt) *Med. adj.* Lessening functional activity or depressing vital force. *—n.* A drug or other substance which reduces vital functions.

de·pressed (di·prest′) *adj.* 1 Sad; dejected. 2 Lowered in position; pressed or kept down. 3 Flattened from above; sunk below the general surface, as the solid part of a plant body. 4 *Ornithol.* Broader than high, as the bill of a flycatcher.

depressed area A region characterized by economic depression, unemployment, a low standard of living, etc.

de·press·ing (di·pres′ing) *adj.* Disheartening; causing sadness or low spirits; sad. **— de·press′ing·ly** *adv.*

de·pres·sion (di·presh′ən) *n.* 1 The act of depressing, or the state of being depressed; low spirits or vitality; dejection; melancholy. 2 That which is depressed; a low or hollow place. 3 A decline in business or trade; also, the period of time during which this inactivity prevails. 4 *Meteorol.* Low atmospheric pressure; also, a region of low atmospheric pressure. 5 *Astron.* The vertical angular distance of a heavenly body below the horizon: opposed to *altitude.* 6 The angular distance of an object below the horizontal plane through the point of observation: the opposite of *elevation.* 7 *Psychiatry* A lowering of vital powers; melancholy; especially, psychopathic melancholy leading to mental disorders. 8 *Music* Flatting of a tone.

de·pres·sive (di·pres′iv) *adj.* Tending to or causing depression. **—de·pres′sive·ly** *adv.* **— de·pres′sive·ness** *n.*

de·pres·so·mo·tor (di·pres′ō·mō′tər) *adj. Physiol.* Diminishing the capacity for movement; retarding motor activity. *—n. Med.* An agent that lowers the activity of the motor centers, as a bromide.

de·pres·sor (di·pres′ər) *n.* 1 One who or that which depresses. 2 *Physiol.* A depressor nerve. 3 *Anat.* One of several muscles which depress or contract a part. 4 *Surg.* An instrument for pressing down a part.

depressor nerve *Physiol.* An afferent nerve connected with the heart, which controls blood pressure.

dep·ri·va·tion (dep′rə·vā′shən) *n.* The act of depriving, or the state of being deprived; loss; want. Also **de·priv·al** (di·prī′vəl). See synonyms under LOSS.

de·prive (di·prīv′) *v.t.* **·prived, ·priv·ing** 1 To take something away from; dispossess; divest. 2 To keep from acquiring, using, or enjoying. 3 *Obs.* To put an end to. [< OF *depriver* < L *de-* completely + *privare* strip, remove] **—de·priv′a·ble** *adj.*

De Pro·fun·dis (dē prō·fun′dis) The 130th Psalm: so called from the first words of the Latin version. [< L, out of the depths]

de·pro·gram (dē·prō′gram) *v.t.* **-gramed** or **-grammed, -gram·ing** or **-gram·ming** To try to convince (a person) to forsake something learned well or accepted, esp. a religious belief.

de pro·pri·o mo·tu (dē prō′prē·ō mō′tōō) *Latin* Of its own accord.

dep·side (dep′sīd, -sid) *n. Chem.* One of a group of aromatic compounds formed from phenol carboxylic acids: found chiefly in lichens or made synthetically. [< Gk. *depsein* soften, tan + -IDE]

Dept·ford (det′fərd) A metropolitan borough of SE London.

depth (depth) *n.* 1 The state or degree of being deep; extent or distance downward, inward, or backward. 2 A deep place. 3 The innermost part. 4 Profundity of thought or feeling; utmost extent; immensity; extremity. 5 The quality of being deep, crafty, or scheming. 6 The quality of being dark in shade, or rich in color. 7 The quality of being low-pitched in tone. [ME *depthe*]

depth bomb or **charge** See under BOMB.

depth-sound·er (depth′soun′dər) *n.* An instrument for measuring the depth of water by sending sound waves and receiving their echoes from the bottom.

dep·u·rate (dep′yə·rāt) *v.t.* & *v.i.* **·rat·ed, ·rat·ing** To free or become free from morbid matter or impurities. [< Med. L *depuratus,* pp. of *depurare* < *de-* completely + *purus* pure] **—dep′u·ra′tion** *n.* **—dep′u·ra′tor** *n.*

dep·u·ra·tive (dep′yə·rā′tiv) *adj.* Purifying; purgative. *—n.* A purifying agent. Also **dep·u·rant** (dep′yə·rənt).

dep·u·ta·tion (dep′yə·tā′shən) *n.* 1 A person or persons acting for another; a delegation. 2 The act of deputing, or the state of being deputed. 3 *Brit.* A forestry license granted to a gamekeeper.

de·pute (di·pyōōt′) *v.t.* **·put·ed, ·put·ing** 1 To appoint as an agent, deputy, or delegation; send with authority. 2 To transfer, as authority, to another. [< OF *deputer* < LL *deputare* < *de-* away + *putare* think]

dep·u·tize (dep′yə·tīz) *v.* **·tized, ·tiz·ing** *v.t.* To appoint as a deputy. *—v.i.* To act as a deputy.

dep·u·ty (dep′yə·tē) *n. pl.* **·ties** 1 One appointed to act for another; representative agent. 2 A member of a legislative assembly in certain countries. See synonyms under DELEGATE. [< F *député,* pp. of *députer* < OF *deputer* DEPUTE]

De Quin·cey (di kwin′sē), **Thomas,** 1785–1859, English essayist.

de·rac·i·nate (di·ras′ə·nāt) *v.t.* **·nat·ed, ·nat·ing** To pull up by the roots; eradicate. [< F *déraciner* < *dé-* away (< L *dis-*) + *racine* a root < L *radix*] **—de·rac′i·na′tion** *n.*

de·raign (di·rān′) *v.t. Obs.* To determine or maintain (a claim, right, etc.) by judicial argument or wager of battle. [< OF *deraisnier* < *de-* down (< L *de-*) + *raisnier* reason < L *ratio, -onis* reason] **—de·raign′ment** *n.*

de·rail (dē·rāl′) *v.t.* To cause to leave the rails, as a train. *—v.i.* To leave the rails. [< F *dérailler* < *dé-* from + *rail* a rail] **—de·rail′ment** *n.*

de·range (di·rānj′) *v.t.* **·ranged, ·rang·ing** 1 To disturb the arrangement or order of; disarrange; disorder. 2 To unbalance the reason of; craze. 3 To disturb the condition, action, or functions of. See synonyms under DISPLACE. [< F *déranger* < *dé-* away (< L *dis-*) + *ranger* RANGE, *v.*]

de·ranged (di·rānjd′) *adj.* 1 Insane. 2 Disordered.

de·range·ment (di·rānj′mənt) *n.* 1 The act of deranging, or state of being deranged. 2 Any severe mental disorder; insanity. See synonyms under INSANITY.

de·ray (di·rā′) *n. Obs.* Confusion; disorder; boisterous revelry. [< OF *desrei* < *desreer* disorder < *des-* away (< L *dis-*) + *rei* order]

der·by (dûr′bē) *n. pl.* **·bies** A stiff, felt hat with curved brim and round crown: in England called a *bowler.* [< DERBY]

Der·by (dûr′bē, *Brit.* där′bē) 1 An annual horse race for three-year-olds run at Epsom Downs in Surrey, England: named for the founder, the 12th Earl of Derby (1780). 2 Any horse race of similar importance; especially, the Kentucky Derby.

Der·by (dûr′bē, *Brit.* där′be) A county in central England; 1,006 square miles; its county seat, Derby. Also **Der′by·shire** (-shir).

Der·by (dûr′bē, *Brit.* där′bē), **Earl of** English title traditionally dating from 1138; held by the Stanley family from the 15th century to the present.

de rè·gle (də re′gl′) *French* According to rule; in proper form.

de·reg·u·late (di·reg′yə·lāt) *v.t.* **-lat·ed, -lat·ing** To remove regulations or restrictions from.

de·re·ism (dir′ē·iz′əm) *n. Psychol.* Mental activity freed of ordinary logic, the facts of experience, or the realities of the external world: common in dreams and in certain mental disorders. [< DE- + L *res* thing + -ISM] **—de′re·is′tic** *adj.* **— de′re·is′ti·cal·ly** *adv.*

der·e·lict (der′ə·likt) *adj.* 1 Neglectful of obligation; unfaithful; remiss. 2 Deserted or abandoned. *—n.* 1 That which is deserted or abandoned. 2 Any property which is abandoned at sea, as a deserted wreck. 3 Land exposed or gained by receding of the sea. 4 One who betrays a trust. 5 A person outside the pale of respectability. [< L *derelictus,* pp. of *derelinquere* < *de-* completely + *relinquere* abandon]

der·e·lic·tion (der′ə·lik′shən) *n.* 1 Neglect or wilful omission; failure in duty. 2 Voluntary abandonment of a charge or property. 3 The state or fact of being abandoned. 4 *Law* a A gain of land by a permanent receding of water. b The land thus gained.

de re·rum na·tu·ra (dē rir′əm nə·tōōr′ə, nə·tyōōr′ə) *Latin* Concerning the nature of things.

de re·tour (də rə·tōōr′) *French* Back again; returned.

de·ride (di·rīd′) *v.t.* **·rid·ed, ·rid·ing** To treat with scornful mirth; ridicule. See synonyms under MOCK, RIDICULE. [< L *deridere* < *de-* completely + *ridere* laugh, mock] **—de·rid′er** *n.* **— de·rid′ing·ly** *adv.*

de ri·gueur (də rē·gœr′) *French* Necessary according to etiquette; required by good form.

de·ris·i·ble (di·riz′ə·bəl) *adj.* Open to derision.

de·ri·sion (di·rizh′ən) *n.* 1 The act of deriding; ridicule; mockery; scornful laughter. 2 An object of ridicule or scorn. See synonyms under BANTER, RIDICULE, SCORN. [< L *derisio, -onis* < *deridere.* See DERIDE.]

de·ri·sive (di·rī′siv) *adj.* Expressive of or characterized by derision. Also **de·ri·so·ry** (di·rī′sər·ē). **—de·ri′sive·ly** *adv.* **—de·ri′sive·ness** *n.*

der·i·va·tion (der′ə·vā′shən) *n.* 1 The act of deriving, or the condition of being derived. 2 The tracing of a word from its original form and meaning; also, a statement of the information thus obtained. 3 Origin; descent; extraction. 4 *Math.* a The process of forming a derivative. b The act of deriving an equation or reaching a conclusion expressed as an equation. **— der′i·va′tion·al** *adj.*

de·riv·a·tive (di·riv′ə·tiv) *adj.* Coming or acquiring by derivation; of or pertaining to derivation or evolution; derived; not original or basic. *—n.* 1 That which is derived. 2 *Gram.* A word developed from a basic word, as by the addition of a prefix or suffix or by phonetic change: "Functional" is a *derivative* of "function." 3 *Chem.* a A compound formed or regarded as being formed from another, usually by partial replacement. b Any organic compound containing a specified radical: a benzene *derivative.* 4 *Music* A chord derived from another by inversion, or from the harmonics of an assumed root: often used in the plural. 5 *Math.* The instantaneous rate of change of a function with reference to a variable. **— de·riv′a·tive·ly** *adv.*

de·rive (di·rīv′) *v.* **·rived, ·riv·ing** *v.t.* 1 To draw or receive, as from a source, principle, or root; be descended from. 2 To deduce, as from a premise; draw, as a conclusion. 3 To trace the derivation of (a word). 4 *Chem.* To obtain (a compound) from another as by partial replacement. 5 *Obs.* To cause to come; bring: with *on, to,* or *upon.* — *v.i.* 6 To have derivation; originate. [< L *derivare* < *de-* from + *rivus* stream] **—de·riv′a·ble** *adj.* **— de·riv′er** *n.*

de·rived unit (di·rīvd′) *Physics* A unit based on or derived from any primary unit of mass, length, time, etc.

derm (dûrm) *n.* 1 *Anat.* The sensitive and vascular or true skin. 2 The skin in general: also **dermis.** Also **der·ma** (dûr′mə). [< Gk. *derma* skin]

-derm suffix Skin: *endoderm.* [< Gk. *derma* skin]

DERM
a. The true derm.

der·mal (dûr′məl) *adj.* Of or pertaining to the skin or epidermis, or, properly, to the corium; cutaneous: *dermal* affections. Also **der′mic.**

dermal body *Zool.* Any of the structures characterized by a glandular or sensory function which are present in the dermis and partly in the epidermis of some marine worms.

dermal layer *Zool.* A single layer of cells covering the outer surface of a sponge, through which the calcareous needle-shaped spicules project.

der·map·ter·ous (dər·map′tər·əs) *adj. Entomol.* Of or pertaining to an order *(Dermaptera)* of small, elongate, terrestrial, and mostly nocturnal insects with a pair of large, forcepslike, caudal appendages and chewing mouth parts: they are wingless or with one or two pairs of inconspicuous wings; the earwigs. [< DERM(O)- + Gk. *a-* without + *pteron* wing]

der·ma·ti·tis (dûr′mə·tī′tis) *n. Pathol.* Inflammation of the skin. [< DERMAT(O) + -ITIS]

dermato- *combining form* Skin: *dermatology.* Also, before vowels, **dermat-.** [< Gk. *derma, dermatos* skin]

Der·ma·to·bi·a (dûr′mə·tō′bē·ə) *n.* A genus of insects (family *Oestridae*) whose larvae live under the skin of animals, causing painful swellings; gadflies; botflies. [< NL < Gk. *derma, dermatos* skin + *bios* life]

der·ma·to·bi·a·sis (dûr′mə·tō·bī′ə·sis) *n.* Infection by the larva of *Dermatobia.* [< DERMATOB(IA) + -IASIS]

der·mat·o·gen (dər·mat′ə·jən, dûr′mə·tō′jən) *n. Bot.* The outermost layer of cells in plants, forming the permanent epidermal tissue: also called *protoderm.*

der·ma·to·glyph·ics (dûr′mə·tō·glif′iks) *n.* **1** The study of the surface ridges of the skin, especially of the palm and the sole. **2** Ink impressions of such ridges taken for identification purposes. [< DERMATO- + Gk. *glyphein* carve]

der·ma·toid (dûr′mə·toid) *adj.* Dermoid.

der·ma·tol·o·gist (dûr′mə·tol′ə·jist) *n.* One who studies or is skilled in dermatology.

der·ma·tol·o·gy (dûr′mə·tol′ə·jē) *n.* The branch of medical science that relates to the skin and its diseases. [< DERMATO- + -LOGY] **—der·ma·to·log·i·cal** (dûr′mə·tə·loj′i·kəl) *adj.*

der·ma·top·a·thy (dûr′mə·top′ə·thē) *n.* Any skin disease.

der·ma·to·phyte (dûr′mə·tō·fīt′) *n. Bot.* A plant living parasitically upon the skin, as certain fungi which produce ringworm, favus, etc. **—der′ma·to·phyt′ic** (-fit′ik) *adj.*

der·ma·to·plas·ty (dûr′mə·tō·plas′tē) *n. Surg.* The replacement of destroyed skin by flaps or skin grafts.

der·mis (dûr′mis) See DERM.

dermo- *combining form* Dermato-. Also, before vowels, **derm-.** [< Gk. *derma* skin]

der·moid (dûr′moid) *adj.* Like skin. *—n. Pathol.* A cystic tumor enclosing skin tissue or any skin-like substance. [< DERM(O)- + -OID]

der·mo·phy·to·sis (dûr′mō·fī·tō′sis) *n.* Athlete's foot. [< DERMO- + -PHYTE + -OSIS]

der·mo·skel·e·ton (dûr′mō·skel′ə·tən) *n. Zool.* A structure formed by the hardening of integument, as in crustaceans, insects, etc.; exoskeleton.

der·ni·er (dûr′nē·ər, *Fr.* der·nyā′) *adj.* Last; final. [< F]

der·nier cri (der·nyā′ krē′) *French* **1** The last word. **2** The latest fashion.

der·nier res·sort (der·nyā′ rə·sôr′) *French* Last resort.

der·o·gate (der′ə·gāt) *v.* **·gat·ed, ·gat·ing** *v.i.* **1** To take away; detract, as from reputation, honor, or powers: with *from*: The charge cannot *derogate* from his honor. **2** To do something derogatory to one's character or position; degenerate. *—v.t.* **3** *Archaic* To take away so as to cause loss or impairment. **4** *Obs.* To disparage. *—adj.* (der′ə·git, -gāt) Derogated. [< L *derogatus,* pp. of *derogare* < *de-* away + *rogare* ask, propose a law] **—der′o·gate·ly** *adv.*

der·o·ga·tion (der′ə·gā′shən) *n.* **1** The act of derogating; detraction; disparagement. **2** The act of limiting in application, as a law, authority, etc.

de·rog·a·tive (di·rog′ə·tiv) *adj.* Tending to derogate or detract; derogatory. **—de·rog′a·tive·ly** *adv.*

de·rog·a·to·ry (di·rog′ə·tôr′ē, -tō′rē) *adj.* Lessening in good repute; detracting in estimation; disparaging. **—de·rog′a·to′ri·ly** *adv.* **—de·rog′a·to′ri·ness** *n.*

der·rick (der′ik) *n.* **1** An apparatus, as a mast with a hinged boom, or a framework, for hoisting and swinging heavy weights into place. **2** The framework over the mouth of an oil well or similar drill hole. [after *Derrick,* 17th c. London hangman]

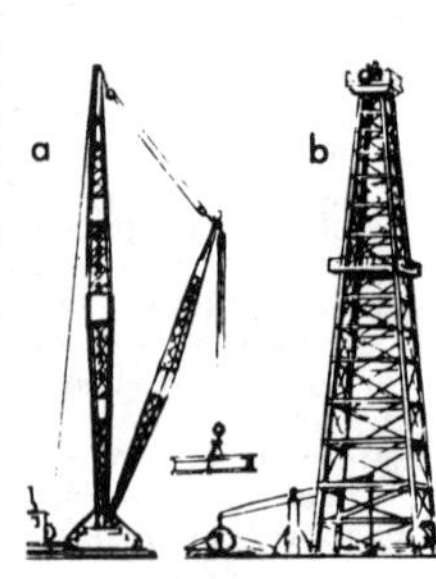

DERRICKS
a. Hoisting derrick.
b. Oil well derrick.

der·rid (der′id) *n.* An extremely toxic, resinous alkaloid obtained from a species of derris *(Derris elliptica)*: used as an arrow poison by the Malays. Also **der·ride** (der′īd).

der·ri·ère (der′ē·er′, *Fr.* de·ryâr′) *n. French* The rear; hind parts; buttocks.

der·ring-do (der′ing·do͞o′) *n.* Courageous deeds; daring action. [ME *dorryng don* daring to do; mistaken for a noun phrase by Spenser]

der·rin·ger (der′in·jər) *n.* A pistol having a short barrel and a large bore. [after Henry *Derringer,* 19th c. U.S. gunsmith, who invented it]

der·ris (der′is) *n.* Any plant of a genus *(Derris)* of woody, climbing plants of the East Indies; especially, *D. tripliata* and *D. elliptica,* whose roots yield rotenone. Also **derris root.** [< NL < Gk., a covering]

der·ry (der′ē) *n. pl.* **·ries** A meaningless word used as a refrain in old songs; hence, a set of verses; a ballad. Also **der′ry-down′.**

Der·ry (der′ē) See LONDONDERRY.

der Tag (der täk′) *German* The day: signifying the day Germany begins to establish her supremacy; hence, any important moment.

der·vish (dûr′vish) *n.* **1** A Mohammedan mendicant friar; a fakir. **2** A member of certain fanatical tribes of Upper Egypt. [< Turkish < Persian *darvish*]

Der·went (dûr′wənt) **1** A river in Yorkshire, England, flowing 60 miles NW to the Ouse River. **2** A river in Derbyshire, England, flowing 60 miles SE to the Trent River. **3** A river in Cumberland, England, flowing 35 miles NW to Solway Firth. **4** A river in southern Tasmania, flowing 120 miles SE to the Tasman Sea.

Der·went·wa·ter (dûr′wənt·wô′tər) A lake in south Cumberland, England. Also **Der′went Wa′ter.**

DES Diethylstilbestrol.

Des·a·gua·de·ro (des′ä·gwä·thā′rō) A river in western Bolivia, flowing 200 miles SE to Lake Poopó.

de·salt (dē·sôlt′) *v.t.* To remove the salt from, as sea water, to make potable. **—de·salt′er** *n.*

des·cant (des′kant) *n.* **1** The act of discussing; a series of remarks. **2** *Music* **a** A varied melody or song. **b** Formerly, an ornamental variation of the main subject or song. **c** A counterpoint above the plain song. **d** The composition or singing of such counterpoint or variations. **e** The upper part in part music, especially the soprano. *—v.i.* (des·kant′, dis-) **1** To discourse at length; hold forth: with *on* or *upon.* **2** To make a descant; sing. Also spelled *discant.* [< AF < Med. L *discantus* < L *dis-* away + *cantus* a song < *canere* sing]

Des·cartes (dā·kärt′), **René,** 1596–1650, French mathematician and philosopher.

de·scend (di·send′) *v.i.* **1** To move from a higher to a lower point; go or come down; sink. **2** To slope or incline downward, as a path. **3** To stoop; lower oneself. **4** To come down by inheritance; be inherited. **5** To be derived by heredity: with *from.* **6** To come or arrive in an overwhelming manner, as from above; attack: with *on* or *upon.* **7** To pass, as from the general to the particular. **8** *Astron.* To move southward or toward the horizon, as a star. *—v.t.* **9** To move from an upper to a lower part of; go down, as a ladder. See synonyms under FALL. [< OF *descendre* < L *descendere* < *de-* down + *scandere* climb]

de·scen·dant (di·sen′dənt) *n.* One who is descended lineally from another; offspring. *—adj.* Descendent. [< F, ppr. of *descendre. See* DESCEND.]

de·scen·dent (di·sen′dənt) *adj.* **1** Proceeding downward; descending. **2** Issuing by descent, as from an ancestor. [< L *descendens, -entis,* ppr. of *descendere.* See DESCEND.]

de·scend·er (di·sen′dər) *n.* **1** One who or that which descends. **2** *Printing* **a** The part of a letter that reaches into the bottom of the body of the type. **b** Any of such letters, as *j, g, q,* etc.

de·scend·i·ble (di·sen′də·bəl) *adj.* **1** That can be descended. **2** That can pass by descent; inheritable. Also **de·scend′a·ble.**

de·scen·sive (di·sen′siv) *adj.* Inclined to descend.

de·scent (di·sent′) *n.* **1** The act of descending. **2** Decline; deterioration; fall. **3** A descending way; declivity; slope. **4** Lineage; birth; extraction. **5** Descendants; issue. **6** A hostile visitation; invasion. **7** The transmission of an estate by inheritance. **8** A generation in the scale of genealogy. See synonyms under AFFINITY, KIN. [< F *descente* < *descendre.* See DESCEND.]

Des·chutes River (dā·sho͞ot′) A river in central Oregon, flowing NE 240 miles to the Columbia River.

de·scribe (di·skrīb′) *v.t.* **·scribed, ·scrib·ing** **1** To give an account of; represent, with spoken or written words. **2** To draw the figure of; delineate; outline. **3** To descry: an erroneous form. See synonyms under CIRCUMSCRIBE, RELATE. [< L *describere* < *de-* down + *scribere* write] **—de·scrib′a·ble** *adj.* **—de·scrib′er** *n.*

de·scrip·tion (di·skrip′shən) *n.* **1** The act of describing; a portrayal or explanation; a drawing or tracing. **2** A group of attributes constituting a class; sort; kind; nature. See synonyms under DEFINITION, REPORT. [< OF *description* < L *descriptio, -onis* < *describere.* See DESCRIBE.]

de·scrip·tive (di·skrip′tiv) *adj.* **1** Characterized by or containing description; serving to describe. **2** Designating a science or branch of a science concerned with the classification of material; taxonomical. **3** *Gram.* Having the function of describing: a *descriptive* adjective. See synonyms under GRAPHIC. **—de·scrip′tive·ly** *adv.* **—de·scrip′tive·ness** *n.*

descriptive geometry That application of geometry in which the representation of solids is projected upon two planes so that their metrical properties can be accurately deduced.

descriptive linguistics See under LINGUISTICS.

descriptive science Any science in which the emphasis is placed upon the classification and description of the material with which it deals: distinguished from *exact science* and *normative science.*

de·scry (di·skrī′) *v.t.* **·scried, ·scry·ing** **1** To discover with the eye, as in the distance or through obscurity; discern; detect. **2** To discover or find out by observation or investigation. See synonyms under DISCERN, DISCOVER, LOOK. [< OF *descrier* < *des-* away (< L *dis-*) + *crier* cry] **—de·scri′er** *n.*

Des·de·mo·na (dez′də·mō′nə) The heroine of Shakespeare's *Othello.*

des·e·crate (des′ə·krāt) *v.t.* **·crat·ed, ·crat·ing** To divert from a sacred to a common use; profane. See synonyms under VIOLATE. [< DE- (def. 4) + L *sacratus,* pp. of *sacrare* make holy < *sacer* holy] **—des′e·crat′er** or **des′e·cra′tor** *n.*

des·e·cra·tion (des′ə·krā′shən) *n.* The act of profanation; condition of being desecrated; violation.

de·seg·re·gate (dē·seg′rə·gāt) *v.t.* **·gat·ed, ·gat·ing** To eliminate racial segregation in (schools, armed forces, public transportation, etc.).

de·seg·re·ga·tion (dē′seg·rə·gā′shən) *n.* **1** The act of ending segregation of races, as of Negroes and whites, in schools and public facilities. **2** The condition resulting from such action.

de·sen·si·tize (dē·sen′sə·tīz) *v.t.* **·tized, ·tiz·ing** **1** To make less sensitive. **2** *Phot.* To reduce the sensitiveness to light. **3** *Physiol.* To lessen the reactive power of (an organ or tissue) to a stimulus, as an allergen, serum, etc. **—de·sen′si·ti·za′tion** *n.* **—de·sen′si·tiz′er** *n.*

des·e·ret (dez′ə·ret′) *n.* The honey bee: used as a mystic word in the *Book of Mormon.*

Des·e·ret (dez′ə·ret′) A proposed State of the United States, organized in 1849 by a convention of Mormons: refused recognition by Congress, which instead set up Utah Territory in 1850.

des·ert[1] (dez′ərt) *n.* **1** A region so lacking in rainfall, moisture, and vegetation as to be uninhabitable by any considerable population. **2** Any region which is uncultivated and desolate because of deficient moisture, barren soil, or permanent frost. —*adj.* **1** Of or like a desert; barren; waste. **2** *Obs.* Deserted; forsaken. [<OF *deserte* <LL *desertum* <L, pp. neut. of *deserere* <*de-* away + *serere* join]

de·sert[2] (di·zûrt′) *n.* **1** The state of deserving reward or punishment; merit or demerit. **2** *Often pl.* That which is deserved or merited. **3** A meritorious or worthy act; meritoriousness. [<OF <*deservir.* See DESERVE.]

de·sert[3] (di·zûrt′) *v.t.* **1** To forsake or abandon, with or without right. **2** To forsake in violation of one's oath or orders, as a service, post, etc. —*v.i.* **3** To abandon one's post, duty, etc. See synonyms under ABANDON. [<F *déserter* <LL *desertare,* freq. of *deserere.* See DESERT[1].]

de·sert·er (di·zûr′tər) *n.* One who forsakes a service, duty, party, or friends; especially, an absconding soldier or sailor.

des·ert·i·fi·ca·tion (dez′ər·tə·fə·kā′shən) *n.* The process of becoming a desert.

de·ser·tion (di·zûr′shən) *n.* **1** The act of deserting. **2** The state of being deserted; desolation.

desert rat *Slang* **1** In the western United States, a person who has spent a long time in the desert. **2** In World War II, a soldier of the Seventh British Armored Division, which fought in the North African campaigns of 1941–42.

de·serve (di·zûrv′) *v.* **·served, serv·ing** *v.t.* To be entitled to or worthy of, by either merit or demerit.—*v.i.* To be worthy. [<OF *deservir* <L *deservire* <*de-* completely + *servire* serve] — **de·serv′er** *n.*

de·served (di·zûrvd′) *adj.* Earned; merited; suited to one's efforts or shortcomings. — **de·serv·ed·ness** (di·zûr′vid·nis) *n.*

de·serv·ed·ly (di·zûr′vid·lē) *adv.* According to desert; justly.

de·serv·ing (di·zûr′ving) *adj.* Worthy; meritorious. —*n.* Desert; merit or demerit. — **de·serv′ing·ly** *adv.* —**de·serv′ing·ness** *n.*

de·sex (dē seks′) *v.t.* Desexualize.

de·sex·u·al·ize (dē sek′shōō·ə·līz) *v.t.* **-ized, -iz·ing 1** to remove sexual characteristics from. **2** to remove the reproductive organs from. —**de·sex′u·al·i·za′tion** *n.*

des·ha·bille (dez′ə·bēl′) See DISHABILLE.

des·ic·cant (des′ə·kənt) *adj.* Producing dryness; desiccating, as a medicine or chemical agent. —*n.* A desiccant agent or substance.

des·ic·cate (des′ə·kāt) *v.* **·cat·ed, ·cat·ing** *v.t.* **1** To exhaust or remove the moisture from, as for preserving. **2** To dry thoroughly. —*v.i.* **3** To become dry. [<L *desiccatus,* pp. of *desiccare* <*de-* completely + *siccare* dry out <*siccus* dry] — **des′ic·ca′tion** *n.*

des·ic·cat·ed (des′ə·kā′tid) *adj.* **1** *Brit.* Dehydrated: *desiccated* soup. **2** Shriveled; dried up.

des·ic·ca·tive (des′ə·kā′tiv) *adj.* Drying. —*n.* A drying agent for external application.

des·ic·ca·tor (des′ə·kā′tər) *n.* **1** One who or that which desiccates. **2** An apparatus for drying meat, vegetables, etc. **3** A tightly covered glass or porcelain vessel having a device for absorbing moisture: used to hold substances to be dried.

de·sid·er·ate (di·sid′ə·rāt) *v.t.* **·at·ed, ·at·ing** To feel desire or need for; feel the lack of. [<L *desideratus,* pp. of *desiderare.* See DESIRE.] — **de·sid′er·a′tion** *n.*

de·sid·er·a·tive (di·sid′ə·rā′tiv) *adj.* Having, implying, or expressing desire. —*n.* **1** A desideratum. **2** *Ling.* A verb derived from another verb and indicating desire to perform the action expressed in the original verb, as Latin *esurio* I wish to eat, I am hungry, from *edo* I eat.

de·sid·er·a·tum (di·sid′ə·rā′təm) *n. pl.* **·ta** (-tə) Something not possessed, but needed or regarded as desirable; a want felt. [<L]

de·sign (di·zīn′) *v.t.* **1** To make, draw, or prepare preliminary plans or sketches of. **2** To plan and make with art or skill, as a structure or work of art. **3** To form or make (plans, schemes, etc.) in the mind; conceive; invent. **4** To intend; purpose. **5** *Archaic* To mark out; designate. —*v.i.* **6** To make drawings or plans; be a designer. **7** To plan mentally; conceive. —*n.* **1** An arrangement of forms or colors, or both, intended to be wrought out for use or ornament in or on various materials; a pattern; preliminary sketch; coordination of details. **2** The art of designing; artistic invention; the artistic idea as executed; original work in the graphic or plastic arts. **3** A fixed purpose or intention; plot; scheme. **4** The adaptation of means to an end; plan; contrivance. **5** The object or reason; final purpose. [<MF *désigner* designate <L *designare.* See DESIGNATE.] — **de·sign′a·ble** *adj.*

Synonyms (noun): aim, device, end, intent, intention, object, plan, project, proposal, purpose, scheme. *Design* refers to the adaptation of means to an *end,* the correspondence and coordination of parts, or of separate acts, to produce a result; *intent* and *purpose* overleap all particulars, and fasten on the *end* itself. *Intention* is simply the more familiar form of the legal and philosophical *intent. Plan* relates to details of form, structure, and action, in themselves; *design* considers these same details all as a means to an *end.* The *plan* of a campaign may be for a series of sharp attacks, with the *design* of thus surprising and overpowering the enemy. A man comes to a fixed *intention* to kill his enemy; he forms a *plan* to entrap him into his power, with the *design* of then compassing his death; as the law cannot read the heart, it can only infer the *intent* from the evidences of *design. Intent* denotes a straining, stretching forth toward an *object, purpose* simply the placing it before oneself. *Intention* contemplates the possibility of failure; *purpose* looks to assured success, *intent* or *intention* refers especially to the state of mind of the actor, *purpose* to the result of the action. Compare AIM, END, IDEA, MODEL, PROJECT, PURPOSE, REASON.

des·ig·nate (dez′ig·nāt) *v.t.* **·nat·ed, ·nat·ing 1** To indicate or make recognizable by some mark, sign, or name. **2** To name or entitle; characterize. **3** To select or appoint for a specific purpose, duty, office, etc. See synonyms under CIRCUMSCRIBE. —*adj.* (dez′ig·nit, -nāt) Designated; selected. [<L *designatus,* pp. of *designare* <*de-* completely + *signare* mark <*signum* a sign] — **des′ig·na′tive** *adj.* —**des′ig·na′tor** *n.*

designated hitter In baseball, a batter designated to bat in the place of the pitcher, who pitches throughout the game but does not bat.

des·ig·na·tion (dez′ig·nā′shən) *n.* **1** The act of designating. **2** A distinctive mark, name, or title. **3** Import, as of a word; character; description. See synonyms under NAME.

de·sign·ed·ly (di·zī′nid·lē) *adv.* By design; purposely; intentionally.

des·ig·nee (dez′ig·nē′) *n.* A person designated. [<F *désigné,* pp. of *désigner* DESIGN]

de·sign·er (di·zī′nər) *n.* **1** One who forms designs; a contriver; schemer. **2** One who invents and prepares useful, decorative, or artistic designs. See synonyms under CAUSE.

de·sign·ing (di·zī′ning) *n.* **1** The act or art of making designs or sketches. **2** The act of plotting or scheming. —*adj.* Artful; scheming. See synonyms under INSIDIOUS. —**de·sign′ing·ly** *adv.*

de·sil·ver·ize (dē·sil′və·rīz) *v.t.* **·ized, ·iz·ing** To remove the silver from.

des·i·nence (des′i·nəns) *n.* **1** A termination or ending. **2** *Gram.* A formative suffix. [<MF *désinence* <L *desinentia* <*desinere* <*de-* away + *sinere* leave]

de·sip·i·ence (di·sip′ē·əns) *n.* Silliness; foolishness; trifling. Also **de·sip′i·en·cy.**

de·sip·i·ent (di·sip′ē·ənt) *adj.* Nonsensical; foolish. [<L *desipiens, -entis,* ppr. of *desipere* <*de-* away + *sapere* know, be wise]

de·sir·a·ble (di·zīr′ə·bəl) *adj.* Worthy or likely to be desired or wanted; worth having. See synonyms under PROFITABLE. —**de·sir′a·bil′i·ty, de·sir′a·ble·ness** *n.* —**de·sir′a·bly** *adv.*

de·sire (di·zīr′) *v.t.* **·sired, ·sir·ing 1** To wish or long for; covet; crave. **2** To express a wish for; ask for; request. —*n.* **1** An earnest wishing for something; longing; craving; yearning. **2** A request; wish; prayer. **3** An object desired. **4** Appetite; passion; lust. [<OF *desirer* <L *desiderare,* ? <*de-* from + *sidus, sideris* star; with ref. to astrology] —**de·sir′er** *n.*

Synonyms (noun): appetency, appetite, aspiration, concupiscence, coveting, craving, hankering, inclination, longing, proclivity, propensity, wish. *Inclination* is the mildest of these terms; it is a quiet, or even a vague or unconscious, tendency. Even when we speak of a strong or decided *inclination* we do not express the intensity of *desire. Desire* has a wide range, from the highest objects to the lowest; *desire* is for an object near at hand, or near in thought, and viewed as attainable; a *wish* may be for what is remote or uncertain; or even for what is recognized as impossible. *Craving* is stronger than *hankering; hankering* may be the result of a fitful and capricious *appetite*; *craving* may be the imperious and reasonable demand of the whole nature. *Longing* is a reaching out with deep and persistent demand for that which is viewed as now distant but at some time attainable; as, the captive's *longing* for release. *Coveting* ordinarily denotes wrong *desire* for that which is another's. Compare APPETITE, FANCY, INCLINATION. *Antonyms*: see synonyms for ANTIPATHY.

de·sir·ous (di·zīr′əs) *adj.* **1** Having desire; experiencing a wish or craving; eager. **2** *Obs.* Exciting desire; desirable.

de·sist (di·zist′) *v.i.* To cease, as from an action or proceeding; forbear; stop: often with *from.* See synonyms under CEASE, END, REST. [<L *desistere* <*de-* from + *sistere* stop, cease] — **de·sis′tance** *n.*

desk (desk) *n.* **1** A table or case specially adapted for writing or studying. **2** A stand for public reading or preaching; pulpit. [<Med. L *desca* <LL *discus.* Doublet of DAIS, DISH, DISK.]

des·man (des′mən) *n. pl.* **·mans** (-mənz) An aquatic, shrew-like, insectivorous mammal (family *Talpidae*), having musk-secreting glands and valued for its fur; especially, *Desmana moschata* of SE Russia and *D. pyrenaica* of the Pyrenees. [<Sw. *desman* musk]

DESMAN
(Body to 10 inches: tail about 6 inches)

des·mid (des′mid) *n.* Any of a family *(Desmidiaceae)* of minute, bright-green, unicellular, mainly solitary, fresh-water algae. The individual is usually divided into symmetrical halves or semi-cells connected by an isthmus. [<NL *desmidium,* the typical genus <Gk. *desmos* a band, chain] —**des·mid·i·a·ceous** (des·mid′ē·ā′shəs) *adj.* —**des·mid′i·an** *adj.*

des·moid (des′moid) *adj. Anat.* Resembling a ligament; ligamentous; also, fibrous: a *desmoid* tumor. —*n. Pathol.* A tough, very hard fibroma. [<Gk. *desmos* band + -OID]

Des Moines (də moin′, -moinz′) The capital of Iowa.

Des Moines River A river in Minnesota and Iowa, flowing 500 miles SE to the Mississippi.

des·mot·ro·pism (des·mot′rə·piz′əm) *n. Chem.* A form of tautomerism in organic compounds in which two molecules may have atoms of the same number, kind, and valence, and arranged in the same position, but with the shifting double bond permitting the independent existence of two types of the compound. [<Gk. *desmos* band + *tropos* turning] —**des·mo·trop·ic** (des′mə·trop′ik, -trō′pik) *adj.*

Des·mou·lins (dā·mōō·lan′), **Camille Benoît,** 1760-94, French revolutionist.

Des·na (dyis′nä) A river in western European U.S.S.R., flowing 737 miles SW to the Dnieper.

des·o·late (des′ə·lit) *adj.* **1** Destitute of inhabitants, dwellings, etc.; laid waste; deserted; abandoned. **2** Lonely; solitary. **3** Without friends; forlorn; sorrowful; afflicted; gloomy. See synonyms under BLEAK[1], SAD. —*v.t.* (des′ə·lāt) **·lat·ed, ·lat·ing 1** To deprive of inhabitants. **2** To lay waste, devastate. **3** To make sorrowful, wretched, or forlorn. 4 To forsake; abandon. [<L *desolatus,* pp. of *desolare* <*de-* completely + *solus* alone] **—des′o·late·ly** *adv.* **—des′o·late·ness** *n.* **—des′o·lat′er, des′o·la′tor** *n.*

des·o·la·tion (des′ə·lā′shən) *n.* 1 The state or condition of being desolate; loneliness; dreariness; sadness; affliction; grief. 2 A desolate region; a waste. 3 The act of making desolate; devastation.

Desolation Island See KERGUELEN ISLANDS.

de·sorp·tion (dē·sôrp′shən) *n. Chem.* The liberation or removal of a substance, usually gaseous, from the surface of adsorbing material: opposed to *adsorption.*

De So·to (də sō′tō), **Hernando,** 1499?–1542, Spanish explorer; discovered the Mississippi River 1541.

de·spair (di·spâr′) *v.i.* To lose or abandon hope; be or become hopeless: with *of.* —*v.t. Obs.* To lose hope or faith in. —*n.* 1 Utter hopelessness and discouragement. 2 That which causes despair or which is despaired of. [<OF *desperer* <L *desperare* <*de-* away + *sperare* hope <*spes* hope] **—de·spair′ing** *adj.* **—de·spair′ing·ly** *adv.*

Synonyms (noun): desperation, despondency, discouragement, hopelessness. *Discouragement* is the result of so much repulse or failure as wears out courage. *Discouragements* too frequent and long continued may produce a settled *hopelessness. Hopelessness* is negative, and may result from simple apathy; *despondency* and *despair* are more emphatic and decided. *Despondency* is an incapacity for the present exercise of hope; *despair* is the utter abandonment of hope. *Despondency* relaxes energy and effort and is always attended with sadness or distress; *despair* may produce a stony calmness, or it may lead to *desperation. Desperation* is energized *despair,* vigorous in action, reckless of consequences. *Antonyms*: anticipation, assurance, cheer, confidence, courage, elation, encouragement, expectancy, expectation, hope, hopefulness, trust.

des·patch (di·spach′) See DISPATCH.

des·patch·er (di·spach′ər) See DISPATCHER.

des·per·a·do (des′pə·rä′dō, -rā′dō) *n. pl.* **·does** or **·dos** A desperate character; a ruffian. [<OSp., pp. of *desperar* <L *desperare.* See DESPAIR.]

des·per·ate (des′pər·it) *adj.* 1 Without care for danger; reckless, as from despair. 2 Resorted to in a last extremity; instigated by or denoting despair; hazardous; frantic; furious. 3 Regarded as almost irremediable; despaired of. 4 Utterly, hopelessly bad; outrageous. 5 Hopeless of recovery; irrecoverable: said especially of a money claim. 6 *Obs.* Despairing. [<L *desperatus,* pp. of *desperare.* See DESPAIR.] **—des′per·ate·ly** *adv.* **—des′per·ate·ness** *n.*

des·per·a·tion (des′pə·rā′shən) *n.* 1 The state of being desperate. 2 The act of despairing. 3 The recklessness of despair; blind fury. See synonyms under DESPAIR.

Des·piau (des·pyō′), **Charles,** 1874–1946, French sculptor.

des·pi·ca·ble (des′pi·kə·bəl, di·spik′ə·bəl) *adj.* Capable of being, or deserving to be, despised; contemptible; mean; vile. See synonyms under BASE², PITIFUL. [<LL *despicabilis* <*despicere.* See DESPISE.] **—des′pi·ca·bil′i·ty, des′pi·ca·ble·ness** *n.* **—des′pi·ca·bly** *adv.*

de·spise (di·spīz′) *v.t.* **·spised, ·spis·ing** To regard as contemptible or worthless; disdain; scorn. See synonyms under ABHOR. [<OF *despis-,* stem of *despire* <L *despicere* <*de-* down + *specere* look at] **—de·spis′a·ble** *adj.* **—de·spis′er** *n.*

de·spite (di·spīt′) *n.* 1 An act of defiance, malice, or injury. 2 Extreme malice; hatred; spite. 3 *Obs.* Defiance. See synonyms under SCORN *n.* **—in despite of** Notwithstanding; in opposition or contradiction to: He seized my hand *in despite of* my efforts to the contrary. —*prep.* In spite of; notwithstanding: They will fight on, *despite* impediments. See synonyms under NOTWITHSTANDING. Also **de·spight′.** —*v.t.* **·spit·ed, ·spit·ing** *Obs.* 1 To despise. 2 To offend. [<OF *despit* <L *despectus* a looking down, contempt <*despicere.* See DESPISE.]

de·spite·ful (di·spīt′fəl) *adj. Archaic* Full of spite; malicious; malignant; offensive. **—de·spite′ful·ly** *adv.* **—de·spite′ful·ness** *n.*

des·pit·e·ous (des·pit′ē·əs) *adj. Archaic* Stirred with malicious scorn or hate; despiteful. **—des·pit′e·ous·ly** *adv.*

Des Plaines River (des plānz′) A river in Wisconsin and Illinois, flowing 110 miles SW to the Illinois River.

de·spoil (di·spoil′) *v.t.* To strip or deprive of something by or as by force; plunder. [<OF *despoillier* <L *despoliare* <*de-* completely + *spoliare* rob <*spolium* plunder] **—de·spoil′er** *n.* **—de·spoil′ment** *n.*

de·spo·li·a·tion (di·spō′lē·ā′shən) *n.* The act of despoiling, or state of being despoiled or plundered. [<LL *despoliatio, -onis* <*despoliare.* See DESPOIL.]

de·spond (di·spond′) *v.i.* To lose spirit, courage, or hope; be depressed. —*n. Obs.* Despondency. [<L *despondere* <*de-* away + *spondere* promise] **—de·spond′ing·ly** *adv.*

de·spon·dent (di·spon′dənt) *adj.* Dejected in spirit; disheartened. Also **de·spond′ing.** See synonyms under SAD. **—de·spon′den·cy, de·spon′dence** *n.* **—de·spon′dent·ly** *adv.*

des·pot (des′pət, -pot) *n.* 1 An absolute monarch; autocrat; a hard master; tyrant. 2 In Oriental countries a title, originally of a Byzantine emperor; later, of various subordinate rulers: applied also to the bishops and patriarchs of the Greek Church. See synonyms under MASTER. [<OF <Gk. *despotēs* a master]

des·pot·ic (di·spot′ik) *adj.* Of or like a despot or despotism; tyrannical. See synonyms under ABSOLUTE, ARBITRARY, IMPERIOUS. **—des·pot′i·cal** *adj.* **—des·pot′i·cal·ly** *adv.* **—des·pot′i·cal·ness** *n.*

des·pot·ism (des′pə·tiz′əm) *n.* 1 Absolute power; autocracy. 2 Any tyrannical control.

des·pot·ize (des′pə·tīz) *v.i.* **·ized, ·iz·ing** To be despotic; play the tyrant.

des·pu·mate (des′pyōō·māt, di·spyōō′māt) *v.* **·mat·ed, ·mat·ing** *v.t.* 1 To skim. 2 To throw off as scum. —*v.i.* 3 To throw or work off impurities in froth or scum. [<L *despumatus,* pp. of *despumare* <*de-* away + *spumare* skim <*spuma* scum] **—des′pu·ma′tion** *n.*

des·qua·mate (des′kwə·māt) *v.i.* **·mat·ed, ·mat·ing** *Pathol.* To peel or scale off, as the epithelial cells in certain skin ailments. [<L *desquamatus,* pp. of *desquamare* <*de-* away + *squama* a scale]

des·qua·ma·tion (des′kwə·mā′shən) *n. Pathol.* The scaling off of the cuticle, as in measles and scarlatina.

Des·sa·lines (des·sȧ·lēn′), **Jean Jacques,** 1758–1806, emperor of Haiti 1804–06: called "Jacques I."

Des·sau (des′ou) A city in Saxony-Anhalt, Germany.

des·sert (di·zûrt′) *n.* A service of something sweet, as pie, cake, pudding, fruit, etc., at the close of lunch or dinner. [<F <*desservir* clear a table <*des-* away + *servir* serve]

des·sert·spoon (di·zûrt′spōōn′) *n.* A spoon intermediate in size between a teaspoon and a tablespoon, holding about 8 cubic centimeters. **—des·sert′spoon′ful** *n.*

des·sia·tine (des′yə·tēn) *n.* A Russian unit of area, equal to 2.698 acres. [<Russian *desyatina*]

des·ti·na·tion (des′tə·nā′shən) *n.* 1 A predetermined end. 2 The point to which a journey, or the course of anything, is directed; goal. 3 A destining; appointment.

des·tine (des′tin) *v.t.* **·tined, ·tin·ing** 1 To design for or appoint to a distinct purpose or end. 2 To determine the future of, as by destiny or fate. See synonyms under ALLOT. [<F *destiner* <L *destinare* make fast, ult. <*de-* completely + *stare* stand]

des·tined (des′tind) *adj.* Bound for an appointed place; assigned to go to a place designated.

Des·ti·nies (des′tə·nēz) In classical mythology, the Fates or Parcae.

Des·tinn (des′tin), **Emmy,** 1878–1930, Czech operatic soprano: real name *Kittl.*

des·ti·ny (des′tə·nē) *n. pl.* **·nies** 1 That to which any person or thing is destined; fortune; doom. 2 Inevitable necessity; divine decree; fate. See synonyms under NECESSITY. [<OF *destinée* <*destiner.* See DESTINE.]

des·ti·tute (des′tə·tōōt, -tyōōt) *adj.* 1 Not having or possessing; entirely lacking: with *of.* 2 Being in want; extremely poor. 3 *Obs.* Desolate; forsaken. [<L *destitutus,* pp. of *destituere* abandon <*de-* down + *statuere* set, place]

des·ti·tu·tion (des′tə·tōō′shən, -tyōō′-) *n.* The state or condition of being destitute; extreme poverty. See synonyms under POVERTY.

des·tri·er (des′trē·ər, des·trir′) *n. Archaic* A war horse. [<AF *destrer,* OF *destrier* <LL *(equus) dextrarius* (horse) led by the right hand <L *dexter* right]

de·stroy (di·stroi′) *v.t.* 1 To ruin utterly; consume; dissolve. 2 To demolish; raze; tear down. 3 To put an end to; do away with. 4 To kill. 5 To make ineffective; counteract. See synonyms under ABOLISH, ANNUL, BREAK, DEMOLISH, EXTERMINATE, SUBVERT. [<OF *destruire,* ult. <L *destruere* <*de-* down + *struere* build]

de·stroy·er (di·stroi′ər) *n.* 1 One who or that which destroys. 2 A speedy war vessel, smaller than a cruiser, and equipped with guns, torpedo tubes, depth bombs, and anti-aircraft batteries: widely used as an escort vessel. 3 A self-propelled anti-tank gun: also **tank destroyer.**

DESTROYER, U.S. NAVY, WORLD WAR II

destroyer escort A U.S. Navy vessel smaller and slower than a destroyer and equipped for anti-submarine warfare.

de·struct (di·strukt′) *Aerospace n.* The act of destroying a defective missile or rocket after launch. —*v.t.* & *v.i.* To destroy a defective missile or rocket after launch.

de·struc·ti·ble (di·struk′tə·bəl) *adj.* Liable to destruction; capable of being destroyed. **—de·struc′ti·bil′i·ty** *n.* **—de·struc′ti·ble·ness** *n.*

de·struc·tion (di·struk′shən) *n.* 1 The act of destroying, or state of being destroyed; demolition; ruin. 2 That which destroys. See synonyms under LOSS, RUIN. [<OF <L *destructio, -onis* <destruere. See DESTROY.]

de·struc·tion·ist (di·struk′shən·ist) *n.* 1 One who favors destruction, or the overthrow of existing conditions. 2 An anarchist.

de·struc·tive (di·struk′tiv) *adj.* 1 Tending or fitted to destroy; causing destruction. 2 Pernicious; ruinous. See synonyms under NOISOME, PERNICIOUS. **—de·struc′tive·ly** *adv.* **—de·struc′tive·ness** *n.*

destructive distillation A process in which a complex organic substance such as wood or coal is decomposed by heat in the absence of air and the volatile components are recovered by condensation.

de·struc·tiv·i·ty (dē′struk·tiv′ə·tē) *n.* The state or quality of being destructive.

de·struc·tor (di·struk′tər) *n.* A furnace or retort for burning refuse.

des·ue·tude (des′wə·tōōd, -tyōōd) *n.* 1 The cessation of use. 2 A condition of disuse. [<MF *désuétude* <L *desuetudo* <*desuescere* <*de-* away + *suescere* be used]

de·sul·fur·ize (dē·sul′fə·rīz) *v.t.* **·ized, ·iz·ing** To remove sulfur from. Also **de·sul′fur, de·sul′fur·ate, de·sul′phur·ize.** **—de·sul′fur·i·za′tion** *n.* **—de·sul′fur·iz′er** *n.*

des·ul·to·ry (des′əl·tôr′ē, -tō′rē) *adj.* 1 Passing abruptly and irregularly from one thing to another; fitful; changeable; unmethodical. 2 Starting suddenly as if by a leap; not connected with what precedes. See synonyms under CURSORY, IRREGULAR. [<L *desultorius* <*desultor* a leaper <*de-* down + *salire* leap, jump] **—des′ul·to′ri·ly** *adv.* **—des′ul·to′ri·ness** *n.*

de·tach (di·tach′) *v.t.* 1 To unfasten and make separate; disconnect; disunite. 2 To separate and send off for a special service, duty, etc., as a regiment or a ship. See synonyms under ABSTRACT. [<F *détacher* <*dé-* away (<L *dis-*) + OF *tache* nail <Gmc.] **—de·tach′a·bil′i·ty** *n.* **—de·tach′a·ble** *adj.* **—de·tach′er** *n.*

de·tached (di·tacht′) *adj.* 1 Separated from others; disconnected; disunited. 2 *Mil.* Designated to special duty elsewhere than with the unit to which assigned, with or without transfer of administration. 3 Pertaining to relief from assignment or attachment and assumption of another status. 4 In painting, standing alone in the foreground or distinctly separate from other objects. 5 Aloof; hence, unbiased.

detached retina *Pathol.* A disconnection of the inner layers of the retina from the pigment layer.

de·tach·ment (di·tach′mənt) *n.* **1** A detaching; separation. **2** Something detached, as a body of troops for special service. **3** Dissociation from surroundings or worldly interest; aloofness.

de·tail (di·tāl′, dē′tāl) *n.* **1** A separately considered particular or item; minor part; accessory. **2** *Mil.* A small detachment assigned to some subordinate service; also, the person or persons assigned. **3** In art and architecture, a minor part essential to the completeness and finish of a work, yet secondary and accessory. See synonyms under CIRCUMSTANCE. **—in detail** Item by item; with particularity. [<*v.*] —*v.t.* (di·tāl′) **1** To report or narrate minutely; enter into or give the details of. **2** *Mil.* (often dē′tāl) To select and send off for a special service, duty, etc. See synonyms under RELATE. [<F *détailler* cut into pieces <*dé-* completely + *tailler* cut up]

detail drawing Drawing of special or typical parts or features of a structure, machine, or design, made to a large scale or of full size.

de·tain (di·tān′) *v.t.* **1** To restrain from proceeding; stop; delay. **2** To keep back; withhold. **3** To hold in custody. See synonyms under RETAIN. [<OF *detenir* <L *detinere* <*de-* away + *tenere* hold] **—de·tain′ment** *n.*

de·tain·er (di·tā′nər) *n.* **1** One who detains, stops, or withholds. **2** *Law* **a** A process for recovering possession of lands or goods wrongfully held. **b** A writ directing the continued holding of a prisoner in custody pending an additional action. **—forcible detainer** The seizure by violence, or keeping possession of by threats, force, or the display of arms, of lands or tenements without authority of law.

de·tect (di·tekt′) *v.t.* **1** To discover, perceive, or find, as something obscure: to *detect* an error in spelling. **2** To expose or uncover, as a crime, fault, or a criminal. **3** *Telecom.* To rectify (a high-frequency carrier wave) to the desired lower frequency; to demodulate. See synonyms under DISCOVER. [<L *detectus*, pp. of *detegere* <*de-* away + *tegere* cover] **—de·tect′a·ble** or **·i·ble** *adj.* **—de·tect′er** *n.*

de·tec·ta·phone (di·tek′tə·fōn) *n.* A wiretapping device for the interception and transmission of telephone messages.

de·tec·tion (di·tek′shən) *n.* **1** The act of detecting; discovery. **2** *Telecom.* Any method of operating on a modulated signal wave so as to obtain the signal imparted to it: a process of demodulation of incoming electrical signals.

de·tec·tive (di·tek′tiv) *adj.* **1** Skilled in or fitted for detection; employed to detect. **2** Belonging or pertaining to detectives and their work. —*n.* A person, often a policeman, whose work is to investigate crimes, discover evidence, capture criminals, etc.

de·tec·tor (di·tek′tər) *n.* **1** One who or that which detects. **2** A device for detecting, as for showing low water in a boiler, indicating the presence of torpedoes under water, etc. **3** *Electr.* A device for discovering the presence of electric waves, as a coherer; also, a portable galvanometer. **4** *Telecom.* A demodulator or a device for obtaining the signal from a modulated carrier.

de·tent (di·tent′) *n. Mech.* A stop or checking device, as a pin, lever, etc., on a ratchet wheel or the like. [<F *détente* <*détendre* slacken <*dé-* away (<L *dis-*) + *tendre* stretch <L *tendere*]

dé·tente (dā·tänt′) *n. French* An easing, as of discord between nations.

de·ten·tion (di·ten′shən) *n.* **1** The act of detaining. **2** The state of being detained; restraint; custody; delay. [<L *detentio, -onis* <*detinere*. See DETAIN.] **—de·ten′tive** *adj.*

detention camp A camp at which recruits or prisoners of war are held to determine whether they have communicable diseases.

de·ter (di·tûr′) *v.t.* **·terred, ·ter·ring** To prevent or restrain by fear, difficulty, danger, etc., from acting or proceeding. [<L *deterrere* <*de-* away + *terrere* frighten] **—de·ter′ment** *n.*

de·terge (di·tûrj′) *v.t.* **·terged, ·terg·ing** **1** To cleanse of morbid or dead matter, as a wound. **2** To wipe off; purge away. [<L *detergere* <*de-* away + *tergere* wipe]

de·ter·gent (di·tûr′jənt) *adj.* Having cleansing qualities; purging. —*n.* **1** A cleansing substance, as soap or an antiseptic. **2** *Chem.* Any of a class of surface-active compounds having strong cleansing effects. **—de·ter′gence, de·ter′gen·cy** *n.*

de·te·ri·o·rate (di·tir′ē·ə·rāt′) *v.t.* & *v.i.* **·rat·ed, ·rat·ing** To make or become worse; reduce in quality, value, etc.; degenerate. See synonyms under CORRUPT, IMPAIR. [<L *deterioratus*, pp. of *deteriorare* <*deterior* worse] **—de·te′ri·o·ra′tion** *n.* **—de·te′ri·o·ra′tive** *adj.*

de·ter·mi·na·ble (di·tûr′mi·nə·bəl) *adj.* **1** That may be accurately found out, settled, or decided. **2** *Law* Liable to be put an end to; terminable.

de·ter·mi·nant (di·tûr′mə·nənt) *adj.* Determinative. —*n.* **1** That which influences to determine. **2** *Math.* A set of algebraic quantities arranged in a square matrix and operated upon according to special rules for the solution of various linear systems of equations. **3** *Biol.* A former name introduced by Weismann for one of the hypothetical secondary units of germ plasm or hereditary substance regulating the origin and the development of cells and systems of cells.

de·ter·mi·nate (di·tûr′mə·nit) *adj.* **1** Definitely limited or fixed; specific; distinct. **2** Predetermined; positive. **3** Known or fixed, as a mathematical quantity. **4** *Bot.* Limited in extent, as an inflorescence or cyme. **5** Determined; intended; determining; decisive. **—de·ter′mi·nate·ly** *adv.* **—de·ter′mi·nate·ness** *n.*

de·ter·mi·na·tion (di·tûr′mə·nā′shən) *n.* **1** The act of determining; a firm resolve. **2** The quality of being earnest and decided; firmness. **3** Judicial decision; authoritative opinion or conclusion. **4** The ascertaining exactly of the character, amount, dimensions, or proportion of a thing; the result of such investigation. **5** *Logic* The making of a notion definite or more definite by the addition of a qualifying or limiting idea; specification; also, an attribute which determines. **6** *Biol.* **a** The classification of plants and animals. **b** The process whereby the cells of a developing organism become differentiated in structure and function: sex *determination.* **7** *Physiol.* Tendency or increased flow, as of blood, to a part. **8** The exercise of decisive force or power: *determination* of the will toward an object. **9** *Obs.* A limiting or putting an end to.

Synonyms: decision, resolution, resolve. *Decision* is literally a cutting off, or cutting short, of debate or questioning; *determination* is a setting of the limits within which one must act; *resolve* is a separating of the essential act from all that might cause doubt or hesitation. *Resolve* always refers to a single act; *resolution* may have the same meaning, or it may refer to the habit of mind which readily forms and adheres to a *resolve.* *Decision* and *determination* especially mark the beginning of action; *resolution* holds out to the end. See AIM, PURPOSE. Compare synonyms for DESIGN. *Antonyms*: doubt, faltering, fickleness, hesitancy, hesitation, indecision, instability, irresolution, vacillation, wavering.

de·ter·mi·na·tive (di·tûr′mə·nā′tiv, -mə·nə·tiv) *adj.* Tending or having power to determine or fix; deciding; shaping. —*n.* **1** That which determines. **2** *Gram.* A demonstrative pronoun. **3** *Ling.* In certain languages, an element affixed to a word which modifies or determines its meaning, as *-sc-* in Latin *calesco* I grow warm, from *caleo* I am warm. **—de·ter′mi·na′tive·ly** *adv.* **—de·ter′mi·na′tive·ness** *n.*

de·ter·mine (di·tûr′min) *v.* **·mined, ·min·ing** *v.t.* **1** To settle or decide, as an argument, question, or debate. **2** To ascertain or fix, as after thought or observation. **3** To cause to reach a decision. **4** To regulate; fix or decide causally: Demand *determines* supply. **5** To give aim, purpose, or direction to. **6** To set bounds to; limit in extent, variety, etc. **7** *Logic* To limit or define by adding differences. **8** To limit; terminate: usually in legal usage. —*v.i.* **9** To come to a decision; resolve. **10** To come to an end: usually in legal usage. See synonyms under PURPOSE. [<OF *determiner* <L *determinare* <*de-* completely + *terminare* end <*terminum* a limit]

de·ter·mined (di·tûr′mind) *adj.* Resolute; settled; determinate. See synonyms under FIRM, OBSTINATE. **—de·ter′mined·ly** *adv.* **—de·ter′mined·ness** *n.*

de·ter·min·er (di·tûr′mə·nər) *n.* **1** A person or thing that determines. **2** *Gram.* Any of a class of words, including articles and possessive adjectives, whose presence in a phrase, often before a descriptive adjective, indicates that the head word is a noun or substantive. In *his old coat,* "his" is a determiner.

de·ter·min·ism (di·tûr′mə·niz′əm) *n. Philos.* The doctrine that man's choices, decisions, and actions are decided by antecedent causes, inherited or environmental, acting upon his character: opposed to *free will.* **—de·ter′min·ist** *adj.* & *n.* **—de·ter′min·is′tic** *adj.*

de·ter·rent (di·tûr′ənt) *adj.* Tending or serving to deter. —*n.* Something that deters. **—de·ter′rence** *n.*

de·ter·sion (di·tûr′zhən) *n.* A cleansing, as of a wound. [<LL *detersio, -onis* <*detergere.* See DETERGE.]

de·ter·sive (di·tûr′siv) *adj.* Cleansing; detergent. —*n.* A cleansing or purging medicine or agent.

de·test (di·test′) *v.t.* To hate; dislike with intensity; abhor. See synonyms under ABHOR. [<MF *détester* <L *detestari* denounce <*de-* away + *testis* a witness] **—de·test′er** *n.* **—de·test′a·bil′i·ty** *n.* **—de·test′a·ble** *adj.* **—de·test′a·ble·ness** *n.* **—de·test′a·bly** *adv.*

de·tes·ta·tion (dē′tes·tā′shən) *n.* **1** Extreme dislike; hatred; abhorrence. **2** An act or thing detested. See synonyms under ABOMINATION, ANTIPATHY, HATRED.

de·throne (dē·thrōn′) *v.t.* **·throned, ·thron·ing** To remove from the throne; depose. **—de·throne′ment** *n.* **—de·thron′er** *n.*

det·i·nue (det′i·nyōō) *n. Law* An action to recover personal property wrongfully detained; the writ used in such action; also, the act of detaining wrongfully. [<OF *detenue*, pp. of *detenir.* See DETAIN.]

Det·mold (det′mōlt) A city in North Rhine-Westphalia, Germany; former capital of Lippe.

det·o·nate (det′ə·nāt, dē′tə-) *v.* **·nat·ed, ·nat·ing** *v.t.* To cause to explode suddenly and with violence. —*v.i.* To explode suddenly with a loud report. [<L *detonatus*, pp. of *detonare* <*de-* down + *tonare* thunder]

detonating powder A powder, chiefly of the mercury fulminates, which explodes violently when heated or struck: used chiefly to fire other explosives.

det·o·na·tion (det′ə·nā′shən, dē′tə-) *n.* A violent and sudden explosion resulting from the instantaneous combustion of a mixture, compound, or substance.

det·o·na·tor (det′ə·nā′tər, dē′tə-) *n.* Any contrivance, as a primer or fuze, for detonating the main charge of a projectile, bomb, etc.

de·tor·sion (dē·tôr′shən) *n.* The act of twisting back or removing torsion. [<DE- + TORSION]

de·tort (dē·tôrt′) *v.t. Obs.* To pervert; distort. [<L *detortus*, pp. of *detorquere* <*de-* away + *torquere* twist]

de·tour (dē′tōōr, di·tōōr′) *n.* A roundabout way; any turning aside from a direct route or course of action; specifically, a byroad substituted for part of a main road temporarily impassable. —*v.t.* & *v.i.* To go or cause to go by a roundabout way. [<F *détour* <*détourner* <*dé-* away + *tourner* turn]

de·tox·i·cate (dē·tok′sə·kāt) *v.t.* **·cat·ed, ·cat·ing** To reduce or destroy the toxic properties of (a substance). [<DE- + (IN)TOXICATE] **—de·tox′i·ca′tion** *n.* **—de·tox′i·cant** (-kənt) *n.*

de·tract (di·trakt′) *v.t.* **1** To take away; withdraw. **2** *Obs.* To disparage. —*v.i.* **3** To take away a part, especially from a reputation, enjoyment, honor, etc. [<L *detractus*, pp. of *detrahere* <*de-* away + *trahere* draw, pull] **—de·trac′tive** *adj.* **—de·tract′ing·ly** *adv.* **—de·trac′tor, de·trac′ter** *n.*

de·trac·tion (di·trak′shən) *n.* The act of detracting; slander; defamation. See synonyms under SCANDAL.

de·trac·to·ry (di·trak′tər·ē) *adj.* Defamatory.

de·train (dē·trān′) *v.t.* & *v.i.* To leave or cause to leave a railway train. **—de·train′ment** *n.*

det·ri·ment (det′rə·mənt) *n.* **1** Something that impairs or injures, or causes damage or loss. **2** Injury or loss. See synonyms under INJURY, LOSS. [< L *detrimentum* < *deterere* < *de-* away + *terere* rub]

det·ri·men·tal (det′rə·men′təl) *adj.* Injurious; hurtful. See synonyms under BAD, NOISOME. — **det′ri·men′tal·ly** *adv.*

de·tri·tion (di·trish′ən) *n.* The act of rubbing or wearing off particles.

de·tri·tus (di·trī′təs) *n.* **1** *Geol.* Loose fragments or particles separated from masses of rock by erosion, glacial action, and other mechanical forces. **2** Any mass of disintegrated material; debris. [< L < *deterere.* See DETRIMENT.] — **de·tri′tal** *adj.*

De·troit (di·troit′) A port on the Detroit River in SE Michigan.

Detroit River A river 31 miles long, connecting Lake St. Clair with Lake Erie and forming part of the boundary between the United States and Canada.

de trop (də trō′) *French* Too much; not wanted; superfluous.

de·trude (di·trōōd′) *v.t.* **·trud·ed, ·trud·ing 1** To thrust down or out. **2** To push down forcibly. [< L *detrudere* < *de-* away + *trudere* thrust] — **de·tru′sion** *n.* **—de·tru′sive** *adj.*

de·trun·cate (di·trung′kāt) *v.t.* **·cat·ed, ·cat·ing** To shorten by cutting off a part; cut off. [< L *detruncatus,* pp. of *detruncare* < *de-* from + *truncare* lop] **—de′trun·ca′tion** *n.*

Det·ting·en (det′ing·ən) A village in NW Bavaria; scene of a French defeat by English and German forces, 1743.

de·tu·mes·cence (dē′tōō·mes′əns, -tyōō-) *n.* *Physiol.* **1** The subsidence of any swelling in an organ or part. **2** Subsidence of the erectile tissue of the genitals following the orgasm. — **de′tu·mes′cent** *adj.*

Deu·ca·li·on (dōō·kā′lē·ən, dyōō-) In Greek mythology, a son of Prometheus who, with his wife Pyrrha, was the only survivor of a deluge sent by Zeus to punish the world's wickedness: they renewed the human race by throwing stones behind them, those thrown by Deucalion becoming men, those by Pyrrha, women.

deuce[1] (dōōs, dyōōs) *n.* **1** Two; especially, a card or side of a die having two spots. **2** In tennis, a condition of the score when it is tied at 40 or at five games each and either side must win two successive points for the game or two successive games for the set. [< F *deux* < L *duo* two]

deuce[2] (dōōs, dyōōs) *n.* The devil; plague: a mild oath used with or without the article in exclamation, signifying disgust or surprise at an unpleasant occurrence. [Prob. < LG *de duus* the deuce (lowest throw at dice)]

deuce-ace (dōōs′ās′, dyōōs′-) *n.* A low throw at dice (ace and deuce); hence, poor luck.

deu·ced (dōō′sid, dyōō′-, dōōst, dyōōst) *adj.* Devilish; confounded; exceeding. —*adv.* Deucedly.

deu·ced·ly (dōō′sid·lē, dyōō′-) *adv.* Extremely; devilishly; confoundedly.

De·us (dē′əs, dā′ōōs) *n. Lat.* God.

de·us ex mach·i·na (dē′əs eks mak′ə·nə) **1** In classical drama, a god brought to the stage in a mechanical device to intervene in the action. **2** Any unexpected event, person, or circumstance worked into a play or novel to resolve a problem. **3** Contrived or providential salvation. [< L, a god from a machine]

De·us vo·bis·cum (dē′əs vō·bis′kəm) *Latin* God be with you.

De·us vult (dē′əs vult′) *Latin* God wills it: the battle cry of the First Crusade.

deu·ter·ag·o·nist (dōō′tər·ag′ə·nist, dyōō′-) *n.* The actor next in importance to the protagonist in the ancient Greek drama. [< Gk. *deuteragōnistēs* < *deuteros* second + *agōnistēs* actor]

deu·ter·a·no·pi·a (dōō′tər·ə·nō′pē·ə, dyōō′-) *n.* *Pathol.* An eye defect which results in an inability to see the color green. Also **deu′ter·a·nop′si·a** (-nop′sē·ə). [< DEUTER(O)- + Gk. *an-* without + *ops* eye]

deu·te·ric (dōō·tir′ik, dyōō-) *adj. Chem.* Pertaining to an acid containing deuterium.

deu·ter·ide (dōō′tə·rīd, dyōō′-) *n. Chem.* Any compound of deuterium with an element or radical.

deu·te·ri·um (dōō·tir′ē·əm, dyōō-) *n.* The isotope of hydrogen having twice the mass of ordinary hydrogen. Symbol, D or [2]H: also called *heavy hydrogen.* [< NL < Gk. *deuteros* second]

deuterium oxide Heavy water.

deutero- *combining form* Second; secondary: *deuterogamy.* Also, before vowels, **deuter-.** [< Gk. *deuteros* second]

deu·ter·o·ca·non·i·cal (dōō′tər·ō·kə·non′i·kəl, dyōō′-) *adj.* Pertaining to or constituting a second canon: applied to the books or parts of books of the Old and New Testament whose authenticity and inspiration were at first contested and afterward admitted by the Roman Catholic Church; in Protestant churches, the contested parts of the Old Testament are considered extracanonical. See APOCRYPHA.

deu·ter·og·a·mist (dōō′tər·og′ə·mist, dyōō′-) *n.* One who marries a second time.

deu·ter·og·a·my (dōō′tər·og′ə·mē, dyōō′-) *n.* A second marriage. [< DEUTERO- + Gk. *gamos* marriage]

Deu·ter·o-I·sa·iah (dōō′tər·ō·ī·zā′ə, dyōō′-) The presumed author of *Isaiah* xl-lxvi, a post-exilian Hebrew writer.

deu·ter·on (dōō′tər·on, dyōō′-) *n. Physics* The nucleus of a deuterium atom. [< NL < Gk., neut. sing. of *deuteros* second]

Deu·ter·on·o·my (dōō′tər·on′ə·mē, dyōō′-) The fifth book of the Pentateuch, which contains a second statement of the Mosaic law. [< Gk. *deuteronomion* < *deuteros* second + *nomos* law]

deu·ter·op·a·thy (dōō′tər·op′ə·thē, dyōō′-) *n.* *Med.* A disease associated with but secondary to another disease. [< DEUTERO- + -PATHY] — **deu·ter·o·path·ic** (dōō′tər·ō·path′ik, dyōō′-) *adj.*

deuto- *combining form* Deutero-.

deu·to·plasm (dōō′tə·plaz′əm, dyōō′-) *n. Biol.* The nutritive material formed within the cytoplasm of a cell; the food yolk of an ovum or egg cell. Also **deu·ter·o·plasm** (dōō′tər·ō·plaz′əm, dyōō′-). **—deu′to·plas′mic** or **·plas′tic** *adj.*

Deutsch·land (doich′länt) The German name for GERMANY.

Deutsch·land ü·ber al·les (doich′länt ü′bər ä′les) *German* Germany above all: a nationalist song and slogan.

deut·zi·a (dōōt′sē·ə, doit′-) *n.* Any of a genus (*Deutzia*) of ornamental shrubs having clusters of pink or white flowers. [< NL < Johann van der *Deutz,* 1743–1784, Dutch horticulturist]

de·va (dā′və) *n.* In Hindu mythology, a god or good spirit. Also **dev** (dāv). [< Skt.]

de Va·le·ra (dev′ə·lâr′ə, dā′və·lir′ə), **Éamon,** 1882–1975, Irish statesman born in the United States; prime minister 1937–48, 1951–54, 1957–59; president 1959–73.

de·val·u·ate (dē·val′yōō·āt) *v.t.* **·at·ed, ·at·ing 1** To reduce or annul the value or worth of. **2** To establish the value of (a currency) at some point below par. Also **de·val′ue. —de·val′u·a′tion** *n.*

De·va·na·ga·ri (dā′və·nä′gə·rē) *n.* The script of the educated classes in northern, western, and central India, in which Sanskrit and much of the literature of the modern Indic languages are written: also called *Nagari.*

dev·as·tate (dev′ə·stāt) *v.t.* **·tat·ed, ·tat·ing** To lay waste, as by war, fire, flood, etc.; destroy; ravage. [< L *devastatus,* pp. of *devastare* < *de-* completely + *vastare* lay waste < *vastus* waste] — **dev′as·tat′ing** *adj.* **—dev′as·tat′ing·ly** *adv.* — **dev′as·ta′tor** *n.*

dev·as·ta·tion (dev′ə·stā′shən) *n.* The act of devastating or condition of having been devastated; waste; desolation; ravage.

deve (dēv) *v.i. Brit. Dial.* To dive.

dev·el (dev′əl) *v.t. Scot.* To strike with a heavy blow. —*n.* A stunning blow.

de·vel·op (di·vel′əp) *v.t.* **1** To expand or bring out the potentialities, capabilities, etc., of; cause to come to completeness or perfection. **2** To expand; enlarge upon, as an idea. **3** To make more extensive or productive, as atomic power. **4** *Phot.* **a** To bring to view by means of a developer (the latent image) produced on a sensitized surface by means of light. **b** To subject (a plate or film) to a developer. **5** *Biol.* To cause to evolve to a higher stage, as in function or structure. **6** *Music* To elaborate on (a theme). **7** *Math.* To expand (an expression) in the form of a series. **8** *Geom.* To change the form of (a surface) as if by bending or unbending. **9** *Obs.* To disclose; reveal. —*v.i.* **10** To increase in capabilities, maturity, etc. **11** To advance from a lower to a higher state; grow; evolve. **12** To disclose itself; become apparent: The plot of a novel *develops.* Also **de·vel′ope.** See synonyms under AMPLIFY. [< F *développer* < *de-* away (< L *dis-*) + OF *voluper* fold] **—de·vel′op·a·ble** *adj.*

de·vel·op·er (di·vel′əp·ər) *n.* **1** One who or that which develops. **2** One who builds housing, shopping centers, etc., on a speculative basis. **3** *Phot.* A chemical bath or reagent used for making a latent image visible on a photographic plate.

de·vel·op·ment (di·vel′əp·mənt) *n.* **1** Gradual evolution or completion; also, the result of such an evolution or completion. **2** *Biol.* The series of changes by which an individual plant or animal passes from a lower to a higher state of being or from an embryonic condition to maturity. See synonyms under EDUCATION, PROGRESS. — **de·vel·op·men·tal** (di·vel′əp·men′təl) *adj.* — **de·vel′op·men′tal·ly** *adv.* **—de·vel′op·men′ta·ry** (-tər·ē) *adj.*

Dev·e·reux (dev′ə·rōō), **Robert** See ESSEX, EARL OF.

de·vest (di·vest′) *v.t.* **1** *Law* To take away, as a title or estate. **2** *Obs.* To remove vesture from; divest; strip. [< OF *devester, desvestir* < *de-* from (< L *dis-*) + *vestir* clothe < L *vestire* < *vestis* a garment]

De·vi (dā′vē) The Hindu goddess Shakti, consort of Siva. [< Skt., goddess]

de·vi·ate (dē′vē·āt) *v.* **·at·ed, ·at·ing** *v.i.* **1** To turn aside from a straight or appointed way or course; wander; diverge. **2** To differ, as in thought or belief. —*v.t.* **3** To cause to turn aside. See synonyms under BEND[1], WANDER. [< LL *deviatus,* pp. of *deviare* < *de-* from + *via* a road] — **de′vi·a′tor** *n.* **—de·vi·a·to·ry** (dē′vē·ə·tôr′ē, -tō′rē) *adj.*

de·vi·a·tion (dē′vē·ā′shən) *n.* **1** The act of deviating, or its result. **2** Variation or deflection from a straight line, from a prescribed course, or from a customary method or standard. **3** *Stat.* The difference between one value in a series of observations and the arithmetic mean of the series.

de·vi·a·tion·ism (dē′vē·ā′shən·iz′əm) *n.* In Communist ideology, departure from currently established party doctrine or policy. **—de′vi·a′tion·ist** *n.*

de·vice (di·vīs′) *n.* **1** Something invented and constructed for a special purpose; contrivance. **2** A plan or scheme; an artifice; stratagem; plot. **3** A fanciful design or pattern, as in embroidery or ornamentation. **4** A motto or emblem, as on a shield. **5** The act, state, or power of devising; inventive skill. **6** Expressed desire; inclination: now only in the phrase *left to one's own devices.* **7** *Obs.* Design or style of anything; cast of mind. **8** *Obs.* A spectacle; show; masque. See synonyms under ARTIFICE, DESIGN, PROJECT. [< OF *devis* intention, will < *diviser,* infl. by OF *devise* emblem, design. See DEVISE.]

dev·il (dev′əl) *n.* **1** *Sometimes cap.* In Jewish and Christian theology, the prince and ruler of the kingdom of evil; Satan. **2** Any subordinate evil spirit; a demon. **3** In Christian Science usage, Evil; a lie; error; neither corporeality nor mind; opposite of Truth; a belief in sin, sickness, and death; animal magnetism or hypnotism. **4** A wicked or malignant person. **5** A wretched fellow: poor *devil.* **6** A person of great energy, daring, or effrontery. **7** A machine for any of various purposes, as for cutting or tearing up rags. **8** A printer's apprentice or errand boy: also **printer's devil. 9** An expletive used profanely or humorously: with *the.* **10** In English law, a junior barrister who prepares a case for a senior, receiving little or no pay. **—between the devil and the deep blue sea** Between equally bad alternatives; in a dilemma. **—the devil to pay** Trouble to be expected as a consequence. **—to give the devil his due** To acknowledge the ability or success of even a bad or disliked person, antagonist, etc. —*v.t.* **dev·iled** or **·illed, dev·il·ing** or **·il·ling 1** To prepare for eating by seasoning highly and sometimes broiling or frying. **2** To make fiendish. **3** To cut up, as cloth, in a devil. **4** To annoy or harass excessively; tease. [OE *dēofol* < LL *diabolus* < Gk. *diabolos* a slanderer; later, the devil < *diaballein* slander < *dia-* across + *ballein* throw]

dev·il·fish (dev′əl·fish′) *n. pl.* **·fish** or **·fish·es 1** Any of a family *(Mobulidae)* of very large top-swimming rays having a pair of fins projecting from the head with which they sweep small prey into the mouth. Also called *devil ray, manta, manta ray.* **2** The octopus.

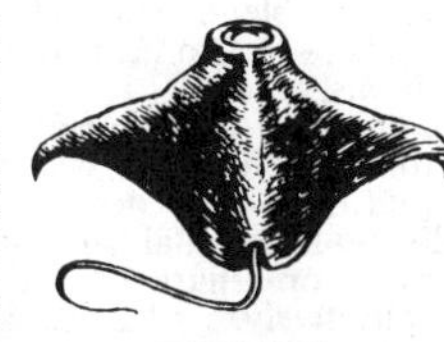
DEVILFISH
(Often 20 feet in breadth)

devil grass Any of the several spreading, injurious grasses.

dev·il·ish (dev′əl·ish, dev′lish) *adj.* **1** Having the qualities of the devil; diabolical; malicious. **2** *Colloq.* Excessive; enormous. —*adv. Colloq.* Excessively; very. See synonyms under INFERNAL. **—dev′il·ish·ly** *adv.* **—dev′il·ish·ness** *n.*

dev·il·kin (dev′əl·kin) *n.* An imp; a little devil.

dev·il-may-care (dev′əl·mā·kâr′) *adj.* Careless; reckless; rollicking.

dev·il·ment (dev′əl·mənt) *n.* Mischief; impish action or tricks.

dev·il-on-two-sticks (dev′əl·on·to͞o′stiks′) *n.* The spool or top used in the game diabolo.

dev·il·ry (dev′əl·rē) *n. pl.* **·ries 1** Malicious mischief; deviltry. **2** Evil magic or art; demonology.

devil's advocate 1 A Roman Catholic official whose duty is to raise objections to a candidate for beatification or canonization. **2** One who argues perversely or for a bad cause.

dev·il's-darn·ing-nee·dle (dev′əlz·där′ning·nēd′l) *n.* **1** A dragonfly. **2** The Venus's-comb. Also **dev′il-darn′ing-nee′dle.**

dev·il's-food cake (dev′əlz·fo͞od′) A rich, reddish-brown chocolate cake.

Devil's Island A rocky island off the Atlantic coast of northern French Guiana; formerly a French penal colony: French *Île du Diable.*

devil's tattoo A drumming or pounding with the feet or hands.

dev·il·try (dev′əl·trē) *n. pl.* **·tries 1** Wanton and malicious mischief, or the spirit inciting it **2** Devilry.

dev·il·wood (dev′əl·wo͝od′) *n.* The American olive *(Osmanthus americanus),* a small tree of the southern Atlantic states, with a fine-grained, hard wood.

de·vi·ous (dē′vē·əs) *adj.* **1** Winding or leading away from a straight course; rambling. **2** Straying from the way of duty. See synonyms under IRREGULAR. [< L *devius* < *de-* from + *via* way] **—de′vi·ous·ly** *adv.* **—de′vi·ous·ness** *n.*

de·vis·a·ble (di·vī′zə·bəl) *adj.* **1** *Law* That can be devised, or given by will. **2** That can be contrived or invented.

de·vi·sal (di·vī′zəl) *n.* The act of contriving or of bequeathing; a devising.

de·vise (di·vīz′) *v.* **·vised, ·vis·ing** *v.t.* **1** To form in the mind; invent; contrive; plan. **2** *Law* To transmit (real estate) by will. **3** *Obs.* To separate; distribute. **4** *Obs.* To imagine; guess. —*v.i.* **5** To form a plan. —*n. Law* **1** A gift of lands by will. **2** The act of bequeathing lands. **3** A will, or a clause in a will conveying real estate. [< OF *deviser* divide, distinguish, contrive < L *dividere* < *dis-* apart + *videre* see] **—de·vis′er** *n.*

de·vi·see (di·vī′zē′, dev′ə·zē′) *n. Law* The person to whom a devise is made.

de·vi·sor (di·vī′zər, -zôr) *n. Law* One who gives by will.

de·vi·tal·ize (dē·vī′təl·īz) *v.t.* **·ized, ·iz·ing 1** To deprive of vital power or of the power to sustain life. **2** To destroy the vitality of; make weak. **—de·vi′tal·i·za′tion** *n.*

de·vi·ta·min·ize (dē′vī′tə·min·īz′) *v.t.* **·ized, ·iz·ing** To deprive of vitamins.

de·vit·ri·fi·ca·tion (dē·vit′rə·fi·kā′shən) *n.* The conversion of glassy to crystalline or lithoidal texture by slow crystallization after solidification.

de·vit·ri·fy (dē·vit′rə·fī) *v.t.* **·fied, ·fy·ing 1** To remove the glassy quality of. **2** To render opaque and hard like porcelain by long-continued great heat: said of glass. [< DE- from + VITRIFY]

de·vo·cal·ize (dē·vō′kəl·īz) *v.t.* **·ized, ·iz·ing** *Phonet.* To deprive of voice or of vocal quality. **—de·vo′cal·i·za′tion** *n.*

de·voiced (dē·voist′) *adj. Phonet.* Unvoiced.

de·void (di·void′) *adj.* Not possessing; destitute: with *of.* [ME *devoided,* pp. of obs. *devoid* empty out < OF *devoidier* < *de-* down (< L *de-*) + *voidier* VOID]

de·voir (də·vwär′, dev′wär) *n.* **1** Service or duty. **2** *pl.* Respectful attentions: to pay one's *devoirs* to. [< OF *deveir* < L *debere* owe]

dev·o·lu·tion (dev′ə·lo͞o′shən) *n.* **1** The act of delivering to another; a passing to a successor. **2** *Biol.* **a** A Degeneration: opposed to *evolution.* **b** Involution. **c** Catabolism. **3** The delegation or surrender of the powers of a central government to local authorities. [< Med. L *devolutio, -onis* < *devolvere.* See DEVOLVE.]

de·volve (di·volv′) *v.* **·volved, ·volv·ing** *v.t.* **1** To cause to pass to a successor or substitute. **2** *Archaic* To roll down. —*v.i.* **3** To pass from a possessor to a successor or substitute: with *to, on,* or *upon.* [< L *devolvere* < *de-* down + *volvere* roll] **—de·volve′ment** *n.*

Dev·on (dev′ən) *n.* A valuable breed of small, hardy cattle originating in Devon, England.

Dev·on (dev′ən) A county in SW England; 2,611 square miles; county seat, Exeter. Also **Dev′on·shire** (-shir).

De·vo·ni·an (di·vō′nē·ən) *adj.* **1** Of or pertaining to Devon or Devonshire in England. **2** *Geol.* Of or pertaining to the Devonian period. —*n.* **1** A person born or residing in Devonshire. **2** The Devonian period or its characteristic rock system.

Devonian period *Geol.* The fourth of the periods in the Paleozoic era, following the Silurian, and succeeded by the Mississippian, or Lower Carboniferous, period. See chart under GEOLOGY. [from *Devon,* England; with ref. to rocks and fossils first found there]

Dev·on Island (dev′ən) An island of the Northwest Territories, Canada, in Baffin Bay; 21,606 square miles.

de·vote (di·vōt′) *v.t.* **·vot·ed, ·vot·ing 1** To give or apply (attention, time, or oneself) completely to some activity, purpose, etc. **2** To set apart; dedicate; consecrate. **3** *Obs.* To doom. [< L *devotus,* pp. of *devovere* < *de-* away + *vovere* vow] **—de·vote′ment** *n.*

de·vot·ed (di·vō′tid) *adj.* **1** Feeling or showing devotion; ardent; zealous; devout. **2** Set apart, as by a vow; consecrated. **3** *Obs.* Doomed. See synonyms under ADDICTED, FAITHFUL, HOLY. **—de·vot′ed·ly** *adv.* **—de·vot′ed·ness** *n.*

dev·o·tee (dev′ə·tē′) *n.* One zealously devoted, especially to religious observances; a votary; zealot. **—dev′o·tee′ism** *n.*

de·vo·tion (di·vō′shən) *n.* **1** The state of being devoted, as to religious faith or duty; zeal. **2** Strong attachment or affection expressing itself in earnest service. **3** *Usually pl.* An act of worship; prayer. **4** The act of devoting. See synonyms under ALLEGIANCE, ATTACHMENT, ENTHUSIASM, FIDELITY, FRIENDSHIP, LOVE, PRAYER, RELIGION. **—de·vo′tion·al** *adj.* **—de·vo′tion·al·ism** *n.* **—de·vo′tion·al·ly** *adv.*

De Vo·to (də vō′tō), **Bernard Augustine,** 1897–1956, U.S. author and critic.

de·vour (di·vour′) *v.t.* **1** To eat up greedily and voraciously. **2** To destroy; waste: The disease *devoured* him. **3** To take in greedily with the senses: He *devoured* the book. **4** To engross the attention of. **5** To engulf; absorb. [< OF *devorer* < L *devorare* < *de-* down + *vorare* gulp, swallow]. **—de·vour′er** *n.* **—de·vour′ing** *adj.* **—de·vour′ing·ly** *adv.* **—de·vour′ing·ness** *n.*

de·vout (di·vout′) *adj.* **1** Earnestly religious; pious; reverent. **2** Warmly devoted; heart-felt; sincere. **3** Containing or expressing devotion, especially religious devotion. [< OF *devot* < L *devotus.* See DEVOTE.] **—de·vout′ly** *adv.* **—de·vout′ness** *n.*

De Vries (də vrēs′), **Hugo,** 1848–1935, Dutch botanist.

dew (do͞o, dyo͞o) *n.* **1** Moisture condensed from the atmosphere in small drops upon the cool surfaces of plants and other bodies. **2** Anything moist, gentle, or refreshing as dew or suggesting the freshness of dewy morning: the *dew* of sleep, the *dew* of youth. **3** Moisture generally, especially that which appears in minute drops, as perspiration, tears, etc. —*v.t.* To wet with or as with dew; bedew. ◆ Homophone: *due.* [OE *dēaw*] **—dew′less** *adj.*

de·wan (di·wän′, -wôn′) *n.* In India and Moslem countries, any of various government officials: also spelled *deewan, diwan.* [< Persian *dīwān.* See DIVAN.]

Dew·ar (dyo͞o′ər), **Sir James,** 1842–1923, Scottish chemist; invented the **Dewar vessel** or **flask,** a double-walled glass vessel for holding liquid air, etc.

dew·ber·ry (do͞o′ber′ē, -bər·ē, dyo͞o′-) *n. pl.* **·ries 1** The fruit of the low blackberry (genus *Rubus*). **2** The plant bearing it.

dew·claw (do͞o′klô′, dyo͞o′-) *n.* **1** A rudimentary toe in some dogs. **2** The false rudimentary hoof above the true hoof of hogs, deer, etc. **—dew′clawed′** *adj.*

dew·drop (do͞o′drop′, dyo͞o′-) *n.* A drop of dew.

De Wet (də vet′), **Christian Rudolph,** 1854–1922, Boer general and statesman.

Dew·ey (do͞o′ē, dyo͞o′ē), **George,** 1837–1917, U.S. admiral. **—John,** 1859–1952, U.S. philosopher, psychologist, and educator. **—Melvil,** 1851–1931, U.S. librarian. **—Thomas Edmund,** 1902–1971, governor of New York 1943–54.

dew·fall (do͞o′fôl′, dyo͞o′-) *n.* **1** The formation of dew. **2** The time of evening when dew appears.

De Witt (di wit′), **Cornelius,** 1623–72, Dutch statesman and naval officer. **—Jan,** 1625–1672, Dutch statesman; brother of the preceding.

dew·lap (do͞o′lap′, dyo͞o′-) *n.* **1** The pendulous skin under the throat of cattle. **2** Something likened to a dewlap, as the wattles of a turkey, or the flaccid skin sometimes seen under the chin of an aged person. [ME *dewlappe* < *dew,* origin uncertain + *lappe,* OE *læppe* lobe, fold] **—dew′lapped′** *adj.*

Dew line A chain of radar stations in North America at about the 70th parallel, maintained by the United States in cooperation with Canada. Also DEW line. [< *D(istant) E(arly) W(arning)*]

dew point *Meteorol.* **1** The temperature at which dew forms or condensation occurs. **2** The temperature at which a given mass of air will have a relative humidity of 100.

dew pond *Brit.* A pond especially built to hold water in dry weather: replenished by the condensation of dew and mist.

Dews·bur·y (dyo͞oz′bər·ē) A county borough of Southern Yorkshire, England.

dew·worm (do͞o′wûrm′, dyo͞o′-) *n. Canadian* A nightcrawler.

dew·y (do͞o′ē, dyo͞o′ē) *adj.* **dew·i·er, dew·i·est 1** Moist, as with dew. **2** Of, like, or yielding dew. **3** Appearing as if covered with dewdrops. **—dew′i·ness** *n.*

dex·ter (dek′stər) *adj.* **1** Right-hand; right. **2** *Her.* On the wearer's right, the spectator's left. **3** Auspicious; favorable; propitious. [< L, right]

Dex·ter (dek′stər) A masculine personal name.

dex·ter·i·ty (dek·ster′ə·tē) *n.* **1** Readiness and skill in using the hands; expertness. **2** Mental quickness, adroitness, or skill. [< L *dexteritas, -tatis* skill, aptness < *dexter* on the right]

Synonyms: adroitness, aptitude, cleverness, expertness, readiness, skill. *Adroitness* and *dexterity* might each be rendered "right-handedness"; but *adroitness* carries more of the idea of eluding, parrying, or checking some hostile movement, or taking advantage of another in controversy; *dexterity* conveys the idea of doing, accomplishing something readily and well, without reference to any action of others. We speak of *adroitness* in fencing, boxing, or debate; of *dexterity* in horsemanship, in the use of tools, weapons, etc. *Aptitude* is a natural *readiness,* which by practice may be developed into *dexterity. Skill* is more exact to line, rule, and method than *dexterity. Dexterity* can not be communicated; *skill* to a very great extent can be imparted. Compare ABILITY, ADDRESS, INGENUITY, POWER.

dex·ter·ous (dek′strəs, -stər·əs) *adj.* **1** Possessing dexterity; skilful or adroit; artful. **2** Done with dexterity. Also **dex·trous** (dek′-

strəs). See synonyms under CLEVER, GOOD, HAPPY. —**dex′ter·ous·ly, dex′trous·ly** *adv.* —**dex′ter·ous·ness, dex′trous·ness** *n.*

dex·trad (dek′strad) *adv. Anat.* On or toward the right hand or side. [<L *dexter* right + *ad* to]

dex·tral (dek′strəl) *adj.* **1** Of, pertaining to, or situated on the right side; right-hand or right-handed. **2** Propitious; favorable: said of omens. —**dex′tral·ly** *adv.* —**dex·tral·i·ty** (dek·stral′ə·tē) *n.*

dex·tran (dek′stran) *n. Biochem.* A white, gumlike substance produced by bacterial action in milk, molasses, beet juice, etc.: used as a substitute for blood plasma in the treatment of severe burns and shock. [<DEXTR(O)- + -AN(E)]

dex·trin (dek′strin) *n. Biochem.* An amorphous, colorless, water-soluble, dextrorotatory carbohydrate formed by the action of acids, heat, or diastase on starch: used as a substitute for gum arabic. Also **dex·trine** (dek′strin, -strēn). [<DEXTR(O)- + IN]

dextro– *combining form* Turned or turning to the right: used especially in chemistry and physics, as in *dextrorotatory.* Also, before vowels, **dextr–.** [<L *dexter* right]

dex·tro·ro·ta·tion (dek′strə·rō·tā′shən) *n. Optics* Clockwise rotation of the plane of polarization of light.

dex·tro·ro·ta·to·ry (dek′strə·rō′tə·tôr′ē, -tō′·rē) *adj. Chem.* Causing the plane of polarization of light to rotate to the right or clockwise: said of certain crystals and compounds: opposed to *levorotatory.* Also **dex·tro·gy·rate** (dek′strə·jī′rāt), **dex·tro·ro·ta·ry** (dek′strə·rō′·tər·ē).

dex·trorse (dek′strôrs, dek·strôrs′) *adj. Bot.* Rising spirally toward the right: opposed to *sinistrorse*; said of the morning-glory. Also **dex·tror′sal.** [<L *dextrorsum, dextrovorsum* <*dexter* right + *vertere* turn] —**dex′·trorse·ly** *adv.*

dex·trose (dek′strōs) *n. Biochem.* The dextrorotatory form of glucose. Also called **dex·tro·glu·cose** (dek′strə·glōō′kōs) [<DEXTR(O)- + (GLUC)OSE]

dey (dā) *n.* **1** The title of a governor of Algiers before the French conquest of 1830. **2** Formerly, the title of a ruler of Tunis or Tripoli. [<F <Turkish *dāī,* orig. uncle]

Dezh·nev (dyezh′nif), **Cape** The northeasternmost point of Asia, on Chukchi Peninsula in the Bering Strait: also *East Cape.*

de·zinc·i·fi·ca·tion (dē·zing′kə·fi·kā′shən) *n. Metall.* The removal of zinc by corrosive action from the surface of an alloy of zinc and copper.

Dhah·ran (dä·rän′) An oil town in eastern Saudi Arabia: also *Zahran.*

dhak (däk, dôk) *n.* A tree of India and Burma (*Butea monosperma*) having trifoliolate leaves and bright orange-red flowers. [<Hind.]

dhar·ma (där′mə, dûr′-) *n.* **1** In Hinduism and Buddhism, right behavior; conformity to law; hence, truth and righteousness. **2** In Buddhism, the law which, together with Buddha and Sangha, forms the three Ratnas or treasures of Buddhism. [<Skt., law]

Dhar·ma (där′mə, dûr′-) In Hindu mythology, a wise man whose numerous offspring personify the virtues and certain religious practices.

dhar·na (där′nə, dûr′-) *n.* In India, a method of claiming justice by refusing food or starving to death while sitting before the gate or door of the oppressor, to the end that the death shall be upon the oppressor's head. Also **dhur′na.** [<Hind. *dharnā*]

Dhau·la·gi·ri (dou′lə·gir′ē) A peak in the central Nepal Himalayas; 26,810 feet.

Dhi·ban (thē·bän′, dē-) A village in central Jordan where the Moabite Stone was discovered. Also **Di·ban′.**

dhole (dōl) *n.* A red-coated wild dog of SE Asia (genus *Cuon*) that hunts in packs and attacks even large game. [Origin uncertain]

DHOLE (About 30 inches high at the shoulder)

dho·ti (dō′tē) *n. pl.* **·tis** A loincloth worn by Hindu men; also the cloth for this. Also **dhoo·ti** (dōō′tē). [<Hind. *dhotī* a loincloth]

dhour·ra, dhoo·ra (dōōr′ə) See DURRA.

dhow (dou) *n.* An Arabian coasting vessel with a sharp prow and high poop, usually having one mast and lateen rigging. [<Arabic *dāw*]

DHOW

dhu (dōō) *adj.* Black: used in Celtic names of places and persons: Roderick *Dhu* (black Roderick). [<Irish *dubh* black]

di–[1] Reduced var. of DIS–[1].

di–[2] *prefix* **1** Twice; double: *digraph.* **2** *Chem.* Containing two atoms, molecules, radicals, etc.: *dichloride.* Also, before *s, dis–,* as in *dissyllable.* [Gk. *di-* <*dis* twice]

dia– *prefix* Through; across; between: *diagonal.* Also, before vowels, **di–.** [<Gk. *dia-* through]

di·a·base (dī′ə·bās) *n. Geol.* A granular igneous rock, composed essentially of plagioclase, and characterized by the feldspar having crystallized before the augite: sometimes called *dolerite.* [<Gk. *diabasis* a crossing over <*dia-* across + *bainein* go] —**di′a·ba′sic** *adj.*

di·a·be·tes (dī′ə·bē′tis, -tēz) *n. Pathol.* A disease associated with inadequate production of insulin by the pancreas and ordinarily characterized by excessive urinary secretion containing an abnormal quantity of sugar. In the form distinguished as **diabetes mel·li·tus** (mə·lī′təs), there is also emaciation with excessive hunger and thirst. [<NL <Gk. *diabētēs* a passer through <*dia-* through + *bainein* go]

di·a·bet·ic (dī′ə·bet′ik, -bē′tik) *adj. Med.* Of, pertaining to, or affected by diabetes. Also **di′a·bet′i·cal.** —*n.* One who has diabetes.

di·a·ble·rie (dē·ä′blə·rē, *Fr.* dyȧ·blə·rē′) *n.* **1** Demonology. **2** Fantastic and perverse behavior; deviltry; impishness. **3** Sorcery. Also **di·a′ble·ry.** [<F <*diable* devil]

Di·a·blo Crater (dē·ä′blō) See METEOR CRATER.

di·a·bol·ic (dī′ə·bol′ik) *adj.* Of, pertaining to, or like the devil; satanic; fiendish; infernal. Also **di′a·bol′i·cal.** [<Gk. *diabolikos* <*diabolos.* See DEVIL.] —**di′a·bol′i·cal·ly** *adv.* —**di′a·bol′i·cal·ness** *n.*

di·ab·o·lism (dī·ab′ə·liz′əm) *n.* **1** Conduct befitting or inspired by the devil; devilishness. **2** Possession by the devil or devils. **3** In occultism, the conjuration or raising of evil spirits; sorcery. **4** A system of belief or doctrine in which devils are worshiped. **5** A devilish nature or disposition. —**di·ab′·o·list** *n.*

di·ab·o·lize (dī·ab′ə·līz) *v.t.* **·lized, ·liz·ing** **1** To render devilish or diabolical. **2** To bring under diabolical influence. **3** To represent as devilish.

di·ab·o·lo (dē·ab′ə·lō) *n.* A game played with a spool or top (called *devil-on-two-sticks*) which is spun on a cord tied to two sticks, thrown into the air, and caught again on the cord. [<Ital. <LL *diabolus.* See DEVIL.]

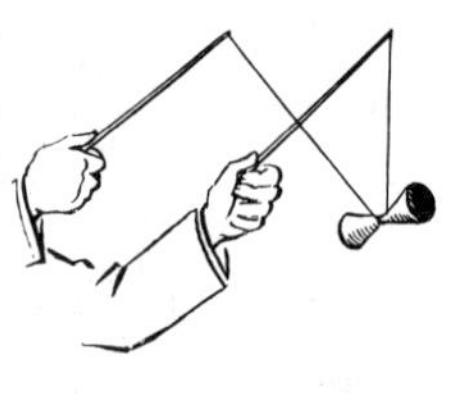

DIABOLO

di·a·caus·tic (dī′ə·kôs′tik) *adj. Optics* Denoting a caustic curve formed by refracted rays: opposed to *catacaustic.* —*n.* **1** A diacaustic curve. **2** Formerly, a burning glass for cauterization. [<DIA- + CAUSTIC (def. 3)]

di·ac·e·tyl·mor·phine (dī·as′ə·təl·môr′fēn) *n.* Heroin.

di·a·chron·ic (dī′ə·kron′ik) *adj.* **1** Existing through time. **2** *Ling.* Pertaining to the study of the historical development of a language in any of its aspects. See SYNCHRONIC.

di·ach·y·lon (dī·ak′ə·lon) *n. Med.* **1** A plaster formed by combining lead oxide, olive oil, and water; lead or litharge plaster. **2** A mixture of mucilaginous vegetable juices, gums, etc., formerly used in making plasters and salves. Also **diachylon plaster, di·ach′·y·lum** (-ə·ləm). [<Med. L *diachylum* <L *diachylon* <Gk. *dia chylōn* made of juices; orig. referring to an ointment made of vegetable juices]

di·ac·id (dī·as′id) *adj. Chem.* **1** Capable of combining with two molecules of a monoacid or with one of a diacid: said of bases and alcohols. **2** Having two hydrogen atoms replaceable by radicals or atoms: said of acids. —*n.* An acid containing two hydrogen atoms.

di·ac·o·nal (dī·ak′ə·nəl) *adj.* Of, pertaining to, or befitting a deacon or the diaconate. [<LL *diaconus* deacon]

di·ac·o·nate (dī·ak′ə·nit, -nāt) *n.* **1** The office, rank, or tenure of a deacon. **2** Deacons collectively. [<LL *diaconatus*]

di·a·crit·ic (dī′ə·krit′ik) *n.* **1** A mark, point, or sign attached to a letter to indicate its exact phonetic value, or to distinguish it from another letter: also **diacritical mark.** For a complete listing of the diacritics used in this book, see page xx. **2** A differential diagnosis. —*adj.* Of or pertaining to a diacritic. [<Gk. *diakritikos* distinguishing <*diakrinein* <*dia-* between + *krinein* distinguish]

di·a·crit·i·cal (dī′ə·krit′i·kəl) *adj.* **1** Marking a difference; distinguishing; distinctive. **2** Indicating certain variations of sounds or of form. **3** *Electr.* Denoting a current sufficient to magnetize a solenoid core to half-saturation. —**di′a·crit′i·cal·ly** *adv.*

di·ac·tin·ic (dī′ak·tin′ik) *adj.* Capable of transmitting actinic or chemical rays: said of a body or substance. —**di·ac′tin·ism** *n.*

di·a·del·phous (dī′ə·del′fəs) *adj. Bot.* Having the stamens combined by their filaments so as to form two sets or bundles. Also **di′a·del′phi·an.** [<Gk. *di-* two + *adelphos* brother]

DIADELPHOUS STAMENS Common in papilionaceous flowers in this arrangement.

di·a·dem (dī′ə·dem) *n.* **1** A symbol of royalty worn upon the head; a crown. **2** Regal power; sovereignty. —*v.t.* To decorate with or as with a diadem; crown. [<OF *diademe* <L *diadema* <Gk. *diadēma* <*dia-* across + *deein* bind]

di·aer·e·sis (dī·er′ə·sis), **di·ae·ret·ic** (dī′ə·ret′ik) See DIERESIS, etc.

di·a·ge·ot·ro·pism (dī′ə·jē·ot′rə·piz′əm) *n. Bot.* Transverse or oblique geotropism: an arrangement of plant organs at right angles to the direction of gravitation. [<DIA- + GEOTROPISM] —**di·a·ge·o·trop·ic** (dī′ə·jē′ə·trop′ik, -trō′pik) *adj.*

Dia·ghi·lev (dyä′gi·lef), **Sergei Pavlovich,** 1872–1929, Russian ballet producer.

di·ag·nose (dī′əg·nōs′, -nōz′) *v.* **·nosed, ·nos·ing** *v.t.* To examine or distinguish by diagnosis. —*v.i.* To make a diagnosis of a person, disease, etc.

di·ag·no·sis (dī′əg·nō′sis) *n.* **1** *Med.* **a** The art or act of discriminating between diseases and of distinguishing them by their characteristic symptoms. **b** A summary of symptoms and the conclusion arrived at. **2** *Biol.* Scientific discrimination between similar or related things or conditions for the purpose of accurate classification. [<Gk. *diagnōsis* <*diagignōskein* <*dia-* between + *gignōskein* know] —**di·ag·nos·tic** (dī′əg·nos′tik) *adj.* —**di′ag·nos′ti·cal·ly** *adv.*

di·ag·nos·ti·cian (dī′əg·nos·tish′ən) *n.* One who is versed in diagnosis.

di·ag·nos·tics (dī′əg·nos′tiks) *n.* The science or recognized principles of diagnosis.

di·ag·o·nal (dī·ag′ə·nəl) *adj.* **1** Crossing obliquely; oblique. **2** Marked by oblique lines or the like. **3** *Geom.* **a** Joining two non-adjacent or reentering angles of a figure: a *diagonal* line. **b** Joining, as a plane, two non-adjacent edges of a solid. —*n.* **1** *Geom.* A straight line or plane passing from one angle, as of a square, to any other angle not adjacent. **2** A fabric woven with diagonal ridges or lines: also **diagonal cloth.** **3** Anything running diagonally. [<L *diagonalis* <*diagonios* <*dia-* across + *gonia* angle] —**di·ag′o·nal·ly** *adv.*

Di·ag·o·ras (dī·ag′ə·rəs) Greek poet and philosopher of the fifth century B.C.: called "the Atheist."

di·a·gram (dī′ə·gram) *n.* **1** A line drawing, mechanical plan, or outline, as distinguished from a perspective drawing. **2** A rough projection, map, chart, etc. **3** A figure drawn to aid in demonstrating a geometrical proposition or to illustrate geometrical relations. **4** An outline figure intended to represent any object or area, or to show the relation between parts or places, or to illustrate the value or relations of quantities, forces, etc. **5** A graph. —*v.t.* **·gramed** or **·grammed, ·gram·ing** or **·gram·ming** **1** To represent by diagram. **2** To illustrate by a diagram. [<Gk. *diagramma* <*dia-* across + *graphein* write] —**di·a·gram·mat·ic** (dī′ə·grə·mat′ik) or **·i·cal** *adj.* —**di′a·gram·mat′i·cal·ly** *adv.*

diagram factor *Mech.* In the cylinder of a steam engine, the ratio between the actual average pressure and the ideal pressure as shown on an indicator diagram.

di·a·graph (dī′ə·graf, -gräf) *n.* A protractor and scale combined for drawing diagrams. [<DIA- + -GRAPH]

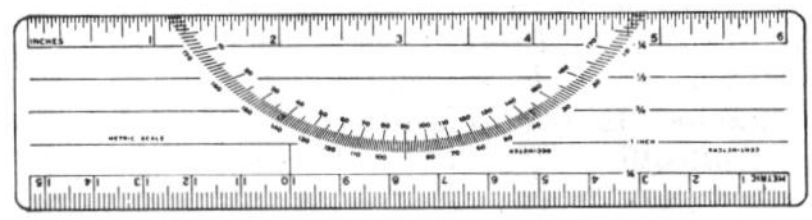

DIAGRAPH

di·a·he·li·ot·ro·pism (dī′ə·hē′lē·ot′rə·piz′əm) *n.* *Bot.* A turning of plant organs so as to assume a position transverse to the light; transverse heliotropism. —**di·a·he·li·o·trop·ic** (dī′ə·hē′lē·ə·trop′ik, -trō′pik) *adj.*

di·al (dī′əl, dīl) *n.* **1** Any graduated circular plate or face, as of a watch, clock, gage, mariner's compass, or radio receiving set. **2** A plate bearing letters and numbers, used to make connections in an automatic telephone system. **3** A device for indicating time by means of the shadow of a gnomon or style thrown upon a graduated plate; a sundial. **4** A compass; especially, a miner's compass for underground surveying. **5** *Obs.* Any timepiece. —*v.t.* & *v.i.* **di·aled** or **di·alled, di·al·ing** or **di·al·ling** **1** To measure or survey with a dial. **2** To turn or adjust a dial; indicate on a dial. **3** To call by means of a telephone. **4** To adjust a radio or television set to (a station, program, etc.). [<Med. L *dialis* daily <L *dies* day] —**di′al·er, di′al·ler** *n.* —**di′al·ist, di′al·list** *n.*

di·a·lect (dī′ə·lekt) *n.* **1** A variety of speech distinguished from the standard or literary language by variations of idiom, vocabulary, phonology, and morphology peculiar to a particular geographical location: the Southern *dialect* of American English. **2** A manner of speech adopted by the members of a class, trade, or profession; jargon; cant: the *dialect* of the cultured. **3** An imperfect use of the standard language by those to whom another language is native. **4** A language developed from a root language, retaining recognizable elements of the parent but having distinctive vocabulary, pronunciation, forms, and idiom; a linguistic branch: The Romance languages are *dialects* of Latin. See synonyms under LANGUAGE. [<MF *dialecte* <L *dialectus* <Gk. *dialektos* discourse, way of speaking <*dialegesthai* <*dia-* across + *legesthai* speak]

di·a·lec·tal (dī′ə·lek′təl) *adj.* Of or characterized by a dialect. Abbr. *dial.*

dialect atlas A collection of linguistic maps marking areas showing a uniformity of dialectal characteristics of pronunciation, vocabulary, syntax, etc.: also called *linguistic atlas.*

di·a·lec·tic (dī′ə·lek′tik) *adj.* **1** Formerly, dialectal. **2** Pertaining to dialectics; logical; argumentative. Also **di′a·lec′ti·cal.** —*n.* **1** *Usually pl.* The art or practice of examining logically, as by a method of question and answer. **2** A specific mode of argument. [<OF *dialectique* <L *dialectica* <Gk. *dialektika (technē)* (art) of discourse <*dialektos.* See DIALECT.]

dialectical materialism A socio-economic theory introduced by Karl Marx and Friedrich Engels, according to which history and the forms of society are interpreted as the result of conflicts between social classes arising from their relations to the means of production.

di·a·lec·ti·cian (dī′ə·lek·tish′ən) *n.* **1** A logician. **2** One who specializes in the study of dialects.

di·a·lec·ti·cism (dī′ə·lek′tə·siz′əm) *n.* **1** The character or nature distinguishing a dialect. **2** A dialectal word or peculiarity. **3** The practice of dialectics.

di·a·lec·tol·o·gy (dī′ə·lek·tol′ə·jē) *n.* The study of dialects.

di·al·ing (dī′əl·ing) *n.* **1** The act of using a dial. **2** The measurement of time by sundials; the art of making sundials. **3** Underground surveying with a dial, especially in mines. Also **di′al·ling.**

di·al·lage (dī′ə·lij) *n.* A brown, gray, or green, thin-foliated variety of pyroxene, crystallizing in the monoclinic system. [<F <Gk. *diallagē* an interchange <*dia-* across + *allassein* change]

di·al·o·gism (dī·al′ə·jiz′əm) *n.* **1** A dialogue or discussion; especially, a discourse with oneself. **2** *Logic* An inference with a single premise and disjunctive conclusion.

di·al·o·gist (dī·al′ə·jist) *n.* One who writes or takes part in a dialogue. —**di·a·lo·gis·tic** (dī′ə·lō·jis′tik) or **·ti·cal** *adj.*

di·al·o·gize (dī·al′ə·jīz) *v.i.* **·gized, ·giz·ing** To carry on a dialogue.

di·a·logue (dī′ə·lôg, -log) *n.* **1** A conversation in which two or more take part. **2** A literary work in which two or more characters are represented as conversing. **3** An exchange of opinions or ideas; free interchange of different points of view; discussion: to propose a *dialogue* among the Christian churches. See synonyms under CONVERSATION. —*v.* **·logued, ·logu·ing** *v.t.* To express in dialogue form. —*v.i.* To carry on a dialogue. Also **di′a·log.** [<F <*dialogus* <Gk. *dialogos* <*dialegesthai.* Related to DIALECT.] —**di′a·logu′er, di′a·log′er** *n.* —**di′a·log′ic** (dī′ə·loj′ik) or **·i·cal** *adj.*

dial telephone A telephone on which a required number may be called by manipulation of a dial bearing letters and numbers.

dial tone The low, steady, humming tone indicating to the user of a dial telephone that a call may be put through, or that a connection has been broken. Compare BUSY SIGNAL.

di·al·y·sis (dī·al′ə·sis) *n.* *pl.* **·ses** (-sēz) **1** *Bot.* Separation of parts previously or normally joined together. **2** *Chem.* The separating of solutions of mixed substances of unequal diffusibility by means of moist membranes or septa; specifically, the separation of a colloid from a substance in true solution. See OSMOSIS. [<Gk. *dialysis* <*dialyein* <*dia-* completely + *lyein* loosen] —**di·a·lyt·ic** (dī′ə·lit′ik) *adj.* —**di′a·lyt′i·cal·ly** *adv.*

di·a·lyze (dī′ə·līz) *v.t.* **·lyzed, ·lyz·ing** *Chem.* To subject to or prepare by dialysis; separate by dialysis.

di·a·lyz·er (dī′ə·lī′zər) *n.* *Chem.* An apparatus used for dialysis, especially a membranous septum stretched over a gutta-percha ring.

di·a·mag·net·ic (dī′ə·mag·net′ik) *adj.* *Physics* **1** Pertaining to or designating the property of substances tending to lie at right angles to the poles of a magnet. **2** Having a negative magnetic susceptibility, or a permeability less than that of a vacuum, as bismuth or copper. —*n.* A substance that possesses such properties. —**di′a·mag′net·ism** *n.* —**di′a·mag·net′·i·cal·ly** *adv.*

Di·a·man·ti·na (dē′ə·mañ·tē′nə) A city in eastern Brazil. Formerly **Te·ju·co** (te·hōō′kō).

Di·a·man·ti·na River (dē′ə·mən·tē′nə) A river in east central Australia, flowing 468 mi. SW.

di·am·e·ter (dī·am′ə·tər) *n.* **1** A straight line passing through the center of a figure or body and terminated at the boundaries thereof. **2** The length of such a line. **3** The thickness of an object as measured by such a line. [<OF *diametre* <L *diametrus* <Gk. *diametros* <*dia-* through + *metron* measure]

di·a·met·ri·cal (dī′ə·met′ri·kəl) *adj.* **1** Of or pertaining to a diameter; coinciding with a diameter: also **di·am·e·tral** (dī·am′ə·trəl). **2** Of or pertaining to the ends of a diameter; directly opposite, and as far removed as possible: also **di′a·met′ric.**

di·a·met·ri·cal·ly (dī′ə·met′rik·lē) *adv.* **1** In the manner of a diameter. **2** Irreconcilably: *diametrically* opposed.

di·am·ine (dī·am′ēn, -in, dī′ə·mēn, -min) *n.* *Chem.* Any of a group of compounds containing two amino radicals; a double amine. Also **di·am·in** (dī·am′in, dī′ə·min).

dia·mond (dī′mənd, dī′ə-) *n.* **1** A mineral of great hardness and refractive power, consisting of carbon crystallized in the isometric system under great pressure and temperature. When pure it is a valuable gem with a beautiful display of prismatic colors, especially when cut. See list below. **2** A natural crystal face of this stone, used in cutting glass, etc. **3** *Geom.* A figure bounded by four equal straight lines, and having two of the angles acute and two obtuse; a rhomb or lozenge. **4** *Printing* A size of type next above brilliant; 4- or 4 1/2-point. **5** A lozenge-shaped spot on a playing card, or a card or (in the plural) suit so marked. **6** The square enclosed by the lines between the bases on a baseball field. —*v.t.* To adorn with or as with diamonds. [<OF *diamant* <LL *daimas, -antis,* alter. of L *adamas.* Doublet of ADAMANT.] —**dia′mond·ed** *adj.*

FORMS OF CUT DIAMONDS
a.b.c. Brilliant cut.
d. Marquise cut.
e. Pitt or regent cut.
f. Kohinor cut.
g. Double rose (side view) cut.
h. Rose cut.
i. Briolette cut.

—**Cullinan diamond** The world's largest diamond, 3,106 metric carats, discovered in South Africa, 1905, and named for Sir T. M. Cullinan: cut into several pieces, one set in the British scepter, one in the crown: presented to King Edward VII and renamed by King George V the **Star of Africa.**

—**Great Mogul diamond** An Indian diamond found about 1650 and said to have weighed 787 carats: named when the diamond was part of the treasure of the Mogul court. The second largest diamond, it has since disappeared.

—**Hope diamond** A blue diamond, the largest and most celebrated of the colored diamonds, 44.5 carats: named for Sir H. T. Hope, one of its owners.

—**Jonker diamond** The world's fourth largest diamond, 726 metric carats, found in South Africa in 1934 by Jacobus Jonker.

—**Koh-i-nor diamond** One of the British crown jewels, 186 carats in original cutting, dating back earlier than the 14th century: from the Persian meaning "mountain of light."

—**Vargas diamond** The world's third largest diamond, 726.6 metric carats, found in Brazil in 1938: named for President G. D. Vargas of Brazil.

dia·mond-back (dī′mənd·bak′, dī′ə-) *n.* **1** An edible turtle *(Malaclemys centrata)* inhabiting salt marshes of the southern United States, having diamond-shaped markings on the shell: also **diamond-back terrapin.** **2** A large rattlesnake *(Crotalus adamanteus)* of the SE United States, having diamond-shaped markings on the back: also **dia′mond-rat′tler.**

Diamond, Cape A promontory on the Saint Lawrence River in the city of Quebec, Canada.

Diamond Head A promontory on the SE shore of Oahu, Hawaii.

Diamond Mountains A mountain range of central Korea; highest peak, 5,374 feet. *Korean* **Kum·gang-San** (kōōm·gäng·sän).

Diamond State Nickname of DELAWARE.

Di·an·a (dī·an′ə) A feminine personal name. Also **Di·an** (dī′an), **Di·ane** (dī·an′, *Fr.* dyàn). [<L]

—**Diana** In Roman mythology, goddess of the hunt, virginity, and the moon: identified with the Greek *Artemis.* Hence, the moon.

—**Diana of Poitiers,** 1499–1566, mistress of Henry II of France.

—**Diana of the Ephesians** An Asiatic goddess of fertility, confused with the Roman Diana. *Acts* xix 21.

di·an·drous (dī·an′drəs) *adj.* *Bot.* Having two stamens. [<NL *diandrus* <Gk. *di-* two + *anēr, andros* man, male]

di·a·net·ics (dī′ə·net′iks) *n.* A system and technique of psychotherapy based on the total recall of all sensory, motor and emotional experiences, including the prenatal: developed around 1950 by L. Ron Hubbard, U.S. engineer. [? <DIANOETIC] — **di′a·net′ic** *adj.*

di·a·no·et·ic (dī′ə·nō·et′ik) *adj. Logic* Of or pertaining to a rational or discursive faculty or its products or acts; intellectual; discursive. — *n.* Logic as treating of reasoning. [<Gk. *dianoētikos* of thinking < *dia-* through + *noeein* think < *nous* mind]

di·an·thus (dī·an′thəs) *n.* Any plant of an extensive genus *(Dianthus)* of ornamental herbs of the pink family, as the carnation and the sweet william. [<NL <Gk. *Dios* of Zeus + *anthos* flower]

di·a·pa·son (dī′ə·pā′zən, -sən) *n.* **1** The basal melodic tone of a pipe organ; also, the stop producing it. In the **open diapason** the pipes are of metal and open at the top; in the **stopped diapason** the pipes are of wood and closed at the top. **2** A tuning fork, or the standard pitch given by a tuning fork. **3** In old Greek music, an octave. **4** *Archaic* Comprehensive or fundamental harmony; universal concord. [<L <Gk. *dia pasōn (chordōn)* through all (the notes)]

di·a·pe·de·sis (dī′ə·pə·dē′sis) *n. Pathol.* The passing of leucocytes through intact blood vessels into the adjoining tissue: noted especially during inflammation. [<NL <Gk. *diapēdēsis* < *dia-* through + *pedaein* leap, throb] — **di′a·pe·det′ic** (-det′ik) *adj.*

di·a·per (dī′ə·pər) *n.* **1** In the Middle Ages, a fine figured silken or linen cloth. **2** In art and architecture, a form of surface decoration, consisting of a system of reticulations, each of which contains a flower pattern, geometric design, etc., either carved or painted. **3** A soft, absorbent, bleached cotton fabric, of plain or birdseye weave: used for toweling, babies' breechcloths, etc. **4** A baby's breechcloth; waistcloth. — *v.t.* **1** To decorate with a repeated figure or similar figures. **2** To put a diaper on. [<OF *diapre,* earlier *diaspre* <Med. Gk. *diaspros* < *dia-* completely + *aspros* white]

A DIAPER PATTERN *(def. 2)*

di·a·pha·ne·i·ty (dī′ə·fə·nē′ə·tē) *n.* Translucency.

di·a·pha·nom·e·ter (dī′ə·fə·nom′ə·tər) *n.* An instrument for observing and measuring the transparency of materials, as fluids, paper, milk, etc., by means of transmitted light. [<Gk. *diaphanēs* transparent + -METER]

di·aph·a·no·scope (dī·af′ə·nə·skōp′) *n. Med.* A device for illuminating cavities of the body to facilitate medical examination and treatment. [<Gk. *diaphanēs* transparent + -SCOPE] — **di·aph·a·nos·co·py** (dī·af′ə·nos′kə·pē) *n.* — **di·aph·a·no·scop·ic** (dī·af′ə·nə·skop′ik) *adj.*

di·aph·a·nous (dī·af′ə·nəs) *adj.* Showing light through its substance; transparent; translucent. See synonyms under CLEAR. [<Med. L *diaphanus* <Gk. *diaphanēs* < *dia-* through + *phainein* show] — **di·aph′a·nous·ly** *adv.* — **di·aph′a·nous·ness** *n.*

di·aph·o·ny (dī·af′ə·nē) *n. pl.* **·nies** **1** *Music* The parallel movement of voices at definite intervals from one another. **2** Anciently, dissonance: opposed to *symphony.* [<LL *diaphonia* dissonance <Gk. *diaphōnia* < *dia-* across + *phoneein* sound < *phonē* a sound] — **di·a·phon·ic** (dī′ə·fon′ik) *adj.* — **di′a·phon′·ics** *n.*

di·a·pho·re·sis (dī′ə·fə·rē′sis) *n. Med.* Copious perspiration. [<LL <Gk. *diaphorēsis* < *diaphorein* perspire < *dia-* across, through + *phorein* carry]

di·a·pho·ret·ic (dī′ə·fə·ret′ik) *adj. Med.* Producing perspiration. — *n.* Any drug or agent that causes or increases perspiration. Also **di′a·pho·ret′i·cal.**

di·a·phragm (dī′ə·fram) *n.* **1** *Anat.* An important muscle used in respiration, situated between the thoracic and abdominal cavities; the midriff. **2** Any dividing membrane or partition. **3** Any device supposed to resemble a diaphragm in shape, appearance, or elasticity, as the thin vibrating disk of a telephone or phonograph, or the flexible rubber sheet of a vacuum brake. **4** The porous cup of a voltaic cell. **5** *Optics* A perforated disk whose aperture may be reduced in order to cut off marginal rays in a camera or telescope. — *v.t.* To act upon or furnish with a diaphragm. [<L *diaphragma* <Gk. < *dia-* across + *phragma* a fence] — **di·a·phrag·mat·ic** (dī′ə·frag·mat′ik) *adj.* — **di′a·phrag·mat′i·cal·ly** *adv.*

di·aph·y·sis (dī·af′ə·sis) *n. pl.* **·ses** (-sēz) *Anat.* **1** The shaft of a long bone or the part that ossifies from the center. **2** Any prominent part of a bony process, or a ligament, of the knee joint. [<NL <Gk., a growing through < *dia-* through + *phyein* grow, produce] — **di·a·phys·i·al** (dī′ə·fiz′ē·əl) *adj.*

di·a·poph·y·sis (dī′ə·pof′ə·sis) *n. pl.* **·ses** (-sēz) *Anat.* The superior or articular part of the transverse process of a vertebra. [<DI(A) + APOPHYSIS] — **di·ap·o·phys·i·al** (dī′ap·ə·fiz′·ē·əl) *adj.*

Di·ar·bekr (dē·är′bek′ər) See DIYARBEKIR.

di·ar·chy (dī′är·kē) *n. pl.* **·chies** A form of government in which two persons are jointly invested with supreme power, as William and Mary in England: also spelled *dyarchy.* [<DI-[2] + -ARCHY]

di·a·rist (dī′ə·rist) *n.* One who keeps a diary.

di·ar·rhe·a (dī′ə·rē′ə) *n. Pathol.* Morbidly frequent and fluid evacuation of the bowels. Also **di′ar·rhoe′a.** [<L *diarrhoea* <Gk. *diarrhoia* < *dia-* through + *rheein* flow] — **di′ar·rhe′·al** or **·rhoe′al, di′ar·rhe′ic** or **·rhoe′ic, di′ar·rhet′ic** or **·rhoet′ic** (-ret′ik) *adj.*

di·ar·thro·sis (dī′är·thrō′sis) *n. pl.* **·ses** (-sēz) *Anat.* A freely movable joint in which the ends of the bones are surrounded by a capsule and covered by cartilage. [<NL <Gk. *diarthrosis* < *dia-* completely + *arthrosis* an articulation < *arthron* a joint] — **di′ar·thro′·di·al** (-dē·əl) *adj.*

di·a·ry (dī′ə·rē) *n. pl.* **·ries** **1** A record of daily events; especially, a personal record of one's activities, experiences, or observations; a journal. **2** A book for keeping such record. [<LL *diarium* <L *dies* a day]

Di·as (dē′əs), **Bartholomeu,** 1445?–1500, Portuguese navigator; discovered Cape of Good Hope: also *Diaz.*

Di·as·po·ra (dī·as′pər·ə) *n.* **1** The dispersion of the Jews among the Gentiles after the Babylonian exile. **2** The Jews or Jewish communities so dispersed. **3** In the New Testament, the Jewish Christians living outside Palestine. I *Pet.* i 1. [<Gk., a dispersion < *dia-* completely + *speirein* sow, scatter]

di·a·spore (dī′ə·spôr, -spōr) *n.* A variously colored, translucent to subtranslucent aluminum hydroxide, AlO·OH. [<Gk. *diaspora* a dispersion (see DIASPORA); so called from its rapid decrepitation and dispersion when heated]

di·a·stal·sis (dī′ə·stal′sis) *n. pl.* **·ses** (-sēz) *Physiol.* A downward-thrusting contraction wave forming part of the peristaltic action of the digestive tube. [<NL <Gk. *dia-* through + *stellein* place, send] — **di′a·stal′·tic** *adj.*

di·a·stase (dī′ə·stās) *n. Biochem.* A white, amorphous enzyme that converts starch and glycogen into dextrin and sugar (chiefly maltose): found in germinating grain and in various parts of plants and in animal fluids, as saliva, pancreatic juice, etc.; an amylase. [<F <Gk. *diastasis* a separation < *dia-* apart + *histanai* set, cause to stand] — **di′a·sta′sic, di′a·stat′ic** (-stat′ik) *adj.*

di·as·ter (dī·as′tər) *n. Biol.* **1** That stage of cell division in which the chromosomes have separated to form two groups of starlike radiations at the poles. **2** One of the groups of radiations so formed. [<DI-[2] + Gk. *aster* star]

di·as·to·le (dī·as′tə·lē) *n.* **1** *Physiol.* The regular expansion or dilatation of the heart and of the arteries: opposed to *systole.* **2** *Zool.* A corresponding motion in protozoans and in parts of other animal organisms. **3** In Greek and Latin prosody, the lengthening of a syllable naturally short. Compare SYSTOLE. [<LL <Gk. *diastolē* a separation, lengthening < *dia-* apart + *stellein* send, put] — **di·as·tol·ic** (dī′ə·stol′ik) *adj.*

di·as·tro·phism (dī·as′trə·fiz′əm) *n. Geol.* **1** The process of deformation of the earth's crust, producing continents and ocean beds, plateaus, mountains, valleys, folds, and faults. **2** Any deformation so caused. [<Gk. *diastrophē* < *dia-* across + *strephein* turn] — **di·a·stroph·ic** (dī′ə·strof′ik) *adj.*

di·a·tes·sa·ron (dī′ə·tes′ə·ron) *n.* **1** In ancient music, a perfect fourth. **2** A harmony of the four Gospels arranged to make one continuous narrative. [<OF <L <Gk. *dia tessarōn* made of four]

di·a·ther·man·cy (dī′ə·thûr′mən·sē) *n. Physics* The property of being transparent to infrared rays, or of transmitting them. Also **di′a·ther′·mance, di′a·ther′ma·cy** (-mə·sē). [<F *diathermansie* <Gk. *dia-* through + *thermansis* a heating] — **di·a·ther·ma·nous** (dī′ə·thûr′mə·nəs) *adj.*

di·a·ther·mize (dī′ə·thûr′mīz) *v.t.* **·mized, ·miz·ing** To apply diathermy to.

di·a·ther·my (dī′ə·thûr′mē) *n. Med.* Application of heat to the deeper tissues of the body by means of high-frequency electric currents; thermopenetration. Also **di·a·ther·mi·a** (dī′ə·thûr′mē·ə). [<NL *diathermia* <Gk. *dia-* through + *thermē* heat]

di·ath·e·sis (dī·ath′ə·sis) *n.* **1** *Med.* A predisposition to certain forms of disease: a gouty *diathesis.* **2** Any mental or physical predisposition. [<NL <Gk. *diathēsis* an arrangement, disposition < *dia-* apart + *tithenai* place] — **di·a·thet·ic** (dī′ə·thet′ik) *adj.* — **di′a·thet′i·cal·ly** *adv.*

di·a·tom (dī′ə·təm, -tom) *n.* A marine and fresh-water plankton, unicellular or colonial, belonging to the family *Chlorophyceae* of microscopic green algae, characterized by bivalve walls containing silica. [<NL *diatoma* <Gk. *dia-* through + *temnein* cut] — **di·a·to·ma·ceous** (dī′ə·tə·mā′shəs) *adj.*

diatomaceous earth The siliceous skeletons of diatoms, dried and used in the manufacture of dynamite, pottery, abrasives, glaze, etc.; kieselguhr. Also **di·at·o·mite** (dī·at′ə·mīt).

di·a·tom·ic (dī′ə·tom′ik) *adj. Chem.* **1** Containing only two atoms: a *diatomic* molecule. **2** Containing two replaceable univalent atoms. **3** Bivalent.

di·a·ton·ic (dī′ə·ton′ik) *adj. Music* Designating the regular tones of a major or minor key (or scale), in distinction from chromatic or occasional tones; having eight tones to an octave. [<MF *diatonique* <LL *diatonicus* <Gk. *diatonikos* < *dia-* through + *teinein* stretch] — **di′a·ton′i·cal·ly** *adv.*

di·a·tribe (dī′ə·trīb) *n.* An abusive discourse; denunciation; invective. [<F <L *diatriba* <Gk. *diatribē* a wearing away of time < *dia-* through + *tribein* rub]

di·at·ro·pism (dī·at′rə·piz′əm) *n. Bot.* The propensity of some plant organs to arrange themselves transversely to the line of action of an external stimulus. [<DIA- + TROPISM] — **di·a·trop·ic** (dī′ə·trop′ik) *adj.*

Dí·az (dē′äts), **Armando,** 1861–1928, Italian general; commander in chief of the Italian Army in World War I.

Di·az (dē′əs), **Bartholomeu** See DIAS.

Dí·az (dē′äs), **Porfirio,** 1830–1915, president of Mexico 1877–80, 1884–1911; overthrown by revolution.

Dí·az de Bi·var (dē′äth thā bē·vär′) See CID.

Diaz de la Pe·ña (dyàz də là pā·nyà′), **Narcisse Virgile,** 1808–76, French painter.

di·a·zine (dī′ə·zēn, -zin, dī·az′in) *n. Chem.* One of three isomeric cyclic hydrocarbon compounds, the ring of which contains two nitrogen and four carbon atoms. Also **di·a·zin** (dī′ə·zin, dī·az′in). [<DIAZ(O)- + -IN]

di·az·o (dī·az′ō, dī·ā′zō) *adj. Chem.* Pertaining to or designating any of a group of very reactive compounds in which two nitrogen atoms are united to a hydrocarbon radical: used in dyestuff manufacture. In compounds, **diazo–** or, before vowels, **diaz–,** as in *diazomethane, diazine.* [<DI-[2] + AZO(TE)]

di·a·zole (dī′ə·zōl, dī·az′ōl) *n. Chem.* Any member of a class of heterocyclic hydrocarbon compounds, the ring of which contains two nitrogen and three carbon atoms. [<DIAZ(O)- + -OLE[1]]

di·az·o·meth·ane (dī·az′ō·meth′ān, dī·ā′zō-) *n. Chem.* An odorless, poisonous, yellow gas, CH_2N_2, used in organic syntheses.

di·a·zo·ni·um (dī′ə·zō′nē·əm) *n. Chem.* A basic organic radical which forms aromatic nitrogen compounds. [<DIAZ(O)- + (AMM)ONIUM]

diazonium salt *Chem.* Any of a group of salts formed by the action of nitrous acid at low temperature upon a salt of a primary aromatic amine.

di·az·o–re·ac·tion (dī·az′ō·rē·ak′shən, dī·ā′zō-)

n. Med. A reaction, especially in typhoid fever, in which the urine becomes deep red in color when treated with certain reagents.

di·az·o·tize (dī·az′ə·tīz) *v.t.* **·tized, ·tiz·ing** *Chem.* To bring about chemical reactions or changes that form a diazo compound or derivative. **—di·az′o·ti·za′tion** *n.*

di·ba·sic (dī·bā′sik) *adj. Chem.* **1** Containing two atoms of hydrogen replaceable by a base or basic radical, as sulfuric acid. **2** Of or derived from such an acid: said of salts. **—di·ba·sic·i·ty** (dī′bā·sis′ə·tē) *n.*

dib·ble[1] (dib′əl) *n.* A gardeners' pointed tool for planting seeds, setting slips, etc. **—***v.t.* **·bled ·bling 1** To make holes in (soil) with a dibble. **2** To plant or set (seeds, etc.) with a dibble. Also **dib·ber** (dib′ər). [? < *dib,* var. of DAB[3]]

dib·ble[2] (dib′əl) *v.i. Brit. Dial.* **1** In angling, to dip the bait gently into the water. **2** To dabble; tamper. Also **dib.** [Freq. of *dib,* var. of DAB[3]]

di·bran·chi·ate (dī·brang′kē·it, -āt) *n.* Any of an order *(Dibranchiata)* of cephalopods including the squids and octopuses, with 8 or 10 sucker-bearing arms surrounding the mouth, 2 internal gills, and a sac and siphon for emitting an inky liquid. **—***adj.* Of or pertaining to the *Dibranchiata.* [<NL *dibranchiata* <Gk. *di-* two + *branchia* gills]

di·bro·mide (dī·brō′mīd, -mid) *n. Chem.* A compound containing two atoms of bromine.

di·bro·mo·gal·lic acid (dī′brō·mə·gal′ik) Gallobromal.

di·car·box·yl·ic acid (dī·kär′bok·sil′ik) *Chem.* An organic compound having two carboxyl radicals.

di·cast (dī′kast, dik′ast) *n.* In ancient Athens, one of the citizens selected annually to serve as a judge of the high court: also called *heliast.* [<Gk. *dikastēs* < *dikē* justice] **—di·cas′tic** *adj.*

dice (dīs) *n. pl. of* **die 1** Small cubes of bone, ivory, or composition, having the sides marked with spots from one to six. **2** A game played with such cubes. **—poker dice** Dice marked with card faces from nine to ace inclusive. **—***v.* **diced, dic·ing** *v.t.* **1** To cut into small cubes. **2** To decorate with a dice-like pattern. **3** To gamble away or win with dice. **—***v.i.* **4** To play at dice. [See DIE[2]] **—dic′er** *n.* **—dic′ing** *n.*

dice box A box used for shaking and throwing dice.

DICE *(def. 1)*

di·cen·tra (dī·sen′trə) *n.* **1** Any plant of a genus *(Dicentra)* of low, delicate, perennial herbs, with a raceme of nodding, rose-colored or yellow, heart-shaped flowers, as the bleeding heart and dutchman's-breeches. [<NL < Gk. *dikentros* < *di-* two + *kentron* a spur]

di·ceph·a·lous (dī·sef′ə·ləs) *adj.* Having two heads.

dic·er·ous (dis′ər·əs) *adj.* Having two horns or antennae. [<Gk. *dikeros* < *di-* two + *keras* horn]

di·cha·si·um (dī·kā′zhē·əm, -zē·əm) *n. pl.* **·si·a** (-zhē·ə, -zē·ə) *Bot.* A cymose inflorescence in which two lateral branches grow from the primary axis below the flower, each branch repeating the division; a two-parted cyme. [<NL <Gk. *dichasis* a division < *dicha* in two] **—di·cha′si·al** *adj.*

di·chlor·a·mine (dī·klôr′ə·mēn) *n. Chem.* A yellowish-white, crystalline compound, $C_7H_7SO_2NCl_2$, used as an antiseptic in treating wound infection. [<DI-[2] + CHLOR- + -AMINE]

di·chlor·eth·yl sulfide (dī′klôr·eth′əl) See MUSTARD GAS.

di·chlo·ride (dī·klôr′īd, -id, -klō′rīd, -rid) *n. Chem.* A compound having two atoms of chlorine combined with an element or radical; a bichloride. Also **di·chlo·rid** (dī·klôr′id, -klō′rid).

di·chlor·o·di·phen·yl·tri·chlor·o·eth·ane (dī·klôr′ō·dī·fen′il·trī·klôr′ō·eth′ān) *n.* DDT.

dicho- *combining form* In two; in pairs: *dichotomy.* Also, before vowels, **dich-.** [<Gk. < *dicha* in two < *dis* twice]

di·chog·a·my (dī·kog′ə·mē) *n. Bot.* A condition, brought about by the maturity at different times of the anthers and stigmas, for promoting intercrossing between hermaphrodite flowers: distinguished from *homogamy.* [<DICHO- + -GAMY] **—di·chog′a·mous** *adj.*

di·chot·o·mize (dī·kot′ə·mīz) *v.* **·mized, ·miz·ing** *v.t.* **1** To cut or part into two sections; subdivide or separate and classify into pairs. **2** *Astron.* To exhibit as a half disk, as the moon. **—***v.i.* To be or become separated into two parts. **—di·chot′o·mi·za′tion** *n.*

di·chot·o·mous (dī·kot′ə·məs) *adj.* **1** Pertaining to or involving dichotomy. **2** Dividing into two parts or branches. Also **di·cho·tom·ic** (dī′kə·tom′ik). **—di·chot′o·mous·ly, di′cho·tom′i·cal·ly** *adv.*

di·chot·o·my (dī·kot′ə·mē) *n. pl.* **·mies 1** The state of being divided in two; division into two parts or into two branches; division by pairs. **2** *Logic* The division of a class into two mutually exclusive subclasses, one positive and the other negative, as minerals into gold and not-gold. **3** *Astron.* The aspect of the moon, Mercury, or Venus, at first and last quarter, when half the apparent disk is illuminated. **4** *Bot.* **a** A forking in pairs, as the stem of a plant; successive bifurcation. **b** A system of branching in which each successive axis forks or bifurcates into two equally developed branches. [<Gk. *dichotomia* < *dicho-* in two + *temnein* cut]

di·chro·ic (dī·krō′ik) *adj.* **1** Of, pertaining to, or exhibiting dichroism. **2** Dichromatic. Also **di·chro·it·ic** (dī′krō·it′ik).

di·chro·ism (dī′krō·iz′əm) *n.* **1** *Physics* The property of showing different colors when viewed in different directions, exhibited by doubly refracting crystals. **2** *Chem.* The property of being differently colored in different degrees of concentration: shown by some solutions. [<Gk. *dichroos* two-colored < *di-* two + *chrōs* color]

di·chro·ite (dī′krō·īt) *n.* The mineral iolite. [<Gk. *dichroos* two-colored + -ITE[1]]

di·chro·mate (dī·krō′māt) *n. Chem.* A compound containing two chromium atoms: potassium *dichromate.*

di·chro·mat·ic (dī′krō·mat′ik) *adj.* **1** Having either of two colors. **2** *Zool.* Having two color phases: said of certain birds and insects, etc., that, apart from changes due to age or sex, exhibit a coloration differing from the normal. **3** *Pathol.* Affected with blue-, green-, or red-blindness; able to see only two of the three primary colors.

di·chro·ma·tism (dī·krō′mə·tiz′əm) *n.* The state of being dichromatic, especially with reference to colorblindness. Also **di·chro′mism.**

di·chro·mic (dī·krō′mik) *adj.* **1** Containing two atoms of chromium, or their equivalents. **2** Dichromatic.

dichromic acid *Chem.* A dibasic acid, $H_2Cr_2O_7$, known only through its salts, the dichromates or bichromates.

Dich·tung und Wahr·heit (dikh′tŏŏng ŏŏnt vär′hīt) *Ger.* "Poetry and Truth": the title of Goethe's autobiography.

di·chro·scope (dī′krə·skōp) *n.* An instrument for examining or exhibiting dichroism, as of crystals. Also **di·chro·o·scope** (dī·krō′ə·skōp). [<Gk. *dichroos* two-colored + -SCOPE] **—di·chro·scop·ic** (dī′krə·skop′ik) *adj.*

dick (dik) *n. U.S. Slang* A detective.

Dick (dik) A masculine nickname: diminutive of RICHARD.

Dick (dik), **George Frederick,** born 1881, and his wife, **Gladys,** born 1881, U.S. physiologists.

dick·cis·sel (dik·sis′əl) *n.* A bunting *(Spiza americana)* of the Mississippi region, distinguished by its black throat and lively call. Also **dick·sis′sel.** [Imit.]

dick·ens (dik′ənz) *n. Colloq.* The devil: a euphemistic expletive.

Dick·ens (dik′ənz), **Charles,** 1812–70, English novelist.

Dick·en·si·an (di·ken′zē·ən) *adj.* Of or characteristic of Charles Dickens, his writing, or his style; especially, denoting a literary style in which odd characters from ordinary life are portrayed humorously and kindly.

dick·er (dik′ər) *n. U.S.* **1** A petty trade; a bargain. **2** A political deal. **—***v.t.* & *v.i.* **1** To trade by haggling or bartering, especially on a small scale. **2** In politics, to bargain; work toward a deal. [ME *dyker,* OE (unrecorded) *dicor* a lot of ten, esp. skins or hides, ult. <L *decuria* a group of ten]

dick·ey (dik′ē) *n.* **1** A detachable article of clothing, as a false shirt front, or sweater front; also, a bib; pinafore. **2** A driver's outside seat on a carriage; also, one behind the body, for servants. **3** A donkey. **4** *Colloq.* Any small bird. Also **dick′y.** [<*Dicky,* double dim. of RICHARD]

Dick·in·son (dik′ən·sən), **Emily Elizabeth,** 1830–86, U.S. poet. **—John,** 1732–1808, American statesman.

Dick test *Med.* A test of susceptibility to or immunity from scarlet fever, consisting of subcutaneous injections of streptococcus toxins of the disease. [after George and Gladys *Dick*]

di·cli·nous (dī′kli·nəs, dī·klī′-) *adj. Bot.* Having stamens in one flower and pistils in another; unisexual. [<DI-[2] + Gk. *klinē* bed]

di·cli·ny (dī′kli·nē, dī·klī′nē) *n. Bot.* The condition of being diclinous.

di·cot·y·le·don (dī′kot·ə·lēd′n, dī·kot′-) *n. Bot.* **1** A plant having two cotyledons or seed leaves. **2** A member of the class *Dicotyledones.*

di·cot·y·le·do·nous (dī′kot·ə·lē′də·nəs, dī·kot′-) *adj. Bot.* Belonging or pertaining to the largest, most important subclass *(Dicotyledones)* of angiosperms or flowering plants, characterized by having seeds with two cotyledons. It embraces the majority of deciduous trees and of herbs and shrubs.

di·crot·ic (dī·krot′ik) *adj. Physiol.* Having an abnormal heartbeat, with a double pulse beat to each systole of the heart. Also **di·cro·tal** (dī·krō′təl),**di·cro·tous** (dī′krə·təs). [<Gk. *dikrotos* < *di-* two + *krotos* beat] **—di·cro·tism** (dī′krə·tiz′əm) *n.*

dic·ta (dik′tə) Plural of DICTUM.

Dic·ta·phone (dik′tə·fōn) *n.* A type of phonographic instrument that records and reproduces words spoken into its mouthpiece, as for transcription by a stenographer: a trade name.

dic·tate (dik′tāt, dik·tāt′) *v.* **·tat·ed, ·tat·ing** *v.t.* **1** To utter or read aloud (something) to be recorded by another, as by writing. **2** To give, impose, or prescribe authoritatively, as commands, terms, rules, etc. **—***v.i.* **3** To utter aloud something to be recorded by another. **4** To give orders. **—***n.* (dik′tāt) **1** An authoritative suggestion or prompting; a rule, precept, or maxim. **2** A positive order. [<L *dictatus,* pp. of *dictare,* freq. of *dicere* say, speak]

Synonyms (verb): command, decree, direct, enjoin, order, prescribe, require. See SPEAK. *Antonyms*: accept, follow, obey, submit, yield.

dic·ta·tion (dik·tā′shən) *n.* **1** The act of dictating. **2** The matter or material dictated. **3** Arbitrary control. **—dic·ta′tion·al** *adj.*

dic·ta·tor (dik′tā·tər, dik·tā′tər) *n.* **1** One invested with absolute power, especially in a state in time of emergency. **2** One who dictates or prescribes. **3** In ancient Rome, a chief magistrate with supreme authority, appointed by the Senate in cases of emergency for a term of about six months. **—dic′ta·tor·ship′** *n.* **—dic·ta′tress** *n. fem.*

dic·ta·to·ri·al (dik′tə·tôr′ē·əl, -tō′rē-) *adj.* Given to dictating; overbearing. See synonyms under ARBITRARY, DOGMATIC, IMPERIOUS. **—dic′ta·to′ri·al·ly** *adv.* **—dic′ta·to′ri·al·ness** *n.*

dic·tion (dik′shən) *n.* **1** The use, choice, and arrangement of words and modes of expression. **2** The manner of speaking or of any vocal expression; enunciation. [<L *dictio, -onis* speech < *dicere* say, speak]

Synonyms: expression, language, phrase, phraseology, style, verbiage, vocabulary, wording, words. An author's *diction* is strictly his choice and use of words, with no special reference to thought; *expression* regards the words simply as the vehicle of the thought. *Phrase* and *phraseology* apply to words or combinations of words which are somewhat technical; as, in legal *phraseology*; in military *phrase. Diction* is general; *wording* is limited; we speak of the *diction* of an author or of a work, the *wording* of a proposition, of a resolution, etc. *Verbiage* is wordiness. *Style* includes *diction, expression,* rhetorical figures such as metaphor and simile, the effect of an author's prevailing tone of thought, of his personal traits—in short, all that makes up the clothing of thought in words. Compare LANGUAGE.

dic·tion·ar·y (dik′shən·er′ē) *n. pl.* **·ar·ies 1** A book containing the words of a language, or of a department of knowledge, arranged alphabetically, usually with their syllabication, pronunciation, definition, and etymology; lexicon; wordbook. **2** A similar work having definitions or equivalents in another language: a German-English *dictionary.* [<Med. L *dictionarium* a collection of words and phrases <*dictio.* See DICTION.]

Dic·to·graph (dik′tə·graf, -gräf) *n.* A sensitive telephonic device used to transmit or overhear conversations: a trade name.

dic·tum (dik′təm) *n. pl.* **dic·ta** (-tə) **1** An authoritative, dogmatic, or positive utterance; a pronouncement. **2** *Law* An opinion by a judge on a point not essential to the decision on the main question in the case on trial. **3** A popular saying; a maxim. See synonyms under ADAGE. [<L <*dicere* say]

dic·ty·nid (dik′tə·nid) *n.* One of a family (*Dictynidae*) of spiders that build their webs of a curled thread and in irregular forms. [<NL <Gk. *diktyon* a net]

Di·cu·ma·rol (dī·ko͞o′mə·rôl, -rol, -kyo͞o′-) *n.* Proprietary name for a derivative of coumarin: used to delay the coagulation of blood.

did (did) Past tense of DO[1].

Did·a·che (did′ə·kē) *n.* The teaching of the Twelve Apostles: the title of the oldest church manual, written in the second century. [<Gk., a teaching]

di·dac·tic (dī·dak′tik, di-) *adj.* **1** Pertaining to or of the nature of teaching; intended to instruct; expository. **2** Morally instructive; preceptive. **3** Overly inclined to teach; pedantic. Also **di·dac′ti·cal.** [<Gk. *didaktikos* apt to teach <*didaskein* teach] **—di·dac′ti·cal·ly** *adv.* **—di·dac′ti·cism** *n.*

di·dac·tics (dī·dak′tiks, di-) *n.* The science or art of instruction or education.

di·dap·per (dī′dap′ər) *n.* A dabchick. [Short for *divedapper*]

did·dle[1] (did′l) *v., Colloq.* **·dled, ·dling** *v.t.* To cheat. *—v.i.* To dawdle; pass time idly. Also *daddle.* [? <DIDDLE[2]] **—did′dler** *n.*

did·dle[2] (did′l) *v.i.* **·dled, ·dling** To jerk up and down or back and forth; jiggle. [Var. of dial. *didder,* ME *diddiren* quiver, shake, tremble]

Di·de·rot (dē·drō′), **Denis** 1713–84, French philosopher, critic, and encyclopedist.

didg·er·i·du (dij′ər·rē·doo′) *n. Austral.* An aboriginal musical instrument, a foot to eight feet long, that amplifies a nasal whine. [<native Australian]

did·na (did′nə) *Scot.* Did not.

did·n't (did′nt) Did not: a contraction.

di·do (dī·dō) *n. pl.* **·dos** or **·does** *Colloq.* An extravagant action; caper; antic. [Origin unknown]

Di·do (dī′dō) In Roman legend, a Tyrian princess, founder and queen of Carthage. In the *Aeneid,* she falls in love with Aeneas when he lands in Carthage after his flight from Troy, and kills herself when he leaves her.

di·drach·ma (dī·drak′mə) *n. pl.* **·mas** or **mae** (-mē) **1** A double drachma in ancient Greece. **2** The earliest Roman silver coin. [<Gk. <*di-* two + *drachma* a drachma]

didst (didst) *Archaic* Second person singular past tense of DO[1]: used with *thou.*

di·dy (dī′dē) *n. pl.* **·dies** *Colloq.* A baby's diaper. [<DIAPER]

di·dym·i·um (dī·dim′ē·əm, di-) *n.* A mixture of the elements neodymium and praseodymium of the lanthanide series, found in cerite and formerly regarded as one of the elements. [<NL <Gk. *didymos* double]

did·y·mous (did′ə·məs) *adj.* **1** *Bot.* Twin; formed in pairs; growing double, as umbelliferous fruits. **2** Double, as markings. [<Gk. *didymos* double]

die[1] (dī) *v.i.* **died, dy·ing 1** To suffer death; pass from life; expire. **2** To suffer the pains of death: The coward *dies* a thousand deaths. **3** To lose energy or power; pass: with *away: down,* or *out.* **4** To cease to exist; fade away, The smile *died* on his lips. **5** To become extinct: with *out* or *off.* **6** To become indifferent or insensible: with *to:* to *die* to the world. **7** To desire exceedingly, as if to death: He's *dying* to meet her. **8** To stop functioning, as an engine. **9** To faint or swoon. **10** *Theol.* To suffer spiritual death. **—to die game** To die fighting. ◆Homophone: *dye.* [<ON *deyja*]

Synonyms: cease, decease, decline, depart, expire, perish, wither. *Die* is applied to anything which has the appearance of life; an echo, a strain of music, a tempest, a topic, an issue, *dies. Expire* is a softer word for *die;* it is used figuratively of things that *cease* to exist by reaching a natural limit; as, a lease *expires;* the time has *expired.* To *perish* is oftenest used of death by privation or exposure; sometimes, of death by violence. Knowledge and fame, art and empires, may be said to *perish;* the word denotes destruction and decay. *Antonyms:* begin, exist, flourish, grow, live, survive.

die[2] (dī) *n. pl.* **dice** *for defs.* **1** *and* **2 dies** *for defs.* **3** *to* **6. 1** A small cube used in games. See DICE. **2** A cast, as in playing dice; stake; hazard. **3** *Mech.* **a** A hard metal pattern for stamping or cutting out some object; specifically, one of a pair between which a metal blank is forced or forged into a special shape, as a spoon. **b** One of a pair of such patterns, one cameo and the other intaglio, between which a sheet of metal is embossed. **c** A block or counter having an orifice through which a punch passes. Also **die plate. 4** A tool for cutting screw threads on a nut, bolt, etc. **5** The cubical part of a pedestal. **6** Any small cubical block or body. **—the die is cast** The choice is made that commits one to an irrevocable course of action *—v.t.* To cut or stamp with or as with a die. ◆Homophone: *dye.* [<OF *de* <L *datum* something given]

die·back (dī′bak′) *n.* Arrested or retarded development in the twigs of certain woody plants, due to parasites or to being winter-killed: also called *twig blight.*

Di·e·go (dē·ā′gō) A Spanish form of JAMES.

die-hard (dī′härd′) *n.* **1** One who fights to the last. **2** One who obstinately refuses to abandon or modify his views; especially, a political conservative who obstinately opposes a winning liberal measure.

di·el·drin (dī·el′drin) *n.* A toxic chlorinated hydrocarbon, $C_{12}H_8Cl_6O$, stereoisomeric with endrin and likewise used as a pesticide.

di·e·lec·tric (dī′ə·lek′trik) *Electr. adj.* **1** Nonconducting. **2** Capable of sustaining an electric field, as by induction. Also **di′e·lec′tri·cal.** *—n.* A dielectric substance, medium or material. **—di′e·lec′tri·cal·ly** *adv.*

Dien Bien Phu (dyen byen fo͞o) A town in North Vietnam; besieged and captured from the French by Vietnamese forces in 1954.

di·en·ceph·a·lon (dī′en·sef′ə·lon) *n. Anat.* That part of the brain forming the posterior part of the prosencephalon, from which are developed the pineal body, the pituitary, and other structures of the third ventricle; the interbrain or middle brain: also called *thalamencephalon.* [<NL <Gk. *di(a)-* between + *enkephalos* brain]

-diene *suffix Chem.* Denoting an open-chain unsaturated hydrocarbon compound having two double bonds: *butadiene.* [<DI-[2] + -ENE]

Di·eppe (dē·ep′, *Fr.* dyep) A port on the English Channel in northern France.

di·er·e·sis (dī·er′ə·sis) *n. pl.* **·ses** (-sēz) **1** Two dots (¨) placed over the second of two adjacent vowels that are to be pronounced separately. **2** The separation of syllables or vowels by dots. **3** In the pronunciations in this book, a diacritic used over *a* to indicate the vowel sound in *palm* (päm). See also ü, Foreign Sounds page xx. **4** The coincidence of the end of a metrical foot with the end of a word in a verse. Also spelled *diaeresis.* Compare SYNERESIS. [<LL *diaeresis* <Gk. *diairesis* a division <*diaireein* <*dia-* apart + *haireein* seize] **—di·e·ret·ic** (dī′ə·ret′ik) *adj.*

di·es (dī′ēz) *n. pl.* **di·es** (dī′ēz) *Latin* Day.

die·sel engine (dē′zəl) An internal-combustion engine, in which crude oil, used as fuel, is ignited by the heat resulting from the high compression of air drawn into the cylinder. Also **Diesel engine.** [after Rudolf *Diesel,* 1858–1913, German inventor]

Di·es I·rae (dī′ēz ī′rē) The name of a famous medieval Latin hymn on the Day of Judgment, used as the sequence in masses for the dead: so called from its opening words; literally, Day of Wrath. [<L]

di·e·sis (dī′ə·sis) *n.* **1** *Music* The difference in tone between a major and a minor semitone, represented by the ratio of vibrations 125:128; also, an interval smaller than a half-step. **2** In Greek music, one of several intervals varying from a semitone to a quartertone. **3** *Printing* The double dagger (‡): a reference mark for the third in a series. [<L <Gk. <*diïenai* <*dia-* through + *hienai* send]

di·es non ju·rid·i·cus (dī′ēz non′ jo͞o·rid′ə·kəs) *Latin Law* A day on which courts are not in session. Also **di′es non′.**

Diest (dēst) A town in north central Belgium.

die·stock (dī′stok′) *n. Mech.* A double-handled holder for a die used to cut threads on screws, bolts, etc.

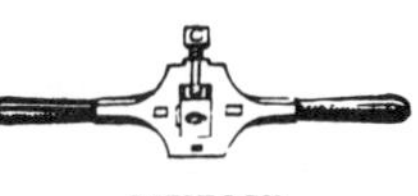
DIESTOCK

di·et[1] (dī′ət) *n.* **1** A regulated course of eating and drinking; a specially prescribed regimen. **2** The daily fare; victuals. **3** *Obs.* Allowance of food; ration. See synonyms under FOOD. *—v.t.* **1** To regulate or restrict the food and drink of. *—v.i.* **2** To take food and drink according to a regimen; eat discriminatingly. **3** To take food; eat. [<OF *diete* <L *diaeta* <Gk. *diaita* a way of living] **—di′et·er** *n.*

di·et[2] (dī′ət) *n.* **1** A legislative assembly. **2** *Scot.* A single session, as of a court; a day appointed for a session. [<Med. L *dieta* <L *dies* a day]

Di·et (dī′ət) *n.* **1** The legislature of certain countries. **2** The semiannual meeting of the estates of the Holy Roman Empire: often distinguished by the name of the city where it was held: the *Diet* of Worms.

di·e·tar·y (dī′ə·ter′ē) *n. pl.* **·tar·ies 1** A system or regimen of dieting. **2** A standard or regulated allowance of food. *—adj.* Pertaining or relating to diet: also **di·e·tet·ic** (dī′ə·tet′ik), **di′e·tet′i·cal. —di′e·tet′i·cal·ly** *adv.*

Diet·bold (dēt′bōlt) A German form of THEOBALD.

di·e·tet·ics (dī′ə·tet′iks) *n.* The branch of hygiene that treats of diet and dieting and the feeding of individuals or of great numbers.

di·eth·y·lene glycol (dī·eth′ə·lēn) *Chem.* An organic compound, $O(CH_2CH_2OH)_2$, used as an anti-freeze mixture and as an agent in many chemical processes for the production of solvents, plastics, explosives, etc.

di·eth·yl·stil·bes·trol (dī·eth′əl·stil·bes′trōl) *n. Biochem.* A synthetic compound, $C_{18}H_{20}O_2$, having estrogenic and carcinogenic properties.

di·e·ti·tian (dī′ə·tish′ən) *n.* One skilled in the principles of dietetics and in their practical application in health and disease. Also **di·e·tet·ist** (dī′ə·tet′ist), **di′e·ti′cian.**

diet kitchen 1 An institution, usually connected with a dispensary or hospital, that provides food for the invalid poor. **2** A kitchen where special diets are prepared and from which they are served under the supervision of a dietitian who gives student nurses dietetic training.

Dieu a·vec nous (dyœ′ à·vek′ no͞o′) *French* God with us.

Dieu et mon droit (dyœ′ ā môn′ drwà′) *French* God and my right: motto of the royal arms of Great Britain.

Dieu vous garde (dyœ′ vo͞o′ gȧrd′) *French* God protect you.

dif- Assimilated var. of DIS-.

dif·fer (dif′ər) *v.i.* **1** To be unlike in quality, degree, form, etc.; often with *from.* **2** To disagree; dissent: often with *with.* **3** To quarrel: sometimes with *over* or *about.* [<OF *differer* <L *differre* <*dis-* apart + *ferre* carry. Doublet of DEFER[1].]

dif·fer·ence (dif′ər·əns, dif′rəns) *n.* **1** The state or quality of being other or unlike, or that in which two things are unlike; dissimilarity; variation. **2** A mark or peculiarity which distinguishes. **3** A disagreement in sentiment or opinion; controversy; quarrel. **4** A separate treatment; discrimination. **5** *Math.* The result obtained by subtracting one number from another. **6** *Logic* The specific difference; differentia. **7** In commerce, a margin that has become payable. **8** *Her.* A device in blazons to distinguish persons bearing the same arms. *—v.t.* **·enced, ·enc·ing 1** To make or mark as different; distinguish; discriminate. **2** *Her.* To add a mark of difference to.

Synonyms (noun): contrariety, contrast, disagreement, discrepancy, discrimination, disparity, dissimilarity, dissimilitude, distinction, divergence, diversity, inconsistency, inequality, unlikeness, variation. A *difference* is in the things compared; a *discrimination* is in our judgment of them; a *distinction* is in our definition or description or mental image of them. Careful *discrimination* of real *differences* results in clear *distinctions*. *Disparity* is stronger than *inequality*, implying that one thing falls far below another; as, the *disparity* of our achievements when compared with our ideals. *Dissimilarity* is between things sharply contrasted; there may be a *difference* between those almost alike. There is a *discrepancy* in accounts that fail to balance. *Diversity* involves more than two objects; *variation* is a *difference* in the condition or action of the same object at different times. *Antonyms*: agreement, consonance, harmony, identity, likeness, resemblance, sameness, similarity, uniformity, unity.

dif·fer·ent (dif′ər·ənt, dif′rənt) *adj.* **1** Not the same; distinct; other: A *different* clerk is there now. **2** Marked by a difference; completely or partly unlike; dissimilar. **3** Unusual. See synonyms under CONTRARY. [<F *différent* <L *differens, -entis*, ppr. of *differre*. See DIFFER.] **—dif′fer·ent·ly** *adv.* **—dif′fer·ent·ness** *n.* ◆ **different from, than, to** In American usage, *from* is established as the idiomatic preposition to follow *different*; when, however, a clause follows the connective, *than* is gaining increasing acceptance: a result *different than* (= *from that which* or *from what*) had been expected. This last is established British usage, which also accepts *to* on a par with *from*: She is *different to* her sister.

dif·fer·en·ti·a (dif′ə·ren′shē·ə) *n.* *pl.* **·ti·ae** (-shi·ē) *Logic* A specific difference; a characteristic attribute distinguishing a species from others of the same genus. [<L, neut. pl. of *differens*. See DIFFERENT.]

dif·fer·en·ti·a·ble (dif′ə·ren′shē·ə·bəl) *adj.* **1** That can be differentiated. **2** *Math.* Belonging to or having a differential coefficient. **—dif′fer·en′ti·a·bil′i·ty** *n.*

dif·fer·en·tial (dif′ə·ren′shəl) *adj.* **1** Relating to, making, or marked by a difference. **2** Distinctive; discriminative. **3** *Math.* Pertaining to or involving differentials or differentiation. **4** *Mech.* Characterized by a construction in which a movement is obtained by the difference in two motions in the same direction. See DIFFERENTIAL GEAR. **—*n.*** **1** *Math.* **a** An infinitesimal increment of a quantity: indicated by the symbol Δ . **b** The derivative of a function multiplied by the increment of the independent variable. **2** A differential rate. **3** *Mech.* A differential gear. **4** *Electr.* One of two resistance coils the current of which flows in a direction opposite to that of the other. **—dif′fer·en′tial·ly** *adv.*

differential calculus See under CALCULUS.

differential coefficient *Math.* The ratio of the infinitesimal increase of a function to that of a variable on which the function depends; a derivative. Also **differential quotient.**

differential equation *Math.* An equation in which derivatives or differentials of an unknown function appear.

differential gear or **gearing** *Mech.* A coupling consisting of an epicyclic train used to connect shafts, as in the driving axle of an automobile, so that a rigid union is effected when moving in a straight line, but permitting of independent motion when describing a curve.

DIFFERENTIAL GEAR
a. Drive shaft. *b.* Drive-shaft gear. *c.* Axles. *d.* Ring gear. *e.* Epicyclic train of gears.

differential windlass See under WINDLASS.

dif·fer·en·ti·ate (dif′ə·ren′shē·āt) *v.* **·at·ed, ·at·ing** *v.t.* **1** To constitute a difference between; mark off. **2** To perceive and indicate the differences of or between. **3** *Biol.* To cause to be unlike; develop differences in. **4** *Math.* To derive the differential of (a function). —*v.i.* **5** To discriminate; perceive a difference. **6** To become specialized; acquire a distinct character. See synonyms under CONTRAST.

dif·fer·en·ti·a·tion (dif′ə·ren′shē·ā′shən) *n.* **1** The process of making or becoming different. **2** *Biol.* **a** Progressive change from the general to the special, as in all organs and tissues in course of development. **b** The setting apart of special organs for special work: distinguished from ordinary cellular growth in that the cells produced by division are dissimilar to the parent cells. **3** *Logic* Distinction on grounds of difference; discrimination. **4** *Math.* The finding of a differential.

dif·fi·cile (dif′ə·sēl′, *Fr.* dē·fē·sēl′) *adj. French* Difficult; especially, difficult to deal with or please.

dif·fi·cult (dif′ə·kult, -kəlt) *adj.* **1** Hard to do or be done; arduous; troublesome to understand; perplexing. **2** Hard to persuade, overcome, or satisfy; intractable; exacting. [Back formation <DIFFICULTY] **—dif′fi·cult·ly** *adv.*

Synonyms: arduous, exhausting, hard, laborious, onerous, severe, toilsome, trying. *Arduous* applies to that which involves great and sustained exertion; great learning can only be won by *arduous* toil. Anything is *hard* that involves tax and strain whether of the physical or mental powers. *Difficult* is not used of that which merely taxes physical force; a dead lift is called *hard* rather than *difficult*; that is *difficult* which involves skill, sagacity, or address, with or without a considerable expenditure of physical force; a geometrical problem may be *difficult* to solve, a mountain *difficult* to ascend. *Hard* may be active or passive; a thing may be *hard* to do or *hard* to bear. *Arduous* is always active. That which is *laborious* or *toilsome* requires the steady application of labor or toil till accomplished; *toilsome* is the stronger word. That which is *onerous* is mentally burdensome or oppressive. See ARDUOUS, HARD, OBSCURE, SQUEAMISH, TROUBLESOME. *Antonyms*: easy, facile, light, pleasant, slight, trifling, trivial.

dif·fi·cul·ty (dif′ə·kul′tē, -kəl-) *n.* *pl.* **·ties** **1** The state or quality of being difficult or of presenting or constituting an obstacle to achievement or mastery. **2** An obstacle; hindrance; something difficult to effect or to understand. **3** Reluctance; objection. **4** A quarrel. **5** *Usually pl.* Financial embarrassment; a strait; trouble: generally in the plural. See synonyms under IMPEDIMENT. [<L *difficultas, -tatis* < *difficilis* < *dis-* away, not + *facilis* easy < *facere* do, make]

dif·fi·dence (dif′ə·dəns) *n.* Self-distrust; shyness; modesty.

dif·fi·dent (dif′ə·dənt) *adj.* **1** Affected or possessed with self-distrust; timid; shy; modest. **2** *Obs.* Distrustful of others; doubtful. [<L *diffidens, -entis*, ppr. of *diffidere* < *dis-* away + *fidere* trust < *fides* faith] **—dif′fi·dent·ly** *adv.*

dif·fract (di·frakt′) *v.t.* **1** To separate into parts. **2** To subject to diffraction. [<L *diffractus*, pp. of *diffringere* < *dis-* away + *frangere* break] **—dif·frac′tive** *adj.* **—dif·frac′tive·ly** *adv.* **—dif·frac′tive·ness** *n.*

dif·frac·tion (di·frak′shən) *n.* *Physics* **1** A deviation of rays of light from a straight course when partially cut off by any obstacle or passing near the edges of an opening, or through a minute hole, generally accompanied by prismatic colors due to interference. Diffraction is a phenomenon accompanying all forms of wave motion, its effect being more marked as the wavelength increases. It is best shown by **diffraction gratings,** plates of glass or polished metal ruled closely with parallel lines, by means of which **diffraction spectra** are obtained. **2** A similar deviation of sound waves in passing the angle or edge of a large body.

dif·fuse (di·fyōōz′) *v.t.* & *v.i.* **·fused, ·fus·ing** **1** To pour or send out so as to spread in all directions; spread abroad; circulate; permeate. **2** To subject to or spread by diffusion. See synonyms under SPREAD. —*adj.* (di·fyōōs′) **1** Characterized by redundance; prolix; verbose. **2** Widely spread out; extended. [<L *diffusus*, pp. of *diffundere* < *dis-* away, from + *fundere* pour] **—dif·fuse·ly** (di·fyōōz′lē) *adv.* **—dif·fuse·ness** (di·fyōōs′nis) *n.*

dif·fus·er (di·fyōō′zər) *n.* **1** One who or that which diffuses. **2** A device for diffusing the heat of a thermoelectric battery, or changing the characteristics of a liquid flow. **3** A reflector placed above an arc lamp to aid in the uniform distribution of the light. Also **dif·fu′sor.**

dif·fus·i·ble (di·fyōō′zə·bəl) *adj.* Capable of being diffused. **—dif·fus′i·bil′i·ty, dif·fus′i·ble·ness** *n.*

dif·fu·sion (di·fyōō′zhən) *n.* **1** The act or process of diffusing, or the state of being diffused; a scattering; dissemination; dispersion; circulation. **2** Prolixity; diffuseness of verbal expression. **3** The scattering and criss-crossing of light rays, producing general illumination rather than direct radiation. **4** *Physics* The intermingling by thermal agitation of the atoms or molecules of two substances initially unmixed but in contact. **5** *Anthropol.* The transmission of culture traits from one area, group, or people to another.

dif·fu·sive (di·fyōō′siv) *adj.* Having the property of diffusing; tending to diffuse; spreading abroad. **—dif·fu′sive·ly** *adv.* **—dif·fu′sive·ness** *n.*

dig (dig) *v.* **dug** (*Archaic* **digged**), **dig·ging** *v.t.* **1** To break up, turn up, or remove (earth, etc.), as with a spade, claws, or the hands. **2** To make or form by or as by digging. **3** To take out or obtain by digging: to *dig* clams. **4** To thrust or force into or against, as a tool, heel, or elbow. **5** To discover or bring out by careful effort or study: often with *up* or *out*: to *dig* up evidence of political corruption. **6** *U.S. Slang* To understand. —*v.i.* **7** To break or turn up earth, etc. **8** To force or make a way by or as by digging. **9** *U.S. Colloq.* To work hard and steadily; plod. **—to dig in** **1** To dig trenches. **2** To entrench (oneself). **3** *Colloq.* To begin to work intensively. —*n. Colloq.* **1** A thrust; poke. **2** A sarcastic remark; jibe; slur. **3** An archeological excavation. **4** *U.S.* A hard-working student. [<OF *diguer* <Gmc. Akin to DIKE.]

di·gam·ma (dī·gam′ə) *n.* The original, but early disused, sixth letter in the Greek alphabet [Ϝ], equivalent in sound to *W*, but in form to *F*. [<Gk. <*di-* two + *gamma* the letter G] **—di·gam·mat·ed** (dī·gam′ā·tid) *adj.*

dig·a·my (dig′ə·mē) *n.* A second, legal marriage. [<LL *digamia* <Gk. <*di-* two + *gamos* a marriage] **—dig′a·mist** *n.* **—dig′a·mous** *adj.*

di·gas·tric (dī·gas′trik) *adj.* *Anat.* **1** Having fleshy ends and a central tendon, as one of the muscles that depress the lower jaw. **2** Having two bellies. [<DI-[2] + Gk. *gastēr* belly]

Dig·by (dig′bē), **Sir Kenelm**, 1603–65, English naval commander, diplomat, and philosopher.

di·gen·e·sis (dī·jen′ə·sis) *n.* *Biol.* Reproduction by two methods, a sexual followed by an asexual; alternation of generations. [<DI-[2] + GENESIS] **—di·ge·net·ic** (dī′jə·net′ik) *adj.*

di·gest (di·jest′, dī-) *v.t.* **1** To convert (food) into chyme in the stomach and intestines; prepare for assimilation. **2** To take in or assimilate mentally. **3** To arrange in systematic form, usually by condensing; summarize and classify. **4** To tolerate patiently; endure. **5** *Chem.* **a** To expose to heat or moisture so as to become softened or decomposed. **b** To treat, as wood, etc., with chemical agents under pressure so as to obtain a desired result. **6** *Obs.* To distribute; disperse. —*v.i.* **7** To be assimilated, as food. **8** To assimilate food. **9** To be subjected to heat, moisture, chemical agents, or pressure. —*n.* (dī′jest) **1** A systematic arrangement, as of writings; classified and abridged summary, as of news; compilation. **2** *Law* A compilation of statutes systematically arranged under proper heads and titles; a brief synopsis of the adjudications of courts as recorded in the original reports. See synonyms under ABRIDGEMENT. [<L *digestus*, pp. of *digerere* < *dis-* away + *gerere* carry]

Digest, The The body of Roman laws collected by order of Justinian; the Pandects.

di·ges·tant (di·jes′tənt, dī-) *n.* Any drug which assists digestion. —*adj.* Digestive.

di·gest·er (dī·jes′tər, di-) *n.* **1** One who makes

a digest, analysis, or summary. 2 A digestant. 3 A strong, closed vessel in which substances may be exposed to the action of water or other liquids at temperatures above their boiling points, to soften or decompose them or to extract some ingredient.

di·gest·i·ble (di·jes'tə·bəl, dī-) *adj.* Capable of being digested or assimilated. **—di·gest'i·bil'i·ty** *n.* **—di·gest'i·bly** *adv.*

di·ges·tion (di·jes'chən, dī-) *n.* 1 *Physiol.* a The process of dissolving and chemically changing food in the stomach, so that it can be assimilated by the blood and furnish nutriment to the body. b The power to digest; the digestive functions. 2 Mental reception and assimilation. 3 Exposure of a substance to heat and moisture preparatory to a chemical or other operation; solution. 4 Any absorption and assimilation, as of carbon dioxide, or of insects and other animal matter, by plants.

di·ges·tive (di·jes'tiv, dī-) *adj.* Pertaining or conducing to digestion. *—n.* A medicine to aid digestion.

dig·ger (dig'ər) *n.* 1 One who or that which digs. 2 A digger wasp. 3 Any implement or part of a machine for lifting and turning the soil or excavating. 4 *Colloq.* A soldier from Australia or New Zealand.

Dig·ger (dig'ər) *n.* Originally, one of a tribe of agricultural North American Indians of Utah; later, an Indian of any tribe of the American Northwest known to subsist chiefly on roots; hence, applied to various tribes of different linguistic stocks.

digger wasp A wasp (family *Sphecidae*) which digs a hole in the ground for its nest, especially the common American genera, *Sphex* or *Ammophila,* and *Bembidula.* For illustration see INSECT (beneficial).

dig·ging (dig'ing) *n.* 1 The act of one who or that which digs. 2 A shallow excavation made by a miner in search for ore.

diggings (dig'ingz) *n. pl.* 1 A mining region; especially a mining region having many exploratory excavations. 2 The materials dug out of such a region. 3 *Brit. Colloq.* Quarters; lodgings.

dight (dīt) *v.t.* **dight** or **dight·ed, dight·ing** *Obs.* 1 To dress, adorn; equip. 2 To prepare. 3 *Dial.* To cleanse; winnow. *—n.* A rub or wipe in order to dry or clean. [OE *dihtan* arrange, prepare <L *dictare.* See DICTATE.]

dig·it (dij'it) *n.* 1 A finger or toe. 2 Any one of the ten Arabic numeral symbols, 0 to 9: so named from counting upon the fingers. 3 *Astron.* The twelfth part of the diameter of the sun or moon. 4 An old English measure of length, equal to about three fourths of an inch. [<L *digitus* finger]

dig·i·tal (dij'ə·təl) *adj.* 1 Of, pertaining to, or like the fingers or digits. 2 Digitate. 3 Showing information, such as numerals, by means of electronics: *digital* watches. *—n.* A key of the piano or organ. **—dig'i·tal·ly** *adv.*

digital computer An electronic computing machine which receives problems and processes the answers in numerical form, especially one using the binary system. Compare *analog computer.*

dig·i·tal·in (dij'ə·tal'in, -tā'lin) *n.* 1 A crystalline, poisonous glucoside, $C_{36}H_{56}O_{14}$, contained in the leaves of the foxglove, of which it is the active principle. 2 Any of several different extracts of foxglove.

dig·i·tal·is (dij'ə·tal'is, -tā'lis) *n.* 1 Any of a genus *(Digitalis)* of tall, Old World herbs of the figwort family, including *D. purpurea,* the foxglove, often cultivated: sometimes called *fairy gloves.* 2 The dried leaves of foxglove, containing several glucosides, some of which are used as a heart tonic. [<NL <L, finger-shaped <*digitus* finger]

dig·i·tal·ism (dij'ə·təl·iz'əm) *n. Pathol.* The effect on the body resulting from the excessive administration of digitalis.

dig·i·tate (dij'ə·tāt) *adj.* 1 *Bot.* Having parts, as leaflets, arranged like the fingers of a hand. 2 *Zool.* Having fingerlike processes. [<L *digitatus* <*digitus* finger] **—dig'i·tat·ed** *adj.* **—dig'i·tate·ly** *adv.*

dig·i·ta·tion (dij'ə·tā'shən) *n.* 1 The state of being digitate. 2 A fingerlike process.

digiti- *combining form* Finger; toe: *digitiform.* [<L *digitus* finger, toe]

dig·i·ti·form (dij'ə·tə·fôrm') *adj.* Having the form or arrangement of a finger or fingers.

dig·i·ti·grade (dij'ə·tə·grād') *adj. Zool.* Walking on the toes, without resting on the whole sole of the foot, as dogs, cats: opposed to *plantigrade.*

dig·i·tox·in (dij'ə·tok'sin) *n.* A powerful form of digitalin. [<DIGI(TALIS) + TOXIN]

di·glot (dī'glot) *adj.* 1 Composed in two languages. 2 Speaking or writing two languages; bilingual. *—n.* A diglot version or book. [<Gk. *diglōttos* <*di-* two + *glōtta* tongue]

dig·ni·fied (dig'nə·fīd) *adj.* 1 Characterized by or invested with dignity; stately. 2 Invested with dignities; promoted in rank; honored. See synonyms under GRAND. **—dig'ni·fied·ly** *adv.*

dig·ni·fy (dig'nə·fī) *v.t.* **·fied, ·fy·ing** 1 To impart or add dignity to; honor; ennoble. 2 To give a high-sounding name to. [<OF *dignefier* <Med. L *dignificare* <*dignus* worthy + *facere* make]

dig·ni·tar·y (dig'nə·ter'ē) *n. pl.* **·tar·ies** One having high official position; especially, a churchman of rank above a canon or priest.

dig·ni·ty (dig'nə·tē) *n. pl.* **·ties** 1 Grave or stately bearing: stateliness. 2 High rank; title, office, or position; distinction, especially in the church. 3 A dignitary; persons of high rank collectively. 4 The state or quality of being excellent, worthy, or honorable. 5 Grade of elevation; rank. [<OF *digneté* <L *dignitas, -tatis* <*dignus* worthy]

di·graph (dī'graf, -gräf) *adj.* Consisting of two letters which represent only one sound. *—n.* A union of two characters representing a single sound, as *oa* in *boat, sh* in *she.* Compare LIGATURE, DIPHTHONG.

di·graph·ic (dī·graf'ik) *adj.* 1 Pertaining to a digraph. 2 Written in two different alphabets or characters.

di·gress (di·gres', dī-) *v.i.* To turn aside from the main subject in speaking or writing; ramble; wander. See synonyms under WANDER. [<L *digressus,* pp. of *digredi* <*di-* away, apart + *gradi* go, step]

di·gres·sion (di·gresh'ən, dī-) *n.* 1 The act of digressing. 2 That which digresses; any part of a discourse or writing that deviates from the main subject. 3 Deviation; divergence. **—di·gres·sion·al** *adj.*

di·gres·sive (di·gres'iv, dī-) *adj.* Given to or marked by digression. **—di·gres'sive·ly** *adv.* **—di·gres'sive·ness** *n.*

Di·gul (dē'gōōl) A river in Netherlands New Guinea, flowing 400 miles SW to the Arafura Sea. Also **Di'goel.**

di·he·dral (dī·hē'drəl) *adj.* 1 Two-sided; formed by or having two plane faces. 2 *Aeron.* Having two or more plane faces: said of an airplane. [<DI-[2] + Gk. *hedra* base]

dihedral angle See under ANGLE.

di·hy·dro·mor·phi·none hydrochloride (dī·hī'drō·môr'fə·nōn) A white, crystalline derivative of morphine, $C_{17}H_{19}O_3N \cdot HCl$, a narcotic and analgesic of great potency: sometimes used as a substitute for morphine.

Di·jon (dē·zhôn') A city in eastern France.

dik-dik (dik'dik') *n.* A small NE African antelope (genera *Madoqua* and *Rhynchotragus*) about a foot tall. [<native name]

DIK-DIK

dike (dīk) *n.* 1 An embankment to protect low land from inundation. 2 A bank formed by the excavation of a ditch; a causeway. 3 A low wall of stone or turf for dividing or enclosing land. 4 *Mining* A fissure which has been filled with solid material other than the ore through which it cuts. 5 *Geol.* A mass of igneous rock filling a fissure in other rocks, into which it has been intruded. *—v.t.* **diked, dik·ing** 1 To surround or furnish with a dike. 2 To drain by ditching. Also spelled *dyke.* [OE *dīc.* Related to DITCH.] **—dik·ing, dik'er** *n.*

di·lac·er·ate (di·las'ə·rāt, dī-) *v.t.* **·at·ed, ·at·ing** To tear asunder; rip to pieces. [<L *dilaceratus,* pp. of *dilacerare* <*dis-* apart + *lacerare* tear, rip] **—di·lac'er·a'tion** *n.*

Di·lan·tin (dī·lan'tin) *n.* Proprietary name for a brand of diphenylhydantoin sodium.

di·lap·i·date (di·lap'ədāt) *v.t.* & *v.i.* **·dat·ed, ·dat·ing** To fall or cause to fall into partial ruin or decay. [<L *dilapidatus,* pp. of *dilapidare* <*dis-* away + *lapidare* throw stones <*lapis, idis* stone] **—di·lap'i·dat·ed** *adj.* **—di·lap'i·da'tion** *n.*

di·la·tant (dī·lā'tənt, di-) *adj.* Having the property of increasing in volume when changed in shape; dilating. *—n.* A dilating substance or instrument. **—di·la'tan·cy** *n.*

di·la·tate (dī·lā'tit, di-) Dilated.

di·la·ta·tion (dī'lə·tā'shən, dil'ə-) *n.* 1 The act or process of dilating. 2 The state of being dilated. 3 That which is dilated. 4 *Pathol.* An excessive enlargement of an organ, orifice, or part. 5 *Med.* A restoration to normal functioning of a small passageway, as in the throat or rectum.

di·late (dī·lāt', di-) *v.* **·lat·ed, ·lat·ing** *v.t.* 1 To make wider, larger or expanded; cause to swell or spread. *—v.i.* 2 To expand, become larger or wider. 3 To speak or write diffusely; enlarge; expatiate: with *on* or *upon.* See synonyms under AMPLIFY. [<L *dilatare* spread out <*dis-* apart + *latus* wide] **—di·lat'a·ble** *adj.* **—di·lat'a·ble·ness, di·lat'a·bil'i·ty** *n.* **—di·lat'a·bly** *adv.*

di·la·tive (dī·lā'tiv, di-) *adj.* Tending to dilate; causing expansion or distention.

dil·a·tom·e·ter (dil'ə·tom'ə·tər) *n.* An apparatus for measuring the expansion of substances, whether due to mechanical or chemical action. [<DILATE + -(O)METER] **—dil'a·tom'e·try** *n.*

di·la·tor (dī·lā'tər, di-) *n.* 1 One who or that which dilates. 2 *Med.* An instrument for opening or expanding a wound, aperture, or cavity. Also **di·la·ta·tor** (dī'lə·tā'tər, dil'ə-), **di·lat'er.**

dil·a·to·ry (dil'ə·tôr'ē, -tō'rē) *adj.* 1 Given to or characterized by delay; tardy; slow. 2 Tending to cause delay. See synonyms under SLOW, TEDIOUS. **—dil'a·to'ri·ly** *adv.* **—dil'a·to'ri·ness** *n.*

Di·lau·did (dī·lô'did) *n.* Proprietary name for a brand of dihydromorphinone hydrochloride.

dil·do (dil'dō) *n. Archaic* A meaningless refrain or burden in old ballads and songs; also, a ballad or song. [? <obs. *dildoe* a phallus]

di·lem·ma (di·lem'ə) *n.* 1 A necessary choice between equally undesirable alternatives, a perplexing predicament. 2 *Logic* A syllogistic argument which presents an antagonist with two (or more) alternatives, but is equally conclusive against him, whichever alternative he chooses. **—the horns of a dilemma** The equally undesirable alternatives between which a choice must be made. [<LL <GK. *dilēmma* <*di-* two + *lēmma* a premise] **—dil·em·mat·ic** (dil'ə·mat'ik) *adj.*

dil·et·tan·te (dil'ə·tan'tē, dil'ə·tänt') *n. pl.* **·ti** or **·tes** 1 A person who interests himself in a subject merely for amusement or superficially. 2 A person who loves the arts. *—adj.* Pertaining to or like a dilettante. [<Ital., ppr. of *dilettare* delight <L *delectare*] **—dil'et·tan'tish, dil'et·tan'tē·ish** *adj.*

dil·et·tan·te·ism (dil'ə·tan'tē·iz'əm, dil'ə·tän'·tiz·əm) *n.* The attitude or characteristics of a dilettante; a superficial approach or interest. Also **dil'et·tan'tism.**

Di·li (dil'ē) The capital of Portuguese Timor. Also **Dil'ly.**

dil·i·gence (dil'ə·jəns, *for def. 3 also Fr.* dē·lē·zhäns') *n.* 1 Assiduous application; industry. 2 Proper heed or attention; meticulous care. 3 A Continental, four-wheeled, public stagecoach, divided into three compartments and having a driver's seat on top: used especially in 18th-century France: also **dil·ly** (dil'ē). See synonyms under INDUSTRY.

DILIGENCE

dil·i·gent (dil'ə·jənt) *adj.* 1 Possessed of or showing diligence; industrious. 2 Done or pursued diligently; painstaking: *diligent* search. See synonyms under ACTIVE, BUSY, INDUSTRIOUS. [<OF <L *diligens, -entis* attentive; orig. ppr. of *diligere* choose] **—dil'i·gent·ly** *adv.*

dill (dil) *n.* 1 An Old World annual of the parsley family (genus *Anethum*) with long-stalked umbels of yellow flowers and aromatic, pungent, medicinal seeds: referred to as *anise* in the Bible. 2 The seeds or leaves of this plant. [OE *dile*]

dill pickle A cucumber pickled in vinegar and flavored with dill.

dil·ly (dil′ē) *n.* 1 The daffodil. 2 *Colloq.* A good one; lulu. [Short for DAFFODIL]

dil·ly-bag (dil′ē·bag′) *n. Austral.* 1 An aborigine's string bag. 2 Any small bag for general carrying purposes.

dil·ly–dal·ly (dil′ē·dal′ē) *v.i.* **–dal·lied, –dal·ly·ing** To waste time, especially in indecision or vacillation; loiter or trifle. [Varied reduplication of DALLY]

dil·u·ent (dil′yo͞o·ənt) *adj.* 1 Serving to dilute, weaken, or thin by admixture; diluting. 2 Having the property of dissolving, solvent. — *n.* That which dilutes. [<L *diluens, -entis,* ppr. of *diluere.* See DILUTE.]

di·lute (di·lo͞ot′, dī–) *v.t.* **·lut·ed, ·lut·ing** 1 To make weaker or more fluid by admixture. 2 To weaken; to reduce the intensity, strength, or purity of (a color, drug, etc.) by admixture. — *adj.* (*also* dī′lo͞ot, -lyo͞ot) Weak; diluted. [<L *dilutus,* pp. of *diluere* < *dis-* away + *luere* wash]

di·lu·tion (di·lo͞o′shən, dī·lyo͞o′shən) *n.* 1 The act of diluting or weakening by admixture. 2 The state of being diluted. 3 Something diluted.

di·lu·vi·al (di·lo͞o′vē·əl) *adj.* 1 Of or pertaining to a flood, especially the Noachian deluge. 2 *Geol.* Produced by a deluge or by floods; consisting of or related to diluvium. Also **di·lu′vi·an.**

di·lu·vi·um (di·lo͞o′vē·əm) *n. Geol.* Coarse rock material transported and deposited by glaciers; glacial drift. [<NL <L, a flood < *diluere* wash away. See DILUTE.]

dim (dim) *adj.* **dim·mer, dim·mest** 1 Obscure from faintness of light or from lack of visual or mental perception; indistinct; shadowy; misty; also, faint, as a sound. 2 Not seeing or perceiving clearly; purblind; obtuse. 3 Lacking luster; tarnished. See synonyms under DARK, FAINT, OBSCURE. — *v.t.* & *v.i.* **dimmed, dim·ming** To render or grow dim; fade. [OE *dim(m)*] — **dim′ly** *adv.* — **dim′ness** *n.*

dime (dīm) *n.* A silver coin, one tenth of a dollar. [<OF *disme* <L *decima* a tenth part < *decem*]

di·men·hy·drin·ate (dī′mən·hī′drə·nāt) *n. Chem.* A white, crystalline, odorless compound, $C_{17}H_{22}NO$, resembling the antihistamines in action.

dime novel A cheap, sensational novel, usually paper-backed, originally costing a dime.

di·men·sion (di·men′shən) *n.* 1 Any measurable extent or magnitude, as length, breadth, or thickness. 2 Importance; extent; bulk. 3 *pl.* Material parts, as of the human body; proportions. 4 *Math.* A factor used to characterize a term: $a^2 b^3 c^4$ is a term of nine *dimensions,* counting all the exponents. See synonyms under MAGNITUDE. [<MF <L *dimensio, -onis* < *dis-* apart + *metiri* measure] — **di·men′sion·al** *adj.*

di·mer (dī′mər) *n. Chem.* A compound formed by the polymerization of two molecules of the same substance. [<DI-[2] + Gk. *meros* part]

di·mer·cap·rol (dī′mər·kap′rol) *n. Chem.* A colorless liquid compound, $C_3H_8OS_2$, containing two sulfhydryl radicals: used in medicine for the treatment of poisoning by arsenic, gold, and mercury. Also called *BAL.* [<DI-[2] + MERCAP(TAN) + PR(OPANE) + -OL[1]]

dim·er·ous (dim′ər·əs) *adj.* 1 Composed of two members or parts. 2 *Bot.* Composed of two members in each circle or whorl: frequently written *2-merous.* 3 *Entomol.* Having two-jointed tarsi. — **dim′er·ism** *n.*

dime store A five- and ten-cent store.

dim·e·ter (dim′ə·tər) *n.* In prosody, a verse of two metrical feet. [<DI-[2] + -METER]

di·meth·yl (dī·meth′əl) *n. Chem.* An alkyl radical, $(CH_3)_2$, generally occurring in combination with other compounds: used in the making of drugs, dyestuffs, solvents, etc.

di·met·ric (dī·met′rik) *adj.* Tetragonal.

di·mid·i·ate (di·mid′ē·āt) *adj. Bot.* Divided in half; lop-sided: said of plants appearing to lack half of a member, or with halves functionally or structurally different. — *v.t.* **·at·ed, ·at·ing** To cut in half. [<L *dimidiatus,* pp. of *dimidiare* halve < *dimidium* a half < *dis-* apart + *medius* middle] — **di·mid′i·a′tion** *n.*

di·min·ish (di·min′ish) *v.t.* 1 To make smaller or less; lessen; decrease. 2 *Music* To lessen (an interval) by a half-step. — *v.i.* 3 To grow or become smaller or less; dwindle; decrease. See synonyms under ABATE, IMPAIR, RETRENCH. [Fusion of ME *diminuen* lessen (<OF *diminuer* <L *diminuere* < *de-* down + *minuere* lessen < *minus* less) and ME *menusen* <OF *menusier* MINISH] — **di·min′ish·a·ble** *adj.*

di·min·ish·ing return (di·min′ish·ing) *Econ.* The theory that an added increment of capital or labor, exceeding a fixed amount, causes a proportionately lower increase in production.

di·min·u·en·do (di·min′yo͞o·en′dō) *Music adj.* & *adv.* Gradually lessening in volume of sound: expressed by *dim., dimin.,* or the sign ⟩. — *n. pl.* **·dos** Diminution, as in force; a diminuendo passage in music. Also called *decrescendo.* [<Ital., ppr. of *diminuire* lessen <L *diminuere.* See DIMINISH.]

dim·i·nu·tion (dim′ə·no͞o′shən, -nyo͞o′-) *n.* 1 The act of diminishing, or the condition of being diminished: reduction. 2 *Music* The repetition of a theme in notes of one half or one quarter the time value of those first used: opposite of *augmentation.* [<AF *diminucium* <L *diminutio, deminutio, -onis* < *diminuere.* See DIMINISH.]

di·min·u·tive (di·min′yə·tiv) *adj.* 1 Of relatively small size; small; little. 2 Diminishing or tending to diminish. 3 Expressing diminished size: said of certain suffixes. — *n.* 1 A word formed from another to express diminished size, or familiarity, affection, etc.: Johnny is a *diminutive* of John, Tom of Thomas, etc. Abbr. *dim.* 2 Anything very small; a very small variety or form of anything. See synonyms under LITTLE, MINUTE.

dim·is·so·ry (dim′ə·sôr′ē, -sō′rē, də·mis′ər·ē) *adj.* 1 Sending away; dismissing to another jurisdiction: said of episcopal letters. 2 Granting leave to go away. [<LL *dimissorius* <L *dimittere* DISMISS]

Di·mi·trov (dē·mē′trôf), **Georgi,** 1882–1949, Bulgarian Communist leader.

dim·i·ty (dim′ə·tē) *n. pl.* **·ties** A sheer cotton fabric woven with stripes, cords, or checks: used for dresses, curtains, etc. [<Ital. *dimito* <Gk. *dimitos* having a double thread < *di-* two + *mitos* thread]

dim·mer (dim′ər) *n.* 1 Anything that dims. 2 *Electr.* An adjustable rheostat used for varying the intensity of illumination in a lamp system.

Dim·net (dēm·ne′), **Ernest,** 1866–1954, French writer: known as *Abbé Dimnet.*

di·morph (dī′môrf) *n.* A form exhibiting dimorphism.

di·mor·phism (dī·môr′fiz·əm) *n.* 1 The quality of existing in two different forms. 2 *Bot.* The existence of two distinct forms of the same organ on the same plant, or on the same species of plant. 3 *Zool.* A difference in form, color, etc., between individuals of the same species, characterizing two distinct types. 4 *Physics* Crystallization of the same substance in two forms. 5 *Ling.* The existence of a word in two different forms in the same language, as *dent* and *dint, card* and *chart;* a doublet. [<Gk. *dimorphos* < *di-* two + *morphē* form] — **di·mor′phic, di·mor′phous** *adj.*

dim–out (dim′out′) *n.* A form of modified lighting in a city or throughout a certain area to prevent or eliminate night-glow: used as a military safety measure. Compare BLACK–OUT.

dim·ple (dim′pəl) *n.* A slight depression on the cheek or chin, or on any smooth surface. — *v.t.* & *v.i.* **dim·pled, dim·pling** To mark with dimples; form dimples. [ME *dympull;* origin uncertain] — **dim′ply** *adj.*

dim·wit (dim′wit′) *n. Slang.* A stupid or simple-minded person. — **dim′wit′ted** *adj.*

din[1] (din) *n.* A loud continuous noise or clamor; a rattling or clattering sound. See synonyms under NOISE. — *v.* **dinned, din·ning** *v.t.* 1 To assail with confusing noise. 2 To urge or press with repetition or insistence. — *v.i.* 3 To make a din. [OE *dyne*]

din[2] (din) *adj. Scot.* Dun.

Di·nah (dī′nə) A feminine personal name. [<Hebrew, judgment]

di·nar (di·när′) *n.* 1 A gold coin of medieval Arabia, especially one issued by the caliphs of Damascus. 2 An Iranian money of account. 3 A silver coin of Yugoslavia. [<Arabic *dīnār* <LGk. *dēnarion* <L *denarius* DENARIUS]

Di·nar·ic Alps (di·nar′ik) The SE division of the eastern Alps, in Yugoslavia along the eastern coast of the Adriatic; highest peak, 8,174 feet.

Dinaric race A tall, brachycephalic people inhabiting the regions along the northern Adriatic: also called *Adriatic race.*

Din·dings (din′dingz) The coastal district of western Perak, Malaya, with adjoining islands; formerly a British possession; 190 square miles.

din·dle (din′dəl, din′əl) *v.t.* & *v.i.* **din·dled, din·dling** *Scot.* & *Brit Dial.* To tingle with pain, as from cold; vibrate. — *n.* A tingling; thrill.

d'In·dy (daṅ·dē′), **(Paul Marie Théodore) Vincent,** 1851–1931, French composer.

dine (dīn) *v.* **dined, din·ing** *v.i.* 1 To eat dinner. 2 To eat any meal. — *v.t.* 3 To entertain at dinner. — **to dine out** To take a meal away from home. [<F *dîner* <OF *disner* <L *dis-* away + *jejunus* fast] — **din′ing** *adj.* & *n.*

din·er (dī′nər) *n.* 1 One who dines. 2 A railroad dining-car. 3 A restaurant built in the form of a railroad car.

di·ner·ic (dī·ner′ik) *adj. Chem.* Of or relating to the surface separating two contiguous liquids in the same container. [DI-[2] + Gk. *nēros* liquid]

di·ne·ro (dē·nā′rō) *n. pl.* **·ros** 1 A Peruvian silver coin, one tenth of a sol. 2 *U.S. Slang* Money. [Sp., penny <L *denarius* DENARIUS]

di·nette (dī·net′) *n.* 1 An alcove where meals are served. 2 A little dinner. [<F]

di·neu·tron (dī·no͞o′tron, -nyo͞o′-) *n. Physics* A transitory atomic particle believed to consist of two neutrons produced by tritons in a nuclear reaction and acting as a unit under certain special conditions.

ding (ding) *v.t.* 1 To ring; sound, as a bell. 2 *Colloq.* To instill by constant iteration; din. 3 *U.S. Slang* & *Brit. Dial.* To beat; strike. — *v.i.* 4 To ring or sound. 5 *Colloq.* To speak with constant iteration. — *n.* The sound of a bell or a sound like it. [Imit. Cf. ON *dengja* hammer, Dan. *dænge* bang, beat]

ding·bat (ding′bat′) *n. Colloq.* 1 Any small object, especially one hurled at another object. 2 A small thing, the name of which is unknown or unrecalled. 3 *Printing* An ornament. [< dial. *ding* knock, dash + BAT[1]]

DINGBATS (*def. 3*)

ding–dong (ding′dong′, -dông′) *n.* 1 The peal of a bell. 2 Any monotonous repetition. 3 A device in a clock for striking the quarter-hours. — *adj.* 1 Characterized by successive blows. 2 *Colloq.* Energetically and closely contested, as a race. [Imit.]

din·ghy (ding′gē, ding′ē) *n. pl.* **·ghies** 1 Any of various kinds of small rowing boats, as a small, clinker-built skiff, a ship's boat, etc. 2 A sleeping car for railway employees. Also **din′gey, din′ghy, din′gy.** [<Hind. *dīngī,* boat]

din·gle (ding′gəl) *n.* 1 A narrow valley; glen. 2 *U.S. Dial.* The enclosed weather porch of a house. See synonyms under VALLEY. [ME *dingel;* origin unknown]

din·go (ding′gō) *n. pl.* **din·goes** The native wild dog (*Canis dingo*) of Australia, having a foxlike face, bushy tail, and reddish-brown color. [< native name]

ding·us (ding′əs) *n. Slang* A thing or device: said of something the name of which is unknown or forgotten. [<Afrikaans < *ding* a thing]

Ding·wall (ding′wôl, -wəl) The county town of Ross and Cromarty county, Scotland.

din·gy (din′jē) *adj.* **din·gi·er, din·gi·est** Of a dusky color, as if soiled; dull; tarnished; grimy; shabby. [Origin uncertain] — **din′gi·ly** *adv.* — **din′gi·ness** *n.*

din·ing-car (dī′ning·kär′) *n.* A railway car in which meals are served en route.

din·ing-room (dī′ning·ro͞om′, -ro͝om′) *n.* A room in which meals are served.

dinitro– *combining form Chem.* Having two

nitro groups, NO_2, as certain isomeric compounds.

di·ni·tro·ben·zene (dī·nī′trō·ben′zēn) *n. Chem.* One of three isomeric compounds, $C_6H_4(NO_2)_2$, that crystallizes in colorless flexible needles, formed by heating benzene with a mixture of nitric and sulfuric acids.

di·ni·tro·cre·sol (dī·nī′trō·krē′sōl) *n. Chem.* A poisonous, orange, coal-tar dye, $C_7H_6O_5N_2$: sometimes used as a substitute for true saffron and in insecticides and rat-killers.

di·ni·tro·phe·nol (dī·nī′trō·fē′nōl) *n. Chem.* Any of six isomeric nitrogen compounds, $C_6H_4O_5N_2$: used in the manufacture of dyes.

dink (dingk) *Scot. v.t.* To dress; array. *—adj.* Neat; trim; tidy. [Origin uncertain]

Din·ka (ding′kä) *n.* **1** A member of a Negroid tribe of the southern Sudan. **2** The Sudanic language of this tribe.

dink·ey (ding′kē) *n. Colloq.* A small engine used for shunting freight. [< DINKY]

dink·um (ding′kəm) *adj. Austral. Colloq.* True; vouched for; honest. Also **dink·y·die** (-kē·dī′).

dink·y (ding′kē) *adj.* **dink·i·er, dink·i·est** *Colloq.* Tiny; insignificant. [< DINK + -Y]

din·mont (din′mənt) *n. Brit. Dial.* A wether between its first and second shearings. [Origin uncertain]

Din·mont (din′mənt) See DANDIE DINMONT.

din·na (din′nə) *Scot.* Do not.

din·ner (din′ər) *n.* **1** The principal meal of the day. **2** A banquet in honor of a notable person or event. **3** A formal feast. [< F *dîner.* See DINE.]

dinner coat or **jacket** A tuxedo jacket.

din·ner·ware (din′ər·wâr′) *n.* The dishes used in a household for serving food.

dino- *combining form* Terrible; huge: *dinosaur.* [< Gk. *deinos* terrible]

di·noc·er·as (dī·nos′ər·əs) *n. Paleontol.* A gigantic, extinct, herbivorous mammal of the Tertiary period (order *Amblypoda*), having three pairs of protuberances on the upper surface of the head. [< DINO- + Gk. *keras* horn]

di·no·saur (dī′nə·sôr) *n. Paleontol.* One of a group of reptiles (orders *Saurischia* and *Ornithischia*) existing on all the continents, but extinct by the end of the Mesozoic period. They varied in size from small, two-footed, pigeonlike carnivores to gigantic, four-footed, aquatic and terrestrial forms, many of them heavily armored, of both herbivorous and carnivorous habits. [< DINO- + Gk. *sauros* lizard] **—di′no·sau′ri·an** *adj.* & *n.*

di·no·there (dī′nə·thir) *n. Paleontol.* One of an extinct Miocene genus (*Dinotherium*) of elephantlike mammals having a pair of huge tusks extending downward from the lower jaw. [< DINO- + Gk. *thēr* wildbeast]

dint (dint) *n.* **1** A small depression made by a blow; a dent. **2** Active agency; force; efficacy: by *dint* of. *—v.t.* To make a dent or dint in; to drive in forcibly. [OE *dynt* blow]

Din·wid·die (din′wid·ē), **Robert,** 1690?–1770, English colonial governor of Virginia.

di·o·bol (dī·ō′bəl) *n.* A silver coin of ancient Greece equal to two obols. See OBOLUS. Also **di·ob·o·lon** (dī·ob′ə·lon). [< Gk. *diōbolon* < *di-* two + *obolos* an obol]

di·oc·e·san (dī·os′ə·sən, dī′ə·sē′sən) *adj.* Of or pertaining to a diocese. *—n.* A bishop in charge of a diocese.

di·o·cese (dī′ə·sēs, -sis) *n.* The territory or the churches under a bishop's jurisdiction. [< OF *diocise* < Med. L *diocesis* < L *dioecesis* a district < Gk. *dioikēsis,* orig. management of a house < *dia-* completely + *oikeein* dwell, manage]

Di·o·cle·tian (dī′ə·klē′shən), **Gaius Aurelius Valerius,** 245–313, Roman emperor, 284–305.

di·ode (dī′ōd) *n. Electronics* A vacuum tube which permits the stream of electrons to pass in one direction only, from the cathode to the anode; a rectifier. [< DI(A)- + Gk. *hodos* a road, way]

di·oe·cious (dī·ē′shəs) *adj. Bot.* Having the male and female organs borne by different individuals, as a plant with stamens and pistils in separate individuals: also spelled *diecious.* Also **di·oi·cous** (dī·oi′kəs). [< DI-[2] + Gk. *oikia* house, dwelling] **—di·oe′cious·ly** *adv.* **—di·oe′cious·ness** *n.*

di·oes·trum (dī·es′trəm, -ēs′-) *n. Zool.* The period of calm in the estrus or mating cycle of animals. [< NL < Gk. *dia-* between + *oistros* passion, frenzy] **—di·oes′trous** *adj.*

Di·og·e·nes (dī·oj′ə·nēz), 412–323 B.C., Greek Cynic philosopher, reputed to have lived in a tub to show his austerity and to have sought for an honest man at midday with a lantern.

Di·o·mede Islands (dī′ə·mēd) Two small islands, one Russian, one American, in the Bering Strait midway between Siberia and Alaska.

Di·o·me·des (dī′ə·mē′dēz) **1** In Greek legend, a king of Argos at the siege of Troy who aided Odysseus in the theft of the Palladium. **2** In Greek mythology, a Thracian king who was fed to his own man-eating horses by Hercules.

di·o·nae·a (dī′ə·nē′ə) *n.* The Venus flytrap. [< NL < Gk. *Diōnē* Dione]

Di·o·ne (dī·ō′nē) In Greek mythology, one of the Oceanids, mother of Aphrodite by Zeus.

di·o·nism (dī′ə·niz′əm) *n.* Normal love between the sexes; heterosexuality: opposed to *uranism.* [< Gk. *Diōnē* Dione]

Di·o·nys·i·a (dī′ə·nish′ē·ə, -nis′-) *n. pl.* Any of the Greek festivals in honor of Dionysus, especially those at Athens connected with the origins of Greek drama. Also **Di′o·nys′i·acs.** — **Di′o·nys′i·ac, Di·o·ny·si·a·cal** (dī′ə·nə·sī′ə·kəl), **Di′o·nys′ian** *adj.* **—Di′o·ny·si′a·cal·ly** *adv.*

Di·o·nys·ian era or **period** (dī′ə·nish′ən, -nis′ē·ən) A period of 532 Julian years, employed to compute the date of Easter. [after *Dionysius Exiguus*]

Di·o·nys·i·us (dī′ə·nish′ē·əs, -nis′-) A masculine personal name. Also *Ital.* **Di·o·ni′gio** (dē′ō·nē′jō), *Ger.* **Di·o·nys** (dē′ə·nēs′), *Pg., Sp.* **Di·o·ny·si·o** (dē′ō·nē′sē·ō), *Gk.* **Di·o·ny·si·os** (dē′ō·nē′sē·ôs). [< Gk., belonging to Dionysus]

—Dionysius Name of two tyrants of Syracuse: **The Elder,** 430–367 B.C., and **The Younger,** 395?–343? B.C.

—Dionysius Exiguus, died 545?, Christian theologian; calculated traditional date of Christ's birth. See CHRISTIAN ERA.

—Dionysius of Alexandria, Saint, theologian of the third century.

—Dionysius of Halicarnassus, 68–7 B.C., Greek historian and rhetorician.

Di·o·ny·sus (dī′ə·nī′səs) In Greek mythology, son of Zeus and Semele, a fertility god especially associated with the vine: identified with the Roman *Bacchus.* See DIONYSIA. Also **Di′o·ny′sos.**

Di·o·phan·tus of Alexandria (dī′ə·fan′təs) Third century A.D., Greek mathematician, inventor of **Diophantine analysis** and **Diophantine equations,** algebraic processes for finding integers that satisfy equations with unknown quantities.

di·op·side (dī·op′sīd, -sid) *n.* A grayish-white or grayish-green variety of pyroxene. [< F < Gk. *di-* two + *opsis* view]

di·op·tase (dī·op′tās) *n.* A vitreous, emerald-green, transparent to translucent, hydrous copper silicate, crystallizing in the hexagonal system. [< F < Gk. *dia-* through + *optos* visible]

di·op·ter (dī·op′tər) *n. Optics* The unit for measuring the refractive power of a lens, expressed as the reciprocal of its focal length in meters: a convergent lens of 1 meter focal length has a power of +1 diopter; a divergent lens, of −1 diopter. Also **di·op′tre, di·op′try.** [< MF *dioptre* < L *dioptra* < Gk., an optical instrument]

di·op·tom·e·ter (dī′op·tom′ə·tər) *n.* An optical instrument for measuring refraction and accommodation of the eye. [< DI(A)- + OPTOMETER] **—di′op·tom′e·try** *n.*

di·op·tric (dī·op′trik) *adj. Optics* **1** Aiding the vision by refraction, as a lens. **2** Of or pertaining to dioptrics. **3** Of or pertaining to a diopter, or the system of numbering optical glasses metrically. Also **di·op′tri·cal.** [< Gk. *dioptrikos* belonging to the use of the dioptra < *dioptra* diopter]

di·op·trics (dī·op′triks) *n.* The branch of optics treating of light-refraction by transparent media.

di·o·ra·ma (dī′ə·rä′mə, -ram′ə) *n.* **1** A painting, or a series of paintings, for exhibition, in which, by the use of cloth transparencies and arrangements of lights, alterations in the pictures are produced in view of the spectators. **2** A group of modeled figures, for exhibition, set in a naturalistic foreground blended into a painted background. **3** A building in which such a picture or group is exhibited. [< Gk. *dia-* through + *horama* a sight] **—di·o·ram·ic** (dī′ə·ram′ik) *adj.*

di·o·rite (dī′ə·rīt) *n.* A granular, crystallized, igneous rock composed of feldspar and hornblende. Also **di′o·ryte.** [< F < Gk. *diorizein* divide < *dia-* through + *horos* limit] **—di·o·rit·ic** (dī′ə·rit′ik) *adj.*

Di·os·cu·ri (dī′ə·skyŏŏr′ī) *n. pl.* Castor and Pollux. [< Gk. *Dioskouroi* < *Dios* of Zeus + *kouros* boy, son]

di·os·mo·sis (dī′os·mō′sis, -oz-) *n.* Osmosis.

Di·os·po·lis (dī·os′pə·lis) A Greek name for THEBES, Egypt.

di·ox·ane (dī·ok′sān) *n. Chem.* A colorless liquid derivative of glycol, $C_4H_8O_2$, having a pleasant, faint odor: used as a solvent for resins, oils, waxes, and organic compounds. [< DI-[2] + OX(A)- + -ANE[2]]

di·ox·ide (dī·ok′sīd, -sid) *n. Chem.* An oxide containing two atoms of oxygen to the molecule. Also **di·ox·id** (dī·ok′sid).

di·ox·in (dī·ok′sən) *n.* An extremely toxic and mutagenic, fat-soluble compound produced inadvertently in the large-scale manufacture of polychlorinated biphenyls.

dip (dip) *v.* **dipped, dip·ping** *v.t.* **1** To put or let down into a liquid momentarily and then take out. **2** To obtain or lift up and out by scooping, bailing, etc.: to *dip* crackers from a barrel, or water from a boat. **3** To lower and then raise, as a flag in salute. **4** To baptize by immersion. **5** To plunge (animals) into a disinfectant so as to rid of insects, germs, etc. **6** To dye by immersion. **7** *Chem.* to coat (a metallic surface) by immersion in a solution of readily decomposed salt. **8** To make (candles) by repeatedly immersing wicks in wax or tallow. **9** *Obs.* To wet. **10** *U.S. Colloq.* To apply snuff to the gums and teeth. *—v.i.* **11** To plunge into and come out of water or other liquid, especially briefly and quickly. **12** To plunge one's hand or a receptacle into water, etc., or into a container, especially so as to take something out. **13** To sink or go down suddenly. **14** To incline downward; go down; decline. **15** *Geol.* To lie at an angle to the horizon, as rock strata. **16** *Aeron.* To drop rapidly and then climb. **17** To engage in or inquire into something slightly or superficially; dabble. **18** To read here and there, as in a book or magazine; browse. **—to dip into** To take a part of (something held in reserve, saved, etc.): to *dip into* one's savings account. See synonyms under IMMERSE. *—n.* **1** The act of dipping; a plunge; bath; depression. **2** A liquid into which something is to be dipped. **3** Inclination, as of the magnetic needle. **4** A candle made by dipping a wick repeatedly into melted tallow. **5** Magnetic dip. **6** *Geol.* Position, other than horizontal, or rock strata; also, the angle between strata and the horizontal plane. **7** *Aeron.* A rapid drop of an airplane followed by a climb. **8** *Colloq.* A pickpocket. **9** A small amount of snuff taken into the mouth on a moistened brush. **10** An antiseptic solution in which sheep are dipped to kill parasites: also called *sheep dip.* [OE *dyppan.* Related to DEEP.]

di·pet·al·ous (dī·pet′əl·əs) *adj. Bot.* Having two petals: also *bipetalous.*

di·phase (dī′fāz′) *adj. Electr.* **1** Having two phases: said of a current compounded of two alternating currents, the maxima and minima of which differ from one another by 90 degrees. **2** The circuit carrying such a current or the generator producing it. Also **di·phas·ic** (dī·fā′zik).

di·phen·yl (dī·fen′əl, dī·fē′nəl) *n.* Biphenyl.

di·phen·yl·a·mine (dī·fen′əl·ə·mēn′, -am′in, -fē′nəl-) *n. Chem.* A crystalline aromatic amine, $(C_6H_5)_2NH$, obtained by heating aniline hydrochloride with aniline: used as a stabilizer and in the manufacture of dyestuffs. Also **di·phen′·yl·am′in** (-am′in).

di·phen·yl·am·ine·chlor·ar·sine (dī·fen′əl·am′·in·klôr′är′sēn, -sin, -fē′nəl-) *n.* Adamsite.

di·phen·yl·cy·an·ar·sine (dī·fen′əl·sī′ə·när′sēn, -sin, -fē′nəl-) *n. Chem.* A lung irritant compound, $(C_6H_5)_2AsCN$, with an odor of garlic and bitter almonds: used in chemical warfare.

di·phen·yl·hy·dan·toin sodium (dī·fen′əl·hī·dan′tō·in, -fē′nəl-) *Chem.* A white, odorless, slightly bitter compound, $C_{15}H_{11}N_2O_2Na$: used in the treatment of epileptic convulsions. Also called *Dilantin.*

di·pho·ni·a (dī·fō′nē·ə, -fōn′yə, di-) *n.* A speech condition in which the same voice produces two distinct tones; double voice. [<NL <Gk. *di-* two + *phōnē* sound]

di·phos·gene (dī·fos′jēn) *n. Chem.* A chemical warfare agent, $C_2O_2Cl_4$, an oily liquid with a suffocating odor and a destructive effect on the lungs.

diph·the·ri·a (dif·thir′ē·ə, dip-) *n. Pathol.* An acute contagious disease, caused by the Klebs–Loeffler bacillus (*Corynebacterium diphtheriae*) and characterized by inflammation, usually of the pharynx, the formation of a false membrane on mucous surfaces, and toxemia. [< NL <F *diphthérie* <Gk. *diphthera* leather, membrane]

diph·the·rit·ic (dif′thə·rit′ik, dip-) *adj. Pathol.* 1 Pertaining to diphtheria. 2 Resembling, or having symptoms characteristic of diphtheria. Also **diph·the′ri·al, diph·the′ric.**

diph·thong (dif′thông, -thong, dip′-) *n.* 1 *Phonet.* A combination of two vowels in one syllable, whether written with two letters, as *oi* in *coil* and *ou* in *doubt*, or with a single letter, as *i* in *fine* and *a* in *bate*. 2 In popular usage, either of the ligatures æ, œ, pronounced as a single sound, but which were true diphthongs in classical Latin. See DIGRAPH, TRIGRAPH. [<F *diphthongue* <LL *diphthongus* <Gk. *diphthongos* <*di-* two + *phthongos* sound] — **diph·thon′gal** *adj.* — **diph·thong′ic** *adj.*

diph·thong·ize (dif′thông·īz, -thong-, dip′-) *v.* **·ized, ·iz·ing** *v.t.* 1 To make a diphthong of; combine with another sound in a diphthong. 2 To pronounce as a diphthong. — *v.i.* 3 To become a diphthong. — **diph′thong·i·za′tion, diph′thong·a′tion** *n.*

di·phyl·lous (dī·fil′əs) *adj. Bot.* Two–leaved. [<DI- + Gk. *phyllon* leaf]

diph·y·o·dont (dif′ē·ō·dont′) *adj. Zool.* Having two sets of teeth, one deciduous, the second permanent. [<Gk. *diphyēs* double + *odous, odontos* tooth]

di·plex (dī′pleks) *adj. Telecom.* 1 Pertaining to the transmission of two simultaneous telegraph messages over one wire in the same direction. 2 Designating a method for the simultaneous transmission or reception of two radio signals. Compare DUPLEX. [<DI-[2] + (DU)PLEX]

diplo– *combining form* Double: *diplococcus.* Also, before vowels, **dipl–.** [<Gk. *diploos* double]

dip·lo·car·di·a (dip′lə·kär′dē·ə) *n. Anat.* A condition in which the right and left sides of the heart are distinctly separated, as by a fissure. [<DIPLO- + Gk. *kardia* heart] — **dip′lo·car′·di·ac** (-ak) *adj.*

dip·lo·coc·cus (dip′lə·kok′əs) *n. pl.* **·coc·ci** (-kok′sī) 1 A cell or micro–organism consisting of two cells united. 2 *Bacteriol.* Any of a genus (*Diplococcus*) of parasitic bacteria, Gram–positive, usually encapsulated and occurring in pairs or chains, including *D. pneumoniae*, the infective agent of lobar pneumonia. See illustration under BACTERIA.

Dip·lo·doc·i·dae (dip′lə·dos′ə·dē) *n. pl. Paleontol.* A family of sauropod, herbivorous dinosaurs of huge size, fossil in the Upper Jurassic rocks of Wyoming and Colorado. The family has but a single genus, **Di·plod·o·cus** (di·plod′ə·kəs), a mounted skeleton of which is 84 1/2 feet long and 14 feet high. [<NL <Gk. *diploos* double + *dokos* a beam]

dip·lo·e (dip′lō·ē) *n. Anat.* The reticulate bony tissue between the two walls of the cranial bones. [<NL <Gk., a fold]

dip·loid (dip′loid) *adj.* 1 Twofold or doubled. 2 *Biol.* Having two sets of chromosomes in the somatic cells, as of all higher organisms. — *n.* 1 A cell having double the haploid number of chromosomes. 2 An isometric crystal with 24 trapezoidal planes.

di·plo·ma (di·plō′mə) *n.* 1 A writing, usually under seal, granting some privilege or authority, or bestowing some honor; especially, the official certificate of graduation in arts, medicine, law, etc., bestowed by a college or university. 2 An instrument authorizing a person to practice a profession. 3 An official document; charter. [<L <Gk. *diplōma* paper folded double, a letter]

di·plo·ma·cy (di·plō′mə·sē) *n. pl.* **·cies** 1 The art, science, or practice of conducting negotiations between nations. 2 Tact, shrewdness, or skill in conducting any affair. [<F *diplomatie* <*diplomate* DIPLOMAT]

dip·lo·mat (dip′lə·mat) *n.* One employed or skilled in diplomacy. [<F *diplomate* <*diplomatique* <NL *diplomaticus* <L *diploma* DIPLOMA]

dip·lo·mat·ic (dip′lə·mat′ik) *adj.* 1 Of or pertaining to diplomacy. 2 Characterized by special tact in negotiation; wary; adroit; tactful. 3 Pertaining to diplomatics. Also **dip′lo·mat′i·cal.** See synonyms under POLITIC. — **dip′lo·mat′i·cal·ly** *adv.*

diplomatic agent 1 Any person who carries on the diplomatic relations of the state he represents in the country to which he has been appointed. See also AMBASSADOR, PLENIPOTENTIARY, MINISTER RESIDENT under RESIDENT, CHARGÉ D'AFFAIRES. 2 A diplomatic representative of the lowest rank, accredited to a country that does not have full sovereignty. 3 An agent who represents a sovereign or head of state for some special purpose.

diplomatic corps Collectively, the heads of foreign diplomatic missions and their staffs at the capital of any country.

diplomatic immunity Exemption of diplomatic agents or representatives, their staffs and premises, from the ordinary processes of local law.

dip·lo·mat·ics (dip′lə·mat′iks) *n.* 1 The science of deciphering ancient documents, charters, etc. 2 Diplomacy.

di·plo·ma·tist (di·plō′mə·tist) *n.* 1 A diplomat. 2 One remarkable for tact and shrewd management.

di·plo·pi·a (di·plō′pē·ə) *n. Pathol.* A derangement of the visual axes whereby two distinct impressions are received from a single object; double vision. Also **dip·lo·py** (dip′·lə·pē). [<NL <Gk. *diploos* double + *ops* eye] — **di·plop·ic** (di·plop′ik) *adj.*

dip·lo·pod (dip′lə·pod) *n. Zool.* Any of a class (*Diplopoda*) of segmented terrestrial arthropods; the millipedes. [<NL *Diplopoda* <Gk. *diploos* double + *pous, podos* foot]

di·plo·sis (di·plō′sis) *n. Genetics* The union of two haploid sets of chromosomes by syngamy of the male and female gametes. [<DIPL(O)- + -OSIS]

dip·lo·some (dip′lə·sōm) *n. Biol.* A small, paired body in the cell, as a double centriole within the centrosome.

dip·lo·so·mi·a (dip′lə·sō′mē·ə, -sōm′yə) *n. Pathol.* An abnormal joining of two bodies. Also **dip·lo·so·ma·tia** (dip′lə·sō·mā′shə, -shē·ə). [<NL <Gk. *diploos* double + *sōma* body]

dip·lo·ste·mo·nous (dip′lə·stē′mə·nəs) *adj. Bot.* Having twice as many stamens as petals. [<DIPLO- + Gk. *stēmōn* thread (used for *stēma* a stamen)]

dip needle An inclinometer (def. 2), used in magnetic compasses.

dip·no·an (dip′nō·ən) *n.* Any of a group (*Dipnoi*) of fishes with regular gills, a single or double lung, and nostrils inside as well as outside the mouth; a lungfish. — *adj.* Of or pertaining to the *Dipnoi*. [<NL <Gk. *dipnoos* <*dis-* two + *pnoē* breath]

dip·o·dy (dip′ə·dē) *n. pl.* **·dies** In prosody, a dimeter. [<L *dipodia* <Gk. <*dis-* two + *pous, podos* foot]

di·pole (dī′pōl′) *n.* 1 *Physics* Any material system having two electric charges, equal in magnitude but of unlike sign, as the proton and electron of a hydrogen atom, or two equal but opposite magnetic poles. 2 *Chem.* A molecule exhibiting polar separation of positive and negative charges.

dip·per (dip′ər) *n.* 1 A long–handled, bowl–shaped utensil, used principally for dipping water, as from a larger vessel into a smaller one. 2 Any of several American birds, so called because they are quick divers; specifically, the dabchick or pied–billed grebe, the small bufflehead duck of North America, and the water ouzel.

Dip·per (dip′ər) *n.* 1 *Astron.* The Big Dipper. 2 A Dunker or member of any other immersionist religious sect: a contemptuous use.

dip·py (dip′ē) *adj. Slang.* Insane; queer; eccentric.

dip·sas (dip′səs) *n. pl.* **dip·sa·des** (dip′sə·dēz) 1 A serpent whose bite was fabled to produce extreme thirst. 2 Any of several tropical colubrine snakes (subfamily *Dipsadomorphinae*). [<L <Gk. <*dipsa* thirst]

dip·sey (dip′sē) *adj.* Deep-sea. — *n. pl.* **·sies** 1 A sinker for a fishing line. 2 A line equipped with a number of hooks and sinkers used for bottom fishing. Also **dip′sie, dip′sy.** [Alter. of DEEP–SEA]

dip·so·ma·ni·a (dip′sə·mā′nē·ə) *n.* An uncontrollable craving for alcoholic drink. [<Gk. *dipsa* thirst + -MANIA]

dip·so·ma·ni·ac (dip′sə·mā′nē·ak) *adj.* Pertaining to or affected by dipsomania: a *dipsomaniac* diathesis: also **dip·so·ma·ni·a·cal** (dip′sə·mə·nī′ə·kəl) — *n.* A person affected with dipsomania; a confirmed drunkard.

dip·ter·al (dip′tər·əl) *adj.* 1 *Archit.* Having or resembling a double peristyle or colonnade. 2 Dipterous. [<L *dipteros* <Gk. *dipteros.* See DIPTEROUS.]

dip·ter·an (dip′tər·ən) *n.* A dipterous insect. Also **dip′ter·on** (-on).

dip·ter·ous (dip′tər·əs) *adj.* 1 *Entomol.* Of or pertaining to an order (*Diptera*) of insects having a single pair of membranous wings with a posterior pair of balancers and a sucking proboscis, including the flies, gnats, mosquitoes, etc. 2 *Bot.* Two–winged, as a seed or fruit. [<Gk. *dipteros* two–winged <*di-* twice + *pteron* wing]

dip·tych (dip′tik) *n.* 1 A double tablet; especially, two tablets of wood, metal, or ivory, hinged together and covered on the inside with wax, on which the ancient Greeks and Romans wrote with a stylus. 2 A cover for a book, resembling this. 3 A double picture or design on a pair of hinged tablets or panels. [<LL *diptycha* <Gk., pair of tablets; orig. neut. pl. of *diptychos* folded <*di-* twice + *ptyssein* fold]

DIPTYCH (*def. 3*)

Di·rac (di·rak′), **Paul Adrien Maurice,** born 1902, British physicist.

Dirac electron *Physics* The positively charged electron as conceived in terms of the wave mechanics formulated by P. A. M. Dirac: now identified as the positron.

dire (dīr) *adj.* **dir·er, dir·est** Extremely calamitous; dreadful; terrible. See synonyms under AWFUL. [<L *dirus* fearful] — **dire′ful** *adj.* — **dire′ly** *adv.* — **dire′ness** *n.*

di·rect (di·rekt′, dī-) *v.t.* 1 To control or conduct the affairs of; manage; govern. 2 To order or instruct with authority; command: often with a clause as object. 3 *Music* To lead as a conductor. 4 To tell (someone) the way. 5 To cause to move, face, or go in a desired direction; aim: He *directed* his gaze toward her. 6 To indicate the destination of, as a letter. 7 To intend, as remarks or insults, to be heard by a person; address: Did you *direct* that remark at me? — *v.i.* 8 To give commands or guidance. 9 To lead performances, musicians, etc. See synonyms under DICTATE, GOVERN, LEAD, REGULATE. — *adj.* 1 Having or being the straightest course; straight; shortest; nearest. 2 Free from intervening agencies or conditions; immediate; exact; in the speaker's words: *direct* discourse. 3 Straightforward, as in meaning, statement or intention; unambiguous; candid; plain. 4 Of succession, lineal: opposed to *collateral*. 5 *Electr.* **a** Continuous as opposed to alternating, as a current. **b** Having the same direction as the primary: said of an induced current: opposed to *inverse*. 6 *Astron.* Designating motion on the celestial sphere from west toward east, in the direction of the sun's movement among the stars: opposed to *retrograde*. 7 *Chem.* Of or pertaining to dyes applied to fabrics without the use of mordants; substantive. See synonyms under IMMEDIATE, RIGHT. — *adv.* By direct course: directly. — *n.* *Music* A mark (⩘or⩘⩗) at the end of a line or page of music indicating the position of

the first note on the next. [<L *directus*, pp. of *dirigere* <*dis-* apart + *regere* set straight]
di·rect–ac·tion (di·rekt′ak′shən, dī-) *adj. Mech.* Having no transmitting mechanism, such as gearwheels, between the part driven and the power that drives it.
direct action An attempt by labor to enforce the granting of its demands by means of demonstrations, strikes, sabotage, or the like.
direct current See under CURRENT.
direct discourse See under DISCOURSE.
direct dye See under DYE.
di·rec·tion (di·rek′shən, dī-) *n.* **1** The position of one point in relation to another without reference to the intervening distance. **2** The trend of a line or of a course of motion, as determined by its spatial relation with some fixed standard of reference; loosely, the trend of a line or course as determined by its extremity. **3** Tendency; aim. **4** The act of directing, governing, or ordering; superintendence; administration. **5** Instruction; command; order. **6** The name and residence of a person; address. **7** *Music* A sign, phrase, or word, in a score designating the proper mood, intensity, etc., of a passage.
Synonyms: aim, bearing, course, inclination, tendency, way. The *direction* of an object is the line of motion or of vision toward it, or the line in which the object is moving, considered from one's own standpoint. *Way*, literally the road or path, comes naturally to mean the *direction* of the road or path. *Bearing* is direction with reference to another object or to the points of the compass. *Course* is the direction of a moving object; *inclination*, that toward which an object leans; *tendency*, that toward which anything stretches or reaches out; *tendency* is stronger and more active than *inclination*. See AIM, CARE, INCLINATION, ORDER, OVERSIGHT.
di·rec·tion·al (di·rek′shən·əl, dī-) *adj.* **1** Pertaining to direction in space. **2** *Telecom.* **a** Adapted for indicating from which of several directions signals are received. **b** Describing an antenna which radiates or receives radio waves more effectively in or from some directions than from others.
di·rec·tion–find·er (di·rek′shən·fīn′dər, dī-) *n. Telecom.* A receiving device with which, by the use of a loop antenna, the direction of radio signals may be determined.
di·rec·tive (di·rek′tiv, dī-) *n.* **1** An order or regulation. **2** The document or the vehicle through which the order is transmitted: applied especially to governmental and military pronouncements. — *adj.* **1** That directs or points out, rules, or governs. **2** Responsive to direction.
di·rect·ly (di·rekt′lē, dī-) *adv.* **1** In a direct line or manner. **2** Without medium, agent, or go-between. **3** Immediately; as soon as possible. **4** Exactly; precisely. See synonyms under IMMEDIATELY. — *conj. Brit.* As soon as.
direct mail Mail sent directly to individuals that promotes the sale of merchandise or services or solicits contributions.
di·rect·ness (di·rekt′nis, dī-) *n.* The quality of being direct; straightness; straightforwardness.
direct object See under OBJECT.
Di·rec·toire (dē·rek·twär′) *n.* The Directory. — *adj.* Of the time, modes, or fashions of the French Directory (1795–99): A *Directoire* gown is characterized by a high waist, low rounded neckline, and puffed sleeves.
di·rec·tor (di·rek′tər, dī-) *n.* **1** One who or that which directs; specifically, a member of a governing body, as of a club or corporation. **2** A conductor of an orchestra. **3** One who supervises a dramatic production. **4** In the Roman Catholic Church, a spiritual guide. **5** *Mil.* An apparatus that systematically computes firing data for use against moving enemy targets. Also **di·rect′er.** See synonyms under MASTER. — **di·rec′tress** *n. fem.*
di·rec·tor·ate (di·rek′tər·it, dī-) *n.* **1** A body of directors. **2** The office or power of a director. Also **di·rec′tor·ship.**
di·rec·to·ri·al (di·rek′tôr′ē·əl, -tō′rē-, dī-) *adj.* **1** That directs; directive. **2** Pertaining to a director or directorate.
di·rec·to·ry (di·rek′tər·ē, dī-) *n. pl.* **·ries 1** An alphabetical or classified list, as of the names and addresses of the inhabitants or business houses of a city. **2** A collection of rules; especially a book of directions for church worship, as the ordinal of the Roman Catholic Church, or the rules adopted by the Scottish General Assembly in 1645, still observed in the Presbyterian Church. **3** A body of directors. — *adj.* Containing directions.
Di·rec·to·ry (di·rek′tər·ē, dī-) *n.* The five men who were the executives of the French government after the downfall of the Convention, October 26, 1795, to November 9, 1799.
di·rec·trix (di·rek′triks, dī-) *n. pl.* **·tri·ces** (-tri·sēz) or **·trix·es 1** *Mil.* In gunnery, the median line in the plane of fire. **2** *Geom.* A line which so determines the motion of another line, or of a point, that the latter shall describe some surface or curve.
dire·ful (dīr′fəl) *adj.* Most dire; dreadful; terrible. See synonyms under AWFUL, FRIGHTFUL. — **dire′ful·ly** *adv.* — **dire′ful·ness** *n.*
dirge (dûrj) *n.* **1** A song, tune, lament, or wail expressing grief and mourning. **2** A hymn or choral service at a funeral. [<L *dirige* (imperative of *dirigere* DIRECT), the first word of the antiphon (*Psalms* v 8) of matins in the Latin burial office] — **dirge′ful** *adj.*
dir·i·ga·tion (dir′ə·gā′shən) *n.* **1** The power of controlling or modifying involuntary bodily functions, such as the pulse, temperature, or digestion. **2** The exercise of that power. [<L *dirigere* DIRECT + -ATION]
dir·i·gi·ble (dir′ə·jə·bəl) *adj.* **1** That may be directed or controlled: a *dirigible* balloon.

A RIGID TYPE OF DIRIGIBLE

2 *Aeron.* Designating an airship, the outer envelope of which is of elongated form, provided with a propelling system, cars, rudders, and stabilizing surfaces. The form of the envelope may be **nonrigid**, by the pressure of the contained gases assisted by the car-suspension system; **rigid**, by a framework contained within the envelope; or **semirigid**, by means of attachment to an exterior girder construction containing the cars. — *n.* An airship. [<L *dirigere* DIRECT + -IBLE] — **dir′i·gi·bil′i·ty** *n.*
dir·i·go (dir′i·gō) *Latin* I direct: motto of the State of Maine.
dir·i·ment (dir′ə·mənt) *adj.* Rendering absolutely void; nullifying. [<L *dirimens, -entis*, ppr. of *dirimere* <*dis-* apart + *emere* take]
diriment impediment of marriage A sufficient cause for rendering a marriage null and void: a Roman Catholic usage.
dirk (dûrk) *n.* A dagger or poniard. — *v.t.* To stab with a dirk. [Origin unknown]
dirl (dirl, dûrl) *v.t.* & *v.i. Scot.* To tingle; vibrate.
dirn·dl (dûrn′dəl) *n.* **1** A woman's dress with a full skirt gathered to a tight bodice. **2** Such a skirt without the bodice: also **dirndl skirt.** [<G *dirndl* girl]
dirt (dûrt) *n.* **1** Any foul or filthy substance; refuse; trash. **2** Loose earth; garden loam. **3** Uncleanness in action or speech; abuse or obscenity. **4** In placer mining, washed-down material or detritus containing precious metal: called **pay dirt** when it yields more than enough to compensate for working. — *adj.* Made of earth: a *dirt* road. [Metathetical var. of earlier *drit* <ON, dirt, bird droppings]
dirt–cheap (dûrt′chēp′) *adj.* & *adv. U.S. Colloq.* Very inexpensive; as cheap as dirt.
dirt–eat·ing (dûrt′ē′ting) *n.* Geophagy.
dirt farmer *U.S. Colloq.* A farmer who does his own work: opposed to *gentleman farmer.*
dirt·y (dûr′tē) *adj.* **dirt·i·er, dirt·i·est 1** Unclean; foul; imparting dirt; filthy. **2** Base; despicable; contemptible; also, mean or unkind. **3** Impure; not clear: said of colors. **4** Uncomfortable or disagreeable to the traveler, as weather or roads. **5** Obscene. See synonyms under FOUL. — *v.t.* & *v.i.* **dirt·ied, dirt·y·ing** To make or become dirty or soiled. — **dirt′i·ly** *adv.* — **dirt′i·ness** *n.*
dirty work 1 *Colloq.* Trickery; deceit; foul play. **2** A difficult job or the most difficult part of a job.
Dis (dis) **1** In Roman mythology, god of the lower world: identified with *Pluto.* **2** The kingdom of the dead: identified with the Greek *Hades.*
dis–[1] *prefix* **1** Apart; away from: *disembody, dislodge, dismiss, dissolve.* **2** The reverse of or the undoing of (what is expressed in the rest of the word): *disarm, disband, disconnect, disrobe, disown.* **3** Deprivation of some quality, power, rank, etc.: *disable, disbar, discolor, disenfranchise.* **4** Not: *disadvantageous, disloyal, distasteful.* **5** Completely; thoroughly (simple intensive with an already negative word): *disannul.* Also: *di–* before *b, d, l, m, n, r, s, v,* and usually before *g,* as in *digress, direct, diverge* (in Late Latin this was often changed back to the full form, as in *dismiss, disrupt*); *dif–* before *f,* as in *differ.* The living English prefix is always in the form *dis–.* [<L *dis-*, sometimes replacing OF *des-* (see DE-)]
dis–[2] *prefix* Var. of DI-[2]. [<Gk. *dis* twice]
dis·a·bil·i·ty (dis′ə·bil′ə·tē) *n. pl.* **·ties 1** That which disables. **2** Lack of ability; inability. **3** Legal incapacity or inability to act.
disability clause In insurance policies, a clause waiving premiums upon certain disabilities of the policyholders.
dis·a·ble (dis·ā′bəl) *v.t.* **·a·bled, ·a·bling 1** To render incapable or unable; cripple; impair. **2** To render legally incapable, as of inheriting property, etc. — **dis·a′ble·ment** *n.*
dis·a·bled (dis·ā′bəld) *adj.* Incapacitated.
dis·a·buse (dis′ə·byo͞oz′) *v.t.* **·a·bused, ·a·bus·ing** To rid of a false notion or impression.
di·sac·cha·ride (dī·sak′ə·rīd, -rid) *n. Biochem.* One of a series of carbohydrates, as lactose and maltose, constituting the chief ingredients of sugarcane and milk: on hydrolysis, they yield two monosaccharides. Also **di·sac′cha·rid** (-rid). [<DI-[2] + SACCHARIDE]
dis·ac·cord (dis′ə·kôrd′) *n.* The state of being inharmonious; disagreement; incongruity. — *v.t.* To disagree; refuse assent. [<OF *desacorder* <*des-* away + *acorder* ACCORD]
dis·ac·cus·tom (dis′ə·kus′təm) *v.t.* To free of a habit or of anything to which one has been habituated. — **dis′ac·cus′tomed** *adj.* — **dis′ac·cus′tomed·ness** *n.*
dis·ad·van·tage (dis′əd·van′tij, -vän′-) *n.* **1** That which hinders, prevents, or is prejudicial to success. **2** Prejudice to interest, reputation, credit, or other good; loss; drawback; injury. **3** A state of inferiority; unfavorable condition: The army was at a *disadvantage.* See synonyms under INJURY, LOSS. — *v.t.* **·taged, ·tag·ing** To injure the interest of; prejudice; hinder. [<OF *désavauntage* <*dés-* away (<L *dis-*) + *avauntage* ADVANTAGE]
dis·ad·van·taged (dis′əd·van′təjd) *adj.* Having less than what is regarded as basic or minimal for decent living, as money, social position, etc.; underprivileged.
dis·ad·van·ta·geous (dis·ad′vən·tā′jəs) *adj.* Attended with disadvantage; detrimental; inconvenient. — **dis·ad′van·ta′geous·ly** *adv.* — **dis·ad′van·ta′geous·ness** *n.*
dis·af·fect (dis′ə·fekt′) *v.t.* To destroy or weaken the affection or loyalty of; alienate.
dis·af·fect·ed (dis′ə·fek′tid) *adj.* Alienated in feeling or loyalty; estranged. See synonyms under INIMICAL. — **dis′af·fect′ed·ly** *adv.*
dis·af·fec·tion (dis′ə·fek′shən) *n.* Discontent; disloyalty; estrangement.
dis·af·fil·i·ate (dis′ə·fil′ē·āt) *v.t.* & *v.i.* **·at·ed, ·at·ing** To sever affiliation (with).
dis·af·firm (dis′ə·fûrm′) *v.t.* **1** To deny; contradict. **2** *Law* **a** To reverse; set aside, as a decision. **b** To repudiate; disclaim, as a contract. — **dis′af·firm′ance, dis·af·fir·ma·tion** (dis·af′ər·mā′shən) *n.*
dis·af·for·est (dis′ə·fôr′ist, -for′-) *v.t.* **1** In English law, to reduce from the privileges of a forest to common ground. Compare AFFOREST. **2** To clear of forests. [<Med. L *disafforestare* <*dis-* away + *afforestare* AFFOREST]
dis·a·gree (dis′ə·grē′) *v.i.* **·a·greed, ·a·gree·ing 1** To vary in opinion; differ; dissent. **2** To quarrel. **3** To fail to agree or harmonize, as facts. **4** To be unfavorable or injurious in action or effect, as food or climate: with *with.* [<OF *desagreer* <*des-* away (<L *dis-*) + *agreer* AGREE]
dis·a·gree·a·ble (dis′ə·grē′ə·bəl) *adj.* Repugnant to taste, sentiment, opinion, or the senses; not agreeable; displeasing; unpleasant. — **dis′a·gree′a·ble·ness, dis′a·gree′a·bil′i·ty** *n.* — **dis′a·gree′a·bly** *adv.*

dis·a·gree·ment (dis′ə·grē′mənt) *n.* Failure to agree; dissimilarity; variance; unsuitableness; incongruity; altercation; quarrel. See synonyms under DIFFERENCE, QUARREL.

dis·al·low (dis′ə·lou′) *v.t.* **1** To refuse to allow or permit. **2** To reject as untrue or invalid. See synonyms under PROHIBIT. [<OF *desalouer* < *des-* away (<L *dis-*) + *alouer* ALLOW] — **dis′al·low′a·ble** *adj.* — **dis′al·low′ance** *n.*

dis·an·nul (dis′ə·nul′) *v.t.* To annul completely. — **dis′an·nul′ment** *n.*

dis·a·noint (dis′ə·noint′) *v.t.* To invalidate the consecration of.

dis·ap·pear (dis′ə·pir′) *v.i.* **1** To pass from sight or view; fade away; vanish. **2** To cease to exist. — **dis′ap·pear′ance** *n.*

disappearing carriage *Mil.* A mechanism by which coastal artillery of large caliber is raised above a protective embankment before firing and automatically lowered behind it after the discharge.

dis·ap·point (dis′ə·point′) *v.t.* **1** To fail to fulfil the expectation, hope, or desire of (a person). **2** To prevent the fulfilment of (a hope or plan); frustrate. [<OF *desappointer* < *des-* away (<L *dis-*) + *appointer* APPOINT] — **dis′ap·point′ed** *adj.* — **dis′ap·point′ed·ly** *adv.*

dis·ap·point·ment (dis′ə·point′mənt) *n.* **1** The state, condition, or sense of being disappointed. **2** That which disappoints: failure; frustration. See synonyms under CHAGRIN, MISFORTUNE.

dis·ap·pro·ba·tion (dis·ap′rə·bā′shən) *n.* Disapproval; unfavorable judgment. — **dis·ap·pro·ba·to·ry** (dis·ap′rə·bə·tôr′ē, -tō′rē) *adj.*

dis·ap·prov·al (dis′ə·pro͞o′vəl) *n.* The act of disapproving; the withholding of approval; disapprobation. See synonyms under ANIMADVERSION.

dis·ap·prove (dis′ə·pro͞ov′) *v.* **·proved, ·prov·ing** *v.t.* **1** To regard with disfavor or censure; condemn. **2** To refuse assent to; decline to approve. — *v.i.* **3** To have or express an unfavorable opinion: often with *of.* — **dis′ap·prov′ing** *adj.* — **dis′ap·prov′ing·ly** *adv.*

dis·arm (dis·ärm′) *v.t.* **1** To deprive of weapons. **2** To render harmless; make unable to do damage, attack, or defend. **3** To allay or reduce, as suspicion or antagonism. — *v.i.* **4** To lay down arms. **5** To reduce or restrict the size of armed forces. [<OF *desarmer* < *des-* away (<L *dis-*) + *armer* arm <L *armare* < *arma* arms]

dis·ar·ma·ment (dis·är′mə·mənt) *n.* **1** The act of disarming. **2** The reduction or limitation of armed forces or of certain types of weapons.

dis·arm·ing (dis·är′ming) *adj.* Removing suspicion or anger.

dis·ar·range (dis′ə·rānj′) *v.t.* **·ranged, ·rang·ing** To disturb the arrangement of. See synonyms under DISPLACE. — **dis′ar·range′ment** *n.*

dis·ar·ray (dis′ə·rā′) *n.* **1** Want of array or regular order; disorder; confusion. **2** Scantiness of dress; negligent or disordered dress. — *v.t.* **1** To impair the order of; throw into disorder, as an army. **2** To undress.

dis·ar·tic·u·late (dis′är·tik′yə·lāt) *v.* **·lat·ed, ·lat·ing** *v.t.* To separate the joints of. — *v.i.* To become separated or unjointed. — **dis′·ar·tic′u·la′tion** *n.* — **dis′ar·tic′u·la′tor** *n.*

dis·as·sem·ble (dis′ə·sem′bəl) *v.t.* **·bled, ·bling** To take apart.

dis·as·sem·bly (dis′ə·sem′blē) *n.* A state of being separated into component parts; a disassembling.

dis·as·so·ci·ate (dis′ə·sō′shē·āt) *v.t.* **·at·ed, ·at·ing** To dissociate. — **dis′as·so′ci·a′tion** *n.*

dis·as·ter (di·zas′tər, -zäs′-) *n.* **1** Crushing misfortune; a calamity; a terrible accident. **2** *Obs.* An evil portent; especially, in astrology, the inimical aspect or action of a star or planet. See synonyms under ACCIDENT, BLOW, MISFORTUNE. [<MF *désastre* < *des-* away + *astre* a star <L *astrum* <Gk. *astron*]

dis·as·trous (di·zas′trəs, -zäs′-) *adj.* **1** Occasioning or accompanied by disaster; calamitous. **2** Threatening disaster; ill-boding; gloomy; dismal; ill-starred. — **dis·as′trous·ly** *adv.* — **dis·as′trous·ness** *n.*

dis·a·vow (dis′ə·vou′) *v.t.* To refuse to acknowledge; disclaim responsibility for or approval of; disown; repudiate. See synonyms under RENOUNCE. [<OF *desavouer* < *des-* away (<L *dis-*) + *vouer* AVOW]

dis·a·vow·al (dis′ə·vou′əl) *n.* A disowning; denial; repudiation.

dis·band (dis·band′) *v.t.* To break up the organization of; remove from military service. — *v.i.* To break up; scatter; cease to be an organization. [<MF *desbander* < *des-* away (<L *dis-*) + *bander* tie < *bande* a band] — **dis·band′ment** *n.*

dis·bar (dis·bär′) *v.t.* **·barred, ·bar·ring** To deprive of the status of a lawyer; expel from the bar. — **dis·bar′ment** *n.*

dis·be·lief (dis′bi·lēf′) *n.* A conviction that a statement is untrue; positive unbelief. See synonyms under DOUBT.

dis·be·lieve (dis′bi·lēv′) *v.t.* & *v.i.* **·lieved, ·liev·ing** To refuse to believe; deem false. — **dis′be·liev′er** *n.*

dis·bos·om (dis·bo͝oz′əm) *v.t.* To reveal, as a secret; unbosom; confess.

dis·branch (dis·branch′, -bränch′) *v.t.* **1** To deprive of branches, as a tree; prune; trim. **2** To cut off, as a branch.

dis·bur·den (dis·bûr′dən) *v.t.* **1** To relieve (someone or something) of a burden; unload. **2** To unload or get rid of (a burden). — *v.i.* **3** To put off a load or burden; unburden. Also *Obs.* **dis·bur′then** (-thən). — **dis·bur′den·ment** *n.*

dis·burse (dis·bûrs′) *v.t.* **·bursed, ·burs·ing** To pay out; expend. [<OF *desbourser* < *des-* away (<L *dis-*) + *bourse* a purse] — **dis·burs′a·ble** *adj.* — **dis·burs′er** *n.*

dis·burse·ment (dis·bûrs′mənt) *n.* **1** The act of disbursing. **2** That which is expended; money paid out.

disc (disk) *n.* **1** A phonograph record. **2** *Biol.* A disk (def. 2). [Var. of DISK]

disc·al (dis′kəl) *adj.* Of, pertaining to, or like a disk.

dis·calced (dis·kalst′) *adj.* Having the shoes off; bare-footed: applied especially to those religious orders whose members go unshod or wear sandals. [<L *discalceatus* < *dis-* not + *calceatus* a shoe, orig. pp. of *calceare* shoe]

dis·cant (dis′kant, dis·kant′) See DESCANT.

dis·card (dis·kärd′) *v.t.* **1** To cast aside as useless or undesirable; reject; dismiss. **2** In card games, to throw out (a card or cards) from one's hand; also, to play (a card, other than a trump, of a different suit from the suit led). — *v.i.* **3** In card games, to throw out a card or cards from one's hand. See synonyms under RENOUNCE. — *n.* (dis′kärd) **1** The act of discarding. **2** A card or cards discarded. **3** A person or thing cast off or dismissed.

dis·case (dis·kās′) *v.t.* **·cased, ·cas·ing** To remove the case or covering of; unsheathe.

dis·cept (di·sept′) *v.i.* To dispute or debate. [<L *disceptare* < *dis-* away + *ceptare,* freq. of *capere* take] — **dis′cep·ta′tion** *n.*

dis·cern (di·zûrn′, di·sûrn′) *v.t.* **1** To perceive, as with sight or mind; recognize; apprehend. **2** To discriminate mentally; recognize as separate and different. — *v.i.* **3** To distinguish; discriminate. [<OF *discerner* <L *discernere* < *dis-* apart + *cernere* separate] — **dis·cern′er** *n.*

Synonyms: descry, discriminate, distinguish, perceive, recognize. What we *discern* we see apart from all other objects; what we *discriminate* we judge apart; what we *distinguish* we mark apart, or *recognize* by some special mark or manifest difference. We *descry* (originally *espy*) what is difficult to discover. Compare DISCOVER, KNOW, LOOK.

dis·cern·i·ble (di·zûr′nə·bəl, -sûr′-) *adj.* Capable of being discerned; perceivable. See synonyms under EVIDENT. — **dis·cern′i·ble·ness** *n.* — **dis·cern′i·bly** *adv.*

dis·cern·ing (di·zûr′ning, -sûr′-) *adj.* Quick to discern; discriminating; penetrating. See synonyms under ACUTE, ASTUTE, INTELLIGENT, KNOWING, SAGACIOUS. — **dis·cern′ing·ly** *adv.*

dis·cern·ment (di·zûrn′mənt, -sûrn′-) *n.* **1** The act or process of discerning. **2** The mental power of discerning; keenness of judgment; insight. See synonyms under ACUMEN, UNDERSTANDING, WISDOM.

dis·cerp (di·sûrp′) *v.t. Obs.* **1** To tear or pluck to pieces. **2** To disjoin; separate; divide. [<L *discerpere* < *dis-* apart + *carpere* pluck] — **dis·cerp′ti·ble** *adj.* — **dis·cerp′tion** *n.*

dis·charge (dis·chärj′) *v.* **·charged, ·charg·ing** *v.t.* **1** To unload; remove the contents of: to *discharge* a ship. **2** To remove or send forth: to *discharge* passengers or cargo. **3** To send forth; emit (fluid). **4** To shoot or fire, as a gun, bow, shot, or arrow. **5** To dismiss from office; fire. **6** To release; set at liberty, as a prisoner, soldier, or patient. **7** To relieve of duty or obligation: to *discharge* a jury. **8** To perform or fulfil the functions and duties of (a trust, office, etc.). **9** To pay (a debt) or meet and satisfy (an obligation or duty). **10** In dyeing, to remove (color) from textiles. **11** *Obs.* To free of blame or accusation. **12** *Electr.* To free of an electrical charge. — *v.i.* **13** To get rid of a load, burden, etc. **14** To go off, as a cannon. **15** To give or send forth contents: The wound *discharges* constantly. **16** *Electr.* To lose a charge of electricity. See synonyms under ABSOLVE, ACCOMPLISH, BANISH, CANCEL, DELIVER, PAY, RELEASE. — *n.* (*also* dis′chärj) **1** The act of removing a load or charge. **2** A firing of a weapon; a release of a missile. **3** An emission; ejection; an issuing forth. **4** The rate or amount of outflow. **5** That which is discharged or released, as blood from a wound. **6** A relieving or freeing from burden or obligation. **7** The payment of a debt. **8** Fulfilment; execution: the *discharge* of one's duty. **9** Release or dismissal from service, employment, or custody. **10** Something which releases or dismisses, as a certificate separating one from military service. **11** *Electr.* **a** The equalization of difference of potential between terminals of a condenser or of a current source, when connected by a conductor, or placed in very near contact. **b** The removal of an electrostatic charge, as from a Leyden jar, a battery, etc. [<OF *deschargier* < *des-* away (<L *dis-*) + *chargier* CHARGE] — **dis·charge′a·ble** *adj.* — **dis·charg′er** *n.*

dis·ci·ple (di·sī′pəl) *n.* One who accepts and follows a teacher or a doctrine; a pupil or learner. **2** One of **the disciples,** the twelve chosen companions and apostles of Jesus. See synonyms under ADHERENT, CONVERT. — *v.t.* **·pled, ·pling 1** To cause to become a disciple; convert. **2** *Obs.* To train; teach. [OE *discipul* <L *discipulus* < *discere* teach; infl. in form by OF *diciple, disciple* <L *discipulus*] — **dis·ci′ple·ship** *n.*

Disciples of Christ A religious body that originated in Pennsylvania in 1809, in connection with the labors of Thomas and Alexander Campbell, holding to Christian union on the basis of the Bible alone, rejecting creeds and party names, and practicing immersion and weekly communion: also called *Christians.*

dis·ci·pli·nal (dis′ə·plī′nəl, dis′ə·plin·əl) *adj.* Of or pertaining to discipline.

Dis·ci·plin·ant (dis′ə·plin·ənt) *n.* One of a former Spanish religious order whose members publicly scourged and otherwise tortured themselves; a Flagellant.

dis·ci·pli·nar·i·an (dis′ə·plə·nâr′ē·ən) *n.* One who disciplines; one strict in discipline; a martinet. — *adj.* Disciplinary.

dis·ci·pli·nar·y (dis′ə·plə·ner′ē) *adj.* Of, relating to, or having the nature of discipline; employed in discipline.

dis·ci·pline (dis′ə·plin) *n.* **1** Systematic training or subjection to authority; especially, the training of the mental, moral, and physical powers by instruction and exercise. **2** The result of this; subjection; habit of obedience. **3** Training resulting from misfortune, troubles, etc. **4** Punishment for the sake of training; correction; chastisement. **5** A system of rules, or method of practice, as of a church. **6** The studies collectively embraced in a course of learning. **7** The self-scourging of some ascetics of the Roman Catholic Church; also, a scourge. See synonyms under EDUCATION. — *v.t.* **·plined, ·plin·ing 1** To train to obedience or subjection. **2** To drill; educate. **3** To punish or chastise. See synonyms under CHASTEN, TEACH. [<OF <L *disciplina* instruction < *discipulus* DISCIPLE] — **dis′ci·plin·a·ble** *adj.* — **dis′ci·plin·er** *n.*

dis·cis·sion (di·sish′ən, -sizh′-) *n.* **1** A cutting into a part. **2** *Surg.* An operation to relieve a soft cataract by lacerating the capsule of the lens. [<LL *discissio, -onis* < *dis-* apart + *scindere* cleave, cut]

disc jockey An announcer on a radio program that presents recorded music, usually interspersed with comments and commercials.

dis·claim (dis·klām′) *v.t.* **1** To disavow any claim to, connection with, or responsibility for; disown; reject. **2** To reject or deny the claim or authority of; deny. **3** *Law* To renounce a right or claim to. —*v.i.* **4** *Law* To renounce or repudiate a legal claim. See synonyms under RENOUNCE. [< AF *desclamer* < *des-* away (< L *dis-*) + *clamare* cry]

dis·claim·er (dis·klā′mər) *n.* **1** One who disclaims. **2** A disclaiming act, notice, or instrument.

dis·cla·ma·tion (dis′klə·mā′shən) *n.* A disavowal.

dis·close (dis·klōz′) *v.t.* **·closed, ·clos·ing 1** To expose to view; lay bare; uncover. **2** To make known; divulge; open. **3** *Obs.* To open. See synonyms under CONFESS, DISCOVER, INFORM, PUBLISH. [< OF *desclos-*, stem of *desclore* close] —**dis·clos′er** *n.*

dis·clo·sure (dis·klō′zhər) *n.* **1** The act or process of disclosing. **2** Anything disclosed.

dis·co (dis′kō) *n.* A discothèque. —*v.i.* **·coed, ·co·ing** To dance to music at a disco.

dis·cob·o·lus (dis·kob′ə·ləs) *n.* A discus thrower. Also **dis·cob′o·los.** —**the Discobolus** A famous Greek statue of a discus thrower, attributed to Myron. [< L < Gk. *diskobolos* < *diskos* a discus + *ballein* throw]

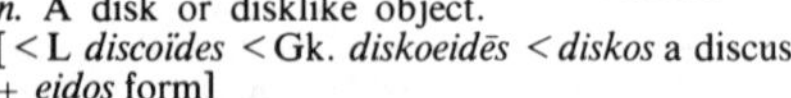

DISCOBOLUS After statue by Myron in the Vatican.

dis·coid (dis′koid) *adj.* **1** *Zool.* Having the form of a disk, as certain univalve shells with the whorls coiled in one plane. **2** Pertaining to, like, or forming a disk or disks. **3** *Bot.* Disk-shaped; rayless, as the tubular central florets of a composite flower, such as the sunflower: also **dis·coi′dal.** —*n.* A disk or disklike object. [< L *discoïdes* < Gk. *diskoeidēs* < *diskos* a discus + *eidos* form]

dis·col·or (dis·kul′ər) *v.t.* To give an unnatural color to; stain. —*v.i.* To become stained, faded, or of a changed color. Also *Brit.* **dis·col′our.** [< OF *descolorer* < *des-* away (< L *dis-*) + *colorer* color < L *colorare* < *color* a color]

dis·col·or·a·tion (dis·kul′ə·rā′shən) *n.* **1** The act or process of discoloring; a discolored state or appearance; changed hue or aspect. **2** A stain or discolored spot or part. Also **dis·col′or·ment.**

dis·com·fit (dis·kum′fit) *v.t.* **1** To defeat the plans or purposes of; frustrate. **2** To rout; vanquish. See synonyms under CONQUER. —*n. Obs.* Rout. [< OF *desconfit*, pp. of *desconfire* < *des-* away (< L *dis-*) + *confire* < L *conficere*. See CONFECT.]

dis·com·fi·ture (dis·kum′fi·chər) *n.* The act of discomfiting or the state of being discomfited: defeat. See synonyms under RUIN.

dis·com·fort (dis·kum′fərt) *n.* **1** The state of being positively uncomfortable; disturbance; disquietude. **2** That which causes an uncomfortable condition. See synonyms under PAIN. —*v.t.* **1** To make uneasy; trouble. **2** *Obs.* To dishearten; dismay. [< OF *desconfort* < *desconforter* < *des-* away (< L *dis-*) + *conforter* COMFORT]

dis·com·fort·a·ble (dis·kum′fər·tə·bəl) *adj.* **1** Uncomfortable. **2** *Archaic* Producing discomfort.

dis·com·mend (dis′kə·mend′) *v.t.* **1** To express disapproval of. **2** To speak of dissuasively. **3** *Obs.* To cause to be regarded unfavorably. —**dis′com·mend′a·ble** *adj.* —**dis′com·men·da′·tion** *n.*

dis·com·mode (dis′kə·mōd′) *v.t.* **·mod·ed, ·mod·ing** To cause inconvenience to; trouble; disturb. [< DIS-[1] + L *commodus* convenient]

dis·com·mod·i·ty (dis′kə·mod′ə·tē) *n. pl.* **·ties 1** The state, fact, or quality of being inconvenient, troublesome, or injurious. **2** Something that causes annoyance, inconvenience, trouble, or loss.

dis·com·mon (dis·kom′ən) *v.t. Law* To change from the condition of a common, as land; make private property of.

dis·com·pose (dis′kəm·pōz′) *v.t.* **·posed, ·pos·ing 1** To disturb the composure of; make uneasy; ruffle; agitate. **2** To disorder or disarrange; derange. See synonyms under ABASH.

dis·com·po·sure (dis′kəm·pō′zhər) *n.* Agitation; disorder; perturbation.

dis·co·my·cete (dis′kə·mī·sēt′) *n. pl.* **·cetes** (-sēts) *Bot.* Any of a group *(Discomycetes)* of fungi belonging to the *Ascomycetes;* a cup fungus. [< NL < Gk. *diskos* disk + *mykēs, mykētos* fungus]

dis·con·cert (dis′kən·sûrt′) *v.t.* **1** To disturb the self-possession or composure of; confuse; upset. **2** To throw into confusion; frustrate, as a plan. See synonyms under ABASH. [< MF *disconcerter* < *dis-* apart + *concerter* agree] —**dis′con·cert′ing** *adj.* —**dis′con·cert′ing·ly** *adv.* —**dis′con·cer′tion, dis′con·cert′ment** *n.*

dis·con·cert·ed (dis′kən·sûr′tid) *adj.* Confused; perturbed; discomposed. —**dis′con·cert′ed·ly** *adv.* —**dis′con·cert′ed·ness** *n.*

dis·con·form·i·ty (dis′kən·fôr′mə·tē) *n. pl.* **·ties** Lack of conformity; nonconformity.

dis·con·nect (dis′kə·nekt′) *v.t.* To undo or dissolve the connection of; disunite; separate. —**dis′con·nec′tion,** *Brit.* **dis′con·nex′ion** *n.*

dis·con·nect·ed (dis′kə·nek′tid) *adj.* **1** Not connected; disjointed. **2** Incoherent; rambling. —**dis′con·nect′ed·ly** *adv.* —**dis′con·nect′ed·ness** *n.*

dis·con·so·late (dis·kon′sə·lit) *adj.* **1** Destitute of consolation; inconsolable; sad. **2** Marked by gloominess; cheerless; saddening. See synonyms under SAD. [< Med. L *disconsolatus* < *dis-* not + *consolatus*, pp. of *consolari* CONSOLE[1]] —**dis·con′so·late·ly** *adv.* —**dis·con′so·late·ness** *n.*

dis·con·so·la·tion (dis·kon′sə·lā′shən) *n.* The state of being disconsolate.

dis·con·tent (dis′kən·tent′) *n.* Lack of content; dissatisfaction; uneasiness: also **dis′con·tent′ed·ness, dis′con·tent′ment.** —*v.t.* To render discontented; dissatisfy. —**dis′con·tent′ing** *adj.*

dis·con·tent·ed (dis′kən·ten′tid) *adj.* Ill at ease; dissatisfied. —**dis′con·tent′ed·ly** *adv.*

dis·con·tin·u·ance (dis′kən·tin′yōō·əns) *n.* **1** The act of discontinuing, or state of being discontinued; interruption or intermission. **2** Discontinuity. **3** *Law* The interruption of a suit, as by failure of the plaintiff to follow it up: distinguished from *dismissal.*

dis·con·tin·ue (dis′kən·tin′yōō) *v.* **·tin·ued, ·tin·u·ing** *v.t.* **1** To break off or cease from; stop. **2** To cease using, receiving, etc.: to *discontinue* a newspaper. **3** *Law* To abandon (a suit, etc.) by discontinuance. —*v.i.* **4** To come to an end; stop. See synonyms under ABANDON, CEASE, SUSPEND. [< OF *discontinuer* < Med. L *discontinuare* < *dis-* not + L *continuare* CONTINUE] —**dis′con·tin′u·a′tion** *n.* —**dis′con·tin′u·er,** *Law* **dis′con·tin′u·or** *n.*

dis·con·ti·nu·i·ty (dis′kon·tə·nōō′ə·tē, -nyōō′-) *n.* **1** Lack of continuity. **2** A gap, as in a structure or electric current.

dis·con·tin·u·ous (dis′kən·tin′yōō·əs) *adj.* Not continuous; characterized by interruptions or breaks. —**dis′con·tin′u·ous·ly** *adv.* —**dis′con·tin′u·ous·ness** *n.*

disc·o·phile (dis′kə·fīl) *n.* A collector, student, and connoisseur of phonograph recordings. [< L *discus* a plate, disk + -PHILE]

dis·cord (dis′kôrd) *n.* **1** Variance or strife; lack of agreement; contention. **2** *Music* A combination of dissonant sounds; lack of harmony. **3** A harsh or disagreeable medley of noises; dissonance. —*v.i.* To be out of accord or harmony; disagree; clash. [< OF *descord* < *descorder* disagree < L *discordare* < *discors* at variance < *dis-* away + *cor, cordis* heart]

dis·cor·dance (dis·kôr′dəns) *n.* **1** A discordant state or quality. **2** A discord. Also **dis·cor′dan·cy.**

dis·cor·dant (dis·kôr′dənt) *adj.* **1** Contradictory; inconsistent. **2** Quarrelsome. **3** Not harmonious; dissonant. **4** *Geol.* Lacking in conformity, as in the direction or sequence of rock strata. See synonyms under CONTRARY, HETEROGENEOUS, INCONGRUOUS. [< OF *descordant*, ppr. of *descorder.* See DISCORD.] —**dis·cor′dant·ly** *adv.*

Dis·cor·di·a (dis·kôr′dē·ə) The Roman goddess of discord.

dis·co·thèque (dis·kə·tek′) *n.* A night club offering recorded music for dancing instead of music played by a band of live musicians. [< F, lit., record library]

dis·count (dis′kount) *n.* **1** An amount counted off or deducted from a sum owing or to be paid: ten per cent *discount* for cash. **2** The interest allowed and deducted from the face amount for advancing money on negotiable paper. **3** The act of discounting. **4** The rate of discount. —**at a discount** At less than the face value; below par; hence, not in esteem. —**true** or **arithmetical discount** That interest at a given rate and term which, added to the principal received, gives the face value of the discounted paper. —*v.t.* (dis′kount, dis·kount′) **1** To set aside or deduct, as a portion of an amount owed; make an allowance of. **2** To buy or sell (a bill or note) for face value less the amount of interest to be accumulated before maturity. **3** To disregard; take no account of. **4** To believe only part of; allow for exaggeration in. **5** To take into account beforehand; diminish by anticipation, especially so as to lessen value, effect, enjoyment, etc. —*v.i.* **6** To lend money, deducting the interest beforehand. [< MF *descompte, desconte* < OF *descompter* < Med. L *discomputare* < *dis-* away + *computare* COMPUTE] —**dis′count·a·ble** *adj.* —**dis′count·er** *n.*

dis·coun·te·nance (dis·koun′tə·nəns) *v.t.* **·nanced, ·nanc·ing 1** To look upon with disfavor; disapprove or discourage. **2** To abash; disconcert. —*n. Obs.* Disapprobation; abashment. [< MF *descontenancer* < *des-* away (< L *dis-*) + *contenancer* favor < *contenance* COUNTENANCE]

dis·cour·age (dis·kûr′ij) *v.t.* **·aged, ·ag·ing 1** To deprive of courage; dispirit; dishearten. **2** To deter or dissuade with *from.* **3** To obstruct; hinder: Malnutrition *discourages* growth. **4** To attempt to repress or prevent by disapproval. [< OF *descoragier* < *des-* away (< L *dis-*) + *corage* courage] —**dis·cour′ag·er** *n.* —**dis·cour′ag·ing** *adj.* —**dis·cour′ag·ing·ly** *adv.*

dis·cour·age·ment (dis·kûr′ij·mənt) *n.* **1** The act of discouraging, or the state of being discouraged. **2** That which discourages. See synonyms under DESPAIR.

dis·course (dis′kôrs, dis·kôrs′) *n.* **1** Connected communication of thought sequence; continuous expression or exchange of ideas. **2** Familiar conversation; talk. **3** Formal expression of thought, oral or written; a long treatise or dissertation; a sermon. **Direct discourse** is spoken or written language quoted in the exact words of the speaker or writer, as in *I will go,* and is contrasted with **indirect discourse,** in which his words are reported with change of person or tense, as in *he said he would go.* **4** An act, the exercise, or the power of analytical and consecutive thought; ratiocination. See synonyms under CONVERSATION, SPEECH. —*v.* (dis·kôrs′) **·coursed, ·cours·ing** *v.i.* **1** To set forth one's thoughts and conclusions concerning a subject: with *on* or *upon.* **2** To converse; confer. —*v.t.* **3** *Obs.* To discuss. [< OF *discours* < L *discursus* < *dis-* apart + *cursus* a running < *currere* run] —**dis·cours′er** *n.*

dis·cour·te·ous (dis·kûr′tē·əs) *adj.* Showing discourtesy; rude. See synonyms under BLUFF[2]. —**dis·cour′te·ous·ly** *adv.* —**dis·cour′te·ous·ness** *n.*

dis·cour·te·sy (dis·kûr′tə·sē) *n. pl.* **·sies** Rude behavior; impoliteness.

dis·cov·er (dis·kuv′ər) *v.t.* **1** To find or gain knowledge of, especially for the first time. **2** *Archaic* To act or speak so as to expose or betray, especially unwittingly. **3** *Archaic* To remove the covering of; reveal; disclose. **4** *Obs.* To distinguish, as black from white. [< OF *descovrir* < *des-* away (< L *dis-*) + *covrir* COVER] —**dis·cov′er·a·bil′i·ty** *n.* —**dis·cov′er·a·ble** *adj.* —**dis·cov′er·er** *n.*

Synonyms: ascertain, descry, detect, discern, disclose, expose, find, invent. Of human actions or character, *detect* is used almost without exception of what is evil; *discover* may be used in either the good or the bad sense, oftener in the good; he was *detected* in a fraud; real merit is sure to be *discovered.* In scientific language, *detect* is used of delicate indications that appear in course of careful watching; as, a slight fluttering of the pulse could be *detected.* We *discover* what has existed but has not been known to us; we *invent* combinations or arrangements not before in use. *Find* is the most general word for every means of coming to know what was not before certainly known. Compare CATCH, KNOW. *Antonyms:* see synonyms for HIDE.

dis·cov·ert (dis·kuv′ərt) *adj.* **1** *Law* Not under

the bonds of matrimony; not covert; unmarried: said of a widow, divorcée, or spinster. 2 *Obs.* Uncovered; revealed. [<OF *descovert,* pp. of *descovrir* DISCOVER]

dis·cov·er·y (dis·kuv′ər·ē) *n. pl.* **·er·ies** 1 The act of discovering; disclosure. 2 Something discovered.

Discovery Bay An inlet of the Indian Ocean in SE Australia.

Discovery Day Columbus Day.

dis·cre·ate (dis′krē·āt′) *v.t.* **·at·ed, ·at·ing** To undo (what has been created); destroy; annihilate. — **dis′cre·a′tion** *n.*

dis·cred·it (dis·kred′it) *v.t.* 1 To disbelieve. 2 To injure the credit or reputation of; dishonor. 3 To show to be unworthy of belief or confidence. — *n.* 1 The act of discrediting. 2 The state of being discredited or disbelieved. 3 Lack of credit; impaired reputation; dishonor. See synonyms under ABASE, DISPARAGE.

dis·cred·it·a·ble (dis·kred′it·ə·bəl) *adj.* Hurtful to credit or reputation; disreputable. — **dis·cred′it·a·bly** *adv.*

dis·creet (dis·krēt′) *adj.* 1 Wise in avoiding errors or in selecting the best means to accomplish a purpose. 2 Judicious; prudent; careful. See synonyms under POLITIC. ◆ Homophone: *discrete.* [<OF *discret* <LL *discretus* learned, orig. pp. of *discernere* discern] — **dis·creet′ly** *adv.* — **dis·creet′ness** *n.*

dis·crep·an·cy (dis·krep′ən·sē) *n. pl.* **·cies** A disagreement or difference; state or point of variance; inconsistency. Also **dis·crep′ance.** See synonyms under DIFFERENCE.

dis·crep·ant (dis·krep′ənt) *adj.* Inharmoniously different; opposite; inconsistent; contrary; discordant. See synonyms under INCONGRUOUS. [<OF <L *discrepans, -antis* < *dis-* away + *crepare* creak, make a noise]

dis·crete (dis·krēt′) *adj.* 1 Disconnected from others; distinct or separate. 2 Made up of distinct parts or separate units; discontinuous. 3 Denoting opposition or contrariety. 4 *Bot.* Separate; not coalescent, as leaves; distinct; segregate: opposed to *confluent.* ◆ Homophone: *discreet.* [Var. of DISCREET] — **dis·crete′ly** *adv.* — **dis·crete′ness** *n.*

dis·cre·tion (dis·kresh′ən) *n.* 1 Cautious and correct judgment; prudence; sagacity; the quality of being discreet. 2 Liberty of action; freedom in the exercise of judgment. 3 *Law* The act or the liberty of deciding according to justice and propriety, and one's idea of what is right and proper under the circumstances, without wilfulness or favor. 4 *Obs.* Distinction or separation; disjunction. See synonyms under ADDRESS, PRUDENCE, WISDOM. — **at discretion** At will; according to one's own judgment. [<OF <L *discretio, -onis* < *discretus* discrete]

dis·cre·tion·al (dis·kresh′ən·əl) *adj.* Discretionary. — **dis·cre′tion·al·ly** *adv.*

dis·cre·tion·ar·y (dis·kresh′ə·ner′ē) *adj.* 1 Exercisable at or left to discretion. 2 Uncontrolled legally except by discretion.

dis·crim·i·nate (dis·krim′ə·nāt) *v.* **·nat·ed, ·nat·ing** *v.i.* 1 To treat someone or something with partiality: with *against* or *in favor of:* to *discriminate* against a group or in favor of a relative. 2 To observe a difference; make a distinction: with *between.* — *v.t.* 3 To discern the difference in or between. 4 To make or constitute a difference in or between: The meter *discriminates* one poem from the other. See synonyms under CONTRAST, DISCERN, KNOW. — *adj.* (-nit) 1 Noting differences; discriminating. 2 Discriminated. [<L *discriminatus,* pp. of *discriminare* < *discrimen, -inis* < *dis-* apart + *crimen* a judgment] — **dis·crim′i·nate·ly** *adv.* — **dis·crim′i·nate·ness** *n.*

dis·crim·i·nat·ing (dis·krim′ə·nā′ting) *adj.* 1 Having power to distinguish keenly: a *discriminating* intellect. 2 Serving to distinguish: a *discriminating* mark. 3 Establishing distinction or inequality. See synonyms under ASTUTE. — **dis·crim′i·nat′ing·ly** *adv.*

dis·crim·i·na·tion (dis·krim′ə·nā′shən) *n.* 1 The act or power of discriminating; the discernment of distinctions. 2 Differential treatment; bias: *discrimination* against minorities. 3 The state or condition of being discriminated; distinction; sometimes, unjust distinction. See synonyms under DIFFERENCE.

dis·crim·i·na·tive (dis·krim′ə·nā′tiv) *adj.* 1 Discriminating. 2 Distinctive or characteristic. Also **dis·crim′i·na·to′ry** (-nə·tôr′ē, -tō′rē). — **dis·crim′i·na′tive·ly** *adv.*

dis·crown (dis·kroun′) *v.t.* To deprive of a crown; dethrone.

dis·cur·sive (dis·kûr′siv) *adj.* Passing from one subject to another; wandering away from the point or theme; digressive. [<L *discursus.* See DISCOURSE.] — **dis·cur′sive·ly** *adv.* — **dis·cur′sive·ness** *n.*

dis·cus (dis′kəs) *n. pl.* **dis·cus·es** or **dis·ci** (dis′ī) 1 A heavy circular plate thrown in athletic contests: originally, in Greek and Roman games, of stone or metal; quoit. 2 The exercise of throwing this plate. For illustration see DISCOBOLUS. 3 *Biol.* A disc. [<L <Gk. *diskos*]

dis·cuss (dis·kus′) *v.t.* 1 To treat of in conversation or in writing; talk about; argue the faults and merits of. 2 *Colloq.* To test by eating or drinking, as a meal. 3 In civil law, to exhaust proceedings against (the principal debtor) before proceeding against the surety or sureties. See synonyms under DISPUTE, EXAMINE. [<L *discussus,* pp. of *discutere* discuss, orig. < *dis-* apart + *quatere* shake] — **dis·cuss′i·ble** *adj.*

dis·cuss·ant (dis·kus′ənt) *n.* One who takes part in a discussion; an active participant in a symposium.

dis·cus·sion (dis·kush′ən) *n.* 1 The act of discussing; argumentative examination; debate. See synonyms under ALTERCATION, QUARREL, SPEECH. 2 *Obs.* The scattering or dispersion of any effusion, tumor, or swelling in the body. [<OF <LL *discussio, -onis* < *discutere.* See DISCUSS.]

dis·cus·sive (dis·kus′iv) *Obs. adj.* Possessing the property of dispersing tumors and the like. — *n.* A medicine that disperses tumors. Also **dis·cu·tient** (dis·kyōō′shənt).

dis·dain (dis·dān′) *v.t.* 1 To consider unworthy of one's regard or notice; treat with contempt or scorn. 2 To reject as beneath oneself; scorn. — *n.* A feeling of superiority and dislike; proud contempt. See synonyms under ARROGANCE, SCORN. [<OF *desdeignier* < *des-* away (<L *dis-*) + *deignier* DEIGN]

dis·dain·ful (dis·dān′fəl) *adj.* Filled with or expressing disdain; scornful. See synonyms under HAUGHTY. — **dis·dain′ful·ly** *adv.* — **dis·dain′ful·ness** *n.*

dis·ease (di·zēz′) *n.* 1 Disturbed or abnormal structure or physiological action in the living organism as a whole, or in any of its parts. 2 A morbid condition resulting from such disturbance. 3 Any disturbed or abnormal condition in organic substances, as wines, liquors, etc.; a taint. 4 *Obs.* Uneasiness; inconvenience; discomfort; discontent. — *v.t.* **·eased, ·eas·ing** 1 To cause disease in; disorder; derange. 2 *Obs.* To make uneasy; distress. [<AF, OF *desaise* < *des-* away (<L *dis-*) + *aise* EASE] — **dis·eased′** *adj.*

Synonyms (noun): affection, ailment, complaint, disorder, distemper, illness, indisposition, infirmity, malady, sickness, unhealthiness, unsoundness. *Disease* is the general term for deviation from health; in a more limited sense it denotes some definite morbid condition; *disorder* and *affection* are rather partial and limited; as, a nervous *affection;* a *disorder* of the digestive system. Although *sickness* was generally used in English speech and literature, till the close of the eighteenth century at least, for every form of physical *disorder,* there is now a tendency to restrict the words *sick* and *sickness* to nausea, and to hold *ill* and *illness* as the proper words to use in a general sense. We speak of trifling *ailments,* a slight *indisposition,* a serious or a deadly *disease;* a slight or severe *illness;* an insidious, serious, severe, or deadly *disease.* *Complaint* is a popular term, which may be applied to any degree of ill health, slight or severe. *Infirmity* denotes a chronic or lingering weakness or disability, as blindness or lameness. See ILLNESS. *Antonyms*: health, robustness, sanity, soundness, strength, sturdiness, vigor.

dis·em·bark (dis′em·bärk′) *v.t.* & *v.i.* To put or go ashore from a ship; land; unload. [<MF *desembarquer* < *des-* away (<L *dis-*) + *embarquer* EMBARK] — **dis·em′bar·ka′tion, dis′em·bark′ment** *n.*

dis·em·bar·rass (dis′em·bar′əs) *v.t.* To free from embarrassment. — **dis′em·bar′rass·ment** *n.*

dis·em·bed (dis′em·bed′) *v.t.* **·bed·ded, ·bed·ding** To extract (a thing embedded).

dis·em·bel·lish (dis′em·bel′ish) *v.t.* To strip of embellishment.

dis·em·bod·y (dis′em·bod′ē) *v.t.* **·bod·ied, ·bod·y·ing** To free from the body; free from physical existence. — **dis′em·bod′i·ment** *n.*

dis·em·bogue (dis′em·bōg′) *v.t.* & *v.i.* **·bogued, ·bo·guing** 1 To pour out or discharge (waters) at the mouth; empty: said of rivers, streams, etc. 2 *Obs.* To sail out of a river, bay, or harbor. [<Sp. *desembocar* < *des-* out (<L *dis-*) + *embocar* put into the mouth <L *in-* into + *bucca* mouth] — **dis′em·bogue′ment** *n.*

dis·em·bos·om (dis′em·bŏŏz′əm) *v.t.* & *v.i.* To reveal (a secret); to disburden (oneself) of a secret.

dis·em·bow·el (dis′em·bou′əl, -boul′) *v.t.* **·bow·eled** or **·bow·elled, ·bow·el·ing** or **·bow·el·ling** 1 To take out the bowels of; eviscerate. 2 To remove the contents of. — **dis′em·bow′el·ment** *n.*

dis·en·a·ble (dis′en·ā′bəl) *v.t.* **·bled, ·bling** To disable; make unfit.

dis·en·chant (dis′en·chant′, -chänt′) *v.t.* To free from enchantment; disillusion. [<OF *desenchanter* < *des-* away (<L *dis-*) + *enchanter* ENCHANT] — **dis′en·chant′er** *n.* — **dis′en·chant′ment** *n.*

dis·en·cum·ber (dis′en·kum′bər) *v.t.* To free from encumbrance or burden. [<OF *desencombre, desencombrer* < *des-* away (<L *dis-*) + *encombrer* ENCUMBER] — **dis′en·cum′berment, dis′en·cum′brance** *n.*

dis·en·dow (dis′en·dou′) *v.t.* To take away an endowment or endowments from. — **dis′en·dow′er** *n.* — **dis′en·dow′ment** *n.*

dis·en·fran·chise (dis′en·fran′chīz) *v.t.* **·chised, ·chis·ing** To disfranchise. — **dis′en·fran′chisement** (-chiz·mənt) *n.*

dis·en·gage (dis′en·gāj′) *v.t.* & *v.i.* **·gaged, ·gag·ing** To set or be free from engagement, entanglement, or occupation; become detached; withdraw. See synonyms under RELEASE. — **dis′en·gaged′** *adj.* — **dis′en·gag′ed·ness** *n.*

dis·en·gage·ment (dis′en·gāj′mənt) *n.* 1 The act of disengaging, or the state of being disengaged; extrication. 2 Freedom from toil or care; leisure; ease.

dis·en·tail (dis′en·tāl′) *v.t. Law* To free from or break the entail of, as an estate. — **dis′en·tail′ment** *n.*

dis·en·tan·gle (dis′en·tang′gəl) *v.t.* **·gled, ·gling** To free or relieve of entanglement or perplexity; unravel. — **dis′en·tan′gle·ment** *n.*

dis·en·thral (dis′en·thrôl′) *v.t.* **·thralled, ·thral·ling** To release from or as from thraldom; set free: also spelled *disinthral.* Also **dis′en·thrall′.** — **dis′en·thral′ment** or **dis′en·thrall′ment** *n.*

dis·en·throne (dis′en·thrōn′) *v.t.* To dethrone; depose. — **dis′en·throne′ment** *n.*

dis·en·ti·tle (dis′en·tīt′l) *v.t.* **·tled, ·tling** To take away the title from; deprive of a right.

dis·en·tomb (dis′en·tōōm′) *v.t.* To exhume; disinter. — **dis′en·tomb′ment** *n.*

dis·en·train (dis′en·trān′) *v.t.* & *v.i.* To detrain, as troops.

dis·en·trance (dis′en·trans′, -träns′) *v.t.* **·tranced, ·tranc·ing** To arouse from a trance.

dis·en·twine (dis′en·twīn′) *v.t.* & *v.i.* **·twined, ·twin·ing** To untwine; disentangle.

di·sep·a·lous (dī·sep′ə·ləs) *adj. Bot.* Having two sepals. [<DI-[2] + SEPALOUS]

dis·es·tab·lish (dis′es·tab′lish) *v.t.* 1 To deprive of established character. 2 To withdraw state patronage from: to *disestablish* a church. — **dis′es·tab′lish·ment** *n.*

dis·es·teem (dis′es·tēm′) *v.t.* To feel a lack of esteem for; regard slightingly or with dislike; disapprove of. — *n.* Lack of esteem.

di·seuse (dē·zœz′) *n. French* A woman entertainer performing dramatic impersonations, monologs, etc.

dis·fa·vor (dis·fā′vər) *n.* 1 Lack of favor; disapproval; dislike. 2 The state of being discountenanced, disliked, or opposed; odium. 3 An unkind act. 4 *Obs.* Ugliness; homeliness. — *v.t.* To treat or regard without favor;

add,āce,câre,pälm; end,ēven; it,īce; odd,ōpen,ôrder; tŏŏk,pōōl; up,bûrn; ə = a in *above,* e in *sicken,* i in *clarity,* o in *melon,* u in *focus;* yōō = u in *fuse;* oi,oil; ou,pout; ch,check; g,go; ng,ring; th,thin; th,this; zh,vision. Foreign sounds à,œ,ü,kh,ń; and ◆: see page xx. < from; + plus; ? possibly.

discountenance; oppose. Also *Brit.* **dis·fa′vour.**

dis·fea·ture (dis·fē′chər) *v.t.* **·tured, ·tur·ing** To mar the features of; disfigure; deface.

dis·fig·ure (dis·fig′yər) *v.t.* **·ured, ·ur·ing** To mar or destroy the figure or beauty of; render unsightly; deform. [<OF *desfigurer* <*des-* away (<L *dis-*) + *figurer* <L *figurare* form, fashion <*figura* a shape] **—dis·fig′ur·er** *n.* **—dis·fig′ured** *adj.* **—dis·fig′ure·ment, dis·fig′u·ra′tion** *n.*

dis·for·est (dis·fôr′ist, -for′-) *v.t.* **1** To clear of forest; deforest. **2** *Law* To disafforest. **—dis·for′es·ta′tion** *n.*

dis·fran·chise (dis·fran′chīz) *v.t.* **·chised, ·chis·ing 1** To deprive of a privilege, right, or grant. **2** To dispossess of a citizen's privileges, as of the ballot. **—dis·fran′chis·er** *n.* **—dis·fran′chise·ment** (-chiz·mənt) *n.*

dis·frock (dis·frok′) *v.t.* To unfrock.

dis·fur·nish (dis·fûr′nish) *v.t. Obs.* To strip of furniture, equipment, or belongings. [<OF *desfourniss-*, stem of *desfournir* <*des-* away (<L *dis-*) + *fournir* FURNISH] **—dis·fur′nish·ment** *n.*

dis·gorge (dis·gôrj′) *v.t.* **·gorged, ·gorg·ing 1** To throw out, as from the throat or stomach; eject; vomit. **2** To give up unwillingly, especially something wrongfully obtained. —*v.i.* **3** To throw up; vomit. [<OF *desgorger* <*des-* from (<L *dis-*) + *gorge* throat]

dis·grace (dis·grās′) *v.t.* **·graced, ·grac·ing 1** To bring reproach or shame upon. **2** To dismiss from favor; treat with dishonor. —*n.* **1** Disfavor. **2** Infamy; ignominy. **3** That which disgraces. See synonyms under ABASE, BLEMISH, STAIN. [<MF *disgracier* <Ital. *disgraziare* <*disgrazia* <*dis-* away (<L *dis-*) + *grazia* <L *gratia* favor] **—dis·grac′er** *n.*

dis·grace·ful (dis·grās′fəl) *adj.* Characterized by or causing disgrace; shameful. See synonyms under FLAGRANT, INFAMOUS. **—dis·grace′ful·ly** *adv.* **—dis·grace′ful·ness** *n.*

dis·grun·tle (dis·grun′təl) *v.t.* **·grun·tled, ·grun·tling** To disappoint and make discontented; cause to sulk.

dis·guise (dis·gīz′) *v.t.* **·guised, ·guis·ing 1** To change the appearance of; hide or conceal the identity of, as by a mask. **2** To obscure or cover up the actual nature or character of by false representation; dissemble; misrepresent. See synonyms under HIDE[1], MASK[1]. —*n.* **1** The act of disguising, or the state of being disguised. **2** Something that disguises, alters the appearance of, or renders difficult of recognition. See synonyms under PRETENSE. [<OF *desguisier* <*des-* down (<L *de-*) + *guise* GUISE] **—dis·guis′ed·ly** (-id·lē) *adv.* **—dis·guis′er** *n.*

dis·gust (dis·gust′) *v.t.* **1** To affect with physical nausea; offend the senses of. **2** To offend the sensibilities of; affect with loathing or aversion. —*n.* Strong aversion or repugnance. See synonyms under ABOMINATION, ANTIPATHY. [<MF *desgouster* <*des-* away (<L *dis-*) + *gouster* taste <L *gustare*]

dis·gust·ed (dis·gus′tid) *adj.* Affected with loathing or disgust. **—dis·gust′ed·ly** *adv.* **—dis·gust′ed·ness** *n.*

dis·gust·ful (dis·gust′fəl) *adj.* **1** Disgusting. **2** Full of or characterized by disgust. **—dis·gust′ful·ly** *adv.* **—dis·gust′ful·ness** *n.*

dis·gust·ing (dis·gus′ting) *adj.* Serving or fitted to provoke disgust; odious; revolting. **—dis·gust′ing·ly** *adv.*

dish (dish) *n.* **1** A concave or hollow vessel for serving food at meals; anything of similar shape. **2** The amount of food served in a dish: also **dish′ful.** **3** Food prepared in a special way. **4** Concavity. —*v.t.* **1** To place in a dish or dishes; serve as food: often with *up* or *out.* **2** To make concave. **3** *Slang* To ruin; cheat. —*v.i.* **4** To become concave; sink in. [<OE *disc* <L *discus.* Doublet of DAIS, DESK, DISK.]

dis·ha·bille (dis′ə·bēl′) *n.* **1** A state of being partially or negligently dressed, as in night clothes. **2** The clothes or garments worn in this state. Also spelled *deshabille.* [<F *déshabillé,* pp. of *deshabiller* undress <*des-* away (<L *dis-*) + *habiller* dress]

dis·hal·low (dis·hal′ō) *v.t.* To render unhallowed; profane; desecrate.

dis·har·mo·nize (dis·här′mə·nīz) *v.t. & v.i.* **·nized, ·niz·ing** To render or be discordant; make or be inharmonious. **—dis·har′mo·nism** *n.*

dis·har·mo·ny (dis·här′mə·nē) *n. pl.* **·nies** Lack of harmony; incongruity; discord. **—dis·har·mo·ni·ous** (dis′här·mō′nē·əs) *adj.* **—dis′·har·mo′ni·ous·ly** *adv.*

dish·cloth (dish′klôth′, -kloth′) *n.* A cloth used in washing dishes. Also **dish′clout′** (-klout′), **dish′rag′** (-rag′).

dishcloth gourd A loofah.

dis·heart·en (dis·här′tən) *v.t.* To weaken the spirit or courage of; dispirit; discourage. See synonyms under ABASH. **—dis·heart′en·ing** *adj.* **—dis·heart′en·ing·ly** *adv.* **—dis·heart′en·ment** *n.*

dished (disht) *adj.* **1** Shaped like a dish; concave. **2** Of wheels, slanted inward at the bottom. **3** *Slang* Worn out; exhausted.

dis·her·i·son (dis·her′ə·zən) *Obs. n.* The act of depriving of an inheritance. —*v.t.* To disinherit. [<OF *desheriteisun* <L *dis-* away + *hereditas* inheritance]

dis·her·it (dis·her′it) *v.t. Obs.* To disinherit. [<OF *desheriter* <LL *dis-* away + *hereditare* inherit <L *heres, -edis* an heir]

di·shev·el (di·shev′əl) *v.t.* **·eled** or **·elled, ·el·ing** or **·el·ling** To disorder (the hair); disarrange (the dress) [<MF *descheveler* <*des-* away (<L *dis-*) + *chevel* hair <L *capillus*] **—di·shev′el·ment** *n.*

dish-faced (dish′fāst′) *adj.* Having a round, flat face.

dis·hon·est (dis·on′ist) *adj.* **1** Lacking in honesty; untrustworthy. **2** Characterized by dishonesty; fraudulent; See synonyms under BAD[1], IMMORAL. [<OF *deshoneste* <LL *dis-* away + *honestus* honest] **—dis·hon′est·ly** *adv.*

dis·hon·es·ty (dis·on′is·tē) *n. pl.* **·ties 1** The quality of being dishonest. **2** Fraud or violation of trust; a dishonest action.

dis·hon·or (dis·on′ər) *v.t.* **1** To deprive of honor; disgrace; insult. **2** To violate the chastity of; seduce. **3** To decline or fail to pay, as a note. See synonyms under ABASE, BLEMISH, DISPARAGE, POLLUTE, STAIN. —*n.* **1** Lack of honor or of honorable character. **2** Degradation. **3** Insult; reproach; stain. **4** Refusal or failure to pay a note, etc., when due. Also *Brit.* **dis·hon′our.** See synonyms under SCORN. [<OF *deshonor* <L *dis-* away + *honor* HONOR] **—dis·hon′or·er** *n.*

dis·hon·or·a·ble (dis·on′ər·ə·bəl) *adj.* **1** Characterized by or bringing dishonor or reproach; discreditable; mean; ignoble: a *dishonorable* motive or act. **2** Lacking honor or honorableness: a *dishonorable* lawyer. **3** In a state of dishonor or disesteem; dishonored: a *dishonorable* grave. See synonyms under INFAMOUS. **—dis·hon′or·a·ble·ness** *n.* **—dis·hon′or·a·bly** *adv.*

dish·pan (dish′pan′) *n.* A pan for washing dishes.

dish·wash·er (dish′wosh′ər, -wôsh′-) *n.* A person or machine that washes dishes.

dish·wa·ter (dish′wô′tər, -wot′-) *n.* Water in which dishes are to be or have been washed.

dis·il·lu·sion (dis′i·lōō′zhən) *v.t.* To free from illusion or delusion; disenchant. Also **dis′·il·lu′sion·ize.** —*n.* The act of freeing or state of being freed from illusion. Also **dis′il·lu′sion·ment.**

dis·il·lu·sive (dis′i·lōō′siv) *adj.* Tending to dispel an illusion.

dis·im·pris·on (dis′im·priz′ən) *v.t.* To free from prison or imprisonment. **—dis′im·pris′on·ment** *n.*

dis·in·cen·tive (dis′in sen′tiv) *n.* Something that deters, or reduces incentive.

dis·in·cli·na·tion (dis·in′klə·nā′shən) *n.* Distaste; aversion; unwillingness.

dis·in·cline (dis′in·klīn′) *v.t. & v.i.* **·clined, ·clin·ing** To make or be unwilling or averse.

dis·in·cor·po·rate (dis′in·kôr′pə·rāt) *v.t.* **·rat·ed, ·rat·ing 1** To free from incorporation; deprive of chartered rights or character, as a company. **2** To separate from a corporation.

dis·in·fect (dis′in·fekt′) *v.t.* **1** To purify from infection. **2** To free from morbid or pathogenic matter, as a wound, clothing, etc. See synonyms under CLEANSE.

dis·in·fec·tant (dis′in·fek′tənt) *adj.* Disinfecting. —*n.* A substance used to disinfect or to destroy the germs of infectious and contagious diseases, as chlorine, carbolic acid, etc.

dis·in·fec·tion (dis′in·fek′shən) *n.* The act of disinfecting; fact or state of being disinfected.

dis·in·fest (dis′in·fest′) *v.t.* To exterminate vermin from; delouse. **—dis·in′fes·ta′tion** *n.*

dis·in·fla·tion (dis′in·flā′shən) *n. Econ.* The process, usually governmental, of attempting to reduce the price level, or to hold it steady, through restrictions of credit and other monetary measures, resulting in a decline in industrial production and reduced pressure on foreign exchange reserves: distinguished from *deflation* by a lesser depressant effect in the economy.

dis·in·for·ma·tion (dis·in′fər·mā′shən) *n.* False, misleading information deliberately disseminated.

dis·in·gen·u·ous (dis′in·jen′yōō·əs) *adj.* Not sincere or ingenuous; artful; deceitful. **—dis′in·gen′u·ous·ly** *adv.* **—dis′in·gen′u·ous·ness** *n.*

dis·in·her·it (dis′in·her′it) *v.t.* To deprive of an inheritance. **—dis′in·her′i·tance** *n.*

dis·in·hume (dis′in·hyōōm′) *v.t.* **·humed, ·hum·ing** To exhume; disinter.

dis·in·te·grate (dis·in′tə·grāt) *v.* **·grat·ed,·grat·ing** *v.t.* To break or reduce into component parts or particles; destroy the wholeness of. —*v.i.* To become reduced to fragments or particles; crumble. **—dis·in′te·gra·ble** (-grə·bəl) *adj.* **—dis·in′te·gra′tor** *n.*

dis·in·te·gra·tion (dis·in′tə·grā′shən) *n.* **1** The act of disintegrating, or the state of being disintegrated; a crumbling away. **2** *Geol.* The gradual decay and wasting, as of rocks under elemental action. **3** *Physics* The disappearance of an initial quantity of any radioactive element due to its conversion into another element as a result of the changes in nuclear properties attendant on the emission of alpha or beta particles.

dis·in·ter (dis′in·tûr′) *v.t.* **·terred, ·ter·ring 1** To dig up, as from a grave; exhume. **2** To bring to light or life as if from a grave. [<MF *désenterrer* <*des-* away + *enterrer* INTER] **—dis′in·ter′ment** *n.*

dis·in·ter·est (dis·in′tər·ist, -trist) *n.* **1** Lack of interest; indifference. **2** Freedom from bias; impartiality.

dis·in·ter·est·ed (dis·in′tər·is·tid, -tris·tid, -tə·res′-) *adj.* **1** Free from self-interest or bias; unselfish; impartial. **2** Loosely, uninterested. See synonyms under GENEROUS. **—dis·in′ter·est·ed·ly** *adv.* **—dis·in′ter·est·ed·ness** *n.*

dis·in·thral, dis·in·thrall (dis′in·thrôl′) See DISENTHRAL, etc.

dis·ject (dis·jekt′) *v.t.* To split apart forcibly; separate; break asunder. [<L *disjectus,* pp. of *disjicere* <*dis-* apart + *jacere* throw]

dis·join (dis·join′) *v.t.* To keep apart; undo or prevent the joining of; separate. —*v.i.* To become divided or separated. [<OF *desjoindre* <*des-* away (<L *dis-*) + *joindre* JOIN]

dis·joint (dis·joint′) *v.t.* **1** To put out of joint; dislocate. **2** To take apart; disconnect the pieces of. **3** To destroy the coherence, connections, or sequence of; disorder. —*v.i.* **4** To break into parts; become out of joint. —*adj. Obs.* Out of joint; disconnected. [<OF *desjoint,* pp. of *desjoindre.* See DISJOIN.] **—dis·joint′ly** *adv.*

dis·joint·ed (dis·join′tid) *adj.* Dislocated; disconnected; incoherent. **—dis·joint′ed·ly** *adv.* **—dis·joint′ed·ness** *n.*

dis·junct (dis·jungkt′) *adj.* **1** *Entomol.* Having the head, thorax, and abdomen separated by constrictions. **2** Not connected; detached. Compare illustrations under INSECT. [<L *disjunctus,* pp. of *disjungere* <*dis-* away + *jungere* join]

dis·junc·tion (dis·jungk′shən) *n.* **1** Sundering; separation: also **dis·junc′ture.** **2** *Biol.* The moving apart of each pair of homologous chromosomes during the anaphase of cell mitosis.

dis·junc·tive (dis·jungk′tiv) *adj.* **1** Helping or serving to disjoin. **2** *Gram.* Expressing separation or disjoining, as certain conjunctions, as *either—or, else, otherwise,* etc. —*n.* **1** That which disjoins. **2** *Gram.* A disjunctive conjunction. **3** A Hebrew character used to separate words and clauses in sentences. **4** *Logic* A disjunctive proposition. **—dis·junc′tive·ly** *adv.*

disk (disk) *n.* **1** A flat plate of any material that is circular, or approximately circular; also, any surface that is flat and circular, or apparently so: the *disk* of a planet. **2** *Biol.* Any approximately flat circular outgrowth, organ, or structure of a planet or animal: in this sense usually spelled *disc.* **3** In the Roman Catholic Church, a paten or plate for the eucharistic bread. **4** A quoit or discus. See Illustration under DISCOBOLUS. **5** *Agric.*

A disk harrow. 6 *Astron.* The figure of a heavenly body, irrespective of its actual form. 7 A disc (def. 1). —**winged disk** In Egyptian art, the disk or symbol of the sun, supported by

EGYPTIAN WINGED DISK

two uraei and the expanded wings of a vulture: also **sun disk.** [<L *discus* <Gk. *diskos* disk, platter. Doublet of DAIS, DESK, DISH.]

disk brake A brake in which a pad of durable, heat-resistant material is pressed against a metal disk: also called *spot brake.*

disk flower Any of the small, tubular florets, usually containing both stamens and pistil, that make up the central disk of a composite flower head. Also **disk floret.**

DISK HARROW
Number and type of disks may be varied for different types of plowing.

disk harrow *Agric.* A harrow consisting of a series of rolling, saucer-shaped disks set on edge and at an angle along one or more axles.

Dis·ko (dis′kō) A Danish island in Davis Strait, west of Greenland; 3,312 square miles. Also **Dis′co.**

disk wheel A wheel with a continuous, flat, convex, or concave outer surface from hub to rim, used on many automobiles.

dis·like (dis·līk′) *v.t.* **·liked, ·lik·ing** To regard with aversion or antipathy. See synonyms under ABHOR. —*n.* Distaste; repugnance; aversion. See synonyms under ANTIPATHY, HATRED. —**dis·lik′a·ble** *adj.* —**dis·lik′er** *n.*

dis·lo·cate (dis′lō·kāt, dis·lō′kāt) *v.t.* **·cat·ed, ·cat·ing** 1 *Anat.* To put out of joint, as a bone. 2 To put out of proper place or order; displace; disarrange. [<Med. L *dislocatus,* pp. of *dislocare* <*dis-* away + L *locare* set, place <*locus* a place]

dis·lo·ca·tion (dis′lō·kā′shən) *n.* 1 *Anat.* The partial or complete displacement of one or more of the bones of a joint. 2 The act of displacing or disarranging, or the resulting condition; disarrangement; disorder. 3 *Geol.* A fault in or a shifting of rocks, generally followed by a displacement on either side. 4 *Physics* A disturbance of the normal atomic or molecular configuration in a crystal, revealed by changes in crystal properties.

dis·lodge (dis·loj′) *v.* **·lodged, ·lodg·ing** *v.t.* To remove or drive out, as from an abode, hiding place, or fortification. —*v.i.* To leave a place of abode; move. See synonyms under BANISH. [<OF *desloger, deslogier* <*dis-* away + *loger* LODGE] —**dis·lodg′ment,** *Brit.* **dis·lodge′ment** *n.*

dis·loy·al (dis·loi′əl) *adj.* False to one's allegiance or obligations; faithless. See synonyms under PERFIDIOUS. [<OF *desloial* <*des-* not (<L *dis-*) + *loial* LOYAL] —**dis·loy′al·ly** *adv.*

dis·loy·al·ty (dis·loi′əl·tē) *n. pl.* **·ties** 1 The state of being disloyal; unfaithfulness; inconstancy. 2 A disloyal action.

dis·mal (diz′məl) *adj.* 1 Producing or expressing depression or gloom of feeling; cheerless; mournful. 2 Relating to adversity or trouble; direful; horrible. 3 Calamitous; ill-omened. See synonyms under DARK, SAD. —*n.* 1 *Colloq.* Usually *pl.* Gloomy feelings; depression. 2 *U.S.* A piece of swampy land along or near the southern Atlantic coast. Also **dismal swamp.** [<L *dies mali* evil or unpropitious days] —**dis′mal·ly** *adv.* —**dis′mal·ness** *n.*

Dismal Swamp A coastal swamp in SE Virginia and NE North Carolina; 20 miles long.

dis·man·tle (dis·man′təl) *v.t.* **·tled, ·tling** 1 To strip of furniture, equipments, or defenses. 2 To take apart; reduce to pieces. 3 *Obs.* To divest of clothing. [<MF *desmanteller* <*des-* away + *manteller* cover with a cloak <*mantel* a cloak] —**dis·man′tle·ment** *n.*

dis·mast (dis·mast′, -mäst′) *v.t. Naut.* To destroy or bring down the masts of; deprive of masts.

dis·may (dis·mā′) *v.t.* To paralyze with fear; deprive of courage and the ability to act; daunt utterly. See synonyms under FRIGHTEN. —*n.* A state of overwhelming embarrassment and fright; consternation; terror. See synonyms under ALARM, CHAGRIN, FEAR, FRIGHT. [ME *dismayen,* prob. <OF. Cf. OF *dismayé* dismayed.]

disme (dēm) *n. Obs.* A tenth part; a tithe. [<OF. See DIME.]

dis·mem·ber (dis·mem′bər) *v.t.* 1 To cut or pull limb from limb or part from part. 2 To divide; separate into parts and distribute, as an empire. [<OF *desmembrer* <L *dis-* apart + *membrum* a limb, member] —**dis·mem′ber·ment** *n.*

dis·miss (dis·mis′) *v.t.* 1 To put out of office or service by an act of authority; discharge. 2 To cause or allow to depart; send away. 3 To put away or aside; reject; put beyond consideration. 4 *Law* To send out of court; reject without further hearing: The case was *dismissed.* See synonyms under BANISH. [<LL *dismissus* <*dis-* away + *missus,* pp. of *mittere* send] —**dis·miss′i·ble** *adj.* —**dis·mis′so·ry, dis·mis′sive** *adj.*

dis·mis·sal (dis·mis′əl) *n.* 1 Removal from office; a dismissing; discharge. 2 A notice of discharge. Also **dis·mis′sion** (-mish′ən).

dis·mount (dis·mount′) *v.i.* 1 To get off or alight from a horse, etc. —*v.t.* 2 To remove from a mounting, as a cannon or a jewel. 3 To come down; descend. 4 To take (a machine) to pieces. 5 To remove from or deprive of horses. —*n.* The act or manner of dismounting. —**dis·mount′a·ble** *adj.*

dis·na (diz′nə) *Scot.* Does not.

Disney (diz′nē), **Walt,** 1901–1966, U.S. producer of animated cartoons: full name Walter Elias Disney.

Dis·ney·land (diz′nē·land′) *n.* 1 A large amusement park near Los Angeles, California. 2 Any fantastic or unreal place. [after Walt *Disney*]

dis·o·be·di·ent (dis′ə·bē′dē·ənt) *adj.* Neglecting or refusing to obey; refractory. See synonyms under REBELLIOUS. [<OF *desobedient* <L *dis-* not + *obediens, -entis* OBEDIENT] —**dis′o·be′di·ence** *n.* —**dis′o·be′di·ent·ly** *adv.*

dis·o·bey (dis′ə·bā′) *v.t.* & *v.i.* To refuse or fail to obey. [<OF *desobeir* <LL *dis-* away + *obedire* OBEY] —**dis′o·bey′er** *n.*

dis·o·blige (dis′ə·blīj′) *v.t.* 1 To neglect or refuse to oblige. 2 *Colloq.* To discommode or inconvenience. 3 To slight; affront. [<OF *desobliger* <L *dis-* not + *obligare* OBLIGE] —**dis·ob′li·ga′tion** *n.*

dis·o·blig·ing (dis′ə·blī′jing) *adj.* Not disposed to oblige; unaccommodating. —**dis′o·blig′ing·ly** *adv.* —**dis′o·blig′ing·ness** *n.*

di·so·di·um (dī·sō′dē·əm) *adj. Chem.* Characterized by the presence of two sodium atoms in one molecule. —**di·so′dic** *adj.*

dis·or·der (dis·ôr′dər) *n.* 1 The state of being disarranged; disorderliness. 2 Hence, disregard or neglect of orderliness. 3 A disturbance of the peace; an infraction of law or discipline; minor uprising or tumult. 4 Derangement of the bodily or mental functions; disease. 5 *Obs.* Agitation. —*v.t.* 1 To throw out of order; disarrange. 2 To disturb the natural functions of, as body or mind; unsettle; derange. 3 *Obs.* To agitate. [<OF *desordre* <L *dis-* away from, out of + *ordo* order]

Synonyms (noun): anarchy, clutter, confusion, disturbance, irregularity. See DISEASE, ILLNESS, TUMULT. *Antonyms*: method, order, regularity, system.

dis·or·dered (dis·ôr′dərd) *adj.* 1 Having no order or arrangement; confused. 2 Mentally deranged.

dis·or·der·ly (dis·ôr′dər·lē) *adj.* & *adv.* 1 Being in or causing disorder; not orderly; without order. 2 Lawless; disreputable. See synonyms under IRREGULAR, TURBULENT. —*n. pl.* **·lies** A disorderly person; offender against public order: a term used in police courts. —**dis·or′der·li·ness** *n.*

disorderly conduct *Law* A minor offense against public peace and order.

disorderly house An establishment run for illegal purposes, as prostitution, gambling, etc.

dis·or·di·nate (dis·ôr′də·nit) *adj. Obs.* Inordinate; without moderation. [<OF *desordené,* pp. of *desordener* <*des-* away (<L *dis-*) + *ordener* ORDAIN]

dis·o·ri·ent (dis·ôr′ē·ənt, -ō′rē-) *v.t.* 1 To cause to lose the sense of direction. 2 *Psychol.* To cause to lose appreciation of spatial, temporal, or human relationships. [<F *désorienter* <*des-* away (<L *dis-*) + *orienter* ORIENT] —**dis·o′ri·en·ta′tion** *n.*

dis·own (dis·ōn′) *v.t.* To refuse to acknowledge or to admit responsibility for or ownership of; deny; repudiate. See synonyms under RENOUNCE.

dis·par·age (dis·par′ij) *v.t.* **·aged, ·ag·ing** 1 To speak of slightingly; undervalue. 2 To bring discredit or dishonor upon. [<OF *desparagier* match unequally <*des-* down, away (<L *dis-*) + *parage* equality, rank] —**dis·par′ag·er** *n.* —**dis·par′ag·ing·ly** *adv.*

Synonyms: belittle, decry, depreciate, discredit, dishonor, lower, underestimate, underrate, undervalue. To *decry* is to cry down, in some noisy, public, or conspicuous manner. A witness or a statement is *discredited*; the currency is *depreciated*; a good name is *dishonored* by unworthy conduct; we *underestimate* in our own minds; we may *underrate* or *undervalue* in statement to others. To *disparage* is to *belittle* by damaging comparison or suggestion. These words are used, with few exceptions, of things such as qualities, merits, attainments, etc. See ASPERSE. *Antonyms*: see synonyms for PRAISE.

dis·par·age·ment (dis·par′ij·mənt) *n.* 1 The act of depreciating, aspersing, slighting, or undervaluing; derogation. 2 A condition of low estimation or valuation; a reproach; disgrace. 3 An unjust classing or comparison with that which is of less worth; degradation.

dis·pa·rate (dis′pə·rit) *adj.* That cannot be compared; dissimilar; radically different; different in essential qualities. [<L *disparatus,* pp. of *disparare* <*dis-* apart + *parare* make ready; infl. in meaning by L *dispars, -partis* unequal] —**dis′pa·rate·ly** *adv.* —**dis′pa·rate·ness** *n.*

dis·pa·ra·tion (dis′pə·rā′shən) *n. Pathol.* An optical distortion, consisting of double images of objects within or beyond the focal point of the eyes.

dis·par·i·ty (dis·par′ə·tē) *n. pl.* **·ties** The state of being dissimilar; inequality; difference. [<MF *disparité* <L *dis-* apart + *paritas* equality]

dis·park (dis·pärk′) *v.t. Obs.* 1 To throw open, as a private park; convert to other uses. 2 To release from enclosure.

dis·part[1] (dis·pärt′) *v.t.* & *v.i.* To divide; separate into pieces or parts. [<Ital. *dispartire* <L *dis-* away + *partire* divide <*pars, partis* a part, share]

dis·part[2] (dis·pärt′) *n. Mil.* 1 The difference between the semidiameters of the base ring and the muzzle of a cannon. 2 A piece upon the top of a cannon's muzzle to raise the line of sight parallel with the axis of the bore; a muzzle sight: also **dis·part′-sight′.** [Origin uncertain]

dis·part·ment (dis·pärt′mənt) *n.* The act of disparting; also, a division; separation.

dis·pas·sion (dis·pash′ən) *n.* Freedom from passion or emotion; lack of bias.

dis·pas·sion·ate (dis·pash′ən·it) *adj.* Free from passion; unprejudiced. See synonyms under CALM, SOBER. —**dis·pas′sion·ate·ly** *adv.* —**dis·pas′sion·ate·ness** *n.*

dis·patch (dis·pach′) *v.t.* 1 To send off, especially on official business or for special purposes. 2 To transact with promptness; finish quickly. 3 To execute; kill summarily. —*v.i.* 4 *Obs.* To make haste. See synonyms under KILL. —*n.* 1 The act of dispatching; a forwarding to some destination: usually with the implication of promptness or celerity: the *dispatch* of a messenger. 2 A message sent by special means and with haste, as by telegraph; especially, a communication on public matters sent by one official to another. 3 Quick transaction, as of business; the prompt performance and completion of work; expedition; speed. 4 The act of killing; a putting to death. 5 An organization or conveyance for the speedy transmission of money, goods, or messages: I will send it by *dispatch.* 6 *Obs.* Dismissal; deliverance; riddance. Also, in diplomatic use, spelled *despatch.* [<Ital. *dispacciare,* ? ult. <LL *dis-* away, not + *pactare* fasten, fix] —**dis·patch'ful** *adj.*

dispatch boat A fast vessel for carrying government dispatches.

dis·patch·er (dis·pach'ər) *n.* **1** One who dispatches. **2** One who directs the movement of trains, trucks, etc., and maintains records of such movement: also spelled *despatcher.*

dis·pel (dis·pel') *v.t.* **·pelled, ·pel·ling** To scatter in various directions; break up and drive away; disperse. [<L *dispellere* <*dis-* away + *pellere* drive]

dis·pend (dis·pend') *v.t. Obs.* To spend; also, to spend lavishly; squander. [<OF *despendre* <L *dispendere.* See DISPENSE.]

dis·pen·sa·ble (dis·pen'sə·bəl) *adj.* **1** That can be dispensed with. **2** That can be distributed or administered to others. **3** That can be removed by or made the subject of dispensation; pardonable. —**dis·pen'sa·bil'i·ty, dis·pen'sa·ble·ness** *n.*

dis·pen·sa·ry (dis·pen'sər·ē) *n. pl.* **·ries** A place or establishment, often public, where medicines are compounded and dispensed gratis or at a nominal price.

dis·pen·sa·tion (dis'pən·sā'shən) *n.* **1** The act of dispensing; a dealing out; distribution. **2** That which is bestowed on or appointed to one from a higher power. **3** The divine arrangement and administration of the affairs of the world: the *dispensation* of Providence. **4** A specific plan: a special *dispensation* of nature. **5** Special exemption granted from the requirements of a law, rule, or obligation; specifically, in the Roman Catholic Church, exemption by express ecclesiastical authority from an obligation incurred at the free will of the individual. Compare INDULGENCE. **6** *Theol.* One of the several systems or bodies of law in which at different times God has revealed his mind and will to man, or the continued state of things resulting from the operation of one of these systems: the Mosaic *dispensation*; also, the period during which a particular revelation of God's mind and will has been directly operative on mankind: during the Christian *dispensation.* [<OF <L *dispensatio, -onis* <*dispensare.* See DISPENSE.] —**dis'pen·sa'tion·al** *adj.*

dis·pen·sa·tor (dis'pen·sā'tər) *n.* One who dispenses or distributes; a dispenser.

dis·pen·sa·to·ry (dis·pen'sə·tôr'ē, -tō'rē) *adj.* Of or pertaining to dispensing or dispensation: also **dis·pen'sa·tive.** —*n. pl.* **·ries** A book in which medicinal substances are described; a pharmacopoeia.

dis·pense (dis·pens') *v.* **·pensed, ·pens·ing** *v.t.* **1** To give or deal out in portions; distribute. **2** To compound and give out (medicines). **3** To administer, as laws. **4** To relieve or excuse; absolve. —*v.i.* **5** To grant exemption or dispensation. See synonyms under APPORTION. —**to dispense with** To waive the observance of; relinquish; forgo. [OF *despenser* <L *dispensare,* freq. of *dispendere* <*dis-* away + *pendere* weigh]

dis·pens·er (dis·pen'sər) *n.* One who dispenses, manages, or administers.

dis·peo·ple (dis·pē'pəl) *v.t.* **·pled, ·pling** To depopulate. —**dis·peo'ple·ment** *n.* —**dis·peo'·pler** *n.*

di·sper·mous (dī·spûr'məs) *adj. Bot.* Two-seeded. [<DI-[2] + Gk. *sperma* seed]

di·sper·my (dī·spûr'mē) *n. Biol.* The fecundation of one egg with two spermatozoa. —**di·sper'mic** *adj.*

dis·per·sal (dis·pûr'səl) *n.* The act or fact of scattering or dispersing; dispersion.

dis·perse (dis·pûrs') *v.* **·persed, ·pers·ing** *v.t.* **1** To cause to scatter and go off in various directions. **2** To dispel; dissipate: The sun *dispersed* the mists. **3** To spread abroad; diffuse. **4** To separate (light) into its component spectral colors. —*v.i.* **5** To scatter and go off in various directions; dissipate. See synonyms under SPREAD. [<MF *disperser* <L *dispersus,* pp. of *dispergere* <*dis-* away + *spargere* scatter] —**dis·pers'i·ble** *adj.* —**dis·per'sive** *adj.*

dis·persed (dis·pûrst') *adj.* **1** Scattered; dissipated. **2** Placed near together but in a random manner. —**dis·pers'ed·ly** (-id·lē) *adv.*

disperse phase *Chem.* In a colloid system, that constituent which is dispersed in the medium: gold particles are the *disperse phase* of colloidal gold. See COLLOID. Also **dispersed phase.**

dis·pers·er (dis·pûr'sər) *n.* One who or that which disperses.

dis·per·sion (dis·pûr'zhən, -shən) *n.* **1** The act of dispersing; the state or result of being dispersed; also **dis·per'sal.** **2** *Mil.* The dispersed pattern of hits made by bombs dropped under the same conditions, or by bullets or shells shot from one gun with the same firing data. **3** *Physics* **a** The separation of light rays of different colors by the action of a prism or lens. **b** The process of sorting out emissions, as of electrons, in accordance with the values or magnitudes of selected properties, physical, chemical, electrical, etc. **4** *Chem.* The condition of the components making up a colloid system: distinguished from *solution.* **5** *Stat.* The arrangement of a series of values around the median or mean of a distribution.

dis·per·soid (dis·pûr'soid) *n. Chem.* A colloid system.

dis·pir·it (dis·pir'it) *v.t.* To render cheerless or hopeless; depress; dishearten. —**dis·pir'it·ed·ly** *adv.* —**dis·pir'it·ed·ness** *n.* —**dis·pir'it·ing·ly** *adv.*

dis·pir·it·ment (dis·pir'it·mənt) *n.* **1** The act of dispiriting, or the state of being dispirited; dejection. **2** That which dispirits, as a sorrow.

dis·pit·e·ous (dis·pit'ē·əs) *adj.* Remorseless; without pity.

dis·place (dis·plās') *v.t.* **·placed, ·plac·ing** **1** To remove or shift from the proper place. **2** To take the place of; supplant. **3** To remove from a position or office; discharge. **4** *Chem.* To release from combination: Zinc *displaces* the hydrogen of an acid. **5** *Obs.* To banish. [<OF *desplacer* <*des-* away (<L *dis-*) + *placer* place]

Synonyms: confuse, derange, disarrange, disturb, jumble, mislay, misplace, remove, unsettle. Objects are *displaced* when moved out of the place they have occupied; they are *misplaced* when they are put into a place where they should not be. One may know where to find what he has *misplaced*; what he has *mislaid* he cannot locate. *Antonyms*: adjust, array, assort, classify, dispose, group, order, place, sort.

dis·placed person (dis·plāst') Any inhabitant forced by military action or calamity to flee his country or leave his home. Abbr. *DP*

dis·place·ment (dis·plās'mənt) *n.* **1** The act of displacing, or the state of being displaced. **2** *Astron.* An apparent change of position, as of a star. **3** *Physics* **a** The weight of water displaced by a body floating in it, this weight being equal to the weight of the body. **b** The quantity of air displaced by an airplane, balloon, etc. **4** The relation between the position of a moving object at any time and its original position. **5** Electric displacement. **6** *Geol.* A fault. **7** *Psychoanal.* Substitution of a secondary, harmless, or unimportant element for a primary and significant one, as in a dream, for purposes of concealment.

displacement law *Physics* **1** The principle that an atom deprived of one of its electrons acquires the physicochemical properties of the element preceding it in the periodic table. See ELECTROMOTIVE SERIES. **2** The statement that radioactive emission of an alpha particle lowers the atomic number of the element by 2, while emission of a beta particle raises the atomic number by 1.

displacement ton See under TON.

dis·plant (dis·plant', -plänt') *v.t.* **1** To take (a plant) from the ground; uproot. **2** *Obs.* To dislodge; displace. [<OF *desplanter* <L *dis-* away + *plantare* plant] —**dis'plan·ta'·tion** *n.*

dis·play (dis·plā') *v.t.* **1** To show; make apparent to the eye or the mind. **2** To show off; exhibit ostentatiously. **3** To unfold; unfurl, as a flag or sail. **4** In printing, to give special prominence to, as by size, style, or spacing of type. See synonyms under FLAUNT. —*n.* **1** The act of spreading out, unfolding, exhibiting, or bringing to the view or to the mind. **2** Ostentatious show. **3** *Printing* A style of type calculated to attract attention. **4** The matter so displayed. See synonyms under OSTENTATION, SPECTACLE. [<OF *despleier* <LL *displicare.* Doublet of DEPLOY.]

dis·please (dis·plēz') *v.* **·pleased, ·pleas·ing** *v.t.* To cause displeasure in or annoyance to; vex; offend. —*v.i.* To cause displeasure or annoyance. See synonyms under AFFRONT, PIQUE[1]. [<OF *desplaisir, desplaire,* ult. <L *displicere* <*dis-* not + *placere* please] —**dis·pleas'ing** *adj.* —**dis·pleas'ing·ly** *adv.*

dis·pleas·ure (dis·plezh'ər) *n.* **1** The state of being displeased; dissatisfaction; vexation; indignant disapproval. **2** An annoyance; offense. See synonyms under ANGER, OFFENSE, PIQUE[1].

dis·plode (dis·plōd') *v.t.* & *v.i.* **·plod·ed, ·plod·ing** *Obs.* To explode. [<L *displodere* <*dis-* apart + *plaudere* clap, burst] —**dis·plo'sion** *n.*

dis·plume (dis·plōōm') *v.t.* **·plumed, ·plum·ing** *Obs.* To deplume.

dis·pone (dis·pōn') *v.t.* & *v.i.* **·poned, ·pon·ing** *Obs.* To arrange; dispose. [<L *disponere.* See DISPOSE.]

dis·port (dis·pôrt', -pōrt') *v.i.* To gambol; display oneself sportively. —*v.t.* To amuse or display (oneself). See synonyms under ENTERTAIN. —*n.* Diversion; pastime; sport. [<OF *desporter* <L *dis-* away + *portare* carry]

dis·pos·a·ble (dis·pō'zə·bəl) *adj.* Subject to disposal; free to be used as occasion may require.

dis·po·sal (dis·pō'zəl) *n.* **1** The act of disposing; arrangement; order; distribution. **2** A getting rid of, a transfer, as by gift or sale. **3** Power of control, outlay, management, or distribution.

dis·pose (dis·pōz') *v.* **·posed, ·pos·ing** *v.t.* **1** To put in order; arrange properly by sequence or interrelation. **2** To incline or influence the mind of; give a tendency to. **3** To put or set in a particular place or location. **4** *Archaic* To prepare; make ready. —*v.i.* **5** To arrange or settle something. —**to dispose of** **1** To settle; finish. **2** To throw away. **3** To get rid of by selling or giving. —*n. Obs.* **1** Disposal. **2** Order; arrangement. **3** Disposition; deportment. [<OF *disposer* <*dis-* apart (<L *dis-*) + *poser.* See POSE.] —**dis·posed'** *adj.*

dis·pos·er (dis·pō'zər) *n.* One who disposes or orders.

dis·po·si·tion (dis'pə·zish'ən) *n.* **1** The act of disposing; arrangement, as of troops. **2** Distribution; state or manner of disposal; final settlement. **3** Control; power: usually with *at*: at his *disposition.* **4** Natural tendency; temper or temperament; characteristic spirit; bent; propensity. **5** Natural tendency of animate or inanimate things. **6** *Archit.* Arrangement, as of plan, perspective, etc.: distinguished from *distribution.* See synonyms under APPETITE, CHARACTER, INCLINATION, MIND, WILL[1]. [<F <L *dispositio, -onis* <*dis-* away + *ponere* place] —**dis·pos·i·tive** (dis·poz'ə·tiv) *adj.*

dis·pos·sess (dis'pə·zes') *v.t.* To deprive (someone) of possession, as of a house or land; eject; oust. [<OF *despossesser* <*des-* away (<L *dis-*) + *possesser* POSSESS] —**dis'pos·ses'·sion** (-zesh'ən) *n.* —**dis'pos·ses'sor** *n.*

dis·pos·ses·so·ry (dis'pə·zes'ər·ē) *adj.* Referring to or partaking of dispossession.

dis·po·sure (dis·pō'zhər) *n. Obs.* **1** Disposal; direction. **2** Disposition; arrangement. **3** Nature; temperament.

dis·praise (dis·prāz') *v.t.* **·praised, ·prais·ing** To speak of with disapproval or censure; disparage. —*n.* The expression of unfavorable opinion; disparagement; censure. [<OF *despreisier* <*dis-* not (<L *dis-*) + *preisier* PRAISE] —**dis·prais'er** *n.* —**dis·prais'ing·ly** *adv.*

dis·pread (dis·pred') *v.t.* & *v.i.* **·pread, ·pread·ing** To spread out or abroad; diffuse; expand: also spelled *disspread.*

dis·prize (dis·prīz') *v.t.* **·prized, ·priz·ing** *Obs.* To think of little value; hold in low esteem. [OF *despriser,* var. of *despreisier.* See DESPRAISE.] —**dis·priz'ing·ly** *adv.*

dis·proof (dis·prōōf') *n.* Refutation; confutation.

dis·prop·er·ty (dis·prop'ər·tē) *v.t. Obs.* To dispossess.

dis·pro·por·tion (dis'prə·pôr'shən, -pōr'-) *n.* Want of due relative proportion; lack of symmetry; also, inadequacy. —*v.t.* To make of unsuitable size or proportions. [<F]

dis·pro·por·tion·a·ble (dis'prə·pôr'shən·ə·bəl, -pōr'-) *adj.* Unsuitable; inadequate.

dis·pro·por·tion·ate (dis'prə·pôr'shən·it, -pōr'-) *adj.* Out of proportion with regard to size, form, or value; disproportioned. Also **dis′·pro·por′tion·al.** —**dis′pro·por′tion·ate·ly, dis′·pro·por′tion·al·ly** *adv.* —**dis′pro·por′tion·ate·ness** *n.*

dis·prove (dis·pro͞ov′) *v.t.* **·proved, ·prov·ing** To prove (a statement, claim, etc.) to be false or erroneous; refute. [<OF *desprouver* < *des-* not (<L *dis-*) + *prouver* prove] —**dis·prov′·a·ble** *adj.* —**dis·prov′al** *n.*

dis·put·a·ble (dis·pyo͞o′tə·bəl, dis′pyo͞o·tə·bəl) *adj.* That can be disputed; controvertible; doubtful. —**dis·put′a·bil′i·ty** *n.* —**dis·put′a·bly** *adv.*

dis·pu·tant (dis′pyo͞o·tənt, dis·pyo͞o′tənt) *adj.* Engaged in controversy; disputing. —*n.* One who disputes. [<L *disputans, -antis,* ppr. of *disputare.* See DISPUTE.]

dis·pu·ta·tion (dis′pyo͞o·tā′shən) *n.* **1** The act of disputing; controversy; discussion; argumentation. **2** A rhetorical or logical exercise; a scholastic debate. See synonyms under ALTERCATION. [<L *disputatio, -onis* < *disputare.* See DISPUTE.]

dis·pu·ta·tious (dis′pyo͞o·tā′shəs) *adj.* Characterized by or pertaining to dispute. —**dis′·pu·ta′tious·ly** *adv.* —**dis′pu·ta′tious·ness** *n.*

dis·put·a·tive (dis·pyo͞o′tə·tiv) *adj.* Disputatious. —**dis·put′a·tive·ly** *adv.*

dis·pute (dis·pyo͞ot′) *v.* **·put·ed, ·put·ing** *v.t.* **1** To argue about; discuss. **2** To question the validity, genuineness, etc., of; controvert. **3** To strive for; contest for, as a prize. **4** To resist; oppose. —*v.i.* **5** To argue. **6** To quarrel; wrangle. —*n.* **1** A controversial discussion; a verbal contest. **2** An altercation; wrangle; quarrel. See synonyms under ALTERCATION, FEUD, QUARREL. [<OF *desputer* <L *disputare* < *dis-* away + *putare* think] —**dis·put′er** *n.*

Synonyms (verb): antagonize, argue, battle, combat, contend, contest, controvert, debate, discuss, oppose, quarrel, question, reason, wrangle. Persons may *contend* either from mere ill will or self-interest, or from the highest motives; "that ye should earnestly *contend* for the faith which was once delivered to the saints," *Jude* 3. To *controvert* is to *argue* wholly on the negative side, urging considerations against an opinion, proposition, or the like. One may *argue* and *discuss* without an opponent. We may *question* or *discuss* a proposition without reference to any one's advocacy of it, but to *contend, debate,* or *dispute* implies an opponent. A *dispute* may be personal, fractious, and petty; a *debate* is formal and orderly; if otherwise, it becomes a mere *wrangle.* Compare ARGUE, CONTEND, QUESTION, REASON.

dis·qual·i·fi·ca·tion (dis·kwol′ə·fə·kā′shən) *n.* **1** The act of debarring a person from participation in a contest or enterprise, or from sharing in the prizes or rewards, due to an infraction of rules or other irregularity. **2** The state of being disqualified; lack of requisite qualities or training. **3** That which disqualifies.

dis·qual·i·fy (dis·kwol′ə·fī) *v.t.* **·fied, ·fy·ing** **1** To render unqualified or unfit; incapacitate; disable. **2** To pronounce unqualified or ineligible; especially, in sports, to deprive (a competitor) of a prize for rule infractions; also, to debar from further competition for such infractions.

dis·qui·et (dis·kwī′ət) *n.* An unsettled or disturbed condition; lack of quiet; restlessness; uneasiness: also **dis·qui′et·ness, dis·qui′e·tude** (-to͞od, -tyo͞od). See synonyms under ALARM, ANXIETY, FEAR. —*v.t.* To make anxious or uneasy; disturb; alarm. —*adj. Rare* Restless; uneasy; impatient. —**dis·qui′et·ly** *adv.*

dis·qui·et·ing (dis·kwī′ət·ing) *adj.* Causing disquiet; making uneasy.

dis·qui·si·tion (dis′kwi·zish′ən) *n.* A systematic treatise or discourse; dissertation. [<L *disquisitio, -onis* an investigation < *dis-* from + *quaerere* seek, ask]

dis·quis·i·tor (dis·kwiz′ə·tər) *n.* One who makes disquisitions: an investigator.

Dis·rae·li (diz·rā′lē), **Benjamin,** 1804–81, Earl of Beaconsfield, English statesman and novelist; prime minister 1867, 1874–80. —**Isaac,** 1766–1848, English writer; father of the preceding.

dis·rate (dis·rāt′) *v.t.* **·rat·ed, ·rat·ing** To lower in rating or rank, as a petty officer; degrade.

dis·re·gard (dis′ri·gärd′) *v.t.* **1** To pay no attention to; ignore. **2** To treat as undeserving of consideration, respect, or attention; slight. —*n.* Want of regard; neglect; slight. See synonyms under NEGLECT, SLIGHT. —**dis′re·gard′er** *n.* —**dis′re·gard′ful** *adj.*

dis·rel·ish (dis·rel′ish) *v.t.* To dislike; have a distaste for. —*n.* **1** A feeling of slight repugnance; distaste or dislike. **2** Lack of palatableness; the quality of being displeasing or distasteful.

dis·re·mem·ber (dis′ri·mem′bər) *v.t. U.S. Dial.* To be unable to recall; forget.

dis·re·pair (dis′ri·pâr′) *n.* The state of being out of repair.

dis·rep·u·ta·ble (dis·rep′yə·tə·bəl) *adj.* Being in or causing ill repute; disgraceful. See synonyms under INFAMOUS. —**dis·rep′u·ta·ble·ness** *n.* —**dis·rep′u·ta·bly** *adv.*

dis·re·pute (dis′ri·pyo͞ot′) *n.* Lack or loss of reputation; ill repute. Also *Obs.* **dis·rep′u·ta′·tion.**

dis·re·spect (dis′ri·spekt′) *n.* Lack of respect; discourtesy. —*v.t.* To treat or regard with lack of respect.

dis·re·spect·a·ble (dis′ri·spek′tə·bəl) *adj.* Wanting respectability; disreputable. —**dis′re·spect′a·bil′i·ty** *n.*

dis·re·spect·ful (dis′ri·spekt′fəl) *adj.* Wanting in respect; discourteous. —**dis′re·spect′ful·ly** *adv.* —**dis′re·spect′ful·ness** *n.*

dis·robe (dis·rōb′) *v.t.* & *v.i.* **·robed, ·rob·ing** To undress. —**dis·robe′ment** *n.*

dis·root (dis·ro͞ot′, -ro͝ot′) *v.t.* **1** To tear up by the roots. **2** To tear from the foundation.

dis·rupt (dis·rupt′) *v.t.* & *v.i.* To burst or break asunder. —*adj. Obs.* Burst asunder; rent. [<L *disruptus,* pp. of *disrumpere* < *dis-* apart + *rumpere* burst] —**dis·rupt′er, dis·rup′tor** *n.*

dis·rup·tion (dis·rup′shən) *n.* **1** The act of bursting or tearing asunder. **2** The state of being so torn. See synonyms under RUPTURE.

dis·rup·tive (dis·rup′tiv) *adj.* Producing, resulting from, or attending disruption; rending; bursting. —**dis·rup′tive·ly** *adv.*

disruptive discharge *Electr.* A strong discharge in an insulating medium caused by breakdown under electrostatic stress.

diss (dis) *n.* The fibrous stems of a reedlike Mediterranean plant (*Ampelodesma mauritanicus*): used for making hats, paper, cordage, etc. [<Arabic *dīs*]

dis·sat·is·fac·tion (dis′sat·is·fak′shən) *n.* A dissatisfied state or feeling; discontent.

dis·sat·is·fac·to·ry (dis′sat·is·fak′tər·ē) *adj.* Giving dissatisfaction or discontent; unsatisfactory. —**dis′sat·is·fac′to·ri·ness** *n.*

dis·sat·is·fy (dis·sat′is·fī) *v.t.* **·fied, ·fy·ing** To fail to satisfy; disappoint; displease.

dis·seat (dis·sēt′) *v.t.* To unseat.

dis·sect (di·sekt′) *v.t.* **1** To cut apart or divide, as an animal body or a plant, in order to examine the structure; anatomize. **2** To analyze critically; examine. See synonyms under CUT. [<L *dissectus,* pp. of *dissecare* < *dis-* apart + *secare* cut]

dis·sect·ed (di·sek′tid) *adj.* **1** Cut in pieces; separated at the joints. **2** *Geol.* Cut into ridges, as a plateau. **3** *Bot.* Deeply cut into lobes or segments, as a leaf.

dis·sec·tion (di·sek′shən) *n.* **1** The act of dissecting. **2** A dissected object; an anatomical preparation. **3** A critical analysis.

dis·sec·tor (di·sek′tər) *n.* **1** One who dissects. **2** An instrument used in dissecting.

dis–seize (dis·sēz′) *v.t.* **–seized, –seiz·ing** *Law* To oust from the possession of an estate in freehold, usually unlawfully. Also **dis–seise′.** [<AF *disseisir,* OF *dessaisir* < *des-* away (<L *dis-*) + *saisir* SEIZE] —**dis–sei′zor** (-zər, -zôr), **dis–sei′sor** *n.*

dis–sei·zee (dis′sē·zē′, dis·sē′zē′) *n.* One who is dis–seized. Also **dis′–seis·ee′.**

dis–sei·zin (dis·sē′zin) *n. Law* The unlawful entry upon the freehold of another and wrongful ouster of him from possession. Also **dis–sei′sin, dis–seiz·ure** (dis·sē′zhər). [<AF *disseisine* < *disseisir.* See DIS–SEIZE.]

dis·sem·blance (di·sem′bləns) *n. Obs.* **1** Dissimilarity. **2** Dissimulation.

dis·sem·ble (di·sem′bəl) *v.* **·bled, ·bling** *v.t.* **1** To conceal or disguise the true nature of (intentions, feelings, etc.) so as to deceive; dissimulate. **2** To pretend not to notice; ignore. **3** *Obs.* To feign. —*v.i.* **4** To conceal one's true nature, intentions, etc.; act hypocritically. See synonyms under HIDE[1], MASK[1]. [Earlier *dissimule* <OF *dissimuler* <L *dissimulare* < *dis-* not, away + *similis* alike; infl. in form by RESEMBLE] —**dis·sem′·bler** *n.* —**dis·sem′bling·ly** *adv.*

dis·sem·i·nate (di·sem′ə·nāt) *v.t.* **·nat·ed, ·nat·ing** To spread about; scatter, as seed in sowing; promulgate. See synonyms under SPREAD. [<L *disseminatus,* pp. of *disseminare* < *dis-* away + *seminare* sow < *semen* seed] —**dis·sem′i·na′tion** *n.* —**dis·sem′i·na′tive** *adj.* —**dis·sem′i·na′tor** *n.*

dis·sem·i·nule (di·sem′ə·nyo͞ol) *n. Bot.* A seed fruit modified for migration. [<DISSEMIN(ATE) + -ULE]

dis·sen·sion (di·sen′shən) *n.* Angry or violent difference of opinion; discord; strife. See synonyms under ALTERCATION, QUARREL.

dis·sent (di·sent′) *v.i.* **1** To differ in thought or opinion; disagree; to withhold approval or consent. **2** To refuse adherence to an established church. —*n.* **1** The act or state of dissenting; disagreement. **2** Refusal to conform to an established church; nonconformity. [<L *dissentire* < *dis-* apart + *sentire* think, feel]

dis·sent·er (di·sen′tər) *n.* **1** One who dissents or disagrees; one who declares his disapproval or disagreement. **2** *Often cap.* A Protestant who refuses assent to the doctrines, or compliance with the usages, of an established or state church, especially the Church of England: opposed to *conformist.* See synonyms under HERETIC.

dis·sen·tient (di·sen′shənt) *adj.* Dissenting; expressing disagreement. —*n.* A dissenter. [<L *dissentiens, -entis,* ppr. of *dissentire.* See DISSENT.]

dis·sent·ing (di·sen′ting) *adj.* Disagreeing; avowing or expressing disagreement or dissent. —**dis·sent′ing·ly** *adv.*

dis·sen·tious (di·sen′shəs) *adj. Rare* Contentious; quarrelsome. —**dis·sen′tious·ly** *adv.*

dis·sep·i·ment (di·sep′ə·mənt) *n.* **1** *Bot.* A partition, as one of those that divide a compound pericarp into two or more cells. **2** *Zool.* A horizontal plate between the vertical septa in corals. [<L *dissaepimentum* < *dis-* apart + *saepire* fence in < *saepes* a fence, a hedge]

dis·ser·tate (dis′ər·tāt) *v.i.* **·tat·ed, ·tat·ing** *Obs.* To discourse or write in a learned or formal manner. Also *Obs.* **dis·sert′.** [<L *dissertatus,* pp. of *dissertare,* freq. of *disserere* < *dis-* apart + *serere* join, connect] —**dis′ser·ta′tive** *adj.* —**dis′ser·ta′tor** *n.*

dis·ser·ta·tion (dis′ər·tā′shən) *n.* An extended and argumentative treatise or discourse; disquisition; thesis. See synonyms under SPEECH.

dis·serve (dis·sûrv′) *v.t.* **·served, ·serv·ing** To serve or to treat badly; do an ill turn to.

dis·serv·ice (dis·sûr′vis) *n.* Ill service; an ill turn.

dis·serv·ice·a·ble (dis·sûr′vis·ə·bəl) *adj.* Disadvantageous; detrimental; unserviceable.

dis·sev·er (di·sev′ər) *v.t.* **1** To divide; separate. **2** To separate into parts. —*v.i.* **3** To separate; part. [<AF *deseverer,* OF *dessevrer* <L *disseparare* < *dis-* apart + *separare* SEPARATE] —**dis·sev′er·ance, dis·sev′er·ment** *n.*

dis·si·dence (dis′ə·dəns) *n.* Disagreement; dissent.

dis·si·dent (dis′ə·dənt) *adj.* Dissenting; differing. —*n.* A dissenter. [<L *dissidens, -entis,* ppr. of *dissidere* < *dis-* apart + *sedere* sit]

dis·sil·i·ent (di·sil′ē·ənt) *adj.* **1** Springing or flying open. **2** *Bot.* Bursting asunder, as the dry pod of the jewelweed. [<L *dissiliens, -entis,* ppr. of *dissilire* < *dis-* apart + *salire* leap] —**dis·sil′i·ence** or **dis·sil′i·en·cy** *n.*

dis·sim·i·lar (di·sim′ə·lər) *adj.* Unlike, different: often with *to.* See synonyms under CONTRARY, HETEROGENEOUS. —**dis·sim′i·lar·ly** *adv.*

dis·sim·i·lar·i·ty (di·sim′ə·lar′ə·tē) *n. pl.* **·ties** Unlikeness; difference. See synonyms under DIFFERENCE.

dis·sim·i·late (di·sim′ə·lāt) *v.t.* & *v.i.* **·lat·ed, ·lat·ing** **1** To make or become unlike. **2**

add, āce, câre, pälm; end, ēven; it, īce; odd, ōpen, ôrder; to͝ok, po͞ol; up, bûrn; ə = a in *above,* e in *sicken,* i in *clarity,* o in *melon,* u in *focus;* yo͞o = u in *fuse;* oi, oil; ou, pout; ch, check; g, go; ng, ring; th, thin; t͟h, this; zh, vision. Foreign sounds à, œ, ü, kh, ṅ; and ♦: see page xx. < from; + plus; ? possibly.

Phonet. To undergo or cause to undergo dissimilation. [<DIS-[1] + L *similis* alike]

dis·sim·i·la·tion (di·sim′ə·lā′shən) *n.* **1** The act or process of making or becoming dissimilar. **2** *Phonet.* The process whereby one of two or more identical or similar sounds in a word is changed or omitted, as in the pronunciation (lī′ber′ē) for *library,* or the English form *turtle* from Latin *turtur.*

dis·si·mil·i·tude (dis′si·mil′ə·to͞od, -tyo͞od) *n.* Lack of resemblance; unlikeness. [<L *dissimilitudo* <*dissimilis* <*dis-* not + *similis* alike]

dis·sim·u·late (di·sim′yə·lāt) *v.t.* & *v.i.* **·lat·ed, ·lat·ing** To conceal (intentions, feelings, etc.) by pretense; dissemble. [<L *dissimulatus,* pp. of *dissimulare.* See DISSEMBLE.] **—dis·sim′u·la′tive** *adj.* **—dis·sim′u·la′tor** *n.*

dis·sim·u·la·tion (di·sim′yə·lā′shən) *n.* False pretense; hypocrisy. See synonyms under DECEPTION, HYPOCRISY, PRETENSE.

dis·si·pate (dis′ə·pāt) *v.* **·pat·ed, ·pat·ing** *v.t.* **1** To disperse or drive away; dispel. **2** To disintegrate; destroy or dissolve utterly. **3** To squander; spend lavishly and wastefully. —*v.i.* **4** To become dispersed; scatter. **5** To engage in excessive or dissolute pleasures. See synonyms under SQUANDER. [<L *dissipatus,* pp. of *dissipare* <*dis-* away + *supare* throw]

dis·si·pat·ed (dis′ə·pā′tid) *adj.* **1** Wasted; scattered. **2** Pursuing pleasure to excess; dissolute. **—dis′si·pat′ed·ly** *adv.* **—dis′si·pat′·ed·ness** *n.*

dis·si·pa·tion (dis′ə·pā′shən) *n.* **1** The act of dissipating or state of being dissipated. **2** Excessive indulgence, especially in vicious pleasures. **3** Distraction, as of the mind, or anything that distracts. See synonyms under EXCESS.

dis·si·pa·tive (dis′ə·pā′tiv) *adj.* **1** Having a tendency to dissipate or disperse, or pertaining to such a tendency. **2** Of or pertaining to dissipation. **3** Tending to a dissipated life.

dis·so·cia·ble (di·sō′shə·bəl, -shē·ə-) *adj.* **1** Not well assorted or associated; incongruous; unsociable. **2** Capable of being separated or dissociated. **3** Unsociable. **—dis·so′cia·bil′·i·ty, dis·so′cia·ble·ness** *n.* **—dis·so′cia·bly** *adv.*

dis·so·cial (di·sō′shəl) *adj.* Unsocial; unfriendly.

dis·so·cial·ize (di·sō′shəl·īz) *v.t.* **·ized, ·iz·ing** To make dissocial.

dis·so·ci·ate (di·sō′shē·āt) *v.* **·at·ed, ·at·ing** *v.t.* **1** To break the association of; disconnect; separate. **2** To regard as separate in concept or nature. **3** *Chem.* To resolve by dissociation. —*v.i.* **4** To break an association. **5** *Chem.* To undergo dissociation. [<L *dissociatus,* pp. of *dissociare* <*dis-* apart + *sociare* join together <*socius* a companion] **—dis·so′ci·a′tive** *adj.*

dis·so·ci·a·tion (di·sō′sē·ā′shən, -shē·ā′-) *n.* **1** The act of dissociating; state of separation. **2** *Chem.* **a** The resolution of a compound into simpler constituents by a change in physical state, as by heat or pressure, with recombination when the original conditions are restored. **b** Electrolytic dissolution. **3** *Psychiatry* A mental disorder in which one or several groups of ideas become split off from the main body of the personality and are not accessible to conscious control: contrasted with *association.*

dis·sol·u·ble (di·sol′yə·bəl) *adj.* **1** Separable into parts. **2** Capable of being dissolved or decomposed. [<L *dissolubilis* <*dissolvere.* See DISSOLVE.] **—dis′sol·u·bil′i·ty, dis·sol′u·ble·ness** *n.*

dis·so·lute (dis′ə·lo͞ot) *adj.* Abandoned; profligate. See synonyms under IMMORAL, IRREGULAR. [<L *dissolutus,* pp. of *dissolvere.* See DISSOLVE.] **—dis′so·lute·ly** *adv.* **—dis′so·lute·ness** *n.*

dis·so·lu·tion (dis′ə·lo͞o′shən) *n.* **1** The act or state of dissolving; disintegration. **2** *Chem.* Decomposition; separation into elements or components. **3** Liquefaction. **4** Separation; breaking up, as of an assembly or corporation, or of a partnership, in accordance with the articles of co-partnership, or by the death or incompetence of a partner, or by the decree of a court. **5** Death, the separation of soul and body.

dis·so·lu·tive (dis′ə·lo͞o′tiv) *adj.* **1** Dissolving. **2** Pertaining to or characterized by physical or mental dissolution.

dis·solve (di·zolv′) *v.* **·solved, ·solv·ing** *v.t.* **1** To change (a substance) from a solid to a fluid condition. **2** To cause to pass into or combine with a solution; melt; liquefy. **3** To end the existence, functions, or meetings of: to *dissolve* Parliament. **4** To end or conclude (a relationship or association): to *dissolve* a partnership or a marriage. **5** *Law* To set aside; annul, as an injunction. **6** To disunite. —*v.i.* **7** To pass into or as into a liquid state; melt; become fluid. **8** To come to an end; disperse, as a meeting. **9** To fade away; vanish, as an image. **10** In motion pictures, to change gradually from one picture or scene to another, the two overlapping in the process. See synonyms under MELT. —*n.* In motion pictures and television, the slow emergence of one scene out of another, caused by the lapping of a fade-in over a fade-out; a lap-dissolve. [<L *dissolvere* <*dis-* apart + *solvere* loosen] **—dis·solv′a·ble** *adj.* **—dis·sol′vent** *adj.* & *n.*

dis·solv·er (di·zol′vər) *n.* One who or that which dissolves; specifically, a device for producing a dissolving view.

dissolving view A series of magic-lantern slides, each of which appears to fade gradually into the next when successively projected on a screen.

dis·so·nance (dis′ə·nəns) *n.* **1** A discordant mingling of sounds; discord. **2** *Music* A combination of tones regarded as displeasing and requiring resolution. **3** Harsh disagreement; incongruity; discord. Also **dis′so·nan·cy.**

dis·so·nant (dis′ə·nənt) *adj.* **1** Harsh in sound; inharmonious. **2** Naturally hostile; incongruous. **3** *Music* Having the quality of dissonance. [<L *dissonans, -antis,* ppr. of *dissonare* <*dis-* away + *sonare* sound] **—dis′·so·nant·ly** *adv.*

dis·spread (dis·pred′) See DISPREAD.

dis·suade (di·swād′) *v.t.* **·suad·ed, ·suad·ing** **1** To change or alter the plans of (a person) by persuasion or advice: with *from.* **2** *Obs.* To advise against (a course of action). See synonyms under ADMONISH. [<L *dissuadere* <*dis-* away + *suadere* persuade] **—dis·suad′er** *n.*

dis·sua·sion (di·swā′zhən) *n.* **1** The act of dissuading. **2** A dissuasive. See synonyms under COUNSEL. [<L *dissuasio, -onis* <*dissuadere.* See DISSUADE.]

dis·sua·sive (di·swā′siv) *adj.* Tending or intended to dissuade. —*n.* A dissuading argument, fact, or consideration. **—dis·sua′sive·ly** *adv.* **—dis·sua′sive·ness** *n.*

dis·syl·lab·i·fy (dis′i·lab′ə·fī, dis′si-) *v.t.* **·fied, ·fy·ing** To make dissyllabic: also spelled *disyllabify.* Also **dis·syl·la·bize** (di·sil′ə·bīz, dis·sil′-).

dis·syl·la·ble (di·sil′ə·bəl, dis′sil′ə·bəl) *n.* A word of two syllables: also spelled *disyllable.* [<F <L *disyllabus* <Gk. *disyllabos* <*dis-* twofold + *syllabos* SYLLABLE] **—dis′syl·lab′ic** *adj.* **—dis′syl·lab′i·fi·ca′tion** *n.*

dis·sym·me·try (dis·sim′ə·trē) *n.* Lack of symmetry. **—dis′sym·met′ric** or **·ri·cal** *adj.* **—dis′sym·met′ri·cal·ly** *adv.*

dis·taff (dis′taf, -täf) *n. pl.* **dis·taffs** or *Rare* **dis·taves** (dis′tāvz) **1** A rotating vertical staff that holds the bunch of flax or wool for use in spinning by hand. **2** Figuratively, woman, as the holder of a distaff; also, woman's work or domain. [OE *distæf* <*dis* bundle of flax + *stæf* staff]

distaff side **1** The maternal branch of a family. **2** Women collectively. Compare SPINDLE SIDE, SPEAR SIDE.

dis·tain (dis·tān′) *v.t. Archaic* **1** To stain; dye. **2** To sully, disgrace. [<OF *desteindre* <*des-* completely (<L *dis-*) + *teindre* <L *tingere* stain, dye]

dis·tal (dis′təl) *adj. Biol.* Relatively remote from the center of the body or the point of attachment; peripheral: opposed to *proximal.* [<DIST(ANT) + -AL[1]] **—dis′tal·ly** *adv.*

dis·tance (dis′təns) *n.* **1** Length of separation in space, or, by extension, in time. **2** The state of being distant; separation; remoteness; a remote point. **3** Reserve; haughtiness; coldness. **4** Separation in rank, relationship, or succession. **5** In art, the part of a picture that represents distant objects. **6** *Music* The interval between two notes. **7** In horse racing, an interval measured back from the winning post to a point on the course marked by a flag or post, called the **distance post.** To be allowed to run in succeeding heats of the race, a horse must reach the distance post before the winning horse reaches the finish line. —*v.t.* **·tanced, ·tanc·ing** **1** To leave behind, as in a race; outstrip; excel. **2** To separate by a space. **3** To cause to appear distant.

dis·tant (dis′tənt) *adj.* **1** Separated in space or time; far apart; not closely related in qualities or in position; far away; remote. **2** Reserved or unapproachable; formal. **3** Indistinct; faint. **4** Not obvious or plain; indirect. See synonyms under ALIEN, HAUGHTY. [<F <L *distans, -antis,* ppr. of *distare* <*dis-* apart + *stare* stand] **—dis′tant·ly** *adv.*

dis·taste (dis·tāst′) *n.* **1** Aversion to food or drink; disrelish. **2** Alienation; disapproval; dislike. See synonyms under ANTIPATHY. —*v.t. Rare* **1** To dislike. **2** To displease; cause the dislike of.

dis·taste·ful (dis·tāst′fəl) *adj.* **1** Causing distaste; disagreeable. **2** Denoting distaste: a *distasteful* glance. **—dis·taste′ful·ly** *adv.* **—dis·taste′ful·ness** *n.*

dis·tel·fink (dis′təl·fingk) *n.* A highly stylized bird design, used on Pennsylvania Dutch furniture, fabrics, etc. Also **dis′tle·fink.** [<G, a goldfinch]

dis·tem·per[1] (dis·tem′pər) *n.* **1** Any of several infectious diseases of animals, especially a catarrhal affection of puppies associated with a filtrable virus. **2** An improper or disordered temper; ill humor. **3** Political or civil disturbance; riot; disorder. [<*v.*] —*v.t.* **1** To disturb or derange the faculties or functions of; disorder. **2** To ruffle; disturb. [<Med. L *distemperare* <*dis-* away + *temperare* regulate, mix]

dis·tem·per[2] (dis·tem′pər) *n.* **1** A pigment mixed with a vehicle (as yolk of eggs or glue) soluble in water, used chiefly for mural decoration and scene painting. **2** The art or process of painting with such materials, or a painting executed in them. —*v.t.* **1** To mix, as colors, for distemper painting. **2** To color or paint with distemper. —*adj.* Of or pertaining to internal decoration done with distemper. [<OF *destemprer* <Med. L *distemperare* <*dis-* apart + *temperare* mix, mingle, soak]

dis·tem·per·a·ture (dis·tem′pər·ə·chər) *n.* **1** Disorder; sickness. **2** Disarrangement; perturbation.

dis·tend (dis·tend′) *v.t.* & *v.i.* To expand; swell; dilate, as from or by pressure from within. [<L *distendere* <*dis-* apart + *tendere* stretch]

dis·ten·si·ble (dis·ten′sə·bəl) *adj.* Capable of being distended. **—dis·ten′si·bil′i·ty** *n.*

dis·tent (dis·tent′) *adj. Obs.* Distended.

dis·ten·tion (dis·ten′shən) *n.* **1** The act of distending. **2** The state of being distended. Also **dis·ten′sion.** [<L *distentio, -onis* <*distendere.* See DISTEND.]

dis·tich (dis′tik) *n.* In prosody, a couplet; a two-line stanza considered as a unit. [<L *distichon* <Gk., neut. sing. of *distichos* <*di-* two + *stichos* row, line]

dis·ti·chous (dis′ti·kəs) *adj. Bot.* Disposed in two longitudinal rows on opposite sides of a common axis, as leaves. [<L *distichus* <Gk. *distichos.* See DISTICH.] **—dis′ti·chous·ly** *adv.*

dis·til (di·stil′) *v.* **·tilled, ·til·ling** *v.t.* **1** To subject to or as to distillation, so as to purify, concentrate, or refine. **2** To extract volatile substances from by distillation: to *distil* corn. **3** To extract or produce by distillation: to *distil* whisky. **4** To give forth or send down in drops: The clouds *distil* rain. —*v.i.* **5** To undergo distillation. **6** To exude in drops; trickle; drip. Also **dis·till′.** [<L *distillare,* var. of *destillare* <*de-* down + *stillare* drop, trickle] **—dis·til′la·ble** *adj.*

dis·til·late (dis′tə·lit, -lāt) *n.* The condensed product separated by distillation. [<L *distillatus,* pp. of *distillare.* See DISTILL.]

dis·til·la·tion (dis′tə·lā′shən) *n.* **1** The act of distilling; separation of the more volatile parts of a substance from those less volatile by vaporizing and subsequently condensing, as by heating in a retort or still and cooling in a retort or worm. **2** The purification or rectification of a substance by this process. **3** The substance separated by distilling; a distillate. **4** The essential or abstract quality of anything.

dis·til·ler (dis·til′ər) *n.* **1** One who distils; a maker and seller of distilled liquors. **2** A condenser used in distilling.

dis·til·ler·y (di·stil′ər·ē) *n. pl.* **·ler·ies** An establishment for distilling, especially for producing alcoholic liquors by distillation.

dis·til·ment (di·stil′mənt) *n.* Distillation. Also **dis·till′ment.**

dis·tinct (dis·tingkt′) *adj.* **1** Clear to the senses or mind; plain; unmistakable. **2** Clearly standing apart, as in space or thought, from other objects; evidently not identical; observably or decidedly different. **3** Standing apart by itself; disjoined; unconnected. **4** Using or marked by clear vision and understanding; not obscure nor confused: a man of *distinct* ideas. **5** *Poetic* Adorned; variegated. See synonyms under CLEAR, EVIDENT, MANIFEST, PARTICULAR, PLAIN[1]. [<L *distinctus,* pp. of *distinguere.* See DISTINGUISH.] —**dis·tinct′ly** *adv.* —**dis·tinct′ness** *n.*

dis·tinc·tion (dis·tingk′shən) *n.* **1** A distinguishing mark or quality; a characteristic difference; also, the relation of difference between objects having distinguishing marks or qualities. **2** The act of distinguishing; discrimination. **3** Heed or regard to differences, as of rank or character. **4** A mark of honor; superiority; honorable position. See synonyms under CHARACTERISTIC, DIFFERENCE, FAME.

dis·tinc·tive (dis·tingk′tiv) *adj.* **1** Characteristic; distinguishing. See synonyms under PARTICULAR. **2** *Ling.* Relevant. —**dis·tinc′·tive·ly** *adv.* —**dis·tinc′tive·ness** *n.*

dis·tin·gué (dis′tang·gā′, *Fr.* dēs·tan·gā′) *adj.* Distinguished; having an air of distinction [<F, pp. of *distinguer.* See DISTINGUISH.] —**dis′·tin·guée′** *adj. fem.*

dis·tin·guish (di·sting′gwish) *v.t.* **1** To mark as different; indicate or constitute the differences of or between. **2** To recognize as separate or distinct; discriminate. **3** To divide into classes or categories classify. **4** To bring fame, celebrity, or credit upon. **5** To apperceive by one of the physical senses. —*v.i.* **6** To make or discern differences; discriminate: often with *among* or *between.* See synonyms under DISCERN, KNOW. [<F *distinguer* (<L *distinguere* separate) + -ISH[2]] —**dis·tin′guish·a·ble** *adj.* —**dis·tin′guish·a·bly** *adv.* —**dis·tin′·guish·er** *n.*

dis·tin·guished (di·sting′gwisht) *adj.* Conspicuous; eminent. See synonyms under EMINENT, ILLUSTRIOUS.

Distinguished Flying Cross *U.S.* A military decoration in the form of a bronze cross on which is superimposed a four-bladed propeller: awarded to members of the Air Force for exceptional heroism while participating in an aerial flight. Abbr. *D.F.C.*

Distinguished Service Cross *U.S.* A decoration in the form of a bronze cross with an eagle on the center and "For Valor" on a scroll below: awarded to members of the armed forces who display extraordinary heroism in connection with military operations against an armed enemy. Abbr. *D.S.C.*

A Distinguished Service Cross — B Distinguished Service Medal — C Distinguished Flying Cross

Distinguished Service Medal *U.S.* A decoration in the form of a bronze, gold, and blue enamel medal, awarded to members of the Army, Navy, Air Force, or merchant marine for exceptionally meritorious service involving responsibility. Abbr. *D.S.M.*

dis·tin·guish·ing (di·sting′gwish·ing) *adj.* Constituting difference or distinction; characteristic.

dis·tin·guish·ment (di·sting′gwish·mənt) *n.* *Obs.* Observation of difference.

dis·tome (dis′tōm) *n.* One of a genus *(Distoma)* of trematode, parasitic worms: also called *flukes.* [<NL<Gk. *di-* two + *stoma* mouth]

dis·tort (dis·tôrt′) *v.t.* **1** To twist or bend out of shape; make crooked or misshapen. **2** To twist the meaning of, misrepresent; pervert. See synonyms under PERVERT. [<L *distortus,* pp. of *distorquere* <*dis-* apart + *torquere* twist] —**dis·tort′er** *n.* —**dis·tort′ed** *adj.* —**dis·tort′ed·ly** *adv.* —**dis·tort′ed·ness** *n.*

dis·tor·tion (dis·tôr′shən) *n.* **1** The act of distorting. **2** A deformity; perversion. **3** *Optics* An imperfect image due to a defective lens or retina. **4** *Telecom.* A change in the wave form of a signal caused by non-uniform transmission at different frequencies. **5** *Psychoanal.* The process whereby certain objectionable elements of the mental life are altered so as to make them acceptable to the conscious ego. Compare CENSORSHIP (def. 2). —**dis·tor′tion·al** *adj.*

dis·tract (dis·trakt′) *v.t.* **1** To draw or divert (the mind, etc.) in a different direction. **2** To turn or draw (the mind or attention) in various directions; bewilder; confuse. **3** To make frantic; craze. See synonyms under PERPLEX. [<L *distractus,* pp. of *distrahere* <*dis-* away + *trahere* draw] —**dis·tract′i·ble** *adj.* —**dis·tract′ing, dis·trac′tive** *adj.*

dis·tract·ed (dis·trak′tid) *adj.* **1** Bewildered or harassed. **2** Mentally deranged; mad. See synonyms under INSANE. —**dis·tract′ed·ly** *adv.*

dis·trac·tion (dis·trak′shən) *n.* **1** A drawing off or diversion of the mind, as from some object or from troubles or cares. **2** Mental disturbance or confusion; perplexity. **3** Strong agitation, excitement, or distress; wild or violent grief. **4** Mental aberration; frenzy; madness. **5** Anything that distracts; a disturbing or diverting object or cause; an interruption or diversion. See synonyms under PERPLEXITY.

dis·train (dis·trān′) *v.t. Law* **1** To take and detain (personal property) by distress as security for a debt, claim, etc. **2** To subject (a person) to distress. —*v.i.* **3** To impose a distress. [<OF *destreindre* <L *distringere* <*dis-* completely + *stringere* draw tight, compress] —**dis·train′a·ble** *adj.* —**dis·train′er** or **dis·train′or** *n.* —**dis·train′ment** *n.*

dis·train·ee (dis′trā·nē′) *n. Law* A person whose property has been distrained.

dis·traint (dis·trānt′) *n. Law* The act or process of distraining.

dis·trait (dis·trā′, *Fr.* dēs·tre′) *adj.* Absent-minded. [<F, pp. of *distraire* <L *distrahere.* See DISTRACT.] —**dis·traite** (dis·trāt′, *Fr.* dēs·tret′) *adj. fem.*

dis·traught (dis·trôt′) *adj.* In a state of distraction. [Var. of earlier *distract,* pp. of DISTRACT]

dis·tress (dis·tres′) *v.t.* **1** To inflict suffering upon; cause agony, anxiety, or worry to; afflict. **2** To constrain by suffering or pain. **3** *Law* To distrain. See synonyms under PERSECUTE. —*n.* **1** Acute or extreme suffering or its cause; pain; trouble. **2** An afflicted, wretched, or exhausted condition; dangerous situation. **3** *Law* Distraint; goods taken by distraint. See synonyms under AGONY, GRIEF, MISFORTUNE, PAIN, POVERTY. [<AF *destresser,* OF *destrecier* <LL *districtiare* <L *distringere.* See DISTRAIN.] —**dis·tress′ful** *adj.* —**dis·tress′·ful·ly** *adv.* —**dis·tress′ful·ness** *n.* —**dis·tress′·ing·ly** *adv.*

dis·trib·u·tar·y (dis·trib′yoo·ter′ē) *n. pl.* **·tar·ies** A river branch flowing away from the main branch and not returning to it: opposed to *tributary.*

dis·trib·ute (dis·trib′yoot) *v.t.* **·ut·ed, ·ut·ing** **1** To divide and deal out in shares; apportion; allot. **2** To divide and classify; categorize: to *distribute* plants into orders. **3** To scatter or spread out, as in an area or over a surface. **4** To divide and arrange into distinctive parts or functions. **5** *Logic* To use (a term) in its full extension, so as to include all members of the class which it names. **6** *Printing* To separate (type) and return the letters to the proper boxes. See synonyms under ALLOT, APPORTION, SPREAD. [<L *distributus,* pp. of *distribuere* <*dis-* away + *tribuere* give, allot] —**dis·trib′ut·a·ble** *adj.*

dis·trib·ut·er (dis·trib′yə·tər) *n.* **1** One who or that which distributes; specifically, a marketing agent. **2** A device used in distribution, as in an automobile or a Linotype machine. Also **dis·trib′u·tor** (-tər, -tôr).

dis·tri·bu·tion (dis′trə·byōō′shən) *n.* **1** The act of distributing; apportionment; arrangement; disposition. **2** That which is distributed. **3** The state or manner of being distributed. **4** *Archit.* The arrangement and interdependence of interior subdivisions, etc., as distinguished from *disposition.* **5** In commerce, the total of all steps involved in the delivery of goods from producer to consumer, including such items as sales methods, transport, storage, financing, accounting, etc.

distribution curve A frequency curve.

dis·trib·u·tive (dis·trib′yə·tiv) *adj.* **1** Serving or tending to distribute; pertaining to distribution. **2** Denoting individual action or consideration. **3** *Gram.* Denoting objects or groups composed of individuals acting individually: The *distributive* pronouns "each," "every," "either," and "neither" are called *distributive* adjectives when they modify nouns. **4** Expressing the act of taking singly: the Latin *distributive* numeral "bini" (two by two). **5** *Logic* Indicating or effecting the distribution of a term. —*n.* A distributive pronoun, adjective, or numeral, as *each, every,* etc. —**dis·trib′u·tive·ly** *adv.* —**dis·trib′·u·tive·ness** *n.*

dis·trict (dis′trikt) *n.* **1** A portion of territory specially set off or defined, as for judicial, political, educational, or other purposes. **2** A subdivision of the United States or of one State having its own Federal or State court. **3** Any region of space; a tract. See synonyms under LAND. —*v.t.* To divide into districts. [<MF <Med. L *districtus* jurisdiction <L *distringere.* See DISTRAIN.]

district attorney The prosecuting officer of a Federal or State judicial district. See PROSECUTING ATTORNEY under ATTORNEY.

district judge A judge who presides over a Federal or State district court.

District of Columbia A Federal district, capital of the United States, coextensive with the city of Washington on the Potomac River; 69 square miles: abbr. DC

Dis·tri·to Fe·de·ral (dēs·trē′tō fā′th ā·räl′) The Spanish form of FEDERAL DISTRICT (Mexico City).

dis·trust (dis·trust′) *v.t.* To feel no trust for or confidence in; doubt; suspect. —*n.* Doubt; suspicion; discredit. See synonyms under DOUBT.

dis·trust·ful (dis·trust′fəl) *adj.* **1** Entertaining doubt or distrust. **2** Wanting in confidence; diffident; modest. —**dis·trust′ful·ly** *adv.* —**dis·trust′ful·ness** *n.*

dis·turb (dis·tûrb′) *v.t.* **1** To destroy or interfere with the repose, tranquility, or peace of. **2** To agitate the mind of; disquiet; trouble. **3** To upset the order, system, or progression of: She has *disturbed* the rhythm of my days. **4** To interrupt; break in on. **5** To cause inconvenience to. See synonyms under DISPLACE. [<OF *destorber* <L *disturbare* <*dis-* completely + *turbare* disorder] —**dis·turb′er** *n.*

dis·tur·bance (dis·tûr′bəns) *n.* **1** A change, or alteration, whether as the result of internal or external action, from a condition of order, repose, or peace to one of agitation or disorder. **2** The act of effecting this change. **3** A tumult or commotion by which the public peace is disturbed. **4** A disordered condition of the mind; mental agitation, distraction, or confusion. See synonyms under ALTERCATION, ANXIETY, DISORDER, TUMULT. [<OF *destorbance* <*destorber.* See DISTURB.]

dis·tyle (dis′tīl) *adj. Archit.* Having two columns; specifically, referring to a portico in antes. See ANTA. —*n.* A building so constructed. [<DI-[2] + Gk. *stylos* pillar]

di·sul·fate (dī·sul′fāt) *n. Chem.* **1** A pyrosulfate. **2** A bisulfate. Also **di·sul′phate.**

di·sul·fide (dī·sul′fīd) *n. Chem.* A sulfide containing two atoms of sulfur to the molecule: also *bisulfide.* Also **di·sul′fid** (-fid), **di·sul′·phide.**

di·sul·fu·ric (dī′sul·fyoor′ik) *adj. Chem.* Pyrosulfuric.

disulfuric acid *Chem.* Pyrosulfuric acid.

dis·un·ion (dis·yōōn′yən) *n.* **1** The state of being disunited; severance; rupture. **2** A condition of disagreement; breach of concord.

dis·un·ion·ist (dis·yōōn′yən·ist) *n.* **1** An advocate of disunion. **2** In U.S. history, one who, before and during Civil War of 1861, favored the dissolution of the Union.

3 In English history, an opponent of the Act of Union with Ireland of 1801. Compare UNIONIST. —**dis·un′ion·ism** *n.*

dis·u·nite (dis′yōō·nīt′) *v.* **·nit·ed, ·nit·ing** *v.t.* 1 To break the union of; separate; disjoin; part. 2 To alienate; estrange, as friends. —*v.i.* 3 To come apart. [<L *dis-* apart + *unus* one]

dis·use (dis·yōōs′) *n.* The state of being excluded or retired from use; desuetude: also **dis·us′age** (-ij). —*v.t.* (dis·yōōz′) **·used, ·us·ing** To cease to use or practice; discontinue.

dis·u·til·i·ty (dis′yōō·til′ə·tē) *n.* Injuriousness; harmfulness.

dis·u·til·ize (dis·yōō′təl·īz) *v.t. Rare* **·ized, ·iz·ing** To destroy the usefulness of.

dis·val·ue (dis·val′yōō) *v.t.* **·val·ued, ·val·u·ing** To treat as of little value; disparage.

di·syl·lab·i·fy (di′si·lab′ə·fī) See DISSYLLABIFY.

di·syl·la·ble (di·sil′ə·bəl) See DISSYLLABLE.

dis·yoke (dis·yōk′) *v.t.* **·yoked, ·yok·ing** To unyoke.

di·ta (dē′tə) *n.* A Philippine forest tree (*Alstonia scholaris*) of the dogbane family. The wood is used in making furniture, and a substitute for quinine is obtained from the bark. Also **di′taa.** [< native name]

di·tat De·us (dī′tat dē′əs) *Latin* God enriches: motto of Arizona.

ditch (dich) *n.* A narrow trench in the ground, as for drainage; an irrigation trench. —*v.t.* 1 To dig or lay a ditch or ditches in. 2 To run or throw into a ditch; derail. 3 *U.S. Slang* To abandon; get rid of. —*v.i.* 4 To make a ditch or ditches. [OE *dīc.* Related to DIKE.]

ditch·er (dich′ər) *n.* 1 One who digs ditches. 2 A machine for digging ditches.

di·the·ism (dī′thē·iz′əm) *n. Theol.* The doctrine that maintains the existence of two coequal gods or powers of good and evil; Manicheism. [<DI-[2] + Gk. *theos* god] —**di′·the·ist** *n.* —**di′the·is′tic** *adj.*

dith·er (dith′ər) *v.i.* To tremble; shake; vibrate. —*n.* 1 A trembling; vibration; state of nervousness or anxiety. 2 *pl. Colloq.* An attack of nerves. [Var. of earlier *didder* tremble, shake; origin uncertain] —**dith′er·y** *adj.*

di·thi·on·ic (dī′thī·on′ik, dith′ē-) *adj. Chem.* Hyposulfuric. [<DI-[2] + Gk. *theion* sulfur]

dith·y·ramb (dith′ə·ram, -ramb) *n.* 1 In ancient Greece, a wild, passionate choric hymn sung in honor of Dionysus. 2 A metrical composition resembling this. 3 A wild or vehement speech or writing. Also **dith′y·ram′·bus.** [<L *dithyrambus* <Gk. *dithyrambos*] —**dith′y·ram′bic** (-ram′bik) *adj.*

Dit·mars (dit′märz), **Raymond Lee,** 1876–1942, U.S. herpetologist.

dit·ta·ny (dit′ə·nē) *n. pl.* **·nies** 1 A perennial American herb of the mint family (*Cunila origanoides*), with small, purplish or lilac blossoms; the stonemint. 2 Any of various plants of the mint family, as the **Cretan dittany** (*Origanum dictamnus*). 3 Fraxinella. [<OF *ditan, dictamne* <L *dictamnus* <Gk. *diktamon,* ? from *Diktē,* a mountain in Crete where it grew]

dit·to (dit′ō) *n. pl.* **·tos** The same thing repeated; the aforesaid: often written *do.,* or expressed by two inverted commas, called **ditto marks,** beneath the word intended to be duplicated. —*adv.* As before; likewise. —*v.t.* **·toed, ·to·ing** To copy; duplicate. [<Ital. *detto, ditto* aforesaid <L *dictum.* See DICTUM.]

dit·to·gram (dit′ō·gram) *n.* One letter or more unconsciously repeated in the copying of a manuscript. Also **dit′to·graph** (-graf, -gräf). [<Gk. *dittos* double + -GRAM]

dit·tog·ra·phy (di·tog′rə·fē) *n.* 1 The absent-minded repetition of letters or words by a copyist. 2 A passage or reading resulting from such repetition. [<Gk. *dittos* double + -GRAPHY] —**dit′to·graph′ic** *adj.*

dit·ty (dit′ē) *n. pl.* **·ties** 1 A short, simple song; lay. 2 *Obs.* A refrain. [<OF *dittié, ditié* <L *dictatum* a thing said <*dictare.* See DICTATE.]

dit·ty–bag (dit′ē·bag′) *n.* A sailor's bag for needles, thread, personal belongings, etc. [Origin uncertain]

dit·ty–box (dit′ē·boks′) *n.* 1 A small box used in place of a ditty-bag. 2 A motion-picture cameraman's repair kit.

Di·u (dē′ōō) A district of Portuguese India, comprising the island of Diu off the coast of NW. India, with the continental dependencies of Gogola and Simbor; total, 14 square miles. See PORTUGUESE INDIA.

di·u·re·sis (dī′yōō·rē′sis) *n. Pathol.* Excessive excretion of urine. [<NL <Gk. *dia-* thoroughly + *ourēsis* urination]

di·u·ret·ic (dī′yōō·ret′ik) *adj.* Stimulating the secretion and flow of urine: also **di′u·ret′i·cal.** —*n.* A diuretic medicine.

di·ur·nal (dī·ûr′nəl) *adj.* 1 Happening every day; daily; also, performed in a day: a planet's *diurnal* revolution. 2 Done in or pertaining to the daytime: opposed to *nocturnal.* 3 *Med.* Increasing in violence by day, as the symptoms of a disease. 4 *Bot.* Expanding by day and closing at night, as certain flowers. 5 Lasting only one day; ephemeral. See synonyms under DAILY. —*n.* 1 *Eccl.* A service book containing the offices for prime, tierce, sext, nones, vespers, and compline. 2 A diurnal bird or insect. 3 *Obs.* A journal; diary. 4 *Obs.* A daily newspaper. [<L *diurnalis* <*diurnus* daily <*dies* day. Doublet of JOURNAL.] —**di·ur′nal·ly** *adv.*

div (div) *v. Scot.* A corruption of the auxiliary verb *do.*

di·va (dē′və) *n. pl.* **·vas** or **·ve** (-vā) A celebrated female operatic singer; a prima donna. [<Ital., fem. of *divo* divine <L *divus*]

di·va·gate (dī′və·gāt) *v.i.* **·gat·ed, ·gat·ing** 1 To wander or stray aimlessly. 2 To digress. [<L *divagatus,* pp. of *divagari* <*dis-* away + *vagari* wander] —**di′va·ga′tion** *n.*

di·va·lent (dī·vā′lənt, div′ə-) See BIVALENT.

di·van (di·van′, dī′van) *n.* 1 A cushioned or pillowed place for reclining; a couch. 2 A café; smoking-room. 3 An Oriental governmental council; a council chamber. 4 A collection of poems usually written by one man: also spelled *diwan.* [<Turkish *dīvān* <Persian *dēvān,* orig. a collection of poems, a register; later, a council, a chamber, a bench]

di·var·i·cate (di·var′ə·kāt, dī-) *v.t.* & *v.i.* **·cat·ed, ·cat·ing** To branch off or cause to branch off; diverge. —*adj.* (di·var′ə·kit, -kāt, dī-) Branching off; widely diverging. [<L *divaricatus,* pp. of *divaricare* <*dis-* apart + *varicare* straddle <*varicus* straddling] —**di·var′i·cate·ly** *adv.* —**di·var′i·ca′tor** *n.*

di·var·i·ca·tion (di·var′ə·kā′shən, dī-) *n.* 1 The act of branching off or diverging; a forking. 2 *Biol.* A crossing or intersection of fibers at different angles. 3 *Obs.* A divergence of opinion.

dive (dīv) *v.* **dived** (*U.S. Colloq.* **dove**), **dived, div·ing** *v.i.* 1 To plunge, usually headfirst, into water, etc. 2 To submerge, as a submarine. 3 To plunge the body, hand, or an object into something, usually so as to obtain a part: He *dived* into the candy. 4 To enter suddenly or abruptly: He *dived* into the forest. 5 To descend at a steep angle and at high speed: The hawk *dived* toward the earth. 6 To work under water as a diver. 7 To become engrossed or deeply involved: to *dive* into politics. —*v.t.* 8 To thrust or plunge (the body, hand, or an object) into something. 9 To cause (an airplane) to descend at a steep angle. —*n.* 1 A plunge headforemost into or as into water. 2 A steep downward plunge of an airplane. 3 *Colloq.* A disreputable resort; den. [Blend of OE *dūfan* dive and *dȳfan* immerse]

dive bomber See BOMBER.

div·er (dī′vər) *n.* 1 One who dives. 2 One whose work is to explore, or gather objects under water. 3 A bird that dives, especially any of several species of loon. 4 In the West Indies, a grebe.

di·verge (di·vûrj′, dī-) *v.* **·verged, ·verg·ing** *v.i.* 1 To extend or lie in different directions from the same point: opposed to *converge.* 2 To vary from a typical form; differ. 3 *Math.* To fail to converge toward a limit: said of an infinite series, the sum of whose terms has no limit. —*v.t.* 4. To make divergent, cause to fork. See synonyms under BEND, WANDER. [<NL *divergere* <*dis-* apart + *vergere* incline]

di·ver·gence (di·vûr′jəns, dī-) *n.* 1 The act of diverging. 2 *Meteorol.* An atmospheric condition in which there is a net outflow of air from a given region. —**di·ver′gen·cy** *n.*

di·ver·gent (di·vûr′jənt, dī-) *adj.* 1 Ever going farther apart. 2 Varying. 3 Differing; conflicting; deviating. 4 Producing divergence. Also **di·verg′ing.** [<NL *divergens, -entis* ppr. of *divergere* DIVERGE] —**di·ver′gent·ly** *adv.*

di·vers (dī′vərz) *adj.* 1 More than one, but not a great number; several; sundry. 2 *Archaic* Of different kinds; various. See synonyms under MANY. [<OF <L *diversus* different; orig. pp. of *divertere.* See DIVERT.]

◆ *Divers* implies severalty; *diverse,* difference. Hence we say: "The Evangelists narrate events in *divers* manners" but "The views of the two parties were quite *diverse.*"

di·verse (di·vûrs′, dī-, dī′vûrs) *adj.* 1 Differing essentially; distinct. 2 *Obs.* Capable of various forms; multiform. [<L *diversus.* See DIVERS.] —**di·verse′ly** *adv.*

di·ver·si·fi·ca·tion (di·vûr′sə·fə·kā′shən, dī-) *n.* 1 Variation; variety. 2 The act of branching out into diverse lines of activity: product *diversification.*

di·ver·si·form (di·vûr′sə·fôrm, dī-) *adj.* Of different forms.

di·ver·si·fy (di·vûr′sə·fī, dī-) *v.t.* **·fied, ·fy·ing** To make diverse; impart variety to.

di·ver·sion (di·vûr′zhən, -shən, dī-) *n.* 1 The act of diverting. 2 *Mil.* An attack or feint intended to divert enemy troops from the point where a full-scale attack is to be made. 3 That which diverts; amusement; recreation. See synonyms under ENTERTAINMENT, SPORT.

di·ver·si·ty (di·vûr′sə·tē, dī-) *n. pl.* **·ties** 1 The state of being diverse; dissimilitude. 2 Variety: a *diversity* of interests. See synonyms under CHANGE, DIFFERENCE.

diver's palsy See CAISSON DISEASE.

di·vert (di·vûrt′, dī-) *v.t.* 1 To turn aside; deflect, as in direction, course, interest, or purpose. 2 To draw off the attention of. 3 To amuse; entertain. See synonyms under ENTERTAIN, RELAX. [<L *divertere* <*dis-* apart + *vertere* turn] —**di·vert′er** *n.* —**di·vert′ing** *adj.* —**di·vert′ing·ly** *adv.*

di·ver·tic·u·lum (dī′vər·tik′yə·ləm) *n. pl.* **·la** (-lə) *Anat.* A blind pouch or structure which has arisen or developed from another larger one, as the cecum, the air bladder of a fish, or the lungs of a vertebrate, all of which arise from the intestinal canal. [<L *diverticulum, deverticulum* a by-path <*divertere.* See DIVERT.] —**di′ver·tic′u·lar** *adj.*

di·ver·ti·men·to (di·ver′ti·men′tō) *n. pl.* **·ti** (-tē) *Music* 1 A light and graceful instrumental composition in several movements. 2 A potpourri. [<Ital., diversion]

di·ver·tisse·ment (dē·ver·tēs·mäṅ′) *n.* 1 A brief performance, often a ballet, between the acts of a play. 2 *Music* A divertimento. 3 A diversion; amusement. [<F, diversion]

Di·ves (dī′vēz) 1 A rich man in a parable. *Luke* xvi 19–31; hence, in general, a rich, worldly man. 2 Crassus. [<L, rich]

di·vest (di·vest′, dī-) *v.t.* 1 To strip, as of clothes, ornaments, or equipment. 2 To dispossess; deprive, as of office, rights, or honors. [<Med. L *divestire, disvestire* <OF *desvestir.* See DEVEST.]

di·vest·i·ture (di·ves′tə·chər, dī-) *n.* 1 The act of divesting, or the state of being divested. Also **di·vest′ment.** 2 *Law* The act of taking from one the possession of his property. Also **di·ves′ture** (-ves′chər).

di·vide (di·vīd′) *v.* **·vid·ed, ·vid·ing** *v.t.* 1 To cut or separate into parts. 2 To distribute in shares; portion out. 3 To separate into classes; categorize. 4 To separate; keep apart. 5 To form the partition or boundary between. 6 To graduate with lines; calibrate. 7 *Math.* **a** To subject to division. **b** To be an exact divisor of. 8 To cause to disagree; cause discord among. —*v.i.* 9 To be or come apart; separate. 10 To differ in opinion; disagree. 11 *Brit. Govt.* To vote in two groups, one for and one against a measure. 12 To share. See synonyms under ALLOT, APPORTION. —*n.* 1 *Geol.* A mountain range or area of high land separating one drainage system from another; a watershed. 2 The boundary line between life and death. 3 *Colloq.* The division of profits, booty or spoils. [<L *dividere* separate] —**di·vid′a·ble** *adj.*

di·vid·ed (di·vī′did) *adj.* 1 Parted; disunited. 2 *Bot.* Having incisions or indentations extending to the base or the midrib, as in certain leaves.

di·vi·de et im·pe·ra (div′ə·dē et im′pər·ə) *Latin* Divide and rule.

div·i·dend (div′ə·dend) *n.* 1 A quantity divided, or to be divided, into equal parts. 2 A sum of money to be distributed according to some fixed scheme, as profit on shares, share of surplus or assets, etc. [<L *dividendum*

thing to be divided < *dividere* separate, divide]

di·vid·er (di·vī′dər) *n.* **1** One who or that which divides, separates, or apportions. **2** *pl.* Compasses for measuring or setting off distances.

div·i·div·i (div′ē·div′ē) *n.* **1** A small tropical American tree *(Caesalpinia coriaria)*. **2** Its astringent, reddish-brown, curved pods, used for dyeing and tanning. **3** A prickly shrub or small tree of tropical America *(Caesalpinia spinosa)* whose pods are similarly used. [<Sp. <Tupian]

di·vid·u·al (di·vij′o͞o·əl) *adj. Obs.* **1** Shared with others; divided. **2** Separate; fragmentary. [<L *dividuus* divisible < *dividere* divide] — **di·vid′u·al·ism** *n.* — **di·vid′u·al·ly** *adv.*

div·i·na·tion (div′ə·nā′shən) *n.* **1** The act or art of trying to foretell the future or the unknown. **2** A forecast; augury. **3** A successful or clever guess.

di·vin·a·to·ry (di·vin′ə·tôr′ē, -tō′rē) *adj.* Of or pertaining to divination; conjectural.

di·vine (di·vīn′) *adj.* **1** Pertaining to, proceeding from, or of the nature of God or of a god; sacred. **2** Addressed or offered up to God in service or adoration; religious; holy. **3** Altogether excellent or admirable; godlike. **4** Pertaining to a deity or to divinity or theology. — *n.* One versed in divinity; a theologian; clergyman. — *v.* **·vined, ·vin·ing** *v.t.* **1** To foretell or prophesy, supposedly with supernatural aid. **2** To surmise or conjecture intuitively; guess. **3** *Obs.* To portend; presage. — *v.i.* **4** To practice divination. See synonyms under AUGUR, GUESS, PROPHESY. [<OF *devin, divin* <L *divinus* < *divus* < *deus* a god] — **di·vine′ly** *adv.* — **di·vine′ness** *n.* — **di·vin′er** *n.*

Divine Comedy A narrative poem in 100 cantos, written (1307–1321) in Italian by Dante Alighieri and dealing with the poet's imaginary journey through HELL, PURGATORY, and PARADISE. *Italian* **Di·vi·na Com·me·dia** (dē·vē′nä kōm·mā′dyä).

divine right of kings Royal authority considered as God-given.

diving beetle Any aquatic, predacious beetle of the family *Dytiscidae*: the larva is called *water tiger*.

diving bell A hollow, watertight vessel, open below and supplied with air under pressure, in which divers may be lowered into and work under water.

diving board A springboard.

diving rudder See ELEVATOR (def. 5).

diving suit A waterproof garment with detachable helmet worn by divers doing underwater work, supplied with air from the surface or from portable tanks.

divining rod A forked twig, usually of witch hazel, held by the tips and believed to bend downward when carried over unrevealed sources of water, mineral deposits, etc.: so called for its assumed supernatural power. See RHABDOMANCY.

di·vin·i·ty (di·vin′ə·tē) *n. pl.* **·ties** **1** The quality or character of being divine. **2** A lesser deity. **3** Theology. **4** An attribute, virtue, or quality assumed to be divine. **5** A being who partakes of the divine nature or qualities. — **the Divinity** The Deity; God. [<OF *devinité* theology <L *divinitas, -tatis* godhead, deity < *divinus* DIVINE]

divinity school A college or school of theology.

div·i·nize (div′ə·nīz) *v.t.* **·nized, ·niz·ing** To make or treat as divine. — **div′i·ni·za′tion** *n.*

di·vis·i·ble (di·viz′ə·bəl) *adj.* **1** Capable of being divided. **2** *Math.* Admitting of division without a remainder. — **di·vis′i·bil′i·ty, di·vis′i·ble·ness** *n.* — **di·vis′i·bly** *adv.*

di·vi·sion (di·vizh′ən) *n.* **1** The act of dividing. **2** A part; section. **3** Separation; disagreement; discord. **4** That which separates, divides, or makes different. **5** *Math.* The operation of finding how often one quantity is contained in another, or the ratio of one to another: opposed to *multiplication*. **6** *Mil.* A large tactical and administrative unit. In the U.S. Army it is larger than a brigade and smaller than a corps and is under the command of a major general. **7** In the U.S. Navy, a group of three battleships, four cruisers, or two aircraft-carriers, under the command of a rear admiral; or four destroyers, commanded by a captain; also, a portion of a ship's company. **8** A voting of a legislative body, specifically by going into affirmative and negative lobbies, as in the British Parliament. **9** *Music* A series of notes sung to one syllable as a showy or brilliant passage. **10** *Zool.* A category of animals having common characters but of no established rank in taxonomy. **11** *Bot.* A category of plants analogous to a phylum in zoology. See synonyms under PART. [<OF <L *divisio, -onis* < *dividere* divide]

di·vi·sion·al (di·vizh′ən·əl) *adj.* Pertaining to dividing or to a division. Also **di·vi′sion·ar′y.**

di·vi·sive (di·vī′siv) *adj.* **1** Causing or expressing division. **2** Causing discord.

di·vi·sor (di·vī′zər) *n. Math.* That by which a number or quantity is divided. — **common divisor** A number or quantity that is contained in another number or quantity without leaving a remainder.

di·vorce (di·vôrs′, -vōrs′) *n.* **1** Legal dissolution of a marriage relation. **2** Hence, severance; separation. **3** A decree dissolving a marriage. — *v.* **·vorced, ·vorc·ing** *v.t.* **1** To free by legal process from the relationship of husband and wife. **2** To sunder; sever; separate. **3** To obtain a legal divorce from. — *v.i.* **4** To get a divorce. [<F <L *divortium* < *divertere* divert] — **di·vorce′ment** *n.* — **di·vorc′er** *n.*

di·vor·cé (di·vôr′sā′, -vōr′-, di·vôr′sā, -vōr′-) *n.* A divorced man. — **di·vor·cée′** *n. fem.* [<F, pp. of *divorcer* divorce]

di·vor·cee (di·vôr′sē′, -vōr′-) *n.* A divorced person.

div·ot (div′ət) *n.* **1** A piece of turf cut from the sod by the stroke of a golf club. **2** *Scot.* An oblong piece of turf or sod used for thatching, etc.

di·vul·gate (di·vul′gāt) *v.t.* **·gat·ed, ·gat·ing** To make known; publish. [<L *divulgatus*, pp. of *divulgare*. See DIVULGE.] — **di·vul′gat·er** *n.* — **di·vul·ga·tion** (div′əl·gā′shən) *n.*

di·vulge (di·vulj′) *v.t.* **·vulged, ·vulg·ing** **1** To tell, as a secret; disclose; reveal. **2** *Obs.* To proclaim publicly. See synonyms under INFORM[1], PUBLISH, SPREAD. [<L *divulgare* < *dis-* away + *vulgare* make public] — **di·vulge′ment** *n.* — **di·vulg′er** *n.*

di·vul·gence (di·vul′jəns) *n.* A revelation; disclosure.

di·vul·sion (di·vul′shən) *n.* **1** The act of plucking or pulling apart. **2** A rupturing or dilating. [<L *divulsio, -onis* < *dis-* apart + *vellere* pull] — **di·vul′sive** *adj.*

div·vy (div′ē) *Slang n. pl.* **·vies** A share; dividend. — *v.t.* **·vied, ·vy·ing** To divide. Also **divvy up.** [Short for DIVIDE]

di·wan[1] (di·wän′, -wôn′) See DEWAN.

di·wan[2] (di·wän′, -wôn′) *n.* Divan (def. 4).

Dix (diks), **John Adams,** 1798–1879, U.S. general and statesman. — **Dorothy** Pseudonym of *Elizabeth Meriwether Gilmer,* 1870–1951, U.S. journalist.

Dix·ie (dik′sē) **1** Traditionally, those States which comprised the southern Confederacy during the Civil War; hence, the southern United States: also **Dixie Land.** **2** A song composed by D. D. Emmett in 1859, adopted by the Confederate Army as a marching song.

Dix·ie·crat (dik′sē·krat) *n.* A member of the U.S. Democratic party who rejected the plank of civil liberties of the party platform and its candidate for the presidency, especially one from the southern States who voted for the States' Rights party candidates. [<DIXIE + (DEMO)CRAT; coined during the 1948 presidential campaign]

Dix·ie·land (dik′sē·land′) *n.* A style of jazz in two-beat or four-beat rhythm, originally played in New Orleans and other cities in the South.

dix·it (dik′sit) *n.* A statement or a declaration made upon personal authority. [<L, he has said]

Dix·on (dik′sən), **Thomas,** 1864–1946, U.S. novelist.

Di·yar·be·kir (dē·yär′be·kir′) A city on the Tigris in eastern Turkey: also *Diarbekr.*

diz·en (diz′ən, dī′zən) *v.t.* To deck out; bedizen. [<MDu. *disen* put flax on a distaff] — **diz′en·ment** *n.*

diz·zy (diz′ē) *adj.* **·zi·er, ·zi·est** **1** Having a feeling of whirling and confusion, with a tendency to fall; giddy. **2** Causing or caused by giddiness; having vertigo. **3** *Colloq.* Thoughtless; capricious; silly; stupid. — *v.t.* **·zied, ·zy·ing** To make giddy; confuse. [OE *dysig* foolish] — **diz′zi·ly** *adv.* — **diz′zi·ness** *n.*

Djai·lo·lo (jī·lō′lō) See HALMAHERA.

Dja·kar·ta (jä·kär′tä) See JAKARTA.

Dja·ko·vi·ca (dyä·kō′vit·sä) A town in SW Serbia, Yugoslavia: also *Dyakovitsa.* Formerly **Dja·ko·va** (dyä′kô·vä).

djeb·el (jeb′əl) See JEBEL.

Dji·bou·ti (ji·bo͞o′tē) A port on the Gulf of Aden, capital of French Somaliland: also *Jibuti.*

djin·ni (ji·nē′) See JINNI, etc.

Djok·ja·kar·ta (jōk′yə·kär′tə) See JOGJAKARTA.

D-lay·er (dē′lā′ər) *n.* A region of the atmosphere lying just below the Heaviside layer and capable of reflecting very long radio waves.

D-line (dē′līn′) *n. Physics* One of the two closely associated yellow lines in the emission spectrum of sodium.

Dmi·tri (dmē′trē) Russian form of DEMETRIUS.

Dne·pro·dzer·zhinsk (dnye′prə·dzer·zhinsk′) A city on the Dnieper in Ukrainian S.S.R. Formerly **Ka·men·sko·ye** (kä′myin·sko͝o′yə).

Dne·pro·ges (dnye·prô·ges′) A village in Ukrainian S.S.R. on the Dnieper, site of the largest dam (200 feet high, 1/2 mile long) and hydroelectric power station in Europe: formerly *Dneprostroi.*

Dne·pro·pe·trovsk (dnye′prə·pə·trôfsk′) A city in SW Ukrainian S.S.R., on the Dnieper: formerly *Ekaterinoslav.* Also **Dnie′pro·pe·trovsk′.**

Dne·pro·stroi (dnye′prə·stroi′) A former name for DNEPROGES.

Dnie·per (dnye′pər, nē′pər) A river in western U.S.S.R., flowing 1,420 miles SW to the Black Sea. Also **Dne′pr.**

Dnies·ter (dnyes′tər, nēs′tər) A river in western U.S.S.R., flowing 876 miles SE to the Black Sea: Rumanian *Nistru.* Also **Dnes′tr.**

do[1] (do͞o) *v.* Present: *sing.* **do, do** (*Archaic* **thou do·est** or **dost), does** (*Archaic* **do·eth** or **doth),** *pl.* **do;** past: **did** (*Archaic* **thou didst);** *pp.* **done;** *ppr.* **do·ing** *v.t.* **1** To perform, as an action; execute or fabricate, as a piece of work. **2** To finish; complete. **3** To deal with or take care of: to *do* chores. **4** To cause or produce; bring about: to *do* good or evil. **5** To exert; put forth: He *did* his best. **6** To work at as one's occupation. **7** To translate. **8** To present (a play, etc.): They are *doing* Hamlet tonight. **9** To play the part of: to *do* Ophelia. **10** To cover; travel: to *do* a mile in four minutes. **11** To visit; make a tour of: to *do* the Louvre. **12** To serve; be sufficient for: Five dollars will *do* me. **13** To extend; render: to *do* homage. **14** To solve; work out, as a problem. **15** To serve, as a term in prison. **16** *Colloq.* To cheat; swindle. — *v.i.* **17** To exert oneself; be active; strive: to *do* or die. **18** To conduct or behave oneself. **19** To fare; get along: I *did* badly in the race. **20** To suffice; serve the purpose. — **to do away with** **1** To throw away; discard. **2** To kill; destroy. — **to do by** To act toward. — **to do for** **1** To provide for; care for. **2** *Colloq.* To ruin; kill. — **to do in** *Slang* To kill. — **to do over** *Colloq.* To redecorate. — **to do to death** To execute; kill. — **to do up** **1** To wrap or tie up, as a parcel. **2** To roll up or arrange, as the hair. **3** To clean; repair. **4** To tire out. — **to make do** To get along with whatever is available. — *auxiliary* As an auxiliary, *do* is used: **1** Without specific meaning in negative, interrogative, and inverted constructions: I *do* not want it; *Do* you want to leave?; Little *did* he know. **2** To add force to imperatives: *Do* hurry. **3** To express emphasis: I *do* believe you. **4** As a substitute for another verb to avoid repetition: I will not affirm, as some *do*; Did he come? Yes, he *did.* — *n.* **1** *Colloq.* A trick; cheat: It is a regular *do.* **2** Deed; duty: chiefly in the phrase *to do one's do.* **3** *Colloq.* Festivity. **4** *Obs.* Bustle; stir. [OE *dōn*]

Synonyms (verb): accomplish, achieve, actualize, commit, complete, consummate, discharge, effect, execute, finish, fulfil, perform, perpetrate, realize, transact. *Do* is the one comprehensive word which includes this whole list. We may say of the least item of daily work, "It is *done,*" and of the grandest human achievement, "Well *done!*" To *discharge* is to *do* what is given in charge, expected, or required; we may say to *do* or to *discharge* one's duty, the duty or duties of one's office, station, position, etc., where *discharge* is the more formal and technical word, signifying to *perform* to the last and utmost all that is required. *Commit,* as applied to actions, is used only of those that are bad, whether grave or trivial; *perpetrate* is used chiefly of aggravated crimes, or, somewhat humorously, of blunders. A man may *commit* a sin, a trespass, or a murder; *perpetrate* an outrage or a felony. *Perform* is used generally in a good sense; as, to *perform* a task, a duty, a service, etc. Compare PERFORM, under ACCOMPLISH. We *finish* a garment or a letter, *complete* an edifice or a life work, *consummate* a bargain or a crime, *discharge* a duty, *effect* a purpose, *execute* a command, *fulfil* a promise, *perform* our daily tasks, *realize* an ideal, *accomplish* a design, *achieve* a victory. Compare ACCOMPLISH, MAKE, TRANSACTION. *Antonyms*: baffle, defeat, destroy, fail, frustrate, mar, miscarry, miss, neglect, ruin, spoil.

do[2] (dō) *n. Music* The first of the syllables commonly used in solmization; the keynote of any key. [< Ital.]

do·a·ble (do͞o′ə·bəl) *adj.* Capable of being done.

do-all (do͞o′ôl′) *n.* A general helper; factotum.

doat·y (dō′tē) *adj.* Stained by decay: *doaty* birch. Also spelled *doty.* [Var. of DOTY] **—doat′i·ness** *n.*

dob·ber[1] (dob′ər) *n.* A dabchick. [Origin uncertain]

dob·ber[2] (dob′ər) *n. U.S.Dial.* A float on a fishing line. [< Du., float, cork]

dob·bin (dob′in) *n.* A horse, especially a plodding or patient one; a workhorse. [from *Dobbin,* var. of *Robin* < Robert]

dob·by (dob′ē) *n. pl.* **·bies** A mechanical attachment on a loom for weaving small designs, known as **dobby weave.** [Dim. of *Dobbin.* See DOBBIN.]

Do·bell's solution (dō′belz) A solution of phenol, borax, sodium bicarbonate, and glycerin, used as a spray for throat and nasal infections. [after H. B. *Dobell,* 1828–1917, English physician]

Dö·be·rei·ner (dœ′bə·rī′nər), **Johann Wolfgang,** 1780–1849, German chemist.

Do·ber·man pin·scher (dō′bər·mən pin′shər) See PINSCHER.

do·bie (dō′bē) *n. pl.* **·bies** *SW U.S.* Adobe. Also **do′by.** [Aphetic var. of ADOBE]

Do·bie (dō′bē), **James Frank,** 1888–1964, U.S. writer and folklorist.

do·bla (dō′blä) *n.* An ancient Spanish gold coin. [< Sp. < *doble* double < L *duplus*]

do·blon (də·blōn′) *n. pl.* **·blo·nes** (-blō′nās) A former Spanish and Spanish-American gold coin. See also DOUBLOON. [< Sp. *doblón*]

do·bra (dō′brə) *n.* Any of several former Portuguese gold coins. [< Pg. < *dobre* double < L *duplus*]

Do·bru·ja (dô′bro͞o·jä) A region of SE Rumania and NE Bulgaria along the Black Sea; 9,000 square miles. Also **Do′bru·dja,** *Rumanian* **Do·bro·gea** (dô′brô·jä), *Bulgarian* **Do·bru·dzha** (dô′bro͞o·jä).

dob·son (dob′sən) *n.* The hellgrammite. [? from *Dobson,* a surname]

Dob·son (dob′sən), **(Henry) Austin,** 1840–1921, English poet.

dobson fly A large, North American, megalopterous insect *(Corydalis cornutus),* the adult of the hellgrammite or dobson.

Dob·zhan·sky (dôb·zhän′skē), **Theodosius,** 1900–1975, U.S. geneticist, born in Russia.

do·cent (dō′sənt) *n.* A person licensed to teach in a university, but without regular faculty rank; a tutor. [< G *(Privat)dozent* < L *docens, -entis,* ppr. of *docere* teach] **—do′cent·ship** *n.*

doch-an-dor·is (dôkh′ən·dor′is) *n. Scot.* A stirrup-cup. Also **doch′-an-dor′ach** (-əkh) or **-dor′·och.**

doch·ter (dôkh′tər) *n. Scot.* Daughter.

doc·ile (dos′əl, *Brit.* dō′sīl) *adj.* **1** Amenable to training; easy to manage; tractable. **2** Easily worked or handled. [< MF < L *docilis* able to be taught < *docere* teach] **—doc′ile·ly** *adv.* **—do·cil·i·ty** (dō·sil′ə·tē, do-) *n.*

Synonyms: amenable, compliant, gentle, manageable, obedient, pliable, pliant, submissive, tame, teachable, tractable, yielding. One who is *docile* is easily taught; one who is *tractable* is easily led; one who is *pliant* is easily bent in any direction; *compliant* represents one as inclined or persuaded to agreement with another's will. Compare DUTY. *Antonyms*: determined, dogged, firm, inflexible, intractable, obstinate, opinionated, resolute, self-willed, stubborn, unyielding, wilful.

dock[1] (dok) *n.* **1** An artificial basin for vessels. **2** The space between two adjoining piers or wharves; also, the piers themselves; hence, a wharf. **3** The front portion of a theater beneath the stage. *—v.t.* To bring (a vessel) into a dock. *—v.i.* To come into a dock. [< MDu. *docke*]

dock[2] (dok) *n.* **1** The stump of a tail. **2** A leather case to cover a horse's tail when doubled. *—v.t.* **1** To cut off the end of (a tail, etc.); clip. **2** To take a part from (wages, etc.). **3** To clip short the tail of. **4** To take a part from the wages of. [Cf. LG *dokke* bundle]

dock[3] (dok) *n.* An enclosed space for prisoners on trial in a criminal court. [< Flemish *dok* cage]

dock[4] (dok) *n.* **1** Any of various plants of the sorrel or buckwheat family (genus *Rumex*) or the **sour dock** *(R. acetosa),* a troublesome weed. **2** Any plant resembling these. [OE *docce*]

dock·age[1] (dok′ij) *n.* **1** A charge for docking. **2** Provision for docking a vessel. **3** The act of docking.

dock·age[2] (dok′ij) *n.* **1** Curtailment, as of wages; reduction. **2** Waste matter in grain, easily separated by cleaning.

dock·er (dok′ər) *n.* A dock laborer; a longshoreman.

dock·et (dok′it) *n.* **1** A condensed statement of a document, generally minuted upon the back of the same; summary; abstract. **2** *Law* An entry on the records of a court of the principal steps taken in a case; the registry of judgments of a court; also, the book in which such entries are made or such judgments registered. **3** A calendar of the cases to be called at any time of the court; a trial docket; hence, any calendar of business, as in an ecclesiastical assembly. **4** A tag or label attached to a parcel ready for delivery. *—v.t.* **1** To place, as a cause or announcement, on a calendar or program to determine order of precedence or a routine of procedure. **2** To make an abstract of (a case) and keep for record. **3** To make a minute on the back of; endorse. **4** To attach a docket, tag, or label to. [Origin uncertain]

dock·mack·ie (dok′mak·ē) *n.* A shrub *(Viburnum acerifolium)* of the United States and Canada, with slender cymes of white flowers and crimson fruit. [< N. Am. Ind.]

dock·wal·lop·er (dok′wol′əp·ər) *n. Slang* A worker on docks or wharves.

dock·yard (dok′yärd′) *n.* **1** A place for collecting and storing naval material, and for building or repairing ships. **2** *Brit.* A navy yard.

doc·tor (dok′tər) *n.* **1** A qualified practitioner of medicine or surgery in any of its branches. **2** A person who has received a diploma of the highest degree in a faculty, as of divinity, law, literature, etc. **3** *Mech.* A device in a machine, for doing some special work; specifically, an auxiliary or donkey engine. **4** A long knife for distributing and removing color on a printing roller. **5** A steel edge on a calender roll to scrape off dirt. **6** On sailing vessels, the steward or the cook. **7** *Colloq.* The cook in a logging camp or on shipboard. **8** Among primitive people, a medicine man, wizard, or conjurer. **9** Any of several varieties of brightly colored, artificial flies, used for fishing. **10** *Obs.* A person of great learning qualified to instruct. *—v.t. Colloq.* **1** To prescribe for or treat medicinally. **2** To repair. **3** To alter; falsify, as evidence. *—v.i. Colloq.* **4** To practice medicine. **5** To take medicine or undergo medicinal treatment. [< L, a teacher < *docere* teach] **—doc′tor·al** *adj.*

doc·tor·ate (dok′tər·it) *n.* The degree, status, or title of a doctor.

doc·tri·naire (dok′trə·nâr′) *adj.* Theoretical; visionary. *—n.* One whose views are derived from theories rather than from facts; a scholastic or impractical theorist. **—doc′tri·nair′ism** *n.*

doc·tri·nal (dok′trə·nəl, *also Brit.* dok·trī′nəl) *adj.* **1** Pertaining to or characterized by doctrine. **2** Having to do with teaching; instructive. See synonyms under DOGMATIC. **—doc′·tri·nal·ly** *adv.*

doc·tri·nar·i·an (dok′trə·nâr′ē·ən) *n.* A doctrinaire. **—doc′tri·nar′i·an·ism** *n.*

doc·trine (dok′trin) *n.* **1** That which is taught or set forth for acceptance or belief; that which is held to be true by any person, sect, or school; especially, in religion, a tenet, or body of tenets; belief; dogma. **2** *Obs.* Instruction; teaching. [< OF < L *doctrina* teaching < *docere* teach]

Synonyms: article, belief, dogma, precept, principle, teaching, tenet. *Doctrine* primarily signifies that which is taught; *principle,* the fundamental basis on which the *teaching* rests. A *doctrine* is reasoned out, and may be defended by reasoning; a *dogma* rests on authority, as of the decision of the church, etc. A *doctrine* or *dogma* is a statement of some one item of *belief*; a *creed* is a summary of *doctrines* or *dogmas. Dogma* has commonly the signification of a *belief* arrogantly asserted. *Tenet* is simply that which is held, and is applied to a single item of *belief.* Compare FAITH, LAW.

doc·u·dra·ma (dok′yə·drä′mə, -dra′-) *n.* A television drama or series based on fact but presented in the style of a documentary.

doc·u·ment (dok′yə·mənt) *n.* **1** An original piece of written or printed matter conveying authoritative information or evidence. **2** One of the several papers affixed to a documentary bill and testifying to or effecting the transfer of goods, as a bill of lading, certificate of insurance, etc. **3** A documentary. **4** *Obs.* A cautionary example. **5** *Obs.* Instruction. **6** *Obs.* Evidence. See synonyms under RECORD. *—v.t.* **1** To furnish with documents. **2** To prove by documentary evidence. **3** To supply with references and notes to authoritative material: to *document* a text. [< OF < L *documentum* a lesson < *docere* teach] **—doc′u·men′tal** *adj.*

doc·u·men·tal·ist (dok′yə·men′təl·ist) *n.* A specialist in the assembling, classifying, and organizing of documents; an archivist with special training in the field of documentation.

doc·u·men·tar·i·an (dok′yə·men·târ′ē·ən) *n.* **1** One who believes in the importance and value of documents. **2** An advocate of the documentary treatment of the subject of motion pictures, television, etc.

doc·u·men·ta·ry (dok′yə·men′tər·ē) *adj.* Of, pertaining to, supported by, or based upon documents: also **doc′u·men′tal.** *—n. pl.* **·ries** A motion-picture film that records or exhibits a phase of regional, social, or cultural life without fictionalization.

doc·u·men·ta·tion (dok′yə·men·tā′shən) *n.* **1** The preparation or supplying of documents, references, records, etc. **2** The documents thus furnished. **3** The act of citing sources in a literary work.

dod·der[1] (dod′ər) *v.i.* To tremble or totter, as from age. [Cf. ME *didder* tremble]

dod·der[2] (dod′ər) *n.* Any of several leafless, twining herbs of the genus *Cuscuta,* parasitic on various plants to which they adhere by suckers. [ME *doder*]

dod·dered (dod′ərd) *adj.* **1** Having lost the top or branches through age or decay: said of trees. **2** Shattered; infirm. [ME *dodden* clip]

dod·der·ing (dod′ər·ing) *adj.* Shaky; infirm; hence, senile.

dodeca- *combining form* Twelve; of or having twelve: *dodecagon.* Also, before vowels, **dodec-.** [< Gk. *dōdeka* twelve]

do·dec·a·gon (dō·dek′ə·gon) *n. Geom.* A figure, especially a plane figure, with twelve sides and twelve angles. [< Gk. *dōdekagōnon*] **—do·de·cag·o·nal** (dō′de·kag′ə·nəl) *adj.*

do·dec·a·he·dron (dō′dek·ə·hē′drən) *n. pl.* **·drons** or **·dra** (-drə) A solid bounded by twelve regular faces. [< Gk. *dōdekaedron,* neut. sing. of *dōdekadros* < *dōdeka* twelve + *hedra* seat] **—do′·dec·a·he′dral** *adj.*

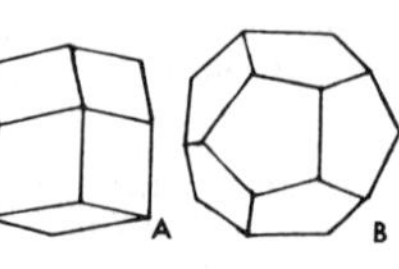

DODECAHEDRON
A. Simple. *B.* Pentagonal.

Do·dec·a·nese (dō·dek′ə·nēs′, -nēz′, dō′dek·ə-) A Greek island group in the SE Aegean; total, 1,044 square miles; capital, Rhodes. *Greek* **Do·de·ka·ne·sos** (thō′the·kä′nē·sôs).

do·dec·a·phon·ic (dō'dek·ə·fon'ik) *adj. Music* Twelve–tone.

dodge (doj) *v.* **dodged, dodg·ing** *v.t.* **1** To avoid, as a blow, by a sudden turn or twist. **2** To evade, as a duty or issue, by cunning or trickery. —*v.i.* **3** To move quickly to one side or change position suddenly, as to avoid a blow. **4** To practice trickery; be deceitful. —*n.* An act of dodging; evasion; hence, a trick to deceive or cheat; any trick. See synonyms under ARTIFICE. [Origin unknown]

Dodge (doj), **Mary Elizabeth,** 1838–1905, *née* Mapes, U.S. author and editor.

dodg·er (doj'ər) *n.* **1** One who dodges; a tricky fellow. **2** A small handbill. **3** A cooked cake of Indian meal; corn dodger.

Dodg·son (doj'sən), **Charles Lutwidge,** 1832–1898, English mathematician and author of *Alice in Wonderland*: pseudonym, *Lewis Carroll.*

do·do (dō'dō) *n. pl.* **·does** or **·dos** A large, extinct bird (genus *Rapheco*) of Mauritius and Réunion, about the size of a turkey, with rudimentary, functionless wings. [<Pg. *doudo* foolish]

Do·do·na (dō·dō'nə) An ancient town in Epirus, Greece; seat of a temple of Zeus and of the oldest of Greek oracles. —**Do·do·nae·an** or **Do·do·ne·an** (dō'də·nē'ən), **Do·do'ni·an** *adj.*

Dods·ley (dodz'lē), **Robert.** 1703–64, English author and bookseller.

doe (dō) *n.* The female of the deer, antelope, hare, rabbit, or kangaroo. ◆ Homophone: *dough.* [OE *dā*]

Doe·nitz (dœ'nits), **Karl,** born 1891, German admiral; successor to Hitler at the fall of the Third Reich in 1945.

do·er (dōō'ər) *n.* One who acts, does, or performs; an agent. See synonyms under AGENT.

does (duz) Present tense, third person singular, of DO.

doe·skin (dō'skin') *n.* **1** The skin of a doe, especially when dressed. **2** A heavy, twilled, cotton fabric napped on one side; also, a heavy, short–napped, woolen fabric resembling doeskin.

does·n't (duz'ənt) Does not: a contraction.

doff (dof, dôf) *v.t.* **1** To take off or remove, as clothing. **2** To take off (the hat) in salutation. **3** To throw away; discard. [Contraction of DO OFF] —**doff'er** *n.*

dog (dôg, dog) *n.* **1** A domesticated carnivorous mammal *(Canis familiaris),* of world–wide distribution and many varieties, noted for its adaptability and its devotion to man. ◆ Collateral adjective: *canine.* **2** One of various other species of the family *Canidae,* as the dingo, etc. **3** The male of the dog and various other animals of the *Canidae*: a *dog* fox. **4** In the western United States, a prairie dog. **5** *Mech.* Any small device that holds or grips; a catch, detent, or pawl. **6** The hammer of a firearm. **7** An andiron. **8** *Meteorol.* A sundog or fog dog. **9** A fellow; man–about–town: a gay *dog.* **10** A scoundrel; rascal. **11** *U.S. Slang* A hot dog. **12** *pl. Slang* Feet. —**dead dog** *Slang* A person or thing of no use or value. —**to put on the dog** *U.S. Slang* To make a pretentious display. —*adv.* Very; utterly: used in combination: *dog–tired.* —*v.t.* **dogged, dog·ging 1** To follow persistently; hound; hunt. **2** To fasten with or as with a dog or catch. [OE *dogga*]

DOG
Nomenclature for anatomical parts

Dog (dôg, dog) **1** Either of two southern constellations, called *Canis Major* and *Canis Minor.* See CONSTELLATION. **2** Sirius, the Dog Star.

dog–ape (dôg'āp', dog'-) *n.* A baboon or similar ape.

dog·bane (dôg'bān', dog'-) *n.* Any of a genus *(Apocynum,* family *Apocynaceae)* of smooth, reddish–stemmed herbs about 3 feet high, having an acrid, milky juice; especially, the **hemp dogbane** *(A. cannabinum),* used in medicine as a cardiac tonic, and the **spreading dogbane** *(A. androsaemifolium)* of North America.

dog·ber·ry (dôg'ber'ē, dog'-) *n. pl.* **·ries 1** The European dogwood *(Cornus sanguinea).* **2** Its fruit. **3** The chokeberry. **4** The bearberry (genus *Arctostaphylos).* **5** The English dog rose.

Dog·ber·ry (dôg'ber'ē, dog'-) In Shakespeare's *Much Ado About Nothing,* a smug, egotistical constable.

dog biscuit A hard biscuit made with meat scraps, ground bones, etc., for feeding dogs.

dog·bri·er (dôg'brī'ər, dog'-) *n.* The dog rose.

dog–cart (dôg'kärt', dog'-) *n.* **1** A one–horse vehicle, usually two–wheeled, with two seats set back to back and, originally, an enclosed space for dogs beneath the rear seat. **2** A cart hauled by one or more dogs.

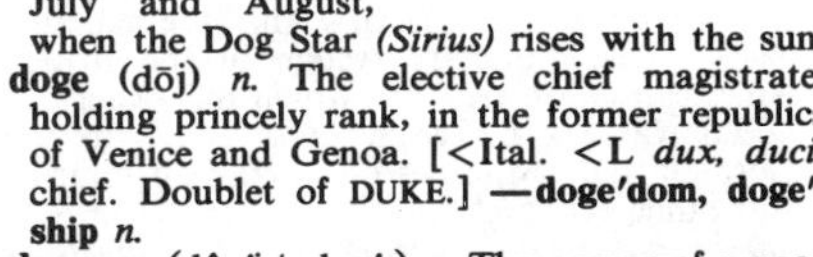
DOG–CART

dog–catch·er (dôg'·kach'ər, dog'-) *n.* A person licensed by a town or city to pick up and impound stray dogs.

dog–cheap (dôg'·chēp', dog'-) *adj.* Absurdly or exceedingly cheap.

dog days The hot, sultry season in July and August, when the Dog Star *(Sirius)* rises with the sun.

doge (dōj) *n.* The elective chief magistrate, holding princely rank, in the former republics of Venice and Genoa. [<Ital. <L *dux, ducis* chief. Doublet of DUKE.] —**doge'dom, doge'·ship** *n.*

dog–ear (dôg'ir', dog'-) *n.* The corner of a page of a book, turned down to mark a place or by careless use. —*v.t.* To turn or fold down the corner of (a page). Also *dog's–ear.* —**dog'–eared'** *adj.*

dog·face (dôg'fās', dog'-) *n. U.S. Slang* A soldier in the U.S. Army; especially, a private.

dog·fen·nel (dôg'fen'əl, dog'-) *n.* **1** Mayweed. **2** The heath aster.

dog·fight (dôg'fīt', dog'-) *n.* **1** A fight between or as between dogs. **2** *Mil.* Combat at close quarters between aircraft or tanks.

dog·fish (dôg'fish', dog'-) *n. pl.* **·fish** or **·fish·es** One of various small, littoral sharks, as the common spiny dogfish *(Squalus acanthias)* of North American waters, and the smooth dogfish (genus *Mustelus).*

dog fox 1 A male fox. **2** The corsac.

dog·ged (dôg'id, dog'-) *adj.* Silently or sullenly persistent; stubborn; obdurate. See synonyms under MOROSE, OBSTINATE. —**dog'ged·ly** *adv.* —**dog'ged·ness** *n.*

dog·ger (dôg'ər, dog'-) *n. Naut.* A two–masted fishing vessel, broad of beam and having a fish–well in the center, used in the North Sea. [ME *doggere*; origin uncertain]

Dogger Bank A submerged sand shoal in the North Sea between Denmark and England; scene of a German naval defeat of World War I (1915).

dog·ger·el (dôg'ər·əl, dog'-) *n.* Trivial, awkwardly written verse, usually comic or burlesque in effect. —*adj.* Of or composed of such verse. Also **dog'grel.** [ME; origin unknown] —**dog'ger·el·ist** *n.*

dog·ger·el·ize (dôg'ər·əl·īz, dog'-) *v.i.* **·ized, ·iz·ing** To write doggerel.

dog·ger·y (dôg'ər·ē, dog'-) *n. pl.* **·ger·ies 1** Dogs collectively. **2** Canaille; the mob; riff-raff. **3** Doglike conduct.

dog·gish (dôg'ish, dog'-) *adj.* **1** Like a dog; snappish. **2** *Colloq.* Showily fashionable; pretentious. —**dog'gish·ly** *adv.* —**dog'gish·ness** *n.*

dog·go (dôg'ō, dog'-) *adv. Slang* In a place of concealment; in hiding: to lie *doggo.*

dog–gone (dôg'gôn', dog'gon') *U.S. Colloq. v.t.* **–goned, –gon·ing** To damn: a euphemism. —*interj.* Damn!; darn!: a mild oath. [? Alter. of *God damn*]

dog·gy (dôg'ē, dog'-) *adj.* **·gi·er, ·gi·est 1** Of or pertaining to dogs; doglike: a *doggy* smell. **2** *Colloq.* Admirable; fashionable; attractive. —*n. pl.* **·gies** A dog, especially a little or pet dog. Also **dog'gie.**

doggy bag A bag containing leftover food which a restaurant customer may carry home for his dog.

dog house 1 A kennel. **2** The caboose on a freight train. —**in the dog house** *Slang* Out of favor.

do·gie (dō'gē) *n.* In the western United States, a stray or motherless calf: also spelled *dogy.* [Origin unknown]

dog in the manger One who will neither enjoy a thing himself nor permit others to.

dog Latin 1 Barbarous or incorrect Latin. **2** A schoolboy jargon imitating Latin.

dog–leg·ged (dôg'leg'id, -legd', dog'-) *adj.* Having a bend like a dog's hind leg: said of stairs, etc. Also **dog'–leg'.**

dog·ma (dôg'mə, dog'-) *n. pl.* **·mas** or **·ma·ta** (-mə·tə) **1** *Theol.* A doctrine or system of teachings of religious truth as maintained by the Christian church or any portion of it; hence, a statement of religious faith or duty formulated by a body possessing or claiming authority to decree or decide. **2** Doctrine asserted and adopted on authority, as distinguished from that which is the result of one's own reasoning or experience; a dictum. **3** Any settled opinion or conviction; an accepted principle, maxim, or tenet. See synonyms under DOCTRINE. [<L <Gk. *dogma, -atos* opinion, tenet<*dokeein* think]

dog·mat·ic (dôg·mat'ik, dog-) *adj.* **1** Marked by positive and authoritative assertion; stating opinions without evidence. **2** Hence, arrogant. **3** Like or pertaining to dogma. Also **dog·mat'i·cal.** —**dog·mat'i·cal·ly** *adv.* —**dog·mat'i·cal·ness** *n.*

Synonyms: arrogant, authoritative, dictatorial, doctrinal, domineering, imperious, magisterial, opinionated, overbearing, positive, self–opinionated, systematic. *Dogmatic* is technically applied to that which is formally enunciated by adequate authority; *doctrinal* to that which is stated in the form of doctrine to be taught or defended. Outside of theology, *dogmatic* has generally an offensive sense; a *dogmatic* statement is one for which the author does not trouble himself to give a reason, either because of the strength of his convictions, or because of his contempt for those whom he addresses; thus *dogmatic* is, in common use, allied with *arrogant* and kindred words. See IMPERIOUS.

dog·mat·ics (dôg·mat'iks, dog-) *n. pl. (construed as singular) Theol.* The systematic exposition of religious dogmas. Also **dogmatic theology.**

dog·ma·tism (dôg'mə·tiz'əm, dog'-) *n.* **1** Positive or arrogant assertion, as of belief, without proof. **2** *Philos.* An uncritical faith in the presumptions of reason or a priori principles: opposed to *scepticism.*

dog·ma·tize (dôg'mə·tīz, dog'-) *v.* **·tized, ·tiz·ing** *v.i.* To express oneself dogmatically. —*v.t.* To declare or assert as a dogma. —**dog'ma·tist** *n.* —**dog'ma·ti·za'tion** *n.* —**dog'ma·tiz'er** *n.*

do–good·er (dōō'good'ər) *n.* An idealistic philanthropist or reformer: a derisive term.

dog rose The wild brier *(Rosa canina)* of European hedges and thickets, bearing single pink flowers and fruits known as *hips.*

dog's–ear (dôgz'ir', dogz'-) See DOG–EAR.

dog sled A sled drawn by one or more dogs. Also **dog sledge.**

dog's–let·ter (dôgz'let'ər, dogz'-) *n.* A name for the letter *r,* especially when pronounced with a trill. [Trans. of L *litera canina,* so called because it resembles a dog's growl]

dog's life *Colloq.* A wretched existence.

dog's–tail (dôgz'tāl', dogz'-) *n.* An Old World perennial grass (genus *Cynosurus*) with flat leaves and spikelets in dense clusters, especially the **crested dog's–tail** (*C. cristatus*), naturalized in eastern North America: also *dogtail.*

Dog's Tail The constellation Ursa Minor.

Dog Star The star Sirius (Alpha of the constellation Canis Major).

dog's–tongue (dôgz′tung′, dogz′-) *n.* Hound's-tongue.

dog's–tooth violet (dôgz′tōōth′, dogz′-) *n.* **1** A spring–flowering European herb of the lily family (*Erythronium dens–canis*) bearing yellow, purple, or white flowers: also called *adder's–tongue.* **2** One of various American plants, as *Erythronium albidum,* bearing pinkish flowers, and the yellow–flowered *E. americanum.* Also **dogtooth violet.**

dog tag 1 A pendant or small metal plate for the collar of a dog, usually indicating ownership. **2** *Colloq.* A soldier's identification tag, worn around the neck.

dog·tail (dôg′tāl′, dog′-) See DOG'S-TAIL.

dog–tired (dôg′tīrd′, dog′-) *adj. Colloq.* Very tired.

dog·tooth (dôg′tōōth′, dog′-) *n.* **1** A human canine tooth or eyetooth. **2** An English architectural ornament, popular in the 13th century, generally composed of four radiating leaves, suggesting a dog's tooth. Also **dog tooth.**

dog–town (dôg′toun′, dog′-) *n.* In the western U.S., a colony of prairie dogs; also, land occupied by prairie dogs.

dog–trot (dôg′trot′, dog′-) *n.* A regular and easy trot.

dog–vane (dôg′vān′, dog′-) *n. Naut.* A small vane of bunting, cork, and feathers placed on the weather gunwale of a vessel to indicate direction of wind.

dog–watch (dôg′woch′, -wôch′, dog′-) *n. Naut.* One of two watches aboard ship, each of two hours, between 4 to 6 and 6 to 8 p.m.

dog·wood (dôg′wōōd′, dog′-) *n.* Any of certain trees or shrubs (family *Cornaceae*); specifically, the European **red dogwood** (*Cornus sanguinea*) and the **flowering** or **Virginia dogwood** (*C. florida*) of the United States, with large decorative pinkish–white flowers.

do·gy (dō′gē) See DOGIE.

Do·ha (dō′hə) Capital of Qatar sheikdom.

Doh·na·nyi (dō′nä·nyē), **Ernst von,** born 1877, Hungarian composer.

doiled (doild) *adj. Brit. Dial.* Stunned; dazed; confused. [Var. of ME *dold,* orig. pp. of *dollen* make dull]

doi·ly (doi′lē) *n. pl.* **·lies** A small, matlike, ornamental napkin, used under dishes, as a decoration, etc.: also spelled *doyley, doyly.* [after *Doily* or *Doyley,* 17th c. English draper]

do·ings (dōō′ingz) *n.pl.* Proceedings; acts; course of conduct. See synonyms under ACT, TRANSACTION, WORK.

Doi·sy (doi′zē), **Edward Adelbert,** born 1893, U.S. biochemist.

doit (doit) *n.* Formerly, a small copper coin of the Netherlands; a trifle. [<Du. *duit* coin]

doit·ed (doi′tid, -tit) *adj. Scot.* Foolish from or as from dotage; senile.

dokh·ma (dok′mə) *n.* See TOWER OF SILENCE.

dol (dol) *n.* A unit of pain intensity, corresponding to a barely perceptible sensation from the application of heat rays to the skin, with a maximum for any given subject of about 10 dols. [<L *dolor* pain]

do·lab·ri·form (dō·lab′rə·fôrm) *adj. Bot.* Ax- or hatchet–shaped, as leaves, etc. [<L *dolabra* ax + (I)FORM]

dol·ce (dōl′chā) *adj. Music* Smooth and sweet in performance. —*adv. Music* Sweetly; softly. —*n.* A soft–toned organ stop. [<Ital. <L *dulcis* sweet]

dol·ce far nien·te (dōl′chā fär nyen′te) *Italian* Pleasant idleness; literally, (it is) sweet to do nothing.

Dol·ci (dōl′chē), **Carlo,** 1616–86, Italian painter.

dol·drums (dol′drəmz) *n. pl.* **1** Those parts of the ocean near the equator where calms or baffling winds prevail. **2** A becalmed state. **3** A dull, depressed, or bored condition of mind; the dumps. [Cf. ME *dold,* pp. of *dollen* make dull]

dole[1] (dōl) *n.* **1** That which is doled out; a small portion; a gratuity. **2** Specifically, a sum of money officially paid to an unemployed person for sustenance; in Great Britain, government relief for the unemployed, instituted 1911, consisting of weekly payments from a special fund contributed by workers, employers, and government: so called since 1918. **3** *Obs.* Lot; portion. —*v.t.* **doled, dol·ing** To dispense in small quantities; distribute: usually with *out.* [OE *dāl.* Related to DEAL[2].]

dole[2] (dōl) *n. Obs.* Grief; mourning. [<OF *dol* <LL *dolium* grief < *dolere* feel pain]

Dole (dōl), **Sanford Ballard,** 1844–1926, U.S. jurist; president of the republic of Hawaii 1894–98; first governor of the Territory of Hawaii 1900–03.

dole·ful (dōl′fəl) *adj.* Melancholy; mournful. Also **dole′some.** [<DOLE[2]] —**dole′ful·ly** *adv.* —**dole′ful·ness** *n.*

dol·er·ite (dol′ə·rīt) *n.* **1** A coarse, crystalline basalt, containing labradorite and augite: sometimes used interchangeably with *diabase.* **2** *U.S.* Any dark, greenish igneous rock not readily identified by visual examination. [<Gk. *doleros* deceptive < *dolos* deceit + -ITE[1]; so called because not easily identified] —**dol′er·it′ic** (-rit′ik) *adj.*

Dol·gel·ly (dol·geth′lē, -gel′ē) The county town of Merioneth, Wales.

dol·i·cho·ce·phal·ic (dol′i·kō·sə·fal′ik) *adj.* Having a long skull, the breadth less than one third of the length, the cephalic index being 75.9 or less: distinguished from *brachycephalic.* Also **dol′i·cho·ceph′a·lous** (-sef′ə·ləs). [<Gk. *dolichos* long + *kephalē* head] —**dol′·i·cho·ceph′al** *adj. & n.* —**dol′i·cho·ceph′a·lism, dol′i·cho·ceph′a·ly** *n.*

dol·i·cho·mor·phic (dol′i·kō·môr′fik) *adj.* Longilineal.

doll (dol) *n.* **1** A child's toy representing a person; a puppet. **2** A pretty but superficial woman. **3** A pretty child. **4** *Slang* Any girl or woman. Also *dolly.* —*v.t. & v.i. Slang* To dress up; dress elaborately: with *up.* [from *Doll,* a nickname for Dorothy.] —**doll′ish** *adj.* —**doll′ish·ly** *adv.* —**doll′ish·ness** *n.*

dol·lar (dol′ər) *n.* **1** The standard monetary unit of the United States and of various other countries which use the $ sign for their coinage, as Canada and Argentina. Specifically, a U.S. silver coin, of the legal value of 100 cents, authorized in 1792 by Congress. **2** A U.S. gold piece, coined 1849–90. **3** A U.S. legal tender note, either a greenback or a silver certificate. **4** The Spanish milled dollar (first coined 1728) or piece–of–eight, the metallic basis of the monetary system in the British American colonies, from which the American dollar was taken. **5** A loose term for the German thaler, the peso, the Haitian gourde, and other coins. [< earlier *daler* <LG <G *taler, thaler,* contraction of *Joachimstaler* money of Joachimstal, Bohemian city where first coined]
—**Hong Kong dollar, British dollar, Straits Settlements dollar** Coins issued by the British for use in parts of the Commonwealth.
—**Levant dollar** or **Maria Theresa dollar** A silver coin issued for trade purposes by Austria since 1780.
—**trade dollar** A U.S. special silver dollar, heavier than normal and of special composition, used in Oriental trade, 1885–87.

dol·lar–a–year man (dol′ər·ə·yir′) One who serves as a government employee for the minimum legal salary.

dollar diplomacy 1 The policy of utilizing the financial interests or power of a country as a means of strengthening its foreign relations. **2** A policy of subordinating all other considerations to the foreign trade and financial interests of a country.

dol·lar·fish (dol′ər·fish′) *n. pl.* **·fish** or **·fish·es 1** A spiny–finned butterfish of oval, compressed form (genus *Poronatus*), common on the Atlantic coast of the United States. **2** The moonfish.

dollar mark or **sign** The sign ($) meaning dollar or dollars when placed before a number.

Doll·fuss (dôl′fōōs), **Engelbert,** 1892–1934, Austrian premier 1932–34; assassinated.

Döl·ling·er (dœl′ing·ər), **Johann Joseph Ignaz von,** 1799–1890, German Roman Catholic theologian; excommunicated for opposition to certain dogmatic teachings.

dol·ly (dol′ē) *n. pl.* **·lies 1** A doll: child's word. **2** *Mining* A contrivance for stirring ore while it is being washed. **3** *Austral.* A rude ore–crushing device. **4** *Mech.* A block or other extension placed on a pile to lengthen it while being driven. **5** A tool for holding one end of a rivet while a head is formed at the other. **6** A small narrow–gage locomotive for use in switching. **7** A light hand truck, with wheels or rollers, used for moving heavy loads, as books, boxes, lumber, etc. **8** *Brit. Dial.* A wooden instrument for beating or stirring clothes while washing. **9** A low, wheeled platform on which a motion–picture or television camera is set. —*v.t.* **·lied, ·ly·ing 1** To crush or concentrate (ore) with a dolly. **2** *Brit. Dial.* To stir or wash (clothes) with a dolly. —*v.i.* **3** To move a television or motion–picture camera toward a scene or subject: with *in.* [from *Dolly,* a nickname for Dorothy]

Dolly Var·den (vär′dən) **1** A dress with a printed or figured design, worn over a petticoat of a plain color. **2** A woman's large, flower–trimmed hat. **3** A salmonoid fish (*Salvelinus malma*) of the Rocky Mountain streams, having red spots on the back and sides and resembling the eastern brook trout: also **Dolly Varden trout.** [after *Dolly Varden,* a character in Dickens' *Barnaby Rudge*]

dol·man (dol′mən) *n. pl.* **dol·mans 1** A long Turkish outer garment. **2** A woman's coat with dolman sleeves or capelike arm pieces. **3** The capelike uniform jacket of a hussar. [<F *doliman* <Turkish *dōlāmān* long robe]

dolman sleeve A sleeve on a coat or dress, tapering from a wide opening at the armhole to a narrow one at the wrist.

dol·men (dol′men) *n.* A megalithic, sepulchral monument of large unhewn stones set on end and covered with a single huge stone or several stones, so as to form a small chamber and often covered with earth. Compare CROMLECH. [<F, prob. <Cornish *tolmen* hole of stone]

DOLMEN

dol·o·mite (dol′ə·mīt) *n.* A brittle calcium magnesium carbonate, occurring abundantly in white to pale–pink rhombohedral crystals. Many so–called marbles are dolomites. [after D. de *Dolomieu,* 1750–1801, French geologist] —**dol′o·mit′ic** (-mit′ik) *adj.*

Dol·o·mites (dol′ə·mīts) An eastern division of the Alps in northern Italy; highest peak, 10,964 feet. Also **Dolomite Alps.**

do·lor (dō′lər) *n. Poetic* Sorrow; anguish. Also *Brit.* **do′lour.** [<L, pain]

dol·or·im·e·try (dol′ə·rim′ə·trē) *n.* The measurement of the intensity of pain in terms of dols. [<L *dolor, -oris* pain + -METRY]

do·lo·ro·so (dō′lə·rō′sō) *adj. & adv. Music* With sorrow or a plaintive quality. [<Ital., sorrowful]

do·lor·ous (dō′lər·əs, dol′ər-) *adj.* Expressing or causing sorrow or pain; pathetic. —**do′lor·ous·ly** *adv.* —**do′lor·ous·ness** *n.*

do·lose (də·lōs′, dō′lōs) *adj. Law* Characterized by criminal intent, as speech or action. [<L *dolosus* < *dolus* fraud]

Dolph (dolf) Diminutive of ADOLPHUS. Also **Dol·phus** (dol′fəs).

dol·phin (dol′fin) *n.* **1** Any of various cetaceans (family *Delphinidae*), with beaklike snouts; specifically, the common dolphin (*Delphinus delphis*), about seven feet long, of the Mediterranean and temperate Atlantic; and the **bottle–nosed dolphin** (*Turiops truncatus*) of the American Atlantic coast: loosely called *porpoise.* **2** Either of two fish of the genus *Coryphaena* of southern waters; especially, the edible *C. hippurus*: also called *dorado.* **3** *Naut.* **a** A spar or block of wood attached to an anchor and used for small boats to ride by. **b** A mooring post or buffer, or a series of such posts contiguous to each other. **c** A group of protective rope fenders just beneath the gunwale of a boat. —*adj.* Of or pertaining to devices having a fancied resemblance to the dolphin. [<OF *daulphin* <L *delphinus* <Gk. *delphis, -inos*]

THE COMMON DOLPHIN

Dol·phin (dol′fin) The constellation Delphinus. See CONSTELLATION.

dol·phin–strik·er (dol′fin·strī′kər) *n. Naut.* **1** The spearlike point of the martingale boom. **2** The martingale boom.

dolt (dōlt) *n.* A stupid person; blockhead; dunce. [ME *dold* dulled, stupid] **—dolt′ish** *adj.* **—dolt′ish·ly** *adv.* **—dolt′ish·ness** *n.*

Dom (dom) *n.* **1** In Portugal and Brazil, a title of respect given to a gentleman: used with the given name. **2** A title given to certain Roman Catholic monks and other church dignitaries. [<Pg. <L *dominus* master]

-dom *suffix of nouns* **1** State or condition of being: *freedom.* **2** Rank of; domain of: *kingdom.* **3** The totality of those having a certain rank, state or condition: *Christendom.* [OE *-dōm* < *dōm* state]

Do·magk (dō′mäk), **Gerhard,** 1895–1964, German chemist.

do·main (dō·mān′) *n.* **1** A territory over which dominion is exercised; commonwealth; province. **2** A department, as of knowledge; range; scope. **3** A manor. **4** Absolute proprietorship in land. **5** Dominion; empire; rule. [<MF *domaine* <OF *demeine, demaine* <L *dominicum,* neut. sing. of *dominicus* of a lord < *dominus* lord. Doublet of DEMESNE.] **—do·ma·ni·al** (dō·mā′nē·əl) *adj.*

dome (dōm) *n.* **1** *Archit.* The vaulted roof of a rotunda; a cupola. **2** Any cuplike covering, vertical extension, or dome–shaped top. **3** A majestic building; specifically, following Italian and German usage, a cathedral. **4** In the orthorhombic, monoclinic, and triclinic crystal systems, a form whose faces intersect the vertical axis and one lateral axis. When the face is parallel to the shorter axis, it is called a *brachydome*; when parallel to the longer axis, a macrodome. **—*v.* domed, dom·ing** *v.t.* **1** To furnish or cover with a dome. **2** To shape like a dome. **—*v.i.*** **3** To rise or swell upward like a dome. [<F *dôme* <Ital. *duomo* cupola <L *domus* house]

Do·me·ni·chi·no (dō·mā′nē·kē′nō), 1581–1641, Italian painter: original name *Domenico Zampieri.*

domes·day (do͞omz′dā′) *n.* Doomsday.

Domesday Book A book containing the record of the statistical survey of England, made in 1085–86 by order of William the Conqueror: also spelled *Doomsday Book.*

do·mes·tic (də·mes′tik) *adj.* **1** Belonging to the house or household; concerning or relating to the home or family. **2** Given to the concerns of home; fond of or adapted to family life, duties, or employments; devoted to housekeeping. **3** Domesticated; tame. **4** Of or pertaining to one's own state or country; produced at home; not foreign; home–made. **—*n.*** **1** A family servant. **2** *pl.* Home–made fabrics or cloth: sometimes restricted to cotton goods. [<L *domesticus* < *domus* house] **—do·mes′ti·cal·ly** *adv.*

do·mes·ti·cate (də·mes′tə·kāt) *v.* **·cat·ed, ·cat·ing** *v.t.* **1** To train for domestic use; tame. **2** To civilize. **3** To cause to feel at ease or at home, make domestic. **—*v.i.*** **4** To become domestic. Also **do·mes′ti·cize.** [<Med. L *domesticatus,* pp. of *domesticare* live in a house <L *domus* house] **—do·mes′ti·ca′tion** *n.*

do·mes·tic·i·ty (dō′mes·tis′ə·tē) *n. pl.* **·ties** **1** The state of being domestic; fondness of home and family. **2** A household habit or affair.

domestic science Home economics.

do·mi·cal (dō′mi·kəl, dom′i-) *adj.* Of or like a dome, or characterized by a dome or domes. **—do′mi·cal·ly** *adv.*

dom·i·cile (dom′ə·səl, -sīl) *n.* **1** A settled place of abode; home, house, or dwelling. **2** The place where a person has his legal abode. See synonyms under HOME, HOUSE. **—*v.* ·ciled, ·cil·ing** *v.t.* To establish in a place of abode. **—*v.i.*** To have one's abode; dwell: also **dom′·i·cil′i·ate.** Also **dom′i·cil.** [<F <L *domicilium* < *domus* house]

dom·i·cil·i·ar·y (dom′ə·sil′ē·er′ē) *adj.* Pertaining to a fixed or a private residence.

dom·i·nance (dom′ə·nəns) *n.* **1** Control; ascendancy. **2** *Genetics* The condition of having or exhibiting only one of a pair of contrasting genetic characteristics. Also **dom′i·nan·cy.**

dom·i·nant (dom′ə·nənt) *adj.* **1** Ruling; governing; predominant. **2** *Genetics* Designating a character transmitted by one parent of a hybrid offspring, in which it appears to the masking of the contrasted character transmitted by the other parent: opposed to *recessive.* **—*n.*** *Music* The fifth tone of a diatonic scale. [<F <L *dominans, -antis,* ppr. of *dominare* DOMINATE]

dom·i·nate (dom′ə·nāt) *v.* **·nat·ed, ·nat·ing** *v.t.* **1** To exercise control over; govern. **2** To tower above; loom over: The city *dominates* the plain. **—*v.i.*** **3** To have control; hold sway. [<L *dominatus,* pp. of *dominare* rule, dominate < *dominus* lord] **—dom′i·na′tive** *adj.* **—dom′i·na′tor** *n.*

dom·i·na·tion (dom′ə·nā′shən) *n.* **1** Control; dominion. **2** *pl. Theol.* The fourth order in the hierarchy of heavenly beings: also called *dominions.*

dom·i·ne (dom′ə·nē, dō′mə-) *n. Obs.* A title of address meaning lord or master. [<L, vocative of *dominus* lord]

dom·i·neer (dom′ə·nir′) *v.t.* & *v.i.* **1** To rule arrogantly or insolently; tyrannize; bully. **2** To tower or loom (over or above). [<Du. *domineren* <F *dominer* <L *dominus* lord]

dom·i·neer·ing (dom′ə·nir′ing) *adj.* Overbearing. See synonyms under ARBITRARY, DOGMATIC, IMPERIOUS. **—dom′i·neer′ing·ly** *adv.*

Dom·i·nic (dom′ə·nik) A masculine personal name. Also **Dom′i·nick.** [<L, of the Lord]

Dom·i·nic (dom′ə·nik), **Saint,** 1170–1221, Spanish friar; founded the Dominican Order: original name *Domingo de Guzmán.*

Dom·i·ni·ca (dom′ə·nē′kə, də·min′i·kə) A British colony in the Windward Islands; 305 square miles; capital, Roseau.

do·min·i·cal (də·min′i·kəl) *adj.* **1** Relating to Christ as the Lord. **2** Relating to Sunday as the Lord's day. **—*n.*** **1** A church edifice. **2** A dominical letter. **3** One who celebrates the Christian Sunday: opposed to *Sabbatarian.* **4** *Obs.* The veil worn by women when attending divine service in the Roman Catholic Church; also, a Sunday dress. [<LL *dominicalis* of the Lord <L *dominicus* < *dominus* lord]

dominical letter One of the first seven letters of the alphabet, used in the ecclesiastical calendar to designate the Sundays in a given year, and to aid in determining the date of Easter.

Do·min·i·can (də·min′i·kən) *adj.* **1** Of or pertaining to St. Dominic. **2** Belonging to a monastic order or institution following the rule of St. Dominic. **3** Of the Dominican Republic. **—*n.*** **1** A member of a mendicant monastic order (*Black Friars*) founded in 1216 by St. Dominic: officially called *Fratres Praedicatores* or *Preaching Friars.* **2** A native of the Dominican Republic.

DOMINICAN FRIAR

Dominican Republic A republic occupying the eastern part of Hispaniola; 19,129 square miles; capital, Santo Domingo· formerly *Ciudad Trujillo. Spanish* **Re·pú·bli·ca Do·mi·ni·ca·na** (rā·po͞o′blē·kä dō·mē′nē·kä′nä).

dom·i·nie (dom′ə·nē) *n.* **1** *Scot.* A schoolmaster. **2** *U.S.* A minister of the Dutch Reformed Church. **3** *Colloq.* Any minister. [Var. of DOMINE]

do·min·ion (də·min′yən) *n.* **1** Sovereign authority; sway. **2** *Law* The right of absolute possession and use; ownership; dominium. **3** A country under a particular government. **4** Formerly, a self–governing member of the Commonwealth of Nations. **5** *pl.* Domination (def. 2). [<F <L *dominium* < *dominus* lord]

Dominion Day In Canada, the anniversary of the federation of Canada into a dominion (July 1, 1867): a legal holiday.

Dom·i·nique (dom′ə·nēk′) *n.* An American breed of domestic fowls, with gray–barred plumage, yellow legs, and rose comb. Also **Dom′i·nick.** [<F, Dominica]

do·min·i·um (də·min′ē·əm) *n. Law* The absolute right of ownership and control of property, especially of land: *dominium* in fee simple. [<L < *dominus* lord]

dom·i·no[1] (dom′ə·nō) *n. pl.* **·noes** or **·nos** **1** A small mask for the eyes. **2** A loose robe, hood and mask worn at masquerades. **3** A person wearing this. **4** A hooded garment forming an outer ecclesiastical vestment. [<MF, a clerical garment <L *dominus* lord]

dom·i·no[2] (dom′ə·nō) *n. pl.* **·noes** or **·nos** **1** A small, flat block, as of wood or plastic, divided on one side into halves, each left blank or marked with usually one to six dots. **2** *pl.* A game played with a set (usually 28) of such pieces, the object being to match the halves having the same number of dots: construed as singular. **—*adj.*** Describing the view or political theory that a series of events is unavoidably contingent on the occurrence of an initial event, as a row of dominoes collapses when the first is toppled: the *domino* theory of Communist aggrandizement.

dom·i·nus (dom′ə·nəs) *n. pl.* **·ni** (-nī) *Latin* Master; sir: a title formerly given to a clergyman, knight, or lord of a manor. Compare DOMINE.

Dom·i·nus (dom′ə·nəs) *n. Latin* The Lord.

Dom·i·nus vo·bis·cum (dom′ə·nəs vō·bis′kəm) *Latin* The Lord be with you.

Do·mi·tian (də·mish′ən), A.D. 51–96, Roman emperor 81–96: full name *Titus Flavius Domitianus Augustus.*

Dom·re·my (dôṅ·rə·mē′) A village in NE France; birthplace of Joan of Arc. Also **Dom·re·my′–la–Pu·celle′** (-la·pü·sel′).

don[1] (don) *n.* **1** A Spanish gentleman or nobleman. **2** An important personage. **3** *Colloq.* In English universities a head, residential fellow, or tutor of a college. [<Sp. <L *dominus* lord]

don[2] (don) *v.t.* **donned, don·ning** To put on, as a garment. [Contraction of *do on*]

Don (don) *n.* Seignior; sir: a title of respect or address, used with the given name in Spain and Spanish–speaking countries.

Don (don) Short for DONALD.

Don (don) **1** A river in south central Russian S.F.S.R., flowing 1,222 miles south to the Sea of Azov: ancient *Tanais.* **2** A river in Aberdeenshire, Scotland, flowing 82 miles east to the North Sea. **3** A river in southern Yorkshire, England, flowing 70 miles to the Ouse.

do·na (dō′nə) *n.* A Portuguese lady.

do·ña (dō′nyä) *n.* A Spanish lady.

Do·na (dô′nə) *n.* The Portuguese form of DOÑA.

Do·ña (dō′nyä) *n.* Lady; madam: the feminine title corresponding to *Don.* [<Sp. <L *domina* mistress]

Don·ald (don′əld) A masculine personal name. [<Celtic, proud chief]

Do·nar (dō′när) In Teutonic mythology, the god of thunder: identified with the Norse *Thor.*

do·nate (dō′nāt) *v.t.* **·nat·ed, ·nat·ing** To bestow as a gift, especially to a cause; present; contribute. [<L *donatus,* pp. of *donare* give < *donum* a gift] **—do′na·tor** *n.*

Do·na·tel·lo (dō′nä·tel′lō), 1386–1466, Italian sculptor: original name *Donato di Niccolò di Betto Bardi.*

do·na·tion (dō·nā′shən) *n.* **1** The act of donating. **2** That which is donated; a gift; grant; offering. See synonyms under GIFT.

Don·a·tism (don′ə·tiz′əm) *n.* The principles of the Donatists.

Don·a·tist (don′ə·tist) *n.* One of a fourth–century, schismatic sect of North Africa. [<Med. L *Donatista,* after *Donatus,* North African bishop and founder of the sect] **—Don′a·tis′tic** or **·ti·cal** *adj.*

don·a·tive (don′ə·tiv, dō′nə·tiv) *adj.* Belonging by deed of gift. **—*n.*** A donation; gift.

Do·nau (dō′nou) The German name for the DANUBE.

Don·cas·ter (dong′kas·tər, *Brit.* -kəs-) A county borough in south Yorkshire.

done (dun) Past participle of DO[1]. **—*adj.*** **1** Completed; finished; ended; agreed. **2** Cooked sufficiently.

do·nee (dō·nē′) *n.* One who receives a gift. [<DON(OR) + -EE]

done for **1** Tired; exhausted. **2** Finished; put out of the running; ruined. **3** Dead or about to die.

Don·e·gal (don′i·gôl, don′i·gôl′) A county in Ulster province, Ireland; 1,865 square miles; county seat, Lifford.

Do·nets (do·nets′, *Russian* dô·nyets′) A river in SW European U.S.S.R., flowing 631 miles SE to the Don.

Donets Basin A principal industrial region of the U.S.S.R., SW of the lower Donets; 10,000 square miles. Also **Don·bas** (don·bäs′), **Don·bass′.**

don·ga (dong′gə) *n. Afrikaans* The dry bed of a stream.

don·go·la (dong′gə·lə) *n.* Sheepskin, goatskin, or calfskin tanned by the use of mineral and vegetable substances (called the **dongola process**), producing a finish resembling kid. Also **Dongola kid, Dongola leather.** [from DONGOLA, where originally made]

Don·go·la (dong′gə·lə) A town on the Nile in Northern Province, Sudan; former capital of the **Christian Kingdom of Dongola** (6th to 14th centuries).

Do·ni·zet·ti (don′ə·zet′ē, *Ital.* dō′nē·dzet′tē), **Gaetano,** 1797–1848, Italian operatic composer.

don·jon (dun′jən, don′-) *n.* The principal tower or keep of a medieval castle. Also **don′jon-keep′.** [Archaic var. of DUNGEON]

DONJON
Chateau de Viviennes, France

Don Juan (don jōō′·ən, *Sp.* dôn hwän′) **1** A legendary Spanish nobleman and seducer of women, the hero of many poems, operas, plays, etc. **2** Any rake or seducer.

don·key (dong′kē, dung′-) *n.* **1** An ass. **2** A stupid or stubborn person. [? from DUNCAN]

donkey engine A small subsidiary engine for pumping, hoisting, etc.

don·na (don′ə, *Ital.* dôn′nä) *n.* An Italian lady. [<Ital. <L *domina* lady]

Don·na (don′ə, *Ital.* dôn′nä) *n.* Lady; madam: a title of respect or address, used with the given name in Italy and Italian-speaking countries.

Don·nan (don′ən), **Frederick George,** 1870–1956, English chemist.

Donne (dun), **John,** 1573?–1631, English poet and clergyman.

don·nerd (don′ərd) *adj. Scot.* **1** Stupid; dunderheaded. **2** Dazed; stunned. Also **don′·nered, don′nert** (-ərt).

don·nish (don′ish) *adj.* **1** Of, characteristic of, or pertaining to the dons of an English university. **2** Formal; distant; pedantic. — **don′·nish·ness** *n.*

Don·ny·brook Fair (don′ē·brŏŏk′) **1** An annual fair formerly held at Donnybrook, Ireland: abolished in 1855 because of its disorder. **2** Any disorderly gathering or free-for-all fight.

do·nor (dō′nər) *n.* **1** A giver; donator. **2** One who gives his blood for transfusion, or tissue, skin, etc., for surgical grafting, for another. [<AF *donour,* OF *doneur* <L *donator* <*donare* give]

do-noth·ing (dōō′nuth′ing) *n.* An idler; procrastinator. — *adj.* Idle; indolent, procrastinating.

Don·o·van (don′ə·vən), **William Joseph,** 1883–1959, U.S. lawyer and general: known as *Wild Bill Donovan.*

Don Quix·ote (don kwik′sət, ki·hō′tē; *Sp.* dôn kē·hō′tā) **1** The hero of Cervantes' romance of that name, a satire on chivalry, written in 1605 and followed by a continuation in 1615. **2** Anyone who naively undertakes to do extravagantly romantic things. Also **Don Qui·jo′te.** See QUIXOTIC.

don·sie (don′sē) *adj. Scot.* **1** Neat; trim: a *donsie* lass. **2** Sickly: feeble. **3** Unfortunate; unlucky. Also **don′cie.**

don't (dōnt) Do not: a contraction.

don·zel (don′zəl) *n. Obs.* A young attendant, page, or gallant. [<Ital. *donzello* <LL *domnicellus,* dim. of *dominus* lord]

doo·dad (dōō′dad) *n. Colloq.* **1** A doo-hickey. **2** A small ornament; bauble.

doo·dle^{1} (dōōd′l) *v.t.* **·dled, ·dling** To play (the bagpipe). [<G *dudeln*]

doo·dle^{2} (dōōd′l) *v.i. Colloq.* To draw pictures, symbols, etc., abstractedly, on whatever material comes to hand, while the mind is otherwise occupied. — *n.* The drawings or symbols so made. [Cf. dial. E *doodle* be idle, trifle]

doo·dle-bug (dōōd′l·bug′) *n.* **1** Any device supposed to be able to detect the location of minerals, water, etc. **2** *Entomol.* The larva of the ant-lion. For illustration see under INSECT (beneficial). **3** Loosely, any droning insect, as the tumblebug. **4** *Colloq.* A robot plane. See under BOMB. [? <dial. E *doodle* an idler, a fool + BUG]

doo·dle·sack (dōōd′l·sak′) *n.* A bagpipe. [<G *dudelsack*]

doo-hick·ey (dōō′hik′ē) *n. Colloq.* Any contrivance or device, the name of which is not known or immediately recalled; doodad. Also, **doo′-hick′us, doo′hink′ey.**

dook (dŏŏk) *v.t.* & *v.i. Scot.* To plunge; bathe; duck.

dool (dōōl) *n. Scot.* Dole; sorrow; grief.

doo·lee (dōō′lē) *n. Anglo-Indian* A light litter; a palanquin. Also **doo′lie, doo′ly.** [<Hind. *dōlī,* dim. of *dōlā* litter <Skt.]

Doo·lit·tle (dōō′lit′l), **Hilda,** 1886–1961, U.S. poet: pen name *H. D.* — **James Harold,** born 1896, U.S. general.

doom (dōōm) *v.t.* **1** To pronounce judgment or sentence upon; condemn. **2** To destine to a disastrous fate. **3** To decree as a penalty. See synonyms under CONDEMN. [<*n.*] — *n.* **1** The act of dooming, or the state of being doomed. **2** Death; ruin; sad or evil destiny. **3** Judicial decision; condemnation; sentence. **4** The Last Judgment. **5** *Obs.* An enactment; decree. — **crack of doom** The signal for the Last Judgment: also **day of doom** [OE *dōm*]

doom palm A palm of northern Africa *(Hyphaene thebaica),* the fruit of which has the flavor of gingerbread: also called *gingerbread tree*: also spelled *doum palm.* [<F *doum* <Arabic *dawm*]

dooms·day (dōōmz′dā′) *n.* The day of the Last Judgment, or of any final judgment: also spelled *domesday.* [OE *domesdæg* judgment day <*dōm* doom + *dæg* day]

Doomsday Book See DOMESDAY BOOK.

doom·ster (dōōm′stər) *n. Scot. Law* The court announcer, who announced the judgment, or doom, of the court.

doon (dōōn) *adv.* & *prep. Scot.* Down.

Doon (dōōn) A river in Ayreshire, Scotland, flowing 27 miles NW through **Loch Doon** to the Firth of Clyde.

door (dôr, dōr) *n.* **1** A hinged or sliding frame used for closing or opening an entrance or exit, as to a house. **2** Doorway. **3** Any means or avenue of exit or entrance; passageway; access. See synonyms under ENTRANCE. [Fusion of OE *duru* pair of doors and *dor* a gate]

door·bell (dôr′bel′, dōr′-) *n.* A device at the entrance to a building or apartment to sound a signal within.

door check A device, usually operated by compressed air, for closing a door automatically and for preventing it from being slammed.

door·jamb (dôr′jam′, dōr′-) *n.* The vertical piece at the side of a doorway supporting the lintel.

door·keep·er (dôr′kē′pər, dōr′-) *n.* A guardian or keeper of a door; a minor official of an organized meeting or assembly.

door·knob (dôr′nob′, dōr′-) *n.* The handle for turning the catch to open a door.

door·man (dôr′man′, -mən, dōr′-) *n. pl.* **·men** (-men′, -mən) An attendant at the door of a hotel, apartment house, etc., who assists persons entering and leaving the building.

door·mat (dôr′mat′, dōr′-) *n.* A mat placed at an entrance for wiping off mud and moisture from the shoes.

Doorn (dōrn) A village in central Netherlands; residence of William II of Germany, 1919–41.

door·nail (dôr′nāl′, dōr′-) *n.* A nail or stud against which a knocker is struck. — **dead as a doornail** Quite dead.

door·plate (dôr′plāt′, dōr′-) *n.* A metal plate on a door, with the occupant's name, address, etc. Also **door plate.**

door·post (dôr′pōst′, dōr′-) *n.* The post on either side of a doorway: also **door post.**

door·sill (dôr′sil′, dōr′-) *n.* The sill or threshold of a door: also **door sill.**

door·step (dôr′step′, dōr′-) *n.* A step or one of a series of steps leading to a door.

door·stop (dôr′stop′, dōr′-) *n.* A device to keep a door open or to prevent it from slamming.

door·way (dôr′wā′, dōr′-) *n.* The passage for entrance and exit into and out of a building, room, etc.

door·yard (dôr′yärd′, dōr′-) *n.* A yard around, or especially in front of, a house.

doot (dōōt) *v.* & *n. Scot.* Doubt.

dop (dop) *n.* A small metal cup on a long stem or holder in which a gemstone is held while being cut or polished. [<Du., lit., shell]

dope (dōp) *n.* **1** *Slang* Any potentially harmful narcotic used for inducing euphoria. **2** *Slang* A dope fiend. **3** A drug given to a race horse to influence its speed. **4** *Slang* Information as to the condition, past performance, etc., of a race horse. **5** *Slang* Any information; also, a calculation or forecast based on it; hence, confidential or inside information. **6** Any thick liquid or semifluid, as an article of food, a lubricant, etc.; specifically, axle grease. **7** An absorbent material for holding a thick liquid, as cotton waste, or a substance for holding nitroglycerin, as in dynamite. **8** *Aeron.* Any material used in treating the cloth surface of airplane members to increase strength or produce or maintain tautness. **9** *Slang* A stupid person. — *v.t.* **1** To give or administer dope to (a race horse). **2** *Slang* To stupefy or exhilarate as by a drug: often with *up.* — **to dope out** *U.S. Slang* **1** To plan, as a course of action. **2** To figure out; solve. [<Du. *doop* dipping sauce <*doopen* dip]

dope fiend *Slang* A habitual user of a narcotic drug.

dope ring A combination of persons trafficking illegally in narcotics.

dope sheet *Slang* An information sheet on horses in the day's races, giving their pedigree, past performance, etc.

do·pey (dō′pē) *adj.* **·pi·er, ·pi·est** *Slang* Stupid from or as if from narcotics; dull; heavy.

Dop·pel·gäng·er (dôp′əl·geng′ər) *n. German* **1** A person exactly like another; a double. **2** A wraith, especially of a person not yet dead. Also *doubleganger.*

Dop·pler (dôp′lər), **Christian Johann,** 1803–1853, Austrian physicist and mathematician.

Doppler effect *Physics* The change in the frequency of a sound, light, or radio wave due to the motion of the observer or of the source toward or away from one another. Also **Doppler shift.** [after C. J. *Doppler*]

dor^{1} (dôr) *n.* **1** A black European dung beetle (genus *Geotrupes*), known by its droning flight. **2** The June beetle. For illustration see under INSECT (injurious). Also **dor beetle, dor bug, dorr, dorr beetle.** [OE *dora* bumblebee]

dor^{2} (dôr) *n. Obs.* A trick; deception; humbug. [? <ON *dār* scoff]

Do·ra (dôr′ə, dō′rə) Short for DOROTHY, EUDORA, or THEODORA.

do·ra·do (də·rä′dō) *n.* A fish of the genus *Coryphaena.* See DOLPHIN. [<Sp., gilded <LL *deauratus,* pp. of *deaurare* <*de-* completely + *aurum* gold]

Do·ra·do (də·rä′dō) *n.* A southern constellation, the Swordfish. See CONSTELLATION.

Dor·cas society (dôr′kəs) A women's society, usually connected with a church, for supplying garments to the poor. [after *Dorcas,* a female disciple. See *Acts* ix 36.]

Dor·ches·ter (dôr′ches·tər, -chis-) A municipal borough, capital of Dorset, England.

Dor·dogne (dôr·dôn′y′) A river in central and SW France, flowing 305 miles SW to the Garonne.

Dor·drecht (dôr′drekht) A town in SW Netherlands: also *Dort.*

Dore (dôr), **Monts** (môn) The highest range of the Auvergne Mountains in central France. Also **Mas·sif du Mont-Dore** (mà·sēf′ dü môn dôr′).

Do·ré (dô·rā′), **(Paul) Gustave,** 1833–83, French painter, illustrator, and engraver.

do·ri·a (dôr′ē·ə, dō′rē·ə) *n.* An East Indian cotton fabric with stripes of varying widths. [<Hind. *doriyā* <*dor* thread, stripe]

Do·ri·an (dôr′ē·ən, dō′rē-) *n.* A member of one of the four major tribes of ancient Greece. The Dorians settled in the Peloponnesus about 1100 B.C. — *adj.* Doric.

Dor·ic (dôr′ik, dor′-) *adj.* **1** Relating to or characteristic of Doris or its inhabitants: also *Dorian.* **2** *Archit.* Constructed in accordance with the earliest and simplest of the three orders of Greek architecture: called the **Doric order.** For illustration see under ARCHITECTURE, CAPITAL. —*n.* **1** A dialect of ancient Greek, spoken by the Dorians in northern Greece, the Peloponnesus, Crete, Sicily, etc.: used by Pindar and many other lyric poets. **2** A rustic dialect of English.

Dor·i·cism (dôr′ə·siz′əm, dor′-) *n.* A Doric idiom or peculiarity of speech. Also **Do·rism** (dôr′iz·əm, dō′riz-).

Do·rin·da (də·rin′də) A feminine personal name. [<Gk., gift]

Dor·is (dôr′is, dor′-) A feminine personal name. [<Gk., the Dorian girl]

—**Doris** In Greek mythology, wife of Nereus and mother of the Nereids.

Dor·is (dôr′is, dor′-) **1** A small mountainous district of west central Greece, traditionally the home of the Dorians. **2** An ancient district on the coast of SW Asia Minor, consisting of Dorian settlements.

Dor·king (dôr′king) *n.* One of a breed of domestic fowls, characterized by five toes on each foot and a large, heavy body. [from *Dorking,* a town in Surrey, England]

dorm (dôrm) *n. Colloq.* A dormitory (def. 2). [Short for DORMITORY]

dor·man·cy (dôr′mən·sē) *n.* A state of torpidity; lethargy; inactivity.

dor·mant (dôr′mənt) *adj.* **1** Being in a state of, or resembling, sleep; torpid. **2** *Bot.* Resting, as plants or parts of plants in winter. **3** *Geol.* Quiescent; not erupting: said of a volcano. **4** Inactive; unused. **5** Not asserted or enforced, as claims. **6** *Her.* In the attitude of sleep. Compare COUCHANT, RAMPANT. [< OF, ppr. of *dormir* <L *dormire* sleep]

dor·mer (dôr′mər) *n.* **1** *Archit.* **a** A vertical window in a small gable rising from a sloping roof: also **dormer window. b** The roofed projection or gable in which this window is set. **c** A sleeper or beam. **2** *Archaic* A sleeping room. [<OF *dormeor* <L *dormitorium.* See DORMITORY.]

DORMER WINDOW

dor·mi·to·ry (dôr′mə·tôr′ē, -tō′rē) *n. pl.* **·ries** **1** A large room in which many persons sleep. **2** A building providing sleeping and living accommodations, especially at a school, college, or resort. [<L *dormitorium* < *dormire* sleep]

dor·mouse (dôr′·mous′) *n. pl.* **·mice** One of the various small, arboreal, Old World, squirrel-like rodents (family *Gliridae*). [? <F *dormir* sleep <L *dormire* + MOUSE]

DORMOUSE (2 to 3 inches long)

dor·my (dôr′mē) *adj.* In golf, being as many holes ahead of an opponent as there are holes still to play. Also **dor′·mie.** [<dial. E *dorm* doze, ult. <L *dormire* sleep; so called because no further effort is needed]

dor·nick (dôr′nik) *n.* A heavy damask cloth, used for hangings, carpets, etc. Also **dor′nock** (-nək). [<Flemish *Doornik* Tournai, where originally made]

Dor·noch (dôr′nokh, -nəkh) The county seat of Sutherlandshire, Scotland.

Dor·o·thy (dôr′ə·thē, dor′-) A feminine personal name. Also **Dor·o·the·a** (dôr′ə·thē′ə, dor′-; *Dan., Du., Ger., Sw.* dō′rō·tā′ä), *Fr.* **Do·ro·thée** (dô·rə·tā′), *Ital., Sp.* **Do·ro·te·a** (dō′rō·tā′ä). [<Gk., gift of God]

dorp (dôrp) *n.* A village. [<Du. Akin to THORP.]

Dor·pat (dôr′pät) The German name for TARTU.

dorr (dôr) See DOR[1].

Dorr (dôr), **Thomas Wilson,** 1805–54, U.S. politician; instigated **Dorr's Rebellion** to set up a government in Rhode Island in 1842.

dor·sad (dôr′sad) *adv. Anat.* Toward the back. [<L *dorsum* back + *ad* toward]

dor·sal (dôr′səl) *adj.* **1** *Zool.* Of, pertaining to, on, or near the back: opposed to *ventral.* **2** *Bot.* Pertaining to the under surface, as of a leaf. **3** *Phonet.* Describing those consonants produced with the back of the tongue, as (k) in *cool.* —*n.* Dossal. [<Med. L *dorsalis* <L *dorsum* back] —**dor′sal·ly** *adv.*

dorsal fin The long, unpaired fin along the backbone of fish and other aquatic vertebrates. For illustration see FISH.

Dor·set (dôr′sit) A county in SW England; 973 square miles; capital, Dorchester. Also **Dor′set·shire** (-shir).

Dor·set (dôr′sit), **Earl of** See SACKVILLE.

Dorset Horn A large-horned breed of English sheep, having a tightly textured fleece of medium length.

dorsi- *combining form* **1** On, to, or of the back: *dorsiferous.* **2** Dorso-. [<L *dorsum* back]

dor·sif·er·ous (dôr·sif′ər·əs) *adj. Bot.* Borne on the back, as the sori of ferns. [<DORSI- + -FEROUS]

dor·si·ven·tral (dôr′si·ven′trəl) *adj.* **1** *Bot.* Having distinct surfaces on both sides, as most leaves. **2** Dorsoventral.

dorso- *combining form* Dorsal; dorsal and: *dorsoventral.* [<L *dorsum* back]

dor·so·ven·tral (dôr′sō·ven′trəl) *adj. Zool.* Extending from the back to the ventral side. —**dor′so·ven′tral·ly** *adv.*

dor·sum (dôr′səm) *n. pl.* **·sa** (-sə) *Anat.* **1** The back. **2** Any part of an organ corresponding to or resembling a back. See illustration under BIRD. **3** *Phonet.* The back of the tongue. [<L]

Dort (dôrt) A shortened form of DORDRECHT. Also **Dordt.**

Dort·mund (dôrt′mənd, *Ger.* dôrt′mo͝ont) A city in North Rhine-Westphalia, West Germany, in the Ruhr valley.

dort·y (dôr′tē) *adj. Scot.* Sulky; haughty.

Do·rus (dō′rus) In Greek legend, son of Hellen and ancestor of the Dorians.

do·ry[1] (dôr′ē, dō′rē) *n. pl.* **·ries** A deep, flat-bottomed rowboat with a sharp prow and flat triangular stern, adapted for rough weather: used especially by North Atlantic fishermen. [< native Honduran name]

DORY

do·ry[2] (dôr′e, dō′rē) *n. pl.* **·ries** **1** The wall-eyed pike. **2** The john dory. [<F *dorée,* pp. fem. of *dorer* gild <LL *deaurare.* See DORADO.]

dor·y·line ant (dôr′ē·līn′, dō′rē-) The driver ant.

dos-à-dos (dō·zà·dō′) *adv. French* Back to back. —*n. pl.* **dos-à-dos** (-dōz′, *Fr.* -dō′) **1** An open vehicle, sofa, etc., made so the occupants sit back to back. **2** (dō′sē·dō′) In square dances, a call directing the dancers to pass each other back to back.

dos·age (dō′sij) *n.* **1** The administering of medicine in prescribed quantity. **2** The total amount to be given. **3** The process of adding sugar, liqueur, etc., to wines to improve quality and flavor or to increase strength.

dose (dōs) *n.* **1** The quantity of medicine prescribed to be taken at one time; also, the quantity and strength of X-rays or other radiation to be taken in a certain period of time. **2** Anything disagreeable given as a prescription or infliction. **3** A determinate quantity or portion of whatever tends to benefit or reform individuals or society. —*v.* **dosed, dos·ing** *v.t.* **1** To give medicine to in a dose or doses. **2** To give, as medicine or drugs, in doses. **3** To perform the process of dosage upon: said of wines. —*v.i.* **4** To take medicines. [<MF <L *dosis* <Gk., orig., a giving] —**dos′er** *n.*

do·sim·e·ter (dō·sim′ə·tər) *n. Med.* An instrument for measuring the dosage of X-rays; also called quantimeter. [<Gk. *dosis* a dose + -METER]

do·sim·e·try (dō·sim′ə·trē) *n. Med.* **1** The accurate measurement of doses. **2** A method for the regular administration of alkaloids of definite strength, usually in granular form. —**do·si·met·ric** (dō′si·met′rik) *adj.*

Dos Pas·sos (dōs pas′ōs), **John,** 1896–1970, U.S. novelist.

doss (dos) *n. Brit. Slang* **1** A sleeping place; a bed; especially, a bed in a cheap lodging house (**doss house**). **2** Sleep. [<F *dos* back <L *dorsum*] —**doss′er** *n.*

dos·sal (dos′əl) *n.* A hanging of silk, etc., for the back of an altar, throne, etc.: also spelled *dorsal.* Also **dos′sel.** [<Med. L *dossalis,* var. of *dorsalis* of the back <L *dorsum*]

dos·ser (dos′ər) *n.* **1** A rich hanging for a hall or church. **2** A pannier. [<OF *dossier* < *dos* back <L *dorsum*]

dos·si·er (dos′ē·ā, dos′ē·ər; *Fr.* dô·syā′) *n.* A collection of memoranda, papers, documents, etc., relating to a particular matter or person. [<F, bundle of papers]

dos·sil (dos′əl) *n.* **1** A plug or spigot. **2** *Printing* A cloth roll for wiping ink from an engraved plate. **3** A soft pledget for cleaning out a wound. [<OF *dosil* <LL *duciculus,* dim. of *dux, ducis* a leader]

Dos·so Dos·si (dôs′sō dôs′sē), 1479?–1542, Italian painter: original name *Giovanni de Luteri.*

dost (dust) Do: obsolescent or poetic second person singular, present tense of DO: used with *thou.*

Dos·to·ev·ski (dôs′tô·yef′skē), **Feodor Mikhailovich,** 1821–81, Russian novelist. Also **Dos′to·yev′sky.**

dot[1] (dot) *n.* **1** A minute, round, or nearly round mark; a speck, spot, or point. **2** In writing and printing, a small spot used as a part of a letter, in punctuation, etc. **3** *Music* A point, written after a note or rest, which lengthens its value by half. **4** A little lump; clot. **5** A precise moment of time: on the *dot.* **6** *Telecom.* A signal of shorter duration than the dash, with which it is combined in the transmission of messages in the Morse or any similar code. —*v.* **dot·ted, dot·ting** *v.t.* **1** To mark with a dot or dots. **2** To spread or scatter like dots. **3** To diversify with, or delineate by means of, dots. —*v.i.* **4** To make a dot or dots. —**to dot one's i's and cross one's t's** To be or to make one's work perfect in every detail. [OE *dott* head of a boil]

dot[2] (dot) *n.* A woman's marriage portion; dowry. [<F <L *dos, dotis*] —**do·tal** (dōt′l) *adj.*

Dot (dot), **Dot·ty** (dot′ē) Diminutives of DOROTHY.

do·tage (dō′tij) *n.* **1** Feebleness of mind, as a result of old age; senility. **2** Foolish and extravagant affection; also, any object of it. **3** A feeble or foolish fancy of a dotard. [<DOTE + -AGE]

do·tard (dō′tərd) *n.* One in his dotage. Also **do′tant.**

do·ta·tion (dō·tā′shən) *n.* **1** The act of making or apportioning a dowry. **2** An endowment, as of a public institution. [<OF <L *dotatio, -onis* < *dotare* endow]

dote[1] (dōt) *v.i.* **dot·ed, dot·ing** **1** To lavish extreme fondness: with *on* or *upon.* **2** To be in one's dotage. [ME *doten.* Cf. MDu. *doten* be silly.] —**dot′er** *n.*

dote[2] (dōt) *n.* A form of decay in wood fibers. [<DOTE[1]]

doth (duth) Do: obsolescent or poetic third person singular, present tense of DO.

dot·ing (dō′ting) *adj.* **1** Extravagantly or foolishly fond. **2** Feeble-minded; driveling. **3** Decaying from age: said of plants. —**dot′·ing·ly** *adv.* —**dot′ing·ness** *n.*

dot-se·quen·tial (dot′si·kwen′shəl) *adj.* Pertaining to a system of color television in which the three primary colors are dissected, projected, transmitted, and received in sequence as a series of dots interwoven to produce the image in its original form. Compare FIELD-SEQUENTIAL, LINE-SEQUENTIAL.

dot·ted (dot′id) *adj.* **1** Marked or flecked with dots: spotted. **2** Distinguished by a dot or dots.

dotted line On a document, the line to carry the signature: to sign on the *dotted line.*

dotted swiss A sheer, crisp, cotton fabric, having either lappet or swivel dots.

dot·ter (dot′ər) *n.* One who or that which makes dots.

dot·ter·el (dot′ər·əl) *n.* **1** A migratory plover (genus *Eudromias*) of northern Europe and Asia, noted for the ease with which it can be taken. **2** A person easily deceived; dupe. Also **dot′trel** (-rəl). [< ME *dotrelle.* Related to DOTE[1].]

dot·tle (dot′l) *n.* The unconsumed tobacco left in a pipe after smoking. Also **dot′tel.** [? Dim. of DOT]

dot·ty (dot′ē) *adj.* **·ti·er, ·ti·est 1** Consisting of or marked with dots. **2** *Colloq.* Of unsteady or feeble gait; hence, slightly demented; imbecile.

do·ty (dō′tē) *adj.* **·ti·er, ·ti·est** Decayed: said of trees, etc. Compare DOATY. [< DOTE[2]]

Dou (dou), **Gerard** See DOW, GERARD.

Dou·ai (dōō·ā′, *Fr.* dwā) A town in northern France. Formerly **Dou·ay′.**

Douay Bible See under BIBLE.

doub·le (dub′əl) *adj.* **1** Having two of a sort together; being in pairs; coupled. **2** Twice as large, much, strong, heavy, valuable, or many. **3** Twofold; hence, ambiguous, deceitful, or two-faced. **4** Doubled; folded. **5** *Bot.* Having the petals increased in number: said of flowers. **6** In musical instruments, making tones an octave lower. —*n.* **1** Something that is twice as much. **2** A fold or plait. **3** A person or thing that closely resembles another; hence, an apparition or wraith. **4** A backward turn, as of a hunted fox; a trick or stratagem. **5** A player or singer who understudies the part of a principal artist, so as to be able to supply his or her place in case of illness, etc.; an understudy. **6** *pl.* A tennis game between two pairs of players; also, two successive faults in tennis. **7** *Eccl.* A feast at which the antiphon is said both before and after the psalms. **8** In baseball, a two-base hit. **9** A domino piece bearing the same number of pips on each half. **10** In card playing, the act of doubling. See DOUBLE (*v.* def. 13). **11** A double star. **—on** (or **at**) **the double** In double-quick time: a military command. —*v.* **doub·led, doub·ling** *v.t.* **1** To make twice as great in number, size, value, force, etc.; increase by adding an equal amount. **2** To fold or bend one part of upon another; make of two thicknesses: usually with *over, up, back,* etc. **3** To do over again; repeat. **4** To be twice the quantity or number of. **5** To act or be the double of. **6** In baseball, to advance (a base runner) by hitting a double: He *doubled* him home. **7** *Naut.* To sail around: to *double* a cape. **8** *Music* To add the upper or lower octave to. —*v.i.* **9** To become double; increase by an equal amount. **10** To turn and go back on a course: often with *back.* **11** To act or perform in two capacities. **12** In baseball, to hit a double. **13** In bridge, to declare each trick in the suit last bid by an opponent to be of twice the normal value in points: done in the expectation of defeating the hand and thereby exacting an increased penalty. **—to double in brass** *U.S. Slang* To take more than one part in anything, as in addition to one's specialty: originally said of musicians. **—to double up 1** To bend over or cause to bend over, as from pain or laughter. **2** To fold or clench, as a fist. **3** To share one's quarters, bed, etc., with another. **4** In baseball, to complete a double play upon. —*adv.* **1** In twofold degree; twice. **2** In twice the quantity. **3** Deceitfully. Also **doub′ly** *adv.* [< OF *duble* < L *duplus* double]

Double, meaning two, twofold, or twice, may appear as a combining form in hyphemes, as in:

double-action	**double-rivet**
double-barrel	**double-riveted**
double-bitt	**double-shot**
double-bitted	**double-space**
double-handed	**double-spacing**
double-leaded	**double-thread**
double-leaf	**double-tooth**
double-lock	**double-track**
double-locking	**double-voiced**

doub·le-banked (dub′əl·bangkt′) *adj. Naut.* **1** Having two men at each oar. **2** Having two tiers of oars: said of oar-propelled boats or ships.

double bar *Music* A double vertical line on a staff, indicating the end of a piece of music or of a section of it.

doub·le-bar·reled (dub′əl·bar′əld) *adj.* **1** Having two barrels, as a shotgun. **2** Doubly powerful or effective: *double-barreled* oratory. **3** Ambiguous as to meaning.

doub·le-bass (dub′əl·bās′) *n. Music* The largest and deepest toned of the stringed instruments played with a bow: also called *bass viol, contrabass, string bass.* —*adj.* Contrabass.

doub·le-bas·soon (dub′əl·bə·sōōn′) *n.* An instrument of the oboe family, an octave below the ordinary bassoon in pitch.

double bed A bed wide enough for two people: usually about 54 inches across.

doub·le-blind (dub′əl·blīnd′) *adj.* Describing a method of minimizing bias in conducting experiments with human subjects by concealing from both researchers and subjects the identity of those receiving the treatment under investigation and those acting as a control, who receive a superficially similar treatment.

double boiler A cooking utensil consisting of two pots, one fitting into the other so that food placed in the upper pot is cooked by boiling water in the lower one.

doub·le-breast·ed (dub′əl·bres′tid) *adj.* Having two rows of buttons and fastening so as to provide a double thickness of cloth across the breast: said of a coat or vest.

double chin A fat, fleshy fold under the chin.

double coconut The sea coconut.

double concave Concavo-concave.

double convex Convexo-convex.

doub·le-cross (dub′əl·krôs′, -kros′) *Slang v.t.* To betray by not acting, or by failing to act, as promised; be treacherous to; cheat. —*n.* (-krôs, -kros′) The act of or an instance of cheating or betraying an associate. **—doub′le-cross′er** *n.*

double dagger See under DAGGER.

double date *Colloq.* An appointment made by two couples.

doub·le-date (dub′əl·dāt′) *v.t.* & *v.i.* **-dat·ed, -dat·ing** To make or go out on a double date (with).

doub·le-deal·er (dub′əl·dē′lər) *n.* One who acts with duplicity.

doub·le-deal·ing (dub′əl·dē′ling) *adj.* Treacherous; deceitful. —*n.* Treachery; duplicity. See synonyms under DECEPTION.

doub·le-deck·er (dub′əl·dek′ər) *n.* **1** *Naut.* A vessel with two decks above the water line. **2** A vehicle with an upper deck. **3** A bed containing two decks. **4** A sandwich made with three slices of bread and two layers of filling.

dou·ble-dig·it (dub′əl·dij′it) *adj.* Being at least 10 percent: *double-digit* inflation.

double drum A bass drum.

doub·le-du·ty (dub′əl·dōō′tē, -dyōō′-) *adj.* **1** Built to stand twice as much wear or use. **2** Serving a dual function.

double eagle A gold coin of the United States with a face value of $20: withdrawn from circulation in 1934.

doub·le-edged (dub′əl·ejd′) *adj.* **1** Having two cutting edges. **2** Applicable both for as well as against.

dou·ble-en·ten·dre (dōō·blän·tän′dr′) *n.* A word or phrase of double meaning, the less obvious one often of doubtful propriety. [Alter. of F *double entente*]

dou·ble en·tente (dōō·blän·tänt′) *French* Double meaning; equivocal sense.

double entry A method of bookkeeping in which every transaction is made to appear as both debtor and creditor. **—doub′le-en′try** *adj.*

doub·le-faced (dub′əl·fāst′) *adj.* **1** Having two faces. **2** Having a pattern on each side: said of a fabric. **3** Deceitful; hypocritical: a *double-faced* friend.

double feature A program of two full-length motion pictures.

doub·le-first (dub′əl·fûrst′) *n.* In British universities, a degree with the highest honors in two subjects; also, a student who obtains such a degree.

doub·le·gang·er (dub′əl·gang′ər) *n.* A Doppelgänger.

doub·le-head·er (dub′əl·hed′ər) *n.* **1** A long, heavy train pulled by two engines. **2** Two games, especially of baseball, played in succession on the same day by the same two teams.

double indemnity A clause in a life insurance policy by which a payment of double the face value of the policy is made in the event of accidental death.

doub·le-joint·ed (dub′əl·join′tid) *adj. Anat.* Characterized by a form of diarthrosis in which the bones move freely backward and forward.

doub·le-mind·ed (dub′əl·mīn′did) *adj.* **1** Unsettled; wavering. **2** Deceitful.

doub·le·ness (dub′əl·nis) *n.* **1** The state or quality of being double. **2** Duplicity.

doub·le-park (dub′əl·pärk′) *v.t.* & *v.i.* To park (a motor vehicle) alongside another already parked along the curb. **—doub′le-park′ing** *n.*

double play In baseball, a play in which two base runners are put out.

double pneumonia Pneumonia affecting both lungs.

doub·le-quick (dub′əl·kwik′) *n.* In the U.S. Army, a rate of march of 180 steps a minute: now usually called *double-time.* —*v.t.* & *v.i.* To march or cause to march at this pace.

doub·le-reed (dub′əl·rēd′) *n. Music* A wind instrument with a reed consisting of two segments united at the lower end and separated at the upper end. —*adj.* **1** Having such a reed. **2** Designating a group of instruments having such a reed, as the oboe, bassoon, etc.

doub·le-rip·per (dub′əl·rip′ər) *n.* A coasting sled composed of two small bobs or pairs of runners connected lengthwise by a long seat or board. Also **doub′le-run′ner.**

double salt *Chem.* **1** Any salt which yields two different anions or cations when hydrolyzed. **2** A molecular combination of two simple salts.

double standard A standard of conduct permitting greater sexual liberty to men than to women.

double star See under STAR.

doub·le-sur·faced (dub′əl·sûr′fist) *adj.* Having two surfaces.

doub·let (dub′lit) *n.* **1** One of a pair of like things; a pair or couple. **2** A short, close-fitting, outer garment, with or without sleeves, worn by men from the 15th to 17th centuries. **3** An imitation gem consisting of a real stone cemented to a piece of glass colored to simulate the imitated gem; also, a paste jewel mounted with a thin face of a genuine jewel. **4** *Ling.* One of a pair of words derived from the same original but entering a language through different routes, as *regal* and *royal.* **5** *Usually pl.* A pair of dice that, when thrown, show on the upper surface the same number of spots: He threw *doublets.* **6** *Optics* A pair of lenses joined so as to eliminate the distortion caused by either lens used alone. [< OF, something folded, orig. dim. of DOUBLE]

DOUBLET (*def. 2*)

doub·le-take (dub′əl·tāk′) *n.* A delayed reaction, with visible evidence of surprise, to a joke or situation.

double talk 1 A manner of speech, adopted to confuse the listener, in which meaningless syllable combinations are substituted for expected words. **2** Ambiguous talk meant to deceive.

doub·le-think (dub′əl·thingk′) *n.* **1** The capacity to hold contradictory opinions in full knowledge of their contradiction. **2** Confused thought. Also **dou′ble·think′.**

doub·le-time (dub′əl·tīm′) See DOUBLE-QUICK.

doub·le-tongue (dub′əl·tung′) *v.i.* **-tongued, -tongu·ing** To apply the tongue rapidly to the teeth and hard palate alternately, as in executing a staccato passage for the flute or cornet.

doub·le-tongued (dub′əl·tungd′) *adj.* Characterized by duplicity of speech.

doub·le-tree (dub′əl·trē′) *n.* The bar or cross piece to the ends of which two swingletrees are fastened.

doub·ling (dub′ling) *n.* **1** The act of one who or that which doubles. **2** Something doubled over or together; a fold; plait. **3** *Her.* The fur lining of a mantle or robe.

doub·loon (du·blōōn′) *n.* A former Spanish gold coin worth about $16. See DOBLA, DOBLON. [< Sp. *doblón,* aug. of *doble* double; orig. worth two pistoles]

doub·ly (dub′lē) See DOUBLE *adv.*

Doubs (dōō) A river in eastern France, flowing 270 miles NE to the Saône.

doubt (dout) *v.t.* **1** To hesitate to accept as true; hold as uncertain; disbelieve. **2** *Obs.* To be apprehensive of; fear. —*v.i.* **3** To be in doubt; be uncertain. **4** To be mistrustful. —*n.* **1** Lack of certain knowledge; uncertainty regarding the truth or reality of something. **2** A matter or case of dubitation; indecision. **3** A question requiring settlement, an objection. **4** *Obs.* Fear; dread. [<OF *duter, douter* <L *dubitare*; spelling refashioned after L] —**doubt′a·ble** *adj.* —**doubt′er** *n.*

Synonyms (verb): distrust, mistrust, surmise, suspect. To *doubt* is to lack conviction. Incompleteness of evidence may compel one to *doubt*, or some perverse bias of mind may so incline him. *Distrust* may express simply a lack of confidence. *Mistrust* and *suspect* imply that one is almost assured of positive evil; one may *distrust* himself or others; he *suspects* others. *Mistrust* is rarely used of persons, but only of motives, intentions, etc. *Distrust* is always serious: *mistrust* is often used playfully. Compare DOUBT *n.*, QUESTION, SUPPOSE. *Antonyms*: believe, trust.

Synonyms (noun): disbelief, distrust, hesitancy, hesitation, incredulity, indecision, irresolution, misgiving, perplexity, question, scruple, suspense, suspicion, uncertainty. *Doubt* is lack of conviction; *disbelief* is conviction to the contrary; *unbelief* refers to a settled state of mind. *Perplexity* seeks a solution; *doubt* may be content to linger unresolved. Any improbable statement awakens *incredulity*. As regards practical matters, *uncertainty* applies to the unknown or undecided; *doubt* implies some negative evidence. *Suspense* regards the future, and is eager and anxious; *uncertainty* may relate to any period, and be quite indifferent. *Misgiving* is ordinarily in regard to the outcome of something already done or decided; *hesitation, indecision,* and *irresolution* have reference to something that remains to be decided or done and are due oftener to infirmity of will than to lack of knowledge. *Distrust* and *suspicion* apply especially to the motives, character, etc., of others, and are more decidedly adverse than *doubt*. *Scruple* relates to matters of conscience and duty. See PERPLEXITY, QUESTION. *Antonyms*: assurance, belief, certainty, confidence, conviction, decision, determination, persuasion, reliance, resolution, resolve, trust.

doubt·ful (dout′fəl) *adj.* **1** Subject to, entertaining, or admitting of doubt. **2** Uncertain; undecided; contingent. **3** Indistinct; vague; ambiguous. **4** Questionable; dubious. See synonyms under EQUIVOCAL, IRRESOLUTE, PRECARIOUS. —**doubt′ful·ly** *adv.* —**doubt′ful·ness** *n.*

Doubting Thomas A confirmed or habitual skeptic. *John* xx 25.

doubt·less (dout′lis) *adj.* **1** Confident; fearless. **2** Indubitable; certain. —*adv.* Without doubt; unquestionably: also **doubt′less·ly.**

douce (do͞os) *adj. Scot.* Sober; sedate; not frivolous. —**douce′ly** *adv.* —**douce′ness** *n.*

dou·cet (do͞o′sit) *n. Obs.* **1** A sweet pastry. **2** A dowcet. [<F, dim. of *douce* sweet <L *dulcis*]

dou·ceur (do͞o·sœr′) *n.* **1** A small present; bribe; tip. **2** Sweetness of manners. **3** *Obs.* A compliment. [<F <L *dulcor, -oris* sweetness < *dulcis* sweet]

douche (do͞osh) *n.* **1** A jet of water or vapor sprayed on or into the body for medicinal or hygienic reasons. **2** The instrument for administering it. **3** A bath taken by making use of these facilities. —*v.t.* & *v.i.* **douched, douch·ing** To give or take a douche. [<F <Ital. *doccia* a water pipe, ult. <L *ducere* lead]

dough (dō) *n.* **1** A soft mass of moistened flour or meal, mixed for cooking into bread, cake, etc. **2** Any soft pasty mass. **3** *Slang* Money. ◆ Homophone: *doe.* [OE *dāh*] —**dough′y** *adj.*

dough·boy (dō′boi′) *n.* **1** A dumpling of raised dough. **2** *U.S. Colloq.* An infantry soldier: also **dough′foot′** (-fo͝ot′).

dough·face (dō′fās′) *n. U.S.* **1** A mask or false face. **2** In American history, a Northern politician who was accused of truckling to the slave power during the period of anti-slavery agitation.

dough·nut (dō′nut) *n.* A small cake made of dough raised by baking powder or yeast and fried in deep fat; a fried cake: usually cut with a hole in the center before frying.

dought (dout) *Scot.* Past tense of DOW.

dough·ty (dou′tē) *adj.* **·ti·er, ·ti·est** *Archaic* Brave; valiant; redoubtable: now chiefly in humorous use. See synonyms under BRAVE. [OE *dohtig*] —**dough′ti·ly** *adv.* —**dough′ti·ness** *n.*

Dough·ty (dou′tē), **Charles Montagu,** 1843–1926, English traveler and author.

Doug·las (dug′ləs) Capital of the Isle of Man.

Doug·las (dug′ləs) Name of a family prominent in Scottish history; especially, **Sir William the Hardy,** first Lord of Douglas, died 1298?, a follower of Wallace; his son, **Sir James the Good,** 1286–1330: known as *Black Douglas,* follower of Robert the Bruce; **James,** 1358–1388, second Earl of Douglas and Mar; **Gawin,** 1474?–1522, Scottish poet. —**Lewis Williams,** born 1894, U.S. diplomat. —**Stephen Arnold,** 1813–61, U.S. senator; opposed Lincoln in a series of debates, 1858. —**William Orville,** born 1898, U.S. jurist, associate Supreme Court justice 1939–75.

Douglas fir A large timber tree *(Pseudotsuga taxifolia)* of the pine family, growing on the Pacific Coast of the United States: often called *red fir, Oregon fir.* Also called **Douglas hemlock, Douglas pine, Douglas spruce.** [after David *Douglas,* 1798–1834, Scottish botanist]

Doug·las-Home (dug′ləs·hyo͞om′), **Sir Alec (Frederick),** former Earl of Home, born 1903, British statesman; prime minister, 1963–1964.

Doug·lass (dug′ləs), **Frederick,** 1817–95, U.S. Negro abolitionist and diplomat.

Dou·kho·bors (do͞o′kə·bôrz′) See DUKHOBORS.

dou·kit (do͞o′kit) *adj. Scot.* Ducked. Also spelled *dookit.*

Dou·ma (do͞o′mä) See DUMA.

Dou·mergue (do͞o·merg′), **Gaston,** 1863–1937, French statesman; president 1924–31.

doum palm (do͞om) The doom palm.

doun (do͞on) *adv. Scot.* Down.

doup (doup, do͞op) *Scot.* The end; butt end.

dou·pi·on (do͞o′pē·ən) *n.* **1** Silk thread of uneven weight and thickness, spun from two cocoons in close contact with each other. **2** A fabric made from such thread, as pongee, nankeen, or shantung. Also **doup·pi·on·i** (do͞o′pē·on′ē, -ō′nē). Also *dupion, dupioni.* [<F <Ital. *doppione,* aug. of *doppio* double <L *duplus*]

dour (do͝or) *adj. Scot.* Hard; unyielding; sullen. [<L *durus*] —**dour′ly** *adv.* —**dour′ness** *n.*

dou·ra (do͝or·ə) See DURRA.

dou·ri·cou·li (do͝or′i·ko͞o′lē) *n.* A small, bushy-tailed, arboreal monkey (genus *Aotes*) of South America, having large eyes adapted for nocturnal vision. [<S. Am. Ind.]

dou·rine (do͞o·rēn′) *n.* An infectious disease of horses and asses transmitted through sexual contact by a parasitic micro-organism *(Trypanosoma equiperdum)*: also called *equine syphilis.* [<F <Arabic *darin* unclean]

Dou·ro (dō′ro͞o) A river in Spain and Portugal, flowing 475 miles west to the Atlantic: Spanish *Duero.*

douse[1] (dous) *v.* **doused, dous·ing** *v.t.* **1** To plunge into water or other liquid; dip suddenly; duck. **2** To drench with water or other liquid. —*v.i.* **3** To become drenched or immersed. See synonyms under IMMERSE. —*n.* A ducking or drenching. Also spelled *dowse.* [Origin unknown]

douse[2] (dous) See DOWSE[2].

douse[3] (dous) *v.t.* **doused, dous·ing** **1** To strike; give a blow to. **2** *Naut.* To take in or haul down quickly, especially a sail. **3** *Colloq.* To take off, as clothes. **4** *Colloq.* To put out; extinguish. [Cf. MDu. *dossen* beat, strike]

douse[4] (do͞os) *Scot.* See DOUCE.

d'ou·tre mer (do͞o′tr′ mâr′) *French* From beyond the sea.

douze·pers (do͞oz′pârz′) *n. pl. sing.* **·par** (-pâr′) **1** In medieval legend, the twelve knights of Charlemagne. **2** In French history, the twelve chief spiritual and temporal peers. [<OF *douze pers* twelve peers]

DO·VAP (dō′vap) *n.* A method for determining the course and velocity of high-altitude, long-range rockets by radio waves whose return frequencies are interpreted on the principle of the Doppler effect. [DO(PPLER) V(ELOCITY) A(ND) P(OSITION)]

dove[1] (duv) *n.* **1** A pigeon; especially, the mourning dove, turtledove, etc. **2** *Eccl.* A symbol of the Holy Spirit. **3** A symbol of peace. **4** One who seeks to resolve a war primarily by means of limited military action, negotiation, or unilateral withdrawal: opposed to *hawk*[1] (def. 4). **5** Any gentle, innocent creature. [Cf. ON *dūfa*]

dove[2] (dōv) *U.S. Colloq.* & *Brit. Dial.* Past tense of DIVE.

dove·cot (duv′kot′) *n.* A house for tame pigeons; generally, a houselike box set on a pole or on the roof or side of a building. Also **dove′cote′** (-kōt′, -kot′).

dove hawk The goshawk.

dove·kie (duv′kē) *n.* **1** The little auk *(Alle alle)*, an arctic bird about 7 1/2 inches long, black above, white below. **2** The black guillemot. Also **dove′key.**

Do·ver (dō′vər) **1** A port in eastern Kent, England, on the **Strait of Dover** (French *Pas de Calais*), a strait 21 miles wide at the eastern end of the English Channel. **2** The capital of Delaware.

Dover's powder *Med.* An anodyne diaphoretic compounded of ipecacuanha, opium, and sugar of milk. [after Thomas *Dover,* 1660–1742, English physician]

dove·tail (duv′tāl′) *n.* **1** A manner of joining boards, timbers, etc., by interlocking wedge-shaped tenons and spaces. **2** The joint so made. —*v.t.* & *v.i.* **1** To join by means of a dovetail or dovetails. **2** To fit in closely or aptly.

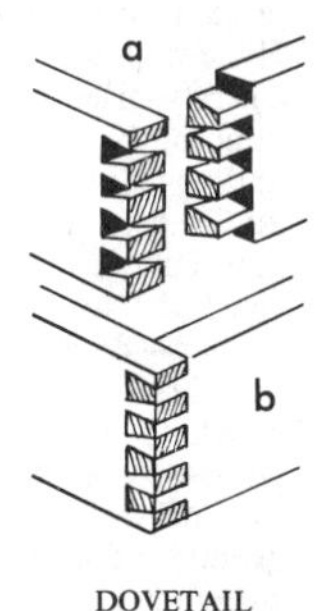

DOVETAIL JOINT
a. Before joining.
b. Joined.

dov·ish (duv′ish) *adj.* Disposed to rely on conciliation to resolve a war: opposed to *hawkish.*

Dow (dou), **Gerard,** 1613–1675, Dutch painter. Also spelled *Dou.*

dow·a·ger (dou′ə·jər) *n.* **1** In English law, a widow holding property or title derived from her late husband. **2** *Colloq.* Any elderly lady of dignified bearing. [<OF *douagere* < *douage* a dower]

dow·cet (dou′sit) *n. Obs.* A testicle of a deer: also spelled *doucet.* [Var. of DOUCET]

Dow·den (dou′dən), **Edward,** 1843–1913, Irish critic and Shakespearean scholar.

dow·dy (dou′dē) *adj.* **·di·er, ·di·est** Ill-dressed; not neat or fashionable; in bad taste; shabby. Also **dow′dy·ish.** —*n. pl.* **·dies** **1** A slatternly woman. **2** A fruit pie baked in a deep dish. [ME *doude* a slut; origin unknown] —**dow′·di·ly** *adv.* —**dow′di·ness** *n.*

dow·el (dou′əl) *n.* **1** A pin or peg, usually cylindrical, for joining together two adjacent pieces, as parts of a barrelhead: distinguished from a *tenon.* **2** A piece of wood built or driven into a wall, to which to nail finishings: also **dowel pin.** —*v.t.* **·eled** or **·elled, ·el·ing** or **·el·ling** To fasten or furnish with dowels. [<MLG *dovel* plug]

DOWELS

dow·er (dou′ər) *n.* **1** A widow's life portion (usually a third) of her husband's lands and tenements. **2** The sum of one's natural gifts; endowment. —*v.t.* **1** To provide with a dower. **2** To endow, as with a talent or quality. [OF *douaire* <LL *dotarium* <L *dos, dotis* a dowery] —**dow′er·less** *adj.*

dow·er·y (dou′ər·ē) See DOWRY.

dowf (douf, do͞of) *adj. Scot.* Dull; stupid.

dow·ie (dou′ē, dō′ē) *adj. Scot.* Dull; spiritless; mournful; in poor health. Also **dow′y.**

Do·wie (dou′ē), **John Alexander,** 1847–1907, Scottish religious leader in America.

dow·itch·er (dou′ich·ər) *n.* **1** The gray snipe *(Limnodromus griseus)* of eastern North America. **2** A related bird, the long-billed *dowitcher (L. griseus scolopaceus).* [<N. Am. Ind.]

dowl (doul) *n.* **1** A filament of a feather. **2** Down or a fiber of down. Also **dowle.** [Origin uncertain]

down[1] (doun) *adv.* **1** From a higher to a lower place, level, position, etc.: Come *down* from that ladder! **2** In or into a lower place, position, etc.: The cattle put their heads *down.* **3** On or to the ground: The house burned *down.* **4** To or toward the south: Come *down* to Florida this winter. **5** To or in an outlying or distant place: life *down* on the farm. **6** Below the horizon: The sun went *down.* **7** From an upright to a prone or prostrate position: to knock a man *down.* **8** From a former or earlier time or owner: This necklace came *down* to me from my ancestors. **9** To or toward the end; away from the start: Read from the beginning *down* to chapter five. **10** To a smaller bulk, greater density, heavier consistency, etc.: The mixture boiled *down* to a hard crust. **11** To or into a less active or violent state: The tumult died *down.* **12** To a diminished pitch or volume: Turn the radio *down!* **13** To a lower rate, price, demand or amount: The market has gone *down.* **14** Into or in an attitude or state of close application, intensity, earnestness, etc.: to get *down* to work; to track *down* a clue. **15** In a depressed mental or emotional state: His troubles had him *down.* **16** In or into ill health: He came *down* with a fever. **17** In or into a degraded, inferior, or helpless state; in subjection: His competitors kept him *down.* **18** Completely; entirely: used as an intensive: loaded *down* with honors. **19** In cash, as at the time of purchase: half the price *down* and the rest in instalments. **20** On or as on paper or other material for writing: Take *down* his words. **21** *Naut.* To or toward the lee side of a vessel: to put the helm *down.* **—down with** (Let us) do away with or overthrow: an exclamation of disfavor or disapproval. *—adj.* **1** Going, facing, or directed toward a lower position or place: the *down* side of the subway station. **2** In a lower place; on the ground: The wires are *down* because of the storm. **3** Gone, brought, or paid down: a *down* payment. **4** Downcast; dejected. **5** Bedridden: He is *down* with a cold. **6** In games, behind an opponent's score by (a number of) points, goals, strokes, etc.: opposed to *up.* **7** In football, not in play. **—down and out 1** In boxing, knocked out. **2** Disabled, destitute, or socially outcast. Also **down′-and-out′. —down on** Opposed to as from anger, ill will, or enmity. *—v.t.* **1** To knock, throw, or put *down*; subdue. **2** To swallow; gulp *down.* *—v.i.* **3** *Rare* To go, fall, or sink *down.* See synonyms under CONQUER. *—prep.* **1** In a descending direction along, upon, or in: The logs floated *down* the river. **2** From an earlier to a later period in the duration of: The story has remained the same *down* the ages. *—n.* **1** A downward movement; a descent. **2** A reverse of fortune: the ups and *downs* of life. **3** In football, any of the four consecutive plays during which a team must advance the ball at least ten yards in order to maintain possession of it. [OE *dūne,* aphetic var. of *adūne* <*of dune* from the hill]

down[2] (doun) *n.* **1** The fine, soft plumage of birds under the feathers, especially that on the breast of water birds. **2** The first feathering of a bird. **3** The soft hairs that first appear on the human face. **4** *Bot.* Soft, short hairs; pubescence, as on plants or fruits. **5** Any feathery, fluffy substance. [<ON *dunn*]

down[3] (doun) *n.* **1** A hill having a broad, treeless, grass-grown top; also, the open space on its top. **2** *pl.* Turf-covered, undulating tracts of upland. **3** A dune. [OE *dūn.* Akin to DUNE.]

Down (doun) A county of eastern Ulster province, Ireland; 952 square miles; county seat, Downpatrick.

dow•na (dou′nə) *Scot.* Cannot. See DOW.

down•beat (down′bēt′) *n. Music* **1** The first accent of each measure. **2** The downward gesture made by the conductor to indicate this accent.

down-bow (doun′bō′) *n.* In stringed instruments, a downward stroke of the bow across the strings: opposite of *up-bow.*

down•cast (doun′kast′, -käst′) *adj.* **1** Directed downward or to the ground: a *downcast* look. **2** Low in spirits; dejected; depressed. See synonyms under SAD. *—n.* A shaft down which a ventilating air current passes.

down•come (doun′kum′) *n.* **1** A downfall, especially a sudden one. **2** A downcomer.

down•com•er (doun′kum′ər) *n.* **1** The pipe which receives the outpourings from the eaves of a roof; leader. **2** A pipe in a mine which conveys combustible gases downward. **3** A circulating tube in water-tube boilers.

Down East New England, especially Maine. **— down′-east′** *adj.*

down•er (doun′ər) *n. Slang* Any of various drugs that depress the central nervous system, as barbiturates.

Downes (dounz), **(Edwin) Olin,** 1886–1955, U.S. music critic.

down•fall (doun′fôl′) *n.* **1** A falling or flowing downward. **2** A sudden, heavy fall of rain. **3** A fall; disgrace. **4** A trap operating as by the descent of a weight; a deadfall. See synonyms under RUIN.

down•fallen (doun′fô′lən) *adj.* Fallen; ruined.

down•grade (doun′grād′) *n.* A descending slope, as of a hill or road. **—on the down•grade** Declining in health, reputation, status, etc. *—adj.* Downhill. *—v.t.* **•grad•ed, •grad•ing** To reduce in status, salary, etc.

down•haul (doun′hôl′) *n. Naut.* A rope for hauling down certain sails, as a jib, staysail, etc.

down-heart•ed (doun′här′tid) *adj.* Dejected, discouraged; low-spirited. **—down′heart′ed•ly** *adv.* **—down′heart′ed•ness** *n.*

down•hill (doun′hil′, doun′hil′) *adj.* Descending; sloping. *—adv.* With a downward direction; toward the bottom of a hill. **—to go downhill** To decline, as in success.

Down•ing Street (dou′ning) **1** A street in Westminster, London; site of the official residence of the Prime Minister (No. 10). **2** The British Government or cabinet.

down-lead (doun′lēd′) *n. Brit.* A lead-in.

down payment In instalment buying, the initial payment on a purchase.

down•play (doun′plā′) *v.t.* To play down.

down•pour (doun′pôr′, -pōr′) *n.* A copious and heavy fall of rain.

down•right (doun′rīt′) *adj.* **1** Straight to the point; unequivocal; plain; outspoken. **2** Directed downward. **3** Thorough; utter; absolute. *—adv.* **1** Directly downward. **2** Without doubt or qualification. **3** In the extreme; utterly. See synonyms under FLAT[1]. **—down′right′ly** *adv.* **— down′right′ness** *n.*

Downs (dounz), **The 1** A sheltered roadstead in the English Channel off the SE coast of Kent. **2** Two parallel ranges of low chalk hills in southern England.

down•spout (doun′spout′) *n.* A pipe for draining rain water, etc., from a roof or from a gutter along a roof.

Down's syndrome (dounz) *Pathol.* Congenital mental and physical retardation due to a chromosomal anomaly, accompanied by variable signs including a flat face and pronounced epicanthic folds: also called *Mongolism.* [<J.L.H. *Down,* 1828–96, Eng. physician]

down•stage (doun′stāj′) *n.* The half of a stage, from left to right, that is nearest to the audience. *—adj.* Belonging or pertaining to the front half of a stage. *—adv.* Toward, near, or on the front half of a stage.

down•stairs (doun′stârz′) *adj.* Below the stairs; on a lower floor. *—n.* The downstairs region of a building. *—adv.* Down the stairs; toward a lower floor.

down•stream (doun′strēm′) *adj.* & *adv.* In the direction of the current; down the stream.

down•take (doun′tāk′) *n.* A downward air passage: the *downtake* to the blowers of a boiler.

down•throw (doun′thrō′) *n.* The act of throwing down, or the state of being overthrown or prostrated.

down•time (doun′tīm′) *n.* The time during working hours when a machine, computer, section, or entire factory is not functioning.

down•town (doun′toun′) *adj.* **1** Of or in the part of a city or town geographically lower than the other parts: opposed to *uptown.* **2** Of, in, or characteristic of the chief business section of a city or town. *—adv.* To, toward, or in the geographically lower or chief business part of a town or city. *—n.* The downtown section of a town or city.

down-trod•den (doun′trod′n) *adj.* Trodden under foot; oppressed. Also **down′-trod.**

down•turn (doun′tûrn′) *n.* A downward turn or decline, as in popularity or in a state's economy.

down under Australia or New Zealand.

down•ward (doun′wərd) *adj.* **1** Descending or tending from a higher to a lower level (literally or figuratively). **2** Descending from that which is more remote. *—adv.* **1** From a higher to a lower position. **2** From that which is more remote, as in place or time. **3** Toward the extremities. Also **down′ward•ly, down′wards** *adv.*

down•y (doun′ē) *adj.* **down•i•er, down•i•est 1** Of, pertaining to, like, or covered with down. **2** Soft; quiet; soothing. **—down′i•ness** *n.*

downy mildew Grape rot.

dow•ry (dou′rē) *n. pl.* **•ries 1** The property a wife brings to her husband in marriage. **2** *Archaic* A reward paid for a wife. *Gen.* xxxiv 12. **3** Any endowment or gift. Also spelled *dowery.* [<AF *dowarie,* var. of OF *douaire* DOWER]

dowse[1] (dous) See DOUSE[1].

dowse[2] (douz) *v.i.* **dowsed, dows•ing** To search for water, minerals, etc., with a dowsing-rod: also spelled *douse.* [Origin uncertain] **—dows′er** *n.*

dows•ing-rod (dou′zing•rod′) *n.* A divining-rod.

dox•ol•o•gy (dok•sol′ə•jē) *n. pl.* **•gies 1** A hymn or verse of praise to God: specifically applied to a stanza beginning "Praise God, from whom all blessings flow." **2** A formula of praise, used as the closing words of a sermon. **—greater doxology** The Gloria in excelsis. **—lesser doxology** The Gloria Patri. [<Med. L *doxologia* <Gk. <*doxa* praise + *legein* speak] **—dox•o•log•i•cal** (dok′sə•loj′i•kəl) *adj.* **—dox′o•log′i•cal•ly** *adv.*

dox•y[1] (dok′sē) *n. pl.* **dox•ies** *Slang* A mistress or paramour; a prostitute. Also **dox′ie.** [<MDu. *docke* a doll]

dox•y[2] (dok′sē) *n.* A doctrine; belief, especially a religious one. [<*-doxy,* as in *orthodoxy, heterodoxy*]

doy•en (doi′ən, *Fr.* dwä•yaṅ′) *n.* The eldest or senior member of a group. [<F <L *decanus.* See DEAN.] **—doy•enne** (doi′en, *Fr.* dwä•yen′) *n. fem.*

Doyle (doil), **Sir Arthur Conan,** 1859–1930, English physician and novelist; known for his *Sherlock Holmes* stories.

doy•ley, doy•ly (doi′lē) See DOILY.

D'Oy•ly Carte (doi′lē kärt′) See CARTE.

doze (dōz) *v.* **dozed, doz•ing** *v.t.* To spend or pass (time) listlessly or in a doze: to *doze* one's hours away. *—v.i.* To sleep unsoundly or lightly; nap; be drowsy. *—n.* A light, unsound sleep. [<Scand. Cf. Dan. *döse* make dull.] **—doz′er** *n.*

doz•en[1] (duz′ən) *n.* Twelve things of a kind, collectively. **—a long dozen** Thirteen. [<OF *dozeine* <*douze* twelve <L *duodecim* <*duo* two + *decim* ten] **—doz′enth** *adj.*

doz•en[2] (dō′zən) *v.t.* & *v.i. Scot.* To stun; daze; make or become torpid.

do•zy (dō′zē) *adj.* **•zi•er, •zi•est** Drowsy; soporific. **—do′zi•ly** *adv.* **—do′zi•ness** *n.*

drab[1] (drab) *adj.* **1** Dull; colorless. **2** Of the color drab. **3** Made of drab. [<*n.*] *—n.* **1** A yellow-gray color. **2** A special kind of cloth so colored. [<F *drap* cloth <LL *drappus,* ? <Gmc.] **— drab′ly** *adv.* **—drab′ness** *n.*

drab[2] (drab) *n.* A slattern; a slut. *—v.i.* **drabbed, drab•bing** To associate with drabs. [Cf. Irish *drabog* a slattern]

drab[3] (drab) *n.* In the manufacture of salt, a box for draining salt. [Origin unknown]

drab•bet (drab′it) *n. Brit.* A coarse linen fabric of drab color.

drab•ble (drab′əl) *v.t.* & *v.i.* **•bled, •bling** To draggle. [<LG *drabbeln* walk in water or mud, splash]

dra•cae•na (drə•sē′nə) *n.* One of various tropical shrubs and small trees (genera *Dracaena* and *Cordyline*) of the lily family, widely distributed in the Old World and grown as an ornamental plant. [<NL <Gk. *drakaina,* fem. of *drakōn* a dragon]

drachm (dram) *n. Brit.* **1** A dram. **2** A drachma. [<F *drachme* <L *drachma* DRACHMA]

drach•ma (drak′mə) *n. pl.* **•mas** or **•mae** (-mē) **1** The modern gold monetary unit of Greece, equivalent to 100 lepta. **2** An ancient Greek silver coin. **3** An ancient Greek unit of weight. [<L *drachma* <Gk. *drachmē* a handful. Doublet of DRAM.]

Dra•co (drā′kō) A northern constellation, the Dragon. See CONSTELLATION.

Dra•co (drā′kō) An archon of Athens about 621 B.C.; reputed author of the first Athenian written code of laws.

Dra•co•ni•an (drā·kō′nē·ən) *adj.* Pertaining to Draco or his laws; hence, inflexible; severe.

dra•con•ic (drā·kon′ik) *adj.* Of or resembling a dragon. [<L *draco, -onis* <Gk. *drakōn* + -IC]

Dra•con•ic (drā·kon′ik) *adj.* **1** Draconian. **2** Pertaining to the constellation Draco. Also **Dra•con′i•cal.** — **Dra•con′i•cal•ly** *adv.*

draff (draf) *n.* Refuse grain from breweries and distilleries; also, lees or dregs. [Prob. <ON *draf*]

draff•ish (draf′ish) *adj.* Worthless. Also **draff′y, draft′y.**

draft (draft, dräft) *n.* **1** A current of air. **2** The act of drinking or inhaling, as a liquid or air; also, that which is so drawn into the mouth or throat in one drink or gulp. **3** *Naut.* The depth to which a vessel sinks in the water. **4** The act of drawing or drawing out, or the fact of being drawn; also, that which is drawn or drawn out, or its weight or resistance; a haul; pull; drag; a load. **5** The result of a drawing, as of a net in fishing. **6** A plan; outline; sketch. See synonyms under SKETCH. **7** A writing of articles or propositions as framed or drawn up, but not adopted or enacted. **8** An order drawn by one party or person on another for the payment of money to a third. **9** An order for money drawn by one bank and payable at another to the person designated in the order; a bill of exchange. **10** A damper, door, or other device for controlling the airflow in a furnace, stove, etc. **11** A military or naval conscription; levy. **12** That which tends to reduce or exhaust by drawing away a part: a *draft* on one's time, strength, etc. **13** An allowance on the invoices of goods for samples drawn from the packages. **14** *Metall.* The bevel given to the pattern for a casting so that it may be drawn from the mold without injuring the latter; in general, a taper given to an article or part. **15** The total sectional area of the openings in a turbine wheel, or the area of the opening of a sluicegate. **16** A line or border chiseled on a stone to guide in its dressing. **17** A ravine; a gully. **18** *pl.* Draughts. — **on draft** Ready to be drawn, as beer, etc., from a cask or the like. — *v.t.* **1** To outline in writing; sketch; delineate. **2** To select and draw off, as for military service; conscript. **3** In weaving, to pull through the heddles. **4** To draw off or away. **5** To cut a draft on (a stone). — *adj.* **1** Suitable or used for pulling heavy loads: a *draft* animal. **2** Not bottled, as beer; drawn from a cask. Also (*esp. for n. defs. 1, 2, 3, 5, 10, and adj. 2*) *draught.* [ME *draht* <OE *dragan* draw] — **draft′er** *n.* — **draft′i•ness** *n.*

draft board An official, local board of civilians which selects qualified men for compulsory service in the U.S. armed forces.

draft dodger One who avoids or attempts to avoid conscription into military service.

draft•ee (draf·tē′, dräf-) *n.* A person drafted for service in the armed forces.

drafts•man (drafts′mən, dräfts′-) *n. pl.* **•men** (-mən) **1** One who draws or prepares plans, designs, deeds, conveyances, etc.: also spelled *draughtsman.* **2** A draughtsman. — **drafts′•man•ship** *n.*

draft•y (draf′tē, dräf′-) *adj.* **draft•i•er, draft•i•est** Having or exposed to drafts. Also spelled *draughty.* — **draft′i•ly** *adv.* — **draft′i•ness** *n.*

drag (drag) *v.* **dragged, drag•ging** *v.t.* **1** To pull along by main force; haul. **2** To sweep or search the bottom of, as with a net or grapnel; dredge. **3** To catch or recover, as with a grapnel or net. **4** To draw along heavily and wearily. **5** To harrow (land). **6** To protract; continue tediously: often with *on* or *out.* **7** To introduce (an irrelevant subject or matter) into a discussion, argument, etc. —*v.i.* **8** To be pulled or hauled along; trail to or as to the ground. **9** To move heavily or slowly: The procession *dragged* along. **10** To lag behind: The tenor *dragged* in his part. **11** To pass slowly, as time. **12** To operate a dredge. **13** To cause a feeling of clutching or tugging: Worry *dragged* at him. See synonyms under DRAW. — **to drag one's feet** *U.S. Colloq.* To act or work with deliberate slowness. — *n.* **1** The act of dragging or that which drags or is dragged, as a grapple, a dredge, a dragnet; a brake or shoe for causing a carriage wheel to drag, as in going down a hill; a runnerless sled; a dragrope, as of a gun; hence, any clog or impediment. **2** A long, high, four-wheeled carriage; a four-in-hand coach. **3** A slow or difficult movement: to walk with a *drag.* **4** An artificial scent used in hunting, as an aniseed bag. **5** The scent or trail of a fox before it is found and started by the hounds: so called because originally the fox was hunted by the line of scent left by it on its return from a predatory expedition. **6** A draghunt. **7** *Aeron.* That component of the total air force acting on a body which is parallel to the relative wind: said of aircraft in flight. **8** The last of a herd of cattle; the stragglers. **9** *Slang* Influence resulting in special favors; pull. **10** *Slang* A puff of a cigarette. **11** *U.S. Slang* A dull, boring person or thing. **12** *U.S. Slang* Women's clothing worn by a man. [OE *dragan*; infl. in form by ON *draga.* Related to DRAW.]

DRAG
One type of drag; others are open-topped; usually drawn by four horses.

drag-driv•er (drag′drī′vər) *n.* The cowboy who drives the stragglers at the end of a herd.

drag•gle (drag′əl) *v.* **•gled, •gling** *v.t.* **1** To make soiled or wet by dragging in mud or over damp ground; muddy. — *v.i.* **2** To become wet or soiled; drag in the mud. **3** To follow slowly; lag. [Freq. of DRAG]

drag•gle•tail (drag′əl·tāl′) *n.* An untidy person.

drag•gle•tailed (drag′əl·tāld′) *adj.* Bedraggled from or as if from having the garments trailing in the wet or mud.

drag•hound (drag′hound′) *n.* A hound trained to follow an artificial scent.

drag•hunt (drag′hunt′) *n.* A hunt in which an artificial scent is used.

drag•line (drag′līn′) *n.* A guiderope; dragrope.

drag•link (drag′lingk′) *n. Mech.* A link for connecting crankshafts, as a main-shaft crank with an inner paddle shaft in a marine engine.

drag•net (drag′net′) *n.* **1** A net to be drawn along the bottom of the water or along the ground, for taking fish or small animals. **2** Any device or plan by which a criminal can be caught.

Dra•go doctrine (drä′gō) A doctrine proposed in 1902, stating that an international debt does not justify armed intervention by the creditor power. [after Luis M. *Drago,* 1859–1921, Argentine statesman]

drag•o•man (drag′ə·mən) *n. pl.* **•mans** (-mənz) or **•men** (-mən) An interpreter or agent for travelers in the Near East. [<F <LGk. *dragoumanos* <Arabic *tarjumān* translator]

drag•on (drag′ən) *n.* **1** A fabulous, serpentlike, winged monster. **2** In the Authorized Version, a word variously understood as a large reptile, a marine monster, a jackal, etc. **3** A fierce or overbearing person; especially, a duenna. **4** *Bot.* A plant of the arum family. **5** A short, large-bored firearm of the 17th century. **6** *Zool.* A small, arboreal, Asian lizard (genus *Draco*) capable of making long glides between trees by means of winglike expansions of the skin which are supported by the elongated and extensible hind ribs; a flying lizard. [<F <L *draco, -onis* <Gk. *drakōn* serpent]

DRAGON LIZARD
(From 12 to 15 inches long)

Drag•on (drag′ən) A northern constellation, Draco. See CONSTELLATION.

drag•on•et (drag′ən·it) *n.* **1** The yellow gurnard. **2** A small dragon. [<OF, dim. of *dragon* a dragon]

drag•on•fly (drag′ən·flī′) *n. pl.* **•flies** A predatory insect (order *Odonata*), having a slender body, four finely veined wings, large eyes, and strong jaws: also called *darning needle, devil's-darning-needle.* For illustration see under INSECT (beneficial).

drag•on•head (drag′ən·hed′) *n.* Any of a genus (*Dracocephalum*) of hardy annual or perennial herbs of the mint family.

drag•on•nade (drag′ə·nād′) *n.* **1** In French history, the quartering of dragoons on French Protestant families by Louis XIV as a means of persecution. **2** Any military persecution. [<F <*dragon* dragoon]

drag•on•root (drag′ən·rōōt′, -rŏŏt′-) *n.* The green dragon.

drag•on's–blood (drag′ənz·blud′) *n.* One of various reddish-brown resins used as a pigment, especially those obtained from the fruit of a Malayan rattan palm (*Daemonorops draco*) and from the dragon tree.

drag•on's–head (drag′ənz·hed′) *n.* **1** A dragonhead. **2** *Astron.* One of the two points where the ecliptic is intersected by the moon's or planet's orbit. The symbol of the first is ☊; that of the second, which is called **dragon's-tail,** is ☋ , and is used only in astrology.

dragon tree *n.* A gigantic tree of the Canary Islands (*Dracaena draco*), yielding dragon's-blood.

dragon withe A West Indian climbing plant (genus *Banisteriopsis* or *Heteropteris*], bearing winged fruit: the roots of some species have been used as an adulterant of ipecac.

dra•goon (drə·gōōn′) *n.* **1** In some European armies, a cavalryman. **2** *Obs.* A soldier who served on horseback or on foot as occasion required. **3** *Obs.* Dragon (def. 5). — *v.t.* **1** To harass by dragoons. **2** To coerce; browbeat. [<F *dragon* dragon (def. 5)]

drag race In racing hot-rod automobiles, a timed test of acceleration over a straight, measured course, usually one kilometer in length.

drag•rope (drag′rōp′) *n.* **1** A rope with chain and hook attached, used as a brake on a gun carriage. **2** A guiderope. **3** A rope dragged by a balloon over the ground to check speed and control height of ascent.

drag•sail (drag′sāl′) *n. Naut.* A driftsail or sea anchor made from a sail. Also **drag′sheet′** (-shēt′).

drai•gle (drā′gəl) *v.t.* & *v.i. Scot.* To draggle.

drain (drān) *v.t.* **1** To draw off gradually, as a fluid; cause to run off. **2** To draw water or any fluid from: to *drain* a swamp. **3** To empty; drink completely. **4** To filter. **5** To exhaust; use up: to *drain* one's vitality; to *drain* a region of resources. — *v.i.* **6** To flow off or leak away gradually. **7** To become empty. — *n.* **1** The act of draining. **2** Continuous strain, leak, or outflow. **3** A pipe or trench for draining; a drainpipe. **4** *Surg.* An appliance to facilitate the discharge of matter from a wound. **5** *pl.* Draff. [OE *drēahnian* strain out] — **drain′er** *n.*

drain•age (drā′nij) *n.* **1** The act or means of draining; a system of drains. **2** That which is drained off; waste water. **3** The area drained; drainage basin. **4** *Surg.* The gradual drawing off of morbid fluids from deep-seated wounds or abscesses.

drainage basin A large surface area whose waters are drained off into a principal river system.

drain•pipe (drān′pīp′) *n.* Pipe used for draining.

drake[1] (drāk) *n.* **1** A male duck. **2** A flat stone used in the game of ducks and drakes. [Cf. dial. G *draak*]

drake[2] (drāk) *n.* **1** A mayfly, used as bait in angling: also **drake′fly′.** **2** A small brass cannon of the 17th and 18th centuries. **3** *Obs.* A dragon, or an ancient standard bearing a dragon for its emblem. [OE *draca* <L *draco.* See DRAGON.]

DRAKE (*def. 1*)

Drake (drāk), **Sir Francis,** 1540–96, English admiral and circumnavigator of the globe.

Dra•kens•berg (drä′kənz·bûrg) A mountain range in South Africa; highest peak, 11,425 feet: also *Quathlamba.*

Drake Passage (drāk) A strait joining the South Pacific and the South Atlantic between Cape Horn and the South Shetland Islands.

dram (dram) *n.* **1** An apothecaries' weight equal to 60 grains, 3.88 grams, or one eighth of an ounce. 2 An avoirdupois measure equal to 27.34 grains, 1.77 grams, or one sixteenth of an ounce. 3 A drachma. 4 A drink of spirits: a *dram* of whisky. 5 In pharmacy, a fluid dram. 6 A small portion; a bit. **—fluid dram** A measure of capacity equal to one eighth of an ounce, 60 minims, or 3.69 cubic centimeters. Also **fluid drachm**: sometimes spelled *fluidram, fluidrachm.* —*v.t.* & *v.i.* **drammed, dram·ming** To use intoxicants freely; to treat to liquor. [<OF *drame* <L *drachma.* Doublet of DRACHMA.]

dra·ma (drä'mə, dram'ə) *n.* 1 A literary composition that tells a story, usually representing human conflict by means of dialog and action to be performed upon the stage; a play. 2 Stage representations collectively; the art or profession of writing, acting, or producing plays; the institution of the theater: often with *the.* 3 A series of actions, events, or purposes, considered collectively as possessing dramatic quality. [<LL, a play <Gk., a deed, an action <*draein* act, do]

Dra·ma (drä'mə) A town in Macedonia, NE Greece. Ancient **Dra·bes·cus** (drä·bes'kəs).

Dram·a·mine (dram'ə·mēn) *n.* Proprietary name of a brand of dimenhydrinate.

dra·mat·ic (drə·mat'ik) *adj.* Of, connected with, or like the drama; especially, involving conflict. Compare LYRIC. Also **dra·mat'i·cal.** —**dra·mat'i·cal·ly** *adv.*

dra·mat·ics (drə·mat'iks) *n. pl.* 1 Dramatic performance, especially by amateurs: construed as plural. 2 The art of staging or acting plays: construed as singular or plural.

dram·a·tis per·so·nae (dram'ə·tis pər·sō'nē) *Latin* The characters of a play; also, a list of these.

dram·a·tist (dram'ə·tist) *n.* One who writes plays.

dram·a·ti·za·tion (dram'ə·tə·zā'shən, -tī·zā'-) *n.* 1 The act or process of dramatizing. 2 A dramatized version.

dram·a·tize (dram'ə·tīz) *v.t.* **·tized, ·tiz·ing** 1 To present in dramatic form; convert for stage use. 2 To tell, represent, or interpret (events, one's personality, etc.) in a theatrical manner. Also *Brit.* **dram'a·tise.**

dram·a·turge (dram'ə·tûrj) *n.* The author of a drama, especially one who also directs and oversees the performance of it; a playwright. Also **dram'a·tur'gist.** [<F <Gk. *dramatourgos* <*drama, -atos* a play + *ergein* work]

dram·a·tur·gic (dram'ə·tûr'jik) *adj.* Of or pertaining to dramaturgy; histrionic; befitting the stage. Also **dram'a·tur'gi·cal.**

dram·a·tur·gy (dram'ə·tûr'jē) *n.* The art of making dramas and placing them properly on the stage; dramatic composition and representation.

dram·shop (dram'shop') *n.* A saloon; bar.

Drang nach Ost·en (dräng näkh ôs'tən) *German* The policy of extending German political, cultural, and economic influence southeastward through the Balkans into the Near East; literally, drive to the east.

drank (drangk) Past tense of DRINK.

drant (dränt, drônt) *Scot.* & *Brit. Dial. v.t.* & *v.i.* To drawl or drone in speaking or singing; also, to spend time tediously. —*n.* A drawl. Also DRAUNT.

drap (drap) *v.* & *n. Scot.* Drop.

drape (drāp) *v.* **draped, drap·ing** *v.t.* 1 To cover or adorn in a graceful fashion, as with drapery or clothing. 2 To arrange (drapery, etc.) in graceful folds. —*v.i.* 3 To hang in folds. —*n.* 1 *Usually pl.* Drapery; curtain. 2 The way in which cloth hangs, as in clothing. [<F *draper* weave <*drap* cloth]

drap·er (drā'pər) *n.* 1 *Brit.* A dealer in cloth or dry goods. 2 Originally, a manufacturer of cloth.

Dra·per (drā'pər), **Henry,** 1837–82, U.S. astronomer. —**John William,** 1811–82, U.S. chemist, physiologist, and historian; born in England.

drap·er·y (drā'pər·ē) *n. pl.* **·er·ies** 1 Loosely hanging attire or its arrangement, especially on figures in art. 2 Hangings; curtains, tapestry, etc. 3 *Brit.* The business of a draper. 4 Cloth in general.

drap·pie (drap'ē) *n. Scot.* A little drop. Also **drap'py.**

dras·tic (dras'tik) *adj.* Acting vigorously; extreme; violently effective. —*n.* A powerful medicine; a strong purgative. [<Gk. *drastikos* effective <*draein* act, do] —**dras'ti·cal·ly** *adv.*

drat (drat) *interj.* An exclamation of anger or annoyance. —*v.t.* Confound; damn: *Drat* him! [Alter. of *God rot*] —**drat'ted** *adj.*

draught (draft, dräft), etc. See DRAFT, etc.

draught·board (draft'bôrd', -bōrd', dräft'-) A checkerboard.

draughts (drafts, dräfts) *n. pl. Brit.* The game of checkers: also spelled *drafts.* See CHECKERS.

draughts·man (drafts'mən, dräfts'-) *n. pl.* **·men** (-mən) 1 A piece in the game of draughts. 2 Draftsman.

draunt (dränt, drônt) See DRANT.

Dra·va (drä'vä) A river in south central Europe, flowing 450 miles SE to the Danube: *German* **Drau** (drou). Also **Dra've** (drä'və).

drave (drāv) Obsolete past tense of DRIVE.

Dra·vid·i·an (drə·vid'ē·ən) *n.* 1 One belonging to the most ancient indigenous race of southern India. 2 A non-Indo-European family of agglutinative languages spoken primarily in southern India and northern Ceylon, including Tamil, Malayalam, Kanarese, and Telugu. —*adj.* Of the Dravidians or their languages: also **Dra·vid'ic.**

draw (drô) *v.* **drew, drawn, draw·ing** *v.t.* 1 To cause to move to or with the mover by means of strength, force, etc.; pull; haul. 2 To acquire or obtain, as from a receptacle: to *draw* water. 3 To cause to flow forth: to *draw* blood or tears. 4 To cause to come forth; induce: to *draw* praise, laughter, criticism, etc. 5 To take or pull off, on, or out, as gloves or a sword: She *drew* off her gloves. 6 To get or receive; earn, as a salary or interest. 7 To take out; remove, as money from a bank. 8 To deduce; extract by mental process; formulate: to *draw* a conclusion or comparison. 9 To attract; allure: Honey *draws* flies. 10 To close, as against light; shut, as curtains, a bag, etc. 11 To elicit; bring out, as truth or information. 12 To stretch out; manufacture by stretching or hammering, as wire or dies. 13 To disembowel: to *draw* a chicken. 14 To take in; inhale, as breath. 15 To drain of contents, as a pond. 16 To win (a prize) in a lottery; to obtain, as by chance. 17 *Naut.* To require (a specified depth) to float: said of vessels. 18 To depict, as a sketch or diagram; to describe pictorially or verbally; delineate. 19 To write out; draft, as a check or deed: often with *up.* 20 In card games, **a** To ask for or take an additional card or cards. **b** To force (a card or cards) to be played: to *draw* trumps. 21 In billiards, to cause (the cue ball) to recoil after contact. 22 In cricket, to deflect (the ball) by a slight turn of the bat. 23 In curling, to play (the stone) gently. 24 To leave undecided, as a game or contest. —*v.i.* 25 To exert a pulling force. 26 To come or go: to *draw* near or away. 27 To exercise or exert an attracting influence. 28 To pull out or unsheathe a weapon. 29 To shrink; tauten; become contracted, as a wound. 30 To cause redness and irritation of the skin, as a poultice or blister. 31 To obtain money, supplies, etc., from some source. 32 To produce a current of air: The fire *draws* well. 33 To end a contest without decision; tie. 34 *Naut.* To fill or swell out with wind: The sails are *drawing* now. 35 In hunting, **a** To track game by scent. **b** To approach game slowly after pointing: said of hounds. —**to draw a blank** To be unsuccessful. —**to draw a** (or **the**) **long bow** To exaggerate. —**to draw and quarter** In medieval executions: **a** To disembowel and dismember after hanging. **b** To tie each of the victim's arms and legs to a different horse and whip the horses in different directions. —**to draw back** To recoil, as from an unfavorable situation. —**to draw fire** To be a target of attack. —**to draw first blood** 1 In dueling, to inflict the first wound. 2 To score first in any contest or competition. —**to draw on** 1 To rely upon or make requirements of: He *drew on* his reputation. 2 To lure or entice. 3 To approach its end: The evening is *drawing on.* —**to draw out** 1 To protract; prolong. 2 To cause (someone) to give information or express opinions. —**to draw the line** To fix the limit; refuse to go further. —**to draw up** 1 To put in required legal form, as a will or deed. 2 To overtake: He *drew up* with the leader. 3 To form in ranks; marshal, as troops. 4 To straighten (oneself); stiffen, as in anger or resentment. —*n.* 1 An act of drawing or state of being drawn; also, that which is drawn. 2 An indecisive contest; a tie game. 3 The movable section of a drawbridge. 4 Anything that draws; specifically, an exhibition that attracts a crowd. 5 A drawn chance or ticket, as in a lottery. 6 A quantity drawn. 7 The act of drawing a revolver or knife: quick on the *draw.* 8 In various card games, cards dealt or drawn after the discard. 9 A ravine or coulee. [OE *dragan*]

Synonyms (verb): allure, attract, drag, entice, haul, incline, induce, lead, lure, pull, tow, tug. One object *draws* another when it moves it toward itself or in the direction of its own motion by the exertion of adequate force, whether slight or powerful. To *attract* is to exert a force that tends to *draw,* while it may produce no actual motion; all objects are *attracted* toward the earth, but they may be sustained from falling. To *drag* is to *draw* against strong resistance; as, to *drag* a sled over bare ground, or a carriage up a steep hill. To *pull* is to exert a *drawing* force, whether adequate or inadequate; as, the fish *pulls* on the line; a dentist *pulls* a tooth. To *tug* is to *draw,* or try to *draw,* a resisting object with a continuous straining motion. To *haul* is to *draw* somewhat slowly a heavy object; as, to *haul* a seine; to *haul* logs. One vessel *tows* another. In the figurative sense, *attract* is more nearly akin to *incline, draw* to *induce.* We are *attracted* by one's appearance, *drawn* to his side. See ACTUATE, ALLURE, INFLUENCE. *Antonyms*: alienate, estrange, push, rebuff, reject, repel, repulse. See synonyms for DRIVE.

draw·back (drô'bak') *n.* 1 Anything that checks or hinders progress, success, prosperity, enjoyment, contentment, etc.; a disadvantage. 2 An allowance, consisting in a total or partial paying back, as of duties previously paid on imported articles on their being exported, or as of freight paid to a railway company; rebate.

draw·bar (drô'bär') *n.* A projecting bar or heavy beam beneath the body of a locomotive, railway car, or tractor, and used as a coupling.

draw·bore (drô'bôr', -bōr') *n.* In carpentry, a hole passing through a tenon and the cheeks of its mortise, to enable the former to be drawn up to its shoulder by driving in a pin (called a **drawbore pin**).

draw·bridge (drô'brij') *n.* A bridge of which the whole or a part may be raised, let down, or drawn aside.

DRAWBRIDGE

draw·ee (drô'ē') *n.* One on whom an order for the payment of money is drawn.

draw·er (drô'ər) *n.* 1 One who draws. 2 One who draws a bill of exchange, money order, etc. 3 (drôr) A sliding receptacle, as in a bureau, table, etc. 4 A draftsman. 5 *Archaic* A tapster.

draw·ers (drôrz) *n. pl.* A trouserlike undergarment.

draw·ing (drô'ing) *n.* 1 The act of one who or that which draws. 2 A picture, sketch, delineation, or design. 3 The art of representing objects by lines; delineation. 4 *pl. Brit.* The receipts of sales in a shop or other establishment. 5 A small quantity of tea for steeping. See synonyms under PICTURE, SKETCH.

drawing account An account, by a business firm, which shows the payments to a partner, employee, or salesman advanced against his expected income, salary or commission.

drawing board A smooth, flat board to which paper or canvas is attached for drawing.

draw·ing-card (drô'ing·kärd') *n.* Any feature that attracts a crowd.

draw·ing-room (drô'ing·ro͞om', -ro͝om') *n.* 1 A room for reception of company. 2 A reception held or the company assembled in such a room. **3** *Brit.* A court reception. **4** *U.S.* A small private room in a sleeping-car on a train. [Short for WITHDRAWING ROOM]

draw·knife (drô′nīf′) *n. pl.* **·knives** (-nīvz′) A knife with a handle at each end, used for cutting with a drawing motion. Also **draw′·ing-knife′.**

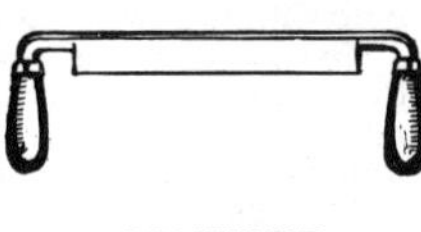

DRAWKNIFE

drawl (drôl) *v.t.* & *v.i.* To speak or pronounce slowly; to lengthen speech sounds, especially vowels. — *n.* The act of drawling; the attenuation of sounds giving an impression of slowness of speech: said of the patterns of speech in part of the southern United States. [Cf. Du. *dralen* loiter] — **drawl′er** *n.* — **drawl′ing·ly** *adv.* — **drawl′y** *adj.*

drawn (drôn) *adj.* **1** Equally contested; undecided, as a game. **2** Eviscerated: a *drawn* fowl. **3** Having all iron removed by magnets: said of brass filings. **4** Subjected to a process of elongation: hard-*drawn* wire. **5** Haggard: His face looked *drawn.*

drawn butter Butter melted and prepared as a sauce.

drawn work Ornamental openwork made by pulling out threads of fabric and embroidering or hemstitching the edges of the openings thus made. For illustration see HEMSTITCH.

draw·plate (drô′plāt′) *n.* **1** The plate on a locomotive to which the drawbar is attached. **2** *Mech.* A hard plate with holes of successively diminishing diameters for drawing out metal rods or wire.

draw·shave (drô′shāv′) *n.* A drawknife.

draw·string (drô′string′) *n.* A string, ribbon, or cord run through a casing or hem, which pulls together, contracts the size of, or closes an opening. Also **drawing string.**

draw·tube (drô′to͞ob′, -tyo͞ob′) *n. Optics* The tube, consisting of two sliding parts, containing the lenses of a microscope.

dray (drā) *n.* **1** A strong, heavy vehicle, usually low for convenience in loading heavy articles. **2** A rude sledge. — *v.t.* To transport by means of a dray. [Cf. OE *dræge* dragnet < *dragan* draw]

dray·age (drā′ij) *n.* **1** The act of conveying in a dray. **2** The charge for draying.

dray horse A horse for drawing a dray; a cart horse.

dray·man (drā′mən) *n. pl.* **·men** (-mən) A man who drives a dray.

Dray·ton (drā′tən), **Michael,** 1563–1631, English poet.

dread (dred) *v.t.* & *v.i.* **1** To anticipate with great fear or anxiety. **2** *Obs.* To be in awe (of). — *adj.* **1** Causing great fear; terrible. **2** Exciting awe or reverential fear. See synonyms under AWFUL. — *n.* **1** Unconquerable fright; shrinking horror; terrifying anticipation. **2** Fear joined to deep respect; awe. See synonyms under ALARM, ANXIETY, FEAR, FRIGHT, VENERATION. [ME *dreden* <OE *andrædan* < *and* against + *drædan* fear] — **dread′less** *adj.*

dread·ful (dred′fəl) *adj.* **1** Inspiring dread or awe; terrible. **2** Awful. See synonyms under AWFUL, FRIGHTFUL. — *n.* A sensational novelette, or a periodical that prints melodramatic stories: a penny *dreadful.* Compare DIME NOVEL. — **dread′ful·ly** *adv.* — **dread′ful·ness** *n.*

dread·nought (dred′nôt′) *n.* **1** One of a class of heavily armed battleships formerly used in the British navy, typified by the *Dreadnought,* of 17,900 tons and carrying an armament of 10 12-inch guns and 24 quick-firing guns. **2** Any battleship of great size carrying large-caliber guns. **3** A heavy cloth or a garment made of it. **4** One who fears nothing. Also **dread′naught′.**

dream (drēm) *n.* **1** A train of thoughts or images passing through the mind in sleep. **2** A mental condition similar to that of one sleeping; abstracted imagining; daydreaming. **3** A visionary idea, anticipation, or fancy; also, anything real having a dreamlike quality. **4** *Psychoanal.* A medium for the expression during sleep of various aspects of the ego and superego typically withdrawn from consciousness but, when recorded and analyzed, having some value in the diagnosis, interpretation, and treatment of certain maladjustments of the personality. — *v.* **dreamed** or **dreamt** (dremt), **dream·ing** *v.t.* **1** To see or imagine in a dream. **2** To imagine or envision as in a dream. **3** To while away, as in idle reverie. — *v.i.* **4** To have a dream or dreams. **5** To have a vague idea or conception of something. — **to dream up** *Colloq.* To concoct or create, especially by artistic invention or unbridled fancy. See synonyms under MUSE. [OE *drēam;* infl. in meaning by ON *draum* a dream] — **dream′ful** *adj.* — **dream′ful·ly** *adv.* — **dream′·less** *adj.* — **dream′less·ly** *adv.*

Synonyms (noun): daydream, fancy, fantasy, hallucination, illusion, reverie, romance, trance, vision. A *dream* is strictly a train of thoughts, fantasies, and images passing through the mind during sleep; a *vision* may occur when one is awake and in clear exercise of the senses and mental powers; *vision* is often applied to something seen by the mind through supernatural agency, whether in sleep or wakefulness, conceived as more real and authoritative than a *dream*; a *trance* is an abnormal state, which is different from normal sleep or wakefulness. A *reverie* is a purposeless drifting of the mind when awake, under the influence of mental images; a *daydream* that which passes before the mind in such condition. A *fancy* is some image presented to the mind, often in the fullest exercise of its powers. *Hallucination* is the seeming perception of non-existent objects, as in insanity or delirium. In the figurative sense, we speak of *dreams* of fortune, *visions* of glory, with little difference of meaning except that the *vision* is thought of as fuller and more vivid. We speak of a *trance* of delight when the emotion almost sweeps one away from the normal exercise of the faculties. Compare DELUSION. *Antonyms*: certainty, fact, reality, realization, substance, verity.

dream·er (drē′mər) *n.* **1** One who dreams. **2** A visionary.

dream·ing (drē′ming) *n. Austral.* An aboriginal totemic site; also, a totem.

dream·land (drēm′land′) *n.* The realm of dreams.

dream·time (drēm′tīm′) *n. Austral.* The aboriginal concept of Creation; the beginning.

dream world A world of illusions.

dream·y (drē′mē) *adj.* **dream·i·er, dream·i·est** **1** Of, causing, pertaining to, or given to dreams. **2** Appropriate to dreams; shadowy; vague; also, soothing; soft. **3** Filled with dreams; visionary. See synonyms under IMAGINARY, ROMANTIC, VAIN. — **dream′i·ly** *adv.* — **dream′i·ness** *n.*

drear (drir) *adj. Poetic* Dreary.

drear·y (drir′ē) *adj.* **drear·i·er, drear·i·est** **1** Causing or manifesting sadness, loneliness, or gloom; dismal. **2** Causing or showing weariness; monotonous; lifeless; dull. **3** Sorrowful. See synonyms under BLEAK[1], SAD, TEDIOUS. [OE *drēorig* sad, bloody < *drēor* gore] — **drear′i·ly** *adv.* — **drear′i·ness** *n.* — **drear′i·some** *adj.*

dredge[1] (drej) *n.* An appliance for bringing up mud, silt, etc., from under water; a dredging machine. — *v.* **dredged, dredg·ing** *v.t.* **1** To clear or widen by means of a dredge. **2** To remove, catch, or gather by a dredge. — *v.i.* **3** To use a dredge. [ME *dreg.* Akin to DRAW.]

FLOATING DREDGE

dredge[2] (drej) *v.t.* **1** To sprinkle or dust with flour before cooking. **2** To sift; sprinkle. [< earlier *dragie* a sweetmeat <OF ? ult. <Gk. *tragema, -atos* a condiment]

dredg·er[1] (drej′ər) *n.* **1** One who dredges. **2** A dredging machine. **3** A boat engaged in dredging.

dredg·er[2] (drej′ər) *n.* In cookery, a box with a perforated lid used for sprinkling flour, etc.: also called **dredging box.**

dredg·ing (drej′ing) *n.* **1** The act of using a dredge. **2** That which is dredged.

dree (drē) *v.t.* & *v.i. Scot.* To suffer; endure: also spelled *driech.* — **to dree one's weird** *Scot* To endure one's fate.

dreel (drēl) *v.t. Scot.* To drill.

dreep (drēp) *v.i. Brit. Dial.* **1** To drip. **2** To droop; lose heart or courage. Also **drepe.** [Var. of DRIP]

dreg·gy (dreg′ē) *adj.* **·gi·er, ·gi·est** Containing dregs; full of dregs; foul. — **dreg′gi·ness** *n.* — **dreg′gish** *adj.*

dregs (dregz) *n. pl.* **1** The sediment of liquids, especially of beverages. **2** Worthless residuum; the coarse part: the *dregs* of society. **3** *sing.* The remaining part; residuum. See synonyms under WASTE. [<ON *dreggjar*]

Drei·bund (drī′bo͝ont) *n.* A triple alliance; specifically, that of Germany, Austria-Hungary, and Italy (1882–1915). [<G < *drei* three + *bund* alliance]

Drei·ser (drī′sər, -zər), **Theodore,** 1871–1945, U. S. novelist.

drench (drench) *v.t.* **1** To wet thoroughly; soak. **2** In veterinary medicine, to administer a potion to; force to swallow a draft. — *n.* **1** A liquid medicine, administered by compulsion, as to a horse. **2** A large draft or quantity of fluid. **3** A water solution for drenching. **4** The act of drenching; also, that which drenches. [OE *drencan* cause to drink] — **drench′er** *n.*

Drep·a·num (drep′ə·nəm) The ancient name for TRAPANI.

Dres·den (drez′dən, *Ger.* drās′dən) *n.* A fine china made in Dresden, Germany.

Dres·den (drez′dən, *Ger.* drās′dən) The capital of Saxony, east central Germany, on the Elbe.

dress (dres) *v.* **dressed** or **drest, dress·ing** *v.t.* **1** To clothe; supply with clothing. **2** To trim or decorate; adorn, as a Christmas tree or a store window. **3** To treat medicinally, as a wound or sore. **4** To comb and arrange (hair). **5** To curry (a horse). **6** To prepare (stone, timber, fabrics, etc.) for use or sale. **7** To clean (fowl, game, fish, etc.) for cooking. **8** To till, trim, or prune. **9** To put in proper alinement, as troops. **10** *Colloq.* To scold; reprove severely: usually with *down.* — *v.i.* **11** To put on or wear clothing, especially formal clothing. **12** To come into proper alinement. — **to dress ship** To display the national colors, all signal flags, and bunting, as in honor of an individual or event. — **to dress up** To put on or wear formal attire or clothing more elaborate than usually worn. — *n.* **1** Covering for the body; clothes collectively; especially, elegant or fashionable attire. **2** The art of dressing correctly. **3** A gown or frock of a woman or child. **4** Full dress as opposed to business attire, etc. **5** External appearance; guise. **6** Dressing or size, as of leather. — *adj.* **1** Of, pertaining to, or suitable for making dresses: *dress* goods. **2** To be worn on formal occasions: a *dress* suit, *dress* uniform. [<OF *dresser,* ult. <L *directus.* See DIRECT.]

Synonyms (noun): apparel, array, attire, clothes, clothing, costume, garb, garments, habiliments, habit, raiment, robes, uniform, vestments, vesture. *Clothing* denotes the entire covering of the body, taken as a whole; *clothes* and *garments* view it as composed of separate parts. *Clothes, clothing,* and *garments* may be used of inner or outer covering; all the other words in the list (with possible rare exceptions in the case of *raiment*) refer to the outer *garments. Array, raiment,* and *vesture* are archaic or poetic; so, too, is *habit,* except in technical use to denote a lady's riding *dress.* The word *vestments* is now rare, except in ecclesiastical use. *Apparel* and *attire* are most frequently used of somewhat complete and elegant outer *clothing. Dress* may be used, specifically, for a woman's gown, and in that sense may be either rich or shabby; but in the general sense it denotes outer *clothing* which is meant to be elegant, complete, and appropriate to some social or public occasion; as, full *dress,* court *dress,* evening *dress,* etc. *Dress* has now largely displaced *apparel* and *attire. Garb* denotes the *clothing* characteristic of some class, profession, or the like; as, the *garb* of a priest. *Costume* is chiefly used for that which befits an assumed character; as, a theatrical *costume*; we sometimes speak of a national *costume,* etc. See HABIT. *Antonyms*: bareness, disarray, dishabille, exposure, nakedness, nudity, undress.

dres·sage (dres′ij, *Fr.* dre·säzh′) *n.* **1** In equitation, the act of guiding a mount through a set of paces or maneuvers by imperceptible movements on the part of the rider, usually for exhibition purposes. **2** The technique of training a horse to respond to such movements.

dress circle A section of seats in a theater or concert hall, usually comprising the first gallery behind and above the orchestra: so called because originally reserved for patrons in evening dress.

dress coat The coat of a man's dress suit.

dressed (drest) *adj.* **1** Prepared, as animal skins, for use; tanned, dyed, softened, etc. **2** Prepared for use, as lumber or stone. **3** Prepared for cooking, as fowl. **4** Clothed; especially, wearing formal dress.

dress·er[1] (dres′ər) *n.* **1** One who dresses something, as shop windows, leather, etc. **2** One who assists another to dress. **3** One who dresses well or in a particular way: a fancy *dresser.* **4** *Brit.* A surgical assistant assigned to dress and bandage wounds.

dress·er[2] (dres′ər) *n.* **1** A chest of drawers supporting a swinging mirror, useful in a dressing-room. **2** A cupboard for dishes. **3** *Obs.* A table on which meat is dressed. [OF *dresseur* < *dresser* dress]

dress goods Fabrics for dresses.

dress·ing (dres′ing) *n.* **1** The act of dressing. **2** That with which anything, as a wound, is dressed. **3** A seasoned sauce served with salads and vegetables; also, a stuffing for fowl or meats. **4** *pl. Archit.* Moldings around the wall openings in a brick building. **5** The mechanical preparation of ore for smelting. **6** *Colloq.* A beating or scolding. **7** The preparation for use of skins, lumber, stone, etc. **8** Fertilizer.

dress·ing-down (dres′ing·doun′) *n. U.S. Colloq.* **1** A reprimand. **2** A beating.

dressing gown A loose gown worn while dressing or in undress.

dress·ing-room (dres′ing·ro͞om′, -ro͝om′) *n.* A room used for dressing, as backstage in a theater.

dressing station *Mil.* A medical field station for giving immediate aid to the wounded.

dress·ing-ta·ble (dres′ing·tā′bəl) *n.* A small table equipped with a mirror and used in making one's toilet; a vanity.

dress·mak·er (dres′mā′kər) *n.* One who makes women's dresses, etc. —*adj.* Not severely tailored, but having soft, dressy, or feminine lines: a *dressmaker* suit.

dress parade A formal military parade in dress uniform.

dress rehearsal The last rehearsal of a play before the public performance, in full costume and using all properties.

dress shield A crescent-shaped piece of fabric with waterproof lining, worn to protect clothes from underarm perspiration.

dress suit A man's suit, usually black, for formal evening wear, characterized by a low-cut vest and an open coat with long, wide lapels, cut to the hips in front, curving into a bifurcated tail, extending almost to the knee: also called *full-dress suit.*

dress·y (dres′ē) *adj.* **dress·i·er, dress·i·est** *Colloq.* **1** Fond of dress. **2** Showy; elegant. —**dress′i·ness** *n.*

drew (dro͞o) Past tense of DRAW.

Drew (dro͞o), **John,** 1853–1927, U.S. actor.

Drex·el (drek′səl), **Anthony Joseph,** 1826–1893, U.S. banker and philanthropist.

Drey·fus (drā′fəs, drī′-; *Fr.* dre·füs′), **Alfred,** 1859–1935, French army officer falsely accused and convicted of treason, 1894 and 1899; his innocence was fully established on retrial in 1906.

drib (drib) *v.t.* **dribbed, drib·bing** *Obs.* **1** To let fall in drops. **2** To do or say (something) little by little. [Var. of DRIP]

drib·ble (drib′əl) *v.t.* & *v.i.* **·bled, ·bling** **1** To fall or let fall in drops; drip. **2** To drool; drivel. **3** In basketball, to propel (the ball) by bouncing with the hands. **4** In soccer, to propel (the ball) by successive pushes or kicks with the feet. —*n.* **1** A small quantity of a liquid falling in drops or flowing in a scanty and broken stream. **2** *Scot.* Showery or drizzly weather. **3** In basketball and soccer, the act of dribbling. [Freq. of DRIB] —**drib′·bler** *n.*

drib·let (drib′lit) *n.* **1** A small piece, part, or sum. **2** A drop or clot formed as if by dribbling: money paid in *driblets.* Also **drib′·blet.**

drid·dle (drid′l) *v.i. Scot.* To waste time and strength to no purpose; dawdle; loiter.

driech (drēkh) See DREE.

dried (drīd) Past tense and past participle of DRY.

dri·er (drī′ər) *n.* **1** One who or that which dries. **2** A substance added to paint, etc., to make it dry more quickly. **3** A mechanical device for drying: also spelled *dryer.*

dri·er (drī′ər), **dri·est** (drī′ist) Comparative and superlative of DRY.

Driesch (drēsh), **Hans Adolf Eduard,** 1867–1941, German biologist.

drift (drift) *n.* **1** That which is driven or carried onward by a current: a *drift* of clouds across the sky. **2** A heap of any matter piled up by wind or sea. **3** A course along which or an end toward which anything moves on; tendency; meaning: the *drift* of a discourse. **4** A driving; an urgent force; hence, controlling power or influence. **5** A number of objects moving onward by one force; especially, anything floating or moving with the current of a river or stream, as logs, trees, etc.; driftwood. **6** A ford. **7** The fact or condition of being driven; the action of drifting. **8** A boring tool. **9** *Geol.* Material which has been transported by moving masses of ice or by running water created by glaciers, and deposited over portions of the earth's surface. **10** *Mining* A horizontal or nearly horizontal passage in a mine; also, the direction of a passage or gallery. **11** The direction of a current. **12** *Naut.* Leeway; the distance which a vessel is driven from her direct course by wind or sea or other causes. **13** A fishing net that drifts with the tide; a drift net. **14** *Aeron.* The angular difference between the long axis of an aircraft and the line of its flight path: also **drift angle.** **15** The movement of a herd of cattle, as before a storm. See synonyms under HEAP, INCLINATION, PURPOSE, STREAM. —*v.t.* **1** To carry along, as on a current. **2** To cause to pile up in heaps, as snow or sand. —*v.i.* **3** To float or be carried along, as by a current. **4** To wander. **5** To accumulate in heaps. [ME <OE *drīfan* drive]

drift·age (drif′tij) *n.* **1** The operation or process of drifting. **2** Anything carried by currents of wind or sea.

drift anchor A sea anchor.

drift·bolt (drift′bōlt′) *n.* A drivebolt.

drift·er (drif′tər) *n.* **1** One who or that which drifts. **2** A fishing boat used for fishing with drift nets. **3** *Colloq.* A person having no settled home or occupation.

drift fence A fence to halt the drifting of cattle.

drift-me·ter (drift′mē′tər) *n. Aeron.* An instrument for measuring the drift of an aircraft and also for taking bearings from ground objects. Also **drift′-in′di·ca′tor** (-in′də·kā′tər).

drift sail *Naut.* A drag sail.

drift tube *Electronics* A cylindrical enclosure forming part of a klystron in which electrons or other charged particles are maintained at a constant potential and velocity.

drift·wood (drift′wo͝od′) *n.* Wood floated or drifted by water, especially that cast ashore by the sea.

drift·y (drif′tē) *adj.* Forming or full of drifts; drifting.

drill[1] (dril) *n.* **1** A boring tool for metal or other hard substance. **2** The art or action of training in military exercises; hence, thorough and regular discipline in any branch of knowledge, activity, or industry. See synonyms under PRACTICE. **3** *Zool.* A mollusk (*Urosalpinx cinereus*) which kills oysters by drilling holes in their shells. —*v.t.* **1** To pierce or bore with or as with a drill. **2** To bore (a hole). **3** To train in military exercises. **4** To instruct by methodical exercises. **5** To impart by methodical exercises: He *drilled* the lessons into his students. —*v.i.* **6** To use a drill. **7** To engage in military exercises. **8** To engage in methodical exercises. See synonyms under PIERCE, TEACH. [<Du. *dril, drille* < *drillen* bore]

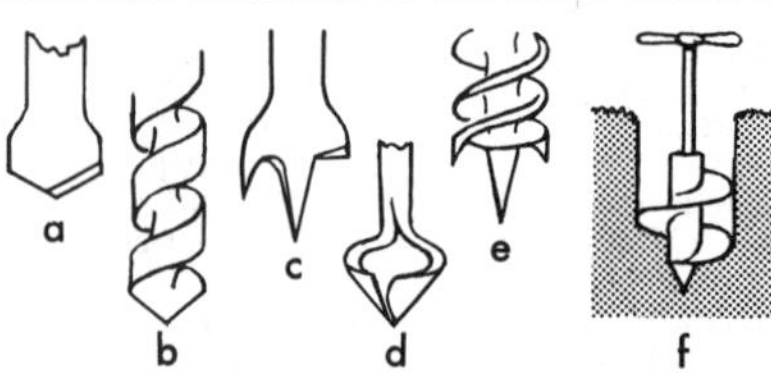

DRILLS

a. V-drill (metal). *b.* Twist drill (metal). *c.* Center bit (wood). *d.* Countersink (wood or metal). *e.* Twist bit (wood). *f.* Earth borer.

drill[2] (dril) *Agric. n.* **1** A machine for planting seeds in rows. **2** A small furrow in which seeds are sown. **3** A row of seeds so planted. —*v.t.* To plant in rows: to *drill* a field; to *drill* seeds. —*v.i.* To sow or plant in drills. [Origin uncertain]

drill[3] (dril) *n.* Heavy, twilled linen or cotton cloth. Also **drill′ing.** [Short for *drilling* <G *drilich* cloth with three threads <L *trilix* < *tres* three + *licium* thread]

drill[4] (dril) *n.* A black-faced baboon of West Africa (genus *Papio*), similar to the mandrill. For illustration see MANDRILL. [? < native name]

drill·er (dril′ər) *n.* **1** One who or that which drills. **2** A drilling machine.

drill·ing (dril′ing) *n.* **1** Material excavated by a drill. **2** The act of one who drills; the act of using a drill.

drill·mas·ter (dril′mas′tər, -mäs′tər) *n.* A trainer in military or gymnastic exercises.

drill·press (dril′pres′) *n.* An upright drilling machine for working in metal.

drill·stock (dril′stok′) *n.* A holder for a drill. See DRILL[1] (def. 1).

dri·ly (drī′lē) See DRYLY.

Drin (drēn) A river in Albania, flowing 65 miles west into the Adriatic: ancient **Dri·lo** (drī′lō). *Albanian* **Dri·ni** (drē′nē).

Dri·na (drē′nä) A river in east Bosnia, Yugoslavia, flowing 285 miles north to the Sava.

drink (dringk) *v.* **drank** (*Obs.* **drunk**), **drunk** (*Obs.* **drunk·en**), **drink·ing** *v.t.* **1** To take into the mouth and swallow, as water. **2** To soak up or absorb (a liquid or moisture). **3** To take in eagerly through the senses or the mind: often with *in.* **4** To drink the health of; toast. **5** To swallow the contents of. —*v.i.* **6** To swallow a liquid. **7** To drink alcoholic liquors, especially to excess or habitually; tope. **8** To drink a toast: with *to.* —*n.* **1** Any liquid that is or may be swallowed; a beverage. **2** Alcoholic liquor. **3** The practice of drinking to excess. **4** As much as is or may be taken at one time; a draft. —**in drink** Overcome by liquor. [OE *drincan*]

drink·a·ble (dringk′ə·bəl) *adj.* Capable of or suitable for use as a drink; potable. —*n.* *Usually pl.* A beverage.

drink·er (dringk′ər) *n.* **1** One who drinks. **2** One who drinks alcoholic liquors habitually.

Drinker respirator An iron lung. [after Philip *Drinker,* born 1894, U.S. Public Health engineer]

Drink·wa·ter (dringk′wô′tər, -wot′ər), **John,** 1882–1937, English poet and playwright.

drip (drip) *n.* **1** A falling, or letting fall, in drops. **2** Dripping; that which drips. **3** *Archit.* A projecting molding over an opening for a window or a door. **4** Condensed moisture, as in gas pipes. **5** *U.S. Slang* A person regarded as socially inept. —*v.t.* & *v.i.* **dripped, drip·ping** To fall or let fall in drops. [OE *dryppan*]

drip coffee Coffee made by letting boiling water seep slowly through a strainer containing finely ground coffee beans.

drip-dry (drip′drī′) *adj.* Designating or pertaining to a garment or fabric that is treated to dry quickly after being hung while dripping wet, to retain its shape, and to require little or no ironing. —*v.i.* **-dried, -dry·ing** To dry after being hung while dripping wet: said especially of drip-dry garments or fabrics.

drip·ping (drip′ing) *n.* **1** That which falls in drops. **2** *Usually pl.* Fat exuded from meat in cooking. **3** The act of falling in drops; also, the sound so produced.

dripping pan A pan for receiving drippings or holding meat in roasting.

drip·stone (drip′stōn′) *n. Archit.* A label or projecting molding over a window or door.

drive (drīv) *v.* **drove, driv·en, driv·ing** *v.t.* **1** To push or propel onward with force; urge or press forward; impel. **2** To force to act or work; urge on by or as by coercion: He *drives* his workers too hard. **3** To bring to a state or condition as if by coercion: Failure *drove* him to despair. **4** To cause to penetrate or pass through: often with *in*: to *drive* in a nail. **5** To form by penetrating or passing through: to *drive* a well. **6** To control the movements or direction of: to *drive* an automobile. **7** To transport in a vehicle. **8** To carry on or complete (trade, a bargain, etc.) with energy. **9** In sports, to strike and propel (a ball) with force. **10** *Mech.* To provide power for: The wind *drives* the generator. **11** In hunting, **a** To chase (game) from cover or into traps, nets, etc. **b** To search (an area) in such a manner. **12** *Mining* To excavate (a tunnel) horizontally. — *v.i.* **13** To move forward or onward rapidly or with force: The ship *drove* before the wind. **14** To operate or travel in a vehicle: We all *drove* together into town. **15** To have an object or intention: with *at*: What are you *driving* at? **16** To aim a blow: with *at*. — **to drive home 1** To force in all the way, as a nail. **2** To make clear or evident; complete. — **to let drive at** To aim or discharge a shot, blow, missile, etc. — *n.* **1** The act of driving. **2** A road for driving; also, an approach for vehicles to a private house or other building. **3** A journey or excursion in an automobile or other vehicle. **4** Urgent pressure, as of business. **5** A hunt by driving; a drove or drift, as of cattle; a round-up; also, any objects driven, collectively. **6** A special sale at reduced price. **7** *Mil.* An advance of troops in mass against an enemy so as to break through defenses and drive back the defenders. **8** In golf, a stroke from the tee made with a wooden club; the distance traveled by the ball. **9** In certain games, as baseball, cricket, croquet, etc., the act of driving the ball, or the stroke by which the ball is driven; also, the flight of the ball. **10** *Mining* A driven tunnel. **11** *Mech.* A driving gear; a means of transmitting power, as from the motor of an automobile to the wheels. **12** Energy; vitality; also, aggressiveness. **13** Logs felled in the winter to be floated downstream in the spring. **14** The mass of logs floating down a river or stream. **15** An organized money-raising campaign: a Red Cross *drive*. See synonyms under WAY. [OE *drīfan*]

Synonyms (verb): compel, impel, propel, push, repel, repulse, resist, ride, thrust. To *drive* is to move an object with some force or violence before or away from oneself; it is the direct reverse of *draw, lead*, etc. A man leads a horse by the halter, *drives* him with whip and rein. One may be *driven* to a thing or from it; hence, *drive* is a synonym equally for *compel* or for *repel* or *repulse*. *Repulse* is stronger and more conclusive than *repel*; one may be *repelled* by the very aspect of the person whose favor he seeks, but is not *repulsed* except by the direct refusal or ignoring of his suit. It is common to speak of *driving* in a car, *riding* upon a horse; though many good authorities use *ride* in the older and broader sense as signifying to be supported and borne along by any means of conveyance. Compare ACTUATE, BANISH, COMPEL, INFLUENCE, PUSH. *Antonyms*: see synonyms for DRAW.

drive·bolt (drīv′bōlt′) *n.* **1** A tool for driving bolts home. **2** A bolt used to drive out another bolt: also called *driftbolt*.

drive-in (drīv′in′) *n.* A restaurant, shop, motion-picture theater, etc., serving patrons seated in their automobiles. — *adj.* So constructed as to allow service to the occupants of automobiles.

driv·el (driv′əl) *v.* **driv·eled** or **driv·elled, driv·el·ing** or **driv·el·ling** *v.i.* **1** To let saliva flow from the mouth; slobber. **2** To flow like saliva. **3** To talk or act in a foolish or stupid manner. — *v.t.* **4** To let flow from the mouth. **5** To say in a foolish manner. — *n.* **1** An involuntary flow of saliva from the mouth. **2** Senseless talk; twaddle. [OE *dreflian*] — **driv′el·er** or **driv′el·ler** *n.*

driv·en (driv′ən) Past participle of DRIVE.

driven well A well made by driving a pipe into the ground until the perforated tip reaches a stratum where water is found. Compare illustration under ARTESIAN WELL. Also **drive·well** (drīv′wel′).

driv·er (drī′vər) *n.* **1** One who or that which drives; a coachman; locomotive engineer; the operator of any motor vehicle. **2** *Mech.* Any of various machine parts which communicate motion; especially, the driving wheel of a locomotive; also, in power transmission, any wheel which moves another, as distinguished from the follower; a driving wheel. See illustration under ECCENTRIC. **3** *Naut.* A four-cornered fore-and-aft sail; a spanker. **4** A wooden-headed golf club with full-length shaft, somewhat supple, for driving the greatest distances from the tee. See illustration under GOLF CLUB. **5** The overseer of a group of laborers. **6** One who works on a log drive. **7** A carriage horse.

Dri·ver (drī′vər), **Samuel Rolles,** 1846–1914, English Hebraic and Biblical scholar and critic.

driver ant Any of a subfamily *(Dorylinae)* of carnivorous, stinging ants of tropical Africa and South America (genera *Dorylus* and *Eciton*), which live in temporary nests and raid the countryside in huge armies: also called *legionary ant, doryline ant.*

drive shaft *Mech.* A shaft for transmitting power from an engine to the working parts of machinery, especially one connecting the transmission with the rear axle of an automobile.

drive train A mechanical system for transmitting motion from the source of power to its point of application, as the engine, transmission, drive shaft, differential gearing, axles, and driving wheels of an automobile: also called *power train.*

drive·way (drīv′wā′) *n.* **1** A private road providing access to a building or house. **2** A road.

driv·ing (drī′ving) *adj.* **1** Transmitting power: a *driving* wheel. **2** Active and energetic: a *driving* personality.

driving wheel 1 One of the large wheels of a locomotive which converts the energy of steam into motion. **2** Any wheel used to communicate motion to any part of a machine.

driz·zle (driz′əl) *v.t.* & *v.i.* **·zled, ·zling** To rain steadily in fine drops. — *n.* A light rain. [? Freq. of ME *dresen*, OE *drēosan* fall] — **driz′zly** *adj.*

drod·dum (drod′əm) *n. Scot.* The breech.

dro·ger (drō′gər) *n.* **1** A small, West Indian coasting vessel, with long masts and lateen sails. **2** Any clumsy coasting vessel. [<MF *drogueur* <MDu. *drogher* < *droogen* dry; orig. a ship which caught and dried fish]

Dro·ghe·da (drô′ə·də, dro′hē·də) A port on the Boyne river, county town of County Louth, Ireland; Cromwell massacred its inhabitants in 1649.

Dro·go·byez (drô′gə·bich) A city in SE Poland. *Polish* **Dro·ho′bycz** (drô·hō′bēch).

drogue (drōg) *n.* **1** *Naut.* A floating anchor, usually made of spars and strong canvas, dragged from the stern to reduce yawing. **2** The drag attached to the end of a harpoon line. **3** *Meteorol.* A tapered fabric bag, open at both ends, to show the direction of the wind: also called *windsock*. **4** *Aeron.* A parachute or similar device used to slow down or stabilize an aircraft in flight. [? Related to DRAG]

droit (droit, *Fr.* drwȧ) *n.* **1** A legal right or claim of ownership, as distinguished from possession; also, that to which one has a legal claim. **2** Right in general; law; justice; equity. **3** *pl.* Customs duties. [<F, a right <LL *directum* <L *dirigere* set straight]

droit des gens (drwȧ dā zhäṅ′) *French* Law of nations; international law.

droits of Admiralty (droits) Rights to the property of an enemy, once belonging to the office of admiral of England. These droits now go into the public treasury.

droit·u·ral (droi′chər·əl) *adj.* Relating to a right of ownership as distinguished from possession.

droll (drōl) *adj.* Facetiously or humorously odd; comical; ludicrous; funny; queer. See synonyms under HUMOROUS, JOCOSE, ODD, QUEER, RIDICULOUS. — *n.* **1** A jester; a funny fellow. **2** A farce. **3** A comical tale. — *v.i.* To jest; play the jester. [<MF *drôle* a jester] — **drol′ly** *adv.*

droll·er·y (drō′lər·ē) *n. pl.* **·er·ies 1** Comical speech or manners; buffoonery; oddity. **2** The quality of being droll; facetiousness; humor. **3** A jest; a facetious or amusing story. **4** *Obs.* A comic picture, drawing, performance, or exhibition. See synonyms under WIT[1].

Drôme (drōm) A river in SE France, flowing 63 miles NW to the Rhône.

-drome *combining form* Racecourse; place for running: *hippodrome*. [<Gk. *dromos* a running]

drom·e·dar·y (drom′ə·der′ē) *n. pl.* **·dar·ies 1** The swift, one-humped Arabian camel *(Camelus dromedarius)* trained for riding. For illustration see CAMEL. [<OF *dromedaire* <LL *dromedarius* <L *dromas* <Gk., a running]

dro·mo·ma·ni·a (drō′mə·mā′nē·ə, mān′yə, drom′ə-) *n. Psychiatry* An abnormal desire to travel: also called *periomania.* [<Gk. *dromos* a running + -MANIA]

drom·on (drom′ən, drum′-) *n.* A swift medieval warship propelled by both oars and sails. Also **drom·ond** (drom′ənd, drum′-). [<AF *dromund*, OF *dromon* <LL *dromon* <LGk. *dromōn* < *dromos* a running]

dro·mo·pho·bi·a (drō′mə·fō′bē·ə, -fōb′yə, drom′ə-) *n. Psychiatry* A morbid fear of crossing streets. [<Gk. *dromos* a running + -PHOBIA] — **dro′mo·pho′bic** *adj.*

dro·mos (drō′məs) *n. pl.* **dro·moi** (-moi) **1** In ancient Greece and Rome, a racecourse. **2** An entrance passage or avenue, as the walled passages leading to the tombs at Mycenae. [<Gk., a running]

-dromous *combining form* Running: *catadromous*. [<-DROME + -OUS]

drone[1] (drōn) *v.* **droned, dron·ing** *v.i.* **1** To make a dull, monotonous, humming sound; hum. **2** To speak in a slow, dull, tone. — *v.t.* **3** To say in a slow, dull tone. — *n.* **1** A dull, monotonous, humming sound, as of a bee. **2** One of the single-note reed pipes of the bagpipe: distinguished from *chanter*; also, a bagpipe or similar instrument. See illustration under BAGPIPE. **3** *Music* A sustained bass commonly of one note. **4** A drawling speaker. [ME *dronen* < *drone* a male bee]

drone[2] (drōn) *n.* **1** A stingless male bee, that gathers no honey. **2** Hence, an idler. **3** *Aeron.* An unmanned airplane piloted by remote control. — *v.* **droned, dron·ing** *v.t.* To spend idly. — *v.i.* To live in idleness; be indolent. [OE *dran*] — **dron′ism** *adj.*

dron·go (drong′gō) *n.* A crowlike, insectivorous bird *(Dicrurus forficatus)* of the East Indies and Africa, with a long, forked tail and dark plumage. Also **drongo shrike.** [<Malagasy]

drool (dro͞ol) *v.t.* & *v.i.* To drivel; slaver. — *n.* **1** Spittle. **2** *Colloq.* Foolish talk; stuff and nonsense. [Contraction of DRIVEL]

droop (dro͞op) *v.i.* **1** To sink down; hang downward. **2** To lose vigor or vitality. **3** To become dejected; lose spirit. — *v.t.* **4** To allow to hang or sink down. See synonyms under FALL. — *n.* A sinking or hanging down; specifically, the bending under its own weight of the long barrel of an artillery gun. [<ON *drūpa*] — **droop′ing** *adj.* — **droop′ing·ly** *adv.*

droop·y (dro͞o′pē) *adj.* **droop·i·er, droop·i·est** Forlorn; drooping; tending to droop. — **droop′·i·ness** *n.*

drop (drop) *n.* **1** A globule of liquid; also, a very small quantity of anything, as of a beverage. **2** Anything that resembles or hangs like a drop of liquid, or that is made in drops or by dropping; a pendant earring, small piece of candy, etc. **3** A fall; the distance fallen; a sudden change of level; descent. **4** Any one of various contrivances that drop or depend, or are employed in lowering, as the drop curtain of a theater; also, in the theater, a drop scene. **5** *Mech.* **a** A forging machine. **b** A press used for forging, stamping, etc. **6** A trap door; especially, the platform of a gallows. **7** *pl.* Any liquid medicine given by the drop. **8** *Naut.* The vertical depth of a course on its central line. **9** A letter-drop. **10** A fall in prices: Stocks took a *drop*. — **at the drop of a** (or **the**) **hat** At once; with little or no hesitation or provocation. — **to have the drop on** To have the advantage over; specifically, to have (a person) covered with a gun before he can draw his. — *v.* **dropped, drop·ping** *v.t.* **1** To let fall in drops. **2** To let fall in any way; release and let fall; lower. **3** To give birth to: said of animals. **4** To say as if casually or incidentally: to *drop* a hint. **5** To write and send (a note, etc.) hastily and informally. **6** To bring down or cause to fall, as by tackling, striking, or shooting. **7** To stop treating of or associating with: to *drop* a subject or a friend. **8** To leave at a specific place, as from a ship or vehicle. **9** To omit (a syllable, letter, or word): He *dropped* the *von* from his name. **10** To sprinkle with drops. **11** *Slang* To lose (money or the like), as in gambling. **12** *U.S.* To discharge (an employee); to dismiss (a student). **13** *Naut.* To outdistance; sail away from. — *v.i.* **14** To fall in drops, as a liquid. **15** To fall rapidly; come down. **16** To fall down exhausted, injured, or dead. **17** To crouch, as a hunting dog at sight of game. **18** To come to an end; cease; stop. **19** To fall into some state or condition: to *drop* into a habit. **20** To fall behind or to the rear: often with *behind* or *back.* See synonyms under FALL. — **to drop down** To move down a stream or along a coast, as a vessel. — **to drop in** To happen in, as for a call. — **to drop out** To leave; withdraw from. [OE *dropa*]

drop curtain A theater curtain lowered in front of the stage between the acts.

drop·forge (drop′fôrj′) *v.t.* **·forged, ·forg·ing** To forge (metal) between dies by a machine employing the mechanical force of a dropped weight. — **drop′forg′ing** *n.*

drop hammer A machine for forging, stamping, etc., in which a heavy weight sliding between vertical guides strikes blows at regular intervals or at the will of the operator.

drop·kick (drop′kik′) *n.* In football, a kick given the ball just as it is rebounding after being dropped. — **drop′kick′er** *n.*

drop–kick (drop′kik′) *v.t.* & *v.i.* To kick (a football) in the manner of a dropkick.

drop leaf A hinged section of a table that may be folded down when not in use. — **drop′–leaf′** *adj.*

drop·let (drop′lit) *n.* A little drop.

drop–let·ter (drop′let′ər) *n.* A letter delivered by the same office in which it is posted.

drop·light (drop′līt′) *n.* **1** An attachment to a side fixture or an overhead chandelier by which a lamp can be raised or lowered at will. **2** The light thus raised or lowered.

drop·out (drop′out′) *n.* **1** A student who leaves school or college after attendance is no longer compulsory, or before graduation. **2** One who abandons any undertaking before completing it.

drop·per (drop′ər) *n.* **1** One who or that which drops. **2** *Agric.* A machine that cuts grain and drops it in bundles at intervals. **3** A glass tube with a suction bulb at one end and a narrow orifice at the other, for dispensing a liquid in drops.

drop·ping (drop′ing) *n.* **1** The act of falling or letting fall in drops. **2** *Usually pl.* Falling drops, or that which has fallen in drops. **3** *pl.* The dung of animals.

drop press A drop hammer.

drop scene A scene, usually across the entire stage, dropped like a curtain.

drop shot Gunshot made by dropping molten metal from a height into water.

drop·si·cal (drop′si·kəl) *adj.* Resembling, relating to, or affected with dropsy. — **drop′·si·cal·ly** *adv.*

drop·sied (drop′sēd) *adj.* Afflicted with dropsy; swollen.

drop·sonde (drop′sond′) *n. Meteorol.* A radiosonde dropped by parachute from an airplane above terrain not suitable for ground stations. [<DROP + F *sonde* a sounding]

drop·sy (drop′sē) *n.* **1** *Pathol.* An abnormal accumulation of serous fluid in cellular tissue as in some body cavity. **2** A disease of certain plants, due to an excess of water. [Short for HYDROPSY]

drop·wort (drop′wûrt′) *n.* **1** A perennial plant *(Filipendula hexapetala)* of the rose family, with interruptedly pinnate leaves and white or reddish, odorless flowers. **2** Any of a genus *(Oenanthe)*, of apiaceous plants, as the hemlock dropwort. **3** A North American marsh plant *(Oxypolis rigidior)* of the parsley family.

drosh·ky (drosh′kē, drôsh′kē) *n. pl.* **·kies** **1** A light, open, four-wheeled Russian carriage. **2** Any of several similar carriages. Also **dros′·ky.** [<Russian *drozhki,* dim. of *drogi* wagon]

DROSHKY

dro·soph·i·la (drō·sof′ə·lə, drə-) *n. pl.* **·lae** (-lē) Any of a genus *(Drosophila)* of fruit flies, especially *D. melanogaster,* used for research in genetics and heredity. See FRUIT FLY. [<NL <Gk. *drosos* dew + *phileein* love]

dross (drôs, dros) *n.* **1** *Metall.* Refuse or impurity in melted metal; slag; cinders. **2** Waste matter; refuse. See synonyms under WASTE. [OE *drōs*] — **dross′i·ness** *n.* — **dross′y** *adj.*

drought (drout) *n.* **1** Long–continued dry weather; want of rain. **2** Scarcity; dearth. **3** Thirst. Also **drouth** (drouth). [OE *drugoth.* Related to DRY.]

drought·y (drou′tē) *adj.* Marked by or suffering from drought or thirst; thirsty. Also **drouth·y** (drou′thē). — **drought′i·ness, drouth′·i·ness** *n.*

drouk (dro͝ok) *v.t. Scot.* **1** To wet through and through; saturate; soak. **2** To overcome.

drouk·it (dro͞o′kit) *adj. Scot.* Drenched.

drove[1] (drōv) Past tense of DRIVE.

drove[2] (drōv) *n.* **1** A number of animals driven or herded for driving. **2** A moving crowd of human beings. **3** A stone mason's broad–edged chisel: also called **drove chisel.** **4** The surface of stone smoothed by a drove: also called **drove′work′.** See synonyms under FLOCK[1]. — *v.t.* **·droved, drov·ing** **1** To drive (cows, etc.) for some distance; work as a drover. **2** To dress (stone) with a broad–edged chisel. [OE *drāf.* Related to DRIVE.]

drov·er (drō′vər) *n.* **1** One who drives animals in droves to market; a cattle–dealer. **2** A small fishing boat equipped with a drift net.

drown (droun) *v.t.* **1** To kill by immersion and suffocation in water or other liquid. **2** To flood; deluge. **3** To overwhelm; overpower; extinguish. — *v.i.* To die by immersion and suffocation in water or other liquid. [ME *drūnen, drounen*; origin uncertain]

drowse (drouz) *v.* **drowsed, drows·ing** *v.i.* **1** To be sleepy; doze; be listless. — *v.t.* **2** To make sleepy. **3** To pass (time) in drowsing. — *n.* The state of being half asleep; a doze. [OE *drūsian* become sluggish]

drow·sy (drou′zē) *adj.* **·si·er, ·si·est** **1** Heavy with sleepiness; dull. **2** Lulling; soporific. See synonyms under SLOW. — **drow′si·ly** *adv.* — **drow′si·ness** *n.*

drow·sy·head (drou′zē·hed′) *n. Obs.* Drowsiness; sleepiness. Also **drow′si·head′.**

drub (drub) *v.t.* **drubbed, drub·bing** **1** To beat, as with a stick; cudgel; thrash. **2** To vanquish; overcome. **3** To stamp (the feet). — *n.* A blow; thump. [? <Arabic *ḍarb* a beating <*ḍaraba* beat] — **drub′ber** *n.*

drub·bing (drub′ing) *n.* **1** A thrashing; a beating. **2** Defeat.

drudge (druj) *v.i.* **drudged, drudg·ing** To toil; work hard and slavishly at menial tasks. — *n.* One who toils at menial tasks. [Prob. related to OE *drēogan* work, labor]

drudg·er·y (druj′ər·ē) *n.* *pl.* **·er·ies** Dull, wearisome, or menial work. See synonyms under TOIL, WORK.

drug (drug) *n.* **1** Any substance, other than food, intended for use in the diagnosis, cure, mitigation, treatment, or prevention of disease in man or other animals. **2** Any article or substance recognized in the U.S. pharmacopoeia. **3** Any narcotic; also, any substance or chemical agent, exclusive of food, employed for other than medical reasons to obtain a given physiological effect or to satisfy a craving. **4** A commodity that is overabundant or in excess of demand: a *drug* on the market. — *v.t.* **drugged, drug·ging** **1** To mix drugs with (food, drink, etc.), especially narcotic or poisonous drugs. **2** To administer drugs to. **3** To stupefy or poison with or as with drugs; overcome: *drugged* with sleep. [<MF *drogue*; ult. origin unknown]

drug addict One addicted to a habit–forming drug.

drug·get (drug′it) *n.* **1** A coarse woolen or wool and cotton fabric for rugs, etc. **2** A rug made of such material. **3** A kind of dress fabric; woolen rep. [<MF *droguet*]

drug·gist (drug′ist) *n.* **1** One who compounds prescriptions and sells drugs; a pharmacist. **2** A dealer in drugs.

drug·store (drug′stôr′, -stōr′) *n.* A place where prescriptions are compounded, and drugs and miscellaneous merchandise are sold; a pharmacy.

dru·id (dro͞o′id) *n.* One of an order of priests or teachers of religion in ancient Gaul, Britain, and Ireland. [<MF *druide* <L *druidae, druides* <Celtic] — **dru′id·ess** (-is) *n. fem.*

dru·id·i·cal (dro͞o·id′i·kəl) *adj.* Of or pertaining to the druids. Also **dru·id′ic.**

dru·id·ism (dro͞o′id·iz′əm) *n.* The religious system of ancient Gaul, Britain, and Ireland, administered by the druids; also, its ceremonies, rites, and philosophy. Also **dru′id·ry** (-rē).

drum[1] (drum) *n.* **1** A hollow cylinder of wood or metal, with skin or vellum stretched upon ringlike frames fitted over each end, kept taut with hoops and cords, and played by beating the head or the heads with drumsticks; also, the sound produced by beating this instrument. **2** The body of a banjo, tambourine, etc. **3** *Anat.* The tympanum, or middle ear. **4** A drummer. **5** Anything resembling a drum in shape, as a cylindrical receptacle for oil, fruit, fish, etc. **6** The drumfish. **7** Any mechanical construction or device shaped like a drum. **8** *Obs.* A social gathering; formerly, a crowded and noisy fashionable card party at a private house. — *v.* **drummed, drum·ming** *v.t.* **1** To perform on or as on a drum. **2** To expel in disgrace: usually with *out.* **3** To summon by beating a drum. **4** To force into the mind or upon the attention by constant repetition. — *v.i.* **5** To beat a drum. **6** To beat on anything continuously or rhythmically. **7** To make a loud, beating noise: said especially of the wings of certain birds, as partridge or grouse. — **to drum up** To seek or solicit: to *drum* up trade. [Prob. <MDu. *tromme*]

HOISTING DRUM

drum[2] (drum) *n.* **1** *Scot.* & *Irish* A hill or elevation. **2** A drumlin.

drum·beat (drum′bēt′) *n.* The sound of a drum; also, the action of beating a drum.

drum·ble (drum′bəl) *v.i. Obs.* To move sluggishly. [< obs. *drumble,* var. of *dummel* stupid <DUMB]

drum brake A brake in which a shoe lined with a durable, heat–resistant material is pressed outward against the inner rim of a drum.

drum·fire (drum′fīr′) *n.* Gunfire so rapid and continuous as to sound like drums; continuous firing.

drum·fish (drum′fish′) *n.* *pl.* **·fish** or **·fishes** **1** A sciaenoid fish *(Pogonias cromis)* of the North American Atlantic coast which makes a drumming sound, especially in the breeding season. **2** Any of similar fishes, as the fresh–water drum *(Aplodinotus grunniens)* of the Great Lakes and the Mississippi.

drum·head (drum′hed′) *n.* **1** The membrane stretched over the end of a drum, especially the end that is beaten. **2** *Naut.* The circular top of a capstan. See illustration under CAPSTAN. **3** *Anat.* The tympanic membrane; the eardrum. See illustration under EAR. **4** An Australian grasstree.

drumhead court martial See under COURT MARTIAL.

drum·lin (drum′lin) *n. Geol.* A compact, elongated, oval mound of glacial drift, usually unstratified and having its longer axis in the direction of the local glacial movement. [<Irish *druim*]

drum major One who instructs or leads a band or drum corps.

drum ma·jor·ette (mā′jə·ret′) A woman who leads or precedes a marching band or accompanies such a band while twirling a baton.

drum·mer (drum′ər) *n.* **1** One who or that which drums. **2** *U.S.* A traveling salesman.

drum·mock (drum′ək) *n. Scot.* Raw oatmeal and water.

Drum·mond (drum′ənd), **Henry,** 1851–97, Scottish evangelical author and lecturer. — **William,** 1585–1649, Scottish poet. — **William Henry,** 1854–1907, Canadian physician and poet, born in Ireland.

Drummond light **1** The calcium light. **2** A type of heliostat. [after T. *Drummond,* 1797–1840, Scottish engineer, who invented it]

drum·stick (drum′stik′) *n.* **1** A stick for beating a drum. **2** The lower joint of the leg of a cooked fowl.

drunk (drungk) Past participle of DRINK; former past tense. — *adj.* **1** Inebriated; intoxicated; figuratively, saturated; satiated; glutted: *drunk* with slaughter. **2** *Obs.* Drenched. — *n. Colloq.* **1** A spree; fit of drunkenness. **2** A drunken person; a case of drunkenness.

drunk·ard (drungk′ərd) *n.* One who habitually drinks to intoxication; a sot.

drunk·en (drungk′ən) *adj.* **1** Given to, resulting from, or characterized by drunkenness; drunk; tipsy. **2** Saturated. — **drunk′·en·ly** *adv.* — **drunk′en·ness** *n.*

drunt (drunt) *n. Scot.* Pettishness; a huff; ill humor.

dru·pa·ceous (dro͞o·pā′shəs) *adj. Bot.* Of, like, or bearing drupes.

drupe (dro͞op) *n. Bot.* A soft, fleshy fruit enclosing a hard-shelled stone or seed, as in the peach or cherry. See illustration under FRUIT. [<NL *drupa* <L *drupa (oliva)* an overripe (olive) <Gk. *druppa*]

drupe·let (dro͞op′lit) *n. Bot.* A little drupe, as in a raspberry or blackberry. Also **dru·pel** (dro͞o′pəl), **dru·pe·ole** (dro͞o′pē·ōl).

Dru·ry Lane (dro͝or′ē) A street in London, known in the 17th and 18th centuries for its theaters.

druse (dro͞oz) *n. Geol.* A cavity lined with crystals of the same minerals as the rock enclosing them: distinguished from *geode.* [<G] — **drus′y, drused** *adj.*

Druse (dro͞oz) *n.* One of a fanatical religious sect of Syrians. [<Arabic *Durūz,* pl., after Ismail al-*Darazi,* who founded the sect] — **Dru·si·an** (dro͞o′zē·ən), **Dru′se·an** *adj.*

Dru·sus (dro͞o′səs) Name of two Roman generals: **Nero Claudius Drusus Germanicus,** 38–9 B.C., brother of the Emperor Tiberius; and **Drusus Caesar,** 15? B.C.–A.D. 23, son of the Emperor Tiberius.

dry (drī) *adj.* **dri·er, dri·est** **1** Lacking moisture; not wet or damp; not fresh; not green, as wood; also, lacking lubrication, as bearings. **2** Thirsty. **3** Lacking interest; lifeless; dull. **4** Slyly jocose or satirical; shrewd, as wit. **5** Free from sweetness: said of wines; also, denoting any wine having 14 percent or less of alcohol. **6** Subject to or in favor of a prohibitory liquor law: a *dry* town. **7** Not giving milk: a *dry* cow. **8** Not liquid; solid: said of merchandise, etc. **9** Tearless: said of the eyes. **10** Characterized by absence of bloodshed. **11** Without butter: said of toast. **12** Wanting in cordiality; not genial. — *v.* **dried, dry·ing** *v.t.* **1** To make dry; rid of moisture. **2** To cure or preserve, as meat, fish, etc., by evaporation or desiccation. — *v.i.* **3** To become dry. — **to dry up** **1** To cease or cause to cease flowing. **2** *Colloq.* To stop talking. — *n. pl.* **dries** **1** A state or condition of dryness; especially, a drought. **2** *Often cap. Colloq.* A prohibitionist. [OE *drȳge*] — **dry′ly, dri′ly** *adv.* — **dry′·ness** *n.*

dry·ad (drī′əd, -ad) *n.* In Greek mythology a wood nymph. [<L *dryas, -adis* <Gk. < *drys, dryos* an oak tree] — **dry·ad′ic** *adj.*

dry·as·dust (drī′əz·dust′) *n.* An uninteresting, pedantic writer or speaker; a dull pedant. — **dry′-as-dust′** *adj.*

dry battery See under BATTERY.

dry-bone ore (drī′bōn′) Smithsonite.

dry cell See under CELL.

dry·clean (drī′klēn′) *v.t.* To clean (clothing, etc.) with solvents other than water, such as carbon tetrachloride, etc. Also **dry′cleanse′.** — **dry′clean′er** *n.* — **dry′clean′ing** *n.*

Dry·den (drīd′n), **John,** 1631–1700, English poet, critic, and dramatist; poet laureate 1670–88.

dry distillation See under DISTILLATION.

dry·dock (drī′dok′) *n.* A structure, either floating or stationary, into which a ship is floated for repairs or cleaning. Gates and pumps operate to remove the enclosed water for convenience in working. — *v.t.* & *v.i.* To put in or go into drydock.

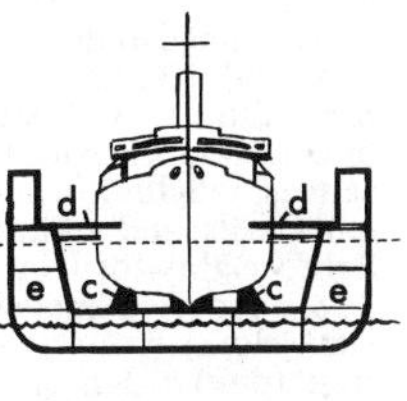

FLOATING DRYDOCK
a. Water line at the time ship is floated into dock.
b. Water line after water is pumped out of dock.
c. Block supports for ship.
d. Shoring for side support.
e. Watertight compartments.

dry·er (drī′ər), **dry·est** (drī′ist) See DRIER, DRIEST.

dry-eyed (drī′īd′) *adj.* Tearless; not weeping.

dry-farm·ing (drī′·fär′ming) *n.* In an arid or dry country, the raising of crops without irrigation, mainly by saving the moisture of the soil and by raising drought-resisting crops. — **dry′-farm′er** *n.*

dry fog *Meteorol.* Haze formed from a suspension of fine dust or smoke particles in the atmosphere.

dry·foot (drī′fo͝ot′) *adv.* **1** With dry feet. **2** *Obs.* By scent of the foot.

dry-goods (drī′go͝odz′) *n. pl.* Textile fabrics, as distinguished from groceries, hardware, etc.

Dry Ice Solid carbon dioxide used as a refrigerant: a trade name.

dry·ing (drī′ing) *adj.* **1** Able to draw out or absorb moisture; causing evaporation; absorbent. **2** Becoming dry rapidly, as certain oils.

dry kiln A heated oven or chamber for drying and seasoning lumber.

dry law A law prohibiting the sale of spirituous liquors.

dry measure A unit or system of units for measuring the volume of dry commodities, as fruits, grain, etc. The principal customary U.S. units are as in the table below. See also METRIC SYSTEM.

2 pints (pt., pts.)	=	1 quart (qt., qts.)
8 quarts	=	1 peck (pk., pks.)
4 pecks	=	1 bushel (bu.)

dry·nurse (drī′nûrs′) *v.t.* **·nursed, ·nurs·ing** **1** To nurse without suckling. **2** To coach or give hints to, as in or concerning the duties of an office. — *n.* **1** A nurse who nourishes and rears a child without suckling it. **2** One who cares for another; particularly, one who instructs his superior in the latter's duties.

Dry·o·pi·the·cus (drī′ō·pi·thē′kəs) *Paleontol. n.* Any of a genus of extinct apes of the Miocene and Pliocene epochs: closely related types are *Sivapithecus* and *Proconsul.* [NL <Gk. *drys, dryos* an oak tree + *pithēkos* a monkey, ape]

dry·point (drī′point′) *n.* **1** A fine etching needle used to incise copperplate in fine lines, without the use of acid or etching ground. **2** A line or work thus engraved, or the method thus used.

dry-rot (drī′rot′) *n.* **1** A fungous disease of timber, causing it to crumble into powder. **2** A disease of potato tubers and other vegetables. **3** Inward and gradual corruption, as of morals.

dry-run (drī′run′) *n.* **1** *Mil.* Practice in aiming and firing weapons without using live ammunition. **2** Any rehearsal or practice exercise.

dry·salt (drī′sôlt′) *v.t.* To preserve (food) by salting and removing moisture.

dry·salt·er (drī′sôl′tər) *n.* **1** One who deals in dried and salted meats, pickles, etc. **2** *Brit.* A dealer in chemical preparations, dyestuffs, etc. — **dry′salt′er·y** *n.*

dry-shod (drī′shod′) *adj.* & *adv.* Having the shoes or feet dry; without getting the feet wet: to cross a ford *dry-shod.*

dry socket *Dent.* A morbid condition of a tooth socket after extraction of a tooth, resulting from the disintegration of a blood clot without the formation of pus and accompanied by a foul odor and severe pain.

Dry Tor·tu·gas (tôr·to͞o′gəz) A group of Florida islets west of the Marquesas Keys.

dry wash **1** Laundry which has been washed and dried, but not ironed. **2** *U.S.* A gully or arroyo which contains water only after a heavy rain.

du·ad (do͞o′ad, dyo͞o′-) *n.* A pair of units. [<Gk. *dyas, -ados* the number two]

du·al (do͞o′əl, dyo͞o′-) *adj.* **1** Denoting or relating to two. **2** Composed of two, as of two natures; twofold; binary. — *n. Gram.* In some languages, as Sanskrit and Greek, the form of the noun or verb indicating its application to two persons or things; the dual number: distinguished from *singular* and *plural.* ◆ Homophone: *duel.* [<L *dualis* < *duo* two] — **du·al·i·ty** (do͞o·al′ə·tē, dyo͞o-) *n.*

Du·a·la (do͞o·ä′lä) *n.* **1** One of a Bantu people inhabiting the Cameroons, West Africa. **2** Their language.

Dual Alliance An alliance (1879) between Germany and Austria-Hungary against Russia.

du·al·ism (do͞o′əl·iz′əm, dyo͞o′-) *n.* **1** The state of being twofold; duality. **2** A system or theory which asserts a twofoldness of nature, being, or operation; specifically, **theological dualism,** or the doctrine that there are two eternal and opposing principles, or beings, one good and the other evil; **philosophical dualism,** or the theory that the nature of the universe is twofold, *i.e.,* comprised of mind and matter, as opposed either to idealistic or materialistic monism; **psychological** or **psychophysical dualism,** the theory that the body and mind of man are two different existences but are placed by the order of nature in a most intimate system of correlations or interactions; or **ethical dualism,** the system of morals which demands and justifies one kind of conduct toward one's fellows in the same social group and another kind of conduct toward other men. **3** *Gram.* The expression of the condition of duality.

du·al·ist (do͞o′əl·ist, dyo͞o′-) *n.* A believer in some form of dualism.

du·al·is·tic (do͞o′əl·is′tik, dyo͞o′-) *adj.* **1** Of or pertaining to dualism. **2** Having a dual nature. — **du′al·is′ti·cal·ly** *adv.*

du·al-pur·pose (do͞o′əl·pûr′pəs, dyo͞o′-) *adj.* Having two functions or uses.

Duar·te (dwer′tā) Portuguese form of EDWARD.

dub[1] (dub) *v.t.* **dubbed, dub·bing** **1** To confer knighthood upon by tapping on the shoulder with a sword. **2** To name or style; entitle. **3** To smooth or rub; dress, as timber. [OE *dubbian*]

dub[2] (dub) *v.t.* & *v.i.* **dubbed, dub·bing** **1** To push or thrust. **2** To beat (a drum). — *n.* **1** A blow. **2** A beat of a drum. [Prob. imit.]

dub[3] (dub) *Slang n.* A clumsy, blundering person; a poor or second-rate player in any game. — *v.t.* **dubbed, dub·bing** To bungle. [? <DUB[2]]

dub[4] (dub) *n. Scot.* A pool; puddle.

dub[5] (dub) *v.t.* **dubbed, dub·bing** To re-record (a sound record) in order to change volume or frequency. — **to dub in** **1** In motion pictures, to insert (a new sound track) into a film. **2** To blend (new sounds, music, etc.) into the sound track of a film, or into a radio or television broadcast. [Short for DOUBLE]

dub-a-dub (dub′ə·dub′) *n.* **1** Drumbeating, or a similar sound. **2** A drummer. [Imit.]

du Bar·ry (do͞o bar′ē, dyo͞o; *Fr.* dü bȧ·rē′), **Comtesse,** 1746?–93, Jeanne Bécu, mistress of Louis XV; guillotined.

Du·bawnt River (do͞o·bônt′) A river in north central Canada, flowing 580 miles NE through **Dubawnt Lake** (1,600 square miles) to the Thelon River.

dub·bing[1] (dub′ing) *n.* **1** Material for softening leather and making it waterproof. **2** Pieces of wood, etc., for filling up deep depressions or interstices in a wall before plastering. **3** The material of the body of a fishing fly. [<DUB[1]]

dub·bing[2] (dub′ing) *n.* The re-recording of a sound record, in whole or in part, where a change in volume levels or frequency characteristics is necessary; especially, the synchronized conversion of a motion-picture sound track from the language of the original cast into some other language. [<DUB[5]]

Dub·he (do͞ob′he) The star Alpha in the constellation Ursa Major: the larger of the two

stars which together make the Pointer toward the Pole Star.
du·bi·e·ty (dōō·bī′ə·tē, dyōō-) *n.* The state of being doubtful or dubious; doubt; doubtfulness. Also **du·bi·os·i·ty** (dōō′bē·os′ə·tē, dyōō′-). [<LL *dubietas, -tatis* < *dubius* doubtful]
du·bi·ous (dōō′bē·əs, dyōō′-) *adj.* **1** Unsettled in judgment or opinion; in a state of doubt; doubtful. **2** Being a subject or matter of doubt; causing doubt. **3** Of uncertain result; not yet settled; problematic. **4** Of questionable propriety; open to objections, especially of a moral kind, or to suspicion; questionable. **5** Being the occasion of doubt; difficult of explanation; equivocal. See synonyms under EQUIVOCAL, PRECARIOUS. [<L *dubiosus* < *dubium* doubt] —**du′bi·ous·ly** *adv.* —**du′bi·ous·ness** *n.*
du·bi·ta·ble (dōō′bə·tə·bəl, dyōō′-) *adj.* Doubtful; debatable. —**du′bi·ta·bly** *adv.*
du·bi·tate (dōō′bə·tāt, dyōō′-) *v.i.* **·tat·ed, ·tat·ing** *Rare* To doubt. [<L *dubitatus,* pp. of *dubitare* doubt] —**du′bi·ta′tion** *n.*
du·bi·ta·tive (dōō′bə·tā′tiv, dyōō′-) *adj.* Tending to or expressing doubt; also, hesitating. —**du′bi·ta′tive·ly** *adv.*
Dub·lin (dub′lin) **1** The capital of Ireland, a port on the Liffey river at **Dublin Bay,** an inlet of the Irish Sea on the eastern coast of Ireland: Irish *Baile Atha Cliath.* **2** A county of Leinster province, eastern Ireland: 356 square miles; county seat, Dublin.
Dub·no (dōōb′nô) A city in Ukrainian S.S.R.
Du·bois (dü·bwä′), **Théodore,** 1837–1924, French composer.
Du Bois (dōō bois′), **William Edward Burghardt,** 1868–1963, U.S. educator and writer.
Du Bois-Rey·mond (dü bwä′rā·môṅ′), **Emil,** 1818–96, German physiologist.
du·bon·net (dōō′bə·nā′) *n.* A reddish purple, the color of Dubonnet.
Du·bon·net (dōō′bə·nā′, *Fr.* dü·bô·ne′) *n.* A fortified French red wine: a trade name.
Du·brov·nik (dōō′brôv·nik) A port on the Adriatic in SW Yugoslavia: Italian *Ragusa.*
Du·buque (də·byōōk′) A city in eastern Iowa on the Mississippi.
du·cal (dōō′kəl, dyōō′-) *adj.* Of or pertaining to a duke or a duchy. [<MF <LL *ducalis* < *dux* leader] —**du′cal·ly** *adv.*
Du Cange (dü käṅzh′), **Charles du Fresne,** 1610–88, French historian and philologist.
duc·at (duk′ət) *n.* **1** One of several European coins of varying value, the first struck by Roger II of Sicily. **2** A former coin of Venice and Holland. **3** *Slang* A ticket, usually for the theater or a sports event. [<MF <Ital. *ducato* <LL *ducatus,* orig. a duchy < *dux* leader]
Duc·cio di Buo·nin·se·gna (dōōt′chō dē bwô′·nēn·sā′nyä), 1260?–1339?, Italian painter.
du·ce (dōō′chā) *n. Ital.* A leader; commander. —**il Duce** The title assumed by Benito Mussolini as leader of the Italian Fascists.
Du Chail·lu (dü shà·yü′), **Paul Belloni,** 1835–1903, U.S. explorer in Africa, born in France.
Du·champ (dü·shäṅ′), **Marcel,** 1887–1968, French painter.
duch·ess (duch′is) *n.* **1** The wife or widow of a duke. **2** The female sovereign of a duchy. [<OF *duchesse* <LL *ducissa* <L *dux* leader]
duch·y (duch′ē) *n. pl.* **duch·ies** The territory or dominion of a duke; a dukedom. [<OF *duché* <L *dux* leader]
duck[1] (duk) *n.* **1** A web-footed, short-legged, broad-billed water bird of the *Anatidae* family comprising fresh-water and wood ducks *(Anatinae),* the sea and bay ducks *(Fuligulinae),* and the mergansers *(Merginae).* ◆ Collateral adjective: *anatine.* **2** The female of this bird: distinguished from *drake.* **3** The flesh of this bird. **4** *Colloq.* A dear; darling. **5** *Slang* A person; a fellow. [OE *duce,* lit. diver]

AMERICAN MALLARD DUCK
(About 23 inches in length)

duck[2] (duk) *v.t.* & *v.i.* **1** To plunge suddenly under water; dive. **2** To lower quickly; bob, as the head. **3** To dodge; evade (a blow or punishment). **4** To avoid (a duty, person, etc.). **5** To move quickly and abruptly: He *ducked* through the crowd. See synonyms under IMMERSE. —*n.* A sudden downward movement, as of the head; a bob or nod; also, a quick plunge under water. [ME *duken, douken* dive, ult. <Gmc.]
duck[3] (duk) *n.* **1** A strong tightly woven linen or cotton fabric with a plain weave, similar to canvas; sailcloth: heavier weights are used for tents, sails, and military and naval equipment; light weights for trousers, middy blouses, etc. **2** *pl.* Trousers made of this fabric. [<Du. *doek* cloth]
duck[4] (duk) *n. Mil.* An amphibious military vehicle of World War II, having a watertight body and equipped with a propeller and a rudder for use when traveling on water. [<DUKW, code word for this type of vehicle]
duck·bill (duk′bil′) *n.* The platypus.
duck·board (duk′bôrd′, -bōrd′) *n.* A board or section of boarding laid over a wet floor or muddy ground to form a raised surface for walking.
duck·er[1] (duk′ər) *n.* **1** One who or that which ducks. **2** A diving bird.
duck·er[2] (duk′ər) *n.* **1** A duck hunter. **2** One who rears ducks.
duck-foot·ed (duk′fŏŏt′id) *adj.* With the back toe pointing nearly forward: applied to poultry.
duck hawk The American peregrine falcon.
duck·ing (duk′ing) *n.* **1** The act of plunging into water; a wetting. **2** The act of dodging or bobbing down, as to escape a blow. **3** Duck hunting.
ducking stool A stool on which the culprit was tied and plunged into water; a cucking stool: formerly used as a punishment in New England, especially for quarrelsome women.
duck·ling (duk′ling) *n.* A young duck.
duck·mole (duk′mōl′) *n.* The platypus.
duck·pin (duk′pin′) *n.* A pin 9 inches high and 3 1/2 inches in diameter at the body: used in the game of tenpins called **duckpins.**
ducks and drakes A game in which one skims or skips flat stones, shells, etc., along the surface of water. —**to make** (or **play**) **ducks and drakes** To throw away or squander: with *of* or *with.*
duck·weed (duk′wēd′) *n.* **1** Any of several small, disk-shaped, aquatic plants (genus *Lemna*) common in streams and ponds in the United States. **2** A somewhat larger plant of the same family, the large duckweed *(Spirodela polyrhiza).* Also **duck′meat′.**
duck·y (duk′ē) *adj. Slang* Delightful; darling; dear.
duct (dukt) *n.* **1** Any tube, canal, or passage by which a fluid is conveyed. **2** *Anat.* A tubular passage for fluid, especially one by which a secretion is carried away from a gland: the nasal *duct.* **3** *Electr.* A tubular channel for carrying electric power, telegraph or telephone cables. [<L *ductus* a leading < *ducere* lead]
duc·tile (duk′til) *adj.* **1** Capable of being hammered into thin layers or of being drawn out into wire, as certain metals. **2** Easily led; tractable; pliant. [<F <L *ductilis* < *ducere* lead] —**duc·til′i·ty, duc′tile·ness** *n.*
duct·less gland (dukt′lis) See ENDOCRINE GLAND.
dud[1] (dud) *n. Colloq.* **1** A garment. **2** *pl.* Clothing; especially, old clothes. **3** *pl.* Belongings in general. [ME *dudde* a cloak; origin uncertain]
dud[2] (dud) *n.* **1** *Mil.* A shell that fails to explode. **2** *Colloq.* Any person or thing that is inadequate or fails to operate. [<Du. *dood* dead]
dud·die (dud′ē) *adj. Scot.* Clothed in duds; poor; ragged; torn. Also **dud′dy.**
dude (dōōd, dyōōd) *n.* **1** *U.S.* A fop; an affected man. **2** A city person, especially one from the eastern United States who is vacationing on a ranch. [Coined 1883, ? < *duds* clothing] —**dud′ish** *adj.* —**dud′ism, dud′ishness** *n.*
du·deen (dōō·dēn′) *n. Irish* A short-stemmed tobacco pipe. [<Irish *dūidīn,* diminutive of *dūd* a smoking pipe]
dude ranch A ranch operated as a resort for tourists.
Dude·vant (düd·väṅ′), **Baroness** See SAND, GEORGE.
dudg·eon[1] (duj′ən) *n.* Sullen displeasure; resentment. [Origin unknown]
dudg·eon[2] (duj′ən) *n.* **1** The root of the boxwood tree, formerly used for dagger hilts. **2** Any mottled or veined wood. **3** *Obs.* A wooden hilt of a dagger; a dudgeon dagger. [<AF *digeon;* ult. origin unknown]
Dud·ley (dud′lē), **Joseph,** 1647–1720, American colonial governor. —**Robert** See LEICESTER. —**Thomas,** 1576–1653, administrator in Massachusetts Bay colony; father of Joseph.
Dud·ley (dud′lē) A county borough of Worcestershire, England.
due (dōō, dyōō) *adj.* **1** Owing and demandable; owed; especially, payable because of the arrival of the time set or agreed upon. **2** That should be rendered or given; justly claimable; appropriate. **3** Suitable; lawful; sufficient; regular. **4** Appointed or expected to arrive; having had time to arrive. **5** That may be charged or attributed; ascribable; owing: with *to*: The delay was *due* to rain. ◆ *Due to* as a preposition, though widely used, is still questioned by some, who would substitute for it *because of* or *on account of: Because of* (not *due to*) rain, we were delayed. —*n.* **1** That which is owed or rightfully required; a debt or obligation. **2** *pl.* Legal charge or fee: club *dues.* —*adv.* **1** Directly; exactly: *due* east. **2** Duly. ◆ Homophone: *dew.* [<OF *deü,* pp. of *devoir* owe <L *debere*]
due bill A written acknowledgment of indebtedness.
du·el (dōō′əl, dyōō′-) *n.* **1** A prearranged combat between two persons, usually fought with deadly weapons in the presence of witnesses or seconds. **2** A struggle between two contending parties. —*v.t.* & *v.i.* **du·eled** or **·elled, du·el·ing** or **·el·ling** To fight or fight with, in a duel. ◆ Homophone: *dual.* [<F <Ital. *duello* <L *duellum,* var. of *bellum* war] —**du′el·er, du′el·ler** *n.* —**du′el·ist, du′el·list** *n.*
du·el·ing (dōō′əl·ing, dyōō′-) *n.* The act of fighting a duel. Also **du′el·ling.**
du·en·na (dōō·en′ə, dyōō-) *n.* An elderly woman who watches over a young woman in Spanish and Portuguese families; hence, a chaperon. [<Sp. <L *domina* lady. Doublet of DAME.]
Due·ro (dwā′rō) The Spanish name for DOURO.
du·et (dōō·et′, dyōō-) *n.* A musical composition for two voices or performers. [<Ital. *duetto,* dim. of *duo* a duet <L *duo* two]
duff[1] (duf) *v.t.* **1** *Brit. Colloq.* To fix or change so as to give the appearance of truth or right to; to fake or cheat. —*v.i.* **2** *Austral.* To steal cattle or horses, especially in large numbers. [? Back formation from *duffer*]
duff[2] (duf) *n.* **1** A thick flour pudding boiled in a bag. **2** The litter of dead leaves, broken branches, etc., accumulated in a forest. **3** Small or fine coal. [Var. of DOUGH]
duf·fel (duf′əl) *n.* **1** A woolen fabric; a heavyweight kersey. **2** Outfit; supplies; especially, camping outfit. Also **duf′fle.** [from *Duffel,* a town near Antwerp]
duffel bag A sack, usually of canvas or duck, used to carry clothing and personal possessions.
duf·fer (duf′ər) *n.* **1** *Colloq.* One who performs in an incompetent or perfunctory manner. **2** *Brit. Dial.* A peddler or hawker; especially, one who sells spurious or flashy articles. **3** *Slang* Any counterfeit or sham. **4** *Austral.* A stealer of horses or cattle. [Origin uncertain]
duf·fle coat (duf′əl) A heavy woolen outer coat, usually knee-length and hooded. Also **duf′fel coat.** [Var. of DUFFEL]
Du·fy (dü·fē′), **Raoul,** 1878–1953, French painter.
dug[1] (dug) Past tense and past participle of DIG.
dug[2] (dug) *n.* A teat or udder. [Cf. Dan. *dægge* suckle]
Du Gard (dü gàr′), **Roger Martin,** 1881–1958, French novelist.
du·gong (dōō′gong) *n.* An aquatic, herbivorous mammal (genus *Dugong*) of the East Indies and Australia, having flippers in front, a paddlelike tail, and tusks which in the male grow to large size: also called *sea cow.* [<Malay *duyong*]

DUGONG
(From 9 to 12 feet in length; 450 to 2000 pounds)

dug-out (dug′out′) *n.* 1 A canoe formed of a hollowed log. See illustration under CANOE. 2 A rude dwelling excavated in a hillside; a cave. 3 An underground shelter against bombs and shells, or for protection from tornadoes, etc. 4 A low, boxlike structure facing a baseball diamond, to shelter the players when not at bat or in the field.

Du Gues·clin (dü ge·klaṅ′), **Bertrand,** 1320?–1380, French soldier; constable of France.

Du·ha·mel (dü·à·mel′), **Georges,** 1884–1966, French author.

dui·ker·bok (dī′kər·bok′) *n.* A small antelope (genus *Cephalophus*) widely distributed over southern and tropical Africa, with short conical horns set far back, a tufted head, and very short tail. Also **dui′ker, dui′ker·buck′.** [<Du. < *duiker* ducker, diver + *bok* buck; from its habit of plunging through thickets]

Duis·burg (düs′bo͝orkh) A city on the Rhine in North Rhine-Westphalia, West Germany. Formerly **Duis′burg-Ham′born** (-häm′bôrn).

Du·kas (dü·kà′), **Paul,** 1865–1935, French composer.

duke (do͞ok, dyo͞ok) *n.* 1 An English temporal peer of the highest rank, yielding precedence to a prince of the blood or an archbishop, and ranking above a marquis or a bishop. 2 A Continental noble or prince of corresponding rank. 3 A reigning prince of less importance than a king ruling over a duchy or a small state. 4 Formerly, a powerful semi-independent vassal. — *v.i.* **duked, duk·ing** To play the duke. [<F *duc* <L *dux* leader]

Duke (do͞ok, dyo͞ok), **Benjamin Newton,** 1855–1929, and his brother **James Buchanan,** 1856–1925, U.S. tobacco magnates.

duke·dom (do͞ok′dəm, dyo͞ok′-) *n.* 1 A duchy. 2 The dignity or title of a duke.

dukes (do͞oks, dyo͞oks) *n. pl. Slang* The fists. [Short for *Duke of Yorks,* orig. riming slang for forks; later fingers, hands, fists]

Du·kho·bors (do͞o′kō·bôrz) *n. pl.* A religious sect of Russian peasants who emigrated from Russia in 1895 to escape persecution, and settled in western Canada and Cyprus. Also spelled *Doukhobors.* [<Russian *dukhobortsy* < *dukh* spirit + *bortsy* wrestlers]

Du·la·wan (do͞o·lä′wän) A municipality in south central Mindanao, Philippines. Also **Du·la′uan.**

dul·cet (dul′sit) *adj.* 1 *Obs.* Sweet to the taste. 2 Sweet or melodious to the ear; soothing. — *n.* An organ stop resembling the dulciana, but an octave higher in tone. [<DOUCET, refashioned after L *dulcis* sweet]

dul·ci·an·a (dul′sē·an′ə) *n.* An organ stop of soft and delicate tone. [<Med. L *dulciana* <L *dulcis* sweet]

dul·ci·fy (dul′sə·fī) *v.t.* **·fied, ·fy·ing** 1 *Obs.* To make sweet. 2 To please; mollify. — **dul′ci·fi·ca′tion** *n.*

dul·ci·mer (dul′sə·mər) *n.* 1 A stringed instrument played with two padded hammers. 2 A wind instrument. *Dan.* iii 10. [<OF *doulcemer, doulcemele* ? <L *dulcemelos* <*dulcis* sweet + *melos* a song <Gk.]

DULCIMER

dul·cin·e·a (dul·sin′ē·ə, dul′sə·nē′ə) *n.* A sweetheart; ladylove. [after *Dulcinea* del Toboso, character in *Don Quixote*]

Dul·heg·gia (dul·hej′ə) See CALENDAR (Mohammedan).

du·li·a (do͞o·lī′ə, dyo͞o-) *n. Theol.* A secondary kind of worship, as distinguished from *latria,* or supreme worship: used in the sense of *veneration* of the saints and angels. [<Gk. *douleia* service < *doulos* slave]

Dul·kaa·da (dul·kä′də) See CALENDAR (Mohammedan).

dull (dul) *adj.* 1 Not sharp or keen; having a blunt edge or point. 2 Not acute or intense: *dull* pain. 3 Not quick, as in thought; sluggish; listless; stupid; lacking in perception, sensibility, or responsiveness. 4 Not brisk or active. 5 Not bright or spirited; wearisome; boring; sad. 6 Lacking luster; cloudy; dim. 7 Of sounds, indistinct; heavily muffled. See synonyms under BLUNT, FLAT, HEAVY, LIFELESS, NUMB, SAD, SLOW, TEDIOUS. — *v.t.* & *v.i.* To make or become dull. [ME *dul.* Akin to OE *dol* foolish.] — **dull′ish** *adj.* — **dul′ly** *adv.* — **dul′ness, dull′ness** *n.*

dull·ard (dul′ərd) *n.* A dull or stupid person.

Dul·les (dul′əs), **John Foster,** 1888–1959, U.S. lawyer and statesman; secretary of state 1952–1959.

Du·long and Pe·tit's law (dü·lôṅ′, pe·tēz′) *Physics* A statement that the specific heat of any solid element, multiplied by the atomic weight is nearly a constant (approximately, 6.4). [after P. L. *Dulong,* 1785–1838; A. T. *Petit,* 1791–1820, French physicists]

du·lo·sis (do͞o·lō′sis, dyo͞o-) *n. Entomol.* A form of slavery practiced by certain genera of ants. [<NL <Gk. *doulōsis* enslavement] — **du·lot′·ic** (-lot′ik) *adj.*

dulse (duls) *n.* A reddish-brown seaweed (*Rhodymenia palmata*) eaten in Ireland, Scotland, and elsewhere as a vegetable. Also **dulce.** [<Irish *duileasg*]

Du·luth (də·lo͞oth′, do͞o-) A port on Lake Superior in NE Minnesota.

du·ly (do͞o′lē, dyo͞o′-) *adv.* In accordance with what is due; fitly; becomingly; regularly; in due time or manner.

Du·ma (do͞o′mä) *n.* The former Russian national assembly elected indirectly by the people; created by an imperial ukase in 1905: also spelled *Douma.* [<Russian]

Du·mas (do͞o·mä′, do͞o′mä; *Fr.* dü·mà′), **Alexandre** Name of two French writers: **Dumas père,** 1803–70, novelist and dramatist, and his son **Dumas fils,** 1824–95, dramatist and novelist.

Du Mau·ri·er (do͞o′môr′ē·ā, dyo͞o′-), **Daphne,** born 1907, English novelist. — **George,** 1834–1896, English illustrator and novelist born in France; grandfather of the preceding.

dumb (dum) *adj.* 1 Unable to make articulate sounds; having no power of speech: deaf and *dumb.* 2 Refraining from speaking; not using words or sounds; mute; silent. 3 Not having usual characteristics, symptoms, accompaniments, or powers; latent: *dumb* ague or chill. 4 *U.S. Colloq.* Stupid. 5 *Naut.* Having no sails: a *dumb* barge. See synonyms under TACITURN. [OE; in def. 4, infl. by cognate G *dumm* stupid] — **dumb′ly** *adv.* — **dumb′ness** *n.*

dumb ague A form of chills and fever in which the symptoms of the disease are concealed or obscure.

Dum·bar·ton (dum·bär′tən) A county of western Scotland; 240 square miles; county seat, Dumbarton. Also **Dum·bar′ton·shire** (-shir).

Dum·bar·ton Oaks (dum′bär·tən, dum·bär′·tən) An estate near Washington, D.C., at which conferences leading to proposals for an international organization were held, August–October 1944.

dumb·bell (dum′bel′) *n.* 1 A gymnastic implement consisting of a handle with a weighted ball at each end. 2 *U.S. Slang* A stupid person.

dumb·found (dum′found′) *v.t.* To strike dumb, confuse; confound. Also **dumb′found′er.** [Blend of DUMB and CONFOUND]

dumb show 1 Gestures and signs without words; pantomime. 2 In early English drama, pantomime representation of part of the action of a play.

dumb·wait·er (dum′wā′tər) *n.* A movable serving table or elevator for carrying things from one room or floor to another.

dum·dum bullet (dum′dum′) A small-arms bullet having a soft point or a jacket which has been cut across at the point so that it will mushroom on impact and tear a gaping wound. [from *Dumdum,* a town near Calcutta, India, where first made]

Dum·fries (dum·frēs′) A county in southern Scotland; 1,073 square miles; capital, Dumfries. Also **Dum·fries′shire** (-shir).

dum·my (dum′ē) *n. pl.* **dum·mies** 1 *Colloq.* One who is dumb; a mute; hence, a stupid person; dolt. 2 A silent person, as an actor without a speaking part. 3 A figure used by a ventriloquist. 4 A comparatively noiseless steam locomotive without a blast pipe. 5 A dumbwaiter. 6 A thing made to represent something else; a model; a figure on which clothes can be displayed. 7 A figure stuffed with straw or sawdust, used in bayonet practice; also, a similar figure used by football players in tackling practice. 8 In certain card games, an exposed hand played by the opposite player; also, the player to whom that hand has been dealt. 9 A person who represents another in a transaction, but who poses as acting for himself; a straw man. 10 *Printing* A model book, usually blank, made up as a pattern. — **double dummy** Whist or bridge as played by two persons, each playing two hands, one of which is exposed. — *adj.* 1 Sham; counterfeit. 2 Silent. 3 Having no explosive charge: *dummy* ammunition. 4 Made to resemble some object, but having no real use; artificial: a *dummy* door. — *v.t.* **dum·mied, ·my·ing** To lay out (printed matter) as a guide for making up. — **to dummy up** *U.S. Slang* To become silent. [<DUMB]

du·mor·ti·er·ite (do͞o·môr′tē·ə·rīt′, dyo͞o-) *n.* An aluminum borosilicate mineral resembling lapis lazuli: used in the making of refractories and high-grade porcelain dielectrics and sometimes cut as a gemstone. [after E. *Dumortier,* French paleontologist]

dump[1] (dump) *v.t.* 1 To drop or throw down abruptly or heavily. 2 To empty out, as from a container. 3 To empty (a container), as by overturning. 4 To throw (goods or commodities) on a market, especially a foreign market, in quantity and at low prices. 5 To get rid of; throw away. — *v.i.* 6 To fall or drop. 7 To unload goods or commodities. 8 To unload. — *n.* 1 A dumping ground; especially, a place where city refuse is dumped. 2 That which is dumped. 3 A place where ammunition, stores, or supplies are held for rapid distribution. 4 *U.S. Slang* A poor, ill-kept dwelling or place; also, lodgings. 5 A leaden counter used by boys in various games. 6 Something short, thick, and heavy. 7 *Brit.* A large globular sweetmeat; a bull's-eye. 8 A coin more or less thick and shapeless. [ME <Scand. Cf. Norw. *dumpa* fall suddenly.] — **dump′er** *n.*

dump[2] (dump) *n.* 1 *pl.* A gloomy state of mind; melancholy. 2 *Obs.* A slow, melancholy dance, or the music for it. [Cf. MD *domp* mental haze]

dump·ish (dump′ish) *adj.* Depressed in spirits; sad; morose. — **dump′ish·ly** *adv.* — **dump′ish·ness** *n.*

dump·ling (dump′ling) *n.* 1 A small piece of pie crust or biscuit dough filled with fruit and baked or steamed. 2 A small mass of dough dropped into boiling soup or stew. 3 A short, stocky person or animal.

dump truck A truck for hauling gravel, coal, etc., which unloads by tilting back the cargo bin and opening the tailboard.

dump·y[1] (dump′ē) *adj.* **dump·i·er, dump·i·est** Sullen or discontented; sulky; gloomy or cast down.

dump·y[2] (dump′ē) *adj.* **dump·i·er, dump·i·est** Short and thick; stocky. — **dump′i·ly** *adv.* — **dump′i·ness** *n.*

dumpy level A surveyor's level consisting of a short telescope rigidly attached to the spindle connecting it with the horizontally rotating table.

Dum·yat (do͝om·yät′) The Arabic name for DAMIETTA.

dun[1] (dun) *v.t.* & *v.i.* **dunned, dun·ning** To press (a debtor) for payment; importune; pester. — *n.* 1 One who duns. 2 A demand for payment. [Prob. var. of DIN[1]]

dun[2] (dun) *adj.* Of a grayish-brown or reddish-brown color. — *n.* 1 Dun color. 2 A dun-colored horse. 3 *Obs.* A nickname for an old horse; a jade. 4 A dun fly. — *v.t.* **dunned, dun·ning** 1 To make dun-colored. 2 *U.S.* To cure (fish) by salting and packing in a dark place. [OE *dunn*]

dun[3] (dun) *n.* In ancient Ireland and Scotland, a fort or fortified dwelling, encircled by earthworks or mounds: surviving in place names, as *Dundalk, Dundee,* etc. [<Irish *dūn* hill]

Dü·na (dü′nä) The German name for the DVINA.

Dü·na·burg (dü′nä·bo͝orkh) The German name for DAUGAVPILS.

Du·na·jec (do͞o·nä′yets) A river in south Poland, flowing 128 miles east to the Vistula.

Du·nant (dü·näṅ′), **Jean Henri,** 1828–1910, Swiss author; founded the International Red Cross Society, 1864.

Du·nă·rea (dōō′nə·ryä) The Rumanian name for the Danube.

Dun·bar (dun·bär′) A burgh on the North Sea, Scotland; scene of Cromwell's victory over the Scots, 1650.

Dun·bar (dun′bär), **Paul Laurence,** 1872–1906, U.S. Negro poet. **—William,** 1465?–1530?, Scottish monk and poet.

Dun·can (dung′kən) A masculine personal name. [<Scottish Gaelic, brown chief] **—Duncan,** died 1040, king of Scotland murdered by Macbeth; portrayed in Shakespeare's *Macbeth.*

Dun·can (dung′kən), **Isadora,** 1878–1927, U.S. dancer.

Duncan Phyfe See PHYFE, DUNCAN.

dunce (duns) *n.* A stupid or ignorant person. [after Johannes *Duns* Scotus]

dunce cap A conical paper cap formerly placed on the head of a dull-witted pupil.

dunch (dunch, dōōnch) *v.t. Scot.* To nudge or shove with the elbow; jog. —*n.* A push with the elbow; a jog; a powerful blow.

Dun·ci·ad (dun′sē·ad) *n.* A satirical poem (Books I–III published in 1728, Book IV in 1742) by Alexander Pope.

Dun·dee (dun·dē′) A port on the Firth of Tay, a burgh of south Angus county, Scotland.

Dun·dee (dun·dē′), **Viscount,** 1649?–89, John Graham of Claverhouse, Scottish soldier; foe of the Covenanters.

dun·der·head (dun′dər·hed′) *n.* A blockhead; dunce. Also **dun′der·pate′** (-pāt′). [<dial. E (Scottish) *dunder* rumble, boom + HEAD] — **dun′der·head′ed** *adj.*

dune (dōōn, dyōōn) *n.* A hill of loose sand heaped up by the wind: usually near a shore; a down. [<F <MDu. Akin to DOWN³.]

Dun·e·din (dun·ē′din) 1 A port in SE South Island, New Zealand. 2 The Gaelic name for EDINBURGH.

Dun·ferm·line (dun·fûrm′lin) A burgh in SW Fifeshire, Scotland.

dun·fish (dun′fish′) *n. U.S.* Codfish cured by dunning.

dun fly An artificial fly variously imitative of the mayfly, used in angling.

dung¹ (dung) *n.* 1 Animal excrement; feces; manure. 2 Anything foul. —*v.t.* To cover or enrich with or as with dung. [OE] —**dung′y** *adj.*

dung² (dung, dōōng) *adj. Scot.* Knocked; beaten; hence, finished; exhausted.

dun·ga·ree (dung′gə·rē′) *n.* 1 A coarse cotton cloth, originally from the East Indies, used for sailors' working clothes, tents, sails, etc. 2 *pl.* Working clothes made of this fabric. [<Hind. *dungrī*]

dung beetle Any of various scarabaeid beetles that breed in dung, as the tumblebug and the sacred scarab of Egypt. Also **dung chafer.**

dun·geon (dun′jən) *n.* 1 A dark underground prison. 2 A donjon. For illustration see DONJON. See synonyms under HOLE. [<OF *donjon* <Gmc.]

dung·hill (dung′hil′) *n.* 1 A heap of manure. 2 Figuratively, a vile abode or condition. —*adj.* From or of the dunghill; ignoble.

dun·ie·was·sal (dōō′nē·wos′əl) *n. Scot.* 1 A yeoman; contemptuously, a farmer of the lower class. 2 A gentleman; especially, a younger son of a family of rank. Also **dun′nie·was′sal.**

dun·ite (dun′īt) *n.* A variety of peridotite either wholly composed of olivine or with a small amount of chromite or ilmenite. [from *Dun* Mountain, New Zealand]

dunk (dungk) *v.t.* & *v.i.* To dip or sop (bread, doughnuts, etc.) into tea, coffee, soup, etc., while eating. [<G *tunken* dip] —**dunk′er** *n.*

Dun·ker (dung′kər) *n.* One of a body of German-American Baptists, practising triple immersion and opposed to military service and the taking of legal oaths: officially called *German Baptist Brethren.* Also **Dun′kard.** [<G *tunker* < *tunken* dip]

Dun·kirk (dun′kûrk) A port on the North Sea in northern France; scene of evacuation of British forces (more than 300,000 men) to Britain, May 26–June 4, 1940, World War II. *French* **Dun·kerque** (dœn·kerk′).

Dun Laoghai·re (dun lâr′ē) The principal port for Dublin. Formerly **Dun·lea′ry** (dun·lir′ē) or **King′ston.**

dun·lin (dun′lin) *n.* The red-backed sandpiper (*Pelidna alpina*) of the northern hemisphere.

Dun·lop (dun′lop, dun·lop′), **John Boyd,** 1840–1921, Scottish inventor.

dun·nage (dun′ij) *n.* 1 *Naut.* Mats and battens used to protect cargo on board ship. 2 A layer of planks placed under stored goods to protect them from contact with the ground. 3 Sailors' baggage. 4 Camp equipment. [Origin uncertain]

Dunne (dun), **Finley Peter,** 1867–1936, U.S. journalist and humorist.

dun·nite (dun′īt) *n.* A shock-resistant explosive composed largely of ammonium picrate: used in armor-piercing projectiles: also called *explosive D.* [after Major B. W. *Dunn,* 1860–1936, U.S. inventor]

Du·nois (dü·nwȧ′), **Jean,** 1403–68, French commander under Joan of Arc, natural son of the Duke of Orléans: called the "Bastard of Orléans."

Dun·sa·ny (dun·sā′nē), **Lord,** 1878–1957, Edward John Moreton Drax Plunkett, 18th Baron Dunsany, Irish writer.

Dun·si·nane (dun′sə·nān′, dun′sə·nān) A hill in SE Perthshire, Scotland: reputed scene of Macbeth's defeat, 1054.

Duns Sco·tus (dunz skō′təs), **Johannes,** 1265–1308, Franciscan monk; scholastic philosopher: called also "the Subtile Doctor."

Dun·stan (dun′stən), **Saint,** 924?–988, English Benedictine monk and statesman; abbot of Glastonbury; archbishop of Canterbury 959–988.

dunt (dunt, dōōnt) *n.* 1 *Scot. Dial.* A blow or thwack. 2 An injury from such a blow.

du·o (dōō′ō, dyōō′ō) *n. pl.* **du·os** or **du·i** (-ē) *Music* An instrumental duet. [<Ital.]

duo- *combining form* Two: *duogravure.* [<L *duo* two]

du·o·dec·i·mal (dōō′ō·des′ə·məl, dyōō′-) *adj.* Pertaining to twelve; reckoning by twelves. —*n.* 1 One of the numbers used in duodecimal arithmetic; a twelfth. 2 *pl.* A method of computing by twelves instead of by tens. [<L *duodecimus* twelfth < *duodecim* twelve]

du·o·dec·i·mo (dōō′ō·des′ə·mō, dyōō′-) *adj.* 1 Having twelve pages or leaves to one sheet of printing paper. 2 Being about 4 1/2 by 7 1/2 inches in size: said of a page or book. Written also *12 mo, 12°.* —*n. pl.* **·mos** 1 The size of a page folded twelve to a sheet; also, a page or a book of this size. 2 *Music* An interval of a twelfth. [<L *(in) duodecimo* (in) twelfth]

du·o·dec·u·ple (dōō′ō·dek′yōō·pəl, dyōō′-) *adj.* Consisting of twelve; having twelve parts or members; twelvefold; also, taken by twelves. —*n.* A number or sum twelve times as great as another. [<L *duodecim* twelve; infl. in form by DECUPLE]

du·o·de·cu·pli·cate (dōō′ō·de·kyōō′plə·kit, dyōō′-) *adj.* 1 Twelvefold. 2 Raised to the twelfth power. —*v.t.* (-kāt) **·cat·ed, ·cat·ing** To multiply by twelve. —*n.* One of twelve like things. —**du′o·de·cu′pli·cate·ly** *adv.*

du·o·den·a·ry (dōō′ō·den′ər·ē, -dē′nər·ē, dyōō′-) *adj.* 1 Pertaining to or determined by the number twelve. 2 Denoting or belonging to a system of arithmetical numeration of which the base is twelve. [<L *duodenarius* containing twelve]

du·o·de·ni·tis (dōō′ə·də·nī′tis, dyōō′-) *n. Pathol.* Inflammation of the duodenum. [<DUODEN(O)- + -ITIS]

duodeno- *combining form* Of or pertaining to the duodenum. Also, before vowels, **duoden-.** [<Med. L *duodenum* the duodenum]

du·o·de·num (dōō′ə·dē′nəm, dyōō′-, dōō·od′ə·nəm) *n. pl.* **·na** (-nə) *Anat.* That part of the small intestine extending from the pylorus to the jejunum. [<Med. L *duodenum (digitorum)* of twelve (fingers) < *duodecim* twelve; with ref. to its length] —**du′o·de′nal** *adj.*

du·o·gra·vure (dōō′ō·grə·vyōōr′, -grā′vyər, dyōō′-) *n.* 1 A process in photoengraving in which two plates are used to produce a print in two shades of one color. 2 A print made by this process. Also **du·o·graph** (dōō′ə·graf, -gräf, dyōō′-).

du·o·log (dōō′ə·lôg, -log, dyōō′-) *n.* A literary composition for two speakers; dialog. Also **du′o·logue.** [<DUO- + (MONO)LOG]

duo·mo (dwô′mō) *n. pl.* **·mi** (-mē) *Italian* A cathedral.

du·o·tone (dōō′ə·tōn′, dyōō′-) *n.* A duogravure; any illustration in two tones of the same color.

du·o·type (dōō′ə·tīp′, dyōō′-) *n.* A picture produced from two halftones, the plates being from one negative, but dissimilar in etching.

dup (dup) *v.t. Obs.* To open. [Contraction of *do up*]

dupe¹ (dōōp, dyōōp) *n.* One misled through credulity; a victim of deception. —*v.t.* **duped, dup·ing** To make a dupe of; impose upon; deceive; trick. See synonyms under DECEIVE. [<OF <L *upupa* a hoopoe (a bird thought to be stupid)] —**dup′a·bil′i·ty** *n.* —**dup′a·ble** *adj.* —**dup′er** *n.*

dupe² (dōōp, dyōōp) *n.* In motion pictures, a negative film made from the positive, as a source for further positives. [Short for DUPLICATE]

dup·er·y (dōō′pər·ē, dyōō′-) *n. pl.* **·er·ies** The act or practice of duping; the condition of being deceived.

du·pi·on (dōō′pē·ən), **du·pi·on·i** (dōō′pē·on′ē, -ō′nē) See DOUPION.

du·ple (dōō′pəl, dyōō′-) *adj.* 1 Double; twofold. 2 Having two beats to a measure, as 2-2 or 2-4 time. [<L *duplus.* See DOUBLE]

Du·pleix (dü·pleks′), **Joseph François,** 1697–1763, Marquis Dupleix, governor of early French settlements in India.

Du·ples·sis-Mor·nay (dü·ple·sē′môr·nā′) See MORNAY.

duple time See under TIME.

du·plex (dōō′pleks, dyōō′-) *adj.* 1 Having two parts; double; twofold. 2 Having different faces, as some kinds of paper. 3 *Mech.* Working mechanically in two ways, whether in opposite directions along the same line, upon two things, by two similar parts, or by two separate operations at once. 4 *Biol.* Double, or with twice the number of parts; twinned. —*n.* A duplex house or apartment. [<L < *duo* two + stem of *plicare* fold] —**du·plex′i·ty** *n.*

duplex apartment An apartment having rooms on two floors instead of on one.

duplex house A house having two one-family units.

duplex telegraphy Telegraphy adapted to the sending of two messages simultaneously over a single wire and in opposite directions.

du·pli·cate (dōō′plə·kit, dyōō′-) *adj.* 1 Made or done exactly like an original. 2 Growing in pairs; double. 3 Replayed by other players with the same cards as originally dealt: *duplicate* whist. See also DUPLICATE BRIDGE under BRIDGE². —*n.* A double or counterpart; something that exactly corresponds to an original from which it is made; a copy: originally one of two, now one of any number of like objects considered in their relation to the original and not to one another. —*v.t.* (dōō′plə·kāt, dyōō′-) **·cat·ed, ·cat·ing** 1 To make an exact copy of; reproduce exactly. 2 To double; make twofold. 3 To repeat, as an action or effort; do a second time. See synonyms under IMITATE. [<L *duplicatus,* pp. of *duplicare* double < *duplex* twofold] —**du′pli·cate·ly** *adv.*

Synonyms (noun): copy, counterpart, facsimile, imitation, likeness, replica, reproduction, transcript. A *copy* is as nearly like the original as the copyist has power to make it; a *duplicate* is exactly like the original; a carbon *copy* of a typewritten document must be a *duplicate*; we may have an inaccurate *copy,* but never an inaccurate *duplicate.* A *facsimile* is like the original in appearance; a *duplicate* is the same as the original in substance and effect; a *facsimile* of the Declaration of Independence is not a *duplicate.* A *facsimile* of a key might be quite useless; a *duplicate* will open the lock. A *counterpart* exactly corresponds to another object, but perhaps without design, while a *copy* is intentional. An *imitation* is always thought of as inferior to the original; as, an *imitation* of Milton. A *replica* is a *copy* of a work of art by the maker of the original. In law, a *transcript* is an official *copy,* authenticated by the signature of the proper officer, and by the seal of the appropriate court. *Antonyms*: archetype, model, original, pattern, prototype.

du·pli·ca·tion (dōō′plə·kā′shən, dyōō′-) *n.* The act of duplicating, or the state of being duplicated; doubling. —**du′pli·ca′tive** *adj.*

du·pli·ca·tor (dōō′plə·kā′tər, dyōō′-) *n.* 1 One who makes anything in duplicate. 2 A contrivance or device for making duplicates, as written or typewritten matter or a drawing.

du·pli·ca·ture (dōō′plə·kā′chər, dyōō′-) *n. Biol.* A doubling or folding, as of a membrane.

du·plic·i·ty (dōō·plis′ə·tē, dyōō-) *n. pl.* **·ties** 1 Tricky deceitfulness; double-dealing. 2 *Obs.* The state of being two; doubleness. See synonyms under DECEPTION, FRAUD. [<OF *duplicité* <LL *duplicitas, -tatis* doubleness < *duplex* twofold] —**du·plic′i·tous** *adj.*

du Pont (do͞o·pont′, dyo͞o-; *Fr.* dü pôɴ′) Family of U.S. industrialists, founded by **Éleuthère Irénée,** 1771–1834, who established the E.I. Du Pont de Nemours Company. —**Samuel Francis,** 1803–65, rear admiral, nephew of the preceding.

du Pont de Ne·mours (do͞o pont′ də nə·mo͝or′, dyo͞o pont′; *Fr.* dü pôɴ′ də nə·mo͝or′), **Pierre Samuel,** 1739–1817, French economist and statesman.

Du·que de Ca·xi·as (do͞o′kə thə kə·shē′əs) A city in SE Brazil: also *Caxias.*

Du·quesne (do͞o·kān′, dyo͞o-), **Fort** A French fort, taken by the English and renamed FORT PITT, on present site of Pittsburgh.

du·ra[1] (do͝or′ə, dyo͝or′ə) *n.* **1** Duramen. **2** The dura mater.

du·ra[2] (do͝or′ə) See DURRA.

du·ra·bil·i·ty (do͝or′ə·bil′ə·tē, dyo͝or′-) *n.* **1** The quality of being durable. **2** The power of long resistance to decay or change. Also **du′ra·ble·ness.** —**du′ra·bly** *adv.*

du·ra·ble (do͝or′ə·bəl, dyo͝or′-) *adj.* Able to continue long in the same state; lasting. See synonyms under PERMANENT. [<OF <L *durabilis* <*durare* endure < *durus* hard]

du·rain (do͞o·rān′, dyo͞o-) *n. Geol.* Bituminous coal having bands of a dense, hard, granular structure, often flecked with thin streaks of brighter material. [<L *durus* hard + (FUS-AIN]

du·ral (do͝or′əl, dyo͝or′-) *adj.* Of, pertaining to, or derived from the dura mater.

Du·ral·u·min (do͞o·ral′yə·min, dyo͞o-) *n.* A light, strong alloy of aluminum and copper, with addition of magnesium and manganese: a trade name.

du·ra ma·ter (do͝or′ə mā′tər, dyo͝or′ə) *Anat.* The tough fibrous membrane forming the outermost covering of the brain and spinal cord. [<Med. L <L *dura* hard + *mater* mother, trans. form Arabic]

du·ra·men (do͞o·rā′min, dyo͞o-) *n. Bot.* The heartwood of an exogenous stem or tree trunk; the darker central portion of the wood, comprised of dead tissue, surrounded by the alburnum. See illustration under EXOGEN. [<L, a ligenous vine branch]

dur·ance (do͝or′əns, dyo͝or′-) *n.* **1** Personal restraint; imprisonment. **2** *Obs.* Duration; continuance. [<OF, duration <*durer* last <L *durare.*

Du·ran·go (do͞o·räng′gō) A state in northern Mexico; 47,691 square miles; capital, Durango.

Du·ran·te (do͞o·rän′tā) See DANTE.

du·ra·tion (do͞o·rā′shən, dyo͞o-) *n.* **1** The period of time during which anything lasts. **2** Continuance; time in general. [<LL *duratio, -onis* <*durare* endure]

dur·a·tive (do͝or′ə·tiv, dyo͝or′-) *adj.* Gram. Designating an aspect of the verb that expresses the action as incomplete or continuing; imperfective. —*n.* The durative aspect, or a verb in this spect.

Du·raz·zo (do͞o·rät′tsō) The chief port of Albania, on the Adriatic: ancient *Dyrrhachium.* Albanian *Durres.*

Dur·ban (dûr′bən) A port and the largest city of KwaZulu/Natal province, Republic of South Africa.

dur·bar (dûr′bär) *n.* Anglo-Indian **1** Formerly a reception or levee given by a native ruler or officer of rank in British India; a state levee. **2** The room in which such a levee is held; court; hall of audience. **3** Formerly, the executive officer or government of a native state, as distinguished from the British resident officials. [<Hind. <Persian *darbār* court <*dar* door + *bār* assembly]

dure (do͝or, dyo͝or) *Obs. v.t. & v.i.* To endure. —*adj.* Severe; hard; rough. [<L *durare* <*durus* hard]

Dü·rer (dü′rər, **Albrecht,** 1471–1528, German painter and engraver.

du·ress (do͝or′is, dyo͝or′-, do͞o·res′, dyo͞o-) *n.* Constraint by force or fear; compulsion; imprisonment. Also **du·resse′.** See synonyms under *fetter.* [<OF *duresse* hardness, constraint <L *duritia* <*durus* hard]

D'Ur·fey (dûr′fē), **Thomas,** 1653–1723, English dramatist and humorous song writer.

Dur·ham (do͝or′əm) *n.* One of a breed of horthorned beef cattle. [from *Durham,* England]

Dur·ham (do͝or′əm) **1** A county of NE England; 1,015 square miles; county seat, Durham. **2** A city in north central North Carolina.

du·ri·an (do͝or′ē·ən) *n.* **1** A tall forest tree *(Durio zibethinus)* cultivated throughout the Malay Peninsula. **2** The fruit of this tree, often ten inches in length with thick, spiny rind, and custard-like pulp having a fetid odor. The seeds are eaten roasted like chestnuts. Also **du′ri·on.** [<Malay <*duri* a thorn]

DURIAN FRUIT AND BLOSSOM (The tree about 80 feet in height)

dur·ing (do͝or′ing, dyo͝or′-) *prep.* **1** Throughout the time, existence, or action of: The noise continued *during* the night. **2** In the course of; at some period in: He interrupted *during* the speech. [Orig. ppr. of DURE]

durk (dûrk) *n.* Scot. Dirk. Also **durke.**

dur·mast (dûr′mast, -mäst) *n.* **1** The valuable dark, tough, elastic wood of the European oak *(Quercus petraea).* **2** The tree itself. [Origin uncertain]

du·ro (do͝or′rō) *n. pl.* **·ros** The Spanish and Spanish-American silver dollar. [< Sp. *(peso) duro* hard (peso) <L *durus* hard]

Du·roc (dü·rôk′), **Géraud Christophe Michel,** 1772–1813, Duc de Friuli, French general under Napoleon.

dur·ra (do͝or′ə) *n.* A grain sorghum of southern Asia and northern Africa; Indian millet: also spelled *dhoura, doura, dura.* Also **durr** (do͝or). [<Arabic *dhura*]

Dur·res (do͝or′rəs) Albanian name for DURAZZO.

durst (dûrst) Archaic past tense of DARE.

du·rum (do͝or′əm, dyo͝or′-) *n.* A species of wheat *(Triticum durum)* widely grown for macaroni and spaghetti products; introduced into the United States from southern Russia and the Mediterranean. [<L, neut. sing. of *durus* hard]

Du·ru·y (dü·rü·ē′) **Victor,** 1811–94, French historian.

Du·se (do͞o′ze), **Eleonora,** 1859–1924, Italian actress.

dusk (dusk) *n.* **1** A state between darkness and light; twilight. **2** Swarthiness; shadowiness. —*adj.* **1** Somewhat dark or obscure by reason of failing or feeble light; dim. **2** Dark in color; swarthy. —*v.t. v.i.* To make, grow, or appear shadowy or dim; darken. [OE *dox*]

dusk·i·ness (dus′kē·nis) *n.* Moderate darkness.

dusk·y (dus′kē) *adj.* **dusk·i·er, dusk·i·est 1** Somewhat dark; dim; obscure; swarthy. **2** Gloomy; dejected. Also **dusk′ish.** See synonyms under DARK. —**dusk′i·ly** *adv.*

dusky glider The greater glider.

dusky grouse A blue grouse *(Dendrogapus obscurus).*

Düs·sel·dorf (düs′əl·dôrf) A city on the Rhine in North Rhine-Westphalia.

dust (dust) *n.* **1** Any substance, as earth, reduced to powder. **2** A cloud of pulverized earth; hence, figuratively, a bewildering cloud of words, arguments, etc.; confusion; controversy. **3** Gold dust. **4** A dead body; remains. **5** The earth; the grave; figuratively, downfall or humiliation. **6** *Brit.* Rubbish; anything worthless; ashes and household sweepings. See synonyms under BODY. —**to bite the dust** To fall wounded or dead. — **to make the dust fly 1** To act or go with energy and speed. **2** To create a fuss. —**to throw dust in one's eyes** To deceive; mislead. —*v.t.* **1** To wipe or brush dust from. **2** To sprinkle with powder, etc. **3** To soil with dust. —*v.i.* **4** To wipe or brush dust from furniture, etc. **5** *Slang* To hurry away: often with *off* or *out.* See synonyms under CLEANSE. [OE *dūst*] —**dust′·less** *adj.*

dust·bin (dust′bin′) *n.* Brit. A container for trash, garbage, or ashes.

Dust Bowl A desert region in the south central United States where the eroded topsoil of fallow lands has been blown away by dust storms. Also **dust bowl.**

dust devil *Meteorol.* A small whirlwind, often of great intensity, which lifts dust, leaves, straw, and other light material to heights of two or three hundred feet in dry or desert areas.

dust·er (dus′tər) *n.* **1** One who or that which dusts. **2** A cloth or brush for removing dust; a receptacle for sprinkling a powder. **3** A garment or covering to protect from dust.

dust jacket A removable covering for a book, usually of paper, and often bearing printed matter.

dust·man (dust′mən) *n. pl.* **·men** (-mən) **1** *Brit.* One whose business is the removal of ashes, refuse, etc., from yards and houses. **2** The sandman.

dust·pan (dust′pan′) *n.* An implement, resembling a short-handled shovel, into which dust from a floor is swept.

dust·proof (dust′pro͞of′) *adj.* Capable of excluding dust.

dust·storm (dust′stôrm′) *n.* A windstorm carrying clouds of dust along with it. Also **dust storm.**

dust·y (dus′tē) *adj.* **dust·i·er, dust·i·st 1** Covered with or as with dust. **2** Of the color of dust. **3** Powdered, like dust. —**dust′i·ly** *adv.* — **dust′i·ness** *n.*

dusty pink A very light dull red.

Dutch (duch) *adj.* **1** Belonging or relating to, or characteristic of the Netherlands or its people. **2** *Archaic* Belonging or relating to the Teutonic or German peoples. **3** *Slang* German: A humorous or derogatory use. —*n.* **1** The people of the Netherlands: with *the.* **2** *Slang* The Germans: with *the.* **3** The Low German, West Germanic language of the Netherlands. Abbr. *Du.* —**Middle Dutch** The pre-Reformation, literary language of Flanders, Brabant, and Limburg. Abbr. *MDu.* —**to beat the Dutch** *Slang* **1** To exceed in causing surprise; surpass in strangeness. **2** To overcome stubborn resistance. **3** Excessively; extremely: adverbial use. —**to get in Dutch** *Slang* To incur disapproval. —**to go Dutch** *U.S. Colloq.* To have each participant pay his own expenses. —**to talk like a Dutch uncle** To talk with severity and kindness at the same time. [<MDu. *dutsch* Germanic, Dutch]

Dutch Belted A breed of dairy cattle originating in the Netherlands and characterized by a wide white band around the middle of the body.

Dutch Borneo See BORNEO.

Dutch cheese 1 A hard, round, skim-milk cheese; also, cottage cheese. **2** The common mallow.

Dutch courage Temporary courage inspired by or as by intoxicating drink; also, the drink itself.

Dutch door A door divided horizontally in the middle, thus allowing the opening of one half or of both.

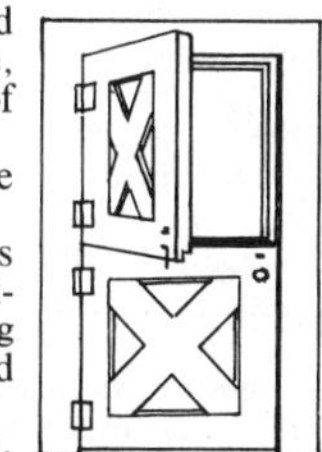
DUTCH DOOR

Dutch East Indies See NETHERLANDS EAST INDIES.

Dutch elm disease A fungus disease of elms which attacks the leaves, causing defoliation, decay, and death.

Dutch foil, Dutch gold, Dutch leaf See DUTCH METAL.

Dutch Guiana See SURINAM.

Dutch Harbor A village and United States naval base on a small island off Unalaska Island, Aleutian Islands.

dutch·man (du ch′mən) *n. pl.* **·men** (-mən) **1** A piece inserted in a crevice to fill it or hide bad fitting, or to take the place of a defective piece cut out or a piece broken. **2** A shim. **3** A stick placed transversely in a load of logs to serve as a brace. **4** A buried log, or the like, serving as an anchor; a deadman.

Dutch·man (duch′mən) *n. pl.* **·men** (-mən) **1** A native of the Netherlands. **2** A Dutch ship. **3** *Slang* A German.

dutch·man's-breech·es (duch′mənz·brich′iz) *n.* A low woodland herb *(Dicentra cucullaria)* of the fumitory family, with widely spreading spurs suggesting the name. Also **dutch′ mans-breech′es.**

dutch·man's-pipe (duch′mənz·pīp′) *n.* A climbing shrub *(Aristolochia durior)* of the Mississippi Valley, which has a calyx tube shaped like the bowl of a meerschaum pipe.

Dutch metal A malleable alloy of copper, tin, and zinc, used in the form of thin leaves as a substitute for gold leaf in bookbinding, toymaking, etc.; tombac.

Dutch New Guinea See NETHERLANDS NEW GUINEA.

Dutch oven **1** A brick oven heated by fire within it and cooking by the heat retained when the embers are removed. **2** A shallow, iron, lidded baking pot, heated by surrounding or covering it with coals. **3** A tin or sheet-steel oven used in front of an open fire, cooking by reflected heat.

Dutch treat *U.S. Colloq.* Entertainment at which each person pays his own bill.

Dutch uncle A very frank and severe critic or advisor.

Dutch West Indies See NETHERLANDS WEST INDIES.

du·te·ous (do͞o′tē·əs, dyo͞o′-) *adj.* Rendering due respect and obedience; dutiful. **—du′te·ous·ly** *adv.* **—du′te·ous·ness** *n.*

du·ti·a·ble (do͞o′tē·ə·bəl, dyo͞o′-) *adj.* Subject to impost duty.

du·tied (do͞o′tēd, dyo͞o′-) *adj. U.S.* Subjected to taxes or customs duties.

du·ti·ful (do͞o′ti·fəl, dyo͞o′-) *adj.* **1** Performing the duties of one's position; submissive to superiors; obedient. **2** Expressive of respect or of a sense of duty; respectful. See synonyms under GOOD, MORAL. **—du′ti·ful·ly** *adv.* **—du′ti·ful·ness** *n.*

Du·tra (do͞o′trə), **Eurico Gaspar,** born 1885, Brazilian general; president of Brazil 1946–1951.

du·ty (do͞o′tē, dyo͞o′-) *n. pl.* **·ties** **1** That which one is bound, by any natural, legal, or moral obligation, to pay, do, or perform. **2** Specific obligatory service or function, as of a soldier, sailor, etc.: He is on sea *duty.* **3** The obligation to do that which is prescribed or required, especially by the moral law; moral obligation; right action. **4** An impost or customs tax, as upon goods imported, exported, or consumed. **5** *Agric.* **a** The quantity of water necessary, in artificial irrigation, to supply adequately a definite surface of land. **b** The acreage which a stated amount of water will adequately serve: called **duty of water.** **6** *Mech.* **a** The efficiency of or useful work done by an engine or motor under stated conditions. **b** The efficiency of a steam engine expressed in terms of its capacity to lift a definite weight one foot high while consuming a certain quantity of coal. **7** A formal expression of respect. **—customs duty** A tax levied on imports (or exports) for purposes of revenue or, more commonly, for the protection of domestic manufacturers. [<AF *duete* <*du* DUE]

Synonyms: accountability, business, function, obligation, office, responsibility, right, righteousness. Etymologically, *duty* is that which is owed or due; *obligation,* that to or by which one is bound; *right,* that which is correct, straight, or in the direct line of truth and goodness; *responsibility,* that for which one must answer. *Duty* and *responsibility* are thought of as to some person or persons; *right* is impersonal. One's *duty* may be to others or to himself; his *obligations* and *responsibilities* are to others. *Duty* arises from the nature of things; *obligation* and *responsibility* may be created by circumstances, as by one's own promise, or by the acceptance of a trust, etc. We speak of a parent's *duty,* a debtor's *obligation*; or of a child's *duty* of obedience, and a parent's *responsibility* for the child's welfare. *Right* is that which accords with the moral system of the universe. *Righteousness* is *right* incarnated in action. In a more limited sense, *right* may be used of what one may rightly claim, and so be the converse of *duty.* It is the creditor's *right* to demand payment, and the debtor's *duty* to pay. Compare BUSINESS, TAX, VIRTUE.

du·ty-free (do͞o′tē·frē′, dyo͞o′-) *adj.* & *adv.* Free from customs duties.

du·um·vir (do͞o·um′vər, dyo͞o-) *n. pl.* **·virs** or **·vi·ri** (vi·rī) One of two ancient Roman magistrates holding an office jointly. [<L <*duo* two + *vir* man] **—du·um′vi·ral** *adj.*

du·um·vi·rate (do͞o·um′və·rit, dyo͞o-) *n.* **1** The joint office of duumviri. **2** A combination of two men; government by a pair of associated officials.

Du·veen (do͞o·vēn′), **Joseph,** 1869–1939, first Baron Duveen of Millbank, English art dealer.

Du·ve·neck (do͞o′və·nek), **Frank,** 1848–1919, U.S. painter, sculptor, and art instructor.

du·ve·tyn (do͞o′və·tēn, do͞o′və·tēn′) *n.* Twill-weave fabric with a napped surface, made of wool, rayon, cotton, or silk, or combinations of fibers. Also **du′ve·tine, du′ve·tyne.** [<F *duvet* down]

dux (duks) *n. pl.* **du·ces** (do͞o′sēz, dyo͞o′-) or **dux·es** **1** *Scot.* The head or leader of a class in a school. **2** *Music* The subject or principal melody of a fugue. [<L, leader]

Dvi·na (dvē′nə) **1** A river in northern European Russian S.F.S.R., flowing 455 miles NW to **Dvina Bay** (also *Archangel Bay*), an inlet of the White Sea; also *Northern Dvina.* **2** A river in west European U.S.S.R. and Latvia, flowing 633 miles SW to the Gulf of Riga: German **Dü·va** (dü′vä): also *Western Dvina.*

Dvinsk (dvēnsk) The Russian name for DAUGAVPILS.

Dvoř·ák (dvôr′zhäk), **Antonín,** 1841–1904, Czech composer.

dwarf (dwôrf) *n.* A person, animal, or plant that is unnaturally small; especially, an adult human being less than four feet tall. —*v.t.* **1** To prevent the natural development of; stunt. **2** To cause to appear small by comparison. —*v.i.* **3** To become stunted; grow smaller. —*adj.* Smaller than others of its kind; diminutive; stunted. [OE *dweorh*]

dwarf alder The smaller alder-leafed buckthorn *(Rhamnus alnifolia).*

dwarf chestnut The chinkapin.

dwarf cornel A woody perennial herb (genus *Cornus*) of the dogwood family, especially the bunchberry.

dwarf·ish (dwôr′fish) *adj.* Like a dwarf; diminutive; stunted. **—dwarf′ish·ly** *adv.* **—dwarf′ish·ness** *n.*

dwarf mallow See under MALLOW.

dwarf star See under STAR.

dwell (dwel) *v.i.* **dwelt** or **dwelled, dwell·ing** **1** To have a fixed abode; reside. **2** To linger, as on a subject; pause, expatiate: with *on* or *upon.* **3** To remain; continue in a state or place. See synonyms under ABIDE. —*n.* **1** The short cessation of motion of a part of a machine to effect its allotted service. **2** *Obs.* Stoppage; delay; pause. [OE *dwellan* mislead, hinder, stay] **—dwell′er** *n.*

dwell·ing (dwel′ing) *n.* A residence; domicile; abode. See synonyms under HOME, HOUSE.

dwelling house A house built for habitation; a domicile. In law it may embrace the dwelling itself and such buildings as are used in connection with it.

Dwight (dwīt), **Timothy,** 1752–1817, American author and educator; president of Yale University 1795–1817.

dwin·dle (dwin′dəl) *v.t.* & *v.i.* **·dled, ·dling** To diminish or become less; make or become smaller; decline. [Freq. of DWINE]

dwine (dwīn) *v.i. Scot.* or *Obs.* To pine or waste away; languish. [OE *dwinan* waste away] **—dwin′ing** *adj.*

Dy *Chem.* Dysprosium (symbol Dy).

dy·ad (dī′ad) *adj.* **1** *Chem.* Having a combining power of two; bivalent. **2** Dyadic. —*n.* **1** A pair of units; duad. **2** *Chem.* An atom, radical, or element that has a combining power of two. See VALENCE. **3** *Biol.* **a** One of a pair of chromosomes, especially in the prophases of the second division in the formation of gametes. See TETRAD. **b** A secondary unit made up of an aggregate of monads. [<L *dyas, dyadis* <Gk. *dyas* the number two]

dy·ad·ic (dī·ad′ik) *adj.* **1** Of or pertaining to a dyad. **2** Based on or relating to the number 2; binary.

Dy·ak (dī′ak) *n.* **1** One of the aboriginal people of Borneo, linguistically akin to the Malays, but differing from them in stature, type, and culture. **2** The Indonesian language of these people. Also spelled *Dayak.*

Dya·ko·vit·sa (dyä·kō′vit·sä) See DJAKOVICA.

dy·ar·chy (dī′är·kē) See DIARCHY.

Dyce (dīs), **Alexander,** 1798–1869, Scottish editor.

dye (dī) *v.* **dyed, dye·ing** *v.t.* **1** To fix a color by soaking in liquid coloring matter. **2** To stain; tinge. —*v.i.* **3** To take or give color: This cloth *dyes* badly. See synonyms under STAIN. —*n.* A fluid or coloring matter used for dyeing; also, the color or hue so produced. According to the method of application, dyes are classified as *substantive,* or *direct,* when they color by simple immersion; *adjective,* or *mordant,* when a fixing agent is used; *ingrain,* or *ice,* when deposited by chemical reaction; *vat,* when applied in an alkali-soluble state and oxidized; and *sulfur,* when used in a sodium sulfide bath followed by oxidation. ◆Homophone: *die.* [OE *dēagian* <*deag* dye, color]

dye·house (dī′hous′) *n.* A building in which dyeing is done.

dyed-in-the-wool (dīd′in·thə·wo͝ol′) *adj.* **1** Dyed before being woven. **2** Thoroughgoing; complete.

dye·ing (dī′ing) *n.* The act, process, or trade of fixing colors in cloth or the like.

dy·er (dī′ər) *n.* One who or that which dyes; especially, a person engaged in the business of dyeing.

Dy·er (dī′ər), **John,** 1700?–58, English poet.

dy·er's-broom (dī′ərz·bro͞om′, -bro͝om′) *n.* A shrubby plant *(Genista tinctoria)* yielding a yellow dye which with woad becomes a permanent green; woadwaxen: also called *dyeweed.* Also **dyer's-green·weed** (dī′ərz-grēn′·wēd′).

dy·er's-weed (dī′ərz·wēd′) *n.* Any of several plants that yield dyeing matter, such as dyer's woad *(Isatis tinctoria).*

dye·stuff (dī′stuf′) *n.* Any material used for dyeing.

dye·weed (dī′wēd′) *n.* Dyer's-broom.

dye·wood (dī′wo͝od′) *n.* A wood that yields dyestuff, such as logwood.

dy·ing (dī′ing) *adj.* **1** Becoming dead; near to death; expiring; closing. **2** Destined to die; mortal; perishable. **3** Relating to death; given, uttered, or manifested just before death.

dyke (dīk) See DIKE.

dyna- *combining form* Power: *dynameter.* Also, before vowels, **dyn-.**

dy·nam·e·ter (dī·nam′ə·tər) *n. Optics* A device for measuring the magnifying power of telescopes. [<DYNA- + METER]

dy·nam·ic (dī·nam′ik) *adj.* **1** Of or pertaining to forces not in equilibrium, or to motion as the result of force: opposed to *static.* **2** Pertaining to or characterized by mechanical force. **3** Producing or involving activity or action of any kind; motive; efficient; causal. **4** Mentally or spiritually energetic, forceful, or powerful: a *dynamic* leader. **5** Of or pertaining to musical dynamics. Also **dy·nam′i·cal.** [<Gk. *dynamikos* powerful <*dynamis* power] **—dy·nam′i·cal·ly** *adv.*

dy·nam·ics (dī·nam′iks) *n. pl. (construed as singular in defs. 1,2, and 4)* **1** The branch of physics that treats of the motion of bodies and the effects of forces in producing motion, and of the laws of the motion thus produced *(kinetics)*: opposed to *statics.* **2** The science that treats of the action of forces, whether producing equilibrium or motion; in this sense including both statics and kinetics. **3** The forces producing or governing activity or movement of any kind; also, the methods of such activity: spiritual *dynamics.* **4** *Music* **a** The words, symbols, etc., used to indicate degrees of loudness: also **dynamic marks.** **b** The act or technique of producing varying degrees of loudness.

dy·na·mism (dī′nə·miz′əm) *n.* **1** *Philos.* One of various doctrines that endeavor to explain the phenomena of the universe, chiefly or wholly, in terms of force or energy. **2** *Psychol.* Any of various psychic forces, as repression, sublimation, etc., acting to produce certain effects upon behavior or the personality: also called *mechanism.* **—dy′na·mist** *n.* **—dy′na·mis′tic** *adj.*

dy·na·mite (dī′nə·mīt) *n.* **1** An explosive composed of nitroglycerin held in an absorbent substance. **2** *Slang* Anything wonderful or spectacular: The news was *dynamite*! —*v.t.* **·mit·ed, ·mit·ing** **1** To blow up or shatter with or as with dynamite. **2** To charge with dynamite; as a mine. [<Gk. *dynamis* power]

dy·na·mit·er (dī′nə·mī′tər) *n.* **1** An expert user of dynamite. **2** One who uses or advocates the destructive use of dynamite, especially for political or revolutionary purposes. Also **dy′na·mit′ist.**

dy·na·mo (dī′nə·mō) *n. pl.* **·mos** A machine for the conversion of mechanical energy into

DYNAMO

electrical energy through the agency of electromagnetic induction. Compare GENERATOR and ELECTRIC MOTOR. [Short for DYNAMOELECTRIC MACHINE]

dynamo- *combining form* Force; power: *dynamograph.* [<Gk. *dynamis* power]

dy·na·mo·e·lec·tric (dī′nə·mō·i·lek′trik) *adj.* Pertaining to the relation between electricity and mechanical force. Also **dy′na·mo·e·lec′·tri·cal.**

dy·na·mog·e·ny (dī′nə·moj′ə·nē) *n. Physiol.* Production of increased nervous activity; the reinforcing effect of sensorial stimuli upon muscular action. [<DYNAMO- + -GENY]

dy·nam·o·graph (dī·nam′ə·graf, -gräf) *n.* A recording dynamometer; specifically, one used to register muscular power. Also **dy′no·graph.**

dy·na·mom·e·ter (dī′nə·mom′ə·tər) *n.* An instrument for measuring force exerted or power expended, as by a machine. [<DYNAMO- + -METER] **—dy·na·mo·met·ric** (dī′nə·mō·met′rik) or **·ri·cal** *adj.*

dy·na·mom·e·try (dī′nə·mom′ə·trē) *n.* The act or art of measuring the expenditure of power.

dy·na·mo·path·ic (dī′nə·mō·path′ik) *adj. Med.* Having an effect upon the character or course of bodily functions.

dy·na·mo·tor (dī′nə·mō′tər) *n.* A dynamoelectric machine having one field magnet, one armature core, and two armature windings, each having a commutator and being insulated from the other.

dy·nast (dī′nast, -nəst) *n.* A monarch; ruler. [<L *dynastes* <Gk. *dynastēs* <*dynasthai* be powerful]

dy·nas·ty (dī′nəs·tē) *n. pl.* **·ties** A succession of sovereigns in one line of family descent governing the same country; also, the length of time during which one family is in power. **—dy·nas·tic** (dī·nas′tik) or **·ti·cal** *adj.* **—dy·nas′ti·cal·ly** *adv.*

dy·na·tron (dī′nə·tron) *n. Electronics* A four-electrode vacuum tube designed to utilize the secondary emission of electrons to decrease the plate current as the plate voltage increases; used as an oscillator in radio. [<DYNA- + (ELEC)TRON]

dyne (dīn) *n. Physics* The fundamental unit of force in the cgs system that, if applied to a mass of one gram, would give it an acceleration of one centimeter per second per second. Abbr. *d., D.* [<F <Gk. *dynamis* power]

Dyr·ra·chi·um (di·rā′kē·əm) Ancient name for DURAZZO.

dys- *combining form* Bad; defective; difficult; hard: *dysphasia, dyspnea*: opposed to *eu-*. [<Gk. *dys-* bad, difficult]

dys·cra·si·a (dis·krā′zhē·ə, -zhə) *n. Pathol.* **1** A depraved condition of the system and especially of the blood, due to constitutional disease. **2** General bad health. [<Med. L <Gk. *dyskrasia* bad temperament <*dys-* bad + *krasia* mixture] **—dys·cra′si·al, dys·cras·ic** (dis·kraz′ik, -kras′-) *adj.*

dys·cra·site (dis′krə·sīt) *n.* A silver-white, opaque silver antimonide, Ag_3Sb, found massive and in orthorhombic crystals. [<Gk. *dyskrasia* bad mixture + -ITE[1]]

dys·e·mi·a (dis·ē′mē·ə) *n. Pathol.* A morbid or vitiated condition of the blood, especially as due to mineral poisoning. Also **dys·ae′mi·a.** [<NL <Gk. *dys-* hard + *haima* blood]

dys·en·ter·y (dis′ən·ter′ē) *n. Pathol.* A severe inflammation of the mucous membrane of the large intestine, attended with bloody evacuations, griping pains, and some fever; bloody flux. [<OF *dysenterie* <L *dysenteria* <Gk. <*dys-* bad + *enteron* intestine] **—dys′en·ter′ic** or **·i·cal** *adj.*

dys·es·the·si·a (dis′əs·thē′zhē·ə, -zhə) *n. Pathol.* Loss of sensation, partial or complete; numbness. Also **dys′aes·the′si·a.**

dys·func·tion (dis·fungk′shən) *n.* Deterioration of the natural action of (anything); malfunction.

dys·gen·ic (dis·jen′ik) *adj.* Relating to or causing the biological impairment or deterioration of a strain or race, especially man: opposite of *eugenic.*

dys·gen·ics (dis·jen′iks) *n. pl.* (*construed as singular*) The science dealing with the factors operating to produce biological, and especially genetic, deterioration in the offspring of animals.

dys·ge·og·e·nous (dis′jē·oj′ə·nəs) *adj. Bot.* Growing on soils, such as granite or hard rocks generally, which do not readily yield a detritus: said of plants. [<DYS- + Gk. *gē* earth, soil + -GENOUS]

dys·ki·ne·si·a (dis′ki·nē′zhē·ə, -zhə) *n. Pathol.* Loss or impairment of the power of voluntary movement. [<Gk. *dyskinēsia* <*dys-* hard + *kinesis* movement] **—dys′ki·net′ic** *adj.*

dys·lex·i·a (dis·lek′sē·ə) *n. Pathol.* Loss of the ability to read due to a central brain lesion. [<NL <Gk. *dys-* hard + *lexis* speech, word]

dys·lo·gis·tic (dis′lō·jis′tik) *adj.* Conveying disapproval or censure: opposed to eulogistic. [<DYS- + (EU)LOGISTIC] **—dys′lo·gis′ti·cal·ly** *adv.*

dys·men·or·rhe·a (dis·men′ə·rē′ə) *n. Pathol.* Difficult or painful menstruation. Also **dys·men′or·rhoe′a.** [<NL <Gk. *dys-* hard + *mēn, mēnos* month + *rheein* flow]

dys·pep·sia (dis·pep′shə, -sē·ə) *n.* Difficult or painful digestion, generally chronic. [<L <Gk. <*dys-* hard + *peptein* cook, digest]

dys·pep·tic (dis·pep′tik) *adj.* **1** Relating to, of the nature of, or suffering from dyspepsia; hence, morbid; querulous. **2** Tending to produce dyspepsia; indigestible. Also **dys·pep′ti·cal.** *—n.* A dyspeptic person. **—dys·pep′ti·cal·ly** *adv.*

dys·pha·gi·a (dis·fā′jē·ə) *n. Pathol.* Great difficulty in swallowing due to some constriction of the muscles of the throat. [<NL <Gk. *dys-* hard + *phagein* eat] **—dys·phag′ic** (-faj′·ik) *adj.*

dys·pha·sia (dis·fā′zhə, -zhē·ə) *n.* Partial aphasia or incoherent speech due to a brain lesion. **—dys·pha′sic** *adj.* [<NL <Gk. *dys-* hard + *phasis* utterance]

dys·pho·ni·a (dis·fō′nē·ə) *n. Psychiatry* Difficulty in uttering articulate sounds; harsh, abnormal, or indistinct vocalization. [<NL <Gk. *dysphōnia* roughness of sound <*dys-* hard + *phōnē* sound] **—dys·phon′ic** (-fon′ik) *adj.*

dys·pho·ri·a (dis·fôr′ē·ə, -fō′rē·ə) *n. Pathol.* A chronic feeling of illness and discontent: opposite of *euphoria.* [<NL <Gk. *dysphoria* <*dys-* hard + *phoreein* suffer]

dys·phot·ic (dis·fot′ik, -fō′tik) *adj.* Dimly illumined, as the bottom of a deep canyon or the sea depths. *—n.* Any plant or animal adapted to such surroundings. [<Gk. *dys-* hard, defective + *phōs, phōtos* light]

dysp·noe·a (disp·nē′ə) *n. Pathol.* Labored, difficult breathing. Also **dysp·ne′a.** [<NL <L *dyspnoea* <Gk. *dyspnoia* <*dys-* hard + *pneein* breathe] **—dysp·noe′al** or **·ic, dysp·ne′al** or **·ic** *adj.*

dys·pro·si·um (dis·prō′sē·əm, -shē-) *n.* A rare-earth element (symbol Dy, atomic number 66) difficult to separate from its oxide. See PERIODIC TABLE. [<NL <Gk. *dysprositos* <*dys-* hard + *prosienai* approach]

dys·tax·i·a (dis·tak′sē·ə) *n. Pathol.* Muscular tremor, resulting from disorder of the spinal cord. [<NL <Gk. *dys-* hard, defective + *taxis* arrangement]

dys·tel·e·ol·o·gy (dis·tel′ē·ol′ə·jē, -tē′lē-) *n.* The doctrine of purposelessness or of the absence ofa final cause: opposed to *teleology.* **—dys·tel′e·o·log′i·cal** (-ē·ə·loj′i·kəl) *adj.*

dys·tro·phy (dis′trə·fē) *n.* Defective or perverted nutrition. Also **dys·tro·phi·a** (dis·trō′·fē·ə). [<NL *dystrophia* <Gk. *dys-* hard, defective + *trophē* nourishment]

dys·tro·py (dis′trə·pē) *n. Psychiatry* Abnormal behavior, however caused. [<DYS- + Gk. *tropē* a turning, change] **—dys·trop′ic** (-trop′·ik) *adj.*

dys·u·ri·a (dis·yŏŏr′ē·ə) *n. Pathol.* Difficult, painful, or incomplete urination. [<LL <Gk. *dysouria* <*dys-* hard + *ouron* urine] **—dys·u′ric** *adj.*

Dyu·sham·be (dyŏŏ·shäm′bə) The former name for STALINABAD.

dy·vour (dē′vər) *n. Scot.* A bankrupt or insolvent debtor; specifically, one who assigns all his property to his creditors.

Dzaoud·zi (dzoud′zē) Capital of the Comoro Islands.

Dzau·dzhi·kau (dzou·jē′kou) A city on the Terek, capital of North Ossetian Autonomous S.S.R.: formerly *Ordzhonikidze.*

Dzer·dzhinsk (dyer·zhinsk′) A city on the Oka in European Russian S.F.S.R.

Dzhu·ga·shvi·li (jŏŏ′gä·shvē′lē), **Iosif** See STALIN.

dzig·ge·tai (dzig′ə·tī) *n.* A species of Mongolian wild ass: also spelled *chigetai.* [<Mongolian *dschiggetei* long-eared]

E

e, E (ē) *n. pl.* **e's, E's** or **es, Es, ees** (ēz) **1** The fifth letter of the English alphabet: from Phoenician *he,* through Hebrew *he,* Greek *epsilon,* and Roman *E.* **2** Any sound of the letter *e.* See ALPHABET.
—symbol **1** *Music* **a** The third tone in the natural scale of C, *mi;* the pitch of this tone, or the note representing it. **b** The scale built upon E. **2** *Math.* The limit of the expression $(1 + 1/n)^n$, as *n* increases without limit: 2.7182818284+: the base to which Napierian logarithms are calculated: written *e.*

e- Reduced var. of EX-.

E·a (ā′ä) In Babylonian mythology, one of the supreme deities and god of the waters. He was the bestower of the arts and sciences, healer of the sick, and the supposed creator of mankind.

each (ēch) *adj.* Being one of two or more individuals that together form an aggregate; every. *—pron.* Every one of any number or aggregation considered individually; each one. See synonyms under EVERY. *—adv.* For or to each person, article, etc.; apiece: one dollar *each.* [OE *ælc* <*a* ever + *gelic* alike]

each other A compound reciprocal pronoun used in oblique cases: They saw *each other.*

that is, Each saw the other. The possessive case is *each other's*.

Ead·mund (ed′mənd), **Ead·ward** (ed′wərd) See EDMUND, etc.

Eads (ēdz), **James Buchanan,** 1820–87, U.S. civil engineer.

ea·ger[1] (ē′gər) *adj.* **1** Impatiently anxious for something. **2** Showing insistent or intense feeling or desire. **3** *Obs.* Sour; tart; pungent. [<OF *aigre* <L *acer* sharp] **—ea′ger·ly** *adv.* **—ea′ger·ness** *n.*
Synonyms: animated, anxious, ardent, avid, burning, desirous, earnest, enthusiastic, fervent, glowing, hot, impatient, impetuous, importunate, intense, intent, keen, longing, vehement, yearning, zealous. One is *eager* who impatiently desires to accomplish some end; one is *earnest* with a desire that is less impatient, but more deep, resolute, and constant; one is *anxious* with a desire that foresees rather the pain of disappointment than the delight of attainment. One is *eager* for the gratification of any appetite or passion; he is *earnest* in conviction, purpose, or character. *Eager* usually refers to some specific and immediate satisfaction, *earnest,* to something permanent and enduring; the patriotic soldier is *earnest* in his devotion to his country, *eager* for a decisive battle. See ARDENT, HOT. Compare ENTHUSIASM. *Antonyms*: apathetic, calm, careless, cold, cool, dispassionate, frigid, heedless, indifferent, negligent, phlegmatic, purposeless, regardless, stolid, stony, stupid, unconcerned, uninterested, unmindful, unmoved.

ea·ger[2] (ē′gər, ā′-) *n.* A sudden flood of the tide in an estuary: also *eagre.* See BORE[2]. [Prob. OE *ēa* river + *gār* storm]

eager beaver *Slang* A person exceedingly zealous or diligent.

ea·gle (ē′gəl) *n.* **1** Any of various species of very large diurnal predatory birds of the family Accipitridae of worldwide distribution, notable for keen sight and strong flight. ◆ Collateral adjective: *aquiline.* **2** A gold coin of the United States, value $10, weight 258 grains: withdrawn from circulation 1934. **3** A Roman military standard, bearing the image of an eagle; also adopted as a standard by France during the two empires. **4** Any article in the design of which an eagle is prominent. **5** In golf, two strokes less than par in playing a hole. [<OF *egle, aigle* <L *aquila*]

Ea·gle (ē′gəl) The constellation Aquila. See CONSTELLATION.

ea·gle-eyed (ē′gəl·īd′) *adj.* Keen-sighted like an eagle.

eagle owl A large predatory European owl *(Bubo bubo).*

eagle ray Any of a family (Myliobatidae) of rays having the eyes and spiracles at the sides of the head and usually bearing a single dorsal spine on the long, whiplike tail.

Eagle Scout A Boy Scout of the highest rank.

ea·gle·stone (ē′gəl·stōn′) *n.* A yellow clay ironstone occurring as hollow oval nodules.

ea·glet (ē′glit) *n.* A young eagle.

ea·gle·wood (ē′gəl·wŏŏd′) See AGALLOCH.

ea·gre (ē′gər, ā′-) See EAGER[2].

Ea·ker (ā′kər), **Ira Clarence,** born 1896, U.S. aviator and general.

Ea·kins (ā′kinz), **Thomas,** 1844–1916, U.S. painter.

eal·dor·man (ôl′dər·mən) *n.* The chief officer of a shire in pre-Norman England. Also **eal′·der·man.** [Var. of ALDERMAN]

Ealh·wi·ne (alkh′wi·ne) See ALCUIN.

Eal·ing (ē′ling) A municipal borough of Middlesex, England, west of London.

EAM In World War II, a Greek underground organization formed to resist German domination, consisting of leftist groups. [<Modern Gk. *E(thniko) A(peleftherotiko) M(etopo)* National Liberation Front]

Eames (āmz), **Emma,** 1865–1952, U.S. prima donna.

ear[1] (ir) *n.* **1** The organ of hearing: in man and other mammals it consists of an *auricle* and external auditory *meatus* for collecting sounds, a *tympanum,* containing the *ossicles* for transmitting them, and a *labyrinth* that includes the *cochlea* for delivering them to the end organs of the auditory nerve. ◆ Collateral adjective: *aural.* **2** The sense of hearing; especially, nice perception of musical sounds. **3** Attentive consideration; heed. **4** Anything like the external ear, as a projecting

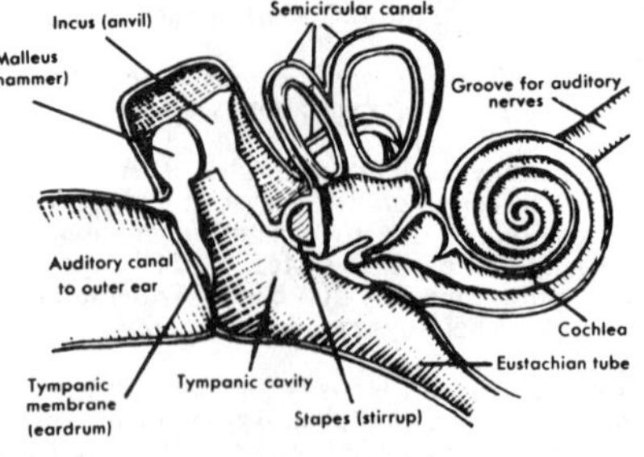

NOMENCLATURE: FRONTAL SECTION OF HUMAN EAR

piece, handle, etc. **5** The external ear alone. **6** *pl.* Spiritual understanding. **—about one's ears** Surrounding one on all sides, as falling objects. **—by the ears** In close struggle or conflict; at variance; as in **to set by the ears,** to cause discord between. **—up to the ears** *Colloq.* Almost covered, as one sinking; almost at the end of one's resources. [OE *ēare*] **—ear′less** *adj.*

ear[2] (ir) *n.* The fruit-bearing part of a cereal plant; the head. **—in** (or **on**) **the ear** On the cob, as corn; unhusked, as grain. *—v.i.* To form ears, as grain. [OE *ēar*]

ear[3] (ir) *v.t. Obs.* To till with a plow. [OE *erian*]

ear·ache (ir′āk′) *n.* Pain in the middle or internal ear; otalgia.

ear·cap (ir′kap′) *n.* A cap with tabs that cover the ears.

ear cup A device, fitted over the ear in a soundproof military helmet, to detect sounds, as of enemy aircraft.

ear·drop (ir′drop′) *n.* An earring with a pendant.

ear·drum (ir′drum′) *n.* The tympanum or the tympanic membrane.

ear dust *Anat.* Otoconia.

eared (ird) *adj.* Having ears or earlike appendages; auriculate.

eared seal Any of a family *(Otariidae)* of seals; the sea lion and the fur seals.

ear·flap (ir′flap′) *n.* One of a pair of adjustable earmuffs permanently attached to a cap.

ear·ful (ir′fŏŏl′) *n. U.S. Colloq.* **1** Something heard or overheard and considered enough or too much: Did you get an *earful*? **2** Surprising or important news. **3** A scolding.

Ear·hart (âr′härt), **Amelia,** 1898–1937, U.S. aviatrix; wife of George P. Putnam.

ear·ing (ir′ing) *n. Naut.* A small line used to fasten the corners of a sail to a yard. [<EAR[1]]

earl (ûrl) *n.* A member of the British nobility next above a viscount. *Earl* is the equivalent of the Norman *count,* in Norman French, and the wife of an earl is still called *countess.* [OE *eorl* nobleman]

Earl (ûrl) A masculine personal name.

ear·lap (ir′lap′) *n.* **1** The external ear; especially, the lobes. **2** An earflap.

earl·dom (ûrl′dəm) *n.* The dignity, prerogative, or territory of an earl.

earl marshal A British officer of state, originally *marshal of England,* who attends the sovereign when Parliament is opened or closed, etc.

ear·lobe (ir′lōb′) *n.* The soft fleshy protuberance at the lower part of the external ear.

ear·lock (ir′lok′) *n.* A lock of hair curling over or near the ear; a lovelock.

ear·ly (ûr′lē) *adj.* **·li·er, ·li·est 1** Being near the beginning of any stated period of time or definite course of existence; being or occurring among the first in a series; ancient. **2** Being or occurring sooner than is usual or necessary. **3** About to be or happen; soon to occur. [<*adv.*] *—adv.* **1** At or near the beginning of a period of time. **2** In good time or season. **—early on** Near the beginning. [OE *ǣrlīce* <*ǣr* sooner + *-līce* -ly] **—ear′li·ness** *n.*

Ear·ly (ûr′lē), **Jubal Anderson,** 1816–94, Confederate general.

early bird *Colloq.* **1** One who arrives early. **2** An early morning riser.

ear·mark (ir′märk′) *v.t.* **1** To make a mark of identification on. **2** To mark an animal's ear. **3** To set aside for special purposes, as money. *—n.* An owner's mark on an animal's ear; any mark of identification.

ear-mind·ed (ir′mīn′did) *adj.* Having a marked preference for auditory images in the various mental processes. **—ear′-mind′ed·ness** *n.*

ear·mold (ir′mōld′) *n.* A plastic mold to be worn in the ear as a means of conducting sound from the earphone of a hearing aid.

ear·muff (ir′muf′) *n.* One of a pair of adjustable coverings for the ears, worn as a protection against cold.

earn[1] (ûrn) *v.t.* **1** To receive, as salary or wages, for labor or exertion. **2** To merit as a result, reward, or punishment; deserve: He *earned* our condemnation. **3** To bring in (interest, etc.) as gain or profit. See synonyms under GAIN[1], GET, OBTAIN. ◆ Homophones: *erne, urn.* [OE *earnian*] **—earn′er** *n.*

earn[2] (ûrn) *v.t.* & *v.i. Brit. Dial.* To curdle, as milk. ◆ Homophones: *erne, urn.*

ear·nest[1] (ûr′nist) *adj.* **1** Intent and direct in purpose; zealous; fervent: of persons. **2** Marked by deep feeling or conviction; heart-felt; hearty: of words or acts. **3** Requiring careful consideration; serious; important. See synonyms under EAGER, SERIOUS. *—n.* Seriousness; reality, as opposed to pretense or trifling. **—in earnest** With full and serious intent; real and intended. [OE *eorneste*] **—ear′nest·ly** *adv.* **—ear′nest·ness** *n.*

ear·nest[2] (ûr′nist) *n.* **1** Money paid in advance to bind a bargain. **2** An assurance of something to come; pledge. See synonyms under SECURITY. [Prob. <OF *erres* <L *arra, arrhabo* <Gk. *arrhabōn* <Hebrew *'ērābōn;* infl. by EARNEST[1]]

earn·ing (ûr′ning) *n. Usually pl.* That which is earned; compensation; wages; salary.

ear·phone (ir′fōn′) *n.* **1** A headphone. **2** That part of an electronic hearing aid which transmits sound by air conduction through the earmold.

ear·plug (ir′plug′) *n.* A wax or plastic mold inserted into the ear to exclude water or noise, as in swimming or sleeping.

ear·ring (ir′ring′) *n.* A ring or hook usually with a pendant, worn at the ear.

ear shell An ear-shaped shell. See ABALONE.

ear·shot (ir′shot′) *n.* The distance at which sounds may be heard.

ear-split·ting (ir′split′ing) *adj.* Painfully loud or high-pitched; deafening.

ear·stone (ir′stōn′) *n.* An otolith.

earth (ûrth) *n.* **1** The solid portion or surface of the globe; ground. **2** Soil as distinguished from rock. **3** Those who inhabit the globe; the world at large. **4** The hole of a burrowing animal. **5** *Electr.* **a** The ground that forms part of an electric circuit. **b** A fault in a telegraphic or telephonic line, caused by connection of the conductor with the ground; also such connection. **6** Any natural soft soil, as clay and ocher. **7** *Chem.* A rare earth. **8** Temporal and transient interests and pursuits as contrasted with those that are spiritual; material things; worldly matters. **9** *Obs.* A locality upon the earth; country. See synonyms under LAND. **—down to earth** Realistic; unfanciful. **—to run to earth** To hunt down and find, as a fox. *—v.t.* **1** To bank up or protect with earth, as plants, flowers, etc. **2** To chase, as a fox, into a burrow or hole. **3** *Electr.* To ground. *—v.i.* **4** To burrow or hide in the earth, as a fox. [OE *eorthe*]

Earth (ûrth) **1** The third planet in order of distance from the sun and fifth in order of size among the planets. It has an area of 196,400,000 square miles, a mass of 6.57 sextillion tons (6.57 $\times 10^{21}$), a mean diameter of 7,918 miles, and a mean solar distance of 93,000,000 miles. ◆ Collateral adjectives: *telluric, terrestrial.* **2** The abode of man, considered as distinct from Heaven and Hell.

earth-bor·er (ûrth′bôr′ər, -bō′rər) *n.* An auger for boring into the ground.

earth-born (ûrth′bôrn′) *adj.* **1** Born out of the earth; of earthly origin. **2** Of terrestrial birth, as distinguished from celestial origin. **3** Springing from earthly or temporal considerations; mean or ignoble.

earth-bound (ûrth′bound′) *adj.* **1** Having only material interests. **2** Firmly fixed in or on the earth.

earth color Any of several pigments or paints

prepared from naturally occurring earth materials, as umber, ocher, chalk.

earth current 1 *Electr.* A direct current induced in the earth by grounded currents near powerhouses and thought responsible for the corrosion of the lead sheaths of cables, etc. 2 An electrical current, variable in strength, duration, and direction, which circulates within the earth's crust.

earth·en (ûr′thən) *adj.* Made of earth or baked clay; earthly.

earth·en·ware (ûr′thən·wâr′) *n.* Pottery, especially of inferior grade, as distinguished from porcelain and stoneware.

earth flax 1 Asbestos. 2 Amianthus.

earth inductor *Electr.* An induction coil which may be sharply rotated in the earth's magnetic field in order to determine the intensity of the field by the strength of the induced current as read on a galvanometer.

earth inductor compass A form of earth inductor designed to aid the pilot of an aircraft in maintaining a correct flight path with reference to the earth's magnetic field.

earth·i·ness (ûr′thē·nis) *n.* The quality of being earthy or like earth.

earth·light (ûrth′līt′) *n.* 1 Light sometimes visible at night, not directly attributable to sun, moon, or stars. 2 Earthshine.

earth·ling (ûrth′ling) *n.* A worldling or mortal.

earth·ly (ûrth′lē) *adj.* 1 Pertaining to the earth or the world of the present; material; secular; worldly; carnal. 2 *Colloq.* Possible; imaginable: of no *earthly* use. **—earth′li·ness** *n.*

earth·nut (ûrth′nut′) *n.* 1 The tuber of any one of several sedges. 2 The peanut. 3 Either of two European herbs (genus *Carum*) of the parsley family, as the caraway. 4 A truffle.

earth pea The hog peanut.

earth plate *Electr.* A ground plate.

earth·quake (ûrth′kwāk′) *n.* A vibration or sudden undulation of a portion of the earth's crust, caused by the splitting or faulting of a mass of rock or by volcanic or other disturbances. ◆Collateral adjective: *seismic*.

earth return *Electr.* The return path through the earth of an electric circuit which is completed by it: also called *ground-return circuit*.

earth·shine (ûrth′shīn′) *n. Astron.* Sunlight reflected from the earth so as to illuminate slightly those parts of the moon not in the direct rays of the sun.

earth·star (ûrth′stär′) *n.* A fungus (genus *Geaster*) having the outer coat distinct from the inner and split into several reflexed divisions suggestive of a star.

earth·ward (ûrth′wərd) *adv.* Toward the earth: also **earth′wards.** *—adj.* Moving toward the earth.

earth wax Ozocerite.

earth·work (ûrth′wûrk′) *n.* 1 *Mil.* An offensive or defensive fortification made largely or wholly of earth. 2 *Engin.* An operation or work, as a cutting or an embankment, requiring the removal of or filling in with earth. 3 Anything similar to a military earthwork.

earth·worm (ûrth′wûrm′) *n.* 1 A burrowing terrestrial annelid (family *Lumbricidae*), useful for enriching the soil. 2 A weak and insignificant or sordid person.

earth·y (ûr′thē) *adj.* **earth·i·er, earth·i·est** 1 Of, pertaining to, or like earth or soil; made of earth. 2 Unrefined; coarse.

ear trumpet An instrument made to collect and concentrate sound. Compare HEARING AID.

ear·wax (ir′waks′) *n.* A waxy substance secreted by the glands lining the passages of the external ear; cerumen.

ear·wig (ir′wig′) *n.* 1 An insect (family *Forficulidae*) with horny, short (or absent) forewings and a caudal pair of forceps: erroneously believed to enter the human ear. For illustration see under INSECT(injurious). 2 Loosely, in the United States, a small centipede. 3 *Obs.* A secret informer. *—v.t.* **·wigged, ·wig·ging** To influence by secret and stealthy counsel; to insinuate against by or as by whispering in the ear. [OE *earwicga*]

ease (ēz) *n.* 1 Freedom from pain, agitation, or perplexity; comfort. 2 Freedom from or absence of apparent effort; facility. 3 Freedom from affectation or constraint. *—v.* **eased, eas·ing** *v.t.* 1 To relieve the mentalor physical pain or oppression of; comfort. 2 To make less painful or oppressive: This will *ease* your pain. 3 To lessen the pressure, weight, tension, etc., of: to *ease* an axle. 4 To move, lower, or put in place gradually and with care. 5 *Colloq.* To rob: with *of* : a humorous usage: He was *eased* of his wallet. 6 *Rare* To facilitate. *—v.i.* 7 To diminish in severity, speed, etc.: often with *up* or *off* : The pain *eased.* **—to ease away** (or **off**) To move away slightly, as one ship from another. **—to ease the helm** *Naut.* To put the helm a trifle to midships so as to reduce the strain on the rudder. [<OF *aise* <LL *adjacens, -entis* neighboring. See ADJACENT.] **—ease′ful·ly** *adv.* **—ease′ful·ness** *n.*

Synonyms (noun) : easiness, expertness, facility, knack, readiness. *Ease* may be either of condition or of action; *facility* is always of action; *readiness* is of action or of expected action. One lives at *ease* who has no pressing cares; one stands at *ease,* moves or speaks with *ease,* when wholly without restraint. *Facility* is always active; *readiness* may be active or passive; the speaker has *facility* of expression, *readiness* of wit. *Ease* of action may imply merely the possession of ample power; *facility* always implies practice and skill. *Readiness* in the active sense includes much of the meaning of *ease* with the added idea of promptness or alertness. *Easiness* applies to the thing done, rather than to the doer. *Expertness* applies to the more mechanical processes of body and mind; we speak of the *readiness* of an orator, but of the *expertness* of a gymnast. Compare COMFORTABLE, DEXTERITY, POWER. *Antonyms*: annoyance, awkwardness, constraint, difficulty, discomfort, disquiet, trouble, uneasiness, vexation, worry.

ease·ful (ēz′fəl) *adj.* Causing or promoting ease or quiet; comfortable; peaceful.

ea·sel (ē′zəl) *n.* A folding frame for supporting a picture, panel, etc. [<Du. *ezel* easel, orig. an ass]

ease·ment (ēz′mənt) *n.* 1 *Law* The incorporeal privilege or right of making limited use of another's adjacent property, as for access over a road or path, or for a telephone line, water pipe, or the like. 2 Relief. 3 Anything that gives ease or relief.

eas·i·ly (ē′zə·lē) *adv.* In an easy manner; readily; quietly.

eas·i·ness (ē′zi·nis) *n.* The state of being at ease, or of being easy to do or accomplish.

east (ēst) *n.* 1 The point of the compass at which the sun rises at the equinox, directly opposite *west.* See COMPASSCARD. 2 Any direction, region, or part of the horizon near that point. **—Far East** Eastern Asia, including China, Japan, and adjacent islands. **—Middle East** 1 The region generally including the countries of SW Asia lying west of Pakistan and India. 2 *Brit.* This region with the exception of Turkey and including India, Pakistan, Burma, Tibet, Libya, Ethiopia, and Somaliland. **—Near East** 1 The countries lying east of the Mediterranean, mostly in SW Asia, including Turkey, Syria, Lebanon, Israel, Jordan, Saudi Arabia, etc., and sometimes the Balkans and Egypt. 2 *Brit.* The Balkans. **—the East** 1 The part of the earth including Asia and the adjacent islands; the Orient. 2 In the United States: **a** The region eastward of the Mississippi and north of the Ohio. **b** The region east of the Allegheny Mountains and north of Maryland. *—adj.* 1 To, toward, facing, or placed in the east; eastern. 2 Coming from the east: the *east* wind. 3 Near the altar of a church as seen from the nave. *—adv.* In or toward the east; in an easterly direction. *—v.i.* To go or turn toward the east; proceed in an easterly direction. [OE]

East (ēst), **Edward Murray,** 1879–1938, U.S. biologist.

East Africa Protectorate A former name of KENYA.

East An·gli·a (ang′glē·ə) An old Anglo-Saxon kingdom in SE England, comprising Norfolk and Suffolk counties.

East Bengal See under BENGAL.

east-bound (ēst′bound′) *adj.* Going eastward. Also **east′bound′.**

East·bourne (ēst′bôrn, -bərn) A county borough in SE Sussex, England.

east by north One point north of east on the mariner's compass. See COMPASS CARD.

east by south One point south of east on the mariner's compass. See COMPASS CARD.

East Cape See DEZHNEV, CAPE.

East China Sea The NE part of the China Sea, bounded by Korea, Japan, Taiwan, and China.

east·er (ēs′tər) *v.i. Obs.* To shift to the east, as the wind.

East·er (ēs′tər) *n.* 1 A Christian festival commemorating the resurrection of Christ. 2 The day on which this festival is celebrated, the Sunday immediately after the first full moon that occurs on or after March 21: also **Easter Day.** [OE *Eastre* goddess of spring]

Easter egg A decorated egg, or imitation of an egg, given as a present at Easter.

Easter Island A Chilean island in the South Pacific; 45 1/2 square miles; known for its numerous stone monuments of undetermined origin: native name *Rapa Nui.* Spanish **Is·la de Pas·cua** (ēs′lä thā päs′kwä).

east·er·ling (ēs′tər·ling) *n. Obs.* A native of the East; an Oriental.

east·er·ly (ēs′tər·lē) *adj.* 1 Situated, moving, or directed toward the east; eastward. 2 Coming from the east: said of winds. *—adv.* Toward the east: also **east′ern·ly.**

Easter Monday The day following Easter.

east·ern (ēs′tərn) *adj.* 1 Of, pertaining to, from or situated in the east. 2 *Usually cap.* Pertaining to the East. 3 Moving to or from the east; easterly.

Eastern Church See GREEKCHURCH.

Eastern Empire The Byzantine Empire.

East·ern·er (ēs′tərn·ər) *n. U.S.* One who dwells in the eastern part of the United States.

Eastern Ghats See GHATS.

eastern hemisphere See under HEMISPHERE.

east·ern·most (ēs′tərn·mōst′) *adj.* Farthest east.

Eastern (Roman) Empire The Byzantine Empire.

Eastern Samoa See SAMOA.

Eastern Shore The eastern coast of Chesapeake Bay; especially, the tidewater region of Maryland.

Eastern Standard Time See STANDARD TIME. Abbr. *E.S.T.*

Eastern Turkestan See under TURKESTAN.

East·er·tide (ēs′tər·tīd′) *n.* 1 The season of Easter; a period extending in various churches from Easter to Ascension Day, Whitsunday, or Trinity Sunday. 2 The week beginning with and immediately following Easter [<EASTER + TIDE[1] (def. 4)]

East Flanders A province of NW Belgium; 1,147 square miles; capital, Ghent. *Flemish* **Oost-Vlaan· de·ren** (ôst′vlän′də·rən).

East Germanic See under GERMANIC.

East Germany See under GERMANY.

East Ham A county borough in SW Essex, England.

East India Company The name of various mercantile associations organized in the 17th and 18th centuries by Europeans to carry on trade with the East Indies: notably the British, Dutch, and French companies.

East Indies 1 The islands of the Malay Archipelago. 2 SE Asia. 3 *Archaic* India. Also **East India. —East Indian.**

east·ing (ēs′ting) *n.* 1 *Naut.* The distance traversed by a ship running on an easterly course. 2 The distance eastward from a given meridian. 3 A shifting or moving toward the east.

East Liverpool A city on the Ohio River in eastern Ohio.

East London A port in Eastern Cape Province, Republic of South Africa. *Afrikaans* **Oos-Lon·den** (ōs′lôn′də).

East Lo·thi·an (lō′thē·ən) A county of SE Scotland; 267 square miles; county seat, Haddington. Formerly **Had·ding·ton·shire** (had′·ing·tən·shir′).

East·man (ēst′mən), **George,** 1854–1932, U.S. pioneer in photography. **—Max,** 1883–1969, U.S. editor and writer.

East Midland See under MIDLAND.

east-north·east (ēst′nôrth′ēst′) *adj., adv., n.*

Midway between east and northeast. See COMPASS CARD.
Eas·ton (ēs′tən) A city on the Delaware River in eastern Pennsylvania.
East Orange A city in NE New Jersey.
East Pakistan See PAKISTAN.
East Prussia A former province of Prussia in NE Germany; capital, Königsberg: German *Ostpreussen.*
East Riding An administrative division of SE Yorkshire, England; 1,172 square miles.
East River A navigable tidal strait in SE New York, connecting Long Island Sound and New York Bay and separating Manhattan Island from Long Island; 16 miles long.
East Semitic See under SEMITIC.
east–south·east (ēst′south′ēst′) *adj., adv.,* & *n.* Midway between east and southeast. See COMPASS CARD.
East St. Louis A city in SW Illinois on the Mississippi River.
east·ward (ēst′wərd) *adj.* Running, tending, or situated in an easterly direction. —*adv.* Toward the east: also **east′wards.** Also **east′·ward·ly.**
eas·y (ē′zē) *adj.* **eas·i·er, eas·i·est 1** Not involving great exertion, discomfort, or difficulty. **2** Free from discomfort or anxiety; comfortable. **3** Possessed of a sufficient competence. **4** Free from embarrassment or affectation; natural. **5** Yielding; indulgent. **6** Gentle; tractable. **7** Causing no disquiet or discomfort; not burdensome. **8** Self–indulgent. **9** Not straitened or tight, as money. **10** To be paid in small instalments: *easy* terms. **11** Not having much current: *easy* water. —**to go easy on** To be moderate in the use of; also, to be tactful about. —**to live on easy street** To be in good financial circumstances. [<OF *aisé,* pp. of *aiser, aisier* put at ease]
easy chair A large, comfortable chair, usually padded or stuffed.
eas·y–go·ing (ē′zē·gō′ing) *adj.* **1** Not inclined to effort or worry; complacently unconcerned. **2** Moving at an easy pace, as a horse.
easy mark *Colloq.* A person easily fooled or victimized.
eat (ēt) *v.* **ate** or *Brit.* **eat** (et), **eat·en, eat·ing** *v.t.* **1** To take (food) into the mouth and swallow. **2** To consume or destroy by or as by eating: often with *away* or *up.* **3** To wear into or away; corrode; rust. **4** To make (a way or hole) by or as by gnawing or chewing. —*v.i.* **5** To take in food; have a meal. **6** To bore into or corrode something: with *through* or *into.* —**to eat crow** To accept what one had been against; submit to humiliation. —**to eat humble pie** To make humble apologies. —**to eat one's words** To retract what one has said. —**to eat up 1** To consume completely. **2** To pass over rapidly: to *eat up* the miles. [OE *etan*] —**eat′er** *n.*
eat·a·ble (ē′tə·bəl) *n.* Something edible: often in the plural. —*adj.* Fit to be eaten; edible.
eat·age (ē′tij) *n. Brit.* Pasturage, especially that obtained from aftermath. Compare EDDISH.
eat·er·y (ē′tər·ē) *n. U.S. Slang* An eating house.
eat·ing (ē′ting) *n.* **1** The act of taking food. **2** Food: Brook trout are good *eating.*
Ea·ton (ē′tən), **Theophilus,** 1590–1658, English colonial administrator in America; first governor of New Haven Colony 1636–58.
eats (ēts) *n. pl. U.S. Slang* Food.
eau (ō) *n. pl.* **eaux** (ō) Water: a word designating various perfumes, cordials, medicinal waters, etc. [<F <L *aqua* water]
Eau Claire (ō klâr′) A city in west central Wisconsin.
eau de Co·logne (ō′ də kə·lōn′) See COLOGNE.
eau de vie (de vē′) *French* Brandy; literally, water of life.
eaves (ēvz) *n. pl.* The projecting edge of a roof. [OE *efes* edge]
eaves·drip (ēvz′drip′) *n.* An ancient law forbidding the erection of a building so close to a boundary line that the eaves would drip on the land of another.
eaves·drop (ēvz′drop′) *v.i.* **·dropped, ·drop·ping** To listen, or try to listen, secretly, as to a private conversation. —*n.* **1** Water that drops from the eaves. **2** The line near the wall of a house made by such droppings. Also **eave′·drop′.** [< *eavesdrop, n.*; with ref. to one who listens within the eavesdrop] —**eaves′drop′per** *n.* —**eaves′drop′ping** *n.*

ebb (eb) *v.i.* **1** To recede, as the tide. **2** To decline; fail. —*n.* **1** The reflux of tidewater to the ocean; low tide: opposed to *flood*: also **ebb tide. 2** Decrease; condition or period of decline. See synonyms under ABATE. [OE *ebbian*]
Eb·e·ne·zer (eb′ə·nē′zər) *n.* **1** In the Bible, a stone set up by Samuel to commemorate a victory of the Israelites: 1 *Sam.* vii 12. **2** Any memorial of divine help and deliverance. **3** A masculine personal name. [<Hebrew *eben ha- 'ēzer* stone of help]
E·bers (ā′bərz), **Georg,** 1837–98, German novelist and Egyptologist.
E·bert (ā′bərt), **Friedrich,** 1871–1925, first president of the German republic 1919–25.
E·bi·o·nite (ē′bē·ə·nīt′) *n.* One of a party in the early church, second to fourth century, chiefly made up of Pharisees and Essenes. Compare NAZARENE. [<L *ebionita* <Hebrew *'ebyōn* poor] —**E′bi·o·nit′ic** (-nit′ik) *adj.*
Eb·lis (eb′lis) In Moslem mythology, the chief of the evil jinn, who, refusing to worship Adam, were cast out of heaven: also called *Iblees.* [<Arabic *Iblis* <Gk. *Diabolos* devil]
E–boat (ē′bōt′) *Brit.* A fast German torpedo boat. [< *e(nemy) boat*]
eb·on (eb′ən) *adj.* **1** Of ebony. **2** Very black. —*n.* Ebony.
eb·on·ite (eb′ən·īt) *n.* Black vulcanite, or hard rubber.
eb·on·ize (eb′ən·īz) *v.t.* **·ized, ·iz·ing** To stain or polish, as wood, in imitation of ebony.
eb·on·y (eb′ən·ē) *n. pl.* **·on·ies 1** A hard, heavy wood, usually black, used for cabinetwork, etc. It is furnished by various species of a tropical genus *(Diospyros)* of hardwood trees. **2** Any tree of this genus, especially *D. ebenum* of Ceylon and Southern India. —*adj.* Made of ebony; ebonylike. [<L *hebeninus* <Gk. *hebeninos* of ebony < *ebenos* ebony <Egyptian *hebni*]
Eb·or·a·cum (eb′ə·rā′kəm) Ancient Roman name for York, England.
e·brac·te·ate (ē·brak′tē·āt) *adj. Bot.* Without bracts. [<NL *ebracteatus* <L *ex-* without + *bractea* plate, bract]
e·bri·e·ty (i·brī′ə·tē) *n. Obs.* Drunkenness; inebriety. [<F *ébrieté* <L *ebrietas, -tatis* < *ebrius* drunken]
e·bri·os·i·ty (ē′brē·os′ə·tē) *n. Obs.* Habitual intoxication.
E·bro (ē′brō, *Sp.* ā′brō) A river in NE Spain, flowing over 500 miles SE to the Mediterranean.
e·bul·lient (i·bul′yənt) *adj.* **1** Bubbling over with enthusiasm. **2** In a boiling condition; boiling. [<L *ebulliens, -entis,* ppr. of *ebullire* < *ex-* out + *bullire* boil] —**e·bul′lient·ly** *adv.* —**e·bul′lience, e·bul′lien·cy** *n.*
eb·ul·lism (eb′ə·liz′əm) *n. Pathol.* The bubbling out or vaporizing of body fluids when their boiling point drops below the normal temperature of 98°F.: a condition associated with high–altitude space travel. [<L *ebullire* boil out]
eb·ul·li·tion (eb′ə·lish′ən) *n.* **1** The bubbling of a liquid; boiling. **2** Any sudden or violent agitation. [<L *ebullitio, -onis* < *ebullire.* See EBULLIENT.]
eb·ur·nat·ed (eb′ər·nā′tid) *adj.* Condensed and hardened like bone.
eb·ur·na·tion (eb′ər·nā′shən) *n. Pathol.* **1** Ossification of joint cartilage. **2** Condensation of a bone structure to the hardness of ivory. [<L *eburnus* ivory + -ATION]
e·bur·ne·an (ē·bûr′nē·ən) *adj.* Of or pertaining to ivory. Also **e·bur′ni·an.** [<L *eburnus* ivory]
ec– Var. of EX–[2].
e·cad (ē′kad) *n. Ecol.* A habitat plant form or modification due to non–inherited adaptation to unusual environment. [<EC(OLOGY) + -AD]
E·car·di·nes (ē·kär′də·nēz) *n. pl.* An order of brachiopods with hornlike or calcareous shells joined only by muscles: formerly called *Inarticulata.* [<NL <L *e-* away + *cardo, cardinis* hinge]
é·car·té (ā′kär·tā′) *n.* A game of cards for two persons. [<F, pp. of *écarter* discard]
Ec·bat·a·na (ek·bat′ə·nə) The capital of ancient Media, on the present site of HAMADAN, Iran.
ec·bol·ic (ek·bol′ik) *adj. Med.* Causing contraction of the uterus and thus inducing abortion or promoting parturition. —*n.* An ecbolic drug. [<Gk. *ekbolē* a casting out (< *ex-* out + *ballein* throw) + -IC]

Ec·ce Ho·mo (ek′sē hō′mō, ek′e) **1** Behold the Man!: the words of Pilate (*John* xix 5). **2** An artistic or other representation of Christ crowned with thorns.
ec·cen·tric (ek·sen′·trik) *adj.* **1** Departing from the usual custom or practice; peculiar; erratic. **2** Not in the center. **3** *Math.* Not having the same center: said of circles, ellipses, spheres, etc.: opposed to *concentric.* **4** Not being a perfect circle, as an ellipse. **5** Of or pertaining to an eccentric. **6** Not holding to an identical purpose. **7** Removed or apart from a nerve center. **8** *Colloq.* Odd or unconventional to a degree short of mental unbalance: said of persons whose actions are considered peculiar to a marked degree. See synonyms under IRREGULAR, ODD, QUEER. —*n.* **1** *Mech.* A disk mounted out of center on a driving shaft, bound to it by a key, and surrounded by a collar or strap connected with a rod, effecting a crank motion. **2** One who or that which is eccentric. **3** *Math.* A circle not having the same center as another that partly coincides with it: also spelled *excentric.* [<LL *eccentricus* <Gk. *ekkentros* < *ek-* out, away + *kentron* center] —**ec·cen′tri·cal** *adj.* —**ec·cen′tri·cal·ly** *adv.*

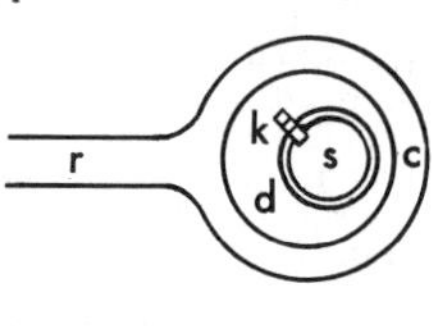

ECCENTRIC
r. Driving shaft, eccentric to center of disk *d. k.* Key binding disk to shaft. *c.* Collar connecting with rod *r.*

ec·cen·tric·i·ty (ek′sen·tris′ə·tē) *n. pl.* **·ties 1** The state or quality of being eccentric; oddity. **2** An odd or capricious act. **3** The distance between the centers of two eccentric circles or objects. **4** The condition or quality of being eccentric. **5** *Math.* The ratio of the distance between the focus and the center of a conic to half of its transverse axis; formerly, the distance itself. Also spelled *excentricity.*
ec·chy·mosed (ek′i·mōzd) *adj. Med.* Discolored by reason of a contusion, as in the case of a black eye.
ec·chy·mo·sis (ek′i·mō′sis) *n. pl.* **·ses** (-sēz) *Med.* A discoloration, as a black–and–blue spot, resulting from the rupture of small blood vessels by a blow or contusion. [<NL <Gk. *ekchymōsis* < *ek-* out + *chymos* humor (def. 4)] —**ec′chy·mot′ic** (-mot′ik) *adj.*
Ec·cles (ek′əlz), **Marriner Stoddard,** born 1890, U. S. banker and economist.
ec·cle·si·a (i·klē′zhē·ə, -zē·ə) *n. pl.* **·si·ae** (-ē) **1** The popular or legislative assembly in Athens and other ancient Greek states in which every free citizen could vote. **2** A body of Christians organized for worship and religous work; a church; congregation. [<L <Gk. *ekklēsia* < *ekkaleein* < *ek-* out + *kaleein* call]
ec·cle·si·arch (i·klē′zē·ärk) *n.* A church ruler, especially one in high authority. [<ECCLESIA + Gk. *archos* chief]
Ec·cle·si·as·tes (i·klē′zē·as′tēz) One of the books of the Old Testament, formerly attributed to King Solomon. [<Gk. *ekklēsiastēs,* trans. of Hebrew *qōhēleth* a preacher]
ec·cle·si·as·tic (i·klē′zē·as′tik) *adj.* Ecclesiastical. —*n.* **1** One officially set apart for the service of the church; a cleric; a churchman: used chiefly in episcopal communions. **2** In early church history, a member of the established or orthodox church, as distinguished from heretics and unbelievers. [<Gk. *ekklēsiastikos* for the assembly < *ekklēsia* assembly]
ec·cle·si·as·ti·cal (i·klē′zē·as′ti·kəl) *adj.* Of or pertaining to the church, especially considered as an organized and governing power: distinguished from *civil.* Abbr. *Eccl.* —**ec·cle′si·as′ti·cal·ly** *adv.*
ec·cle·si·as·ti·cism (i·klē′zē·as′tə·siz′əm) *n.* **1** Devotion to the principles of the church or to its privileges and forms. **2** The spirit that leads to such devotion. **3** Systematically exercised ecclesiastical authority.
Ec·cle·si·as·ti·cus (i·klē′zē·as′ti·kəs) One of the books of the Old Testament Apocrypha, resembling in form the Proverbs of Solomon: accepted as canonical by the Roman Catholic Church: called also *The Wisdom of Jesus, the Son of Sirach.*
ec·cle·si·ol·a·try (i·klē′zē·ol′ə·trē) *n.* Worship of the church; extreme veneration for the authority, forms, and traditions of the church.

[<Gk. *ekklēsia* church + *latreia* worship] — **ec·cle′si·ol′a·ter** *n.*

ec·cle·si·ol·o·gy (i·klē′zē·ol′ə·jē) *n.* **1** The study of the organization, government, liturgy, and ritual of the Christian church. **2** The study of church architecture and decoration. —**ec·cle′·si·o·log′ic** (-zē·ə·loj′ik) or **·i·cal** *adj.*

ec·dem·ic (ek·dem′ik) *adj. Med.* Of or pertaining to diseases originating at a distance: opposed to *endemic.* [<EC- + Gk. *dēmos* people]

ec·de·mo·ma·ni·a (ek·dē′mə·mā′nē·ə, -mān′yə) *n. Psychiatry* A morbid compulsion to wander away from home. Also **ec·de′mo·no·ma′ni·a.** [<EC- + Gk. *dēmos* folk, people + -MANIA]

ec·dys·i·ast (ek·diz′ē·ast, -əst) *n.* A strip-teaser. Also **ek·dys′i·ast.** [<Gk. *ekdysis* a shedding of the skin; coined by H. L. Mencken in 1940]

ec·dy·sis (ek′di·sis) *n. pl.* **·ses** (-sēz) The act of casting off an integument, as in serpents and insects. [<NL <Gk. <*ek-* off + *dyein* dress, clothe]

e·ce·sis (i·sē′sis) *n. Ecol.* The adjustment of a plant to a new habitat; the establishment of a migrant organism. [<NL <Gk. *oikēsis* a dwelling]

ec·go·nine (ek′gə·nēn, -nin) *n. Chem.* A white, bitter crystalline alkaloid, $C_9H_{15}O_3N \cdot H_2O$, resulting from the decomposition of cocaine by hydrochloric acid. [<Gk. *ekgonos* born of, sprung from + -INE[2]]

ec·hard (ek′härd) *n. Ecol.* The non-available water of the soil: opposed to *chresard.* [Gk. *echthos* outside + *ardeia* irrigation]

eche (ēch) *v.t. Obs.* To increase or enlarge. [OE *ēcan*]

E·che·ga·ray y Ei·za·guir·re (ā′chā·gä·rī′ ē ā′thä·gir′rā), **José,** 1832–1916, Spanish dramatist.

ech·e·lon (esh′ə·lon) *n.* **1** A staggered troop, fleet, or airplane formation, one rank, ship, or airplane behind the other, but extending farther toward one flank than the preceding rank, ship, or airplane: often V-shaped. **2** *Mil.* **a** One of the different fractions of a command arranged from front to rear, to which a particular combat mission is assigned: assault *echelon,* support *echelon.* **b** One of the various subdivisions from front to rear of a military headquarters: forward *echelon,* rear *echelon.* **c** A military unit regarded as having a distinct function: command *echelon,* first *echelon* maintenance, etc. **3** *Optics* A diffraction grating made of glass plates so constructed that each overlaps the one below, forming a stairlike pattern. —*v.t.* & *v.i.* To form in echelon. [<F *échelon* <*échelle* ladder <L *scala*]

ECHELON (*def. 1*)

ech·e·lon·ment (esh′ə·lon·mənt) *n.* The act of forming or the state of being formed into echelons, including those of formation, position, or function.

e·chid·na (i·kid′nə) *n. pl.* **·nae** (-nē) An egg-laying monotreme of Australia, etc. *(Echidna aculeata),* having a vermiform tongue, tubular snout with nostrils near the tip, fossorial feet, and strong spines intermixed with fur; a spiny ant-eater. [<NL<Gk., adder]

ECHIDNA
(About 15 inches in body length)

ech·i·na·ce·a (ek′ə·nā′shē·ə) *n.* A genus of hardy perennial plants of the composite family native in the United States; the root of *E. angustifolia* has medicinal properties. [<NL <Gk. *echinos* hedgehog]

ech·i·nate (ek′ə·nāt) *adj.* Set or armed thickly with prickles; bristly; spiny. Also **ech′i·nat′ed.**

e·chi·ni·form (i·kī′nə·fôrm) *adj.* Having the form of a sea urchin.

echino- *combining form* Spiny; prickly: *echinoderm*: also, before vowels, **echin-.** Also **echini-.** [<Gk. *echinos* hedgehog]

e·chi·no·derm (i·kī′nə·dûrm) *n.* Any of a phylum (Echinodermata) of coelomate, bottom-dwelling marine animals, as starfishes, sea cucumbers, etc., characterized by pentamerous radial symmetry, a skeleton of calcite plates just beneath the skin, and a water-vascular system which serves primarily for locomotion. —**e·chi′no·der′ma·tous** (-dûr′mə·təs), **e·chi′no·der′mal** *adj.*

e·chi·noid (i·kī′noid) *n.* Any of a class *(Echinoidea)* of echinoderms, including sea urchins, sand dollars, etc. —*adj.* Echiniform. —**ech·i·noi·de·an** (ek′i·noi′dē·ən) *adj.* & *n.*

ech·i·nop·sine (ek′ə·nop′sēn, -sin) *n.* An alkaloid, $C_{10}H_9ON$, obtained from the globe thistle (genus *Echinops*) and similar in action to strychnine. [<NL *Echinops,* genus of the globe thistle + -INE]

e·chi·nus (i·kī′nəs) *n. pl.* **·ni** (-nī) **1** *Archit.* The cushion of the capital of a Doric column, or the corresponding part in some other order. For illustration see under CAPITAL. **2** A sea urchin or echinoid. **3** A hedgehog. [<L <Gk. *echinos* hedgehog, sea urchin]

Ech·mi·a·dzin (ech′mē·ä·dzēn′) A city of central Armenian S.S.R.; former capital of Armenia: also *Ejmiadzin, Etchmiadzine.*

ech·o (ek′ō) *n. pl.* **·oes 1** The sound produced by the reflection of sound waves from an opposing surface. **2** Reproduction of another's views or thoughts; a close imitation. **3** Prompt response. **4** The repetition of a musical phrase in soft tone; an echo-stop; an echo-organ. **5** A verse construction wherein one line repeats the last syllable or syllables of the line preceding. **6** *Telecom.* A retarded sound wave in radio reception; a signal received in addition to or later than the expected one. **7** In bridge, the play of a conventional card after a lead, to inform one's partner. —*v.t.* **1** To repeat or send back (sound) by echo: The walls *echoed* the shot. **2** To repeat the words, opinions, etc., of. **3** To repeat (words, opinions, etc.) in imitation of another. —*v.i.* **4** To give back sound; reverberate. **5** To be repeated or given back; resound. [<L <Gk. *ēchō*] —**ech′o·er** *n.*

Ech·o (ek′ō) In Greek mythology, a nymph who, because of her unrequited love for Narcissus, pined away until only her voice was left.

ech·o·gram (ek′ō·gram) *n.* A pictorial representation, as of an organ or other structure within the body, of objects under water, etc., detected by means of reflected ultrasound. Also called *sonogram.*

e·cho·ic (e·kō′ik) *adj.* Pertaining to echoism or onomatopoeia.

ech·o·ism (ek′ō·iz′əm) *n.* Word-making by the repetition or imitation of a sound heard; onomatopoeia.

ech·o·la·li·a (ek′ō·la′lē·ə) *n. Psychiatry* The senseless repetition of words. [<NL <Gk. *ēchō* echo + *laleein* babble]

ech·o·lo·ca·tion (ek′ō·lō·kā′shən) *n.* The determination of the distance and position of objects by the interpretation of sound waves transmitted to and returned from them. Compare RADAR, SONAR.

ech·o·or·gan (ek′ō·ôr′gən) *n.* A group of pipes or stops of a pipe organ, set apart from the main instrument, and enclosed for echo effects.

ech·o·stop (ek′ō·stop′) *n.* On a pipe organ, a stop with pipes enclosed so as to echo the tones produced.

Eck (ek), **Johann,** 1486–1543, German Roman Catholic theologian: original name *Johann Mayer.*

Eck·er·mann (ek′ər·man), **Johann Peter,** 1792–1854, German writer.

Eck·hart (ek′härt), **Johannes,** 1260–1327?, German Dominican mystic and pantheist: known as *Meister Eckhart.* Also **Eck′ardt.**

é·clair (ā·klâr′, i·klâr′) *n.* A small oblong pastry shell filled with custard or whipped cream and usually iced with chocolate. [<F, lit., flash of lightning]

é·clair·cisse·ment (ā·klâr·sēs·mäṅ′) *n. French* The clearing up of something obscure; a full explanation.

ec·lamp·si·a (ek·lamp′sē·ə) *n. Pathol.* A sudden convulsive seizure, without loss of consciousness, especially during pregnancy or childbirth. [<NL <Gk. *eklampsis* <*ek-* forth + *lampein* shine]

é·clat (ā·klä′, i·klä′) *n.* **1** Showiness of achievement; brilliancy; splendor. **2** Renown; celebrity; glory. [<F <*éclater* burst out]

ec·lec·tic (ek·lek′tik, ik-) *adj.* **1** Selecting or made by selection from different systems or sources. **2** Having broad views; liberal. **3** Composed of selections: an *eclectic* review. Also **ec·lec′ti·cal.** —*n.* One who practices selection from all systems or sources, as in philosophy or medicine. [<Gk. *eklektikos* <*ek-* out + *legein* select] — **ec·lec′ti·cal·ly** *adv.*

ec·lec·ti·cism (ek·lek′tə·siz′əm, ik-) *n.* **1** An eclectic method or system. **2** A system of philosophy composed of doctrines selected from different sources. **3** That which is conceived or formed eclectically.

e·clipse (i·klips′) *n.* **1** *Astron.* The dimming or elimination of light reaching an observer from a heavenly body. A **lunar eclipse** is caused by the passage of the moon through the earth's shadow; a **solar eclipse** by the passage of the moon between the sun and the observer. **2** Any hiding or obscuring. See ANNULAR ECLIPSE.

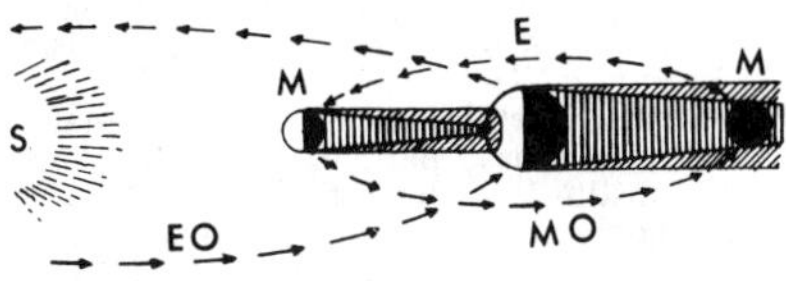

ECLIPSE
S. Sun. *E.* Earth. *M.* Moon. *EO.* Earth's orbit. *MO.* Moon's orbit.

When the moon passes between the sun and the earth, it causes an eclipse of the sun. this solar eclipse being total to observers within the umbra (darker shaded portions) of the moon's shadow and partial to those within the penumbra (lighter portions). When the moon passes through the earth's shadow, earth observers witness a total or partial lunar eclipse.

—*v.t.* **e·clipsed, e·clips·ing 1** To cause an eclipse of; darken. **2** To obscure the beauty, fame, worth, etc., of; overshadow. [<OF <L *eclipsis* <Gk. *ekleipsis* <*ek-* out + *leipein* leave]

eclipsing variable See under STAR.

e·clip·sis (i·klip′sis) *n.* **1** Ellipsis. **2** In the Celtic languages, a phonetic change undergone by the initial consonant of a word under the influence of a preceding word or form. [<L. See ECLIPSE.]

e·clip·tic (i·klip′tik, ē-) *n.* **1** *Astron.* **a** That plane, passing through the center of the sun, which contains the orbit of the earth: also **plane of the ecliptic. b** The great circle in which this plane intersects the celestial sphere; the apparent path of the sun around the celestial sphere. **2** A great circle on a terrestrial globe drawn tangent to the tropics, used when a terrestrial globe is employed for a celestial. —**fixed ecliptic** A fixed plane in the position of the ecliptic at some standard epoch. —*adj.* Pertaining to eclipses or to the ecliptic. — **e·clip′ti·cal** *adj.* —**e·clip′ti·cal·ly** *adv.*

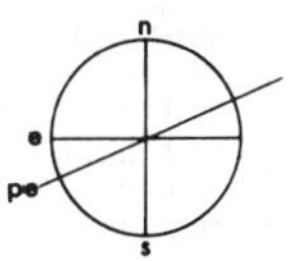

PLANES OF THE ECLIPTIC
n. s. North, south poles. *e.* Equator. *pe.* Plane. *ns.* Greenwich meridian.

ec·lo·gite (ek′lə·jīt) *n.* A rock consisting of red garnet, greenish pyroxene, and emerald-green smaragdite. [<Gk. *eklogē* selection <*ek-* out + *legein* select]

ec·logue (ek′lôg, -log) *n.* **1** A poem containing discourses or dialogs, with shepherds as principal speakers. **2** A short pastoral poem; bucolic. Also **ec′log.** [<F *églogue* <L *ecloga* <Gk. *eklogē.* See ECLOGITE.]

e·clo·sion (i·klō′zhən) *n.* **1** *Biol.* The process of hatching from an egg. **2** *Entomol.* The emergence of the mature insect from the pupa. [<F *éclosion* <*éclore* be hatched]

ec·o·cide (ek′ō·sīd) *n.* The disruption of an ecosystem, as by the reckless introduction of an agent or process that destroys some key element in the system. —**ec′o·cid′al** *adj.*

é·cole (ā·kôl′) *n. French* School.

e·col·o·gy (i·kol′ə·jē) *n.* **1** That division of

biology which treats of the relations between organisms and their environment; bionomics. **2** The study of human populations and of their reciprocal relations in terms of physical environment, spatial distribution, and cultural characteristics. [<Gk. *oikos* home + -LOGY] **—ec'o·log'ic** (ek'ə·loj'ik) or **·i·cal** *adj.* **—ec'·o·log'i·cal·ly** *adv.* **—e·col'o·gist** *n.*

e·con·o·met·ric (i·kon'ə·met'rik) *adj.* Pertaining to a system of analysis of economic affairs using a specialized statistical technique for large masses of assembled data.

e·con·o·met·rics (i·kon'ə·met'riks) *n.* The application of the principles of mathematical analysis to economic problems, specifically those pertaining to business and finance. [<ECONOMY + -METRICS] **—e·con'o·met'ric** *adj.*

ec·o·nom·ic (ek'ə·nom'ik, ē'kə-) *adj.* **1** Relating to the science of economics; pertaining to money matters or wealth. **2** Economical. **3** Of practical utility: *economic* botany. **4** *Obs.* Pertaining to the management of household affairs. [<L *oeconomicus* <Gk. *oikonomia.* See ECONOMY.]

ec·o·nom·i·cal (ek'ə·nom'i·kəl, ē'kə-) *adj.* **1** Careful and provident in management; not wasteful nor extravagant; frugal; saving. **2** Managed with prudence or practical vision. **3** Economic. **—ec'o·nom'i·cal·ly** *adv.*

economic determinism The theory that all human activities, particularly political and social institutions, have their ultimate origin in economic conditions and motivation.

ec·o·nom·ics (ek'ə·nom'iks, ē'kə-) *n. pl.* (*Construed as singular*) The science that treats of the production and distribution of wealth.

e·con·o·mist (i·kon'ə·mist) *n.* **1** One who is proficient in economics. **2** A manager of domestic or pecuniary resources. **3** One who is careful and thrifty in management.

e·con·o·mize (i·kon'ə·mīz) *v.* **·mized, ·miz·ing** *v.t.* To use thriftily. *—v.i.* To be frugal or economical. Also *Brit.* **e·con'o·mise.** See synonyms under RETRENCH. **—e·con'o·miz'er** *n.*

e·con·o·my (i·kon'ə·mē) *n. pl.* **·mies** **1** Disposition to save or spare; carefulness in outlay; freedom from extravagance or waste; frugality: *economy* of words, *economy* in dress. **2** Cheapness of operation, relative or absolute, as expressed in steam, fuel, or money. **3** The management of household matters: usually with a qualifying adjective: domestic *economy.* **4** Any practical system in which means are adjusted to ends, especially in the natural world: the *economy* of nature, the animal *economy,* the *economy* of a plant. **5** The practical adjustment, organization, or administration of affairs or resources, especially of industrial resources of a state: political *economy.* **6** A method of divine management of human affairs or a system of laws and regulations, rites, and ceremonies; specifically, any particular method of divine government: the Mosaic *economy.* **7** The handling and presentation of doctrine in a judicious manner. See synonyms under FRUGALITY, LEGISLATION. [<L *oeconomia* <Gk. *oikonomia* < *oikos* house + *nemein* manage]

e·con·o·my-sized (i·kon'ə·mē·sīzd') *adj.* Large-sized: a term used in consumer advertising. Also **e·con'o·my-size'.**

e·co·spe·cies (ē'kə·spē'shēz, ek'ə-) *n. Ecol.* A species of plant, natural or cultivated, highly adapted to its habitat. [<Gk. *oikos* home, habitat + SPECIES]

ec·o·sys·tem (ek'ō·sis'təm) *n. Ecol.* A community of organisms and their nonliving environment. [<Gk. *oikos* habitat + SYSTEM]

e·co·tone (ē'kə·tōn, ek'ə-) *n. Ecol.* A zone where two different forms of vegetable life compete. [<Gk. *oikos* habitat + *tonos* stress]

e·co·tope (ē'ka·tōp, ek'ə-) *n. Ecol.* A specialized habitat within a larger region. [<Gk. *oikos* habitat + *topos* place]

e·co·type (ē'ka·tīp, ek'ə-) *n. Ecol.* A biotype adapted for life in a particular kind of habitat. [<Gk. *oikos* habitat + TYPE]

é·cra·seur (ā·krà·zœr') *n. Surg.* An instrument in the form of a fine chain, wire, or cord, for tightening around a tumor, etc., as a means of removal. [<F < *écraser* crush]

ec·ru (ek'rōō, ā'krōō) *adj.* **1** Unbleached. **2** Having the color of unbleached linen or of hemp. *—n.* **1** The color of unbleached linen; a light-yellowish brown. **2** Goods made of unbleached linen. Also **é'cru.** [<F <OF *escru* <L *ex-* thoroughly + *crudus* raw]

ec·sta·size (ek'stə·sīz) *v.t.* & *v.i.* **·sized, ·siz·ing** To fill with, or go into, a feeling of ecstasy; enrapture.

ec·sta·sy (ek'stə·sē) *n. pl.* **·sies** **1** The state of being beside oneself through some extravagant and overpowering emotion or mental exaltation: an *ecstasy* of joy. **2** An enrapturing or transporting influence; a rapture. **3** In mysticism, the state of trance supposed to accompany inspiration. **4** Religious rapture. **5** *Obs.* Madness. See synonyms under ENTHUSIASM, HAPPINESS, RAPTURE. [<OF *extasie* <LL *ecstasis* <Gk. *ekstasis* distraction < *ek-* out + *histanai* place]

ec·stat·ic (ek·stat'ik) *adj.* Pertaining to or of the nature of ecstasy; transporting; enraptured: also **ec·stat'i·cal.** *—n.* **1** A person subject to ecstasies or trances; an enthusiast. **2** *pl.* Rapturous emotions. **—ec·stat'i·cal·ly** *adv.*

ec·thy·ma (ek·thī'mə) *n. pl.* **·thym·a·ta** (-thim'·ə·tə) *Pathol.* A virus disease characterized by the formation on the skin of ulcerating pustules whose discharge produces vesicular lesions. [<Gk. *ekthyma* pustule < *ek-* out + *thuein* seethe]

ecto- *combining form* Without; outside; external: *ectoderm.* Also, before vowels, **ect-.** [<Gk. *ekto-* < *ektos* outside]

ec·to·blast (ek'tə·blast) *n. Biol.* The embryonic stage of the ectoderm. **—ec'to·blas'tic** *adj.*

ec·to·derm (ek'tə·dûrm) *n. Biol.* **1** The outer layer of the integument of a multicellular organism. **2** The outer germ layer of the embryo, from which the epithelial structures of the surface of the body and the nervous system develop by the process of gastrulation: often called *exoderm.* **—ec'to·der'mal, ec'to·der'mic** *adj.*

ec·to·en·zyme (ek'tō·en'zīm, -zim) *n. Biochem.* An enzyme which functions outside of the cell and acts directly upon the surrounding blood or tissue: opposed to *endoenzyme,* and often spelled *exoenzyme.* Also **ec'to·en'zym** (-zim).

ec·tog·e·nous (ek·toj'ə·nəs) *adj. Biol.* Having the power of development without a host: said of certain parasitic organisms, as bacteria. Also **ec·to·gen·ic** (ek'tə·jen'ik).

ec·tog·o·ny (ek·tog'ə·nē) *n.* The influence supposed to be exerted upon the mother by a developing embryo. [<ECTO- + Gk. *gonē* child]

ec·to·mere (ek'tə·mɪr) *n. Biol.* One of the blastomeres derived from the segmentation of the ovum during the development of the ectoderm. **—ec'to·mer'ic** (-mer'ik) *adj.*

ec·to·mor·phic (ek'tə·môr'fik) *adj.* Denoting a physical and personality type associated with the body structure as developed from the ectodermal layer of the embryo, and characterized by predominance of the nervous system. Compare ENDOMORPHIC and MESOMORPHIC.

-ectomy *combining form* Removal of a part by cutting out: used in surgical terms to indicate certain kinds of operations; as, *appendectomy.* [<Gk. *ektomē* < *ek-* out + *temnein* cut]

ec·to·par·a·site (ek'tə·par'ə·sīt) *n. Biol.* A parasite that lives upon the exterior of its host, as a louse.

ec·to·phyte (ek'tə·fīt) *n.* An ectoparasite which attacks plants.

ec·to·pi·a (ek·tō'pē·ə) *n. Pathol.* Displacement of parts or organs, especially when congenital. [<NL <Gk. *ek-* out, from + *topos* place] **—ec·top'ic** (-top'ik) *adj.*

ec·to·plasm (ek'tə·plaz'əm) *n.* **1** *Biol.* The firm outer layer of the cytoplasm of a unicellular organism or of a plant cell. **2** The substance alleged to emanate from the body of a spiritualist medium during a trance: also called *teleplasm.* **—ec'to·plas'mic** *adj.*

ec·to·sarc (ek'tə·särk) *n. Biol.* The ectoplasm of protozoans. [<ECTO- + Gk. *sarx* flesh]

ec·tos·to·sis (ek'tos·tō'sis) *n. Pathol.* Ossification around the exterior of a cartilage. [<ECT(O)- + OST(EO)- + -OSIS]

ec·to·troph·ic (ek'tə·trof'ik, -trō'fik) *adj. Bot.* Nourished by the outside (of roots): said of certain fungi. [<ECTO- + Gk. *trophikos* < *trephein* grow, nourish]

ec·trog·e·ny (ek·troj'ə·nē) *n. Pathol.* The loss or absence, usually congenital, of an organ or part of the body. [< *ectro-* absence (<Gk. *ektrōsis* an abortion) + -GENY] **—ec·tro·gen·ic** (ek'trə·jen'ik) *adj.*

ec·tro·pi·um (ek·trō'pē·əm) *n. Anat.* A turning outward, partial or complete, of a part, as an eyelid, or the lips of the neck of the womb. Also **ec·tro'pi·on.** [<NL <Gk. *ektropion* < *ektropos* < *ek-* out + *trepein* turn]

ec·type (ek'tīp) *n.* **1** An imitation or reproduction of an original: opposed to *prototype* and distinguished from *replica.* **2** *Archit.* A figure or other work in relief. **3** A reproduction, in a world of time and sense, of an eternal and non-sensuous idea: contrasted with *archetype.* **4** *Psychiatry* A physical or mental constitution that varies markedly from the average. [<Gk. *ektypos* < *ek-* out + *typos* < *typtein* stamp] **—ec'ty·pal** *adj.*

é·cu (ā·kü') *n. pl.* **é·cus** (ā·kü') *French* A former coin and monetary unit of European countries, commonly called a crown, and having a wide range of values.

Ec·ua·dor (ek'wə·dôr) A republic in NW South America; 108,478 square miles; capital, Quito. **—Ec'ua·do're·an, Ec'ua·do'ri·an** *adj.* & *n.*

ec·u·men·i·cal (ek'yōō·men'i·kəl) *adj.* **1** Of or pertaining to the habitable world; general; universal. **2** Belonging to or accepted by the Christian church throughout the world: an *ecumenical* council. Also spelled *oecumenical.* Also **ec'u·men'ic.** [<LL *oecumenicus* <Gk. *oikoumenikos* < *oikoumenē* (*gē*) the inhabited (world) < *oikeein* dwell] **—ec'u·men'i·cal·ly** *adv.*

ec·u·men·ism (ek'yōō·men'iz·əm) *n.* The beliefs, principles, or practices of those who desire and work for world-wide unity and co-operation among all Christian churches. Also **ec·u·men·i·cal·ism** (ek'yōō·men'ə·kəl·iz·əm), **ec·u·men·i·cism** (ek'yōō·men'ə·siz'əm).

ec·ze·ma (ek'sə·mə, eg'zə·mə, eg·zē'mə) *n. Pathol.* An inflammatory disease of the skin attended by itching, watery discharge, and the appearance of lesions. [<Gk. *ekzema* < *ek-* out + *zeein* boil] **—ec·zem'a·tous** (-zem'ə·təs) *adj.*

Ed (ed) Diminutive of EDGAR, EDMUND, EDWARD, EDWIN.

-ed[1] *suffix* Used in the past tense of regular verbs: *walked, killed, played.* [OE *-ede, -ode, -ade*]

-ed[2] *suffix* **1** Used in the past participles of regular verbs: *clothed, washed.* **2** Forming adjectives from adjectives in *-ate,* with the same general meaning: *bipinnated.* [OE *-ed, -ad, -od*]

-ed[3] *suffix* **1** Having; possessing; characterized by: *toothed, green-eyed.* **2** Like; resembling: *bigoted.* [OE *-ede*]

e·da·cious (i·dā'shəs) *adj.* Given to eating; voracious; devouring. [<L *edax, edacis* < *edere* eat] **—e·da'cious·ly** *adv.*

e·dac·i·ty (i·das'ə·tē) *n.* Excess in eating; gluttony. Also **e·da'cious·ness.**

E·dam (ē'dəm, ē'dam) A town in NW Netherlands.

Edam cheese A mild curd cheese, originally produced in Edam, made in a round, flattened mold and usually coated with red paraffin.

e·daph·ic (i·daf'ik) *adj. Ecol.* Of, pertaining to, or affected by the state or condition of the soil rather than by climate; indigenous; local. [<Gk. *edaphos* ground]

Ed·da (ed'ə) Either of two collections of Old Icelandic or Old Norse literature: the **Elder Edda,** also called the **Poetic Edda,** containing mythological and heroic poetry of the 10th–13th centuries; and the **Younger Edda** or **Prose Edda,** a commentary on Norse mythology and composition by Snorri Sturluson (1178–1241). [<ON] **—Ed·da·ic** (e·dā'ik), **Ed'dic** *adj.*

ed·der (ed'ər) *Brit. Dial. n.* **1** A hedge. **2** Light, supple wood used to bind together the tops of hedges. *—v.t.* To fasten or bind with edders. [OE *eodor* a hedge]

Ed·die (ed'ē) Diminutive of EDGAR, EDMUND, EDWARD, EDWIN.

Ed·ding·ton (ed'ing·tən), **Sir Arthur Stanley,** 1882–1944, English astronomer, astrophysicist, and author.

ed·dy (ed'ē) *n. pl.* **·dies** **1** A whirl or backward-circling current of water or air; a whirlpool. **2** Figuratively, a turning aside or departure from the main current of thought or life. See synonyms under STREAM. *—v.t.* & *v.i.* **·died, ·dy·ing** To move, or cause to move, in or as in an eddy. [Prob. <ON *idha*]

Ed·dy (ed'ē), **Mary Baker,** 1821–1910, U.S. religious leader; founder of the Church of Christ, Scientist.

eddy current See under CURRENT.

Ed·dy·stone Rocks (ed'i·stōn') A dangerous

reef in the English Channel, 14 miles SSW of Plymouth; site of **Eddystone Lighthouse.**

E·de (ā′dā) A town of SW Nigeria.

e·del·weiss (ā′dəl·vīs) *n.* A small perennial alpine herb of the composite family *(Leontopodium alpinum),* with white woolly leaves suggesting a flower, and dense terminal cymes. [<G <*edel* noble + *weiss* white]

EDELWEISS (Plant about 4 inches high over all)

e·de·ma (i·dē′mə) *n. pl.* **·ma·ta** (-mə·tə) *Pathol.* A morbid accumulation of serous fluid in various organs or tissues of the body, as the pleural cavity or the retina: also spelled *oedema.* [<NL < Gk. *oidēma* a tumor < *oidein* swell] **—e·dem·a·tous** (i·dem′ə·təs), **e·dem′a·tose** (tōs) *adj.*

E·den (ēd′n) **1** In the Bible, the garden that was the first home of Adam and Eve: often *Paradise.* **2** Any delightful region or abode; a paradise.

E·den (ēd′n), **Sir (Robert) Anthony,** 1897–1977, English statesman; prime minister 1955–1957.

e·den·tate (ē·den′tāt, i·den′-) *adj.* **1** Toothless. **2** Of or pertaining to an order of placental mammals *(Edentata* or *Xenarthra),* some of which lack teeth, including sloths, ant–eaters, and armadillos. **—*n.*** **1** One of the *Edentata.* **2** A creature without teeth. [<L *edentatus* <*ex-* without + *dens, dentis* tooth]

e·den·tu·lous (ē·den′chŏŏ·ləs, i·den′-) *adj.* Having no teeth. Also **e·den′tu·late** (-lit, -lāt).

E·des·sa (i·des′ə) Ancient name for URFA. **—E·des′san** *adj.*

e·des·tin (i·des′tin) *n. Biochem.* A crystalline protein found in the castor–oil bean, hemp seed, and other seeds. [<Gk. *edestos* edible + -IN]

Ed·fu (ed′fōō) A town on the Nile in Upper Egypt; site of several temples and ruins: also *Idfu.*

Ed·gar (ed′gər, *Ger.* et′gär) A masculine personal name. Also *Ital.* **Ed·ga·ro** (ed·gä′rō), *Lat.* **Ed·ga·rus** (ed·gä′rŏŏs).

edge (ej) *n.* **1** The thin, sharp cutting part of a blade. **2** Sharpness; acuteness. **3** An abrupt border or margin; verge, brink; rim: the *edge* of a cliff. **4** A bounding or dividing line: the *edge* of a plain. See synonyms under BANK[1], BOUNDARY, MARGIN. **—on edge 1** Nervous; irritable. **2** Keenly eager. **—*v.*** **edged, edg·ing** *v.t.* **1** To put a cutting edge on; sharpen. **2** To put an edging or border on. **3** To move cautiously sidewise: to *edge* one's way through a mob. **4** To move by degrees; inch: to *edge* one's chair closer. **5** *U.S. Colloq.* To defeat by a slight margin: The home team just *edged* the visitors. **—*v.i.*** **6** To move sidewise. **7** To move by degrees: to *edge* away. [OE *ecg*] **—edged** *adj.* **—edge′·less** *adj.*

Edge·hill (ej′hil′) A ridge in southern Warwickshire, England; site of a battle between Charles I and Parliamentary forces, 1642.

edge tool 1 Any sharp, cutting tool. **2** A tool for making an edging, or finishing an edge.

edge·wise (ej′wīz′) *adv.* With the edge forward; on, by, with, along, or in the direction of the edge. Also **edge′ways′.**

Edge·worth (ej′wərth), **Maria,** 1767–1849, English novelist.

edg·ing (ej′ing) *n.* **1** Anything serving as or attached to an edge; trimming. **2** The making, dressing, or ornamenting of edges.

edg·y (ej′ē) *adj.* **1** Brought out too sharply; edgelike, as the outlines of a sculptured figure. **2** Irritable; sharp–tempered; eager. **—edg′i·ness** *n.*

edh (eth) *n.* The name of the letter ð, capital Ð, used in Old English to represent both voiceless and voiced *th,* as in *thin, then;* and in Icelandic and in phonetic writing to represent voiced *th,* as in *then:* also spelled *eth.* Compare THORN (*n.* def. 5).

ed·i·ble (ed′ə·bəl) *adj.* Fit to eat. **—*n.*** *Usually pl.* Something suitable for food. [<LL *edibilis*< L *edere* eat] **—ed′i·bil′i·ty** *n.*—**ed′i·ble·ness** *n.*

e·dict (ē′dikt) *n.* **1** That which is uttered or proclaimed by authority as a rule of action; a public ordinance emanating from a sovereign and having the force of law. **2** Any proclamation of command or prohibition. See synonyms under LAW. [<L *edictum,* pp. neut. of *edicere* <*ex-* out + *dicere* say] **—e·dic′tal** *adj.* **—e·dic′tal·ly** *adv.*

ed·i·fice (ed′ə·fis) *n.* A large structure of impressive architecture; a building. See synonyms under HOUSE. [<F *édifice* <L *aedificium* <*aedes* building + *facere* make] **—ed·i·fi·cial** (ed′ə·fish′əl) *adj.*

ed·i·fy (ed′ə·fī) *v.t.* **fied, fy·ing** To build up or strengthen, especially in morals or religion; instruct; improve; enlighten. [<OF *edifier* <L *aedificare* <*aedes* building + *facere* make] **—ed′i·fi·ca′tion** *n.* **—ed′i·fi′er** *n.* **—ed′i·fy′ing** *adj.* **—ed′i·fy′ing·ly** *adv.*

e·dile (ē′dīl) See AEDILE.

Ed·in·burgh (ed′ən·bûr′ə) The capital of Scotland on the Firth of Forth: Gaelic *Dunedin.*

E·dir·ne (e·dir′ne) See ADRIANOPLE.

Ed·i·son (ed′ə·sən), **Thomas Alva,** 1847–1931, U.S. inventor.

ed·it (ed′it) *v.t.* **1** To manage the preparation and publication of (a newspaper, etc.). **2** To compile, arrange and emend for publication: to *edit* memoirs or letters. **3** To correct and prepare (a manuscript, copy, etc.) for publication. [<L *editus,* pp. of *edere* <*ex-* out + *dare* give]

E·dith (ē′dith) A feminine personal name. Also *Ital.* **E·di·ta** (ā′dē·tä), *Lat.* **Ed·i·tha** (ed′i·tä). [OE, rich war]

E·dith Cav·ell Mountain (ē′dith kav′əl) A mountain in Jasper National Park, Alberta, Canada; 11,033 feet.

e·di·tion (i·dish′ən) *n.* **1** A published form of a literary work, or a copy of the form so published. **2** The total number of copies of a book, magazine, newspaper, etc., issued at one time.

é·di·tion de luxe (ā·dē·syôṅ′ də lüks′) *French* An elaborate and costly edition, often limited.

e·di·ti·o prin·ceps (i·dish′ē·ō prin′seps) *Latin* First edition, especially of a work printed from manuscript for the first time in the early years of printing.

ed·i·tor (ed′i·tər) *n.* **1** One who prepares manuscripts, copy, etc., for publication. **2** One having charge of a publication.

ed·i·to·ri·al (ed′i·tôr′ē·əl, -tō′rē-) *adj.* Of or pertaining to or emanating from an editor. **—*n.*** An article in a journal, or periodical, presumably written by the editor or by his subordinate, and published as an official argument or expression of opinion; a leading article. **—ed′i·to′ri·al·ly** *adv.*

ed·i·to·ri·al·ize (ed′i·tôr′ē·əl·īz′, -tō′rē-) *v.t.* & *v.i.* **·ized, iz·ing 1** To express opinions on (a subject) editorially. **2** To insert editorial opinions into (a news item, etc.).

editorial plural The editorial "we": the first person plural substituted for the first person singular in editorial writing.

editor in chief *pl.* **editors in chief** The chief editor of a publication; the one responsible for carrying out policies.

ed·i·tor·ship (ed′i·tər·ship′) *n.* The office and duties of an editor.

Ed·mon·ton (ed′mən·tən) **1** A northern suburb of London. **2** The capital of Alberta province, Canada.

Ed·mund (ed′mənd, *Ger.* et′mŏŏnt) A masculine personal name. Also *Du.* **Ed·mond** (et′·mōnt), *Fr.* **Ed·mond** (ed·môṅ′), *Ital.* **Ed·mon·do** (ed·mōn′dō), *Pg., Sp.* **Ed·mun·do** (*Pg.* ed·mŏŏn′dŏŏ, *Sp.* -dō). [OE, rich protector]

—Edmund II, 989–1016; king of England 1016: known as *Ironside.* Also spelled *Eadmund.*

Ed·na (ed′nə) A feminine personal name. [< Hebrew, rejuvenation]

E·do (e·dō) A former name for TOKYO.

E·dom (ē′dəm) See IDUMAEA.

E·dom·ite (ē′dəm·īt) *n.* A descendant of Esau, or an inhabitant of Edom. **—E′dom·it′ish** *adj.*

É·douard (ā·dwår′) French form of EDWARD. Also *Ital.* **E·doar·do** (ā·dwär′dō).

ed·u·ca·ble (ej′oo·kə·bəl) *adj.* Capable of being educated.

ed·u·cate (ej′oo·kāt) *v.t.* **·cat·ed, ·cat·ing 1** To develop or train the mind, capabilities, and character of by or as by formal schooling or instruction; teach. **2** To train for some special purpose: He was *educated* for the ministry. **3** To develop and train (taste, special ability, etc.). **4** To provide schooling for. See synonyms under TEACH. [<L *educatus,* pp. of *educare* bring up <*educere.* See EDUCE.] **—ed′u·cat′a·ble** *adj.*

ed·u·cat·ed (ej′ŏŏ·kā′tid) *adj.* **1** Developed and informed by education; instructed; trained. **2** Having a cultivated mind, speech, manner, etc. See synonyms under INTELLIGENT.

ed·u·ca·tion (ej′ŏŏ·kā′shən) *n.* **1** The systematic development and cultivation of the natural powers, by inculcation, example, etc. **2** Instruction and training in an institution of learning. **3** The knowledge and skills resulting from such instruction and training. **4** Teaching as a system, science, or art; pedagogy. **5** The training of animals. **6** The culture of bees, bacteria, etc. **—Education, Office of** See UNITED STATES OFFICE OF EDUCATION. **—ed′u·ca′tion·al** *adj.* **—ed′u·ca′tion·al·ly** *adv.* **—ed′u·ca′tion·ar′y** *adj.*

Synonyms: breeding, cultivation, culture, development, discipline, information, instruction, knowledge, learning, nurture, reading, schooling, study, teaching, training, tuition. *Education* (L. *educere,* to lead or draw out) is the systematic *development* and *cultivation* of the mind and other natural powers. It begins in the nursery, continues through school, and also through life, whether we will or not. *Instruction,* the impartation of *knowledge* by others is but a part of education. *Teaching* is the more familiar and less formal word for *instruction. Training* refers not merely to the impartation of *knowledge,* but to the exercising of one in actions with the design to form habits. *Discipline* is systematic and rigorous *training,* with the idea of subjection to authority and perhaps of punishment. *Tuition* is the technical term for *teaching* as the business of an instructor or as in the routine of a school. We speak of the *teaching, training,* or *discipline,* rather than of the *education* or *tuition* of a dog or a horse. Compare KNOWLEDGE, LEARNING, NURTURE, REFINEMENT, WISDOM. *Antonyms:* ignorance, illiteracy. Compare synonyms for IGNORANT.

ed·u·ca·tion·al·ist (ej′ŏŏ·kā′shən·əl·ist) *n.* **1** One interested in educational forms or methods; one employed in educational pursuits; a practical educator. **2** One versed in educational theories or devoted to educational interests: also **ed′u·ca′tion·ist.**

ed·u·ca·tive (ej′ŏŏ·kā′tiv) *adj.* Instructive; developing; educating.

ed·u·ca·tor (ej′ŏŏ·kā′tər) *n.* A teacher. **—ed′u·ca·to′ry** (-tôr′ē, -tō′rē) *adj.*

e·duce (i·dōōs′, i·dyōōs′) *v.t.* **e·duced, e·duc·ing 1** To call forth; draw out; evoke. **2** To develop or formulate, as from data or experimentation. [<L *educere* <*ex-* out + *ducere* lead] **—e·duc′i·ble** *adj.* **—e·duc·tive** (i·duk′·tiv) *adj.* **—e·duc′tor** *n.*

e·duct (ē′dukt) *n.* **1** That which is educed; something brought out or developed from another. **2** *Chem.* A substance or body derived from another body in which it originally existed, as opposed to a *product* resulting from chemical change.

e·duc·tion (i·duk′shən) *n.* **1** The act or process of educing. **2** An educt. **3** The act of exhausting, as an engine cylinder, of steam: used in various self–explaining compounds, as **eduction pipe:** now superseded by *exhaust.*

E·dui·no (ā·dwē′nō) Italian form of EDWIN.

e·dul·co·rate (i·dul′kə·rāt) *v.t.* **·rat·ed, ·rat·ing 1** To correct the acidity or acridity of; soften; sweeten. **2** *Chem.* To cleanse or free from soluble acids, salts, etc., by washing with water. [<L *edulcoratus,* pp. of *edulcorare* <*ex-* out + *dulcis* sweet] **—e·dul′co·ra′tion** *n.* **—e·dul′co·ra′tive** *adj.*

Ed·ward (ed′wərd) A masculine personal name. Also *Du., Ger.* **E·duard** (ā′dwärt), *Ital., Pg., Sp.* **E·duar·do** (ā·dwär′dō, *Pg.* -dŏŏ), *Dan.* **Ed·vard** (ed′värth). [OE, rich guardian]

—Edward, 1330–76, prince of Wales; fought at Crécy and Poitiers; son of Edward III: called the "Black Prince."

—Edward, 1004?–66, king of England 1042–1066: known as *Edward the Confessor.*

— **Edward I,** 1239–1307, king of England 1272–1307: known as *Edward Longshanks.*
— **Edward II,** 1284–1327, king of England 1307–27; defeated by Bruce at Bannockburn, 1314; murdered.
— **Edward III,** 1312–77, king of England 1327–77; defeated the Scots and French.
— **Edward IV,** 1442–83, king of England 1461–70, 1471–83; overthrew the Lancastrians.
— **Edward V,** 1470?–83, king of England 1483; murdered in the Tower.
— **Edward VI,** 1537–53, king of England 1547–53; son of Henry VIII and Jane Seymour.
— **Edward VII,** 1841–1910, king of England 1901–10.
— **Edward VIII,** 1894–1972, succeeded his father George V as king of England, Jan. 20, 1936; abdicated Dec. 10, 1936; became the Duke of Windsor.

Edward, Lake A lake in Africa, situated between Uganda and Belgian Congo; 830 square miles: also *Albert Lake.*

Ed·ward·i·an (ed·wär′dē·ən) *adj.* **1** *Law* Relating to Edward I as regards the writs founded on the statute of Gloucester, which enforced the law that a grant in fee simple by a tenant for life, or in dower, caused forfeiture of the entire estate. **2** *Archit.* Indicating the style of the time of the first three Edwards. **3** *Eccl.* Pertaining to the adoption of a new ritual and important changes in church management, under Edward VI. **4** Relating to Edward VII, his reign and especially the literature, manners, and decorative styles characterizing this period.

Ed·wards (ed′wərdz), **Jonathan,** 1703–58, American theologian and preacher.

Edwards Plateau A SE extension of the Great Plains in SW Texas; elevation, 2,500 feet.

Ed·win (ed′win; *Dan.* ed′vin, *Ger.* et′vin) A masculine personal name. Also *Lat.* **Ed·wi·nus** (ed·vī′nəs). [OE, rich friend]
— **Edwin,** 583?–633, king of Northumbria.

ee (ē) *n. Scot.* An eye.

-ee *Suffix of nouns* **1** A person who undergoes the action or receives the benefit of the main element: *payee:* often used in legal terms and opposed to *-er, -or,* as in *grantor, grantee.* **2** A person who is described by the main element: *absentee.* [AF *-é,* suffix of pp. <L *-atus*]

eel (ēl) *n. pl.* **eels** or **eel 1** A voracious teleost fish belonging to the order *Apodes,* having an elongated snakelike body, usually without scales or pelvic fins, and of both marine and fresh-water habitat; especially the **American eel** *(Anguilla bastoniensis)* and the **European eel** *(A. anguilla).* **2** Any of certain other eel-like fishes, as the lamprey, frequently called the lamprey eel, electric eel, etc. **3** An eelworm. [OE *ǣl*] — **eel′y** *adj.*

AMERICAN EEL
(Average length under 3 feet, maximum 4 feet)

eel·grass (ēl′gras′, -gräs′) *n.* An herb *(Zostera marina)* of the pondweed family, of grasslike appearance, and growing wholly under water: used as a sound insulator, for packing, etc.

eel·pot (ēl′pot′) *n.* A form of basket for trapping eels.

eel·pout (ēl′pout′) *n. pl.* **·pouts** or **·pout** A marine fish with an eel-like body tapering backward. *Zoarces anguillaris* is the American and *Z. viviparus* the European eelpout. [OE *ǣlepute*]

eel·worm (ēl′wûrm′) *n.* **1** A threadworm or nematode, especially *Ascaris lumbricoides,* parasitic in the human digestive tract. **2** The vinegar eel.

een (ēn) *n. Scot.* Eyes.

e'en (ēn) *adv. Poetic* Even. — *n. Poetic & Dial.* Evening.

-eer *suffix of nouns and verbs* **1** One who is concerned with, works with, or produces: *engineer:* now often used disdainfully, as in *pamphleteer.* **2** Be concerned with: *electioneer.* [<F *-ier* <L *-arius*]

e'er (âr) *adv. Poetic* Ever.

ee·rie (ē′rē, ir′ē) *adj.* **1** Inspiring fear or awe; weird. **2** Affected by fear; awed. Also **ee′ry.** [ME *eri* timid, var. of *erg* <OE *earg*] — **ee′ri·ly** *adv.* — **ee′ri·ness** *n.*

Ees·ti (ās′tē) The Estonian name for ESTONIA.

ef- Assimilated var. of EX-[1].

E·fa·te (e·fä′tē) A central island of the New Hebrides group; 200 square miles: also *Vaté.*

ef·fa·ble (ef′ə·bəl) *adj.* That can be uttered or explained. [<L *effabilis* <*ex-* out + *fari* speak]

ef·face (i·fās′) *v.t.* **·faced, ·fac·ing 1** To rub out, as written characters; erase; cancel. **2** To obliterate or destroy, as a memory. **3** To make (oneself) inconspicuous or insignificant. See synonyms under CANCEL. [<F *effacer* <L *ex-* out + *facies* face] — **ef·face′a·ble** *adj.* — **ef·face′ment** *n.* — **ef·fac′er** *n.* — **ef·fa′cive** *adj.*

ef·fect (i·fekt′) *n.* **1** A result or product of some cause or agency; a consequence. **2** Practical efficiency. **3** The substance of a statement; gist. **4** Active operation; execution. **5** Fact or reality: following *in.* **6** *pl.* Movable goods. **7** Useful work performed by a machine. **8** A mental state or attitude resulting from observation or external impression: the *effect* of a picture. See synonyms under ACT, CONSEQUENCE, END, OPERATION, PRODUCT. — *v.t.* **1** To bring about; produce as a result; cause. **2** To achieve; accomplish. [<L *effectus,* pp. of *efficere* <*ex-* out + *facere* do, make] — **ef·fect′er** *n.* — **ef·fect′i·ble** *adj.*

Synonyms (verb): accomplish, achieve, close, complete, conclude, consummate, do, end, execute, finish, fulfil, perform, produce, realize. *Effect, execute, consummate,* and *realize* all signify to embody in fact what was before in thought. One may *realize* that which he has done nothing to *bring about;* he may *realize* the dreams of youth by inheriting a fortune; but he cannot *effect* his early designs except by *doing* the utmost that is necessary to make them fact. *Effect* includes all that is *done* to *accomplish* the intent; *execute* refers rather to the formal steps; *consummate* is limited quite sharply to the concluding act. Care must be taken to distinguish between *effect* and *affect.* An officer *executes* the law when he proceeds against its violators; a purchase is *consummated* when the money is paid and the property delivered. *Execute* refers more commonly to the commands of another, *effect* and *consummate* to one's own designs; as, The commander *effected* the capture of the fort, because his officers and men promptly *executed* his commands. See ACCOMPLISH, DO[1], MAKE.

ef·fec·tive (i·fek′tiv) *adj.* **1** Producing, or adapted to produce, an effect; efficient. **2** Impressive; moving, as oratory. **3** In force, as a law. **4** Ready, as an army. — *n.* **1** One who is fit for duty. **2** The number of men available for active service: a war *effective* of 250,000. **3** That which effects; a cause. **4** Silver or gold currency, as distinguished from paper; coin. See synonyms under EFFICIENT, POWERFUL. — **ef·fec′tive·ly** *adv.* — **ef·fec′tive·ness** *n.*

ef·fec·tor (i·fek′tər) *n. Physiol.* A specialized structure at the periphery of a motor nerve, as a muscle or gland, serving to transform efferent nerve impulses into physical action, or to innervate them. Compare RECEPTOR.

ef·fec·tu·al (i·fek′chōō·əl) *adj.* **1** Possessing or exercising adequate power to produce a designed effect; completely efficient; efficacious: *effectual* measures. **2** In force; legal, as a rule or law. See synonyms under POWERFUL. [<OF *effectuel* <LL *effectualis* <*effectus.* See EFFECT.] — **ef·fec′tu·al′i·ty** (-al′ə·tē) *n.* — **ef·fec′·tu·al·ness** *n.*

ef·fec·tu·al·ly (i·fek′chōō·əl·ē) *adv.* With effect; actually; truly.

ef·fec·tu·ate (i·fek′chōō·āt) *v.t.* **·at·ed, ·at·ing** To make effectual; effect. [<F *effectuer* <L *effectus.* See EFFECT.] — **ef·fec′tu·a′tion** *n.*

ef·fem·i·na·cy (i·fem′ə·nə·sē) *n.* The quality of being effeminate; womanishness.

ef·fem·i·nate (i·fem′ə·nit) *adj.* Having womanish traits or qualities; unmanly; voluptuous; delicate. See synonyms under FEMININE. [<L *effeminatus,* pp. of *effeminare* <*ex-* out + *femina* a woman] — **ef·fem′i·nate·ly** *adv.* — **ef·fem′i·nate·ness** *n.*

ef·fen·di (i·fen′dē) *n.* A title of respect in Turkey: sir; master. [<Turkish *efendi,* ult. <Gk. *authentēs* master]

ef·fer·ent (ef′ər·ənt) *adj. Physiol.* Carrying or carried outward, as impulses from the central nervous system to muscles, the cells of glands, etc.; discharging: opposed to *afferent.* — *n.* **1** An efferent duct, vessel, or nerve. **2** A stream carrying off water, as from a pond. [<L *efferens, -entis,* ppr. of *efferre* <*ex-* out + *ferre* carry]

ef·fer·vesce (ef′ər·ves′) *v.i.* **·vesced, ·vesc·ing 1** To bubble up; give off bubbles of gas, as water charged with carbon dioxide. **2** To come away in bubbles, as a gas. **3** To show exhilaration or lively spirits. [<L *effervescere* <*ex-* out + *fervescere* boil, inceptive of *fervere* be hot]

ef·fer·ves·cence (ef′ər·ves′əns) *n.* **1** The escape of bubbles of gas from a liquid otherwise than by boiling, or the condition of a substance resulting therefrom. **2** A bubbling up: the *effervescence* of a carbonate with an acid. **3** Irrepressible excitement or emotion. Also **ef′fer·ves′cen·cy.** [<L *effervescens, -entis,* ppr. of *effervescere.* See EFFERVESCE.]

ef·fer·ves·cent (ef′ər·ves′ənt) *adj.* **1** Giving off bubbles of gas; coming off in bubbles, as gas from a liquid. **2** Effervescing, or having the property of effervescing. — **ef′fer·ves′ci·ble** *adj.* — **ef′fer·ves′cive** *adj.*

ef·fete (i·fēt′) *adj.* Worn out and incapable of further production, as an animal, a plant, or soil; exhausted; barren. [<L *effetus* <*ex-* out + *fetus* a breeding] — **ef·fete′ness** *n.*

ef·fi·ca·cious (ef′ə·kā′shəs) *adj.* Producing or capable of producing an intended effect; having efficacy. See synonyms under EFFICIENT, POWERFUL. [<L *efficax, -cacis* <*efficere.* See EFFECT.] — **ef′fi·ca′cious·ly** *adv.* — **ef′fi·ca′·cious·ness** *n.*

ef·fi·ca·cy (ef′ə·kə·sē) *n. pl.* **·cies** Power to produce an effect; effective energy. See synonyms under POWER, WEIGHT.

ef·fi·cien·cy (i·fish′ən·sē) *n. pl.* **·cies 1** The character of being efficient; effectiveness. **2** The ratio of the work done or energy expended by an organism or machine to the energy supplied in the form of food or fuel. Also **ef·fi′·cience.** See synonyms under ABILITY, POWER.

ef·fi·cient (i·fish′ənt) *adj.* **1** Acting or having power to act effectually; competent: an *efficient* leader. **2** Productive of effects; causative. — *n.* **1** A qualified person; specifically, in the British Army, a volunteer certified for his qualifications. **2** An efficient cause. [<L *efficiens, -entis,* ppr. of *efficere.* See EFFECT.] — **ef·fi′cient·ly** *adv.*

Synonyms (adj.): effective, effectual, efficacious. That is *effective* which accomplishes an intended effect with emphasis, decision, and certainty; that is *effectual* which acts with such finality as to leave no more to be done. A person may be said to be *efficient* in general character or action; as, an *efficient* businessman; he may be called *effective* in some special relation; as, an *effective* speaker; the *efficient* person is habitually energetic, industrious, sagacious, and alert; a man may be an *effective* speaker on occasion who is not *efficient* in ordinary life. *Efficacious* and *effectual* are not used of persons. *Antonyms:* awkward, dull, feckless, feeble, fruitless, idle, ineffective, ineffectual, inefficacious, inefficient, inoperative, negligent, powerless, remiss, unavailing, useless, vain.

efficient cause The immediate force or agent in the performance of work.

ef·fi·gy (ef′ə·jē) *n. pl.* **·gies 1** A figure representing a person, as in sculpture or numismatics. **2** A representation of a person who has incurred odium. — **to burn** (or **hang**) **in effigy** To burn or hang publicly an image of a person who is hated. [<F *effigie* <L *effigies* <*ex-* out + *fingere* fashion] — **ef·fig·i·al** (e·fij′ē·əl) *adj.*

ef·fla·tion (i·flā′shən) *n.* That which is blown or breathed forth; an emanation. [<L *efflatus* <*ex-* out + *flare* blow]

ef·fleu·rage (e·flœ·räzh′) *n. French* A gentle rubbing with the palm of the hand; massage.

ef·flo·resce (ef′lô·res′, -lō-) *v.i.* **·resced, ·resc·ing 1** *Bot.* To blossom, bloom, or flower. **2** *Chem.* **a** To become powdery, wholly or in part, and lose crystalline structure through loss of water of crystallization on exposure to the air. **b** To become covered with a crust of saline particles left by evaporation, as the ground. [<L *efflorescere* <*ex-* thoroughly + *florescere* bloom <*flos, floris* a flower]

ef·flo·res·cence (ef′lô·res′əns, -lō-) *n.* **1** *Bot.* The time or act of flowering. **2** *Pathol.* A rash on the skin. **3** The process, act, or result of efflorescing. **4** A crystalline deposit on the surface of a mineral or on the face of a stone wall. Also **ef′flo·res′cen·cy.**

ef·flo·res·cent (ef′lô·res′ənt, -lo-) *adj.* **1** *Bot.* Blossoming out; blooming. **2** Tending or liable to effloresce. **3** *Chem.* **a** Forming into white threads or powder. **b** Covered with efflorescence. [<L *efflorescens, -entis,* ppr. of *efflorescere.* See EFFLORESCE.]

ef·flu·ence (ef′lo͞o·əns) *n.* A flowing out; emanation. Also **ef′flu·en·cy.**

ef·flu·ent (ef′lo͞o·ənt) *adj.* Flowing out. —*n.* **1** Sewage after purification treatment. **2** An outflow, as of water from a lake or stream. [<L *effluens, -entis,* ppr. of *effluere* < *ex-* out + *fluere* flow]

ef·flu·vi·um (i·flo͞o′vē·əm) *n. pl.* **·vi·a** (-vē·ə) **1** An invisible emanation. **2** A noxious or ill-smelling exhalation from decaying matter: commonly in the plural: the *effluvia* from foul drains. **3** A theoretic imponderable agent formerly regarded as the source of the electric and magnetic forces of certain substances. [<L, a flowing out] —**ef·flu′vi·al, ef·flu′vi·ous** *adj.*

ef·flux (ef′luks) *n.* An outflow; effluence; emanation; effluvium. [<L *effluxus* < *ex-* out + *fluere* flow]

ef·flux·ion (i·fluk′shən) *n.* **1** A flowing forth; hence, lapse, as of time. **2** That which flows forth; emanation, outpouring.

ef·fort (ef′ərt) *n.* **1** A voluntary exertion of power; strenuous endeavor; attempt. **2** A result or display of consciously directed power; an achievement. **3** *Mech.* Force exerted against the inertia of a body. See synonyms under ENDEAVOR, INDUSTRY. [<F < *efforcer* <L *ex-* out + *fortis* strong]

ef·fort·less (ef′ərt·lis) *adj.* Showing or making no effort; easy. —**ef′fort·less·ly** *adv.*

ef·front·er·y (i·frun′tər·ē) *n. pl.* **·er·ies** Insolent assurance; audacity; impudence. [<F *effronterie* <OF *esfront* shameless <L *effrons* < *ex-* out + *frons, frontis* forehead, face]

Synonyms: assurance, audacity, boldness, brass, hardihood, impudence, insolence, shamelessness. *Audacity,* in the sense here considered, is a reckless defiance of law, decency, public opinion, or personal rights, claims, or views, approaching the meaning of *impudence* or *shamelessness,* but always carrying the thought of the personal risk that one disregards in such defiance; the merely *impudent* or *shameless* person may take no thought of consequences; the *audacious* person recognizes and recklessly braves them. *Hardihood* defies and disregards the rational judgment of men. *Effrontery* (L *effrons* bare-faced, shameless) adds to *audacity* and *hardihood* the special element of defiance of considerations of propriety, duty, and respect for others, yet not to the extent implied in *impudence* or *shamelessness. Impudence* disregards what is due to superiors: *shamelessness* defies decency. *Boldness* is forward-stepping courage, spoken of with reference to the presence and observation of others; *boldness,* in the good sense, is courage viewed from the outside; but the word is frequently used in an unfavorable sense to indicate a lack of proper sensitiveness and modesty. Compare ASSURANCE, BRAVE, IMPUDENCE. *Antonyms*: bashfulness, coyness, diffidence, modesty, sensitiveness, shrinking, shyness, timidity.

ef·fulge (i·fulj′) *v.t.* & *v.i.* **·fulged, ·fulg·ing** To shine forth; radiate. [<L *effulgere* < *ex-* out + *fulgere* shine]

ef·ful·gence (i·ful′jəns) *n.* A shining forth brilliantly; beaming brightness; splendor. [<L *effulgens, -entis,* ppr. of *effulgere.* See EFFULGE.] —**ef·ful′gent** *adj.* —**ef·ful′gent·ly** *adv.*

ef·fuse (i·fyo͞os′) *adj.* **1** *Bot.* Spreading loosely, as the panicle of the common rush, or spreading flat, as the plant body of some thallophytic epiphytes. **2** *Bacteriol.* Profuse, as a thin spreading film of bacteria in a culture. **3** *Entomol.* Composed of loosely joined parts; not compact, as an insect's body. **4** *Zool.* Having the lips separated by a groove, as a shell; expanded. **5** *Obs.* Poured out freely; profuse. —*v.* (i·fyo͞oz′) **·fused, ·fus·ing** *v.t.* **1** To pour forth; shed. —*v.i.* **2** To emanate; exude. **3** *Physics* To flow through a porous diaphragm or aperture under pressure: said of gases. [<L *effusus,* pp. of *effundere* < *ex-* out + *fundere* pour]

ef·fu·sion (i·fyo͞o′zhən) *n.* **1** The act or process of pouring forth, or that which is poured forth. **2** An outpouring, as of fancy or sentiment: applied ironically to literary compositions. **3** Sentimental demonstration. **4** *Pathol.* The pouring out of the blood or other fluid, as into the cellular tissue. **5** *Physics* The flow of gases under pressure through openings in the container.

ef·fu·sive (i·fyo͞o′siv) *adj.* **1** Overflowing with sentiment; demonstrative; gushing. **2** Pouring forth; shedding abroad: with *of.* —**ef·fu′sive·ly** *adv.* —**ef·fu′sive·ness** *n.*

effusive rocks *Geol.* Volcanic material poured out and solidified on the surface of the earth.

Ef·ik (ef′ik) *n. pl.* **Ef·ik 1** One of a Negro people inhabiting Nigeria. **2** The language of these people, showing Sudanic characteristics.

eft[1] (eft) *n.* **1** A newt. **2** Formerly, a small lizard. [OE *efeta*]

eft[2] (eft) *adv. Obs.* Again; afterwards. [OE]

eft·soon (eft′so͞on′) *adv. Obs.* Soon afterward or again; hence, speedily; quickly; also, often. Also **eft′soons′.** [OE *eftsona* immediately afterwards]

e·gad (i·gad′, ē·gad′) *interj.* By God!: a mild oath. [Prob. alter. of *ah, God!*]

Eg·a·di Islands (eg′ə·dē) An island group in the Mediterranean off western Sicily; total, 15 square miles: ancient *Aegates*: also *Aegadian Islands, Aegadean Islands.*

e·gal (ē′gəl) *Obs. adj.* Equal. —*n.* An equal. [<F *égal*]

e·gal·i·tar·i·an (i·gal′ə·târ′ē·ən) *n.* One who believes in or works for equal rights. —*adj.* Equalitarian. [<F *égalitaire*] —**e·gal′i·tar′i·an·ism** *n.*

é·ga·li·té (ā·gȧ·lē·tā′) *n. French* Equality.

Eg·bert (eg′bərt) A masculine personal name. Also *Ital.* **Eg·ber·to** (eg·ber′tō), *Lat.* **Eg·ber·tus** (eg·bûr′təs). [OE, bright sword]
—**Egbert,** 775?–839; king of Wessex 802–839; king of England 827–839.

E·ger (ā′gər) A river in Bavaria and western Bohemia, flowing 159 miles east to the Elbe: Czech *Ohře.*

E·ge·ri·a (i·jir′ē·ə) **1** In Roman legend, an Italian nymph who was the wife and adviser of Numa, second king of Rome. **2** Any woman adviser.

e·gest (ē·jest′) *v.t.* To eject or void, as feces or perspiration; excrete. [<L *egestus,* pp. of *egerere* < *ex-* out + *gerere* carry]

e·ges·ta (ē·jes′tə) *n.* Excreta: opposed to *ingesta.* [<L, neut. pl. of *egestus.* See EGEST.]

e·ges·tion (ē·jes′chən) *n.* The expulsion or voiding of digested matter; defecation.

e·ges·tive (ē·jes′tiv) *adj.* Excretory: opposed to *ingestive.*

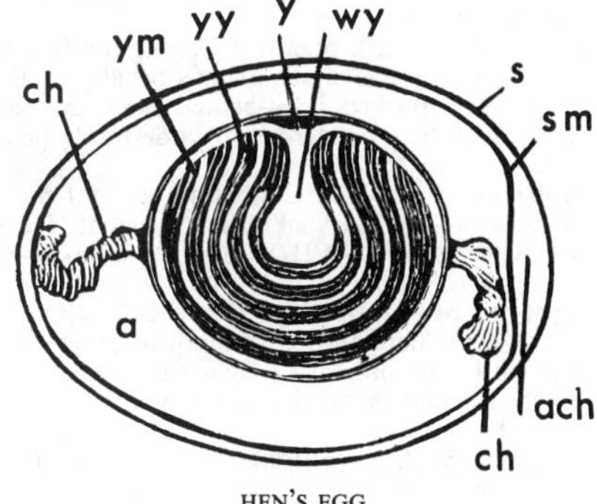

HEN'S EGG

ch.	Chalazae.	*s.*	Shell.
ym.	Yolk membrane.	*sm.*	Shell membrane.
yy.	Yellow food yolk.	*ach.*	Air chamber.
y.	Germinal vesicle.	*a.*	Albumin, or white of the egg.
wy.	White yolk.		

egg[1] (eg) *n.* **1** A reproductive body containing the germ and the food yolk of birds, insects, reptiles, or fishes, enclosed in a membranous or shell-like covering. **2** In common usage, such a body, especially that of the domestic fowl. See also illustration under EMBRYOLOGY, FROG. **3** The female reproductive cell of animals which, when fertilized, becomes a *zygote*; an ovum or germ cell. **4** Something like or likened to an egg. **5** Figuratively, that which contains a germ. —*v.t.* **1** To mix or cover with eggs. **2** *U.S.* To pelt with eggs. —*v.i.* **3** To collect birds' eggs. —**lay an egg** *U.S. Slang* To fail: said of a play, joke, etc. [<ON]

egg[2] (eg) *v.t.* To instigate or incite; urge: usually with *on.* [<ON *eggja*]

egg-and-an·chor (eg′ənd·ang′kər) *n. Archit.* An ornamental molding carved with series of alternate egg-shaped and anchor-shaped, or dart- or tongue-shaped figures. Also **egg′-and-dart′, egg′-and-tongue′.**

EGG-AND-ANCHOR MOLDING

egg-beat·er (eg′bē′tər) *n.* A kitchen utensil for beating an egg after it has been removed from the shell.

eg·ger (eg′ər) *n.* **1** Any of several European moths (genera *Lasiocampa* and *Eriogaster*). **2** The tent caterpillar. Also called **eg′ger moth.** Also spelled **eg′gar.** [Prob. <EGG, with ref. to the shape of the cocoon]

egg·head (eg′hed′) *n. U.S. Slang* An intellectual; a highbrow: usually slightly derisive.

egg-lay·ing (eg′lā′ing) *adj.* Oviparous.

Eg·gle·ston (eg′əl·stən), **Edward,** 1837–1902, U. S. clergyman and novelist. —**George Cary,** 1839–1911, U. S. writer; brother of preceding.

Egg·mühl (ek′mül) See ECKMÜHL.

egg·nog (eg′nog′) *n.* A drink made of beaten eggs and milk with sugar and nutmeg and sometimes with brandy, rum, or other liquor. [<EGG + NOG[2] (def. 1)]

egg·plant (eg′plant′, -plänt′) *n.* **1** A widely cultivated herb (*Solanum melongena*) of the nightshade family, with large egg-shaped edible fruit. **2** The fruit, used as a vegetable. **3** A very dark blackish-purple; the color of the skin of the eggplant.

egg·shell (eg′shel′) *n.* **1** The hard, brittle, outer envelope of an egg. **2** A light ivory shade; the color commonly associated with that of a hen's egg. **2** A very thin and delicate porcelain: also **eggshell china, eggshell porcelain.**

egg tray A tray to hold eggs in an incubator. See illustration under INCUBATOR.

egg white The albumen of an egg as distinguished from the yolk: also *white of egg.*

E·gi·di·us (i·jid′ē·əs, *Du., Ger.* ā·gē′dē·o͝os) Dutch and German form of GILES. Also *Fr.* **É·gide** (ā·zhēd′), *Ital.* **E·gi·dio** (ā·jē′dyō).

e·gis (ē′jis) See AEGIS.

eg·lan·tine (eg′lən·tīn, -tēn) *n.* Either of two roselike plants, the sweetbrier, and the dog rose. Also *Obs.* **eg·la·tere** (eg′lə·tir′). [<F *églantine* <OF *aiglent,* ult. <L *acus* needle]

Eg·mont (eg′mont) An extinct volcano on North Island, New Zealand; 8,260 feet: Maori *Taranaki.*

Eg·mont (eg′mont, *Flemish* ekh′mônt), **Lamoral,** 1522–68, Count of Egmont, Flemish general and statesman.

e·go (ē′go, eg′ō) *n. pl.* **e·gos 1** Self, considered as the seat of consciousness. **2** In philosophy, the entire man, body and mind. **3** *Psychol.* The self, considered as the aggregate of all conscious acts and states, whether organized or sporadic, but having a unity and continuity differentiating it from all others. **4** *Psychoanal.* The superficial conscious part of the id, developed in response to the physical and social environment. **5** In metaphysics, the permanent real being to whom all the conscious states and attributes belong. **6** *Colloq.* Self-centeredness; egotism; conceit. [<L, I]

e·go·cen·tric (ē′gō·sen′trik, eg′ō-) *adj.* **1** Self-centered; reacting to all things from a personal point of view; caring only for self or personal interests. **2** *Philos.* Proceeding from self as the center, as one's knowledge of the nature of the outside world. —**e′go·cen·tric′·i·ty** (-sen·tris′ə·tē) *n.*

e·go·ism (ē′gō·iz′əm, eg′ō-) *n.* **1** In ethics, the doctrine that the supreme end of human conduct is the perfection or happiness of the ego, or self, and that all virtue consists in the pursuit of self-interest; also, that part of the theory or practice of conduct or duty that has reference to oneself, as distinguished from *altruism.* **2** Selfishness. **3** Egotism. See synonyms under EGOTISM.

e·go·ist (ē′gō·ist, eg′ō-) *n.* One who advocates or practices egoism.

e·go·is·tic (ē′gō·is′tik, eg′ō-) *adj.* **1** Characterized by inordinate regard for self. **2** Of or pertaining to self. **3** Egotistic. Also **e′go·is′ti·cal.** — **e′go·is′ti·cal·ly** *adv.*

e·go·ma·ni·a (ē′gō·mā′nē·ə, -mān′yə, eg′ō-) *n.* Abnormal or excessive egotism. —**e′go·ma′·ni·ac** *n.* & adj.

E·gor·evsk (yi·gôr′yifsk) See YEGORYEVSK.

e·go·tism (ē′gə·tiz′əm, eg′ə-) *n.* The habit or practice of thinking and talking much of oneself, or the spirit that leads to this practice; self-exaltation.

Synonyms: conceit, egoism, self-assertion, self-conceit, self-confidence, self-consciousness, self-esteem, vanity. *Egoism* is the giving the "I" undue supremacy in thought; *egotism* is giving the "I" undue prominence in speech and action. *Self-assertion* is the claim of what one believes to be his due; *self-conceit* is an overestimate of one's own powers or deserts. *Self-consciousness* (as here considered) is the keeping of one's thoughts upon oneself, with the constant anxious question of what others will think. *Vanity* is an overweening admiration of self, craving equal admiration from others. *Self-esteem* is more solid and better founded than *self-conceit*; but is ordinarily a weakness, and never has the worthy sense of *self-confidence.* Compare ASSURANCE, PRIDE. *Antonyms*: bashfulness, deference, diffidence, humility, modesty, self-distrust, self-forgetfulness, shyness, unobtrusiveness, unostentatiousness.

e·go·tist (ē′gə·tist, eg′ə-) *n.* One characterized by egotism. —**e′go·tis′ti·cal** *adj.* —**e′go·tis′·ti·cal·ly** *adv.*

e·gre·gious (i·grē′jəs, -jē·əs) *adj.* **1** Flagrant; outstanding in bad or evil qualities. **2** *Obs.* Prominent; protuberant. See synonyms under EXTRAORDINARY, NOTORIOUS. [<L *egregius,* outstanding <*ex-* out + *grex, gregis* herd] —**e·gre′gious·ly** *adv.* —**e·gre′gious·ness** *n.*

e·gress (ē′gres) *n.* **1** A going out; passing forth, as from a building. **2** A place of exit. **3** *Astron.* The end of the apparent passage of a small body over the face of a larger one, as the end of an eclipse. Also **e·gres′sion.** [<L *egressus* <*ex-* out + *gradi* go]

e·gret (ē′grit) *n.* **1** A heron characterized, in the breeding season, by long and loose plumes drooping over the tail, and usually white plumage; especially, the American egret (*Casmerodius albus*), and the snowy egret (*Egretta thula*). **2** A plume or tuft of its feathers, called an *aigrette.* [Var. of AIGRET]

SNOWY EGRET
(Length of body about 2 feet)

E·gypt (ē′jipt) A republic of NE Africa; 386,186 square miles, of which about 12,000 square miles are cultivated; capital, Cairo; divided into **Lower Egypt,** the Nile Delta, and **Upper Egypt,** the Nile Valley between a point a few miles south of Cairo and the Sudan. Officially *Arab Republic of Egypt.*

E·gyp·tian (i·jip′shən) *adj.* Of or pertaining to Egypt, its people, or their culture. —*n.* **1** One of the people of Egypt, ancient or modern. **2** The Hamitic language of Egypt, in its final stage called Coptic, and superseded, about 1500, by Arabic. **3** *Obs.* A gipsy.

Egyptian blue A blue pigment made from a mixture of copper silicates and widely used by the early Egyptians, Cretans, and Romans: now imitated by coal-tar colors.

Egyptian hallel See HALLEL.

E·gyp·tian·ize (i·jip′shən·īz) *v.t.* & *v.i.* **·ized, ·iz·ing** To make or act like an Egyptian or the Egyptians.

Egyptian lily See under CALLA.

E·gyp·tol·o·gist (ē′jip·tol′ə·jist) *n.* A student of or one versed in Egyptology. Also **E′gyp·tol′o·ger.**

E·gyp·tol·o·gy (ē′jip·tol′ə·jē) *n.* The science or scientific investigation or study of the antiquities of Egypt. —**E·gyp·to·log·ic** (ē·jip′tə·loj′ik), or **·i·cal** *adj.*

eh (ā, e) *interj.* What: used as an interrogative.

Eh·ren·breit·stein (ā′rən·brīt′shtīn) A fortress on the Rhine opposite Coblenz, Germany: called *Gibraltar of the Rhine.*

Eh·ren·burg (ā′rən·bŏŏrkh), **Ilya Grigorievich,** 1891–1967, U.S.S.R. writer.

Ehr·lich (âr′likh), **Paul,** 1854–1915, German bacteriologist.

ei·dent (ī′dənt) *adj. Scot.* Diligent; industrious. Also spelled *eydent.*

ei·der (ī′dər) *n.* A large sea duck of northern regions (genus *Somateria*), having plumage mostly white above and black below. Also **eider duck.** [<ON *œdhr-* in *œdhar-dūn* eider down; infl. in form by Sw. *eider* eider]

Ei·der (ī′dər) A river in NW Germany, flowing 117 miles NE to the North Sea.

eider down 1 The down of the eider used for stuffing pillows and quilts. **2** A warm, lightweight cotton or woolen fabric with a woolen nap. [<ON *œdhar-dūn*]

ei·det·ic (ī·det′ik) *adj. Psychol.* Of or pertaining to the faculty, voluntary or otherwise, of clearly visualizing objects previously seen. [<Gk. *eidētikos* pertaining to images]

eidetic imagery *Psychol.* The phenomenon of visual reproduction of previously seen objects: usually associated with pre-adolescent children.

ei·do·graph (ī′də·graf, -gräf) *n.* An instrument for copying drawings, usually on a reduced scale. [<Gk. *eidos* form + -GRAPH]

ei·do·lon (ī·dō′lən) *n. pl.* **·la** (-lə) **1** A representation; image. **2** A phantom. [<Gk. *eidōlon* image]

Ei·fel (ī′fəl) A desolate plateau region of western Germany between the Rhine, the Moselle, and the Ardennes; 2,447 feet high.

Eif·fel (ī′fəl, *Fr.* ā·fel′), **Alexandre Gustave,** 1832–1923, French engineer; pioneer in aerodynamics.

Eiffel Tower An iron tower in Paris, 984.25 feet high: designed for the Exposition of 1889 by A. G. Eiffel.

eight (āt) *n.* **1** The cardinal number following seven and preceding nine, or any of the symbols (8, viii, VIII) used to represent it. ◆ Collateral adjective: *octonary.* **2** Anything made up of eight units or members, as the crew of a racing shell, or a playing card with eight pips. —*adj.* Being or consisting of one more than seven; twice four. [OE *eahta*]

Eight, The A group of U.S. painters who opposed sentimentalism and academicism, but who varied widely in their individual work. The group, organized in 1908, included Davies, Glackens, Henri, Lawson, Luks, Prendergast, Shinn, and Sloan.

eight ball A black pool ball bearing a figure 8, and, in certain games, incurring a penalty on the player who pockets it. —**behind the eight ball** *U.S. Slang* In a dangerous or undesirable position.

eight·een (ā′tēn′) *adj.* Consisting of eight more than ten. —*n.* **1** The sum of ten and eight. **2** The symbols (18, xviii, XVIII) representing this number. [OE *eahtatēne*]

eight·een·mo (ā′tēn′mō′) See OCTODECIMO.

eight·eenth (ā′tēnth′) *adj.* Eighth in order after the tenth: the ordinal of *eighteen.* —*n.* One of eighteen equal parts; the quotient of a unit divided by eighteen.

Eighteenth Amendment An amendment to the Constitution of the United States prohibiting the manufacture, sale, and transportation of intoxicating liquors for beverage purposes: ratified in 1919 and put into effect, January, 1920: repealed in 1933 by the Twenty-first Amendment.

eight·fold (āt′fōld′) *adv.* So as to be eight times as many or as great; octuplicate. —*adj.* **1** Consisting of eight parts. **2** Eight times as many or as great.

eighth (ātth, āth) *adj.* **1** Next in order after the seventh. **2** Being one of eight equal parts. —*adv.* In the eighth order, place, or rank: also, in formal discourse, **eighth′ly.** —*n.* An eighth number or part.

eighth note *Music* A quaver.

eight·i·eth (ā′tē·ith) *adj.* **1** Tenth in order after the seventieth. **2** Being one of eighty equal parts. —*n.* **1** One of eighty equal parts. **2** That which follows the seventy-ninth.

eight·score (āt′skôr′, -skōr′) *adj.* & *n.* Eight times twenty.

eight·y (ā′tē) *adj.* Consisting of ten more than seventy. —*n.* **1** Eight times ten. **2** The symbols (80, lxxx, LXXX) representing this number. [OE *eahtatig*]

eight·y-nin·er (ā′tē·nī′nər) *n.* One of the Oklahoma homestead settlers of 1889.

ei·gon (ī′gon) *n. Med.* A compound of iodine with certain protein substances: used as an antiseptic.

Eijk·man (īk′män), **Christian,** 1858–1930, Dutch physician; pioneer in nutrition.

ei·kon (ī′kon) See ICON.

eild (ēld) *n. Scot.* Eld; old age.

eild·ing (ēl′ding) *n. Scot.* Elding; fuel; rubbish.

Ei·leen (ī·lēn′) Irish form of HELEN.

-ein Var. of -IN.

Eind·ho·ven (īnt′hō·vən) A city in south Netherlands.

ein·korn (īn′kôrn) *n.* A variety of wheat *(Triticum monococcum)* with narrow, slender curved spikelets usually bearing only one fertile floret; one-grained wheat: cultivated especially in central Europe. [<G; trans. of NL *monococcum,* species name <Gk. *monos* one + *kokkos* grain]

Ein·stein (īn′stīn), **Albert,** 1878–1955, mathematical physicist, developed the theory of relativity; born in Germany, active in Switzerland and the United States.

ein·stein·i·um (īn·stīn′ē·əm) *n.* A synthetic transuranium element (symbol Es, atomic number 99) originally detected in the debris of a thermonuclear explosion, the most stable isotope having a half-life of 276 days. See PERIODIC TABLE. [after Albert *Einstein*]

Eint·ho·ven (int′hō·vən), **Willem,** 1860–1927, Dutch physiologist.

Eir·e (âr′ə) A former name for the REPUBLIC OF IRELAND.

Eire·ann (âr′ən) *adj. Irish* Of Ireland.

Ei·re·ne (ī·rā′nə) Greek form of Irene.

Ei·sen·ach (ī′zə·näkh) A city in Thuringia, central Germany.

Ei·sen·how·er (ī′zən·hou′ər), **Dwight David,** 1890–1969, president of the United States 1953–61; supreme commander of Allied forces in invasion of Europe, World War II.

Ei·sen·stadt (ī′zən·shtät) The capital of Burgenland, Austria.

Ei·ser·nes Tor (ī′zer·nəs tôr′) The German name for IRON GATE.

eis·tedd·fod (ā·steth′vod, es·teth′-) *n. pl.* **·fods** or **·fod·au** (-vod′ī) An annual assembly of bards, in Wales, to foster national, musical, and literary interests. Also **eis·tedd′vod.** [<Welsh, session <*eistedd* sit] —**eis′tedd·fod′ic** *adj.*

ei·ther (ē′thər, ī′-) *adj.* **1** One or the other of two: Use *either* foot on the pedal. **2** Each of two; one and the other: on *either* side. See synonyms under EVERY. —*pron.* One of two; one or the other. —*conj.* In one of two or more cases, indeterminately or indifferently: used as a disjunctive correlative introducing a first alternative, the second and any other being preceded by *or*: *Either* I shall go *or* he will come. —*adv.* At all; any more so: used after the denial of an alternative: He could not speak, and I could not *either.* [OE *œgther*]

ei·ther-or (ē′thər·ôr′, ī′thər-) *adj.* Offering a choice between two alternatives, with other possibilities excluded.

e·jac·u·late (i·jak′yə·lāt) *v.* **·lat·ed, ·lat·ing** *v.t.* **1** To say vehemently and suddenly. **2** To throw out suddenly; eject, as fluids from the body. —*v.i.* **3** To exclaim. See synonyms under CALL, EXCLAIM. [<L *ejaculatus,* pp. of *ejaculari* <*ex-* out + *jaculari* throw] —**e·jac′u·la′tive** *adj.* —**e·jac′u·la′tor** *n.*

e·jac·u·la·tion (i·jak′yə·lā′shən) *n.* **1** The uttering of brief, sudden exclamations; an exclamation. **2** *Eccl.* A brief prayer; a short, pious utterance. **3** *Physiol.* The forceful expulsion of semen during the orgasm; an emission.

e·jac·u·la·to·ry (i·jak′yə·lə·tôr′ē, -tō′rē) *adj.* **1** In the form or of the nature of an ejaculation; exclamatory. **2** Pertaining to or using ejaculation, in any sense.

e·ject (i·jekt′) *v.t.* **1** To throw or drive out by sudden force; expel. **2** To evict. See synonyms under BANISH. —*n.* (ē′jekt) *Psychol.* A perception, mental state, etc. (of another) inferred as an entity by one's own consciousness, but which is essentially inaccessible to consciousness. [< L *ejectus*, pp. of *ejicere* < *ex-* out + *jacere* throw] **—e·jec′tor** *n.*

e·jec·ta (i·jek′tə) *n. pl.* Matter or refuse that has been cast out, as by a volcano or the body. Also **e·jec·ta·men·ta** (i·jek′tə·men′tə). [< L, neut. pl. of *ejectus*. See EJECT.]

e·jec·ta·ble (i·jek′tə·bəl) *adj.* Capable of being ejected.

e·jec·tion (i·jek′shən) *n.* **1** The act of ejecting; expulsion. **2** Matter ejected. **—e·jec′tive** *adj.* **—e·jec′tive·ly** *adv.*

e·ject·ment (i·jekt′mənt) *n.* **1** A casting out; eviction. **2** *Law* An action to recover posession of real estate, with damages for wrongful withholding; also, the writ by which this action is instituted.

ejector seat A pilot's seat which can be catapulted from an aircraft, thus enabling the pilot to bail out at high speeds.

e·ji·do (ā·hē′thō) *n.* A communal farm, specifically in Mexico. [< Sp.]

Ej·mi·a·dzin (ech′mē·ä·dzēn′) See ECHMIADZIN.

E·ka·te·ri·na (ā′kä·tə·rē′nə) Russian form of CATHERINE.

E·ka·te·rin·burg (ye·kä′tye·rin·bo͝orkh′) A former name for SVERDLOVSK.

E·ka·te·ri·no·dar (ye·kä′tye·rē′nô·där) A former name for KRASNODAR.

E·ka·te·ri·no·slav (ye·kä′tye·rē′nô·släf) A former name for DNEPROPETROVSK.

eke[1] (ēk) *v.t.* **eked, ek·ing 1** To supplement; make small additions to; piece out: usually with *out.* **2** To obtain or produce (a living) with difficulty. **3** *Obs.* To protract; lengthen; increase. *—n. Obs.* An addition, as to a bell rope; postscript; appendix. [Var. of ECHE]

eke[2] (ēk) *adv. & cong. Archaic* Likewise; also. [OE *ēac*]

e·kis·tics (i·kis′tiks) *n. pl.* (*construed as sing.*) The study of human settlements, including area planning and the relationship between communities. [< Gk. *oikos* habitat + -ICS] **—e·kis′tic** *adj.*

ek·ka (ek′ə) *n.* A one-horse vehicle used in India. [< Hind. *ekkā* < *ek* one]

El (el) *n.* An elevated railroad. Also *L.* [Short for ELEVATED]

el- Assimilated var. of EN-[2].

e·lab·o·rate (i·lab′ə·rāt) *v.* **·rat·ed, ·rat·ing** *v.t.* **1** To create and work out with care and in detail: to *elaborate* a system. **2** To produce by labor; make. *—v.i.* **3** To speak or write so as to embellish a matter, subject, etc., with additional details; be more specific: with *on* or *upon.* *—adj.* (-ər·it) Developed in detail with care or painstaking; carefully wrought out; done with thoroughness or exactness. [< L *elaboratus*, pp. of *elaborare* < *e-* out + *laborare* work] **—e·lab′o·rate·ly** *adv.* **—e·lab′o·rate·ness** *n.* **—e·lab′o·ra′tion** *n.* **—e·lab′o·ra′tive** *adj.* **—e·lab′o·ra′tor** *n.*

e·lae·o·lite (i·lē′ə·līt) *n.* A coarsely crystallized or massive opaque variety of nephelite with a resinous luster: also spelled *eleolite.* [< Gk. *elaion* oil + -LITE]

el·ae·op·tene (el′ē·op′tēn) *n. Chem.* The liquid hydrocarbon or terpene constituent of an essential oil: distinguished from *stearoptene.* [< Gk. *elaion* oil + *ptenos* flying]

El·a·gab·a·lus (el′ə·gab′ə·ləs) See HELIOGABALUS.

e·la·in (i·lā′ən) See OLEIN.

E·laine (i·lān′) A feminine personal name. [See HELEN]

—Elaine In Arthurian legend, any of several ladies; especially, the mother of Sir Galahad.

elaio- *combining form* Oil: *elaioplast.* Also **elaeo-.** [< Gk. *elaion* olive oil]

el·ai·o·plast (el′ē·ō·plast) *n. Bot.* One of the highly refractive oil-secreting protoplasmic granules found near the nuclei of plant cells: also spelled *eleoplast.*

E·lam (ē′ləm) An ancient country of SW Asia between the Persian Gulf and the Caspian Sea. *Gen.* x 22: also *Susiana.*

E·lam·ite (ē′ləm·īt) *n.* **1** One of the ancient inhabitants of Elam. **2** An extinct, unrelated, agglutinative language, or group of languages, spoken in Elam: also **E·lam·it·ic** (ē′ləm·it′ik): also called *Susian.* *—adj.* Of or pertaining to Elam, its inhabitants or their language: also **E′lam·it′ic, E′lam·it′ish** (-ī′tish).

é·lan (ā·läṅ′) *n.* Ardor; dash; vivacity. [< F < *élancer* < *é-* out + *lancer* dart, throw]

e·land (ē′lənd) *n.* A large oxlike African antelope with twisted horns (genus *Taurotragus*); especially; the common eland (*T. oryx*), of SE Africa. [< Du., elk]

ELAND

élan vi·tal (vē·tȧl′) *French* Literally, life force; vital energy; in Bergson's philosophy, the creative life impulse of all evolution. Compare VITALISM.

el·a·phine (el′ə·fīn, -fin) *adj.* **1** Of or pertaining to a genus (*Elaphodus*) of deer native in China. **2** Describing the antlers characteristic of this genus. [< L *elaphus* < Gk, *elaphos* a stag]

el·a·pine (el′ə·pīn, -pin) *adj. Zool.* Of or pertaining to a subfamily (*Elipinae*) of tropical snakes, including many of the most venomous species, as the coral snake, cobra, and harlequin snake. [< NL < Gk. *elaps*, var. of *ellops*, a kind of serpent]

e·lapse (i·laps′) *v.i.* **e·lapsed, e·laps·ing** To slip by; pass away: said of time. [< L *elapsus*, pp. of *elabi* < *e-* out, away + *labi* glide]

El A·raish (el ä·rīsh′) The Arabic name for LARACHE.

e·las·mo·branch (i·las′mō·brangk, i·laz′-) *n.* Any of a subclass (Elasmobranchii) of fishes having cartilaginous skeletons and lamellate gills, including sharks and rays. *—adj.* Pertaining to or belonging to the subclass Elasmobranchii. [< NL < Gk. *elasmos* metal plate + *branchia* gills]

e·las·tance (i·las′təns) *n. Electr.* The reciprocal of capacitance. [< ELAST(ICITY) + -ANCE]

e·las·tic (i·las′tik) *adj.* **1** Spontaneously returning to a former size, shape, or configuration after being altered from it; springy; accommodating. **2** Capable of quick recovery, as from misfortune or depression; buoyant. **3** Increasing or diminishing readily in response to a changing stimulus, demand, or other causative influence: an *elastic* price, one that soars or drops quickly owing to sudden variations in demand. **4** Capable of expansion and contraction, as a gas; flexible. *—n.* A strip, cord, or piece of india rubber or of webbing made elastic by india-rubber threads woven therein, used as a band, suspender, etc.; specifically, a garter. [< NL *elasticus* < Gk. *elastikos* driving, propulsive < *elaunein* drive] **—e·las′ti·cal·ly** *adv.*

e·las·tic·i·ty (i·las′tis′ə·tē, ē′las-) *n.* **1** *Physics* That property of matter by virtue of which a body tends to resist deformation, returning to a former or normal size, shape, or configuration, after being deflected, compressed, expanded, twisted or drawn. **2** The rebounding quality of bodies; resilience; springiness: the *elasticity* of the air. **3** The tendency to recover from depression or misfortune; buoyancy.

e·las·tin (i·las′tin) *n. Biochem.* The protein substance, of high glycine and leucine content, which is found in tendons, cartilage, connective tissue, and bone.

e·las·to·mer (i·las′tə·mər) *n. Chem.* One of a class of polymerized compounds characterized by elastic, rubberlike properties, as the synthetic rubbers and various plastics. [< ELAST(IC) + *-o-* + Gk. *meros* part]

e·late (i·lāt′) *v.t.* **·lat·ed, ·lat·ing** To raise the spirits of; excite. *—adj.* Exalted or triumphant; exultant. [< L *elatus*, pp. for *efferre* < *ex-* out + *ferre* bear] **—e·lat′ed** *adj.* **—e·lat′ed·ly** *adv.* **—e·lat′ed·ness** *n.*

El·a·te·a (el′ə·tē′ə) An ancient city of Phocis, Greece.

el·a·ter (el′ə·tər) *n.* **1** *Entomol.* **a** A click beetle or elaterid. **b** A spring or terminal bristlelike abdominal appendage of a springtail or podurid insect. **2** *Bot.* **a** In the horsetail family of plants (*Equisetaceae*), one of the four club-shaped membranous bands attached at a single point on a spore formed by the splitting of the outer coat. **b** A sterile, elastic, spirally twisted filament for the dispersion of spores, as in liverworts, puffballs, and slime molds. [< NL < Gk. *elatēr* < *elaunein* drive]

e·lat·er·id (i·lat′ər·id) *adj.* Of or pertaining to a family (*Elateridae*) of beetles with serrate antennae, including the click beetles or snapping beetles. *—n.* An elaterid beetle. [< NL < Gk. *elatēr.* See ELATER.]

e·lat·er·in (i·lat′ər·in) *n. Chem.* A bitter crystalline compound, $C_{20}H_{28}O_5$, contained in elaterium and having a powerful cathartic effect. [< ELATER(IUM) + -IN]

e·lat·er·ite (i·lat′ə·rīt) *n.* An elastic, resinous, dark-brown, subtranslucent mineral hydrocarbon, found in soft masses. [< obs. *elater* elasticity (< Gk. < *elaunein* drive) + -ITE[1]]

el·a·te·ri·um (el′ə·tir′ē·əm) *n.* **1** The squirting cucumber (*Ecballium elaterium*). **2** A purgative derived from its juice. **3** A greenish to gray strongly cathartic substance contained in the juice of the fruit of the squirting cucumber. [< L < Gk. *elatērion* a purgative < *elaunein* drive]

E·lath (ē′lath) **1** A port at the southern extremity of Israel on the Gulf of Aqaba. **2** The ancient name for AQABA.

e·la·tion (i·lā′shən) *n.* Exalted feeling, as from pride or joy; exultation.

E-lay·er (ē′lā′ər) *n.* The Heaviside layer.

El·ba (el′bə) The largest island of the Tuscan Archipelago; 86 square miles; a sovereign principality under the exiled Napoleon I, 1814–15.

El·be (el′bə) A river of central Europe, flowing 691 miles NW to the North Sea near Hamburg. *Czechoslovakian* **La·be** (la′be).

El Be·kaa (el bē·kä′) Bekaa. Also **El Bi·ka′, El Bi·qa′.**

El·ber·feld (el′bər·felt) See WUPPERTAL.

El·bert (el′bərt) A masculine personal name. Also *Lat.* **El·ber·tus** (el·bûr′təs).

Elbert, Mount A peak in central Colorado, highest in the United States Rockies; 14,431 feet.

El·bing (el′bing) A port in northern Poland on the Vistula estuary. *Polish* **El′blag** (el′blôngk).

el·bow (el′bō) *n.* **1** The joint at the bend of the arm; also, the joint resembling an elbow in the shoulder or hock of a quadruped. Compare illustration under HORSE. **2** Any outward bend resembling an elbow, as a short angular pipe fitting, or a projection on the side of a chair or sofa on which to rest the arm. *—v.t.* **1** To push or jostle with or as with the elbows. **2** To make (one's way) by such pushing. *—v.i.* **3** To make one's way by pushing or jostling. [OE *elboga*]

elbow grease *Colloq.* Steady application; hard work.

elbow room Ample room; scope for activity or occupation.

El·brus (el′bro͞os) A peak in the Caucasus Mountains in NW Georgian S.S.R. and the highest peak in Europe; 18,481 feet.

el·buck (el′buk) *n. Scot.* Elbow.

El·burz (el·bo͝orz′) A mountain range in northern Iran; highest peak, 18,603 feet.

El Ca·ney (el kä·nā′) A town in east Cuba; scene of an American victory over Cuban forces (1898) in the Spanish-American War: also *Caney.*

El Cap·i·tan (el kap·i·tan′) A peak in the Yosemite Valley, California; 7,564 feet.

El·che (el′chā) A city in eastern Spain.

eld (eld) *n. Archaic* Old times; antiquity; old age. [OE *eldo* old age]

el·der[1] (el′dər) *n.* **1** A shrub (genus *Sambucus*) of the honeysuckle family, with white flowers and purple-black or red berries; the roots of some species contain a very poisonous alkaloid, but the flowers and berries are often used in medicine. **2** Any one of various trees or plants resembling elder: the poison *elder* (*Rhus vernix*). [OE *ellærn*]

eld·er[2] (el′dər) *adj.* **1** Having lived longer; earlier born. **2** Senior: alternative comparative of *old.* **3** Earlier in time. **4** Prior in rank. *—n.* **1** A prince or head of a tribe or family. **2** A church officer or minister. **3** An older or aged person. 4 An ancestor. [OE *eldra*] — **eld′er·ship** *n.*

el·der·ber·ry (el′dər·ber′ē, -bər·ē) *n. pl.* **·ber·ries** The drupe of the common elder.

eld·er·ly (el′dər·lē) *adj.* Somewhat old; approaching old age.

eld·est (el′dist) *adj.* First-born; oldest; superlative of OLD. See ELDER[2].

eldest hand The first player in a card game; the player on the dealer's left; in poker, the age: opposed to *younger hand.*

el·ding (el′ding) *n. Scot.* Firewood; fuel.

El Do·ra·do (el də·rä′dō) 1 A legendary South American realm rich in gold and jewels: the object of the early Spanish conquerors and of many European explorers. 2 Any region of the western United States conceived of as promising wealth and opportunity to the adventurous, particularly California during and after the gold rush of 1848–49. 3 Any region rich in gold or opportunity. 4 A golden opportunity. Also **El′do·ra′do.**

E·le·a (ē′lē·ə) An ancient town in Lucania, Italy, where the Eleatic school of philosophy was founded.

El·ea·nor (el′ə·nər, -nôr) A feminine personal name. Also *Lat.* **El·e·a·no·ra** (el′ē·ə·nôr′ə, -nō′rə), *Dan., Ger.* **E·le·o·no·re** (ā·lā′ə·nō′rə), *Ital.* **E·le·o·no·ra** (ā·lā·ə·nō′rä). [See HELEN] — **Eleanor of Aquitaine,** 1122–1204, divorced wife of Louis VII of France; married Henry II of England: also **Eleanor of Guienne.** —**Eleanor of Castile,** died 1290, wife of Edward I of England. —**Eleanor of Provence,** died 1291, wife of Henry III of England.

El·e·at·ic (el′ē·at′ik) *adj.* Pertaining to or characteristic of Elea or the school of philosophy founded there by Xenophanes and Parmenides. —*n.* 1 A native of Elea. 2 A disciple of the Eleatic school of philosophy, which developed the conception of the universal unity of being. [< L *Eleaticus* < *Elea* ELEA] —**El′e·at′i·cism** *n.*

El·e·a·zar (el′ē·ā′zər, *Du.* ā′lā·ä′zär) A masculine personal name. Also **El′e·a′zer,** *Fr.,* **É·lé·a·zar** (ā·lā·á·zär′), *Ital.* **E·le·a·za·ro** (ā·lā·äd′zä· rō), *Sp.* **E·le·á·za·ro** (ā′lā·ä′thä·rō). [< Hebrew, God's help, or God is helper]

el·e·cam·pane (el′i·kam·pān′) *n.* 1 A tall perennial herb of the composite family (*Inula helenium*), having large leaves, yellow flowers, and a mucilaginous root yielding a tonic. 2 A coarse candy flavored with an extract made from the root of this herb. [< Med. L *enula* elecampane + *campana* of the field]

e·lect (i·lekt′) *v.t.* 1 To choose for an office by vote. 2 To take by choice or selection. 3 *Theol.* To choose or set aside for eternal life. —*v.i.* 4 To make a choice. —*adj.* 1 Elected to office, but not yet in charge: used as the second element in compounds, as president-*elect.* 2 *Theol.* Chosen of God for salvation; of saintly or divine character. 3 Selected; chosen; picked out. —*n.* 1 *Theol.* A person, or body of persons, chosen of God for salvation or for special service. 2 One who is favored or preferred. [< L *electus,* pp. of *eligere* < *ex-* out + *legere* choose]

e·lec·tion (i·lek′shən) *n.* 1 The selecting of a person or persons for office, as by ballot. 2 A popular vote on any question. 3 A choice, as between alternatives; choice in general. 4 In Calvinism, the predestination of some individuals to be saved from God's wrath and punishment. See synonyms under ALTERNATIVE.

e·lec·tion·eer (i·lek′shən·ir′) *v.i.* 1 To endeavor to win an election. 2 To canvass for votes.

e·lec·tive (i·lek′tiv) *adj.* 1 Of or pertaining to a choice by vote. 2 Obtained or bestowed by election. 3 Exerting the privilege of choice. 4 Subject to choice; optional. 5 *Chem.* Having a tendency to attract and combine with some substances and not with others: *elective* absorption. —*n.* An optional study in a fixed college curriculum. — **e·lec′·tive·ly** *adv.* —**e·lec′tive·ness** *n.*

e·lec·tor (i·lek′tər) *n.* 1 One who elects; a person qualified to vote at an election. 2 *U.S.* A presidential elector. 3 One of the great princes who formerly (12th to 18th century) had the right of electing the Holy Roman Emperor. —**presidential electors** The persons chosen by the several States and the District of Columbia to elect the president and vice president of the United States. The District of Columbia has three electors; each State sends a number equal to its total of senators and representatives.

e·lec·tor·al (i·lek′tər·əl) *adj.* Pertaining to, of, or comprising electors.

electoral college The whole corporate body of the presidential electors chosen at one election, although they never meet as a body; also, those of a single State, which do meet: a popular, unofficial term, first used informally in 1821.

e·lec·tor·ate (i·lek′tər·it) *n.* 1 Those who elect; the mass of voters. 2 The rank or territory of an elector in the Holy Roman Empire.

e·lec·tor·ess (i·lek′tər·is) *n.* 1 A woman qualified to vote at an election. 2 The wife or widow of an elector of the Holy Roman Empire. Also **e·lec′tress** (-tris).

E·lec·tra (i·lek′trə) 1 In Greek legend, a daughter of Agamemnon and Clytemnestra who persuaded her brother Orestes to kill their mother and their mother's lover Aegisthus to avenge their father's murder. 2 One of the Pleiades. Also *Elektra.*

Electra complex *Psychoanal.* A compulsive, strongly repressed sexual attachment of the daughter to her father: the female analog of the *Oedipus complex.*

e·lec·tret (i·lek′trit) *n.* A dielectric, usually rod-shaped, which may be strongly charged with positive electricity at one pole and with negative electricity at the other: it is the electrical analog of the magnet. [< ELECTR(ICITY) + (MAGN)ET]

e·lec·tric (i·lek′trik) *adj.* 1 Relating to, derived from, produced, or operated by electricity. 2 Containing, producing, or carrying electricity. 3 Spirited; magnetic; thrilling. Also **e·lec′tri·cal.** — *n.* 1 A street car, train, or other vehicle run by electricity. 2 Any substance or material, as amber or resin, which can be given an electric charge by rubbing. [< NL *electricus* < L *electrum* amber < Gk. *ēlektron*] —**e·lec′tri·cal·ly** *adv.*

electrical transcription See under TRANSCRIPTION (def. 3).

electric breeze 1 A stream of ions repelled from an electrified point. 2 A brush discharge as used in therapeutics.

electric calamine Hemimorphite

electric cell Any of a large variety of devices consisting of two dissimilar metals or materials immersed in an electrolyte, capable of generating an electric charge by chemical action.

ELECTRIC CELL
c. Carbon (positive pole).
z. Zinc (negative pole).

electric chair 1 A chair used for electrocuting criminals by sending a high voltage of electricity through the body of the person fastened into it. 2 Hence, the death penalty.

electric clock Any of variously designed clocks which are actuated by electricity in any way; especially, a clock operated by plugging in on an alternating current transmitting electromagnetic impulses from a master clock.

electric current A stream of electrons flowing through a conducting body; it is usually measured and expressed in terms of amperes, coulombs, and volts. See ELECTRON.

electric displacement The theoretical movement of the electricity in a dielectric as a result of changes in the electric field where the latter is located.

electric eel A cyprinoid, eel-like fish (*Electrophorus electricus*) of tropical America, which sometimes reaches a length of six feet, carrying in its tail organs capable of delivering powerful electric shocks.

electric energy The capacity possessed by electricity for doing work.

electric eye A photoelectric cell.

electric field A field of force surrounding a charged object or a moving magnet.

electric fish Any fish having organs capable of imparting an electric shock.

electric furnace 1 A furnace in which high temperatures are obtained by the use of an electric arc or by induction from a central power station. 2 A smelting furnace in which the heat is produced by an electric current.

e·lec·tri·cian (i·lek′trish′ən, ē′lek-) *n.* 1 One versed in the science of electricity. 2 An inventor, maker, or repairer of electrical apparatus.

e·lec·tric·i·ty (i·lek′tris′ə·tē, ē′lek-) *n.* 1 A fundamental property of matter, associated with atomic particles whose movements, free or controlled, lead to the development of fields of force and the generation of kinetic or potential energy. The electron is the basic unit of *negative* electricity, and the proton of *positive* electricity. Any accumulation of one kind of electricity in excess of an equivalent of the opposite kind is called a *charge* and is measured in appropriate units. A charge fixed at one point or within a circumscribed field of force, as a Leyden jar, is *static* electricity; a charge which flows through a conductor is *current* electricity. 2 The property of many substances, as amber, fur, glass, etc., mutually to attract or repel each other when subjected to friction. 3 The science which deals with the phenomena, laws, theory, and application of this property.

electric light 1 Illumination produced by electricity. 2 The lamp, tower, or other device used for electric illumination, especially the bulb.

electric machine 1 An apparatus for generating static electricity, as by friction. 2 A dynamo.

electric motor A machine for transforming electric energy into mechanical power: distinguished from *dynamo.*

Electric Peak The highest peak in the Gallatin Range, SW Montana; 11,155 feet.

electric ray Any of a family (Torpedinidae) of rays with usually round bodies and short tails having an organ in each winglike fin that delivers an electric shock as a means of stunning prey or of defense against predators. Also called *crampfish, numbfish, torpedo.*

e·lec·tri·fy (i·lek′trə·fī) *v.t.* **·fied, ·fy·ing** 1 To act upon, charge with, or subject to electricity. 2 To equip, as a house, for the use of electricity. 3 To adapt for operation by electric power, as a railroad. 4 To arouse; startle; thrill. — **e·lec′tri·fi′a·ble** *adj.* —**e·lec′tri·fi·ca′·tion** *n.* — **e·lec′tri·fi′er** *n.*

e·lec·trine (i·lek′trin) *adj.* 1 Made of electrum. 2 Made of or related to amber. —*n.* An imaginary substance, supposed by some to be the basis of electricity. [< Gk. *ēlektrinos* < *ēlektron* amber]

e·lec·trize (i·lek′trīz) *v.t.* **·trized, ·triz·ing** To electrify. —**e·lec′tri·za′tion** *n.*

e·lec·triz·er (i·lek′trī·zər) *n.* One who or that which electrizes.

e·lec·tro (i·lek′trō) *n. pl.* **·tros** 1 An electrotype. 2 Electroplating. —*v.t.* **·troed, ·tro·ing** To make an electrotype of; electroplate. [Short for ELECTROTYPE]

electro- *combining form* 1 Electric; by, with, or of electricity: *electrocardiogram.* 2 Electrolytic: *electroanalysis.* Also, before vowels, sometimes **electr-.** [< Gk. *ēlektron* amber]

e·lec·tro·a·cous·tics (i·lek′trō·ə·kōō′stiks) *n.* The branch of acoustics which studies the design, operation, and efficiency of equipment used in the electrical and electronic transmission of sound, as microphones, loudspeakers, soundtrack apparatus, tape-recorders, etc. — **e·lec′tro·a·cous′tic** *adj.*

e·lec·tro·a·nal·y·sis (i·lek′trō·ə·nal′ə·sis) *n.* An analysis by and in accordance with the methods of electrolysis.

e·lec·tro·bi·ol·o·gy (i·lek′trō·bī·ol′ə·jē) *n.* The study of electrical phenomena associated with the functioning and behavior of living organisms.

e·lec·tro·bi·os·co·py (i·lek′trō·bī·os′kə·pē) *n.* The determination of the presence of absence of life in an organism by means of suitably applied electric currents. —**e·lec′tro·bi′o·scop′·ic** (-bī′ə·skop′ik) *adj.*

e·lec·tro·cap·il·lar·i·ty (i·lek′trō·kap′i·lar′ə·tē) *n.* That change in the surface tension between two conducting liquids in contact which occurs when an electric current is passed between them.

e·lec·tro·car·di·o·gram (i·lek′trō·kär′dē·ə·gram′) *n. Med.* A graph indicating electromotive variations in the action of the heart.

e·lec·tro·car·di·o·graph (i·lek′trō·kär′dē·ə·graf′, -gräf′) *n. Med.* An instrument for recording the electric current produced by the action of the heart muscle: used in the diagnosis of diseases affecting the heart. **—e·lec·tro·car·di·og·ra·phy** (i·lek′trō·kär′dē·og′rə·fē) *n.*

e·lec·tro·chem·is·try (i·lek′trō·kem′is·trē) *n.* The branch of chemistry that treats of electricity as active in effecting chemical change. — **e·lec′tro·chem′i·cal** *adj.* **—e·lec′tro·chem′i·cal·ly** *adv.* **—e·lec′tro·chem′ist** *n.*

e·lec·tro·co·ag·u·la·tion (i·lek′trō·kō·ag′yə·lā′·shən) *n.* The destructive coagulation of protoplasmic material or of living tissue, healthy or morbid, by the passage through it of an electric current.

e·lec·tro·co·ma (i·lek′trō·kō′mə) *n.* Coma induced by electroshock therapy.

e·lec·tro·cul·ture (i·lek′trō·kul′chər) *n.* The stimulation of the growth, development, and maturing of plants by electrical means, especially by static electricity and fields of force in the atmosphere.

e·lec·tro·cute (i·lek′trə·kyōōt) *v.t.* **·cut·ed, ·cut·ing 1** To execute in the electric chair. **2** To kill by electricity. [<ELECTRO- + (EXE)CUTE] — **e·lec′tro·cu′tion** *n.*

e·lec·trode (i·lek′trōd) *n. Electr.* Either of the two conducting elements through which a current leaves or enters an electrolytic cell, vacuum tube, electric arc or furnace, or any non-metallic conductor; an anode or cathode. Compare illustration under ELECTRIC CELL. [<ELECTR(O) + -ODE[1]]

e·lec·tro·de·pos·it (i·lek′trō·di·poz′it) *v.i.* To deposit chemically, as metal from a solution, by means of an electric current. —*n.* That which is so deposited. **—e·lec′tro·dep′o·si′tion** (-dep′ə·zish′ən, -dē′pə-) *n.*

e·lec·tro·des·ic·ca·tion (i·lek′trō·des′ə·kā′·shən) *n.* The destruction of animal tissues by means of controlled high-frequency electric-spark discharges: also called *fulguration.*

e·lec·tro·dy·nam·ic (i·lek′trō·dī·nam′ik) *adj.* Relating to the forces of attraction and repulsion produced by electric currents. **—e·lec′tro·dy·nam′i·cal·ly** *adv.*

e·lec·tro·dy·nam·ics (i·lek′trō·dī·nam′iks) *n.* The branch of physics which deals with the forces of electrical attraction and repulsion and with the energy transformations of magnetic fields and electric currents.

e·lec·tro·dy·na·mom·e·ter (i·lek′trō·dī′nə·mom′ə·tər) *n.* An instrument for measuring electrical current, voltage, or power, in which the deflecting force arises from the interaction of two wire coils carrying currents.

e·lec·tro·en·ceph·a·lo·gram (i·lek′trō·en·sef′ə·lə·gram′) *n.* A record of electrical impulses and changes in the brain: important in the diagnosis of certain diseases, as epilepsy. **—e·lec′tro·en·ceph′a·lo·graph′** (-graf′,-gräf′) *n.*

e·lec·tro·en·ceph·a·log·ra·phy (i·lek′trō·en·sef′ə·log′rə·fē) *n.* **1** The art and technique of recording electrical changes in the brain. **2** The science of interpreting these changes in the diagnosis of epilepsy and other incapacitating brain diseases.

e·lec·tro·en·dos·mo·sis (i·lek′trō·en′dos·mō′·sis) *n.* The diffusion of fluids through permeable membranes or diaphragms by the application of an electrical potential.

e·lec·tro·form (i·lek′trō·fôrm′) *v.t.* To produce (shaped objects) by the electrolytic deposition of metal upon a mold.

e·lec·tro·form·ing (i·lek′trō·fôr′ming) *n.* The production of metal tubing, medals, and the like by the electrolytic deposition of metal upon a mold of the desired shape or pattern.

e·lec·tro·gas·tro·gram (i·lek′trō·gas′trə·gram) *n. Med.* The record of an electrogastrograph.

e·lec·tro·gas·tro·graph (i·lek′trō·gas′trə·graf, -gräf) *n. Med.* A device for indicating electrical changes caused by muscular contractions of the stomach.

e·lec·tro·graph (i·lek′trō·graf, -gräf) *n.* **1** The linear record of an electrometer. **2** An apparatus for tracing a design to be etched for use in printing wallpaper, calico, etc. **3** A roentgenogram. **—e·lec′tro·graph′ic** *adj.* **—e·lec·trog·ra·phy** (i·lek′trog′rə·fē, ē′lek-) *n.*

e·lec·tro·ki·net·ic (i·lek′trō·ki·net′ik) *adj.* Pertaining to or caused by electricity in motion.

e·lec·tro·ki·net·ics (i·lek′trō·ki·net′iks) *n.* That branch of electrical science which treats of the motion of electricity and the forces producing or regulating it: opposed to *electrostatics.*

e·lec·tro·ky·mo·gram (i·lek′trō·kī′mə·gram) *n.* The record made by an electrokymograph.

e·lec·tro·ky·mo·graph (i·lek′trō·kī′mə·graf, -gräf) *n. Med.* An instrument for measuring the action of the heart by means of X-rays which project the heart shadow upon a fluorescent screen used in conjunction with a photocell.

e·lec·tro·lier (i·lek′trə·lir′) *n.* A fixture, usually ornamental, for holding electric lamps. [<ELECTRO- + (CHANDE)LIER]

e·lec·tro·lu·mi·nes·cence (i·lek′trō·lōō′mə·nes′·əns) *n.* **1** Light produced by the agency of electricity. **2** The emission of a soft, uniformly diffused light from phosphor powders embedded in the surface of a panel of glass or other insulating material which is directly subjected to the action of an alternating electric field. — **e·lec′tro·lu′mi·nes′cent** *adj.*

e·lec·trol·y·sis (i·lek′trol′ə·sis) *n.* **1** The decomposing of a chemical compound by passing an electric current through it. **2** The use of an electrified needle to destroy the roots of unwanted body hair. [<ELECTRO- + -LYSIS]

e·lec·tro·lyte (i·lek′trə·līt) *n.* **1** A substance, usually in solution, which will transmit an electric current by the formation of ions. **2** A solution which conducts an electric current between the electrodes of a cell, accompanied by the release of a gas or the deposition of a solid. [<ELECTRO- + Gk. *lytos* loosed <*luein* loosen] — **e·lec·tro·lyt·ic** (i·lek′trə·lit′ik) or **·i·cal** *adj.* — **e·lec′tro·lyt′i·cal·ly** *adv.*

e·lec·tro·lyze (i·lek′trə·līz) *v.t.* **·lyzed, ·lyz·ing** To decompose by electric current. **—e·lec′·tro·ly·za′tion** *n.* **—e·lec′tro·lyz′er** *n.*

e·lec·tro·mag·net (i·lek′trō·mag′nit) *n.* A core of soft iron or the like, which temporarily becomes a magnet during the passage of an electric current through a coil of wire surrounding it. — **e·lec′tro·mag·net′ic** (-mag·net′ik) or **·i·cal** *adj.* — **e·lec′tro·mag·net′i·cal·ly** *adv.*

e·lec·tro·mag·net·ism (i·lek′trō·mag′nə·tiz′əm) *n.* **1** Magnetism developed by electricity. **2** That science which treats of the relations between electricity and magnetism and the phenomena due to these relations. Also **e·lec′tro·mag·net′ics.**

e·lec·tro·met·al·lur·gy (i·lek′trō·met′ə·lûr′jē, -mə·tal′ər·jē) *n.* The art or science of electrolytically depositing metals, or of separating them from their ores or alloys by electrolysis or the electric furnace. **—e·lec′tro·met′al·lur′gi·cal** *adj.*

e·lec·trom·e·ter (i·lek′trom′ə·tər, ē′lek-) *n.* An instrument for measuring the voltage in an electric circuit by the electrostatic forces exerted between two charged bodies.

e·lec·trom·e·try (i·lek′trom′ə·trē, ē′lek-) *n.* The science or art of making electrical measurements. **—e·lec·tro·met·ric** (i·lek′trō·met′rik) or **·ri·cal** *adj.*

e·lec·tro·mo·tion (i·lek′trə·mō′shən) *n.* **1** The passage of an electric current in a voltaic circuit. **2** Motion produced by electricity employed as power.

e·lec·tro·mo·tive (i·lek′trə·mō′tiv) *adj.* Producing, or tending to produce an electric current; distinguished from *magnetomotive.*

electromotive force That which tends to produce the flow of electricity from one point to another; difference of potential between the terminals of an electrolyte, voltaic cell, or other conducting medium; voltage.

electromotive series An arrangement of the elements in a series such that each will, in general and under suitable conditions, replace from its compounds any element listed after it. See table below for the series of metals, from the most active to the least active. Also called *displacement, activity,* or *electrochemical series.*

ELECTROMOTIVE SERIES OF THE METALS

1. Potassium	10. Chromium	19. Arsenic
2. Barium	11. Iron	20. Bismuth
3. Strontium	12. Cadmium	21. Antimony
4. Calcium	13. Cobalt	22. Mercury
5. Sodium	14. Nickel	23. Silver
6. Magnesium	15. Tin	24. Gold
7. Aluminum	16. Lead	25. Platinum
8. Manganese	17. Hydrogen	
9. Zinc	18. Copper	

e·lec·tro·mo·tor (i·lek′trə·mō′tər) *n.* **1** An electric motor. **2** Any electric source, as a voltaic cell.

e·lec·tro·my·o·gram (i·lek′trō·mī′ə·gram) *n.* The tracing made by an electromyograph.

e·lec·tro·my·o·graph (i·lek′trō·mī′ə·graf, -gräf) *n. Med.* An instrument for determining the location and extent of nerve lesions by the application of an electric stimulus to muscles whose responses are converted into both sound and visual records. **—e·lec′tro·my·og′ra·phy** (-mī·og′rə·fē) *n.* **e·lec′tro·my′o·graph′i·cal** *adj.*

e·lec·tron (i·lek′tron) *n.* An electrically charged particle of the atom: it carries the unit charge of negative electricity, estimated at 4.8×10^{-10}cgs electrostatic units, and has a mass approximately one eighteen-hundredth (more exactly 1/1837) of that of the proton. Electrons are emitted in the form of beta particles and cathode rays. **—free electron** An electron not permanently bound to any atom and free to move within the limits of a given substance or material, as in a galvanic current. [<Gk. *ēlektron* amber]

e·lec·tro·nar·co·sis (i·lek′trō·när·kō′sis) *n. Psychiatry* Narcosis induced by the passing of a very mild electric current between two electrodes attached to the sides of the head: used in the treatment of schizophrenia and related mental disorders.

e·lec·tro·neg·a·tive (i·lek′trō·neg′ə·tiv) *adj.* **1** Appearing, as an element in electrolysis, at the positive electrode. **2** Having the property of becoming negatively electrified by contact with or the chemical action of another element.

electron gun An apparatus, usually in the form of a slender tube with thermionic filaments and focusing and accelerating electrodes, used in television for directing a steady stream of electrons in a given direction.

e·lec·tron·ic (i·lek′tron′ik, ē′lek-) *adj.* **1** Of or pertaining to electrons. **2** Operating or produced by the movement of free electrons or other carriers of electric charge, as in an electron tube. **3** Pertaining to electronics. — **e·lec′tron′i·cal·ly** *adv.*

e·lec·tron·ics (i·lek′tron′iks, ē′lek-) *n. pl. (Construed as singular)* The study of the properties and behavior of electrons under all conditions, especially with reference to technical and industrial applications.

electron lens A distribution of an electric field surrounding the path of an electron beam such that the beam may be concentrated in a focus similar to that of an optical lens.

electron microscope A microscope which uses high-voltage streams of electrons in order to bring into visibility objects not accessible to the relatively large wavelengths of visible light used by the most powerful optical microscopes.

electronic music Music based on an arrangement of electronically produced, organized, or altered sounds, recorded on tape.

e·lec·tro·nog·ra·phy (i·lek′trō·nog′rə·fē) *n.* A method of printing without pressure between paper and the inked surface, by means of an applied electric charge which ionizes the ink particles, causing them to migrate to the oppositely charged printing surface. [<ELECTRON + -(O)GRAPHY]

electron optics A method for the control of electron beams or rays by properly adjusted magnetic or electric fields so that the flow of electrons will simulate the effect of light rays in an optical instrument.

electron shell *Physics* The orbital arrangement of electrons outside the nucleus of an atom.

electron tube A high vacuum tube in which a stream of electrons is emitted from a heated cathode and subjected to the controlling action of a grid which amplifies and directs the current.

electron volt A unit of energy equal to that acquired by an electron which passes through a potential difference of one volt: equal to 1.602 $\times 10^{-12}$erg: also called *equivalent volt.*

e·lec·tro·op·tics (i·lek′trō·op′tiks) *n. Physics* The study of the modification of optical phenomena by the application of an electric field.

e·lec·trop·a·thy (i·lek′trop′ə·thē, ē′lek-) *n. Med.* The treatment of disease by means of electricity. **—e·lec′tro·path′ic** (-trə·path′ik) *adj.* **—e·lec′tro·path′i·cal·ly** *adv.*

e·lec·tro·pho·re·sis (i·lek′trō·fə·rē′sis) *n. Chem.*

The slow movement of colloidal particles suspended in a fluid, when under the influence of an electric field.

e·lec·troph·o·rus (i·lek′trof′ər·əs, ē′lek-) *n. pl.* **·ri** (-rī) An instrument for generating static electricity by induction: commonly a flat disk of resin, to which may be applied another of wood coated with tinfoil. Also **e·lec·tro·phore** (i·lek′trə·fôr, -fōr).

e·lec·tro·phren·ic (i·lek′trə·fren′ik) *adj. Med.* Describing a method of artificial respiration by the electrical stimulation of one or both of the phrenic nerves.

e·lec·tro·phys·i·ol·o·gy (i·lek′trō·fiz′ē·ol′ə·jē) *n.* The study of the electric phenomena of living organs. — **e·lec′tro·phys′i·o·log′i·cal** (-fiz′ē·ə·loj′i·kəl) *adj.*

e·lec·tro·plate (i·lek′trə·plāt′) *v.t.* **·plat·ed, ·plat·ing** To coat with metal by electrolysis, the object being immersed in a solution of a salt of the metal in connection with the negative pole of a battery or dynamo. —*n.* An electroplated article. — **e·lec′tro·plat′er** *n.*

e·lec·tro·plat·ing (i·lek′trə·plā′ting) *n.* **1** The act or process of depositing metal by electric means. **2** The coat of metal so deposited.

e·lec·tro·pos·i·tive (i·lek′trō·poz′ə·tiv) *adj.* **1** Appearing at the negative electrode: said of an element in electrolysis. **2** Having the property of becoming positively electrified by contact or chemical action.

e·lec·tro·scis·sion (i·lek′trō·sizh′ən) *n. Surg.* The cutting or division of tissues by an electrically operated knife.

e·lec·tro·scope (i·lek′trə·skōp) *n.* An instrument for detecting the presence of electricity upon a conductor by the attraction or repulsion of pith balls or strips of gold leaf. See illustration. — **e·lec′tro·scop′ic** (-skop′ik) *adj.*

ELECTROSCOPE
Metallic pole *(m)*, electrically charged by *(e)*, conducts the impulse to strips *(s)* that acquire the charge and move apart in electrostatic repulsion.

e·lec·tro·shock (i·lek′trō·shok′) *n. Psychiatry* A shock to the nervous system of a mental patient, produced by a carefully regulated electric current passed through the head.

e·lec·tro·stat·ics (i·lek′trō·stat′iks) *n.* That branch of electrical science which treats of the phenomena of electricity at rest or of frictional electricity: opposed to *electrokinetics.* — **e·lec′tro·stat′ic** or **·i·cal** *adj.* — **e·lec′tro·stat′i·cal·ly** *adv.*

electrostatic unit An electric charge which, concentrated at one point in a vacuum, would repel with a force of 1 dyne an equal and like charge placed 1 centimeter away.

e·lec·tro·ste·nol·y·sis (i·lek′trō·sti·nol′ə·sis) *n.* The depositing of metallic particles in the pores of a high-resistance membrane by electrolysis.

e·lec·tro·tax·is (i·lek′trō·tak′sis) *n. Biol.* **1** That property of protoplasm which makes it susceptible to the influence of an electric stimulus, as shown by the direction of movements. **2** Any similar property in simple organisms. Also **e·lec′trot′ro·pism** (i·lek′trot′rə·piz′əm, ē′lek-). — **e·lec′tro·tac′tic** (-tak′tik) *adj.*

e·lec·tro·tech·nics (i·lek′trō·tek′niks) *n.* The science of the methods, processes, and operations by which electricity is applied in the industrial arts. — **e·lec′tro·tech′nic** (-nik) or **·ni·cal** *adj.*

e·lec·tro·ther·a·peu·tics (i·lek′trō·ther′ə·pyōō′·tiks) *n.* The treatment of disease by electricity, or the laws, etc., of such treatment. Also **e·lec′tro·ther′a·py** (-ə·pē). — **e·lec′tro·ther′a·peu′tic** (-tik) or **·ti·cal** *adj.*

e·lec·tro·ther·a·pist (i·lek′trō·ther′ə·pist) *n.* A practitioner of electrotherapeutics. Also **e·lec′·tro·ther′a·peu′tist.**

e·lec·trot·o·nus (i·lek′trot′ə·nəs, ē′lek-) *n. Physiol.* The change in the activity of a nerve or muscle induced by a voltaic current. [<NL <ELECTRO- + Gk. *tonos* tension] — **e·lec·tro·ton·ic** (i·lek′trō·ton′ik) *adj.*

e·lec·tro·type (i·lek′trō·tīp′) *n.* **1** A metallic copy of any surface, as a coin, made by electric deposition, especially one of a page of type for printing. **2** An impression from an electrotyped cut. **3** The process of electrotyping; electrotypy. —*v.t.* **·typed, ·typ·ing** To make an electrotype of.

e·lec·tro·typ·er (i·lek′trō·tī′pər) *n.* One who electrotypes. Also **e·lec′tro·typ′ist.**

e·lec·tro·typ·ic (i·lek′trō·tip′ik) *adj.* Pertaining to or made by electrotyping.

e·lec·tro·typ·ing (i·lek′trō·tī′ping) *n.* The act or business of forming electrotypes. Also **e·lec′tro·typ′y** (-tī′pē).

e·lec·tro·va·lence (i·lek′trō·vā′ləns) *n. Chem.* A bond formed by the complete transfer of electrons from the atoms of one element of a compound to the atoms of another element: distinguished from *covalence.*

e·lec·tro·va·lent (i·lek′trō·vā′lənt) *adj. Chem.* Designating a compound formed by electrovalence.

e·lec·trum (i·lek′trəm) *n.* **1** German silver or other like alloy. **2** Anciently, amber. **3** Native gold containing a large percentage of silver. [<L <Gk. *ēlektron* amber]

e·lec·tu·ar·y (i·lek′chōō·er′ē) *n. pl.* **·ar·ies** A medicine mixed with honey or sirup to form a paste. [<LL *electuarium* <Gk. *ekleikton* <*ek* out + *leichein* lick]

el·ee·mos·y·nar (el′ə·mos′ə·nər, el′ē·ə-) *n.* **1** One who gives charity. **2** The supervisor of the distribution of papal charities. **3** *Obs.* Almoner.

el·ee·mos·y·nar·y (el′ə·mos′ə·ner′ē, el′ē·ə-) *adj.* **1** Of or pertaining to charity or alms; existing for the relief of the poor. **2** Charitable; nonprofit: *eleemosynary* institutions. **3** Aided by or dependent upon charity: the *eleemosynary* classes. —*n. pl.* **·nar·ies** A recipient of charity. [<Med. L *eleemosynarius* <*eleemosyna* ALMS]

el·e·gance (el′ə·gəns) *n.* **1** The state or quality of being elegant or refined. **2** Anything elegant. Also **el′e·gan·cy.**

el·e·gant (el′ə·gənt) *adj.* **1** Marked by refinement, grace, or symmetry, as of action, form or structure; also, possessing or exhibiting refined taste. **2** Possessing a fine sense of beauty or fitness. **3** *Colloq.* Excellent; capital. **4** Marked by completeness and simplicity; appropriate: an *elegant* solution. [<F *élégant* <L *elegans, -antis* fastidious] — **el′e·gant·ly** *adv.*

Synonyms: dainty, exquisite. *Elegant* (Latin *elegans,* select) refers to the lighter, finer elements of beauty in form or motion, but is often misused as a general term of approval. *Exquisite* denotes the utmost perfection of the *elegant* in minute details; we speak of an *elegant* garment, and *exquisite* lace. *Exquisite* is also applied to intense keenness of any feeling; as, *exquisite* delight; *exquisite* pain. *Dainty,* at its best, applies to what is at once slight, delicate, and pleasing; in its extreme use, it may apply to sensibilities or feelings too delicate for the demands of practical life, overnice, squeamish. See BEAUTIFUL, CHOICE, FINE[1], POLITE. *Antonyms*: common, coarse, harsh, rude.

el·e·gi·ac (el′ə·jī′ək, i·lē′jē·ak) *adj.* **1** Pertaining to elegies. **2** Of the nature of an elegy; sad; plaintive. **3** In ancient prosody, written in distichs consisting of hexameter and pentameter. Also **el′e·gi′a·cal.** —*n.* **1** A poet who writes in the tone or in the meter of the elegy. **2** *pl.* Verse composed in the elegiac spirit or form.

el·e·gist (el′ə·jist) *n.* A writer of funeral songs; one who writes in elegiac verse. Also **e·le·gi·ast** (i·lē′jē·ast), **el·e·gi·og·ra·pher** (el′ə·jē·og′rə·fər).

e·le·git (i·lē′jit) *n. Law* **1** A writ of execution, issued on the election of a judgment creditor, directing the sheriff to turn over to him the debtor's attachable goods, and, if these be insufficient, half the debtor's land, the latter to be held till the rents and profits shall extinguish the debt. **2** The right secured by this writ. [<L]

el·e·gize (el′ə·jīz) *v.t.* & *v.i.* **·gized, ·giz·ing** To mourn or commemorate in elegaic form.

el·e·gy (el′ə·jē) *n. pl.* **·gies** **1** A funeral song. **2** A meditative poem with sorrowful theme. **3** A classical poem written in elegiac verse. [<F *élégie* <L *elegia* <Gk. *elegeia* <*elegos* a song]

E·lek·tra (i·lek′trə) See ELECTRA.

el·e·ment (el′ə·mənt) *n.* **1** A component or essential part; especially, a simple part of anything complex; a constituent; ingredient. **2** *pl.* First principles or fundamental ideas; rudiments. **3** *Eccl.* The bread and wine of the Lord's Supper. **4** An ultimate and essential principle in the make-up of anything; essential constituent; anciently, one of the substances —earth, air, fire, and water—supposed to make up all things: still in popular use: the fury of the *elements,* the devouring *element.* **5** The natural sphere or environment: The *element* of fishes is water. **6** *Physics* One of a limited number of substances each of which is com-

TABLE OF CHEMICAL ELEMENTS
(See also PERIODIC TABLE OF ELEMENTS.)

NAME	Symbol	Atomic No.	NAME	Symbol	Atomic No.	NAME	Symbol	Atomic No.
Actinium	Ac	89	Gold *(aurum)*	Au	79	Polonium	Po	84
Aluminum	Al	13	Hafnium	Hf	72	Potassium *(kalium)*	K	19
Americium	Am	95	Helium	He	2	Praseodymium	Pr	59
Antimony *(stibium)*	Sb	51	Holmium	Ho	67	Promethium	Pm	61
Argon	A	18	Hydrogen	H	1	Protactinium	Pa	91
Arsenic	As	33	Indium	In	49	Radium	Ra	88
Astatine	At	85	Iodine	I	53	Radon	Rn	86
Barium	Ba	56	Iridium	Ir	77	Rhenium	Re	75
Berkelium	Bk	97	Iron *(ferrum)*	Fe	26	Rhodium	Rh	45
Beryllium	Be	4	Krypton	Kr	36	Rubidium	Rb	37
Bismuth	Bi	83	Lanthanum	La	57	Ruthenium	Ru	44
Boron	B	5	Lawrencium	Lw	103	Samarium	Sm	62
Bromine	Br	35	Lead *(plumbum)*	Pb	82	Scandium	Sc	21
Cadmium	Cd	48	Lithium	Li	3	Selenium	Se	34
Calcium	Ca	20	Lutetium	Lu	71	Silicon	Si	14
Californium	Cf	98	Magnesium	Mg	12	Silver *(argentum)*	Ag	47
Carbon	C	6	Manganese	Mn	25	Sodium *(natrium)*	Na	11
Cerium	Ce	58	Mendelevium	Md	101	Strontium	Sr	38
Cesium	Cs	55	Mercury			Sulfur	S	16
Chlorine	Cl	17	*(hydrargyrum)*	Hg	80	Tantalum	Ta	73
Chromium	Cr	24	Molybdenum	Mo	42	Technetium	Tc	43
Cobalt	Co	27	Neodymium	Nd	60	Tellurium	Te	52
Columbium	(Cb)		Neon	Ne	10	Terbium	Tb	65
See NIOBIUM			Neoytterbium			Thallium	Tl	81
Copper *(cuprum)*	Cu	29	See YTTERBIUM			Thorium	Th	90
Curium	Cm	96	Neptunium	Np	93	Thulium	Tm	69
Dysprosium	Dy	66	Nickel	Ni	28	Tin *(stannum)*	Sn	50
Einsteinium	Es	99	Niobium	Nb	41	Titanium	Ti	22
Erbium	Er	68	Niton See RADON			Tungsten		
Europium	Eu	63	Nitrogen	N	7	See WOLFRAM		
Fermium	Fm	100	Nobelium	No	102	Uranium	U	92
Fluorine	F	9	Osmium	Os	76	Vanadium	V	23
Francium	Fr	87	Oxygen	O	8	Wolfram	W	74
Gadolinium	Gd	64	Palladium	Pd	46	Xenon	Xe	54
Gallium	Ga	31	Phosphorus	P	15	Ytterbium	Yb	70
Germanium	Ge	32	Platinum	Pt	78	Yttrium	Yt	39
Glucinum See BERYLLIUM			Plutonium	Pu	94	Zinc	Zn	30
						Zirconium	Zr	40

posed entirely of atoms having an invariant nuclear charge and none of which may be decomposed by ordinary chemical means, as gold, carbon, sodium, etc. See Table, page 408. **7** One of the primary parts of an organism; also, a cell or morphological unit. **8** One of a number of parts composing a symmetrical whole. **9** *Geom.* One of the forms or data which together compose a figure, as a line, a point, a plane, a space. **10** *Math.* **a** An infinitely small portion of a magnitude; a generatrix. **b** A term in an algebraic expression. **11** One of the dissimilar substances in a voltaic cell or battery, etc. **12** A group or class of people distinguished from a larger group to which it belongs by its own peculiar beliefs, attitudes, behavior, etc.: the conservative *element* in the party; a rowdy *element* in the crowd. See synonyms under PART, PARTICLE. **— to be in one's element** To be in pleasing surroundings or be engaged in activities in which one excels. [<L *elementum* first principle]

el·e·men·tal (el'ə·men'təl) *adj.* **1** Pertaining to the fundamental or basic constituent of anything; primary; simple. **2** Having to do with rudiments or first principles. **3** Pertaining to or like one of the four elements of ancient physics, fire, air, earth, and water. **4** Pertaining to the forces, phenomena, or powers of physical nature, often as personified: *elemental* spirits. **5** Comparable to the great primal powers of nature: *elemental* storms. **6** Of or pertaining to chemical elements, or one of the chemical elements; uncompounded. **— el'·e·men'tal·ly** *adv.*

el·e·men·ta·ry (el'ə·men'tər·ē) *adj.* **1** Of, pertaining to, or being an element or elements, in any sense. **2** Treating of the first principles of anything; rudimentary: an *elementary* analysis. **3** Having the nature of an infinitesimal part of a quantity or magnitude. **— el'e·men'·ta·ri·ly** *adv.* **— el'e·men'ta·ri·ness** *n.*

elementary education Public school and private education beyond kindergarten and preceding secondary school, from six to eight years in length, dealing with the fundamentals of education.

elementary school See under SCHOOL.

el·e·mi (el'ə·mē) *n.* Any one of several gum resins obtained from tropical trees of various genera, especially Manila elemi, from the pili tree of the Philippines: used in drugs and varnishes. [<Sp. *elemi,* ? <Arabic *al-lāmī*]

E·le·na (*Sp., Ital.* ā·lā'nä) See HELEN.

e·len·chus (i·leng'kəs) *n. pl.* **·chi** (-kī) **1** The contradictory opposite of a proposition; hence, a refuting argument; a refutation. **2** A false refutation; sophism. Also **e·lench** (i·lengk'). [<L <Gk. *elenchos* a cross-examination] **— e·len'chic** or **·chi·cal, e·lenc'·tic** or **·ti·cal** *adj.*

e·le·o·lite (i·lē'ə·līt) See ELAEOLITE.

el·e·o·plast (el'ē·ə·plast') See ELAIOPLAST.

el·e·phant (el'ə·fənt) *n.* **1** A massively built, almost hairless ungulate mammal of Asia and Africa (family *Elephantidae*), the largest of existing land animals, having a flexible proboscis or trunk, and the upper incisors developed as tusks valued as the chief source of ivory. There are two genera: the small-eared Asian elephant, *Elephas Maximus* and the African elephant, *Loxodonta africana,* with large flapping ears. **2** Something unwieldy, burdensome, or hard to dispose of. See WHITE ELEPHANT. **3** A size of paper, 23 by 38 inches. [<OF *olifant* <L *elephantus* <Gk. *elephas, -antos* ivory; ult. origin unknown]

AFRICAN ELEPHANT
(Height at the shoulder rarely above 11 feet; the Indian elephant slightly smaller; the cows, 7 to 9 feet)

El·e·phan·ta (el'ə·fan'tə) An island in Bombay Harbor; site of Brahmanic caves carved in hillside (main hall, eighth century) and statues.

Elephant Butte Dam The main unit of the Rio Grande reclamation project in SW New Mexico; 306 feet high; 1,674 feet long; impounding **Elephant Butte Reservoir.**

elephant ear The taro.

elephant foot A South African twining vine (*Testudinaria elephantipes*) of the yam family, having a conical, cormlike stem covered with a barky substance which, becoming deeply cracked, forms large angular protuberances like those on the shell of a tortoise (whence the name *tortoise plant*): often cultivated in greenhouses. Also called *Hottentot bread.* Also **el'e·phant's-foot'.**

el·e·phan·ti·a·sis (el'ə·fən·tī'ə·sis) *n. Pathol.* The final chronic stage of a filariasis caused by the presence in the blood and lymph of a parasitic nematode worm (*Wuchereria bancrofti*). It is characterized by a thickening and hardening of the skin, together with an enormous enlargement of the part affected, usually the lower extremities. [<L <Gk. <*elephas* elephant]

el·e·phan·tine (el'ə·fan'tēn, -tin, -tīn) *adj.* **1** Pertaining to an elephant. **2** Enormous; unwieldy.

El·eu·sin·i·a (el'yōō·sin'ē·ə) *n. pl.* The Athenian festival and mysteries in honor of Demeter and Persephone, formerly held at Eleusis. [<Gk.]

El·eu·sin·i·an (el'yōō·sin'ē·ən) *adj.* Of or pertaining to Eleusis or the Eleusinia.

Eleusinian mysteries The secret religious rites, which were probably originated by the Thracians at Eleusis and later absorbed by the Athenian state religion.

E·leu·sis (i·lōō'sis) In Greek mythology, the son of Mercury.

E·leu·sis (i·lōō'sis) A port on the **Bay of Eleusis** in east central Greece, on the site of an ancient Attic city. See ELEUSINIA. Modern Greek **E·lev·sis** (â'lâf·sēs').

El·eu·the·ri·a (el'yōō·thir'ē·ə) *n.* A quadrennial festival kept by the Greeks after the battle of Plataea in honor of Zeus Eleutherios (the Deliverer). [<Gk.]

el·e·vate (el'ə·vāt) *v.t.* **·vat·ed, ·vat·ing** **1** To raise; lift up. **2** To raise in rank, status, position, etc.; promote. **3** To raise the spirits of; cheer; inspire. **4** To raise the pitch or loudness of. **5** To raise the moral character or intellectual nature of, as a conversation. See synonyms under HEIGHTEN, PROMOTE, RAISE. [<L *elevatus,* pp. of *elevare* <*ex-* out + *levare* lighten]

el·e·vat·ed (el'ə·vā'tid) *adj.* **1** Lofty in situation; high: an *elevated* plateau. **2** Lofty in character; sublime: *elevated* sentiments. See synonyms under GRAND, HIGH. **—** *n. Colloq.* An overhead railroad.

el·e·va·tion (el'ə·vā'shən) *n.* **1** The act of elevation; exaltation. **2** An elevated place. **3** *Archit.* A geometrical drawing of the upright parts of a structure, as shown in blueprints and scale drawings. **4** *Eccl.* **a** The raising of the eucharistic elements: also **elevation of the Host. b** The music of voice or instrument that accompanies the elevation of the Host. **5** Height above the sea level. **6** *Astron.* The angular distance of a celestial body above the horizon. See synonyms under HEIGHT, RAMPART.

el·e·va·tor (el'ə·vā'tər) *n.* **1** One who or that which elevates. **2** A hoisting mechanism for grain. **3** A warehouse where grain is elevated and distributed. **4** A movable platform or cage in a building, for carrying freight or passengers up or down. **5** *Aeron.* An auxiliary airfoil, by the tilting or dipping of which the ascent or descent of the airplane is regulated: also called *diving rudder.* See illustration under AIRPLANE.

é·lève (ā·lev') *n. French* Pupil; scholar.

e·lev·en (i·lev'ən) *adj.* Consisting of one more than ten. **—** *n.* **1** The cardinal number preceding twelve and following ten. **2** Any of the symbols (11, xi, XI) representing this number. **3** A team or side of eleven players, as in cricket or football. [OE *endleofan*]

e·lev·en·fold (i·lev'ən·fōld') *adj.* Consisting of eleven; eleven times as great or as much; undecuplicate.

e·lev·enth (i·lev'ənth) *adj.* **1** Next in order after the tenth. **2** Being one of eleven equal parts. **—** *n.* **1** One of eleven equal parts. **2** The quotient of a unit divided by eleven: five is one *eleventh* of fifty-five. **3** In a series, the unit or thing after the tenth.

eleventh hour The latest possible time; the last opportunity.

el·e·von (el'ə·von) *n. Aeron.* A combined aileron and elevator, used in certain types of airplanes. [<ELEV(ATOR) + (AILER)ON]

elf (elf) *n. pl.* **elves** (elvz) **1** In folklore, a dwarfish, mischievous sprite. **2** A dwarf or diminutive person: a pet name for a lively child. [OE *ælf.* Akin to OAF.]

El Fai·yum (el fī·ōōm') See FAIYUM.

elf·child (elf'chīld') *n.* A child believed to have been left by elves in place of one that they have stolen; a changeling.

El Fer·rol del Cau·di·llo (el fer·rōl' thel kou·thē'lyō) A port in NW Spain. Formerly **El Fer·rol'.**

elf·in (el'fin) *adj.* Relating or belonging to elves. **—** *n.* **1** An elf. **2** A sportive child.

elf·ish (el'fish) *adj.* Relating to elves; mischievous. **— elf'ish·ly** *adv.* **— elf'ish·ness** *n.*

elf-land (elf'land') *n.* The supposed home of the elves; fairyland.

elf-lock (elf'lok') *n.* A lock of hair tangled as if by elves; a straggling lock.

El·gar (el'gär), **Sir Edward,** 1857–1934, English composer.

El·gin (el'gin) **1** A burgh, county town of Morayshire, Scotland. **2** A former name for MORAYSHIRE: also **El'gin·shire** (-shir). **3** (el'·jin) A city in NE Illinois.

Elgin marbles A collection of Greek sculpture in the British Museum, formerly on the Acropolis at Athens. [after the Earl of *Elgin,* who had the collection brought to England, 1803–12]

El Gi·zeh (el gē'zə) See GIZA.

El·gon (el'gon), **Mount** An extinct volcano on the Uganda-Kenya border NE of Lake Victoria; 14,178 feet.

El Gre·co (el grā'kō, grek'ō) See under GRECO.

El Ha·sa (el hä'sə) See HASA, EL.

E·li (ē'lī) A Biblical high priest and judge. 1 *Sam.* iv 13–18. [<Hebrew, the highest]

E·li·a (ē'lē·ə) Pen name of Charles Lamb.

E·li·as (i·lī'əs) See ELIJAH.

e·lic·it (i·lis'it) *v.t.* To draw out or forth, as by some attraction or inducement; bring to light: to *elicit* truth. [<L *elicitus,* pp. of *elicere* <*ex-* out + *lacere* entice] **— e·lic'i·ta'tion** *n.* **— e·lic'i·tor** *n.*

e·lide (i·līd') *v.t.* **e·lid·ed, e·lid·ing** **1** To omit (a vowel or syllable) in writing or pronouncing a word. **2** To suppress; omit; ignore. **3** *Law* To annul. [<L *elidere* <*ex-* out + *laedere* strike] **— e·lid'i·ble** *adj.*

el·i·gi·ble (el'ə·jə·bəl) *adj.* Capable of being chosen or elected; worthy of acceptance. **—***n.* One who is eligible in any sense. [<F *éligible* <L *eligere.* See ELECT.] **— el'i·gi·bil'i·ty, el'i·gi·ble·ness** *n.* **— el'i·gi·bly** *adv.*

E·li·hu (el'ə·hyōō) A masculine personal name. [See ELIJAH]

— Elihu A young man who visits Job. *Job* xxxii–xxxvii.

E·li·jah (i·lī'jə) A masculine personal name. Also **E·li'as.** [<Hebrew, Jehovah is my God]

—Elijah A prophet of Jehovah in the time of Ahab, ninth century B.C.

e·lim·i·nate (i·lim'ə·nāt) *v.t.* **·nat·ed, ·nat·ing** **1** To expel; get rid of. **2** To disregard as irrelevant or incorrect; ignore. **3** *Physiol.* To void; excrete. **4** *Math.* To remove (a quantity) from a system of algebraic equations. [<L *eliminatus,* pp. of *eliminare* <*ex-* out + *limen* a threshold]

e·lim·i·na·tion (i·lim'ə·nā'shən) *n.* **1** The act of eliminating. **2** The state of being cast out or expelled. **— e·lim'i·na'tive** *adj.* **— e·lim'i·na'tor** *n.* **— e·lim'i·na·to'ry** (-tôr'ē, -tō'rē) *adj.*

El·i·nor (el'ə·nər, -nor) See ELEANOR.

El·i·ot (el'ē·ət), **Charles William,** 1834–1926, U.S. educator; president of Harvard 1869–1909. **— George** Pen name of Mary Ann Evans, 1819–80, English novelist. **— John,** 1604–90, American clergyman; apostle to the Indians. **—Sir John,** 1592–1632, English statesman and champion of liberty. **— T(homas) S(tearns),** 1888–1965, U.S. poet, dramatist and essayist; became a British subject.

E·liph·a·let (i·lif'ə·lit) A masculine personal name. Also **E·liph'a·lat** (-lat). [<Hebrew, God delivers]

E·lis (ē′lis) A nome of west central Greece; 1,178 square miles, in part the ancient country and city of Elis. Modern Greek **I·lí·a** (ē·lyē′ä).

E·lis·a·beth (i·liz′ə·bəth) See ELIZABETH.

E·lis·a·beth·ville (i·liz′ə·bəth·vil′) A former name for LUBUMBASHI.

E·li·sha (i·lī′shə) A masculine personal name. [<Hebrew, God is salvation]
— **Elisha,** ninth century B.C., a Jewish prophet of Jehovah; successor of Elijah.

e·li·sion (i·lizh′ən) *n.* **1** The eliding or striking out of a part of a word, as in "o'er" for "over." **2** A suppression of a part. [<L *elisio, -onis* < *elidere.* See ELIDE.]

e·lite (ā·lēt′, i·lēt′) *n.* **1** The choicest part, as of a society, army, etc.; the pick. **2** A size of typewriter type, equivalent to 10-point, with 12 characters to the inch. Also **é·lite′.** [<F *élite* <Med. L *electa* choice <L *eligere.* See ELECT.]

Élite Guard The Schutzstaffel.

e·lix·ir (i·lik′sər) *n.* **1** A sweetened alcoholic medicinal preparation; a cordial; formerly a compound tincture. **2** An imaginary liquid or soluble substance by means of which alchemists once hoped to change base metals into gold. **3** An imaginary cordial supposed to be capable of sustaining life indefinitely: also *Obs.* **elixir vi·tae** (vī′tē). **4** The essential principle; concentrated essence. [<Med. L <Arabic *al-iksīr* <Gk. *xerion* medicated powder < *xeros* dry]

E·liz·a·beth (i·liz′ə·bəth) A feminine personal name. Also **E·li·za** (i·lī′zə), **E·lis·a·beth** (i·liz′ə·bəth, *Dan., Du., Ger.* ā·lē′zä·bet), *Fr.* **É·li·sa·beth** (ā·lē·zà·bet′), *Ital.* **E·li·sa·bet·ta** (ā·lē′zä·bet′tä). [<Hebrew, God has sworn]
— **Elizabeth,** the mother of John the Baptist. *Luke* ii 5–14.
— **Elizabeth,** born 1900, Elizabeth Angela Marguerite Bowes-Lyon, wife of George VI of England, king 1937–52.
— **Elizabeth,** pseudonym of Countess Elizabeth Mary Russell. See RUSSELL.
— **Elizabeth, Saint,** 1207–31, Hungarian princess; queen of Thuringia 1221–27.
— **Elizabeth I,** 1533–1603, queen of England 1558–1603; daughter of Henry VIII and Anne Boleyn.
— **Elizabeth II,** born 1926, Elizabeth Alexandra Mary, queen of Great Britain 1952– ; daughter of George VI; married to Prince Philip.
— **Elizabeth Pe·trov·na** (pe·trôv′nə), 1709–62, empress of Russia 1741–62.

E·liz·a·beth (i·liz′ə·bəth) A port in NE New Jersey.

E·liz·a·be·than (i·liz′ə·bē′thən, -beth′ən) *adj.* Relating to Elizabeth I of England, or to her era. — *n.* **1** An Englishman who lived during the reign of Elizabeth. **2** An author who wrote during her reign or during the reign of James I.

Elizabethan sonnet See under SONNET.

Elizabeth River A short, branching river of SE Virginia.

E·liz·a·beth·ville (i·liz′ə·bəth·vil′) See ELISABETHVILLE.

E·li·za·vet·pol (ye·lē′sä·vet·pôl′y′) Former name of KIROVABAD.

elk (elk) *n. pl.* **elks** or **elk** **1** A large deer of northern Europe and Asia (genus *Alces*), with palmated antlers and the upper lip forming a proboscis for browsing upon trees. **2** The American wapiti. [ME *elke* <OE *elh*]

ELK
(Height at the shoulder up to 7 feet)

Elk (elk) A town in NE Poland. *German* **Lyck** (lēk).

El Kha·lil (el kä·lēl′, khä-) The Arabic name for HEBRON.

elk·hound (elk′hound′) *n.* A sporting dog of Norwegian origin, of medium size, with a short, robust body and thick gray coat.

Elk Mountains A range of the Rocky Mountains in west central Colorado; highest peak, 14,259 feet.

ell[1] (el) *n.* A measure of length now rarely used; in England, 45 inches, or 1.114 meters. [OE *eln* an arm's length]

ell[2] (el) *n.* Anything shaped like the letter L, as an addition at right angles to one side of a house. Also **el.**

El·las (el′əs) The modern Greek name for GREECE.

El·len (el′ən) A feminine personal name. [See HELEN]

El·ler·y (el′ər·ē), **William,** 1727–1820, American lawyer; signer, for Rhode Island, of the Declaration of Independence.

Elles·mere Island (elz′mir) An island in NE Franklin District, Northwest Territories, Canada; 77,392 square miles.

El·lice Islands (el′is) An island group SE of the Gilbert Islands, comprising a district of the Gilbert and Ellice Islands colony; total, 9 1/2 square miles: formerly **Lagoon Islands.**

El·lick (el′ik) Diminutive of ALEXANDER.

El·li·ott (el′ē·ət), **Maxine,** 1871–1940, stage name of the U. S. actress *Jessie Dermot.*

el·lipse (i·lips′) *n. Geom.* **1** A plane curve such that the sum of the distances from any point of the curve to two fixed points, called *foci,* is a constant. **2** A conic section. [<L *ellipsis.* See ELLIPSIS.]

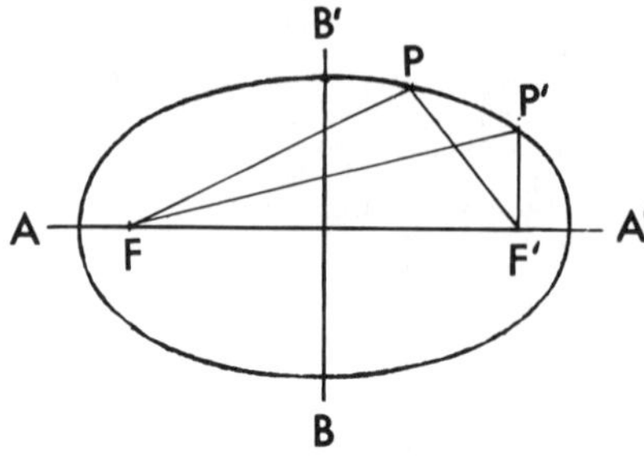

ELLIPSE
A–A′ Major axis. *B–B′* Minor axis.
F, F′ Foci. *P, P′* Points on curve.
FP + PF′ = FP′ + P′F′

el·lip·sis (i·lip′sis) *n. pl.* **·ses** (-sēz) **1** The omission of a word or words necessary to complete a sentence or expression. **2** Marks indicating omission, such as . . . or * * * . Also *eclipsis.* [<L <Gk. *elleipsis* < *en-* in + *leipsis* a leaving < *leipein* leave]

el·lip·soid (i·lip′soid) *n. Geom.* A solid of which every plane section is an ellipse or a circle. — *adj.* Resembling a compressed sphere or ellipsoid: also **el·lip·soi·dal** (ē′lip·soid′l).

el·lip·tic (i·lip′tik) *adj.* **1** Of, pertaining to, or shaped like an ellipse; oblong with rounded ends. **2** Characterized by ellipsis; shortened. Also **el·lip′ti·cal.** — **el·lip′ti·cal·ly** *adv.*

el·lip·tic·i·ty (el′ip·tis′ə·tē, i·lip′-) *n.* **1** The state of being elliptic. **2** The degree of deviation of an ellipse from a circle.

El·lis (el′is), **Alexander John,** 1814–90, English philologist and phoneticist. — **(Henry) Havelock,** 1859–1939, English psychologist and author.

El·lis Island (el′is) An island in upper New York Bay; formerly site of the chief United States immigration station.

el·lit·or·al (i·lit′ər·əl) *adj.* Of or pertaining to that part of the ocean from a depth of below 120 feet to as far as the light will penetrate.

Ells·worth (elz′wərth), **Lincoln,** 1880–1951, U. S. polar explorer. — **Oliver,** 1745–1807, American jurist.

ell·wand (el′wänd′) *n.* A measuring stick one ell in length.

elm (elm) *n.* **1** A deciduous shade tree of America, Europe, and Asia (genus *Ulmus*), with a broad, spreading, or overarching top: *U. americana* is the American elm and *U. fulva* the slippery elm. **2** The wood of this tree.

El·man (el′mən), **Mischa,** 1891–1967, U. S. violinist born in Russia.

elm-bark beetle (elm′bärk′) Any of various beetles (family *Scolytidae*) destructive of elm trees, especially a European species (*Scolytus multistratus*) introduced into America, which acts as the carrier of a parasitic fungus.

El Mis·ti (el mēs′tē) A volcano in southern Peru; 19,110 feet.

elm-leaf beetle (elm′lēf′) A coleopterous insect (*Galerucella xanthomelaena* or *luteola*), yellowish-green with dark lateral spots: introduced from Europe. Both larvae and adults are injurious to elm trees.

elm·y (el′mē) *adj.* Consisting of or abounding in elm trees.

E·lo·bey (ā′lō·bā′), **Great** and **Little** Two islands in the Bight of Biafra, comprising part of Spanish Guinea; total, 1 1/2 square miles.

el·o·cu·tion (el′ə·kyōō′shən) *n.* **1** The art of correct intonation, and inflection, in public speaking or reading. **2** Manner of utterance. [<L *elocutio, -onis* < *eloqui* < *ex-* out + *loqui* speak] — **el′o·cu′tion·ar′y** *adj.*

el·o·cu·tion·ist (el′ə·kyōō′shən·ist) *n.* One who is skilled in or teaches elocution; especially, one who gives public elocutionary readings.

é·loge (ā·lōzh′, *Fr.* ā·lôzh′) *n.* A biographical and eulogistic memoir or panegyric. Also **el·o·gy** (el′ō·jē). [<F <Med. L *eulogium* a eulogy; infl. in form by L *elogium* an inscription]

E·lo·him (e·lō·him′, -lō′·him) God: Hebrew name used in the Old Testament. [<Hebrew *'Elōhīm,* pl. of *'Elōah* God]

E·lo·hist (e·lō′hist) *n.* The author of those portions of the Hexateuch that are characterized by the use of *Elohim* for God instead of *Yahweh* or *Jehovah.* Compare YAHWIST.

El·o·his·tic (el′ō·his′tik) *adj.* **1** Of or pertaining to those portions of the Hexateuch where *Elohim* occurs in the Hebrew text and not *Yahweh* or *Jehovah.* **2** Written by the Elohist.

e·loin (i·loin′) *v.t. Law* To remove beyond the jurisdiction of; carry away, as property. Also **e·loign′.** [<OF *esloignier* carry off <LL *elongare.* See ELONGATE.] — **e·loin′er, e·loign′er** *n.* — **e·loin′ment, e·loign′ment** *n.*

E·lo·i·sa (ā′lō·ē′zä) Italian form of LOUISE.

e·lon·gate (i·lông′gāt, i·long′-) *v.t.* & *v.i.* **·gat·ed, ·gat·ing** To make or grow longer; lengthen. — *adj.* Elongated. See synonyms under PROTRACT. [<LL *elongatus,* pp. of *elongare* <*ex-* away + *longe* far off]

e·lon·ga·tion (ē′lông·gā′shən, ē′long-) *n.* **1** The act of elongating, or the state of being elongated. **2** An addition or appendage that adds to the length of something. **3** An extension or continuation.

e·lope (i·lōp′) *v.i.* **e·loped, e·lop·ing** **1** To run away with a lover, usually to get married. **2** To abscond; run off. [<AF *aloper.* Cf. OE *ahleapen* flee] — **e·lope′ment** *n.* — **e·lop′er** *n.*

el·o·quence (el′ə·kwəns) *n.* **1** Lofty, impassioned, and convincing utterance. **2** The quality of being eloquent, moving, forceful, or persuasive. See synonyms under SPEECH.

el·o·quent (el′ə·kwənt) *adj.* **1** Possessed of or manifesting eloquence. **2** Persuasive; convincing. **3** Visibly expressive of emotion. [<L *eloquens, -entis* ppr. of *eloqui.* See ELOCUTION.] — **el′o·quent·ly** *adv.*

El Pas·o (el pas′ō) A city on the Rio Grande in western Texas.

El Pa·so del Nor·te (el pä′sō thel nōr′tā) A former name of CIUDAD JUÁREZ.

El·phin·stone (el′fin·stōn, -stən), **Mountstuart,** 1779–1859, British historian and statesman. — **William,** 1431–1514, Scottish prelate; founded Aberdeen University.

El·sa (el′sə) A feminine personal name. Also *Dan., Ger.* **El·se** (el′zə), *Du.* **Els·ye** (els′yə). [See ALICE]
— **Elsa** The heroine of Wagner's opera *Lohengrin.*

El Sal·va·dor (el sal′və·dôr, *Sp.* el säl′vä·thōr′) A republic in western Central America; 13,176 square miles; capital, San Salvador. — **Sal′va·dor′an, Sal′va·do′ri·an,** *adj.* & *n.*

El·sass (el′zäs) The German name for ALSACE.

El·sass-Lo·thring·en (el′zäs·lō′tring·ən) The German name for ALSACE-LORRAINE.

else (els) *adv.* **1** In a different place, time, or way; elsewhere. **2** If the case or facts were different; otherwise; besides; instead. — *adj.* Additional; different: somebody *else*: What *else* can I do? — *conj.* If not; under other conditions. [OE *elles*]
◆ The expressions *someone else, anyone else, everyone else, somebody else,* etc., are in good usage treated as substantive phrases and have the possessive inflection upon the *else*: *somebody else's* umbrella.

else·where (els′hwâr′) *adv.* In or to another place or places; somewhere or anywhere else.

El·sie (el′sē) A feminine personal name. [See ALICE]

El·si·nore (el′sə·nôr, -nōr) A port on Zealand Island, Denmark; scene of Shakespeare's *Hamlet*: Danish *Helsingør.*

e·lu·ci·date (i·lo͞o′sə·dāt) *v.t.* **·dat·ed, ·dat·ing** To throw light upon; clear up; make plain. See synonyms under INTERPRET. [<LL *elucidatus,* pp. of *elucidare* < *ex-* out + *lucidus* clear] **—e·lu′ci·da′tive, e·lu′ci·da·to′ry** (-də·tôr′ē, -tō′rē) *adj.* **—e·lu′ci·da′tor** *n.*

e·lu·ci·da·tion (i·lo͞o′sə·dā′shən) *n.* The act of of elucidating; an illustration.

e·lude (i·lo͞od′) *v.t.* **e·lud·ed, e·lud·ing 1** To avoid or escape from by dexterity or artifice. **2** To escape the notice or understanding of: Your meaning *eludes* me. See synonyms under ESCAPE. [<L *eludere* < *ex-* out + *ludere* play] **—e·lud′i·ble** *adj.*

E·lul (e·lo͞ol′, *Hebrew* el′o͝ol) A Jewish month nearly corresponding to September. See CALENDAR (Hebrew).

e·lu·sion (i·lo͞o′zhən) *n.* The act of eluding or escaping; evasion. [<Med. L *elusio, -onis* <L *eludere.* See ELUDE.]

e·lu·sive (i·lo͞o′siv) *adj.* **1** Tending to slip away or escape; hard to understand; baffling. **2** Hard to grasp or keep: the *elusive* dream of wealth. Also **e·lu′so·ry** (-sər·ē). **—e·lu′sive·ly** *adv.* **—e·lu′sive·ness** *n.*

e·lute (i·lo͞ot′) *adj. Entomol.* Having indistinct or barely visible markings: said especially of insects. [<L *elutus,* pp. of *eluere* < *ex-* away + *luere* wash]

e·lu·tri·ate (i·lo͞o′trē·āt) *v.t.* **·at·ed, ·at·ing 1** To purify by washing. **2** To separate, as finer from coarser powder, by washing and straining or decanting. [<L *elutriatus,* pp. of *elutriare* wash off] **—e·lu′tri·a′tion** *n.*

e·lu·vi·a·tion (i·lo͞o′vē·ā′shən) *n.* The process, mechanical or chemical, of removing the fine particles of soil from an area. [<L *eluvies* a washing away + -ATION]

e·lu·vi·um (i·lo͞o′vē·əm) *n. Geol.* A deposit of soil and dust particles remaining where they were formed by the decomposition of rock masses. [<NL <L *eluvies* <*eluere.* See ELUTE.] **—e·lu′vi·al** *adj.*

Él·ve·hjem (el·vā′əm), **Conrad Arnold,** born 1901, U. S. physiologist and biochemist.

el·ver (el′vər) *n.* A young eel. [Var. of *eelfare* the journey of young eels upstream <EEL + FARE]

elves (elvz) Plural of ELF.

elv·et (el′vit) *n. Rare* A little elf.

elv·ish (el′vish) *adj.* Elfish; prankish. Also **elv′an.** **—elv′ish·ly** *adv.*

E·ly (ē′lē) An urban district in the **Isle of Ely,** an administrative county of Cambridgeshire, England; site of a 12th century cathedral.

El·y·ot (el′ē·ət, el′yət), **Sir Thomas,** 1490?–1546, English scholar, diplomat, and lexicographer.

É·ly·sée (ā·lē·zā′) *n.* The residence in Paris of the president of France.

E·ly·sian (i·lizh′ən, -ē·ən) *adj.* **1** Belonging to, or like, Elysium. **2** Supremely blessed or happy.

E·ly·si·um (i·lizh′ē·əm, i·liz′-) **1** In Greek mythology, the abode of the blessed dead, represented as in Hades, or in the Islands of the Blest in the Western Ocean: also **Elysian Fields. 2** A place or a condition of supreme delight; a paradise. [<L <Gk. *ēlysion (pedion)* the Elysian (field)]

el·y·tra (el′ə·trə) Plural of ELYTRON.

el·y·troid (el′ə·troid) *adj.* Sheathlike; like an elytron.

el·y·tron (el′ə·tron) *n. pl.* **·tra** *Entomol.* One of the thickened forewings of certain insects, as beetles; a wing cover: usually in the plural for the wing pair. Also **el′y·trum** (-trəm). [<Gk. *elytron* case < *eiluein* wrap up]

El·ze·vir (el′zə·vir) *adj.* **1** Belonging or related to Louis Elzevir, his successors, or their firm. **2** Denoting the type face used by the Elzevirs in their books. **—***n.* **1** A book printed by the Elzevirs. **2** A compact, modern printing type.

El·ze·vir (el′zə·vir), **Louis,** 1540?–1617, Dutch printer; founder of a 17th century publishing house celebrated for fine editions of the classics.

El·ze·vir·an (el′zə·vir′ən) *adj.* Of or pertaining to the Elzevirs. **—***n.* A collector of Elzevirs. Also **El′ze·vir′i·an.**

em (em) *n.* **1** The name of the thirteenth letter in the English alphabet, written M or m. **2** *Printing* The square of the body size of a type; especially, a pica *em,* about 1/6 of an inch, used as a standard unit of measurement: originally, the space occupied by the letter M in a font.

em-[1] *prefix* Var. of EN-[1], used before the labials *b, p,* and *m,* as in *embody, empower,* etc.

em-[2] Assimilated var. of EN-[2].

'em (əm, m) *pron. Colloq.* Them. [OE *heom* dative pl. of *he* he]

E·ma (ā′mä) Spanish form of EMMA.

e·ma·ci·ate (i·mā′shē·āt) *v.t.* **·at·ed, ·at·ing** To make abnormally lean; cause to lose flesh. [<L *emaciatus,* pp. of *emaciare* waste away < *ex-* out + *macies* leanness] **—e·ma′ci·a′·tion** *n.*

e·ma·ci·at·ed (i·mā′shē·ā′tid) *adj.* Very thin; wasted away.

em·a·nant (em′ə·nənt) *adj.* Issuing from a source; emanating. [<L *emanans, -antis,* ppr. of *emanare.* See EMANATE.]

em·a·nate (em′ə·nāt) *v.i.* **·nat·ed, ·nat·ing 1** To come or flow forth, as from a source. **2** to take rise; originate; emerge. [<L *emanatus,* pp. of *emanare* < *ex-* out + *manare* flow]

em·a·na·tion (em′ə·nā′shən) *n.* **1** The act of issuing or flowing forth from some origin or source. **2** That which proceeds from an origin or source; efflux; effluence. **3** The pantheistic doctrine that all existing things have been created as effluxes of the Divine Essence; hence, an outcome or product of such a process. **4** *Physics* An inert gaseous product of disintegration in certain radioactive substances, as radon and thoron. **—em′a·na′tive** *adj.* **—em′a·na′tive·ly** *adv.*

e·man·ci·pate (i·man′sə·pāt) *v.t.* **·pat·ed, ·pat·ing 1** To release from bondage or slavery, or any physical or spiritual oppression or authority; liberate; set free. **2** In Roman law, to free (a child) from its father's control. [<L *emancipatus,* pp. of *emancipare* < *ex-* out + *manus* hand + *capere* taken] **—e·man′ci·pa·to′ry** (-pə·tôr′ē, -tō′rē) *adj.* **—e·man′ci·pa′tive** *adj.* **—e·man′ci·pa′tor** *n.*

e·man·ci·pa·tion (i·man′sə·pā′shən) *n.* **1** The act of emancipating, or the state of being emancipated. **2** Liberation from bondage, disability, or dependence, or from any injurious or undue restraint or influence: *emancipation* from evil associations. **3** In Roman law, the enfranchisement of a minor by his father. See synonyms under LIBERTY.

Emancipation Proclamation A proclamation issued by President Abraham Lincoln on January 1, 1863, declaring free all Negro slaves in the seceded States: reinforced by the 13th Amendment (1865), which freed the slaves in eight other States.

E·man·u·el (i·man′yo͞o·əl, -el; *Ger.* ā·mä′·no͞o·el) See EMMANUEL. Also *Ital.* **E·ma·nu·e·le** (ā·mä′no͞o·ā′lā).

e·mar·gi·nate (i·mär′jə·nit, -nāt) *adj. Bot.* Having the margin interrupted or notched; specifically, notched at the summit: said of leaves, petals, etc. Also **e·mar′gi·nat′ed.** [<L *emarginatus,* pp. of *emarginare* < *ex-* off, away + *margo, -inis* border, edge]

e·mas·cu·late (i·mas′kyə·lāt) *v.t.* **·lat·ed, ·lat·ing 1** To deprive of procreative power; castrate; geld. **2** To deprive of strength; weaken; make effeminate. **3** To impair by cutting down or censoring, as a literary work. **—***adj.* (i·mas′kyə·lit) Emasculated; weakened. [<L *emasculatus,* pp. of *emasculare* < *ex-* away + *masculus* male] **—e·mas′cu·la′tion** *n.* **—e·mas′cu·la′tive** *adj.* **—e·mas′cu·la′tor** *n.* **—e·mas′cu·la·to′ry** (-tôr′ē, -tō′rē) *adj.*

em·ball (im·bôl′) *v.t. Obs.* To ensphere.

em·balm (im·bäm′) *v.t.* **1** To preserve from decay, as a dead body, by treatment with balsams, antiseptic preparations, drugs, and chemicals. **2** To perfume. **3** To preserve from oblivion. Also spelled *imbalm.* [<F *embaumer* < *em-* in (<L *in-*) + *baume* <OF *basme* BALM]

em·balm·er (im·bä′mər) *n.* **1** One who embalms the dead. **2** Anything that preserves from decay.

em·balm·ment (im·bäm′mənt) *n.* The act of embalming.

em·bank (im·bangk′) *v.t.* To confine or protect by a bank, dike, or the like.

em·bank·ment (im·bangk′mənt) *n.* **1** A protecting or supporting bank. **2** The process of strengthening by a bank. See synonyms under RAMPART.

em·bar (im·bär′) *v.t.* **·barred, ·bar·ring 1** To enclose within bars; fasten in. **2** To stop; check, as by a bar. **—em·bar′ment** *n.*

em·bar·ca·de·ro (im·bär′kə·dâr′ō) *n. SW U.S.* A wharf or landing place. [<Sp. < *embarcar* embark]

em·bar·ca·tion (em′bär·kā′shən) See EMBARKATION.

em·bar·go (im·bär′gō) *n. pl.* **·goes 1** A prohibition by the sovereign power of a nation temporarily restraining vessels from leaving or entering its ports. **2** Authoritative stoppage of foreign commerce or of any special trade. **3** Any imposed impediment; a check or hindrance; specifically, in railroad operation, a notice forbidding massing of cars at specified places. **—***v.t.* **·goed, ·go·ing** To lay an embargo upon. [<Sp. < *embargar* < *em-* in (<L *in-*) + *bargar* <LL *barra* a bar]

em·bark (im·bärk′) *v.t.* **1** To put or take aboard a vessel. **2** To invest (money) or involve (a person) in a venture. **—***v.i.* **3** To go aboard a vessel, as for a voyage. **4** To engage in a venture. [<F *embarquer* <LL *imbarcare* < *in-* in + *barca* boat] **—em·bark′ment** *n.*

em·bar·ka·tion (em′bär·kā′shən) *n.* The act of embarking. Also spelled *embarcation.*

embarkation center A military establishment near a port for the care of troops about to embark.

em·bar·ras des ri·chesses (äṅ·bà·rä′ dā rē·shes′) *French* An encumbrance of wealth; hence, the burden of obligations and circumstances that accompany wealth.

em·bar·rass (im·bar′əs) *v.t.* **1** To make ill at ease, self-conscious, and uncomfortable; abash; disconcert. **2** To involve in difficulties, especially in business. **3** To hamper; encumber. **4** To render difficult; complicate. [<F *embarrasser* < *em-* in (<L *in-*) + *barre* <OF BAR] **—em·bar′rass·ing** *adj.* **—em·bar′·rass·ing·ly** *adv.*

Synonyms: abash, confuse, discomfit, disconcert, faze, hamper, hinder, impede, rattle. *Embarrass* implies some influence which impedes freedom of thought, speech, or action and refers to persons and things they plan to do. One is *embarrassed* in the presence of others, and because of their presence. *Confusion* is of the intellect, *embarrassment* of the feelings. A witness may be *embarrassed* by annoying personalities, so as to become *confused* in statements. As applied to mental action, a solitary thinker may be *confused* by some difficulty in a subject, or by some mental defect. *Rattle* is a colloquialism which implies a disorganization of one's mental processes. *Faze* is an Americanism usually found in negative expressions, but sometimes carries the implications of *abash* and *rattle*; as, Nothing can *faze* him. *Hamper* is used either literally or figuratively; as, *hampered* by debt; encumbered. *Hinder* is used in the sense of obstruction; as, Adverse winds *hindered* the ship. Compare ABASH, HINDER, INVOLVE, OBSTRUCT, PERPLEX. *Antonyms*: assure, cheer, compose, embolden, encourage, help, relieve, sustain.

em·bar·rass·ment (im·bar′əs·mənt) *n.* **1** The state of being embarrassed. **2** That which embarrasses.

em·bas·sa·dor (im·bas′ə·dər, -dôr) See AMBASSADOR.

em·bas·sage (em′bə·sij) *n. Obs.* **1** The sending, business, office, or message of an ambassador or an embassy. **2** The body of ambassadors or embassy itself.

em·bas·sy (em′bə·sē) *n. pl.* **·sies 1** An ambassador together with his suite; the person or body of persons deputed for a mission from one government to another. **2** The mission or office of an envoy or ambassador. **3** The official residence of an ambassador and his suite. [Var. of earlier *ambassy* <OF *ambassé* <Med. L *ambactia,* ult. <Celtic]

em·bathe (em·bāth′) *v.t.* **·bathed, ·bath·ing** To bathe; drench; immerse: also spelled *imbathe.*

em·bat·tle[1] (em·bat′l) *v.t.* **·tled, ·tling** To form in line of battle; prepare or equip for battle. [<OF *embataillier* < *en-* in (<L *in-*) + *bataille* BATTLE]

em·bat·tle[2] (em·bat′l) *v.t.* **·tled, ·tling** To furnish with battlements. [<EM-[1] + BATTLE in obs. sense of "fortify" <OF *bastiller* build]

em·bat·tled (em·bat′ld) *adj.* **1** Drawn up in battle array; ready for battle. **2** Made the scene of a muster or battle. **3** Having battlements.

em·bat·tle·ment (em·bat′l·mənt) *n.* **1** A battlement. **2** The fortifying, as of a wall, with battlements. For illustrations see BATTLEMENT.

em·bay (em·bā′) *v.t.* **1** To put or force into a bay, as a ship. **2** To shut in by arms of land.

em·bay·ment (em·bā′mənt) *n.* **1** A bay or large inlet. **2** The process of forming a bay.

em·bed (im·bed′) *v.t.* **·bed·ded, ·bed·ding 1** To place in or as in a bed. **2** To set firmly in surrounding matter. **3** To hold in the mind; keep in memory. Also spelled *imbed.* —**em·bed′ment** *n.*

em·bel·lish (im·bel′ish) *v.t.* **1** To beautify by adding ornamental features; decorate. **2** To heighten the interest of, as a story, by adding fictitious details: See synonyms under ADORN, GARNISH. [<OF *embelliss-,* stem of *embellir* beautify <*em-* in (<L *in-*) + *bel* beautiful <L *bellus*]

em·bel·lish·ment (im·bel′ish·mənt) *n.* **1** The act of adorning. **2** An ornament; ornamentation.

em·ber (em′bər) *n.* **1** A live coal or an unextinguished brand. **2** *pl.* A dying fire. [OE *ǣmerge*]

Ember days *Eccl.* A three-day period of fasting and prayer observed quarterly on the Wednesday, Friday, and Saturday after the first Sunday in Lent, after Whitsunday, after September 14, and after December 13. [OE *ymbrene, ymbryne* circuit, cycle <*ymb* around + *ryne* a running]

Ember week A week including Ember days.

em·bez·zle (im·bez′əl) *v.t.* **·zled ·zling 1** To appropriate fraudulently to one's own use. **2** *Obs.* To misappropriate secretly; make off with. See synonyms under STEAL. [<AF *embesiler* <*em-* in + *besiler* destroy] —**em·bez′zle·ment** *n.* —**em·bez′zler** *n.*

em·bit·ter (im·bit′ər) *v.t.* To render bitter, unhappy, or resentful. —**em·bit′ter·ment** *n.*

em·blaze (em·blāz′) *v.t.* **·blazed, ·blaz·ing** To emblazon. [EM- + BLAZE[3]] —**em·blaz′er** *n.*

em·bla·zon (em·blā′zən) *v.t.* **1** To adorn with or as with heraldic designs; decorate. **2** To adorn magnificently; set off in resplendent colors. **3** To extol; celebrate the fame or virtues of. —**em·bla′zon·er** *n.* —**em·bla′zon·ment** *n.*

em·bla·zon·ry (em·blā′zən·rē) *n. pl.* **·ries 1** The act or art of emblazoning. **2** Heraldic devices, collectively; any brilliantly colored representation or embellishment. See under ESCUTCHEON.

em·blem (em′bləm) *n.* **1** An object suggesting something which it does not directly represent; a figurative representation; symbol. **2** A distinctive badge; ensign. **3** An allegorical picture, usually having a motto. **4** *Obs.* An inlaid or inserted ornament. —*v.t. Rare* To emblematize. [<L *emblema* inlaid work <Gk. *emblēma* an insertion <*em-* in + *ballein* throw]

Synonyms: attribute, figure, sign, symbol, token, type. An *emblem* has some natural fitness to suggest that for which it stands; a *symbol* has been chosen or agreed upon to suggest something else, with or without natural fitness; a *sign* does actually suggest the thing with or without reason, and with or without intention or choice. A *symbol* may be also an *emblem.* On the other hand, the same thing may be both a *sign* and a *symbol*; a letter of the alphabet is a *sign* which indicates a sound; but letters are often used as mathematical, chemical, or astronomical *symbols.* A *token* is some object given or act done as a pledge or expression of feeling or intent; a ring, the natural *emblem* of eternity, and also its accepted *symbol,* is frequently given as a *token* of friendship or love. Compare FIGURE, IMAGE, LETTER, SIGN.

em·blem·at·ic (em′blə·mat′ik) *adj.* Of, pertaining to, or serving as an emblem; symbolic. Also **em′blem·at′i·cal.** —**em′blem·at′i·cal·ly** *adv.*

em·blem·a·tize (em·blem′ə·tīz) *v.t.* **·tized, ·tiz·ing 1** To serve as an emblem of. **2** To represent by a symbol or emblem.

em·ble·ments (em′blə·mənts) *n. pl. Law* **1** Growing crops produced by the labor of the cultivator of the soil. **2** The right to or profits from such crops. [<OF *emblaement* <*emblaer,* sow with grain <LL *imbladare* <*in-* in + *bladum* grain]

em·blem·ize (em′blə·mīz) *v.t.* **·ized, ·iz·ing** To represent by an emblem; make into an emblem.

em·bod·i·ment (im·bod′i·mənt) *n.* **1** The act or process of embodying, the state of being embodied, or that which embodies; incarnation. **2** A concrete example: She is the *embodiment* of wit.

em·bod·y (im·bod′ē) *v.t.* **·bod·ied, ·bod·y·ing 1** To invest with or as with a body; incarnate; make corporeal. **2** To collect into one whole; incorporate. **3** To express concretely.

em·bold·en (im·bōl′dən) *v.t.* To make bold; give courage to. See synonyms under ABET, ENCOURAGE.

em·bo·lec·to·my (em′bə·lek′tə·mē) *n. Surg.* Removal of an embolus. [<EMBOL(US) + -ECTOMY]

em·bol·ic (em·bol′ik) *adj.* **1** *Pathol.* Of, pertaining to, or caused by embolism or an embolus: *embolic* abscesses. **2** Embolismic. **3** *Biol.* Growing or pushing inward: *embolic* invagination.

em·bo·lism (em′bə·liz′əm) *n.* **1** *Pathol.* The stopping up of a vein or artery, as by a blood clot or foreign particle. **2** Intercalation, as of days, for the adjustment of the calendar. [<LL *embolismus* <Gk. *embolismos* intercalary <*embolos.* See EMBOLUS.]

em·bo·lis·mic (em′bə·liz′mik) *adj.* **1** Of or pertaining to embolism or intercalation. **2** Adjusted by intercalation; intercalated.

embolismic year The period covered by 13 lunar months or 384 days; the year in which there is an intercalation.

em·bo·lo·la·li·a (em′bə·lō·lā′lē·ə) *Psychiatry* The interspersing of speech or writing with meaningless words or phrases. Also **em′bo·lo·pha′si·a** (-fā′zhē·ə). [<NL <Gk. *embolos* peg + *lalia* talk, speech]

em·bo·lus (em′bə·ləs) *n. pl.* **·li** (-lī) **1** Anything inserted or shaped for insertion, as a wedge, sucker of a pump, plunger, or piston. **2** *Pathol.* Any solid body (as a piece of fibrin or a blood clot) that forms an obstruction in a blood vessel. [<L <Gk. *embolos* peg <*en-* in + *ballein* throw]

em·bon·point (äṅ·bôṅ·pwaṅ′) *n. French* Marked corpulence; plumpness; stoutness.

em·bor·der (em·bôr′dər) *v.t.* To furnish with a border.

em·bos·om (em·bo͝oz′əm, -bo͞o′zəm) *v.t.* **1** To take to the bosom; embrace. **2** To cherish. **3** To shelter; enclose.

em·boss[1] (im·bôs′, -bos′) *v.t.* **1** To cover or adorn (a surface) with raised figures, designs, etc. **2** To raise or represent (designs, figures, etc.) from or upon a surface. **3** To decorate sumptuously. [<OF *embocer* <*em-* in + *boce* a boss] —**em·boss′er** *n.* —**em·boss′ment** *n.*

em·boss[2] (im·bôs′, -bos′) *v.t. Obs.* **1** To cover with foam; fleck. **2** To drive, as a hunted animal, into a thicket; press to extremity; tire out. **3** To conceal. [ME *embose,* ? <EN-[1] + OF *bois* woods, thicket]

em·bossed (im·bôst′, -bost′) *adj.* **1** Ornamented with raised figures. **2** *Obs.* Swollen; puffed up.

em·boss·ing (im·bôs′ing, -bos′-) *n.* In textiles, the process of raising design from the surface, so that it stands out in relief: usually done, in making embossed damask, seersucker, etc., by passing a resin-impregnated fabric between hot, engraved metal rollers, but for velvet and plush effected by shearing high pile to different levels or by pressing parts flat.

em·bou·chure (äm·bo͞o·sho͝or′, *Fr.* äṅ·bo͞o·shür′) *n.* **1** The mouth, as of a river or stream; point of discharge. **2** Any opening resembling a mouth: the *embouchure* of a cannon or embrasure. **3** A mouthpiece, or the place where the mouth is applied. **4** Position or adjustment of the lips, tongue, and other organs in playing a wind instrument or in vocalization. [<F <*emboucher* <*em-* in (<L *in-*) + *bouche* mouth <L *bucca* cheek]

em·bow (em·bō′) *v.t.* To bend or curve like a bow; arch. —**em·bow′ment** *n.*

em·bowed (em·bōd′) *adj.* Bent like a bow; curved outward; arched: an *embowed* window.

em·bow·el (em·bou′əl, -boul′) *v.t.* **·eled** or **·elled, ·el·ing** or **·el·ling 1** To disembowel; figuratively, to rend. **2** To embed deeply: *emboweled* in the earth. [Def. 1 <OF *enboweler,* alter. of *esboueler* <*es-* out (<L *ex-*) + *boel* BOWEL; def. 2 <EN-[1] + BOWEL]

em·bow·er (em·bou′ər) *v.t.* & *v.i.* To cover, shelter, or rest in or as in a bower.

em·brace[1] (im·brās′) *v.* **·braced, ·brac·ing** *v.t.* **1** To take or infold in the arms; hug. **2** To accept willingly; adopt, as a religion or doctrine. **3** To avail oneself of: to *embrace* an offer. **4** To surround; encircle. **5** To include; contain. **6** To take in visually or mentally. **7** To have sexual intercourse with. —*v.i.* **8** To hug each other. —*n.* The act of embracing; a clasping in the arms; a hug. [<OF *embracer* <LL *in-* in + *bracchia* arm] —**em·brace′ment** *n.* —**em·brac′er** *n.*

Synonyms (verb): adopt, clasp, comprehend, comprise, contain, encircle, enclose, encompass, entwine, environ, espouse, grasp, hold, hug, surround. See CARESS. *Antonyms*: disown, exclude, refuse, reject, repel, repulse.

em·brace[2] (em·brās′) *v.t.* **·braced, ·brac·ing** *Law* To influence, or attempt to influence, corruptly. [Back formation from EMBRACER]

em·brac·er (em·brā′sər) *n. Law* One guilty of embracery. Also **em·brace′or.** [<OF *embraceor* <*embraser* kindle, incite <*em-* in + *braise* charcoal]

em·brac·er·y (em·brā′sər·ē) *n. Law* The act of influencing or trying to influence, corrupt, or bribe a jury, judge, etc.

em·branch·ment (em·branch′mənt, -bränch′-) *n.* A branching out or off, as of an arm of a river; a branch, ramification, or division.

em·bran·gle (em·brang′gəl) *v.t.* **·gled, ·gling** To entangle; complicate; confuse. [<EM-[2] + dial. *brangle* brawl] —**em·bran′gle·ment** *n.*

em·bra·sure (em·brā′zhər) *n.* **1** An opening in a wall, as for a cannon. **2** *Archit.* **a** The sloping or beveling of an opening in a wall, as of a window or door, so as to enlarge its interior profile. **b** The opening itself, or the space within it. For illustrations see BASTION, BATTLEMENT. [<F <*embraser* widen <*em-* in (<L *in-*) + *braser* bevel]

em·brit·tle (em·brit′l) *v.t.* **·tled, ·tling** To make brittle, as steel by sudden cooling.

em·brit·tle·ment (em·brit′l·mənt) *n.* A deterioration of the lining metal of steam boilers, due to the presence of excess sodium carbonate in the water.

em·bro·cate (em′brō·kāt) *v.t.* **·cat·ed, ·cat·ing** To moisten and rub, as with liniment or oil. [<Med. L *embrocatus,* pp. of *embrocare* <*embrocha* an ointment <Gk. *embrochē*]

em·bro·ca·tion (em′brō·kā′shən) *n.* **1** The application of a soothing liniment to any part of the body. **2** The liniment or preparation so used.

em·broi·der (im·broi′dər) *v.t.* **1** To ornament with designs in needlework. **2** To execute in needlework. **3** To embellish or adorn; exaggerate, as a narrative with fictitious details. —*v.i.* **4** To make embroidery. [<EN-[1] + BROIDER] —**em·broi′der·er** *n.*

em·broi·der·y (im·broi′dər·ē) *n. pl.* **·der·ies 1** Ornamental needlework, or the art of producing such work. **2** Any variegated or elaborate decoration or ornamentation; embellishment.

em·broil (em·broil′) *v.t.* **1** To involve in dissension or strife. **2** To throw into uproar or tumult. **3** To render complicated or confused; entangle. See synonyms under INVOLVE. [<F *embrouiller* <*em-* in (<L *in-*) + *brouiller* confuse]

em·broil·ment (em·broil′mənt) *n.* The act or result of embroiling; strife.

em·brown (em·broun′) *v.t.* & *v.i.* **1** To make or become brown or dusky. **2** To darken.

em·bry·ec·to·my (em′brē·ek′tə·mē) *n. Surg.* An operation for removing an embryo through an incision in the abdomen.

em·bry·o (em′brē·ō) *n. pl.* **·os 1** The germ or rudimentary form of anything in its earliest stage; specifically, the germ of an organism before it has developed its distinctive form. **2** The germ of a viviparous animal in the first stages of its existence (in the human species the first two months). **3** *Bot.* The rudimentary plant within the seed, which makes its appearance soon after fertilization of the ovule by the pollen and then passes through a period of rest until the germination or sprouting of the seed. Also **em′bry·on** (-on). —**in embryo** In an undeveloped or incipient stage or state; not yet developed or advanced, as a project or undertaking. For illustrations see under EGG, EMBRYOLOGY, FROG. —*adj.* Pertaining to an embryo; rudimentary: also **em′bry·al.** [<Gk. *embryon* <*en-* in + *bryein* swell]

embryo- *combining form* Embryo; embryonic: *embryogenesis.* Also, before vowels, **embry-.** [<Gk. *embryon* embryo]

em·bry·o·gen·e·sis (em′brē·ō·jen′ə·sis) *n.* The development of an organism from its embryonic stage. Also **em·bry·og·e·ny** (em′brē·oj′ə·nē) —**em′bry·o·gen′ic** or **·ge·net′ic** (-jə·net′ik) *adj.*

em·bry·ol·o·gy (em′brē·ol′ə·jē) *n.* The science which deals with the origin, structure, and

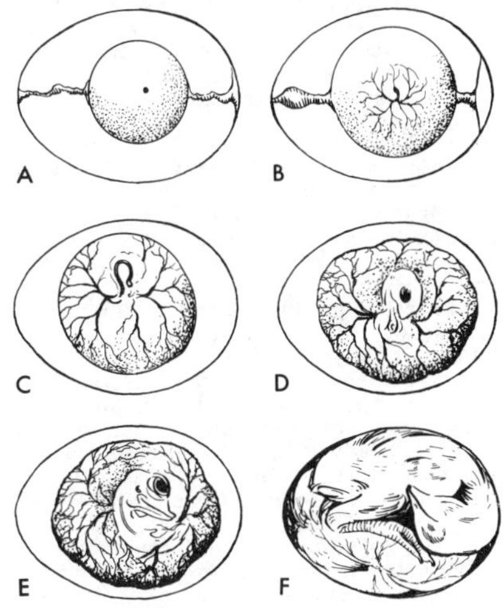

EMBRYOLOGY OF A CHICKEN
A. Before incubation, a germinal disk shown by small black spot. *B.* Three-day-old embryo, showing blood vessels radiating from heart. *C.* The fourth day. *D.* The fifth day. *E.* The seventh day. *F.* The nineteenth day, when chick absorbs remaining yolk. The chick hatches on the twenty-first day.

development of the embryo. —**em′bry·o·log′i·cal** (-ə·loj′i·kəl) *adj.* —**em′bry·o·log′i·cal·ly** *adv.* —**em′bry·ol′o·gist** *n.*

em·bry·o·nal (em′brē·ə·nəl) *adj.* Of or pertaining to an embryo or embryonic stage; embryonic.

em·bry·on·ic (em′brē·on′ik) *adj.* **1** Of, pertaining to, or like an embryo. **2** Undeveloped.

embryo sac *Bot.* The sac, formed of one cell, rarely more, within the nucleus of the ovule of flowering, seed-producing plants, containing the embryonal vesicle.

em·bry·o·scope (em′brē·ə·skōp′) *n.* A device for observing embryonic development, especially in the eggs of birds. —**em·bry·os·co·py** (em′brē·os′kə·pē) *n.*

em·cee (em′sē′) *Colloq. n.* Master of ceremonies. —*v.i.* & *v.t.* **em·ceed, em·cee·ing** To act or direct as master of ceremonies. [<*M(aster of) C(eremonies)*]

Em·den (em′dən) A port on the Ems at the North Sea, Lower Saxony, Germany.

eme (ēm) *n. Brit. Dial.* An uncle; also, a friend, or neighbor. [OE *ēam*]

e·meer (ə·mir′) See EMIR.

Em·e·line (em′ə·līn, -lēn) A feminine personal name. [<Gmc., industrious ruler]

e·mend (i·mend′) *v.t.* **1** To make corrections or changes in the form or wording of (a literary work, etc.), especially after scholarly study. **2** To free from faults; correct. Also **e·men·date** (ē′men·dāt). [<L *emendare* <*ex-* out + *menda* a fault] —**e·mend′a·ble** *adj.*

Synonyms: amend, correct, rectify, redress, reform, remedy, revise. *Amend, emend, correct,* and *mend* all imply the *correction* of an evil. To *amend* is to *rectify* defects by positive means, generally by adding or altering, as to *amend* a law. *Emend* means negatively to remove particular faults in a literary work by alteration of letters, single words, or passages.

e·men·da·tion (ē′men·dā′shən, em′ən-) *n.* A correction or alteration. [<L *emendatio, -onis* <*emendare.* See EMEND.] —**e′men·da′tor** *n.* —**e·mend·a·to·ry** (i·men′də·tôr′ē, -tō′rē) *adj.*

em·er·ald (em′ər·əld, em′rəld) *n.* **1** A bright-green variety of beryl, which when clear and nearly flawless is one of the most highly valued gems. **2** In the Bible, an unidentified precious stone. **3** A rich and vivid green. **4** One of various green moths. **5** *Printing* A size of type intermediate between minion and nonpareil. —**Oriental emerald** A valuable transparent variety of corundum. —*adj.* **1** Pertaining to or like the emerald. **2** Of a rich green color. [<OF *emeraude, esmeraldus* <L *smaragdus.* Doublet of SMARAGD.]

emerald green A brilliant green, highly poisonous pigment made from copper and arsenic.

Emerald Isle Ireland: probably so called because of the rich green of its landscape.

emerald nickel Zaratite.

e·merge (i·mûrj′) *v.i.* **e·merged, e·merg·ing** **1** To rise, as from a fluid. **2** To come forth into view or existence; become noticeable or apparent. [<L *emergere* <*ex-* out + *mergere* dip]

e·mer·gence (i·mûr′jəns) *n.* **1** The process or result of emerging. **2** *Bot.* An outgrowth, as a prickle or hair growing from the tissue under the epidermis of a plant.

e·mer·gen·cy (i·mûr′jən·sē) *n. pl.* **·cies** A sudden condition or state of affairs calling for immediate action.

e·mer·gent (i·mûr′jənt) *adj.* **1** Rising or emerging, as from a fluid or from concealment. **2** Coming unexpectedly; urgent. **3** *Biol.* New and unforeseen in the evolution of plant and animal organisms. —*n.* That which emerges; the result of a natural process. [<L *emergens, -entis,* ppr. of *emergere* EMERGE]

emergent evolution A philosophical theory stated by C. Lloyd Morgan and S. Alexander differentiating between two types of evolutionary products: *resultants,* which are predictable from previously existing conditions; and *emergents,* such as new species and new manifestations of life which are not predictable from the known laws of matter.

e·mer·i·tus (i·mer′ə·təs) *adj.* Retired from active service (as on account of age), but retained in an honorary position: pastor *emeritus.* [<L, pp. of *emerere* <*ex-* out + *merere* deserve]

em·er·od (em′ər·od) *n. Obs.* **1** A tumor; boil; hemorrhoid. **2** In the Bible, an infectious disease, perhaps bubonic plague. 1 *Sam.* v 6. Also **em′er·oid.** [Var. of HEMORRHOID]

e·mersed (ē·mûrst′) *adj. Bot.* Standing above and out of water, as the stems and leaves of aquatic plants. [<L *emersus,* pp. of *emergere* EMERGE]

e·mer·sion (ē·mûr′shən, -zhən) *n.* **1** The act or process of emerging. **2** *Astron.* The rising out of or from behind something, as the moon from the earth's shadow during an eclipse.

Em·er·son (em′ər·sən), **Haven,** 1874–1957, U.S. physician; public health administrator. —**Ralph Waldo,** 1803–82, U.S. essayist, philosopher, and poet.

em·er·y (em′ər·ē, em′rē) *n.* A very hard, black or grayish-black variety of corundum mixed with magnesite and other minerals; used as an abrasive. [F *émeri* <OF *esmeril* <LL *smericulum* <Gk. *smēris* emery powder]

Em·er·y (em′ər·ē) A masculine personal name. Also *Fr.* **É·me·ri** (ām·rē′). [<Gmc., work ruler]

emery bag A small bag, often the size and shape of a strawberry, filled with emery powder: used to keep needles clean of rust.

emery board A small, flat board covered with powdered emery, used in manicuring.

emery cloth Cloth coated with powdered emery, used for fine abrading and polishing.

Em·e·sa (em′ə·sə) Ancient name for HOMS.

em·e·sis (em′ə·sis) *n. Pathol.* Vomiting. [<NL <Gk. <*emeein* vomit]

e·met·ic (i·met′ik) *adj.* Tending to produce vomiting. —*n.* A medicine used to induce vomiting. [<Gk. *emetikos* <*emeein* vomit]

em·e·tine (em′ə·tēn, -tin) *n. Chem.* A white crystalline alkaloid, $C_{29}H_{40}O_4N_2$, from the ipecacuanha root, used in certain conditions of amebic dysentery. Also **em′e·tin** (-tin). [<Gk. *emetos* vomiting + -INE[2]]

e·meu, e·mew (ē′myōō) See EMU.

é·meute (i·myōōt′, *Fr.* ā·mœt′) *n. French* A seditious or mutinous outbreak; riot; tumult.

-emia *combining form Med.* Blood; condition of the blood: used in names of diseases: *leukemia.* Also spelled *-aemia.* [<Gk. *haima* blood]

em·i·grant (em′ə·grənt) *adj.* Moving from one place or country for the purpose of settling in another: opposed to *immigrant.* —*n.* **1** A person who leaves one country, or section of a country, to settle in another. **2** A person from the eastern United States who went west to settle new lands. [<L *emigrans, -antis,* ppr. of *emigrare.* See EMIGRATE.]

emigrant trail A road made by the constant travel of emigrants to the West.

em·i·grate (em′ə·grāt) *v.i.* **·grat·ed, ·grat·ing** To go from one country, or section of a country, to settle in another. [<L *emigratus,* pp. of *emigrare* <*ex-* out + *migrare* move]

Synonyms: immigrate, migrate. To *migrate* is to change one's dwelling place, usually with the idea of repeated change, or of periodical return; it applies to wandering tribes of men, and to many birds and animals. *Emigrate* and *immigrate* carry the idea of a permanent change of residence to some other country or some distant region; the two words are used distinctively of human beings, and apply to the same person and the same act, according to the side from which the action is viewed. A person *emigrates from* the land he leaves, and *immigrates to* the land where he takes up his abode.

em·i·gra·tion (em′ə·grā′shən) *n.* **1** The act of emigrating. **2** Emigrants collectively.

Emigration Road The Oregon Trail.

é·mi·gré (em′ə·grā, *Fr.* ā·mē·grā′) An emigrant; especially one who fled during the French or Russian revolutions. [<F, pp. of *émigrer* <L *emigrare* EMIGRATE]

E·mil (ā′məl, ē′məl, em′əl) A masculine personal name. Also **E·mile** (ā·mēl′), *Fr.* **É·mile** (ā·mēl′). [<L, ? <Gmc., labor]

E·mil·ia–Ro·ma·gna (ā·mē′lyä·rō·mä′nyä) A region of north central Italy; 8,542 square miles; capital, Bologna. Formerly **E·mi′lia.**

Em·i·ly (em′ə·lē) A feminine personal name. Also *Fr.* **É·mi·lie** (ā·mē·lē′), *Ger.* **E·mi·li·e** (e·mē′lē·ə), *Ital., Pg., Sp.* **E·mi·lia** (ā·mē′·lyä). [<L, ? <Gmc., labor]

é·min·cé (ā·maṅ·sā′) *n. French* Meat cut into thin slices, cooked, and served with a sauce.

em·i·nence (em′ə·nəns) *n.* **1** A lofty place; a hill. **2** An exalted rank, condition, or degree. **3** A title of honor applied to cardinals of the Roman Catholic Church. Also **em′i·nen·cy.** See synonyms under FAME, HEIGHT. [<L *eminentia* <*e-* forth + *minere* project]

em·i·nent (em′ə·nənt) *adj.* **1** High in station, merit, or esteem; distinguished; prominent; conspicuous: an *eminent* scholar. **2** Rising above other things; high in relative position; lofty: an *eminent* tower. [<L *eminens, -entis,* ppr. of *eminere* project] —**em′i·nent·ly** *adv.*

Synonyms: conspicuous, distinguished, famed, famous, known, lofty, noted, prominent, remarkable, signal. See CELEBRATED, HIGH, ILLUSTRIOUS, PARAMOUNT. *Antonyms*: common, commonplace, inferior, low, mean, ordinary.

eminent domain *Law* The right or power of the state to take private property for public use or to control its use, usually at an adequate compensation.

e·mir (ə·mir′) *n.* **1** Any independent prince or commander in the Moslem East, especially in Arabia. **2** A descendant of Mohammed through Fatima, his favorite daughter. **3** A high Turkish official. Also spelled *emeer.* [<Arabic *amīr* ruler]

e·mir·ate (ə·mir′it) *n.* The jurisdiction of an emir.

em·is·sar·y (em′ə·ser′ē) *n. pl.* **·sar·ies** **1** A person sent on a mission as an agent or representative of a government, as to negotiate or gather information. **2** A secret agent; spy. **3** *Archaic* A channel, as for water: also **em·is·sa·ri·um** (em′ə·sā′rē·əm). **4** *Archaic* An excretory or connecting canal in the body. See synonyms under SPY. —*adj.* Sent forth or out. [<L *emissarius* <*emittere.* See EMIT.]

e·mis·sion (i·mish′ən) *n.* **1** The act of emitting or that which is emitted. **2** *Electronics* The ejection of electrons from the heated cathode or filament of a vacuum tube. **3** *Med.* A discharge of body fluids, especially semen.

[<L *emissio, -onis* <*emittere.* See EMIT.]
emission spectrum *Physics* The spectrum of a substance indicating the type of radiation which it emits: distinguished from *absorption spectrum.*
e·mis·sive (i·mis′iv) *adj.* Sending or sent out or forth; emitting.
emissive power *Physics* The rate at which a body at a given temperature will radiate energy per unit of surface area.
em·is·siv·i·ty (em′ə·siv′ə·tē) *n. Physics* Emissive power or rate; specifically, the total emissive power of a radiating surface, expressed as a ratio to that of a black body of identical area and temperature.
e·mit (i·mit′) *v.t.* **e·mit·ted, e·mit·ting** **1** To send or give out; discharge. **2** To utter (sounds, oaths, etc.). **3** To promulgate, as a law or decree. **4** To put into circulation, as paper money. [<L *emittere* <*ex-* out + *mittere* send] —**e·mit′ter** *n.*
Em·ma (em′ə; *Fr.* e·mȧ′, *Ger.* em′ä, *Ital.* em′mä) A feminine personal name. [<Gmc., grandmother]
—**Emma, Queen,** 982–1052, wife of Ethelred the Unready; after his death she married Canute; mother of Edward the Confessor.
Em·man·u·el (i·man′yōō·əl, *Fr.* ā·mȧ·nü·el′) A masculine personal name. See also EMANUEL, IMMANUEL. [<Hebrew, God with us]
Em·me·line (em′ə·līn, -lēn) See EMELINE.
em·men·a·gog (i·men′ə·gôg, -gog) *n.* Any medicine or substance that stimulates or renews the menstrual flow. Also **em·men′a·gogue.** [<Gk. *emmēna* the menses < *agōgos* leading <*agein* lead]
em·mer (em′ər) *n.* Amelcorn. [< dial. G]
em·met (em′it) *n. Archaic* An ant. [OE *ǣmete.* Related to ANT.]
Em·met (em′it), **Robert,** 1778–1803, Irish patriot; hanged by the British.
em·me·tro·pi·a (em′ə·trō′pē·ə) *n.* The normal state of the eye as regards the power of accommodation or refraction. [<NL <Gk. *emmetros* <*en-* in + *metron* measure + *ōps* eye] —**em′me·trop′ic** (-trop′ik) *adj.*
Em·my (em′ē) *n.* A gold-plated statuette awarded annually since 1949 by the Academy of Television Arts and Sciences for exceptional performances and productions on television. [Alter. of *immy,* short for *image* orthicon tube. See under ORTHICON.]
em·o·din (em′ə·din) *n. Chem.* An orange-red crystalline glucoside, $C_{15}H_{10}O_5$, obtained from rhubarb, senna, aloes, and various other related plants: used as a cathartic. [<NL *(Rheum) emodi,* a species of rhubarb (<Gk. *ēmōdos* Himalaya) + -IN]
em·ol·les·cence (em′ə·les′əns) *n.* The state or degree of softness in which a body begins to lose its shape, as in melting; incipient fusion. [<E- + L *mollescere* become soft + -ENCE]
e·mol·li·ate (i·mol′ē·āt) *v.t.* **·at·ed, ·at·ing** *Obs.* To render soft; make effeminate.
e·mol·lient (i·mol′yənt, -ē·ənt) *adj.* Softening or relaxing; soothing. —*n. Med.* A softening or soothing external application. Also *mollient.* [<L *emolliens, -entis,* ppr. of *emollire* <*ex-* thoroughly + *mollire* soften <*mollis* soft]
e·mol·u·ment (i·mol′yə·mənt) *n.* **1** The compensation, salary, fees, perquisites, advantage, gain, or profit arising from an office or employment. **2** General advantage; gain; profit. See synonyms under PROFIT. [<L *emolimentum* <*emolere* <*ex-* out + *molere* grind]
e·mote (i·mōt′) *v.i.* **e·mot·ed, e·mot·ing** *Colloq.* To exhibit an exaggerated emotion, as in acting a melodramatic role: a humorous use. [Back formation <EMOTION]
e·mo·tion (i·mō′shən) *n.* **1** Any strong manifestation or disturbance of the conscious or the unconscious mind, typically involuntary and often leading to complex bodily changes and forms of behavior; an act or state of excited feeling: *emotions* of fear. **2** The power of feeling, with or without a corresponding trend of activities; sensibility; sentiment. **3** *Obs.* Unusual or disturbed motion. See synonyms under FEELING, SENSATION, WARMTH. [<L *emotio, -onis* <*emovere* <*ex-* out + *movere* move]
e·mo·tion·al (i·mō′shən·əl) *adj.* **1** Of, pertaining to, or expressive of emotion. **2** Having capacity for emotion. **3** Moving or suited to move the feelings or passions: an *emotional* poem. —**e·mo′tion·al·ly** *adv.*
e·mo·tion·al·ism (i·mō′shən·əl·iz′əm) *n.* **1** The expression of emotion. **2** The disposition or tendency to see and judge all things from an emotional point of view. **3** The act or habit of appealing to the emotions.
e·mo·tion·al·ist (i·mō′shən·əl·ist) *n.* **1** One whose feelings are easily excited or wrought upon. **2** One who aims to influence others through the emotions. **3** In ethics, one who bases his theory of conduct on the emotions, as in making pleasure or happiness the supreme end. **4** One who uses emotional methods in art, in religion, or in the promotion of any project.
e·mo·tion·al·i·ty (i·mō′shən·al′ə·tē) *n.* The state or quality of being emotional.
e·mo·tion·al·ize (i·mō′shən·əl·īz′) *v.t.* **·ized, ·iz·ing** To make emotional; treat in an emotional manner. —**e·mo′tion·al·i·za′tion** *n.*
e·mo·tive (i·mō′tiv) *adj.* **1** Tending to excite emotion. **2** Expressing or characterized by or inducing emotion: *emotive* eloquence. —**e·mo′tive·ly** *adv.* —**e·mo′tive·ness, e·mo·tiv·i·ty** (ē′mō·tiv′ə·tē) *n.*
em·pale (im·pāl′) See IMPALE.
em·pan·el (im·pan′əl), etc. See IMPANEL, etc.
em·path·ic (em·path′ik) *adj.* Characterized by or pertaining to empathy. —**em·path′i·cal·ly** *adv.*
em·pa·thize (em′pə·thīz) *v.t.* & *v.i.* **·thized, ·thiz·ing** To regard with or feel empathy.
em·pa·thy (em′pə·thē) *n.* **1** *Psychol.* A strong imaginative or emotional projection of one's self into a work of art; esthetic appreciation. **2** *Psychoanal.* The mental identification of the ego with the character and experiences of another person. [<Gk. *empatheia* <*en-* in + *pathos* feeling; trans. of G *Einfühlung*]
Em·ped·o·cles (em·ped′ə·klēz) Greek poet and philosopher of the fifth century B.C.
em·pen·nage (em′pi·nij, *Fr.* äṅ·pe·näzh′) *n. Aeron.* The tail parts of an airplane, used to steer or steady it. See illustration under AIRPLANE. [<F <*empenner* provide with feathers <*em-* in (<L *in-*) + *penne* <L *pinna* feather]
em·per·or (em′pər·ər) *n.* **1** The sovereign of an empire. **2** One of various moths, as the **emperor moth** *(Samia cecropia),* or butterflies, as the **purple emperor** *(Apatura iris),* or the **tawny emperor** *(Asterocampa clyton),* etc. [<OF *empereor* <L *imperator* commander < *imperare* order]
emperor goose A small goose of the Alaskan coasts *(Philacte canagica)* with barred plumage, a short neck, and short wings.
em·per·y (em′pər·ē) *n. pl.* **·per·ies** *Poetic* **1** Sovereignty; dominion. **2** The domain of an emperor. [OF *emperie* <L *imperium* empire]
em·pha·sis (em′fə·sis) *n. pl.* **·ses** (-sēz) **1** A stress laid upon some word or words in speaking or reading: indicated in print or writing by underscoring or underlining, by italics, or by accent marks. **2** The act of emphasizing; distinctiveness; stress of thought or importance; significance. [<L <Gk. <*en-* in + *phainein* show]
em·pha·size (em′fə·sīz) *v.t.* **·sized, ·siz·ing** To make especially distinct or prominent; put stress on; give emphasis to.
em·phat·ic (im·fat′ik) *adj.* **1** Speaking or spoken with emphasis or stress. **2** Conveying or expressing emphasis; habitually forceful and decisive; striking; forcible; positive. Also **em·phat′i·cal.** [<Gk. *emphatikos,* var. of *emphantikos* <*emphainein.* See EMPHASIS.] —**em·phat′i·cal·ly** *adv.*
em·phy·se·ma (em′fə·sē′mə, -zē′mə) *n. Pathol.* A puffed condition of body tissues or organs caused by the infiltration of air; especially, a condition of the lungs marked by difficulty in breathing because of enlargement and consequent loss of elasticity of the alveoli, or air sacs. [<NL <Gk. *emphysēma* an inflation <*en-* in + *physaein* blow] —**em′phy·sem′a·tous** (-sem′ə·təs, -zēm′ə·təs) *adj.*
em·phy·teu·sis (em′fə·tyōō′sis) *n.* In ancient Roman law, a perpetual lease of lands and tenements in consideration of annual rent and improvements thereon; an improving lease. [<LL <Gk. <*en-* in + *phyteuein* plant]
em·piece·ment (em·pēs′mənt) *n.* In sewing, an insertion.
em·pire (em′pīr) *n.* **1** A state, or union of states, governed by an emperor. **2** A union of dispersed territories, dominions, colonies, states, and unrelated peoples under one foreign rule. **3** Wide and supreme dominion. —**Holy Roman Empire** Certain portions of the old Roman Empire of the West together with the Frankish possessions of Charlemagne, who was crowned emperor by Pope Leo III at Rome in 800. In 962 the real Holy Roman-German Empire began. It became extinct in 1806, when Francis II resigned the elective imperial crown for the hereditary one of Austria. [<F <L *imperium* rule, authority]
Em·pire (em′pīr) *adj.* **1** Of, belonging to, or characterizing an empire, especially the French Empire, 1804–15, under Napoleon I. **2** Designating a simple and dignified type of furniture introduced at the time of the first French Empire by Percier, Fontaine, and others. **3** (also, *Fr.* äṅ·pēr′) Designating a type of woman's costume of the first French Empire, marked by high waistline, short décolleté bodice, and straight, loose skirt.
Empire Day Former name of COMMONWEALTH DAY.
Empire State Nickname of NEW YORK.
em·pir·ic (em·pir′ik) *n.* **1** One who uses trial-and-error methods; one who believes experiment is the source of knowledge. **2** *Archaic* A quack or charlatan. —*adj.* Empirical. [<L *empiricus* <Gk. *empeirikos* < *empeiria* experience <*en-* in + *peira* a trial]
Em·pir·ic (em·pir′ik) *n.* Among the ancient Greeks, one of a school of physicians maintaining that experiment was the one requisite.
em·pir·i·cal (em·pir′i·kəl) *adj.* **1** Relating to or based on experience or observation. **2** Relying entirely or to excess upon direct, repeated, and uncritically accepted experience: opposed to metempirical. **3** Given to or skilled in experiments. **4** *Archaic* Generalizing hastily from limited facts; hence, befitting a charlatan. Also **em·pir′ic.** —**em·pir′i·cal·ly** *adv.*
em·pir·i·cism (em·pir′ə·siz′əm) *n.* **1** Empirical character, method, or practice. **2** Belief in experiment and repudiation of theory; quackery. **3** *Philos.* The doctrine that all knowledge is derived from experience through the senses. —**em·pir′i·cist** *n.*
em·place·ment (im·plās′mənt) *n.* **1** The position assigned to guns or to a battery within a fortification; also, a gun platform or the like. **2** A setting in place; location. [<F]
em·plane (im·plān′) *v.t.* & *v.i.* To board or put aboard an airplane.
em·plas·tic (im·plas′tik) *adj.* Glutinous. —*n.* **1** A constipating medicine. **2** An adhesive substance. [<Gk. *emplastikos* <*em-* in + *plassein* mold, form]
em·ploy (im·ploi′) *v.t.* **1** To hire; engage the services of. **2** To provide work and livelihood for; have as employees. **3** To make use of as a means or instrument: to *employ* cunning. **4** To devote or apply: to *employ* one's energies in research. —*n.* The state of being employed; service. [<F *employer* <L *in-* in + *plicare* fold. Doublet of IMPLY.] —**em·ploy′a·ble** *adj.* —**em·ployed′** *adj.*

Synonyms (verb): engage, engross, hire, use. In general terms it may be said that to *employ* is to devote to one's purpose, to *use* is to render subservient to one's purpose; what is *used* is viewed as more absolutely an instrument than what is *employed*; a merchant *employs* a clerk; he *uses* pen and paper; hence, *use,* as applied to persons, inclines to the derogatory sense; as, The conspirators *used* him as a go-between. That which is *used* is often consumed in the *using*; as, We *used* twenty tons of coal last winter; in such cases we could not substitute *employ.* A person may be *employed* in his own work or in that of another; in the latter case the service is always understood to be for pay. In this connection *employ* is a word of more dignity than *hire*; a general is *employed* in his country's service; a mercenary adventurer is *hired* to fight; *hire* now implies that the one *hired* works directly and primarily for the pay. See OCCUPY, RETAIN.
em·ploy·ee (im·ploi′ē, em′ploi·ē′) *n.* One who works for another in return for a salary, wages, or other consideration. Also **em·ploy′e.**
em·ploy·er (im·ploi′ər) *n.* **1** One who employs. **2** A person or business firm that employs workmen, servants, etc., for wages.
em·ploy·ment (im·ploi′mənt) *n.* **1** The act of employing, or the state of being employed. **2** The work upon which one is or may be engaged; occupation; trade. See synonyms under BUSINESS, EXERCISE, WORK.

employment agency An office or bureau that puts employers in contact with people seeking work: also **employment bureau.**

em·poi·son (em·poi′zən) *v.t.* **1** To envenom; corrupt. **2** *Obs.* To poison. —**em·poi′son·ment** *n.*

Em·po·ri·a (em·pôr′ē·ə, -pō′rē·ə) A city in eastern Kansas.

em·po·ri·um (em·pôr′ē·əm, -pō′rē-) *n. pl.* **·ri·ums** or **·ri·a** (-ē·ə) **1** A store carrying general merchandise. **2** The chief mart of a wide territory. **3** A bazaar. [< L < Gk. *emporion* a market < *emporos* merchant, traveler < *en-* in + *poros* journey]

em·pov·er·ish (im·pov′ər·ish) See IMPOVERISH.

em·pow·er (im·pou′ər) *v.t.* **1** To authorize; delegate authority to. **2** To enable; permit. See synonyms under PERMIT.

em·press (em′pris) *n.* **1** A woman who rules an empire. **2** The wife or widow of an emperor. [< OF *emperesse,* fem. of *emperere,* var. of *empereor* EMPEROR]

Empress Augusta Bay An inlet of the South Pacific in SW Bougainville, Solomon Islands.

em·presse·ment (äṅ·pres·mäṅ′) *n. French* Animated earnestness; demonstrative cordiality.

em·prise (em·prīz′) *n. Archaic* **1** Enterprise; adventure. **2** Chivalric or martial prowess. Also **em·prize′**. [< OF, orig. pp. of *emprendre* undertake < L *in-* in + *prehendere* take]

emp·tings (emp′tingz) *n. pl. U.S.* The lees of beer, etc., used as yeast. Also **emp′tins.** [< obs. *empt* empty]

emp·ty (emp′tē) *adj.* **·ti·er, ·ti·est 1** Having nothing within; containing nothing; void; vacant: often with reference to particular, usual, or proper contents, as food or inhabitants: an *empty* pitcher. **2** Without force, weight, value, or meaning: *empty* protestations, *empty* promises. **3** Without substance or significance; hollow; unreal; unsubstantial. **4** Destitute of intelligence, ideas, manners, etc.; senseless; inane; frivolous; contemptible: *empty* talk. **5** Being without supplies, etc.; unsupplied; unsatisfied; unfed. **6** Not carrying or drawing anything: *empty* hands. **7** Having no fruit; barren. **8** *Colloq.* Hungry. See synonyms under BLANK, FLAT[1], VACANT, VAIN. —*v.* **emp·tied, emp·ty·ing** *v.t.* **1** To make empty. **2** To transfer the contents of as if to another place or container: He *emptied* the bucket onto the fire. **3** To transfer (the contents) as if to another place or container: He *emptied* the milk into the street. **4** To remove (the contents): often with *out*: He *emptied* out the water. —*v.i.* **5** To become empty. **6** To discharge or pour out: The river *empties* into the bay. —*n. pl.* **emp·ties** A boat, barge, freight car, tank, etc., containing or transporting nothing. [OE *ǣmetig* < *ǣmetta* leisure] —**emp′ti·ly** *adv.* —**emp′ti·ness** *n.*

emp·ty-hand·ed (emp′tē·han′did) *adj.* Having or carrying nothing.

emp·ty-head·ed (emp′tē·hed′id) *adj.* Without sense or discretion; foolish; brainless.

Empty Quarter The English name for the RUB AL KHALI.

em·pur·ple (em·pûr′pəl) *v.t.* **·pled, ·pling** To tinge or color with purple: also spelled *impurple.*

em·py·e·ma (em′pi·ē′mə, -pī-) *n. Pathol.* A collection or formation of pus, especially in the pleural cavity, often associated with various bacterial infections. [< NL < Gk. *empyēma* suppuration < *en-* in + *pyon* pus]

em·pyr·e·al (em·pir′ē·əl, em′pə·rē′əl, -pī-) *adj.* **1** Of or pertaining to the highest region of heaven; celestial. **2** Most highly refined; originally, formed of light or fire. —*n.* The empyrean. [< Med. L *empyreus* < Gk. *empyros* in the fire < *en-* in + *pyr* fire]

em·py·re·an (em′pə·rē′ən, -pī-) *n.* **1** The ancient supposed region of pure fire; the highest heaven. **2** Hence, the abode of God and the angels. **3** The upper sky. Also **em′py·rae′um.** —*adj.* Empyreal.

em·py·reu·ma (em′pə·rōō′mə, -pī-) *n.* The disagreeable odor produced when organic substances are decomposed by heat in a closed vessel. [< Gk. *empyreuma* covered live coal < *empyros.* See EMPYREAL.] —**em·py·reu·mat·ic** (em′pə·rōō·mat′ik) or **·i·cal** *adj.*

Ems (emz, *Ger.* āms) **1** A resort town in Rhineland-Palatinate, western Germany: also **Bad Ems. 2** A river of NW Germany, flowing 250 miles NE to the North Sea.

e·mu (ē′myōō) *n.* A large ostrichlike Australian bird (genus *Dromiceius*), with neck and most of the head feathered: also spelled *emeu, emew.* [Prob. < Pg. *ema* ostrich]

EMU
(About 5 feet tall; second largest living bird)

em·u·late (em′yə·lāt) *v.t.* **·lat·ed, ·lat·ing 1** To try to equal or surpass. **2** To rival with some success. [< L *aemulatus,* pp. of *aemulari* rival < *aemulus* jealous] —**em′u·la′tive** *adj.* —**em′u·la′tive·ly** *adv.* —**em′u·la′tor** *n.*

em·u·la·tion (em′yə·lā′shən) *n.* **1** Effort or ambition to equal or excel another in any act or quality. **2** *Obs.* Selfish rivalry and strife.

Synonyms: ambition, competition, opposition, rivalry. We speak of *competition* in business, *emulation* in scholarship, *rivalry* in love, politics, etc.; *emulation* of excellence, success, achievement; *competition* for a prize. *Competition* may be friendly; *rivalry* is commonly hostile. See AMBITION, COMPETITION.

e·mul·gent (i·mul′jənt) *adj.* Milking out or straining. —*n.* Any preparation to aid an excretory organ or duct. [< L *emulgens, -entis,* ppr. of *emulgere* < *ex-* out + *mulgere* milk]

em·u·lous (em′yə·ləs) *adj.* **1** Eager or striving to equal or excel another; competitive. **2** *Obs.* Envious; jealous. —**em′u·lous·ly** *adv.* —**em′u·lous·ness** *n.*

e·mul·si·fy (i·mul′sə·fī) *v.t.* **·fied, ·fy·ing** To make or convert into an emulsion. —**e·mul′si·fi·ca′tion** *n.* —**e·mul′si·fi′er** *n.*

e·mul·sion (i·mul′shən) *n.* **1** A liquid mixture in which a fatty or resinous substance is suspended in minute globules, as butter in milk. **2** Any milky liquid. **3** *Phot.* A substance, as a silver salt, held in suspension in collodion or gelatin, and used to coat dry plates. **4** *Physics* A colloid system, consisting of the globules or particles of one liquid finely dispersed in another. See COLLOID [< LL *emulsio, -onis* < L *emulgere.* See EMULGENT.]

e·mul·sive (i·mul′siv) *adj.* **1** Capable of emulsifying. **2** Of the nature of an emulsion; softening. **3** Producing oil on being pressed.

e·munc·to·ry (i·mungk′tər·ē) *adj.* Serving to discharge excrementitious matter. —*n. pl.* **·ries** An organ for removing waste matter, as the kidneys, intestines, etc. [< NL *emunctorius* < L *emunctorium* a snuffer < *emungere* < *ex-* out + *mungere* blow the nose]

em·yd (em′id) *n.* A fresh-water tortoise of North America *(Emys blandingii)* having a black carapace covered with pale yellow spots. Also called *Blanding's turtle.* Also **em·yde** (em′īd). [< Gk. *emys, emydos*]

en (en) *n.* **1** The name of the fourteenth letter in the English alphabet, written N or n. **2** *Printing* A space half the width of an em.

en-[1] *prefix* Forming transitive verbs: **1** (from nouns) To cover or surround with; to place into or upon: *encircle.* **2** (from adjectives and nouns) To make; cause to be or to resemble: *enable, enfeeble.* **3** (from verbs) Often with simple intensive force, or used to form transitive verbs from intransitives: *enact, encompass.* Also, **em-** before *b, p,* and sometimes *m,* as in *embark.* Many words in *en-* have variant forms in *in-* because of the confusion between Old French *en-,* Latin *in-,* and native English *in-.* Compare IN-[2] and IN-[3]. [< OF < L *in-* < *in* in, into]

en-[2] *prefix* In, into; on: *endemic.* Also: *el-* before *l,* as in *ellipse; em-* before *b, m, p, ph,* as in *embolism, empathy; er-* before *r,* as in *errhine.* [< Gk. *en-* < *en* in, into]

-en[1] *suffix* Forming verbs: **1** (from adjectives) Cause to be; become: *deepen, harden.* **2** (from nouns) Cause to have; gain: *hearten, strengthen.* [OE *-nian*]

-en[2] *suffix of adjectives* Made of; resembling: *woolen, brazen.* [OE]

-en[3] *suffix* Used in the past participles of many strong verbs: *broken, beaten.* [OE]

-en[4] *suffix* Used in the plural of certain nouns: *oxen, children.* [OE *-an,* plural ending of the weak declension]

-en[5] *suffix* Small; little: *chicken, kitten.* [OE]

en·a·ble (in·ā′bəl) *v.t.* **·bled, ·bling 1** To make able; give means or power to. **2** To make possible or more easy.

en·a·bling act (in·ā′bling) *Law* **1** An act enabling persons or corporations to do what before was not allowed. **2** *U.S.* A Congressional act allowing the people of a territory to prepare a constitution for statehood.

en·act (in·akt′) *v.t.* **1** To make into a law. **2** To carry out in action; perform. **3** To represent in or as in a play. —**en·act′a·ble** *adj.* —**en·ac′tor** *n.*

en·ac·tive (in·ak′tiv) *adj.* Tending or having efficacy to enact or establish; enacting: the *enactive* clause of a bill.

en·act·ment (in·akt′mənt) *n.* **1** A law enacted; a statute. **2** The act of establishing a law. See synonyms under LAW.

en·ac·to·ry (in·ak′tər·ē) *adj.* Connected with the enactment of law: sometimes opposed to *declaratory,* and then meaning that the law does not simply interpret another law.

en·ac·ture (in·ak′chər) *n. Obs.* An action; effect; fulfilment.

en·a·lid (en′ə·lid) *n. Bot.* A plant growing on the sea bottom, as eelgrass. [< Gk. *enalios* (< *en-* in + *hals, halos* the sea) + ID[1]]

en·al·la·ge (en·al′ə·jē) *n.* In rhetoric, the use of one part of speech, gender, etc., for another. [< L < Gk. *enallagē* exchange < *en-* in + *allassein* change]

en·am·el (in·am′əl) *n.* **1** A semi-opaque, vitreous material that is applied by fusion to gold, silver, copper, or other metals, or to porcelain, either as a decoration in colors or to form a surface for encaustic painting; also, as a lining for culinary and chemical vessels. **2** A work executed in such material: a fine cloisonné *enamel.* **3** One of various glossy lacquers or varnishes used for leather, paper, etc. **4** A kind of cosmetic or paint for the face, supposed to imitate exactly the natural gloss of the complexion. **5** *Anat.* The layer of hard, glossy, calcareous material forming the exposed outer covering of the teeth and protecting the dentine. —*v.t.* **·eled** or **·elled, ·el·ing** or **·el·ling 1** To cover or inlay, with enamel. **2** To surface with or as with enamel. **3** To adorn with different colors, as if with enamel. [< AF *enamyller* < *en-* on + *amayl,* OF *esmail* enamel < Gmc.] —**en·am′el·er, en·am′el·ler** *n.* —**en·am′el·ist, en·am′el·list** *n.*

en·am·el·ing (in·am′əl·ing) *n.* **1** The art or occupation of one who enamels. **2** The ornamentation or coating of enamel. Also **en·am′el·ling.**

◆en·am·el·ware (in·am′əl·wâr′) *n.* Enameled kitchen utensils.

en·am·or (in·am′ər) *v.t.* To inspire with ardent love: used chiefly in the past participle, and followed by *of* or *with.* Also *Brit.* **en·am′our.** [< OF *enamourer* < *en-* in (< L *in-*) + *amour* love < L *amor*] —**en·am′ored** *adj.*

en·an·ti·o·mer (en·an′tē·ə·mər) *n.* Enantiomorph. —**en·an·ti·o·mer·ic** (en·an′tē·ə·mer′ik) *adj.*

en·an·ti·o·morph (en·an′tē·ə·môrf′) *n.* Either of a pair of molecular or crystalline forms which are mirror images of each other. —**en·an′ti·o·morph′ism** *n.* —**en·an′ti·o·mor′phous** *adj.* [< Gk. *enantios* opposite + *morphē* form]

en·an·ti·op·a·thy (en·an′tē·op′ə·thē) *n.* **1** *Pathol.* A morbid condition or disease which is hostile to or preventive of another. **2** The curing of one disease by inducing another. Also **en·an·ti·o·path·i·a** (en·an′tē·ə·path′ē·ə). [< Gk. *enantios* opposite + -PATHY] —**en·an′ti·o·path′ic** (-tē·ə·path′ik) *adj.*

en ar·rière (äṅ nȧ·ryâr′) *French* In the rear; behind.

en·ar·thro·sis (en′är·thrō′sis) *n. Anat.* An articulation in which the rounded head of a bone is received into a corresponding cavity; a ball-and-socket joint, as the hip joint. [< NL < Gk. *enarthrōsis* < *enarthros* jointed < *en-* in + *arthron* a joint] —**en′ar·thro′di·al** (-dē·əl) *adj.*

e·nate (ē′nāt, i·nāt′) *adj.* **1** Growing out. **2** Related on the mother's side: distinguished from *agnate.* —*n.* A relative on the mother's side. [< L *enatus,* pp. of *enasci* < *ex-* out + *nasci* be born] **—e·nat·ic** (i·nat′ik) *adj.*

e·na·tion (i·nā′shən) *n. Bot.* An excessive development in plants, consisting in the formation of supplementary lobes or excrescences, usually on the upper surface of other organs, as scales on petals.

en a·vant (äṅ nȧ·väṅ′) *French* Forward; onward.

en bloc (äṅ blôk′) *French* In one piece; as a whole; in the lump.

en broche (äṅ brôsh′) *French* Served on skewers: quail *en broche.*

en·cae·ni·a (en·sē′nē·ə, -sēn′yə) See ENCENIA.

en·cage (in·kāj′) *v.t.* **·caged, ·cag·ing** To shut up in a cage: also spelled *incage.*

en·camp (in·kamp′) *v.i.* To go into camp; live in a camp. *—v.t.* To place in a camp.

en·camp·ment (in·kamp′mənt) *n.* **1** The act of pitching a camp. **2** A camp, or the persons occupying it.

en·car·nal·ize (in·kär′nəl·īz) *v.t.* **·ized, ·iz·ing 1** To invest with flesh and blood; to embody. **2** To make gross or sensual.

en·case (in·kās′) See INCASE.

en casse·role (äṅ kȧs·rôl′) *French* Prepared and served in a casserole.

en·caus·tic (en·kôs′tik) *adj.* **1** Painted and having the hues fixed by heat. **2** Painted in wax and burnt in. *—n.* The art of encaustic painting. [< L *encausticus* < Gk. *enkaustikos* < *en-* in + *kaiein* burn]

encaustic painting A method of painting statues or architectural details with hot, colored wax or with cold, colored wax later fused with hot irons.

en·cave (in·kāv′) *v.t.* **·caved, ·cav·ing** To put in or as in a cave.

-ence *suffix of nouns* Forming nouns of action, quality, state or condition from adjectives in *-ent,* as in *diffidence, prominence.* Compare -ENCY. See note under -ANCE. [< F *-ence* < L *-entia,* a suffix used to form nouns from present participles; or directly < L]

en·ceinte[1] (en·sānt′, *Fr.* äṅ·saṅt′) *adj.* With child; pregnant. [< F < LL *incincta,* pp. of *incingere* unbind < *in-* not + *cingere* bind]

en·ceinte[2] (en·sānt′, *Fr.* äṅ·saṅt′) *n.* **1** A girdle of works encircling a fortified place. **2** The place they encircle. **3** A close or precinct, as of an abbey or cathedral. [< F < *enceindre* < L *incingere* < *in-* on + *cingere* bind]

En·cel·a·dus (en·sel′ə·dəs) In Greek mythology, a giant who revolted against the gods; buried under Mt. Etna.

en·ce·ni·a (en·sē′nē·ə, -sēn′yə) *n. pl. (sometimes sing.)* **1** A ceremony at Oxford University, held every year in June, in commemoration of founders and benefactors. **2** A yearly celebration to commemorate the dedication of a temple or church, particularly of the Temple at Jerusalem. Also spelled *encaenia.* [< L *encaenia* < Gk. *enkainia* a feast of dedication < *en-* in + *kainos* new]

en·ce·phal·ic (en′sə·fal′ik) *adj.* **1** Of or pertaining to the encephalon. **2** Situated within the cranial cavity.

en·ceph·a·li·tis (en′sef·ə·lī′tis, en·sef′-) *n. Pathol.* Inflammation of the brain; brain fever. **—en′ceph·a·lit′ic** (-lit′ik) *adj.*

encephalitis le·thar·gi·ca (li·thär′ji·kə) *Pathol.* An acute, frequently epidemic, viral encephalitis, deeply involving the central nervous system, and accompanied by widely varying symptoms, including fever, lethargy, and numerous sensory disturbances. Also called *sleeping sickness.*

en·ceph·a·li·za·tion (en·sef′ə·lə·zā′shən, -lī·zā′-) *n. Biol.* **1** The developmental processes resulting in the formation of the head. **2** The gradual association of various physiological functions, sensory and motor, with localized areas in the brain.

encephalo- *combining form* Brain: *encephalogram.* Also, before vowels, **encephal-.** [< Gk. *enkephalos* brain < *en-* in + *kephalē* head]

en·ceph·a·lo·cele (en·sef′ə·lə·sēl′) *n. Pathol.* Hernia of the brain, usually through a traumatic or congenital fissure in the skull.

en·ceph·a·lo·di·al·y·sis (en·sef′ə·lō·dī·al′ə·sis) *n. Pathol.* Softening of the brain. [< ENCEPHALO- + Gk. *dialysis* dissolution]

en·ceph·a·lo·gram (en·sef′ə·lə·gram′) *n.* An X-ray photograph of the brain, obtained by replacing the cerebral fluid by air, oxygen, or helium. **—en·ceph′a·log′ra·phy** (-log′rə·fē) *n.*

en·ceph·a·lol·o·gy (en·sef′ə·lol′ə·jē) *n.* The study of the anatomy, physiology, and pathology of the brain. **—en·ceph′a·lol′o·gist** *n.*

en·ceph·a·lo·ma (en·sef′ə·lō′mə) *n. pl.* **·ma·ta** (-mə·tə) *Pathol.* A growth upon the brain; a brain tumor.

en·ceph·a·lo·ma·la·ci·a (en·sef′ə·lō·mə·lā′shē·ə) *n. Pathol.* Morbid softening of the brain. [< ENCEPHALO- + Gk. *malakos* soft]

en·ceph·a·lo·my·e·li·tis (en·sef′ə·lō·mī′ə·lī′tis) *n. Pathol.* One of a number of inflammatory diseases affecting the brain and the spinal cord. [< ENCEPHALO- + MYEL(O)- + -ITIS]

en·ceph·a·lon (en·sef′ə·lon) *n. pl.* **·la** (-lə) *Anat.* The brain. Also **en·ceph′a·los.** [< NL < Gk. *enkephalos*] **—en·ceph′a·lous** *adj.*

en·ceph·a·lop·a·thy (en·sef′ə·lop′ə·thē) *n. Pathol.* Any degenerative disease of the brain. **—en·ceph·a·lo·path·ic** (en·sef′ə·lə·path′ik) *adj.*

en·chafe (in·chāf′) *v.t. Obs.* **1** To heat. **2** To irritate; stir up.

en·chain (in·chān′) *v.t.* **1** To bind with or as with a chain. **2** To hold fast or captive, as attention.

en·chain·ment (in·chān′mənt) *n.* The act of enchaining, or the state of being enchained.

en·chant (in·chant′, -chänt′) *v.t.* **1** To put a magic spell upon; bewitch. **2** To delight; charm completely. **3** *Obs.* To mislead; delude. See synonyms under CHARM[1], RAVISH. [< F *enchanter* < L *incantare* < *in-* in + *cantare* sing] **—en·chant′ing** *adj.* **—en·chant′ing·ly** *adv.*

en·chant·er (in·chan′tər, -chän′-) *n.* One who enchants; a magician.

en·chant·ment (in·chant′mənt, -chänt′-) *n.* **1** The act of enchanting, or the state of being enchanted. **2** Illusive charm.

en·chant·ress (in·chan′tris, -chän′-) *n.* **1** A sorceress. **2** An attractive or fascinating woman.

en·chase (en·chās′) *v.t.* **·chased, ·chas·ing 1** To incase in a setting, as a jewel in gold. **2** To enrich or decorate with engraved, chased, or inlaid work. **3** To engrave or work (figures, designs, etc.). [< F *enchâsser* < *en-* in (< L *in-*) + *châsse* case < L *capsa*]

en·chi·la·da (en′chi·lä′də) *n. SW U.S.* A Mexican dish composed of a rolled tortilla stuffed with meat or cheese and flavored with chile. [< Sp.]

en·chi·rid·i·on (en′kī·rid′ē·ən, -kə-) *n. pl.* **·i·ons** or **·i·a** (-ē·ə) A handbook; specifically, a manual of devotions. [< Gk. *encheiridion* < *en-* in + *cheir* hand + *-idion,* dim. suffix]

en·chon·dro·ma (en′kon·drō′mə) *n. pl.* **·ma·ta** (-mə·tə) or **·mas** *Pathol.* A cartilaginous tumor; chondroma. [< NL < Gk. *en-* in + CHONDR(O) + -OMA] **—en·chon·drom·a·tous** (en′kon·drom′ə·təs, -drō′mə-) *adj.*

en·cho·ri·al (en·kôr′ē·əl, -kō′rē-) *adj.* Peculiar to a country; native; popular; indigenous. Also **en·chor·ic** (en·kôr′ik, -kor′-), **en·cho′ri·ous, en′cho·ris′tic.** [< Gk. *enchorios* native < *en-* in + *chōra* country]

en·chy·ma (eng′kə·mə) *n. Physiol.* The formative juice of tissues elaborated from chyme. [< NL < Gk. *enchyma* infusion < *en-* in + *chyma* fluid < *cheein* pour]

en·ci·na (en·sē′nə) *n.* **1** The California live oak *(Quercus agrifolia).* **2** The live or holm oak *(Q. virginiana).* [< Sp. < LL *ilicina* < L *ilex, ilicis* an oak] **—en·ci′nal** (-sī′nəl) *adj.*

en·ci·pher (en·sī′fər) *v.t.* To convert (a message, report, etc.) from plain text into cipher.

en·cir·cle (en·sûr′kəl) *v.t.* **·cled, ·cling 1** To form a circle around. **2** To go around; make a circuit of. See synonyms under EMBRACE[1], TWIST. **—en·cir′cle·ment** *n.*

en·clasp (en·klasp′, -kläsp′) *v.t.* To hold in or as in a clasp; embrace.

en·clave (en′klāv) *n.* **1** Part of a country surrounded by the territory or possessions of a foreign government, as East Prussia after World War I. **2** A substance removed from its normal place in the body and enclosed in another organ or tissue. Also **en·cla′vure** (-klā′vyər). *—v.t.* **·claved, ·clav·ing** To surround, as a region or country, with the territories of another country. [< F < *enclaver* enclose < LL *inclavare* < *in-* in + *clavis* key]

en·clit·ic (en·klit′ik) *adj.* **1** *Gram.* Attached to and dependent on a preceding word in stress and accent, as *ge* in Greek and *-que* in Latin. Such forms yield their own accent and generally change that of the word to which they are attached, usually causing a secondary accent to be laid on the final syllable of the latter. The particles *de, ge,* and *te* in Greek and *-que, -ne,* and *-ve* in Latin are examples. **2** *Anat.* Having the planes of the fetal head inclined to those of the maternal pelvis: opposed to *synclitic.* *—n.* An unaccented word attached to a preceding accented word. [< LL *encliticus* < Gk. *enklitikos* < *en-* on + *klinein* lean]

en·close (in·klōz′) *v.t.* **·closed, ·clos·ing 1** To close in; fence in. **2** To place in a cover, envelope, etc. **3** To place, as a check, in a cover, envelope, etc., with a letter or message. **4** To surround; trap. Also spelled *inclose.* See synonyms under CIRCUMSCRIBE, EMBRACE[1]. [< EN-[1] + CLOSE, after OF *enclos,* pp. of *enclore* shut in] **—en·clos′er** *n.*

en·clo·sure (in·klō′zhər) *n.* **1** The act of enclosing, or the state of being enclosed. **2** An enclosed object or space. **3** That which encompasses, encloses, or shuts in, as a fence, wall, case, or wrapper. **4** The fencing in of land. **5** Clausura. Also spelled *inclosure.* See synonyms under BOUNDARY.

en·code (en·kōd′) *v.t.* **·cod·ed, ·cod·ing** To transform a message, document, etc., from plain text into code. **—en·cod′ing** *n.*

en·co·mi·ast (en·kō′mē·ast) *n.* A eulogist; panegyrist. **—en·co′mi·as′tic** or **·ti·cal** *adj.*

en·co·mi·um (en·kō′mē·əm) *n. pl.* **·mi·ums** or **·mi·a** (-me·ə) A formal expression of praise; a eulogy. See synonyms under EULOGY, PRAISE. [< L < Gk. *enkōmion* a eulogy]

en·com·pass (in·kum′pəs) *v.t.* **1** To form a circle around; encircle. **2** To surround, either protectively or hostilely; shut in. **3** *Obs.* To outwit. See synonyms under EMBRACE[1]. **—en·com′pass·ment** *n.*

en·core (äng′kôr, -kōr, än′-) *v.t.* **·cored, ·cor·ing** To call for a repetition of (a performance) or by (a performer). *—n.* **1** The call for a repetition, as of some part of a performance. **2** The repetition itself. *—adv.* Again; once more. [< F]

en·coun·ter (in·koun′tər) *n.* **1** A coming together, especially when casual or unexpected. **2** A hostile meeting, contest; battle. **3** *Obs.* Manner of meeting; address. See synonyms under BATTLE, COLLISION. *—v.t.* **1** To meet accidentally; come upon. **2** To meet in conflict; face in battle. **3** To be faced with (opposition, difficulties, etc.). *—v.i.* **4** To meet accidentally or in battle. See synonyms under ATTACK. [< OF *encontrer* < LL *incontrare* < *in-* in + *contra* against]

en·cour·age (in·kûr′ij) *v.t.* **·aged, ·ag·ing 1** To inspire with courage, hope, or resolution. **2** To help or foster; be favorable toward. [< OF *encoragier* < *en-* in (< L *in-*) + *corage* COURAGE] **—en·cour′ag·er** *n.*

Synonyms: animate, arouse, cheer, countenance, embolden, excite, forward, hearten, impel, inspire, inspirit, instigate, promote, prompt, rally, reassure, stimulate. See ABET, AID, CHERISH, CONSOLE[1], HELP, PROMOTE.

en·cour·age·ment (in·kûr′ij·mənt) *n.* **1** The act of encouraging, or the state of being encouraged; incitement; stimulation. **2** That which encourages.

en·cour·ag·ing (in·kûr′ij·ing) *adj.* Giving, or tending to give, courage or confidence. See synonyms under AUSPICIOUS. **—en·cour′ag·ing·ly** *adv.*

en·crim·son (en·krim′zən) *v.t.* To make crimson; redden.

en·cri·nite (en′krə·nīt) *n. Paleontol.* A fossil crinoid, especially one with cylindrical stem and developed arms. Also *crinite.* [< NL *Encrinus,* name of the genus (< Gk. *en-* in + *krinon* lily) + -ITE[1]]

en·croach (in·krōch′) *v.i.* **1** To intrude upon the possessions or rights of another by or as by stealth; trespass: with *on* or *upon.* **2** To advance or make inroads beyond the proper or usual limits, extent, etc.: The water is *encroaching* on the land. [< OF *encrochier* < *en-* in + *croc* a hook] **—en·croach′er** *n.*

en·croach·ment (in·krōch′mənt) *n.* **1** Entrance upon the rights or domain of another; especially, gradual intrusion. **2** That which is gained or seized by encroaching. See synonyms under AGGRESSION, ATTACK, INVASION.

en·crust (in·krust′), etc. See INCRUST, etc.

en·crypt (en·kript′) *v.t.* To convert (a message) from plain text into a cryptogram. **—en·cryp·tion** (en·krip′shən) *n.*

en·cul·tu·ra·tion (in·kul′chə·rā′shən) *n. Sociol.* The processes whereby individuals are conditioned by, adjusted to, and integrated with the cultural norms prevalent in the society of which they are members. — **en·cul'tu·ra'tive** *adj.*

en·cum·ber (in·kum'bər) *v.t.* **1** To obstruct or hinder in action or movement, as with a burden; impede. **2** To obstruct or make hard to use; block: The decks were *encumbered* with fallen spars. **3** To weigh down or burden with a duty, financial obligations, mortgages, etc. Also spelled *incumber.* See synonyms under HINDER[1]. [<OF *encombrer* <LL *incombrare* < *in-* in + *combrus* an obstacle]

en·cum·brance (in·kum'brəns) *n.* **1** That which encumbers. **2** *Law* Any lien or liability attached to real property. **3** One's wife, child, or dependent. Also spelled *incumbrance.* See synonyms under IMPEDIMENT, LOAD. [<OF *encombrance* < *encombrer.* See ENCUMBER.]

en·cum·branc·er (in·kum'brən·sər) *n.* One who holds a legal claim or burden on an estate: also spelled *incumbrancer.*

-ency *suffix of nouns* A variant of -ENCE, as in *decency, urgency,* used to form words expressing quality, state or condition, the earlier form being reserved largely for nouns of action. [<L *-entia*]

en·cyc·li·cal (en·sik'li·kəl, -sī'kli-) *adj.* Intended for general circulation; circular: said of letters: also **en·cyc'lic.** — *n. Eccl.* A circular letter addressed by the pope to all the bishops, dealing with matters affecting the church in general. [<LL *encyclicus* <Gk. *enkyklios* general, common < *en-* in + *kyklos* circle]

en·cy·clo·pe·di·a (en·sī'klə·pē'dē·ə) *n.* **1** A work containing information on all subjects, or exhaustive of one subject; a cyclopedia. **2** A work of this kind by some of the intellectual leaders of the French Revolution, the French Encyclopedists. **3** The entire circle of knowledge. Also **en·cy'clo·pae'di·a.** [<NL *encyclopaedia* <Gk. *enkyklopaideia,* a misreading for *enkyklios paideia* a general education]

en·cy·clo·pe·dic (en·sī'klə·pē'dik) *adj.* Pertaining to, of the character of, or proper to an encyclopedia; comprehending a wide range of topics. Also **en·cy'clo·pae'dic, en·cy'clo·pe'di·ac** or **en·cy·clo·pe·di·a·cal** (en·sī'klə·pi·dī'ə·kəl), **en·cy'clo·pe'di·al, en·cy'clo·pe'di·an.**

en·cy·clo·pe·dism (en·sī'klə·pē'diz·əm) *n.* **1** The work or art of compiling encyclopedias; an encyclopedic quality. **2** The doctrines of the French Encyclopedists. Also **en·cy'clo·pae'·dism.**

en·cy·clo·pe·dist (en·sī'klə·pē'dist) *n.* **1** A writer for or compiler of an encyclopedia. **2** One whose studies embrace all sciences. Also **en·cy'clo·pae'dist.** — **French Encyclopedist** One of the writers of the *Encyclopédie ou Dictionnaire raisonné des sciences, des arts, et des métiers* (1751–65): among these were the two editors, Diderot and D'Alembert, and a number of contributors, of whom Voltaire and Rousseau are the best known.

en·cyst (en·sist') *v.t.* & *v.i. Biol.* To envelop or become enclosed in a cyst, sac, etc. — **en·cyst'ed** *adj.*

en·cyst·ment (en·sist'mənt) *n. Biol.* A process by which certain protozoans, after retraction of the pseudopodia or other processes, become enclosed in a cyst, usually preparatory to reproduction, but also for protection against desiccation or putrefaction, in hibernation, etc. Also **en'cys·ta'tion.**

end (end) *n.* **1** The terminal point or part of any material object that has length. **2** The part of an object that is near either extremity. **3** The point in time at which some process ceases; hence, the conclusion of any work or operation. **4** The farthest limit of the space occupied by any extended object. **5** The purpose in view. **6** An inevitable or natural consequence. **7** The close of life. **8** A fragment; remnant. **9** A player stationed at the end of a line, as in football. **10** In archery, a unit of shooting toward a butt; in England, three arrows; in the United States, six. — **at loose ends** In an unsettled or confused state. — **in the end** At last. — **to the end that** In order that. — *v.t.* **1** To bring to a finish or termination; conclude. **2** To be the end of. **3** To cause the death of; kill. — *v.i.* **4** To come to an end. **5** To die. [OE *ende*]

Synonyms (noun): accomplishment, achievement, bound, boundary, cessation, close, completion, conclusion, consequence, consummation, design, effect, expiration, extent, extremity, finale, finis, finish, fulfilment, goal, intent, issue, limit, outcome, period, point, purpose, result, termination, terminus, tip, utmost, uttermost. The *end* is the terminal part of a material object that has length; the *extremity* is distinctively the terminal *point,* and may thus be but part of the *end* in the general sense of that word; the *extremity* is viewed as that which is most remote from some center, or some mean or standard position; the southern *end* of South America includes all Patagonia, the southern *extremity* or *point* is Cape Horn. *Tip* has nearly the same meaning as *extremity,* but is said of small or slight and tapering objects; as, the *tip* of the finger; *point* in such connections is said of that which is drawn out to exceeding fineness or sharpness, as the *point* of a needle, a fork, or a sword; *extremity* is said of something considerable; we do not speak of the *extremity* of a needle. A *goal* is an *end* sought or striven for, as in a race. For the figurative senses of *end* and its associated words, compare the synonyms for the verb END; also for AIM, CONSEQUENCE, DESIGN, EVENT, PURPOSE, REASON. *Antonyms*: see synonyms for BEGINNING.

Synonyms (verb): cease, close, complete, conclude, desist, expire, finish, quit, terminate, top. That *ends,* or is *ended,* of which there is no more, whether or not more was intended or needed; that is *closed, completed, concluded,* or *finished* which has come to an expected or appropriate end. A tumult in the audience may cause a speech to be *ended* when it is neither *closed, completed,* nor *finished,* nor, in the strict sense, *concluded.* An argument may be *closed* with nothing proved; when an argument is *concluded* all that is deemed necessary to prove the point has been stated. To *finish* is to do the last thing there is to do. To *terminate* may be to bring either to an arbitrary or to an appropriate end; as, He *terminated* his remarks abruptly; The spire *terminates* in a cross. A thing *stops* that comes to rest from motion; or the motion *stops* or *ceases* when the object comes to rest; *stop* frequently signifies to bring or come to a sudden and decided cessation of motion, progress, or action of any kind. Compare ABOLISH, CEASE, EFFECT, FINISH, TRANSACT. *Antonyms*: commence, found, inaugurate, initiate, institute, open, originate, start, undertake. Compare INSTITUTE *(verb).*

end–all (end'ôl') *n.* The end of everything or that which ends everything.

en·dam·age (en·dam'ij) *v.t.* **·aged, ·ag·ing** To cause damage to; injure.

en·dam·age·ment (en·dam'ij·mənt) *n. Obs.* Injury.

en·da·me·ba (en'də·mē'bə) *n.* Any of a genus *(Endamoeba)* of protozoan organisms, some species of which are parasitic on man, especially *E. histolytica,* a causative agent in dysentery and liver abscess: also spelled *entamoeba.* Also **en'da·moe'ba.** ◆ [<END(O)- + AMEBA]

en·dan·ger (en·dān'jər) *v.t.* To expose to danger.

en·dar·te·ri·tis (en·där'tə·rī'tis) *n. Pathol.* Inflammation of the endarterium.

en·dar·te·ri·um (en'där·tir'ē·əm) *n. Anat.* The innermost coat of an artery. [<NL <Gk. *endo-* within + *artēria* an artery]

end·brain (end'brān') *n.* The telencephalon.

end·brush (end'brush') *n. Physiol.* The tufted branching fibrils forming the termination of many nerve cells.

en·dear (in·dir') *v.t.* **1** To make dear or beloved. **2** *Obs.* To win or secure the affection of.

en·dear·ing (in·dir'ing) *adj.* **1** Making dear or beloved. **2** Manifesting affection; caressing. — **en·dear'ing·ly** *adv.*

en·dear·ment (in·dir'mənt) *n.* **1** Something, as an act, that expresses or attracts affection; an utterance of fondness; a caress. **2** The act of endearing, or the state of being endeared; hence, affection; love.

en·deav·or (in·dev'ər) *n.* An attempt or effort to do or attain something; earnest exertion for an end. — *v.t.* To make an effort to do or effect; try: usually with an infinitive as object. — *v.i.* To make an effort; strive: usually with *at, after,* or *for.* Also *Brit.* **en·deav'our.** [ME *endeveren* <EN[1] + DEVOIR. Cf. F *se mettre en devoir* make it one's duty, set about]

Synonyms (noun): attempt, effort, essay, exertion, struggle, trial. *Effort* denotes the voluntary putting forth of power to attain or accomplish some specific thing; it reaches toward a definite end; *exertion* is a putting forth of power without special reference to an object. Every *effort* is an *exertion,* but not every *exertion* is an *effort. Attempt* is more experimental than *effort, endeavor* less strenuous but more continuous. An *effort* is a single act, an *endeavor* a continued series of acts. A *struggle* is a violent *effort* or strenuous *exertion.* An *essay* is an *attempt, effort,* or *endeavor* made as a test of the powers of the one who makes it. See AIM, ATTEMPT.

Synonyms (verb): attempt, essay, strive, try, undertake. To *attempt* is to take action somewhat experimentally with the hope and purpose of accomplishing a certain result; to *endeavor* is to *attempt* strenuously and with firm and enduring purpose. To *attempt* expresses a single act; to *endeavor,* a continuous exertion; we say, I will *endeavor* (not I will *attempt*) while I live. To *attempt* is with the view of accomplishing; to *essay* with a view of testing our own powers. To *undertake* is to accept or take upon oneself as an obligation, as some business, labor, or trust; the word often implies complete assurance of success: as, I will *undertake* to produce the witness. To *strive* suggests little of the result, much of toil, strain, and contest, in seeking it; I will *strive* to fulfil your wishes, that is, I will spare no labor and exertion to do it. *Try* is the most comprehensive of these words. The original idea of testing or experimenting is not thought of when a man says "I will *try.*" To *attempt* suggests giving up, if the thing is not accomplished at a stroke; to *try* implies using other means and studying out other ways if not at first successful. *Try* is more earnest; *endeavor* is more mild and formal. *Antonyms*: abandon, dismiss, drop, neglect, omit, overlook.

en·deav·or·er (in·dev'ər·ər) *n.* One who endeavors.

en·dec·a·gon (en·dek'ə·gon), etc. See HENDECAGON, etc.

En·de·cott (en'di·kot, -kət), **John,** 1589–1665, English colonial governor of Massachusetts. Also spelled **En'di·cott.**

en·dem·ic (en·dem'ik) *adj.* **1** Peculiar to or prevailing in or among some (specified) country or people. **2** *Ecol.* Indigenous or native to a restricted area: said of plants and animals: opposed to *ecdemic.* **3** *Pathol.* Pertaining to a disease confined to or characteristic of a given locality, as distinguished from an epidemic or sporadic disease. Also **en·de·mi·al** (en·dē'mē·əl), **en·dem'i·cal.** [<Gk. *endēmos* native < *en-* in + *dēmos* people]

en·de·mic·i·ty (en'də·mis'ə·tē) *n. Ecol.* The condition of growing in only one natural area, or of being restricted in distribution to a given locality. Also **en'de·mism.**

end·er (en'dər) *n.* One who or that which brings something to an end.

En·der·bur·y Island (en'dər·ber'ē) One of the Phoenix Islands, comprising a condominium (1939) of Great Britain and the United States; 2 square miles.

En·der·by Land (en'dər·bē) A region on the coast of Antarctica south of the continent of Africa.

en·der·mic (en·dûr'mik) *adj. Med.* Acting by being absorbed in or through the skin. [<EN-[2] + Gk. *derma* skin] — **en'der·mism** *n.*

en dés·ha·bil·lé (äṅ dā·zà·bē·yā') *French* In dishabille.

En·di·an·dra (en'dē·an'drə) *n.* A genus of close-grained, straight-fibered hardwood trees of the laurel family native to Australia, bearing large globular fruit, especially *E. glauca,* with an aromatic teaklike wood.

end·ing (en'ding) *n.* **1** The act of bringing or coming to an end; also, an end; extremity. **2** One or more letters or syllables added to the base of a word, especially to indicate an inflection.

en·dive (en′dīv, än′dēv) *n.* **1** An herb *(Cichorium endivia)* allied to chicory. There are many varieties, divided into two groups, the **curled** or **narrow-leaved endive** (variety *crispa)* and the **broad-leaved endive** (variety *latifolia).* **2** The blanched leaves of this herb, used as a salad. [< F < L *intibus* endive]

end·less (end′lis) *adj.* **1** Enduring everlastingly; eternal. **2** Having no end in space; boundless; infinite. **3** Continually recurring; incessant. **4** Forming a closed loop or circle; continuous. See synonyms under ETERNAL, IMMORTAL, PERPETUAL. **—end′less·ly** *adv.* **—end′less·ness** *n.*

end·long (end′lông′, -lŏng′) *adv.* **1** Lengthwise; at full length. **2** Continuously. **3** On end; perpendicularly.

end man In a minstrel troupe, one who sits at either end of the company as grouped upon the stage, and who engages in comic dialogs with the interlocutor.

end·most (end′mōst′) *adj.* Placed or being at the extreme end; most remote; farthest.

endo- *combining form* Within; inside: *endocarp.* Also, before vowels, **end-.** [< Gk. < *endon* within]

en·do·blast (en′dō·blast) *n. Biol.* The hypoblast: also spelled *entoblast.* **—en′do·blas′tic** *adj.*

en·do·car·di·ac (en′dō·kär′dē·ak) *adj. Anat.* **1** Situated or being within the heart. **2** Of or pertaining to the endocardium. Also **en′do·car′di·al.**

en·do·car·di·tis (en′dō·kär·dī′tis) *n. Pathol.* Inflammation of the endocardium. **—en′do·car·dit′ic** (-dit′ik) *adj.*

en·do·car·di·um (en′dō·kär′dē·əm) *n. Anat.* The delicate endothelial membrane lining the chambers of the heart. [< NL < Gk. *endo-* within + *kardia* heart]

en·do·carp (en′dō·kärp) *n. Bot.* The inner layer of a pericarp, as the hard inner part of a cherry stone.

en·do·cen·tric (en′dō·sen′trik) *adj. Ling.* Denoting a syntactic construction which as a unit has the same function as any one of its component parts, as the phrase *healthy boys and girls* in *healthy boys and girls eat well*: opposed to *exocentric.*

en·do·cho·ri·on (en′dō·kôr′ē·ən, -kō′rē-) *n.* **1** *Anat.* The inner chorion associated with the fetal membrane. **2** *Entomol.* The inner layer of the chorion or shell, covering an insect egg.

en·do·crine (en′dō·krin, -krīn) *adj.* **1** Producing an internal secretion. **2** Pertaining to or produced by an endocrine gland or glands. **3** Hormonal. Also **en′do·cri′nal** (-krī′nəl), **en·doc·ri·nous** (en·dok′rə·nəs), **en′do·crin′ic** (-krin′·ik). *—n.* The secretion of an endocrine gland; a hormone. [< ENDO- + Gk. *krinein* separate]

endocrine gland Any of numerous ductless, hormone-secreting structures in various sites in the body which release secretions into surrounding tissue and thence into the bloodstream, either directly or through the lymphatic system.

ENDOCRINE GLANDS

Name	*Location*
Adrenals (2)	Anterior to the kidneys
Gonads	Sex glands collectively
Ovaries (2)	Paired sex glands of the female
Pancreas	Upper abdominal cavity
Parathyroids	In pairs, near the thyroid
Pineal	Attached to the brain, near the pituitary
Pituitary	In the floor of the skull
Testes (2)	Paired sex glands of the male
Thymus	Above the heart
Thyroid	Paired lobes, one on each side of the trachea

en·do·cri·nol·o·gy (en′dō·kri·nol′ə·jē, -krī-) *n.* That branch of medicine which treats of the anatomy, physiology, and pathology of the endocrine glands and the properties and functions of the various internal secretions. **—en′do·cri·nol′o·gist** *n.*

en·do·cyte (en′dō·sīt) *n. Biol.* A foreign substance found inside a cell.

en·do·cyt·ic (en′dō·sit′ik) *adj. Biol.* Pertaining to the contents of a cell.

en·do·derm (en′dō·dûrm) *n. Biol.* **1** The innermost of the germ layers of the embryo. **2** The inner layer of the integument of an organism. Also spelled *entoderm.*

en·do·der·mis (en′dō·dûr′mis) *n. Bot.* A sheath of one or more layers of modified parenchymatous cells between the cortex and the central zone of the stem or root in plants: also spelled *entoderm.* [< ENDODERM, on analogy with *epidermis*] **—en′do·der′mal, en′do·der′mic** *adj.*

en·do·don·tics (en′dō·don′tiks) *n.* The branch of dentistry which is concerned with the prevention, diagnosis, and treatment of diseases of the tooth pulp, as root canal work. Also **en′do·don′tia** (-don′shə), **en′do·don′tol′o·gy** (-don′tol′ə·jē). [< ENDO- + Gk. *odous, odontos* a tooth + -ICS] **—en′do·don′tist** *n.*

en·do·en·zyme (en′dō·en′zīm, -zim) *n. Biochem.* An enzyme or ferment acting from within the cell, as zymase: opposed to *ectoenzyme.* Also **en′do·en′zym** (-zim).

en·dog·a·my (en·dog′ə·mē) *n.* **1** *Anthropol.* The custom of marriage within the group, class, caste, or tribe; inbreeding: opposed to *exogamy.* **2** *Bot.* The fertilization of plants by pollination between two flowers on the same plant. — **en·dog′a·mous, en·do·gam·ic** (en′dō·gam′ik) *adj.*

en·do·gen (en′dō·jen) *n. Bot.* A plant that increases by the growth of new vascular and cellular tissue among that already formed; a monocotyledon: opposed to *exogen.*

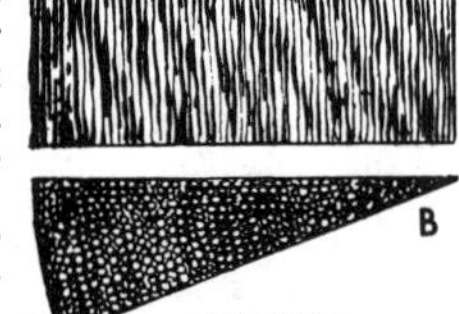

ENDOGEN
A. Vertical section.
B. Cross-section.

en·dog·e·nous (en·doj′ə·nəs) *adj.* Originating or produced internally; due to internal causes. — **en·dog′e·nous·ly** *adv.*

en·dog·e·ny (en·doj′ə·nē) *n.* **1** Growth from within; specifically, endogenous cell formation. **2** Endogamy.

en·do·lymph (en′dō·limf) *n. Anat.* The serous fluid that fills the membranous labyrinth of the ear.

en·do·me·tri·um (en′dō·mē′trē·əm) *n. Anat.* The mucous membrane which lines the uterus. [< NL < Gk. *endo-* within + *mētra* womb] — **en′do·me′tri·al** *adj.*

en·dom·e·try (en·dom′ə·trē) *n.* The measurement of cavities; specifically of the interior of body organs, as the cranium. **—en·do·met·ric** (en′dō·met′rik) or **·ri·cal** *adj.*

en·do·mix·is (en′dō·mik′sis) *n. Biol.* The periodic reorganization of the nucleus in certain unicellular organisms which reproduce asexually, as paramecium; a form of parthenogenesis: distinguished from *amphimixis.* [< ENDO- + Gk. *mixis* intercourse]

en·do·morph (en′dō·môrf) *n. Mineral.* A mineral enclosed within another, as a crystal of tourmaline in quartz.

en·do·mor·phic (en′dō·môr′fik) *adj.* **1** *Mineral.* **a** Of or pertaining to an endomorph. **b** Occuring on the inside; produced by endomorphism. **2** Pertaining to a physical and personality type associated with the development of the endodermal layer of the embryo, and characterized by predominance of the abdominal system. Compare ECTOMORPHIC and MESOMORPHIC.

en·do·morph·ism (en′dō·môr′fiz·əm) *n. Geol.* The changes produced in igneous rocks by the action upon them of underlying and intrusive magmatic material.

en·do·par·a·site (en′dō·par′ə·sīt) *n. Biol.* A parasite that lives in the internal parts of its host, as an intestinal worm. **—en′do·par′a·sit′ic** (-sit′ik) *adj.*

en·do·path·ic (en′dō·path′ik) *adj. Pathol.* Pertaining to those diseases originating from within the organism. **—en·dop·a·thy** (en·dop′·ə·thē) *n.*

en·do·phyte (en′dō·fīt) *n. Bot.* A plant living within another organism, usually as a parasite, as certain algae and fungi. Also spelled *entophyte.* **—en′do·phy′tal** *adj.* **—en′do·phyt′ic** (-fit′ik) *adj.* **—en′do·phyt′i·cal·ly** *adv.*

en·doph·y·tous (en·dof′ə·təs) *adj.* Living within wood, as the larvae of certain insects.

en·do·plasm (en′dō·plaz′əm) *n. Biol.* The inner granular portion of the cytoplasm of the cell, enclosing the nucleus. Also **en·do·sarc** (en′dō·särk). **—en′do·plas′mic** *adj.*

en·dop·o·dite (en·dop′ə·dīt) *n. Biol.* The inner, variously modified branch of the shaft or stem of an appendage, as in the thoracic region of a lobster, crab, or other decapod. [< ENDO- + Gk. *pous, podos* foot + -ITE[1]]

end organ *Physiol.* Any organ adapted for the reception or delivery of nervous stimuli.

en·dor·phin (en·dôr′fin) *n.* Any of several peptides produced by the brain and having a morphinelike effect. [< ENDO- + (M)ORPHIN(E)]

en·dorse (in·dôrs′) *v.t.* **·dorsed, ·dors·ing 1** To write upon the back of; especially, to write one's name on the back of (a check, draft, etc.) to assign it or to guarantee its payment; to write one's name on the back of (a check, etc.) in exchanging the document for the cash it represents. **2** To indicate receipt of (a sum) by signing one's name. **3** To give sanction to. See synonyms under ACKNOWLEDGE, AFFIRM, CONFESS, JUSTIFY, RATIFY. Also spelled *indorse.* [< OF *endosser* < Med.L *indorsare* < L *in-* on + *dorsum* back; partially refashioned after L] — **en·dors′a·ble** *adj.* **—en·dors′er, en·dor′sor** *n.*

en·dor·see (en′dôr·sē′, in·dôr′sē) *n.* One to whom transference by endorsement is made.

en·dorse·ment (in·dôrs′mənt) *n.* **1** The writing of one's name on the back of a note, check, etc. **2** The act of ratification; approval. **3** The act or method by which bills, notes, and other negotiable instruments are transferred. **4** Any writing on the back of a document. **5** A rider attached to an insurance policy to modify the original contract. Also spelled *indorsement.*

en·do·scope (en′də·skōp) *n. Med.* An instrument for viewing the inside of a body cavity or hollow organ, especially the womb, rectum, urethra, and bladder. **—en·dos·co·py** (en·dos′·kə·pē) *n.*

en·do·skel·e·ton (en′dō·skel′ə·tən) *n. Zool.* The internal supporting structure of an animal, characteristic of all vertebrates; all of the skeleton not of dermal origin: opposed to *exoskeleton.* **—en′do·skel′e·tal** *adj.*

en·dos·mo·sis (en′dos·mō′sis, -doz-) *n. Chem.* **1** Osmosis in that direction in which the fluid traverses the septum most rapidly. **2** Osmosis from an outer vessel to one within it. Also **en′dos·mose′** (-mōz′). **—en′dos·mot′ic** (-mot′ik) *adj.*

en·do·sperm (en′dō·spûrm) *n. Bot.* The albumen of a seed; nutritive substance within the embryo sac of an ovule.

en·do·spore (en′dō·spôr, -spōr) *n. Bot.* **1** A spore formed within the membrane of a cell. **2** The delicate inner layer of the wall of a spore: also **en′do·spo′ri·um. 3** An asexual spore produced by certain bacteria: opposed to *arthrospore.* **—en·dos·po·rous** (en·dos′pər·əs) *adj.*

en·dos·te·um (en·dos′tē·əm) *n. pl.* **·te·a** (-tē·ə) *Anat.* The thin, vascular membrane lining the medullary cavity of a bone. [< NL < Gk. *endo-* within + *osteon* bone]

en·dos·to·sis (en′dos·tō′sis) *n. Biol.* Ossification that takes place between cartilage cells.

en·do·style (en′dō·stīl) *n. Zool.* In ascidians, a longitudinal fold of the endoderm of the pharyngeal cavity, projecting into the blood cavity. [< ENDO- + -STYLE[2]]

en·do·sym·bi·o·sis (en′dō·sim′bē·ō′sis) *n.* Symbiosis in which one of the symbiontic partners lives within the body of the other.

en·do·the·ci·um (en′dō·thē′sē·əm) *n. pl.* **·ci·a** (-sē·ə) *Bot.* **1** The inner lining of the cell of an anther. **2** The internal lining of the capsule of mosses. [< NL < Gk. *endo-* within + *thēkion* a small case]

en·do·the·li·o·ma (en′dō·thē′lē·ō′mə) *n. pl.* **·ma·ta** (-mə·tə) or **·mas** *Pathol.* A tumorous growth developed in or from the endothelium.

en·do·the·li·um (en′dō·thē′lē·əm) *n. pl.* **·li·a** (-lē·ə) *Anat.* A membrane, composed of flat, thin cells, that lines blood vessels, lymphatic tubes, and cavities. [< NL < Gk. *endo-* within + *thēlē* nipple] **—en′do·the′li·al** *adj.* — **en′do·the′li·oid, en·doth·e·loid** (en·doth′loid) *adj.*

en·do·therm (en′də·thûrm) *n.* An animal that maintains a uniform temperature independent of and usually higher than the ambient temperature; a warm-blooded animal.

en·do·ther·mic (en′dō·thûr′mik) *adj.* **1** *Chem.* Pertaining to, attended by, or produced from the absorption of heat; heat-absorbing: *endothermic* combination or reaction: opposed to *exothermic.* 2 *Zool.* Warm-blooded. Also **en′do·ther′mal.**

en·do·tox·in (en′dō·tok′sin) *n. Bacteriol.* A toxic product liberated by the disintegration of certain bacteria which fails to induce the formation of an antitoxin in an animal organism. — **en′do·tox′ic** *adj.*

en·do·troph·ic (en′dō·trof′ik, -trō′fik) *adj. Bot.* Relating to the condition of fungi which live in and feed upon the internal cells of plant parts, such as roots.

en·dow (in·dou′) *v.t.* **1** To bestow a permanent fund or income upon. **2** To furnish or equip, as with talents or natural gifts: usually with *with.* **3** *Obs.* To provide with a dower. Also spelled *indow.* [<OF *endouer* <*en-* in (<L *in-*) + *douer* <L *dotare* give]

en·dow·ment (in·dou′mənt) *n.* **1** Money or property given for the permanent use of an institution, person, or object. **2** Any natural gift, as talent or beauty. **3** The act of endowing. Also spelled *indowment.*

endowment insurance See under INSURANCE.

end papers In bookbinding, those papers, plain or variously colored and decorated, placed at the front and back of a book, one leaf being pasted to the binding or cover, the others acting as flyleaves.

end·plate (end′plāt′) *n.* **1** *Electronics* One of the electrodes of a vacuum tube, carrying a negative potential to prevent the escape of electrons at the anode. **2** *Physiol.* The termination of a motor nerve, usually embedded in muscle fiber.

end product The final product, result, or outcome of any rocess.

en·drin (en′drin) *n.* A toxic chlorinated hydrocarbon, $C_{12}H_8OCl_6$, used as a pesticide and tending to persist in fats in the food chain.

end table A small table to be placed beside chairs, at the end of a sofa, etc.

en·due (in·dōō′, -dyōō′) *v.t.* **·dued, ·du·ing 1** To provide or endow, as with some quality or power: with *with.* **2** To put on; don. **3** To clothe; garb. Also spelled *indue.* [Fusion of OF *enduire* introduce <L *inducere* (see INDUCE) and OF *enduire* clothe <L *induere*; infl. in meaning by ENDOW]

en·dur·a·ble (in·dōōr′ə·bəl, -dyōōr′-) *adj.* That can be endured; bearable.

en·dur·ance (in·dōōr′əns, -dyōōr′-) *n.* **1** The capacity or power to endure; ability to suffer pain, distress, hardship, or any very prolonged stress without succumbing; patient fortitude. **2** The act or experience of enduring or suffering. **3** *Obs.* Hardship. See synonyms under FORTITUDE.

en·dure (in·dōōr′, -dyōōr′) *v.* **·dured, ·dur·ing** *v.t.* **1** To bear or undergo, as pain, grief, or injury, especially without yielding; withstand; suffer. **2** To tolerate; put up with. —*v.i.* **3** To last; continue to be. **4** To suffer without yielding; hold out. [<OF *endurer* <L *indurare* <*in-* in + *durare* harden <*durus* hard]

Synonyms: abide, afford, allow, bear, brook, permit, suffer, support, sustain, tolerate, undergo. *Bear* is the most general of these words; it is metaphorically to hold up or keep up a burden of care, pain, grief, annoyance, or the like, without sinking, lamenting, or repining. *Allow* and *permit* involve large concession of the will; whispering is *allowed* by the schoolteacher who does not forbid nor censure it; a state *tolerates* a religion which it would be glad to suppress. To *endure* is to *bear* with strain and resistance, but with conscious power; *endure* conveys a fuller suggestion of contest and conquest than *bear.* One may choose to *endure* the pain of a surgical operation rather than take anesthetics; he *permits* the thing to come which he must brace himself to *endure* when it comes. To *afford* is to be equal to a pecuniary demand, that is, to be able to *bear* it. *Abide* combines the senses of await and *endure*; as, I will *abide* the result. Compare ABIDE, LIVE, PERSEVERE, PERSIST, STAND, SUPPORT. *Antonyms*: break, despair, droop, fail, faint, fall, falter, sink, succumb, surrender, yield.

en·dur·ing (in·dōōr′ing, -dyōōr′-) *adj.* **1** Lasting; permanent. **2** Long-suffering. See synonymsunder PERMANENT, PERPETUAL. —**en·dur′ing·ly** *adv.* —**en·dur′ing·ness** *n.*

end·wise (end′wīz′) *adv.* **1** With the end foremost or uppermost. **2** On end; so as to present the end toward the spectator or some object. **3** Lengthwise; from end to end. Also **end′ways′** (-wāz′).

En·dym·i·on (en·dim′ē·ən) In Greek legend, a beautiful young shepherd loved by Selene and granted eternal youth and sleep at her request.

-ene *suffix Chem.* **1** Denoting an open-chain, unsaturated, hydrocarbon compound having one double-bond: *ethylene.* **2** Denoting an aromatic compound of the benzene series.

E·ne·as (i·nē′əs) A masculine personal name. Also *Fr.* **E·née** (ā·nā′), See AENEAS. [<Gk., praiseworthy]

en ef·fet (äṅ nef·fe′) *French* In effect; consequently; substantially.

en·e·ma (en′ə·mə) *n. pl.* **·mas** or **e·nem·a·ta** (e·nem′ə·tə) *Med.* **1** A liquid injected into the rectum for cleansing or nutritive purposes. **2** The injection of such a liquid. **3** The apparatus for such an injection. [<Gk. <*enienai* <*en-* in + *hienai* send]

en·e·my (en′ə·mē) *n. pl.* **·mies 1** One who cherishes resentment or malicious purpose toward another; an adversary; foe. **2** One of a hostile army or nation. **3** A hostile nation or military force collectively. —*adj.* **1** Of or pertaining to a hostile army or power. **2** *Obs.* Unfriendly; hostile. [<OF *enemi* <L *inimicus* <*in-* not + *amicus* friend]

Synonyms (noun): adversary, antagonist, competitor, foe, opponent, rival. An *enemy* in private life is one who is moved by hostile feeling with active disposition to injure; but in military language all who fight on the opposite side are called *enemies* or collectively "the *enemy*," where no personal animosity may be implied; *foe,* which is rather a poetical and literary word, implies intensely hostile spirit and purpose. An *antagonist* is one who opposes and is opposed actively and with intensity of effort; an *opponent,* one in whom the attitude of resistance is the more prominent; a *competitor,* one who seeks the same object for which another is striving; *antagonists* in wrestling, *competitors* in business, *opponents* in debate may contend with no personal ill will; *rivals* in love, ambition, etc., rarely avoid inimical feeling. *Adversary* now commonly denotes one who not only opposes another in fact, but does so with hostile spirit or perhaps out of pure malignity. Compare synonyms for AMBITION. *Antonyms*: abettor, accessory, accomplice, ally, friend, helper, supporter.

enemy alien An alien living or interned in a country which is at war with his own country.

en·er·ge·sis (en′ər·jē′sis) *n. Bot.* The chemical and physical changes which set free the energy produced by the respiratory processes in plant cells. [<NL <Gk. *energeein* be active]

en·er·get·ic (en′ər·jet′ik) *adj.* **1** Having or displaying energy. **2** Acting with prompt, rapid, and effective force; forceful and efficient; strenuous. Also **en′er·get′i·cal.** [<Gk. *energētikos* <*energeein* be active] —**en′er·get′i·cal·ly** *adv.*

en·er·get·ics (en′ər·jet′iks) *n. pl. (construed as singular)* **1** The science of the laws and phenomena of energy in all its forms. **2** The philosophic doctrine which attributes all natural phenomena to the action of energy.

en·er·gid (i·nûr′jid) *n. Biol.* The cytoplasm and nucleus of a cell considered as a unit. [<Gk. *energos* active + -ID[1]]

en·er·gize (en′ər·jīz) *v.* **·gized, ·giz·ing** *v.t.* To give energy, force, or strength to; activate. —*v.i.* To be in operation; be active. —**en′er·giz′er** *n.*

en·er·gu·men (en′ər·gyōō′mən) *n.* One who is supposed to be possessed by evil spirits; a demoniac; hence, a fanatical enthusiast. [<LL *energumenus* <Gk. *energoumenos,* ppr. of *energeein* be active]

en·er·gy (en′ər·jē) *n. pl.* **·gies 1** The power by which anything acts effectively to move or change other things or accomplish any result. **2** Habitual tendency to and readiness for effective action. **3** Power in active exercise; force in operation. **4** *Physics* The capacity of doing work and of overcoming inertia, as by heat, light, radiation, or mechanical and chemical forces. **Potential energy** is that due to the position of one body relative to another; **kinetic energy** is manifested by bodies in motion. The units of energy and work are mutually convertible, and energy itself is regarded as functionally related to the mass and velocity of a material system. See QUANTUM. **5** Vigor and forcefulness of style or expression. See synonyms under POWER, WARMTH. [<LL *energia* <Gk. *energeia* <*energēs* <*en-* on + *ergon* work]

energy level *Physics* Any of several discrete states which an electron may assume within an atom, transition between which is associated with the emission of quanta: also called *quantum state.*

en·er·vate (en′ər·vāt) *v.t.* **·vat·ed, ·vat·ing** To deprive of nerve, energy, or strength; weaken. — *adj.* (i·nûr′vit) Rendered feeble or effeminate; weakened. [<L *enervatus,* pp. of *enervare* weaken <*ex-* out + *nervus* a sinew] —**en′er·va′tor** *n.*

en·er·va·tion (en′ər·vā′shən) *n.* The act of enervating, or the state of being enervated; debility.

en·face (en·fās′) *v.t.* **·faced, ·fac·ing** To write or print on the face of. —**en·face′ment** *n.*

en fa·mille (äṅ fȧ·mē′y′) *French* Within the family; at home; informally.

en·fant per·du (äṅ·fäṅ′ per·dü′) *French* A soldier assigned to a position of extreme danger; literally, a lost child.

en·fant ter·ri·ble (äṅ·fäṅ′ te·rē′bl′) *French* A precocious child given to disconcerting remarks; literally, a terrible child.

en·fee·ble (en·fē′bəl) *v.t.* **·bled, ·bling** To render feeble. See synonyms under IMPAIR. —**en·fee′ble·ment** *n.* —**en·fee′bler** *n.*

en·feoff (en·fēf′, -fef′) *v.t.* **1** *Law* To invest with a fee or fief. **2** *Obs.* To surrender, as a vassal; give over, as oneself. Also spelled *infeoff.* [<OF *enfeoffer* <*en-* in + *fief* FIEF]

en·feoff·ment (en·fēf′mənt, -fef′-) *n.* The act or instrument by which an estate in fee is transferred: also spelled *infeoffment.*

en·fet·ter (en·fet′ər) *v.t.* To enchain.

En·field (en′fēld) A town in northern Middlesex, England.

Enfield rifle A .30-caliber, bolt-action, breech-loading magazine rifle used by the U.S. Army and by the British: officially, Lee Enfield. [from *Enfield,* England, where it was first manufactured]

en·fi·lade (en′fə·lād′) *Mil. v.t.* **·lad·ed, ·lad·ing** To fire or be in a position to fire down the length of, as a trench or column of troops. [<*n.*] —*n.* **1** Gunfire that can rake lengthwise a line of troops, etc. **2** A position exposed to a raking fire. [<F <*enfiler* thread <*en-* in + *fil* thread]

en·fin (äṅ·faṅ′) *adv. French* Finally; in conclusion.

en·fleu·rage (äṅ′flœ·räzh′) *n.* The extraction of perfumes by exposing odorless fats to the exhalations of the more delicate flowers. [<F <*enfleurer* <*en-* in + *fleur* flower]

en·fold (in·fōld′), etc. See INFOLD, etc.

en·force (in·fôrs′, -fōrs′) *v.t.* **·forced, ·forc·ing 1** To compel obedience to, as laws. **2** To compel (performance, obedience, etc.) by physical or moral force. **3** To make convincing; give weight to, as an argument. **4** *Obs.* To force; coerce. See synonyms under EXECUTE. [<OF *enforcier* <LL *infortiare* <*in-* in + *fortis* strong] — **en·force′a·ble** *adj.* —**en·forc′er** *n.*

en·force·ment (in·fôrs′mənt, -fōrs′-) *n.* The act of enforcing, or the state of being enforced; compulsory execution; compulsion.

en·frame (in·frām′) *v.t.* **·framed, ·fram·ing** To enclose in or as in a border or a frame. **·en·frame′ment** *n.*

en·fran·chise (en·fran′chīz) *v.t.* **—chised, ·chis·ing 1** To endow with a franchise, as the right to vote. **2** To set free, as from bondage. **3** *Law* In England, to convert (a copyhold estate) into a freehold, either by payment in gross or by setting a fixed annual rent charge. [<OF *enfranchiss-,* stem of *enfranchir* <*en-* in + *franc* free. See FRANK.]

en·fran·chise·ment (en·fran′chiz·mənt) *n.* The act of enfranchising, or the state of being enfranchised.

En·ga·dine (eng′gə·dēn) The valley of the Inn in eastern Switzerland; a resort center; 60 miles long.

en·gage (in·gāj′) *v.* **·gaged, ·gag·ing** *v.t.* **1** To bind by a promise, pledge, etc. **2** To promise to marry; betroth: usually in the passive. **3** To hire, as a lawyer, or his services; secure the use of, as a room. **4** To hold the interest or attention of. **5** To hold (interest or attention); occupy. **6** To occupy or take up the extent, energies, etc., of: How do you *engage* your time? **7** To win over; attract: to *engage* affections. **8** To begin a battle with: We *engaged* the enemy. **9** *Mech.* To mesh or interlock. — *v.i.* **10** To bind oneself by a promise, pledge, etc. **11** To devote or occupy oneself: to *engage* in research. **12** To begin a battle. **13** *Mech.* To mesh. See synonyms under BIND, EMPLOY, INTEREST, OCCUPY, RETAIN. [<F *engager* < *en-* in + *gager* pledge]

en·gaged (in·gājd′) *adj.* **1** Affianced. **2** Occupied or busy. **3** Partially sunk or built into another part of a structure, or so appearing. **4** *Mech.* Geared together; driven by gearing. **5** Involved in a contest or conflict. See synonyms under BUSY, INDUSTRIOUS.

en·gage·ment (in·gāj′mənt) *n.* **1** The act of engaging. **2** The condition of being engaged; a betrothal. **3** Something that engages or binds; an obligation; agreement; promise; contract. **4** An entering into or being in battle; a battle. **5** *Mech.* The state of being in gear. **6** *pl.* Pecuniary obligations. **7** A salaried position. See synonyms under BATTLE, CONTRACT.

en·gag·ing (in·gā′jing) *adj.* Attracting interest; winning. See synonyms under AMIABLE. — **en·gag′ing·ly** *adv.*

en gar·çon (äṅ gȧr·sôṅ′) *French* In bachelorhood.

en garde (äṅ gȧrd′) *French* On guard. See under GUARD.

en·gar·land (en·gär′lənd) *v.t.* To encircle with or as with garlands; wreathe.

Eng·els (eng′əls), **Friedrich,** 1820–95, German socialist and author; associate of Karl Marx.

en·gen·der (in·jen′dər) *v.t.* **1** To cause to exist; produce. **2** *Rare* To beget. — *v.i.* **3** To come into being. See synonyms under PRODUCE, PROPAGATE. [<OF *engendrer* <L *ingenerare* < *in-* in + *genus, generis* race]

en·gild (en·gild′) *v.t.* To gild or brighten.

en·gine (en′jin) *n.* **1** A machine by which energy is applied to the doing of work, notably one that converts heat energy into mechanical work: a steam *engine,* gas *engine,* etc. **2** A locomotive, taken as a whole. **3** Any large mechanism or material contrivance for producing some effect, especially of destruction or disintegration: an *engine* of war. **4** Any agency or instrumentality designedly employed. [<OF *engin* <L *ingenium* < *in-* in + *gen-,* root of *gignere* beget]

en·gine-driv·er (en′jin·drī′vər) *n. Brit.* A locomotive engineer.

en·gi·neer (en′jə·nir′) *n.* **1** One versed in or practicing any branch of engineering. **2** One who runs or manages an engine; engine-driver. **3** A manager; inventor; plotter. **4** A member of the division of an army which constructs forts and bridges, clears and builds roads, etc. Also *Obs.* **en′gin·er.** — *v.t.* **1** To put through or manage by contrivance: to *engineer* a scheme. **2** To plan and superintend as engineer: to *engineer* an aqueduct.

en·gi·neer·ing (en′jə·nir′ing) *n.* **1** The art of designing, building, or using engines and machines, or of designating and constructing public works or the like. The general art is now subdivided into numerous branches, dealing chiefly with the application of scientific knowledge for purposes useful to man: chemical *engineering,* civil *engineering,* electrical *engineering,* hydraulic *engineering,* mining *engineering.* **2** Painstaking management; maneuvering.

en·gine·ry (en′jin·rē) *n.* **1** *Mil.* **a** Engines of war. **b** Their management. **2** Engines collectively. **3** An artful scheme. **4** Any powerful agency.

en·gi·nous (en′jə·nəs) *adj. Obs.* Tricky; crafty; deceitful. [<OF *engineus* <L *ingeniosus* INGENIOUS]

en·gird (en·gûrd′) *v.t.* **·girt** or **·gird·ed, ·gird·ing** To gird about; encompass; surround.

en·gir·dle (en·gûr′dəl) *v.t.* **·dled, ·dling** To encircle; girdle.

en·gla·cial (en·glā′shəl) *adj.* **1** Embedded within glacier ice. **2** Occurring in a glacier.

Eng·land (ing′glənd) The southern part and largest political division of Great Britain, south of Scotland and east of Wales; 50,874 square miles; capital, London: Latin *Anglia.* See COMMONWEALTH OF NATIONS, GREAT BRITAIN, UNITED KINGDOM.

SOVEREIGNS OF ENGLAND, GREAT BRITAIN, AND THE UNITED KINGDOM

	Began to reign
SOVEREIGNS OF ENGLAND[1]	
ANGLO-SAXON LINE	A.D.
Egbert	800
Ethelwulf (son)	836
Ethelbald (son)	857
Ethelbert (brother)	860
Ethelred I (brother)	866
Alfred *the Great* (brother)	871
Edward *the Elder* (son)	901
Athelstan (son)	925
Edmund I (brother)	940
Edred (brother)	946
Edwy (nephew)	955
Edgar (brother)	957
Edward *the Martyr* (son)	975
Ethelred II, *the Unready* (half-brother)	979
Edmund II, *Ironside* (son)	1016
DANISH LINE	
Canute (son of Sweyn, a Viking)	1017
Harold I, *Harefoot* (son)	1036
Hardicanute (half-brother)	1039
SAXON LINE (RESTORED)	
Edward *the Confessor* (son of Ethelred II)	1041
Harold II (son of Earl Godwin)	1066
NORMAN LINE	
William I	1066
William II (son)	1087
Henry I (brother)	1100
Stephen (nephew)	1135
PLANTAGENET LINE	
Henry II (grandson of Henry I)	1154
Richard I (son)	1189
John (brother)	1199
Henry III (son)	1216
Edward I (son)	1272
Edward II (son)	1307
Edward III (son)	1327
Richard II (grandson)	1377
HOUSE OF LANCASTER	
Henry IV (grandson of Edward III)	1399
Henry V (son)	1413
Henry VI (son)	1422
HOUSE OF YORK	
Edward IV (great-great-grandson of Edward III)	1461
Edward V (son)	1483
Richard III (uncle)	1483
HOUSE OF TUDOR	A.D.
Henry VII (great-great-great-grandson of Edward III)	1485
Henry VIII (son)	1509
Edward VI (son)	1547
Mary I (half-sister)	1553
Elizabeth I (half-sister)	1558
SOVEREIGNS OF GREAT BRITAIN	
STUART LINE	
James I of England or VI of Scotland (son of Mary Queen of Scots, great-granddaughter of Henry VII)	1603
Charles I (son)	1625
COMMONWEALTH (during which Oliver Cromwell ruled as Lord Protector 1653–58, being succeeded by Richard Cromwell, his son, 1658–59; a year of anarchy followed)	
STUART LINE (RESTORED)	
Charles II (son of Charles I)	1660
James II (brother)	1685
HOUSE OF ORANGE	
William III (nephew) and Mary II (daughter of James II)	1688
STUART LINE	
Anne (daughter of James II)	1702
HOUSE OF HANOVER	
George I (great-grandson of James I)	1714
George II (son)	1727
SOVEREIGNS OF THE UNITED KINGDOM[2]	
George III (grandson)[3]	1760
George IV (son)	1820
William IV (brother)	1830
Victoria (niece of William IV)	1837
SAXE-COBURG LINE	
Edward VII (son)	1901
HOUSE OF WINDSOR[4]	
George V (son)	1910
Edward VIII (son): abdicated	1936
George VI (brother)	1936
Elizabeth II (daughter)	1952

[1]The British Sovereign has, from Norman times, been advised in the conduct of the government by a Committee of his *Privy Council,* known later as the *Cabinet.* See these words. [2]United, 1801. [3]Son of Frederick, Prince of Wales, who died 1751. [4]Created by Royal Proclamation July 17, 1917. Relationship is to previous sovereign, unless otherwise stated.

Eng·land·er (ing′glən·dər) *n.* A native of England.

Eng·lish (ing′glish) *adj.* **1** Of, pertaining to, or derived from England or its people. **2** Expressed in or belonging to the English language. — *n.* **1** The people of England collectively: with *the.* **2** The Low German, West Germanic language spoken by the people of the British Isles and most of the British Commonwealth, and of the United States, its territories, and possessions. — **Old English** or **Anglo-Saxon,** the English language from about A.D. 450 to A.D. 1150, consisting of the Kentish, West Saxon, Mercian, and Northumbrian dialects: represented by the epic poem *Beowulf* and the writings of Alfred the Great. The language in this period is synthetic in form and consists of an almost purely Germanic vocabulary. Abbr. *OE* — **Middle English,** the language of England after the Norman Conquest, from about 1150 to 1500: represented by the works of Chaucer. The characteristics of this period are the gradual loss of inflections accompanied by a stabilizing of word order, extensive borrowings from Latin, French, and the Low German languages, and the rise of the East Midland dialect as the standard. Abbr. *ME* — **Modern English,** the English language after 1500. **3** An English rendering or equivalent: "John" is the *English* of the French "Jean." **4** The English pronunciation, style, syntax, vocabulary, etc., of a particular region, time, or person: Chaucerian *English,* American *English.* **5** *Printing* A size of type between pica and great primer: about 14 points; also, a type face resembling German text: more commonly called **Old English.** **6** In billiards, a horizontal twist or spin given to the cue ball by striking it on one side; by the British called *side:* also applied in other games to the spin given to a ball. — **king's English** Spoken or written English considered as correct by official (or the king's) authority: also **queen's English.** — **plain English** A direct simple statement: This is the *plain English* of it. — *v.t.* **1** To translate into English. **2** To make English; Anglicize, as a foreign word. **3** In billiards and other games, to apply English to (a ball). [OE *Englisc* <*Engle* the Angles]

English bulldog See under BULLDOG.

English Channel An arm of the Atlantic between England and France, connecting the North Sea with the Atlantic Ocean: French *La Manche.*

English coach dog A Dalmatian.

English daisy See under DAISY.

English horn A woodwind instrument, with a pitch a fifth lower than an oboe: also called *cor anglais.*

Eng·lish·ism (ing′glish·iz′əm) *n.* **1** An English

peculiarity or idiom; Briticism. **2** Devotion to what is English in speech, manners, customs, etc.

Eng·lish·man (ing′glish·mən) *n. pl.* **·men** (-mən) **1** A native or citizen of England. **2** An English ship. Also **Eng′lish·er.**

Eng·lish·man's tie *Naut.* A strong knot for heavy ropes.

English Revolution See under REVOLUTION.

Eng·lish·ry (ing′glish·rē) *n.* **1** People of English birth or descent collectively: applied especially to the English in Ireland. **2** The condition or fact of being an Englishman.

English setter See under SETTER.

English sonnet See under SONNET.

English sparrow See under SPARROW (def. 1).

English springer spaniel See under SPANIEL.

Eng·lish·wom·an (ing′glish·wo͝om′ən) *n. pl.* **·wom·en** (-wim′in) A woman of English birth; also, one who is English by naturalization, marriage, or domicile.

en·globe (en·glōb′) *v.t.* **·globed, ·glob·ing 1** To ensphere. **2** To take up or assimilate within a globular body: An ameba *englobes* nutriment.

en·glut (en·glut′) *v.t. Obs.* **1** To swallow up; gulp down. **2** To satiate; glut.

en·gorge (en·gôrj′) *v.t.* **·gorged, ·gorg·ing 1** To fill with blood, as an artery. **2** To devour or swallow greedily. [< F *engorger* < *en-* in + *gorge* throat]

en·gorge·ment (en·gôrj′mənt) *n.* **1** The act of feeding voraciously or swallowing greedily. **2** The condition of being engorged, as an organ with blood. **3** *Pathol.* Excessive fullness of an organ, passage, or tissue; congestion.

en·graft (en·graft′, -gräft′) *v.t.* **1** To graft (a cion) to another type of tree or plant for propagation. **2** To implant; set firmly. Also spelled *ingraft.* — **en·graft′ment** *n.*

en·grail (en·grāl′) *v.t.* To ornament the edge of with a series of concave notches; indent the edge of. [< OF *engresler* indent as by hailstones < *en-* in + *gresle* hail] **—en·grailed′** *adj.*

en·grain (in·grān′) *v.t.* **1** To ingrain. **2** To grain in imitation of wood.

en·gram (en′gram) *n. Psychol.* **1** A memory picture latent in consciousness. **2** The trace or impression assumed in a certain theory of mnemonics to be left in cells subjected to a constantly repeated stimulus. [< EN-[2] + -GRAM]

en·grave (in·grāv′) *v.t.* **·graved, ·grav·ing 1** To carve or etch figures, letters, etc., into (a surface). **2** To impress deeply. **3** To cut (pictures, lettering, etc.) into metal, stone, or wood, for printing. **4** To print from plates made by such a process. See synonyms under INSCRIBE. [< EN-[1] + GRAVE[3]; cf. F *engraver*]

en·grav·er (in·grā′vər) *n.* **1** A person who engraves. **2** One whose occupation is to make engravings.

en·grav·ing (in·grā′ving) *n.* **1** The act or art of cutting designs on a plate. **2** An engraved design on a plate. **3** A picture or design printed from an engraved plate; a print. See synonyms under PICTURE.

en·gross (in·grōs′) *v.t.* **1** To occupy completely; absorb. **2** To copy legibly; make a formal transcript of. **3** To monopolize, as the supply of a marketable product. See synonyms under ABSORB, EMPLOY. [< AF *engrosser* < LL *ingrossare* write large < *in-* in + *grossus* large] — **en·gross′ing** *adj.* **—en·gross′ing·ly** *adv.*

en·gross·ment (in·grōs′mənt) *n.* **1** The act of engrossing. **2** Something engrossed, as a deed or charter. **3** The state of being wholly occupied with something.

en·gulf (in·gulf′) *v.t.* **1** To swallow up in or as in a gulf. **2** To bury or overwhelm completely.

en·hance (in·hans′, -häns′) *v.t.* **·hanced, ·hanc·ing** To make higher or greater, as in reputation, cost, beauty, quality, etc. See synonyms under AGGRAVATE, HEIGHTEN, INCREASE. [< AF *enhauncer,* prob. var. of OF *enhaucer* < *en-* in, on + *haucer* lift, ult. < L *altus* high]

en·hance·ment (in·hans′mənt, -häns′-) *n.* Increase; advance.

en·har·mon·ic (en′här·mon′ik) *Music adj.* **1** Having intervals less than a half-step. **2** Pertaining to that perfectly true intonation which is violated on keyed instruments to avoid complexity: C-sharp and D-flat are not the same in the *enharmonic* scale, though they are on the pianoforte. **3** Relating to that Greek scale whose intervals were quartertones and major thirds: distinguished from the *diatonic* and *chromatic* tetrachords. *—n.* **1** An enharmonic chord or note. **2** *pl.* Music distinguished by enharmonic intervals. [< L *enharmonicus* < Gk. *enharmonikos* < *en-* in + *harmonia* HARMONY] **—en′har·mon′i·cal** *adj.* **—en′har·mon′i·cal·ly** *adv.*

e·ni·ac (ē′nē·ak) *n.* An electronically operated calculating machine designed to solve complicated mathematical problems at high speed: a trade name. [< E(LECTRONIC) N(UMERICAL) I(NTEGRATOR) A(ND) C(OMPUTER)]

E·nid (ē′nid) A feminine personal name. [< Celtic, soul]
—Enid In Arthurian legend and Tennyson's *Idylls of the King,* a lady of Arthur's court, the wife of Geraint.

e·nig·ma (i·nig′mə) *n.* **1** An obscure or ambiguous saying; a riddle. **2** Anything that puzzles or baffles. See synonyms under RIDDLE. [< L *aenigma* < Gk. *ainigma* < *ainissesthai* speak in riddles < *ainos* tale]

en·ig·mat·ic (en′ig·mat′ik) *adj.* Of or like an enigma; ambiguous; puzzling. Also **en′ig·mat′i·cal.** See synonyms under EQUIVOCAL, MYSTERIOUS. **—en′ig·mat′i·cal·ly** *adv.*

e·nig·ma·tist (i·nig′mə·tist) *n.* A maker or propounder of riddles.

e·nig·ma·tize (i·nig′mə·tīz) *v.i.* **·tized, ·tiz·ing** To make or propound riddles; speak enigmatically.

E·ni·sei (yen·i·sā′) See YENISEI.

en·isle (en·īl′) *v.t.* **·isled, ·isl·ing** *Poetic* **1** To place on an island; isolate. **2** To make an island of.

E·ni·we·tok (en′i·wē′tok, i·nē′wi·tôk) An atoll in the Marshall Islands; U.S. proving grounds (1948) for atomic weapons.

en·jambe·ment (in·jam′mənt, -jamb′-; *Fr.* äṅ·zhäṅb·mäṅ′) *n.* In prosody, the running over of a sentence or thought from one couplet or line to the next, without a pause at the end of the line or verse division. Also **en·jamb′ment.** [< F < *enjamber* encroach < *en-* in + *jambe* leg]

en·join (in·join′) *v.t.* **1** To order authoritatively and emphatically; direct (a person or group) to a course of action, conduct, etc. **2** To impose (a condition, course of action, etc.) on a person or group. **3** To forbid or prohibit, especially by judicial order or injunction. See synonyms under DICTATE. [< OF *enjoindre* < L *injungere* < *in-* on + *jungere* join] **—en·join′er** *n.*

en·joy (in·joi′) *v.t.* **1** To experience joy or pleasure in; receive pleasure from the possession or use of. **2** To have the use or benefit of. **—to enjoy oneself** To be happy; receive pleasure from an experience, party, etc. See synonyms under ADMIRE, REJOICE. [< OF *enjoir* < *en-* in (< L *in-*) + *joir* < L *gaudere* rejoice] **—en·joy′a·ble** *adj.* **—en·joy′a·ble·ness** *n.* **—en·joy′a·bly** *adv.* — **en·joy′er** *n.*

en·joy·ment (in·joi′mənt) *n.* **1** The act or state of enjoying; pleasure. **2** Something that gives joy or satisfaction. See synonyms under COMFORT, ENTERTAINMENT, HAPPINESS, SATISFACTION.

en·keph·a·lin (en·kef′ə·lin) *n.* A neurohormone elaborated by the pituitary and acting as an endogenous opiate.

en·keph·a·lin·er·gic (en·kef′ə·li·nûr′jik) *adj.* Effecting the release or activation of enkephalin.

en·kin·dle (en·kin′dəl) *v.t.* **·dled, ·dling 1** To set on fire; kindle. **2** To stir to action; excite; inflame. **—en·kin′dler** *n.*

en·lace (in·lās′) *v.t.* **·laced, ·lac·ing 1** To bind or wrap with or as with laces. **2** To intertwine; entangle. Also spelled *inlace.* [< F *enlacer* < *en-* in + *lacer* < OF *las* LACE] **—en·lace′ment** *n.*

en·large (in·lärj′) *v.* **·larged, ·larg·ing** *v.t.* **1** To make greater or larger; increase the amount or extent of; expand. **2** *Phot.* To increase the size of (a photograph) by projection printing. *—v.i.* **3** To become greater or larger; increase; widen. **4** To express oneself in greater detail or at greater length; expatiate: with *on* or *upon.* See synonyms under ADD, AMPLIFY, INCREASE. [< OF *enlarger* < *en-* in + *large* large] **—en·larg′er** *n.*

en·large·ment (in·lärj′mənt) *n.* **1** The act of making or growing larger; also, the state of being enlarged; an addition or extension. **2** Increase of range or capacity; expansion; dilatation: *enlargement* of the mind. **3** A photograph made larger than its original negative. **4** *Obs.* A setting at liberty. **5** Fullness of statement. See synonyms under ACCESSION, INCREASE.

en·light·en (in·līt′n) *v.t.* **1** To impart intellectual or spiritual knowledge to; cause to know or understand; teach. **2** *Obs.* To light up. See synonyms under TEACH. **—en·light′en·er** *n.*

en·light·ened (in·līt′nd) *adj.* **1** Having or exhibiting enlightenment. **2** Having reached the highest stage of civilization.

en·light·en·ment (in·līt′n·mənt) *n.* **1** The act or result of enlightening, or the state of being enlightened. **2** Great moral and intellectual advancement. See synonyms under WISDOM.

En·light·en·ment (in·līt′n·mənt) *n.* A philosophical movement of the 18th century, characterized by rationalistic methods and skepticism of established dogmas.

en·link (en·lingk′) *v.t.* To unite by or as by links; connect closely. **—en·link′ment** *n.*

en·list (in·list′) *v.t.* **1** To engage for service, as in the army or navy. **2** To gain the help or interest of (a person or his services). *—v.i.* **3** To enter military or naval services voluntarily. **4** To join in some venture, cause, etc. See synonyms under ENROL, RECRUIT.

en·list·ed man (in·lis′tid) Any member of the armed forces who is not a commissioned officer or warrant officer; a private, seaman, or a noncommissioned officer.

en·list·ment (in·list′mənt) *n.* **1** The act of enlisting or the state of being enlisted; voluntary enrolment. **2** The document binding one enlisted. **3** The term for which one enlists.

en·li·ven (in·lī′vən) *v.t.* **1** To make lively, cheerful, or sprightly. **2** To make active or vigorous; stimulate. See synonyms under ENTERTAIN. — **en·li′ven·er** *n.*

en masse (en mas′, *Fr.* äṅ mȧs′) In a mass or body; all together. [< F]

en·mesh (en·mesh′) *v.t.* To ensnare or entangle in or as in a net: also spelled *inmesh.*

en·mi·ty (en′mə·tē) *n. pl.* **·ties 1** The spirit of an enemy; hostility. **2** The state of being an enemy; a hostile condition. [< OF *enemistié,* ult. < L *inimicus* hostile < *in-* not + *amicus* a friend]

Synonyms: acrimony, animosity, antagonism, bitterness, hatred, hostility, malevolence, malice, malignity, rancor, spite. *Enmity* is the state of being an enemy or the feeling and disposition characterizing an enemy (compare ENEMY). *Animosity* denotes a feeling more active and vehement, but often less enduring and determined, than *enmity. Hostility* is *enmity* in action; the term *hostilities* between nations denotes actual armed collision. *Bitterness* is a resentful feeling arising from a belief that one has been wronged; *acrimony* is a kindred feeling, but deeper and more persistent, and may arise from the crossing of one's wishes or plans by another, where no injustice or wrong is felt. *Antagonism* does not necessarily imply *enmity,* but ordinarily suggests a shade, at least, of hostile feeling. *Malice* is a disposition or intent to injure others, for the gratification of some evil passion; *malignity* is intense and violent *enmity, hatred,* or *malice.* Compare synonyms for ACRIMONY, ANGER, FEUD, HATRED. *Antonyms*: agreement, alliance, amity, concord, friendship, harmony, kindliness, kindness, regard, sympathy.

ennea- *combining form* Nine: *enneagon.* [< Gk. *ennea* nine]

en·ne·ad (en′ē·ad) *n.* The number nine; any system or group containing nine objects. [< Gk. *enneas, enneados*]

en·ne·a·gon (en′ē·ə·gon) *n. Geom.* A figure, especially a plane figure, with nine sides and nine angles.

en·ne·a·he·dron (en′ē·ə·hē′drən) *n. pl.* **·drons** or **·dra** (-drə) *Geom.* A solid bounded by nine surfaces. **—en′ne·a·he′dral** *adj.*

en·ne·an·drous (en′ē·an′drəs) *adj. Bot.* Having nine stamens.

en·ne·a·style (en′ē·ə·stīl′) *adj. Archit.* Having nine columns. [< ENNEA- + Gk. *stylos* a pillar]

En·nis·kil·len (en′is·kil′ən) County town of Fermanagh, Ireland.

En·ni·us (en′ē·əs), **Quintus,** 239–169 B.C., Roman epic poet.

en·no·ble (i·nō′bəl, en-) *v.t.* **·bled, ·bling** 1 To make honorable or noble in nature, quality, etc. 2 To confer a title of nobility upon. [<F *ennoblir* < *en-* in (<L *in-*) + *noble* NOBLE] — **en·no′bler** *n.*

en·no·ble·ment (i·nō′bəl·mənt, en-) *n.* 1 The act of ennobling; also, elevation to the rank of a noble. 2 Anything that ennobles or exalts.

Enns (enz, *Ger.* ens) A river in central Austria, flowing 160 miles NE to the Danube.

en·nui (än′wē, *Fr.* äṅ·nwē′) *n.* A feeling of listless weariness resulting from satiety, boredom, inactivity, etc. — *v.t.* **en·nuied, en·nuy·ing** To oppress with tedium and lack of interest; bore. [<F <OF *enui* <L *in odio.* See ANNOY.]

en·nuy·é (äṅ·nwē·ā′) *French adj.* Oppressed with ennui; mentally satiated, wearied, or bored. — *n.* A person afflicted with ennui. — **en·nuy·ée′** *adj.* & *n. fem.*

E·noch (ē′nək, *Fr.* e·nôk′) A masculine personal name. Also *Lat.* **E·no·chus** (i·nō′kəs). Also *Henoch.* [<Hebrew, dedicated]
— **Enoch** The eldest son of Cain. *Gen.* iv 17.
— **Enoch** The father of Methuselah. *Gen.* v 21.

e·nol (ē′nōl, -nol) *n. Chem.* An organic compound in which a hydroxyl group is joined with a doubly linked carbon atom. [Prob. <Gk. *en,* neut. of *heis* one + -OL[1]]

e·nol·o·gy (i·nol′ə·jē) *n.* The science or study of wines. Also *oenology, oinology.* [<Gk. *oinos* wine + -LOGY] — **e·no·log·i·cal** (ē′nə·loj′·i·kəl) *adj.*

e·norm (i·nôrm′) *adj. Obs.* Enormous; huge. [<F <L *enormis* < *ex-* out + *norma* a pattern]

e·nor·mi·ty (i·nôr′mə·tē) *n. pl.* **·ties** 1 The state of being outrageous or extremely wicked. 2 A great or flagrant instance of wickedness or depravity; an outrageous offense; atrocity.

e·nor·mous (i·nôr′məs) *adj.* 1 Excessive or extraordinary in size, amount, or degree. 2 Wicked above measure; atrocious. See synonyms under FLAGRANT, IMMENSE, LARGE. — **e·nor′mous·ly** *adv.* — **e·nor′mous·ness** *n.*

E·nos (ē′nəs) A masculine personal name. [<Hebrew, man]
— **Enos** A son of Seth. *Gen.* iv 26.

e·no·sis (e·nō′sis) *n.* Union, especially as proposed between Cyprus and Greece. [<Gk. *énōsis* union]

e·nough (i·nuf′) *adj.* Adequate for any demand or need; sufficient. —*n.* An ample supply; a sufficiency. — *adv.* So as to be sufficient; sufficiently. — *interj.* It is enough; stop. [OE *genoh, genog*]

Synonyms (adj.): ample, sufficient. *Enough* is relative, denoting a supply equal to a given demand. A temperature of 70° Fahrenheit is *enough* for a living-room; of 212° *enough* to boil water; neither is *enough* to melt iron. *Sufficient* is an equivalent of the Saxon *enough,* with no perceptible difference of meaning, but only of usage, *enough* being the more blunt, homely, and forcible word, while *sufficient* is in many cases the more elegant or polite. *Sufficient* usually precedes its noun; *enough* preferably follows. See AMPLE.

e·nounce (i·nouns′) *v.t.* **e·nounced, e·nounc·ing** 1 To make a formal statement of; announce. 2 To give verbal expression to; utter; enunciate. [<F *énoncer* <L *enuntiare.* See ENUNCIATE.] — **e·nounce′ment** *n.*

e·now[1] (i·nou′) *adj., n.,* & *adv. Archaic* Enough. [Var. of ENOUGH]

e·now[2] (ē·nōō′) *adv. Brit. Dial.* Presently; by and by. [? Short for *even now*]

en pas·sant (äṅ pȧ·säṅ′) 1 By the way; in passing. 2 In chess, applied to the taking of a pawn that, in its first move, passes over a square commanded by a hostile pawn. [<F]

en·phy·tot·ic (en′fī·tot′ik) *adj. Bot.* Of regular occurrence in a locality: said of certain fungus diseases of plants. [<Gk. *en-* in + *phyton* plant]

en·plane (en·plān′) *v.i.* **·planed, ·plan·ing** To board an airplane.

en·quire (in·kwīr′), **en·quir·y** (in·kwīr′ē), etc. See INQUIRE, etc.

en·rage (in·rāj′) *v.t.* **·raged, ·rag·ing** To throw into a rage; infuriate. See synonyms under INCENSE. [<OF *enrager* < *en-* in + *rage* RAGE]

en rap·port (äṅ rȧ·pôr′) *French* In sympathetic relation; in accord.

en·rapt (in·rapt′) *adj.* Overpowered by emotion.

en·rap·ture (in·rap′chər) *v.t.* **·tured, ·tur·ing** To bring into a state of rapture; delight extravagantly. See synonyms under CHARM[1], RAVISH, REJOICE.

en·rav·ish (en·rav′ish) *v.t.* To enrapture.

en·reg·is·ter (en·rej′is·tər) *v.t.* To put on record; enrol; register. [<F *enregistrer*]

en re·gle (äṅ re′gl′) *French* According to rule; in due order.

en re·vanche (äṅ rə·väṅsh′) *French* In return; by way of compensation; in revenge.

en·rich (in·rich′) *v.t.* 1 To make rich; increase the wealth of. 2 To make fertile, as soil. 3 To increase or enhance the level, quality, etc., of: to *enrich* a poem with images. 4 To increase the food value of, as bread. 5 To increase the beauty of; adorn. [<OF *enricher* < *en-* in + *riche* rich] — **en·rich′er** *n.*

en·rich·ment (in·rich′mənt) *n.* 1 The act or process of making rich or richer. 2 That which enriches. 3 A decoration; ornament.

En·ri·ghet·ta (än′rē·get′tä) Italian form of HENRIETTA. Also *Sp.* **En·ri·que·ta** (än′rē·kā′tä).

en·ring (en·ring′) *v.t.* 1 To enclose with or as with a ring; encircle. 2 To adorn with rings; put a ring on.

en·robe (en·rōb′) *v.t.* **·robed, ·rob·ing** To put a robe on; attire.

en·rob·er (en·rō′bər) *n.* An automatic machine for applying icing to cakes, cookies, etc.

en·rol (in·rōl′) *v.* **·rolled, ·rol·ling** *v.t.* 1 To write or record (a name) in a roll; register; list. 2 To enlist. 3 To place on record; record, as a document or decree. 4 To roll up; wrap. —*v.i.* 5 To place one's name on a list; register oneself. Also **en·roll′.** [<OF *enroller* < *en-* in + *rolle* ROLL]

Synonyms: enlist, enter, incorporate, initiate, list, register. Compare RECORD *(noun). Antonyms*: disband, dismiss, expel, refuse, reject.

en·rol·ment (en·rōl′mənt) *n.* 1 The act of enrolling. 2 An enrolled entry; a record. Also **en·roll′ment.**

en·root (en·rōōt′, -rŏŏt′) *v.t.* To cause to take root; implant deeply: used chiefly in the past participle.

en route (än rōōt′, *Fr.* äṅ rōōt′) On the road; on the way.

ens (enz) *n. pl.* **en·ti·a** (en′shē·ə) In scholastic philosophy, the abstract conception of being, or being as absolute, without regard to any question of actual existence. [<LL, orig. ppr. formed from *esse* be]

en·sam·ple (en·sam′pəl, -säm′-) *Archaic v.* & *n.* Example.

en·san·guine (en·sang′gwin) *v.t.* **·guined, ·guin·ing** To cover or stain with or as with blood.

En·sche·de (en′skhe·dā′) A town in eastern Netherlands.

en·sconce (en·skons′) *v.t.* **·sconced, ·sconc·ing** 1 To fix securely or comfortably in some place; settle snugly. 2 To shelter; hide.

en·seal (en·sēl′) *v.t. Obs.* To seal up; put a seal upon. [<OF *enseeler* < *en-* in + *seel* SEAL]

en·sem·ble (än·säm′bəl, *Fr.* äṅ·säṅ′bl′) *n.* 1 The parts of a thing viewed as a whole; general effect. 2 A combination of clothing and accessories that match or harmonize in color. 3 *Music* The union of soloists and chorus in a concerted number. 4 The scene in a play, usually the last, that includes the entire cast. [<F <L *insimul* < *in-* in + *simul* at the same time]

en·sep·ul·cher (en·sep′əl·kər) *v.t.* **·chered, ·cher·ing** To put into or as into a sepulchre; entomb. Also **en·sep′ul·chre.**

en·shrine (in·shrīn′) *v.t.* **·shrined, ·shrin·ing** 1 To place in or as in a shrine. 2 To cherish devoutly; hold sacred. — **en·shrine′ment** *n.*

en·shroud (en·shroud′) *v.t.* To cover as with a shroud; conceal.

en·si·form (en′sə·fôrm) *adj. Bot.* Sword-shaped, as certain leaves. [<L *ensis* sword + -FORM]

en·sign (en′sīn) *n.* 1 A distinguished flag or banner; especially, a national standard or naval flag. 2 (en′sən) In the U.S. Navy or Coast Guard, a commissioned officer of the lowest grade, ranking with a second lieutenant in the U.S. Army, Air Force, or Marine Corps. 3 In the British Army, until 1871, a commissioned officer who carried the flag of a regiment or company. 4 A badge or symbol, as of office. 5 *Obs.* A signal. [<F *enseigne* <L *insignia* < *in-* in + *signum* mark]

en·sign·cy (en′sən·sē) *n. pl.* **·cies** The function, rank, or commission of an ensign. Also **en′sign·ship.**

en·si·lage (en′sə·lij) *n.* 1 The process of preserving succulent fodder in closed pits or silos. 2 The fodder thus preserved: also called *silage.* — *v.t.* **·laged, ·lag·ing** To store in a silo for preservation: also **en·sile** (en·sīl′). [<F < *ensiler* < *en-* in + *silo* SILO]

en·sky (en·skī′) *v.t.* **·skied, ·sky·ing** To fix or place in the sky or in heaven: used in the passive.

en·slave (in·slāv′) *v.t.* **·slaved, ·slav·ing** To make a slave of; dominate. — **en·slave′ment** *n.* — **en·slav′er** *n.*

en·snare (en·snâr′) *v.t.* **·snared, ·snar·ing** To catch in a snare; trick. Also spelled *insnare.* See synonyms under CATCH, DECEIVE.

en·sor·cel (en·sôr′səl) *v.t. Obs.* To bewitch. Also **en·sor′cell.** [<OF *ensorceler*]

en·soul (en·sōl′) *v.t.* 1 To endow with a soul. 2 To receive or put into the soul. Also spelled *insoul.*

en·sphere (en·sfir′) *v.t.* **·sphered, ·spher·ing** 1 To enclose in a sphere. 2 To give the form of a sphere to.

en·sta·tite (en′stə·tīt) *n. Mineral.* A variety of orthorhombic pyroxene low in iron oxide: a constituent of many basic igneous rocks. [<Gk. *enstatēs* adversary + -ITE[1]; so called from its refractory nature]

en·steep (en·stēp′) *v.t. Obs.* To steep; plunge under water.

en·sue (en·sōō′) *v.i.* **·sued, ·su·ing** 1 To follow; occur afterward or subsequently. 2 To follow as a consequence; result. [<OF *ensu-,* stem of *ensuivre* <L *insequor* < *in-* on, in + *sequi* follow]

en suite (äṅ swēt′) *French* In a series, set, or succession.

en·sure (in·shŏŏr′) See INSURE.

en·swathe (en·swāth′) *v.t.* **·swathed, ·swath·ing** To enwrap, as in swaddling clothes; swathe: also spelled *inswathe.* — **en·swathe′ment** *n.*

-ent *suffix of nouns and adjectives* 1 Having the quality, or performing the action of (the main element): *potent.* 2 One who or that which performs the action of (the main element): *superintendent.* Compare -ANT. [<F *-ent* <L *-ens, -entis,* suffix of present participle]

ent- See ENTO-.

en·tab·la·ture (en·tab′lə·chər) *n. Archit.* 1 The uppermost member of a classical order or columnar system, consisting of the architrave, frieze, and cornice. 2 A projecting frieze or cornice of several members, as on the front of an edifice. 3 A platform. [<MF <Ital. *intavolatura* < *in-* in + *tavola* base, table <L *tabula*]

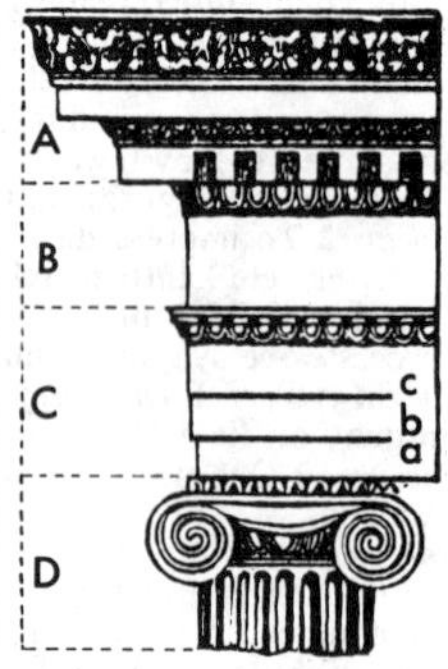

ENTABLATURE
A. Cornice. *B.* Frieze. *C.* Architrave. *D.* Capital on shaft. *a, b, c.* Fasciae.

en·ta·ble·ment (en·tā′bəl·mənt) *n. Archit.* 1 An entablature. 2 The series of platforms supporting a statue above the dado and base. [<F < *en-* in, on + *table* TABLE]

en·tail (in·tāl′) *v.t.* 1 To impose or result in (labor, concentration, etc.) as a necessary consequence. 2 *Law* To restrict the inheritance of (real property) to an unalterable succession of heirs. 3 To leave (anything) to an unalterable succession of heirs. — *n.* 1 Anything transmitted as an inalienable inheritance. 2 An estate in fee limited to a particular class of heirs, as eldest sons. 3 The act or custom of thus limiting inheritance. [<EN-[1] + TAIL[2]] — **en·tail′ment** *n.*

en·tame (en·tām′) *v.t. Obs.* To tame.

en·ta·moe·ba (en′tə·mē′bə) See ENDAMEBA.

en·tan·gle (in·tang′gəl) *v.t.* **·gled, ·gling** 1 To catch in or as in a snare; hamper. 2 To make tangled; snarl; interlace; complicate. 3 To involve in difficulties; perplex; embarrass. See synonyms under INVOLVE, PERPLEX. — **en·tan′gled** *adj.* — **en·tan′gler** *n.*

en·tan·gle·ment (in·tang′gəl·mənt) *n.* 1 Something that entangles; a snare; complication. 2 The act of entangling, or the state of being entangled.

en·ta·sis (en′tə·sis) *n.* **1** *Archit.* A slight convex curve in the vertical outlines of the shaft of a pilaster or of a column. **2** *Physiol.* Spasmodic contraction of a muscle; a tonic spasm: also **en·ta·si·a** (en·tā′zhē·ə). [<NL <Gk. *entasis* a stretching < *enteinein* < *en-* in + *teinein* stretch] — **en·tas·tic** (en·tas′tik) *adj.*

En·teb·be (en·teb′ē) A city in central Uganda, on Lake Victoria.

en·tel·e·chy (en·tel′ə·kē) *n. pl.* **·chies** *Philos.* **1** In Aristotle's metaphysics, completed realization, as distinguished from potentiality. **2** In the philosophy of Driesch, Bergson, etc., the non-physicochemical principle, or vital force, assumed to be responsible for life and growth. [<L *entelechia* <Gk. *entelecheia* actuality < *en telei echein* be complete]

ENTELLUS
(Body length 2 1/2 to 3 feet)

en·tel·lus (en·tel′əs) *n.* The hanuman or East Indian bearded monkey (genus *Presbytis*). [<NL, appar. after a character in the *Aeneid*]

en·tente (än·tänt′, *Fr.* än·tänt′) *n.* An understanding. [<F]

entente cor·diale (kôr·dyȧl′) Cordial understanding; in politics, friendliness between governments; especially, **Entente Cordiale,** the alliance between France and England, formed in 1904; enlarged to include Russia in 1907, and then called the **Triple Entente.** [<F]

en·ter (en′tər) *v.t.* **1** To come or go into. **2** To make a way into; penetrate; pierce. **3** To set or insert in: to *enter* a wedge. **4** To become a member of; join. **5** To begin; pass within the limits of; start: to *enter* middle age. **6** To obtain admission; enrol, as in a school or competition. **7** To write or record, as in a list, book, etc. **8** To report (goods, a vessel, etc.) to the customhouse. **9** *Law* **a** To place on the records of a court, as evidence, a plea, or an appearance. **b** To go upon or into feloniously or as a trespasser. **c** To file for title to (public lands). —*v.i.* **10** To come or go inward; make an entrance. **11** To come onto the stage: *Enter* the queen, weeping. —**to enter into 1** To begin; start. **2** To become a party to; engage in: to *enter into* a discussion. **3** To take an interest in; join in: to *enter into* the plans for a party. **4** To form a part of; be a constituent of: Oxygen *enters into* many compound bodies. **5** To consider or discuss: to *enter into* the particulars. —**to enter on** (or **upon**) To begin; set out on: to *enter upon* a career of dissipation. [<F *entrer* <L *intrare* < *intra* within]

en·ter·al·gi·a (en′tə·ral′jē·ə) *n. Pathol.* Intestinal neuralgia.

en·ter·ec·to·my (en′tə·rek′tə·mē) *n. Surg.* Excision of a portion of an intestine.

en·ter·ic (en·ter′ik) *adj.* **1** Of or pertaining to the intestine. **2** Having an intestine. [<Gk. *enterikos* < *enteron* intestine < *entos* within]

enteric fever Typhoid fever.

entering edge *Aeron.* The forward or leading edge of an airplane wing.

en·ter·i·tis (en′tə·rī′tis) *n. Pathol.* Inflammation of the intestines, particularly of the small intestine.

entero– *combining form* Intestine. Also, before vowels, **enter–.** [<Gk. *enteron* intestine]

en·ter·o·cep·tor (en′tə·rō·sep′tər) See INTEROCEPTOR.

en·ter·o·gas·trone (en′tə·rō·gas′trōn) *n. Biochem.* A hormone obtained from the mucous lining of the upper intestine and having the power to inhibit the action of the gastric juices. [<ENTERO- + GASTR(O)- + (HORM)ONE]

en·ter·o·ci·ne·sia (en′tə·rō·si·nē′zhə) *n. Physiol.* Peristalsis. [<ENTERO- + Gk. *kinēsis* movement] —**en′ter·o·ci·net′ic** (-si·net′ik) *adj.*

en·ter·o·ki·nase (en′tə·rō·kī′nās, -kin′ās) *n. Biochem.* An intestinal enzyme which converts trypsinogen into trypsin.

en·ter·o·lith (en′tə·rō·lith′) *n. Pathol.* An intestinal concretion; a bezoar.

en·ter·ol·o·gy (en′tə·rol′ə·jē) *n.* The study of the intestines.

en·ter·on (en′tə·ron) *n. pl.* **·ter·a** (-tər·ə) *Anat.* The entire intestine or alimentary canal; the gut. [<NL <Gk.]

en·ter·op·to·sis (en′tə·rop·tō′sis) *n. Pathol.* Prolapse of the intestines. [<NL <Gk. *enteron* intestine + *ptosis* < *piptein* fall] —**en′ter·op′·tic** *adj.*

en·ter·o·scope (en′tər·ə·skōp′) *n. Med.* An instrument equipped with an electric light for examining the intestines. —**en·ter·os·co·py** (en′tə·ros′kə·pē) *n.*

en·ter·o·sta·sis (en′tə·rō·stā′sis) *n. Pathol.* A stoppage of food in the intestinal passages; intestinal stasis.

en·ter·o·stax·is (en′tə·rō·stak′sis) *n. Pathol.* Gradual hemorrhage through the mucous membrane of the intestine. [<ENTERO- + Gk. *staxis* < *stazein* drip]

en·ter·os·to·my (en′tə·ros′tə·mē) *n. Surg.* The formation of a permanent artificial opening through the abdominal wall into the intestine.

en·ter·ot·o·my (en′tə·rot′ə·mē) *n. Surg.* Any cutting operation upon the intestines.

en·ter·o·tox·e·mi·a (en′tə·rō·tok·sē′mē·ə) *n.* Severe intestinal poisoning of sheep caused by the toxins of certain bacteria, especially *Clostridium perfringens.*

en·ter·prise (en′tər·prīz) *n.* **1** Any projected task or work; an undertaking. **2** Boldness, energy, and invention in practical affairs. [<F *enterprise* < *entreprendre* < *entre-* between (<L *inter-*) + *prendre* take <L *prehendere*]

en·ter·pris·ing (en′tər·prī′zing) *adj.* Energetic and progressive. —**en′ter·pris′ing·ly** *adv.*

en·ter·tain (en′tər·tān′) *v.t.* **1** To hold the attention of; amuse; divert. **2** To extend hospitality to; receive as a guest. **3** To take into consideration, as a proposal. **4** To keep or bear in mind; maintain: to *entertain* a grudge. **5** *Obs.* To keep up; maintain. —*v.i.* **6** To receive and care for guests: to *entertain* lavishly. [<F *entretenir* < *entre-* between (<L *inter-*) + *tenir* < *tenere* hold] —**en′ter·tain′·a·ble** *adj.* —**en′ter·tain′er** *n.*

Synonyms: amuse, beguile, cheer, delight, disport, divert, enliven, gratify, interest, occupy, please, recreate. To *entertain,* in the sense here considered, is to engage and pleasantly occupy the attention; to *amuse* is to occupy the attention in an especially bright and cheerful way, often with that which excites merriment or laughter; as, He *entertained* us with an *amusing* story. To *divert* is to turn from serious thoughts or laborious pursuits to something that lightly and agreeably occupies the mind; one may be *entertained* or *amused* who has nothing serious or laborious from which to be *diverted.* To *recreate,* literally to re-create, is to engage mind or body in some pleasing activity that restores strength and energy for serious work. To *beguile* is, as it were, to cheat into cheer and comfort by something that insensibly draws thought or feeling away from pain or disquiet. We *beguile* a weary hour, *cheer* the despondent, *divert* the preoccupied, *enliven* a dull evening or company, *gratify* our friends' wishes, *entertain, interest, please* a listening audience, *occupy* idle time, *disport* ourselves when merry, *recreate* when worn with toil; we *amuse* ourselves or others with whatever pleasantly passes the time without special exertion, each according to his taste. See ACCOMMODATE, CHERISH, INTEREST. *Antonyms*: annoy, bore, busy, disquiet, distract, disturb, tire, weary.

en·ter·tain·ing (en′tər·tā′ning) *adj.* Of a character to entertain; amusing; diverting. —**en′·ter·tain′ing·ly** *adv.* —**en′ter·tain′ing·ness** *n.*

en·ter·tain·ment (en′tər·tān′mənt) *n.* **1** The act of receiving and caring for guests; hospitable accommodation in the inn or dwelling of a host; the furnishing of food, lodging, and service to a guest. **2** A source or means of amusement; a diverting performance, especially a public performance, as a concert, drama, or the like. **3** Pleasure afforded by an amusing act or spectacle; amusement. **4** A social party; also, the refreshments provided for guests. **5** *Obs.* Maintenance; employment; service.

Synonyms: amusement, cheer, delight, diversion, enjoyment, frolic, fun, merriment, pastime, pleasure, recreation, sport. *Entertainment* and *recreation* imply thought and mental occupation, but in an agreeable, refreshing way; they are therefore words of a high order. *Entertainment* is used of somewhat mirthful, mental delight; *recreation* may, and usually does, combine the mental with the physical. *Amusement* and *pastime* are nearly equivalent, the latter probably the lighter word; many slight things may be *pastimes* which we should hardly dignify by the name of *amusements. Sports* are almost wholly on the physical plane, while involving a certain grade of mental action. *Cheer* may be very quiet, as the *cheer* of a bright fire to an aged traveler; *merriment* suggests liveliness and laughter; *fun* and *frolic* are apt to be boisterous. Compare ENTERTAIN, FROLIC, SPORT. *Antonyms*: ennui, fatigue, labor, lassitude, toil, weariness, work.

en·thal·py (en·thal′pē, en′thəl·pē) *n. Physics* The quantity of heat in a substance or physical system per unit of mass; heat content. [<Gk. *enthalpein* < *en-* in + *thalpein* warm]

en·thet·ic (en·thet′ik) *adj.* **1** Introduced from without. **2** *Med.* Communicated by inoculation: said of infectious diseases. [<Gk. *enthetikos* fit for implanting < *en-* in + *tithenai* put]

en·thral (in·thrôl′) *v.t.* **·thralled, ·thral·ling 1** To keep spellbound; fascinate; charm. **2** To put or keep in thraldom; enslave. Also spelled *inthral.* Also **en·thrall′.** —**en·thral′·ment, en·thrall′ment** *n.*

en·throne (in·thrōn′) *v.t.* **·throned, thron·ing 1** To put upon a throne. **2** To invest with sovereign or ecclesiastical power. **3** To exalt; revere. Also spelled *inthrone.* —**en·throne′·ment** *n.*

en·thuse (in·thōōz′) *v.t.* & *v.i.* **·thused, ·thus·ing** *U.S. Colloq.* To make enthusiastic; yield to or display enthusiasm. [Back formation from ENTHUSIASM]

en·thu·si·asm (in·thōō′zē·az′əm) *n.* **1** Earnest and fervent feeling; ardent zeal for a person or cause. **2** *Archaic* Exalted or ecstatic feeling; also, irrational religious ecstasy; divine fury or frenzy; possession. **3** An object of great interest to a person. [<LL *enthusiasmus* <Gk. *enthusiasmos,* ult. < *entheos, enthous* inspired < *en-* in + *theos* god]

Synonyms: ardor, devotion, eagerness, earnestness, ecstasy, excitement, extravagance, fanaticism, fervency, fervor, frenzy, inspiration, intensity, passion, rapture, transport, vehemence, warmth, zeal. The old meaning of *enthusiasm* implies a pseudo-*inspiration,* an almost frantic *extravagance* in behalf of something supposed to be an expression of the divine will. This sense remains as the controlling one in the kindred noun *enthusiast. Enthusiasm* has now chiefly the meaning of an earnest and commendable *devotion,* an intense and eager interest. *Zeal* is burning *earnestness,* always tending to vigorous action with all the *devotion* of *enthusiasm,* but often without its hopefulness. Compare WARMTH. *Antonyms*: calculation, calmness, caution, coldness, deadness, dulness, indifference, lukewarmness, policy, prudence, timidity, wariness.

en·thu·si·ast (in·thōō′zē·ast) *n.* One prone to or moved by enthusiasm; an ardent adherent; zealot.

en·thu·si·as·tic (in·thōō′zē·as′tik) *adj.* Given to enthusiasm; ardent; zealous. Also **en·thu′·si·as′ti·cal.** See synonyms under EAGER, SANGUINE. —**en·thu′si·as′ti·cal·ly** *adv.*

en·thy·meme (en′thə·mēm) *n. Logic* An argument in which one of the premises of the syllogism is not stated. [<L *enthymema* <Gk. *enthymēma* < *enthymeesthai* think < *en-* in + *thymos* mind]

en·tice (in·tīs′) *v.t.* **·ticed, ·tic·ing** To lead on or attract by arousing hope of pleasure, profit, etc.; allure. See synonyms under ALLURE, CHARM[1], DRAW, PERSUADE. [<OF *enticier* arouse <L *in-* in + *titio* a firebrand] —**en·tic′er** *n.* —**en·tic′ing** *adj.* —**en·tic′ing·ly** *adv.*

en·tice·ment (in·tīs′mənt) *n.* **1** The act of enticing. **2** State of being enticed. **3** That which entices; allurement.

en·tire (in·tīr′) *adj.* **1** Complete in all its parts; undivided; whole. **2** Free from admixture; unalloyed; pure. **3** *Bot.* Having the margin of a leaf not serrated, as a tiger lily. **4** Consisting of only one piece. **5** Uncastrated: an *entire* horse. See synonyms under PERFECT, RADICAL. —*n.* The whole; the entirety. [<OF *entier* <L *integer.* See INTEGER.] —**en·tire′ly** *adv.* —**en·tire′ness** *n.*

en·tire·ty (in·tīr′tē) *n. pl.* **·ties 1** The state or condition of being entire; completeness. **2** That which is entire; a whole. See synonyms under AGGREGATE.

en·ti·tle (in·tīt′l) *v.t.* **·tled, ·tling 1** To give a right to demand or expect; authorize or qualify: His position *entitles* him to do it. **2** To give a name or designation to. **3** To give (a person) a title designating rank, honor, etc. Also spelled *intitle.* [<AF *entitler,* OF *entituler* <LL *intitulare* <*in-* in + *titulus* a title]

en·ti·ty (en′tə·tē) *n. pl.* **·ties 1** Anything that exists or may be supposed to exist· being. **2** A fact or conception regarded as complete in itself. [<L *entitas, -tatis* <*ens,* ppr. of *esse* be]

ento– *combining form* Within, interior: *entozoic.* Also, before vowels, *ent–*

en·to·blast (en′tō·blast), **en·to·blas·tic** (en′tō·blas′tik) See ENDOBLAST, etc.

en·to·derm (en′tō·dûrm) See ENDODERM.

en·toil (in·toil′) *v.t. Obs.* To ensnare.

en·tomb (in·tōōm′) *v.t.* **1** To place in or as in a tomb; bury. **2** To serve as a tomb for. Also spelled *intomb.* See synonyms under BURY, HIDE. [<OF *entoumber* <*en-* in + *tombe* a tomb] **—en·tomb′er** *n.* **—en·tomb′ment** *n.*

entomo– *combining form* Insect: *entomogenous.* Also, before vowels, **entom–.** [<Gk. *entoma* insects, orig. neut. pl. of *entomos* cut up <*en-* in + *temnein* cut; with ref. to their body structure]

en·to·mog·e·nous (en′tə·moj′ə·nəs) *adj. Bot.* Growing in or upon insects, as certain fungi.

en·to·mol·o·gist (en′tə·mol′ə·jist) *n.* A student of or one versed in entomology.

en·to·mol·o·gize (en′tə·mol′ə·jīz) *v.i.* **·gized, ·giz·ing 1** To study insects. **2** To collect insects for scientific study.

en·to·mol·o·gy (en′tə·mol′ə·jē) *n.* The branch of zoology that treats of insects. **—en·to·mo·log·i·cal** (en′tə·mə·loj′i·kəl) or **·log′ic** *adj.* **—en′to·mo·log′i·cal·ly** *adv.*

en·to·moph·a·gous (en′tə·mof′ə·gəs) *adj.* Feeding on insects.

en·to·moph·i·lous (en′tə·mof′ə·ləs) *adj. Bot.* Insect–loving: said of those flowers that are especially adapted for pollination by the agency of insects.

en·to·moph·i·ly (en′tə·mof′ə·lē) *n. Bot.* The condition or state of being pollinated by insects. [<ENTOMO- + Gk. *philos* loving]

en·to·mos·tra·can (en′tə·mos′trə·kan) *adj.* Designating a subclass *(Entomostraca)* of crustaceans, chiefly marine, including the branchiopods, copepods, etc. **—***n.* A member of this subclass. [<ENTOM(O) + Gk. *ostrakon* shell]

en·to·phyte (en′tō·fīt) See ENDOPHYTE.

en·top·ic (en·top′ik) *adj. Med.* Situated or occurring in its normal place: opposed to *ectopic.* [<Gk. *entopos* in a place <*en-* in + *topos* place]

en·top·tic (en·top′tik) *adj. Med.* **1** Of or pertaining to the interior of the eye. **2** Describing visual perception dependent on the eye itself, and not on anything external to it: *entoptic* phenomena. [<ENT- + Gk. *optikos* optic] **—en·top′ti·cal·ly** *adv.*

en·top·tics (en·top′tiks) *n.* The science of the eye with reference to its interior functions and the phenomena of visual perception.

en·to·sarc (en′tō·särk) See ENDOPLASM.

en·tot·ic (en·tot′ik) *adj. Med.* Of or pertaining to the interior of the ear. Compare illustration under EAR. [<ENT- + Gk. *ous, otos* ear]

en·tou·rage (än′tōō·räzh′, *Fr.* äṅ·tōō·räzh′) *n.* **1** Associates, companions, or attendants collectively, especially of a person of rank. **2** Environment. [<F <*entourer* surround <*entour* around]

en·to·zo·an (en′tə·zō′ən) *n.* Any of a branch *(Entozoa)* of metazoans, chiefly parasitic worms, characterized by the possession of a gut cavity and a two–layered cell arrangement. **—***adj.* Entozoic. [<ENTO- + Gk. *zōon* animal]

en·to·zo·ic (en′tə·zō′ik) *adj. Biol.* **1** Living within another animal. **2** Of, pertaining to, or caused by entozoans. Also **en′to·zo′al, en′·to·zo′i·cal.**

en·tr′acte (än·trakt′, *Fr.* äṅ·träkt′) *n.* **1** The time between any two acts of a play or opera. **2** A musical interlude, dance, or the like, performed between acts. [<F]

en·trails (en′trālz, -trəlz) *n. pl.* The internal parts, especially the intestines, of an animal. [<F *entrailles* <LL *intralia* intestines]

en·train[1] (en·trān′) *v.t. Physics* To draw along after itself: Steam *entrains* water. [<F *entrainer* <*en-* away (<L *inde*) + *trainer* drag]

en·train[2] (en·trān′) *v.t.* & *v.i.* To put or go aboard a railway train. **—en·train′ment** *n.*

en·tram·mel (en·tram′əl) See TRAMMEL.

en·trance[1] (en′trəns) *n.* **1** The act of entering, in any sense. **2** A passage into a house or other enclosed space. **3** The right or power of entering; entrée. **4** The entry of a vessel at a port. **5** The point or moment at which an actor first enters a scene. **6** *Obs.* Commencement; beginning. [<OF <*entrer* ENTER]

Synonyms: access, accession, adit, admission, admittance, door, doorway, entry, gate, gateway, ingress, inlet, introduction, opening, penetration, portal. *Entrance* refers merely to the fact of passing from without to within some enclosure; *admission* and *admittance* refer to entering by consent given or opportunity allowed. We may effect or force an *entrance,* but not *admittance* or *admission*; those we gain, procure, obtain, secure, win. *Admittance* refers to place; *admission* refers also to position, privilege, favor, friendship, etc. *Entrance* is also used figuratively for setting out upon some career, or becoming a member of some organization, profession, etc. *Antonyms*: departure, egress, ejection, exclusion, exit, expulsion, refusal, rejection, withdrawal.

en·trance[2] (in·trans′, -träns′) *v.t.* **·tranced, ·tranc·ing 1** To fill with rapture or wonder; delight; charm. **2** To put into a trance. See synonyms under CHARM[1], RAVISH. **—en·trance′·ment** *n.* **—en·tranc′ing** *adj.* **—en·tranc′ing·ly** *adv.*

en·trant (en′trənt) *adj.* Entering; admitting. **—***n.* **1** One who enters; a beginner. **2** One who competes in a contest.

en·trap (in·trap′) *v.t.* **·trapped, ·trap·ping 1** To catch in or as in a trap. **2** To trick into danger or difficulty; deceive; ensnare. See synonyms under CATCH, DECEIVE. **—en·trap′ment** *n.*

en·treas·ure (in·trezh′ər) *v.t.* **·ured, ·ur·ing** To store in a treasury; treasure up.

en·treat (in·trēt′) *v.t.* **1** To beg of abjectly; beseech; implore. **2** To ask for earnestly. **3** *Obs.* To act toward; treat. **—***v.i.* **4** To ask earnestly. See synonyms under ASK, PLEAD, PRAY. [<OF *entraiter* <*en-* in + *traiter* TREAT] **—en·treat′ing·ly** *adv.* **—en·treat′ment** *n.*

en·treat·y (in·trē′tē) *n. pl.* **·treat·ies** An earnest request; supplication. See synonyms under PETITION.

en·tre·chat (äṅ·trə·shà′) *n. French* In ballet, a leap upward in which the dancer repeatedly crosses his feet while in the air.

en·tre·côte (äṅ·trə·kōt′) *n. French* Rib steak.

en·trée (än′trā, *Fr.* äṅ·trā′) *n.* **1** The act or privilege of entering; entrance; admission. **2** The principal course at a dinner or luncheon. **3** Formerly, a subordinate dish served between the fish and meat courses or directly before the main course. [<F, orig. pp. of *entrer* ENTER]

en·tre·mets (än′trə·mā, *Fr.* äṅ·trə·me′) *n. pl.* **·mets** (-māz, *Fr.* -me′) *French* A dish served between the main courses of a meal or as a side dish.

en·trench (in·trench′) *v.t.* **1** To fortify or protect with or as with a trench or trenches. **2** To establish firmly: The idea was *entrenched* in his mind. **—***v.i.* **3** To encroach or trespass: with *on* or *upon.* Also spelled *intrench.*

en·trench·ment (in·trench′mənt) *n.* **1** A breastwork of earth, especially one with a ditch. **2** Any defense or protection. **3** The act of entrenching, or the state of being entrenched. **4** Encroachment. Also spelled *intrenchment.*

en·tre nous (äṅ′tr′ nōō′) *French* Between ourselves; confidentially.

en·tre·pôt (än′trə·pō, *Fr.* äṅ·trə·pō′) *n.* A depot or storehouse. [<F <*entreposer* <*entre-* between (<L *inter-*) + *poser.* See POSE[1].]

en·tre·pre·neur (än′trə·prə·nûr′, *Fr.* äṅ·trə·prə·nœr′) *n.* **1** One who undertakes to start and conduct an enterprise or business, assuming full control and risk. **2** One who originates and manages entertainments, especially musical productions; an impresario. [<F <*entreprendre.* See ENTERPRISE.]

En·tre Rí·os (en′trā rē′ōs) A province of eastern Argentina; 28,487 square miles; capital, Paraná.

en·tre·sol (en′tər·sol, *Fr.* äṅ·trə·sôl′) *n.* A half story or mezzanine, especially one next above the ground floor. [<F]

en·tro·pi·on (en·trō′pē·on) *n. Anat.* A turning inward of the edge of the eyelid or of any similar structure. [<NL <Gk. *entropē.* See ENTROPY.]

en·tro·py (en′trə·pē) *n.* **1** *Physics* An index of the degree in which the total energy of a thermodynamic system is uniformly distributed and is thus unavailable for conversion into work. **2** In information theory, a measure of the uncertainty of our knowledge. [<Gk. *entropia,* var. of *entropē* a turning <*en-* in + *trepein* turn]

en·truck (en·truk′) *v.i.* To board a truck.

en·trust (in·trust′) *v.t.* **1** To give over (something) for care, safekeeping, or performance: I will *entrust* this task to you. **2** To place something in the care or trust of; trust, as with a duty, responsibility, etc. Also spelled *intrust.* See synonyms under COMMIT.

en·try (en′trē) *n. pl.* **·tries 1** The act of coming or going in; entrance. **2** A place of entrance; a small hallway. **3** The act of entering anything in a register, list, etc., or the item, name, or statement entered. **4** The act of reporting at a customhouse, as prescribed by law, the arrival of a ship in port and the nature of her cargo. **5** The act of assuming actual possession of lands or tenements by entering upon them. **6** A contestant listed for a race, prize competition, etc. See synonyms under ENTRANCE[1], RECORD. [<F *entrée* <*entrer.* See ENTER.]

en·try·man (en′trē·mən) *n. pl.* **·men** (-mən) *U.S.* One who takes action for an entry upon, that is, for legal possession of, a portion of the public land; a homesteader.

en·try·way (en′trē·wā′) *n.* A way of entrance; entry.

en·twine (in·twīn′) *v.t.* & *v.i.* **·twined, ·twin·ing** To twine around; twine or twist together: also spelled *intwine.* See synonyms under EMBRACE[1], TWIST.

en·twist (in·twist′) *v.t.* To twist; intertwine: also spelled *intwist.*

e·nu·cle·ate (i·nōō′klē·āt, -nyōō′-) *v.t.* **·at·ed, ·at·ing 1** To shell, as a kernel. **2** *Surg.* To extract, as a tumor, eyeball, etc.; to extract from a sac without cutting. **3** To explain clearly; disclose. **4** *Biol.* To remove the nucleus from, as a cell. **—***adj.* (-it, -āt) Without a nucleus. [<L *enucleatus,* pp. of *enucleare* <*ex-* out + *nucleus* kernel] **—e·nu′·cle·a′tor** *n.*

e·nu·cle·a·tion (i·nōō′klē·ā′shən, -nyōō′-) *n. Surg.* The operation of extracting a tumor in its entirety.

e·nu·mer·ate (i·nōō′mə·rāt, -nyōō′-) *v.t.* **·at·ed, ·at·ing 1** To name one by one; list. **2** To count or ascertain the number of. See synonyms under CALCULATE. [<L *enumeratus,* pp. of *enumerare* <*ex-* out + *numerare* count] **—e·nu′mer·a′tive** *adj.*

e·nu·mer·a·tion (i·nōō′mə·rā′shən, -nyōō′-) *n.* **1** Detailed mention of things in succession; a catalog; a census. **2** The act of ascertaining a number by counting. See synonyms under RECORD.

e·nu·mer·a·tor (i·nōō′mə·rā′tər, -nyōō′-) *n.* One who enumerates; specifically, one of the minor officials employed in taking a census.

e·nun·ci·a·ble (i·nun′sē·ə·bəl, -shē-) *adj.* That may be enunciated, in any sense. **—e·nun′ci·a·bil′i·ty** *n.*

e·nun·ci·ate (i·nun′sē·āt, -shē-) *v.* **·at·ed, ·at·ing** *v.t.* **1** To pronounce or articulate (words), especially clearly and distinctly. **2** To state with exactness, as a theory or dogma. **3** To announce or proclaim. **—***v.i.* **4** To utter or pronounce words. See synonyms under ANNOUNCE, SPEAK. [<L *enunciatus,* pp. of *enunciare* <*ex-* out + *nunciare* announce <*nuntius* a messenger] **—e·nun′ci·a′tive, e·nun′ci·a·to′ry** (-ə·tôr′ē, -tō′rē) *adj.* **—e·nun′ci·a′tive·ly** *adv.* **—e·nun′ci·a′tor** *n.*

e·nun·ci·a·tion (i·nun′sē·ā′shən, -shē-) *n.* **1** The utterance or mode of utterance of vocal sounds. **2** Definite statement.

en·ure (in·yōōr′) See INURE.

en·u·re·sis (en′yə·rē′sis) *n. Pathol.* Incontinence of urine. [<NL <Gk. *enoureein* <*en-* in + *oureein* urinate]

en·vel·op (in·vel′əp) *v.t.* **·oped, ·op·ing 1** To wrap; enclose. **2** To hide from sight or understanding; obscure. **3** To surround. Also

en·vel′ope. [<OF *enveloper* < *en-* in + *voluper* fold] — **en·vel′op·er** *n.*

en·ve·lope (en′və·lōp, än′-) *n.* **1** A case or wrapper of paper with gummed edges, for enclosing a letter or the like. **2** Any enclosing covering; a wrapper. **3** *Aeron.* The outer fabric covering of an aerostat. **4** *Biol.* The enclosing membrane of an organ. **5** *Electronics* The glass or metal casing of a vacuum tube. **6** *Geom.* A curve or surface to which another curve or surface, varying or moving according to any law, is invariably tangent. **7** *Astron.* A curved sheet of nebulous matter rising and expanding from the nucleus of a comet on the side toward the sun. Also **en′·ve·lop.** [<F *enveloppe* < *envelopper* <OF *enveloper* ENVELOP]

en·vel·op·ment (in·vel′əp·mənt) *n.* **1** The act of enveloping, or the state of being enveloped. **2** That which envelops; a covering; envelope the seed and its *envelopment.*

en·ven·om (en·ven′əm) *v.t.* **1** To impregnate with venom; poison. **2** To render vindictive; embitter. [<OF *envenimer* < *en-* in + *venim* venom]

en vé·ri·té (äṅ vā·rē·tā′) *French* In truth; verily.

En·ver Pa·sha (en·ver′ pä·shä′), 1881–1922, Turkish general.

en·vi·a·ble (en′vē·ə·bəl) *adj.* Adapted to excite envy; covetable. — **en′vi·a·bly** *adv.*

en·vi·ous (en′vē·əs) *adj.* **1** Having, showing, or cherishing envy; characterized or caused by envy; grudging: an *envious* feeling. **2** *Obs.* Jealous; emulous. **3** *Obs.* Spiteful. [<AF <OF *envieus* <L *invidiosus.* Doublet of INVIDIOUS.] — **en′vi·ous·ly** *adv.* — **en′vi·ous·ness** *n.*

Synonyms: jealous, suspicious. One is *envious* who cherishes selfish ill will toward another because of his superior success, endowments, possessions, or the like. A person is *envious* of that which is another's, and to which he himself has no right or claim; he is *jealous* of intrusion upon that which is his own, or to which he maintains a right or claim. An *envious* spirit is always bad; a *jealous* spirit may be good or bad, according to its object and tendency. A free people must be *jealous* of their liberties if they would retain them. One is *suspicious* of another from unfavorable indications or from a knowledge of wrong in his previous conduct, or even without reason. Compare DOUBT. *Antonyms:* contented, friendly, kindly, satisfied, trustful.

en·vi·ron (in·vī′rən) *v.t.* To be or extend around; encircle; surround. See synonyms under EMBRACE[1]. [<F *environner* < *environ* about]

en·vi·ron·ment (in·vī′rən·mənt, -ərn-) *n.* **1** Whatever encompasses. **2** *Biol.* The aggregate of all external and internal conditions affecting the existence, growth, and welfare of organisms. **3** One's surroundings or external circumstances collectively. **4** The act of environing, or the state of being environed. — **en·vi′ron·men′tal** *adj.*

en·vi·ron·ment·al·ist (in·vī′rən·men′təl·ist) *n.* **1** One who advocates preservation of the environment, as from commercial exploitation. **2** One who attaches more importance to environment than to heredity as a determinant in the development of a person or a group. — **en·vi′ron·men′tal·ism** *n.*

en·vi·rons (in·vī′rənz) *n. pl.* The surrounding region; outskirts; suburbs. [<F < *environ* about]

en·vis·age (en·viz′ij) *v.t.* **·aged, ·ag·ing** **1** To face; look into the face of. **2** To form a mental image of; visualize. — **en·vis′age·ment** *n.*

en·vi·sion (en·vizh′ən) *v.t.* To see or foresee in the imagination: to *envision* the future.

en·voi (äṅ·vwä′) See ENVOY[1].

en·voy[1] (en′voi) *n.* **1** A diplomatic agent. See PLENIPOTENTIARY. **2** A diplomat dispatched on a special mission. **3** Any one entrusted with a mission; a commissioner. [<F *envoyé,* pp. of *envoyer* send <OF *envoiier* < *en voie* on the way]

en·voy[2] (en′voi) *n.* **1** A postscript to or the closing lines of a poem: generally printed *l'envoi.* **2** *Obs* The act of sending a message. [<OF *envoye* < *envoiier.* See ENVOY[1].]

en·vy (en′vē) *v.* **·vied, ·vy·ing** *v.t.* **1** To regard enviously. **2** To feel envy because of; begrudge. **3** To covet; desire; want. — *v.i.* **4** To feel or show envy. — *n. pl.* **·vies** **1** Selfish and unfriendly grudging of what another enjoys; in a mild sense, the longing for a good possessed by another, without ill will toward the possessor. **2** An object of envy. **3** *Obs.* Hatred; ill will. [<F *envie* <L *invidia* < *in-* on + *videre* see, look] — **en′vi·er** *n.* — **en′vy·ing·ly** *adv.*

en·wind (en·wīnd′) *v.t.* To wind or coil around.

en·womb (en·wōōm′) *v.t.* To hold in the womb; conceal as in a womb.

en·wrap (en·rap′) *v.t.* **·wrapped, ·wrap·ping** To wrap in a cover; hence, to envelop: also spelled *inwrap.* — **en·wrap′ment** *n.*

en·wreathe (en·rēth′) *v.t.* **·wreathed, ·wreath·ing** To wrap or encircle with or as with a wreath: also spelled *inwreathe.*

E·ny·o (ē·nī′ō) **1** In Greek mythology, the goddess of war: later identified with the Roman *Bellona.* **2** One of the Graeae.

en·zo·ot·ic (en′zō·ot′ik) *adj.* Endemic among animals, as a disease. [<Gk. *en-* in + *zōon* animal]

en·zyme (en′zīm, -zim) *n. Biochem.* A complex organic substance, usually a protein, produced by cells and having the power to initiate or accelerate specific chemical reactions in the metabolism of plants and animals; a ferment; an organic catalyst: also called *biocatalyst.* Also **en′zym** (-zim). [<L <Gk. *enzymos* leavened < *en-* in + *zymē* leaven] — **en·zy·mat·ic** (en′zī·mat′ik, -zi-) *adj.*

en·zy·mol·o·gy (en′zī·mol′ə·jē) *n.* The branch of biochemistry which treats of the structure, properties, and functions of enzymes.

en·zy·mol·y·sis (en′zī·mol′ə·sis) *n.* The chemical change induced by the action of enzymes. Also **en′zy·mo′sis** (-mō′sis).

eo– *combining form* Earliest; early part of: used in geology, paleontology, archeology, etc. [<Gk. *ēōs* dawn, daybreak]

E·o·an·thro·pus (ē′ō·an·thrō′pəs, -an′thrə-) *n.* A spurious type of early man *(E. dawsoni)* based on incompatible skull fragments found by Charles Dawson and others in Pleistocene gravel beds near Piltdown, England, between 1909 and 1915; exposed in 1953 as a fossil artifact combining a modern skull with the jaw of an orangutan. Also called *Dawn man, Piltdown man.* [<NL <Gk. *ēōs* dawn + *anthropos* man]

e·o·bi·ont (ē′ō·bī′ənt) *n.* A living organism; specifically, one produced by biopoesis. [<EO- + Gk. *biōn, biontos* ppr. of *bioein* live]

E·o·cene (ē′ə·sēn) *Geol. adj.* Of, pertaining to, or existing in the Lower Tertiary period of the Cenozoic era, following the Paleocene and succeeded by the Oligocene. — *n.* The second epoch of the Cenozoic era, associated with a warm climate and the rise of mammals. See chart under GEOLOGY. [<EO- + Gk. *kainos* new]

e·o·cli·max (ē′ō·klī′maks) *n. Ecol.* The climax of the period of dominance of a given plant population. See EOSERE.

E·o·gene (ē′ə·jēn) *adj. Geol.* Of or pertaining to the Paleocene, Eocene, and Oligocene epochs of the Cenozoic era; Paleogene.

E·o·hip·pus (ē′ō·hip′əs) *n. Paleontol.* A genus of primitive, now extinct, small, four-toed horses, connected through a complete series of succeeding types with the present horse; associated with the lower Eocene of the western United States. [<EO- + Gk. *hippos* horse]

e·o·li·an (ē·ō′lē·ən) See AEOLIAN.

E·o·li·an (ē·ō′lē·ən), **E·ol·ic** (ē·ol′ik), etc. See AEOLIAN, etc.

e·ol·i·pile (ē·ol′ə·pīl) *n.* **1** A reaction engine consisting of a hollow sphere upon trunnions, usually above a boiler connected with it. At right angles to its trunnions, two or more radial pipes project from the sphere, their openings so disposed that the forcible ejection of steam rotates the sphere in the opposite direction. **2** One of various devices working on the same principle, as for operating toys, etc. Also **e·ol′o·pile**: often spelled *aeol-* or *-pyle.* [<L *aeolipilae* an instrument for investigating the nature of the wind <*Aeolus* god of the winds + *pila* a ball]

EOLIPILE

e·o·lith (ē′ə·lith) *n.* A stone tool of the earliest form; a celt. For illustration see CELT. [<EO- + Gk. *lithos* stone]

E·o·lith·ic (ē′ə·lith′ik) *adj. Anthropol.* Of or pertaining to a period of protohuman culture extending from the late Pliocene to the first glacial epoch of the Pleistocene and followed by the Paleolithic period: known only by the rudest implements of bone and chipped stone.

e·o·li·trop·ic (ē′ə·lə·trop′ik) See ANISOTROPIC.

e·on (ē′on) *n.* **1** An incalculable period of time; an age; eternity. **2** *Geol.* A time interval including two or more eras. Also spelled *aeon.* [<L *aeon* <Gk. *aiōn* age]

e·o·ni·an (ē·ō′nē·ən) *adj.* Pertaining to or lasting for eons; everlasting: also spelled *aeonian.*

e·o·nism (ē′ə·niz′əm) *n.* The adoption by a male of female habits, clothing, etc.; transvestitism. [after Chevalier Charles *d'Éon,* 1728–1810, French diplomat]

E·os (ē′əs) In Greek mythology, the goddess of the dawn, daughter of Hyperion: identified with the Roman *Aurora.*

e·o·sere (ē′ə·sir) *n. Ecol.* The total development of a particular vegetation, such as ferns, conifers, etc., throughout a geological period that was dominated by plant population.

e·o·sin (ē′ə·sin) *n. Chem.* **1** A reddish coloring matter, $C_{20}H_8Br_4O_5$, derived from coal tar: used for dyeing, for making red ink and pink lakes, and as a stain in microscopical work. **2** Any of several analogous dyes derived from coal tar. Also **e′o·sine** (-sin, -sēn). [<Gk. *eos* dawn + -IN] — **e′o·sin′ic** *adj.*

e·o·sin·o·phile (ē′ə·sin′ə·fīl, -fil) *n. Biol.* A micro-organism, cell, or cell substance with a special affinity for eosin stains or acid stains in general. — **e·o·si·noph·i·lous** (ē′ō·si·nof′ə·ləs), **e′o·sin′o·phil′ic** (-fil′ik) *adj.*

Eöt·vös balance (œt′vœsh) *Physics* An extremely sensitive torsion balance designed to detect and measure local irregularities in gravity: used in geophysics research. [after Roland von *Eötvös,* 1848–1919, Hungarian physicist]

-eous *suffix* Of the nature of: *vitreous.* [<L *-eus*]

E·o·zo·ic (ē′ə·zō′ik) *adj. Geol.* Of or pertaining to the upper portion of the Pre-Cambrian period, immediately underlying the Paleozoic, and showing the first signs of invertebrate life. [<EO- + Gk. *zōē* life]

ep– Var. of EPI–.

e·pact (ē′pakt) *n. Astron.* **1** The excess of the solar year over 12 lunar months, generally about 11 days. **2** The number of days in the age of the moon on the first day of any particular year. [<LL *epacta* <Gk. *epaktē,* fem. sing., added < *epi-* upon + *agein* lead]

E·pam·i·non·das (i·pam′ə·non′dəs), 418?–362 B.C., Theban general and statesman.

ep·arch (ep′ärk) *n.* **1** The chief administrator of a Grecian eparchy. **2** In the Greek Church, a metropolitan or bishop. — **ep·ar′chi·al** *adj.*

ep·ar·chy (ep′är·kē) *n. pl.* **·chies** **1** In ancient Greece, a district corresponding to a Roman province, under the jurisdiction of an eparch. **2** In modern Greece, a governmental subdivision of the country. **3** In the Greek Church, an ecclesiastical province or diocese. [<Gk. *eparcheia* < *eparchos* < *epi-* on + *archein* rule]

ep·au·let (ep′ə·let) *n.* **1** *Mil.* A fringed shoulder ornament of commissioned officers: no longer used in the British Army; used in the U.S. Army and Navy with full dress. **2** A shoulder ornament of women's dresses designed to give the effect of width to the shoulder line. Also **ep′au·lette.** [<F *épaulette,* dim. of *épaule* shoulder, OF *espale* <L *spatula*; from its having been used as a device to hold a shoulder belt or protect the shoulder bearing a musket. See SPATULA.]

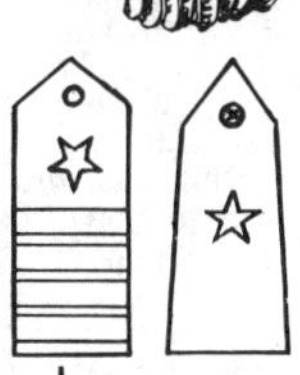

EPAULETS
United States
a. Full dress, 1812.
b. Captain, Navy.
c. Brigadier General, Army.

é·pée (ā·pā′) *n.* A dueling sword with a sharp point and no cutting edge. [<F <OF *espee* <L *spatha* a broad, flat blade <Gk. *spathē*]

é·pée·ist (ā·pā′ist) *n.* A skilled or expert swordsman or fencer.

e·pei·ro·gen·ic (i·pī′rō·jen′ik) *adj. Geol.* Of, pertaining to, or designating continent-making movements of the earth's crust, or the rising and sinking of vast areas: also spelled *epirogenic.* Also **e·pei′ro·ge·net′ic** (-jə·net′ik). [<Gk. *ēpeiros* mainland + -GENIC]

ep·ei·rog·e·ny (ep′ī·roj′ə·nē) *n. Geol.* The process of the formation of a continent or of the greater masses that compose a continent: also spelled *epirogeny.* See DIASTROPHISM.

ep·en·ceph·a·lon (ep′en·sef′ə·lon) *n. pl.* **·la** (-lə) *Anat.* **1** The hind brain. **2** The cerebellum. — **ep·en·ce·phal·ic** (ep′en·si·fal′ik) *adj.*

ep·en·dy·ma (ep·en′di·mə) *n. Anat.* The tissue lining the central cavities of the brain and spinal cord and derived from the original epithelium of the neural tube. [<NL <Gk. < *epi-* upon + *endyma* a garment] — **ep·en′dy·mal** *adj.*

ep·en·the·sis (ep·en′thə·sis) *n. pl.* **·ses** (-sēz) **1** The intrusion of a letter or syllable within a word, as the *d* in *thunder* (Old English *thunor*). **2** The phonetic change resulting from the transference of a semivowel to the syllable preceding, as (in the Greek) in changing *karjo* to *kairo.* [<LL <Gk. < *epi-* upon + *en-* in + *tithenai* place] — **ep·en·thet·ic** (ep′·en·thet′ik) *adj.*

e·pergne (i·pûrn′, ā·pârn′) *n.* An ornamental centerpiece for a dinner table, often consisting of several grouped dishes for fruit, sweets, flowers, etc. [? <F *épargne* economy, thrift]

É·per·nay (ā·per·nā′) A town on the Marne in northern France.

E·pe·us (i·pē′əs) In Greek mythology, the builder of the wooden horse, used by the Greeks to enter and destroy Troy. See TROJAN HORSE.

ep·ex·e·ge·sis (ep·ek′sə·jē′sis) *n.* Something added by way of further elucidation; fuller statement or explanation. [<Gk. *epexēgēsis* < *epi-* upon + *exēgēsis.* See EXEGESIS.]

ep·ex·e·get·ic (ep·ek′sə·jet′ik) *adj.* Explanatory of or additional to a preceding explanation; of the nature of epexegesis. Also **ep·ex′e·get′i·cal.** — **ep·ex′e·get′i·cal·ly** *adv.*

eph– Var. of EPI–.

e·phah (ē′fə) *n.* An ancient Jewish measure of capacity, a little over a bushel, dry measure. Also **e′pha.** [<Hebrew]

ep·har·mone (ep·här′mōn) *n. Ecol.* A plant form differing from the normal through influences of the environment in which it lives. [<EPHARMONY]

ep·har·mo·ny (ep·här′mə·nē) *n. Ecol.* The growth and form of plants as determined by their adaptability to environmental influences, or the harmony between the structure of a plant and the external factor. Also **ep′har·mo′sis** (-mō′sis). [<EP(H)- outside + HARMONY]

e·phe·bic (e·fē′bik) *adj.* **1** Of or pertaining to an ephebus. **2** Of or relating to the adult stages of an organism.

e·phe·bus (e·fē′bəs) *n. pl.* **·bi** (-bī) In ancient Greece, especially Attica, a free-born youth between 18 and 20 years of age, who, having passed an examination, was entered on the list of his tribe. Also **e·phe′bos.** [<L <Gk. *ephēbos* youth < *epi-* upon + *hēbē* youth]

e·phed·rine (e·fed′rin, ef′ə·drēn) *n. Chem.* An alkaloid, $C_{10}H_{15}ON$, isolated from plants of the genus *Ephedra,* and also made synthetically; used as a cardiac depressant and for asthma. Also **e·phed·rin** (i·fed′rin, ef′ə·drin). [<NL *Ephedra,* a genus of plants + -INE[2]]

e·phem·er·a (i·fem′ər·ə) *n. pl.* **·as** or **·ae** (-ē) **1** An ephemerid or mayfly. **2** Anything of very short life or duration. [<Gk. *ephēmeros* for a day < *epi-* on + *hēmera* day]

e·phem·er·al (i·fem′ər·əl) *adj.* **1** Living one day only, as certain insects. **2** Transitory. See synonyms under TRANSIENT. — *n.* Anything lasting for a very short time. — **e·phem′·er·al·ly** *adv.*

e·phem·er·id (i·fem′ər·id) *n.* Any of a widespread order *(Ephemerida)* of insects with aquatic early stages and a very short-lived adult stage; of fragile build, with two or three long caudal filaments, hind wings reduced in size, and vestigial mouth parts; a mayfly, dayfly, or shadfly. [<NL *Ephemeridae* <Gk. *ephēmeros.* See EPHEMERA.]

e·phem·er·is (i·fem′ər·is) *n. pl.* **eph·e·mer·i·des** (ef′ə·mer′ə·dēz) **1** A table showing the calculated positions and motions of a heavenly body, or of several such bodies, from day to day or at regular intervals. **2** A collection of such tables, or an annual publication giving such tables: an astronomical almanac. **3** Ephemera. **4** *Obs.* A diary or other diurnal record of events. [<L, a diary <Gk. *ephēmeris* < *ephēmeros.* See EPHEMERA.]

e·phem·er·on (i·fem′ər·on) *n. pl.* **·er·a** (-ər·ə) **1** An ephemerid, or ephemera. **2** Anything short-lived.

E·phe·sian (i·fē′zhən) *adj.* Of or pertaining to Ephesus. — *n.* **1** A citizen of Ephesus. **2** *Rare* A jovial comrade; boon companion.

E·phe·sians (i·fē′zhənz) **1** The people of Ephesus. **2** The New Testament epistle to the church at Ephesus.

Eph·e·sus (ef′ə·səs) An ancient Greek city in western Asia Minor; site of a great temple of Diana.

Eph·i·al·tes (ef′ē·al′tēz) *n.* In Greek mythology, the demon supposed to inflict nightmares; hence, any nightmare.

eph·od (ef′od, ē′fod) *n.* A Jewish priestly vestment. *Ex.* xxviii 31. [<Hebrew *ēphōd* < *āphad* clothe]

eph·or (ef′ôr, -ər) *n. pl.* **·ors** or **·o·ri** (-ə·rī) **1** In ancient Greece, one of a body of supervising magistrates at Sparta and other Doric towns. **2** In modern Greece, a supervisor of public works. [<L *ephorus* <Gk. *ephoros* < *epi-* over + *hor-,* root of *horaein* see]

E·phra·im (ē′frē·əm, ē′frəm) **1** In the Old Testament, Joseph's second son, who obtained the birthright. *Gen.* xlvi 20. **2** The tribe descended from him. *Josh.* xiv 4.

E·phra·im (ē′frē·əm, ē′frəm) **1** A hilly region of Palestine between the Mediterranean and the Plain of Jezreel, occupied by the Ephraimites: also **Mount Ephraim, the Hills of Ephraim.** **2** The kingdom of Israel.

E·phra·im·ite (ē′frē·əm·īt) *n.* A descendant of Ephraim or a member of the tribe of Ephraim.

ep·i (ep′ē) *n.* **1** A short spur of a railroad, sometimes used for mounting coastal artillery. **2** (ā·pē′) *Archit.* A protection for the apex of a spire or sharply pointed roof; a finial. [<F, lit., ear of grain <L *spica*]

EPI

epi– *prefix* **1** Upon; above; among; outside: *epidermis.* **2** Besides; over; in addition to: *epilog.* **3** Near; close to; beside: *epifocal.* Also: *ep–,* before vowels. as in *eponym*; *eph–,* before an aspirate, as in *ephemeral.* [<Gk. *epi-, ep-, eph-* <*epi* upon, on]

ep·i·blast (ep′ə·blast) *n.* **1** *Biol.* The outermost of the germ layers of the embryo; the ectoderm. **2** *Bot.* A small scalelike appendage in front of the embryo in the seed of certain grasses. — **ep′i·blas′tic** *adj.*

ep·i·bol·ic (ep′ə·bol′ik) *adj. Biol.* Of, pertaining to, or exhibiting epiboly: *epibolic* invagination.

e·pib·o·ly (e·pib′ə·lē) *n. Biol.* The inclusion of one set of segmenting cells within another by means of the more rapid division of the latter. Also **e·pib′o·lism.** [<Gk. *epibolē* < *epi-* upon + *ballein* throw]

ep·ic (ep′ik) *n.* A poem celebrating in stately, formal verse the achievements of heroes, gods, and demigods: also **heroic epic.** Homer's *Iliad* and *Odyssey,* Vergil's *Aeneid* are famous classical epics; the Hindu *Mahabharata* and *Ramayana,* and the Babylonian *Creation Epic* are among the world's greatest, as are also the medieval French *Chanson de Roland* and the 12th century Spanish *Poema del Cid.* The conscious **art epic** is typified by Milton's *Paradise Lost.* — *adj.* Of, pertaining to, or like an epic; grand; noble; heroic: also **ep′i·cal.** [<Gk. *epikos* < *epos* word] — **ep′i·cal·ly** *adv.*

ep·i·ca·lyx (ep′ə·kā′liks, -kal′iks) *n. pl.* **·ca·lyx·es** or **·ca·ly·ces** (-kā′lə·sēz, -kal′ə-) *Bot.* An external involucel or accessory calyx outside the true calyx of a flower. Compare illustration under INVOLUCEL.

ep·i·can·thic fold (ep′ə·kan′thik) *Anat.* A vertical fold of skin on the nasal side of the eyelid whose presence gives the slant-eyed effect noted chiefly in certain Mongoloid peoples. Also **ep′i·can′thus.** [<NL *epicanthus* <Gk. *epi-* upon + *kanthos* corner of the eye]

ep·i·car·di·um (ep′ə·kär′dē·əm) *n. pl.* **·di·a** (-dē·ə) *Anat.* The portion of the pericardium that is directly united with the substance of the heart. [<NL <Gk. *epi-* upon + *kardia* heart] — **ep′i·car′di·ac** (-ak), **ep′i·car′di·al** *adj.*

ep·i·carp (ep′ə·kärp) *n. Bot.* The outer layer of a pericarp. Compare illustration under FRUIT.

ep·i·ce·di·um (ep′ə·sē′dē·əm) *n. pl.* **·di·a** (-dē·ə) A dirge; funeral hymn; lament. [<L <Gk. *epikēdeion,* neut. sing. of *epikēdeios* funereal < *epi-* upon + *kēdos* care, funeral]

ep·i·cene (ep′ə·sēn) *adj.* **1** Of common gender. **2** Belonging to or partaking of the characteristics of both sexes. **3** Loosely, sexless. — *n.* **1** A noun that includes both sexes, as *bird, rat.* **2** A person who exhibits characteristics of both sexes. Also **ep′i·coene.** [<L *epicoenus* <Gk. *epikoinos* < *epi-* upon + *koinos* common] — **ep′i·cen′ism** *n.*

ep·i·cen·ter (ep′ə·sen′tər) *n. Geol.* The point or area on the earth's surface vertically above the focus or point of origin of an earthquake. Also **ep′i·cen′trum.** — **ep′i·cen′tral** *adj.*

ep·i·cot·yl (ep′ə·kot′l) *n. Bot.* That part of the young stem of a plant seedling above the cotyledons. [<EPI- + COTYL(EDON)]

e·pic·ri·sis[1] (i·pik′rə·sis) *n. pl.* **·ses** (-sēz) **1** An elaborate or detailed literary criticism. **2** *Med.* Critical discussion and analysis of a disease subsequent to its termination. [< Gk. *epikrisis* < *epi-* upon + *krinein* judge]

ep·i·cri·sis[2] (ep′ə·krī′sis) *n. pl.* **·ses** (-sēz) *Med.* A supplementary crisis in a disease. [<EPI- + CRISIS]

ep·i·crit·ic (ep′ə·krit′ik) *adj. Physiol.* Of or pertaining to nerve fibers in the skin which are responsive to very delicate variations in touch and temperature stimuli: opposed to *protopathic.* [<Gk. *epikritikos* < *epikrisis.* See EPICRISIS[1].]

Ep·ic·te·tus (ep′ik·tē′təs) Greek Stoic philosopher, first century A.D.

ep·i·cure (ep′ə·kyo͝or) *n.* One given to refined indulgence in the pleasures of the table; originally, a sensualist. [after *Epicurus*] — **ep′·i·cu·re′an** (-kyo͝o·rē′ən) *adj.* & *n.* — **ep′i·cu·re′·an·ism** *n.* — **ep′i·cur·ism** *n.*

Ep·i·cu·re·an (ep′ə·kyo͝o·rē′ən) *adj.* Pertaining to the Greek philosopher Epicurus or to his doctrine. — *n.* A follower of Epicurus.

Ep·i·cu·re·an·ism (ep′ə·kyo͝o·rē′ən·iz′əm) *n.* The doctrine or spirit of the philosophy of Epicurus.

Ep·i·cu·rus (ep′ə·kyo͝or′əs), 342?–270? B.C., Greek philosopher who maintained that freedom from pain and peace of mind constitute the chief good, to be gained by self-control and the pursuit of virtue: mistakenly regarded as the philosopher of pleasure and indulgence of the senses.

ep·i·cy·cle (ep′ə·sī′kəl) *n.* **1** In the Ptolemaic cosmogony, a small circle whose center moves on the circumference of a larger circle (the deferent) concentric with the earth, while its own circumference forms the orbit of a planet. **2** *Geom.* A circle that rolls upon the exterior or interior of the circumference of another circle. [<L *epicyclus* <Gk. *epikyklos* < *epi-* upon + *kyklos* a circle] — **ep′i·cy′clic** (-sī′klik, -sik′lik), **ep′i·cy′cli·cal** *adj.*

EPICYCLE
c. Earth.
e. Epicycle.
d.d.d. Deferent.
p. Planet.

epicyclic train *Mech.* A train of gear wheels in which, in addition to the motions of the wheels about their respective axes, one has a fixed axis about which the other axes revolve.

ep·i·cy·cloid (ep′ə·sī′kloid) *n. Math.* The curve traced by a point on the circumference of a circle which rolls without slipping upon the outside of the circumference of a fixed circle.

ep·i·cy·cloi·dal (ep′ə·sī·kloid′l) *adj.* Having the form of part of an epicycloid; tracing an epicycloid.

epicycloidal wheel One of the wheels in an epicyclic train.

ep·i·dem·ic (ep′ə·dem′ik) *adj.* Affecting many in a community at once: also **ep′i·dem′i·cal.** —*n.* **1** *Med.* A disease temporarily prevalent in a community or throughout a large area. **2** Any widespread excitement, influence, etc. [<F *épidémique* <*épidémie* a plague <LL *epidemia* <Gk. *epidēmia* <*epi-* upon + *dēmos* people] —**ep′i·dem′i·cal·ly** *adv.* —**ep·i·de·mic·i·ty** (ep′ə·də·mis′ə·tē) *n.*

ep·i·de·mi·ol·o·gist (ep′ə·dē′·mē·ol′ə·jist, -dem′·ē-) *n.* A specialist in epidemic diseases.

ep·i·de·mi·ol·o·gy (ep′ə·dē′mē·ol′ə·jē, -dem′ē-) *n.* That branch of medicine which treats of the origin, nature, pathology, and prevention of epidemic diseases. —**ep′i·de′mi·o·log′ic** (-dē′·mē·ə·loj′ik) or **·i·cal** *adj.*

ep·i·der·mis (ep′ə·dûr′mis) *n.* **1** *Anat.* The outer, non-vascular covering of the skin, overlying the corium; the cuticle. **2** Any integument or tegumentary covering. **3** *Bot.* The outermost layer of cells covering the surface of a plant when there are several layers of tissue. Also **ep′i·derm.** [<NL <Gk. <*epi-* upon + *derma* skin] —**ep′i·der′mal, ep′i·der′mic** *adj.*

ep·i·der·moid (ep′ə·dûr′moid) *adj.* Resembling epidermis. Also **ep′i·der·moi′dal.**

ep·i·di·a·scope (ep′ə·dī′ə·skōp) *n.* A device for projecting the images of opaque or transparent objects upon a screen: also called *aphengoscope.* [<EPI- + DIA- + -SCOPE]

ep·i·did·y·mec·to·my (ep′ə·did′ə·mek′tə·mē) *n.* *Surg.* Removal of the epididymis.

ep·i·did·y·mis (ep′ə·did′ə·mis) *n. pl.* **ep·i·di·dym·i·des** (ep′ə·di·dim′ə·dēz) *Anat.* An oblong body composed of the convoluted efferent duct of the testis, at the posterior part of that organ. [<NL <Gk. <*epi-* upon + *didymos* testicle] —**ep′i·did′y·mal** *adj.*

ep·i·dote (ep′ə·dōt) *n.* A monoclinic, greenish-to-black, aluminum calcium silicate. [<F *épidote* <Gk. *epididonai* <*epi-* upon + *didonai* give; from the large base of its crystals] —**ep′i·dot′ic** (-dot′ik) *adj.*

ep·i·do·ti·za·tion (ep′ə·dō′tə·zā′shən, -tī·zā′-) *n.* Metamorphic alteration into epidote.

ep·i·fo·cal (ep′ə·fō′kəl) *adj.* *Geol.* Of, pertaining to, or situated near the focus of an earthquake; epicentral.

ep·i·gam·ic (ep′ə·gam′ik) *adj.* *Biol.* Attractive to the opposite sex, especially during the mating season: said of animal coloration.

ep·i·gas·tric (ep′ə·gas′trik) *adj.* *Anat.* **1** Relating to the anterior walls of the abdomen. **2** Of or pertaining to the epigastrium or the abdomen generally. Also **ep′i·gas′tri·al.**

ep·i·gas·tri·um (ep′ə·gas′trē·əm) *n. pl.* **·tri·a** (-trē·ə) *Anat.* The upper part of the abdomen, especially the region over the stomach and its walls. See illustration under ABDOMINAL. [<NL <Gk. *epigastrion,* neut. sing. of *epigastrios* <*epi-* upon + *gastēr* stomach]

ep·i·ge·al (ep′ə·jē′əl) *adj.* **1** *Bot.* Epigeous. **2** *Zool.* Keeping close to ground, as certain insects. Also **ep′i·ge′an.**

ep·i·gene (ep′ə·jēn) *adj.* *Geol.* **1** Produced or occurring at the surface of the earth: *epigene* disintegration, *epigene* rocks: contrasted with *hypogene.* **2** Pseudomorphous; irregular; changed from its original formation: said of crystals. [<F *épigène* <Gk. *epigenēs* <*epi-* on, upon + *gen-,* root of *gignesthai* be born]

ep·i·gen·e·sis (ep′ə·jen′ə·sis) *n.* **1** *Biol.* The theory that the structure, organization, and development of new organisms, as in embryos, is the result of the successive interactions between male and female cells subsequent to fertilization: opposed to the doctrines of *preformation* and *syngenesis.* **2** *Geol.* An alteration in the character of rocks due to external forces or agents. **3** *Med.* An accessory or secondary symptom of a disease. —**ep′i·ge·net′ic** (-jə·net′ik) *adj.*

e·pig·e·nous (i·pij′ə·nəs) *adj.* *Bot.* Growing on the surface, especially the upper surface, as fungi on leaves. [<EPIGENE + -OUS]

ep·i·ge·ous (ep′ə·jē′əs) *adj.* *Bot.* Related or pertaining to plants or plant parts which appear above the surface of the ground, especially applied to cotyledons. [<Gk. *epigeios* <*epi-* upon + *gē* earth]

ep·i·glot·tis (ep′ə·glot′is) *n.* *Anat.* The leaf-shaped cartilaginous lid, at the base of the tongue, that covers the trachea, or windpipe, during the act of swallowing. [<NL <Gk. *epiglōttis* <*epi-* upon + *glōtta* tongue] —**ep′·i·glot′tal** *adj.*

E·pig·o·ni (i·pig′ə·nī) *n. pl.* In Greek legend, the descendants of the Seven against Thebes, who attacked Thebes successfully ten years later.

ep·i·gram (ep′ə·gram) *n.* **1** A pithy, caustic, or thought-provoking saying. **2** A short, pithy poem, especially one ending with a caustic point. [<L *epigramma* <Gk., an inscription <*epi-* upon + *graphein* write] —**ep′·i·gram′ma·tism** *n.* —**ep′i·gram′ma·tist** *n.*

ep·i·gram·mat·ic (ep′ə·grə·mat′ik) *adj.* Pertaining to or marked by epigram; witty; pointed; antithetical. Also **ep′i·gram·mat′i·cal.** —**ep′i·gram·mat′i·cal·ly** *adv.*

ep·i·gram·ma·tize (ep′ə·gram′ə·tīz) *v.* **·tized, ·tiz·ing** *v.t.* To make an epigram of; express in an epigram. —*v.i.* To write or speak in epigrams; make an epigram.

ep·i·graph (ep′ə·graf, -gräf) *n.* **1** A carved inscription on a monument, tomb, etc. **2** The superscription prefixed to a book or chapter. [<Gk. *epigraphē* <*epi-* upon + *graphein* write] —**ep′i·graph′ic** or **·i·cal** *adj.* —**ep′i·graph′i·cal·ly** *adv.*

e·pig·ra·phy (i·pig′rə·fē) *n.* The science that treats of the study, interpretation, etc., of inscriptions or epitaphs. —**e·pig′ra·pher, e·pig′·ra·phist** *n.*

e·pig·y·nous (i·pij′ə·nəs) *adj.* *Bot.* Having floral organs adnate to and near the summit of the ovary. [<EPI- + -GYNOUS] —**e·pig′y·ny** *n.*

ep·i·lep·sy (ep′ə·lep′sē) *n.* *Pathol.* A chronic nervous affection characterized by sudden loss of consciousness, sometimes accompanied by paroxysmic seizures of varying intensity and duration: primarily a symptom complex associated with various neuropsychiatric disorders. See also GRAND MAL, PETIT MAL. Also **ep′i·lep′si·a.** [<OF *epilepsie* <LL *epilepsia* <Gk. *epilēpsia* <*epi-* upon + *lambanein* seize]

ep·i·lep·tic (ep′ə·lep′tik) *adj.* Pertaining to or affected with epilepsy. —*n.* One affected with epilepsy. —**ep′i·lep′ti·cal·ly** *adv.*

ep·i·lep·toid (ep′ə·lep′toid) *adj.* Having the character of or resembling epilepsy. —*n.* One affected with a disorder resembling epilepsy.

ep·i·log (ep′ə·lôg, -log) *n.* **1** The conclusion of a discourse. **2** A short poem or speech to the audience delivered by an actor after the conclusion of a play. **3** The close of a novel or a narrative or dramatic poem. Also **ep′i·logue.** [<F *epilogue* <L *epilogus* <Gk. *epilogos* a peroration <*epi-* upon, in addition + *legein* say] —**ep′i·log′ic** (-loj′ik) or **·i·cal** *adj.* —**ep′i·lo·gis′tic** (-lō·jis′tik) *adj.*

e·pil·o·gize (i·pil′ə·jīz) *v.* **·gized, ·giz·ing** *v.i.* To utter an epilog, as to a play. —*v.t.* To give an epilog to. Also **ep′i·log,** *Brit.* **e·pil′·o·gise.**

ep·i·me·ron (ep′ə·mē′ron) *n. pl.* **·ra** (-rə) *Entomol.* The posterior division of the pleuron in the thorax of an insect. Also **ep′i·me′rum.** [<NL <Gk. *epi-* upon, besides + *mēros* thigh] —**ep′i·me′ral** *adj.*

Ep·i·me·the·us (ep′ə·mē′thē·əs) In Greek mythology, a Titan, the brother of Prometheus and husband of Pandora.

ep·i·mor·pha (ep′ə·môr′fə) *n. pl.* *Zool.* Larvae having all their segments fully formed before hatching. [<NL <Gk. *epi-* on, upon + *morphē* form]

ep·i·mor·pho·sis (ep′ə·môr·fō′sis) *n.* *Biol.* The proliferation of new tissue preceding the regeneration of a part, as in many invertebrate animals.

É·pi·nal (ā·pē·nál′) A town on the Moselle in eastern France.

ep·i·nas·ty (ep′ə·nas′tē) *n.* *Bot.* Downward curvature of a plant member, induced by a more active growth on its upper side. [<EPI- + Gk. *nastos* compact] —**ep′i·nas′tic** *adj.*

ep·i·neph·rine (ep′ə·nef′rin, -rēn) *n.* A hormone, $CaH_{13}NO_3$, secreted by the adrenal medulla, which stimulates heart action and causes constriction of blood vessels, thus increasing blood pressure. Also *Brit. adrenaline.* [<EPI- + Gk. *nephros* kidney]

ep·i·neu·ri·um (ep′ə·no͞or′ē·əm, -nyo͞or′-) *n. pl.* **·ri·a** (-ē·ə) *Anat.* The sheath of connective tissue that surrounds a nerve trunk. [<NL <Gk. *epi-* upon + *neuron* nerve, sinew] —**ep′i·neu′ri·al** *adj.*

ep·i·no·sis (ep′ə·nō′sis) *n.* **1** *Pathol.* A morbid condition subordinate to an original and primary illness. **2** *Psychoanal.* A secondary illness or disorder exploited by the patient to gain relief from the primary affliction and to obtain further sympathy. [<EPI- + Gk. *nosos* illness] —**ep′i·no′sic** *adj.*

ep·i·on·tol·o·gy (ep′ē·on·tol′ə·jē) *n.* The study of the geographic distribution of plants. [<Gk. *epiōn, -ontos,* ppr. of *epienai* (<*epi-* upon + *ienai* go) + -LOGY] —**ep′i·on′to·log′i·cal** (-tə·loj′·i·kəl) *adj.* —**ep′i·on·tol′o·gist** *n.*

Ep·i·pa·le·o·lith·ic (ep′ə·pā′lē·ə·lith′ik) *adj.* *Anthropol.* Mesolithic.

ep·i·pet·a·lous (ep′ə·pet′ə·ləs) *adj.* *Bot.* Inserted or growing on a petal, as a stamen.

e·piph·a·ny (i·pif′ə·nē) *n. pl.* **·nies** A bodily manifestation, as of a deity. [<OF *epiphanie* <Gk. *epiphainein* manifest <*epi-* upon + *phainein* show]

E·piph·a·ny (i·pif′ə·nē) *n.* *Eccl.* A festival, observed on January 6, commemorating the manifestation of Christ to the Gentiles, represented by the Magi: also called *Twelfth Day.*

ep·i·phe·nom·e·non (ep′ə·fə·nom′ə·non) *n. pl.* **·nom·e·na** (-nə) A phenomenon which is secondary to or a by-product of one or more other phenomena; one which is a mere accompaniment of some effect and exerts no causal influence on the effect.

ep·i·phyl·lous (ep′ə·fil′əs) *adj.* *Bot.* Situated or growing upon a leaf, especially with reference to stamens inserted on a perigonium. Also **ep′i·phyl′line** (-īn, -ēn). [<EPI- + Gk. *phyllon* leaf]

e·piph·y·sis (i·pif′ə·sis) *n. pl.* **·ses** (-sēz) *Anat.* **1** The extremity of a long bone, originally separated from it by cartilage but later consolidated with it by ossification. **2** The pineal body. [<NL <Gk., an outgrowth <*epi-* upon + *phyein* grow] —**ep·i·phys·i·al** (ep′ə·fiz′ē·əl), **ep′i·phys′e·al** *adj.*

ep·i·phyte (ep′ə·fīt) *n.* *Bot.* **1** A plant growing nonparasitically upon another plant or on a nonliving support and deriving nutrients and moisture from the air; also called *air plant, aerophyte.* **2** A plant, as a fungus, parasitic upon the exterior surface of an animal. —**ep′i·phyt′ic** (-fit′ik) or **·i·cal** *adj.*

ep·i·phy·tot·ic (ep′ə·fī·tot′ik) *adj.* Having or characterized by a wide-spreading plant disease. Compare EPIDEMIC, EPIZOOTIC.

ep·i·po·di·um (ep′ə·pō′dē·əm) *n. pl.* **·di·a** (-dē·ə) *Zool.* A lateral part of the foot in certain mollusks. [<NL <Gk. *epipodios* on the feet <*epi-* upon + *pous, podos* foot]

E·pi·rus (i·pī′rəs) A region of NW Greece on the Ionian Sea, formerly an independent kingdom and republic. Also **E·pei′rus.**

e·pis·co·pa·cy (i·pis′kə·pə·sē) *n. pl.* **·cies** **1** Government of a church by bishops. **2** A bishop's state or office. **3** The body of bishops collectively. [<LL *episcopatus* <*episcopus* BISHOP]

e·pis·co·pal (i·pis′kə·pəl) *adj.* **1** Of or pertaining to bishops. **2** Having a government vested in bishops; characterized by episcopacy. **3** Advocating or supporting episcopacy. [<LL *episcopalis* <*episcopus* BISHOP] —**e·pis′co·pal·ly** *adv.*

E·pis·co·pal (i·pis′kə·pəl) *adj.* Belonging or pertaining to the Protestant Episcopal Church, or to any church in the Anglican communion.

Episcopal Church See PROTESTANT EPISCOPAL CHURCH.

e·pis·co·pa·li·an (i·pis′kə·pā′lē·ən, -pāl′yən) *n.* An advocate of episcopacy. —*adj.* Pertaining to or favoring episcopal government.

E·pis·co·pa·li·an (i·pis′kə·pā′lē·ən, -pāl′yən) *n.* A member of the Protestant Episcopal Church. —*adj.* Episcopal. —**E·pis′co·pa′li·an·ism** *n.*

e·pis·co·pal·ism (i·pis′kə·pəl·iz′əm) *n.* That view of the constitution of the church that places the supreme power in the hands of a body of bishops, and recognizes no single supreme head, as the pope, with ordinary jurisdiction over the whole church.

e·pis·co·pate (i·pis′kə·pit, -pāt) *n.* **1** The office, dignity, or term of office of a bishop. **2** A bishopric. **3** Bishops collectively.

ep·i·sode (ep′ə·sōd) *n.* **1** An incident or story in a literary work, separable from, yet related to it. **2** A notable incident or action occurring as a break in the regular course of events. **3** An intermediate passage in a musical composition whereby the development of the subject is for a time suspended for the sake of variety and relief. **4** A portion of a Greek tragedy occurring between two choric songs. See synonyms under EVENT. [<Gk. *epeisodion* < *epeisodios* coming in besides < *epi-* upon + *eisodos* entrance < *eis-* into + *hodos* way, road] — **ep′i·sod′ic** (-sod′ik) or **·i·cal, ep′i·so′·dal** or **·di·al** *adj.* — **ep′i·sod′i·cal·ly** *adv.*

ep·i·spas·tic (ep′ə·spas′tik) *adj.* Raising blisters; blistering. — *n.* A blistering medicament. [<NL *epispasticus* <Gk. *epispastikos* < *epi-* on + *spaein* draw]

ep·i·sperm (ep′ə·spûrm) *n. Bot.* The outer covering of a seed. — **ep′i·sper′mic** *adj.*

ep·i·spore (ep′ə·spôr, -spōr) *n. Bot.* The outer integument or coat of a spore.

e·pis·ta·sis (i·pis′tə·sis) *n.* **1** *Genetics* The masking of one factor in Mendelian inheritance by another not allelomorphic to it. **2** *Med.* The stoppage of a hemorrhage or other fluid discharge of the body. [<NL <Gk., a stoppage < *epi-* upon + *histanai* stand]

ep·i·stat·ic (ep′ə·stat′ik) *adj. Genetics* **1** Pertaining to the dominance of one factor over another not of the same allelomorphic pair. **2** Possessing such a factor: opposed to *hypostatic.*

ep·i·stax·is (ep′ə·stak′sis) *n. Pathol.* Nosebleed. [<NL <Gk. *epistaxis* < *epi-* upon + *stazein* drop, drip]

e·pis·te·mol·o·gy (i·pis′tə·mol′ə·jē) *n.* That department of philosophy which investigates critically the nature, grounds, limits, and criteria, or validity, of human knowledge; theory of cognition. [<Gk. *epistēmē* knowledge + -LOGY] — **e·pis·te·mo·log·i·cal** (i·pis′·tə·mə·loj′i·kəl) *adj.* — **e·pis′te·mo·log′i·cal·ly** *adv.* — **e·pis′te·mol′o·gist** *n.*

e·pis·tle (i·pis′əl) *n.* **1** A written message; communication; letter: more formal than *letter,* and especially applied to ancient epistolary writings of sacred character or of literary excellence: the Pauline *epistles.* **2** *Eccl. Usually cap.* A selection, usually from an apostolic epistle, read in the communion service of the Greek, Roman, and Anglican churches. [OE *epistol* <L *epistola* <Gk. *epistolē* < *epi-* on + *stellein* send]

e·pis·tler (i·pis′lər) *n.* **1** One who writes epistles. **2** *Eccl.* The reader of the Epistle at the Eucharist; the subdeacon. Also **e·pis′to·ler** (-tə·lər).

e·pis·to·lar·y (i·pis′tə·ler′ē) *adj.* Belonging or suitable to correspondence by letter; included in or maintained by letters: also **ep·is·tol·ic** (ep′is·tol′ik), **ep′is·tol′i·cal.** — *n. pl.* **·lar·ies** A book containing the epistles of a liturgy.

e·pis·tro·phe (i·pis′trə·fē) *n.* **1** In rhetoric, that form of repetition in which successive clauses or sentences end with the same word. **2** A musical refrain. **3** *Bot.* The arrangement of chlorophyll granules (as on the upper and under walls of leaf cells) when exposed to diffused light. [<EPI- + Gk. *strophe* turning about]

ep·i·style (ep′ə·stīl) *n. Archit.* An architrave.

ep·i·taph (ep′ə·taf, -tāf) *n.* **1** An inscription on a tomb or monument in honor or in memory of the dead. See EPIGRAPH. **2** A sentiment in prose or verse written as for inscription on a tomb. [<L *epitaphium* a eulogy <Gk. *epitaphios* at a tomb < *epi-* upon, at + *taphos* a tomb] — **ep′i·taph′ic** (-taf′ik), **ep′i·taph′i·al** *adj.*

e·pit·a·sis (i·pit′ə·sis) *n.* In Greek drama, the main action of a play, wherein the plot develops, leading on to the catastrophe: opposed to *protasis.* [<NL <Gk., an intensifying < *epiteinein* intensify < *epi-* in addition + *teinein* stretch]

ep·i·tha·la·mi·um (ep′ə·thə·lā′mē·əm) *n. pl.* **·mi·a** (-mē·ə) A nuptial poem or song. Also **ep′i·tha·la′mi·on.** [<L <Gk. *epithalamion* < *epi-* at + *thalamos* a bridal chamber]

ep·i·the·li·oid (ep′ə·thē′lē·oid) *adj. Biol.* Resembling epithelium or epithelial tissue.

ep·i·the·li·o·ma (ep′ə·thē′lē·ō′mə) *n. pl.* **·o·ma·ta** (-ō′mə·tə) or **·o·mas** *Pathol.* A tumor originating in or affecting epithelial tissue; specifically, cancer of the skin. — **ep·i·the·li·om·a·tous** (ep′ə·thē′lē·om′ə·təs) *adj.*

ep·i·the·li·um (ep′ə·thē′lē·əm) *n. pl.* **·li·ums** or **·li·a** (-lē·ə) *Biol.* A membranous tissue consisting of one or more layers of cells of various types and sizes, compactly joined and serving to line the canals, cavities, and ducts of the body as well as all free surfaces exposed to the air. [<NL <Gk. *epi-* upon + *thēlē* nipple]

ep·i·thet (ep′ə·thet) *n.* **1** A phrase or word used adjectively to express some characteristic attribute or quality. **2** An expressive surname or nickname, as Harry *Hotspur, Old Hickory.* Also **e·pith·e·ton** (i·pith′ə·ton). See synonyms under NAME. [<L *epitheton* <Gk. < *epitithenai* attribute < *epi-* upon + *tithenai* place] — **ep′i·thet′ic** or **·i·cal** *adj.*

e·pit·o·me (i·pit′ə·mē) *n.* **1** A typical example; embodiment: the *epitome* of arrogance. **2** An extreme example; climax or culmination. **3** A concise summary; abridgement. See synonyms under ABBREVIATION, ABRIDGMENT. [<L <Gk. *epitomē* < *epi-* upon + *temnein* cut] — **ep·i·tom·ic** (ep′ə·tom′ik) or **·i·cal** *adj.* — **e·pit′o·mist** or **e·pit′o·miz′er** or *Brit.* **e·pit′o·mis′er** *n.*

e·pit·o·mize (i·pit′ə·mīz) *v.t.* **·mized, ·miz·ing** **1** To abridge. **2** To be an epitome of. Also *Brit.* **e·pit′o·mise.** See synonyms under ABBREVIATE.

ep·i·trite (ep′ə·trīt) *n.* In ancient prosody, a foot of three long syllables and one short. [<LL *epitritos* <Gk. *epitritos* containing one and one third < *epi-* upon + *tritos* third]

ep·i·troch·le·a (ep′ə·trok′lē·ə) *n. Anat.* The bony prominence on the inner side of the humerus at its lower end; the inner condyle.

ep·i·zeux·is (ep′ə·zōōk′sis) *n.* That form of figurative repetition in which a word is repeated without any intervening words or clauses. Example: He is brave—brave beyond measure. [<LL <Gk. < *epizeugnunai* < *epi-* upon + *zeugnunai* yoke, join]

ep·i·zo·on (ep′ə·zō′on) *n. pl.* **·zo·a** (-zō′ə) An animal parasite living on the outside of the body.

ep·i·zo·ot·ic (ep′ə·zō·ot′ik) *adj.* Common to or affecting many animals at the same time: said especially of diseases. — *n.* An epizootic disease: also **ep′i·zo′o·ty** (-zō′ə·tē).

e plu·ri·bus u·num (ē plŏŏr′ə·bəs yōō′nəm) *Latin* One out of many; motto of the United States.

ep·och (ep′ək, *Brit.* ē′pok) *n.* **1** A point in the onward course of history from which succeeding years are counted: Atomic energy marks an *epoch* in history. **2** An interval of time or a series of years, regarded as a whole, memorable for extraordinary events and far-reaching results; any definite period of history. **3** *Geol.* A minor subdivision of time; a time interval less than a period: the Pleistocene *epoch.* See chart under GEOLOGY. **4** *Astron.* A moment of time when a planet reaches a certain known position with reference to the sun. [<Gk. *epochē* a stoppage, point of time < *epi-* upon + *echein* have]

ep·och·al (ep′ə·kəl) *adj.* Creating or marking an epoch.

ep·och-mak·ing (ep′ək·mā′king, *Brit.* ē′pok-) *adj.* Opening up a new era, as in history, science, culture, etc.

ep·ode (ep′ōd) *n.* **1** That part of a Pindaric ode following the strophe and antistrophe. **2** A species of lyric poem, in which a longer verse is followed by a shorter one. [<F *épode* <L *epodos* <Gk. *epōidos* an incantation < *epi-* in addition + *aidein* sing]

ep·o·nym (ep′ə·nim) *n.* **1** A personage assumed as the founder and name-giver of a race, state, or city; also, the name of that personage. **2** A name or phrase formed from the name of a person to designate a people, period, scientific theory, disease, etc. **3** A high official in ancient Assyria, whose name was given to the year during which he held office. [<Gk. *epōnymos* < *epi-* upon + *onyma* name]

e·pon·y·mist (i·pon′ə·mist) *n.* One from whom an eponym is derived.

e·pon·y·mous (i·pon′ə·məs) *adj.* Pertaining to an eponym. Also **ep·o·nym·ic** (ep′ə·nim′ik).

e·pon·y·my (i·pon′ə·mē) *n.* **1** The year or period of office of an eponym. **2** Eponymic nomenclature.

ep·o·pee (ep′ə·pē, ep′ə·pē′) *n.* **1** An epic poem. **2** Epic poetry in general. Also **ep′o·poe′ia.** [<F *épopée* <Gk. *epopoiia* epic poetry < *epos* word, song + *poieein* make]

ep·opt (ep′opt) *n.* In ancient Greece, one of the initiated; hence, one to whom all the secrets of any body of mysteries have been revealed. [<LL *epopta* <Gk. *epoptes* < *epi-* upon + *op-,* stem of *horaein* see, look] — **ep·op′tic** *adj.*

ep·os (ep′os) *n.* **1** An epopee. **2** Unwritten narrative poetry; a series of heroic events. [<L <Gk., word, song]

e·pox·y (i·pok′sē) *n. Chem.* The radical -O-, especially as bonded to different atoms already joined in different ways to form the durable **epoxy resins** much used for varnishes and adhesives.

Ep·ping (ep′ing) An urban district of western Essex, England, on the edge of **Epping Forest** which once included all Essex, now a public park of 5,600 acres.

ep·si·lon (ep′sə·lon) *n.* The fifth letter and second vowel of the Greek alphabet (Ε, ε), equivalent to English short *e.* As a numeral it denotes 5. [<Gk. *epsilon* < *e* e + *psilon* simple]

Ep·som (ep′səm) A town in north central Surrey, England, famous for its racecourse on **Epsom Downs** where the Derby and other races are run.

Epsom salts A hydrous magnesium sulfate, used as a purge or to reduce inflammation. Also **Epsom salt.**

Ep·stein (ep′stīn), **Sir Jacob,** 1880–1959, English sculptor born in the United States.

Ep·worth League (ep′wərth) An American youth organization in the Methodist Church.

eq·ua·bil·i·ty (ek′wə·bil′ə·tē, ē′kwə-) *n.* Evenness, as of temper or action. Also **eq′ua·ble·ness.**

eq·ua·ble (ek′wə·bəl, ē′kwə-) *adj.* Of uniform condition or movement; steady; even; not readily disturbed: an *equable* disposition. [<L *aequabilis* < *aequare* make equal] — **eq′·ua·bly** *adv.*

e·qual (ē′kwəl) *adj.* **1** Of the same degree with another or with each other, as in magnitude or value; neither greater nor less. **2** Equable. **3** Adequate for the purpose; commensurate. **4** *Archaic* Equitable; just. **5** Having the same rank, rights, or importance. **6** Level. **7** Uniform in operation: *equal* laws. See synonyms under ADEQUATE, ALIKE. — *v.t.* **e·qualed** or **e·qualled, e·qual·ing** or **e·qual·ling** **1** To be or become equal to. **2** To do or produce something equal to. **3** To recompense in full. **4** *Obs.* To make equal; equalize. — *n.* A person or thing equal to another; a person of the same rank or condition. [<L *aequalis* < *aequus* even] — **e′qual·ly** *adv.* — **e′qual·ness** *n.*

e·qual·i·tar·i·an (i·kwol′ə·târ′ē·ən) *adj.* Of or pertaining to the doctrine that all men are equal. — *n.* A believer in this doctrine.

e·qual·i·ty (i·kwol′ə·tē) *n. pl.* **·ties** **1** The state of being equal. **2** Exact agreement; uniformity.

Equality State Nickname of WYOMING.

e·qual·i·za·tion (ē′kwəl·ə·zā′shən, -ī·zā′-) *n.* **1** The act of equalizing. **2** An equal state.

equalization fund A fund established for the purpose of equalizing payments, income, taxes, etc., of different economic classes.

e·qual·ize (ē′kwəl·īz) *v.t.* **·ized, ·iz·ing** **1** To make equal. **2** To render uniform. Also *Brit.* **e′qual·ise.**

e·qual·iz·er (ē′kwəl·ī′zər) *n.* **1** One who or that which equalizes. **2** *Mech.* A device for equalizing pressure or strain between parts of a structure, as the springs and wheels of a locomotive. **3** *Electr.* **a** A conductor of low resistance used to join the currents of two generators and equalize their voltage. **b** Any contrivance for equalizing the pull of electromagnets. **4** *U.S. Slang* A revolver.

equal rights Equality of rights, especially between men and women.

e·quan·gu·lar (i·kwang′gyə·lər) *adj.* Equiangular.

e·qua·nim·i·ty (ē′kwə·nim′ə·tē, ek′wə-) *n.* Evenness of mind or temper; composure; calmness. [<L *aequanimitas, -tatis* < *aequus* even + *animus* mind]

e·quan·i·mous (i·kwan′ə·məs) *adj.* Even-tempered.

e·quate (i·kwāt′) *v.t.* **e·quat·ed, e·quat·ing** **1** To make equal; treat or consider as equivalent. **2** *Math.* To indicate the equality of; express as an equation. **3** To reduce to an average;

correct so as to reduce to a common standard [<L *aequatus,* pp. of *aequare* make even <*aequus* even]

e·qua·tion (i·kwā′zhən, -shən) *n.* **1** The process or act of making equal; equal division; equality. **2** *Math.* A statement expressing (usually by the symbol =) the equality of two quantities. **3** *Chem.* A symbolic representation of a chemical reaction, as $Na_2CO_3 + H_2SO_4 = Na_2SO_4 + CO_2 + H_2O$. The first member includes the substances reacting; the second, the products. The sum of the quantities of the two members must be equal. — **e·qua′·tion·al** *adj.* — **e·qua′tion·al·ly** *adv.*

equation of payments The determination of the time at which several sums of money, due at various times, should be due, if all are paid at once.

e·qua·tor (i·kwā′tər) *n.* **1** A great circle of the earth, a planet, etc., lying at right angles to its axis and equidistant from the poles. **2** Any similar circle, as of the sun, a planet, etc. **3** The celestial equator. [<LL (*circulus*) *aequator* equalizer (circle); so called because day and night are equal when the sun crosses the equator]

EQUATOR
e. Equator.
n. North pole.
s. South pole.

e·qua·to·ri·al (ē′kwə·tôr′ē·əl, -tō′rē-) *adj.* Relating to, near, or determined by an equator: *equatorial* climate. — *n. Astron.* A telescope turning on two axes at right angles to each other, the principal one being parallel to the axis of the earth.

Equatorial Islands See LINE ISLANDS.

equatorial plate *Biol.* In cell division, the group of chromosomes collected into a disk midway between the centrosomes, just prior to the anaphase: also called *nuclear plate.* See MITOSIS, also illustration under CELL.

eq·uer·ry (ek′wə·rē) *n. pl.* **·ries** **1** An officer having charge of the horses of a prince or nobleman. **2** An officer of the royal household of England, who occasionally attends upon the sovereign or a royal prince. Also **eq′uer·y.** [<F *écurie* stable <OF *escurie,* ult. <Gmc.; infl. by L *equus* a horse]

e·ques·tri·an (i·kwes′trē·ən) *adj.* **1** Pertaining to horses or horsemanship; skilled in horsemanship. **2** Representing as on horseback. **3** Composed of or pertaining to knights. — *n.* One skilled in horsemanship. [<L *equester, -tris* <*eques* a horseman <*equus* a horse]

e·ques·tri·an·ism (i·kwes′trē·ən·iz′əm) *n.* Horsemanship.

e·ques·tri·enne (i·kwes′trē·en′) *n.* A woman skilled in horsemanship.

equi– *combining form* Equal; equally: *equidistant.* [<L *aequus* equal]

e·qui·an·gu·lar (ē′kwē·ang′gyə·lər) *adj.* Having equal angles.

equiangular spiral Logarithmic spiral.

e·qui·dis·tant (ē′kwə·dis′tənt) *adj.* Equally distant. — **e′qui·dis′tance** *n.*

e·qui·lat·er·al (ē′kwə·lat′ər·əl) *n.* A side of equal length with another, or a figure with equal sides. — *adj.* Having all the sides equal. — **e′qui·lat′er·al·ly** *adv.*

equilateral hyperbola *Math.* A rectangular hyperbola.

e·qui·len·in (ē′kwə·len′in) *n. Biochem.* A sex hormone obtained from the urine of pregnant mares: a derivative of estrone. [<L *equus* horse]

e·quil·i·brant (i·kwil′ə·brənt) *n. Physics* A force or system of forces which, applied to a body, counteracts another force or system and produces equilibrium. [<F *équilibrant,* ppr. of *équilibrer* balance <*équilibre* <L *aequilibrium* equilibrium]

e·qui·li·brate (ē′kwə·lī′brāt, i·kwil′ə-) *v.t.* & *v.i.* **·brat·ed, ·brat·ing** **1** To bring into or be in a state of equilibrium. **2** To counterpoise. [<L *aequilibratus* level <*aequus* equal + *libratus* level <*libra* a balance] — **e′qui·li·bra′tion** *n.*

e·qui·li·bra·tor (ē′kwə·lī′brā·tər, i·kwil′ə-) *n.* A device for establishing equilibrium.

e·quil·i·brist (i·kwil′ə·brist) *n.* One skilled in balancing, as a rope-walker. — **e·quil′i·bris′tic** *adj.*

e·qui·lib·ri·um (ē′kwə·lib′rē·əm) *n.* **1** A state of balance produced by the counteraction of two or more forces; equipoise. **2** *Physics* A condition of balance among forces acting within or upon a body or material system such that there is no change in the state of rest or motion of the system. **3** *Chem.* The state in a chemical process when the components no longer react among themselves or react in such a way as to maintain a balanced condition. **4** Equal balance of the mind between conflicting or differing motives or reasons; hence, fairness of judgment; well-balanced state. Also **e′qui·lib′ri·ty.** [<L *aequilibrium* <*aequus* equal + *libra* a balance]

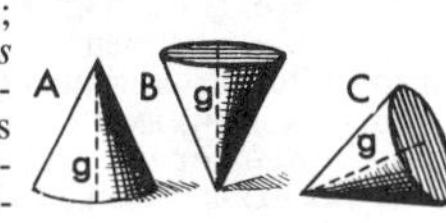

EQUILIBRIUM
A. Stable. *B.* Unstable. *C.* Neutral.
g. Center of gravity.

e·qui·mul·ti·ple (ē′kwə·mul′tə·pəl) *adj.* Produced by multiplying by the same number. — *n.* One of two or more products of different quantities by the same multiplier.

e·quine (ē′kwīn) *adj.* Of, pertaining to, or like a horse. — *n.* A horse, or a related animal. [<L *equinus* <*equus* horse]

equine syphilis Dourine.

e·qui·noc·tial (ē′kwə·nok′shəl) *adj.* **1** Occurring at or near the time when the sun crosses the celestial equator. **2** Of or pertaining to the equinox, or equality of day and night. **3** *Bot.* Opening and closing at regular hours: said of certain flowers, as the four-o'clock. **4** Of or pertaining to the equator or equatorial regions. — *n.* **1** *Meteorol.* A severe storm occurring usually at or near the equinox: also called, locally, *line storm.* **2** The equator. See EQUINOX. [<L *aequinoctialis* <*aequinox* EQUINOX]

equinoctial line The celestial equator.

equinoctial points The points of intersection of the equator and the ecliptic; the equinoxes.

equinoctial time Time reckoned from the moment at which the sun passes the vernal equinox.

e·qui·nox (ē′kwə·noks) *n.* One of two opposite points at which the sun crosses the celestial equator, when the days and nights are equal; also, the time of this crossing (about Mar. 21, the **vernal** or **spring equinox,** and Sept. 21, the **autumnal equinox**). [<L *aequinox* <*aequus* equal + *nox* night]

e·quip (i·kwip′) *v.t.* **e·quipped, e·quip·ping** **1** To furnish or fit out with whatever is needed for any purpose or undertaking. **2** To dress or attire; array. [<F *équiper* <OF *esquiper,* prob. <ON *skipa* outfit a vessel <*skip* a ship]

eq·ui·page (ek′wə·pij) *n.* **1** The equipment for a camp, army, etc. **2** A carriage, with its horses, attendants, etc. **3** Imposing display; retinue. **4** *Archaic* A complete set, as of toilet articles, silverware, etc.; also, a case containing such a set. [<F <*équiper* EQUIP]

e·qui·par·ti·tion (ē′kwə·pär·tish′ən) *n. Physics* **1** The balanced arrangement of atoms, as in a crystal. **2** That state of the molecules in a gas where they keep the same average distance apart under the same pressure. Also **equipartition of energy.**

e·quip·ment (i·kwip′mənt) *n.* **1** The act or process of equipping. **2** The state of being equipped or furnished. **3** Whatever constitutes an outfit for some special purpose or service. **4** Personal acquirements, as of an instructor, a diplomatist, etc. **5** The rolling stock and apparatus for operating a railroad or other transportation system, as distinguished from stations, trackage, and personnel.

equipment bond A railroad bond for which the rolling stock only is pledged.

equipment note A note issued to a railroad for the sole purpose of purchasing equipment, as locomotives, etc.

equipment trust The deed of trust securing an equipment bond.

e·qui·poise (ē′kwə·poiz, ek′wə-) *n.* **1** Equality or equal distribution, as of weight and power; equilibrium. **2** A counterpoise.

e·qui·pol·lence (ē′kwə·pol′əns) *n.* The state or quality of being equipollent. Also **e′qui·pol′·len·cy.**

e·qui·pol·lent (ē′kwə·pol′ənt) *adj.* **1** Equal in weight, power, effect, etc.; equivalent. **2** Equivalent in meaning and force. **3** Equal and parallel. — *n.* An equivalent. [<F *équipollent* <L *aequipollens, -entis* <*aequus* equal + *pollere* be strong]

e·qui·pon·der·ance (ē′kwə·pon′dər·əns) *n.* Equality of weight; equipoise. — **e′qui·pon′·der·ant** *adj.*

e·qui·pon·der·ate (ē′kwə·pon′də·rāt) *v.t.* **·at·ed, ·at·ing** **1** To counterbalance. **2** To make balanced. [<Med. L *aequiponderatus,* pp. of *aequiponderare* <L *aequus* equal + *ponderare* weigh]

e·qui·po·ten·tial (ē′kwə·pō·ten′shəl) *adj.* **1** Having equal power or influence. **2** *Electr.* Of equal potential at all points.

e·qui·prob·a·ble (ē′kwə·prob′ə·bəl) *adj.* Having an equal chance of occurring or being selected, as any one of a group of numbers, objects, events, etc., forming part of a random array. Compare CHANCIFY. — **e′qui·prob′a·bil′i·ty** *n.*

eq·ui·se·tum (ek′wə·sē′təm) *n. pl.* **·se·ta** (-sē′·tə) Any of a widely distributed genus (*Equisetum*) of rushlike, non-seed-bearing plants; the horsetail. [<NL <L *equus* horse + *saeta* bristle]

e·qui·so·nance (ē′kwə·sō′nəns) *n. Music* The consonance which exists between octaves.

e·qui·so·nant (ē′kwə·sō′nənt) *adj.* In ancient and medieval music, of like or equal sound, as a tone and its octave.

eq·ui·ta·ble (ek′wə·tə·bəl) *adj.* **1** Characterized by equity, or fairness and just dealing; impartial. **2** *Law* Of or pertaining to the principles of right and justice as administered by courts of equity, having relation to the system of rules and remedies enforced by those courts, as distinguished from courts of common law. **3** Within the cognizance of a court of equity. See synonyms under HONEST, JUST, RIGHT. [<F *équitable* <*équité* EQUITY] — **eq′ui·ta·ble·ness** *n.* — **eq′ui·ta·bly** *adv.*

eq·ui·tant (ek′wə·tənt) *adj. Bot.* Overlapping or riding, as leaves folded forward. [<L *equitans, -antis,* pp. of *equitare* ride on horseback <*eques, -itis* horseman <*equus* horse]

eq·ui·ta·tion (ek′wə·tā′shən) *n.* **1** Horsemanship. **2** The art of riding on horseback. [<L *equitatio, -onis* <*equitare.* See EQUITANT.]

eq·ui·tes (ek′wə·tēz) *n. pl.* The equestrian order of knights in ancient Rome, consisting originally of the mounted soldiers. [<L, pl. of *eques* horseman]

eq·ui·ty (ek′wə·tē) *n. pl.* **·ties** **1** Fairness or impartiality; justness. **2** Something that is fair or equitable. **3** *Law* **a** Justice administered between litigants which is based on natural reason or ethical judgment. **b** That field of jurisprudence superseding the legal remedies of statute law and common law when these are considered inadequate or inflexible for the purposes of justice to the parties concerned. **c** A right recognized by a court of equity. **4** Value in excess of mortgage or other liens. See synonyms under JUSTICE. [<F *équité* <L *aequitas, -tatis* <*aequus* equal]

equity of redemption The equitable right accorded to a mortgagor to redeem his mortgaged premises on payment of the sum due, notwithstanding that the time appointed for payment has passed.

e·quiv·a·lence (i·kwiv′ə·ləns) *n.* **1** The state of being equivalent or of having equal values. **2** *Chem.* The property of having equal valences. **3** Valence. Also **e·quiv′a·len·cy.**

e·quiv·a·lent (i·kwiv′ə·lənt) *adj.* **1** Equal in value, force, meaning, or the like. **2** Equal in area or volume. **3** *Chem.* Having the same valence or the same combining weight. See synonyms under ALIKE, IDENTICAL, SYNONYMOUS. — *n.* **1** That which is equivalent; something equal in value, power, or effect. **2** *Chem.* **a** A number or amount representing one of the relative weights in which elements unite with each other to form compounds, or replace other elements in compounds. **b** The combining weight of an element, compound, or radical, or that weight which combines with or displaces

8 parts of oxygen or 1.008 parts of hydrogen. [<LL *aequivalens, -entis* ppr. of *aequivalere* <*aequus* equal + *valere* be worth] —**e·quiv′a·lent·ly** *adv.*

equivalent volt An electron volt.

e·quiv·o·cal (i·kwiv′ə·kəl) *adj.* **1** Having a doubtful meaning; susceptible of different interpretations. **2** Of uncertain significance, origin, character, or value; questionable. [<LL *aequivocus* ambiguous <*aequus* equal + *vox* voice] —**e·quiv′o·cal·ly** *adv.* —**e·quiv′o·cal·ness** *n.*

Synonyms: ambiguous, doubtful, dubious, enigmatic, enigmatical, indefinite, indeterminate, indistinct, obscure, perplexing, questionable, suspicious, uncertain. *Ambiguous* is applied only to spoken or written statements; *equivocal* has other applications. A statement is *ambiguous* when it causes the mind of the reader or hearer to fluctuate between two meanings, which would fit the language equally well; it is *equivocal* when it would naturally be understood in one way, but is capable of a different interpretation; an *equivocal* expression is, as a rule, intentionally deceptive, while an *ambiguous* utterance may result merely from a lack of clear thought or of adequate expression. That which is *enigmatical* must be guessed like a riddle. That is *doubtful* which is fairly open to doubt; that is *dubious* which has become the subject of doubts so grave as scarcely to fall short of condemnation; as a *dubious* reputation. *Questionable* may be used nearly in the sense either of *dubious* or of *doubtful*; a *questionable* statement is one that must be proved before it can be accepted. A *suspicious* character gives reason to be suspected; a *suspicious* temper is inclined to suspect the others, with or without reason. Compare CLEAR, PRECARIOUS. *Antonyms*: certain, clear, distinct, evident, indisputable, indubitable, lucid, manifest, obvious, perspicuous, plain, unambiguous, unequivocal, unquestionable, unquestioned.

e·quiv·o·cate (i·kwiv′ə·kāt) *v.i.* **·cat·ed, ·cat·ing** To use ambiguous language with intent to deceive. [<LL *aequivocatus*, pp. of *aequivocare* call by the same name <*aequivocus*. See EQUIVOCAL.]

e·quiv·o·ca·tion (i·kwiv′ə·kā′shən) *n.* **1** The act of equivocating. **2** A fallacy arising from the employment of a word of doubtful meaning. —**e·quiv′o·ca′tor** *n.* —**e·quiv′o·ca·to′ry** (-kə·tôr′ē, -tō′rē) *adj.*

eq·ui·voke (ek′wə·vōk) *n.* **1** An ambiguous term or expression; an equivocal word or phrase. **2** An equivocation. **3** A play upon words; pun. Also **eq′ui·voque.**

E·quu·le·us (i·kwōō′lē·əs) A southern constellation, near Aquarius. See CONSTELLATION.

er– Assimilated var. of EN–[2].

–er[1] *suffix of nouns* **1** A person or thing that performs the action of the root verb: *checker.* **2** A person concerned with or practicing a trade or profession: *glover.* **3** One who lives in or comes from: *New Yorker.* **4** A person, thing, or action related to or characterized by: *three-decker.* ◆ Nouns of agency are generally formed in English by adding **–er** to a verb, as in *leader,* but some such nouns, on analogy with those from French or Latin, are formed with **–or.** There is no definite rule regarding the use of these suffixes. [OE *-ere, -are*]

–er[2] *suffix of nouns* A person or thing concerned with, or related to: *jailer.* [<AF *-er,* OF *-ier* <L *-arius, -arium*]

–er[3] *suffix* More: used in the comparative degree of adjectives and adverbs: *harder, later.* [OE *-ra, -or*]

–er[4] *suffix* Repeatedly: used in frequentative verbs: *stutter.* [OE *-rian*]

–er[5] *suffix* Denoting the action expressed by the root word: *waiver*: used mostly in legal terms. [<F *-er,* infinitive ending]

e·ra (ir′ə, ē′rə) *n.* **1** A historical period or reckoning of years, dating from some important event or fixed point of time; a period running from a fixed epoch established as the basis of a chronology. **2** A period of time characterized by some coextensive phenomenon or order of things, or social, intellectual, or physical conditions, etc. **3** A date or event from which time is reckoned; a time or age marked by a remarkable event; the beginning of a period; an epoch: the Christian *era.* **4** *Geol.* A division of geological history of highest rank: the Cenozoic *era.* See chart under GEOLOGY. [<LL *aera* counters; orig. pl. of *aes* brass, money]

e·ra·di·ate (i·rā′dē·āt) *v.t.* & *v.i.* **·at·ed, ·at·ing** To radiate. —**e·ra′di·a′tion** *n.*

e·rad·i·cate (i·rad′ə·kāt) *v.t.* **·cat·ed, ·cat·ing** **1** To pull up by the roots; root out. **2** To destroy utterly; extirpate; erase. See synonyms under ABOLISH, EXTERMINATE. [<L *eradicatus,* pp. of *eradicare* <*e-* out + *radix, -icis* a root] —**e·rad′i·ca·ble** (-ə·kə·bəl) *adj.* —**e·rad′i·ca′tor** *n.*

e·rad·i·ca·tion (i·rad′ə·kā′shən) *n.* Extirpation; extermination.

e·rad·i·ca·tive (i·rad′ə·kā′tiv) *adj.* Serving or tending to eradicate.

Era of Good Feeling The period of President Monroe's administration (1817–24), characterized by an absence of political dissension

e·rase (i·rās′) *v.t.* **e·rased, e·ras·ing** **1** To obliterate, as by scraping or rubbing out; efface. **2** *U.S. Slang* To kill. See synonyms under CANCEL. [<L *erasus,* pp. of *eradere* <*e-* out + *radere* scrape] —**e·ras′a·ble** *adj.*

e·ras·er (i·rā′sər) *n.* **1** One who or that which erases. **2** A sharp tool or a rubber for removing pencil or ink marks. **3** An oblong device of wood, felt, etc., for removing chalk marks.

e·ra·sion (i·rā′zhən) *n.* **1** The act of erasing; erasure. **2** *Surg.* The operation of scraping away diseased material; specifically, that of laying open a diseased joint and removing morbid tissue by scraping.

E·ras·mus (i·raz′məs, *Dan., Du., Ger.* ā·räs′mōōs; *Lat.* e·räs′məs) A masculine personal name. Also *Fr.* **É·rasme** (ā·råsm′), *Ital., Sp.* **E·ras·mo** (*Ital.* ā·räz′mō, *Sp.* ā·räs′mō). [<Greek, lovely]

E·ras·mus (i·raz′məs), **Desiderius,** 1466?–1536, Dutch scholar: original name *Geert Geerts.*

E·ras·tian·ism (i·ras′chən·iz′əm, -tē·ən-) *n.* The doctrine that the church is entirely subservient to the authority of the state. [after Thomas *Erastus,* to whom this doctrine is improperly attributed] —**E·ras′tian** *adj.* & *n.*

E·ras·tus (i·ras′təs), **Thomas,** 1524–83, Swiss Protestant theologian.

e·ra·sure (i·rā′shər, -zhər) *n.* **1** The act of erasing or the state of being erased. **2** Anything erased.

Er·a·to (er′ə·tō) The Muse of lyric and love poetry.

Er·a·tos·the·nes (er′ə·tos′thə·nēz), 276?–195? B.C., Greek astronomer and geographer.

Er·ber·to (er·ber′tō) Italian form of HERBERT.

Er·bil (ir′bil) A town in northern Iraq on the site of ancient Arbela. Also **Ar·bil** (ir′bil).

er·bi·um (ûr′bē·əm) *n.* A metallic element (symbol Er) of the lanthanide series, first isolated in crude form by C. G. Mosander in 1843. It is found in gadolinite and some other minerals. See ELEMENT. [<NL <*(Ytt)erby,* town in Sweden where first found]

Er·ci·yas Da·ği (er′jē·yäs′ dä·ï′) A mountain in central Turkey; 12,848 feet: ancient *Argaeus.* Formerly **Er′ji·as′.**

Erck·mann–Cha·tri·an (erk·mån′shå·trē·äṅ′) Joint pseudonym of **Émile Erckmann,** 1826–1899, and **Alexandre Chatrian,** 1826–90, French literary collaborators.

ere (âr) *Archaic* & *Poetic prep.* Prior to; before in time. —*conj.* **1** Earlier than; before. **2** Sooner than; rather than. [OE *ǣr*]

Er·e·bus (er′ə·bəs) In Greek mythology, a dark region under the earth through which the shades of the dead pass on their way to Hades.

Er·e·bus (er′ə·bəs), **Mount** A volcano on Ross Island, Antarctica; 13,200 feet.

Er·ech·the·um (er′ək·thē′əm) A temple to the tutelary deities of Athens on the Acropolis, completed about 407 B.C. and famous as an example of Ionic architecture. *Greek* **Er′ech·thei′on** (-thī′on).

E·rech·theus (i·rek′thyōōs, -thē·əs) A legendary king of Athens, honored at the Erechtheum.

e·rect (i·rekt′) *v.t.* **1** To construct, as a house; build. **2** To assemble the parts of; set up. **3** To set upright; lift up: to *erect* a flagpole. **4** To construct or establish; formulate, as a theory. **5** *Geom.* To draw upon a given base, as a geometrical figure. **6** *Optics* To cause (an inverted image) to become upright. **7** *Obs.* To raise to a higher position; exalt. See synonyms under CONSTRUCT, INSTITUTE, RAISE. —*adj.* **1** Upright in position, form, or person; vertical. **2** Directed upward. **3** Free from depression or humiliation. **4** Attentive; alert. [<L *erectus,* pp. of *erigere* <*e-* out + *regere* make straight] —**e·rect′ly** *adv.* —**e·rect′ness** *n.*

e·rec·tile (i·rek′təl, -til) *adj.* Susceptible of erection: *erectile* feathers. Also **e·rect′a·ble.** —**e′rec·til′i·ty** *n.*

e·rec·tion (i·rek′shən) *n.* **1** The act or process of building or constructing; also, the state of being erected. **2** A raising to and fixing in an upright position; a setting up. **3** A building or structure. **4** *Physiol.* **a** The raising up or stiffening of a part through the accumulation of blood in erectile tissue. **b** The state of being so raised and stiffened.

e·rec·tive (i·rek′tiv) *adj.* Tending to erect or raise.

e·rec·tor (i·rek′tər) *n.* **1** One who or that which erects. **2** *Anat.* Any of various muscles which stiffen or hold up a part of the body.

ere·long (âr′lông′, -long′) *adv.* Before much time has passed; soon.

er·e·ma·cau·sis (er′ə·mə·kô′sis) *n.* *Biochem.* The process of gradual decay by oxidation in animal or vegetable matter when in contact with air and moisture. [<NL <Gk. *ērema* slightly + *kausis* a burning <*kaiein* burn]

e·re·mic (i·rē′mik) *adj.* *Ecol.* Designating plant communities adapted to deserts and steppes. [<Gk. *erēmos* deserted]

er·e·mite (er′ə·mīt) *n.* A hermit. [<LL *eremita* <LGk. *erēmitēs* <*erēmia* a desert <*erēmos* deserted] —**er·e·mit·ic** (er′ə·mit′ik) or **·i·cal, er′e·mit′ish** (-mī′tish) *adj.*

er·e·mo·phil·i·a (er′ə·mō·fil′ē·ə, -fēl′yə) *n.* *Psychiatry* A morbid craving for solitude. [<NL <Gk. *erēmos* deserted + -PHILIA]

er·e·mo·phyte (er′ə·mō·fīt′) *n.* *Ecol.* Any individual of a society of desert plants. [<Gk. *erēmos* deserted + -PHYTE]

ere·now (âr′nou′) *adv.* Before this time; heretofore.

e·rep·sin (i·rep′sin) *n.* *Biochem.* An enzyme or group of associated enzymes found in the intestinal and pancreatic juices of animals: it splits peptones into amino acids and ammonia. Also **e·rep′tase** (-tās). [<L *ereptus,* pp. of *eripere* set free + *-sin,* as in *pepsin*] —**e·rep′tic** *adj.*

er·e·thism (er′ə·thiz′əm) *n.* *Physiol.* Abnormal excitability or irritability in any part of the body. [<Gk. *erethismos* <*erethizein* irritate] —**er′e·this′mic** *adj.*

ere·while (âr′hwīl′) *adv.* *Archaic* Some time ago; heretofore. Also **ere′whiles′.**

Er·furt (er′fōōrt) A city in Thuringia, central Germany.

erg (ûrg) *n.* *Physics* In the cgs system, the unit of work and of energy, being the work done in moving a body one centimeter against the force of one dyne. See UNIT. Also **er·gon** (ûr′gon). [<Gk. *ergon* work]

er·gas·the·ni·a (ûr′gəs·thē′nē·ə, -thēn′yə) *n.* A condition of debility and exhaustion from overwork. —**er′gas·then′ic** (-then′ik) *adj.*

er·ga·tes (ûr′gə·tēz) *n.* *Entomol.* A worker ant. [<Gk. *ergatēs* workman]

er·go (ûr′gō) *conj.* & *adv.* *Latin* Hence; therefore. [<L]

ergo– *combining form* Work; of or related to work: *ergometer.* Also, before vowels, **erg–.** [<Gk. *ergon* work]

er·go·gen·ic (ûr′gō·jen′ik) *adj.* Tending to increase the quantity of work done under given conditions.

er·go·graph (ûr′gō·graf, -gräf) *n.* *Physiol.* An instrument for registering on a moving drum the movement of a finger or a contracting muscle in doing work: used as an index of mental excitement, fatigue, etc.

er·gom·e·ter (ûr·gom′ə·tər) *n.* *Physiol.* An apparatus, as a geared bicycle wheel, for measuring the metabolism rate or the amount of energy expended in doing work.

er·go·nom·ics (ûr′gə·nom′iks) *n.* The study of the relationship between man and his working environment, with special reference to anatomical, physiological, and psychological factors; human engineering. [<ERGO- + (ECO)NOMICS] —**er′go·nom′ic** *adj.*

er·go·phile (ûr′gō·fil, -fil) *n.* A lover of work.

er·gos·ter·ol (ûr·gos′tə·rōl) *n.* *Biochem.* An inert sterol, $C_{28}H_{44}O$, obtained from ergot, yeast, and certain other plants: irradiation by sunlight or ultraviolet light converts it into vitamin D_2. [<ERGO(T) + STEROL]

er·got (ûr′gət) *n.* **1** A fungus (*Claviceps purpurea*) that sometimes takes the place of the grain in rye and other grasses; it yields several alkaloids which are used medicinally in parturition. 2 The disease of rye and other cereal grasses caused by this growth. 3 The dried sclerotia of rye ergot, used in medicine to contract muscle fibers, especially those of the uterus, in order to check hemorrhage. [<F <OF *argot* spur of a cock] —**er'got·ed** *adj.*

er·got·in·ine (ûr·got'ə·nēn, -nin) *n. Chem.* A crystalline alkaloid, $C_{35}H_{39}N_5O_5$, obtained from ergot; used in medicine.

er·got·ism (ûr'gə·tiz'əm) *n.* 1 *Pathol.* A morbid condition produced by excessive doses of ergot; poisoning from ergotized grain. 2 The formation of ergot in grasses.

Er·hard (er'härt), **Ludwig,** 1897–1977, German statesman; chancellor of the West German Republic, 1963–66.

Er·ic (er'ik) A masculine personal name. [< Scand., ever king]

—**Eric the Red** Scandinavian navigator; discovered and colonized Greenland around 983.

er·i·ca·ceous (er'ə·kā'shəs) *adj. Bot.* Of or relating to the heath family *(Ericaceae)* of trees, shrubs, or herbs, natives of temperate or cold climates, including the azalea, rhododendron, wintergreen, mountain laurel, etc. [<NL *Ericaceae* <*Erica*, name of a genus <L *erica* heath <Gk. *ereikē*]

Er·ic·son (er'ik·sən), **Leif** Norse rover; son of Eric the Red; probable discoverer of North America about A.D. 1000. Also **Er'ics·son.**

Er·ics·son (er'ik·sən), **John,** 1803–89, U.S. engineer born in Sweden; invented the screw propeller.

E·rid·a·nus (i·rid'ə·nəs) A southern constellation, containing the bright star Achernar. See CONSTELLATION. [<L, the Po river]

E·rie (ir'ē) A port in Pennsylvania on Lake Erie.

E·rie (ir'ē) *n. pl.* **E·rie** or **E·ries** One of a tribe of North American Indians of Iroquoian stock, formerly inhabiting the southern shores of Lake Erie.

Erie, Lake The southernmost and fourth largest of the Great Lakes; 241 by 57 miles; 9,940 square miles.

Erie Canal A historic waterway in New York, extending 350 miles from Buffalo on Lake Erie to Albany on the Hudson River; now part of the *New York State Barge Canal.*

E·rig·e·na (i·rij'ə·nə), **Johannes Scotus** Irish philosopher of the ninth century.

e·rig·er·on (i·rij'ə·ron) *n.* Any plant of a large genus *(Erigeron)* of mainly North American weedy herbs of the composite family, usually bearing solitary heads with numerous violet, purple, or white ray flowers. Certain species, as *E. canadensis,* yield **oil of erigeron,** used as a hemostatic drug. [<L, groundsel <Gk. *ērigerōn* <*ēri* early + *gerōn* old man; with ref. to a hoary growth on some species]

Er·in (âr'in, ir'in) *Poetic* Ireland.

er·i·na·ceous (er'ə·nā'shəs) *adj.* Of or like a hedgehog. [<L *erinaceus* hedgehog]

e·rin·go (i·ring'gō) See ERYNGO.

E·rin·y·es (i·rin'i·ēz) *pl. of* **E·rin·ys** (i·rin'is, i·rī'·nis) In Greek mythology, the Furies. [<L <Gk. *Erinys*]

er·i·om·e·ter (er'ē·om'ə·tər) *n.* An instrument for measuring by diffraction the diameters of very small objects. [<Gk. *erion* wool, fibre + -METER] —**er'i·om'e·try** *n.*

E·ris (ir'is, er'is) In Greek mythology, the sister of Ares, and goddess of discord.

e·ris·tic (e·ris'tik) *adj.* 1 Relating to controversy. 2 Prone to dispute: also **e·ris'ti·cal.** —*n.* 1 A person given to controversy. 2 A scholar of Euclid's Eristic or Megarian school of philosophy. [<Gk. *eristikos* <*eris* strife]

E·ri·tre·a (er'i·trē'ə) An autonomous state in eastern Africa on the Red Sea, federated with Ethiopia; formerly an Italian colony; 45,754 square miles; capital, Asmara. —**Er'i·tre'an** *adj. & n.*

Er·i·van (er'i·vän'y') The capital of Armenian S.S.R.: Armenian *Yerevan.*

Er·land·er (er'län·dər), **Tage Fritiof,** born 1901, Swedish political leader.

Er·lang·en (er'läng·ən) A city in north central Bavaria, Germany.

Er·lan·ger (der·län·zhā'), **Baron Frederic d',** 1868–1943, British composer born in France.

Er·lang·er (ûr'lang·ər), **Joseph,** 1874–1965, U.S. physiologist.

Er·len·mey·er flask (ûr'lən·mī'ər) A conical glass flask with a narrow neck and very broad base, extensively used in laboratory work in chemistry, physiology, and medicine. [after Emil *Erlenmeyer,* 1825–1909, German chemist]

erl·king (ûrl'king') *n.* In Teutonic folklore, the king of the elves, malicious toward children.

Er·man·no (er·män'nō) The Italian form of HERMAN.

er·mine (ûr'min) *n.* 1 A long-bodied, slender, voracious weasel (genus *Mustela*) of the northern hemisphere; the stoat, especially in its winter dress, which is white, with a black tail tip. 2 Its fur, used in Europe for the facings of official robes, as of judges. 3 The judicial office or its ideal purity. [<OF *(h)ermine,* ? <Gmc.] —**er'mined** *adj.*

ERMINE
(Body: 9 to 12 inches; tail: 3 to 3 1/2 inches)

ermine moth A moth *(Yponomeuta padella),* whose larvae destroy the foliage of apple and related trees.

er·myte (er'mīt) *n. Obs.* A hermit.

erne (ûrn) *n.* A sea eagle (genus *Haliaetus*). Also **ern.** ◆ Homophones: *earn, urn.* [OE *earn*]

Er·nest (ûr'nist, *Fr.* er·nest') A masculine personal name. Also *Dan., Ger., Sw.* **Ernst** (ernst), *Du.* **Er·nes·tus** (er·nes'to͝os), *Ital., Sp.* **Er·nes·to** (er·nes'tō). [<Gmc., serious]

Ernst (ûrnst; *Ger.* ernst), **Max,** born 1891, German painter, in the U.S. since 1941.

e·rode (i·rōd') *v.* **e·rod·ed, e·rod·ing** *v.t.* 1 To eat or wear into or away. 2 *Geol.* To wear down, as rocks, soil, etc., by the action of wind, water, and other agencies; also, to form, as a canyon, by such action. —*v.i.* 3 To become eroded. [<L *erodere* <*e-* off + *rodere* gnaw]

e·ro·dent (i·rōd'nt) *adj.* 1 Causing erosion. 2 Caustic, as certain drugs. —*n.* A caustic drug; that which erodes or burns away. [<L *erodens, -entis,* ppr. of *erodere.* See ERODE.]

e·rog·e·nous (i·roj'ə·nəs) *adj.* Producing erotic feeling; exciting sexual desire. Also **er·o·gen·ic** (er'ə·jen'ik). [<Gk. *erōs* love, + -GENOUS]

Er·os (ir'os, er'os) 1 In Greek mythology, the god of love, youngest of the gods, son of Aphrodite and Zeus, Ares, or Hermes; identified with the Roman *Cupid.* 2 *Astron.* An asteroid of the sixth magnitude, discovered in 1898, and used in determination of the distance of the sun from the earth. 3 *Psychoanal.* **a** The libido. **b** The sum total of the life-preserving and self-preserving instincts: opposed to *Thanatos.*

e·rose (i·rōs') *adj.* 1 Appearing as if gnawed. 2 *Bot.* Having an irregularly toothed margin, as some leaves. [<L *erosus,* pp. of *erodere.* See ERODE.]

e·ro·sion (i·rō'zhən) *n.* 1 *Geol.* The wearing away of materials, as rocks by wind and water; denudation. 2 *Med.* The eating away of body tissue, bone, etc.

e·ro·sive (i·rō'siv) *adj.* 1 Having the power or property of gnawing or wearing away. 2 Acting by erosion: an *erosive* acid.

e·rot·ic (i·rot'ik) *adj.* Of or pertaining to passionate love; amorous; amatory: also **e·rot'·i·cal.** —*n.* 1 An amatory poem. 2 A theory or science of love: also **e·rot'ics.** 3 An erotic person. [<Gk. *erōtikos*<*erōs* love] —**e·rot'·i·cal·ly** *adv.*

e·rot·i·ca (i·rot'i·kə) *n. pl.* Erotic pictures, books, etc. [<Gk. *erōtika,* neut. pl. of *erōtikos* EROTIC]

e·rot·i·cism (i·rot'ə·siz'əm) *n.* Erotic tendency or character.

er·o·tism (er'ə·tiz'əm) *n.* 1 Eroticism. 2 *Psychoanal.* Sexual life in all its phases of physical and mental development and manifestations.

e·ro·to·ma·ni·a (i·rō'tə·mā'nē·ə, i·rot'ə-) *n.* 1 *Psychiatry* A morbid propensity to love or make love; uncontrollable sexual desire. 2 Melancholia caused by love.

err (ûr) *v.i.* **erred, err·ing** 1 To make a mistake; be wrong. 2 To go astray morally; sin. 3 *Obs.* To wander; stray. See synonyms under WANDER. [<OF *errer* <L *errare* wander]

er·ran·cy (er'ən·sē) *n.* 1 The condition of erring or of containing errors. 2 Liability to err.

er·rand (er'ənd) *n.* 1 A trip or journey made to carry a message or do a commission. 2 The object of a going or coming; the business or commission to be done or message to be given by a messenger. [OE *ærende* message, news]

er·rant (er'ənt) *adj.* 1 Roving or wandering. 2 Erring; erratic. 3 *Obs.* See ARRANT. [<OF *errant,* ppr. of *errer* travel <L *iter* a journey; infl. by OF *errant* <*errer* wander. See ERR.] —**er'rant·ly** *adv.*

er·rant·ry (er'ənt·rē) *n.* The vocation, conduct, or career of a knight errant; knight-errantry.

er·ra·re hu·ma·num est (e·rä'rē hyo͞o·mā'·nəm est) *Latin* To err is human.

er·ra·ta (i·rā'tə, e·rä'tə) Plural of ERRATUM.

er·rat·ic (i·rat'ik) *adj.* 1 Not conforming to rules or standards; irregular; eccentric. 2 Wandering; straying. 3 *Geol.* Transported from the original site by natural agencies: *erratic* rocks or gravel. Also **er·rat'i·cal.** See synonyms under IRREGULAR, QUEER. [<L *erraticus* <*errare* wander] —**er·rat'i·cal·ly** *adv.*

er·ra·tum (i·rā'təm, e·rä'-) *n. pl.* **·ra·ta** (-rā'tə, -rä'tə) An error, as in writing or printing. [< L]

er·rhine (er'īn, -in) *adj. Med.* Promotive of sneezing and nasal discharges. —*n.* A medicine to be snuffed; a sternutatory. [<NL *errhinum* <Gk. *errhinon* <*en-* in + *rhis, rhinos* nose]

err·ing (ûr'ing, er'ing) *adj.* 1 Sinning; doing wrong. 2 In error; wrong. —**err'ing·ly** *adv.*

er·ro·ne·ous (ə·rō'nē·əs, e·rō'-) *adj.* Marked by error; incorrect; mistaken. —**er·ro'ne·ous·ly** *adv.* —**er·ro'ne·ous·ness** *n.*

er·ror (er'ər) *n.* 1 The condition of erring, or going astray from the truth, especially in matters of opinion or belief; also, deviation from a right standard of judgment or conduct, as through ignorance or inadvertence; mistake. 2 Something done, said, or believed wrongly; a deviation from correctness or accuracy, or from truth. 3 Any misplay in baseball which prolongs the batsman's time at bat or permits a base runner to make one or more bases. Misplays, as a passed ball or a wild pitch, made by catcher or pitcher, are not scored as *errors.* 4 A violation or neglect of duty; transgression; sin. 5 *Math.* **a** The difference between the observed value of a magnitude and the true or mean value as determined by a series of measurements of the same quantity. **b** Any deviation from the true or mean value not due to gross blunders of observation and measurement. 6 In Christian Science, the contradiction of truth; a belief without understanding; that which seems and is not. [<OF <L < *errare* wander]

Synonyms: balk, blunder, fallacy, falsity, fault, hallucination, mistake, omission, oversight, unsoundness. See DELUSION, FOIBLE.

ers (ûrs) *n.* See under VETCH. [<F <L *ervum*]

er·satz (er·zäts') *n.* A substitute; equivalent; replacement, usually inferior to the original product or material. —*adj.* Substitute. [<G <*ersetzen* replace]

Erse (ûrs) *n.* 1 Scottish Gaelic. 2 Irish Gaelic. [Var. of IRISH]

Er·skine (ûr'skin), **John,** 1695–1768, Scottish jurist. —**John,** 1879–1951, U.S. educator and writer. —**Lord Thomas,** 1750–1823, first Baron of Restormel, lord chancellor of England.

erst (ûrst) *Archaic adv.* 1 Formerly; long ago; once. 2 In the beginning. —*adj.* First. [OE *ǣrest*]

erst·while (ûrst'hwīl') *adj.* Former. —*adv. Archaic* Formerly.

er·u·bes·cence (er'o͞o·bes'əns) *n. Med.* The process or condition of growing red; redness; blush. Also **er'u·bes'cen·cy.** [<LL *erubescentia* <L *erubescere* blush] —**er'u·bes'cent** *adj.*

e·ruct (i·rukt') *v.t. & v.i.* To belch. Also **e·ruc'·** [<L *eructare* <*e-* out + *ructare* belch]

e·ruc·ta·tion (i·ruk'tā'shən, ē'ruk-, er'ək-) *n.* 1 The act of belching. 2 That which is thrown off in belching. [<L *eructatus,* pp. of

eructare. See ERUCT.] **—e·ruc·ta·tive** (i·ruk′tə·tiv) *adj.*

er·u·dite (er′yo͞o·dīt, er′o͞o-) *adj.* Very learned; scholarly. [<L *eruditus,* pp. of *erudire* instruct <*e-* out + *rudis* untrained] **—er′u·dite·ly** *adv.* **—er′u·dite·ness** *n.*

er·u·di·tion (er′yo͞o·dish′ən, -o͞o-) *n.* **1** Extensive knowledge of history, literature, languages, etc.; accomplished scholarship. **2** *Obs.* The act of instructing. See synonyms under KNOWLEDGE, LEARNING, WISDOM. **—er′u·di′tion·al** *adj.*

e·ru·gi·nous (i·ro͞o′jə·nəs) *adj.* See AERUGINOUS. [<L *aeruginosus* <*aerugo, -inis* copper rust <*aes* copper]

e·rum·pent (i·rum′pənt) *adj. Bot.* Bursting forth, as if through the epidermis, as the spore clusters of certain fungi. [<L *erumpens, -entis,* ppr. of *erumpere.* See ERUPT.]

e·rupt (i·rupt′) *v.i.* **1** To cast forth smoke, lava, etc., suddenly and with violence: The volcano *erupted.* **2** To be thrown forth: Steam is *erupting* from the volcano. **3** *Dent.* To become visible in the mouth, as teeth. *—v.t.* **4** To cause to burst forth. [<L *eruptus,* pp. of *erumpere* <*e-* out + *rumpere* burst]

e·rup·tion (i·rup′shən) *n.* **1** A breaking forth with violence; bursting out. **2** That which bursts forth, as lava from a volcano. **3** A breaking out, as in a rash. **4** Any sudden outbreak, as of armed forces.

e·rup·tive (i·rup′tive) *adj.* Pertaining or tending to eruption. **—e·rup′tive·ly** *adv.* **—e·rup′tive·ness** *n.*

Er·vine (ûr′vin), **St. John Greer,** 1883–1971, Irish novelist and playwright.

-ery *suffix of nouns* **1** A business, place of business, or place where something is done: *brewery.* **2** A place or residence for: *nunnery.* **3** A collection of goods, wares, etc.: *pottery*; or things pertaining to: *popery.* **4** The qualities, principles, or practices of: *snobbery.* **5** An art, trade, or profession: *cookery.* **6** A state, or condition of being: *slavery.* Also *-ry,* as in *jewelry.* [<OF *-erie* <*-ier* (<L *-arius*) + *-ie* <L *-ia.* See -ARY, -Y[2].]

Er·y·man·thi·an Boar (er′ə·man′thē·ən) In Greek mythology, a savage boar captured alive by Hercules.

Er·y·man·thus (er′ə·man′thəs), **Mount** A mountain between Arcadia and Achaea in Greece. **—Er′y·man′thi·an** *adj.*

e·ryn·go (i·ring′gō) *n.* **1** Any of various coarse herbs of the genus *Eryngium*: the roots are used in medicine. **2** *Obs.* The candied root of sea eryngo *(E. maritimum),* formerly deemed an aphrodisiac. Also spelled *eringo.* [? Alter. of Ital. *eringio* <L *eryngion* <Gk. *eryngion* <*eryngos*]

er·y·sip·e·las (er′ə·sip′ə·ləs, ir′ə-) *n. Pathol.* An acute inflammatory disease of the skin, due to infection by various strains of streptococcus and accompanied by fever. [<NL <Gk., ? <*erysis* a reddening + *pella* skin] **—er·y·si·pel·a·tous** (er′ə·si·pel′ə·təs, ir′ə-), **er′y·sip′e·lat′ic** (-lat′ik), **er′y·sip′e·lous** *adj.*

er·y·sip·e·loid (er′ə·sip′ə·loid, ir′ə-) *n. Pathol.* A localized dermatitis caused by infection with a bacterium (genus *Erysipelothrix*).

Er·y·thei·a (er′ə·thē′ə) **1** In classical geography, the westernmost point of the known world: an island beyond the pillars of Hercules. **2** One of the Hesperides.

er·y·the·ma (er′ə·thē′mə) *n. Pathol.* **1** A superficial skin disease characterized by abnormal redness, but without swelling or fever. **2** Abnormal redness of the cheek in hectic fever. [<NL <Gk. *erythēma* redness <*erythros* red] **—er′y·them′a·tous** (-them′ə·təs, -thē′mə-), **er′y·the·mat′ic** (-thi·mat′ik), **er′y·the′mic** *adj.*

Er·y·thrae (er′i·thrē) An ancient Ionian city in Asia Minor. Also **Er′y·thræ.** **—Er′y·thrae′an** *adj.* & *n.*

Er·y·thrae·an Sea (er′i·thrē′ən) An ancient name for the RED SEA.

er·y·thre·an (er′i·thrē′ən) *adj.* Red. Also **er′y·thrae′an.** [<L *erythraeus* <Gk. *erythraios* <*erythros* red]

e·ryth·rin (i·rith′rin) *n. Chem.* A crystalline compound, $C_{20}H_{22}O_{10}$, contained in various lichens, as *Rocella tinctoria,* from which it is extracted by milk of lime. Also **e·ryth′rine.**

e·ryth·rism (i·rith′riz·əm) *n.* **1** Morbid fondness for red. **2** Abnormal or excessive redness, especially when exhibited by certain dichromatic birds, as the screech owl, which has two distinct plumage phases, one grayish and the other red. **—er·y·thris·mal** (er′ə·thriz′məl), **er′y·thris′tic** *adj.*

e·ryth·rite (i·rith′rīt) *n.* **1** A crimson and peach-red transparent, hydrous cobalt arsenate, found amorphous and also crystallized in the monoclinic system; cobalt bloom. **2** Erythritol.

e·ryth·ri·tol (i·rith′rə·tōl, -tol) *n. Chem.* Any of three isomeric compounds, $C_4H_{10}O_4$, contained in certain algae and lichens, especially one occurring as a white, crystalline saccharide alcohol.

erythro- *combining form* Red: *erythrocyte.* Also, before vowels, **erythr-.** [<Gk. *erythros* red]

e·ryth·ro·blast (i·rith′rō·blast) *n. Anat.* One of the colored ameboid cells from which the red corpuscles of the blood are believed to be developed: found in the red marrow of bones.

e·ryth·ro·ca·tal·y·sis (i·rith′rō·kə·tal′ə·sis) *n.* Destruction of red blood corpuscles by phagocytes.

e·ryth·ro·chlo·ro·pi·a (i·rith′rō·klôr′ə·pē′ə, -klō′rə-) *n. Pathol.* A visual defect which allows correct perception only of red and green. Also **e·ryth′ro·chlo·rop′si·a** (-klô·rop′sē·ə, -klō·rop′-). [<ERYTHRO- + CHLOR(O)- + -OPIA]

e·ryth·ro·cyte (i·rith′rō·sīt) *n. Anat.* A red blood cell, formed in the red bone marrow and, in all mammals, lacking a nucleus: it contains hemoglobin and transports oxygen to all tissues of the body. **—e·ryth′ro·cyt′ic** (-sit′ik) *adj.*

e·ryth·ro·cy·tom·e·ter (i·rith′rō·sī·tom′ə·tər) *n.* A device for counting erythrocytes.

e·ryth·ro·cy·to·sis (i·rith′rō·sī·tō′sis) *n. Pathol.* An excessive increase in the number of red blood corpuscles in the circulatory system.

e·ryth·ro·dex·trin (i·rith′rō·dek′strin) *n. Biochem.* A dextrin produced by the action of saliva on starch: it turns red on contact with iodine.

er·y·throl (er′ə·thrōl, -thrôl) *n.* A crystalline alkaloid, $C_4H_{10}O_4$, found in certain lichens: the compound **erythrol tetranitrate** is used medicinally as a substitute for amyl nitrite and nitroglycerin in heart ailments, and also in explosives as a detonator.

e·ryth·ro·me·lal·gi·a (i·rith′rō·mə·lal′jē·ə) *n. Pathol.* A nervous disease of the extremities, characterized by persistent redness on the soles of the feet or palms of the hands, with burning pain. [<ERYTHRO- + Gk. *melos* limb + -ALGIA]

er·y·throph·i·lous (er′ə·throf′ə·ləs) *adj. Biol.* Having an affinity for red coloring matter.

e·ryth·ro·pho·bi·a (i·rith′rō·fō′bē·ə) *n.* A morbid fear of the color red; specifically, fear of blushing. **—e·ryth′ro·pho′bic** *adj.*

e·ryth·ro·phyll (i·rith′rō·fil) See ANTHOCYANIN.

Erz·ber·ger (erts′ber·gər), **Matthias,** 1875–1921, German political leader; signer of the armistice at Compiègne, 1918.

Erz·ge·bir·ge (erts′gə·bir′gə) A mountain range on the Bohemia-Saxony border; highest peak, 4,080 feet: English *Ore Mountains.*

Er·zu·rum (er′zə·ro͞om) A province of NE Turkey; 9,244 square miles; capital, Erzurum. Also **Er′ze·rum.**

Es *Chem.* Einsteinium (symbol Es).

es- *prefix* Out: used in words borrowed into English from Old French: *escape, escheat.* It was often later refashioned to *ex-* after Latin, as in *exchange,* formerly *eschange.* [<OF <L *ex-.* See EX-[1].]

-es[1] An inflectional ending used to form the plural of nouns ending in a sibilant *(glasses, fuses, fishes)* or an affricate *(witches, judges).* After such consonants it is pronounced as a separate syllable; after vowels, as in *potatoes,* it merely extends the syllable. [OE *-as*]

-es[2] An inflectional ending used to form the third person singular present indicative of verbs ending in a sibilant, affricate, or vowel: *goes, kisses, poaches.* [ME *-es*]

E·sai·as (*Lat.* e·sä′yəs; *Dan.* ā·sī′äs; *Ger.* ā·zä′·yäs) See ISAIAH.

E·sau (ē′sô) A masculine personal name. Also *Fr.* **E·sa·u** (ā·zä·ü′), *Lat.* **E·sa·vus** (e·sä′vəs). [<Hebrew, hairy]

—Esau Eldest son of Isaac; sold his birthright to his brother Jacob. *Gen.* xxv 25.

es·ca·drille (es′kə·dril′, *Fr.* es·kȧ·drē′y′) *n.* **1** In France, a unit of six military airplanes. **2** A squadron of naval vessels. [<F, dim. of *escadre* a squadron; infl. by Sp. *escuadrilla,* dim. of *escuadra* a squadron; both ult. <L *ex-* completely + *quadrare* make square < *quattuor* four]

es·ca·lade (es′kə·lād′) *v.t.* **·lad·ed, ·lad·ing** To attack and force a way into or over (a fort, rampart, etc.) by means of ladders. *—n.* An attack by escalading. [<F <Sp. *escalada* <*escalar* climb <L *scala* a ladder]

Es·ca·lan·te (äs′kä·län′tā) A municipality in NE Negros island, Philippines.

es·ca·late (es′kə·lāt) *v.t.* & *v.i.* **·lat·ed, ·lat·ing** **1** To ascend or raise on an escalator. **2** To increase or be increased in a gradual manner. **3** To determine the upward trend of material and labor costs in adjusting (price contracts). [Back formation from ESCALATOR] **—es′ca·la′tion** *n.*

Es·ca·la·tor (es′kə·lā′tər) *n.* A moving stairway, built on the endless-chain principle, used in stores, railroad stations, etc.: a trade name. [<ESCAL(ADE) + (ELEV)ATOR]

escalator clause A clause in a contract stipulating an increase or decrease in wages, prices, etc., under certain specified conditions.

es·cal·lop (e·skol′əp, -skal′-), **es·cal·op** See SCALLOP.

es·ca·pade (es′kə·pād) *n.* **1** An act in reckless disregard of propriety; a mischievous prank. **2** An escape from restraint. **3** *Obs.* A plunging or kicking, as of a horse. [<F <Sp. *escapada* <*escapar* escape]

es·cape (ə·skāp′, e·skāp′) *v.* **es·caped, es·cap·ing** *v.t.* **1** To get away from; flee from, as guards or prison. **2** To avoid, as harm or evil. **3** To be uttered involuntarily; slip from: No cry *escaped* him. **4** To slip away from or elude (notice or recollection); fail to be understood or remembered. *—v.i.* **5** To get free from or avoid arrest, custody, danger, etc. **6** To elude notice or recollection. **7** To come forth; emerge; leak: Gas is *escaping* from the stove. **8** *Bot.* To grow wild, as a newly introduced plant. *—n.* **1** A successful flight from, or evasion of, custody, pursuit, danger, injury, or annoyance. **2** Mental relief from monotony, anxiety, etc.: literature of *escape.* **3** Issue, as of a fluid; leakage. **4** *Bot.* Any plant formerly cultivated that now grows wild in fields. **5** *Obs.* An outburst; sally. **6** *Obs.* An inadvertence; act of transgression. [<AF *escaper* <L *ex-* out + *cappa* a cloak] **—es·cap′er** *n.*

Synonyms (verb): abscond, avoid, decamp, depart, elude, evade, flee, fly, shun. To *escape* is to get away clear; to *flee* or *fly* is to attempt it, with or without success; to *abscond* is both to *flee* and to hide, or at least to seek concealment and obscurity. To *escape* may be noble and worthy; to *abscond* is ordinarily an act of cowardice and guilt. See AVOID.

escape cock *Mech.* **1** A cock or bearing in a watch to support the escape wheel. **2** A cock or faucet in an engine cylinder to draw off condensed steam.

escape hatch A means of exit, as from an aircraft, submarine, etc., for use in emergencies.

escape lung A respiratory device for underwater breathing, especially in escaping from submarines: it consists of a tightly fitting mask with a nose clamp, connected with an oxygen-filled rubber chamber and a canister of powdered charcoal or other adsorbent material.

escape mechanism *Psychol.* The process whereby the mind evades its problems, anxieties, responsibilities, etc.

es·cape·ment (ə·skāp′mənt, e·skāp′-) *n.* **1** *Mech.* A device used in timepieces for securing a uniform movement, consisting of an escape wheel and a detent or lock, through which periodical impulses are imparted to the balance wheel, to keep it in oscillation, and to which, in turn, motion is imparted by the return movement of the balance wheel actuated by a mainspring or a weight. **2** *Obs.* The act of escaping; an escape or a means of escape; a vent.

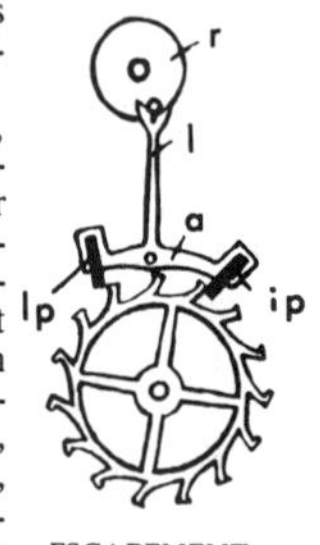

ESCAPEMENT OF A WATCH
a. Anchor.
l. Lever or fork.
ip. Impulse pallet.
lp. Locking pallet.
r. Roller.

escape wheel A toothed wheel in an escapement: also called *scape wheel.* See illustration under PENDULUM.

es·cap·ist (ə·skā′pist, e·skā′-) *adj.* Offering or intended to offer relief from unpleasant or monotonous realities of life: *escapist* drama; *escapist* novels. —*n.* One who seeks to avoid the realities of life. —**es·cap′ism** *n.*

es·car·got (es·kȧr·gō′) *n. French* A snail, especially one of an edible variety.

es·carp (es·kärp′) *n.* The inner wall or side of the ditch at the foot of a rampart: distinguished from *counterscarp,* the further or outer side. See illustration under BASTION. —*v.t.* **1** To cause to slope steeply. **2** To provide with a scarp. [<F <Ital. *scarpa* a scarp]

es·carp·ment (es·kärp′mənt) *n.* **1** A precipitous artificial slope about a fortification or position. **2** A steep slope; the precipitous face of a more or less extended line of cliffs: sometimes called *scarp.*

Es·caut (es·kō′) The French name for the SCHELDT.

-esce *suffix of verbs* To become or grow; begin to be or do (what is indicated by the main element): *phosphoresce.* [<L *-escere,* suffix of inceptive verbs]

-escence *suffix of nouns* Forming nouns of state or quality corresponding to adjectives in *-escent*: *effervescence.* [<L *-escentia*]

-escent *suffix of adjectives* Beginning to be, have, or do (what is indicated by the main element): *effervescent.* [<L *-escens, -escentis,* suffix of ppr. of inceptive verbs]

esch·a·lot (esh′ə·lot, esh′ə·lot′) *n. Rare* A shallot. [<F *eschalotte,* dim. of *eschaloigne* an onion]

es·char (es′kär) *n. Med.* The dry crust produced by mortification or cauterization; a slough or scab. [<L *eschara* <Gk. *eschara* a hearth]

es·cha·rot·ic (es′kə·rot′ik) *adj. Med.* Able to destroy living tissue and form an eschar; caustic. —*n.* A powerful caustic.

es·cha·tol·o·gy (es′kə·tol′ə·jē) *n.* The branch of theology that treats of death, resurrection, immortality, the end of the world, final judgment, and the future state. [<Gk. *eschatos* last + -LOGY] —**es′cha·to·log′ic** (-tə·loj′ik) or **·i·cal** *adj.* —**es′cha·tol′o·gist** *n.*

es·cheat (es·chēt′) *Law v.t.* & *v.i.* To revert, or cause to revert, to the state or crown. —*n.* **1** The reversion of lands, in the United States to the state, in England to the crown, in default of heirs or devisees. **2** In feudal law, reversion of an estate to the lord of the fee on failure of heirs or service. **3** Forfeiture of property, real or personal, for default; confiscation. [<OF *eschete, escheoite* <*escheoir* <*es-* out (<L *ex-*) + *cheoir* <*cadere* fall] —**es·cheat′a·ble** *adj.* —**es·cheat′age** *n.*

Esch·en·bach (esh′ən·bäkh), **Wolfram von** See WOLFRAM VON ESCHENBACH.

es·chew (es·chōō′) *v.t.* To shun, as something unworthy or injurious. [<OF *eschiver,* ult. <Gmc. Akin to SHY[1].] —**es·chew′al** *n.*

Esch·scholt·zi·a (e·shōlt′sē·ə, e·sholt′-, esh·kolt′-) *n.* A genus of smooth herbs of the poppy family with dissected leaves and long-peduncled yellow flowers of western North America. The California poppy is the best known. [<NL, after J. F. von *Eschscholtz,* 1793–1831, German naturalist]

es·co·pette (es′kō·pet′) *n. SW U.S.* A short carbine. Also **es′co·pe′ta** (-pā′tə), **es′co·pet′, es′co·pate′** (-pāt′). [<Sp. *escopeta*; infl. in form by F *escopette* a musket]

Es·co·ri·al (es·kôr′ē·əl, -kō′rē-; *Sp.* es′kō·ryäl′) *n.* A monastery, church, and royal residence built by Philip II in the 16th century, 27 miles NW of Madrid. Also **Es·cu·ri·al** (es·kyōōr′ē·əl).

es·cort (es·kôrt′) *v.t.* To accompany; go with, as from courtesy or to protect; conduct; convoy. See synonyms under LEAD. [<*n.*] —*n.* (es′kôrt) **1** A guard accompanying a person or property in transit, for protection, surveillance, as compulsion, or as a mark of respect. **2** Safeguard; protection. **3** A companion at a social affair. [<F *escorte* <Ital. *scorta* <*scorgere* lead <L *ex-* out + *corrigere.* See CORRECT.]

es·cri·toire (es′kri·twär′) *n.* A secretary; writing desk. [<OF <LL *scriptorium* place for writing <*scribere* write] —**es′cri·to′ri·al** (-tôr′ē·əl, -tō′rē-) *adj.*

es·croll (es·krōl′) *n.* **1** *Her.* A scroll. **2** *Obs.* An escrow. Also **es·crol′.** [<OF *escroele,* dim. of *escroe.* See ESCROW.]

es·crow (es′krō, es·krō′) *n. Law* An instrument, under seal, placed in the hands of a third person for delivery to the grantee on some condition, the instrument being of no effect until delivery. [<AF *escrowe,* OF *escroe* a scroll <Gmc.]

es·cu·age (es′kyōō·ij) *n.* In feudal law, a military tax paid in lieu of knight service; originally, shield service or personal military duty, a form of feudal tenure. [<AF <OF *escu* <L *scutum* a shield]

es·cu·do (es·kōō′dō; *Pg.* es·kōō′thōō, *Sp.* es·kōō′thō) *n. pl.* **·dos** **1** The monetary unit of Portugal, containing 100 centavos. **2** An obsolete Spanish silver coin equal to ten reals. [<Pg. <L *scutum* shield]

Es·cu·la·pi·an (es′kyōō·lā′pē·ən) See AESCULAPIAN.

es·cu·lent (es′kyə·lənt) *adj.* Suitable for food; edible. —*n.* Anything suitable for food, especially a plant that is edible. [<L *ēsculentus* <*esca* food]

es·cutch·eon (i·skuch′ən) *n.* **1** *Her.* The surface, usually shield-shaped, upon which armorial bearings are displayed; a heraldic shield. See under FIELD. **2** Any shield-shaped surface or device. **3** *Entomol.* The scutum of the mesothorax in certain insects. **4** An ornamented plate about a keyhole, or one to which a door knocker is attached. **5** *Naut.* That part of a ship's stern on which her name is inscribed. [<AF *escuchon* <L *scutum* shield]

ESCUTCHEON
Divisions of shield:
a. Dexter chief.
b. Middle chief.
c. Sinister chief.
d. Dexter flank.
e. Fess point.
f. Sinister flank.
g. Dexter base.
h. Middle base.
i. Sinister base.
j. Honor point.
k. Nombril point.

Es·dra·e·lon (ez′drə·ē′lən) See JEZREEL, PLAIN OF.

Es·dras (ez′drəs, *Fr.* ez·drȧs′) **1** Variant of EZRA. **2** The name of the first two books of the Old Testament Apocrypha.

-ese *suffix of nouns and adjectives* **1** A native or inhabitant of: *Milanese.* **2** The language or dialect of: *Chinese.* **3** Originating in; denoting the inhabitants or language of: *Tirolese.* **4** In the manner or style of: *journalese.* [<OF *-ese* <L *-ensis*]

E·se·nin (yi·syä′nyin), **Sergei Aleksandrovich,** 1895–1925, Russian poet.

es·er·ine (es′ə·rēn, -rin) See PHYSOSTIGMINE.

Es·fa·han (is′fə·hän′) See ISFAHAN.

E·sher (ē′shər) An urban district of NE Surrey, England.

es·ker (es′kər) *n. Geol.* A ridge of glacial gravel, deposited by a subglacial stream between banks of ice. Also **es′kar.** [<Irish *escir* ridge]

E·skils·tu·na (ā′shils·tōō′nä) A city in eastern Sweden.

Es·ki·mo (es′kə·mō) *n. pl.* **·mos** **1** One of a Mongoloid people indigenous to the Arctic coasts of North America, Greenland, and NE Siberia. **2** The language of the Eskimos, belonging to the Eskimo-Aleut family. Also spelled *Esquimau.* [<Dan. <F *Esquimaux* <N. Am. Ind., eaters of raw flesh]

Es·ki·mo-Al·e·ut (es′kə·mō·al′ē·ōōt) *n.* A family of polysynthetic languages spoken along the shores of Greenland, the coasts of Labrador, in the Hudson Bay area, along the entire Arctic coast of North America, in western and northern Alaska, the Chukchi peninsula of NE Siberia, and the Aleutian Islands: possibly related to the Altaic languages.

Es·ki·mo·an (es′kə·mō′ən) *adj.* Of, pertaining to, or designating the Eskimo people or their language. Also **Es′ki·mau′an.**

Eskimo dog One of a breed of large, sturdy, broad-chested dogs used by the Eskimos to draw sledges.

Es·ki·se·hir (es′kē·she·hir′) A province of west central Turkey; 5,245 square miles; capital, Eskisehir. Also **Es′ki·she·hir′.**

es·ne (es′nē) *n. Obs.* An Anglo-Saxon domestic slave. [OE]

e·soph·a·gos·to·my (i·sof′ə·gos′tə·mē) *n. Surg.* The forming of an artificial opening into the esophagus. [<ESOPHAGUS + -STOMY]

e·soph·a·gus (i·sof′ə·gəs) *n. pl.* **·gi** (-jī) *Zool.* The tube in vertebrate and invertebrate animals through which food passes from the mouth to the stomach: also *oesophagus.* [<NL <Gk. *oisophagos*] —**e·so·phag·e·al** (ē′sō·faj′ē·əl, i·sof′ə·jē′əl), **e·soph′a·gal** (-ə·gəl) *adj.*

E·so·pi·an (i·sō′pē·ən) See AESOPIAN.

es·o·ter·ic (es′ə·ter′ik) *adj.* **1** Confined to a select circle; confidential. **2** Adapted exclusively for the initiated and enlightened few; abstruse; profound: opposed to *exoteric.* [<Gk. *esōterikos* inner <*esō* inside] —**es′o·ter′i·cal·ly** *adv.*

ESP Extrasensory perception.

es·pa·drille (es′pə·dril′, *Fr.* es·pȧ·drē′y′) *n.* A canvas shoe soled with rope: used in sports and in mountain-climbing. [<F]

es·pal·ier (es·pal′yər) *n.* **1** A trellis on which small fruit trees, shrubs, etc., are trained to grow flattened out. **2** A tree or row of plants trained on a wall or framework. —*v.t.* To train on or furnish with an espalier, as small trees. [<F <Ital. *spalliera* <*spalla* a shoulder]

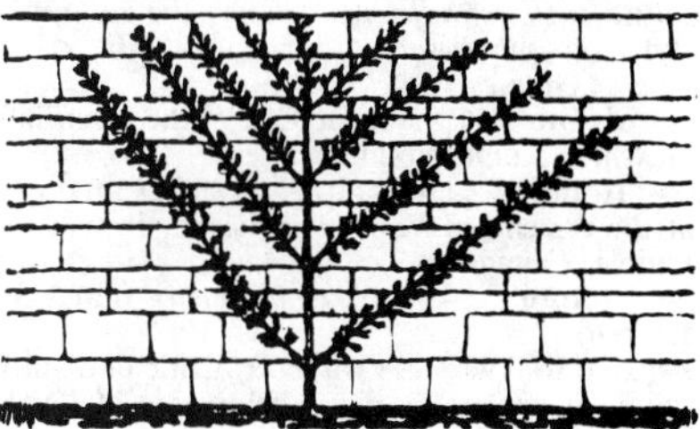

ESPALIER
A tree espaliered against a wall.

Es·pa·ña (es·pä′nyä) The Spanish name for SPAIN.

es·par·cet (es·pär′set, es′pär·set′) *n. Obs.* Sainfoin. Also **es·par′cette, es·par′sette.** [<F]

Es·par·te·ro (es′pär·tā′rō), **Baldomero,** 1792–1879, Spanish statesman and general.

es·par·to (es·pär′tō) *n.* A hardy perennial rush-like grass (genera *Lygeum* and *Stipa*) of sandy regions in northern Africa and southern Spain: used for weaving and for making a grade of paper. Also **esparto grass.** [<Sp. <L *spartum* <Gk. *sparton* a fiber rope <*spartos* esparto]

es·pe·cial (es·pesh′əl) *adj.* **1** Exceptional; noteworthy. **2** Particular or individual; special. [<OF <L *specialis* <*species* kind, type]

es·pe·cial·ly (es·pesh′əl·ē) *adv.* Preeminently; particularly.

es·per·ance (es′pər·əns) *n. Obs.* Hope. [<F *espérance*]

Es·pe·ran·to (es′pə·rän′tō) *n.* An artificial language designed for universal use, invented by Ludwig Zamenhof, a Russian scholar, and published in 1887. Its vocabulary, as far as was found practicable, consists of words common to every important European language, spelled more or less phonetically. [after Dr. *Esperanto* (Dr. Hopeful), pen name of inventor] —**Es′pe·ran′tism** *n.* —**Es′pe·ran′tist** *n.*

es·pi·al (es·pī′əl) *n.* **1** The action of a spy. **2** A watching in secret; concealed observation. **3** *Obs.* A company of spies, or a spy. **4** The catching or being caught sight of.

es·piè·gle (es·pye′gl′) *adj. French* Roguish; playful.

es·piè·gle·rie (es·pye·glə·rē′) *n. French* Roguishness; bantering.

es·pi·o·nage (es′pē·ə·nij, -näzh; *Fr.* es·pyô·näzh′) *n.* **1** The practice of spying; excessive or offensive surveillance. **2** The employment and activities of spies and secret agents in time of war. [<F *espionnage* <*espier* espy]

Es·pí·ri·to San·to (is·pē′rē·tōō sun′tōō) A coastal state in eastern Brazil; 15,780 square miles; capital, Vitória.

Es·pí·ri·tu San·to (es·pē′rē·tōō sän′tō) The largest island of the New Hebrides group; 1,875 square miles: also *Marina.*

es·pla·nade (es′plə·nād′, -näd′) *n.* A level open space, as before a fortress or along a waterside, for promenading, driving, etc. [<F <Sp.

esplanada < *explanar* < L *explanare* < *ex-* out + *planus* level]

es·pon·toon (es·pon′tōōn) See SPONTOON.

es·pou·sal (es·pou′zəl) *adj.* Of or pertaining to a betrothal or marriage. —*n.* **1** The act of espousing; plighting of troths; betrothal; marriage. **2** The adoption, as of a cause or principle.

es·pouse (es·pouz′) *v.t.* **·poused, ·pous·ing 1** To take as a spouse; marry. **2** To promise or give in marriage. **3** To make one's own; adopt, as a cause or doctrine. **4** *Obs.* To pledge; commit. See synonyms under EMBRACE. [< OF *espouser* < L *sponsare* < *sponsus.* See SPOUSE.] —**es·pous′er** *n.*

es·prin·gal (es·pring′gəl) *Obs.* See SPRINGAL[1].

es·prit (es·prē′) *n.* Spirit; wit. [< F < L *spiritus*]

esprit de corps (də kôr) *French* The spirit of the group; morale; especially, common devotion of members to a group.

es·py (es·pī′) *v.t.* **es·pied, es·py·ing 1** To catch sight of (something distant or hidden); see; descry. **2** *Obs.* To observe closely; explore; spy. [< OF *espier* < Gmc.]

-esque *suffix of adjectives* Like; in the manner or style of: *picturesque, arabesque.* [< F < Ital. *-esco* < Gmc.]

Es·qui·line (es′kwə·līn) *n.* One of the seven hills on which Rome is built.

Es·qui·malt (es·kwī′môlt) A naval base and port at the SE end of Vancouver Island, British Columbia, Canada.

Es·qui·mau (es′kə·mō) *n. pl.* **·maux** (mōz) See ESKIMO.

es·quire (es·kwīr′, es′kwīr) *n.* **1** A title of dignity, office, or courtesy ranking below that of *knight.* In the United States, the title is given specially to lawyers and justices of the peace, but occasionally to any man as a mark of respect. **2** In England, a landed proprietor; squire. **3** A gentleman who escorts a lady in public. —*v.t.* (es·kwīr′) **es·quired, es·quir·ing 1** *Rare* To squire. **2** To address as or raise to the title of esquire. [< OF *esquier* < LL *scutarius* shield-bearer < *scutum* a shield]

ess (es) *n. pl.* **ess·es 1** The letter *S, s.* **2** Anything shaped like an *S.* [< L *es* letter *s*]

-ess *suffix* Female: *goddess, lioness*: used to form the feminine of many nouns. [< F *-esse* < LL *-issa* < Gk.]

es·say (e·sā′) *v.t.* **1** To try to do or accomplish; attempt. **2** To test the nature, quality, etc., of. See synonyms under ENDEAVOR. [Var. of ASSAY, *v.*] —*n.* (e·sā′, es′ā) **1** (es′ā) A literary composition on some special subject, analytical, expository, critical, or reflective and personal, commonly briefer and less complete and formal than a *treatise*; latterly, any dissertation on a particular subject, a form of pure representative discourse. **2** An endeavor; attempt; effort. **3** *Obs.* An assay. **4** In philately, a rejected or unused design for a stamp. See synonyms under ENDEAVOR, PROOF. [< OF *essai.* Doublet of ASSAY, *n.*]

es·say·ist (es′ā·ist) *n.* **1** A writer of essays. **2** *Rare* One who makes an attempt.

Es·sen (es′ən) A city in North Rhine-Westphalia, Germany, in the Ruhr valley.

es·sence (es′əns) *n.* **1** The intrinsic nature of anything; that which makes a thing what it is. **2** Being or existence in the abstract. **3** A being, especially a spiritual being. **4** A solution, as of an essential oil in alcohol. **5** The active principle of a plant or medicinal substance. **6** Perfume; scent. [< F < L *essentia* < *esse* be]

Es·sene (es′ēn) *n.* One of an ascetic sect of Jews formed about the second century B.C.: their beliefs in voluntary poverty, community of property, celibacy, and a high degree of personal holiness influenced early Christianity. [< L *Esseni* the Essenes < Gk. *Essēnoi*] —**Es·se′ni·an, Es·sen·ic** (e·sen′ik) *adj.*

es·sen·tial (ə·sen′shəl) *adj.* **1** Of or pertaining to the essence or intrinsic nature of anything; substantial; basal; characteristic. **2** Indispensable, necessary, or highly important, as to success or completeness; absolutely requisite; cardinal. **3** Constituting, containing, or derived from the essence or any distinguishing constituent, as of a plant; constitutive: *essential* oils. **4** Having real existence; real; actual: distinguished from *accidental.* **5** Having the appearance or properties of an essence. See synonyms under INHERENT, NECESSARY, RADICAL. —*n.* **1** That which is essential or characteristic. **2** A necessary element, organ, or part. See synonyms under NECESSITY. [< LL *essentialis* < *essentia.* See ESSENCE.] —**es·sen′ti·al′i·ty** (-shē·al′ə·tē) *n.* —**es·sen′tial·ly** *adv.* —**es·sen′tial·ness** *n.*

essential amino acid Any of some eight amino acids that must be present in the human diet because they are required for protein synthesis but are not themselves synthesized in the human body.

essential oil Any of a group of volatile oils which give to plants their characteristic odors and are used in the making of perfumes and flavors.

Es·se·qui·bo (es′ə·kwē′bō) The largest river of British Guiana, flowing 600 miles north to the Atlantic.

Es·sex (es′iks), **Earl of,** 1567?–1601, Robert Devereux, English courtier; favorite of Elizabeth I; beheaded for treason.

Es·sex (es′iks) A county of SE England north of the Thames estuary; 1,528 square miles; county seat, Chelmsford.

Es·sie (es′ē) Diminutive of ESTHER.

Ess·ling (es′ling) A town east of Vienna, Austria; site of Napoleon's defeat by Austrian forces, 1809.

Ess·ling·en (es′ling·ən) A city in Baden-Württemberg, Germany. Also **Ess·ling·en-am-Neck·ar** (-äm·nek′är).

es·soin (i·soin′) *n.* **1** In English law, an excuse for non-appearance in court, or the allegation of such excuse. **2** The person so excused. **3** *Obs.* Excuse; delay. —*v.t.* To excuse for not appearing at court. Also **es·soign′.** [< OF *essoine, essoigne* < *essoignier* < Med. L *exsoniare* < *ex-* out + *soniare* < *sonia* excuse]

es·so·nite (es′ə·nīt) *n.* Cinnamon stone: also called *hessonite.* [< Gk. *hēssōn* lesser, inferior + -ITE[1]; because softer than similar minerals]

-est[1] *suffix* Most: used in the superlative degree of adjectives and adverbs: *hardest, latest.* [OE *-ast, -est, -ost*]

-est[2] An archaic inflectional ending used in the second person singular present and past indicative, with *thou: eatest, walkest.* Also, in contracted forms, *-st,* as in *hast, didst.*

es·tab·lish (es·tab′lish) *v.t.* **1** To settle or fix firmly; make stable or permanent. **2** To set up; found, as an institution or business. **3** To set up; install (oneself or someone else) in business, a position, etc.: to *establish* oneself in an apartment. **4** To make firm; build up securely: to *establish* a reputation. **5** To put into effect permanently; ordain, as laws. **6** To gain acceptance for; prove, as a theory or argument. **7** To appoint (a church) as a national or state institution. **8** In card games, to gain command of (a suit). See synonyms under CONFIRM, INSTITUTE, MAKE, RATIFY, SET, SETTLE. [< OF *establiss-*, stem of *establir* < L *stabilire* < *stabilis* STABLE[1]] —**es·tab′lish·er** *n.*

established church A church maintained by the state and receiving financial support out of public funds, as the Church of England or the Presbyterian Church of Scotland.

es·tab·lish·ment (es·tab′lish·mənt) *n.* **1** The act of establishing. **2** The state of being established, in any sense of the word. **3** Anything established. **4** A household; a family residence, with its grounds and equipment. **5** An organized staff of servants or employees, together with the building in which they are located. **6** A place of business, together with its equipment. **7** An organized civil, military, or navel force. **8** The act of recognizing a church as a state church. **9** A church so recognized. **10** A settlement in life; particularly, a fixed allowance or income. —**the Establishment** Those collectively who occupy positions of influence and status in a society.

es·ta·cade (es′tə·kād′, -käd′) *n. Mil.* A stockade or dike of piles in a morass, sea, or river, to prevent any enemy's approach; also, any defensive work of stakes or piles. Also **es′ta·ca′do** (-kä′dō). [< F < Sp. *estacada* < *estaca* stake, post]

E·sta·cio (e·stä′syōō) Portuguese form of EUSTACE.

es·ta·fette (es′tə·fet′) *n.* A mounted courier. [< F *estafette* < Ital. *staffetta,* dim. of *staffa* stirrup < OHG *stapho* step]

Es·taing (des·taṅ′), **Charles Hector, Count d',** 1729–94, French admiral.

es·ta·mi·net (es·tȧ·mē·nā′) *n. French* A drinking place; wineshop; a café.

es·tan·cia (es·tän′syä) *n. SW U.S.* A large estate or cattle ranch. [< Sp.]

es·tate (es·tāt′) *n.* **1** One's entire property; a tract of land. **2** Property left after death. **3** Condition or state; social standing; rank; dignity. **4** A class or order of persons in a state. **5** *Brit.* The lords spiritual, lords temporal, and commons. **6** *Law* The degree, nature, and amount of one's lawful interest in any property. **7** *Obs.* Pomp; display. See synonyms under PROPERTY. —**third estate** The commons, as distinguished from the clergy and the nobles, the **first** and the **second estates.** —*v.t. Obs.* To set up in or as in an estate. [< OF *estat* < L *status* STATE]

es·tate-bot·tled (es·tāt′bot′ld) *adj.* Referring to wine bottled by the vineyard owner or producer.

Estates of the Realm 1 The Parliament of Scotland: so called before the union with England in 1707. **2** Throughout feudal Europe, the three estates: clergy, nobility and commons.

Es·te (es′tā) Italian princely family of Ferrara, notably **Alfonso d'Este I,** 1476–1534, his brother **Ipollito I, Cardinal d'Este,** 1479–1520, and their sisters, **Isabella d'Este,** 1474–1539, Marchioness of Mantua, and **Beatrice d'Este,** 1475–97, Duchess of Milan, patronesses of the arts.

Es·te·ban (es·tā′bän) Spanish form of STEPHEN. Also *Pg.* **Es·te·vão** (es·te·vouṅ′).

es·teem (es·tēm′) *n.* **1** Favorable opinion or estimation on the basis of worth, especially that based on moral characteristics; respect; regard. **2** Character that commands respect or consideration; estimableness: a person of *esteem.* **3** *Obs.* Estimation or judgment of merit or demerit; opinion; estimation. [< *v.*] —*v.t.* **1** To value highly; regard as having worth or excellence. **2** To think to be; deem; consider: to *esteem* one fortunate. [< F *estimer* < L *aestimare* value]

Synonyms (noun): estimate, estimation, favor, regard, respect. *Esteem* for a person is a favorable opinion on the basis of worth, especially of moral worth, joined with a feeling of interest in and attraction toward the person. *Regard* for a person is the mental view or feeling that springs from a sense of his excellence, with a cordial and hearty friendliness. *Regard* is more personal and less distant than *esteem,* and adds a special kindliness; *respect* is a more distant word than *esteem. Respect* may be wholly on one side, while *regard* is commonly mutual; *respect* in the fullest sense is given to what is lofty, worthy, and honorable, or to a person of such qualities; but we may pay *respect* to station or office, regardless of the person holding it. *Estimate* has more of calculation; as, My *estimate* of the man, or of his abilities, is very high. *Estimation* involves the idea of appraisal, and is especially used of the feeling entertained by numbers of people; as, He stood high in public *estimation.* Compare ESTEEM *verb,* ATTACHMENT, FRIENDSHIP, LOVE, REGARD. *Antonyms*: abhorrence, antipathy, aversion, contempt, dislike, hatred, loathing, repugnance.

Synonyms (verb): appreciate, calculate, consider, deem, estimate, hold, prize, regard, think, value. *Esteem* and *estimate* alike imply to set a certain mental value upon, but *esteem* is less precise and mercantile than *calculate* or *estimate.* We *esteem* a jewel precious; we *estimate* it to be worth so much money. In popular usage *esteem,* as said of persons, denotes a union of respect and kindly feeling and, in the highest sense, of moral approbation; as, one whom I highly *esteem.* To *appreciate* anything is to be deeply or keenly sensible of or sensitive to its qualities or influence; as, to *appreciate* beauty or harmony; to *appreciate* one's services. To *prize* is to set a high value on for something more than merely commercial reasons. To *regard* (F *regarder* look at, observe) is to have a certain mental view favorable or unfavorable; as, I *regard* him as a friend; or, I *regard* him as a villain; *regard* has a distinctively favorable sense as applied to institutions, proprieties, duties, etc., but does not share the use of the noun *regard* as applied to persons; we *regard* the Sabbath; we *regard* a person's feelings; we have a *regard* for the person. See ADMIRE, APPRECIATE, LIKE. Compare ESTEEM *noun. Antonyms*: see synonyms for ABHOR.

Es·telle (es·tel′) See STELLA. Also *Sp.* **Es·tel·la** (es·tel′lä). [< L, star]

es·ter (es′tər) *n. Chem.* Any of a class of organic compounds formed by the reaction of an acid with an alcohol: they include oils, natural fats, and waxes, and are important in the manufacture of explosives, plastics, rayon, etc. [Coined by Leopold Gmelin, 1788–1853, German chemist]

es·ter·ase (es′tə·rās) *n. Biochem.* A hydrolytic enzyme having the power of accelerating the breakdown of esters, as the lipases.

Es·ter·ha·zy (es·ter·á·zē′), **Marie Charles Ferdinand,** 1847–1923, French army officer; forger of the documents in the Dreyfus case.

es·ter·i·fi·ca·tion (es·ter′ə·fə·kā′shən) *n. Chem.* The formation of an ester by the direct action of an acid on an alcohol in the presence of hydrogen ions, and accompanied by the removal of water.

es·ter·i·fy (es·ter′ə·fī) *v.t.* & *v.i.* **·fied, ·fy·ing** To make or change into an ester.

Es·ther (es′tər; *Fr.* es·târ′, *Ger.* es′tər) A feminine personal name. Also *Ital., Sp.* **Es·ter** (*Ital.* es′tər, *Sp.* es·târ′), *Ital.* **Es·ter·re** (es·ter′·rā), *Lat.* **Es·the·ra** (es·thē′rə). [<Persian, star] — **Esther** Queen of Ahasuerus (Xerxes); heroine of the Old Testament book of Esther.

es·the·sia (es·thē′zhə, -zhē·ə) *n. Physiol.* The capacity or state of feeling or sensation; sensibility: also *aesthesia, aesthesis.* Also **es·the′·sis** (-sis). [<NL <Gk. *aisthēsis* a feeling, sensation]

es·the·si·om·e·ter (es·thē′zē·om′ə·tər) *n.* An instrument for measuring the degrees of discriminative sensitiveness to touch.

es·thete (es′thēt) *n.* A votary of the beautiful; a possessor of or a pretender to fine taste and artistic culture: also spelled *aesthete.* [<Gk. *aisthetēs* one who feels]

es·thet·ic (es·thet′ik) *adj.* 1 Pertaining to beauty, taste, or the fine arts; artistic. 2 Appreciating or loving the beautiful. Also **es·thet′i·cal.** —*n.* 1 The philosophy of the beautiful; the principles underlying beauty. 2 Esthetics. Also spelled *aesthetic.* [<Gk. *aisthētikos* perceptive] —**es·thet′i·cal·ly** *adv.*

es·the·ti·cian (es′thə·tish′ən) *n.* One devoted to esthetics; an expert in matters of taste.

es·thet·i·cism (es·thet′ə·siz′əm) *n.* Devotion to beauty in its sensuous forms; also, the principles or spirit of those devoted to beauty in its sensuous forms.

es·thet·ics (es·thet′iks) *n. pl.* (*construed as singular*) 1 The science of beauty and taste. 2 Knowledge of the fine arts and art criticism. Also spelled *aesthetics.*

Es·tho·ni·a (es·thō′nē·ə) See ESTONIA.

Es·tienne (es·tyen′) A French family of printers and scholars, especially **Henri,** 1528–98, and **Robert,** 1503–59.

es·ti·ma·ble (es′tə·mə·bəl) *adj.* 1 Deserving of esteem. 2 That may be estimated or calculated. 3 Valuable. —**es′ti·ma·ble·ness** *n.* —**es′ti·ma·bly** *adv.*

es·ti·mate (es′tə·māt) *v.* **·mat·ed, ·mat·ing** *v.t.* 1 To form an approximate opinion of (size, amount, number, etc.); calculate roughly. 2 To form an opinion about; judge, as character. —*v.i.* 3 To make or submit an estimate. See synonyms under APPRECIATE, CALCULATE, ESTEEM. —*n.* (es′tə·mit) 1 A valuation based on opinion or roughly made from imperfect or incomplete data; a calculation not professedly exact; appraisement; also, a statement, as by a builder, in regard to the cost of certain work. 2 Carefully weighed judgment; formal opinion: an *estimate* of a person's character. [<L *aestimatus,* pp. of *aestimare* value] —**es′ti·ma′tive** *adj.* —**es′ti·ma′tor** *n.* —**es′ti·ma·to′ry** (-mə·tôr′ē, -tō′rē) *adj.*

es·ti·ma·tion (es′tə·mā′shən) *n.* 1 The act of estimating. 2 The conclusion arrived at; an estimate. 3 Esteem; regard. See synonyms under ATTACHMENT, ESTEEM.

Es·ti·mé (es·tē·mā′), **Dumarsais,** 1900–1953, president of Haiti 1946–50.

e·stip·u·late (ē·stip′yə·lit) See EXSTIPULATE.

es·ti·val (es′tə·vəl, es·tī′-) *adj.* Of or pertaining to summer; appearing in summer: also spelled *aestival.* [<LL *aestivalis* <L *aestas* summer]

es·ti·vate (es′tə·vāt) *v.i.* **·vat·ed, ·vat·ing** 1 To pass the summer. 2 To pass the summer in torpor: said of certain animals. Compare HIBERNATE. Also spelled *aestivate.* [<L *aestivatus,* pp. of *aestivare* < *aestas* summer] —**es′·ti·va′tor** *n.*

es·ti·va·tion (es′tə·vā′shən) *n.* 1 The act of spending the summer. 2 *Zool.* The dormancy in summer of certain animals. 3 *Bot.* The disposition of the parts of a flower in the bud; prefloration. Also spelled *aestivation.*

es·toile (es·toil′, -twäl′) *n.* A heraldic star, having six, eight, or more points. [<OF <L *stella* star]

Es·to·ni·a A republic, northern-most of the Baltic states of NE Europe; 17,400 square miles; capital, Tallinn; pop. 1,600,000. Formerly the **Estonian Soviet Socialist Republic** (1940–1991). Estonia separated from the Soviet Union on August 20, 1991. It received a seat in the United Nations on September 17, 1991.

Es·to·ni·an (es·tō′nē·ən) *adj.* Of or pertaining to Estonia. —*n.* 1 One of a Finnish people inhabiting Estonia and other districts. 2 The Finno-Ugric language of this people.

es·top (es·top′) *v.t.* **·topped, ·top·ping** 1 *Law* To prevent by estoppel. 2 *Obs.* To bar; plug. [<AF *estopper,* OF *estoper* <OF *estoupe* tow <L *stuppa*] —**es·top′page** (-ij) *n.*

es·top·pel (es·top′əl) *n.* 1 *Law* An impediment to a right of action, whereby one is forbidden to contradict or deny one's own previous statement or act. 2 Prohibition.

es·to·vers (es·tō′vərz) *n. pl. Law* 1 Necessaries or supplies allowed by law, as wood taken by a tenant for his own use. 2 Alimony allowed to a wife separated from her husband; also, a widow's allowance. [<OF *estover* < *estovoir* be necessary]

es·trange (es·trānj′) *v.t.* **·tranged, ·trang·ing** 1 To make (someone previously friendly or affectionate) indifferent or hostile; alienate, as affections. 2 To remove or dissociate (oneself, etc.): to *estrange* oneself from society. [<OF *estranger* <L *extraneare* < *extraneus.* See STRANGE.]

es·trange·ment (es·trānj′mənt) *n.* The act of estranging, or the condition of being estranged.

es·tray (es·trā′) *n.* 1 *Law* A stray or unclaimed domestic animal. 2 Something which has gone astray. —*v.t.* To go astray. [<OF *estraié,* pp. of *estraier.* See STRAY.]

es·treat (es·trēt′) *Brit. Law n.* An exact copy of a record or writing, especially of fines and amercements on court rolls. —*v.t.* 1 To copy from the records of a court for prosecution. 2 To levy (a fine, etc.) under estreat of record; exact, as a fine. [<AF *estrete,* OF *estrait,* pp. of *estraire* <L *extrahere.* See EXTRACT.]

Es·tre·ma·du·ra (es′trə·mə·dŏŏr′ə) 1 (esh′trə·mə·dōō′rə) A province of central Portugal; 2,064 square miles; capital, Lisbon. 2 (*Sp.* es′trā·mä·thōō′rä) A historic region of western Spain bordering on Portugal, comprising Cáceres (**Upper Estremadura**) and Badajoz (**Lower Estremadura**) provinces; 16,059 square miles: Spanish *Extremadura.*

es·tridge (es′trij) *n. Obs.* Ostrich.

es·tri·ol (es′trē·ōl, -ol) *n. Biochem.* An estrogen, $C_{18}H_{24}O_3$, found in the urine of pregnant women: also *oestriol.* [<ESTRUS + -OL[1]]

es·tro·gen (es′trə·jən) *n. Biochem.* Any of several hormones found in the ovarian fluids of the mammalian female and exercising a more or less specific and critical influence on the sexual cycle: also called *oestrin.* [<ESTRUS + -GEN] —**es′tro·gen′ic** *adj.*

Es·tron (es′tron) *n. Chem.* A synthetic fiber made of cellulose acetate: used to distinguish from the regenerated cellulose products known as rayon: a trade name.

es·trone (es′trōn) *n. Biochem.* An estrogen, $C_{18}H_{22}O_2$, present in the ovary, adrenal glands, urine and placental tissue: also *oestrone.* [<ESTRUS + -ONE]

es·trus (es′trəs, ēs′-) *n.* 1 *Zool.* The peak of the sexual cycle in animals, culminating in ovulation; heat or rut, especially in female mammals. 2 A violent or passionate impulse, craving, or stimulus; specifically, erotic desire. Also spelled *oestrus, oestrum.* [<L *oestrus* frenzy, passion <Gk. *oistros* a gadfly] —**es′tru·al** *adj.*

es·tu·ar·y (es′chōō·er′ē) *n. pl.* **·ar·ies** The wide mouth of a river where it is met and invaded by the sea, especially in a depression of the coast. [<L *aestuarium* < *aestus* tide] —**es′·tu·ar′i·al** (-âr′ē·əl), **es′tu·ar′i·an, es·tu·a·rine** (es′chōō·ə·rin, -rīn) *adj.*

es·tu·fa (es·tōō′fä) *n. SW U.S.* 1 A council chamber and religious meeting place in Pueblo villages, wholly or partly underground and containing a perpetual religious fire. 2 A stove. [<Sp., stove]

e·su·ri·ent (i·sŏŏr′ē·ənt) *adj.* Hungry; greedy; eager for food. [<L *esuriens, -entis,* ppr. of *esurire* be greedy < *edere* eat] —**e·su′ri·ence, e·su′ri·en·cy** *n.* —**e·su′ri·ent·ly** *adv.*

-et *suffix* Small; little: *islet:* often without appreciable force, as in *sonnet.* [<F]

e·ta (ā′tə, ē′-) *n.* 1 The seventh letter and third vowel of the Greek alphabet (H,η): corresponding to English *e* long. As a numeral it denotes 8. 2 Symbol for the viscosity of fluids. [<Gk. *eta* <Phoenician *hēth*]

e·tae·ri·o (i·tē′rē·ō) *n. pl.* **·ri·os** *Bot.* An aggregate fruit, such as the strawberry. Also **e·tae′ri·um.** [<Gk. *hetairia* society < *hetairos* companion]

é·ta·gère (ā·tà·zhâr′) *n.* An ornamental stand with shelves; a what-not. [<F < *étage* stage]

et a·li·i (et ā′lē·ī) *Latin* And others: abbreviated *et al.*

et·a·lon (et′ə·lon) *n. Physics* An interferometer for studying the fine lines of a spectrum by means of multiple reflection between parallel, half-silvered plates of glass or quartz arranged at fixed distances. [<F *étalon* a standard (def. 4)]

et·a·mine (et′ə·mēn) *n.* A loosely woven, buntinglike fabric. Also **et′a·min** (-min). [<F *étamine*]

é·tape (ā·tàp′) *n.* 1 A public warehouse. 2 A halting place. 3 Supplies allotted to troops during a march. 4 The distance marched in one day. [<F <OF *estaple* <MDu. *stapel* a warehouse]

et cet·er·a (et set′ər·ə, set′rə) And other things; and the rest; and so forth. Also **et caet′er·a.** Abbr. *etc.* and *&c.* [<L]

etch (ech) *v.t.* 1 To engrave by means of acid or other corrosive fluid, especially for making a design on a plate for printing. 2 To outline or sketch by scratching lines with a pointed instrument. [<Du. *etsen* <G *ätzen* <MHG *etzen,* causative of *ezzen* eat] —**etch′·er** *n.*

etch figure *Physics* The pattern etched on a crystal or metal surface by a reagent, valuable in indicating molecular structure.

etch·ing (ech′ing) *n.* 1 A process of engraving in which lines are scratched with a needle on a plate covered with wax or other coating, and the parts exposed are subjected to the biting of an acid. 2 A figure or design formed by etching. 3 An impression from an etched plate.

Etch·mi·a·dzin (ech′mē·ə·dzēn′) See ECHMIADZIN.

E·te·o·cles (i·tē′ə·klēz) In Greek legend, a son of Oedipus and Jocasta. See SEVEN AGAINST THEBES.

e·ter·nal (i·tûr′nəl) *adj.* 1 Having neither beginning nor end of existence; infinite in duration. 2 Having no end; everlasting. 3 Continued without interruption; perpetual. 4 Independent of time or its conditions, or of the things that are perishable; unchangeable; immutable. 5 Of or pertaining to eternity. 6 Appearing interminable; perpetual; incessant: often implying weariness or disgust: George and his *eternal* jokes. —*n.* One who or that which is everlasting: usually in the plural. —**the Eternal** God. [<OF <LL *aeternalis* < *aeternus* < *aevum* an age] —**e·ter′·nal·ly** *adv.* —**e·ter′nal·ness, e·ter·nal·i·ty** (ē′tər·nal′ə·tē) *n.*

Synonyms (adj.): deathless, endless, eonian, everlasting, everliving, fadeless, immortal, imperishable, interminable, never-ending, never-failing, perennial, perpetual, timeless, unceasing, undying, unending, unfading, unfailing. *Eternal* strictly signifies without beginning or end; *everlasting* applies to that which may or may not have beginning, but can never cease; *endless,* without end, in its utmost reach, is not distinguishable from *everlasting,* but is constantly used in inferior senses, especially in mechanics, as in the phrases "an *endless* screw," "an *endless* chain." *Everlasting, endless,* and *interminable* are used in a limited sense of protracted, indefinite, but not infinite duration; as, the *everlasting* hills; *endless* debates; *interminable* quarrels. *Immortal* applies to that which now has life and is forever exempt from death. *Timeless* carries the fullest idea of *eternal*, as above and beyond time, and not to be measured by it. See IMMORTAL, INFINITE, PERPETUAL.

Eternal City Rome.

e·terne (i·tûrn′) *adj. Archaic* or *Poetic* Eternal.

e·ter·ni·ty (i·tûr′nə·tē) *n. pl.* **·ties** **1** Infinite duration or existence. **2** An endless or limitless time. **3** Immortality. **4** That which is eternal or immortal. [< OF *eternité* < L *aeternitas, -tatis*]

Eternity Cape A mountainous headland on the Saguenay River, Quebec, Canada; 1,700 feet high.

e·ter·nize (i·tûr′niz) *v.t.* **·nized, ·niz·ing** **1** To make eternal. **2** To perpetuate the fame of; immortalize. Also *Brit.* **e·ter′nise.** —**e·ter′·ni·za′tion** *n.*

e·te·sian (i·tē′zhən) *adj. Meteorol.* Annually periodic, as certain northerly Mediterranean summer winds. [< L *etesius* < Gk. *etēsios* < *etos* a year]

eth (eth) See EDH.

-eth[1] An archaic inflectional ending used in the third person singular present indicative of some verbs: *eateth, drinketh.* Also, in contracted forms, *-th,* as in *hath, doth.* [OE *-ath, -eth, -oth*]

-eth[2] *suffix* Var. of -TH[2].

E·than (ē′thən) A masculine personal name. [< Hebrew, firmness]

eth·ane (eth′ān) *n. Chem.* A colorless, odorless, gaseous compound, C_2H_6, of the paraffin series contained in the gases given off by petroleum and in illuminating gas; an alkane or saturated hydrocarbon of the methane series. [< ETHER]

eth·a·nol (eth′ə·nōl, -nol) *n.* Alcohol (def. 1); an organic compound, C_2H_5OH, representing the second member of the homologous series of alcohols of the general formula $C_nH_{2n+1}OH$. Also called *ethyl alcohol, grain alcohol.*

Eth·el (eth′əl) A feminine personal name. [< Gmc., noble]

Eth·el·bert (eth′əl·bûrt), 552–616, king of Kent, converted by Augustine in 597. Also spelled *Æthelbert.*

Eth·el·dre·da (eth′əl·drā′də), **Saint** A British abbess of the seventh century: also called *Saint Audrey.*

Eth·el·red II (eth′əl·red), 968–1016, king of England 979?–1016: called "Ethelred the Unready." Also spelled *Æthelred.*

eth·ene (eth′ēn) *n.* Ethylene.

e·ther (ē′thər) *n.* **1** *Chem.* **a** A colorless, mobile, volatile, aromatic liquid compound, ethyl oxide, $(C_2H_5)_2O$, made by the action of sulfuric acid on alcohol: used as an anesthetic and solvent. **b** Any of a group of organic compounds in which an oxygen atom is joined with two organic radicals. **2** A solid or semisolid, perfectly elastic medium formerly assumed to pervade all of space and to be responsible for the transmission of light, heat, gravitational effects, and all forms of energy and radiation. **3** The upper air. Also spelled *aether* (for defs. 2 and 3). [< L *aether* sky < Gk. *aithēr* < *aithein* burn, shine]

e·the·re·al (i·thir′ē·əl) *adj.* **1** Having the nature of ether or air. **2** Light; airy; fine; subtle; exquisite. **3** Existing in or belonging to the ether or upper air; aerial; heavenly. **4** Of or pertaining to ether. See synonyms under AIRY. —**e·the′·re·al′i·ty, e·the′re·al·ness** *n.* —**e·the′re·al·ly** *adv.* —**e·the′re·ous** *adj.*

e·the·re·al·ize (i·thir′ē·əl·īz) *v.t. & v.i.* **·ized, ·iz·ing** To make or become ethereal; spiritualize. —**e·the′re·al·i·za′tion** *n.*

Eth·er·ege (eth′ə·rij), **Sir George,** 1635–91, English dramatist.

e·ther·i·fy (i·ther′ə·fī) *v.t.* **·fied, ·fy·ing** *Chem.* To form ether from (an alcohol). —**e·ther′i·fi·ca′tion** *n.*

e·ther·ize (ē′thə·rīz) *v.t.* **·ized, ·iz·ing** **1** To subject to the influence of ether; anesthetize. **2** To change into ether. —**e′ther·i·za′tion** *n.* —**e′ther·iz′er** *n.*

eth·ic (eth′ik) *adj.* Ethical; moral. —*n.* **1** The philosophy of morals; ethics: now in revived use by some philosophical writers instead of *ethics.* **2** The standard of character set up by any race or nation. [< L *ethicus* < Gk. *ēthikos* < *ethos* character]

eth·i·cal (eth′i·kəl) *adj.* **1** Pertaining or relating to ethics. **2** Treating of morals. **3** In accordance with right principles, as defined by a given system of ethics or professional conduct. See synonyms under MORAL. —**eth′i·cal′i·ty, eth′i·cal·ness** *n.* —**eth′i·cal·ly** *adv.*

eth·i·cize (eth′ə·sīz) *v.t.* **·cized, ·ciz·ing** To make ethical; treat ethically.

eth·ics (eth′iks) *n. pl.* (*construed as singular in defs.* **1** and **3**) **1** The study and philosophy of human conduct, with emphasis on the determination of right and wrong: one of the normative sciences. **2** The basic principles of right action. **3** A work or treatise on morals.

E·thi·op (ē′thē·op) *Archaic adj.* Ethiopian; Negro; black. —*n.* An Ethiopian. [< L *Aethiops* < Gk. *Aithiops,* ? < *aithein* burn + *ops* face]

E·thi·o·pi·a (ē′thē·ō′pē·ə) **1** A native empire in eastern Africa; 350,000 square miles; capital, Addis Ababa; annexed by Italy, 1936; recovered by British forces, 1941: also *Abyssinia.* **2** An ancient country south of Egypt.

E·thi·o·pi·an (ē′thē·ō′pē·ən) *adj.* **1** Of or pertaining to Ethiopia, or to the Ethiopians. **2** Of or pertaining to a group of Hamitic languages spoken in Abyssinia and regions to the south. **3** *Ecol.* Designating a zoogeographical region including Africa south of the Sahara, southern Arabia, and Madagascar. —*n.* **1** A native of modern Abyssinia. **2** A member of the Ethiopian race. **3** A blackamoor. **4** **a** The Hamitic language of Abyssinia and the regions to the south; Cushitic. **b** Ethiopic.

Ethiopian race An old designation of a division of mankind, applied to all the African Negro and Negrito peoples.

E·thi·op·ic (ē′thē·op′ik) *n.* The ancient Semitic language of Abyssinia, developed by Arabian invaders and still used in the services and records of the Christian Abyssinian Church: also called *Geez.* —*adj.* Ethiopian.

eth·moid (eth′moid) *n. Anat.* A bone, cubical in man, composed of thin plates and situated at the base of the skull, behind the nose. —*adj.* Of or pertaining to the ethmoid; sievelike. [< Gk. *ēthmoeidēs* < *ēthmos* sieve + *eidos* form] —**eth·moi′dal** *adj.*

eth·narch (eth′närk) *n.* In ancient Rome, a governor of a nation or people; viceroy. [< Gk. *ethnarchēs* < *ethnos* nation + *archein* rule]

eth·nar·chy (eth′när·kē) *n. pl.* **·chies** **1** The office or jurisdiction of an ethnarch. **2** The territory ruled by him.

eth·nic (eth′nik) *adj.* **1** Of or pertaining to race, races, or peoples. **2** Pertaining to groups or stocks of mankind as having certain physical, mental, or cultural characteristics in common, and usually but not necessarily living within a given geographic area; ethnological. **3** Belonging distinctively to a race. **4** Pertaining to peoples neither Jewish nor Christian; gentile; heathen; pagan. Also **eth′ni·cal.** —*n. Colloq.* A member of a minority ethnic group, esp., in the U.S., a non-black minority. [< Gk. *ethnikos* < *ethnos* nation] —**eth′ni·cal·ly** *adv.*

ethno- *combining form* Race, nation; peoples: *ethnogenic, ethnozoology.* Also, before vowels, **ethn-.**

eth·no·bi·ol·o·gy (eth′nō·bī·ol′ə·jē) *n.* The study of human societies in relation to their biological environment, especially as regards plant life and food supply; human ecology.

eth·no·bot·a·ny (eth′nō·bot′ə·nē) *n.* The study of plants in relation to the needs and customs of a given ethnic group or people. —**eth′no·bo·tan′i·cal** (-bə·tan′i·kəl) *adj.* —**eth′no·bot′a·nist** *n.*

eth·no·cen·trism (eth′nō·sen′triz·əm) *n. Sociol.* The concept, formulated by W. G. Sumner, that the attitudes, beliefs, and customs of one's own group, nation, or people are of central importance and a basis for judging all other groups. —**eth′no·cen′tric** *adj.*

eth·no·gen·ic (eth′nō·jen′ik) *adj.* **1** Of or pertaining to the origin of races and ethnic groups. **2** Producing races or peoples.

eth·nog·e·ny (eth·noj′ə·nē) *n.* The department of ethnology that deals with the origin of races and ethnic groups.

eth·nog·ra·pher (eth·nog′rə·fər) *n.* One who studies or is proficient in ethnography. Also **eth·nog′ra·phist.**

eth·no·graph·ic (eth′nō·graf′ik) *adj.* Of or pertaining to ethnography; descriptive of races and peoples. Also **eth′no·graph′i·cal.** —**eth′no·graph′i·cal·ly** *adv.*

eth·nog·ra·phy (eth·nog′rə·fē) *n.* **1** The branch of anthropology that considers man geographically and descriptively, treating of the subdivision of races and peoples, the causes of migration, etc. **2** Formerly, ethnology.

eth·no·lin·guis·tics (eth′nō·ling·gwis′tiks) *n.* The study, through linguistic methodology, of the relation between language and ethnology.

eth·nol·o·gist (eth·nol′ə·jist) *n.* A student of or an expert in ethnology.

eth·nol·o·gy (eth·nol′ə·jē) *n.* The science of the subdivisions and families of men, their origins, characteristics, distribution, and physical and linguistic classification. —**eth·no·log·i·cal** (eth′·nō·loj′i·kəl) or **eth′no·log′ic** *adj.* —**eth′no·log′·i·cal·ly** *adv.*

eth·no·zo·ol·o·gy (eth′nō·zō·ol′ə·jē) *n.* The study of a regional fauna in relation to the needs, uses, and customs of a given people or ethnic community. —**eth′no·zo′o·log′i·cal** (-zō′·ə·loj′i·kəl) *adj.* —**eth′no·zo·ol′o·gist** *n.*

e·thog·ra·phy (i·thog′rə·fē) *n.* A description of the moral attributes and customs of mankind. [< Gk. *ēthos* character + -GRAPHY]

e·thol·o·gy (i·thol′e·jē) *n.* **1** The scientific study of animal behavior. **2** The science of the formation of human character. [< Gk. *ēthos* character + -LOGY] —**e·tho·log·ic** (ē′thə·loj′ik) or **·i·cal** *adj.*

e·thos (ē′thos) *n.* **1** The characteristic spirit, disposition, or tendency of a people or community regarded as an endowment and as expressed in their customs. **2** The genius or spirit of an institution or a system. **3** The essential characteristics, or ideal attributes, of a work, or period in art or literature, or the type to which the art or period corresponds, as opposed to what is merely emotional, incidental, and transient. Compare PATHOS. [< Gk. *ēthos* character]

eth·yl (eth′il) *n. Chem.* **1** A univalent hydrocarbon radical, C_2H_5, of the paraffin series, denoting the presence of the radical in any of numerous compounds widely used in industry, medicine, and the arts: *ethyl* acetate, *ethyl* cellulose, etc. **2** Any gasoline treated with tetraethyl lead to reduce knock. [< ETHER + -YL] —**eth·yl′ic** *adj.*

Eth·yl (eth′il) *n.* An anti-knock motor fuel containing tetraethyl lead ethylene dibromide: a trade name.

ethyl alcohol Ethanol.

eth·y·late (eth′ə·lāt) *v.t.* **·lat·ed, ·lat·ing** To treat or combine so as to cause the introduction of ethyl or its compounds. —**eth′y·la′tion** *n.* —**eth′y·lat′ed** *adj.*

eth·yl·di·chlor·ar·sine (eth′əl·dī′klôr·är′sēn) *n. Chem.* A colorless, pungent, liquid compound, $C_2H_5AsCl_2$, used in chemical warfare as a lung irritant and vesicant.

eth·y·lene (eth′ə·lēn) *n.* A flammable, unsaturated gaseous compound, C_2H_4, used in manufacturing numerous organic chemicals and in medicine. Also called *ethene, olefiant gas.*

ethylene dibromide *Chem.* A volatile liquid hydrocarbon, $C_2H_4Br_2$, having an odor resembling that of chloroform: used in the making of ethyl gas.

ethylene glycol See GLYCOL.

eth·yl·u·re·thane (eth′əl·yŏŏr′ə·thān) *n. Chem.* Urethan.

eth·yne (eth′īn) *n.* Acetylene.

É·tienne (ā·tyen′) French form of STEPHEN.

e·ti·o·late (ē′tē·ə·lāt′) *v.t. & v.i.* **·lat·ed, ·lat·ing** To whiten, or become white, as a plant or person kept from sunlight. [< F *étioler* < OF *estieuler* grow up in stalks, ? ult. < L *stipula* straw]

e·ti·o·la·tion (ē′tē·ə·lā′shən) *n.* A blanching or yellowing, specifically in plants deprived of light or deficient in chlorophyll.

e·ti·ol·o·gy (ē′tē·ol′ə·jē) *n.* **1** The science of efficient, as distinguished from final, causes. **2** That department of medicine that treats of the causes of disease. **3** The giving of a cause or reason for anything; also, the reason itself. Also spelled *aetiology.* [< LL *aetiologia* < Gk. *aitiologia* < *aitia* cause + *logos* word, study] —**e·ti·o·log·i·cal** (ē′tē·ə·loj′i·kəl) *adj.* —**e′ti·o·log′i·cal·ly** *adv.* —**e′ti·ol′o·gist** *n.*

et·i·quette (et′ə·ket, -kət) *n.* The usages of polite society or professional intercourse. [< F < OF *estiquette.* Doublet of TICKET.]

Et·na (et′nə) A volcano in eastern Sicily; 10,740 feet: ancient *Aetna*. — **Et·ne·an** (et·nē′·ən) *adj.*

é·toile (ā·twäl′) *n.* A lustrous satin fabric with plain or changeable surface. [<F, star]

E·ton (ēt′n) An urban district opposite Windsor on the Thames river, England: seat of **Eton College,** a public school.

E·to·ni·an (i·tō′nē·ən) *n.* One who is or has been a student at Eton College.

Eton jacket 1 A short black broadcloth jacket cut off square at the hips and generally worn with a wide overlapping stiff collar, the **Eton collar**: originally used by the boys of Eton College. 2 A jacket, similar in cut, worn by women. Also **Eton coat.**

E·tru·ri·a (i·trŏŏr′ē·ə) An ancient country of west central Italy. — **E·tru′ri·an** *adj.* & *n.*

E·trus·can (i·trus′kən) *adj.* Belonging or relating to ancient Etruria or to its people, or their language, civilization, or art. — *n.* 1 One of the ancient people of Etruria. 2 The extinct language of the Etruscans, as yet unclassified, but apparently not of the Indo-European family.

et se·quens (et sē′kwənz) *pl.* **et se·quen·ti·a** (si·kwen′shē·ə) *Latin* And the following. Abbr. *et seq.*

-ette *suffix* 1 Little, small: *kitchenette.* 2 Resembling; like; imitating: *leatherette.* 3 Feminine: *farmerette.* [<F *-ette,* fem. of *-et,* dim. suffix]

et·tle (et′l) *Scot. v.t* & *v.i.* To aim; intend. — *n.* 1 Intention; aim. 2 Opportunity.

Et·trick Forest (et′rik) A grazing area including Selkirk, Scotland, formerly part of the forest covering SE Scotland.

et tu, Bru·te (et tōō brōō′tā) *Latin* And thou, Brutus!: exclamation attributed to Caesar when he saw his friend Brutus among his assassins.

é·tude (ā′tōōd, -tyōōd; *Fr.* ā·tüd′) *n. Music* 1 A composition designed to illustrate some phase of technique. 2 A composition meant to be played for its esthetic effect, but also exemplifying some aspect of technical virtuosity. [<F. See STUDY.]

é·tui (ā·twē′) *n.* *pl.* **é·tuis** A case for carrying small articles. Also **et·wee′.** [<F]

et·y·mo·log·i·cal (et′ə·mə·loj′i·kəl) *adj.* Relating to or based upon the study of etymology. Also **et′y·mo·log′ic.** —**et′y·mo·log′i·cal·ly** *adv.*

et·y·mo·log·i·con (et′ə·mə·loj′i·kon) *n.* *pl.* **·ca** (-kə) An etymological dictionary or a treatise on the derivation of words. [<LL <Gk. *etymologikon* of an etymologist]

et·y·mol·o·gist (et′ə·mol′ə·jist) *n.* A student of or one versed in the derivations, form changes, and meanings of words.

et·y·mol·o·gize (et′ə·mol′ə·jīz) *v.t.* & *v.i.* **·gized, ·giz·ing** To trace or give the derivation of (a word or words).

et·y·mol·o·gy (et′ə·mol′ə·jē) *n.* *pl.* **·gies** 1 The history of a word as indicated by breaking it down into basic elements, or by tracing it back to the earliest known form or root, with all its changes in form and meaning; also, a statement of this. 2 The study of the derivation of words. See FOLK ETYMOLOGY. [<F *etymologie* <L *etymologia* <Gk. <*etymon* original meaning + *logos* word, study]

et·y·mon (et′ə·mon, -mən) *n.* *pl.* **·mons** or **·ma** (-mə) 1 The radical or root form of a word. 2 The primitive signification of a word. [<L <Gk., original meaning; orig. neut. sing. of *etymos* true, genuine]

Et·zel (et′səl) In the *Nibelungenlied,* the king of the Huns who married Kriemhild after Siegfried's death: identified with *Attila.*

eu- *prefix* Good; well; easy; agreeable: *euphony, eupnea*: opposed to *dys-*. [<Gk. *eu-* <*eus* well]

Eu·bac·te·ri·a·les (yōō′bak·tir′ē·ā′lēz) *n. pl.* A large and highly diversified order of bacteria, including many of the disease-producing genera, as the cholera, typhoid, anthrax, and dysentery groups. See illustration under BACTERIA. [<NL *Eubacterium,* one of an order of bacteria <Gk. *eu-* good, typical + *bacterium* BACTERIUM]

Eu·boe·a (yōō·bē′ə) The largest Greek island in the Aegean, off central Greece; 1,457 square miles; capital, Chalcis: Greek *Evvoia,* Italian *Negroponte.* Also **Eu·bœ′a.**

eu·caine (yōō·kān′, yōō′kə·in) *n. Chem.* Either of two important compounds similar in effect to cocaine, but less toxic, used for local anesthesia, known as **eucaine A** and **eucaine B.** [<EU- + (CO)CAINE]

eu·ca·lypt (yōō′kə·lipt) *n.* A tree of the genus *Eucalyptus.* — **eu′ca·lyp′tic** *adj.*

eu·ca·lyp·te·ol (yōō′kə·lip′tē·ōl, -ol) *n. Chem.* A crystalline compound, $C_{10}H_{16}·2HCl$, with a camphorlike odor, derived from eucalyptol. Also **eucalyptene hydrochloride.**

eu·ca·lyp·tol (yōō′kə·lip′tōl, -tol) *n.* A colorless camphoraceous liquid compound, $C_{10}H_{18}O$, contained in eucalyptus oil: used as an antiseptic and expectorant: also called *cineol.* [<EUCALYPT(US) + -OL[2]]

eu·ca·lyp·tus (yōō′kə·lip′təs) *n.* *pl.* **·lyp·ti** (-tī) or **·lyp·tus·es** Any of a genus *(Eucalyptus)* of large, chiefly Australian evergreen trees of the myrtle family: widely used as timber, for ornamental purposes, and in the preparation of drugs, especially the volatile, pungent, essential **oil of eucalyptus.** [<NL <Gk. *eu-* well + *kalyptos* covered <*kalyptein* cover; from the covering of the buds]

eu·cha·ris (yōō′kə·ris) *n.* Any plant of a small genus *(Eucharis)* of bulbous South American plants of the amaryllis family, with elliptic or ovate leaves and white, fragrant flowers in umbels. [<NL <Gk. *eucharis* agreeable <*eu-* good + *charis* grace]

Eu·char·ist (yōō′kə·rist) *n.* 1 A Christian sacrament in which bread and wine are consecrated, distributed, and consumed in commemoration of the passion and death of Christ. 2 The consecrated bread and wine of this sacrament. See synonyms under SACRAMENT. [<OF *eucariste* <LL *eucharistia* <Gk. <*eu-* well + *charizesthai* give thanks] — **eu′cha·ris′tic** or **·ti·cal** *adj.*

eu·char·is·tial (yōō′kə·ris′chəl) *n.* A pyx (def. 1).

eu·chre (yōō′kər) *n.* 1 A card game for two to four players, played with 32 cards, one side in choosing trumps being required to take three to five tricks to win. See BOWER[2]. 2 An instance of euchring an opponent or of being euchred. — *v.t.* **eu·chred** (-kərd), **eu·chring** 1 In the game of euchre, to defeat (the trump-making side) by taking three tricks. 2 *Colloq.* To outwit or defeat. [Origin uncertain]

Eu·cken (oi′kən), **Rudolf Christoph,** 1846–1926, German philosopher.

eu·clase (yōō′klās) *n.* A very brittle pale-green silicate of beryllium and aluminum, used rarely as a gem. [<EU- + Gk. *klasis* breaking <*klaein* break]

Eu·clid (yōō′klid) 1 An Athenian geometer who lived about 300 B.C. 2 The work on geometry written by him. 3 An elementary textbook of geometry. 4 Impersonally, the science of geometry or its principles.

Eu·clid·e·an (yōō·klid′ē·ən) *adj.* Of or pertaining to Euclid; accordant with the axioms and postulates of his geometry. Also **Eu·clid′i·an.**

eu·de·mon (yōō·dē′mən) *n.* A benevolent spirit or genius. Also **eu·dae′mon.** [<Gk. *eudaimōn* fortunate <*eu-* well + *daimōn* spirit]

eu·de·mo·ni·a (yōō′də·mō′nē·ə) *n.* A state of complete well-being, as defined by the philosophy of Aristotle; good fortune; true happiness, as arising from a rational satisfaction. Also **eu′dae·mo′ni·a, eu·de′mo·ny.** [<Gk. *eudaimonia* <*eudaimōn.* See EUDEMON.]

eu·de·mon·ic (yōō′də·mon′ik) *adj.* Of, pertaining to, or tending to produce happiness; conceived or done for the sake of happiness: *eudemonic* morals. Also **eu′de·mon′i·cal.**

eu·de·mon·ics (yōō′də·mon′iks) *n.* 1 The branch of ethics that discusses happiness. 2 Means of comfort or happiness. 3 Eudemonism.

eu·de·mon·ism (yōō·dē′mən·iz′əm) *n.* Any of several philosophical theories which maintain that man's greatest good exists in some form of mental or spiritual happiness. See HEDONISM. — **eu·de′mon·ist** *n.* — **eu·de′mon·is′tic** or **·ti·cal** *adj.* — **eu·de′mon·is′ti·cal·ly** *adv.*

eu·di·om·e·ter (yōō′dē·om′ə·tər) *n. Chem.* A graduated glass vessel used in the volumetric analysis of gases. [<Gk. *eudios* clear, fine + -METER; orig. used to measure the amount of oxygen in the air] — **eu·di·o·met·ric** (yōō′·dē·ə·met′rik) or **·ri·cal** *adj.* — **eu′di·o·met′ri·cal·ly** *adv.* — **eu′di·om′e·try** *n.*

Eu·dist (yōō′dist) *n.* One of a French missionary order founded in 1643 by Jean Eudes.

Eu·do·ra (yōō·dôr′ə, -dō′rə) A feminine personal name. Also *Fr.* **Eu·dore** (œ·dôr′). [<Gk., good gift]

Eu·ga·ne·an Hills (yōō·gā′nē·ən) A range in northern Italy; highest point 1,978 feet. *Italian* **Col·li E·u·ga·ne·i** (kôl′lē ā′ōō·gä·nä′ē).

Eu·gene (yōō·jēn′) A masculine personal name. Also *Fr.* **Eu·gène** (œ·zhen′), *Ger.* **Eu·gen** (oi′·gān, oi·gān′), *Ital., Pg., Sp.* **E·u·ge·nio** (*Ital.* ā′ōō·jā′nyō, *Pg.* ā′ōō·zhe′nyōō, *Sp.* ā′ōō hā′·nyō), *Du., Sw.* **Eu·ge·ni·us** (*Du.* œ·kā′nē·əs, *Sw.* ā′ōō·gā′nē·əs). [<Gk., well-born]

Eu·gène of Savoy (œ·zhen′), **Prince,** 1663–1736, François Eugène de Savoie-Carignan, Austrian general.

Eu·ge·ni·a (yōō·jē′nē·ə; *Ger.* oi·gā′nē·ä, *Ital.* ā′ōō·jā′nyä; *Sp.* ā′ōō·hā′nyä) A feminine personal name. Also **Eu·ge·nie** (yōō·jē′nē), *Fr.* **Eu·gé·nie** (œ·zhā·nē′). See EUGENE.
— **Eugénie,** 1826–1920, Eugénie Marie de Montijo de Guzmán, empress of France 1853–70, wife of Napoleon III.

eu·gen·ic (yōō·jen′ik) *adj.* 1 Relating to the development and improvement of human stocks. 2 Well-born. Also **eu·gen′i·cal.** [<Gk. *eugenēs* well-born (<*eu-* well + *genos* race) + -IC] — **eu·gen′i·cal·ly** *adv.*

eu·gen·ics (yōō·jen′iks) *n. pl.* *(construed as singular)* The science and art of improving human breeds by so applying the ascertained principles of genetics and inheritance as to secure a desirable combination of physical characteristics and mental traits in the offspring of suitably mated parents. [Coined by Sir Francis Galton in 1883]

eu·ge·nist (yōō′jə·nist, yōō·jen′ist) *n.* A student or advocate of eugenics. Also **eu·gen·i·cist** (yōō·jen′ə·sist).

eu·ge·nol (yōō′jə·nōl, -nol) *n. Chem.* A colorless oil, $C_{10}H_{12}O_2$, of spicy odor and burning taste contained in oil of cloves, oil of bay, and other oils: used medicinally and in the manufacture of vanillin. [<EUGEN(IA) + -OL[2]]

Eu·gle·na (yōō·glē′nə) *n. Zool.* A genus of microscopic fresh-water protozoans (class *Mastigophora*) having one flagellum and a red eyespot or stigma, especially *E. viridis,* noted for its green chromatophores. [<NL <Gk. *eu-* well + *glēnē* eyeball]

eu·he·mer·ism (yōō·hē′mə·riz′əm, -hem′ə-) *n.* The rationalistic system of **Euhemerus,** a Sicilian philosopher of the fourth century B.C., who explained mythology as the deification of earth-born kings and heroes, and denied the existence of divine beings. — **eu·he′mer·ist** *n.* — **eu·he′mer·is′tic** *adj.* — **eu·he′mer·is′ti·cal·ly** *adv.*

eu·he·mer·ize (yōō·hē′mə·rīz, -hem′ə-) *v.t.* **·ized, ·iz·ing** To explain (myths) by euhemerism.

Eu·la·li·a (yōō·lā′lē·ə, *Ital., Sp.* ā′ōō·lä′lyä) A feminine personal name. Also *Fr.* **Eu·la·lie** (œ·là·lē′). [<Gk., fair speech]

Eu·ler (oi′lər), **Leonhard,** 1707–83, Swiss mathematician and physicist. — **Eu·le·ri·an** (oi·lir′ē·ən) *adj.*

Eu·ler-Chel·pin (oi′lər·kel′pin), **Hans August von,** born 1873, Swedish chemist born in Germany.

eu·lo·gi·a (yōō·lō′jē·ə) *n.* 1 In the Greek Church, unconsecrated bread which is blessed and distributed to non-communicants after the Eucharist. 2 In patristic writings, the Eucharist itself. [<LL <Gk. See EULOGY.]

eu·lo·gist (yōō′lə·jist) *n.* One who speaks in high or extravagant praise; the author of a eulogy. Also **eu′lo·giz′er.**

eu·lo·gize (yōō′lə·jīz) *v.t.* **·gized, ·giz·ing** To speak or write a eulogy about; to praise highly. Also *Brit.* **eu′lo·gise.** See synonyms under PRAISE. — **eu·lo·gis·tic** (yōō′lə·jis′tik) or **·ti·cal, eu·lo·gi·ous** (yōō·lō′jē·əs) *adj.* —**eu′lo·gis′ti·cal·ly** *adv.*

eu·lo·gy (yōō′lə·jē) *n.* *pl.* **·gies** A spoken or written laudation of a person's life or character; praise. Also **eu′lo·gism, eu·lo·gi·um** (yōō·lō′jē·əm). [<Gk. *eulogia* praise <*eu-* well + *legein* speak] —**eu·log·ic** (yōō·loj′ik) *adj.* — **eu·log′i·cal·ly** *adv.*

Synonyms: applause, commendation, encomium, laudation, panegyric, praise. *Panegyric* is *commendation* expressed *to* an assembly, and *applause* is *commendation* expressed *by* an assembly. *Eulogy* is now used almost in the very sense of *panegyric,* a laudatory address before an audience; as Blaine's *eulogy* on Garfield; *eulogy,* however, is regarded as more discriminating than *panegyric,* which is unstinted *praise.* Compare APPLAUSE, PRAISE. *Antonyms:* abuse, calumny, denunciation, detraction, invective, obloquy, philippic, slander, vilification, vituperation.

Eu·men·i·des (yōō·men·ə·dēz) *n. pl.* The Furies. [< Gk., the kind ones]

Eu·nice (yōō′nis) A feminine personal name. Also *Lat.* **Eu·ni·ce** (yōō·nī′sē). [< Gk., happy victory]

Eu·no·mi·an (yōō·nō′mē·ən) *n.* A follower of **Eunomius,** a fourth century heretic who held that Christ was created by God, and a wholly subordinate being.

eu·nuch (yōō′nək) *n.* An emasculated man, formerly employed as a harem attendant or an Oriental palace official. [< L *eunuchus* < Gk. *eunouchos* chamber attendant < *eunē* bed + *echein* keep, guard]

eu·nuch·oid (yōō′nək·oid) *adj.* Having the appearance of a eunuch.

eu·on·y·mus (yōō·on′ə·məs) *n.* Any of a widely distributed genus *(Euonymus)* of shrubs or small trees having inconspicuous flowers and many-colored fruits; especially, the wahoo: also spelled *evonymus.* [< L *euonymos* < Gk. *euōnymos* < *eu-* well + *onyma* name]

eu·pa·to·ri·um (yōō′pə·tôr′ē·əm, -tō′rē-) *n.* Any plant of the large, principally American genus *(Eupatorium)* of herbaceous or shrubby plants of the composite family, the thoroughworts, with mainly aromatic or bitter leaves and numerous corymbose heads of small flowers, as the joe-pye-weed, the boneset, the white snakeroot, and hemp agrimony. [< NL < Gk. *eupatorion* agrimony; named after Mithridates VI, called *Eupator* < *eu-* good + *patēr* father]

eu·pat·rid (yōō·pat′rid, yōō′pə·trid) *adj.* Of or pertaining to the eupatridae; of patrician birth. —*n.* One of the eupatridae; a patrician.

eu·pat·ri·dae (yōō·pat′rə·dē) *n. pl.* The hereditary aristocracy of early Attica. [< Gk. *eupatridēs* of noble father < *eu-* good + *patēr* father]

Eu·pen (oi′pən) A town on the Belgian-German frontier; ceded to Belgium under the Treaty of Versailles.

eu·pep·si·a (yōō·pep′sē·ə, -shə) *n.* Healthy digestion: opposed to *dyspepsia.* Also **eu·pep·sy** (yōō′pep·sē, yōō·pep′-). [< NL < Gk. < *eu-* good + *pepsia* digestion]

eu·pep·tic (yōō·pep′tik) *adj.* **1** Pertaining to good digestion. **2** Promoting digestion. **3** Optimistic; sanguine.

Eu·phe·mi·a (yōō·fē′mē·ə; *Ger.* oi·fā′mē·ä; *Ital., Sp.* ā′ōō·fā′myä) A feminine personal name. Also *Fr.* **Eu·phé·mie** (œ·fā·mē′). [< Gk., of good report]

eu·phe·mism (yōō′fə·miz′əm) *n.* A mild or agreeable expression substituted for a realistic description of something disagreeable. [< Gk. *euphēmismos* < *euphēmizein* < *eu-* well + *phēmizein* < *phanai* speak] —**eu′phe·mist** *n.* —**eu′·phe·mis′tic** or **·ti·cal** *adj.* —**eu′phe·mis′ti·cal·ly** *adv.*

eu·phe·mize (yōō′fə·mīz) *v.t.* & *v.i.* **·mized, ·miz·ing** To say in euphemistic form; express oneself euphemistically. —**eu′phe·miz′er** *n.*

eu·phon·ic (yōō·fon′ik) *adj.* Agreeable in sound; pertaining to euphony; euphonious. Also **eu·phon′i·cal.** —**eu·phon′i·cal·ly** *adv.* —**eu·phon′i·cal·ness** *n.*

eu·pho·ni·ous (yōō·fō′nē·əs) *adj.* Pleasant in sound, as a word; characterized by euphony. —**eu·pho′ni·ous·ly** *adv.* —**eu·pho′ni·ous·ness** *n.*

eu·pho·ni·um (yōō·fō′nē·əm) *n. Music* **1** A bass and tenor brass wind instrument, producing a mellower tone than the baritone saxhorn, and having the same range (E to B flat). **2** A musical instrument consisting of glass tubes connected by steel bars. [< NL < Gk. *euphōnos.* See EUPHONY.]

eu·pho·nize (yōō′fə·nīz) *v.t.* **·nized, ·niz·ing** To make euphonious. —**eu′pho·nism** *n.*

eu·pho·ny (yōō′fə·nē) *n. pl.* **·nies 1** Agreeableness of sound. **2** Pleasant-sounding combination or arrangement of words. See synonyms under METER. [< Gk. *euphōnia* < *euphōnos* < *eu-* good + *phonē sound*]

eu·phor·bi·a (yōō·fôr′bē·ə) *n.* Any plant of a large and widely distributed genus *(Euphorbia)* of herbs of the spurge family, characterized by their milky juice and various medicinal properties. [< NL < L *euphorbea* < Gk. *euphorbion;* named after *Euphorbos,* a Greek physician] —**eu·phor′bi·a′ceous, eu·phor′bi·al** *adj.*

eu·pho·ri·a (yōō·fôr′ē·ə, -fō′rē-) *n.* **1** Physical comfort or well-being. **2** *Psychiatry* An exaggerated buoyancy and sense of bodily health. [< NL < Gk. *euphoria* < *eupherein* be well] —**eu·phor·ic** (yōō·fôr′ik, -for′-) *adj.*

eu·pho·ri·ant (yōō·fôr′ē·ənt, -fō′rē-) *n. Med.* A drug or other agent which induces euphoria.

eu·phot·ic (yōō·fot′ik) *adj. Ecol.* Of or pertaining to the receipt of the maximum amount of sunlight: The *euphotic* zone. [< Gk. *eu-* well + *phōs, phōtos* light]

eu·phra·sy (yōō′frə·sē) *n.* Eyebright. [< Med. L *euphrasia* < Gk, delight < *eu-* well + *phrēn* mind]

Eu·phra·tes (yōō·frā′tēz) A river of SW Asia, rising in eastern Turkey and flowing 1,700 miles SW to the Persian Gulf.

eu·phroe (yōō′frō, -vrō) *n. Naut.* A long wooden block having several holes through which to reeve a cord: used in adjusting an awning on shipboard, also sometimes in tightening tent ropes: also spelled *uphroe.* [< Du. *juffrouw,* orig., a maiden]

Eu·phros·y·ne (yōō·fros′ə·nē, -froz′-) One of the Graces.

eu·phu·ism (yōō′fyōō·iz′əm) *n.* **1** An affectation of elegance in writing; a high-flown periphrastic style, such as that of John Lyly. **2** An instance of such a style. **3** Affected elegance in dress, etc. [after *Euphues,* character created by John Lyly] —**eu′phu·ist** *n.* —**eu′phu·is′tic** or **·ti·cal** *adj.* —**eu′phu·is′ti·cal·ly** *adv.*

eu·phu·ize (yōō′fyōō·īz) *v.t.* **·ized, ·iz·ing** To speak or write in an affected style.

eu·plas·tic (yōō·plas′tik) *adj. Biol.* Readily transformable into organic tissue. —*n.* Matter thus transformable. [< Gk. *euplastos* easily molded < *eu-* well + *plassein* form]

eu·ploid (yōō′ploid) *adj. Genetics.* Having a number of chromosomes that is an exact multiple of the haploid number. —*n.* A euploid cell or organism. —**eu·ploid·y** *n.*

eup·ne·a (yōōp·nē′ə) *n. Med.* Easy, natural breathing, normal respiration: opposed to *dyspnea.* Also **eup·noe′a.** [< EU- + Gk. *pnoia* breath < *pneein* breathe]

Eur·a·sia (yōō·rā′zhə, -shə) The land mass comprising the continents of Europe and Asia.

Eur·a·sian (yōō·rā′zhən, -shən) *adj.* **1** Pertaining to both Europe and Asia. **2** Of European and Asian descent. —*n.* A half-caste of mixed European and Asian parentage. Also **Eur·a·si·at·ic** (yōō·rā′zhē·at′ik, -shē-), **Eu·ro·pa·sian** (yōōr′ə·pā′zhən, -shən).

eu·re·ka (yōō·rē′kə) *interj.* I have found (it): attributed to Archimedes on his discovery of a method of determining the ratio of weight to volume: the motto of the State of California. [< Gk. *heurēka*]

Eure (œr) A river in NW France, flowing 112 miles to the Seine.

eu·rhyth·mics (yōō·rith′miks) See EURYTHMICS.

eu·rhyth·my (yōō·rith′mē) See EURYTHMY.

Eu·rip·i·des (yōō·rip′ə·dēz), 480–406 B.C., Greek tragic dramatist.

eu·ri·pus (yōō·rī′pəs) *n. pl.* **·pi** (-pī) **1** An arm of the sea where the tide rushes in strong, shifting currents. **2** A scene or occasion of violent changes. [< L < Gk. *euripos* a strait < *eu-* well + *rhipē* rush]

Eu·ro·com·mu·nism (yōōr′ō·kom′yə·niz·əm) *n.* A form of Communism practiced in some Western European countries that emphasizes the importance of democratic methods.

Eu·ro·dol·lar (yōōr′ō·dol′ər) *n. Econ.* A U.S. dollar on deposit outside the United States, especially in one of the western European countries. [< EUR(OPE) + DOLLAR]

Eu·ro·pa (yōō·rō′pə) **1** In Greek mythology, a Phoenician princess abducted to Crete by Zeus in the guise of a bull, where she bore Minos, Rhadamanthus, and Sarpedon. **2** A female figure representing Europe.

Eu·rope (yōōr′əp) A continent comprising a vast western peninsula of the Eurasian land mass; about 3,800,000 square miles, or excluding European U.S.S.R. and Turkey about 1,902,600 square miles.

Eu·ro·pe·an (yōōr′ə·pē′ən) *adj.* Relating to or derived from Europe or its inhabitants. —*n.* A native of Europe.

European Economic Community A customs union of France, Italy, West Germany, and the Benelux nations. Also **European Common Market.**

Eu·ro·pe·an·ize (yōōr′ə·pē′ən·īz) *v.t.* **·ized, ·iz·ing** To make European in characteristics, views, culture, etc. —**Eu′ro·pe′an·i·za′tion** *n.*

European plan The system of hotel-keeping by which lodging and service are charged for separately from meals, these being furnished to order. Compare AMERICAN PLAN.

eu·ro·pi·um (yōō·rō′pē·əm) *n.* A rare metallic element (symbol Eu, atomic number 63) of the lanthanide series. See PERIODIC TABLE. [< NL < L *Europa* Europe]

Eu·rus (yōōr′əs) In Greek mythology, the god of the east or southeast wind. [< L < Gk. *Euros* east wind]

eury- *combining form* Wide; broad: *eurychoric.* [< Gk. *eurys* wide]

Eu·ry·a·le (yōō·rī′ə·lē) One of the Gorgons.

eu·ry·ce·phal·ic (yōōr′i·sə·fal′ik) *adj. Anat.* Broad-headed. Also **eu′ry·ceph′a·lous** (-sef′·ə·ləs).

eu·ry·cho·ric (yōōr′i·kôr′ik, -kō′rik) *adj. Ecol.* Of or pertaining to a wide distribution in varying climates, as plant species. [< EURY- + Gk. *chōros* country]

Eu·ryd·i·ce (yōō·rid′ə·sē) In Greek mythology, the wife of Orpheus. See ORPHEUS.

eu·ryg·na·thous (yōōr′ig·nā′thəs) *adj. Anat.* Having a wide upper jaw. Also **eu′ryg·na′thic.** [< EURY- + Gk. *gnathos* jaw]

eu·ry·on (yōōr′ē·on) *n. Anat.* The point on either side of the head above the ear having the greatest lateral projection: the distance between the two euryons is a measure of the head width. [< Gk. *eurys* broad]

eu·ryp·ter·id (yōō·rip′tər·id) *n. Paleontol.* Any member of an extinct Silurian order *(Eurypterida)* of very large aquatic arthropods related to the *Arachnida* and to the king crab. —*adj.* Belonging to this order. [< NL *Eurypterida* < Gk. eurys broad + *pteron* wing]

Eu·rys·the·us (yōō·ris′thē·əs) In Greek legend, a king of Argos who imposed the twelve labors upon Hercules.

eu·ry·ther·mic (yōōr′i·thûr′mik) *adj. Biol.* Designating plant or animal organisms capable of withstanding a wide range of temperature conditions, as bacteria. [< EURY- + Gk. *thermē* heat]

eu·ryth·mics (yōō·rith′miks) *n.* A method of free-style rhythmical bodily movements in interpretation of musical compositions: devised by Émile Jaques-Dalcroze (1860–1950), Swiss composer. Also spelled *eurhythmics.*

eu·ryth·my (yōō·rith′mē) *n.* Harmony and just proportion. Also spelled *eurhythmy.* [< L < Gk. *eurythmia* harmony < *eu-* well + *rhythmos* rhythm] —**eu·ryth′mic** or **·mi·cal** *adj.*

Eus·den (yōōz′dən), **Laurence,** 1688–1730, English poet; poet laureate 1718–30.

Eu·se·bi·an (yōō·sē′bē·ən) *adj.* **1** Of or pertaining to Eusebius Pamphili, bishop of Caesarea: the *Eusebian* canons. **2** Of or pertaining to Eusebius, bishop of Constantinople, a leader of the Arians. —*n.* A follower of Eusebius.

Eu·se·bi·us (yōō·sē′bē·əs), 264?–340?, bishop of Caesarea: called "the father of church history": surnamed *Pamphili.*

Eu·se·bi·us (yōō·sē′bē·əs), died A.D. 341, Arian bishop of Nicomedia and Constantinople.

eu·sol (yōō′sōl, -sol) *n.* A chlorinated antiseptic solution for wound treatment. [< E(DINBURGH) U(NIVERSITY) SOL(UTION)]

eu·spo·ran·gi·ate (yōō′spə·ran′jē·āt) *adj. Bot.* Having sporangia developed from a group of cells, instead of from a single cell. [< EU- + SPORANGIA]

Eus·tace (yōōs′tis) A masculine personal name. Also *Du.* **Eu·sta·ti·us** (oi·stä′sē·əs), *Fr.* **Eu·stache** (œ·stàsh′), *Ger.* **Eu·sta·thi·us** (oi·stä′·tē·ōōs), *Ital.* **E·u·sta·zi·o** (ā′ōō·stä′dzē·ō), *Lat.* **Eu·sta·chi·us** (yōō·stā′kē·əs), *Sp.* **E·u·sta·quio** (ā′ōō·stä′kyō), *Pg.* **E·sta·cio** (e·stä′syōō). [< Gk., happy in harvest]

Eu·sta·chi·an (yōō·stā′kē·ən, -shē·ən, -shən) *adj.* Of, pertaining to, or named for Eustachio.

Eustachian tube *Anat.* A passage between the pharynx and the inner ear; it forms the auditory canal and serves to equalize air pressure between the inner ear, the tympanic cavity of the middle ear, and the external air.

See illustration under EAR. [after Bartolommeo *Eustachio*]

E·u·sta·chio (ā′o͞o′stä′kyō), **Bartolommeo,** 1520–74, Italian anatomist.

eu·tax·it·ic (yo͞o′tak·sit′ik) Of or pertaining to ore deposits occurring in stratified form: opposed to *ataxitic.*

eu·tax·y (yo͞o·tak′sē) *n.* Good arrangement; orderly disposition. [< Gk. *eutaxia* < *eu-* good + *taxis* arrangement < *tassein* arrange]

eu·tec·tic (yo͞o·tek′tik) *adj. Chem.* Melting readily or at a low temperature: said of an alloy or a solution that has the lowest possible fusing point, usually below that of any of the components taken separately. —*n.* A eutectic substance, as an alloy. [< GK. *eutēktos* < *eu-* well, easily + *tēkein* fuse]

eu·tec·toid (yo͞o·tek′toid) *adj. Chem.* Like a eutectic; formed at the lowest temperature.

eu·tel·e·gen·e·sis (yo͞o·tel′ə·jen′ə·sis) *n. Biol.* Artificial insemination. [< EU- + TELE- + GENESIS] —**eu·tel′e·gen′ic, eu·tel′e·ge·net′ic** *adj.*

Eu·ter·pe (yo͞o·tûr′pē) The Muse of lyric song and music. —**Eu·ter′pe·an** *adj.*

eu·tha·na·si·a (yo͞o′thə·nā′zhē·ə, -zhə) *n.* **1** Painless, peaceful death. **2** The deliberate putting to death of a person suffering from a painful and incurable disease; mercy killing. Also called *active euthanasia.* **3** Death resulting from the cessation of heroic measures to prolong a life. Also called *passive euthanasia.* [< Gk. < *eu-* easy + *thanatos* death]

eu·then·ics (yo͞o·then′iks) *n. pl. (construed as singular)* **1** The science of improving the human race by external influences, apart from considerations of heredity. **2** The science which aims at securing the most favorable environmental conditions for the growth of plants and animals. Compare EUGENICS. [< GK. *euthenia* well-being] —**eu′the·nist** *n.*

Eu·the·ri·a (yo͞o·thir′ē·ə) *n.* A subclass of mammals characterized by a highly developed placenta and lengthy prenatal development of off-spring: includes man and most of the mammalian types: formerly called *Monodelphia.* [< NL < Gk. *eu-* good, typical + *thērion* animal]

eu·troph·ic (yo͞o·trof′ik, -trō′fik) *adj. Ecol.* Of a lake or other body of water, characterized by an advanced stage of eutrophication; rich in nutrients; mature. [< Gk. *eutrophos* well-nourished]

eu·troph·i·ca·tion (yo͞o·trof′ə·kā′shən, -trō′fə-) *n. Ecol.* The process by which a body of water, as a lake, matures and ages, characterized by an environment growing progressively richer in mineral and organic nutrients, resulting in a seasonally recurring depletion in oxygen that is ultimately incompatible with animal life. [< EU-TROPHIC + -ATION]

eux·e·nite (yo͞ok′sə·nīt) *n.* A brilliant, metallic-vitreous, brownish-black mineral crystallizing in the orthorhombic system and valuable as a source of certain rare elements, as titanium, germanium, cerium. [< Gk. *euxenos* hospitable + -ITE[1], because it often contains rare elements]

Eux·ine Sea (yo͞ok′sin, -sīn) See BLACK SEA.

E·va (ē′və; *Du., Ger., Ital., Pg., Sp.* ā′vä; *Sw.* e′vä) A feminine personal name. Also **Eve** (ēv), *Fr.* **Ève** (ev). [See EVE]

e·vac·u·ant (i·vak′yo͞o·ənt) *adj. Med.* Producing evacuation; cathartic, diuretic, or emetic. —*n.* Something that assists evacuation.

e·vac·u·ate (i·vak′yo͞o·āt) *v.* **·at·ed, ·at·ing** *v.t.* **1** *Mil.* **a** To give up or abandon possession of; withdraw from, as a fortress or city. **b** To withdraw (troops, inhabitants, etc.) from a threatened area or place. **2** To make empty; vacate. **3** To remove the contents of. **4** *Physiol.* To discharge or eject, as from the bowels. —*v.i.* **5** To withdraw, as from a threatened area or place. [< L *evacuatus,* pp. of *evacuare* < *e-* out + *vacuare* make empty < *vacuus* empty] — **e·vac′u·a′tive, e·vac′u·a·to′ry** (-tôr′ē, -tō′rē) *adj.* — **e·vac′u·a′tor** *n.*

e·vac·u·a·tion (i·vak′yo͞o·ā′shən) *n.* **1** The act of evacuating or making empty: the *evacuation* of a fort. **2** *Physiol.* That which is evacuated or ejected by excretory passages, especially by the bowels. **3** The act of making void or null, as a contract.

e·vac·u·ee (i·vak′yo͞o·ē′) *n.* One who has been removed from or has abandoned his home.

e·vade (i·vād′) *v.* **e·vad·ed, e·vad·ing** *v.t.* **1** To escape or get away from by tricks or cleverness; save oneself from: to *evade* pursuers or a crisis. **2** To avoid or get out of; get around: to *evade* a question or a duty. **3** To baffle; elude: The facts *evade* explanation. —*v.i.* **4** To practice evasion. **5** *Rare* To escape; get away. See synonyms under ESCAPE. [< L *evadere* < *e-* out + *vadere* go] — **e·vad′a·ble, e·vad′i·ble** *adj.* —**e·vad′er** *n.*

e·vag·i·nate (i·vaj′ə·nāt) *v.t.* **·nat·ed, ·nat·ing** *Biol.* To turn inside out, as a tubular organ; protrude by eversion; unsheathe. [< LL *evaginatus,* pp. of *evaginare* < *e-* out + *vagina* a sheath] — **e·vag′i·na′tion** *n.*

e·val·u·ate (i·val′yo͞o·āt) *v.t.* **·at·ed, ·at·ing 1** To find or determine the amount, worth, etc., of; appraise. **2** *Math.* To determine the numerical value of. [< F *évaluer* < *e-* out (< L *ex*) + *valuer* < OF *valoir.* See VALUE.]

e·val·u·a·tion (i·val′yo͞o·ā′shən) *n.* Accurate appraisal of value.

Ev·an (ev′ən) A masculine personal name. [< Celtic, young warrior]

ev·a·nesce (ev′ə·nes′) *v.t.* **·nesced, ·nesc·ing** To disappear by degrees; vanish gradually. [< L *evanescere* < *e-* out + *vanescere* vanish < *vanus* empty] —**ev′a·nes′ci·ble** *adj.*

ev·a·nes·cent (ev′ə·nes′ənt) *adj.* Passing away, or liable to pass away, gradually or imperceptibly. See synonyms under TRANSIENT. [< F *évanescent* < L *evanescens, -entis,* ppr. of *evanescere.* See EVANESCE.] —**ev′a·nes′cence** *n.* —**ev′a·nes′cent·ly** *adv.*

e·van·gel[1] (i·van′jəl) *n.* **1** The message of redemption through Jesus Christ; the Christian gospel. **2** *Usually cap.* One of the four Gospels of the New Testament. **3** Any good news or glad tidings. [< OF *evangile* < LL *evangelium* < Gk. *euangelion* good news < *eu-* good + *angellein* announce]

e·van·gel[2] (i·van′jəl) An evangelist. [< MGk. *euangelos* < *eu-* good + *angelos* messenger]

e·van·gel·i·cal (ē′van·jel′i·kəl, ev′ən-) *adj.* **1** In or agreeing with the four Gospels or the teachings of the New Testament. **2** Denoting the adherents of a school of Protestant theology stressing the divine inspiration, authority, and sufficiency of the Scriptures, the fallen state of man, salvation by faith in the redeeming work of Christ, and spiritual regeneration, and denying in whole or in part the efficacy of the sacraments and the authority of the church. **3** *U.S.* Loosely, orthodox; Trinitarian in belief. **4** Zealous or fervent: *evangelical* preaching. **5** Pertaining to the work of an evangelist; evangelistic: *evangelical* labors. —*n.* A member of an evangelical church, or of an evangelical party within a church, as of the Low Church party in Anglicanism. Also **e′van·gel′ic.** [< LL *evangelicus* < Gk. *euangelikos* < *euangelion.* See EVANGEL[1].] —**e′van·gel′i·cal·ism, e′van·gel′i·cism** *n.* —**e′van·gel′i·cal·ly** *adv.* — **e′van·gel′i·cal·ness, e·van·ge·lic·i·ty** (i·van′jə·lis′ə·tē) *n.*

Evangelical and Reformed Church A presbyterial Protestant denomination, first organized in 1934, and, since 1957, a part of the *United Church of Christ.*

Evangelical Counsel See COUNSEL OF PERFECTION.

E·van·ge·line (i·van′jə·lin, -līn, -lēn) A feminine personal name. [< Gk., bearer of glad tidings] — **Evangeline** The heroine of Longfellow's poem of this name.

e·van·gel·ism (i·van′jə·liz′əm) *n.* **1** The zealous preaching or spreading of the gospel. **2** The work of an evangelist.

e·van·gel·ist (i·van′jə·list) *n.* **1** *Usually cap.* One of the four writers of the New Testament Gospels; Matthew, Mark, Luke, or John. **2** An itinerant or missionary preacher; a revivalist. **3** In the Mormon Church, a patriarch.

e·van·gel·is·tic (i·van′jə·lis′tik) *adj.* **1** Pertaining to an evangelist. **2** Evangelical. **3** Seeking or suited to evangelize. —**e·van′gel·is′ti·cal·ly** *adv.*

e·van·gel·ize (i·van′jəl·īz) *v.* **·ized, ·iz·ing** *v.t.* **1** To preach the gospel to. **2** To convert to Christianity. —*v.t.* **3** To preach as an evangelist. — **e·van′gel·i·za′tion** *n.* —**e·van′gel·iz′er** *n.*

Ev·ans (ev′ənz), **Sir Arthur John,** 1851–1941, English archeologist. —**Herbert McLean, 1882–1971, U.S.** anatomist and embryologist. — **Maurice,** born 1901, English actor. —**Robley Dunglison,** 1846–1912, U.S. admiral. —**Rudulph,** 1878–1960, U.S. sculptor.

Ev·ans·ton (ev′ən·stən, -ənz·tən) A city on Lake Michigan, Illinois; a northern suburb of Chicago.

Ev·ans·ville (ev′ənz·vil′) A city on the Ohio River in SW Indiana.

e·vap·o·ra·ble (i·vap′ər·ə·bəl) *adj.* Capable of being converted into vapor. —**e·vap′o·ra·bil′i·ty** *n.*

e·vap·o·rate (i·vap′ə·rāt) *v.* **·rat·ed, ·rat·ing** *v.t.* **1** To convert into vapor, usually by application of heat; vaporize. **2** To remove moisture from by a drying or heating process; to concentrate (fruit, milk, etc.) by evaporation. —*v.i.* **3** To become vapor; pass off as vapor. **4** To yield vapor. **5** To vanish; disappear. [< LL *evaporatus,* pp. of *evaporare* < *e-* out, away + *vapor.* See VAPOR.] — **e·vap′o·ra′tive** *adj.*

evaporated milk Cow's milk, unsweetened, with much of its water content removed.

e·vap·o·ra·tion (i·vap′ə·rā′shən) *n.* **1** The act or process of changing or being changed into vapor, specifically, at temperatures below the boiling point. **2** A rising of or passing off in vapor. **3** The act of drying or concentrating. **4** The result of evaporation; vapor.

e·vap·o·ra·tor (i·vap′ə·rā′tər) *n.* An apparatus for drying substances, as fruits, by evaporation.

e·vap·o·rim·e·ter (i·vap′ə·rim′ə·tər) *n.* An apparatus for testing the rate of evaporation of a liquid; an atmometer. Also **e·vap′o·rom′e·ter.**

Ev·arts (ev′ərts), **William Maxwell,** 1818–1901, U.S. lawyer and statesman.

e·va·sion (i·vā′zhən) *n.* The act, means, or result of evading; equivocation; subterfuge. [< LL *evasio, -onis* < *evadere.* See EVADE.]

e·va·sive (i·vā′siv) *adj.* Tending or seeking to evade; marked by evasion; elusive. —**e·va′·sive·ly** *adv.* —**e·va′sive·ness** *n.*

eve (ēv) *n.* **1** *Poetic* Evening. **2** The evening before a church festival or saint's day: Christmas *Eve.* **3** The time immediately preceding some event. [Var. of EVEN[2]]

Eve (ēv) A feminine personal name. [< Hebrew, life]

—**Eve** The wife of Adam and the mother of all mankind. *Gen.* iii 20.

e·vec·tics (i·vek′tiks) *n. pl* (*construed as singular*) **1** The art of developing health, physical vigor, strength, and energy. **2** Hygiene. [< Gk. *euektikē* (*technē*) (skill) of good health < *eu echein* be well]

e·vec·tion (i·vek′shən) *n. Astron.* The largest inequality in the motion of the moon, due to the action of the sun, which causes periodic changes in the eccentricity of the moon's orbit. [< LL *evectio, -onis* < *evehere* < *e-* out + *vehere* carry] — **e·vec′tion·al** *adj.*

Ev·e·li·na (ev′ə·lī′nə, -lē′-) A feminine personal name. Also **Ev′e·line** (-līn, -lēn, -lin). [< Celtic, pleasant]

Ev·e·lyn (ev′ə·lin, ēv′lin) A feminine, or (especially British) masculine, personal name. [< L, hazelnut]

Eve·lyn (ēv′lin), **John,** 1620–1706, English diarist; one of the founders of the Royal Society.

e·ven[1] (ē′vən) *adj.* **1** Free from inequalities or irregularities; level; uniform. **2** Divisible by 2 without remainder: said of numbers. **3** On the same level or line. **4** Without advantage on either side; of the same character; equal; fair; impartial. **5** Unvarying in disposition, action, or quality. **6** Whole or entire: said of money, numbers, etc.: *even* dollars. See synonyms under FLAT, HORIZONTAL, JUST, LEVEL, SMOOTH. —**of even date** *Law* Of identical date. —**on an even keel** Smoothly: from a nautical phrase applied to a ship with the same draft of water forward and aft. —**to get even** To get revenge; retaliate. —*adv.* **1** To a like degree; at the very time; so far or so much as; exactly; precisely; fully; quite: used to express emphasis, surprise, concession, or extension to what might not be expected: *even* to the end, intelligible *even* to a child. **2** As much as; yet: They would not believe the report, nor *even* the evidence. **3** Smoothly; regularly;

evenly: His verses ran *even.* **4** *Obs.* Exactly. — *v.t.* & *v.i.* **1** To make or become even or level; balance: often with *up.* **2** To make or become equal; equalize. [OE *efen* level] — **e′ven·ly** *adv.* — **e′ven·ness** *n.*

e·ven[2] (ē′vən) *n. Archaic* **1** Evening. **2** The eve before a church festival, an event, etc. [OE *æfen*]

e·ven·fall (ē′vən·fôl′) *n.* Early evening; twilight; dusk.

e·ven-hand·ed (ē′vən·han′did) *adj.* Treating all alike; impartial. — **e′ven-hand′ed·ly** *adv.* — **e′ven-hand′ed·ness** *n.*

even if Although; notwithstanding.

eve·ning (ēv′ning) *n.* **1** The closing part of the day and beginning of the night; in a strict sense, from sunset till dark; in common speech, the latter part of the day and the earlier part of the night, until bedtime: used also adjectively: *evening* prayer. ◆ Collateral adjective: *vesperal.* **2** *U.S. Dial.* Afternoon until dark. **3** A closing or declining part of any state or period: the *evening* of life. [OE *ǣfnung* < *ǣfnian* grow to evening]

evening dress Formal evening wear, especially of men.

evening gown A woman's formal dress for evening wear.

Evening Prayer In the Anglican Church, an order of worship prescribed for use in the evening: also called *evensong, vespers.*

evening primrose **1** A stout, erect American biennial herb *(Oenothera biennis),* with conspicuous yellow flowers opening in the evening. **2** Any other species of this genus.

eve·nings (ēv′ningz) *adv.* During the evening: They played bridge *evenings.*

evening star A bright planet when visible in the west just after sunset: especially applied to Venus: also called *Hesperus* and *Vesper.*

e·ven-mind·ed (ē′vən·mīn′did) *adj.* Characterized by equanimity; fair; just.

e·ven·song (ē′vən·sông′, -song′) *n.* **1** *Eccl.* The service of Evening Prayer, or the time, usually near sunset, of saying it. **2** A song or hymn sung at evening. [OE *ǣfensang*]

e·vent (i·vent′) *n.* **1** Anything that happens or comes to pass. **2** The result or outcome of any action. **3** A contingent occurrence or state of things. **4** One incident in a series, as of games. **5** *Philos.* Anything that occurs, usually manifesting changes and lasting only a relatively short time: thus opposed to *object,* which endures. [<OF <L *eventus* < *e-* out + *venire* come] — **e·vent′less** *adj.*

Synonyms: case, chance, circumstance, consequence, contingency, end, episode, fact, fortune, incident, issue, occurrence, outcome, possibility, result, sequel. Etymologically, the *incident* is that which falls in, the *event* that which comes out; *event* is thus greater and more signal than *incident*; we speak of trifling *incidents,* great *events*; *incidents* of daily life, *events* of history. *Circumstance* agrees with *incident* in denoting a matter of relatively slight importance, but implies a more direct connection with the principal matter as indicated in the phrase "circumstantial evidence." An *occurrence* is, etymologically, that which we run against, without thought of its origin, connection, or tendency. An *episode* is connected with the main course of *events,* like an *incident* or *circumstance,* but is of more independent interest and importance. *Outcome* is the Saxon, and *event* the Latin for expressing the same original idea. *Consequence* and *result* express more of logical connection, and are more comprehensive. The *end* may be simple cessation; the *event* is what has been accomplished; the *event* of a war is victory or defeat; the *end* of the war is reached when a treaty of peace is signed. Since the future is contingent, *event* comes to have the meaning of a *contingency*; as, In the *event* of his death, the policy will at once fall due. Compare CIRCUMSTANCE, CONSEQUENCE, END.

e·vent·ful (i·vent′fəl) *adj.* Attended or characterized by important or noteworthy events; also, momentous. — **e·vent′ful·ly** *adv.* — **e·vent′ful·ness** *n.*

e·ven·tide (ē′vən·tīd′) *n. Poetic* Evening time.

e·ven·tu·al (i·ven′chōō·əl) *adj.* **1** Pertaining to or being a result; consequential; ultimate. **2** Dependent upon a final contingency. — **e·ven′tu·al·ly** *adv.*

e·ven·tu·al·i·ty (i·ven′chōō·al′ə·tē) *n. pl.* **·ties** **1** The character of happening contingently or as a result. **2** A consequential event or issue.

e·ven·tu·ate (i·ven′chōō·āt) *v.t.* **·at·ed, ·at·ing** **1** To have a particular event or issue; result. **2** To be the event or issue; happen. — **e·ven′·tu·a′tion** *n.*

ev·er (ev′ər) *adv.* **1** At any time; in any case: better than *ever.* **2** In any degree: Run as fast as *ever* you can. **3** Under all circumstances; invariably; always. [OE *ǣfre*]

Ever may appear as a combining form in hyphemes or solidemes; as in:

ever-abiding	**ever-growing**
ever-active	**ever-increasing**
ever-admiring	**everliving**
everbearing	**ever-loving**
ever-blazing	**ever-moving**
ever-blessed	**ever-new**
everblooming	**ever-present**
ever-burning	**ever-ready**
ever-celebrated	**ever-recurrent**
ever-changeful	**ever-renewed**
ever-changing	**ever-renewing**
ever-circling	**ever-strong**
ever-constant	**ever-varying**
ever-deepening	**ever-widening**
ever-dying	**ever-willing**
ever-esteemed	**ever-winding**
ever-expanding	**ever-wise**
ever-faithful	**ever-young**

ever and anon Now and then; at one time and at another; repeatedly.

Ev·er·est (ev′ər·ist), **Mount** A peak of the Himalayas in eastern Nepal, the highest recorded point of the earth's surface; 29,002 feet. *Tibetan* **Cho·mo·lung·ma** (chō′mō·lōōng′·mä).

Ev·er·ett (ev′ər·it), **Edward,** 1794–1865, U.S. scholar, statesman, and orator.

Ev·er·ett (ev′ər·it) A port on Puget Sound in NW Washington.

ev·er·glade (ev′ər·glād) *n.* A tract of low swampy land covered with tall grass. — **The Everglades** A swampy subtropical region of southern Florida; 100 miles long, 50–75 miles wide.

Everglades National Park A government reservation in the southern part of the Everglades; 1,719 square miles; established 1947.

Everglade State Nickname of FLORIDA.

ev·er·green (ev′ər·grēn′) *adj.* Retaining verdure throughout the year: opposite of *deciduous.* — *n.* **1** A tree or other plant which retains its foliage throughout the year, as the pine, fir, hemlock, laurel, etc. **2** A branch or twig of an evergreen plant or tree, or the plant, used for decoration: Christmas *evergreens.*

evergreen oak Any of various live oaks of the United States; especially, *Quercus nigra* of the South, and encina.

Evergreen State Nickname of WASHINGTON.

ev·er·last·ing (ev′ər·las′ting, -läs′-) *adj.* **1** Lasting forever; eternal. **2** Interminable; incessant. — *n.* **1** Past or future endless duration; eternity. **2** A plant, the flowers of which retain their form and color when dried, as the cudweed. **3** Prunella, a durable woolen material. **4** A game of cards. See synonyms under ETERNAL, IMMORTAL. — **the Everlasting** The Eternal; God. — **ev′er·last′ing·ly** *adv.* — **ev′er·last′ing·ness** *n.*

ev·er·more (ev′ər·môr′, -mōr′) *adv.* During all time; always.

e·ver·si·ble (i·vûr′sə·bəl) *adj.* Capable of being everted.

e·ver·sion (i·vûr′zhən) *n.* A turning outward or inside out. [<L *eversio, -onis* < *evertere.* See EVERT.]

ever so Exceedingly, very: He is *ever so* strong. See NEVER SO.

e·vert (i·vûrt′) *v.t.* To turn inside out; turn outward. [<L *evertere* < *e-* out + *vertere* turn] — **e·ver·tile** (i·vûr′til) *adj.*

e·ver·tor (i·vûr′tər) *n. Anat.* A muscle which serves to rotate an organ or a part outward.

eve·ry (ev′rē, ev′ər·ē) *adj.* **1** Each individual or part, as of an aggregate whole; all taken one by one. **2** All possible; very great: Show him *every* consideration. **3** *Obs.* All: with plural noun. — *pron. Law* Every one; each. [ME <OE *ǣfre* ever + *ǣlc* each]

Synonyms (adj.): all, any, both, each, either. *Any* makes no selection and may not reach to the full limits of *all*; *each* and *every* make no exception or omission, and must extend to *all*; *all* sweeps in the units as part of a total, *each* and *every* proceed through the units to the total. A promise made to *all* omits none; a promise made to *any* may not reach *all*; a promise made to *every* one is so made that no individual shall fail to be aware of it; a promise made to *each* is made to the individuals personally, one by one. *Each* divides, *both* unites; if a certain sum is given to *each* of two persons, *both* (together) receive twice the amount; a man may fire *both* barrels of a gun by a single movement; if he fires *each* barrel, he discharges them separately. *Either* denotes one of two, indefinitely to the exclusion of the other; *either* is also in good, but somewhat rare, use, in the sense of *each* or *both* of two, taken separately and indifferently; as, on *either* side of the river.

eve·ry·bod·y (ev′rē·bod′ē, -bud′ē) *pron.* Every person; everyone.

◆ **everybody, everyone** *Everybody,* like *everyone,* calls for a singular verb and singular pronouns of reference: *Everybody* here *has* had *his* turn.

eve·ry·day (ev′rē·dā′, -dā′) *adj.* **1** Suitable for every day; ordinary; *everyday* clothes. **2** Happening every day. **3** Having general utility; practicable. See synonyms under GENERAL, USUAL.

every now and then Occasionally; intermittently. Also **every now and again.**

every once in a while Every now and then.

eve·ry·one (ev′rē·wun′, -wən) *pron.* Everybody; every person: *Everyone* likes ice-cream. See note under EVERYBODY.

every one Each individual person or thing out of the whole number, excepting none: *Every one* of the men is ill.

every so often At more or less regular intervals.

eve·ry·thing (ev′rē·thing′) *pron.* Each one in a collection or number of things, none being omitted; whatever exists; whatever pertains to some specified person, thing, place, condition, etc. — *n.* That which is of the highest importance or which includes all things: Health is *everything* to the worker.

eve·ry·where (ev′rē·hwâr′) *adv.* **1** At or in every place. **2** Wherever.

every which way *U.S. Colloq.* In every way; in all directions.

Eve's-cup (ēvz′kup′) *n.* An insectivorous American pitcherplant *(Sarracenia flava)* with trumpet leaves, crimson throat, and yellow flowers.

Eve·sham (ēv′shəm, ē′shəm, ē′səm) A municipal borough in SE Worcester, England; scene of Edward I's victory over Simon de Montfort, 1265.

e·vict (i·vikt′) *v.t.* **1** To expel (a tenant) by legal process; dispossess; put out. **2** To recover, as property, by legal process. See synonyms under BANISH. [<L *evictus,* pp. of *evincere* < *e-* out + *vincere* conquer] — **e·vic′·tion** *n.* — **e·vic′tor** *n.*

ev·i·dence (ev′ə·dəns) *n.* **1** That which makes evident or clear, whether taken singly or collectively. **2** Any ground or reason for knowledge or certitude in knowledge. **3** Proof, whether immediate or derived by inference. **4** A fact or body of facts on which a proof, belief, or judgment is based. **5** *Law* That by means of which a fact is established: distinguished from *proof,* which is the result of evidence, and *testimony,* which is evidence given orally. **6** Evidentness; clearness. See synonyms under CERTAINTY, DEMONSTRATION, PROOF, TESTIMONY. — **circumstantial evidence** Evidence consisting of circumstances which furnish reasonable ground for believing or deciding as to the existence of fact, or the guilt or innocence of an accused person. — **in evidence** Present; at hand; to be seen; conspicuous. — *v.t.* **·denced, ·denc·ing** **1** To make evident; show clearly; display. **2** To support by one's testimony; attest.

ev·i·dent (ev′ə·dənt) *adj.* Plain, manifest, or clear, as to the mind or the senses; obvious. [<L *evidens, -entis,* ppr. of *evidere* < *e-* out + *videre* see] — **ev′i·dent·ly** *adv.*

Synonyms: apparent, clear, conspicuous, discernible, distinct, glaring, indubitable, manifest, obvious, open, overt, palpable, patent, perceptible, plain, tangible, transparent, unmistakable, visible. That is *apparent* which clearly appears to the senses or to the mind as soon as the attention is directed toward it;

that is *evident* of which the mind is made sure by some inference that supplements the facts of perception: The marks of a struggle were *apparent* in broken shrubbery and trampled ground, and the finding of a mutilated body and a rifled purse made it *evident* that robbery and murder had been committed. That is *manifest* which we can lay the hand upon; *manifest* is thus stronger than *evident*, as touch is more absolute than sight. That is *obvious* which is directly in the way so that it cannot be missed; as, The application of the remark was *obvious*. *Visible* applies to all that can be perceived by the sense of sight, whether the noonday sun, a ship on the horizon, or a microscopic object. *Discernible* applies to that which is dimly or faintly *visible*, requiring strain and effort in order to be seen; as, The ship was *discernible* through the mist. That is *conspicuous* which stands out and attracts the attention. *Palpable* and *tangible* express more emphatically the thought of *manifest*. See APPARENT, CLEAR, MANIFEST, NOTORIOUS. *Antonyms*: concealed, covert, dark, hidden, impalpable, impenetrable, imperceptible, invisible, latent, obscure, occult, secret, undiscovered, unimagined, unknown, unseen, unsuspected, veiled.

ev·i·den·tial (ev′ə·den′shəl) *adj.* **1** Of the nature of or furnishing evidence. **2** Based or relying on evidence. —**ev′i·den′tial·ly** *adv.*

e·vil (ē′vəl) *adj.* **1** Morally bad; contrary to divine or righteous law; wrong or wicked; sinful or depraved. **2** Possessing injurious nature or qualities; unwholesome; noxious. **3** Characterized by calamity, trouble, or sorrow. **4** Of ill repute. See synonyms under BAD[1], IMMORAL, PERNICIOUS. —*n.* **1** Wicked conduct or disposition as showing depravity or as being destructive of good; sinfulness as injurious; moral depravity. **2** Something that harms or hurts; that which hinders prosperity, diminishes welfare, or prevents the enjoyment of a good; affliction. **3** King's evil. See synonyms under ABOMINATION, INJURY, SIN. —*adv.* In an evil manner. [OE *yfel*] —**e′vil·ly** *adv.* —**e′vil·ness** *n.*

e·vil-do·er (ē′vəl·dōō′ər) *n.* A wicked person. —**e′vil-do′ing** *n.*

evil eye In folklore, an eye having the power to cast an evil spell on a person or animal, or able to blight or cause the death of anything on which its glance falls, with or without the intent and ill will of the possessor. —**e′vil-eyed′** *adj.*

Ev·ill (ev′il), **Sir Douglas Claude Strathern,** born 1892, British air marshal.

e·vil-mind·ed (ē′vəl-mīn′did) *adj.* **1** Having an evil disposition; malicious. **2** Apt to interpret actions, language, intentions, etc., in the worst sense. See synonyms under MALICIOUS. —**e′vil-mind′ed·ly** *adv.* —**e′vil-mind′ed·ness** *n.*

Evil One Satan.

e·vince (i·vins′) *v.t.* **e·vinced, e·vinc·ing** **1** To show plainly or certainly; make evident; display. **2** *Obs.* To conquer. [<L *evincere*. See EVICT.] —**e·vin′ci·ble** *adj.* —**e·vin′ci·bly** *adv.*

e·vin·cive (i·vin′siv) *adj.* Capable of proving; convincing.

ev·i·ra·tion (ev′i·rā′shən) *n.* **1** Castration. **2** *Psychiatry* A paranoid condition in which a man develops the conviction that he is a woman, especially in relation to sexual behavior and personality traits. [<L *e-* out + *vir* man + -ATION]

e·vis·cer·ate (i·vis′ə·rāt) *v.t.* **·at·ed, ·at·ing** **1** To disembowel. **2** To remove the essential or vital parts of (anything). —*adj.* (i·vis′ə·rit) *Surg.* Disemboweled: an *eviscerate* abdomen. [<L *evisceratus*, pp. of *eviscerare* <*e-* out + *viscera* entrails]

ev·i·ta·ble (ev′ə·tə·bəl) *adj.* That may be escaped, avoided, or shunned; avoidable. [<L *evitabilis* <*evitare* <*e-* out + *vitare* shun]

e·vite (i·vīt′) *v.t. Obs.* To avoid. [<L *evitare*. See EVITABLE.]

ev·o·ca·ble (ev′ə·kə·bəl) *adj.* Capable of being evoked or called forth.

ev·o·ca·tion (ev′ə·kā′shən) *n.* **1** A calling forth or out; summoning, as of memories, etc. **2** Specifically, the summoning of a spirit, or of the dead, from a grave. **3** The formula used in such a summons. **4** In civil law, the transference of a suit from a lower to a higher court. [<L *evocatio, -onis* <*evocare*. See EVOKE.]

e·voc·a·tive (i·vok′ə·tiv, -vō′kə-) *adj.* Evoking; calling forth; fitted or calculated to evoke or call forth.

ev·o·ca·tor (ev′ə·kā′tər) *n.* One who summons up spirits.

ev·o·e (ev′ō·ē) *interj.* A cry of Bacchanals. Also **ev′o·he.** [<L <Gk. *euoi*]

e·voke (i·vōk′) *v.t.* **e·voked, e·vok·ing** **1** To call or summon forth; elicit, as an emotion or reply. **2** To summon up (spirits) by or as by spells. [<L *evocare* <*e-* out + *vocare* call]

ev·o·lute (ev′ə·lōōt) *n. Math.* A curve which is the locus of the center of curvature of another curve, its *involute*, and therefore tangent to all its normals; a curve that is the envelope of all the normals of another curve. [<L *evolutus*, pp. of *evolvere*. See EVOLVE.]

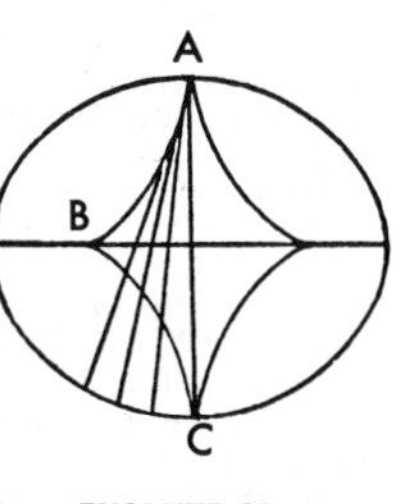

EVOLUTE OF AN ELLIPSE

ABC is the evolute of ellipse *ADC*. Cord *AC*, if fastened at *A* and swung so as to encompass *AB*, will describe arc *CD* of the ellipse.

ev·o·lu·tion (ev′ə·lōō′shən) *n.* **1** The act or process of unfolding; development or growth, usually in slow stages and from simpler forms to those which are more complex: the *evolution* of the telephone. **2** *Biol.* **a** The doctrine that all forms of life originated by descent, with gradual or abrupt modifications, from preexisting forms which themselves trace backward in a continuing series to the most rudimentary organisms. **b** The series of changes by which a given type of organism has acquired the physiological and structural characteristics differentiating it from other types; phylogeny. **3** The old theory of preformation, that the germ contains all the parts of the mature organism in minute form; development from such a germ: opposed to *epigenesis*. **4** *Math.* The operation of extracting a root. **5** A move or maneuver, as of troops. **6** *Philos.* The cosmological theory that accounts for the universe and its contents by the combination of separate and diffused atoms existing originally in a condition of absolute homogeneity. **7** A movement forming one of a series of complex motions; hence, any intricate or involved form: the *evolutions* of the labyrinth. **8** Anything evolved; also, a series unfolded. —**ev′o·lu′tion·al** *adj.* —**ev′o·lu′tion·al·ly** *adv.* —**ev′o·lu′tion·ism** *n.* —**ev′o·lu′tion·ist** *adj.* & *n.*

ev·o·lu·tion·ar·y (ev′ə·lōō′shən·er′ē) *adj.* Pertaining or relating to evolution, in any sense.

e·volve (i·volv′) *v.* **e·volved, e·volv·ing** *v.t.* **1** To unfold or expand. **2** To work out; develop: to *evolve* a plan. **3** *Biol.* To develop, as by a differentiation of parts or functions, to a more highly organized condition. **4** To give or throw off (vapor, heat, etc.); emit. —*v.i.* **5** To undergo the process of evolution. **6** To open out; develop. [<L *evolvere* unroll <*e-* out + *volvere* roll] —**e·volv′a·ble** *adj.* —**e·volv′ent** *adj.* & *n.* —**e·volve′ment** *n.* —**e·volv′er** *n.*

e·von·y·mus (i·von′ə·məs) See EUONYMUS.

e·vul·sion (i·vul′shən) *n.* A plucking out; forcible extraction. [<L *evulsio, -onis* <*e-* out + *vellere* pluck]

Ev·voia (ev·vyä′) The Greek name for EUBOEA.

ev·zone (ev′zōn) *n.* A modern Greek soldier, one of a corps picked from the mountainous regions. [<Modern Gk. *euzōnoi* <Gk. *euzōnos* well-girdled <*eu-* well + *zōnē* belt]

E·wald (i′väl), **Johannes,** 1743–81, Danish poet and dramatist: also *Evald.*

ewe (yōō, *Dial.* yō) *n.* A female sheep. ◆ Homophone: *yew*. [OE *eowu*]

E·we (ā′wā, ā′vā) *n.* **1** One of a tribe of African Negroes of the Slave Coast. **2** The Sudanic language of this tribe.

ewe lamb The one highly valued possession of a person who has little else; a beloved or an only child.

Ew·ell (yōō′əl), **Richard Stoddert,** 1817–72, American Confederate general.

ewe-neck (yōō′nek′) *n.* A neck, as of some horses, thin and bowed backward, like that of a ewe. —**ewe′-necked′** *adj.*

ew·er (yōō′ər) *n.* A wide-mouthed pitcher, sometimes with a lid. [<OF *aiguier* <L *aquaria* vessel for water <*aqua* water]

PERSIAN EWER

E·wig·keit (ā′vikh·kīt) *n. German* Eternity.

E·wig-Weib·li·che, das (däs ā′vikh·vīp′likh·ə) *n. German* The eternal feminine.

Ew·ing (yōō′ing), **Sir James Alfred,** 1855–1935, Scottish physicist and engineer. —**Juliana Horatia,** 1841–85, *née* Gatty, English author of juvenile literature.

ex[1] (eks) *prep.* **1** In finance, without the right to have or to participate in; excluding: said of stocks, as *ex* bonus, *ex* dividend, etc. **2** In commerce, free out of; not subject to charge until taken out of, as *ex* elevator, *ex* ship, *ex* store, etc. **3** *U.S.* From, but not having graduated with a given class: *ex* '54. [<L *ex-* out]

ex[2] (eks) *n. pl.* **ex·es** The letter X, x.

ex-[1] *prefix* **1** Out; out of: *exit, exhale.* **2** Remove from; free from: *exonerate.* **3** Thoroughly: *exasperate, excruciate.* **4** Without; not having: *excaudate.* **5** Once; formerly (hyphenated): *ex-president.* Also: *e-* before consonants except *c, f, p, q, s, t,* as in *edentate, erode, evade; ef-* before *f,* as in *efferent.* [<L *ex-* <*ex* from, out of]

ex-[2] *prefix* Out of; from; forth: *exodus.* Also, before consonants, *ec-*, as in *eclipse.* [<Gk. *ex-, ek-* <*ex* out]

ex-[3] Var. of EXO-.

ex·ac·er·bate (ig·zas′ər·bāt) *v.t.* **·bat·ed, ·bat·ing** **1** To make more sharp or severe; aggravate (feelings, a disease, pain, etc.). **2** To embitter or irritate (someone). [<L *exacerbatus*, pp. of *exacerbare* <*ex-* completely + *acerbus* bitter, harsh]

ex·ac·er·ba·tion (ig·zas′ər·bā′shən) *n.* **1** The act of exacerbating, or the state of being exacerbated. **2** *Pathol.* Increased severity, as in the symptoms of a disease.

ex·act (ig·zakt′) *adj.* **1** Perfectly conformed to a standard; nicely adjusted; strictly accurate or correct. **2** Precise: the *exact* sum. **3** Accurately or precisely conceived or expressed; characterized by definite knowledge or principles; rigorously determined; definite: *exact* thinking. **4** Capable of yielding results of high precision and accuracy: an *exact* instrument. See synonyms under CORRECT, JUST, MINUTE, PARTICULAR, PRECISE. —*v.t.* **1** To compel the yielding or payment of; extort. **2** To demand; insist upon as a right. **3** To require; call for: The task will *exact* great effort. See synonyms under DEMAND. [<L *exactus*, pp. of *exigere* determine <*ex-* out + *agere* drive. Related to EXAMINE.] —**ex·act′a·ble** *adj.* —**ex·act′er, ex·ac′tor** *n.*

ex·act·ing (ig·zak′ting) *adj.* Making unreasonable or inconsiderate demands; taxing; arduous. See synonyms under HARD, IMPERIOUS. —**ex·act′ing·ly** *adv.* —**ex·act′ing·ness** *n.*

ex·ac·tion (ig·zak′shən) *n.* **1** The act of exacting; extortion. **2** Something exacted; a compulsory levy. See synonyms under TAX.

ex·act·ly (ig·zakt′lē) *adv.* **1** In an exact manner; precisely. **2** Yes indeed; quite so.

ex·act·ness (ig·zakt′nis) *n.* The condition or quality of being accurate and precise. Also **ex·act′i·tude** (-tōōd, -tyōōd).

exact science A science the data of which are susceptible to precise formulation and rigorous mathematical analysis, especially one that permits accurate prediction of future events within its prescribed field, as physics or astronomy: distinguished from *descriptive science, normative science.*

ex·ag·ger·ate (ig·zaj′ə·rāt) *v.* **·at·ed, ·at·ing** *v.t.* **1** To describe or represent beyond the bounds of truth; overstate. **2** To increase or enlarge immoderately. —*v.i.* **3** To use exaggeration. See synonyms under INCREASE. [<L *exaggeratus*, pp. of *exaggerare* <*ex-* out + *agger* mound, heap] —**ex·ag′ger·at′ed** *adj.* —**ex·ag′ger·at′ed·ly** *adv.* —**ex·ag′ger·at′ing·ly** *adv.* —**ex·ag′ger·a′tor** *n.*

ex·ag·ger·a·tion (ig·zaj′ə·rā′shən) *n.* The act

of exaggerating; overstatement; hyperbole. See synonyms under CARICATURE.

ex·ag·ger·a·tive (ig·zaj′ə·rā′tiv) *adj.* Tending to or marked by exaggeration. Also **ex·ag′ger·a·to′ry** (-tôr′ē, -tō′rē). —**ex·ag′ger·a′tive·ly** *adv.* —**ex·ag′ger·a′tive·ness** *n.*

ex·alt (ig·zôlt′) *v.t.* **1** To raise on high; lift up; elevate. **2** To raise in rank, character, honor, etc. **3** To glorify or praise; pay honor to. **4** To fill with delight, pride, etc. **5** To increase the force or intensity of, as colors. See synonyms under HEIGHTEN, PROMOTE, RAISE. [<L *exaltare* < *ex-* out + *altus* high] —**ex·alt′er** *n.*

ex·al·ta·tion (eg′zôl·tā′shən) *n.* **1** The act of exalting. **2** The state of being exalted. **3** Promotion; elevation, political, social, or spiritual: used specifically of promotion to the papal office. **4** Intensification. **5** A mental state distinguished by ecstatic joy, abnormal optimism, or delusions of grandeur. See synonyms under HEIGHT. [<F <LL *exaltatio, -onis* < *exaltare.* See EXALT.]

ex·alt·ed (ig·zôl′tid) *adj.* **1** Raised up or aloft; elevated. **2** Raised in rank, position, or dignity. **3** Dignified; sublime: *exalted* poetry. **4** Intensely joyous or abnormally elated. —**ex·alt′ed·ly** *adv.* —**ex·alt′ed·ness** *n.*

ex·am (ig·zam′) *n. Colloq.* An examination.

ex·a·men (ig·zā′men) *n.* **1** A scrutiny or searching of conscience. **2** *Eccl.* An examination, as for ordination. [<L. See EXAMINE.]

ex·am·i·nant (ig·zam′ə·nənt) *n.* An examiner.

ex·am·i·na·tion (ig·zam′ə·nā′shən) *n.* **1** The act or process of examining or being examined; careful scrutiny or inquiry; investigation; inspection. **2** A testing of knowledge, progress, skill, qualifications, etc: an *examination* in history, civil service *examination.* **3** *Law* Inquiry by means of interrogation or testimony; the result of such inquiry; testimony reduced to writing. See synonyms under INQUIRY. [<F <L *examinatio, -onis* < *examinare.* See EXAMINE.] —**ex·am′i·na′tion·al** *adj.*

ex·am·ine (ig·zam′in) *v.t.* **·ined, ·in·ing 1** To inspect or scrutinize with care; investigate critically. **2** To test by questions or exercises as to qualifications, fitness, etc., as a pupil. **3** To question in order to elicit facts, etc. **4** To assay; analyze. [<OF *examiner* <L *examinare* < *examen* a testing < *ex-* out + *ag-*, root of *agere* drive. Related to EXACT.] —**ex·am′in·a·ble** *adj.* —**ex·am′i·na·to′ri·al** (-tôr′ē·əl, -tō′rē-) *adj.* —**ex·am′i·nee′** *n.* —**ex·am′in·er** *n.*

Synonyms: canvass, consider, criticize, discuss, explore, inspect, interrogate, investigate, observe, overhaul, ponder, question, ransack, scrutinize, search, study, test, try, view, weigh. See CONSIDER, INQUIRE, REVIEW. Compare synonyms for DELIBERATE.

ex·am·ple (ig·zam′pəl, -zäm′-) *n.* **1** A thing or person suitable to be used as a model. **2** An instance of something to be avoided; an act, especially a punishment, serving or designed to serve as a warning. **3** A sample; specimen. **4** An instance serving to illustrate a rule. **5** A problem to be solved. **6** That with which something may be compared; precedent; parallel. —*v.t. Obs.* **1** To exemplify. **2** To teach by example. [<OF, earlier *essample* <L *exemplum* something taken out < *eximere* < *ex-* out + *emere* buy. Doublet of SAMPLE.]

Synonyms (noun): archetype, exemplar, exemplification, ideal, model, pattern, precedent, prototype, sample, specimen, standard, type, warning. From its original sense of *sample* or *specimen* (L *exemplum*), *example* derives the seemingly contradictory meanings, on the one hand of a *pattern* or *model,* and on the other hand of a *warning*—a *sample* or *specimen* of what is to be followed, or of what is to be shunned. An *example,* however, may be more than a *sample* or *specimen* of any class; it may be the very *archetype* or *prototype* to which the whole class must conform. *Example* comes nearer to *model* than to the necessary exactness of the *pattern.* In its application to a person or thing, *exemplar* can scarcely be distinguished from *example*; but *example* is most frequently used for an act, or course of action, for which *exemplar* is not used; as, one sets a good (or a bad) *example.* An *exemplification* is an illustrative working out in action of a principle or law, without any reference to its being copied or repeated; an *example* guides, an *exemplification* illustrates or explains. Compare ARCHETYPE, MODEL, PRECEDENT, SAMPLE.

ex·an·i·mate (ig·zan′ə·mit, -māt) *adj.* **1** Deprived of life; inanimate. **2** Having no animation; dispirited; spiritless. [<L *exanimatus,* pp. of *exanimare* kill < *ex-* out + *animus* breath, life]

ex·an·i·ma·tion (ig·zan′ə·mā′shən) *n.* Real or apparent death; swooning.

ex an·i·mo (eks an′i·mō) *Latin* From the heart; sincerely.

ex·an·the·ma (ek′san·thē′mə) *n. pl.* **·them·a·ta** (-them′ə·tə, -thē′mə·tə) *Pathol.* A breaking out upon the skin; a rash, or a disease accompanied by rash, as smallpox or measles; specifically, usually in the plural, the eruptive fevers. [<LL <Gk. *exanthēma* a blossoming < *ex-* out + *anthos* a flower] —**ex·an·the·mat·ic** (ek·san′thi·mat′ik), **ex′an·them′a·tous** (-them′ə·təs) *adj.*

ex·arch (ek′särk) *n.* **1** A provincial governor under the Byzantine Empire. **2** In the Greek Church, the deputy of a patriarch. **3** Formerly, in the Greek Church, a metropolitan or patriarch; later, a bishop ranking below a patriarch. [<LL *exarchus* <Gk. *exarchos* < *ex-* out + *archein* rule] —**ex·ar·chate** (ek′·sär·kāt, ik·sär′kāt) *n.*

ex·as·per·ate (ig·zas′pə·rāt) *v.t.* **·at·ed, ·at·ing 1** To irritate exceedingly; enrage. **2** To make worse; intensify; inflame. See synonyms under AFFRONT, INCENSE. [<L *exasperatus,* pp. of *exasperare* < *ex-* out + *asper* rough] —**ex·as′per·at′er** *n.* —**ex·as′per·at′ing** *adj.* —**ex·as′per·at′ing·ly** *adv.*

ex·as·per·a·tion (ig·zas′pə·rā′shən) *n.* **1** The act of exasperating, in any sense; especially, provocation of extreme anger. **2** The state of being exasperated; extreme anger; rage. **3** Aggravation, as of a disease. See synonyms under ANGER.

Ex·cal·i·bur (eks·kal′ə·bər) In Arthurian legend, the sword of King Arthur: also called *Caliburn.* Also **Ex·cal′i·bar.** [<OF *Escalibor* <Med. L *Caliburnus* <Celtic]

ex cap·i·te (eks kap′i·tē) *Latin* Out of the head; from memory; by heart.

ex ca·the·dra (eks kə·thē′drə, kath′i-) *Latin* Officially; with authority. See CATHEDRA.

ex·cau·date (eks·kô′dāt) *adj. Zool.* Having no tail.

ex·ca·vate (eks′kə·vāt) *v.t.* **·vat·ed, ·vat·ing 1** To make a hole or cavity in; hollow or dig out. **2** To form or make by hollowing, digging out, or scooping. **3** To remove by digging or scooping out, as soil. **4** To uncover by digging, as ruins. [<L *excavatus,* pp. of *excavare* < *ex-* out + *cavus* hollow]

ex·ca·va·tion (eks′kə·vā′shən) *n.* **1** A digging out. **2** A cavity or hollow formed by excavating. See synonyms under HOLE.

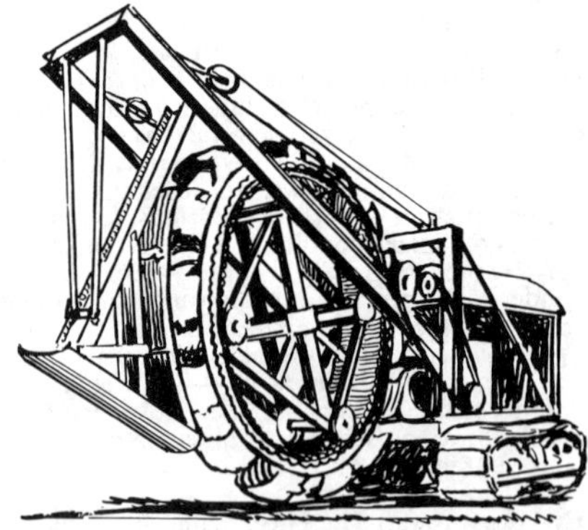

EXCAVATOR
Side view of 27-ton ditch excavator operated by one man.

ex·ca·va·tor (eks′kə·vā′tər) *n.* **1** One who or that which excavates. **2** A steam shovel or dredging machine.

ex·ceed (ik·sēd′) *v.t.* **1** To go or be beyond; surpass, as in quantity, quality, measure, or value. **2** To go beyond the limit or extent of: to *exceed* one's income. —*v.i.* **3** To be superior; surpass others. [<F *excéder* <L *excedere* < *ex-* out, beyond + *cedere* go]

ex·ceed·ing (ik·sē′ding) *adj.* Greater than usual; surpassing; extraordinary. —*adv. Obs.* Exceedingly.

ex·ceed·ing·ly (ik·sē′ding·lē) *adv.* To a greater degree than usual; extremely.

ex·cel (ik·sel′) *v.t.* & *v.i.* **·celled, ·cel·ling** To go beyond or above; outdo; surpass (another or others). See synonyms under LEAD. [<OF *exceller* <L *excellere* rise]

ex·cel·lence (ek′sə·ləns) *n.* **1** Possession of eminently good qualities; great merit, virtue, or goodness. **2** A superior trait. See synonyms under VIRTUE. Also **ex′cel·len·cy.**

Ex·cel·len·cy (ek′sə·lən·sē) *n. pl.* **·cies** An honorary title of various high officials, specifically used of the governors of Massachusetts and New Hampshire: also used to address a foreign president or minister of foreign affairs or a foreign ambassador.

ex·cel·lent (ek′sə·lənt) *adj.* **1** Having good qualities in a high degree; superior in worth or value. **2** *Obs.* Eminent; excelling. [<OF <L *excellens, -entis,* ppr. of *excellere* rise]

Synonyms: admirable, capital, choice, fine, first-class, first-rate, precious, prime, select, superior, transcendent, valuable, worthy. That which is *excellent* excels, but an object that is *valuable* or a man who is *worthy* so far excels the majority of persons or things that these words have become close synonyms for *excellent.* See CHOICE, FINE, GOOD, MORAL. *Antonyms*: bad, base, defective, deficient, good-for-nothing, imperfect, inferior, mean, poor, unworthy, useless, valueless, vile, worthless.

ex·cel·lent·ly (ek′sə·lənt·lē) *adv.* Surpassingly.

ex·cel·si·or (ik·sel′sē·ər) *n.* **1** A packing material composed of long, fine, wood shavings. **2** *Printing* An old size of type, equivalent to 3 points. [<a trade name]

Ex·cel·si·or (ek·sel′sē·ôr) Upward: motto of the State of New York. [Compar. of L *excelsus* high]

ex·cen·tric (ek·sen′trik) See ECCENTRIC.

ex·cept (ik·sept′) *v.t.* To leave or take out; exclude; omit. —*v.i.* To object; take exception: with *to.* —*prep.* With the exception of; excluding; leaving out; save; but: Tell no one *except* me. —*conj. Archaic* If not that; unless: *except* a man be born again. [<F *excepter* <L *exceptare,* freq. of *excipere* < *ex-* out + *capere* take] —**ex·cep′tor** *n.*

ex·cept·ing (ik·sep′ting) *prep.* Except; excluding. —*conj. Archaic* Unless.

ex·cep·tion (ik·sep′shən) *n.* **1** That which is excluded, as from a list. **2** The act of excepting; exclusion. **3** A captious objection, complaint, or quibble. **4** *Law* A formal objection to the decision of a court during trial. —**to take exception** To take offense; object.

ex·cep·tion·a·ble (ik·sep′shən·ə·bəl) *adj.* Open to exception or objection. —**ex·cep′tion·a·bly** *adv.*

ex·cep·tion·al (ik·sep′shən·əl) *adj.* Unusual or uncommon; superior. See synonyms under IRREGULAR. —**ex·cep′tion·al·ly** *adv.*

ex·cep·tive (ik·sep′tiv) *adj.* **1** Of the nature of an exception. **2** Captious.

ex·cerpt (ek′sûrpt) *n.* An extract from written or printed matter. —*v.t.* (ik·sûrpt′) To take out, as a passage or quotation; extract. See synonyms under QUOTE. [<L *excerptus,* pp. of *excerpere* < *ex-* out + *carpere* pluck, seize] —**ex·cerp′tion** *n.* —**ex·cerp′tive** *adj.* —**ex·cerp′tor** *n.*

ex·cess (ik·ses′) *n.* **1** That which passes the ordinary, reasonable, or required limit. **2** Inordinate gratification of appetite. **3** The amount by which one thing is greater than another; overplus. —*adj.* (*also* ek′ses) Being above a stipulated amount; extra. [<OF *exces* <L *excessus* a departure < *excedere.* See EXCEED.]

Synonyms (noun): dissipation, exorbitance, extravagance, intemperance, lavishness, overplus, prodigality, profusion, redundance, redundancy, superabundance, superfluity, surplus, waste, wastefulness. *Excess* is more than enough of anything, and, since this in many cases indicates a lack either of judgment or of self-control, the word is used frequently in an unfavorable sense. Careless expenditure in *excess* of income is *extravagance*; we may have also *extravagance* of language, professions, etc. As *extravagance* is *excess* in outlay, *exorbitance* is *excess* in demands, especially in pecuniary demands. *Overplus* and *superabundance* denote in the main a satisfactory, and *superfluity* an undesirable, *excess*; *lavishness* and *profusion,* a generous or bountiful *excess. Surplus* has none of the unfavorable meaning that often attaches to *excess*; a *surplus* is that which remains over after all demands are met. *Redundance* or *redundancy* refers chiefly to literary style, denoting an *excess* of words or matter. *Excess* in the moral sense is expressed by *dissipation, prodigality, intemperance,* etc. *Antonyms*: dearth, defect, deficiency, destitution, economy, failure, frugality, inadequacy, insufficiency, lack, need, poverty, scantiness, shortcoming, want.

ex·ces·sive (ik·ses′iv) *adj.* Being in, tending to, marked by excess; immoderate; extreme. See synonyms under IMMODERATE, REDUNDANT. — **ex·ces′sive·ly** *adv.* — **ex·ces′sive·ness** *n.*

excess profits Net profits beyond the normal average for a period of years.

ex·change (iks·chānj′) *n.* **1** The act of giving or receiving one thing as an equivalent for another; a trade; a bartering: an *exchange* of prisoners. **2** Interchange: an *exchange* of wit, remarks, etc. **3** The mutual giving and receiving of equivalents in money, goods, or labor. **4** The system by which titles to commodities in distant localities are transferred by means of credits, drafts, etc. **5** The rate of exchange. **6** The percentage of difference between currencies of values at two given places. **7** Bills, drafts, etc., presented to a clearing house for settlement. **8** A transition from one experience or condition to another. **9** That which is given or received by interchange, as a periodical or an advertisement exchanged for another. **10** A place where merchants or brokers effect exchanges: a stock *exchange.* See CURB[1]. **11** A central telephone office. **12** *Physics* The mutual interaction between the electrons, protons, and other components of the same or different atoms. **13** *Brit.* A labor exchange. See synonyms under INTERCOURSE. — **bill of exchange** A written order or request from one person to another for the payment of money to a third, the amount to be charged to the drawer of the bill. — **par of exchange** The comparison of value in gold of the monetary units of two different countries. — **rate of exchange** The price at which a bill drawn in one country upon a drawee in another country may be sold where drawn. — *v.* **·changed, ·chang·ing** *v.t.* **1** To give or part with for something regarded as of equal value, etc.: to *exchange* francs for dollars. **2** To give and receive in turn; reciprocate. **3** To replace by or give up for something else: to *exchange* poverty for wealth. — *v.i.* **4** To be given or taken in exchange: American money *exchanges* well. **5** To make an exchange. See synonyms under CHANGE. [<AF *eschaunge* <LL *excambium* < *excambiare* < *ex-* out + *cambiare* exchange] — **ex·change′a·bil′i·ty** *n.* — **ex·change′a·ble** *adj.* — **ex·change′a·bly** *adv.*

ex·cheq·uer (iks·chek′ər, eks′chek·ər) *n.* **1** The treasury of a state. **2** *Colloq.* Finances; pecuniary resources. [<OF *eschequier.* See CHECKER.]

Ex·cheq·uer (iks·chek′ər, eks′chek·ər) *n.* **1** The administrative department of the British government having the management of the public revenue. **2** In England, an ancient common law court taking cognizance of matters connected with the public revenue. In 1873, this **Court of Exchequer** was made a division of the High Court of Justice, and in 1881 this division was merged in the Queen's Bench division.

ex·cip·i·ent (ik·sip′ē·ənt) *n. Med.* Any inert substance used to give drug preparations a suitable form or pleasant taste. [<L *excipiens, -entis,* ppr. of *excipere.* See EXCEPT.]

ex·cise[1] (ik·sīz′, ek′sīz) *n.* **1** An indirect tax on commodities manufactured, produced, sold, used, or transported within a country, including license fees for various sports, trades, or occupations. **2** *Brit.* A branch of the department of the civil service having charge of the inland revenue taxes and duties. See synonyms under TAX. — *v.t.* (ik·sīz′) **·cised, ·cis·ing** To levy an excise upon. [<MDu. *excijs, accijs* <OF *acceis* <L *ad-* to + *census* a tax] — **ex·cis′a·ble** *adj.*

ex·cise[2] (ik·sīz′) *v.t.* **·cised, ·cis·ing** To cut out or off; remove; extirpate; expunge. [<L *excisus,* pp. of *excidere* < *ex-* out + *caedere* cut] — **ex·ci·sion** (ik·sizh′ən) *n.*

ex·cise·man (ik·sīz′mən) *n. pl.* **·men** (-mən) *Brit.* A revenue officer.

ex·cit·a·bil·i·ty (ik·sī′tə·bil′ə·tē) *n.* **1** The quality of being excitable; susceptibility to excitement. **2** *Physiol.* Sensitiveness to stimuli.

ex·cit·a·ble (ik·sī′tə·bəl) *adj.* **1** Easily excited; high-strung. **2** *Physiol.* Susceptible to stimuli. See synonyms under ARDENT, IMPETUOUS. — **ex·cit′a·ble·ness** *n.* — **ex·cit′a·bly** *adv.*

ex·ci·tant (ik·sī′tənt, ek′sə·tənt) *n.* A drug that excites or stimulates. — *adj.* Adapted or tending to excite or stimulate: also **ex·ci′ta·tive, ex·ci′ta·to′ry** (-tôr′ē, -tō′rē). [<L *excitans, -antis,* ppr. of *excitare.* See EXCITE.]

ex·ci·ta·tion (ek′sī·tā′shən) *n.* **1** A state of disturbance or agitation; excitement. **2** *Physics* **a** The deflection of an electron from its normal orbit in an atom to one of higher energy content: also called *activation.* **b** The electrification or magnetization of a substance. **3** *Biol.* The action of a stimulus on a plant or animal organism. [<F <L *excitatio, -onis* < *excitare.* See EXCITE.]

ex·cite (ik·sīt′) *v.t.* **·cit·ed, ·cit·ing** **1** To arouse (a feeling, interest, etc.) into being or activity; evoke: to *excite* admiration or jealousy. **2** To arouse feeling in; stimulate the emotions of: to *excite* someone to hatred. **3** To cause action in; stir to activity or motion: Wine *excites* the tongue. **4** To bring about; stir up: to *excite* a riot. **5** *Physiol.* To cause increased activity in; stimulate (muscles or nerves). **6** *Electr.* To initiate or develop a magnetic field in, as a dynamo. **7** *Physics* To raise an atom or molecule to a higher energy or quantum state, as by heat, radiation, or electron bombardment. See synonyms under ACTUATE, ENCOURAGE, INFLUENCE, INTEREST, PROMOTE, STIR. [<OF *exciter* <L *excitare,* freq. of *exciere* < *ex-* out + *ciere* arouse, stir up] — **ex·cit′ed** *adj.* — **ex·cit′ed·ly** *adv.*

ex·cite·ment (ik·sīt′mənt) *n.* **1** The act of exciting; stimulation. **2** That which excites. **3** The state of being excited, agitated, or aroused; disturbance; agitation. Also *excitation.* See synonyms under ENTHUSIASM, WARMTH.

ex·cit·er (ik·sī′tər) *n.* **1** One who or that which excites, stimulates, or rouses: an *exciter* of the people. **2** *Electr.* **a** An auxiliary generator which supplies energy for the field magnets of a dynamo. **b** A machine which generates electric waves of definite length by means of sparks.

ex·cit·ing (ik·sī′ting) *adj.* Of a nature to excite; stirring; rousing. — **ex·cit′ing·ly** *adv.*

ex·ci·to·mo·tor (ik·sī′tə·mō′tər) *n.* Any agent or drug which increases the activity of the motor centers. — *adj.* Exciting motion, but without sensation or volition: also **ex·ci′to·mo′to·ry** (-mō′tər·ē). [< *excito-* stimulating (<EXCITE) + MOTOR]

ex·ci·tor (ik·sī′tər) *n. Physiol.* An afferent nerve connected with the spinal division of the nervous system. Also **ex·cit′er.**

ex·claim (iks·klām′) *v.t.* & *v.i.* To say or cry out abruptly; speak vehemently, as in surprise or anger. [<F *exclamer* <L *exclamare* < *ex-* out + *clamare* cry] — **ex·claim′er** *n.*

Synonyms (verb): call, ejaculate. We may *exclaim* by mere interjections, or by connected words. To *ejaculate* is to throw out brief, disconnected, but coherent utterances of joy, regret, and of appeal, petition, prayer; such devotional utterances are named "ejaculatory prayer." See CALL.

ex·cla·ma·tion (eks′klə·mā′shən) *n.* **1** Clamorous or passionate outcry. **2** An abrupt or emphatic expression; an interjection. **3** An exclamation mark.

exclamation mark A point, note, or mark (!) placed after an interjection or exclamation to indicate its character. Also **exclamation point.**

ex·clam·a·tive (iks·klam′ə·tiv) *adj.* Exclamatory. — *n.* A word, phrase, or sound uttered under emotional stress; an ejaculation.

ex·clam·a·to·ry (iks·klam′ə·tôr′ē, -tō′rē) *adj.* **1** Of the nature of exclamation. **2** Given to or characterized by the use of exclamation.

ex·clave (eks′klāv) *n.* A minor part of a country disjoined from the main part and lying within an alien territory. Compare ENCLAVE. [<EX- + (EN)CLAVE]

ex·clo·sure (iks·klō′zhər) *n. Ecol.* An area set apart from its surroundings as a means of studying the characteristics of a region under controlled conditions. [<EX- + (EN)CLOSURE]

ex·clude (iks·klōōd′) *v.t.* **·clud·ed, ·clud·ing** **1** To keep from entering; shut out, as from a place or group. **2** To refuse to notice, consider, or allow for; leave out: opposed to *include.* **3** To put out; eject. [<L *excludere* < *ex-* out + *claudere* close] — **ex·clud′a·ble** *adj.* — **ex·clud′er** *n.*

ex·clu·sion (iks·klōō′zhən) *n.* **1** The act of excluding. **2** The state of being excluded. **3** That which is excluded. [<L *exclusio, -onis* < *excludere.* See EXCLUDE.] — **ex·clu′sion·ism** *n.* — **ex·clu′sion·ist** *n.*

exclusion principle *Physics* The principle, discovered by W. Pauli, which states that no two electrons in a molecular or atomic system can simultaneously have all four quantum numbers identical.

ex·clu·sive (iks·klōō′siv) *adj.* **1** Intended for or possessed by a single group or individual; not shared: *exclusive* fishing rights; *exclusive* information. **2** Restricting membership or patronage; fastidiously reluctant to accept outsiders; hence, snobbish: an *exclusive* club. **3** Singly devoted; undivided: *exclusive* attention to music. **4** Not including; not comprising: usually followed by *of*: *exclusive* of fees. **5** Not counting the specified terminal points: 20 to 30 *exclusive* (including 21 through 29 and excluding 20 and 30): opposed to *inclusive.* — **ex·clu′sive·ly** *adv.* — **ex·clu′sive·ness** *n.*

ex·cog·i·tate (iks·koj′ə·tāt) *v.t.* **·tat·ed, ·tat·ing** To think out carefully; invent; devise. [<L *excogitatus,* pp. of *excogitare* < *ex-* out + *cogitare* think]

ex·cog·i·ta·tion (iks·koj′ə·tā′shən) *n.* **1** The act of excogitating; invention. **2** That which is thought out. — **ex·cog′i·ta′tive** *adj.*

ex·com·mu·ni·ca·ble (eks′kə·myōō′ni·kə·bəl) *adj.* Punishable by or deserving excommunication.

ex·com·mu·ni·cate (eks′kə·myōō′nə·kāt) *v.t.* **·cat·ed, ·cat·ing** **1** To punish by an ecclesiastical sentence of exclusion from the sacraments and communion of the church. **2** To expel in disgrace from any organization. — *adj.* Excommunicated. — *n.* An excommunicated person. [<LL *excommunicatus,* pp. of *excommunicare* < *ex-* out + *communicare* share < *communis* common] — **ex′com·mu′ni·ca′tor** *n.*

ex·com·mu·ni·ca·tion (eks′kə·myōō′nə·kā′shən) *n.* The act of excommunicating, or the state of having been excommunicated; a cutting off of an offender from all privileges of church membership.

ex·com·mu·ni·ca·tive (eks′kə·myōō′nə·kā′tiv, -kə·tiv) *adj.* Favoring or decreeing excommunication.

ex·com·mu·ni·ca·to·ry (eks′kə·myōō′ni·kə·tôr′ē, -tō′rē) *adj.* Causing or of the nature of excommunication.

ex·co·ri·ate (ik·skôr′ē·āt, -skō′rē-) *v.t.* **·at·ed, ·at·ing** **1** *Physiol.* To strip off the skin or covering of; flay; abrade; gall. **2** To denounce scathingly. [<L *excoriatus,* pp. of *excoriare* < *ex-* out, off + *corium* skin] — **ex·co′ri·a′tion** *n.*

ex·cre·ment (eks′krə·mənt) *n.* Refuse matter discharged from an animal body; feces. [<L *excrementum* < *excernere.* See EXCRETE.] — **ex′cre·men′tal, ex′cre·men′ta·ry, ex′cre·men·ti′tial** (-tish′əl), **ex′cre·men·ti′tious** (-tish′əs) *adj.*

ex·cres·cence (iks·kres′əns) *n.* **1** An unnatural or disfiguring outgrowth, as a wart on the human body or a nutgall on the oak. **2** Any unnatural addition, outgrowth, or development. **3** A natural outgrowth, as hair.

ex·cres·cen·cy (iks·kres′ən·sē) *n. pl.* **·cies** Excrescence; especially, an abnormal outgrowth.

ex·cres·cent (iks·kres′ənt) *adj.* **1** Of the nature of or pertaining to an excrescence; superfluous. **2** *Phonet.* Intrusive. [<L *excrescens, -entis,* ppr. of *excrescere* < *ex-* out + *crescere* grow]

ex·cre·ta (iks·krē′tə) *n. pl.* **1** *Physiol.* All useless matter eliminated from the bodily system, especially that which has entered into the constitution of the body and is removed in urine or sweat. **2** Noxious or worthless matter generated in a plant body by destructive

metabolism. [<NL <L <*excernere*. See EXCRETE.] — **ex·cre′tal** *adj.*
ex·crete (iks·krēt′) *v.t.* **·cret·ed, ·cret·ing** To throw off or eliminate, as waste matter, by normal discharge from an organism or any of its tissues. [<L *excretus*, pp. of *excernere* <*ex-* out + *cernere* separate]
ex·cre·tion (iks·krē′shən) *n.* **1** The act of excreting. **2** Matter excreted, particularly sweat, urine, and the juices exuded from certain plants: distinguished from *secretion.*
ex·cre·tive (iks·krē′tiv) *adj.* Having the function or power to excrete. Also **ex·cre·to·ry** (eks′krə·tôr′ē, -tō′rē).
ex·cru·ci·ate (iks·krōō′shē·āt) *v.t.* **·at·ed, ·at·ing** To inflict extreme pain or agony upon; torture. [<L *excruciatus*, pp. of *excruciare* <*ex-* completely + *cruciare* torture <*crux, crucis* cross] — **ex·cru′ci·a′tion** *n.*
ex·cru·ci·at·ing (iks·krōō′shē·ā′ting) *adj.* Causing or inflicting intense pain; agonizing. — **ex·cru′ci·at′ing·ly** *adv.*
ex·cul·pate (eks′kəl·pāt, ik·skul′-) *v.t.* **·pat·ed, ·pat·ing** To declare free from blame; prove innocent of guilt or fault; exonerate. See synonyms under JUSTIFY. [<EX-[1] + L *culpatus*, pp. of *culpare* blame <*culpa* a fault] — **ex·culp′a·ble** *adj.*
ex·cul·pa·tion (eks′kəl·pā′shən) *n.* **1** The act of freeing, or of attempting to free, from blame; vindication. **2** The state of being freed from blame.
ex·cul·pa·to·ry (ik·skul′pə·tôr′ē, -tō′rē) *adj.* Tending to or resulting in exculpation; vindicatory.
ex cu·ri·a (eks kyōōr′ē·ə) *Latin* Out of court.
ex·cur·rent (ik·skûr′ənt) *adj.* **1** Running or passing out. **2** *Biol.* Running through to the surface, summit, or tip, as the midrib of a leaf, or the canal of a sponge. [<L *excurrens, -entis*, ppr. of *excurrere* <*ex-* out + *currere* run]
ex·cur·sion (ik·skûr′zhən, -shən) *n.* **1** A short journey, usually for pleasure. **2** A boat or train trip at reduced rates, accommodating groups of excursionists to specified points. **3** A body of excursionists collectively. **4** A digression; deviation. **5** A running out or going forth. **6** *Physics* Half the amplitude of vibration; the movement of a vibrating or oscillating body from its mean to either of its extreme states or positions. **7** *Astron.* The apparent movement to and fro of a heavenly body, as of a satellite about its primary. See synonyms under JOURNEY. [<L *excursio, -onis* <*excurrere*. See EXCURRENT.]
ex·cur·sion·ist (ik·skûr′zhən·ist, -shən-) *n.* One who makes an excursion.
excursion ticket A round-trip ticket at a reduced rate.
ex·cur·sive (ik·skûr′siv) *adj.* **1** Given to making excursions; wandering. **2** Desultory; erratic; digressive. — **ex·cur′sive·ly** *adv.* — **ex·cur′sive·ness** *n.*
ex·cur·sus (eks·kûr′səs) *n. pl.* **·sus·es** or **·sus** **1** A supplemental dissertation added to a work. **2** A wandering off; digression. [<L, a going out <*excurrere*. See EXCURRENT.]
ex·cus·al (ik·skyōō′zəl) *n. Rare* The act of excusing.
ex·cuse (ik·skyōōz′) *v.t.* **·cused, ·cus·ing** **1** To pardon and overlook (a fault, offense, etc.); regard as unimportant. **2** To try to free (someone) from blame; seek to remove blame from: I *excused* myself to him. **3** To offer a reason or apology for (an error, fault, etc.); try to obtain pardon for or minimize. **4** To be or serve as a reason for; justify: His energy does not *excuse* his lateness. **5** To release from attendance, a duty, promise, etc. **6** To refrain from exacting or enforcing, as a demand or claim. See synonyms under JUSTIFY, PALLIATE, PARDON. — *n.* (ik·skyōōs′) **1** A plea in extenuation of an offense, neglect, or failure. **2** The act of excusing. **3** A reason for excusing. See synonyms under APOLOGY, PRETENSE. [<OF *excuser* <L *excusare* <*ex-* out, away + *causa* charge, accusation] — **ex·cus′a·ble** *adj.* — **ex·cus′a·ble·ness** *n.* — **ex·cus′a·bly** *adv.* — **ex·cus′er** *n.*
ex de·lic·to (eks di·lik′tō) *Latin* From the crime.
ex·e·cra·ble (ek′sə·krə·bəl) *adj.* Worthy of execration; abominable; accursed; appallingly bad. — **ex′e·cra·bly** *adv.*
ex·e·crate (ek′sə·krāt) *v.* **·crat·ed, ·crat·ing** *v.t.* **1** To curse, or call down evil upon. **2** To detest; abhor. — *v.i.* **3** To utter curses. [<L *execratus*, pp. of *execrari* curse <*ex-* out + *sacrare* devote to a god <*sacer* holy, accursed] — **ex′e·cra′tor** *n.*
ex·e·cra·tion (ek′sə·krā′shən) *n.* **1** The act of execrating. **2** An imprecation; malediction; a curse. **3** An accursed thing. See synonyms under ABOMINATION, IMPRECATION, OATH. — **ex′e·cra′tive** *adj.*
ex·ec·u·tant (ig·zek′yə·tənt) *n.* One who executes or performs; specifically, a skilled musical performer.
ex·e·cute (ek′sə·kyōōt) *v.t.* **·cut·ed, ·cut·ing** **1** To do or carry out fully: to *execute* an order. **2** To put in force; administer, as a law. **3** To put to death by legal sentence. **4** *Law* To make legal or valid by fulfilling all requirements of law. **5** To do or perform, as a maneuver or a musical work. **6** To produce, as according to a preconceived plan or design: to *execute* a portrait in oils. [<L *executus*, var. of *exsecutus*, pp. of *exsequi* <*ex-* out + *sequi* follow] — **ex′e·cut′a·ble** *adj.* — **ex′e·cut′er** *n.*
Synonyms: administer, do, enforce, perform. To *execute*, is to follow through to the end, put into absolute and final effect in action; to *administer* is to conduct as one holding a trust, as a minister and not an originator; the sheriff *executes* a writ; the trustee *administers* an estate, a charity, etc.; to *enforce* is to put into effect by force, actual or potential. To *administer* the laws is the province of a court of justice; to *execute* or *enforce* the laws is the province of a sheriff, marshal, constable, or other executive officer; to *administer* the law is to declare or apply it; to *execute* the law is to put it in force; for this *enforce* is the more general word, *execute* the more specific. *Administer* passes by a natural transition to signify *inflict, dispense,* and blows, medicine, etc., are said to be *administered. Enforce* signifies also to present and urge home by intellectual and moral force; as, to *enforce* a precept or a duty. Compare ACCOMPLISH, EFFECT, KILL, MAKE.
ex·e·cu·tion (ek′sə·kyōō′shən) *n.* **1** The act of executing. **2** *Law* A judicial writ, as for the seizure of goods, etc. **3** The act of carrying into effect or enforcing any legislative or judicial act or decree. **4** The signing, as of a deed. **5** The infliction of capital punishment. **6** Style of performance; technical skill, as in music or art. **7** Effective work: said especially of warlike operations. See synonyms under ACT, OPERATION.
ex·e·cu·tion·er (ek′sə·kyōō′shən·ər) *n.* One who executes a death sentence.
ex·ec·u·tive (ig·zek′yə·tiv) *adj.* **1** Having the function, power, or skill of executing or performing. **2** Having ability or aptitude for directing or controlling. **3** Connected with or pertaining to direction or control; carrying into effect; administrative, as distinguished from *judicial* and *legislative*: an *executive* department of the government. Compare JUDICIAL, LEGISLATIVE. **4** Adroit or dexterous in execution. — *n.* **1** An official personage or body charged with the administration of a government: applied in the United States to the president and to governors. **2** The executive branch of government. **3** A director of a business or other organization.
executive agreement *U.S.* An international agreement concluded by the president and not requiring Senate ratification.
Executive Mansion **1** The White House, Washington, D.C.: the official residence of the president of the United States. **2** The residence of the governor of a State.
executive officer *U.S.* The principal officer assisting a commanding officer. Compare CHIEF OF STAFF (def. 2).
executive session A session of the U.S. Senate, closed to the public and convened to consider confidential business.
ex·ec·u·tor (ig·zek′yə·tər) *n.* **1** *Law* A person nominated by the will of another to execute the will. **2** One who executes, in any sense.
ex·ec·u·to·ri·al (ig·zek′yə·tôr′ē·əl, -tō′rē-) *adj.* **1** Executive. **2** In Scots law, of or pertaining to the execution of a judicial writ.
ex·ec·u·to·ry (ig·zek′yə·tôr′ē, -tō′rē) *adj.* **1** Pertaining to execution; executive; administrative. **2** *Law* That is to be executed or put into effect; especially, becoming operative on a future contingency: an *executory* consideration, contract, or devise.
ex·ec·u·trix (ig·zek′yə·triks) *n. fem. pl.* **ex·ec·u·trix·es** or **ex·ec·u·tri·ces** (-trī′sēz) *Law* A female executor.

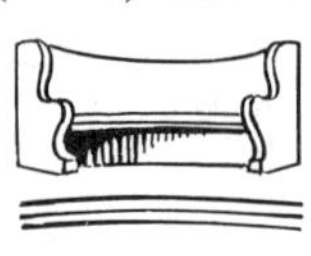
EXEDRA

ex·e·dra (ek′sə·drə, ik·sē′drə) *n. pl.* **·drae** (-drē) *Archit.* **1** In classical antiquity, a range of permanent seats, or a platform with seats, by the roadside, in a court, or otherwise placed, built of masonry and often curved in plan, intended for rest and conversation. **2** A curved seat, accommodating several persons, for use in the open air. **3** An apse, niche, window recess, or the like. [<L <Gk. *exedra* <*ex-* out + *hedra* a seat]
ex·e·ge·sis (ek′sə·jē′sis) *n. pl.* **·ses** (-sēz) Explanation of the language and thought of a literary work; especially, Biblical exposition or interpretation. [<Gk. *exēgēsis* <*exegeesthai* explain <*ex-* out <*hegeesthai* <*agein* lead]
ex·e·gete (ek′sə·jēt) *n.* One skilled in interpretation, as of the Bible. Also **ex′e·ge′tist.**
ex·e·get·ic (ek′sə·jet′ik) *adj.* Pertaining to exegesis; expository; explanatory. [<Gk. *exēgētikos* <*exēgēsis*. See EXEGESIS.] — **ex′e·get′i·cal·ly** *adv.*
ex·e·get·ics (ek′sə·jet′iks) *n. pl.* (*construed as singular*) **1** The science of exegesis. **2** The science of the interpretation of the Bible.
ex·em·plar (ig·zem′plər, -plär) *n.* **1** A model, pattern, or original, to be copied or imitated. **2** The mental conception or image of something to be produced. **3** A specimen or transcript; especially, a specimen copy of a book or writing. **4** A typical example; archetype. See synonyms under EXAMPLE. [<OF *exemplaire* <L *exemplarium* <*exemplum* EXAMPLE; infl. in form by L *exemplar* typical <*exemplum*]
ex·em·pla·ry (ig·zem′plər·ē) *adj.* **1** Serving or fitted to serve as a model or example worthy of imitation; commendable: *exemplary* conduct. **2** Serving as or furnishing a warning example: *exemplary* damages; a most *exemplary* punishment. **3** Serving to exemplify; illustrative. — **ex·em′pla·ri·ly** *adv.* — **ex·em′pla·ri·ness** *n.*
ex·em·pli·fi·ca·tion (ig·zem′plə·fə·kā′shən) *n.* **1** The act of exemplifying. **2** An example. **3** *Law* A certified copy. See synonyms under EXAMPLE, SAMPLE.
ex·em·pli·fy (ig·zem′plə·fī) *v.t.* **·fied, ·fy·ing** **1** To show by example; illustrate. **2** *Law* **a** To prove by an attested copy. **b** To make an authenticated transcript from, as a public record. [<Med. L *exemplificare* <*exemplum* EXAMPLE + *facere* make] — **ex·em′pli·fi·ca′tive** *adj.*
ex·em·pli gra·ti·a (ig·zem′plē grā′shē·ə) *Latin* By way of example: abbreviated *e.g.* or *ex. gr.*
ex·empt (ig·zempt′) *v.t.* **1** To free or excuse from some obligation to which others are subject; grant immunity to: to *exempt* one from military service. **2** *Obs.* To take or put away; remove. See synonyms under ABSOLVE, RELEASE. — *adj.* **1** Free, clear, or excused, as from some liability, restriction, or burden. **2** *Obs.* Remote; separated. See synonyms under FREE. — *n.* A person who is exempted, as from military service. [<L *exemptus*, pp. of *eximere* <*ex-* out + *emere* buy, take] — **ex·empt′i·ble** *adj.*
ex·emp·tion (ig·zemp′shən) *n.* **1** The act of exempting. **2** The state of being exempt; a dispensation giving freedom from duty or penalty; freedom or immunity from some liability, requirement, or evil: *exemption* from punishment. See synonyms under RIGHT.
ex·en·ter·ate (eks·en′tə·rāt) *v.t.* **·at·ed, ·at·ing** *Surg.* To eviscerate. [<L *exenteratus*, pp. of *exenterare* <*ex-* out + Gk. *enteron* intestine] — **ex·en′ter·a′tion** *n.*
ex·e·qua·tur (ek′sə·kwā′tər) *n.* In international law, the official recognition given to a consul or commercial agent by the government of the country in which he is to exercise his functions. [<L, let him perform]
ex·e·quy (ek′sə·kwē) *n. pl.* **·quies** **1** *pl.* Funeral ceremonies; obsequies. **2** A funeral procession. [<OF *exequies* <L *exequiae* <*exequi, exsequi*. See EXECUTE.]
ex·er·cise (ek′sər·sīz) *v.* **·cised, ·cis·ing** *v.t.* **1** To subject to drills, systematic movements, etc., so as to train or develop (troops, muscles, the mind, etc.). **2** To make use of; employ: to

exercise caution or a right. 3 To perform or execute, as the duties of an office. 4 To wield; exert, as influence or authority. 5 To do habitually; make a habit of: used reflexively or in the passive: to be *exercised* in good works. 6 To occupy the mind of; especially, to make anxious; worry. — *v.i.* 7 To take exercise. 8 To undergo training. [< *n.*] — *n.* 1 A putting into use, action, or practice. 2 Activity for health, development, or training. 3 An act of speaking, reading, etc., as at a school exhibition or religious meeting: usually in the plural. 4 An act of worship; a religious service. 5 A lesson assigned to a student; also, the written or oral fulfilment of that assignment. [<OF *exercice* <L *exercitium* < *exercere* practice < *ex-* out, away + *arcere* restrain] — **ex′er·cis′a·ble** *adj.*

Synonyms (noun): act, action, activity, application, employment, exertion, occupation, operation, performance, practice, use. See ACT, PRACTICE. *Antonyms*: idleness, inaction, inactivity, relaxation, rest.

ex·er·cised (ek′sər·sīzd) *adj.* Harassed; agitated, excited.

ex·er·cis·er (ek′sər·sī′zər) *n.* 1 One who exercises. 2 An apparatus for the exercise of the body.

ex·er·ci·ta·tion (ig·zûr′sə·tā′shən) *n.* 1 An exercise, as a disciplinary mental act. 2 Exercise or practice. [<OF <L *exercitatio, -onis* < *exercitare,* freq. of *exercere.* See EXERCISE.]

ex·ergue (ig·zûrg′, ek′sûrg) *n.* The space beneath the principal design on the reverse of a coin or medal, with date, place of coining, etc. [<F <Gk. *ex* out + *ergon* work]

ex·ert (ig·zûrt′) *v.t.* 1 To put forth or put in action, as strength, force, or faculty; bring into strong or vigorous action. 2 *Obs.* To push or thrust forth. — **to exert oneself** To put forth effort. [<L *exertus,* var. of *exsertus,* pp. of *exserere* thrust out < *ex-* out + *serere* bind] — **ex·er′tive** *adj.*

ex·er·tion (ig·zûr′shən) *n.* The act of putting some power or faculty into vigorous action; a strong effort. See synonyms under ACT, ENDEAVOR, EXERCISE, INDUSTRY, WORK.

ex·e·sion (ig·zē′zhən, -shən) *n. Pathol.* The slow superficial destruction of organic tissues, especially bone, by the action of abscesses and other agencies. [<L *exesus,* pp. of *edere* eat + -ION]

Ex·e·ter (ek′sə·tər) The county seat of Devonshire, England. A native of Exeter is known as an *Exonian.*

ex·e·unt (ek′sē·ənt, -o͝ont) They go out: a stage direction. [<L]

exeunt om·nes (om′nēz) All go out: a stage direction. [<L]

ex fac·to jus (eks fak′tō jo͞os) *Latin* The law arises out of the fact.

ex·fo·li·ate (eks·fō′lē·āt) *v.t.* & *v.i.* **·at·ed, ·at·ing** 1 To remove scales or splinters (from). 2 To peel or scale off in thin flakes, as the bark of a tree. 3 *Geol.* To split off in scales or sheets, as a heated mineral or weathered rock. [<LL *exfoliatus,* pp. of *exfoliare* < *ex-* off + *folium* a leaf] — **ex·fo′li·a′tive** *adj.*

ex·fo·li·a·tion (eks·fō′lē·ā′shən) *n.* 1 A scaling or peeling off, as of bark, skin, bone, or flakes of mineral. 2 Matter scaled off or exfoliated.

ex·ha·lant (eks·hā′lənt, ig·zā′-) *adj.* Having the property of exhaling. — *n.* Anything exhaled or which exhales; specifically, a duct used for exhaling. [<F <L *exhalans, -antis,* pp. of *exhalare* EXHALE]

ex·ha·la·tion (eks′hə·lā′shən, eg′zə-) *n.* 1 A breathing out; anything exhaled. 2 An emitted vapor or fume; evaporation; expiration. [<L *exhalatio, -onis* < *exhalare* EXHALE]

ex·hale (eks·hāl′, ig·zāl′) *v.* **·haled, ·hal·ing** *v.i.* 1 To expel air or vapor; breathe out. 2 To pass off or rise as a vapor or effluence; evaporate. — *v.t.* 3 To breathe forth or give off, as gas, vapor, or an aroma. 4 To draw off; cause to evaporate: Heat *exhales* the earth's moisture. [<F *exhaler* <L *exhalare* < *ex-* out + *halare* breathe] — **ex·hal′a·ble** *adj.*

ex·haust (ig·zôst′) *v.t.* 1 To make tired; wear out completely. 2 To drain of resources, strength, etc.; use up. 3 To draw off, as gas, steam, etc., from or as from a container. 4 To empty (a container) of contents; drain. 5 To study, treat of, or develop thoroughly and completely: to *exhaust* a subject. 6 In pharmacy, to remove the essential principles of by means of a solvent, thus leaving an inert remainder. — *v.i.* 7 To pass out as the exhaust: The steam *exhausts* from the pipe. See synonyms under ABSORB. — *n.* 1 The fluid discharged or escaping from the cylinder of a steam engine after expansion. 2 The formation of air currents by creating a partial vacuum. 3 The device used in flour mills to conduct dust particles away by means of air currents. 4 The escape of the waste gases from the cylinders of an internal-combustion engine; also, more loosely, the muffler which regulates this escape. 5 Foul air escaping from an apartment by a special register or pipe. 6 Emission. [<L *exhaustus,* pp. of *exhaurire* < *ex-* out + *haurire* draw] — **ex·haust′er** *n.* — **ex·haust′i·bil′i·ty** *n.* — **ex·haust′i·ble** *adj.*

ex·haust·ed (ig·zôs′tid) *adj.* 1 Used up; consumed; spent. 2 Emptied: an *exhausted* cask. 3 Depleted of essential ingredients: said specifically of soil. 4 Deprived of air; having a vacuum. 5 Weakened; tired out. — **ex·haust′ed·ly** *adv.*

ex·haust·ing (ig·zôs′ting) *adj.* Producing or tending to produce exhaustion; wearying; weakening.

ex·haus·tion (ig·zôs′chən) *n.* 1 The act or process of exhausting. 2 The state of being exhausted. 3 Deprivation of strength or energy.

ex·haus·tive (ig·zôs′tiv) *adj.* 1 Having the effect or tendency to exhaust, as by thorough and complete discussion. 2 Covering all points or items, as in an investigation or discussion. — **ex·haus′tive·ly** *adv.* — **ex·haus′tive·ness** *n.*

ex·haust·less (ig·zôst′lis) *adj.* Inexhaustible. — **ex·haust′less·ly** *adv.* — **ex·haust′less·ness** *n.*

exhaust steam Steam which has already performed work: distinguished from *live steam.*

exhaust velocity The velocity of exhaust gases at the moment of their expulsion from an internal-combustion engine, jet engine, rocket motor, or the like.

ex·hib·it (ig·zib′it) *v.t.* 1 To present to view; display. 2 To show or reveal: to *exhibit* ill will. 3 To present for public inspection or entertainment, as a product, play, etc. 4 *Law* To present formally or officially, as evidence. 5 *Med.* To administer, as a remedy. — *v.i.* 6 To place something on display. See synonyms under FLAUNT. — *n.* 1 Any object or objects exhibited. 2 *Law* A document or object marked for use as evidence. 3 A showing or manifestation; especially, a written statement of the condition of anything. [<L *exhibitus,* pp. of *exhibere* < *ex-* out + *habere* hold, have] — **ex·hib′i·tor, ex·hib′it·er** *n.*

ex·hi·bi·tion (ek′sə·bish′ən) *n.* 1 The act of exhibiting; display. 2 Anything exhibited; a show; especially, a public showing of works of art, athletic prowess, cattle, agricultural or manufactured products, etc. 3 An examination of students before an audience. 4 A display of student work. 5 *Brit.* A bursary. See synonyms under SPECTACLE. [<OF *exhibicion* <L *exhibitio, -onis* < *exhibere.* See EXHIBIT.]

ex·hi·bi·tion·er (ek′sə·bish′ən·ər) *n.* 1 *Brit.* A student maintained in a university by a donated allowance. 2 An exhibitor.

ex·hi·bi·tion·ism (ek′sə·bish′ən·iz′əm) *n.* 1 The tendency to display one's personal qualities in a manner that will attract attention. 2 *Psychiatry* The tendency, usually compulsive, to obtain sexual gratification by public exposure of one's body or genitalia. — **ex′hi·bi′tion·ist** *n.*

ex·hib·i·tive (ig·zib′ə·tiv) *adj.* 1 Representative. 2 Serving for exhibition.

ex·hib·i·to·ry (ig·zib′ə·tôr′ē, -tō′rē) *adj.* Pertaining to exhibition; exhibiting; tending to exhibit.

ex·hil·a·rant (ig·zil′ər·ənt) *adj.* Causing exhilaration. — *n.* Something that exhilarates. [<F <L *exhilarans, -antis,* ppr. of *exhilarare.* See EXHILARATE.]

ex·hil·a·rate (ig·zil′ə·rāt) *v.t.* **·rat·ed, ·rat·ing** To induce a lively or enlivening feeling in; enliven; cheer; stimulate. See synonyms under REJOICE. [<L *exhilaratus,* pp. of *exhilarare* gladden < *ex-* completely + *hilarare* < *hilaris* glad] — **ex·hil′a·rat′ing** *adj.* — **ex·hil′a·rat′ing·ly** *adv.* — **ex·hil′a·ra′tor** *n.*

ex·hil·a·ra·tion (ig·zil′ə·rā′shən) *n.* The act of exhilarating, or the state of being exhilarated; animation; enlivenment; stimulation. — **ex·hil′a·ra′tive, ex·hil′a·ra·to′ry** (-tôr′ē, -tō′rē) *adj.*

ex·hort (ig·zôrt′) *v.t.* To urge by earnest appeal or argument; advise or caution strongly. — *v.i.* To utter exhortation. [<L *exhortari* < *ex-* completely + *hortari* urge]

ex·hor·ta·tion (eg′zôr·tā′shən, ek′sər-) *n.* 1 The act or practice of exhorting; attempt to arouse or incite, as by appeal, argument, or admonition. 2 That which is spoken in exhorting; admonition; earnest advice. See synonyms under COUNSEL. [<L *exhortatio, -onis* < *exhortari.* See EXHORT.]

ex·hort·a·tive (ig·zôr′tə·tiv) *adj.* Containing or serving for exhortation. Also **ex·hort′a·to′ry** (-tôr′ē, -tō′rē).

ex·hort·er (ig·zôr′tər) *n.* One who exhorts; especially, a sensational religious speaker.

ex·hu·ma·tion (eks′hyo͞o·mā′shən) *n.* The digging up of that which has been buried; disinterring; especially, the disinterring of a human body.

ex·hume (ig·zyo͞om′, iks·hyo͞om′) *v.t.* **·humed, ·hum·ing** To dig out of the earth, as a dead body; disinter. [<F *exhumer* <Med. L *exhumare* <L *ex-* out + *humus* ground]

ex·i·gen·cy (ek′sə·jən·sē) *n. pl.* **·cies** 1 The state of being urgent or exigent; pressing need or demand. 2 A case requiring immediate attention, assistance, or remedy. 3 A critical period or condition; a pressing necessity. Also **ex′i·gence.** See synonyms under NECESSITY.

ex·i·gent (ek′sə·jənt) *adj.* 1 Demanding immediate aid or action; urgent. 2 Feeling the need; requiring; exacting. [<L *exigens, -entis,* ppr. of *exigere.* See EXACT.]

ex·i·gi·ble (ek′sə·jə·bəl) *adj.* That may be exacted, demanded, or required; demandable.

ex·ig·u·ous (ig·zig′yo͞o·əs, ik·sig′-) *adj.* Small; slender; diminutive. [<L *exiguus* scanty] — **ex·i·gu·i·ty** (ek′sə·gyo͞o′ə·tē), **ex·ig′u·ous·ness** *n.*

ex·ile (eg′zīl, ek′sīl) *n.* 1 Banishment from one's home or native land; expatriation. 2 One driven or wandering away from country or home; an expatriate. — **the Exile** The Babylonian captivity of the Jews. — *v.t.* **ex·iled, ex·il·ing** To expel from and forbid to return to a native land or home; banish. See synonyms under BANISH. [<OF *exil, essil* <L *exsilium* < *ex-* out + *sal-,* root of *salire* leap] — **ex·il·ic** (eg·zil′ik, ek·sil′ik) *adj.*

ex·ist (ig·zist′) *v.i.* 1 To have actual being or reality; be. 2 To continue to live or be: Animal life cannot *exist* without oxygen. 3 To be present; occur: This species now *exists* only in Australia. See synonyms under LIVE. [<F *exister* <L *existere* < *ex-* out + *sistere* be located < *stare* stand]

ex·is·tence (ig·zis′təns) *n.* 1 Being; the state or fact of being, or continuing to be, whether as substance, essence, personality, or consciousness: a brief or an endless *existence,* real or idle *existence.* 2 Possession or continuance of animate or vital being; life: a fight for *existence.* 3 Anything that exists or has the quality of objectivity; an entity; actuality.

ex·is·tent (ig·zis′tənt) *adj.* Having being or existence. — *n.* That which exists. See synonyms under ALIVE. [<L *existens, -entis,* ppr. of *existere.* See EXIST.]

ex·is·ten·tial (eg′zis·ten′shəl) *adj.* 1 Of or pertaining to existence. 2 Expressing or stating the fact of existence. — **ex′is·ten′tial·ly** *adv.*

ex·is·ten·tial·ism (eg′zis·ten′shəl·iz′əm) *n.* 1 A movement in 20th century philosophy, influenced in its development by Kierkegaard and Nietzsche and popularized in France by Sartre, emphasizing the active participation of the will, rather than the reason, in confronting the problems of a non-moral or absurd universe. Man is defined in existentialism as the sum total of his acts rather than his intentions or potentialities, and exists in order to will himself to act. 2 A cult of nihilism and pessimism popularized in France after World War II, supposedly based on the doctrines of Sartre and other existentialist writers. — **ex′is·ten′tial·ist** *adj.* & *n.*

ex·it (eg′zit, ek′sit) *n.* 1 A way or passage

out; egress. 2 The departure of an actor from the stage. 3 Any departure, as that from the scenes of life; death. —*v.i.* 1 To go out. 2 (He or she) goes out: a stage direction. [<L *exitus* <*exire* <*ex-* out + *ire* go]

ex li·bris (eks lī′bris, lē′-) *Latin* From the books (of): used as an inscription or label on a book, followed by the owner's name; hence, a bookplate.

Ex·moor (eks′mo͝or) A plateau in west Somersetshire and NE Devonshire, England, 30 square miles.

ex mo·re (eks mō′rē) *Latin* According to custom.

Ex·mouth (eks′məth) A channel port in SE Devonshire, England.

ex ne·ces·si·ta·te re·i (eks ni·ses′ə·tā′tē rē′ī) *Latin* From the necessity of the case; the case demands.

exo- *combining form* Out; outside; external: *exocarp.* Also, before vowels, *ex-.* [<Gk. *exo-, ex-* <*exō* outside]

ex·o·bi·ol·o·gy (ek′sō·bī·ol′ə·jē) *n.* 1 The scientific investigation of extraterrestrial life. 2 The study of the effects of space travel on terrestrial organisms. **—ex′o·bi·o·log′i·cal** *adj.*

ex·o·car·di·a (ek′sō·kär′dē·ə) *n. Pathol.* A displacement of the heart from its normal position. [<NL <Gk. *exo-* out + *kardia* heart]

ex·o·car·di·ac (ek′sō·kär′dē·ak) *adj.* Situated outside the heart. Also **ex′o·car′di·al.**

ex·o·carp (ek′sō·kärp) *n. Bot.* The outer wall of a fruit covering, when it is possible to distinguish more than one; epicarp. Compare ENDOCARP and illustrations under FRUIT.

ex·o·cen·tric (ek′sō·sen′trik) *adj. Ling.* Denoting a syntactic construction which as a unit functions differently from any of its component parts, as *Jim works hard* is an *exocentric* construction: opposed to *endocentric.*

ex·o·derm (ek′sō·dûrm) *n.* The ectoderm.

ex·od·ic (ek·sod′ik) *adj.* 1 Of or pertaining to an exodus. 2 Efferent.

ex·o·don·tia (ek′sō·don′shə, -shē·ə) *n.* The branch of dentistry concerned with the extraction of teeth. [<NL <Gk. *ex-* out + *odōn, odontos* a tooth] **—ex′o·dont′ist** *n.*

ex·o·dus (ek′sə·dəs) *n.* A going forth, or departure, as of a multitude, from a place or country. **—the Exodus** The departure of the Israelites from Egypt under the guidance of Moses, described in **Exodus,** the second book of the Old Testament. [<L <Gk. *exodos* <*ex-* out + *hodos* way]

ex·o·en·zyme (ek′sō·en′zīm, -zim) See ECTOENZYME.

ex of·fi·ci·o (eks ə·fish′ē·ō) *Latin* by virtue of or because of office or position.

ex·og·a·my (eks·og′ə·mē) *n.* 1 The custom of certain peoples forbidding any man to marry within his own tribe or clan. 2 Marriage outside of one's tribe, clan, or family: opposed to *endogamy.* 3 *Biol.* The union of two protozoans of different ancestry, with fusion of nuclei, as the commencement of a new cycle of growth. **—ex·og′a·mous, ex·o·gam·ic** (ek′sō·gam′ik) *adj.*

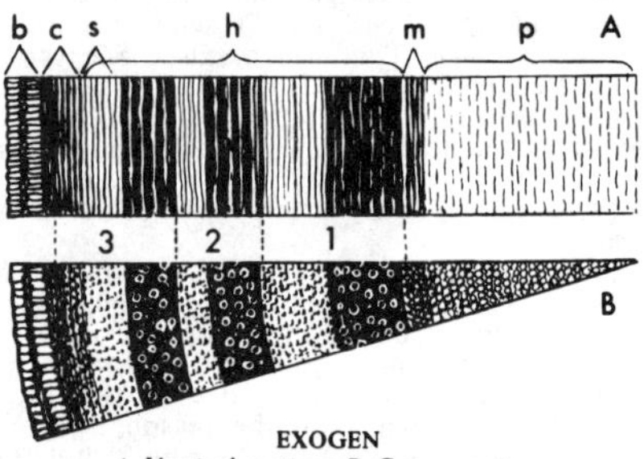

EXOGEN
A. Vertical section; *B.* Cross-section; showing growth rings for three successive years at *1, 2, 3.*
b. Bark. *s.* Sapwood (alburnum). *m.* Medullary sheath. *c.* Cambium layer. *h.* Heartwood (duramen). *p.* Pith.

ex·o·gen (ek′sə·jən) *n. Bot.* A plant which increases in size by successive concentric additions or rings beneath the bark and outside the previous growth; a dicotyledon: opposed to *endogen.*

ex·og·e·nous (eks·oj′ə·nəs) *adj.* 1 Originating outside the organism. 2 Due to external causes. 3 Growing by addition at the outer surface. **—ex·og′e·nous·ly** *adv.*

ex·on·er·ate (ig·zon′ə·rāt) *v.t.* **·at·ed, ·at·ing** 1 To free from accusation or blame; acquit; exculpate. 2 To relieve or free from a responsibility or the like. See synonyms under ABSOLVE, JUSTIFY. [<L *exoneratus,* pp. of *exonerare* <*ex-* out, away + *onus, oneris* burden] **—ex·on′er·a′tion** *n.* **—ex·on′er·a′tive** *adj.*

Ex·o·ni·an (ek·sō′nē·ən) *n.* A native or inhabitant of Exeter. —*adj.* Of or pertaining to Exeter.

ex·o·path·ic (ek′sō·path′ik) *adj. Pathol.* Of or resulting from causes external to the organism: an *exopathic* disease.

ex·oph·thal·mic (ek′sof·thal′mik) *adj.* Pertaining to, of the nature of, accompanied by, or affected with exophathlmos.

exophthalmic goiter *Pathol.* A disease characterized by enlargement of the thyroid gland, protrusion of the eyeballs, anemia, and palpitation of the heart; Basedow's disease: also called *Graves' disease.*

ex·oph·thal·mos (ek′sof·thal′məs) *n. Pathol.* Undue protrusion of the eyeball. Also **ex′oph·thal′mus.** [<NL <Gk., with prominent eyes <*ex-* out + *ophthalmos* eye]

ex·o·ra·ble (ek′sər·ə·bəl) *adj.* Capable of being persuaded or moved by entreaty; capable of relenting. [<L *exorabilis* <*ex-* out, away + *orare* pray] **—ex′o·ra·bil′i·ty** *n.*

ex·or·bi·tance (ig·zôr′bə·təns) *n.* Excessiveness in degree or amount; extravagance; a tendency to be exorbitant. Also **ex·or′bi·tan·cy.** See synonyms under EXCESS.

ex·or·bi·tant (ig·zôr′bə·tənt) *adj.* 1 Going beyond usual and proper limits, as in price or demand; excessive; extravagant. 2 Out of the realm of the law; illegal. See synonyms under IMMODERATE. [<LL *exorbitans, -antis,* ppr. of *exorbitare* go astray <*ex-* out + *orbita* a track] **—ex·or′bi·tant·ly** *adv.*

ex·or·cise (ek′sôr·sīz) *v.t.* **·cised, ·cis·ing** 1 To cast out (an evil spirit) by prayers or incantations. 2 To free of an evil spirit. 3 *Obs.* To summon or conjure up, as a demon. Also **ex′or·cize.** [<OF *exorciser* <LL *exorcizare* <Gk. *exorkizein* <*ex-* out + *horkos* an oath]**—ex′or·cis′er** or **·ciz′er** *n.*

ex·or·cism (ek′sôr·siz′əm) *n.* 1 The act of casting out or exorcising evil spirits. 2 *Obs.* The act or formula of calling or conjuring up the devil or a spirit. **—ex′or·cis′mal** *adj.* **—ex′or·cist** *n.*

ex·or·di·um (ig·zôr′dē·əm, ik·sôr′-) *n. pl.* **·di·ums** or **·di·a** (-dē·ə) The introductory part, as of a discourse; a prelude. [<L *exordiri* <*ex-* out + *ordiri* begin] **—ex·or′di·al** *adj.*

ex·o·re·ic (ek′sə·rē′ik) *adj.* Pertaining to or designating a region whose surface drainage reaches the oceans, as the greater part of North and South America. [<EXO- + Gk. *rheein* flow]

ex·o·skel·e·ton (ek′sō·skel′ə·tən) *n. Biol.* An external skeleton; any bony or horny external covering, armor, or structure of hardened integument, especially in invertebrates; dermoskeleton: opposed to *endoskeleton.*

ex·os·mo·sis (ek′sos·mō′sis, -soz-) *n. Chem.* 1 Osmosis in that direction in which the fluid crosses the septum most slowly. 2 Osmosis from an inner to an outer vessel; opposed to *endosmosis.* Also **ex′os·mose. —ex′os·mot′ic** (-mot′ik) *adj.* **—ex·os′mic** *adj.*

ex·o·sphere (ek′sō·sfir) *n.* The outermost region of the earth's atmosphere, beginning at a height of about 400 miles.

ex·o·spore (ek′sō·spôr, -spōr) *n. Bot.* 1 The outer wall of a spore. 2 An outer coat of the spores of certain fungi.

ex·os·to·sis (ek′sos·tō′sis) *n. pl.* **·ses** (-sēz) *Pathol.* An excessive bony outgrowth or tumor formed on either the outer or the inner surface of a bone or on a cartilage. [<NL <Gk. <*ex-* out + *osteon* bone]

ex·o·ter·ic (ek′sə·ter′ik) *adj.* 1 Adapted or intelligible, as a doctrine, to those outside the inner circle of disciples, or to the uninitiated; suitable for popular comprehension: opposed to *esoteric.* 2 External. Also **ex′o·ter′i·cal.** [<LL *exotericus* <Gk. *exōterikos* <*exōterō,* comparative of *exō* outside] **—ex′o·ter′i·cal·ly** *adv.* **—ex′o·ter′i·cism** *n.*

ex·o·ther·mic (ek′sō·thûr′mik) *adj. Chem.* Designating those reactions which are accompanied by the liberation of heat: opposed to *endothermic.* Also **ex·o·ther′mal.** [<EXO- + Gk. *thermē* heat]

ex·ot·ic (ig·zot′ik) *adj.* Belonging by nature or origin to another part of the world; brought in from abroad; foreign; strange: an *exotic* flower. —*n.* Something not native, as a plant, person, word, etc. [<L *exoticus* <Gk. *exōtikos* foreign <*exō* outside] **—ex·ot′i·cal·ly** *adv.* **—ex·ot′i·cism** *n.*

ex·o·tox·in (ek′sō·tok′sin) *n. Biochem.* A toxin formed within and excreted by an organism which is not itself toxic: distinguished from *endotoxin.* **—ex′o·tox′ic** *adj.*

ex·pand (ik·spand′) *v.t.* 1 To increase the range, scope, volume, size, etc., of: to *expand* a business. 2 To spread out by unfolding or extending; open: The peacock *expands* his tail. 3 To write or develop in full the details or form of, as a thought, argument, etc. —*v.i.* 4 To grow larger, wider, etc.; unfold; increase. See synonyms under AMPLIFY, SPREAD. [<L *expandere* <*ex-* out + *pandere* spread. Doublet of SPAWN.] **—ex·pand′er** *n.*

expanding bit *Mech.* A bit which can be adjusted to bore holes of varying size.

ex·panse (ik·spans′) *n.* That which lies spread out; a vast continuous area or stretch: the blue *expanse* of heaven. [<L *expansum* <*expandere.* See EXPAND.]

ex·pan·si·ble (ik·span′sə·bəl) *adj.* Capable of being expanded; expansile. **—ex·pan′si·bil′i·ty** *n.*

ex·pan·sile (ik·span′səl) *adj.* 1 Capable of expanding or of causing expansion. 2 Capable of being expanded.

ex·pan·sion (ik·span′shən) *n.* 1 The act of expanding, in any sense. 2 The condition or state of being expanded. 3 The amount of increase in size, scope, or the like. 4 That which is expanded; an expanded continuation or result; an extended surface; an expanded part; an enlargement. 5 The extent or space over or through which a thing expands; hence, extent in general; unlimited space; expanse; immensity. 6 *Physics* Increase of volume, as of steam in an engine cylinder when cut off from connection with the supply of pressure, or of the exploding gas in an internal-combustion engine. 7 *Math.* Development of a mathematical function into a series; also, the full expression as developed: the *expansion* of $(a + b)^3$ into $a^3 + 3a^2b + 3ab^2 + b^3$.

expansion bolt *Mech.* A bolt fitted with a split sleeve or other expansible member, by which it may be secured in a hole in masonry and the like.

ex·pan·sion·ism (ik·span′shən·iz′əm) *n.* Belief in or advocacy of a policy of expansion, as of commerce, currency, or territory. **—ex·pan′sion·ist** *n.*

ex·pan·sive (ik·span′siv) *adj.* 1 Capable of enlarging or being expanded; tending to expand; causing or characterized by expansion. 2 Presenting an expanse; extending; extensive. 3 Comprehensive; broad in mind or sympathies; liberal. 4 Amiable and effusive: an *expansive* personality. **—ex·pan′sive·ly** *adv.* **—ex·pan′sive·ness** *n.*

expansive delusion *Psychiatry* A delusion of wealth, power, etc., accompanied by euphoria.

ex par·te (eks pär′tē) *Latin* Emanating from or in the interest of one side only. [<L]

ex·pa·ti·ate (ik·spā′shē·āt) *v.i.* **·at·ed, ·at·ing** 1 To speak or write in a lengthy manner; elaborate: with *on* or *upon.* 2 *Rare* To roam at large; range widely or unrestrainedly. See synonyms under AMPLIFY. [<L *ex(s)patiatus,* pp. of *ex(s)patiari* <*ex-* out + *spatiari* walk <*spatium* space] **—ex·pa′ti·a′tion** *n.* **—ex·pa′ti·a′tor** *n.* **—ex·pa′ti·a·to′ry** (-tôr′ē, -tō′rē) *adj.*

ex·pa·tri·ate (eks·pā′trē·āt) *v.t.* **·at·ed, ·at·ing** 1 To drive (a person) from his native land; exile; banish. 2 To withdraw (oneself) from one's native land. —*n.* (-it, -āt) One exiled. —*adj.* Banished; exiled. [<Med. L *expatriatus,* pp. of *expatriare* <*ex-* out + *patria* native land] **—ex·pa′tri·a′tion** *n.*

ex·pect (ik·spekt′) *v.t.* 1 To look forward to as certain or probable; anticipate in thought. 2 To look for as right, proper, or necessary; require. 3 *Colloq.* To presume; suppose. 4 *Obs.* To wait for. See synonyms under ABIDE, ANTICIPATE. [<L *ex(s)pectare* <*ex-* out + *spectare* look at]

ex·pec·tan·cy (ik·spek′tən·sē) *n. pl.* **·cies** 1

The act or state of expecting; expectation. 2 An object of expectation. 3 *Law* The state of being expected; abeyance: an estate in *expectancy.* See synonyms under ANTICIPATION. Also **ex·pec′tance.**

ex·pec·tant (ik·spek′tənt) *adj.* 1 Waiting or looking forward in expectation. 2 Awaiting the birth of a child: an *expectant* mother. —*n.* One who is anticipating confidently. [<OF <L *ex(s)pectans, -antis,* ppr. of *ex-(s)pectare.* See EXPECT.] —**ex·pec′tant·ly** *adv.*

ex·pec·ta·tion (ek′spek·tā′shən) *n.* 1 The act of looking confidently for something; expectancy. 2 Anticipation; prospect of good to come, as of wealth: often plural. 3 Something expected. 4 The present value of a probability. See synonyms under ANTICIPATION. [<L *ex(s)pectatio, -onis* <*ex(s)pectare.* See EXPECT.]

ex·pec·ta·tive (ik·spek′tə·tiv) *adj.* Contingent.

ex·pect·ing (ik·spek′ting) *adj.* Pregnant; also, due to give birth.

ex·pec·to·rant (ik·spek′tər·ənt) *adj.* Relating to or promotive of expectoration. —*n.* A medicine to promote expectoration. [<L *expectorans, -antis,* ppr. of *expectorare.* See EXPECTORATE.]

ex·pec·to·rate (ik·spek′tə·rāt) *v.t.* & *v.i.* **·rat·ed, ·rat·ing** 1 To discharge, as phlegm, by hawking or coughing up and spitting from the mouth. 2 To spit. [<L *expectoratus,* pp. of *expectorare* <*ex-* out + *pectus, -oris* breast]

ex·pec·to·ra·tion (ik·spek′tə·rā′shən) *n.* The act of expectorating; also, matter expectorated.

ex·pe·di·en·cy (ik·spē′dē·ən·sē) *n. pl.* **·cies** 1 The quality of being proper, suitable, and advantageous under given circumstances; advantageousness; fitness. 2 That which is most practicable, all things considered. 3 In ethics, the doing of what is useful, politic, or advantageous, regardless of justice or right. See synonyms under PROFIT, UTILITY. Also **ex·pe′di·ence.**

ex·pe·di·ent (ik·spē′dē·ənt) *adj.* 1 Serving to promote a desired end; suitable under the circumstances; contributing to personal advantage; advisable. 2 Pertaining to utility or advantage rather than principle. 3 *Obs.* Speedy; expeditious. —*n.* 1 That which furthers or promotes an end. 2 A device; shift. [<OF <L *expediens, -entis,* ppr. of *expedire.* See EXPEDITE.] —**ex·pe′di·ent·ly** *adv.*

Synonyms (adj.): advantageous, beneficial, convenient, favorable, paying, profitable, sensible, suitable, useful, wise, worthwhile. See PROFITABLE. Compare synonyms for PROFIT, UTILITY. *Antonyms*: absurd, ill-adapted, ill-considered, ill-devised, ill-judged, inexpedient, irrational, reckless, unsuitable, unwise.

ex·pe·di·en·tial (ik·spē′dē·en′shəl) *adj.* Of or pertaining to expediency.

ex·pe·dite (ek′spə·dīt) *v.t.* **·dit·ed, ·dit·ing** 1 To speed up the process or progress of; facilitate. 2 To do quickly. 3 To send or issue officially; dispatch. See synonyms under PUSH. —*adj.* Prompt; expeditious. [<L *expeditus,* pp. of *expedire* <*ex-* out + *pes, pedis* foot]

ex·pe·dit·er (ek′spə·dī′tər) *n.* One who or that which expedites; especially, one who facilitates the delivery of goods. Also **ex′pe·di′tor.**

ex·pe·di·tion (ek′spə·dish′ən) *n.* 1 A journey, march or voyage, generally of several or many persons, for a definite purpose: an Arctic *expedition.* 2 The body of persons engaged in such a journey, march, or voyage, together with their equipment. 3 The quality of being expeditious; speed; dispatch. See synonyms under JOURNEY.

ex·pe·di·tion·ar·y (ek′spə·dish′ən·er′ē) *adj.* Of the nature of, for the purpose of, or constituting an expedition.

expeditionary force A force of men equipped for military service abroad.

ex·pe·di·tious (ek′spə·dish′əs) *adj.* Accomplished with energy and dispatch; quick; speedy. See synonyms under ACTIVE. —**ex′·pe·di′tious·ly** *adv.* —**ex′pe·di′tious·ness** *n.*

ex·pel (ik·spel′) *v.t.* **·pelled, ·pel·ling** 1 To drive out by force or authority; force out. 2 To dismiss, as a pupil from a school; eject. See synonyms under BANISH, EXTERMINATE. [<L *expellere* <*ex-* out + *pellere* drive, thrust] —**ex·pel′la·ble** *adj.*

ex·pel·lant (ik·spel′ənt) *adj.* Of a nature or having the power to expel: expelling: *expellant* treatment in medicine. —*n.* That which expels, as a purgative. Also **ex·pel′lent.** [<OF <L *expellens, -entis,* ppr. of *expellere.* See EXPEL.]

ex·pel·lee (ek′spel·ē′) *n.* One who has been expelled.

ex·pend (ik·spend′) *v.t.* To pay out or spend; use up. [<L *expendere* <*ex-* out + *pendere* weigh]

ex·pend·a·ble (ik·spen′də·bəl) *adj.* That may be expended; capable of being, or to be, consumed, used, or sacrificed, as men and materiel in warfare.

ex·pen·di·ture (ik·spen′də·chər) *n.* 1 The act of expending; outlay; disbursement. 2 That which is expended; expense. See synonyms under EXPENSE, PRICE. [<Med. L *expenditus,* irreg. pp. of *expendere.* See EXPEND.]

ex·pense (ik·spens′) *n.* 1 The laying out or expending, as of money or other resources; expenditure. 2 Loss: at the *expense* of health. 3 Money expended; outlay. 4 Anything requiring expenditure. [<AF <LL *expensa* <*expendere.* See EXPEND.]

Synonyms: cost, expenditure, outgo, outlay. The *cost* of a thing is whatever one surrenders or gives up for it, intentionally or unintentionally, or even unconsciously; *expense* is what is laid out by calculation or intention. We say, "He won his fame at the *cost* of his life"; "I know it to my *cost*"; we speak of a joke at another's *expense*; at another's *cost* would seem to make it a more serious matter. There is a tendency to use *cost* of what we pay for a possession, *expense* of what we pay for a service; we speak of the *cost* of goods, the *expense* of manufacture. *Outlay* is used of some definite *expenditure,* as for the purchase of supplies; *outgo* of a steady drain or of incidental *expenses.* See PRICE. *Antonyms*: gain, income, proceeds, product, profit, profits, receipt, receipts, return, returns.

ex·pen·sive (ik·spen′siv) *adj.* Causing or involving much expense; costly. —**ex·pen′sive·ly** *adv.* —**ex·pen′sive·ness** *n.*

ex·pe·ri·ence (ik·spir′ē·əns) *n.* 1 Knowledge derived from one's own action, practice, perception, enjoyment, or suffering; experimental knowledge; especially, the state of such knowledge in an individual as an index of wisdom or skill: He is a lawyer of *experience.* 2 Something undergone, enjoyed, etc. 3 Spiritual exercise of mind; conversion. 4 Every form of knowledge due to one's immediate observation; also, the sum total of such knowledge in the life of an individual. 5 Length, duration, or state of occupation with or employment in a particular study, business, or work. See synonyms under ACQUAINTANCE, KNOWLEDGE. —*v.t.* **·enced, ·enc·ing** To undergo personally; feel. See synonyms under KNOW. —**to experience religion** To undergo a change of heart; be converted. [<OF <L *experientia* <*experiri* try out]

ex·pe·ri·enced (ik·spir′ē·ənst) *adj.* Taught by experience; practiced; skilled.

experience meeting A religious meeting for prayer and the relation of personal religious experiences.

experience table In life insurance, a mortality table based on the records and reports of one or more companies.

ex·pe·ri·en·tial (ik·spir′ē·en′shəl) *adj.* Pertaining to or acquired by experience; empirical. —**ex·pe′ri·en′tial·ly** *adv.*

ex·per·i·ment (ik·sper′ə·mənt) *n.* 1 An act or operation designed to discover, test, or illustrate a truth, principle, or effect; a test, especially one intended to confirm or disprove something which is still in doubt. 2 The conducting of such operations or tests. 3 Something undergoing the test of actual experience, as opposed to that whose practicability or usefulness has been fully demonstrated: often used depreciatively: Your boasted institutions are but an *experiment.* 4 *Obs.* Experience. —*v.i.* (-ment) To make experiments; make a test or trial. [<OF <L *experimentum* <*experiri* try out] —**ex·per′i·ment′er** *n.*

ex·per·i·men·tal (ik·sper′ə·men′təl) *adj.* 1 Pertaining to, growing out of, or known by methods of controlled testing and direct observation under stated conditions: *experimental* science: opposed to *speculative.* 2 Designating or pertaining to that which is learned by experience: distinguished from *theoretical.* —**ex·per′i·men′tal·ism** *n.* —**ex·per′i·men′tal·ist** *n.* —**ex·per′i·men′tal·ly** *adv.*

ex·per·i·men·ta·tion (ik·sper′ə·men·tā′shən) *n.* The act or practice of experimenting. —**ex·per′i·men′ta·tive** (-men′tə·tiv) *adj.*

experiment station A place where agricultural experiments are developed and conducted with a view to improvement in methods and products.

ex·pert (ek′spûrt) *n.* 1 One who has special skill or knowledge; a specialist. 2 In the U.S. Army, the highest of three grades for skill in the use of small arms. 3 A soldier having this grade. Compare MARKSMAN, SHARPSHOOTER. —*adj.* (*also* ik·spûrt′) 1 Skilful as the result of practice; dexterous; marked by skill. 2 Proceeding from an expert. See synonyms under CLEVER, GOOD. [<L *expertus,* pp. of *experiri* try out] —**ex·pert′ly** *adv.* —**ex·pert′·ness** *n.*

ex·per·tise (ek′spər·tēz′) *n. French* An evaluation or assessment by an expert.

ex·pi·a·ble (ek′spē·ə·bəl) *adj.* That may be expiated or atoned for.

ex·pi·ate (ek′spē·āt) *v.t.* **·at·ed, ·at·ing** To atone for; make amends for. [<L *expiatus,* pp. of *expiare* <*ex-* completely + *piare* appease <*pius* pious] —**ex′pi·a′tor** *n.*

ex·pi·a·tion (ek′spē·ā′shən) *n.* 1 The active means of expiating, or of making reparation or satisfaction, as for offense or sin. 2 The removing of guilt by suffering punishment; atonement. ◆ Collateral adjective: *piacular.* See synonyms under PROPITIATION. —**ex′pi·a·to′ry** (-tôr′ē, -tō′rē) *adj.*

ex·pi·ra·tion (ek′spə·rā′shən) *n.* 1 The natural termination of anything, as of a lease or a period of time. 2 The act of breathing out, as air from the lungs: opposed to *inspiration.* 3 The outbreathing of life; death. 4 That which is expired. 5 The sound made in respiration. See synonyms under END. [<L *expiratio, -onis* <*expirare.* See EXPIRE.]

ex·pir·a·to·ry (ik·spī′rə·tôr′ē, -tō′rē) *adj.* Pertaining to, or used for, the expiration of breath.

ex·pire (ik·spīr′) *v.* **·pired, ·pir·ing** *v.i.* 1 To exhale one's last breath; die. 2 To die out, as the embers of a fire. 3 To come to an end; terminate, as a contract or magazine subscription. 4 To breathe out air from the lungs; exhale. —*v.t.* 5 To breathe out from the lungs. 6 *Obs.* To emit (a vapor or odor). See synonyms under DIE, END. [<L *ex(s)pirare* <*ex-* out + *spirare* breathe] —**ex·pir′er** *n.*

ex·pi·ry (ik·spī′rē) *n. pl.* **·ries** 1 End; termination. 2 *Archaic* Death.

ex·plain (ik·splān′) *v.t.* 1 To make plain or clear; make understandable. 2 To give a meaning to; interpret. 3 To give reasons for; state the cause or purpose of. —*v.i.* 4 To give an explanation. See synonyms under INTERPRET. [<L *explanare* <*ex-* out + *planare* make level <*planus* flat] —**ex·plain′·a·ble** *adj.*

ex·pla·na·tion (ek′splə·nā′shən) *n.* 1 The act or means of explaining; elucidation. 2 Meaning; significance; sense. 3 The process of settling a disagreement, or reconciling a difference, by explaining the circumstances; reconciliation. See synonyms under DEFINITION. [<L *explanatio, -onis* <*explanare.* See EXPLAIN.]

ex·plan·a·to·ry (ik·splan′ə·tôr′ē, -tō′rē) *adj.* Serving or tending to explain. Also **ex·plan′a·tive.** —**ex·plan′a·to′ri·ly** *adv.*

ex·plant (iks·plant′, -plänt′) *v.t.* To place outside its habitat, as an organ of the body or bacteria in a medium, for purposes of observation and study.

ex·ple·tive (eks′plə·tiv) *n.* 1 An interjection, often profane. 2 A word or syllable employed for rhetorical or rhythmical effect. 3 Something serving to fill out. —*adj.* Added for emphasis; redundant: also **ex′ple·to′ry** (-tôr′ē, -tō′rē). [<LL *expletivus* <L *expletus,* pp. of *explere* <*ex-* completely + *plere* fill]

ex·pli·ca·ble (eks′pli·kə·bəl, *frequently* iks·plik′·ə·bəl) *adj.* Capable of explanation.

ex·pli·cate (eks′plə·kāt) *v.t.* **·cat·ed, ·cat·ing** To clear from obscurity; explain. See synonyms under INTERPRET. [<L *explicatus,* pp. of

explicare < *ex-* out + *plicare* fold] — **ex'pli·ca'tor** *n.*

ex·pli·ca·tion (eks'plə·kā'shən) *n.* **1** Explanation, especially of a passage in any text, or definition, as of a word, by unfolding what is implied in it. **2** The act or process of explicating. **3** A detailed description.

ex·pli·ca·tive (eks'plə·kā'tiv) *adj.* **1** Serving to unfold or explain. **2** Analytic. Also **ex'pli·ca·to'ry** (-tôr'ē, -tō'rē).

ex·plic·it (ik·splis'it) *adj.* **1** Plainly expressed, or that plainly expresses. **2** Having no disguised meaning or reservation; definite; open; unreserved. **3** *Logic* Brought out definitely in words; not merely implied: opposed to *implicit.* [<L *explicitus,* var. of *explicatus.* See EXPLICATE.] — **ex·plic'it·ly** *adv.* — **ex·plic'·it·ness** *n.*

Synonym: express. Both *explicit* and *express* are opposed to what is merely implicit or implied. See IMPLICIT. That which is *explicit* is unfolded, so that it may not be obscure, doubtful, or ambiguous; that which is *express* is uttered or stated so decidedly that it may not be forgotten nor overlooked. An *explicit* statement is too clear to be misunderstood; an *express* command is too emphatic to be disregarded. Compare CLEAR, PLAIN, PRECISE. *Antonyms*: ambiguous, doubtful, implicit, implied, indefinite, indeterminate, uncertain.

ex·plode (ik·splōd') *v.* **·plod·ed, ·plod·ing** *v.t.* **1** To cause to expand violently or pass suddenly from a solid to a gaseous state: to *explode* gunpowder. **2** To cause to burst or blow up violently and with noise: to *explode* a bomb. **3** To disprove utterly; refute: to *explode* a theory. **4** *Phonet.* To pronounce with an explosion. **5** *Obs.* To drive from the stage, as an actor. — *v.i.* **6** To be exploded, as gunpowder. **7** To burst into pieces or fragments; blow up. **8** To make a noise as if bursting: to *explode* with laughter. [<L *explodere,* orig. drive off the stage, hiss < *ex-* out + *plaudere* clap] — **ex·plod'er** *n.*

ex·plo·dent (ik·splōd'nt) *n. Phonet.* A plosive.

ex·ploit (eks'ploit, ik·sploit') *n.* A deed or act, especially one marked by heroism, daring, skill, or brilliancy. See synonyms under ACT. — *v.t.* (ik·sploit') **1** To use for one's own advantage; take advantage of: Rulers often *exploit* the people. **2** To put to use; make use of: to *exploit* water power. [<OF *esploit* <L *explicitum,* neut. sing. of *explicitus.* See EXPLICIT.] — **ex·ploit'a·ble** *adj.*

ex·ploi·ta·tion (eks'ploi·tā'shən) *n.* **1** The act of exploiting. **2** Selfish employment for one's own use or advantage.

ex·ploit·a·tive (ik·sploi'tə·tiv) *adj.* Tending or serving to exploit.

ex·ploi·ter (ik·sploi'tər) *v.t.* To turn to one's use or advantage illegitimately; exploit. — *n.* One who exploits.

ex·plo·ra·tion (eks'plə·rā'shən) *n.* **1** The act of exploring; especially, geographical research in unknown regions. **2** The examination of internal organs or parts. [<L *exploratio, -onis* < *explorare.* See EXPLORE.]

ex·plor·a·to·ry (ik·splôr'ə·tôr'ē, ik·splō'rə·tō'·rē) *adj.* Of, for, or relating to exploration. Also **ex·plor'a·tive.**

ex·plore (ik·splôr', -splōr') *v.* **·plored, ·plor·ing** *v.t.* **1** To search through or travel in or over, as new lands, for discovery. **2** To look into carefully; scrutinize. **3** *Med.* To examine: to *explore* a wound with a probe. — *v.i.* **4** To make explorations. See synonyms under EXAMINE. [<L *explorare* investigate < *ex-* out + *plorare* cry out]

ex·plor·er (ik·splôr'ər, -splō'rər) *n.* **1** One who explores; especially, one who travels in a new or strange region. **2** Any device with which to explore or examine; a probe.

Ex·plor·er The first U. S. artificial satellite, launched from Cape Canaveral, Fla., Jan. 31, 1958; maximum height about 1600 miles; weight, 30.8 lbs.; orbital velocity, 18,000 mph.

ex·plo·sion (ik·splō'zhən) *n.* **1** The act of exploding; rapid combustion or other similar process, usually causing a loud report. **2** The power stroke of an internal-combustion engine. **3** *Physiol.* The sudden discharge of a neural cell or group of cells. **4** A sudden and violent outbreak as of physical forces or of human emotion. **5** *Phonet.* Plosion. [<L *explosio, -onis* < *explodere.* See EXPLODE.]

ex·plo·sive (ik·splō'siv) *adj.* **1** Pertaining to explosion. **2** Liable to explode or to cause explosion. **3** *Phonet.* Plosive. — *n.* **1** *Physics* Any substance or mixture of substances which, on impact or by ignition, reacts by a violent rearrangement of its molecules accompanied by the sudden expansion of gases and the liberation of relatively large amounts of thermal energy. **2** *Phonet.* A plosive consonant. — **ex·plo'sive·ly** *adv.* — **ex·plo'sive·ness** *n.*

explosive D Dunnite.

ex·po·nent (ik·spō'nənt) *n.* **1** One who or that which explains, interprets, or expounds. **2** *Logic* An illustrative example of a general proposition. **3** *Math.* Any number or symbol placed as a superscript to the right of a quantity to indicate a power or the reciprocal or root of a power: thus, $3^2 = 3 \times 3$; $3^{-2} = 1/3^2$; $3^{\frac{1}{2}} = \sqrt{3}$. **4** Any person or thing that represents the character or principles of something: Franklin was the *exponent* of American principles in France. [<L *exponens, -entis,* ppr. of *exponere* indicate < *ex-* out + *ponere* place] — **ex·po·nen·tial** (ek'spō·nen'shəl) *adj.* — **ex'po·nen'tial·ly** *adv.*

ex·po·ni·ble (ik·spō'nə·bəl) *adj.* Needing explanation, as in logic, when propositions must be restated to be intelligible. — *n.* An exponible statement.

ex·port (ik·spôrt', -spōrt', eks'pôrt, -pōrt) *v.t.* To carry or send, as merchandise or raw materials, to other countries for sale or trade. — *n.* (eks'pôrt, -pōrt) **1** The act of exporting; exportation. **2** That which is exported; especially, merchandise sent from one country to another: usually in the plural. — *adj.* Of or pertaining to exports or exportation. [<L *exportare* < *ex-* out + *portare* carry] — **ex·port'a·ble** *adj.* — **ex·port'a·bil'i·ty** *n.* — **ex·port'er** *n.*

ex·por·ta·tion (ek'spôr·tā'shən, -spōr-) *n.* **1** The act or practice of exporting. **2** An export commodity.

ex·pose (ik·spōz') *v.t.* **·posed, ·pos·ing** **1** To lay open, as to harm, attack, ridicule, censure, etc. **2** To leave open to the action of a force or influence. **3** To present to view; show; display: The dress *exposed* her shoulders. **4** To cause to be known; make public, as a conspiracy or crime. **5** To lay open or make known the crimes, faults, etc., of (a person): to *expose* a traitor. **6** To abandon so as to cause the death of: to *expose* an unwanted child. **7** *Phot.* To admit light to (a sensitized film or plate). **8** In the Roman Catholic Church, to show for adoration or worship, as the Host. See synonyms under DISCOVER. [<MF *exposer* < *ex-* out + *poser.* See POSE[1].] — **ex·po'sal** *n.* — **ex·pos'er** *n.*

ex·po·sé (ek'spō·zā') *n.* **1** An undesirable or embarrassing disclosure or exposure. **2** A revelation or disclosure of something to the public, as corruption, political graft, social injustice, etc. — *adj.* Given to exposing discreditable things: an *exposé* magazine. [<F, pp. of *exposer.* See EXPOSE.]

ex·posed (ik·spōzd') *adj.* **1** In plain view. **2** Uncovered; open to or unprotected from, as the elements.

ex·po·si·tion (eks'pə·zish'ən) *n.* **1** A public exhibition of the arts, products, achievements, etc., of a specific region, country, or group, as a world's fair. **2** An explanation; commentary. **3** Rhetorical analysis. **4** The part of a dramatic composition that unfolds the plot. **5** In the Roman Catholic Church, a service in which the blessed sacrament is exposed for adoration. **6** *Music* The initial presentation or statement of the themes of a movement; especially, in a fugue, the introduction of the several parts or voices. See synonyms under DEFINITION. [<OF <L *expositio, -onis* < *exponere.* See EXPONENT.]

ex·pos·i·tor (ik·spoz'ə·tər) *n.* One who expounds.

ex·pos·i·to·ry (ik·spoz'ə·tôr'ē, -tō'rē) *adj.* Conveying, containing, or pertaining to exposition. Also **ex·pos'i·tive.**

ex post fac·to (eks pōst fak'tō) Arising or enacted after the fact but retroacting upon it; retroactive; retrospective. [<L]

ex·pos·tu·late (ik·spos'chə·lāt) *v.i.* **·lat·ed, ·lat·ing** To reason earnestly with a person, against some action: usually with *with.* [<L *expostulatus,* pp. of *expostulare* < *ex-* out + *postulare* demand] — **ex·pos'tu·la'tor** *n.*

ex·pos·tu·la·tion (ik·spos'chə·lā'shən) *n.* The act of expostulating; dissuasion. — **ex·pos'tu·la'tive** *adj.* — **ex·pos'tu·la'tive·ly** *adv.*

ex·pos·tu·la·to·ry (ik·spos'chə·lə·tôr'ē, -tō'rē) *adj.* Conveying, containing, or pertaining to expostulation.

ex·po·sure (ik·spō'zhər) *n.* **1** The act or process of exposing, or the state of being exposed in any sense; disclosure of the hitherto hidden truth, usually discreditable, about a person or situation. **2** An open situation or position in relation to the sun, elements, or points of the compass; outlook; aspect: The house had a southern *exposure.* **3** In ancient Greece and Rome, the practice of abandoning sickly and deformed (and often female) infants. **4** *Phot.* The act of submitting a sensitized plate or film to the action of actinic rays. **5** *Geol.* The portion of a rock mass exposed to view. **6** *Law* Offensive public display of one's body.

exposure meter *Phot.* An instrument which shows the correct film exposure required for best results.

ex·pound (ik·spound') *v.t.* **1** To set forth in detail; state; declare, as a doctrine or theory. **2** To explain the meaning or significance of; interpret. See synonyms under INTERPRET. [<OF *espondre* <L *exponere.* See EXPONENT.] — **ex·pound'er** *n.*

ex·press (ik·spres') *v.t.* **1** To put (thought or opinion) into spoken or written words. **2** To make apparent; reveal: His actions *express* his anger. **3** To represent in art, poetry, etc.; depict by symbols: The rose *expresses* love. **4** *Math.* To represent by a figure, symbol, letter, etc. **5** *U.S.* To send by express. **6** To press out; squeeze out, as juice or moisture. **7** To force out by or as by pressure. **8** To send or cause to be sent by express, as a package. — **to express oneself** **1** To make known one's thoughts. **2** To give expression to one's imagination or emotions, especially in artistic activity. See synonyms under SPEAK. — *adj.* **1** Set forth distinctly; explicit; plain; direct. **2** Specially prepared; adapted to a specific purpose: There was *express* provision for strangers. **3** Done, traveling, or carried with speed or in haste: an *express* train. **4** Exactly resembling an original: an *express* likeness. **5** Of or pertaining to an express company. See synonyms under EXPLICIT. — *adv.* With speed; not stopping at local stations: This train runs *express.* — *n.* **1** A system of transportation for trunks, small parcels, packages, etc., by organized corporations. **2** The packages, parcels, etc., sent by this system. **3** Any means of rapid transmission. **4** A message; dispatch; special communication sent with speed. **5** A messenger bearing dispatches; a courier. **6** An express rifle. **7** An express train. [<OF *expresser* <L *ex-* out + *pressare* < *premere* press]

ex·press·age (ik·spres'ij) *n.* **1** The transportation of goods by special system. **2** Amount charged for carrying by express.

express company A business company that operates a system for the rapid transportation of trunks, packages, and other articles.

ex·press·er (ik·spres'ər) *n.* **1** One who sends anything by express. **2** One who or that which presses out a juice or the like.

ex·press·i·ble (ik·spres'ə·bəl) *adj.* Capable of being expressed. — **ex·press'i·bly** *adv.*

ex·pres·sion (ik·spresh'ən) *n.* **1** The act or mode of uttering or representing, as by language or gesture. **2** Any act or object by which some truth or idea is conveyed: the *expression* of pleasure. **3** That which is uttered; a saying; any embodiment of a thought: a common *expression* among doctors. **4** Outward aspect; especially, the ensemble of the face as indicating the feelings, etc.; look. **5** The quality of having proper expressive methods; the effective utterance of thought or feeling; expressiveness. **6** The development or revelation of character and sentiment in art, music, etc., by shadings, nuances, variations in style. **7** A pressing out. **8** *Math.* A group of characters, numbers, and symbols composing a statement. Also *Obs.* **ex·pres'sure.** See synonyms under AIR, DICTION, LANGUAGE, TERM. [<F <L *expressio, -onis* < *exprimere* < *ex-* out + *premere* press] — **ex·pres'sion·less** *adj.*

Ex·pres·sion·ism (ik·spresh'ən·iz'əm) *n.* A movement in the arts, originating in Europe at about the time of World War I, which had as its object the free expression of the inner experience of the artist rather than the realistic representation of appearances. — **ex·pres'·sion·ist** *n.* & *adj.* — **ex·pres'sion·is'tic** *adj.*

ex·pres·sis ver·bis (ek·spres′is vûr′bis) *Latin* In express terms.
ex·pres·sive (ik·spres′iv) *adj.* **1** Of, pertaining to, or characterized by expression. **2** Conveying or containing expression, in any sense of the word. **3** Manifesting special significance or force. See synonyms under MOBILE. —**ex·pres′sive·ly** *adv.* —**ex·pres′sive·ness** *n.*
express letter *Brit.* A special delivery letter.
ex·press·ly (ik·spres′lē) *adv.* With definitely stated intent or application; exactly and unmistakably; in direct terms: The condition was *expressly* named.
ex·press·man (ik·spres′mən) *n. pl.* **·men** (-mən) An employee of an express company; a driver or deliveryman on an express truck.
express money order A money order issued by an express company.
express rifle A modern sporting rifle with a large charge of powder and a light bullet of large caliber, for use at close range.
express train A train operated at high speed with few stops.
ex·press·way (ik·spres′wā′) *n.* A road designed for rapid travel.
ex pro·fes·so (eks prō·fes′ō) *Latin* Openly; avowedly; professedly.
ex·pro·pri·ate (eks·prō′prē·āt) *v.t.* **·at·ed, ·at·ing 1** To take from the owner, especially for public use. **2** To deprive of ownership or property. [<LL *expropriatus,* pp. of *expropriare* < *ex-* out + *proprium* property < *proprius* one's own] —**ex·pro′pri·a′tor** *n.*
ex·pro·pri·a·tion (eks·prō′prē·ā′shən) *n.* **1** The act, process, or result of expropriating. **2** The act of taking land for public use by right of eminent domain.
ex pro·pri·is (eks prō′prē·is) *Latin* From one's own resources.
ex pro·pri·o mo·tu (eks prō′prē·ō mō′to͞o) *Latin* Of its (or his) own accord; voluntarily.
ex·pul·sion (ik·spul′shən) *n.* **1** The act of expelling; forcible ejection. **2** The state of being expelled. [<L *expulsio, -onis* < *expellere.* See EXPEL.] —**ex·pul′sive** *adj.*
ex·punc·tion (ik·spungk′shən) *n.* The act of expunging; erasure. [<L *expunctio, -onis* < *expungere.* See EXPUNGE.]
ex·punge (ik·spunj′) *v.t.* **·punged, ·pung·ing** To blot or scratch out, as from a record or list; obliterate; efface. See synonyms under CANCEL. [<L *expungere* < *ex-* out + *pungere* prick] —**ex·pung′er** *n.*
ex·pur·gate (eks′pər·gāt) *v.t.* **·gat·ed, ·gat·ing** To clear, as a book, of whatever is considered objectionable, immoral, etc. [<L *expurgatus,* pp. of *expurgare* < *ex-* out + *purgare* cleanse] —**ex′pur·ga′tion** *n.* —**ex′pur·ga′tor** *n.* —**ex·pur·ga·to·ry** (ik·spûr′gə·tôr′ē, -tō′rē) *adj.*
ex·pur·ga·to·ri·al (ik·spûr′gə·tôr′ē·əl, -tō′rē-) *adj.* Pertaining to expurgation; purifying.
ex·qui·site (eks′kwi·zit, ik·skwiz′it) *adj.* **1** Characterized by fineness and delicacy; dainty in make or quality; satisfying to the esthetic faculties; refined; delicately beautiful. **2** Having unusually refined perception or judgment; delicately sensitive and accurate; of keen esthetic discrimination; nice; fastidious: *exquisite* taste. **3** Causing or marked by intense or extreme emotion; exciting or fitted to excite extreme pleasure or pain; intense or poignant: *exquisite* rapture or pain. **4** *Obs.* Very careful; curious. **5** *Obs.* Particular; choice. See synonyms under BEAUTIFUL, CHOICE, DELICIOUS, ELEGANT, FINE. —*n.* A person very dainty in dress or manners; a fop; dandy; dude. [<L *exquisitus,* pp. of *exquirere* < *ex-* out + *quarere* seek] —**ex′qui·site·ly** *adv.* —**ex′qui·site·ness** *n.*
ex·san·guine (eks·sang′gwin) *adj.* Having no blood; anemic.
ex·scind (ek·sind′) *v.t.* To cut out; sever. [<L *exscindere* < *ex-* out + *scindere* cut]
ex·se·cant (eks′sē′kənt, -kant) *n. Trig.* A function of an angle expressible as the secant of the angle minus one. See TRIGONOMETRICAL FUNCTIONS. [<EX(TERIOR) SECANT]
ex·sect (ek·sekt′) *v.t.* To cut out. [<L *exsectus,* pp. of *exsecare* < *ex-* out + *secare* cut] —**ex·sec′tion** *n.*
ex·sert (ek·sûrt′) *v.t.* To push out; protrude. [<L *exsertus.* See EXERT.] —**ex·ser′tile** (-til) *adj.* —**ex·ser′tion** *n.*
ex·sert·ed (ek·sûr′tid) *adj. Bot.* Protruding from surrounding parts, as the stamens or style beyond the mouth of some tubular corollas; thrust out; unsheathed.
ex·sic·ca·tae (ek′sə·kā′tē) *n. pl.* Dried specimens of plants, especially in numbered sets for herbariums. [<L, fem. pl. of *exsiccatus.* See EXSICCATE.]
ex·sic·cate (ek′sə·kāt) *v.t.* & *v.i.* **·cat·ed, ·cat·ing** To dry up or out. [<L *exsiccatus,* pp. of *exsiccare* < *ex-* out + *siccus* dry] —**ex·sic·cant** (ek·sik′ənt) *adj.* & *n.* —**ex′sic·ca′tion** *n.* —**ex′sic·ca′tive** *adj.* —**ex′sic·ca′tor** *n.*
ex·sic·ca·ti (ek′sə·kā′tī) *n. pl.* Dried specimens of fungi, especially in numbered sets for herbariums. [<L, masc. pl. of *exsiccatus.* See EXSICCATE.]
ex·stip·u·late (eks·stip′yə·lit, -lāt) *adj. Bot.* Destitute of stipules: also *estipulate.*
ex·stro·phy (ek′strə·fē) *n. Pathol.* The turning of an inner part outward, as the bladder. [<Gk. *ex-* out + *strephein* turn]
ex·suf·fli·cate (eks·suf′lə·kit, -kāt) *adj. Obs.* Inflated; empty; frivolous. [Cf. L *exsufflare* blow on]
ex·tant (ek′stənt, ik·stant′) *adj.* **1** Still existing and known; living. **2** *Obs.* Standing out; manifest; conspicuous. [<L *ex(s)tans, -antis,* ppr. of *exstare* < *ex-* out + *stare* stand]
ex·tem·po·ral (ik·stem′pər·əl) *adj. Obs.* or *Archaic* Extemporaneous; extemporary. —**ex·tem′po·ral·ly** *adv.*
ex·tem·po·ra·ne·ous (ik·stem′pə·rā′nē·əs) *adj.* **1** Done or made with little or no preparation; composed or uttered on the spur of the moment; unpremeditated. **2** Given to speaking without notes. [<LL *extemporaneus* < *ex-* out + *tempus, temporis* time] —**ex·tem′po·ra′ne·ous·ly** *adv.* —**ex·tem′po·ra′ne·ous·ness** *n.*
Synonyms: extemporary, extempore, impromptu, improvised, offhand, unpremeditated. *Extemporaneous,* originally signifying *of* or *from the time* or *occasion,* has come to mean done or made with but little (if any) preparation, and is now chiefly applied to addresses of which the thought has been prepared, and only the language and incidental treatment left to the suggestion of the moment, so that an *extemporaneous* speech is understood to be one that is not read or recited; *impromptu* keeps its original sense, denoting something that springs from the instant. *Offhand* is still more emphatic as to the readiness and freedom of the utterance. *Unpremeditated* is graver and more formal, denoting absolute want of preparation, but is too heavy a word to be applied to such apt, ready utterance as is generally designated by *impromptu.* *Antonyms*: elaborated, premeditated, prepared, read, recited, studied, written.
ex·tem·po·rar·y (ik·stem′pə·rer′ē) *adj.* **1** Extemporaneous. **2** Made for the occasion; extemporized: an *extemporary* shelter. —**ex·tem′po·rar′i·ly** *adv.* —**ex·tem′po·rar′i·ness** *n.*
ex·tem·po·re (ik·stem′pər·ē) *adj.* Done on the spur of the moment; extemporaneous; unstudied; offhand. —*adv.* Without special preparation; extemporaneously. See synonyms under EXTEMPORANEOUS. [<L *ex tempore* out of the time]
ex·tem·po·rize (ik·stem′pə·rīz) *v.t.* & *v.i.* **·rized, ·riz·ing** To do, make, or compose without preparation; improvise. —**ex·tem′po·ri·za′tion** *n.* —**ex·tem′po·riz′er** *n.*
ex·tend (ik·stend′) *v.t.* **1** To open or stretch to full length. **2** To cause to stretch to a specified point, in a given direction, or for a given distance; make longer. **3** To cause to last until or for a specified time; continue. **4** To widen or enlarge the range, area, scope, meaning, etc., of: to *extend* the duties of an office. **5** To hold out or put forth, as the hand. **6** To give or offer to give: to *extend* hospitality. **7** To straighten, as a leg or arm. **8** In business, to put off the date of completion or payment of, as a contract or debt, beyond that originally set. **9** *Law* **a** *Brit.* To assess; appraise. **b** To seize under a writ of extent. —*v.i.* **10** To be extended; stretch. **11** To reach, as in a specified direction: This road *extends* west. —**to extend oneself** To put forth great effort. See synonyms under ADD, AMPLIFY, INCREASE, PROTRACT, SPREAD. [<L *extendere* < *ex-* out + *tendere* stretch] —**ex·tend′i·ble** *adj.*
ex·tend·ed (ik·sten′did) *adj.* **1** Covering a great extent of time or space. **2** Pulled or stretched out. **3** Broad in proportion to height: said of type: an *extended* letter. —**ex·tend′ed·ly** *adv.*
ex·ten·si·ble (ik·sten′sə·bəl) *adj.* That may be extended. —**ex·ten′si·bil′i·ty, ex·ten′si·ble·ness** *n.*
ex·ten·sile (ik·sten′sil) *adj.* Extensible.
ex·ten·sion (ik·sten′shən) *n.* **1** The act or process of extending. **2** An annex; addition. **3** That property of matter by virtue of which it occupies space. **4** *Logic* The capacity of a general concept to cover the specific classes or individual things connoted by it; the degree of applicability belonging to a notion. **5** *Surg.* Traction of a fractured or dislocated limb in order to replace its parts. **6** *Anat.* The straightening of a limb: opposed to *flexion.* **7** The act of a creditor allowing to a debtor further time in which to pay a debt. See synonyms under ACCESSION, APPENDAGE, INCREASE. [<L *extensio, -onis* < *extendere.* See EXTEND.]
ex·ten·si·ty (ik·sten′sə·tē) *n.* **1** The quality of extension; extensiveness. **2** *Psychol.* An element of sensation yielding the spatial qualities of perception.
ex·ten·sive (ik·sten′siv) *adj.* **1** Extended widely in space, time, or scope; great; wide. **2** Designating a method of land cultivation in which the crop depends on the area treated rather than (as in *intensive* agriculture) on the fertilization and care of a restricted area. **3** Of or pertaining to extension. See synonyms under LARGE. —**ex·ten′sive·ly** *adv.* —**ex·ten′sive·ness** *n.*
ex·ten·som·e·ter (eks′ten·som′ə·tər) *n. Mech.* A micrometer by which to measure the expansion of a body, as a bar of metal. Also **ex′ten·sim′e·ter.**
ex·ten·sor (ik·sten′sər, -sôr) *n. Anat.* A muscle that causes extension. Compare FLEXOR.
ex·tent (ik·stent′) *n.* **1** The dimension or degree to which anything is extended; compass; reach; size; range; also, the limit to which anything reaches. **2** Size within given bounds: the *extent* of his power. **3** *Law* A writ directing the appraisal of lands at their yearly value, and their delivery to a creditor for a limited time to satisfy his claim. **4** *Logic* Extension (def. 4). **5** Any continuous magnitude, as of a line, surface, or solid. See synonyms under END, MAGNITUDE. [<L *extentus,* pp. of *extendere.* See EXTEND.]
ex·ten·u·ate (ik·sten′yo͞o·āt) *v.t.* **·at·ed, ·at·ing 1** To represent as less blameworthy; make excuses for. **2** To cause to seem less serious or blameworthy. **3** *Rare* To make thin or weak; attenuate. **4** *Obs.* To diminish in estimation; depreciate; detract from. [<L *extenuatus,* pp. of *extenuare* weaken < *ex-* out + *tenuis* thin] —**ex·ten′u·at′ing** *adj.* —**ex·ten′u·a′tor** *n.*
ex·ten·u·a·tion (ik·sten′yo͞o·ā′shən) *n.* The act of extenuating, in any sense; palliation; excuse. —**ex·ten′u·a′tive** *adj.* & *n.* —**ex·ten′u·a·to′ry** (-tôr′ē, -tō′rē) *adj.*
ex·te·ri·or (ik·stir′ē·ər) *adj.* **1** External; outlying. **2** Manifest to the senses. **3** Acting from without. **4** Pertaining to foreign countries; foreign. —*n.* **1** That which is outside; external features or qualities. **2** Hence, the sum of observable qualities or traits: one's physiognomy, demeanor, general appearance, or outward conduct. [<L *exterior,* compar. of *exterus* outside] —**ex·te′ri·or·ly** *adv.*
exterior angle See under ANGLE.
ex·te·ri·or·i·za·tion (ik·stir′ē·ər·ə·zā′shən) *n. Psychiatry* The act or process of turning the thoughts and emotions away from the self and toward the external world: used in the treatment of schizophrenia and related mental disorders.
ex·ter·mi·nate (ik·stûr′mə·nāt) *v.t.* **·nat·ed, ·nat·ing** To destroy entirely; annihilate. Also *Obs.* **ex·ter′mine.** [<L *exterminatus,* pp. of *exterminare* < *ex-* out + *terminus* a boundary] —**ex·ter′mi·na·ble** *adj.* —**ex·ter′mi·na′tive, ex·ter′mi·na·to′ry** (-tôr′ē, -tō′rē) *adj.*
Synonyms: annihilate, banish, demolish, destroy, eradicate, expel, extirpate, overthrow, remove, uproot. The word *exterminate* is applied to groups or masses of men or animals; individuals are said to be *banished, expelled,*

destroyed, etc. *Eradicate* is primarily applied to numbers or groups of plants; a single tree may be *uprooted,* but is not said to be *eradicated.* To *extirpate* is to *destroy* the very stock, so that the race can never be restored; we speak of *eradicating* a disease, of *extirpating* a cancer, *exterminating* wild beasts or hostile tribes; we seek to *eradicate* or *extirpate* vice. See ABOLISH. *Antonyms*: augment, beget, cherish, colonize, develop, foster, increase, plant, populate, propagate, replenish, settle.

ex·ter·mi·na·tion (ik·stur′mə·nā′shən) *n.* The act or process of exterminating; annihilation.

extermination camp A death camp.

ex·ter·mi·na·tor (ik·stûr′mə·nā′tər) *n.* **1** Someone or something that exterminates. **2** A person whose business is destroying rodents, insects, etc. **3** A chemical preparation used to destroy rodents, insects, etc.

ex·tern (eks′tûrn) *n.* **1** *Brit.* A pupil who does not live at the school he attends; a day scholar. **2** A member of the house staff of a hospital who does not reside in the institution; opposed to *intern.* Also **ex′terne.** — *adj.* (ik·stûrn′) *Obs.* External. [<F *externe* <L *externus* outer < *ex* out]

ex·ter·nal (ik·stûr′nəl) *adj.* **1** Situated or occurring outside of the subject; being on or relating to the exterior. **2** Visible from the outside; hence, often, superficial: *external* polish. **3** Belonging to the material or phenomenal world as distinguished from the mind that perceives it; objective. **4** Relating to the surface of the body: an *external* disease. **5** Pertaining to or coming from foreign lands or people; foreign: *external* traffic. **6** Extraneous; extrinsic. — *n.* **1** An exterior or outer part. **2** *pl.* Outward symbols, as of religion. [<L *externus* outer < *ex* out] — **ex·ter′nal·ly** *adv.*

ex·ter·nal–com·bus·tion (ik·stûr′nəl·kəm·bus′·chən) *adj.* Pertaining to or designating a type of engine in which ignition of the fuel–air mixture takes place outside the engine cylinder.

ex·ter·nal·ism (ik·stûr′nəl·iz′əm) *n.* **1** *Philos.* The doctrine that only things which are the objects of sense perception have reality, or can be known to have it; phenomenalism. **2** Devotion to externals, especially in matters of religion.

ex·ter·nal·i·ty (ek′stər·nal′ə·tē) *n.* **1** Location on the outside, or as on a surface outside. **2** Regard for or devotion to externals.

ex·ter·nal·ize (ik·stûr′nəl·īz) *v.t.* **·ized, ·iz·ing** **1** To give shape to; embody. **2** To make outwardly real. — **ex·ter′nal·i·za′tion** *n.*

ex·ter·o·cep·tor (ek′stər·ō·sep′tər) *n. Physiol.* A peripheral sense organ that responds to stimulation from external agents, as in sight, hearing, touch, etc. Compare INTEROCEPTOR. [<L *exterus* external + (RE)CEPTOR] — **ex′·ter·o·cep′tive** *adj.*

ex·ter·ri·to·ri·al (eks′ter·ə·tôr′ē·əl, -tō′rē-) *adj.* Extraterritorial. — **ex′ter·ri·to′ri·al′i·ty** *n.* — **ex′ter·ri·to′ri·al·ly** *adv.*

ex·tinct (ik·stingkt′) *adj.* **1** Extinguished; inactive; quenched: an *extinct* volcano. **2** Exterminated; no longer existing: an *extinct* animal or species. **3** Void; lapsed: an *extinct* title. See synonyms under LIFELESS. [<L *ex(s)tinctus,* pp. of *ex(s)tinguere* EXTINGUISH]

ex·tinc·tion (ik·stingk′shən) *n.* **1** The act of extinguishing or state of being extinguished; extinguishment. **2** A putting an end to something; a destroying; complete destruction; annihilation. **3** A quenching or slaking, as of quicklime with water. **4** *Physics* A diminution in the intensity of radiation due to absorption by or scattering in the medium; also, the stopping of incident X–rays by the outer layers of atoms in a crystal.

ex·tinc·tive (ik·stingk′tiv) *adj.* Calculated to extinguish; extinguishing.

ex·tin·guish (ik·sting′gwish) *v.t.* **1** To put out; quench, as a fire. **2** To make extinct; wipe out. **3** To obscure or throw into the shade; eclipse. **4** *Law* To cause to end and become extinct; pay off and satisfy in full. See synonyms under ANNUL, SUBVERT. [<L *ex(s)tinguere* < *ex-* completely + *stinguere* quench] — **ex·tin′guish·a·ble** *adj.* — **ex·tin′guish·er** *n.* — **ex·tin′guish·ment** *n.*

ex·tir·pate (ek′stər·pāt, ik·stûr′-) *v.t.* **·pat·ed, ·pat·ing** To root out or up; eradicate; destroy wholly. See synonyms under ABOLISH, EXTERMINATE. [<L *ex(s)tirpatus,* pp. of *ex(s)tirpare* < *ex-* out + *stirps* stem, root] — **ex·tir′pa·ble** *adj.* — **ex′tir·pa′tion** *n.* — **ex′tir·pa′tive** *adj.* — **ex′tir·pa′tor** *n.* — **ex·tir·pa·to·ry** (ik·stûr′·pə·tôr′ē, -tō′rē) *adj.*

ex·tol (ik·stōl′, -stol′) *v.t.* **·tolled, ·tol·ling** To praise in the highest terms; magnify. See synonyms under ADMIRE, PRAISE. Also **ex·toll′.** [<L *extollere* < *ex-* out, up + *tollere* raise] — **ex·tol′ler** *n.* — **ex·tol′ment** or **ex·toll′ment** *n.*

ex·tort (ik·stôrt′) *v.t.* To obtain from a person by violence, threat, oppression, or abuse of authority; wring; wrest. See synonyms under STEAL. [<L *extortus,* pp. of *extorquere* < *ex-* out + *torquere* twist] — **ex·tort′er** *n.* — **ex·tor′tive** *adj.*

ex·tor·tion (ik·stôr′shən) *n.* **1** The act or practice of extorting. **2** That which has been extorted. **3** *Law* The offense, committed by an official, of taking money under color of his office, with the consent of the victim, either where none is due, in excess of what is due, or before it is due. — **ex·tor′tion·er** or **·ist** *n.*

ex·tor·tion·ar·y (ik·stôr′shən·er′ē) *adj.* Practicing extortion.

ex·tor·tion·ate (ik·stôr′shən·it) *adj.* Characterized by extortion; oppressive. — **ex·tor′·tion·ate·ly** *adv.*

ex·tra (eks′trə) *adj.* Being over and above what is required; additional. — *n.* **1** Something beyond what is usual or required. **2** A copy or an edition of a newspaper issued for some special purpose, or at a time different from that of the regular edition. **3** In cricket, any run resulting from a by, leg–by, no–ball, or wide. **4** Something of a special quality. **5** An actor, not a member of the regular cast, hired for a special scene, as a mob scene, or for a small part. — *adv.* Unusually. [<L, outside, beyond]

extra– *prefix* Beyond; outside; outside the scope of: *extraordinary* beyond the ordinary; *extra–oral* outside the mouth. [<L *extra-* < *extra* < *exter* on the outside < *ex* out]

Extra– may appear as a prefix in hyphemes or solidemes, as in:

extra–alimentary
extra–American
extra–analogical
extra–articular
extra–artistic
extra–atmospheric
extra–axillar
extra–axillary
extra–Britannic
extrabuccal
extrabureau
extracapsular
extracarpal
extracathedral
extracellular
extracerebral
extra–Christian
extracivic
extraclassroom
extraclaustral
extracloacal
extracollegiate
extraconscious
extraconstellated
extraconstitutional
extracorporeal
extracorpuscular
extracosmic
extracosmical
extracranial
extracultural
extracurial
extracutaneous
extradecretal
extradialectal
extradural
extra–embryonic
extra–European
extrafascicular
extrafloral
extrafocal
extrafoliaceous
extraformal
extragastric
extragenital
extraglacial
extragovernmental
extragrammatical
extrahepatic
extrahistoric
extrahistorical
extrahuman
extra–industrial
extra–insular
extra–intellectual
extra–Judaical
extrajugal
extrajural
extralegal
extraligamentous
extralimitary
extralogical
extramanorial
extramarine
extramarital
extramatrimonial
extramedial
extramental
extrametaphysical
extrametropolitan
extramodal
extramolecular
extramoral
extramoralist
extramusical
extranational
extranatural
extranormal
extranuclear
extra–ocular
extra–official
extra–oral
extra–orbital
extra–organismal
extra–ovate
extra–ovular
extraparental
extraparliamentary
extraparochial
extrapatriarchal
extrapelvic
extraperiodic
extraperiosteal
extraperitoneal
extraphenomenal
extraphysiological
extrapituitary
extraplanetary
extrapleural
extraprostatic
extrapulmonary
extrarenal
extraretinal
extrasacerdotal
extrascholastic
extrascriptural
extra–Scriptural
extrasensible
extrasocial
extrasolar
extrasomatic
extraspectral
extraspherical
extraspinal
extrastate
extrasyllabic
extrasyllogistic
extratabular
extratellurian
extratemporal
extraterrene
extraterrestrial
extrathoracic
extratracheal
extratropical
extra–university
extra–urban
extravaginal
extravisceral
extrazodiacal

ex·tra–bold (eks′trə·bōld′) *adj. Printing* Denoting a very heavy face of type.

ex·tra–ca·non·i·cal (eks′trə·kə·non′i·kəl) *adj.* Being outside the canon; non–canonical: *extra–canonical* writings.

ex·tra–con·densed (eks′trə·kən·denst′) *adj. Printing* Extremely narrow in proportion to the height: said of type.

ex·tract (ik·strakt′) *v.t.* **1** To draw or pull out by force: to *extract* a tooth. **2** To obtain from a substance by pressing, treatment with chemicals, etc. **3** To draw out or obtain as if by such process; derive, as instruction or pleasure. **4** To copy out; select for quotation. **5** *Math.* To calculate (the root of a number). See synonyms under QUOTE. — *n.* (eks′trakt) **1** Something extracted or drawn out. **2** A selection from a book; a passage quoted. **3** The portion of a plant or substance removed by solvents and used in drug preparations in solid, powdered, or liquid form. [<L *extractus,* pp. of *extrahere* < *ex-* out + *trahere* draw, pull] — **ex·tract′a·ble** or **ex·tract′i·ble** *adj.*

ex·trac·tion (ik·strak′shən) *n.* **1** The act of extracting. **2** That which is extracted. **3** Lineage; descent.

ex·trac·tive (ik·strak′tiv) *adj.* **1** That extracts or tends to extract. **2** Capable of extraction. — *n.* **1** Something capable of being extracted. **2** That portion of an extract which becomes insoluble.

ex·trac·tor (ik·strak′tər) *n.* **1** One who or that which extracts. **2** The device in a firearm or cannon which withdraws a spent round of ammunition from the chamber prior to ejection.

ex·tra–cur·ric·u·lar (eks′trə·kə·rik′yə·lər) *adj.* Of or pertaining to those activities which are not a part of the curriculum, but which form an important part of school or college life, as athletics, fraternities, campus publications, etc. Also **ex′tra–cur·ric′u·lum.**

ex·tra·dit·a·ble (eks′trə·dī′tə·bəl) *adj.* Liable to or warranting extradition.

ex·tra·dite (eks′trə·dīt) *v.t.* **·dit·ed, ·dit·ing** **1** To deliver up, as to another state or nation. **2** To obtain the extradition of. [Back formation from EXTRADITION]

ex·tra·di·tion (eks′trə·dish′ən) *n.* The surrender of an accused person by a government to the justice of another government, or of a prisoner by one authority to another. [<F <L *extraditio, -onis* < *ex-* out + *traditio* a surrender. See TRADITION.]

ex·tra·dos (eks·trā′dos) *n. Archit.* The exterior curve of an arch. For illustration see under ARCH. [<F < *extra-* EXTRA- + *dos* the back <L *dorsum*]

ex·tra·ga·lac·tic (eks′trə·gə·lak′tik) *adj. Astron.* Beyond the Galaxy.

ex·tra–ju·di·cial (eks′trə·jōō·dish′əl) *adj.* Happening out of court; out of the jurisdiction of the proper court. — **ex′tra·ju·di′cial·ly** *adv.*

ex·tra·mun·dane (eks′trə·mun′dān, -mun·dān′) *adj.* Existing outside of our world or beyond the limits of the material universe.

ex·tra·mu·ral (eks′trə·myŏŏr′əl) *adj.* **1** Situated without or beyond the walls, as of a fortified city. **2** Beyond the boundaries of an educational institution: *extramural* games: opposed to *intramural.*

ex·tra·ne·ous (ik·strā′nē·əs) *adj.* Not intrinsic or essential to matter under consideration; foreign. [<L *extraneus* foreign. Doublet of STRANGE.] — **ex·tra′ne·ous·ly** *adv.* — **ex·tra′ne·ous·ness** *n.*

ex·traor·di·nar·y (ik·strôr′də·ner′ē; *esp. for def. 3,* eks′trə·ôr′də·ner′ē) *adj.* **1** Being beyond or out of the common order, course, or method. **2** Exceeding the ordinary degree; not ordinary; unusual; remarkable: an *extraordinary* accident. **3** Employed for a special purpose or on an exceptional occasion; special: an envoy *extraordinary.* **4** *Optics* Designating that component of a plane–

polarized ray of light which, on passing through a doubly refracting crystal, has different speeds in different directions. [<L *extraordinarius* <*extra* beyond + *ordo, ordinis* order] —**ex·traor′di·nar′i·ly** *adv.*

Synonyms: amazing, egregious, marvelous, monstrous, peculiar, preposterous, prodigious, remarkable, signal, singular, strange, striking, uncommon, unprecedented, unusual, unwonted, wonderful, See ODD, RARE[1]. *Antonyms*: common, commonplace, frequent, natural, ordinary, unimportant, usual.

extraordinary session A special session of the U. S. Congress.

ex·trap·o·late (eks·trap′ə·lāt, eks′trə·pə·lāt′) *v.t.* & *v.i.* **·lat·ed, ·lat·ing 1** *Math.* To estimate those values of a magnitude or a function which lie beyond the range of known or determined values: distinguished from *interpolate.* **2** To infer (a possibility) beyond the strict evidence of a series of facts, events, observations, etc. [<EXTRA- + (INTER)POLATE]

ex·trap·o·la·tion (eks·trap′ə·lā′shən, eks′trə·pə·lā′shən) *n.* **1** *Math.* The assignment of values beyond either limit of the known range of values of a function or quantity. **2** Conjecture based on but not strictly validated by a given range of facts, events, etc. **3** Any instance of extrapolating.

ex·tra–pro·fes·sion·al (eks′trə·prə·fesh′ən·əl) *adj.* Being outside the usual limits of professional duty or interest.

ex·tra·sen·so·ry (eks′trə·sen′sər·ē) *adj. Psychol.* **1** Of or pertaining to phenomena outside of or beyond normal sensory perception. **2** Designating those powers of perception not yet scientifically explained in relation to any of the senses, as telepathy, clairvoyance, etc. Compare PARAPSYCHOLOGY.

ex·tra·ter·ri·to·ri·al (eks′trə·ter′ə·tôr′ē·əl, -tō′rē-) *adj.* **1** Exempt from territorial jurisdiction; not subject to the laws of one's abode: the *extraterritorial* rights of an ambassador. **2** Of or pertaining to things beyond the national territory: *extraterritorial* possessions. —**ex′tra·ter′ri·to′ri·al·ly** *adv.*

ex·tra·ter·ri·to·ri·al·i·ty (eks′trə·ter′ə·tôr′ē·al′ə·tē, -tō′rē-) *n.* In international law, the state or privilege of freedom from (local) territorial jurisdiction, accorded to foreign sovereigns, to diplomatic representatives, their suites, and to a certain extent their dwellings.

ex·traught (eks·trôt′) *adj. Obs.* **1** Extracted. **2** Distraught. [Var. of EXTRACT]

ex·tra–u·ter·ine (eks′trə·yōō′tər·in, -tə·rīn) *adj.* Situated or occurring externally to the uterus.

ex·trav·a·gance (ik·strav′ə·gəns) *n.* **1** An extravagant act or group of such acts; especially, undue expenditure of money; lavishness: prodigality; excess. **2** Overly exaggerated statement or language. **3** Ridiculous action. Also **ex·trav′a·gan·cy.** See synonyms under ENTHUSIASM, EXCESS.

ex·trav·a·gant (ik·strav′ə·gənt) *adj.* **1** Exceeding ordinary limits; needlessly free or lavish in expenditure. **2** Immoderate; fantastic; unrestrained, as language or behavior. **3** Excessive; exorbitant. **4** *Obs.* Straying beyond bounds; wandering abroad. See synonyms under IMMODERATE, ROMANTIC. [<MF <Med. L *extravagans, -antis,* ppr. of *extravagari* <L *extra-* outside + *vagari* wander] —**ex·trav′a·gant·ly** *adv.* —**ex·trav′a·gant·ness** *n.*

ex·trav·a·gan·za (ik·strav′ə·gan′zə) *n.* **1** A lavish or fantastic composition in literature, music, or the drama; especially, a spectacular musical comedy. **2** Any extravagant utterance or act. See synonyms under CARICATURE. [< Ital. *estravaganza* extravagance, ult. <Med. L *extravagari.* See EXTRAVAGANT.]

ex·trav·a·gate (ik·strav′ə·gāt) *v.i.* **·gat·ed, ·gat·ing 1** To roam at will. **2** To exceed proper bounds. [<Med. L *extravagatus,* pp. of *extravagari.* See EXTRAVAGANT.]

ex·trav·a·sate (ik·strav′ə·sāt) *v.* **·sat·ed, ·sat·ing** *v.t.* **1** *Pathol.* To cause or allow the escape of from the proper vessels, as blood or air. **2** *Geol.* To gush out, as lava. —*v.i.* **3** *Pathol.* To filter or ooze into surrounding tissues, as blood from an artery or vein following a bruise. [<EXTRA- + L *vas* a vessel + -ATE[2]]

ex·trav·a·sa·tion (ik·strav′ə·sā′shən) *n.* **1** The state or process of being extravasated. **2** The substances extravasated.

ex·tra·vas·cu·lar (eks′trə·vas′kyə·lər) *adj. Anat.* **1** Situated outside the vascular system. **2** Having no blood vessels; non–vascular.

ex·tra·ver·sion (eks′trə·vûr′zhən, -shən), **ex·tra·vert** (eks′trə·vûrt) See EXTROVERSION, EXTROVERT.

Ex·tre·ma·du·ra (es′trā·mä·thōō′rä) The Spanish name for ESTREMADURA.

ex·treme (ik·strēm′) *adj.* **1** At or to the farthest limit; outermost; utmost. **2** Last; final. **3** In the utmost degree; far removed from the normal or average: *extreme* joy; *extreme* poverty. **4** Immoderate or radical: *extreme* opinions. —*n.* **1** The utmost or highest degree: the *extreme* of cruelty. **2** Either of two ends (of a line, series, scale, etc.): *extremes* of temperature. **3** *Math.* The first or last term of a proportion or series. **4** *Logic* **a** Either the subject or predicate of a proposition, distinguished from the copula. **b** Either of the two terms of a syllogism which, separated in the premises, are joined in the conclusion. [<OF <L *extremus,* superl. of *exterus* outside] —**ex·treme′ly** *adv.* —**ex·treme′ness** *n.*

extreme unction See under UNCTION.

ex·trem·ism (ik·strē′miz·əm) *n.* A tendency to extremes.

ex·trem·ist (ik·strē′mist) *n.* One who supports or advocates extreme measures or holds extreme views.

ex·trem·i·ty (ik·strem′ə·tē) *n. pl.* **·ties 1** The utmost or farthest point; termination, end, or edge. **2** The greatest degree. **3** Desperate distress or need. **4** *pl.* Extreme measures. **5** *Usually pl.* The end part of a limb or appendage. See synonyms under END, NECESSITY.

ex·tri·cate (eks′trə·kāt) *v.t.* **·cat·ed, ·cat·ing 1** To free from hindrance, difficulties, etc.; disentangle. **2** To cause to be given off; evolve, as gas or moisture. See synonyms under RELEASE. [<L *extricatus,* pp. of *extricare* <*ex-* out + *tricae* troubles] —**ex·tri·ca·ble** (eks′tri·kə·bəl) *adj.* —**ex′tri·ca·bly** *adv.*

ex·tri·ca·tion (eks′trə·kā′shən) *n.* **1** The act or process of extricating. **2** The act of evolving; disengagement.

ex·trin·sic (ek·strin′sik) *adj.* **1** Being outside of the nature of an object or case; not inherent or included in a thing; not essential: opposed to *intrinsic.* **2** *Anat.* Originating beyond the limits of a body or limb: *extrinsic* muscles. **3** Irrelevant; extraneous. Also **ex·trin′si·cal.** [<F *extrinsèque* <L *extrinsecus* outwardly <*exter* outside + *secus* besides] —**ex·trin′si·cal·ly** *adv.* —**ex·trin′si·cal·ness** *n.*

ex·trorse (eks·trôrs′) *adj. Bot.* Turned outward, as an anther from the axis of a flower. Also **ex·tror′sal.** [<F <LL *extrorsus* outwards <*extra* outside + *versus* towards]

ex·tro·ver·sion (eks′trō·vûr′zhən, -shən) *n.* **1** *Psychol.* The turning of one's interests toward the outside world or toward persons other than oneself; the quality of finding interest and pleasure in outside interests; opposed to *introversion.* Also *extraversion.* **2** *Anat.* Exstrophy. [<*extro-* outwards (<EXTRA-) + L *versio, -onis* a turning <*vertere* turn]

ex·tro·vert (eks′trō·vûrt) *n.* A person highly adapted to living in and deriving satisfaction from the external world: opposed to *introvert.* Also *extravert.*

ex·trude (ik·strōōd′) *v.* **·trud·ed, ·trud·ing** *v.t.* **1** To force, thrust, or push out; expel. **2** To force (a plastic, metal, or other substance) through a shaped opening in order to give it a desired cross–section. —*v.i.* **3** To protrude. [<L *extrudere* <*ex-* out + *trudere* thrust]

ex·tru·sion (ik·strōō′zhən) *n.* **1** The act or process of extruding; expulsion. **2** *Geol.* An overflow of lava upon the earth's surface through conduits or fissures in the rocks; effusion.

ex·tru·sive (ik·strōō′siv) *adj.* **1** Tending to extrude. **2** *Geol.* Extruded, as outflows of igneous rocks.

ex·u·ber·ance (ig·zōō′bər·əns) *n.* **1** Abounding variety or copiousness. **2** Superabundance: an *exuberance* of imagination. Also **ex·u′ber·an·cy.**

ex·u·ber·ant (ig·zōō′bər·ənt) *adj.* **1** Effusive; overflowing; lavish. **2** Marked by plentifulness; producing copiously. See synonyms under FERTILE, REDUNDANT. [<L *exuberans, -antis* <*ex-* completely + *uberare* be fruitful <*uber* rich] —**ex·u′ber·ant·ly** *adv.*

ex·u·ber·ate (ig·zōō′bə·rāt) *v.i.* **·rat·ed, ·rat·ing** *Rare* To be exuberant.

ex·u·date (eks′yōō·dāt) *n. Biol.* Any substance which filters through the walls of living cellular tissue and is available for removal or extraction, as gums and resins. [<L *ex(s)udatus,* pp. of *ex(s)udare.* See EXUDE.]

ex·u·da·tion (eks′yōō·dā′shən) *n.* **1** The act or process of exuding. **2** That which is exuded.

ex·ude (ig·zōōd′, ik·sōōd′) *v.t.* & *v.i.* **·ud·ed, ·ud·ing** To give off or come forth gradually; ooze or trickle forth, as sweat. [<L *ex(s)udare* <*ex-* out + *sudare* sweat]

ex·ult (ig·zult′) *v.i.* To rejoice in or as in triumph; take great delight. [<F *exulter* <L *ex(s)ultare,* freq. of *exsilire* leap up <*ex-* out + *salire* leap] —**ex·ult′ing·ly** *adv.*

ex·ul·tant (ig·zul′tənt) *adj.* **1** Rejoicing triumphantly. **2** Denoting great joy. [<L *ex(s)ultans, -antis,* ppr. of *ex(s)ultare.* See EXULT.] —**ex·ul′tant·ly** *adv.*

ex·ul·ta·tion (eg′zul·tā′shən, ek′sul-) *n.* The act or state of exulting; triumphant joy. Also **ex·ul′tance, ex·ul′tan·cy.** [<L *ex(s)ultatio, -onis* <*ex(s)ultare.* See EXULT.]

ex·urb (eks′ûrb′) *n.* A residential area outside a city beyond the suburbs, usually characterized by relative affluence. [<EX- + *-urb* (on analogy with *suburb*) <L *urbs* city] —**ex·urb·an** (eks·ûr′bən) *adj.*

ex·ur·ban·ite (eks·ûr′bən·īt) *n.* One living outside a city in a usually affluent residential area beyond the suburbs, and who commutes to work in the city.

ex·ur·bi·a (eks·ûr′bē·ə) *n.* Exurbs collectively.

ex·u·vi·ae (ig·zōō′vi·ē, ik·sōō′-) *n. pl.* Parts cast off or shed by animals. [<L <*exuere* cast off, undress] —**ex·u′vi·al** *adj.*

ex·u·vi·ate (ig·zōō′vē·āt, ik·sōō′-) *v.t.* & *v.i.* **·at·ed, ·at·ing** To cast off or shed (skin, shell, etc.); slough; molt. —**ex·u′vi·a′tion** *n.*

ex vi ter·mi·ni (eks vī tûr′mə·nī) *Latin* By force of the term.

ey·as (ī′əs) *n.* A young hawk; nestling. [ME *nyas* <F *niais* <L *nidus* a nest; in ME *a nyas* became *an eyas*]

Eyck (īk), **Hubert van,** 1366?–1426, and **Jan van,** 1385?–1440, Flemish painters, brothers; traditional inventors of oil painting.

-ey Var. of -Y[1].

ey·dent (ī′dənt) See EIDENT.

eye[1] (ī) *n.* **1** The organ of vision in animals; especially, the human eye, a nearly spherical mass set in a cavity of the skull and consisting of the cornea, iris, pupil, lens, with associated muscles and optic nerve, also the eyelids, eyelashes, and eyebrows. **2** Ocular perception; sight. **3** Capacity for seeing or discerning. **4** Attentive observation; watchful care. **5** A particular look or expression; mien. **6** Mental or moral vision; estimation; also, regard; desire. **7** Anything that resembles the human organ of sight, or its socket, in shape, place, or office: the *eye* of a needle, the *eye* of a potato, apple, gooseberry, dahlia, etc. **8** *Meteorol.* The calm central area of an advancing hurricane or cyclone: also **eye of the storm.** —**to keep an eye out** or **peeled** To watch for; keep alert. —**to lay eyes on** To see. —*v.t.* **eyed, ey·ing** or **eye·ing 1** To look at carefully; scrutinize. **2** To make a hole in, like the eye of a needle. ◆ Homophones: *aye, I.* [OE *ēage*]

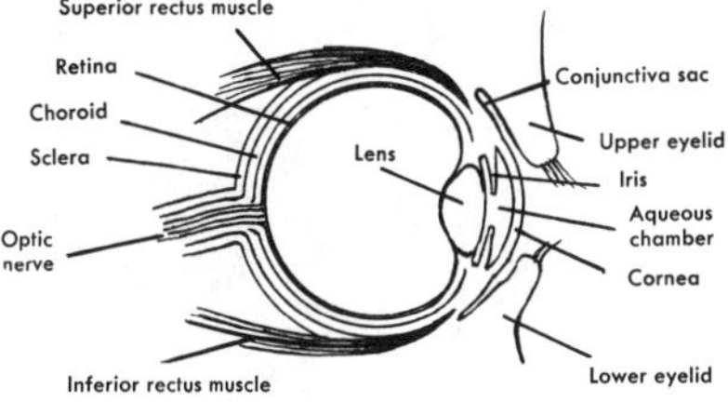

CROSS–SECTION OF THE HUMAN EYE

eye[2] (ī) *n.* A brood, as of pheasants. ◆ Homophones: *aye, I.* [ME *nye* <OF *ni* <L *nidus* a nest: in ME *a nye* was altered to *an eye*]

eye agate A variety of agate with concentric banding which, on cutting and polishing, resembles an eye.

eye•ball (ī′bôl′) *n.* The globe or ball of the eye.

eye bank *Med.* A collection of healthy corneas stored at very low temperatures, for use in transplanting on eyes which have been seriously injured by accident or disease.

eye•bar (ī′bär′) *n. Engin.* A heat-treated steel bar of high tensile strength, usually rectangular in cross-section, with holes punched in the terminal heads for attachment to other structural members, as suspension cables, trusses, etc.

eye•beam (ī′bēm′) *n.* A quick look or glance of the eye.

eye•bolt (ī′bōlt′) *n. Mech.* Any of various forms of bolt having, in place of a head, an eye or ring to receive a rope, hook, etc.

eye•bright (ī′brīt′) *n.* **1** A low annual herb of the figwort family *(Euphrasia officinalis),* formerly used in eye lotions. **2** The red or scarlet pimpernel.

eye•brow (ī′brou′) *n.* **1** The arch over the eye. **2** Its covering, especially the hairs. ◆ Collateral adjective: *superciliary.*

eyebrow pencil A cosmetic pencil used to outline or darken the eyebrows.

eye•cup (ī′kup′) *n.* **1** A small cup of glass or metal, with rim curved to fit the eye, used in applying lotions. **2** *Anat.* An embryonic structure which develops into the retina.

eyed (īd) *adj.* **1** Having eyes: often in composition: *evil-eyed, tender-eyed.* **2** Having eyelike spots, as the peacock's tail; ocellated.

eye•ful (ī′fo͝ol′) *n.* **1** A stare or glance involving full scrutiny of the subject. **2** *Slang* A person, particularly a woman, who is striking in appearance.

eye•glass (ī′glas′, ī′gläs′) *n.* **1** *pl.* A pair of lenses resembling spectacles without bows; a pincenez: frequently called **glass′es. 2** Any lens used to assist vision; a monocle. **3** The glass nearest the eye in a telescope or microscope. **4** An eyecup.

eye•ground (ī′ground′) *n. Anat.* The fundus, or inner side of the back of the eyeball, especially as seen in an ophthalmoscope.

eye•hole (ī′hōl′) *n.* **1** A round opening through which to pass a pin, hook, rope, or the like. **2** A hole or crevice through which one may look; peephole. **3** The socket containing the eye.

eye•hook (ī′ho͝ok′) *n.* A hook permanently attached to a reinforced ring at the end of a rope, chain, etc. See illustration under HOOK.

eye•lash (ī′lash′) *n.* One of the stiff curved hairs growing from the edge of the eyelids. ◆ Collateral adjective: *ciliary.*

eye•less (ī′lis) *adj.* Lacking eyes; deprived of sight.

eye•let (ī′lit) *n.* **1** A small hole or opening; a little eye or aperture. **2** A hole made in canvas, leather, paper, or the like, either bushed with metal or worked around with buttonhole stitch. **3** A metal ring for protecting such a perforation: also **eye′let-ring′. 4** *Entomol.* An ocellus. —*v.t.* To make eyelets in. [< F *oeillet,* dim. of *oeil* an eye]

eye•let•eer (ī′lə•tir′) *n.* An instrument for making eyelet holes; a stiletto.

eye•lid (ī′lid′) *n.* One of the curtains of loose integument that cover the eyeballs in front. ◆ Collateral adjective: *palpebral.*

eye-o•pen•er (ī′ō′pən•ər) *n. U.S.* **1** Anything that opens the eyes, actually or figuratively. **2** An incredible tale or piece of news. **3** *Colloq.* Something enabling one to comprehend what was before a mystery or unheeded. **4** *Colloq.* A drink of liquor, especially one taken early in the morning.

eye•piece (ī′pēs′) *n. Optics* The lens or combination of lenses nearest the eye in a telescope or microscope.

eye rime A rime not phonetically correct, but composed of words similar in spelling: as in *good, flood; move, love.*

eye•ser•vant (ī′sûr′vənt) *n.* One who does his duty only when watched. Also **eye′serv′er.**

eye•ser•vice (ī′sûr′vis) *n.* **1** Duty performed only when the worker is being watched. **2** Admiring glances.

eye shadow A cosmetic preparation, tinted blue, green, black, etc., applied to the eyelids to enhance the eyes.

eye•shot (ī′shot′) *n.* Reach or scope of the eye; view; sight.

eye•sight (ī′sīt′) *n.* **1** The power or sense of sight. **2** Extent of vision; view.

eye•some (ī′səm) *adj.* Pleasant to look at.

eye•sore (ī′sôr′, ī′sōr′) *n.* **1** A diseased place on or near the eye. **2** Anything that offends the sight.

eye speculum An instrument for retracting the eyelids and holding them apart.

eye•splice (ī′splīs′) *n. Naut.* A loop formed by bending back the end of a rope and splicing it into the rope.

eye•spot (ī′spot′) *n. Biol.* **1** One of the rudimentary visual organs of many invertebrates, consisting of a few pigment cells overlaying a nerve filament sensitive to light. **2** The rudimentary eye in an embryo. **3** An ocellus. **4** An eyelike marking.

eye•stalk (ī′stôk′) *n. Zool.* A stalk or peduncle that supports an eye, as in lobsters and crabs.

eye•stone (ī′stōn′) *n.* A small smooth calcareous disk with one side convex, used to remove foreign substances from the eye.

eye•strain (ī′strān′) *n.* An affection caused by excessive or improper use of the eyes.

eye•string (ī′string′) *n. Anat.* A muscle or tendon that holds or moves the eye.

eye•tooth (ī′to͞oth′) *n. pl.* **eye•teeth** One of the upper canine teeth. **—to cut one's eyeteeth** To grow old enough to gain wisdom by experience.

eye•wash (ī′wosh′, ī′wôsh′) *n.* **1** A medicinal wash for the eye. **2** *Slang* Nonsense; bunk.

eye•wa•ter (ī′wô′tər, ī′wot′ər) *n.* **1** The natural water that forms in the eye; tears. **2** A medicated lotion for the eyes.

eye•wink•er (ī′wingk′ər) *n.* An eyelash.

eye•wit•ness (ī′wit′nis) *n.* One who has seen a thing or an occurrence with his own eyes and hence can give testimony about it.

eye worm A nematode worm *(Thelazia californiensis),* whitish in color and about half an inch long, which lives underneath the eyelids and in the tear ducts, causing inflammation and discomfort: parasitic on dogs, sheep, cats, and man.

Ey•lau (ī′lou) A former name for BAGRATIONOVSK. *German* **Preuss•isch Ey•lau** (proi′sish ī′lou).

ey•ra (ī′rə) *n.* The jaguarundi. [< Tupian]

eyre (âr) *n. Obs.* **1** A circuit or journey. **2** A court of circuit judges. **—justices in eyre** Judges who prior to the time of Edward III rode a circuit periodically to hold court in the English shires. [< OF *erre* < L *iter* journey]

Eyre (âr), **Lake** A salt lake in northern South Australia, often dry; 3,430 square miles.

Eyre Peninsula (âr) A peninsula of southern South Australia, between Spencer's Gulf and the Great Australian Bight. Also **Eyre's Peninsula.**

ey•ry, ey•rie (âr′ē, ir′ē) See AERIE.

Eysk (āsk) See EISK.

E•zé•chias (ā•zā•kyäs′) French form of HEZEKIAH. Also *Ital.* **E•ze•chia** (ā•dzā′kyä), *Sp.* **E•ze•quí•as** (ā′thā•kē′äs).

E•ze•ki•el (i•zē′kē•əl, -kyəl; *Du., Ger.* ā•sā′kē•äl) A masculine personal name. Also spelled *Hesekiel.* Also *Fr.* **É•zé•chiel** (ā•zā•kyel′), *Sp.* **E•ze•quiel** (ā′thā•kyel′). [< Hebrew, strength of God]
—**Ezekiel** A major Hebrew prophet of the sixth century B.C.; also, a book of the Old Testament written by him.

E•ze•ki•el (i•zē′kē•əl, -kyəl), **Moses Jacob,** 1844–1917, U.S. sculptor and musician.

Ez•ra (ez′rə) A masculine personal name. [< Hebrew, rising light or helper]
—**Ezra** Hebrew high priest of the fifth century B.C., who originated public preaching, and who wrote, in part, the Old Testament **book of Ezra.** Also *Esdras.*

F

f, F (ef) *pl.* **f's, F's** or **fs, Fs, effs** (efs) *n.* **1** The sixth letter of the English alphabet, from Phoenician *vau,* through Hebrew *vau,* Greek *digamma,* which was early dropped from the Greek alphabet, but was restored by the Romans. **2** The sound of the letter *f,* usually a voiceless labiodental fricative. See ALPHABET. —*symbol* **1** *Music* **a** The fourth tone in the musical scale of C; the pitch of this tone, or the note representing it. **b** The scale built upon F. **c** The bass clef in musical notation. **2** *Chem.* Fluorine (symbol F). **3** *Genetics* A filial generation, usually followed by a subscript numeral, as F_1, F_2, for the first, second, etc., filial generation offspring of a given mating. **4** In education, a grade meaning failure, or, sometimes, fair.

fa (fä) *n.* The fourth tone of any key in music, or of the so-called natural key. [< Ital.]

fa' (fô) *n. Scot.* **1** Lot; luck. **2** Share. **3** Fall. Also spelled *faw.*

fa•ba•ceous (fə•bā′shəs) *adj. Bot.* Designating a very large family *(Leguminosae;* formerly *Fabaceae)* of herbs, shrubs, and trees, characterized by stipulate leaves, irregular flowers, and fruits that are true pods or legumes; the bean or pea family. [< L *fabaceus* leguminous < *faba* a bean]

Fa•bi•an (fā′bē•ən) *adj.* Designating a policy like that of Quintus Fabius Maximus Verrucosus (died 203 B.C.), who, in the Second Punic War with Hannibal, acquired the nickname *Cunctator* or Delayer, because he avoided direct engagements and used dilatory tactics, thereby foiling his antagonist; hence, practicing the policy of delay. —*n.* A member of the Fabian Society. **—Fa′bi•an•ism** *n.* **—Fa′•bi•an•ist** *n.* & *adj.*

Fabian Society An English association of socialists, formed in 1884, including many able writers on economics, having as their object the achievement of socialism by easy stages.

fa•ble (fā′bəl) *n.* **1** A brief story or tale embodying a moral and introducing persons, animals, or inanimate things as speakers and actors. **2** A foolish or improbable story; fabrication. **3** *Archaic* The plot of an epic or dramatic poem. **4** Common talk. See synonyms under ALLEGORY, FICTION. —*v.t.* & *v.i.* **fa•bled, fa•bling** To invent or tell (fables or stories); fabricate; lie. [< OF < L *fabula* < *fari* say, speak] **—fa′bler** *n.*

fa•bled (fā′bəld) *adj.* **1** Recorded in fable; made famous by fable. **2** Existing only in fable; mythical.

fab•li•au (fab′lē•ō, *Fr.* fà•blē•ō′) *n. pl.* **•aux** (-ōz, *Fr.* -ō′) A short, comic or gay tale, usually in eight-syllable verse: the genre which arose in France in the 12th and 13th centuries. [< F, ult. < OF *fable.* See FABLE.]

Fabre (fā′bər, *Fr.* fà′br′), **Jean Henri,** 1823–1915, French entomologist.

fab•ric (fab′rik) *n.* **1** A woven, felted, or knitted material, as cloth, felt, hosiery, or lace; also, the material used in its making. **2** Something that has been fabricated, constructed, or put together; any complex construction. **3** An edifice: St. Paul's, that noble *fabric.* **4** The manner of construction; workmanship; texture: cloth of a very intricate *fabric.* **5** *Geol.* The texture or structure of igneous rock. See synonyms under FRAME. [< OF *fabrique* < L *fabrica* a workshop < *faber* a workman. Doublet of FORGE.]

fab·ri·cant (fab′rə·kənt) *n.* A manufacturer; maker. [<F <L *fabricans, -antis,* ppr. of *fabricare.* See FABRICATE.]

fab·ri·cate (fab′rə·kāt) *v.t.* **·cat·ed, ·cat·ing** **1** To make or manufacture; build. **2** To make by combining parts; assemble. **3** To invent, as lies or reasons; concoct. See synonyms under CONSTRUCT, MAKE. [<L *fabricatus,* pp. of *fabricare* construct <*faber* a workman] — **fab′ri·ca′tor** *n.*

fab·ri·ca·tion (fab′rə·kā′shən) *n.* **1** The art of fabricating. **2** Something fabricated, as a structure or contrivance. **3** A contrived or trumped-up story; a falsehood. See synonyms under DECEPTION, FICTION, LIE.

Fab·ri·koid (fab′rə·koid) *n.* A fabric with cloth base but pyroxylin surface, impervious to water or other fluid: a trade name.

fab·u·list (fab′yə·list) *n.* **1** A composer of fables. **2** One who falsifies or fabricates.

fab·u·lize (fab′yə·līz) *v.i.* **·lized, ·liz·ing** To compose or relate fables or stories. Also *Brit.* **fab′·u·lise.** [<L *fabula* a fable + -IZE]

fab·u·lous (fab′yə·ləs) *adj.* **1** Belonging to fable; fictitious; mythical. **2** Passing the limits of belief; incredible. — **fab′u·lous·ly** *adv.* — **fab′u·lous·ness** *n.*

fa·çade (fə·säd′, fa-; *Fr.* fà·sàd′) *n.* **1** *Archit.* The front or chief face of a building. **2** The front, visible part, or most conspicuous part of an institution, often designed to convey a favorable impression of the whole. [<F <*face* a face, on analogy with Ital. *facciata,* both ult. <L *facies* a face]

face (fās) *n.* **1** The anterior portion of the head, in which the eyes, nose, and mouth are situated, comprising in man the surface between the top of the forehead and the bottom of the chin, and extending laterally from ear to ear. **2** The surface, or most important surface, of anything; a front or working surface; that side or edge presented to view, or to any particular adjustment for operating; a side or surface of a solid: the *face* of a dam, one of the *faces* of a crystal, the *face* of a playing card, the *face* of a molar tooth. **3** The façade. **4** The flat portion of a propeller blade. **5** The flat or rounded striking surface of a hammer. **6** The long outer slope of a bastion; also, that part of the line of defense ending with the curtain and the angle of the shoulder. **7** *Mining* **a** The end of a drift or tunnel. **b** The sharply defined and more important joint in coal running at right angles to the plane of stratification. **8** *Printing* **a** The impression surface of a type body or of a printing plate. **b** The letter or other character cut on the type, or the size or style of the character cut on the type. **9** The dial of a clock or watch. **10** The obverse of a coin, or medal, which bears the effigy; occasionally the reverse side. **11** The inscribed side of a document, or printed side of a sheet. **12** One of the sides of any military formation, as of a square. **13** The external aspect or appearance; look; show; outward effect or impression: He put a bold *face* on the matter. **14** Personal force, influence, opinion, or will, as if expressed in the countenance: He set his *face* steadily against it. **15** Personal presence; immediate cognizance; sight: before the *face* of, to one's *face.* **16** *Colloq.* Effrontery; audacity; assurance. **17** The value as expressed on the written or printed surface: said of any commercial paper, as a note or bond. **18** In golf, the striking side of a club head; the side or slope of a hillock or bunker. — **in the face of** **1** In the presence of; confronting. **2** In opposition to; in defiance of; in spite of. — **to save face** To save one's reputation or standing; protect one's dignity in the opinion of others. — **to lose face** To lose standing or reputation. — **to make faces** To grimace. — *v.* **faced, fac·ing** *v.t.* **1** To bear or turn the face toward; front upon: The house *faces* the street. **2** To cause to turn in a given direction, as soldiers. **3** To meet face to face; confront, as with courage or boldness: to *face* great odds. **4** To realize or be aware of: to *face* facts. **5** To cover with a layer or surface of another material: to *face* brick with stucco or a garment with silk. **6** To make smooth the surface of; dress: to *face* stone. **7** To turn face upward, as a playing card. — *v.i.* **8** To be turned or placed with the face in a given direction: The house *faces* west. **9** To turn in a given direction: The soldiers *faced* right. See synonyms under OPPOSE. — **to face down** To abash or disconcert by a bold stare or audacious manner. — **to face out** To see to completion or endure, as by a persevering manner. — **to face the music** *U.S. Slang* To accept the consequences. — **to face up to** **1** To meet with courage; confront. **2** To realize: become aware of. [<F, ult. <L *facies* a face] — **face′a·ble** *adj.*

face card A playing card bearing the picture of a king, queen, or knave.

face·hard·en (fās′här′dən) *v.t. Metall.* To harden the surface of (steel, iron, etc.), by the addition of carbon in conjunction with great heat.

face-height (fās′hīt′) *n. Anat.* The distance between the gnathion and the nasion. Also **face′-length′.**

face-lift·ing (fās′lif′ting) *n.* An operation that removes or tightens sagging tissues or muscles in the face; plastic surgery of the face.

face pack A cosmetic paste having a mud, clay, or meal base compounded with certain astringents, bleaches, etc., applied thickly to the face and allowed to dry like a mask: also called *beauty pack, facial mask.*

face·plate (fās′plāt′) *n. Mech.* A disk that holds and rotates work, as on a lathe or boring mill.

face powder A cosmetic powder usually having a talc or rice-starch base, applied to the face to dull shiny skin, cover blemishes, etc.

fac·er (fā′sər) *n.* **1** *Colloq.* A blow in the face, as in boxing; hence, any stunning check. **2** *Colloq.* A difficult, challenging, or elusive problem; a poser. **3** *Mech.* An attachment to a machine tool to hold a cutter in facing or surfacing.

fac·et (fas′it) *n.* **1** One of the small plane surfaces cut upon a diamond or other gem. For illustration see DIAMOND. **2** *Archit.* A flat projecting fillet between the flutes of a column. **3** *Zool.* A unit of a compound eye in insects and crustaceans; also, the surface or cornea of such an eye. **4** One side, view, or phase of a subject or of a person's mind or character. **5** *Anat.* A small flat surface on a bone. **6** *Dent.* A flat abraded spot on a tooth: also **fac′ette.** — *v.t.* **fac·et·ed** or **·et·ted, fac·et·ing** or **·et·ting** To cut or work a facet or facets upon. [<F *facette,* dim. of *face* FACE]

fa·cete (fə·sēt′) *adj. Archaic* Clever; witty; humorous. [<L *facetus* splendid, facetious]

fa·ce·ti·ae (fə·sē′shi·ē) *n. pl.* **1** Facetious sayings collectively. **2** Coarsely witty books. [<L]

fa·ce·tious (fə·sē′shəs) *adj.* Indulging in, characterized by, or marked by wit or humor; jocular; jocose; waggish; witty; funny; humorous. See synonyms under HUMOROUS, JOCOSE, MERRY. [<L *facetia* wit + -OUS] — **fa·ce′tious·ly** *adv.* — **fa·ce′tious·ness** *n.*

face value See under VALUE.

fa·cial (fā′shəl) *adj.* Of, near, or affecting the face. — *n. Colloq.* A massage or other treatment of the face for the purpose of enhancing health and beauty of facial skin.

facial angle *Anat.* The angle subtended between the line representing the face-height and the axis of the skull from the edge of central incisors to the auricular point.

FACIAL ANGLE
a. Glabella.
c. Edge of central incisors.
f. Auricular point.
acf. Facial angle.

facial index A number expressing the ratio of the breadth to the length of the face.

facial mask A face pack.

facial nerve *Anat.* The seventh cranial nerve, one of a pair which actuate the muscles controlling facial expression.

fa·ci·end (fā′shē·end) *n. Math.* An operand. [<L *faciendum,* neut. gerundive of *facere* do]

-facient *suffix* Causing; making: *sorbefacient.* [<L *faciens, -entis,* ppr. of *facere* do]

fa·ci·es (fā′shi·ēz) *n.* **1** The general aspect or external appearance of anything. **2** *Geol.* The aggregate of the characteristics which determine the origin, composition, and mode of formation of rock deposits. **3** *Med.* The expression of the face in a given disease. **4** A surface. [<L, face, appearance]

fac·ile (fas′il) *adj.* **1** Easy of performance. **2** Easily gained; readily mastered. **3** Easily moved or persuaded; pliant; yielding. **4** Ready or quick in performance; dexterous; skilful. [<F <L *facilis* easy to do <*facere* do] — **fac′ile·ly** *adv.* — **fac′ile·ness** *n.*

fa·ci·le prin·ceps (fas′ə·lē prin′seps) *Latin* Unquestionably first or foremost.

fa·ci·lis de·scen·sus A·ver·no (fas′ə·lis di·sen′səs ə·vûr′nō) or **A·ver·ni** (ə·vûr′nī) *Latin* Easy is the descent into Avernus (hell).

fa·cil·i·tate (fə·sil′ə·tāt) *v.t.* **·tat·ed, ·tat·ing** To make easier or more convenient. — **fa·cil′i·ta′tion** *n.*

fa·cil·i·ty (fə·sil′ə·tē) *n. pl.* **·ties** **1** Ease or readiness in doing; dexterity. **2** Readiness of compliance; pliancy. **3** *pl.* Any aid or convenience: *facilities* for travel. **4** A place or office equipped to fulfill a special function: a government *facility.* [<L *facilitas, -tatis* ability <*facere* do]

fac·ing (fā′sing) *n.* **1** A covering in front serving any purpose. **2** A covering plate or layer in front, for ornament or protection against wear or corrosion, or to alter the contour. **3** The lining of a garment on parts exposed by being turned back, as the lapel of a coat or a hem, cuff, etc. **4** Any heavy, durable fabric used for this. **5** An improvement to the appearance of a food product, as by the addition of coloring matter. **6** *Mech.* A smooth, machined surface for attachment to another part. **7** *pl.* The different-colored collars and cuffs on a military uniform, often indicative of the branch of the service.

fac·sim·i·le (fak·sim′ə·lē) *n.* An exact copy or reproduction, often differing in scale but always identical or closely imitative in detail, material, etc. See synonyms under DUPLICATE. — *adj.* **1** Exactly copied or reproduced; exactly similar or corresponding: a *facsimile* autograph. **2** Producing exact copies or facsimiles. [<L *fac simile* make like]

facsimile telegraph An apparatus for telegraphing messages, designs, drawings, etc., in facsimile. Compare TELAUTOGRAPH.

fact (fakt) *n.* **1** Anything that is done or happens, as an act or deed. **2** Anything actually existent. **3** Any statement strictly true; truth; reality. **4** *pl. Law* The issues raised by the pleadings and evidence in an action and upon which the jury must base their verdict. **5** *Obs.* A thing done; a deed; performance. See synonyms under CIRCUMSTANCE, EVENT, PROOF. [<L *factum* <*facere* do. Doublet of FEAT.]

fact-find·ing (fakt′fīn′ding) *n.* The ascertainment of facts or conditions. —*adj.* Collecting facts and information: a *fact-finding* commission.

fac·tice (fak′tis) *n.* A fluffy, rubberlike material obtained by vulcanizing linseed oil with sulfur or sulfur chloride. [<F <L *factitius.* See FACTITIOUS.]

fac·tion (fak′shən) *n.* **1** A number of persons combined for a common purpose. **2** A party within a party; an irregular association of partisans; a cabal. **3** Violent opposition, as to a government; turbulence; dissension. See synonyms under CABAL. [<F <L *factio, -onis* <*facere* do. Doublet of FASHION.] — **fac′tion·ist,** *Obs.* **fac′tion·ar′y** *n.*

fac·tion·al (fak′shən·əl) *adj.* Of or pertaining to a faction. — **fac′tion·al·ism** *n.*

fac·tious (fak′shəs) *adj.* Given to, characterized by, or promoting faction; turbulent; partisan. See synonyms under PERVERSE. — **fac′tious·ly** *adv.* — **fac′tious·ness** *n.*

fac·ti·tious (fak·tish′əs) *adj.* **1** Artificial; conventional; affected; unnatural. **2** Proceeding from or created by art as opposed to nature. [<L *factitius* artificial <*facere* do] — **fac·ti′tious·ly** *adv.* — **fac·ti′tious·ness** *n.*

Synonyms: affected, artificial, manufactured, pretended, sham, simulated, spurious.

fac·ti·tive (fak′tə·tiv) *adj. Gram.* Pertaining to or designating a verb which takes, in addition to an object, a characterizing complement. Examples: They elected *him president*; He called *John* a *villain.* [<NL *factitivus*

<*factitare,* freq. of *facere* do] **—fac′ti·tive·ly** *adv.*

fac·tor (fak′tər) *n.* **1** *Math.* One of two or more quantities that, when multiplied together, produce a given quantity. **2** One of several elements or causes that produce a result. **3** *Brit.* A commission merchant; agent. **4** *Scot.* A bailiff or steward; also, a person legally appointed to care for forfeited property. **5** *U.S.* In some States, a garnishee. **6** A specialized commercial banker who finances manufacturers and dealers, accepting receivables as collateral. **7** The unit of heredity. See GENE. **8** *Physiol.* An element important in metabolism and nutrition, as a vitamin, enzyme, or hormone. **9** The agent controlling one of the remaining posts of the Hudson's Bay Company. See synonyms under AGENT. **—*v.t.*** **1** To manage as a factor. **2** *Math.* To resolve into factors; factorize. [<L, maker <*facere* make]

fac·tor·age (fak′tər·ij) *n.* **1** A factor's commission. **2** The conduct of a factor's business.

fac·to·ri·al (fak·tôr′ē·əl, -tō′rē-) *n. Math.* The product of a series of consecutive positive integers from 1 to a given number; thus, *factorial* four (written 4! or ⌊4) = 1 × 2 × 3 × 4 = 24. **—*adj.*** Pertaining to a factor or a factorial.

fac·tor·ize (fak′tə·rīz) *v.t.* **·ized, ·iz·ing** **1** *Law* To garnishee. **2** *Math.* To convert into factors. **—fac′tor·i·za′tion** *n.*

fac·tor·ship (fak′tər·ship) *n.* **1** The business of a factor or a factory. **2** A body of factors.

fac·to·ry (fak′tər·ē) *n. pl.* **·ries** **1** An establishment devoted to the manufacture of something, including the building or buildings and machinery necessary to such manufacture; a manufactory. **2** A business establishment in charge of factors or agents in a foreign country.

fac·to·tum (fak·tō′təm) *n.* An employee hired to do all kinds of work. [<Med. L <*fac,* sing. imperative of *facere* do + *totum* everything]

fac·tu·al (fak′chōō·əl) *adj.* Pertaining to, containing, or consisting of facts; literal and exact; genuine.

fac·tu·al·ly (fak′chōō·əl·ē) *adv.* In factual form; actually.

fac·u·la (fak′yə·lə) *n. pl.* **·lae** (-lē) *Astron.* A small spot on the sun brighter than the rest of the photosphere. [<L, dim. of *fax* torch]

fac·ul·ta·tive (fak′əl·tā′tiv) *adj.* **1** Producing or imparting faculty or power; enabling; qualifying. **2** Endowing with authority or power, but allowing the use of it at option or contingently. **3** Empowering but not requiring one to perform some act; providing, as a law, for optional action: distinguished from *obligative.* **4** *Biol.* Having the power to exist in and become adapted to changed conditions, as aerobic bacteria, which may become anaerobic: distinguished from *obligate.* **5** Related or pertaining to a faculty or faculties.

fac·ul·ty (fak′əl·tē) *n. pl.* **·ties** **1** Any mode of bodily or mental behavior regarded as implying a natural endowment or acquired power: the *faculty* of seeing, feeling, reasoning. **2** Any special form of skill, or unusual ability, whether natural or acquired; knack; turn; native facility. **3** One of the native complex capacities or powers into which the older psychology analyzed, and to which it ascribed, the phenomena of conscious mental life: the *faculty* of perception, memory, thought, etc. **4** The members of any one of the learned professions, collectively: the *faculty* of law or medicine. **5** The body of instructors in a university, college, or higher educational institution. **6** A department of learning or instruction at a university: the English *faculty.* **7** In the Roman Catholic Church, the right to perform certain ecclesiastical functions, bestowed by a prelate upon a subordinate; formerly, also, power or privilege in general bestowed or otherwise obtained: chiefly in the plural. **8** Ability to do or manage: executive skill and efficiency, especially in domestic matters: a housekeeper of notable *faculty.* **9** Pecuniary resources; means. See synonyms under ABILITY. [<OF *faculté* <L *facultas, -tatis* <*facilis.* See FACILE.]

fad (fad) *n.* A passing fancy or fashion; hobby. [Cf. dial. E *fad* be busy with trifles] **—fad′dist** *n.*

fad·dle (fad′l) *Brit. Dial. v.t.* & *v.i.* **·dled, ·dling** To dandle; toy; trifle. **—*n.*** A toy; trifle; fad.

fad·dom (fad′əm) *v.t. Scot.* To fathom; measure.

fad·dy (fad′ē) *adj.* **·di·er, ·di·est** *Colloq.* Full of, given to, or like fads. Also **fad′dish.**

fade (fād) *v.* **fad·ed, fad·ing** *v.i.* **1** To lose brightness or clearness; become indistinct; dim. **2** To lose freshness, vigor, youth, etc.; wither; wane. **—*v.t.*** **3** To cause to fade. **4** *U.S. Slang* In dice, to cover (a bet). **—to fade in** In motion pictures, to come into view gradually. **—to fade out** In motion pictures, to disappear gradually. See synonyms under DIE[1]. [<OF *fader* <*fade* pale, insipid]

fade–a·way (fād′ə·wā′) *n.* In baseball, a slow, curved ball, seemingly pitched fast, that breaks inward toward the batter.

fade–in (fād′in′) *n.* A gradual appearance of a motion–picture sequence on the screen, often, as by double exposure, etc., replacing a preceding sequence.

fade·less (fād′lis) *adj.* Unfading. See synonyms under ETERNAL. **—fade′less·ly** *adv.*

fade–out (fād′out′) *n.* A gradual disappearance of a motion–picture sequence on the screen.

fad·er (fā′dər) *n.* In motion pictures, a potentiometer for the control of sound volume in reproduction, or for controlling the amount of light in developing the film.

fad·ing (fā′ding) *n. Telecom.* A lessening in the strength of electromagnetic signals owing to increased distance from the transmitting station, atmospheric condition, or mechanical defect.

fae·ces (fē′sēz), **fae·cal** (fē′kəl), etc. See FECES, etc.

Fa·en·za (fä·en′zə, *Ital.* fä·en′dzä) A city in north central Italy: ancient *Faventia.*

fa·er·ie (fā′ə·rē, fâr′ē) *n.* **1** The imaginary world inhabited by fairies. **2** *Archaic* A fairy. **—*adj. Archaic*** Of or pertaining to fairies or fairyland. [See FAIRY]

Faerie Queene An allegorical romance of chivalry by Edmund Spenser, planned in twelve books, of which only six were published (1590–96).

Faer·oe Islands (fâr′ō) A group of 21 Danish islands in the North Atlantic; 540 square miles; capital, Thorshavn: also *Faroe Islands.* Also **Faer′oes,** *Danish* **Faer·ö·er·ne** (fer·œ′er·nə).

Faf·nir (fäv′nir, fäf′-) In Norse mythology, the dragon who guards the hoard of the Nibelungs; slain by Sigurd. Also **Faf′ner.**

fag (fag) *v.* **fagged, fag·ging** *v.i.* **1** To weary oneself by working. **2** To work or serve as a fag. **—*v.t.*** **3** To tire out by hard work. **4** To make a fag of. **—*n.*** **1** One who does menial service for another, as in English public schools. **2** A piece of drudgery. **3** *Slang* A cigarette. **4** *Slang* A male homosexual. [? Alter. of *flag*[3]] **—fag′ger** *n.*

fa·ga·ceous (fə·gā′shəs) *adj. Bot.* Of or pertaining to a large family *(Fagaceae)* of trees and shrubs having alternate simple leaves, sterile flowers, and one–celled, one–seeded nuts; the beech family. [<NL *Fagaceae,* the beech family <L *fagus* a beech]

fag–end (fag′end′) *n.* **1** The frayed end, as of a rope. **2** A remnant or last part, usually of slight utility.

fag·got (fag′ət) *n.* **1** See FAGOT. **2** *Slang* A male homosexual. [Origin unknown]

Fa·gin (fā′gin) In Dickens's *Oliver Twist,* an old thief–trainer into whose hands Oliver fell.

fag·ot (fag′ət) *n.* **1** A bundle of sticks, twigs, or branches, as used for fuel. **2** A bundle of pieces of wrought iron or steel to be worked over. **—*v.t.*** **1** To make a fagot of. **2** To ornament by fagoting. Also *faggot.* [<F]

fag·ot·ing (fag′ət·ing) *n.* A mode of ornamenting textile fabrics, in which a number of threads of a material are drawn out and the cross–threads tied together in the middle; in basketry, hemstitching. Also **fag′got·ing.**

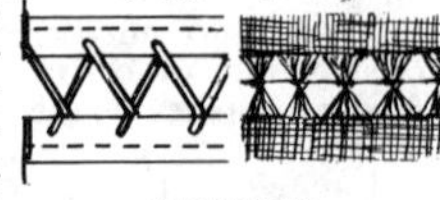

FAGOTING
Hemstitch Drawn work

fahl·band (fäl′band′, *Ger.* fäl′bänt′) *n. Geol.* A band or stratum of rock containing metallic sulfides. [<G <*fahl* pale + *band* band]

Fahr·en·heit (far′ən·hīt, *Ger.* fär′ən·hīt) *adj.* **1** Designating a temperature scale in which zero is the temperature of a mixture of equal weights of snow and common salt; the freezing point of water is 32° and the boiling point 212°, all under standard atmospheric pressure. **2** Noting a thermometer graduated to this scale. Abbr. *F.* or *Fahr.* See TEMPERATURE. [after Gabriel Daniel *Fahrenheit,* 1686–1736, German physicist]

fa·ience (fī·äns′, fā-; *Fr.* fà·yäns′) *n.* A variety of majolica, usually highly decorated. [<F, pottery from Faenza]

fail (fāl) *v.i.* **1** To be unsuccessful; be unable. **2** To be deficient or wanting, as in ability, faithfulness, etc.; prove disappointing: He *failed* in his duty. **3** To give out: His strength *failed.* **4** To become extinct; die out. **5** To fade away; disappear: The light *failed* rapidly. **6** To weaken gradually, as in illness or death. **7** To become insolvent; go bankrupt. **8** To receive a failing grade. **—*v.t.*** **9** To prove to be inadequate or of no help to; abandon; forsake: My courage *fails* me. **10** To leave undone or unfulfilled; neglect: with infinitive as object: He *failed* to carry out orders. **11** In education: **a** To receive a failing grade in (a course or test). **b** To assign a failing grade to (a pupil). See synonyms under FALL, SUSPEND. **—*n.*** Failure: in the phrase *without fail.* [<OF *faillir* <L *fallere* to deceive]

fail·ing (fā′ling) *n.* A minor fault; foible; infirmity. See synonyms under FOIBLE. **—*adj.*** **1** Characterized by failure. **2** Diminishing; weakening. **—fail′ing·ly** *adv.*

faille (fāl, fīl; *Fr.* fà′y′) *n.* An untwilled silk dress fabric having a light grain or cord. [<F]

fail–safe (fāl′sāf′) *adj.* **1** Utilizing a system that makes automatic adjustments in the event of operational failure to assure satisfactory performance. **2** *Mil.* Describing a system that automatically prevents a nation's own military aircraft from carrying out planned bombing missions without specific confirming authority.

fail·ure (fāl′yər) *n.* **1** The act of failing, cessation of supply, power, etc.: *failure* of sight. **2** A becoming bankrupt or proving unsuccessful in business or in any profession or trade. **3** Neglect or non–performance. **4** That which fails; anything unsuccessful. **5** One who fails conspicuously or in some specific effort. See synonyms under LOSS, MISFORTUNE, NEGLECT. [Earlier *failer* <AF, orig. var. of OF *faillir.* See FAIL.]

fain (fān) *adj. Archaic & Poetic* **1** Reluctantly willing; content. **2** Glad; rejoiced. **3** Eager; desirous. **—*adv.*** Gladly: with *would* and infinitive: He would *fain* depart. ◆ Homophones: *fane, feign.* [OE *fægen*]

fai·naigue (fə·nāg′) *v.t.* & *v.i.* **·naigued, ·nai·guing** *Dial.* To finagle; revoke; cheat. [? <FEIGN] **—fai·nai′guer** *n.*

fai·né·ant (fā′nē·ənt, *Fr.* fe·nā·äṅ′) *adj.* Ineffective; lazy; useless. **—*n.*** An idler; a do-nothing. [<F <*faire* do + *néant* nothing]

faint (fānt) *v.i.* **1** To lose consciousness; swoon: often with *away.* **2** *Archaic* To fail in courage or hope. **3** *Obs.* To become weak. See synonyms under FALL. [<*adj.*] **—*adj.*** **1** Lacking in purpose, courage, or energy; timid. **2** Ready to faint; weak. **3** Evincive of weakness, feebleness, or lack of purpose; slight. **4** Indistinct; feeble; dim. **—*n.*** A swoon; syncope: also **faint′ing.** ◆ Homophone: *feint.* [<OF, pp. of *faindre* FEIGN] **—faint′er** *n.* **—faint′ish** *adj.* **—faint′ish·ness** *n.* **—faint′ly** *adv.* **—faint′ness** *n.*

Synonyms (adj.): dim, exhausted, faded, faint–hearted, faltering, fatigued, feeble, half–hearted, ill–defined, indistinct, irresolute, languid, listless, purposeless, timid, weak, wearied, worn. *Faint,* with the general sense of lacking strength or effectiveness, covers a wide range of meaning, signifying overcome by physical weakness or exhaustion, or lacking in purpose, courage, or energy, as said of persons; or lacking definiteness or distinctness of color or sound, as said of written characters, voices, or musical notes. A person may be *faint* when physically *wearied,* or when overcome by fear; he may be a *faint* adherent because naturally *feeble* or *purposeless,* or because *half–hearted* in the cause; he may be a *faltering* supporter because naturally *irresolute* or because *faint–hearted* and *timid* in view of perils that threaten, a *listless* worker, through want of mental energy and purpose. Written characters may be *faint* or *dim,* either because originally written with poor ink, or because they have become *faded* by time and exposure. *Antonyms:* bright, brilliant, clear, conspicuous, daring, energetic, fresh, hearty, resolute, strong, sturdy, vigorous.

faint–heart·ed (fānt′här′tid) *adj.* Timorous;

cowardly. **—faint′-heart′ed·ly** *adv.* **—faint′-heart′ed·ness** *n.*

faints (fānts) *n. pl.* The dilute and impure spirit produced during the first and last stages of the distillation of whisky: also spelled *feints.*

fair[1] (fâr) *adj.* **1** Free from clouds; not obscure; sunshiny; clear. Compare def. 13. **2** Open; distinct. **3** Free from spot or blemish. **4** Showing no partiality, prejudice, or favoritism; hence, just, upright; honest. **5** Having light or clear color or hue; not dark or sallow: *fair* hair or complexion. **6** Pleasing to the eye or the mind; comely; beautiful. **7** Nearly or fully up to the average; moderately satisfactory or excellent; passably good or large: a *fair* crop. **8** Easily legible; well-formed and distinct: a *fair* print; a *fair* handwriting. **9** Apparently good and plausible, but not sincere: *fair* promises. **10** Accurately trimmed; even; regular; flowing: said of timbers, lines, or the like. **11** In games and sports, according to rule: a *fair* tackle, *fair* walking. **12** In a favorable direction: *fair* wind. **13** *Meteorol.* Having the sky cloudless to half covered with clouds; no aspect of rain, snow, or hail; fine; bright; sunny. **14** Properly open to attack: He is *fair* game. See synonyms under BEAUTIFUL, CANDID, GOOD, HONEST, JUST[1], PURE, RIGHT. —*adv.* **1** In a spirit of justice and reason: fairly, justly; honestly: deal *fair* with me. **2** In clear view; distinctly: *fair* in sight. **3** Favorably; fortunately; happily; to bid *fair.* **4** Politely; kindly; plausibly: to speak *fair.* **5** *Obs.* Deliberately; quietly. —*v.t.* To make smooth, as timbers. —*v.i. Dial.* To become fair or clear: said of weather. —*n.* **1** A fair one; sweetheart. **2** Women: with *the*: also *the fair sex.* **3** *Obs.* Good fortune; good luck. **4** *Obs.* Beauty. **—for fair** For sure. ◆ Homophone: *fare.* [OE *fæger*] **—fair′ness** *n.*

fair[2] (fâr) *n.* **1** An exhibit and sale of fancywork, etc., for the especial benefit of some object. **2** An occasional or periodical exhibit of agricultural products, manufactures, or other articles of value or interest: a county *fair,* an industrial *fair.* **3** A stated or regular market; a gathering of buyers and sellers. ◆ Homophone: *fare.* [<OF *feire* <L *feria* a holiday]

fair-and-square (fâr′ənd·skwâr′) *adj.* Thoroughly fair-dealing and honest. —*adv.* In a straightforward way; honestly.

Fair·banks (fâr′bangks), **Douglas,** 1883–1939, U.S. film actor.

Fair·banks (fâr′bangks) A town in east central Alaska, the northern terminus of the Alaska Highway.

fair catch **1** In football, the catch of a kicked ball by a defensive player who has signaled that he will not attempt a runback, and who therefore may not be tackled or interfered with without penalty. **2** In Rugby football, a ball caught in a manner that entitles the catching team to an extra kick.

fair copy **1** The copy of a document made after final corrections and revisions. **2** The state of such a copy.

fair cow *Austral. Slang.* Cow (def. 2).

Fair Deal The domestic program and policies of the administration of President Truman, as set forth in his State of the Union message to the U.S. Congress, January 5, 1949.

fair fa′ (faw) *Scot.* Good luck to.

fair-faced (fâr′fāst′) *adj.* **1** Having a fair face. **2** Specious.

Fair·fax (fâr′faks), **Thomas,** 1612–71, third Baron Fairfax, English Parliamentary leader.

fair green In golf, a fairway.

fair·ground (fâr′ground′) *n.* The ground or enclosure in which a fair is held.

fair-haired (fâr′hârd′) *adj.* **1** Flaxen-haired. **2** Favorite.

fair·ing[1] (fâr′ing) *n. Aeron.* **1** In airplanes, an auxiliary structure designed to reduce drag, or head resistance, of the part to which it is attached. Also called *fillet.* **2** The operation of shaping the contour of a part to obtain maximum aerodynamic efficiency. [<FAIR[1] (def. 10) + -ING[3]]

fair·ing[2] (fâr′ing) *n. Archaic* A present bought at a fair; reward. Also *Scot.* **fair′in.**

fair·ish (fâr′ish) *adj.* Moderately good, well, or large; passable.

fair lead *Naut.* **1** Such direction of a rope as will prevent it from chafing or fouling. **2** A protective guide for a rope, usually a ring or a perforated board through which rigging is passed.

fair-lead·er (fâr′lē′dər) *n. Naut.* A perforated block or a cringle for giving a rope a fair lead.

fair·ly (fâr′lē) *adv.* **1** In a just manner; equitably; properly. **2** Moderately; tolerably: a *fairly* tall building. **3** Positively; completely: The crowd *fairly* roared. **4** Clearly; distinctly. **5** *Obs.* Handsomely; courteously. **6** *Obs.* Softly; gently.

fair-mind·ed (fâr′mīn′did) *adj.* Free from bias or bigotry; open to reason; honest-minded. **—fair′mind′ed·ness** *n.*

Fair Oaks A locality east of Richmond, Virginia; scene of an indecisive Civil War battle, 1862: also *Seven Pines.*

fair play **1** Fairness in playing, contending, debating, etc. **2** The ideal and practice of justice, unaffected by prejudice or partiality.

fair sex Women.

fair shake *Slang* A fair chance or treatment.

fair-spo·ken (fâr′spō′kən) *adj.* Having grace of speech; plausible.

fair-trade (fâr′trād′) *v.t.* **-trad·ed, -trad·ing** To set a price no less than the manufacturer's minimum price on (a branded or trademarked product). —*adj.* Of or pertaining to such a price.

fair·wa·ter (fâr′wô′tər, -wot′ər) *n.* A streamlined covering of metal or plastic shaped to fit over the superstructures of a submarine as a protection against the mechanical and chemical action of sea water.

fair·way (fâr′wā′) *n.* **1** The proper course through a channel or harbor. **2** That part of a links or golf course, between the several tees and putting greens, on which the grass is constantly kept short: also called *fair green.*

fair-weath·er (fâr′weth′ər) *adj.* **1** Suitable for or restricted to fair weather, as a racetrack. **2** Useful or dependable only in favorable circumstances; not helpful in adversity: *fair-weather* friends.

Fair·weath·er (fâr′weth′ər), **Mount** Highest peak (15,300 feet) of the **Fairweather Range** in SE Alaska.

fair·y (fâr′ē) *n. pl.* **fair·ies** **1** An imaginary being, ordinarily of small and graceful human form, capable of working good or ill to mankind. **2** *Slang* A male homosexual. —*adj.* **1** Of or pertaining to fairies. **2** Resembling fairies. Also *Obs. faery* or *faerie.* [<OF *faerie* enchantment <*fae.* See FAY[2].] **—fair′y·like′** *adj.*

fairy gloves Digitalis; foxglove.

fair·y·hood (fâr′ē·ho͝od) *n.* **1** Enchantment by fairies. **2** Fairy nature or characteristics. **3** The race of fairies.

fair·y·ism (fâr′ē·iz′əm) *n.* **1** Belief in fairies; fairy lore. **2** Resemblance to fairies or to their supposed habitations, customs, or characteristics.

fair·y·land (fâr′ē·land′) *n.* The fancied abode of the fairies.

fairy rings Circles in lawns or pastures, usually caused by the spreading of the mycelia of certain fungi, but popularly said to be made by fairies.

fairy stone **1** A fossil sea urchin or echinite. **2** A stone arrowhead. **3** A variously shaped concretion found in alluvial clays in Scotland.

fairy tale **1** A tale about fairies; an imaginative or legendary story. **2** An incredible statement.

fairy wand Blazing star (def. 1).

Fai·sal (fī′səl) See FEISAL.

fait ac·com·pli (fe·tȧ·kôṅ·plē′) *French* A thing done beyond recall or opposition; literally, an accomplished fact.

faith (fāth) *n.* **1** Belief without evidence. **2** Confidence in or dependence on a person, statement, or thing as trustworthy. ◆ Collateral adjective: *fiducial.* **3** Belief in God or the testimony of God as revealed in Scripture. **4** A doctrine or system of doctrines, propositions, etc., held to be true: the Christian *faith.* **5** Anything given adherence or credence: a man's political *faith.* **6** Allegiance or loyal adherence to something; faithfulness: to pledge *faith* in a venture. **—bad faith** Deceit; dishonesty. **—in faith** Indeed; truly. **—in good faith** Honestly; with honorable intentions. **—to break faith** **1** To betray one's principles or beliefs. **2** To fail to keep a promise. **—to keep faith** **1** To adhere to one's principles or beliefs. **2** To keep a promise. —*interj.* In truth; indeed. [<OF *feit, feid* <L *fides* < *fidere* trust]

Synonyms (noun): assent, assurance, belief, confidence, conviction, credence, credit, creed, doctrine, opinion, reliance, trust. *Belief,* as an intellectual process, is the acceptance of something as true on other grounds than personal observation and experience. We give *credence* to a report, *assent* to a proposition or to a proposal. *Belief* is stronger than *credence*; *credence* might be described as a prima-facie *belief*; *credence* is a more formal word than *belief,* and seems to imply somewhat more of volition; we speak of giving *credence* to a report, but not of giving *belief.* Goods are sold on *credit*; we give one *credit* for good intentions. *Conviction* is a *belief* established by argument or evidence; *assurance* is *belief* beyond the reach of argument; as, the Christian's *assurance* of salvation. *Faith* is a union of *belief* and *trust. Faith* is often personal; *belief* may be quite impersonal, but as soon as a *belief* is strong enough to be followed by definite action, the *belief* becomes *faith.* In religion it is common to distinguish between intellectual *belief* of religious truth, as any other truth might be believed, and *belief* of the heart, or saving *faith.* Compare FIDELITY, OPINION, RELIGION, TRUST. *Antonyms*: denial, disbelief, dissent, distrust, doubt, incredulity, infidelity, misgiving, rejection, skepticism, suspicion, unbelief.

faith cure **1** The alleged cure of disease by virtue of prayer, with faith in its efficacy. **2** The procedure, prescribed acts, etc., to effect such cure.

faith·ful (fāth′fəl) *adj.* **1** True or trustworthy in the performance of duty, especially in the fulfilment of promises, obligations, vows, and the like: a *faithful* servant, *faithful* to one's agreement. **2** True in detail; accurate in correspondence, or exact in description: a *faithful* copy. **3** Truthful; worthy of belief or confidence: a *faithful* witness, a *faithful* saying. **4** Full of faith; strong or firm in faith: *faithful* convictions. **—the faithful** **1** In the early church, all true believers in God. **2** The members in good standing of the Christian church, or any part of it. **3** In Islam, the followers of Mohammed. **4** The devoted members of a group or organization. **—faith′ful·ly** *adv.* **—faith′ful·ness** *n.*

Synonyms: devoted, firm, incorruptible, loyal, staunch, sure, true, trustworthy, trusty, unwavering. A person is *faithful* who will keep faith, whether with or without power to aid or serve; a person or thing is *trusty* that possesses such qualities as to justify the fullest confidence and dependence. We may speak of a *faithful* but feeble friend; we say a *trusty* agent, a *trusty* steed, a *trusty* sword. See HONEST, MORAL. *Antonyms*: capricious, faithless, false, fickle, unfaithful, untrue, untrustworthy.

faith healer One who heals by faith cures.

faith·less (fāth′lis) *adj.* **1** Untrue to promise or obligation; unfaithful; disloyal. **2** Tending or calculated to delude; deceptive and unreliable. **3** Lacking in or devoid of faith, especially in the Christian religion. See synonyms under PERFIDIOUS. **—faith′less·ly** *adv.* **—faith′less·ness** *n.*

fai·tor (fā′tər) *n. Obs.* A deceiver or rogue; an impostor. Also **fai′tour.** [<AF *faitour* <L *factor* a doer. See FACTOR.]

Fai·yum (fī·yo͞om′) A province of Upper Egypt; 686 square miles; capital, Faiyum: also *Fayum, El Faiyum.*

Fai·za·bad (fī′zə·bad, fī′zä·bäd′) **1** A town in NE Afghanistan. **2** A city in east central Uttar Pradesh, India: formerly *Fyzabad.*

Fa·ka·ra·va (fä′kə·rä′və) The second largest of the Tuamotu islands, French Oceania. Formerly *Wittgenstein Island.*

fake[1] (fāk) *n. Colloq.* Anything or any person not genuine; a counterfeit. —*adj.* Spurious. —*v.* **faked, fak·ing** *v.t.* **1** To make up and attempt to pass off as genuine: to *fake* a pedigree. **2** To simulate; feign: to *fake* gratitude. **3** To improvise, as in music or a play. —*v.i.* **4** To practice faking. [? Var.

of obs. *feague, feak* <Du. *vegen* beat, dust off]

fake[2] (fāk) *n. Naut.* A single coil or turn of a rope or cable. —*v.t.* **faked, fak·ing** To coil, as a rope. [Origin uncertain]

fak·er (fā′kər) *n. Colloq.* **1** A street vendor or other person who sells fakes or notions. **2** One who originates a fake, humbug, or swindling contrivance.

fak·er·y (fā′kər·ē) *n. pl.* **·er·ies** *Colloq.* The practice of faking; a deceptive imitation.

fa·kir (fə·kir′, fā′kər) *n.* **1** A Mohammedan ascetic, religious mendicant, or mendicant priest. **2** Loosely, a Hindu Yogi or mendicant devotee. Also **fa·keer** (fə·kir′). [<Arabic *faqīr* poor]

fa–la (fä′lä, fə·lä′) *n.* **1** A refrain in old songs. **2** An old simple style of part song. Also spelled *fal–la.*

Fa·laise (fâ·lez′) A town in NW France, ancient seat of the Dukes of Normandy; scene of heavy fighting (1944) in World War II.

Fa·lange (fā′lanj, fə·lanj′; *Sp.* fä·läng′hā) The official fascist party of Spain. [<Sp., a phalanx]

Fa·lan·gist (fə·lan′jist) *n.* A member of the fascist party in Spain.

fal·ba·la (fal′bə·lə) *n. Obs.* A furbelow; flounce. [<F; ult. origin uncertain]

fal·cate (fal′kāt) *adj.* Sickle– or scythe–shaped: also **fal′cat·ed.** —*n.* A sickle–shaped figure. [<L *falcatus* <*falx, falcis* sickle] —**fal·ca′·tion** *n.*

fal·chion (fôl′chən, -shən) *n.* A sword of the Middle Ages with a broad and slightly curved blade; hence, poetically, any sword. [<OF *fauchon,* ult. <L *falx, falcis* a sickle]

fal·ci·form (fal′sə·fôrm) *adj.* Curved like a sickle; falcate.

fal·con (fôl′kən, fô′-, fal′-) *n.* **1** A diurnal bird of prey (genus *Falco*) used by falconers; especially, the peregrine falcon (*F. peregrinus*), with long, pointed wings, the hobby, merlin, or gerfalcon. **2** A falconine bird, whether used in falconry or not, having the upper mandible toothed, and circular nostrils, as a kestrel, duck hawk, prairie falcon (*F. mexicanus*), or sparrow hawk. **3** A small cannon of the 15th–17th centuries, firing a shot of around six pounds. [<OF *faucon, falcun* <LL *falco, -onis* <L *falx, falcis* a sickle]

FALCON

fal·con·er (fôl′kən·ər, fô′-, fal′-) *n.* One who breeds, trains or hunts with falcons for sport.

fal·co·net (fôl′kə·net, fô′-, fal′-) *n.* **1** A little falcon. **2** A small cannon of the 16th century.

fal·con–gen·tle (fôl′kən·jen′təl, fô′-, fal′-) *n.* **1** The European goshawk. **2** A female falcon. Also **fal′con–gen′til.**

fal·co·ni·form (fal·kō′nə·fôrm) *adj. Ornithol.* Belonging to the order of birds (*Falconiformes*) which includes the vultures, hawks, falcons, and eagles.

fal·co·nine (fal′kə·nīn, -nin) *adj.* Falconlike.

fal·con·ry (fôl′kən·rē, fô′-, fal′-) *n.* The training or using of falcons for sport.

fal·cu·la (fal′kyə·lə) *n.* **1** A sharp, curved claw, as in birds of prey. **2** *Anat.* A sickle–shaped process of the dura mater between the lobes of the cerebellum: also called *falx cerebelli.* [<L, dim. of *falx* a sickle]

fal·de·ral (fal′də·ral) *n.* **1** Any trifling fancy or conceit; foolish nonsense. **2** A gew–gaw; a trifling ornament. **3** A meaningless refrain used in old English songs. Also *Scot. folderol.*

fald·stool (fôld′stōōl′) *n.* **1** A desk at which the litany is read, as in the Church of England. **2** A folding seat, stool, or chair, especially one used by a king, or by a bishop when performing pontifical acts away from his cathedral, or in the presence of a superior. **3** A camp stool. [<Med. L *faldistolium* <OHG *faldstuol* a folding stool]

Fa·lie·ri (fä·lyā′rē), **Marino,** 1278?–1355, doge of Venice 1354–55: also **Fa·lie·ro** (fä·lyā′rō).

Fa·lis·can (fə·lis′kən) *adj.* Of or pertaining to the **Fa·lis·ci** (fə·lis′ī), an ancient people of southern Etruria. —*n.* **1** One of the Falisci. **2** Their Italic language, closely related to Latin.

Fa·lis·co–La·tin·i·an (fə·lis′kō·lə·tin′ē·ən) *n.* A branch of the Italic subfamily of Indo–European languages, including Latin and its modern descendants (French, Italian, Spanish, Portuguese, Rumanian, etc.), and ancient Faliscan.

Fal·ken·hayn (fäl′kən·hīn), **Erich von,** 1861–1922, German chief of staff 1914–16.

Fal·kirk (fôl′kûrk, fô′-) A town in Stirlingshire, Scotland; scene of English defeat of Scottish forces under Wallace, 1298.

Falk·land Island Dependencies (fôk′lənd) The territories in the South Atlantic administered by Great Britain along with the Falkland Islands, including South Georgia, the South Shetland, South Orkney, and South Sandwich islands, and Palmer Peninsula in Antarctica.

Falk·land Islands (fôk′lənd) A British crown colony in the South Atlantic, 4,618 square miles; capital, Stanley. *Spanish* **Is·las Mal·vi·nas** (ēs′läs mäl·vē′näs).

Falk·ner (fôk′nər), **William** See FAULKNER.

fall (fôl) *v.* **fell, fall·en, fall·ing** *v.i.* **1** To drop from a higher to a lower place or position because of removal of support or loss of hold or attachment. **2** To drop from an erect to a less erect or prone position: He *fell* to his knees. **3** To collapse; come down: The bridge *fell.* **4** To become less in height, number, force, volume, value, etc. **5** To descend or become less in rank, estimation, importance, etc. **6** To be wounded or slain, as in battle. **7** To be overthrown; lose power, as a government. **8** To be taken or captured: The fort *fell.* **9** To yield to temptation; sin. **10** To hit; land: The bombs *fell* short. **11** To slope downward: The road *falls* into the valley. **12** To hang down; droop. **13** To begin and continue: Night *fell.* **14** To pass into a state or condition: to *fall* asleep. **15** To experience or show dejection: His face *fell.* **16** To come or happen by chance or lot: Suspicion *fell* on him. **17** To happen; occur: Hallowe'en *falls* on Tuesday. **18** To pass by right or inheritance, as an estate. **19** To be uttered as if accidentally: An oath *fell* from his lips. **20** To be born, as a lamb. **21** To happen or come at a specific place: The accent *falls* on the last syllable. **22** To be classified or divided: with *into.* —*v.t.* **23** *U.S.* To fell or cut down, as a tree. —**to fall afoul** (or **foul**) **of** **1** To collide with, as a vessel. **2** To quarrel or argue with. —**to fall away** **1** To become lean or emaciated. **2** To die; decline. —**to fall away from** To renounce allegiance to. —**to fall back** To recede; retreat. —**to fall back on** (or **upon**) **1** *Mil.* To retreat to. **2** To resort to; have recourse to. —**to fall behind** **1** To drop back; lose ground. **2** To be in arrears. —**to fall down on** *U.S. Slang* To fail in. —**to fall flat** To fail to produce the intended effect or result. —**to fall for** *U.S. Colloq.* **1** To be deceived by. **2** To fall in love with. —**to fall in** *Mil.* To take proper place in a formation or group. —**to fall in with** **1** To meet and accompany. **2** To agree with; conform to. —**to fall off** **1** To leave or withdraw. **2** To become less: Attendance is *falling off.* **3** *Naut.* To veer to leeward from the former course. —**to fall on** (or **upon**) **1** To attack; assail. **2** To find; discover. —**to fall out** **1** To quarrel. **2** To happen; result. **3** *Mil.* To leave ranks. —**to fall through** To come to nothing; fail. —*adj.* **1** Of or pertaining to autumn; happening, or for use in, the fall of the year: *fall* weather, *fall* planting, a *fall* coat. **2** *Slang* Easily duped: a *fall* guy. —*n.* **1** The act, process, or result of falling, in any sense of the word: the *fall* of Adam, a *fall* in price, the *fall* of Rome. **2** *Usually pl.* A waterfall; cataract; cascade. **3** A flowing or discharge, as of one stream or body of water into another. **4** That which falls or is caused to fall; also, the amount of descent. **5** *Often cap.* The season coming between summer and winter; autumn. **6** A falling band or ruff for the neck; also, a veil. **7** In wrestling, the throwing of or being thrown by one's opponent, or the method of doing it. **8** That which acts by falling, as a *deadfall.* **9** In music and oratory, a cadence; a sinking of tone or decrease of volume of sound. **10** A hoisting rope, or the part of a hoisting rope or tackle to which power is applied or by which power is exerted; the rope of a tackle or purchase. **11** The birth of animals. See synonyms under RUIN. —**the fall of man** The disobedience of Adam and Eve. [OE *feallan*]

Synonyms (*verb*): decline, descend, droop, drop, fail, faint, lapse, set, sink, subside. See HAPPEN. *Antonyms*: ascend, climb, mount, rise, soar.

fal–la (fä′lä, fə·lä′) See FA–LA.

Fal·la (fä′lyä), **Manuel de,** 1876–1946, Spanish composer.

fal·la·ci·a (fə·lā′shē·ə, -shə) *n. Psychiatry* An illusion or hallucination: *fallacia* optica, an optical illusion. [<L. See FALLACY.]

fal·la·cious (fə·lā′shəs) *adj.* Of, pertaining to, embodying, or involving a fallacy; deceptive; misleading; delusive. —**fal·la′cious·ly** *adv.* —**fal·la′cious·ness** *n.*

fal·la·cy (fal′ə·sē) *n. pl.* **·cies** **1** Anything that deceives the mind or eye; deception. **2** A flaw in reasoning; fallaciousness. **3** *Logic.* Any reasoning, exposition, argument, etc., contravening the canons of logic. See synonyms under DELUSION, ERROR. [<L *fallacia* <*fallax, fallacis* deceptive <*fallere* deceive]

fal·lal (fal·lal′) *n.* **1** An ornament or trinket; gew–gaw. **2** Pretentiousness. Also **fal·lal′er·y.** [Cf. FALBALA]

fall dandelion An herb (*Leontodon autumnalis*) of the composite family having yellow flowers.

fall·en (fô′lən) *adj.* **1** Having come down by falling. **2** Overthrown; disgraced; ruined.

fall·er (fô′lər) *n.* **1** One who or that which falls. **2** A machine or part that acts by falling.

fall·fish (fôl′fish′) *n. pl.* **·fish** or **·fish·es** **1** A fresh–water cyprinoid fish (genus *Semotilus*) of eastern North America, about 18 inches long, bluish above, with silvery sides. **2** One of various other cyprinoids, as the **red fallfish** (*Notropis rubricroceus*).

fall guy *Slang* A dupe; gullible person.

fal·li·ble (fal′ə·bəl) *adj.* **1** Liable to error or mistake. **2** Liable to be misled or deceived. **3** Liable to be erroneous, incorrect, or false. [<Med. L *fallibilis* <*fallere* deceive] —**fal′·li·bil′i·ty, fal′li·ble·ness** *n.* —**fal′li·bly** *adv.*

falling band A 16th or 17th century broad linen or lace collar or ruff worn over the shoulders; Vandyke.

fall·ing–leaf (fô′ling·lēf′) *n. Aeron.* A flight maneuver in which an airplane loses altitude by a series of lateral oscillations resembling those of a falling leaf.

fall·ing–sick·ness (fô′ling·sik′nis) *n. Rare* Epilepsy. Also **fall′ing–e′vil.**

falling star A shooting star; a meteor. Also **falling stone.**

fall line The brink of a plateau, as indicated by waterfalls.

Fal·lo·pi·an tube (fə·lō′pē·ən) *Anat.* One of a pair of long, slender ducts in mammals, serving as a passage for the ovum from the ovary to the uterus.

Fal·lo·pi·o (fä·lō′pē·ō), **Gabriello,** 1523?–62, Italian anatomist.

fall–out (fôl′out′) *n. Physics* **1** The descent of minute particles of radioactive material resulting from the explosion of an atomic or thermonuclear bomb. **2** The particles themselves. **3** Any incidental result; unplanned or unpredictable consequences. Also **fall′out′.**

fal·low[1] (fal′ō) *adj.* Left unseeded after being plowed; uncultivated. —*n.* **1** Land left unseeded after plowing; also, cleared woodland. **2** The act or system of plowing or working land and leaving it unseeded for a time. —*v.t.* & *v.i.* To make, keep, or become fallow. [OE *fealga* fallow land] —**fal′low·ness** *n.*

fal·low[2] (fal′ō) *adj.* Pale–yellow or pale–red. [OE *fealu* tawny]

fallow crop A crop alternated with the main crop to nourish the soil.

fallow deer A European deer (genus *Dama*), about 3 feet high at the shoulders and spotted white in the summer.

FALLOW DEER

Fall River A city in SE Massachusetts.

fall term **1** A court session beginning in the fall. **2** A school session beginning in the fall.

fall·way (fôl′wā′) *n.* A hoistway through several floors, as of a warehouse.

Fal·mouth (fal′məth) A port in SW Cornwall, England.

false (fôls) *adj.* **1** Contrary to truth or fact. **2** Deceptive; counterfeit; artificial; not real or genuine. **3** Incorrect; irregular. **4** Lying; dishonest; faithless; treacherous. **5** Supplementary; substitutive. **6** Out of tune. See synonyms under BAD, COUNTERFEIT, PERFIDIOUS. —*adv. Obs.* Falsely. [<OF *fals, faus* <L *falsus,* orig. pp. of *fallere* deceive] **—false′·ly** *adv.* **—false′ness** *n.*

False Bay (fôls) An inlet of the Atlantic in Western Cape Province, Republic of South Africa.

false bottom 1 A partition that appears to be the bottom, as of a trunk, drawer, etc., forming a secret compartment beneath it. **2** The base of a drinking glass formed in such a way as to give a deceptive notion of the capacity of the glass.

false cirrus *Meteorol.* Cirrus formed from the upper frozen parts of a cumulonimbus cloud, often spreading out from the summit of a thundercloud.

false colors 1 The flag of a country not one's own. **2** Deceptive presentation of fact; pretense.

false face A covering for the face; mask.

false foxglove Any of several widely distributed plants of the figwort family (genus *Aureolaria*) bearing bright yellow flowers.

false glottis The space between the false vocal cords. See VOCAL CORD.

false-heart·ed (fôls′här′tid) *adj.* Having a false heart; treacherous; deceitful.

false hellebore See under HELLEBORE.

false·hood (fôls′o͝od) *n.* **1** Lack of accord to fact or truth; untruthfulness. **2** An intentional untruth; a lie. **3** Act of lying; falsification, **4** An untrue belief or idea. See synonyms under DECEPTION, FICTION, LIE.

false imprisonment The forcible detention of a person contrary to law.

false keel *Naut.* A supplementary keel attached to the bottom of the true keel of a vessel.

false pretenses Wilful misrepresentations made to cheat and defraud; swindling.

false ribs *Anat.* Ribs that do not unite directly with the sternum; in man, there are five on each side. See RIB.

false step 1 A stumble. **2** An error or blunder in behavior. See FAUX PAS.

fal·set·tist (fôl·set′ist) *n.* One who speaks or sings in falsetto.

fal·set·to (fôl·set′ō) *n. pl.* **·tos 1** The artificial tones of the voice, higher than the chest voice or natural voice. **2** A singer possessing such a voice. —*adj.* Having the quality of the falsetto; shrill; artificial. [<Ital., dim. of *falso* false]

false vampire Any of a group of large Old World bats (families *Nycteridae* and *Megadermidae*) wrongly supposed to suck blood.

false·work (fôls′wûrk′) *n.* **1** A temporary scaffolding to facilitate the erection of a permanent structure. **2** That part of a structure designed to improve its shape or increase its efficiency, but without carrying any of the fundamental stresses, as an airplane fairing.

fals·ies (fôl′sēz) *n. pl. Colloq.* Pads worn within a brassière to give the breasts a fuller appearance.

fal·si·fi·ca·tion (fôl′sə·fə·kā′shən) *n.* **1** The act or process of falsifying. **2** *Law* The intentional alteration of a record, an account, or any document, so as to render it untrue. Compare SURCHARGE.

fal·si·fy (fôl′sə·fī) *v.* **·fied, ·fy·ing** *v.t.* **1** To misrepresent; tell lies about. **2** To prove to be false; disprove; **3** *Law* To tamper with, as a document. **4** In prosody, to alter (an accent in a poem) from the usual form or rule. —*v.i.* **5** To tell falsehoods; lie. See synonyms under PERVERT. [<F *falsifier* <LL *falsificare* <L *falsificus* making false <*falsus* FALSE + *facere* make] **—fal′si·fi′er** *n.*

fal·si·ty (fôl′sə·tē) *n. pl.* **·ties 1** The quality of being false. **2** A false statement, thing, or appearance. See synonyms under ERROR.

Fal·staff (fô′staf, -stäf), **Sir John** A jovial, witty solider, fat, boastful, and mendacious, in Shakespeare's *Henry IV* and *The Merry Wives of Windsor.* **—Fal·staff′i·an.**

Fal·ster (fäl′sər) A Danish island in the Baltic Sea; 198 square miles.

falt·boat (fält′bōt′) *n.* A collapsible, kayaklike boat, seating one person, propelled by a double-bladed paddle; used chiefly on rivers: also *foldboat.* [<G *faltboot* folding boat]

fal·ter (fôl′tər) *v.i* **1** To be hesitant or uncertain; waver; give way. **2** To stumble; move unsteadily. **3** To speak haltingly; stammer. —*v.t.* **4** To utter haltingly. —*n.* A faltering hesitation; a trembling. [? <ON *faltrask* be encumbered] **—fal′ter·er** *n.* **—fal′ter·ing** *adj.* **—fal′ter·ing·ly** *adv.*

falx cer·e·bel·li (falks ser′ə·bel′ī) See FALCULA.

Fa·ma·gu·sta (fä′mä·go͞os′tä) A port of **Famagusta Bay,** an inlet of the Mediterranean in eastern Cyprus.

fame (fām) *n.* **1** Public or general reputation; renown. **2** *Obs.* Report; rumor. —*v.t.* **famed, fam·ing 1** To speak of widely; celebrate. **2** To make famous. [<F <L *fama* report, reputation <*fari* speak]

Synonyms (noun): celebrity, credit, distinction, eminence, glory, honor, laurels, notoriety, renown, reputation, repute. *Fame* is the widely disseminated report of a person's character, deeds, or ability, and is oftenest used in the favorable sense. *Reputation* and *repute* are more limited than *fame,* and may be either good or bad. *Notoriety* is evil *repute* or a dishonorable counterfeit of *fame. Eminence* and *distinction* may result from rank, station, or character. *Celebrity* is limited in range; we speak of local *celebrity,* or world-wide *fame. Fame* in its best sense may be defined as the applause of numbers; *renown,* as such applause worthily won: we speak of the conqueror's *fame,* the patriot's *renown. Glory* and *honor* are of good import; *honor* may be given for qualities or acts that should not win it, but it is always given as for something good and worthy; we speak of an evil *fame,* but not of evil *honor; glory* has a more exalted and often a sacred sense. *Antonyms:* contempt, contumely, discredit, disgrace, dishonor, disrepute, humiliation, ignominy, infamy, oblivion, obscurity, shame.

Fa·meuse (fə·myo͞oz′, *Fr.* fà·mœz′) *n.* An early winter apple, striped with deep red, and having tender white flesh; also called *snow apple.* [<F, famous]

fa·mil′ial (fə·mil′yəl) *adj.* **1** Of, pertaining to, involving, or associated with the family. **2** *Genetics* Transmitted within the family, as certain hereditary diseases. [<L *familia* family]

fa·mil·iar (fə·mil′yər) *adj.* **1** Having close knowledge; well acquainted; thoroughly versed; followed by *with.* **2** Having the relation of an intimate or near friend; arising from or characterized by close acquaintance; not distant; informal. **3** Exercising undue intimacy; forward; intrusive. **4** Well known, as from habitual use or long acquaintance; common; frequent; customary. **5** Domesticated; attached: said of animals. See synonyms under COMMON, GENERAL, HABITUAL, USUAL. —*n.* **1** An intimate friend. **2** A person with whom one frequently associates. **3** A spirit supposed to attend and obey a sorcerer: also **familiar spirit. 4** A servant of a prelate of the Roman Catholic Church, or the inquisition. [<L *familiaris* of the family <*familia*◆family] **—fa·mil′iar·ly** *adv.*

fa·mil·i·ar·i·ty (fə·mil′ē·ar′ə·tē, -mil′yar′-) *n. pl.* **·ties 1** The state or condition of being familiar; intimacy; intimate knowledge or acquaintance, as with a subject. **2** Conduct implying familiar intimacy. **3** *Often pl.* Offensively familiar conduct. See synonym under ACQUAINTANCE, ASSOCIATION.

fa·mil·iar·ize (fə·mil′yə·rīz) *v.t.* **·ized, ·iz·ing 1** To make (oneself or someone) accustomed or familiar. **2** To cause to be well known or familiar. **—fa·mil′iar·i·za′tion** *n.*

fam·i·lis·ter·y (fam′ə·lis′tər·ē) *n. pl.* **·ter·ies 1** A communal dwelling. **2** A group of families living together in one building and sharing facilities. [<F *familistère* <*familie* family + *(phalan)stère* PHALANSTERY]

fam·i·ly (fam′ə·lē, fam′lē) *n. pl.* **·lies 1** A group of persons, consisting of parents and their children. **2** The children as distinguished from the parents. **3** A group of persons forming a household, including servants, etc.; a household. **4** A succession of persons connected by blood, name, etc.; a house, line; clan, tribe; race. **5** Distinguished or ancient lineage with its traditions; descent. **6** *Biol.* A taxonomic category higher than a genus; for animals, family names end in *-idae,* for plants, in *-aceae.* **7** Any class or group of like or related things. **8** *Ling.* A grouping of languages, such as Indo-European, assumed from certain shared characteristics, to be descended from a common parent: often subdivided into *subfamily, branch,* and *group.* —*adj.* Of, belonging to, or suitable for a family. [<L *familia* family <*famulus* servant]

family circle The members of a family.

fam·i·ly-cir·cle (fam′ə·lē·sûr′kəl, fam′lē) *n.* The upper balcony in a theater, containing inexpensive seats.

family name A surname, as distinguished from a *personal* or *Christian name.*

family planning Control by means of contraceptive measures of the timing and number of births in a family.

family tree 1 A relational diagram of a family showing its ancestors and various branches of descendants. **2** The ancestors and descendants of a family, collectively.

fam·ine (fam′in) *n.* **1** A wide-spread scarcity of food; dearth. **2** A great scarcity of anything: a water *famine.* **3** Starvation. [<OF <L *fames* hunger]

famine fever Typhus.

fam·ish (fam′ish) *v.t.* & *v.i.* To suffer or die, or to cause to suffer or die, from lack of nourishment; starve. [Earlier *fame* <F *afamer;* refashioned after verbs in *-ish,* as *banish, finish,* etc.] **—fam′ish·ment** *n.*

fa·mous (fā′məs) *adj.* **1** Having fame or celebrity; renowned. **2** *Colloq.* Admirable, excellent. See synonyms under EMINENT, ILLUSTRIOUS. **—fa′mous·ly** *adv.* **—fa′mous·ness** *n.*

fam·u·lus (fam′yə·ləs) *n. pl.* **·li** (-lī) An assistant or servant; specifically, the assistant or amanuensis of a scholar or the familiar of a magician. [<L, servant]

fan[1] (fan) *n.* **1** An implement or device for agitating the air; specifically, a light, flat implement, often collapsible, spreading a wedge-shaped sheet from a stem or point, with a stock or handle. **2** One of various implements or machines for stirring up currents of air or doing something similar. **3** A kind of basket formerly used for winnowing grain, by tossing the grain in the air. **4** A winnowing machine. **5** A small sail or vane to keep the sails of a windmill at right angles to the wind. **6** A propeller; also, one of its blades. **7** Something that excites or stimulates. —*v.* **fanned, fan·ning** *v.t.* **1** To move or stir (air) with or as with a fan. **2** To direct air upon; cool or refresh with or as with a fan. **3** To move or stir to action; excite, as fire or rage. **4** To winnow (grain or chaff). **5** To spread like a fan. **6** In baseball, to cause (a batter) to strike out —*v.i.* **7** To spread out like a fan. **8** In baseball, to strike out. [OE *fann* <L *vannus* winnowing fan]

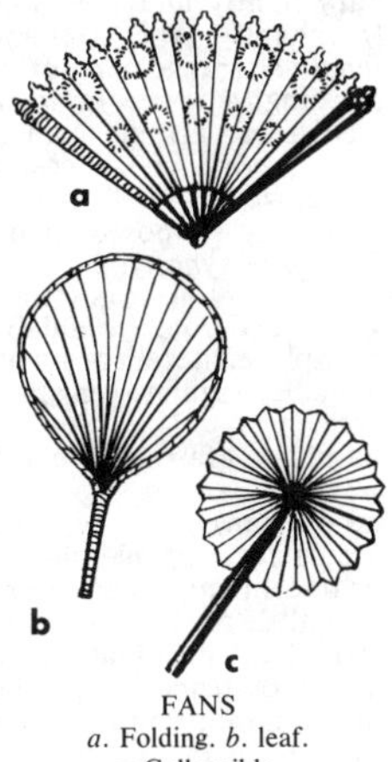

FANS
a. Folding. *b.* leaf. *c.* Collapsible.

fan[2] (fan) *n. Colloq.* **1** An enthusiastic devotee of any sport or diversion, as of baseball or of motion pictures; a fanatic. **2** An ardent admirer, usually of a public character, writer, artist, etc. [? <*the fancy* (see under FANCY)]

fa′n (fän) *adj. Scot.* Fallen.

Fan·ar (fan′ər) PHANAR.

fa·nat·ic (fə·nat′ik) *adj.* Actuated by extravagant or intemperate zeal; inordinately and unreasonably enthusiastic: also **fa·nat′i·cal.** —*n.* One who is motivated by intemperate zeal; one who is moved by a frenzy of enthusiasm; especially, a religious zealot. [<L *fanaticus* inspired <*fanum* a temple] **—fa·nat′i·cal·ly** *adv.*

fa·nat·i·cism (fə·nat′ə·siz′əm) *n.* The spirit or conduct of a fanatic; unreasonable zeal. Also **fa·nat′i·cal·ness.**

Synonyms: bigotry, credulity, intolerance, superstition. *Fanaticism* is extravagant or even frenzied zeal; *bigotry* is obstinate and unreasoning attachment to a cause or creed; *fanaticism* and *bigotry* usually include *intolerance,* which is unwillingness to tolerate beliefs or opinions contrary to one's own; *superstition* is ignorant and irrational religious belief. *Credulity* is not distinctively religious, but is a general readiness to believe without sufficient evidence, with a proneness to accept the marvelous. *Bigotry* has not the capacity to reason fairly, *fanaticism* has not the patience, *superstition* has not the knowledge and mental discipline, *intolerance* has not the disposition. *Bigotry, fanaticism,* and *superstition* are perversions of the religious sentiment; *credulity* and *intolerance* often accompany skepticism or atheism. Compare FNTHUSIASM, FRENZY. *Antonyms*: cynicism, free–thinking, indifference, latitudinarianism.

fa·nat·i·cize (fə·nat′ə·sīz) *v.t.* & *v.i.* **·cized, ·ciz·ing** To make or to become fanatical; act like a fanatic.

fan·ci·er (fan′sē·ər) *n.* **1** A breeder and seller of birds or animals. **2** One having a taste for special objects; an amateur. **3** A dreamer; visionary.

fan·ci·ful (fan′si·fəl) *adj.* **1** Proceeding from or produced by fancy; ideal; odd; curious in appearance. **2** Existing only in the fancy; unreal; visionary. **3** Whimsical. **— fan′ci·ful·ly** *adv.* **— fan′ci·ful·ness** *n.*

Synonyms: chimerical, fantastic, grotesque, imaginative, visionary. That is *fanciful* which is dictated or suggested by fancy independently of more serious considerations; the *fantastic* is the *fanciful* with the added elements of whimsicalness and extravagance. The *fanciful* swings away from the real or the ordinary lightly and pleasantly, the *fantastic* extravagantly, the *grotesque* ridiculously. A *fanciful* arrangement of objects is commonly pleasing, a *fantastic* arrangement is striking, a *grotesque* arrangement is laughable. A *fanciful* theory or suggestion may be clearly recognized as such; a *visionary* scheme is erroneously supposed to have a basis in fact. Compare synonyms for DREAM, IDEA, IDEAL, IMAGINARY, IMAGINATION, ROMANTIC. *Antonyms*: accurate, calculable, calculated, commonplace, literal, ordinary, prosaic, real, reasonable, regular, sensible, solid, sound, sure, true.

fan·ci·less (fan′si·lis) *adj.* Lacking fancy; unimaginative.

fan·cy (fan′sē) *n. pl.* **·cies 1** The power or act of forming pleasing, graceful, whimsical, or odd mental images, or of combining them with little regard to rational processes of construction; imagination in its lower form; hence, in former usage, the re–imaging faculty of the mind; fantasy. **2** Any product of the exercise of this faculty; an imaginary notion, representation, or image; whimsical notion; vagary. **3** A baseless or visionary idea; notion; illusion. **4** An unreasoned liking or fondness, resulting from caprice; preference. **5** A pet pursuit; an object sought after to gratify the taste or a whim without regard to utility; a hobby; fad. **6** Taste exhibited in production; artistic invention; design: The edifice showed a cultivated *fancy.* **7** *Obs.* A specter; phantom. **8** *Obs.* Love. **— the fancy** The votaries collectively of any special art, sport, or amusement. **—** *adj.* **·ci·er, ·ci·est 1** Adapted to please the fancy; ornamental; decorative: *fancy* embroidery. **2** Evolved from the fancy; imaginary; ideal. **3** Capricious; whimsical; fanciful. **4** In commerce, of higher grade than the average; choice; characterized by variety, excellence, or special request: *fancy* fruits. **5** Extravagant; exorbitant: *fancy* prices. **6** Selectively bred to a type, as an animal. **7** Performed with exceptional grace and skill: the *fancy* bowing of a violinist. **—** *v.t.* **·cied, ·cy·ing 1** To imagine; picture. **2** To take a fancy to; like. **3** To believe without proof or conviction; suppose. **4** To breed, as animals, for conventional points of symmetry or beauty. [Short for FANTASY]

Synonyms (noun): belief, caprice, conceit, conception, desire, humor, idea, image, imagination, inclination, liking, mood, predilection, supposition, vagary, whim. An intellectual *fancy* is a mental *image* or picture founded upon slight or whimsical association or resemblance; a *conceit* has less of the picturesque and more of the theoretic than a *fancy.* An intellectual *fancy* or *conceit* may be pleasing or amusing, but is never worth serious discussion. An emotional or personal *fancy* is a capricious *belief, idea,* or *liking* formed with slight reason or judgment, and liable to fade as lightly as it was formed. Compare synonyms for DREAM, IDEA, IMAGINATION, INCLINATION, THOUGHT[1], WHIM. *Antonyms*: actuality, certainty, fact, reality, truth, verity.

fancy ball A ball at which fancy dress is worn. Also **fan′cy–dress′ ball.**

fancy dress Masquerade costume. **— fan′cy–dress′** *adj.*

fan·cy-free (fan′sē·frē′) *adj.* Not in love.

fancy man *Slang* A man supported by a woman, especially by a prostitute.

fancy woman A mistress or a prostitute.

fan·cy·work (fan′sē·wûrk′) *n.* Embroidery, tatting, crocheting, lacework, etc.

fan·dan·go (fan·dang′gō) *n. pl.* **·gos 1** A Spanish dance in triple time, usually accompanied by castanets. **2** The music for this dance. **3** A dancing party or ball. [<Sp.]

fan delta An alluvial cone.

fane (fān) *n.* A sanctuary; temple. ◆ Homophones: *fain, feign.* [<L *fanum* temple]

fa·ne·ga (fä·nā′gä) *n.* A Spanish dry measure equal to a little more than 1 1/2 bushels, but variable in Latin–American countries. Also **fan·ga** (fäng′gä). [<Sp.]

fa·ne·ga·da (fä′nā·gä′thä) *n.* A Spanish unit of area, equal to 6.92 acres or 7,449 square feet.

Fan·euil Hall (fan′əl, fan′yəl) A public hall and market house built in Boston, Mass., by **Peter Faneuil,** 1700–43, a merchant. Called the "Cradle of American Liberty" because it was used by Revolutionary patriots.

fan·fare (fan′fâr′) *n.* A flourish, as of trumpets; a noisy parade or demonstration. [<F]

fan·fa·ron (fan′fə·ron) *n. Obs.* **1** A swaggering boaster; a bully. **2** A fanfare. [<F <Sp. *fanfarrón* <Arabic *farfār* talkative]

fan·fa·ron·ade (fan′fə·rə·nād′) *n.* A blustering, ranting, or vainglorious speech or style; a boastful or bullying manner; rodomontade. **—** *v.i.* **·ad·ed, ·ad·ing** To swagger; bluster. [<F <Sp. *fanfarronada* <*fanfarrón.* See FANFARON.]

fang (fang) *n.* **1** A long pointed tooth or tusk by which an animal seizes, holds, or tears its prey, as the canine tooth of a boar or dog. **2** One of the long, curved, hollow or grooved, usually erectile teeth with which a venomous serpent injects its poison into its victim. **3**

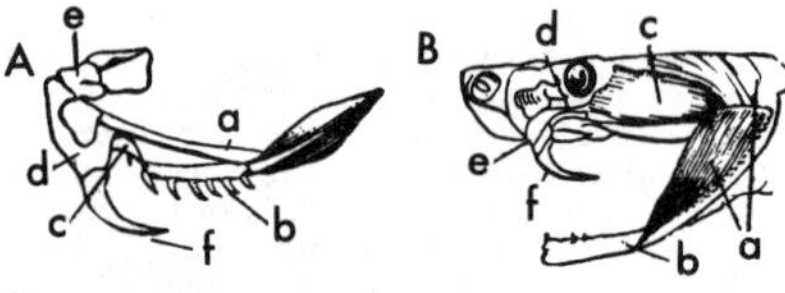

FANGS OF THE RATTLESNAKE

A. Fang and accompanying bones: *f.* fang; *a.* external pterygoid; *b.* internal pterygoid; *c.* palatal; *d.* superior maxillary; *e.* lacrimal. *B.* Muscles related to the venom gland and fang: *f.* fang; *a.* anterior temporal muscles; *b.* internal pterygoid; *c.* venom gland; *d.* the fang, half erected; *e.* point where the venom enters the channel of the fang.

One of various pointed or incurved objects, organs, or devices, especially for clutching or holding fast, as the root of a tooth or the claw or talon of a bird. **—** *v.t.* **1** *Obs.* To seize or take hold of. **2** To sink fangs into. [OE *fang* catching, seizing] **— fanged** (fangd) *adj.* **— fang′less** *adj.* **— fang′like′** *adj.*

fan·gle (fang′gəl) *n. Rare* A fashion; novelty: new fads and *fangles.* [<NEWFANGLED, incorrectly taken as *new* + *fangle*]

fan·ion (fan′yən) *n. Archaic* A small flag. [< OF, var. of *fanon.* See FANON.]

fan·jet (fan′jet′) *n.* A turbofan (def. 2).

fan·light (fan′līt′) *n.* **1** A fan window. **2** *Brit.* A transom.

fan mail Complimentary letters to public performers, as actors, musicians, and the like.

fan·nel (fan′əl) *n.* A fanon. [<Med. L *fanula,* dim. of *fano.* See FANON.]

fan·ner (fan′ər) *n.* **1** One who or that which fans. **2** A ventilating fan or fan blower.

Fan·ning Island (fan′ing) Headquarters of the Line Islands district of the Gilbert and Ellice Islands colony; 12 square miles.

fan·ny (fan′ē) *n. U.S. Slang* The buttocks.

Fan·ny (fan′ē) Diminutive of FRANCES.

fan·on (fan′ən) *n. Eccl.* **1** A maniple or napkin used by a celebrant at mass. **2** A cape worn only by the pope, as he presides at solemn pontifical mass. Also **fan·o** (fan′ō), **fan·um** (fan′əm). [<OF *fanon* <Med. L *fano, -onis* a banner, napkin <Gmc.]

fan palm Any palm with fan–shaped leaves; especially, the talipot palm of Ceylon and the Malabar Coast, having immense leaves; the palmetto of Florida; and the California or Washington fan palm (*Washingtonia filifera*), occurring in California and Lower California.

fan·tail (fan′tāl′) *n.* **1** A variety of domestic pigeon having fanlike tail feathers. **2** An Australian or Oriental flycatcher (genus *Rhipidura*) having fanlike tail feathers. **3** A fan–shaped joint or mortise. **4** Any end or tail shaped like a fan. **5** Any of certain species of fancy–bred goldfish, having double anal and dorsal fins. **6** *Naut.* The overhanging stern of some vessels.

FANTAIL PIGEON

fan–tailed (fan′tāld′) *adj.* Having the tail feathers arranged like a fan or capable of expansion like a fan, as the flycatcher.

fan–tan (fan′tan′) *n.* **1** A Chinese gambling game, played with coins or other small objects, which the players cover, and then bet on what the remainder will be when the pile has been divided by four. **2** A game of cards played in sequence, the winner being the person who gets rid of his cards first. [<Chinese *fan t'an* repeated divisions]

fan·ta·si·a (fan·tā′zē·ə, -zhə, fan′tə·zē′ə) *n.* **1** A fanciful, irregular, fantastic composition, not observing strict musical forms. **2** A piece of orchestral music less formal than an overture; also, a prelude to an organ fugue. [<Ital., a fancy]

fan·ta·size (fan′tə·sīz) *v.* **·sized, ·siz·ing** *v.i.* **1** To imagine or daydream about fantastic events. **—** *v.t.* **2** To create in fantasy, as in daydreaming. **— fan′ta·sist** *n.*

fan·tasm (fan′taz·əm) *n.* **1** An imaginary appearance; a phantom. **2** A mental image; fancy. Also spelled *phantasm.* See synonyms under DELUSION. [<Gk. *phantasma.* Doublet of PHANTOM.]

fan·tas·ma·go·ri·a (fan·taz′mə·gôr′ē·ə, -gō′rē·ə) *n.* **1** A changing, incoherent series of apparitions or fantasms. **2** An exhibition of pictures projected on a screen and made to increase or diminish in size rapidly while continually in focus. Also **fan·tas′ma·go′ry:** also spelled *phantasmagoria.* [<NL <Gk. *phantasma* an apparition + prob. *agora* assembly, crowd] **— fan·tas′ma·go′ri·al, fan·tas′ma·gor′ic** (-gôr′ik, -gor′-) or **·i·cal** *adj.*

fan·tas·mal (fan·taz′məl) *adj.* Of or like a fantasm; unreal or illusive. Also **fan·tas′mic.**

fan·tast (fan′tast) *n.* **1** One who believes in or advocates a fantastic delusion as a true doctrine. **2** A dreamer or visionary. [<Med. L *phantasta* <Gk. *phantastēs* a boaster <*phantazein* boast]

fan·tas·tic (fan·tas′tik) *adj.* **1** Of an odd appearance; grotesque. **2** Capricious; whimsical: a *fantastic* imagination. **3** Of the nature of fantasy; fanciful; illusory. See synonyms under FANCIFUL, ODD, QUEER, ROMANTIC. **—** *n.* One who is fantastic in conduct or appearance: also *Obs.* **fan·tas′ti·co.** Also **fan·tas′ti·cal.** [<Med. L *fantasticus* <L *phantasticus* <Gk. *phantastikos* <*phantastēs.* See FANTAST.] **— fan·tas′ti·cal·ly** *adv.* **— fan·tas′ti·cal·ness** *n.*

fan·tas·ti·cal·i·ty (fan·tas′ti·kal′ə·tē) *n.* **1** The quality of being fantastic. **2** Anything which is fantastic or grotesque.

fan·ta·sy (fan′tə·sē, -zē) *n. pl.* **·sies 1** A fantastic notion or mental image; fancy. **2** A fantastic design, as in embroidery. **3** *Psychol.* The form of representation that brings before the mind a sequence of images serving to fulfil a need not gratified in the real world; a daydream. **4** *Music* A fantasia. **5** A capricious mood. See synonyms under

DREAM, IDEA, IMAGINATION. — *v.t.* **·sied, ·sy·ing** To imagine; conceive. Also spelled *phantasy.* [<F *fantasie* <L *phantasia* <Gk., appearance <*phainein* show]

Fan·tin-La·tour (fäṅ·taṅ'là·tōōr'), **Henri,** 1836–1904, French painter.

fan·toc·ci·ni (fän'tə·chē'nē) *n. pl.* **1** Marionettes. **2** A puppet show. [<Ital. <*fantoccio* puppet <*fante* child]

fan·tom (fan'təm) See PHANTOM.

fan tracery *Archit.* Bar tracery, diverging like a fan to form a section of fan vaulting rising from a capital or corbel, as in Henry VII's chapel, Westminster.

fan vaulting *Archit.* A system of vaulting in which the ribs spread out like a fan: used in later English Gothic.

fan window *Archit.* A semicircular window containing a sash with bars radiating from the middle of its base.

fan·wort (fan'wûrt') *n.* An American aquatic plant (*Cabomba caroliniana*) which occurs in the southern United States; one of the water-lily family: also called *fishgrass.*

far (fär) *adv.* **1** At a remote or distant point or place; so as to be a long way off: *far* distant. **2** To a great distance; so as to reach to a point a long way off; so as to occupy or cover an extent of time or space: How *far* did Caesar march? **3** To a great degree; by much; very greatly: *far* wiser than their ancestors. **4** From afar; from a long distance: a *far*-traveled guest. —**by far** In a great degree; by much. —*adj.* **far·ther** or **fur·ther, far·thest** or **fur·thest**: see FARTHER. **1** Situated at a great distance in space or time; being a long way off; remote: He went into a *far* country. **2** Extending widely or at length; reaching a long way. **3** Being the more distant of two: the *far* end of the garden. **4** Advanced; progressed, as in age. [OE *feor*]

far·ad (far'əd, -ad) *n. Electr.* The unit of capacitance; the capacitance of a condenser that retains one coulomb of charge with one volt difference of potential. [after Michael *Faraday*]

far·a·day (far'ə·dā) *n. Electr.* The quantity of electricity required in electrolysis to liberate one unit equivalent weight of an element, equal to 96,500 coulombs per gram equivalent. [after Michael *Faraday*]

Far·a·day (far'ə·dā), **Michael,** 1791–1867, English chemist and physicist; discovered electromagnetic induction.

fa·rad·ic (fə·rad'ik) *adj.* Pertaining to or caused by induced electric currents. Also **far·a·da·ic** (far'ə·dā'ik).

far·a·dism (far'ə·diz'əm) *n.* **1** The electricity of an induced current. **2** *Med.* The treatment of a nerve or muscle with a faradic current.

far·a·dize (far'ə·dīz) *v.t.* **·dized, ·diz·ing** To stimulate (a nerve, muscle, etc.) by faradic currents. —**far'a·di·za'tion** *n.* —**far'a·diz'er** *n.*

far·ad·me·ter (far'əd·mē'tər, -ad-) *n.* An instrument, usually graded in microfarads, for measuring the strength of an induced electric current.

far and away By a great deal; emphatically.

far·an·dine (far'ən·dīn) *n.* A fabric of silk mixed with hair or wool, used during the 17th century. [<F *ferrandine,* after *Ferrand* de Lyon, its inventor]

far·an·dole (far'ən·dōl, *Fr.* fà·ràṅ·dôl') *n.* A rapid dance in which the participants whirl in a circle, alternately facing in and out.

far and wide Everywhere; in every place. Also **far and near.**

far-a·way (fär'ə·wā') *adj.* **1** Distant: a *faraway* town. **2** Absent-minded; abstracted.

farce (färs) *n.* **1** A short comedy with exaggerated effects and incidents. **2** A ridiculous proceeding; an absurd failure. —*v.t.* **farced, farc·ing 1** To fill out with witticisms, jibes, etc., as a play. **2** *Obs.* To fill with dressing; stuff, as a fowl. [<F, orig. stuffing <*farcer* stuff <L *farcire*] —**far·cial** (fär'shəl) *adj.*

far·ceur (fär·sœr') *n.* One who writes or acts a farce; a jester; wag. Also **farc·er** (fär'sər). [<F]

far·ci·cal (fär'si·kəl) *adj.* Of, pertaining to, or of the nature of a farce; absurd. See synonyms under RIDICULOUS. —**far'ci·cal·ly** *adv.* —**far'ci·cal·ness, far'ci·cal'i·ty** *n.*

far·cy (fär'sē) *n.* A contagious disease, primarily of the horse, characterized by pustular eruptions; glanders. [Var. of obs. *farcin* <F <L *farcimimum,* a disease of horses]

far·cy-bud (fär'sē·bud') *n.* A swollen gland, as in glanders..

far·del (fär'dəl) *n. Archaic* A bundle; pack; burden. [<OF, dim. of *farde* <Arabic *fardah* a bundle]

fare (fâr) *v.i.* **fared, far·ing 1** To be in a specified state; get on. **2** To turn out; happen. **3** To eat; be supplied with food. **4** *Archaic* To go; travel. —*n.* **1** Passage money. **2** A passenger carried for hire. **3** Food and drink; diet; eatables. See synonyms under FOOD. ◆ Homophone: *fair.* [OE *faran* go, travel]

Far East See under EAST.

fare·box (fâr'boks') *n.* A box into which passengers boarding a street car or bus deposit their fares.

far·er (fâr'ər) *n.* One who travels: most commonly in compounds, as *wayfarer,* etc.

fare·well (fâr'wel') *n.* **1** A parting salutation; a good-by; adieu. **2** The act of taking leave; parting. —*inter.* (fâr'wel') May you fare well; may you prosper: now used only at parting. —*adj.* Parting; closing; valedictory. —*v.t. Poetic* To take leave of. —**to a fare-you-well** *U.S. Colloq.* Completely; with finality: beaten *to a fare-you-well*: also **to a fare-thee-well.** [Earlier *fare well.* See FARE.]

Synonyms (noun): adieu, congé, good-by, leave-taking, valediction, valedictory. *Good-by* is the homely and hearty parting salutation, *farewell* the formal, English word at parting. *Adieu,* from the French, is still more ceremonious than *farewell*; *congé,* also from the French, is commonly contemptuous or supercilious, and equivalent to dismissal. *Valediction* is a learned word never in popular use. A *valedictory* is a public farewell to a company or assembly.

Farewell, Cape The most southerly point of Greenland.

far-fetched (fär'fecht') *adj.* **1** Brought in only by laborious or strained effort. **2** Neither natural nor obvious.

far-flung (fär'flung') *adj.* Having great range; extending over great distances.

Far·go (fär'gō) A city on the Red River in SE North Dakota.

fa·ri·na (fə·rē'nə) *n.* **1** A meal or flour obtained chiefly from cereals, nuts, potatoes, or Indian corn, and used as a breakfast food. **2** Starch. **3** A mealy powder found on certain insects. [<L <*far* spelt]

Fa·ri·na (fä·rē'nä), **Salvatore,** 1846–1918, Italian novelist.

far·i·na·ceous (far'ə·nā'shəs) *adj.* **1** Consisting or made of farina. **2** Containing or yielding starch. **3** Mealy.

far·i·nose (far'ə·nōs) *adj.* **1** Yielding farina: *farinose* plants. **2** *Bot.* Covered with or as if with a white meal-like powder, as the under side of the leaves of certain primroses.

far·kle·ber·ry (fär'kəl·ber'ē) *n. pl.* **·ries** A shrub or small tree (*Vaccinium arboreum*) of the heath family, with globose black berries. [Origin uncertain]

farl (färl) *n. Scot.* A fourth part, as of a cake. Also **farle.**

Far·ley (fär'lē), **James Aloysius,** born 1888, U.S. political leader.

farm (färm) *n.* **1** A tract of land forming a single property and devoted to agriculture, stock-raising, dairying, or some allied activity. **2** A tract of water used for the cultivation of marine life: an oyster *farm.* **3** *Obs.* **a** The system of farming out revenues or taxes. **b** A fixed annual sum paid as a rent or tax. **4** In baseball, a minor-league club used by a major-league club for training its recruits. —*v.t.* **1** To cultivate (land). **2** To take a lease of, as the use of a business or the collection of taxes, for a fixed rental, retaining the profits. **3** To let at a fixed rental, as lands, collection of taxes, etc.: usually with *out*: to *farm* out taxes. **4** To let out the services of (a person) for hire. **5** To agree to maintain or care for at a fixed price, as paupers. **6** To arrange for (work) to be performed by persons or a firm not in the main organization; subcontract: with *out.* **7** In baseball, to place (a player) with a minor-league team for training: often with *out.* —*v.i.* **8** To practice farming; be a farmer. [<F *ferme* <Med. L *firma* a fixed payment <L *firmare* fix, settle <*firmus* firm]

Far·man (fär·mäṅ'), **Henri,** 1874?–1934, French airplane manufacturer and pioneer aviator.

Farm Bureau A local organization of farmers in the United States, forming a unit in the **American Farm Bureau Federation,** dealing with farm problems.

farm·er (fär'mər) *n.* **1** One who follows the occupation of farming; an agriculturist. **2** One who collects revenues for a percentage or commission.

Far·mer (fär'mər), **Fannie Merritt,** 1857–1915, U.S. cookery expert.

farm·er·ette (fär'mə·ret') *n. Colloq.* A woman or girl who farms.

farmer general *pl.* **farmers general** A member of a privileged class in France before the revolution of 1789, who farmed or leased the public revenues. —**farm'er-gen'er·al·ship** *n.*

Farm·er-La·bor party (fär'mər·lā'bər) A minor U. S. political party, 1919–23: active since 1923 in Minnesota.

farm·er·y (fär'mər·ē) *n. Brit.* The buildings, yards, etc., of a farm.

farm·hand (färm'hand') *n.* One who works for wages on a farm. Also **farm laborer.**

farm·house (färm'hous') *n.* The homestead on a farm, commonly occupied by the farmer's family.

farm·ing (fär'ming) *n.* The act of one who farms; the management of or labor on a farm; agriculture. See synonyms under AGRICULTURE. —*adj.* Engaged in, suitable for, or used for, agriculture: a *farming* region, *farming* implements.

farm·stead (färm'sted) *n.* A farm and the buildings on it. Also **farm'stead·ing.**

farm·yard (färm'yärd') *n.* A space surrounded by farm buildings, and enclosed for confining stock, etc.

Far·ne·se (fär·nā'sā) The name of an old Italian family. —**Alessandro** See Paul III. —**Alessandro,** 1545–92, general; governor of the Netherlands.

far·ne·sol (fär'nə·sōl, -sol) *n. Chem.* An alcohol with a delicate fragrance, $C_{15}H_{25}O$, extracted from the flowers of the acacia and from various essential oils: used in perfumery. [<NL (*Acacia*) *farnesiana,* a species of acacia + -OL[1]]

far·o (fâr'ō) *n.* A game of cards in which the players bet against the dealer as to the order in which certain cards will appear. [alter. of *Pharaoh,* ? from a picture originally on one of the cards]

Fa·ro (fä'rōō) The southernmost city of Portugal, capital of Algarve province.

faro bank 1 A house or establishment for playing faro. **2** The proprietor's fund risked in the game.

Far·oe Islands (fâr'ō) See FAEROE ISLANDS.

Far·o·ese (fâr'ō·ēz', -ēs') *n.* **1** A native or the natives of the Faeroe Islands. **2** The North Germanic language spoken in these islands: also **Far'o·ish.**

far-off (fär'ôf', -of') *adj.* Situated at a great distance; remote.

fa·rouche (fà·rōōsh') *adj. French* **1** Fierce. **2** Sullen. **3** Shy.

Fa·rouk I (fə·rōōk'), 1920–1965, king of Egypt 1936–52; abdicated. Also *Faruk.*

far-out (fär'out') *adj.* **far·ther-out, far·thest-out** *Slang* Advanced, unconventional, or avant-garde.

far-point (fär'point') *n. Physiol.* The farthest point at which the eye, under conditions of relaxation, can see objects distinctly: greatest in normal and hypermetropic vision.

Far·quhar (fär'kwər, -kər), **George,** 1678–1707, British dramatist.

far·ra·go (fə·rā'gō, -rä'-) *n. pl.* **·goes** A confused mixture; medley: a *farrago* of nonsense. [<L, salad, mixture <*far* spelt] —**far·rag·i·nous** (fə·raj'ə·nəs) *adj.*

Far·ra·gut (far'ə·gət), **David Glasgow,** 1801–1870, U.S. naval officer; Union admiral in the Civil War.

Far·rar (fə·rär'), **Geraldine,** 1882–1967, U.S. operatic soprano.

far-reach·ing (fär'rē'ching) *adj.* **1** Producing effects that extend far; having profound consequences: a *far-reaching* decision. **2** Reaching far either in time or in space.

Far·rell (far′əl), **James Thomas,** 1904–1979, U. S. novelist.

far·ri·er (far′ē·ər) *n. Brit.* **1** One who shoes horses. **2** A veterinary surgeon. [<OF *ferrier* <L *ferrarius* <*ferrum* iron]

far·ri·er·y (far′ē·ə·rē) *n. pl.* **·er·ies** The business or shop of a farrier.

far·row[1] (far′ō) *n.* **1** A litter of pigs. **2** *Obs.* A little pig. —*v.t. & v.i.* To give birth to (young): said of swine. [OE *fearh* young pig]

far·row[2] (far′ō) *adj.* Not producing young during a given year, as a cow. [Cf. Flemish *varvekoe* cow no longer fertile]

Fars (färs) A former province of southern Iran on the Persian Gulf, coextensive with ancient Persis. Also **Far·si·stan** (fär′sē·stän′).

Far·sa·la (fär′sä·lä) See PHARSALA.

far–see·ing (fär′sē′ing) *adj.* **1** Seeing afar. **2** Having foresight.

far–sight·ed (fär′sī′tid) *adj.* **1** Able to see things at a distance more clearly than things near at hand; hypermetropic. **2** Far-seeing; prescient, as a statesman. —**far′–sight′ed·ly** *adv.* —**far′–sight′ed·ness** *n.*

fart (färt) *n.* An anal emission of intestinal gases, especially when audible: now a vulgar term. [<*v.*] —*v.i.* To emit gas in such a way. [ME *farten.* Cf. OHG *ferzan*]

far·ther (fär′thər) Comparative of FAR. —*adj.* More distant in space; more advanced. —*adv.* **1** To or at a more forward or distant point in space. **2** At a more forward stage; more fully or completely. [Var. of FURTHER; infl. in form by *far*]

◆ **farther, further** *Farther* is used only with reference to literal, spatial distance; *further* is employed in figurative senses involving time, degree, or quantity: *further* in the future; *further* (=additional) damage. Because it is often hard to tell whether the meaning is spatial or figurative, *further* is also used where some might prefer *farther*: We drove no *further* that day.

Farther India See INDOCHINA.

far·ther·most (fär′thər·mōst′) *adj.* Farthest.

far·thest (fär′thist) Superlative of FAR. —*adj. & adv.* Most distant or advanced in space. [Var. of FURTHEST; infl. by *far*]

far·thing (fär′thing) *n.* **1** One fourth of an English penny, at par value, about one half of a cent. **2** A small trifle. [OE *feorthing* < *feortha* a fourth]

far·thin·gale (fär′thing·gāl) *n.* A woman's hoop skirt of the 16th and 17th centuries: so called because distended by hoops of green osier, willow, or rattan. [<OF *verdugale,* alter. of Sp. *verdugado* <*verdugo* a rod, hoop]

FARTHINGALE

Faruk (fə·ro͞ok′) See FAROUK.

Fas (fäs) The Arabic name for FEZ.

fas·ces (fas′ēz) *n. pl.* In ancient Rome, a bundle of rods enclosing an ax, borne by lictors before consuls and other magistrates as a symbol of power. [<L] —**fas·ci·al** (fash′ē·əl) *adj.*

fas·ci·a (fash′ē·ə) *n. pl.* **·ci·ae** (-i.ē) **1** *Anat.* Condensed connective tissue forming sheets or layers, for the investment of organs or the insertion of muscles. **2** *Archit.* A flat member or broad volute; a jutting brick course in any story of a building except the uppermost. See illustration under ENTABLATURE. **3** Something that binds together, as a fillet; a band. **4** A bandage. **5** A distinct band of color, as in certain plants and animals. [<L, a band] —**fas′·ci·al** *adj.*

fas·ci·ate (fash′ē·āt) *adj.* **1** Bound with a fascia or belt. **2** Characterized by fasciation. **3** Marked with transverse bands: said of insects. Also **fas′ci·at′ed.** [<L *fasciatus* <*fascia* a band] —**fas′ci·ate′ly** *adv.*

fas·ci·a·tion (fash′ē·ā′shən) *n.* **1** The act of securing or fastening by fasciae. **2** The state of being fasciate or of bearing fasciate marking. **3** *Bot.* A flat, ribbonlike malformation in plants, sometimes due to an accumulated surplus of food materials.

fas·ci·cle (fas′i·kəl) *n.* **1** A small collection; bundle; cluster; group. **2** *Anat.* A bundle of fibers in the body; a fasciculus. **3** *Bot.* A cluster or bundle, as of leaves, flowers, or stalks, which proceed from a common point. **4** A number of sheets of printed work bound together. [<L *fasciculus,* dim. of *fascia* a bundle]

fas·cic·u·lar (fə·sik′yə·lər) *adj.* Of or pertaining to a fascicle.

fas·cic·u·late (fə·sik′yə·lit) *adj.* Composed of or growing in bundles. Also **fas′ci·cled, fas·cic′u·lat′ed** —**fas·cic′u·late′ly** *adv.* —**fas·cic′·u·la′tion** *n.*

fas·cic·u·lus (fə·sik′yə·ləs) *n. pl.* **·li** (-lī) A fascicle; especially, a bundle of nerve fibers.

fas·ci·nate (fas′ə·nāt) *v.* **·nat·ed, ·nat·ing** *v.t.* **1** To attract irresistibly, as by beauty or other qualities; captivate. **2** To hold spellbound, as by terror or awe. **3** *Obs.* To bewitch. —*v.i.* **4** To be fascinating. See synonyms under CHARM. [<L *fascinatus,* pp. of *fascinare* charm <*fascinum* a spell] —**fas′ci·nat′ing** *adj.* —**fas′ci·nat′ing·ly** *adv.*

fas·ci·na·tion (fas′ə·nā′shən) *n.* **1** The act of fascinating. **2** The state of being fascinated. **3** Enchantment; charm.

fas·ci·na·tor (fas′ə·nā′tər) *n.* **1** A person who fascinates. **2** A covering for the head of silk, lace, or crocheted net worn by women.

fas·cine (fas·ēn′, fə·sēn′) *n.* A bundle of sticks tied together and used in building earthworks and fortifications, filling ditches, etc. [<F <L *fascina* <*fascis* bundle]

fas·cism (fash′iz·əm) *n.* Any authoritarian, anti-democratic, anti-communist system of government in which economic control by the state, militaristic nationalism, propaganda, and the crushing of opposition by means of secret police emphasize the supremacy of the state over the individual. [<Ital. *fascismo* < *fascio* political club <L *fascis* a bundle] —**fas′cist** *n.* —**fa·scis′tic** *adj.* —**fa·scis′ti·cal·ly** *adv.*

Fas·cism (fash′iz·əm) *n.* The system of one-party government, developed by the Fascisti in Italy, which exercised a centralized autocratic control over the activities of all individuals, especially through the economic agency of state corporations.

Fas·cist (fash′ist) *n.* One of the Fascisti.

Fa·scis·ti (fə·shis′tē, *Ital.* fä·shē′stē) *n. pl. of* **Fa·scis′ta** The members of a totalitarian, syndicalist society in Italy, formed in 1919 under Benito Mussolini to oppose socialism and communism: in control of the government, 1922–43. [<Ital. <*fascio* a political club; meaning infl. by L *fasces* a bundle of rods. See FASCES.] —**Fas′cism,** *Italian* **Fa·scis·mo** (fä·shēs′mō) *n.*

fash (fash) *v.t. & v.i. Scot.* To worry; fret: to *fash* one's wits. —*n.* Worry; annoyance; vexation.

fash·ion (fash′ən) *n.* **1** The prevailing mode, especially in dress; the usage of polite society. **2** Manner of doing a thing; method; way. **3** The make or shape of a thing; external appearance; form. **4** Fashionable people, collectively. **5** Common practice or custom; usage. **6** A thing that is fashionable. See synonyms under AIR, CUSTOM, HABIT. —**after a fashion** In a way; not thoroughly, well, or enthusiastically: also **in a fashion.** —*v.t.* **1** To give shape or form to; frame; mold; make. **2** To conform; accommodate; fit. See synonyms under ADAPT, MAKE. [<AF *fachon,* var. of OF *façon* <L *factio, -onis.* Doublet of FACTION.]

fash·ion·a·ble (fash′ən·ə·bəl) *adj.* **1** Conforming to the current edicts of fashion. **2** Established and approved by the prevailing custom or polite usage. **3** Of, pertaining to, or like persons of fashion. —*n.* A person of fashion. —**fash′ion·a·ble·ness** *n.* —**fash′ion·a·bly** *adv.*

fash·ioned (fash′ənd) *adj.* **1** Made; shaped; formed: carefully *fashioned.* **2** Of a certain style or fashion: usually compounded, as old-*fashioned.*

fash·ion·er (fash′ən·ər) *n.* One who forms, molds, or puts together anything, according to a pattern or model.

fash·ion·mon·ger (fash′ən·mung′gər, -mong′-) *n.* **1** One whose life is devoted to following and spreading modes and fashions. **2** An exquisite; a dandy. —**fash′ion·mon′ger·ing, fash′·ion·mon′ging** *adj. & n.*

fashion plate **1** A picture representing the prevailing fashions in wearing apparel. **2** *Colloq.* One whose attire is perfect, according to the current mode.

Fa·sho·da (fə·shō′də) A town in south central Sudan, on the White Nile; scene of an encounter that led to an Anglo-French diplomatic crisis, the **Fashoda Incident** (1898): modern *Kodok.*

fasht (fasht) *Scot.* Troubled; wearied.

fast[1] (fast, fäst) *adj.* **1** Firm in place; not easily moved. **2** Firmly secured or bound. **3** Constant; steadfast. **4** Unfadable: said of colors. **5** Resistant: *acid-fast.* **6** Sound or deep, as sleep. **7** Acting or moving quickly; swift. **8** Performed quickly: *fast* work. **9** Adapted to, or suitable for, quick movement: a *fast* track. **10** Requiring rapidity of action or motion: a *fast* schedule. **11** Indicating a time in advance of the true time: The clock is *fast.* **12** Given to dissipation or moral laxity: *fast* living. **13** *Phot.* Intended for short exposure, as a high-velocity shutter or a highly sensitive film. —*adv.* **1** Firmly; fixedly; securely. **2** Soundly: *fast* asleep. **3** Quickly; rapidly; swiftly. **4** In quick succession: His thoughts came *fast.* **5** Dissipatedly; recklessly: to live *fast.* **6** *Archaic* Near: *fast* by. —*n.* **1** Something which is firm or fixed, as shore ice. **2** A mooring line. [OE *fæst*]

fast[2] (fast, fäst) *v.i.* **1** To abstain from food. **2** To go without food, wholly or in part, as in observance of a religious duty. —*n.* **1** Abstinence from food, partial or total, or from prescribed kinds of food, particularly as a religious duty. **2** A period prescribed for religious fasting and other observances: opposed to *feast.* [OE *fæstan*]

fast and loose Originally, a cheating game; hence, **to play fast and loose,** to act in a tricky or untrustworthy fashion.

fast·back (fast′bak′, fäst′-) *n.* **1** An automobile's continuous, downward-sloping roof from windshield to rear bumper. **2** An automobile having such a design.

fast day A day set apart for religious fasting appointed by civil or ecclesiastical authority.

fast·en (fas′ən, fäs′-) *v.t.* **1** To attach or secure to something else; connect. **2** To make fast; secure: to *fasten* a door. **3** To direct, as attention or the eyes, steadily. **4** To cause to cling or be attributed: to *fasten* blame. —*v.i.* **5** To take fast hold; cling: usually with *on.* **6** To become firm or attached. See synonyms under BIND. [OE *fæstnian* <*fæst* fixed] —**fast′en·er** *n.*

fast·en·ing (fas′ən·ing, fäs′-) *n.* **1** The act of making fast. **2** That which fastens, as a bolt. See synonyms under LOCK.

fast–food (fast′fo͞od′) *adj.* Serving quickly prepared foods, such as hamburgers, frankfurters, french-fried potatoes, etc.

fas·tid·i·ous (fas·tid′ē·əs) *adj.* Hard to please; overnice; squeamish. See synonyms under SQUEAMISH. [<L *fastidiosus* <*fastidium* disgust] —**fas·tid′i·ous·ly** *adv.* —**fas·tid′i·ous·ness** *n.*

fas·tig·i·ate (fas·tij′ē·it, -āt) *adj.* **1** Tapering toward a point. **2** *Zool.* Forming a conical bundle. **3** *Bot.* Nearly parallel and pointing upward, as the branches of a Lombardy poplar. [<L *fastigium* top + -ATE[1]]

fast·ness (fast′nis, fäst′-) *n.* **1** A fortress; stronghold. **2** The state of being firm or fixed; security. **3** Rapidity. **4** Dissipation. See synonyms under FORTIFICATION.

fat (fat) *adj.* **fat·ter, fat·test** **1** Having much or superfluous flesh; corpulent; obese. **2** Containing much oil, grease, etc. **3** Broad: said of a ship's quarter, of type bodies, etc. **4** *Printing* Profitable, because containing a large proportion of open space, illustrations, etc.: said of type matter or copy for it: also spelled *phat.* **5** Stupid; sluggish; dull. **6** Prosperous; thriving; flourishing. **7** Rich in products or in profits; rewarding: *fat* lands, a *fat* office. **8** Resinous; as *fat* wood. **9** Well-filled: a *fat* larder. **10** Plump, well-nourished, and healthy, as cattle. See synonyms under CORPULENT. —*n.* **1** *Biochem.* A gray to white, greasy, easily melted compound contained in certain specialized cells of plants and animals, and forming an important food reserve as well as a source of hormones, vitamins, and other products essential in metabolism. **2** The richest or most desirable part of anything: the *fat* of the land. **3** *Chem.* Any of various compounds of carbon, oxygen, and hydrogen which are glycerol esters of certain acids, as stearic, palmitic, etc.; they include waxes, lipids, and sterols, are insoluble in water, and in the pure state are generally colorless, odorless, and tasteless. — **the fat is in the fire** The mischief is done. — *v.t.* & *v.i.* **fat·ted, fat·ting** To fatten. [OE *fæt*] — **fat'ly** *adv.* — **fat'ness** *n.*

fa·tal (fāt'l) *adj.* 1 Bringing or connected with death or ruin; destructive; deadly. 2 Portentous; ominous. 3 Fraught with or determining fate or destiny; fateful. 4 *Obs.* That must be; inevitable. [<L *fatalis* <*fatum* FATE]

fa·tal·ism (fā'təl·iz'əm) *n.* 1 *Philos.* The doctrine that every event is predetermined by fate and inevitable. 2 A disposition to accept every event as preordained.

fa·tal·ist (fā'təl·ist) *n.* A believer in fatalism. — **fa'tal·is'tic** *adj.* — **fa'tal·is'ti·cal·ly** *adv.*

fa·tal·i·ty (fā·tal'ə·tē, fə-) *n. pl.* **·ties** 1 A state of being fated. 2 Destiny; a decree of fate. 3 A disastrous or fatal event; death. 4 Tendency to danger or disaster. See synonyms under NECESSITY.

fa·tal·ly (fā'təl·ē) *adv.* 1 In a disastrous manner; ruinously; mortally. 2 According to the decrees of fate.

fa·ta mor·ga·na (fä'tə môr·gä'nə) A mirage, especially as observed on the coast of Sicily, poetically attributed to the fairy, **Fata Morgana.** See MORGAN LE FAY.

fat·back (fat'bak') *n.* 1 The menhaden. 2 The American striped mullet. 3 Unsmoked salt pork.

fat·bird (fat'bûrd') *n.* 1 The pectoral sandpiper (*Pisobia melanota*). 2 The guacharo.

fat-body (fat'bod'ē) *n. Entomol.* The tissue of oily cells closely associated with the nutritive and metabolic functions of insects.

fat cat *U.S. Slang* A wealthy individual who is considered a potential source for large political campaign contributions.

fat-cell (fat'sel') *n. Biol.* One of a class of nucleated cells filled with fatty matter. See illustration under HAIR.

fat chance *U.S. Slang* Not much chance.

fate (fāt) *n.* 1 Predetermined and inevitable necessity; that power which is thought to determine one's future, success or failure, etc. 2 Destiny; fortune; lot. 3 Evil destiny; doom; destruction; death. 4 Outcome; final result. See synonyms under NECESSITY. — *v.t.* **fat·ed, fat·ing** To predestine: obsolete except in passive. [<L *fatum,* orig. neut. sing. of *fatus,* pp. of *fari* speak]

fat·ed (fā'tid) *adj.* Determined by fate; destined; doomed.

fate·ful (fāt'fəl) *adj.* 1 Fraught with fate. 2 Fatal. 3 Controlled by fate. — **fate'ful·ly** *adv.* — **fate'ful·ness** *n.*

Fates (fāts) In Greek mythology, three goddesses who control human destiny: Clotho spins the thread of life, Lachesis decides its length, and Atropos severs it: identified with the Roman *Parcae*: also *Destinies.*

fat·head (fat'hed') *n. U.S. Slang* A dullard; dunce. — **fat'-head'ed** *adj.*

fa·ther (fä'thər) *n.* 1 The male human parent. 2 Any male ancestor; forefather. 3 A patriarch; an aged and reverend man or honored official. 4 **a** In the Roman Catholic and, sometimes, in the Anglican Church, a priest: often used as a title and capitalized when preceding a name. **b** A church dignitary, as a bishop or abbot. 5 *Eccl.* Any one of the early historical or doctrinal writers of the Christian Church. 6 An author; founder. 7 *Brit.* The oldest member of a class or body; doyen. 8 One who bears a paternal relationship toward another. 9 A member of the ancient Roman Senate. 10 *pl.* The chiefs of a city or assembly. — *v.t.* 1 To beget as a father. 2 To found, create, or make. 3 To acknowledge as one's offspring. 4 To act as a father to. 5 To take or accept the responsibility of. [OE *fæder*] — **fa'ther·like'** *adj.* & *adv.*

Fa·ther (fä'thər) *n.* The Deity; God; the first person in the Trinity.

father confessor A priest of the Roman Catholic Church or of any other church to whom the members confess their faults and sins; hence, any one in whom one confides.

fa·ther·hood (fä'thər·hŏŏd) *n.* The state of being a father.

fa·ther-in-law (fä'thər·in·lô') *n. pl.* **fa·thers-in-law** The father of one's husband or wife.

fa·ther·land (fä'thər·land') *n.* The land of one's birth.

fa·ther·less (fä'thər·lis) *adj.* Not having a living father.

father-long-legs (fä'thər·lông'legz', -long'-) *n.* 1 A daddy-long-legs. 2 The crane fly.

fa·ther·ly (fä'thər·lē) *adj.* 1 Of, pertaining to, or like a father. 2 Manifesting the affection of a father; paternal. — **fa'ther·li·ness** *n.*

Father of History Herodotus.

Father of Medicine Hippocrates.

Father of the Constitution James Madison.

Father's Day A memorial day, observed in honor of fathers, on the third Sunday in June.

Fathers of the Church The teachers and defenders of Christianity during its first seven centuries.

fath·om (fath'əm) *n. pl.* **·oms** or **·om** A measure of length, 6 feet, or 1.829 meters: used principally in marine and mining measurements. — *v.t.* 1 To find the depth of; sound. 2 To get to the bottom of; understand; interpret. [OE *fæthm* the span of two arms outstretched] — **fath'om·a·ble** *adj.*

fa·thom·e·ter (fə·thom'ə·tər) *n.* A device for registering ocean depths by measuring the time required for the transmission and reflection of sound waves.

fath·om·less (fath'əm·lis) *adj.* Unfathomable.

fa·tid·ic (fə·tid'ik) *adj.* Able to prophesy; oracular. Also **fa·tid'i·cal.** [<L *fatidicus* <*fatum* FATE + *dicere* speak]

fat·i·ga·ble (fat'ə·gə·bəl) *adj.* Capable of causing or experiencing fatigue; tiring; wearying.

fat·i·gate (fat'ə·gāt) *adj. Obs.* Fatigued; exhausted. [<L *fatigatus,* pp. of *fatigare* tire]

fa·tigue (fə·tēg') *n.* 1 Exhaustion of strength by toil; weariness. 2 Wearing toil. 3 *Physiol.* **a** A condition of lessened activity of an organism or any of its parts, resulting from prolonged exertion. **b** A diminished susceptibility to stimulation of the central nervous system, affecting primarily the junction between nerve and muscle fibers. 4 *Metall.* The failure of metals under prolonged or repeated stress, characterized by local deformation of structure. 5 Fatigue duty. 6 *pl.* Strong, durable clothes worn on fatigue duty. — *v.t.* & *v.i.* **·tigued, ·ti·guing** To weary; tire out. [<F <*fatiguer* tire <L *fatigare*]

fatigue duty Common labor done by soldiers.

Fat·i·ma (fat'i·mə, fə·tē'mə), 606?–632, the only daughter of Mohammed.

Fat·i·ma (fat'i·mə, fə·tē'mə) The seventh wife and widow of Bluebeard.

Fat·i·ma (fat'ē·mə) A village in central Portugal, a Roman Catholic pilgrimage center since 1917.

Fat·i·mid (fat'i·mid) *n.* 1 A descendant of Fatima, daughter of Mohammed. 2 One of a North African Arab dynasty (909–1171). — *adj.* 1 Pertaining to or descended from Fatima. 2 Of or pertaining to the Fatimid dynasty. Also **Fat'i·mite** (-mīt).

fat·ling (fat'ling) *adj.* Fat; plump. — *n.* A young animal fattened for slaughter.

Fat·shan (fät'shän') A former name for NAMHOI. Also **Fa·chan** (fä'shän').

fat-sol·u·ble (fat'sol'yə·bəl) *adj. Biochem.* That may be dissolved in fat, as certain vitamins.

fat·ten (fat'n) *v.* **fat·tened, fat·ten·ing** *v.t.* 1 To make fat or plump. 2 To make (land) fertile or productive. 3 To make rich or richer. — *v.i.* 4 To become fat. — **fat'ten·er** *n.*

fat·tish (fat'ish) *adj.* Somewhat fat. — **fat'tish·ness** *n.*

fat·trels (fat'rəlz) *n. pl. Scot.* The ends of a ribbon; gathers in dressmaking.

fat·ty (fat'ē) *adj.* **fat·ti·er, fat·ti·est** Fat; unctuous. — **fat'ti·ly** *adv.* — **fat'ti·ness** *n.*

fatty acid *Chem.* A derivative of the paraffin series formed by oxidizing one of the monatomic alcohols. The physical characteristics of the higher complex fatty acids, as palmitic and stearic acids, give the name to the group.

fatty degeneration *Pathol.* A condition in which the efficient cells in an organ are enveloped in or replaced by fat.

fa·tu·i·ty (fə·tōō'ə·tē, -tyōō'-) *n.* 1 Obstinate or conceited folly. 2 Imbecility; idiocy; feeble-mindedness. [<F *fatuité* <L *fatuitas, -tatis* <*fatuus* foolish] — **fa·tu'i·tous** *adj.*

fat·u·oid (fach'ōō·oid) *n.* A species of wild oat (*Avena fatua*) resembling the cultivated variety; it is frequently a troublesome weed.

fat·u·ous (fach'ōō·əs) *adj.* 1 Stubbornly blind or foolish; idiotic. 2 Baseless; illusory, like the will-o'-the-wisp. [<L *fatuus* foolish] — **fat'u·ous·ly** *adv.* — **fat'u·ous·ness** *n.*

fat-witt·ed (fat'wit'id) *adj.* Of a dull wit; stupid.

fau·bourg (fō'bŏŏrg, *Fr.* fō·bōōr') *n.* A suburb; originally, a quarter of a city outside the old wall. [<F]

fau·cal (fô'kəl) *adj. Anat.* Of or pertaining to the fauces; produced in the fauces; deeply guttural. Also **fau·cial** (fô'shəl).

fau·ces (fô'sēz) *n. pl. Anat.* The parts bordering on the opening between the back of the mouth and the pharynx. [<L]

fau·cet (fô'sit) *n.* A spout fitted with a valve, for drawing liquids through a pipe. [<OF *fausset,* prob. <*fausser* break into, damage <L *falsare* <*falsus* FALSE]

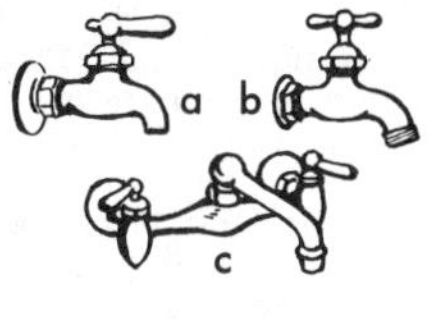

TYPES OF FAUCETS
a. Sink. *b.* Hose.
c. Mixing.

faugh (fô) *interj.* An exclamation of disgust, contempt, or rejection.

fauld (fôld, fäd) *v.t. Scot.* To fold. — *n.* 1 The working arch of a furnace; a tymp arch. 2 *Scot.* Fold.

Faulk·ner (fôk'nər), **William,** 1897–1962, U.S. novelist: also spelled *Falkner.*

fault (fôlt) *n.* 1 A slight offense; failure; negligence. 2 Whatever impairs excellence; an imperfection or defect in a person or thing; failure; blemish. 3 *Geol.* **a** A dislocation of a stratum or vein of ore which breaks its continuity. **b** A displacement or break in the continuity of rock masses, caused by disturbances of the earth's crust and resulting in a wide variety of surface features. 4 A missing or losing of the trail or scent: said of hunting dogs. 5 *Electr.* A deflection or leak in a current, due to abnormal connection of circuits or defective insulation of a conductor. 6 In tennis, rackets, etc., a failure by the server to drive the ball into the proper part of his opponent's court; also, a failure by the server to have both feet on the ground behind the service line in serving: usually called **foot fault.** 7 *Obs.* Default; lack. See synonyms under BLEMISH, ERROR, OFFENSE. — **at fault** 1 In the wrong. 2 Worthy of blame. 3 Off the scent. 4 Hence, at a loss; in a quandary. — **in fault** Blameworthy. — **to a fault** Exceedingly; excessively: generous *to a fault.* — *v.t.* 1 *Rare* To find fault with; blame. 2 *Geol.* To cause a fault in. — *v.i.* 3 *Archaic* To commit a fault; err. 4 *Geol.* To crack or fracture so as to produce a fault. [<OF *faute,* ult. <L *fallere* deceive] — **fault'ful·ly** *adv.* — **fault'ful·ness** *n.*

FAULT (*def. 3*)

fault-current (fôlt'kûr'ənt) *n. Electr.* A current flowing from conductor to ground or to another conductor because of faulty connections.

fault·find·er (fôlt'fīnd'dər) *n.* 1 A person given to complaining or finding fault; one who is excessively critical. 2 An instrument designed to locate leaks in electric current. — **fault'find'ing** *adj.* & *n.*

fault·less (fôlt'lis) *adj.* Without fault; flawless. See synonyms under CORRECT, INNOCENT, PERFECT. — **fault'less·ly** *adv.* — **fault'less·ness** *n.*

fault plane *Geol.* The fracture along which faulting occurs, commonly a curved surface.

fault·y (fôl'tē) *adj.* **fault·i·er, fault·i·est** 1 Having faults or blemishes. 2 Characterized by faults of conduct. 3 *Obs.* Guilty of faults; blamable. — **fault'i·ly** *adv.* — **fault'i·ness** *n.*

faun[1] (fôn) *n.* In Roman mythology, a deity of the woods and herds, half-human, with pointed ears and goat's feet; a satyr. ◆ Homophone: *fawn.* [<L *Faunus,* a rural god]

faun[2] (fôn, fän) *Scot.* Fallen.

fau·na (fô′nə) *n. pl.* **fau·nas** or **fau·nae** (-nē) **1** The animals living within a given area or environment or during a stated period: distinguished from *flora.* **2** A treatise upon a fauna. See synonyms under ANIMAL. [<NL, after L *Fauna,* a rural goddess] **—fau′nal** *adj.* **—fau′nal·ly** *adv.*

Fau·na (fô′nə) See BONA DEA.

Fau·nus (fô′nəs) In Roman mythology, a god of nature, patron of agriculture: identified with the Greek *Pan.*

Faure (fôr), **Élie,** 1873–1937, French art critic and historian.

Fau·ré (fô·rā′), **Gabriel Urban,** 1845–1924, French composer.

fause (fôs) *adj. Scot.* False.

Faust (foust) In medieval legend, an old philosopher who sells his soul to the devil, Mephistopheles, for wisdom and power. Also **Faust′us.**

Faus·ta (fous′tə), **Flavia Maximiana,** 289?–326, Roman empress; wife of Constantine the Great.

Faus·tine (fô′stēn, *Fr.* fôs·tēn′; *Ger.* fous·tē′·nə) A feminine personal name. Also **Faus·ti·na** (fôs·tē′nə, *Ital.* fous·tē′nā). [<L, lucky]

Faus·tus (fôs′təs, *Ger.* fous′tōōs) A masculine personal name. [<L. See FAUSTA.]

faut (fôt, fät) *v.* & *n. Scot.* Fault. Also **faute.**

fau·teuil (fō′til, *Fr.* fō·tœ′y′) *n.* An upholstered armchair. [<F <OF *faudeteuil* <Med. L *faldistolium* FALDSTOOL]

Fauves (fōv), **Les** (lā) A group of French painters, including Derain, Dufy, Matisse, and Vlaminck, who, about 1906, revolted from what they regarded as the limitations of Impressionism as well as from those of academic art. [<F, wild beasts] **—Fau′vism** *n.* **—Fau′vist** *n.*

faux pas (fō pä′) *French* A false step; mistake; error; especially, a breach of etiquette.

Fa·ven·ti·a (fə·ven′shē·ə, -shə) Ancient name for FAENZA.

fa·ve·o·late (fə·vē′ə·lāt) *adj.* Pitted; honeycombed; alveolate. Also **fa·vose** (fā′vōs, fə·vōs′). [<NL *faveolus,* dim. of *favus* a honeycomb <L + -ATE[1]]

fa·vo·ni·an (fə·vō′nē·ən) adj. **1** Of or pertaining to Favonius, the west wind, promoter of vegetation. **2** Auspicious.

fa·vor (fā′vər) *n.* **1** An act or course of generosity; kind and favorable feeling; privilege granted. **2** The state or condition of being favored or approved. **3** Favoritism; bias; partiality. **4** Kind permission. **5** Convenience; facility. **6** Something given as a token; a gage. **7** A letter, especially a business letter. **8** That which is favored. **—in favor of 1** On the side of. **2** To the benefit of; payable to. *—v.t.* **1** To look upon with favor or kindness; like. **2** To treat with partiality; show preference for. **3** To make easier; facilitate. **4** To be in favor of; support; help. **5** To do a favor for; oblige. **6** To use carefully; spare, as a lame foot. **7** *Colloq.* To look like; resemble. See synonyms under INDULGE. Also *Brit.* **fa′vour.** [<L *favere* favor] **—fa′vor·er** *n.*

Synonyms (noun): benefit, blessing, boon, civility, concession, condescension, countenance, gift, grace, kindness, patronage, predilection, preference, regard. A *favor* is a *benefit* or *kindness* that one is glad to receive, but cannot demand or claim, hence always indicating good will or *regard* on the part of the person by whom it is conferred. See ESTEEM, FRIENDSHIP, GIFT, MERCY. *Antonyms*: disapproval, disfavor, dislike, harm, hostility, hurt, injury, insult, repulse.

fa·vor·a·ble (fā′vər·ə·bəl) *adj.* **1** Convenient; advantageous. **2** Friendly; propitious. Also *Brit.* **fa′vour·able.** See synonyms under AMICABLE, AUSPICIOUS, CONVENIENT, EXPEDIENT, FRIENDLY, GOOD, PROPITIOUS. **—fa′vor·a·ble·ness** *n.* **—fa′vor·a·bly** *adv.*

fa·vored (fā′vərd) *adj.* **1** Having an aspect or appearance; in compounds: ill-*favored.* **2** Wearing a favor. **3** Befriended; aided; privileged. See synonyms under FORTUNATE.

fa·vor·ite (fā′vər·it) *adj.* Regarded with special favor; preferred. *—n.* **1** A person or animal that is considered to have the best chance of success in a race or other contest. **2** A person or thing particularly liked or favored. Also *Brit.* **fa′vour·ite.** [<OF *favorit* <Ital. *favorito,* pp. of *favorire* favor <L *favor*]

favorite son A man favored by his native State; especially, a political leader honored by receiving from his constituents a nomination for high office, as the presidency.

fa·vor·it·ism (fā′vər·ə·tiz′əm) *n.* **1** A disposition to favor unfairly or unreasonably. **2** The state or condition of being a favorite. Also *Brit.* **fa′vour·it·ism.**

fa·vus (fā′vəs) *n. Pathol.* A contagious disease as of the scalp, caused by a parasitic fungus *(Achorion schönleinii)* and producing yellow flattened scabs and baldness; scaldhead. [<L, honeycomb]

Fawkes (fôks), **Guy** See under GUY FAWKES DAY.

fawn[1] (fôn) *v.i.* **1** To show cringing fondness, as a dog: often with *on* or *upon.* **2** To show affection or seek favor by or as by cringing. ◆ Homophone: *faun.* [OE *fahnian,* var. of *fægnian* rejoice] **—fawn′er** *n.* **—fawn′ing** *adj.* & *n.* **—fawn′ing·ly** *adv.* **—fawn′ing·ness** *n.*

fawn[2] (fôn) *n.* **1** A young deer; a buck or doe in its first year. **2** The color of a fawn. *—adj.* Fawn-colored. ◆ Homophone: *faun.* [<OF *faon,* ult. <L *fetus* offspring]

fawn-col·ored (fôn′kul′ərd) *adj.* Light-yellowish brown.

faw·sont (fô′sənt) *adj. Scot.* Proper; decent: also spelled *fausant.*

fay[1] (fā) *v.t.* & *v.i.* To fit or join closely; lie closely together, as two timbers. *—n.* A fitting smoothly, as of one plank to another. [OE *fegan*]

fay[2] (fā) *n.* A fairy. [<OF *fae* <L *fata* the Fates, pl. of *fatum* fate]

fay[3] (fā) *n. Obs.* Faith: by my *fay.* [<OF *fei,* var. of *feid* FAITH]

Fay (fā) A feminine personal name. Also **Faye.** [<OF, faith]

Fa·yal (fə·yäl′) An island of the central Azores; 64 square miles; chief town Horta.

fay·al·ite (fā′əl·it, fī·äl′īt) *n.* A black magnetic iron silicate crystallizing in the orthorhombic system. [from *Fayal* + -ITE[1]]

Fa·yûm (fī·yōōm′) See FAIYUM.

faze (fāz) *v.t.* **fazed, faz·ing** *U.S. Colloq.* To worry; disturb; disconcert. Also *fease, feaze, feeze.* ◆ Homophone: *phase.* [Var. of dial. E *fease,* OE *fēsian* frighten]

fa·zen·da (fä·zeṅ′dȧ) *n.* In Brazil: **1** A hacienda. **2** An industrial enterprise for the production of coffee, cotton, or sugarcane. [<Pg. <*fazer* do]

Fe *Chem.* Iron (symbol Fe). [L *Ferrum*]

feal (fēl) *adj. Archaic* Faithful. [<OF, var. of *feeil* <L *fidelis* loyal]

fe·al·ty (fē′əl·tē) *n. pl.* **·ties 1** Fidelity, as of a vassal to his lord. **2** Devoted faithfulness; loyalty. See synonyms under ALLEGIANCE, FIDELITY. [<OF *feaute, feaulte* <L *fidelitas.* Doublet of FIDELITY.]

fear (fir) *n.* **1** An emotion excited by threatening evil or impending pain, accompanied by a desire to avoid or escape it; apprehension; dread. **2** Uneasiness about a thing; solicitude accompanied with dread. **3** That which causes fear. **4** Alarming character; formidableness. **5** Reverence for constituted authority, especially when accompanied by obedience thereto: the *fear* of God. *—v.t.* **1** To be afraid of; be fearful of. **2** To look upon with awe or reverence; venerate: to *fear* God. **3** To be anxious about; be apprehensive about. *—v.i.* **4** To be afraid; feel fear. **5** To be anxious or doubtful. [OE *fǣr* peril, sudden attack] **—fear′er** *n.*

Synonyms (noun): affright, apprehension, awe, consternation, dismay, disquiet, dread, fright, horror, misgiving, panic, terror, timidity, trembling, tremor, trepidation. *Fear* is the generic term denoting an emotion excited by threatening evil with a desire to avoid or escape it; *fear* may be sudden or lingering, in view of present, of imminent, or of distant and only possible danger; in the latter sense *dread* is oftener used. *Horror* (etymologically a shivering or shuddering) denotes a shuddering *fear* accompanied by abhorrence, or such a shock to the feelings and sensibilities as may exist without *fear,* as when one suddenly encounters some ghastly spectacle; we say of a desperate but fettered criminal, "I looked upon him with *horror.*" Where *horror* includes *fear,* it is *fear* mingled with abhorrence. (See ABHOR.) *Timidity* is a quality, habit, or condition, a readiness to be affected with *fear.* A person of great *timidity* is constantly liable to needless *alarm* and even *terror. Dread* is terrifying anticipation of evil, and is lingering and oppressive. *Dismay* is a helpless sinking of heart in view of some overwhelming peril or sorrow, actual or prospective. *Dismay* is more reflective, enduring, and despairing than *fright*; a horse is subject to *fright* or *terror,* but not to *dismay. Awe* is a reverential *fear.* Compare ALARM, ANXIETY, FRIGHT. *Antonyms*: see synonyms for FORTITUDE. Compare BRAVE.

Fear (fir), **Cape** A promontory in North Carolina near the mouth of the **Cape Fear River,** flowing 200 miles south to the Atlantic Ocean.

fear·ful (fir′fəl) *adj.* **1** Experiencing fear; afraid; apprehensive. **2** Timid; timorous. **3** Inspiring fear; terrible. **4** Caused by fear: *fearful* tremblings. **5** Full of awe and reverential fear. **6** *Colloq.* Very bad; appalling. See synonyms under AWFUL, FRIGHTFUL. **—fear′ful·ly** *adv.* **—fear′ful·ness** *n.*

fear·less (fir′lis) *adj.* Being without fear. See synonyms under BRAVE. **—fear′less·ly** *adv.* **—fear′less·ness** *n.*

fear·naught (fir′nôt′) *n.* **1** A fearless individual. **2** A heavy shaggy woolen goods; dreadnaught. Also **fear′nought′.**

fear·some (fir′səm) *adj.* **1** Causing fear; alarming. **2** Timid; frightened. **—fear′some·ly** *adv.* **—fear′some·ness** *n.*

fea·sance (fē′zəns) *n. Law* Performance of a duty; fulfilling a condition. [<AF *fesance* <*faire* do <L *facere*]

fease (fāz) See FAZE.

fea·si·ble (fē′zə·bəl) *adj.* **1** That may be done; practicable. **2** Open to being dealt with successfully. [<OF *faisable* <*faire* do <L *facere*] **—fea′si·bil′i·ty, fea′si·ble·ness** *n.* **—fea′si·bly** *adv.*

fea·sor (fē′zər) *n. Law* A doer; one who does a tort or wrong. See TORT. [<OF]

feast (fēst) *n.* **1** A sumptuous repast. **2** Anything affording great pleasure or enjoyment. **3** A day set aside for the commemoration of some person or event with rejoicing; a festival or joyous anniversary: opposed to *fast.* *—v.t.* **1** To give a feast for; entertain lavishly. **2** To delight; gratify: He *feasted* his eyes on her beauty. *—v.i.* **3** To partake of a feast; eat heartily. **4** To dwell delightedly, as on beauty. [<OF *feste* <L *festa,* neut. pl. of *festus* joyful] **—feast′er** *n.*

feast·ful (fēst′fəl) *adj.* Festive; sumptuous.

Feast of Dedication See HANUKKAH.

Feast of Lanterns 1 A Chinese festival held at the first full moon of every year (January–February): so called from the practice of hanging colored lanterns at every door and every grave. **2** The Japanese festival, Bon.

feat (fēt) *n.* **1** A notable act or performance, as one displaying skill, endurance, or daring; an achievement. **2** *Obs.* An act of any kind. See synonyms under ACT. *—adj. Obs.* **1** Dexterous; neat; ingenious. **2** Fit; befitting. [<OF *fait* <L *factum.* See FACT.]

feath·er (feth′ər) *n.* **1** One of the horny, elongated structures which form the body covering of birds and provide the flight surface for their wings. It consists of a central *shaft* composed of a hollow part near the body called the *quill* and a distal solid part, the *rachis,* along each side of which is a series of processes, the *barbs.* The barbs are provided with a fringe of smaller processes, the *barbules,* which in turn are equipped with *barbicels,* or hooklets, the whole composing the *vane* of the feather. **2** Something resembling a feather, as in mechanisms; a tongue, wedge, or fin. **3** Kind; class or species: birds of a *feather.* **4** Frame of mind; mood; spirits. **5** In rowing, the act of feathering. **6** The wake of the periscope of a submarine. **7** An irregular flaw in a gem. **8** The hairy fringe on the backs of the legs and on

FEATHER
a. Aftershaft.
b. Shaft.
c. Barbs.

the tail of some dogs. **9** *pl.* Plumage; by extension, dress or attire. **10** A fin or guide on the shaft of an arrow. **11** Anything light or trivial: A *feather* would upset him. **— a feather in one's cap** An achievement to be proud of; a thing to one's credit. **— in full feather** In full force; fully equipped. **— in high, fine,** or **good feather** In a cheerful or confident frame of mind. **—** *v.t.* **1** To fit with a feather, as an arrow. **2** To cover, adorn, or fringe with feathers. **3** To join by a tongue and groove. **4** In rowing, to turn (the oar blade) as it comes from the water until it is horizontal or nearly horizontal, thus offering the least resistance while reaching for a new stroke. **5** *Aeron.* To turn one edge of (the propeller blade) into the wind, thus minimizing drag. **—** *v.i.* **6** To grow or become covered with feathers. **7** To move, spread, or expand like feathers. **8** To feather an oar or propeller blade. **— to feather one's nest** To provide well for one's own future while acting as the agent of another. [OE *fether*]

feath·er·bed (feth′ər·bed′) *v.i.* **·bed·ded, ·bed·ding** To force the employment of unneeded workmen or the slowing of work so as to reduce unemployment: said of labor unions. **— feath′er·bed′ding** *n.*

feath·er·bone (feth′ər·bōn′) *n.* A substitute for whalebone, prepared from the quills of feathers of turkeys and chickens.

feath·er·brain (feth′ər·brān′) *n.* A light-headed or weak-minded person. **— feath′er-brained** *adj.*

feath·ered (feth′ərd) *adj.* **1** Provided with feathers or featherlike appendages. **2** Winged; swift.

feath·er-edge (feth′ər·ej′) *n.* A very thin edge, as in a wedge-shaped board or on a millstone. **— feath′er-edged′** *adj.*

feather grass **1** An ornamental grass (*Stipa pennata*) of southern Europe, having a feathered beard. **2** A related species (*S. comata*) of the western United States, sometimes called *needle grass.*

feath·er·head (feth′ər·hed′) *n.* A giddy, frivolous person. **— feath′er-head′ed** *adj.*

feath·er·less (feth′ər·lis) *adj.* Without feathers.

feather palm Any of various palms having feather-shaped or pinnate leaves.

feather star One of a genus (*Comatula*) of free-swimming crinoids with plumelike arms.

feath·er·stitch (feth′ər·stich′) *n.* A kind of decorative stitch, resembling a feather, made by taking one or more short stitches alternately on either side of a straight line. **— feath′er·stitch′ing** *n.*

feath·er-veined (feth′ər·vānd′) *adj. Bot.* Having the veins all proceeding from opposite sides of a midrib.

feath·er·weight (feth′ər·wāt′) *n.* **1** A boxer or wrestler weighing from 118 to 126 pounds. **2** The least weight allowed to a race horse in a handicap. **3** A person weighing very little; hence, anyone of little ability or importance. **—** *adj.* Of little weight; insignificant; unimportant.

feath·er·wood (feth′ər·wo͝od′) *n.* A hickorylike, hardwood timber tree of Australia (*Polyosma cunninghami*).

feath·er·y (feth′ər·ē) *adj.* Covered with or resembling feathers; light, soft, or fluffy. **— feath′er·i·ness** *n.*

fea·ture (fē′chər) *n.* **1** Any part of the human face. **2** *pl.* The whole face. **3** A salient point. **4** A magazine or newspaper article or story on a special subject. **5** A full-length motion picture. **6** *Archaic* Make; shape; form. See synonyms under CHARACTERISTIC, CIRCUMSTANCE. **—** *v.t.* **fea·tured, fea·tur·ing** **1** To make a feature of, as in a newspaper story. **2** To be a feature of. **3** To portray or outline the features of. **4** *U.S. Slang* To imagine; fancy. **5** *Colloq.* To resemble; favor. [<OF *faiture* <L *factura* <*facere* do] **— fea′ture·less** *adj.*

fea·tured (fē′chərd) *adj.* **1** Chiseled; shaped or fashioned. **2** Having or exhibiting features. **3** Given special prominence.

fea·ture-length (fē′chər·length′) *adj.* Full-length: said especially of a motion picture.

feaze (fāz) See FAZE.

Fe·be (fē′bē) The Italian form of PHOEBE.

Fe·bold Fe·bold·son (fē′bōld fē′bəld·sən) In American folklore, a Swedish pioneer plainsman, defier of tornadoes, Indians, politicians, and extreme heat or cold.

febri- *combining form* Fever: *febrifuge.* Also, before vowels, **febr-.** [<L *febris* fever]

fe·bric·i·ty (fə·bris′ə·tē) *n.* The condition of being feverish.

fe·bric·u·la (fə·brik′yə·lə) *n.* A light and passing fever. [<L, little fever]

feb·ri·fa·cient (feb′rə·fā′shənt) *n.* A substance that produces fever. **—** *adj.* Producing or promoting fever.

fe·brif·ic (fə·brif′ik) *adj.* **1** Causing fever. **2** Feverish. Also **fe·brif′er·ous.**

feb·ri·fuge (feb′rə·fyo͞oj) *n.* A medicine efficacious in reducing or removing fever. [<FEBRI- + L *fugere* flee] **— fe·brif·u·gal** (fə·brif′yə·gəl) *adj.*

fe·brile (fē′brəl, feb′rəl) *adj.* Pertaining to fever; caused by or indicating fever; feverish. [<F *fébrile* <L *febrilis* <*febris* fever]

Feb·ru·ar·y (feb′ro͞o·er′ē) The second month of the year, having twenty-eight, or, in leap years, twenty-nine days. See LEAP YEAR. [<F *Februarius (mensis)* (month) of purification <*februa,* a Roman purificatory festival, celebrated on Feb. 15]

fe·ces (fē′sēz) *n. pl.* **1** Animal excrement; ordure. **2** Any foul refuse matter or sediment. Also spelled *faeces.* [<L *faex, faecis* sediment] **— fe·cal** (fē′kəl) *adj.*

Fech·ner (fekh′nər), **Gustav Theodor,** 1801–1887, German scientist and psychophysicist.

fecht (fekht) *v.* & *n. Scot.* Fight.

fe·cial (fē′shəl) See FETIAL.

feck (fek) *Scot. adj.* Hardy; vigorous. **—** *n.* **1** Power; strength; vigor. **2** Amount, quantity, number, or value. **3** The main part: also called **maist feck.** [Aphetic var. of EFFECT]

feck·et (fek′it) *n. Scot.* An undervest or sleeveless shirt.

feck·less (fek′lis) *adj.* Feeble; good-for-nothing; irresponsible. **— feck′less·ly** *adv.* **— feck′less·ness** *n.*

feck·ly (fek′lē) *adv. Scot.* For the most part; mostly.

fec·u·la (fek′yə·lə) *n. pl.* **·lae** (-lē) **1** Starch, especially as extracted by washing farinaceous pulp; also called **amylaceous fecula.** **2** The sediment or dregs precipitated from an infusion. [<L *faecula* crust of wine, orig. dim. of *faex* dregs]

fec·u·lence (fek′yə·ləns) *n.* **1** The condition or quality of being feculent; foulness; muddiness. **2** That which is feculent; dregs. Also **fec′u·len·cy.**

fec·u·lent (fek′yə·lənt) *adj.* Turbid or foul from impurities; fecal. [<L *faeculentus* <*faecula.* See FECULA.]

fe·cund (fē′kund, fek′und) *adj.* Fruitful; fertile; prolific. [<OF *fecond* <L *fecundus*]

fe·cun·date (fē′kən·dāt, fek′ən-) *v.t.* **·dat·ed, ·dat·ing** **1** To make fruitful or fecund. **2** To impregnate; fertilize. [<L *fecundatus,* pp. of *fecundare* fertilize <*fecundus* fruitful] **— fe′cun·da′tion** *n.*

fe·cun·di·ty (fi·kun′də·tē) *n.* Productiveness; fruitfulness.

fed (fed) Past tense and past participle of FEED.

Fe·da·la (fə·dä′lə) A city in NW Morocco.

Fe·da·yeen (fe·dä′yēn) *n.* In Arab states, a commando. [<Arabic *fidayim,* pl. of *fidayi* one who ransoms or redeems his country < *fida* redemption <*faday* redeem]

fed·er·a·cy (fed′ər·ə·sē) *n. pl.* **·cies** A confederacy.

fed·er·al (fed′ər·əl) *adj.* **1** *Govt.* Of or pertaining to a form of government in which certain states agree by compact to grant control of common affairs to a central authority but retain individual control over internal affairs. **2** Of or pertaining to a union or central authority so established. **3** Favoring or supporting a government formed by a union of several states. **4** Relating to, arising from, or founded upon a league or covenant. **—** *n.* An advocate of federalism. [<F *fédéral* <L *foedus, -eris* a compact, league] **— fed′er·al·ly** *adv.*

Fed·er·al (fed′ər·əl) *adj.* **1** Of, pertaining to, owned or used by, or representing the United States of America: a *Federal* building, the *Federal* Bureau of Investigation. **2** Supporting the Union cause in the American Civil War of 1861–65: the *Federal* forces. **—** *n.* One who favored or fought for the Union cause in the American Civil War.

Federal Bureau of Investigation A branch of the Department of Justice which investigates all violations of Federal laws other than those specifically assigned to other agencies: popularly the FBI.

Federal Capital Territory A former name for the AUSTRALIAN CAPITAL TERRITORY.

Federal Communications Commission An agency of the U.S. government which supervises wire, radio, and television communication in the interest of maximum efficiency and public service.

Federal District A district reserved by a country for the location of the national government; in Argentina, including Buenos Aires, 74 square miles; in Brazil, including Rio de Janeiro, 154 square miles; in Mexico, including Mexico City, 573 square miles; in Venezuela, including Caracas, 745 square miles; in the United States, the District of Columbia, including Washington, 61 square miles. Spanish and Portugese *Distrito Federal.*

fed·er·al·ism (fed′ər·əl·iz′əm) *n.* **1** The doctrine of federal union in government. **2** *Cap.* The principles of the Federal party.

fed·er·al·ist (fed′ər·əl·ist) *n.* An advocate of federalism.

Fed·er·al·ist (fed′ər·əl·ist) *n.* One who supported the federal union of the American colonies and the adoption of the Constitution of the United States; a member of the Federal party. **— The Federalist** A series of 85 essays by Alexander Hamilton, John Jay, and James Madison, explaining, and recommending for ratification, the Constitution of the United States.

fed·er·al·is·tic (fed′ər·əl·is′tik) *adj.* Of or pertaining to federalists or federalism.

fed·er·al·ize (fed′ər·əl·īz) *v.t.* **·ized, ·iz·ing** To bring together under federal compact or government. **— fed′er·al·i·za′tion** *n.*

Federal party A political party (1787–1830) originally under the leadership of Alexander Hamilton, which advocated the adoption of the United States Constitution and the formation of a strong national government.

Federal Power Commission An agency of the U.S. government which supervises the development and utilization of power resources on Federal property, regulates the activities of public utilities engaged in interstate commerce, and provides for a uniform system of accounts in the management of electric power enterprises.

Federal Republic of Germany See under GERMANY.

Federal Reserve System A banking system created by the **Federal Reserve Act** (1913) and controlled by a **Federal Reserve Board** of eight members, established to provide an elastic currency and to concentrate the national banking resources in a system of twelve **Federal reserve banks,** each designed to regulate and aid the member banks in its respective **Federal reserve district.** The **Federal reserve cities** are Boston, New York, Philadelphia, Cleveland, Richmond, Atlanta, Chicago, St. Louis, Minneapolis, Kansas City, Dallas, and San Francisco.

Federal Territory A former name for the AUSTRALIAN CAPITAL TERRITORY.

Federal Trade Commission An agency of the U.S. government which enforces Federal laws against unfair trade practices, as price-fixing, false advertising claims, etc.

fed·er·ate (fed′ə·rāt) *v.t.* & *v.i.* **·at·ed, ·at·ing** To unite in a federation. **—** *adj.* Leagued; confederate; federal. [<L *foederatus,* pp. of L *foederare* <*foedus, -eris* a league]

Federated Malay States Former collective name for the states of Negri Sembilan, Pahang, Perak, and Selangor, now incorporated in Malaysia.

fed·er·a·tion (fed′ə·rā′shən) *n.* **1** The act of uniting under a federal government. **2** A federated body; league. **3** A national union. See synonyms under ALLIANCE, ASSOCIATION.

Federation of Malaya See MALAYA, FEDERATION OF

Federation of Rhodesia and Nyasaland See RHODESIA.

fed·er·a·tive (fed′ər·ə·tiv, fed′ə·rā′tiv) *adj.* Pertaining to federation; federal. **—fed′er·a′·tive·ly** *adv.*

Fe·de·ri·ca (fā′dā·rē′kä) Italian form of FREDERICA.

Fe·de·ri·co (fā′dā·rē′kō) Italian, Portuguese, and Spanish forms of FREDERICK. Also *Ital.* **Fe·de·ri·go** (fā′dā·rē′gō).

fe·do·ra (fə·dôr′ə, -dō′rə) *n.* A low hat, usually of soft felt, with the crown creased lengthwise. [after *Fédora,* a play by V. Sardou]

fee (fē) *n.* **1** A payment, as for professional service. **2** A charge for a special privilege, as admission to an entertainment or membership in a society or club. **3** A gratuity. **4** *Law* An estate of inheritance, either in *fee-simple,* in which the heir has unqualified ownership and power of disposition, or in *fee-tail,* in which inheritance is limited to a man and his heirs or to certain classes of heirs. **5** In feudal law, a fief. **6** Ownership; property. See synonyms under SALARY. *—v.t.* **feed, fee·ing 1** To give a fee to; tip, as a waiter. **2** *Scot.* To hire. **3** *Obs.* To bribe. [<AF, var. of OF *fé, fief* <Med. L *feudum* FEUD[2]]

fee·ble (fē′bəl) *adj.* **fee·bler, fee·blest 1** Lacking muscular power; frail; infirm. **2** Lacking strength for support or resistance; weak: a *feeble* barrier. **3** Lacking force, energy, or vigor. See synonyms under FAINT, LITTLE, MEAGER, PUSILLANIMOUS. [<OF *feble* <*fleible* weak <L *flebilis* tearful <*flere* weep. Related to FOIBLE.] **—fee′ble·ness** *n.* **—fee′blish** *adj.* **—fee′bly** *adv.*

fee·ble-mind·ed (fē′bəl·mīn′did) *adj.* **1** Deficient in will or understanding; irresolute; imbecile. **2** *Psychol.* In the United States, designating all grades of mental deficiency and backwardness, from the moron to the idiot. **—fee′ble-mind′ed·ly** *adv.* **—fee′ble-mind′ed·ness** *n.*

feed (fēd) *n.* **1** Anything that is used for food; especially, food for domestic animals; fodder, such as hay and grain. **2** The amount of food given to an animal at one time. **3** The motion that carries material into a machine or work toward a tool. **4** The machinery by which motion of the work toward the tool or of the tool toward the work is produced. **5** The material supplied to a machine to be operated upon or consumed, as wool to a carding engine or water to a boiler. **6** *Colloq.* A meal. See synonyms under FOOD. [< *v.*] *—v.* **fed, feed·ing** *v.t.* **1** To give food to; supply with food. **2** To give as food. **3** To furnish with what is necessary for the continuance, growth, or operation of: to *feed* a furnace. **4** To supply (what is necessary) for operation, manufacture, etc.: to *feed* steel to a factory. **5** To enlarge; increase, as if by causing to grow: Compliments *feed* his vanity. **6** To cue an actor with (lines). **7** In sports, to hand or throw (the ball or puck) to a player who will try for a goal, etc. *—v.i.* **8** To take food; eat: said of animals. **9** To subsist; depend: usually with *on*: to *feed* on hopes. [OE *fēdan*]

feed·back (fēd′bak′) *n.* **1** *Electronics* The transfer of a portion of the energy from the output circuit of an electronic system to the input circuit; when properly controlled and in correct phase, it is positive or regenerative; reversed or improper forms anywhere in the system are negative or degenerative. **2** A similar energy transfer occurring in certain biological processes, as in the transmission of stimuli along an interconnected system of nerve fibers.

feed·bag (fēd′bag′) *n.* A bag for feeding horses, hung over the muzzle.

feed·er (fē′dər) *n.* **1** One who or that which feeds, as a person or appliance for supplying material to a machine. **2** A person, animal, or plant that takes in nourishment. **3** Anything that supplies the wants, or increases the importance, of something else, as a tributary stream, a branch railroad, a small vein in a mine, running into a main lode. **4** One who fattens livestock for market. **5** An animal intended for intensive feeding in preparation for slaughter, or an animal that is on such feed. **6** A plant root. **7** A large box or container for feed for animals. **8** *Electr.* A conductor or group of conductors between different generating or distributing units of a power system.

feed·lift (fēd′lift′) *n.* The emergency feeding of stranded livestock by supplies dropped from airplanes in regions isolated from ground assistance by storms, blizzards, and extreme cold.

feed·lot (fēd′lot′) *n.* An area where cattle are penned and fattened up prior to their being shipped to market.

feed pipe A pipe for the distribution of liquid or gas.

feed pump A device for forcing water into a steam boiler.

feed·stock (fēd′stok′) *n.* Any raw material supplied to machine or factory that processes it into manufactured products.

feed·stuff (fēd′stuf′) *n.* Fodder, as grain (corn, oats, etc.) or alfalfa for domestic animals.

fee-fi-fo-fum (fē′fī′fō′fum′) *n.* **1** Nonsense words of a giant in the tale of *Jack the Giant-Killer.* **2** Any jargon or mummery.

feel (fēl) *v.* **felt, feel·ing** *v.t.* **1** To touch; examine by touching or handling. **2** To perceive or become aware of by the senses: to *feel* the prick of a pin. **3** To be conscious of the effects of: to *feel* the weight of a storm. **4** To be conscious of mentally; experience: to *feel* joy. **5** To have the emotions stirred by; be affected by: to *feel* a slight. **6** To be convinced of intellectually; believe in: to *feel* the need for reform. *—v.i.* **7** To have perception as if by the sense of touch: I *feel* cold. **8** To seem; appear: The air *feels* humid to me. **9** To have the emotions or opinions stirred: I *feel* strongly about the matter. **10** To make examination with or as with the hands; grope: to *feel* around a room. **—to feel like** *Colloq.* To have a desire or inclination for: to *feel like* a swim. **—to feel one's oats** *Colloq.* To act in a high-spirited manner. **—to feel out 1** To examine the possibilities of (a situation). **2** To talk to (a person) so as to determine opinions, ideas, etc. **—to feel up to** To feel able to do. *—n.* **1** The sense of touch. **2** Sensation; perception by touch. **3** Perception in general as accompanied with feeling: the *feel* of joy. **4** The quality of a thing that is perceived by the touch: Fur has a soft *feel.* [OE *fēlan*]

feel·er (fē′lər) *n.* **1** One who or that which feels. **2** *Zool.* An antenna; tentacle. **3** *Bot.* A tendril of a vine. **4** An indirect approach; a trial venture.

feel·ing (fē′ling) *n.* **1** The sense of touch or immediate contact, as aroused by stimulating receptors in the skin, muscles, or internal organs. **2** The fact or the power of perceiving the qualities of the objects arousing the sensations: the *feeling* of a glassy or metallic surface. **3** The collective state or general tone of consciousness due to more or less complex and obscure combinations of classes of sensations: a rested *feeling,* etc. **4** Any emotion as apart from the body; mental stirring; emotion; sentiment; presentiment: to express *feelings* of sympathy: The *feeling* of the meeting was hostile. **5** Sensitiveness, or the capacity to feel deeply; refined sensibility shown in tenderness or ready sympathy; by extension, sentimentality: a woman of *feeling,* to hurt one's *feelings.* **6** *Psychol.* The affective, emotional aspect of all mental life and its phenomena, as distinguished from the intellectual and voluntary, or active, aspects. **7** That quality by which expression is given to the emotions, and which should actuate a painter in the conception and execution of his design; sympathetic expression in art. *—adj.* **1** Possessed of warm sensibilities; sympathetic. **2** Marked by, or indicating deep sensibility or fervor and earnestness; hence, affecting. **—feel′ing·ly** *adv.*

Synonyms (noun): consciousness, emotion, impression, passion, pathos, sensation, sense, sensibility, sensitiveness, sentiment, tenderness. See IMPULSE, LOVE, SENSATION.

fee-sim·ple (fē′sim′pəl) *n.* *Law* An estate of inheritance free from condition.

feet (fēt) Plural of FOOT. **—feet′less** *adj.*

fee-tail (fē′tāl′) *n.* *Law* An estate limited to a person and the heirs of his body, or to a particular class of them.

feeze (fēz, fāz) See FAZE.

feign (fān) *v.t.* **1** To make a false show of; simulate; pretend. **2** To invent deceptively, as excuses. **3** To make up or imagine, as myths or stories. *—v.t.* **4** To pretend; dissimulate. See synonyms under ASSUME, PRETEND. ◆ Homophones: *fain, fane.* [<OF *feindre* <L *fingere* shape] **—feign·ed·ly** (fā′·nid·lē), **—feign′ing·ly** *adv.* **—feign′er** *n.*

feint (fānt) *n.* **1** A deceptive appearance or movement; a ruse or pretense. **2** In boxing, fencing, war, etc., an apparent or pretended blow or attack meant to divert attention from an attack to be made on another part. **3** *pl.* Faints. *—v.i.* To make a feint. *—adj. Obs.* Feigned; pretended. ◆ Homophone: *faint.* [<F *feinte* <*feindre.* See FEIGN.]

Fei·sal I (fī′səl), 1885–1933, king of Iraq 1921–1933. **—Feisal II,** 1935–58, king of Iraq 1939–58. Also spelled *Faisal.*

feist (fīst) *n.* A fice.

feis·ty (fīs′tē) *adj.* *U.S. Colloq.* Frisky; meddlesome; spunky.

feld·spar (feld′spär, fel′-) *n.* Any one of a group of crystalline rock-forming materials which consist of silicates of aluminum with potassium, sodium, or calcium: sometimes spelled *felspar.* Also **feld′spath** (-spath). [Partial trans. of G *feldspat* <*feld* field + *spat* spar[1]] **—feld·spath′ic, feld·spath′ose** *adj.*

feld·spath·oid (feld·spath′oid) *n.* One of a group of rock-forming minerals, as leucite, nepheline, sodalite, etc.; in general, silicates of aluminum and potassium or sodium, which act like the feldspars in the formation of igneous rocks.

Fel·li·ci·a (fə·lish′ē·ə, -lish′ə; *Ital.* fā·lē′chē·ä) A feminine personal name. Also **Fel·li′ci·ty,** *Fr.* **Fé·li·cie** (fā·lē·sē′) or **Fé·li·ci·té** (fā·lē·sē·tā′), *Sp.* **Fe·li·ci·dad** (fā·lē·thē·thäth′). [<L, happy]

fe·li·cif·ic (fē′lə·sif′ik) *adj.* Producing happiness. [<L *felix* happy + -FIC]

fe·lic·i·tate (fə·lis′ə·tāt) *v.t.* **·tat·ed, ·tat·ing 1** To wish joy or happiness to; congratulate. **2** *Rare* To make happy. *—adj.* Made happy. [<L *felicitatus,* pp. of *felicitare* <*felix* happy]

fe·lic·i·ta·tion (fə·lis′ə·tā′shən) *n.* **1** The act of felicitating. **2** Congratulation.

fe·lic·i·tous (fə·lis′ə·təs) *adj.* **1** Marked by or producing felicity. **2** Happy in operation or effect; appropriate; apt. See synonyms under HAPPY. **—fe·lic′i·tous·ly** *adv.* **—fe·lic′i·tous·ness** *n.*

fe·lic·i·ty (fə·lis′ə·tē) *n. pl.* **·ties 1** A state of great and well-founded happiness, comfort, and content; good fortune; blissfulness. **2** Something causing happiness; a source of content or satisfaction. **3** Happy faculty or turn; tact or knack. **4** A clever, happy, or apt expression. See synonyms under HAPPINESS. [<L *felicitas, -tatis* <*felix* happy]

fe·lid (fē′lid) *n.* Any member of a family of carnivores *(Felidae),* the cat family, including the lion, tiger, leopard, puma, lynx, etc., and the domestic cat. [<NL <L *felis* a cat]

fe·line (fē′līn) *adj.* **1** Of or pertaining to cats or catlike animals. **2** Catlike; sly. *—n.* A cat; one of the cat family. [<L *felinus* <*felis* cat] **—fe′line·ly** *adv.* **—fe′line·ness, fe·lin·i·ty** (fə·lin′ə·tē) *n.*

Fe·li·pa (fā·lē′pä) Spanish and Portuguese form of PHILIPPA.

Fe·li·pe (fā·lē′pā) Spanish form of PHILIP. Also *Pg.* **Fe·lip·pe** (fə·lē′pe).

Fe·lix (fē′liks, *Dan., Du., Ger., Sp.* fā′lēks) A masculine personal name. Also *Fr.* **Fé·lix** (fā·lēks′), *Ital.* **Fe·li·ce** (fā·lē′chā), *Pg.* **Fe·liz** (fe·lēs′). [<L, happy, fortunate, prosperous]

fell[1] (fel) *v.t.* **1** To cause to fall; cut down. **2** In sewing, to finish with a flat seam. *—n.* **1** A seam made by joining edges, folding them under, and stitching flat. **2** The end of the web in weaving. **3** The timber cut down during one season. [OE *fellan*] **—fell′a·ble** *adj.*

fell[2] (fel) Past tense of FALL.

fell[3] (fel) *adj.* **1** Characterized by fierceness or cruelty; inhuman; barbarous. **2** Hideous. **3** *Scot.* Strong; sharp; heroic: *fell* liquor. **4** *Scot.* Huge; immense. [<OF, cruel, orig. nominative of *felon.* See FELON.]

fell[4] (fel) *n.* **1** Hair; a growth of hair. **2** A hide or pelt. [OE, hide]

fell[5] (fel) *n.* *Scot. & Brit. Dial.* **1** A tract of waste land; a moor. **2** A barren hill or upland level.

fel·lah (fel′ə) *n. pl.* **fel·lahs** or **fel·la·heen** or **·hin** (fel′ə·hēn′) A peasant; laborer, as in Egypt. [<Arabic *fellāh*]

fell·er (fel′ər) *n.* **1** One who or that which fells. **2** A sewing machine attachment for the felling of seams.

fell field An area of scattered dwarf plants,

chiefly cryptogams, usually in very cold zones or on mountains above the timber line.

fell·mon·ger (fel′mung′gər, -mong′-) *n.* A dealer in fells, or skins and furs. — **fell′mon′·ger·ing, fell′mon′ger·y** *n.*

fell·ness (fel′nis) *n.* Great cruelty; ruthlessness.

fel·loe (fel′ō) *n.* A felly. ◆ Homophone: *fellow.*

fel·low (fel′ō) *n.* **1** A man; boy. **2** A person or individual; one: A *fellow* can't work day and night. **3** A companion; mate; a counterpart or one of a pair; an equal. **4** An inferior or worthless person. **5** A trustee or member of the corporation in some educational institutions. **6** A member of a society. **7** A graduate or student of a university holding a fellowship or stipend awarded for excellence in and the further pursuit of a special field of study. See FELLOWSHIP. **8** *Colloq.* A girl's beau. See synonyms under ASSOCIATE. — *v.t.* **1** To make or proclaim an equal to another. **2** To produce an equal to; match. — *adj.* Joined or associated; associate; having the same relation to something. ◆ Homophone: *felloe.* [OE *fēolaga* business partner <*feoh* property + *lag-*, stem of *lecgan* lay]

Fellow may appear as the first element in two-word phrases, with the adjectival meaning.

fellow Christian	**fellow passenger**
fellow citizen	**fellow prisoner**
fellow conspirator	**fellow soldier**
fellow countryman	**fellow student**
fellow employee	**fellow townsman**
fellow man	**fellow worker**

fellow creature A being of the same kind; any person or animal created by the same creator.

fellow feeling A sympathetic understanding.

fellow servant **1** One of a group of servants hired by the same master. **2** *Law* One of a group in common employment, in such relationship to each other that each accepts the liability of safety or danger to himself as depending upon the care or negligence of every other.

fel·low·ship (fel′ō·ship) *n.* **1** The state of being a companion or fellow; association; communion; friendly intercourse: the *fellowship* of students. **2** The condition of being sharers or partakers; community of interest, condition, or feeling; joint interest or experience: *fellowship* in prosperity or adversity. **3** A body of persons associated by reason of a community of taste, views, or interests; a company. **4** A position to which graduate members of a college may be elected, carrying with it certain privileges. **5** A foundation, as in a college or university, the income of which is bestowed upon a student, to aid him in pursuing further studies. **6** The rules for determining the shares of partners in the gains or losses of a business; partnership. See synonyms under ACQUAINTANCE, ASSOCIATION, INTERCOURSE. — *v.* **·shiped** or **·shipped, ·ship·ing** or **·ship·ping** *v.t.* To admit to religious fellowship. — *v.i. U.S.* To unite with others in fellowship.

fellow traveler A person who favors the ideology or program of a political party (specifically, the Communist party) without membership in the party.

fel·ly[1] (fel′ē) *n. pl.* **fel·lies** A segment of the rim of a wooden wheel, in which the spokes are inserted; also, sometimes, the entire rim: also spelled *felloe.* [OE *felg*]

fel·ly[2] (fel′ē) *adv. Archaic* Harshly; fiercely.

fe·lo de se (fē′lō də sē, fel′ō) *pl.* **fe·lo·nes de se** (fel′ō·nēz) or **fe·los de se** *Law Latin* **1** A suicide; self-murderer. **2** The act of suicide. [<Med. L *felo* felon + *de* of + *se* self]

fel·on[1] (fel′ən) *n.* **1** One who has committed a felony. **2** *Obs.* A criminal or depraved person. — *adj.* **1** Obtained by felony. **2** Wicked; criminal; treacherous. [<OF, base, ult. <L *fellare* suck (in obscene sense)]

fel·on[2] (fel′ən) *n. Pathol.* Inflammation of the cellular tissue and periosteum, as on a finger; a whitlow. [Origin uncertain]

fe·lo·ni·ous (fə·lō′nē·əs) *adj.* **1** Showing criminal purpose; malicious; villainous. **2** Like or involving legal felony. See synonyms under CRIMINAL. — **fe·lo′ni·ous·ly** *adv.* — **fe·lo′ni·ous·ness** *n.*

fel·on·ry (fel′ən·rē) *n.* A body of felons; a convict population, as of a penal colony.

fel·o·ny (fel′ə·nē) *Law n. pl.* **·nies** **1** In common law, an offense the punishment of which carried with it the forfeiture of lands or goods, or both. **2** One of the highest class of offenses, variously limited by common law or by statute, and punishable by imprisonment or death. Included are treason, murder, rape, robbery, arson, etc., and punishment is in a State prison.

In modern usage, and especially in American law, forfeiture of estate for crime being generally abolished, the word is used, as defined above, as distinct from *misdemeanor,* an offense of minor degree, punishable by fine or imprisonment in a county jail. Hence, *felony* is now a generic term that denotes a general class or grade of offenses, usually those of greater enormity.

felony murder A murder perpetrated during the commission of a crime of arson, rape, robbery, or burglary.

fel·site (fel′sīt) *n.* A cryptocrystalline mixture of quartz and feldspar: the groundmass of the quartz porphyries, and often the product of devitrification. Also **fel′stone** (-stōn). [<G. *fels* rock] — **fel·sit·ic** (fel·sit′ik) *adj.*

fel·spar (fel′spär) see FELDSPAR.

felt[1] (felt) Past tense and past participle of FEEL.

felt[2] (felt) *n.* **1** A fabric made by compacting wool, fur, or hair, or a mixture thereof, by mechanical or chemical action, moisture, and heat. **2** A piece of material so made; also, some article manufactured therefrom. **3** A thick fabric made of asbestos by weaving or other process. **4** In papermaking, one of two woolen or cotton blankets on which the sheet is carried and between which it is pressed on passing through the rolls of the machine. — *adj.* Made of felt. — *v.t.* **1** To make into felt. **2** To overlay with felt. — *v.i.* **3** To become matted together. [OE]

felt·ing (fel′ting) *n.* **1** The process by which, or the materials of which, felt is made. **2** Felt in quantity.

fe·luc·ca (fə·luk′ə, fe-) *n.* A small, swift Mediterranean vessel propelled by lateen sails and by oars. [<Ital. <Arabic *falūkah*]

FELUCCA

fe·male (fē′māl) *adj.* **1** Of or pertaining to the sex that brings forth young or produces ova. **2** Characteristic of a woman; feminine. **3** *Bot.* Designating a plant which has a pistil but no stamen; pistillate; capable of being fertilized and producing fruit. **4** *Mech.* Denoting some object having a correlative known as the male; specifically, a part having a hollow or bore into which the correlative may enter. **5** *Obs.* Effeminate. See synonyms under FEMININE. — *n.* **1** A person or animal of the female sex. ◆ The use of the word to mean a woman is a survival of an old English usage now regarded with disfavor by good speakers and writers. But *female* is correctly used as the correlative of *male,* whether the latter be expressed or not: "Statistics of population show that there is an excess of *females* in many cities." **2** A pistillate plant. [<OF *femelle* <L *femella,* dim. of *femina* woman]

female rime A feminine rime.

female suffrage See under SUFFRAGE.

feme (fem) *n. Law* **1** A wife: a baron and *feme.* **2** *Obs.* A woman. [<OF]

feme cov·ert (kuv′ərt) *Law* A married woman.

feme sole (sōl) *Law* **1** A single woman, unmarried, widowed, or divorced. **2** A married woman who is independent of her husband in controlling her property.

feme-sole trader (fem′sōl′) *Law* A married woman in business on her own account, independently of her husband. Also **feme-sole merchant.**

fem·i·na·cy (fem′ə·nə·sē) *n. pl.* **·cies** Feminine qualities; female nature. [<L *femina* woman]

fem·i·nal·i·ty (fem′ə·nal′ə·tē) *n.* The quality of being female; womanliness. Also **fem′i·ne′i·ty** (-nē′ə·tē). [<OF *feminal* <L *femina* a woman]

fem·i·nie (fem′ə·nē) *n. Archaic* Women collectively; womankind; also, the Amazons. [<OF]

Fem·i·nie (fem′ə·nē) *Archaic* The country of the Amazons.

fem·i·nine (fem′ə·nin) *adj.* **1** Belonging to or characteristic of womankind; having qualities, as modesty, delicacy, tenderness, tact, etc., normally characteristic of women. **2** Lacking in manly qualities; effeminate. **3** *Gram.* Applicable to females only or to objects classified with them. — *n.* **1** Women, or a woman. **2** *Gram.* A word belonging to the feminine gender. [<L *femininus* <*femina* a woman] — **fem′i·nine·ly** *adv.* — **fem′i·nine·ness** *n.*

Synonyms (adj.): effeminate, female, womanish, womanly. We apply *female* to the sex, *feminine* to the qualities, especially the finer physical or mental qualities that distinguish the *female* sex in the human family, or to the objects appropriate for or especially employed by them. A *female* voice is the voice of a woman; a *feminine* voice may belong to a man. *Womanish* denotes the undesirable, *womanly* the admirable or lovely qualities of woman. *Womanly* tears would suggest respect and sympathy, *womanish* tears a touch of contempt. The word *effeminate* is always used reproachfully, and only of men as possessing *womanish* traits such as are inconsistent with true manliness. *Antonyms*: See synonyms for MASCULINE.

feminine ending **1** The termination of an iambic verse (line of poetry) with an unaccented final syllable. **2** *Gram.* A termination or final syllable indicating feminine gender.

feminine rime Rime of the two final syllables of two or more verses in which the accent falls on the next to the last syllable, as in Keats's *Endymion,*

A thing of beauty is a joy forever:
Its loveliness increases; it will never . . .

fem·i·nin·i·ty (fem′ə·nin′ə·tē) *n.* **1** The quality or state of being feminine. **2** Women collectively. Also **fe·min′i·ty.**

fem·i·nism (fem′ə·niz′əm) *n.* **1** The doctrine which declares the equality of the sexes and advocates equal social, political, and economic rights for women. **2** *Med.* The existence of female characteristics in the male. — **fem′i·nist** *n.* — **fem′i·nis′tic** *adj.*

fem·i·nize (fem′ə·nīz) *v.t.* & *v.i.* **·nized, ·niz·ing** To make or become effeminate or feminine. — **fem′i·ni·za′tion** *n.*

femme (fâm) *n. French* **1** A woman; wife. **2** *Law* Feme.

femme de cham·bre (də shäṅ′br′) *French* A chambermaid.

fem·o·ral (fem′ər·əl) *adj. Anat.* Pertaining to the femur or thigh: the *femoral* artery.

fe·mur (fē′mər) *n. pl.* **fe·murs** or **fem·o·ra** (fem′·ər·ə) **1** *Anat.* The long bone that forms the chief support of the thigh; thigh bone; thigh. **2** *Entomol.* The third, strongest, and most prominent segment of the leg in insects, situated between the trochanter and the tibia. Compare illustration under KNEE JOINT. [<L, thigh]

fen[1] (fen) *n.* A marsh; bog. — **The Fens** A low, flat district in Cambridgeshire, Norfolk, Huntingdonshire, and Lincolnshire, England. [OE *fenn*]

fen[2] (fen) *Scot. v.t.* & *v.i.* To defend; work hard to exist; struggle to live. — *n.* A struggle for one's self; a shift.

fence (fens) *n.* **1** An enclosing structure of rails, pickets, wires, or the like. **2** A defense; shield; bulwark. **3** The art of using weapons in self-defense; especially, the skilful use of the épée, rapier, or saber; hence, skill in repartee or debate. **4** *Mech.* A guard, guide, or gage. **5** A receiver of stolen goods, or the place where such goods are received. See synonyms under RAMPART. — **on the fence** Undecided or non-committal as to opposing opinions, parties, etc. — **worm fence** A zigzag fence of rails crossed at their ends: varieties of this fence are known as *panel, serpent, snake,* and *Virginia rail fence.* — *v.* **fenced, fenc·ing** *v.t.* **1** To enclose with or as with a fence. **2** To separate with or as with a fence. **3** *Archaic* To protect; shield. **4** *Obs.* To keep out; ward off. — *v.i.* **5** To engage in the art of fencing. **6** To attempt to avoid giving direct answers; parry. **7** To deal in stolen goods. See synonyms under CIRCUMSCRIBE. [Aphetic var. of DEFENSE]

fence·less (fens′lis) *adj.* Having no fence; unenclosed or unguarded; hence, defenseless. — **fence′less·ness** *n.*
fenc·er (fen′sər) *n.* **1** One who fences, as with foil or sword. **2** A horse good at leaping fences. **3** One who builds or mends fences.
fence-rid·er (fens′rī′dər) *n.* One who rides along fences on a cattle ranch to find and repair breaks: also called a *line-rider.*
fence-sit·ter (fens′sit′ər) *n. Colloq.* A person remaining neutral, usually waiting to see which side will win.
fence-view·er (fens′vyōō′ər) *n.* In New England, a township official in charge of the inspection and erecting of fences, and the settling of line disputes.
fenc·i·ble (fen′sə·bəl) *adj. Scot.* Capable of defending or of being defended. —*n. Archaic* A soldier enlisted for home service only.
fenc·ing (fen′sing) *n.* **1** The art of attacking and defending as with a foil or sword. **2** Skilful debate or the parrying of prying questions. **3** Material for fences; fences collectively.
fend (fend) *v.t.* **1** To ward off; parry: usually with *off.* **2** *Archaic* To defend. —*v.i.* **3** To offer resistance; parry. **4** *Colloq.* To provide or get along: with *for*: to *fend for* oneself. [Aphetic var. of DEFEND]
fend·er (fen′dər) *n.* **1** One who or that which fends or wards off. **2** A metal guard before an open fire, to keep burning coals from falling onto the floor. **3** *Naut.* Any timber, rope plaiting, or other device hanging against or lying along a vessel's side as a protection from injury. **4** A plate of pressed steel over the wheels of a motor vehicle; a mudguard.
Fé·ne·lon (fā·nə·lôn′), **François de Salignac de la Mothe,** 1651–1715, French ecclesiastic and writer.
fen·es·tel·la (fen′is·tel′ə) *n. pl.* **·lae** (-ē) *Archit.* **1** A small window. **2** A niche in the wall to the side of the altar of a Roman Catholic church, containing a piscina and often the credence. [< L, dim. of *fenestra* window]
fe·nes·tra (fə·nes′trə) *n. pl.* **·trae** (-trē) **1** *Anat.* A windowlike aperture in the body: the **fenestra ovalis,** the opening between the tympanum and the vestibule of the middle ear, closed by the foot of the stapes. See illustration under EAR. **2** *Entomol.* A transparent, glassy spot, as in the wings of some insects. [< L] —**fe·nes′tral** *adj.*
fe·nes·trate (fə·nes′trit, -trāt) *adj.* **1** Having windows or windowlike openings. **2** Having transparent spots. Also **fe·nes′trat·ed.** [< L *fenestratus,* pp. of *fenestrare* furnish with windows < *fenestra* window]
fen·es·tra·tion (fen′is·trā′shən) *n.* **1** The design or arrangement of the windows of a building. **2** A fenestral or fenestrated state. **3** *Surg.* The operation of perforating: *fenestration* of the semicircular canals.
Feng·kieh (fung′jye′) A city on the Yangtze in south central China. Formerly **Kwei·chow** (gwā′jō′).
Feng·tien (fung′tyen′) The former name for MUKDEN.
Fe·ni·an (fē′nē·ən, fēn′yən) *n.* **1** A member of an Irish society called the Fenian Brotherhood, formed in New York in 1857 to seek independence for Ireland. **2** One sympathizing with the Fenian Brotherhood. **3** One of the Fianna, the warriors of Fionn MacCumal, Irish chieftain of the second and third centuries. —*adj.* Of or belonging to, composed of, or characteristic of the Fenians or the Fianna. [< Irish *Fiann,* a legendary Irish warrior; infl. by OIrish *fene* an Irishman]—**Fe′ni·an·ism** *n.*
Fenian cycle A body of Old Irish tales dealing with the expoits of Fionn MacCumal and his warriors, called the Fianna, in the second and third centuries A.D.
fen·land (fen′land′) *n.* Low, boggy land; marsh.
fen·nec (fen′ek) *n.* A small, fawn-colored African fox *(Vulpes zenda)* having very large, pointed ears. [< Arabic *fanak*]
fen·nel (fen′əl) *n.* **1** A tall, stout European herb *(Foeniculum vulgare)* of the parsley family, with finely dissected leaves and yellow flowers: cultivated in the United States for use in sauces and for its aromatic seeds. **2** The seeds of this plant. **—giant fennel** An Old World herb *(Ferula communis)* of the parsley family, sometimes attaining a height of 15 feet. [OE *fenugl, fenol* < L *faeniculum* fennel, dim. of *faenum* hay]
fen·nel·flow·er (fen′əl·flou′ər) *n.* **1** An ornamental annual herb (genus *Nigella)* of the crowfoot family; ragged lady. **2** The nutmeg flower *(N. sativa),* the seeds of which are used as seasoning.
fen·ny (fen′ē) *adj.* Marshy; boggy. Also **fen′nish.**
Fen·rir (fen′rir) In Norse mythology, a monster wolf, the son of Loki. He is kept chained by the gods, but will break loose at Ragnarok, swallow Odin, and be killed by Vidar, Odin's son. Also **Fen′rer, Fen·ris·wolf** (fen′ris·wōōlf′).
fent (fent) *n. Brit.* **1** A remnant or flawed piece of fabric. **2** *Dial.* A slit or vent in a garment. [< F *fente* < *fendre* split < L *findere*]
fen·u·greek (fen′yōō·grēk′) *n.* **1** An Old World herb *(Trigonella foenum-graecum)* of the pea family, having strong-scented leaves and mucilaginous seeds. **2** The seeds, used in medicine and as curry powder. [OE *feno-graecum* < L *faenum Graecum* Greek hay]
feod (fyōōd), **feo·dal** (fyōōd′l), etc. See FEUD, etc.
Fe·o·dor (fā′ə·dôr) Polish and Russian form of THEODORE.
feoff (fef, fēf) *Law v.t.* **feoffed, feoff·ing** To give or grant a fief to; enfeoff. —*n.* A fief; fee. [< AF *feoffer,* OF *fieffer* < *fief* FIEF]
feoff·ee (fef·ē′, fēf·ē′) *n. Law* One to whom a feoffment is made.
feof·fer (fef′ər, fēf′-) *n.* One who grants a feoffment. Also **feof′for.**
feoff·ment (fef′mənt, fēf′-) *n.* **1** A grant of lands in fee by deed with delivery. **2** The accompanying deed.
-fer *combining form* One who or that which bears: *conifer.* [< L < *ferre* bear]
fe·ra·cious (fə·rā′shəs) *adj.* Fruitful; fertile. [< L *ferax, feracis* < *ferre* bear] —**fe·rac·i·ty** (fə·ras′ə·tē) *n.*
fe·ral (fir′əl) *adj.* **1** Undomesticated; existing in a wild state; savage. **2** Pertaining to or characteristic of the wild state. Also *ferine.*
Fer·ber (fûr′bər), **Edna,** 1887–1968, U.S. novelist and playwright.
fer-de-lance (fâr′də·läns′) *n.* A venomous crotaline snake *(Bothrops atrox)* of tropical South America and Martinique, related to the copperhead. [< F, iron head of a lance]
Fer·di·nand (fûr′di·nand, *Du., Ger.* fer′dē·nänt; *Fr.* fâr·dē·nän′) A masculine personal name. Also *Ital.* **Fer·di·nan·do** (fer′dē·nän′dō). [< Gmc., ? brave life]
—Ferdinand I, died 1065, king of Castile and Leon.
—Ferdinand I, 1503–64, king of Bohemia and Hungary; Holy Roman Emperor 1556–64.
—Ferdinand II, 1578–1637, king of Bohemia and Hungary; Holy Roman Emperor 1619–1637; grandson of preceding; involved in the Thirty Years' War.
—Ferdinand III, 1608–57, king of Bohemia and Hungary; Holy Roman Emperor 1637–57; son of Ferdinand II; signed Peace of Westphalia, 1648.
—Ferdinand V, 1452–1516, king of Castile and Aragon; established the Inquisition at Seville; expelled the Jews and Moors; promoted the expeditions of Columbus and Vespucci. Known as *Ferdinand the Catholic.*
—Ferdinand VII, 1784–1833, king of Spain 1808, 1814–33.
fere[1] (fir) *adj. Obs.* Able; strong; healthy. [< ON *foer(r)*]
fere[2] (fir) *n. Obs.* A companion: also spelled *feer.* [ME, OE *gefera.* Related to FARE.]
Fer·en·czi (fer′ən·tsē), **Sandor,** 1873–1933, Hungarian psychoanalyst.
fer·e·to·ry (fer′ə·tôr′ē, -tō′rē) *n. pl.* **·ries 1** A portable shrine for the relics of saints; a reliquary. **2** The place in a church where the shrine is kept; a fixed shrine. [Alter. of earlier *fertre* < OF *fiertre* < L *feretrum* < Gk. *pheretron* < *pherein* bear]

FERETORY *(def. 1)*

Fer·ga·na (fer·gä′nə) A city in Uzbek S.S.R.
Fer·gus (fûr′gəs) A masculine personal name. [< Celtic, man's strength]
Fer·gu·son (fûr′gə·sən), **Samuel,** 1810–86, Irish poet and antiquary.
fe·ri·a (fir′ē·ə) *n. pl.* **·ri·ae** (-i·ē) **1** Any day of the week except Sunday, if not a church feast day. **2** *pl.* Holidays; festivals. [< L, holiday] —**fe′ri·al** *adj.*
fe·rine (fir′īn, -in) *adj.* Feral. [< L *ferinus* < *fera* wild beast] —**fe′rine·ly** *adv.*
Fe·rin·gi (fə·ring′gē) *n.* In the Orient, a European: among the Hindus, a European, usually in a disparaging sense, or specifically, an Indian-born Portuguese. Also **Fe·ren′ghi, Fe·rin′gee, Fe·rin′ghee, Fe·rin′ghi.** [< Persian *farangi* < Arabic *faranji* a Frank]
fer·i·ty (fer′ə·tē) *n.* Wildness; fierceness; cruelty. [< L *feritas, -tatis* < *ferus* wild, fierce]
fer·ly (fûr′lē) *adj. Obs.* Fearful or wonderful; surprising; sudden. —*n. pl.* **·lies 1** *Scot. & Brit. Dial.* A wonder or marvel; also, wonder; surprise. **2** A fault or weakness. —*v.t. & v.i.* **fer·lied, fer·ly·ing** *Scot. & Brit. Dial.* To surprise, wonder. Also **fer′lie.** [OE *færlic* sudden < *fœr* sudden danger]
Fer·man·agh (fər·man′ə) A county in SW Northern Ireland, once in Ulster; 653 square miles; county town, Enniskillen.
fer·ma·ta (fer·mä′tä) *n. Music* A pause of indeterminate length. Also *German* **fer·ma·te** (fer·mä′tə). [< Ital.]
Fer·ma·tian (fər·mā′shən) *adj.* Of or pertaining to **Pierre de Fer·mat** (fer·mà′), 1601–65, French mathematician, or to the method of mathematical induction used by him.
Fer·mat's spiral (fûr′mats) A parabolic spiral.
fer·ment (fûr′ment) *n.* **1** A substance productive of fermentation, as yeast; an enzyme. **2** Fermentation. **3** Excitement or agitation. —*v.t. & v.i.* (fər·ment′) **1** To undergo fermentation or produce fermentation in; work. **2** To stir with anger; agitate or be agitated by emotions or passions. [< F < L *fermentum* < *fervere* boil] — **fer·ment′a·ble** or **·i·ble** *adj.* —**fer·ment′·a·bil′i·ty** *n.*
fer·men·ta·tion (fûr′mən·tā′shən) *n.* **1** *Chem.* The gradual decomposition of organic compounds induced by the action of living organisms, by enzymes, or by chemical agents; specifically, the conversion of glucose into ethyl alcohol through the action of zymase. **2** Commotion, agitation, or excitement.
fer·ment·a·tive (fər·men′tə·tiv) *adj.* Causing, capable of causing, or caused by fermentation; fermenting.
fer·mi (fer′mē, fûr′-) *n. Physics* A unit for the measurement of the radii of atomic particles, equal to 10^{-13} centimeter. [after E. *Fermi*]
Fer·mi (fer′mē), **Enrico,** 1901–54, Italian nuclear physicist active in the United States.
fer·mi·um (fer′mē·əm, fûr′-) *n.* A synthetic radioactive element (symbol Fm, atomic number 100) produced by neutron bombardment of plutonium and by other nuclear reactions, first identified in residue from a thermonuclear explosion. See PERIODIC TABLE. [after E. *Fermi*]
fern[1] (fûrn) *n.* Any of a widely distributed class *(Filicineae)* of flowerless, seedless pteridophytic plants, having roots and stems and feathery leaves (fronds) which carry the reproductive spores in clusters of sporangia called *sori*: related to the horsetails and club-mosses. See SORUS. [OE *fearn*] —**fern′·like′** *adj.*
fern[2] (fûrn) *Obs. adj.* Former. — *adv.* Formerly; in olden times. [OE *fyrn*]

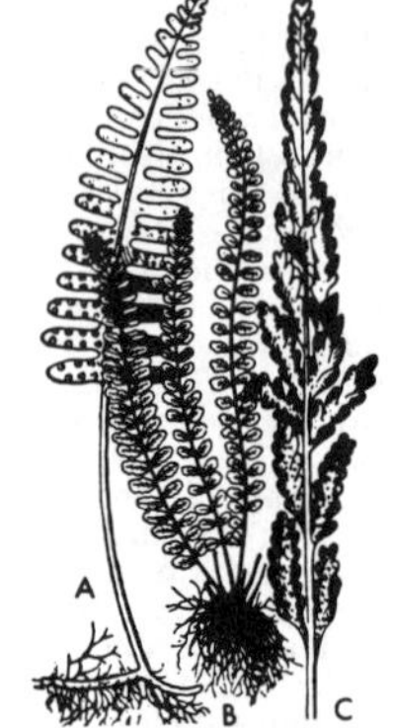

FERNS
A. Polypodium: rootstock and frond.
B. Asplenium trichomanes: fronds.
C. Osmunda cinnamomea: fertile frond.

Fer·nán·dez (fer·nän′däth), **Juan,** 1536?–1602?, Spanish navigator.
Fer·nan·do (fer·nän′·dō) Italian and Spanish form of FERDINAND. Also *Pg.* **Fer·não** (fer·noun′).

Fer·nan·do de No·ro·nha (fer·nän′do͞o de nō·rō′nyə) An island in the South Atlantic comprising a federal territory of Brazil; 7 square miles.

Fernando Po (pō) An island in the Bight of Biafra, comprising a district of Spanish Guinea; 779 square miles; capital, Santa Isabel. *Spanish* **Fer·nan′do Pó·o** (pō′ō).

fern·er·y (fûr′nər·ē) *n. pl.* **·er·ies** A place in which ferns are grown.

fern seed The reproductive spores of the fern which were formerly supposed to render one carrying them invisible.

fern·wort (fûrn′wûrt′) *n.* Any pteridophyte or fern.

fern·y (fûr′nē) *adj.* Of, pertaining to, abounding in, or resembling ferns.

fe·ro·cious (fə·rō′shəs) *adj.* **1** Of a fierce and savage nature; rapacious. **2** Very intense: *ferocious* heat. See synonyms under FIERCE, GRIM. [<L *ferox, ferocis* <*ferus* wild beast] **— fe·ro′cious·ly** *adv.* **— fe·ro′cious·ness** *n.*

fe·roc·i·ty (fə·ros′ə·tē) *n. pl.* **·ties** The state or quality of being ferocious or savage; fierce cruelty.

-ferous *combining form* Bearing or producing: *coniferous.* [<-FER + -OUS]

fer·ral·i·um (fə·ral′ē·əm) *n.* A medicine or drug containing iron; a chalybeate. [Erroneous sing. of NL *ferralia* <L *ferralis* containing iron <*ferrum* iron]

Fer·rand (fe·räṅ′) French form of FERDINAND. Also *Ital.* **Fer·ran·do** (fer·rän′dō).

Fer·ra·ra (fə·rä′rə, *Ital.* fer·rä′rä) A city in north central Italy in the Po delta. **— Fer·ra·rese** (fer′ə·rēz′, -rēs′) *adj.* & *n.*

fer·rate (fer′āt) *n. Chem.* A salt of the hypothetical ferric acid, especially **sodium ferrate,** Na_2FeO_4, a deep-red or purple, unstable solution.

fer·re·ous (fer′ē·əs) See FERROUS.

Fer·re·ro (fer·rā′rō), **Guglielmo,** 1871–1942, Italian historian.

fer·ret[1] (fer′it) *n.* **1** A small, red-eyed domesticated polecat of Europe (genus *Mustela*), about 14 inches long: used to hunt rodents and other vermin. **2** A black-footed weasel of the western United States (*M. nigripes*), which preys on prairie dogs. **—** *adj.* Ferretlike; red, like the eyes of a ferret. **—** *v.t.* **1** To drive out of hiding with a ferret. **2** To search out by careful investigation: with *out.* **3** To hunt with ferrets. **—** *v.i.* **4** To hunt by means of ferrets. **5** To search. [<OF *fuiret,* dim. of *fuiron* <LL *furon* robber <*fur* a thief] **— fer′ret·er** *n.* **— fer′ret·y** *adj.*

FERRET

fer·ret[2] (fer′it) *n.* A narrow ribbon or tape, used for binding fabrics, etc. Also **fer′ret·ing.** [<Ital. *fioretto,* dim. of *fiore* a flower <L *flos, floris*]

fer·ret[3] (fer′it) *n.* A glassmaker's iron rod for trying the melted material. [<F, dim. of *fer* iron <L *ferrum*]

ferret badger A stout-bodied carnivore (genus *Helictis*) of SE Asia.

ferri- *combining form Chem.* Containing iron in the ferric condition: *ferricyanide.* [Var. of FERRO-]

fer·ri·age (fer′ē·ij) *n.* **1** The act of ferrying; conveyance by ferry. **2** The toll charged for ferrying.

fer·ric (fer′ik) *adj. Chem.* **1** Pertaining to iron. **2** Pertaining to or designating compounds of iron in its higher valence. [<L *ferrum* iron + -IC]

ferric acetate *Chem.* A reddish-brown powder, $FeO_5H_7C_4$, widely used as an ingredient in many chemicals as a mordant, and in certain drug preparations.

ferric oxide Hematite.

ferric sulfate *Chem.* A compound of iron, $Fe_2(SO_4)_3$, uniting with water in the form of colorless crystals: used alone or as iron alum in tanning and dyeing.

fer·ri·cy·an·ic (fer′ə·sī·an′ik) *adj. Chem.* Of or pertaining to a compound of iron in its higher valence and cyanogen: *ferricyanic* acid, $H_3Fe(CN)_2$.

fer·ri·cy·a·nide (fer′ə·sī′ə·nīd, -nid) *n. Chem.* A salt containing the trivalent negative ion radical $Fe(CN)_6$, as potassium ferricyanide, $K_3Fe(CN)_6$.

fer·rif·er·ous (fə·rif′ər·əs) *adj.* Yielding iron, as rocks.

Fer·ris wheel (fer′is) A giant, vertical, power-driven wheel that revolves on a stationary axle and bears swinging observation cars for passengers. Also **ferris wheel.** [after G. W. G. *Ferris,* 1859–96, U.S. engineer]

fer·rite (fer′īt) *n.* **1** *Geol.* Indeterminable reddish decomposition products in altered igneous rocks, presumably containing iron. **2** *Chem.* Any compound, such as franklinite (zinc ferrite), considered as a derivative of the ferric hydroxide, $Fe(OH)_3$. **3** *Metall.* The pure metallic constituent in iron and steel. [<L *ferrum* iron + -ITE[1]]

Fer·ro (fer′rō) A former name for HIERRO.

ferro- *combining form* **1** Derived from, containing, or alloyed with iron: *ferromanganese.* **2** *Chem.* Containing iron in the ferrous condition: *ferrocyanide.* [<L *ferrum* iron]

fer·ro·al·loy (fer′ō·al′oi, -ə·loi′) *n. Metall.* An alloy of iron with certain other metals used in the making of special steels, as nickel, manganese, chromium, etc.

fer·ro·cal·cite (fer′ō·kal′sīt) *n.* A variety of calcite containing ferrous carbonate.

fer·ro·chrome (fer′ō·krōm′) *n. Metall.* An alloy of iron and chromium: used in the production of especially hard steel. Also **fer′ro·chro′mi·um.**

fer·ro·con·crete (fer′ō·kon′krēt, -kon·krēt′) *n.* Concrete containing metal bars or rods disposed through the mass in such a way as to increase its tensile strength and durability: also called *reinforced concrete.*

fer·ro·cy·an·ic (fer′ō·sī·an′ik) *adj. Chem.* Designating a compound obtained by the treatment of ferrocyanide with acid: *hydroferrocyanic* acid, $H_4Fe(CN)_6$.

fer·ro·cy·a·nide (fer′ō·sī′ə·nīd, -nid) *n. Chem.* A compound containing the tetravalent radical $Fe(CN)_6$: potassium *ferrocyanide,* $K_4Fe(CN)_6$.

Fer·rol (fer·rōl′) See EL FERROL DEL CAUDILLO.

fer·ro·mag·ne·sian (fer′ō·mag·nē′shən) *adj. Geol.* Relating to rocks rich in iron and magnesium, as pyroxene.

fer·ro·mag·net·ic (fer′ō·mag·net′ik) *adj. Physics* **1** Acting in a magnetic field as or like iron; also, extremely magnetic. **2** Formerly, paramagnetic. **— fer′ro·mag′ne·tism** *n.*

fer·ro·man·ga·nese (fer′ō·mang′gə·nēs, -nēz) *n.* An alloy of iron, containing 50 percent or more of manganese and being rich in carbon: used in making tough steel.

fer·ro·mo·lyb·de·num (fer′ō·mə·lib′də·nəm) *n.* An alloy of iron and molybdenum: used in the manufacture of a special steel.

fer·ro·nick·el (fer′ō·nik′əl) *n.* An alloy of iron containing at least 25 percent of nickel and practically free from carbon.

fer·ro·sil·i·con (fer′ō·sil′ə·kən) *n.* An alloy of silicon and iron added to iron when molten, to increase the proportion of silicon.

fer·ro·tung·sten (fer′ō·tung′stən) *n.* An alloy of iron and tungsten: used in the manufacture of high-speed tool steel.

fer·ro·type (fer′ō·tīp′) *n.* A tintype.

fer·rous (fer′əs) *adj. Chem.* Of or pertaining to bivalent iron, where its combining value is lowest: *ferrous* chloride, $FeCl_2$: also spelled *ferreous.* [<L *ferrum* iron + -OUS]

ferrous carbonate A compound, $FeCO_3$, precipitated as a white solid, uniting readily with the free oxygen of the air; also found as a mineral, which is an important iron ore.

ferrous sulfate A compound, $FeSO_4 \cdot H_2O$, which unites with free oxygen to form ferric sulfate. See COPPERAS.

ferrous sulfide A compound, FeS, formed either as a black solid precipitated by the action of an iron salt solution with an alkaline sulfide, or as a brittle solid from the union of sulfur and iron under heat: a source of hydrogen sulfide.

fer·ro·va·na·di·um (fer′ō·və·nā′dē·əm) *n.* An alloy of iron and vanadium: used in the manufacture of a special steel.

fer·ru·gi·nous (fə·ro͞o′jə·nəs) *adj.* **1** Of or like iron. **2** Rust-colored. [<L *ferruginus* <*ferrugo, -inis,* iron rust <*ferrum* iron]

ferruginous thrush The brown thrasher.

fer·rule (fer′əl, -o͞ol, -o͞ol) *n.* **1** A metal ring or cap, as on the end of a cane or around the handle of a tool. **2** A bushing or thimble. **3** The frame of a slate. **4** A ferule. **—** *v.t.* **·ruled, ·rul·ing** To furnish with a ferrule. [Earlier *verrel* <OF *virelle* <L *viriola,* dim. of *viriae* bracelets; infl. in form by L *ferrum* iron]

fer·ry (fer′ē) *n. pl.* **·ries** **1** Transportation by boat or airplane across a body of water. **2** The place of crossing a river, bay, strait, or the like by boat. **3** The legal right to run a ferry and to charge toll for transporting passengers and goods. **4** A boat for such transportation; a ferryboat. **— trail ferry** A raft connected with a cable crossing a stream and so adjusted as to utilize the force of the current for motive power. [<*v.*] **—** *v.* **fer·ried, fer·ry·ing** *v.t.* **1** To carry across a body of water in a boat. **2** To cross (a river, bay, etc.) in a boat. **3** To bring or take (an airplane or vehicle) to a point of delivery under its own power. **—** *v.i.* **4** To cross a body of water in a boat or by ferry. [OE *ferian* carry, convey]

fer·ry·boat (fer′ē·bōt′) *n.* A boat, often double-ended, used to transport passengers, vehicles, goods, etc., across a river, bay, strait, etc.

fer·ry·man (fer′ē·mən) *n. pl.* **·men** (-mən) **1** One who has charge of a ferry: also **fer′ry·mas′ter. 2** A member of the crew of a ferry.

ferry slip A landing dock for a ferryboat.

fer·tile (fûr′təl) *adj.* **1** Producing or capable of producing abundantly; fruitful or prolific; rich; productive; inventive. **2** Reproducing or capable of reproducing. **3** *Bot.* **a** Bearing or capable of producing fruit; capable of fertilizing or of being fertilized, as perfect anthers and pistils. **b** Productive of spore-bearing organs: said of ferns, etc. **4** *Biol.* Capable of growth or development; productive: said of seeds or eggs. **5** Causing or imparting productiveness: *fertile* rains. **6** Produced abundantly; plentiful. [<OF *fertil* <L *fertilis* <*ferre* bear] **— fer′tile·ly** *adv.*

Synonyms: exuberant, fecund, fruitful, luxuriant, productive, prolific, rich, teeming.

Fertile Crescent **1** Originally, the arc-shaped area in the Near and Middle East in which agriculture was supposedly first practiced. **2** A similar region extending from the Levant to modern Iraq.

fer·til·i·ty (fər·til′ə·tē) *n.* **1** The state or quality of being fertile. **2** Procreative capacity; fruitfulness. **3** Quickness; readiness. Also **fer′tile·ness.**

fer·til·i·za·tion (fûr′təl·ə·zā′shən) *n.* **1** The act or process of fertilizing or rendering productive. **2** *Biol.* The fusion of two gametes or of the sperm or male cell with an egg, to form a new individual, the zygote. **3** *Bot.* Pollination. **4** The treatment of soils to increase their crop productivity.

fer·til·ize (fûr′təl·īz) *v.t.* **·ized, ·iz·ing** **1** To render fertile or fruitful. **2** To impregnate an egg, ovum, or seed. **3** To enrich, as soil. **— fer′til·iz′a·ble** *adj.*

fer·til·iz·er (fûr′təl·īz′ər) *n.* **1** One who or that which fertilizes. **2** A fertilizing material applied to soil, as guano, manure, etc.

fer·u·la (fer′yo͝o·lə, -o͞o·lə) *n. pl.* **·lae** (-lē) or **·las** **1** Any of a large genus (*Ferula*) of chiefly Mediterranean herbs of the parsley family, with dissected leaves and umbels of yellow flowers. Several species supply important medicinal products, as asafetida, galbanum, and sumbul or muskroot. **2** A ferule; rod. **3** A scepter, especially that of the Byzantine emperors. [<L, giant fennel, whip, rod]

fer·u·la·ceous (fer′yo͝o·lā′shəs, -o͞o-) *adj.* Pertaining to reeds or canes; having a stalk like a reed.

fer·ule (fer′əl, -o͞ol) *n.* **1** A flat stick or ruler sometimes used for punishing children. **2** Punishment; discipline. **—** *v.t.* **fer·uled, fer·ul·ing** To punish with a ferule. [<L *ferula* FERULA]

fer·vent (fûr′vənt) *adj.* **1** Ardent in feeling; fervid. **2** Burning, or very hot. See synonyms under ARDENT, EAGER, HOT. [<L *fervens, -entis,* pp. of *fervere* be hot] **— fer′ven·cy** *n.* **— fer′vent·ly** *adv.* **— fer′vent·ness** *n.*

fer·vid (fûr′vid) *adj.* **1** Burning with zeal or eagerness; vehement. **2** Hot; glowing; fiery. [<L *fervidus* hot, violent <*fervere* be hot]

— fer·vid′i·ty, fer′vid·ness *n.* **— fer′vid·ly** *adv.*

Fer·vi·dor (fûr′vi·dôr, *Fr.* fer·vē·dôr′) See under CALENDAR (Republican).

fer·vor (fûr′vər) *n.* **1** Ardor, or intensity of feeling; zeal. **2** Heat; warmth. Also *Brit.* **fer′vour.** See synonyms under ENTHUSIASM, WARMTH. [<OF <L, heat, passion <*fervere* be hot]

Fès (fes) See FEZ.

Fes·cen·nine (fes′ə·nīn, -nin) *adj.* Relating to the ancient festivals attributed to Fescennium, a town in Etruria, and to the rude jests and licentious verses that characterized the festivals; hence, obscene; indelicate.

fes·cue (fes′kyōō) *n.* **1** Any of a genus *(Festuca)* of slender, tough grasses, valuable for pasturage. **2** A twig or straw formerly used to point out the letters to children learning to read. [<OF *festu* <L *festuca* a stalk, straw]

fess (fes) *n. Her.* A horizontal band across the middle of the shield and having a breadth equal to one third of the field. Compare illustration under ESCUTCHEON. Also **fesse.** [<OF *fesse* <L *fascia* band]

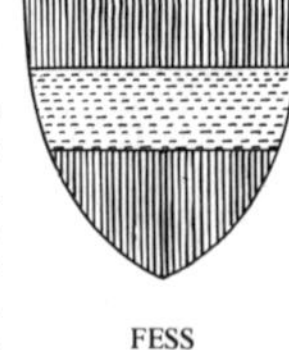

FESS

Fes·sen·den (fes′ən·dən), **William Pitt,** 1806–1869, U.S. statesman.

fess·wise (fes′wīz′) *adv. Her.* Horizontally. Also **fesse′wise′.**

fes·tal (fes′təl) *adj.* Pertaining to a festival, feast, or holiday; festive. [<OF <L *festum* a feast] **— fes′tal·ly** *adv.*

fes·ter (fes′tər) *v.i.* **1** To generate morbid matter; ulcerate. **2** To become embittered; rankle. **3** To decay; rot. **—** *v.t.* **4** To cause to fester or rankle. [< *n.*] **—** *n.* **1** The act of festering; rankling. **2** An ulcerous sore. [<OF *festre* <L *fistula* ulcer]

fes·ti·na len·te (fes·tī′nə len′tē) *Latin* Make haste slowly.

fes·ti·nate (fes′tə·nāt) *Obs. v.t.* & *v.i.* **fes·ti·nat·ed, fes·ti·nat·ing** To hasten. **—** *adj.* Quick; speedy. [<L *festinatus,* pp. of *festinare* hasten] **— fes′ti·nate·ly** *adv.*

fes·ti·na·tion (fes′tə·nā′shən) *n.* **1** *Psychiatry* Involuntary haste in walking, as in certain nervous diseases. **2** Haste.

fes·ti·val (fes′tə·vəl) *adj.* **1** Of, pertaining to, or suitable to a feast. **2** *Obs.* Joyous; merry. **—** *n.* **1** A period of feasting or celebration, as an anniversary. **2** A season devoted periodically to some form of entertainment. **3** An entertainment, as a supper, bazaar, etc., to raise funds for some charitable or other purpose: a church *festival.* [<OF <Med. L *festivalis* <L *festivus* FESTIVE]

fes·tive (fes′tiv) *adj.* Pertaining or suited to a feast; gay; joyful. [<L *festivus* <*festum* feast] **— fes′tive·ly** *adv.* **— fes′tive·ness** *n.*

fes·tiv·i·ty (fes·tiv′ə·tē) *n. pl.* **·ties** A festive celebration; social enjoyment or merriment; gaiety; merrymaking. See synonyms under FROLIC, REVEL.

fes·toon (fes·tōōn′) *n.* **1** A decorative garland or band hanging in a curve between two points. **2** An ornamental carving resembling a wreath or garland. **—** *v.t.* **1** To decorate with festoons. **2** To fashion into festoons. **3** To link together by festoons. [<F *feston* <Ital. *festone* <*festa* a feast <L *festus*] **— fes·toon′y** *adj.*

fes·toon·er·y (fes·tōōn′ər·ē) *n.* A system, method, or arrangement of festoons.

fet (fet) *v.t. Obs.* **fet·ted, fet·ting** To fetch. [OE *fetian*]

fe·tal (fēt′l) *adj.* Pertaining to the fetus: also spelled *foetal.*

fetal rickets Achondroplasia.

fe·ta·tion (fē·tā′shən) *n.* Pregnancy: also spelled *foetation.*

fetch[1] (fech) *v.t.* **1** To go after and bring back. **2** To cause to come; draw; bring, as a reply. **3** To heave (a sigh); to utter (a groan). **4** To bring as a price; sell for. **5** To execute; perform, as a leap or other movement. **6** *Colloq.* To captivate; charm. **7** *Naut.* To reach or arrive at. **8** *Colloq.* To strike or deliver, as a blow. **—** *v.i.* **9** To go after and bring things back. **10** In hunting, to retrieve game. **11** *Naut.* **a** To take a course. **b** To reach or get. **— to fetch and carry** To perform menial tasks; be a servant. **— to fetch up** To rear; bring up. **—** *n.* **1** The act of fetching. **2** The distance something is brought. **3** A stratagem. [OE *feccan,* var. of *fetian.* See FET.]

fetch[2] (fech) *v.t. Scot.* To pull by fits and starts.

fetch[3] (fech) *n.* The apparition of one still living; a wraith. [Origin uncertain]

fetch·er (fech′ər) *n.* One who or that which goes and brings.

fetch·ing (fech′ing) *adj. Colloq.* Calculated to attract; taking; fascinating. **— fetch′ing·ly** *adv.*

fête (fāt) *n.* A festival; holiday. **—** *v.t.* **fêt·ed, fêt·ing** To honor with festivities; give a feast or celebration for. [<F <OF *feste.* See FEAST.]

fête cham·pê·tre (fet shäṅ·pe′tr′) *French* An open-air festival.

fet·e·ri·ta (fet′ə·rē′tə) *n.* A variety of sorghum introduced as fodder in the United States: also called *Sudan durra.* [< native Sudanese name]

fe·tial (fē′shəl) *adj.* Pertaining to the fetiales or to their office. **—** *n.* One of the fetiales. Also spelled *fecial.*

fe·ti·a·les (fē′shē·ā′lēz) *n. pl.* A college of twenty priests or heralds in ancient Rome who conducted the negotiations and the ceremonies attending declarations of war and peace. [<L; ult. origin unknown]

fe·ti·cide (fē′tə·sīd) *n.* **1** *Law* The felonious killing of an unborn child. **2** The intentional production of abortion. Also spelled *foeticide.* [<L *fetus* fetus + -CIDE] **— fe′ti·ci′dal** *adj.*

fet·id (fet′id) *adj.* Emitting an offensive odor: also spelled *foetid.* See synonyms under NOISOME, ROTTEN. [<L *fetidus* <*fetere* stink] **— fet′id·ly** *adv.* **— fet′id·ness** *n.*

fetid hellebore Helleboraster.

fe·tip·a·rous (fə·tip′ər·əs) *adj.* Bringing forth undeveloped young, as marsupials: also spelled *foetiparous.* [<L *fetus* fetus + -PAROUS]

fe·tish (fē′tish, fet′ish) *n.* **1** A natural object believed to be the dwelling of a spirit, or to represent a spirit that may be induced or compelled magically to help and safeguard the possessor, and to protect him from harm or disease: an object of worship among savages. **2** Any object of devotion or blind affection. Also **fe′tich.** [<F *fétiche* <Pg. *feitiço* a charm, orig. an adj. <L *factitius* artificial]

fe·tish·ism (fē′tish·iz′əm, fet′ish-) *n.* **1** The belief in, devotion to, or worship of fetishes, or rites used in fetish-worship. **2** The mental state which characterizes such worship; superstition. **3** *Psychiatry* Sensual or sexual pleasure derived from fixing the attention on a part of the body or on a piece of wearing apparel belonging to a person. Also **fe′tich·ism. — fe′tish·ist** *n.* **— fe′tish·is′tic** *adj.*

fet·lock (fet′lok′) *n.* **1** The tuft of hair above a horse's hoof. **2** The projection and the joint at this place. See illustration under HORSE. [ME *fitlok, fetlak,* prob. <LG. Cf. Du. *vitlok.*]

fe·tor (fē′tər, -tôr) *n.* A stench: also spelled *foetor.* [<L]

fet·ter (fet′ər) *n.* A shackle for the ankles or a rope that binds, etc.; hence, anything that confines. **—** *v.t.* **1** To fasten fetters upon; shackle. **2** To prevent the activity of; restrain. [OE *feter, fetor.* Related to FOOT.]

Synonyms (noun): bondage, bonds, chains, custody, durance, duress, gyves, handcuffs, imprisonment, irons, manacles, shackles. *Bonds* may be of cord, leather, or any other substance that can bind; *chains* are of linked metal. *Manacles* and *handcuffs* are for the hands, *fetters* are primarily chains or jointed iron fastenings for the ankles; *gyves* may be for either. A *shackle* is a metallic ring, clasp, or braceletlike fastening for encircling and restraining a limb: commonly one of a pair, used either for hands or feet. *Bonds, fetters,* and *chains* are used in a general way for almost any form of restraint. *Gyves* is now wholly poetic, and the other words are mostly restricted to the literary style; *handcuffs* is the specific and *irons* the general term in popular usage; as, The prisoner was put in *irons. Bonds, chains,* and *shackles* are frequently used in the metaphorical sense of restraint.

fetter bone The first phalanx or great pastern of a horse's foot, just below the fetlock. See illustration under HORSE.

fet·ter·bush (fet′ər·bŏŏsh′) *n.* **1** An evergreen shrub *(Lyonia lucida)* of the heath family, with alternate leaves and fragrant white flowers, of the southern United States. **2** A related shrub *(Pieris floribunda),* with white, bell-shaped flowers.

fet·ter·lock (fet′ər·lok′) *n.* A fetlock.

fet·tle (fet′l) *v.t.* **fet·tled, fet·tling 1** *Metall.* To line or cover with a refractory material: to *fettle* the hearth of a puddling furnace. **2** *Brit. Dial.* To put in repair or good condition. **3** To beat; thrash. **—** *n.* **1** State of repair; condition. **2** The fettling used in a furnace. **— fine fettle** Good condition; high spirits. [ME *fetlen* prepare, lit., gird up <OE *fetel* a belt]

fet·tling (fet′ling) *n. Metall.* Iron ore, cinder, or other oxidizing agents, used to cover the hearth of a puddling furnace before charging it.

fet·tuc·ci·ne (fet′ə·chē′nē) *n.pl. (construed as sing. or pl.)* Flat noodles, often prepared with butter, cheese, heavy cream, etc. Also **fet′tu·ci′ne, fet′tu·ci′ni.** [<Ital., lit., dim. of *fettucia* ribbon]

fe·tus (fē′təs) *n. pl.* **fe·tus·es** The young in the womb of viviparous animals in the later stages of development; specifically, in women, from the end of the second month, prior to which it is called the *embryo;* unborn offspring: also spelled *foetus.* [<L]

feu (fyōō) *n.* **1** Tenure of lands based on agricultural service, or rent in grain or money: distinguished from *ward-holding,* the military tenure of the country; also, a perpetual lease at a stipulated rent. **2** The ground so held. **3** A piece of land held in fee. **—** *v.t.* In Scots law, to grant (land) upon feu. [<OF, var. of *fé.* See FEE.]

feud[1] (fyōōd) *n.* **1** Vindictive strife or hostility between families or clans, commonly hereditary. **2** Any quarrel or conflict. **—** *v.i.* To engage in a feud; quarrel bitterly. [ME *fede* <OF <OHG *fehida* hatred, revenge] **— feud′·ist** *n.*

Synonyms: animosity, bitterness, contention, contest, controversy, dispute, dissension, enmity, hostility, quarrel, strife. A *feud* is *enmity* between families, clans, or parties, with acts of *hostility* mutually retaliated and avenged; *feud* is rarely used of individuals, never of nations. While all the other words of the group may refer to that which is transient, a *feud* is long-enduring, and often hereditary. *Dissension* is used of a number of persons, of a party or other organization. *Bitterness* is in feeling only; *enmity* and *hostility* involve will and purpose to oppose or injure. Compare QUARREL.

feud[2] (fyōōd) *n. Law* Land held of a superior on condition of rendering service; a fief: also spelled *feod.* [<Med. L *feudum* <Gmc.]

feu·dal (fyōō′dəl) *adj.* **1** Pertaining to the relation of lord and vassal, or to the feudal system. **2** Relating to or of the nature of a feud or fee. **— feu′dal·ly** *adv.*

feu·dal·ism (fyōō′dəl·iz′əm) *n.* The medieval European system of land tenure on condition of military aid and other services. **— feu′dal·is′tic** *adj.*

feu·dal·ist (fyōō′dəl·ist) *n.* One learned in the laws of feudalism.

feu·dal·i·ty (fyōō·dal′ə·tē) *n.* **1** The condition or quality of being feudal; the practice and principles of feudalism. **2** A fief.

feu·dal·ize (fyōō′dəl·īz) *v.t.* **·ized, ·iz·ing** To bring under the feudal system; render feudal. **— feu′dal·i·za′tion** *n.*

feudal system A politico-social system in force throughout Europe from the 9th to the 15th century, founded on the tenure of feuds, or fiefs, given as compensation for military services rendered by chiefs and by them sublet by allotments to their subordinates and vassals.

feu·da·ry (fyōō′dər·ē) *adj.* Relating to a feudal tenure. **—** *n. pl.* **·ries** One holding land by feudal tenure; a vassal.

feu·da·to·ry (fyōō′də·tôr′ē, -tō′rē) *adj.* Holding or held by feudal tenure. **—** *n. pl.* **·ries 1** A feud or fief. **2** A vassal.

feud·ist[1] (fyōō′dist) *n.* **1** One versed in feudal law; a writer on feudalism. **2** One subject to feudal law. **3** The holder of a feud.

feud·ist[2] (fyōō′dist) *n. U.S.* One who takes part in a feud or quarrel.

Feu·er·mann (foi′ər·män), **Emanuel,** 1902–42, Austrian violoncellist active in the United States.

Feu·illant (fœ·yäṅ′) *n.* **1** A reformed Cistercian of the order instituted by Jean de la Barrière and approved by the pope in 1586: so called from the monastery of Feuillants in Languedoc. **2** A member of a club of conservative royalists in the French Revolution of 1789: named from the convent of the Feuillants, where it met.

Feuil·let (fœ·ye′), **Octave,** 1821–90, French novelist and dramatist.

feuil·le·ton (fœ·yə·tôṅ′) *n.* **1** The part of a French newspaper devoted to light literature, criticism, etc.: usually a space across the foot of the page. **2** An article or critique. **3** A serialized article or story. [<F <*feuillet,* dim. of *feuille* a leaf <L *folium*] **— feuil′le·ton·ism** *n.* **— feuil′le·ton·ist** *n.* **— feuil′le·ton·is′·tic** *adj.*

feu·ter·er (fyōō′tər·ər) See FEWTERER.

fe·ver (fē′vər) *n.* **1** Body temperature above the normal; pyrexia. **2** A disorder marked by high temperature, rapid pulse, increased tissue-destruction, loss of appetite, restlessness, and delirium. ◆ Collateral adjective: *febrile.* **3** Emotional excitement; great interest, enthusiasm, or urge. **—** *v.t.* To affect with fever. [OE *fēfer* <L *febris* <*fervere* be hot] **— fe′·vered** *adj.*

fever blister A form of herpes affecting the lips. Also **fever sore.**

fe·ver·bush (fē′vər·bŏŏsh′) *n.* **1** The benjamin-bush. **2** The winterberry.

fe·ver·few (fē′vər·fyōō′) *n.* An erect bushy herb (*Chrysanthemum parthenium*) of the composite family, bearing white-rayed flowers, once used to make a medicinal tea. [OE *feferfuge* <LL *febrifugia* <L *febris* fever + *fugare* put to flight]

FEVERFEW
(Plants from 1 1/2 to 3 feet tall)

fever heat 1 Body temperature in excess of the normal; in man, above 98.6 degrees Fahrenheit. **2** A condition of great excitement or interest.

fe·ver·ish (fē′vər·ish) *adj.* **1** Affected with fever. **2** Eager; hot; impatient. **— fe′ver·ish·ly** *adv.* **— fe′ver·ish·ness** *n.*

fe·ver·ous (fē′vər·əs) *adj.* Feverish. **— fe′ver·ous·ly** *adv.*

fever therapy Pyretotherapy.

fever tree 1 The bluegum tree (*Eucalyptus globulus*) from which eucalyptol is obtained. **2** An American tree (*Pinckneya pubens*), with a bark of tonic and febrifugal properties.

fe·ver·weed (fē′vər·wēd′) *n.* Any of a genus (*Eryngium*) of herbs of the parsley family having medicinal uses.

fe·ver·wort (fē′vər·wûrt′) *n.* A perennial weedy herb (*Triosteum perfoliatum*) of the honeysuckle family having brownish-purple flowers and a nauseous odor. Its root is a purgative and emetic. Also **fe′ver·root′** (-rōōt′, -rŏŏt′).

few (fyōō) *adj.* Small or limited in number; not many. **—** *n.* A small number; some: Give me a *few.* **— the few** The minority. **— quite a few** An appreciable number. ◆ **fewer, less** See LESS (def. 3). [OE *fēawe*]

few·ness (fyōō′nis) *n.* The state of being few; scarcity.

few·ter·er (fyōō′tər·ər) *n. Obs.* A keeper of hounds, especially greyhounds: also spelled *feuterer.* [Alter. of AF *veutrier,* OF *veutre,* ult. <L *vertragum* a greyhound <Celtic]

few·trils (fyōō′trilz) *n. pl. Brit. Dial.* Trifling or unimportant things, as small articles of furniture.

fey[1] (fā) *adj. Scot.* **1** Fated or foredoomed to death, particularly to a sudden death. **2** Seeming to be fated or doomed.

fey[2] (fā) *adj.* **1** Affected by association with the fairies; enchanted, under a spell; hence, out of touch with reality. **2** Visionary; touched in the head. [<F *fé,* pp. of *féer* enchant <*fee, fae.* See FAY[2].]

fez (fez) *n.* A brimless felt cap, usually red with a black tassel, formerly worn by the Turks. [<F <Turkish *fes,* after *Fez* in Morocco, where these caps were formerly manufactured] **— fezzed** *adj.*

Fez (fez) A city in NE Morocco: also *Fès:* Arabic *Fas.*

Fez·zan (fe·zan′) The SW district of Libya; 280,000 square miles; capital, Sebha.

fi·a·cre (fē·ä′kər, *Fr.* fyà′kr′) *n.* A small four-wheeled public carriage; a French hackney coach. [<F, after Hotel St. *Fiacre,* a Parisian inn]

fi·an·cé (fē′än·sā′, fē·än′sā; *Fr.* fē·äṅ·sā′) *n. masc.* An affianced or betrothed person. [<F] **— fi′an·cée′** *n. fem.*

Fi·an·na Eir·eann (fē′ə·nə âr′in) The Fenians of Ireland.

fi·ar (fē′ər) *n.* In Scots law, one who holds the fee-simple to land or an estate.

fi·as·co (fē·as′kō) *n. pl.* **·cos** or **·coes** A complete or humiliating failure. [<Ital., a flask; semantic development uncertain]

fi·at (fē′at, -ət) *n.* **1** A positive and authoritative command that something be done; an order or decree. **2** Authorization. [<L, let it be done]

fi·at lux (fī′ət luks′) *Latin* Let there be light.

fiat money Irredeemable paper money made legal tender by law.

fib (fib) *n.* A petty falsehood. **—** *v.i.* **fibbed, fib·bing** To tell a fib. [? Alter. of FABLE] **— fib′ber** *n.*

fi·ber (fī′bər) *n.* **1** A fine filament. **2** A slender or threadlike component of a substance, as of wood, or spun glass. **3** An individual filament, as of wool or cotton. **4** A structure composed of filaments; especially, any natural or synthetic material that may be separated into threads for spinning, weaving, etc.: the *fiber* of hemp, flax, rayon, or wool, etc. **5** *Bot.* **a** A slender, elongated, and thickened cell in the strengthening tissue of plants. **b** A filamentous wool; also, a rootlet. **6** The texture of anything. **7** Character; nature; make-up: a woman of strong *fiber.* Also **fi′bre.** [<F *fibre* <L *fibra* fiber] **— fi′bered** *adj.* **— fi′ber·less** *adj.*

fi·ber·board (fī′bər·bôrd′, -bōrd′) *n.* A tough, pliable, water-resistant material made of wood or other plant fibers compressed and rolled into sheets of varying thickness.

Fi·ber·glas (fī′bər·glas′, -gläs′) *n.* A flexible, non-flammable, moisture- and rot-proof material made of glass spun into filaments: it is widely used for textiles, insulators, mats, filters, etc.: a trade name.

fiber leather Leatherboard.

fiber optics A branch of optics concerned with optical fibers and their applications.

fiber silk An imitation of silk woven from the fibrils of cellulose.

fi·bri·form (fī′brə·fôrm) *adj.* **1** Having a fibrous form or structure. **2** Resembling fiber.

fi·bril (fī′brəl) *n.* **1** A minute fiber, especially a nerve or muscle filament. **2** *Bot.* A root hair. [<NL *fibrilla,* dim. of L *fibra* fiber]

fi·bril·la (fī·bril′ə) *n. pl.* **·lae** (-ē) *Biol.* One of the filamentous structures found in the cytoplasm of cells and thought to be essential in cell development and function. [<NL, dim. of L *fibra* a fiber]

fi·bril·lar (fī′brə·lər) *adj.* Of, pertaining to, resembling, or composed of fibers or fibrils. Also **fi′bril·lar′y.**

fi·bril·late (fib′rə·lāt, fī′brə-) *v.i.* **·lat·ed, ·lat·ing** *Pathol.* To undergo fibrillation.

fi·bril·la·tion (fī′brə·lā′shən, fī′brə-) *n.* **1** The formation of fibers. **2** *Physiol.* A localized twitching of certain muscle fibers. **3** *Pathol.* Rapid, irregular, uncoordinated contractions of the muscle fibers of the heart.

fi·bril·lif·er·ous (fī′brə·lif′ər·əs) *adj.* Fibril-bearing.

fi·bril·li·form (fī·bril′ə·fôrm) *adj.* Having the form of fibrils.

fi·bril·lose (fī′brə·lōs) *adj.* Composed of fibers or fibrils.

fi·brin (fī′brin) *n.* **1** *Biochem.* An insoluble protein which forms an interlacing network of fibers in clotting blood, with resulting coagulation of the plasma and separation of the serum. **2** The fibrous portion of flesh. **3** *Bot.* Gluten, or vegetable fibrin.

fi·brin·o·gen (fī·brin′ə·jən) *n. Biochem.* A complex protein of the globulin group, found in blood plasma and in other body fluids. It is associated with a ferment, thrombin, in the formation of fibrin during the process of coagulation. **— fi′brin·o·gen′ic, fi·bri·nog·e·nous** (fī′brə·noj′ə·nəs) *adj.*

fi·bri·no·ly·sin (fī′brə·nō·lī′sin) *n. Biochem.* A toxic substance having the power to liquefy human fibrin. It is formed by the action of certain pathogenic bacteria, as staphylococci.

fi·bri·no·sis (fī′brə·nō′sis) *n. Pathol.* A condition of excess fibrin in the blood.

fi·bri·nous (fī′brə·nəs) *adj.* Possessed of the properties, characteristics, or nature of fibrin.

fibro– *combining form* Related to or composed of fibrous tissue; having a fibrous structure: *fibrovascular.* Also, before vowels, **fibr–.** [<L *fibra* fiber]

fi·broid (fī′broid) *adj.* Of the nature of fiber; fibrous: as a *fibroid* tumor.

fi·bro·in (fī′brō·in) *n. Biochem.* A white, lustrous protein, forming the principal ingredient in natural silk and spider webs.

fi·bro·ma (fī·brō′mə) *n. pl.* **·ma·ta** (-mə·tə) *Pathol.* A fibrous tumor. **— fi·bro′ma·tous** *adj.*

fi·bro·sis (fī·brō′sis) *n. Pathol.* Morbid increase of fibrous tissue in the body; fibroid degeneration, as of the blood capillaries.

fi·brous (fī′brəs) *adj.* Composed of, or having the character of fibers.

fi·bro·vas·cu·lar (fī′brə·vas′kyə·lər) *adj. Bot.* Composed or consisting of woody fibers and vessels, as **fibrovascular tissue,** a tissue composed of elongated, thick-walled, and generally fusiform elements, as wood and bast.

fib·u·la (fib′yōō·lə) *n. pl.* **·lae** (-lē) **1** *Anat.* The outer of the two bones forming the lower part of the leg or hind limb; the calf bone. ◆ Collateral adjective: *peroneal.* **2** An ancient type of ornamental brooch, fastening somewhat like a safety pin. [<L, a clasp <*figere* fasten] **— fib′u·lar** *adj.*

-fic *suffix* Making, rendering, or causing: *beatific, scientific.* [<L *-ficus* <*facere* make, render]

-fication *suffix* The making, rendering, or causing to be of a certain sort of character: *beatification, glorification.* [<L *-ficatio, -onis* <*-ficare* <*facere* make]

fice (fīs) *n.* A small dog of mixed breed, but usually terrierlike: also spelled *feist, fist.* [Short for *fisting dog* <obs. *fist* break wind]

fiche (fēsh) *n.* Microfiche.

Fich·te (fikh′tə), **Johann Gottlieb,** 1762–1814, German philosopher. **— Fich′te·an** *adj.* & *n.*

Fich·te·an·ism (fikh′tē·ə·niz′əm) *n.* The philosophy of J. G. Fichte, a pure idealism, based upon the self or ego as the only reality.

fi·chu (fish′ōō, *Fr.* fē·shü′) *n.* **1** A triangular piece of light material worn about the neck. **2** A three-cornered cape worn with the ends crossed or tied in front. [<F *ficher* put on hastily]

fick·le (fik′əl) *adj.* Inconstant in feeling or purpose; changeful; capricious. [OE *ficol* crafty] **— fick′le·ness** *n.*

Synonyms: capricious, changeable, changeful, crotchety, fitful, inconstant, irresolute, mutable, shifting, unstable, unsteady, vacillating, variable, veering, wavering, whimsical. See IRRESOLUTE, MOBILE. *Antonyms*: constant, decided, determined, firm, fixed, immutable, invariable, reliable, resolute, steadfast.

fi·co (fē′kō) *n. pl.* **·coes 1** *Archaic* A trifle; a fig's worth. **2** *Obs.* A gesture of contempt made by thrusting the thumb between two fingers or into the mouth. [<Ital. <L *ficus* a fig]

fic·tile (fik′til) *adj.* **1** Made of molded earth or clay; pertaining to pottery. **2** Capable of being molded; plastic. [<L *fictilis* <*fingere* form]

fic·tion (fik′shən) *n.* **1** The act of feigning or imagining that which does not exist or is not actual. **2** That which is feigned or imagined, as opposed to that which is actual. **3** The department of literature that embraces fictitious narrative, including romances, novels, short stories, art epics, etc. See NOVEL. **4** A legal assumption, for the furtherance of justice, that a certain thing which is or may be false is true. **5** *Obs.* The act of fashioning; also, a device; fabric. **6** *Obs.* Pretense; deceit. [<F <L *fictio, -onis* a making <*fingere* form]

Synonyms: allegory, apolog, fable, fabrication, falsehood, figment, invention, legend, myth, novel, romance, story. *Fiction* is now chiefly used of a prose work in narrative form in which the characters are partly or wholly imaginary, and which is designed to portray human life, with or without a practical lesson; a *romance* portrays what is picturesque or striking, as a mere *fiction* may not do; *novel* is a general name for any continuous fictitious narrative, especially a love story. The moral of the *fable* is expressed formally; the lesson of the *fiction,* if any, is inwrought. A *fiction* is studied; a *myth* grows up without intent. A *legend* may be true, but cannot be historically verified; a *myth* has been received as true at some time. A *fabrication* is designed to deceive; it is a less odious word than *falsehood,* but is really stronger, as a *falsehood* may be a sudden unpremeditated statement, while a *fabrication* is a series of statements carefully studied and fitted together in order to deceive; the *falsehood* is all false; the *fabrication* may mingle the true with the false. A *figment* is something imaginary which the one who utters it may or may not believe to be true; we say, "That statement is a *figment* of his imagination." The *story* may be either true or false, and covers the various senses of all the words in the group. *Apolog,* a word simply transferred from Greek into English, is the same as *fable.* Compare ALLEGORY. *Antonyms*: certainty, fact, history, literalness, reality, truth, verity.

fic·tion·al (fik′shən·əl) *adj.* Belonging to fiction; ideal. — **fic′tion·al·ly** *adv.*

fic·tion·ist (fik′shən·ist) *n.* One who writes fiction.

fic·ti·tious (fik·tish′əs) *adj.* **1** Belonging to or of the nature of fiction. **2** Counterfeit; false; assumed. See synonyms under COUNTERFEIT, ROMANTIC. — **fic·ti′tious·ly** *adv.* — **fic·ti′tious·ness** *n.*

fic·tive (fik′tiv) *adj.* **1** Of the nature of a figment; imaginary. **2** Having to do with the creation of fiction: *fictive* ability. — **fic′tive·ly** *adv.*

Fi·cus (fī′kəs) *n.* A large genus of plants, mostly tropical trees, shrubs, and vines, belonging to the mulberry family and including the fig, banyan, and rubber plant. [<L, a fig tree]

fid (fid) *n. Naut.* **1** A supporting bar; a crosspiece to hold a topmast in place. **2** A large tapering wooden pin used for stretching eyes in rigging, opening ropes when splicing, etc. [Origin uncertain]

FIDS

-fid *combining form Bot.* Divided into; split: *pinnatifid.* [<L *-fidus* <*findere* split]

fid·dle (fid′l) *n.* **1** A violin. **2** *Naut.* A rack or frame used at table on board ship in rough weather to keep the dishes in place. — *v.* **fid·dled, fid·dling** *v.i.* **1** To play on a fiddle. **2** To pass the time in trifling matters. **3** To toy with an object. — *v.t.* **4** To play (an air, tune, etc.) on a fiddle. **5** To trifle; fritter: to *fiddle* time away. [OE *fithele,* found in *fithelere* a fiddler. Akin to VIOL.]

fiddle block *Mech.* A pulley block with two sheaves, the larger one above the smaller.

fiddle bow A bow³ (def. 4).

fid·dle-de-dee (fid′l·dē′dē′) *interj. & n.* Nonsense. [Fanciful var. of FIDDLE]

fid·dle-fad·dle (fid′l·fad′l) *v.i.* **-fad·dled, -fad·dling** **1** To trifle. **2** To talk nonsense. — *n.* Idle talk; nonsense. [Varied reduplication of FIDDLE]

fid·dle·head (fid′l·hed′) *n.* **1** *Naut.* An ornament just above a ship's cutwater, resembling the convoluted head of a fiddle. **2** *Canadian* An edible fern shoot. Also **fid′dle·neck′** (-nek′).

fid·dler (fid′lər) *n.* **1** One who plays a fiddle. **2** A fiddler crab. — **to pay the fiddler** To suffer the consequences.

fiddler crab A small burrowing crab (genus *Uca*) the male of which flourishes its enlarged claw as if fiddling: found on the Atlantic coast of the United States.

FIDDLER CRAB
(Carapace about 1/2 to 1 inch in width)

fid·dle·stick (fid′l·stik′) *n.* **1** A fiddle bow. **2** A trifling or absurd thing.

fid·dle·sticks (fid′l·stiks′) *interj.* Nonsense!

fid·dle·wood (fid′l·wo͝od′) *n.* Any one of several species of trees of the vervain family (*Citharexylum* and allied genera): used in tropical America for building.

fi·de·i·com·mis·sar·y (fī′de·ī·kom′ə·ser′ē) *n. Law* A beneficiary in a trust estate, or one for whose benefit a trust has been created. [<L *fidei commissarius*] — **fi′de·i·com′mis·sar′i·ly** *adv.* — **fi′de·i·com·mis′sion** *n.* — **fi′de·i·com·mis′sion·er** *n.*

fi·de·i·com·mis·sum (fī′de·ī·kə·mis′əm) *n. pl.* **·sa** In Roman and civil law, a devise or bequest coupled with a request to the party named to give the property to a third party who could not hold directly under the will; a trust estate. [<L <*fidei,* dat. of *fides* faith + *commissum,* pp. neut. sing of *committere* entrust to]

Fi·de·i De·fen·sor (fī′dē·ī di·fen′sôr) *Latin* Defender of the Faith: a title of the British sovereign.

fi·de·jus·sion (fī′də·jush′ən) *n. Law* The condition of being bound as surety for another; suretyship. [<L *fideiussio, -onis* <*fideiubere* <*fide,* ablative sing. of *fides* faith + *iubere* order] — **fi′de·jus′so·ry** (-jus′ər·ē) *adj.*

Fi·de·li·a (fi·dē′lē·ə, -dēl′yə) A feminine personal name. [<L, faithful]

fi·del·i·ty (fī·del′ə·tē, fə-) *n. pl.* **·ties** **1** Faithfulness in the discharge of duty or of obligation. **2** Hearty allegiance to those to whom one is bound in affection or honor; loyalty; devotion: matrimonial *fidelity, fidelity* to a father or friend. **3** Strict adherence to truth or fact; reliability; veracity. **4** *Electronics* A measure of the accuracy and freedom from distortion with which a sound-reproducing system, as radio, will receive and transmit the input signals; it may be high, medium, or low. [<F *fidelité* <L *fidelitas, -tatis* <*fides* faith]

Synonyms: allegiance, constancy, devotion, faith, faithfulness, fealty, honesty, integrity, loyalty, truth, truthfulness. See ALLEGIANCE. *Antonyms*: disloyalty, infidelity, treachery, treason.

fidg·et (fij′it) *v.i.* **1** To move about restlessly. **2** To toy with something nervously. — *v.t.* **3** To make restless; worry. — *n.* **1** Nervous restlessness: often in the plural: to have the *fidgets.* **2** A restless person; one who fidgets. [< obs. *fidge* move about; ultimate origin unknown] — **fidg′et·y** *adj.* — **fidg′et·i·ness** *n.*

fi·du·cial (fi·do͞o′shəl, -dyo͞o′-) *adj.* **1** Of the nature of or indicating faith or practical confidence. **2** Of the nature of a trust; fiduciary. **3** *Physics* Fixed as a basis of measurement or reference: the *fiducial* point of a scale. [<L *fiducialis* <*fiducia* trust] — **fi·du′cial·ly** *adv.*

fi·du·ci·ar·y (fi·do͞o′shē·er′ē, -shə·rē, -dyo͞o′-) *adj.* **1** Pertaining to a position of trust or confidence; confidential: a *fiduciary* relation, as that of an attorney, guardian, or trustee. **2** Unwavering; trustful; undoubting. **3** Relying on the confidence of the public as for paper currency or value. **4** Held in trust. — *n. pl.* **·ar·ies** *Law* A person who holds a thing in trust; a trustee.

Fi·dus A·cha·tes (fī′dəs ə·kā′tēz) See ACHATES.

fie (fī) *interj.* An expression of impatience or disapproval. [<OF *fi, fy* <L *fi,* an expression of disgust]

fief (fēf) *n.* A landed estate held under feudal tenure; a fee: also spelled *feoff.* [<OF <Med. L *feudum* FEUD²]

fiel (fēl) *adj. Scot.* Snug; comfortable.

field¹ (fēld) *n.* **1** A piece of cleared land set apart and enclosed for tillage or pasture. ◆ Collateral adjective: *campestral.* **2** A plot of land set apart for a particular use: the potter's *field.* **3** A region of the countryside considered as yielding some natural product: the *coalfields* of Pennsylvania. **4** *Mil.* **a** A sphere of action or place of contest. **b** A battleground. **c** A battle: a hard-fought *field.* **5** Open or unenclosed countryside: the beast of the *field.* **6** Any wide or open expanse: the *fields* of ocean. **7** Sphere of study, investigation or practice. **8** In painting, the surface of canvas upon which the figures of a composition are set. **9** That portion of the face of a coin or medal which is not occupied by the type or principal figure. **10** The ground of each section of a flag: a blue *field* with white stars. **11** In games, the plot of ground on which the game is played; especially, in baseball, the outfield, or part outside the diamond; in baseball and cricket, the fielders collectively. For illustration see BASEBALL. **12** *Her.* The whole surface of the escutcheon upon which the charges and bearings are depicted, or of each separate coat when the shield contains quarterings or impalements. See illustration under ESCUTCHEON. **13** *Physics* **a** A portion of space at every point of which force is exerted. **b** The force exerted therein: the magnetic *field,* a *field* of force. **14** *Optics* The space or apparent surface within which objects are seen in a telescope or other optical instrument. **15** The participants in a hunt; all the competitors in a contest or race; also, the contestants exclusive of the favorites in the betting. — **to keep the field** **1** To hold one's ground against all opposers. **2** To continue active operations. — *adj.* **1** Of, pertaining to, or found in the fields: *field* flowers. **2** Used in, or for use in, the fields: a *field* gun. **3** Played on a field: *field* sports. — *v.t.* In baseball, cricket, etc. **1** To catch and return (a ball in play). **2** To put (a player or team) on the field. — *v.i.* **3** In baseball, cricket, etc., to play as a fielder. [OE *feld*]

field² (fyeld) See FJELD.

Field (fēld), **Cyrus West,** 1819–92, U.S. merchant; laid the first transatlantic cable, 1858, and a second in 1866. — **Eugene,** 1850–95, U.S. poet and journalist. — **Marshall,** 1834–1906, U.S. merchant.

field artillery Light or heavy artillery so mounted as to be freely movable, and suitable for use with troops in the field. Hence, **Field Artillery,** a branch of the U.S. Army.

field battery A battery of field artillery, containing usually four or six guns.

field book A surveyor's or naturalist's notebook.

field cap See OVERSEAS CAP.

field coil An insulated coil for exciting a field magnet.

field colors **1** Small flags used for marking the position for companies and regiments, especially in peacetime field maneuvers, reviews, parades, etc. **2** Any regimental headquarters flags, used in field service.

field corn Any of several kinds of Indian corn used for feeding livestock.

field day **1** A day when army troops are taken to the field for exercise and maneuvers. **2** In the navy, a day for general cleaning up. **3** A school holiday devoted to athletic sports. **4** Any day of display, excitement, celebration, or success. **5** A day of outdoor scientific excursion.

field·er (fēl′dər) *n.* In baseball, cricket, etc., a player stationed in the field to stop, or catch, and return the balls. Compare illustration under BASEBALL.

fielder's choice In baseball, the decision by a player to attempt to retire a base runner rather than the batter, the latter being credited with a time at bat but not with a hit.

field events The jumping, vaulting, and casting contests at an athletic meet: distinguished from *track events.*

field·fare (fēld′fâr′) *n.* A European thrush (*Turdus pilaris*), deep brown above, with a pearl-gray head and black tail, streaked on the breast and throat with blackish-brown. [OE *feldeware,* ? misspelling of *feldefare* (<*feld* field + *faran* go); or <*feld* field + *warian* dwell]

field glass **1** A small, portable, terrestrial telescope, monocular or binocular; a spyglass. **2** A field lens.

field goal **1** In football, a goal scored from scrimmage by means of a dropkick or placement kick. **2** In basketball, a goal scored with the ball in active play.

field gun A cannon mounted on wheels for rapid movement in operations by troops in the field; a fieldpiece.

field hand An agricultural laborer.

field hockey See under HOCKEY.

field hospital A hospital established on a field of battle; also, its medical officers and attendants, with their equipment for service.

field ice Ice formed in fields or floes: distinguished from *icebergs.*

Field·ing (fēl′ding), **Henry,** 1707–54, English novelist and playwright.

field intensity *Electr.* A measure of the direction and magnitude of the force exerted upon a unit charge at a given point.

field jacket A lightweight, cotton, waterproof jacket of olive-drab worn by soldiers in the field.

field kitchen A portable unit used to cook food for soldiers in the field; also, the site at which the unit is set.

field lark **1** The American meadowlark. **2** The English skylark. **3** Any of various larklike birds, as the pipit.

field lens *Optics* The anterior of the two lenses in the eyepiece of a telescope or microscope, whose purpose is to enlarge the field of view.

field magnet **1** The magnet of a magneto-electric or dynamoelectric machine, which produces the *magnetic field.* **2** A small magnet, commonly of horseshoe shape, used in determining the existence of iron ore in minerals.

field marshal A general officer of high rank in the armies of several European nations.

field martin The kingbird.

field mouse A mouse inhabiting fields and meadows, as the common European vole *(Microtus agrestis)* and the small short-tailed vole of North America *(M. pennsylvanicus)*: also called *meadow mouse.*

field music **1** The drummers, buglers, fifers, etc., who play for military troops on the march, sound regimental calls, etc. **2** The music produced by them.

field notes **1** A surveyor's notes detailing a survey. **2** A naturalist's notes taken in the field.

field officer An officer intermediate between a company and a general officer; a major, lieutenant colonel, or colonel.

field of force See FIELD[1] (def.13).

field of honor **1** The ground where a duel is fought. **2** A battlefield.

field·piece (fēld′pēs′) *n.* A cannon mounted on wheels, for use in field battles.

field plover **1** The upland plover. **2** The golden plover.

fields·man (fēldz′mən) *n. pl.* **·men** (-mən) In cricket, a fielder.

field spaniel See under SPANIEL.

field sparrow A small light-breasted American sparrow *(Spizella pusilla).*

field sports **1** Outdoor sports, especially hunting, shooting, and racing. **2** Athletic games played on the field, as opposed to races, hurdles, etc., on the track.

field·stone (fēld′stōn′) *n.* Loose stone found near a construction site and used in building. — *adj.* Consisting of or having the appearance of fieldstone: a *fieldstone* house.

field stop An opening in an opaque screen, generally circular, for determining the size of the field of view of an optical instrument.

field strength *Electr.* The magnitude of a field, expressed as a vector quantity in volts per unit length at a given point.

field trial A trial or test of hunting dogs in field performance.

field trip A trip outside the classroom for purposes of first-hand observation and study.

field winding *Electr.* The winding of the field-magnet coils of a dynamoelectric machine.

field·work (fēld′wûrk′) *n.* A temporary fortification thrown up in the field.

field work Observations or performance in the field, as by scientists, surveyors, etc.

fiend (fēnd) *n.* **1** An evil spirit; a devil; demon. **2** An intensely malicious or wicked person; one having a cruel, diabolical spirit. **3** *Colloq.* One unduly devoted to some theory or occupation; one exceptionally interested in and clever or talented in a certain subject: an algebra *fiend*; a crank; monomaniac: a fresh-air *fiend.* **4** *Colloq.* One morbidly addicted to the use of a narcotic drug or some deleterious habit: a cocaine *fiend.* **5** An implacable enemy; foe. — **the Fiend** Satan; the devil. [OE *fēond* enemy, devil]

fiend·ish (fēn′dish) *adj.* Of, pertaining to, or resembling a fiend or his conduct; diabolical. — **fiend′ish·ly** *adv.* — **fiend′ish·ness** *n.*

fient (fēnt) *n. Scot.* Fiend.

fient a haet (ə hāt) *Scot.* Devil a bit; nothing at all.

fier (fir) *adj. Scot.* Sound; healthy: also spelled *fere.*

fierce (firs) *adj.* **1** Having a violent and cruel nature or temper; savage; ferocious. **2** Violent in action; furious. **3** Vehement; passionate; extreme. **4** *Slang* Very bad; atrocious. [<OF *fers, fiers,* nominative sing. of *fier* proud <L *ferus* wild] — **fierce′ly** *adv.* — **fierce′·ness** *n.*

Synonyms: ferocious, fiery, furious, impetuous, raging, savage, uncultivated, untrained, violent, wild. *Fierce* signifies having a *furious* and cruel nature, or being in a *furious* and cruel mood. It applies to that which is intensely excited at the moment, or liable to intense and sudden excitement. *Ferocious* refers to a state or disposition; that which is *fierce* flashes or blazes; that which is *ferocious* steadily burns; we speak of a *ferocious* animal, a *fierce* passion. A *fiery* spirit with a good disposition is quickly excitable in a good cause, but may not be *fierce* or *ferocious. Savage* signifies *untrained, uncultivated. Ferocious* always denotes a tendency to violence; it is more distinctly bloodthirsty than the other words; a person may be deeply, intensely cruel, and not at all *ferocious*: a *ferocious* countenance expresses habitual ferocity; a *fierce* countenance may express habitual fierceness, or only the sudden anger of the moment. That which is *wild* is simply unrestrained; the word may imply no anger or harshness; as *wild* delight, *wild* alarm. See ARDENT, GRIM. *Antonyms*: affectionate, docile, gentle, harmless, kind, mild, patient, peaceful, submissive, tame, tender.

fi·e·ri fa·ci·as (fī′ə·rī fā′shē·əs) *Law* A writ of execution commanding a levy on goods, etc., to satisfy a judgment; literally, that you cause to be done. [<L]

fier·y (fīr′ē, fī′ər·ē) *adj.* **fier·i·er, fier·i·est** **1** Of or pertaining to fire; having the appearance of or containing fire; glowing; glaring; burning; hot: a *fiery* furnace. **2** Of the nature of ardor, rage, or animation; passionate; impetuous; fervid; spirited: a *fiery* disposition. **3** Inflammable: a *fiery* gas in a coal mine. See synonyms under ARDENT, FIERCE, HOT, IMPETUOUS. — **fier′i·ly** *adv.* — **fier′i·ness** *n.*

fiery cross See under CROSS *n.*

fiery hunter A large, black ground beetle of the United States *(Calosoma calidum)* with small coppery spots on the wing covers. For illustration see under INSECT (beneficial).

Fie·so·le (fye′zō·lā), **Fra Giovanni da** See ANGELICO, FRA.

Fie·so·le (fye′zō·lā) A town in central Italy near Florence. Ancient **Fae·su·lae** (fē′zyŏŏ·lē).

fi·es·ta (fē·es′tə, *Sp.* fyes′tä) *n.* A feast day; holiday. [<Sp. <L *festa.* See FEAST.]

fife (fīf) *n.* A small, shrill-toned, flute-like, martial wind instrument. — *v.t.* & *v.i.* **fifed, fif·ing** To play on a fife. [<G *pfeife* pipe <OHG *pfifa* < (assumed) LL *pipa* <L *pipare* peep, chirp. Doublet of PIPE.] — **fif′er** *n.*

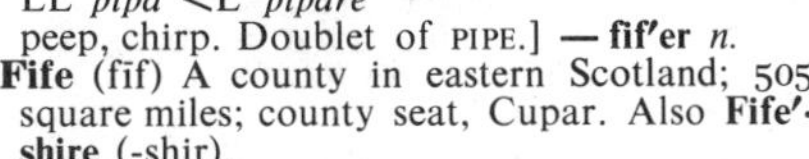

FIFE

Fife (fīf) A county in eastern Scotland; 505 square miles; county seat, Cupar. Also **Fife′·shire** (-shir).

fife rail *Naut.* A railing around a mast for holding belaying pins, etc.

fif·teen (fif′tēn′) *adj.* Consisting of five more than ten; quindecimal. — *n.* **1** The sum of ten and five: a cardinal number. **2** Any of the symbols (15, xv, XV) representing this number. [OE *fiftēne*]

fif·teenth (fif′tēnth′) *adj.* **1** Fifth in order after the tenth: the ordinal of *fifteen.* **2** Being one of fifteen equal parts: a *fifteenth* share. — *n.* **1** One of the fifteen equal parts of anything. **2** The quotient of a unit divided by fifteen.

Fifteenth Amendment An amendment to the Constitution of the United States, providing that the right of citizens to vote shall not be denied or abridged on account of "race, color, or previous condition of servitude. . . ."

fifth (fifth) *adj.* **1** Next in order after the fourth: the ordinal of *five.* **2** Being one of five equal parts: a *fifth* part. — *n.* **1** One of five equal parts of anything. **2** The quotient of a unit divided by five. **3** *Music* **a** The interval between any note and the fifth note above it in the diatonic scale, counting the starting point as one (see SCALE[2]). **b** A note separated by this interval from any other, considered in relation to that other; specifically, the fifth above the keynote; the dominant. **4** One fifth of a U.S. gallon used as a measure of spirituous liquors. — *adv.* In the fifth order, place, or rank: also, in formal discourse, **fifth′ly.**

Fifth Amendment An amendment to the Constitution of the United States, providing that no person "shall be compelled in any criminal case to be a witness against himself. . . ."

Fifth Avenue A street running north and south in Manhattan borough of New York City, famous for the elegance of its shopping district and its wealthy residential sections.

fifth column A group, within a city or country, of civilian sympathizers with an enemy, who act as spies, saboteurs, and propagandists: first applied to Franco agents and sympathizers in Madrid by Gen. Emilio Mola (1887–1937), who led four armed columns against that city in 1936.

fifth-col·um·nist (fifth′kol′əm·nist) *n.* A member of a fifth column.

fifth wheel **1** A horizontal metallic circle or segment of a circle attached to the upper side of the fore axle of a carriage or wagon to give support to the body in turning; a circle iron. **2** An additional wheel carried with a vehicle as a replacement in case of accidents. **3** A superfluous thing or person.

fif·ti·eth (fif′tē·ith) *adj.* **1** Tenth in order after the fortieth: the ordinal of *fifty.* **2** Being one of fifty equal parts of a thing. — *n.* **1** One of fifty equal parts. **2** The quotient of a unit divided by fifty.

fif·ty (fif′tē) *adj.* Consisting of ten more than forty or five times ten. — *n. pl.* **fif·ties** **1** The sum of ten and forty; five times ten. **2** Any of the symbols (50, l, L) representing this number. [OE *fiftig*]

fif·ty-fif·ty (fif′tē·fif′tē) *adj. Colloq.* Sharing equally, as benefits: *fifty-fifty* partners in business.

fig[1] (fig) *n.* **1** The small, edible, pear-shaped fruit of a tree (genus *Ficus*), cultivated in warm climates. **2** The tree *(F. carica)* that bears the fruit. **3** Any tree or plant bearing a fruit somewhat like the fig, or the fruit of such a tree or plant. **4** One of several Australian trees and shrubs of the fig family, as *F. macrophylla,* used as fodder for cattle. **5** A petty matter; trifle. **6** An insulting gesture; a fico. — *v.t. Obs.* To make a fico at; insult. [<OF *fige, figue* <L *ficus* a fig]

fig[2] (fig) *v.t.* **figged, fig·ging** *Colloq.* To dress; deck; rig. — *n.* **1** Figure; dress; array: in full *fig.* **2** Condition. [Var. of obs. *feague* whip <G *fegen* polish]

fig-eat·er (fig′ē′tər) *n.* **1** A large velvety-green scarabaeid beetle *(Cotinis nitida)* common in the southern United States, injurious to ripe fruits. **2** The beccafico. **3** The grape-eater.

fight (fīt) *v.* **fought, fight·ing** *v.t.* **1** To struggle against in battle or physical combat. **2** To struggle against in any manner. **3** To carry on or engage in (a battle, duel, court action, etc.). **4** To make (one's way) by struggling. **5** To maneuver or handle, as troops or a gun, in battle. **6** To cause to fight, as dogs or gamecocks. — *v.i.* **7** To take part in battle or physical combat. **8** To struggle in any manner. See synonyms under CONTEND. — **to fight shy of** To avoid meeting (an opponent or an issue) squarely. — **to fight it out** To fight until a final decision is reached. — *n.* **1** Strife or struggle between adversaries; battle; conflict; combat. **2** Strife to attain an object in spite of difficulties or opposition. **3** Power or disposition to fight; pugnacity. **4** *Obs.* A temporary bulwark or screen on a ship when in action, to conceal the men. See synonyms under BATTLE. [OE *feohtan*]

fight·er (fī′tər) *n.* **1** One who fights; a combatant; warrior. **2** A pugnacious or spirited person. **3** *Mil.* A fast, highly maneuverable airplane designed to hunt out and destroy enemy planes in the air.

fight·er-bomb·er (fī′tər·bom′ər) *n. Mil.* An aircraft which combines the functions of the fighter and the bomber.

fighter command A division of the U.S. Air Force intermediate between a wing and an air force, used for interception of enemy aircraft and for support of air and ground offensive forces.

fighter plane A pursuit plane.

fight·ing (fī′ting) *adj.* **1** Qualified, equipped, trained, or ready to fight; active in war or battle. **2** Of, pertaining to, suitable for, engaged in, or used for conflict. — *n.* Strife; struggle; battle; conflict.

fighting chance A bare possibility of success, contingent on a hard struggle.

fighting cock A gamecock.
fighting fish A brightly colored Siamese aquarium fish *(Betta splendens)*, the males of which are noted for their nesting habits and pugnacity.
fighting top On war vessels, a platform at the lower masthead for the fire-control lookout, or for light anti-aircraft guns.
Figl (fē′gəl), **Leopold,** 1902–1965, Austrian agrarian and politician; acting president of Austria 1950–51.
fig marigold Any of several species of a South African genus of herbs *(Mesembryanthemum)* yielding a fig-shaped fruit.
fig·ment (fig′mənt) *n.* **1** Something imagined or feigned; a fiction. **2** *Obs.* An object molded or shaped. [<L *figmentum* anything made, <*fingere* form]
Fi·gue·ro·a (fē′gā·rō′ä), **Francisco de,** 1536?–1620, Spanish poet.
fig·u·line (fig′yŏŏ·lin, -līn) *adj.* **1** Capable of being used in the manufacture of porcelain or earthenware. **2** Made or molded as in potter's clay. **—** *n.* **1** Fictile ware; any object made of potter's clay, especially if decorated. **2** Potter's clay. [<L *figulinus* <*figulus* potter <*fingere* form]
fig·ur·a·ble (fig′yər·ə·bəl) *adj.* Capable of being brought to or retained in a fixed form or shape.
fig·ur·al (fig′yər·əl) *adj.* **1** Represented by or consisting of figures or delineation. **2** *Music* Figurate.
fig·u·rant (fig′yŏŏ·rant, *Fr.* fē·gü·räṅ′) *n.* **1** An accessory character on the stage. **2** A nonfeatured ballet dancer. [<F, ppr. of *figurer* figure] **— fig·u·rante** (fig′yŏŏ·rant′, -ränt′; *Fr.* fē·gü·räṅt′) *n. fem.*
fig·ur·ate (fig′yər·it) *adj.* **1** Having a definite or characteristic figure or shape; resembling anything of definite form. **2** *Music* Florid; figured. [<L *figuratus,* pp. of *figurare* form <*figura.* See FIGURE.]
fig·ur·a·tion (fig′yə·rā′shən) *n.* **1** The act or process of shaping something or of marking with a figure or figures. **2** External form or shape. **3** *Music* Ornamentation or variation, as by addition of passing notes; also, the preparation of a figured bass. **4** *Obs.* A type or symbol.
fig·ur·a·tive (fig′yər·ə·tiv) *adj.* **1** Not literal; metaphorical; symbolic. **2** Ornate; florid. **3** Of or pertaining to the representation of form or figure. **4** Representing by means of a form or figure; emblematic. **— fig′ur·a·tive·ly** *adv.* **— fig′ur·a·tive·ness** *n.*
fig·ure (fig′yər, *Brit.* fig′ər) *n.* **1** The visible form of any person or thing; fashion; shape; outline; appearance; hence, any visible object thus recognized. **2** The representation or likeness of the form of a person or other object, as in wax or marble, in a painting or drawing, upon a fabric, or as embodied in a diagram or illustration; a cut. **3** A combination of lines, points, surfaces, or solids representing an object or illustrating a condition or relation, or simply for decoration; a diagram, drawing, or pattern. **4** *Geom.* **a** A surface enclosed by lines, as a square, triangle, etc.: called a **plane figure. b** A space enclosed by planes or surfaces, as a cube, sphere, etc.: called a **solid figure. 5** Any person, thing, or act that figures or prefigures, or is a type of some other or future thing or person. **6** Any personage or character, especially one who is active or conspicuous; one who plays a prominent part. **7** The appearance that a person or his conduct makes: to make a sorry *figure.* **8** A character representing a number: the *figure* 5; hence, amount stated in numbers; price; value: to sell goods at a high *figure.* **9** One of the regular movements or divisions of a dance, in which a certain set of steps or evolutions is completed. **10** Something conjured up by the imagination; a fancy; fantasm; imagination; idea. **11** A form of expression that deviates intentionally from the ordinary mode of speech for the sake of more powerful, pleasing, or distinctive effect; pictorial or poetic language. **12** An intentional deviation from ordinary form or construction, as in syntax, euphony, or prosody. **13** *Logic* The character of a syllogism with reference to the places occupied by the middle term in the major and minor premises. **14** *Music* **a** Any short succession of notes, either as melody or a group of chords, which produces a single, complete, and distinct impression; a musical phrase. **b** A theme or melody repeated throughout a whole movement as an accompaniment or bond of connection. **c** A numeral written in connection with the bass to show the unwritten harmony of a piece. **15** A horoscope; the diagram of the aspects of the astrological houses. **—** *v.* **fig·ured, fig·ur·ing** *v.t.* **1** To make an image, picture, or other representation of; depict. **2** To form an idea or mental image of; imagine. **3** To ornament or mark with a design. **4** To compute numerically; calculate. **5** To express metaphorically; symbolize. **6** *Colloq.* To think; believe; predict. **7** *Music* **a** To embellish, as by adding passing notes. **b** To mark with figures above or below the staff, indicating accompanying chords. **—** *v.i.* **8** To be conspicuous; appear prominently. **9** To make computations; do arithmetic. **— to figure on** (or **upon**) **1** To think over; consider. **2** To plan; expect. **— to figure out** To reckon; ascertain; solve. [<F <L *figura* <*fingere* form] **— fig′ur·er** *n.*
Synonyms (noun): appearance, aspect, attribute, comparison, delineation, diagram, drawing, emblem, form, illustration, image, likeness, metaphor, simile, similitude, shape, symbol, type. *Figure* is the general term, including all representation of *form* to the eye, as in drawing, painting, or sculpture, and also the *form* itself that may be so represented. *Figure* is also the general word for representation of anything to the mind, as by *illustration, metaphor,* or *symbol.* An *image* is a visible representation, especially in sculpture, having or supposed to have a close resemblance to that which it represents. We speak of one object as the *type* of the class whose characteristics it exhibits, as in the case of animal or vegetable *types.* An *attribute* in art is some accessory used to characterize a *figure* or scene; the *attribute* is often an emblem or symbol; thus the eagle is the *attribute* of St. John as an *emblem* of lofty spiritual vision. Compare ALLEGORY, ATTRIBUTE, EMBLEM, FORM, IMAGE, SIGN, SIMILE.
fig·ured (fig′yərd) *adj.* **1** Adorned or marked with figures or designs: *figured* cottons. **2** Represented by figures; pictured. **3** *Music* **a** Figurate. **b** Indicated by figures, as a bass.
figure eight 1 *Aeron.* A flight maneuver which consists in tracing the figure eight above the ground, with two conspicuous points as the pivots around which to describe each loop. **2** A similar maneuver in ice skating. **3** A style of knot. See illustration under KNOT.
fig·ure·head (fig′yər·hed′) *n.* **1** *Naut.* A carved or ornamental figure on the prow of a vessel. **2** A person having nominal leadership but without real power, responsibility, or authority.

FIGUREHEAD

figure of speech An expression, usually within a sentence, which deviates from simple, normal speech to produce a fanciful or vivid impression, as simile, metaphor, personification, etc.
fig·u·rine (fig′yə·rēn′) *n.* A small, painted, single figure or an attached group of figures, especially in terra cotta or ivory; a statuette. [<F <Ital. *figurina,* dim. of *figura* <L. See FIGURE.]
fig·wort (fig′wûrt′) *n.* **1** A plant (genus *Scrophularia*) with small, dark-colored flowers, formerly supposed to cure scrofula. **2** Any plant of the figwort family *(Scrophulariaceae).*
Fi·ji (fē′jē) A British colony in the South Pacific SW of Samoa, comprising the **Fiji Islands,** 7,056 square miles: capital, Suva; and the dependency of Rotuma.
Fi·ji (fē′jē) *n.* **1** One of the native people of the Fiji Islands, mostly Melanesian with Polynesian admixture. **2** The Melanesian language of the Fijis.
Fi·ji·an (fē′jē·ən) *adj.* Of Fiji, its people, or their language. **—** *n.* A Fiji.
fike (fīk) See FYKE[1].
fil·a·gree (fil′ə·grē) See FILIGREE.
fil·a·ment (fil′ə·mənt) *n.* **1** A fine thread, fiber, or fibril. **2** Any threadlike structure or appendage. **3** *Bot.* The stalk or support of an anther. **4** *Electr.* The slender wire of tungsten, carbon, or other material, which, when an electric current is passed through it in a vacuum, is heated to a brilliant glow and produces light. See illustration under INCANDESCENT LAMP. **5** *Electronics* A similar wire, forming the cathode of a vacuum tube, from which electrons are emitted under the action of heat. **6** *Ornithol.* The barb of a feather. [<F <LL *filamentum* <*filare* spin <*filum* a thread]
fil·a·men·tous (fil′ə·men′təs) *adj.* Like, consisting of, or bearing filaments; threadlike. Also **fil′a·men′ta·ry.**
fi·lar (fī′lər) *adj.* **1** Of, pertaining to, or characterized by a thread or threads; threadlike. **2** *Optics* Having fine threads across the field of view, as in a microscope equipped with a *filar* micrometer for measuring the sizes of objects under examination. [<L *filum* a thread + -AR[1]]
fi·lar·i·a (fi·lâr′ē·ə) *n. pl.* **·i·ae** (-i·ē) A nematode or threadworm (family *Filariidae*) parasitic in the blood and intestines of man and other animals; especially *Wuchereria bancrofti,* the causative agent of elephantiasis, and the Guinea worm. [<NL <L *filum* a thread] **— fi·lar′i·al, fi·lar′i·an** *adj.*
fil·a·ri·a·sis (fil′ə·rī′ə·sis) *n. Pathol.* **1** Infection with nematode worms. **2** The disease so caused, affecting chiefly the lymph glands and connective tissues.
fil·a·ture (fil′ə·chər) *n.* **1** The act or process of forming threads or of reeling off raw silk from cocoons. **2** An apparatus, machine, or establishment for reeling silk, etc. [<F <L *filare* spin <*filum* a thread]
fil·bert (fil′bərt) *n.* **1** The edible nut of the European or the Oriental hazel *(Corylus avellana)*; and also, sometimes, of the American hazel *(C. americana* and *C. cornuta).* **2** The bushy shrub or small tree that bears the nut. [Earlier *filbert nut* <dial. F *noix de filbert* nut of Philibert, after St. *Philibert,* near whose feast (Aug. 22) these nuts ripen]
filch (filch) *v.t.* To steal slyly and in small amounts; pilfer. See synonyms under STEAL. [Origin uncertain] **— filch′er** *n.*
file[1] (fīl) *n.* **1** Any device, as a pointed wire, to keep papers in order for reference; also, a cabinet, drawer, or the like, in which papers are filed. **2** A collection of papers or documents arranged systematically for reference. **3** Any orderly succession or line of men or things; especially a line or row of men standing or marching one behind another: distinguished from *rank;* a small detachment; corporal's guard. **4** Place or standing on a list for advancement, as in the army. **5** A roll; list. **6** A vertical row of squares running directly across a chessboard from one player to the other. **— single file** An arrangement of persons or things one behind another in a single line: also *Indian file.* **—** *v.* **filed, fil·ing** *v.t.* **1** To put on file in systematic order, as papers for reference. **—** *v.i.* **2** To march in file, as soldiers. **3** To make an application, as for a job. [Fusion of F *fil* thread and *file* a row, both ult. <L *filum* a thread] **— fil′er** *n.*
file[2] (fīl) *n.* **1** A hard steel abrading or smoothing instrument with ridged cutting surfaces. **2** Figuratively, anything used to abrade, smooth, or polish. **3** *Brit. Slang* A shrewd or artful person. **—** *v.t.* **filed, fil·ing 1** To cut, smooth, or sharpen with a file. **2** To remove with a file: with *away* or *off:* to *file away* rust. [OE *fīl*] **— fil′er** *n.*
file[3] (fīl) *v.t. Archaic* To defile; sully. [OE *-fȳlan,* found in *befȳlan* befoul]
file card A wire brush for cleaning the teeth of files.
file clerk An employee who maintains files and records.
file-clos·er (fīl′klō′zər) *n.* In close order drill, a non-commissioned officer at the rear of a rank who sees that the leader's commands are executed.
file·fish (fīl′fish′) *n.* **·fish** or **·fish·es 1** Any of certain fish (family *Balistidae*) with roughly granulated skin, especially the triggerfish. **2** Any of certain fish (family *Monacanthidae*) with prickly scales.
file-lead·er (fīl′lē′dər) *n.* The front man in a military file; hence, any recognized or official leader.
Fi·le·mo·na (fē′lā·mō′nä) Italian feminine form of PHILEMON.
fil·e·mot (fil′ə·mot) *adj. Archaic* Having the

color of a dead or faded leaf. —*n. Obs.* The color of a dead or faded leaf. [Alter. of F *feuillemorte* dead leaf]

fi·lé powder (fi·lā′) A sassafras seasoning and thickening for sauces and gravies.

fi·let (fi·lā′, fil′ā; *Fr.* fē·le′) *n.* 1 Net lace having a square mesh. 2 Fillet (def. 2 and 3). [<F. See FILLET.]

LACE FILET

filet de sole (də sôl′) *French* Fillet of sole.

fi·let mi·gnon (fi·lā′min·yon′) A small fillet of beef cooked with a garnish of bacon. [<F]

fil·i·al (fil′ē·əl, fil′yəl) *adj.* 1 Of, pertaining to, or befitting a son or daughter; due to parents. 2 *Genetics* Pertaining to a generation following the parental. The first filial generation is designated F_1, the second F_2, etc. [<LL *filialis* <L *filius* a son] —**fil′i·al·ly** *adv.*

fil·i·ate (fil′ē·āt) *v.t.* **·at·ed, ·at·ing** To affiliate. [<LL *filiatus,* pp. of *filiare* have a son <*filius* son]

fil·i·a·tion (fil′ē·ā′shən) *n.* 1 The relation of a child to a parent. 2 *Law* The judicial determination of parentage; affiliation. 3 Causal connection or relationship; descent. 4 The formation of offshoots, as of a language.

fil·i·beg (fil′ə·beg) *n.* A kilt of the modern fashion, as distinguished from the earlier great kilt, which covered the body: also spelled *philabeg, philibeg.* [<Scottish Gaelic *feileadh* kilt + *beag* little]

fil·i·bus·ter (fil′ə·bus′tər) *n.* 1 *U.S.* A member of a legislative body who attempts to obstruct legislation by prolonged speaking to consume time; hence, any such prolonged speech. 2 A freebooter or buccaneer; pirate. 3 An adventurer who takes part in an unlawful military expedition into a foreign country. —*v.i.* 1 *U.S.* To obstruct legislation by long speeches and constant delay. 2 To act as a freebooter or adventurer. —*v.t.* 3 *U.S.* To block passage of (legislation) by constant delay. [<Sp. *filibustero* <Du. *vrijbuiter* freebooter] —**fil′i·bus′ter·er** *n.* —**fil′i·bus′trous** *adj.*

fil·i·cide (fil′ə·sīd) *n.* 1 One who kills his child. 2 The act of killing one's child. [<L *filius* a son + -CIDE] —**fil′i·ci′dal** *adj.*

Fil·i·cin·e·ae (fil′ə·sin′i·ē) *n. pl.* A large class of pteridophyte plants; the ferns. [<NL *filicineus* <*Filicales,* an order of ferns <L *filix, filicis* a fern]

fil·i·coid (fil′ə·koid) *adj.* Resembling a fern; fernlike: a *filicoid* pattern. See illustration under FROST. [<L *filix, filicis* a fern + -OID]

Fi·li·de (fē′lē·dā) Italian form of PHYLLIS.

fil·i·form (fil′ə·fôrm) *adj.* Threadlike; filamentous; thready. [<L *filum* thread + -FORM]

fil·i·gree (fil′ə·grē) *n.* 1 Delicate ornamental work formed of intertwisted gold or silver wire. 2 Anything fanciful and delicate, but purely ornate. —*adj.* Made of or adorned with filigree; fanciful; ornate. —*v.t.* **·greed, ·gree·ing** To adorn with filigree; work in filigree. Sometimes spelled *filagree* or *fillagree.* Also *Obs.* **fil′i·grain.** [Short for *filigreen,* var. of *filigrane* <F <Ital. *filigrana* <L *filum* thread + *granum* a grain]

fil·ing (fī′ling) *n.* 1 The act or process of using a file. 2 A particle removed by a file.

Fi·lip (*Pol.* fē′lēp; *Rus.* fē·lēp′; *Sw.* fil′ip) Polish, Russian, and Swedish form of PHILIP. Also *Ital.* **Fi·lip·po** (fē·lēp′pō).

Fil·i·pi·no (fil′ə·pē′nō) *n. pl.* **·nos** A native or inhabitant of the Philippines. —*adj.* Of or pertaining to the Philippines.

Fi·lip·pa (fē·lēp′pä) Italian form of PHILIPPA. Also **Fi·lip·pi·na** (fē′lēp·pē′nä).

fill (fil) *v.t.* 1 To make full; put as much in as possible. 2 To occupy to capacity; pack. 3 To abound in. 4 To stop up or plug: to *fill* a tooth. 5 To supply with what is necessary or ordered: to *fill* a prescription. 6 To occupy (an office or position). 7 To put someone into (an office or position): to *fill* the governorship with a good man. 8 To feed to fullness; to satisfy; glut. 9 *Engin.* To build up or make full, as an embankment or a ravine, by adding fill. 10 *Naut.* **a** To distend (a sail): said of the wind. **b** To trim (a yard) so the wind will distend the sail. —*v.i.* 11 To become full. See synonyms under SATISFY. —**to fill in** 1 To fill up, as an excavation. 2 To insert (something), as into a blank space. 3 To insert something into (a blank space). 4 *Colloq.* To be a substitute. 5 To fill in on. —**to fill in on** *Colloq.* To tell or bring (someone) up to date on additional details or facts. —**to fill out** 1 To become fuller or more rounded. 2 To make complete, as a document. —**to fill the bill** *Colloq.* To do or be what is wanted or needed. —*n.* 1 That which fills or is sufficient to fill; a full supply. 2 An embankment, especially a section of a road or railroad bed built up by filling in with stone, gravel, etc., over low ground. 3 The stone, gravel, etc., used to make such an embankment. [OE *fyllan* fill]

fille de joie (fē′y′ də zhwä′) *French* A prostitute.

filled gold (fild) A layer of gold rolled upon base metal and not merely electroplated on it.

filled milk Milk in which vegetable oils replace the normal cream content.

fill·er[1] (fil′ər) *n.* 1 One who or that which fills. 2 Any substance used for filling. 3 A composition for filling pores or holes in wood, before painting or varnishing. 4 Tobacco used for the inside of cigars and for plug tobacco. 5 Any device which conducts a substance into a receptacle, as a funnel or a conduit to a reservoir. 6 A brief piece of writing, usually an unimportant item, used to fill space in a newspaper or magazine.

fil·lér[2] (fēl′lâr) *n. sing. & pl.* A Hungarian coin, the hundredth part of a forint. [<Hungarian]

fil·let (fil·lit, *usually for defs. 2 and 3* fil′ā) *n.* 1 A narrow band or ribbon for binding the hair. 2 A strip of lean meat. 3 A flat slice of fish without the bone. 4 A thin band, strip, or engraved line. 5 *Archit.* **a** A small band or molding, usually rectangular, narrow, and flat, used to separate or ornament larger moldings or members. **b** The narrow ridge or strip between the flutes of a column or filling any similar function; a facet. **c** A strip or molding fastened to a wall or the like. 6 *Physiol.* An important nerve tract by which sensory impressions are conveyed to the higher cerebral centers. 7 *Her.* A diminutive ordinary occupying the lower fourth part of the chief. 8 The loins of a horse. 9 Fairing[1] (def. 1). —*v.t.* 1 To bind or adorn with a fillet or band. 2 (also fil′ā, fi·lā′) To slice into fillets; cook as a fillet. [<F *filet,* dim. of *fil* a thread <L *filum*]

fill-in (fil′in′) *n.* 1 A person or thing included to fill a gap or omission. 2 *Colloq.* A summary of facts given to complete one's understanding of a situation.

fill·ing (fil′ing) *n.* 1 The act of making or becoming full. 2 Something used to fill a cavity or vacant space: a *filling* of gold for a tooth. 3 In weaving, the weft or woof, which crosses the warp. 4 A custard, jelly, or fruit-and-nut mixture placed between layers of a cake.

filling station A station for supplying gasoline, oil, and other necessaries to automobiles.

fil·lip (fil′əp) *n.* 1 A sudden flip of a finger from contact with the thumb; a quick snap or blow with the end of a finger. 2 Anything which serves as an incitement or gives impulse, as to an ambition. —*v.t.* 1 To strike by or as by a fillip; snap with the finger. 2 To project or impel, as by a fillip. —*v.i.* To make a fillip. [Var. of FLIP]

fil·li·peen (fil′ə·pēn′) See PHILOPENA.

fil·lis·ter (fil′is·tər) *n. Mech.* 1 A plane for making grooves. 2 A rabbet on a sash bar, for receiving the edge of the glass and the putty. 3 A type of screw with a round head. [Origin unknown]

Fill·more (fil′môr), **Millard,** 1800–74, president of the United States 1850–53.

fil·ly (fil′ē) *n. pl.* **fil·lies** A young mare. [<ON *fylia* <*fōli* foal]

film (film) *n.* 1 A thin coating, layer, or membrane. 2 *Phot.* **a** A thin coating of a light-sensitive emulsion laid on a glass plate or on a flexible base, for making photographs. **b** The base itself. 3 A motion picture. 4 A delicate filament, as of a cobweb. 5 *Pathol.* A morbid growth on the cornea of the eye. —*v.t.* 1 To cover or obscure by or as by a film. 2 To photograph on a film; especially, to take motion pictures of. —*v.i.* 3 To become covered or obscured by a film. 4 To take motion pictures. [OE *filmen* membrane]

film pack *Phot.* A set of films so packaged that it may be safely handled in daylight, each individual film being exposed in turn.

film·strip (film′strip′) *n.* A length of film containing frames of still pictures which are projected on a screen, usually as a visual aid in lectures.

film·y (fil′mē) *adj.* **film·i·er, film·i·est** Like a film; cloudy; obscure; also, gauzy; thin; unsubstantial. —**film′i·ly** *adv.* —**film′i·ness** *n.*

fil·o·plume (fil′ə·plōōm′, fī′lə-) *n. Ornithol.* A thread feather. [<L *filum* thread + *pluma* plume]

fi·lose (fī′lōs) *adj.* Having a threadlike appendage. [<L *filum* thread + -OSE[1]]

fils (fēs) *n. French* Son: used after a surname to distinguish father *(père)* from son: Dumas *fils.*

fil·ter (fil′tər) *n.* 1 Any device or porous substance, as paper, cloth, fine clay, or charcoal, used as a strainer for clearing or purifying fluids. Compare illustration under FUNNEL. 2 *Electr.* A device which permits the passage of currents of certain frequencies and limits the flow of certain others, such as a **band filter,** which passes currents neither above nor below a given range, a **high-pass filter,** which selects certain high-frequency currents and a **low-pass filter,** which permits the flow of certain low-frequency currents; also used in power transmission. 3 *Phot.* A colored screen of glass, or of other translucent material, placed in front of a camera lens to control the kind and relative intensity of light waves in an exposure. —*v.t.* 1 To pass (liquids) through a filter; strain. 2 To separate (solid matter) from liquid by a filter. —*v.i.* 3 To pass through a filter. 4 To move slowly; leak out, as news. See synonyms under PURIFY. ◆ Homophone: *philter.* [<OF *filtre* <Med. L *fĕltrum.* Related to FELT[2].] —**fil′ter·a·bil′i·ty, fil·tra·bil·i·ty** (fil′trə·bil′ə·tē), **fil′ter·a·ble·ness** *n.* —**fil′ter·a·ble, fil·tra·ble** (fil′·trə·bəl) *adj.*

filter bed A reservoir with a sand or gravel bottom for purifying large quantities of water.

filter feeder Any aquatic organism that feeds on small organisms which are strained out of the surrounding water as it is channeled through a specialized sieve or filtering system.

filter paper A soft porous paper suitable for filtering.

filth (filth) *n.* 1 Anything that soils, or makes foul; that which is foul or dirty. 2 Moral defilement; obscenity. [OE *fȳlth*]

filth·y (fil′thē) *adj.* **filth·i·er, filth·i·est** Of the nature of or containing filth; foul; obscene. See synonyms under FOUL. —**filth′i·ly** *adv.* —**filth′·i·ness** *n.*

filtrable virus See under VIRUS.

fil·trate (fil′trāt) *v.t.* **·trat·ed, ·trat·ing** To filter. —*n.* The liquid or other substance separated by filtration. [<NL *filtratus,* pp. of *filtrare* <Med. L *filtrum* a filter]

fil·tra·tion (fil·trā′shən) *n.* 1 The act or process of filtering. 2 The separation of liquids from solids. 3 The sterilization of liquids by the mechanical removal of bacteria and other impurities.

filtration plant A place equipped with large filters, through which the water supply of a city passes to be purified.

fi·lum (fī′ləm) *n. pl.* **·la** (-lə) *Anat.* A thread or threadlike structure. [<NL <L]

fim·ble (fim′bəl) *n.* The male hemp plant, which is generally harvested before the female plant. [<Du. *femel* <F *(chanvre) femelle* female (hemp)]

fim·bri·a (fim′brē·ə) *n. Zool.* A fringe or fringelike structure, as around the mouth of a tube or duct in certain animals. [<NL <L, a fringe]

fim·bri·ate (fim′brē·āt) *v.t.* **·at·ed, ·at·ing** *Biol.* To furnish with a fringe or border; fringe. —*adj.* (-it) Having such a fringe or border. —**fim′bri·a′tion** *n.*

fim·bri·at·ed (fim′brē·ā′tid) *adj.* Having a fringe or fringelike processes; fimbriate.

fim·bril·late (fim·bril′it) *adj. Biol.* Having a fine fringe or border. [<NL *fimbrilla,* dim. of *fimbra* a fringe]

fin[1] (fin) *n.* **1** A membranous extension from the body of a fish or other aquatic animal, serving to propel, balance, or steer it in the water. For illustrations see FISH, RORQUAL. **2** Any finlike or projecting part, appendage, or attachment. **3** *Naut.* A finlike appendage to a submarine boat or the like; a fin keel. **4** *Aeron.* A fixed supplementary surface of an aircraft, usually vertical: a tail *fin.* See illustration under AIRPLANE. **5** A projecting rib on a radiator or on the cylinder of an internal-combustion engine. **6** Any finlike part, as on a rocket, bomb, etc. **7** A flipper (def. 2). **8** *Mech.* The projecting ridge of a metal casting at the line of junction with the mold. —*v.* **finned, fin·ning** *v.t.* To cut up or trim off the fins of (a fish). —*v.i.* To beat the water with the fins, as a whale when dying. [OE *finn*]

fin[2] (fīn) *v.t.* & *v.i. Scot.* To find.

fin·a·ble (fī′nə·bəl) *adj.* **1** Liable to or involving a fine. **2** Capable of being refined or purified. Also *fineable.*

fi·na·gle (fi·nā′gəl) *v.* **·gled, ·gling** *Colloq. v.t.* **1** To get (something) by trickery or deceit. **2** To cheat or trick (someone). —*v.i.* **3** To use trickery or deceit; be sly. **4** In card games, to renege. [Var. of FAINAIGUE] —**fi·na′gler** *n.*

fi·nal (fī′nəl) *adj.* **1** Pertaining to, or coming at or as, the end; ultimate; last. **2** Precluding, or making unnecessary, further action or controversy; conclusive; decisive. **3** Relating to or consisting in the end or purpose aimed at: a *final* cause. —*n.* **1** Something that is terminal, last, or final; that which makes an end; a finale. **2** The last, deciding match in a tournament or series of games. **3** The last examination of a term in a school or college. [<F <L *finalis* <*finis* end]

final cause The object or end to be reached by an action or process; purpose.

fi·na·le (fi·nä′lē, -nal′ē; *Ital.* fē·nä′lā) *n.* **1** The last act, part, or scene; end. **2** The last movement in a musical composition. See synonyms under END. [<Ital., final]

fi·nal·ist (fī′nəl·ist) *n.* In athletics, a contestant who takes part in the final round, as of a tournament, race, etc.

fi·nal·i·ty (fī·nal′ə·tē) *n. pl.* **·ties** **1** The state or quality of being final. **2** A final, conclusive, or decisive act, determination, offer, etc. **3** *Philos.* The doctrine of final causes, that design actuates the universe; teleology. **4** The belief that there can be no progress or change.

fi·nal·ize (fī′nəl·īz) *v.t.* **·ized, ·iz·ing** **1** To bring to a state of completion, as a transaction, sale, or agreement. **2** To put into final or complete form.

fi·nal·ly (fī′nəl·ē) *adv.* **1** At or in the end; ultimately. **2** Lastly. **3** Completely; irrecoverably.

fi·nance (fi·nans′, fī′nans) *n.* **1** The science of monetary affairs. **2** *pl.* Monetary affairs; pecuniary resources; funds; revenue; income. —*v.t.* **·nanced, ·nanc·ing** **1** To manage the finances of. **2** To supply the money for. [<OF, payment <*finer* settle <*fin* end. See FINE[2].]

finance bill Legislation to raise revenue for the government.

fi·nan·cial (fi·nan′shəl, fī-) *adj.* **1** Of or pertaining to finance; monetary. **2** Of or pertaining to those dealing professionally with money and credit. —**fi·nan′cial·ly** *adv.*

Synonyms: fiscal, monetary, pecuniary. These words all relate to money, receipts, or expenditures. *Monetary* relates to actual money, coin, currency; as, the *monetary* system; a *monetary* transaction is one in which money is transferred. *Pecuniary* refers to that in which money is involved, but less directly; we speak of one's *pecuniary* affairs or interests, with no special reference to the handling of cash. *Financial* applies especially to governmental revenues or expenditures, or to private transactions of considerable moment; we speak of a *pecuniary* reward, a *financial* enterprise; we give a needy person *pecuniary* (not *financial*) assistance. *Fiscal* applies to the state treasury or public finances or accounts; it is common to speak of the *fiscal* rather than the *financial* year.

fin·an·cier (fin′ən·sir′) *n.* One skilled in or occupied with financial affairs; a capitalist. —*v.t.* & *v.i.* To finance.

fin·back (fin′bak′) *n.* A rorqual. Also **finback whale.**

finch (finch) *n.* A small, seed-eating bird (family *Fringillidae*), as a bunting, sparrow, grosbeak, bullfinch, goldfinch, greenfinch, canary, chaffinch, or weaverbird. ◆ Collateral adjective: *fringilline.* [OE *finc*]

find (fīnd) *v.* **found, find·ing** *v.t.* **1** To come upon unexpectedly; discover. **2** To perceive or discover; come upon by search or examination. **3** To learn or become aware of by experience. **4** To recover (something lost). **5** To reach; arrive at; attain. **6** To give a decision upon: The judge *found* him in contempt. **7** To gain or recover the use of: He *found* his tongue. **8** To furnish; provide. —*v.i.* **9** To arrive at and express a judicial decision: to *find* for the plaintiff. See synonyms under DISCOVER. —**to find fault** To complain of some defect or deficiency. —**to find oneself** **1** To become aware of one's special ability or vocation. **2** To fare in health; feel. —**to find out** To detect or discover, as a thief. —**to find out about** To learn the truth concerning. —*n.* A finding; a thing found or discovered; especially, a valuable discovery. [OE *findan*]

find·er (fīn′dər) *n.* **1** One who or that which finds. **2** *Astron.* A small telescope by the side of a large one, used to locate a particular object for astronomical observation. **3** *Phot.* A supplementary lens attached to a camera, to locate the object in the field of view.

fin de siè·cle (fañ də sye′kl′) *French* End of the century; specifically, the close of the 19th century, viewed as a period of transition in social and moral values.

fin-de-siè·cle (fañ·də·sye′kl′) *adj. French* Decadent.

find·ing (fīn′ding) *n.* **1** The act of finding; that which is found; discovery. **2** *Law* A conclusion arrived at before an official or a court. **3** Support; expense.

find·ings (fīn′dingz) *n. pl.* **1** Small tools and supplies which a workman provides for himself. **2** Sewing essentials, as thread, needles, tape, buttons, etc.; notions. **3** *Law* Conclusions as to matters of fact arrived at through testimony heard before an official or a court.

fine[1] (fīn) *adj.* **fin·er, fin·est** **1** Excellent in quality; admirable; superior. **2** Suggesting lightness; light or delicate; not coarse, gross, or dull; subtle; thin; keen. **3** Showy in appearance or style; pretentious; ostentatious. **4** Delicate of perception; refined; sensitive; nice. **5** Refined, as sirup. **6** Having a high or specified degree of purity, as gold or silver. **7** Distinguished or noteworthy. **8** Enjoyable; pleasant. **9** Trained to the highest point of efficiency: said of an athlete, a horse, etc. **10** Cloudless; rainless. —*adv.* **1** *Colloq.* Very much; finely; well; excellently. **2** In billiards, in a manner producing a fine carom, etc. —*v.t.* & *v.i.* **fined, fin·ing** To make or become purified, thin, or slender. [<OF *fin* perfected <LL *finus,* a back formation <L *finire* complete <*finis* end] —**fine′ly** *adv.*

Synonyms (adj.): beautiful, clarified, clear, comminuted, dainty, delicate, elegant, excellent, exquisite, gauzy, handsome, keen, minute, nice, polished, pure, refined, sensitive, sharp, slender, slight, small, smooth, splendid, subtile, subtle, tenuous, thin. *Fine* denotes that which has been brought to a full end, finished, consummated. From this root-sense many derived meanings branch out, causing words quite remote from each other to be synonyms of *fine.* That which is truly finished is *excellent* of its kind, and *beautiful,* if a thing that admits of beauty; as a *fine* house, *fine* trees, a *fine* woman, a *fine* morning. If it is a thing that admits of the removal of impurities, it is not finished till these are removed, and hence *fine* signifies *clarified, clear, pure, refined*; as, *fine* gold. That which is finished is apt to be *polished, smooth* to the touch, minutely exact in outline; hence *fine* comes to be a synonym for all words like *dainty, delicate, exquisite*; as, *fine* manners, a *fine* touch, *fine* perceptions. As that which is *delicate* is apt to be small, by an easy extension of meaning *fine* becomes a synonym for *slender, slight, minute, comminuted*; as, a *fine* thread, *fine* sand; or for *filmy, tenuous, thin*; as, a *fine* lace, *fine* wire; and as a *thin* edge is *keen* and *sharp, fine* becomes also a synonym for these words; as, a *fine* point, a *fine* edge. Compare BEAUTIFUL, EXCELLENT, MINUTE, TASTEFUL. *Antonyms*: big, blunt, clumsy, coarse, great, heavy, huge, immense, large, rude, stout, thick.

fine[2] (fīn) *n.* **1** A pecuniary penalty; the money so required, or anything forfeited as a penalty. **2** In English law, an amicable adjustment of a suit either actual or fictitious; a final agreement as for the possession of lands. **3** *Obs.* End; conclusion; death. —**in fine** Finally. —*v.t.* **fined, fin·ing** To punish by fine; exact a fine from. [<OF *fin* settlement <L *finis* end]

fine[3] (fēn) *n. French* A drink of brandy, especially one served with meals.

fi·ne[4] (fē′nā) *n. Music* A mark denoting the end; finis. [<Ital.]

fine·a·ble (fī′nə·bəl) See FINABLE.

fine arts See under ART[1].

Fi·ne·as (fē′nā·äs′) Spanish form of PHINEAS. Also *Ital.* **Fi·ne·o** (fē·nā′ō).

fine-cut (fīn′kut′) *n.* A kind of smoking or chewing tobacco, finely shredded.

fine-draw (fīn′drô′) *v.t.* **·drew, ·drawn, ·draw·ing** **1** To sew or close up, as a tear, so that the joining is imperceptible. **2** To draw out, as wire, to an extreme degree of fineness.

fine-drawn (fīn′drôn′) *adj.* Drawn out finely; hence, developed very subtly or too subtly.

fine-frame (fīn′frām′) *n.* A special frame used in making high-grade yarns of Sea Island cotton.

fine-grained (fīn′grānd′) *adj.* Having a close, fine grain, as in texture or surface: said of some leathers and woods.

fine·ness (fīn′nis) *n.* **1** The state or quality of being fine. **2** The degree of subdivision of the particles of a powder or other granular substance. **3** The purity of an alloy, especially one containing gold or silver, expressed in parts per thousand.

fin·er·y (fī′nər·ē) *n. pl.* **·er·ies** Showy or fine clothes or decoration.

fines herbes (fēn ârb) *French* A mixture of herbs used to season soups, stews, etc.

fine-spun (fīn′spun′) *adj.* **1** Drawn or spun out to an extreme degree of tenuity. **2** Subtle.

fi·nesse (fi·nes′) *n.* **1** Subtle contrivance; artifice; stratagem. **2** Dexterity; artfulness; skill. **3** In card-playing, an attempt on the part of a player to take a trick with a lower card when he holds a higher (as a queen when he holds the ace), in the hope that the opposing hand yet to play will not hold a taking card (as the king). See synonyms under ARTIFICE, DECEPTION. —*v.* **fi·nessed, fi·ness·ing** *v.t.* **1** To change or bring about by finesse. **2** In card games, to play as a finesse. —*v.i.* **3** To use finesse. **4** In card games, to make a finesse. [<F <*fin* FINE[1]]

fine-toothed comb (fīn′tōōtht′) A comb with fine teeth very close together. —**to go over with a fine-toothed comb** To search carefully; leave no part unsearched or unexamined.

fine·top (fīn′top′) *n.* Redtop.

fin·fish (fin′fish′) *n.* True fish: not shellfish.

fin-foot·ed (fin′fŏŏt′id) *adj.* **1** Having webbed feet. **2** Having lobate toes.

Fin·gal (fing′gəl) Hero of the spurious Ossianic poems, *Fingal* and *Temora,* by James Macpherson. See FIONN MACCUMAL.

Fingal's Cave A basaltic cavern on Staffa island, Inner Hebrides, Scotland; 227 feet long, 66 feet high.

fin·gan (fin·gän′) See FINJAN.

fin·gent (fin′jənt) *adj.* Forming; making; molding. [<L *fingens, -entis,* ppr. of *fingere* form]

fin·ger (fing′gər) *n.* **1** One of the digits of the hand, usually excluding the thumb. **2** Any small projecting piece or part, like a finger, as a lever. **3** A measure of length; the length of the middle finger. **4** A measure of depth, equal to the width of the finger. **5** That part of a glove which covers a finger. —**to burn one's fingers** To suffer the consequences of meddling or interfering. —**to have a finger in the pie** To take part in some matter. —**to have at one's finger tips** To have ready and available knowledge of. —**to put one's finger on** To identify or indicate correctly. —**to put the finger on** *U.S. Slang* **1** To betray to the police. **2** To indicate (the victim) of a planned crime. —**to twist around one's (little) finger** To be able to influence or manage with ease. —*v.t.* **1** To touch or handle with the fingers; toy with. **2** To steal; purloin. **3** *Music* **a** To play (an instrument) with the fingers. **b** To mark the notes of (music) showing which fingers are to be used. **4** *U.S. Slang* **a** To betray. **b** To point out (the victim) of a planned crime. —*v.i.* **5** To touch or feel anything with the fingers. **6** *Music* **a** To use the fingers on a musical instrument in a certain manner. **b** To be arranged for playing by the fingers: said of instruments. [OE]

fin·ger·board (fing′gər·bôrd′, -bōrd′) *n.* **1** A guideboard bearing a pointing finger. **2** In stringed instruments, the strip of wood upon which the strings are pressed by the fingers of the player. **3** In instruments of the piano or organ class, a keyboard.

fin·ger·bowl (fing′gər·bōl′) *n.* A bowl containing water for cleansing the fingers at the table after eating.

fin·ger·breadth (fing′gər·bredth′) *n.* The breadth of a finger, from 3/4 inch to one inch.

fin·gered (fing′gərd) *adj.* **1** Having fingers; digitate. **2** Having figures to mark the fingering, as in music.

fin·ger·er (fing′gər·ər) *n.* One who fingers; a pilferer.

finger hole 1 A hole in any object into which a finger may be fitted, as in a bowling ball. **2** One of a series of holes in various wind instruments, as a flute, oboe, etc., over which the finger is manipulated in order to change the tones. **3** One of a series of small holes in a dial telephone.

fin·ger·ing[1] (fing′gər·ing) *n.* **1** The act of touching or feeling with the fingers. **2** *Music* **a** The act or order of using the fingers in playing an instrument, as the flute or piano. **b** The notation indicating what fingers are to be used.

fin·ger·ing[2] (fing′gər·ing) *n.* A finely twisted woolen yarn of medium weight, used for knitting and crocheting. Also **fingering yarn.**

Finger Lakes A group of long, narrow glacial lakes in west central New York.

fin·ger·ling (fing′gər·ling) *n.* **1** A young fish, especially a salmon or trout, no bigger than a man's finger. **2** A being of very small size. Compare THUMBLING. **3** *Obs.* A glove finger; a finger covering; a thimble.

finger mark A mark or stain left by a finger.

fin·ger-marked (fing′gər·märkt′) *adj.* Smudged with finger marks.

fin·ger·nail (fing′gər·nāl′) *n.* The horny growth on the end and along the upper surface of a finger.

finger painting A technique of applying paint to wet paper with the fingers and palms to form a design or picture.

fin·ger·post (fing′gər·pōst′) *n.* A guidepost in the shape of a pointing finger.

fin·ger·print (fing′gər·print′) *n.* An impression of the skin pattern on the inner surface of a finger tip: especially used in the identification of criminals, in the military, naval, and police services, and in various commercial transactions. —*v.t.* To take the fingerprints of. See synonyms under MARK[1]. —**fin′ger·print′ing** *n.*

FINGERPRINT
The whorl type of print.

finger stall A cover to protect a finger.

finger wave A wave in the hair, shaped and set with the fingers, without the use of instruments.

fin·i·al (fin′ē·əl) *n.* **1** *Archit.* An ornament at the apex of a spire, pinnacle, or the like. **2** Any terminal part pointing upward. [<L *finis* end + -IAL]

FINIAL

fin·i·cal (fin′i·kəl) *adj.* Overnice or fastidious in dress, manners, and the like. Also **fin′ick·ing, fin′ick·y, fin′i·kin.** See synonyms under SQUEAMISH. [<FINE[1]] —**fin′i·cal·ly** *adv.* —**fin′·i·cal·ness** *n.*

fin·i·cal·i·ty (fin′ə·kal′ə·tē) *n.* **1** The characteristic of being finical. **2** That which is finical.

fin·ing (fī′ning) *n.* **1** The process of making fine. **2** The removal of gas bubbles from fused glass. **3** The purification and clarifying of wines. **4** Any substance used in clarifying liquids.

fi·nis (fī′nis, fin′is) *n.* *pl.* **fi·nis·es** *Latin* The end.

fin·ish (fin′ish) *v.t.* **1** To complete or bring to an end; come to the end of. **2** To perfect finally or in detail, as a portrait. **3** To use up; dispose of. **4** *Colloq.* To kill or destroy. **5** *Colloq.* To defeat; make powerless. —*v.i.* **6** To reach or come to an end; stop. **7** *Obs.* To die. —*n.* **1** The conclusion or last stage of anything. **2** The process or effect of perfecting or beautifying anything: the *finish* of a statue; cloth of a fine *finish.* **3** Perfection in speech or manner; social poise. **4** The joinery and cabinetwork necessary to complete the interior of a building. **5** That which finishes or completes. **6** A material, as oil, used in finishing. See synonyms under END. [<OF *feniss-*, stem of *fenir* end <L *finire* <*finis* an end]

Synonyms (verb): accomplish, achieve, close, complete, conclude, elaborate, end, perfect, polish, terminate. In addition to its meaning of *completing* by which it is synonymous with *close, conclude, end, terminate,* etc., *finish* has come to denote the bringing to perfection of every minutest detail, especially of superficial elegance, refinement, or beauty, and is thus a close synonym of *elaborate, perfect, polish,* etc., as in the expression, to add the *finishing* touches. Compare END *v.* *Antonyms*: begin, commence, found, inaugurate, initiate, institute, open, originate, start, undertake. Compare synonyms for BEGIN.

fin·ished (fin′isht) *adj.* **1** Carried to a high degree of perfection; polished. **2** Ended; concluded. **3** Completed; done. See synonyms under PERFECT, RIPE.

fin·ish·er (fin′ish·ər) *n.* One who or that which finishes, completes, ends, or perfects anything.

fin·ish·ing (fin′ish·ing) *n.* The final operation or set of operations in any manufacturing process: the *finishing* of furs, etc.

finishing school See under SCHOOL.

Fin·is·terre (fin′is·târ′, *Sp.* fē′nēs·ter′rā), **Cape** A headland in Galicia, the most westerly point of Spain.

fi·nite (fī′nīt) *adj.* **1** Having bounds, ends, or limits, as opposed to that which is infinite. **2** That may be determined, counted, or measured. **3** Subject to creature limitations, especially those that affect human life. **4** *Gram.* Limited by number and person: said of verb forms that can serve as predicates in sentences: distinguished from infinitives, participles, and gerunds that have no such limitations. **5** *Math.* **a** That may be equaled or exceeded by counting: said of numbers. **b** Limited and determinate, in theory or by observation; not infinite or infinitesimal: said of a magnitude. —*n.* Finite things collectively, or that which is finite: usually with *the.* [<L *finitus* limited; orig. pp. of *finire* end] —**fi′·nite·ly** *adv.* —**fi′nite·ness** *n.*

fin·i·tes·i·mal (fin′ə·tes′ə·məl) *adj. Math.* Denoted by the ordinal of a finite number. [<FINITE + *-esimal,* as in *centesimal* <L *-esimus,* suffix of ordinal numbers]

fin·i·tude (fin′ə·to͞od, -tyo͞od, fī′nə-) *n.* The mode or fact of being finite; limitation. [<L *finitus* limited]

fin·jan (fin′jən) *n.* A small handleless coffee cup of Asia Minor: also spelled *fingan.* [< Arabic]

fink (fingk) *n. U.S. Slang* A non-working strikebreaker. [? <FINGER, *v.* (def. 4)]

fin keel See under KEEL.

Fin·land (fin′lənd) A republic of northern Europe, NE of the Baltic Sea; 130,091 square miles; capital, Helsinki: Finnish *Suomi.*

Finland, Gulf of An eastern arm of the Baltic Sea, between Finland and the U.S.S.R.

Fin·land·er (fin′lən·dər) *n.* A native or naturalized inhabitant of Finland.

Fin·lay (fin′lē, *Sp.* fin·lī′), **Carlos Juan,** 1833–1915, Cuban physician and biologist.

Finlay River (fin′lē) The chief tributary of the Peace River, flowing 210 miles SE through northern British Columbia.

Finn (fin) See FIONN MACCUMAL.

Finn (fin) *n.* **1** A native or inhabitant of Finland. **2** A member of a people speaking a Finnic language. [OE *Finnas* Finns]

fin·nan had·die (fin′ən had′ē) Smoked haddock. Also **fin′nan had·dock** (had′ək). [<*Findhorn haddock,* from *Findhorn,* a Scottish town where originally prepared]

finned (find) *adj.* Having fins or finlike extensions.

Finn·ic (fin′ik) *n.* A branch of the Finno-Ugric subfamily of Uralic languages, including Finnish, Estonian, and Lapp. —*adj.* Finnish.

fin·nick·ing (fin′i·king), **fin·nick·y** (fin′i·kē) See FINICAL.

Finn·ish (fin′ish) *adj.* Of or pertaining to Finland, the Finns, or their language. —*n.* The Uralic language of the Finns.

Fin·no-U·gric (fin′ō·o͞o′grik, -yo͞o′grik) *n.* A subfamily of the Uralic languages, embracing the Finnic (Finnish, Estonian, Lapp, etc.) and Ugric (Magyar, Ostyak, Vogul) branches. —*adj.* Pertaining to the Finns and the Ugrians, or to their languages. Also **Fin′no-U′gri·an.**

fin·ny (fin′ē) *adj.* **1** Having fins; fishlike. **2** Abounding in fish.

fi·no·chi·o (fi·nō′kē·ō) *n.* A variety of fennel (*Foeniculum vulgare dulce*) whose young sweet shoots are esteemed as a food and salad. [<Ital. *finocchio* <L *faeniculum* FENNEL]

fin ray One of the cartilaginous or bony rods supporting the membrane of a fish's fin: also called *ray.*

Fin·sen light (fin′sən) A strong actinic light obtained either from an electric lamp or by passing sunlight through an ammoniacal solution of copper sulfate: used in treating certain skin diseases. [after N. R. *Finsen,* 1860–1904, Danish physician, its originator]

Fin·ster·aar·horn (fin′stər·är′hôrn) The highest peak of the Bernese Alps, Switzerland; 14,026 feet high.

Fio·na Mc·Leod (fē′nə mə·kloud′) Pseudonym of William Sharp.

Fionn Mac·Cumal (fin mə·ko͞ol′) The hero of the Fenian cycle of Old Irish legend, a chieftain of third century Ireland; father of the poet Ossian. Also spelled *Finn.*

fiord (fyôrd, fyōrd) *n.* A long and narrow arm of the sea, with high rocky banks: also spelled *fjord.* [<Norw. *fjord*]

fip·pence (fip′əns) *n. Brit.* Fivepence.

fip·pen·ny (fip′ə·nē, fip′nē) Short for FIVEPENNY.

fippenny bit *U.S.* A Spanish or Mexican silver piece current before the Civil War at about 6 cents.

fip·ple (fip′əl) *n.* A plug with a lip, as in certain wind instruments, such as the *fipple* flute. [? <ON *flipi* lip of a horse]

fi·que (fē′kā) *n.* A succulent plant of the amaryllis family (*Furcraea macrophylla*) native in tropical America, yielding a fiber similar to jute. [<Sp.]

fir (fûr) *n.* **1** An evergreen tree of the pine family (genus *Abies*), cone-bearing and resinous, especially the balsam fir (*A. balsamea*). **2** Its wood. ◆ Homophone: *fur.* [OE *fyrh*]

Fir·bolg (fir′bul·əg) Literally, men of the leather boats: one of a legendary pre-Celtic people of Ireland, defeated and run out by the Fomorians. [<Irish *fir* men + *bolg* leather coracle]

Fir·dau·si (fir·dou′sē) Pseudonym of Abul Kasim Mansur, 939?–1020, Persian epic poet. Also **Fir·du·si** (fir·do͞o′sē).

fire (fīr) *n.* **1** The evolution of heat and light by combustion. **2** The combustion thus manifested, especially the flame, or the fuel as burning. **3** A destructive burning, as of a building. **4** The discharge of firearms. **5** A spark or sparks; a light, luster, or flash. **6** Intensity of feeling or action; ardor; passion; vivacity. **7** Any raging evil; affliction; trial. **8** Fever. **9** A combustible device or substance for producing fire or for display; fireworks. **10** Lightning. **11** *Poetic* A luminous object in the sky, as a star or meteor. **12** Torture or death by or as by burning;

also, any severe trial. **13** *Obs.* A North American Indian term for a family or a nation; hence, by transference, one of the United States, especially one of the first thirteen. **— colored fire** A mixture of combustibles, as sulfur with a mineral salt that yields a colored light when burning: used for signals, fireworks, etc. **— Greek fire** An incendiary composition, used by the Byzantine Greeks to fire enemy ships: said to ignite on contact with water. **— on fire** Burning; ablaze; hence, ardent; zealous. **— under fire** Exposed to gunshot or artillery fire; hence, under attack of any kind. **—** *v.* **fired, fir·ing** *v.t.* **1** To set on fire; cause to burn. **2** To tend the fire of; put fuel in: to *fire* a furnace. **3** To bake, as pottery, in a kiln. **4** To cure, as tobacco, by exposure to heat. **5** To cauterize. **6** To inflame the emotions or passions of; excite. **7** To discharge, as a gun or bullet. **8** *Colloq.* To impel or hurl, as with force: to *fire* questions. **9** To cause to glow or shine. **10** *U.S. Colloq.* To discharge peremptorily from employment. **—** *v.i.* **11** To take fire; become ignited. **12** To discharge firearms. **13** To discharge a missile. **14** To become inflamed or excited. **15** To tend a fire. **16** To become blotched or yellow: said of flax and grain. See synonyms under INCENSE[1]. **— to fire away** To begin; start. **— to fire up** **1** To start a fire, as in a furnace. **2** To become enraged. [OE *fȳr*]

Synonyms (noun): blaze, burning, combustion, conflagration, flame. *Combustion* is the essential fact which is at the basis of that assemblage of visible phenomena which we call *fire, combustion* being the continuous chemical combination of a substance with some element, as oxygen, evolving heat, and extending from slow processes, such as those by which the heat of the human body is maintained, to the processes producing the most intense light also, as in a blast furnace, or on the surface of the sun. *Fire* is always attended with light, as well as heat; *blaze, flame,* etc., designate the mingled light and heat of a *fire. Combustion* is the scientific, *fire* the popular term. A *conflagration* is an extensive *fire.* Compare LIGHT[1].

fire-ac·tion (fīr′ak′shən) *n.* The fire of small arms or artillery estimated as a force in attack or defense.

fire alarm **1** An alarm calling attention to a fire or its whereabouts. **2** An apparatus for giving an alarm of fire, especially a telegraphic alarm.

fire-and-brim·stone (fīr′ən·brim′stōn′) *adj.* Impassioned; also, threatening hell: a *fire-and-brimstone* sermon.

fire ant A destructive, mound-building red ant *(Solenopsis geminata)* common in the SE United States: its sting is very painful and often fatal to animals.

fire·arm (fīr′ärm′) *n.* Any weapon from which a missile, as a bullet, is hurled by an explosive: usually restricted to small arms.

fire at will **1** The command given to riflemen or to gun crews to fire independently of each other and of their commanding officer. **2** The act of so firing.

fire·back (fīr′bak′) *n.* **1** The rear wall of a furnace or fireplace. **2** One of various Asian pheasants, having the plumage of the back a bright metallic red.

fire·ball (fīr′bôl′) *n.* **1** A sack of canvas filled with combustibles. **2** A meteor brighter than the planet Venus. **3** Ball-shaped lightning. **4** *Physics* The dense, mushroom-shaped or globular mass of radioactive debris and fall-out material produced by the explosion of an atomic or thermonuclear bomb.

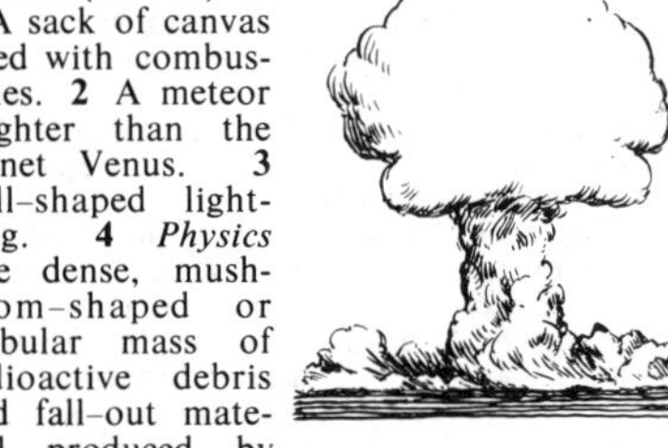

FIREBALL *(def. 4)*

fire balloon **1** A balloon inflated with hot air supplied by fire from underneath, particularly a paper toy balloon carrying a lighted ball or sponge. **2** A balloon carrying inflammable explosives or fireworks, to ignite at a certain height.

fire beetle Any of various elaterid beetles (genus *Pyrophorus*) of the West Indies, especially the cucubano *(P. luminosus),* which emits a greenish light from two spots near the head and a red light from the abdomen.

fire·bird (fīr′bûrd′) *n.* Any of various, small, brilliantly colored birds, as the Baltimore oriole, the vermilion flycatcher, and the scarlet tanager.

fire·blight (fīr′blīt′) *n.* A serious bacterial disease of various pome fruits, caused by *Erwina amylovora* and attacking blossoms, leaves, twigs, and fruit.

fire·board (fīr′bôrd′, -bōrd′) *n.* A board to close a fireplace not in use; chimney board.

fire boat A steamboat provided with fire-extinguishing apparatus: used to protect shipping and wharves.

fire·box (fīr′boks′) *n.* The chamber in which the fuel of a locomotive, furnace, etc., is burnt.

fire·brand (fīr′brand′) *n.* **1** A burning or glowing piece of wood or other substance. **2** An incendiary; a mischief-maker.

fire·brat (fīr′brat′) *n.* A small, wingless, scaly insect *(Thermobia domestica)* which inhabits warm houses and is destructive of wallpaper, clothing, and starchy materials: related to the silverfish. For illustration see under INSECT (injurious).

fire·break (fīr′brāk′) *n.* A strip of plowed or cleared land made to prevent the spread of fire in woods or on a prairie.

fire·brick (fīr′brik′) *n.* A brick made of fireclay, used for lining furnaces.

fire brigade A company of firemen.

fire·bug (fīr′bug′) *n. U.S. Colloq.* An incendiary; a pyromaniac.

fire bug The harlequin bug.

fire·clay (fīr′klā′) *n.* A refractory material, usually finely powdered aluminum silicate, mixed with iron oxide, lime, and other constituents to improve its fire-resistant qualities.

fire company **1** A company of men employed to extinguish fires. **2** A fire-insurance company.

fire control *Mil.* The control of artillery fire by automatic instruments and technical supervision.

fire·crack·er (fīr′krak′ər) *n.* A firework made of a small paper cylinder charged with gunpowder.

fire-cure (fīr′kyŏŏr′) *v.t.* **-cured, -cur·ing** To season with the heat and smoke of an open fire, as tobacco; to smoke.

fire·damp (fīr′damp′) *n.* **1** A combustible gas (chiefly methane) which enters mines from coal seams. **2** The explosive mixture formed by this gas and air.

fire department That part of the public service, including buildings, fire-extinguishing apparatus, and men, devoted to the prevention or extinguishment of fires.

fire·dog (fīr′dôg′, -dog′) *n.* An andiron.

fire·drake (fīr′drāk′) *n.* A fire-breathing dragon of Germanic mythology; specifically, the dragon that killed Beowulf. Also **fire′drag′on** (-drag′ən). [OE *fȳrdraca* <*fȳr* fire + *draca* a dragon]

fire drill **1** The drilling of a fire company. **2** Drilling, as of pupils in a school, to accustom them to proper action in case of fire.

fire-eat·er (fīr′ē′tər) *n.* **1** A juggler who pretends to eat fire. **2** A hot-headed person eager to fight or quarrel.

fire engine A heavy motor truck equipped with fire-fighting apparatus, especially power-driven pumps for throwing water and chemicals under high pressure.

fire escape A ladder or other device attached to the outside of a building and furnishing a means of escape from a burning building.

fire extinguisher A portable fire-fighting apparatus containing certain chemicals that are ejected by pressure through a short hose.

fire·fang (fīr′fang′) *v.i.* To deteriorate by oxidation, as cheese. [<FIRE + FANG, *v.*]

fire·find·er (fīr′fīn′dər) *n.* An instrument consisting of a map with an azimuth circle, an alidade, spirit level, and other accessories: used by forest rangers to locate the position of a fire.

fire·flaught (fīr′flôt′, -fläkht′) *n. Scot.* **1** A flash of lightning. **2** The aurora borealis.

fire·fly (fīr′flī′) *n. pl.* **·flies** Any of various phosphorescent, night-flying beetles (family *Lampyridae*); specifically, the North American genera *Photinus* and *Photuris,* whose females and phosphorescent larvae are called *glowworms.*

Fire·foam (fīr′fōm′) *n.* A thick foamlike substance, formed by the chemical union of aluminum sulfate and sodium bicarbonate with other materials, which smothers a fire: a trade name.

fire·guard (fīr′gärd′) *n.* **1** A space in fields, grasslands, woods, and forests, cleared of all combustible matter and serving as a protection against the spread of fire. **2** A metal screen placed before an open fire as a guard against sparks.

fire·house (fīr′hous′) *n.* A building for the housing of fire-fighting equipment and personnel.

fire insurance Insurance covering loss resulting from fire.

fire-i·rons (fīr′ī′ərnz) *n.* Poker, shovel, and tongs.

fire·less (fīr′lis) *adj.* Having no fire.

fireless cooker An insulated container in which hot foods may be placed to finish cooking or to be kept warm.

fire·light (fīr′līt′) *n.* The light from a fire, as a campfire.

fire line **1** A firebreak. **2** A barrier made by police against approach to a burning building.

fire·lock (fīr′lok′) *n.* An old form of musket discharged by any device for producing sparks; a flintlock.

fire·man (fīr′mən) *n. pl.* **·men** (-mən) **1** One who aids in extinguishing fires; a member of a professional fire-fighting company or crew. **2** One who tends the firing on a locomotive; a stoker.

fire-new (fīr′nōō′, -nyōō′) *adj. Archaic* Fresh from the fire; brand-new.

Fi·ren·ze (fē·ren′tzā) The Italian name for FLORENCE.

fire opal See under OPAL.

fire·pan (fīr′pan′) *n.* **1** A brazier; a grate. **2** The priming receptacle of a flintlock gun.

fire·pink (fīr′pingk′) *n.* A catchfly *(Silene virginica)* of the eastern United States, with crimson or scarlet flowers.

fire·place (fīr′plās′) *n.* A recess or structure in or on which a fire is built; especially that part of a chimney that opens into a room.

fire·plug (fīr′plug′) *n.* A hydrant for use in case of fire.

fire point A flash point.

fire·pow·er (fīr′pou′ər) *n. Mil.* **1** Capacity for delivering fire, as from the guns of a ship, battery, etc. **2** The total amount of fire delivered by a given weapon or unit.

fire·proof (fīr′prōōf′) *adj.* **1** Made resistant against fire; incombustible. **2** Of a nature to protect from fire. **—** *v.t.* To make resistant to fire.

fir·er (fīr′ər) *n.* **1** One who kindles fires. **2** An incendiary. **3** A stoker. **4** One who fires a weapon.

fire-reel (fīr′rēl′) *n. Canadian* A fire engine.

fire·room (fīr′rōōm′, -rōōm′) *n.* The boiler-room on a steamship, where the firing of the furnace is done; stokehole.

fire sale A sale of goods reduced in price because of slight damage by fire.

fire screen A fireguard (def. 2).

fire ship A ship filled with combustibles, fired and floated toward an enemy for the purpose of destroying ships, bridges, etc.

fire·side (fīr′sīd′) *n.* The hearth or space about the fireplace; hence, the place of family cheer. See synonyms under HOME.

fireside chat An informal talk, over a radio network, on subjects of national interest; specifically, one given by President Franklin D. Roosevelt.

fire station A firehouse.

fire·stone (fīr′stōn′) *n.* **1** Flint or pyrites used for striking fire. **2** A stone that will withstand the action of fire.

fire surface That part of the surface of a boiler which is exposed to the fire; the heating surface.

fire·thorn (fīr′thôrn′) *n.* An evergreen, typically thorny shrub (genus *Pyracantha*) of the rose family, bearing white flowers and a scarlet or orange fruit, and cultivated as an ornamental hedge plant.

fire·tow·er (fīr′tou′ər) *n.* A watchtower, usually in a wooded area, from which a fire can be seen and reported.

fire•trap (fīr′trap′) *n.* A building notoriously inflammable, or one not provided with an escape for use in case of fire.
fire•wall (fīr′wôl′) *n.* **1** A fireproof wall designed to block the progress of a fire. **2** *Aeron.* A bulkhead of fire-resistant material placed between the engine compartment of an aircraft and the rest of the structure to limit the spread of fire from the engines.
fire•war•den (fīr′wôr′dən) *n.* An officer who has charge of the prevention and extinguishing of fires.
fire•wa•ter (fīr′wô′tər, -wot′ər) *n.* Whisky: a term first used by the North American Indians.
fire•weed (fīr′wēd′) *n.* **1** The willow herb. **2** The jimsonweed.
fire•wood[1] (fīr′wŏŏd′) *n.* Wood used, or fit to use, as fuel.
fire•wood[2] (fīr′wŏŏd′) *n.* An ironwood *(Cyrilla racemiflora)* of Central America and the SE United States.
fire•works (fīr′wûrks′) *n.* **1** A case or cases containing combustibles and explosives, producing brilliant or colored light or scintillations in burning. **2** A pyrotechnic display.
fire•worm (fīr′wûrm′) *n.* **1** A glowworm. **2** The larva of a tortricid moth *(Rhopobota naevana),* which devours the leaves of the cranberry, leaving the plant apparently burned.
fire-wor•ship (fīr′wûr′ship) *n.* The worship of fire as a deity.
fir•ing (fīr′ing) *n.* **1** The act or process of applying fire or intense heat to anything, as in stoking, burning, baking, or vitrifying, as bricks or pottery in a kiln; also, in cauterizing. **2** The discharge of firearms. **3** Fuel, as wood or coal.
firing line **1** The line of active engagement in battle. **2** The main body of troops in action within effective rifle range of the enemy. **3** The foremost position in any activity.
firing pin That part of a firearm or a fuze which, on being actuated, strikes the primer or detonator. See illustration under BOMB (aerial).
firing squad A military or naval detachment selected to show honor to a deceased person by firing over his grave, or to execute a sentence of death by shooting.
firing tread A banquette tread; banquette.
fir•kin (fûr′kən) *n.* **1** A wooden vessel for lard, etc. **2** An English measure equal to one fourth of a barrel, or 40.9 liters: in the United States, 34.068 liters. [ME *ferdekyn* <MDu. *vierde* fourth + -KIN]
fir•lot (fûr′lot) *n.* An old Scottish dry measure, used also on the Isle of Man: from 1 to 1 1/2 bushels.
firm[1] (fûrm) *adj.* **1** Solidly compacted; unyielding; solid. **2** Fixedly settled; difficult to move; stable. **3** Strong, steadfast, or determined in character; vigorous; resolute; enduring. **4** Solid; not liquid or gaseous. **5** Not fluctuating widely, as prices. — *v.t.* & *v.i.* **1** To make or become firm, solid, or compact. **2** *Obs.* To confirm; establish. —*adv.* Solidly; resolutely; fixedly: to stand *firm* against the foe. [<L *firmus*] — **firm′ly** *adv.* — **firm′ness** *n.*
Synonyms (adj.): close, compact, decided, determined, established, fast, fixed, hard, immovable, immutable, resolute, robust, rugged, secure, solid, stable, steadfast, steady, strong, sturdy, unchanging, unfailing, unfaltering, unshaken. See FAITHFUL, HARD, IMPLICIT, OBSTINATE.
firm[2] (fûrm) *n.* **1** A union of two or more persons for the purpose of conducting business; a commercial, industrial, or financial partnership; a business house. **2** The style or title under which such a house carries on business; firm name. [<Ital. *firma* a signature <L *firmare* confirm <*firmus* firm]
fir•ma•ment (fûr′mə•mənt) *n.* The expanse of the heavens; sky. [<L *firmamentum* a support <*firmare* make firm] — **fir′ma•men′tal** *adj.*
fir•man (fûr′mən, fər•män′) *n. pl.* **•mans** A special decree or edict of an Oriental sovereign; a grant or license. Also **fir′maun.** [<Persian *fermān* a command]
firm•er (fûr′mər) *adj.* Designating a cutting tool with a thin, narrow blade, for manual use in shaping wood. — *n.* A firmer chisel or gouge. For illustration see under GOUGE.
firm power Electric power from a generating station available for use under all conditions.
firn (firn) *n.* *Meteorol.* Snow, partly consolidated into ice, found in Alpine regions; névé. [<G <*firn,* adj., of last year]
fir•ry (fûr′ē) *adj.* Pertaining to the fir; made of fir; wooded with firs.
first (fûrst) *adj.* **1** Preceding all others in the order of numbering: the ordinal of *one.* **2** Prior to all others in time; earliest. **3** Nearest or foremost in place from a given point. **4** Highest or foremost in character, rank, etc.; leading; chief; best. — **at (the) first blush** On first presentation; at first thought, without mature consideration. — **at first hand** Directly from the original source; without intervening assistance. — *n.* **1** That which comes or is first; the beginning. **2** *Music* The leading or upper part, voice, or instrument; also, a unison. **3** In English universities, the highest rank in examinations for honors; also, one taking the highest rank. **4** A winning position in a contest. **5** The first day of a month; the first year in a period or reign. **6** *pl.* The best grade of certain commercial products, as butter, sugar, etc. — **at first** (or **from the first**) At the beginning or origin. — *adv.* **1** Before all others in order, as in counting, time, place, or rank; also, in formal discourse, **first′ly.** **2** Before, or in preference to, some proposed act or anticipated event; sooner: He will never confess: he would die *first.* **3** For the first time. [OE *fyrst,* superlative of *fore* before]
Synonyms (adj.): chief, earliest, foremost, front, highest, leading, original, primary, primeval, primitive, primordial, principal, pristine, supreme. *Antonyms*: hindmost, inferior, insignificant, last, least, lowest, secondary, subordinate, subsequent, subservient, subsidiary, trifling, trivial, unimportant.
first aid Treatment given in any emergency while awaiting qualified medical or surgical attention. — **first-aid** (fûrst′ād′) *adj.*
first base In baseball, the base first reached by the runner, at the right-hand angle of the infield. Compare illustration under BASEBALL. — **to get to first base** *U.S. Slang* To succeed in the first phase of an enterprise.
first-born (fûrst′bôrn′) *adj.* First brought forth; eldest; first, best, or highest; preeminent. — *n.* The child first born; an heir; also, a first product or result.
First Cause **1** God as uncaused, the original source and creator of all things. **2** In Aristotelian philosophy, prime mover.
first-class (fûrst′klas′, -kläs′) *adj.* **1** Belonging to the first class; of the highest rank or the best quality. **2** Consisting of sealed letters or other sealed matter transmitted by the post: *first-class* mail. **3** Pertaining to, for, or using, the most luxurious accommodations on a steamer, train, plane, etc.
First Day Sunday: name used by the Society of Friends.
first floor **1** *U.S.* The ground floor. **2** The floor just above the ground floor: a designation used generally in Great Britain, on the Continent, and occasionally in the United States.
first-fruit (fûrst′fro͞ot′) *n., usually pl.* **1** The first gatherings of a season's produce. *Ex.* xxiii 19. **2** The first outcome, effects, results, or rewards of anything.
first-hand (fûrst′hand′) *adj.* Obtained direct from the origin or producer; without intermediary. — *adv.* Direct from the original source.
First Lady The wife of the President of the United States or if he has no wife, the lady chosen by him to be the hostess of the White House.
first•ling (fûrst′ling) *n.* The first of anything; especially, the first-born of a flock. — *adj.* First produced.
first•ly (fûrst′lē) See under FIRST.
first mortgage A mortgage having priority over all other liens.
first night The first public performance of a play or opera; also, the night of this performance. — **first-night** (fûrst′nīt′) *adj.*
first-night•er (fûrst′nī′tər) *n.* One who habitually attends opening performances; anyone present at an opening performance.
first officer In the merchant marine, a first mate.
first papers Papers declaring intent to become a citizen of the United States: first step in the naturalization of a foreigner.
first-rate (fûrst′rāt′) *adj.* Of the first or finest class, quality, or character. — *adv.* In a high degree; well; excellently. — **first′-rat′er** *n.*
first water **1** The finest quality and purest luster: said of gems, especially of diamonds and pearls. **2** The utmost excellence of anything.
First World War See WORLD WAR I in table under WAR.
firth (fûrth) *n.* *Scot.* An arm of the sea: also spelled *frith.*
Firth of Forth See FORTH, FIRTH OF.
Firth of Tay See TAY RIVER.
fisc (fisk) *n.* The treasury of a state; any treasury. [<F <L *fiscus* a purse]
fis•cal (fis′kəl) *adj.* **1** Of or pertaining to the treasury or finances of a government. **2** Financial. — *n.* In Spain, Portugal, and some other countries in Europe, a public prosecutor.
fiscal agent A person or company representing another financially.
fiscal year See under YEAR.
Fisch•er (fish′ər), **Emil,** 1852–1919, German chemist. — **Hans** 1881–1945, German chemist.
fish (fish) *n. pl.* **fish** or (with reference to different species) **fish•es** **1** A vertebrate, cold-blooded craniate animal with permanent gills, belonging to the superclass *Pisces* in the phylum *Chordata*; adapted solely for aquatic life, it has a typically elongate, tapering body, usually covered with scales and provided with

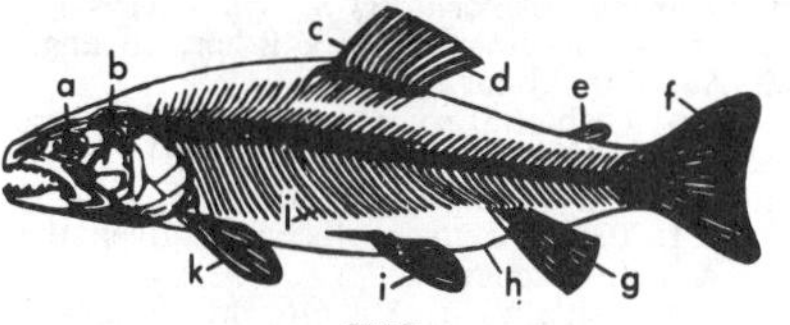

FISH
(Anatomical features of a trout)
a Eye socket. *b* Brain case. *c* Dorsal fin. *d* Fin ray. *e* Adipose fin. *f* Caudal fin. *g* Anal fin. *h* Anus. *i* Ventral fin (also called abdominal, thoracic, or jugular, according to its deviation from normal position). *j* Ribs. *k* Pectoral fin.

fins for locomotion. ◆ Collateral adjective: *piscine.* **2** Loosely, any animal habitually living in the water. **3** The flesh of a fish used as food. **4** *Naut.* **a** A strip used to strengthen or mend a spar, rail joint, etc., or to join parts. **b** An apparatus for weighing anchor; anchor tackle: also called **fish tackle.** **5** A person with fishlike characteristics, such as cold-bloodedness, stupidity, etc. — **to have other fish to fry** To have other business to do. — *adj.* Pertaining to, like, consisting of, or made from, fish: *fish* market, *fish* beam, *fish* glue; also, for fish: *fish* bowl, *fish* sauce. — *v.t.* **1** To catch or try to catch fish in (a body of water). **2** To catch or try to catch (fish, eels, etc.). **3** To search for by dragging, diving, etc. **4** To grope for and bring out: usually with *up* or *out.* **5** *Naut.* **a** To repair or strengthen by strips fastened lengthwise: to *fish* a spar. **b** To bring the flukes of (an anchor) to the gunwale or rail. — *v.i.* **6** To catch or try to catch fish. **7** To try to get something in an artful or indirect manner: usually with *for*: to *fish* for compliments. — **to fish or cut bait** To make a choice, as of joining or being left out of an enterprise. — **to fish out** To exhaust of fish. [OE *fisc*] — **fish′a•ble** *adj.*
Fish Either of two star groups regarded as together composing the constellation Pisces. See CONSTELLATION.
Fish (fish), **Hamilton,** 1808–93, governor of New York; secretary of state under President Grant 1869–77.
fish and chips *Brit.* Fish fillets and potatoes sliced and French-fried.
fish ball A fried ball or cake made of chopped

fish (often salt codfish) mixed with mashed potatoes. Also **fish cake.**
fish beam A beam cut with a downward bulge, like the belly of a fish.
fish·ber·ry (fish′ber′ē) *n. pl.* **·ber·ries** The berry of an East Indian vine *(Anamirta cocculus),* yielding picrotoxin. Also called *cocculus indicus.*
fish·bolt (fish′bōlt′) *n.* A bolt for securing fishplates at a fish joint.
fish·bone (fish′bōn′) *n.* **1** A bone of a fish. **2** *Mil.* A network of subterranean passages constructed by military engineers for purposes of defense, attack, and as listening posts close to enemy positions.
fish bowl (fish′bōl′) *n.* A bowl, usually glass, serving as a small aquarium for fish.
fish crow A crow *(Corvus ossifragus)* of the Atlantic coast of the United States that feeds mainly on fish.
fish–cul·ture (fish′kul′chər) *n.* The artificial breeding of fishes; pisciculture. **— fish′–cul′·tur·ist** *n.*
fish–di·vert·er (fish′di·vûr′tər) *n.* An electrical device for generating currents in selected areas of water, as power dams, irrigation ditches, etc., for the purpose of diverting fish from entering them.
fish·er (fish′ər) *n.* **1** One who fishes; a fisherman. **2** A weasel-like carnivore *(Martes pennanti)* of eastern North America, related to the martens. **3** The dark–brown fur of this animal. ◆ Homophone: *fissure.*
Fisher (fish′ər), **Dorothy Canfield** See CANFIELD. **— Herbert Albert Laurens,** 1865–1940, English historian. **— Irving,** 1867–1947, U.S. economist. **— Sir John Arbuthnot,** 1841–1920, Baron of Kilverstone, English admiral, first sea lord 1904–10, 1914–15.
fish·er·man (fish′ər·mən) *n. pl.* **·men** (-mən) **1** One who catches fish; a fisher; an angler. **2** A fishing boat.
fish·er·y (fish′ər·ē) *n. pl.* **·er·ies** **1** The operation or business of catching fish; fishing industry. **2** A place for fishing. **3** *Law* The right to fish in a given place at a given time. **4** A fish–hatchery.
fish·gig (fish′gig′) *n.* A staff with prongs for spearing fish. [<FISH + GIG²]
fish·grass (fish′gras′, -gräs′) *n.* Fanwort.
fish–hatch·er·y (fish′hach′ər·ē) *n. pl.* **·er·ies** A place designed for the artificial propagation, hatching, and nurture of fish.
fish hawk The osprey.
fish hook A hook, usually barbed, for catching fish.
fish·ing (fish′ing) *n.* **1** The operation or the sport of catching or trying to catch fish. **2** A right of, a place for, fishing; a fishery. ◆ Collateral adjective: *piscatorial.*
fish·ing–frog (fish′ing·frog′, -frôg′) *n.* The angler (def. 1).
fishing line A line or cord used in catching fish with a hook. Also **fish line.**
fishing tackle Rod, reel, line, leader, hooks, and harness, used in fishing.
fish joint A splice made by fastening two rails together by fishplates bolted across the meeting ends.
fish knife **1** A broad knife, often with a serrated edge, for serving fish. **2** A heavy knife for scaling and dressing fish.
fish ladder A chute or series of steps in a dam, covered with flowing water, to facilitate the upstream migrations of fish: also called *fishway.*
fish·meal (fish′mēl′) *n.* **1** Ground dried fish: used in soups. **2** Ground fish waste: used as fertilizer.
fish·mon·ger (fish′mung′gər, -mong′-) *n.* A dealer in fish.
fish·net (fish′net′) *n.* **1** A net for catching fish. **2** A similar net for holding camouflage materials in place.
fish owl A large Asian or African owl (genera *Ketupa* and *Scotopelia*), feeding mostly on fish.
fish·plate (fish′plāt′) *n.* One of the iron plates used in forming a fish joint.
fish·pole (fish′pōl′) *n.* A long, flexible rod to which a line and hook are attached for catching fish.
fish·pot (fish′pot′) *n.* A basketlike trap for catching fish, eels, or lobsters.
fish·pound (fish′pound′) *n.* A weir.
fish·skin (fish′skin′) *n.* The skin of a fish or marine animal, as of a dogfish or shark (used for abrading), of a porpoise (tanned for leather), or the like.
fishskin disease Ichthyosis.
fish·spear (fish′spir′) *n.* **1** A spear for catching or killing fish; a fishgig. **2** A lance for bleeding captured whales.
fish story *Colloq.* An extravagant or incredible narrative.
fish tackle A tackle used to raise an anchor to the gunwale of a ship by means of an iron hook.
fish·tail (fish′tāl′) *adj.* Like the tail of a fish in shape or in action. **—** *v.i. Aeron.* To swing the tail of an aircraft from side to side as a retarding action: also called *yaw.*
fishtail kick In swimming, a kick in which both legs are drawn up and then thrust simultaneously backward while held together.
fish–tracks (fish′traks′) *n. pl. Physics* Visible trails made by the particles activated in a cloud chamber.
fish warden A local officer to enforce laws relating to the protection of fish or fisheries.
fish·way (fish′wā′) *n.* A fish ladder.
fish–well (fish′wel′) *n.* A compartment, as in the hold of a fishing smack, open to the water beneath, used for storing live fish.
fish·wife (fish′wīf′) *n. pl.* **·wives** (-wīvz′) **1** A woman who sells fish. **2** An abusive virago.
fish·y (fish′ē) *adj.* **fish·i·er, fish·i·est** **1** Suggestive of, pertaining to, or like fish. **2** Abounding in fish. **3** *Colloq.* Of the nature of a fish story; incredible. **4** Vacant of expression; dull, as the eyes; lacking luster. **— fish′·i·ly** *adv.* **— fish′i·ness** *n.*
Fiske (fisk), **Bradley Allen,** 1854–1942, U.S. admiral and inventor. **— John,** 1842–1901, U.S. philosopher and historian. **— Minnie Maddern,** 1865–1932, *née* Davey, U. S. actress.
fis·sate (fis′āt) *adj.* Deeply cleft; fissured.
fissi– *combining form* Split; cleft: *fissiparous.* Also, before vowels, **fiss–.** [<L *fissus,* pp. of *findere* split]
fis·sile (fis′əl) *adj.* **1** Capable of being split or separated into layers. **2** Tending to split. [<L *fissilis* <*findere* split] **— fis·sil·i·ty** (fi·sil′ə·tē) *n.*
fis·sion (fish′ən) *n.* **1** The act of splitting or breaking apart. **2** *Biol.* Spontaneous division of a cell or organism into new cells or organisms, especially as a mode of reproduction; cell division. **3** *Physics* The disintegration of the nucleus of a radioactive atom initiated by bombardment with nucleons or gamma rays, leading to the formation of nuclei of more stable atoms and the release of energy. **4** In astrophysics, the breaking up of a large gaseous body into separate masses subject to mutual attraction: regarded as the possible origin of binary and double stars. [<L *fissio, -onis* <*fissus,* pp. of *findere* split] **— fis′sion·a·ble** *adj.*
fission fungus A bacterium; any member of the group *Schizomycetes* of the *Thallophyta* division of plants.
fis·si·pal·mate (fis′i·pal′māt) *adj.* Partially web–footed. **— fis′si·pal·ma′tion** *n.*
fis·sip·a·rous (fi·sip′ər·əs) *adj. Biol.* **1** Reproducing by fission. **2** Separating by fission. **— fis·sip′a·rous·ly** *adv.*
fis·si·ped (fis′i·ped) *adj.* Having the toes separated: also **fis·sip·e·dal** (fi·sip′ə·dəl, fis′i·ped′l), **fis′si·pe′di·al** (-pē′dē·əl). **—** *n. Zool.* Any of a suborder *(Fissipedia)* of terrestrial carnivores with separate toes, as cats, bears, etc. [<LL *fissipes, -pedis*]
fis·si·ros·tral (fis′i·ros′trəl) *adj. Ornithol.* Having a wide beak deeply cleft, as swifts, nighthawks, etc.
fis·sle (fis′əl) *Scot. v.i.* **·sled, ·sling** To rustle; bustle about; also, to fidget. **—** *n.* Fuss; bustle.
fis·sure (fish′ər) *n.* **1** A narrow opening, cleft, crevice, or furrow. **2** Cleavage. **3** *Anat.* **a** Any cleft or furrow of the body, as between the lobes of the liver or the bones of the skull. **b** One of the furrows on the surface of the brain. See synonyms under BREACH. **—** *v.t.* & *v.i.* **fis·sured, fis·sur·ing** To crack; split; cleave. ◆ Homophone: *fisher.* [<L *fissura* <*findere* split]
fissure of Sylvius The Sylvian fissure.
fist¹ (fist) *n.* **1** The hand closed tightly, as for striking; the clenched hand; also, grip, clutch. **2** *Colloq.* The hand. **3** *Colloq.* Handwriting. **4** *Printing* An index mark (☞). **—** *v.t.* **1** To strike with the fist. **2** *Naut.* To grasp with the fist. [OE *fȳst*] **— fist′ful** *n.*
fist² (fīst) See FICE.
fist·ic (fis′tik) *adj.* Pertaining to the fist; pugilistic.
fist·i·cuff (fis′ti·kuf) *v.t.* & *v.i.* To beat or fight with the fist. **—** *n.* **1** A cuff with the fist. **2** *pl.* A pugilistic encounter.
fist·i·cuff·er (fis′ti·kuf′ər) *n.* A pugilist; boxer.
fis·tu·la (fis′chŏŏ·lə) *n. pl.* **·las** or **·lae** (-lē) **1** *Pathol.* Any abnormal opening or duct leading into a natural canal, hollow organ, or other part of the body. **2** A deep–seated suppurative inflammation, as in the withers of horses, ordinarily resulting from a bruise. **3** *Obs.* A reed or pipe. **— gastric fistula** An opening into the stomach through the abdominal wall, usually of traumatic origin. [<L, a pipe] **— fis′tu·lar** *adj.*
fis·tu·lous (fis′chŏŏ·ləs) *adj.* **1** Cylindrical and hollow like a reed. **2** Of or pertaining to a fistula. Also **fis′tu·late** (-lit, -lāt), **fis′tu·lat′ed.**
fist·wise (fist′wīz′) *adj.* & *adv.* Like a fist.
fit¹ (fit) *adj.* **fit·ter, fit·test** **1** Adapted to an end, aim, or design; adequate; competent; qualified. **2** Conformed to a standard, suitable; appropriate. **3** In a state of preparation; ready. **4** In good physical condition and training: originally a sporting use. **5** Suitable to the person or occasion; convenient; becoming; proper. See synonyms under ADEQUATE, APPROPRIATE, BECOMING, COMPETENT, CONVENIENT, GOOD, RIPE. **—** *v.* **fit·ted** or **fit, fit·ting** *v.t.* **1** To be suitable for: Dark days *fit* dark deeds. **2** To be of the right size and shape for. **3** To make or alter to the proper size or purpose: to *fit* a suit. **4** To provide with what is suitable or necessary: to *fit* a ship for sea. **5** To prepare or make qualified or ready: His experience *fits* him for the position. **6** To put in place carefully or exactly: to *fit* an arrow to a bow. **—** *v.i.* **7** To be suitable or proper. **8** To be of the proper size, shape, etc.: This shoe *fits.* See synonyms under ADAPT, ACCOMMODATE, TEMPER. **—** *n.* **1** An adjustment or agreement in size, form, or the like; suitability; adaptation. **2** A making ready; preparation. **3** *Mech.* **a** A part upon which something fits snugly; specifically, that part of a car axle upon which the wheel is forced. **b** The closeness or completeness of contact in machine parts, usually classified as loose, free, medium, snug, and wringing. **4** That which fits, as a piece of clothing. [ME *fyt*; origin uncertain] **— fit′ly** *adv.* **— fit′ness** *n.* **— fit′·ter** *n.*
fit² (fit) *n.* **1** A sudden onset of an organic or functional disorder, often attended by convulsions, as in epilepsy; spasm. **2** A sudden overmastering emotion or feeling; a mood: a *fit* of rage. **3** Impulsive and irregular exertion or action: a *fit* of industry. **— by fits** (or **by fits and starts**) Spasmodically; irregularly. [OE *fitt* struggle]
fit³ (fit) *n.* **1** A song, story, or ballad. **2** A division of a ballad or song. [OE *fitt*]
fit⁴ (fit) *n. Scot.* A foot; step.
fitch¹ (fich) *n.* A fitchew or its fur. [<MDu. *vitsche* a polecat]
fitch² (fich) *n. Archaic.* A vetch: commonly in the plural. The plural form in the Bible represents two different Hebrew words, meaning in *Isa.* xxviii 25, 27, black cumin, and in *Ezek.* iv 9, spelt. [Var. of VETCH]
Fitch (fich), **John,** 1743–98, U.S. inventor; pioneer in steam navigation. **— (William) Clyde,** 1865–1909, U.S. playwright.
fitch·ew (fich′ōō) *n.* **1** The polecat of Europe. **2** The fur of this animal: also called *fitch.* Also **fitch′et** (-it), **fitch′ole** (-ōl). [<OF *fissel, fissau.* Cf. MDu. *fisse, vitsche.*]
fit·ful (fit′fəl) *adj.* Occurring in fits; marked by fits; spasmodic; capricious; unstable. See synonyms under FICKLE, IRREGULAR, IRRESOLUTE. **— fit′ful·ly** *adv.* **— fit′ful·ness** *n.*
fit·tie–lan′ (fit′i·län′, -lôn′) *n. Scot.* The near horse of the hind pair in a plow team; the horse that walks on the unplowed part of the land.
fit·ting (fit′ing) *adj.* Fit or suitable for any purpose; proper; appropriate. **—** *n.* **1** The act of adjusting or connecting properly. **2** A fixture or a piece of apparatus. **3** Anything designed as an accessory to any system of working parts in a machine: usually in the plural. See synonyms under ADEQUATE, BE-

LONGING, JUST. — **fit′ting·ly** *adv.* — **fit′ting·ness** *n.*

fit to kill *Colloq.* Excessively: He laughed *fit to kill.*

Fitz– *prefix* Son of: an element in surnames, as in *Fitzgerald*: formerly used in forming the surnames of illegitimate children of royalty. [<AF, var. of OF *fiz, filz* <L *filius* son]

Fitz·Ger·ald (fits′jer′əld), **Edward,** 1809–83, English poet; translator of the *Rubáiyát* of Omar Khayyám.

Fitz·ger·ald (fits′jer′əld), **F(rancis) Scott,** 1896–1940, U.S. novelist.

Fiu·me (fyōō′mā) The Italian name for RIJEKA.

Fiu·mi·ci·no (fyōō′mē·chē′nō) Modern name for the Rubicon.

five (fīv) *n.* **1** The cardinal number following four and preceding six, or any of the symbols (5, v, V) used to represent it. **2** Anything made up of five units or members, as a basketball team, or representing five, as a playing card having five spots, or a five-dollar bill. ◆ Collateral adjective: *quinary.* — *adj.* Being five. [OE *fīf*]

five– and ten–cent store (fīv′ən·ten′sent′) A store selling miscellaneous articles priced at five and ten cents: extended to include stores selling articles priced from five cents to one dollar or more. Also called *dime store.* Also **five′–and–ten′, five–and–dime** (fīv′ən·dīm′).

Five Civilized Nations or **Tribes** The Cherokee, Chickasaw, Choctaw, Creek, and Seminole tribes of Oklahoma.

five–fin·gers (fīv′fing′gərz) *n.* **1** Any of several plants, as cinquefoil, bird's-foot trefoil, oxlip, Virginia creeper. **2** A starfish with five arms.

five·fold (fīv′fōld′) *adj.* Made up of five; five times as much or as great; quintuplicate. — *adv.* In a fivefold manner or degree.

Five Forks A locality in SE Virginia; scene of a Federal victory in the Civil War, April 1, 1865.

five hundred A card game developed from euchre, with the joker as high card and 500 points for game.

Five Nations Five confederated tribes of Iroquois Indians within the borders of the State of New York; namely, Mohawks, Oneidas, Onondagas, Cayugas, and Senecas. These five tribes, together with a sixth, the Tuscaroras, which returned from self-exile in 1712, formed the famous *Six Nations* of American history.

five·pence (fīv′pəns, *Brit. Colloq.* fip′əns) *n.* **1** Five English pennies. **2** Formerly, an American half-dime.

five·pen·ny (fīv′pə·nē, *Brit. Colloq.* fip′ən·ē) *adj.* **1** Worth five pence. **2** Having a length of 1 3/4 inches: a *fivepenny* nail.

fiv·er (fī′vər) *n. Colloq.* **1** A five-dollar bill or a five-pound note. **2** Anything counting five, as a hit in cricket permitting five runs, etc.

fives[1] (fīvz) *n. pl. Brit.* A game similar to handball.

fives[2] (fīvz) See VIVES.

five–spot (fīv′spot′) *n.* A small delicate annual herb (*Nemophila maculata*) of the waterleaf family, with white purple-spotted flowers: common in California.

Five–Year Plan (fīv′yir′) A plan for national economic development: a term originating with the first of such plans adopted by the U.S.S.R. in 1928.

fix (fiks) *v.t.* **1** To make firm or secure; attach securely; fasten. **2** To set or direct (attention, gaze, etc.) steadily: He *fixed* his eyes on the door. **3** To look at steadily or piercingly: He *fixed* her with his eyes. **4** To attract and hold; get, as attention or regard. **5** To decide definitely; settle: The decision *fixed* his fate. **6** To decide or agree on; determine: We *fixed* a date for the next meeting. **7** To place firmly in the mind. **8** To lay, as blame or responsibility, on. **9** *U.S.* To repair. **10** To arrange or put in order; adjust, as clothing or the hair. **11** *U.S.* To make ready and cook (food or a meal). **12** *U.S. Colloq.* To arrange or influence the outcome, decision, etc., of (a race, game, jury, etc.) by bribery or collusion: to *fix* a race. **13** To prepare (specimens) for microscopic study. **14** *Chem.* To cause to form a non-volatile or solid compound. **15** *Phot.* To bathe (a film or plate) in chemicals which remove substances still sensitive to light, thus preventing fading. **16** To regulate or stabilize (wages, prices, etc.). — *v.i.* **17** To become firm or fixed. **18** *Colloq.* To intend or prepare: I'm *fixing* to go. — **to fix on** To decide upon; choose. — **to fix up** *Colloq.* **1** To repair. **2** To arrange or put in order. **3** To supply the needs of. — *n.* **1** *Colloq.* A position of embarrassment; dilemma. **2** *Naut.* A ship's position as decided by reference to certain fixed points on shore or to astronomical observations; location. **3** On a chart or map, the point of intersection of two or more bearings, which serve to establish the position of an aircraft on its course. [<Med. L *fixare* fasten <L *fixus,* pp. of *figere* fasten] — **fix′·a·ble** *adj.*

Synonyms (verb): See BIND, CONFIRM, SET, SETTLE. The best usage avoids such expressions as "*Fix* the furniture in the room," "*Fix* the books on the shelves," when the meaning is *set* or *arrange* them. We *fix* a statue on its pedestal, a stone in the wall. *Fix* in the sense of *repair* is a convenient American and British colloquialism, rooted in popular use. In the United States, to *fix* a thing is to do to or with it whatever is needed to make it answer its purpose; to *fix* a furnace is to put it in working order by whatever process.

fix·ate (fik′sāt) *v.t* & *v.i.* **·at·ed, ·at·ing 1** To render fixed; become fixed. **2** To fix or concentrate, as the eyes or attention, upon something. **3** To render constant or unchanged. **4** *Psychoanal.* To concentrate the libido on a particular object, blocking further development or new attachment. [<Med. L *fixatus,* pp. of *fixare.* See FIX.]

fix·a·tion (fik·sā′shən) *n.* **1** The act of fixing, or the state of being fixed; stability. **2** *Chem.* **a** A state of non-volatility in a chemical compound, or the entering into such a state. **b** The making permanent of a dye or color. **c** The conversion of free nitrogen from the air into useful compounds; any similar process applied to an oil or a gas. **3** *Psychoanal.* An excessive concentration of the libido on a particular object, as the exaggerated attachment of a child for one of its parents, manifested in periods of adult emotional stress in some types of psychosis or psychoneurosis. **4** A sustained focusing of the eyes upon a definite object. **5** *Bacteriol.* The prevention of hemolysis by the action of the complement.

fix·a·tive (fik′sə·tiv) *adj.* Serving to render permanent. — *n.* **1** That which serves to render permanent, as a mordant or varnish. **2** In art, a solution applied to pastel and crayon pictures to reduce fragility.

fixed (fikst) *adj.* **1** Of an established, unchanging, or permanent character; settled; lasting; stable. **2** Keeping nearly the same relative position. **3** Without days of grace: said of bills, notes, etc. **4** Attached; not locomotory: said of plants and certain organisms. **5** Equipped: all *fixed* for camp. **6** Settled; located: *fixed* in a new home. **7** *U.S. Colloq.* Bribed: a *fixed* jury. **8** *U.S. Colloq.* Provided with money, possessions, etc.: He's well *fixed.* — **fix·ed·ly** (fik′sid·lē) *adv.* — **fix′ed·ness** *n.*

fixed bridge Any bridge constructed on permanent supports: distinguished from a *pontoon bridge.*

fixed charge A charge that cannot be changed or escaped; specifically, such a charge payable at fixed intervals.

fixed idea *Psychiatry* An obsessional idea, often delusional, which tends to influence a person's whole attitude or mental life: also *idée fixe.*

fixed oil *Chem.* An oil, as olein, which leaves a permanent greasy stain, and cannot be volatilized without decomposition.

fixed star *Astron.* A self-luminous celestial body far beyond the bounds of our solar system: so called because such bodies preserve the same relative positions as observed from the earth.

fix·er (fik′sər) *n. U.S. Colloq.* An adjuster; specifically, a person who bribes or influences a jury, an election board, etc.

fix·ing (fik′sing) *n.* **1** The act of fastening, securing, repairing, solidifying, deciding, etc. See FIX. **2** *Phot.* The process of treating a developed picture so that it will not be changed by the further action of light. **3** *pl. U.S. Colloq.* Furnishings, ornaments, or trappings of any kind. **4** *pl. U.S. Colloq.* Foods prepared as accompaniments to a main dish.

fix·i·ty (fik′sə·tē) The state of being fixed; permanent character or condition; fixedness; stability.

fix·ture (fiks′chər) *n.* **1** Anything fixed firmly in its place; gas *fixtures.* **2** One who or that which is regarded as permanently fixed. **3** *Law* **a** Personal articles or chattels affixed to a freehold which may be removed by the tenant only without injury to the realty: also **movable fixtures. b** Anything affixed to a freehold of such a permanent nature as to be a legal part thereof: also **immovable fixtures.** [<FIXURE; infl. in form by *mixture*]

fix·ure (fik′shər) *n. Obs.* Fixed condition; firmness. [<LL *fixura* a fastening <L *figere* fasten]

Fi·zeau (fē·zō′), **Armand Hippolyte Louis,** 1819–96, French physicist.

fiz·gig (fiz′gig′) *n.* **1** A silly flirt; a giddy girl. **2** A firework that makes a fizzing noise when ignited. [? <FIZZ + GIG[1]]

fizz (fiz) *v.i.* To make a hissing noise. — *n.* **1** A hissing noise. **2** An effervescing beverage. **3** *Brit.* Champagne. Also **fiz.** [Imit.] — **fizz′y** *adj.*

fiz·zle (fiz′əl) *v.i.* **fiz·zled, fiz·zling 1** To make a hissing noise, as wet wood or gunpowder when burning. **2** *Colloq.* To fail, especially after a good start. — **to fizzle out** To become a failure. — *n.* **1** A spluttering; fizzing. **2** A person, an attempt, or an undertaking that fails or comes to nothing; an ignominious failure, as in a recitation. [Freq. of obs. *fise* break wind]

fjeld (fyeld) *n.* In Scandinavian countries, a high, barren plateau or tableland: also spelled *field.*

fjord (fyôrd) See FIORD.

flab (flab) *n.* Flabby body tissue. [Back formation <FLABBY]

flab·ber·gast (flab′ər·gast) *v.t. Colloq.* To astound; confound, as by extraordinary news. [? Blend of FLABBY and AGHAST] — **flab′ber·gas·ta′tion** *n.*

flab·by (flab′ē) *adj.* **·bi·er, ·bi·est 1** Lacking muscle or healthy fiber; flaccid. **2** Lacking in moral or intellectual vigor; languid; feeble. [Var. of *flappy* <FLAP + -Y[1]] — **flab′bi·ly** *adv.* — **flab′bi·ness** *n.*

fla·bel·late (flə·bel′it, -āt) *adj. Zool.* Fan-shaped: *flabellate* antennae.

flabelli– *combining form* Fan-shaped: *flabelliform.* [<L *flabellum* a fan, orig. dim. of *flabrum* a breeze <*flare* blow]

fla·bel·li·form (flə·bel′ə·fôrm) *adj.* Fan-shaped; flabellate.

fla·bel·lum (flə·bel′əm) *n. pl.* **·la** (-ə) **1** A fan, especially one used ceremonially in the Greek and Roman Catholic churches. **2** Any fan-shaped structure. **3** *Anat.* A group of fibers radiating from the corpus striatum of the brain. [<L, fan]

flac·cid (flak′sid) *adj.* Lacking firmness or elasticity; having no resistance; flabby. [<F *flaccide* <L *flaccidus* <*flaccus* limp] — **flac′·cid·ly** *adv.* — **flac·cid′i·ty, flac′cid·ness** *n.*

flack (flak) *n. Slang* A press agent.

fla·con (flà·kôṅ′) *n. French* A stoppered bottle or flask.

flaf·fin (flăf′in) *n. Scot.* Fluttering; flapping.

flag[1] (flag) *n.* **1** A piece of cloth commonly bearing a device and attached to a staff or halyard: used as a standard, symbol, or signal. See COLOR, ENSIGN, GUIDON, PENNANT, STANDARD. **2** The bushy part of the tail of a dog, as that of a setter. **3** *pl. Ornithol.* The long feathers on the leg of a hawk or other bird of prey; also, those on the second joint of a bird's wing. **4** The tail of a deer. — **black flag** A flag with a black field surmounted by white skull and crossbones, traditionally flown by pirate ships; the Jolly Roger.— **Christian flag** A flag with a white field (peace) and a blue canton (sincerity), emblazoned with a red cross: adopted by most Protestant churches. — **papal flag** A yellow-and-white banner, in which the crossed keys of Saint Peter surmounted by the papal triple crown occupy the center of the white half. — **service flag** A flag with red border and white center on which one or more blue or gold stars are sewn, each representing a man or woman in or formerly in the armed forces. —*v.t.* **flagged, flag·ging 1** To mark out or adorn with flags. **2** To signal with a flag. **3** To send (information) by signals. **4** To decoy, as deer, by or as by waving a flag. —**to flag down** To cause to stop, as a train, by signaling with a flag or with a waving motion. [? <FLAG[2]] —**flag′ger** *n.* —**flag′gy** *adj.*

flag[2] (flag) *n.* **1** One of various monocotyledonous plants of the genus *Iris,* having sword-shaped leaves and growing in moist places; especially, the **yellow flag** of Europe *(I. pseudacorus)* and the common **blue flag** *(I. versicolor)* of the United States, the State flower of Tennessee. **2** The leaf of a flag. —*v.t.* **flagged, flag·ging** To calk the seams of (a cask) with flags or rushes. [Cf. Du. *vlag* iris]

flag[3] (flag) *v.i.* **flagged, flag·ging 1** To grow spiritless or languid; become tired or weak. **2** To hang down; become limp. [? <obs. *flack* flutter; infl. by OF *flaquir* droop <*flac* droopy <L *flaccus*]

flag[4] (flag) *n.* Split stone for paving; a flagstone. —*v.t.* **flagged, flag·ging** To pave with flagstones. [<ON *flaga* slab of stone. Akin to FLAKE.] —**flag′ger** *n.*

Flag Day A holiday commemorating the day, June 14, 1777, on which Congress proclaimed the Stars and Stripes the national standard of the United States.

flag·el·lant (flaj′ə·lənt, flə·jel′ənt) *n.* A zealot given to whipping or scourging himself, to secure pardon from sin: also **flag′el·la′tor.** —*adj.* Using a scourge; scourging; practicing flagellation. [<L *flagellans, -antis,* ppr. of *flagellare* scourge <*flagellum* a whip]

flag·el·late (flaj′ə·lāt) *v.t.* **·lat·ed, ·lat·ing** To whip; scourge. —*adj. Biol.* **1** Having or producing flagella or whiplike processes, or runnerlike branches. **2** Shaped like a flagellum. Also **flag′el·lat′ed** *adj.* [<L *flagellatus,* pp. of *flagellare.* See FLAGELLANT.]

flag·el·la·tion (flaj′ə·lā′shən) *n.* **1** A scourging, specifically as an incitement of abnormal sexual desire. **2** A massaging by strokes or blows. **3** Self-scourging as a means of religious discipline. **4** *Biol.* The development of flagella by certain protozoan organisms.

fla·gel·li·form (flə·jel′ə·fôrm) *adj.* Long, slender, and flexible, like a whiplash. [<L *flagellum* a whip + -FORM]

fla·gel·lum (flə·jel′əm) *n. pl.* **·la** (-ə) **1** *Biol.* A lashlike appendage, as the terminal part of an antenna in insects, or the mobile process of a protozoan. **2** A scourge. [<L, whip]

flag·eo·let (flaj′ə·let′) *n.* **1** A musical instrument resembling the flute, but blown at the end instead of at the side. It usually has six finger holes and a mouthpiece with a fipple.

FLAGEOLET

2 An organ stop. [<F, dim. of OF *flageol*; ult. origin uncertain]

Flagg (flag), **James Montgomery,** 1877–1960, U.S. artist and illustrator.

flag·ging[1] (flag′ing) *adj.* Growing weak; becoming languid or exhausted; failing; drooping.

flag·ging[2] (flag′ing) *n.* **1** A pavement of flagstones; flagstones collectively. **2** The act of paving with flagstones.

flag·gy[1] (flag′ē) *adj.* **·gi·er, ·gi·est** Lax; languid; limp. —**flag′gi·ness** *n.*

flag·gy[2] (flag′ē) *adj.* **·gi·er, ·gi·est** Resembling or consisting of flagstones; laminate.

flag·gy[3] (flag′ē) *adj.* **·gi·er, ·gi·est** Covered with irises.

fla·gi·tious (flə·jish′əs) *adj.* **1** Flagrantly wicked; atrocious; heinous. **2** Guilty of extraordinary vice; extremely criminal. See synonyms under CRIMINAL, FLAGRANT. [<L *flagitiosus* <*flagitium* disgraceful act] —**fla·gi′tious·ly** *adv.* —**fla·gi′tious·ness** *n.*

flag-lil·y (flag′lil′ē) *n. pl.* **-lil·ies** The American blue iris; blue flag.

flag·man (flag′mən) *n. pl.* **·men** (-mən) One who carries a flag, as for signaling trains on a railway.

flag officer Formerly, the captain of a flagship; now, the commander of a fleet or squadron, entitled to fly the flag of his command, as a fleet admiral, admiral, vice admiral, or rear admiral.

flag of truce A white flag displayed to the enemy to denote that a conference is desired; also, the bearer of the flag, or a vessel bearing such a flag.

flag·on (flag′ən) *n.* **1** A vessel with a handle and a spout, and often having a hinged lid, used to serve liquors at table. **2** A large wine bottle. [<OF *flacon, flascon* <Med. L *flasco, -onis* <Gmc.]

flag·pole (flag′pōl′) *n.* A pole of some length on which a flag is displayed.

fla·gran·cy (flā′grən·sē) *n. pl.* **·cies** Notoriousness; heinousness. Also **fla′grance.**

fla·grant (flā′grənt) *adj.* **1** Openly scandalous; notorious; heinous. **2** *Obs.* Burning; blazing; also, raging. [<L *flagrans, -antis,* ppr. of *flagrare* blaze, burn] —**fla′grant·ly** *adv.*

Synonyms: atrocious, disgraceful, enormous, flagitious, heinous, monstrous, nefarious, outrageous, scandalous, shameful, shocking. *Antonyms*: see synonyms for EXCELLENT.

fla·gran·te de·lic·to (flə·gran′tē di·lik′tō) *Latin* In the act of committing a crime; literally, while the crime was blazing.

flag·ship (flag′ship′) *n.* The ship in a naval formation that carries a flag officer and displays his flag. See FLAG OFFICER.

flag-smut (flag′smut′) *n.* A disease of wheat, caused by the smut fungus *Ustilago tritici* affecting the leaves and culms.

Flag·stad (flag′stad, *Norw.* fläg′stä), **Kirsten,** 1895–1963, Norwegian soprano active in the United States.

flag·staff (flag′staf′, -stäf′) *n.* A staff on which a flag is hung or displayed.

Flag·staff (flag′staf, -stäf) A city in north central Arizona.

flag station A station on a railway at which a train stops only on signal. Also **flag stop.**

flag·stone (flag′stōn′) *n.* **1** A broad, flat stone suitable for pavements. **2** Any fine-grained rock from which such slabs may be split. [<FLAG[4] + STONE]

flail (flāl) *n.* **1** An implement consisting of a wooden bar (the swingle) hinged or tied to a handle, for separating grain by beating. **2** A medieval weapon with spiked iron swingle. —*v.t.* & *v.i.* To beat with or as with a flail; use a flail; thresh. [OE *flygel,* prob. <L *flagellum* a whip]

FLAIL *(def. 2)*

flail joint *Pathol.* A disorder characterized by excessive mobility of a limb, usually after resection of a joint.

flair (flâr) *n.* **1** Discernment; talent; aptitude. **2** Inclination; fondness; strong liking. **3** *Colloq.* A showy or dashing style: to wear clothes with *flair.* [<OF <*flairer* smell, ult. <L *fragrare*]

flak (flak) *n.* **1** Anti-aircraft fire. **2** *U.S. Colloq.* Criticism: political *flak.* [<G *fl(ieger)* aircraft + *a(bwehr)* defense + *k(anonen)* guns]

flake[1] (flāk) *n.* **1** A small flat fragment or loosely cohering mass; a thin piece or chip of anything; scale; fleck. **2** A carnation having stripes of any single color on a white ground. **3** A gleam of light; flash. **4** *Naut.* The flat coil of a stowed cable; a fake. —*adj. Anthropol.* Denoting that form of Paleolithic stone implement shaped from the thin flakes chipped off the core of a large lump. —*v.t.* & *v.i.* **flaked, flak·ing 1** To peel off in flakes. **2** To form into flakes. **3** To spot or become spotted with flakes. [ME <Scand. Akin to FLAG[4].]

flake[2] (flāk) *n.* **1** A light staging or platform for drying fish. **2** A flap on a saddle to keep the rider's knee from the horse. [<ON *flaki* hurdle]

flake[3] (flāk) *v.* **flaked, flak·ing** *Slang v.i.* **1** To retire or go to sleep, as from exhaustion: usually with *out.* —*v.t.* **2** To fatigue; exhaust: usually with *out.*

flake-white (flāk′hwīt′) *n.* Pure white lead in scales used by artists as a pigment.

flak·ing (flā′king) *n.* **1** The operation of making flint flakes by chipping, as for gunlocks. **2** The breaking away of small bits of paint or plaster from covered surfaces.

flak·y (flā′kē) *adj.* **flak·i·er, flak·i·est** Resembling or consisting of flakes; easily separable into flakes. —**flak′i·ly** *adv.* —**flak′i·ness** *n.*

flam (flam) *n. Colloq.* **1** A false pretense; sham; falsehood. **2** A freak or whim. **3** An appoggiatura on the drum. —*v.t.* **flammed, flam·ming** *U.S. Colloq.* To deceive by imposture; to flim-flam. [Short for FLIM-FLAM]

flam·beau (flam′bō) *n. pl.* **·beaux** (-bōz) **1** A burning torch, as one made of a bundle of wicks covered with wax; any torch. **2** A large decorated candlestick. **3** A large sugar-boiling kettle. [<F <*flambe* <OF *flamme* FLAME]

Flam·bor·ough Head (flam′bûr′ə) A chalk peninsula and lighthouse in eastern Yorkshire, England.

flam·boy·ant (flam·boi′ənt) *adj.* **1** Characterized by extravagance; showy; bombastic. **2** Bursting into flame; blazing. **3** Having a wavy edge, as of flame. [<F, ppr. of *flamboyer* <OF *flambeier* <*flambe* FLAME] —**flam·boy′·ance, flam·boy′an·cy** *n.* —**flam·boy′ant·ly** *adv.*

flamboyant architecture A highly florid style of French Gothic architecture.

FLAMBOYANT ARCHITECTURE

flame (flām) *n.* **1** A stream of vapor or gas made luminous by heat; gas or vapor in combustion. **2** An appearance or color like that of a blaze; glow; brilliancy; a red-yellow color, called **flame-scarlet. 3** Excitement, as from rage, strife, or passionate desire. **4** An ardent affection; passionate love. **5** *Slang* A sweetheart. See synonyms under FIRE, LIGHT[1]. —*v.* **flamed, flam·ing** *v.i.* **1** To give out flame; blaze; burn. **2** To light up or burn as if on fire; flash: His face *flamed* with rage. **3** To become enraged or excited (with anger, indignation, etc.): He *flamed* with indignation. —*v.t.* **4** To subject to heat or fire. **5** *Obs.* To inflame; excite. See synonyms under BURN. [<OF *flamme, flambe* <L *flamma* a flame] —**flam′ing** *adj.* —**flam′ing·ly** *adv.*

flame arc An electric arc produced and maintained between two carbons impregnated with mineral salts.

fla·men (flā′men) *n. pl.* **fla·mens** or **flam·in·es** (flam′ə·nēz) In ancient Rome, a priest devoted to the service of a particular god. [<L]

fla·men·co (flə·meng′kō, -men′-, flä-) *n.* A style of singing and dancing practiced by the Gipsies of Andalusia; also, a song or dance in this style. [<Sp., Flemish, because the Gipsies were thought to be from Flanders]

flame·out (flām′out′) *n.* The sudden extinguishing of the flame in a jet engine caused by an excess of fuel.

flame test *Chem.* The determination of the presence of an element or certain of its compounds, by holding the substance in the flame of a Bunsen burner and noting the resulting color.

flame-throw·er (flām′thrō′ər) *n. Mil.* A weapon that throws a stream of burning napalm or other gasoline mixture.

fla·min·go (flə·ming′gō) *n. pl.* **·gos** or **·goes** A long-necked, small-bodied wading bird (genus *Phoenicopterus*) of a pink or red color, having very long legs, webbed feet, and a bent bill. [<Pg. *flamingo* or Sp. *flamenco,* ult. <L *flamma* flame + Gmc. *-enc* -ING[3]]

FLAMINGO (From 4 to 4 1/2 feet standing height over-all)

Fla·min·i·an Way (flə·min′ē·ən) One of the chief ancient Roman roads from Rome to Cisalpine Gaul, built in 220 B.C. by Gaius Flaminius: Latin *Via Flaminia.*

Flam·i·ni·nus (flam′ə·nī′nəs), **Titus Quinctius,** 230?–174 B.C., Roman general.

Fla·min·i·us (flə·min′ē·əs), **Gaius,** died 217 B.C., Roman statesman.
flam·ma·ble (flam′ə·bəl) *adj.* Combustible; inflammable.
Flam·ma·rion (flȧ·mȧ·ryôn′), **Nicolas Camille,** 1842–1925, French astronomer and writer.
flam·y (flā′mē) *adj.* **flam·i·er, flam·i·est** Relating to, composed of, or resembling flame.
flan (flan, *Fr.* flän) *n.* **1** A piece of metal ready to be made into a coin by receiving the stamp or the die; a blank. **2** A tart filled with cheese, cream, or fruit; also a custard or soufflé. [<F]
flanch (flanch, flänch) *n. Her.* A subordinary on the right or left side of the fess point of an escutcheon. Also **flanque** (flank). See illustration under ESCUTCHEON. [<OF *flanche,* var. of *flanc* flank]
flan·dan (flan′dan) *n. Archaic* A woman's cap or headdress with long hanging flaps. [Origin unknown]
Flan·ders (flan′dərz) A former county in the Low Countries, divided into: **1** Belgian Flanders, *Flemish* **Vlaan·de·ren** (vlän′də·rən), comprising the provinces of **East Flanders,** *Flemish* **Oost-Vlaan·de·ren** (ōst′vlän′də·rən); 1,147 square miles, capital, Ghent; and **West Flanders,** *Flemish* **West-Vlaan·de·ren** (vest′·vlän′də·rən); 1,249 square miles; capital, Bruges; and **2** French Flanders, *French* **Flan·dre** (flän′dr′), a region and former province of northern France.
flâ·ne·rie (flän·rē′) *n. French* Lounging; idling.
flâ·neur (flä·nœr′) *n. French* A dawdler; idler.
flange (flanj) *n.* **1** A spreading or flaring part. **2** A projecting rim or edge, as on a car wheel, a section of pipe, length of shafting, etc. **3** A tool used to shape flanges. — *v.* **flanged, flang·ing** *v.t.* To supply with a flange. — *v.i.* To have or take the form of a flange. [Prob. <OF *flangir* bend]
flank (flangk) *n.* **1** The hinder part of an animal's side, between the ribs and the hip. See illustration under HORSE. **2** *Entomol.* The side of an insect's thorax; the pleura. **3** The side, or the lateral portion or anything, especially of a military or naval force, or of a marching column. **4** That part of a bastion between the curtain and the face, or any part of a fortification that defends another work by a fire along its face; also, the lateral part of a fortification. See illustration under BASTION. — **by the right** or **left flank** A drill command preparatory to the marching maneuver in which every marcher makes a 90-degree turn to the right or left. — *v.t.* **1** To stand or be on one or both sides of. **2** *Mil.* **a** To get around and in back of (an enemy position or unit); turn the flank of. **b** To attack or threaten the flank of. **c** To guard the flank of (a friendly position or unit). — *adj.* **1** Pertaining to the flank or side. **2** Cut from the side, or situated at the side: a *flank* steak. **3** Coming from or toward the side: a *flank* attack. [<F *flanc* <Gmc.]
flank·er (flang′kər) *n.* **1** One of a body of troops thrown out to protect the flank or side of a marching column. **2** An addition to a fortification built at an angle to protect the main fortification, or to command the flank of an attacking enemy.
flan·nel (flan′əl) *n.* **1** A loosely-woven fabric of cotton, or of cotton and wool, with soft, naplike surface. **2** Plain cloth in the first stage of manufacture. **3** *pl.* Clothing made of flannel. — *v.t.* **·neled** or **·nelled, ·nel·ing** or **·nel·ling** To wrap in or rub with flannel. [Prob. <Welsh *gwlanen* flannel < *gwlan* wool] — **flan′nel·ly** *adj.*
flannel cake A pancake.
flan·nel·et (flan′əl·et′) *n.* A cotton fabric similar to flannel: plain, figured, or striped: used for underwear, etc. Also **flan′nel·ette′.**
flap (flap) *n.* **1** A broad, limber, and loosely hanging part or attachment. **2** The act of flapping. **3** An implement for brushing away flies. **4** *Surg.* A piece of skin or flesh cut away except at its base. **5** The flapping tongue of a valve. **6** *pl.* A disease of the lips of horses. **7** *Aeron.* A movable hinged section along the rear or trailing edge of a wing of an airplane, used to increase drag. **8** *Slang* An agitated or tempestuous reaction. [< *v.*] — *v.* **flapped, flap·ping** *v.t.* **1** To move by beating: to *flap* the wings. **2** To move with a flapping sound. **3** To strike with something flat and flexible. — *v.i.* **4** To beat the wings or move by beating the wings. **5** To move to and fro, as if blown by the wind. **6** *Slang* To lose one's composure. [Imit.]
flap·doo·dle (flap′do͞od′l) *n. Slang.* Boastful talk; twaddle; nonsense. [Arbitrary coinage]
flap·drag·on (flap′drag′ən) *n.* **1** A game in which raisins or other edibles are snatched by the players out of burning spirits and swallowed. **2** One of the articles thus used.
flap·jack (flap′jak′) *n.* A griddle cake.
flap·per (flap′ər) *n.* **1** One who or that which flaps or slaps, or calls attention. **2** A young bird unable to fly. **3** A flipper. **4** *Colloq.* A young girl, especially, in the 1920's, given to exaggerated styles and to sophisticated conduct.
flare (flâr) *v.* **flared, flar·ing** *v.i.* **1** To blaze or burn with a brilliant, wavering light, as a candle in the wind. **2** To break out in sudden or violent emotion: often with *up* or *out.* **3** To open or spread outward: A ship's bows *flare.* — *v.t.* **4** To cause to flare. **5** To signal (information) with flares. — *n.* **1** A large, bright, but unsteady and flickering light; unsteady glare. **2** A widening or spreading outward, as of the sides of a funnel. Compare illustrations under FUNNEL. **3** *Phot.* Unwanted light falling on the image plane in a camera projector or printer due to reflection of light between the lens surface or the interior of the lens barrel. **4** A brilliant brief burst of flame or light used as a signal or guide or as illumination. **5** Any sudden display, as of temper. See synonyms under LIGHT. [? Blend of FLY[1] and BARE[1]]
flare·back (flâr′bak′) *n.* Flame caused by ignition of gases released by opening the breech of a gun after firing.
flare-up (flâr′up′) *n.* **1** A sudden outburst of flame or light. **2** A sudden outbreak of anger.
flash (flash) *v.i.* **1** To break forth with light or fire suddenly and briefly: Lightning *flashed* across the sky. **2** To gleam; glisten: Their helmets *flashed* in the sun. **3** To be in view fleetingly; move very quickly: A train *flashed* by. **4** To come suddenly; be known or perceived in an instant: The memory *flashed* into my mind. **5** *Colloq.* To make a display. — *v.t.* **6** To send forth (fire, light, etc.) in brief flashes; cause to flash: His sword *flashed* fire in the sun. **7** To send or communicate with great speed: to *flash* news. **8** *Colloq.* To show or display briefly or ostentatiously: to *flash* a badge. **9** In glassmaking: **a** To cover with a thin coating of colored glass. **b** To apply (colored glass) as a coating. See synonyms under BURN[1]. — *n.* **1** A sudden and transient blaze; gleam. **2** A sudden outburst, as of wit, anger, etc. **3** A moment; instant. **4** Display; pomp; specifically, a vulgar display. **5** The coating of glass which is flashed upon other glass. **6** A mixture of capsicum, caramel, etc.: used in adulterating liquors. **7** A reservoir and sluiceway in a stream for storing water to float boats over a shoal. **8** A brief news dispatch sent right after the event, usually as a preliminary to fuller coverage. **9** *Archaic* Thieves' jargon. See synonyms under LIGHT[1]. — **a flash in the pan 1** An explosion of the powder in the pan of a flintlock that does not discharge the weapon. **2** Hence, any abortive attempt, or weak outburst. — *adj.* **1** Obtained by flashlight, as a photograph. **2** Flashy; smart; sporty. **3** *Archaic* Of, pertaining to, or used by thieves: *flash* slang. [ME *flaschen;* prob. imit.]
flash·back (flash′bak′) *n.* **1** In fiction, drama, motion pictures, etc., a break in continuity made by the presentation of a scene, episode, or event occurring earlier. **2** The scene, episode, or event so presented.
flash·board (flash′bôrd′, -bōrd′) *n.* A board at the top of a dam to increase the height of water: also called *flushboard.*
flash bulb A photoflash bulb.
flash·cube (flash′kyo͞ob′) *n.* A small, rotatable cube containing four flash bulbs for use with a camera.
flash·er (flash′ər) *n.* **1** One who or that which flashes. **2** A device for intermittently opening and closing an electric circuit connected with incandescent lamps: used in advertising signs, etc.
flash flood A sudden, rushing flood of short duration.
flash house A house frequented by thieves, etc., where stolen goods are received.
flash·ing (flash′ing) *n.* **1** The act of one who flashes, in any sense. **2** A reheating of imperfectly formed glassware. **3** The twirling of a hollow globe of heated glass to spread it into a flat disk. **4** The fusing of a thin coating of colored glass on plain glass. **5** A lap joint, or a turned-up flange, usually of metal, to keep a roof watertight at an angle or where it joins a chimney, etc. **6** The act of flushing, as a stream or sewer. **7** The operation of perfecting the vacuum in a lamp bulb or vacuum tube by suddenly increasing the voltage passing through the filaments or cathode. — *adj.* Emitting flashes. — **flash′·ing·ly** *adv.*

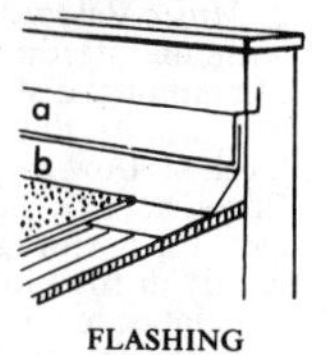

FLASHING
a, b. Parts of a lap joint.

flash lamp A lamp for taking flashlight photographs.
flash·light (flash′līt′) *n.* **1** *U.S.* A light, as in a lighthouse, shown only at regular intervals. **2** A brief and brilliant light for taking photographs. **3** A small portable electric light. Also **flash light.**
flash·o·ver (flash′ō′vər) *n. Electr.* A disruptive leakage of current through or around an insulator.
flash point The lowest temperature at which the vapors of petroleum or other combustible liquids will give a flash or slight explosion on exposure to a flame.
flash spectrum *Astron.* In a total eclipse of the sun, the instantaneous emission of bright lines in the spectrum of the chromosphere at the moment of totality.
flash·y (flash′ē) *adj.* **flash·i·er, flash·i·est 1** Flashing; bright for a moment. **2** Pretentious and cheap; showy; tawdry. — **flash′i·ly** *adv.* — **flash′i·ness** *n.*
flask[1] (flask, fläsk) *n.* **1** A small bottle or similar vessel. **2** A small container, often of metal, for carrying liquids or liquor on the person. **3** A metal or horn vessel used by hunters to carry gunpowder. **4** A thin long-necked glass bottle covered with straw, as for oil. **5** A frame for holding a founding mold. **6** Any of variously shaped receptacles of glass or other material, used in laboratory work. **7** The commercial unit for the measurement and sale of mercury, equal to 76 pounds. **8** The iron container in which mercury is sold. [<F *flasque* <Med. L *flasca,* var. of *flasco.* See FLAGON.]
flask[2] (flask, fläsk) *n. Mil.* **1** The side plates forming the trail of a gun carriage. **2** *Obs.* The bed of a gun carriage. [<F *flasque* cheek of a gun carriage]
flas·ket (flas′kit, fläs′-) *n.* **1** A shallow basket, as for laundry. **2** A small flask.
flat[1] (flat) *adj.* **flat·ter, flat·test 1** Having a surface that is a horizontal plane, or nearly so; level; without unevenness or inclination. **2** Without prominences or depressions; not curved or round or uneven: a *flat* country. **3** Lying prone upon the ground; prostrate; hence, overthrown; ruined. **4** Not qualified or softened in any way; positive; absolute: a *flat* refusal. **5** Deficient in distinctness, form, or interesting qualities; monotonous; stupid; tasteless; dull; insipid: a *flat* sermon, a *flat* market, *flat* wine. **6** *Music* Below pitch; minor or diminished: a *flat* third; having flats in the signature: a *flat* key. **7** *Phonet.* **a** Designating the vowel sound in *man,* as opposed to the sound in *calm.* **b** Of consonants, voiced: opposed to *sharp.* **8** Without gloss, as a painted surface. **9** Uniform in tint. **10** Lacking in contrast; without distinguishing light and shadow: an effect often aimed at in mural-painting. **11** Of a golf club, having the head set at a very obtuse angle to the shaft. **12** *Gram.* Having no inflectional or distinguishing ending or mark, as an adverb not ending in *-ly,* or a noun used as an adjective without the addition of

a characterizing suffix, as in such expressions as to breathe *deep*, the *sister* arts, etc. **13** Not varying with changing conditions; uniform: a *flat* rate. **14** Wanting in tonal quality: said of a sound or accent. — *adv.* **1** In a level state or position; so as to be flat; flatly. **2** *Music* Below the true pitch. **3** In finance, without interest. **4** Exactly; precisely: used of amounts, distances, and the like: It weighed ten pounds *flat*. — *n.* **1** A plane surface; a level. **2** Low meadowland over which the tide flows, never completely submerged by water: used for pasturage or planting. **3** Shoal: commonly in the plural. **4** Anything that is flat; the flat side of a thing. **5** *Music* A tone a half step lower than a tone from which it is named, represented by the character ♭. **6** A strip of high, level land. **7** An oblong wooden frame covered with canvas; a unit of a box-set of stage scenery. **8** A platform car. **9** A flat-bottomed boat, used for transporting heavy cargoes; a flatboat. **10** A deflated automobile tire. **11** A shallow, earth-filled tray for earlier seed germination to advance the flowering period. — *v.* **flat·ted, flat·ting** *v.t.* **1** To make flat. **2** *Music* To lower (a tone) in playing or composing, especially by a semitone. — *v.i.* **3** To become flat. **4** *Music* To sing or play below pitch. [ON *flatr*] — **flat′ly** *adv.* — **flat′ness** *n.*

Synonyms (adj.): absolute, characterless, downright, dull, empty, even, horizontal, insipid, level, lifeless, mawkish, pointless, spiritless, stupid, tame, vapid. As a dead level is monotonous and uninteresting, we have a *flat* joke, a *flat* remark, for one that is *dull, insipid, pointless.* As what is perfectly *level* is without variation or relief, we have a *flat* refusal, in the sense of what is *absolute.* See HORIZONTAL, LEVEL, SMOOTH.

◆ *Flat* is the first element in many self-explaining compound adjectives: *flat*-billed, *flat*-bottomed, *flat*-breasted, etc.

flat[2] (flat) *n.* **1** A set of rooms on one floor, for the occupancy of a family; apartment. **2** A house containing such flats. [Var. of obs. *flet*, a floor OE *flet*; infl. by FLAT[1]]

flat·boat (flat′bōt′) *n.* A large boat with a flat bottom much in use on rivers for freighting merchandise: also *flat.* Also **flat′bot′tom** (-bot′əm).

flat-bot·tomed (flat′bot′əmd) *adj.* Having the bottom flat: usually said of boats.

flat car A railroad freight car, usually without sides or covering; a platform car. Also *flat.*

flat·fish (flat′fish′) *n. pl.* **·fish** or **·fish·es** Any of an order *(Heterosomata)* of fishes having a compressed body with unsymmetrical sides and with both eyes on one side, as the flounder, halibut, sole, etc.

flat·foot (flat′fo͝ot′) *n.* **1** *Pathol.* The deformed condition of a foot caused by a falling of the arch. **2** *pl.* **flat·feet** *Slang* A policeman.

flat foot A foot having a flat sole.

flat-foot·ed (flat′fo͝ot′id) *adj.* **1** Having flat feet. **2** Uncompromising; resolute; positive. — **flat′-foot′ed·ly** *adv.*

Flat·head (flat′hed′) *n.* **1** One of the Salishan tribe of North American Indians. **2** One of the Chinook Indians.

flat·i·ron (flat′ī′ərn) *n.* An iron with a smooth, polished surface for smoothing cloth by the action of heat and pressure.

flat knot A reef knot.

flat·ling (flat′ling) *adj. Obs.* Given with the flat side of a weapon; hence, oppressive, crushing. — *adv.* **1** *Brit. Dial.* Positively; peremptorily. **2** *Scot.* Flatlong. Also **flat′lings.**

flat·long (flat′lông) *adv. Obs.* With the flat side, as of a sword.

flat-nose (flat′nōz′) *adj.* Designating a type of pliers whose gripping surfaces meet along a common edge. See illustration under PLIERS.

flat silver Silver spoons, knives, forks, etc., collectively, as distinguished from silver bowls, pitchers, goblets, etc.

flat·ten (flat′n) *v.t.* & *v.i.* **1** To make or become flat or flatter. **2** To make or become prostrate. — **to flatten out** **1** To make or become flat or flatter. **2** *Aeron.* To change or become changed in angle of flight so as to fly horizontally, as after diving or climbing. — **flat′ten·er** *n.*

flat·ter[1] (flat′ər) *v.t.* **1** To praise unduly or insincerely. **2** To try to win over or gain the favor of by flattery. **3** To play upon the hopes or vanity of; beguile. **4** To please or gratify: She *flattered* me by saying "Yes." **5** To represent too favorably: The picture *flatters* her. — *v.i.* **6** To use flattery. See synonyms under CARESS, PRAISE, PUFF. — **to flatter oneself** To believe: I *flatter* myself that my gifts are acceptable. [<OF *flater* fawn, caress. Akin to FLAT[1].] — **flat′ter·er** *n.* — **flat′ter·ing** *adj.* — **flat′ter·ing·ly** *adv.*

flat·ter[2] (flat′ər) *n.* **1** One who or that which flattens. **2** A flat-holed drawplate through which watch springs, skirt wire, etc., are drawn. **3** A flat-faced hammer used by blacksmiths.

flat·ter·y (flat′er·ē) *n. pl.* **·ter·ies** **1** The act or practice of the flatterer. **2** Undue or insincere compliment; adulation. See synonyms under PRAISE. [<OF *flaterie* <*flater* fawn, caress]

Flat·ter·y (flat′ər·ē), **Cape** A high promontory and lighthouse at the entrance to Juan de Fuca Strait, NW Washington.

flat·ting (flat′ing) *n.* **1** The act, process, or operation of making or becoming flat or smooth. **2** A method of applying paint so that it will dry without gloss.

flat·tish (flat′ish) *adj.* Rather flat.

flat-top (flat′top′) *n.* A U.S. naval aircraft-carrier.

FLAT-TOP — AN AIRCRAFT-CARRIER

flat·u·lence (flach′ə·ləns, -yo͞o-) *n.* **1** The accumulation of gas in the stomach and bowels. **2** Windiness; vanity. Also **flat′u·len·cy.** [<F, ult. <L *flatus* a blowing <*flare* blow] — **flat′u·lent, flat′u·ous** *adj.* — **flat′u·lent·ly** *adv.*

fla·tus (flā′təs) *n. pl.* **·tus·es** **1** A breath; puff of wind. **2** Windiness; wind or gas in the stomach or bowels. **3** The condition of being puffed out with wind; inflation. [<L <*flare* blow]

flat·ware (flat′wâr′) *n.* **1** Dishes that are more or less flat, as plates and saucers, taken collectively: distinguished from *hollowware.* **2** Table utensils, as knives, forks, and spoons.

flat·wise (flat′wīz′) *adv.* With the flat side downward or next to another object. Also **flat′ways′** (-wāz′).

flat·work (flat′wûrk′) *n.* Household linen which can be ironed out on a mangle, as sheets, tablecloths, napkins, towels, etc.

flat·worm (flat′wûrm′) *n.* Any flat-bodied worm, as a tapeworm, fluke, planarian, etc.

Flau·bert (flō·bâr′), **Gustave,** 1821–80, French novelist.

flaunt (flônt) *v.i.* **1** To make an ostentatious or gaudy display; parade impudently: to *flaunt* through the streets. **2** To wave or flutter freely. — *v.t.* **3** To show or display in an ostentatious or impudent manner. — *n.* **1** The act of flaunting. **2** A boast; vaunt. [ME *flant* <Scand. Cf. Norw. *flanta* gad about.] — **flaunt′er** *n.*

Synonyms (verb): boast, display, exhibit, flourish, flutter, parade, vaunt, wave.

flaunt·ing (flôn′ting) *adj.* Making a parade or ostentatious display; jaunty and gay. Also **flaunt′y.** — **flaunt′ing·ly** *adv.*

flau·tist (flô′tist) *n.* One who plays the flute; a flutist.

fla·ves·cent (flə·ves′ənt) *adj.* Turning yellow; yellowish. [<L *flavescens, -entis,* ppr. of *flavescere* become yellow <*flavus* yellow]

Fla·vi·an (flā′vē·ən) *adj.* Of or pertaining to the emperor Titus Flavius Vespasianus (Vespasian) or to his sons and successors Titus and Domitian.

fla·vin (flā′vən) *n.* **1** *Biochem.* One of a group of yellow pigments widely distributed in plant and animal tissues and constituting an important element of the vitamin B_2 complex, as ribo*flavin.* **2** Quercetin. [<L *flavus* yellow + -IN]

fla·vism (flā′viz·əm) *n.* The condition or state of being yellow.

fla·vone (flā′vōn, flə·vōn′, flav′ōn) *n.* A colorless, crystalline, vegetable pigment, $C_{15}H_{10}O_2$, the parent substance of certain yellow dyes, as quercetin, etc. [<L *flavus* yellow + -ONE]

fla·vo·pro·te·in (flā′vō·prō′tē·in, -tēn) *n. Biochem.* An enzyme chemically linked with a protein and serving to oxidize nutrients in animal cells. [<FLAVIN + PROTEIN]

fla·vo·pur·pu·rin (flā′vō·pûr′pyə·rin) *n. Chem.* A crystalline coal-tar dye, $C_{14}H_8O_5$, isomeric with purpurin and similar to alizarin except that it produces colors with a yellowish tinge. [<L *flavus* yellow + PURPURIN]

fla·vor (flā′vər) *n.* **1** The quality of a thing as affecting the sense of taste or the senses of taste and smell; odor; scent. **2** The characteristic taste of a thing, especially if pleasant. **3** Distinctive quality or characteristic: the *flavor* of speech. **4** Flavoring. — *v.t.* To give flavor or any distinguishing quality to. Also, *Brit.,* **fla′vour.** [<OF *flaor, fleur,* prob. ult. <L *flare* blow; *v* added on analogy with *savor*] — **fla′vor·y** *adj.*

fla·vor·ing (flā′vər·ing) *n.* A substance, as an essence or extract, for giving a flavor to anything.

fla·vor·ous (flā′vər·əs) *adj.* Pleasantly flavored; savory. See synonyms under RACY.

fla·vous (flā′vəs) *adj.* Nearly pure yellow.

flaw[1] (flô) *n.* **1** An inherent defect, as in construction or constitution; especially, a defect that destroys or impairs strength, force, or legal validity; weak spot. **2** A crack; fissure: a *flaw* in a casting. See synonyms under BLEMISH, BREACH. — *v.t.* & *v.i.* To make flaws in; become cracked or defective. [? <ON *flaga* slab of stone] — **flaw′less** *adj.* — **flaw′less·ness** *n.* — **flaw′less·ly** *adv.*

flaw[2] (flô) *n.* **1** A sudden squall of wind; a transient but violent windstorm. **2** *Obs.* A tumult. [Prob. <ON *flaga* gust]

flaw·y (flô′ē) *adj.* Having flaws; defective.

flax (flaks) *n.* **1** An annual plant (genus *Linum*) with stems about two feet high and blue flowers, having a mucilaginous seed, called *flaxseed* or *linseed,* and an inner bark which yields the flax of commerce. **2** The soft fiber obtained from the bark of the flax plant, used in the manufacture of linen. **3** Any plant resembling flax. — *v.t.* & *v.i.* To beat or thrash. — **to flax around** *U.S. Colloq.* To stir about busily. — **to flax out** *U.S. Colloq.* **1** To knock out; beat, as in a fight. **2** To become fatigued or exhausted. [OE *fleax*]

FLAX

flax·en (flak′sən) *adj.* **1** Of, pertaining to, or made of flax. **2** Like flax. **3** Of a light golden color.

Flax·man (flaks′mən), **John,** 1755–1826, English sculptor and draughtsman.

flax·seed (flaks′sēd′, flak′-) *n.* **1** The mucilaginous seed borne by the common flax; linseed: used medicinally for soothing and softening. **2** A low European herb of the flax family, having similar seed vessels.

flax·wort (flaks′wûrt′) *n.* Any plant of the flax family *(Linaceae).*

flax·y (flak′sē) *adj.* Like flax; fair; flaxen.

flay (flā) *v.t.* **1** To strip off the skin from, as by flogging. **2** To pillage; rob. **3** To attack with scathing criticism. [OE *flēan*] — **flay′er** *n.*

F-layer (ef′lā′ər) See APPLETON LAYER.

flea (flē) *n.* **1** A wingless insect (order *Siphonaptera*), parasitic upon a mammal or a bird, and having a compressed body, limbs adapted for leaping, and a head armed with piercing mandibles and a suctorial proboscis. For illustration see under INSECT (injurious). ◆ Collateral adjective: *pulicene.* **2** One of several small beetles or crustaceans that jump like fleas, as a beach flea or sand hopper. ◆ Homophone: *flee.* [OE *flēa.* Akin to FLEE.] — **a flea in one's** (or **the**) **ear** A warning; caution; sometimes, an irritating reply or rebuff.

flea·bane (flē′bān′) *n.* One of various plants of the composite family, especially *Erigeron philadelphicus* of the U.S., supposed to repel fleas.

flea•bite (flē′bīt′) *n.* **1** The bite of a flea. **2** Any trifling wound or discomfort. **3** A minute quantity.

flea-bit•ten (flē′bit′n) *adj.* **1** Bitten by a flea. **2** White, flecked with bay or sorrel spots: said of the color of a horse.

fleam (flēm) *n.* **1** A surgeon's lancet. **2** The angle made by the cutting edge of a saw tooth with the plane of the blade. [<OF *flieme,* ult. <LL *flebotomum* <Gk. *phlebotomon.* See PHLEBOTOMY.]

flea market A market, often outdoors, for the sale of a wide assortment of old or second-hand articles, antiques, etc.

flea•wort (flē′wûrt′) *n.* **1** A European plant (genus *Inula*) of the composite family: a reputed repellent of fleas. **2** A plant *(Plantago psyllium)* of the plantain family, whose seeds are used medicinally.

flèche (flesh) *n. Archit.* Any spire; more particularly, one over the intersection of the nave and transepts. [<F, lit., arrow]

fleck (flek) *n.* A dot or speck; a spot; dapple. —*v.t.* To mark with spots or flecks. [Cf. ON *flekkr* spot] **—fleck′less** *adj.* **—fleck′y** *adj.*

Fleck•er (flek′ər), **Herman James Elroy,** 1884–1915, English poet.

flec•tion (flek′shən) *n.* **1** The act of bending or turning. **2** A curved or bent part. **3** A turning as of the eye; glance; cast. **4** *Anat.* Flexion. **5** *Gram.* Inflection. Also, for defs. 1–3, *Brit. flexion.* [<L *flexio, -onis* <*flectere* bend]

flec•tion•al (flek′shən•əl) *adj.* Pertaining to flection or inflection, especially that of words by declension, etc. ◆ In anatomy and physiology the form *flexional* is preferred.

fled (fled) Past tense and past participle of FLEE[1].

fledge (flej) *v.* **fledged, fledg•ing** *v.t.* **1** To furnish with feathers, as an arrow. **2** To bring up (a young bird) until ready for flight. —*v.i.* **3** To grow enough feathers for flight. [<obs. *fledge* ready to fly, ME *flegge,* OE *-flycge* in *unflycge* not ready to fly]

fledg•ling (flej′ling) *n.* **1** A young bird just fledged. **2** A tyro; an inexperienced person. Also **fledge′ling.**

fledg•y (flej′ē) *adj.* **fledg•i•er, fledg•i•est** Feathery; downy; feathered.

flee[1] (flē) *v.* **fled, flee•ing** *v.i.* **1** To run away, as from danger, harm, or enemies. **2** To move away quickly; disappear. **3** To move swiftly; leave abruptly. —*v.t.* **4** To run away from; avoid or try to avoid. **5** To leave or go away from abruptly: to *flee* the country. See synonyms under ESCAPE, FLY[1]. ◆ Homophone: *flea.* [OE *flēon.* Akin to FLEA.]

flee[2] (flē, flā) *Scot. v.t.* & *v.i.* To fly; let fly. —*n.* A fly: also spelled *flie.*

fleece (flēs) *n.* **1** The coat of wool covering a sheep. **2** The entire coat of wool sheared from a sheep. **3** Anything resembling a fleece in quality or appearance. **4** A textile fabric with a soft silky pile, used for linings, etc.; also, the nap. **5** Meat from the ribs of buffalo. **6** Bear fat, used as food. —*v.t.* **fleeced, fleec•ing 1** To shear the fleece from. **2** To swindle; defraud. **3** To cover or fleck as with fleece. [OE *flēos*] **—fleece′a•ble** *adj.*

fleec•er (flē′sər) *n.* One who fleeces; especially, one who takes by fraud.

fleech (flēch) *v.t. Scot.* To cajole; coax. —*n.* Flattery.

fleec•y (flē′sē) *adj.* **fleec•i•er, fleec•i•est** Pertaining to, like, or covered with a fleece. **—fleec′i•ly** *adv.*

fleer (flir) *v.t.* To jeer at; deride. —*v.i.* To laugh or grin coarsely or scornfully; sneer. —*n.* **1** Derision or scorn. **2** A leer. [Prob. <Scand. Cf. Norw. *flira* laugh, grin.] **—fleer′ing** *adj.* **—fleer′ing•ly** *adv.*

fleet[1] (flēt) *v.i.* **1** To move swiftly. **2** *Naut.* To change place; shift. **3** *Archaic* To fade. **4** *Obs.* To float. —*v.t.* **5** *Rare* To cause to pass quickly; while away. **6** *Naut.* To change the position of, as a cable. —*adj.* **1** Moving, or capable of moving, swiftly; rapid; swift; nimble. **2** Passing; evanescent. **3** *Brit. Dial.* Thin; shallow. [OE *flēotan* float] **—fleet′ly** *adv.* **—fleet′ness** *n.*

fleet[2] (flēt) *n.* **1** A number of vessels in company or under one command; especially ships of war. **2** The entire number of vessels belonging to one government; a navy. **3** The number of vessels in one command: the Pacific *fleet.* **4** A number of vessels, aircraft, or vehicles, collectively, engaged in the same activity, or operated as a unit: a fishing *fleet,* a *fleet* of trucks. [OE *flēot* ship]

fleet[3] (flēt) *n. Dial.* An inlet, creek, or sewer: now chiefly an element in place names: *Fleet* Street. [OE *flēot* estuary]

Fleet Admiral See ADMIRAL OF THE FLEET.

fleet•ing (flē′ting) *adj.* Passing quickly; transitory. See synonyms under TRANSIENT.

Fleet Prison A former debtors' prison in London. Also **the Fleet.**

Fleet Street An old street in London, center of the newspaper and printing business; hence, London journalism.

fleg (fleg) *Scot. v.t.* To frighten. —*v.i.* To flee. —*n.* A stroke.

Flem•ing (flem′ing) *n.* A native of Flanders; one of Flemish blood and speech, of Dutch descent. [<MDu. *Vlaming*]

Flem•ing (flem′ing), **Sir Alexander,** 1881–1955, British bacteriologist; discovered penicillin. **—Sir John Ambrose,** 1849–1945, English electrical engineer.

Flem•ish (flem′ish) *adj.* Of or pertaining to Flanders, its people, literature, or language. —*n.* **1** Flemings collectively: with the definite article. **2** The language of Flanders, belonging to the Low German branch of the Germanic languages. [<MDu. *Vlaemisch*]

Flens•burg (flens′bo͝ork) A port in NW Germany near the Danish border.

flense (flens) *v.t.* **flensed, flens•ing** To strip the blubber or the skin from, as a whale or a seal. Also **flench** (flench). [<Dan. *flense*] **—flens′er** *n.*

flesh (flesh) *n.* **1** The portion of an animal body that consists of the softer tissues; especially, the muscular part of the body, but the fats being often included: distinguished from the fluids, bones, and integuments. **2** Animal food or meat as distinguished from vegetable; in a restricted sense, the meat of mammals and birds as distinguished from fish. **3** The material part of man as distinguished from the spiritual; the body as opposed to the soul. **4** Mankind in general; the human race. **5** In Scriptural and theological use, human nature; specifically, the carnal nature of man as affected with evil inclinations. **6** Desire for the gratification of sensual passions. **7** *Poetic* Kind-heartedness; gentleness of nature. **8** The outer appearance or color of a person's body: a man of dark *flesh.* **9** Animal life as a whole. **10** The soft, pulpy parts of fruits and vegetables, as distinguished from skin, etc. **11** The color of the skin of a white person; flesh-colored. **12** Kin; family stock. **—in the flesh 1** In person. **2** Alive. **—own flesh and blood** One's own family, relations, or descendants. —*v.t.* **1** To plunge, as a sword, into the flesh, especially for the first time. **2** To inure or initiate, as troops, by giving a first experience of warfare. **3** To incite, as hawks for hunting, with a first experience of killing. **4** To scrape the flesh from, as a hide. **5** To invest or pad out with flesh. **6** To make fat or fleshy. —*v.i.* **7** To become fat or fleshy. **—flesh out** To give substance or the appearance of reality to; develop fully: to *flesh out* an idea.[OE *flǣsc*]

flesh-col•ored (flesh′kul′ərd) *adj.* Having the color of the skin of a white person; pinkish.

flesh•er (flesh′ər) *n.* **1** One who strips the flesh from hides; also, an instrument used for this. **2** *Scot.* A butcher.

flesh fly A carnivorous dipterous insect (genus *Sarcophaga*) that deposits its eggs or larvae in animal matter.

flesh•i•ness (flesh′ē•nis) *n.* Plumpness; corpulence.

flesh•ing (flesh′ing) *n.* The process of cleaning the inner side of hides and skins of adhering flesh and fat.

flesh•ings (flesh′ingz) *n. pl.* Flesh-colored tights.

flesh•li•ly (flesh′li•lē) *adj. Rare* Sensually

flesh•li•ness (flesh′lē•nis) *n.* **1** Sensuality. **2** Fleshiness.

flesh•ly (flesh′lē) *adj.* **•li•er, •li•est 1** Pertaining to the body; corporeal. **2** Sensual; carnal. **3** Fleshy; fat; plump. —*adv.* In a fleshly manner.

flesh•mon•ger (flesh′mung′gər, -mong′-) *n.* **1** A dealer in meat; butcher. **2** A procurer.

flesh•pot (flesh′pot′) *n.* **1** A pot to cook flesh in. **2** *pl.* Any form of indulgence; luxury; soft living.

flesh wound A superficial wound not injuring the bones or vital organs.

flesh•y (flesh′ē) *adj.* **flesh•i•er, flesh•i•est 1** Having much flesh; plump; corpulent; fat. **2** Pertaining to flesh or to carnal nature; composed of flesh. **3** Consisting of firm pulp; succulent, as a peach or an apple.

fletch (flech) *v.t.* To provide with feathers, as arrows; fledge. [Alter. of FLEDGE; infl. by *fletcher*]

fletch•er (flech′ər) *n. Archaic* One who fletches arrows; an arrowmaker. [<OF *flechier, flecher* <*fleche* arrow]

Fletch•er (flech′ər), **John,** 1579–1625, English dramatist; collaborated with Beaumont. **—John Gould,** 1886–1950, U.S. poet.

Fletch•er•ism (flech′ə•riz′əm) *n.* **1** The doctrine that perfect health requires complete mastication of food. **2** The practice of this doctrine. [after Horace *Fletcher,* 1849–1919, U.S. dietician]

Fletch•er•ize (flech′ə•rīz) *v.t.* **•ized, •iz•ing** To masticate until converted into pulp.

Fletsch•horn (flech′hôrn) A peak in southern Switzerland; 13,121 feet.

fleur-de-lis (flœr′də•lē′, -lēs′) *n. pl.* **fleurs-de-lis** (-də•lēz′) **1** The iris. **2** A heraldic device, the bearing of the former royal family of France. Also **fleur′-de-lys′.** [<F, flower of lily]

FLEUR-DE-LIS

fleured (flœrd) *adj.* Decorated with fleurs-de-lis.

Fleu•rus (flœ•rüs′) A town in south central Belgium; scene of Spanish defeat in 1622, French victories in 1690, 1794.

fleu•ry (flo͞o′rē) *adj. Her.* Terminating in the three leaves of, or strewed with, the fleur-de-lis; specifically, tipped with a fleur-de-lis: said of the arms of a cross. For illustration see under CROSS.

flew[1] (flo͞o) See FLUE[1].

flew[2] (flo͞o) Past tense of FIY[1].

flew•it (flo͞o′it) *n. Scot.* A box on the ears; a slap.

flews (flo͞oz) *n. pl.* The large chops or hanging parts of the upper lip of certain dogs: term used especially of hounds. See illustration under DOG. [Origin unknown] **—flewed** *adj.*

flex (fleks) *v.t.* & *v.i.* **1** To bend. **2** To contract, as a muscle. —*n.* **1** A bend; flexure. **2** *Brit.* A length of pliant, usually insulated, copper wire, as for an electric plug-in connection. [<L *flexus,* pp. of *flectere* bend]

flex•i•ble (flek′sə•bəl) *adj.* **1** Capable of being bent, turned, or twisted, without breaking. **2** Pliant; plastic. **3** Tractable; yielding; compliant. Also **flex•ile** (flek′sil). **—flex′i•bil′i•ty, flex′i•ble•ness** *n.* **—flex′i•bly** *adv.*

flex•ion (flek′shən) *n.* **1** *Anat.* The bending or turning of a part, as a limb, muscle, etc.: opposed to *extension.* **2** *Brit.* Flection (defs. 1–3).

Flex•ner (fleks′nər), **Abraham,** 1866–1959, U.S. educator. **—Simon,** 1863–1946, bacteriologist, brother of the preceding.

flex•or (flek′sər) *n. Anat.* A muscle that operates to bend a joint.

flex•time (fleks′tīm′) *n.* The system of allowing workers to arrange working hours according to their own convenience.

flex•u•ose (flek′sho͞o•ōs) *adj.* **1** *Bot.* Bending gently to and fro in opposite directions, as certain plants; zigzag. **2** Flexuous. [<L *flexuosus* <*flexus* bent. See FLEX.]

flex•u•ous (flek′sho͞o•əs) *adj.* **1** Winding or turning about; having bends or turns. **2** Unsteady; wavering. **3** Flexuose. [<L *flexuosus* <*flexus;* see FLEX] **—flex•u•os•i•ty** (flek′sho͞o•os′ə•tē), **flex′u•ous•ness** *n.* **—flex′u•ous•ly** *adv.*

flex•u•ral (flek′shər•əl) *adj.* Of or pertaining to bending or curving.

flex•ure (flek′shər) *n.* **1** A bending; the state of being bent or flexed. **2** A bent part; turn; curve; fold.

fley (flā) *Scot. v.t.* To frighten; affright. —*n.* A fright.
fli·aum (flī'ôm) *n.* The orange rockfish *(Sebastodes pinniger)* of the American Pacific coast. [Origin uncertain]
flib·ber·ti·gib·bet (flib'ər·tē·jib'it) *n.* An impulsive, flighty, or gossipy person. Also **flib'ber·di·gib'bit, flib'ber·ty·gib'bet.** [Imit.]
flich·ter (flikh'tər) *Scot. v.i.* To flutter; flicker. —*n.* A flicker.
flick[1] (flik) *v.t.* **1** To strike with a quick, light stroke, as with a whip or finger. **2** To throw or remove with such a motion: to *flick* dust. **3** To cause to move, as a whip, in a quick, darting manner. —*v.i.* **4** To move in a quick, darting manner: His fist *flicked* out. **5** To flutter. [<*n.*] —*n.* **1** A quick, light stroke, as with a whip. **2** The sound of such a stroke. **3** A streak or splash. [Imit.]
flick[2] (flik) *n. Slang* A movie. [Short for FLICKER[1]]
flick·er[1] (flik'ər) *v.i.* **1** To burn or shine with an unsteady or wavering light. **2** To move quickly or jerkily, as lightning. **3** To flutter the wings. —*v.t.* **4** To cause to flicker. —*n.* **1** A waving or fluctuating light. **2** A flickering or fluttering motion. See synonyms under LIGHT[1]. **3** In motion pictures, the effect of discontinuity due to faulty projection. [OE *flicorian* move the wings] —**flick'·er·ing** *adj.* —**flick'er·ing·ly** *adv.* —**flick'er·y** *adj.*
flick·er[2] (flik'ər) *n.* A woodpecker, especially the golden-winged woodpecker *(Colaptes auratus)* of eastern North America. [Imit.]
flick·er·tail (flik'ər·tāl') *n.* A medium-sized ground squirrel *(Citellus richardsonii)* with a buff-to-grayish coat and a bushy tail, black above and brown beneath: common in Montana and North Dakota.
Flickertail State Nickname of NORTH DAKOTA.
flicks (fliks) *n. pl. Brit. Slang* Motion pictures.
flied (flīd) Past tense and past participle of FLY[1] (def. 7).
fli·er (flī'ər) *n.* **1** That which flies; a flying bird, airplane, or the like; a fugitive. **2** An aviator or airman. **3** A rapidly moving piece in a machine. **4** *U.S.* A printed handbill. **5** A single step in a straight flight of stairs; in the plural, a straight flight. **6** A bus or express train with a fast schedule. **7** *Colloq.* A venture, as in the stock market. Also spelled *flyer.*
flight (flīt) *n.* **1** The act, process, or power of flying; swift movement of any kind. ◆ Collateral adjective: *volar.* **2** The distance traveled, as by a projectile. **3** A group or flock flying through the air together. **4** The art of traveling through the air in aircraft. **5** A single trip of an airplane. **6** In the U.S. Air Force, a tactical unit of two or more aircraft. **7** A soaring and sustained effort or utterance. **8** An ascent or continuous series (of stairs or steps). **9** A light, slender arrow for shooting at long distances: also **flight arrow.** **10** In angling, a device for whirling the bait rapidly. **11** The act of fleeing or escaping. See synonyms under CAREER. —**to put to flight** To cause to flee or run; defeat decisively; rout. —*v.i. Obs.* To migrate or move in flights, as birds. [OE *flyht*] —**flight'·less** *adj.*
flight attendant An employee of an airline who attends passengers on board an aircraft, as a steward or stewardess.
flight deck The top deck of an aircraft-carrier, on which aircraft land and takeoff.
flight engineer *Aeron.* The crew member of an airplane in charge of mechanical performance during flight.
flight feather *Ornithol.* One of the strong, stiff feathers that are essential to the flight of a bird.
flight formation *Aeron.* A maneuver in which two or more aircraft fly in a definite pattern with reference to the complete unit.
flight line *Aeron.* The part of an airfield adjacent to the hangars, where aircraft are serviced, parked, etc.
flight officer *U.S.* In World War II, a specially created rank in the Air Force, corresponding to a warrant officer in grade.
flight path *Aeron.* The path traced out by the center of gravity of an aircraft with reference to the earth.
flight plan *Aeron.* The essential details of a proposed aircraft flight, including type of airplane, points of departure and arrival, cruising altitude, course, speed, etc.
flight-re·cord·er (flīt'ri·kôr'dər) *n. Aeron.* An automatic electronic device for recording temperature and pressure changes in an aircraft in flight: used primarily on test flights.
flight station *Aeron.* The compartment of a large airplane containing equipment for controlling mechanical performance during flight, and manned by crew members other than the pilot.
flight strip *Aeron.* An auxiliary landing field for aircraft.
flight·y (flī'tē) *adj.* **flight·i·er, flight·i·est** **1** Given to light-headed fancies or caprices; volatile. **2** Slightly delirious. **3** Fleeting; passing swiftly. —**flight'i·ly** *adv.* —**flight'i·ness** *n.*
flim-flam (flim'flam) *Colloq. v.t.* **-flammed, -flam·ming** To deceive; swindle; trick. —*adj.* Shifty; deceptive; tricky. —*n.* **1** Nonsense. **2** A deception; sham; pretense; specifically, a process of cheating a person when making change. [Cf. Norw. *flim* a lampoon, *flimta* mock] —**flim'-flam'mer** *n.* —**flim'-flam'mer·y** *n.*
flim·sy (flim'zē) *adj.* **·si·er, ·si·est** Lacking substantial texture or structure; thin and weak; ineffective. —*n. pl.* **flim·sies** **1** A thin paper used for carbon copies. **2** A dispatch or article received on thin paper. [<FILM, by metathesis; infl. in form by *clumsy, tipsy,* etc.] —**flim'si·ly** *adv.* —**flim'si·ness** *n.*
flinch (flinch) *v.i.* **1** To shrink back, as from pain or danger; waver; wince. **2** In croquet, to allow the foot to slip from one's ball during the action of driving an opponent's ball from the field of play. —*n.* Any act of shrinking back, wavering, or wincing. [<OF *flenchir,* var. of *flechir* bend; ult. origin uncertain] —**flinch'er** *n.* —**flinch'ing·ly** *adv.*
flin·der (flin'dər) *n.* A small fragment; splinter; shred: usually in the plural. [Cf. Norw. *flindra* splinter]
Flin·ders Island (flin'dərz) Largest of the Furneaux group; 802 square miles.
Flinders Ranges A mountain range in eastern South Australia; highest peak, 3,900 feet.
Flinders River A river in northern Queensland, Australia, flowing 520 miles NW to the Gulf of Carpentaria.
F lines Fraunhofer's lines.
fling (fling) *v.* **flung, fling·ing** *v.t.* **1** To cast or throw with violence; hurl. **2** To cast off; discard. **3** To put abruptly or violently, as if by throwing: They *flung* him into prison. **4** To put (oneself) into something completely or with energy: He *flung* himself into the battle. **5** To throw to the ground, as in wrestling; overthrow. **6** To send forth; emit, as a fragrance. —*v.i.* **7** To move, rush, or flounce, as with anger or contempt. **8** To make abusive remarks; speak bitterly or critically. **9** To kick and plunge: said of horses. —*n.* **1** The act of casting out, down, or away; a throw. **2** A sneering insinuation; aspersion. **3** A kick, flounce, leap, or the like. **4** Free range for action or indulgence; dash; swagger. **5** A lively Scotch dance. [ME *flingen* <Scand. Cf. ON *flegja* beat.] —**fling'er** *n.*
fling·ing-tree (fling'ing·trē') *n. Scot.* **1** A flail. **2** A timber hung between horses in a stall.
flint (flint) *n.* **1** A dull-colored variety of quartz resembling chalcedony but more opaque; it is very hard, and produces a spark when struck with steel. **2** A piece of such stone, shaped for some purpose, as for striking fire. **3** Anything very hard, obdurate, or cruel. —*v.t.* To provide with a flint. [OE]
Flint (flint) **1** A city in central Michigan. **2** A county in NE Wales; 256 square miles; county town, Mold: also **Flint'shire** (-shir).
Flint (flint), **Austin,** 1812–86, U.S. physician. —**Austin,** 1836–1915, U.S. physiologist and physician; son of the preceding.
flint corn A kind of Indian corn *(Zea mays indurata),* having especially hard smooth kernels which do not shrivel.
flint glass See under GLASS.
flint·lock (flint'lok') *n.* **1** A gunlock in which a flint was used to ignite the powder in the pan. **2** A firearm equipped with such a gunlock.
flint paper A paper covered with powdered flint, resembling sandpaper.
Flint River (flint) A river in western Georgia, flowing 330 miles south to the Chattahoochee to form the Apalachicola.
flint·y (flin'tē) *adj.* **flint·i·er, flint·i·est** **1** Made of, containing, or resembling flint. **2** Hard; cruel; obdurate. See synonyms under HARD. —**flint'i·ly** *adv.* —**flint'i·ness** *n.*
flip (flip) *v.* **flipped, flip·ping** *v.t.* **1** To throw or put in motion with a jerk; flick. **2** To toss, as a coin or cigarette, by or as by a fillip. —*v.i.* **3** To move abruptly or with a jerk. **4** To make a fillip; strike lightly and quickly. —*n.* **1** A quick movement of the hand or finger; sudden toss; snap; fillip; flick. **2** A drink made with some liquor, as sherry, mixed with egg, sugar, and spices. —*adj. Colloq.* Pert; saucy; impertinent. [Imit.]
flip-flop (flip'flop') *n.* **1** A somersault or handspring. **2** In advertising presentations, an easel device permitting display cards to be flipped over the top. [Varied reduplication of FLIP]
flip·pant (flip'ənt) *adj.* **1** Light, pert, and trifling; shallow and impertinent. **2** *Obs.* Fluent; free of speech. [<FLIP, *v.* + -ANT] —**flip'pan·cy, flip'pant·ness** *n.* —**flip'pant·ly** *adv.*
flip·per (flip'ər) *n.* **1** A limb used to swim with, as by seals, turtles, etc. **2** *Usually pl.* One of a pair of rubber shoes having a long, flat, paddlelike piece projecting beyond the toes, used by skin divers and other swimmers: also called *fin.* **3** *Slang* The hand.
flip side The back or second side of a phonograph record, esp. the side with the recording of lesser importance.
flirt (flûrt) *v.i.* **1** To play at courtship; try to attract attention or admiration; coquet. **2** To trifle; toy: to *flirt* with danger. **3** To move with sudden jerky motions. —*v.t.* **4** To toss or throw with a jerk. **5** To move briskly or back and forth. —*n.* **1** A person, especially a woman, who coquets; a trifler. **2** The act of flirting; a flirting motion; fling. [Imit.] —**flirt'er** *n.* —**flirt'y** *adj.*
flir·ta·tion (flər·tā'shən) *n.* Insincere lovemaking. Also **flirt'ing.** —**flir·ta'tious** *adj.* —**flir·ta'tious·ly** *adv.* —**flir·ta'tious·ness** *n.*
flirt·gill (flûrt'gil') *n. Obs.* A forward or frivolous girl.
flit (flit) *v.* **flit·ted, flit·ting** *v.i.* **1** To move or fly rapidly and lightly; dart; skim. **2** To pass away, as time. **3** *Dial.* To leave; depart. **4** *Scot. & Brit. Dial.* To move from one dwelling to another. —*v.t.* **5** *Scot.* To transfer; move. See synonyms under FLY[1]. —*n.* A flitting motion or action; flutter. [<ON *flytja* remove, move] —**flit'ter** *n.* —**flit'ting** *n.*
flitch (flich) *n.* **1** A side (of a hog) salted and cured; side of bacon. **2** A strip or steak cut from the side of certain fishes, smoked or adapted for smoking. **3** In carpentry, one of the parts of a compound beam. **4** A length of stripped log from whose circumference thin sheets of veneer are cut; also, the sheet so cut. —*v.t.* To cut into flitches. [OE *flicce*]
flite (flīt) *Scot. v.t. & v.i.* **flit·ed, flit·ing** **1** To scold; quarrel. **2** To wrangle with (a person). —*n.* A quarreling; railing; scolding. Also spelled *flyte.* —**flit'ing** *n.*
flit·ter[1] (flit'ər) *n.* A thin bit or bits of tin, brass, or the like, used in decorative work. [Alter. of obs. *fitters* pieces, fragments]
flit·ter[2] (flit'ər) *v.t. & v.i.* To flutter; flit. [Freq. of FLIT]
flit·ter·mouse (flit'ər·mous') *n. pl.* **·mice** (-mīs') A bat. [Cf. G *fledermaus*]
fliv·ver (fliv'ər) *Slang v.i.* To fail. —*n.* **1** A cheap motorcar. **2** Hence, anything small of its kind or of low price. [Origin unknown]
float (flōt) *v.i.* **1** To rest on the surface of a liquid. **2** To drift on or as on the surface of a liquid; move gently. **3** To move or drift without purpose or destination. **4** To hover; stay vaguely: The image *floated* in his mind. —*v.t.* **5** To cause to rest on the surface of a liquid. **6** To put in circulation; place on sale: to *float* a loan. **7** To find support for, as a business venture. **8** To irrigate; flood. **9** To smooth the surface of (soft plaster). —*n.* **1** An object, as a ball, that floats on a liquid or buoys up something, as a cork on a bait line or a hollow ball in a cistern. **2** One of various devices or appliances, as a plasterer's spreading trowel, a shoemaker's rasp, etc. **3** A truck or wheeled platform, decorated for display in

a pageant. **4** *Naut.* A dock or basin in which a ship is floated. For illustration see DRYDOCK. **5** *Geol.* Rock or rocky debris detached from the original formation. **6** *Aeron.* That portion of the landing gear of a seaplane which provides buoyancy when it is resting on the surface of the water. **7** In banking, time drafts and out-of-town checks in transit for collection. See TRANSIT. **8** A mechanical device for elevating performers above the stage in spectacular plays; also, the footlights. **9** The passage of a filling thread under or over several warp threads without engaging them. **10** *Electr.* A voltage equalizer; storage battery. **11** *Biol.* A hollow or inflated organ that supports an animal in water. **12** A milk shake with a ball of ice-cream floating in it. [OE *flotian* float] **—float'a·ble, float'y** *adj.*

Synonym (verb): swim. An object *floats* which is upborne in a fluid without action; a living being *swims* when borne up, or borne onward, in a liquid by action; one wearied with *swimming* may rest himself by *floating*; a cork *floats* on water; the hawk seems to *float* in the upper air. *Antonyms*: drown, sink.

float·age (flō'tij), **float·a·tion** (flō·tā'shən) See FLOTAGE, etc.

float·board (flōt'bôrd', -bōrd') *n.* One of the paddles of a water wheel or of a paddle wheel.

float·er (flō'tər) *n.* **1** One who or that which floats; a float. **2** *U.S.* An unattached voter, especially one whose vote may be bought; also, one who votes fraudulently elsewhere than in his own district.

float-feed (flōt'fēd') *adj. Mech.* Furnished with a feed controlled by a float, as the carburetor of an internal-combustion engine.

float·ing (flō'ting) *adj.* **1** Buoyed up or carried along by a liquid or gas; borne on the surface of a liquid. **2** Unattached to moorings or anchorage; afloat. **3** Moving about; not settled; fluctuating. **4** Not funded; due at various times and in various sums: said of an indebtedness. **5** Not invested permanently; in circulation; available: said of funds or capital.—*n.* **1** The act, operation, or process of floating, in any sense of the verb. **2** A second coat of plastering.

floating axle *Mech.* In an automobile, a live axle which floats in a housing: it supports none of the weight, its sole function being to transmit propelling power to the wheels.

floating debt The general unfunded indebtedness of a state or a corporation.

floating dock A double caisson having a floored open space between air chambers: used for lifting a vessel out of water by pumping the water out of the air chambers. Also **floating drydock.**

float·ing-heart (flō'ting·härt') *n.* An aquatic herb (genus *Nymphoides*), with floating heart-shaped leaves.

float·ing-island (flō'ting·ī'lənd) *n.* A dessert consisting of boiled custard with the beaten whites of eggs or whipped cream floating on the surface.

floating kidney *Pathol.* An abnormal condition, usually congenital, in which the kidneys are movable or unstable in position: also called *movable kidney, wandering kidney.*

floating ribs See RIB.

floc (flok) *n.* A tiny flaky mass, as in smoke; a chemical precipitate: also spelled *flock.* [Short for FLOCCULE]

floc·cil·la·tion (flok'si·lā'shən) *n. Pathol.* A delirious picking at the bedclothes by a patient. [< NL *floccillus,* dim. of *floccus* lock of wool + ATION]

floc·cose (flok'ōs, flo·kōs') *adj.* **1** Woolly. **2** *Bot.* Having tufts of soft hairs or wool. [< LL *floccosus* < *floccus* lock of wool]

floc·cu·late (flok'yə·lāt) *v.t.* & *v.i.* **·lat·ed, ·lat·ing 1** To gather or be joined together in small lumps, as some soils. **2** To collect in flaky masses, as the particles of a finely divided precipitate. **3** To form large masses, as clouds. —*adj.* (-lit) Having a tuft of stiff hairs or a flocculus. **—floc'cu·la'tion** *n.*

floc·cule (flok'yōōl) *n.* **1** A loose tuft, like wool. **2** *Chem.* One of the flakes in a flocculent precipitate. **3** A small flocculent mass. Also **floc·cus** (flok'əs). [< NL *flocculus,* dim. of *floccus* lock of wool]

floc·cu·lent (flok'yə·lənt) *adj.* **1** Resembling wool; woolly. **2** Of, pertaining to, or like the down of a young bird. **3** Covered with a soft waxy secretion, as certain insects. **4** Coalescing in flakes, as the clumping together of microscopic particles in a liquid. **—floc'cu·lence, floc'cu·len·cy** *n.* **—floc'cu·lent·ly** *adv.*

floc·cu·lus (flok'yə·ləs) *n. pl.* **·li** (-lī) **1** A little flake; floccule. **2** A small tuft of wool or woollike hairs. **3** *Astron.* One of the gaseous cloudlike masses in the chromosphere of the sun. **4** *Anat.* One of a pair of small lateral lobes in the cerebellum of the higher vertebrates. [< NL. See FLOCCULE.]

flock[1] (flok) *n.* **1** A company or collection of animals, as sheep, goats, or birds. **2** The persons belonging to a congregation, church, parish, or diocese. **3** An unorganized company of persons; a crowd. —*v.i.* To assemble or go in flocks, crowds, etc.; congregate. [OE *flocc*]

Synonyms (noun): bevy, brood, company, covey, drove, gam, group, hatch, herd, litter, lot, pack, set, swarm. *Group* is the general word for any gathering of a small number of objects, whether of persons, animals, or inanimate things. The individuals in a *brood* or *litter* are related to each other; those in the other *groups* may not be. *Brood* is used chiefly of fowls and birds, *litter* of certain quadrupeds which bring forth many young at a birth; we speak of a *brood* of chickens, a *litter* of puppies. *Bevy* is used of birds, and figuratively of any bright and lively *group* of women or children, but rarely of men. *Flock* is applied to birds and to some of the smaller animals; *herd* is confined to the larger animals; we speak of a *bevy* of quail, a *covey* of partridges, a *flock* of blackbirds, or a *flock* of sheep, a *gam* of whales, a *herd* of cattle, horses, buffaloes, or elephants, a *pack* of wolves, a *pack* of hounds, a *swarm* of bees. A collection of animals driven or gathered for driving is called a *drove.*

flock[2] (flok) *n.* **1** Finely ground wool, felt or vegetable fiber; wool dust. **2** A tuft of wool, or the like. **3** Short refuse wool, used as stuffing and in upholstery. **4** A tufted or flakelike mass, especially if produced by precipitation: also spelled *floc.* —*v.t.* To cover or fill with flock, as a cushion. [Prob. < OF *floc* < L *floccus* lock of wool]

flock paper Wallpaper sized and covered or figured with flock; velvet paper.

flock·y (flok'ē) *adj.* **flock·i·er, flock·i·est** Resembling flock; floccose.

Flod·den (flod'n) A small hill in north Cumberland, England, surrounded by **Flodden Field,** scene of the defeat of James IV of Scotland by English forces, 1513.

floe (flō) *n.* A tabular mass, or a collection of such masses, of floating ice. ◆ Homophone: *flow.* [< ON *flo* a layer]

flog (flog, flôg) *v.t.* **flogged, flog·ging** To beat with a whip, rod, etc.; to whip. See synonyms under BEAT. —*n.* A sound resembling the impact of a blow; also, the act of flogging. [? < L *flagellare*] **—flog'ger** *n.* **—flog'ging** *n.*

flong (flong) *n.* A sheet of specially prepared paper used for making a stereotype mold or matrix. [Var. of FLAN]

flood (flud) *n.* **1** An unusually large flow of water; freshet; inundation; deluge. ◆ Collateral adjective: *diluvial.* **2** The coming in of the tide; the tide at its height; high tide: also called *flood tide.* **3** A copious flow or stream, as of sunlight, lava, etc.; abundant or excessive supply. **4** Any great body of water; the sea; a river. **5** A stage light that throws a broad beam. **—the Flood** or **Noah's flood** See under DELUGE. —*v.t.* **1** To cover or inundate with a flood; deluge. **2** To fill or overwhelm as with a flood: They *flooded* him with advice. **3** To supply with too much: He *flooded* the engine with gasoline. —*v.i.* **4** To rise to a flood; overflow. **5** To flow in a flood; gush. [OE *flōd*] **—flood'er** *n.*

flood control The use of dikes, dams, tunnels, artificial channels, and other engineering techniques as a means of regulating and controlling flood waters.

flood·gate (flud'gāt') *n.* **1** *Engin.* A gate for regulating the flow of water, as a raceway. **2** Any free vent for an outpouring, as of wrath or tears.

flood·light (flud'līt') *n.* Artificial illumination of great brilliancy and broad beam; specifically, a lighting unit equipped with a highpowered projector, enveloping the desired object in a broad flood of light.

flood plain An area of flat country bordering a stream and subject to flooding in periods of high water.

flood tide See FLOOD *n.* (def. 2).

floor (flôr, flōr) *n.* **1** The surface in a room or building upon which one walks. **2** The space between two adjacent levels of a building; a story. **3** Any natural area made smooth or level, corresponding in character or use to a floor; also, the surface of something built, as a bridge. **4** In any parliamentary body, the part of the hall occupied by its members; hence, the right or privilege to address the house during a given time and to the exclusion of other speakers. **5** The main business hall of an exchange. **6** *Naut.* The vertical plates between the inner and outer bottoms of a ship extending from one side (bilge) to the other. **7** The bottom limit of anything; specifically, the lowest price charged for a given thing. —*v.t.* **1** To cover or provide with a floor. **2** To throw or knock down; overthrow. **3** *Colloq.* To silence; defeat. **4** *Colloq.* To baffle; confound. [OE *flōr*] **—floor'er** *n.*

floor·age (flôr'ij, flō'rij) *n.* The area of a floor; floor space.

floor·board (flôr'bôrd', flōr'bōrd') *n.* A board in a floor; flooring.

floor·cloth (flôr'klôth', -kloth', flōr'-) *n.* **1** Any fabric used to cover floors, as oilcloth. **2** A cloth used to clean a floor.

floor·ing (flôr'ing, flō'ring) *n.* **1** Material for the making of a floor. **2** Floors collectively. **3** A floor.

floor leader A party leader in either house of the U.S. Congress, in charge of party organization and many of the privileges of the floor.

floor plan An architectural plan of the rooms and other spaces on one floor of a building.

floor show Entertainment consisting of dancing, singing, etc., presented on the dance floor of a night club or cabaret.

floor·walk·er (flôr'wô'kər, flōr'-) *n.* In a retail store, one who oversees the employees on a floor, directs customers, etc.

flooz·y (flōō'zē) *n. pl.* **flooz·ies** *Slang* A dissolute young woman; a tart. [Cf. FLOSSY]

flop (flop) *v.* **flopped, flop·ping** *v.i.* **1** To move or beat about with or as with thuds. **2** To fall loosely and heavily: to *flop* to the ground. **3** *Colloq.* To fail. —*v.t.* **4** To cause to strike, slap, or drop with or as with a thud. —*n.* **1** The sound or act of flopping. **2** *Colloq.* An utter failure, or a person who has failed. [Var. of FLAP] **—flop'per** *n.* **— flop'py** *adj.* **—flop'pi·ly** *adv.* **—flop'pi·ness** *n.*

flop·house (flop'hous') *n.* A cheap lodging house or hotel.

floppy disc A small, flexible recording disc on which data may be stored in the memory of a digital computer.

flo·ra (flôr'ə, flō'rə) *n. pl.* **·ras** or **·rae** (-ē) **1** The aggregate of plants indigenous to a country or district: distinguished from *fauna.* **2** A work systematically describing such plants. [< NL, after L *Flora,* goddess of flowers]

Flo·ra (flôr'ə, flō'rə) A feminine personal name. Also *Fr.* **Flore** (flôr). [< L, flower]

—Flora In Roman mythology, the goddess of flowers and spring.

flo·ral (flôr'əl, flō'rəl) *adj.* Of, like, or pertaining to flowers.

Flo·ral (flôr'əl, flō'rəl) *adj.* Of, belonging, or relating to Flora.

floral envelope *Bot.* The corolla and calyx of a flower.

Flo·ré·al (flôr'ē·əl, *Fr.* flô·rā·àl') See CALENDAR (Republican).

Flor·ence (flôr'əns, flor'-) A city on the Arno in central Italy: Italian *Firenze.* Ancient **Flo·ren·ti·a** (flō·ren'shē·ə).

Flor·ence (flôr'əns, flor'-; *Fr.* flô·räṅs') A feminine personal name. Also *Dan., Ger., Sw.*

Flo·renz (flô·rents′), *Du.* **Flo·ren·ti·a** (flô·ren′tsē·ä), *Sp.* **Flo·ren·cia** (flō·ren′thyä). [< L, blooming]

Florence flask 1 A round or pear-shaped bottle of thin glass in which liquids are heated. **2** A straw-covered glass flask in which olive oil or wine is imported from Italy.

flor·en·tine (flôr′ən·tēn, -tīn, flor′-) *n.* A stout and durable kind of silk dress goods.

Flor·en·tine (flôr′ən·tēn, -tīn, flor′-) *adj.* Of or pertaining to the city of Florence, Italy. —*n.* An inhabitant or native of Florence.

Flo·res (flō′res) **1** One of the Lesser Sunda Islands, east of Sumbawa; 6,000 square miles. **2** (flō′rish) An island in the western Azores; 57 square miles.

flo·res·cence (flô·res′əns, flō-) *n. Bot.* **1** The state of being in blossom. **2** Inflorescence. For illustrations see INFLORESCENCE. [< NL *florescentia* < L *florescere,* inceptive of *florere* bloom]—**flo·res′cent** *adj.*

Flo·res Sea (flō′res) A part of the Indian Ocean between Sulawesi and the Lesser Sunda Islands.

flo·ret (flôr′it, flō′rit) *n.* **1** A little flower. **2** *Bot.* One of the small individual flowers that make up a cluster or head, as in sunflowers, dandelions, etc., of the composite family. **3** A silk yarn or floss. [< OF *florete,* dim. of *flor* a flower < L *flos, floris*]

Flo·rey (flôr′ē, flō′rē), **Sir Howard Walter,** 1898–1968, British pathologist born in Australia.

Florey unit The Oxford unit.

Flo·ri·an·ó·po·lis (flôr′ē·ən·op′ə·lis, flō′rē-) A port in southern Brazil, capital of Santa Catarina state. Formerly **Des·têr·ro** (dish·tär′·rōō).

flo·ri·at·ed (flôr′ē·ā′tid, flō′rē-) *adj.* Decorated with flower designs.

flo·ri·cul·ture (flôr′ə·kul′chər, flō′rə-) *n.* The cultivation of flowers or ornamental plants. See synonyms under AGRICULTURE. [< L *flos, floris* a flower + CULTURE]—**flo′ri·cul′tur·al** *adj.* —**flo′ri·cul′tur·al·ly** *adv.* —**flo′ri·cul′tur·ist** *n.*

flor·id (flôr′id, flor′-) *adj.* **1** Having a bright color; of a lively reddish hue. **2** Excessively ornate. **3** Blooming; flowery. **4** Full of ornamental musical phrases. [< L *floridus* flowery < *flos, floris* a flower]—**flo·rid·i·ty** (flə·rid′ə·te), **flor′id·ness** *n.* —**flor′id·ly** *adv.*

Flor·i·da (flôr′ə·də, flor′-) The southernmost Atlantic State of the United States; 58,560 square miles; capital, Tallahassee; entered the Union March 3, 1845: nickname, *Everglade State.* Abbr. FL —**Flo·rid·i·an** (flô·rid′ē·ən, flō-, flo-), **Flor·i·dan** (flôr′-, flor′-) *adj.* & *n.*

Florida Keys A chain of islands curving 150 miles SW around the tip of the Florida peninsula from Virginia Key to Key West.

Florida moss Spanish moss.

Florida, Straits of A passage separating the southern tip of Florida from the Bahamas and Cuba.

flo·rif·er·ous (flô·rif′ər·əs, flō-) *adj.* Bearing flowers. [< L *florifer* bearing flowers + -OUS]

flor·in (flôr′in, flor′·in) *n.* **1** The unit of value of the Netherlands: also called *guilder.* **2** A British silver coin, equal to one tenth of a pound, or two shillings. **3** A gold coin first issued in England in 1343. **4** A coin first issued by Florence, made of gold, and weighing about 54 grains: also **flor′ence.** **5** Any of several ancient coins of England, Tuscany, Germany, etc. [< OF < Ital. *fiorino* < *fiore* a flower; so called from the figure of a lily stamped on it]

FLORIN (Obverse)

Flo·ri·o (flôr′ē·ō, flō′rē·ō), **John,** 1553?–1625, English writer; translator of Montaigne's *Essays.*

flo·rist (flôr′ist, flō′rist, flor′ist) *n.* A grower of or dealer in flowers.

-florous *combining form Bot.* Having (a specified number, kind, etc., of) flowers: *uniflorous.* [< L *-florus* < *flos, floris* a flower]

flo·ru·it (flôr′yōō·it, flō′rōō·it) *Latin* He (or she) flourished.

flos fer·ri (flos′ fer′ī) A variety of aragonite, suggesting coral. [< L, flower of iron]

floss[1] (flôs, flos) *n.* **1** Floss silk. **2** The silk of some plants, as Indian corn. **3** The stray silk on the outside of cocoons of silkworms and of spiders. **4** A flossy surface; fluff. [< OF *flosche*]

floss[2] (flôs, flos) *n. Metall.* A slag that floats on molten metal. [< G *flosz*]

Flos·sie (flôs′ē, flos′ē) Diminutive of FLORENCE.

floss silk A soft, downy silk fiber suitable for embroidery.

floss·y (flôs′ē, flos′ē) *adj.* **floss·i·er, floss·i·est** **1** Of, pertaining to, or like floss; light; downy. **2** *Colloq.* Elegant; fine; beautiful.

flo·tage (flō′tij) *n.* **1** Things that float, collectively. **2** The capacity of anything to buoy up or to float. Also spelled *floatage.*

flo·ta·tion (flō·tā′shən) *n.* **1** The act or state of floating. **2** The science of bodies that float. **3** The act of floating or financing, as of an issue of bonds, etc., by bankers. **4** *Metall.* A method of separating pulverized ores by placing them in a froth of oils and chemicals in water, and applying a current of air so that the valuable ore particles float on or adhere to the surface. Also spelled *floatation.*

flotation gear *Aeron.* A buoyant apparatus attached to an aircraft to enable it to float when forced to alight on water.

flo·til·la (flō·til′ə) *n.* **1** A fleet of small vessels; a small fleet. **2** In the U.S. Navy, an organized group of destroyers, composed of two or more squadrons. **3** In the U.S. Army, a seagoing unit for laying mines. [< Sp., dim. of *flota* a fleet]

Flo·tow (flō′tō), **Friedrich von,** 1812–83, German opera composer.

flot·sam (flot′səm) *n.* **1** *Law* Goods cast or swept from a vessel into the sea and found floating. Compare JETSAM, LAGAN. **2** Any objects floating on the sea. **3** Hence, vagrants or unattached persons: the *flotsam* of society. Also spelled **flot′san** (-sən), **flot′son.** [< AF *floteson* < *floter* float < OE *flotian*]

flounce[1] (flouns) *n.* A gathered or plaited strip on a skirt. —*v.t.* **flounced, flounc·ing** To furnish with flounces. [Var. of FROUNCE]

flounce[2] (flouns) *v.i.* **flounced, flounc·ing** **1** To move or go with exaggerated tosses of the body, as in anger or petulance. **2** To plunge; founder: said of animals. —*n.* The act of flouncing; a fling. [< Scand. Cf. dial. Sw. *flunsa* plunge.]

flounc·ing (floun′sing) *n.* Material for flounces; also, flounces collectively.

floun·der[1] (floun′dər) *v.i.* **1** To struggle clumsily; move awkwardly as if mired or injured. **2** To proceed, as in speech or action, in a clumsy or confused manner; muddle. —*n.* A stumbling or struggling motion. [? Blend of FLOUNCE[2] and FOUNDER[2]]—**floun′der·ing·ly** *adv.*

floun·der[2] (floun′dər) *n.* **1** One of certain species of flatfish, valued as a food fish; especially, the winter flounder *(Pseudopleuronectes americanus)* of the North Atlantic coast, and the California flounder *(Platichthys stellatus).* **2** Any of several flat fish other than sole. [< AF *floundre,* prob. < Scand. Cf. Sw. *flundra.*]

flour (flour) *n.* **1** The ground and bolted substance of wheat. **2** The finely ground particles of any specified cereal: rye *flour.* **3** Any finely powdered substance. **4** Loose, finely crystallized saltpeter, used in making gunpowder. —*v.t.* **1** To make into flour; pulverize, as wheat. **2** *Metall.* To break up into minute particles: to *flour* mercury in the amalgamating process. **3** To sprinkle or cover with flour. [Var. of FLOWER]—**flour′y** *adj.*

flour·ish (flûr′ish) *v.i.* **1** To grow or fare well or prosperously; thrive. **2** To be at the peak of success or development; be at the height or in the prime: Alchemy *flourished* in the Middle Ages. **3** To move with sweeping motions; be displayed or waved about: Swords *flourished* in the air. **4** To write with sweeping or ornamental strokes. **5** *Music* **a** To play a showy passage. **b** To sound a fanfare. **6** *Obs.* To blossom. —*v.t.* **7** To wave about or brandish; flaunt, as a weapon or flag. **8** To embellish, as with ornamental lines or figures. —*n.* **1** An ornamental mark or design, especially a sweeping stroke, as in writing or embroidery; anything done for display alone. **2** The act of brandishing or waving. **3** A musical passage for display; fanfare. See synonyms under OSTENTATION. [< OF *floriss-,* stem of *florir* < L *florere* bloom]—**flour′ish·er** *n.* —**flour′ish·ing** *adj.* —**flour′ish·ing·ly** *adv.*

Synonyms (verb): advance, blossom, flower, gain, grow, increase, prosper, thrive. See FLAUNT, GAIN[1], SUCCEED. *Antonyms:* see synonyms for FALL.

flout (flout) *v.t.* To show or express scorn or contempt for; scoff at. —*v.i.* To express one's contempt; mock; jeer. See synonyms under MOCK. —*n.* A gibe; scoff; mockery. [Prob. ME *flouten* play the flute, deride]—**flout′er** *n.* —**flout′ing·ly** *adv.*

flow (flō) *v.i.* **1** To move along in a stream, as water or other fluid. **2** To move along, as with the qualities of a liquid: The crowd *flowed* through the gates. **3** To stream forth; proceed from a source. **4** To move with continuity and pleasing rhythm, as verse or music. **5** To fall or lie in waves, as garments or hair. **6** To be full or too full; abound; overflow: The creeks are *flowing* with gold. **7** To come in or rise, as the tide: opposed to ebb. —*v.t.* **8** To flood; inundate. **9** *Obs.* To cause to flow. —*n.* **1** The act of flowing, or that which flows; also, a continuous stream or current. **2** The incoming of the tide. **3** The quantity, as of water, that passes through an orifice or by a given point in a given time. **4** A copious outpouring. **5** Any easy, gentle movement, as of speech. ◆Homophone: *floe.* [OE *flowan*]—**flow′ing** *adj.* & *n.* —**flow′ing·ly** *adv.* —**flow′ing·ness** *n.*

flow·age (flō′ij) *n.* **1** The act of flowing or overflowing, or the state of being overflowed. **2** Liquid which flows or overflows. **3** *Physics* Deformation of a solid body by intermolecular movement like that of a viscous fluid: distinguished from or opposed to *fracture.*

flow·chart (flō′chärt′) *n.* A diagram showing all the steps in a logical sequence, as in a computer program.

flow·er (flou′ər, flour) *n.* **1** *Bot.* **a** The organ, or the combination of organs of reproduction in a plant; blossom; bloom. **b** In mosses, the reproductive organs with their enveloped or associated leaves. **2** A blooming plant. **3** The brightest, finest, choicest part, period, or specimen of anything. **4** Any flower-like ornament. **5** A flowery figure of speech. **6** *pl.* A very light powder obtained by sublimation and usually a metallic oxide: *flowers* of antimony; flour (def. 3). —*v.i.* **1** To put forth blossoms; bloom. **2** To come to full development; be at the full: The Renaissance *flowered* in Italy. —*v.t.* **3** To decorate with flowers or a floral pattern. [< OF *flour, flor* < L *flos, floris* a flower]—**flow′er·er** *n.* —**flow′er·less** *adj.* —**flow′er·y** *adj.* —**flow′er·i·ly** *adv.* —**flow′er·i·ness** *n.*

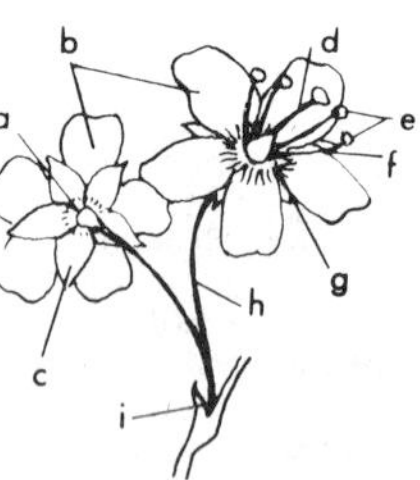

FLOWER
a. Calyx. *b.* Petal. *c.* Sepal. *d.* Pistil. *e.* Pollen. *f.* Stamen. *g.* Corolla. *h.* Pedicel. *i.* Bract.

flow·er·age (flou′ər·ij, flou′rij) *n.* **1** The act or state of flowering. **2** An ornamentation of flowers, or flowers collectively.

flower bed A plot of ground in which flowers are planted.

flow·er-de-luce (flou′ər·də·lōōs′, flour′-) *n. pl.* **flow·ers-de-luce** A flower of the iris variety. FLEUR-DE-LIS.

flow·er·et (flou′ər·it, flou′rit) *n.* A small flower, or a floret.

flower girl 1 A girl who sells flowers. **2** A small girl who carries flowers before the bride in a wedding procession.

flower head *Bot.* A dense headlike cluster of sessile florets.

flowering maple A plant *(Abutilon striatum)* with maplelike leaves and orange flowers veined in dark crimson: also called *redvein maple.*

flow·er-of-an-hour (flou′ər·uv·ən·our′, flour′-) *n.* The bladder ketmia.

flower pot A pot for holding growing plants.

flowers of benzoin See BENZOIN[1].

flow·me·ter (flō′mē′tər) *n.* An apparatus designed to measure the rate of flow of a liquid or a gas through any part of a transmitting system.

flown[1] (flōn) Past participle of FLY[1].

flown[2] (flōn) *adj.* **1** Coated, as a glaze, with color freely blended or flowed. **2** Eased off; slack, as a sheet. [<obs. pp. of FLOW]

flow relay *Electr.* A relay circuit adjusted to operate under specified conditions of flow in a gas or liquid.

flow-sheet (flō′shēt′) *n.* A diagram, chart, or expository outline showing the successive operations through which material progresses in a manufacturing process.

Floyd (floid) A masculine personal name. [<Welsh, gray]

flu (floo͞) *n. Colloq.* Influenza: a contraction.

flub (flub) *U.S. Colloq. v.t. & v.i.* **flubbed, flub·bing** To do or manage (something) badly; botch or bungle: to *flub* one's chance. —*n.* A blunder; failure. [Origin unknown]

flub·dub (flub′dub) *n.* **1** Drivel; twaddle; flapdoodle. **2** *Printing* An insignificant stock ornament. [Imit.] —**flub·dub′ber·y** *n.*

fluc·tu·ant (fluk′cho͞o·ənt) *adj.* **1** Showing fluctuation. **2** Moving or shaped like a wave.

fluc·tu·ate (fluk′cho͞o·āt) *v.* **·at·ed, ·at·ing** *v.i.* **1** To change or vary often and in an irregular manner; waver; be unsteady. **2** To move with successive rise and fall; undulate. —*v.t.* **3** To cause to fluctuate. [<L *fluctuatus,* pp. of *fluctuare* wave <*fluctus* a wave <*fluere* flow] —**fluc′tu·a·bil′i·ty** *n.* —**fluc′tu·a·ble** *adj.*

Synonyms: hesitate, oscillate, swerve, undulate, vacillate, vary, veer, waver. To *fluctuate* is to move like a wave with alternate rise and fall. A pendulum *oscillates;* waves *fluctuate* or *undulate;* a light or a flame *wavers;* a frightened steed *swerves* from his course; a tool or weapon *swerves* from the mark or line; the temperature *varies;* the wind *veers* when it suddenly changes its direction. That which *veers* may steadily hold the new direction; that which *oscillates, fluctuates, undulates,* or *wavers* returns upon its way. As regards mental states, he who *hesitates* sticks (L *haerere*) on the verge of decision; he who *wavers* does not stick to a decision; he who *vacillates* decides now one way, and now another; one *vacillates* between contrasted decisions or actions; he may *waver* between decision and indecision, or between action and inaction. Persons *hesitate, vacillate, waver;* feelings *fluctuate* or *vary.* Compare SHAKE. *Antonyms*: abide, adhere, persist.

fluc·tu·a·tion (fluk′cho͞o·ā′shən) *n.* **1** Frequent irregular change; varying movement or action. **2** A rising and falling, as of prices. **3** *Biol.* A variation in an organism which is not inherited.

flue[1] (floo͞) *n.* **1** A channel or passage for smoke, air, or gases of combustion; a chimney. **2** An organ pipe of flute or diapason quality. **3** Any of several types of fishing nets. Also spelled *flew.* [Origin uncertain]

flue[2] (floo͞) *n.* Any fine, flocklike refuse of wool or the like; lint; down. [<Flemish *vluwe* down]

flue[3] (floo͞) *n.* A fluke; barb, as of a harpoon, feather, or anchor. [Cf. Sw. *fly*]

flue gas The by-product of combustion in a heating system, consisting mostly of nitrogen, with varying proportions of carbon dioxide, oxygen, and, under improper conditions, carbon monoxide.

flu·ent (floo͞′ənt) *adj.* **1** Ready in speaking or writing; voluble; copious. **2** Marked by fluency; flowing; smooth. **3** Flowing freely; mobile; changeable. [<L *fluens, -entis,* ppr. of *fluere* flow] —**flu′en·cy** (-sē), **flu′ent·ness** *n.* —**flu′ent·ly** *adv.*

flue pipe *Music* An organ pipe in which the tone is produced by a current of air striking an aperture or flue.

flue stop *Music* A stop controlling the flue pipes of an organ.

flue·y (floo͞′ē) *adj.* Containing or like flue or lint; downy; fluffy.

fluff[1] (fluf) *n.* **1** Nap or down. **2** Anything downy or fluffy. **3** *Colloq.* An error made in reading or speaking (lines): said of actors, etc. —*v.t.* **1** To shake or pound so as to cause to puff out and become fluffy. **2** *Colloq.* To make an error in reading or speaking (lines). —*v.i.* **3** To become fluffy. **4** *Colloq.* To make a fluff (def. 3). [? Blend of FLUE[2] + PUFF]

fluff[2] (fluf) *n.* A flash, as of loose powder; puff. [Imit.]

fluff·y (fluf′ē) *adj.* **fluff·i·er, fluff·i·est** Downy; feathery. —**fluff′i·ly** *adv.* —**fluff′i·ness** *n.*

fluffy glider A flying phalanger *(Petaurus australis)* of Australia: also called *yellow-bellied glider.*

Flü·gel·horn (floo͞′gəl·hôrn′, *Ger.* flü′gəl·hôrn′) *n.* A brass wind instrument similar in pitch and design to a cornet yet mellower in tone. [<G *flügel* wing + *horn* a horn; so called from its shape]

flu·id (floo͞′id) *adj.* Capable of flowing; liquid or gaseous. —*n.* A substance that yields to any force tending to change its form; a liquid or gas. [<F *fluide* <L *fluidus* <*fluere* flow] —**flu·id′ic** *adj.* —**flu·id′i·ty, flu′id·ness** *n.* —**flu′id·ly** *adv.*

Synonyms (noun): gas, liquid. In comparison with the substance, *fluid,* a *liquid* is a body in a state in which the particles move freely among themselves, but remain in one mass, keeping the same volume, but taking always the form of the containing vessel; a *liquid* is an inelastic *fluid;* a gas is an elastic *fluid* that tends to expand to the utmost limits of the containing space. All *liquids* are *fluids,* but not all *fluids* are *liquids;* air and all the *gases* are *fluids,* but they are not *liquids* under ordinary circumstances, even if capable of being reduced to a *liquid* form by special means, as by cold and pressure. Water at the ordinary temperature is at once a *fluid* and a *liquid. Antonym*: solid.

fluid dram or **drachm** See under DRAM.

fluid drive An automobile transmission in which a driving rotor, turning in oil, transmits driving force to a driven rotor by forcing it to rotate in response to the action of the oil: usually automatically operated. Also called *hydraulic transmission.*

flu·id·ex·tract (floo͞′id·eks′trakt) *n.* A solution in alcohol of the active principle of a vegetable drug so prepared that 1 cubic centimeter has the strength of 1 gram of the dry drug.

fluid ounce See under OUNCE (def. 1).

fluid pressure See under PRESSURE.

flu·i·dram (floo͞′i·dram′) See FLUID DRAM under DRAM. Also **flu′i·drachm′.**

fluid wax Any liquid wax obtained from the oils of marine animals.

fluke[1] (flo͝ok) *n.* **1** *Naut.* The part of an anchor that holds to the ground. **2** One of the lobes of the tail of a whale. **3** A barb on a harpoon, arrow, etc. [? <FLUKE[2]]

FLUKE[1] *(def. 3)*

fluke[2] (flo͝ok) *n.* **1** A leaflike, parasitic, trematode worm infesting sheep, and also man and other animals: also called **fluke worm. 2** A flatfish or flounder. [OE *flōc*]

fluke[3] (flo͝ok) *n.* **1** A lucky stroke or accident, as in billiards, etc. **2** *Colloq.* An accidental failure or disappointment, as from a capricious wind in sailing. [Origin unknown]

fluk·y (floo͞′kē) *adj.* **fluk·i·er, fluk·i·est 1** Occurring by lucky chance. **2** Variable; capricious, as wind. Also **fluk′ey.**

flume (floo͞m) *n.* **1** A conduit, as for a millwheel. **2** A narrow passage through which a torrent passes. **3** A chute. —*v.t.* **flumed, flum·ing 1** To drain away or divert by means of a water chute or conduit, as in mining. **2** To move or transport, as logs, by means of a flume. See synonyms under STREAM. [<OF *flum* <L *flumen* river <*fluere* flow]

flu·mi·nous (floo͞′mə·nəs) *adj.* Of or pertaining to rivers; watered by streams. [<L *flumen, -inis* a river]

flum·mer·y (flum′er·ē) *n. pl.* **·mer·ies 1** A light dish made of flour or cornstarch; blanc-mange. **2** A glutinous refuse product of the manufacture of wheat starch. **3** Originally, a dish of oatmeal steeped in water and turned sour; pap. **4** Hence, anything vapid or insipid; empty compliment; flimsy show; humbug. [<Welsh *llymru*]

flum·mox (flum′əks) *v.t. Slang* To confuse; confound; perplex. [Cf. dial. E *flummocks* maul, mangle]

flump (flump) *v.t. & v.i. Colloq.* To drop heavily and clumsily; flop. —*n.* The act of flumping or the sound so produced. [Imit.]

flung (flung) Past tense and past participle of FLING.

flunk (flungk) *U.S. Colloq. v.t.* **1** To fail in, as an examination. **2** To give a failing grade to. —*v.i.* **3** To fail, as in an examination. **4** To back out; give up. —**to flunk out** To leave or cause to leave a class, school, or college because of failure in studies. —*n.* A complete failure; a giving up. [? Blend of FLINCH and FUNK]

flunk·y (flung′kē) *n. pl.* **flunk·ies 1** An obsequious fellow; servile imitator; toady. **2** A servant in livery. Also **flunk′ey.** [? Alter. of *flanker* <FLANK, *v.*] —**flunk′y·ism** *n.*

fluo- See FLUORO-.

flu·o·bo·rate (floo͞′ō·bôr′āt, -bō′rāt) *n. Chem.* **1** The negative ion BO_2Fe_2. **2** Any compound containing this ion.

flu·o·phos·phate (floo͞′ō·fos′fāt) *n. Chem.* A double salt of hydrofluoric and phosphoric acids.

flu·or (floo͞′ər, -ôr) *n.* Fluorite. [<NL <L, a flowing <*fluere* flow; a trans. of G *flusse*]

fluor- Var. of FLUORO-.

flu·or·an (floo͞′ə·ran) *n. Chem.* A crystalline anhydride, $C_{20}H_{12}O_3$, fluorescing in solution, formed as a by-product in making phenolphthalein. Also **flu′or·ane** (-ə·rān).

flu·or·ap·a·tite (floo͞′ə·rap′ə·tīt) *n.* Apatite in which fluorine but little or no chlorine is present.

flu·o·rate (floo͞′ə·rāt, -rit) *n. Chem.* **1** The negative ion FO_3. **2** Any compound containing this ion.

flu·o·resce (floo͞′ə·res′) *v.i.* **·resced, ·resc·ing** To become fluorescent; exhibit fluorescence. [Back formation <FLUORESCENCE]

flu·o·res·ce·in (floo͞′ə·res′ē·in) *n. Chem.* A dark-red crystalline compound, $C_{20}H_{12}O_5$, obtained by heating phthalic anhydride, and subsequent separation: used in medicine and in the making of dyestuffs. Also **flu′o·res′ce·ine** (-ēn).

flu·o·res·cence (floo͞′ə·res′əns) *n. Physics* **1** The property of certain substances to absorb radiation of a particular wavelength and to re-emit it as light of a different, usually greater, wavelength; the emitted radiation persists only as long as the stimulus is active: distinguished from *phosphorescence.* **2** The light so produced. [<FLUOR(SPAR); coined on analogy with OPALESCENCE]

flu·o·res·cent (floo͞′ə·res′ənt) *adj.* Having or exhibiting fluorescence.

fluorescent lamp An electric-discharge lamp, usually tubular in shape, containing a metallic vapor which becomes luminous on the passing of the current and energizes a layer of fluorescent material coating the tube.

fluorescent screen A surface of glass coated with a fluorescent material, as platinocyanide; it fluoresces on exposure to electron bombardment and is used in cathode-ray vacuum tubes.

flu·or·ic (floo͞·ôr′ik, -or′-) *adj.* Pertaining to, derived from, or containing fluorine or fluorite.

fluor·i·date (flo͝or′ə·dāt, floo͞′ə·ri·dāt) *v.t.* **·dat·ed, ·dat·ing** To add sodium fluoride to (drinking water), especially as a means of preventing tooth decay. —**fluor′i·da′tion** *n.*

flu·o·ride (floo͞′ə·rīd, -rid) *n. Chem.* A binary compound of fluorine and another element. Also **flu′o·rid** (-rid).

fluor·i·dize (flo͝or′ə·dīz, floo͞′ə·ri·dīz) *v.t.* **·dized, ·diz·ing** To treat (teeth) with a fluoride, especially as a preventive of tooth decay. —**fluor′i·di·za′tion** *n.*

flu·o·rim·e·ter (floo͞′ə·rim′ə·tər) *n. Physics* An absorbing screen used to measure the intensity of fluorescence from different sources, as X-rays, radium, etc.

flu·o·ri·na·tion (floo͞′ər·i·nā′shən, flo͝or′ə–) *n.* The act or process of introducing fluorine into an organic compound.

flu·o·rine (floo͞′ə·rēn, -rin) *n.* A pale yellow, toxic, corrosive gaseous element (symbol F, atomic number 9), the most electronegative and reactive of all elements. See PERIODIC TABLE.

flu·o·rite (flo͞o′ə·rīt) *n.* A cleavable, isometric, variously colored calcium fluoride, CaF_2: used as a flux in making steel and glass: also called *fluor, fluorspar.*

fluoro- *combining form* **1** *Chem.* Indicating the presence of fluorine in a compound. **2** Fluorescence: *fluoroscope*: also, before vowels, *fluor-*, as in *fluoride.*

flu·o·ro·car·bon (flo͞o′ə·rō·kär′bən) *n. Chem.* Any of a group of very stable compounds in which hydrogen has been replaced by fluorine: used as solvents, lubricants, and insulators.

flu·or·o·chem·i·cal (flo͞o′ə·rō·kem′ə·kəl) *n.* Any of various chemicals containing fluorine, as the fluorocarbons.

flu·or·om·e·try (flo͞o′ə·rom′ə·trē) *n.* The measurement of the color and intensity of fluorescence.

fluor·o·scope (flo͝or′ə·skōp, flo͞o′ər·ə-) *n.* A device for observing, by means of some fluorescent substance, the shadows of objects enclosed in media opaque to ordinary light, but transparent to X-rays. **—fluor′o·scop′ic** (-skop′ik) *adj.*

fluor·os·co·py (flo͝or·os′kə·pē, flo͞o′ə·ros′-) *n.* Examination conducted by means of a fluoroscope.

flu·or·o·sis (flo͞o′ə·rō′sis, flo͞o·rō′-) *n. Pathol.* Chronic poisoning with fluorine.

flu·or·spar (flo͞o′ôr·spär′, flo͞o′ər-) *n.* Fluorite.

flu·o·sil·i·cate (flo͞o′ə·sil′ə·kāt, -kit) *n. Chem.* A salt of silicic acid.

flu·o·si·lic·ic (flo͞o′ə·sə·lis′ik) *adj.* **1** Of, pertaining to, or containing fluorine and silicon. **2** Designating a colorless suffocating gaseous compound, **fluosilicic acid,** H_2SiF_6, formed by the action of hydrofluoric acid on silica.

flur·ry (flûr′ē) *v.* **·ried, ·ry·ing** *v.t.* To bewilder or confuse; agitate; fluster. *—v.i.* To move in a flurry. [< *n.*] *—n. pl.* **flur·ries 1** A sudden commotion; nervous agitation. **2** Flutter; hurry. **3** A light gust of wind. **4** A light snowfall or rain. **5** The spasmodic contortions of a dying whale. See synonyms under TUMULT. [Blend of FLUTTER and HURRY]

flush[1] (flush) *v.i.* **1** To become red in the face or overspread with color; redden; blush. **2** To flow and spread suddenly; rush: The blood *flushes* in his veins. **3** To be washed out or cleansed by a sudden flow of water. *—v.t.* **4** To cause to color, as with a rush of blood; make red or florid. **5** To encourage; excite: *flushed* with victory. **6** To wash out by a flow of water, as a sewer or an obstacle. *—n.* **1** A heightened color; warm glow; blush. **2** Sudden elation or excitement. **3** A sudden blossoming out; growth; bloom. **4** A sudden gush or flow of water. *—adj.* **1** Full of life; vigorous. **2** Powerful and direct, as a blow. *—adv.* In a direct manner; squarely; straight. [? < FLUSH[4]; infl. in meaning by *flash, flow, bluish,* etc.] **—flush′er** *n.*

flush[2] (flush) *adj.* **1** Having the surfaces in the same plane; level. **2** *Printing* Set even with the left edge of the type page; having no indention. **3** *Naut.* Of or pertaining to a ship with an upper deck extending in one level from stern to stern. **4** Full; copious. **5** Well supplied with money; spending freely. *—v.t.* To make level or straight. *—n.* **1** A level or unbroken surface. **2** Abundance. *—adv.* **1** With level, unbroken surface or form. **2** *Printing* Without indention; straight. [? < FLUSH[1]]

flush[3] (flush) *n.* In some card games, a hand of cards all of one color; specifically, in poker, of one suit. **—royal flush** A hand of cards containing the ace, king, queen, jack, and ten of one suit. **—straight flush** A poker hand having all the cards of the same suit and in sequence. [Cf. F *flux, flus* < L *fluxus* A flow]

flush[4] (flush) *v.t. & v.i.* To drive or to be startled from cover; start up, as birds. *—n.* The act of startling a bird; also a bird or birds startled from cover. [ME *flusschen;* origin uncertain]

flush·board (flush′bôrd′, -bōrd′) *n.* A flashboard.

Flush·ing (flush′ing) **1** A port in SW Netherlands, on the English Channel: Dutch *Vlissingen.* **2** A section of the Borough of Queens, New York City, including **Flushing Meadow,** site of the 1939–40 World's Fair and headquarters of the United Nations, 1946–51.

flus·ter (flus′tər) *v.t. & v.i.* To make or become confused, agitated, or befuddled. *—n.* Confusion of mind; flurry; intoxication. [Cf. Icel. *flaustr* hurry]

flus·trate (flus′trāt) *v.t.* **·trat·ed, ·trat·ing** To fluster; befuddle. Also **flus′ter·ate.** [< FLUSTER + -ATE[1]] **—flus′ter·a′tion, flus·tra′tion** *n.*

flute (flo͞ot) *n.* **1** A tubular wind instrument of small diameter with holes along the side. **2** A flute stop in an organ; flue. **3** *Archit.* A groove, usually of semicircular section, as in a column. **4** A corrugation; crimping. **5** A tall, slender wineglass. *—v.* **flut·ed, flut·ing.** *—v.i.* **1** To play on a flute. **2** To produce a flutelike sound. *—v.t.* **3** To sing or utter with flutelike tones. **4** To make flutes in, as a column. [< OF *flaüte*] **—flut′y** *adj.*

FLUTE

flut·ed (flo͞o′tid) *adj.* **1** Having parallel grooves or flutes. **2** Having the tone of a flute.

flut·er (flo͞o′tər) *n.* **1** A flutist. **2** One who or that which makes fluted work.

flut·ing (flo͞o′ting) *n.* **1** A flute or groove. **2** Flutes or grooves collectively. **3** The act of making a flute, as by carving a column: the reverse of *reeding.* **4** A crimp, as in the ruffle of a woman's dress.

flut·ist (flo͞o′tist) *n.* A flute-player: also called *flautist.*

flut·ter (flut′ər) *v.i.* **1** To wave or flap rapidly and irregularly, as in the wind. **2** To flap the wings rapidly, in or as in erratic flight. **3** To move or proceed with irregular motion: to *flutter* to the ground. **4** To move about lightly and quickly; flit. **5** To be excited or nervous, as with hope, fear, or expectation. *—v.t.* **6** To cause to flutter. **7** To excite; fluster. See synonyms under SHAKE. *—n.* **1** The act of vibrating or quivering. **2** Agitation; confused or tumultous emotion. **3** An up-and-down motion of the feet used in various swimming strokes, especially the crawl. **4** *Aeron.* A periodic oscillation set up in any part of an airplane by mechanical disturbances and maintained by inertia, structural characteristics, etc. **5** Tremololike pulsations in the sound track of a motion picture, due to rapid fluctuations in motor speed. **6** *Pathol.* An abnormally rapid but rhythmical contraction of the atria of the heart; also **auricular flutter.** [OE *flotorian*] **—flut′ter·er** *n.* **—flut′ter·y** *adj.*

flutter kick In swimming, a kick, usually performed with the crawl stroke, in which the legs are kept almost straight while being moved up and down rapidly.

flu·vi·al (flo͞o′vē·əl) *adj.* **1** Of, pertaining to or formed by a river. **2** Existing in a river. Also **flu·vi·at·ic** (flo͞o′vē·at′ik), **flu·vi·a·tile** (flo͞o′vē·ə·til). [< L *fluvialis* < *fluvius* river]

fluvio- *combining form* River: *fluviograph.* [< L *fluvius* a river]

flu·vi·o·graph (flo͞o′vē·ə·graf′, -gräf′) *n.* A mechanical contrivance for measuring the rise and fall of a river.

flu·vi·o·ma·rine (flo͞o′vē·ō′mə·rēn′) *adj.* Formed by or pertaining to the joint action of the sea and flowing streams, as delta deposits.

flux (fluks) *n.* **1** A continuous flowing or discharge: a thermal or electrical *flux.* **2** The act or process of melting. **3** *Pathol.* A morbid discharge of fluid matter from the body. **4** *Metall.* A substance that promotes the fusing of minerals or metals, as borax. **5** Any readily fusible glass or enamel used as a base or ground in ceramic work. **6** *Physics* The rate of flow or transfer of water, heat, electricity, etc. **7** A state of constant movement: the *flux* of the tide. See synonyms under STREAM. **—bloody flux** Dysentery. *—v.t.* **1** To make fluid; melt; fuse. **2** To treat, as metal, with a flux. **3** *Obs.* To purge. *—v.i.* **4** *Obs.* To flow; move. [< F < L *fluxus* < *fluere* flow] **—flux·a′tion** *n.*

flux density *Physics* The induction of lines of electrical or magnetic force per unit section.

flux·ion (fluk′shən) *n.* **1** The act of flowing or melting; that which flows or melts; continuous change. **2** *Math. Obs.* The rate of variation of a changing quantity; also, a differential. **3** *Pathol.* An abnormal or excessive flow of body fluids.

flux·ion·al (fluk′shən·əl) *adj.* **1** *Obs.* Of or pertaining to mathematical fluxions. **2** *Obs.* Of a nature to flow. Also **flux′ion·ar′y.** **—flux′·ion·al·ly** *adv.*

fly[1] (flī) *v.* **flew** or **flied** (def. 7), **flown, fly·ing** *v.i.* **1** To move through the air by using wings, as a bird. **2** To move through the air in an aircraft; travel by aircraft. **3** To move through the air with speed, as an arrow or bullet. **4** To wave or move in the air, as a flag. **5** To pass swiftly: The years *flew* by. **6** To move swiftly or with violence: The door *flew* open. **7** In baseball, to bat a fly. **8** To take flight; flee. **9** In hawking, to hunt with or as with a hawk. *—v.t.* **10** To cause to wave or float in the air. **11** To operate (an aircraft). **12** To pass over in an aircraft: to *fly* the Atlantic. **13** To transport by aircraft. **14** To flee from. **15** In hawking, to hunt with a hawk. **—to fly at** To attack. **—to fly in the face of** To defy openly. **—to fly out** In baseball, to be retired by batting a ball which is caught by an opposing player before it touches the ground. *—n. pl.* **flies. 1** An object or device that moves or swings rapidly through the air, or has some relation to such motion. **2** A speed-regulating device, as of vanes upon a rotating shaft, used in music boxes, in the striking part of clocks. **3** *Printing* A long-fingered frame oscillating quickly upon a horizontal axis, taking the sheets from the tapes or cylinder of a printing press and delivering them flat upon a pile. **4** A knitting-machine latch. **5** The length of a flag measured from the staff to its farthest edge, as distinguished from the *hoist.* **6** That part of a flag farthest from the staff, or beyond the canton. **7** The revolving part of a vane that shows the direction of the wind. **8** *Mech.* **a** A flywheel, a weighted arm, or other mechanical device involving the flywheel principle. **b** The heavily weighted lever which enables a fly press to acquire momentum. **c** A fly press. **9** A strip or lap on a garment, to cover the buttons or other fasteners; hence, something used to cover or connect; a flap, as of a bootee. **10** An upper covering to a ridge-pole tent; also, the flap at the entrance of a tent. **11** The condition or movement of a ball when sent flying through the air as in baseball; also, the ball thus flying. **12** Waste cotton. **13** The act or state of flying; flight. **14** A public carriage; also, a delivery wagon. **15** In a theater, the space above the stage and behind the proscenium containing the borders, the mechanism for handling and setting the scenery, the overhead lights, etc. **—on the fly** While flying; while in the air; in haste. [OE *flēogan*]

Synonyms (verb): flee, flit, haste, hasten, run, soar, speed. See ESCAPE.

fly[2] (flī) *n. pl.* **flies 1** One of various small dipterous insects (family *Muscidae*), especially the common housefly *(Musca domestica).* **2** Any of various other flying insects not of the family *Muscidae*: the Spanish *fly,* or the *mayfly.* **3** A fish hook concealed by feathers, etc., to imitate some insect. **4** *pl.* **flys** A light carriage. [OE *flȳge*]

fly[3] (flī) *adj. Slang* Sharp; wide-awake.

fly·a·gar·ic (flī′ə·gar′ik, -ag′ə·rik) *n.* A common species of poisonous mushroom *(Amanita muscaria)* with a brightly colored pileus. Also **fly-am·a·ni·ta** (-am′ə·nī′tə).

fly·a·way (flī′ə·wā′) *adj.* Disposed to flightiness; fluttering; restless; giddy. *—n.* A person or thing that is flighty, swift, or elusive.

fly·blow (flī′blō′) *n.* The egg or young larva of a blowfly. *—v.t. & v.t.* **·blew, ·blown, ·blow·ing 1** To taint (food) with flyblows. **2** To spoil.

fly·blown (flī′blōn′) *adj.* Tainted with flyblows.

fly·boat (flī′bōt′) *n.* **1** A large flat-bottomed Dutch coasting boat. **2** A narrow English canal boat. **3** Any very swift vessel.

fly book A booklike case for holding artificial flies.

fly-by (flī′bī′) *n. pl.* **-bys** The passage of a spacecraft relatively near a heavenly body, as for obtaining photographs of its surface.

fly-by-night (flī′bī·nīt′) *adj.* Financially precarious or irresponsible. *—n.* One who is financially insecure or untrustworthy; one who cheats a creditor by decamping at night.

fly·catch·er (flī′kach′ər) *n.* Any of a large order of perching birds *(Passeriformes)* that feed upon insects; especially, the American tyrant flycatcher (family *Tyrannidae*) and the Old World flycatcher (family *Muscicapidae*)–**least flycatcher** A small American flycatcher; the chebec *(Empidonax minimus).*

fly·er (flī′ər) See FLIER.

fly-fish (flī′fish′) *v.i.* To fish with artificial flies as bait. **—fly′-fish′ing** *n.*

fly·flap·per (flī′flap′ər) *n.* A device for whisking flies.

fly·frame (flī′frām′) *n.* Any of several machines used to draw and twist textile fibers preparatory to spinning, as a roving frame.

fly-front (flī′frunt′) *adj.* Having a fly that covers buttons or a zipper.

fly·ing (flī′ing) *adj.* **1** Intended or adapted for swift or easy motion, or motion through the air; moving with or as with wings. **2** Moving rapidly or continuously; hurried: a *flying* bird or trip. **3** Floating or suspended so as to float in the air: a *flying* banner. **4** Extending or being beyond the ordinary; extra: a *flying* jib. —*n.* **1** The act of flight; flight, as of a bird or an aircraft. **2** *pl.* Loose material, as fibers, floating in the air. —**instrument flying** Navigation of an aircraft by means of instruments alone: also called **blind flying.**

flying boat A large seaplane, supported on water by its own hull rather than by floats.

flying bomb See under BOMB.

flying buttress *Archit.* A rampant arch extending from a wall or pier to a supporting abutment, usually receiving the thrust of another arch on the other side of the wall.

flying cadet An aviation cadet.

flying circus **1** In World War I, a squadron of fighter planes. **2** Aerial acrobatics performed by several planes. **3** The group giving such a performance.

flying colors Outward signs of victory or success: an allusion to passing through combat without striking the colors.

flying column *Mil.* A body of troops equipped to move swiftly and operate independently of the main force.

flying doctor *Austral.* A physician serving with the Royal Flying Doctor Service, which since 1928 has been providing medical care in remote inland places.

Flying Dutchman **1** A spectral Dutch ship supposed to be seen near the Cape of Good Hope in stormy weather: an omen of bad luck. **2** The captain of this ship, doomed to sail the seas forever for his sins: subject of an opera (1843) by Richard Wagner.

flying fatigue Aeroneurosis.

flying field *Aeron.* A field with a graded portion for taking off and landing and an unimproved area for flying operations.

flying fish A fish (family *Exocoetidae*) of warm and temperate seas, with large pectoral fins that enable it to glide through the air for short distances.

fly·ing-fox (flī′ing·foks′) *n.* A large fruit-eating bat, especially a genus *(Pteropus)* of the warmer parts of the Old World, with foxlike snout.

flying frog A ranoid tree frog *(Rhacophorus pardalis)* of Borneo, having elongated, webbed toes which serve as supports during leaps.

flying gurnard A marine fish (family *Dactylopteridae*) having very long horizontal pectoral fins divided into a smaller upper and a longer lower or posterior portion and able to flutter for short distances in the air.

flying jib, flying-jib boom See under JIB[1].

flying lemur An insect-eating mammal (genus *Cynocephalus*) having the fore and hind limbs connected by a fold of skin, by the aid of which it makes flying leaps: native of East Indies: also called *colugo.*

flying lizard A dragon (def. 6).

flying machine **1** An aircraft which is sustained by aerodynamic forces; an airplane. **2** An airship.

fly·ing-mare (flī′ing·mâr′) *n.* In wrestling, a throw accomplished by seizing an opponent's wrist, turning around and jerking the opponent over one's shoulder.

flying officer An officer who belongs to the crew of an aircraft, as a pilot, navigator, bombardier, or the like.

flying phalanger Any of several arboreal marsupials (genera *Acrobates, Petaurus, Schoinobates*) of Australia and New Guinea, having folds of skin along the sides that enable them to make long, gliding leaps. Also called *glider, gliding possum, possum glider.*

flying saucer Any of various oddly shaped objects alleged to have been seen flying at high altitudes; an unidentified flying object (UFO).

flying squirrel A squirrel (genus *Glaucomys*) having on each side a fold of skin forming a parachute, by the help of which the animal can make long sailing leaps.

FLYING SQUIRREL
(Head and body about 5 inches long; tail, 4 inches)

flying start **1** In racing, the passing of the starting post at full speed. **2** Any rapid beginning.

flying trip A quick, hurried trip.

flying wing **1** An airplane without a fuselage. **2** *Canadian* In football, a player whose position varies behind the line of scrimmage.

fly·leaf (flī′lēf′) *n. pl.* **·leaves** A blank leaf at the beginning or end of a book, pamphlet, or similar printed matter.

fly·net (flī′net′) *n.* **1** A net worn by horses to keep off flies. **2** Any netting, as in a window, for excluding insects.

fly-o·ver (flī′ō′vər) *n.* A public display of military aircraft as a demonstration of strength, variety of types, and maneuverability; a military air show. Also **fly′-past′** (-past′).

fly·pa·per (flī′pā′pər) *n.* An adhesive paper, or one impregnated with poison, for catching or killing flies.

fly press A press for stamping and punching metal blanks, equipped with a hand screw and a heavily weighted cross arm.

fly·speck (flī′spek′) *n.* **1** The dot made by the excrement of a fly. **2** Any slight speck. —*v.t.* To mark with flyspecks.

fly·stone (flī′stōn′) *n.* Cobalt, used as a poison for flies, worms, etc., when ground and mixed with sugar and water.

fly·trap (flī′trap′) *n.* **1** A trap for catching flies. **2** An insectivorous plant, as the pitcher plant and the Venus flytrap.

fly·weight (flī′wāt′) *n.* A boxer weighing 112 lbs. or less: the lightest weight class.

fly·wheel (flī′hwēl′) *n.* A heavy wheel whose weight resists sudden changes of speed, thus securing uniform motion in the working parts of an engine or machine.

Fm *Chem.* Fermium (symbol Fm).

F N 300 A gas-operated, clip-fed rifle designed in Belgium and manufactured in England, having a bore of 7.62 mm, and capable of full automatic fire at 650 to 700 rounds per minute. It supersedes the Lee Enfield as the standard British service weapon. [from *F(abrique) N(ationale d'Armes de Guerre),* where it was designed]

F-num·ber (ef′num′bər) *n. Phot.* A number obtained by dividing the focal length of a lens by its effective diameter: the smaller the F-number, the wider the aperture and the shorter the exposure required: also called *F-stop.* Also **F, F/, F:, f, f/, f·.**

Fo (fō) Buddha: the Chinese name.

foal (fōl) *n.* The young of an equine animal; a colt. —*v.t.* & *v.i.* To give birth to (a foal). [OE *fola*]

foam (fōm) *n.* **1** A collection of minute bubbles forming a frothy mass. **2** *Chem.* A colloid system of gas dispersed in liquid. **3** Frothy saliva or sweat. **4** The white crest of a breaking wave; hence, the sea. **5** Figuratively, rage or fury. —*v.i.* To gather, produce, or form foam; froth. —*v.t.* To cause to foam. [OE *fam*] **—foam′less** *adj.*

foam·flow·er (fōm′flou′ər) *n.* A hardy herbaceous perennial *(Tiarella cordifolia)* of the saxifrage family, with purple or red flowers and decorative foliage.

Foam·ite (fō′mīt) *n.* A fire-extinguishing substance composed of licorice in a solution of bicarbonate of soda; in contact with flame it yields a heavy foam which smothers the fire: a trade name.

foam rubber Natural or synthetic rubber which has been treated with various chemicals and expanded into a cellular structure adapted for a wide range of uses as an insulating and buoyancy material and in upholstery.

foam·y (fō′mē) *adj.* **foam·i·er, foam·i·est** Covered with or full of foam; foamlike. **—foam′i·ly** *adv.* **—foam′i·ness** *n.*

fob[1] (fob) *n.* **1** A watch pocket in the waistband of trousers. **2** A chain or ribbon hanging from it; also, an ornament on a watch chain or ribbon. [Cf. dial. G *fuppe* a pocket]

fob[2] (fob) *v.t.* **fobbed, fob·bing** *Archaic* To cheat; trick: also spelled *fub.* **—to fob off** **1** To dispose of or palm off by craft or deceit. **2** To put off; attempt to placate, as with promises. [? < FOB[1]]

fo·cal (fō′kəl) *adj.* Pertaining to, at, or limited to a certain point or focus.

focal epilepsy Jacksonian epilepsy.

focal infection *Pathol.* An infection originating in and often spreading from a circumscribed region of the body.

fo·cal·ize (fō′kəl·īz) *v.t.* & *v.i.* **·ized, ·iz·ing** **1** To adjust or come to a focus; focus. **2** *Med.* To confine or be confined to a small area, as an infection. **—fo′cal·i·za′tion** *n.*

focal length *Optics* The distance from the second principal plane of a lens or mirror to the point where rays from a distant object converge. Also **focal distance.**

Foch (fôsh), **Ferdinand,** 1851–1929, marshal of France; commander in chief (1918) of the Allied Armies on the western front in World War I.

fo'c's'le (fōk′səl) *n. Naut.* Forecastle.

fo·cus (fō′kəs) *n. pl.* **·cus·es** or **·ci** (-sī) **1** *Optics* **a** The point to which a system of light rays converges after passage through a lens or other optical arrangement, or after reflection from a mirror. **b** The point from which such rays appear to diverge. **c** The place where a visual image is clearly formed, as in the eye or a camera. The point of convergence of the rays is called the **real focus;** the point where diverging rays would meet if their directions were reversed is called the **virtual focus.** **2** *Physics* The meeting point of any system of rays, beams, or waves: an acoustic *focus.* **3** *Geom.* **a** One of two points, the sum or difference of whose distances to a conic section is a constant. **b** A point in some other curve, having similar properties. **4** Any central point: the *focus* of an earthquake. —*v.t.* & *v.i.* **fo·cused** or **fo·cussed, fo·cus·ing** or **fo·cus·sing** **1** To adjust the focus of (the eye or an optical instrument). **2** To bring or come to a focus or point, as rays. [< L, hearth] **—fo′cal** *adj.*

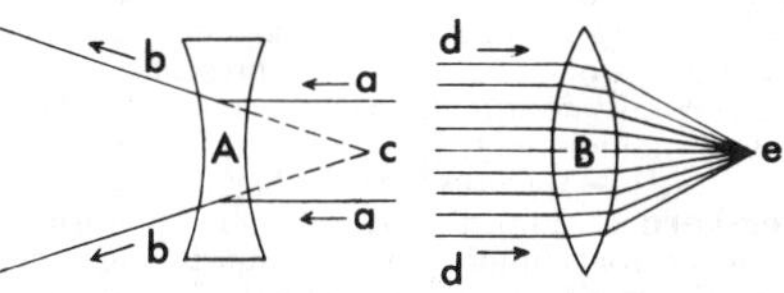

FOCI
A. Concavo-concave lens—showing light rays *a, a,* refracting as at *b, b,* and forming the virtual focus at *c.*
B. Convexo-convex lens—showing light rays *d, d,* converging to the principal focus at *e.*

fod·der (fod′ər) *n.* Coarse feed, for horses, cattle, etc., as the stalks and leaves of field corn. See synonyms under FOOD. —*v.t.* To supply with fodder. [OE *fōdor*]

fodg·el (foj′əl) *adj. Scot.* Fat; corpulent; squat.

foe (fō) *n.* **1** One actively hostile. **2** A hostile force; an enemy; adversary. **3** One who or that which opposes or injures; anything injurious or detrimental. See synonyms under ENEMY. [Fusion of OE *fah* hostile and *gefa* an enemy]

foehn (fœn) *n. Meteorol.* A warm and dry southerly wind of Alpine valleys: also spelled *föhn, fön.* [< dial. G *föhn* < L *Favonius,* the west wind]

foe·man (fō′mən) *n. pl.* **·men** (-mən) An active or open enemy.

foe·tal (fē′təl), **foe·ta·tion** (fē·tā′shən), **foe·tus** (fē′təs), etc. See FETAL, etc.

fog[1] (fog, fôg) *n. Agric.* **1** Dead or decaying grass. **2** Aftermath (def. 2). Also *foggage.*

[ME *fogge,* prob. <Scand. Cf. Norw. *fogg* long grass on wet ground.] **— fog'gy** *adj.*

fog[2] (fog, fôg) *n.* **1** Condensed watery vapor suspended in the atmosphere at or near the earth's surface. **2** *Chem.* A colloid system of the liquid-in-gas type (see COLLOID SYSTEM). **3** *Meteorol.* Any hazy condition of the atmosphere, or the material causing it: a dust *fog.* **4** Bewilderment; obscurity. **5** *Phot.* A coating obscuring a developed photographic plate. **— *v.* fogged, fog·ging** *v.t.* **1** To surround with or as with fog. **2** To confuse; bewilder. **3** *Phot.* To cloud (a plate) with a fog. **—** *v.i.* **4** To become foggy. [Prob. back formation <*foggy,* in the sense "marshy" <FOG[1]; infl. in meaning by Dan. *fog* spray]

Fo·gaz·za·ro (fō'gät·tsä'rō), **Antonio,** 1842–1911, Italian novelist and poet.

fog bank A mass of fog seen at a distance, especially at sea.

fog·bound (fog'bound', fôg'-) *adj.* Detained by fog; prevented because of fog from traveling, sailing, flying, etc.

fog·bow (fog'bō', fôg'-) *n. Meteorol.* A white or very faintly colored arc of light seen opposite the sun in fog.

fog chamber A cloud chamber. See under CHAMBER.

fog dog A clearing spot in a fog bank, indicating the lifting of the fog: also called *sea dog.*

fog·fruit (fog'fro͞ot', fôg'-) *n.* An American creeping plant (genus *Lippia*) of the vervain family bearing closely bracted heads of bluish-white flowers, especially *L. lanceolata.*

fog·gage (fog'ij, fôg'-) *n.* **1** Long grass, left standing over winter, for feeding cattle in the spring. **2** The privilege of pasturing cattle on fog; also, such pasturing.

Fog·gia (fôd'jä) A city in southern Italy.

fog·gy (fog'ē, fôg'ē) *adj.* **fog·gi·er, fog·gi·est** **1** Full of or marked by the presence of fog. **2** Mentally confused; obscure; cloudy. **3** *Phot.* Fogged; indistinct. See synonyms under THICK. [<FOG[1]] **— fog'gi·ly** *adv.* **— fog'gi·ness** *n.*

fog·horn (fog'hôrn', fôg'-) *n.* **1** A horn or whistle for sounding a warning during a fog on the water: also **fog'-sig'nal, fog'-whis'tle.** **2** Hence, a powerful, harsh voice.

fo·gy (fō'gē) *n. pl.* **fo·gies** A person of old-fashioned notions. **—** *adj.* Old-fashioned; out-of-date; fusty. Also **fo'gey, fo'gie.** [? <FOGGY] **— fo'gy·ish** *adj.* **— fo'gy·ism** *n.*

fogy pay *U.S. Mil. Slang* Longevity pay. Also **fo'gey pay.**

foh (fô) *interj.* An exclamation of contempt, dislike, or disgust. [Var. of FAUGH]

föhn (fœn) See FOEHN.

foi·ble (foi'bəl) *n.* **1** A personal weakness; slight fault of character. **2** The portion of a sword blade or foil blade from the middle to the point: distinguished from *forte.* [<F, obs. var. of *faible* FEEBLE]

Synonyms: defect, error, failing, frailty, imperfection, infirmity, peccadillo, weakness.

foil[1] (foil) *v.t.* **1** To prevent the success of; balk; frustrate; baffle. **2** In hunting, to cross and recross (a scent or trail) so as to confuse pursuers. See synonyms under BAFFLE, HINDER[1]. **—** *n.* **1** *Archaic* A thwarting; frustration. **2** In wrestling, an incomplete fall. **3** An animal's trail. [<OF *fouler, fuler* crush, trample down <LL *fullare* full cloth <*fullo* a fuller]

foil[2] (foil) *n.* **1** Metal in very thin pliable sheets or leaves. **2** A leaf of bright metal placed by jewelers beneath an inferior gem to heighten the color or luster. **3** Anything serving to adorn or set off by contrast something different or superior. **4** The reflecting amalgam on the back of a mirror. **5** *Archit.* A leaflike division in ornamentation; a lobe, as in tracery. A group of three foils is called *trefoil*; of four, *quatrefoil*; of five, *cinquefoil*; etc. **6** *Obs.* A leaf. **—** *v.t.* **1** To apply foil to; cover with foil. **2** To intensify or set off by contrast. **3** *Archit.* To adorn, as windows, with foils. [<OF <L *folium* leaf]

FOILS (*def. 5*)
Foliated tracery in Gothic window, Grace Church Chantry, New York.

foil[3] (foil) *n.* **1** A blunted rapierlike implement, sometimes having a button on its end, used in fencing. **2** The art of fencing. [Origin uncertain]

foiled (foild) *adj.* Having foils, as a window.

foils·man (foilz'mən) *n. pl.* **·men** (-mən) A fencer; one skilled in fencing.

foin (foin) *Obs. v.i.* To lunge or thrust, with or as with a weapon. **—** *n.* A thrust or pass with a weapon. [<OF *foine* a fishspear <L *fuscina*]

Fo·ism (fō'iz·əm) *n.* Chinese Buddhism. [<Fo] **— Fo'ist** *n.*

foi·son (foi'zən) *n. Archaic* **1** Power, strength. **2** *pl.* Resources. **3** Abundance. [<OF, a pouring out <L *fusio, -onis* <*fundere* pour]

foist (foist) *v.t.* **1** To put in or introduce slyly or improperly: to *foist* a candidate on a party. **2** To pass off (something spurious) as genuine. [Prob. <dial. Du. *vuisten* hold in the hand, palm]

Fo·kine (fô·kēn', *Russ.* fô'kin), **Michel,** 1880–1942, U.S. choreographer born in Russia.

Fok·ker (fok'ər), **Anthony H. G.,** 1890–1939, Dutch airplane designer active in Germany and the United States.

fold[1] (fōld) *v.t.* **1** To turn back (something) upon itself one or more times. **2** To bring down upon itself; close; collapse: to *fold* an umbrella; to *fold* wings. **3** To place together and interlock: to *fold* one's hands. **4** To wrap up; enclose. **5** To mix, as beaten egg whites or whipped cream, into other ingredients, by gently turning one part over the other with a spoon: with *in.* **6** To embrace; enfold: She *folded* him in her arms. **—** *v.i.* **7** To come together in folds. **8** *U.S. Slang* To fail; close: often with *up.* **—** *n.* **1** One part doubled over another; a plait; ply; a lap; also, the space between two folded-over parts. **2** The crease made by folding. **3** *Geol.* A smooth bend or flexure in a layer of rock; an anticline or syncline. **4** That which envelops; an embrace. [OE *fealdan*]

fold[2] (fōld) *n.* **1** A pen, as for sheep. **2** A flock of sheep. **3** Any group needing care, as the congregation of a church. **4** *Brit. Dial.* A farmstead. **—** *v.t.* To shut up in a fold, as sheep. [OE *fald*]

-fold *suffix* **1** Having (a specified number of) parts: a *threefold* blessing. **2** (A specified number of) times as great, or as much: to reward *tenfold.* [OE *-feald* <*fealdan* fold]

fold·boat (fōld'bōt') *n.* A faltboat.

fold·er (fōl'dər) *n.* **1** One who or that which folds. **2** A timetable or other printed paper that may be readily folded or readily spread out. **3** A large envelope or binder for loose papers.

fol·de·rol (fol'də·rol) See FALDERAL.

fold·ing (fōl'ding) *n.* The gathering or keeping of sheep in a fold.

fo·li·a (fō'lē·ə) Plural of FOLIUM.

fo·li·a·ceous (fō'lē·ā'shəs) *adj.* **1** Of the nature or form of a leaf. **2** Leaflike. **3** Having leaves; foliate. [<L *foliaceus* <*folium* a leaf]

fo·li·age (fō'lē·ij) *n.* **1** Any growth of leaves; leaves collectively. **2** A representation of leaves, flowers, and branches, used in architectural ornamentation. [Earlier *foillage* <F *feuillage* <*feuille* a leaf <L *folium*; refashioned after the Latin form]

fo·li·aged (fō'lē·ijd) *adj.* Having, or ornamented with, foliage.

foliage green Any of several shades of dark, dull green; a color like that of the leaves of trees in the summer.

fo·li·ar (fō'lē·ər) *adj.* Of, pertaining to, consisting of, or resembling leaves.

fo·li·ate (fō'lē·āt, -it) *adj.* **1** Having leaves; leafy; leaf-shaped. **2** Decorated with leaf-shaped ornaments; beaten into leaf. **— *v.* ·at·ed, ·at·ing** *v.t.* **1** To beat or form into a leaf or thin plate, as gold. **2** To coat or back with metal foil. **3** To number the leaves of (a book). **4** *Archit.* To adorn or ornament with foils or foliage. **—** *v.i.* **5** To split into leaves or laminae. **6** To put forth leaves. [<L *foliatus* leafy <*folium* a leaf] **— fo'li·at'ed** *adj.*

fo·li·a·tion (fō'lē·ā'shən) *n.* **1** *Bot.* **a** The leafing-out of plants. **b** The disposition of leaves in a bud. **2** The act or process of making into thin sheet metal or foil, or of covering or backing with foil, as a mirror. **3** *Archit.* Decoration or enrichment with cusps, lobes, or foliated tracery; also, one of such ornaments. **4** The state of being foliaceous or foliated. **5** *Geol.* A crystalline segregation of certain minerals in a rock, in dominant planes. **6** The numbering of the leaves of a book, etc., instead of its pages. Also **fo·li·a·ture** (fō'lē·ə·cho͝or').

fo·lic acid (fō'lik) *Biochem.* A nitrogen-containing acid having vitaminlike properties and often included in the vitamin-B complex. It is found abundantly in green leaves, and in mushrooms, yeast, and some animal tissues.

fo·li·o (fō'lē·ō, fōl'yō) *n. pl.* **·li·os** **1** A sheet of paper folded once or of a size adapted to folding once. **2** A book, or the like, composed of sheets folded but once; hence, a book of the largest size. **3** The size of a book so made up. **4** A page of a book; sometimes, in bookkeeping, two opposite pages numbered alike. **5** *Printing* The number of a page. **6** *Law* A certain number of words (72–100), recognized as a unit for estimating the length of a document. **7** A leaf of manuscript or of a book. **8** A holder made of heavy paper for protecting sheets of manuscript, music, etc. **—** *adj.* Consisting of or resulting from a sheet or sheets folded once; having two leaves, hence, four pages. **—** *v.t.* To number the pages or locate the folios of (a book or manuscript) consecutively. [<L, ablative sing. of *folium* a leaf]

fo·li·o·late (fō'lē·ə·lāt') *adj. Bot.* Of, pertaining to, or composed of leaflets: used in composition: *bifoliolate,* composed of two leaflets. [<L *foliolum,* dim. of *folium* a leaf + -ATE[1]]

fo·li·ose (fō'lē·ōs) *adj.* Bearing leaves or leaflike appendages. [<L *foliosus* <*folium* a leaf]

-folious *suffix* Leaflike or leafy: used in the formation of adjectives. [<L *foliosus* <*folium* leaf]

fo·li·um (fō'lē·əm) *n. pl.* **·li·ums** or **·li·a** (-lē·ə) **1** *Usually pl.* A thin layer or stratum, especially of rocks. **2** *Geom.* A segment of a curve closed by its node; a loop. [<L, a leaf]

folium of Descartes *Geom.* A plane cubic curve with one loop, a node, and two branches asymptotic to the same line.

folk (fōk) *n. pl.* **folk** or **folks** **1** A people; nation; race. **2** *Usually pl.* People of a particular group or class: old *folks*; poor *folks*; town *folk.* **3** *pl. Colloq.* People in general: *Folks* say; *folks* disagree. **4** *pl. Colloq.* One's family or relatives. **—** *adj.* Originating among or characteristic of the common people of a district or country. [OE *folc*]

Folk, in the adjectival use, may appear as the first element in two-word phrases; as in:

folk air	**folk faith**	**folk song**
folk art	**folk life**	**folk speech**
folk belief	**folk literature**	**folk story**
folk custom	**folk music**	**folk tale**
folk dance	**folk name**	**folk tune**

Folke·stone (fōk'stən) A port and resort in Kent, England.

Fol·ke·ting (fōl'kə·ting) *n.* The lower branch of the Danish Rigsdag or legislature. Also **Fol'ke·thing.**

folk etymology **1** Modification of an unfamiliar word resulting from an incorrect analysis of the elements, causing it to assume the shape or pronunciation of better known forms, as *agnail* (in Middle English, a painful nail) became *hangnail.* **2** Nonscientific word derivation. Also called *popular etymology.*

folk·free (fōk'frē') *adj.* Having the lawful rights of a freeman.

folk·land (fōk'land') *n.* In old English law, land of the folk or people, of the community, or of the nation, held by folkright: distinguished from *bookland,* requiring written title. [OE *folcland*]

folk laws The laws of the common people; specifically, the laws of the Salian Franks.

folk·lore (fōk'lôr', -lōr') *n.* **1** The traditions, beliefs, customs, sayings, stories, etc., preserved among the common people. **2** The study of folk cultures. **— folk'lor'ist** *n.*

folk·mote (fōk'mōt') *n.* In early English history, a general assembly of the people of a town, county, etc. Also **folk'moot'** (-mo͞ot'). [OE *folcmōt* <*folc* folk + *mōt* meeting]

folk·right (fōk'rīt') *n.* The common law of the people; the public right.

folk·sy (fōk'sē) *adj.* **·si·er, ·si·est** *Colloq.* Friendly; sociable; unpretentious.

folk·ways (fōk′wāz′) *n. pl.* The traditional habits, customs, and behavior of a given group, tribe, or nation. [Coined by W. G. Sumner]

fol·li·cle (fol′i·kəl) *n.* **1** *Anat.* A small cavity or saclike structure in certain parts of the animal body, having a protective or secretory function: a hair *follicle.* See illustration under HAIR. **2** *Bot.* **a** A dry seed vessel of one carpel. **b** A small bladder on the leaves of some mosses. [<L *folliculus,* dim. of *follis* bag]

fol·lic·u·lar (fə·lik′yə·lər) *adj.* **1** Of, pertaining to, or like a follicle. **2** Affecting the follicles, as of the pharynx.

fol·lic·u·lat·ed (fə·lik′yə·lā′tid) *adj.* Having a follicle or a cocoon; follicular. Also **fol·lic′u·late** (-lit).

fol·lies (fol′ēz) *n. pl. of* **folly** A theatrical performance having no plot sequence, consisting of many elaborate scenes of music and dance; revue.

fol·low (fol′ō) *v.t.* **1** To go or come after and in the same direction. **2** To succeed in time or order. **3** To seek to overtake or capture; pursue. **4** To accompany; attend. **5** To hold to the course of: to *follow* a road. **6** To conform to; act in accordance with. **7** To move or act in the cause of; be under the leadership or authority of: He *follows* Plato. **8** To work at as a profession or livelihood; employ oneself in: men who *follow* the sea. **9** To come after as a consequence or result: The effect *follows* the cause. **10** To use or take as a model; imitate: to *follow* an example. **11** To watch or observe closely; be attentive to: to *follow* sports. **12** To understand the course, sequence, or meaning of, as an explanation. **13** To strive after; try to attain or obtain: to *follow* one's star. — *v.i.* **14** To move or come after or in the direction of something preceding in time, sequence, or motion. **15** To attend; understand: Do you *follow*? **16** To come as a result or consequence. — **to follow out 1** To follow to the end, as an argument. **2** To comply with, as orders or instructions. — **to follow suit 1** In card games, to play a card of the suit led. **2** To follow another's example. — **to follow through 1** To swing to the full extent of the stroke after having struck the ball, as in tennis or golf. **2** To perform fully; complete. — **to follow up 1** To pursue closely. **2** To achieve more by acting upon what has already been achieved, as an advantage. — *n.* The act of following; specifically, a stroke in billiards that causes the cue ball, after impact, to follow the object ball. [OE *folgian*]

Synonyms (verb): accompany, attend, chase, copy, ensue, heed, imitate, obey, observe, practice, pursue, result, succeed. A servant *follows* or *attends* his master, a victorious general may *follow* the retiring enemy merely to watch and hold him in check; he *chases* or *pursues* with intent to overtake and attack; the chase is closer and hotter than the pursuit. (Compare synonyms for HUNT.) One event may *follow* another either with or without special connection; if it *ensues,* there is some orderly connection; if it *results* from another, there is some relation of effect, consequence, or inference. A clerk *observes* his employer's directions. A child *obeys* his parent's commands, *follows* or *copies* his example, *imitates* his speech and manners. The compositor *follows* copy; the incoming official *succeeds* the outgoing official. See IMITATE. *Antonyms*: anticipate, direct, flee, guide, lead, pass, precede, surpass.

fol·low·er (fol′ō·ər) *n.* **1** One who or that which follows; an adherent, imitator, or attendant. **2** *Mech.* A part of a machine put into action by another part, as a driven pulley. **3** *Brit. Colloq.* An admirer; a beau.

fol·low·ing (fol′ō·ing) *adj.* **1** Next in order; succeeding or ensuing. **2** That is about to follow, be recounted, be mentioned, or the like. — *n.* A body of adherents, attendants, or disciples.

fol·low-through (fol′ō·thrōō′) *n.* **1** In some sports, the continuing and completion of a motion, as the swing of the racket, club, or bat after contact with the ball. **2** Any continuing or completion.

fol·low-up (fol′ō·up′) *adj.* Pertaining to steady or repeated action or to a second or immediately following action or thing; reinforcing; supplementary. — *n.* A supplementary letter or visit to a business prospect, urging favorable action on a previous proposal.

fol·ly (fol′ē) *n. pl.* **·lies 1** The condition or state of being foolish, or deficient in understanding; foolish conduct, idea, or act. **2** The result of a ruinous undertaking or enterprise, as a costly and useless structure left unfinished; also, any extravagant structure or undertaking, considered as showing the bad judgment of the originator. **3** An object of foolish or vicious attention or pursuit. **4** Immoral conduct; sin. See synonyms under IDIOCY. [<F *folie* <*fol* fool]

Fol·som culture (fol′səm) *Anthropol.* A supposed prehistoric North American culture represented by typically Neolithic artifacts discovered near Folsom, northeastern New Mexico.

Folsom point *Anthropol.* One of various chipped points, first found near Folsom, New Mexico, in 1925.

Fo·mal·haut (fō′məl·hôt) The bright star Alpha in the constellation of Piscis Austrinus; magnitude, 1.3.

fo·ment (fō·ment′) *v.t.* **1** To stir up or instigate; incite, as rebellion or discord. **2** To treat with warm water or medicated lotions; apply a poultice to. See synonyms under PROMOTE. [<F *fomenter* <LL *fomentare* <*fomentum* a poultice <*fovere* warm, keep warm] — **fo·ment′er** *n.*

fo·men·ta·tion (fō′mən·tā′shən) *n.* **1** The act of fomenting, warming, or cherishing. **2** The use of any warm, moist application, as a poultice; also, the lotion applied. **3** Instigation or incitement, as to mutiny.

fo·mes (fō′mēz) *n. pl.* **fom·i·tes** (fom′i·tēz, fō′·mi-) *Med.* An object or substance other than food capable of transmitting an infection, as bedding, clothes, etc. [<L, tinder]

Fo·mor·i·an (fə·môr′ē·ən, -mō′rē-) *n.* In Old Irish mythology, one of a people who dwelt under the sea and ravaged Ireland: generally associated with the powers of evil. [<Irish *fomhor* pirate]

Fön (fœn) See FOEHN.

fond[1] (fond) *adj.* **1** Disposed to love or to regard with pleasure, tenderness, or desire; enamored: followed by *of,* formerly by *on.* **2** Loving or affectionate; devotedly attached: sometimes with an implication of unwise tenderness or weak indulgence. **3** Cherished or regarded with affection; doted on. **4** *Archaic.* Foolish or simple; silly. See synonyms under FRIENDLY. [Earlier *fonned,* pp. of obs. *fon* be foolish]

fond[2] (fond, *Fr.* fôṅ) *n.* A groundwork or background, especially of lace. [<F <L *fundus* bottom]

fon·dant (fon′dənt, *Fr.* fôṅ·däṅ′) *n.* A soft, molded confection. [<F, orig. ppr. of *fondre* melt]

fon·dle (fon′dəl) *v.* **·dled, ·dling** *v.t.* **1** To handle lovingly; caress. **2** *Obs.* To pamper; coddle. — *v.i.* **3** To display fondness, as by caressing. See synonyms under CARESS. [Freq. of obs. *fond* caress] — **fon′dler** *n.*

fon·dling (fond′ling) *n.* One who or that which is fondled.

fond·ly (fond′lē) *adv.* **1** In a fond manner; tenderly; dotingly. **2** Credulously. **3** *Obs.* Foolishly.

fond·ness (fond′nis) *n.* **1** Extravagant or foolish affection. **2** Strong preferment, liking or relish. **3** *Obs.* Foolishness.

fon·du (fôṅ·dü′) *adj. French* Melting into or blending gradually with one another, as colors.

fon·due (fon·dōō′, *Fr.* fôṅ·dü′) *n.* A dish made of grated cheese, melted with eggs, butter, etc. [<F]

Fon·se·ca (fōn·sā′kä), **Gulf of** An inlet of the Pacific in Salvador, Honduras, and Nicaragua.

font[1] (font) *n.* **1** A receptacle for the water used in baptizing. **2** A receptacle for holy water. **3** A fountain; hence, origin; source. [OE <LL *fons, fontis* a fountain]

font[2] (font) *n.* A full assortment of printing type of a particular face and size: also *Brit. fount.* [<F *fonte* <*fondre* melt]

Fon·taine·bleau (fôṅ·ten·blō′) A town in central France in the **Forest of Fontainebleau;** site of the **Palace of Fontainebleau,** a former residence of French kings, now a museum.

font·al (fon′təl) *adj.* Pertaining to a font or fountain, and hence to an origin or source.

fon·ta·nel (fon′tə·nel′) *n.* **1** *Anat.* A soft, pulsating, unossified area in the fetal and infantile skull. **2** *Surg.* An artificial opening for the discharge of body fluids; a seton. Also **fon′ta·nelle′.** [<F *fontanelle,* dim. of *fontaine.* See FOUNTAIN.]

Fon·tanne (fon·tan′), **Lynn,** born 1887?, U.S. actress born in England; wife of Alfred Lunt.

Fon·te·noy (fon′tə·noi, *Fr.* fôṅ·tə·nwä′) **1** A village in western Belgium; scene of a French victory over British forces, 1745. **2** A village of north central France; scene of a victory of Charles II of France, 841: also **Fon·te·nailles** (fôṅ·tə·nä′y′), **Fon·ta·net** (fôṅ·tà·ne′).

Foo·chow (fōō′chou′, *Chinese* fōō′jō′) A port in SE China; capital of Fukien province: formerly *Minhow.* Also **Fu′chow′.**

food (fōōd) *n.* **1** That which is eaten or drunk or absorbed for the growth and repair of organisms and the maintenance of life; nourishment; nutriment; aliment. **2** Nourishment taken in solid as opposed to liquid form: *food* and drink. **3** That which increases, keeps active, or sustains. [OE *fōda*]

Synonyms: aliment, diet, fare, feed, fodder, forage, nourishment, nutriment, nutrition, pabulum, provender, regimen, sustenance, viands, victuals. *Food* is, in the popular sense, whatever one eats in contradistinction to what one drinks. Thus we speak of *food* and drink, of wholesome, unwholesome, or indigestible *food*; in a more scientific sense whatever, when taken into an organism, serves to build up structure or supply waste may be termed *food*; thus we speak of liquid *food,* plant *food,* etc.; in this wider sense *food* is closely synonymous with *nutriment, nourishment,* and *sustenance. Victuals* is a plain, homely word for whatever may be eaten; we speak of choice *viands,* cold *victuals. Diet* refers to the quantity and quality of *food* habitually taken, with reference to preservation of health. *Regimen* considers *food* as taken by strict rule, in which use it is closely synonymous with *diet,* but applies more widely to the whole ordering of life. *Fare* is a general word for all table supplies, good or bad; as, sumptuous *fare*; wretched *fare. Feed, fodder,* and *provender* are used only of the food of the lower animals, *feed* denoting anything consumed, but more commonly grain, *fodder* denoting hay, corn stalks, or the like, sometimes called long *feed*; *provender* is dry *feed,* whether grain or hay, straw, etc. *Forage* denotes any kind of *food* suitable for horses and cattle, primarily as obtained by a military force in scouring the country, especially an enemy's country. Compare NUTRIMENT.

Food and Drug Administration A division of the U.S. Department of Health, Education, and Welfare, which enforces laws relating to the purity, standards, branding, and labeling of foods, drugs, and cosmetics.

food chain *Ecol.* The relationship of organisms considered as food sources or consumers or both, as the relationship of a flowering plant to a bee to a bird.

Foo dog (fōō) A lion dog (def. 1): a western commercial term. [<Chinese *Foo,* var. of *Fo* Buddha + dog]

food·stuff (fōōd′stuf′) *n.* Anything used as nourishment, or entering into the composition of food: often in the plural.

foo·fa·raw (fōō′fə·rô) *n. Colloq.* **1** Gaudy trimmings; tinsel. **2** Nonsense. [Origin unknown]

fool[1] (fōōl) *n.* **1** A person lacking in understanding, judgment, or common sense; a simpleton. **2** A person, fantastically dressed and equipped, formerly kept at court and in great households to make sport; a professional jester. **3** One who is fooled or made a fool of; butt; victim. **4** *Obs.* An idiot; imbecile. **5** *Obs.* One without spiritual wisdom; wicked person. — *v.i.* To act like a fool; be foolish or playful. — *v.t.* To make a fool of; impose upon; deceive. — **to fool around** *U.S. Colloq.* **1** To waste time on trifles. **2** To

hang about idly. —**to fool away** *Colloq.* To spend foolishly; squander, as money. —**to fool with** 1 To meddle with. 2 To joke with. 3 To play with. —*adj. Colloq.* 1 Stupid: that *fool* cook. 2 Foolish: a *fool* story. [<F *fou* <L *follis* a bellows; later, a windbag, a simpleton]
fool[2] (fōōl) *n.* Crushed stewed fruit with whipped cream. [Prob. <FOOL[1]]
fool·er·y (fōō′lə·rē) *n. pl.* **·er·ies** Foolish conduct; anything foolish.
fool·har·dy (fōōl′här′dē) *adj.* Bold without judgment; reckless; rash. See synonyms under IMPRUDENT. —**fool′har′di·ly** *adv.* —**fool′har′·di·ness** *n.*
fool·ing (fōō′ling) *n.* 1 Playing the fool; jesting. 2 Loitering.
fool·ish (fōō′lish) *adj.* 1 Showing folly; wanting in judgment. 2 Resulting from folly or stupidity. 3 *Archaic* Insignificant; small; humble. See synonyms under ABSURD, CHILDISH. —**fool′ish·ly** *adv.* —**fool′ish·ness** *n.*
fool·proof (fōōl′prōōf′) *adj.* So simple as to be understood or operated by a fool; so constructed as to operate smoothly and safely no matter how ignorant the operator.
fools·cap (fōōlz′kap′) *n.* 1 A size of writing paper about 13 by 16 inches, making when folded a page 13 by 8 inches. 2 *Brit.* A size of printing paper 13 1/2 by 17 inches: so called from the watermark of a fool's cap and bells used by old papermakers. 3 A fool's cap.
fool's cap 1 A pointed, belled cap, formerly worn by jesters. 2 A dunce's cap of this shape: formerly used as a punishment for school children.
fool's errand A profitless undertaking.
fool's gold Pyrite, a gold-colored mineral.
fool's paradise A state of deceptive happiness based on vain hopes or delusions.
fool's-parsley (fōōlz′pärs′lē) *n.* A fetid, poisonous herb (*Aethusa cynapium*) naturalized in NE United States and eastern Canada: so called because it resembles parsley: also **fool's′-cic′e·ly** (fōōlz′sis′ə·lē).
foot (fŏŏt) *n. pl.* **feet** 1 The terminal segment of the limb of a vertebrate animal upon which it rests in standing or moving. ◆ Collateral adjective: *pedal.* 2 Any part serving as or likened to a foot. 3 Anything corresponding in form, use, or position to the foot. 4 The part of a boot or stocking which receives the wearer's foot. 5 A part in a sewing machine, to hold the fabric down: also called **presser foot.** 6 *Naut.* The lower edge of a four-sided sail. 7 The lowest part; bottom; base; foundation; also, the last row, line, or series; the inferior part or end. 8 A measure of length, equivalent to 12 inches, or 30.48 centimeters. 9 Soldiers, collectively, who march and fight on foot: distinguished from *horse* (cavalry). 10 A primary measure of poetic rhythm, corresponding to a *bar* in music. —**on foot** 1 Walking; not riding. 2 Happening; going on; proceeding. —**to put one's foot down** To be decisive or determined. —**to put one's foot in it** To get into a difficulty or scrape. —**under foot** 1 Under the feet; hence, in the way. 2 On the ground: wet *under foot.* —*v.i.* 1 To go afoot; walk. 2 To move the foot to music; dance. 3 *Naut.* To move or sail faster. —*v.t.* 4 To move on or through by walking or dancing; set foot on. 5 To furnish with a foot, as a stocking. 6 To add, as a column of figures, and place the sum at the bottom. 7 *Colloq.* To pay, as a bill. —**to foot it** To walk, run, or dance. —**to foot up** To amount to when counted or added. [OE *fōt*]

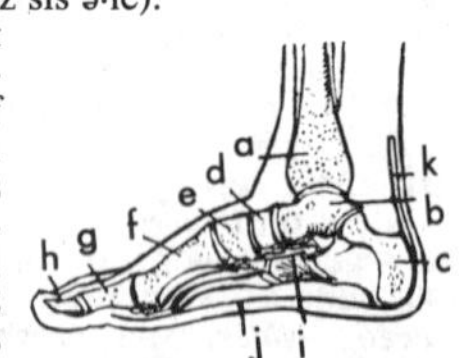

LONGITUDINAL SECTION OF HUMAN FOOT
a. Tibia.
b. Astragal.
c. Calcaneum.
d. Navicular.
e. Internal cuneiform bone.
f. First metatarsal.
g, h. Phalanges of great toe.
i. Inferior ligament.
j. Plantar fasciae, supporting the plantar arch.
k. Achilles' tendon.

foot·age (fŏŏt′ij) *n.* 1 Length in running feet, as of lumber, of tunneling or mining, or of film in a motion picture. 2 Payment at a rate of so much a foot for work done.
foot-and-mouth disease (fŏŏt′ən·mouth′) A contagious, febrile disease of domestic animals, in which ulcers are formed about the mouth and hoofs. It is caused by a filtrable virus.
foot·ball (fŏŏt′bôl′) *n.* 1 *U.S.* A game played between two teams, properly of eleven men each, on a field with goals at each end, points being scored by running or passing an ellipsoidal leather ball across the opponent's goal line, or kicking it between the goal posts placed on or behind the goal line. 2 The ball itself. 3 *Brit.* **a** Soccer. **b** Rugby football. 4 Any person, idea, etc., bandied or shunted back and forth.

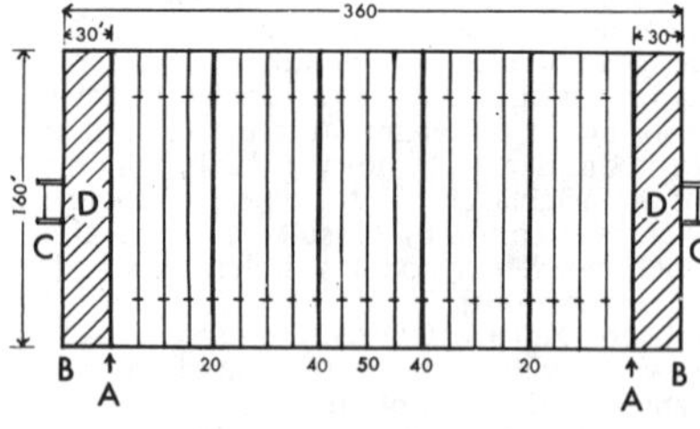

FOOTBALL PLAYING FIELD
A. Goal lines. *C.* Goal posts.
B. End lines. *D.* End zones.
The field of play is marked off in guidelines spaced 5 yards apart and so identified, as 20-yard line, etc.

foot·board (fŏŏt′bôrd′, -bōrd′) *n.* 1 Something to rest the feet upon. 2 An upright piece at the foot of a bedstead.
foot·boy (fŏŏt′boi′) *n.* A page.
foot brake A brake operated by pressure of the foot.
foot·breadth (fŏŏt′bredth′) *n.* The breadth of a foot, as a measure.
foot·bridge (fŏŏt′brij′) *n.* A bridge for persons on foot.
foot-can·dle (fŏŏt′kan′dəl) *n.* The illumination on one square foot of surface, all points of which are at a distance of one foot from one international candle. —**apparent foot-candle** See FOOT-LAMBERT.
foot·cloth (fŏŏt′klôth′, -kloth′) *n.* 1 A carpet to walk upon on occasions of ceremony. 2 *Obs.* A caparison for a horse.
foot·ed (fŏŏt′id) *adj.* Having a foot or feet: four-*footed*; also, shaped like a foot.
foot·er (fŏŏt′ər) *n.* 1 A person who goes on foot. 2 A person or thing having a certain number of feet in height or length: a six-*footer.*
foot·fall (fŏŏt′fôl′) *n.* The sound of a footstep; a footstep.
foot·gear (fŏŏt′gir′) *n.* Footwear.
foot·guard (fŏŏt′gärd′) *n.* A horse's boot.
foot·hill (fŏŏt′hil′) *n.* A low hill at the base of a mountain.
foot·hold (fŏŏt′hōld′) *n.* 1 A firm support for the foot. 2 Secure footing. 3 Established position.
foot·ing (fŏŏt′ing) *n.* 1 A place to stand or walk on; hence, position or condition; especially, secure position. 2 An established mode of mutual consideration and treatment. 3 The adding of a column or columns of figures, or the sum thus obtained. 4 A footstep; tread; especially, measured tread; dancing. 5 The act of adding a foot to anything; that which is added as a foot. 6 A strong foundation of greater lateral dimensions than the wall, embankment, or structural member which it supports.
foot ladder A ladder with flat steps to place the feet upon.
foot-lam·bert (fŏŏt′lam′bərt) *n.* A unit of brightness, equal to the brightness of a uniformly diffusing surface which emits or reflects one lumen per square foot: also called *apparent foot-candle.*
foot·le (fŏŏt′l) *Colloq. v.t. & v.i.* **foot·led, foot·ling** To talk or act in a silly or foolish manner. —*adj.* Nonsensical: also **foot′ling.** —*n.* Foolish talk; nonsense. [Origin uncertain]
foot·less (fŏŏt′lis) *adj.* 1 Having no feet. 2 Having no footing or basis. 3 *Colloq.* Awkward; inept.
foot·lights (fŏŏt′līts′) *n. pl.* 1 Lights in a row near the front of the stage, as in a theater. 2 The stage.
foot·ling (fŏŏt′ling) *adj. & adv.* 1 Foolish; trifling. 2 Having or with the feet foremost: said of a position of the fetus at birth.
foot·lock·er (fŏŏt′lok′ər) *n.* A small trunk, usually used by soldiers for personal belongings and clothing.
foot·log (fŏŏt′lôg′, -log′) *n.* A log across a stream from bank to bank, on which a person may cross.
foot·loose (fŏŏt′lōōs′) *adj.* Free to travel or rove around; not bound to any person or duty; unattached.
foot·man (fŏŏt′mən) *n. pl.* **·men** (-mən) 1 A male servant in livery who attends a carriage, answers the door, waits at table, etc. 2 *Obs.* A pedestrian.
foot·mark (fŏŏt′märk′) *n.* A footprint. See synonyms under TRACE.
foot·note (fŏŏt′nōt′) *n.* A note at the foot of a page or column.
foot·pace (fŏŏt′pās′) *n.* 1 A slow pace. 2 A staircase landing. 3 A dais.
foot·pad (fŏŏt′pad′) *n.* A highwayman or robber on foot.
foot·path (fŏŏt′path′, -päth′) *n.* A path for persons on foot.
foot-pound (fŏŏt′pound′) *n.* The work done in moving a pound's weight one foot against gravity: a unit of mechanical work.
foot-pound·al (fŏŏt′poun′dəl) *n.* A measure of the work done in moving through one foot against a force of one poundal.
foot·print (fŏŏt′print′) *n.* An impression left by a foot. See synonyms under MARK, TRACE.
foot·rest (fŏŏt′rest′) *n.* A stool, chair extension, etc., for supporting the feet.
foot·rope (fŏŏt′rōp′) *n. Naut.* 1 A rope stretched under a yard for sailors to stand on while reefing or furling. 2 A boltrope sewed to the lower edge of a sail.
foot-rot (fŏŏt′rot′) *n.* An infectious disease of sheep, characterized by inflammation of the foot, progressive degeneration of the tissues, ill-smelling discharges, and lameness: caused by any of several micro-organisms, bacterial or of fungous origin.
foots (fŏŏts) *n. pl.* Settlings or sediment, as of molasses or oil.
foot soldier An infantryman.
foot·sore (fŏŏt′sôr′, -sōr′) *adj.* Having sore feet, as from walking.
foot·stalk (fŏŏt′stôk′) *n. Bot.* 1 The petiole of a leaf, or the peduncle of a flower. 2 A stem or part supporting the body or an organ; a pedicel.
foot·stall (fŏŏt′stôl′) *n.* 1 *Archit.* The base or pedestal of a column or pillar. 2 The stirrup of a side-saddle.
foot·step (fŏŏt′step′) *n.* 1 The impression or mark of a foot; footprint; track. 2 The action of a foot in stepping. 3 The sound of a step; tread; footfall. See synonyms under TRACE.
foot·stock (fŏŏt′stok′) *n. Mech.* In turning or boring machinery, a tailstock or loose headstock.
foot·stone (fŏŏt′stōn′) *n.* The stone at the foot of a grave.
foot·stool (fŏŏt′stōōl′) *n.* A low stool for the feet.
foot·stove (fŏŏt′stōv′) *n.* A metal container for live coals, enclosed in a box having a perforated top: used for warming the feet.
foot-ton (fŏŏt′tun′) *n.* The work done in raising a long ton a distance of one foot against the force of gravity.
foot·wall (fŏŏt′wôl′) *n.* 1 *Mining* The layer of rock lying just beneath a vein of ore. 2 *Geol.* That side of an inclined fault that lies below the hanging wall.
foot·wash·ing (fŏŏt′wosh′ing, -wôsh′-) *n.* The washing of one another's feet as an act of humility: a religious ceremony performed by certain sects in remembrance of the washing of the disciples' feet by Jesus.
foot·way (fŏŏt′wā′) *n.* A path or passage for pedestrians; footpath.
foot·wear (fŏŏt′wâr′) *n.* Clothing for the feet; boots, shoes, socks, stockings.
foot·work (fŏŏt′wûrk′) *n.* Use or control of the feet, as in boxing or tennis.
foot-worn (fŏŏt′wôrn′, -wōrn′) *adj.* 1 Weary with walking. 2 Worn by the feet, as a path.
foot·y (fŏŏt′ē) *adj.* **foot·i·er, foot·i·est** *Colloq.* Foolish; insignificant; worthless. [<F *foutu,* pp. of *foutre* damn]
foo·zle (fōō′zəl) *v.t. & v.i.* **·zled, ·zling** To do

awkwardly; fumble. —*n.* A misstroke or misplay, especially in golf. [Cf. dial. G *fuseln* work badly]—**foo′zler** *n.*

fop (fop) *n.* A man affectedly fastidious in dress or deportment; a dandy. [Cf. Du. *foppen* cheat]

fop·ling (fop′ling) *n.* A petty fop.

fop·per·y (fop′ər·ē) *n. pl.* **·per·ies** The conduct or practices of a fop. Also **fop′pish·ness.**

fop·pish (fop′ish) *adj.* Characteristic of a fop; dandified. —**fop′pish·ly** *adv.*

for (fôr, *unstressed* fər) *prep.* **1** To the extent of: The ground is flat *for miles.* **2** Through the duration or period of: The coupon is good *for* a week. **3** To the number or amount of: a check *for* six dollars. **4** At the price or payment of: He bought the hat *for* ten dollars. **5** On account of; as a result of: He is respected *for* his ability. **6** In honor of; by the name of: He is called Walter *for* his grandfather. **7** Appropriate to: a time *for* work. **8** In place or instead of: using a book *for* a desk. **9** In favor, support, or approval of: a vote *for* peace. **10** In the interest or behalf of: My lawyers will speak *for* me. **11** Tending toward, as with longing or desire: a passion *for* jewelry; an eye *for* bargains. **12** As affecting (in a particular way): good *for* your health. **13** Belonging, given, attributed, or assigned to: a package *for* you; the reason *for* going. **14** In proportion to: big *for* his age. **15** As the equivalent to or requital of: blow *for* blow. **16** In spite of: I believe in it *for* all your sophistry! **17** In order to reach or go toward: He left *for* his office. **18** In order to become, find, keep, or obtain: suing *for* damages; looking *for* a hat. **19** At (a particular time or occasion): We agreed to meet *for* Easter. **20** In the character of; as being, seeming, or supposed to be: We took him *for* an honest man. —**for . . . to . . .** To have: The child pulled at her skirt *for* her *to* notice him. —**O (Now,** etc.**) for** . . . ! Would that I had!: O *for* a horse! —*conj.* **1** In view of the reason that; seeing that: It is no easy matter to decide, *for* its elements are complex. **2** Owing to the fact that; because: He could not leave, *for* he was expecting a visitor. See synonyms under BECAUSE. [OE]

for- *prefix* **1** Away; off (in a privative sense); past: *forget, forgo.* **2** Very; extremely: *forlorn.* [OE *for-, fær-*]

for- See also words beginning FORE-.

for·age (fôr′ij, for′-) *n.* **1** Any food suitable for horses or cattle. **2** The act of foraging or seeking food. —*v.* **for·aged, for·ag·ing** *v.t.* **1** To strip of provisions; search through for supplies; ravage. **2** To provide with forage. **3** To obtain or provide by or as by foraging. —*v.i.* **4** To search for food or supplies. **5** To search: usually with *out* or *for.* **6** To make a foray. See synonyms under FOOD. [<F *fourrage* <OF *feurre* <Gmc.]—**for′ag·er** *n.*

forage cap *Brit.* A small, undress military cap.

foraging ant Any of various tropical ants (family *Formicidae*) that make forays for food in large bodies; especially, the driver ant and army ant of Africa, and the tropical American legionary ant (genus *Eciton*).

Fo·rain (fô·raṅ′, **Jean Louis,** 1852–1931, French painter.

For·a·ker, Mount (fôr′ə·kər, for′-) A peak in south central Alaska; 17,280 feet.

fo·ra·men (fô·rā′mən) *n. pl.* **·ram·i·na** (-ram′ə·nə) *Anat.* **1** An orifice or short passage, as in a bone. **2** An opening; aperture. [<L <*forare* bore]

foramen magnum *Anat.* The large orifice by which the spinal cord passes into the skull and becomes continuous with the medulla oblongata.

for·a·min·i·fer (fôr′ə·min′ə·fər, for′-) *n.* One of a large order *(Foraminifera)* of rhizopods usually having a typically calcareous or chitinous shell perforated by many minute apertures. They are chiefly marine and virtually microscopic. [<L *foramen, -inis* a hole +*-fer* having <*ferre* bear]—**fo·ram·i·nif·er·al** (fə·ram′ə·nif′ər·əl), **fo·ram·i·nif′er·ous** *adj.*

for·as·much as (fôr′əz·much′) **1** Seeing or considering that; since; because. **2** *Obs.* So far as. Also **for as much as.**

for·ay (fôr′ā, for′ā) *v.t.* & *v.i.* To ravage; pillage; raid. —*n.* A marauding expedition; raid. See synonyms under INVASION. [Prob. back formation <*forayer* a raider <OF *forrier* <*forre,* var. of *feurre* FORAGE]

forb (fôrb) *n.* A weed, in the range stockman's usage; a non-grasslike herb. [Appar. <Gk. *phorbē* fodder]

for·bade, for·bad (fər·bad′, fôr-) Past tense of FORBID.

for·bear[1] (fôr·bâr′, fər-) *v.* **·bore, ·borne, ·bear·ing** *v.t.* **1** To refrain or abstain from; avoid (an action) voluntarily. **2** *Archaic* To put up with; endure. —*v.i.* **3** To abstain or refrain. **4** To be patient or act patiently. See synonyms under REFRAIN. [OE]—**for·bear′er** *n.*

for·bear[2] (fôr′bâr′) See FOREBEAR.

for·bear·ance (fôr·bâr′əns, fər-) *n.* **1** The act of forbearing; patient endurance of offenses. **2** *Law* A refraining from claiming or enforcing a right. **3** A refraining from retaliation or retribution. See synonyms under MERCY, PATIENCE, RESPITE.

for·bear·ing (fôr·bâr′ing, fər-) *adj.* Disposed to forbear; patient.

Forbes–Rob·ert·son (fôrbz′rob′ərt·sən), **Sir Johnston,** 1853–1937, English actor.

for·bid (fər·bid′, fôr-) *v.t.* **for·bade** or **for·bad, for·bid·den** or **for·bid, for·bid·ding** **1** To command (a person) not to do, use, enter, etc. **2** To prohibit the use or doing of; interdict. **3** To make impossible. See synonyms under PROHIBIT. [OE *forbēodan*]—**for·bid′dance** *n.* —**for·bid′der** *n.*

for·bid·den (fər·bid′n, fôr-) *adj.* Not allowed; prohibited.

Forbidden City **1** Lhasa, Tibet. **2** A walled section of Peking, China, containing the royal palaces of the former Chinese Empire.

forbidden fruit **1** In the Bible, the fruit of the tree of knowledge of good and evil, forbidden to Adam and Eve. **2** Prohibited pleasure.

for·bid·ding (fər·bid′ing, fôr-) *adj.* **1** Such as to repel; unfriendly and repellent in manner. **2** Repulsive, or causing aversion: a *forbidding* countenance. —**for·bid′ding·ly** *adv.* —**for·bid′·ding·ness** *n.*

for·bore (fôr·bôr′, -bōr′) Past tense of FORBEAR[1].

for·borne (fôr·bôrn′, -bōrn′) Past participle of FORBEAR[1].

for·by (fôr·bī′) *adv.* & *prep. Scot.* **1** Besides; over and above. **2** Near; hard by. **3** Past, in time. Also **for·bye′.**

force (fôrs, fōrs) *n.* **1** *Physics* Anything that changes or tends to change the state of rest or motion in a body: the fundamental cgs unit of force is the dyne. **2** The action of one body upon another; any operating energy. **3** Any moral, social, or political cause, or aggregate of causes. **4** Power or energy as lodged in an individual agent. **5** Power or energy considered as exerting constraint or compulsion; coercion. **6** The capacity to convince or move; weight; import. **7** Binding effect; efficacy. **8** An organized or aggregated body of individuals; especially, a military aggregate; an army; troop or naval unit. **9** Rhetorical vigor; energy; animation; strength. **10** A group of workers. See synonyms under ARMY, IMPULSE, OPERATION, POWER. —**coercive** or **coercitive force** *Physics* The power of resisting magnetization or demagnetization. —**the force** The police of a certain district. —*v.t.* **forced, forc·ing** **1** To compel to do something by or as by force; coerce; constrain. **2** To get or obtain by or as by force: to *force* an answer. **3** To bring forth or about by or as by effort: to *force* a smile. **4** To drive or move despite resistance; press: to *force* the enemy back. **5** To assault and capture, as a fortification. **6** To break open, as a door or lock. **7** To make, as a passage or way, by force. **8** To press or impose upon someone as by force: to *force* one's opinion on someone. **9** To exert to or beyond the utmost; strain, as the voice. **10** To stimulate the growth of artificially, as plants in a hothouse. **11** To rape. **12** *Obs.* To put in force, as a law. **13** In baseball: **a** To put out (a base runner) who has been compelled by another baserunner to leave one base for the next. **b** To allow (the base runner on third base) to score by walking the batter when the bases are full. **c** To allow (a run) in such a manner. **14** In card games: **a** To compel (a player) to trump a trick by leading a suit of which he has none. **b** To play so as to compel (a player) to reveal the strength of his hand. **c** To compel a player to play (a particular card). [<F <L *fortis* brave, strong]—**force′a·ble** *adj.* —**forc′er** *n.*

forced (fôrst, fōrst) *adj.* **1** Compulsory. **2** Strained; affected: *forced* gaiety. **3** Speeded up, with few or no pauses: a *forced* march.

forced draft A current of air artificially supplied as to a furnace.

forced feeding Compulsory feeding of a person.

forced landing *Aeron.* The landing of an aircraft because of adverse weather conditions, mechanical failure, or the like.

forced oscillations *Electr.* Oscillations imposed upon an electrical system by outside forces which determine the amplitude and frequency of the oscillation. Compare FREE OSCILLATION.

force-feed (fōrs′fēd′, fōrs′-) *n.* The supply of lubricating oil under pressure to an internal-combustion engine.

force·ful (fôrs′fəl, fōrs′-) *adj.* Acting with force; strong; effective. —**force′ful·ly** *adv.* —**force′ful·ness** *n.*

force ma·jeure (má·zhœr′) *French* **1** Superior and irresistible force. **2** *Law* The virtual equivalent of *act of God* or *inevitable accident.*

force·meat (fôrs′mēt′, fōrs′-) *n.* Finely chopped, seasoned meat served separately or used as stuffing. [<*force,* alter. of FARCE, *v.* +MEAT]

force-out (fôrs′out′, fōrs′-) *n.* In baseball, an out made when a runner, forced from his base, fails to reach the next base before it is tagged by a fielder holding the ball.

for·ceps (fôr′səps) *n.* **1** A pair of pincers for grasping and manipulating small or delicate objects: used by watchmakers, surgeons, dentists, etc. **2** *Anat.* A bundle of fibers uniting the corpus callosum with the cerebral hemispheres of the brain. **3** A pincerslike structure. [<L <*formus* warm +*capere* take]

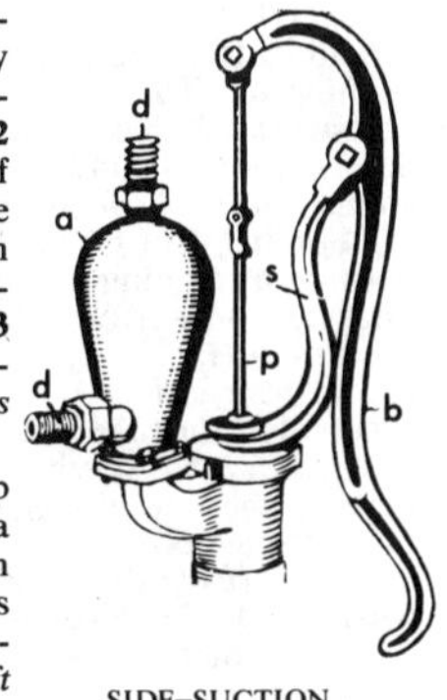

SIDE–SUCTION FORCE PUMP
a. Air chamber. *b.* Brake. *d, d.* Discharge pipes. *p.* Piston rod. *s.* Stand.

force pump A pump that delivers fluid at a pressure greater than that at which it is received: distinguished from *lift pump.*

for·ci·ble (fôr′sə·bəl) *adj.* **1** Accomplished by force. **2** Energetic; cogent. See synonyms under POWERFUL, RACY. —**for′ci·ble·ness** *n.* —**for′ci·bly** *adv.*

ford (fôrd, fōrd) *n.* A place in a stream that can be crossed in a vehicle or by wading. —*v.t.* **1** To go on foot or in a vehicle across (a stream, river, etc.). **2** To drive across a river or stream at a ford, as cattle, etc. [OE *ford*]—**ford′a·ble** *adj.* —**ford′less** *adj.*

Ford (fôrd, fōrd), **Ford Madox,** 1873–1939, English writer: original surname Hueffer. —**Gerald Rudolph,** born 1913, 38th president of the United States 1974-1977. —**Henry,** 1863–1947, U.S. automobile manufacturer. —**John,** 1586?–1639?, English dramatist.

for·do (fôr·do͞o′) *v.t.* **·did, ·done, ·do·ing** *Archaic* **1** To kill; destroy. **2** To ruin; undo. Also spelled *foredo.* [OE *fordōn*]

for·done (fôr·dun′) *adj. Archaic* Worn out with fatigue; exhausted.

fore (fôr, fōr) *adj.* **1** Preceding in place or time; forward; antecedent; prior. **2** Situated at or toward the front in relation to something else. —*n.* **1** The foremost part; the leading place. **2** *Naut.* The foremast. —**to the fore** **1** To or at the front; into prominence or conspicuous view. 2 At hand; available. 3 Alive; still active. —*prep.* & *conj. Archaic* or *Dial.* Before. —*adv.* 1 *Naut.* At or toward the bow of a ship. 2 Before; forward; in front. —*interj.* In golf, a warning to any person who stands in the way of a stroke or of the ball. [OE]

fore–[1] See also words beginning FOR–.

fore–[2] *prefix* 1 Prior in time, place, or rank; as in:

fore–acquaint, **fore–adapt**, **fore–age**, **fore–announce**, **fore–answer**, **fore–assign**, **forebeing**, **forebless**, **forecited**, **foreconclude**, **foreman**, **forenotice**, **foreparent**, **fore–quoted**, **foresignify**

2 Front; in or at the front; as in:

forebay, **forebody**, **foreboom**, **forecabin**, **fore–edge**, **fore–end**

[OE *fore-, for-* before]

fore–and–aft (fôr′ən·aft′, fōr′-) *adj.* & *adv. Naut.* Lying or going in the direction of the ship's length; also, toward both bow and stern; in or at the bow and stern.

fore–and–aft rigged *Naut.* Fitted with sails whose forward edge (luff) is set on travelers attached to the mast: distinguished from *square–rigged.* See SCHOONER (def. 1).

fore–and–after (fôr′ən·af′ter, fōr′-) *n. Naut.* 1 Anything set along the length of a ship, as a hatch beam. 2 A vessel having only fore–and–aft sails.

fore·arm[1] (fôr·ärm′, fōr-) *v.t.* To arm beforehand.

fore·arm[2] (fôr′ärm′, fōr′-) *n.* 1 The part of the arm between the elbow and the wrist. ◆ Collateral adjective: *cubital.* 2 A wooden grip on the barrel of a gun to guard the firer's hand against being burned.

fore·bear (fôr′bâr′, fōr′-) *n.* An ancestor. [<Earlier *fore-be-er,* one who has existed formerly]

fore·bode (fôr·bōd′, fōr-) *v.t.* & *v.i.* **·bod·ed, ·bod·ing** 1 To have a premonition of (evil or harm). 2 To portend; presage; foretell. See synonyms under AUGUR. [<FORE- + BODE[2]] —**fore·bode′ment** *n.* —**fore·bod′er** *n.*

fore·bod·ing (fôr·bō′ding, fōr-) *n.* The apprehension of coming misfortune. See synonyms under ANTICIPATION, ANXIETY.

fore·brace (fôr′brās′, fōr′-) *n. Naut.* A brace of the foreyard.

fore·brain (fôr′brān′, fōr′-) *n. Anat.* 1 The first embryonic cerebral vesicle, from which develop the interbrain and endbrain. 2 The prosencephalon.

fore·cast (fôr′kast′, -käst′, fōr′-) *v.t.* **·cast, ·cast·ing** 1 To calculate or plan beforehand. 2 To predict; foresee. 3 To foreshadow. See synonyms under ANTICIPATE, AUGUR. —*n.* 1 *Meteorol.* An antecedent calculation or determination, especially in regard to weather conditions over a short period of time on the basis of charted data. 2 Previous contrivance; also, plan. 3 Forethought; foresight. 4 A prophecy. See synonyms under ANTICIPATION, PRUDENCE.

fore·cast·er (fôr′kas′tər, -käs′-, fōr′-) *n.* One who forecasts, as the weather.

fore·cas·tle (fôr′kas′əl, -käs′-, fōr′-, fōk′səl) *n. Naut.* 1 The forward part of a ship. 2 In a merchant vessel, the forward part or compartment with living quarters for common sailors. Also spelled *fo'c's'le.*

fore·close (fôr·klōz′, fōr′-) *v.* **·closed, ·clos·ing** *v.t.* 1 *Law* **a** To deprive (a mortgager in default) of the right to redeem mortgaged property. **b** To take away the power to redeem (a mortgage or pledge). 2 To shut out; exclude. —*v.i.* 3 To foreclose a mortgage. [<OF *forclos,* pp. of *forclore* exclude <*for-* outside (<L *fors*) + *clore* <L *claudere* close] —**fore·clos′a·ble** *adj.* —**fore·clo′sure** (-klō′zhər) *n.*

fore·con·scious (fôr·kon′shəs, fōr-) *n.* The preconscious.

fore·course (fôr′kôrs′, fōr′kōrs′) *n. Naut.* In a square–rigged vessel, the foresail.

fore·court (fôr′kôrt′, fōr′kōrt′) *n.* In tennis, handball, etc., the zone nearest the net or wall.

fore·date (fôr·dāt′, fōr-) *v.t.* **·dat·ed, ·dat·ing** To antedate.

fore·deck (fôr′dek′, fōr′-) *n. Naut.* The forward part of a deck, especially of an upper deck.

fore·do (fôr·do͞o′, fōr-) See FORDO.

fore·doom (fôr·do͞om′, fōr-) *v.t.* To doom in advance; condemn beforehand. —*n.* (fôr′·do͞om′, fōr′-) Doom in advance.

fore·fa·ther (fôr′fä′thər, fōr′-) *n.* An ancestor, especially a remote ancestor.

Forefathers' Day The anniversary of the landing of the Pilgrims at Plymouth, Mass. (Dec. 21, 1620), usually celebrated on Dec. 22, through an error in changing from the Old Style calendar to the New Style.

fore·feel (fôr·fēl′, fōr-) *v.t.* **·felt, ·feel·ing** To have a premonition of; feel before.

fore·foot (fôr′fo͝ot′, fōr′-) *n. pl.* **·feet** 1 A front foot. 2 *Naut.* The bow or cutwater of a vessel.

fore·front (fôr′frunt′, fōr′-) *n.* The foremost part or position.

fore·gath·er (fôr·gath′ər, fōr-) See FORGATHER.

fore·glimpse (fôr′glimps′, fōr′-) *n.* A glimpse of the future, or a glance ahead at the outset.

fore·go[1] (fôr·gō′, fōr-) See FORGO.

fore·go[2] (fôr·gō′, fōr-) *v.t.* & *v.i.* **fore·went, fore·gone, fore·go·ing** To go before or precede in time, place, etc. [OE *foregān*]

fore·go·er (fôr·gō′ər, fōr-) *n.* One who or that which precedes; especially, the leader of a dog team.

fore·go·ing (fôr·gō′ing, fōr-) *adj.* Occurring previously; antecedent. See synonyms under ANTECEDENT.

fore·gone (fôr′gôn′, -gon′, fōr′-) *adj.* Determined already; previous. —**fore′gone′ness** *n.*

foregone conclusion 1 A conclusion determined in advance of the evidence. 2 An obvious, foreseen, or foreseeable result.

fore·ground (fôr′ground′, fōr′-) *n.* That part of a landscape or picture nearest the spectator.

fore·gut (fôr′gut′, fōr′-) *n. Zool.* In vertebrates, the anterior part of the embryonic alimentary canal.

fore·hand (fôr′hand′, fōr′-) *adj.* 1 Done prior to. 2 Front. 3 Of or pertaining to a tennis stroke made to the right of the body (when the player is right–handed): distinguished from *backhand.* —*n.* 1 The part of a horse in front of the rider. 2 Superiority; advantage. 3 A forehand tennis stroke; also, the position in playing such a stroke.

fore·hand·ed (fôr′han′did, fōr′-) *adj.* 1 Done in good time; early. 2 Having money saved; thrifty. 3 In tennis, forehand. 4 Referring to the forehand or foreparts of a horse. —**fore′hand′ed·ness** *n.*

fore·head (fôr′id, -hed, for′-) *n.* 1 The upper part of the face, between the eyes and the natural line of the hair. ◆ Collateral adjective: *frontal.* 2 The front part of a thing.

for·eign (fôr′in, for′-) *adj.* 1 Belonging to, situated in, or derived from another country; not native; alien. 2 Connected with other countries; bearing a relation to other countries. 3 Of, pertaining to, or resulting from some person or thing aside from that under discussion. 4 *Biol.* Occurring in that place or body in which it is not normally or organically found. 5 Having only remote relation or no relation; not pertinent; irrelevant. 6 *Law* Not subject to the laws or jurisdiction of a country; extraterritorial. 7 *Obs.* Outside one's family circle. See synonyms under ALIEN. [<F *forain,* ult. <L *foras* out of doors]

foreign affairs International affairs in relation to the home government.

foreign bill A bill of exchange drawn in one country or state and made payable in another: also called **foreign draft.**

for·eign-born (fôr′in·bôrn′, for′-) *adj.* Born in another country; not native.

for·eign·er (fôr′in·ər, for′-) *n.* A native or citizen of a foreign country. See synonyms under ALIEN.

foreign exchange 1 The transaction of monetary affairs, payment of debts, etc., between residents of different countries. 2 The value of the money of one country in terms of the money of another; also, the difference between this and par.

for·eign·ism (fôr′ən·iz′əm, for′-) *n.* 1 The state of being foreign. 2 A foreign peculiarity, idiom, or custom.

foreign legion A military unit of foreign volunteers serving in a national army.

Foreign Legion A volunteer infantry regiment of the French army composed chiefly, in its enlisted ranks, of non–French troops and originally serving in North Africa. Also **French Foreign Legion.**

foreign mission 1 A group of people organized and sent to spread religious teaching, medical knowledge, etc., in a foreign country. 2 A group of government representatives sent to a foreign country on diplomatic or other business.

for·eign·ness (fôr′in·nis, for′-) *n.* 1 The state or quality of being foreign. 2 Absence of connection or relation; extraneousness.

foreign office A department or bureau of a government in charge of foreign affairs; also, the building in which it is housed. Also **Foreign Office.**

fore·judge[1] (fôr·juj′, fōr-) See FORJUDGE.

fore·judge[2] (fôr·juj′, fōr-) *v.t.* **·judged, ·judg·ing** To prejudge; pass judgment on before hearing the evidence.

fore·know (fôr·nō′, fōr-) *v.t.* **·knew, ·known, ·know·ing** To know beforehand. —**fore·know′a·ble** *adj.*

fore·knowl·edge (fôr′nol′ij, fōr′-) *n.* Knowledge of a thing before it manifests itself or of an event before it takes place; prescience.

fore·la·dy (fôr′lā′dē, fōr′-) *n. pl.* **·la·dies** A forewoman.

fore·land (fôr′land, fōr′-) *n.* 1 A projecting point of land; a cape. 2 Territory situated in front: opposed to *hinterland.*

fore·lay (fôr·lā′, fōr-) *v.t.* **·laid, ·lay·ing** *Dial.* To plan or lay down beforehand.

fore·leg (fôr′leg′, fōr′-) *n.* A front leg of a quadruped. Also **fore leg.**

fore·lock[1] (fôr′lok′, fōr′-) *n.* A lock of hair growing over the forehead.

fore·lock[2] (fôr′lok′, fōr′-) *n. Mech.* An iron pin or wedge passed through the end of a bolt or the like, to prevent its withdrawal; linchpin; key.

fore·look (fôr′lo͝ok′, fōr′-) *n. U.S.* A look into the future.

fore·man (fôr′mən, fōr′-) *n. pl.* **·men** (-mən) 1 The overseer of a body of workmen. 2 The head man; chief man; especially, the spokesman of a jury. See synonyms under MASTER. —**fore′man·ship** *n.*

fore·mast (fôr′mast′, -mäst′, -məst, fōr′-) *n. Naut.* The foremost mast of a vessel.

fore·mast·man (fôr′mast′mən, -mäst′-, fōr′-) *n. pl.* **·men** (-mən) An ordinary sailor.

fore·most (fôr′mōst, -məst, fōr′-) *adj.* First in place, time, rank, or order; chief. See synonyms under FIRST, PARAMOUNT. —*adv.* In the first place; soonest; first. [OE *formest*]

fore·name (fôr·nām′, fōr-) *v.t.* **·named, ·nam·ing** To name before; mention previously. —*n.* (fôr′nām′, fōr′-) A name placed before the family name or surname; a prenomen. —**fore′named′** *adj.*

fore·noon (fôr′no͞on′, fōr′-, fôr·no͞on′, fōr-) *n.* The period of daylight preceding midday; the morning.

fo·ren·sic (fə·ren′sik) *adj.* 1 Pertaining to courts of justice or to public disputation; argumentative; rhetorical. 2 Relating to or used in legal proceedings: *forensic* medicine. Also **fo·ren′si·cal.** [<L *forensis* <*forum* market place, forum] —**fo·ren′si·cal·ly** *adv.*

fore·or·dain (fôr′ôr·dān′, fōr′-) *v.t.* To ordain beforehand; predestinate.

fore·or·dain·ment (fôr′ôr·dān′mənt, fōr′-) *n.* Foreordination.

fore·or·di·na·tion (fôr·ôr′də·nā′shən, fōr-) *n.* Predestination; predetermination. See PREDESTINATION.

fore·part (fôr′pärt′, fōr′-) *n.* The first part in time, place, or sequence.

fore·past (fôr′past′, -päst′, fōr′-) *adj. Rare* Past; bygone. Also **fore′passed′.**

fore·peak (fôr′pēk′, fōr′-) *n. Naut.* The extreme forward part of a ship's hold within the angle of the bow under the lowest deck.

fore·quar·ter (fôr′kwôr′tər, fōr′-) *n.* The front portion of a side of beef, etc., including the leg and adjacent parts.

fore·rank (fôr′rangk′, fōr′-) *n.* The front or first rank.

fore·reach (fôr·rēch′, fōr-) *v.t. Naut.* 1 To gain upon or pass, as a ship. —*v.i.* 2 To move forward suddenly and unexpectedly. 3 To gain.

fore·run (fôr·run′, fōr-) *v.t.* **·ran, ·run, ·run·ning** 1 To be the precursor of; foreshadow; herald. 2 To run in advance of; precede. 3 To forestall.

fore·run·ner (fôr·run′ər, fōr-, fôr′run′ər, fōr′-) *n.*, **1** A precursor; predecessor; ancestor. **2** One who or that which runs before; a herald; a harbinger. **3** A portent or prognostic. **— the Forerunner** John the Baptist. See synonyms under HERALD.

fore·said (fôr′sed′, fōr′-) *adj.* Aforesaid.

fore·sail (fôr′sāl′, -səl, fōr′-, fō′səl) *n. Naut.* **1** A square sail, bent to the foreyard; the lowest sail on the foremast of a square-rigged vessel. **2** The fore-and-aft sail on a schooner's foremast, set on a boom and gaff. **3** The forestaysail of a cutter or sloop.

fore·see (fôr·sē′, fōr-) *v.t.* **fore·saw, fore·seen, fore·see·ing** To see beforehand; anticipate. **— fore·see′a·ble** *adj.* **— fore·seer′** *n.*

fore·shad·ow (fôr·shad′ō, fōr-) *v.t.* To suggest or indicate beforehand; prefigure. **—** *n.* The indistinct representation or indication of something to come. **— fore·shad′ow·er** *n.*

fore·sheet (fôr′shēt′, fōr′-) *n. Naut.* **1** A rope holding one of the clews of a foresail. **2** *pl.* The forward space in a boat.

fore·shore (fôr′shôr′, fōr′shōr′) *n.* That part of a shore uncovered at low tide.

fore·short·en (fôr·shôr′tən, fōr-) *v.t.* In drawing, to reduce the lines or parts of (a drawing, etc.) so as to create the illusion of depth and distance while retaining the proper proportions of size and extent. **— fore·short′en·ing** *n.*

fore·show (fôr·shō′, fōr-) *v.t.* **·showed, ·shown, ·show·ing** To show or indicate beforehand; prophesy. Also *Archaic* **fore·shew′** (-shō).

fore·side (fôr′sīd′, fōr′-) *n.* **1** The front. **2** Land along the shore.

fore·sight (fôr′sīt′, fōr′-) *n.* **1** The act or capacity of foreseeing; a looking forward. **2** Thoughtful care for the future. See synonyms under ANTICIPATION, PRUDENCE, WISDOM. **—fore′sight′ed** *adj.* **—fore′sight′ed·ness** *n.*

fore·skin (fôr′skin′, fōr′-) *n.* The prepuce.

fore·spur·rer (fôr·spûr′ər, fōr-) *n. Obs.* One who rides in advance as a herald.

for·est (fôr′ist, for′-) *n.* **1** A large tract of land covered with a natural growth of trees and underbrush. ◆ Collateral adjective: *sylvan.* **2** In English law, wild land generally belonging to the crown and kept for the protection of game. **—** *adj.* Of, pertaining to, or inhabiting woods or forest. **—** *v.t.* To overspread or plant with trees; make a forest of. [<OF <Med. L *(silva) foresta* an unenclosed (wood) <*foris* outside]

for·est·age (fôr′is·tij, for′-) *n. Brit.* **1** *Law* Tribute payable to a forester. **2** A forester's service to the king.

fore·stall (fôr·stôl′, fōr-) *v.t.* **1** To hinder, prevent, or guard against by taking preventive measures. **2** To deal with, think of, or realize beforehand; anticipate. **3** To affect (the market) in one's favor by buying up or diverting goods. **4** *Obs.* To intercept. See synonyms under PREVENT. [OE *foresteall* an ambush] **— fore·stall′er** *n.* **— fore·stall′ing** *n.*

for·est·a·tion (fôr′is·tā′shən, for′-) *n.* **1** Forest extension; the planting of, or conversion of land into, forests. **2** Practical forestry.

fore·stay (fôr′stā′, fōr′-) *n. Naut.* A guy from the head of the foremast to the stem.

fore·stay·sail (fôr′stā′sāl′, -səl, fōr′-) *n. Naut.* A triangular sail in front of the foremast, hoisted on the forestay: in some rigs called *foresail.*

forest cover The sum total of vegetation in a forest; more especially, herbs, shrubs, and the litter of leaves, branches, fallen trees, and decayed vegetable matter composing the **forest floor.**

for·est·ed (fôr′is·tid, for′-) *adj.* Covered with trees or woods.

for·est·er (fôr′is·tər, for′-) *n.* **1** One skilled in the science of forestry; one in charge of a forest, its timber, or its game. **2** Any forest dweller. **3** A spotted moth (family *Agaristidae*) of the United States; especially, the velvety-black eight-spotted forester *(Alypia octomaculata).* **4** The great gray kangaroo of Australia *(Macropus giganteus).*

For·es·ter (fôr′is·tər, for′-), **C(ecil) S(cott),** 1899–1966, English novelist.

forest fly A small, dipterous insect *(Hippobosca equina)* widely distributed in the Old World, infesting horses, mules, camels, and related quadrupeds: also called *horse tick.*

Forest Hills A section of New York City on Long Island, site of the national lawn tennis tournaments.

forest reserve A tract of forest land set aside by government order for protection and cultivation.

for·est·ry (fôr′is·trē, for′-) *n.* The science of planting, developing, and managing forests.

Forest Service A branch of the Department of Agriculture which administers the National Forests, directs forest research, and promotes the conservation of forest resources.

fore·taste (fôr·tāst′, fōr-) *v.t.* **·tast·ed, ·tast·ing** To have some experience or taste of beforehand. See synonyms under ANTICIPATE. **—** *n.* (fôr′tāst′, fōr′-) A taste or brief experience beforehand. See synonyms under ANTICIPATION.

fore·tell (fôr·tel′, fōr-) *v.t.* & *v.i.* **·told, ·tell·ing** To tell or declare in advance; predict; prophesy. See synonyms under AUGUR, PROPHESY. **— fore·tell′er** *n.*

fore·think (fôr·thingk′, fōr-) *v.t. Rare* To think over or out in advance; anticipate.

fore·thought (fôr′thôt′, fōr′-) *adj.* Devised or thought of in advance; planned. **—** *n.* **1** Consideration beforehand; deliberate planning. **2** Prudent care for the future. See synonyms under ANTICIPATION, CARE, PRUDENCE. **— fore·thought′ful** *adj.* **— fore·thought′ful·ly** *adv.* **— fore·thought′ful·ness** *n.*

fore·time (fôr′tīm′, fōr′-) *n.* Time gone by; the past.

fore·to·ken (fôr·tō′kən, fōr-) *v.t.* To foreshow or presage; foreshadow. **—** *n.* (fôr′tō′kən, fōr′-) A token in advance.

fore·tooth (fôr′to͞oth′, fōr′-) *n.* *pl.* **·teeth** An incisor.

fore·top (fôr′top′, fōr′-; *for def. 3, also* fôr′təp, fōr′-) *n.* **1** The forelock; especially of a horse. **2** The front part of a wig. **3** *Naut.* A platform at the head of the lower section of a foremast.

fore·top·gal·lant (fôr′top·gal′ənt, -tə-, fōr′-) *adj. Naut.* Of, pertaining to, or designating the mast, sail, yard, etc., immediately above the foretopmast.

fore·top·gal·lant·mast (fôr′top·gal′ənt·mast′, -mäst′, -məst, -tə-, fōr′-) *n. Naut.* The mast or section of a mast above the foretopmast.

fore·top·man (fôr′top′mən, fōr′-) *n.* *pl.* **·men** (-mən) *Naut.* A sailor assigned to duty on the upper parts of a foremast.

fore·top·mast (fôr·top′mast′, -mäst′, -məst, fōr-) *n. Naut.* The section of a mast above the foretop.

fore·top·sail (fôr·top′sāl′, -səl, fōr-) *n.* The sail set on the foretopmast.

for·ev·er (fôr·ev′ər, fər-) *adv.* **1** Throughout eternity; to the end of time; everlastingly. **2** Incessantly. Also *Brit.* **for ever.**

forever and a day To all eternity: emphatic form.

for·ev·er·more (fôr·ev′ər·môr, -mōr, fər-) *adv.* For all time and eternity; forever: emphatic form.

fore·warn (fôr·wôrn′, fōr-) *v.t.* To caution beforehand; inform or instruct in advance. **— fore·warn′ing** *n.*

fore·wom·an (fôr′wo͝om′ən, fōr′-) *n.* *pl.* **·wom·en** (-wim′in) A woman who oversees other employees.

fore·word (fôr′wûrd′, fōr′-) *n.* An introduction; preface.

fore·yard[1] (fôr′yärd′, fōr′-) *n. Naut.* The lowest yard on the foremast of a square-rigged vessel.

fore·yard[2] (fôr′yärd′, fōr′-) *n.* A front yard of a house, temple, etc.

for·fairn (fôr·fârn′, fōr-) *adj. Scot.* Tired out; forlorn.

For·far (fôr′fər, -fär) **1** A former name for ANGUS county, Scotland: also **For′far·shire** (-shir). **2** The county town of Angus county, Scotland.

for·feit (fôr′fit) *v.t.* To incur the loss of through some fault, omission, error, or offense. [<*n.*] **—** *adj.* Forfeited. **—** *n.* **1** A thing lost by way of penalty for some default. **2** *pl.* Any game in which some piece of personal property is taken as a fine for a breach of the rules, and is redeemable by some playful penalty; also, the articles so taken. **3** Forfeiture. [<OF *forfait* a misdeed <Med. L *foris factum* <*foris* outside + *factum.* See FACT.] **— for′feit·a·ble** *adj.* **— for′feit·er** *n.*

for·fei·ture (fôr′fi·chər) *n.* **1** The act of forfeiting. **2** That which is forfeited.

for·fend (fôr·fend′) *v.t. Archaic* **1** To ward off, prevent. **2** To forbid. Also spelled *forefend.*

for·fi·cate (fôr′fi·kit) *adj.* Deeply furcate, or forked, as the tail of a frigate bird. [<L *forfex, forficis* scissors + -ATE[1]]

for·gat (fôr·gat′, fər-) *Archaic* Past tense of FORGET.

for·gath·er (fôr·gath′ər) *v.i.* **1** To meet or gather together; assemble. **2** To meet or encounter, especially by chance. **3** To associate; converse socially. Also spelled *foregather.*

for·gave (fôr·gāv′, fər-) Past tense of FORGIVE.

forge[1] (fôrj, fōrj) *n.* **1** An open fireplace or hearth with forced draft, for heating metal ready for hammering or shaping. **2** A smithy. **3** A place where metal is refined. **—** *v.* **forged, forg·ing** *v.t.* **1** To shape by heating and hammering, as a horseshoe; beat or stamp into shape. **2** To fashion or form in any way; invent. **3** To make, alter, or imitate with intent to defraud. **—** *v.i.* **4** To commit forgery. **5** To work as a smith. [<OF, ult. <L *fabrica.* Doublet of FABRIC.] **— forged** *adj.*

FORGE
a. Blower. *b.* Hood. *c.* Water tank. *d.* Coal bed.
The blower keeps fuel burning steadily by forced draft under the fire bed.

forge[2] (fôrj, fōrj) *v.t.* & *v.i.* **forged, forg·ing** To move, go, or impel slowly forward. [? Alter. of FORCE]

forg·er (fôr′jər, fōr′-) *n.* **1** One who counterfeits or commits forgery. **2** A smith. **3** A fabricator.

for·ger·y (fôr′jər·ē, fōr′-) *n.* *pl.* **·ger·ies** **1** The act of falsely making or materially altering, with intent to defraud, any writing which, if genuine, might be of legal efficacy or the foundation of a legal liability. **2** The act of counterfeiting coin. **3** A spurious article bearing a false signature, as a painting, sculpture, or book. **4** *Obs.* The exercise of invention.

Synonym: counterfeiting. Imitating or altering a coin or note which passes as currency or money is *counterfeiting*; the making of a fraudulent writing, or the material alteration of a genuine writing with intent to defraud, is *forgery*; the changing of the figures in a genuine note or check, the unauthorized appending of another's signature, the transferring of a genuine signature to a document for which it was not intended, are all instances of *forgery*; the making of spurious coins, the raising of government notes, bonds, etc., to higher values, are instances of *counterfeiting.*

for·get (fər·get′, fôr-) *v.* **for·got** (*Archaic* **for·gat**), **for·got·ten** or **for·got, for·get·ting** *v.t.* **1** To be unable to recall (something previously known) to the mind; fail or cease to remember. **2** To fail (to do something) unintentionally; neglect. **3** To fail to take through forgetfulness; leave behind accidentally. **4** To lose interest in or regard for; overlook purposely; disregard or slight: I will never *forget* you. **5** To leave unmentioned; fail to think of. **—** *v.i.* **6** To lose remembrance of something. **— to forget oneself** **1** To be unselfish. **2** To lose self-control and act in an unbecoming manner. **3** To lose consciousness. **4** To be lost in thought. [OE *forgietan*] **— for·get′ter** *n.*

for·get·ful (fər·get′fəl, fôr-) *adj.* **1** Having little power to retain or recall. **2** Neglectful; inattentive; careless. **3** *Obs.* Producing forgetfulness or oblivion. **— for·get′ful·ly** *adv.* **— for·get′ful·ness** *n.*

for·ge·tive (fôr′jə·tiv, fōr-) *adj. Archaic* Creative; inventive. [? <*forge*[1], *v.*]

for·get-me-not (fər·get′mē·not′) *n.* A small herb (genus *Myosotis*) of the borage family, with blue, rose, or white flowers. One species (*M. alpestris*) is the official flower of Alaska Territory.

forget-me-not blue The color of the forget-me-not, a light, dusty blue.

for·get·ta·ble (fər·get′ə·bəl, fôr-) *adj.* That may be forgotten. Also **for·get′a·ble.**

for·gie (fər·gē′) *v.t.* & *v.i. Scot.* To forgive.

forg·ing (fôr′jing, fōr′-) *n.* A tool or implement that has been forged.

for·give (fər·giv′, fôr-) *v.* **for·gave, for·giv·en, for·giv·ing** *v.t.* **1** To grant pardon for or remission of (something); cease to demand the penalty for. **2** To grant freedom from penalty to (someone). **3** To cease to blame or feel resentment against. **4** To remit, as a debt. — *v.i.* **5** To show forgiveness; grant pardon. See synonyms under ABSOLVE, PARDON. [OE *forgiefan*] — **for·giv′a·ble** *adj.* — **for·giv′er** *n.*

for·give·ness (fər·giv′nis, fôr-) *n.* **1** The act of forgiving; pardon. **2** A disposition to forgive. See synonyms under MERCY.

for·giv·ing (fər·giv′ing, fôr-) *adj.* Disposed to forgive; merciful. See synonyms under CHARITABLE, HUMANE, MERCIFUL. — **for·giv′ing·ly** *adv.* — **for·giv′ing·ness** *n.*

for·go (fôr·gō′) *v.t.* **for·went, for·gone, for·go·ing** **1** To refrain from. **2** To give up; go without. **3** *Obs.* To overlook; neglect. Also spelled *forego.* See synonyms under ABANDON. [OE *forgān* pass over] — **for·go′er** *n.*

for·got (fər·got′, fôr-) Past tense and alternative past participle of FORGET.

for·got·ten (fər·got′n, fôr-) Past participle of FORGET.

fo·rint (fôr′int, *Hungarian* fô·rēnt′) *n.* The basic monetary unit of Hungary since 1946, subdivided into 100 fillér.

for·jes·kit (fər·jes′kit) *adj. Scot.* Exhausted by labor.

for·judge (fôr·juj′) *v.t.* **·judged, ·judg·ing** *Law* **1** To deprive, as of a right, by judgment of court. **2** To expel (an attorney or officer) from court for some offense. Sometimes spelled *forejudge.* [<OF *forjugier* <*fors-* outside (<L *foris*) + *jugier* <L *judicare* judge]

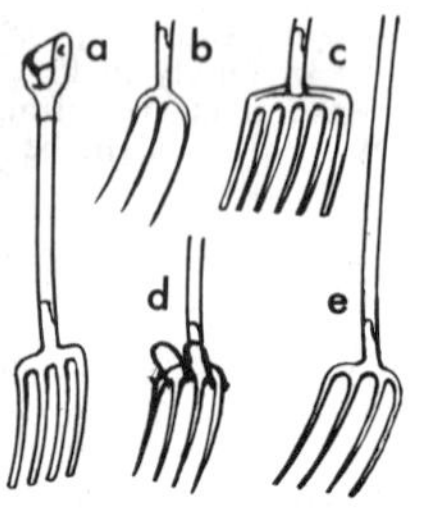

fork (fôrk) *n.* **1** A utensil consisting of a handle and two or more tines or prongs, used for handling food at the table or in cooking. **2** A pronged agricultural or mechanical implement for tossing, turning, carrying, digging, lifting, etc.: a *pitchfork.* **3** Anything of like use or shape. **4** An offshoot: diverging branch. **5** The angular opening or place of division. **6** The point at which two roads or streams unite. **7** Each of the roads or streams: the west *fork;* also, the ground in the angle made by the junction of two streams. **8** A dilemma. **9** The barb of an arrow. — *v.t.* **1** To make fork-shaped. **2** To pierce, pitch, or dig with or as with a fork. **3** In chess, to attack (two pieces) simultaneously. — *v.i.* **4** To branch; bifurcate: The trail *forked.* — **to fork out** (or **over** or **up**) *Slang* To pay or hand over. [OE *forca* <L *furca*]

a b c d e

FARM FORKS
a. Spading fork.
b. Hay fork.
c. Ensilage fork.
d. Barley fork.
e. Manure fork.

forked (fôrkt, fôr′kid) *adj.* **1** Having a fork, or shaped like a fork. **2** Diverging into two branches: *forked* lightning. — **fork′ed·ly** *adv.* — **fork′ed·ness** *n.*

forked tongue A lying or treacherous tongue.

fork·y (fôr′kē) *adj.* Like a fork; forked; bifurcate.

For·lì (fôr·lē′) A city in north central Italy on the Montone. Ancient **Fo·rum Liv·i·i** (fôr′əm liv′ē·ī, fō′rəm).

for·lorn (fər·lôrn, fôr-) *adj.* **1** Left in distress without help or hope; deserted. **2** Miserable; pitiable. **3** Lonely; dreary. [Orig. pp. of obs. *forlese* lose, abandon, OE *forleosan*] — **for·lorn′ly** *adv.* — **for·lorn′ness** *n.*

forlorn hope **1** A desperate enterprise. **2** Those who undertake a hopeless task, as the members of a storming party. [<Du. *verloren hoop* lost troop]

form (fôrm) *n.* **1** The outward or visible shape of a body as distinguished from its substance or color. **2** *Philos.* The intelligible structure of a thing, which determines its substance or species, as distinguished from its matter. **3** A body, especially of a living being. **4** A mold or frame for shaping. **5** A specific structure, condition, or appearance: carbon in the *form* of diamonds; disease in all its *forms.* **6** A specific type or species of a larger group: democracy as a *form* of government. **7** In art, music, and literature, style and manner, as opposed to content. **8** System; order; formal procedure: to convene as a matter of *form.* **9** Behavior or conduct according to custom, ceremony, or decorum; formality; manners. **10** Manner or fashion of doing something: He swam in good *form.* **11** Fitness in respect to health, spirits, training, etc.: The horse was in good *form* for the race. **12** A formula or draft; a specimen document used as a guide in drawing up others. **13** A document with spaces left for the insertion of information: an application *form.* **14** The lair of an animal, especially of a hare. **15** A cotton bud. **16** A long bench without a back. **17** *Brit.* A grade or class in a school. **18** *Printing* The body of type and cuts secured in a chase. Also *Brit.* **forme.** **19** *Gram.* Any of the various shapes assumed by a word in a particular context, as *talk, talks, talked, talking.* **20** *Ling.* A linguistic form. See BOUND FORM, FREE FORM. — *v.t.* **1** To give shape to; mold; fashion. **2** To construct in the mind; devise: to *form* a plan. **3** To combine into; organize into: The men *formed* a club. **4** To develop; acquire, as a habit or liking. **5** To give a specific or exemplified shape or character to: He *formed* his ideals on those of Wilson. **6** To go to make up; be an element of: Guesswork *forms* the larger part of his theory. **7** To shape by discipline or training; mold: Education *forms* the mind. **8** *Gram.* To construct (a word) by adding or combining elements: to *form* an adverb by adding *-ly* to an adjective. — *v.i.* **9** To take shape; assume a specific form or arrangement. **10** To begin to exist. See synonyms under CONSTRUCT. [<OF *fourme* <L *forma*]

Synonyms (noun): appearance, aspect, ceremonial, ceremony, configuration, conformation, contour, fashion, figure, formality, method, mode, mold, observance, outline, rite, ritual, shape. See BODY, FIGURE, FRAME.

-form *combining form* Like; in the shape of: *ensiform.* [<L *-formis* -like <*forma* form]

for·mal[1] (fôr′məl) *adj.* **1** Made, framed, or done in accordance with regular and established forms and methods, or with proper dignity and impressiveness; orderly. **2** Of or pertaining to established forms or methods. **3** Of or pertaining to the external appearance or form as opposed to real substance: *formal* religion; perfunctory. **4** Having outward show, but lacking reality; outward; mechanical. **5** Having regard to or done in accordance with a scrupulous observance of social forms, customs, and etiquette; punctilious; ceremonious; conventional. **6** Of or pertaining to the form as opposed to the content of logical reasoning. **7** *Philos.* Of or pertaining to the characteristic composition of anything; essential instead of material.

for·mal[2] (fôr·mal′) *n.* Methylal.

for·mal·de·hyde (fôr·mal′də·hīd) *n. Chem.* A colorless pungent gas, CH_2O, obtained variously by the partial oxidation of methyl alcohol: used as an antiseptic, reagent, preservative, and disinfectant, for which it is prepared by solution in water or absorption into porous materials. It is also the basis of many important plastic materials, such as Bakelite, Formica, etc. Also **for·mal′de·hyd** (-hid). [<FORM(IC) + ALDEHYDE]

for·mal·ism (fôr′məl·iz′əm) *n.* **1** Scrupulous observance of prescribed forms, especially in religious worship, social life, art, etc. **2** An instance of such observance. **3** Gestalt or configuration psychology. — **for′mal·ist** *n.* — **for′mal·is′tic** *adj.*

for·mal·i·ty (fôr·mal′ə·tē) *n. pl.* **·ties** **1** The state or character of being formal, precise, stiff, or elaborately ceremonious. **2** Adherence to standards and rules; ceremony; conventionality. **3** A proper order of procedure. **4** Form without substance or meaning. See synonyms under FORM.

for·mal·ize (fôr·məl·īz) *v.* **·ized, ·iz·ing** *v.t.* **1** To make formal. **2** To give form to; reduce to form. — *v.i.* **3** To be formal; act formally. — **for′mal·i·za′tion** *n.* — **for′mal·iz′er** *n.*

formal logic The branch of logic which deals only with the formal structure of propositions and with the operations by which conclusions are deduced from them; the art of deductive reasoning.

for·mal·ly (fôr′mə·lē) *adv.* **1** In accordance with forms; in a formal manner; stiffly. **2** In an authorized manner.

for·mat (fôr′mat) *n.* The form, size, type face, margins, and general style of a book or other publication, when printed and bound; especially, its shape and size as determined by the number of times the original sheet forming the leaves has been folded. [<F <L (*liber*) *formatus* a (book) made up <*formare* form]

for·mate (fôr′māt) *n. Chem.* A salt or ester of formic acid.

for·ma·tion (fôr·mā′shən) *n.* **1** The act or process of forming or of making by the combination of materials; also, the taking on of specific form; development. **2** Manner in which anything is shaped or composed. **3** The disposition of military troops as in column, line, or square. **4** Anything that is formed. **5** *Geol.* **a** Earthy or mineral deposits, or rock masses, named with reference to mode of origin. **b** A series of associated rocks, having similar conditions of origin. **6** *Ecol.* A fully developed plant association in a given area.

form·a·tive (fôr′mə·tiv) *adj.* **1** Competent, serving, or aiding to form; capable of being formed or influenced; plastic. **2** Pertaining to formation. **3** *Gram.* Serving to form words. — *n. Gram.* **1** An element, as an affix, added to the root of a word to give it a new and special grammatical form. **2** A word formed by the addition of a new element to, or a modification of, the root.

form class A group of linguistic forms having certain syntactical characteristics in common, as all words functioning as the subjects of sentences in English.

form drag *Physics* That component of fluid resistance which is due to the form of the object moving through it and which may be reduced or neutralized by streamlining.

For·men·te·ra (fôr′men·tā′rä) Smallest of the major islands of the Balearic group; 37 square miles.

form·er[1] (fôr′mər) *n.* One who or that which forms or molds; a maker; pattern.

for·mer[2] (fôr′mər) *adj.* Going before in time; previously mentioned; preceding; ancient. — **the former** The first of two mentioned persons or things: opposed to *the latter.* See synonyms under ANTECEDENT, ANTERIOR, CAUSE. [ME *formere,* a back formation <*foremost*]

for·mer·ly (fôr′mər·lē) *adv.* **1** Some time or a long time ago; heretofore. **2** *Obs.* At a time immediately preceding the present; just now.

for·mic (fôr′mik) *adj.* **1** Pertaining to or derived from ants. **2** Derived from formic acid. [<L *formica* ant]

For·mi·ca (fôr·mī′kə, fôr′mə·kə) *n.* A thermosetting phenolic resin used in transparent or colored sheets as wallboard, table tops, paneling, etc.; a trade name.

formic acid *Chem.* A colorless corrosive liquid compound, HCOOH, with a penetrating odor, found in the bodies of ants and spiders, in the hairs and other parts of certain caterpillars, and in stinging nettles, and made commercially by the reaction of carbon monoxide with sodium hydroxide.

for·mi·cant (fôr′mə·kənt) *adj.* **1** Antlike. **2** *Med.* Pertaining to the feeble, creeping motion of the pulse noted in certain conditions.

for·mi·car·y (fôr′mə·ker′ē) *n. pl.* **·car·ies** A nest of ants, consisting of galleries and chambers excavated in the earth and covered by a mound of debris.

for·mi·cate (fôr′mə·kāt) *v.i.* **·cat·ed, ·cat·ing** To swarm; collect in swarms, as ants. [<L *formicatus,* pp. of *formicare* crawl <*formica* an ant]

for·mi·ca·tion (fôr′mə·kā′shən) *n. Med.* An

itching sensation like the creeping of ants.
for·mi·ci·a·sis (fôr′mə·sī′ə·sis) *n. Pathol.* The itching, swollen condition following ant bite.
for·mi·da·ble (fôr′mi·də·bəl) *adj.* **1** Exciting fear; felt as dangerous to encounter. **2** Difficult to accomplish. [<MF <L *formidabilis* <*formidare* fear] —**for′mi·da·ble·ness** *n.* —**for′mi·da·bly** *adv.*
Synonyms: dangerous, redoubtable, redoubted, terrible, tremendous. That which is *formidable* is worthy of fear if encountered or opposed; as, a *formidable* array of troops, or of evidence. *Formidable* is a word of more dignity than *dangerous,* and suggests more calm and collected power than *terrible*; *formidable* is less overwhelming than *tremendous.* A loaded gun is *dangerous*; a battery of artillery is *formidable.* A *dangerous* man is likely to do mischief, and needs watching; a *formidable* man may not be *dangerous* if not attacked; an enraged maniac is *terrible*; the force of ocean waves in a storm, the silent pressure in the ocean depths, are *tremendous.* *Antonyms*: contemptible, despicable, feeble, harmless, helpless, powerless, weak.
form·less (fôrm′lis) *adj.* Without form; shapeless. —**form′less·ly** *adv.* —**form′less·ness** *n.*
For·mo·sa (fôr·mō′sə) **1** A former name for TAIWAN. **2** A province of northern Argentina; 28,778 square miles; capital, Formosa.
For·mo·san (fôr·mō′sən) *n.* **1** A native or inhabitant of the island of Formosa (Taiwan). **2** The Indonesian language of the Malay aborigines of Formosa. —*adj.* Of or pertaining to Formosa, its people, or their Indonesian language.
Formosa Strait The channel between China and Taiwan. *Chinese* **Tai·wan Hai·hsia** (tī′wän′ hī′shyä′).
for·mu·la (fôr′myə·lə) *n. pl.* **·las** or **·lae** (-lē) **1** An exact method or form of words prescribed as a guide for thought, action, expression, or statement; fixed rule or set form. **2** A medical prescription. **3** *Math.* A rule or combination expressed in algebraic or symbolic form. **4** *Chem.* A symbolic representation of the nature, composition, and structure of a chemical compound. The principal types are: the **empirical formula,** giving the quantitative values of the constituents, as H_2SO_4, sulfuric acid; the **structural formula,** showing the linkages of each atom, as CH_3CH_3, ethane; and the **graphic formula,** showing the spatial relations of the constituents, as

$$\begin{matrix} & H & & H & \\ & | & & | & \\ H- & C & - & C & -OH \\ & | & & | & \\ & H & & H & \end{matrix}$$ ethyl alcohol C_2H_6O, or CH_3CH_2OH.

5 A confession of religious faith, or a formal statement of doctrine. See synonyms under LAW, RULE. [<L, dim. of *forma* form]
for·mu·lar·ize (fôr′myə·lə·rīz) *v.t.* **·ized, ·iz·ing** To formulate.
for·mu·lar·y (fôr′myə·ler′ē) *adj.* Stated in or as in a formula; formal. —*n. pl.* **·lar·ies** **1** A collection of forms, formulas, etc.: a *formulary* of drugs. **2** Specifically, a church ritual. **3** A prescribed form; formula.
for·mu·late (fôr′myə·lāt) *v.t.* **·lat·ed, ·lat·ing** **1** To express in a formula, or as a formula. **2** To put or state in exact, concise, and systematic form. —**for′mu·la′tion** *n.* —**for′·mu·la′tor** *n.*
for·mu·lism (fôr′myə·liz′əm) *n.* Observance or use of, or adherence to, formulas. —**for′mu·lis′tic** *adj.*
for·mu·lize (fôr′myə·līz) *v.t.* & *v.i.* **·lized, ·liz·ing** To formulate. —**for′mu·li·za′tion** *n.* —**for′·mu·li′zer** *n.*
for·myl (fôr′mil) *n. Chem.* The univalent radical CHO, constituting the base of formic acid. [<FORM(IC) + -YL]
For·nax (fôr′naks) A southern constellation near Eridanus. See CONSTELLATION.
for·ni·cate[1] (fôr′nə·kit) *adj. Archit.* Arched; vaulted. [<L *fornicatus* <*fornix, -icis* an arch]
for·ni·cate[2] (fôr′nə·kāt) *v.i.* **·cat·ed, ·cat·ing** To commit fornication. [<L *fornicatus,* pp. of *fornicare* <*fornix, -icis* a vault, brothel] —**for′ni·ca′tor** *n.*
for·ni·ca·tion (fôr′nə·kā′shən) *n.* **1** Illicit sexual intercourse of unmarried persons. **2** In Scriptural use: **a** Adultery or harlotry, or incest. **b** Idolatry.
for·nix (fôr′niks) *n. pl.* **for·ni·ces** (-nə·sēz) **1** *Anat.* **a** A vaulted or reflected surface. **b** The bands of white fibers beneath the corpus callosum of the brain, connecting the two hemispheres of the cerebellum. **2** *Archit.* A vault or arch, commonly one within a building. [<L, vault]
For·rest (fôr′ist, for′-), **Edwin,** 1806–72, U.S. tragic actor. —**Nathan Bedford,** 1821–77, American Confederate general.
For·res·tal (fôr′is·tôl, for′-), **James Vincent,** 1892–1949, U.S. banker; first U.S. secretary of defense 1947–49.
for·rit (fôr′it, for′-) *adv. Scot.* Forward.
for·sake (fər·sāk′, fôr-) *v.t.* **for·sook, for·sak·en, for·sak·ing** **1** To leave or withdraw from; renounce. **2** To abandon; desert. **3** *Obs.* To reject. See synonyms under ABANDON. [OE *forsacan*]
For·se·ti (fôr′se·tē) In Norse mythology, the god of justice; son of Balder. Also **For′se·te.**
for·sooth (fər·sōōth′, fôr-) *adv.* In truth; certainly: chiefly ironical. [OE *forsōth*]
for·speak (fôr·spēk′) *v.t. Scot.* & *Brit. Dial.* **1** To bewitch. **2** *Obs.* To forbid.
for·spent (fôr·spent′) *adj.* Tired out; exhausted: also spelled *forespent.* [Orig. pp. of *forspend* exhaust, OE *forspendan*]
For·ster (fôr′stər), **E(dward) M(organ),** 1879–1970, English novelist.
for·swear (fôr·swâr′) *v.* **·swore, ·sworn, ·swear·ing** *v.t.* **1** To renounce upon oath; repudiate; abjure. **2** To deny upon oath. —*v.i.* **3** To swear falsely; commit perjury. —**to forswear oneself** To swear falsely. See synonyms under ABANDON, RENOUNCE. [OE *forswerian* swear falsely]
for·sworn (fôr·swôrn′, -swōrn′) *adj.* Perjured.
For·syth (fôr·sīth′), **Alexander John,** 1769–1843, Scottish clergyman and inventor.
for·syth·i·a (fôr·sith′ē·ə, -sī′thē·ə, fər-) *n.* One of a genus *(Forsythia)* of slender shrubs of the olive family native to China and Japan. Two species, *F. viridissima* and *F. suspensa,* are widely cultivated as ornamental plants. [after Wm. *Forsyth,* 1737–1804, British botanist, who brought the shrub from China]
fort (fôrt, fōrt) *n.* A single enclosed military work capable of independent defense; any fortification held by a garrison; a fortification: fortress. [<F, orig. an adj. <L *fortis* strong]
For·ta·le·za (fôr′tə·lā′zə) A port in eastern Brazil, capital of Ceará state.
fort·a·lice (fôr′tə·lis) *n.* An outwork of a fortification; a small fort. [<Med. L *fortalitia* <*fortis* strong]
Fort Dear·born (dir′bôrn) A military post established in 1803 on the present site of Chicago, Illinois.
Fort–de–France (fôr·də·fräns′) A port, the capital of Martinique.
Fort Don·el·son National Military Park (don′əl·sən) A locality in NW Tennessee on the Cumberland River; site of a Confederate defeat, 1862. See FORT HENRY.
Fort Du·quesne (dōō·kān′, dyōō-) An 18th century French trading post on the later site of Pittsburgh, Pennsylvania. See FORT PITT.
forte[1] (fôrt) *n.* **1** That which one does most readily or excellently. **2** The strongest part of a sword blade: distinguished from *foible.* [<F *fort.* See FORT.]
for·te[2] (fôr′tā, -tē) *Music n.* A musical chord or passage to be performed loudly. —*adj.* & *adv.* Loud: often as a direction to the player. [<Ital., strong <L *fortis*]
Fort Fish·er (fish′ər) An earthwork near the mouth of the Cape Fear River in North Carolina; besieged and captured by Union forces in the Civil War, 1865.
Fort Fred·e·ri·ca National Monument (fred′·ə·rē′kə) A locality on St. Simons Island, SE Georgia; site of the ruins of an English fort built in 1736 by John Oglethorpe.
forth (fôrth, fōrth) *adv.* **1** Forward in place, time, or order. **2** Outward, as from seclusion. **3** Away; out, as from a place of origin; abroad. —*prep. Archaic* Forth from; out of. [OE, forwards]
Forth (fôrth, fōrth), **Firth of** The estuary, extending 51 miles to the North Sea, of the **Forth,** a river that flows 65 miles east in SE Scotland. The estuary is spanned by **Forth Bridge;** 3,770 feet, 8,295 feet with approaches.
forth·com·ing (fôrth′kum′ing, fōrth′-) *adj.* Ready or about to appear. —*n.* A coming forth.
Fort Hen·ry (hen′rē) A fort in NW Tennessee on the Tennessee River, 12 miles from Fort Donelson; captured by Northern forces, 1862.
forth·right (fôrth′rīt′, fōrth′-) *adj.* Straightforward; direct. —*n. Archaic* A direct path or course. —*adv.* **1** Straightforwardly; with directness or frankness. **2** At once; straightway.
forth·with (fôrth′with′, -with′, fōrth′-) *adv.* Without delay; immediately.
for·ti·eth (fôr′tē·ith) *adj.* **1** Tenth in order after the thirtieth: the ordinal of *forty.* **2** Being one of forty equal parts. —*n.* One of forty equal parts of anything; the quotient of a unit divided by forty.
for·ti·fi·ca·tion (fôr′tə·fə·kā′shən) *n.* **1** The act, art, or science of fortifying. **2** A military defensive work; a fort. **3** A strengthening of any kind.
Synonyms: castle, citadel, fastness, fort, fortress, stronghold. *Fortification* is the general word for any artificial defensive work; a *fortress* is a *fortification* of especial size and strength, regarded as permanent, and ordinarily an independent work; a *fort* or *fortification* may be temporary; a *fortification* may be but part of a defensive system; we speak of the *fortifications* of a city. A *citadel* is a *fortification* within a city, or the fortified inner part of a city, or a *fortress* within which a garrison may be placed to overawe the citizens, or to which the defenders may retire if the outer works are captured; the medieval *castle* was the fortified residence of a king or baron. *Fort* is the common military term for a detached fortified building or enclosure of moderate size occupied or designed to be occupied by troops. The *fortifications* of a modern city usually consist of a chain of *forts.* Any defensible place, whether made so by nature or by art, is a *fastness* or *stronghold.* See RAMPART.
for·ti·fied (fôr′tə·fīd) *adj.* **1** Strengthened; said especially of wines whose alcoholic content has been increased by the addition of brandy. **2** Enriched, as bread.
for·ti·fy (fôr′tə·fī) *v.* **·fied, ·fy·ing** *v.t.* **1** To provide with defensive works; strengthen against attack. **2** To give physical or moral strength to; invigorate or encourage. **3** To confirm; corroborate. **4** To strengthen the structure of; reenforce. **5** To strengthen, as wine, by adding alcohol. **6** To enrich (food) by adding minerals, vitamins, etc. —*v.i.* **7** To raise defensive works. [<F *fortifier* <L *fortificare* <*fortis* strong + *facere* make] —**for′·ti·fi′a·ble** *adj.* —**for′ti·fi′er** *n.*
for·tis (fôr′tis) *Phonet. adj.* Strongly articulated: opposed to *lenis.* —*n.* A consonant, usually a stop, pronounced with tension of the speech organs or with strong plosion. [<L, strong]
for·tis·si·mo (fôr·tis′ə·mō, *Ital.* fôr·tēs′sē·mō) *adj.* & *adv. Music* Very loud. [<Ital., superl. of *forte* strong]
for·ti·tude (fôr′tə·tōōd, -tyōōd) *n.* **1** Strength of mind to meet or endure unfalteringly pain, adversity, or peril; patient and constant courage. **2** *Obs.* Physical strength or force. [<F <L *fortitudo* <*fortis* strong]
Synonyms: courage, endurance, heroism, resolution. *Fortitude* (L. *fortis,* strong) is the strength or firmness of mind or soul to endure pain or adversity patiently and determinedly. *Fortitude* has been defined as "passive *courage,*" which is a good definition, but not complete. *Fortitude* might be termed "still *courage,*" or "enduring *courage*"; it is that quality which is able not merely to endure pain or trial, but steadily to confront dangers that cannot be actively opposed, or against which one has no adequate defense; it takes *courage* to charge a trench, *fortitude* to withstand an enemy's fire. *Resolution* is of the mind; *endurance* is

partly physical; it requires *resolution* to resist temptation, *endurance* to resist hunger and cold. Compare COURAGE, PATIENCE.

for·ti·tu·di·nous (fôr′tə·to͞o′də·nəs, -tyo͞o′-) *adj.* Having or showing courage and endurance.

Fort Knox (noks) A military reservation in north central Kentucky; site (since 1936) of Federal gold bullion depository.

Fort–La·my (fôr·là·mē′) The capital of Chad in north central Africa.

Fort Mc·Hen·ry National Monument (mək·hen′rē) A fort in the harbor of Baltimore, Maryland. Its bombardment by the British, Sept. 13, 1814, was the occasion of Francis Scott Key's writing *The Star Spangled Banner.*

Fort Meigs (megz) A former fort on the Maumee River, NW Ohio; unsuccessfully besieged by British and Indian forces, 1813.

Fort Mims (mimz) A stockade near Mobile, Alabama, site of an Indian massacre, Aug. 30, 1813.

Fort Mon·roe (mən·rō′) A military post in SE Virginia at the entrance to Hampton Roads. Also **Fortress Monroe.**

Fort Moul·trie (mōl′trē, mo͞ol′-, mo͞o′-) A fort in Charleston harbor, South Carolina; scene of battles in the Revolutionary War and in the Civil War. See MOULTRIE, WILLIAM.

Fort Ni·ag·a·ra (nī·ag′ər·ə, -ag′rə) A fort at the mouth of the Niagara River in New York; scene of battles in 1759, 1812, and 1813.

fort·night (fôrt′nīt′, -nit′) *n.* A period of two weeks; fourteen days. [OE *fēowertēne* fourteen + *niht* nights]

fort·night·ly (fôrt′nīt′lē) *adj.* Occurring, coming, or issued every fortnight. —*adv.* Once a fortnight.

Fort Peck Dam (pek) One of the world's largest earth-fill dams, in the Missouri River, NE Montana; 250 feet high, 4 miles long; on **Fort Peck Reservoir,** the second largest in the United States; 383 square miles.

Fort Pick·ens (pik′ənz) A fort at the entrance to Pensacola harbor, NW Florida.

Fort Pitt (pit) The British name for FORT DUQUESNE after they captured it from the French in 1758: on the present site of Pittsburgh.

Fort Pulaski National Monument (po͞o·las′·kē) A fort in the mouth of the Savannah River, built in 1829.

for·tress (fôr′tris) *n.* A large permanent fort; a stronghold; castle. See synonyms under DEFENSE, FORTIFICATION. —*v.t.* To furnish or strengthen with a fortress; fortify. [<OF *forteresse* <L *fortis* strong]

Fort Smith (smith) A city on the Arkansas River in western Arkansas.

Fort Sum·ter National Monument (sum′tər) A fort in Charleston harbor, South Carolina; object of a Confederate attack, Apr. 12, 1861, that began the Civil War.

for·tu·i·tism (fôr·to͞o′ə·tiz′əm, -tyo͞o′-) *n.* The doctrine that phenomena or events come to pass by chance rather than in accordance with intelligent design or natural law. —**for·tu′i·tist** *n.* & *adj.*

for·tu·i·tous (fôr·to͞o′ə·təs, -tyo͞o′-) *adj.* **1** Occurring by chance; casual; accidental. **2** Fortunate; lucky. See synonyms under INCIDENTAL. [<L *fortuitus* <*fors* chance] —**for·tu′i·tous·ly** *adv.* —**for·tu′i·tous·ness** *n.*

for·tu·i·ty (fôr·to͞o′ə·tē, -tyo͞o′-) *n.* *pl.* **·ties** Chance occurrence; also, chance. See synonyms under ACCIDENT, HAZARD.

For·tu·na (fôr·to͞o′nə, -tyo͞o′-) In Roman mythology, the goddess of chance: identified with the Greek *Tyche.*

for·tu·nate (fôr′chə·nit) *adj.* **1** Happening by a favorable chance; lucky. **2** Favored with good fortune. —**for′tu·nate·ly** *adv.* —**for′tu·nate·ness** *n.*

Synonyms: favored, happy, lucky, prospered, prosperous, successful. A man is *successful* in any case if he achieves or gains what he seeks; he is known as a *successful* man if he has achieved or gained worthy objects of endeavor; he is *fortunate* or *lucky* if advantages have come to him without or beyond his direct planning or achieving. *Lucky* is the more common and colloquial, *fortunate* the more elegant word; *fortunate* is more naturally applied to the graver matters, as we speak of the *fortunate,* rather than the *lucky,* issue of a great battle; *lucky* more strongly emphasizes the element of chance, as when we speak of a *lucky* hit, a *lucky* guess, or of one as "born under a *lucky* star." *Favored* is used in a religious sense, implying that one is the object of divine favor. *Happy,* in this connection, signifies possessed of the means of happiness. One is said to be *happy* or *prosperous* whether his prosperity be the result of fortune or of achievement; *prospered* rather denotes the action of a superintending Providence. See AUSPICIOUS, HAPPY. *Antonyms*: broken, crushed, fallen, ill-starred, miserable, unfortunate, unhappy, unlucky, woeful, wretched.

for·tune (fôr′chən) *n.* **1** Chance or luck as the cause of changes in human affairs: often personified. **2** That which befalls one as his lot; good or bad luck. **3** Future destiny; fate: to tell *fortunes.* **4** Good luck; success; prosperity. **5** An amount of wealth; usually great wealth. See synonyms under EVENT. —*v.* **·tuned, ·tun·ing** *v.t.* *Rare* To bestow wealth upon. —*v.i.* To happen; occur by chance. [<OF <L *fortuna* <*fors* chance] —**for′tune·less** *adj.*

for·tune-hunt·er (fôr′chən·hun′tər) *n.* One who seeks to obtain wealth by marriage. —**for′tune-hunt′ing** *n.*

for·tune-tell·er (fôr′chən·tel′ər) *n.* One who claims to foretell events in a person's future. —**for′tune-tell′ing** *n.* & *adj.*

Fort Wayne (wān) A city in NE Indiana.

Fort Worth (wûrth) A city in northern Texas.

for·ty (fôr′tē) *adj.* Consisting of ten more than thirty, or of four times ten. —*n.* *pl.* **·ties** **1** The sum of ten and thirty; four times ten: a cardinal number. **2** Any of the symbols (40, xl, XL) representing this number. **3** *U.S.* Forty acres, or one-sixteenth of a section of land. [OE *fēowertig*]

for·ty-nin·er (fôr′tē·nī′nər) *n.* *U.S.* An adventurer or pioneer who went to California in 1849, the year of the gold rush.

Forty Thieves See ALI BABA.

forty winks *Colloq.* A short nap.

fo·rum (fôr′əm, fō′rəm) *n.* *pl.* **·rums** or **·ra** (-rə) **1** The public market place of an ancient Roman city, where popular assemblies met, and most legal and political business was transacted. **2** A tribunal; a court. **3** An assembly for free discussion of public affairs. [<L]

for·ward (fôr′wərd) *adj.* **1** At, or belonging to, the fore part, as of a ship. **2** Directed toward a position in front; onward: a *forward* course. **3** For deferred delivery: a *forward* purchase. **4** Advanced toward maturity or completion; specifically, precocious. **5** Bold; presumptuous. **6** Advanced; extreme; said of opinions or actions. —*adv.* **1** Toward the future. **2** Toward the front; ahead; onward. **3** At or in the fore part, as of a ship. **4** To a prominent position; forth; into view: to come *forward*; to bring *forward* an idea. Also *forwards.* —**forward of** In advance of. —*n.* **1** In American football, one of the players in the front line who attack in advance of the backfield and try to thwart the opponents. **2** In basketball, soccer, hockey, etc., one of those players who lead the attack and specialize in making goals. —*v.t.* **1** To help onward or ahead; promote. **2** To send; transmit; especially, to send (mail) on to a new address. **3** To prepare (a book) for finishing by covering, etc. See synonyms under ENCOURAGE, PROMOTE. [OE *foreweard*]

forward delivery Delivery at a future time.

for·ward·er (fôr′wər·dər) *n.* **1** A person, firm, or corporation whose business it is to receive goods for transportation and send them to their destination; a forwarding merchant or agent. **2** One who carries or promotes anything, as a reform.

for·ward·ly (fôr′wərd·lē) *adv.* **1** In a forward or front position. **2** In a forward manner; eagerly; boldly.

for·ward·ness (fôr′wərd·nis) *n.* **1** Presumption; overeagerness to put oneself forward; boldness; brazenness. **2** Willing readiness; eagerness. **3** State of being forward or in advance; precocity.

forward pass See under PASS.

forward quotation A price set for goods to be delivered at a future time.

for·wards (fôr′wərdz) See FORWARD *adv.*

for·why (fôr′hwī′) *Obs.* *adv.* Why; wherefore. —*conj.* Because.

for·worn (fôr·wôrn′) *adj.* *Archaic* Worn out: also spelled *foreworn.* [Orig. pp. of obs. *forwear* exhaust]

for·zan·do (fôr·tsän′dō) See SFORZANDO.

Fos·ca·ri (fôs·kä′rē), **Francesco,** 1372?–1457, doge of Venice; waged three wars with Milan.

Fos·dick (foz′dik), **Harry Emerson,** 1878–1969, U.S. clergyman and writer.

foss (fôs, fos) *n.* An artificial ditch or moat, as in a fortification. Also **fosse.** [<F *fosse* <L *fossa* <*fodire* dig]

fos·sa (fôs′ə, fos′ə) *n.* *pl.* **fos·sae** (-ē) *Anat.* A shallow depression or cavity in the body. [<L. See FOSS.]

fos·sette (fô·set′, fo-) *n.* *French* **1** A dimple. **2** *Anat.* A small depression, as in the crown of a tooth. [<F, dim. of *fosse.* See FOSS.]

fos·sick (fôs′ik, fos′-) *v.i.* *Austral.* **1** *Mining* To search for gold in abandoned mines, waste heaps, etc.; also, to search for surface gold. **2** To rummage about for something: used with *about* or *around.* [Cf. dial. E *fussock* bustle] —**fos′sick·er** *n.*

fos·sil (fos′əl, fôs′-) *n.* *Paleontol.* **1** The actual remains of plants or animals, preserved in the rocks of the earth's crust; also, material evidences of early organisms, as in petrified forms, coprolites, casts, impressions, imprints, etc. **2** *Geol.* One of certain inorganic objects or substances which in extinct or mineralized forms preserve in themselves records of the natural activities or phenomena of ancient geological ages, as solidified ripple marks. **3** Buried records of human activities, even within historic times. **4** *Colloq.* A person or thing that is behind the times, antiquated, or out of date. —*adj.* **1** Dug out of the earth; petrified. **2** Of or like a fossil; outworn; antiquated. [<F *fossile* <L *fossilis* dug up <*fossa.* See FOSS.]

fos·sil·if·er·ous (fos′əl·if′ər·əs) *adj.* Containing fossils.

fos·sil·ize (fos′əl·īz) *v.* **·ized, ·iz·ing** *v.t.* **1** To change into a fossil; petrify. **2** To make antiquated or out of date. —*v.i.* **3** To become a fossil. **4** To search for or gather fossil specimens. —**fos′sil·i·za′tion** *n.*

fos·so·ri·al (fo·sôr′ē·əl, -sō′rē-) *adj.* **1** Digging; burrowing: a *fossorial* animal. **2** Adapted for or used in digging in the earth, as the legs and other organs of the moles, armadillos, etc. [<LL *fossorius* <L *fodire* dig]

fos·ter (fôs′tər, fos′-) *v.t.* **1** To rear; bring up, as a child. **2** To promote the growth of; forward; help: to *foster* genius. **3** To keep as if affectionately; cherish; nurse: to *foster* a grudge. **4** *Obs.* To provide with food. See synonyms under AID, CHERISH, HELP, PROMOTE. —*adj.* Having the relation of, in the sense of giving, sharing, or receiving nourishment, shelter, affection, and care, but unrelated by blood; as in

foster brother	**foster father**	**foster parent**
foster child	**foster land**	**foster sister**
foster daughter	**foster mother**	**foster son**

[OE *fostrian* nourish] —**fos′ter·age** *n.* —**fos′·ter·er** *n.* —**fos′tress** *n. fem.*

Fos·ter (fôs′tər, fos′-), **Sir Michael,** 1836–1907, English physiologist. —**Stephen Collins,** 1826–64, U. S. song writer. —**William Zebulon,** 1881–1961, U. S. labor leader and former Communist party chairman.

fos·ter·ling (fôs′tər·ling, fos′-) *n.* A foster child.

Foth·er·in·ghay Castle (foth′ər·ing·gā′) A castle in Northamptonshire, England; scene of imprisonment and execution of Mary Queen of Scots.

Fou·cault (fo͞o·kō′), **Jean Bernard Léon,** 1819–68, French physicist.

Foucault current See under CURRENT.

Fouc·quet (fo͞o·ke′) See FOUQUET.

fou·droy·ant (fo͞o·droi′ənt, *Fr.* fo͞o·drwà·yäṅ′) *adj.* **1** Sudden and overwhelming, as lightning. **2** *Pathol.* Beginning in an aggravated form, as a disease. [<F, ppr. of *foudroyer* strike with lightning <*foudre* lightning]

fought (fôt) Past tense and past participle of FIGHT.

fought·en (fôt′n) *Archaic* Past participle of FIGHT.

foul (foul) *adj.* **1** Offensive or loathsome to the physical, moral, or esthetic sense; filthy. **2** Obstructing, entangling or injuring by anything that clogs or is harmful; contrary; disagreeable. **3** Impeded or encumbered by something detrimental; clogged; entangled; encumbered; a *foul* chimney, a *foul* anchor. **4** Not according to justice or rule; unfair.

5 *Printing* **a** Full of errors; inaccurate; dirty. **b** Having the characters badly mixed; said of a type case. 6 Unfavorable; unlucky: a *foul* wind. 7 *Obs.* Ugly; homely. 8 In baseball, of or pertaining to a foul ball or foul line. — *n.* 1 An act of fouling, colliding, or becoming entangled. 2 A breach of rule in various sports and games. 3 In baseball, a foul ball. — *adv.* In a foul manner. — *v.t.* 1 To make foul or dirty; befoul. 2 To clog or choke, as a drain. 3 To entangle; snarl, as a rope in a pulley. 4 *Naut.* To cover or encumber (a ship's bottom) with barnacles, seaweed, etc. 5 To collide with. 6 To dishonor; disgrace. 7 In sports, to commit a foul against. 8 In baseball, to bat (the ball) outside of the foul lines. — *v.i.* 9 To become foul or dirty. 10 To become clogged or encumbered. 11 To become entangled. 12 To collide. 13 In sports, to violate a rule. 14 In baseball: **a** To bat a foul ball. **b** To be retired by batting a foul ball which is caught before it strikes the ground: usually with *out.* — **to foul up** *Slang* To bungle; make a mess (of). ◆ Homophone: *fowl.* [OE *ful*]

Synonyms (adj.): defiled, dirty, filthy, gross, impure, indelicate, muddy, nasty, obscene, odious, offensive, soiled, stained, sullied, unclean, vile. See BAD, NOISOME. *Antonyms*: see synonyms for PURE.

fou·lard (fo͞o·lärd′) *n.* 1 A lightweight, washable silk fabric, usually printed, used for dresses, ties, etc. 2 A highly mercerized cotton or rayon fabric in imitation of this. [<F <Swiss F *foulat* <OF *fouler.* See FOIL[1].]

foul ball In baseball, a ball batted so that it falls outside the foul lines.

foul line 1 In baseball, a line drawn from home plate through first or third base to the limits of the field. 2 In basketball, the line from which foul shots are made. 3 In bowling, tennis, etc., any line limiting the area of play or action.

foul·ly (foul′lē) *adv.* 1 In a foul manner. 2 Undeservedly: *foully* maligned.

foul-mouthed (foul′mouthd′, -moutht′) *adj.* Using abusive, profane, or obscene language.

foul·ness (foul′nis) *n.* 1 The state or quality of being foul. 2 Foul matter.

foul play 1 Unfairness; in games and sports, a violation of rule. 2 Any unfair or treacherous conduct, often with the implication of murder.

foul shot In basketball, a free throw awarded a player who has been fouled by an opposing player, and if successful scored as one point.

foul tip In baseball, a pitched ball swung at by the batter and glancing off the bat into the catcher's hands: the batter is retired if there are two strikes against him.

fou·mart (fo͞o′märt) *n.* The European polecat; the fitchew. Also **fou·li·mart** (fo͞o′lē·märt). [ME *fulmard,* OE *fūl* foul + *mearth* marten]

found[1] (found) *v.t.* 1 To lay the foundation of; establish on a foundation or basis: to *found* a theory. 2 To give origin to; establish; set up: to *found* a college or a family. — **to found on** 1 To form and base one's opinion. 2 To rest as on a foundation. [<OF *fonder* <L *fundare* <*fundus* base, bottom] — **found′er** *n.*

found[2] (found) *v.t.* 1 To cast, as iron, by melting and pouring into a mold. 2 To make by casting molten metal. [<F *fondre* <L *fundere* pour]

found[3] (found) Past tense and past participle of FIND. — *adj.* Provided with food, lodging, equipment, etc. — **and found** Plus board and lodging, as part payment.

foun·da·tion (foun·dā′shən) *n.* 1 The act of founding or establishing. 2 That on which anything is founded and by which it is supported or sustained. 3 A fund for the permanent maintenance of an institution; an endowment. 4 An endowed institution. 5 A structure upon which a building or a machine is erected, usually wholly or principally of masonry; that part of a building below the surface of the ground, or the portion that constitutes a base; sometimes, a platform, on which the upper portions rest. 6 An inner, fitted lining of a garment. 7 Theatrical grease-paint applied to the face, hands, etc., before adding the final make-up details. — **foun·da′·tion·al** *adj.*

foundation garment A girdle or corset, often combined with a brassière.

foundation sire In horse breeding, the named stallion from which the genealogy of all horses of a given breed is traced.

found·er[1] (foun′dər) *n.* One who makes metal castings.

foun·der[2] (foun′dər) *v.i.* 1 *Naut.* To fill with water and sink. 2 To collapse; cave in; fail. 3 To stumble; go lame, as a horse. 4 To have founder. — *v.t.* 5 *Naut.* To cause to sink. 6 To cause to go lame. — *n.* 1 Inflammation of the tissue in the foot of a horse, commonly due to overfeeding: also called *laminitis.* 2 Act of foundering. [<OF *fondrer* sink <*fond* bottom <L *fundus*]

foun·der·ous (foun′dər·əs) *adj.* Causing to founder; miry; swampy.

founders' shares Shares of stock, often privileged to extra dividends, issued to the promoters or founders of a company as payment for organizing expenses and reward for initiative.

found·ing (foun′ding) *n.* The business of making articles of cast iron, brass, etc.

found·ling (found′ling) *n.* A deserted infant of unknown parentage. [ME *fundeling* <*funde,* pp. of *find* + -LING[1]]

foun·dry (foun′drē) *n. pl.* **·dries** 1 An establishment in which articles are cast from metal. 2 The act or operation of founding. Also **foun′der·y.**

foundry proof *Printing* A final proof of composed type before stereotyping or electrotyping.

fount[1] (fount) *n.* A fountain; hence, any source. [<F *font* <L *fons, fontis* fountain]

fount[2] (fount) See FONT[2].

foun·tain (foun′tən) *n.* 1 A spring or jet of water issuing from the earth; especially, the source of a stream. ◆ Collateral adjective: *fontal.* 2 The origin or source of anything. 3 A jet or spray of water forced upward artificially, to provide water for drinking, cooling the air, or display. 4 A structure designed for such a jet to rise and fall in. 5 A reservoir or supply chamber for holding oil, ink, etc., as in a lamp, printing press, or inkstand. 6 A soda fountain. See synonyms under BEGINNING, CAUSE. [<OF *fontaine* <LL *fontana,* orig. fem. singular of *fontanus* of a spring <*fons, fontis* fountain]

foun·tain·head (foun′tən·hed′) *n.* 1 The source of a stream. 2 Any primal source or originating cause.

Fountain of Youth A legendary fountain said to have the power of rejuvenation: sought by Ponce de León and others in Florida and the West Indies.

fountain pen A pen having a reservoir for ink within the holder.

Fou·qué (fo͞o·kā′), **Friedrich H. K.,** 1777–1843, Baron de la Motte, German poet and dramatist.

Fou·quet (fo͞o·ke′), **Jean,** 1416?–80?, French painter. — **Nicolas,** 1615–80, Marquis de Belle Isle, French statesman. Also spelled *Foucquet.*

Fou·qui·e·ri·a (fo͞o′kē·ir′ē·ə) *n.* A genus of thorny shrubs, native to Mexico and the southern United States.

four (fôr, fōr) *adj.* Consisting of one more than three; twice two; quaternary. — *n.* 1 The cardinal number following three and preceding five, or any of the symbols (4, iv, IV) used to represent it. 2 Anything made up of four units or members; especially, a crew of four oarsmen, a team of four horses, a playing card with four pips, etc. [OE *feower*]

four bits *U.S. Slang* Fifty cents.

four·chette (fo͞or·shet′) *n.* 1 A forked piece between glove fingers, uniting the front and back parts. 2 *Ornithol.* The furculum or wishbone of a bird. 3 The frog of a horse. 4 *Anat.* A fold of mucous membrane forming the posterior commissure of the vulva. [<F, dim. of *fourche* a fork <L *furca*]

four-cy·cle (fôr′sī′kəl, fōr′-) A cycle of operation in an engine in which fuel is taken into the cylinder, compressed, burned, and exhausted in four successive strokes.

four-di·men·sion·al (fôr′di·men′shən·əl, fōr′-) *adj.* 1 Having, or pertaining to, four dimensions. 2 *Math.* Relating to a system or a set of magnitudes whose elements can be completely defined only by four coordinates.

Four·drin·i·er (fo͞or·drin′ē·ər) *adj.* Of, pertaining to, or designating a papermaking machine, the first to make a continuous web: invented by Louis Robert of France and patented by him there, but improved in England by Henry and Sealy Fourdrinier early in the 19th century. — *n.* A Fourdrinier machine.

four-eyed fish (fôr′īd′, fōr′-) The anableps.

four-flush (fôr′flush′, fōr′-) *n.* A valueless poker hand containing four cards of one suit and one of another. — *v.i.* 1 To bet on a hand containing four cards of one suit but lacking the fifth. 2 *Slang* To bluff.

four-flush·er (fôr′flush′ər, fōr′-) *n. Slang* A bluffer; one whose abilities and performance are less than his pretensions or promises.

four·fold (fôr′fōld′, fōr′-) *adj.* Made up of four; quadruplicate. — *n.* That which is four times as many or as much. — *adv.* In quadrupled measure.

four-foot·ed (fôr′fo͝ot′id, fōr′-) *adj.* Having four feet; quadruped.

Four Forest Cantons, Lake of the See LAKE OF LUCERNE.

Four Freedoms Freedom of speech and religion and freedom from want and fear: the world-wide goals of U.S. foreign policy stated by President F. D. Roosevelt in a message to Congress, January 6, 1941.

four·gon (fo͞or·gôn′) *n. French* A covered wagon or van for carrying baggage, military supplies, etc.

four-hand·ed (fôr′han′did, fōr′-) *adj.* 1 Having four hands; quadrumanous, as monkeys. 2 Needing four hands, as certain games, a piano duet, etc.

Four-H Club (fôr′āch′, fōr′-) A youth organization, sponsored by the Department of Agriculture, offering education in home economics and agriculture: so called because it aims to improve the head, heart, hands, and health of its members. Also **4-H Club.**

four hundred The most exclusive social group of a place: a term originally applied to the wealthiest set in New York by Ward McAllister.

Fou·rier (fo͞o·ryā′), **François Marie Charles,** 1772–1837, French socialist. — **Jean Baptiste Joseph,** 1768–1830, French mathematician and physicist.

Fou·ri·er·ism (fo͞or′ē·ə·riz′əm) *n.* The social reform system advocated by F. M. C. Fourier about 1815, proposing small, voluntary cooperative groups for economic production and maintenance, the achievement of social justice, and the fulfilment of individual desires. — **Fou′ri·er·ist, Fou′ri·er·ite′** *n.*

four-in-hand (fôr′in·hand′, fōr′-) *adj.* 1 Consisting of a four-horse team driven by one person. 2 Designating a necktie tied in a slipknot with the ends hanging vertically. — *n.* 1 A four-horse team driven by one person; also, a vehicle drawn by four horses. 2 A four-in-hand necktie.

four-leafed rose (fôr′lēft′, fōr′-) *Geom.* The polar curve of equation $r = a \sin 2\theta$: a curve of four symmetrical loops with the node at the origin.

four-let·ter word (fôr′let′ər, fōr′-) Any of several short words considered profane or obscene.

four-mast·ed (fôr′mas′tid, -mäs′-, fōr′-) *adj. Naut.* Having four masts. — **four′-mast′er** *n.*

Four·nier d'Albe (fo͞or′nyā dalb′), **Edmund Edward,** 1868–1933, English physicist.

four-o'clock (fôr′ə·klok′, fōr′-) *n.* 1 An ornamental herb from Peru (*Mirabilis jalapa*) with flowers of a great variety of color that bloom from late afternoon till the next morning. 2 The Australian friarbird.

four·pence (fôr′pəns, fōr′-) *n.* 1 The sum of four English pennies; also, a silver piece of that value. 2 A silver coin used before the Civil War, worth 6 1/4 cents; the Spanish half-real: called *fourpence halfpenny* in New England, *fippenny bit* in Pennsylvania and elsewhere.

four-post·er (fôr′pōs′tər, fōr′-) *n.* A bedstead with four tall posts at the corners.

four·ra·gère (fo͞o·rà·zhâr′) *n.* A braided, metal-tipped cord awarded to individual soldiers or to a unit of troops for distinguished service;

and worn around the left shoulder. [<F]

four·score (fôr′skôr′, fōr′skōr′) *adj.* & *n.* Four times twenty; eighty.

four·some (fôr′səm, fōr′-) *adj.* Consisting of four: said of anything in which four are needed to take part together. —*n.* **1** A game, especially of golf, in which four players take part, two on each side; also the players. **2** Any group of four.

four·square (fôr′skwâr′, fōr′-) *adj.* **1** Having four equal sides and angles; square. **2** Hence, firm; solid; also, sincere; without guile. —*n.* An object having four equal sides; a square.

four·teen (fôr′tēn′, fōr′-) *adj.* Consisting of four more than ten, or of twice seven. —*n.* **1** The sum of ten and four; twice seven. **2** Any symbol (14, xiv, XIV) representing this number. [OE *fēowertēne*]

Fourteen Points The peace aims set forth by President Woodrow Wilson in an address, January 8, 1918, ten months before the end of World War I. Also **Fourteen Peace Points.**

four·teenth (fôr′tēnth′, fōr′-) *adj.* **1** Fourth in order after the tenth. **2** Being one of fourteen equal parts. —*n.* **1** One of fourteen equal parts of anything; the quotient of a unit divided by fourteen. **2** A fourteenth person, thing, or group.

fourth (fôrth, fōrth) *adj.* **1** Next in order after the third. **2** Being one of four equal parts. —*n.* **1** One of four equal parts of anything; the quotient of a unit divided by four; a quarter. **2** A fourth person, thing, or group. **3** *Music* **a** The interval between any note and the fourth note above it in a diatonic scale, counting the starting point as one. **b** A note at this interval above or below any other, considered in relation to that other; specifically, the fourth above the keynote; the subdominant. **c** Two notes at this interval written or sounded together; the consonance thus produced. See INTERVAL. **—the Fourth** July 4th; Independence Day. —*adv.* In the fourth order, rank, or place: also, in formal discourse, *fourthly.* ◆ Homophone: *forth.*

fourth-class (fôrth′klas′, -kläs′, fōrth′-) *adj.* Designating mail matter consisting of merchandise, and carried at the lowest rate.

fourth dimension **1** *Math.* A hypothetical, usually spatial dimension in addition to height, width, and thickness. **2** In the theory of relativity, the temporal coordinate of space time. — **fourth′-di·men′sion·al** *adj.*

fourth estate **1** The newspapers; journalism, in general. **2** *Brit.* The reporters' gallery in the House of Commons.

fourth·ly (fôrth′lē, fōrth′-) *adv.* In the fourth place. See under FOURTH.

Fourth of July *U.S.* Independence Day.

Fourth Republic The republic formed in France in 1945.

four-wheel (fôr′hwēl, fōr′-) *adj.* **1** Having four wheels. **2** Affecting or controlling all four wheels: *four-wheel* drive.

Fou·ta Djal·lon (fōō′tä jä·lôn′) See FUTA JALLON.

fo·ve·a (fō′vē·ə) *n. pl.* **·ve·ae** (-vi·ē) *Anat.* A shallow rounded depression: the central *fovea* of the retina directly in the axis of vision; a fossa. [<L, a small pit] **—fo′ve·al** *adj.*

fo·ve·ate (fō′vē·āt, -it) *adj.* Having foveae; covered with little pits.

fo·ve·o·la (fə·vē′ə·lə) *n. pl.* **·lae** (-lē) A small fovea or pit. Also **fo·ve·ole** (fō′vē·ōl), **fo′ve·o·let** (-let). [<L, dim. of *fovea* a small pit]

fo·ve·o·late (fō′vē·ə·lāt) *adj.* Having foveolae or little pits. Also **fo′ve·o·lat′ed.**

fowl (foul) *n. pl.* **fowl** or **fowls** **1** The common domestic cock, hen, or chicken. **2** The flesh of fowls, especially of the full-grown domestic hen. **3** Poultry in general. **4** Birds collectively: wild *fowl.* **5** *Obs.* Any bird. —*v.i.* To catch or hunt wild fowl. ◆ Homophone: *foul.* [OE *fugol*] — **fowl′er** *n.*

fowl cholera An infectious intestinal disease, chronic or acute, of domestic fowl caused by a pathogenic bacterium, *Pasteurella avicida.*

Fowl·er (fou′lər), **Henry Watson**, 1858–1933, English lexicographer.

harles James**Fowler's solution** An aqueous solution of potassium arsenite containing arsenious acid: very poisonous: used in medicine as an alterative and tonic. [after Thomas *Fowler,* 1736–1801, English physician]

Fow·liang (fō′lyäng′, fōō′-) A city in NE Kiangsi province, SE China: formerly *Kingtehchen.*

fowl·ing (fou′ling) *n.* The hunting of birds for sport or food.

fowling net A net for catching birds.

fowl·ing-piece (fou′ling·pēs′) *n.* A light gun for bird-shooting.

fowl pox A disease affecting many species of domestic fowl and wild birds, characterized by skin lesions, tissue injuries, and sometimes diphtheria symptoms of the mucous membrane: caused by certain strains of filtrable viruses.

fowl tick A hardy, bloodsucking tick *(Argas persicus)* parasitic on fowls, especially prevalent in the SW United States.

fowl typhoid A sporadic disease of domestic fowl caused by the bacterium *Shigella gallinarum.*

fox (foks) *n.* **1** A burrowing canine mammal (family *Canidae,* genus *Vulpes*) having a long, pointed muzzle and long bushy tail, commonly reddish-brown in color, noted for its cunning. The common **European red fox** *(V. vulpes)* is reddish-brown above and white beneath, with a white-tipped tail. It inhabits a burrow, and preys on poultry, rabbits, etc. The **North American red fox** *(V. fulva)* is a similar species of which the **cross fox** (having a dark cross mark on its back) and **black** or **silver fox** are color varieties. The **gray fox** *(Urocyon cinereoargenteus)* is found from Pennsylvania southward, and differs in habits from the red. ◆ Collateral adjective: *vulpine.* **2** The fur of the fox. **3** A sly, crafty person. **4** A small rope made by hand of two or more rope yarns. **5** *Obs.* A sword. —*v.t.* **1** To trick; outwit. **2** To make drunk; intoxicate. **3** To stain, as paper or timber, with a reddish color. **4** To make sour, as beer, in fermenting. **5** To repair or mend, as shoes, with new uppers. —*v.i.* **6** To become drunk. **7** To become sour. **8** To become reddish in color. [OE]

NORTH AMERICAN RED FOX
(Average length 2 feet; tail, 13 inches; height, 13 inches)

Fox (foks) *n.* One of an Algonquian tribe of North American Indians, formerly inhabiting the neighborhood of Green Bay, Wisconsin: combined with the Sacs, 1760.

Fox (foks), **Charles James,** 1749–1806, English statesman; opposed American policy of George III. **—George,** 1624–91, English preacher; founded the Society of Friends. **—Henry,** 1705–74, first Baron Holland, British statesman. — **John Williams,** 1863–1919, U.S. novelist.

fox·bane (foks′bān′) *n.* A European herb *(Aconitum lycoctonum)* of the crowfoot family; wolf's-bane.

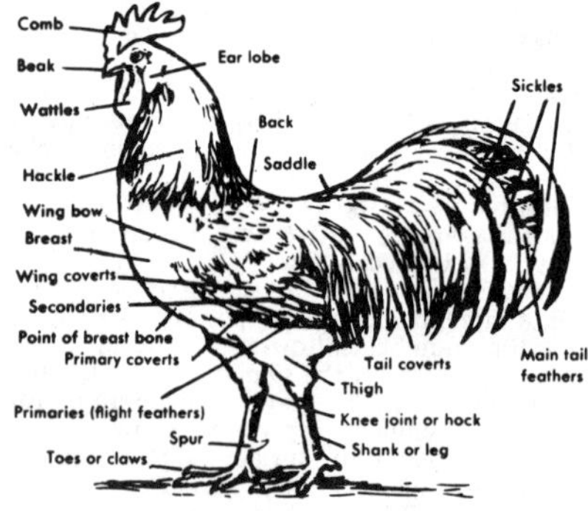

FOWL
Nomenclature for anatomical parts.

fox·ber·ry (foks′ber′ē) *n. pl.* **·ries** The cowberry.

fox brush The tail of a fox.

fox·chase (foks′chās′) *n.* A fox hunt.

Foxe (foks), **John,** 1516–87, English divine and historian. **—Richard,** 1448?–1528, English prelate and statesman; also **Fox.**

Foxe Basin An arm of the Atlantic between Melville Peninsula and Baffin Island.

fox earth The burrow of a fox.

foxed (fokst) *adj.* **1** Discolored by decay: applied to timber. **2** Having light-brown stains or spots, as the paper of books, prints, etc. **3** Repaired or ornamented with a foxing, as the upper leather of a shoe.

fox·fire (foks′fīr′) *n.* The phosphorescent light emitted by foxed or rotten wood.

fox·fish (foks′fish′) *n. pl.* **·fish** or **·fish·es** **1** The dragonet. **2** The fox shark.

fox·glove (foks′gluv′) *n.* Any plant of a genus *(Digitalis)* of the figwort family, especially the English variety *(D. purpurea),* having flowers in long one-sided racemes; the leaves are a source of digitalis.

ENGLISH FOXGLOVE
(From 2 1/2 to 5 feet tall)

fox grape Either of two species of American grapes, called the **northern fox grape** *(Vitio labrusca)* and the **southern fox grape** *(V. rotundifolia).*

fox·hole (foks′hōl′) *n.* A shallow pit dug by a combatant as cover against enemy fire: so called from the earth burrow of a fox.

fox·hound (foks′hound′) *n.* One of a breed of large, strong, very swift dogs trained for fox-hunting.

fox·hunt (foks′hunt′) *n.* The hunting of foxes with hounds. Also **fox hunt.**

fox·hunt·ing (foks′hun′ting) *n.* The sport of hunting foxes with hounds. **—fox′hunt′er** *n.*

fox·ing (fok′sing) *n.* A piece of leather put on the upper leather of a shoe along the edge next to the sole.

Fox Islands (foks) The easternmost group of the Aleutian Islands.

fox shark The thresher shark *(Alopias vulpes),* having a powerful tail as long as its body: also called *foxfish.*

fox·skin (foks′skin′) *n.* **1** The dressed skin of a fox. **2** A fur cap made of such skin.

fox squirrel Any of several large North American arboreal squirrels; especially *Sciurus niger.*

fox·tail (foks′tāl′) *n.* **1** The tail of a fox. **2** Any of various species of grass bearing a dense spike of flowers like a fox's tail; especially the meadows foxtail *(Alopecurus pratensis).*

fox terrier See under TERRIER.

fox·trot (foks′trot′) *n.* **1** A pace between a trot and a walk: used of horses. **2** A modern dance step of syncopated two-four time.

fox·wood (foks′wŏŏd′) *n.* Decayed or foxed wood.

fox·y (fok′sē) *adj.* **fox·i·er, fox·i·est** **1** Of or like a fox; crafty. **2** Reddish-brown in color. **3** Discolored; foxed. **4** Soured; improperly fermented, as wine. **5** Defective, as in quality. **6** Denoting a wild flavor found in wine made from some American grapes. **—fox′i·ness** *n.*

foy (foi) *n. Dial.* A feast given before one goes on a journey. [<MDu. *foie,* prob. <OF *voie* <L *via* a road, way]

foy·er (foi′ər, -ā; *Fr.* fwȧ·yā′) *n.* **1** A public room or lobby, as in a theater or hotel. **2** An entrance room in a house. [<F <LL *focarium* hearth <*focus*]

Foynes (foinz) A town in County Limerick, Ireland; site of a transoceanic airport superseded by Shannon after World War II. *Irish Gaelic* **Faeng.**

Fr *Chem.* Francium (symbol Fr).

Fra (frä) *n.* Brother: a friar's title. [<Ital., short for *frate* <L *frater* brother]

Fra Angelico See ANGELICO, FRA.

fra·cas (frā′kəs) *n.* A noisy fight; brawl. See synonyms under ALTERCATION, QUARREL. [<F <Ital. *fracasso* an uproar <*fracassare* shatter]

Fra·ca·sto·ro (frä′käs·tō′rō), **Girolamo,** 1483–1553, Italian physician and poet.

frac·tion (frak′shən) *n.* **1** A disconnected part; fragment; hence, a tiny bit. **2** *Math.* A quantity less than a unit, or one expressed as the sum of a number of aliquot parts of a unit. See list of principal kinds of fractions below. **3** *Obs.* The act of breaking. **4** A piece of land smaller than the standard unit of measurement. **5** *Chem.* One of the components separated from a substance by fractional distillation: Naphtha is a *fraction* of petroleum. —*v.t.* To set or separate into fractions. See synonyms under PART. [<OF <L *fractio, -onis* <*fractus,* pp. of *frangere* break]

—common fraction A fraction expressed by two numbers, a denominator, indicating the number of equal parts into which the unit is to be divided, and a numerator, indicating

the number of those parts to be taken. Also called **vulgar fraction.**
—complex fraction A fraction in which either the numerator or the denominator is a fraction. Also called **compound fraction.**
—continued fraction A fraction whose denominator is another integer plus another fraction, and so on.
—decimal fraction A fraction whose denominator is any power of 10 and which may be expressed in decimal form, as 7/10 (0.7), 3/100 (0.03), etc.
—improper fraction A fraction in which the numerator exceeds the denominator.
—partial fraction One of a set of fractions whose algebraic sum is a given fraction.
—proper fraction A fraction in which the numerator is less than the denominator.
—similar fraction Any of a group of fractions having a common denominator or the same number of decimal places.
—simple fraction A fraction in which both numerator and denominator are integers.
—unit fraction A fraction whose numerator is unity.

frac·tion·al (frak′shən·əl) *adj.* **1** Pertaining to or constituting a fraction. **2** Broken; small. **3** *Chem.* Designating a process or method of separating a complex of substances into component parts on the basis of specific differences in selected properties, as solubility, boiling point, crystallization, etc.

fractional currency Money or coins of any denomination less than the standard monetary unit: in the United States, less than a dollar.

fractional distillation *Chem.* The separation of the various components of a mixture, as petroleum, by distillation into fractions having more or less fixed properties but not necessarily being definite compounds: also **frac′tion·a′tion.**

frac·tion·al·ism (frak′shə·nə·liz·əm) *n.* A tendency to fractionalize.

frac·tion·al·ize (frak′shə·nə·līz) *v.t.* **·ized, ·iz·ing** To divide into parts or fractions.

fractional section A piece of land of less than 640 acres, having topographical irregularities.

fractional township A tract of land of more or less than 36 sections, having various topographical irregularities.

frac·tion·ate (frak′shən·āt) *v.t.* **·at·ed, ·at·ing** To subject to fractional distillation.

fractionating column *Chem.* A long vertical tube divided into segments and attached to a still for the fractional distillation of liquid mixtures: also called *dephlegmator.*

frac·tion·ize (frak′shən·īz) *v.t.* & *v.i.* **·ized, ·iz·ing** To divide into fractions. **—frac′tion·i·za′tion** *n.*

frac·tious (frak′shəs) *adj.* Disposed to rebel; restive; unruly; peevish. See synonyms under FRETFUL, PERVERSE, RESTIVE. **—frac′tious·ly** *adv.* **—frac′tious·ness** *n.*

frac·tog·ra·phy (frak·tog′rə·fē) *n.* The microscopic study of the fractures and other structural defects occurring in metals. [<L *fractus* broken + -GRAPHY] **—frac·to·graph·ic** (frak′tə·Jean graf′·ik) *adj.*

frac·tur (fräk·tōōr′) See FRAKTUR.

frac·ture (frak′chər) *n.* **1** The act, mode, or result of breaking, or the state of being broken. **2** A break. **3** The breaking of a bone; a break in a bone. **—comminuted fracture** A fracture in which the bone is splintered or crushed. **—compound fracture** One leading to an open wound, often exposing the bone. **—impacted fracture** One in which the broken parts are driven into each other. **—simple fracture** One without any break in the skin: also **closed fracture. 4** A rupture; crack. **5** The characteristic appearance of the freshly broken surface of a mineral, as a conchoidal *fracture.* —*v.t.* & *v.i.* **·tured, ·tur·ing** To break or be broken; crack. See synonyms under BREAK, RUPTURE. **—frac′tur·a·ble** *adj.* **—frac′·tur·al** *adj.*

frae (frā) *prep. Scot.* From.

frae·num (frē′nəm) See FRENUM.

frag·ile (fraj′əl) *adj.* Easily broken; frail; delicate. [<L *fragilis* <*frangere* break. Doublet of FRAIL.] **—frag′ile·ly** *adv.* **—fra·gil·i·ty** (frə·jil′·ə·tē), **frag′ile·ness** *n.*
Synonyms: breakable, brittle, delicate, frail, frangible, infirm, slight, tender, weak.

frag·ment (frag′mənt) *n.* A part broken off; a small detached portion. See synonyms under PART. [<F <L *fragmentum* fragment, remnant]

frag·men·tar·y (frag′mən·ter′ē) *adj.* Composed of fragments; broken; incomplete. Also **frag·men′tal. —frag′men·tar′i·ly** *adv.* **—frag′men·tar′i·ness** *n.*

frag·men·ta·tion (frag′mən·tā′shən) *n.* **1** The breaking up into fragments. **2** The scattering in all directions of the fragments of an exploding grenade, shell, or bomb. **3** *Biol.* In cell division, the breaking up of one or more chromosomes into pieces smaller than the normal.

fragmentation bomb See under BOMB.

frag·ment·ed (frag′mən·tid) *adj.* Broken into pieces or fragments.

frag·ment·ize (frag′mən·tīz) *v.t.* **·ized, ·iz·ing** To break into small pieces.

Fra·go·nard (frȧ·gō·när′), **Jean Honoré,** 1732–1806, French painter.

fra·grance (frā′grəns) *n.* The state or quality of being fragrant; a sweet odor. Also **fra′gran·cy.**

fra·grant (frā′grənt) *adj.* Having an agreeable or sweet smell. [<L *fragrans, -antis,* ppr. of *fragrare* smell sweet] **—fra′grant·ly** *adv.*

frail[1] (frāl) *n.* **1** A basket made of rushes: used for containing dried fruits, and as a measure. **2** The weight measure of raisins in such a basket, about 50 pounds avoirdupois. [<OF *fraiel* basket]

frail[2] (frāl) *adj.* **1** Delicately constituted; easily broken or destroyed. **2** Easily tempted; liable to be led astray. See synonyms under FRAGILE. [<OF *fraile* <L *fragilis.* Doublet of FRAGILE.] **—frail′ly** *adv.*

frail·ty (frāl′tē) *n. pl.* **·ties 1** The state of being frail. **2** A fault or moral weakness. Also **frail′ness.** See synonyms under FOIBLE.

fraim (frām) See FREM.

fraise (frāz) *n.* **1** A defense of pointed stakes planted in a rampart horizontally or in an inclined position. **2** A ruff of the kind worn in Europe in the 16th century. [<F <*fraiser* curl, ult. <Gmc.]

frai·ter (frā′tər) *n. Obs.* A monastery or convent dining-room: also spelled *frater.* Also **frai′tor.** [<OF *fraitur,* short for *refreitor* <Med. L *refectorium* a dining-hall]

frak·tur (fräk·tōōr′) *n.* A form of Latin letter formerly widely used in German printing, characterized by thin shape, pointed ends, and bristling serifs: also spelled *fractur.* See ALPHABET. [<G <L *fractura* a breaking]

fram·be·si·a (fram·bē′zhē·ə, -zē·ə, -zhə) *n.* Yaws. Also **fram·boe′si·a.** [<NL <F *framboise* a raspberry]

frame (frām) *v.* **framed, fram·ing** *v.t.* **1** To surround with or put in a frame. **2** *Colloq.* To incriminate falsely. **3** To put together; build, as a house. **4** To put in words; utter: to *frame* a reply. **5** To draw up; put in proper form: to *frame* a law. **6** To think out; arrange; conceive, as a plan or theory. **7** To shape or adapt to a purpose; dispose: to *frame* oneself to obedience. —*v.i.* **8** *Obs.* To move; go. See synonyms under CONSTRUCT, MAKE. —*n.* **1** Something composed or constructed of parts, whether physical or mental, united and adjusted to one another in a system; a construction. **2** The general arrangement or constitution of a thing. **3** Structure or build, as of a person. **4** The supporting and formative parts of a structure, put together so as to sustain and give shape to the whole. **5** A machine characterized by a wooden framework or structure: a silk *frame.* **6** A case or border made to enclose or surround a thing. **7** A mental state or condition; mood. **8** In tenpins and bowling, a division of the game during which a player bowls at one setting of the pins. **9** The triangular frame in which the balls in a pool game are bunched ready for the break. **10** One of the complete exposures in a roll of motion-picture film. **11** In television, a single complete scanning of the field of view by the electronic or other scanning device. **12** Form; proportion. **13** The act of contriving or inventing. **14** *Colloq.* A frame-up. [OE *framian* benefit]
Synonyms (noun): fabric, form, framework, order, structure, system. See BODY, FORM, TEMPER.

frame frequency In television, the number of frames per second completed by the scanning spot.

frame house A house built on a wooden framework covered on the outside by shingles, boards, stucco, etc.

fram·er (frā′mər) *n.* One who or that which frames; a maker.

frame-up (frām′up′) *n. Colloq.* **1** Anything prearranged. **2** A conspiracy to convict a person on a false charge.

frame·work (frām′wûrk′) *n.* A skeleton structure for supporting or enclosing something.

fram·ing (frā′ming) *n.* **1** A framework. **2** The act of erecting or making a frame; the act of composing or drawing up. **3** *Colloq.* The act of conspiring against.

fram·mit (fram′it) *adj. Scot.* Foreign; strange.

franc (frangk) *n.* **1** A French coin, originally silver and once valued at about 19 1/2 cents: equivalent to 100 centimes: the monetary unit of France. **2** The corresponding monetary unit of Belgium, Switzerland, etc. **3** A French gold piece, first coined in 1360; also, a silver piece, first coined in 1575. [<OF *Franc(orum rex)* king of the Franks, the motto on the first of these coins]

France (frans, fräns), **Anatole** Pseudonym of Jacques Anatole Thibault, 1844–1924, French novelist and critic.

France (frans, fräns) A republic in western Europe; 212,659 square miles; capital, Paris. Abbr. *Fr.*

Fran·ces (fran′sis, frän′-) A feminine personal name. Compare FRANCIS. Also **Fran·cis·ca** (*Dan., Du., Pg.* frän·sēs′kä; *Ger.* frän·tsēs′kä; *Sp.* frän·thēs′kä), *Ital.* **Fran·ces·ca** (frän·ches′·kä), *Sw.* **Fran·cis·ka** (frän·sis′kä), *Fr.* **Fran·çoise** (fräṅ·swȧz′) or **Fran·cisque** (fräṅ·sēsk′).

Fran·ces·ca (frän·ches′kä), **Piero della** See under PIERO.

Fran·ces·ca da Ri·mi·ni (frän·ches′kä dä rē′mē·nē), died 1205?, Italian lady; killed, together with her lover, Paolo, by her husband, Giovanni the Lame: immortalized by Dante.

Franche-Com·té (fräṅsh·kôṅ·tā′) A region and former province of eastern France. Also **Free County of Burgundy.**

fran·chise (fran′chīz) *n.* **1** A political or constitutional right reserved to or vested in the people, as the right of suffrage. **2** *Law* A special privilege emanating from the government by legislative or royal grant and vested in an individual person or in a body politic and corporate; a right to do something, as run a railroad, a bus line, etc. **3** The territory or boundary of a special privilege or immunity. **4** Authorization granted by a manufacturer to distributor or retailer to sell his products. See synonyms under RIGHT. —*v.t. Obs.* To enfranchise. [<OF <*franc, franche* free]

Fran·cis (fran′sis, frän′-) A masculine personal name. Also **Fran·cis·cus** (*Dan., Du.* frän·sēs′kəs; *Ger.* frän·tsēs′kəs), *Fr.* **Fran·çois** (fräṅ·swȧ′), *Ital.* **Fran·ces·co** (frän·ches′kō), *Pg., Sp.* **Fran·cis·co** (*Pg.* frän·sēs′kōō, *Sp.* frän·thēs′kō). Compare FRANCES. [<Gmc., free]
—Francis I, 1494–1547, king of France 1515–1547.
—Francis II, 1768–1835, Holy Roman Emperor 1792–1806, emperor of Austria 1804–35.
—Francis Ferdinand, 1863–1914, archduke of Austria; assassinated.
—Francis Joseph, 1830–1916, emperor of Austria 1848–1916. Also *Ger.* **Franz Josef.**
—Francis of Assisi, Saint, 1182–1226, Italian mendicant; founder of the Franciscan order.
—Francis of Sales, Saint, 1567–1622, French prelate; founded the Order of Visitation, 1610. See SALESIAN.
—Francis Xavier, Saint See XAVIER.

Fran·cis·can (fran·sis′kən) *n.* A member of the mendicant order *(Gray Friars* or *Minorites)* founded in 1209 by St. Francis of Assisi. The three branches of the order are *Capuchins, Conventuals,* and *Observantines.* See also POOR CLARE. —*adj.* **1** Of or pertaining to St. Francis. **2** Belonging to a religious order or institution following the rule of St. Francis.

fran·ci·um (fran′sē·əm) *n.* A short-lived radioactive metallic element (symbol Fr, atomic number 87) occurring as a decay product of actinium and having a half-life of 22 minutes. See PERIODIC TABLE. [after FRANCE]

Franck (frängk), **César Auguste,** 1822–90, French composer born in Belgium. **—James,** 1882–1964, German physicist.

Fran·co (fräng′kō) Italian and Spanish form of FRANCIS.

Fran·co (frang′kō, *Sp.* fräng′kō), **Francisco,** 1892–1975; chief of state 1939–75.

Franco- *combining form* French: *Franco-Prussian.* [< L *Francus* a Frank]

Fran·co-Ger·man War (frang′kō·jûr′mən) See FRANCO-PRUSSIAN WAR in table under WAR.

fran·co·lin (frang′kə·lin) *n.* An Old World, now chiefly Asian, partridge (genus *Francolinus*), having richly colored plumage and a rather long tail and bill. [< F < Ital. *francolino*]

Fran·co·ni·a (frang·kō′nē·ə) A medieval duchy in south Germany, divided into the present administrative districts of Lower, Middle, and Upper Franconia. *German* **Fran·ken** (fräng′·kən) **—Fran·co′ni·an** *adj. & n.*

Fran·co·phile (frang′kə·fil) *n.* A non-French admirer of France or of French customs, etc. *—adj.* Kindly disposed toward France. — **Fran′co·phil′i·a** (-fil′ē·ə) *n.*

Fran·co·phobe (frang′kə·fōb) *n.* A person who fears or dislikes France or French things. *—adj.* Fearful of France. **—Fran′co·pho′bi·a** *n.*

Fran·co-Prus·sian War (frang′kō·prush′ən) See table under WAR.

franc-ti·reur (fräṅ·tē·rœr′) *n. pl.* **francs-ti·reurs** (fräṅ·tē·rœr′) A French soldier, one of the sharpshooters of a light infantry force. [< F < *franc* free + *tireur* shooter < *tirer* shoot]

fran·gi·ble (fran′jə·bəl) *adj.* Easily broken; brittle; fragile. [< OF < L *frangere* break] — **fran′gi·bil′i·ty, fran′gi·ble·ness** *n.*

fran·gi·pan·i (fran′ji·pan′ē, -pä′nē) *n.* **1** A perfume derived from or resembling that of the West Indian red jasmine *(Plumera rubra).* **2** The plant. Also **fran′gi·pane** (-pān). [after Marquis *Frangipani,* who created the perfume]

Fran·glais (frang·glā′) *n.* The French language as used by speakers who utilize many English borrowings. [< F *français* French + *anglais* English]

frank (frangk) *adj.* **1** Candid and open; ingenuous. **2** *Obs.* Giving freely; generous. **3** *Law* Free, in the sense of privileged, exempt, or unhindered in action. See synonyms under BLUFF, CANDID, HONEST. *—v.t.* **1** To mark, as a letter or package, so as to be sent free of charge. **2** To send, as a letter, free of charge. **3** To convey free of charge. **4** *Chiefly Brit.* To mark or stamp (mail) by machine (a **franking machine**) to indicate that postage has been paid. *—n.* **1** The right to send mail matter free. **2** The package so sent. **3** The signature that authenticates it: extended commercially to telegrams, etc. [< OF *franc* frank, free] — **frank′ly** *adv.* **—frank′ness** *n.* **—frank′er** *n.*

Frank (frangk) A masculine personal name; also shortened form of FRANCIS, FRANKLIN.

Frank (frangk) *n.* **1** A member of one of the Germanic tribes settled on the Rhine early in the Christian era. **2** In the Near East, any European. [< L *Francus* a Frank < Gmc., a spear (cf. OE *franca* lance); named from their weapon]

Frank (frangk), **Glenn,** 1877–1940, U.S. educator. **—Waldo David,** 1889–1967, U.S. writer.

Frank·en·stein (frangk′ən·stīn) *n.* **1** The hero of Mary Wollstonecraft Shelley's *Frankenstein,* a medical student who fashions a man monster which commits numerous atrocities and finally slays its maker. **2** Any person destroyed by his own handiwork. **3** Loosely, Frankenstein's monster. **4** Any work or created thing that gets beyond the control of the inventor and causes his destruction.

Frank·fort (frangk′fərt) The capital of Kentucky.

Frankfort on the Main (mān) A city in Hesse, West Germany; birthplace of Goethe. *German* **Frank·furt** or **Frank·furt-am-Main** (frängk′fo͞ort·äm·mīn′).

Frankfort on the O·der (ō′dər) A city in Brandenburg, East Germany. *German* **Frank·furt** or **Frank·furt-an-der-O·der** (frängk′fo͞ort·än·dər·ō′dər).

frank·furt·er (frangk′fər·tər) *n.* A highly seasoned sausage of mixed meats. Compare WIENERWURST. Also **frank′fort·er, frankfurt** (or **frankfort) sausage.** [after *Frankfurt,* Germany]

Frank·furt·er (frangk′fər·tər), **Felix,** 1882–1965, U.S. jurist born in Austria; associate justice of the Supreme Court, 1939–1962.

frank·in·cense (frangk′in·sens) *n.* An aromatic gum or resin from various trees of East Africa, especially *Boswellia carteri*: used as an incense and in medicine as a stimulant and expectorant: also called *olibanum.* [< OF *franc* pure + *encens* incense]

Frank·ish (frang′kish) *adj.* Of or pertaining to the Franks, or, in the Near East, to Europeans in general. *—n.* The language spoken by the Franks, belonging to the western branch of the Germanic languages.

frank·lin (frangk′lin) *n.* In late medieval England, a freeholder; a non-noble landholder ranking below the gentry. [ME *frankeleyn* < Med. L *francus* free]

Frank·lin (frangk′lin), **Benjamin,** 1706–90, American patriot, writer, scientist, and diplomat; signer of the Declaration of Independence. **—Sir John,** 1786–1847, English Arctic explorer.

Frank·lin (frangk′lin) **1** A temporary state, 1784–88, comprising lands of western North Carolina ceded to Congress in 1784; now part of eastern Tennessee. **2** The northernmost district of Northwest Territories, Canada; 541,753 square miles.

frank·lin·ite (frangk′lin·īt) *n.* A metallic, iron-black, slightly magnetic oxide of zinc, iron, and manganese, crystallizing in the isometric system: a valuable ore of zinc. [after *Franklin,* N. J., where it is found]

Franklin stove An open-faced cast-iron stove resembling a fireplace: invented by Benjamin Franklin.

FRANKLIN STOVE

frank·ly (frangk′lē) *adv.* Candidly; openly.

frank·pledge (frangk′plej′) *n.* **1** In old English law, a system of mutual suretyship that required all men to combine in groups of ten to stand as sureties for one another's good behavior. **2** A member of such a group. **3** One such group; a tithing.

Frans (fräns) Swedish and Dutch form of FRANCIS.

fran·tic (fran′tik) *adj.* Manifesting, or caused by, excessive excitement; frenzied. See synonyms under INSANE. [< OF *frenetique* < LL *phreneticus* < Gk. *phrenitikos* delirious < *phrenitis* delirium < *phrēn* mind] **—fran′ti·cal·ly, fran′tic·ly** *adv.* — **fran′tic·ness** *n.*

Frants (fränts) Danish form of FRANCIS.

Franz (fränts) German form of FRANCIS.

Franz Jo·sef Land (fränts jō′zəf, *Ger.* fränts yō′zəf) An archipelago in the Arctic Ocean, the most northerly land of the eastern hemisphere; annexed by the U.S.S.R. in 1926: also *Fridtjof Nansen land. Russian* **Zem·lya Fran·tsa Io·si·fa** (zyim·lyä′ frän′tsä ō′zyi·fä).

frap (frap) *v.t.* **frapped, frap·ping** *Naut.* To draw or bind firmly. [< OF *fraper* strike]

frap·pé (fra·pā′) *U.S. adj.* **frap·pée** *fem.* Iced; chilled. *—n.* **1** A fruit juice frozen to a mush. **2** A liqueur or other beverage poured over shaved ice. [< F, pp. of *frapper* chill]

Fra·ser River (frā′zər) The chief river of British Columbia, flowing 850 miles SW to the Gulf of Georgia.

frat (frat) *n. U.S. Colloq.* A college fraternity.

fratch (frach) *v.i. & n. Brit. Dial.* Quarrel.

fra·ter[1] (frā′tər) *n.* A brother; a comrade. [< L]

fra·ter[2] (frā′tər) *n. Obs.* a fraiter.

fra·ter·nal (frə·tûr′nəl) *adj.* **1** Pertaining to or befitting a brother; brotherly. **2** Of or pertaining to a fraternal order or association. [< L *fraternus* < *frater* brother] **—fra·ter′nal·ism** *n.* — **fra·ter′nal·ly** *adv.*

fraternal society An organization for the attainment of some mutual benefit. Also **fraternal association** or **order.**

fraternal twins *Genetics* Twins that develop from separately fertilized ova and thus are as distinct in hereditary characteristics as though born at different times. They may be of the same or opposite sex: distinguished from *identical* twins.

fra·ter·ni·ty (frə·tûr′nə·tē) *n. pl.* **·ties 1** The condition or relation of brotherhood; brotherly affection. **2** An organization, for social or other purposes, of men students of American colleges, usually having Greek letter names and secret rites, and represented by chapters in many in

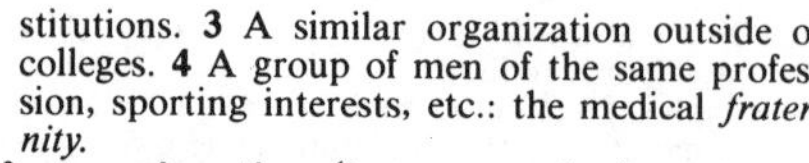

stitutions. **3** A similar organization outside of colleges. **4** A group of men of the same profession, sporting interests, etc.: the medical *fraternity.*

frat·er·ni·za·tion (frat′ər·nə·zā′shən) *n.* The act of fraternizing; specifically, intercourse between occupying military forces and civilians, often in contravention of regulations.

frat·er·nize (frat′ər·nīz) *v.* **·nized, ·niz·ing** *v.i.* **1** To be friendly or fraternal. **2** To be friendly with the enemy or with the people of an occupied or conquered territory; especially, to have sexual relations with women of such a territory. *—v.t.* **3** To bring into fraternal association. — **frat′er·niz′er** *n.*

Fra·tres Ar·va·les (frā′trēz är·vā′lēz) The Arval Brethren.

Fratres Mi·no·res (mī·nôr′ēz, -nō′rēz) See MINORITE.

Fratres Prae·di·ca·tor·es (prē′dik·ə·tôr′ēz, -tō′rēz) See DOMINICAN.

frat·ri·ci·dal (frat′rə·sī′dəl) *adj.* Of, pertaining to, or guilty of fratricide.

frat·ri·cide (frat′rə·sīd) *n.* **1** One who kills his brother. **2** The killing of a brother. [Def. 1 < F < L *fratricida* < *frater* brother + *caedere* kill; def. 2 < F < L *fratricidium*]

Frau (frou) *n. pl.* **Frau·en** (-ən) *German* A married woman; a wife; a lady: as a title, the German equivalent of *Mistress, Mrs.*

fraud (frôd) *n.* **1** Deception in order to gain by another's loss; craft; trickery; guile. **2** One who acts fraudulently; a cheat. **3** A deceptive or spurious thing. **4** *Law* Any artifice or deception practiced to cheat, deceive, or circumvent another to his injury. [< OF *fraude* < L *fraus, fraudis* deceit] **—fraud′ful** *adj.* **—fraud′ful·ly** *adv.* **—fraud′less** *adj.* **fraud′·less·ly** *adv.* — **fraud′less·ness** *n.*

Synonyms: artifice, cheat, cheating, deceit, deception, dishonesty, duplicity, imposition, imposture, swindle, swindling, treachery, treason, trick. A *fraud* is an act of deliberate *deception* with the design of securing something by taking unfair advantage of another. *A deceit* or *deception* may be designed merely to gain some end of one's own, with no intent of harming another; an *imposition* is intended to take some small advantage of another, or simply to make another ridiculous. An *imposture* is designed to obtain money, credit, or position to which one is not entitled, and may be practiced by a street beggar or by the pretender to a throne. All action that is not honest is *dishonesty,* but the term *dishonesty* is generally applied in business, politics, etc., to deceitful practices which are not distinctly criminal. *Fraud* includes *deceit,* but *deceit* may not reach the gravity of *fraud;* a *cheat* is of the nature of *fraud,* but of a petty sort; a *swindle* is more serious than a *cheat,* involving larger values and more flagrant *dishonesty. Fraud* is commonly actionable at law; *cheating* and *swindling* are for the most part out of the reach of legal proceedings. Compare ARTIFICE, DECEPTION, TREACHERY. *Antonyms*: fairness, honesty, integrity, truth, uprightness.

fraud·u·lence (frô′jə·ləns) *n.* The quality to being fraudulent; unfairness. Also **fraud′u·len·cy.**

fraud·u·lent (frô′jə·lənt) *adj.* Proceeding from, characterized by, or practicing fraud. See synonyms under BAD, COUNTERFEIT. **—fraud′·u·lent·ly** *adv.*

fraught (frôt) *adj.* **1** Involving; full of. **2** *Archaic* Freighted; laden. *—n. Obs.* Freight; cargo. [Orig. pp. of obs. *fraught* load, ult. < MDu. *vrachten*]

Frau Hol·le (frou hôl′ə) See HOLDA.

Fräu·lein (froi′līn) *n. German* An unmarried woman; a young woman: as a title, the German equivalent of *Miss.*

Fraun·ho·fer (froun′hō′fər), **Joseph von,** 1787–1826, German optician and physicist; mapped dark lines of the spectrum.

Fraunhofer's lines A series of groups of dark lines in the spectrum of the sun and other stars, each group appearing to the eye as a single transverse line: also called *F lines.*

frax·i·nel·la (frak′sə·nel′ə) *n.* A Eurasian herb *(Dictamnus albus)* of the rue family with white flowers and a powerful odor: also called *dittany* and *gas plant.* [< NL, dim. of L *fraxinus* ash tree]

fray[1] (frā) *n.* A fight; an affray. *—v.t. Obs.* To frighten. *—v.i. Obs.* To fight. [Aphetic var. of AFFRAY]

fray[2] (frā) *v.t. & v.i.* To wear, rub, or become

worn, as by friction; ravel. —*n.* A fretted spot in a cloth, etc. [<F *frayer* <L *fricare* rub]

Fra·zer (frā′zər), **Sir James George,** 1854–1941, Scottish anthropologist.

fra·zil (frə·zil′, fraz′əl, frā′zəl) *n.* Ice of a granular, spicular, or platelike shape formed in agitated or flowing water. Also **frazil ice.** [Cf. F *fraisil* cinders]

fraz·zle (fraz′əl) *Colloq. v.t. & v.i.* **·zled, ·zling** **1** To fray or become frayed; fret, or tatter. **2** To tire out; weary. —*n.* Frayed ends; state of being frayed. —**beat to a frazzle** Beat into shreds and tatters; hence, overcome completely. —**worn to a frazzle** Worn to shreds; hence, tired out; utterly exhausted. [? Blend of FRAY[2] + obs. *fasel* ravel]

freak (frēk) *n.* **1** A sudden causeless change of mind; a whim. **2** A malformation; monstrosity. **3** *Slang* One given to the use of drugs, especially illegal drugs. **4** *Slang* One who is very unconventional. **5** *Slang* One who is very enthusiastic about something: an opera *freak.* —*adj.* Strange; abnormal. —**to freak out** *Slang* **1** To experience, often unpleasantly, the effects of drugs, especially psychedelic drugs. **2** To behave as though one were under the influence of a psychedelic drug. [Origin unknown] —**freak′y** *adj.*

freak·ish (frē′kish) *adj.* Inclined to freaks; eccentric; also, like a freak, capricious; prankish. —**freak′ish·ly** *adv.* —**freak′ish·ness** *n.*

freath (frēth, frēth) *n. & v. Scot.* Lather; froth.

Fré·chette (frā·shet′), **Louis Honoré,** 1839–1908, Canadian journalist and poet.

freck·le (frek′əl) *n.* A small, brownish, or dark-colored spot on the skin. —*v.* **freck·led, freck·ling** *v.t.* To mark or cover with freckles. —*v.i.* To become marked with freckles. [ME *fracel,* var. of *frekne* <ON *freknur* freckles]

freck·led (frek′əld) *adj.* Marked with freckles. Also **freck′ly.**

Fred (fred) Shortened form of FREDERICK, ALFRED, WILFRED.

Fred·er·i·ca (fred′ə·rē′kə) A feminine personal name. Compare FREDERICK. Also *Pg., Sp.* **Fre·de·ri·ca** (frā′dā·rē′kä), *Fr.* **Fré·dé·rique** (frā·dā·rēk′).

Fred·er·ick (fred′ər·ik, -rik) **1** A masculine personal name. **2** Name of many European monarchs. Also **Fred′er·ic,** *Fr.* **Fré·dé·ric** (frā·dā·rēk′), *Dan.* **Fre·der·ik** (freth′ə·rēk), *Du.* **Fre·de·rik** (frā′dā·rēk). See also FEDERICO, FRIEDRICH. [<Gmc., peaceful ruler]

—**Frederick I,** 1121–90, Holy Roman Emperor 1152–90: known as *Barbarossa* (Redbeard).

—**Frederick I,** 1657–1713, elector of Brandenburg 1688–1701; first king of Prussia 1701–13.

—**Frederick II,** 1194–1250, Holy Roman Emperor 1215–50.

—**Frederick II,** 1712–86, king of Prussia 1740–86: known as **Frederick the Great.**

—**Frederick III,** 1415–93, Holy Roman Emperor 1440–93; king of Germany as Frederick IV.

—**Frederick William,** 1620–88, elector of Brandenburg 1640–88; secured Prussian independence: called "the Great Elector."

—**Frederick William I,** 1688–1740, king of Prussia 1713–40; succeeded Frederick I.

—**Frederick William II,** 1744–97, king of Prussia 1786–97; succeeded Frederick II.

—**Frederick William III,** 1770–1840, king of Prussia 1797–1840.

—**Frederick William IV,** 1795–1861, king of Prussia 1840–61.

Fred·er·icks·burg (fred′riks·bûrg, fred′ər·iks-) A city in NE Virginia; scene of Confederate victory in the Civil War, 1862.

Fred·er·ic·ton (fred′ər·ik·tən, fred′rik-) The capital of New Brunswick province, Canada.

Fre·der·iks·berg (fred′ər·iks·bûrg, fred′riks-; *Dan.* freth′ə·rēks·berkh′) The chief suburb of Copenhagen, Denmark, comprising a separate commune.

free (frē) *adj.* **fre·er, fre·est** **1** Not bound by restrictions, physical, governmental, or moral; exempt from arbitrary domination or distinction; independent. **2** Not enslaved or in bondage. **3** Not believing in or permitting slavery. **4** Self-determining, whether as implying the absence of control through external causes in the form of physical forces, legal commands, or moral influences, or as asserting the mysterious and inexplicable spontaneity of the self as possessed of so-called *free* will. **5** Having, conferring, or characterized by political liberty; not subject to despotic or arbitrary rule; living under a government based on the consent of the people: a *free* nation. **6** Liberated, by reason of age, from the authority of parents or guardians: At 21 years a man is *free.* **7** Invested with certain franchises; enjoying certain immunities; given or allowed all privileges of: *free* of the city. **8** Exempt from or not subject to; not dominated by; clear of: followed by *from,* or rarely by *of.* **9** Characterized by disregard of conventionality, ceremony, or formality; accessible; frank; ingenuous. **10** Characterized by disregard of duty or propriety; forward; impertinent, indelicate or immodest; careless; immoderate; reckless. **11** Without impediment or restraint; moving or ranging at will; not repressed, checked, or hampered; unobstructed; unrestricted; unconstrained. **12** Without restriction; especially, without charge or cost; open; gratuitous: *free* seats. **13** Employing or giving unrestrainedly or without parsimony; liberal; profuse; generous; also, not obtained by solicitation. **14** Expending energy without stint; ready and prompt in action or movement without urging; ready; spirited. **15** Not closely bound to an original or pattern, nor limited by strict technical rules; exercising some liberty or discretion: a *free* choice, a *free* translation. **16** Not attached, bound, or fixed; capable of moving; loose: the *free* end of a rope. **17** Uncombined chemically: *free* hydrogen. **18** Available: *free* energy. **19** *Naut.* Favorable: applied to winds more than six points from being dead ahead. **20** Of or pertaining to a freeman: opposed to *base.* —*adv.* **1** Gratuitously. **2** Freely; willingly. **3** With the wind more than six points from being dead ahead. —*v.t.* **freed, free·ing** **1** To make free; release from bondage, obligation, worry, etc. **2** To clear or rid of obstruction or hindrance; disentangle; disengage. See synonyms under ABSOLVE, DELIVER, RELEASE. [OE *frēo*] —**free′ly** *adv.*

Synonyms (adj.): clear, emancipated, exempt, independent, unchecked, unconfined, unfettered, unhindered, unimpeded, unobstructed, unrestrained, untrammeled. See GENEROUS. *Antonyms:* bound, clogged, dependent, enslaved, fettered, hindered, impeded, restrained, restricted, shackled, subdued, subjected, subjugated.

-free *combining form* Free of; devoid of: *carefree, duty-free.*

free agency The power or capacity of a personality to act freely without constraint of his will. See WILL.

free agent A person regarded as self-determining and thus capable of responsible choice, and whose actions are determined by his own unconstrained will.

free alongside ship or **vessel** Delivered without charge to the pier where a ship is docked: abbreviated *f.a.s.*

free-and-eas·y (frē′ənd·ē′zē) *adj.* Unconventional; unrestrained.

free association **1** *Psychol.* An association of ideas unrestricted by definite control or limiting factors. **2** *Psychoanal.* A method of revealing unconscious processes by encouraging a spontaneous and unselective association of ideas.

free balloon A balloon floating freely in the atmosphere, its height controlled only by ballast and regulation of gas content.

free·bie (frē′bē) *n. Slang* Anything, as a ticket to a sports event, that is given free.

free·board (frē′bôrd′, -bōrd′) *n.* **1** *Naut.* The side of a vessel between the water line and the main deck. **2** The distance between the underframe of an automobile and the ground.

free·boot (frē′bo͞ot′) *v.i.* To act as a freebooter.

free·boot·er (frē′bo͞o′tər) *n.* One who plunders; especially a pirate or buccaneer. [<MDu. *vrijbuiter* < *vrij* free + *buit* booty]

free·boot·y (frē′bo͞o′tē) *n. Obs.* **1** Spoil; loot. **2** Pillaging.

free-born (frē′bôrn′) *adj.* Not born in servitude.

free city A city having an independent government, as certain German cities, that at one time were virtually small republics.

free coinage The mintage of certain specified bullion that may be offered at the mint by any person, with or without a fixed charge.

free companion See FREE LANCE (def. 1).

free company A company of medieval mercenaries.

freed·man (frēd′mən) *n. pl.* **·men** (-mən) An emancipated slave, especially an emancipated American Negro after the Civil War. —**freed′·wom′an** *n. fem.*

free·dom (frē′dəm) *n.* **1** Exemption or liberation from slavery or imprisonment. **2** Exemption from political restraint or autocratic control; independence. **3** Liberty of choice or action. **4** *Philos.* The state of the will as the first cause of human actions; self-determination in rational beings. **5** Exemption; immunity: *freedom* from want; *freedom* from arrest. **6** Exemption or release from obligations, ties, etc. **7** Ease; facility. **8** Frankness or familiarity in speech or manner. **9** The right to enjoy the privileges of membership or citizenship: *freedom* of the city. **10** Unrestricted use: He had *freedom* of the library. **11** Ease of motion. See synonyms under LIBERTY. —**free′dom·less** *adj.* [OE *frēodōm*]

freedom of the press The right freely to publish without censorship or other government interference, usually restricted in practice by laws barring obscenity, sedition, and libel.

freedom of the seas Exemption from seizure at sea in war, by armed vessels of belligerents, of all private property of neutrals except contraband of war.

free electron See under ELECTRON.

free energy *Physics* That portion of the energy of a physicochemical system that is available to perform work.

free enterprise See PRIVATE ENTERPRISE.

free fight A general fight; a free-for-all.

free-for-all (frē′fər·ôl′) *n.* A fight, game, or competition, open to all comers.

free form *Ling.* A morpheme which can occur meaningfully in isolation: opposed to *bound form.*

free gold **1** Gold held by the U.S. Treasury over and above that in the gold reserve. **2** Pure gold found loose, as in placer mining.

free·hand (frē′hand′) *adj.* Executed with the hand without aid of measurements or drawing instruments: *freehand* drawing.

free hand Authority to act on one's own.

free-hand·ed (frē′han′did) *adj.* **1** Having the hands free or unrestricted. **2** Open-handed; generous. —**free′-hand′ed·ness** *n.*

free-heart·ed (frē′här′tid) *adj.* Generous; frank; open-hearted.

free·hold (frē′hōld′) *n.* **1** An estate in lands. **2** Land held without limitations or conditions; absolute ownership of an estate. —**free′hold′er** *n.*

free lance **1** A medieval soldier who sold his services to any state or cause. **2** One who writes, performs, or offers services without being regularly employed. **3** One who supports a cause or causes independently and without personal allegiance.

free-lance (frē′lans′, -läns′) *v.i.* **-lanced, -lanc·ing** To serve or work as a free lance. —*adj.* Working or acting as a free lance.

free list **1** A list of goods not subject to tariff charges. **2** A list of persons admitted free.

free-liv·er (frē′liv′ər) *n.* One addicted to personal indulgence, as in eating and drinking.

free-liv·ing (frē′liv′ing) *adj.* **1** Given to easy-going or self-indulgent habits of life. **2** *Zool.* Having or characterized by freedom of movement; motile.

free·load (frē′lōd′) *v.i. Slang* To act as a freeloader.

free·load·er (frē′lō′dər) *n. Slang* One who attends social gatherings for free food and drink.

free love The doctrine or custom of free choice in sexual relations, without the constraint of legal marriage or any permanent obligations.

free·man (frē′mən) *n. pl.* **·men** (-mən) **1** A man who is free; one not a slave or serf. **2** An inhabitant of a city. **3** In English law, a person admitted to the freedom of a corporate town or borough or of any other corporate body and hence having full rights and privileges. **4** In feudal law, an allodial proprietor, as distinct from a vassal. **5** In old English law, a freeholder, as distinct from a villein. **6** In colonial America, a freeholder and hence, in most colonies, an enfranchised citizen.

Free·man (frē′mən), **Douglas Southall,** 1886–1953, U.S. editor and historian. — **Edward Augustus,** 1823–92, English historian. — **Mary Eleanor,** 1852–1930, *née* Wilkins, U.S. writer.

free·mar·tin (frē′mär′tən) *n.* A female calf twinned with a male calf and generally barren. [Origin uncertain]

free·ma·son (frē′mā′sən) *n.* In the Middle Ages, a stonemason belonging to a craft guild that had secret signs and passwords, and that admitted as honorary members persons not connected with their craft, who were designated *accepted masons.*

Free·ma·son (frē′mā′sən) *n.* A member of an extensive secret order or fraternity, dating from the Middle Ages, the members denoting themselves *Free and Accepted Masons.* — **Free·ma·son·ic** (frē′mə·son′ik) *adj.* — **Free′ma′·son·ry** *n.*

free·ma·son·ry (frē′mā′sən·rē) *n.* Instinctive sympathy or community of interests.

free·ness (frē′nis) *n.* The state of being free.

free on board Put on board a train, ship, or other freight or baggage carrier, without charge: abbreviated *f.o.b.*

free oscillations *Electr.* Oscillations within a circuit of a frequency determined by the inductance and capacity of the circuit uninfluenced by impressed voltages. Compare FORCED OSCILLATIONS.

free path *Physics* The distance traveled by a particle, as an ion, electron, or molecule, before colliding with another.

free port **1** A port open to all trading vessels on equal terms. **2** The whole or part of a port area where no customs duties are levied on goods intended for transshipment rather than for import.

free press An uncensored press; newspapers, magazines, etc., not accountable to a government for the news or opinions they print.

free ship **1** A ship belonging to a neutral power, and hence free from liability to seizure in time of war. **2** A ship that, while foreign built, may receive U.S. registry when owned by a citizen or citizens of the United States.

free·si·a (frē′zhē·ə, -sē·ə, -zhə) *n.* A South African plant (genus *Freesia*) of the iris family, having bell-shaped, various colored, fragrant flowers. [<NL, after E. M. *Fries,* 1794–1878, Swedish botanist]

free silver The free and unlimited coinage of silver, particularly at a fixed ratio to gold, as 16 to 1 (advocated by a section of the Democratic party in 1896). — **free′-sil′ver** *adj.*

Free-soil (frē′soil′) *adj. U.S.* Of or pertaining to the Free-soil party, organized in 1848 to oppose the extension of slavery. — **Free′-soil′er** *n.*

free-spo·ken (frē′spō′kən) *adj.* Unreserved or frank in speech. — **free′spo′ken·ly** *adv.* — **free′·spo′ken·ness** *n.*

Free State **1** Before the Civil War, any State where slavery did not exist or was forbidden. **2** The Irish Free State.

free·stone (frē′stōn′) *adj.* Having a pit from which the pulp easily separates, as a plum or peach. — *n.* **1** Any stone, as sandstone or limestone, easily wrought for building purposes. **2** A peach easily freed from its pit.

free-style (frē′stīl′) *adj.* In competitive swimming, using or marked by the freedom to use whichever stroke the swimmer chooses. — *n.* Free-style swimming.

free-swim·mer (frē′swim′ər) *n.* A fish that swims habitually near the surface.

free-swim·ming (frē′swim′ing) *adj. Zool.* Swimming freely, as an aquatic animal: said especially of certain organisms that are attached or immovable during other stages of their development.

free·think·er (frē′thing′kər) *n.* An independent thinker; especially, one who forms his own religious beliefs without regard to church authority. — **free′think′ing** *adj.* & *n.*

free thought Thought or belief, especially in religious matters, based on reason alone and uninfluenced by authority or dogma.

Free·town (frē′toun) A port, capital of Sierra Leone.

free trade **1** Commerce between different countries free from restrictions or burdens, as tariff or customs; specifically, commerce not subjected to restrictions, discriminations, or favors of any kind designed to influence its normal course. **2** The practice, policy, or system of unrestricted trade. **3** The trade system of a country whose duties are levied only for revenue and without regard to their effect on home industries. Compare PROTECTION, PROTECTIVE TARIFF. **4** *Archaic* or *Obs.* Smuggling.

free-trad·er (frē′trā′dər) *n.* An advocate of or believer in free trade.

free verse Verse depending for its poetic effect upon irregular rhythmical pattern, either absence or irregularity of rime, and the use of cadenced speech rhythms rather than conventional verse forms; vers libre.

free·war·ren (frē′wôr′ən, -wor′-) *n.* In English law, the exclusive right of killing game within warren.

free water Soil water in excess of that absorbed by the soil: also called *gravity water.*

free·way (frē′wā′) *n.* A multiple-lane road designed for rapid transportation.

free wheel *Mech.* **1** A form of automotive transmission including a clutch which allows the driving shaft to run freely when its speed exceeds that of the engine shaft. **2** A brake device attached to the rear wheel of a bicycle which permits wheel motion without pedal action. — **free′-wheel′ing** *n.* & *adj.*

free will **1** The power of self-determination regarded as a special faculty. **2** *Philos.* The doctrine that man is entirely unrestricted in his ability to choose between good and evil: opposed to *determinism.*

free-will (frē′wil′) *adj.* Made, done, or given of one's own free choice; voluntary.

freeze (frēz) *v.* **froze, fro·zen, freez·ing** *v.i.* **1** To become converted from a fluid to a solid state by loss of heat; become ice. **2** To become stiff or hard with cold, as wet clothes. **3** To be very cold: It's *freezing* in here! **4** To become covered or obstructed with ice. **5** To adhere by freezing: It *froze* to the ground. **6** To be damaged or killed by freezing or frost. **7** To become motionless, as if frozen. **8** To be chilled or made motionless, as if by fear or other emotion. **9** To become formal or unyielding in manner. — *v.t.* **10** To change into ice; cause to become frozen. **11** To make stiff or hard by freezing the moisture of. **12** To cover or obstruct with ice. **13** To damage or kill by freezing or frost. **14** To make or hold motionless or in position. **15** To chill or make motionless, as if by fear, awe, or other emotion; frighten; discourage. **16** To fix or stabilize (prices, stocks, wages, etc.) so as to prevent change, as by government order. **17** *Med.* To anesthetize: to *freeze* a tooth. — **to freeze to** (or **onto**) **1** To keep close or cling to (a person). **2** To hold on to. — **to freeze out** *U.S. Colloq.* To exclude or drive away, as by unfriendliness or severe competition. — *n.* **1** The act of freezing or the state of being frozen. **2** A spell of freezing weather. **3** The stabilizing or fixing of prices, labor, etc., in order to prevent profiteering, migration of workers, etc. ◆ Homophone: *frieze.* [OE *frēosan*]

freeze-out (frēz′out′) *n.* **1** A kind of poker game in which each player drops out as soon as all his money is lost, the last player winning all. **2** An exclusion, as by unfriendliness, outwitting, or trickery.

freez·er (frē′zər) *n.* **1** That which freezes. **2** A refrigerator within which a low temperature is maintained for the purpose of preserving or freezing foods, etc. **3** An apparatus containing ice or brine, for freezing ice-cream.

freeze-up (frēz′up′) *n.* The freezing over of lakes, rivers, streams, etc., in severe winter weather; also, such weather.

freezing mixture Any mixture, as of salt and ice, that can lower the temperature of surrounding bodies or substances to various levels below the freezing point.

freezing point *Physics* The temperature at which a liquid passes into the solid state under given pressure; for fresh water at sea-level pressure this temperature is 32 degrees above zero Fahrenheit, or zero degrees Celsius. Compare MELTING POINT.

free zone A section of a port or city for the receipt and storage of goods, duty-free.

Frei·berg (frī′bûrg, *Ger.* frī′berkh) A city in the former state of Saxony, SE East Germany.

Frei·burg (frī′bûrg, *Ger.* frī′bo͝orkh) **1** A city in SW Germany: also **Freiburg-im-Breis·gau** (im brīs′gou). **2** The German name for FRIBOURG.

freight (frāt) *n.* **1** *U.S. & Can.* **a** The service of transporting commodities by land, air, or water; specifically, ordinary transportation as opposed to *express.* **b** The commodities so transported. **2** *Brit.* **a** The service of transporting commodities by air or water. **b** The commodities so transported. In Great Britain, commodities transported by land are known as *goods.* **3** The price paid for the transportation of commodities. **4** *U.S. & Can.* A freight train: in Great Britain, called a *goods* train. — **dead freight** Money paid for cargo space, as on shipboard, that was not used. — *v.t.* **1** To load with commodities for transportation. **2** To load; burden. **3** To send or transport as or by freight. [<MDu. *vrecht,* var. of *vracht.* See FRAUGHT.]

freight·age (frā′tij) *n.* **1** A cargo; lading. **2** The price charged or paid for carrying goods. **3** The transportation of merchandise.

freight car A railway car for carrying freight.

freight·er (frā′tər) *n.* **1** One who has freight transported. **2** One who contracts to transport freight for others; especially, the charterer of a ship for carrying merchandise. **3** One engaged in transporting merchandise by fleets or trains of vehicles. **4** A freight-carrying vessel or aircraft.

freight train *U.S.* A railroad train comprised of freight cars.

Fré·jus (frā·zhüs′), **Pointe de** An Alpine peak on the Franco-Italian border; 9,659 feet; crossed by the **Fréjus Pass** at 8,370 feet.

frem (frem) *Scot. adj.* Alien; strange. — *n.* A stranger. Also **fremd** (fremd), **frem·it** (frem′·it), **fremt** (fremt): sometimes spelled *fraim.*

Fre·man·tle (frē′man·təl) A port in SW Western Australia.

fre·mes·cent (frə·mes′ənt) *adj. Obs.* Growing increasingly noisy; tumultuous. [<L *fremere* roar + -ESCENT]

frem·i·tus (frem′i·təs) *n. pl.* **·tus** *Pathol.* A palpable vibration, as of the wall of the chest; resonant thrill. [<L, a roar]

Fré·mont (frē′mont), **John Charles,** 1813–90, U.S. explorer, general, and politician.

Frem·stad (frem′städ), **Olive,** 1872–1951, U.S. soprano born in Sweden.

fre·na·tor (frē′nā·tər) *n. Anat.* Anything which checks or restrains body motion. [<L, a tamer <*frenare* curb, restrain]

french (french) *v.t.* To prepare (chops or rib roasts) by trimming the meat from the ends of the bones.

French (french), **Daniel Chester,** 1850–1931, U. S. sculptor. — **Sir John Denton Pinkstone,** 1852–1925, first Earl of Ypres, British field marshal in World War I.

French (french) *adj.* Pertaining to, from, or characteristic of France, its people, or their language. — *n.* **1** The people of France collectively: with *the.* **2** The Romance language of France, belonging to the Italic subfamily of Indo-European languages. — **Old French** The French language from about 850 to 1400, directly descended from Vulgar Latin as it developed in Gaul. Old French had two especially important dialects, the *langue d'oïl,* spoken north of the Loire, and the *langue d'oc* (Provençal), spoken south of it. Modern French is derived from the former, with the central French dialect of Paris as the standard. Abbr. *OF* — **Middle French** The French language as spoken from about 1400 to 1600. Abbr. *MF* — **Modern French** The language of France after 1600. Abbr. *F* [OE *Frencisc* <*Franca* a Frank]

French Academy An association of forty scholars, writers, and intellectuals, known as "The Immortals," established in 1685 by Cardinal Richelieu to exercise control over the French language and literature. *French* **A·ca·dé·mie Fran·çaise** (à·kà·dā·mē′ frän·sez′).

French and Indian War That part of the war between France and England, 1754–60, waged in America, in which the French received support from Indian allies.

French blue Ultramarine.

French Broad River A river in western North Carolina and eastern Tennessee, flowing 204 miles north to the Tennessee River.

French bulldog A breed of small, compact, bat-eared bulldog, generally of a dark or brindle color, developed in France.

French Canada 1 The province of Quebec. 2 French-Canadians collectively.

French-Ca·na·di·an (french′kə·nā′dē·ən) *n.* A French settler in Canada or a descendant of French settlers in Canada.

French casement A casement for a French window.

French chop A rib chop of lamb with the top of the bone scraped bare.

French Community A political association that includes France, Central African Republic, Chad, Congo Republic, Dahomey, Gabon Republic, Ivory Coast Republic, Malagasy Republic, Mauritania, Republic of Niger, Senegal, and Republic of the Upper Volta, together with the French overseas departments and territories.

French cuff A cuff of a sleeve turned back and secured to itself with a link.

French curve An instrument used by draftsmen and architects for drawing curves.

French disease Syphilis.

French doors A pair of adjoining doors, often set with glass panes, attached to opposite door jambs and opening in the middle.

French dressing A salad dressing consisting of olive oil, spices, vinegar, salt, etc.

French Equatorial Africa A former group of French overseas territories in west central Africa. Formerly **French Congo**. See CENTRAL AFRICAN REPUBLIC, CHAD, CONGO REPUBLIC, GABON REPUBLIC.

French-fried (french′frīd′) *adj.* Cooked by frying crisp in deep fat.

French gray A light, clear, somewhat greenish gray.

French Gui·an·a (gē·an′ə) An overseas department of France on the NE coast of South America, including the inland Territory of Inini; 34,740 square miles; capital, Cayenne. *French* **Guy·ane Fran·çaise** (gē·än′ frän·sez′).

French heel A high, forward-slanting heel, used on women's dress shoes.

French horn A keyed, brass wind instrument with long twisted tube whose diameter increases gradually from the mouthpiece to a widely flaring bell shape: developed from the hunting horn.

FRENCH HORN

French·i·fy (fren′chə·fī) *v.t.* **·fied, ·fy·ing** To make French in form or characteristics.

French India Formerly, the overseas territories of France in India, consisting of the settlements of Chandernagore, Karikal, Mahé, Pondicherry, and Yanam, with adjoining territory; total, 193 square miles; capital, Pondicherry. *French* **É·ta·blisse·ments fran·çais dans l'Inde** (ā·tà·blēs·män′ frän·sā′ dän lañd′).

French Indochina A former name for INDOCHINA (def. 2).

French leave An informal, unauthorized, or hurried departure.

French·man (french′mən) *n. pl.* **·men** (-mən) A native or citizen of France; one of the French people. — **French′wom′an** *n. fem.*

French Morocco A former French protectorate and associated state in the French Union, in NW Africa: since 1956 a part of the sultanate of Morocco.

French North Africa A former name for Algeria, French Morocco, and Tunisia.

French Polynesia A French overseas territory spread over a wide area of the South Pacific, comprising Gambier, Tubuai, Marquesas, and Society Islands, and Tuamotu Archipelago; 1,575 square miles; capital, Papeete, on Tahiti; *French* **Po·ly·né·sie Fran·çaise** (pô·lē·nä·zē′ frän·sez′). Formerly called **French Oceania**, *French* **Établissements français de l'Océanie.**

French pancake A very thin, rolled pancake, usually covered with preserved fruit, sugar, and cinnamon.

French pastry A rich fancy pastry often having a filling of whipped cream, custard, or preserved fruits.

French Revolution See under REVOLUTION.

French roof A modified mansard roof.

French seam A seam sewed on both sides so that no raw edges are exposed.

French Shore The parts of the Newfoundland coast included in various British treaties granting rights to French fishermen from 1713 to 1904.

French Somaliland See SOMALILAND, FRENCH.

French Sudan See MALI.

French telephone A handset telephone, with the receiver and the transmitter mounted on one handle.

French toast Bread dipped in a batter of beaten eggs and milk, and fried in shallow fat.

French Togoland See TOGO.

French Union A former political association of France, its overseas departments and territories, and other associated states and territories. See also FRENCH COMMUNITY.

French West Africa A former group of French overseas territories comprised in the western bulge of Africa. See DAHOMEY, GUINEA, IVORY COAST REPUBLIC, MALI, MAURITANIA, REPUBLIC OF NIGER, REPUBLIC OF SENEGAL, REPUBLIC OF THE UPPER VOLTA.

French West Indies Islands in the Caribbean, comprising two overseas departments of France: Martinique and Guadeloupe.

French windows A casement window with adjoining sashes attached to opposite jambs and opening in the middle.

FRENCH WINDOW

French·y (fren′chē) *Colloq. adj.* **·i·er, ·i·est** Having or assuming French characteristics. — *n. pl.* **French·ies** A Frenchman.

Fre·neau (fre·nō′), **Philip,** 1752–1832, American poet.

fre·net·ic (frə·net′ik) *adj.* Frenzied, frantic; also, pertaining to mental disorder: also **fre·net′i·cal.** — *n.* A frantic or mentally disordered person; a phrenetic. [Var. of PHRENETIC] — **fre·net′i·cal·ly** *adv.*

fre·num (frē′nəm) *n. pl.* **·na** (-nə) *Anat.* A restraining band or fold; the *frenum* of the tongue: also spelled *fraenum.* [<L, bridle]

fren·zied (fren′zēd) *adj.* Affected with frenzy or madness; frantic.

fren·zy (fren′zē) *n. pl.* **·zies** Violent agitation; fury; madness; delirium. — *v.t.* **·zied, ·zy·ing** To throw into frenzy; make frantic. [<OF *frenesie* <LL *phrenesis* <LGk. *phrenēsis,* var. of *phrenitis* delirium < *phrēn* mind]

Synonyms (noun): fanaticism, fury, insanity, madness, mania, raving. See ENTHUSIASM, INSANITY. *Antonyms*: composure, coolness, equanimity, equipoise, sanity, sobriety.

Fre·on (frē′on) *n. Chem.* Any of a group of stable, colorless, non-toxic, non-flammable organic compounds of chlorine and fluorine used as solvents, refrigerants, and propellants for aerosol insecticides: a trade name.

fre·quence (frē′kwəns) *n.* Frequency.

fre·quen·cy (frē′kwən·sē) *n. pl.* **·cies** 1 The property or state of being frequent. 2 *Physics* The number of occurrences of a periodic quantity, as waves, vibrations, oscillations, in a unit of time; usually expressed as cycles per second. 3 *Stat.* A ratio expressing the number of times a given case, value, or score occurs in a total of relevant classified data: the *frequency* of marriage in a specified population. 4 *Ecol.* The relative number of plant and animal species in a given region.

frequency band *Telecom.* A channel included between certain specified wavelengths for the efficient transmission of radio, television, and other forms of electromagnetic signals.

frequency bridge *Electr.* A device similar to the Wheatstone bridge, used in the measurement of alternating-current frequencies.

frequency condition *Physics* The state of an atom or molecule in which it may emit radiation of a given frequency.

frequency curve *Stat.* A graphic representation of the frequencies of the values of specified variables as presented in a **frequency distribution** table and arranged by order of magnitude: also called *distribution curve.* See HISTOGRAM.

frequency level *Physics* A logarithmic expression of the tone interval between a given sound frequency and a reference keynote; one octave has a frequency level of unity.

frequency meter An instrument, calibrated in cycles, kilocycles, or megacycles, for measuring the wavelength or frequency of radio signals.

frequency modulation *Telecom.* A system of radio transmission in which the carrier wave is varied by the modulation signal in frequency rather than in amplitude. This system can utilize narrower channels than does the amplitude modulation system and is exceptionally free of static and other atmospheric disturbances.

fre·quent (frē′kwənt) *adj.* 1 Occurring or appearing often. 2 Repeating or inclined to repeat often; reiterating; persistent. 3 *Obs.* Crowded; full; thronged. — *v.t.* (fri·kwent′) 1 To visit often. 2 To be in or at often or habitually. [<L *frequens, -entis* crowded] — **fre·quent′er** *n.*

Synonyms (adj.): common, constant, general, numerous, recurrent, recurring, repeated, returning, usual. See COMMON, GENERAL, MANY, USUAL. *Antonyms*: few, occasional, rare, scanty, solitary, uncommon, unusual.

fre·quen·ta·tion (frē′kwən·tā′shən) *n.* The practice of frequenting or resorting; frequent visiting.

fre·quen·ta·tive (fri·kwen′tə·tiv) *Gram. adj.* Denoting repeated or habitual action: a *frequentative* verb. — *n.* An iterative or frequentative verb.

fre·quent·ly (frē′kwənt·lē) *adv.* Often; repeatedly; at short intervals.

frère (frâr) *n. pl.* **frères** (frâr) *French* 1 Brother. 2 Friar; monk.

fres·co (fres′kō) *n. pl.* **·coes** or **·cos** 1 The art of painting on a surface of plaster, especially while the plaster is still fresh. 2 A picture so painted. — *v.t.* **fres·coed, fres·co·ing** To paint in fresco. [<Ital., fresh] — **fres′co·er, fres′co·ist** *n.*

fresh[1] (fresh) *adj.* 1 Newly made, obtained, received, etc.: *fresh* coffee; *fresh* footprints. 2 New; recent: *fresh* news. 3 Additional; further: *fresh* supplies. 4 Not salted, pickled, smoked, etc. 5 Not spoiled, stale, musty, etc. 6 Not faded, worn, etc.: *fresh* colors; *fresh* memories. 7 Not salt: *fresh* water. 8 Pure; refreshing: *fresh* air. 9 Appearing healthy or youthful. 10 Not fatigued; active. 11 Inexperienced; unsophisticated. 12 *Meteorol.* Moderately rapid and strong; specifically designating a breeze (No. 5) or a gale (No. 8) of the Beaufort scale. 13 Having a renewed supply of milk: said of a cow that has recently calved. — *n.* 1 A freshet. 2 A pool or stream of fresh water. 3 A fresh-water stream running into tidewater; also the adjoining lands. [OE *fersc,* infl. by OF *freis,* both ult. <Gmc.] — **fresh′ly** *adv.* — **fresh′ness** *n.*

Synonyms (adj.): blooming, bright, cool, green, new, novel, recent, renewed, ruddy, undimmed, unfaded, unimpaired, unskilled, untarnished, untried, unworn, verdant, vigorous, young, youthful. See MODERN, NEW. *Antonyms*: blasé, decayed, dim, dull, exhausted, faded, jaded, moldy, musty.

fresh[2] (fresh) *adj. Slang* Forward; presumptuous. [<G *frech* impudent]

fresh-air (fresh′âr′) *adj.* Fond of, providing, or organized to provide fresh or uncontaminated air.

fresh·en (fresh′ən) *v.t.* 1 To make fresh, vigorous, or less salty. 2 *Naut.* To relieve (a hawser or rope) by changing the position of the part exposed to chafing. — *v.i.* 3 To become fresh. 4 To have a calf: said of cows. 5 To come into milk. — **fresh′en·er** *n.*

fresh·et (fresh′it) *n.* 1 A sudden flood in a

stream; an inundation. **2** A fresh-water stream flowing into the sea.

fresh·man (fresh′mən) *n. pl.* **·men** (-mən) A student in the first year of the course in a college, high school, etc.

fresh-wa·ter (fresh′wô′tər, -wot′ər) *adj.* **1** Pertaining to or living in fresh water. **2** Experienced in sailing on fresh water only; hence, untrained; of no experience. **3** Inland; not situated on the coast. **4** *U.S.* Not well known; somewhat provincial: a *fresh-water* college. **5** Untrained; unskilled.

fres·nel (frā·nel′) *n. Physics* A unit of wave frequency, equal to 10^{12} cycles per second. [after A. J. *Fresnel*]

Fres·nel (frā·nel′), **Augustin Jean,** 1788–1827, French physicist.

fres·no (frez′nō) *n. pl.* **·noes** or **·nos** A wide, shallow, scooplike, metal scraper for moving earth. Also **fresno scraper.** [after *Fresno,* Cal., where first made]

Fres·no (frez′nō) A city in central California.

fret[1] (fret) *v.* **fret·ted, fret·ting** *v.t.* **1** To irritate; worry; annoy. **2** To wear or eat away, as by chafing or gnawing; corrode; fray. **3** To form or make by wearing away. **4** To make rough; agitate: to *fret* the surface of a pond. —*v.i.* **5** To be angry, troubled, or irritated; chafe. **6** To be worn or eaten away. **7** To become rough or agitated. See synonyms under PIQUE. —*n.* **1** The act of fretting. **2** An abrasion, corrosion, or wearing away. **3** An abraded, worn, or eroded spot. **4** A state of irritation, ill temper, or vexation. [OE *fretan* devour]

fret[2] (fret) *n.* A ridge on a musical instrument, as a guitar, against which the strings may be stopped. —*v.t.* **fret·ted, fret·ting** To provide with frets, as of a stringed instrument. [Cf. OF *frete* ring]

fret[3] (fret) *n.* **1** Ornamental work in relief,

TYPES OF FRET

done by carving, cutting, or embossing; in a broad sense, perforated or interlaced ornamental work in wood or stone or in painting. **2** An ornament characterized by angular interlocked or interlacing lines. **3** A headdress of wire of precious metal, often ornamented with gems: worn by women in medieval times. —*v.t.* **fret·ted, fret·ting** To ornament with fretwork; embroider with gold or silver thread. [Prob. <OF *frette* a lattice, trellis]

fret·ful (fret′fəl) *adj.* Inclined to fret; peevish; worrying; agitated. —**fret′ful·ly** *adv.* —**fret′ful·ness** *n.* —**fret·some** *adj.*

Synonyms (adj.): complaining, cross, fractious, fretting, impatient, irritable, peevish, pettish, petulant, snappish, snarling, testy, touchy, vexed, waspish, worried, worrying. See RESTIVE. *Antonyms*: forbearing, genial, gentle, kind, lovely, loving, meek, mild, patient, sweet, uncomplaining.

fret saw A saw with a long, narrow blade and fine teeth: used for fretwork, scroll-work, etc.

fret·ty (fret′ē) *adj.* **·ti·er, ·ti·est** **1** Fretful; peevish. **2** *Colloq.* Rubbed; inflamed, as a sore.

FRET SAW

fret·work (fret′-wûrk′) *n.* **1** Interlaced ornamental work composed of frets. **2** Perforated architectural work. **3** Variable movement, as of light and shade.

Freud (froid, *Ger.* froit), **Sigmund,** 1856–1939, Austrian neurologist; founder of modern theory of psychoanalysis.

Freu·di·an (froi′dē·ən) *adj.* Of, pertaining to, or conforming to the teachings of Sigmund Freud, especially regarding the cause and cure of neurotic and psychotic disorders, and the significance of dreams. —*n.* One who upholds the theories of Freud. —**Freu′di·an·ism** *n.*

Frey (frā) In Norse mythology, the god of rain and sunshine, and specifically of fruitfulness and prosperity. Also **Freyr** (frār).

Frey·a (frā′ə) In Norse mythology, the goddess of love; daughter of Njord and sister of Frey. Compare FRIGG. Also **Frey′ja.**

Frey·tag (frī′täkh), **Gustav,** 1816–95, German novelist and historian.

fri·a·ble (frī′ə·bəl) *adj.* Easily crumbled or pulverized. [<F <L *friabilis* < *friare* crumble] —**fri′a·bil′i·ty, fri′a·ble·ness** *n.*

fri·ar (frī′ər) *n.* **1** A brother or member of one of the mendicant religious orders, as the Augustinians, Carmelites (*White Friars*), Dominicans (*Black Friars*), or Franciscans (*Gray Friars*). **2** *Printing* An area on a printed sheet or page containing too little ink: opposed to *monk.* [<OF *frere* <L *frater* brother]

fri·ar·bird (frī′ər·bûrd′) *n.* An Australian honey-eating bird (genus *Philemon*) having a bare head: also called *four-o'clock.*

friar's balsam A soothing balsam, composed of benzoin, myrrh, aloe, balsam of Tolu, and other ingredients dissolved in alcohol.

fri·ar's-lan·tern (frī′ərz·lan′tərn) *n.* The will-o'-the-wisp.

Friar Tuck In medieval English legend, a jovial priest; associate of Robin Hood.

fri·ar·y (frī′ər·ē) *n. pl.* **·ar·ies** **1** A monastery of a mendicant order. **2** The institution of friars. See synonyms under CLOISTER. —*adj.* Pertaining to friars or to a monastery.

frib·ble (frib′əl) *v.* **frib·bled, frib·bling** *v.t.* To waste; fritter away. —*v.i.* To act in a frivolous way; trifle. —*adj.* Of little importance; frivolous. —*n.* **1** Trifling action. **2** A trifler. [Cf. FRIVOLOUS] —**frib′bler** *n.* —**frib′bling** *adj.*

Fri·bourg (frī′bûrg, *Fr.* frē·bōōr′) A city in west central Switzerland: German *Freiburg.*

fric·an·deau (frik′ən·dō′) *n. pl.* **·deaux** (-dōz) A cutlet of veal or other meat, roasted or braised and served with sauce. Also **fric′·an·do′.** [<F]

fric·as·see (frik′ə·sē′) *n.* A dish of meat cut small, stewed, and served with gravy. —*v.t.* **·seed, ·see·ing** To make into a fricassee. [<F *fricassé,* orig. pp. of *fricasser* sauté]

fric·a·tive (frik′ə·tiv) *Phonet. adj.* Describing those consonants that are produced by the forced escape and friction of the breath through a narrow aperture, as (f), (v), (th). —*n.* A consonant so produced. Also called *spirant.* [<NL *fricativus* <L *fricare* rub]

Frick (frik), **Henry Clay,** 1849–1919, U.S. industrialist and philanthropist.

fric·tion (frik′shən) *n.* **1** The rubbing together of two bodies. **2** Resistance to motion due to the contact of two surfaces moving relatively to each other. **3** Lack of harmony; conflict of opinions; disagreement. [<F <L *frictio, -onis* < *fricare* rub] —**fric′tion·al** *adj.* —**fric′·tion·al·ly** *adv.*

Synonyms: abrasion, attrition, chafing, fretting, grating, grinding, interference, rubbing, wearing.

friction clutch *Mech.* Any of various arrangements for transferring the motion of one system of parts to another by regulating the frictional contact between designated elements. Also **friction coupling.**

friction drive *Mech.* A drive in which motion is obtained by the frictional contact of surfaces, one being connected with the power system, the other with the transmission system.

friction fabric Fabric impregnated with rubber: used in the making of automobile tires. Also **friction stock.**

friction gear *Mech.* Any machine element that transmits power by frictional contact between surfaces, as of rotating wheels, disks, etc.

friction layer *Meteorol.* That portion of the atmosphere, from 1,500 to 3,000 feet altitude, in which air flow is strongly affected by the rotational friction of the earth.

friction loss Loss of power through friction, as in the contact surfaces of a machine, the surface tension of flowing water in pipes, etc.

friction match A match tipped with a chemical mixture that ignites by friction.

friction tape Cotton tape impregnated with an adhesive, moisture-resisting compound: used in electrical and mechanical work.

friction test A test for determining the amount of power absorbed by a specified lubricant.

Fri·day (frī′dē, -dā) The sixth day of the week. —**Good Friday** The Friday before Easter. [OE *Frigedæg* Frigg's day; trans. of LL *Veneris dies* day of Venus]

Fri·day (frī′dē, -dā) In Defoe's *Robinson Crusoe,* Crusoe's native servant, whom he saves from death on a Friday.

Fridt·jof Nan·sen Land (frit′yôf nän′sən) An unofficial name for FRANZ JOSEF LAND.

fried (frīd) Past tense and past participle of FRY.

fried cake A cruller or doughnut fried in deep fat.

Fried·e·ri·ke (frē′də·rē′kə) German form of FREDERICA.

Fried·land (frēd′land, *Ger.* frēt′länt) The former German name for PRAVDINSK.

Fried·rich (frēd′rikh) German form of FREDERICK.

friend (frend) *n.* **1** One who cherishes kind regard for another person; an intimate and trustworthy companion. **2** One who regards a thing with favor; a promoter. **3** An adherent; ally; one of the same nation or party. See synonyms under ASSOCIATE. —*v.t. Obs.* To befriend. [OE *frēond*]

Friend (frend) *n.* A member of the Society of Friends; a Quaker. —**Friend′ly** *adj.*

friend·ed (fren′did) *adj.* Having friends; with friends.

friend·less (frend′lis) *adj.* Having no friends; forlorn. —**friend′less·ness** *n.*

friend·ly (frend′lē) *adj.* **·li·er, ·li·est** **1** Pertaining to or like a friend; befitting friendship; amicable. **2** Propitious; favorable. —**friend′li·ly, friend′ly** *adv.* —**friend′li·ness** *n.*

Synonyms: accessible, affable, affectionate, amicable, brotherly, companionable, complaisant, cordial, favorable, fond, genial, hearty, kind, kindly, loving, neighborly, sociable, social, tender, well-disposed. *Friendly,* as said of persons, signifies having the disposition of a friend; as said of acts, it signifies befitting or worthy of a friend. The adjective *friendly* does not reach the full significance of the nouns "friend" and "friendship"; one may be *friendly* to those who are not his friends, and to be in *friendly* relations often signifies little more than not to be hostile. *Affable* and *accessible* are distinctively used of public and eminent persons, who might, if disposed, hold themselves at a distance from others. *Companionable* and *sociable* refer to manner and behavior, *cordial* and *genial* express genuine kindliness of heart and warmth of feeling. We speak of a *cordial* greeting, a *favorable* reception, a *neighborly* call, a *sociable* visitor, an *amicable* settlement, a *kind* interest, a *friendly* regard, a *hearty* welcome. The Saxon *friendly* is stronger than the Latin *amicable. Fond* is commonly applied to an affection that becomes, or at least appears, excessive. *Affectionate, devoted,* and *tender* are almost always used in a high and good sense; as, an *affectionate* son; a *devoted* friend; "the *tender* mercy of our God," *Luke* i 78. See AMICABLE, GOOD, PROPITIOUS. Compare FRIENDSHIP. *Antonyms*: adverse, alienated, antagonistic, bellicose, belligerent, cold, contentious, disaffected, distant, estranged, frigid, hostile, ill-disposed, indifferent, inimical, unfriendly, unkind, warlike.

Friendly Islands See TONGA ISLANDS.

friend·ship (frend′ship) *n.* **1** Mutual regard cherished by kindred minds. **2** The state or fact of being friends.

Synonyms: affection, amity, attachment, comity, consideration, devotion, esteem, favor, friendliness, love, regard. *Friendship* is a deep, quiet, enduring *affection,* founded upon mutual respect and *esteem. Friendship* is always mutual; one may have friendly feelings toward an enemy, but while there is hostility or coldness on one side there cannot be *friendship* between the two. *Friendliness* is a quality of friendly feeling, without the deep and settled *attachment* implied in the state of *friendship. Comity* is mutual, kindly courtesy, with care of each other's right, and *amity* a friendly feeling and relation not necessarily implying special *friendliness*; as, the *comity* of nations, or *amity* between neighboring countries. *Affection* may be purely natural; *friendship* is a growth. *Friendship* is more intellectual and less emotional than *love*; it is easier to give reasons for *friendship* than for *love*; *friendship* is more calm and quiet, *love* more fervent, often rising to intensest passion.

Compare ACQUAINTANCE, ASSOCIATION, ATTACHMENT, LOVE. *Antonyms*: see synonyms for BATTLE, ENMITY, FEUD, HATRED.

fri·er (frī′ər) See FRYER.

Frie·sian (frē′zhən) See FRISIAN.

Fries·land (frēz′lənd, -land) The most northerly province of the Netherlands; 1,249 square miles; capital, Leeuwarden. Ancient **Fri·sia** (frizh′ə).

frieze[1] (frēz) *n. Archit.* **1** The middle division of an entablature. It may be flat and plain, as in the Roman Tuscan order; conventionally ornamented, as in the Greek Doric; or highly enriched with sculpture. For illustration see ENTABLATURE. **2** Any ornamented horizontal band or strip in a wall. ◆ Homophone: *freeze.* [<F *frise* <Med. L *frisium,* ? ult. <L *Phrygium (opus)* Phrygian (work, ornament)]

frieze[2] (frēz) *n.* A coarse woolen cloth with shaggy nap, now made almost exclusively in Ireland. — *v.t.* **friezed, friez·ing** *Obs.* To produce a nap on. ◆ Homophone: *freeze.* [<MF *frise* <*friser* curl]

FRIGATE

frig·ate (frig′it) *n.* **1** A sailing war vessel, in use from 1650 to 1840, smaller than a ship of the line but larger than a corvette. **2** A modern anti-submarine warship, somewhat larger than the 600-ton corvette; used to escort merchant convoys. **3** Originally, a light and swift vessel of the Mediterranean, propelled by both oars and sails. [<F *frégate* <Ital. *fregata*]

frigate bird Either of two species of large raptorial birds (genus *Fregata*) with great powers of flight, having the upper mandible hooked and extraordinarily long wings and tail feathers: also called *man-of-war bird.*

Frigg (frig) In Norse mythology, the wife of Odin and goddess of marriage: often confused with *Freya.* Also **Frig′ga.**

fright (frīt) *n.* **1** Sudden and violent alarm or fear. **2** *Colloq.* Anything ugly, ridiculous, or shocking in appearance, producing aversion or alarm. — *v.t. Poetic* To frighten. [OE *fryhto*]

Synonyms (noun): affright, dismay, dread, fear, horror, panic, terror. *Affright, fright,* and *terror* are always sudden, and in actual presence of that which is terrible; *fear* may be controlled by force of will; *fright* and *terror* overwhelm the will; *terror* paralyzes; *fright* may cause wild or desperate action. *Fright* is largely a matter of the nerves; *fear* of the intellect and the imagination; *terror* of all the faculties, bodily and mental. *Panic* is a sudden *fear* or *fright,* affecting numbers at once; vast armies or crowded audiences are liable to *panic* upon slight occasion. In a like sense we speak of a financial *panic.* Compare ALARM, FEAR.

fright disease A nervous disorder of dogs, characterized by sporadic attacks of running and barking, with manifestations of great fear: also called *running fits, canine hysteria.*

fright·en (frīt′n) *v.t.* **1** To throw into a state of fear or fright; terrify; scare. **2** To drive by scaring: with *away* or *off.* — **fright′en·er** *n.* — **fright′en·ing** *adj.* — **fright′en·ing·ly** *adv.*

Synonyms: affright, alarm, appal, browbeat, cow, daunt, dismay, intimidate, scare, terrify. The sudden rush of an armed madman may *frighten*; the quiet leveling of a highwayman's pistol *intimidates.* A savage beast is *intimidated* by the keeper's whip. Employers may *intimidate* their employees from voting contrary to their will by threat of discharge. To *browbeat* or *cow* is to bring into a state of submissive fear; to *daunt* is to give pause or check to a violent, threatening, or even a brave spirit. To *scare* is to cause sudden, unnerving fear; to *terrify* is to awaken fear that is overwhelming. To *appal* (literally to make *pale*) is to overcome momentarily by some staggering or chilling fear or shocked repugnance; to *dismay* (literally to deprive of power) is to cause a sinking fear, make faint with dread or terror. Compare ALARM, FRIGHT.

fright·ened (frīt′nd) *adj.* Terrified; alarmed.

fright·ful (frīt′fəl) *adj.* Apt to induce terror; shocking. — **fright′ful·ly** *adv.* — **fright′ful·ness** *n.*

Synonyms: alarming, appalling, awful, direful, dreadful, fearful, hideous, horrible, horrid, portentous, shocking, terrible, terrific, terrifying. See AWFUL.

frig·id (frij′id) *adj.* **1** Of low temperature; cold. **2** Lacking in warmth of feeling; stiff, formal, and forbidding. **3** Lacking in sexual feeling or response: said of women. Compare IMPOTENT. [<L *frigidus* <*frigere* be cold] — **frig′id·ly** *adv.* — **frig′id·ness** *n.*

Frig·id·aire (frij′i·dâr′) *n.* An electric refrigerator: a trade name.

fri·gid·i·ty (fri·jid′ə·tē) *n.* **1** Coldness; formality. **2** Sexual unresponsiveness. Compare IMPOTENCE.

frigid zone See under ZONE.

frig·o·rif·ic (frig′ə·rif′ik) *adj.* Producing cold; chilling. Also **frig′o·rif′i·cal.** [<F *frigorifique* <L *frigorificus* <*frigor* cold + *facere* make]

fri·jole (frē′hōl, *Sp.* frē·hō′lā) *n. pl.* **·joles** (-hōlz, *Sp.* -hō′lās) A bean or beanlike seed (genus *Phaseolus*) used as food by Latin-American peoples. Also **fri′jol.** [<Sp.]

frill (fril) *n.* **1** An ornamental band of textile fabric, especially of lace or fine lawn, gathered in folds on one edge, the other edge being left loose; a flounce; ruffle. **2** *pl.* Affected airs and manners; fripperies, as of dress. **3** *Zool.* A ruff or frill-like part, appendage, or fold, as of elongated feathers on the neck of some birds, of long hairs on the neck of some dogs, and of membrane on the frilled lizard. **4** *Bot.* A thin membrane surrounding the stem of certain fungi near the pileus or hood, as in *Agaricus*: also called *armilla.* **5** *Phot.* A loosening and bulging of a plate or film around the edges, caused by uneven action of the emulsion; frilling. — *v.t.* **1** To make into a frill. **2** To put frills on. — *v.i.* **3** *Phot.* To wrinkle at the edges, as a gelatin film. [Origin uncertain] — **frill′er** *n.* — **frill′y** *adj.*

frilled lizard A large arboreal lizard (*Chlamydosaurus kingii*) of Australia, about three feet long, and having on each side of the neck a broad erectile membrane.

frill·ing (fril′ing) *n.* Gathered trimming in general; ruffles; frills.

Fri·maire (frē·mâr′) See under CALENDAR (Republican).

Friml (frim′əl), **Rudolf,** 1881–1972, Czech composer, active in the United States.

fringe (frinj) *n.* **1** An ornamental border or trimming of pendent cords, loose threads, or tassels. **2** Any fringelike border, edging, or margin. **3** Any outer or bounding portion: a *fringe* of shrubs in a garden, a *fringe* of land seen in the distance. **4** *Optics* One of the alternate light and dark bands produced by the interference of light, as in diffraction. — *v.t.* **fringed, fring·ing** **1** To ornament with or as with a fringe. **2** To serve as a fringe or border for. [<OF *frenge* <L *fimbria* a fringe]

fringe bell A Japanese stemless evergreen herb (*Schizocodon soldanelloides*) with toothed leaves and deep-rose flowers blue or white near the edges.

fringe benefit Any of various benefits received from an employer apart from salary, as insurance, pension, vacation, etc.

fringed gentian See under GENTIAN.

fringed orchis An orchid of the hardy terrestrial group (genus *Habenaria*) with tuberous roots and flowers having a fringed lip.

fringe lily A perennial herb of the lily family (genus *Thysanotus*) having clusters of purple flowers with fringed edges, native in Western Australia, but now found in California. Also **fringed violet.**

fringe tree A small tree (*Chionanthus virginicus*) of the olive family of the eastern United States with dark-blue drupes and white flowers; the dried root bark has medicinal properties.

frin·gil·line (frin·jil′īn, -in) *adj.* **1** Finchlike. **2** Of or pertaining to a family (*Fringillidae*) of small birds of which the finches and sparrows are characteristic. [<L *fringilla,* a small bird + -INE[1]]

fring·y (frin′jē) *adj.* **fring·i·er, fring·i·est** Resembling fringe; having a fringe.

frip·per·y (frip′ər·ē) *n. pl.* **·per·ies** **1** Mean or worthless things; trumpery; tawdry finery; gew-gaws. **2** *Obs.* Cast-off or old clothes. **3** *Obs.* Traffic in old clothes, or a place where they are sold. [<F *friperie* <OF *freperie* <*frepe* a rag]

Fris·bee (friz′bē) *n.* A light plastic disk used in play by being tossed with a spin from person to person: a trade name. Also **fris′·bee.**

Frisch·es Haff (frish′əs häf′) The German name for VISTULA LAGOON.

Fris·co (fris′kō) *Colloq.* San Francisco, California.

fri·sé (fri·zā′) *n.* An upholstery or rug fabric faced with a thick pile of uncut loops or of cut and uncut loops in design. [<F, orig. pp. of *friser* curl]

fri·sette (fri·zet′) See FRIZETTE.

fri·seur (frē·zœr′) *n. French* A hairdresser.

Fris·ian (frizh′ən, -ē·ən) *adj.* **1** Of or pertaining to the Dutch province of Friesland, its people, or their language. **2** Of or pertaining to the Frisii, an ancient Germanic tribe of the Netherlands. — *n.* **1** A native or inhabitant of modern Friesland. **2** A member of the tribe of the ancient Frisii. **3** The Low German, West Germanic language of the Frisians, closely related to English. Also *Friesian.*

Frisian Islands An island chain of the North Sea, divided into three major groups, the **West, North,** and **East Frisian Islands.**

frisk (frisk) *v.t.* **1** To move briskly or playfully. **2** *U.S. Slang* To search (someone) for concealed weapons, smuggled goods, etc., by running the hand rapidly over his clothing. **3** *U.S. Slang* To steal from in this way. — *v.i.* **4** To leap about playfully; gambol; frolic. — *n.* **1** A playful skipping about. **2** *U.S. Slang* A frisking or searching. [<obs. *frisk* lively <F *frisque*; ult. origin unknown] — **frisk′er** *n.*

Synonyms (verb): caper, dance, frolic, gambol, play, sport. See LEAP. *Antonyms*: droop, mope, muse, repose, rest.

fris·ket (fris′kit) *n. Printing* **1** A light frame to hold the printing surface between the tympan and the form of a platen press. **2** A similar frame attached to a hand press of the Washington type. [<F *frisquette*]

frisk·y (fris′kē) *adj.* **frisk·i·er, frisk·i·est** Lively or playful. See synonyms under RESTIVE. — **frisk′i·ly** *adv.* — **frisk′i·ness** *n.*

frit (frit) *v.t.* **frit·ted, frit·ting** To decompose and partly melt: to *frit* glassmaking materials before final fusion. — *n.* **1** An imperfectly vitrified mass, formed in making glass. **2** The material from which soft fictile wares are made. **3** A partially fused composition used as a basis for glazes. Also **fritt.** [<F *fritte* <Ital. *fritta,* pp. of *friggere* fry]

frit fly A small fly (*Oscinosoma frit*), very destructive of cereal grains.

frith (frith) *n. Scot.* A firth.

frit·il·lar·y (frit′ə·ler′ē) *n. pl.* **·lar·ies** **1** One of a genus (*Fritillaria*) of arctic or north-temperate bulbous plants of the lily family in which the flowers are checkered with pale and dark purple. **2** One of various butterflies (*Argynnis, Dione,* and related genera) having wings checkered with black and light brown, whose caterpillars feed on the violet and related plants. [<NL *Fritillaria* <L *fritillus* a dice box; from its checkered markings]

frit·ter[1] (frit′ər) *v.t.* **1** To waste or disperse little by little: usually with *away.* **2** To break or tear into small pieces. [<*n.*] — *n.* A small piece or fragment: a shred. [Cf. OF *fraiture* <L *fractura* <*frangere* break]

frit·ter[2] (frit′ər) *n.* A small fried cake, often

containing fruit or pieces of meat. [<F *friture* <L *frigere* fry]

Fritz (frits) Shortened form of FRIEDRICH.

Fri·u·li (frē·ōō′lē) A historical region of northern Italy on the Adriatic, now partly in Yugoslavia.

Fri·u·li·an (frē·ōō′lē·ən) *n.* **1** One of a people of Celtic origin inhabiting the region of Friuli. **2** The Rhaeto-Romanic dialect of these people.

friv·ol (friv′əl) *v.* **friv·oled** or **friv·olled, friv·ol·ing** or **friv·ol·ling** *Colloq. v.i.* To behave frivolously; trifle. — *v.t.* To fritter: with *away.* [Back formation <FRIVOLOUS] — **friv′ol·er, friv′ol·ler** *n.*

fri·vol·i·ty (fri·vol′ə·tē) *n.* *pl.* **·ties** **1** The quality or condition of being frivolous. **2** A frivolous act, thing, or practice. See synonyms under LEVITY.

friv·o·lous (friv′ə·ləs) *adj.* **1** Void of significance or reason; petty; trivial; unimportant. **2** Characterized by lack of seriousness, sense, or reverence; trifling; silly. [<L *frivolus* silly] — **friv′o·lous·ly** *adv.* — **friv′o·lous·ness** *n.*

fri·zette (fri·zet′) *n.* A frizz of hair, worn as a bang.

frizz[1] (friz) *v.t.* & *v.i.* **frizzed, frizz·ing** **1** To form into tight, crisp curls, as the hair. **2** To make or form into small, tight tufts or knots, as the nap of cloth. — *n.* **1** That which is frizzed, as hair. **2** The condition of being frizzed. Also **friz.** [Var. of FRIEZE[2], *v.*] — **friz′·zer, friz′er** *n.* — **frizz′i·ly** *adv.* — **frizz′i·ness** *n.*

frizz[2] (friz) *v.t.* & *v.i.* **frizzed, friz·zing** To fry with a sizzling noise. [<FRY + imit. suffix]

friz·zle[1] (friz′əl) *v.t.* & *v.i.* **friz·zled, friz·zling** **1** To fry or cook with a sizzling noise. **2** To make or become curled or crisp, as by frying. [Blend of FRY and SIZZLE; ? infl. by FRIZZLE[2]]

friz·zle[2] (friz′əl) *v.t.* & *v.i.* **friz·zled, friz·zling** To form into tight, crisp curls, as the hair. [? Freq. of FRIEZE[2], *v.*]

fro (frō) *adv.* Away from; back: used in the phrase *to-and-fro.* — *prep. Scot.* From. [<ON *fra* from]

Fro·bish·er (frō′bish·ər), **Sir Martin,** 1535?–1594, English navigator and explorer.

Frobisher Bay An inlet of the Atlantic in SE Baffin Island.

frock (frok) *n.* **1** The principal outer garment of women and girls; a dress. **2** A monk's robe, long and very loose. **3** A coarse loose outer garment worn by laborers, brewers, butchers, etc. **4** A woolen jersey worn by sailors. **5** In English military service, an undress regimental coat. **6** A frock coat. — *v.t.* **1** To furnish with or clothe in a frock. **2** To invest with ecclesiastic office. [<OF *froc*; ult. origin uncertain]

frock coat A coat for men's wear, usually double-breasted, having knee-length skirts.

froe (frō) *n.* A cleaving knife with the blade at right angles to the handle, used for riving staves, shingles, etc. Also spelled *frow.* [Appar. <FROWARD, in sense "turned away," with ref. to the blade]

Froe·bel (frā′bəl, *Ger.* frœ′bəl), **Friedrich Wilhelm August,** 1782–1852, German educator; founder of the kindergarten system.

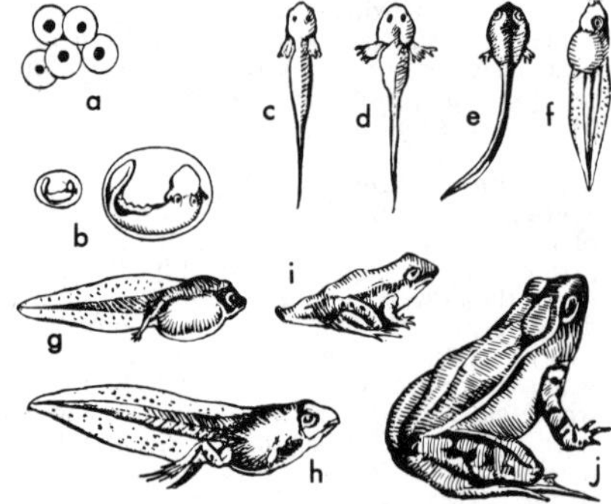

STAGES IN THE DEVELOPMENT OF THE FROG
a. Eggs. *b.* Embryo. *c–h.* Development of the tadpole. *i.* Young frog. *j.* Adult frog.

frog (frog, frôg) *n.* **1** One of a genus (*Rana*) of small, tailless, amphibious, web-footed animals; especially, the North American bullfrog (*R. catesbina*), the leopard frog (*R. pipiens*), and the green edible European frog (*R. esculenta*). Frogs are distinguished from the toads in having smooth skin, webbed feet, and greater leaping and swimming powers. **2** Any of several arboreal frogs (family *Ranidae*), as the tree *frog,* flying *frog.* **3** The triangular prominence in the sole of a horse's foot. **4** A section of a railway track where one rail crosses or diverges from another. **5** A metal device used to stop the action in a power loom when the warp becomes entangled with the shuttle. **6** A small bundle of certain types of Cuban, Puerto Rican, or other imported tobaccos, having a V-shaped notch at the ends where the heaviest part of the stems has been removed. **7** An ornamental fastening on a cloak or a coat. **8** The loop of a scabbard. **9** *Slang* A Frenchman: a derogatory term. — **a frog in one's throat** A slight laryngeal hoarseness. — *v.i.* **frogged, frog·ging** To hunt frogs. [OE *frogga*] — **frog′like′** *adj.*

frog·bit (frog′bit′, frôg′-) *n.* **1** A little aquatic European plant (*Hydrocharis morsus-ranae*) which floats on water and bears white flowers. **2** An American plant (*Limnobium spongia*) of the same family (*Hydrocharitaceae*), found in stagnant water. Also **frog's′-bit′.**

frog–eye (frog′ī′, frôg′ī′) *n.* **1** A fungus disease affecting the leaves of apple trees and caused by various species of a fungus (*Physalospora*). **2** Any similar leaf blight of fungus origin characterized by concentric whitish spots. — **frog′–eyed′** *adj.*

frog fish The angler: so called from its wide mouth.

frog·ger·y (frog′ər·ē, frôg′-) *n.* *pl.* **·ger·ies** **1** A place frequented by frogs, or one where frogs are raised. **2** A collection of frogs.

frog·gy (frog′ē, frôg′ē) *adj.* **·gi·er, ·gi·est** Of, pertaining to, or abounding in frogs. — **frog′·gi·ness** *n.*

frog·hop·per (frog′hop′ər, frôg′-) *n.* A broad, squat leafhopping insect (family *Cercopidae*); the nymphs of many species are enclosed in a frothy mass; a spittle insect. See FROG SPIT.

frog kick In swimming, a kick in which both legs are drawn up with the heels together and the knees apart, then simultaneously thrust backward.

frog lily The yellow waterlily (*Nuphar advena*).

frog·man (frog′mən, -man′, frôg′-) *n.* *pl.* **·men** (-mən, -men′) One who is dressed in a waterproof suit and equipped with a portable diving unit and various implements for underwater military or naval reconnaissance.

frog·mouth (frog′mouth′, frôg′-) *n.* **1** An East Indian nocturnal bird (genus *Podargus*) with very broad, deeply cleft bill: found also in Australia and locally named *mopoke.* **2** The snapdragon.

frog spit **1** *Entomol.* The frothy exudation from the nymphs of a froghopper; cuckoo spit; toad spittle. **2** *Bot.* A green fresh-water alga whose filaments clump in foamlike floating masses.

Froh·man (frō′mən), **Charles,** 1860–1915, U. S. theatrical manager.

Frois·sart (froi′särt, *Fr.* frwȧ·sȧr′), **Jean,** 1337?–1410?, French chronicler.

frol·ic (frol′ik) *n.* **1** A scene of gaiety. **2** A gay or sportive outburst or act; a prank. **3** A gathering for social merriment; a party. **4** A gathering of neighbors to do or finish some kind of work; a bee: a harvesting *frolic.* [< *adj.*] — *v.i.* **frol·icked, frol·ick·ing** To play merrily; gambol. — *adj.* Full of or characterized by mirth or playfulness; sportive; merry. [<Du. *vrolijk* merry <MDu. *vro* glad] — **frol′ick·er** *n.* — **frol′ick·y** *adj.*

Synonyms (*noun*): amusement, caper, carousal, entertainment, festivity, fun, gambol, game, gaiety, lark, merrymaking, prank, spree, sport. See AMUSEMENT, ENTERTAINMENT, SPORT.

frol·ic·some (frol′ik·səm) *adj.* Full of frolic; playful. Also **frol′ick·y.** See synonyms under AIRY, MERRY. — **frol′ic·some·ly** *adv.* — **frol′·ic·some·ness** *n.*

from (frum, from; *unstressed* frəm) *prep.* **1** Starting at (a particular place or time): the plane *from* Chicago; busy *from* six until nine. **2** Out of (something serving as a holder or container): She drew a pistol *from* her purse. **3** Not near to or in contact with: far *from* the madding crowd. **4** Out of the control or authority of: released *from* custody. **5** Out of the totality of: six cigarettes *from* the pack. **6** As being other or another than: He couldn't tell me *from* my brother. **7** As being in adverse relation to: *from* grave to gay. **8** Because of: having as the foundation, origin, or cause: Skill comes *from* practice. **9** With (some person, place, or thing) as the instrument, maker, or source: a note *from* your mother; silks *from* Rome. [OE *fram, from*]

fro·men·ty (frō′mən·tē) See FRUMENTY.

frond (frond) *n. Bot.* **1** A leaflike expansion in which the functions of stem and leaf are not fully differentiated, as the so-called leaf of ferns and seaweeds. See illustration under FERN. **2** The leaf of a palm. [<L *frons, frondis* leaf]

Fronde (frônd) *n.* A political party established in France during the minority of Louis XIV, opposing the court and Cardinal Mazarin, and precipitating the civil wars of 1648, 1650, and 1651. [<F, a sling]

frond·ed (fron′did) *adj.* Provided with fronds; leafy.

fron·des·cence (fron·des′əns) *n. Bot.* **1** The period or act of leafing. **2** Leaves collectively. — **fron·des′cent** *adj.*

fron·dif·er·ous (fron·dif′ər·əs) *adj.* Frond-bearing.

front (frunt) *n.* **1** The fore part or side of anything: opposed to *back.* **2** The position directly before a person or thing: the steps in *front* of the church. **3** A face of a building; usually the face on the entrance side. **4** The foremost ground occupied by an army; battle zone. **5** Land facing a road, body of water, etc.; frontage. **6** *Brit.* A promenade facing a beach. **7** In the theater, the audience part of the auditorium. **8** *Archaic* The forehead; by extension, the face. **9** Bearing or attitude in facing a problem, etc.: a bold *front.* **10** Bold assurance; effrontery. **11** *Colloq.* An outward semblance of wealth or position. **12** A person chosen for his prestige to serve as an official, usually titular, of an organization; a figurehead. **13** A person, group, or business serving as a cover for underhanded activities. **14** A coalition of diverse forces working for a common political or ideological aim: a labor *front.* **15** A dickey (def. 1); also, a large cravat. **16** In hotels, the bellhop first in line: generally used as a call to the desk. **17** *Meteorol.* The boundary, diffuse or sharp, which separates masses of cold air and warm air. **18** *Phonet.* The part of the tongue immediately behind the blade and directly below the hard palate. — *adj.* **1** Of or pertaining to the front; situated in front. **2** Considered from the front: a *front* view. **3** *Phonet.* Describing those vowels produced with the front of the tongue raised toward the hard palate, as (ē) in *feed.* See synonyms under ANTERIOR, FIRST. — *v.t.* **1** To have the front opposite to or in the direction of; face. **2** To confront; meet face to face; defy. **3** To furnish with a front. **4** To serve as a front for. — *v.i.* **5** To have the front or face turned in a specific direction. [<OF <L *frons, frontis* forehead]

front·age (frunt′tij) *n.* **1** Linear extent of front: the *frontage* of a lot. **2** The fact or action of facing in a certain direction; outlook; exposure.

fron·tal[1] (frun′təl) *adj.* Pertaining to the front or to the forehead. — *n. Anat.* A bone of the anterior part of the skull, forming the skeleton of the forehead. [<NL *frontalis* <L *frons, frontis* forehead] — **fron′tal·ly** *adv.*

fron·tal[2] (frun′təl) *n.* **1** A front part. **2** Something to cover the front or forehead. **3** *Eccl.* A movable hanging to cover the front of an altar. **4** *Archit.* A small pediment or other front piece above a minor door or window. [<OF *frontel* <LL *frontale* <*frons, frontis* forehead, front]

front bench *Brit.* In the House of Commons, the seats closest to the Speaker, reserved for the party leaders.

front·ed (frun′tid) *adj.* **1** Having a front. **2** Formed in line.

Fron·te·nac (fron′tə·nak, *Fr.* frônt·nȧk′), **Comte Louis de Buade de,** 1620–98, French governor of Canada.

fron·tier (frun·tir′) *n.* **1** The part of a nation's territory that abuts upon another country; the border; confines. **2** That portion of a country bordering on the wilderness, newly or thinly settled by pioneer settlers. **3** Any region of thought or knowledge not yet explored: a *frontier* of science. **4** *Obs.* A fort. See synonyms under BOUNDARY. — *adj.* Of, from, inhabiting, situated on, or characteristic of a frontier. [<OF *frontiere* <*front* FRONT]

fron·tiers·man (frun·tirz′mən) *n. pl.* **·men** (-mən) One who lives on the frontier or on or beyond the borders of civilization. Also **fron·tier′man.**

fron·tis·piece (frun′tis·pēs′, fron′-) *n.* **1** An illustration in the front of a book. **2** An ornamental front; a façade. [Earlier *frontispice* <F <Med. L *frontispicium* face <L *frons, frontis* forehead + *specere* look at; infl. in form by *piece*]

front·less (frunt′lis) *adj.* Without a front.

front·let (frunt′lit) *n.* **1** A band worn on the forehead. **2** The forehead of a bird or animal when distinguished by color or the like. **3** A frontstall. [<OF *frontelet,* dim. of *frontel.* See FRONTAL.]

front line The foremost line of battle.

fronto– *combining form* **1** *Anat.* Pertaining to the frontal bone or frontal region of the skull. **2** *Meteorol.* Pertaining to a front. [<L *frons, frontis* forehead, front]

front office The main office, or office of the highest ranking executive, in an organization.

fron·to·gen·e·sis (frun′tō·jen′ə·sis) *n. Meteorol.* The development of a boundary between cold air and warm air masses, or the intensification of an already existing boundary.

fron·tol·y·sis (frun·tol′ə·sis) *n. Meteorol.* The disappearance or subsidence of a front: opposed to *frontogenesis.*

fron·to·ma·lar (frun′tō·mā′lər) *adj. Anat.* Pertaining to the frontal and cheek bones.

fron·tón (frən·tōn′) *n.* The court in which jai alai is played. [<Sp.]

front–page (frunt′pāj′) *adj.* Of great significance or importance; meriting placement on the front page of a publication.

Front Range The easternmost range of the Rocky Mountains, in Colorado and Wyoming; highest peak, 14,225 feet.

front·stall (frunt′stôl′) *n. Obs.* A perforated headplate for a horse.

frore (frôr, frōr) *adj. Archaic* Frosty; frozen. [Early pp. of FREEZE]

frosh (frosh) *n. pl.* **frosh** *U.S. Slang* A college freshman.

frost (frôst, frost) *n.* **1** Minute crystals of ice

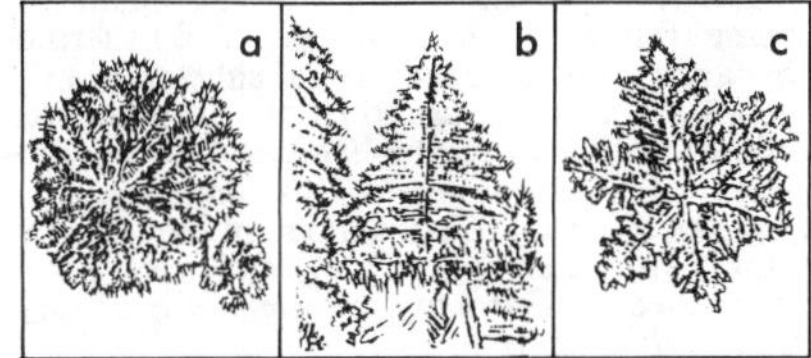

FROST PATTERNS
a. Spongiform. *b.* Filicoid. *c.* Stellate.

formed directly from atmospheric water vapor; frozen dew; hoarfrost. **2** Freezing weather; the **degree of frost** is the number of degrees below the freezing point. **3** The formation of ice; frozen moisture within a porous substance. **4** Coldness and austerity of manner. **5** *Slang* A failure. — *v.t.* **1** To cover with frost. **2** To damage or kill by frost. **3** To apply frosting to. [OE] — **frost′less** *adj.*

Frost (frôst, frost), **Robert Lee,** 1875–1963, U. S. poet and essayist.

frost·bite (frôst′bīt′, frost′-) *n.* The gangrenous condition of having some part of the body, as the ears or fingers, partially frozen. — *v.t.* **·bit, ·bit·ten, ·bit·ing** To injure, as a part of the body, by partial freezing. — **frost′bit′ten** *adj.*

frost·ed (frôs′tid, fros′-) *adj.* **1** Covered with frost or frosting. **2** Presenting a surface resembling frost, as an iced cake or matted electric bulb. **3** Frostbitten.

frost·fish (frôst′fish′, frost′-) *n. pl.* **·fish** or **·fish·es** The tomcod.

frost·flow·er (frôst′flou′ər, frost′-) *n.* A small bulbous plant of the lily family (*Milla biflora*) with scape 6–18 inches high, bearing starlike, fragrant, white, waxy flowers; native in southwestern U. S.

frost fog A pogonip.

frost·ing (frôs′ting, fros′-) *n.* **1** A mixture of sugar, egg white or fat, and flavoring of various kinds, used to coat or cover a cake; also called *icing.* **2** The rough surface produced on metal, glass, etc., in imitation of frost. **3** Coarsely powdered glass, etc., used for decorative work.

frost itch A complaint affecting certain persons only in winter and usually in dry climates; a form of pruritis: also called *winter itch.*

frost line The depth to which frost penetrates the ground, expressed in terms of a single season, a seasonal average, or the maximum attained.

frost·weed (frôst′wēd′, frost′-) *n.* A cistaceous plant, the rockrose (*Crocanthemum canadense*). Also **frost′wort′** (-wûrt′).

frost·work (frôst′wûrk′, frost′-) *n.* **1** Hoarfrost deposited upon exposed objects in delicate tracery. **2** Any surface ornamentation in imitation of such effect.

frost·y (frôs′tē, fros′-) *adj.* **frost·i·er, frost·i·est** **1** Attended with frost; freezing: *frosty* weather. **2** Affected or covered by or like frost. **3** Lacking in warmth of manner; chilling; distant. **4** Having white hair; hoary. — **frost′i·ly** *adv.* — **frost′i·ness** *n.*

froth (frôth, froth) *n.* **1** A mass of bubbles resulting from fermentation or agitation; a colloid system of gas dispersed in a liquid. **2** Any foamy excretion or exudation; foam. **3** Any light, unsubstantial matter; vain or senseless display of wit; idle pleasure; vanity. — *v.t.* **1** To cause to foam. **2** To cover with froth. **3** To give forth in the form of foam. — *v.i.* **4** To form or give off froth; foam. [<ON *frodha*]

froth·er (frô′thər, froth′ər) *n.* **1** One who or that which froths. **2** A substance or chemical agent used to develop the foam in the flotation process of separating minerals from their ores.

froth·ing–a·gent (frô′thing·ā′jənt, froth′ing-) *n. Chem.* Any substance, as saponin or oleic acid, which will produce froth in an agitated liquid.

froth·y (frô′thē, froth′ē) *adj.* **froth·i·er, froth·i·est** **1** Consisting of, covered with, or full of froth. **2** As unsubstantial as froth; empty; pretentious; trivial. — **froth′i·ly** *adv.* — **froth′i·ness** *n.*

Froude (fro͞od), **James Anthony,** 1818–94, English historian.

frou–frou (fro͞o′fro͞o′) *n.* **1** A rustling, as of silk; the swish of a woman's dress. **2** *Colloq.* Affected elegance; fanciness. [<F]

frounce (frouns) *v.t.* & *v.i.* **frounced, frounc·ing** **1** To curl. **2** *Archaic* To wrinkle; pleat. — *n.* *Archaic* Affectation; empty pretence. [<OF *froncier* <*fronce* a fold, ? <Gmc.]

frou·zy (frou′zē) See FROWZY.

frow[1] (frou) *n.* **1** A Dutch or German woman. **2** A wife; a married woman. [<MDu. *frouwe* woman, lady]

frow[2] (frō) See FROE.

fro·ward (frō′ərd, -wərd) *adj.* Disobedient; intractable; perverse. [<FRO + WARD] — **fro′ward·ly** *adv.* — **fro′ward·ness** *n.*

frown (froun) *v.i.* **1** To contract the brow, as in displeasure or concentration; scowl. **2** To look one's displeasure or disapproval: with *on* or *upon.* — *v.t.* **3** To make known (one's displeasure, disgust, etc.) by contracting one's brow. **4** To silence, rebuke, etc., by or as by a frown. — *n.* **1** A wrinkling of the brow, as in dislike, anger or abstraction; a scowl. **2** Hence, any manifestation of displeasure or lack of favor. [<OF *froignier,* prob. <Gmc.] — **frown′er** *n.* — **frown′ing** *adj.* — **frown′ing·ly** *adv.*

frowst·y (frous′tē) *adj. Brit. Colloq.* Musty; stuffy. [Cf. OF *frouste* decayed]

frow·zled (frou′zəld) *adj.* Unkempt; disheveled.

frow·zy (frou′zē) *adj.* **·zi·er, ·zi·est** Slovenly in appearance; unkempt; untidy. Also **frou′zy, frow′sy.** [? Akin to FROWSTY]

froze (frōz) Past tense of FREEZE.

fro·zen (frō′zən) *adj.* **1** Congealed, benumbed, or killed by cold; having become, or overspread with, ice. **2** Subject to extreme cold, as a climate or region. **3** Quick–frozen, as *frozen* food. **4** *Econ.* Arbitrarily maintained at a given level: said of prices, wages, employment status, etc.

frozen assets Property still valuable but not readily available for conversion into cash.

frozen sleep *Med.* A form of therapy that consists in putting the patient to sleep and lowering the body temperature to from 70° to 90° F.: also called *cryotherapy.*

Fruc·ti·dor (fruk′ti·dôr, *Fr.* frük·tē·dôr′) See under CALENDAR (Republican).

fruc·tif·er·ous (fruk·tif′ər·əs) *adj.* Fruit–bearing.

fruc·ti·fy (fruk′tə·fī) *v.* **·fied, ·fy·ing** *v.t.* To make fruitful; fertilize. — *v.i.* To bear fruit. [<F *fructifier* <L *fructificare* <*fructus* fruit + *facere* do, make] — **fruc′ti·fi·ca′tion** *n.*

fruc·tose (fruk′tōs) *n.* A very sweet, levorotatory monosaccharide, $C_6H_{12}O_6$, occurring in sugar cane and fruits: also called *fruit sugar, levulose.*

fruc·tu·ous (fruk′cho͞o·əs) *adj.* Productive; fertile; fruitful. [<OF <L *fructuosus* <*fructus* fruit]

fru·gal (fro͞o′gəl) *adj.* **1** Exercising economy; saving; sparing. **2** Marked by economy; meager; stinted. [<L *frugalis* <*frugi* temperate, orig. dative singular of *frux* food] — **fru′gal·ly** *adv.*

fru·gal·i·ty (fro͞o·gal′ə·tē) *n. pl.* **·ties** **1** Strict economy; thrift. **2** Wise and sparing use: *frugality* of praise. Also **fru′gal·ness.**

Synonyms: economy, miserliness, parsimoniousness, parsimony, providence, prudence, saving, scrimping, sparing, thrift. *Economy* is a wise and careful administration of the means at one's disposal; *frugality* is a withholding of expenditure, or *sparing* of supplies or provision, to a noticeable and often to a painful degree; *parsimony* is excessive and unreasonable *saving* for the sake of *saving. Frugality* exalted into a virtue to be practiced for its own sake, instead of as a means to an end, becomes the vice of *parsimony. Miserliness* is the denying oneself and others the ordinary comforts or even necessaries of life, for the sake of hoarding. *Prudence* and *providence* look far ahead, and sacrifice the present to the future, saving as much as may be necessary for that end. (See PRUDENCE.) *Thrift* seeks not merely to save, but to earn. *Economy* manages, *frugality* saves, *providence* plans, *thrift* at once earns and saves, with a view to wholesome and profitable expenditure at a fitting time. See ABSTINENCE. *Antonyms:* abundance, bounty, extravagance, liberality, luxury, opulence, riches, waste, wealth.

fru·giv·o·rous (fro͞o·jiv′ər·əs) *adj.* Fruit–eating. [<L *frux, frugis* fruit + -VOROUS]

fruit (fro͞ot) *n.* **1** *Bot.* **a** The edible, pulpy mass covering the seeds of various plants and

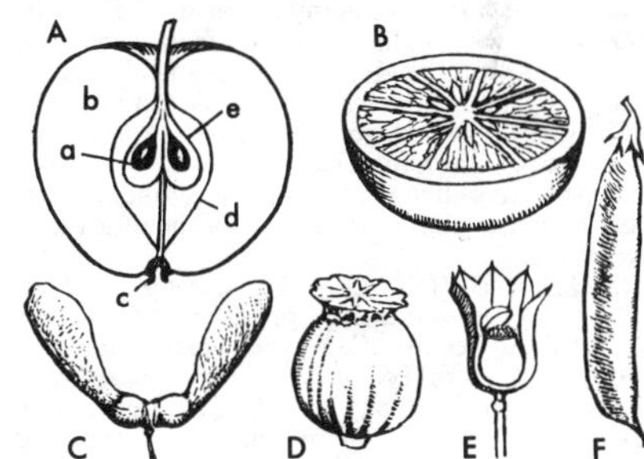

FRUIT
A. Cross–section of an apple:
a. Seeds. *b.* Pulp. *c.* Limb of calyx. *d.* Core. *e.* Carpels.
B. Cross–section of an orange.
C. Schizocarpous fruit of the maple.
D. Ripe capsule of a poppy.
E. Pyxis of henbane with outer carpel removed.
F. Legume of pea.

trees. They are classified as *fleshy,* as gourds, melons, oranges, apples, pears, berries, etc.; *drupaceous,* as cherries, peaches, plums, apricots, and others containing stones; *dry,* as nuts, capsules, achenia, follicles, legumes, etc. **b** In flowering plants, the mature seed vessel and its contents, together with such accessory or external parts of the inflorescence as seem to be integral with them. **c** In cryptogams, the spores with their enveloping or accessory organs. **2** Any vegetable product used as food, or otherwise serviceable to man, as grain, cotton, or flax; also, such products collectively: the *fruits* of the earth. **3** That which is produced, as the young of man or animals. **4** The consequence or result of any action; any outcome, effect, or result: the *fruit* of evil, the *fruits* of industry. — *v.t.* & *v.i.* To bear or make bear fruit. [<OF <L *fructus* <*frui* enjoy]

Synonym (noun): vegetable. In the botanical sense not only apples, pears, peaches, tomatoes, figs, etc., but all berries, nuts, grains, beans, peas, pumpkins, squashes, cucumbers, and melons, as well as pine cones, the samaras or winged seeds of the maple, ash, or elm, and many other products, are *fruits*. Popular usage, however, is narrower. The *grains* have been dropped, and the tendency is to drop *nuts* also, so that a *fruit* is now generally understood to be the fleshy and juicy product of some plant, usually tree or shrub (and nearly always containing the seed), which, when ripe, is edible without cooking, and adapted for use as a dessert as well as a salad. The quince, however, while usually cooked before eating, is classed among *fruits*, and we sometimes speak of poisonous *fruits* as the *berries* of the nightshade. A *vegetable*, in the popular sense, is any part of a herbaceous plant commonly used for culinary purposes, and may consist of the *root*, as in the beet and turnip; the *stem*, as in the asparagus, celery, and rhubarb; a *tuber*, or underground stem, as in the potato; the *foliage*, as in cabbage and spinach, or of that which is botanically the *fruit*, as in the tomato, bean, pea, and eggplant. See synonyms under HARVEST, PRODUCT.

fruit·age (fro͞o′tij) *n.* **1** Fruit collectively. **2** The state, process, or time of producing fruit. **3** Any result or effect of action; consequence.

frui·tar·i·an (fro͞o·târ′ē·ən) *n.* One whose food consists mainly of fruits, with or without milk and nuts. — **frui·tar′i·an·ism** *n.*

fruit cake A cake containing fruit, generally raisins, currants, and citron.

fruit–cup (fro͞ot′kup′) *n.* A mixture of cut fruits, fresh or preserved, served in a cup or glass.

fruit dot Sorus.

fruit·ed (fro͞o′tid) *adj.* Bearing or containing fruit.

fruit·er (fro͞o′tər) *n.* **1** A vessel that carries fruit. **2** A fruit–bearing tree.

fruit·er·er (fro͞o′tər·ər) *n. Brit.* A dealer in fruits.

fruit fly 1 One of various flies of the family *Trypetidae* whose larvae attack fruit, especially a member of the destructive tropical genera, *Ceratitis* and *Anastrepha*. **2** A pomace fly *(Drosophila melanogaster)* whose larvae feed on ripe or overripe fruit and whose various species have been used in fundamental researches on the mechanism of genetics and heredity.

fruit·ful (fro͞ot′fəl) *adj.* **1** Bearing fruit or offspring abundantly; prolific; productive. **2** Bringing results. See synonyms under FERTILE. — **fruit′ful·ly** *adv.* — **fruit′ful·ness** *n.*

fru·i·tion (fro͞o·ish′ən) *n.* **1** The bearing of fruit. **2** The yielding of natural or expected results; realization; fulfilment. **3** Enjoyment. [<OF <LL *fruitio, -onis* enjoyment <*frui* enjoy]

fruit·less (fro͞ot′lis) *adj.* **1** Yielding no fruit; barren. **2** Yielding no good results; useless; idle. See synonyms under USELESS, VAIN. — **fruit′less·ly** *adv.* — **fruit′less·ness** *n.*

fruit rot Leaf rot.

fruit sugar Fructose.

fruit tree A tree, particularly a cultivated tree, producing an edible, succulent fruit.

fruit·y (fro͞o′tē) *adj.* **fruit·i·er, fruit·i·est** Like fruit in taste, flavor, etc. — **fruit′i·ness** *n.*

fru·men·ta·ceous (fro͞o′mən·tā′shəs) *adj.* **1** Belonging to the cereals. **2** Resembling or made of cereal grain. [<LL *frumentaceus* <*frumentum* grain]

fru·men·ty (fro͞o′mən·tē) *n.* A seasoned dish of hulled wheat boiled in milk: also spelled *fromenty, furmenty*. [<OF *frumentée* <L *frumentum* grain]

frump (frump) *n.* A dowdily dressed, sometimes ill–tempered, woman. [? <MDu. *frompelen*, var. of *verrompelen* wrinkle]

frump·ish (frum′pish) *adj.* **1** Dowdy; old–fashioned in dress. **2** Ill–tempered; morose. Also **frump′y.**

Frun·ze (fro͞on′ze) The capital of Kirghiz S.S.R. in Soviet Central Asia. Formerly **Pish·pek** (pish′pek).

frus·trate (frus′trāt) *v.t.* **·trat·ed, ·trat·ing 1** To keep (someone) from doing or achieving something; baffle the efforts or hopes of. **2** To keep, as plans or schemes, from being fulfilled; thwart; bring to naught. See synonyms under BAFFLE, HINDER. — *adj.* **1** Without effect; vain; null; void. **2** Frustrated; baffled. [<L *frustratus*, pp. of *frustrari* disappoint <*frustra* in vain] — **frus′trat·er** *n.* — **frus′tra·tive** *adj.*

frus·tra·tion (frus·trā′shən) *n.* State of being frustrated or thwarted; bafflement.

frus·tule (frus′cho͞ol) *n.* The siliceous shell of a diatom. [<F <LL *frustulum*, dim. of *frustum* a bit, small piece]

frus·tum (frus′təm) *n. pl.* **·tums** or **·ta** (-tə) **1** *Geom.* **a** That which is left of a solid after cutting off the upper part: said of a cone or a pyramid. **b** That part of a solid included between any two planes, or, in the case of a sphere, that part between two parallel planes. **2** *Archit.* A fragment; a broken shaft of a column. [<L, fragment]

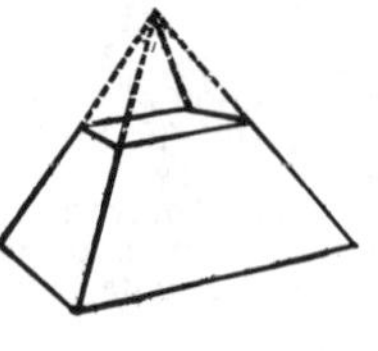

FRUSTUM OF A PYRAMID

fru·tes·cent (fro͞o·tes′ənt) *adj.* **1** Somewhat shrubby. **2** Becoming a shrub. [<L *frutex* a shrub + -ESCENT] — **fru·tes′cence** *n.*

fru·ti·cose (fro͞o′ti·kōs) *adj.* Of, pertaining to, or having the characteristics of a true shrub. [<L *fruticosus* <*frutex, fruticis* a shrub]

fry[1] (frī) *v.t.* & *v.i.* **fried, fry·ing 1** To cook or be cooked in hot fat, usually over direct heat. **2** *Obs.* To vex; worry; be agitated. — *n. pl.* **fries 1** A dish of anything fried. **2** A social occasion, usually a picnic, at which foods are fried and eaten: a fish *fry*. **3** The viscera or testes of an animal fried and served for the table: calf's *fry* (pluck), pig's *fry* (liver), lamb's *fries* (testes). [<F *frier* <L *frigere*]

fry[2] (frī) *n. pl.* **fry 1** Very young fish. **2** The young of other animals, especially when spawned or littered in large numbers. **3** Small adult fish. **4** A multitude or quantity of persons or objects of little importance. [<ON *friō* seed]

Fry (frī), **Christopher,** born 1907, English dramatist.

fry·er (frī′ər) *n.* **1** One who or that which fries. **2** A young chicken, suitable for frying. **3** A high–power electric lamp for use in color photography. Also spelled *frier*.

frying pan A shallow metal pan, with a long handle, for frying food.

F–stop (ef′stop′) *n.* F–number.

fu′ (fo͞o) *adj. Scot.* Full; intoxicated.

Fu·ad I (fo͞o·äd′), 1868–1936, sultan 1917–22, and king 1922–36, of Egypt: original name *Ahmed Fuad*.

fub (fub) See FOB[2].

fub·sy (fub′zē) *adj.* **·si·er, ·si·est** Plump.

fuch·sia (fyo͞o′shə, -shē·ə) *n.* **1** A plant (genus *Fuchsia*) of the evening–primrose family, with red, pink, white, or purple drooping, four–petaled flowers. **2** A perennial herb, the California fuchsia *(Zauschneria californica)*, with scarlet flowers. **3** A bright bluish–red, the typical color of the fuchsia. [after Leonhard *Fuchs*, 1501–66, German botanist]

fuch·sin (fo͝ok′sin) *n. Chem.* A crystalline coal–tar product, superficially green in the solid state, but deep red in solution. Obtained by treating rosaniline with hydrochloric acid, it is used as a dye and in printing. Also called *magenta*. Also **fuch′sine** (-sin, -sēn). [<FUCHSIA + -IN]

fu·coid (fyo͞o′koid) *adj.* **1** Resembling or belonging to seaweeds; of the family *Fucaceae* which includes the rockweeds. **2** Containing fucoids or impressions of them. Also **fu·coi′·dal, fu′cous.** — *n.* **1** A large, coarse, olive–brown seaweed. **2** A plant, either living or fossil, that resembles a seaweed.

fu·co·xan·thin (fyo͞o′kō·zan′thin) *n. Biochem.* The reddish–brown pigment found in red algae: also called *phycophaein*.

fu·cus (fyo͞o′kəs) *n. pl.* **·ci** (-sī) or **·cus·es 1** Any of a genus *(Fucus)* of algae, typified by certain large olive–brown seaweeds, known as *rockweed* or *bladderwrack*. **2** *Obs.* A paint or dye. [<L]

fud·dle (fud′l) *v.* **·dled, ·dling** *v.t.* To confuse or make stupid with drink. — *v.i.* To tipple. [Cf. dial. G *fuddeln* swindle]

fud·dy–dud·dy (fud′ē·dud′ē) *n. Colloq.* **1** An old–fashioned person. **2** A faultfinding, fussy person. [Origin uncertain]

fudge (fuj) *n.* **1** A soft confection made of butter, sugar, chocolate, etc. **2** Humbug; nonsense: commonly used as a contemptuous interjection. **3** An attachment to a rotary newspaper press, for printing late news, usually in a different color from the remainder of the publication. **4** The news so printed. — *v.t.* **fudged, fudg·ing** To make, adjust, or fit together in a clumsy or dishonest manner. [Origin uncertain]

Fu·e·gi·an (fyo͞o·ē′jē·ən, fwā′jē·ən) *adj.* Of or pertaining to Tierra del Fuego or to its native people. — *n.* An Indian of Tierra del Fuego.

Fuehr·er (fyo͞or′ər, *Ger.* fü′rər) *German* Leader: a title of distinction applied to Adolf Hitler by his adherents. Also **Führ′er.**

fu·el (fyo͞o′əl) *n.* **1** Combustible matter, as wood or coal, used to feed a fire. **2** Whatever feeds or sustains any expenditure, outlay, passion, or excitement. — *v.t.* & *v.i.* **fu·eled** or **fu·elled, fu·el·ing** or **fu·el·ling** To supply with or take in fuel. [<OF *fouaille* <LL *focalia* <*focus* hearth] — **fu′el·er, fu′el·ler** *n.*

fuel cell Any of various devices for the generation of electrical energy from the chemical energy of continuously supplied fuels, chiefly hydrogen and oxygen, in contact with a suitable electrolyte.

fuel injection The providing of fuel to an engine by direct injection into the cylinders for the purpose of obtaining precise distribution of the fuel.

fuel tank A tank for holding fuel.

Fuer·te·ven·tu·ra (fwer′tā·ven·to͞o′rä) The second largest of the Canary Islands; 666 square miles.

fuff (fuf) *v.t.* & *v.i. Scot.* To puff.

fu·ga·cious (fyo͞o·gā′shəs) *adj.* **1** Having a fugitive tendency; transitory; volatile. **2** *Bot.* Falling very early, as the petals of a poppy. [<L *fugax, fugacis* <*fugere* flee] — **fu·ga′·cious·ly** *adv.* — **fu·ga′cious·ness** *n.*

fu·gac·i·ty (fyo͞o·gas′ə·tē) *n.* **1** The quality of being transitory; fugaciousness. **2** In thermodynamics, the tendency of a substance in a heterogeneous mixture to escape from a given phase in order to reestablish chemical equilibrium. **3** The amount of this tendency.

Fug·ger (fo͝og′ər) The name of a wealthy family of merchants and financiers who flourished in Germany in the 16th century.

fu·gi·o (fyo͞o′jē·ō) *n.* A copper coin, issued 1787, bearing the word *fugio* beside a meridian sun; the Franklin cent: the first U. S. coinage authorized by Congress. [<L, I flee]

FUGIO

fu·gi·tive (fyo͞o′jə·tiv) *adj.* **1** Fleeing or having fled, as from pursuit, danger, arrest, etc.; escaping or escaped; runaway. **2** Not fixed or lasting; transient; fading or liable to fade; evanescent. **3** Treating of subjects of passing interest; occasional. See synonyms under TRANSIENT. — *n.* **1** One who or that which flees, as from pursuit, danger, bondage, restraint, or duty; a runaway or deserter. **2** An exile or refugee. [<F *fugitif* <L *fugitivus* <*fugere* flee] — **fu′gi·tive·ly** *adv.* — **fu′gi·tive·ness** *n.*

fu·gle (fyo͞o′gəl) *v.i.* **·gled, ·gling** *Rare* **1** To act as fugleman. **2** To make signals.

fu·gle·man (fyo͞o′gəl·mən) *n. pl.* **·men** (-mən) **1** A soldier who stands in front of a line or body of men and leads them in military exercises; a file–leader. **2** One who leads or sets an example in anything. [<G *flügelmann* <*flügel* wing + *mann* man]

fugue (fyo͞og) *n. Music* **1** A form, or sometimes a complete composition in strict polyphonic style in which a theme is introduced by one part, harmonized by contrapuntal rule, and reintroduced throughout. **2** *Psychiatry* An interval of flight from reality, during which an individual will assume a personality and perform actions in themselves rational but entirely forgotten upon the return of normal consciousness: a form of amnesia. [<F <Ital. *fuga* <L, a flight] **—fug′al** *adj.*

Fu·ji (fōō·jē) The highest peak of Japan, an extinct volcano on Honshu island: 12,300 feet. Also **Fu·ji-no-ya·ma** (fōō·jē·nō·yä·mä), **Fu·ji·san** (fōō·jē·sän), **Fu·ji·ya·ma** (fōō·jē·yä·mä).

Fu·kien (fōō′kyen′) A province of SE China; 45,000 square miles; capital, Foochow. Also **Fu′-chien′.**

Fu·ku·o·ka (fōō·kōō·ō·kä) A city on northern Kyushu island, Japan.

-ful *suffix* **1** Full of; characterized by: *joyful.* **2** Able to; tending to: *fearful.* **3** Having the character of: *manful.* **4** The quantity or number that will fill: *cupful.* [OE *-full, -ful* <*full* full] ◆ Nouns ending in **-ful** form the plural by adding *-s*, as in *cupfuls, spoonfuls.*

Fu·la (fōō′lä) *n.* **1** One of a Moslem people of the Egyptian Sudan, basically of Hamitic stock but mixed with Negro, having straight or curly hair, aquiline features, and light reddish-brown complexion. **2** The Sudanic language of these people. Also **Fu′lah.**

Ful·bright Act (fŏŏl′brīt) A Congressional act of 1946 that provides for a large part of the proceeds from the sale of United States war surplus property in foreign countries to be used for financing the mutual exchange of students, teachers, and other cultural workers: named for James William Fulbright, born 1905, U. S. senator.

ful·crum (fŏŏl′krəm) *n. pl.* **·crums** or **·cra** (-krə) **1** The support on or against which a lever rests. **2** Any prop or support. **3** *Zool.* In many ganoid fishes one of the rows of spinelike scales arranged along the forward edge of the median and paired fins: usually in the plural. [<L, bed post <*fulcire* prop up]

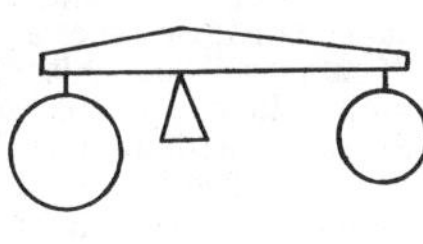
FULCRUM

Ful·da (fŏŏl′dä), **Ludwig,** 1862–1939, German writer.

ful·fil (fŏŏl·fil′) *v.t.* **ful·filled, ful·fil·ling** **1** To perform, as a duty or command. **2** To bring into effect or to consummation. **3** To finish; come to the end of. **4** To fill the requirements of; satisfy, as the conditions of a contract. Also **ful·fill′.** See synonyms under EFFECT, KEEP. [OE *fullfyllan*] **—ful·fil′ler** *n.* **—ful·fil′ment, ful·fill′ment** *n.*

ful·gent (ful′jənt) *adj.* Beaming or shining brightly; radiant; gleaming; effulgent; resplendent. [<L *fulgens, -entis,* ppr. of *fulgere* gleam] **—ful′gen·cy** *n.* **—ful′gent·ly** *adv.*

ful·gid (ful′jid) *adj.* **1** Fulgent. **2** Fiery red. [<L *fulgidus* <*fulgere* gleam]

ful·gor (ful′gər) *n. Archaic* Dazzling brightness. Also **ful′gour.** [<L <*fulgere* gleam]

ful·gu·rant (ful′gyər·ənt) *adj.* Flashing; lightninglike.

ful·gu·rate (ful′gyə·rāt) *v.i.* **·rat·ed, ·rat·ing** To flash or throw out flashes, as of lightning. [<L *fulguratus,* pp. of *fulgurare* lighten <*fulgur* lightning]

ful·gu·rat·ing (ful′gyə·rā′ting) *adj.* Flashing; emitting flashes; darting; lancinating: *fulgurating* pains.

ful·gu·ra·tion (ful′gyə·rā′shən) *n.* **1** The act of flashing or lightening. **2** The sensation of stabbing pain. **3** Lightning stroke. **4** Destruction of animal tissue by electric sparks.

ful·gu·rite (ful′gyə·rīt) *n.* **1** A vertical tube with fused walls, formed in sand or rock by the passage of lightning. **2** An explosive: a type of dynamite.

ful·gu·rous (ful′gyər·əs) *adj.* Flashing, moving, or acting like lightning.

ful·ham (fŏŏl′əm) *n. Archaic* **1** A fraudulent or loaded die. **2** *Usually pl.* Any sham or fraud. Also **ful′lam.** [? from *Fulham,* a section of London once frequented by gamblers]

fu·lig·i·nous (fyōō·lij′ə·nəs) *adj.* **1** Like soot or smoke; also, sooty-brown. **2** Dark, as if shrouded in smoke. [<L *fuliginosus* <*fuligo, -inis* soot] **—fu·lig′i·nous·ly** *adv.*

full[1] (fŏŏl) *adj.* **1** Containing or having all that can or should be admitted; having no empty or vacant space; filled. **2** Abounding in something; also, engrossed or excited as with some thought: with *of.* **3** Perfectly sufficient or complete. **4** Ample in extent or volume; well-filled or rounded out; plump. **5** Having the disk wholly illuminated, as the moon. **6** Filled or satisfied with food or drink; hence, intoxicated. **7** Filled with emotion or with knowledge. **8** High, as the tide. **9** Possessing depth or volume: said of sounds. **10** Unblended; pure: said of color. **11** Having plenty of body: said of wines, etc. **12** Distended by wind, as a sail. **13** Having folds or plaits: a *full* skirt. See synonyms under AMPLE, IMPLICIT. **—***n.* **1** The highest state, point, or degree. **2** The phase (of the moon) when the whole disk is illuminated. **—***adv.* **1** Without abatement, diminution, qualification, etc.; fully; completely; to the utmost extent. **2** Very: to run *full* fast. **—***v.t.* To make full; gather, as a sleeve. **—***v.i.* To become full. [OE *ful*] **—full′ness, ful′ness** *n.* **—ful′ly** *adv.*

The adjective is the first element of many compound adjectives, as:

full-armed	**full-fed**	**full-opening**
full-bearded	**full-flowering**	**full-resounding**
full-built	**full-leaved**	**full-shouldered**
full-chested	**full-mouthed**	**full-strength**

full[2] (fŏŏl) *v.t.* & *v.i.* To make or become thicker and more compact, by shrinking: said of cloth. [Back formation <FULLER, *n.*]

full and by *Naut.* Close to the wind but with the sails full.

full·back (fŏŏl′bak′) *n.* In American football, one of the backfield, originally the player farthest from the line of scrimmage.

full-blood (fŏŏl′blud′) *n.* A person or animal of unmixed breed.

full blood **1** The condition of being thoroughbred: an Indian of *full blood.* **2** The relationship between kindred of any degree who possess to the full the degree of kinship named. **—full′-blood′** *adj.*

full-blood·ed (fŏŏl′blud′id) *adj.* **1** Having a large supply of blood; plethoric. **2** Of pure or unmixed blood; thoroughbred.

full-blown (fŏŏl′blōn′) *adj.* **1** Fully expanded or blossomed out. **2** Fully matured, perfected, or attired. **3** Filled with wind.

full-dress (fŏŏl′dres′) *adj.* **1** Characterized by or requiring full dress: a *full-dress* dinner. **2** Formal and thoroughgoing: a *full-dress* debate.

full dress Costume worn at court receptions or at formal social gatherings.

full·er[1] (fŏŏl′ər) *n.* One who fulls and cleanses cloth. [OE *fullere* <L *fullo*]

full·er[2] (fŏŏl′ər) *n.* **1** A blacksmith's tool with a round edge, used in grooving or spreading hot iron; a form of swage. **2** A groove made by a fuller. **—***v.t.* To groove or crease by the use of a fuller: to *fuller* a bayonet blade. [? <FULL[1], *v.*]

Full·er (fŏŏl′ər), **George,** 1822–84, U. S. painter. **—Melville Weston,** 1833–1910, jurist, chief justice of the U. S. Supreme Court 1888–1910. **—(Sarah) Margaret,** 1810–50, Marchioness Ossoli, U. S. writer. **—Thomas,** 1608–61, English divine and author.

Full·er·board (fŏŏl′ər·bôrd′, -bōrd′) *n.* A cardboard used as insulating material and for other protective purposes in the electrical industry: a trade name. Also called *electrical pressboard, presspahn.*

fuller's earth A soft earthy material occurring in nature as an impure hydrous aluminum silicate: it is used as a filter and in removing grease from cloth and wool, and also in medicine, as a dusting powder and, with glycerin, in poultices.

ful·ler's-tea·sel (fŏŏl′ərz·tē′zəl) *n.* A stout coarse herb *(Dipsacus fullonum)* resembling a thistle, with opposite connate leaves, and oblong heads of flowers.

full·er·y (fŏŏl′ər·ē) *n. pl.* **·er·ies** A place where cloth is fulled; a fulling mill.

full-fashioned (fŏŏl′fash′ənd) *adj.* Knitted to conform to the shape of the lower leg, the human figure, etc.: said of hosiery and sweaters.

full-fledged (fŏŏl′flejd′) *adj.* **1** Full-feathered. **2** Fully developed; having gone into full operation. **3** Of full rank.

full house In poker, three of a kind and a pair, a hand next in value below four of a kind. Also **full hand.**

fulling mill **1** A machine for fulling woolen cloth. **2** A mill where cloth is fulled.

full moon **1** The moon when it shows its whole disk illuminated. **2** The time when this occurs.

full-rigged (fŏŏl′rigd′) *adj. Naut.* Completely equipped, with three or more masts, each fully supplied with square sails.

full-scale (fŏŏl′skāl′) *adj.* **1** Unreduced; scaled to actual size: a *full-scale* drawing. **2** All-out: a *full-scale* attack.

full stop A period.

full swing Unrestrained liberty or license; free course. **—in full swing** Going on vigorously and unrestrainedly.

full-time (fŏŏl′tīm′) *adj.* Requiring all one's working hours.

full-track (fŏŏl′trak′) *adj.* Designating a vehicle, as a tank, which rides entirely on and is steered by an endless belt on each side. Compare HALF-TRACK.

ful·mar (fŏŏl′mər) *n.* A large sea bird *(Fulmarus glacialis)* of the Arctic; also, the **giant fulmar** *(Macronectes giganteus)* of southern seas. [<ON *full mar* stinking mew]

ful·mi·nant (ful′mə·nənt) *adj.* **1** Fulminating. **2** Beginning suddenly, as a fever.

ful·mi·nate (ful′mə·nāt) *v.* **·nat·ed, ·nat·ing** *v.i.* **1** To explode or detonate violently. **2** To shout accusations, threats, etc.; denounce. **3** *Rare* To thunder and lighten. **—***v.t.* **4** To cause to explode violently. **5** To shout (accusations, threats, etc.). **—***n. Chem.* **1** A salt of fulminic acid, that explodes under percussion. **2** A mixture containing such a salt. [<L *fulminatus,* pp. of *fulminare* lighten <*fulmen, fulminis* lightning] **—ful′mi·na′tion** *n.* **—ful′mi·na′tor** *n.* **—ful′mi·na·to′ry** (-tôr′ē, -tō′rē) *adj.*

fulminating compound A fulminate. Also **fulminating powder.**

ful·mine (ful′min) *v.t.* & *v.i.* **·mined, ·min·ing** To fulminate. [<F *fulminer* <L *fulminare.* See FULMINATE.]

ful·min·ic (ful·min′ik) *adj.* Relating to or producing a detonation.

fulminic acid *Chem.* An isomer of cyanic acid, CNOH, that unites with bases to form explosive salts, called fulminates.

ful·mi·nous (ful′mə·nəs) *adj.* Of, pertaining to, or like thunder and lightning.

ful·some (fŏŏl′səm, ful′-) *adj.* **1** Offensive and distasteful because excessive: *fulsome* praise. **2** Coarse; indelicate. [<FULL, *adj.* + -SOME; infl. by FOUL] **—ful′some·ly** *adv.* **—ful′some·ness** *n.*

Ful·ton (fŏŏl′tən), **John Farquhar,** 1899–1960, U. S. physiologist. **—Robert,** 1765–1815, U. S. inventor; launched first steamboat 1803.

ful·vous (ful′vəs) *adj.* Reddish-yellow; tawny. [<L *fulvus*]

fu·mar·ic (fyōō·mar′ik) *adj. Chem.* Of, pertaining to, or occurring in fumitory plants: *fumaric* acid, $C_4H_4O_4$.

fu·ma·role (fyōō′mə·rōl) *n.* A small hole from which volcanic vapors issue. [<F *fumerolle* <LL *fumariolum,* dim. of *fumarium* chimney <*fumus* smoke]

fu·ma·to·ri·um (fyōō′mə·tôr′ē·əm, -tō′rē-) *n. pl.* **·ri·ums** or **·ri·a** An airtight chamber or apparatus for an arboretum, etc., to contain gases or the like, with which to destroy insects, fungous scales, etc. [<NL <L *fumare* smoke <*fumus* smoke]

fu·ma·to·ry (fyōō′mə·tôr′ē, -tō′rē) *adj.* Of or pertaining to smoking. **—***n.* A fumatorium.

fum·ble (fum′bəl) *v.* **fum·bled, fum·bling** *v.i.* **1** To feel about blindly or clumsily; grope: with *for, at, with,* or *after.* **2** In sports, to fail to catch or hold the ball. **—***v.t.* **3** To handle clumsily or awkwardly. **4** In sports, to fumble (the ball). **—***n.* The act of fumbling. [Prob. <Scand. Cf. Sw. *fumla* grope] **—fum′bler** *n.*

fume (fyōōm) *n.* **1** Reek; smoke. **2** Vapor, visible or invisible, especially as having narcotic or choking qualities. 3 Any odorous smoke or vapor. 4 Furious anger. 5 Incense; aromatic smoke. — *v.* **fumed, fum·ing** *v.i.* 1 To give off smoke, vapor, etc. 2 To pass off in a mist or vapor. 3 To express or show anger, irritation, etc. — *v.t.* 4 To expose to or treat or fill with fumes, smoke, etc. [<OF *fum* <L *fumus* smoke] — **fum′er** *n.* — **fum′·ing** *adj.*

fumed (fyōōmd) *adj.* Treated with fumes: said especially of wood coated with filler and then exposed to chemical fumes: *fumed* oak.

fume fading The fading of synthetic dyes in textiles exposed to certain chemical fumes. Also called *gas fading.*

fu·met (fyōō′met) *n. Obs.* 1 The odor of long-kept game. 2 The savory odor of meats while cooking. Also **fu·mette′.** [<F <L *fumus* smoke]

fu·mi·gant (fyōō′mə·gənt) *n.* Any substance, as hydrogen cyanide, whose vapors are capable of destroying vermin, rats, insects, etc., in an enclosed space; a gaseous disinfectant or insecticide.

fu·mi·gate (fyōō′mə·gāt) *v.t.* **·gat·ed, ·gat·ing** 1 To subject to smoke or fumes, as for disinfection. 2 *Archaic* To perfume. [<L *fumigatus,* pp. of *fumigare* smoke <*fumus* smoke + *agere* drive] — **fu′mi·ga′tion** *n.* — **fu′·mi·ga′tor** *n.*

fu·mi·to·ry (fyōō′mə·tôr′ē, -tō′rē) *n. pl.* **·ries** Any of a genus (*Fumaria*) of climbing herbs; especially, a low herb (*F. officinalis*) with terminal racemes of rose-colored flowers, used medicinally as an alterative and tonic. [<F *fumeterre* <Med. L *fumus terrae* smoke of the earth]

fu·mu·lus (fyōō′myə·ləs) *n. Meteorol.* A delicate, almost invisible veil of cloud that may form at all heights from cirrus to stratus: most observable in low latitudes and on hot days. [<NL, dim. of *fumus* smoke]

fum·y (fyōō′mē) *adj.* **fum·i·er, fum·i·est** Yielding or containing fumes; smoky; vaporous. — **fum′i·ly** *adv.* — **fum′i·ness** *n.*

fun (fun) *n.* 1 That which excites merriment; frolic; sport; amusement. 2 Drollery; jocularity; a joke. 3 Frolicsome doings; also, the mirth and enjoyment derived therefrom. See synonyms under ENTERTAINMENT, LAUGHTER, SPORT, WIT. — **to make fun of** To ridicule. — **for** or **in fun** Not seriously; sportively, jokingly. — *v.i.* **funned, fun·ning** *Colloq.* To indulge in fun; make sport; jest. [< obs. *fonnen* befool]

Fu·na·fu·ti (fōō′nə·fōō′tē) The island headquarters of the Gilbert Islands district of the Gilbert and Ellice Islands colony; one square mile.

fu·nam·bu·list (fyōō·nam′byə·list) *n.* A performer on a tight or slack rope. [<L *funambulus* <*funis* rope + *ambulare* walk] — **fu·nam′bu·la·to′ry** (-tôr′ē, -tō′rē) *adj.* — **fu·nam′·bu·lism** *n.*

Fun·chal (fōōn·shäl′) 1 A port, capital of Madeira. 2 An administrative district of Portugal comprising Madeira.

func·tion (fungk′shən) *n.* 1 The specific, natural, or proper action that belongs to an agent. 2 One's appropriate or assigned business, duty, part, or office. 3 The proper employment of faculties or powers. 4 The normal action of any organ or set of organs: the respiratory *function.* 5 A public or official ceremony or formal entertainment. 6 *Math.* A quantity whose value is dependent on the value of some other quantity. 7 *Ling.* The part played by a linguistic element in a form or construction. See synonyms under DUTY. — *v.i.* 1 To perform as expected or required; operate properly. 2 To perform the rôle of something else. 3 *Ling.* To perform a specific function. [<OF <L *functio, -onis* <*fungi* perform]

func·tion·al (fungk′shən·əl) *adj.* 1 Of or belonging to the proper office or work of an agent or agency. 2 Designed for or suited to a particular operation or use: *functional* architecture. 3 *Med.* Affecting only the functions of an organ or part; not structural or organic: a *functional* disease. — **func′tion·al·ly** *adv.*

func·tion·al·ism (fungk′shən·əl·iz′əm) *n.* In art, architecture, etc., a doctrine that holds function to be of prime importance, modifying such factors as form and structure so that they may contribute the utmost to the effective functioning of the finished product. — **func′·tion·al·ist** *n.*

functional shift *Ling.* The assuming of a new syntactic function by a word, without a change in form, as when an adjective serves as a noun in English.

func·tion·ar·y (funk′shən·er′ē) *n. pl.* **·ar·ies** A public official.

function word *Ling.* A word which is used to indicate the function of, or the relationship between, other words in a phrase or sentence, as a preposition or conjunction.

fund (fund) *n.* 1 A sum of money or stock of convertible wealth employed in, set aside for, or available for a business enterprise or other purpose; specifically, the quick capital or available assets of a business firm or corporation. 2 *pl.* Money lent to government; a funded debt. 3 A reserve store; an ample stock: a *fund* of humor. 4 *pl.* Money in general: out of *funds.* 5 *Obs.* Bottom. See synonyms under STOCK, MONEY. — *v.t.* 1 To convert into a more or less permanent debt bearing a fixed rate of interest: to *fund* a public debt. 2 To furnish a fund for the payment of the principal or interest of (a debt). 3 To make a fund of; amass. [<L *fundus* bottom] — **fund′a·ble** *adj.*

fun·da·ment (fun′də·mənt) *n.* 1 A fundamental principle or element. 2 The part on which the body rests in sitting; the buttocks; also, the anus. 3 *Geog.* The natural features of a region considered in the aggregate and as unmodified by human action. 4 *Obs.* Foundation. [<L *fundamentum* <*fundus* bottom]

fun·da·men·tal (fun′də·men′təl) *adj.* 1 Relating to or constituting a foundation; indispensable; basal. 2 *Geol.* Located at the bottom; constituting the lowest stratum or formation: *fundamental* rock. 3 *Music* Radical: applied to the lowest note of a chord, considered as being its foundation or root. 4 *Physics* Designating that component of a wave form or other periodic oscillation on which all harmonic frequencies are based. See synonyms under RADICAL. — *n.* 1 Anything that serves as the foundation or basis of a system of belief, as a truth, law, or principle; a primary and necessary truth; an essential. 2 *Music* The note on which a chord is formed. 3 *Physics* That frequency on which a harmonic or group of harmonics is based. — **fun′·da·men′tal·ly** *adv.*

fun·da·men·tal·ism (fun′də·men′təl·iz′əm) *n.* 1 The belief that all statements made in the Bible are literally true. 2 In the United States, a movement among Protestants holding that such belief is essential to Christian faith: opposed to *modernism.* — **fun′da·men′tal·ist** *n.*

fun·dus (fun′dəs) *n. Anat.* The rounded base, bottom, or farther end or part of any hollow organ: the *fundus* of the eye. [<L]

Fun·dy (fun′dē), **Bay of** An inlet of the Atlantic between Nova Scotia and New Brunswick and NE Maine; its tides are among the highest in the world, rising to 70 feet.

Fü·nen (fü′nən) German name for FYN.

fu·ner·al (fyōō′nər·əl) *n.* 1 The rites and ceremonies preceding and accompanying burial; obsequies. 2 A gathering or procession of persons on the occasion of a burial. — *adj.* Pertaining to, suitable for, or used at a funeral. [<OF *funeraille* <Med. L *funeralia,* neut. pl. of *funeralis* <*funus, funeris* a burial rite]

fu·ne·re·al (fyōō·nir′ē·əl) *adj.* Pertaining to or suitable for a funeral; mournful; lugubrious. [<L *funereus* <*funus* FUNERAL] — **fu·ne′·re·al·ly** *adv.*

fu·nest (fyōō·nest′) *adj. Rare* Portending or causing death or evil; fatal; doleful. [<F *funeste* <L *funestus* <*funus* FUNERAL]

Fünf·kir·chen (fünf′·kēr′khən) The German name for PÉCS.

fun·gal (fung′gəl) *adj.* Fungous. — *n.* A fungus.

Fun·gi (fun′jī) *n. pl.* One of the subdivisions of the *Thallophyta:* non-flowering plants of wide distribution and great variety, devoid of chlorophyll, reproducing chiefly by asexual means and obtaining nourishment either as *parasites* on living organisms or as *saprophytes* on dead organic matter. They include the molds, mildews, rusts, and mushrooms, and are subdivided into bacteria or fission fungi (*Schizomycetes*), slime fungi (*Myxomycetes*), algal fungi (*Phycomycetes*), ascus fungi (*Ascomycetes*), basidium fungi (*Basidomycetes*), and the Fungi Imperfecti, not yet classified. [See FUNGUS]

fungi– *combining form* Fungus: *fungicide.* Also, before vowels, **fung–.** [<L *fungus* a mushroom]

fun·gi·ble (fun′jə·bəl) *adj.* 1 Capable of being replaced in kind, as movables. 2 That may be measured, counted, or weighed. — *n.* 1 Anything fungible. 2 *Law* A thing of which one portion may be taken or used in the place of another portion to fulfil an obligation. [<Med. L *fungibilis* <*fungi* perform] — **fun′·gi·bil′i·ty** *n.*

fun·gi·cide (fun′jə·sīd) *n.* Anything that kills fungi or destroys their spores; especially, any chemical compound used for this purpose. — **fun′gi·ci′dal** *adj.*

fun·gi·form (fun′jə·fôrm) *adj.* Having a form or a head like that of a mushroom or fungus.

fun·goid (fung′goid) *adj.* Resembling a mushroom or fungus. — *n.* A fungus.

fun·gous (fung′gəs) *adj.* 1 Pertaining to or of the nature of a fungus; spongy. 2 Springing up suddenly. 3 Bearing or containing fungi.

fun·gus (fung′gəs) *n. pl.* **fun·gus·es** or **fun·gi** (fun′jī) 1 Any of the *Fungi* group of thallophytic plants, comprising the mushrooms, puffballs, molds, smuts, etc. 2 A soft, spongy growth on an animal body. [<L, a mushroom. Akin to SPONGE.]

fu·ni·cle (fyōō′ni·kəl) *n. Anat.* 1 A small cord, ligature, or fiber. 2 A funiculus. [<L *funiculus,* dim. of *funis* a rope]

fu·nic·u·lar (fyōō·nik′yə·lər) *adj.* 1 Pertaining to, consisting of, or like a funicle. 2 Pertaining to a cord or funiculus. 3 Operated by a cable, cord, or rope: a *funicular* railway. — *n.* A cable railway. Also **funicular railway.**

fu·nic·u·late (fyōō·nik′yə·lit, -lāt) *adj.* 1 *Bot.* Provided with funicles. 2 *Zool.* Forming a narrow ridge.

fu·nic·u·lus (fyōō·nik′yə·ləs) *n. pl.* **·li** (-lī) 1 A small cord, rope, or the like. 2 *Anat.* The umbilical cord. 3 *Bot.* The cord or stalk that connects the ovule or seed with the peridium of a plant. [<L]

funk (fungk) *n. Colloq.* Cowardly fright; panic. — *v.t.* 1 To shrink from; be afraid of. 2 To frighten; scare. — *v.i.* 3 To shrink through fear or aversion; try to back out. [Cf. Flemish *fonck* fear]

Funk (fungk), **Casimir,** 1884–1967, Polish biochemist. — **Charles Earle,** 1881–1957, U.S. lexicographer. — **Isaac Kauffman,** 1838–1912, U. S. publisher and lexicographer; founder of *The Literary Digest;* editor in chief of the *Standard Dictionary* and *New Standard Dictionary of the English Language.*

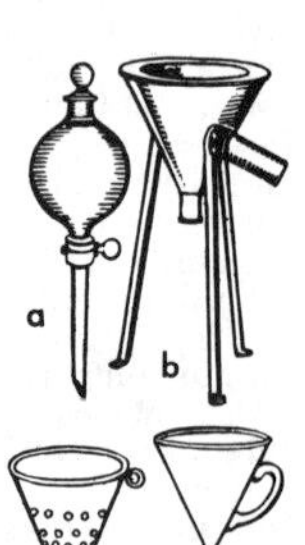

FUNNELS
a. Separatory funnel.
b. Hot filtration funnel.
c. Filter funnel.
d. Glass funnel, with olivary tip.

fun·nel (fun′əl) *n.* 1 A wide-mouthed conical vessel, terminating in a tube, for filling close-necked vessels with liquids: also called *tunnel.* 2 A smoke pipe, chimney, or flue. 3 A smokestack on a steamship. 4 Any funnel-like part or process: the *funnel* cell in a leaf. — *v.t.* & *v.i.* **·neled** or **·nelled, ·nel·ing** or **·nel·ling** To pass or move through or as through a funnel; focus. [Earlier *fonel,* ult. <L *infundibulum* <*infundere* pour <*in-* into + *fundere* pour]

fun·nies (fun′ēz) *n. pl. U.S. Colloq.* Comic strips.

fun·ny (fun′ē) *adj.* **·ni·er, ·ni·est** 1 Affording fun; comical; ludicrous; laughable. 2 *Colloq.* Puzzling; strange; unusual. — **fun′ni·ly** *adv.* — **fun′ni·ness** *n.*

Synonyms: amusing, comical, diverting, droll, facetious, farcical, grotesque, humorous, jocose, jocular, jolly, jovial, laughable, ludicrous, merry, mirthful, odd, queer, ridiculous, whimsical, witty. Compare AMUSE. *Antonyms*: see synonyms for SAD.

funny bone The part of the humerus where the ulnar nerve is exposed at the elbow; crazy bone.

funny paper *U.S. Colloq.* A newspaper supplement containing comic strips.
Fun·ston (fun′stən), **Frederick,** 1865–1917, U. S. general.
Fun·za (fo͞on′sä) See BOGOTÁ (def. 2).
fur (fûr) *n.* 1 The soft, fine, hairy coat covering the skin of many mammals. 2 *pl.* or *collective sing.* Skins of fur-bearing animals, as ermine, sable, beaver, etc.; also, apparel made of them. 3 Any fuzzy covering, as coating on the tongue. 4 A piece of wood nailed under a bent rafter to straighten it. [< *v.*] — **to make the fur fly** To attack a person or thing vigorously; fight. —*v.t.* **furred, fur·ring** 1 To cover, line, or trim with fur. 2 To clothe with fur. 3 To cover with a coating, as of scum. 4 To apply furring to, as for lathing. ◆ Homophone: *fir.* [<OF *forrer* line with fur <Gmc.]
fu·ran (fyo͝or′·an, fyo͞o·ran′) *n. Chem.* A colorless liquid heterocyclic hydrocarbon, C_4H_4O, obtained from pine tar and an important source of furfural: also *furfuran.* Also **fu·rane** (fyo͝or′ān). [Short for *furfurane* <L *furfur* bran + -AN(E)[2]]
fur·be·low (fûr′bə·lō) *n.* 1 A plaited flounce, ruffle, or similar ornament. 2 Hence, any ornament in feminine dress. — *v.t.* To decorate elaborately or fussily. [Alter. of FALBALA]
fur·bish (fûr′bish) *v.t.* 1 To make bright by rubbing; burnish. 2 To restore to brightness or beauty; renovate: often with *up.* See synonyms under GARNISH. [<OF *forbiss-*, stem of *forbir* <OHG *furban* clean] — **fur′bish·er** *n.*
fur·cal (fûr′kəl) *adj.* Forked; branched; furcate.
fur·cate (fûr′kāt) *v.i.* **·cat·ed, ·cat·ing** To separate into diverging parts; fork. —*adj.* Forked: also **fur′cat·ed.** [<Med. L *furcatus* cloven <*furca* fork] — **fur′cate·ly** *adv.* — **fur·ca′tion** *n.*
fur·crae·a (fər·krē′ə) *n.* One of a genus (*Furcraea*) of tropical American plants of the amaryllis family; especially *F. macrophylla,* which yields a valuable fiber. See FIQUE. [<NL, after A. F. *Fourcroy,* 1755–1809, French chemist]
fur·cu·lum (fûr′kyə·ləm) *n. pl.* **·la** (-lə) The united clavicles of a bird; the wishbone. [< NL, incorrectly formed as dim. of *furca* fork]
fur·fur (fûr′fər) *n. pl.* **·fur·es** (-fə·rēz) Dandruff, or branlike scales of skin; scurf. [<L, bran] — **fur′fur·a′ceous** *adj.*
fur·fur·al (fûr′fə·ral) *n. Chem.* A colorless liquid heterocyclic aldehyde, $C_5H_4O_2$, obtained by distillation of the pentose sugars occurring in corncobs, oat hulls, and other agricultural waste products: widely used as a solvent and reagent in the dyestuffs, plastics, and other industries. Also **fur′fur·ol** (-ôl, -ol). [<L *furfur* bran + AL(DEHYDE)]
fur·fu·ran (fûr′fə·ran) *n.* Furan.
fu·ri·bund (fyo͝or′i·bund′) *adj. Rare* Filled with rage or fury; raging. [<L *furibundus* <*furere* rage]
Fu·ries (fyo͝or′ēz) *n. pl.* In Greek and Roman mythology, the three goddesses who take vengeance on unpunished criminals—Alecto, Megaera, and Tisiphone: also called *Erinyes, Eumenides.*
fu·ri·o·so (fyo͞o′rē·ō′sō) *adj. Music* With fury or vehemence. [<Ital.]
fu·ri·ous (fyo͝or′ē·əs) *adj.* 1 Full of fury; raging; frantic. 2 Wildly rushing; violent; tempestuous; as waves, a storm, etc. See synonyms under FIERCE. [<L *furiosus* <*furere* rage] — **fu′ri·ous·ly** *adv.* — **fu′ri·ous·ness** *n.*
furl (fûrl) *v.t.* To roll up and make secure, as a sail to a spar. — *v.i.* To become furled. — *n.* 1 The act of furling. 2 Something furled. [<F *ferler* <OF *fermlier* <*ferm* close (<L *firmus*) + *lier* bind <L *ligare*]
fur·long (fûr′lông, -long) *n.* A measure of length, one eighth of a mile, 220 yards, or 201.168 meters. [OE *furlang* <*furh* furrow + *lang* long]
fur·lough (fûr′lō) *n.* An authorized leave of absence of more than three days granted to an enlisted man in the army or navy. Compare LEAVE, PASS. —*v.t.* To grant a furlough to. [<Du. *verlof*]
furm (fûrm) *n. Scot.* A form; bench.
fur·men·ty (fûr′mən·tē), **fur·me·ty** (fûr′mə·tē), **fur·mi·ty** See FRUMENTY.
fur·nace (fûr′nis) *n.* 1 A structure or apparatus containing a chamber for heating, fusing, hardening, etc., by means of a fire beneath, as for melting metal, baking pottery, evaporating water, etc. 2 A large stove in the basement or cellar of a house, equipped with conduits for heating the upper rooms. See ELECTRIC FURNACE. [<OF *fornais* <L *fornax, fornacis* <*furnus* oven]
Fur·neaux Islands (fûr′nō) An Australian island group between Australia and Tasmania; 1,031 square miles.
Fur·ness (fûr′nis), **Horace Howard,** 1833–1912, U. S. scholar.
fur·nish (fûr′nish) *v.t.* 1 To equip, or fit out, as with fittings or furniture. 2 To supply; provide. See synonyms under ACCOMMODATE, GIVE, PRODUCE, PROVIDE. [<OF *furniss-*, stem of *furnir* <OHG *frumjan* provide] — **fur′nish·er** *n.*
fur·nish·ing (fûr′nish·ing) *n.* 1 *pl.* Fixtures or fittings, as hardware for cabinetwork, etc. 2 The act of supplying with furniture.
fur·ni·ture (fûr′nə·chər) *n.* 1 That with which anything is furnished or supplied; equipment or outfit; specifically, movable household articles, such as chairs, tables, bureaus. 2 Ornamental appendages or external adjuncts that serve to complete anything. 3 *Printing* The strips and blocks of wood or metal, made in multiples of picas, which are locked between the page forms and the chase. 4 *Obs.* The action of providing for, equipping, or furnishing. [<F *fourniture* <*fournir* FURNISH]
Fur·ni·vall (fûr′nə·vəl), **Frederick James,** 1825–1910, English philologist.
fu·ror (fyo͝or′ôr) *n.* 1 Fury. 2 Great excitement or enthusiasm. 3 An object of enthusiasm; a fad; a craze. 4 Religious frenzy. Also **fu·rore** (fyo͝or′ôr, fyo͞o·rôr′ē, -rō′rē). [<L *furor* <*furere* rage]
fu·ror lo·quen·di (fyo͝or′ōr lō·kwen′dī) *Latin* Enthusiasm for speaking.
furor po·et·i·cus (pō·et′i·kəs) *Latin* Poetic frenzy.
furor scri·ben·di (skri·ben′dī) *Latin* Enthusiasm for writing.
fur·phy (fûr′fē) *Austral.* A rumor; canard. [after *Furphy,* a foundry owner]
furred (fûrd) *adj.* 1 Bearing fur; also, trimmed with fur. 2 Provided with furring.
fur·ri·er (fûr′ē·ər, -yər) *n.* A dealer in furs or fur goods; a dresser of furs for garments.
fur·ri·er·y (fûr′ē·ər·ē) *n. pl.* **·er·ies** 1 Furs in general. 2 The business of a furrier.
fur·ring (fûr′ing) *n.* 1 Fur, or fur trimmings. 2 A coating or scale, as on the inner surface of boiler pipes; also, the process of removing it. 3 Pieces of wood attached to a surface, as for lathing. 4 The act of applying or adjusting, as pieces of wood or metal for lathing.
fur·row (fûr′ō) *n.* 1 A trench made in the earth by a plow. 2 One of the grooves in the face of a millstone. 3 Any groove or wrinkle. 4 *Obs.* A plowed field. —*v.t.* 1 To make furrows in; plow. 2 To make wrinkles in, as the brow. — *v.i.* 3 To become wrinkled. [OE *furh*] — **fur′row·er** *n.*
fur·ry (fûr′ē) *adj.* 1 Of or like fur. 2 Covered with or clad in fur. — **fur′ri·ness** *n.*
fur seal An eared seal that yields a fur of great commercial value, especially *Callorhinus alascanus,* the Alaska fur seal of the Pribilof Islands. See SEAL[2].
Fürth (fürt) A city in Bavaria, Germany.
fur·ther (fûr′thər) Comparative of FAR. —*adj.* 1 More distant or advanced in time or degree. 2 Wider or fuller; additional. 3 More distant in space; farther. See note under FARTHER. — *adv.* 1 More remotely; farther. 2 In addition; besides; also. See synonyms under YET. — *v.t.* To help forward; promote. See synonyms under PROMOTE. [OE *furthra*] — **fur′ther·er** *n.*
fur·ther·ance (fûr′thər·əns) *n.* 1 The act of furthering; advancement. 2 That which furthers.
fur·ther·more (fûr′thər·môr′, -mōr′) *adv.* In addition; moreover.
fur·ther·most (fûr′thər·mōst′) *adj.* Furthest or most remote.
fur·ther·some (fûr′thər·səm) *adj.* Tending to further or advance; promotive; helpful.
fur·thest (fûr′thist) Superlative of FAR. — *adj.* 1 Most distant, remote, or advanced in time or degree. 2 Most distant in space. — *adv.* 1 At or to the greatest distance in time or degree. 2 Farthest.
fur·tive (fûr′tiv) *adj.* Stealthy or sly; stolen; secret; elusive. See synonyms under SECRET. [<F *furtif* <L *furtivus* stolen <*fur* a thief] — **fur′tive·ly** *adv.* — **fur′tive·ness** *n.*
fu·run·cle (fyo͝or′ung·kəl) *n.* A boil or inflammatory sore caused by bacterial infection of the subcutaneous tissue. [<L *furunculus,* dim. of *fur* thief] — **fu·run·cu·lar** (fyo͞o·rung′kyə·lər) *adj.* — **fu·run′cu·lous** *adj.*
fu·ry (fyo͝or′ē) *n. pl.* **·ries** 1 A state of violent anger; ungovernable rage. 2 A storm of anger; a fit of raving passion. 3 Violent action or agitation; impetuosity; fierceness; frenzy. 4 Intense passion of any kind; inspiration; enthusiasm. 5 A person of violent temper, especially a turbulent woman; termagant. See synonyms under ANGER, FRENZY, VIOLENCE. [<L *furia* <*furere* rave]
furze (fûrz) *n.* A spiny evergreen shrub (*Ulex europaeus*) of the bean family, having many branches and yellow flowers: also called *gorse, whin.* [OE *fyrs*] — **furz′y** *adj.*
fu·sain (fyo͞o·zān′, *Fr.* fü·zaṅ′) *n.* 1 A crayon of fine charcoal, or a drawing made with it. 2 One of the constituents of bituminous coal, consisting of patches and wedges of fibrous strands; mineral charcoal. [<F, spindle tree <L *fusus* spindle]
Fu·san (fo͞o·sän) Japanese name for PUSAN.
fus·cous (fus′kəs) *adj.* Grayish-brown or tawny; dusky. [<L *fuscus* dusky]
fuse[1] (fyo͞oz) *n.* 1 *Electr.* A protective device of fusible metal set in a circuit so as to be directly heated and destroyed by the passage of an excess current through it. 2 A textile cord, ribbon, or the like impregnated with combustible material for communicating fire to explosives, as in mining, blasting, and pyrotechnics; black match: distinguished from *fuze.* [<Ital. *fuso* <L *fusus* a spindle]
fuse[2] (fyo͞oz) *v.t.* & *v.i.* **fused, fus·ing** 1 To liquefy by heat; melt. 2 To join or cause to join as if by melting together. See synonyms under MELT, MIX, UNITE. [<L *fusus,* pp. of *fundere* pour]
fu·see (fyo͞o·zē′) *n.* 1 A wooden match having a bulb of inflammable material at its end and not extinguishable by wind. 2 A flare used as a railroad signal. 3 *Mech.* A spirally grooved cone, as in a watch or a spring clock, about which is wrapped a chain or cord, which is also wound about a cylindrical barrel containing or driven by a spiral spring. Its use is to give the spring increasing leverage as its power lessens by unwinding. Also spelled *fuzee.* [<F *fusée* <Med. L *fusata* <L *fusus* spindle]
fu·se·lage (fyo͞o′sə·lij, -läzh, -zə-) *n. Aeron.* The main structural framework of an airplane which supports the power plant, cockpit, fuel container, wings, cargo, crew and passenger space, etc. See illustration under AIRPLANE. [<F, ult. <L *fusus* a spindle]
fu·sel oil (fyo͞o′zəl, -səl) A volatile, poisonous, oily liquid, consisting largely of amyl alcohol, and having a disagreeable odor and taste, obtained when corn, potato, or grape spirits are rectified: used as a solvent in various chemical processes. Also **fu′sel.** [<G *fusel* inferior spirits]
Fu·shih (fo͞o′shir′) See YENAN.
Fu·shun (fo͞o′sho͞on′) A city in south central Manchuria, near Mukden.
fu·si·bil·i·ty (fyo͞o′zə·bil′ə·tē) *n.* Quality of being fusible, or the degree of this quality.
fu·si·ble (fyo͞o′zə·bəl) *adj.* Capable of being fused or melted by heat. — **fu′si·ble·ness** *n.* — **fu′si·bly** *adv.*
fusible metal Any alloy, as one containing bismuth, which melts at a comparatively low temperature. Also **fusible alloy.**
fu·si·form (fyo͞o′zə·fôrm) *adj.* Tapering from the middle toward each end; spindle-shaped. [<L *fusus* spindle + -FORM]
fu·sil (fyo͞o′zəl) *n.* A flintlock musket: also spelled *fuzil.* [<F <OF *foisil* a steel for striking sparks, ult. <L *focus* a hearth]
fu·sile (fyo͞o′zəl, -səl, -sīl) *adj.* 1 Made by melting or casting. 2 *Obs.* Capable of being fused. [<L *fusilis* <*fundere* pour]

fu·si·liers (fyōō′zə·lirz′) *n. pl.* A title borne by certain British infantry regiments: from soldiers who formerly carried fusils. Also **fu′si·leers′.**

fu·sil·lade (fyōō′zə·lād′) *n.* A simultaneous discharge of firearms. —*v.t.* **·lad·ed, ·lad·ing** To attack or kill by a fusillade. Also **fu′si·lade′.** [<F <*fusiller* shoot <*fusil* a musket]

fu·sion (fyōō′zhən) *n.* **1** The act of blending, or the state of being blended throughout. **2** The act of coalescing of two political parties, or the state of coalescence: also used attributively: a *fusion* ticket. **3** The act or process of changing, or the state of being in the course of change, from a solid into a liquid by the agency of heat; melting. **4** A state of fluidity due to the action of heat. **5** *Physics* A thermonuclear reaction in which the nuclei of a light element undergo transformation into those of a heavier element, with the release of great energy: the reverse of *fission.* **6** *Ling.* A coalescing of two originally distinct words because of a similarity in form and meaning, as in the development of the verb *bid* from the Old English verbs *biddan* "ask" and *bēodan* "command." See synonyms under ALLIANCE. [<L *fusio, -onis* <*fundere* pour]

fu·sion·ism (fyōō′zhən·iz′əm) *n.* The doctrine, advocacy, or practice of fusion in politics. —**fu′sion·ist** *n.*

fusion welding A process of joining metal parts by applying high temperatures to the contact surfaces, thus bonding them together without the use of rivets or other mechanical means.

fuss (fus) *n.* **1** Disturbance about trivial matters; trouble; ado. **2** One who worries about trifles: also **fuss′er.** See synonyms under QUARREL. —*v.i.* To make a fuss or bustle over trifles. —*v.t.* To bother or perplex with trifles. [Origin unknown]

fuss–budg·et (fus′buj′it) *n. Colloq.* A nervous, fussy person.

fuss·y (fus′ē) *adj.* **fuss·i·er, fuss·i·est 1** Inclined to fuss; fidgety; fretful. **2** Troublesome to do or make. —**fuss′i·ly** *adv.* —**fuss′i·ness** *n.*

fust (fust) *n. Obs.* A musty, rank smell. —*v.i.* To become musty or moldy in taste or smell. [<OF *fust* cask]

fus·ta·nel·la (fus′tə·nel′ə) *n.* A short white skirt worn by men in modern Greece. Also **fus′ta·nelle′** (-nel′). [<Ital.]

fus·tian (fus′chən) *n.* **1** Formerly, a kind of stout cloth made of cotton and flax; now, a coarse, twilled cotton fabric, such as corduroy or velveteen. **2** Pretentious verbiage; bombast. —*adj.* **1** Made of fustian. **2** Pompous, bombastic. [<OF *fustaine* <Med. L *(pannus) fustaneus* (<L *fustis* a cudgel), trans. of Gk. *xylinon* wooden <*xylon* wood]

fus·tic (fus′tik) *n.* **1** The wood of a tropical tree *(Chlorophora tinctoria)* used as a yellow dyestuff; yellow wood. **2** Any of several other woods used for dyeing. [<F *fustoc* <Sp. < Arabic *fustug,* prob. <Gk. *pistakē* pistachio]

fus·ti·gate (fus′tə·gāt) *v.t.* **·gat·ed,·gat·ing** To beat with a stick; cudgel: now in humorous use. [<L *fustigatus,* pp. of *fustigare* <*fustis* club + *agere* do, drive] —**fus′ti·ga′tion** *n.*

fus·tin (fus′tin) *n.* **1** The coloring matter of fustic and sumac. **2** *Chem.* A glucoside, $C_{36}H_{26}O_{14}$, from the wood of the smoke tree. [<FUST(IC) + -IN]

fust·y (fus′tē) *adj.* **fust·i·er, fust·i·est 1** Musty; moldy; rank. **2** Old–fashioned; fogeyish. —**fust′i·ly** *adv.* —**fust′i·ness** *n.*

fu·thark (fōō′thärk) *n.* The runic alphabet. Also **fu′tharc, fu′thorc** (-thôrk), **fu′thork.** [from the first six letters, *f, u, þ (th), a* (or *o*), *r, c*]

fu·tile (fyōō′təl, -til; *Brit.* -tīl) *adj.* **1** Of no avail; done in vain; useless. **2** Frivolous; trivial: *futile* chatter. See synonyms under USELESS, VAIN. [<F <L *futilis* pouring out easily, useless] —**fu′tile·ly** *adv.* —**fu′tile·ness** *n.*

fu·til·i·tar·i·an (fyoo·til′ə·târ′ē·ən) *adj.* Convinced of the futility of human enterprise. —*n.* One so convinced.

fu·til·i·ty (fyōō·til′ə·tē) *n. pl.* **·ties 1** The quality of being ineffective or useless. **2** Unimportance; triviality. **3** A futile act, event, thing, etc.

fut·tock (fut′ək) *n. Naut.* One of the curved or crooked timbers in the built–up rib or frame of a wooden ship. [? Alter, of FOOT HOOK]

futtock shrouds *Naut.* Shrouds extending from the outer extremities of the crosstrees to a band in the mast below.

Fu·tu·na (fōō·tōō′nə) See WALLIS AND FUTUNA ISLANDS.

fu·tur·al (fyōō′chər·əl) *adj.* Of or pertaining to the future or futures.

fu·ture (fyōō′chər) *n.* **1** The time yet to come. **2** Prospects or outlook. **3** Any security sold or bought upon agreement for future delivery: usually plural: to deal in *futures.* **4** *Gram.* **a** A verb tense denoting action that will take place at some time to come. **b** A verb in this tense. —*adj.* **1** Such as will or may be hereafter. **2** Pertaining to or expressing time to come. **3** Pertaining to the state of the soul after death: the *future* life. [<OF *futur* <L *futurus,* future participle of *esse* be]

fu·ture·less (fyōō′chər·lis) *adj.* Having or knowing no future; lacking foresight or forethought.

future life Spiritual existence after death.

future perfect *Gram.* The verb tense expressing an action completed before a specified future time. Example: He *will have finished* by tomorrow.

future shock A state of stress and disorientation brought on by a quick succession of changes, esp. in new standards of behavior and values.

fu·tur·ism (fyōō′chə·riz′əm) *n.* A movement in art, music, and literature originating in Italy in 1910, and aiming at originality, intensity, and force unhampered by tradition. —**fu′·tur·ist** *n.*

fu·tu·ri·ty (fyōō·tŏŏr′ə·tē, -tyŏŏr′-) *n. pl.* **·ties 1** Time to come; the future. **2** The state of being future. **3** The people of the future. **4** A future possibility **5** A futurity race.

futurity race *U.S.* A horse race for which entry nominations long precede the running.

futurity stakes *U.S.* Stakes to be raced for, long after the entries or nominations are made.

fuze (fyōōz) *n.* A mechanical or electrical device that initiates the explosive charge of a shell, bomb, grenade, etc.: distinguished from *fuse* (def. 2). —**all–ways fuze** A fuze, used especially on mortar shells, which detonates the explosive charge on contact, regardless of the position of the projectile. —**non–delay fuze** A fuze which detonates on impact. [Var. of FUSE[1]]

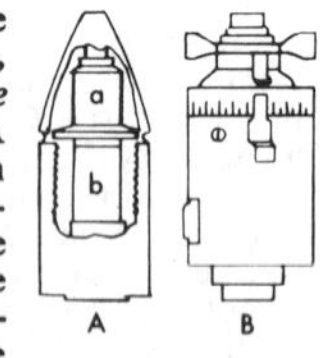

FUZES
A. Artillery VT (proximity) fuze: *a.* Radio unit. *b.* Battery.
B. Aerial bomb time fuze.

fu·zee (fyōō·zē′) See FUSEE.

fu·zil (fyōō′zəl) See FUSIL.

fuzz (fuz) *n.* **1** Loose, light, or fluffy matter. **2** A mass or coating of such matter. **3** *Slang* A policeman or the police. —*v.t.* & *v.i.* To cover or become covered with fuzz. [Origin unknown]

fuzz·y (fuz′ē) *adj.* **fuzz·i·er, fuzz·i·est 1** Covered with fuzz. **2** Lacking sharpness: said of motion–picture sound track on visual inspection. **3** Having distorted sound: said of recorded music, especially of high frequencies. —**fuzz′i·ly** *adv.* —**fuzz′i·ness** *n.*

-fy *suffix of verbs* **1** Make; form into: *deify.* **2** Cause to be; become: *liquefy.* [<OF *-fier* < L *-ficare* <*facere* do, make]

fyke[1] (fīk) *Scot. n.* **1** Uneasiness; fidgetiness; fidget. **2** Fussy, unnecessary, or annoying exactness, or any crotchety peculiarity. —*v.t.* & *v.i.* To fidget. Also spelled *fike.*

fyke[2] (fīk) *n.* A fish trap consisting of several successive conical nets with wide–stretched mouths; a bag net; bow net. Also **fyke net.** [<Du. *fuik* bow net]

fyl·fot (fil′fot) *n.* The swastika. [<FILL, *v.* + FOOT; so called because used to fill in the foot or base of stained glass windows]

Fyn (fün) A Danish island in the Baltic Sea; 1,149 square miles: German *Fünen.* Also **Fyen.**

fyrd (fûrd, fird) *n.* An army or military force in England before the Norman conquest. [OE]

Fy·za·bad (fī′zä·bäd) A former spelling of FAIZABAD.

G

g, G (jē) *n. pl.* **g's, G's** or **gs, Gs, gees** (jēz) **1** The seventh letter of the English alphabet: from Phoenician *gimel,* through Greek *gamma,* Roman *G.* **2** A sound of the letter *g.* See ALPHABET. —*symbol* **1** *Music* **a** The fifth, or dominant, tone in the scale of C major. **b** The pitch of this tone. **c** A printed or written note representing it. **d** A scale built upon G. **e** The treble clef. **2** *Physics* The acceleration of a body due to gravity, about 32 feet per second per second: written in lower case.

G–1, G–2, G–3 See under GENERAL STAFF.

gab[1] (gab) *n. Colloq.* Idle talk; loquacity. —*v.i.* **gabbed, gab·bing** To talk much or idly; chatter. [Prob. <ON *gabba* mock]

gab[2] (gab) *n. Mech.* A hook, as on a rod conveying the motion of an eccentric. For illustration see ECCENTRIC. [Cf. Flemish *gabbe* a notch]

gab[3] (gab, gäb) *n. Scot.* The mouth.

gab·ar·dine (gab′ər·dēn, gab′ər·dēn′) *n.* **1** A firm, twilled, worsted fabric, having a diagonal raised weave, used for coats, suits, etc. **2** A similar, softer fabric of mercerized cotton. **3** A gaberdine. [Var. of GABERDINE]

gab·bart (gab′ərt) *n. Scot.* A vessel used for inland trade; a lighter. Also **gab′bard** (-ərd).

gab·ble (gab′əl) *v.* **·bled, ·bling** *v.i.* **1** To talk rapidly and incoherently; babble. **2** To utter rapid, cackling sounds, as geese. —*v.t.* **3** To utter rapidly and incoherently. —*n.* **1** Noisy and incoherent or foolish talk. **2** Cackling, as of geese. See synonyms under BABBLE. [Freq. of GAB[1]] —**gab′bler** *n.*

gab·bro (gab′rō) *n. pl.* **·bros** *Geol.* Any of a class of igneous rocks of granular texture, consisting essentially of pyroxene, usually augite or diallage, and plagioclase. [<Ital.] —**gab′broid** *adj.*

gab·by (gab′ē) *adj. Colloq.* **·bi·er, ·bi·est** Given to talk; loquacious.

ga·belle (gə·bel′) *n.* In old English and French law, a tax, excise, impost, or duty; specifically, in French history, a tax on salt, abolished in 1790. Also **ga·bel′.** [<F <Med. L *gabella* < *gablum* tax <Gmc.] —**ga·belled′** *adj.*

gab·er·dine (gab′ər·dēn, gab′ər·dēn′) *n.* **1** A loose, coarse coat or frock. **2** A long, loose, coarse cloak worn by Jews in medieval times. **3** Gabardine. [<Sp. *garbardina* <MHG *wallevart* a pilgrimage]

gab·er·lun·yie (gäb′ər·lün′yē,-lōōn′-) *n. Scot.* A beggar who carries a bag or pouch; a mendicant. Also **gab′er·lun′zie** (-lun′zē).

Ga·bès (gä′bes) A port on the **Gulf of Gabès** (ancient *Syrtis Minor*), an inlet of the Mediterranean on the SE coast of Tunisia.

gab·fest (gab′fest) *n. Slang* A "feast" of talking; prolonged empty talk; also, an occasion marked by prolonged talking. [<GAB[1] + G *fest* feast]

ga·bi·on (gā′bē·ən) *n.* A bottomless wicker

basket or cylinder, to be stuffed with sand or earth to form a fortification, foundation, etc. [< F < Ital. *gabbione,* aug. of *gabbia* a cage < L *cavea* cage] **—ga·bi·oned** *adj.*

ga·bi·on·ade (gā′bē·ən·ād′) *n.* A defensive work formed principally of gabions. Also **ga′bi·on·nade′.**

ga·ble (gā′bəl) *n. Archit.* **1** The upper part of an end wall, above the level of the eaves, beneath the end of a ridge roof that is not hipped or returned on itself: commonly triangular. **2** The entire end wall of a building; a gable end. —*v.t.* & *v.i.* **ga·bled, ga·bling** To build or be built with gables; form or end in gables. [< OF, prob. < ON *gafl* gable] **—ga′bled** *adj.*

GABLES

gable end *Archit.* The triangular wall between the eaves and the apex of the roof on the end of a building having a gable.

gable roof A ridge roof terminating in a gable at each end.

gable window A window in a gable, or one having a gable top.

Ga·bon (gȧ·bôṅ) An estuary tributary to the Gulf of Guinea in western Gabon; 40 miles long.

Gabon Republic An independent republic of the French Community on the west coast of equatorial Africa; 102,290 square miles; capital, Libreville; formerly a French overseas territory. Also **Ga·boon** (gə·bōōn′), **Ga·bun′.** **—Ga′bon·ese′** (-nēz, -nēs) *adj.* & *n.*

Ga·bo·riau (gȧ·bô·ryō′), **Emile,** 1835–73, French novelist.

Ga·bri·el (gā′brē·əl, *Fr.* gȧ·brē·el′; *Ger., Sw.* gä′brē·äl; *Pg., Sp.* gä′brē·äl′) A masculine personal name. Also *Ital.* **Ga·bri·el·lo** (gä′·brē·el′lō). [< Hebrew, hero of God]

—Gabriel In the Bible, an archangel, appearing as the messenger of God. *Dan.* viii 16, *Luke* i 26.

ga·bri·elle (gā′brē·el′) *n.* A flowing house dress of flimsy material. [from a proper name]

Ga·bri·lo·witsch (gä′vri·lô′vich), **Ossip,** 1878–1936, Russian pianist and conductor.

gad[1] (gad) *v.i.* **gad·ded, gad·ding** To roam abroad idly; ramble; stray. —*n.* The act of gadding. [? Back formation from obs. *gadling* vagabond] **—gad′der** *n.*

gad[2] (gad) *n.* **1** A punch or metal-pointed tool for breaking up ore or rock; also, a percussion drill. **2** A goad for driving cattle; any small rod or switch. **3** A large nail, spike, or wedge. —*v.t.* **gad·ded, gad·ding 1** To break up with a gad. **2** To use a gad or rod upon. [< ON *gaddr* goad, spike]

Gad (gad) *interj.* & *n. Archaic* God: a variant form used euphemistically in oaths.

Gad (gad) In the Bible, Jacob's seventh son; also, the tribe descended from him, or its territory east of Jordan. *Gen.* xxx 11.

gad·a·bout (gad′ə·bout′) *n.* One who gads habitually. —*adj.* Fond of gadding.

Gad·a·ra (gad′ə·rə) An ancient city of Palestine SE of the Sea of Galilee. **—Gad·a·rene** (gad′·ə·rēn, gad′ə·rēn′) *adj.* & *n.*

gad·bee (gad′bē′) *n.* A gadfly.

Ga·del·ic (gə·del′ik, -dē′lik) See GOIDELIC.

gad·fly (gad′flī′) *n. pl.* **·flies 1** A large fly (family *Tabanidae*) that torments cattle and horses. **2** A botfly or warblefly. **3** A restless, annoying busybody. [< GAD[2] + FLY]

gadg·et (gaj′it) *n.* **1** Any small mechanical device or contrivance, especially one of which the name cannot be recalled. **2** In glassmaking, a tool for grasping a piece of ware in the course of treatment. [Origin uncertain]

gadg·e·teer (gaj′ə·tir′) *n.* A habitual user or contriver of gadgets.

gadg·et·ry (gaj′ət·rē) *n.* **1** The devising of gadgets. **2** Gadgets collectively.

Gadhel (gāl) See GAEL.

ga·doid (gā′doid) *adj.* Of or pertaining to a large family *(Gadidae)* of chiefly marine fishes with soft fins, somewhat elongated bodies, large mouths, and wide gill openings. The family includes the codfish, hake, and haddock. —*n.* One of the *Gadidae.* Also **ga′did.** [< NL *gadus* codfish < Gk. *gados,* a kind of fish + -OID]

gad·o·lin·ite (gad′ə·lin·īt′) *n.* A black, vitreous silicate ore which yields gadolinium and other rare-earth elements.

gad·o·lin·i·um (gad′ə·lin′ē·əm) *n.* A metallic element (symbol Gd, atomic number 64) of the lanthanide series, having six naturally occurring stable isotopes and one weakly radioactive isotope. See PERIODIC TABLE. [after John *Gadolin,* 1760–1852, Finnish chemist]

ga·droon (gə·drōōn′) See GODROON.

Gads·den (gadz′dən), **James,** 1788–1858, U.S. soldier and diplomat; by treaty with Mexico, 1853, secured for the United States a tract (45,535 square miles) known as the **Gadsden Purchase,** now part of Arizona and New Mexico.

gad·wall (gad′wôl) *n. pl.* **·walls** or **·wall** A large fresh-water duck *(Chaulelasmus streperus)* of the northern hemisphere, with black and white markings and numerous fine lamellae on the bill: highly esteemed as game. [Origin unknown]

gae[1] (gā) *v.i. Scot.* **gaed, gaen, gae·ing** To go: also spelled *gay.*

gae[2] (gā) *Scot.* Past tense of GIVE.

Gae·a (jē′ə) In Greek mythology, the goddess of earth, mother and wife of Uranus, and mother of the Titans, etc.: identified with the Roman *Tellus*: also called *Gaia, Ge.* Also **Gæ′a.** [< Gk. *Gaia* Earth]

Gae·dhel·ic (gə·del′ik, -dē′lik) See GOIDELIC.

Gaek·war (gīk′wär, jēk′-) *n.* Title of the native ruler of Baroda, India: also spelled *Gaikwar, Guicowar.* [< Marathi *Gāekvād,* a family name; lit., cowherd]

Gael (gāl) *n.* One of the Celtic people of Ireland, the Scottish Highlands, and the Isle of Man: also spelled *Gadhel.* [< Scottish Gaelic *Gaidheal*]

Gael·ic (gā′lik) *adj.* Belonging or relating to the Celtic Gaels, or to their languages. —*n.* **1** The languages of the Gaels; namely, Irish *(Irish Gaelic),* Manx, and, specifically, the speech of the Scottish Highlanders *(Scottish Gaelic).* **2** The Goidelic branch of the Celtic languages.

gaet (gāt) *n. Scot.* Manner; way; gait: also spelled *gait.*

gaff[1] (gaf) *n.* **1** A sharp iron hook at the end of a pole, for landing a large fish. **2** *Naut.* A spar for extending the upper edge of a fore-and-aft sail. **3** A gamecock's steel spur. —*v.t.* **1** To strike or land with a gaff: to *gaff* a sailfish. **2** *Brit. Slang* To trick; cheat. **—to stand the gaff** *U.S. Colloq.* To endure hardship, ridicule, or pain without complaining or quitting; be game. [< OF *gaffe,* prob. < Celtic]

gaff[2] (gaf) *n.* **1** Loud, rude talk; raillery. **2** An outburst of laughter; a guffaw. [Cf. OE *gafspræc* ribald talk]

gaff[3] (gaf) *n. Brit. Slang* A cheap theater or low-priced place of amusement. [Origin unknown]

gaffe (gȧf) *n. French Colloq.* A clumsy mistake; a blunder; faux pas.

gaf·fer (gaf′ər) *n.* **1** An old man: correlative of *gammer;* an aged rustic: now contemptuous. **2** *Brit.* A foreman of laborers. **3** *U.S. Slang* The chief electrician in a motion-picture studio. [Alter. of GODFATHER]

gaff-headed (gaf′hed′id) *adj. Naut.* Having a gaff rig.

gaff rig *Naut.* A type of rig consisting of a fore-and-aft sail with the head supported by a gaff. **—gaff′-rigged′** *adj.*

gaff-top·sail (gaf top′səl, -sāl) *n. Naut.* A light sail set above a gaff and having its foot extended thereby.

Gaf·sa (gaf′sə) A town in south central Tunisia; site of prehistoric discoveries; scene of first engagement (February, 1943) between American and German forces in the Tunisian campaign of World War II: ancient *Capsa.*

gag (gag) *n.* **1** Any appliance for completely obstructing the vocal organs or restraining speech; hence, any restraint upon free speech or discussion. **2** Something nauseating. **3** An instrument for holding open the jaws during an operation. **4** An interpolation by an actor in a play; a joke, humorous remark, story, etc.; also, a practical joke. [< *v.*] **—to pull a gag** *U.S. Slang* To perpetrate a hoax; tell an untrue story in a playful spirit. —*v.* **gagged, gag·ging** *v.t.* **1** To keep from speaking or crying out by means of a gag. **2** To keep from speaking or discussing freely, as by force or authority: to *gag* the press. **3** To cause nausea in; cause to retch. **4** *Surg.* To hold open (the mouth) with a gag. **5** *Slang* To make fun of; hoax. **6** *Slang* To introduce one's own words or speeches into (a theatrical role): often with *up.* —*v.i.* **7** To heave with nausea; retch. **8** *Slang* To make jokes or speeches of an improvised nature. [ME *gaggen;* prob. imit.]

ga·ga (gä′gä′) *adj. Slang* Foolish; crazy. [< F (slang), a foolish old man]

Ga·ga·rin (gä·gä′rēn), **Yuri Alekseyevitch,** 1934–1968, U.S.S.R. air force officer; first astronaut to make a successful space flight and first man to orbit the earth, April 12, 1961.

gage[1] (gāj) *v.t.* **gaged, gag·ing 1** To determine the dimensions, amount, force, etc., of by means of a gage. **2** To determine the contents or capacity of, as a cask. **3** To estimate; appraise or judge. **4** To cut or rub (stones or bricks) to uniform size. **5** To mix (plaster) in the right proportions so as to dry in a desired time. —*n.* **1** An instrument for measuring, indicating, or regulating the capacity, quantity, dimensions, power, amount, proportions, etc., of anything. **2** A standard of comparison: the *gage* of the boiler; and, figuratively: the *gage* of his genius. **3** A standard measurement, dimension, quantity, or amount. **4** The distance between rails or between wheel treads, as in a railway. See the adjectives BROAD-GAGE, NARROW-GAGE, and STANDARD-GAGE. **5** The exposed length of a tile, slate, or shingle. **6** The amount of gypsum added to lime plaster to hasten its setting. **7** The composition of plaster of Paris and other substances used in making moldings, decorations, etc. **8** The diameter of the bore of a gun. **9** *Printing* A strip of metal or other material by which the exact space occupied by type of a certain kind, or the length of a page, or the width of a margin, is determined. **10** *Naut.* **a** The position of a vessel with regard to the wind and to another vessel. When to windward of another vessel, a ship is said to have the *weather gage;* when to leeward, the *lee gage.* **b** The draft of a vessel. **11** A measurement standard indicating relative fineness of hose, as determined by the number of needles used per inch. Also spelled *gauge.* [< OF *gauger* measure]

gage[2] (gāj) *v.t.* **gaged, gag·ing** *Archaic* **1** To bind or pledge as a guaranty or forfeit. **2** To wager; stake. —*n.* Something given or thrown down as security for some act, as a gauntlet in token of readiness for combat; a pledge. See synonyms under SECURITY. [< OF *gager* < *gage* a pledge < Gmc. Doublet of WAGE.]

gage[3] (gāj) *n.* One of several varieties of plum, as the *greengage.* [after Sir William *Gage,* 1777–1864, who introduced it into England]

Gage (gāj), **Thomas,** 1721–87, British general and administrator; commanded the British army at Bunker Hill in the Revolutionary War.

gage d'a·mour (gäzh dȧ·mōōr′) *French* Pledge of love.

gag·er (gā′jər) *n.* **1** One who gages. **2** An officer of the revenue service who measures the contents of casks, etc. Also spelled *gauger.*

gag·ger (gag′ər) *n.* **1** One who gags. **2** A piece of iron used to keep a core in its place in a mold.

gag·gle (gag′əl) *v.i.* **gag·gled, gag·gling** To utter the cackle of the goose; gabble. —*n.* **1** A flock of geese. **2** A group, as of talkative women. **3** A cackle. [Imit.]

gag·man (gag′man′) *n. pl.* **·men** (-men′) A professional humorist; one employed to write humorous lines and sketches for stage, screen, radio, etc.

gag rule A rule of parliamentary procedure limiting speech or discussion; especially, a rule adopted by the U.S. Congress in 1836 tabling all matters relating to slavery.

gahn·ite (gän′īt) *n.* A zinc aluminate, subtranslucent to opaque and varying in color from green to black and brown, crystallizing in the isometric system. [after J. G. *Gahn,* 1745–1818, Swedish chemist]

Gai·a (gā′ə, gī′ə) See GAEA.

gai·e·ty (gā′ə·tē) *n. pl.* **·ties 1** The state of being gay; merriment; fun: often used in the plural. **2** Gay appearance; finery; show: *gaiety* of attire. Also spelled *gayety.* See synonyms under FROLIC, HAPPINESS, SPORT. [< F *gaieté* < *gai.* See GAY.]

Gaik·war (gīk′wär) See GAEKWAR.

Gail·lard Cut (gā′lärd, gil·yärd′) A passage about 10 miles from the city of Panama, made in constructing the Panama Canal; 8 miles long, 300 feet wide at the bottom, 45 feet deep: formerly *Culebra Cut.* [after David DuB. *Gaillard,* 1859–1913, American army engineer]

gail·lar·di·a (gā·lär′dē·ə) *n.* Any plant of a genus *(Gaillardia)* of western American herbs of the composite family with alternate resinous dotted leaves and large shiny terminal heads of fragrant yellow or reddish-purple flowers. [after *Gaillard* de Charentonneau, French botanist]

gai·ly (gā′lē) *adv.* In a gay manner; joyously; merrily; showily: also spelled *gayly.*

gain[1] (gān) *v.t.* **1** To obtain by or as by effort; earn. **2** To get in competition; win. **3** To reach; arrive at. **4** To get or undergo as an increase, profit, addition, etc.: to *gain* interest or weight. **5** To get the friendship or support of; win over. —*v.i.* **6** To make progress; increase; improve. **7** To draw nearer or farther away: He *gained* on me steadily. —*n.* **1** That which is obtained as an advantage; a desired acquisition; commercial profit. **2** Amount of increase; accession. **3** The pursuit or the acquisition of riches. **4** *Electronics* The ratio of output to input in a sound-transmitting circuit. See synonyms under PROFIT. [< F *gagner* < OF *gaaignier* < Gmc.]

Synonyms (verb): achieve, acquire, attain, conquer, earn, flourish, get, learn, master, obtain, procure, realize, reap, win. See ACHIEVE, FLOURISH, GET, OBTAIN, REACH. *Antonyms*: forfeit, lose, miss, surrender.

gain[2] (gān) *n.* **1** A groove across a board or plank; a cut to receive a timber, as a girder. **2** A beveled shoulder in a binding joist. —*v.t.* To fasten with notches or gains, or cut gains in, as floor timbers. [Origin uncertain]

gain·er (gā′nər) *n.* **1** One who gains profit or advantage for himself. **2** A fancy dive, consisting of a back somersault from a front-diving take-off.

gain·ful (gān′fəl) *adj.* Yielding profit; lucrative. **—gain′ful·ly** *adv.* **—gain′ful·ness** *n.*

gain·giv·ing (gān′giv′ing) *n. Obs.* Uncertainty of mind; misgiving.

gain·less (gān′lis) *adj.* Profitless. **—gain′·less·ness** *n.*

gain·ly (gān′lē) *adj. Obs.* **1** Well built; comely; graceful. **2** Convenient. [< obs. *gain* fit, favorable (< ON *gegn*) + -LY] **—gain′li·ness** *n.*

gain·say (gān′sā′) *v.t.* **gain·said, gain·say·ing 1** To deny. **2** To contradict; controvert. **3** To speak or act against; oppose. —*n. Rare* A contradiction. [OE *gegn-* against + SAY[2]] **—gain′say′er** *n.*

Gains·bor·ough (gānz′bûr·ō), **Thomas,** 1727–1788, English painter.

'gainst (genst) *prep.* Against: an abbreviated form.

gair (gâr) *n. Scot.* A gore, as in a field. See GORE[2] (def. 1).

gair·ish (gâr′ish), **gair·ish·ly,** etc. See GARISH, etc.

gaist (gāst) *n. Scot.* A ghost.

gait (gāt) *n.* **1** The manner of walking or stepping; carriage of the body in going; walk. **2** The movement of a horse's feet in going, as the canter, pace, trot, run, single-foot, etc. —*v.t.* **1** To train to or cause to take a particular gait: to *gait* a horse. **2** To put in working order; set up: to *gait* a loom. ◆Homophone: *gate.* [< ON *gata* way]

gait·ed (gā′tid) *adj.* Having a (particular) gait.

gai·ter (gā′tər) *n.* **1** A covering for the lower leg or ankle, fastened at the side and usually strapped under the foot. **2** A shoe covering the ankle and having no opening in front and usually elastic sides. **3** An overshoe with a cloth top. [< F *guêtre*]

gaiting pole A device for keeping a horse straight in the shafts of a racing sulky; a pole on which a roller is mounted which rubs against the horse when he swerves.

Ga·ius (gā′əs, gī′-) A Roman praenomen: also *Caius.*

—Gaius Roman jurist of the second century A.D.

gal (gal) *n. U.S. Colloq.* A girl.

ga·la (gā′lə, gal′ə, gä′lə) *n.* A festivity; show. —*adj.* Festive; appropriate for a festive occasion. [< F < Ital., holiday dress]

ga·lac·ta·gog (gə·lak′tə·gôg, -gog) *adj.* Promotive of the flow of milk. —*n.* Any medicine promoting the secretion of milk. Also **ga·lac′·ta·gogue, ga·lac′to·gogue.** [< GALACT(O)- + Gk. *agōgos* producing]

ga·lac·tan (gə·lak′tən) *n. Biochem.* A polymeric anhydride of galactose, found in gums, algae, lichens, agar, and in fruit pectins. [< GALACT(O)- + AN(HYDRIDE)]

ga·lac·tic (gə·lak′tik) *adj. Astron.* Pertaining to the Galaxy or Milky Way.

galactic circle *Astron.* The great circle passing centrally along the Milky Way.

galactic latitude *Astron.* The angular distance of a celestial body from the galactic plane.

galactic plane The plane of the galactic circle.

galactic poles The poles of the galactic circle.

galacto- *combining form* Milk; milky: *galactopoietic.* Also, before vowels, **galact-.** [< Gk. *gala, galaktos* milk]

ga·lac·to·cele (gə·lak′tə·sēl) *n. Pathol.* A tumor of the female breast caused by blockage of a milk duct.

ga·lac·to·lip·in (gə·lak′tō·lip′in) See CEREBROSIDE.

gal·ac·tom·e·ter (gal′ək·tom′ə·tər) *n.* A lactometer.

ga·lac·to·poi·et·ic (gə·lak′tō·poi·et′ik) *adj.* Promoting the secretion of milk. [< GALACTO- + Gk. *poiētikos* capable of making]

ga·lac·to·scope (gə·lak′tə·skōp) *n.* An instrument for testing milk for butterfat content.

ga·lac·tose (gə·lak′tōs) *n. Chem.* A sweet crystalline glucose, $C_6H_{12}O_6$, the dextrorotatory form of which is obtained when milk sugar is treated with dilute acids.

ga·lac·to·se·mi·a (gə·lak′tə·sē′mē·ə) *n. Pathol.* A metabolic disease in which the body is unable to tolerate milk in any form because of the lack of an enzyme which converts galactose into glucose: often fatal in newborn children. [< GALACTOSE + -EMIA]

ga·lac·to·ther·a·py (gə·lak′tō·ther′ə·pē) *n.* Treatment of disease by means of milk.

gala day A holiday; festival.

gala dress Gay costume for gala days.

ga·la·go (gə·lā′gō) *n. pl.* **-gos** Bush baby.

Gal·a·had (gal′ə·had), **Sir** In Arthurian romance, the purest and noblest knight of the Round Table, son of Lancelot and Elaine.

gal·a·lith (gal′ə·lith) *n.* A hard, thermoplastic casein plastic, available in colors, used to make buttons, clips, etc., and for trimming apparel and accessories. Also called *milkstone.* [< Gk. *gala* milk + *lithos* stone]

ga·lan·gal (gə·lang′gəl) *n.* The aromatic rootstocks of various East Indian herbs (genus *Alpinia)* of the ginger family: also spelled *galingale.* [< OF *galingal* < Arabic *khalanjān* < Chinese *Ko-liang-kiang* mild ginger from the province Ko]

gal·an·tine (gal′ən·tēn) *n.* A cold preparation of boned, stuffed, and seasoned chicken, veal, etc., served in its own jelly. [< F]

ga·lan·ty show (gə·lan′tē) A shadow pantomime in miniature, the shadows being cast by figures cut from paper. [Prob. < Ital. *galante* gallant]

Ga·lá·pa·gos Islands (gä·lä′pä·gōs) An Ecuadorian island group 600 miles west of Ecuador; 3,028 square miles: officially *Colón Archipelago.*

Gal·a·ta (gä′lä·tä) A commercial section of Istanbul on the north side of the Golden Horn; originally a Genoese settlement.

gal·a·te·a (gal′ə·tē′ə) *n.* A strong twill cotton fabric, white or striped, used in making women's and children's garments. [after the *Galatea,* a British warship]

Gal·a·te·a (gal′ə·tē′ə) In Greek mythology, an ivory statue of a maiden brought to life by Aphrodite after its sculptor Pygmalion had fallen in love with it.

Ga·la·ti (gä·läts′, -lä′tsē) A city in eastern Rumania on the Danube. Also **Ga·latz′.**

Ga·la·tia (gə·lā′shə, -shē·ə) An ancient country of central Asia Minor, so called from the Gauls who invaded and conquered the region in the third century B.C. *Greek* **Ga·la′tei·a.**

Ga·la·tian (gə·lā′shən) *adj.* Belonging or relating to the ancient Galatia: also **Ga·lat·ic** (gə·lat′ik) —*n.* A native of ancient Galatia. *Gal.* iii 1. — **Epistle to the Galatians** A letter written by the apostle Paul, about A.D. 56, to the Christians of Galatia, and included in the New Testament.

gal·a·vant (gal′ə·vant) See GALLIVANT.

ga·lax (gā′laks) *n.* A stemless evergreen herb *(Galax aphylla)* bearing a raceme of white flowers; its leaves are much used for funeral decoration. [< NL < Gk. *gala* milk]

gal·ax·y (gal′ək·sē) *n. pl.* **·ax·ies 1** *Astron.* Any of the very large systems of stars, nebulae, and other celestial bodies, comparable with but assumed to be independent of our own; an island universe. **2** Any brilliant group, as of persons. [< F *galaxie* < L *galaxias* the Milky Way < Gk. < *gala* milk]

Gal·ax·y (gal′ək·sē) *n. Astron.* The aggregate of all celestial bodies in the universe to which the sun belongs, including the luminous band of stars known as the Milky Way.

Gal·ba (gal′bə, gôl′-), **Servius Sulpicius,** 3 B.C.–A.D. 69, Roman emperor 68–69; killed by his soldiers.

gal·ba·num (gal′bə·nəm) *n.* A bitter and odorous gum resin obtained from certain umbelliferous herbs, especially the giant fennel: used as a stimulant, expectorant, and anti-spasmodic. [< L *galbanum* < Gk. *chalbanē* < Hebrew *ḥelbenah*]

gale[1] (gāl) *n.* **1** A strong wind less violent than a hurricane, but stronger than a stiff breeze (7–10 on the Beaufort scale). **2** In poetic usage, a breeze; zephyr. **3** Figuratively, a noisy outburst: *gales* of merriment. [Origin uncertain]

gale[2] (gāl) *n.* A branching, sweet-smelling marsh shrub (*Myrica gala*) of the eastern United States. See SWEETGALE. [OE *gagel*]

gale[3] (gāl) *n. Brit.* A payment, at certain stated intervals, such as rent, interest, etc. [Var. of GAVEL[3]]

Gale (gāl), **Zona,** 1874–1938, U.S. novelist and playwright.

ga·le·a (gā′lē·ə) *n. pl.* **·le·ae** (-li·ē) **1** *Entomol.* A helmetlike membrane attached to the maxillae of certain insects. **2** *Bot.* The upper sepal of the flower of monkshood. **3** *Anat.* A structure connecting the separate parts of one of the muscles of the scalp. **4** *Med.* A type of bandage for the head. [< L, helmet]

ga·le·ate (gā′lē·āt) *adj.* Covered with, wearing, or having a galea. Also **ga′le·at′ed.**

GALEATE SEPAL A monkshood flower showing galeate upper sepal *(a).*

ga·le·i·form (gā′lē·ə·fôrm) *adj.* Helmet-shaped; resembling a casque or helm. [< L *galea* helmet + *-i-* + -FORM]

Ga·len (gā′lən), **Claudius,** 130?–200?, Greek physician and writer on medicine. — **Ga·len·ic** (ga·len′ik, -le′·nik) or **·i·cal** *adj.*

ga·le·na (gə·lē′nə) *n.* A metallic, lead-gray, cleavable, isometric lead sulfide, PbS: an important ore of lead; lead glance. Also **ga·le·nite** (gə·lē′nīt). [< L, lead ore]

ga·len·i·cal (gə·len′i·kəl, -lē′·ni-) *n.* **1** A medicine or drug prepared in accordance with the principles of Galen. **2** A drug containing a standard proportion of naturally occurring organic substances as distinguished from chemical ingredients.

Ga·len·ism (gā′lən·iz′əm) *n.* The theory or practice of medicine followed by Galen. **—Ga′len·ist** *n.*

ga·le·o·pi·the·cus (gā′lē·ō·pi·thē′kəs) *n.* Any member of a genus *(Galeopithecus,* family *Galeopithecidae)* of insectivorous mammals, as the flying lemur. [< Gk. *galeē* weasel + *pithēkos* ape]

Ga·ler·as Volcano (gä·ler′äs) See PASTO VOLCANO.

gal·er·o·pi·a (gal′ə·rō′pē·ə) *n.* Abnormally clear vision and perception of objects. Also **gal′er·op′si·a** (-op′sē·ə) [< Gk. *galeros* cheerful + *ōps* eye]

Ga·li·bi (gä·lē′bē) *n.* A Carib Indian, especially of the tribes in the Guianas.

Ga·li·cia (gə·lish′ə) **1** (*Polish* gä·lē′tsē·ä) A region in SE Poland and NW Ukrainian S.S.R., formerly an Austrian crownland. **2** (*Sp.* gä·lē′thyä) A region and former kingdom in NW Spain.

Ga·li·cian (gə·lish′ən) *adj.* **1** Of or pertaining to Spanish Galicia, its people, or their language. **2** Of or pertaining to Polish Galicia or its native people. — *n.* **1** A native or inhabitant of Spanish Galicia. **2** The Portuguese dialect spoken in Spanish Galicia. **3** A native of Polish Galicia.

Gal·i·le·an (gal′ə·lē′ən) *adj.* Belonging or relating to Galilee. — *n.* **1** A native or inhabitant of Galilee. **2** A Christian: so called opprobriously in ancient times by the Jews. — **The Galilean** Jesus Christ. Also **Gal′i·lae′an.**

Gal·i·le·an (gal′ə·lē′ən) *adj.* Of or pertaining to Galileo.

Gal·i·lee (gal′ə·lē) A region in northern Palestine.

Galilee, Sea of A fresh-water lake in northern Palestine on the Israel-Jordan border, through which the river Jordan flows: Old Testament *Sea of Chinnereth*; New Testament *Sea of Gennesaret*: also *Lake Tiberias.*

Galilee porch A porch or chapel at the west end of some abbey churches. Also **Gal′i·lee.**

Gal·i·le·o (gal′ə·lē′ō), 1564–1642, Italian astronomer and founder of the science of mechanics; condemned by the Roman Inquisition: full name *Galileo Galilei.*

gal·i·ma·ti·as (gal′ə·mā′shē·əs, -mat′ē·əs) *n.* Confused or meaningless talk; gibberish. [<F]

gal·in·gale (gal′in·gāl) *n.* **1** A tall, perennial, and rare sedge *(Cyperus longus)* of southern England, with aromatic tuberous roots. **2** Galangal. [See GALANGAL]

gal·i·ot (gal′ē·ət) *n.* **1** A small galley propelled by sails and oars. **2** A one- or two-masted Dutch or Flemish merchant vessel. Also spelled *galliot.* [<OF, dim. of *galie* <Med. L *galea* a galley]

gal·i·pe·a (gal′ə·pē′ə) *n.* A tropical American shrub *(Galipea officinalis)* of the rutaceous family which yields angostura bark. [<NL]

gal·i·pot (gal′i·pot) *n.* The white turpentine resin formed on the bark of a pine *(Pinus pinaster)* of southern Europe: when refined it is called *white, yellow,* or *Burgundy pitch*: also spelled *gallipot.* [<F]

gall[1] (gôl) *n.* **1** *Physiol.* The bitter fluid secreted by the liver; bile. **2** Bitter feeling; malignity. **3** Any bitter and trying experience. **4** *Anat.* The sac containing the bile: also *gall bladder.* **5** *U.S. Slang* Cool impudence; effrontery. [OE *gealla*]

gall[2] (gôl) *n.* **1** An abrasion or excoriation, as by the friction of harness on a horse. **2** *Brit.* A blemish. **3** A locality made barren by exhaustion of the soil. **4** *U.S. Dial.* Low-lying wet land. **5** A person or thing that irritates or galls. — *v.t.* **1** To make sore or injure (the skin) by friction; chafe. **2** To vex or irritate. — *v.i.* **3** To be or become chafed or irritated. See synonyms under INCENSE. [Prob. <GALL[1]]

gall[3] (gôl) *n.* **1** An excrescence on plants, caused by insects, bacteria, or a parasitic fungus. The galls of commerce are produced by a gallfly which lays its eggs in the soft twigs of an oak *(Quercus lusitanica)* of western Asia and southern Europe. Galls contain tannin, and are used in inkmaking, dyeing, etc. **2** A similar excrescence on animals. [<F *galle* <L *galla* the gallnut]

Gal·la (gal′ə) *n.* **1** A member of a tribe of Hamitic origin inhabiting Ethiopia. **2** The language of this tribe.

gal·lant (gal′ənt) *adj.* **1** Possessing an intrepid spirit; brave; chivalrous. **2** Stately; imposing; noble. **3** Marked by showiness; gay: said chiefly of attire. **4** (gə·lant′, gal′ənt) Polite and attentive to women; courteous. See synonyms under BRAVE. — *n.* (gal′ənt, gə·lant′) **1** A man of gay and dashing manners; an intrepid youth. **2** A man who pays court to women; also, a man of fashion. — *v.t.* (gə·lant′) **1** To accompany (a woman); escort. **2** To court or dally with (a woman). — *v.i.* **3** To play the gallant. [<OF *galant,* ppr. of *galer* rejoice]

gal·lant·ly (gal′ənt·lē) *adv.* Bravely; politely.

gal·lant·ry (gal′ən·trē) *n. pl.* **·ries** **1** Courage; heroism; chivalrousness. **2** Polite or excessive attention to women. **3** A gallant act or polite speech. **4** The calling or manner of a gallant. **5** Gallants collectively. See synonyms under COURAGE, PROWESS.

gall-ap·ple (gôl′ap′əl) *n.* A gallnut.

Gal·la·tin (gal′ə·tin), **Albert,** 1761–1849, U. S. statesman and financier born in Switzerland.

Gal·la·tin Range (gal′ə·tin) A range of the Rockies in NW Wyoming and SW Montana; highest peak, 11,155 feet.

Gal·lau·det (gal′ə·det′), **Thomas Hopkins,** 1787–1851, U. S. teacher of the deaf and dumb.

gall·ber·ry (gôl′ber′ē) *n. pl.* **·ries** The inkberry.

gall bladder *Anat.* A small, pear-shaped muscular pouch situated beneath the liver in man and serving as a reservoir for bile conducted through the **gall duct.**

Galle (gäl) A port of SW Ceylon: formerly *Point de Galle.*

Gal·le (gäl′ə), **Johann Gottfried,** 1812–1910, German astronomer; discoverer of Neptune, 1846.

GALLEASS

gal·le·ass (gal′ē·as, -əs) *n.* A large galley of the 15th to 17th centuries, carrying three masts and heavily armed: used chiefly in the Mediterranean as a war vessel. [<F *galeace* <Ital. *galeaza,* aug. of *galea* <Med. L. See GALLEY.]

Gal·le·gos Frei·re (gä·yā′gōs frā′rā), **Rómulo,** born 1884, Venezuelan novelist; president of Venezuela 1948.

gal·le·on (gal′ē·ən) *n.* A sailing vessel of the 15th to 17th centuries, usually armed and having three or four decks; especially, the vessel used by Spain in trade with her Central American possessions. [<Sp. *galeón,* aug. of *galea* <Med. L. See GALLEY.]

GALLEON

gal·ler·y (gal′ər·ē) *n. pl.* **·ler·ies** **1** A long, narrow balcony or other passage having balustrades or rails and projecting from the inner or outer wall of a building. **2** *U.S.* In the South, a veranda. **3** A platform with seats which projects from the rear or side walls of a theater, legislative chamber, church, etc., out over the main floor; specifically, in a theater, the highest of such platforms, containing the cheapest seats. **4** The audience occupying the gallery seats; hence, the general public. **5** *Naut.* A balcony projecting from the after part of a ship's hull. **6** A long, narrow room or corridor. **7** A room or building used for the display of works of art. **8** A collection of works of art. **9** A room suggestive of a gallery, used for business purposes: a shooting *gallery*; a photographer's *gallery.* **10** *Mil. & Mining* A horizontal underground passage; a driftway. **11** An underground passage made by an animal. — *v.* **gal·ler·ied, gal·ler·y·ing** *v.t.* To furnish or adorn with a gallery or galleries. — *v.i. Mil.* To make an underground passage. [<F *galerie* <Med. L *galeria,* ? alter. of *galilaea* a Galilee porch]

gal·let (gal′it) *n.* A small piece of stone; a chip. — *v.t.* To fill the joints of (a wall) with bits of stone. [<F *galet* a pebble]

gal·ley (gal′ē) *n. pl.* **·leys** **1** A long, low vessel used in ancient and medieval times, propelled by oars and sails or by oars alone. **2** A large rowboat. **3** The kitchen of a ship; also, the cookstove. **4** *Printing* **a** A long tray, for holding composed type. **b** A proof (**galley proof**) printed from such type. [< OF *galee* <Med. L *galea* <LGk. *galaia*]

galley slave **1** A slave who rowed in a galley. **2** Formerly, a convict sentenced to labor at the oar of a galley. **3** Hence, a drudge; hack.

galley west *adv. U.S. Colloq.* All askew: to knock *galley west.*

gall·fly (gôl′flī′) *n. pl.* **·flies** **1** Any of various small hymenopterous insects (family *Cynipidae*), resembling wasps in appearance, whose larvae promote the growth of galls on plants. Also called *gall wasp.* **2** A gall midge.

Gal·li·a (gal′ē·ə) The Latin name for GAUL.

gal·liard (gal′yərd) *adj. Archaic* Full of gaiety; dashing; jaunty; spirited. — *n.* **1** A dance of brisk movement, popular in the 16th and 17th centuries. **2** The music for such a dance. [<OF *gaillard*]

gal·lic (gal′ik) *adj. Chem.* **1** Of, pertaining to, or derived from the element gallium. **2** Relating to or derived from gallnuts; specifically, designating a white, odorless, crystalline organic compound, **gallic acid,** $C_7H_6O_5 \cdot H_2O$, widely distributed in the vegetable kingdom and used in the making of inks, dyestuffs, paper, etc.

Gal·lic (gal′ik) *adj.* Of or pertaining to ancient Gaul or modern France. [<L *Gallicus* <*Gallus* inhabitant of Gaul]

Gal·li·can (gal′ə·kən) *adj.* Of or pertaining to Gaul or France, or especially to a former party in the Roman Catholic Church there. — *n.* A member of the Gallican party.

Gal·li·can·ism (gal′ə·kən·iz′əm) *n.* The doctrine of the national party in the Roman Catholic Church of France, adopted March 19, 1682, limiting the papal power and extending that of the national church: opposed to *Ultramontanism.*

Gal·li·cism (gal′ə·siz′əm) *n.* A French idiom, as used in any other language.

Gal·li·cize (gal′ə·sīz) *v.t. & v.i.* **·cized, ·ciz·ing** To make or become French in character, language, etc.; Frenchify.

Gal·li-Cur·ci (gäl′lē·ko͝or′chē), **Amelita,** 1889–1963, Italian coloratura soprano active in the United States.

Gal·lié·ni (gà·lyā·nē′), **Joseph,** 1849–1916, French general in World War I.

gal·li·fi·ca·tion (gal′ə·fi·kā′shən) *n.* The production of galls.

gal·li·gas·kins (gal′i·gas′kinz) *n. pl.* **1** Long loose hose, worn in the 16th century. **2** Loose breeches. **3** A sportsman's leather leggings. [Alter. of MF *garguesque,* var. of *greguesque* <Ital. *grechesca,* fem. of *grechesco* Greek]

gal·li·mau·fry (gal′i·mô′frē) *n. pl.* **·fries** **1** A hash or hodgepodge. **2** A confused jumble or medley of any kind. [<F *gallimafrée*; ult. origin unknown]

gal·li·na·cean (gal′ə·nā′shən) *n.* A gallinaceous bird.

gal·li·na·ceous (gal′ə·nā′shəs) *adj.* Of or pertaining to an order of birds *(Galliformes),* including the common hen, turkeys, partridges, etc. [<L *gallinaceus* <*gallina* a hen]

Gal·li·nas Point (gä·yē′näs) A cape in northern Colombia; the northernmost point of South America. *Spanish* **Punta Gallinas.**

gal·li·na·zo (gal′i·nä′zō) *n. pl.* **·zos** or **·zoes** **1** A turkey buzzard. **2** A tropical carrion crow. [<Sp. *gallinaza* vulture, aug. of *gallina* a hen]

gall·ing (gô′ling) *adj.* Chafing and rendering sore; hence, irritating; harrowing: *galling* bondage. — **gall′ing·ly** *adv.*

gal·li·nip·per (gal′ə·nip′ər) *n.* A large mosquito; a cranefly. [Origin uncertain]

gal·li·nule (gal′ə·nyo͞ol, -no͞ol) *n.* Any of several cootlike birds allied to the rails; especially, the **Florida gallinule** *(Gallinula chloropus).* [<NL *gallinula,* dim. of *gallina* a hen]

Gal·li·o (gal′ē·ō) A Roman proconsul in

Achaia in the first century. *Acts* xviii 17. **—careless Gallio** An indifferent or careless person.

gal·li·ot (gal′ē·ət) See GALIOT.

Gal·lip·o·li (gə·lip′ə·lē) A port on **Gallipoli Peninsula** in European Turkey, between the Gulf of Saros and the Dardanelles. Turkish *Gelibolu.*

gal·li·pot[1] (gal′i·pot) *n.* A small earthen jar as for ointments, jam, etc., especially as used by apothecaries. [? <GALLEY + POT, because orig. imported on galleys]

gal·li·pot[2] (gal′i·pot) See GALIPOT.

gal·li·um (gal′ē·əm) *n.* A rare metallic element (symbol Ga, atomic number 31) having a low melting point. See PERIODIC TABLE. [<NL <L *gallus* a cock, trans. of *Lecoq* de Boisbaudran, 1838–1912, its discoverer]

gal·li·vant (gal′ə·vant, gal′ə·vant′) *v.i.* To go about, especially with members of the opposite sex, in search of fun and pleasure; gad: also spelled *galavant, galivant.* [? Alter. of GALLANT]

gal·li·vat (gal′ə·vat) *n.* A large boat propelled by oars and a large, triangular sail: formerly used by Malay pirates. [Ult. <Pg. *galeota* a galley]

gal·li·wasp (gal′i·wosp′, -wôsp′) *n.* **1** A lizard (genus *Diploglossus*) of Jamaica, greatly feared, but harmless. **2** A lizard fish. Also spelled *gallywasp.* [Appar. <GALLEY + WASP; orig. an insect which infested West Indian ships]

gall midge Any of various small, slender, hairy gnats (family *Cecidomyiae*) whose larvae produce galls on plants, especially on those of the composite and willow families. Also **gall′fly′, gall gnat.** For illustration see INSECT (injurious).

gall·nut (gôl′nut′) *n.* The gall of any gall-bearing oak: a source of tannic acid. Also **gall′-ap′ple.**

Gallo- *combining form* French; pertaining to the French or to France: *Gallomania.* [<L *Gallus* a Gaul]

gal·lo·bro·mal (gal′ō·brō′məl) *n. Chem.* An organic compound, $C_7H_4O_5Br_2$, obtained by treating bromine with gallic acid: used in medicine as a sedative and hypnotic.

Gal·lo·ma·ni·a (gal′ə·mā′nē·ə, -mān′yə) *n.* A craze for imitating French manners, fashions, etc. **—Gal′lo·ma′ni·ac** (-ak) *n.*

gal·lon (gal′ən) *n.* **1** An English and American liquid measure of various capacities: the **Winchester** or **wine gallon,** containing 231 cubic inches or four quarts, or 3.78 liters, which is the common standard of the United States; the **imperial gallon** of Great Britain of 277.42 cubic inches, or 4.5459 liters. **2** *Brit.* A dry measure; one eighth of a bushel. [<AF *galon,* ? <Celtic]

gal·lon·age (gal′ən·ij) *n.* Quantity or capacity reckoned in gallons.

gal·loon (gə·lo͞on′) *n.* A narrow braid, tape, or trimming of worsted, silk, or rayon, sometimes of gold or silver thread. [<OF *galon* <*galonner* adorn with ribbons] **—gal·looned′, ga·looned′** *adj.*

gal·loot (gə·lo͞ot′) See GALOOT.

gal·lop (gal′əp) *n.* **1** A gait of a quadruped characterized by a regular succession of leaps, in which the foot sequence is left hind, right hind, left fore, right fore, in repeating sequence. **2** The act of riding, or a ride at a gallop. **3** Speedy and careless action. *—v.i.* **1** To ride at a gallop. **2** To go, run, or move very fast or at a gallop. *—v.t.* **3** To cause to run at a gallop. [<OF *galop* <*galoper* <Gmc. Doublet of WALLOP.] **—gal′lop·er** *n.*

gal·lo·pade (gal′ə·pād′) *n.* **1** A sidewise gallop, or curveting motion. **2** A brisk dance, or the music for it.

gal·lous (gal′əs) *adj. Chem.* Designating a compound containing bivalent gallium: *gallous* bromide.

Gal·lo·way (gal′ə·wā) A district of SW Scotland comprising the counties of Wigtownshire and Kirkcudbrightshire.

Gal·lo·way (gal′ə·wā) *n.* **1** A small horse, originally from Galloway, Scotland, now nearly or quite extinct. **2** A breed of dark cattle from Galloway, Scotland.

gal·low·glass (gal′ō·glas′, -gläs′) *n.* In ancient Ireland, an armed retainer of a chief. Also **gal′lo·glass′.** [<Irish *galloglach* <*gall* stranger + *ōglach* soldier]

gal·lows (gal′ōz) *n. pl.* **·lows·es** or **·lows** **1** A framework consisting of two or more uprights supporting a crossbeam, used for hanging criminals. **2** *Naut.* A similar structure used to support spars on a vessel, or for other purposes: also called *gallows bitts.* [OE *galga*]

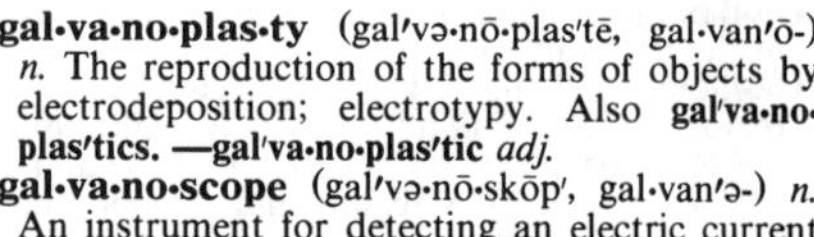

A TYPE OF GALLOWS

gal·lows-bird (gal′·ōz·bûrd′) *n.* One who either has been hanged or deserves hanging.

gal·lows-tree (gal′·ōz·trē′) *n.* A gallows.

gall·stone (gôl′stōn′) *n. Pathol.* A solid substance found in the gall bladder, liver, etc.; biliary calculus.

Gal·lup poll (gal′əp) A sampling or cross-section of public opinion on given subjects, as conducted by George Horace *Gallup,* born 1901, U.S. statistician.

gal·lus·es (gal′əs·əs) *n. pl. U.S. Dial.* Suspenders for trousers. [<GALLOWS]

gall wasp A gallfly.

gal·ly·gas·kins (gal′i·gas′kinz) See GALLIGASKINS.

ga·loot (gə·lo͞ot′) *n. U.S. Slang* An awkward or uncouth fellow: often used as a term of good-natured depreciation: also spelled *galloot.* [Cf. Du. *gelubt* castrated]

gal·op (gal′əp) *n.* **1** A lively dance in double measure. **2** The music for it. Also **gal·o·pade** (gal′ə·pād′). [<F, gallop]

ga·lore (gə·lôr′, -lōr′) *adj.* Very many; abundant: used after its noun. *—n. Obs.* Abundance. *—adv.* In abundance. [<Irish *go leōr,* enough]

ga·losh (gə·losh′) *n.* **1** *Usually pl.* An overshoe reaching above the ankle and worn in stormy weather. **2** *Obs.* A heavy wooden shoe; a clog or patten; hence, any boot or shoe. Also spelled *golosh.* Also **ga·loshe′.** [<F *galoche,* ult. <Gk. *kalopous* wooden shoe]

Gals·wor·thy (gôlz′wûr·thē), **John,** 1867–1933, English novelist and playwright.

Gal·ton (gôl′tən), **Sir Francis,** 1822–1911, English scientist and anthropologist; introduced fingerprint identification in England and established the science of biometrics for the study of heredity. **—Gal·to·ni·an** (gôl·tō′nē·ən) *adj.*

ga·lu·chat (gá·lü·shá′) *n.* **1** Ornamental sharkskin leather, tanned without removal of pebbly surface. **2** A type of sharkskin fabric. [<F]

Gal·va·ni (gäl·vä′nē), **Luigi,** 1737–98, Italian physiologist.

gal·van·ic (gal·van′ik) *adj.* **1** Pertaining to galvanism. **2** Resembling the movement of a limb of a dead animal subjected to an electric current; spasmodic. Also **gal·van′i·cal. —gal·van′i·cal·ly** *adv.*

galvanic battery A battery of primary cells.

galvanic pile A voltaic pile.

gal·va·nism (gal′və·niz′əm) *n.* **1** A flow of electricity as produced by chemical action. **2** *Med.* The therapeutic application of a continuous electric current from voltaic cells. [after Luigi *Galvani* + -ISM] **—gal′va·nist** *n.*

gal·va·nize (gal′və·nīz) *v.t.* **·nized, ·niz·ing** **1** To stimulate to muscular action by electricity. **2** To rouse to action; startle; excite. **3** To coat with metal by galvanic process; electroplate; also, to coat iron with zinc. Also *Brit.* **gal′va·nise. — gal′va·ni·za′tion** *n.* **—gal′va·niz′er** *n.*

galvanized iron Iron coated with zinc, primarily by the electrolytic process.

galvano- *combining form* Galvanic; galvanism; produced by a galvanic current: *galvanometer.*

gal·va·no·cau·ter·y (gal′və·nō·kô′tər·ē) *n. pl.* **·ter·ies** *Med.* The operation or result of cauterizing by electricity.

gal·va·nom·e·ter (gal′və·nom′ə·tər) *n. Electr.* An apparatus for measuring current strength or potential difference. **—gal·va·no·met·ric** (gal′və·nō·met′rik, gal·van′ō-) or **·ri·cal** *adj.*

gal·va·nom·e·try (gal′və·nom′ə·trē) *n.* The science, art, or process of measuring electric currents.

gal·va·no·plas·ty (gal′və·nō·plas′tē, gal·van′ō-) *n.* The reproduction of the forms of objects by electrodeposition; electrotypy. Also **gal′va·no·plas′tics. —gal′va·no·plas′tic** *adj.*

gal·va·no·scope (gal′və·nō·skōp′, gal·van′ə-) *n.* An instrument for detecting an electric current and showing its direction, differing from a galvanometer in being only qualitative. **—gal·va·no·scop·ic** (gal′və·nō·skop′ik, gal·van′ō-) *adj.*

gal·va·nos·co·py (gal′və·nos′kə·pē) *n.* **1** Use of the galvanoscope. **2** *Med.* Diagnosis by galvanism.

gal·va·no·sur·ger·y (gal′və·nō·sûr′jər·ē) *n.* Use of galvanic electricity in surgery.

gal·va·no·tax·is (gal′və·nō·tak′sis) *n.* Electrotaxis. Also **gal·va·not·ro·pism** (gal′və·not′rə·piz′əm).

gal·va·no·ther·my (gal′və·nō·thûr′mē) *n.* Production of heat by galvanism.

Gal·ves·ton (gal′vəs·tən) A port on the NE end of **Galveston Island** in **Galveston Bay,** an inlet of the Gulf of Mexico in SE Texas.

Galveston plan The commission plan of municipal government.

Gal·way (gôl′wā) A maritime county in western Ireland; 2,293 square miles; capital, Galway.

Galway Bay An inlet of the Atlantic Ocean between County Galway and County Clare, Ireland.

Gal·we·gian (gal·wē′jən) *adj.* Of or pertaining to the people or the district of Galloway, Scotland. *—n.* A native or inhabitant of this region.

gal·yak (gal′yak) *n.* A flat fur from the skin of a prematurely born kid or lamb. [<Russian *golyak* bare]

gam[1] (gam) *n.* **1** A herd or school of whales. **2** *U.S. Dial.* An exchange of visits between whaling vessels and crews.*—v.* **gammed, gam·ming** *v.i.* **1** *U.S. Dial.* To visit back and forth while at sea. **2** To come together in a gam: said of whales.*—v.t.* **3** *U.S. Dial.* To make a visit or visits to. [? Var. of GAME[1]]

gam[2] (gam) *n. Slang.* A leg or calf, especially of a woman. [Var. of GAMB]

Ga·ma (gam′ə, *Pg.* gä′mə), **Vasco da,** 1469?–1524, Portuguese navigator; first to sail around Africa and to reach India (1498) by sea.

Ga·ma·li·el (gə·mā′lē·əl, -māl′yəl) A masculine personal name. [<Hebrew, reward of God] — **Gamaliel** A Pharisee; preceptor of the apostle Paul. *Acts* v 34; xxii 3.

ga·mash·es (gə·mash′əz, -mäsh′-) *n. pl. Brit. Dial.* Leggings, or high boots worn by horseback riders. [<F *gamache*]

gamb (gamb) *n.* **1** A leg; shank. **2** *Her.* The entire foreleg of a beast, especially of a lion. [<OF *gambe,* var. of *jambe.* See JAMB.]

gam·ba·do (gam·bā′·dō) *n. pl.* **·dos** or **·does** **1** A legging; gaiter. **2** *pl.* Bootlike leathers attached to a saddle, protecting the feet and serving as stirrups. **3** A curveting, prank, or flourish; antic. Also **gam·bade′** (-bād′). [<Ital. *gamba* leg]

gam·be·son (gam′bə·sən) *n.* A coat of medieval times, made of leather or of cloth stuffed and quilted, worn as armor.[<OF *gambison* <Gmc.]

GAMBESON

Gam·bet·ta (gam·bet′ə, *Fr.* gäṅ·bĕ·tȧ′), **Léon Michel,** 1838–82, French statesman.

Gam·bi·a (gam′bē·ə) An independent state in the Commonwealth of Nations, in western Africa; 4,000 square miles; capital, Bathurst; comprising an enclave along 300 miles of the lower course of the **Gambia River,** a river flowing 700 miles west from French Guinea to the Atlantic: *French* **Gam·bie** (gäṅ·bē′).

Gam·bier Islands (gam′bir) A part of French Oceania at the southern end of the Tuamotu group; 12 square miles; capital, Rikitea on Mangareva: also *Mangareva.*

gam·bir (gam′bir) *n.* Pale catechu, the dried

extract from the leaves and twigs of an Asian woody vine (*Uncaria gambir*): used as an astringent and tonic, and in tanning, dyeing, etc. Also **gam'bi·a** (-bē·ə), **gam'bier.** [<Malay]

gam·bit (gam'bit) *n.* One of various openings in chess, in which a pawn or piece is risked to obtain an attack. [<F <OF *gambet,* a tripping up, ult. <LL *gamba* a leg]

gam·ble (gam'bəl) *v.* **gam·bled, gam·bling** *v.i.* **1** To risk or bet something of value on the outcome of an event, a game of chance, etc. **2** To take a risk to obtain a desired result: He *gambled* on finding the window open. —*v.t.* **3** To wager or bet (something of value). **4** To lose or squander by gaming: usually with *away.* —*n. Colloq.* **1** Any risky or uncertain venture. **2** A gambling venture or transaction. ◆ Homophone: *gambol.* [Cf. ME *gamenen,* OE *gamenian* sport, play] — **gam'bling** *n.*

gam·bler (gam'blər) *n.* One who gambles.

gam·boge (gam·bōj', -bōōzh') *n.* A brownish Oriental gum resin obtained from a tropical tree (*Garcinia hanburyi*), used as a pigment and cathartic. [<NL *gambogium,* from *Cambodia,* where found]

gam·bol (gam'bəl) *v.i.* **·boled** or **·bolled, ·bol·ing** or **·bol·ling** To skip or leap about in play; frolic. See synonyms under FRISK, LEAP. —*n.* A skipping about in sport. See synonyms under FROLIC, SPORT. ◆ Homophone: *gamble.* [Earlier *gambald* <F *gambader* <*gambade* a spring, leap <Ital. *gambata* <*gamba* leg]

gam·brel (gam'brəl) *n.* **1** The hock of an animal. **2** A stick used for hanging meat. **3** *Archit.* A roof having its slope broken by an obtuse angle: also called **gambrel roof.** [<OF *gamberel,* dim. of *gambe* leg <LL *gamba*]

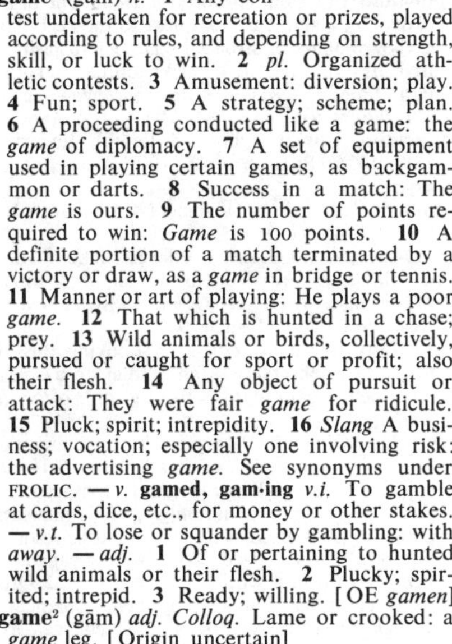
GAMBREL (*def. 3*)

Gam·bri·nus (gam·brī'nəs), 1251–94, duke of Brabant, reputed to be the inventor of lager beer.

game[1] (gām) *n.* **1** Any contest undertaken for recreation or prizes, played according to rules, and depending on strength, skill, or luck to win. **2** *pl.* Organized athletic contests. **3** Amusement: diversion; play. **4** Fun; sport. **5** A strategy; scheme; plan. **6** A proceeding conducted like a game: the *game* of diplomacy. **7** A set of equipment used in playing certain games, as backgammon or darts. **8** Success in a match: The *game* is ours. **9** The number of points required to win: *Game* is 100 points. **10** A definite portion of a match terminated by a victory or draw, as a *game* in bridge or tennis. **11** Manner or art of playing: He plays a poor *game.* **12** That which is hunted in a chase; prey. **13** Wild animals or birds, collectively, pursued or caught for sport or profit; also their flesh. **14** Any object of pursuit or attack: They were fair *game* for ridicule. **15** Pluck; spirit; intrepidity. **16** *Slang* A business; vocation; especially one involving risk: the advertising *game.* See synonyms under FROLIC. —*v.* **gamed, gam·ing** *v.i.* To gamble at cards, dice, etc., for money or other stakes. —*v.t.* To lose or squander by gambling: with *away.* —*adj.* **1** Of or pertaining to hunted wild animals or their flesh. **2** Plucky; spirited; intrepid. **3** Ready; willing. [OE *gamen*]

game[2] (gām) *adj. Colloq.* Lame or crooked: a *game* leg. [Origin uncertain]

game bird Any bird commonly hunted as game, as pheasant, wild duck, or partridge.

game·cock (gām'kok') *n.* A rooster bred and trained for fighting. Also **game cock.**

game fowl **1** One of several breeds of fowl used in cockfighting. **2** Any bird hunted as game.

game·keep·er (gām'kē'pər) *n.* A person having the care of game, as in a preserve or park.

game laws Laws passed by Federal or State legislatures to protect wild game (animals, birds, fish) by setting the season and manner of capture and sale.

game·ly (gām'lē) *adv.* In a game manner; pluckily. Also **gam'i·ly.**

game·ness (gām'nis) *n.* Pluck; bravery; endurance.

game preserve A large tract of land set apart by law as a refuge and natural breeding ground for wild game.

games·man·ship (gāmz'mən·ship) *n.* The art of winning by the use of any and all means available while seeming to honor the recognized dictates of sportsmanship. [Coined by Stephen Potter, born 1900, English writer]

game·some (gām'səm) *adj.* Playful; sportive; gay; merry. —**game'some·ly** *adv.* —**game'·some·ness** *n.*

game·ster (gām'stər) *n.* **1** A gambler. **2** *Obs.* A lewd, lecherous man or woman.

gam·e·tan·gi·um (gam'ə·tan'jē·əm) *n. pl.* **·gi·a** *Bot.* The plant cell or organ in which gametes are produced. [<GAMETE + Gk. *angeion* vessel]

gam·ete (gam'ēt, gə·mēt') *n. Biol.* Either of two mature reproductive cells, an ovum or sperm, which in uniting produce a zygote. [<NL *gameta* <Gk. *gametē* wife, or *gametēs* husband] —**ga·met·ic** (gə·met'ik) *adj.* —**ga·met'i·cal·ly** *adv.*

gameto- *combining form* Gamete: *gametophore.* [<Gk. *gametēs* husband <*gamos* marriage]

ga·me·to·cyte (gə·mē'tə·sīt) *n. Biol.* A cell which produces gametes.

gam·e·tog·e·ny (gam'ə·toj'ə·nē) *n. Biol.* The formation of gametes. Also **gam·e·to·gen·e·sis** (gam'ə·tō·jen'ə·sis). —**gam'e·to·gen'ic** *adj.*

ga·me·to·phore (gə·mē'tə·fôr, -fōr) *n. Bot.* A modified branch or filament which bears reproductive organs or gametes, as in certain liverworts.

ga·me·to·phyte (gə·mē'tə·fīt) *n. Bot.* That phase or generation of a plant which produces the sexual organs: distinguished from the non-sexual form. —**gam·e·to·phyt·ic** (gam'ə·tō·fit'·ik) *adj.*

gam·ic (gam'ik) *adj.* **1** Pertaining to or produced by the congress of the sexes; sexual. **2** *Biol.* Capable of development only after fecundation: *gamic* ova. [<Gk. *gamikos* < *gamos* marriage]

gam·in (gam'in, *Fr.* gà·maṅ') *n.* A neglected boy or girl of city streets; a street Arab. [<F]

gam·ing (gā'ming) *n.* The act or practice of gambling.

gaming table A table furnished with apparatus for gaming; especially, one in a **gaming house.**

gam·ma (gam'ə) *n.* **1** The third letter in the Greek alphabet (Γ, γ): corresponding to *g* (as in *go*). As a numeral it denotes 3. **2** *Physics* A unit of magnetic field intensity, equal to 10^{-5} gauss. **3** A unit of weight, equal to one thousandth of a milligram. **4** *Phot.* A number expressing the degree to which a negative has been developed as compared with the range of light values in the subject photographed. [<Gk.]

gam·ma·cism (gam'ə·siz'əm) *n.* Inability to utter such letters as *g, k;* baby talk.

gam·ma·di·on (gə·mā'dē·ən) *n.* **1** A cross made of four capital gammas; a swastika; a fylfot. **2** A Greek cross formed of four capital gammas all facing outward so that the ends of the arms of the cross are open. Also **gam·ma'tion** (-shən). [<LGk. <*gamma,* the letter G]

gamma globulin A globulin present in blood plasma which contains antibodies effective against certain pathogenic micro-organisms.

gamma rays *Physics* A type of emission from radioactive substances, consisting of electromagnetic radiation of great penetrating power and of wavelengths lying beyond the region of the shortest X-rays.

gamma test *Phot.* A test using a strip of film to determine the degree of density in a photographic image in comparison with the degree of illumination of the object photographed.

gam·mer (gam'ər) *n. Brit. Dial.* An old woman; grandmother: correlative of *gaffer.* [Alter. of GODMOTHER]

gam·mon[1] (gam'ən) *n.* In backgammon, a defeat in which the winner throws all his men before the loser throws off any. —*v.t.* To obtain a gammon over. [? ME *gamen* a game]

gam·mon[2] (gam'ən) *Brit. Colloq. n.* Deceitful nonsense or trickery. —*v.t.* To hoodwink by deceitful talk. —*v.i.* To talk deceitful nonsense. [Origin uncertain] —**gam'mon·er** *n.*

gam·mon[3] (gam'ən) *n.* **1** A cured ham. **2** The bottom part of a flitch of bacon. —*v.t.* To cure by salting and smoking. [<OF *gambon* <*gambe* a leg <LL *gamba*]

gam·mon[4] (gam'ən) *Naut. n.* Gammoning. —*v.t.* To make fast (the bowsprit) to the stem by means of gammoning. [Origin unknown]

gam·mon·ing (gam'ən·ing) *n. Naut.* The rope, chain, or iron lashing that fastens the bowsprit down to the stem of a vessel.

gamo- *combining form* **1** Sexually joined: *gamogenesis.* **2** Fused; united: *gamophyllous.* [<Gk. *gamos* marriage]

gam·o·gen·e·sis (gam'ə·jen'ə·sis) *n. Biol.* Sexual generation.

gam·o·ge·net·ic (gam'ə·jə·net'ik) *adj.* Of, pertaining to, or resulting from gamogenesis. —**gam'o·ge·net'i·cal·ly** *adv.*

gam·o·ma·ni·a (gam'ə·mā'nē·ə, -mān'yə) *n.* An excessive desire to marry.

gam·o·pet·al·ous (gam'ə·pet'əl·əs) *adj. Bot.* Pertaining to a division of dicotyledonous plants in which the flowers possess both calyx and corolla.

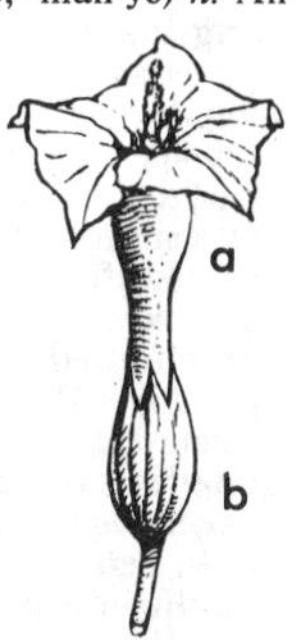

GAMOPETALOUS Gamopetalous corolla (*a*) and gamosepalous calyx (*b*) of the flower of the tobacco plant.

gam·o·phyl·lous (gam'ə·fil'·əs) *adj. Bot.* Having cohering perianth leaves. [<GAMO- + Gk. *phyllon* leaf]

gam·o·sep·al·ous (gam'ə·sep'·ə·ləs) *adj. Bot.* Having the sepals more or less united; monosepalous.

-gamous *combining form* Pertaining to marriage or union for reproduction: used in adjectives corresponding to nouns in *-gamy*: *polygamous.* [<Gk. *gamos* marriage + -OUS]

gamp[1] (gamp) *n. Brit.* A large heavy umbrella: a humorous usage. [With ref. to one carried by Mrs. *Gamp,* a character in Dickens' *Martin Chuzzlewit*]

gamp[2] (gamp) *n.* A long piece of metal with a raised center, fitted to a sewing machine to produce a rounded tuck on fabric. [<F *guimpe.* See GUIMPE]

gam·ut (gam'ət) *n.* **1** *Music* The diatonic scale of musical notes. **2** The whole range of anything: the *gamut* of emotions. [<Med. L *gamma ut* <*gamma,* the first note of the early musical scale + *ut* (later, *do*); the names of the notes of the scale were taken from a medieval Latin hymn: *Ut* queant laxis *Re*sonare fibris, *Mi*ra gestorum *Fa*muli tuorum, *Sol*ve polluti *La*bii reatum, *S*ancte *I*ohannes]

gam·y (gā'mē) *adj.* **gam·i·er, gam·i·est** **1** Having the flavor of game, especially game that has been kept raw until somewhat tainted, as preferred by gourmets. **2** Full of pluck; disposed to fight.

-gamy *combining form* Marriage or union for reproduction: used in anthropology, biology, and sociology: *polygamy.* [<Gk. *gamos* marriage]

gan (gan) *Archaic & Poetic* Began.

Gand (gäṅ) The French name for GHENT.

Gan·dak (gun'duk) A river in Nepal and NW Bihar, India, flowing south 420 miles to the Ganges. Also **Great Gandak.**

gan·der (gan'dər) *n.* **1** A male goose. **2** A dunce. [OE *gandra*]

Gan·der (gan'dər) A town in eastern Newfoundland; site of transatlantic airport, a North American transit point for air services to Europe.

Gan·dhi (gän'dē, gan'-), **Mohandas Karamchand,** 1869–1948, Hindu nationalist leader: known as *Mahatma Gandhi.*

Gan·do (gän'dō) A former emirate including parts of Nigeria and French West Africa. Also **Gan'du** (-dōō).

gan·dou·rah (gän·dōō'rä) *n.* A sleeveless garment resembling a shirt, worn by Arabs in the Near East. Also **gan·dou'ra.** [<Arabic *ghandūrah*]

gan·dy dancer (gan'dē) *U.S.* A railroad laborer. Also **gandy.**

Gan·dzha (gän'jä) A former name for KIROVABAD.

gane (gān) *Scot.* Gone.

ga•nef (gä′nəf) *n. Yiddish* A thief: also spelled *gonof, gonoph.* Also **ga′nof.**

gang[1] (gang) *n.* **1** A number of persons acting or operating together; a group; squad. **2** A group cooperating for evil purposes. **3** A set of tools or other objects of one kind operated together. **4** Gangue. See synonyms under CABAL. —*v.t.* **1** To unite into or as into a gang. **2** *Colloq.* To attack as a group. —*v.i.* **3** To come together as a gang; form a gang. **—to gang up on** *U.S. Slang* To attack or act against together: They *ganged up on* me. [OE *gang* a going < *gangan* go]

gang[2] (gang) *v.i. Scot.* To go.

gang•er (gang′ər) *n. Brit.* The foreman of a gang.

Gan•ges (gan′jēz) A river sacred to the Hindus in northern India and eastern Pakistan, flowing 1,560 miles from the Himalayas to the Bay of Bengal. *Sanskrit* and *Hindi* **Gan•ga** (gung′gä).

gang hook Two or three fish hooks, joined together and attached to one line.

gang•ing (gang′ing) *n. Electronics* A system of coupling two or more coils or condensers of a radio receiving set so that they may be controlled by a single dial.

gang knife A set of knives used to slice fish, etc., into pieces of predetermined length.

gan•gli•at•ed (gang′glē•ā′tid) *adj.* Possessing ganglia. Also **gan′gli•ate** (-it, -āt), **gan•gli•on•at•ed** (gang′glē•ən•ā′tid).

gan•gling (gang′gling) *adj.* Awkwardly tall and loosely built. Also **gan′gly.** [Cf. dial. E *gangrel* a lanky person]

ganglio- *combining form* Ganglion. Also, before vowels, **ganglion-**, as in *ganglionitis.*

gan•gli•oid (gang′glē•oid) *adj.* Resembling a ganglion.

gan•gli•on (gang′glē•ən) *n. pl.* **•gli•ons** or **•gli•a** (glē•ə) *Physiol.* **1** A collection of nerve cells, acting as a center of nervous influence. **2** Any center of energy, activity, or strength. **3** *Pathol.* A hard globular tumor proceeding from a tendon. [< LL < Gk. *ganglion* tumor] **—gan•gli•on•ic** (gang′glē•on′ik) *adj.*

gan•gli•on•ec•to•my (gang′glē•ən•ek′tə•mē) *n. Surg.* Removal of a ganglion.

gan•gli•on•i•tis (gang′glē•ən•ī′tis) *n. Pathol.* Inflammation of a ganglion.

gang•plank (gang′plangk′) *n.* A temporary bridge for passengers between a vessel and a wharf.

gang plow A set of plowshares arranged to work simultaneously.

gan•grel (gang′grəl, -rəl) *n. Scot.* **1** An awkward fellow. **2** A wanderer; vagrant. Also **gan′grell.**

gan•grene (gang′grēn, gang•grēn′) *n. Pathol.* Mortification or death of a part of the body, caused by failure or lack of an adequate blood supply; massive necrosis of the tissue. —*v.t.* & *v.i.* **gan•grened, gan•gren•ing** To cause gangrene in or become affected by gangrene. [< L *gangraena* < Gk. *gangraina*] **—gan′gre•nous** (-grə•nəs) *adj.*

gang saw An arrangement of circular saws geared to one shaft and used to perform several cutting operations simultaneously.

gang•ster (gang′stər) *n.* A member of a gang of toughs, gunmen, or the like. **—gang′ster•dom** *n.*

Gang•tok (gung′tok) The capital of Sikkim protectorate.

gangue (gang) *n. Mining* The non-metalliferous or worthless minerals found in a vein of ore. [< F < G *gang* vein of ore]

gang•way (gang′wā′) *n.* **1** A passageway through, into, or out of any enclosure; especially, a temporary passageway made of planks. **2** *Brit.* An aisle between rows of seats in the British House of Commons, separating members of the government or ex-ministers who are in opposition from the rank and file of their parties. **3** *Naut.* **a** Either side of the upper deck of a ship, from the mainmast to the quarter-deck. **b** An opening in a vessel's bulwarks to afford entrance for passengers or freight; also, a gangplank. **4** *Mining* The main level in a coal mine. **5** The gradient up which logs are conveyed into a sawmill: also called *logway.* —*interj.* Get out of the way! Stand aside! [OE *gangweg*]

gan•is•ter (gan′is•tər) *n.* **1** A very siliceous claystone of the lower coal measures of England, used chiefly for flagging and refractory furnace linings. **2** A mixture of ground quartz and fire clay used in lining Bessemer converters. Also **gan′nis•ter.** [< dial. G *ganster* < MHG, a spark]

gan•net (gan′it) *n.* **1** Any of several large sea birds (family *Sulidae*) related to the pelicans. The common gannet *(Moris bassana)* of the North Atlantic coasts is of a prevailing white color with blackish feet. **2** The wood ibis of Florida. [OE *ganot*]

gan•oid (gan′oid) *adj.* **1** Pertaining to a subclass *(Ganoidei)* of teleost fishes having scales consisting of laminated bone covered with a shiny enamel surface, as sturgeons, bowfins, etc. —*n.* A ganoid fish. [< Gk. *ganos* brightness + -OID]

gant•let[1] (gônt′lit, gant′-) *n.* **1** A punishment wherein the victim runs between two rows of men who strike him with clubs or switches as he passes. **2** A series of risks or unpleasant events. **3** A narrowing of two lines of railway track almost into the space of one, as on a bridge or in a tunnel, without breaking the continuity of either track. **—to run the gantlet** To be exposed to a series of hostile attacks or unpleasant incidents. —*v.t.* To form a gantlet by running together (railway tracks). Also spelled *gauntlet.* [Earlier *gantlope,* alter. of Sw. *gatlopp* a running down a lane]

gant•let[2] (gônt′lit, gant′-) See GAUNTLET[1].

gant•line (gant′līn′) *n. Naut.* A rope rove through a block at the masthead of a vessel for temporary use. [Alter. of *girtline.* See GIRT, LINE]

gan•try (gan′trē) *n. pl.* **•tries** **1** The frame of a traveling crane, or the crane and frame together. **2** A framework for supporting railway signals usually bridging the tracks. **3** A frame to hold a barrel horizontally. Also spelled *gauntry, gauntree.* [Alter. of OF *gantier, chantier* < L *canterius* beast of burden, framework < Gk. *kanthēlios* pack ass]

GANTRY *(def. 1)*

Gan•y•mede (gan′ə•mēd) **1** In Greek mythology, a beautiful shepherd boy of Troy whom Zeus, in the form of an eagle, carried up to Olympus to succeed Hebe as cupbearer to the gods; hence, any boy who serves drinks; a cupbearer. **2** *Astron.* The fourth (commonly called third) and largest satellite of Jupiter. [< Gk. *Ganymēdēs*]

Ga•o (gä′ō) A town in eastern Mali.

gaol (jāl) *n. Brit.* Jail. [Var. of JAIL] **—gaol′er** *n.*

gap (gap) *n.* **1** An opening or parting in anything; aperture; breach; chasm. **2** *Geog.* A deep notch or ravine in a mountain ridge. **3** A break in continuity; an interruption; a period in chronology or a range of phenomena about which nothing is known. **4** *Aeron.* The vertical distance between two supporting planes of an airplane. See synonyms under BREACH, HOLE. —*v.t.* **gapped, gap•ping** To make a breach or opening in. [< ON *gap* gap, abyss < *gapa* gape] **—gap′less** *adj.*

gape (gāp, gap) *v.i.* **gaped, gap•ing** **1** To stare with or as with open mouth, as in awe or surprise. **2** To open the mouth wide, as in yawning. **3** To be or become open wide; present a wide opening. —*n.* **1** The act of gaping. **2** *Zool.* The expanse of the open mouth, as in birds; also, the opening between the shells of a bivalve the edges of which do not naturally shut tight together, as in soft clams. **3** A gap. **—the gapes** **1** A fit of gaping or yawning. **2** A disease of young fowls, caused by the presence of gapeworms obstructing the breathing and causing much gaping. [< ON *gapa*] **—gap′er** *n.*

gape•seed (gāp′sēd′, gap′-, gäp′-) *n.* **1** *Brit.* Anything that causes wonder or astonishment to the ignorant or simple. **2** One who stares in a gaping manner.

gape•worm (gāp′wûrm′, gap′-) *n.* A nematode worm *(Syngamus trachealis)* that causes the gapes.

gap•py (gap′ē) *adj.* Having gaps; disconnected.

gap•y (gā′pē, gap′ē) *adj.* Affected with the gapes.

gar[1] (gär) *n. pl.* **gars** or **gar** Any of several fishes having a spearlike snout and elongate body, including the North American species *(Tylosurus marinus)*; the common European species *(Belone vulgaris),* esteemed as a food fish; and the teleost marine varieties also called *billfishes, needlefishes.* [Short for GARFISH]

gar[2] (gär) *v.t. Scot.* To make; cause.

ga•rage (gə•räzh′, -räj′, *Brit.* gar′ij) *n.* A building in which motor vehicles are stored and cared for. —*v.t.* **ga•raged, ga•rag•ing** To put or keep in a garage. [< F < *garer* protect, ult. < Gmc.]

Gar•a•mond (gar′ə•mond, *Fr.* gȧ•rȧ•môṅ′), **Claude,** died 1561, French printer and type founder.

Gar•and rifle (gar′ənd, gə•rand′) A semi-automatic, gas-operated, .30-caliber rifle adopted by the U.S. Army in World War II. [after J. C. *Garand,* born 1888, U.S. inventor]

garb (gärb) *n.* **1** Style of apparel, especially as characteristic of some office, rank, etc. **2** Clothes. **3** *Obs.* External seeming; appearance; demeanor; manner. **4** *Obs.* Custom; style. See synonyms under DRESS. —*v.t.* To clothe; dress. [< MF *garbe* gracefulness, ult. < Gmc.]

gar•bage (gär′bij) *n.* **1** Animal or household refuse. **2** Low or vile things collectively. [Prob. < AF. Cf. OF *garbe* a sheaf of grain, animal fodder]

gar•ban•zo bean (gär•bän′sō) The Mexican chickpea.

gar•ble (gär′bəl) *v.t.* **gar•bled, gar•bling** **1** To mix up or confuse; make incomprehensible: to *garble* a message. **2** To change or alter the meaning or emphasis of (a document, report, etc.) with intent to mislead or misrepresent. **3** *Obs.* To take the best part of. **4** *Obs.* To cull or sift. See synonyms under PERVERT. —*n.* **1** The act of garbling; a perversion, as of a text. **2** *pl.* Impurities separated from drugs, spices, etc.; refuse; trash. [< Ital. *garbellare* < Arabic *gharbala* sift < *ghirbal* a sieve, ult. < L *cribellum,* dim. of *cribrum* a sieve]

gar•board (gär′bôrd′, -bōrd′) *n. Naut.* One of the planks on a ship's bottom next to the keel. Also **garboard plank** or **strake.** [< Du. *gaarboord*]

gar•boil (gär′boil) *n. Obs.* An uproar; commotion. [< MF *garbouil* < Ital. *garbuglio,* appar. < L *bullire* boil]

Gar•cí•a Lor•ca (gär•thē′ä lôr′kä), **Federico,** 1899–1936, Spanish poet, dramatist, and essayist.

gar•çon (gȧr•sôṅ′) *n. pl.* **•çons** (-sôṅ′) *French* **1** A boy. **2** A waiter. **3** A male servant.

Gar•da (gär′dä), **Lake** The largest lake in Italy, on the Lombardy-Veneto border; 143 square miles: also *Lago di Garda.* Also **La•go di Be•na•co** (lä′gō dē be•nä′kō).

gar•dant (gär′dənt) *adj. Her.* Looking directly toward the observer, as an animal on a shield: also spelled *guardant.* [< F, orig. ppr. of *garder* watch]

gar•den (gär′dən) *n.* **1** A place for the cultivation of flowers, vegetables, or small plants. **2** Hence, any fertile or highly cultivated territory. **3** A piece of ground, commonly with ornamental plants or trees, used as a place of public resort: a botanical *garden.* —*adj.* **1** Grown, or capable of being grown in a garden; hence, hardy. **2** Ordinary; common. **3** Like a garden; ornamental: *garden* spot of the world. —*v.t.* To cultivate as a garden. —*v.i.* To till or work in a garden. [< AF *gardin* < Gmc.]

Gar•den (gär′dən), **Mary,** 1877–1967, U.S. operatic soprano.

garden balsam An ornamental plant *(Impatiens balsamina),* cultivated in many varieties.

gar•den•er (gärd′nər, gär′dən•ər) *n.* One who tends gardens, or is skilled in gardening.

garden heliotrope A species of valerian *(Valeriana officinalis)* having clusters of small pink or white flowers and roots with a penetrating aroma, reputed to have curative properties. Also called *allheal, valerian.*

gar•de•ni•a (gär•dē′nē•ə, -dēn′yə) *n.* Any of a considerable genus *(Gardenia)* of mainly tropical shrubs or trees of the madder family, with large and fragrant yellow or white axillary flowers. The Cape jasmine *(G. jasminoides)* is the best known in cultivation. [< NL, after

Alexander *Garden,* 1730–91, U.S. botanist]

gar·den·ing (gärd′ning, gär′dən·ing) *n.* The art of making and caring for a garden; also, the work involved. See synonyms under AGRICULTURE.

Garden of the Gods An area of curiously eroded sandstone formations in central Colorado.

garden sorrel The common sorrel, or sour dock.

Garden State Nickname of NEW JERSEY.

garde·robe (gärd′rōb) *n.* **1** *Archaic* A locked-up storeroom or wardrobe; also, its contents. **2** A private room, as a bedchamber. [< F < *garder* keep + *robe* a robe]

gar·dez bien (gȧr·dā′ byaṅ′) *French* Take good care (of yourself).

gar·dez la foi (gȧr·dā′ lȧ fwä′) *French* Keep faith.

Gar·di·ner (gärd′nər, gär′də·nər), **Samuel Rawson,** 1829–1902, English historian. **—Stephen,** 1483–1555, English prelate and statesman.

gar·dy·loo (gär′dē·lo͞o′) *n. Scot.* Beware of the water: formerly said in Edinburgh, to warn passers-by to avoid slops thrown from a window.

Gar·eth (gar′ith) The "kitchen-scullion" knight of the Round Table, brother of Gawain.

Gar·field (gär′fēld), **James Abram,** 1831–81, 20th president of the United States, March 4 to September 19, 1881; assassinated.

gar·fish (gär′fish′) *n. pl.* **·fish** or **·fish·es** A fish with a spearlike snout, as a garpike. See GAR[1]. [OE *gar* spear + FISH]

gar·ga·ney (gär′gə·nē) *n.* A teal *(Anas querquedula)* of Europe and Asia, having a broad white line on each side of the head and neck. [< Ital. *garganello*]

Gar·gan·tu·a (gär·gan′cho͞o·ə) The peace-loving giant prince of Rabelais' satirical romance *Gargantua* (1534); mouthpiece for educational reform; possessor of an enormous appetite.

Gar·gan·tu·an (gär·gan′cho͞o·ən) *adj.* Huge; gigantic; prodigious.

gar·get (gär′git) *n.* **1** An infectious bacterial disease of cattle, sheep, and swine, characterized by inflammation of the udder, deficient or contaminated milk, distemper, and other symptoms: also called *mastitis.* **2** The pokeweed. [< OF *gargate* throat < L *gurges* a whirlpool]

gar·gle (gär′gəl) *v.* **gar·gled, gar·gling** *v.t.* **1** To rinse (the throat) with a liquid agitated by air from the windpipe. *—v.i.* **2** To use a gargle. **3** To make a sound as if gargling. *—n.* A liquid for gargling. [< OF *gargouiller* gargle < *gargouille* throat]

GARGOYLES
a. **On cathedral of Amiens, 13th cent.**
b. **On cathedral of St. Eustache, Paris, 16th cent.**
c. **On church of Montmartre, 19th cent.**
d. **On Chrysler Building, New York, 20th cent.**

gar·goyle (gär′goil) *n.* A waterspout, usually carved in a grotesque human or animal figure, projecting from the gutter of a building. Also spelled *gurgoyle.* [< OF *gargouille* throat] — **gar′goyled** *adj.*

gar·i·bal·di (gar′ə·bôl′dē) *n.* A loose blouse resembling those worn by the soldiers of Garibaldi.

Gar·i·bal·di (gar′ə·bôl′dē, *Ital.* gä′rē·bäl′dē), **Giuseppe,** 1807–82, Italian patriot and general; secured unity of Italy.

Gar·i·bal·di·an (gar′ə·bôl′dē·ən) *adj.* Of or pertaining to Giuseppe Garibaldi or his troops. *—n.* One of the soldiers of Giuseppe Garibaldi

Ga·ri·glia·no (gä′rē·lyä′nō) The lower reaches of the Liri.

gar·ish (gâr′ish) *adj.* **1** Marked by a dazzling glare. **2** Displaying a gaudy effect. **3** Extravagantly conceited. Also formerly spelled *gairish.* [Cf. obs. *gaure* stare] **—gar′ish·ly** *adv.* — **gar′ish·ness** *n.*

gar·land (gär′lənd) *n.* **1** A wreath of leaves, flowers, etc., as a token of victory, joy, or honor. **2** A collection of literary gems. **3** A wire framework covered with cloth or burlap strips and used in camouflage. **4** Something resembling a garland or wreath. **5** A strop used to hoist spars. *—v.t.* To deck with or as with a garland. [< OF *garlande*]

Gar·land (gär′lənd), **(Hannibal) Hamlin,** 1860–1940, U.S. writer.

gar·lic (gär′lik) *n.* **1** A hardy bulbous perennial *(Allium sativum)* of the same genus as the onion. **2** Its pungent bulb, used in cooking. [OE *gārlēac* < *gār* spear + *lēac* leek] **—gar′lick·y** *adj.*

gar·ment (gär′mənt) *n.* An article of clothing. See synonyms under DRESS. *—v.t.* To clothe: usually in the past participle. [< OF *garnement* < *garnir* garnish]

Gar·misch-Par·ten·kir·chen (gär′mish·pär′·tən·kir′khən) A resort town in Upper Bavaria, Germany.

Gar·mo Peak (gär′mō) A former name for STALIN PEAK, U.S.S.R.

gar·ner (gär′nər) *v.t.* To gather or store as in a garner; collect. *—n.* **1** A place for the storing of grain; a granary. **2** Any storage place. [< OF *gernier, grenier* < L *granarium* a granary < *granum* grain]

Gar·ner (gär′nər), **John Nance,** 1868–1967, U.S. politician; vice president of the United States 1933–41.

gar·net[1] (gär′nit) *n.* **1** Any of a group of mineral double salts (silicates) of isometric crystalline form and varied composition, used as gemstones and abrasives. **2** A variable deep red color characteristic of certain varieties of garnet, as pyrope and almandine. [< OF *grenat* < Med. L *granatum* < L, a pomegranate; so called from its color]

gar·net[2] (gär′nit) *n. Naut.* A form of tackle or purchase. [Origin uncertain]

Gar·nett (gär′nit), **Constance,** 1862–1946, *née* Black; English translator of Russian literature. — **David,** born 1892, English writer; son of the preceding.

gar·net·ting (gär·net′ing) *n.* A process of reducing wool or cotton shoddy and rags to fibers that can be re-used. [from *Garnett* machine, named after the inventor]

gar·ni·er·ite (gär′nē·ə·rīt′) *n.* An amorphous, apple-green, hydrous silicate of nickel and magnesium, forming an important ore of nickel. [after Jules *Garnier,* French geologist]

gar·nish (gär′nish) *v.t.* **1** To decorate, as with ornaments; embellish. **2** In cookery, to decorate (a dish) with flavorsome or colorful trimmings for the table. **3** *Law* To give warning to (someone) to answer to an action; garnishee. *—n.* **1** Something placed around a dish for ornamentation or a relish. **2** Anything added as an ornament; embellishment. **3** *Obs.* In English jails, a fee collected from a new prisoner by the jailer. [< OF *garniss-,* stem of *garnir* prepare. Akin to WARN.]

Synonyms (verb): adorn, beautify, deck, decorate, dress, embellish, furbish, ornament. See ADORN. *Antonyms*: blemish, deface, denude, disfigure, dismantle, spoil, strip.

gar·nish·ee (gär′nish·ē′) *v.t.* **·eed, ·ee·ing** *Law* **1** To secure by garnishment (any debt or property, in the hands of a third person, which is due or belonging to the defendant in attachment). **2** To warn (a person) by garnishment. *—n. Law* A person warned not to pay or deliver money or effects to a defendant, pending a judgment of a court.

gar·nish·er (gär′nish·ər) One who garnishes or garnishees.

gar·nish·ment (gär′nish·mənt) *n.* **1** The act of garnishing. **2** That which garnishes; embellishment; ornament. **3** *Law* A warning or summons; specifically, a notice not to pay or deliver money or effects to a defendant, but to appear and answer the plaintiff's suit.

gar·ni·ture (gär′ni·chər) *n.* Anything used to garnish; embellishment. [< F < *garnir.* See GARNISH.]

Ga·ronne (gȧ·rôn′) A river in SW France, flowing NW 402 miles to the Gironde.

gar·pike (gär′pīk′) *n. pl.* **·pike** or **·pikes** **1** A large ganoid fish of the fresh waters of eastern North America (family *Lepirosteidae*), having an elongated spearlike snout. **2** A garfish. [< GAR[1] + PIKE]

gar·ret (gar′it) *n.* A story or room directly under a sloping roof. [< OF *garite* a watchtower < *garir* watch, defend < Gmc.]

gar·ret·eer (gar′it·ir′) *n.* One who lives in a garret.

Gar·rick (gar′ik), **David,** 1717–79, English actor and author.

gar·ri·son (gar′ə·sən) *n.* **1** The military force defending a fort, town, etc. **2** The place where such a force is stationed. ◆ Collateral adjective: *presidial.* *—v.t.* **1** To place troops in, as a fort or town, for its defense. **2** To station (troops) in a fort, town, etc. **3** To be the garrison of. [< OF *garison* < *garir* defend < Gmc.]

Gar·ri·son (gar′ə·sən), **Fielding Hudson,** 1870–1935, U.S. medical historian. **—William Lloyd,** 1805–79, U.S. abolitionist.

garrison cap A military cap having a round cloth top and a stiff, shiny visor, worn with the dress uniform.

gar·rote (gə·rot′, -rōt′) *n.* **1** A Spanish instrument for strangling, formerly used as a means of capital punishment. **2** The mode of punishment inflicted by the garrote. **3** Any similar method of strangulation, especially in order to rob. *—v.t.* **gar·rot·ed, gar·rot·ing** **1** To execute with a garrote. **2** To throttle in order to rob. Also **ga·rote′, ga·rotte′, gar·rotte′.** [< Sp. *garotte,* orig. a stick, cudgel < Celtic]

gar·rot·er (gə·rot′ər, -rō′tər) *n.* A strangler; especially, a highwayman who throttles his victim. Also **gar·rot′ter.**

gar·ru·line (gar′o͞o·līn, -lin, -yo͞o-) *adj.* Of or pertaining to a subfamily of corvine birds *(Garrulinae),* which includes the jays. *—n.* Any bird of this subfamily. [< NL < L *garrulus* talkative]

gar·ru·li·ty (gə·ro͞o′lə·tē) *n.* Idle and empty talkativeness.

gar·ru·lous (gar′ə·ləs, -yə-) *adj.* Given to continual and tedious talking; habitually loquacious. [< L *garrulus* talkative] **—gar′ru·lous·ly** *adv.* — **gar′ru·lous·ness** *n.*

Synonyms: chattering, loquacious, talkative, verbose. *Garrulous* signifies given to constant trivial talking. *Chattering* signifies uttering rapid, noisy, and unintelligible, or scarcely intelligible, sounds, whether articulate words or such as resemble them. The *talkative* person has a strong disposition to talk, with or without an abundance of words, or many ideas; the *loquacious* person has an abundant flow of language and much to say on any subject suggested; either may be lively and for a time entertaining; the *garrulous* person is tedious, repetitious, petty, and self-absorbed. *Verbose* is applied to utterances more formal than conversation, as to writings, or public addresses. Compare CIRCUMLOCUTION. *Antonyms*: laconic, reserved, reticent, silent, speechless, taciturn.

gar·ter (gär′tər) *n.* A band worn around the leg to hold a stocking in place; loosely, any stocking supporter. *—v.t.* To support or fasten with a garter. [< AF *gartier* < OF *garet* bend of the knee < Celtic]

Gar·ter (gär′tər) *n.* **1** The distinctive badge of the **Order of the Garter,** the highest order of knighthood in Great Britain. **2** The order itself, or membership therein.

garter snake Any of various small, harmless, viviparous, brightly striped snakes (genus *Thamnophis*): most common of American snakes.

garth (gärth) *n.* **1** The open space or courtyard enclosed by a cloister. **2** *Archaic* A yard; garden. [< ON *gardhr* a yard]

Gar·y (gâr′ē) A city in NW Indiana, on Lake Michigan.

Gar·y (gâr′ē), **Elbert Henry,** 1846–1927, U.S. lawyer and financier.

gas (gas) *n.* **1** *Physics* That fluid form of matter which is compressible within limits, and which, owing to the relatively free movement of its molecules, diffuses readily and is capable of indefinite expansion in all directions. **2** Any gaseous or vaporous mixture other than air: illuminating *gas,* fuel *gas,* etc. **3** A single jet of flame supplied by illuminating gas. **4**

Laughing gas. 5 *Mining* An explosive mixture of atmospheric air with firedamp. 6 *Slang* Empty boasting; chatter. 7 *U.S. Colloq.* Gasoline. 8 Chlorine or some other highly poisonous or asphyxiating substance used in warfare: also **poison gas.** 9 Flatulence. See synonyms under FLUID. —*v.* **gassed, gas·sing** *v.t.* 1 To overcome, affect, or kill by gas or gas fumes. 2 To treat or saturate with gas. 3 To supply with gas or gasoline. 4 To singe so as to free of loose fibers: to *gas* lace. 5 *U.S. Slang* To talk boastfully or nonsensically to. —*v.i.* 6 To give off gas. 7 *U.S. Slang* To talk in an idle or empty manner; boast. [Coined by J. B. van Helmont, 1577–1644, Belgian chemist]

gas alarm 1 A warning of a gas attack. 2 The device by which the warning is given.

gas·a·lier (gas′ə·lir′) See GASOLIER.

gas analysis The qualitative and quantitative determination of gases, especially in regard to their physiological and thermodynamic properties.

gas attack A military attack using asphyxiating or poisonous gases to overcome the enemy, as by bombardment with gas shells.

gas bacillus The micro-organism producing gas gangrene in gunshot wounds, specifically *Bacillus welchii.*

gas·bag (gas′bag′) *n.* 1 An expansible container for holding gas. 2 *Slang* A tiresome, garrulous person.

gas balance An instrument for determining the specific gravity of gases.

gas black Carbon black, produced by carbonizing natural gas: used as a substitute for animal and vegetable carbon.

gas bleaching Bleaching by means of a gas, as by chlorine.

gas bomb A bomb or shell filled with poison gas which is released when the shell explodes. Also **gas shell.**

gas bracket A bracket bearing one or more gas burners.

gas burner A tube or tip, usually attached to a gas fixture, for regulating the flame of the gas consumed.

gas carbon A compact, amorphous carbon deposited in the retorts of gasworks, which is a good conductor of heat and electricity, and is used for battery plates and in the electric arc light. Also **gas coke.**

gas cell 1 *Aeron.* One of the individual compartments containing the gas in an airship: also **gas container.** 2 An electrolytic cell composed of two gas electrodes: also **gas battery.**

gas chamber A chamber in which executions are performed by means of poisonous gas.

gas coal A bituminous coal from which illuminating gas may be made.

Gas·coigne (gas′koin), **George,** 1525?–77, English poet.

gas·con (gas′kən) *n.* A boaster. —*adj.* Boastful; blustering. [<F, a native of Gascony]

Gas·con (gas′kən) *adj.* Of, native of, or pertaining to Gascony. —*n.* A native of Gascony.

gas·con·ade (gas′kə·nād′) *v.i.* **·ad·ed, ·ad·ing** To brag; bluster. —*n.* Boastful or blustering talk, boasting; braggadocio; bluster. [<F *gasconnade* <*gascon* GASCON] —**gas′con·ad′er** *n.*

Gas·co·ny (gas′kə·nē) A region and former province of SW France. *French* **Gas·cogne** (gȧs·kôn′y′).

gas electrode An electrode capable of dissolving a gas or holding it on its surface; it is usually made of finely divided metal and in the solution behaves as a reversible electrode.

gas·e·lier (gas′ə·lir′) See GASOLIER.

gas engine An internal-combustion engine, especially one using illuminating or natural gas.

gas·e·ous (gas′ē·əs, -yəs) *adj.* 1 Having the nature or form of gas; aeriform. 2 Unsubstantial.

gas fading Fume fading.

gas filter A filter for removing solid or liquid particles from a gas.

gas fitter One who fits and puts up gas fixtures.

gas fittings The appliances connected with the introduction and use of gas in a building.

gas fixture A tube, with burners and stopcocks, connected with a gas pipe.

gas focusing *Physics* A method of focusing a stream of electrons through the action of an ionized gas.

gas furnace A furnace in which gas is used for fuel, or one for making gas.

gas gangrene *Pathol.* Gangrene with gas formation in the tissues of gunshot wounds; caused chiefly by anaerobic bacteria, as *Bacillus welchii.*

gas groove *Chem.* A groove formed by a stream of hydrogen or other gas rising continuously along the surface of an electrochemical metallic deposit while it is forming.

gash[1] (gash) *v.t.* To make a long, deep cut in. See synonyms under CUT. —*n.* A long, deep incision; a flesh wound. [Earlier *garse* <OF *garser* scratch]

gash[2] (gäsh) *adj. Scot.* 1 Fluent; intelligent 2 Neat; trim.

gas helmet A gas mask.

gas·hold·er (gas′hōl′dər) See GASOMETER.

gas·house (gas′hous′) *n.* A gasworks: often used figuratively to designate the rowdy district around a gashouse.

gas·i·form (gas′ə·fôrm) *adj.* Gaseous.

gas·i·fy (gas′ə·fī) *v.t. & v.i.* **·fied, ·fy·ing** To make into or become gas. —**gas′i·fi′a·ble** *adj.* —**gas′i·fi·ca′tion** *n.* —**gas′i·fi′er** *n.*

gas jet 1 A burner on a gas fixture. 2 The jet of flame on a gas burner.

Gas·kell (gas′kəl), **Elizabeth Cleghorn,** 1810–1865, *née* Stevenson, English novelist.

gas·ket (gas′kit) *n.* 1 *Mech.* A ring, disk, or plate of packing to make a joint watertight. 2 *Naut.* A rope or cord used to confine furled sails to the yard or boom. Also **gas′kin** (-kin), **gas′king** (-king). [Cf. Ital. *gaschetta* end of rope]

gas·kin (gas′kin) *n.* 1 The hinder part of a horse's leg, between the stifle and the hock. See illustration under HORSE. 2 *pl.* Galligaskins. See GASKET (def. 2). [? <GALLIGASKINS]

gas·light (gas′līt′) *n.* 1 Light produced by gas: also **gas light.** 2 A gas jet or burner. —**gas′light′ing** *n.*

gas liquor A by-product obtained by subjecting soft coal to destructive distillation: the chief source of ammonia.

gas log An imitation log concealing a gas burner, used in a fireplace.

gas main A trunk gas pipe for conveying gas to the service pipes.

gas·man (gas′man′) *n. pl.* **·men** (-men′) 1 One who manufactures or supplies gas for lighting. 2 A gas fitter. 3 *Mining* One who superintends ventilation and guards against firedamp. 4 A man employed by a gas-supplying company to examine and read gas meters, note the amount used, etc.

gas mantle A mantle surrounding the flame of a gas jet, which radiates light when heated.

gas mask A protective headpiece worn to prevent poisoning by noxious fumes or gases.

gas meter An apparatus for measuring the quantity of gas that passes through it.

gas·o·gene (gas′ə·jēn) *n.* 1 A fuel gas made from charcoal. 2 A portable contrivance for producing gas for aerating water. [<F *gazogène*]

gas·o·hol (gas′ə·hôl, -hol) *n.* A mixture of 90 percent gasoline and usu. 10 percent alcohol, used in internal-combustion engines as a petroleum-saving fuel.

gas·o·lier (gas′ə·lir′) *n.* A pendent fixture having branches ending in gas burners: also spelled *gasalier, gaselier.* [<*gaso-* (<GAS) + (CHANDE)LIER]

gas·o·line (gas′ə·lēn, gas′ə·lēn′) *n.* A colorless, volatile, inflammable hydrocarbon product of the distillation of crude petroleum, having a specific gravity of .629 to .667 and boiling at from 75° to 90° C. It is used as fuel, for carbonizing water gases, to propel machinery, and as a solvent for fats. Also **gas′o·lene.** [<GAS + -OL[2] + -INE[2]]

gasoline bomb See FRANGIBLE GRENADE under GRENADE.

gas·om·e·ter (gas·om′ə·tər) *n.* 1 An apparatus for measuring gases, used in chemical manipulations. 2 An apparatus adapted to collecting, holding, or mixing gases; a gas-holder.

gas·om·e·try (gas·om′ə·trē) *n.* The measurement of gases. —**gas·o·met·ric** (gas′ə·met′rik) *adj.*

gas-op·er·at·ed (gas′op′ə·rā′tid) *adj.* Operated by the action of expanding gases: said especially of certain automatic and semi-automatic weapons. See GARAND RIFLE.

gas oven An oven heated by gas.

gasp (gasp, gäsp) *v.i.* 1 To take in the breath suddenly and sharply; breathe convulsively, as from fear or exhaustion. 2 To have great longing or desire: with *for* or *after.* —*v.t.* 3 To say or utter with gasps. —*n.* An act of convulsive and interrupted breathing. [<ON *geispa* yawn]

Gas·par (gäs·pär′) Portuguese and Spanish form of JASPER. Also *Fr.* **Gas·pard** (gȧs·pär′), *Ital.* **Gas·pa·ro** (gäs′pä·rō).

—**Gaspar** Traditional name of one of the three kings, the Magi, who honored the infant Jesus. Also called *Kasper.*

Gas·pé Peninsula (gȧs·pā′) A peninsula of the Province of Quebec, Canada, in the Gulf of St. Lawrence.

gasp·er (gas′pər, gäs′-) *n.* 1 One who or that which gasps. 2 *Brit. Slang* A cigarette.

gas pipe A pipe for carrying gas, especially illuminating gas.

gas plant The herb fraxinella.

gas pot A receptacle containing lacrimatory or other poison gases and used principally in training for chemical warfare.

gas sand Any sandstone that contains or yields natural gas.

gas shaft A corridor to permit the escape of gas released or discharged from the gas cells of an airship.

gas·sing (gas′ing) *n.* 1 Subjection to the action of a gas, as lime to chlorine. 2 The act of poisoning by gas warfare. 3 *Slang* Conversation; especially, idle or boastful talk.

gas station A filling station.

gas·sy (gas′ē) *adj.* **gas·si·er, gas·si·est** 1 Characteristic of or impregnated with gas. 2 *Slang* Addicted to idle chatter or boastful talk.

gast (gast) *v.t. Obs.* To terrify. Compare AGHAST. [OE *gǣstan*]

gas tank 1 A gasometer. 2 A tank for holding gas or gasoline, as the fuel tank of an airplane or motor vehicle.

gastero- *combining form* Gastro-.

gas·ter·o·my·ce·tous (gas′tər·ō·mī·sē′təs) *adj.* Of or pertaining to a subgroup *(Gasteromycetes)* of fleshy fungi having spores enclosed in cavities within the fruit body, as puffballs and earthstars. [<GASTERO- + Gk. *mykēs, mykētos* fungus + -OUS]

Gas·ter·oph·i·lus (gas′tə·rof′ə·ləs) See GASTROPHILUS.

gas thermometer A thermometer which indicates temperature changes by variations in the pressure or volume of a contained gas, usually hydrogen.

gas·tight (gas′tīt′) *adj.* Not permitting the escape of gas.

gas·tral·gi·a (gas·tral′jē·ə) *n.* 1 *Pathol.* Neuralgia in the stomach. 2 Gastric pain.

gas·trec·to·my (gas·trek′tə·mē) *n. Surg.* An operation to remove a portion of the stomach.

gas·tric (gas′trik) *adj.* Of, pertaining to, or near the stomach. Compare illustration under ABDOMINAL.

gastric fever *Pathol.* 1 A bilious remittent fever; harvest fever. 2 Acute dyspepsia.

gastric juice *Biochem.* A thin acid fluid secreted by the glands of the stomach and containing several enzymes; the chief digestive fluid, acting mainly on proteins.

gas·trin (gas′trin) *n. Biochem.* A hormone secreted by the stomach membrane and promoting digestion by activating gastric juices.

gas·tri·tis (gas·trī′tis) *n. Pathol.* Inflammation of the stomach. —**gas·trit·ic** (gas·trit′ik) *adj.*

gastro- *combining form* 1 Stomach: *gastrolith.* 2 Stomach and: *gastroenterology.* Also **gastero-.** [<Gk. *gastēr* stomach]

gas·tro·coel (gas′trə·sēl) *n. Anat.* The archenteron. [<GASTRO- + Gk. *koilia* cavity]

gas·tro·col·ic (gas′trə·kol′ik) *adj. Anat.* Of, pertaining to, or attached to the stomach and the transverse colon.

gas·tro·di·aph·a·ny (gas′trō·dī·af′ə·nē) *n. Med.* Examination of the stomach by means of a small electric light inserted through the esophagus. Also **gas·tro·di·aph·a·nos·co·py** (gas′trō·dī·af′ə·nos′kə·pē). [<GASTRO- + Gk. *diaphanēs* transparent <*dia-* through + *phainein* appear]

gas·tro·en·ter·i·tis (gas′trō·en′tə·rī′tis) *n. Pathol.* Inflammation of the lining membrane of the stomach and bowels. —**gas′tro·en′te·rit′ic** (-tə·rit′ik) *adj.*

gas·tro·en·ter·ol·o·gy (gas′trō·en′tə·rol′ə·jē) *n.* The study of the anatomy, physiology, and pathology of the stomach and intestines. —**gas′tro·en′ter·ol′o·gist** *n.*

gas·tro·en·ter·os·to·my (gas′trō·en′tə·ros′tə·mē) *n. Surg.* An operation by which a passage is formed between the stomach and the intestine.

gas·tro·ga·vage (gas′trō·gə·väzh′) *n. Med.* Artificial feeding through an opening in the abdominal wall to the stomach. Also **gas·tros·to·ga·vage** (gas·tros′tō·gə·väzh′). [<GASTRO- + F *gavage* cramming <*gaver* gorge]

gas·tro·he·pat·ic (gas′trō·hi·pat′ik) *adj. Anat.* Of or pertaining to the stomach and the liver.

gas·tro·in·tes·ti·nal (gas′trō·in·tes′tə·nəl) *adj. Anat.* Of or pertaining to the stomach and the intestines.

gas·tro·lith (gas′trō·lith) *n. Pathol.* A calculus or stony formation in the gastric region.

gas·trol·o·gy (gas·trol′ə·jē) *n.* The study of the anatomy, physiology, and pathology of the stomach.

gas·tron·o·mer (gas·tron′ə·mər) *n.* An epicure. Also **gas·tro·nome** (gas′trə·nōm), **gas·tron′o·mist.**

gas·tro·nom·ic (gas′trə·nom′ik) *adj.* Of or pertaining to gastronomy. Also **gas′tro·nom′i·cal.** —**gas′tro·nom′i·cal·ly** *adv.*

gas·tron·o·my (gas·tron′ə·mē) *n.* The art of good eating; epicurism. [<F *gastronomie* <Gk. *gastronomia* <*gastēr* stomach + *nomos* law]

Gas·troph·i·lus (gas·trof′ə·ləs) *n.* A genus of dipterous insects whose larvae are parasitic on horses, especially *G. intestinalis*; a botfly: also called *Gasterophilus.* [<NL <Gk. *gastēr* stomach + *philos* loving]

gas·tro·pod (gas′trə·pod) *n.* Any of a large and diverse class (Gastropoda) of mollusks usually having a spiral shell and moving by means of a ventral muscular organ, including snails, slugs, limpets, and conches. —*adj.* Of or pertaining to the class of gastropods. [<NL <Gk. *gastēr* stomach + *pous, podos* foot] —**gas·trop·o·dan** (gas·trop′ə·dən), **gas·trop′o·dous** *adj.*

gas·trop·to·sis (gas′trop·tō′sis) *n. Pathol* Prolapse of the stomach. [<GASTRO- + Gk. *ptosis* a falling]

gas·tro·scope (gas′trə·skōp) *n. Med.* An electrical apparatus for illuminating and inspecting the human stomach. —**gas′tro·scop′ic** (-skop′ik) *adj.*

gas·tros·co·py (gas·tros′kə·pē) *n. Med.* An examination of the abdomen to discover disease.

gas·tro·stege (gas′trə·stēj) *n. Zool.* One of the abdominal scales of a reptile. [<GASTRO- + Gk. *stegē* a covering]

gas·trot·o·my (gas·trot′ə·mē) *n. Surg.* An opening of or cutting into the stomach or abdomen, as to remove a foreign substance.

gas·trot·ri·chan (gas·trot′rə·kən) *n.* Any of a class (Gastrotricha) of minute fresh-water animals, possibly related to the rotifers, having spindle-shaped bodies partly or entirely covered with spines, bristles, or scales. [<GASTRO- + Gk. *thrix, trichos* hair]

gas·tro·vas·cu·lar (gas′trō·vas′kyə·lər) *adj. Physiol.* **1** Serving both a circulating and a digestive function. **2** Of or pertaining to organs having such a dual function.

gas·tru·la (gas′trōō·lə) *n. pl.* **·lae** (-lē) *Biol.* That embryonic form of metazoic animals which consists of a two-layered sac enclosing a central cavity or archenteron and having an opening or blastopore at one end. [<NL, dim. of Gk. *gastēr* stomach] —**gas′tru·lar** *adj.*

gas·tru·la·tion (gas′trōō·lā′shən) *n.* The formation of a gastrula.

gas tube *Physics* A vacuum tube in which the pressure of the contained gas or vapor is such as to affect the electrical characteristics of the tube appreciably.

gas turbine A turbine engine in which liquid or gaseous fuel is burned under pressure and the expansion gases sent through a rotor unit connected with a generator.

gas warfare Warfare in which noxious or poisonous gases are dispersed by gas bombs or other means among enemy forces.

gas weld A fusion of metals by use of high-temperature gas flames, mixtures of hydrogen or acetylene with oxygen.

gas well A well from which natural gas flows.

gas·works (gas′wûrks′) *n.* A factory where illuminating gas or heating gas is made.

gat[1] (gat) *Archaic* Past tense of GET.

gat[2] (gat) *n.* A ship channel in an otherwise shallow place. [<ON, an opening]

gat[3] (gat) *n. Slang* A pistol. [Short for GATLING GUN]

gate[1] (gāt) *n.* **1** A movable barrier, commonly swinging on hinges: often distinguished from a door by having openwork. **2** An opening or passageway, as in a barrier, fence, wall, or enclosure, often with its surrounding masonry or woodwork; a portal. **3** *Geog.* A mountain gap or natural passageway. **4** That which gives or affords access: the *gates* of hell. **5** A frame in which a saw (or set of saws) is stretched. **6** *Mech.* A valve controlling the water supply of a water wheel or the like. **7** *Metall.* **a** A pouring hole in a mold. **b** A sprue or waste piece on a casting formed in a pouring hole. **8** A hinge. See illustration under HINGE. **9** The total paid admissions at a sports event; the total attendance. See synonyms under ENTRANCE. —*v.t.* **gat·ed, gat·ing** *Brit.* To keep (a college student) within the gates as a punishment. ◆ Homophone: *gait.* [OE *gatu,* plural of *geat* opening]

gate[2] (gāt) *n. Scot.* **1** Method of doing; manner; way. **2** A course or path. ◆ Homophone: *gait.* [<ON *gata* way]

gate·age (gā′tij) *n.* **1** Use of gates as in controlling the flow of water; also, the gates used. **2** Area of gate opening, as of a turbine gate.

gate·crash·er (gāt′krash′ər) *n. Slang* A person who gains admittance to a function without paying or without an invitation.

gate hinge *Mech.* A type of hinge formed of two detachable sections, one of which pivots on a cylindrical core projecting from the other. See illustration under HINGE.

gate·house (gāt′hous′) *n.* A house beside, over, or at a gate, as a power station, a porter's lodge, or a medieval defensive structure.

gate·keep·er (gāt′kē′pər) *n.* One in charge of a gate. Also **gate′man.**

gate-leg table (gāt′leg′) A table with swinging legs which support drop leaves and fold against the frame when the leaves are let down.

gate money Money paid for admission to a sports event, theatrical performance, etc.

gate-post (gāt′pōst′) *n.* Either of two posts between which a gate swings.

Gates (gāts), **Horatio,** 1728–1806, American general in the Revolution. —**Reginald Ruggles,** 1882–1962, Canadian botanist and geneticist.

Gates·head (gāts′hed) A port on the Tyne in NE Durham, England.

gate·way (gāt′wā′) *n.* **1** An entrance that is or may be closed with a gate. **2** That which is regarded as a means of ingress or egress. **3** The guides of a saw frame. See synonyms under ENTRANCE.

Gath (gath) In the Bible, one of the five cities of the Philistines; the home of Goliath: I *Samuel* v 17.

gath·er (gath′ər) *v.t.* **1** To bring together in one place or group. **2** To bring together from various places, sources, etc. **3** To pick, harvest, or collect. **4** To collect or summon up, as one's energies, for an effort, trial, etc. **5** To acquire or gain in increasing amount or degree: The storm *gathered* force. **6** To come to understand, believe, or infer. **7** To clasp or enfold: to *gather* someone into one's arms. **8** To draw into folds or plaits, as by shirring. **9** To wrinkle (the brow). —*v.i.* **10** To come together. **11** To increase by accumulation. **12** To wrinkle up, as the brow. **13** To come to a head; contract, as a boil. See synonyms under AMASS, CONVOKE. —**to gather up** To pick up and collect together in one place. —*n.* A plait or fold in cloth, held by a thread passing through the folds; a drawing together. [OE *gadrian*] —**gath′er·a·ble** *adj.*

gath·er·er (gath′ər·ər) *n.* **1** One who or that which gathers. **2** A sewing-machine attachment for gathering cloth. **3** One who collects taxes, fees, etc.

gath·er·ing (gath′ər·ing) *n.* **1** The action of that which gathers. **2** An assemblage of people. **3** An accumulation or collection of anything. **4** The contraction of a passage, as in a chimney or drain. **5** A series of gathers. **6** An abscess or boil. **7** In bookbinding, a collection of printed sheets in proper order. See synonyms under ASSEMBLY, COMPANY.

gat·ing (gā′ting) *n.* **1** A form of punishment. See GATE[1] *v.* **2** *Mech.* A gate in a lock tumbler for the passage of the stub.

Gat·ling gun (gat′ling) An early machine-gun having numerous barrels rotating about a central axis, each being loaded and discharged as it was brought to firing position by the turning of a crank. [after R. J. *Gatling,* 1818–1903, U.S. inventor]

Ga·tun (gä·tōōn′) A town in northern Panama Canal Zone. *Spanish* **Ga·tún′.**

Gatun Dam A dam of the Panama Canal at Gatun; 7,700 feet long, 115 feet high; impounding **Gatun Lake,** 163 square miles; 85 feet above sea level.

gauche (gōsh) *adj.* Awkward; clumsy; boorish. [<F, left-handed]

gauche·rie (gōsh·rē′) *n.* **1** An awkward or tactless action. **2** Clumsiness; tactlessness. [<F]

Gau·cho (gou′chō) *n. pl.* **·chos** A native of the South American pampas of mixed Indian and Spanish ancestry; a cowboy. [<Sp.]

gaud (gôd) *n.* An article of vulgar finery. [<OF *gaudir* be merry <L *gaudere* rejoice]

Synonyms: bauble, finery, gew-gaw, gimcrack, kickshaw, toy, trinket, trumpery.

gau·de·a·mus ig·i·tur (gô′dē·ā′məs ij′ə·tər, gou′dā·ä′mōōs ē′gi·tōōr) *Latin* Therefore let us be merry: the first words of a famous medieval student song.

gaud·er·y (gô′dər·ē) *n.* Showy ornament; finery.

Gau·dier-Br·zes·ka (gō·dyā′bər·zes·kà′), **Henri,** 1891–1915, French sculptor.

gaud·y[1] (gô′dē) *adj.* **gaud·i·er, gaud·i·est** Obtrusively brilliant in color: garish; flashy. —**gaud′i·ly** *adv.* —**gaud′i·ness** *n.*

gaud·y[2] (gô′dē) *n. Brit.* A feast or festival; an entertainment; especially, an annual dinner given by a college in one of the English universities. [<L *gaudium* joy]

gauf·fer (gôf′ər) See GOFFER.

gauge (gāj) See GAGE[1].

Gau·guin (gō·gaṅ′), **Paul,** 1848–1903, French painter.

Gaul (gôl) An ancient name for the territory south and west of the Rhine, west of the Alps, and north of the Pyrenees; roughly the area of modern France: Latin *Gallia.* See also CISALPINE GAUL, TRANSALPINE GAUL, TRANSPADANE GAUL.

Gaul (gôl) *n.* **1** A native of ancient Gaul. **2** A Frenchman. [<F *Gaule* <L *Gallus*]

Gau·leit·er (gou′lī·tər) *n. German* A district leader of the Nazi party.

Gaul·ish (gô′lish) *adj.* Of ancient Gaul, its people, or their Celtic language. —*n.* The extinct continental Celtic language of Gaul.

Gaull·ism (gôl′iz′əm) *n.* The policies or philosophy of Charles de Gaulle and his followers. —**Gaull′ist** *adj.* & *n.*

gaul·the·ri·a (gôl·thir′ē·ə) *n.* **1** Any of a large genus (*Gaultheria*) of aromatic shrubs or undershrubs with thick, shining, evergreen leaves and axillary white or rose-colored nodding flowers. The wintergreen is a well-known North American species. **2** Oil of wintergreen: also called **oil of gaultheria.** [<NL, after Dr. Jean-François *Gaultier,* 1708?–56, Canadian physician and botanist]

gaum (gôm) *v.t. Dial.* To smear, as with something sticky. [Var. of GUM]

gaunt (gônt) *adj.* **1** Emaciated, as from lack of food; lank; lean; meager; thin. **2** Grim; desolate. [? <OF *gent* elegant, infl. in meaning by ON *gand* a tall, thin person] —**gaunt′ly** *adv.* —**gaunt′ness** *n.*

Synonyms: emaciated, famished, hungry, lank, lean, meager, pinched, thin, wan, wasted. See MEAGER.

gaunt·let[1] (gônt′lit, gänt′-) *n.* **1** In medieval armor, a leather glove covered with metal plates. **2** A modern glove with long wrist-extension; also, the part of the glove covering the wrist.

GAUNTLET (*def. 1*)

—**to throw** (or **fling**) **down the gauntlet** To challenge to combat or contest. Also spelled *gantlet.* [<OF *gantelet,* dim. of *gant* mitten] — **gaunt′let·ed** *adj.*

gaunt·let[2] (gônt′lit, gänt′-) See GANTLET[1].

gaun·try (gôn′trē), **gaun·tree** See GANTRY.

gaur (gour) *n.* A large wild ox *(Bos gaurus)* of southeastern Asia, having a hump on the dorsal ridge and horns curving backward. [<Hind.]

gauss (gous) *n. pl.* **gauss** *Physics* The cgs unit of magnetic induction, equal to a field exerting a force of one dyne on unit magnetic pole, or 0.7958 ampere-turn per centimeter. [after K. F. *Gauss*]

Gauss (gous), **Karl Friedrich,** 1777–1855, German mathematician.

Gau·ta·ma (gôt′ə·mə, gou′-) See BUDDHA. Also spelled *Gotama.*

Gau·tier (gō·yā′), **Théophile,** 1811–72, French writer.

gauze (gôz) *n.* **1** A light perforated fabric in which the warp threads are crossed or twisted around the filling. **2** Any thin open-woven material: wire *gauze.* **3** A mist; light fog. —*adj.* Resembling or made of gauze. [<MF *gaze,* appar. from *Gaza,* where originally made]

gauz·y (gô′zē) *adj.* **gauz·i·er, gauz·i·est** Thin and diaphanous, like gauze. See synonyms under FINE[1]. —**gauz′i·ly** *adv.* —**gauz′i·ness** *n.*

ga·vage (gə·väzh′, *Fr.* gȧ·väzh′) *n.* **1** A method of fattening poultry by forcing them to swallow a prepared food. **2** *Med.* A method of forcing patients to eat, as through a stomach tube. [<F <*gaver* gorge]

gave (gāv) Past tense of GIVE.

gav·el[1] (gav′əl) *n.* A mallet used by a presiding officer to call for order or attention. [Prob. var. of KEVEL]

gav·el[2] (gav′əl) *n. Brit. Dial.* An unbound bundle of grain. [<AF *gavelle* sheaf]

gav·el[3] (gav′əl) *n.* In old English law, customs duties or tribute; also, rent. [OE *gafol* tribute]

gav·el·kind (gav′əl·kīnd′) *n. Brit.* **1** A tenure of land whereby the lands of a deceased person are divided equally among his sons or nearest heirs; can be alienated by an heir after reaching the age of fifteen; and cannot escheat for felony: a custom once wide-spread in England, but now limited to Kent. **2** Any custom of dividing property equally among male heirs. [<GAVEL[3] + KIND]

gav·e·lock (gav′ə·lok) *n. Brit. Dial.* An iron crowbar. [OE *gafeluc* spear]

ga·vi·al (gā′vē·əl) *n.* The great Indian crocodile *(Gavialis gangeticus),* having long, slender jaws, the upper one knobbed at the end. [<F <Hind. *ghariyal*]

ga·votte (gə·vot′) *n.* **1** A vivacious French dance, resembling the minuet. **2** Music appropriate to such a dance. Also **ga·vot′.** [<F <Provençal *gavoto* Alpine dance <*gavot* an inhabitant of the Alps]

Ga·wain (gä′win, gô′-) The "perfect knight" of Arthurian legend, nephew of King Arthur, appearing in the earliest sources, and in Malory. Also **Ga′waine.**

gawd (gôd), etc. See GAUD, etc.

gawk (gôk) *v.i. Colloq.* To stare or behave awkwardly and stupidly. —*n.* An awkward, stupid fellow. [Cf. dial. E *gawk* left-handed]

gawk·y (gô′kē) *adj.* **gawk·i·er, gawk·i·est** Awkward and dull; clownish; clumsy. See synonyms under AWKWARD. —*n. pl.* **gawk·ies** A gawk. — **gawk′i·ly** *adv.* —**gawk′i·ness** *n.*

gay (gā) *adj.* **1** Filled with or inspiring mirth; merry; sportive. **2** Brilliant; showy. **3** Loving pleasure; wanton. **3** *Slang* Homosexual; also, intended for homosexuals: a *gay* bar. See synonyms under AIRY, CHEERFUL, HAPPY, MERRY, VIVACIOUS, WANTON. —*n. Slang* A homosexual person. —*adv. Scot.* Fairly; considerably: sometimes spelled *gey;* also **gay′lie.** [<OF <Gmc.] —**gay′ness** *n.* —**gay′some** *adj.*

Gay (gā), **John,** 1685–1732, English poet and playwright.

Gay·a (gī′ə) A city and pilgrimage center in central Bihar, India.

gay·al (gā′əl, gə·yäl′) *n.* A semi-domesticated bovine (*Bos frontalis*) of southeastern Asia, very similar to the closely related wild and slightly larger gaur. [<Hind.]

gay·e·ty (gā′ə·tē), **gay·ly** (gā′lē), etc. See GAIETY, GAILY, etc.

Gay-Lus·sac (gā·lü·sák′), **Joseph Louis,** 1778–1850, French chemist and physicist.

Gay-Lussac's law See CHARLES'S LAW.

Gay Nine·ties (nīn′tēz) The decade from 1890 to 1900.

Gay-Pay-Oo (gā′pā′ōō′) See OGPU.

Ga·za (gä′zə) A city in SW Palestine; since 1948 administered with the surrounding coastal district **(Gaza strip)** by Egypt, since 1957, by United Nations. *Arabic* **Ghaz·ze** (gaz′zē).

ga·za·bo (gə·zā′bō) *n. U.S. Slang* An awkward or eccentric man or boy; a queer fellow. [Cf. Sp. *gazapo* a shrewd fellow]

gaze (gāz) *v.i.* **gazed, gaz·ing** To look earnestly and steadily, as in scrutiny, admiration, or concern. —*n.* **1** A continued or intense look. **2** Something gazed at. See synonyms under LOOK. —**at gaze** *Brit.* In a gazing attitude; in the act of looking around with fear or apprehension, as a stag on hearing hounds. [ME *gasen* <Scand. Cf. dial Sw. *gasa* stare.] —**gaz′er** *n.*

ga·ze·bo (gə·zē′bō, -zā′-) *n. pl.* **·bos** or **·boes** A structure commanding a wide view, such as a summerhouse, or projecting window or balcony; a belvedere. [? <GAZE, imitating a Latin form]

gaze·hound (gāz′hound′) *n.* A hound that hunts by sight.

ga·zelle (gə·zel′) *n.* A small, delicately formed antelope of northern Africa and Arabia (genus *Gazella*), with recurved horns and large, gentle eyes. [<OF <Arabic *ghazāl* gazelle]

GAZELLE
(Species vary from 2 to 3 feet in height)

ga·zette (gə·zet′) *n.* **1** A newspaper, or printed account of current events. **2** *Brit.* Any official government journal announcing appointments, promotions, etc. —*v.t. Brit.* **ga·zet·ted, ga·zet·ting** To publish or announce in a gazette. [<F <Ital. *gazzetta* <dial. Ital. (Venetian) *gazeta* a coin, orig. the price of the paper]

gaz·et·teer (gaz′ə·tir′) *n.* **1** A dictionary of geographical names. **2** A writer or contributor of news for a gazette.

Ga·zi·an·tep (gä′zē·än·tep′) A city in southern Turkey in Asia: formerly *Aintab.*

gaz·pa·cho (gäz·pä′chō) *n. pl.* **·chos** A cold Spanish soup made with fresh tomatoes, peppers, olive oil, vinegar, garlic, and spices, to which cucumber and bread are added. [<Sp.]

Gd *Chem.* Gadolinium (symbol Gd).

Gdańsk (gə·dänsk′, *Polish* gdän′y′sk) The Polish name for DANZIG.

Gdy·nia (gə·din′yə, *Polish* gdē′nyä) A port in NW Poland.

Ge (jē, gē) See GAEA.

Ge (zhā) *n.* A large and important South American Indian linguistic stock of eastern and central Brazil: also called *Tapuyan.*

Ge *Chem.* Germanium (symbol Ge).

ge·an·ti·cline (jē·an′tə·klīn) *n. Geol.* A vast upward flexure of the earth's crust: opposed to *geosyncline.* [<Gk. *ge* earth + ANTICLINE] — **ge·an′ti·cli′nal** *adj.* & *n.*

gear (gir) *n.* **1** *Mech.* **a** The moving parts or appliances that constitute a whole or set, serving to transmit motion or change its rate or direction: valve *gear,* reversing *gear.* **b** A cogwheel. **c** The engagement of toothed wheels or other parts in a mechanical assembly. **2** *Naut.* The ropes, blocks, etc., used in working a spar or sail; all the rigging of a ship. **3** Fitness for harmonious and effective action; working relationship: out of *gear.* **4** Any equipment, as dress, vestments, warlike accouterments, harness, tools, or household necessaries. **5** *Archaic* Property; possessions; goods. **6** *Archaic* Arms; armor. —*v.t.* **1** *Mech.* **a** To put into gear. **b** To equip with gears. **c** To connect by means of gears. **2** To regulate so as to match or suit something else: to *gear* production to demand. **3** To put gear on; harness; dress. —*v.i.* **4** To come into or be in gear; mesh. [<ON *gervi* equipment]

gear·box (gir′boks′) *n.* The gears and gearcase comprising the variable transmission of an automobile.

gear·case (gir′kās′) *n. Mech.* A metal housing for the gears of machinery.

gear·ing (gir′ing) *n. Mech.* **1** Power-transmitting gear in general. **2** Working parts collectively. **3** Ropes and tackle.

gear·shift (gir′shift′) *n. Mech.* A device for engaging or disengaging the gears in a power-transmission system.

gear·wheel (gir′hwēl′) *n. Mech.* A cogwheel.

geck (gek) *v.t.* & *v.i. Scot.* & *Brit. Dial.* **1** To show contempt; toss (the head); jeer. **2** *Obs.* To fool; cheat. —*n. Scot.* **1** Scorn or derision; jeer; taunt. **2** An object of contempt or derision; dupe.

geck·o (gek′ō) *n. pl.* **geck·os** or **geck·oes** Any of a family (*Geckonidae*) of small lizards having toes with adhesive disks; wall lizard. [<Malay *gēkoq,* imit. of its cry]

GECKO
(Varies from 4 to over 12 inches in length)

ged (ged) *n. Scot.* A fish, the pike. Also **gedd.**

Ged·des (ged′ēz), **Norman Bel,** 1893–1958, U.S. industrial and stage designer. —**Sir Patrick,** 1854–1932, Scottish biologist.

Gé·dé·on (zhā·dā·ôn′) French form of GIDEON. Also *Ital.* **Ge·de·o·ne** (gā′dā·ō′nā).

Ge·diz (gə·dēz′) A river in western Turkey, flowing 215 miles SW to the Gulf of Smyrna: formerly *Sarabat.*

gee[1] (jē) *n.* The letter G, g, or its sound.

gee[2] (jē) *v.t.* & *v.i.* **1** To turn to the right. **2** To evade; swerve. —*interj.* Turn to the right! a call in driving animals without reins: opposed to *haw*[4]. Also spelled *jee.* [Origin uncertain]

Gee (jē) *interj.* A minced oath: a euphemism for Jesus.

geek (gēk) *n.* A carnival performer who publicly eats or swallows live animals as a sensational spectacle. [Prob. var. of GECK]

Gee·long (jē·lông′) A port in southern Victoria, Australia.

Geel·vink Bay (khāl′vingk) An inlet of the Pacific in NW New Guinea.

gee·pound (jē′pound′) See SLUG (def. 5).

Geer·trui·da (hâr·troi′dä) Dutch form of GERTRUDE.

geese (gēs) Plural of GOOSE[1].

geest (gēst) *n. Geol.* **1** Material derived from rock decay in its natural place. **2** Gravel; especially, alluvium. [<Du., barren, dry soil]

Ge·ez (gē·ez′, gēz) *n.* Ethiopic.

gee·zer (gē′zər) *n. Slang* A queer old person. [Var. of *guiser* mummer <GUISE, *v.* (def. 3)]

Gef·le (yev′lə) See GAVLE.

ge·gen·schein (gā′gən·shīn) *n. Astron.* A patch of faint, hazy light sometimes observable at night on the point of the ecliptic opposite the sun: associated with the zodiacal light. Also called *counterglow.* [<G]

Ge·hen·na (gi·hen′ə) *n.* **1** In the Bible, the valley of Hinnom near Jerusalem, where offal was thrown and fires kept burning to purify the air. **2** A place of torment. **3** In the New Testament, hell; hellfire. [<LL <Gk. *geenna* <Hebrew *gehinnom* valley of *Hinnom*]

Gei·ger (gī′gər), **Hans,** 1882–1945, German physicist.

Gei·ger counter (gī′gər) *Physics* A sensitive instrument for counting ionizing particles in the air, as alpha particles or cosmic rays and also for detecting the amount of radioactivity in a given area. Also called *counting tube.* [after Hans *Geiger*]

Gei·kie (gī′kē), **Sir Archibald,** 1835–1924, English geologist and writer.

gei·sha (gā′shə) *n. pl.* **·sha** or **·shas** A Japanese girl trained to furnish entertainment by singing, dancing, etc. [<Japanese]

Geiss·ler tube (gīs′lər) *Physics* A sealed and partly evacuated glass tube containing electrodes: used for the study of electric discharges through gases. [after Heinrich *Geissler,* 1814–79, German physicist]

gel (jel) *n. Chem.* A colloidal dispersion of a solid in a liquid which may range from the nearly liquid to the solid state, but is typically a semisolid and of a jellylike consistency, as gelatin, mucilage, uncooked egg white, etc. —*v.i.* **gelled, gel·ling** To change into a gel; jellify. [Short for GELATIN]

ge·län·de·sprung (gə·len′də·shprŏŏng) *n.* In skiing, a jump, using both poles, made from a crouching position. [<G <*gelände* level ground + *sprung* jump]

gel·a·tin (jel′ə·tin) *n.* A hard, transparent, tasteless, colloidal protein produced from bones, white connective tissue, and skin of animals. It is soluble in hot water, cooling to a jelly, but insoluble in alcohol or chloroform. Edible gelatin, used for foods, drugs, etc., is a highly refined product of yellowish tint; technical gelatin is used in photography, lithography, in the manufacture of sizing, plastics, etc. Also **gel′a·tine** (-tin, -tēn). [<F *gélatine*, orig. a soup made from fish <Ital. *gelatina* <*gelata* jelly <L. See JELLY.]

ge·lat·i·nate (ji·lat′ə·nāt) *v.t.* & *v.i.* **·nat·ed, ·nat·ing** To change into gelatin or a jellylike substance. **—ge·lat′i·na′tion** *n.*

ge·lat·i·nize (ji·lat′ə·nīz) *v.* **·nized, ·niz·ing** *v.t.* **1** To gelatinate. **2** To treat or coat with gelatin. —*v.i.* **3** To be changed into gelatin or jelly. —**ge·lat′i·ni·za′tion** *n.*

ge·lat·i·noid (ji·lat′ə·noid) *adj.* Like jelly or gelatin. —*n.* A gelatinlike substance.

ge·lat·i·nous (ji·lat′ə·nəs) *adj.* **1** Of the nature of gelatin; like jelly. **2** Of or pertaining to or consisting of gelatin. **—ge·lat′i·nous·ly** *adv.* — **ge·lat′i·nous·ness** *n.*

ge·la·tion (ji·lā′shən) *n.* Solidification, especially by cooling.

geld[1] (geld) *n.* In early English history, a tax or tribute. [OE]

geld[2] (geld) *v.t.* **geld·ed** or **gelt, geld·ing 1** To castrate; emasculate; also, to spay. **2** To deprive of an essential part; weaken. [<ON *gelda* castrate]

Gel·der·land (gel′dər·land, *Du.* hel′dər·länt) A province of eastern and central Netherlands; 1,921 square miles; capital, Arnhem: also *Guelderland, Guelders.*

geld·ing (gel′ding) *n.* A castrated animal, especially a horse.

Ge·lée (zhə·lā′), **Claude** See LORRAIN, CLAUDE.

Ge·li·bo·lu (ge′lē·bō·lo͞o′) The Turkish name for GALLIPOLI.

gel·id (jel′id) *adj.* Very cold; icy; frozen. [<L *gelidus*] **—ge·lid′i·ty** *n.* **—gel′id·ly** *adv.*

gel·se·mine (jel′sə·mīn, -min) *n. Chem.* A white, crystalline, very poisonous alkaloid, $C_{22}H_{26}O_2N_2$, obtained from gelsemium: used as a depressant and mydriatic.

gel·se·mi·um (jel·sē′mē·əm) *n.* **1** The poisonous root of the yellow jasmine *(Gelsemium sempervirens).* **2** A medical preparation made from it. [<NL <Ital. *gelsomino* jasmine]

Gel·sen·kir·chen (gel′zən·kir′khən) A city in the Ruhr valley, North Rhine-Westphalia, Germany.

gelt (gelt) *n. Slang* Money. [<G *geld* money]

gem (jem) *n.* **1** A precious stone, especially when set as an ornament. **2** Anything rare, delicate, and perfect, as a work of literature or art. **3** A carved or engraved semiprecious stone; any jewel. **4** *Printing* A size of type between brilliant and diamond. **5** A light cake somewhat like a muffin. —*v.t.* **gemmed, gem·ming** To adorn with or as with gems. [OE *gim* <L *gemma* jewel]

Ge·ma·ra (gə·mä′rə, -môr′ə) *n.* The second part of the Jewish Talmud, an exposition of the first part (Mishna). [<Aramaic, completion]

gem·el (jem′əl) *adj.* Paired; coupled: a *gemel* window. [<OF <L *gemellus* doubled]

gem·i·nate (jem′ə·nāt) *v.t.* & *v.i.* **·nat·ed, ·nat·ing 1** To make or become double; pair. **2** *Ling.* To double a phoneme, particularly a consonant. —*adj.* (-nit) *Bot.* Occurring in pairs or couples, as leaves. [<L *geminatus,* pp. of *geminare* <*geminus* a twin] **—gem′i·na′tion** *n.*

Gem·i·ni (jem′ə·nī) **1** A constellation, the Twins. See CONSTELLATION. **2** The third sign of the zodiac.

gem·ma (jem′ə) *n. pl.* **·mae** (-ē) *Bot.* **1** A bud. **2** The budlike product of gemmation. [<L]

gem·mate (jem′āt) *adj. Bot.* Bearing buds; reproducing by buds. [<L *gemmatus,* pp. of *gemmare* bud]

gem·ma·tion (jem·ā′shən) *n. Bot.* **1** Reproduction by budlike outgrowth that becomes an independent individual. **2** The period of the expansion of buds.

gem·me·ous (jem′ē·əs) *adj.* Relating to, having the nature of, or resembling gems.

gem·mip·a·rous (jem·ip′ər·əs) *adj. Bot.* Reproducing by, or producing, buds. [<L *gemma* bud + -PAROUS] **—gem·mip′a·rous·ly** *adv.*

gem·mu·la·tion (jem′yo͞o·lā′shən) *n. Biol.* Reproduction by, or formation of, gemmules.

gem·mule (jem′yo͞ol) *n.* **1** *Bot.* A small bud or gemma. **2** *Biol.* One of the minute hypothetical granules that, according to the doctrine of pangenesis, reproduce the cells or organic units from which they are thrown off. **3** *Zool.* A small internal reproductive bud in certain fresh-water sponges. [<LL *gemmula,* dim. of *gemma* bud]

gem·my (jem′ē) *adj.* **1** Full of, set with, or containing gems. **2** Like a gem; bright; sparkling.

gem·ol·o·gy (jem·ol′ə·jē) *n.* The scientific study and investigation of gems. **—gem·o·log·i·cal** (jem′ə·loj′i·kəl) *adj.* **—gem·ol′o·gist** *n.*

ge·mot (gə·mōt′) *n.* In early English history, a public meeting or assembly: the folk *gemot*; a local court. Also **ge·mote′.** [OE *gemōt*]

gems·bok (gemz′·bok) *n. pl.* **·bok** or **·boks** A South African antelope (*Oryx gazella*) having long, sharp, nearly straight horns and a tufted tail. [<Afrikaans <G *gemse* chamois + *bock* a buck]

GEMSBOK
(About 3 feet high at the shoulder; horns to 3 feet)

Gem State Nickname of IDAHO.

gem·stone (jem′stōn′) *n.* A mineral or petrified organic material of a quality suitable for cutting, polishing, and using in jewelry.

ge·müt·lich (gə·müt′likh) *adj. German* Full of good feeling; genial; comfortable.

Ge·müt·lich·keit (gə·müt′likh·kīt) *n. German* Good feeling; a feeling of comfort.

-gen *suffix of nouns* **1** *Chem.* That which produces: *oxygen.* **2** *Biol.* That which is produced: *antigen.* [<F *-gène* <Gk. *-genēs,* <*gen-*, stem of *gignesthai* be born, become]

gen·darme (zhän′därm, *Fr.* zhäṅ·dárm′) *n. pl.* **·darmes** (-därmz, *Fr.* -dárm′) One of a corps of armed police, especially in France. [<F <*gens d'armes* men-at-arms]

gen·darm·e·rie (zhän′där·mə·rē, zhän·därm′·ə·rē; *Fr.* zhäṅ·dárm·rē′) *n.* Gendarmes collectively. Also **gen·darm′e·ry.**

gen·der (jen′dər) *n.* **1** *Gram.* In many languages, as in the Indo-European and Semitic families, a grammatical category of nouns governing the form assumed by the words which modify or refer to them. **Natural gender** corresponds to sex or lack of sex; animate beings are either masculine or feminine, inanimate objects are neuter. This is true of English, which indicates natural gender by pronoun reference (*he, she, it,* etc.), by suffixes and prefixes (*aviator, aviatrix, emperor, empress, he-bear, she-bear,* etc.), or by completely different forms (*cow, bull,* etc.). **Grammatical gender** may have a partial correspondence to sex for animate beings, but sexless objects can be of any gender. Latin and German have three grammatical genders (masculine, feminine, and neuter) often without reference to sex, as seen in Latin *nauta* sailor, which is in a feminine declension. French and Hebrew have two genders, the names of inanimate objects being either masculine or feminine. In some languages, as in the Algonquian family, gender classification is made on another basis entirely—that of animate and inanimate categories. **2** *Colloq.* Sex. **3** *Obs.* A kind; genus. —*v.t.* & *v.i. Obs.* To engender. [<OF *gendre* <L *genus, -eris.* Doublet of GENUS, GENRE.]

gene (jēn) *n. Biol.* The chemically complex unit which is assumed to be the carrier of specific physical characters from parents to offspring, being transmitted through the chromosomes of the gametes and subject to many influences, as mutation, translocation, crossing over, radiation, X-rays, etc.: also called *factor.* [<Gk. *genea* breed, kind]

Gene (jēn) Diminutive of EUGENE.

ge·ne·al·o·gist (jē′nē·al′ə·jist, jen′ē-) *n.* One versed in genealogies.

ge·ne·al·o·gy (jē′nē·al′ə·jē, jen′ē-) *n. pl.* **·gies 1** A record of descent from some ancestor; a list of ancestors and their descendants. **2** Descent in a direct line; pedigree. **3** The science that treats of pedigrees. [<Gk. *genea* race + -LOGY] **—ge·ne·a·log·i·cal** (jē′nē·ə·loj′i·kəl, jen′ē-) *adj.* **—ge′ne·a·log′i·cal·ly** *adv.*

gen·e·ra (jen′ər·ə) Plural of GENUS. [<L]

gen·er·a·ble (jen′ə·ər·bəl) *adj.* Capable of being generated. [<L *generabilis* <*generare* generate]

gen·er·al (jen′ər·əl) *adj.* **1** Pertaining to, including, or affecting all of the whole; not local or particular: a *general* election; a *general* anesthetic. **2** Common to or current among the majority; prevalent: the *general* opinion. **3** Extended in scope, meaning, or content; not restricted in application: a *general* principle. **4** Not limited to a special class; miscellaneous: a *general* cargo. **5** Not detailed or precise: a *general* idea. **6** Usual or customary: one's *general* habit. **7** Dealing with all branches of a business or pursuit; not specialized: a *general* store; a *general* practitioner. **8** Superior in rank: attorney *general.* —*n.* **1** *Mil.* **a** In the U.S. Army, Air Force, or Marine Corps, an officer ranking next above a lieutenant general, equivalent in rank to an admiral in the Navy. **b** Any general officer, as a brigadier general, lieutenant general, etc.: a shortened form. **c** In

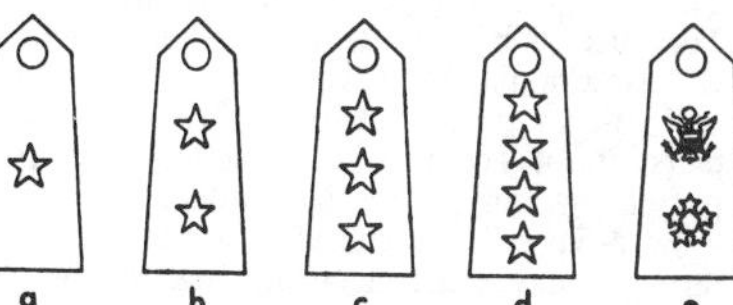

INSIGNIA OF GENERALS—UNITED STATES ARMY
a. Brigadier general. *b.* Major general. *c.* Lieutenant general. *d.* General. *e.* General of the Army.

many foreign armies, an officer of superior grade, usually ranking just below a marshal or field marshal. **2** *Eccl.* The chief of a religious order. **3** A general statement, fact, or principle. **4** *Archaic* The people or the public. **—brigadier general** An officer in the U.S. Army, Air Force, or Marine Corps ranking next above a colonel and next below a major general. **—in general** For the most part; in the main. **—lieutenant general** An officer in the U.S. Army, Air Force, or Marine Corps ranking next above a major general and next below a general. **—major general** An officer in the U.S. Army, Air Force, or Marine Corps ranking next above a brigadier general and next below a lieutenant general. [<OF <L *generalis* of a race or kind <*genus, generis* kind]

Synonyms (adj.): common, commonplace, customary, everyday, familiar, frequent, habitual, normal, ordinary, popular, prevalent, public, universal, usual. *Common* signifies frequently occurring, not out of the regular course, not exceptional; hence, not above the average, not excellent or distinguished; inferior, or even low; it also signifies pertaining to or participated in by two or more persons or things; as, Sorrow is *common* to the race. *General* may signify pertaining equally to all of a class, race, etc., but often signifies pertaining to the greater number, but not necessarily to all. *Universal* applies to all without exception; *general* applies to all with possible or comparatively few exceptions; *common* applies to very many without deciding whether or not they are all. A *common* remark is one we often hear; a *general* experience is one that comes to the majority of people; a *universal* experience is one from which no human being is exempt. Compare COMMON, FREQUENT, HABITUAL, NORMAL, USUAL. *Antonyms*: exceptional, infrequent, odd, peculiar, queer, rare, singular, strange, uncommon, unfamiliar, unknown, unparalleled, unprecedented, unusual.

general agent *Law* One appointed by a principal to act for him solely or particularly.

General Assembly 1 The deliberative body of the United Nations, meeting in annual or special sessions, in which every member nation is represented. **2** *U.S.* The legislature in some States. **3** The highest ecclesiastical governing body of certain denominations.

General Court The legislature in Massachusetts and New Hampshire.
gen·er·al·cy (jen′ər·əl·sē) *n.* Rank, authority, or tenure of office of a general.
general delivery 1 A post-office department that delivers mail to an addressee when called for. 2 Mail so addressed.
general election An election on a set date in which every constituency chooses a representative.
gen·er·al·is·si·mo (jen′ər·əl·is′i·mō) *n. pl.* **·mos** A supreme military or military and naval commander. [< Ital.]
gen·er·al·i·ty (jen′ə·ral′ə·tē) *n. pl.* **·ties** 1 The main part; chief portion; majority: the *generality* of voters. 2 Anything general or not specific; especially, a vague general statement: to deal in *generalities.* 3 The state of being general or generalized. Also **gen·er·al·ty** (jen′ər·əl·tē).
gen·er·al·i·za·tion (jen′ər·əl·ə·zā′shən, -ī·zā′-) *n.* 1 Act of generalizing. 2 A statement or proposition expressed in general terms, applying to a class or numerous members of a class, rather than covering only an individual case; opposite of *particularization.*
gen·er·al·ize (jen′ər·əl·īz′) *v.* **·ized, ·iz·ing** *v.t.* 1 To treat as having general or wide application. 2 To cause to be used or understood generally or widely; popularize. 3 To draw or frame (a general rule or principle) from particular evidence, facts, etc. 4 To draw or frame a general rule or principle from (particular evidence, facts, etc.). —*v.i.* 5 To talk in general rather than particular terms; make generalizations; be vague. 6 To draw general ideas or inferences from particulars.
General Land Office A U.S. government bureau in charge of surveying, selling, and disposing of claims to public land.
gen·er·al·ly (jen′ər·əl·ē) *adv.* 1 For the most part; ordinarily; in most but not all cases. 2 Without going into particulars. 3 So as to include or apply to all; collectively or universally.
general officer Any army officer holding a rank higher than colonel.
General of the Air Force The highest ranking officer of the U.S. Air Force.
General of the Armies A special title and rank conferred upon John J. Pershing in 1919.
General of the Army An officer of the highest rank in the U.S. Army: equivalent to marshal or field marshal in other armies. For insignia see illustration under GENERAL.
general paralysis See under PARESIS.
gen·er·al-pur·pose (jen′ər·əl·pûr′pəs) *adj.* Good for many purposes: A good *general-purpose* horse may be used as a draft horse or for pleasure driving.
general semantics A discipline for human living, formulated by Alfred Korzybski, involving a critical analysis of verbal and non-verbal symbols as these enter into behavioral responses, and a denial of the universality of Aristotelian logic: in practice using a methodology based on modern science, distinguishing carefully between levels of abstraction, between statements and the events they represent, generalizations and the particular, etc., avoiding polarized (either-or) orientations, and emphasizing unity and relationships within wholes.
gen·er·al·ship (jen′ər·əl·ship) *n.* 1 A general's office or rank. 2 A general's military skill or management. 3 Management or leadership of any sort.
general staff 1 A body of officers who direct the military policy and strategy of a national state. 2 A group of officers charged with directing a division or higher unit and operating from a headquarters under a commander in chief.
General Staff In the U.S. Army, the supreme military staff for policy and strategy, consisting of the Chief of Staff, several deputy and assistant Chiefs of Staff, including those heading sections of personnel administration (G-1), military intelligence (G-2), and operations and training (G-3), the Comptroller of the Army, the Director of the Women's Army Corps, and other officers.
gen·er·ate (jen′ə·rāt) *v.t.* **·at·ed, ·at·ing** 1 To produce or cause to be; bring into being. 2 To beget as a parent; procreate. 3 *Geom.* To trace out by motion: A moving point *generates* a line, or a line a surface. See synonyms under PRODUCE, PROPAGATE. [< L *generatus,* pp. of *generare* generate]
gen·er·a·tion (jen′ə·rā′shən) *n.* 1 The process, act, or function of begetting or procreating; reproduction. 2 Production or origination by any process; creation: the *generation* of electricity. 3 A step or degree in natural descent. 4 The period between successive steps in natural descent, usually taken at 30 years in humans. 5 All persons removed in the same degree from an ancestor. 6 A body of persons existing at the same time or period. 7 A body of persons overlapping other existing bodies, but typified by difference in mental, moral, or ethical outlook: the jazz *generation.* 8 The average lifetime of the persons in a community. 9 *Geom.* The formation of a magnitude by the motion of a point, line, or surface. 10 Race or family. 11 Progeny; offspring. —**spontaneous generation** Abiogenesis.
gen·er·a·tive (jen′ə·rā′tiv) *adj.* 1 Of or pertaining to generation. 2 Having the power to produce or originate.
gen·er·a·tor (jen′ə·rā′tər) *n.* 1 One who or that which generates, produces, or originates. 2 An apparatus in which the generation of a gas is effected. 3 A machine that transforms heat or mechanical work directly into electric energy; a dynamo.
gen·er·a·trix (jen′ə·rā′triks) *n. pl.* **gen·er·a·tri·ces** (jen′ər·ə·trī′sēz) 1 *Geom.* A line, point, or figure that generates another figure by its motion. 2 A female that generates or produces.
ge·ner·ic (ji·ner′ik) *adj.* 1 Pertaining to a genus or a class of related things: contrasted with *specific* or *varietal.* 2 Having a general application; abstract; not concrete. Also **ge·ner′i·cal.** [< L *genus, -eris* race, kind + -IC] —**ge·ner′i·cal·ly** *adv.*
gen·er·os·i·ty (jen′ə·ros′ə·tē) *n. pl.* **·ties** 1 The quality of being generous; liberality. 2 A generous act. See synonyms under BENEVOLENCE.
gen·er·ous (jen′ər·əs) *adj.* 1 Giving or bestowing heartily and munificently; munificent: a *generous* contributor. 2 Having noble qualities; honorable; high-minded: a *generous* nature. 3 Abundant; bountiful: a *generous* fare. 4 *Obs.* Of good descent: said either of men or of animals. 5 Having stimulating qualities; strong: *generous* wine. [< F *généreux* < L *generosus* of noble birth < *genus.* See GENUS.] —**gen′er·ous·ly** *adv.* —**gen′er·ous·ness** *n.*

Synonyms: bountiful, chivalrous, disinterested, free, free-handed, free-hearted, liberal, magnanimous, munificent, noble, open-handed, openhearted. *Generous* primarily signifies having the qualities worthy of noble or honorable birth; hence, free and abundant in giving, giving freely, heartily, and unselfishly. As regards giving, *generous* refers rather to the heartiness of the giver; *liberal* to the amount of the gift; a child may show himself *generous* in the gift of an apple, a millionaire makes a *liberal* donation; a *generous* gift, however, is commonly thought of as both ample and hearty. A *munificent* gift is vast in amount, whatever the motive of its bestowal. One may be *free* with another's money; he can be *generous* only with his own. *Disinterested* means without self-interest or selfish motive. One is *magnanimous* by a greatness of soul that rises above all that is poor, mean, or weak, and above resentment of injury or insult. *Antonyms:* avaricious, close, covetous, greedy, ignoble, illiberal, mean, miserly, niggardly, parsimonious, penurious, petty, rapacious, stingy.

Gen·e·see River (jen′ə·sē′) A river in Pennsylvania and western New York, rising in the Alleghenies, which flows 158 miles north to Lake Ontario.
ge·ne·si·al (ji·nē′zē·əl) *adj.* Of or pertaining to reproduction or generation. Also **ge·ne·sic** (ji·nē′zik).
ge·ne·si·ol·o·gy (ji·nē′zē·ol′ə·jē) *n.* The study of the reproduction of organisms. [< GENESIS + -(O)LOGY]
gen·e·sis (jen′ə·sis) *n. pl.* **·ses** (-sēz) 1 The act or mode of originating; creation. 2 Origin; beginning. [< L < Gk. *genēsis* creation, origin]
Gen·e·sis (jen′ə·sis) The first book of the Pentateuch in the Old Testament.
-genesis *combining form* Development; genesis; evolution: *biogenesis.* [< Gk. *genēsis* origin]
gen·et[1] (jen′it, jə·net′) *n.* 1 Any of certain small carnivores (genus *Genetta*) related to the civets but having only rudimentary scent glands. 2 The fur of the genet. Also **ge·nette′.** [< F *genette* < Sp. *gineta* < Arabic *jarnait* genet]

GENET
(Body 1 foot, 10 inches; tail, 1 foot, 6 inches)

gen·et[2] (jen′it) *n.* A jennet.
Ge·nêt (zhə·ne′), **Edmond Charles,** 1763–1834, French diplomat in the United States: also known as *Citizen Genêt.*
ge·neth·li·ac (jə·neth′lē·ak) *adj.* Relating to nativities or their calculation; showing the position of the stars at birth. Also **gen·eth·li·a·cal** (jen′əth·lī′ə·kəl). [< F *généthliaque* < LL *genethliacus* < Gk. *genethliakos* of one's birth] —**gen′eth·li′a·cal·ly** *adv.*
ge·net·ic (jə·net′ik) *adj.* 1 Of, pertaining to, dealing with, or based on genesis. 2 Of or relating to genetics. 3 *Biol.* Designating those characteristics of an organism due to inheritance or to the action of genes. Also **ge·net′i·cal.** [< GENESIS; formed on analogy with *synthetic, antithetic,* etc.] —**ge·net′i·cal·ly** *adv.*
genetic engineering The application of techniques of genetic recombination to produce desired alterations in genetic material.
ge·net·ics (jə·net′iks) *n.* 1 That branch of biology which deals with the interaction of the genes in producing the similarities and differences between individuals related by descent. 2 The science of plant- and animal-breeding. 3 The inherited characteristics of an organism or group of organisms. —**ge·net′i·cist** *n.*
ge·net·o·troph·ic (jə·net′ə·trof′ik, -trō′fik) *adj. Biol.* Pertaining to, exhibiting, or characterized by inherited defects in body chemistry resulting in an inability to assimilate enough of the essential elements in nutrition. [< GENETIC + TROPHIC]
ge·ne·va (jə·nē′və) *n.* Gin, especially Holland gin. [< MDu. *genever* < OF *genevre* gin < L *juniperus* juniper]
Ge·ne·va (jə·nē′və) 1 A canton of SW Switzerland; 107 square miles. 2 A city on the Lake of Geneva; capital of Geneva canton. *French* **Ge·nève** (zhə·nev′); *German* **Genf** (genf).
Geneva, Lake of The largest lake in Switzerland; 224 square miles: also *Lake Leman.*
Geneva bands A pair of linen strips, hanging from the front of the neck: worn with clerical or academic garments.
Geneva Convention A convention for the amelioration of the condition of the wounded and of prisoners in time of war, signed at Geneva, Switzerland, in 1864: also called *Red Cross Convention.*
Geneva cross See under CROSS.
Geneva gown A loose academic gown with large sleeves: used as an ecclesiastical vestment.
Geneva movement *Mech.* The movement effected by a mechanism having its driving wheel so geared as to give intermittent motion to another wheel which is toothed: used in watches, motion-picture projectors, etc.
Ge·ne·van (jə·nē′vən) *adj.* 1 Of or pertaining to Geneva, Switzerland. 2 Of or pertaining to the theology taught there by Calvin; Calvinistic. —*n.* 1 A native or inhabitant of Geneva. 2 A Calvinist.
Gen·e·vese (jen′ə·vēz′, -vēs′) *adj. & n.* Genevan.
Gen·ghis Khan (jen′giz kän′, jeng′gis), 1162–1227, Mongol conqueror of northern China, Iran, etc. Also spelled *Jenghiz.*
gen·ial[1] (jēn′yəl, jē′nē·əl) *adj.* 1 Kindly in disposition; cordial and pleasant in manner. 2 Imparting warmth, comfort, or life; supporting life or growth. 3 *Rare* Exhibiting or relating to genius. See synonyms under BLAND, CHEERFUL, COMFORTABLE, FRIENDLY, GOOD. [< L *genialis* of one's tutelary deity < *genius.* See GENIUS.] —**ge′nial·ly** *adv.*
ge·ni·al[2] (jə·nī′əl) *adj. Anat.* Of, pertaining to, or near the chin. [< Gk. *geneion* chin]
ge·ni·al·i·ty (jē′nē·al′ə·tē) *n.* Kindness of disposition; warmth; friendly cheerfulness.
gen·ic (jen′ik) *adj.* Of, pertaining to, or like a gene or genes; genetic.

-genic *combining form* Related to generation or production: *biogenic.* [<-GEN+-IC]

ge·nic·u·late (jə·nik′yə·lāt, -lit) *adj. Biol.* **1** Having kneelike joints or protuberances. **2** Bent abruptly, like a knee. [<L *geniculatus* <*geniculum,* dim. of *genu* knee]

ge·nie (jē′nē) *n.* A jinni.

Ge·nie (jē′nē) Diminutive of EUGENIA.

ge·ni·i (jē′nē·ī) **1** Plural of GENIUS (defs. 6 and 9). **2** Jinn.

ge·ni·o·plas·ty (jə·nī′ə·plas′tē) *n.* Plastic surgery of the chin and lower cheek.

gen·i·pap (jen′ə·pap) *n.* **1** A tropical American tree *(Genipa americana)* of the madder family. **2** Its edible fruit, about the size of an orange. [<Pg. *genipapo* <native name]

gen·i·tal (jen′ə·təl) *adj.* **1** Of or pertaining to the reproductive organs, or to the process of generation. **2** *Psychoanal.* Of or relating to a stage of psychosexual development in which the genitals are the dominant source of libidinal gratification in the context of mature personal relations with others: compare ANAL, ORAL. [<L *genitalis* of generation <*genitus,* pp. of *gignere* beget]

gen·i·ta·li·a (jen′ə·tā′lē·ə, -tāl′yə) *n. pl.* The genitals. [<L, neut. plural of *genitalis.* See GENITAL.]

gen·i·tals (jen′ə·təlz) *n. pl.* The external organs of generation; sexual organs.

gen·i·ti·val (jen′ə·tī′vəl) *adj.* Pertaining to the genitive case; having a genitive form. —**gen′·i·ti′val·ly** *adv.*

gen·i·tive (jen′ə·tiv) *adj.* **1** Indicating source, origin, possession, or the like. **2** *Gram.* Pertaining to a case in Latin, Greek, etc., corresponding in part to the English possessive. —*n. Gram.* **1** The genitive case. **2** A word in this case. [<L *genitivus* <*gignere* beget]

genito- *combining form* Of or related to the genitals. [<L *genitus,* pp. of *gignere* beget]

gen·i·tor (jen′ə·tər, -tôr) *n. Obs.* A progenitor; a begetter. [<L]

gen·i·to·u·ri·nar·y (jen′ə·tō·yŏŏr′ə·ner′ē) *adj. Anat.* Of or pertaining to the genital and the urinary organs.

gen·ius (jēn′yəs) *n. pl.* **gen·ius·es** *for defs. 2–5, 7, 8;* **ge·ni·i** *for defs. 6 and 9.* **1** Extraordinary intellectual gifts, evidenced in original creation, expression, or achievement. **2** Remarkable aptitude for some special pursuit; a distinguishing natural capacity or tendency: a *genius* for oratory. **3** A person of phenomenal and original powers for productivity in art, science, statesmanship, etc.: such a *genius* as Mozart, Shakespeare, Napoleon, Einstein, etc. **4** The dominant influence or essential animating principle of anything; the prevalent feeling or thought (of a nation or era). **5** A representative type; impersonation; embodiment. **6** In Roman antiquity, a beneficent spirit or demon supposed to accompany one through life, or either of two attendant spirits, one good, the other bad; a guardian or tutelary spirit of a person, place, or thing. **7** Hence, a person having an extraordinary influence over another. **8** The traditions, history, associations, influences, etc., of a locality or place. **9** In Mohammedan folklore, a jinni. [<L, tutelary spirit <*gen-,* stem of *gignere* beget]

Synonyms: talent, talents. *Genius* is exalted intellectual power capable of operating independently of tuition and training, and marked by extraordinary faculty for original creation, invention, discovery, expression, etc. *Talent* is marked mental ability, and in a special sense, a particular and uncommon aptitude for some special mental work or attainment. *Genius* is higher than *talent,* more spontaneous, less dependent upon instruction, less amenable to training; *talent* is largely the capacity to learn, acquire, appropriate, adapt oneself to demand. Compare CHARACTER, INGENUITY, MIND, POWER. *Antonyms:* dulness, folly, imbecility, obtuseness, senselessness, stupidity.

ge·ni·us lo·ci (jē′nē·əs lō′sī, -kē) *Latin* **1** The spirit or guardian deity of the place. **2** The unique quality of a place as felt by an observer.

Gen·nes·a·ret (jə·nes′ə·ret), **Sea of** or **Lake** The New Testament name for the SEA OF GALILEE. Also **Gen·nes′a·reth.**

Gen·o·a (jen′ō·ə) A port in NW Italy on the **Gulf of Genoa,** the northern portion of the Ligurian Sea. *Italian* **Ge·no·va** (je′nō·vä).

gen·o·cide (jen′ə·sīd) *n.* The systematic extermination of racial and national groups: term first used in indictment of German war criminals after World War II. [<Gk. *genos* race, tribe +-CIDE; coined by Raphael Lemkin, 1944.]

Gen·o·ese (jen′ō·ēz′, -ēs′) *adj.* Of or pertaining to Genoa. —*n.* A native or legally constituted citizen of Genoa: used as singular, plural, or collective.

gen·om (jen′om) *n. Biol.* A full set of chromosomes with their associated genes. Also **gen′ome** (-ōm). [<GENE+-OM(E)]

gen·o·type (jen′ə·tīp) *n. Biol.* **1** The genetic constitution of an organism, expressed and latent: contrasted with *phenotype.* **2** A type representative of a group of organisms; the most typical species of a genus. [<Gk. *genos* race, kind +-TYPE]—**gen·o·typ·ic** (jen′ə·tip′·ik) or **·i·cal** *adj.*

-genous *suffix of adjectives* **1** Generating; yielding: *sporogenous.* **2** Produced or generated by: *parthenogenous.* [<-GEN+-OUS]

gen·re (zhän′rə) *n.* **1** A genus, sort, or style; especially, a category of art or literature characterized by a certain form, style, subject matter, or atmosphere. **2** A class of painting or other art portraying everyday life; distinguished from the historical, romantic, etc., style. [<F <L *genus, -eris* race, kind. Doublet of GENDER, GENUS.]

gen·ro (gen·rō) *n. pl.* **gen·ros** One of the Japanese elder statesmen. [<Japanese *genrō* first (of the) elders]

gens (jenz) *n. pl.* **gen·tes** (jen′tēz) **1** *Anthropol.* In primitive society, a body of blood kindred having a common gentile name, and distinguished by a totem or crest. **2** In Roman antiquity, a clan or house composed of several families having a common ancestor; a subdivision of a tribe. [<L]

Gen·san (gen·sän) The Japanese name for WONSAN, Korea.

Gen·ser·ic (jen′sər·ik, gen′-), 406?–77, king of the Vandals; conquered north Africa; sacked Rome, 455.

gent[1] (jent) *adj. Obs.* **1** Of gentle birth; genteel; noble. **2** Neat; pretty. [<OF <L *genitus,* orig. pp. of *gignere* beget]

gent[2] (jent) *n. Slang.* A gentleman.

Gent (gent) The Flemish name for GHENT.

gen·teel (jen·tēl′) *adj.* **1** Well-bred or refined; elegant; polite. **2** Suitable for or pertaining to the station or needs of well-bred persons. **3** Stylish or fashionable. ◆This word is now used chiefly in a somewhat derogatory or humorous sense: *genteel* poverty. See synonyms under POLITE. [<MF *gentil.* Doublet of GENTLE.]—**gen·teel′ly** *adv.* —**gen·teel′ness** *n.*

gen·teel·ism (jen·tēl′iz·əm) *n.* An expression that is pretentious, affected, or overly elegant for what it describes or designates.

gen·tian (jen′shən) *n.* **1** Any of a large genus *(Gentiana)* of European and American flowering herbs, as the **yellow gentian** of Europe *(G. lutea),* the **fringed gentian** of America *(G. crinita),* with blue, conspicuously fringed solitary flowers, and the **closed** or **bottle gentian** *(G. andrewsi),* with purple-blue, non-opening flowers. **2** The root of the yellow gentian, having tonic properties. [<L *gentiana,* appar. after *Gentius,* an Illyrian king]

GENTIAN
a. Bottle or closed.
b. Fringed.

gen·tian·a·ceous (jen′shən·ā′shəs) *adj. Bot.* Belonging to a family *(Gentianaceae)* of annual or perennial herbs, with showy, perfect, regular flowers.

gen·tian·el·la (jen′shən·el′ə) *n.* **1** A European alpine dwarf gentian *(Gentiana acaulis)* having attractive blue flowers. **2** A shade of blue. [<NL, dim. of L *gentiana* GENTIAN]

gentian violet *Chem.* A purple dye of the rosaniline group, used medicinally as an antiseptic and bactericide: also called *methylrosaniline.*

gen·tile (jen′tīl) *adj.* **1** Of or pertaining to a nation, gens, or clan. **2** *Gram.* Denoting racial, national, or local extraction: said of a noun or adjective. **3** Heathen; pagan. —*n.* **1** *Gram.* A noun or an adjective denoting race, country, etc. **2** In Roman law, a member of a gens or clan. [<F *gentil* <LL *gentilis* foreign. Doublet of GENTLE.]

Gen·tile (jen′tīl) *n.* **1** Among the Jews, one of a non-Jewish people; one not a Jew. **2** Among Christians: **a** One who is not a Jew; a pagan. **b** A Christian, especially one formerly a pagan. **3** Among Mormons, a non-Mormon. —*adj.* **1** Pertaining to or characteristic of a non-Jewish people. **2** Belonging to or like Christians, as distinguished from Jews. **3** Of or pertaining to non-Mormons.

gen·ti·lesse (jen′tə·les) *n. Archaic* Gentle birth or manners. [<OF <*gentil.* See GENTLE.]

gen·til·ism (jen′təl·iz′əm) *n.* **1** The character of being Gentile in birth and spirit; formerly, heathenism. **2** Clannishness; attachment to one's gens or tribe.

gen·til·i·ty (jen·til′ə·tē) *n. pl.* **·ties** **1** The quality of being genteel or well-bred; refinement: now often used ironically. **2** Gentle birth; good extraction. **3** Well-born or well-bred persons collectively; gentry. [<OF *gentilite* <L *gentilitas, -tatis* <*gentilis.* See GENTLE.]

gen·tle (jen′təl) *adj.* **1** Belonging to a family distinguished by blood, birth, or station. **2** Befitting one of high birth or station. **3** *Archaic* Noble; chivalrous: a *gentle* knight. **4** Considerate; generously inclined: *gentle* reader. **5** Mild in disposition; refined in manners. **6** Tame; docile: a *gentle* horse. **7** Soft; moderate; not harsh: a *gentle* touch. **8** Not steep, sharp, or abrupt: a *gentle* slope. **9** *Meteorol.* Designating a moderate breeze, No. 3 on the Beaufort scale. —*v.t.* **gen·tled, gen·tling** **1** To make easy to control; tame, as a horse. **2** To make gentle. **3** *Obs.* To raise to the rank of gentility. [<OF *gentil* <L *gentilis* of good birth <*gens, gentis* race, clan. Doublet of GENTEEL, GENTILE.]—**gen′tly** *adv.* —**gen′tle·ness** *n.*

gentle craft **1** Shoemaking. **2** Angling.

gen·tle·folk (jen′təl·fōk′) *n. pl.* Persons of good family and good breeding. Also **gen′tle·folks′.**

gen·tle·man (jen′təl·mən) *n. pl.* **·men** (-mən) **1** A well-bred man with good manners. **2** Any man: in the plural the usual form of address in public assemblies: Ladies and *gentlemen.* **3** *Brit.* A man above a yeoman in social rank. —**fine gentleman** A fashionable gentleman; also a dandy; fop.

gen·tle·man-at-arms (jen′təl·mən·at·ärmz′) *n. pl.* **·men·**(-mən-) *Brit.* One of forty-six gentlemen who attend the sovereign on various state and solemn occasions.

gentleman farmer One who owns a farm, but hires others to work it.

gen·tle·man·ly (jen′təl·mən·lē) *adj.* Pertaining to or befitting a gentleman; courteous; gracious. Also **gen′tle·man·like.**

gentleman of fortune Formerly, a gentleman who sought his fortune in dangerous pursuits; now, an adventurer living by his wits.

gentleman of the road **1** A highwayman. **2** *U.S.* A hobo.

gentleman's agreement An agreement, usually diplomatic or political, and less formal than a treaty or contract, guaranteed only by the honor of the parties involved.

gentleman's gentleman A valet serving a man of social position.

gentle sex Women collectively.

gen·tle·wom·an (jen′təl·wŏŏm′ən) *n. pl.* **·wom·en** (-wim′in) **1** A woman of good birth and social position: a lady. **2** A considerate, gracious, well-mannered woman. **3** Formerly, a woman in attendance on a lady of rank.

Gen·too (jen·tōō′) *n. pl.* **·toos** (-tōōz′) **1** In India, a Hindu, especially a Telugu, as distinguished from a Moslem. **2** The language of the Gentoos. [<Pg. *gentio* gentile <L *gentilis.*]

gen·tri·fi·ca·tion (jen′trə·fə·kā′shən) n. The rebuilding or restoration of deteriorating city residential properties for purchase or use by middle- or upper-class buyers.

gen·try (jen′trē) *n.* **1** People of good position or birth; in England, the upper class exclusive of the nobility. **2** Any specified class of people: commonly an ironical term. **3** *Obs.* Gentle birth or condition. **4** *Obs.* Urbanity; politeness. [Appar. a back formation from GENTRICE, incorrectly taken as a plural]

gen·ty (jen′tē) *adj. Scot.* Shapely; trim; jaunty.

ge·nu (jē′nōō, -nyōō) *n. pl.* **gen·u·a** (jen′yōō·ə) *Anat.* **1** The knee. **2** A kneelike structure, as a bend of the corpus callosum. [<L]

gen·u·flect (jen′yə·flekt) *v.i.* To bend the knee, as in worship. [<Med. L *genuflectere* <*genu* knee + *flectere* bend]

gen·u·flec·tion (jen′yə·flek′shən) *n.* A bending of the knee, as in worship. Also *Brit.* **gen′·u·flex′ion.**

gen·u·ine (jen′yōō·in) *adj.* **1** Of the original or true stock. **2** Authentic; of the authorship claimed. **3** Not spurious, adulterated, or counterfeit. **4** Not affected or hypocritical; frank; sincere; true. See synonyms under AUTHENTIC, HONEST, PURE. [<L *genuinus* innate] — **gen′u·ine·ly** *adv.* — **gen′u·ine·ness** *n.*

ge·nus (jē′nəs) *n. pl.* **gen·e·ra** (jen′ər·ə) **1** *Biol.* A class or category of plants and animals ranking next above the species and next below the family or subfamily. The genus and species names together constitute the scientific name of an organism, the genus name (capitalized) standing first; as *Homo sapiens* for the human species. **2** *Logic* A class of things divisible into two or more subordinate classes, or species. **3** A kind; class. [<L, race, kind]

-geny *combining form* Mode of production of; generation or development of: *anthropogeny, cosmogeny.* [<F *-génie* <L *-genia* <Gk. *-geneia* <*gen-*, stem of *gignesthai* become]

geo– *combining form* Earth; ground; soil: *geocentric, geology.*

ge·o·ben·thos (jē′ə·ben′thəs) *n. Ecol.* That portion of the bottom of a river, stream, or lake which is destitute of vegetation. Compare PHYTOBENTHON. [<GEO- + Gk. *benthos* depth]

ge·o·bi·on (jē′ə·bī′on) *n. Ecol.* A plant community adapted to the land, as distinguished from aquatic communities. [<GEO- + Gk. *bios* life]

ge·o·bot·a·ny (jē′ō·bot′ə·nē) *n.* Phytogeography.

ge·o·cen·tric (jē′ō·sen′trik) *adj.* **1** Relating to the earth as a center. **2** Measured from the earth or the earth's center. — **ge′o·cen′tri·cal** *adj.* — **ge′o·cen′tri·cal·ly** *adv.*

ge·o·cen·tri·cism (jē′ō·sen′trə·siz′əm) *n.* The ancient theory that the earth is the center of the planetary system, or the central object of divine providential care.

ge·o·chem·i·cal (jē′ō·kem′i·kəl) *adj.* Showing the results of both geological and chemical action.

ge·o·chem·is·try (jē′ō·kem′is·trē) *n.* The chemistry of geological processes and of the substances taking part in them; chemical geology.

ge·o·chro·nol·o·gy (jē′ō·krə·nol′ə·jē) *n.* The age of the earth, as determined by the observation and study of geologic, geographic, climatic, and biological processes. — **ge·o·chron·o·log·ic** (jē′ō·kron′ə·loj′ik) or **·i·cal** *adj.*

ge·ode (jē′ōd) *n. Geol.* **1** A stone having a cavity lined with crystals. **2** The cavity in such a stone. [<F *géode* <L *geodes*, a precious stone <Gk. *geōdēs* earthy] — **ge·od·ic** (jē·od′ik) *adj.*

ge·o·des·ic (jē′ə·des′ik) *adj.* Of or pertaining to geodesy. — *n.* A geodesic line.

geodesic line *Math.* The shortest line connecting two points on a given surface.

ge·od·e·sy (jē·od′ə·sē) *n. Math.* The study and measurement of extensive areas of the earth's surface, especially with reference to the determination of the magnitude and figure of the earth: distinguished from *surveying* (of limited areas). [<F *géodésie* <NL *geodaesia* <Gk. *geodaisia* <*gē* earth + *daiein* divide] — **ge·od′e·sist** *n.*

ge·o·det·ic (jē′ə·det′ik) *adj.* **1** Of, pertaining to, determined, or effected by geodesy: a *geodetic* survey. **2** *Aeron.* Denoting a type of aircraft construction in which all parts of the fuselage, wings, and other exposed surfaces are built along the contours where the aerodynamic strain and load stress are greatest. **3** Geodesic. Also **ge′o·det′i·cal.** — **ge′o·det′i·cal·ly** *adv.*

ge·o·dy·nam·ics (jē′ō·dī·nam′iks) *n.* The study of the forces that affect the structure and modifications of the earth. — **ge′o·dy·nam′ic, ge′o·dy·nam′i·cal** *adj.*

Geof·frey (jef′rē) A masculine personal name. See GODFREY. Also *Fr.* **Geof·froi** (zhō·frwä′).
— **Geoffrey of Anjou,** 1113–50, father of Henry II of England: also known as *Geoffrey Plantagenet.*
— **Geoffrey of Monmouth,** 1100?–54?, English chronicler.

Geof·froy Saint–Hi·laire (zhō·frwä′ saṅ·tē·lâr′), **Étienne,** 1772–1844, French zoologist.

ge·og·no·sy (jē·og′nə·sē) *n.* The study of the materials of the earth, their structure, characteristics, and interrelationships; structural geology. [<GEO- + Gk. *gnōsis* knowledge]

ge·o·graph·ic determinism (jē′ə·graf′ik) *Sociol.* The theory that attributes the forms and characteristics of a given society, community, or nation to the molding influence of geographic factors.

geographic mile See under MILE.

ge·og·ra·phy (jē·og′rə·fē) *n. pl.* **·phies** **1** The science that describes the surface of the earth and its associated physical, biological, economic, political, and demographic characteristics, especially in terms of large areas and the complex of interrelationships obtaining among them. **2** The natural aspect, features, etc., of a place or area: the *geography* of the Arctic. [<L *geographia* <Gk. <*gē* earth + *graphein* write, describe] — **ge·og′ra·pher** *n.* — **ge′o·graph′ic** or **·i·cal** *adj.* — **ge′o·graph′·i·cal·ly** *adv.*

ge·oid (jē′oid) *n.* The earth considered as an ellipsoidal solid whose surface coincides with the mean level of the ocean. [<Gk. *geoidēs* earthlike <*gē* earth + *eidos* form]

GEOLOGICAL TIME SCALE

Read from bottom to top.

ERAS	TIME PERIODS ROCK SYSTEMS	TIME EPOCHS ROCK SERIES	APPROX. DURATION MILLION YEARS	APPROX. PERCENT TOTAL AGE	LIFE FORMS
CENOZOIC	QUATERNARY	RECENT PLEISTOCENE	1	2	Rise and dominance of Man.
	UPPER TERTIARY	PLIOCENE MIOCENE	65		Modern animals and plants.
	LOWER TERTIARY	OLIGOCENE EOCENE PALEOCENE			Rapid development of modern mammals, insects, and plants.
MESOZOIC	UPPER CRETACEOUS		75	5	Primitive mammals; last dinosaurs; last ammonites.
	LOWER CRETACEOUS				Rise of flowering plants.
	JURASSIC		45		First birds, first mammals. Diversification of reptiles; climax of ammonites; coniferous trees.
	TRIASSIC		45		Rise of dinosaurs; cycadlike plants; bony fishes.
PALEOZOIC	PERMIAN		45	9	Rise of reptiles. Modern insects. Last of many plant and animal groups.
	PENNSYLVANIAN (CARBONIFEROUS)		75		First reptiles. Amphibians; primitive insects; seed ferns; primitive conifers.
	MISSISSIPPIAN (CARBONIFEROUS)				Climax of shell–crushing sharks. Primitive ammonites.
	DEVONIAN		50		First amphibians, first land snails. Primitive land plants. Climax of brachiopods.
	SILURIAN		20		First traces of land life. Scorpions. First lungfishes. Widespread coral reefs.
	ORDOVICIAN		70		First fish. Climax of trilobites. First appearance of many marine invertebrates.
	CAMBRIAN		50		First marine invertebrates, including trilobites.
PROTEROZOIC (PRE-CAMBRIAN)			About 3,000	84	First signs of life. Algae.
ARCHEOZOIC (PRE-CAMBRIAN)					
Age of oldest dated rocks: about 3,500,000,000 years.					

ge·ol·o·gist (jē·ol′ə·jist) *n.* One versed in geology. Also **ge·ol′o·ger.**

ge·ol·o·gize (jē·ol′ə·jīz) *v.i.* **·gized, ·giz·ing** **1** To study, or discourse on, geology. **2** To make geological investigations, especially in the field.

ge·ol·o·gy (jē·ol′ə·jē) *n. pl.* **·gies** **1** The science that treats of the origin, history, constitution, and structure of the earth, including the operation of the physical forces affecting its development and appearance and the history of living or extinct forms as recorded in the rocks. See Time Scale above. **2** A treatise on this subject. See HISTORICAL GEOLOGY. — **ge·o·log·ic** (jē′ə·loj′ik) or **·i·cal** *adj.* —**ge′o·log′i·cal·ly** *adv.*

ge·o·man·cy (jē′ə·man′sē) *n.* Divination by means of some aspect of the earth, particularly by the observation of points and lines on the earth. —**ge′o·man′cer** *n.* —**ge′o·man′tic** *adj.*

ge·o·med·i·cine (jē′ō·med′ə·sin) *n.* The branch of medicine that treats of the geographic factors of disease.

ge·om·e·ter (jē·om′ə·tər) *n.* One skilled in geometry. Also **ge·om·e·tri·cian** (jē·om′ə·trish′·ən, jē′ə·mə-). [< L *geometres* < Gk. *geōmetrēs* one who measures land]

ge·o·met·ric (jē′ə·met′rik) *adj.* **1** Pertaining to or according to the rules and principles of geometry. **2** Forming, consisting of, or characterized by regular lines, curves, and angles, as the markings on certain insects, or on the primitive pottery of the Mycenaean era, which is recognized by its rectilinear decorations. Also **ge′o·met′ri·cal** — **ge′o·met′ri·cal·ly** *adv.*

geometric progression *Math.* A sequence of terms of which each member except the first is greater than its predecessor by a constant ratio, as 2, 4, 8, 16, 32, 64: distinguished from *arithmetic progression.*

ge·om·e·trid (jē·om′ə·trid) *n.* Any of a family *(Geometridae)* of moths whose larvae are called measuring worms, because they walk by moving their abdominal and anal prolegs, thus forming the body into a loop, giving the impression that they are measuring the space below. [< NL *Geometridae* < L *geometres.* See GEOMETER.]

ge·om·e·trize (jē·om′ə·trīz) *v.i.* **·trized, ·triz·ing 1** To study geometry. **2** To apply geometric methods or principles.

ge·om·e·try (jē·om′ə·trē) *n. pl.* **·tries** The branch of mathematics that treats of space and its relations, especially as shown in the properties and measurement of points, lines, angles, surfaces, and solids. [< OF *geometrie* < L *geometria* < Gk. *geōmetria* < *gē* earth + *metrein* measure]

ge·o·mor·phic (jē′ə·môr′fik) *adj.* **1** Resembling the earth, as in contour. **2** Of or pertaining to the earth's form or the configuration of its surface features.

ge·o·mor·phol·o·gy (jē′ō·môr·fol′ə·jē) *n.* The study of the development, configuration, and distribution of the surface features of the earth; physiographical geology. Also **ge′o·mor·phog′e·ny** (-foj′ə·nē). —**ge′o·mor′pho·log′i·cal** (-fə·loj′i·kəl) *adj.*

ge·on·o·my (jē·on′ə·mē) *n.* The study of the earth in all its geological, physical, chemical, and mechanical aspects; earth science. —**ge·o·nom·ic** (jē′ə·nom′ik) *adj.*

ge·oph·a·gy (jē·of′ə·jē) *n.* Dirt-eating; morbid appetite for dirt, clay, etc. —**ge·oph′a·gism** (-jiz′əm) *n.* —**ge·oph′a·gist** *n.*

ge·o·phys·ics (jē′ə·fiz′iks) *n.* The science that treats of the physical forces and phenomena associated with the earth, and studies the nature of deep-lying areas by means of seismographs, the torsion balance, and various electromagnetic instruments. —**ge′o·phys′i·cal** *adj.* —**ge′o·phys′i·cist** *n.*

ge·o·phyte (jē′ə·fīt) *n. Bot.* An earth-growing plant; especially, one whose buds, mycelia, etc., are deeply buried in the substratum.

ge·o·pol·i·tics (jē′ō·pol′ə·tiks) *n.* **1** The study of geography, geology, climate, and the natural resources of the earth in relation to the development of peoples, cultures, and states. **2** A method of studying geography and power politics in terms of national security in international relations, embracing geography, natural resources, industrial development, and political strength. **3** The former German doctrine of living space as the primary element in, and strongest guaranty of, state power and world domination. See LEBENSRAUM.

ge·o·pon·ic (jē′ə·pon′ik) *adj.* Pertaining to agriculture; hence, rustic. [< Gk. *geōponikos* < *geōponos* a farmer < *gē* earth + *ponos* labor]

ge·o·pon·ics (jē′ə·pon′iks) *n. pl.* The art or science of agriculture.

ge·o·po·ten·tial (jē′ə·pə·ten′shəl) *n. Meteorol.* The potential energy of unit mass, equal to the work required to lift it from the zero potential of sea level to its actual position: applied especially in air-mass analysis.

geor·die (jôr′dē) *n. Scot.* A guinea.

George (jôrj) A masculine personal name. Also *Dan., Ger., Sw.* **Ge·org** (gā′ôrg), *Fr.* **Georges** (zhôrzh) or **Geor·get** (zhôr·zhe′), *Latin* **Geor·gi·us** (jôr′jē·əs). [< Gk., husbandman]
—**George I,** 1660–1727, elector of Hanover; king of England 1714–27.
—**George I,** 1845–1913, king of Greece 1863–1913.
—**George II,** 1683–1760, king of England 1727–60.
—**George II,** 1890–1947, king of Greece 1922–23, 1935–47.
—**George III,** 1738–1820, king of England 1760–1820.
—**George IV,** 1762–1830, king of England 1820–30.
—**George V,** 1865–1936, king of England 1910–36.
—**George VI,** 1895–1952, king of England 1936–52.
—**George, Saint,** martyred 303?, patron saint of England.

George (jôrj) *n.* **1** A jewel carved with the figure of St. George slaying the dragon: one of the insignia of the Knights of the Garter. **2** An old coin minted in England during the reign of Henry VIII, and bearing the figure of St. George.

George (jôrj), **David Lloyd** See LLOYD GEORGE, DAVID. —**Henry,** 1839–97, U.S. economist.

Ge·or·ge (gā·ôr′gā), **Stefan,** 1868–1933, German lyric poet.

George (jôrj), **Lake** A lake in eastern New York, 33 miles long: called *Lake Horicon* in the novels of J. F. Cooper.

George V Coast A region of the coast of Antarctica south of Australia.

George Town A port on Penang Island, capital of Penang State, Malaya.

George·town (jôrj′toun) The capital of Guyana.

geor·gette crepe (jôr·jet′) A sheer, dull fabric with a crepelike surface, originally made of silk: used for blouses, gowns, millinery, etc.: a trade name. [after Mme. *Georgette* de la Plante, French modiste]

Geor·gia (jôr′jə) **1** A southern Atlantic State of the United States; 58,876 square miles; capital, Atlanta; entered the Union Jan. 2, 1788, one of the original thirteen States: nickname, *Cracker State*: abbr. GA **2** A constituent republic of the U.S.S.R. in the southern Caucasus on the Black Sea; 29,400 square miles; capital, Tiflis: Russian *Gruziya*; Georgian *Sakartvelo*: also **Georgian Soviet Socialist Republic.**

Geor·gia (jôr′jə), **Strait of** A channel between the mainland of British Columbia and Vancouver Island; 150 miles long, 20 to 40 miles wide.

Geor·gian (jôr′jən) *adj.* **1** Of or pertaining to the reigns or period of the four Georges in England, 1714–1830, or of George V, 1910–36. **2** Of or pertaining to the State of Georgia. **3** Of or pertaining to Georgia in the U.S.S.R., to the Georgians, or to their language. —*n.* **1** A native or inhabitant of the State of Georgia. **2** One of an ancient mountain people native to the Caucasus; also, one of their modern descendants, a native of the Georgian Republic. **3** The agglutinative South Caucasian language of the Georgians of the Soviet Union. **4** A person belonging to either of the Georgian periods in England, or having Georgian taste.

Geor·gi·an·a (jôr′jē·an′ə) A feminine personal name. Also **Geor·gi·na** (jôr·jē′nə), *Ger.* gā′ôr·gē′·nä), *Fr.* **Geor·gine** (zhôr·zhēn) or **Geor·gette** (zhôr·zhet′). [See GEORGE]

Georgian Bay An inlet in the NE part of Lake Huron, Ontario, Canada; 110 by 50 miles.

Georgia pine 1 The long-leaved southern yellow pine *(Pinus palustris).* **2** The wood of this tree.

geor·gic (jôr′jik) *adj.* Pertaining to husbandry or rural affairs: also **geor′gi·cal.** —*n.* A poem on husbandry. [< L *georgicus* < Gk. *geōrgikos* < *geōrgia* husbandry]

ge·o·stat·ic (jē′ə·stat′ik) *adj.* Of or pertaining to the pressure of the earth.

ge·o·stat·ics (jē′ə·stat′iks) *n.* The statics of rigid bodies in relation to balanced forces on or beneath the earth's surface.

ge·o·strat·e·gist (jē′ō·strat′ə·jist) *n.* A specialist in the problems, objectives, and doctrines of geostrategy.

ge·o·strat·e·gy (jē′ō·strat′ə·jē) *n.* Military strategy as related to and determined by geopolitical factors. [< GEO(POLITICS) + STRATEGY] — **ge′o·stra·te′gic** (-strə·tē′jik) *adj.*

ge·o·stroph·ic (jē′ə·strof′ik) *adj. Meteorol.* Designating a regional drift of air masses caused by the rotation of the earth. Compare CYCLOSTROPHIC. [< GEO- + Gk. *strephein* turn]

ge·o·syn·cline (jē′ə·sin′klīn) *n. Geol.* A massive downward flexure of the earth's crust: opposed to *geanticline.* —**ge′o·syn·cli′nal** *adj.* & *n.*

ge·o·tax·is (jē′ə·tak′sis) *n. Biol.* The arrangement of an organism or any of its parts with respect to the force of gravitation. See GEOTROPISM.

ge·o·tech·nol·o·gy (jē′ō·tek·nol′ə·jē) *n.* The application of the mineral arts and sciences to the improvement of old and development of new methods, techniques, processes, and products, as in ceramics, glassmaking, metallurgy, etc. — **ge′o·tech′no·log′i·cal** (-nə·loj′i·kəl) *adj.* — **ge′o·tech·nol′o·gist** *n.*

ge·o·tec·ton·ic (jē′ō·tek·ton′ik) *adj. Geol.* Relating to the structure of the rock masses of the earth's crust and to their shape, composition, and distribution.

ge·o·ther·mal (jē′ə·thûr′məl) *adj.* Pertaining to or of the earth's internal heat. Also **ge′o·ther′mic.**

ge·ot·ro·pism (jē·ot′rə·piz′əm) *n. Biol.* A tendency exhibited by organisms, especially the roots of growing plants, to turn toward the center of the earth: distinguished from *apogeotropism.* Compare GEOTAXIS. —**ge·o·trop·ic** (jē′ə·trop′ik) *adj.* —**ge′o·trop′i·cal·ly** *adv.*

Ge·ra (gā′rä) A city in Thuringia, S East Germany.

ge·rah (gē′rə) *n.* An ancient Hebrew unit of weight, one twentieth of a shekel. *Ezek.* xlv 12.

Ge·raint (jə·rānt′) In Arthurian legend, one of the knights of the Round Table; husband of Enid. Tennyson used his story in *Idylls of the King.*

Ger·ald (jer′əld) A masculine personal name. [< Gmc., spear ruler]

Ger·al·dine (jer′əl·dēn) A feminine personal name. Also *Fr.* **Gé·ral·dine** (zhā·rál·dēn′). [See GERALD]

ge·ra·ni·a·ceous (ji·rā′nē·ā′shəs) *adj. Bot.* Belonging or pertaining to a family *(Geraniaceae)* of polypetalous herbs, shrubs, and trees, the geranium family, widely scattered in temperate and subtropical regions. [< NL *Geraniaceae* < L *geranium* GERANIUM]

ge·ra·ni·al (ji·rā′nē·əl) *n.* Citral.

ge·ra·ni·ol (ji·rā′nē·ôl, -ōl) *n. Chem.* An oily colorless alcohol of the terpene group, $C_{10}H_{18}O$, a constituent of oil of roses, geranium, citronella, and other plants: used in perfumery and cosmetics.

ge·ra·ni·um (ji·rā′nē·əm) *n.* **1** Any of a widespread genus *(Geranium)* of plants typical of the family Geraniaceae. Also called *cranesbill.* **2** Pelargonium. **3** A very deep pink to vivid red color. [< L < Gk. *geranion* < *geranos* crane]

Ge·rard (ji·rärd′, *Du.* hā′rärt) A masculine personal name: same as GERALD. Also *Fr.* **Gé·rard** (zhā·rár′), *Ital.* **Ge·rar·do** (jā·rär′dō), *Lat.* **Ge·rar·dus** (jə·rär′dəs) [< Gmc., hard spear]

Ge·rard (ji·rärd′), **Ralph Waldo,** born 1900, U.S. physiologist. —**John,** 1545–1612, English surgeon and botanist.

Gé·raud (zhā·rō′) French form of GERALD.

ger·bil (jûr′bil) *n.* Any of a subfamily *(Gerbillinae)* of rodents found in Asia, Africa, and SE Europe, with long hind legs, hairy tail, and narrow incisors. Also **ger·bille′.** [< F *gerbille* < NL *gerbillus,* dim. of *gerbo* a jerboa]

Ger·da (gûr′dä) In Norse mythology, a giantess who was loved by Frey and became his wife: also spelled *Gerd, Gerdh, Gerthr.*

Ge·re·mi·a (jā′rā·mē′ä) Italian form of JEREMIAH.

ge·rent (jir′ənt) *n.* A governing power; ruler;

manager. [<L *gerens, -entis,* ppr. of *gerere* carry on, do]

ge·re·nuk (ge′rə·no͝ok) *n.* An East African antelope *(Lithocranius walleri)* with extremely long legs and a massive head. [<native name]

ger·e·ol·ogy (jer·ē·ol′ə·jē) *n.* Gerontology. Also **ger′a·tol′o·gy** (-ə·tol′ə·jē). [<Gk. *gēras* old age + -LOGY]

ger·fal·con (jûr′fôl′kən, -fô′-) *n.* A large falcon *(Falco rusticolus)* of the Arctic regions, with feathered shanks: also spelled *gyrfalcon.* [<OF *gerfaucon* <OHG *gir* vulture + OF *faucon* a falcon]

Ger·hard (*Dan.* ger′härth, *Du.* kher′ärt, *Sw.* yer′härd) See GERALD. Also *Ger.* **Ger·hart** (ger′härt).

Ger·har·di·ne (ger′här·dē′nə) German form of GERALDINE.

ger·i·at·ric (jer′ē·at′rik) *adj.* Of or pertaining to geriatrics or to old people.

ger·i·a·tri·cian (jer′ē·ə·trish′ən) *n.* A specialist in the diseases of old age. Also **ger·i·at·rist** (jer′ē·at′rist).

ger·i·at·rics (jer′ē·at′riks) *n.* **1** The branch of medicine which deals with the structural changes, physiology, diseases, and hygiene of old age. **2** Gerontology. [<Gk. *gēras* old age + -IATRICS]

Gé·ri·cault (zhā·rē·kō′), **Jean Louis André Théodore,** 1791–1824, French painter.

ger·i·o·psy·cho·sis (jer′ē·ō·sī·kō′sis) *n.* Mental disorder associated with old age; a psychosis of the senile. [<Gk. *gēras* old age + PSYCHOSIS]

ger·kin (gûr′kin) See GHERKIN.

Ger·la·chov·ka (ger·lä·khôf′kä) The former name of STALIN PEAK, Czechoslovakia. *German* **Gerls·dor·fer Spit·ze** (gerls′dôr·fər shpit′sə). Also **Ger·lach** (ger′läkh).

germ (jûrm) *n.* **1** Any rudimentary vital element. **2** *Biol.* **a** The formative protoplasm of an egg or ovum, or of an ovule; a gamete; germ cell. **b** The earliest stage of an organism. **3** *Bot.* A growing point, as a young bud. **4** The primary source of anything; that from which a thing may be developed as from a seed. **5** A micro-organism; especially, one likely to cause disease; a microbe. **6** An embryo. —*adj.* **1** Germinative. **2** Pertaining to or arising from disease germs. [<F *germe* <L *germen* sprig]

ger·man[1] (jûr′mən) *n.* The cotillion, or a dance at which it is the chief feature. [Short for *German* cotillion]

ger·man[2] (jûr′mən) *adj.* Having the same parents or grandparents: used after the noun: cousins *german,* brothers *german.* [<OF *germain* <L *germanus* closely related]

Ger·man (jûr′mən) *n.* **1** A native or citizen of Germany. **2** The West Germanic language of the Germans. —**High German** The standard literary and spoken language used throughout most of Germany and in parts of Switzerland, Austria, and Alsace: also called **New High German.** Abbr. *HG* —**Low German 1** The collective languages of the Low Countries, including Dutch, Flemish, and Frisian, and of the northern lowlands of Germany (Plattdeutsch). **2** The division of West Germanic which includes Dutch, Flemish, Frisian, English, etc. Abbr. *LG* —**Old High German** The language of southern Germany from about 800 to 1100. Abbr. *OHG* —**Middle High German** The High German language from 1100 to 1450, as exemplified in the *Nibelungenlied.* Abbr. *MHG* —**Middle Low German** The low German language from 1100 to 1450. Abbr. *MLG*

German Baptist Brethren The Dunkers: official name.

German cockroach The Croton bug.

German Democratic Republic See under GERMANY.

ger·man·der (jər·man′dər) *n.* **1** A labiate herb (genus *Teucrium*) of the mint family, with pale purple flowers; especially the American germander (*T. canadense*). **2** The germander speedwell. See under SPEEDWELL. [<OF *germandree* <Med. L. *germandra,* alter. of LGk. *chamandrya* <Gk. *chamaidrys* <*chamai* on the ground + *drys* an oak]

ger·mane (jər·mān′) *adj.* **1** In close relationship; relevant; appropriate; pertinent. **2** Akin; german. [See GERMAN[2]]

German East Africa A former German protectorate occupying Tanganyika, 1885–1916.

German Empire See under GERMANY.

ger·man·ic (jər·man′ik) *adj. Chem.* Containing germanium in its higher valence.

Ger·man·ic (jər·man′ik) *adj.* **1** Of or pertaining to a group of early Indo-European tribes living in the region between the Rhine, Danube, and Vistula rivers: later extended to include the Germans, English, Dutch, Flemings, Danes, Scandinavians, and German-Swiss. **2** Relating to the language or customs of any of these people. —*n.* **1** A subfamily of the Indo-European family of languages, divided into the branches **East Germanic,** including Gothic (extinct); **North Germanic** or Scandinavian, including Norwegian, Swedish, Danish, Icelandic, and Faroese; and **West Germanic,** including all the High and Low German languages and dialects, among which are German, Dutch, Flemish, Frisian, English, Yiddish, Plattdeutsch, etc. **2** The prehistoric parent of these languages: called **Primitive Germanic.** Also called *Teutonic.*

Ger·man·i·cus Cae·sar (jər·man′i·kəs sē′zər), 15 B.C.–A.D. 19, Roman general. See also DRUSUS.

Ger·man·ism (jûr′mən·iz′əm) *n.* **1** A German idiom, word, or phrase, or an imitation of German idiom. **2** The characteristic German spirit; admiration of things German; anything copied after German customs, ideas, etc.

ger·ma·ni·um (jər·mā′nē·əm) *n.* A brittle, grayish white crystalline element (symbol Ge, atomic number 32) with a metallic luster, important as a semiconductor in the manufacture of electronic instruments. See PERIODIC TABLE. [<NL <L *Germania* Germany]

Ger·man·ize (jûr′mən·īz) *v.* **·ized, ·z·ing** *v.t.* **1** To cause to conform to German speech, customs, etc. **2** To translate into German. —*v.t.* **3** To adopt German opinions, customs, etc. —**Ger′man·i·za′tion** *n.* —**Ger′man·iz′er** *n.*

German measles Rubella.

Germano- *combining form* German: *Germanophile.*

German Ocean A former name for the NORTH SEA.

Ger·man·o·phile (jər·man′ə·fīl) *n.* One who has love for Germany or what is German.

Ger·man·o·phobe (jər·man′ə·fōb) *n.* One who dislikes Germany or what is German.

ger·man·ous (jûr′mən·əs) *adj. Chem.* Of or pertaining to germanium in its lower valence.

German shepherd A breed of dog having a large, muscular body, a thick, smooth coat, and unusual adaptability to work with policemen, blind persons, etc. Also called *police dog, Alsatian.*

German silver A white alloy of copper, nickel, and zinc, used in cutlery and as a base for plated ware; nickel silver.

German Southwest Africa A former name for South-West Africa. Now NAMIBIA.

German tinder Amadou.

Ger·man·town (jûr′mən·toun) A northern suburb of Philadelphia; scene of Washington's defeat during the Revolutionary War, Oct. 4, 1777.

Ger·ma·ny (jûr′mə·nē) A country of central Europe, known as the *German Empire* 1871–1918, divided in 1949 into: **a** The *Federal Republic of Germany (West Germany);* 84,634 square miles; capital, Bonn; **b** The *German Democratic Republic (East Germany);* 41,700 square miles; capital, Berlin: German *Deutschland,* French *Allemagne.*

ger·mar·i·um (jər·mâr′ē·əm) *n. Zool.* The formative part of the ovary of certain invertebrates, as the flatworm, containing the primary cell elements. [<NL <L *germen* a sprig]

germ cell *Biol.* A cell specialized for reproduction: distinguished from *somatic cell.*

ger·mi·cide (jûr′mə·sīd) *n.* That which is capable of killing germs; any agent used to destroy disease germs or other micro-organisms, as chlorine. [<GERM + -(I)CIDE] —**ger′mi·ci′dal** *adj.*

ger·mi·cul·ture (jûr′mə·kul′chər) *n.* The artificial cultivation of bacteria or disease germs for scientific research. —**ger′mi·cul′tur·ist** *n.*

ger·mi·nal (jûr′mə·nəl) *adj.* Pertaining to or constituting a germ; germinative [<NL *germinalis* <L *germen, -inis* a sprig]

Ger·mi·nal (jûr′mə·nəl, *Fr.* zhâr·mē·näl′) See under CALENDAR (Republican).

germinal disk *Biol.* **1** A disklike area of the blastoderm of eggs of amniotic vertebrates, in which the embryo proper first appears. **2** In meroblastic eggs with much yolk, the disklike protoplasmic part, which undergoes segmentation. Also called *blastodisk.* Compare illustration under EMBRYOLOGY.

germinal vesicle 1 *Biol.* The nucleus of the animal ovum. **2** *Bot.* The oospore within the embryo sac of the ovule of plants.

ger·mi·nate (jûr′mə·nāt) *v.* **·nat·ed, ·nat·ing** *v.i.* To begin to grow or develop; sprout. —*v.t.* To cause to sprout. [<L *germinatus,* pp. of *germinare* sprout] —**ger′mi·na·ble** (-nə·bəl) *adj.* —**ger′mi·nant** *adj.* —**ger′mi·na′tion** *n.* —**ger′mi·na′tor** *n.*

ger·mi·na·tive (jûr′mə·nā′tiv) *adj.* **1** Pertaining to or tending to produce germination; capable of germinating. **2** Capable of growing.

Ger·mis·ton (jûr′məs·tən) A city in Gauteng province, Republic of South Africa.

germ layer *Biol.* One of the three principal layers of cells from which the embryo develops, as the ectoderm, mesoderm, or endoderm.

germ plasm *Biol.* The part of the cell protoplasm which is the material basis of heredity, transferred from one generation to another. Also **germ plasma.**

germ theory 1 *Pathol.* The theory that infectious diseases, as typhoid fever, are caused by bacteria or other micro-organisms. **2** The doctrine of biogenesis.

ger·o·don·tia (jer′ə·don′shə) *n.* The branch of dentistry which specializes in the dental condition of elderly people. [<NL <Gk. *gēras* old age + *odous, odontos* tooth]

Gé·rold (zhā·rō′) French form of GERALD. Also *Ger.* **Ge′rold, Ge·rolt** (gā′rōlt).

Gé·rome (zhā·rōm′), **Jean Léon,** 1824–1904, French painter.

ger·o·mor·phism (jer′ə·môr′fiz·əm) *n. Pathol.* Premature senility and old age. [<Gk. *gēras* old age + *morphē* form + -ISM] —**ger′o·mor′phic** *adj.*

Ge·ro·ni·mo (jā·rô′nē·mō) Italian form of JEROME. —**Ge·ron·i·mo** (jə·ron′ə·mō) An Apache chief, 1829–1909, who led an insurrection against U.S. forces, 1884–86.

ge·ron·tic (ji·ron′tik) *adj.* Senile; of or pertaining to an old person or to old age. [<Gk. *gerontikos* <*gerōn, gerontos* old man]

geronto- *combining form* Old age; pertaining to old people: *gerontology.* Also, before vowels, **geront-.** [<Gk. *gerōn, gerontos* old man]

ger·on·toc·ra·cy (jer′on·tok′rə·sē) *n.* Government by the old; specifically, in certain primitive African cultures, the control of social life by members of the oldest age group. —**ge·ron·to·crat·ic** (ji·ron′tō·krat′ik) *adj.*

ge·ron·to·ge·ic (ji·ron′tō·jē′ik) *adj.* Of or pertaining to the Old World: opposed to *neogeic.* [<GERONTO- + Gk. *gē* earth]

ger·on·tol·o·gy (jer′on·tol′ə·jē) *n.* **1** The scientific study of the processes and phenomena of aging. **2** Geriatrics. —**ger′on·tol′o·gist** *n.*

ger·on·to·pi·a (jer′on·tō′pē·ə) *n.* Senopia.

ge·ron·to·ther·a·py (ji·ron′tō·ther′ə·pē) *n.* The therapeutic management of the disorders and processes associated with aging: distinguished from *geriatrics.*

-gerous *suffix* Bearing or producing: crystalligerous. [<L *gerere* bear + -OUS]

Ger·ry (ger′ē), **Elbridge,** 1744–1814, American statesman; signer of the Declaration of Independence.

ger·ry·man·der (jer′i·man′dər, ger′-) *n.t.* To alter unfairly or abnormally, as the political map of a state, etc. —*n.* An unnatural and arbitrary redistricting of a state or county. [<GERRY + (SALA)MANDER: from the salamander shape of one of the districts formed in Massachusetts while Elbridge Gerry was governor]

Gersh·win (gûrsh′win), **George,** 1898–1937, U.S. composer. —**Ira,** 1896–1983 U.S. lyricist; brother of George.

Ger·tie (gûr′tē) Diminutive of GERTRUDE.

Ger·trude (gûr′tro͞od, *Fr.* zher·trüd′; *Ital.* jer·tro͞o′dä) A feminine personal name. Also *Ger.* **Ger·traud** (ger′trout), *Ger., Sw.* **Ger·trud** (ger′tro͞ot), *Pg.* **Ger·tru·des** (zher·tro͞o′desh), *Sp.* **Ger·trú·dis** (her·tro͞o′dēs). [<Gmc., spear maid]

ger·und (jer′ənd) *n. Gram.* **1** In Latin, a verbal noun used only in the oblique cases of the singular, as furor *scribendi,* a rage for *writing.*

2 In English, a verbal noun ending in *-ing,* functioning as a noun, but capable of taking objects and adverbial modifiers. Example: *Writing* poetry well is an art. [<LL *gerundium* <*gerere* carry on, do] **—ge·rundi·al** (jə·run′dē·əl) *adj.*

ge·run·dive (jə·run′div) *Gram. adj.* Like, pertaining to, or having the nature of the gerund. —*n.* In Latin, a verbal adjective having the gerund stem and used as future passive participle, expressing obligation, fitness, or necessity, as *regendus,* that must or should be ruled, or *amandus,* to be loved, that should be loved, etc. [<LL *gerundivus* <*gerundium* GERUND]

Ge·ry·on (jē′rē·ən, ger′ē-) In Greek mythology, a three-headed monster of Erytheia, killed by Hercules for his herd of red cattle.

Ge·sell (gə·zel′), **Arnold Lucius,** 1880–1961, U.S. psychologist.

ges·so (jes′ō) *n.* **1** A ground of plaster, as gypsum or plaster of Paris, prepared to be painted on. **2** Gypsum or plaster of Paris prepared for use in sculpture. [<Ital. <L *gypsum* GYPSUM]

gest[1] (jest) *n.* **1** *Archaic* A deed; exploit. **2** A tale of adventure; a romance, especially a metrical romance. Also **geste.** ◆ Homophone: *jest.* [<OF <L *gesta* deeds, orig. neut. plural of *gestus,* pp. of *gerere* do]

gest[2] (jest) *n. Archaic* A gesture; carriage; bearing. Also **geste.** ◆ Homophone: *jest.* [<OF *geste* <L *gestus* bearing <*gerere* carry on, do]

gest[3] (jest) *n. Obs.* **1** A halting place. **2** An itinerary, especially of a royal progress. ◆ Homophone: *jest.* [Var. of GIST]

Ge·stalt (gə·shtält′) *n. pl.* **·stalt·en** (-shtält′ən) *Psychol.* An arrangement of separate elements of experience, emotion, etc., in a form, pattern, or configuration so integrated as to appear and function as a unit that is more than a simple summation of its parts. [<G, form]

Gestalt psychology A school of psychology which interprets biological and psychic processes in terms of the action and interplay of closely integrated patterns or *Gestalten*; the observed effect of a Gestalt, as well as the mechanism of its action, cannot be adequately explained through a simple analysis of its constituent parts.

Ge·sta·po (gə·stä′pō) *n.* The secret police of Nazi Germany. [<G *Ge(heime) Sta(ats)-po(lizei)* Secret State Police]

Ges·ta Ro·ma·no·rum (jes′tə rō′mə·nôr′əm, -nō′rəm) A collection of tales compiled in Latin in Europe in the 14th century, used as a source book by Chaucer, Shakespeare, and others. [<L, deeds of the Romans]

ges·tate (jes′tāt) *v.t.* **·tat·ed, ·tat·ing** To carry in the womb during gestation. [<L *gestatus,* pp. of *gestare* carry young]

ges·ta·tion (jes·tā′shən) *n.* Pregnancy; especially, the period of carrying a fetus in the womb from conception until birth. **—ges′ta·to′ry** (-tôr′ē, -tō′rē) *adj.*

ges·tic (jes′tik) *adj.* Of or pertaining to bodily motion, especially dancing. Also **ges′ti·cal.**

ges·tic·u·late (jes·tik′yə·lāt) *v.* **·lat·ed, ·lat·ing** *v.i.* To make motions with the hands or arms, as in speaking. —*v.t.* To express by gestures. [<L *gesticulatus,* pp. of *gesticulari* <*gesticulus,* dim. of *gestus* bearing, gesture] **—ges·tic′u·la′tive** *adj.* **—ges·tic′u·la′tor** *n.*

ges·tic·u·la·tion (jes·tik′yə·lā′shən) *n.* **1** A motion of the body or limbs, designed to illustrate speech; a gesture. **2** The act or art of making gestures. See synonyms under GESTURE. **—ges·tic′u·la·to′ry** (-tôr′ē, -tō′rē) *adj.*

ges·tion (jes′chən) *n. Obs.* Management; operation.

ges·ture (jes′chər) *n.* **1** An expressive motion or action, as of the hand or hands in speaking, used for emphasis or to express some idea or emotion. **2** Such motions collectively, or the art of making them. **3** Something said or done as a mere concession to manners, courtesy, etc. **4** *Obs.* Deportment; posture. —*v.* **·tured, ·tur·ing** *v.i.* To make gestures; gesticulate. —*v.t.* To express by gestures. [<Med. L *gestura* <*gerere* carry on, do] **—ges′tur·er** *n.*

Synonym (noun): gesticulation. *Gesticulation* often conveys the idea of jerky, sudden, or undignified motions; a *gesture* is any expressive movement of the limbs or body.

Ge·sund·heit (gə·zŏŏnt′hīt) *German* (Your) health: a salutation or a toast, or an expression of good will after a sneeze.

get (get) *v.* **got** or *Archaic* **gat, got** or *U.S.* **got·ten, get·ting** *v.t.* **1** To come into possession of; obtain. **2** To go and bring back or obtain: to *get* one's hat. **3** To cause to come, go, move, etc.: to *get* baggage through customs. **4** To take; carry away: *Get* your things out of this house. **5** To prepare; make ready: to *get* breakfast. **6** To cause to be; bring to a state or condition: to *get* the work done. **7** To find out; ascertain by calculation, experiment, etc.: To *get* the range of a gun. **8** To obtain as a result: Divide two into six and you will *get* three. **9** To receive as a reward, punishment, evaluation, etc.: to *get* ten years in jail for robbery. **10** To obtain, receive, or earn (something desired or needed): to *get* permission. **11** To receive as a salary, gift, etc.: What did you *get* for Christmas? **12** To learn by memorizing: to *get* a lesson by heart. **13** To become sick with; contract: to *get* malaria. **14** To board; catch, as a train. **15** To beget: said chiefly of animals. **16** *U.S. Colloq.* To come to an understanding of; comprehend: I *get* the idea. **17** *Colloq.* To possess, or to have as a characteristic: with *have* or *has*: He has *got* quite a temper. See note under GOT. **18** To square accounts with: I'll *get* you yet. **19** *Colloq.* To be obliged or forced to do: with *have* or *has*: I have *got* to go home. See note under GOT. **20** *Colloq.* To strike; hit: That shot *got* him in the arm. **21** *Slang* To puzzle; baffle; also, to cause irritation or pleasure to: His impudence *gets* me. **22** *Archaic* Betake: *Get* thee behind me. —*v.i.* **23** To arrive: When does the train *get* there? **24** To come or go: *Get* in here! **25** To board; enter: to *get* on a train or into a car. **26** To become: arrive at a condition or state: to *get* drunk; to *get* stuck in the mud. **27** To acquire profits or property. **28** *Colloq.* To find time, means, or opportunity: to *get* to go. **—to get about 1** To become known. **2** To move about. **—to get across 1** To make or be convincing or clear, as to an audience. **2** To be successful, as in projecting one's personality, entertaining, etc. **—to get ahead** To succeed; prosper. **—to get along 1** To leave; go. **2** To be successful or fairly successful, as in business. **3** To be friendly; harmonize. **4** To proceed. **5** To grow old or older. **—to get around 1** To become known. **2** To move about. **3** To avoid; circumvent. **4** To flatter, cajole, etc., so as to obtain the favor of. **—to get at 1** To reach; arrive at: to *get at* the truth. **2** To intend; mean: I don't see what you're *getting at.* **3** To apply oneself to: to *get at* a problem. **4** *Colloq.* To bribe; corrupt. **—to get away 1** To escape. **2** To leave; go. **3** To start. **—to get away with** *Slang* To do (something) without discovery, criticism, or punishment. **—to get back at** *Slang* To revenge oneself on. **—to get by 1** To pass: This *got by* the censor. **2** *Colloq.* To manage to survive. **—to get in 1** To arrive. **2** To interject effectively, as a remark or the last word. **—to get off 1** To descend from; dismount. **2** To leave; depart. **3** To be relieved, as of duty. **4** To be released without punishment; escape penalty. **5** To utter: to *get off* a joke. **—to get on 1** To mount, as a horse. **2** To get along. **—to get out 1** To depart. **2** To escape. **3** To become known, as a secret. **4** To publish; issue. **—to get over 1** To recover from, as illness or surprise. **2** To get across. **—to get together 1** To collect, as facts or goods. **2** To meet; assemble. **3** *Colloq.* To come to an agreement. **—to get up 1** To rise, as from sleep. **2** To prepare and arrange; devise. **3** *Colloq.* To dress up; bedeck, as with finery. **4** To acquire or work up knowledge of: to *get up* German for an examination. **5** To climb; ascend. —*n.* **1** The act of begetting, or that which is begotten; breed; progeny: the *get* of the stallion. **2** In tennis, handball, etc., the retrieval of a shot apparently beyond reach. [<ON *geta*] **—get′ta·ble** *adj.*

Synonyms (verb): achieve, acquire, attain, earn, gain, obtain, procure, receive, secure, win. *Get* is a most comprehensive word. A person *gets* whatever he comes to possess or experience, with or without endeavor, expectation, or desire; he *gets* a bargain, a blow, a fall, a fever; he *gains* what he comes to by effort or striving; the swimmer *gains* the shore; a man *acquires* by continuous and ordinarily by slow process; as, One *acquires* a foreign language. A person is sometimes said to *gain* and often to *acquire* what has not been an object of direct endeavor; in the pursuits of trade, he incidentally *gains* some knowledge of foreign countries; he *acquires* by association with others a correct or incorrect accent; he *acquires* a bronzed complexion by exposure to a tropical sun; in such use, what he *gains* is viewed as desirable, what he *acquires* as slowly and gradually resulting. A person *earns* what he gives an equivalent of labor for, but he may not *get* it. On the other hand, he may *get* what he has not *earned*; the temptation to all dishonesty is the desire to *get* a living or a fortune without *earning* it. Compare ATTAIN, GAIN[1], LEARN, MAKE, OBTAIN, PURCHASE, REACH. *Antonyms*: see synonyms for ABANDON.

get-at-a·ble (get′at′ə·bəl) *adj. Colloq.* That one may get at or reach; obtainable; accessible. **—get′-at′-a·bil′i·ty** *n.*

get-a·way (get′ə·wā′) *n.* **1** An escape, as of a criminal or of a fox from covert. **2** The start, as of a horse in a race. Also **get′a·way′.**

geth·sem·a·ne (geth·sem′ə·nē) *n.* A place or time of agony.

Geth·sem·a·ne (geth·sem′ə·nē) A garden outside Jerusalem at the foot of the Mount of Olives; the scene of the agony, betrayal, and arrest of Jesus. *Matt.* xxvi 36. [<Gk. *Gethsēmanē* <Aramaic *gath shemānīm* oil press]

get-rich-quick (get′rich′kwik′) *adj.* Aiming at quick and lucrative gains.

get·ter (get′ər) *n.* **1** One who gets. **2** *Electronics* A substance, as magnesium, placed inside a vacuum tube during manufacture and acting by incandescence to remove any gases left by the vacuum pump. **3** *Electr.* A coating of metal on the filament of a tungsten lamp, designed to prolong its life.

get-to·geth·er (get′tə·geth′ər) *n.* An informal gathering or meeting.

Get·tys·burg (get′iz·bûrg) A town in southern Pennsylvania; scene of a Confederate defeat in the Civil War, July 1–3, 1863.

get-up (get′up′) *n. Colloq.* **1** The manner in which a thing is put together; general appearance; make-up. **2** Style of dress.

Gev *abbr. Physics* Giga (10^9) electron volts.

gew·gaw (gyōō′gô) *adj.* Showy; gaudy. —*n.* A flashy, useless ornament; bauble. See synonyms under GAUD. [ME *giue-goue;* origin uncertain]

gey (gā) *adj. Scot.* Moderate; considerable. —*adv.* Very.

gey·ser (gī′zər) *n.* **1** A natural hot spring from which intermittent jets of steam, hot water, or mud are ejected in a fountainlike column. **2** *Brit.* A gas hot-water heater. [<Icel. *geysir* gusher, name of a hot spring <*geysa* gush]

gey·ser·ite (gī′zər·īt) *n.* A concretionary opaline quartz deposited in various forms around the orifices of geysers and hot springs, sometimes forming terraces.

Ge·zi·ra (je·zē′rə) An irrigated region in east central Sudan between the Blue Nile and the White Nile.

ghaist (gāst) *n. Scot.* A ghost.

Gha·na (gä′nä) An independent state (1957) in the Commonwealth of Nations, comprising the former Gold Coast Colony and the protectorates of Ashanti, Northern Territories, and British Togoland in western Africa; 91,690 square miles; capital, Accra: formerly *Gold Coast.*

ghar·ry (gar′ē) *n. pl.* **·ries** *Anglo-Indian* A wheeled vehicle; a cart or carriage for hire. Also **ghar′ri.** [<Hind. *gārī* cart]

ghast·ly (gast′lē, gäst′-) *adj.* **·li·er, ·li·est 1** Having a haggard, deathlike appearance. **2** Terrifying or shocking. —*adv.* Like a specter; fearfully. [ME *gastlich,* OE *gæstan* terrify + *-lich* LY[1]] **—ghast′li·ness** *n.*

Synonyms (adj.): cadaverous, deathlike, deathly, hideous, pale, pallid, spectral, wan. See PALE². *Antonyms*: blooming, bright, buxom, comely, fresh, ruddy.

ghat (gôt) *n. Anglo-Indian* **1** A stairway on a river bank leading to a temple, or to a landing place or wharf. **2** A mountain pass or a descent from a mountain range. Also **ghaut.** [<Hind. *ghāt*]

Ghats (gôts, gäts), **Eastern** and **Western** The two principal mountain ranges of southern India, parallel to its coasts; average height of the Western Ghats, 3,000 to 5,000 feet; average height of the Eastern Ghats, 1,500 to 2,000 feet.

gha·zi (gä′zē) *n.* **1** In Moslem countries, a hero or champion, especially one who has fought against infidels. **2** In Turkey, an honorary title bestowed on eminent national leaders. [<Arabic, orig. ppr. of *ghazā* fight] **—gha′zism** *n.*

Ghaz·ni (gäz′nē) A city in eastern Afghanistan; former capital of the first Moslem dynasty in Afghanistan.

Ghe·ber (gā′bər, gē′-) *n.* A fire-worshiper or Parsee; a Zoroastrian: so called by Mohammedans: often spelled *Gueber, Guebre.* Also **Ghe′bre.** See GIAOUR. [<F. *guèbre* <Persian *gabr*]

ghee (gē) *n. Anglo-Indian* **1** Clarified butter. **2** A solid white oil obtained from a tree of northern India *(Madhuca butyracea)*, used in soaps and ointments. Also **ghi.** [<Hind. *ghī* <Skt. *ghṛta*]

Gheel (khāl) A city in northern Belgium, known since the 14th century for its community treatment of the insane. Also **Geel.**

Ghent (gent) A city in NW Belgium: Flemish *Gent,* French *Gand.*

gher·kin (gûr′kin) *n.* **1** A small prickly cucumber *(Cucumis anguria)*, used for pickles. **2** Any small, immature cucumber used for pickling: also spelled *gerkin.* [<Du. *agurk* cucumber <G <Slavic, ult. <LGk. *angourion*]

GHERKIN — VINE, FLOWER AND FRUIT

ghet·to (get′ō) *n. pl.* **·tos** or **·ti** (-tē) **1** A part of a city or town, especially in Italy, in which Jews were formerly required to live. **2** A section of a city, often rundown or overcrowded, inhabited chiefly by a minority group that is effectively barred from living in other communities, as because of racial prejudice or for economic or social reasons. [<Ital.]

Ghib·el·line (gib′əl·in, -ēn) *n.* A supporter in Italy of the German emperor (11th–14th centuries); one of the imperial party opposed to the papal party. See GUELF. *—adj.* Of or pertaining to this party. [<Ital. *Ghibellino,* alter. of G *Waiblingen,* an imperial estate] **—Ghib′el·lin·ism** *n.*

Ghi·ber·ti (gē·ber′tē), **Lorenzo,** 1378–1455, Florentine sculptor, painter, and goldsmith.

ghost (gōst) *n.* **1** A disembodied spirit. **2** The soul or spirit. **3** A shadow or semblance; slight trace. **4** A spirit of any kind. **5** *Optics* **a** A false or secondary image, or a spot of light, as from a defect in a lens or instrument. **b** In television, a secondary image, appearing as a doubling of the image to the right, caused by reception of a reflected signal a fraction of a second later than the primary image. **6** *Obs.* The Holy Ghost. **7** *U.S. Slang* An addict to opium-smoking. **8** *Metall.* A narrow band of metal on steel ingots or forgings, harder than the adjoining parts; it becomes more evident on machining: also **ghost line.** See synonyms under SPECTER. **—to give up the ghost.** To die. *—v.t. & v.i.* **1** To haunt as a ghost. **2** *Colloq.* To write as a ghost writer. [OE *gāst* spirit] **—ghost′like′** *adj.*

ghost dance A dance performed by certain North American Indian tribes, in which both sexes take part, believed to bring the dancer into communion with the souls of dead friends.

ghost·ly (gōst′lē) *adj.* **·li·er, ·li·est 1** Pertaining to the soul or religion; spiritual. **2** Pertaining to apparitions; spectral. **—ghost′li·ness** *n.*

ghost town A deserted town; especially, a former boom town now empty and decayed.

ghost-write (gōst′rīt′) *v.i. & v.t.* **-wrote, -writ·ten, -writ·ing** To do literary work credited to another. **—ghost writer.**

ghoul (gōōl) *n.* **1** In Oriental legend, an evil spirit supposed to prey on corpses. **2** A person who robs dead bodies; a grave-robber; body-snatcher. **3** One who delights in morbid and revolting things. [<Arabic *ghūl*] **—ghoul′ish** *adj.* **—ghoul′ish·ly** *adv.* **—ghoul′ish·ness** *n.*

ghur·ry (gûr′ē) *n. pl.* **·ries 1** In India, a clepsydra or water clock; hence, any timepiece. **2** In Hindu custom, the sixtieth part of a day. Also **ghur′rie.** [<Hind. *gharī* <Skt. *ghaṭī*]

ghyll (gil) See GILL

GI (jē′ī′) *n. Colloq.* A soldier, especially an enlisted man, in the U.S. Army *—adj.* Of, pertaining to, or issued by the U.S. Army. See GOVERNMENT ISSUE. Also **G.I.** [<*G(overnment) I(ssue)*]

Gia·cob·be (jä·kôb′bā) Italian form of JACOB.

Gia·co·mo (jä′kō·mō) Italian form of JAMES.

gi·ant (jī′ənt) *n.* **1** In mythology, a being of human form, but of enormous size. **2** Any person or thing of great size, either physically, mentally, or figuratively. **3** Any imaginary person of gigantic size. *—adj.* Gigantic. [<OF *géant* <L *gigas, -antis* <Gk. *gigas, -antos*] **—gi′ant·ess** *n. fem.* **—gi′ant·ship** *n.*

giant cactus A large desert cactus of SW United States *(Cereus giganteus)*, with an erect columnar trunk, sometimes branching, many ribs, strong spines, and flowering tops: also called *saguaro, sahuaro.*

giant fennel See under FENNEL.

giant hyssop See under HYSSOP.

gi·ant·ism (jī′ənt·iz′əm) *n.* **1** The quality or condition of being a giant. **2** Gigantism.

giant kelp A very large, tough and massive seaweed *(Macrocystis pyrifera)* belonging to the brown algae, found mainly in the Pacific.

giant panda See under PANDA.

giant powder A variety of dynamite.

Giant's Causeway A headland on the northern coast of County Antrim, Northern Ireland, consisting of thousands of small basaltic columns of volcanic origin.

giant star See under STAR.

giaour (jour) *n.* An unbeliever; a term of opprobrium applied by Moslems. See GHEBER. [<Turkish *giaur* <Persian *gaur,* var. of *gabr*]

gi·ar·di·a·sis (jē′är·dī′ə·sis) *n. Pathol.* An intestinal disorder attributed to the presence of a parasitic flagellate protozoan, *Giardia lamblia;* flagellate diarrhea. [<NL *Giardia,* a genus name + -IASIS]

gib (gib) *n. Mech.* **1** A wedge-shaped or other piece of metal that holds another in place or adjusts a bearing, etc. **2** A bearing surface, usually of brass, let into the cross-head of a steam engine to reduce friction. *—v.t.* **gibbed, gib·bing** To fasten with a gib or gibs; supply with a gib. [? <GIBBET]

gib·ber¹ (jib′ər, gib′-) *v.i.* To talk rapidly and incoherently; jabber. *—n.* Gibberish. [Imit.]

gib·ber² (gib′ər) *n. Austral.* A boulder; stone. [<native Australian]

gibber country *Austral.* An inland area covered with stones. Also *gibber plain.*

gib·ber·el·lic acid (jib′ə·rel′ik) *Chem.* A fermentation product of gibberellin, $C_{19}H_{22}O_6$, used as a plant-growth regulator.

gib·ber·el·lin (jib′ə·rel′in) *n. Chem.* Any of a group of closely related plant hormones that regulate certain processes in all higher plants, as flowering, germination of seeds, stem elongation, etc. [after *Gibberella fujikuroi,* a pathogenic fungus from which they were first isolated]

gib·ber·ish (jib′ər·ish, gib′-) *n.* Incoherent or unintelligible gabble. See synonyms under LANGUAGE.

gib·bet (jib′it) *n.* An upright timber with a crosspiece projecting at right angles from its upper end, upon which criminals were formerly hanged; hence, any gallows. *—v.t.* **·bet·ed** or **·bet·ted, ·bet·ing** or **·bet·ting 1** To execute by hanging. **2** To hang and expose on a gibbet. **3** To hold up to public contempt. [<OF *gibet,* dim. of *gibe* a staff]

gib·bon (gib′ən) *n.* A slender, long-armed arboreal anthropoid ape of southern Asia (genus *Hylobates*). [<F; ult. origin uncertain]

BLACK–CAPPED GIBBON (Standing erect, usually about 2 1/2 feet)

Gib·bon (gib′ən), **Edward,** 1737–94, English historian.

Gib·bons (gib′ənz), **James,** 1834–1921, U.S. cardinal. **—Orlando,** 1583–1625, English composer.

gib·bos·i·ty (gi·bos′ə·tē) *n. pl.* **·ties 1** The state of being gibbous, or convex. **2** A rounded protuberance; hump.

gib·bous (gib′əs) *adj.* **1** Irregularly rounded; convex, as the moon when less than full and yet more than half full. **2** Humpbacked. **3** *Bot.* Swollen on one side, as the calyx of a lupine. Also **gib·bose** (gib′ōs, gi·bōs′). [<L *gibbosus* <*gibbus* a hump] **—gib′bous·ly** *adv.* **—gib′bous·ness** *n.*

Gibbs (gibz), **Josiah Willard,** 1839–1903, U.S. mathematician and physicist. **—Sir Philip,** 1877–1962, English author and journalist. **—William Francis,** 1886-1967, U.S. naval architect.

gibe¹ (jīb) *v.t. & v.i.* **gibed, gib·ing** To mock; sneer; scoff. See synonyms under MOCK, SCOFF. *—n.* An expression of sarcasm and ridicule. See synonyms under SNEER. Also spelled *jibe.* [Cf. OF *giber* treat roughly in play] **—gib′er** *n.* **—gib′ing·ly** *adv.*

gibe² (jīb) See JIBE¹

Gib·e·on (gib′ē·ən) A city NW of Jerusalem in ancient Palestine.

Gib·e·on·ite (gib′ē·ən·īt) *n.* **1** One of the inhabitants of Gibeon, condemned by Joshua to be "hewers of wood and drawers of water" for the Israelites. *Josh.* ix 27. **2** *Obs.* A drudge; a slave's slave.

gib·let (jib′lit) *n.* One of the edible visceral parts of a fowl, as the gizzard, heart, or liver. [<OF *gibelet* a stew made from game]

Gi·bral·tar (ji·brôl′tər) A British crown colony, fortress, and naval base on the southern coast of Spain: called *Key of the Mediterranean* and identified with one of the *Pillars of Hercules;* 2 1/4 square miles, including the **Rock of Gibraltar** (ancient *Calpe*: also *the Rock*) 1,396 feet high, and dominating the **Strait of Gibraltar,** the passage between Spain and Africa at the western end of the Mediterranean.

Gib·son (gib′sən), **Charles Dana,** 1867–1944, U.S. illustrator.

Gib·son Desert (gib′sən) The central belt of the Western Australian desert, between the Great Sandy Desert and Victoria Desert.

Gibson girl An idealization of the American girl of the 1890's as portrayed by Charles Dana Gibson; also, the style of dress fashionable in that period. **—Gib′son-girl′** *adj.*

gid (gid) *n.* A parasitic disease chiefly affecting sheep and goats, caused by the presence in the brain or spinal cord of the cysticercus of a tapeworm *(Coenurus cerebralis).* [<GIDDY]

gid·dy (gid′ē) *adj.* **·di·er, ·di·est 1** Having a whirling or swimming sensation in the head; dizzy. **2** Tending to cause such a sensation: a *giddy* precipice. **3** Marked by foolish levity or impudence; heedless; fickle. *—v.t. & v.i.* **gid·died, gid·dy·ing** To make or become dizzy or unsteady. [OE *gydig* insane] **—gid′di·ly** *adv.* **—gid′di·ness** *n.*

Gide (zhēd), **André,** 1869–1951, French author. **—Charles,** 1847–1932, French economist.

Gid·e·on (gid′ē·ən) A masculine personal name. [<Hebrew, hewer]

—Gideon An Israelite judge. *Judges* vi 11.

Gid·e·ons (gid′ē·ənz), **The International** A society of American businessmen founded in 1899 to advance the distribution of Bibles in hotels, hospitals, prisons, and public schools.

gie (gē) *v.t. Scot.* To give.

gier-ea·gle (jir′ē′gəl) *n.* A bird of prey, probably the Egyptian vulture *(Neophron percnopterus). Lev.* xi 18. [< Du. *gier* vulture + EAGLE]

Gi·e·ron·y·mus (jē′ə·ron′i·məs) A Latin form of JEROME.

Gies·sen (gē′sən) A city in central Hesse, West Germany.

gif (gif) *conj. Scot. & Brit. Dial.* If. Also **giff.**

gift (gift) *n.* **1** That which is given; a donation; present. **2** The act, right, or power of giving. **3** A natural endowment; aptitude; talent. **4** *Obs.* A bribe; also, an offering. —*v.t.* **1** To bestow or confer upon. **2** To endow with a talent or faculty. [OE < *gifan* give]

Synonyms (noun): benefaction, bequest, boon, bounty, bribe, donation, grant, gratuity, largess, present, tip. A *gift* is that which is voluntarily bestowed without expectation of return or compensation. *Gift* is almost always used in the good sense, *bribe* is the evil sense to signify payment for a dishonorable service under the semblance of a *gift.* A *benefaction* is a charitable *gift,* generally of large amount, and viewed as of enduring value, as an endowment for a college. A *donation* is something, perhaps of great, seldom of trivial value, given to a cause or to a person representing a cause; as, a *donation* to a charity. A *gratuity* is usually of moderate value and is always given as of favor, not of right; as, a *gratuity* to a waiter; commonly called a *tip. Largess* is archaic for a bountiful *gratuity,* usually to be distributed among many, as among the heralds at ancient tournaments. A *present* is a *gift* of friendship, or conciliation, and given as to an equal or a superior. A *boon* is something that has been desired or craved or perhaps asked, or something freely given that meets some great desire. A *grant* is commonly considerable in amount and given by public authority; as, a *grant* of public lands for a college. See FAVOR, SUBSIDY. *Antonyms*: compensation, earnings, guerdon, penalty, remuneration, wages.

gift·ed (gif′tid) *adj.* Endowed with mental power or talent. See synonyms under CLEVER. —**gift′ed·ness** *n.*

gift·ie (gif′tē) *n. Scot.* Faculty; power; gift.

gift of gab *Colloq.* Fluency in speaking.

gift of tongues In the Bible, a miraculous power of speaking in unknown tongues.

Gi·fu (gē·fōō) A city on central Honshu island, Japan.

gig[1] (gig) *n.* **1** A light, two-wheeled, one-seated vehicle drawn by one horse. **2** A machine for raising a nap on a cloth by passing it over cylinders fitted with teasels. **3** *Naut.* A ship's boat in which the oarsmen are seated on alternate thwarts; also, a speedy, light rowboat. —*v.* **gigged, gig·ging** *v.i.* To ride in a gig. —*v.t.* To raise the nap on (cloth). [Origin uncertain]

gig[2] (gig) *n.* **1** A pronged fishspear. **2** An arrangement of four barbless fish hooks fastened back to back and drawn through a school of fish to catch them in the bodies. —*v.t. & v.i.* **gigged, gig·ging** To spear or catch (fish) with a gig. [< FISHGIG]

gig[3] (gig) *Slang n.* A demerit, as in the army, school, etc. —*v.t.* **gigged, gig·ging 1** To give a demerit to. **2** To punish with a gig. [Origin unknown]

giga- *combining form* In systems of measurement, one billion (10^9) times (the specified unit): *gigavolt.*

gi·gan·tesque (jī′gan·tesk′) *adj.* Like or suited to giants.

gi·gan·tic (jī·gan′tik) *adj.* **1** Like a giant; colossal; huge. **2** Tremendous; extraordinary. Also **gi·gan·te·an** (jī′gan·tē′ən). See synonyms under IMMENSE, LARGE. [< L *gigas, -antis* GIANT + -IC]

gi·gan·tism (jī·gan′tiz·əm) *n.* **1** Abnormal size. **2** *Pathol.* Excessive growth of the body due to disturbances in the function and growth of the anterior lobe of the pituitary gland: also called *giantism.* Also **gi′gan·to·so′ma** (-tə·sō′mə).

giganto- *combining form* Gigantic; very large: *gigantocyte.* Also, before vowels, **gigant-.** [< Gk. *gigas, -antos* giant]

gi·gan·to·cyte (jī·gan′tə·sīt) *n. Physiol.* An excessively large erythrocyte.

gi·gan·tom·a·chy (jī′gan·tom′ə·kē) *n.* In classical mythology, the battle of the giants; the war of the giants against Zeus and the Olympian gods. Also **gi·gan·to·ma·chi·a** (jī·gan′tō·mā′kē·ə). [< Gk. *gigantomachia* < *gigas, -antos* giant + *machē* battle]

Gi·gan·to·pith·e·cus (jī·gan′tō·pith′ə·kəs) *n. Paleontol.* A giant hominoid primate of the early Pleistocene, represented only by several very large fossilized molar teeth discovered in Hong Kong apothecary shops between 1935 and 1939. Also **Gi·gant·an·thro·pus** (jī′gan·tan′thrə·pəs). [< NL < Gk. *gigas, -antos* giant + *pithēkos* ape]

gig·gle (gig′əl) *v.i.* **gig·gled, gig·gling** To laugh in a high-pitched, nervous manner; titter. —*n.* A convulsive laugh; titter. [Imit.] —**gig′gler** *n.* —**gig′gle·some** *adj.* —**gig′gling** *adj. & n.* —**gig′gly** *adj.*

gig·let (gig′lit) *n. Brit.* A giddy girl; romp; minx. Also **gig′lot.** [Origin uncertain]

gig·o·lo (jig′ə·lō, *Fr.* zhē·gô·lō′) *n. pl.* **·los** (-lōz, *Fr.* -lō′) **1** A professional male dancer in dance halls, cabarets, or the like, who attends women patrons or visitors. **2** A woman's paid escort. **3** A man who is supported by a woman; a kept man. [< F, prob. < *gigolette* a prostitute]

gig·ot (jig′ət) *n.* **1** A leg of mutton. **2** A sleeve having the shape of a leg of mutton. [< F]

gigue (zhēg) *n. Music* A lively composition often forming the final movement of a suite. [< F. See JIG.]

Gi·hulng·an (hi·hōōlng′än) A municipality on the NE coast of Negros island, Philippines.

Gi·jón (hi·hôn′) A port in Asturias, NW Spain.

Gi·la monster (hē′·lə) A large, poisonous lizard *(Heloderma suspectum)* with a stout orange-and-black body, ranging from southern Utah and Nevada through Arizona and New Mexico into northern Mexico. The beaded lizard *(H. horridum),* an allied form found in Mexico, is also poisonous.

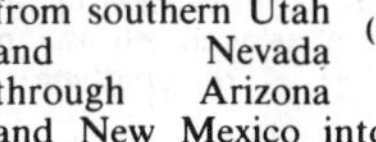

GILA MONSTER (Up to 20 inches over all in length)

Gi·la River (hē′lə) A river in New Mexico and Arizona, flowing 650 miles SW to the Colorado River.

Gila woodpecker A woodpecker *(Centurus uropygialis)* of the SW United States, habitually nesting in the stem of the giant cactus.

gil·bert (gil′bərt) *n. Electr.* The cgs unit of magnetomotive force; equal to 0.7958 ampere-turn. [after William *Gilbert,* 1540–1603, English physicist]

Gil·bert (gil′bərt; *Dan.* gil′bert; *Du.* hil′bərt; *Fr.* zhĕl·bâr′; *Ger.* gĕl′bert) A masculine personal name. Also *Ital.* **Gil·ber·to** (jēl·ber′tō, *Sp.* hĕl·ber′tō), *Lat.* **Gil·ber·tus** (gil·bûr′tus, *Sw.* yil·ber′tōōs). [< Gmc., bright wish]

Gil·bert (gil′bərt), **Cass,** 1859–1934, U.S. architect. —**Sir Humphrey,** 1539?–83, English navigator. —**William,** 1540–1603, English physicist and physician. —**Sir William Schwenck,** 1836–1911, English humorous poet and librettist; collaborator with Sir Arthur Sullivan.

Gilbert and Ellice Islands A British colony in the west central and SW Pacific, comprising Ocean Island, the Gilbert Islands, the Ellice Islands, and several of the Phoenix and Line islands; total, about 375 square miles; headquarters on Tarawa, in the Gilbert Islands.

Gil·ber·ti·an (gil·bûr′tē·ən) *adj.* Pertaining to or resembling the style or humor of Sir W. S. Gilbert.

Gilbert Islands A group of atolls SE of the Marshall Islands, comprising a district of the Gilbert and Ellice Islands colony; 144 square miles; headquarters of the district and the colony, Tarawa.

Gil Blas (zhēl bläs′) The hero and title of a satiric picaresque romance by A. R. Le Sage.

Gil·bo·a (gil·bō′ə) A hilly district at the SE end of the Plain of Jezreel, scene of Saul's defeat and death. I *Sam.* xxxi 2–4.

gild[1] (gild) *v.t.* **gild·ed** or **gilt, gild·ing 1** To coat with or as with gold or gold leaf. **2** To give a pleasing or attractive appearance to; gloss over. **3** *Obs.* To redden or smear (with blood). See synonyms under ADORN. ◆Homophone: *guild.* [OE *gyldan*] —**gild′er** *n.*

gild[2] (gild), **gild·hall** (gild′hôl′), **gild·ry** (gild′rē), etc. See GUILD, etc.

gild·ed (gil′did) *adj.* **1** Thinly overlaid with or as with gold. **2** Fashionable; wealthy.

Gilded Age, the A post-Civil War period (1870–98) of waxing plutocratic accumulation and display in the United States: from *The Gilded Age* (1871), a novel by Mark Twain and Charles Dudley Warner depicting the newly emergent plutocracy with its conspicuous consumption and waste.

gild·er (gil′dər) See GUILDER.

gild·ing (gil′ding) *n.* **1** The art of overlaying a surface thinly with gold. **2** A mixture of finely divided gold, brass, or other substance to simulate gold, and a drying liquid: used as a decorative paint. **3** A specious or superficial appearance. Also **gilt, gild.**

Gil·e·ad (gil′ē·əd) A mountainous region of ancient Palestine east of the Jordan. *Josh.* xii 2.

Gil·e·ad·ite (gil′ē·əd·īt′) *n.* An inhabitant of Gilead. *Judges* xii 4.

Giles (jīlz) A masculine personal name. [< OF < L, having the aegis]

—**Giles** A seventh century hermit and saint; patron of cripples.

Gil·ga·mesh (gil′gə·mesh) A mythical Babylonian king, later identified with the sun-god: hero of the **Gilgamesh epic,** a literary epic written on cuneiform tablets found in the library of Ashurbanipal.

gill[1] (gil) *n.* **1** An organ for breathing the air dissolved in water, consisting, in aquatic vertebrates, as fishes and amphibians, of leaflike or threadlike vascular processes of mucous membrane on either side of the neck. Fishes take in water for the gills through the mouth and force it out mostly through the gill slits. **2** A gill-like part, as the wattle of a fowl. **3** *Bot.* One of the thin radial plates on the under side of the cap of a mushroom. —*v.t.* **1** To catch by the gills, as fish in a gill net. **2** To gut (fish). [ME *gile,* prob. < Scand. Cf. Sw. *gäl* gill.]

gill[2] (jil) *n.* A liquid measure, one fourth of a pint or 0.118 liter: also spelled *jill.* [< OF *gelle* measure for wine]

gill[3] (gil) *n.* **1** A ravine; a deep narrow gully. **2** A brook; narrow mountain stream. Also *ghyll.* [< ON *gil* gorge]

gill[4] (jil) *n.* **1** A girl or woman, especially a wanton one; sweetheart. **2** The ground ivy. [Short for GILLIAN]

gill arch *Zool.* One of the arches in gill-bearing vertebrates that carry the gills. In the higher vertebrates, the gill arches are transformed to perform other functions.

gill cleft Gill slit.

Gil·lette (ji·let′), **King Camp,** 1855–1932, U.S. inventor of safety razor. —**William,** 1855–1937, U.S. actor.

gill filament *Zool.* A threadlike vascular process of the mucous membrane of the gill.

gill fungus Any fungus of the genus *Agaricus*; an agaric.

Gil·li·an (jil′ē·ən) British form of JULIANA.

gil·lie (gil′ē) *n. Scot.* A manservant; attendant; especially one attending a sportsman in the field. Also **gil′ly.**

gil·li·flow·er (jil′ē·flou′ər) *n.* **1** One of various plants of the mustard family, as the common stock, the wallflower, or the rocket. **2** A plant of the pink family, as the clove pink: the Middle English and Elizabethan sense. **3** The feathered gilliflower *(Dianthus plumarius)* and ragged robin. **4** A variety of apple. Also **gil′ly·flow′er.** [Alter. of ME *gilofre* < OF, var. of *girofle* a clove < L *caryophyllum* < Gk. *karyophyllon* a clove tree]

gill net A net, set upright in the water by means of weighted stakes, in the meshes of which fish become entangled by their gills.

gill raker *Zool.* One of a row of processes projecting from the gill arches of fishes and screening the gills from injurious substances.

gill slit Any of a bilateral series of narrow external openings in the pharynx of embryonic chordates which persists throughout life in some aquatic forms, as sharks. Also called *gill cleft, branchial cleft.*

Gil·man (gil′mən), **Daniel Coit,** 1831–1908, U. S. educator.
gil·py (gil′pē) *n. pl.* **·pies** or **·peys** *Scot.* A lively, frolicsome young person of either sex. Also **gil′pey.**
gil·rav·age (gil·rav′ij) *Scot. v.i.* To feast or make merry in riotous fashion. — *n.* Noisy, riotous merriment.
gil·son·ite (gil′sən·īt) See UINTAHITE.
gilt[1] (gilt) Alternative past tense and past participle of GILD. — *adj.* Gilded; yellow like gold. — *n.* **1** The material used in gilding. **2** Superficial or meretricious show. ◆ Homophone: *guilt.*
gilt[2] (gilt) *n.* A young female pig. ◆ Homophone: *guilt.* [<ON *gyltr*]
gilt–edge (gilt′ej′) *adj.* **1** Having the edges gilded: said of leaves of paper either for writing or as bound in a book. **2** Of the best quality or highest price; first-class: *gilt-edge* securities. Also **gilt′-edged′.**
gilt·head (gilt′hed′) *n.* **1** One of various European fishes, as the sea bream *(Pagrus auratus)* of the Mediterranean. **2** A cunner.
gim·bals (jim′bəlz, gim′-) *n. Naut.* A contrivance for allowing a suspended object, as a ship's compass, to tip freely in all directions, thus remaining level, however the ship moves: also spelled *gymbals.* [Alter. of OF *gemelle* twin <L *gemellus,* dim. of *geminus* twin, double]

GIMBALS

gim·crack (jim′krak) *n.* A gew-gaw; bauble. See synonyms under GAUD. — *adj.* Cheap and showy. [Origin uncertain]
gim·crack·er·y (jim′krak·ər·ē) *n.* Worthless ornament or show.
gim·el (gim′əl) *n.* The third Hebrew letter. See ALPHABET.
gim·let (gim′lit) *n.* A small boring tool with a cross-head and a cutter-pointed screw tip. See illustration under AUGER. — *v.t.* To make a hole in with a gimlet. [<OF *guimbelet.* Akin to WIMBLE.]
gim·mick (gim′ik) *n. Slang* **1** A secret device for controlling the movements of a prize wheel. **2** Any tricky device or means. **3** Any contrivance, the name of which is not known or cannot be recalled. [Origin uncertain]
gimp[1] (gimp) *n.* **1** A narrow, flat, ornamental trimming, used for dresses, furniture, etc.: also **gimp′ing.** **2** A coarse thread for forming edges and outlines in pillow lace. — *v.t.* To border with gimp. [Cf. OF *guimpre,* var. of *guipure,* a kind of trimming]
gimp[2] (gimp) *U.S. Slang n.* **1** Lameness; a limp. **2** One who limps; a cripple. — *v.i.* To limp. [Origin unknown]
gin[1] (jin) *n.* An aromatic alcoholic liquor, distilled from various grains and flavored with juniper berries; also, such a liquor with other flavoring. [Short for GENEVA]
gin[2] (gin) *v.t.* & *v.i.* **gan, gin·ning** *Archaic* & *Poetic* To begin.
gin[3] (jin) *n.* **1** A machine for separating cotton fibers from the seeds. **2** A portable hoisting machine. **3** A pump worked by a windmill. **4** A pile driver. **5** A snare or trap. **6** *Obs.* Artifice of any sort. — *v.t.* **ginned, gin·ning** **1** To catch in or as in a gin or trap. **2** To remove the seeds from (cotton) in a gin. [Aphetic var. of OF *engin* ingenuity. See ENGINE.]
gin[4] (gin) *prep. Scot.* By; against (a certain) time. — *conj.* If; whether.
gin[5] (jin) *n. Austral.* An adult aboriginal female. [< native Australian]
gin·gal (jin′gôl), **gin·gall** See JINGAL.
gin·ge·ley (jin′ji·lē) *n.* The sesame. Also **gin′·ge·li, gin′gel·ly, gin′ge·ly.** [<Hind. *jingalī*]
gin·ger (jin′jər) *n.* **1** The pungent, spicy rootstock of a tropical plant *(Zingiber officinale),* either whole or pulverized: used in medicine and cookery. With the outer covering scraped off, the rootstock is called **white ginger,** and is regarded as superior to the East Indian or **black ginger,** in which the covering is not removed. **2** The plant itself. **3** A tawny, sandy, or reddish-brown color. **4** *Colloq.* Something of pungent quality; liveliness; spunk. — *v.t.* **1** To treat or spice with ginger. **2** *Colloq.* To make lively or piquant; enliven: often with *up.* [OE *gingifer* <LL *gingiber* <Gk. *zingiberis,* ult. <Skt.]
ginger ale An effervescent soft drink flavored with ginger.
ginger beer An effervescent drink made with yeast and flavored with ginger, popular in England, Canada, etc.
gin·ger·bread (jin′jər·bred′) *n.* **1** A light sweet cake flavored with ginger. **2** A ginger-flavored cooky cut into odd shapes and ornamented with colored icings. **3** Gaudy or unnecessary ornament. [Alter. of OF *gingembras* preserved ginger <LL *gingiber* GINGER]
gingerbread tree **1** The doom palm. **2** A tree of the rose family of West Africa *(Parinarium macrophylla),* bearing a farinaceous stone fruit called the gingerbread plum.
gingerbread work Cheap and tawdry ornamental work.
gin·ger·ly (jin′jər·lē) *adj.* Cautious, or fastidious, as an act or movement. — *adv.* **1** In a cautious, scrupulous, or fastidious manner. **2** *Obs.* Daintily. [Cf. OF *gensor, gentchur,* compar. of *gent* delicate]
gin·ger·snap (jin′jər·snap′) *n.* A small, flat, brittle cooky or biscuit flavored with ginger and molasses.
gin·ger·y (jin′jər·ē) *adj.* **1** Resembling ginger; spicy; hot-flavored. **2** Having a reddish or sandy color.
ging·ham (ging′əm) *n.* A plain-weave cotton fabric, usually in checks or stripes. [<F *guingan,* ult. <Malay *ginggang* striped]
gin·gi·val (jin·jī′vəl, jin′jə-) *adj.* **1** Of or pertaining to the gums. **2** *Phonet.* Produced with the aid of the gums; alveolar: *gingival* sounds. [<L *gingiva* gum]
gingival line *Pathol.* A line across the gums indicating chronic metal poisoning: in lead poisoning the line has a bluish tinge.
gin·gi·vi·tis (jin′jə·vī′tis) *n. Pathol.* Inflammation of the gums.
gin·gly·mus (jing′glə·məs, ging′-) *n. pl.* **·mi** (-mī) *Anat.* A joint that permits flexion and extension in a single plane, as at the elbow and knee; a hinge joint. [<NL <Gk. *ginglymos* a hinge]
gink (gingk) *n. Slang* An odd or peculiar person; guy. [Cf. dial. E *gink* trick]
gink·go (ging′kō, jing′kō) *n. pl.* **·goes** A deciduous resinous tree *(Ginkgo biloba),* native in China but cultivated in the United States for its fanlike foliage; the maidenhair tree: also spelled *jinkgo.* Also **ging′ko.** [<Japanese]

GINKGO
Branch showing leaf and nut. Regarded as the only surviving member of a family that had flourished millions of years ago, during the time of the dinosaurs.

gin·mill (jin′mil′) *n. Slang* A saloon.
gin·ner (jin′ər) *n.* One who operates a gin.
gin rummy A variety of rummy, in which a player may meld his hand whenever his unmatched cards are worth 10 points or less.
gin·seng (jin′seng) *n.* **1** An herb (genus *Panax*) native in North America and China, having a root of aromatic and stimulant properties, in great esteem in China. **2** The root, or a preparation made from it. [<Chinese *jen shen*]
Giob·be (jôb′bā) Italian form of JOB.
Gio·con·da (jō·kôn′dä), **La** Mona Lisa.
Gior·gia (jôr′jä) Italian form of GEORGIANA.
Gior·gio (jôr′jō) Italian form of GEORGE.
Gior·gio·ne (jôr·jō′nā), 1478?–1511, Venetian painter. Also **Gior·gio′ne da Cas·tel·fran·co** (käs′tel·frän′kō). Original name *Giorgio Barbarelli.*
Gio·si·a·de (jō·zē′ä·dā) Italian form of JOSIAH.
Giot·to (jôt′tō) Italian form of GODFREY.
Giot·to di Bon·do·ne (jôt′tō dē bôn·dō′nā), 1266–1337, Italian painter, architect, and sculptor.
Gio·van·na (jō·vän′nä) Italian form of JOAN.
Gio·van·ni (jō·vän′nē) Italian form of JOHN.
gip[1] (jip) *v.t. Brit.* To gut (fish). [Origin unknown]
gip[2] (jip) See GYP[1].
gi·pon (ji·pon′, jip′on) See JUPON.
gip·si·fy (jip′sə·fī) *v.t.* **·fied, ·fy·ing** To cause to be or to look like a gipsy.
gip·sy (jip′sē) *n. pl.* **·sies** One of any wandering group of people living the gipsy life; an itinerant tinker, farrier, etc. — *v.i.* **·sied, ·sy·ing** To live or wander like a gipsy. — *adj.* Of, pertaining to, or like a gipsy or the Gipsies; unconventional; wandering; Bohemian. Also spelled *gypsy.*
Gip·sy (jip′sē) *n. pl.* **·sies** **1** A member of a wandering, dark-haired, dark-skinned people originating in India and appearing in Europe in the 15th century, now known in every part of the world as itinerant metalworkers, musicians, fortune-tellers, and, formerly, horse dealers. **2** Romany, their language. Also spelled *Gypsy.* [<Earlier *gipcyan,* aphetic var. of *Egypcyan* Egyptian]
gip·sy·ish (jip′sē·ish) *adj.* Like a gipsy; roving; hoydenish. — **gip′sy·ism** *n.*
gipsy moth A European moth *(Porthetria* or *Lymantria dispar)* naturalized in eastern New England about 1869, having larvae highly destructive to foliage: the male is light-brown, the larger female nearly white. For illustration see under INSECT (injurious).
gi·raffe (jə·raf′, -räf′) *n. pl.* **·raffes** or **·raffe** **1** A large spotted African ruminant *(Giraffa camelopardalis),* having a very long neck and limbs; the tallest of the quadrupeds, sometimes attaining a height of 18 feet. **2** A cagelike mine car especially adapted for inclines. [<F, ult. <Arabic *zarāfah*]

GIRAFFE

Gi·raffe (jə·raf′, -räf′) The constellation Camelopard. See CONSTELLATION.
Gi·ral·da (jē·räl′dä) Italian form of GERALDINE.
Gi·ral·da (hē·räl′dä), **La** The square bell tower of the cathedral of Seville, Spain, surmounted by a bronze figure of Faith. [<Sp. *giralda* weathercock in the form of a person]
gir·an·dole (jir′ən·dōl) *n.* **1** A branching chandelier or bracket light. **2** A rotating firework. **3** A rotating water jet. **4** In fortification, a connection of several mines. **5** A pendent piece of jewelry. [<F <Ital. *girandola* < *girare* rotate <L *gyrare.* See GYRATE.]
Gi·rard (ji·rärd′), **Stephen,** 1750–1831, U. S. banker and philanthropist.
gir·a·sol (jir′ə·sōl, -sol) *n.* **1** A bluish-white translucent opal with reddish reflections: also called *fire opal.* **2** Any plant of the sunflower family; especially, the Jerusalem artichoke. Also **gir′a·sole.** [<Ital. *girasole* sunflower < *girare* turn + *sole* sun]
Gi·raud (zhē·rō′) French form of GERALD. Also **Gi·rauld′.**
Gi·raud (zhē·rō′), **Henri Honoré,** 1879–1949, French general in World War II.
Gi·rau·doux (zhē·rō·dōō′), **Jean,** 1882–1944, French novelist and playwright.
gird[1] (gûrd) *v.t.* **gird·ed** or **girt, gird·ing** **1** To surround with a belt or girdle. **2** To encircle; hem in. **3** To prepare (oneself) for action. **4** To clothe; equip; endue, etc. [OE *gyrdan*]
gird[2] (gûrd) *n.* **1** A sarcastic thrust; taunt; gibe; sneer. **2** *Obs.* A cutting stroke; hence, a pang. **3** *Obs.* A spurt. — *v.t.* & *v.i.* To attack with sarcasm; gibe; jeer. [ME *girden;* origin unknown] — **gird′er** *n.*
gird·er (gûr′dər) *n.* **1** A principal horizontal beam, or a compound structure acting as a beam, receiving a vertical load and bearing vertically upon its supports. **2** One who or that which girds or encompasses.

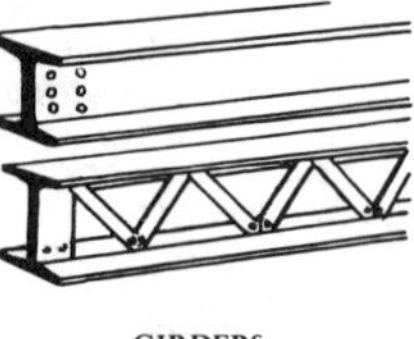
GIRDERS

gird·er·age (gûr′dər·ij) *n.* Girders collectively.
gir·dle[1] (gûr′dəl) *n.* **1** A belt used for girding

a loose garment about the waist; specifically, in ecclesiastical language, the narrow belt adorned with tassels, used to secure the alb; called also *cincture.* 2 Anything which encircles like a belt; especially, a woman's undergarment, more flexible and lighter than a corset, not coming above the waistline. 3 *Obs.* A small band or fillet encompassing a column. 4 *Mining* A thin sandstone stratum in a vein of coal. 5 *Anat.* The ringlike arrangement of bones, by which the limbs of a vertebrate animal are attached to the trunk. 6 The peripheral line of a cut gem, at which it is held in the setting. 7 An encircling cut through the bark of a branch or tree. — *v.t.* **gir·dled, gir·dling** 1 To fasten a girdle or belt around. 2 To encircle; encompass. 3 To make an encircling cut through the bark of (a branch or tree). [OE *gyrdel*]

gir·dle[2] (gûr′dəl) *n. Scot.* A griddle.

gir·dle–cake (gûr′dəl·kāk′) *n. Scot.* A griddle-cake.

gir·dler (gûrd′lər) *n.* 1 One who makes girdles. 2 One who or that which girdles or encircles. 3 *Entomol.* Any insect which cuts through the bark of twigs or branches; especially, the American twig girdler (*Oncideres cingulata*), which severs the twigs of hickory, poplar, and many other trees.

Gir·gen·ti (jir·jen′tē) The former name of AGRIGENTO.

girl (gûrl) *n.* 1 A female infant or child, or a young unmarried woman. 2 A maid servant. 3 A sweetheart. [ME *gurle*; origin uncertain]

girl Friday A female office worker who performs various tasks. [<GIRL + (MAN) FRIDAY]

girl friend *Colloq.* 1 A boy or man's sweetheart, favorite female companion, etc. 2 A female friend.

girl guide A member of an English organization, the **Girl Guides,** resembling the Girl Scouts.

girl·hood (gûrl′hŏŏd) *n.* The state or time of being a girl.

girl·ie (gûr′lē) *adj. Colloq.* Featuring nude or nearly nude women or pictures of them: a *girlie* magazine or show. Also **girl′y.**

girl·ish (gûr′lish) *adj.* Like or pertaining to a girl. See synonyms under YOUTHFUL. — **girl′·ish·ly** *adv.* — **girl′ish·ness** *n.*

girl scout A member of an organization, **Girl Scouts of America,** formed in the United States in 1912 by Juliette Low to develop health, character, etc.

girn (gûrn, girn) *v.i. Scot.* To snarl; growl.

Gi·ronde (jə·rond′, *Fr.* zhē·rôṅd′) An estuary in SW France formed by the Garonne and Dordogne rivers, extending 45 miles to the Bay of Biscay.

Gi·ronde (jə·rond′) The moderate republican party at the time of the first French assembly (1791–93). [from *Gironde,* because its leaders came from this area] — **Gi·ron′dist** (jə·ron′·dist), *Fr.* **Gi·ron·din** (zhē·rôṅ·dăṅ′) *n.* & *adj.*

gir·o·sol (jir′ə·sôl, -sol) See GIRASOL.

girt[1] (gûrt) *v.t.* 1 To gird. 2 To measure the girth of. 3 To fasten with a girth, strap, etc. — *v.i.* 4 To measure in girth. — *n.* Girth. [<GIRD[1]; also partly <*n.*]

girt[2] (gûrt) Past tense and past participle of GIRD[1]. — *adj.* 1 Encircled; bound or fastened with a girth or girdle. 2 *Naut.* Moored with taut cables, so as to prevent swinging by wind or tide, as a vessel. 3 *Entomol.* Braced, as a chrysalis.

girth[1] (gûrth) *n.* 1 A band or strap for fastening a pack or saddle to a horse's back. 2 Anything that girds or binds; a girdle. 3 The circumference of a circular or cylindrical object; especially, the measure around the waist. 4 A circular bandage. — *v.t.* 1 To bind with a girth. 2 To encircle; girdle. 3 To find the girth of. [<ON *gjordh*]

girth[2] (gûrth) See GRITH.

Gis·borne (giz′bərn) A port in eastern North Island, New Zealand.

Gis·sing (gis′ing), **George Robert,** 1857–1903, English novelist.

gist (jist) *n.* 1 The substance or fundamental fact of a matter in law, the essential cause of legal action. 2 The substance or pith of any matter; the point or main idea. [<OF *giste* place of rest <*gesir* lie <L *jacere*]

git·a·lin (jit′ə·lin, jə·tā′lin, -tal′in) *n. Chem.* A glucoside, $C_{35}H_{56}O_{12}$, in crystalline or powdered form, from the leaves of digitalis, similar in action to digitalis. [<(DI)GITAL(IS) + -IN]

gi·ta·no (ji·tä′nō, *Sp.* hē·tä′nō) *n. pl.* **·nos** A Spanish gipsy. [<Sp.]

git·tern (git′ərn) *n.* A medieval musical instrument, like a cithern, but having gut instead of metal strings: predecessor of the guitar. [<OF *guiterne*]

Giu·ba (jōō′bä) The Italian name for JUBA.

Giu·dit·ta (jōō·dēt′tä) Italian form of JUDITH.

Giu·lia·na (jōō·lyä′nä) Italian form of JULIANA.

Giu·lia·no (jōō·lyä′nō) Italian form of JULIAN.

Giu·lio (jōōl′yō) Italian form of JULIUS.

Giu·lio Ro·ma·no (jōōl′yō rō·mä′nō), 1492–1546, Italian painter.

Giu·sep·pe (jōō·sep′pā) Italian form of JOSEPH.

Giu·sep·pi·na (jōō′sep·pē′nä) Italian form of JOSEPHINE. Also **Giu·sep·pa** (jōō·sep′pä).

Gius·ti·na (jōōs·tē′nä) Italian form of JUSTINA.

Gius·to (jōōs′tō) Italian form of JUSTUS.

give (giv) *v.* **gave, giv·en, giv·ing** *v.t.* 1 To transfer the possession or title of to another without compensation of any kind. 2 To transfer to the possession or control of another for a price or equal value. 3 To hand over to another for safekeeping, delivery, etc.: to *give* a letter to a postman. 4 To offer as entertainment: to *give* a play, party, etc. 5 To yield as a product or result: Two plus two *gives* four. 6 To be the cause or source of: The sun *gives* light. 7 To provide or furnish; impart: to *give* evidence; to *give* form to an idea. 8 To express in words; declare: to *give* a ruling or reply. 9 To impose or grant, as a punishment or reward: They *gave* him the death penalty. 10 To emit or show, as a movement, shout, etc. 11 To administer, as medicine. 12 To deal; inflict, as a blow or pain. 13 To concede; yield or grant: to *give* ground; to *give* permission. 14 To devote or sacrifice, as to a cause: to *give* one's time or one's life. — *v.i.* 15 To make gifts. 16 To yield, as from pressure, melting, or thawing; collapse. 17 To be springy or resilient; bend. — **to give away** 1 To bestow as a gift. 2 To bestow (the bride) upon the bridegroom in a marriage ceremony. 3 *Colloq.* To reveal or disclose; betray. — **to give birth (to)** 1 To bear (offspring). 2 To result in. — **to give in** 1 To yield, as in a fight or argument. 2 To collapse, as under stress. — **to give off** To send forth; emit, as odors. — **to give out** 1 To send forth; emit. 2 To serve out or distribute. 3 To make known; publish. 4 To fail; become worn out or exhausted. — **to give over** 1 To hand over, as to another's care. 2 To cease; desist. — **to give rise to** To cause or result in. — **to give tongue** To bark or bay: said of hunting dogs in pursuit. — **to give up** 1 To surrender; cede; hand over. 2 To stop; cease. 3 To desist from as hopeless. 4 To lose all hope for, as a sick person. 5 To devote wholly: to *give* oneself *up* to art. — *n.* The quality of being yielding; elasticity; the process or act of giving way. [Fusion of OE *giefan* and ON *gefa*] — **giv′er** *n.*

Synonyms (verb): bestow, cede, communicate, confer, deliver, furnish, grant, impart, supply. To *give* is primarily to transfer to another's possession or ownership without compensation; in its secondary sense in popular use, it is to put into another's possession by any means and on any terms whatever; a buyer may say "*Give* me the goods, and I will *give* you the money"; we speak of *giving* answers, information, etc., and often of *giving* what is not agreeable to the recipient, as blows, medicine, reproof. To *grant* is to put into one's possession in some formal way, or by authoritative act; as, Congress *grants* lands to a railroad corporation. *Confer* has a similar sense; as, to *confer* a degree or an honor; we *grant* a request or petition, but do not *confer* it. To *impart* is to *give* of that which one still, to a greater or less degree, retains; the teacher *imparts* instruction. To *bestow* is to *give* that of which the receiver stands in especial need; we *bestow* charity.

give–and–take (giv′ən·tāk′) *n.* 1 Fair exchange; equal compromise. 2 Repartee; a flow or exchange of ideas or wit: He is adept at such *give–and–take.*

give–a·way (giv′ə·wā′) *n.* 1 A betrayal to ridicule or detection, often unintentional. 2 That which betrays a secret or a person. — *adj.* Featuring awards of money or prizes: said of a radio or television show.

giv·en (giv′ən) *adj.* 1 Habitually inclined: with *to.* 2 Specified; stated; also, in law, dated. 3 Donated; presented. 4 Admitted as a fact or a premise. — *n.* A datum; premise.

given name The name given at birth or baptism.

give–up (giv′up′) *n.* The practice of splitting a stockbroker's commission with another broker at the direction of the customer.

Gi·za (gē′zə) A city in Upper Egypt on the Nile; site of the pyramids: also *El Gizeh.*

giz·mo (giz′mō) *n. pl.* **·mos** *U.S. Slang* Any gadget. [Origin unknown]

giz·zard (giz′ərd) *n.* 1 The second stomach of birds, in which the food is ground. 2 *Entomol.* The first stomach of insects, provided with horny plates for macerating or sifting food. 3 *Slang* The stomach. [<OF *gezier* <L *gigeria* cooked entrails of poultry]

gla·bel·la (glə·bel′ə) *n. pl.* **·lae** (-ē) *Anat.* The smooth prominence on the forehead just above the nose and between the eyebrows. See illustration under FACIAL ANGLE. [<NL <L, dim. of *glaber* smooth]

gla·brate (glā′brāt) *adj.* 1 Glabrous. 2 Becoming glabrous.

gla·bres·cent (glə·bres′ənt) *adj.* Shedding hair; becoming glabrous.

gla·bri·ros·tral (glā′brē·ros′trəl) *adj. Ornithol.* Having the mouth free from bristles, as some birds. [<L *glaber* smooth + ROSTRAL]

gla·brous (glā′brəs) *adj. Biol.* 1 Without hair or down. 2 Having a smooth surface. [<L *glaber* smooth]

gla·cé (gla·sā′, *Fr.* glȧ·sā′) *adj.* 1 Iced; frozen or cooled. 2 Having a glossy surface resembling ice. 3 Smooth and glossy, as certain leathers. — *v.t.* **·céed, ·cé·ing** 1 To cover with icing. 2 To render smooth and glossy. [<F, pp. of *glacer* freeze <*glace* ice]

gla·cial (glā′shəl) *adj.* 1 Pertaining to or caused by ice masses. 2 Icy, or icily cold. 3 Of or pertaining to the glacial epoch. 4 *Chem.* Crystallizing or assuming an ice-like appearance at ordinary temperature: *glacial* acetic acid. [<F <L *glacialis* <*glacies* ice] — **gla′cial·ly** *adv.*

glacial deposits *Geol.* Unstratified earth materials and debris transported by glaciers and left at the place of melting.

glacial epoch *Geol.* 1 Any portion of geological time characterized by the formation of ice sheets over large portions of the earth's surface. 2 One of four such epochs identified as succeeding one another during the Pleistocene: beginning with the oldest, they are the Günz, the Mindel, the Riss, and the Würm.

gla·cial·ist (glā′shəl·ist) *n.* One who studies geological processes as they are affected by the action of ice.

glacial period The period of time covering the glacial epochs.

gla·ci·ate (glā′shē·āt) *v.t.* **·at·ed, ·at·ing** 1 To cover with glacial ice. 2 To affect or change by glacial action. 3 To convert into ice. [<L *glaciatus,* pp. of *glaciare* freeze <*glacies* ice] — **gla′ci·a′tion** *n.*

gla·cier (glā′shər) *n.* A field of ice, formed in regions of perennial frost from compacted snow, which moves slowly downward over slopes or through valleys until it either melts, as in the lowlands, or breaks off in the form of icebergs on the borders of the sea. [<F <L *glacies* ice] — **gla′ciered** *adj.*

Glacier Bay National Monument A region of SE Alaska on the border of British Columbia; 3,590 square miles; established 1925.

glacier meal See ROCK FLOUR.

glacier milk The milky water of a stream issuing from a glacier and containing suspended silt or finely divided rock particles.

Glacier National Park A mountainous area in NW Montana; 1,560 square miles; established 1910.

glacier theory *Geol.* The theory that large elevated portions of the temperate and frigid zones were covered during the earlier geologic epochs by slowly moving glaciers that transported vast masses of drift to lower latitudes.

gla·ci·ol·o·gy (glā'sē·ol'ə·jē) *n.* That branch of geology which studies the forms, movements, causes, and effects of glaciers. **—gla·ci·o·log·ic** (glā'sē·ə·loj'ik) or **·i·cal** *adj.* **—gla'ci·ol'o·gist** *n.*

gla·cis (glā'sis, glas'is) *n.* A defensive slope in front of a fortification. See illustration under BASTION. [< F, orig. a slippery place < OF *glacier* slip]

Glack·ens (glak'ənz), **William James,** 1870–1938, U. S. painter.

glad (glad) *adj.* **glad·der, glad·dest 1** Having a feeling of joy, pleasure, or contentment; joyful; gratified: often with *of* or *at.* **1** Having an appearance of joy or brightness; gladsome; joyous. **3** Suggestive of or exciting joy: *glad* tidings. See synonyms under HAPPY, MERRY. **—*v.t.* &** *v.i.* **glad·ded, glad·ding** *Obs* .To gladden. [OE *glœd* shining, glad]**—glad'ly** *adv.* **—glad'ness** *n.*

Glad·beck (glät'bek) A city in North Rhine – Westphalia, Germany.

glad·den (glad'n) *v.t. & v.i.* To make or become glad. See synonyms under REJOICE. **—glad' den·er** *n.*

glade (glād) *n.* **1** A clearing or open space in a wood. **2** A smooth tract of uncovered ice, or an unfrozen open space in the ice of a river or lake. **3** An everglade. [Prob. akin to *glad* in obs. sense "bright," "sunny"]

glad eye *Slang* A provocative or flirtatious glance.

glad hand *Slang* A hearty welcome.

glad·i·ate (glad'ē·āt) *adj.* Sword-shaped. [< L *gladius* sword + -ATE[1]]

glad·i·a·tor (glad'ē·ā'tər) *n.* **1** A man who fought with deadly weapons, as in the ancient Roman amphitheater, for popular amusement. **2** Hence, one who engages in any kind of spirited contest. [< L < *gladius* sword]

ROMAN GLADIATORS
a. Retiarius. *c.* Andabata
b. Mirmillon. *d.* Thracian.

glad·i·a·to·ri·al (glad'ē·ə·tôr'ē·əl, -tō'rē-) *adj.* Of or pertaining to gladiators or combats.

glad·i·o·lus (glad'ē·ō'ləs, glə·dī'ə·ləs) *n. pl.* **·lus·es** or **·li** (-lī) **1** Any of a large Old World genus *(Gladiolus)* of plants of the iris family with fleshy bulbs, sword-shaped leaves, and spikes of colored flowers. **2** Its corm or flower. Also **glad·i·o·la** (glad'ē·ō'lə, glə·dī'·ə·lə), **glad'i·ole** (-ōl). [< L, dim. of *gladius* sword]

glad·some (glad'səm) *adj.* **1** Causing, feeling, or expressive of joy; joyous; pleasing. **2** Having a feeling of joy or pleasure: cheerful. See synonyms under MERRY. **—glad'some·ly** *adv.* **— glad'some·ness** *n.*

Glad·stone (glad'stōn, -stən) *n.* **1** A suitcase, generally of leather, hinged in the middle lengthwise so that it may open into halves: also called **Gladstone bag. 2** A four-wheeled pleasure carriage having a driver's seat and two inside seats. [after W. E. *Gladstone*]

Glad·stone (glad'stōn, -stən), **William Ewart,** 1809–98, English statesman and Liberal leader; premier 1868–74; 1880–85; 1886; 1892–1894. **—Glad·sto·ni·an** (glad·stō'nē·ən), **Glad'·stonite** *adj. & n.*

Glag·ol (glag'əl) *n.* An ancient Slavic alphabet: still used in many Roman Catholic dioceses in Dalmatia and Croatia, where Church Slavonic is the liturgical language. [< Russian *glagoly'* a word]**—Glag·o·lit·ic** (glag'ə·lit'ik) *adj.*

glaik (glāk) *n. Scot.* **1** A fraud or trick. **2** A gleam; glance. **3** Mockery; deception.

glaik·it (glā'kit) *adj. Scot.* Unsteady; giddy; silly; stupid. Also **glaik'et.**

glair (glâr) *n.* **1** The white of eggs mixed with vinegar: used as a size in gilding, etc. **2** Any similar viscous matter; anything slimy or slippery. — *v.t.* To treat with glair, as a book cover before gilding. Also **glaire.** ◆Homophone: *glare.* [< F *glaire* < L *clarus* clear]

glair·e·ous (glâr'ē·əs) *adj.* Of the nature of glair; glairy.

glair·y (glâr'ē) *adj.* **1** Like glair. **2** Exhibiting glair. **—glair'i·ness** *n.*

glaive (glāv) *n. Archaic* **1** A weapon consisting of a long blade fastened to a pole and resembling a halberd. **2** A broadsword. [< OF, lance]

glai·zie (glā'zē) *adj. Scot.* Glossy; sleek.

Gla·mor·gan (glə·môr'gən) A county in SE Wales; 813 square miles; county town, Cardiff. Also **Gla·mor'gan·shire** (-shir).

glam·or·ous (glam'ər·əs) *adj.* Radiating glamour; gorgeous. **—glam'or·ous·ly** *adv.*

glam·our (glam'ər) *n.* **1** A delusion wrought by magic spells; charm; enchantment. **2** Any artificial interest or association by which an object is made to appear delusively magnified or glorified; illusion; fascination; witchery. Also **glam'or.** [Scottish alter. of GRAMARY. Related to GRAMMAR.]

glance[1] (glans, gläns) *v.* **glanced, glanc·ing** *v.i.* **1** To strike something at an angle and bounce off. **2** To look quickly or hurriedly. **3** To glint; flash. **4** To make passing reference; allude. **—*v.t.* 5** To cause to strike something at an angle and bounce off. See synonyms under LOOK. **—*n.* 1** A quick or passing look; sudden or transient thought. **2** A momentary gleam. **3** An oblique movement or rebound. **4** In cricket, a stroke with the bat held slanting and thus sending the ball to one side of the wicket. [< OF *glacier* slip, ? infl. by ME *glenten* shine]

glance[2] (glans, gläns) *n.* A mineral, usually a sulfide, having a vitreous sheen: lead *glance.* [Short for *glance ore* < Du. *glanserts* luster ore]

gland (gland) *n.* **1** *Anat.* Any of various organs, composed of specialized epithelial tissue, intended for the secretion of materials essential to the bodily system or for the elimination of waste products: the salivary *glands,* endocrine *glands.* **2** A glandlike structure; a lymph *gland.* **3** *Aeron.* A tube so fitted to the envelope or gas bag of an airship as to allow the passing of a line through it without leakage of air or gas. **4** *Bot.* A special secreting organ in plants. **5** *Mech.* One of various parts of a mechanism that hold something in place; especially, a device for compressing the packing in a stuffing box in order to prevent leakage of a fluid under pressure. [< F *glande* < OF *glandre* < L *glandula,* dim. of *glans, glandis* acorn]

glan·ders (glan'dərz) *n.* A serious contagious disease of horses, mules, and other equines, caused by a bacillus *(Malleomyces mallei)* and characterized by nasal discharges and ulcerative lesions of the lungs and other organs: occasionally found in other animals and in man. When affecting the skin it is called *farcy.* [< OF *glandres,* pl. of *glandre* a gland]**—glan'dered, glan'der·ous** *adj.*

glan·dif·er·ous (glan·dif'ər·əs) *adj.* Acorn-bearing, [< L *glans, glandis* an acorn + -(I)FEROUS]

glan·di·form (glan'də·fôrm) *adj.* Acorn-shaped.

glan·du·lar (glan'jə·lər) *adj.* **1** Pertaining to, bearing, or of the nature of glands. **2** Affecting glands: a *glandular* infection. Also **glan'·du·lous.**

glandular fever Infectious mononucleosis.

glan·dule (glan'jo͞ol) *n.* A small gland.

glans (glanz) *n. pl.* **glan·des** (-dēz) **1** An acorn, or an acornlike part or instrument. **2** *Anat.* The rounded extremity of the penis or clitoris. [< L, an acorn]

glare[1] (glâr) *v.* **glared, glar·ing** *v.i.* **1** To shine with great and dazzling intensity. **2** To gaze or stare fiercely. **3** To be conspicuous or ostentatious. — *v.t.* **4** To express or send forth with a glare. **—*n.* 1** A dazzling light. **2** An intense and piercing look or gaze, usually hostile. **3** Gaudiness; vulgar splendor.See synonyms under LIGHT[1]. ◆ Homophone: *glair.* [ME *glaren* < LG]

glare[2] (glâr) *n.* A glassy, smooth surface. **—*adj.*** Having a glassy, smooth surface. ◆Homophone: *glair.* [? < GLARE[1], *n.*]

glar·ing (glâr'ing) *adj.* **1** Looking or staring fixedly or hostilely. **2** Emitting an excessively brilliant light. **3** Plainly or unpleasantly conspicuous: a *glaring* mistake. **—glar'·ing·ly** *adv.*

Gla·rus (glä'ro͞os) A city in eastern Switzerland.

glar·y[1] (glâr'ē) *adj.* Dazzling; glaring.

glar·y[2] (glâr'ē) *adj. U.S.* Slippery, as ice.

Glas·gow (glas'gō, -kō, gläs'-) A port on the Clyde river, SW Scotland: a native of Glasgow is known as a *Glaswegian.*

Glas·gow (glas'gō), **Ellen,** 1874–1945, U.S. novelist.

glas·nost (glas'nost) *n.* Openness, in present-day Soviet Union, in describing the actual conditions of society. [< Russian]

Glas·pell (glas'pel), **Susan,** 1882–1948, U.S. novelist and dramatist.

glass (glas, gläs) *n.* **1** A hard, amorphous, brittle, usually transparent substance made by fusing one or more of the oxides of silicon, boron, or phosphorus with certain basic oxides, followed by rapid cooling to prevent crystallization. ◆ Collateral adjectives: *hyaline, vitreous.* Principal types are:

—borosilicate glass A tough optical and thermal glass; Pyrex glass.

—bottle glass A soda-lime-silica glass with a greenish color caused by iron impurities.

—crown glass Hard optical sodium-silicate glass of low refraction.

—cut glass Glass ornamented by cutting or grinding on a wheel of stone, iron, or wood into grooves, leaving prismatic or crystal-like elevations between them.

—flint glass Soft optical lead-oxide glass of high refraction.

—ground glass Glass having a smooth, semi-opaque surface that diffuses light.

—lime glass Plate, window, and container glass; made of lime and soda.

—milk glass Opaque milky glass containing cryolite.

—optical glass High-quality glass specialized in refractive and dispersive powers for lenses.

—plate glass Sheets of glass poured, rolled, and polished: used for mirrors and display windows.

—safety glass Glass in two sheets enclosing a film of transparent adhesive plastic tightly pressed between them; laminated glass: often called *shatterproof glass.*

—stained glass Glass colored by the addition of pigments in the form of metallic oxides: used decoratively, as for church windows.

—window glass Ordinary blown glass, flattened from cylinder shapes.

—wire glass Glass sheets reinforced with wire netting. **2** Any fused substance resembling glass. **3** Any article made of glass, as a window pane, a goblet or tumbler, a mirror, spectacles, etc. **4** A telescope; also, a barometer. **5** A glass devised for measuring time by the passage of sand or the like through an orifice. See HOURGLASS. **6** The contents of a glass or drinking vessel: He drank a *glass* of wine. **7** Glassware collectively. **—*v.t.* 1** To enclose with glass. **2** To reflect; mirror. **3** To give a glazed surface to. — *adj.* Made of, relating to, or like glass. [OE *glœs*]

Glass may appear as a combining form in hyphemes and solidemes, or as the first element in two-word phrases; as in:

glass-bottomed	**glass-lined**
glass-clear	**glassmaking**
glass-colored	**glass-painter**
glass-covered	**glass-paneled**
glass-cutter	**glass-sided**
glass-cutting	**glass-staining**
glass-engraving	**glass-topped**
glass-green	**glass wall**
glass-hard	**glass window**

Glass (glas, gläs), **Carter,** 1858–1946, U.S. statesman.

glass bead Any small, solid or hollow sphere of glass.

glass-blow·ing (glas'blō'ing, gläs'-) *n.* The process of blowing viscid molten glass into any desired form. **—glass'-blow'er** *n.*

glass eye An artificial eye made of glass.

glass·ful (glas′fo͝ol, gläs′-) *n. pl.* **·fuls** As much as can be contained in a drinking glass.

glass furnace A furnace for fusing the materials of which glass is made, or one for remelting glass frit and making it ready for working.

glass gall A porous scum of impurities formed on the surface of molten glass.

glass·house (glas′hous′, gläs′-) *n.* **1** A factory where glass is made. **2** *Brit.* A hothouse or greenhouse.

glass·ine (gla·sēn′) *n.* A tough, thin, glazed, almost transparent paper made from thoroughly beaten pulp.

glass·mak·er (glas′mā′kər, gläs′-) *n.* One who makes glass.

glass·man (glas′mən, gläs′-) *n. pl.* **·men** (-mən) **1** One who sells glass or glassware. **2** A glassmaker. **3** A glazier.

glass paper Paper coated with glue and sprinkled with powdered glass: used as an abrasive.

glass snake 1 A slender legless lizard of the southern United States (*Ophisaurus ventralis*) having a very brittle tail. **2** A similar Old World snakelike lizard (*O. apus*).

glass·ware (glas′wâr′, gläs′-) *n.* Articles made of glass.

GLASSWARE FOR MODERN TABLE USE

glass·wool (glas′wo͝ol′, gläs′-) *n.* Fibers of spun glass of wool-like appearance: used in fireproofing fabrics, as insulator material, as a filter, and in draining wounds.

glass·work (glas′wûrk′, gläs′-) *n.* **1** The manufacture of glass articles, etc. **2** Articles made of glass. —**glass′work′er** *n.*

glass·works (glas′wûrks′, gläs′-) *n. sing.* & *pl.* A glass factory.

glass·worm (glas′wûrm′, gläs′-) *n.* The arrowworm.

glass·wort (glas′wûrt′, gläs′-) *n.* Any of several low saline seaside herbs (genus *Salicornia*) whose ashes were formerly used in glassmaking.

glass·y (glas′ē, gläs′ē) *adj.* **glass·i·er, glass·i·est 1** Composed of or like glass; having a hard, fixed appearance. **2** Fixed, blank, and uncomprehending: a *glassy* stare. —**glass′i·ly** *adv.* —**glass′i·ness** *n.*

Glas·ton·bur·y (glas′tən·ber′ē) A municipal borough in central Somersetshire, England; the ruins of its abbey, originally built in the eighth century, are traditionally regarded as on the site of the first Christian church in England.

Glas·we·gi·an (glas·wē′jən, -jē·ən, gläs-) *adj.* Of or pertaining to Glasgow. —*n.* A native or inhabitant of Glasgow.

Glau·ber (glou′bər), **Johann Rudolf,** 1604–1668, German physician and alchemist who discovered muriatic acid and Glauber's salts.

Glauber's salts A white crystalline sodium sulfate, used medicinally as a cathartic. Also **Glauber salt.**

glau·cine (glô′sēn, -sin) *n. Biochem.* A yellowish, bitter, crystalline alkaloid, $C_{21}H_{25}O_4N$, from the sap of the yellow-horned poppy (*Glaucium flavum*): it suspends heart action and inhibits muscular sensibility.

glauco– *combining form* Bluish-gray: *glauconite.* Also, before vowels, **glauc–.** [<Gk. *glaukos* bluish-gray]

glau·co·ma (glô·kō′mə) *n. Pathol.* An affection of the eye characterized by opacity of the vitreous humor and impaired vision that may, if not given early therapeutic treatment, lead to blindness. [<L <Gk. *glaukōma* < *glaukos* bluish-gray] —**glau·com·a·tous** (glô·kom′ə·təs) *adj.*

glau·co·nite (glô′kə·nīt) *n.* An amorphous, olive-green, loosely granular, massive hydrous silicate, chiefly of iron and potassium, found in greensand. [<Gk. *glaukon,* neut. of *glaukos* bluish-gray + -ITE[1]]

glau·cous (glô·kəs) *adj.* **1** Having a yellowish-green color; also, sea green. **2** *Bot.* Covered with a bluish-white bloom, as grapes, blueberries, etc. [<L *glaucus* <Gk. *glaukos* bluish-gray]

glaucous gull See BURGOMASTER (def. 2).

glaucous willow The pussy willow.

glaum (gläm, glôm) *v.i. Scot.* To clutch; grasp.

glaze (glāz) *v.* **glazed, glaz·ing** *v.t.* **1** To fit, as a window, with glass panes. **2** To provide (a building, etc.) with windows. **3** To coat, as pottery, with a glasslike surface applied by fusing. **4** To cover with a glaze, as meat or biscuits. **5** To make glossy, as by polishing. **6** In painting, to cover with a thin, transparent color so as to modify the tone. —*v.i.* **7** To become glassy; take on a glaze. —*n.* **1** A smooth, shining, transparent surface; a glossy coating, or a substance used to produce it, as on pottery or tiles: distinguished from *enamel.* **2** A sheet of ice; an icy surface. **3** Stock or icing cooked to a thin paste and applied to the surface of meat, fish, vegetables, fruits, or nuts. [ME *glasen* <*glas* glass] —**glaz′er** *n.* —**glaz′i·ness** *n.* —**glaz′y** *adj.*

gla·zier (glā′zhər) *n.* **1** One who fits panes of glass. **2** One who applies glaze to pottery. —**gla′zier·y** *n.*

glaz·ing (glā′zing) *n.* **1** A glaze; material used to produce a glaze. **2** The act or art of applying glaze. **3** Window panes collectively; glasswork. **4** The act or art of setting glass.

Gla·zu·nov (glä′zo͞o·nôf), **Alexander,** 1865–1936, Russian composer.

gleam (glēm) *n.* **1** A moderate light; a passing or intermittent glimmer; flash. **2** Something likened to a flash of light: a *gleam* of wit. See synonyms under LIGHT. —*v.i.* **1** To shine or glitter with a gleam or gleams. **2** To appear clearly and briefly, as a signal fire. —*v.t.* **3** To show with a gleam or gleams: His eyes *gleamed* hatred. See synonyms under SHINE. [OE *glǣm.* Akin to GLIM, GLIMMER.]

gleam·y (glē′mē) *adj.* **gleam·i·er, gleam·i·est 1** Sending forth gleams. **2** Characterized by fitful gleams of sunlight; uncertain: said of the weather.

glean (glēn) *v.t.* & *v.i.* **1** To collect (information, facts, etc.) by patient effort. **2** To gather (the leavings) from a field after the crop has been reaped. **3** To gather the leavings from (a field, etc.). [<OF *glener* <LL *glenare* <Celtic] —**glean′er** *n.*

glean·ing (glē′ning) *n.* **1** *pl.* That which is collected by a gleaner; a remaining portion. **2** The act of a gleaner.

gle·ba (glē′bə) *n. pl.* **·bae** (-bē) *Bot.* The chambered spore-bearing tissue within the closed sac or peridium of a puffball fungus. [<NL <L, a clod]

glebe (glēb) *n.* **1** *Brit.* A portion of land attached to an ecclesiastical benefice as part of its endowment. **2** *Poetic* Any field; cultivated land. [<OF <L *gleba* clod]

glede (glēd) *n.* **1** The European kite (genus *Milvus*). **2** Any of several similar birds. Also **gled** (gled). [OE *glida*]

glee[1] (glē) *n.* **1** Mirth; gaiety; merriment. **2** A musical composition for three or more voices, without accompaniment. See synonyms under LAUGHTER. [OE *glēo*] —**glee′some** (-səm) *adj.*

glee[2] (glē) *Scot. v.i.* To squint. —*n.* A squint. Also **gley** (glē, glī).

glee club A musical club or group organized, formerly, to sing glees, now, any songs.

gleed (glēd) *n. Obs.* A coal of fire; flame; cinder. [OE *glēd*]

glee·ful (glē′fəl) *adj.* Feeling or exhibiting glee; mirthful. —**glee′ful·ly** *adv.* —**glee′ful·ness** *n.*

glee·man (glē′mən) *n. pl.* **·men** (-mən) *Archaic* A wandering singer or minstrel.

gleet (glēt) *Pathol. n.* **1 a** A slimy mucous discharge succeeding inflammation of the urethra. **b** A chronic discharge from any mucous membrane. **2** A chronic discharge from the nasal cavities, as in horses. —*v.i.* To emit a thin, watery liquid; ooze. [<OF *glette* mucus, pus] —**gleet′y** *adj.*

gleg (gleg) *adj. Scot.* Quick; nimble; happy. —**gleg′ly** *adv.*

Glei·witz (glī′vits) A city in southern Poland; formerly in Germany. *Polish* **Gli·wi·ce** (glē·vē′tse).

glei·za·tion (glī·zā′shən) *n. Geol.* The process by which moisture acts upon rock materials to produce a greenish or bluish waterlogged soil, often with formation of peat bogs.

glen (glen) *n.* A small, secluded valley. [<Scottish Gaelic *glenn*]

Glen·coe (glen·kō′) A valley in Argyllshire, Scotland; scene of massacre of the MacDonalds by the Campbells and the English, 1692.

Glen·dow·er (glen′do͞or, -dou·ər), **Owen,** 1359?–1416?, Welsh chieftain; rebelled against Henry IV.

Glen·gar·ry (glen·gar′ē) *n.* A woolen Scottish cap, high in front and sloping backward: also called **Glengarry bonnet.** [from *Glengarry,* a valley in Scotland]

Glen More (glen môr′, mōr′) See GREAT GLEN OF SCOTLAND.

Glenn (glen), **John H., Jr.,** born 1921, U. S. Marine Corps officer; first U. S. astronaut to orbit the earth, Feb. 20, 1962.

gle·noid (glē′noid) *adj.* **1** *Anat.* Hollowed like a shallow pit, as the articular cavities or fossae of the scapula and the temporal bone. **2** Having a shallow cavity. [<Gk. *glēnoeidēs* like a socket <*glēnē* a socket]

gli·a·din (glī′ə·din) *n. Biochem.* Any of a group of simple proteins derived from the gluten of wheat, rye, or other grains. [<F *gliadine* <Gk. *glia* glue]

glib (glib) *adj.* **glib·ber, glib·best 1** Speaking with smooth fluency without much thought: a *glib* talker. **2** More facile than sincere: a *glib* compliment. **3** Characterized by easiness or quickness, as of manner. [Cf. obs. *glibbery* <MLG *glibberich* slippery] —**glib′ly** *adv.* —**glib′ness** *n.*

glid·der (glid′ər) *Brit. Dial. adj.* Slippery: also **glid′der·y.** —*v.t.* To make icy or smooth. —*v.i.* To slip. [OE]

glide (glīd) *v.* **glid·ed, glid·ing** *v.i.* **1** To move, slip, or flow smoothly or easily. **2** To pass unnoticed or imperceptibly, as time: often with *by.* **3** *Aeron.* To descend gradually and without the use of motor power: also, to operate or fly in a glider. **4** *Music* & *Phonet.* To produce a glide. —*v.t.* **5** To cause to glide. —*n.* **1** The act of gliding; a gliding motion. **2** *Music* An unbroken passage from tone to tone; a slur. **3** *Phonet.* **a** A transitional sound made in passing from the position of one speech sound to that of another, as the (w) heard between (o͞o) and (a) in *bivouac.* **b** A semivowel. **4** A gliding step in waltzing; also, a waltz in which this movement is used. **5** The movement of a glider. [OE *glīdan*]

glid·er (glī′dər) *n.* **1** One who or that which glides. **2** *Aeron.* An aircraft similar in general structure to an airplane but without an engine, supported by rising currents of air. **3** A couch hung in a metal frame and arranged so as to glide back and forth. **4** *Austral.* A flying phalanger: also **gliding possum.**

GLIDER—TWO-SEATED TRAINER

glid·ing (glī′ding) *n.* The act of one who or that which glides. —*adj.* Having the action or motion of a glide.

gliding angle See under ANGLE.

gliding plane *Mineral.* A plane parallel to which a differential movement of the parts of a crystal can take place without rupture.

gliding range *Aeron.* The greatest distance that can be traveled by an aircraft from a given height under normal gliding conditions. Also **gliding distance.**

gliff (glif) *n. Scot.* **1** A glimpse; a moment. **2** Fright. **3** A look; expression.

glim (glim) *n.* **1** *Slang* A light; a candle. **2** *Scot.* A momentary glance. **3** *Slang* An eye. [Akin to GLEAM]

glim·mer (glim′ər) *v.i.* **1** To shine with a faint,

unsteady light; flicker. 2 To appear fitfully or faintly. —*n.* 1 A faint, unsteady light; a flickering gleam. 2 A momentary apprehension; glimpse; a vague idea: a *glimmer* of the truth. See synonyms under LIGHT[1]. [ME *glimeren* shine. Akin to GLEAM.]

glimpse (glimps) *n.* 1 A momentary view or look. 2 A swift, passing appearance. 3 An inkling. 4 A sudden, passing gleam. —*v.* **glimpsed, glimps·ing** *v.t.* 1 To see for an instant; catch a glimpse of. —*v.i.* 2 To look for an instant; glance. [ME *glimsen* shine faintly. Akin to GLEAM.]

Glin·ka (glēn′kə), **Mikhail Ivanovich,** 1803–1857, Russian composer.

glint (glint) *v.i.* 1 To gleam; glitter. 2 To move quickly; glance aside. —*v.t.* 3 To reflect; shine. —*n.* 1 A gleam; flash. 2 *Scot.* A glimpse. [ME *glinten,* var. of *glenten* shine <Scand. Cf. dial. Sw. *glänta* shine.]

gli·o·ma (glī·ō′mə) *n. pl.* **·ma·ta** *Pathol.* A tumor containing elements similar to neuroglia cells, occurring in connective tissue. [<NL <Gk. *glia* glue + *-ōma* -OMA] —**gli·o·ma·tous** (glī·ō′mə·təs, -om′ə-) *adj.*

gli·o·sa (glī·ō′sə) *n. Anat.* The gray matter which surrounds the central canal of the spinal cord. [<NL <Gk. *glia* glue]

glis·sade (gli·säd′, -sād′) *v.i.* **·sad·ed, ·sad·ing** To slide or glide. —*n.* 1 The act of gliding down a slope, as of ice or snow. 2 A sliding step in dancing; glide. [<F <*glisser* slip]

glis·san·do (gli·sän′dō) *n. pl.* **·di** (-dē) A gliding effect, as in the playing of a run on the piano by sliding a finger rapidly over the keys. [<F *glissant,* ppr. of *glisser* slip + Ital. *-ando,* ppr. suffix]

glis·ten (glis′ən) *v.i.* To sparkle, especially with reflected light; shine; gleam. See synonyms under SHINE. —*n.* A shining, as by reflection from a wet surface. See synonyms under LIGHT[1]. [OE *glisnian* shine] —**glis′ten·ing** *adj.*

glis·ter (glis′tər) *v.i. Archaic* To glitter; glisten. —*n.* Glitter; glistening. [<MDu. *glisteren*]

glitch (glich) *n. Slang* 1 A malfunction or mishap. 2 A sudden shift from normal function, as in electric power. 3 A false or spurious electronic signal. [Prob. <G *glitschen* to slide, slip]

glit·ter (glit′ər) *v.i.* 1 To shine with a gleaming light; sparkle. 2 To be bright or colorful. —*n.* Sparkle; brilliancy. See synonyms under LIGHT[1]. [<ON *glitra*]

glit·ter·y (glit′ər·ē) *adj.* Having, or shining with, a glitter.

gloam (glōm) *v.t.* & *v.i. Scot.* To darken; make or become dusk. —*n. Rare* Twilight.

gloam·ing (glō′ming) *n.* The twilight; dusk. Also *gloam.* [OE *glōmung*]

gloat (glōt) *v.i.* To look with cruel or triumphant satisfaction; think about something with exultation or avarice: usually with *over.* [Cf. ON *glotta* grin]

glob·al (glō′bəl) *adj.* 1 Spherical. 2 Pertaining to or involving the world in its entirety: *global* war. 3 *Pathol.* Entire; all-inclusive: *global* aphasia.

glo·bate (glō′bāt) *adj.* Globe-shaped; spherical; hence, rounded; complete. Also **glo′bat·ed.**

globe (glōb) *n.* 1 A perfectly round body; ball; sphere. 2 The earth: with the definite article. 3 A sphere on which is a map of the earth or of the heavens: also **terrestrial** or **celestial globe.** 4 A hollow globular vessel or the like. 5 Any planetary or celestial body. 6 A ball, usually of gold, borne as an emblem of authority. —*v.t.* & *v.i.* **globed, glob·ing** To form into a globe. [<F <L *globus* ball]

globe daisy See under GLOBULARIN.

globe·fish (glōb′fish′) *n. pl.* **·fish** or **·fish·es** 1 A teleost fish (*Diodon hystrix*) of tropical seas, covered with long, horny spines and able, when disturbed, to inflate its body into a globular form: also called *porcupine fish.* 2 A puffer.

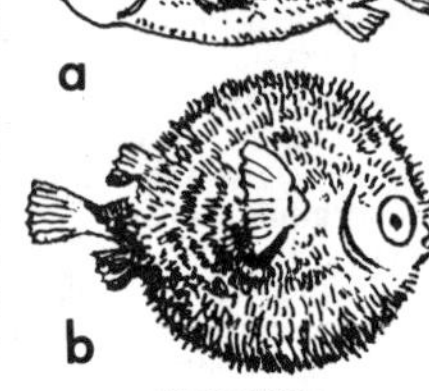

GLOBEFISH
a. Normal. *b.* Inflated.
(About 7 inches long)

globe·flow·er (glōb′flou′ər) *n.* Any of a genus (*Trollius*) of ranunculaceous plants having globular, yellow flowers.

globe-trot·ter (glōb′trot′ər) *n.* A habitual traveler; especially, one who travels all over the world. —**globe′-trot′ting** *n.* & *adj.*

Glo·big·er·i·na (glō·bij′ə·rī′nə) *n.* A genus of small marine foraminifers whose calcareous shells accumulate in vast quantities on the sea bottoms, forming the deposits known as **globigerina ooze.** [<NL <L *globus* a ball + *gerere* bear]

glo·bin (glō′bin) *n. Biochem.* A protein constituent of red blood corpuscles. [<L *globus* a ball + -IN]

glo·boid (glō′boid) *adj.* Having a spherical or globular shape; globate. —*n.* Any globate body or mass.

glo·bose (glō′bōs) *adj.* Spherical. Also **glo′bous** (-bəs). [<L *globosus* <*globus* a ball] —**glo·bose′ness** *n.* —**glo·bos·i·ty** (glō·bos′ə·tē) *n.*

glob·u·lar (glob′yə·lər) *adj.* 1 Spherical. 2 Formed of globules. 3 World-wide.

glob·u·lar·in (glob′yə·lər·in) *n.* A white, bitter powder, $C_{15}H_{20}O_8$, obtained from the leaves of the globe daisy (*Globularia alypum*): a glucoside similar to caffeine in action.

glob·ule (glob′yōōl) *n.* 1 A small globe or spherical particle. 2 A small pill. 3 *Med.* A corpuscle (def. 3). [<F <L *globulus,* dim. of *globus* a ball]

glob·u·li·cide (glob′yə·lə·sīd′) *n.* An agent destructive of red blood corpuscles. —**glob′u·li·ci′dal** *adj.*

glob·u·lif·er·ous (glob′yə·lif′ər·əs) *adj.* 1 Having or containing globules. 2 Containing red blood corpuscles.

glob·u·lim·e·ter (glob′yə·lim′ə·tər) *n.* An instrument for determining the number of red blood corpuscles in a given amount of blood.

glob·u·lin (glob′yə·lin) *n. Biochem.* Any one of a class of simple plant and animal proteins, insoluble in water but soluble in dilute saline solutions. [<GLOBULE]

glob·u·lous (glob′yə·ləs) *adj.* Of the shape of a small globe; globular; spherical. Also **glob′u·lose** (-lōs).

glo·chid·i·ate (glō·kid′ē·āt) *adj. Biol.* Barbed, as hairs and bristles.

glo·chid·i·um (glō·kid′ē·əm) *n. pl.* **·chid·i·a** (-kid′ē·ə) *Zool.* A larva of a mussel with a bivalve embryonic shell provided with hooked processes by which it may attach itself to a fish and there pass a brief phase of its life. [<NL, dim. of Gk. *glōchis* point of an arrow]

glock·en·spiel (glok′ən·spēl) *n.* 1 A portable musical instrument consisting of a series of metal bars tuned in chromatic range and played by striking with two wooden or composition hammers. 2 A set of bells; a carillon. [<G *glocken* bells + *spiel* play]

GLOCKENSPIEL

glom·er·ate (glom′ər·āt, -it) *v.t.* & *v.i. Obs.* **·at·ed, ·at·ing** To gather or wind into a ball or spherical mass. —*adj.* Clustered compactly. [<L *glomeratus,* pp. of *glomerare* collect <*glomus, -eris* a mass]

glom·er·a·tion (glom′ə·rā′shən) *n.* 1 A conglomerated mass. 2 Agglomeration. 3 A ball, or anything made into a ball or rounded mass.

glom·er·ule (glom′ər·ōōl) *n. Bot.* A cymose flower cluster which is condensed into a headlike form. [<F <NL *glomerulus,* dim. of *glomus, -eris* a mass]

glo·mer·u·lus (glə·mer′yə·ləs) *n. pl.* **·li** (-lī) 1 A glomerule. 2 *Anat.* A coil of blood vessels forming a small tuft at the expanded end of each uriniferous tubule. [<NL. See GLOMERULE.]

Glom·ma (glôm′ä) A river in SE Norway, flowing 185 miles south to the Skagerrak. Also **Gla′ma.**

glon·o·in (glon′ō·in) *n.* Nitroglycerin, especially as used in medicine. Also **glon′o·ine** (-in, -ēn). [<GL(YCERIN) + *O,* oxygen, and NO_3, nitric anhydride + -IN]

gloom (glōōm) *n.* 1 Partial or total darkness; heavy shadow. 2 Darkness or depression of the mind or spirits. 3 A dark or gloomy place. 4 *Scot.* A sulky look; frown. [<*v.*] —*v.i.* 1 To look sullen, displeased, or dejected. 2 To be or become dark or threatening. —*v.t.* 3 To make dark, sad, or sullen. ◆ Homophone: *glume.* [ME *glom(b)en* look sad]

gloom·ing (glōō′ming) *n.* 1 Gloaming. 2 A frown; sulky fit.

gloom·y (glōō′mē) *adj.* **gloom·i·er, gloom·i·est** 1 Dark; dismal; obscure. 2 Affected with gloom or melancholy; morose. 3 Productive of gloom or melancholy. See synonyms under DARK, MOROSE, SAD. —**gloom′i·ly** *adv.* —**gloom′i·ness** *n.*

glo·ri·a (glôr′ē·ə, glō′rē·ə) *n.* 1 *Eccl.* A hymn or ascription of praise to God; a doxology. 2 *Eccl. Usually cap.* **a** A movement of the mass, following the Kyrie, during which the *Gloria in excelsis* is sung. **b** In the Anglican and some other churches, a similar section in the Eucharist. 3 A musical setting for a gloria, especially the *Gloria in excelsis.* 4 A gloriole; glory. 5 An ornament for the head in imitation of a gloriole. 6 A mixture of wool and silk or similar material, used as a substitute for silk in covering umbrellas and in dressmaking. [<L, glory]

Gloria in ex·cel·sis (ek·sel′sis) 1 A Latin doxology beginning *Gloria in excelsis*; the greater doxology. 2 An English translation of this. [<LL *Gloria in excelsis (Deo)* Glory (to God) in the highest. See *Luke* ii 14.]

Gloria Pa·tri (pat′rē) 1 A short Latin doxology which begins *Gloria Patri*: the lesser doxology. 2 An English translation of this. [<LL *Gloria Patri* Glory (be) to the Father]

glo·ri·fi·ca·tion (glôr′ə·fə·kā′shən, glō′rə-) *n.* 1 The act of glorifying or exalting. 2 The state of being glorified. 3 *Colloq.* An occasion of jollity; celebration.

glo·ri·fy (glôr′ə·fī, glō′rə-) *v.t.* **·fied, ·fy·ing** 1 To give a glorious or exaggerated appearance to: to *glorify* military life. 2 To give exaggerated praise to; extol. 3 To honor or make glorious by prayer or action; worship. 4 To give glory to; make exalted or blessed. See synonyms under PRAISE. [<OF *glorifier* <LL *glorificare* <L *gloria* glory + *facere* make] —**glo′ri·fi′er** *n.*

glo·ri·ole (glôr′ē·ōl, glō′rē-) *n.* A halo or aureole. [<F <L *gloriola,* dim. of *gloria* glory]

glo·ri·ous (glôr′ē·əs, glō′rē-) *adj.* 1 Full of glory; of exalted honor, dignity, or majesty. 2 Extremely delightful; splendid: a *glorious* time. 3 *Obs.* Resplendent. 4 Eager for glory or distinction; vainglorious. See synonyms under BRIGHT, ILLUSTRIOUS. [<L *gloriosus* <*gloria* glory] —**glo′ri·ous·ly** *adv.* —**glo′ri·ous·ness** *n.*

glo·ry (glôr′ē, glō′rē) *n. pl.* **·ries** 1 Distinguished honor or praise; exalted reputation. 2 Something which occasions praise or renown; an object of praise. 3 Adoration; worshipful praise: give *glory* to God. 4 Splendor; magnificence: the *glory* of Rome. 5 The bliss of heaven: to go to *glory.* 6 A state of exaltation or extreme well-being: He was in his *glory.* 7 Radiance; brilliancy. 8 The emanation of light surrounding the head or the entire figure of a divine being; a nimbus; halo. See synonyms under FAME. —*v.i.* **glo·ried, glo·ry·ing** To rejoice proudly or triumphantly; exult; take pride: with *in.* [<OF *glorie* <L *gloria*]

glo·ry·flow·er (glôr′ē·flou′ər, glō′rē-) *n.* A climbing shrub of the bignonia family, native in Chile and Peru (*Eccremocarpus scaber*), with pinnate leaves and orange, yellow, or scarlet tubular flowers. Also called **glo′ry·vine′** (-vīn′).

glo·ry-lil·y (glôr′ē·lil′ē, glō′rē-) *n.* A climbing plant (genus *Gloriosa*) of the lily family, with solitary red and yellow flowers; especially *G. superba,* whose root yields superbine.

gloss[1] (glôs, glos) *n.* 1 The brightness or sheen of a polished surface. 2 A deceptive or superficial show. —*v.t.* 1 To make smooth or lustrous, as by polishing or buffing. 2 To hide or attempt to hide (errors, defects, etc.) by falsehood or equivocation: with *over.* —*v.i.* 3 To become shiny. [<Scand. Cf. ON *glossi* blaze, spark.] —**gloss′er** *n.*

gloss[2] (glôs, glos) *n.* 1 An explanatory note; especially, a marginal or interlinear note. 2 A glossary. 3 A plausible explanation to cover fault or defect. —*v.t.* 1 To write marginal explanations for (a text, word, etc.); annotate. 2 To excuse or change by false explanations: to *gloss* the truth of a matter. —*v.i.* 3 To make glosses. [<OF *glose* a note <L *glossa* a difficult word (in a text) <Gk. *glōssa* a foreign word; orig., tongue] —**gloss′er** *n.*

Glos·sa (glôs′ə, glos′ə), **Cape** A promontory in SW Albania; ancient *Acroceraunia*: Italian *Capo Linguetta.*

glos·sal (glôs′əl, glos′-) *adj.* Of or pertaining to the tongue; having a tongue; lingual.

glos·sa·rist (glos′ə·rist, glôs′-) *n.* One who writes glosses; also, one who compiles a glossary. Also **glos·sa·tor** (glo·sā′tər, glô-).

glos·sa·ry (glos′ə·rē, glôs′-) *n. pl.* **·ries 1** A lexicon of the obsolete, obscure, or foreign words of a work. **2** Any explanatory vocabulary, as of a science. [<L *glossarium* <*glossa* GLOSS[2]] —**glos·sar·i·al** (glo·sâr′ē·əl, glô-) *adj.*

glos·sec·to·my (glo·sek′tə·mē, glô-) *n. Surg.* Total or partial removal of the tongue or of a glossal lesion.

Glos·si·na (glo·sī′nə, glô-) *n.* An Ethiopian genus of biting flies which includes the tsetse fly, carrier of the infective agent of African sleeping sickness. For illustration see under INSECT (injurious). [<NL <Gk. *glōssa* tongue]

glos·si·tis (glo·sī′tis, glô-) *n. Pathol.* Inflammation of the tongue. —**glos·sit·ic** (-sit′ik) *adj.*

glosso- *combining form* The tongue; pertaining to the tongue: *glossography.* Also, before vowels, **gloss-.** [<Gk. *glōssa* tongue]

glos·sog·ra·phy (glo·sog′rə·fē, glô-) *n.* **1** A description of the tongue. **2** The making of glosses or of glossaries. —**glos·sog′ra·pher** *n.*

glos·so·la·li·a (glôs′ə·lā′lē·ə, glos-) *n.* **1** The gift of tongues. **2** (In some Pentecostal churches) a speaking in sounds that do not correspond linguistically to those of any known language.

glos·sol·o·gy (glo·sol′ə·jē, glô-) *n. Obs.* The science of language; comparative philology: also called *glottology.*

gloss·y (glôs′ē, glos′ē) *adj.* **gloss·i·er, gloss·i·est 1** Having a lustrous surface; polished. **2** Outwardly or speciously fair. See synonyms under SMOOTH. —**gloss′i·ly** *adv.* —**gloss′i·ness** *n.*

glost (glôst, glost) *n.* Lead glaze used in making pottery; also, glazed pottery. [Variant of GLOSS[1]]

-glot *combining form* Able to speak, or written in, a number of languages: *polyglot.* [<Gk. *glōtta,* var. of *glōssa* tongue, language]

glot·tal (glot′l) *adj.* Of, pertaining to, or articulated in the glottis.

glottal stop *Phonet.* A sound produced in the larynx by an instantaneous closure of the glottis, as at the beginning of a cough, or in one pronunciation of *bottle*: not a phoneme in English.

glot·tic (glot′ik) *adj.* **1** Of or pertaining to the tongue. **2** Of, pertaining to, or produced by the glottis; glottal. **3** *Obs.* Linguistic.

glot·tis (glot′is) *n. pl.* **·ti·des** (-ə·dēz) *Anat.* The cleft or opening between the vocal folds at the upper orifice of the larynx, the mouth of the windpipe. [<NL <Gk. *glōttis* <*glōtta* tongue]

glot·tol·o·gy (glo·tol′ə·jē) See GLOSSOLOGY.

Glouces·ter (glos′tər, glôs′-), **Duke of** See under HUMPHREY. —**Richard,** 1452–85, Duke of Gloucester, became king of England 1483, as Richard III.

Glouces·ter (glos′tər, glôs′-) **1** A county in west central England; 1,257 square miles; county town, Gloucester. Also **Glouces′ter·shire** (-shir). **2** A port and resort in NE Massachusetts.

glove (gluv) *n.* A covering for the hand, having a separate sheath for each finger. —**the gloves** Boxing gloves. —*v.t.* **gloved, glov·ing 1** To put gloves on. **2** To cover with or as with a glove. **3** To serve as a glove for. [OE *glōf*]

glov·er (gluv′ər) *n.* A maker of or a dealer in gloves.

Glov·ers·ville (gluv′ərz·vil) A city in central New York; center of leather glove and mitten manufacture.

glow (glō) *v.i.* **1** To give off light and heat, especially without flame; be incandescent. **2** To shine as if greatly heated. **3** To show a strong, bright color; be bright or red, as with heat or animation; blush. **4** To be animated with strong emotion. **5** To be excessively hot; burn. —*n.* **1** The incandescence of a heated substance. **2** Bright color; redness; flush; ruddiness. **3** Fervid heat; strong emotion or ardor. **4** Bodily warmth, as caused by exercise, etc. See synonyms under LIGHT[1], WARMTH. [OE *glōwan*]

glow-dis·charge (glō′dis·chärj′) *n.* The initial luminous electrical discharge in a gas, as observed in neon lamps, etc.

glow·er (glou′ər) *v.i.* **1** To stare with an angry frown; scowl sullenly. **2** *Scot.* To stare. —*n.* The act of glowering; a fierce or threatening stare. Also *Scot.* **glour, glowr.** [? Freq. of obs. *glow* stare] —**glow′er·ing** *adj.* —**glow′er·ing·ly** *adv.*

glow·fly (glō′flī′) *n.* A firefly.

glow·ing (glō′ing) *adj.* Having a glow; ardent; bright; also, enthusiastic. —**glow′ing·ly** *adv.*

glow lamp An incandescent lamp, usually electrical.

glow potential The voltage marking the beginning of a glow-discharge.

glow·worm (glō′wûrm′) *n.* **1** A European beetle (genus *Lampyris*), the larva and wingless female of which display phosphorescent light. **2** The luminous larva of American fireflies.

glox·in·i·a (glok·sin′ē·ə) *n.* Any plant of a genus *(Sinningia),* with opposite leaves and large bell-shaped spotted flowers. [after B. P. *Gloxin,* 18th century German physician]

gloze[1] (glōz) *v.* **glozed, gloz·ing** *v.t.* **1** To explain away; palliate: usually with *over.* **2** *Obs.* To flatter. **3** *Obs.* To explain by notes or glosses. —*v.i.* **4** *Obs.* To make notes or glosses. —*n. Obs.* **1** Specious show; gloss. **2** A note, gloss, or comment. **3** Flattery. [<OF *gloser* explain <*glose* a note <L *glossa.* See GLOSS[2].]

gloze[2] (glōz) *v.t.* & *v.i.* **glozed, gloz·ing** *Rare* To shine; light up; gleam. [Cf. GLOSS[1]]

gloz·ing (glō′zing) *n.* **1** Specious flattery. **2** Annotation.

glu·ca·gon (gloo͞′kə·gon) *n.* A hormone secreted by the pancreas that increases the level of sugar in the blood by stimulating the breakdown of glycogen to glucose.

glu·ci·num (gloo͞·sī′nəm) *n.* The former name for beryllium. [<NL <Gk. *glykys* sweet; because some of its salts are sweet to taste]

Gluck (glo͝ok), **Alma,** 1884–1938, U.S. soprano, born in Rumania. —**Christoph Willibald,** 1714–87, German composer.

glu·co·pro·te·in (gloo͞′kō·prō′tē·in, -tēn) See GLYCOPROTEIN.

glu·cose (gloo͞′kōs) *n. Chem.* **1** Dextrose or grape sugar; a monosaccharide carbohydrate having the formula $C_6H_{12}O_6$. It is widely distributed in plants and animals and is obtained by the hydrolysis of starch and other carbohydrates. It is fermentable but less sweet than cane sugar. **2** A thick yellowish sirup containing dextrose, maltose, and dextrin, obtained by incomplete hydrolysis of starch and used in confectionery, baking, etc. [<Gk. *glykys* sweet + -OSE[2]] —**glu·cos′ic** (-kos′ik) *adj.*

glu·co·side (gloo͞′kə·sīd) See GLYCOSIDE.

glu·co·su·ri·a (gloo͞′kō·so͝or′ē·ə) See GLYCOSURIA.

glue (gloo͞) *n.* **1** A viscid cement or adhesive preparation, usually a form of impure gelatin derived from boiling certain animal substances, as skin, bones, and cartilage, in water. It is a typical colloid. **2** Any of a number of sticky substances. —*v.t.* **glued, glu·ing** To stick or fasten with or as with glue. [<OF *glu* birdlime <LL *glus, glutis*] —**glue′y** *adj.*

glum (glum) *adj.* **glum·mer, glum·mest** Moody and silent; sullen. [Akin to GLOOM] —**glum′ly** *adv.* —**glum′ness** *n.*

glu·ma·ceous (gloo͞·mā′shəs) *adj.* Bearing, or pertaining to, glumes.

glume (gloo͞m) *n. Bot.* A chafflike scale on the lowest bracts of a grass spikelet. ◆ Homophone: *gloom.* [<L *gluma* husk]

glump·y (glum′pē) *adj.* Sullen; sulky; grumpy. [? Blend of GLUM and GRUMPY]

glunch (gloo͞nsh, glunsh) *Scot. v.i.* To frown; look sullen. —*adj.* Sullen and sour. —*n.* A look expressive of displeasure.

glut[1] (glut) *v.* **glut·ted, glut·ting** *v.t.* **1** To fill or supply to excess; satiate; gorge. **2** To supply (the market) with an excessive quantity of an article and bring on a lowering of prices. —*v.i.* **3** To eat gluttonously; gormandize. See synonyms under PAMPER, SATISFY. —*n.* **1** An excessive supply; plethora. **2** A full supply. **3** The condition of being glutted; act of glutting. [<obs. *glut* a glutton <OF *gloutir* swallow <L *glutire*]

glut[2] (glut) *n.* A wooden wedge used in splitting logs. [Cf. dial. *clut* a cleat]

glu·tam·ic acid (gloo͞·tam′ik) *Chem.* An amino acid, $C_5H_9O_4N$, present in many animal and vegetable proteins.

glu·ta·mine (gloo͞′tə·mēn, -min) *n. Biochem.* An amino acid, $C_5H_{10}O_3N_2$, commonly present in animal and vegetable proteins. [<GLUT(EN) + -AMINE]

glu·ta·thi·one (gloo͞′tə·thī′ōn) *n. Biochem.* A peptide of glutamic acid, cystine, and glycine, $C_{10}H_{17}O_6N_3S$, obtained from yeast; found also in muscle tissue, blood, and plants. [<GLUTA(MIC) + THI- + -ONE]

glu·te·al (gloo͞·tē′əl, gloo͞′tē·əl) *adj. Anat.* Of or pertaining to the muscles of the buttocks. [<GLUTEUS]

glu·te·lin (gloo͞′tə·lin) *n. Biochem.* Any of a class of simple proteins found in certain plants, as wheat. [<GLUTEN + *-lin,* an arbitrary ending]

glu·ten (gloo͞t′n) *n.* A mixture of plant proteins found in cereal grains; a tough, sticky substance obtained by washing out the starch from wheat flour: used as an adhesive and thickener. [<L, glue] —**glu′te·nous** *adj.*

gluten bread Bread made from flour rich in gluten and containing little starch.

glu·te·us (gloo͞·tē′əs) *n. pl.* **·te·i** (-tē′ī) *Anat.* Any of three muscles in the region of the buttocks. [<NL <Gk. *gloutos* rump]

glu·ti·nous (gloo͞′tə·nəs) *adj.* **1** Resembling glue; sticky. **2** Pervaded with sticky matter. See synonyms under ADHESIVE. —**glu′ti·nous·ly** *adv.* —**glu′ti·nous·ness** *n.*

glut·ton[1] (glut′n) *n.* **1** One who gluts himself; an excessive eater. **2** One who has an excessive appetite for anything. [<OF *glouton* <L *gluto, -onis* a glutton]

glut·ton[2] (glut′n) *n.* A musteline carnivore, the wolverine *(Gulo luscus),* especially the Old World form. [Trans. of G *vielfrass* great eater]

glut·ton·ize (glut′ən·īz) *v.t.* & *v.i.* **·ized, ·iz·ing** To eat (food) gluttonously.

glut·ton·ous (glut′ən·əs) *adj.* Voracious. —**glut′ton·ous·ly** *adv.*

glut·ton·y (glut′ən·ē) *n. pl.* **·ton·ies** The act or habit of eating to excess.

gly·cer·ic (gli·ser′ik, glis′ər-) *adj.* Of or derived from glycerol.

glyceric acid *Chem.* A colorless, sirupy compound, $C_3H_6O_4$, formed during alcoholic fermentation and by oxidizing glycerol with nitric acid.

glyc·er·ide (glis′ər·īd, -id) *n. Chem.* An ether or ester of glycerol with a fatty acid.

glyc·er·in (glis′ər·in) See GLYCEROL. Also **glyc′er·ine** (-in, -ēn).

glyc·er·ol (glis′ər·ōl, -ol) *n. Chem.* A sweet, oily, nearly colorless trihydric alcohol, $C_3H_8O_3$, formed by decomposition of natural fats with alkalis or superheated steam; also obtained from petroleum products. Also called *glycerin.* [<Gk. *glykeros* sweet + -OL[2]]

glyc·er·yl (glis′ər·il) *n. Chem.* The trivalent glycerol radical C_3H_5. [<GLYCER(IN) + -YL]

gly·cine (glī′sēn, glī·sēn′) *n. Chem.* A sweet, colorless amino acid, $C_2H_5O_2N$, obtained from various proteins. [<Gk. *glykys* sweet + -INE[2]]

gly·co·gen (glī′kə·jən) *n. Biochem.* A white, mealy, amorphous polysaccharide, $(C_6H_{10}O_5)_x$, contained in animal tissues, principally the liver: also called *animal starch.* [<Gk. *glykys* sweet + -GEN]

gly·co·gen·ase (glī′kə·jə·nās′) *n. Biochem.* An enzyme present in the liver which converts glycogen to a saccharide. [<GLYCOGEN + -ASE]

gly·co·gen·ic (glī′kə·jen′ik) *adj.* **1** Relating to the formation of glycogen. **2** Caused by glycogen.

gly·col (glī′kōl, -kol) *n. Chem.* **1** A colorless, sweetish compound, $C_2H_6O_2$, formed by decomposing certain ethylene compounds: used as a solvent, as a freezing mixture, and in the manufacture of explosives, intermediates, etc. **2** Any dihydroxyl alcohol of the glycol group having the general formula $C_nH_{2n}(OH)_2$. [<GLYC(ERIN) + -OL[1]]

gly·col·ic acid (glī·kol′ik) *Chem.* An acid, $C_2H_4O_3$, found in the juice of cane sugar and unripe grapes: also made synthetically.

gly·co·pro·te·in (glī′kə·prō′tē·in, -tēn) *n. Biochem.* Any of a group of proteins containing a carbohydrate group other than nucleic acid, as mucin: also spelled *glucoprotein.* [<Gk. *glykys* sweet + PROTEIN]

gly·co·side (glī′kə·sīd) *n. Chem.* Any of a group of compounds which, when decomposed by dilute acids, alkalis, or certain ferments, yield glucose or some other sugar and a principle, as digitalin, quercetin, salicin, etc.: also spelled *glucoside.* [<GLUCOSE + -IDE]

gly·co·su·ri·a (glī′kə·sŏŏr′ē·ə) *n. Pathol.* A condition, as diabetes mellitus, in which the urine contains glucose: also spelled *glucosuria.* [<NL <F *glycose* glucose + Gk. *ouron* urine] **— gly′co·su′ric** *adj.*

Glyc·yr·rhi·za (glis′i·rī′zə) *n.* A genus of leguminous plants native in southern Europe and central Asia, the roots of which yield the common licorice of commerce. [<Gk. <*glykys* sweet + *rhiza* root]

Glyn (glin), **Elinor,** 1864–1943, *née* Sutherland, English novelist born in Canada.

gly·ox·a·line (glī·ok′sə·lin) *n.* Imidazole. [< GLY(COL) + OXAL(IC) + -INE[2]]

glyph (glif) *n.* **1** *Archit.* A vertical groove or channel, as in a Doric frieze. Compare TRIGLYPH. **2** A picture or carving representing an idea; hieroglyph. [<Gk. *glyphē* a carving <*glyphein* carve] **— glyph′ic** *adj.*

glyph·og·ra·phy (glif·og′rə·fē) *n.* A process for making relief plates for printing by engraving the design on a copperplate covered with a wax film. [<Gk. *glyphē* a carving + -GRAPHY]

Glyp·tal (glip′təl) *n.* A synthetic resin made from phthalic anhydride and glycerol: used as a bonding material, in paints and lacquers, etc.: a trade name.

glyp·tic (glip′tik) *adj.* **1** Pertaining to carving or engraving. **2** Exhibiting figures, as in a mineral. [<Gk. *glyptikos* <*glyphē* a carving]

glyp·tics (glip′tiks) *n. pl.* The art of cutting designs on precious stones, shells, etc.

glyp·to·dont (glip′tə·dont) *n.* Any of a genus *(Glyptodon)* of extinct American armadillos. [<NL *Glyptodon* <Gk. *glyptos* carved + *odous, odontos* a tooth]

GLYPTODONT
(From 12 to 14 feet long)

glyp·to·graph (glip′tə·graf, -gräf) *n.* A design cut on a gem. **— glyp·tog·ra·pher** (glip·tog′rə·fər) *n.* **— glyp′to·graph′ic** *adj.*

glyp·tog·ra·phy (glip·tog′rə·fē) *n.* **1** The art or operation of engraving on gems. **2** The study of engraved gems. [<Gk. *glyptos* carved + -GRAPHY]

G–man (jē′man′) *n. pl.* **–men** (-men′) An operative of the Federal Bureau of Investigation. [<G(OVERNMENT) MAN]

gnar (när) *v.i.* **gnarred, gnar·ring** To snarl or growl. Also **gnarr.** [Imit.]

gnarl[1] (närl) *v.i.* To snarl; growl. [Freq. of GNAR]

gnarl[2] (närl) *n.* A protuberance on a tree; a tough knot. [Back formation from GNARLED]

gnarled (närld) *adj.* Exhibiting gnarls; knotty; cross–grained; distorted. Also **gnarl′y.** [Var. of KNURLED]

gnash (nash) *v.t.* **1** To grind or snap (the teeth) together, as in rage or pain. **2** To bite or chew with grinding teeth. *— v.i.* **3** To grind the teeth together. *—n.* A snap or bite of the teeth. [Var. of obs. *gnast* <Scand. Cf. ON *gnista* gnash.]

gnat (nat) *n.* **1** Any of various small dipterous flies with long, many–jointed antennae, as the buffalo gnats, punkies, and midges. **2** A mosquito. [OE *gnæt*]

gnat·catch·er (nat′kach′ər) *n.* A small American bird (genus *Polioptila*) having a black, white–bordered tail and short wings.

gnath·ic (nath′ik) *adj.* Of or pertaining to the jaw. [<Gk. *gnathos* jaw]

gnathic index A measure of the prominence of the jaw, expressed as the ratio of the distance from nasion to basion taken as 100, to the distance from the basion to the alveolar point. Compare illustration under FACIAL ANGLE.

gna·thi·on (nā′thē·on, nath′ē·on) *n. Anat.* The lower end of the symphysis of the jaw. [<NL, dim. of Gk. *gnathos* the jaw]

gnatho– *combining form* Jaw: *gnathostome.* [<Gk. *gnathos* jaw]

gna·thon·ic (na·thon′ik) *adj.* Fawning; flattering. [after *Gnatho,* a sycophant in Terence's *Eunuchus*]

gnath·o·stome (nath′ə·stōm) *n.* Any of a division *(Gnathostomata)* of vertebrates having mouths provided with jaws.

–gnathous *combining form* Jaw: *prognathous.* [<Gk. *gnathos* jaw + -OUS]

gnaw (nô) *v.t.* **gnawed, gnawed** or **gnawn, gnaw·ing 1** To bite or eat away little by little with or as with the teeth. **2** To make by gnawing: to *gnaw* a hole. **3** To bite on repeatedly: He *gnawed* his lip in rage. **4** To torment or oppress with fear, pain, etc. *— v.i.* **5** To bite, chew, or corrode persistently or continually. **6** To cause constant worry, pain, etc. [OE *gnagan*] **— gnaw′er** *n.*

gnaw·ing (nô′ing) *n.* A constant biting, fretting pain.

gneiss (nīs) *n.* **1** A metamorphic rock consisting essentially of the same components as granite but in which there is a more or less distinctly foliated arrangement of the components, and especially of the mica. **2** Any of a number of highly metamorphic rocks containing feldspar. ◆ Homophone: *nice.* [<G] **— gneiss′ic** *adj.*

gneiss·oid (nīs′oid) *adj.* Resembling gneiss.

gnome[1] (nōm) *n.* **1** In folklore, one of a race of dwarfs believed to live underground as guardians of treasure, mines, etc. **2** The pigmy owl of North America. [<F <NL *gnomus*] **— gnom′ish** *adj.*

gnome[2] (nōm) *n.* A pithy proverbial saying; maxim. [<Gk. *gnōmē* thought, maxim]

gno·mic (nō′mik, nom′ik) *adj.* **1** Dealing in maxims. **2** Expressing a maxim or a universal truth. Also **gno′mi·cal.**

gno·mol·o·gy (nə·mol′ə·jē) *n.* A compilation of or a treatise on gnomic sayings.

gno·mon (nō′mon) *n.* **1** The triangular piece whose shadow points out the time of day on a sundial, or anything, as a pillar, used for a similar purpose. **2** The index of the hour circle of a globe. **3** *Geom.* The figure that remains after a parallelogram has been removed from the corner of a similar but larger parallelogram, as *BCIGDE* or *FCAGHE.* The diagonally opposite parallelograms *ADEB, EHIF,* or *GHED, EFCB,* are called *complements* of each other or of the whole parallelogram. **4** *Math.* One of the terms of an arithmetical series by which polygonal numbers are found: also **gnomonic number.** [<Gk. *gnōmōn* an indicator <*gnō-,* stem of *gignōskein* know]

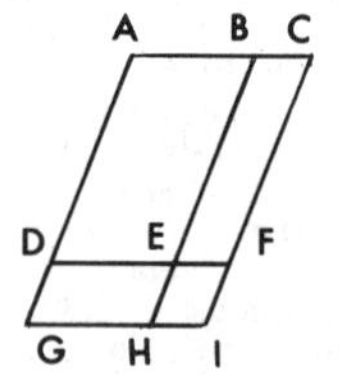

GNOMON

gno·mon·ic (nō·mon′ik) *adj.* **1** Of the nature of a gnomon. **2** Pertaining to the measurement of time by sundials. Also **gno·mon′i·cal.**

gno·mon·ics (nō·mon′iks) *n. pl.* The science of constructing sundials.

–gnomy *combining form* Knowledge or art of judging: *physiognomy.* [<Gk. *gnōmē* judgment]

gno·si·ol·o·gy (nō′sē·ol′ə·jē, nō′zē-) *n.* The branch of philosophy that treats of the sources, limits, and validity of knowledge; the systematic and critical treatment of philosophic principles underlying the activities of the cognitive faculties. [<GNOSIS + -(O)LOGY]

gno·sis (nō′sis) *n.* Cognition; especially, the knowledge of spiritual mysteries; Gnosticism. [<NL <Gk. *gnōsis* knowledge <*gignōskein* know]

–gnosis *combining form Med.* Knowledge; recognition: *prognosis.* [<Gk. *gnōsis* knowledge]

gnos·tic (nos′tik) *adj.* Of, pertaining to, or possessing knowledge; claiming esoteric insight or wisdom. Also **gnos′ti·cal.** [<Gk. *gnōstikos* knowing <*gnōsis.* See GNOSIS.] **— gnos′ti·cal·ly** *adv.*

Gnos·tic (nos′tik) *adj.* Of or pertaining to the Gnostics or Gnosticism. *— n.* An adherent or advocate of Gnosticism.

Gnos·ti·cism (nos′tə·siz′əm) *n.* A philosophical and religious system (first to sixth century) teaching that knowledge rather than faith was the key to salvation.

gnu (nōō, nyōō) *n. pl.* **gnus** or **gnu** A South African antelope (genus *Connochaetes*) having an oxlike head with curved horns, a mane, and a long tail; a wildebeest. Also **gnoo.** ◆ Homophone: *new.* [< Kaffir *nqu*]

GNU
(From 4 to 4 1/2 feet high at the shoulder)

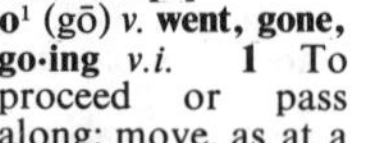

go[1] (gō) *v.* **went, gone, go·ing** *v.i.* **1** To proceed or pass along; move, as at a given speed. **2** To move from a place; leave; depart. **3** To move from one place to another for or as for a purpose: She *went* to dress for dinner. **4** To pass away; disappear; end: The opportunity has *gone.* **5** To be free or freed: They let him *go.* **6** To be in motion or operation; work properly: The watch is *going* now. **7** To extend or reach: The pipe *goes* into the next room. **8** To be, continue, or appear in a specified state or condition: Should these crimes *go* unpunished? **9** To pass into a state or condition; become: to *go* insane. **10** To proceed or end in a specified manner: The election *went* badly for him. **11** To be suitable; have its usual place; fit; belong: The music *goes* with these words. **12** To be considered or ranked: a good lunch, as lunches *go.* **13** To be phrased or expressed; have proper form or order: The song *goes* like this. **14** To emit or produce a specified sound or signal: The chain *goes* clank. **15** To attend; engage oneself in an occupation: to *go* to sea; to *go* fishing. **16** To pass: said of time. **17** To be guided or regulated; conform: to *go* with the times. **18** To be awarded, given, or applied: This *goes* toward canceling the debt. **19** To have recourse; make appeal; resort: to *go* to court. **20** To be known: What name does she *go* by? **21** To be sold or bid for: These shoes will *go* at a high price. **22** To help; tend: This *goes* to prove my argument. **23** To serve as a part; contribute: the graces that *go* to make a lady. **24** To be abolished or surrendered: The poll tax must *go.* **25** To collapse; fail: The walls *went* last in the fire. **26** To subject or put oneself: He *went* to great pains to do it. **27** To die. **28** To be about to do or act: used only in the progressive form and followed by the present infinitive: They were *going* to protest. *— v.t.* **29** To furnish; put up: to *go* bail. **30** To contribute; share: to *go* halves. **31** *Colloq.* To risk or bet; wager. **32** *Colloq.* To put up with; tolerate: I cannot *go* that music. **— to go about 1** To be occupied or busy with. **2** To set about to do (something). **3** *Naut.* To change to the other tack. **— to go around 1** To move about or circulate. **2** To be enough to furnish even shares. **— to go at 1** To attack. **2** To work at. **— to go back on 1** To forsake; be untrue to. **2** To fail to fulfil or abide by. **— to go by 1** To pass. **2** To conform to or be guided by: to *go by* the rules. **— to go for 1** To reach for; try to get: He *went for* his gun. **2** To attack. **3** *Colloq.* To be strongly attracted by. **— to go in for** *Colloq.* **1** To strive for or advocate: to *go in for* social reform. **2** To prefer; have a liking for: to *go in for* classical music. **— to go into 1** To investigate. **2** To take up, as an occupation: He *went into* business for himself. **3** To be contained in: Four *goes into* twelve three times. **— to go in with 1** To join. **2** To share expenses or risks with. **— to go off 1** To explode or be discharged, as a gun. **2** *Colloq.* To succeed; result: How did the party *go off*? **— to go on 1** To act; behave. **2** To happen: What's *going on* here? **3** *Colloq.* To talk aimlessly; chatter. **4** In the theater, to appear on stage. **— to go one better (than)** To surpass by a single degree or quality. **— to go out 1** To cease or be extinguished, as a light. **2** To advance or be drawn forth in sympathy: My heart *goes out* to him. **3** To strike: The union *went out* for higher wages. **4** To become obsolete. **5** To go to social affairs, the theater, etc. **— to go over 1** To turn on its side: The car *went over.* **2** To rehearse; repeat. **3** To examine closely or carefully. **4** *Colloq.* To succeed. **— to go**

through 1 To search thoroughly. 2 To experience; undergo. 3 To practice, as a role or part. 4 To be passed, as legislation. 5 To spend completely; use up: to *go through* a fortune. **— to go through with** To complete; undertake to finish. **— to go together** 1 To be suitable; harmonize. 2 *Colloq.* To keep company, as sweethearts. **— to go under** 1 To be overwhelmed or conquered. 2 To fail, as a business. **— to go up** To increase, as prices or values. **— to go with** 1 To be suitable to; harmonize with. 2 *Colloq.* To keep company with. **— to go without** To do or be without. **— to let go of** 1 To release one's hold of. 2 To abandon one's interest or share in. — *n.* 1 The act of going: the come and *go* of the seasons. 2 *Colloq.* The capacity for energetic action; vigor: He has plenty of *go.* 3 *Colloq.* A try; attempt: to have a *go* at something. 4 *Colloq.* A success: He made a *go* of it. 5 *Colloq.* A bargain. 6 *Colloq.* The fashion; mode: with *the.* 7 *Colloq.* A proceeding; turn of affairs. **— no go** *Colloq.* Useless; hopeless. **— on the go** *Colloq.* Busy; in constant motion. — *adj. Aerospace* Operating or proceeding as planned. [OE *gān*] **— go'er** *n.*

go[2] (gō) *n.* A Japanese game played with counters or stones on the intersections of lines on a board. [<Japanese]

go·a (gō'ə) *n.* A black-tailed gazelle *(Procapra picticaudata)* of the mountains of Tibet. [< Tibetan *dgoba*]

Go·a (gō'ə) A district of the former Portuguese India, on the west coast of India; annexed by India in 1961; 1,394 square miles; capital, New Goa.

goad (gōd) *n.* 1 A point set in the end of a stick for urging oxen or other beasts. 2 Something that spurs or incites. — *v.t.* To prick or drive with or as with a goad; incite. See synonyms under INCENSE[1], PIQUE[1], SPUR. [OE *gād*]

Goad (gōd) See GUDE.

goads·man (gōdz'mən) *n. pl.* **·men** (-mən) A driver of oxen, cattle, etc.

go–a·head (gō'ə·hed') *adj. Colloq.* Disposed to make rapid progress; energetic.

goal (gōl) *n.* 1 A point toward which effort or movement is directed; the objective point or terminus that one is striving to reach; the end aimed at: the *goal* of one's ambition. 2 In any game, race, contest, or competition, a mark, line, post, pole, or the like, made or set up to indicate the limit, winning point, or safety place of the game; in football, a pair of upright posts, **goal posts,** with a crosspiece over which the players strive to kick the ball. 3 In football and similar games, the act of propelling the ball over or past the goal, so as to win a point; also, the point so won. See synonyms under AIM, END. [ME *gol*; origin uncertain]

goal·ie (gō'lē) *n. Colloq.* A goalkeeper.

goal·keep·er (gōl'kē'pər) *n.* In certain games, as hockey, soccer, etc., a player stationed to protect the goal. Also **goal'tend'er.**

go·an·na (gō·an'ə) *n.* Any of several large, predatory, Australian lizards (family *Varanidae*) resembling the iguana, especially the black-and-yellow tree goanna *(Varanus varius).* [Alter. of IGUANA]

Goa powder A bitter yellow powder found in cavities of the Brazilian araroba tree *(Andira araroba)*: used in medicine.

goat (gōt) *n.* 1 A hollow-horned ruminant (genus *Capra*) of rocky and mountainous regions, related to the sheep and including wild and domesticated forms. ◆ Collateral adjective: *hircine.* 2 A lecherous man. 3 *Slang* A scapegoat; the butt of a joke. **—to get one's goat** *Slang* To get a strong reaction (from someone) by teasing, tormenting, etc. [OE *gāt*] **— goat'like'** *adj.*

Goat (gōt) See CAPRICORN under CONSTELLATION.

goat antelope Any of certain ruminant mammals related to the goats and antelopes, as the chamois, Rocky Mountain goat, etc.

goat·beard (gōt'bird') *n.* 1 A European plant, the salsify *(Tragopogon pratensis)* with long, feathery pappus, naturalized in the United States. 2 A perennial herb of the rose family *(Aruncus sylvester)* with long compound panicles of whitish flowers. Also **goats'beard'.**

goat·ee (gō·tē') *n.* A man's beard so trimmed as to resemble the pointed beard of a goat.

goat·fish (gōt'fish') *n. pl.* **·fish** or **·fish·es** 1 A tropical marine fish of the mullet family, having a beardlike appendage below the mouth, especially the European red mullet, esteemed as a food fish. 2 The European filefish.

goat–god (gōt'god') *n.* Pan.

goat·herd (gōt'hûrd') *n.* One who tends goats.

goat·ish (gō'tish) *adj.* Resembling a goat; lustful. **— goat'ish·ly** *adv.* **— goat'ish·ness** *n.*

Goat Island An island in the Niagara River, dividing Niagara Falls into American Falls and Horseshoe (Canadian) Falls.

goat·skin (gōt'skin') *n.* 1 The hide of a goat. 2 Leather made from it.

goats·rue (gōts'ro͞o') *n.* 1 A hardy perennial herb *(Galega officinalis)* of the Old World. 2 An American herb of the pea family *(Tephrosia virginiana).*

goat·suck·er (gōt'suk'ər) *n.* 1 Any of numerous nocturnal, insectivorous birds (family *Caprimulgidae*) with flattened heads and wide mouths, as the whippoorwill or nighthawk. 2 The frogmouth.

goave (gōv) *v.i. Scot.* To stare stupidly.

goav·ing (gō'ving) *adj. Scot.* Staring stupidly; dreaming.

gob[1] (gob) *n.* A small piece, mass, or chunk; a lump. [<OF *gobe* mouthful, lump, ? <Celtic]

gob[2] (gob) *n. Brit.* 1 An abandoned mine-works filled with refuse. 2 Rubbish. [Cf. dial. E *goaf, goave* an empty space from which coal has been mined]

gob[3] (gob) *n. Slang* A sailor of the U.S. Navy. [Origin uncertain]

go·bang (gō'bäng') *n.* A Japanese game played on a checkerboard, usually of 256 squares, the object being to be first to arrange 5 counters in a row on intersecting lines. Also **go'ban'.** [<Japanese *goban* chessboard]

gobbe (gob) *n.* A creeping annual *(Voandzeia subterranea)*, resembling the common peanut: much cultivated in Africa and South America. [< native Cariban name]

gob·bet (gob'it) *n.* 1 A piece or fragment, especially a morsel of cooked meat, highly seasoned. 2 A chunk; lump. 3 *Archaic* A mouthful. [<F *gobet,* dim. of *gobe* GOB[1]]

gob·ble[1] (gob'əl) *v.* **gob·bled, gob·bling** *v.t.* 1 To swallow (food) greedily and in gulps. 2 *U.S. Slang* To seize or acquire in a grasping manner. — *v.i.* 3 To eat greedily and quickly. [<F *gover* bolt, devour] **— gob'bler** *n.*

gob·ble[2] (gob'əl) *n.* The sound made by the turkey cock. **—** *v.i.* **gob·bled, gob·bling** To utter a gobble, as turkeys. [Var. of GABBLE]

gob·ble·dy·gook (gob'əl·dē·go͝ok') *n. Colloq.* Involved, pedantic, repetitious, and pompous jargon, relying heavily upon Latinized expressions and meaningless clichés: applied especially to the language of bureaucrats and professional politicians. [Coined by M. Maverick, U.S. Congressman, about 1940]

gob·bler (gob'lər) *n.* A turkey cock.

Gob·e·lin tapestry (gob'ə·lin, gō'bə-; *Fr.* gō·blaṅ') Any tapestry woven at the Parisian factory of the Gobelins, a family by whom the industry was begun in the 15th century.

go–be·tween (gō'bə·twēn') *n.* One who acts as an agent, assistant, or mediator between other persons in relation to business, intrigue, or other matters; an intermediary.

Go·bi (gō'bē) A desert in central Asia; 500,000 square miles: Chinese *Shamo.* Also **Gobi Desert.**

gob·let (gob'lit) *n.* 1 A drinking vessel with a stem and no handle. 2 A large, shallow bowl or drinking vessel for ceremonious or festive occasions. [<OF *gobelet,* dim. of *gobel* a drinking cup <Celtic]

gob·lin (gob'lin) *n.* A supernatural, grotesque creature regarded as malicious or mischievous. [<OF *gobelin* <Med. L *gobelinus,* ? <Gk. *kobalos* a rogue]

go·bo (gō'bō) *n. pl.* **·bos** 1 A portable sound-absorbing panel used to control sound effects in motion-picture production. 2 A device for shielding the lens of a television camera from the direct rays of light. [Origin uncertain]

gob·stick (gəb'stik') *n.* An implement for removing a hook from a fish's mouth. [< dial. E *gob* the mouth + STICK]

go·by (gō'bē) *n. pl.* **·by** or **·bies** Any of a widely distributed family *(Gobiidae)* of spiny-rayed, chiefly marine fishes having ventral fins united into a funnel-shaped suction disk, as the rock goby *(Gobius paganellus)* and the California blind goby (genus *Typhlogobius*). [<L *gobius* <Gk. *kōbios,* a small fish]

go–by (gō'bī') *n. Colloq.* An intended slight.

go·cart (gō'kärt') *n.* 1 A light framework on rollers designed to support a baby learning to walk. 2 A small, light, baby carriage having the front wheels smaller than the rear. 3 A light carriage.

god (god) *n.* 1 A being regarded as possessing superhuman or supernatural qualities or powers, and made an object of worship or propitiation; a higher intelligence supposed to control the forces of good and of evil; a personification of any of the forces of nature or of some human attribute, interest, or relation; a divinity; deity. 2 Any person or thing exalted as the chief good, or made an object of supreme devotion. 3 Anything that absorbs one's attentions or aspirations: Money is his *god.* 4 The embodiment of some aspect of reality or of some being regarded as the ultimate principle of the universe: the *god* of justice. 5 An image or symbol of a deity; idol. — *v.t. Rare* **god·ded, god·ding** To deify; idolize. [OE]

God (god) The one Supreme Being, self-existent and eternal; the infinite creator, sustainer, and ruler of the universe: conceived of as omniscient, good, and almighty.

Go·da·va·ri (gō·dä'və·rē) A river in central India, flowing about 900 miles to the Bay of Bengal.

god·child (god'chīld') *n.* A child for whom a person becomes sponsor at baptism.

god·daugh·ter (god'dô'tər) *n.* A female godchild.

god·den (god·den') *Brit. Dial.* Good evening: a salutation. [Contraction of *good even*]

god·dess (god'is) 1 A female divinity. 2 Figuratively, a woman surpassingly beloved, good, or beautiful. **— god'dess·hood** *n.*

Go·des·berg (gō'des·berkh) A resort town on the Rhine in North Rhine-Westphalia. Also **Bad Godesberg** (bäd).

go–dev·il (gō'dev'əl) *n.* 1 A dray sled for hauling rocks, logs, etc. 2 A pointed iron weight dropped into the bore of an oil well to explode the charge of dynamite. 3 A railroad handcar used by work gangs. 4 A jointed, flexible device for cleaning a pipeline of obstructions.

god·fa·ther (god'fä'thər) *n.* A man who becomes sponsor for a child at its baptism or confirmation. — *v.t.* To act as a godfather to.

God·frey (god'frē) A masculine personal name. Also *Du.* **God·fried** (gōt'frēt), *Fr.* **Gode·froi** (gôd·frwà'), *Ital.* **Go·de·fre·do** (gō'dā·frā'dō), *Sp.* **Go·do·fre·do** (gō'thō·frā'thō). [<Gmc., peace of God]

— Godfrey of Bouillon, 1061–1100, duke of lower Lorraine; leader of the first crusade, 1096–1100.

God·havn (gôth'houn) A Danish settlement on the southern tip of Disko Island.

god·head (god'hed') *n.* Godhood; divinity.

God·head (god'hed') *n.* The essential nature of God; the Deity.

god·hood (god'ho͝od) *n.* The state or quality of being divine.

Go·di·va (gə·dī'və) The wife of Leofric, 11th century Earl of Mercia, who according to English legend rode naked through Coventry as the condition of the removal of oppressive taxes.

god·less (god'lis) *adj.* Ungodly; atheistical; wicked. See synonyms under PROFANE. **— god'less·ness** *n.*

god·like (god'līk') *adj.* Similar to God or to a god; divine; of supreme excellence or beauty. **— god'like'ness** *n.*

god·ling (god'ling) *n.* A minor divinity.

god·ly (god'lē) *adj.* **·li·er, ·li·est** Filled with reverence and love for God; pious. **— god'li·ly** *adv.* **— god'li·ness** *n.*

god·moth·er (god'muth'ər) *n.* A female sponsor at baptism. — *v.t.* To act as godmother to.

Go·dol·phin (gō·dol'fin), **Sidney,** 1645–1712, first Earl of Godolphin, English statesman.

go·down (gō·doun') *n.* In China and the East Indies, a warehouse. [<Malay *godong* warehouse]

Go·doy (gō·thoi′), **Manuel de,** 1767–1851, Spanish statesman.

god·par·ent (god′pâr′ənt) *n.* A godfather or godmother.

go·droon (gə·drōōn′) *n.* **1** *Archit.* An ornament of notched or carved rounded form. **2** Fluted or oval decoration used in silverwork. Also spelled *gadroon.* [<F *godron* plait] **—go·drooned′·** *adj.*

GODROON

God's acre A burying ground.

God's country *U.S.* A region considered to be a paradise.

god·send (god′send′) *n.* An unexpected stroke of good fortune regarded as sent by God. [Earlier *God's send* <GOD + ME *sande* message]

god·ship (god′ship) *n.* The rank or character of a god; deity.

god·son (god′sun′) *n.* A male godchild.

God·speed (god′spēd′) *n.* God speed you: a wish for a safe journey or for success.

Godt·haab (gôt′hôp) A port in SW Greenland.

Go·du·nov (gô·dōō·nôf′), **Boris,** 1552?–1605, czar of Russia 1598–1605.

God·ward (god′wərd) *adv.* Toward or in connection with God. Also **God′wards.**

God·win (god′win) A masculine personal name. Also **God′wine,** *Du.* **Go·de·wijn** (gō′də·vīn), *Lat.* **God·wi·nus** (god·wī′nəs). [<Gmc., friend of God]
—Godwin, died 1053, earl of the West Saxons, English statesman; chief minister to Edward the Confessor.

Godwin (god′win), **William,** 1756–1836, English philosopher and author.

God·win Aus·ten (god′win ôs′tin) See K2.

god·wit (god′wit) *n.* A curlewlike shore bird (genus *Limosa)* with long legs and a long, tilted bill, as the American marbled godwit *(L. fedoa).* [Origin uncertain]

Goeb·bels (gœb′əls), **Joseph Paul,** 1897–1945, German politician; Nazi minister of propaganda 1933–45.

Goe·ring (gœ′ring) See GORING.

Goe·thals (gō′thəlz), **George Washington,** 1858–1928, U.S. engineer; builder of Panama Canal.

Goe·the (gœ′tə), **Johann Wolfgang von,** 1749–1832, German poet, dramatist, novelist, and statesman.

goe·thite (gō′thīt, gœ′tīt) *n.* An imperfect, adamantine, reddish or blackish-brown ferric hydroxide, crystallizing in the orthorhombic system: also spelled *göthite.* [after *Goethe*]

gof·fer (gof′ər, gôf′-) *n.* **1** A fluting or crimp. **2** A tool used in crimping lace, paper, etc. *—v.t.* **1** To form plaits or flutes in; crimp, as lace or paper. **2** To raise in relief. Also spelled *gauffer.* [<F *gaufrer* crimp cloth <*gaufre* a honeycomb]

Gof·fre·do (gôf·frā′dō) Italian form of GODFREY. Also *Sp.* **Go·fre·do** (gō·frā′thō).

Gog (gog) **and Ma·gog** (mā′gog) In the Bible, the nations, led by Satan, which will war against the kingdom of God. *Rev.* xx 8.

go-get·ter (gō′get′ər) *n. U.S. Colloq.* A hustling, energetic, aggressive person.

gog·gle (gog′əl) *n.* **1** A rolling of the eyes. **2** *pl.* Spectacles, often with colored lenses, and attachments to fit close to the face as protection against strong light, wind, and dust. [<*v.*] *—adj.* Prominent; staring. *—v.* **gog·gled, gog·gling** *v.i.* **1** To roll the eyes about or stare with bulging eyes. **2** To roll sidewise or stare protrusively: said of the eyes. *—v.t.* **3** To roll (the eyes). [ME *gogelen* look aside, prob. <Celtic]

gog·gle-eye (gog′əl·ī′) *n.* A staring eye. **—gog′·gle-eyed′** *adj.*

Gogh (gō, gôk; *Du.* khôkh), **Vincent van** See VAN GOGH.

gog·let (gog′lit) *n.* In the East Indies, a jar or vase of porous pottery for keeping water cool by evaporation: also called *gurglet.* [<Pg. *gorgoleta*]

go-go (gō′gō′) *adj. Slang* **1** Of or describing discothèques, the usually unrestrained, erotic dances performed there, or the dancers, typically young women, who entertain with such dances. **2** Lively, modern, glamorous, etc. **3** In finance, characterized by rapid speculative trading to realize profit quickly. **4** Aggressively enterprising or ambitious [<F *à gogo* joyfully]

Go·gol (gō′gəl, *Russian* gô′gôl), **Nikolai Vasilievich,** 1809–52, Russian novelist.

Gog·ra (gog′rə) A river in Tibet, Nepal, and India, flowing 640 miles, generally south, to the Ganges.

Goi·â·ni·a (goi·a′nē·ə) Capital of Goiás, Brazil.

Goi·ás (goi·äs′) A state of central Brazil; 240,444 square miles: formerly *Goyaz.*

Goi·del·ic (goi·del′ik) *n.* A branch of the Celtic languages including Irish, the Gaelic of the Scottish Highlands, and Manx; Gaelic. *—adj.* Of or pertaining to the Gaels or their languages. Also spelled *Gadelic, Gaedhelic.* Also **Goi·dhel′ic.** [<OIrish *Góidel* a Gael]

go·ing (gō′ing) *n.* **1** The act of departing or moving; leaving. **2** The condition of the ground, paths, or roads. **3** Style of walking; gait. **4** *Obs.* The manner of conducting oneself; deportment. **—goings on** *Colloq.* Behavior; conduct; actions: used to express disapproval. *—adj.* **1** Continuing to function: a *going* concern. **2** Arising from continued operation: the *going* value of a business. **3** In existence: available: the best bargain *going.* **4** Departing; leaving. **—going on** *Colloq.* Approaching (a particular age or time).

goi·ter (goi′tər) *n. Pathol.* **1** A morbid enlargement of the thyroid gland, variously caused, visible as a swelling on the front part of the neck. **2** The condition itself; bronchocele. See also EXOPHTHALMIC GOITER. Also **goi′tre.** [<F, back formation from *goitreux,* ult. <L *guttur* throat] **—goi′trous** *adj.*

goi·tro·gen (goi′trə·jən) *n.* Any substance capable of initiating or promoting a goiter.

Gol·con·da (gol·kon′də) A city in Hyderabad, India, famous in the 16th century for diamond marketing.

Gol·con·da (gol·kon′də) *n.* A mine or other source of wealth. Also **gol·con′da.**

gold (gōld) *n.* **1** A soft, heavy, malleable and ductile metallic element (symbol Au, atomic number 79) found uncombined in nature, resistant to oxidation and to most chemical reagents. See PERIODIC TABLE. **2** The metal in the form of a coin. **3** Wealth; riches. **4** Gilding, or a golden-yellow color. See synonyms under MONEY. *—adj.* Pertaining to, like, made of, containing, or producing gold, or used in mining gold. [OE]

gold-band lily (gōld′band′) See under LILY.

gold basis The basis of values calculated on a gold standard.

gold·beat·er (gōld′bē′tər) *n.* One who makes gold leaf.

gold·beat·er's-skin (gōld′bē′tərz·skin′) *n.* The outer coat of the cecum of the ox, prepared for the use of the goldbeater.

gold·beat·ing (gōld′bē′ting) *n.* The act or operation of making gold leaf by hammering.

gold beetle **1** A leaf beetle *(Coptocycla bicolor)*: so called from its metallic luster. **2** A brilliant beetle (family *Chrysomelidae*) found on the sweet potato.

Gold·berg (gōld′bûrg), **Arthur Joseph,** born 1908, U.S. labor lawyer; secretary of labor 1961–62; associate justice of the Supreme Court 1962–65; U.S. ambassador to the UN, 1965–68.

gold·brick (gōld′brik′) *n.* **1** *Colloq.* A brick or bar of base metal gilded, used by swindlers, or a brick or bar of gold for which something else is substituted in delivery to the purchaser; hence, any swindle: also **gold brick.** **2** *Slang* A soldier or sailor who shirks or tries to shirk work: also **gold′brick′er.** *—v.t. & v.i. Slang* **1** To shirk (work or duty). **2** To cheat.

gold·bug (gōld′bug′) *n.* **1** A gold beetle. **2** *U.S. Colloq.* An advocate of the gold standard.

gold certificate A U.S. Treasury note redeemable in gold at its face value, not now issued.

Gold Coast **1** A former name for GHANA. **2** A section of the African shore line on the Gulf of Guinea between the Ivory Coast and the Slave Coast. **3** *U.S.* Any residential or resort district frequented by rich people.

Gold Coast Colony A former British colony on the coast of western Africa. See GHANA.

gold·dig·ger (gōld′dig′ər) *n.* **1** One who or that which digs for gold. **2** *Colloq.* A woman who uses her personal relations with men to get money and gifts from them.

gold dust Gold in fine particles.

gold·en (gōl′dən) *adj.* **1** Made of or consisting of gold. **2** Having the color or luster of gold; bright-yellow; resplendent. **3** Resembling gold in worth or scarcity; unusually valuable or excellent; rare. **4** Characterized by a condition of great happiness and prosperity: the *golden* age. **—gold′en·ly** *adv.* **—gold′en·ness** *n.*

golden age **1** In Greek and Roman legend, a mythical period when perfect innocence, peace, and happiness reigned. **2** The most flourishing period of a nation's history. **3** In Roman literature, the period (27 B.C. to A.D. 14) of the finest classical writers; hence, in any country, the periods of literature most nearly corresponding to this: also called *Augustan age.*

golden anniversary See under ANNIVERSARY.

golden aster A North American perennial (genus *Chrysopsis)* of the composite family, with yellow-rayed flowers.

Golden Chersonese The Malay Peninsula.

golden eagle A rare eagle *(Aquila chrysaetos)* ranging throughout the Northern Hemisphere, having dark brown feathers tipped with golden brown at the nape.

gold·en·eye (gōl′dən·ī′) *n.* A large sea duck *(Glaucionetta clangula)* having the upper parts black and the lower parts white.

Golden Fleece In Greek legend, a fleece of gold that hung in a sacred grove in Colchis, guarded by a dragon: stolen by Jason with the aid of Medea. See PHRIXUS.

Golden Gate A strait leading from the Pacific Ocean to San Francisco Bay.

gold·en·glow (gōl′dən·glō′) *n.* A summer-flowering, erect herb *(Rudbeckia laciniata)* of the composite family, with showy terminal heads of yellow-rayed flowers.

golden goose In Greek legend, a goose that laid golden eggs, killed by its owner who thought to obtain all of them at once.

Golden Horde See under HORDE.

Golden Horn The crescent-shaped inlet of the Bosporus in Turkey in Europe, forming the harbor of Istanbul.

Golden Legend The name given by Caxton to his translation, published in 1483, of a medieval collection of the lives of the saints, composed in Latin by Jacobus de Voragine, 1230–98, archbishop of Genoa: also called *Legenda Aurea.*

golden mean A wise moderation; the avoidance of extremes.

golden number *Eccl.* A number indicating the place of a year in a Metonic cycle of 19 years, used in calculating the movable feasts.

golden pheasant A vividly colored pheasant *(Chrysolophus pictus)* of China and Tibet.

golden robin The Baltimore oriole.

gold·en·rod (gōl′dən·rod′) *n.* A widely distributed North American biennial or perennial herb (genus *Solidago)* of the composite family, with erect stalks carrying small heads of flowers, usually yellow and sometimes in clusters, blooming in summer and autumn. State flower of Alabama, Kentucky, and Nebraska.

golden rule The rule of life given in *Matt.* vii 12: "Whatsoever ye would that men should do to you, do ye even so to them."

gold·en·seal (gōl′dən·sēl′) *n.* **1** An herb *(Hydrastis canadensis)* of the United States, with a yellow rootstock, a single radical leaf, a hairy stem, and a single greenish-white flower. **2** This plant's rootstock.

golden section **1** In Euclidean geometry, the division of a line segment in extreme and mean ratio. **2** In esthetics, the division of a line or of a figure in which the smaller length or area is to the larger as the larger is to the whole; also, that proportion of a plane figure in which the smaller dimension is to the larger as the larger is to the sum of the dimensions; broadly a ratio of 3:5, thought to be especially pleasing esthetically. In sculpture, this is applied to the proportion of the frontal plane of the figure. In the Petrarchan sonnet, the relationship between the octave and the sestet is very like that of

D E A F B C G H I

GOLDEN SECTION
On line *AB,* square *ABIG* is constructed; *AG* is bisected at *C,* whereby *CD* = *CB,* and square *DEFA* is constructed. Ratio: *DA* : *AG* : : *AG* : *DG.*

the golden section, with the 14 lines divided in a ratio of 8 : 6. (The true section of 14 is 8.65 : 5.35.) In bookbinding, the proportion of an octavo binding also approximates this ratio.
Golden State Nickname of CALIFORNIA.
golden wattle A plant of the genus *Acacia* (especially *A. pycnantha*) related to the mimosa and having yellow flowers: widely distributed in Australasia.
golden wedding Fiftieth wedding anniversary.
gold·en-winged warbler (gōl′dən·wingd′) A North American warbler with yellow wings (*Vermivora chrysoptera*).
gold-ex·change standard (gōld′iks·chānj′) A monetary system based on currency at par in another country that maintains a gold standard.
gold·eye (gōld′ī′) *n.* A small fresh-water fish (*Amphiodon alosoides*) of northern and western North America: also called *Winnipeg goldeye*.
gold-filled (gōld′fild′) *adj.* Denoting an extra heavy or thick plate of gold on a base metal foundation, as in watchmaking.
gold·finch (gōld′finch′) *n.* **1** A European finch (genus *Carduelis*) having a black hood and a yellow patch on the wings. **2** An American finch (*Spinus tristis*) of which the male, in the summer, has a yellow body with black tail.
gold·fin·ny (gōld′fin′ē) *n.* *pl.* **·nies** A bright-colored European wrasse (genus *Ctenolabrus*).
gold·fish (gōld′fish′) *n.* *pl.* **·fish** or **·fish·es** A small carp of golden color (genus *Carassius*), originally of China, now cultivated in many varieties as an ornamental aquarium fish.
gold foil Thin sheets of gold, thicker than gold leaf. **—gold-foil** (gōld′foil′) *adj.*
gold·i·locks (gōl′dē·loks′) *n.* **1** A European herb (*Linosyris vulgaris*) with yellow flower heads. **2** The European buttercup. **3** A girl with golden hair.
gold lace A lace wrought with gold or gilt thread.
gold leaf A very fine leaf made from beaten gold. **—gold-leaf** (gōld′lēf′) *adj.*
Gold·mark (gōld′märk), **Karl,** 1830–1915, Hungarian composer.
gold note A banknote to be paid in gold.
gold number *Chem.* A number expressing the weight in milligrams of a lyophilic colloid (gelatin) just insufficient to prevent a change from red to violet in 10 cc. of colloidal gold to which has been added 1 cc. of a 10 percent solution of sodium chloride.
gold-of-pleas·ure (gōld′əv·plezh′ər) *n.* An erect annual herb (*Camelina sativa*) with long, lanceolate leaves, small, numerous flowers, and obovoid or pear-shaped pods: naturalized from Europe; false flax.
Gol·do·ni (gōl·dō′nē), **Carlo,** 1707–93, Italian dramatist.
gold point **1** That point in the rate of foreign exchange at which bullion can be shipped in payment of accounts without entailing a loss. **2** *Physics* The melting point of gold, 1063° C., used as a reference temperature.
gold reserve **1** Gold held in reserve by the U. S. Treasury to protect and formerly to redeem U. S. promissory notes; established by Congress, 1882. **2** The quantity of gold bullion or coin owned by the central bank of a country.
gold rush A mass movement of people to an area where gold has been discovered.
gold shell A copper-zinc alloy thinly plated with gold and used for making cheap jewelry: also called *Talmi gold.*
gold·smith (gōld′smith′) *n.* A worker in gold. **—gold′smith′er·y** *n.* **—gold′smith′ing** *n.*
Gold·smith (gōld′smith), **Oliver,** 1728–74, English poet, novelist, and dramatist.
goldsmith beetle A large European scarabaeid beetle (*Cetonia aurata*) of a brilliant golden color: also called *rose beetle.*
gold standard A monetary system based on gold of a specified weight and fineness as the unit of value.
gold-star mother (gōld′stär′) A mother of a member of the U. S. armed forces killed in action during wartime.
gold stick **1** An official of the British royal household who attends the sovereign on state occasions. **2** The gilt rod he carries as an emblem of office.
gold·stone (gōld′stōn′) *n.* Aventurine glass having numerous gold specks which give it a jeweled appearance.
gold-thread (gōld′thred) *n.* **1** A North American evergreen herb (*Coptis groenlandica*) of the crowfoot family, with long, bright-yellow, fibrous roots. **2** The roots of this plant.
golf (gôlf, golf) *n.* An outdoor game played on a large course with a small resilient ball and a set of clubs, the object being to direct the ball into a series of variously distributed holes (usually nine or eighteen) in as few strokes as possible. **—*v.i.*** To play golf. [Cf. dial. E (Scottish) *gowf* strike] **—golf′er** *n.*
golf club **1** One of several clubs used in playing golf. **2** An organization of golfers; also, the building and grounds used by them.

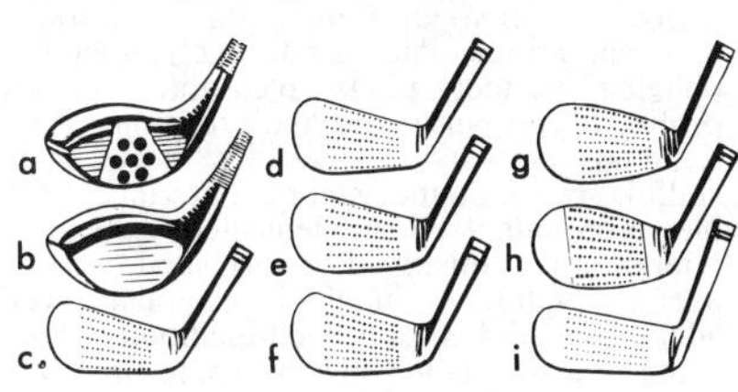

TYPES OF GOLF CLUBS
a. Driver. *b.* Brassie. *c.* No. 2 iron or midiron. *d.* No. 5 iron or mashie. *e.* No. 6 iron. *f.* No 7 iron. *g.* No. 8 iron. *h.* No. 9 iron or niblick. *i.* Putter.

golf links The course over which a game of golf is played. Also **golf course.**
Gol·gi (gôl′jē), **Camillo,** 1844–1926, Italian anatomist.
Golgi apparatus *Biol.* A netlike structure of rod-shaped elements found in the cytoplasm of animal cells. Also **Golgi body.** See illustration under CELL.
gol·go·tha (gol′gə·thə) *n.* **1** A burial place; graveyard; charnel house. **2** Any place of torment or sacrifice. [from *Golgotha*]
Gol·go·tha (gol′gə·thə) A place near Jerusalem where Jesus was crucified. *Matt.* xxvii 33. [<LL <Gk. <Aramaic *gogoltha* skull <Hebrew *gulgōleth*]
gol·iard (gōl′yərd) *n.* One of a class of wandering student jesters of the 12th and 13th centuries who wrote and sang Latin satirical verses. [<OF, a glutton <*gole* gluttony <L *gula*] **—gol·iar·der·y** (gōl·yär′dər·ē) *n.* **—gol·iar′dic** *adj.*
Go·li·ath (gə·lī′əth) A Philistine giant, slain by David. I *Sam.* xvii 4.
gol·li·wog (gol′ē·wog) *n.* **1** A grotesque, black doll. **2** A grotesque person. Also **gol′li·wogg.** [after illustrations drawn (1895) by Florence Upton for a series of children's books]
go·losh (gə·losh′) See GALOSH.
Goltz (gôlts), **Baron Kolmar von der,** 1843–1916, German field marshal of World War I.
gom·broon (gom·brōōn′) *n.* A Persian pottery of a semitransparent white. Also **gom·broon′-ware.** [from a town on the Persian Gulf].
Go·mel (gô′mel) A city in SE Belorussian S.S.R.
Go·me·ra (gō·mā′rä) One of the Canary Islands; 146 square miles.
Gó·mez (gō′mes), **Juan Vicente,** 1857?–1935, Venezuelan general; dictator 1908–35.
Go·mor·rah (gə·môr′ə, -mor′ə) A city on the shore of the Dead Sea, destroyed with Sodom because of the wickedness of its people. *Gen.* xiii 10. Also **Go·mor′rha.**
Gom·pers (gom′pərz), **Samuel,** 1850–1924, U. S. labor leader; president, American Federation of Labor 1886–95, 1896–1924.
gom·pho·sis (gom·fō′sis) *n.* *Anat.* An articulation or union by the firm implantation of one part in a socket situated in another, as the setting of teeth in the jaw or the styloid process in the temporal bone. [<NL <Gk. *gomphos* a bolt]
go·mu·ti (gō·mōō′tē) *n.* **1** The Malayan feather palm (*Arenga pinnata*): a source of palm sugar. **2** A durable, black, hairlike fiber obtained from this palm: valuable for cordage, etc., because it does not rot in water. [<Malay *gumuti*]
gon- Var. of GONO-.
-gon *combining form* Having (a certain number of) angles: *pentagon.* [<Gk. *gonia* an angle]
gon·ad (gon′ad, gō′nad) *n.* *Anat.* A male or female sex gland, in which the gametes develop; an ovary or testis. [<GON- + -AD[1]] **—gon′a·dal, go·na·di·al** (gō·nā′dē·əl), **go·nad·ic** (gō·nad′ik) *adj.*
gon·ad·o·ther·a·py (gon′ə·dō·ther′ə·pē, gə·nad′·ə-) *n.* Treatment of the gonads by the use of sex hormones.
gon·a·do·trop·ic (gon′ə·dō·trop′ik, -trō′pik, gə·nad′ə-) *adj.* Stimulating or nourishing the gonads. Also **gon′a·do·troph′ic** (-trof′ik, -trō′·fik).
gon·ad·ot·ro·pism (gon′əd·ot′rə·piz′əm) *n.* A physical constitution marked by a strong dominance of the gonads.
Go·na·ïves (gə·nà·ēv′), **Gulf of** A wide bay on the west coast of Haiti.
gon·a·poph·y·ses (gon′ə·pof′ə·sēz) *n. pl.* *Entomol.* The genital organs of insects collectively. [<GON- + APOPHYSIS]
Gon·court (gôn·kōōr′), **Edmond Louis Antoine Huot de,** 1822–96, French novelist; collaborator with his brother, **Jules Alfred Huot de,** 1830–70.
Gond (gond) *n.* A Dravidian of the hilly country of central India.
Gon·dar (gon′dər) A city in NW Ethiopia.
Gon·di (gon′dē) *n.* The Dravidian language of the Gonds, closely related to Khond.
gon·do·la (gon′də·lə) *n.* **1** A long, narrow, flat-bottomed Venetian boat, high-peaked at the ends, and rowed with one oar by a gondolier who stands near the stern. **2** A large flat-bottomed river boat of light build. **3** A long, shallow, open freight car. **4** *Aeron.* The car hanging below or attached to a dirigible balloon for the accommodation of engines, crew, or the like. [<Ital. <*gondolar* rock]

TRADITIONAL VENETIAN GONDOLA

gon·do·lier (gon′də·lir′) *n.* The rower of a gondola.
Gond·wa·na (gond·wä′nə) **1** A historical region comprising most of Madhya Pradesh, India. **2** A hypothetical Paleozoic continent believed to have existed in the southern Indian Ocean.
gone (gôn, gon) Past participle of GO. **—*adj.*** **1** Passed beyond help or hope; ruined; lost: a *gone* case. **2** Marked by faintness or weakness: a *gone* sensation. **3** Ended; past; dead. **4** Depressed and hopeless. **—gone on** *Colloq.* In love with.
gone·ness (gôn′nis, gon′-) *n.* A state of weakness or exhaustion.
gon·er (gôn′ər, gon′-) *n.* *Colloq.* A person or thing that is ruined or beyond saving; one who is as good as dead.
Gon·er·il (gon′ər·il) In Shakespeare's *King Lear,* Lear's eldest daughter, a symbol of filial ingratitude.
gon·fa·lon (gon′fə·lən) *n.* An ensign fixed to a revolving frame or a crossyard, generally with two or three streamers; a banderole. Also **gon·fa·non** (gon′fə·nən). [<Ital. *gonfalone* <OHG *gundfano* war banner]
gon·fa·lon·ier (gon′fə·lə·nir′) *n.* **1** A gonfalon-bearer; a chief standard-bearer, as of the Church of Rome. **2** The title of the chief magistrate of Florence, after 1293, and of other Italian medieval republics.
gong (gông, gong) *n.* **1** A metal musical instrument shaped like a shallow dish, sounded by beating. **2** A fixed signal bell of flattened curvature. [<Malay]
Gon·gor·ism (gong′gə·riz′əm) *n.* An ornate and

euphuistic literary style of the type cultivated by the Spanish poet **Luis de Gongora y Argote**,1561– 1627.

go·nid·i·um (gō·nid′ē· əm) *n. pl.* **·nid·i·a** (-ə) *Bot.* **1** In algae, a naked or membranous-coated propagative cell produced asexually. **2** In mosses, a cell filled with green granules. **3** In lichens, one of the green algal cells of a thallus. [<NL, dim. of Gk. *gonos* seed] **—go·nid′i·al** *adj.*

gonio- *combining form* Angle; corner: *goniometry* [<Gk. *gōnia* a corner]

go·ni·om·e·ter (gō′nē· om′ə·tər) *n.* **1** An instrument for measuring angles, as in crystallography, surveying, etc., either by direct contact as in the **contact goniometer,** or more accurately, by utilizing beams of light, as in the **reflecting goniometer. 2** An electrical direction-finder for aircraft. **—go·ni·o·met·ric** (gō′nē·ə·met′rik) or **·ri·cal** *adj.*

go·ni·om·e·try (gō′nē·om′ə·trē) *n.* **1** The art of measuring angles. **2** The branch of trigonometry that treats of angles.

go·ni·on (gō′nē·on) *n.* pl. **·ni·a** (-ə) *Anat.* The tip of the angle of the lower jaw. [<NL <Gk. *gonia* an angle]

go·ni·um (gō′nē·əm) *n. pl.* **·ni·a**(-ə) *Biol.* One of the primitive germ cells which aggregate from male or female sex cells. [<NL] **—gonium** *combining form* Seed; reproductive cell: *sporogonium.* [<Gk. *gonos* seed]

gono- *combining form* Procreative; sexual: *gonophore.* Also, before vowels, *gon-*. [< Gk. *gonos* seed]

gon·o·coc·cus (gon′ə·kok′əs) *n. pl.* **·coc·ci** (-kok′sī) The Gram-negative, strictly parasitic bacterium *(Neisseria gonorrheae)* which causes gonorrhea. [<NL. See GONO-, COCCUS.]

gon·of (gon′əf) *n. Slang* A pickpocket; a thief: also spelled *ganef.* Also **gon′iff, gon′oph.** [<Hebrew *gannābh* thief]

gon·o·phore (gon′ə·fôr, -fōr) *n.* **1** *Bot.* A stalk bearing male and female organs; an elongation of the axis of a flower lifting the stamens and pistil high above the floral envelopes. **2** *Biol.* An accessory generative organ that conveys the generative products, as an oviduct or spermiduct.

gon·o·poi·et·ic (gon′ə·poi·et′ik) *adj. Biol.* Yielding or producing reproductive elements, as ova or spermatozoa.

gon·or·rhe·a (gon′ə·rē′ə) *n. Pathol.* A specific contagious inflammation of the mucous membrane of the genital organs, caused by the gonococcus and accompanied by a discharge of morbid matter. Also **gon′or·rhoe′a.** [<LL <Gk. *gonorrhoia* <*gonos* seed + *rheein* flow]

gon·or·rhe·al (gon′ə·rē′əl) *adj.* Relating to, proceeding from, or affected with, gonorrhea. Also **gon′or·rhoe′al.**

gon·sil (gon′sil) See GUNSEL.

go·ny (gō′nē) See GOONEY.

-gony *combining form* Generation or production of: *cosmogony.* [<L *-gonia* < Gk. <*gonos* seed, reproduction; cf. -GENY]

Gon·za·ga (gôn·tsä′gä) Name of a princely Italian family, rulers of Mantua from the 14th to the 17th century; especially, **Federigo II,** died 1540, duke of Mantua 1519–40; **Luigi,** 1568–91, Jesuit philosopher, canonized as *Saint Aloysius.*

Gon·zá·lez-Vi·de·la (gōn·sä′lās·bē·thä′lä), **Gabriel,** born 1898, Chilean lawyer; president of Chile 1946–52.

goo (gōō) *n. U.S. Slang* Any sticky fluid or semifluid. [? <BURGOO]

goo·ber (gōō′bər) *n. U.S.* A peanut. Also **goober pea.** [<Bantu *nguba*]

good (gŏŏd) *adj.* **bet·ter, best 1** Satisfactory in quality or kind: *good* food; *good* soil. **2** Striking in appearance: a *good* figure. **3** Morally excellent; virtuous. **4** Worthy: in *good* standing; a *good* name; a *good* family. **5** Kind; benevolent. **6** Well-behaved: a *good* child. **7** Proper; desirable: *good* manners. **8** Pleasing; agreeable: *good* company; *good* news. **9** Beneficial; salutary: *good* for business; *good* advice. **10** Favorable; approving a *good* opinion. **11** Skilful; proficient: *good* at arithmetic; a *good* swimmer. **12** Orthodox; conforming: a *good* Democrat. **13** Reliable; safe: a *good* investment. **14** Considerable; rather great in degree, measure, or extent: a *good* supply; a *good* while; a *good* beating. **15** Full: a *good* two miles off. **—as good as** Practically; virtually: It is *as good as* done. **—to make good 1** To compensate for; replace. **2** To carry out; accomplish. **3** To prove; substantiate. **4** To be successful. *—n.* **1** That which is desirable, fit, serviceable, etc.: opposed to the *bad* or *evil.* **2** Benefit; profit; advantage: for the *good* of mankind; to get some *good* out of it. **3** That which is morally or ethically desirable: to do *good.* See synonyms under PROFIT, SERVICE —for good (and all) Finally; for the last time. **—to the good** In excess of assets over liabilities: fifty dollars *to the good.* *—interj.* An exclamation of satisfaction or assent. *—adv. Illit. Dial.* Well. [OE *gōd*] **—good′ ness** *n.*

Synonyms (adj.) : able, adequate, admirable, advantageous, agreeable, beneficial, benevolent, capital, cheerful, cheering, companionable, competent, complete, considerable, convenient, dexterous, dutiful, excellent, expert, fair, favorable, fit, friendly, genial, genuine, godly, gracious, gratifying, holy, honorable, humane, immaculate, kind, lively, merciful, obliging, perfect, pious, pleasant, precious, profitable, proper, ready, real, religious, right, righteous, satisfactory, serious, serviceable, skilful, social, sound, staunch, sterling, suitable, thorough, true, unblemished, unfeigned, unimpeached, unsullied, untarnished, upright, useful, valid, valuable, virtuous, well-adapted, well-disposed, well-qualified, wholesome, worthy. *Good* may at some time be a synonym of almost any adjective in the language implying advantage, benefit, utility, worth, etc. *Good* almost always carries a silent connotation of the connection or purpose with reference to which it is affirmed. A horse that is sound, kind, and serviceable, whether swift, as a racer, or strong and heavy, as a dray horse, is a *good* horse; a ship that is *staunch* and seaworthy is a *good* ship; a use of money that brings in sure and ample returns is a *good* investment; a man of high and true moral character is a *good* man; one of very different character, if brave and skilful in war, is a *good* soldier. Compare AMIABLE, BENEFICIAL, CHOICE, EXCELLENT, HONEST, MORAL, RIGHT, USEFUL, VIRTUOUS, WELL[2]. *Antonyms:* see synonyms for BAD.

good and *Colloq.* **1** Very: He's *good and* hungry. **2** Completely: when I'm *good and* ready.

good book, the The Bible. Also **the Good Book.**

good-by (gŏŏd′bī′) *adj., n. interj. pl.* **-bys** (-bīz′) Farewell; adieu. Also **good-bye.** See synonyms under FAREWELL. [Contraction of GOD BE WITH YOU]

Good Conduct Medal A decoration awarded for efficiency, honor, and fidelity in the U.S. Army: a bronze medal on which is an eagle standing on a closed book.

good fellow A boon companion; any sociable person.

good-fel·low·ship (gŏŏd′fel′ō·ship) *n.* Merry society; companionableness. Also **good′-fel′low·hood** (-hŏŏd).

good for 1 Able or likely to produce: That patch is *good for* ten bushels. **2** Entitling (one) to, or acceptable for: a ticket *good for* ten trips, or *good for* a year. **3** Admitting to: The pass is *good for* any performance.

good-for-nothing (gŏŏd′fər·nuth′ing) *n.* A worthless person. *—adj.* Having no use or value.

Good Friday The Friday before Easter.

good-heart·ed (gŏŏd′här′tid) *adj.* Kind. **—good′heart′ed·ly** *adv.* **—good′heart′ed·ness** *n.*

Good Hope, Cape of A promontory in Western Cape Province, Republic of South Africa.

good humor A cheery, kindly mood or temper.

good-hu·mored (gŏŏd′hyōō′mərd, -yōō′-) *adj.* **1** Having or marked by a cheerful, kindly temper; pleasant. **2** Done or said in a pleasant, kindly way. **—good′hu′mored·ly** *adv.*

good·ish (gŏŏd′ish) *adj.* **1** Somewhat good; not bad; rather good. **2** Of appreciable extent; considerable.

good-look·ing (gŏŏd′lŏŏk′ing) *adj.* Attractive; handsome.

good·ly (gŏŏd′lē) *adj.* **·li·er, ·li·est 1** Having a pleasing appearance or superior qualities; comely; attractive. **2** Large; sizable. **—good′·li·ness** *n.*

good·man (gŏŏd′mən) *n. pl.* **·men** (-mən) *Archaic* **1** Master; Mr.: a familiar appellation of civility for a man below the rank of gentleman. **2** A husband; head of a family.

good-na·tured (gŏŏd′nā′chərd) *adj.* Having a pleasant disposition; not easily provoked. See synonyms under AMIABLE, PLEASANT. **—good′na′tured·ly** *adv.* **—good′na′tured·ness** *n.*

Good Neighbor Policy A policy of the U.S. government for promoting political and economic amity with the Central and South American countries: first enunciated in 1933 by President Franklin D. Roosevelt.

goods (gŏŏdz) *n. pl.* **1** Merchandise: dry *goods,* green *goods;* also, property, especially personal property. **2** A fabric: linen *goods,* dress *goods.* **3** *Colloq.* Qualifications; resources; abilities. **4** *Brit.* Freight: a *goods* train. **—to deliver the goods** To produce what was specified, promised, or expected.

Good Samaritan See under SAMARITAN.

Good Shepherd A designation of Jesus. *John* x 11, 12.

good speed Good luck: a wish for a safe journey or for success.

good-tem·pered (gŏŏd′tem′pərd) *adj.* Of a good disposition. **—good′tem′pered·ly** *adv.*

good usage Standard use: said of diction, phraseology, and idioms acceptable to cultivated speakers and writers of a language. Also **good use.**

good·wife (gŏŏd′wīf′) *n. pl.* **·wives** (-wīvz′) *Archaic* **1** The mistress of the house. **2** A title of respect for a woman: the correlative of *goodman.*

good-will (gŏŏd′wil′) *n.* The prestige and friendly relations with customers built up by a business or member of a profession.

good will 1 A desire for the well-being of others. **2** Benevolence; charity; kindly intent. See synonyms under BENEVOLENCE, FAVOR, FRIENDSHIP.

Good·win Sands (gŏŏd′win) An area of shoals, 10 miles long, in the Straits of Dover, enclosing the Downs.

good·y[1] (gŏŏd′ē) *n.* A term of civility to women of humble station, formerly used in New England. [<GOODWIFE]

good·y[2] (gŏŏd′ē) *Colloq. adj.* Mawkishly good; weakly pious: also **good′y-good′y.** *—n. pl.* **good·ies 1** A weakly good person. **2** A sweetmeat.

Good·year (gŏŏd′yir), **Charles,** 1800–60, U.S. inventor.

goo·ey (gōō′ē) *adj.* **goo·i·er, goo·i·est** *Slang* Like goo; sticky.

goof (gōōf) *n. Slang* A blockhead; simpleton; stupid, foolish person. *—v.i. v.t.* To blunder; botch. [Cf. obs. *goff* a stupid person <F *goffe*] **—goof′y** *adj.* **—goof′i·ly** *adv.* **—goof′i·ness** *n.*

goo·gly (gōō′glē) *n.* In cricket, a ball bowled at a slow pace which breaks one way and then swerves in the other. [Cf. dial. E *goggle* roll, sway]

goo·gol (gōō′gol) *n.* **1** *Math.* The number 10 raised to the hundredth power (10^{100}) or 1 followed by 100 zeros. **2** Any enormous number. [Adopted by E. Kasner, 1878–1955, U.S. mathematician, from a child's word]

goo·gol·plex (gōō′gol·pleks′) *n. Math.* The number 10 raised to the googol power: this is equivalent to the number 1 followed by a googol of zeros.

gook (gŏŏk *for def. 1,* gōōk *for def. 2*) *n.* **1** *Mil. Slang* A Filipino: later applied to Chinese, Koreans, Polynesians, etc.: a contemptuous use. **2** *U.S. Slang* Excessive or gaudy ornamentation. [? <GOO]

goon (gōōn) *n.* U.S. Slang **1** A roughneck; thug; especially, one employed during labor disputes: most commonly used in the phrase **goon squad. 2** A dolt; stupid person. [after a character created by E. C. Segar, 1894–1938, U.S. cartoonist]

goo·ney (gōō′nē) *n.* The black-footed albatross *(Diomedea nigripes)* of Pacific waters, having a sooty-brown plumage, whitish face, and saberlike wings with a spread up to 7 feet: also called *gony.* Also **gooney bird.** [Cf. dial. E *gawney* a fool]

goop (gōōp) *n. U.S. Slang* A rude, clownish, boorish person. [after a nonsensical creature created by Gelett Burgess]

goo·ral (gōō′rəl) See GORAL.

goos·an·der (gōōs·an′dər) *n.* A merganser. [Origin uncertain]

goose[1] (gōōs) *n. pl.* **geese** (gēs) **1** One of a subfamily *(Anserinae)* of wild or domesticated web-footed birds larger than ducks and smaller than swans. See GRAYLAG. ◆Collateral adjective: *anserine.* **2** The female of the goose: distinguished from *gander.* **3** *pl.* **goos·es** A tailor's heavy smoothing iron, having a curved handle. **4** A silly creature; ninny. **5** *Obs.* An old game of chance, played with dice and counters. **—Canada goose** The common North American wild goose *(Branta canadensis),* brownish-gray with black neck and head. **—to cook one's goose** *Colloq.* To spoil one's chances; ruin a person. **—the goose hangs** (or **honks) high** The prospect is good; everything is favorable. [OE *gōs*]

goose[2] (gōōs) *Slang v.t.* **goosed, goos·ing 1** To prod or poke unexpectedly from behind. **2** To accelerate an engine in irregular spurts. **—***n. pl.* **goos·es** A sudden or unexpected prod or poke in the backside. [? Special use of GOOSE[1]]

goose·ber·ry (gōōs'ber'ē, -bər·ē, gōōz'-) *n. pl.* **·ries 1** The tart fruit of a spiny shrub (genus *Grossularia* or *Ribes*). **2** This shrub. **3** A casklike portable frame around which barbed wire is wound in forming entanglements.

goose-egg (gōōs'eg') *n. Slang* A cipher; naught; zero, as in the score of a game.

goose-flesh (gōōs'flesh') *n.* A roughened condition of the skin produced by cold, fear, etc. Also **goose'-pim'ples** (-pim'pəlz), **goose'-skin'** (-skin').

goose·foot (gōōs'fōōt') *n. pl.* **·foots 1** Any plant of a widely distributed genus *(Chenopodium)* of mealy-leaved shrubs and herbs with small green flowers; the pigweed. **2** A plant of the family *(Chenopodiaceae)* of which the goosefoot is typical.

goose·grass (gōōs'gras', -gräs') *n.* Any of various herbs and grasses, especially the cleavers, the silverweed, and a weed common in the West Indies and warmer parts of the United States *(Eleusine indica).*

goose·herd (gōōs'hûrd') *n.* A tender of geese.

goose·neck (gōōs'nek') *n.* **1** A mechanical contrivance curved like a goose's neck. **2** *Naut.* A swivel forming the fastening between a boom and a mast. **3** A curved shaft for a seat on a bicycle. **4** A bent pipe or tube having a swivel joint so that its outer end may be revolved.

goose-step (gōōs'step') *n.* **1** The act of marking time with the feet. **2** A gymnastic exercise, or setting-up drill for the legs, which are alternately lifted and held straight out. **3** In some European armies, a stiff manner of marching on parade, which suggests this exercise. **—***v.i.* To move or march in this manner.

goos·y (gōō'sē) *adj.* **goos·i·er, goos·i·est 1** Like a goose. **2** Appearing like goose-flesh. **3** *Slang* Extremely nervous or ticklish: said of a person. Also **goos'ey. —goos'i·ness** *n.*

go·pher (gō'fər) *n.* **1** A burrowing American rodent (family *Geomyidae*), especially one with large cheek pouches, as the **pocket gopher** (genera *Thomomys* and *Geomys*). **2** One of various western North American ground squirrels, especially *Citellus columbianus* and related forms. **3** A large, nocturnal, burrowing land tortoise *(Gopherus polyphemus)* of the southern United States. [< F *gaufre* a honeycomb]

gopher snake 1 A nonpoisonous burrowing snake *(Drymarchon corais couperi)* of the southern United States: also called *indigo snake.* **2** Any of several nonpoisonous snakes (genus *Pituophis*) of the United States that feed on gophers and other rodents: also called *bull snake.*

Gopher State Nickname of MINNESOTA.

go·pher·wood (gō'fər·wōōd') *n.* **1** Yellowwood. **2** The wood of which Noah's ark was made. *Gen.* vi 14. [< Hebrew *gōfer, gōpher*]

go·ral (gō'rəl) *n. pl.* **·rals** or **·ral** A Himalayan goat antelope (genus *Nemorhedus*) having a short grayish coat speckled with black, short horns, and a white throat: also spelled *gooral.* [< native name]

Gor·ba·chev (gôr'bə·chof), **Mikhail Sergeyevich,** 1931-, first secretary of the Communist party 1985-

gor·cock (gôr'kok') *n.* The moorcock. [Origin uncertain]

Gor·di·an (gôr'dē·ən) *adj.* Pertaining to Gordius, or to the knot tied by him.

Gordian knot 1 The knot tied by Gordius. **2** A difficulty that can be overcome only by the application of unusual or bold measures.

Gor·di·us (gor'dē·əs) An ancient king of Phrygia who tied a knot which, according to an oracle, was to be undone only by the man who should rule Asia: Alexander the Great, unable to untie the knot, cut it in two with his sword.

Gor·don (gôr'dən), **Charles George,** 1833–85, English general; killed at Khartoum: called "Chinese Gordon." **—Lord George,** 1751–93, English political agitator; instigated "No Popery" riots in 1780.

gore[1] (gôr, gōr) *v.t.* **gored, gor·ing** To pierce, as with a tusk or a horn; wound. [ME *goren;* prob. akin to OE *gār* a spear]

gore[2] (gôr, gōr) *n.* **1** A wedge-shaped or triangular piece, as a tapering or triangular piece of land; also, in Maine and Vermont, a minor civil division. **2** A triangular piece of cloth let into a garment, sail, etc.; also, one of the separate fabric sections of a balloon, airship, or parachute. **3** *Naut.* A triangular piece of plank used in fitting a vessel. **—***v.t.* **gored, gor·ing** To cut into triangular or tapering form, as a garment, or the deck of a vessel. [OE *gāra* triangular piece of land]

gore[3] (gôr, gōr) *n.* Blood after effusion, especially clotted blood. [OE *gor* dirt, filth]

Go·rée (gô·rā') An island off the SE tip of Cape Verde, French West Africa; first French stronghold in French West Africa.

Gor·gas (gôr'gəs), **William Crawford,** 1854–1920, U.S. sanitation expert and surgeon general of U.S. Army.

gorge (gôrj) *n.* **1** The throat; gullet. **2** A narrow passage between hills; ravine. **3** The act of gorging, or that which is gorged. **4** The part of a garment about the throat. **5** A jam: an ice *gorge.* **6** An entrance into a bastion or similar part of a fortification; hence, the rear of a redan or other work. For illustration see BASTION. **7** Bait used on a gorge hook. **8** *Colloq.* A full meal. **9** In falconry, the crop of a hawk. See synonyms under VALLEY. **—***v.* **gorged, gorg·ing** *v.t.* **1** To stuff with food; glut. **2** To swallow gluttonously; gulp down. **—***v.i.* **3** To stuff oneself with food. [< OF < L *gurges* a whirlpool]

gorge hook A pair of small fishhooks joined in a heavily leaded shank.

gor·geous (gôr'jəs) *adj.* Conspicuous by splendor of colors; very beautiful; magnificent; resplendent. [< OF *gorgias* elegant; ult. origin uncertain] **—gor'geous·ly** *adv.* **—gor'geous·ness** *n.*

gorg·er (gôr'jər) *n.* **1** One who eats to excess. **2** A heavy haul of fish.

gor·get (gôr'jit) *n.* **1** A piece of armor protecting the junction of the helmet and cuirass. **2** An ornament, often crescent-shaped, worn on the neck or breast. **3** A ruff formerly worn by women. **4** *Zool.* A throat patch distinguished by color or texture. [< OF *gorgete,* dim. of *gorge* throat]

Gor·gi·as (gôr'jē·əs) 485?–380? B.C., Greek orator and sophist.

gor·gon (gôr'gən) *n.* Any hideous object, especially a repulsive-looking woman. [< GORGON]

Gor·gon (gôr'gən) In Greek mythology, one of three sisters (Stheno, Euryale, and Medusa) with serpents for hair, so hideous that they turned the beholder to stone. [< L *Gorgo, -onis* < Gk. *Gorgō* < *gorgos* terrible] ◆

gor·go·ne·an (gôr·gō'nē·ən) *adj.* Of or relating to the Gorgons; Gorgonlike. Also **gor·go'ni·an.**

gor·go·nei·on (gôr'·gə·nē'ən) *n. pl.* **·nei·a** (-nē'ə) In classical mythology, a mask or head of Medusa: an emblem or attribute of Athena, borne as the centerpiece of the aegis and on her shield. Also **gor'go·ne'um** (-nē'əm). [< Gk., neut. of *gorgoneios* of a Gorgon]

GORGONEION
The Gorgon Medusa

gor·gon·ize (gôr'gə n·īz) *v.t.* **·ized, ·iz·ing** To paralyze as if by the Gorgon's spell; petrify or transfix.

Gor·gon·zo·la (gôr'gən·zō'lə) *n.* A white Italian cheese of pressed milk somewhat like Roquefort. [from *Gorgonzola,* a town in Italy]

gor·hen (gôr'hen') *n.* The moorhen; the female red grouse. [See GORCOCK]

go·ril·la (gə·ril'ə) *n.* **1** Any of a dwindling species *(Gorilla gorilla)* of herbivorous great apes native to equatorial Africa, living in a close family groups and having an unearned reputation for aggressiveness due in part to their ritual threat displays, large size, and great strength. **2** *Slang* A tough; a brutal person; especially, a gangster. [< NL < Gk., appar. < native name]

GORILLA
(Weight up to 600 pounds; female about 1/5 less in stature and weight)

Gö·ring (gœ'ring), **Hermann,** 1893–1946, German field marshal and Nazi politician. Also spelled *Goering.*

Go·ri·zia (gō·rē'tsyä) A city in NE Italy on the Yugoslav border. *Slovenian* **Go·ri·ca** (gô·r·ē'tsä).

Gor·ki (gôr'kē), **Maxim** Pseudonym of Alexei Maximovich Pyeshkov, 1868–1936, Russian author.

Gor·ki (gôr'kē) A city on the Volga in west central Russian S.F.S.R.: formerly *Nizhni Novgorod.* Also **Gor'ky.**

Gör·litz (gœr'lits) A manufacturing city on the Neisse river in Saxony, Germany.

Gor·lov·ka (gôr·lôf'kə) A city in eastern Ukrainian S.S.R.

gor·mand (gôr'mənd), etc. See GOURMAND, etc.

gor·mand·ize (gôr'mən·dīz) *v.t.* & *v.i.* **·ized, ·iz·ing** To eat voraciously or gluttonously. **—gor'mand·iz'er** *n.*

Gor·no-Al·tai Autonomous Region (gôr'nō·äl·tī') An administrative division of SE Altai Territory; 35,800 square miles. Formerly **Oi·rot Autonomous Region** (oi'rət).

Gor·no-Ba·dakh·shan Autonomous Region (gôr'nō·bä·däkh·shän') An administrative district of SE Tadzhik S.S.R.; 23,600 square miles.

gorse (gôrs) *n. Brit.* Furze. [OE *gors(t)*] **—gors'y** *adj.*

go·ry (gôr'ē, gō'rē) *adj.* **·ri·er, ·ri·est 1** Covered or stained with gore. **2** Resembling gore. See synonyms under BLOODY. [< GORE[3]] **—go'ri·ness** *n.*

gosh (gosh) *interj.* A minced oath. [Alter. of GOD]

gos·hawk (gos'hôk', gôs'-) *n.* **1** A powerfully built, short-winged hawk (genus *Accipiter*), formerly used in falconry. **2** The eastern goshawk of North America *(Astur atricapillus).* [OE *gōshafoc* < *gōs* a goose + *hafoc* a hawk]

Go·shen (gō'shən) **1** The district in Egypt occupied by the Israelites. *Gen.* xiv 10. **2** A land of plenty.

gos·ling (goz'ling) *n.* **1** A young goose. **2** The pasqueflower. **3** A catkin or ament. **4** A silly erson.

gos·ling-green (goz'ling·grēn') *n.* A yellowish-green color.

gos·pel (gos'pəl) *n.* **1** Good news or tidings, especially the message of salvation preached by Jesus Christ and the apostles; the teaching of the Christian church. **2** *Usually cap.* A portion of the Gospels read during the eucharistic services of some churches. **3** Any doctrine concerning human welfare which is considered of great importance. **4** Anything which is regarded as absolutely true. **—***v.t.* **·peled** or **·pelled, ·pel·ing** or **·pel·ling** *Obs.* To preach the gospel to. **—***adj.* Relating to or agreeing with the gospel; evangelical; veritable. [OE *godspell* good news, trans. of Gk. *euangelion.* See EVANGEL.]

Gos·pel (gos'pəl) *n.* A narrative of Christ's life and teaching as given in one of the first four books of the New Testament.

gos·pel·er (gos'pəl·ər) *n.* **1** An ardent adherent of the Reformation, as distinguished from a Roman Catholic. **2** The cleric who reads the Gospel at a church service. 3 An evangelist; missionary. Also **gos′pel·ler.**

Gos·plan (gôs·plän′) *n.* An economic planning commission of the Soviet Union, established in 1921, one of its functions now being the direction of the Five-Year Plans. [<Russian *gos(udar)* national + *plan* a plan]

gos·po·din (gôs′pô·dēn′) *n. Russian* Mister: since 1917, a courtesy title for non-Russians.

Gos·port (gos′pôrt, -pōrt) A port and municipal borough in SE Hampshire, England: yacht-building center and site of a naval base.

gos·sa·mer (gos′ə·mər) *n.* **1** An exceedingly fine thread or web of spider's silk that may float in the air. **2** A fine fabric like gauze. **3** A thin waterproof outer garment. —*adj.* Thin and light as gauze; flimsy: also **gos′sa·mer·y.** [<ME *gossamer* Indian summer, lit. goose summer; appar. so called because often seen in autumn when geese are in season]

gos·san (gos′ən, goz′-) *n. Mining* Decomposed material, usually reddish or ferruginous, forming the upper part of mineral veins and ore deposits. [<Cornish]

gos·san·if·er·ous (gos′ən·if′ər·əs) *adj.* Yielding or producing gossan.

Gosse (gôs, gos), **Sir Edmund William,** 1849–1928, English poet and critic.

gos·sip (gos′əp) *n.* **1** Familiar or idle talk; groundless rumor; mischievous tattle. **2** One who tattles or talks idly: also **gos′sip·er.** **3** *Archaic* A boon companion. —*v.i.* To talk idly, usually about the affairs of others; be a gossip. —*v.t.* To repeat as gossip. See synonyms under BABBLE. [OE *godsibb* a baptismal sponsor < *god* God + *sib* a relative]

gos·sip·ing (gos′əp·ing) *n.* **1** Gossipy talk; a prating. **2** *Brit.Dial.* A christening.

gos·sip·mong·er (gos′əp·mung′gər, -mong′-) *n.* A zealous spreader of gossip.

gos·sip·y (gos′əp·ē) *adj.* Devoted to gossip; chatty.

gos·soon (go·sōōn′) *n. Irish* A lad; a serving boy. [Alter. of F *garçon* a boy]

got (got) Past tense and past participle of GET. ◆ **have got** In the sense of must, *have got* is in wide colloquial use to add emphasis: I *have* (or *I've*) *got* to leave. In the sense of possess, *have got* is still more common in informal speech: We *have got* (or *We've got*) plenty and intend to keep it. This usage has long been challenged on the grounds (1) that *have got* properly means "have acquired," and (2) that *got* is superfluous, since *have* alone would convey the same meaning. The usage is now defended as acceptable colloquial idiom on the grounds that *have* is so much used as an auxiliary that it has lost much of its primary sense of possess, and *got* therefore serves to restore and emphasize this meaning. When *have* is dropped, and *got* stands alone in the sense of must or of possess, it is illiterate, or at best dialectal, as in "I *got* rhythm" or "All God's chillun *got* wings."

Go·ta·ma (gō′tə·mə) See GAUTAMA.

Gö·te·borg (yœ′tə·bôr′y′) A port in SW Sweden. Also **Goth·en·burg** (got′ən·bûrg, goth′-).

Goth (goth, gôth) *n.* **1** A member of an ancient East Germanic people, originating in the basin of the Vistula, that overran the Roman Empire in the third and fourth centuries: divided into the Ostrogoths, or **East Goths,** and Visigoths, or **West Goths.** **2** A barbarian; rude or uncivilized person. [<LL *Gothi* the Goths < Gk. *Gothoi* <Gothic]

Go·tha (gō′tä) A city in the former state of Thuringia, SW East Germany.

Goth·am (goth′əm, gō′thəm) **1** A village near Nottingham, England, noted in stories for the foolishness of its inhabitants. **2** New York City. —**Goth′am·ite** (-īt) *n.*

Goth·ic (goth′ik) *adj.* **1** Of or pertaining to the Goths or to their language. **2** Rude, barbaric. **3** Of or pertaining to Gothic architecture. **4** *Obs.* Germanic or Teutonic. **5** Romantic; medieval: distinguished from *classic.* —*n.* **1** The East Germanic language of the Goths, known chiefly from fragments of a translation of the Bible made by Bishop Ulfilas in the fourth century: extinct by the ninth century. **2** The pointed style in architecture. —**Goth′i·cal·ly** *adv.*

Gothic arch See POINTED ARCH.

Gothic architecture The pointed type of medieval architecture prevalent in Europe from the full evolution of the Romanesque style until the Renaissance, or roughly from 1200 to 1500.

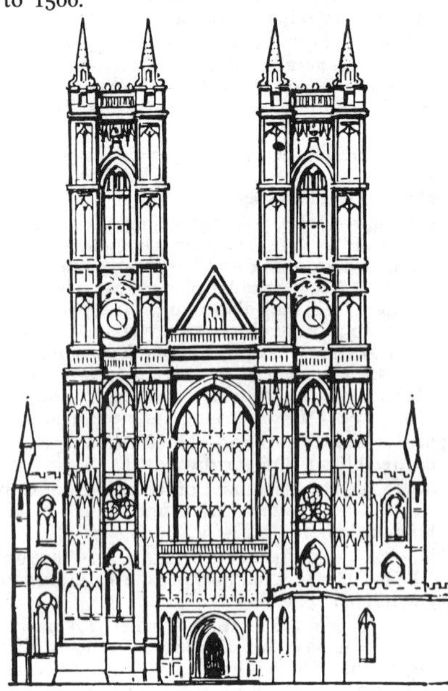

GOTHIC ARCHITECTURE
Westminster Abbey, London, 13th–15th centuries A.D.

Goth·i·cism (goth′ə·siz′əm) *n.* **1** A Gothic idiom. **2** Imitation of or inclination for Gothic architecture. **3** Rudeness of manners; barbarousness.

Goth·i·cize (goth′ə·sīz) *v.t.* **·cized, ·ciz·ing** To make Gothic.

Gothic novel A type of romance developed in the late 18th and early 19th centuries, characterized by the supernatural and grotesque in a medieval setting: first used by Horace Walpole in *"The Castle of Otranto: A Gothic Story,"* 1764.

gothic type **1** *U.S.* A type face having all the strokes of uniform width and without serifs. **2** *Brit.* Black letter.

go·thite (gō′thīt) See GOETHITE.

Got·land (got′lənd, *Sw.* gôt′länd) A Swedish island in the Baltic Sea; 1,224 square miles; chief town, Visby. Formerly **Gott′land, Goth′·land.**

got·ten (got′n) Past participle of GET. ◆ *Gotten,* obsolete in British, is current in American English in the sense of "obtained"; We have *gotten* the necessary funds. *Gotten* is also used in the sense of "become": He has *gotten* fat.

Göt·ter·däm·mer·ung (gœt′ər·dem′ər·ōōng) *German* Twilight of the gods. See RING OF THE NIBELUNG.

Gott·fried (gôt′frēt) German form of GODFREY.

Göt·ting·en (gœt′ing·ən) A city in Lower Saxony, West Germany.

Gott·lieb (gôt′lēp) Danish and German equivalent of THEOPHILUS. [<G, love of God]

Götz von Berlichingen (gœts fôn ber′likh·ing·ən) See BERLICHINGEN, GÖTZ VON.

gouache (gwäsh) *n.* **1** A method of water-color painting with opaque colors mixed with water and gum. **2** A painting executed by this method, or the pigment used for it. [<F <Ital. *guazzo* a spray <L *aquatio* a watering < *aqua* water]

Gou·da cheese (gou′də, gōō′-) A mild cheese similar to Edam cheese.

Gou·dy (gou′dē), **Frederic William,** 1865–1947, U. S. type designer.

gouge (gouj) *n.* **1** A chisel having a curved cutting edge. **2** A groove made, or as made, by it. **3** A layer of soft clay or decomposed rock along the wall of a vein; selvage. **4** A tool for stamping metal. **5** *U.S. Colloq.* Stealing or cheating; also, one who cheats or defrauds. —*v.t.* **gouged, goug·ing** **1** To cut or scoop out with or as with a gouge. **2** To scoop, force, or tear out as with a gouge: to *gouge* out an eye. **3** *U.S. Colloq.* To cheat in a bargain; swindle. [<F <LL *gulbia,* prob. <Celtic] —**goug′er** *n.*

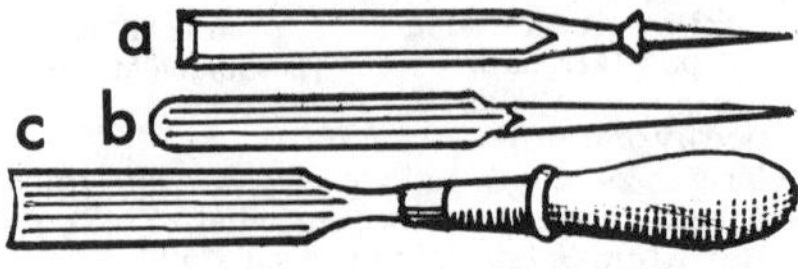

TYPES OF GOUGES
a. Paring. *b.* Turning. *c.* Firmer.

Gou·jon (gōō·zhôn′), **Jean,** 1515?–72?, French sculptor.

gou·lash (gōō′läsh, -lash) *n.* A stew made with beef or veal and seasoned with paprika: generally known as **Hungarian goulash.** Also spelled *gulash.* [<Magyar *gulyas (hus)* shepherd's (meat)]

Gould (gōōld), **Jay,** 1836–92, U. S. financier.

Gou·nod (gōō·nō′), **Charles François,** 1818–1893, French composer.

gou·ra·mi (gōōr′ə·mē) *n. pl.* **·mis** **1** A large, air-breathing, fresh-water Asian fish (*Osphromenus olfax*) which builds nests and is highly esteemed as food. **2** Any of several related fishes cultivated in home aquaria, as the banded gourami (*Colisa fasciata*), the three-spot gourami (*Trichogaster trichopterus*), and the dwarf gourami (*C. lalia*). [< Malay *gurami*]

gourd (gôrd, gōrd, gōōrd) *n.* **1** The melonlike fruit of certain plants of the cucurbit family, having a hard rind, as the pumpkin, squash, etc. **2** The fruit of any of various bottle gourds of the genus *Lagenaria.* **3** The plant that bears this fruit, or a vessel, as a dipper, made of its shell. **4** A hollow die used by gamblers for cheating. [<F *gourde* <L *cucurbita* gourd]

gourde (gōōrd) *n.* The monetary unit of Haiti.

gour·mand (gōōr′mənd, *Fr.* gōōr·män′) *n.* **1** A glutton. **2** Loosely, an epicure. Also spelled *gormand.* [<F, a glutton]

gour·met (gōōr·mā′, *Fr.* gōōr·me′) *n.* An epicure. [<F <OF, a winetaster]

Gour·mont (gōōr·môn′), **Remy de,** 1858–1915, French novelist and critic.

gout (gout) *n.* **1** *Pathol.* A disease of metabolism characterized by inflammation of a joint, as of the great toe, paroxysmal recurrent pain, and an excess of uric acid in the blood. Also called *podagra.* **2** A drop; clot. [<F *goutte* a drop <L *gutta*]

goût (gōō) *n. French* Taste; relish.

goutte (gōōt) *n. Her.* A subordinate ordinary representing a drop or tear. [<F. See GOUT.]

gout·y (gou′tē) *adj.* **gout·i·er, gout·i·est** **1** Affected with gout. **2** Of or pertaining to the gout. **3** Swollen; protuberant. —**gout′i·ly** *adv.* —**gout′i·ness** *n.*

gou·ver·nante (gōō·ver·nänt′) *n. French* **1** A chaperon. **2** A governess; housekeeper.

Gov·an (guv′ən) A suburb of Glasgow, Scotland.

gov·ern (guv′ərn) *v.t.* **1** To rule or control by right or authority: to *govern* a kingdom. **2** To control or influence morally or physically; direct: His ideals *govern* his life. **3** To serve as a rule or regulation for; determine: This decision *governed* the case. **4** To hold back; curb, as one's temper. **5** *Gram.* **a** To regulate (a word) as to form: In *Take me home,* the verb *governs* the pronoun. **b** To require (a particular case, mood, or form): In English, a transitive verb *governs* the objective case of a pronoun. —*v.i.* **6** To exercise authority. [<OF *governer* <L *gubernare* steer <Gk. *kubernaein*] —**gov′ern·a·ble** *adj.*

Synonyms: command, control, curb, direct, influence, manage, reign, restrain, rule, sway. A person *commands* another when he has, or claims, the right to make that other do his will, with power of inflicting penalty if not obeyed; he *controls* another whom he can prevent from doing anything contrary to his will; he *governs* one whom he actually does cause to obey his will. A wise mother, by gentle means, *sways* the feelings and *molds* the lives of her children; to be able to *manage* servants is an important element of good housekeeping. The word *reign,* once so absolute, now simply denotes that one holds the official station of sovereign with or without effective power. See COMMAND, REGULATE. *Antonyms*: comply, obey, submit, yield.

gov·ern·ance (guv′ər·nəns) *n.* **1** Exercise of authority; direction; control. **2** Manner or system of government or regulation.

gov·ern·ess (guv′ər·nis) *n.* A woman employed in a private home to train and instruct children. —*v.i.* To act or serve as a governess.

gov·ern·ment (guv′ərn·mənt, -ər-) *n.* **1** The authoritative direction of the affairs of men in a community; rule and administration. **2** The governing body of a community, considered either as a continuous entity or as the group of administrators currently in power. **3** The form by which a community is managed: democratic *government*; ecclesiastical *government*. **4** A governed territory. **5** Management; control: the *government* of one's behavior. **6** *Gram.* A syntactical relation which requires a word to assume a certain case or mood when related to another word.

gov·ern·men·tal (guv′ərn·men′təl, -ər-) *adj.* Relating or pertaining to government; made by or proceeding from the government. —**gov′ern·men′tal·ly** *adv.*

Government House In British colonies, the official residence of a governor.

Government Issue Something which is furnished by a governmental agency, as uniforms to Army personnel. Abbr. *G.I.*

Government land Land owned by the U. S. government, available to the public at low cost and under specific conditions.

gov·er·nor (guv′ər·nər) *n.* **1** One who governs; especially, the chief executive of a state or colony. **2** *Mech.* A device for regulating the speed of an engine, motor, compressor, etc., usually by the centrifugal force of two or more balls or weights, which so control the motive fluid as to reduce speed: also called *ball-governor.* **3** *Brit. Colloq.* One's father. **4** *Brit. Colloq.* An employer. See synonyms under MASTER.

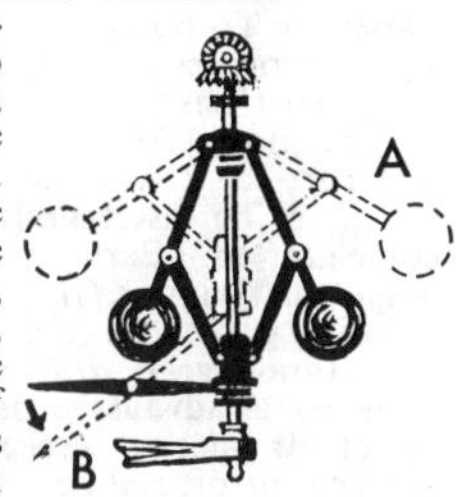

BALL–GOVERNOR
The balls, revolving, raise levers to position *A*, thus reducing excess speed of engine by closing valve at *B*.

governor general A governor who has deputy or lieutenant governors under him: the *governor general* of Canada. Also *Brit.* **gov′er·nor-gen′er·al.** —**gov′er·nor-gen′er·al·ship** *n.*

gov·er·nor·ship (guv′ər·nər·ship) *n.* The office of a governor; his term of office; or the territory under his jurisdiction.

Governors Island A small island at the mouth of the East River, New York Harbor; site of a United States military reservation and historic Fort Jay.

gow·an (gou′ən) *n. Scot.* **1** The English or garden daisy. **2** A yellow flower of any one of several species. Also **gow′un.** —**gow′an·y** *adj.*

gowd (goud) *n. Scot.* Gold. —**gow·den** (gou′dən), **gow′dun** *adj.*

Gow·er (gou′ər, gōr), **John,** 1325?–1408, English poet.

gowf (gouf) *Scot. n.* Golf. —*v.t.* To strike as in playing golf; beat; strike.

gowk (gouk) *n. Scot.* **1** The cuckoo. **2** A fool; simpleton.

gowk·it (gouk′it) *adj. Scot.* Foolish.

gown (goun) *n.* **1** A woman's dress or outer garment, especially when elaborate or costly. **2** A long and loose outer robe worn as a distinctive or official habit, as by clergymen, judges, barristers, professors, or university students, especially in England. See GENEVA GOWN. **3** Any loose outer garment or wrapper, especially when long: a dressing *gown.* **4** *Obs.* Dress; garb: the *gown* of humility. **5** *Obs.* A toga.—*v.t.* & *v.i.* To dress in a gown. [<OF *goune* < Med. L *gunna* a loose robe]

gowns·man (gounz′mən) *n. pl.* **·men** (-mən) **1** One who wears a gown professionally, as a clergyman, a graduate or student in a university, or a barrister. **2** *Brit.* A collegian as distinguished from a townsman: also **gown′·man.**

goy (goi) *n. pl.* **goy·im** (goi′im) *Yiddish* A non-Jew; a Gentile.

Go·ya (gô′yə), **Francisco José de,** 1746–1828, Spanish painter and etcher: full surname *Goya y Lucientes.*

Go·yaz (goi·äs′) A former name for GOIÁS.

Graaf·i·an follicle (grä′fē·ən) *Anat.* The small sac in which the ova are developed in the ovary. Also **Graafian vesicle.** [after Regnier de *Graaf,* 1641–73, Dutch physician and anatomist]

graal (grāl) See GRAIL.

grab[1] (grab) *v.* **grabbed, grab·bing** *v.t.* **1** To grasp or seize forcibly or suddenly. **2** To take possession of violently or dishonestly. —*v.i.* **3** To make a sudden grasp. See synonyms under GRASP. —*n.* **1** The act of grabbing, or that which is grabbed. **2** A dishonest or unlawful taking possession or acquisition. **3** An apparatus for grappling. [Cf. MDu. *grabben* grip] —**grab′ber** *n.*

grab[2] (grab) *n.* A coasting vessel of the East Indies, with two or three masts. [<Arabic *ghurāb*]

grab-bag (grab′bag′) *n.* A bag or box filled with miscellaneous articles, from which one draws something unseen on payment of a price for each grab or draw.

grab·ble (grab′əl) *v.i.* **grab·bled, grab·bling 1** To feel about with the hands; grope. **2** To flounder; sprawl. [Cf. Du. *grabbelen,* freq. of *grabben* grab]

gra·ben (grä′bən) *n. Geol.* A valleylike depression of the land caused by the subsidence of a series of blocks of the earth's crust. [<G, ditch]

grab rope *Naut.* A rope which runs along the side of a vessel for the use of boats coming alongside.

Grac·chi (grak′ī) Two Roman political reformers, **Gaius Sempronius Grac·chus** (grak′əs), 153–121 B.C., and his brother **Tiberius Sempronius Gracchus,** 163–133 B.C.

grace (grās) *n.* **1** Beauty or harmony of form, attitude, etc.; ease and elegance of speech. **2** Any excellence or attractive characteristic, quality, or endowment. **3** Unmerited favor or good will; clemency; hence, any kindness, favor, or service freely rendered. **4** *Theol.* The unmerited love and favor of God in Christ; hence, free gift; the divine influence acting within the heart, to regenerate, sanctify, and keep it; a state of reconciliation to God through Christ; the power or disposition to exercise saving faith and to live the Christian life; any spiritual gift or attainment. See CHARISMA. **5** A short prayer before or after a meal. **6** Something granted in the exercise of favor or discretion and not as of right. **7** A courteous or gracious demeanor; graciousness; demeanor in general. **8** *Music* An ornament or embellishment, as a trill, turn, or the like. **9** *Obs.* Physical virtue or efficiency. See synonyms under FAVOR, MERCY. —**good graces** Favorable regard; friendship. —*v.t.* **graced, grac·ing 1** To add grace and beauty to; adorn. **2** To dignify; honor. **3** *Music* To ornament with grace notes or other embellishments. [<OF <L *gratia* favor]

Grace (grās) *n.* Goodness; clemency: a title applied in Great Britain and Ireland to a duke, duchess, or archbishop, formerly to the sovereign, and used with a possessive adjective: His *Grace.*

Grace (grās) A feminine personal name. [<L, favor]

grâce à Dieu (gräs à dyœ′) *French* Thanks to God.

grace cup A cup passed at the end of a meal for the drinking of the concluding health.

grace·ful (grās′fəl) *adj.* Characterized by grace; elegant; easy; becoming. —**grace′ful·ly** *adv.* —**grace′ful·ness** *n.*

Synonym: beautiful. That which is *graceful* is marked by elegance and harmony, with ease of action, attitude, or posture, or delicacy of form. *Graceful* commonly suggests motion or the possibility of motion; *beautiful* may apply to absolute fixity; a landscape or a blue sky is *beautiful,* but neither is *graceful. Graceful* commonly applies to beauty as addressed to the eye, but we often speak of a *graceful* poem or a *graceful* compliment. *Graceful* applies to the perfection of motion, especially of the lighter motions, which convey no suggestion of stress or strain, and are in harmonious curves. Apart from the thought of motion, *graceful* denotes a pleasing harmony of outline, proportion, etc., with a certain degree of delicacy; a Hercules is massive, an Apollo is *graceful.* We speak of a *graceful* attitude, *graceful* drapery. Compare BEAUTIFUL, BECOMING. *Antonyms*: see synonyms for AWKWARD.

graceful tree frog A tiny frog (*Hyla gracilenta*) of Australia, often kept as a pet.

grace·less (grās′lis) *adj.* Lacking grace, charm, or tact. —**grace′less·ly** *adv.* —**grace′less·ness** *n.*

grace note *Music* An ornamental note introduced as an embellishment, but not actually essential to the harmony or melody; an appoggiatura.

Grac·es (grā′siz) In Greek mythology, three sister goddesses: Aglaia (splendor), Euphrosyne (joy), and Thalia (abundance). Also **the three Graces.**

gra·ci·as (grä′thē·äs, -sē·əs) *interj. Spanish* Thanks.

grac·ile (gras′il) *adj.* Gracefully slender or slight. [<L *gracilis* slender] —**grac′ile·ness, gra·cil·i·ty** (grə·sil′ə·tē) *n.*

Gra·cio·sa (grə·syô′zə) An island in the central Azores; 27 square miles.

gra·ci·os·i·ty (grā′shē·os′ə·tē) *n. Rare* The quality or state of being gracious.

gra·ci·o·so (grā′shē·ō′sō, *Sp.* grä·thyō′sō) *n. pl.* **·sos 1** A clown in Spanish comedy. **2** A low comic character. **3** *Obs.* A favorite. [<Sp., graceful]

gra·cious (grā′shəs) *adj.* **1** Disposed to show grace or favor; full of kindness or love. **2** Courteous and condescending; kind; affable. **3** Possessing or exhibiting divine grace. **4** *Obs.* Happy; fortunate. See synonyms under BLAND, HUMANE, MERCIFUL, POLITE, PROPITIOUS. [<OF <L *gratiosus* <*gratia* favor] —**gra′cious·ly** *adv.* —**gra′cious·ness** *n.*

grack·le (grak′əl) *n.* **1** One of various Old World starlinglike birds (family *Sturnidae*), usually black or black and white, as the myna. **2** An American blackbird; especially, the **purple grackle** (*Quiscalus quiscula*), with vivid iridescent plumage. [<NL *Gracula,* name of a genus <*graculus* a jackdaw]

gra·date (grā′dāt) *v.t.* & *v.i.* **·dat·ed, ·dat·ing** To pass or cause to pass imperceptibly from one shade or degree of intensity to another. —*adj.* Graduated according to size.

gra·da·tion (grā·dā′shən) *n.* **1** Orderly or continuous succession, progression, or arrangement, as according to size, quality, state, rank, or proficiency; regular advance upward or downward, as by steps or degrees. **2** A step, degree, rank, or relative position in an order or series; grade. **3** In art and architecture, a relative subordination or arrangement of parts so as to produce a desired effect; such a blending and variation of color and light as will produce effects of depth, relief, etc. **4** *Ling.* Ablaut. [<F <L *gradatio, -onis* a going by steps <*gradus* a step] —**gra·da′tion·al** *adj.* —**gra·da′tion·al·ly** *adv.*

grad·a·to·ry (grad′ə·tôr′ē, -tō′rē, grā′də-) *adj.* **1** Proceeding by gradations; gradual. **2** Adapted for stepping.

grade (grād) *n.* **1** A degree or step in any scale, as of quality, ability, dignity, etc. **2** A group of persons of the same rank or station: all *grades* of society. **3** Rate or rank in the U. S. armed forces. See page 548. **4** A class of things of the same quality or value: a high *grade* of wool. **5** *U.S.* **a** One of the divisions of an elementary or secondary school covering a year of work. **b** The pupils in such a division. **6** *pl. U.S.* A grade school. **7** A scholastic rating or mark on an examination or in a course. **8** A part of a road, track, or surface inclined to the horizontal. **9** The degree of inclination of a road or the like as compared with the horizontal. **10** *Agric.* An animal (as a cow or sheep) or a class of animals produced by crossing a common or other breed with a pure or better breed. —**at grade** At the same point of grade or inclination: a road crossing another *at grade.* —*v.* **grad·ed, grad·ing** *v.t.* **1** To arrange or classify by grades or degrees, according to size or quality. **2** To assign a grade to. **3** To gradate. **4** To make level or properly inclined: to *grade* a road. **5** To improve by crossbreeding with better stock: often with *up*: to *grade* up a herd of cattle. —*v.i.* **6** To take rank; be of a grade. [<F <L *gradus* step] —**grad′er** *n.*

-grade *combining form Zool.* Manner of walking: *plantigrade.* [<L *gradi* walk]

grade crossing A place where a road crosses a railroad on the same level.

grad·ed (grā′did) *adj.* **1** Leveled, as a road or railroad. **2** Improved by crossbreeding.

grade school An elementary school.

gra·di·ent (grā′dē·ənt) *adj.* **1** Running on legs; adapted for walking or running: a *gradient* animal or automaton, *gradient* feet. **2** Rising or descending gently or by degrees: a *gradient* road. —*n.* **1** A grade: a *gradient* of 1 to 50. **2** An incline; also, a ramp. **3** *Meteorol.* A rate of change in certain elements affecting weather conditions, as pressure, temperature, etc.: usually with reference to horizontal distance. [<L *gradiens, -entis,* ppr. of *gradi* walk]

gra·din (grā′din, *Fr.* grà·dan′) *n.* **1** One of a series of rising seats or steps, as in an amphitheater. **2** A raised step back of an altar; superaltar. Also **gra′dine** (-dēn). [<F <Ital. *gradino,* dim. of *grado* <L *gradus* a step]

gra·di·om·e·ter (grā′dē·om′ə·tər) *n.* **1** A surveyor's instrument for determining grades: also **gra·dom·e·ter** (grā·dom′ə·tər). **2** An instrument for measuring the gradient of the field of gravity in a given locality.

grad·u·al (graj′ōō·əl) *adj.* **1** Proceeding by steps or degrees; moving or changing slowly and regularly; slow. **2** Divided into degrees; graduated. —*n. Eccl.* **1** An antiphon sung at the Eucharist after the epistle. **2** A book containing the music for the sung parts of the Eucharist. *Ital.* **gra·dua·le** (grä·dwä′lā) *n.* [<Med. L *gradualis* <L *gradus* a step] —**grad′u·al·ly** *adv.* —**grad′u·al·ness** *n.*

Synonyms (adj.): continuous, moderate, progressive, regular, slow. See SLOW. *Antonyms*: instant, instantaneous, momentary, prompt, quick, sudden.

grad·u·and (graj′ōō·ənd) *n. Canadian* A student who is about to graduate.

grad·u·ate (graj′ōō·āt) *v.* **·at·ed, ·at·ing** *v.t.* **1** To grant a diploma or degree to upon completion of a course of study, as at a college. **2** To mark in units or degrees, as a thermometer scale; calibrate. **3** To arrange into grades or divisions, as according to size or quality. —*v.i.* **4** To receive a diploma or degree upon completion of a course of study. **5** To change by degrees. —*n.* (graj′ōō·it) **1** One who has been graduated by an institution of learning, or who has completed any prescribed academic or professional course. **2** A graduated vessel used in measuring liquids, etc. —*adj.* (graj′ōō·it) **1** Holding a bachelor's degree: a *graduate* student. **2** Designed for or pertaining to graduate students: a *graduate* school. [<Med. L *graduatus,* pp. of *graduare* <L *gradus* step, degree] —**grad′u·a′tor** *n.*

graduate nurse A nurse who has graduated from a recognized school of nursing.

graduate student A student working toward an advanced degree at a graduate school, as in a university or college.

grad·u·a·tion (graj′ōō·ā′shən) *n.* **1** The act of graduating, as a scale, or state of being graduated, as a series of colors. **2** An equal division or dividing line in a graduated scale. **3** In education, commencement.

gra·dus (grā′dəs) *n.* **1** A dictionary of quantities in prosody. **2** *Music* A collection of graded exercises. [<L *Gradus (ad Parnassum)* step (to Parnassus), title of a Latin dictionary, 1702]

Grae·ae (grē′ē) In Greek mythology, the three daughters of Phorcus who guarded the habitation of the Gorgons and had but one eye and one tooth among them: also spelled *Graiae.* Also **Græ′æ.**

Grae·cia Mag·na (grē′shə mag′nə) In classical geography, the Greek colonies in southern Italy: also *Magna Graecia.* Also **Græ′cia Mag′na.**

Grae·cize (grē′sīz) See GRECIZE.

Graeco- See GRECO-.

Graf (gräf) *n. pl.* **Graf·en** (gräf′ən) A count: title of a German or Swedish nobleman equivalent in rank to an English earl or a French count.

graff (gräf) *n. Scot.* A grave.

graf·fi·to (grə·fē′tō) *n. pl.* **·ti** (-tē) **1** Any design or scribbled motto, etc., drawn on a wall or other exposed surface. **2** *Archeol.* A pictograph scratched on an escarpment, wall, or any other surface. [<Ital. <*graffio* a scratch, ult. <Gk. *graphein* write]

graft[1] (graft, gräft) *n.* **1** *Bot.* **a** A shoot inserted into a tree or plant, so as to become a living part of it. **b** The place where the cion is inserted in a stock. **2** Something amalgamated with a foreign stock: The family was a Spanish *graft* upon an American tree. **3** *Surg.* **a** A juncture between a piece of animal tissue cut from a living person or animal and the tissue of another subject. **b** The piece so implanted. —*v.t.* **1** *Bot.* **a** To insert (a cion or bud) into a tree or plant. **b** To insert a shoot or shoots upon: to *graft* a tree with a new variety. **c** To obtain by such process. **2** *Surg.* To transplant tissue removed from one part, or from one animal, to another. —*v.i.* **3** To insert grafts. **4** To be or become grafted. [Earlier *graff* <OF *grafe* <LL *graphium* stylus <Gk. *grapheion* <*graphein* write] —**graft′age** (-ij) *n.* —**graft′er** *n.*

GRAFTING
a. Method of cutting for ligule-grafting, showing shape of ligule.
b. Graft and stock bound together.
c. Protection of the union by a ball of clay.

graft[2] (graft, gräft) *U.S. n.* **1** The attainment of personal advantage or profit by dishonest or unfair means, especially through one's political or official connections. **2** Anything thus gained. **3** *Austral. Slang* Work. —*v.t.* **1** To obtain by graft. —*v.i.* **2** To practice graft. **3** *Austral. Slang* To work. [Cf. dial. E *graft* work, livelihood] —**graft′er** *n.*

grafting wax A composition of beeswax, tallow, etc., used in grafting to exclude air.

TABLE OF COMPARATIVE GRADES (UNITED STATES ARMED SERVICES)

Army	Air Force	Marine Corps	Navy	Coast Guard
General of the Army	General of the Air Force	(no equivalent)	Admiral of the Fleet	(no equivalent)
General	General	General	Admiral	Admiral
Lieutenant General	Lieutenant General	Lieutenant General	Vice Admiral	Vice Admiral
Major General	Major General	Major General	Rear Admiral (upper half)	Rear Admiral (upper half)
Brigadier General	Brigadier General	Brigadier General	Rear Admiral (lower half)	Rear Admiral (lower half)
Colonel	Colonel	Colonel	Captain	Captain
Lieutenant Colonel	Lieutenant Colonel	Lieutenant Colonel	Commander	Commander
Major	Major	Major	Lieutenant Commander	Lieutenant Commander
Captain	Captain	Captain	Lieutenant	Lieutenant
1st Lieutenant	1st Lieutenant	1st Lieutenant	Lieutenant (Junior Grade)	Lieutenant (Junior Grade)
2nd Lieutenant	2nd Lieutenant	2nd Lieutenant	Ensign	Ensign
Chief Warrant Officer W-4 Chief Warrant Officer W-3 Chief Warrant Officer W-2 Warrant Officer W-1	SAME	SAME	SAME	SAME
Sergeant Major of the Army				
Sergeant Major or Specialist 9	Chief Master Sergeant	Master Gunnery Sergeant Sergeant Major	Master Chief Petty Officer	Master Chief Petty Officer
Master Sergeant First Sergeant or Specialist 8	Senior Master Sergeant	Master Sergeant First Sergeant	Senior Chief Petty Officer	Senior Chief Petty Officer
Sergeant First Class Platoon Sergeant or Specialist 7	Master Sergeant	Gunnery Sergeant	Chief Petty Officer	Chief Petty Officer
Staff Sergeant or Specialist 6	Technical Sergeant	Staff Sergeant	Petty Officer First Class	Petty Officer First Class
Sergeant or Specialist 5	Staff Sergeant	Sergeant	Petty Officer Second Class	Petty Officer Second Class
Corporal or Specialist 4	Airman First Class	Corporal	Petty Officer Third Class	Petty Officer Third Class
Private First Class	Airman Second Class	Lance Corporal	Seaman	Seaman
Private E-2	Airman Third Class	Private First Class	Seaman Apprentice	Seaman Apprentice
Private E-1	Airman Basic	Private	Seaman Recruit	Seaman Recruit

Gra·ham (grā′əm), **John,** 1650?–89, Viscount Dundee, Scottish soldier: called "Graham of Claverhouse." **—Thomas,** 1805–69, Scottish chemist. **—William Franklin,** born 1918, U.S. evangelist: called **Billy Graham.**

Gra·hame (grā′əm), **Kenneth,** 1859–1932, English author.

graham flour Unbolted wheat flour. [after Sylvester *Graham,* 1794–1851, U.S. clergyman and vegetarian]

Graham Land A British name for PALMER PENINSULA. Also **Graham Coast.**

Grai·ae (grā′ē, grī′ē) See GRAEAE.

Gra·ian Alps (grā′ən, grī′-) A section of the Alps on the French-Italian border; highest peak, 13,324 feet.

grail (grāl) *n.* A broad bowl or chalice; specifically, in medieval legend, the **Holy Grail,** or *Sangreal,* the cup used by Jesus at the Last Supper, preserved by Joseph of Arimathea, who received some of Christ's blood into it at the Crucifixion, and brought it to Britain, after which it disappeared because of the impurity of its guardians. Also spelled *graal.* [<OF *graal* <Med. L *gradalis;* ult. origin uncertain]

grain (grān) *n.* **1** Any very small, hard mass: a *grain* of sand; especially, a seed resembling this; a kernel. **2** Any of the common cereals; specifically, the seed or fruit of any cereal, collectively, as wheat, oats, rye, barley, etc. **3** A minute particle. **4** A unit of weight, equal to 1/20 of a scruple apothecary: 1 oz. apothecary or troy contains 480 grains; 1 oz. avoirdupois contains 437.5 grains. **5** A unit of weight for pearls, equal to 1/4 of a metric carat or 50 milligrams. **6** The arrangement of the particles of a body of granular texture; hence, degree of coarseness, roughness, fineness of surface, direction or set of fibers, etc.: the *grain* of wood or leather. **7** The innate quality or character of a thing. **8** The cochineal insect, originally mistaken for a seed; hence, a red or purple dye, or any fast color. **9** *pl.* Refuse grain or malt after brewing. **10** Natural disposition; temper. See synonyms under PARTICLE, TEMPER. **—in grain** or **in the grain** **1** Set; fixed: said of dye. **2** Figuratively, innate; deeply rooted; ineradicable. *—v.t.* **1** To form into grains; granulate. **2** To paint or stain in imitation of the grain of wood, marble, etc. **3** In leather-making: **a** To scrape off hair from with a grainer. **b** To soften or raise the grain or pattern of. *—v.i.* **4** To form grains. [Fusion of OF *grain* a seed and *graine* seed, grain, both <L *granum* a seed]

grain alcohol Alcohol (def. 1), especially if produced by the fermentation of a cereal grain.

Grain Coast The coastal region of Liberia and some of Sierra Leone: so called for its former trade in grains of paradise.

graine (grān) *n.* The eggs of the silkworm. [<F, grain]

grain elevator **1** A warehouse or series of storage tanks for the storage, lifting, and distribution of grain. **2** A system of belt conveyors to carry grain to and from storage bins.

grain·er (grā′nər) *n.* **1** One who imitates the grain of wood with paint. **2** A knife used by tanners for removing hair. **3** A tool or machine used to simulate or raise the grain of wood, leather, etc.

Grain·ger (grān′jər), **Percy Aldridge,** 1882–1961, U.S. composer and pianist born in Australia.

grains (grānz) *n. pl. (often construed as singular)* A strong, iron fish spear with a line attached, having several points half-barbed inwardly. [<ON *grein* division]

grains of paradise The seeds of a West African plant *(Aframomum melegueta)* of the ginger family, used in medicine as an aromatic stimulant: also called *guinea grains.*

grain·y (grā′nē) *adj.* **grain·i·er, grain·i·est** **1** Full of grains or kernels. **2** Of the appearance of wood. **3** Granular. **—grain′i·ness** *n.*

graith (grāth) *Scot. n.* Equipment for any work or undertaking; tackle or tools. *—v.t.* To prepare (equipment for use).

gral·la·to·ri·al (gral′ə·tôr′ē·əl, -tō′rē-) *adj.* Of or pertaining to a former order *(Grallatores)* of long-legged wading birds, including the herons and snipes. [<L *grallator* a stilt-walker <*grallae* stilts]

gram[1] (gram) *n.* The basic unit of mass (or weight) in the metric system, equal to 15.432 grains: originally defined as the mass of 1 cubic centimeter of water at 4° C., but now as one thousandth of the mass of the kilogram at Sèvres, France. See METRIC SYSTEM. Also **gramme.** [<F *gramme* <LL *gramma* <Gk. *gramma* a small weight]

gram[2] (gram) *n.* **1** The chickpea of the East Indies: used as food for men, horses, and cattle. **2** One of various kinds of pulse, as **black gram** *(Phaseolus mungo).* [<Pg. *grão* <L *granum* a seed]

-gram[1] *combining form* Something written or drawn: *telegram.* [<Gk. *gramma* a letter, writing <*graphein* write.]

-gram[2] *combining form* A gram: used in the metric system: *kilogram.* [<GRAM[1]]

Gram (gram, *Dan.* gräm), **Hans Christian Joachim,** 1855–1938, Danish physician.

gra·ma (grä′mə) *n.* Any of various species of low pasture grasses of the western and SW United States, especially **blue grama** *(Bouteloua gracilis).* Also **gram′ma, grama grass, gramma grass.** [<Sp. <L *gramen* grass]

gram·a·ry (gram′ər·ē) *n.* **1** *Archaic* Occult lore; magic. **2** *Obs.* Grammar; erudition. Also **gram′a·rye, gram′ma·rye.** [<OF *gramaire.* See GRAMMAR.]

gram-at·om (gram′at′əm) *n. Chem.* That quantity of an element of which the weight in grams is the same as the atomic weight of the element. Also **gram′-a·tom′ic weight** (-ə·tom′ik).**—gram′-a·tom′ic** *adj.*

gram-e·quiv·a·lent (gram′i·kwiv′ə·lənt) *n.* The weight in grams of a substance which displaces or otherwise reacts with 1.008 gram of hydrogen or combines with 8 grams of oxygen. **—gram-equivalent** *adj.*

gra·mer·cy (grə·mûr′sē) *interj. Archaic* Many thanks; great thanks. [<OF *grand merci* great thanks]

gram·i·cid·in (gram′ə·sīd′n, grə·mis′ə·din) *n. Biochem.* A crystalline bacteriostatic and bactericidal substance isolated from an aerobic spore-forming soil bacterium *(Bacillus brevis).* It is a constituent of tyrothricin and has a powerful selective effect against Gram-positive microorganisms. [<GRAM(-POSITIVE) + -(I)CIDE + -IN]

Gra·min·e·ae (grə·min′i·ē), **Gram·i·na·ce·ae** (gram′i·nā′si·ē) Former name of POACEAE. See POACEOUS. [<L *gramen, -inis* grass]

gra·min·e·ous (grə·min′ē·əs) *adj.* Of, pertaining to, or like grasses; poaceous.

gram·i·niv·or·ous (gram′i·niv′ər·əs) *adj.* Grass-eating.

gram·mar (gram′ər) *n.* **1** The systematic analysis of the classes and structure of words (morphology) and of their arrangements and interrelationships in larger constructions (syntax). **2** Formerly, the study of all aspects of language, as phonology, orthography, syntax, etymology, semantics, and prosody. **3** A system of morphological and syntactical rules and principles assumed for a given language. **4** A treatise or book dealing with such rules. **5** Speech or writing considered with regard to current standard of correctness: He employs poor *grammar.* **6** The elements of any science or art, or a book or treatise dealing with them. [<OF *gramaire* <L *grammatica* <Gk. *grammatikē (technē)* literary (art) <*grammata* literature, orig. plural of *gramma* letter <*graphein* write. Related to GLAMOUR.]

gram·mar·i·an (grə·mâr′ē·ən) *n.* **1** One skilled in grammar. **2** A writer or compiler of grammars. **3** Formerly, a learned humanist. **4** A writer on the principles of an art or science.

gram·mat·i·cal (grə·mat′i·kəl) *adj.* **1** Conforming to the principles of grammar. **2** Of or pertaining to grammar. Also **gram·mat′ic.—gram·mat′i·cal·ly** *adv.* **—gram·mat′i·cal·ness** *n.*

grammatical gender See under GENDER.

gramme (gram) See GRAM[1].

Gramme (gràm), **Zénobe Théophile,** 1826–1901, Belgian electrical scientist.

gram-mol·e·cule (gram′mol′ə·kyōōl) *n. Chem.* That quantity of a substance containing a weight in grams numerically equal to its molecular weight: also called *mol, mole.* Also **gram-mo·lec·u·lar weight** (gram′mə·lek′yə·lər).**—gram′-mo·lec′u·lar** *adj.*

Gram-neg·a·tive (gram′neg′ə·tiv) *adj.* See GRAM'S METHOD.

Gra·mont (grà·môṅ′), **Philibert,** 1621–1707, Comte de Gramont, French courtier, adventurer, and soldier.

Gram·o·phone (gram′ə·fōn) *n.* A type of phonograph; a trade name.

Gram·pi·ans (gram′pē·ənz) A mountain chain in Scotland dividing the Highlands from the Lowlands; highest peak, Ben Nevis, 4,406 feet. Also **Grampian Hills, Grampian Mountains.**

Gram-pos·i·tive (gram′poz′ə·tiv) *adj.* See GRAM'S METHOD.

gram·pus (gram′pəs) *n. pl.* **·pus·es** **1** A large dolphinlike cetacean (genus *Grampus)* found in North Atlantic and North Pacific waters. **2** The killer whale (genus *Orcinus).* [Alter. of obs. *grapeys* <OF *grapois, graspeis* <Med. L *crassus piscis* fat fish]

GRAMPUS
(Killer whale: from 20 to 30 feet in length)

Gram's method A method for the differentiation and classification of bacteria which depends upon the reaction to treatment, first with aniline gentian violet, then with an iodine solution, followed by immersion in alcohol. Those bacteria which are decolorized by the alcohol are *Gram-negative,* and those which retain the purple dye are *Gram-positive.* [after Hans C. J. *Gram*]

gran (gran) *adj. Scot.* Grand.

Gra·na·da (grə·nä′də, *Sp.* grä·nä′thä) **1** A province of southern Spain; 4,438 square miles. **2** Its capital; site of the Alhambra and former capital of a Moorish kingdom.

gran·a·dil·la (gran′ə·dil′ə) *n.* **1** The edible fruit of various species of passionflower *(Passiflora)* of tropical America, especially the giant granadilla *(P. quadrangularis),* oblong, with a soft pulp of a sweet acid flavor. **2** Any plant yielding this fruit. [<Sp., dim. of *granada* a pomegranate]

gran·a·dil·lo (gran′ə·dil′ō) *n.* **1** Any of a large number of tropical American trees, especially a West Indian tree *(Brya ebenus)* yielding a hard, durable wood used in making flutes, clarinets, recorders, etc. **2** The fine-grained rosewood or cocobolo *(Dalbergia retusa),* valued for furniture and cabinetwork. **3** The wood of such trees, especially that used in making musical instruments. Also called *grenadilla, grenadillo.* [<Sp.]

gran·a·ry (grā′nər·ē, gran′ər-) *n. pl.* **·ries** **1** A storehouse for grain. **2** A country or region where grain grows in abundance. [<L *granarium* <*granum* grain]

Gran Ca·na·ria (gräng kä·nä′ryä) One of the Canary Islands; 592 square miles; capital, Las Palmas. Also **Grand Ca·nar·y** (grand′ kə·nâr′ē).

Gran Cha·co (grän chä′kō) An extensive lowland plain of central South America, divided among Paraguay, Bolivia, and Argentina: also **El Chaco.**

grand (grand) *adj.* **1** Of imposing character or aspect; magnificent in proportion, extent, or belongings: *grand* scenery. **2** Characterized by striking excellence or impressive dignity; inspiring: a *grand* oration. **3** Preeminent by reason of great ability or high character; noble; worthy of exalted respect: the *grand* old man. **4** Preeminent in rank or order; also, of prime importance; principal: a *grand* climax. **5** Covering the whole field, or including all details; comprehensive; complete: the *grand* total. **6** *Music* Containing all the parts or movements that belong to a given style of composition. **7** Being one degree of relationship more distant than that ordinarily indicated by the word qualified: used in composition: *grandfather, granduncle, granddaughter, grandniece.* **8** Main; leading: the *grand* hall. *—n. U.S. Slang* One thousand dollars. [<OF <L *grandis*] **—grand′ly** *adv.* **—grand′ness** *n.*

Synonyms (adj.): august, dignified, elevated, exalted, great, illustrious, imposing, impressive, lofty, magnificent, majestic, stately, sublime. Aside from material dimensions, *great* is said of that which is more than ordinarily powerful and influential, *grand* of that which is worthily so; a *great* victory may be simply an overwhelming triumph of might over right. We can speak of a *great* bad man, but not of a *grand* bad man; of a *great,* but not of a *grand,* tyrant. Compare AWFUL, IMPERIAL, LARGE, SUBLIME.

gran•dam (gran′dam, -dəm) *n. Archaic* A grandmother; an old woman. Also **gran′dame** (-dām, -dəm). [<AF *graund dame*]

Grand Army of the Republic An organization of Union army and navy veterans of the Civil War in the United States, organized (1866) in memory of the dead and to aid widows and dependents of the dead.

grand•aunt (grand′ant′, -änt′) *n.* The aunt of one's parent; sister of one's grandparent; a great-aunt.

Grand Banks A submarine shoal in the North Atlantic east and south of Newfoundland; 420 by 350 miles; a major fishing ground.

Grand Canal 1 A large canal in Venice, Italy, comprising the city's main thoroughfare. **2** The longest canal of China, comprising the main north-south waterway of north China; 1,000 miles long.

Grand Canyon A gorge formed by the Colorado River in NW Arizona; about 250 miles long; width, from 4 to 18 miles; depth, about one mile; partly in **Grand Canyon National Park;** 1,008 square miles; established 1919.

grand•child (grand′child′) *n. pl.* **•chil•dren** The child of one's son or daughter.

grand climacteric See under CLIMACTERIC.

Grand Cou•lee (ko͞o′lē) A dry canyon cut by the Columbia River in eastern Washington during the glacial epoch: site of **Grand Coulee Dam,** 550 feet high, 4,300 feet long, forming Franklin D. Roosevelt Lake.

grand•dad (gran′dad′) *n. Colloq.* Grandfather: a childish or familiar term. Also **grand′dad′dy.**

grand•daugh•ter (gran′dô′tər, grand′-) *n.* The daughter of one's child.

grand duchess 1 The wife or widow of a grand duke. **2** A woman holding sovereign rights over a grand duchy. **3** Formerly, in Russia, a daughter of a czar, or a daughter of any of his descendants in the male line.

grand duchy The domain of a grand duke or grand duchess.

grand duke 1 A sovereign who ranks just below a king. **2** In Russia, formerly, a ruler of a principality; later, any brother, son, uncle, or nephew of a czar.

gran•dee (gran•dē′) *n.* A Spanish or Portuguese nobleman of the highest rank. [<Sp. *grande* great]

grande pas•sion (gräṅd′ pä•syôṅ′) *French* Supreme love; great passion.

Grande-Terre (gräṅ•târ′) See GUADELOUPE.

grande toi•lette (gräṅd′ twȧ•let′) *French* Full dress.

gran•deur (gran′jər, -jo͝or) *n.* The quality of being grand; magnificence; sublimity. [<F <*grand* great]

Grand Falls A waterfall on the upper Hamilton River in Labrador; 245 feet high; 200 feet wide.

grand•fa•ther (grand′fä′thər) *n.* The father of one's father or mother. Also **grand′pa′** (-pä′), **grand′pa•pa′** (-pə•pä′). **—grand′fa′ther•ly** *adj.*

Grand Forks A city on the Red River in North Dakota.

gran•dil•o•quence (gran•dil′ə•kwəns) *n.* **1** The quality of being grandiloquent. **2** Lofty or bombastic speech.

gran•dil•o•quent (gran•dil′ə•kwənt) *adj.* Speaking in or characterized by a pompous or bombastic style. Also **gran•dil′o•quous** (-kwəs). [<L *grandiloquus* <*grandis* great + *loqui* speak; infl. in form by ELOQUENT] **—gran•dil′o•quent•ly** *adv.*

gran•di•ose (gran′dē•ōs) *adj.* **1** Having an imposing style; impressive; grand. **2** Affecting grandeur; pompous; bombastic. [<F <Ital. *grandioso* <L *grandis* great] **—gran′di•ose•ly** *adv.* **—gran•di•os•i•ty** (gran′dē•os′ə•tē) *n.*

gran•di•o•so (gran′dē•ō′sō) *adj. & adv. Music* In a grand or imposing manner. [<Ital.]

grand jury See under JURY.

Grand Lac (gräṅ lȧk) The French name for TONLE SAP.

Grand Lama The Dalai Lama.

grand larceny See under LARCENY.

grand mal (gräṅ mȧl′) *Pathol.* An epileptic seizure characterized by severe convulsions followed by coma, often preceded by warning symptoms: distinguished from *petit mal.* [<F, lit. great sickness]

Grand Ma•nan (mə•nan′) An island in Bay of Fundy, SW New Brunswick, Canada; 57 square miles.

grand mer•ci (gräṅ mer•sē′) *French* Many thanks.

grand monde (gräṅ môṅd′) *French* Fashionable society: literally, the great world.

grand•moth•er (grand′muth′ər) *n.* The mother of one's father or mother. Also **grand′ma′** (-mä′), **grand′ma•ma′** (-mə•mä′). **—grand′moth′er•ly** *adj.*

grand•neph•ew (grand′nef′yo͞o, -nev′-, gran′-) *n.* A son of one's nephew or niece; grandson of one's brother or sister.

grand•niece (grand′nēs′, gran′-) *n.* A daughter of one's nephew or niece; granddaughter of one's brother or sister.

Grand Old Party In U.S. politics, the Republican party.

grand opera See under OPERA.

grand•par•ent (grand′pâr′ənt, gran′-) *n.* The parent of one's parent.

grand piano See under PIANO.

grand prix (gräṅ prē′) *French* Grand prize.

Grand Rapids A city in western Michigan.

gran•drelle (gran•drel′) *n.* **1** Two-ply yarn of contrasting colors. **2** A varicolored fabric made of such yarn.

Grand River 1 The former name of a source stream of the Colorado River. **2** A river in southern Iowa and NW Missouri, flowing 215 miles SE to the Missouri. **3** A river in SW Michigan, flowing NW 260 miles to Lake Michigan. **4** A river in NW South Dakota, flowing SE 209 miles to the Missouri. **5** A river in southern Ontario, flowing south 165 miles to Lake Erie.

grand•sire (grand′sīr′) *n.* **1** A grandfather; any male ancestor preceding a father. **2** Any venerable man. Also **grand′sir** (-sûr, gran′-).

grand•son (grand′sun′, gran′-) *n.* The son of one's son or daughter.

grand•stand (grand′stand′, gran′-) *n.* The principal stand on a racecourse; hence, a similar erection for spectators at any public spectacle. *—v.i. U.S. Colloq.* To show off in an attempt to win applause.

grandstand play Anything done to show off, or to win applause.

Grand Teton National Park A glaciated mountainous region of NW Wyoming including part of the Teton Range; 465 square miles; established 1929.

grand tour See under TOUR.

grand•un•cle (grand′ung′kəl) *n.* The uncle of one's father or mother; brother of one's grandparent.

grange (grānj) *n.* **1** *Brit.* A farm, with its dwelling house and appurtenances; specifically, the residence of a gentleman farmer. **2** *Obs.* A granary. **3** Formerly, a farm establishment belonging to a feudal manor or a monastery: the grain paid in as rent or tithes was stored in its granaries. [<AF *graunge,* OF *grange* <Med. L *granea* <L *granum* grain]

Grange (grānj) *n.* **1** The order of Patrons of Husbandry, a nation-wide association of U.S. farmers, founded in 1867 for the furtherance of agricultural interests. **2** One of the subordinate lodges of the Patrons of Husbandry.

grang•er (grān′jər) *n.* **1** A member of a Grange. **2** A countryman. **—grang′er•ism** *n.*

grang•er•ize (grān′jər•īz) *v.t.* **•ized, •iz•ing 1** To illustrate (a book) with prints, engravings, etc., taken from other books. **2** To mutilate (a book) by cutting out the illustrations. [after Rev. James *Granger,* 1723–76, whose *Biographical History of England* (1769) was so illustrated] **—grang′er•ism** *n.* **—grang′er•i•za′tion** *n.* **—grang′er•iz′er** *n.*

grani- *combining form* Grain: *graniform.* [<L *granum* grain]

Gra•ni•cus (grə•nī′kəs) A river in NW Turkey, flowing 45 miles NE to the Sea of Marmara; scene of Alexander the Great's victory over the Persians in 334 B.C. *Turkish* **Ko•ca•baş** (kô•jä•bäsh′).

gra•nif•er•ous (grə•nif′ər•əs) *adj.* Bearing grain.

gran•i•form (gran′ə•fôrm) *adj.* Formed like a grain or a granule.

gran•ite (gran′it) *n.* **1** A hard, coarse-grained, igneous rock composed principally of quartz, feldspar, and mica, of great strength and taking a high polish. **2** Great hardness or rigidity. [<Ital. *granito,* orig. pp. of *granire* make seeds <*grano* a seed <L *granum*] **—gra•nit•ic** (grə•nit′ik) or **•i•cal** *adj.*

granite paper A wove paper containing very short silk threads of different colors.

Granite State Nickname of NEW HAMPSHIRE.

gran•ite•ware (gran′it•wâr′) *n.* **1** A variety of ironware coated with hard, granite-colored enamel. **2** A fine, hard pottery resembling ironstone china.

gran•it•ite (gran′it•īt) *n.* A [illegible] containing biotite.

gran•it•oid (gran′it•oid) *adj.* [illegible] igneous rock of granitelike tex[illegible]

gra•niv•o•rous (grə•niv′ər•ə[illegible] on grain or seeds. **—gran•i•vore** [illegible] *n.*

gran•ny (gran′ē) *n. pl.* **•nies** [illegible] d-mother. **2** An old woman. [illegible] a nurse. **4** A finical, fussy [illegible]y knot. Also **gran′nie.**

granny knot *Naut.* An imperfect sailor's knot, differing from a reef knot in having the second tie crosswise. See illustration under KNOT. Also **granny's knot, granny's bend.**

grano- *combining form* Granitic: *granolith.* [<L *granum* a grain]

gra•no•la (grə•nō′lə) *n.* A mixture of dry cereals, nuts, and raisins, chopped fine and marketed as a health food.

gran•o•lith (gran′ə•lith) *n.* Pulverized granite cement used as artificial stone for paving. **—gran•o•lith•ic** (gran′ə•lith′ik) *adj.*

gran•o•phyre (gran′ə•fīr) *n.* A granite porphyry. [<GRANO- + (POR)PHYRY] **—gran•o•phy•ric** (gran′ə•fī′rik) *adj.*

grant (grant, gränt) *v.t.* **1** To give or accord, as permission, a request, etc. **2** To confer or bestow, as a privilege, charter, favor, etc. **3** To admit as true, especially something not proved, as for the sake of argument; concede. **4** To transfer (property), especially by deed. See synonyms under ACKNOWLEDGE, ALLOT, ALLOW, APPORTION, CONFESS, GIVE. *—n.* **1** The act of granting; a bestowing or conferring. **2** The thing granted; specifically, a piece of land granted to a person, state, etc., by the government. **3** An admission, concession. **4** One of certain tracts of land in New Hampshire, Maine, and Vermont, once belonging to Indian tribes, but allocated to settlers during the 18th century, and the subject of territorial controversy in colonial days. **5** A transfer of real property by deed. See synonyms under GIFT, SUBSIDY. [<AF *graunter, granter,* ult. <L *credens, -entis,* ppr. of *credere* believe] **—grant′a•ble** *adj.* **—grant′er** *n.*

Grant (grant), **Ulysses Simpson,** 1822-85, U.S. general in the Civil War; 18th president of the United States 1869-77.

Gran•ta (gran′tə) See CAM.

grant•ee (gran•tē′, grän-) *n. Law* The person to whom property is transferred by deed, or to whom rights are granted by patent or charter.

grant-in-aid (grant′in•ād′, gränt′-) *n.* A grant made by a central to a local government to assist in some public undertaking.

gran•tor (gran′tər, gran•tôr′, grän-) *n. Law* The person by whom a grant is made; maker of a deed.

gran•u•lar (gran′yə•lər) *adj.* Composed of, like, or containing grains or granules. Also **gran′u•lose** (-lōs), **gran′u•lous** (-ləs).

gran•u•lar•i•ty (gran′yə•lar′ə•tē) *n.* **1** The state or condition of being granular. **2** A coarseness in the silver graining of a motion-picture film.

gran•u•late (gran′yə•lāt) *v.t. & v.i.* **•lat•ed, •lat•ing 1** To make or become granular; form into grains. **2** To become or cause to become rough on the surface by the formation of granules. **—gran′u•lat′ed** *adj.* **—gran′u•la′tor, gran′u•lat′er** *n.*

gran•u•la•tion (gran′yə•lā′shən) *n.* **1** The forming into grains or granules. **2** A granulated surface, or one of the elevations in such surface. **3** *Physiol.* **a** The process of forming new tissue in the healing of wounds. **b** The minute, flesh-colored, breadlike projections so formed. **4** *Astron.* An evanescent mottled appearance observed in the photosphere of the sun, attributed to gaseous convection currents in the outer layers. **—gran′u•la′tive** *adj.*

gran·ule (gran′yo͞ol) *n.* **1** A small grain; particle; corpuscle. **2** *Biol.* One of the small protoplasmic bodies suspended in the cytoplasm of the cell. [<LL *granulum,* dim. of L *granum* grain]

gran·u·lite (gran′yə·līt) *n.* A finely granulated, crystalline, foliated rock composed mainly of quartz and feldspar, but generally carrying garnet. —**gran·u·lit·ic** (gran′yə·lit′ik) *adj.*

gran·u·lo·cyte (gran′yə·lə·sīt) *n.* Any of several types of leukocyte in which the cytoplasm contains granules. —**gran·u·lo·cytic** (gran′yə·lə·sit′ik) *adj.*

gran·u·lo·ma (gran′yə·lō′mə) *n. Pathol.* A tumor composed of granulation tissue.

gran·u·lose (gran′yə·lōs) *n.* That portion of starch granules capable of being changed into sugar by certain ferments: distinguished from *cellulose.*

grape (grāp) *n.* **1** The smooth-skinned, edible, juicy, berrylike fruit of various species of the grapevine, from which most wines are made. **2** Any grapevine yielding this fruit. **3** Figuratively, wine. **4** Grapeshot. **5** A dark-blue color with a slight reddish tint. **6** *pl.* A cluster of nodular excrescences on a horse's fetlock, caused by a parasitic fungus. [<OF, bunch of grapes <*graper* gather grapes <*grape* a hook <Gmc.]

grape-eat·er (grāp′ē′tər) *n.* An Australian fruit-eating bird *(Zosterops lateralis).*

grape·fruit (grāp′fro͞ot′) *n.* A large, round, pale-yellow citrus fruit of tropical regions (*Citrus paradisi* and varieties), cultivated also in the United States.

grape hyacinth A plant (genus *Muscari*) of the lily family, differing from the common hyacinth in having its small blue flowers ovoid or globular and minutely six-toothed.

grape juice The unfermented juice of the grape: used as a beverage.

grape rot A wide-spread and malignant disease of grapes, caused by a parasitic fungus *(Plasmopara viticola)* and characterized by the formation of a milky coating on the leaves, sometimes having the appearance of oil spots: also called *downy mildew.* Also **grape blight.**

grap·er·y (grā′pər·ē) *n. pl.* **·er·ies** A building for the growing of grapes.

grape·shot (grāp′shot′) *n.* A cluster of cast-iron shot, to be discharged from a cannon.

grape·stone (grāp′stōn′) *n.* A seed of the grape.

grape sugar Dextrose: occurring in ripe grapes.

grape·vine (grāp′vīn′) *n.* **1** Any of a genus *(Vitis)* of woody, climbing vines characterized by profuse clusters of berrylike juicy fruit, especially the American species *V. labrusca* and the Old World *V. vinifera.* **2** *U.S. Colloq.* **a** Grapevine telegraph. **b** An unverified report or rumor. **3** *U.S.* Grapevine twist.

grapevine telegraph *U.S.* Any hidden means by which information, rumor, etc., not available through regular channels becomes rapidly widespread.

grapevine twist *U.S.* A complicated figure in dancing used by Negroes of the South: also *grapevine.*

graph (graf, gräf) *n.* **1** A diagram indicating any sort of relationship between two or more things by means of a system of dots, curves, bars, or lines. **2** *Math.* The locus of a point moving in relation to coordinates so that all of its values satisfy a function of an equation. —*v.t.* To trace or represent in the form of a graph. [Short for *graphic formula*]

-graph *combining form* **1** One who or that which writes or records: *phonograph.* **2** A writing or record: *monograph.* [<F *-graphe* <L *-graphus* <Gk. *-graphos* <*graphein* write]

Graph·al·loy (graf′ə·loi′) *n.* A composition consisting of graphite into which bronze or Babbitt metal has been forced by hydraulic pressure: a trade name.

-grapher *combining form* A writer or one engaged in a graphic or kindred art: *bibliographer, photographer.*

graph·ic (graf′ik) *adj.* **1** Of or pertaining to the art of writing, or of indicating by letters or written signs. **2** Describing with pictorial effect; portraying with vividness. **3** Written, engraved, or recorded by means of letters or inscriptions. **4** Having the appearance of written or printed signs: *graphic* granite. **5** *Stat.* Indicating or calculating by lines, areas, diagrams, etc. **6** *Math.* Of or pertaining to the use of plotted

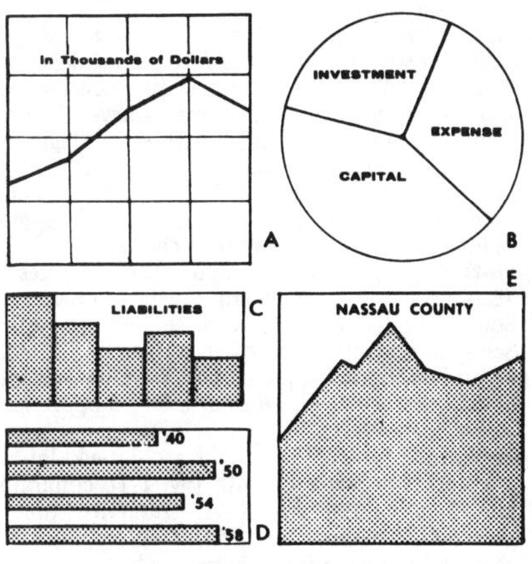

TYPES OF GRAPHS
A. Line graph. *B.* Pie or sector graph.
C. D. Bar graphs. *E.* Area graph.

curves to represent or solve an equation **7** *Geol.* Denoting a rock texture produced by a blending of crystalline constituents in such a way as to give a graphic appearance to a freshly cut section. Also **graph′i·cal.** [<L *graphicus* <Gk. *graphikos* of writing <*graphē* writing] — **graph′i·cal·ly, graph′ic·ly** *adv.*

Synonyms: descriptive, forcible, illustrative, pictorial, picturesque, vivid. See VIVID. *Antonyms*: dreary, dull, flat, monotonous, prosy, stupid, uninteresting.

graphic accent A written or printed sign of emphasis, as in many Spanish words.

graphic arts **1** Those arts involving the use of lines or strokes on a flat surface, as painting, drawing, engraving, etc. **2** Those arts which involve impressions printed on flat surfaces, as printing, lithography, etching, wood-engraving, etc.

graphic gold, graphic tellurium See SYLVANITE.

graph·ics (graf′iks) *n. pl.* The science or art of drawing, particularly of mechanical drawing, or of drawing to mathematical rules as in engineering.

graph·ite (graf′īt) *n.* A soft, black, chemically inert, hexagonal variety of carbon with a metallic luster and oily feel: used as a lubricant and in the making of lead pencils, electrodes, crucibles, etc.: also called *plumbago, black-lead.* [<G *graphit* <Gk. *graphein* write + *-it* -ITE[1]] —**gra·phit·ic** (grə·fit′ik) *adj.*

graph·i·tize (graf′ə·tīz) *v.t.* **·tized, ·tiz·ing** **1** To coat with graphite. **2** To make into graphite by a heating process. —**graph′i·ti·za′tion** (-tə·zā′·shən, -tī·zā′-) *n.*

grapho- *combining form* Of or pertaining to writing: *graphology.* Also, before vowels, **graph-.** [<Gk. *graphē* writing <*graphein* write]

graph·ol·o·gy (graf·ol′ə·jē) *n.* **1** The scientific study and analysis of handwriting, especially with reference to forgeries and questioned documents. **2** The art of interpreting character and personality from the diagnostic peculiarities of handwriting. **3** The study of handwriting as an aid in the diagnosis of diseases of the brain and nervous system. —**graph·o·log·i·cal** (graf′ə·loj′i·kəl) *adj.* —**graph·ol′o·gist** *n.*

graph·o·ma·ni·a (graf′ə·mā′nē·ə, -mān′yə) *n.* A compulsive desire to write.

graph·o·mo·tor (graf′ə·mō′tər) *adj. Med.* Pertaining to or having influence upon the movements required in writing.

Graph·o·phone (graf′ə·fōn) *n.* A type of phonograph: a trade name.

graph·o·spasm (graf′ə·spaz′əm) *n.* Writer's cramp.

graph·o·type (graf′ə·tīp) *n.* **1** A process for producing engravings quickly by drawing with siliceous ink upon a plate faced with chalk afterward brushed away. **2** A plate so made.

graph paper Paper variously ruled to facilitate the drawing of a graph: usually quadrille paper, divided into equal squares.

-graphy *combining form* A written description of: *geography, biography.* [<Gk. *-graphia* <*graphein* write]

grap·lin (grap′lin) *n.* A grapnel. Also **grap′line** (-lin). [Alter. of GRAPNEL]

grap·nel (grap′nəl) *n.* **1** A device for grappling, consisting of several hooks or clamps on one stem, designed to catch hold of any object across which it is thrown or drawn; a grapple. Also *grappling iron.* **2** *Naut.* A boat's anchor with many flukes. See illustration under ANCHOR. [ME *grapenel,* dim. of OF *grapin* a hook]

grap·ple (grap′əl) *v.* **grap·pled, grap·pling** *v.t.* **1** To take hold of; grasp firmly. —*v.i.* **2** To use a grapnel. **3** To seize or come to grips with another, as in wrestling. **4** To deal or contend: with *with*: to *grapple* with a problem. See synonyms under CONTEND, GRASP. [<*n.*] —*n.* **1** A close hold, as in wrestling. **2** A grapnel. [<OF *grappil* grapnel] —**grap′pler** *n.*

grap·pling (grap′ling) *n.* **1** The act of seizing or grasping, or that by which anything is seized and held. **2** A grapnel.

grappling iron A grapnel. Also **grappling hook.**

grap·y (grā′pē) *adj.* Pertaining to, composed of, or resembling grapes.

Gras·mere (gras′mir, gräs′-) A small lake in Westmorland, England.

grasp (grasp, gräsp) *v.t.* **1** To lay hold of with or as with the hand; grip. **2** To seize greedily or eagerly; snatch. **3** To take hold of with the mind; understand. —*v.i.* **4** To make grasping motions. —**to grasp at** **1** To try to seize. **2** To clutch at eagerly or desperately: to *grasp at* straws. —*n.* **1** The act of seizing or attempting to lay hold of something, as with the hand. **2** The ability to seize and hold; possession taken and kept by force. **3** Power of comprehension, or the exercise of this power. [ME *graspen,* metathetic var. of *grapsen* <LG] —**grasp′er** *n.*

Synonyms (verb): catch, clasp, clutch, comprehend, grab, grapple, grip, gripe, hold, seize, snatch, understand. See CATCH, EMBRACE[1]. *Antonyms*: abandon, fail, loose, lose, miss, release, relinquish.

grasp·ing (gras′ping, gräs′-) *adj.* Avaricious. See synonyms under GREEDY. —**grasp′ing·ly** *adv.* — **grasp′ing·ness** *n.*

grass (gras, gräs) *n.* **1** The green plants on which cattle feed. **2** Any of a large natural family of plants *(Poaceae)* with mostly rounded and hollow jointed stems, sheathing leaves, flowers borne on spikelets, and the fruit a seedlike grain, including all the common cereals, canes, bamboos, and a great variety of pasture plants. **3** *pl.* Spires or sprays of grass. **4** Grassland used for pasture; also, ground covered with grass; lawn. **5** Any of numerous plants with foliage suggesting or resembling the true grasses, as the sedges, the rushes, etc. **6** *Slang* Marihuana. —*v.t.* **1** To cover with grass or turf. **2** To feed with grass; pasture. **3** To spread on grass for bleaching by the sun. —*v.i.* **4** To graze on grass. **5** To produce grass; become covered with grass. [OE *græs.* Akin to GREEN, GROW.]

Grasse (gräs), **François Joseph Paul,** 1722–1788, Comte de Grasse, French admiral.

grass finch **1** The vesper sparrow. **2** An Australian weaverbird.

grass·hop·per (gras′hop′ər, gräs′-) *n.* Any of several orthopterous insects, including the locust and katydid (families *Locustidae* and *Tettigonidae*), having powerful hind legs adapted for leaping. The males of most species make a chirping sound with their wings or by friction of the hind legs against parts of the wings or wing covers. For illustration, see under INSECT (injurious).

grass·land (gras′land′, gräs′-) *n.* **1** Land reserved for pasturage or mowing. **2** Land in which grasses predominate, as the American prairies.

grass-of-Par·nas·sus (grås′əv·pär·nas′əs, gräs′) *n.* Any of a genus *(Parnassia)* of smooth perennial herbs of the saxifrage family, bearing handsome white flowers.

grass·plot (gras′plot′, gräs′-) *n.* A plot of

ground covered with grass, sometimes with groups of shrubs, flowers, etc. Also *Obs.* **grass′plat′** (-plat).

grass·quit (gras′kwit, gräs′-) *n.* A small fringilline bird *(Tiaris bicolor* and *T. canora)* of Cuba and the Bahamas.

grass·roots (gras′ro͞ots′, -ro͝ots′, gräs′-) *n.* The rural sections of the country; the hinterland. — *adj.* Of or pertaining to such sections: a *grass-roots* region.

grass snipe The pectoral sandpiper.

grass tree 1 Any of various Australian plants of the lily family (genus *Xanthorrhoea)* having a thick, woody trunk crowned with long grasslike leaves and yielding a fragrant resin. **2** Any of several Australasian plants with grasslike foliage, as the ti.

grass widow A woman separated from her husband by causes other than death.

grass·y (gras′ē, gräs′ē) *adj.* **grass·i·er, grass·i·est** Abounding in, covered with, consisting of, or resembling grass. **—grass′i·ly** *adv.* **—grass′i·ness** *n.*

grat (grat) *Scot.* Past participle of GREET[2].

grate[1] (grāt) *v.* **grat·ed, grat·ing,** *v.t.* **1** To reduce to small particles by rubbing with a rough surface or through a grate. **2** To rub or grind so as to produce a harsh, scraping sound. **3** To annoy; irritate: to *grate* the nerves. **4** *Archaic* To wear or scrape away. *—v.i.* **5** To sound harshly, from or as from scraping or grinding; creak. **6** To have an irritating effect: with *on* or *upon.* *—n.* A harsh, grinding noise. ◆Homophone: *great.* [< OF *grater* < Gmc.]

grate[2] (grāt) *n.* **1** A framework of bars, as to close an opening, or to hold fuel in burning. **2** A perforated metallic plate through which the ores pass after being crushed under stamps. **3** A fireplace. **4** *Obs.* A cage furnished with grates; a place of confinement. *—v.t.* **grat·ed, grat·ing** To fit with a grate or grates. ◆Homophone: *great.* [< Med. L *grata* < Ital. < L *cratis* a lattice]

grate·ful (grāt′fəl) *adj.* **1** Having a due sense of benefits received; thankful. **2** Affording gratification; pleasurable; agreeable. **3** Expressing or denoting thankfulness; indicative of gratitude. [< obs. *grate* pleasing (< L *gratus)* + -FUL] — **grate′ful·ly** *adv.* **—grate′ful·ness** *n.*

Synonyms: obliged, thankful. See AGREEABLE, DELIGHTFUL.

grat·er (grā′tər) *n.* **1** Someone or something that grates. **2** A kitchen utensil used to grate vegetables, cheese, etc.

Gra·ti·an (grā′shē·ən, -shən), 359–83, Roman emperor 375–83: real name *Flavius Gratianus.*

grat·i·fi·ca·tion (grat′ə·fə·kā′shən) *n.* **1** The act of gratifying; a satisfying or pleasing. **2** The state of being gratified; specifically, the satisfaction of sexual craving. **3** *Obs.* That which gratifies; a reward; recompense; gratuity. See synonyms under HAPPINESS, SATISFACTION.

grat·i·fy (grat′ə·fī) *v.t.* **·fied, ·fy·ing 1** To give pleasure or satisfaction to. **2** To satisfy or indulge, as a desire or need. **3** *Obs.* To reward. See synonyms under ENTERTAIN, INDULGE, REJOICE. [< MF *gratifier* < L *gratificari* < *gratus* pleasing + *facere* make] **—grat′i·fi′er** *n.* **—grat′i·fy′ing·ly** *adv.*

gra·tin (grät′n, grat′n; *Fr.* grȧ·taṅ′) See AU GRATIN.

grat·i·nate (grat′ə·nāt) *v.t.* **·nat·ed, ·nat·ing** To prepare with a crust, as of grated bread, and cook until browned and crisp. [< F *gratiner* form a crust]

grat·ing[1] (grā′ting) *n.* **1** A grate. **2** *Physics* An optical device for the dispersion of light waves and the production of spectra, usually consisting of a series of very fine parallel grooves cut in the surface of polished metal or glass, sometimes of a suitably mounted crystal: also called **diffraction grating.**

grat·ing[2] (grā′ting) *adj.* Harsh in sound; rasping; irritating. *—n.* The act or sound of rasping. — **grat′ing·ly** *adv.*

gra·tis (grā′tis, grat′is) *adv.* Without recompense; freely. *—adj.* Given free of charge. [< L, var. of *gratiis* out of kindness, orig. ablative of *gratia* favor]

grat·i·tude (grat′ə·to͞od, -tyo͞od) *n.* The state of being grateful; thankfulness. [< F < LL *gratitudo* < *gratus* pleasing]

Grat·tan (grat′ən), **Henry,** 1746–1820, Irish statesman and orator.

gra·tu·i·tant (grə·to͞o′ə·tənt, -tyo͞o′-) *n.* One who receives a gratuity.

gra·tu·i·tous (grə·to͞o′ə·təs, -tyo͞o′-) *adj.* **1** Given freely without claim or consideration; voluntary. **2** Without cause, provocation, or warrant; uncalled for; unnecessary. **3** *Law* Imposing no obligation based on a legal or valuable consideration. **4** Freely given by nature, without labor on the part of man: opposed to *onerous.* [< L *gratuitus*] **—gra·tu′i·tous·ly** *adv.* **—gra·tu′i·tous·ness** *n.*

gra·tu·i·ty (grə·to͞o′ə·tē, -tyo͞o′-) *n. pl.* **·ties 1** That which is given gratuitously; a present. **2** Something given in return for service, etc.; a tip. See synonyms under GIFT.

grat·u·lant (grach′o͞o·lənt) *adj.* Wishing one joy; congratulatory. [< L *gratulans, -antis,* pp. of *gratulari.* See GRATULATE.]

grat·u·late (grach′o͞o·lāt) *Obs. v.t.* **·lat·ed, ·lat·ing 1** To greet or welcome with joy. **2** To congratulate. *—adj.* Gratifying. [< L *gratulatus,* pp. of *gratulari* rejoice < *gratus* pleasing] — **grat′u·la′tion** *n.* **—grat′u·la·to′ry** *adj.*

Grau·denz (grou′dents) The German name for GRUDZIADZ.

graul (grôl) See GRILSE.

grau·pel (grou′pəl) *n.* Small, compact pellets of snow: often called *soft hail.* [< G, hailstone]

gra·va·men (grə·vā′men) *n. pl.* **·vam·i·na** (-vam′ə·nə) The essence of a charge or grievance; the burden of a complaint. [< Med. L, grievance < L *gravare* burden < *gravis* heavy]

grave[1] (grāv) *adj.* **1** Of momentous import; solemn; important. **2** Serious, as in mind, manner, or speech; dignified; sedate. **3** Sober in color or fashion. **4** *Phonet.* **a** Having the tonal quality of the grave accent, or marked with it, as the vowel *è.* **b** Unaccented, as a syllable. See synonyms under IMPORTANT, SAD, SEDATE, SERIOUS. *—n.* **1** A mark (`) used in French to indicate the open quality of *e* or a distinction in meaning, as in *ou, où;* in English elocution to indicate a falling inflection or the pronunciation of a final *ed,* as in *preparèd;* in Greek to indicate a lowering of the tone from a higher pitch: also **grave accent.** See ACCENT. **2** *Music* A passage or movement in the slowest tempo. [< F < L *gravis* heavy] — **grave′ly** *adv.* **—grave′ness** *n.*

grave[2] (grāv) *n.* **1** An excavation in the earth for the burial of a dead body; a tomb. **2** Hence, death or ruin. **3** The abode of the dead. [OE *græf.* Related to GRAVE[3].] **—grave′less** *adj.*

grave[3] (grāv) *v.t.* **graved, grav·en, grav·ing 1** To engrave; carve with a chisel. **2** To sculpture. **3** To impress deeply, as on the memory. **4** *Brit. Dial.* To dig. **5** *Archaic* To bury. [OE *grafan* dig. Related to GRAVE[2]]

grave[4] (grāv) *v.t.* **graved, grav·ing** *Naut.* To clean, as a ship's bottom, by scraping or burning off seaweed, etc., and coating with pitch. [< OF, beach]

gra·ve[5] (grä′vā) *adv. Music* Slowly and solemnly. [< Ital.]

grave·clothes (grāv′klōz′; -klōthz′) *n. pl.* The clothes or wrappings in which a dead person is interred.

grave·dig·ger (grāv′dig′ər) *n.* One who digs graves.

grav·el (grav′əl) *n.* **1** A mixture of sand and small, usually rounded, pebbles or stones. **2** *Pathol.* A disease characterized by formation in the kidneys of granular concretions. **3** *Obs.* Sand. — *v.t.* **grav·eled** or **grav·elled, grav·el·ing** or **grav·el·ling 1** To cover or fill with gravel. **2** To bring up short, as in embarrassment or confusion. **3** *U.S. Colloq.* To irritate; annoy. **4** *Obs.* To run (a vessel) aground. [< OF *gravele,* dim. of *grave* beach] **—grav′el·ly, grav′el·y** *adj.*

grav·el-blind (grav′əl·blīnd′) *adj.* Almost blind: intermediate between *sandblind* and *stone-blind.*

gravel pit An excavation from which gravel is taken.

gravel road A road surfaced with gravel.

grav·en (grā′vən) *adj.* Carved or cut.

graven image A carved or graven idol.

Grav·en·stein (grav′ən·stēn, -stīn, grä′vən-) *n.* A large yellowish-red apple. [from *Gravenstein,* resort in southern Denmark]

grav·er (grā′vər) *n.* **1** An engraver's burin; also, a sculptor's chisel. **2** An engraver or a stonecarver.

graves (grāvz) See GREAVES.

Graves (grāvz, *Fr.* gräv) *n.* Wine produced in a district of SW France.

Graves (grāvz), **Robert,** born 1895, English poet, critic, and novelist.

Graves' disease *Pathol.* Exophthalmic goiter. [after Robert J. *Graves,* 1797–1853, Irish physician]

Graves·end (grāvz′end′) A port on the Thames river in NW Kent, England.

grave·stone (grāv′stōn′) *n.* A memorial stone, placed at a grave.

Gra·vet·ti·an (grə·vet′ē·ən) *adj. Anthropol.* Denoting a later extension of the Aurignacian culture period, merging with the Solutrean. Also called *Upper Perigordian.*

grave·yard (grāv′yärd′) *n.* A burial place; a cemetery.

graveyard shift A work shift during the late night, generally from midnight to eight in the morning.

grav·id (grav′id) *adj.* Pregnant. [< L *gravidus* < *gravis* heavy] **—grav′id·ly** *adv.* **—grav′id·ness, gra·vid·i·ty** (grə·vid′ə·tē) *n.*

gra·vim·e·ter (grə·vim′ə·tər) *n.* An instrument for determining specific gravity; a type of hydrometer. [< L *gravis* heavy + -METER]

grav·i·met·ric (grav′ə·met′rik) *adj.* **1** Determined by weight, or of a kind usually so determined. **2** Pertaining to measurement by weight. **—grav′i·met′ri·cal·ly** *adv.*

gra·vim·e·try (grə·vim′ə·trē) *n.* The measurement of weight or specific gravity with the gravimeter.

grav·ing (grā′ving) *n.* **1** The act or operation of incising or engraving. **2** *Naut.* The act of cleaning a ship's bottom by burning, scraping, and coating with pitch.

graving dock A drydock for examining, cleaning, and repairing a ship's bottom.

grav·i·pause (grav′ə·pôz) *n.* The region in space where the gravitational field of one celestial body ends, or is neutralized by that of another. [< GRAVI(TY) + PAUSE]

grav·i·sphere (grav′ə·sfir) *n.* The spherical area within which the gravitational field of a body is dominant. [< GRAVI(TY) + SPHERE]

grav·i·tate (grav′ə·tāt) *v.i.* **·tat·ed, ·tat·ing 1** To tend by or as by force of gravity. **2** To move as though drawn by a powerful force. **3** To sink or fall to the lowest level. [< NL *gravitatus,* pp. of *gravitare* press down < *gravis* heavy] — **grav′i·tat′er** *n.* **—grav′i·ta′tive** *adj.*

grav·i·ta·tion (grav′ə·tā′shən) *n.* **1** *Physics* The force whereby any two bodies attract each other in proportion to the product of their masses and inversely as the square of the distance between them. **2** The act of gravitating or its effect. — **grav′i·ta′tion·al** *adj.* **—grav′i·ta′tion·al·ly** *adv.*

grav·i·ty (grav′ə·tē) *n. pl.* **·ties 1** The accelerating tendency of bodies toward the center of the earth. **2** A similar tendency toward the center of any heavenly body. **3** Weight. **4** Gravitation. **5** The quality of being charged with or involving great interests; importance. **6** Dignified reserve; sedateness. **7** Lowness of pitch. **8** Something of grave import; a serious subject. See synonyms under WEIGHT. *—adj.* Employing gravity; worked by gravity: the *gravity* feed of an oil burner. [< F *gravité* < L *gravitas, -tatis* heaviness < *gravis* heavy]

gravity cell *Electr.* A primary cell in which the two electrolytes are kept separate by differences in specific gravity.

gravity fault *Geol.* A downward-sloping fault in which the upper portion or hanging wall appears to have moved under gravity to a level lower than that of the lower portion or footwall.

gra·vure (grə·vyo͝or′) *n.* **1** An engraved copperplate or wooden block used in photogravure. **2** The print made from it. [< F < *graver* engrave]

gra·vy (grā′vē) *n. pl.* **·vies 1** The juice that drips from roasting or baking meat, or a sauce made from it. **2** *U.S. Slang* Any added, easily acquired, or extra payment or income; also, graft; illegally acquired money. **—gravy train** *U.S. Slang* A line of endeavor that is easy and lucrative. [ME *gravey*]

gravy boat A boat-shaped dish in which gravy is served.

gray (grā) *adj.* **1** Of the color of white and black mixed and without brilliancy. **2** Having gray hair; hoary. **3** Hence, old; aged. **4** Wearing a gray habit: a *Gray* Friar. See synonyms under ANCIENT. *—n.* **1** A gray color;

any dull, whitish tint; specifically, an achromatic color; one which may have brilliance but no hue. See COLOR 2 Something gray; specifically, a gray animal. —*v.t.* & *v.i.* To make or become gray. Also *esp. Brit. grey.* [OE *grǣg*] —**gray′ly** *adv.* —**gray′ness** *n.*

Gray (grā) *n.* A soldier of the Confederate Army in the American Civil War; also, collectively, the Confederate Army itself: the Blue and the *Gray.* Compare BLUE.

Gray (grā), **Asa,** 1810–88, U.S. botanist. —**Elisha,** 1835–1901, U.S. electrician and inventor. —**Thomas,** 1716–71, English poet.

gray·back (grā′bak′) *n.* 1 One of various animals, as the gray whale, the hooded crow *(Corvus cornix),* the American sandpiper, etc. 2 *Colloq.* A member of the Confederate Army during the Civil War. 3 *Colloq.* The body louse. Also spelled *greyback.*

gray·beard (grā′bird′) *n.* An old man, or one with a gray beard.

gray eagle The American bald eagle. See under EAGLE.

gray·fish (grā′fish′) *n. pl.* **·fish** or **·fish·es** The dogfish: also spelled *greyfish.*

gray goods Greige.

gray·ish (grā′ish) *adj.* Somewhat gray: also spelled *greyish.*

gray·lag (grā′lag′) *n. pl.* **·lag** or **·lags** the common wild gray goose *(Anser anser)* of Europe: so called because it migrates late. See GOOSE. Also spelled *greylag.*

gray·ling (grā′ling) *n. pl.* **·ling** or **·lings** 1 A small troutlike fish (genus *Thymallus),* with a richly colored, long, high dorsal fin. 2 A North American butterfly *(Minois alope),* with gray and brown markings (subfamily *Satyrinae).* Also spelled *greyling.*

gray market A trade operation involving the selling of scarce goods at exorbitant prices, a practice considered unethical but not necessarily illegal.

gray matter 1 *Anat.* The grayish substance of the brain, composed largely of ganglionic cell bodies and few fibers. 2 *Colloq.* Brains; intelligence.

gray·out grā′out′ *n.* A temporary loss or blurring of vision caused by oxygen deficiency: noted especially in aviators subjected to high acceleration.

gray plover A large plover of nearly cosmopolitan range *(Squatarola squatarola),* having a plumage which is gray in winter and black during the breeding season.

Grays Peak The highest peak of the Front Range in Colorado; 14,274 feet.

Gray·son (grā′sən), **David** Pseudonym of RAY STANNARD BAKER.

gray squirrel See under SQUIRREL.

gray·wacke (grā′wak, -wak·ə) *n. Geol.* A sedimentary rock composed of rounded or subangular grains of quartz, feldspar, etc., or rock fragments in a siliceous, argillaceous, or calcareous cement: also spelled *greywacke.* [<G *grauwacke* gray wacke]

gray whale A whalebone whale *(Rhachianectes glaucus)* of the northern Pacific coast.

gray wolf A large wolf of northern North America; the timber wolf.

Graz (gräts) The second largest city in Austria, capital of Styria.

graze[1] (grāz) *v.* **grazed, graz·ing** *v.i.* 1 To feed upon growing herbage. —*v.t.* 2 To put (cattle, etc.) to feed on growing herbage. 3 To put cattle, etc., to feed on, as a pasture, grass, etc. 4 To tend (cattle, etc.) at pasture. —*n.* The act of cropping or feeding upon growing grass or the like. [OE *grasian* <*græs* grass] —**graz′er** *n.*

graze[2] (grāz) *v.* **grazed, graz·ing** *v.t.* 1 To touch or rub against lightly in passing. 2 To scrape or cut slightly in passing: The bullet *grazed* his arm. —*v.i.* 3 To touch lightly in passing. 4 To scrape slightly. —*n.* 1 A light or passing touch; a scrape or abrasion. 2 *Mil.* The explosion of a bomb or shell immediately upon impact with the gound. [? <GRAZE[1]] —**graz′er** *n.* —**graz′ing·ly** *adv.*

gra·zier (grā′zhər) *n.* 1 One who is engaged in grazing or pasturing cattle, or in raising them for the market. 2 *Austral.* One who occupies grazing land for sheep farming under a lease or license.

gra·zing (grā′zing) *n.* A pasture.

gra·zio·so (grä·tsyō′sō) *adv.* & *adj. Music* With grace. [<Ital.]

grease (grēs) *n.* 1 Animal fat, especially when soft. 2 A thick, oily or unctuous substance resembling animal fat, derived from the distillation of petroleum. 3 Wool, after shearing and before cleansing: also **grease wool.** 4 The condition of wool or furs before being cleansed: wool in the *grease.* 5 A scabrous inflammation of a horse's pastern and fetlock, characterized by an odorous, oily secretion, and, in the later stages, formation of fungoid masses: also called *grease-heel.* 6 Fat or fatness in an animal, as a deer: a hunting term. 7 *Slang* A bribe; money used for bribery. —*v.t.* (grēs, grēz) **greased, greas·ing** 1 To lubricate by smearing with grease; put grease in or on. 2 *Slang* To influence by gifts or bribes: to *grease* the hand or palm. [<OF *graisse,* ult. <L *crassus* fat]

grease cup A receptacle for lubricating oil or grease. Also **grease box, grease cock.**

grease-heel (grēs′hēl′) See under GREASE.

grease-paint (grēs′pānt′) *n.* A paste, with a grease base, used in theatrical make-up.

greas·er (grē′sər, -zər) *n.* 1 One who or that which greases. 2 *Slang* A Mexican or Spanish-American: a contemptuous term.

grease·wood (grēs′wo͝od′) *n.* Any one of various stunted and prickly shrubs of the goosefoot family (genus *Sarcobatus)* found on the alkaline plains of the western United States. Also **grease′bush′** (-bo͝osh′).

greas·y (grē′sē, -zē) *adj.* **greas·i·er, greas·i·est** 1 Smeared or spotted with grease. 2 Containing much grease or fat; unctuous; oily. 3 Resembling grease; smooth. 4 Affected with scabby sores, as a horse's heels. —**greas′i·ly** *adv.* —**greas′i·ness** *n.*

great (grāt) *adj.* 1 Very large; big; immense; vast. 2 Being much more numerous than the average: a *great* army. 3 Extending through a long time; prolonged. 4 Of very considerable degree; extreme: *great* foolishness. 5 Of large or the largest importance; mighty; foremost. 6 Having large mental, moral, or other endowments; eminent; excellent. 7 *Colloq.* Adept; skilled: He's *great* at carpentry. 8 Important; weighty; momentous. 9 Characterized by or showing elevation, as of feeling, act, or aspect; high-minded; magnanimous. 10 *Archaic* Large in or as in pregnancy; teeming; gravid. 11 More remote by a single generation than the relationship indicated by the word qualified: used in combination with a hyphen: *great*-uncle, *great*-grandson. 12 *Colloq.* Excellent: We had a *great* time. 13 Intimately acquainted: *great* friends. See synonyms under GRAND, LARGE, SERIOUS. —*n.* 1 One who is or those who are powerful, noble, influential, or rich: usually with *the.* 2 *pl.* Great go. 3 The mass, lump, or job; the whole: to do work by the *great.* ◆Homophone: *grate.* [OE *grēat*] —**great′ness** *n.*

great ape Any of the large anthropoid apes; a chimpanzee, gorilla, or orangutan.

Great Appalachian Valley A longitudinal chain of lowlands of the Appalachian Mountains extending from Canada to Alabama: also *Great Valley.*

Great Artesian Basin An area of about 680,000 square miles in eastern Australia, chiefly in Queensland, providing artesian wells. Also **Great Australian Basin.**

great auk See under AUK.

great-aunt (grāt′ant′, -änt′) *n.* A grandaunt.

Great Australian Bight A bay of the Indian Ocean in the coast of southern Australia.

Great Barrier Reef The world's largest chain of coral reefs, off the eastern coast of Queensland, Australia, extending about 1,260 miles: also *Barrier Reef.*

Great Basin An inland drainage region in the western United States, between the Wasatch and the Sierra Nevada mountains; 200,000 square miles.

Great Bear Ursa Major. See CONSTELLATION.

Great Bear Lake A lake in western Northwest Territories, Canada; 12,000 square miles; drained by the **Great Bear River,** flowing 100 miles west to the Mackenzie River.

Great Britain The principal island of the United Kingdom, comprising England, Scotland, and Wales; 88,745 square miles; capital, London.

great calorie See under CALORIE.

Great Channel A passage from the Indian Ocean to the Andaman Sea between Sumatra and the Nicobar Islands.

great circle *Geom.* A circle formed on the surface of a sphere by a plane which passes through the center of the sphere, dividing it into two equal parts.

great-cir·cle course (grāt′sûr′kəl) A course, as of a ship or aircraft, plotted along a great circle of the earth.

great·coat (grāt′kōt′) *n.* A heavy overcoat.

Great Commoner Nickname applied to William Pitt, Henry Clay, Thaddeus Stevens, and William Jennings Bryan.

Great Dane One of a breed of close-haired dogs of large size and great strength.

Great Divide See CONTINENTAL DIVIDE.

Great Dividing Range The mountains and plateaus of Australia forming the watershed of rivers flowing to the Coral and Tasman seas and those flowing to the Gulf of Carpentaria and the Indian Ocean.

great·en (grāt′n) *v.t.* & *v.i. Archaic* To make or become great or greater.

Greater Antilles See under ANTILLES.

greater glider A flying phalanger *(Schoinobates volans)* of Australia: also called *dusky glider.*

Greater New York See NEW YORK (def. 2).

Greater Sunda Islands See SUNDA ISLANDS.

Greater Walachia See MUNTENIA.

Great Falls A city in west central Montana.

Great Glen of Scotland A depression extending 60 miles across Scotland, dividing the central from the NW Highlands: also *Glen More.*

great go In British universities, the final examination for a degree.

great-grand·child (grāt′grand′chīld′) *n.* A child of a grandchild.

great-grand·daughter (grāt′gran′dô′tər) *n.* A daughter of a grandchild.

great-grand·father (grāt′grand′fä′thər) *n.* The father of a grandparent.

great-grand·mother (grāt′grand′muth′ər) *n.* The mother of a grandparent.

great gray owl See under OWL.

great gross Twelve gross, as a unit.

great-heart·ed (grāt′här′tid) *adj.* high-spirited; courageous; also, magnanimous.

great horned owl A large American owl *(Bubo virginianus)* with tufted ears that resemble horns: also called *cat owl.*

Great Kar·roo (kə·ro͞o′) A plateau region of S Northern Cape Province, Republic of South Africa: also *Central Karroo.*

Great Khing·an Mountains (king′än′, shing′) See KHINGHAN MOUNTAINS.

Great Lakes A chain of five lakes, the largest group of fresh-water lakes in the world, in central North America on the Canada-United States border: Lakes Superior, Michigan, Huron, Erie, and Ontario; total 94,710 square miles; drained by the Saint Lawrence River.

great laurel The rosebay rhododendron.

great·ly (grāt′lē) *adv.* 1 In a great manner. 2 In or to a great degree.

Great Miami River See MIAMI RIVER.

Great Mogul See under MOGUL.

Great Mother Cybele.

great northern diver See under LOON.

Great Plains A sloping plateau, generally 400 miles wide, in western North America bordering the eastern base of the Rocky Mountains from Canada to New Mexico and Texas.

great power One of the countries exercising

a predominant influence in world affairs.

great primer *Printing* A size of type (18-point).

great Pyr·e·nees (pir′ə·nēz) One of a breed of large dog with a heavy, bearlike head, broad straight back, and long thick coat.

Great Rebellion See CIVIL WAR (ENGLISH) in table under WAR.

Great Rift Valley A great depression of the Near East and eastern Africa, extending from Syria to Mozambique, and traceable by the lakes and seas filling its elongated pockets: also *Rift Valley.*

Great Russian See under RUSSIAN.

Great Sandy Desert The northern belt of the Western Australian desert, north of the Gibson Desert.

Great Salt Lake A salt lake in NW Utah having no outlet and fluctuating in size from 1,000 to 2,000 square miles: also *Salt Lake.*

Great Schism The division in the Roman Catholic Church, 1378–1417, when rival popes ruled at Rome and Avignon.

Great Seal 1 The chief seal of a government, used to authenticate important documents and commissions in the name of the sovereign or highest executive of the government. **2** The Lord Chancellor of England, custodian of the British Great Seal, or his office. See SEAL[1].

Great Slave Lake A lake in southern Northwest Territories, Canada; 11,170 square miles.

Great Slave River See SLAVE RIVER.

Great Smoky Mountains A mountain range in North Carolina and Tennessee; highest point, 6,642 feet; site of **Great Smoky Mountains National Park,** 789 square miles, established 1930. Also **Great Smokies.**

Great St. Bernard Pass See under ST. BERNARD.

great-un·cle (grāt′ung′kəl) *n.* A granduncle.

Great Valley See CENTRAL VALLEY, GREAT APPALACHIAN VALLEY.

Great Victoria Desert See VICTORIA DESERT.

Great Wall of China A monumental wall in northern China, extending 1,500 miles between China proper and Mongolia; 20 feet wide at the base, 12 feet wide at the top; from 15 to 50 feet high; constructed 246–209 B.C.: also *Chinese Wall.*

Great War See WORLD WAR I in table under WAR.

Great Week In the Greek Orthodox Church, the week before Easter.

Great White Father A name used by American Indians for the president of the United States.

great white heron 1 A large white heron *(Ardea occidentalis)* of southern North America. **2** An egret *(Casmerodius albus)* of America and the Old World.

Great White Way The brightly lighted theater district of New York City; specifically, the section near Broadway and Times Square.

Great Yarmouth A port and county borough in SE Norfolk, England, on the North Sea: also *Yarmouth.*

great year See PRECESSION OF THE EQUINOXES.

greave (grēv) *n.* Armor to protect the leg from knee to ankle. [<OF *greve;* ult. origin unknown]

greaves (grēvz) *n. pl.* Pieces of boiled tallow scrap; cracklings; also, dregs of melted tallow: also spelled *graves.* [Akin to LG *greve* refuse of tallow]

grebe (grēb) *n.* Any of a family *(Colymbidae)* of four-toed swimming and diving birds, smaller than loons and of fresh-water habitat, as the **horned grebe** *(Colymbus auritus)* and the **pied-billed grebe,** or dabchick of America. [<F *grebe;* ult. origin uncertain]

Gre·cian (grē′shən) *adj.* Greek. —*n.* **1** A Greek. **2** A scholar of Greek.

Grecian bend 1 An affected posture, fashionable among women in the nineteenth century, in which the body inclined forward from the hips. **2** A type of bustle emphasizing this posture.

Gre·cism (grē′siz·əm) *n.* **1** A Greek idiom. **2** The style or spirit of Greek art, culture, etc. Also spelled *Graecism.*

Gre·cize (grē′sīz) *v.* **·cized, ·ciz·ing** *v.t.* **1** To make Greek in form, character, etc.; Hellenize. **2** To translate into Greek. —*v.i.* **3** To adopt or imitate Greek customs, speech, etc. [<F *gréciser* <L *graecizare* <*Graecus* a Greek]

Greco– *combining form* Greek: *Greco-Roman.* Also spelled *Graeco–.* [<L *Graecus* a Greek]

Gre·co (grā′kō, grek′ō), **El,** 1541–1614, Spanish painter, born in Crete: real name *Domenico Theotocopuli.* [<Sp., the Greek]

Gre·co–Per·sian Wars (grē′kō·pûr′zhən) See table under WAR.

Gre·co–Ro·man (grē′kō·rō′mən) *adj.* Of or pertaining to Greece and Rome together: *Greco-Roman* art, *Greco-Roman* style of wrestling.

gree[1] (grē) *v.t. & v.i. Scot. & Brit. Dial.* To bring or come to agreement.

gree[2] (grē) *n. Obs.* **1** Satisfaction; legal redress. **2** Good will; favor. [<OF *gré,* ult. < L *gratus* pleasing]

gree[3] (grē) *n. Scot. & Archaic* **1** Superiority; victory. **2** The prize of victory.

Greece (grēs) A kingdom of SE Europe; 51,182 square miles; capital, Athens: Greek *Hellas.*

greed (grēd) *n.* Eager and selfish desire; greediness; avarice. [Back formation <GREEDY]

greed·y (grē′dē) *adj.* **greed·i·er, greed·i·est 1** Eager to obtain; avaricious; grasping. **2** Having excessive appetite for food or drink. [OE *grǣdig*] —**greed′i·ly** *adv.* —**greed′i·ness** *n.*

Synonyms: gluttonous, grasping, insatiable, insatiate, ravenous, selfish, voracious. See AVARICIOUS.

gree·gree (grē′grē′) See GRIGRI.

Greek (grēk) *adj.* Pertaining to Greece, its inhabitants, their language, or culture; Grecian; resembling the people of Greece. —*n.* **1** One of the people of ancient Greece; specifically, a member of one of the four major tribes: Achaean, Aeolian, Dorian, and Ionian. **2** One of the people of modern Greece, descended, with admixture, from the ancient Greeks. **3** The Indo-European, Hellenic language of ancient or modern Greece. Ancient, or classical, Greek, from Homer to about A.D. 200, is divided into four literary dialects: Aeolic, Attic, Doric, and Ionic. Abbr. *Gk.* —**Late Greek,** the language from about A.D. 200 to 600, including the patristic writings. See KOINE. Abbr. *LGk.* —**Medieval Greek,** the language of the Byzantine period, from 600 to 1500. Abbr. *Med. Gk.* —**Modern Greek,** the language of Greece since 1500, in its literary form retaining many classical features: also called *Romaic,* especially in its spoken form. **4** Language or things not understood: It's all *Greek* to me. **5** A member of the Greek Church. **6** *Colloq.* A tricky fellow; sharper; rogue. **7** *Archaic* A gay fellow; roisterer: a merry *Greek.* **8** *U.S. Slang* A member of a student fraternity designated by a combination of Greek letters. [<L *Graecus* <Gk. *Graikos* Greek] —**Greek′ish** *adj.*

Greek calends See CALENDS.

Greek Catholic A member of the Greek Church.

Greek Church 1 The Eastern or Oriental Church (officially, the Holy Oriental Orthodox Catholic Apostolic Church), which finally separated from the Roman or Western Church in the 15th century, on doctrinal and liturgical grounds: also **Greek Orthodox Church. 2** The Oriental Church in communion with Rome.

Greek cross See under CROSS.

Greek fire See under FIRE.

Greek Revival A style of architecture developed in the 18th and early 19th centuries, depending for its effect on the use of modified Greek motifs and structural elements.

Gree·ley (grē′lē), **Horace,** 1811–72, U.S. editor and politician.

Gree·ly (grē′lē), **Adolphus Washington,** 1844–1935, U.S. general and Arctic explorer.

green (grēn) *adj.* **1** Having the spectrum color between blue and yellow. **2** In leaf; grass-covered; verdant: *green* hills. **3** Not arrived at perfect or mature form or condition; unripe. **4** Of or due to immature or unskilled judgment or lack of knowledge; inexperienced; also, gullible. **5** Not seasoned or made ready for use; new; fresh; unrefined; raw. **6** Pale-greenish; pale; sickly; wan. **7** Characterized by strength or youthful vigor; flourishing. See synonyms under FRESH. —*n.* **1** The color of spring foliage; the color in the solar spectrum between the blue and the yellow. **2** A grassy level or piece of ground covered with herbage; a common; specifically, a golf putting green, or a whole golf course. **3** A green pigment or substance. **4** *pl.* The leaves and stems of young plants, as dandelion and spinach, used as food: usually boiled. **5** *pl.* Leaves or branches of trees; wreaths. **6** Something green used as an emblem. —*v.t. & v.i.* To become or cause to become green. [OE *grēne.* Akin to GRASS, GROW.] —**green′·ly** *adv.* —**green′ness** *n.*

Green (grēn), **Anna Katharine,** 1846–1935, U.S. writer. —**Hetty Howland,** 1835–1916, *née* Robinson, U.S. financier.—**John Richard,** 1837–83, English historian. —**Julian,** born 1900, French novelist born in America. — **William,** 1873–1952, U.S. labor leader, president of the American Federation of Labor 1924–52.

green algae A class *(Chlorophyceae)* of algae in which the chlorophyll-bearing cells are dominant; especially, *Protococcus viridis,* found as a coating on rocks, trees, fence posts, etc.

Green·a·way (grē′nə·wā), **Kate,** 1846–1901, English painter and illustrator of children's books, whose drawings popularized a style of children's clothes known by her name.

green·back (grēn′bak′) *n.* **1** One of a class of legal-tender notes of the United States: so called because the back is printed in green. **2** The golden plover.

Greenback party A U.S. political party, 1874–84, that advocated the restriction of the currency to Treasury notes. —**Green′back′er** *n.*

Green Bay A city in eastern Wisconsin on the Fox River at the head of **Green Bay,** an inlet of Lake Michigan in Michigan and Wisconsin.

green·belt (grēn′belt′) *n.* A strip of recreational or unoccupied land, encircling a community as a protection against objectionable property uses.

Green Berets The nickname of an elite unit of the U.S. Army, officially called Special Forces.

green·bri·er (grēn′brī′ər) *n.* Any of a genus *(Smilax)* of plants, especially a thorny vine *(S. rotundifolia)* of the United States and Canada, having small greenish flowers.

green comma A butterfly of North America *(Polygonia faunus),* so called from the greenish color and comma-shaped markings on the under side of its hind wings.

green corn Indian corn in the unripe, milky stage: boiled or roasted on the cob for eating.

green crop Green manure.

green dragon An American herb *(Arisaema dracontium)* related to the jack-in-the-pulpit: also called *dragonroot.*

Greene (grēn), **Graham,** born 1904, English novelist. —**Nathanael,** 1742–86, American general in the Revolutionary War. —**Robert,** 1558?–92, English dramatist and pamphleteer.

green earth Native clay containing small amounts of manganese and iron: used as a pigment in dyeing and as a base for some green lakes.

green·er·y (grē′nər·ē) *n. pl.* **·er·ies 1** A place where plants are grown. **2** A verdant mass of plants; verdure.

green-eyed (grēn′īd′) *adj.* **1** Having green eyes. **2** Influenced by jealousy.

green felt A cluster of green algae (genus *Vaucheria).*

green·finch (grēn′finch′) *n.* **1** An Old World finch *(Chloris chloris),* the male of which has green-and-gold plumage. **2** The Texas sparrow *(Arremonops rufivirgatus).*

green fingers Green thumb. —**green′-fin′·gered** *adj.*

green flash A vivid green hue sometimes seen on the upper edge of the sun's disk during sunrise or sunset.

green·fly (grēn′flī′) *n. pl.* **·flies** A green plant louse; an aphid.

green·gage (grēn′gāj′) *n.* A small, green-fleshed plum, originally developed in France. [<GREEN + GAGE[3]]

green gland *Zool.* One of two excretory organs near the head in decapod crustaceans.

green glass The viscid melted glass used for making bottles: also called *bottle glass.*

green gold An alloy of gold, silver, and copper in varying proportions, ranging from 14 to 18 karats in fineness, the deepest shade of green being of 18 karats: used in jewelry.

green·gro·cer (grēn′grō′sər) *n. Brit.* A retailer of fresh vegetables, fruit, etc. —**green′gro′·cer·y** *n.*

green·head (grēn′hed′) *n. pl.* **·heads** or **·head 1** The striped bass. **2** Any of various American horseflies with green eyes *(Tabanus line-*

ola or *T. costalis).* **3** The male mallard duck **4** The scaup duck. **5** The golden plover. **6** The black-bellied plover.

green·heart (grēn′härt′) *n.* A large hardwood tree *(Ocotea rodiaei)* of Guyana and the Pacific coast of the United States, with a tough, durable wood ranging in color from yellowish-green to black: used in shipbuilding: also called *bebeeru.*

green heron A small, wide-ranging American heron *(Butorides virescens)* with a greenish-black head and a white throat.

green·horn (grēn′hôrn′) *n. Colloq.* An inexperienced person. [<GREEN (*adj.* def. 3) + HORN; with ref. to an immature animal]

green·house (grēn′hous′) *n.* A building having glass walls and roof, for the protection or propagation of plants.

greenhouse effect A postulated warming of the earth due to an increase in atmospheric carbon dioxide, which is relatively transparent to incident solar radiation but opaque to reflected radiation at thermal wavelengths.

green·ing (grē′ning) *n.* One of several varieties of apples having a green skin when ripe.

green·ish (grē′nish) *adj.* Somewhat green.

Green·land (grēn′lənd) The largest island in the world, off NE North America, comprising a Danish colony; 840,000 square miles. *Danish* **Grön·land** (grœn′län′).

Greenland Sea The southern Arctic Ocean off NE Greenland and north of Iceland.

green·let (grēn′lit) *n.* A vireo.

green light **1** A green signal used in the control of traffic and indicating that traffic may proceed. **2** *Colloq.* Approval or authorization of an intended action, program, etc.

green·ling (grēn′ling) *n.* Any of a genus *(Hexagrammos)* of large, carnivorous food fishes, found in North Pacific waters.

green lizard **1** A small, harmless, insectivorous lizard *(Anolis carolinensis)* of the southern United States. **2** A slender, long-tailed bright-green lizard *(Lacerta viridis)* of Europe and Asia Minor.

green manure **1** A crop, as of beans, clover, etc., plowed under before ripening to improve the fertility of the soil: also **green crop, green dressing. 2** Unaged stable manure.

green mold See BLUE MOLD.

green monkey A monkey *(Cercopithecus sabaeus)* of West Africa having an olive-greenish coat and a white ruff.

Green Mountain Boys Vermont soldiers of the American Revolution, led by Ethan Allen.

Green Mountains A Vermont range of the Appalachians; highest peak, 4,393 feet.

Green Mountain State Nickname of VERMONT.

green pepper The unripe fruit of the red pepper (genus *Capsicum*): eaten as a vegetable.

green revolution The large-scale development of inexpensive varieties of wheat, rice, and other grains, esp. to improve the economy of underdeveloped countries.

Green River **1** A headstream of the Colorado River, flowing 730 miles south through Wyoming, Colorado, and Utah. **2** A river in central Kentucky, flowing 370 miles NW to the Ohio River.

green·room (grēn′rōōm′, -rŏŏm′) *n.* The common waiting room for performers in a theater when they are off stage.

green·sand (grēn′sand′) *n. Geol.* Either of two sandstone strata of the Cretaceous system: so called from the color imparted to it by the glauconite with which it is mingled: often used as a fertilizer and water softener. See MARL[2].

Greens·bor·o (grēnz′bûr·ō) A city in north central North Carolina.

green·shank (grēn′shangk′) *n.* A European sandpiper *(Tringa nebularia)* with greenish-gray legs and feet.

green·sick·ness (grēn′sik′nis) *n.* Chlorosis.

green soap A soft soap made from linseed oil and the hydroxides of potassium and sodium: used in the treatment of skin diseases.

green·stone (grēn′stōn′) *n.* One of various kinds of compact, igneous rocks to which a green color has been imparted by chlorite, such as diabase and diorite.

green·sward (grēn′swôrd′) *n.* Turf green with grass.

green tea Tea leaves withered and rolled but not allowed to undergo fermentation.

greenth (grēnth) *n. Rare* Verdure.

green thumb Success or skill in making plants grow easily.

Green·ville (grēn′vil) A city in NW South Carolina.

green vitriol Copperas.

Green·wich (gren′ich, -ij, grin-) A metropolitan borough of SE London on the Thames, England; former site of the Royal Observatory; location of the prime meridian.

Greenwich time See under TIME.

Green·wich Village (gren′ich, -ij) A section of New York City on the lower west side of the borough of Manhattan, formerly a village: traditionally frequented by artists, students, and writers.

green·wood (grēn′wŏŏd′) *n.* A forest in leaf.

green woodpecker A European woodpecker *(Picus viridis)* with greenish upper plumage, a scarlet crown, and a fringed band on the cheek. Also called *hickwall, yaffle.*

greet[1] (grēt) *v.t.* **1** To address words of friendliness, courtesy, respect, etc., to, as in speaking or writing. **2** To receive or meet in a specified manner: He was *greeted* with a chorus of boos. **3** To come into the sight or awareness of; appear to: The sea *greeted* their eyes. See synonyms under ADDRESS. [OE *grētan*] **—greet′er** *n.*

greet[2] (grēt) *Scot. v.i.* **grat, greet·ing** To weep. —*n.* A crying; weeping. **—greet′ing** *n.*

greet·ing (grē′ting) *n.* Salutation on meeting, or by letter or message; welcome.

greg·a·rine (greg′ə·rēn, -rin) One of an order *(Gregarinina)* of sporozoans, parasitic in arthropods, insects, crustaceans, etc. [<NL <L *gregarius* gregarious]

gre·gar·i·ous (gri·gâr′ē·əs) *adj.* **1** Having the habit of associating in flocks, herds, or companies; not habitually solitary or living alone. **2** Of or pertaining to a flock; characteristic of a crowd or aggregation. **3** *Bot.* Growing in association, but not matted together, as certain mosses; clustered. [<L *gregarius* < *grex, gregis* a flock] **—gre·gar′i·ous·ly** *adv.* **—gre·gar′i·ous·ness** *n.*

gre·go (grē′gō, grā′-) *n.* A short, hooded cloak of coarse cloth, worn in the Levant. [<Ital. *greco* Greek <L *Graecus*]

Gre·go·ri·an (gri·gôr′ē·ən, -gō′rē-) *adj.* Pertaining to one named Gregory; especially to one of the two popes, Gregory I and Gregory XIII.

Gregorian calendar See under CALENDAR.

Gregorian chant **1** The system of church music ascribed to Gregory I, used as ritual music in the Roman Catholic and some other churches. **2** Any of the traditional melodies of this music.

Greg·o·ry (greg′ər·ē) A masculine personal name: the name of sixteen popes. Also **Greg·or** (greg′ər), *Dan., Ger.* **Gre·gor** (grā′gôr), *Du., Ger.* **Gre·go·ri·us** (grā·gō′rē·ōōs), *Fr.* **Gré·goire** (grā·gwär′), *Ital., Pg., Sp.* **Gre·go·ri·o** (grā·gō′·rē·ō). [<Gk., watchman]

—Gregory I, 540?–604, pope 590–604; reformed the church service: known as **Gregory the Great.**

—Gregory VII, 1015–85, pope 1073–85; deposed by Emperor Henry IV, who appointed an anti-pope 1080: original name *Hildebrand.*

—Gregory XIII, 1502–85, pope 1572–85; reformed the Julian calendar.

—Gregory Naz·i·an·zus (naz′ē·an′zəs), 328?–389?, bishop of Constantinople: called "The Theologian."

—Gregory of Ne·o·cae·sar·e·a (nē′ō·si·zâr′ē·ə), **Saint,** 213?–270?, bishop of Neocaesarea, a city of Pontus, Asia Minor: called "Thaumaturgus."

—Gregory of Nys·sa (nis′ə), **Saint,** 332?–398?, Greek ecclesiastic; bishop of Nyssa.

—Gregory of Tours, 544?–594, Frankish historian and ecclesiastic; bishop of Tours.

Greg·o·ry (greg′ər·ē), **Lady Augusta,** 1852–1932, *née* Persse, Irish playwright. **—James,** 1638–75, Scottish mathematician and inventor.

Greifs·wald (grīfs′vält) A university city in Mecklenburg, northern East Germany.

greige (grā, grāzh) *n.* Cotton, linen, silk, rayon, or wool fabric before dyeing, sizing, or other processing: named for its gray unfinished appearance: also called *gray goods.* [<F *grège* raw, finished; infl. in form by *beige*]

grei·sen (grī′zən) *n.* A crystalline mixture of quartz and mica. [<G]

gre·mi·al (grē′mē·əl) *n.* A silken apron laid on the lap of a bishop when celebrating the Eucharist or anointing. [<L *gremium* lap]

grem·lin (grem′lin) *n.* A mischievous, invisible imp said to ride airplanes and cause mechanical trouble: a coinage of British aviators in World War II. [Origin uncertain]

Gre·na·da (gri·nā′də) An island republic in the West Indies, a member of the Commonwealth of Nations; the southernmost of the Windward Islands; with its dependencies in the Grenadines, 133 sq. mi.; capital, St. George's.

gre·nade (gri·nād′) *n.* **1** A small bomb designed to be thrown by hand (**hand grenade**) or fired from a rifle or launching device, exploding on impact or by the action of a time fuze. **2** A glass bottle containing chemicals for extinguishing a fire. **—frangible grenade** A glass bottle filled with inflammable fluid, as gasoline, which is ignited on striking any object, as an armored vehicle or tank: popularly called *Molotov cocktail* or *gasoline bomb.* [<F, a pomegranate <Sp. *granada* <L *granatus* having seeds <*granum* a eed]

gre·nade-launch·er (gri·nād′lôn′chər) *n.* An attachment to the muzzle of a rifle or other weapon by which grenades are fired.

gren·a·dier (gren′ə·dir′) *n.* **1** Formerly, a soldier assigned to throw grenades. **2** A member of a specially constituted corps or regiment, as the British Grenadier Guards. **3** Any of a family *(Macrouridae)* of deep-sea, soft-finned fishes related to the cod. [<F <*grenade.* See GRENADE.]

gren·a·dil·la (gren′ə·dil′ə), **gren·a·dil·lo** (-dil′ō) See GRANADILLO.

gren·a·dine[1] (gren′ə·dēn′, gren′ə·dēn) *n.* **1** A silk or woolen, loosely woven fabric, usually mixed with cotton: used for curtains. **2** Silk cord made of several twisted strands braided together. [<F, ? after Grenada]

gren·a·dine[2] (gren′ə·dēn′, gren′ə·dēn) *n.* A beverage sirup made from currants or pomegranates. [<F <*grenade* a pomegranate]

Gren·a·dines (gren′ə·dēnz) An island group of the Windward Islands, comprising dependencies of Grenada and St. Vincent; 30 square miles.

Gren·fell (gren′fel), **Sir Wilfred Thomason,** 1865–1940, English physician and author; missionary to Labrador.

Gre·no·ble (grə·nō′bəl, *Fr.* grə·nô′bl′) A city in SE France.

Gren·ville (gren′vil), **George,** 1712–70, English statesman; premier 1763–65. **—Sir Richard,** 1541?–91, English vice admiral: also **Greyn′·ville.**

Gresh·am (gresh′əm), **Sir Thomas,** 1519?–79, English merchant and financier.

Gresh·am's law (gresh′əmz) In political economy, the law that of two forms of currency the inferior or more depreciated tends to drive the other from circulation, owing to the hoarding and exportation of the better form: as commonly stated, "bad money drives out good." Also **Gresham's theorem.** [after Sir Thomas *Gresham*]

gres·so·ri·al (gre·sôr'ē·əl, -sō'rē-) *adj. Zool.* Having legs or feet adapted for walking; ambulatory: a *gressorial* bird or insect. Also **gres·so'ri·ous** (-sôr'ē-, -sō'rē). [< L *gressus,* pp. of *gradi* walk]

Gre·ta (grā'tə, gret'ə; *Ger.* grā'tä) Diminutive of MARGARET.

Gretch·en (grech'ən) See under MARGARET.

Gret·na Green (gret'nə) A village in Dumfriesshire, Scotland, near the English border: former scene of run-away marriages.

Greuze (grœz), **Jean Baptiste,** 1725–1805, French painter.

Grev·ille (grev'il), **Sir Fulke** See BROOKE.

grew (grōō) Past tense of GROW.

Grew (grōō), **Joseph Clark,** 1880–1965, U.S. diplomat.

grew·some (grōō'səm) See GRUESOME.

grey (grā) *adj. Brit.* Gray.

Grey (grā), **Charles,** 1764–1845, Earl Grey, English statesman. —**Sir Edward,** 1862–1933, Viscount Grey of Fallodon, English statesman; foreign secretary 1905–16. —**Lady Jane,** 1537–54, great-granddaughter of Henry VII; made heir to English throne by Edward VI; proclaimed queen 1553; deposed; beheaded.

grey·hound (grā' hound') *n.* **1** One of a breed of tall, slender dogs with a long narow head and smooth short coat: used for hunting and racing. **2** A fast ocean vessel. [OE *grighund*]

GREYHOUND
(About 26 to 28 inches high at the shoulder)

Grey·lock (grā'lok), **Mount** The highest point in Massachusetts, in the Berkshires; 3,505 eet.

grib·ble (grib'əl) *n.* A small isopod, as *Limnoria terebrans* or *L. lignorum,* that bores into and destroys submerged timber. [? Akin to GRUB]

grice (grīs) *n. Scot.* A pig; especially, a suckling pig.

grid (grid) *n.* **1** A grating of parallel bars. **2** A gridiron. **3** *Electr.* A metallic framework employed in a storage cell or battery for conducting the electric current and supporting the active material. **4** *Electronics* An electrode mounted between the cathode and anode of a vacuum tube for the control of electrons: usually in the form of a screen. **5** A system of coordinate lines superimposed upon a map and used as a basis for reference from a designated point. **6** A network of catwalks suspended from the ceiling of a motion-picture studio or other enclosure. **7** *Brit.* A network of high-tension lines for distributing electric power throughout a large area. [Short for GRIDIRON]

grid bias *Electronics* The direct-current potential applied to the grid of a vacuum tube to make it negative with respect to the filament or the cathode: also called *C-bias.*

grid circuit *Electronics* The part of a circuit between the cathode and grid of a vacuum tube.

grid condenser *Electronics* A small condenser connected in series with the grid or control circuit of a vacuum tube.

grid current *Electronics* The current flowing between the grid of a vacuum tube and the cathode.

grid·dle (grid'l) *n.* **1** A shallow pan for baking or frying thin cakes. **2** A cover for a hole in a cookstove. —*v.t.* **grid·dled, grid·dling** To cook on a griddle. [< AF *grédil,* var. of OF *greil* < LL *craticulum,* dim. of *cratis* wickerwork]

grid·dle·cake (grid'l·kāk') *n.* A thin, flat cake baked on a griddle, especially one of thin batter; a pancake.

gride (grīd) *v.t. & v.i.* **grid·ed, grid·ing 1** To grind or scrape harshly; grate. **2** To cut; pierce. —*n.* A harsh cutting, grinding, or hacking. [Metathetic var. of GIRD²]

grid emission *Electronics* The emission of electrons from the overheated grid electrode of a vacuum tube.

grid·i·ron (grid'ī'ərn) *n.* **1** A grated utensil for broiling. **2** Any object resembling or likened to a gridiron, as a football field prepared for the game, or a network of pipe lines, railroad tracks, or the like. **3** The framework above a theater stage supporting the pulleys that raise and lower scenery; a storage space for scenery. [ME *gredire,* var. of *gredile* < AF *grédil* GRIDDLE; infl. by IRON]

grid leak *Electronics* A high-resistance unit connected directly or indirectly between the grid and cathode of a vacuum tube to allow escape of excess negative charges from the grid.

grid line One of the reference lines forming part of the grid on a map or chart.

grid·lock (grid'lok') *n.* A clogged traffic situation which prevents vehicles from moving in any direction.

grid meridian A grid line extending in a north–south direction on the grid: the prime grid meridian usually coincides with the zero meridian of Greenwich.

grid north That direction on a grid map or chart which corresponds with the direction of the North Pole along the meridian of Greenwich.

grid return *Electronics* The connection which allows electrons to flow from the grid to the cathode of a vacuum tube.

grid road *Canadian* A road following a grid line of the original survey.

grid variation The angle between the magnetic and grid meridian at any place, expressed in degrees east or west to show the variation of the magnetic compass-card axis from grid north. Also called *grivation.*

grief (grēf) *n.* **1** Sorrow or mental suffering resulting from loss, affliction, regret, etc. **2** A cause of sorrow; an affliction; grievance. **3** An accident, as in hunting or racing; a mishap. **4** *Obs.* Physical pain; distress; also, a cause of pain. —**to come to grief** To have misfortune; fail. [< OF < *grever* GRIEVE]—**grief'less** *adj.* —**grief'less·ness** *n.*

Synonyms: affliction, agony, distress, melancholy, mourning, regret, sadness, sorrow, tribulation, trouble, woe. *Grief* is acute mental pain resulting from loss, misfortune, or deep disappointment. *Grief* is more acute and less enduring than *sorrow. Sorrow* and *grief* are for definite cause; *sadness* and *melancholy* may arise from a vague sense of want or loss, from a low state of health, or other ill-defined cause; *sadness* may be momentary; *melancholy* is more enduring, and may become chronic. *Affliction* is a deep *sorrow* and is applied also to the misfortune producing such *sorrow; mourning* most frequently denotes *sorrow* publicly expressed. *Antonyms*: see synonyms for HAPPINESS.

grief-strick·en (grēf'strik'ən) *adj.* Overwhelmed or bowed down by sorrow.

Grieg (grēg), **Edvard Hagerup,** 1843–1907, Norwegian composer.

griev·ance (grē'vəns) *n.* **1** That which oppresses, injures, or causes grief and a sense of wrong; a cause of annoyance. **2** A complaint, or a cause for complaint, because of a wrong suffered. **3** *Obs.* Mental or physical pain; also, anger; grief. See synonyms under INJUSTICE.

grieve (grēv) *v.* **grieved, griev·ing** *v.t.* **1** To cause great sorrow or grief to; make sad. **2** *Obs.* To injure or offend. —*v.i.* **3** To feel sorrow or grief; mourn; lament. See synonyms under HURT, MOURN. [< OF *grever* < L *gravare* oppress < *gravis* heavy]—**griev'er** *n.* —**griev'·ing** *adj.* —**griev'ing·ly** *adv.*

griev·ous (grē'vəs) *adj.* **1** Causing grief or sorrow; hard to be borne; oppressive. **2** Causing mischief or destruction; hurtful; injurious. **3** Expressive of or connected with grief or distress: a *grievous* complaint. **4** Severe: a *grievous* pain or illness. **5** Atrocious; heinous: *grievous* sin. See synonyms under HARD, HEAVY. —**griev'ous·ly** *adv.* —**griev'ous·ness** *n.*

griff (grif) *n.* **1** A series of horizontal blades in a reciprocating frame, to raise and lower the shedding mechanism of a Jacquard loom in forming the pattern. **2** Griffe¹. **3** A claw. [< F *griffe* a claw. See GRIFFE¹.]

griffe¹ (grif) *n. Archit.* An ornament in the form of a claw at an angle of the base of a column: also spelled *griff*: also called *spur.* [< F, claw < *griffer* grasp]

griffe² (grif) *n. U.S. Dial.* **1** A person having one Negro and one mulatto parent; also, a mulatto. **2** A person of mixed Negro and American Indian descent. Also **griff, grif'fin** (-in). [< F < Sp. *grifo,* orig. a griffin]

grif·fin¹ (grif'in) *n.* In Greek mythology, a creature with the head and wings of an eagle and the body of a lion: also spelled *griffon.* [< OF *grifoun* < L *gryphus* < Gk. *gryps* griffin]—**grif'fin·esque'** (-esk') *adj.*

STYLIZED HERALDIC GRIFFIN

grif·fin² (grif'in) *n. Anglo-Indian* A newcomer to India from England; greenhorn. [Origin uncertain]

Grif·fith (grif'ith), **D(avid Lewelyn) W(ark),** 1875–1948, U.S. motion-picture producer.

grif·fon (grif'ən) *n.* **1** A griffin. **2** A breed of large sporting dog of European origin, having a gray, wiry coat and long head: also *wire-haired griffon.* Compare BRUSSELS GRIFFON, BELGIAN GRIFFON, BRABANÇON GRIFFON. [< F]

grift·er (grif'tər) *n. U.S. Colloq.* A person given a concession with a circus or carnival to run a freak show or refreshment stand, or operate games of chance, etc. [? < GRAFTER]

grig (grig) *n.* **1** A cricket or grasshopper. **2** A sand eel. **3** A very lively person. [Origin uncertain]

Gri·gnard (grē·nyår'), **Victor,** 1871–1934, French chemist.

gri·gri (grē'grē') *n.* An African Negro talisman or charm; fetish: also spelled *greegree.* [< native name]

grigri man An African Negro witch doctor or magician.

grill (gril) *v.t.* **1** To cook on a gridiron; broil. **2** To torment with heat. **3** *U.S. Colloq.* To cross-examine persistently and searchingly. —*v.i.* To be cooked on a gridiron. —*n.* **1** A gridiron. **2** That which is broiled on a gridiron. **3** A grillroom. **4** The action of grilling. **5** A grille or grating of any kind. [< F *griller* < *gril* < OF *greil.* See GRIDDLE.]—**grill'er** *n.*

gril·lage (gril'ij) *n.* A heavy framework of crossed timbers or steel beams to sustain a foundation, especially on yielding soil. [< F < *grille,* var. of *gril* a grill]

grille (gril) *n.* **1** A grating or screen; especially one of wrought metal, as in a grate for shielding an open door or window. **2** In court tennis, a square opening at the rear of the hazard court. Also **grill.** [< F, var. of *gril.* See GRILL.]

grilled (grild) *adj.* **1** Having a grille. **2** Broiled.

Grill·par·zer (gril'pär·tsər), **Franz,** 1791–1872, Austrian dramatist and poet.

grill·room (gril'rōōm', -rōōm') *n.* A restaurant or eating place where grilling is done or grilled food is served.

grill·work (gril'wûrk') *n.* **1** A grille (def. 1). **2** The design or structure of a grille.

grilse (grils) *n. pl.* **grilse** or **grils·es** A young salmon after its first return to fresh water: also called *graul.* [Origin unknown]

grim (grim) *adj.* **1** Stern and forbidding in aspect or nature; fierce; ferocious. **2** Harsh; severe; dreadful. **3** Unyielding; formidable. [OE]—**grim'ly** *adv.* —**grim'ness** *n.*

Synonyms: ferocious, fierce, hideous, savage, stern, sullen, terrible. *Grim* expresses or suggests a silent but most determined ferocity; as, the *grim* aspect of the executioner. Compare FIERCE. *Antonyms*: benign, genial, gentle, kind, mild, placid, sweet, tender.

gri·mace (gri·mās') *n.* A distortion of the features, either habitual or occasioned by annoyance, disgust, contempt, etc.; a wry face. —*v.i.* **·maced, ·mac·ing** To make grimaces. [< MF < Sp. *grimazo,* prob. < Gmc.]—**gri·mac'er** *n.*

Gri·mal·di (grē·mäl'dē), **Joseph,** 1779–1837, English clown.

Grimaldi man *Anthropol.* A type of early man represented by skeletons found in the caves of Grimaldi near Menton, on the French–Italian border: variously interpreted as ancestral to the Caucasoid or Negroid type.

gri·mal·kin (gri·mal'kin, -môl-) *n.* **1** A cat,

particularly an old female cat. 2 A malevolent old woman. [<GRAY + MALKIN]

grime (grīm) *n.* That which soils; soot; dirt ground into a surface. —*v.t.* **grimed, grim·ing** To make dirty; begrime. [<Flemish *grijm*]

Grimes Golden A variety of golden-yellow eating apple. [after T. P. *Grimes,* c. 1790, who first grew it in W. Virginia]

Grimm (grim), **Jacob Ludwig Karl,** 1785–1862, and his brother **Wilhelm Karl,** 1786–1859, German philologists, noted for their collection of fairy tales.

Grimm's Law A statement by J. L. K. Grimm (earlier enunciated by Rasmus Rask) of the development of the consonants from Indo-European into Germanic. Among the commonest consonantal changes are: Indo-European voiceless plosives *(p, t, k),* represented by Sanskrit *pitár,* Greek *treis,* Latin *centum,* becoming voiceless fricatives *(f, th, h),* as seen in English *father, three, hundred;* Indo-European aspirated voiced plosives *(bh, dh, gh),* represented by Sanskrit *bhrātar,* Sanskrit *dhā,* Latin *hostis* (IE *ghosti-s*), to unaspirated voiced plosives *(b, d, g),* as in English *brother, do, guest;* Indo-European voiced plosives *(b, d, g),* represented by Latin *cannabis,* Greek *damaein,* Latin *ager,* to voiceless plosives *(p, t, k),* as in English *hemp, tame, acre.* A further development in High German accounts for the difference between English *pound,* German *pfund;* English *ten,* German *zehn,* English *make,* German *machen;* English *that,* German *das.* See VERNER'S LAW.

Grims·by (grimz′bē) The largest British fishing port, in northern Lincolnshire, England.

grim·y (grī′mē) *adj.* **grim·i·er, grim·i·est** Full of or covered with grime; dirty. **—grim′i·ly** *adv.* **—grim′i·ness** *n.*

grin[1] (grin) *v.* **grinned, grin·ning** *v.i.* **1** To smile broadly. **2** To draw back the lips so as to show the teeth, as in pain, rage, or foolish laughter. —*v.t.* **3** To express by grinning. —*n.* The act of grinning; a broad smile. [OE *grennian*] **—grin′ner** *n.* **—grin′ning·ly** *adv.*

grin[2] (grin) *n. Archaic* A snare; trap. [OE]

grind (grīnd) *v.* **ground, grind·ing** *v.t.* **1** To sharpen, polish, or shape by friction. **2** To reduce to fine particles, as by crushing or friction; triturate. **3** To rub or press gratingly or harshly: to *grind* one's teeth. **4** To oppress; harass cruelly. **5** To operate by turning a crank, as a coffee mill. **6** To produce by or as by grinding. **7** *Colloq.* To teach laboriously. —*v.i.* **8** To perform the operation of grinding. **9** To undergo grinding; become ground. **10** To rub; grate. **11** *Colloq.* To study or work steadily; drudge. —*n.* **1** The act of grinding, or the sound made by grinding. **2** *Colloq.* Work or study that is tediously and laboriously performed. **3** *Colloq.* A laborious student. [OE *grindan*] **—grind′ing** *adj. n.* **—grind′ing·ly** *adv.*

grin·de·li·a (grin·dē′lē ·ə) *n.* **1** Any plant of an American genus *(Grindelia)* of coarse herbaceous or shrubby plants with sessile, rigid leaves and large heads of yellow flowers. **2** The dried leaves and flowering tops of certain species of this plant *(G. camporum* or *G. humilis), yielding a balsam used in the treatment of asthma, bronchitis, and ivy poisoning. Also called gum plant.* [<NL, after D. H. *Grindel,* Russian botanist]

grind·er (grīn′dər) *n.* **1** One who or that which grinds, as a knife sharpener, coffee mill, etc. **2** A molar tooth.

grind·er·y (grīn′dər·ē) *n. pl.* **·er·ies 1** A place where edged tools or other instruments are ground. **2** *Brit.* Materials and tools used by leatherworkers.

grind·stone (grīnd′stōn′) *n.* **1** A flat circular stone so hung that it can be rotated upon an axis: used for sharpening tools, abrading, etc. **2** A millstone.

grin·go (grin′gō) *n. pl.* **·gos** In Latin America, a foreigner, particularly an American or Englishman: a contemptuous term. [<Am. Sp., gibberish]

Grin·nel (gri·nel′), **Henry,** 1799–1874, U.S. merchant; fitted out Arctic expeditions.

Grin·nell Land (gri·nel′) Formerly, a central section of Ellesmere Island in NE Franklin district, Northwest Territories, Canada.

grip[1] (grip) See GRIPPE.

grip[2] (grip) *n.* **1** The act of grasping firmly; a holding fast; clutch; a firm grasp. **2** A particular mode of grasping hands, as among members of a secret society, for mutual recognition. **3** *U.S.* A valise; gripsack. **4** That part of a thing by which it is grasped. **5** One of various mechanical grasping devices. **6** Ability to seize and hold physically or mentally; intellectual grasping power. **7** *Slang* A stagehand; a scene-shifter. **8** A twinge of pain. —*v.* **gripped** or **gript, grip·ping** *v.t.* **1** To take firm hold of with or as with the hand; hold onto tightly. **2** To join or attach securely with a grip (def. 5). **3** To seize or capture, as the mind; attract and hold the attention or imagination of. —*v.i.* **4** To take firm hold. **5** To take hold of the attention, imagination, etc. See synonyms under CATCH, GRASP. [Fusion of OE *gripe* a grasp and *gripa* handful, both <*gripan* seize. Akin to GROPE.] **—grip′per** *n.* **—grip′ping** *adj.* **—grip′ping·ly** *adv.*

gripe (grīp) *v.* **griped, grip·ing** *v.t.* **1** To seize and hold firmly; grasp; grip. **2** To cause pain in the bowels of, as if by sudden constriction. **3** To cause mental pain to; oppress; grieve. —*v.i.* **4** *U.S. Colloq.* To grumble; complain. **5** To suffer pains in the bowels. **6** *Obs.* To reach for or clutch something firmly. **7** *Naut.* To tend to come up into the wind. See synonyms under CATCH, GRASP. —*n.* **1** A fast or firm hold; grip; control. **2** *pl.* Intermittent pains in the bowels. [OE *gripan*] **—grip′er** *n.* **—grip′y** *adj.*

grippe (grip) *n. Influenza.* Also *grip.* [<F <*gripper* seize] **—grip′py** *adj.*

grip·ple (grip′əl) *adj. Scot.* Tenacious; greedy; covetous.

grip·sack (grip′sak′) *n.* U.S. A traveling bag, valise, or portmanteau.

Gri·qua (grē′kwə, grik′wə) *n.* A half-breed of South Africa of European (usually Dutch) and Hottentot or Bushman parents. [<Afrikaans]

Gri·qua·land East (grē′kwə· land, grik′wə-) Previous Transkeian province in Northern-Cape Province, Republic of South Africa; 6,602 square miles.

Griqualand West Previous Transkeian province in Northern Cape Province, Republic of South Africa; 15,007 square miles; chief city, Kimberley.

Gris (grēs), **Juan,** 1887–1927, Spanish painter.

gri·saille (gri·zāl, *Fr.* grē ·zä′y′) *n.* **1** A style of painting in grayish monochrome, in imitation of bas-relief: especially adapted for decoration. **2** Any object, especially glass, thus painted. [<F <*gris* gray]

Gri·sel·da (gri·zel′də, *Ital.* grē·sel′dä) A feminine personal name. Also **Gris·sel** (gris′əl). [<Gmc., stone heroine] *Griselda* In Boccaccio's *Decameron,* a lady of proverbial virtue and patience: called "Patient Griselda."

gris·e·ous (gris′ē·əs, griz′-) *adj.* Bluish-gray; having a mottled or grizzled grayish color. [<Med. L *griseus*]

gri·sette (gri·zet′) *n.* **1** A Parisian working-girl, especially one of easy, gay manners. **2** A gray woolen dress fabric worn by French working-women. [<F, orig. a gray woolen fabric < *gris* gray]

gris·kin (gris′kin) *n.* Brit. A loin of pork. [<obs. *grice* a pig + -KIN]

gris·ly[1] (griz′lē) *adj.* **·li·er, ·li·est** Savage-looking; fear-inspiring; horrifying. ◆Homophone: *grizzly.* [OE *grislic*] **—gris′li·ness** *n.*

gris·ly[2] (griz′lē) See GRIZZLY.

Gris-Nez (grē·nā′), **Cape** A headland and lighthouse of northern France on the narrowest part of the Strait of Dover.

gri·son (grī′sən, griz′·ən) *n.* A South American carnivore *(Grison vittata)* resembling a weasel. [<F *grison* <*gris* gray]

GRISON
(About 12 to 14 inches in body length)

Gri·sons (grē·zôn′) The largest canton in Switzerland; 2,746 square miles; capital, Chur. *German* **Grau·bün·den** (grou·bün′·dən), *Italian* **Gri·gi·o·ni** (grē·jyō′nē).

grist (grist) *n.* **1** A portion of grain brought to a mill to be ground; hence, that which is ground. **2** A supply; provision. **3** *U.S. Colloq.* A number or quantity of anything: a *grist* of flies. [OE <*grindan* grind]

gris·tle (gris′əl) *n.* Cartilage, especially in meat. [OE] **—gris′tled, gris′tly, gris′ly** *adj.* **—gris′tli·ness, gris′li·ness** *n.*

grist·mill (grist′mil′) *n.* A mill for grinding grain.

grit[1] (grit) *n.* **1** Rough, hard particles; sand or fine gravel. **2** A coarse compact sandstone adapted for grindstones. **3** *U.S.* Firmness of character, especially in pain or danger; pluck; courage. **4** Degree of hardness with openness of texture or composition: applied to burrstone, etc. — *v.* **grit·ted, grit·ting** *v.t.* To grind or press (the teeth) together, as in anger or determination. — *v.i.* To give forth a grating sound. [OE *grēot*]

grit[2] (grit) *n.* **1** Coarse meal. **2** *pl. U.S.* Coarsely ground hominy. [OE *grytte*]

grit[3] (grit) *adj. Scot.* Great; influential.

Grit (grit) *Canadian n.* A member of the Liberal Party. —*adj.* Of or pertaining to the Liberal Party.

grith (grith) *n.* Obs. **1** Security; specifically, in Old English law, **church grith,** the sanctuary or refuge afforded by a church. **2** A place of safety; sanctuary; refuge. Also spelled *girth.* [OE <ON *gridh* home; in pl., asylum]

grit·ty (grit′ē) *adj.* **·ti· er, ·ti·est 1** Like, containing, or consisting of grit. **2** *U.S.* Full of pluck. **—grit′ti·ly** *adv.* **—grit′ti·ness** *n.*

gri·va·tion (gri·vā′shən) *n.* Grid variation.

griv·et (griv′it) *n.* A small monkey *(Cercopithecus aethiops)* of Abyssinia, greenish above, whitish below. [Origin unknown]

Griz·el (griz′əl) See GRISELDA. Also *Scot.* **Griz′zle.**

griz·zle[1] (griz′əl) *v.t. & v.i.* **griz·zled, griz·zling** To become or cause to become gray. [<*adj.*] —*n.* **1** A mixture of white and black; gray. **2** A gray wig. **3** *Obs.* A gray-haired person. — *adj.* Gray. [<OF *grisel* <*gris* gray] **—griz′zled** *adj.*

griz·zle[2] (griz′əl) *v.i.* **griz·zled, griz·zling** *Brit. Colloq.* To grumble or fret continuously. [Freq. of dial. E *grize* grind the teeth]

griz·zly (griz′lē) *adj.* **·zli·er, zli·est** Grayish; somewhat gray: also spelled *grisly.* ◆ Homophone: *grisly*[1]. – *n. pl.* **·zlies** A grizzly bear.

grizzly bear A large, powerful, yellowish or brownish bear *(Ursus horribilis)* of western North America.

groan (grōn) *v.i.* **1** To utter a low, prolonged sound of or as of pain, sorrow, etc.; moan. **2** To be oppressed or overburdened: The people *groaned* under the heavy taxes. —*v.t.* **3** To utter or express with groans. —*n.* A low moaning sound uttered in anguish, distress, or derision. [OE *grānian*] **—groan′er** *n.* **—groan′ ing** *adj. n.* **—groan′ing·ly** *adv.*

groat (grōt) *n.* **1** A former English silver coin of the 14th–17th centuries; fourpence. **2** A trifle. [<MDu. *groot,* orig. great, large]

groats (grōts) *n. pl.* Hulled and crushed oats or wheat; fragments of wheat larger than grits. [OE *grotan*]

gro·cer (grō′sər) *n.* One who deals in supplies for the table, as sugar, tea, coffee, spices, country produce, etc., and in other household articles. [<OF *grossier,* lit., one who trades in grosses, a wholesaler <Med. L *grossarius* < *grossus* gross, great]

gro·cer·y (grō′sər·ē) *n. pl.* **·cer·ies 1** *U.S.* A grocer's store or shop. **2** *pl.* Supplies sold by a grocer.

Grod·no (grôd′nô) A city on the Nieman in western Belorussia; formerly in Poland.

grog (grog) *n.* A mixture of spirits and water; especially, rum and water; hence, any intoxicating drink. [after Old *Grog,* nickname (with ref. to his grogram cloak) of Admiral E. Vernon, 1684–1757, who first rationed it to English sailors]

grog·ger·y (grog′ər·ē) *n. pl.* **·ger·ies** *U.S. Slang* A low drinking place; a grogshop.

grog·gy (grog′ē) *adj.* **·gi·er, ·gi·est 1** Unsteady on the feet or not fully conscious; dazed, as from weakness or exhaustion. **2** Drunk. **—grog′gi·ly** *adv.* **—grog′gi·ness** *n.*

grog·ram (grog′rəm) *n.* Grosgrain. [<F *gros grain.* See GROSGRAIN.]

grog·shop (grog′shop′) *n. Brit.* A low barroom.

groin (groin) *n.* 1 *Anat.* The fleshy hollow where the thigh joins the abdomen. ◆ Collateral adjective: *inguinal.* 2 *Archit.* The line of intersection of two vaults. —*v.t.* To build with or form into groins. [? OE *grynde* abyss, hollow]

groin-rib (groin′·rib′) *n. Archit.* A rib supporting or masking a groin; an ogive.

GROIN–RIBS
In a cathedral vault.

Gro·lier de Ser·vières (grō·lyā′ də ser·vyâr′), **Jean,** 1479–1565, French collector of books and designer of bindings.

Gro·lier design (grō′lē·ər, *Fr.* grō·lyā′) In bookbinding, an ornamental design characterized by geometrical or arabesque figures and leaf sprays in gold lines. Also **Grolier scroll.** [after Jean *Grolier* de Servières]

grom·met (grom′it) *n.* 1 *Naut.* A ring of rope, as on the peak of a sail. 2 A metallic eyelet, as for a mailbag. Also spelled *grummet.* [<F *gromette* <*gourmer* curb]

grom·well (grom′wəl) *n.* 1 A rough grayish herb *(Lithospermum officinale)* of the borage family. 2 Any plant of this genus. [<OF *gromil* <L *gruinum milium* <*gruinum* a crane + *milium* millet]

Gro·my·ko (grō·mē′kō), **Andrei A.,** born 1909, U.S.S.R. Communist leader and diplomat.

Gro·ning·en (grō′ning·ən, *Du.* khrō′ning·ən) A city in northern Netherlands.

groom (grōōm, grŏŏm) *n.* 1 A person who cares for horses in the stable; hostler. 2 A bridegroom. 3 *Archaic* A menial; page; servitor. 4 A dignitary in an English royal household under the chamberlain, having nominal offices to perform. —*v.t.* 1 To take care of; especially, to clean, curry, and brush (a horse). 2 To make neat, clean, and smart. 3 *U.S.* To prepare by training and developing, as for political office: to *groom* a candidate. [ME *grom.* Cf. OF *gromet* a servant.]

groomed (grōōmd, grŏŏmd) *adj.* Brushed and cleaned; cared for: often in combination: ill-*groomed,* well-*groomed.*

grooms·man (grōōmz′mən, grŏŏms′-) *n. pl.* **·men** (-mən) The best man at a wedding.

Groot (grōt), **Gerhard,** 1340–84, Dutch reformer and preacher: known as *Gerardus Magnus.* Also **Groete, Groote.**

groove (grōōv) *n.* 1 A furrow, channel, or long hollow, especially one cut by a tool for something to fit into or work in. 2 A fixed routine in the affairs of life. 3 *U.S. Slang* A satisfying or delightful experience. **—in the groove** *Slang* Acting or performing deftly and smoothly. —*v.* **grooved, groov·ing** *v.t.* 1 To form a groove in. 2 To fix in a groove. 3 *U.S. Slang* To take satisfaction or delight in; dig. —*v.i.* 4 *U.S. Slang* To find satisfaction or delight. [<Du. *groeve.* Akin to GRAVE[2], GRAVE[3].] **—groov′er** *n.*

groov·y (grōō′vē) *adj.* **groov·i·er, groov·i·est** *U.S. Slang* Satisfying; delightful; great; super: a *groovy* feeling; *groovy* people.

grope (grōp) *v.* **groped, grop·ing** *v.i.* To feel about with or as with the hands, as in the dark; feel one's way. —*v.t.* To seek out or find by or as by groping. [OE *grāpian.* Akin to GRIP.] **—grop′er** *n.* **—grop′ing** *adj.*

Gro·pi·us (grō′pē·əs), **Walter,** 1883–1969, German architect active in the United States.

Gros (grō), **Baron Antoine Jean,** 1771–1835, French painter.

gros·beak (grōs′bēk′) *n.* Any of certain species of finches or of other small birds allied to the finches and having a large stout beak, including the **rose-breasted grosbeak** *(Hedymeles ludovicianus)* and the **pine grosbeak** *(Pinicola enucleator)* of North America. [<F *grosbec* large beak]

gro·schen (grō′shən) *n. pl.* **·schen** A former silver coin of Germany and Austria, of small value; also a current Austrian coin, a hundredth part of a schilling.

gros de Lon·dres (grō də lôn′dr′) A heavy silk material having alternating horizontal ribs of varied fineness of yarns or of different colors. [<F, heavy (silk) of London]

gro·ser (grō′zər) *n. Scot.* A gooseberry.

gros·grain (grō′grān) *n.* A closely woven corded silk or rayon fabric, often having a cotton filling, and of dull luster: used for ribbons, collar facings, etc.: also called *grogram.* [<F, large grain]

gross (grōs) *adj.* 1 Conspicuous by reason of size or openness; glaring; flagrant: said of errors, wrongs, faults, untruths, etc. 2 Undiminished by deduction; entire: opposed to *net*: *gross* earnings, *gross* weight. 3 Coarse in meaning or sense; indelicate; obscene: *gross* epithets. 4 Of excessive or repulsive size combined with coarseness; big; fat; bulky: a *gross* woman. 5 Wanting in fineness; coarse in composition or structure: *gross* material. 6 Closely compacted, so as to be thick or dense: *gross* vapors. 7 Wanting in delicacy of perception or sensibility; dull of apprehension or feeling; stupid. 8 Not specific or detailed; general. 9 *Obs.* Palpable; obvious. See synonyms under CORPULENT, FOUL, IMMODEST, THICK, VULGAR. —*n. pl.* **gross** 1 Twelve dozen, as a unit. 2 The greater part; mass; entire amount. **—in gross** or **in the gross** In bulk; all together. —*v.t.* & *v.i.* To make or earn (total profit) before deduction of expenses, taxes, etc. [<OF *gros* <LL *grossus* thick] **—gross′ly** *adv.* **—gross′ness** *n.*

gross national product The total market value of a nation's goods and services, before any deductions or allowances are made.

gros·su·lar·ite (gros′yə·lə·rīt′) *n.* A variety of garnet composed of colorless calcium aluminum silicate and varying from colorless when pure to pale green, gray, pink, or brown, depending on trace impurities. [<NL *grossularia* a gooseberry + -ITE[1]]

Gross·war·dein (grōs′vär·dīn′) The German name for ORADEA.

grosz (grôsh) *n. pl.* **grosz·y** (grôsh′ē) A hundredth part of a zloty. [<Polish]

Grosz (grōs), **George,** 1893–1959, German painter active in the United States.

grot (grot) *n. Poetic* A grotto. [<F *grotte.* See GROTTO.]

Grote (grōt), **George,** 1794–1871, English historian.

gro·tesque (grō·tesk′) *n.* 1 The incongruous, fantastic, or uncouth in art; specifically, painting or sculpture combining human and animal forms with foliage, wreaths, etc. 2 Any disproportionate or ludicrous person, figure, or design. —*adj.* 1 Incongruously composed or ill-proportioned; fantastic; ludicrously or whimsically odd or extravagant. 2 Containing or comprised of incongruous or fantastic details; pertaining to grotesques. See synonyms under FANCIFUL, ODD, RIDICULOUS. [<F <Ital. *grottesco* <*grotta* a grotto, excavation; with ref. to works of art found in excavations of ancient houses] **—gro·tesque′ness** *n.*

gro·tes·que·ry (grō·tes′kə·rē) *n. pl.* **·ries** 1 The quality of being grotesque; grotesqueness. 2 A grotesque object, action, event, etc. 3 A grotesque ornamental style or detail, as in architecture. Also **gro·tes′que·rie.**

Gro·ti·us (grō′shē·əs), **Hugo,** 1583–1645, Dutch jurist and statesman: called the "Father of International Law": originally, *Huig van Groot.*

grot·to (grot′ō) *n. pl.* **·toes** or **·tos** A small cave; an artificial cavernlike retreat. [<Ital. *grotta* <L *crypta.* Doublet of CRYPT.]

grouch (grouch) *U.S. Colloq. v.i.* To grumble; be surly or discontented. —*n.* 1 A discontented, grumbling person. 2 A grumbling, sulky mood. [<OF *groucher* murmur] **—grouch′er** *n.* **—grouch′i·ly** *adv.* **—grouch′i·ness** *n.* **—grouch′y** *adj.*

ground[1] (ground) *n.* 1 The firm, solid portion of the earth at and near its surface. 2 Hence, soil; earth; dirt. 3 Any region or tract of land, especially a portion put to special use: a parade *ground,* hunting *ground,* etc. 4 *Often pl.* A starting point; good reason; basis; sufficient cause: On what *ground* is the argument based?; also, pretext. 5 Position or distance: to gain, hold, or lose *ground.* 6 *pl.* The particles that settle at the bottom of a liquid preparation; dregs. 7 In various arts, some preparative work or part, as a surface to be worked on; in painting, a first coat or color or a surface prepared therewith. 8 *Music* The plain song or air as a basis for development and variation. 9 *Electr.* a A connection of a circuit with the earth. b An object or place to which a ground wire is attached. 10 *Often pl.* Private land; landed estate; especially in the plural, the enclosed spaces immediately appertaining to a mansion. 11 *Often pl.* The base or foundation, as of belief or knowledge. 12 The bottom, as of a lake or the ocean; lowest depth. See synonyms under LAND, REASON. **—to gain ground** 1 To conquer land. 2 To make progress; win favor, position, influence, etc. **—to stand one's ground** To maintain an argument or a purpose. —*adj.* 1 Being on the ground or on a level with it. 2 Fundamental: the *ground* form of a word. 3 Terrestrial: said of birds: the *ground* sparrow, *ground* warbler. 4 Burrowing: the *ground* squirrel, *ground* snake. 5 Growing on the ground; trailing or dwarfed: *ground* ivy, *ground* hemlock. —*v.t.* 1 To put, place, or set on the ground. 2 To fix firmly on a basis; found; establish. 3 To train (someone) in first principles or elements, as of Latin or science. 4 *Aeron.* To cause to stay on the ground. 5 *Naut.* To cause to run aground, as a ship. 6 To furnish (a surface) with a ground or background for painting, etc. 7 *Electr.* To place in connection with the earth, as a circuit. —*v.i.* 8 To come or fall to the ground. 9 In baseball, to be retired on a grounder batted to an opposing player: usually with *out.* 10 *Naut.* To run aground. 11 To sink to the bottom: The bait *grounds.* [OE *grund*]

ground[2] (ground) Past tense and past participle of GRIND.

ground·age (groun′dij) *n. Brit.* A charge for space occupied by a vessel while in port.

ground bait Bait dropped to the bottom to attract fish.

ground bass *Music* A short bass part or phrase repeated continually against varied melody and harmony in the upper parts.

ground beetle Any of various insectivorous beetles of the family *Carabidae,* often found under logs, stones, etc. For illustration see under INSECT (beneficial).

ground bird A field sparrow or vesper sparrow.

ground cherry Any of several plants of the nightshade family (genus *Physalis*), as the Cape gooseberry *(P. peruviana),* having yellow, edible berries, or the common strawberry tomato *(P. pruinosa).*

ground connection *Electr.* A wire or other conductor for grounding a current.

ground cover Low-growing plants, shrubs, and other vegetation.

ground crew *Aeron.* The crew required for the landing, servicing, repairing, and maintenance of aircraft, including the landing crew, mechanics, etc.

ground·er (groun′dər) *n.* 1 One who or that which grounds. 2 In baseball, a batted ball that rolls or bounces along the ground.

ground floor The floor of a building level or almost level with the ground. —*U.S. Colloq.* **to get in on the ground floor** To enter a company or join a business undertaking at its inception and hence receive equal profits with the promoters.

ground fog *Meteorol.* A narrow layer of fog formed over a cool land surface, and not exceeding the height of a man.

ground frost A ground temperature low enough to cause injury to growing plants: usually reckoned at 30° F.

ground gear *Aeron.* The apparatus and equipment needed for the landing of aircraft and their handling while on the ground.

ground glass See under GLASS.

ground hemlock A low, evergreen shrub *(Taxus canadensis)* of the northern United States with long, straggling branches and a red fruit; the American yew: also called *moosegrass.*

ground hog 1 The woodchuck. 2 The aardvark. 3 A sandhog.

ground-hog day (ground′hôg′, -hog′) February 2, Candlemas: according to rural tradition, if the ground hog, emerging after hibernation, sees his shadow on this day, he retreats to his hole, thus indicating six weeks more of winter; if he does not see his shadow it is a sign of an early spring.

ground ivy A creeping herb *(Nepeta hederacea)* with roundish, kidney-shaped, scalloped leaves and bluish-purple flowers.

ground laurel The trailing arbutus.

ground·less (ground′lis) *adj.* Without foundation, reason, or cause. **—ground′less·ly** *adv.* **—ground′less·ness** *n.*

ground·ling (ground′ling) *n.* **1** An animal of terrestrial habits. **2** A plant which creeps on the ground. **3** A fish that keeps to the bottom. **4** Formerly, one of the audience in the pit of a theater; hence, a person of unrefined tastes.

ground loop *Aeron.* An acute, ungovernable turning of an aircraft during a landing or a take-off.

ground·mass (ground′mas′) *n. Geol.* A compact and fine-grained or glassy portion of porphyritic igneous rock, in which the phenocrysts, or larger, distinct crystals, are embedded.

ground·nut (ground′nut′) *n.* **1** The peanut. **2** Any of several plants having edible tubers attached to the roots, as the **ground pea,** a North American wild bean *(Apios americana),* and the dwarf ginseng *(Panax trifolium).* **3** St. Anthony's nut.

ground owl A small, long-legged, terrestrial owl *(Speotyto cunicularia)* common in the western United States, where it digs extensive nesting burrows in open prairie country: also called *burrowing owl.*

ground pine **1** An evergreen, generally creeping plant *(Lycopodium obscurum)*; clubmoss. **2** An evergreen European herb *(Ajuga chamaepitys)*: so called from its resinous odor.

ground pink The moss pink.

ground plan **1** The plan of the ground floor of a building. **2** Any preliminary plan or outline.

ground plate **1** A groundsill. **2** A bedplate, as for railroad ties. **3** *Electr.* A metal plate in the ground forming the earth connection of a circuit.

ground plum **1** A plant *(Astragalus crassicarpus)* of the bean family, found in the western Mississippi valley from Minnesota to Texas. **2** Its thick, fleshy, plum-shaped pod. Also called *milkvetch.*

ground rattlesnake The massasauga.

ground rent Compensation paid each year, or for a term of years, for grounds leased for building or other improvement.

ground-re·turn circuit (ground′ri·tûrn′) See EARTH RETURN.

ground robin The towhee.

ground·sel (ground′səl) *n.* **1** A common herb of the composite family (genus *Senecio*), having yellow tubular flowers. **2** Groundsill. [OE *gundæswelgiæ,* lit., that swallows pus (with ref. to its use in poultices); infl. in form by OE *grund* ground]

groundsel tree A small tree of the North American Atlantic coast *(Baccharis halimifolia),* with showy white or yellow flowers.

ground·sill (ground′sil′) *n.* The lowest horizontal timber in a frame building: also *groundsel.*

ground sparrow Any of various small sparrows that nest on the ground, as the vesper sparrow or the song sparrow.

ground speed *Aeron.* The speed of an airplane with relation to the earth. See AIR SPEED.

ground squirrel **1** A chipmunk. **2** A gopher.

ground state *Physics* That condition of an atom which corresponds to its lowest level of energy and, hence, to its maximum stability.

ground swell A broad, deep swell or heaving of the sea caused by prolonged storm, continuing into calm weather, and frequently reaching open stretches of coast remote from the area of the storm.

ground water Free subsurface water, the top of which is the water table; all water in and saturating the soil.

ground wave A radio wave which travels along the surface of the ground.

ground·ways (ground′wāz′) *n. pl. Naut.* Timbers fixed to the ground and extending fore and aft under the hull of a ship on each side of the keel, to form the surface track on which a ship is launched.

ground wire The wire connecting an electrical apparatus with the ground or with a grounded object.

ground·work (ground′wûrk′) *n.* A fundamental part; basis.

ground zero The point on the ground vertically beneath or above the point of detonation of an atomic or thermonuclear bomb.

group (grōōp) *n.* **1** A number of persons, animals, or things existing or brought together; an assemblage; cluster. **2** In painting or sculpture, an assemblage of figures or objects affording a harmonious unit or design. **3** A number of plants or animals classed together because of certain common characteristics. **4** In the U.S. Air Force, a tactical, maintenance, medical, or administrative subdivision of a wing. **5** In the U.S. Army or Marine Corps, a tactical unit consisting of two or more battalions. **6** *Chem.* **a** A number of connected atoms constituting a part of a molecule: the hydroxyl *group* (OH). **b** A set of elements having similar properties, as in the periodic table. **7** *Geol.* A rock system of highest rank, corresponding with an era in the time scale. **8** An ethnological or linguistic division ranking below a branch. *—v.t.* & *v.i.* To gather or form into a group or groups. [<F *groupe* <Ital. *groppo* knot, lump <Gmc.]

group·er (grōō′pər) *n.* Any of certain serranoid food fishes of warm seas, of *Mycteroperca, Epinephalus,* and related genera. [<Pg. *garupa,* appar. <S. Am. Ind.]

group·ie (grōō′pē) *n. Slang* A fan or supporter, especially a young woman who follows a performer in a rock-and-roll group on tour.

group·ment (grōōp′mənt) *n.* A grouping; specifically, a grouping of battalions or larger units.

grouse[1] (grous) *n. pl.* **grouse** Any of a family *(Tetraonidae)* of game birds of the northern hemisphere, related to the pheasants, smaller than the domestic hen, and having mottled plumage; especially, the **red grouse** *(Lagopus scoticus)* of the British Isles, the **ruffed grouse** or partridge *(Bonasa umbellus)* of the United States, the **pinnated grouse** or prairie chicken *(Tympanuchus cupido),* the **sage grouse** or cock of the plains, the **spruce grouse** or spruce partridge *(Canachites canadensis),* and the capercaillie. [Origin uncertain]

RUFFED GROUSE (From 12 to 17 inches tall)

grouse[2] (grous) *Slang v.i.* **groused, grous·ing** To grumble; grouch. [<OF *grousser* murmur] **—grous′er** *n.* **—grous′ing** *n.*

grout (grout) *n.* **1** A light, semi-liquid cement mortar used to fill joints between stones, bricks or tiles. **2** A finishing coat for surfaces. **3** Coarse meal. **4** *pl.* Groats. **5** *pl.* Dregs; lees; grounds. **6** A wall coating of rough plaster studded with small stones. *—v.t.* To fill, surround, or finish with grout. [OE *grūt* coarse meal] **—grout′er** *n.*

grout·y (grou′tē) *adj.* **1** Turbid, as liquor. **2** *Slang* Cross or surly; sulky.

grove (grōv) *n.* A group of trees, smaller than a forest; a small wood, especially when cleared of underbrush. ◆ Collateral adjective: *nemoral.* [OE *grāf*]

grov·el (gruv′əl, grov′-) *v.i.* **grov·eled** or **grov·elled, grov·el·ing** or **grov·el·ling** **1** To creep or crawl face downward; lie abjectly prostrate. **2** To act with abject humility; abase oneself, as from fear or servility. **3** To take pleasure in what is base or sensual. [Back formation <GROVELING] **—grov′el·er** or **grov′el·ler** *n.*

grov·el·ing (gruv′əl·ing, grov′-) *adj.* Lying prostrate; abject; low; mean; sordid. Also **grov′el·ling.** See synonyms under BASE[2]. [ME *grovelynge, adv.* <*on gruff* face down (<ON *a grufu*) + -LING[2]] **—grov′el·ing·ly** *adv.*

groves of Ac·a·deme (ak′ə·dēm′) See under ACADEME.

grow (grō) *v.* **grew, grown, grow·ing** *v.i.* **1** To increase in size by the assimilation of nutriment; progress toward maturity. **2** To sprout and develop to maturity, as from a seed or spore. **3** To flourish; thrive: Moss *grows* in damp places. **4** To become more in size, quantity, or degree: The storm was *growing.* **5** To become; come to be gradually: She was *growing* angry. **6** To become fixed or attached by or as by growth: The vine *grew* to the wall. *—v.t.* **7** To cause to grow; raise by cultivation. **8** To develop: This crab will *grow* a new shell. **9** To cover with a growth: used in the passive: The hull was *grown* with weeds. **—grow on** To become gradually more pleasing or important to. **—grow up** To reach adult maturity. See synonyms under FLOURISH. [OE *grōwan*] **—grow′er** *n.*

grow·ing-pains (grō′ing·pānz′) *n. pl.* **1** Pains of a rheumatic or neuralgic character sometimes experienced during the period of growth in children. **2** Problems encountered in the early phases of an enterprise.

growl (groul) *n.* **1** The guttural threatening sound made by an angry animal. **2** Angry faultfinding; grumbling. *—v.i.* **1** To utter a growl, as an angry dog. **2** To grumble or find fault in a surly manner. **3** To rumble, as distant thunder. *—v.t.* **4** To express by growling. See synonyms under COMPLAIN. [? <OF *grouler* mumble <Gmc.]

growl·er (grou′lər) *n.* **1** One who or that which growls. **2** *U.S. Slang* A vessel in which beer is carried home from the place of sale. **3** *Brit. Slang* A four-wheeled cab. **4** *Electr.* A device which indicates the presence of a short circuit by a growling sound produced by two field poles arranged as in a motor. **5** An irregular fragment of an iceberg or mass of floe ice large enough to be dangerous to ships.

grown (grōn) *adj.* Mature; fully developed.

grown-up (grōn′up′) *n.* A mature person. *—adj.* (grōn′up′) Adult or like adults.

growth (grōth) *n.* **1** The process of growing; gradual increase of a living organism by natural process; development to maturity or full size. **2** Any gradual increase or development; augmentation; progress. **3** Anything grown or produced, or in the process of growing; product; effect. **4** *Pathol.* A morbid formation: a cancerous *growth.* See synonyms under HARVEST, INCREASE, PROGRESS.

growth industry An industry with a rate of growth or development greater than the rate of growth of the economy as a whole.

growth ring An annual ring.

Groz·ny (grôz′nē) A city east of the Caspian Sea, Russian S.F.S.R. Also **Groz′nyy.**

grub (grub) *v.* **grubbed, grub·bing** *v.i.* **1** To dig in the ground. **2** To do menial labor; toil: to *grub* for a living. **3** To make careful or plodding search; rummage. **4** *Slang* To eat. *—v.t.* **5** To dig from the ground; root out: often with *up* or *out.* **6** To clear (ground) of roots, stumps, etc. **7** *Slang* To provide with food. *—n.* **1** The wormlike larva of certain insects, as of the June beetle and most of the *Hymenoptera.* See illustration under INSECT. **2** One who grubs; a grind or drudge. **3** *Slang* Food. [ME *grubben.* Akin to GRAVE[1], GRAVE[2].]

grub·ber (grub′ər) *n.* **1** One who or that which grubs. **2** A grub hoe. **3** A machine or tool for pulling up stumps.

grub·by (grub′ē) *adj.* **·bi·er, ·bi·est** **1** Dirty; unclean. **2** Full of grubs: specifically used in the western United States of cattle or sheep attacked by the larvae of botflies or warbleflies. **—grub′bi·ly** *adv.* **—grub′bi·ness** *n.*

grub hoe A heavy hoe for digging or for grubbing out stumps; a mattock. See illustration under HOE.

grub·stake (grub′stāk′) *U.S. n.* Money, supplies, or equipment provided a prospector on condition of a share of his finds. *—v.t.* **·staked, ·stak·ing** To supply with a grubstake.

grub·street (grub′strēt′) *adj.* Characteristic of literary hacks or their work; second-rate. *—n.* Inferior authors and literary hacks as a class, or their work.

Grub Street The former name of Milton Street, London, once frequented by needy authors and literary hacks.

grudge (gruj) *v.* **grudged, grudg·ing** *v.t.* **1** To envy the possessions or good fortunes of (another). **2** To give or allow unwillingly and resentfully; begrudge. *—v.i.* **3** *Obs.* To be envious or discontented; grumble. *—n.* **1** Ill will cherished for some remembered wrong. **2** Reluctance; unwillingness. See synonyms under HATRED, PIQUE[1]. [<OF *groucher.* Cf. GROUCH.] **—grudg′er** *n.* **—grudg′ing·ly** *adv.*

Gru·dziądz (grōō′jônts) A city on the Vistula in northern Poland: German *Graudenz.*

grue (gro͞o) *v.i. Scot.* & *Brit. Dial.* To feel dread or horror; shudder. [Akin to Du. *gruwen* shudder]

gru·el (gro͞o′əl) *n.* A semi-liquid food made by boiling meal in water or milk. —**to take one's gruel** To take one's punishment. —*v.t.* **gru·eled** or **gru·elled, gru·el·ing** or **gru·el·ling** To wear out, disable, or exhaust by hard work, punishment, etc. [<OF, meal, ult. <Med. L *grutum* coarse meal <Gmc.] —**gru′el·er** or **gru′el·ler** *n.* —**gru′el·ly** *adj.*

gru·el·ing (gro͞o′əl·ing) *adj.* Severe; exhausting; punishing. —*n.* Punishment; exhausting labor; prolonged and relentless questioning, etc. Also **gru′el·ling.**

grue·some (gro͞o′səm) *adj.* Frightening; grisly: also spelled *grewsome.* [<GRUE + -SOME] —**grue′some·ly** *adv.* —**grue′some·ness** *n.*

gruff (gruf) *adj.* Having a rough or brusque manner, voice, or countenance; harsh; surly. See synonyms under MOROSE. [<Du. *grof* rough] —**gruff′ish, gruff′y** *adj.* —**gruff′ly, gruff′i·ly** *adv.* —**gruff′ness, gruff′i·ness** *n.*

gru-gru (gro͞o′gro͞o′) *n.* **1** Either of two West Indian palms (*Acrocomia aculeata* or *A. sclerocarpa*) the nuts of which yield a butter-like oil used for scenting toilet soap: also **gru-gru palm. 2** The larva of a South American palm weevil (*Rhynchophorus palmarum*), destructive to the gru-gru and other palms and sugarcane, and eaten as a delicacy: also **gru-gru worm.** [<Sp. *grugrú* <Cariban]

grum (grum) *adj.* **grum·mer, grum·mest** *Rare* **1** Morose, sullen, or sour; surly. **2** Guttural; gruff. [Prob. blend of GRIM and GLUM]

grum·ble (grum′bəl) *v.* **grum·bled, grum·bling** *v.i.* **1** To complain in a surly manner; mutter. **2** To make growling sounds in the throat. **3** To rumble, as thunder. —*v.t.* **4** To say with a grumble. See synonyms under COMPLAIN. —*n.* **1** A surly, discontented sound or complaint; murmur. **2** *pl.* An ill-tempered, complaining mood. **3** A rumble. [Cf. Du. *grommelen* <*grommen* growl] —**grum′bler** *n.* —**grum′bling·ly** *adv.* —**grum′bly** *adj.*

Grum·ble·to·ni·an (grum′bəl·tō′nē·ən) *n.* A political nickname for one who opposed the policies of William III of England.

grume (gro͞om) *n.* **1** A viscid, semifluid mass. **2** A clot, as of blood. [<F <L *grumus* little pile]

grum·met (grum′it) See GROMMET.

gru·mose (gro͞o′mōs) *adj. Bot.* Consisting of clustered grains.

gru·mous (gro͞o′məs) *adj.* **1** Like grume; clotted. **2** Grumose.

grumph (grumf) *Scot. v.t.* & *v.i.* To grunt. —*n.* A grunt.

grumph·ie (grum′fē) *n. Scot.* A pig; especially, a sow. Also **grumph′y.**

grump·y (grum′pē) *adj.* **grump·i·er, grump·i·est** Exhibiting surliness or gruffness; cranky. Also **grump′ish.** [Blend of GRUNT and DUMP] —**grump′i·ly** *adv.* —**grump′i·ness** *n.*

grund (gro͝ond) *Scot. v.* & *n.* Ground. Also **grun.**

Grun·dy (grun′dē), **Mrs.** A character in Morton's comedy, *Speed the Plough* (1798): now symbolizing society in general as a censor of morals and manners. —**Grun′dy·ism** *n.*

grun·ion (gro͞on·yōn′) *n.* A silversides (*Leuresthes tenuis*), common on the coast of California. [Prob. <Sp. *gruñón* grunter]

grun·stane (gro͞on′stən) *n. Scot.* A grindstone. Also **grun′stun.**

grunt (grunt) *v.i.* **1** To make the deep, guttural sound of a hog. **2** To make a similar sound, as in annoyance, assent, effort, etc. —*v.t.* **3** To express, as dissent or disapproval, by grunting. See synonyms under COMPLAIN. —*n.* **1** A short, guttural sound, as of a hog. **2** A food fish of warm American seas related to the snappers (*Haemulon* and related genera): so called from the noise it makes when caught. [OE *grunnettan*] —**grunt′er** *n.*

grun·tle (grun′təl) *Brit. Dial. v.i.* To grunt; sulk. —*n.* A grunt; a snout. [Freq. of GRUNT]

grun·yie (gro͞on′yē) *n. Scot.* A snout. Also **grun′zie.**

Grus (grus) A constellation, the Crane. See under CONSTELLATION.

grush·ie (grush′ē, gro͝osh′ē) *adj. Scot.* Growing luxuriantly; thick.

grutch (gruch, gro͝och) *v.t.* & *v.i. Scot.* & *Brit. Dial.* Grudge.

Gru·yère (grē·yâr′, gro͞o-; *Fr.* grü·yâr′) *n.* A light-yellow, whole-milk Swiss cheese, usually without holes. [from *Gruyère,* a town in Switzerland]

Gru·zi·ya (gro͞o′zyē·yə) The Russian name for GEORGIA, U.S.S.R.

gryl·lid (gril′id) *n.* One of a family (*Gryllidae*) of orthopterous insects having the hind legs specialized for jumping, long, slender antennae, and wings frequently reduced or absent; a cricket. —*adj.* Of or pertaining to the *Gryllidae.* [<NL <L *gryllus* a grasshopper <Gk. *gryllos*]

G-string (jē′string′) *n.* **1** A strip of cloth passed between the legs and supported at the waist by a band or cord; a loincloth. **2** A thin strip of cloth, often ornamented with tassels and spangles, worn about the groin and hip by strip-teasers.

gua·cha·ro (gwä′chä·rō) *n.* The oilbird (*Steatornis caripensis*) of South America and Trinidad, of frugivorous and nocturnal habits, from whose young an oil is extracted and used by the natives as butter and for illumination. [<Sp. *guácharo*]

gua·co (gwä′kō) *n.* Any of certain tropical American climbing plants used as antidotes to snake bites; especially, the birthworts (genus *Aristolochia*), closely allied to the Virginia snakeroot, and a climbing Brazilian plant (genus *Mikania*), of the composite family. [<Sp. <native name]

Gua·da·la·ja·ra (gwä′thä·lä·hä′rä) A city of west central Mexico, capital of Jalisco state.

Gua·dal·ca·nal (gwä′dəl·kə·nal′) The largest island in the British Solomon Islands protectorate; 2,500 square miles; scene of first Allied invasion northward in the Pacific in World War II, August, 1943.

Gua·dal·qui·vir (gwä′thäl·kē·vir′) A river in southern Spain, flowing over 360 miles SW to the Gulf of Cadiz.

Gua·da·lupe Hi·dal·go (gwä′də·lo͞op′ hi·dal′gō, *Sp.* gwä′thä·lo͞o′pä ē·thäl′gō) A former town, part of Gustavo A. Madero federal district in south central Mexico; site of the shrine of Our Lady of Guadalupe and of the signing of the treaty ending the Mexican War, 1848.

Gua·da·lupe Mountains (gô′də·lo͞op′, gwä′·də·lo͞op′) A range in SW Texas and southern New Mexico between the Pecos and Rio Grande rivers; highest point, **Guadalupe Peak,** is highest point in Texas, 8,751 feet.

Gua·da·lupe River (gô′də·lo͞op′, gwä′də·lo͞op′) A river in Texas, flowing 458 miles SE to San Antonio Bay.

Gua·de·loupe (gô′də·lo͞op′, *Fr.* gwȧ·də·lo͞op′) An overseas department of France in the Lesser Antilles, comprising the twin islands of Basse-Terre (also called *Guadeloupe*) and Grande-Terre; together 583 square miles; with island dependencies, 639 square miles; capital, Basse-Terre.

Gua·di·a·na (gwä′dē·ä′nə, *Pg.* gwə·thya′nə; *Sp.* gwä·thyä′nä) A river in SW Spain and SE Portugal, flowing west 510 miles to the Gulf of Cádiz.

guai·ac (gwī′ak) *n.* **1** A brown or greenish-brown resin extracted from guaiacum: used in medicine, in making paints and varnishes, etc.: also **guai′a·cum** (-ə·kəm). **2** The Tonka bean.

guai·a·col (gwī′ə·kōl, -kol) *n. Chem.* A colorless fluid or white crystalline compound, $C_7H_8O_2$, obtained by distilling guaiacum, found in hardwood tar, and also made synthetically: its compounds are widely used in medicine. [<GUAIAC(UM) + -OL[2]]

guai·a·cum (gwī′ə·kəm) *n.* **1** Any of a genus (*Guajacum*) of tropical American trees or shrubs of the caltrop family, especially *G. officinale* and *G. sanctum.* **2** The hard, durable, resinous wood of this tree or shrub; lignumvitae. **3** Guaiac. [<NL <Sp. *guayacán* <Taino]

Guai·ra (gwī′rə), **La** See LA GUAIRA.

Gual·te·ri·o (gwäl·tā′rē·ō) Spanish form of WALTER. *Ital.* **Gual·tie·ro** (gwäl·tyâ′rō).

Guam (gwäm) The largest island of the Marianas group, comprising an unincorporated territory of the United States; ceded by Spain in 1898; 217 square miles; capital, Agaña. —**Gua·ma·ni·an** (gwə·mā′nē·ən) *adj.* & *n.*

guan (gwän) *n.* A Central and South American gallinaceous bird (subfamily *Penelopinae*), related to the curassows, having a long tail. [<Sp. <Cariban]

Gua·na·ba·ra Bay (gwu·nə·vä′rə) An inlet of the Atlantic in SE Brazil; Rio de Janeiro is on the SW shore. Also **Río de Janeiro Bay.**

gua·na·co (gwä·nä′·kō) *n. pl.* **·cos** or **·co** A South American ruminant of the llama family (*Lama huanacus*), of light-brown color, passing into white below: also spelled *huanaco.* [<Sp. < Quechua]

GUANACO
(From 4 to 4 1/2 feet high at the shoulder)

Gua·na·jua·to (gwä′·nä·hwä′tō) A state in central Mexico; 11,804 square miles; capital Guanajuato.

gua·nase (gwä′nās) *n. Biochem.* An autolytic enzyme capable of changing guanine into xanthine.

gua·ni·dine (gwä′nə·dēn, -din, gwan′ə-) *n. Chem.* A strongly basic crystalline compound, CH_5N_3, formed by the oxidation of guanine: many of its derivatives are used in the making of plastics, resins, explosives, etc. Also **gua′·ni·din** (-din).

gua·nine (gwä′nēn) *n. Biochem.* A white amorphous compound, $C_5H_5N_5O$, contained in guano, fish scales, muscle tissue, the pancreas: it is also a decomposition product of nucleoproteins. Also **gua′nin** (-nin). [<GUANO + -INE[2]]

gua·no (gwä′nō) *n. pl.* **·nos 1** The accumulated excrement of sea birds found in the dry climate of the Peruvian coast and elsewhere: used as a fertilizer. **2** A manufactured nitrogenous fertilizer; also, decomposing animal remains used as a fertilizer. [<Sp. <Quechua *huanu* dung]

Guan·tá·na·mo (gwän·tä′nä·mō) A city near **Guantánamo Bay,** a sheltered Caribbean inlet, site of a U.S. naval station in SE Cuba.

Guap (wäp) A former spelling of YAP.

Gua·po·ré (gwä·pô·rā′) **1** A river of central South America, forming part of the boundary between Brazil and NE Bolivia and flowing 750 miles NW to the Mamore: also *Iténez.* **2** The former name of RONDÔNIA.

gua·ra·ni (gwä′rä·nē′) *n.* The basic monetary unit of Paraguay, equal to 100 centavos.

Gua·ra·ni (gwä′rä·nē′) *n. pl.* **·nis** or **·ni 1** A member of any of a group of South American Indian tribes, comprising the southern branch of the Tupian stock, and formerly occupying the valleys of the Paraná and the Uruguay. **2** The Tupian language of these tribes. [< Tupian, a warrior]

guar·an·tee (gar′ən·tē′) *n.* **1** A pledge or formal assurance that something will meet stated specifications or that a specified act will be performed. **2** Something given as security. **3** A guarantor. **4** Something which assures a certain outcome: Diligence is a *guarantee* of success. —*v.t.* **·teed, ·tee·ing 1** To certify or vouch for the performance of (something); warrant. **2** To make (oneself) responsible for the obligation of another. **3** To secure against loss or damage. **4** To affirm with certainty; promise; swear: He *guarantees* to be there. [Var. of GUARANTY]

guar·an·tor (gar′ən·tər, -tôr′) *n.* One who or that which guarantees or warrants; one who makes a guaranty or makes himself responsible for the obligation of another.

guar·an·ty (gar′ən·tē) *n. pl.* **·ties 1** A pledge, made in separate contract, to be responsible for the contract, debt, or duty of another person in case of his default or miscarriage. **2** A deposit or security made in place of such a pledge. **3** The assumption of such responsibility by pledge or security. **4** A guarantor. —*v.t.* **·tied, ·ty·ing** To guarantee. [<OF *guarantie* <*guarantir* warrant <*guarant* a warrant <Gmc. Doublet of WARRANTY.]

guard (gärd) *v.t.* **1** To stand guard over (a door, pass, etc.). **2** To watch over so as to keep from harm, loss, etc.; protect. **3** To watch over so as to keep from escaping. **4** To keep a check on; restrain: *Guard* your tongue. **5** *Archaic* To escort. —*v.i.* **6** To take precautions; be on guard. See synonyms under KEEP, PRESERVE, SHELTER. —*n.* **1** One who or that which protects, defends, or secures from loss, injury, or attack; hence, defense; protection; watch. **2** Specifically, a man or a body of men occupied in preserving a person or place from attack, or in controlling prisoners or preventing their escape. **3** Precaution against surprise or attack; care; attention. **4** A posture, attitude, or condition of defense. **5** Any of various protective or defensive devices for wearing, or for attaching to an object, as a machine or implement. **6** *Brit.* A railway official in charge of a train; a conductor. **7** *U.S.* An official employed on elevated and subway trains at points of entrance and egress. **8** In football, one of two line players (the **right guard** and **left guard**) who support the center; also, one of two players in basketball with similar positions and titles. See synonyms under DEFENSE, RAMPART. **—on guard 1** Ready for defense or protection; on the watch, as a military guard. **2** The first position in fencing or in bayonet exercises. Also, *French, en garde.* [<OF *guarden, garder* <Gmc. Akin to WARD.] **— guard′er** *n.*

Guar·da·fui (gwär′dä·fwē′), **Cape** A cape of eastern Africa, at the eastern tip of the Gulf of Aden.

guar·dant (gär′dənt) *Obs. adj.* **1** Exercising guardianship; guarding. **2** Gardant. **—***n.* A guardian. [<OF *gardant,* pp. of *garder* guard]

guard cell *Bot.* A specialized epidermal cell in plants, controlling the pores by which gases enter and pass out from the leaves and young stems.

guard·ed (gär′did) *adj.* Exhibiting caution; circumspect; also, protected. **— guard′ed·ly** *adv.* **— guard′ed·ness** *n.*

guard·house (gärd′hous′) *n.* **1** A quarters and headquarters for military guards. **2** A building for confinement of military personnel convicted of minor offenses or awaiting court martial.

guard·i·an (gär′dē·ən) *n.* **1** *Law* A person who legally has the care of the person or property, or both, of one who is incompetent to act for himself, especially of an infant or minor. **2** One to whom anything is committed for safekeeping or preservation. **3** One who guards; a warden. ◆ Collateral adjective: *custodial.* **—***adj.* Keeping guard; watching; protecting; tutelary. [<OF *guarden* < *guarder* guard. Doublet of WARDEN.] **— guard′i·an·ship** *n.*

guard·rail (gärd′rāl′) *n.* **1** *Naut.* A timber bolted to a ship's side to serve as a fender. **2** On railroads, a beam or rail parallel to a main rail in a track to prevent the wheels from jumping the track: used on curves and other dangerous places. **3** A protective railing around any dangerous place.

guard·room (gärd′ro͞om′, -ro͝om′) *n.* **1** The room occupied by a military guard while on duty. **2** A room where prisoners are kept under guard.

guards·man (gärdz′mən) *n. pl.* **·men** (-mən) **1** A man who serves as a guard. **2** *U.S.* A member of the National Guard.

guard–wire (gärd′wīr′) *n. Electr.* A grounded wire erected near a low–voltage circuit or public crossing as a safeguard against accidental contact with a high–voltage overhead conductor.

Guá·ri·co (gwä′rē·kō) A state in central Venezuela; 25,640 square miles; capital, San Juan de los Morros.

Guar·ne·ri (gwär·nā′rē) Name of a family of Italian violin–makers, notably **Giuseppe Antonio,** 1687?–1745. Also **Guar·nie′ri** (-nyâ′rē).

Guar·ne·ri·us (gwär·nā′rē·əs) *n.* A violin made by a member of the Guarneri family.

Gua·te·ma·la (gwä′tə·mä′lä) A Central American republic south and east of Mexico; 42,042 square miles; capital, Guatemala City. **— Gua′te·ma′lan** *adj.* & *n.*

gua·va (gwä′və) *n.* **1** A small tropical American tree or shrub of the myrtle family (genus *Psidium*). **2** Its fruit, about the size of a crab apple, chiefly used in making guava jelly. [<Sp. *guayaba,* appar. <S. Am. Ind.]

Gua·via·re (gwä·vyä′rā) A river in eastern and central Colombia, flowing 650 miles east to the Orinoco.

Guay·a·quil (gwī′ä·kēl′) A port of western Ecuador on the **Gulf of Guayaquil,** a Pacific bay in SW Ecuador.

gua·yu·le (gwä·yo͞o′lā) *n.* **1** A perennial herb (*Parthenium argentatum*) of the composite family, grown in Mexico, Texas, and California. **2** The resinous latex of this tree, yielding a natural rubber: also **guayule rubber.** [<Sp. <Nahuatl]

gu·ber·na·to·ri·al (go͞o′bər·nə·tôr′ē·əl, -tō′rē-, gyo͞o′-) *adj.* Of or pertaining to a governor or the office of governor. [<L *gubernator* a governor < *gubernare* govern]

gu·ber·ni·ya (go͞o·ber′nē·yä) *n.* **1** In the U.S.S.R., an administrative subdivision under a rural soviet. **2** In Russia before 1917, an administrative division corresponding to a province. [<Russian, ult. <L *gubernare* govern]

guck (guk) *n. U.S. & Canadian Slang* Goo; muck.

gude (güd) *adj. Scot.* Good: also spelled *guid.*

Gude (güd) *n. Scot.* God: also spelled *Goad.*

gude·fa·ther (güd′fä′*th*ər) *n. Scot.* Father–in–law: also spelled *guidfather.*

gude·man (güd′män) *n. Scot.* Husband; the head of a house; goodman: also spelled *guidman.*

gude·wife (güd′wīf′) *n. Scot.* **1** The mistress of a house; goodwife. **2** A landlady.

gudg·eon[1] (guj′ən) *n.* **1** An Old World, carp-like, fresh–water fish (genus *Gobio*), very easily caught. **2** A minnow. **3** A simpleton. **4** Anything swallowed credulously; bait. **—***v.t.* To impose upon; cheat; dupe. [<OF *goujon* <L *gobio,* var. of *gobios.* See GOBY.]

gudg·eon[2] (guj′ən) *n.* **1** *Mech.* The bearing of a shaft, especially when made of a separate piece. **2** A metallic journal piece let into the end of a wooden shaft. [<OF *gougeon* pin of a pulley]

Gud·run (go͝od′ro͞on) **1** In the *Gudrun Lied,* a 13th century German national epic, a princess, daughter of Hettal, king of Denmark. **2** In the *Volsunga Saga,* the daughter of the king of the Nibelungs and wife of Sigurd, later married to Atli. Also spelled *Guthrun.*

Gue·ber (gā′bər), **Gue·bre** See GHEBER.

Guel·der·land (gel′dər·land) See GELDERLAND.

guel·der–rose (gel′dər·rōz′) *n.* The snowball tree, a cultivated variety of cranberry with white flowers. [from *Guelder(land) rose*]

Guel·ders (gel′dərz) See GELDERLAND.

Guelf (gwelf) *n.* **1** A member of a medieval political faction in Italy that supported the papacy in its struggle against the influence of the German emperors: opposed to the *Ghibellines.* **2** A member of a German princely family, founded in the time of Charlemagne by Welf I in Swabia, from which the Hanoverian line of English kings descended. Also **Guelph.** [<Ital. *Guelfo,* ult. after OHG *Welf,* a family name] **— Guelf′i·an, Guelf′ic** *adj.* **— Guelf′ism** *n.*

gue·non (gə·nōn′, *Fr.* gə·nôṅ′) *n.* A long–tailed monkey (genus *Cercopithecus*) found in Mozambique, Africa: its banded hairs give it a mottled appearance. [<F; ult. origin unknown]

guer·don (gûr′dən) *n.* An honorable reward; requital. [<OF <Med. L *widerdonum* <OHG *widarlōn* < *widar* in turn + *lōn* reward] **— guer′don·er** *n.*

Gue·rick·e (gā′rik·ə), **Otto von,** 1602–86, German physicist.

Guer·ni·ca (ger·nē′kä) A town in northern Spain; bombed by German planes in 1937.

guern·sey (gûrn′zē) *n.* A knitted shirt; jersey.

Guern·sey (gûrn′zē) *n.* One of a breed of dairy cattle from the island of Guernsey, Channel Islands.

Guern·sey (gûrn′zē) One of the Channel Islands; 25 square miles.

guerre à mort (gâr à môr′) *French* War to the death.

Guer·re·ro (ger·rā′rō) A state in SW Mexico; 24,885 square miles; capital, Chilpancingo.

guer·ril·la (gə·ril′ə) *n.* One of an irregular, independent band of partisan soldiers. Also **gue·ril′la.** [<Sp. *guerrilla,* dim. of *guerra* a war]

Guesde (ged), **Jules Basile,** 1845–1922, French socialist. **— Guesd′ism** *n.* **— Guesd′ist** *adj.* & *n.*

guess (ges) *v.t.* **1** To form a judgment or opinion of (something) on uncertain or incomplete knowledge; surmise; conjecture. **2** To conjecture correctly: to *guess* the answer. **3** To believe; think: I *guess* we'll be late. **—***v.i.* **4** To form a judgment or opinion on uncertain or incomplete knowledge. **5** To conjecture correctly: How did you *guess*? **—***n.* **1** A tentative opinion or conclusion; a supposition; surmise; conjecture. **2** The act of guessing. [ME *gessen,* prob. <Scand. Cf. Sw. *gissa,* Dan. *gisse* guess.] **— guess′er** *n.*

Synonyms (verb): conjecture, divine, fancy, imagine, suppose, surmise, suspect. See SOLVE, SUPPOSE. *Antonyms*: demonstrate, establish, prove.

Synonyms (noun): conjecture, hypothesis, supposition, surmise. A *guess* is a conclusion from data directly at hand, and held as probable or tentative, while one confessedly lacks material for certainty. A *conjecture* is preliminary and tentative, but more methodical than a *guess*; a *supposition* is more nearly final; a *surmise* is an imagination or a suspicion. *Antonyms*: assurance, certainty, confidence, conviction, demonstration, proof.

guess·ti·mate (ges′tə·mit) *n. U.S. Colloq.* A prediction or extrapolation based, in part, on guesswork.

guess·work (ges′wûrk′) *n.* The process of guessing, or the result obtained thereby; a guess, or guesses collectively.

guest (gest) *n.* **1** A person received and entertained at the house of another; a visitor. **2** A lodger or boarder. **3** A parasitic animal; especially, any of various inquilines or insects living or breeding in the nests of other species: *guest* ants, *guest* wasps, etc. **4** *Obs.* A foreigner; stranger. **—** *v.t.* To entertain as a guest. **—***v.i.* To be a guest. [OE *giest*; infl. in form by ON *gastr* stranger. Akin to HOST[1], HOST[2].]

Guest (gest), **Edgar Albert,** 1881–1959, U. S. humorist and poet.

guest room A room, as in a private home or inn, which is used for the lodging of guests.

guest rope *Naut.* **1** A hawser carried and paid out by a boat so as to connect a vessel with an object towards which it is to be warped. **2** A rope used to assist the towline of a boat in towing; also, a line by which a boat is fastened to a vessel or eased into a gangway. Also **guess rope, guess warp, ges·warp** (ges′·wôrp′).

Gueux (gœ) *n. pl.* The Dutch nobles and burghers who from 1566 resisted the Inquisition and Philip II in the Netherlands. [<F, beggars]

guff (guf) *n.* **1** A sudden or slight gust of air; puff. **2** *Slang* Nonsense; buncombe. [Imit.]

guf·faw (gə·fô′) *n.* A shout of boisterous laughter; horselaugh. **—***v.i.* To utter such laughter. [Imit.]

Gug·gen·heim (go͝og′ən·hīm), **Daniel,** 1856–1930, U. S. industrialist and philanthropist.

Gu·gliel·ma (go͞o·lyel′mä) Italian form of WILHELMINA.

Gu·gliel·mo (go͞o·lyel′mō) Italian form of WILLIAM.

gu·ha (go͞o′hä, go͞o′ä) *n. Pathol.* A type of bronchial asthma endemic on the island of Guam. Also **gu′ja.**

Gui·an·a (gē·an′ə, -ä′nə) A region of NE South America, comprising British and French Guiana, Surinam, and sometimes including northern Brazil and eastern Venezuela. **— the Guianas**: British Guiana, French Guiana, Surinam.

guid (güd) See GUDE.

gui·dance (gīd′ns) *n.* **1** The act, process, or result of guiding. **2** A leading; direction. **3** *Mil.* The principles and techniques of assembling, interpreting, and transmitting intelligence necessary to the maneuvering of guided missiles along their flight paths to the designated targets.

guide (gīd) *v.* **guid·ed, guid·ing** *v.t.* **1** To show the way to; lead or accompany as a guide. **2** To direct the motion or action of, as a vehicle, tool, etc. **3** To lead or direct the affairs, standards, opinions, etc., of: Let these principles *guide* your life. **—***v.i.* **4** To act as a guide. See synonyms under LEAD[1], REGULATE. **—***n.* **1** One who leads or directs another in any path or direction; one who shows the way by accompanying or going in advance; specifically, one who conducts sightseers, or an expert woodsman who conducts hunters, fishermen, etc. **2** Something serving to guide; a guidebook or guidepost. **3** *Mech.*

Any device acting as an indicator or serving to keep a part or object in position or to regulate its operation. **4** *Mil.* A soldier on the flank of a line to mark a pivot or regulate an alinement. See synonyms under RULE. [<OF *guider*] — **guid'a·ble** *adj.* —**guid'er** *n.*

guide·board (gīd'bôrd', -bōrd') *n.* A board bearing directions for travelers, usually at the junction of highways: also called *fingerpost.*

guide·book (gīd'bo͝ok') *n.* A handbook for travelers or tourists, containing descriptions of places, routes, etc.

guided missile *Mil.* An unmanned aerial missile whose course can be altered during flight by mechanisms within it and sometimes under the control of radio signals transmitted from ground stations or from aircraft.

guide·line (gīd'līn') *n.* **1** A line, as a rope, for guiding. **2** A word, phrase, etc., often printed as a guide along the upper margin of printed copy. **3** Any indication of the limits or scope of an undertaking.

guide·post (gīd'pōst') *n.* **1** A post with an attached sign giving directions to travelers, as at a roadside. **2** Anything that guides, directs, or limits; guideline.

guide·rope (gīd'rōp') *n.* **1** *Aeron.* **a** A long rope suspended from a balloon or dirigible and trailed along the ground as a brake and to maintain altitude. **b** Any similar rope for hauling down and mooring an airship; a grab line: also called *trail rope.* **2** A line attached to a rope to hold it in position.

Gui·do d'A·rez·zo (gwē'dō dä·ret'tsō), 990?–1050?, Italian Benedictine monk; musician.

gui·don (gīd'n) *n.* **1** A forked flag carried by mounted troops. **2** The man who carries it. **3** A small flag carried by a unit of the U.S. Army as a company emblem. [<F <Ital. *guidone*]

Gui·do Re·ni (gwē'do rā'nē) See RENI, GUIDO.

Gui·enne (gwē·yen', gē-) A former province of SW France; formerly the kingdom of Aquitaine: also *Guyenne.*

Guil·bert (gēl·bâr') French form of GILBERT.

guild (gild) *n.* **1** A corporation or association of persons engaged in kindred pursuits for mutual protection, aid, etc., known in England from the seventh century. **2** A church or religious association organized for benevolent and other parish work. **3** *Ecol.* **a** One of four groups of plants having characteristic modes of life, namely, the lianas, epiphytes, saprophytes, and parasites. **b** A group of plants which, under certain ecological conditions, adapt themselves in mass to a new locality. Also spelled *gild.* ◆ Homophone: *gild.* [Fusion of OE *gild* payment, *gegyld* association, and ON *gildi* payment] —**guild'ship** *n.* — **guilds'man** *n.*

guil·der (gil'dər) *n.* Gulden: also spelled *gilder.* also called *florin.* [Earlier *guldren,* alter. of Du. *gulden* golden]

Guild·ford (gil'fəd) The county town of Surrey, England.

guild·hall (gild'hôl') *n. Brit.* **1** The hall where a guild meets. **2** A town hall.

Guild·hall (gild'hôl') The hall of the Corporation of the City of London, England.

guild socialism See under SOCIALISM.

guile (gīl) *n.* **1** The act of deceiving, or the disposition to deceive; craft; duplicity; treachery. **2** *Obs.* A stratagem. See synonyms under ARTIFICE, DECEPTION. [<OF <Gmc. ? Akin to WILE.] —**guile'ful** *adj.*

guile·less (gīl'lis) *adj.* Free from guile; artless; frank. See synonyms under CANDID, INNOCENT, PURE. —**guile'less·ly** *adv.* —**guile'less·ness** *n.*

Guil·ford Courthouse (gil'fərd) A national military park in north central North Carolina, scene of a Revolutionary War battle, 1781.

Guil·laume (gē·yōm') French form of WILLIAM. Also *Sp.* **Guil·ler·mo** (gē·lyer'mō), *Pg.* **Guil·her·me** (gē·lyer'mə).

Guil·laume (gē·yōm'), **Charles Édouard,** 1861–1938, French physicist.

Guil·lel·mine (gē·yel·mēn') French form of WILHELMINA. Also **Guil·lel·mette** (-met'), *Sp.* **Guil·lel·mi·na** (gē·lyel·mē'nä).

guil·le·mot (gil'ə·mot) *n.* Any of several narrow-billed auks (genera *Uria* and *Cepphus*), found in northern latitudes; specifically, the **black guillemot** (*C. grylle*) or cuttie, and the murres, including the **foolish guillemot** (*Uria aalge*). [<F, dim. of *Guillaume* William]

guil·loche (gi·lōsh') *n.* An ornament formed by two or more intertwining bands or intersecting lines; an ornamental braid. [<F *guillochis;* ult. origin unknown]

guil·lo·tine (gil'ə·tēn) *n.* **1** The instrument of capital punishment in France, consisting of a weighted knife which falls and beheads the victim: invented by Antoine Louis, 1723–92, French physician. **2** A form of paper-cutting machine. **3** *Surg.* An instrument for cutting the tonsils. —*v.t.* **·tined, ·tin·ing** To behead with the guillotine. [<F, after Dr. J. I. *Guillotin,* 1738–1814, who advocated its use]

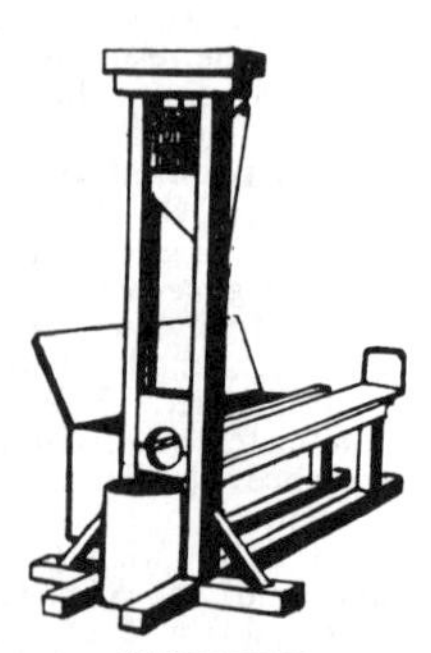

GUILLOTINE
Showing the basket for the body and receptacle for the head.

guilt (gilt) *n.* **1** The state of one who, by violation of law, has made himself liable to or deserving of punishment; culpability. **2** Wrongdoing; wickedness. See synonyms under SIN. ◆ Homophone: *gilt.* [OE *gylt*]

guilt·less (gilt'lis) *adj.* **1** Free from guilt; innocent. **2** Ignorant: with *of.* **3** Devoid: with *of.* See synonyms under INNOCENT, PURE. —**guilt'less·ly** *adv.* —**guilt'less·ness** *n.*

guilt·y (gil'tē) *adj.* **guilt·i·er, guilt·i·est** **1** Having violated a law or rule of duty; liable to penalty. **2** Involving, expressing, feeling, or characterized by guilt. See synonyms under CRIMINAL. — **guilt'i·ly** *adv.* —**guilt'i·ness** *n.*

guin·ea (gin'ē) *n.* **1** A former English gold coin, so called because first coined (1663) from Guinea gold: last issued in 1813; now, money of account: equal to 21 shillings. **2** The guinea fowl.

Guin·ea (gin'ē) **1** A term formerly used to describe a coastal region in western Africa, divided by the Niger delta into **Upper Guinea** and **Lower Guinea.** It was broadly considered to consist of the littoral portions of the British, French, and Portuguese equatorial possessions from Senegal to Angola. **2** The littoral portion of the territory extending from the Niger delta to southern Senegal. See PORTUGUESE GUINEA, SPANISH GUINEA. **3** A republic in west Africa, coextensive with former French Guinea; 95,350 square miles; Capital, Conakry.

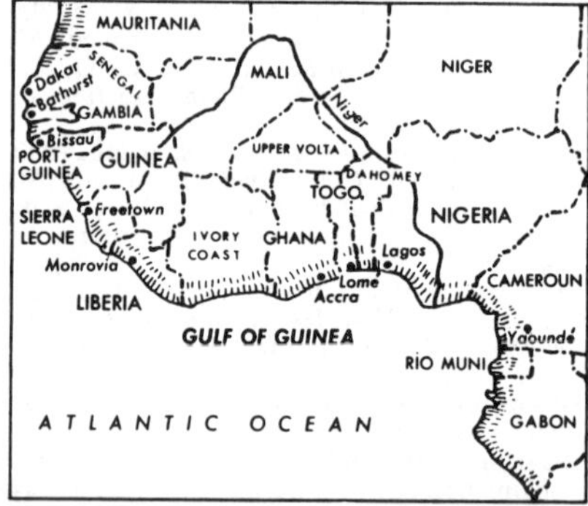

Guinea, Gulf of An inlet of the Atlantic in the western coast of Africa, south of the great bulge of the continent.

Guinea corn Durra.

guinea fowl A gallinaceous bird (*Numida meleagris*) of African origin, having dark-gray plumage speckled with white spots: long domesticated in Europe and America: also *guinea, guinea hen.*

GUINEA FOWL
(About 15 inches tall)

guinea grains Grains of paradise.

guinea grass A hardy, perennial, erect grass (*Panicum maximum*) native to Africa: grown in the southern United States for forage.

guinea green A crystalline substance, $C_{37}H_{35}N_2O_6S_2Na$, dark-green in powder form.

guinea hen **1** A female guinea fowl. **2** A guinea fowl.

Guinea pepper Cayenne pepper.

guinea pig **1** A small, domesticated rodent, usually white, variegated with red and black, having short ears and lacking a visible tail, widely used as an experimental animal in biological and medical research. **2** Any object or victim of experimentation.

Guinea worm A slender, threadlike nematode worm (*Dracunculus medinensis*), common in tropical Africa and Asia. The larva parasitically enters the stomach of man or animal, usually in drinking water, and makes its way to the subcutaneous connective tissue, especially, in man, of the legs and feet.

Guin·e·vere (gwin'ə·vir) In Arthurian legend, Arthur's unfaithful queen, the paramour of Lancelot. Also **Guin'e·ver** (-vər).

gui·pure (gi·pyo͝or', *Fr.* gē·pür') *n.* A lace having no ground mesh, but having the pattern held in place by connecting threads. [<F <*guiper* cover with silk <Gmc.]

guise (gīz) *n.* **1** The external appearance as produced by garb or costume; outward seeming; mien; aspect; habit; dress. **2** The manner; behavior; also, customary manner; fashion; way. **3** A mask or pretense; cover. —*v.* **guised, guis·ing** *v.t.* **1** *Archaic* To dress; costume. **2** *Brit. Dial.* To disguise. —*v.i.* **3** *Brit. Dial.* To go about in disguise or costume. [<OF <Gmc. Akin to WISE[2].]

Guise (gēz, gwēz; *Fr.* gēz, gü·ēz') A French ducal family; specifically, either **François de Lorraine,** 1519–63, second Duc de Guise, French commander; or **Henri de Lorraine,** 1550–88, third Duc de Guise, French commander who instigated the massacre of St. Bartholomew.

Guise (gēz) A town in northern France.

gui·tar (gi·tär') *n.* A musical instrument having a fretted fingerboard and usually six strings, played with the fingers. [<Sp. *guitarra* <Gk. *kithara.* Doublet of CITHARA, ZITHER.]

GUITAR

gui·tar·fish (gi·tär'fish') *n. pl.* **·fish** or **·fish·es** Any of a family (Rhinobatidae) of viviparous, shark-like rays having a long tail and wide body.

guit·guit (gwit'gwit') *n.* Any of several tropical American birds, the honey creepers. [Imit.]

Gui·try (gē·trē'), **Sacha** 1885–1957, French playwright and actor.

Gui·zot (gē·zō'), **François Pierre Guillaume,** 1787–1874, French statesman and historian.

Gu·ja·rat (go͞oj'ə·rät') A fertile plain in northern Bombay State, India. Also **Gu'ze·rat'** (go͞oz'-).

Gu·ja·ra·ti (go͞oj'ə·rä'tē) *n.* The language of the natives of Gujarat, Baroda, and the adjoining states, belonging to the Indic branch of Indo-Iranian languages.

Gujarat States A group of former princely states included since 1949 in various districts of Bombay State, India; 7,493 square miles.

gu·la (gyo͞o'lə) *n. pl.* **·lae** (-lē) **1** *Anat.* The esophagus or gullet. **2** *Ornithol.* The upper part of the throat next the chin, as in a bird. **3** *Entomol.* The ventral part of the neck in insects; also, the submentum in a beetle. [<L, throat] —**gu'lar** *adj.*

gu·lash (go͞o'läsh) See GOULASH.

gulch (gulch) *n. U.S.* A ravine; hollow; gully. [? <dial. *gulch* swallow greedily]

gul·den (go͞ol'dən) *n.* **1** The monetary unit of value in the Netherlands. **2** The Austro-Hungarian florin: a former monetary unit. **3** One of various coins formerly current in Germany and the Netherlands. Also *guilder, gilder.* [<Du. and G, lit., golden]

Gü·lek Bo·ghaz (gü·lek' bō·gäz') A pass over the Taurus mountains in southern Turkey: ancient *Cilician Gates.*

gules (gyo͞olz) *n. Her.* The tincture red: in a blazon without color, indicated by parallel vertical lines. [<OF *gueules* red-dyed ermine fur, ? <L *gula* throat]

gulf (gulf) *n.* **1** The tract of water within an

indentation or curve of the coastline, in size between a bay and a sea. **2** An abyss; chasm. **3** That which engulfs irretrievably; a whirlpool. **4** A wide or impassable space; a separation not easily bridged. —*v.t.* To swallow up as in a gulf; engulf. [<OF *golfe* <Ital. *golfo* <LGk. *kolphos* <Gk. *kolpos* a bay]

Gulf of Lyons See LION, GULF OF THE

Gulf States The States of the United States bordering on the Gulf of Mexico: Florida, Alabama, Mississippi, Louisiana, and Texas.

Gulf Stream The largest of the warm ocean current systems, flowing from the Gulf of Mexico along the coast of the United States to Nantucket, and thence eastward as far as Norway.

gulf·weed (gulf′wēd′) *n.* Any of a genus (*Sargassum*) of brown algae that grow in warm seas and are found drifting in the Gulf Stream and the Sargasso Sea. Also called *sargasso.*

gull[1] (gul) *n.* **1** A long-winged, usually white, web-footed swimming bird (family *Laridae*) having the upper mandible hooked. **2** One of various sea birds related to the gull, as a tern or gannet. [ME <Celtic. Cf. Welsh *gwylan* a gull.]

gull[2] (gul) *n.* **1** A simple, credulous person; dupe. **2** A deceit; fraud; trick. —*v.t.* To deceive; outwit; cheat. [? <obs. *gull* swallow; infl. by ME *goll* a gosling]

Gul·lah (gul′ə) *n.* **1** One of a group of Negroes dwelling on a narrow, coastal strip and outlying islands of South Carolina, Georgia, and NE Florida. **2** The creolized language spoken by these people.

gul·let (gul′it) *n.* **1** *Anat.* The passage from the mouth to the stomach; the esophagus. **2** The throat or neck. **3** A channel for water; ravine; gully. [<OF *goulet,* dim. of *goule* throat <L *gula*]

gul·li·ble (gul′ə·bəl) *adj.* Capable of being easily gulled, duped, or deceived; simple; credulous. Also **gul′la·ble.** —**gul′li·bil′i·ty, gul′la·bil′i·ty** *n.*

Gul·li·ver (gul′ə·vər), **Lemuel** Hero of Jonathan Swift's *Gulliver's Travels* (1726), a political and social satire in four books.

gul·ly[1] (gul′ē) *n. pl.* **·lies** **1** A channel or ravine cut in the earth by running water; narrow ravine. **2** A watercourse. —*v.t.* **gul·lied, gul·ly·ing** To cut or wear a gully in. [Var. of GULLET]

gul·ly[2] (gul′ē) *n. Scot.* A knife.

gulp (gulp) *v.t.* **1** To swallow eagerly and in large amounts: usually with *down.* **2** To keep back as if by swallowing: to *gulp* down a retort. —*v.i.* **3** To gasp or choke as if taking a large drink of liquid. —*n.* The act of gulping, or something gulped down; a swallow; also, the amount swallowed: a *gulp* of milk. [<Du. *gulpen;* of imit. origin] —**gulp′er** *n.* —**gulp′ing·ly** *adv.*

gum[1] (gum) *n.* **1** An amorphous, brittle, colloidal mass resulting from the drying of the exuded sap of trees or shrubs. True gums are complex hydrocarbons; they are usually soluble in water, but not in alcohol, ether, and the oils; but the name is popularly applied also to true resins and to gum resins, especially when used as mucilage, etc. **2** The gum tree. **3** Rubber. **4** *pl. U.S. Dial.* Rubber overshoes; also, automobile tires. **5** A preparation of some natural gum (as cherry gum or balsam of Tolu), or some other tenacious substance, flavored and sweetened for use as a masticatory: also **chewing gum. 6** *U.S. Dial.* A section of a gum tree made into a well-curb, a watering trough, a bin, etc.; also, a beehive made of a similar hollow log. **7** Any sticky, viscous substance. **8** The adhesive wash on the reverse side of postage stamps. —*v.* **gummed, gum·ming** *v.t.* **1** To smear gum. **2** To stiffen or unite with gum. —*v.i.* **3** To exude or form gum. **4** To become stiff and sticky. —**to gum up** *U.S. Slang* To bungle or ruin. [<OF *gomme* <L *gummi* <Gk. *kommi*] —**gum′mer** *n.*

gum[2] (gum) *n. Anat.* The fleshy tissue that covers the alveolar arches of the jaws and invests the necks of the teeth. ◆ Collateral adjective: *gingival.* —*v.t.* **gummed, gum·ming** To chew with the gums: He *gums* his food. [OE *goma* inside of mouth]

gum ammoniac See AMMONIAC[2].

gum arabic The dried, yellowish-white or amber gum from various species of *Acacia,* especially *A. senegal* and *A. arabica,* composed chiefly of the salts of arabic acid: widely used in medicine and the arts.

Gum·bin·nen (go͝om·bin′ən) The former German name for GUSEV.

gum·bo (gum′bō) *n.* **1** Okra. **2** The stratified portion of the lower till of the Mississippi Valley; especially, those soils which form a sticky or soapy mud when wet. **3** Clay encountered in drilling for oil or sulfur. —*adj.* Resembling or pertaining to gumbo soil (see *n.* def. 3). [<Bantu language of Angola]

gum·boil (gum′boil′) *n.* A small boil or abscess formed on the gum.

gum·bo·til (gum′bō·til) *n. Geol.* A gray or brown plastic clay resulting from the prolonged weathering of glacial deposits; the varying thicknesses of its layers sometimes give indications of the length of interglacial periods. [<GUMBO + TILL[4]]

gum·drop (gum′drop′) *n.* A molded sweetmeat, often soft inside, made usually of gum arabic, but sometimes also of gelatin, glucose, etc.

gum elastic Rubber.

gum·lie (gum′lē) *adj. Scot.* Muddy; gloomy. Also **gum′ly.**

gum·ma (gum′ə) *n. pl.* **gum·ma·ta** (gum′ə·tə) or **gum·mas** *Pathol.* A soft tumor occurring in tertiary syphilis. [<NL <L *gummi* gum] —**gum′ma·tous** *adj.*

gum·mif·er·ous (gu·mif′ər·əs) *adj.* Yielding or producing gum.

gum·mite (gum′īt) *n.* A greasy, viscid material of red or yellow color, formed as an alteration product of pitchblende.

gum·mo·sis (gu·mō′sis) *n. Bot.* The extensive change of tissue into gum, as in cherry gum.

gum·my (gum′ē) *adj.* **·mi·er, ·mi·est** Like or covered with gum; sticky; viscous. Also **gum′mous.** See synonyms under ADHESIVE. —**gum′mi·ness** *n.*

gum plant Any of several plants of the western United States (genus *Grindelia*), covered with a glutinous varnish when young. Also **gum weed.**

gump·tion (gump′shən) *n. Colloq.* **1** Ready perception; quick-wittedness; initiative. **2** Shrewd common sense. [<dial. E (Scottish). Cf. ME *gome* care, heed.]

gum resin Any of a kind of combined gum and resin which oozes as a milky juice from incisions in the stems, roots, or branches of certain plants and gradually solidifies in the air.

gum·shoe (gum′sho͞o′) *n.* **1** *U.S. Slang* A detective. **2** *Pl.* Sneakers. **3** A rubber shoe or overshoe. —*adj. U.S. Slang* **1** Done secretly; undercover. **2** Pertaining to detectives. —*v.i.* **·shoed, ·shoe·ing** *U.S. Slang* To go stealthily and noiselessly; sneak.

Gum·ti (go͞om′tē) A river in central Uttar Pradesh, India, flowing SE 500 miles to the Ganges.

gum·tree (gum′trē′) *n.* Any of various species of Australian eucalyptus trees.

gum tree An American gum-producing and hardwood lumber tree, as the sour or black gum and the tupelo.

gum·wood (gum′wo͝od′) *n.* The wood of several Australasian trees (genus *Eucalyptus*), especially the blue gum (*E. globulus*) and the salmon gum (*E. salmonophloia*), now grown in the United States: used for construction and furniture.

gun (gun) *n.* **1** A metal tube for firing projectiles by the force of an explosive, by compressed air, or a spring, together with its stock and other attachments. **2** A piece of ordnance with a flat trajectory. **3** Any portable firearm except a pistol or revolver, as a rifle, musket, carbine, etc. **4** *U.S. Colloq.* A pistol or revolver. **5** The discharge of a cannon, as in firing salutes or signaling. **6** The throttle controlling the action of an internal-combustion engine, as in an automobile or airplane. **7** Any device resembling a gun in shape or operation: a grease *gun.* —*v.* **gunned, gun·ning** *v.i.* **1** To go hunting with a gun. **2** To shoot with a gun. **3** To seek with intent to harm or kill: with *for.* **4** To seek eagerly: with *for:* to *gun* for votes. **5** *U.S. Colloq.* To go or drive at great speed. —*v.t.* **6** *U.S. Colloq.* To shoot (someone). **7** *U.S. Colloq.* To open the throttle of, as an engine, so as to increase the speed of operation. [ME *gonne, gunne* <ON *gunna,* orig. a nickname for *Gunnhildr,* fem. personal name]

gun barrel Barrel (def. 7).

gun·boat (gun′bōt′) *n.* A lightly armed, unarmored naval vessel, used for patrolling rivers and coastal waters.

gun carriage A carriage upon which a cannon is mounted.

gun·cot·ton (gun′kot′n) *n.* A highly explosive compound prepared by treating cotton with nitric and sulfuric acids: also called *nitrocotton.*

gun deck A covered deck carrying the principal battery of a warship.

gun dog A hunting dog; a dog bred and trained to accompany and assist a hunter, as a setter, pointer, etc.

gun·fight (gun′fīt′) *n. U.S.* In the old West, a fight with revolvers or pistols. —**gun′fight′er** *n.* —**gun′fight′ing** *n.*

gun·fire (gun′fīr′) *n.* **1** The firing or discharge of a gun or guns. **2** *Mil.* **a** An artillery action in which guns fire independently of each other, with or without ordered interval. **b** The use of artillery or small arms in warfare, as distinguished from bayonets, or from charge tactics.

gun·flint (gun′flint′) *n.* A piece of flint fitted to the hammer of a flintlock musket.

gung ho (gung′ hō′) *Chinese* Work together: a motto adopted by a body of U.S. Marine raiders in World War II.

gun·lock (gun′lok′) *n.* The mechanism of a gun by which the hammer or needle is driven and the charge exploded. See RIFLE.

gun·man (gun′mən) *n. pl.* **·men** (-mən) **1** *U.S.* A man armed with a gun, especially a criminal or killer. **2** A gunsmith.

gun metal 1 A bronze alloy, composed of nine parts copper to one part tin, formerly much used for smaller cannon, and still used for other purposes. **2** Any other material used in making guns, as gun iron, steel, certain kinds of brass, etc. **3** Any of various alloys treated with sulfur or the like to imitate the color of gun metal: used for metal novelties. **4** A neutral gray color with a bluish tinge: also **gun-met·al gray** (gun′met′l).

gun moll *U.S. Slang* A woman who associates with criminals.

Gun·nar (go͞on′är) In the *Volsunga Saga,* a hero who wins Brynhild as his wife; brother to Gudrun. Compare GUNTHER.

gun·nel[1] (gun′əl) See GUNWALE.

gun·nel[2] (gun′əl) *n. pl.* **·nels** or **·nel** A blenny (fish) of the North Atlantic (*Pholis gunnellus*). [Origin unknown]

gun·ner (gun′ər) *n.* **1** A soldier or sailor who operates a gun or cannon. **2** A member of an aircraft crew who operates a gun mounted on a swivel base. **3** One who hunts game with a gun.

gun·ner·y (gun′ər·ē) *n.* **1** The science and art of operating cannon. **2** The use of artillery. **3** Guns collectively.

gun·ning (gun′ing) *n.* The sport of hunting game with a gun.

Gun·ni·son River (gun′ə·sən) A river of west central Colorado, flowing 180 miles NW to the Colorado River.

gun·ny (gun′ē) *n. pl.* **·nies** **1** Coarse sacking of jute or hemp. **2** A bag or sack made of it: also **gunny bag** or **gunny sack.** [<Hind. *gonī* gunny sack]

gun·pa·per (gun′pā′pər) *n.* A cellulose compound used as an absorbent foundation for the preparation of a form of guncotton.

gun·pow·der (gun′pou′dər) *n.* An explosive mixture of potassium nitrate, charcoal, and sulfur, black or brown in color, used especially in gunnery.

Gunpowder Plot See under GUY FAWKES DAY.

gunpowder tea A fine green tea, each leaf of which is rolled into a tiny round pellet.

gun·room (gun′ro͞om′, -ro͝om′) *n.* **1** A room in which guns are kept. **2** In the British navy, a room for the accommodation of junior officers.

gun·run·ner (gun′run′ər) *n.* One who smuggles

or carries on illegal traffic in firearms and ammunition. — **gun′run′ning** *n.*

gun·sel (gun′səl) *n. Slang* **1** A young armed robber or killer. **2** A young sexual pervert. **3** A callow, unsophisticated youth. Also **gon·sil** (gon′səl). [Origin uncertain]

gun·shot (gun′shot′) *n.* **1** The range or reach of a gun. **2** The act of discharging a firearm. — *adj.* Made by the shot of a gun: a *gunshot* wound.

gun–shy (gun′shī′) *adj.* Afraid of the sound of a gun, as a dog.

gun·sight (gun′sīt′) *n.* A device on a gun which assists in aiming; a sight.

gun·sling·er (gun′sling′ər) *n. U.S. Slang* A gunfighter.

gun·smith (gun′smith′) *n.* One who makes or repairs firearms.

gun·stock (gun′stok′) *n.* The wooden part of a firearm, as a rifle, etc., holding the lock and the barrel.

Gun·ter (gun′tər), **Edmund,** 1581–1626, English mathematician.

Gunter's chain See under CHAIN.

Gun·ther (gŏŏn′tər) In the *Nibelungenlied,* the brother of Kriemhild and husband of Brünhilde: identified with *Gunnar.*

gun·wale (gun′əl) *n. Naut.* **1** The upper wale of a war vessel with apertures for guns. **2** The strake which tops a ship's side or bounds the top plank of the side of a vessel: also spelled *gunnel.* [<GUN + WALE (plank)]

Günz (günts) See GLACIAL EPOCH.

gup·py (gup′ē) *n. pl.* **·pies** A small, tropical, fresh–water fish (genus *Lebistes*), valued as an aquarium fish for the brilliant coloring of the males, and for mosquito control. [after R. J. L. *Guppy,* British scientist]

Gup·ta (gŏŏp′tə) A dynasty, 320?–544?, of North India, founded by Chandragupta II.

gur·gle (gûr′gəl) *v.* **gur·gled, gur·gling** *v.i.* **1** To flow with a bubbling, liquid sound. **2** To make such a sound. — *v.t.* **3** To utter with a gurgling sound. — *n.* A gurgling flow or sound: also **gur′gling.** [Var. of GARGLE]

gur·glet (gûr′glit) See GOGLET.

Gur·kha (gŏŏr′kə) *n.* One of a warlike Rajput people of Hindu religion in Nepal.

gur·nard (gûr′nərd) *n. pl.* **·nards** or **·nard** One of various spiny–finned marine fishes (family *Triglidae*) with mailed cheeks: some species are called *sea robins.* [<F *grognard* grumbler <*grogner* grunt <L *grunnire*]

gur·ney (gûr′nē) *n. pl.* **·neys** A stretcher mounted on wheels. [Origin uncertain]

gu·ru (gōō′rōō) *n. pl.* **·rus** **1** One who provides instruction or spiritual leadership in Hindu mysticism. **2** A teacher or leader regarded as having special knowledge, powers, etc. [<Hind.]

Gus (gus) Diminutive of AUGUSTUS.

Gu·sev (gōō′syəf) A city in Russian S.F.S.R., formerly in East Prussia: former German *Gumbinnen.*

gush (gush) *v.i.* **1** To flow out suddenly and in volume, as tears or blood. **2** To produce a sudden flood, as of blood, tears, etc.: Her eyes *gushed* with tears. **3** *Colloq.* To express oneself with extravagant and affected emotion; be overly enthusiastic. — *v.t.* **4** To pour forth (blood, tears, etc.). — *n.* **1** A sudden outpouring of fluid or of something likened to it, as of sound, or the thing thus emitted. **2** *Colloq.* An extravagant display of sentiment. [ME *guschen,* prob. <Scand. Cf. ON *gusa* gush.] — **gush′i·ness** *n.* — **gush′y** *adj.*

gush·er (gush′ər) *n.* **1** One who or that which gushes. **2** A free–flowing oil well.

gush·ing (gush′ing) *adj.* Flowing freely; sentimental. — **gush′ing·ly** *adv.* — **gush′ing·ness** *n.*

gus·set (gus′it) *n.* **1** A small triangular piece of cloth fitted into a garment to fill an open angle or to give added strength or more room. **2** In metalworking, an angle–iron or bracket for stiffening an angle in construction. **3** A chain–mail connection between two armor plates. — *v.t.* To furnish with a gusset. [<OF *gousset,* dim. of *gousse* a pod, shell]

gust[1] (gust) *n.* **1** A violent blast of wind; rapid fluctuations in the force of a wind near the earth's surface. **2** A sudden outburst of feeling. [<ON *gustr*] — **gust′i·ly** *adv.* — **gust′i·ness** *n.* — **gust′y** *adj.*

gust[2] (gust) *n.* **1** Taste; relish; gratification; gusto. **2** Flavor, as of food. [<L *gustus* taste] — **gust′a·ble** *adj.*

gus·ta·tion (gus·tā′shən) *n.* The act or power of tasting. — **gus·ta·tive** (gus′tə·tiv) *adj.* — **gus′ta·tive·ness** *n.* — **gus′ta·to′ry** (-tôr′ē, -tō′rē) *adj.*

Gus·ta·vo A. Ma·de·ro (gōōs·tä′vō ä mä·thā′·rō) The Federal district of central Mexico including Guadalupe Hidalgo.

Gus·ta·vus (gus·tā′vəs, -tä′-) A masculine personal name. Also *Du.* **Gus·taaf** (khōōs′täf), *Fr.* **Gus·tave** (güs·tàv′), *Ger.* **Gus·tav** (gōōs′·täf), *Ital., Sp.* **Gus·ta·vo** (gōōs·tä′vō), *Sw.* **Gus·taf** (gōōs′täf). [<Gmc., divine staff]

— **Gustavus I,** 1496–1560, king of Sweden who defeated the Danes (king, 1523–60): known as *Gustavus Vasa.*

— **Gustavus II,** 1594–1632, prominent in the Thirty Years' War: known as *Gustavus Adolphus.*

— **Gustavus V,** 1858–1950, king of Sweden 1907–50: known as *Gustaf.*

— **Gustavus VI,** 1882–1973, king of Sweden 1950–1973: known as *Gustaf Adolf.*

gus·to (gus′tō) *n.* **1** Keen enjoyment; relish; zest. **2** Individual taste. See synonyms under RELISH. [<Ital. <L *gustus* taste]

gut (gut) *n.* **1** *pl.* The alimentary canal; an intestine: regarded as indelicate usage. **2** The dried entrails of an animal, used for strings for musical instruments, etc.; catgut. **3** A contracted strait connecting two bodies of water. **4** A strong cord made from fiber drawn out of a silkworm when ready to spin its cocoon, used like catgut for snells, etc. **5** *pl. Slang* Stamina; courage; grit. — *v.t.* **gut·ted, gut·ting** **1** To take out the intestines of; eviscerate. **2** To plunder. **3** To remove or destroy the contents of: The fire *gutted* the interior of the building. — *adj. Slang* **1** Central; basic; fundamental: *gut* issues. **2** Deeply felt, as though physically experienced: a *gut* conviction. [OE *guttas* viscera] — **gut′·ter** *n.*

Gu·ten·berg (gōō′tən·bûrg, *Ger.* gōō′tən·berkh), **Johann,** 1397?–1468, German printer; reputed inventor of movable type. Compare COSTER.

Gutenberg Bible A Vulgate edition printed in Mainz sometime before 1456, generally ascribed to J. Gutenberg and regarded as the first large work printed from movable type.

Guth·run (gŏŏth′rōōn) See GUDRUN.

Gu·tru·ne (gōō·trōō′nə) In Wagner's *Ring des Nibelungen,* the wife of Siegfried and the sister of Gunther.

gut·sy (gut′sē) *adj.* **gut·si·er, gut·si·est** *Slang* Courageous; dauntless; gritty.

gut·ta (gut′ə) *n. pl.* **·tae** (-ē) **1** In pharmacy, a drop. **2** *Archit.* One of the small droplike ornaments, usually in the form of truncated cones, enriching the under part of mutules and regulae of the Doric entablature. [<L]

gut·ta–per·cha (gut′ə·pûr′chə) *n.* The purified and coagulated exudate, grayish–white to red in color, from various sapotaceous Malayan trees (genera *Palaquium* and *Payena*): used as an electrical insulator, a dental plastic, etc. [<Malay *getah* gum + *percha* gum tree]

gut·tate (gut′āt) *adj.* **1** Spotted, as if by colored drops. **2** Containing drops or little round masses likened to drops. Also **gut′tat·ed.** [<L *guttatus* speckled <*gutta* a drop]

gut·té (gōō·tā′) *adj. Her.* Covered with drops. Also **gut·tée′, gut′ty.** [<AF *gutté* <L *guttatus.* See GUTTATE.]

gut·ter (gut′ər) *n.* **1** A channel along the eaves of a house to carry off rain water. **2** A waterway for carrying off surface water, constructed generally at the side of a road or street. **3** Slum areas of a community: language of the *gutter.* **4** Any slight channel, trench, or trough. — *v.t.* **1** To form channels or grooves

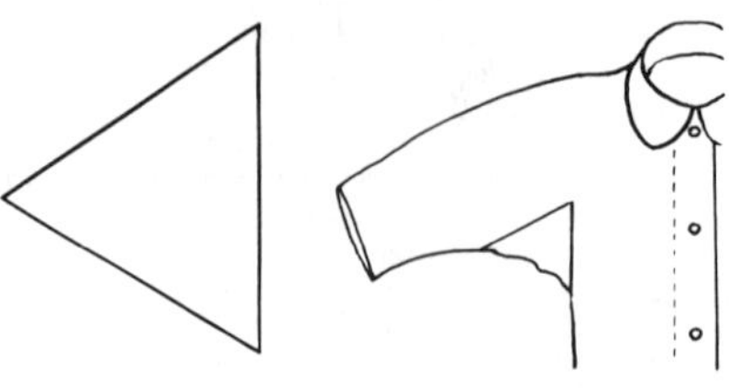

GUSSET *(def. 1)*

in. **2** To furnish with gutters, as a house. **3** To conduct or lead as through a gutter. — *v.i.* **4** To flow in channels, as water. **5** To melt rapidly into streams of wax: said of candles. [<OF *goutiere* <*goute* a drop <L *gutta*] — **gut′ter·y** *adj.*

gut·ter·bird (gut′ər·bûrd′) *n.* **1** A sparrow. **2** A mean or contemptible person.

gut·ter·snipe (gut′ər·snīp′) *n.* A neglected child who runs loose on the streets; a slum child; a street Arab.

gut·tur·al (gut′ər·əl) *adj.* **1** Pertaining to the throat. **2** Produced or formed in the throat; hence, harsh; grating: a *guttural* sound. **3** *Phonet.* Velar. — *n. Phonet.* A velar sound. [<NL *gutturalis* <*guttur* throat] — **gut·tur·al·i·ty** (gut′ə·ral′ə·tē), **gut′tur·al·ness** *n.* — **gut′·tur·al·ly** *adv.*

gut·tur·al·ize (gut′ər·əl·īz′) *v.t.* & *v.i.* **·ized, ·iz·ing** **1** To speak or utter gutturally. **2** *Phonet.* To velarize. — **gut′tur·al·i·za′tion** *n.*

gut·ty (gut′ē) *adj.* **gut·ti·er, gut·ti·est** *Slang* Courageous; strong; plucky.

guy[1] (gī) *n. Naut.* A rope, cord, or the like, as for steadying a mast. — *v.t.* To secure, steady, or guide with a guy. [<OF *guie* <*guier,* var. of *guider* guide]

guy[2] (gī) *n.* **1** *Slang* A person; fellow; man. **2** *Brit.* A person of grotesque appearance. **3** An effigy of Guy Fawkes. See GUY FAWKES DAY. — *v.t.* **guyed, guy·ing** *Slang* To ridicule; make fun of. [after *Guy* Fawkes] — **guy′er** *n.*

Guy (gī, *Fr.* gē) A masculine personal name. Also *Du., Ger., Sp.* **Gui·do** (gē′dō, *Dan., Ital., Sw.* gwē′dō). [<Celtic, sense]

— **Guy de Lusignan** (lü·sē·nyäṅ′), died 1194, French Crusader; king of Jerusalem 1186–92, and of Cyprus.

Guy (gī), **Thomas,** 1644–1724, English philanthropist; founded Guy's Hospital, London, England.

Guy·enne (gwē·yen′, gē-) See GUIENNE.

Guy Fawkes Day (gī′ fôks′) An English celebration, November 5, commemorating the Gunpowder Plot, an abortive conspiracy (1605) led by **Guy Fawkes** (1570–1606) to blow up the Parliament buildings while King James I and Parliament were in assembly.

guy·ot (gē′ō) *n.* A seamount having a flat top: also called *tablemount.* [after A. H. *Guyot,* 1807–84, Swiss-born U.S. geographer]

guz·zle (guz′əl) *v.t.* & *v.i.* **guz·zled, guz·zling** To drink immoderately or frequently. [? <OF *gosiller* <*gosier* throat] — **guz′zler** *n.*

Gwa·li·or (gwä′lē·ôr) A former princely state in central India; 26,008 square miles.

Gwin·nett (gwi·net′), **Button,** 1735?–77, American patriot; signer of Declaration of Independence.

Gwyn (gwin), **Nell,** 1650–87, English actress, mistress of Charles II.

Gyang·tse (gyäng′tse′) A town in southern Tibet.

gybe (jīb) See JIBE[1].

Gy·ges (gī′jēz, jī′-) **1** One of the Hecatoncheires. **2** A king of Lydia, 716–678 B.C., said by Plato to possess a magic ring that could make the wearer invisible.

gym (jim) *n. U.S. Colloq.* **1** A gymnasium. **2** A course in physical training. [Short for GYMNASIUM]

gym·bals (jim′bəlz, gim′-) See GIMBALS.

gym·kha·na (jim·kä′nə) *n. Brit.* An athletic meet, especially for racing; the meeting place. [<Hind. *gend–khana* a racket court; infl. by *gymnastics*]

gym·na·si·arch (jim·nā′zē·ärk) *n.* An official in ancient Greece entrusted with the management of the gymnasia. [<L *gymnasiarchus* <Gk. *gymnasiarchos* <*gymnasion* a gymnasium + *archein* rule]

gym·na·si·um (jim·nā′zē·əm) *n. pl.* **·si·ums** or **·si·a** (-zē·ə) **1** A building or room used for physical education activities and sports, and usually having gymnastic equipment. **2** In ancient Greece, a place where youths met for physical exercise and discussion. [<L <Gk. *gymnasion* <*gymnazein* exercise, train naked <*gymnos* naked]

Gym·na·si·um (gim·nä′zē·ōōm) *n.* In continental Europe, especially Germany, a classical school preparatory to the universities.

gym·nast (jim′nast) *n.* One expert in gymnastics. [<Gk. *gymnastēs* a trainer <*gymnazein.* See GYMNASIUM.]

gym·nas·tic (jim·nas′tik) *adj.* Relating to gymnastics. — **gym·nas′ti·cal·ly** *adv.*

gym·nas·tics (jim·nas′tiks) *n.* **1** Gymnastic exercises for the development of bodily strength and agility. **2** Exercises in a gymnasium, as

distinguished from outdoor athletics. **3** Feats of bodily skill.
gymno- *combining form* Naked: *gymnosperm.* Also, before vowels, *gymn-*. [<Gk. *gymnos* naked]
gym•no•bac•te•ri•um (jim′nō•bak•tir′ē•əm) *n. pl.* **•ri•a** (-ē•ə) A type of bacterium without flagella: distinguished from *trichobacterium.*
gym•no•car•pous (jim′nə•kär′pəs) *adj. Bot.* Provided with naked fruits in flowering plants: said of a fruit without pubescence. Also **gym′•no•car′pic.**
gym•nos•o•phist (jim•nos′ə•fist) *n.* **1** One of an ancient Hindu sect of ascetic philosophers who wore little or no clothing. **2** A nudist. [<L *gymnosophistae,* pl. <Gk. *gymnosophistai* <*gymnos* naked + *sophistēs* a sophist] **—gym•nos′o•phy** *n.*
gym•no•sperm (jim′nə•spûrm′) *n.* One of a class of plants (the *Gymnospermae*) having their ovules and seeds naked, as certain evergreens: distinguished from *angiosperm.* **—gym′no•sper′mous, gym′no•sper′mic** *adj.*
gyn- Var. of GYNO-.
gy•nae•ce•um (jī′nə•sē′əm, jin′ə-) See GYNECEUM.
gynaeco- See GYNECO-.
gy•nan•der (jī•nan′dər, ji-, gī-) *n.* **1** *Biol.* An organism exhibiting bisexual characteristics, usually localized on one or the other side of the midline of the body, as certain insects: also **gy•nan•dro•morph** (jī•nan′drə•môrf, ji-, gī-). **2** A masculine woman. [<Gk. *gynandros* of doubtful sex <*gynē* woman + *anēr, andros* man]
gy•nan•droid (jī•nan′droid, ji-, gī-) *n.* A hermaphrodite with predominantly female characteristics.
gy•nan•dro•mor•phism (jī•nan′drō•môr′fiz•əm, ji-, gī-) *n. Biol.* The occurrence of male and female characteristics in the same individual. **—gy•nan′dro•mor′phic, gy•nan′dro•mor′phous** *adj.*
gy•nan•drous (jī•nan′drəs, ji-, gī-) *adj.* **1** *Bot.* Having the stamens united with or seemingly borne upon the pistil. **2** Exhibiting gynandry.
gy•nan•dry (jī•nan′drē, ji-, gī-) *n.* Hermaphroditism. Also **gy•nan′drism.**
gy•nar•chy (jī′när•kē, jin′är-) *n. pl.* **•chies** Female authority or domination; the supremacy of women; government by a woman or by women. **—gy•nar′chic** *adj.*
gyne (jīn) *n.* The female or queen ant. [<NL <Gk. *gynē* a woman]
gy•ne•ce•um (jī′nə•sē′əm, jin′ə-) *n. pl.* **•ce•a** (-sē′ə) **1** The part of a Greek house reserved for the women, usually the rear. **2** The gynoecium. Also *gynaeceum.* [<L *gynacium* <Gk. *gynaikeion* <*gynē, gynaikos* a woman]
gyneco- *combining form* Female; pertaining to women: *gynecomorphous*: also spelled *gynaeco-*. Also, before vowels, **gynec-**. [<Gk. *gynē, gynaikos* a woman]
gy•ne•coc•ra•cy (jī′nə•kok′rə•sē, jin′ə-) *n. pl.* **•cies** Rule by a woman or by women; female supremacy. [<Gk. *gynaikokratia* <*gynē, gynaikos* a woman + *krateein* rule] **—gy•ne•co•crat** (jī•nē′•kə•krat, ji-) *n.* **—gy•ne•co•crat•ic** (jī′nə•kō•krat′ik, jin′ə-) *adj.*
gy•ne•coid (jī′nə•koid, jin′ə-) *n.* A worker ant capable of laying eggs.
gy•ne•col•o•gy (gī′nə•kol′ə•jē, jī′nə-, jin′ə-) *n.* The study of the female reproductive system and the disorders peculiar to it. **—gy•ne•co•log′i•cal** *adj.* **—gy′ne•col′o•gist** *n.*
gy•ne•co•mor•phous (jī•nē′kō•môr′fəs, jin′ə•kō-, gī-) *adj.* Having the characteristics, shape, or appearance of a female.
gy•ni•at•rics (jī′nē•at′riks, jin′ē-) *n.* The diagnosis and treatment of women's diseases. Also **gy•ni•at•ry** (jī′nē•at′rē, jin′ē-, ji•nī′ə•trē).
gyno- *combining form* **1** Woman; female: *gynophobia.* **2** *Bot. & Med.* Female reproductive organ; ovary; pistil: *gynophore.* Also, before vowels, *gyn-*. [<Gk. *gynē* a woman]
gy•no•base (jī′nə•bās, jin′ə-) *n. Bot.* The conical or flat enlargement of the receptacle of a flower, bearing the gynaecium. **—gy′no•ba′sic, gy′no•ba′seous** (-bā′shəs) *adj.*
gy•noe•ci•um (jī•nē′sē•əm, ji-) *n. Bot.* The female parts of a flower; the pistil or pistils taken as a unit. Compare ANDROECIUM. [<NL <L *gynaeceum.* See GYNECEUM.]
gy•no•gen•e•sis (jī′nō•jen′ə•sis, jin′ō-) *n. Biol.* The development of an egg after fertilization by a sperm whose nucleus is either absent or inactive, as in certain nematodes. **—gy′no•gen′ic** *adj.*
gy•nop•a•thy (jī•nop′ə•thē, ji-) *n.* Any disease of women. **—gy•no•path•ic** (jī′nə•path′ik, jin′ə-) *adj.*
gy•no•phore (jī′nə•fôr, -fōr, jin′ə-) *n. Bot.* A stalk supporting the ovary of certain plants, as in the cleome and some crucifers.
-gynous *combining form* **1** Female; of women: *philogynous.* **2** *Bot.* Denoting location, number, etc., of the pistils: *acrogynous.* [<Gk. *gynē* a woman]
gyp[1] (jip) *U.S. Slang n.* **1** A swindler. **2** A swindling transaction. *—v.t. & v.i.* **gypped, gyp•ping** To cheat or swindle. Also spelled *gip.* [? <GYPSY]
gyp[2] (jip) *n. Brit. Colloq.* A male servant at a university. [<obs. *gippo* a scullion <F *jupeau* tunic]
gyp•soph•i•la (jip•sof′ə•lə) *n.* Any of a large genus (*Gypsophila*) of hardy annual and perennial herbs with sparse foliage and small rosy or white flowers; babysbreath. [<NL <Gk. *gypsos* chalk + *philein* love]
gyp•sum (jip′səm) *n.* Hydrous sulfate of lime, $CaSO_4 \cdot 2H_2O$, occurring in massive, fibrous, foliated, or granular form. The crystalline and usually transparent form is called *selenite;* the massive fine-grained, white or delicately colored variety is called *alabaster;* when calcined, it is called *plaster of Paris.* [<L <Gk. *gypsos* chalk] **—gyp′se•ous** *adj.* **—gyp•sif•er•ous** (jip•sif′ər•əs) *adj.*
Gyp•sy (jip′sē) See GIPSY.
gypsy moth A European moth with mottled light brown or near-white wings (*Porthetria dispar*), which has become established as a destructive pest in the Eastern United States and Canada, its hairy caterpillar devouring the leaves of deciduous trees.
gy•ral (jī′rəl) *adj.* **1** Having a circular, revolving, or whirling motion. **2** Of or pertaining to the convolutions of the brain. **—gy′ral•ly** *adv.*
gy•rate (jī′rāt) *v.i.* **gy•rat•ed, gy•rat•ing 1** To rotate or revolve. **2** To move in a spiral path; whirl, as a cyclone. *—adj. Zool.* Having spiral or convoluted parts. [<L *gyratus,* pp. of *gyrare* gyrate <gyrus a circle <Gk. *gyrus*]
gy•ra•tion (jī•rā′shən) *n.* **1** A rotating whirling or spiral motion; a revolution. **2** A single whorl of a spiral shell.
gy•ra•to•ry (jī′rə•tôr′ē, -tō′rē) *adj.* Gyrating.
gyre[1] (jīr) *n.* **1** A circular or swirling motion. **2** A ring; vortex; a spiral or round form. **3** In oceanography, a ringlike movement of ocean currents set up by variable wind systems acting upon large ocean areas of different chemical and biological properties. [<L *gyrus* a circle]
gyre[2] (jīr) *n. Scot.* An evil spirit; ogre.
gyr•fal•con (jûr′fôl′kən, -fô′-) See GERFALCON.
gy•ro (jī′rō) *n.* A gyroscope or gyrocompass.
gyro- *combining form* Circle, ring, or spiral: *gyroscope.* Also, before vowels, **gyr-**.
gy•ro•com•pass (jī′rō•kum′pəs, -kom′-) *n.* A compass operating on the principle of a gyroscope; an instrument of navigation indicating a change in the direction of a ship or an aircraft by the resistance of a gyroscope to such change.
gyro control 1 *Aeron.* The gyroscope element of an automatic pilot. **2** A gyro stabilizer.
gy•ro•dy•nam•ics (jī′rō•dī•nam′iks, -di-) *n.* The dynamics of rotating bodies.
gy•ro•ho•ri•zon (jī′rō•hə•rī′zən) *n. Aeron.* A gyroscopic instrument designed to simulate the natural horizons and thus indicate the exact lateral and longitudinal position of an aircraft.
gy•ro•mag•net•ic (jī′rō•mag•net′ik) *adj.* Of or pertaining to the magnetic properties of electric charges in rotation, specifically of electron movements in atoms.
gy•ron (jī′ron) *n. Her.* A charge formed by two straight lines meeting in an acute angle at the center of a shield, its fess point. [<F *giron* <OHG *gēro* gusset, triangular piece]
gyro pilot An automatic pilot.
gy•ro•plane (jī′rə•plān′) *n.* An airplane whose chief support is obtained from the rapid rotation of airfoils about a vertical or nearly vertical axis.
gy•ro•scope (jī′rə•skōp) *n.* A heavy rotating wheel, the axis of which is free to turn in any direction, and which can be set to rotate in any plane, independently of forces tending to change the position of the axis. [<F] **—gy′ro•scop′ic** (-skop′ik) *adj.*

GYROSCOPE
Showing possible directional movements.

gyro stabilizer A gyroscopic device which operates to maintain a structural unit in a steady position, as a gun, despite the rolling of a ship or the motion of the vehicle upon which it is mounted.
gy•ro•stat (jī′rə•stat) *n.* A modification of the gyroscope, used to illustrate the dynamics of rotating rigid bodies. [<GYRO(SCOPE) + -STAT]
gy•ro•stat•ic (jī′rə•stat′ik) *adj.* Pertaining to the gyrostat or to the law that a rapidly rotating body tends to keep in the same plane. **—gy′ro•stat′i•cal•ly** *adv.*
gy•ro•stat•ics (jī′rə•stat′iks) *n. pl.* The laws governing the rotation of solid bodies.
gy•rus (jī′rəs) *n. pl.* **•ri** (-rī) *Anat.* A rounded, serpentine ridge between two fissures or sulci; especially, one of the convolutions of the cortex of the brain. [<NL <L *gyrus* a circle]
gyve (jīv) *n. Usually pl.* A fetter for the limbs of prisoners. See synonyms under FETTER. *—v.t.* **gyved, gyv•ing** To bind with fetters; shackle. [ME *give, gyves;* origin uncertain]

H

h, H (āch) *n. pl.* **h's, H's** or **hs, Hs, aitch•es** (ā′chiz) **1** The eighth letter of the English alphabet, from Phoenician *cheth,* which eventually developed into Greek *eta,* Roman *H.* **2** The sound of the letter *h,* a voiceless, glottal fricative. In a few English words of French origin, as heir, honor, hour, etc., initial *h* is still written but not pronounced; usage varies in certain other words, as herb, homage, etc., in which some persons pronounce the *h* and some do not. See ALPHABET. *—symbol Chem.* Hydrogen (symbol H).
ha (hä) *n. & interj.* **1** An exclamation or sound made by a quick expulsion of breath expressing surprise, joy, grief, laughter, etc. **2** A sound indicating hesitation, indecision, etc. Also spelled *hah.*
ha' (hô) *n. Scot.* A hall; principal room.

Ha·a·bai (hä·ä·bī′) An island group of the central Tonga Islands. Also **Ha·a·pai′.**

haaf (häf) *n.* A deep-sea fishing ground off the coast of the Shetland or Orkney Islands. [<ON *haf* sea]

haak (häk) See HAKE.

Haa·kon (hô′ko͝on) The name of several kings of Norway. —**Haakon VII,** 1872–1957, king of Norway 1905–57.

haar (här) *n. Scot.* Mist; especially, a chilly fog.

Haar·lem (här′ləm) A city of western Netherlands; capital of North Holland province: also *Harlem.*

Ha·bak·kuk (hə·bak′ək, hab′ə·kuk) A minor Hebrew prophet of about the seventh century B.C.; also, the book of the Old Testament written by him. Also **Ha·bac′uc.**

Ha·ba·na (ä·vä′nä), **La** The Spanish name for HAVANA.

ha·ba·ne·ra (ä′bä·nā′rä) *n.* **1** A dance of African origin common in Cuba. **2** The slow rhythmic music for this dance. [<Sp., of Havana]

Ha·ba·ne·ro (ä′vä·nā′rō) *n.* A native or inhabitant of Havana, Cuba.

Hab·ba·ni·ya (häb·bä′nē·yə), **Lake** A salt lake of central Iraq; 54 square miles.

ha·be·as cor·pus (hā′bē·əs kôr′pəs) *Law* A writ commanding a person having another in custody to produce the detained person before a court. [<L, (you) have the body]

ha·ben·dum (hə·ben′dəm) *n. pl.* **·da** (-də) *Law* The clause in a deed beginning "to have and to hold" (in Latin, *habendum et tenendum*), which determines what interest or estate is granted by the deed. [<L, gerundive of *habere* have]

Ha·ber (hä′bər), **Fritz,** 1868–1934, German electrochemist; developed the **Haber process** for the fixation of atmospheric nitrogen.

hab·er·dash·er (hab′ər·dash′ər) *n.* **1** A dealer in men's furnishings. **2** *Brit.* A dealer in or peddler of ribbons, trimmings, thread, needles, and other small wares. [Prob. <AF *hapertas* kind of fabric]

hab·er·dash·er·y (hab′ər·dash′ər·ē) *n. pl.* **·er·ies** **1** The goods sold by haberdashers. **2** A haberdasher's shop.

hab·er·geon (hab′ər·jən) *n.* A coat of mail for the breast and neck, shorter than a hauberk. [<OF *haubergeon,* dim. of *hauberc.* See HAUBERK.]

hab·ile (hab′il) *adj.* Skilful; able. [Var. of ABLE; infl. in form by F *habile* able or L *habilis* apt]

ha·bil·i·ment (hə·bil′ə·mənt) *n.* **1** An article of clothing. **2** *pl.* Clothes; garb. See synonyms under DRESS. [<OF *habillement* <*habiller* dress, make fit <L *habilis* fit, apt]

ha·bil·i·tate (hə·bil′ə·tāt) *v.t.* **·tat·ed, ·tat·ing** **1** *U.S.* In the West, to furnish with suitable means of equipment, to work (a mine). **2** *Rare* To dress: clothe. [<Med. L *habilitatus,* pp. of *habilitare* enable <*habilis* fit] —**ha·bil′·i·ta′tion** *n.*

hab·it (hab′it) *n.* **1** A tendency toward an action or condition, which by repetition has become spontaneous. **2** An action so induced; habitual course of action or conduct. **3** Habitual condition, appearance, or temperament; physical or mental make-up. **4** *Biol.* A characteristic mode of growth or aspect of a plant or animal. **5** An outer garment or garments; costume; especially, a woman's dress or costume for horseback riding. **6** The distinctive garment of a religious order. **7** *Psychol.* An acquired response or set of responses; a cultivated tendency. Compare INSTINCT. **8** *Obs.* Intimate acquaintance; familiarity. —*v.t.* **1** To furnish with a habit; clothe; dress. **2** *Obs.* To inhabit. [<OF <L *habitus* condition, dress <*habere* have]

Synonyms (noun): custom, fashion, habitude, practice, routine, rule, system, usage, use, wont. *Habit* is a tendency or inclination toward an action or condition, which by repetition has become easy, spontaneous, or even unconscious, or an action or regular series of actions, or a condition so induced. *Habitude* is habitual relation or association. *Custom* is the uniform doing of the same act in the same circumstance, usually, at least in the origin of the *custom,* for a definite reason; *routine* is the doing of customary acts in a regular and uniform sequence and is more mechanical than *custom.* It is the *custom* of shopkeepers to open at a uniform hour, and to follow a regular *routine* of business until closing time. *Custom* is chiefly used of the action of many; *habit* of the action of one; we speak of the *customs* of society, the *habits* of an individual. *Fashion* is the generally recognized *custom* in the smaller matters, especially in dress. A *rule* is prescribed either by some external authority or by one's own will; as, It is the *rule* of the house; or, my invariable *rule. Practice* is the active doing of something in a systematic way; we do not speak of the *practice,* but of the *habit* of going to sleep. *Wont* is established *usage* or *custom* and now chiefly poetical. Compare CUSTOM, DRESS, MANNER, PRACTICE, USE.

hab·it·able (hab′it·ə·bəl) *adj.* Fit to be inhabited. [<L *habitabilis* <*habitare* inhabit] —**hab·it·a·bil·i·ty** (hab′it·ə·bil′ə·tē), **hab′it·a·ble·ness** *n.* —**hab′it·a·bly** *adv.*

hab·i·tan·cy (hab′ə·tən·sē) *n. pl.* **·cies** *Rare* **1** Inhabitance; residence. **2** Inhabitants collectively.

hab·i·tant (hab′ə·tənt) *n.* **1** An inhabitant. **2** (*Fr.* à·bē·täṅ′) A small rural proprietor, or resident, of French descent, in Canada or Louisiana: also **ha·bi·tan′.** [<F <L *habitans, -antis,* ppr. of *habitare* dwell]

hab·i·tat (hab′ə·tat) *n.* **1** The region where a race, species, or individual naturally or usually lives or is found. **2** Natural environment. [<NL, it dwells]

hab·i·ta·tion (hab′ə·tā′shən) *n.* **1** A place of abode. **2** The act or state of inhabiting. See synonyms under HOME, HOUSE.

hab·i·ted (hab′ə·tid) *adj.* **1** Clothed; arrayed; wearing a habit. **2** *Obs* Habituated.

ha·bit·u·al (hə·bich′o͞o·əl) *adj.* **1** Of, pertaining to, or constituting a habit. **2** Acquired by or resulting from habit, repeated use, or continued causes. **3** Characterized by repeated or constant practice or indulgence; inveterate: a *habitual* liar. [<Med. L *habitualis* <*habitus.* See HABIT.] —**ha·bit′u·al·ly** *adv.* —**ha·bit′u·al·ness** *n.*

Synonyms: accustomed, common, customary, familiar, general, ordinary, regular, stated, usual, wonted. See COMMON, GENERAL, USUAL. Compare synonyms for HABIT. *Antonyms*: exceptional, extraordinary, infrequent, irregular, occasional, rare, unusual, unwonted.

ha·bit·u·ate (hə·bich′o͞o·āt) *v.t.* **·at·ed, ·at·ing** **1** To make familiar by repetition or use; accustom. **2** *U.S. Colloq.* To frequent. [<L *habituatus,* pp. of *habituare* condition] —**ha·bit′u·at′ed** *adj.* —**ha·bit′u·a′tion** *n.*

hab·i·tude (hab′ə·to͞od, -tyo͞od) *n.* **1** Habitual method, state, character, constitution, or tendency; habit. **2** Customary relation or association. **3** Habitual practice. See synonyms under HABIT. [<MF <L *habitudo* condition]

ha·bit·u·é (hə·bich′o͞o·ā′, *Fr.* à·bē·twā′) *n.* A habitual visitor or frequenter of a place. [<F, pp. of *habituer* accustom]

Habs·burg (häps′bo͝orkh) See HAPSBURG.

ha·bu (hä·bo͞o) *n.* A very poisonous crotaline snake (genus *Trimeresurus*) of Okinawa and the Ryukyu archipelago, patterned in green and yellow: related to the American rattlesnake and copperhead. [<Japanese]

ha·chure (ha·sho͝or′, hash′o͝or) *n.* **1** In art, a hatching. **2** In mapmaking, the shading or lines used to indicate hills or elevations. —*v.t.* (ha·sho͝or′) **·chured, ·chur·ing** To mark or indicate with hatchings. [<F *hacher* HATCH[3]]

ha·ci·en·da (hä′sē·en′də, *Sp.* ä·syen′dä) *n.* In Spanish America: **1** A landed estate; a country house. **2** A farming, mining, or manufacturing establishment in the country. [<Am. Sp. <L *facienda* things to be done <*facere* do, make]

hack[1] (hak) *v.t.* **1** To cut or chop crudely or irregularly, as with an ax or sword. **2** To break up, as clods of earth. **3** In basketball, to strike (an opposing player) on the arm. **4** In Rugby football, to kick (an opposing player) in the shins. —*v.i.* **5** To make cuts or notches with heavy, crude blows. **6** To emit short, dry coughs. See synonyms under CUT. —**to hack it** *Slang* To cope with it; do it. —*n.* **1** A gash, cut, or nick made by or as by a sharp instrument. **2** An ax or other tool for hacking. **3** A kick on the shins, as in Rugby football. **4** A short, dry cough. [OE *haccian* cut] —**hack′er** *n.*

hack[2] (hak) *n.* **1** A horse for hire. **2** A horse used for general work or for ordinary riding, as distinguished from one bred or trained for special use. **3** An old, worn-out horse. **4** A hackney coach. **5** A taxicab. **6** A writer who hires himself out for any kind of writing jobs; a literary drudge. —*v.t.* **1** To let out for hire, as a horse. **2** To make stale or trite by constant use; hackney. —*v.i.* **3** *Colloq.* To drive a taxicab. **4** *Brit.* To ride on or move at the pace of a hack (*n.* def. 2). —*adj.* **1** Of or designated for a hack: a *hack* stand. **2** For hire or drudging work: a *hack* horse; a *hack* writer. **3** Done by a hack; requiring drudgery: a *hack* job. **4** Trite; hackneyed. [<HACKNEY]

hack[3] (hak) *n.* **1** A frame or rack on which to dry cheese, fish, bricks, etc. **2** A row of bricks laid out to dry. **3** A pile of green brick. [Var. of HATCH[1]]

hack·a·more (hak′ə·môr, -mōr) *n. U.S.* A special headstall of a halter of rawhide or horsehair used to break colts to respond to a bridle. [Alter. of Sp. *jaquima* halter]

hack·ber·ry (hak′ber′ē, -bər·ē) *n. pl.* **·ries** **1** An American tree (genus *Celtis*) resembling the elm and having small, sweet, edible fruit. **2** The fruit or wood of this tree. Also called *hagberry.* [Var. of *hagberry* <ON *heggr* hedge + BERRY]

hack·but (hak′but) *n.* A harquebus. Also spelled *hagbut.* [<MF *hacquebut* <Du. *hakebus* <*hake* hook + *bus* gun]

hack·ee (hak′ē) *n.* The chipmunk: sometimes spelled *hacky.* [Imit.]

Hack·en·sack (hak′ən·sak) A city in eastern New Jersey, on the **Hackensack River,** which flows 45 miles south to Newark Bay.

hack·er·y (hak′ər·ē) *n. pl.* **·er·ies** *Anglo-Indian* A bullock cart with rude and primitive wooden wheels. [<Hind. *chhakṛā*]

hack·ham·mer (hak′ham′ər) *n.* An implement for dressing grindstones.

hack·le[1] (hak′əl) *n.* **1** One of the long narrow feathers on the neck of a cock, used by anglers in making artificial flies; also, a similar feather on other birds. **2** An artificial feather fly for angling: also **hackle fly.** **3** *pl.* The erectile hairs on the neck and back of a dog: also spelled *heckle.* **4** A hatchel. **5** Unspun fiber, as raw silk. —*v.t.* **hack·led, hack·ling** **1** To furnish (a fly) with a hackle. **2** To hatchel. [See HATCHEL] —**hack′ler** *n.*

hack·le[2] (hak′əl) *v.t.* & *v.i.* **hack·led, hack·ling** To cut or chop roughly or crudely; mangle; hack. [Freq. of HACK[1]]

hack·ly (hak′lē) *adj.* Jagged; rough.

hack·man (hak′mən) *n. pl.* **·men** (-mən) The driver of a hack or public carriage.

hack·ma·tack (hak′mə·tak) *n.* The American larch; tamarack. [<N. Am. Ind.]

hack·ney (hak′nē) *n. pl.* **·neys** **1** One of a breed of driving and saddle horses. **2** A horse kept for hire. **3** A hackney coach. **4** A drudge. —*v.t.* **1** To make trite by constant use. **2** To let out or use as a hackney. —*adj.* Let out for hire; common. [<OF *haquenée* a horse; ult. origin unknown] —**hack′ney·ism** *n.*

hackney coach A coach kept for hire.

hack·neyed (hak′nēd) *adj.* Worn out; made commonplace by frequent use; trite. See synonyms under TRITE.

hack·saw (hak′sô′) *n.* A narrow-bladed, close-toothed saw for cutting metal.

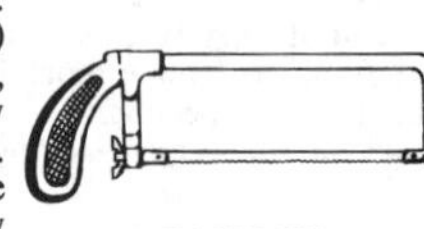
HACKSAW

hack work The work of a literary hack.

had[1] (had) Past tense and past participle of HAVE.

had[2] (had) *v.t. Scot.* To hold.

had better, had liefer, had rather See usage note under HAVE.

had·die (had′ē) *n. Scot.* A haddock.

had·din (had′ən) *n. Scot.* A dwelling; holding.

Had·ding·ton (had′ing·tən) The county seat of East Lothian, Scotland.

had·dock (had′ək) *n. pl.* **·dock** or **·docks** A food fish (*Melanogrammus aeglefinus*) of the North Atlantic, allied to the cod and with a black lateral line and blackish shoulder spot. [ME; origin unknown]

hade (hād) *n. Geol.* The inclination of a fault plane or vein from the vertical; an underlay: also **had′ing.** See FAULT (def. 3). —*v.i.* **had·ed, had·ing** To incline from a vertical position, as a fault plane. [Cf. dial. E *hade* slope]

Ha·des (hā′dēz) **1** In Greek mythology,

brother of Zeus, god of the underworld and lord of the dead: identified with the Greek and Roman *Pluto* and the Roman *Dis.* **2** The kingdom over which Pluto rules, the abode of the dead. See TARTARUS, ORCUS. **3** *Colloq.* A euphemism for HELL. [<Gk. *Haidēs* <*a-* not + *idein* see]

Had·field (had′fēld), **Sir Robert Abbott,** 1858–1940. English metallurgist.

Ha·dhra·maut (hä′drä·mout′, -môt′) A region on the southern coast of Arabia. Also **Ha′dra·maut′.**

hadj (haj) *n.* The pilgrimage to Mecca required of every free Mohammedan at least once in his life. Also spelled *haj, hajj.* See HEGIRA. [<Turkish <Arabic *hajj* pilgrimage. Akin to HEGIRA.]

hadj·i (haj′ē) *n.* **1** A Mohammedan who has made the pilgrimage to Mecca: used also before a name as a title. **2** An Armenian or a Greek who has made a pilgrimage to the holy sepulcher at Jerusalem. Also **hadj′ee.** [<Arabic *hajj* pilgrim]

Had·ley (had′lē), **Henry Kimball,** 1871–1937, U.S. composer.

had·n't (had′nt) Contraction of HAD NOT.

Ha·dri·an (hā′drē·ən), 76–138, Roman emperor 117–138: full name *Publius Aelius Hadrianus*: sometimes called "Adrian."

Ha·dri·an·op·o·lis (hā′drē·ən·op′ə·lis) The ancient name for ADRIANOPLE.

Hadrian's Wall A wall extending from Solway Firth to the Tyne, built by Hadrian, 122–128, to protect Roman Britain from the Picts and Scots.

Had·ru·me·tum (had′rə·mē′təm) The ancient name for SOUSSE.

hae (hā, ha) *v.t. Scot.* To have.

Haeck·el (hek′əl), **Ernst Heinrich,** 1834–1919, German biologist.

Hae·ju (hī·jo͞o) A port of central Korea on the Yellow Sea. *Japanese* **Kai·shu** (kī·sho͞o).

haem-, haemo- See HEMO-.

haema- See HEMA-.

haemat-, haemato- See HEMATO-.

hae·ma·to·cry·al (hē′mə·tō·krī′əl) See HEMATOCRYAL.

hae·ma·to·therm·al (hē′mə·tō·thûr′məl) See HEMATOTHERMAL.

hae·ma·tox·y·lon (hē′mə·tok′sə·lon, hem′ə-) *n.* **1** Any of a genus (*Haematoxylon*) of tropical American trees, especially the logwood or bloodwood tree (*H. campechianum*), whose heartwood supplies a purple-red coloring matter. **2** The wood of this tree. [<NL <Gk. *haima, -atos* blood + *xylon* wood]

haem·or·rhoid (hem′ə·roid), **haem·or·rhoi·dal** See HEMORRHOID, etc.

haen (hān) *Scot.* Past participle of HAE; had.

hae·res (hē′rēz) See HERES.

haf·fet (häf′it) *n. Scot.* Side of the head; temple.

ha·fiz (hä′fiz) *n.* One who has memorized the Koran: a Moslem title of respect. [<Arabic *hāfiz* one who remembers]

Ha·fiz (hä′fiz) Pseudonym of Shams ud-din Mohammed, Persian poet and philosopher of the 14th century.

haf·ni·um (haf′nē·əm) *n.* A metallic element (symbol Hf, atomic number 72) found combined in zirconium ores and used to control fission in nuclear reactors. See PERIODIC TABLE. [<NL, from L *Hafnia* Copenhagen]

haft (haft, häft) *n.* A handle; specifically, the handle of a cutting weapon. —*v.t.* To supply with or set in a haft or handle. Also spelled *heft.* [OE *hæft* handle <*habban* hold, have]

hag[1] (hag) *n.* **1** A forbidding or malicious old woman; an ugly crone. **2** A witch; sorceress; she-devil; a woman in league with the devil. **3** A hagfish. [OE *hægtes* witch] **—hag′gish** *adj.*

hag[2] (hag) *Scot. & Brit. Dial. v.t. & v.i.* **1** To hack or hew. **2** To harass; torment. —*n.* **1** A stroke with a chopping tool; hack. **2** A notch; cut. **3** One man's section of wood for felling. **4** Broken or mossy ground in a bog. **5** Cut branches. Also **hagg.** [<ON *höggva* hew]

Ha·gar (hā′gər) Abraham's concubine, mother of Ishmael. *Gen.* xvi 1.

hag·ber·ry (hag′ber′ē, -bər·ē) *n. pl.* **·ries** The hackberry. [See HACKBERRY]

hag·bush (hag′bo͝osh′) *n.* The azedarach. [? OE *haga* hedge + BUSH]

hag·but (hag′but) *n.* A hackbut.

hag·don (hag′dən) *n.* The shearwater: also calle *haglet, haglin.* Also **hag′del** (-dəl), **hag′den** (-dən). [? <HAG[2] *v.*]

Ha·gen (hä′gən) **1** In the *Nibelungenlied,* Siegfried's murderer. **2** In Wagner's *Götterdämmerung,* the half-brother of Gunther and Gutrune.

Ha·gen (hä′gən) A city in North Rhine-Westphalia, Germany. Also **Ha·gen-in-West·fal·en** (in vest·fäl′ən).

hag·fish (hag′fish′) *n. pl.* **·fish** or **·fish·es** A primitive eel-like marine cyclostome (order or subclass *Myxinoidea*), allied to the lamprey, which bores its way into the bodies of living fishes by means of a rasping suctorial mouth. [<HAG[2], *v.* + FISH]

Hag·ga·dah (hə·gä′də, *Hebrew* hä·gô′dô) *n. pl.* **·doth** (-dōth) **1** A free interpretation or application: specifically, an illustrative anecdote or parable of the Midrash: distinguished from *halacha.* **2** The ritual, including the exposition of the story of the Exodus, read during the Seder on the first two nights of Passover. Also **Ha·ga′dah, Hag·ga′da.** [<Hebrew <*higgid* tell]

hag·gad·ic (hə·gad′ik, -gäd′-) *adj.* Of or pertaining to the Haggadah. Also **ha·gad′ic, hag·gad′i·cal.**

hag·ga·dist (hə·gä′dist) *n.* A haggadic writer or scholar. Also **ha·ga′dist. —hag·ga·dis·tic** (hag′ə·dis′tik), **hag′a·dis′tic** *adj.*

Hag·ga·i (hag′ē·ī, hag′ī) A minor Hebrew prophet of about 520 B.C.; also, the Old Testament book written by him.

hag·gard[1] (hag′ərd) *adj.* **1** Worn and gaunt in appearance. **2** Wild or intractable, as a hawk. —*n.* **1** In falconry, a wild hawk caught in its adult plumage. **2** Hence, an untamed fierce creature. [<OF *hagard* wild <MHG *hag* hedge] **—hag′gard·ly** *adv.* **—hag′gard·ness** *n.*

hag·gard[2] (hag′ərd) *n. Obs.* A wanton woman. [<HAG[1]]

Hag·gard (hag′ərd), **Sir Henry Rider,** 1856–1925, English novelist.

hag·gis (hag′is) *n.* A Scottish dish commonly made of a sheep's heart and liver with onions and suet, mixed with oatmeal and boiled in a sheep's stomach. [ME *hagas* <*haggen* chop + *es* food]

hag·gish (hag′ish) *adj.* Resembling or characteristic of a hag.

hag·gle (hag′əl) *v.* **hag·gled, hag·gling** *v.t.* **1** To cut unskilfully; mangle. **2** To tire or confuse, as by wrangling. —*v.i.* **3** To argue about price or terms. —*n.* The act of haggling or higgling. [Freq. of HAG[2]] **—hag′gler** *n.*

hag·i·ar·chy (hag′ē·är′kē, hā′jē-) *n. pl.* **·chies** A government, or the principle of government, by priests; sacerdotal government. Also **hag·i·oc·ra·cy** (hag′ē·ok′rə·sē, hā′jē-).

hagio- *combining form* Sacred: *hagiography.* Also, before vowels, **hagi-.** [<Gk. *hagios* sacred]

Hag·i·og·ra·pha (hag′ē·og′rə·fə, hā′jē-) *n. pl.* The third of the three ancient divisions of the Old Testament, comprising all books not reckoned in the Law or the Prophets. [<Gk. <*hagios* sacred + *graphein* write]

hag·i·og·ra·phy (hag′ē·og′rə·fē, hā′jē-) *n. pl.* **·phies 1** The writing or study of saints' lives. **2** A collection of biographies of saints. **—hag′i·og′ra·phal** *adj.* **—hag′i·og′ra·pher** *n.* **—hag·i·o·graph·ic** (hag′ē·ə·graf′ik, hā′jē-) or **·i·cal** *adj.*

hag·i·ol·a·try (hag′ē·ol′ə·trē, hā′jē-) *n.* The veneration or invocation of saints. **—hag′i·ol′a·ter** *n.* **—hag′i·ol′a·trous** *adj.*

hag·i·ol·o·gy (hag′ē·ol′ə·jē, hā′jē-) *n. pl.* **·gies 1** A list of saints. **2** A treatise on saints' lives; sacred writings. **—hag·i·o·log·ic** (hag′ē·ə·loj′ik, hā′jē-) *adj.* **—hag′i·ol′o·gist** *n.*

hag·i·o·scope (hag′ē·ə·skōp′, hā′jē-) *n.* An oblique opening in the screen or chancel wall of a medieval church, to permit those in a side chapel or aisle to see the main altar. **—hag′i·o·scop′ic** (-skop′ik) *adj.*

hag·let (hag′lit), **hag·lin** (hag′lin) See HAGDON.

hag-rid·den (hag′rid′n) *adj.* **1** Ridden by a hag or witch. **2** Tormented or distressed by or as by nightmares or hallucinations. **3** By extension, tormented by a woman.

Hague (ág), **Cap de la** A cape of NW France on the English Channel.

Hague (hāg), **The** The de facto capital of the Netherlands: Dutch *'s Gravenhage.*

—Hague Conferences The first international peace conferences, held at The Hague in 1899 (26 states) and 1907 (44 states). The **Hague Conventions,** relating to the conduct of war and to the arbitration of international disputes, were adopted by the conferences, and the **Hague Tribunal** was created by the first. See PERMANENT COURT OF ARBITRATION under COURT.

hah (hä) See HA.

ha-ha (hä′hä) *n.* A hedge or wall set in a ditch, so as not to obstruct the view: also spelled *haw-haw.* [<F *haha*]

Hahn (hän), **Otto,** 1879–1968, German physical chemist.

Hah·ne·mann (hä′nə·män), **(Christian Friedrich) Samuel,** 1755–1843, German physician; founder of homeopathy.

Hah·ne·mann·ism (hä′nə·män·iz′əm) *n.* The original homeopathy. **—Hah·ne·man·i·an** (hä′nə·man′ē·ən, -män′ē-), **Hah′ne·man′ni·an** *adj.*

Hai·da (hī′də) *n.* **1** A member of any of the tribes of North American Indians inhabiting the Queen Charlotte Islands, British Columbia, and Prince of Wales Island, Alaska. **2** The family of languages spoken by these tribes.

Hai·dar·a·bad (hī′dər·ə·bad′) See HYDERABAD.

Hai·dar A·li (hī′dər ä′lē) See HYDER ALI.

Hai·duk (hī′do͝ok) *n.* **1** One of a body of Hungarian mercenaries of the 16th century, of Magyar race, who served the Protestant cause. **2** One of the bandit mountaineers of the Balkans who took part in the struggle for independence against Turkey. Also spelled *Heyduck.* Also **Hai′duck.** [<Hungarian *hajduk* drover]

Hai·fa (hī′fə) A port of NW Israel on the Bay of Acre.

Haig (Hāg), **Douglas,** 1861–1928, first Earl Haig, British field marshal.

haik (hīk, hāk) *n.* An Oriental outside garment made of an oblong woolen cloth. Also **haick.** [<Arabic *hayk* <*hāk* to weave]

HAIK

hai·ku (hī·ko͞o) *n.* A poem in imitation of a Japanese verse form, consisting of three lines of five, seven, five syllables respectively. Also *hokku.* [<Japanese *haikai*]

hai·kwan (hī′kwän′) *n.* The maritime custom duties of China. [<Chinese <*hai* sea + *kuan* gate]

hail[1] (hāl) *n.* **1** Frozen rain or congealed vapor, often falling in pellets during thunderstorms. **2** Figuratively, anything falling thickly and with violence: a *hail* of blows. **3** A hailstorm. —*v.i.* To pour down hail: used impersonally. —*v.t.* To hurl or pour down like hail: to *hail* curses on someone. ◆ Homophone: *hale.* [OE *hægel*] **—hail′y** *adj.*

hail[2] (hāl) *v.t.* **1** To call loudly to in greeting; salute. **2** To call to so as to attract attention: to *hail* a cab. **3** To name as; designate: They *hailed* him captain. —*v.i.* **4** To call out so as to attract attention or give greeting. **—to hail from** To come from; have as one's original home or residence. See synonyms under ADDRESS. —*n.* **1** A call to attract attention; greeting. **2** The distance a shout can be heard: within *hail.* —*interj.* An exclamation of greeting. ◆ Homophone: *hale.* [ME *hailen, heilen* <ON *heilla* <*heill* whole, hale. Akin to HALE[2].] **—hail′er** *n.*

hail[3] (hāl) *adj. Scot.* Healthy; hale; whole.

hail Columbia *U.S. Slang* **1** A severe punishment or reprimand. **2** A beating or drubbing: to give the enemy *hail Columbia.* **3** A rumpus: to raise *hail Columbia.* [Euphemism for HELL]

Hai·le Se·las·sie (hī′lē sə·las′ē, -lä′sē), 1891–1975, emperor of Ethiopia 1930–74; in exile 1936–41.

hail-fel·low (hāl′fel′ō) *adj.* On very familiar or cordial terms. —*n.* A close companion. Also **hail′-fel′low-well′-met′.**

Hail Mary See AVE MARIA.

hail·stone (hāl′stōn′) *n.* A pellet of hail.

hail·storm (hāl′stôrm′) *n.* A storm in which hail falls: also **hail storm.**

hain (hain) *v.t. Scot.* To save; spare; preserve.

Hai·nan (hī′nän′) An island of SE China; 13,000 square miles; separated from the mainland by **Hainan Strait,** an arm of the South China Sea.

Hai·naut (e·nō′) A province of SW Belgium; 1,437 square miles; capital, Mons. *Flemish* **He·ne·gou·wen** (hā′nə·gou′wən).

hain't (hānt) *Illit. & Dial.* Contraction of *have not* or *has not.*

Hai·phong (hī′fong′) A port of North Vietnam.

hair (hâr) *n.* **1** One of the filaments of modified epidermal tissue growing from the skin or outer covering of a mammal. ◆ Collateral adjectives: *capillary, pilar.* **2** Any mass of such filaments, especially that which grows upon the head. **3** Any filamentous process. **4** *Bot.* An outgrowth of the epidermis in plants. **5** Haircloth; specifically, mats woven from horsehair, used in expressing oils, etc. **6** Figuratively, an exceedingly minute, slight, or delicate thing, space, etc. —*adj.* Like, or made of, hair. —**to a hair line** With the utmost exactness. —**to split hairs** To quibble; make petty or excessive distinctions. —**to let down one's hair** To disclose the actual state of one's affairs. —**not to turn a hair** To show or reveal no sign of exhaustion nor a lack of composure. ◆ Homophone: *hare.* [OE *hær*] —**hair′less** *adj.*

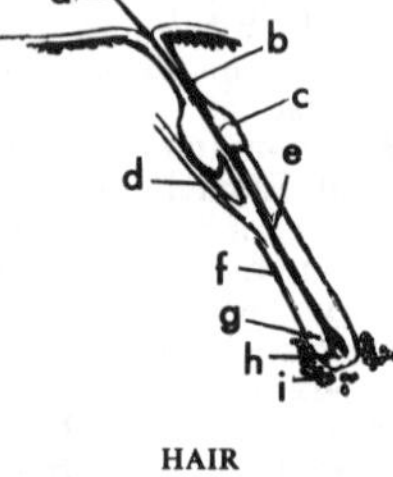

HAIR
Section through the skin: *a.* Shaft. *b.* Root. *c.* Sebaceous gland. *d.* Erector pili muscle. *e.* Root sheath. *f.* Follicle. *g.* Bulb. *h.* Papilla. *i.* Fat-cells.

Hair may appear as a combining form in hyphemes or solidemes, or as the first element in two-word phrases; as in:

hairband	**hairmonger**
hair bleacher	**hairmongering**
hair braid	**hair net**
haircap	**hair oil**
hair carder	**hair powder**
hair clipper	**hair remover**
hair-collecting	**hair restorer**
hair-collector	**hair ribbon**
hair crimper	**hair sorter**
hair curler	**hair straightener**
hair drawer	**hair tonic**
hair dye	**hair wash**
hair dyer	**hair washer**
hair dyeing	**hair waver**
hairlock	**hair-waving**
hair mattress	**hairwork**

hair·bird (hâr′bûrd′) *n.* The chipping sparrow: so called because it lines its nest with hair.

hair·breadth (hâr′bredth′) *n.* A hair's breadth; an extremely small space or distance. —*adj.* Having only the breadth of a hair; very narrow. Also **hairs′-breadth′, hair's′-breadth′.**

hair·brush (hâr′brush′) *n.* A brush used for the hair.

hair cell *Anat.* One of the delicate filamentous cells situated in the organ of Corti in the cochlea, and responsible for the transmission of sound vibrations.

hair·cloth (hâr′klôth′, -kloth′) *n.* A fabric having a warp of either cotton or linen yarn with a horsehair filling.

hair·cut (hâr′kut′) *n.* The act of cutting the hair or the style in which it is cut. —**hair′·cut′ter** *n.* —**hair′cut′ting** *adj. & n.*

hair-do (hâr′do͞o′) *n.* A style of dressing the hair; coiffure.

hair·dress·er (hâr′dres′ər) *n.* One who arranges the hair, especially women's hair. —**hair′·dress′ing** *n.*

hair·line (hâr′līn′) *n.* **1** *Printing* **a** A very thin line on a type face; also, the type itself. **b** A thin rule. **2** A narrow stripe in textile fabrics. **3** The outline of hair on the head.

hair·pin (hâr′pin′) *n.* A U-shaped pin made of wire, bone, celluloid, or the like, for supporting the hair or headdress.

hair-rais·ing (hâr′rā′zing) *adj.* Causing fright or shock. —**hair′-rais′er** *n.*

hair seal The eared seal or sea lion, not valued for its fur.

hair shirt A rough cloth garment of goats' hair worn as a shirt or as a girdle for penance or mortification.

hair space *Printing* The thinnest of the metal spaces for separating letters and words.

hair-split·ting (hâr′split′ing) *n.* Insistence upon minute or trivial distinctions. See synonyms under SOPHISTRY. —*adj.* Drawing excessively nice distinctions. —**hair′-split′ter** *n.*

hair·spring (hâr′spring′) *n.* The fine spring of the balance wheel of a watch.

hairst (hârst) *n. Scot.* Harvest.

hair·streak (hâr′strēk′) *n.* A small butterfly (family *Lycaenidae*) with narrow stripes on the underside of the wings.

hair·stroke (hâr′strōk′) *n.* **1** A very fine stroke in writing. **2** A serif.

hair-trig·ger (hâr′trig′ər) *n.* **1** A trigger so delicately adjusted that a very slight pressure discharges the firearm. **2** A pistol or revolver having such a trigger. —*adj.* Stimulated or set in operation by the slightest provocation.

hair·worm (hâr′wûrm′) *n.* Any of various nematode worms (families *Gordiidae* and *Mermithidae*) which inhabit running water and whose larvae are parasitic in insects: sometimes called *horsehair-snake.*

hair·y (hâr′ē) *adj.* **hair·i·er, hair·i·est** **1** Covered with, made of, or like hair. **2** *Slang* **a** Troublesome; difficult. **b** Dangerous; harrowing. —**hair′i·ness** *n.*

Hai·ti (hā′tē) **1** A republic comprising the western portion of Hispaniola; 10,714 square miles; capital, Port-au-Prince. **2** Former name of HISPANIOLA. *French* **Ha·ï·ti** (à·ē·tē′).

Hai·ti·an (hā′tē·ən, -shən) *adj.* Of or pertaining to Haiti, its people, or their culture. —*n.* **1** A native or inhabitant of Haiti. **2** A French patois spoken by the Haitians: also **Haitian Creole.** **3** Taino.

haj (haj), **hajj** See HADJ.

ha·je (hä′jē) *n.* The African cobra or asp (*Naja haje*). See also illustration under URAEUS. [<Arabic *ḥayyah* snake]

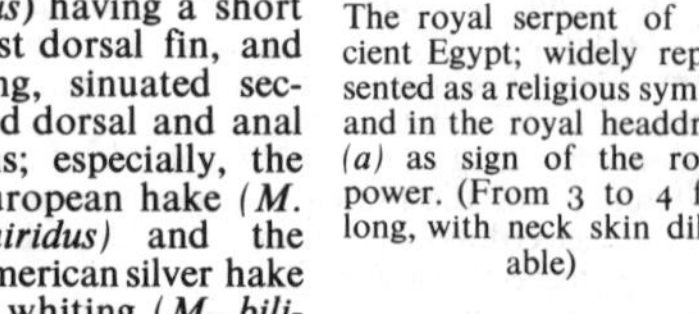

HAJE
The royal serpent of ancient Egypt; widely represented as a religious symbol and in the royal headdress (*a*) as sign of the royal power. (From 3 to 4 feet long, with neck skin dilatable)

haj·i (haj′ē), **haj·ji** See HADJI.

hake (hāk) *n. pl.* **hake** or **hakes** **1** A fish (genus *Merluccius*) having a short first dorsal fin, and long, sinuated second dorsal and anal fins; especially, the European hake (*M. smiridus*) and the American silver hake or whiting (*M. bilinearis*). **2** A North American food fish (genus *Phycis*), the codling. Also spelled *haak.* [OE *hacod* pike <*haca* hook]

Ha·ken·kreuz (hä′kən·kroits) *n.* A swastika: especially as the symbol of Nazism. [<G, lit., hooked cross]

ha·kim (hä·kēm′) *n.* In Moslem countries, a governor; also, a sage or physician. Also **ha·keem′, ha·kem′.** [<Arabic, wise, learned]

Hak·luyt (hak′lo͞ot), **Richard,** 1553?–1616, English historian and geographer.

Ha·ko·da·te (hä·kō·dä·tā) A port on SW Hokkaido island, Japan.

hal- Var. of HALO-.

ha·la·cha (hä′lä·khä′, *Hebrew* hä·lô′khô) *n. pl.* **·choth** (-khōth) In the Talmud, Jewish traditional law embracing minute precepts not found in the written law; the legal part of the Midrash. Compare HAGGADAH. Also **ha′la·kah′.** [<Hebrew *halakāh* a rule to go by <*hālak* walk, go] —**ha·lach·ic** (hə·lak′ik) *adj.*

ha·la·chist (hä′lə·kist, hə·lä′kist) *n.* One who frames from the Biblical laws precepts of the halacha. Also **ha′la·kist.**

ha·la·tion (hā·lā′shən, ha-) *n. Phot.* An appearance somewhat like a halo: caused by the radiation of light from a window or other object in the scene of a photograph, or by reflection of light from the plate; ghost. [< HALO]

hal·berd (hal′bərd) *n.* A weapon in the form of a battle-ax and pike at the end of a long staff. Also **hal′bard, hal′bert** (-bərt). [<OF *hallebarde* <MHG *helmbarte* <*helm* handle + *barte* broad-ax]

hal·ber·dier (hal′bər·dir′) *n.* A soldier armed with a halberd.

hal·cy·on (hal′sē·ən) *n.* **1** A mythical bird, identified with the kingfisher, said to have nested on the sea at the time of the winter solstice, when the sea was supposed to become calm. **2** Any kingfisher of the genus *Halcyon* of Australasia. —*adj.* **1** Of or pertaining to the halcyon. **2** Calm; peaceful. [<L *halcyon,* var. of *alcyon* <Gk. *alkyōn* kingfisher]

halcyon days **1** The seven days before and the seven days after the winter solstice, when the halcyon bred and brought calm, peaceful weather. **2** Any period of peace and tranquillity.

Hal·cy·o·ne (hal·sī′ə·nē) See ALCYONE.

Hal·dane (hôl′dān), **J(ohn) B(urdon) S(anderson),** 1892–1964, English biologist. —**John Scott,** 1860–1936, English physiologist, father of the preceding. —**Richard Burdon,** 1856–1928, Viscount Haldane of Cloan, English philosopher and statesman, brother of John Scott.

hale[1] (hāl) *v.t.* **haled, hal·ing** **1** To drag by force; haul; pull. **2** To compel to go: to *hale* someone into court. ◆ Homophone: *hail.* [Var. of HAUL] —**hal′er** *n.*

hale[2] (hāl) *adj.* **1** Of sound and vigorous health; robust. **2** *Scot.* Free from defect or injury. See synonyms under HEALTHY. ◆ Homophone: *hail.* [OE *hāl.* Related to WHOLE.] —**hale′ly** *adv.* —**hale′ness** *n.*

Hale (hāl), **Edward Everett,** 1822–1909, U. S. clergyman and author. —**George Ellery,** 1868–1938, U. S. astronomer. —**Sir Matthew,** 1609–76, English judge and historian. —**Nathan,** 1755–75, American Revolutionary officer; hanged as a spy by the British.

Ha·le·a·ka·la (hä′lā·ä·kä·lä′) The largest extinct volcanic crater in the world, on eastern Maui island, Hawaii; 10,032 feet high; 19 square miles; 2,000 feet deep.

Ha·le·mau·mau (hä′lā·mou′mou) The fiery pit in the Kilauea crater of Mauna Loa, Hawaii.

Ha·le·vi (hä·lē′vī), **Judah,** 1085?–1140?, Spanish Hebrew poet and Arabic philosopher: also **ha-Le′vi.**

Ha·lé·vy (à·lā·vē′), **Jacques François Fromental Élie,** 1799–1862, French composer. —**Ludovic,** 1834–1908, French playwright and novelist.

half (haf, häf) *n. pl.* **halves** (havz, hävz) One of two equal parts into which a thing is or may be divided, or a quantity equal to such a part. —**to, for, at,** or **on halves** For half the crop or profits: for rent *at halves,* to farm *on halves.* —*adj.* **1** Being one of two equal parts of a thing. **2** Partial; approximately one half of, in amount or value. —*adv.* To the degree or extent of a half; partially. —**not half bad** *Brit.* Actually quite good, don't you know! [OE *hælf*]

Half frequently appears as the first element in hyphenated compounds, with the following meanings:

1 Exactly half; as in:

half-acre	**half-foot**	**half-pounder**
half-barrel	**half-full**	**half-price**
half-century	**half-inch**	**half-rod**
half-circle	**half-liter**	**half-round**
half-day	**half-mile**	**half-thick**
half-dozen	**half-mystic**	**half-timer**
half-fill	**half-pound**	**half-weight**

2 Partial or partially; approximately half; as in:

half-admitted	**half-deserted**	**half-mad**
half-afraid	**half-digested**	**half-make**
half-alive	**half-done**	**half-murder**
half-altered	**half-dressed**	**half-open**
half-angry	**half-drunk**	**half-opened**
half-ashamed	**half-earnest**	**half-raw**
half-awake	**half-eaten**	**half-ripe**
half-belief	**half-ebb**	**half-ruined**
half-believe	**half-educated**	**half-safe**
half-bent	**half-finished**	**half-serious**
half-blind	**half-frozen**	**half-shut**
half-buried	**half-gloom**	**half-sleep**
half-civilized	**half-grown**	**half-spoiled**
half-cleaned	**half-hidden**	**half-strength**
half-clear	**half-human**	**half-submerge**
half-conscious	**half-humorous**	**half-true**
half-crazy	**half-joking**	**half-whisper**
half-dead	**half-knowledge**	**half-wild**

half-and-half (haf′ənd·haf′, häf′ənd·häf′) *adj.* Half of one thing and half of another. —*n.* A mixture of two liquors; specifically, beer and ale. —*adv.* Equally; in two equal divisions.

Hal·fa·ya Pass (häl·fä′yä) A pass through the coastal hills of NW Egypt; scene of heavy fighting in World War II, 1941–42.

half·back (haf′bak′, häf′-) *n.* In American football, either of two players in the backfield, originally stationed half-way between the line and the fullback.

half-baked (haf′bākt′, häf′-) *adj.* **1** Baked on one side or not baked through; doughy. **2** Imperfectly planned or conceived. **3** Raw; immature; unseasoned.

halfbeak (haf′bēk′, häf′-) *n.* A fish (genus *Hemiramphus*), related to the saury, having the lower jaw prolonged into a flat, narrow extension.

half-bind·ing (haf′bīn′ding, häf′-) *n.* A style of bookbinding in which only the back and corners of the volume are covered with leather. —**half′-bound′** (-bound′) *adj.*

half blood **1** *Law* The relationship between persons who have one parent only in common. **2** The condition of being of mixed stock: an Indian of *half blood.*

half-blood (haf′blud′) *n.* **1** A person having only one parent of a specified stock; one whose parents are of different stocks; a half-breed. **2** An animal, as a cow, sheep, etc., of crossed inferior and superior stock. **3** A person of Indian and white, or Negro and white parentage. —*adj.* Being a half-blood or half-breed; in a loose sense, of mixed blood or breed: also **half′-blood′ed.**

half-boot (haf′bōōt′, häf′-) *n.* A boot extending slightly above the ankle.

half-breed (haf′brēd′, häf′-) *n.* **1** One having parents of different blood or ethnic stock: a Canadian *half-breed.* **2** One having a white father and an American Indian mother. **3** An adherent of President Garfield in the factional struggles of 1881 within the Republican party. See STALWART. —*adj.* Half of one breed and half of another; coming of mixed ethnic or racial stock: also **half′-bred′** (-bred′).

half-breed buffalo A catalo.

half-broth·er (haf′bruth′ər, häf′-) *n.* A brother related through only one parent.

half-case (haf′kās′, häf′-) *n.* *Printing* A type case about half the width of the standard upper case.

half-caste (haf′kast′, häf′käst′) *n.* One born of mixed European and Asian blood; also, any half-breed. —*adj.* Of mixed European and other blood.

half-cock (haf′kok′, häf′-) *n.* The position of the hammer of a firearm when partly raised, but not releasable by the trigger. —**to go off at half-cock** **1** To be discharged prematurely. **2** Hence, to act or speak hastily or without deliberation. Also **to go off half-cocked.** —*v.t.* To raise the hammer of (a gun) to the position of half-cock.

half-cracked (haf′krakt′, häf′-) *adj.* Half-witted.

half-crown (haf′kroun′, häf′-) *n.* **1** An English silver coin of the value of 2*s.* 6*d.* **2** *Naut.* A method of passing a rope around a spar.

half-dime (haf′dīm′, häf′-) *n.* A U.S. silver coin worth five cents: first minted, 1792; discontinued, 1873. Also **half′-disme′.**

half-dol·lar (haf′dol′ər, häf′-) *n.* A U.S. silver coin worth fifty cents: first minted, 1794.

half-ea·gle (haf′ē′gəl, häf′-) *n.* A gold coin of the United States having a value of five dollars.

half gainer A backward somersault from the standing position of a front dive.

half hatchet A hatchet, the blade of which is trimmed flush with the wedge of the shaft. See illustration under HATCHET.

half-heart·ed (haf′här′tid, häf′-) *adj.* Showing little interest or enthusiasm. See synonyms under FAINT, IRRESOLUTE. —**half′-heart′ed·ly** *adv.* —**half′-heart′ed·ness** *n.*

half-hitch (haf′hich′, häf′-) *n.* A hitch formed by an overhand knot. See illustration under HITCH.

half-hose (haf′hōz′, häf′-) *n.* Socks or stockings extending halfway to the knee.

half-hour (haf′our′, häf′-) *n.* **1** A period of thirty minutes. **2** The point midway between the hours. —**half′-hour′ly** *adv.*

half leather A style of bookbinding in which the volume has a leather back and muslin sides.

half-length (haf′length′, häf′-) *adj.* Of half the full length, as of a portrait. —*n.* A portrait showing only the upper half of the body.

half-life (haf′līf′, häf′-) *n.* *Physics* The period of time during which half the atoms of a radioactive element or isotope will disintegrate. The half-life of radium is about 1,620 years, at the end of which period the amount remaining will require another 1,620 years to decline by half. Also called *half-value period.* Also **half period.**

half-lift (haf′lift′, häf′-) *n.* A layer of heel leather split to half the standard thickness, and used for close adjustment in built-up heels.

half-light (haf′līt′, häf′-) *n.* A dim, grayish light, as at evening.

half-loop (haf′lōōp′, häf′-) *n.* *Aeron.* A flight maneuver in which an airplane makes one half of a complete loop.

half-mast (haf′mast′, häf′mäst′) *n.* The position of a flag when half-way up the staff, as a tribute of respect to the dead or as a signal of distress. —*v.t.* To put, as a flag, at half-mast. Also called *half-staff.*

half-meas·ure (haf′mezh′ər, häf′-) *n.* An imperfect or inadequate measure or plan.

half-mitt (haf′mit′, häf′-) *n.* A type of mitten extending only to the knuckles. Also **half′-mit′ten.**

half-moon (haf′mōōn′, häf′-) *n.* **1** The moon when half its disk is illuminated. **2** Something similar in shape to a half-moon.

half-nel·son (haf′nel′sən, häf′-) *n.* A wrestling hold in which one arm is passed below the opponent's armpit and the hand is pressed against the back of his neck.

half note *Music* A note held half the measure of a whole note; a minim.

half-pace (haf′pās′, häf′-) *n.* *Brit.* **1** A floor raised above the adjoining level, in a bay window or the like; the raised place at the head of steps on which an altar stands; a dais. **2** A resting place at the end of a flight of stairs; a footpace.

half-pay (haf′pā′, häf′-) *n.* Literally, half of full pay; most commonly, the reduced pay of an officer not in regular service or on the retired list, generally more than half.

half·pen·ny (hā′pən·ē, hāp′nē) *n.* *pl.* **half·pence** (hā′pəns) or **half·pen·nies** (hā′pən·ēz, hāp′nēz) A British copper coin equivalent to one half of a penny.

half-pike (haf′pīk′, häf′-) *n.* A spearing weapon having a staff about half as long as that of the pike.

half pint **1** A measure of capacity equal to one half of a pint. **2** *Slang* A small person.

half relief Mezzo-relievo.

half rime Near rime.

half-roll (haf′rōl′, häf′-) *n.* *Aeron.* The turning of an airplane through an angle of 180° about its long axis.

half-sec·tion (haf′sek′shən, häf′-) *n.* Half a square mile, or 320 acres of land.

half-shot (haf′shot′, häf′-) *adj.* *Slang* **1** Very tired. **2** Half drunk.

half-sis·ter (haf′sis′tər, häf′-) *n.* A sister related through only one parent.

half-sole (haf′sōl′, häf′-) *n.* A tap sole on a shoe, extending only to the shank. —*v.t.* **·soled, ·sol·ing** To repair by attaching a half-sole.

half-sov·er·eign (haf′sov′rin, -suv′rən, häf′-) *n.* A British gold coin of the value of ten shillings: no longer in active circulation.

half-staff (haf′staf′, häf′stäf′) See HALF-MAST.

half-step (haf′step′, häf′-) *n.* **1** *Music.* A semitone. **2** *Mil.* A step of fifteen inches at quick time; in double time, one of eighteen inches.

half-stuff (haf′stuf′, häf′-) *n.* Crude paper pulp before it goes into the papermaking machine.

half-sword (haf′sôrd′, -sōrd′, häf′-) *n.* Half the length of a sword.

half tide The interval midway between high and low tide.

half-tim·bered (haf′tim′bərd, häf′-) *adj.* Built of heavy timbers, with the spaces between filled with masonry or plaster: said of the framework of a house.

half time The middle break in a field or court game played in definite time intervals.

half-time (haf′tīm′, häf′-) *adj.* Requiring half a person's usual working hours.

half-tint (haf′tint′, häf′-) *n.* A tint or tone of color intermediate between two strong tones of different values.

half-ti·tle (haf′tīt′l, häf′-) *n.* **1** The title of a book, usually abridged, printed on the leaf preceding the title page. **2** The title of any part or section of a book printed on the leaf preceding the text proper: often called *mock title.*

halftone (haf′tōn′, häf′-) *n.* **1** An illustration made from a relief plate obtained by photographing an original through a finely ruled glass screen, the lights and shadows appearing when printed as minutely lined or dotted surfaces. **2** A half-tint. **3** *Music* A semitone. —*adj.* Made by the process of printing halftones.

half-track (haf′trak′, häf′-) *adj.* Designating a type of military vehicle propelled by endless tracks, but steered by a pair of wheels in front. —*n.* A half-track vehicle. Compare FULL-TRACK.

half-truth (haf′trōōth′, häf′-) *n.* An assertion that is true as far as it goes, but that omits or conceals part of the truth.

half-val·ue period (haf′val′yōō, häf′-) See HALF-LIFE.

half-vol·ley (haf′vol′ē, häf′-) *n.* In tennis, cricket, etc., a ball, or the return, struck close to the ground, the instant after it bounces.

half-way (haf′wā′, häf′-) *adv.* At or to half the distance. —*adj.* **1** Midway between two points. **2** Partial; inadequate: *half-way measures.*

half-wit (haf′wit′, häf′-) *n.* A feeble-minded person; idiot. —**half′-wit′ted** *adj.*

half-year (haf′yir′, häf′-) *n.* **1** Half of a calendar year, or six months. **2** Half the time regularly used in a year, as of a school year. —**half′-year′ly** *adj.* & *adv.*

hal·i·but (hal′ə·bət, hol′-) *n.* *pl.* **·but** or **·buts** A large flatfish (*Hippoglossus hippoglossus*) of northern seas, much esteemed as food, sometimes attaining a weight of 400 pounds: also spelled *holibut.* [ME *halybutte,* OE *halig* holy + BUT[2]]

hal·ic (hal′ik, hā′lik) *adj.* *Ecol.* Of or pertaining to plant communities associated with saline soils.

Hal·i·car·nas·sus (hal′ə·kär·nas′əs) An ancient Greek city in SW Asia Minor; site of the Mausoleum, one of the Seven Wonders of the Ancient World; modern *Bodrum.*

hal·ide (hal′īd, -id, hā′līd, -lid) *n.* *Chem.* Any compound of a halogen with an element or radical, as a bromide, chloride, etc. —*adj.* Resembling sea salt; haloid. Also **hal·id** (hal′·id, hā′lid).

hal·i·dom (hal′ə·dəm) *n.* *Archaic* **1** Holiness. **2** A holy relic. **3** A holy place; sanctuary. [OE *haligdom* < *halig* holy + -DOM]

Hal·i·fax (hal′ə·faks), **Earl of,** 1881–1959, Edward Frederick Lindley Wood, English statesman.

Hal·i·fax (hal′ə·faks) **1** The capital of Nova Scotia province, Canada; the principal Atlantic port in Canada. **2** A county borough in SW Yorkshire, England. —**Hal·i·go·ni·an** (hal′i·gō′nē·ən) *adj.* & *n.*

hal·i·plank·ton (hal′ə·plangk′tən) *n.* Marine plankton, as opposed to lacustrine plankton.

hal·ite (hal′īt, hā′līt) *n.* A massive or granular, white or variously colored sodium chloride, NaCl; rock salt.

hal·i·to·sis (hal′ə·tō′sis) *n.* A malodorous condition of the breath. [<L *halitus* breath + -OSIS]

hal·i·tus (hal′ə·təs) *n.* **1** The breath. **2** The vapor from a living body or from blood newly drawn. [<L]

hall (hôl) *n.* **1** A passage or corridor in a building. **2** A small room or enclosure at the entry of a house; a vestibule; lobby. **3** A large building or room devoted to public or semipublic business or entertainments. **4** In a university or college, a large building used as a dormitory, classroom building, laboratory, etc. **5** A meeting place for a fraternity or society; also the society itself: Tammany

Hall. 6 *Brit.* A college dining-room; also, the dinner served there. 7 In medieval times, the large main room of a castle or other great house, used for dining, entertaining, and, often, sleeping. 8 The country residence of a baron, squire, etc. See synonyms under HOUSE.◆ Homophone: *haul.* [OE *heall*]

Hall (hôl), **Charles Francis,** 1821–71, U.S. Arctic explorer. **—G(ranville) Stanley,** 1846–1924, U.S. psychologist and editor.

Hal·lam (hal′əm), **Henry,** 1777–1859, English historian.

hal·lan (hal′ən, häl′-) *n. Scot.* A wall or partition in cottages, to screen the occupants from the cold air when the door is opened.

hall bedroom A small bedroom opening into a hall, especially one at the head of a stairway.

Hal·le (häl′ə) A city in SW East Germany, capital of former Saxony-Anhalt state. Also **Hal·le-an-der-Saa·le** (häl′ə·än·dər·zä′lə).

Hal·leck (hal′ək), **Fitz-Greene,** 1790–1867, U.S. poet.

hal·lel (häl′el, hə·lāl′) *n.* In Jewish religious observances, the Psalms from cxiii to cxviii inclusive, chanted at the Passover, Pentecost, and Sukkoth. [<Hebrew *hallēl* praise]

hal·le·lu·jah (hal′ə·lo͞o′yə) *interj.* Praise ye the Lord! *—n.* 1 A musical composition whose principal theme is found in the word *hallelujah.* 2 A flower of the wood sorrel family (*Oxalidaceae*). Also **hal′le·lu′iah.** [<Gk. <Hebrew *hallēlū* praise + *yāh* Jehovah]

Hal·ley (hal′ē), **Edmund,** 1656–1742, English astronomer royal. See under COMET.

hal·liard (hal′yərd) See HALYARD.

hal·lion (hal′yən) *n. Scot.* A rascal, hellion.

hall·mark (hôl′märk′) *n.* 1 An official mark stamped on gold and silver articles in England to guarantee their purity. 2 Any mark or proof of genuineness or excellence. *—v.t.* To stamp with a hallmark. [<Goldsmiths' *Hall,* London, where the assaying and stamping were formerly exclusively done + MARK]

hal·loo (hə·lo͞o′) *interj.* 1 An exclamation to attract attention, express surprise, etc. 2 A shout to incite hounds to the chase. *—n.* A cry of "halloo." *—v.i.* To shout "halloo"; cry out. *—v.t.* 1 To incite or encourage with shouts. 2 To shout to; hail. 3 To shout (something). Also **hal·lo, hal·loa** (hə·lō): also spelled *holla, hollo, holloa, hillo, hilloa, hullo.* [<OF *halloer* pursue noisily]

hal·low (hal′ō) *v.t.* 1 To make holy; consecrate. 2 To look upon as holy; reverence. [OE *halgian* <*halig* holy] **—hal·lowed** (hal′ōd, in liturgical use hal′ō·id) *adj.*

Hal·low·e'en (hal′ō·ēn′) *n.* The evening of Oct. 31, vigil of All Saints' Day. [<(ALL-) HALLOW(S) E(V)EN]

Hal·low·mass (hal′ō·məs) *n. Archaic* The feast of All-hallows or All Saints' Day. Also **Hal′low·mas.** [<(ALL-)HALLOW-MASS]

Hall process A process for the electrolytic reduction of aluminum from its ores. [after C. M. *Hall,* 1863–1914, U.S. inventor]

Hall·statt (häl′shtät) A village of Upper Austria on the SW shore of the **Lake of Hallstatt,** where prehistoric implements were found.

Hall·statt (häl′shtät) *adj.* Pertaining to or denoting the earlier of two principal divisions of the prehistoric Iron Age of Europe, extending from about the ninth to the fifth century B.C. — **Hall·stat′ti·an** (-ē·ən) *adj.*

hall tree A clothestree.

hal·lu·ci·nate (hə·lo͞o′sə·nāt) *v.t.* **·nat·ed, ·nat·ing** To affect or afflict with hallucinations. [<L *hallucinatus,* pp. of *hallucinari, alucinari* wander mentally]

hal·lu·ci·na·tion (hə·lo͞o′sə·nā′shən) *n.* 1 An apparent perception without any corresponding external object. 2 *Psychiatry* Any of numerous sensations, auditory, visual, or tactile, experienced without external stimulus, and caused by mental derangement, intoxication, or fever. See ILLUSION. 3 A mistaken notion. See synonyms under DELUSION, DREAM, ERROR. **—hal·lu·ci·na·to·ry** (hə·lo͞o′sə·nə·tôr′ē, -tō′rē) *adj.*

hal·lu·ci·no·gen (hə·lo͞o′sin·ə·jən) *n.* Any drug or chemical, as peyote, capable of inducing hallucinations.

hal·lu·ci·no·gen·ic (hə·lo͞o′sə·nə·jen′ik) *adj.* 1 Causing or having to do with hallucinations or with a distortion of perception or consciousness: *hallucinogenic* drugs. 2 Of or pertaining to hallucinogens.

hal·lu·ci·no·sis (hə·lo͞o′sə·nō′sis) *n. Psychiatry* A mental or nervous disorder characterized by persistent hallucinations.

hal·lux (hal′əks) *n. pl.* **hal·lu·ces** (hal′yo͞o·sēz) *Biol.* 1 The first or innermost digit of the foot; the great toe. 2 In a bird, the hind toe. [<NL <L *hallex;* infl. by *hallus* thumb]

hall·way (hôl′wā′) *n.* A passage giving entrance to a building or communicating with its various apartments.

halm (hôm) See HAULM.

hal·ma (hal′mə) *n.* In the exercise of the pentathlon, the long jump with weights in the hands. [<Gk. <*halesthai* leap]

Hal·ma·he·ra (häl′mä·hā′rä) An Indonesian island NE of Celebes; 6,870 square miles: also *Djailolo, Jailolo, Jilolo.*

ha·lo (hā′lō) *n. pl.* **·los** or **·loes** 1 *Meteorol.* A luminous circle around the sun or the moon, caused by the refraction of light passing through ice crystals floating in the air. 2 A nimbus; a radiance encircling the head in portrayals of a sacred personage. 3 The ideal brightness with which imagination surrounds an object of affection or sentiment. *—v.t.* To enclose in a halo. — *v.i.* To form a halo. [<L <Gk. *halos* a circular threshing floor]

halo- *combining form* 1 The sea; of or related to the sea: *halophyte.* 2 Related to a halogen. Also, before vowels, *hal-,* as in *haloid.* [<Gk. *hals, halos* salt, the sea]

hal·o·bi·os (hal′ə·bī′əs) *n.* Life in the oceans; marine life collectively. [<HALO- + Gk. *bios* life] — **hal′o·bi·ot′ic** (-bī·ot′ik) *adj.*

hal·o·gen (hal′ə·jən) *n. Chem.* One of certain non-metallic elements belonging to the seventh group in the periodic table, as iodine, fluorine, chlorine, and bromine, which combine directly with metals to form halides. [<Gk. *hals* sea, salt + -GEN] **—ha·log·e·nous** (hə·loj′ə·nəs) *adj.*

hal·o·ge·na·tion (hal′ə·jə·nā′shən) *n. Chem.* The introduction of a halogen into an organic molecule, by substitution or addition.

hal·oid (hal′oid, hā′loid) *adj.* 1 Resembling sea salt. 2 Pertaining to or derived from a halogen. *—n.* A haloid salt.

hal·o·man·cy (hal′ə·man′sē) *n.* Divination by means of salt thrown into a flame: also spelled *alomancy.*

hal·o·per·i·dol (hal′ō·per′ə·dōl, -dôl) *n.* An ataractic drug, $C_{21}H_{23}ClFNO_2$.

ha·loph·i·lous (hə·lof′ə·ləs) *adj. Bot.* Adapted to salt; said of plants growing in saline soil. Also **hal·o·phil** (hal′ə·fil), **hal′o·phile** (-fīl, -fil).

hal·o·phyte (hal′ə·fīt) *n. Bot.* A plant of saline soil, such as those of the genera *Salsola* and *Salicornia,* growing in salt marshes and yielding salt. **—hal′o·phyt′ic** (-fit′ik) *adj.*

Hals (häls), **Frans,** 1580?–1666, Dutch painter.

halse (hôls) *n. Brit. Dial.* The neck. [OE *hals*]

Hal·sey (hôl′zē), **William Frederick,** 1882–1959, U.S. admiral in World War II.

Häl·sing·borg (hel′sing·bôr·y′) A port in SW Sweden.

halt[1] (hôlt) *n.* A complete stop, or cessation of progress in any movement, as of marching troops. **—to call a halt** To put a stop to, or demand that something be stopped. *—v.t. & v.i.* To stop; bring or come to a halt. See synonyms under REST[1], STAND. [<F *halte* <G *halt,* orig. imperative of *halten* stop]

halt[2] (hôlt) *v.i.* 1 To be imperfect; proceed lamely, as verse or logic. 2 To be in doubt; waver. 3 *Archaic* To walk with a limp; hobble. *—adj. Archaic* Crippled; limping in gait; lame. *—n. Archaic* The act of limping; lameness. [OE *healt* lame] **—halt′ing** *adj.* **—halt′ing·ly** *adv.* — **halt′ing·ness** *n.*

hal·ter[1] (hôl′tər) *n.* 1 A strap or rope, especially one with a headstall at one end, by which to hold a horse or other animal. 2 A hangman's rope; hence, death by the rope. 3 A woman's waist designed for exposing the back and arms to the sun, fastened around the neck and waist. *—v.t.* 1 To put a halter on; secure with a halter. 2 To hang (someone). [OE *hælftre*]

hal·ter[2] (hal′tər) *n. pl.* **hal·te·res** (hal·tir′ēz) *Entomol.* One of a pair of small, knobbed, filamentous appendages on each side of the thorax in dipterous insects, replacing the hind wings; a balancer. [<NL <Gk. *haltēres* jumping weights (as used in the halma)]

ha·lutz (khä·lo͞ots′) *n. pl.* **ha·lu·tzim** (khä·lo͞o·tsēm′) A pioneer agriculturist in Israel: also spelled *chalutz.* [<Hebrew *chalutz* a warrior]

halve (hav, häv) *v.t.* **halved, halv·ing** 1 To divide into two equal parts; share equally. 2 To lessen by half; take away half of. 3 In golf, to play (a match or hole) in the same number of strokes as one's opponent. [<HALF]

halves (havz, hävz) Plural of HALF.

ha·ly (hā′lē) *adj. Scot.* Holy.

hal·yard (hal′yərd) *n. Naut.* A rope for hoisting or lowering a sail, a yard, or a flag: also spelled *halliard, haulyard.* [<HALE[1] + YARD[1]]

Ha·lys (hā′lis) Ancient name for KIZIL-IRMAK.

ham (ham) *n.* 1 The thigh of an animal, as a hog, prepared for food. 2 *pl.* The buttocks. 3 The space or region behind the knee joint; the hock of quadrupeds. 4 *Slang* A third-rate actor; one who overdramatizes scenes, or portrays a character in amateur fashion. 5 An amateur radio operator. [OE *hamm*] **—ham′my** *adj.*

Ham (ham) The youngest son of Noah. *Gen.* v 32, ix 24.

Ha·ma (hä′mä) A town in western Syria on the Orontes: *Old Testament* **Ha·math** (hä′mäth). Also **Ha′mah.**

Ha·ma·dan (hä′mä·dän′) A city in western Iran; ancient *Ecbatana.*

ham·a·dry·ad (ham′ə·drī′əd, -ad) *n. pl.* **·ads** or **·a·des** (-ə·dēz) 1 In Greek mythology, a wood nymph whose life was connected with that of the tree she inhabited. 2 The king cobra. [<Gk. *hamadryas, -ados* <*hama* together with + *drys* oak tree]

ha·mal (hə·mäl′, -môl′) *n.* 1 In Oriental countries, one who bears burdens; a porter; a carrier. 2 In India, a man servant: also spelled *hammal.* Also **ha·maul′.** [<Arabic *ḥammāl* <*ḥamala* carry]

Ha·ma·mat·su (hä·mä·mät·so͞o) A city on south central Honshu island, Japan.

Ham·a·me·lis (ham′ə·mē′lis) *n.* A genus of shrubs of the witch hazel family (*Hamamelidaceae*) having alternate simple leaves and heads or spikes of monoecious or polygamous flowers. *H. virginiana* is the common witch hazel. [<NL <Gk. *hammamēlis* tree with pearlike fruit] — **ham·a·me·li·da·ceous** (ham′ə·mē′lə·dā′shəs) *adj.*

Ha·man (hā′mən) The chief minister of Ahasuerus, whose plot against the Jews recoiled upon himself (*Esth.* iii–vii), and who was hanged on a gallows fifty cubits high; hence, the phrase **hanged as high as Haman.**

Ham·ble·to·ni·an (ham′bəl·tō′nē·ən) *n.* 1 One of a famous breed of American trotting horses. 2 The chief harness race for three-year-old trotters, held annually, formerly at Goshen, New York. *—adj.* Of or pertaining to a horse of the Hambletonian breed. [after *Hambletonian,* famous American stud, from Black *Hambleton,* a racecourse in Yorkshire, England]

Ham·born (häm′bôrn) See DUISBURG-HAMBORN.

Ham·bro (häm′brō), **Carl Joachim,** 1885–1964, Norwegian statesman.

ham·burg (ham′bûrg) *n.* Hamburger (defs. 1 and 2). Also **hamburg steak.**

Ham·burg (ham′bûrg) *n.* 1 A European variety of the domestic fowl, having lead-gray legs and a rose-colored comb. 2 A black, sweet and juicy grape, indigenous to the Tyrol and widely cultivated in hothouses throughout the northern latitudes. Also **Ham′burgh.**

Ham·burg (ham′bûrg, *Ger.* häm′bo͝orkh) A state comprising the chief port and second largest city in Germany, at the head of the Elbe estuary in NW Germany; 288 square miles.

ham·burg·er (ham′bûr′gər) *n.* 1 Finely ground beef. 2 Such meat fried or broiled in the form of a patty. Also **hamburger steak:** also called *Salisbury steak.* 3 A sandwich consisting of such meat placed between the halves of a round roll. [from *Hamburg,* Germany]

hame[1] (hām) *n.* One of two curved bars fitted to the collar, that hold the traces of a draft harness. [OE *hama* dress, covering]

hame[2] (hām) *n. Scot.* Home. **—hame′ly** *adj.*

Ha·meln (hä′meln) A town on the Weser in Lower Saxony, West Germany. Also **Ham·e·lin** (ham′ə·lin).

Ham·hung (häm·ho͝ong) A city in North Korea. *Japanese* **Kan·ko.**

Ha·mil·car Bar·ca (hə·mil′kär bär′kə, ham′əl·kär), died in battle 229? B.C., Carthaginian general; father of Hannibal.

Ham·il·ton (ham′əl·tən), **Alexander,** 1757–1804, American statesman; joint author of *The Federalist.* —**Lady Emma,** 1761?–1815, mistress of Lord Nelson. —**Sir William,** 1788–1856, Scottish philosopher. —**Sir William Rowan,** 1805–65, Irish mathematician and astronomer.

Ham·il·ton (ham′əl·tən) **1** A port in southern Ontario, Canada, on Lake Ontario. **2** The chief port and capital of Bermuda, on Bermuda Island. **3** A burgh of Lanarkshire, Scotland.

Ham·il·ton (ham′əl·tən), **Mount** A peak of the Coast Ranges in western California; 4,372 feet; site of the Lick Observatory.

Hamilton River A river in southern Labrador, flowing 600 miles to **Hamilton Inlet,** a bay of the Atlantic.

Ham·ite (ham′īt) *n.* **1** A descendant of Ham, youngest son of Noah. **2** A member of the Caucasoid ethnic stock which from earliest days inhabited NE Africa and the Canary Islands.

Ha·mit·ic (ha·mit′ik) *adj.* Of or pertaining to Ham, or the Hamites, or their languages. —*n.* A North African subfamily of the Hamito-Semitic family of languages, divided into three branches—ancient Egyptian, Libyco-Berber (extinct Libyan and the modern Berber dialects), and the Cushitic languages of Ethiopia and Somaliland.

Ham·i·to-Se·mit·ic (ham′ə·tō·sə·mit′ik) *n.* A large family of languages spoken in northern Africa and part of SW Asia, consisting of the subfamilies *Hamitic* (ancient Egyptian, Libyan, the modern Berber dialects, and the Cushitic languages) and *Semitic* (Akkadian, Phoenician, Aramaic, Syriac, Arabic, Hebrew, Amharic, etc.). The family is characterized grammatically by triliteral or biliteral word bases.

ham·let (ham′lit) *n.* **1** A little village; a cluster of houses in the country. **2** *Brit.* A village without a church of its own. [<OF *hamelet,* dim. of *hamel* <LL *hamellum* village <Gmc.]

Ham·let (ham′lit) In Shakespeare's play of this name, the hero, prince of Denmark, who seeks to avenge the murder of his father at the bidding of his father's ghost.

ham·mal (hə·mäl′, -môl′) See HAMAL.

Hamm (häm) A city in North Rhine-Westphalia, West Germany. Also **Hamm-in-West·fal·en** (häm·in·vest′fäl·ən).

Ham·mar·skjold (häm′är·shüld), **Dag,** 1905–1961, Swedish statesman; secretary general of the United Nations 1953–61.

ham·mer (ham′ər) *n.* **1** A hand implement with a head at right angles to the handle, used for driving nails, pounding, swaging, etc. See under CLAW HAMMER, TACK HAMMER. **2** A machine, as a steam hammer or trip hammer, performing functions similar to those of a heavy hand hammer. **3** A part or piece of a machine or apparatus performing functions similar to those of a hammer: especially, the piece by which a gong or the like is struck. **4** That part of a gunlock which strikes the cap or cartridge. **5** A padded piece that strikes the string of a pianoforte. **6** An auctioneer's mallet. **7** A lever in an internal combustion engine which controls the exhaust. **8** *Anat.* The malleus of the middle ear. **9** A metal ball weighing 16 pounds with a long wire or wooden handle: used for throwing in track meets. —**under the hammer** For sale at auction. —*v.t.* **1** To strike or beat with or as with a hammer; drive, as a nail. **2** To shape or fasten with a hammer. **3** To form or force as if with hammer blows: to *hammer* an idea into his head. —*v.i.* **4** To strike blows with or as with a hammer. [OE *hamer*] —**ham′mer·er** *n.*

hammer and sickle The Communist party emblem, in which a crossed sickle and hammer symbolize the peasant and the worker.

hammer and tongs Forcefully; with vehemence: to go at it *hammer and tongs.*

ham·mer·cloth (ham′ər·klôth′, -kloth′) *n.* The cloth covering a coachman's box. [? Alter. of *hamper cloth*]

hammered work Work in thin metal having the design hammered or beaten by hand, as in repoussé work.

Ham·mer·fest (häm′ər·fest) A city in northern Norway.

ham·mer·har·den (ham′ər·här′dən) *v.t.* To harden (metals) by beating with a hammer.

ham·mer·head (ham′ər·hed′) *n.* **1** The head of a hammer. **2** A heronlike wading bird (order *Ciconiiformes*) native to Africa and Madagascar, with a blunt-pointed beak, clove-brown plumage, and a large crest. **3** A voracious shark (family *Sphynidae*) of warm seas, having a transversely elongated head with the eyes at each end. **4** The hogsucker. **5** An African fruit bat (family *Pteropidae*) with an elongated snout, related to the flying fox.

ham·mer·less (ham′ər·lis) *adj.* Having no hammer visible: said of firearms.

hammer lock A wrestling grip in which the arm is twisted behind the back and upwards.

ham·mer·smith (ham′ər·smith′) *n.* One who works metal with a hammer.

Ham·mer·stein (ham′ər·stīn), **Oscar,** 1847–1919, U. S. theatrical manager born in Germany. —**Oscar,** 1895–1960, U. S. songwriter and librettist; grandson of the preceding.

ham·mer·toe (ham′ər·tō′) *n. Pathol.* A deformity of the toe, usually the second, in which the joint nearest the foot is bent downward.

ham·mock[1] (ham′ək) *n.* A couch of canvas or netting, swung by the ends. [<Sp. *hamaca* < native name]

ham·mock[2] (ham′ək) *n. U.S.* In the South, a thickly wooded tract of fertile land, often elevated: also called *hummock.* [Var. of HUMMOCK]

Ham·mu·ra·bi (hä′mo͝o·rä′bē, ham′ə-) Founder of the first Babylonian dynasty at the beginning of the second millenium B.C.; famous lawgiver who promulgated the **Code of Hammurabi.**

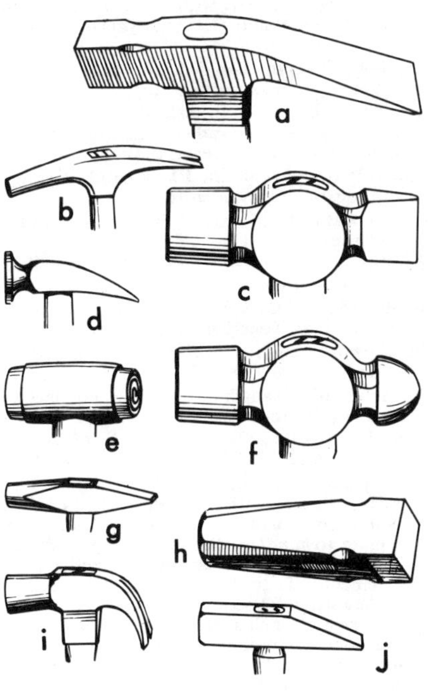

HAMMERS
a. Bricklayer's hammer.
b. Upholsterer's or tack hammer.
c. Machinist's straight-peen.
d. Shoemaker's hammer.
e. Rawhide-faced hammer.
f. Machinist's ball-peen.
g. Riveting hammer.
h. Blacksmith's set-hammer.
i. Claw hammer.
j. Tinner's hammer.

Hamp·den (ham′dən), **John,** 1594–1643, English patriot; refused to pay ship money exacted by Charles I. —**Walter,** stage name of W. H. Dougherty, 1879–1955, U.S. actor.

ham·per[1] (ham′pər) *v.t.* To hinder the movements of; encumber; restrain. —*n.* **1** *Naut.* Necessary but encumbering equipment of a ship, as the rigging. **2** A fetter. See synonyms under EMBARRASS, HINDER. [ME *hampren;* origin uncertain]

ham·per[2] (ham′pər) *n.* A large packing basket, as for food. —*v.t.* To put into hampers. [<OF *hanapier* case to hold a cup or goblet <*hanap* cup <LG. Doublet of HANAPER.]

Hamp·shire (hamp′shir) A county in southern England; 1,650 square miles; capital, Winchester; including the administrative counties of Southampton and the Isle of Wight: shortened form *Hants.*

Hamp·stead (hamp′sted, -stid) A metropolitan borough of London north of the Thames, including **Hampstead Heath,** a public common, once the resort of highwaymen.

Hamp·ton (hamp′tən), **Wade,** 1752?–1835, American Revolutionary officer. —**Wade,** 1818–1902, Confederate general and politician; grandson of the preceding.

Hampton Roads A channel in SE Virginia through which the James, Nansemond, and Elizabeth Rivers flow to Chesapeake Bay; scene of the Civil War engagement of the armored warships "Monitor" and "Merrimac," Mar. 9, 1862.

ham·shack·le (ham′shak′əl) *v.t.* **·led, ·ling** **1** To hobble, as a horse, by connecting the head and forelegs with a short rope or strap, so as to impede movement. **2** To restrain or impede. Also spelled *hapshackle.* [<HAM[1] + SHACKLE]

ham·ster (ham′stər) *n.* A sturdy burrowing rodent. The common hamster (*Cricetus cricetus*) of Europe and Asia has very large cheek pouches and a short tail; it stores up grain in subterranean galleries. [<G]

ham·string (ham′string′) *n.* **1** A tendon of the thigh, back of the knee. **2** The large sinew at the back of the hock of the hind leg of a quadruped. —*v.t.* **·strung, ·string·ing** **1** To cut the hamstring of; cripple; disable. **2** To cripple (a whale) by cutting the fluke-tendons.

Ham·sun (häm′so͞on, ham′sən), **Knut,** 1859–1952, Norwegian novelist.

Ham·tramck (ham·tram′ik) A city of SE Michigan, entirely surrounded by Detroit.

ham·u·late (ham′yə·lāt, -lit) *adj.* **1** Having little hooks, as certain plants. **2** Curved.

ham·u·lus (ham′yə·ləs) *n. pl.* **·li** (-lī) **1** A little hook. **2** A hooklike process of a bone. **3** A hooked barbicel of a feather. [<L]

ham·za (ham′zə) *n.* In Arabic orthography, the sign of the glottal stop, transliterated with an apostrophe.

han (han) *n. Scot.* Hand.

Han (hän) The fifth Chinese dynasty, 207 B.C.–A.D. 220.

Han (hän) **1** A river in east central China, flowing 750 miles SE to the Yangtze. **2** A river in southern China, flowing 210 miles south to the China Sea.

han·a·per (han′ə·pər) *n.* A wicker receptacle for documents or valuables. [<OF *hanapier.* Doublet of HAMPER[2]]

hance (hans) *n.* **1** *Archit.* **a** The haunch of an arch; the lower part of a many-centered arch, above the springing. **b** A small arch joining a straight lintel to its jamb. **2** A break or sudden departure from a natural form; an irregularity, as in a fife rail. [ME, aphetic var. of ENHANCE.]

Han Cities (hän) See WUHAN.

Han·cock (han′kok), **John,** 1737–93, American statesman; signer of the Declaration of Independence. —**Winfield Scott,** 1824–86, U. S. general.

hand (hand) *n.* **1** The part of the forelimb in man and other primates that is attached to the lower extremity of the forearm, and is adapted for grasping; it consists of the carpus, metacarpus, and fingers. **2** The end or distal segment of a limb when serving as a prehensile organ, as in bats. **3** Side or direction: At his right *hand* sat the president. **4** A side or viewpoint of a subject or question: on the one *hand* this and on the other *hand* that. **5** A part or role in doing something: They all had a *hand* in it. **6** *pl.* Possession; control; supervision: The work is in my *hands.* **7** Aid;

assistance: to lend a *hand.* **8** A pledge of betrothal, or a giving in marriage. **9** A manual laborer: a farm *hand.* **10** A person, as the performer of some action or task: a book written by various *hands.* **11** A person, considered with reference to his skill or ability: He was quite a *hand* with the violin. **12** Skill; ability; touch: The painting showed the *hand* of a master. **13** The members of a group or company: All *hands* joined in the sport. **14** A (specified) remove from a source of supply or information: a story heard at second-*hand.* **15** The cards held by a player at one deal; also, the player. **16** The playing of the cards at one deal. **17** Clapping of hands; a round of applause. **18** Handwriting; style of writing: a legible *hand.* **19** A person's signature. **20** Something resembling a hand in appearance or function. **21** The figure ☞ used as an index; fist. **22** The pointer of a clock. **23** A bunch of tobacco leaves on the stem, tied together. **24** A small cluster of bananas. **25** The approximate width of the palm; specifically, four inches: a horse 16 *hands* high. **26** The part of a gunstock grasped by the hand. **27** *Law* A manus. **—a great hand at** or **for** A person specially fond of or clever at. **—at first hand** At the source. **—at hand** Within reach; nearby; convenient. **—at the hand of** From the hand of; by the operation of. **—by hand** With the hands; not aided by machinery. **—to have one's hands full** To have all or more than one can do. **—in hand 1** Delivered in advance; paid in the hand. **2** In process of execution or under consideration: I have the matter *in hand.* **3** Entirely under control **—laying on of hands** The act or ceremony of laying the hands on the head of another for the purpose of consecrating to a special office, or of blessing or healing. **—to lend a hand** To help. **—off one's hands** Out of one's care or control. **—on hand 1** In present or rightful possession: We have too many goods *on hand.* **2** In place; present: He was promptly *on hand.* **—on one's hands** In one's care or possession; entailing responsibility on one. **—out of hand 1** Unruly; lawless: The rioters got *out of hand.* **2** Immediately; without delay; offhand. **—to hand** At hand; close by; readily accessible. **—to wash one's hands of** To take no further responsibility in; dismiss from consideration. *—v.t.* **1** To give, pass, or deliver with or as with the hand; transmit; transfer. **2** To lead or help with the hand. **3** *Naut.* To furl, as sail. **—to hand down 1** To transmit, as to one's heirs or successors. **2** To deliver, as the decision of a court. **—to hand it to** *U.S. Slang* To acknowledge the abilities, success, etc., of. **—to hand on** To pass on; transmit. **—to hand out** To mete out; distribute. **—to hand over** To give up possession of; surrender. [OE *hand*]

Hand (hand), **Learned,** 1872–1961, U.S. jurist.

hand·bag (hand′bag′) *n.* A small, portable bag, as a small satchel or a woman's purse.

hand·ball (hand′bôl′) *n.* **1** A game in which a small ball is struck with the hand and kept bounding against a wall or walls by, usually, two or four players. **2** The rubber ball used in this game.

hand·bar·row (hand′bar′ō) *n.* **1** A litter or stretcher. **2** A wheelbarrow.

hand·bill (hand′bil′) *n.* A small advertising sheet or public notice, usually distributed by hand.

hand·book (hand′bo͝ok′) *n.* A small guidebook or manual.

hand·breadth (hand′bredth′) *n.* The breadth of the hand; a palm. Also *hand's breadth.*

hand car A small open railroad car, propelled by a hand pump or motor, used by section men and other railroad workers.

hand cart A cart pushed by hand.

hand·clasp (hand′klasp′, -kläsp′) *n.* A clasping of a person's hand in greeting, agreement, farewell, etc.

hand·cuff (hand′·kuf′) *n.* One of two manacles connected by a chain, and designed to be locked around the wrists. See synonyms under FETTER. *—v.t.* To put handcuffs on; manacle.

HANDCUFFS

hand·ed (han′did) *adj.* **1** Having hands. **2** Acting or provided with hands: used in combination: right-*handed,* four-*handed.*

hand·ed·ness (han′did·nis) *n.* The tendency of an individual to prefer the use of either the right or the left hand.

Han·del (han′dəl), **George Frederick,** 1685–1759, German composer active in England. Also *Ger.* **Georg Friedrich Hän·del** (hen′dəl).

hand·fast (hand′fast′, -fäst′) *n. Obs.* A contract signified and sealed by clasping hands; hence, a betrothal or marriage contract. *—v.t. Archaic* **1** To grasp with the hand. **2** To betroth. **—hand′fast′ing** *n.*

hand·ful (hand′fo͝ol) *n. pl.* **hand·fuls 1** As much or as many as a hand can hold at once. See -FUL. **2** A comparatively small number or quantity. **3** *Colloq.* Something or someone difficult to control.

hand·gal·lop (hand′gal′əp) *n.* A moderate gallop.

hand glass 1 A mirror intended to be held in the hand. **2** A reading glass. **3** A time glass to measure a ship's log.

hand grenade See under GRENADE.

hand·grip (hand′grip′) *n.* **1** A grip of the hand. **2** *Usually pl.* Close conflict; struggle.

hand·gun (hand′gun′) *n.* A firearm held and fired in one hand, as a pistol.

hand·i·cap (han′dē·kap′) *n.* **1** A condition imposed to equalize the chances of competitors in a race or athletic contest, as the carrying of extra weight, or the requirement of a greater distance or a later start than is assigned to an inferior competitor; also, the weight, etc., so required. **2** A race or contest in which such conditions are imposed. **3** Any disadvantage or hindrance making success in an undertaking more difficult. *—v.t.* **·capped, ·cap·ping 1** To impose a handicap on, as a contestant in a race. **2** To be a handicap to: His leg *handicaps* his movements. [< *hand in cap,* a lottery game in which winners were penalized] **—hand′i·cap′per** *n.*

hand·i·craft (han′dē·kraft′, -kräft′) *n.* **1** Skill and expertness in working with the hands. **2** A trade calling for such skill. See synonyms under BUSINESS. [OE *handcræft*]

hand·i·crafts·man (han′dē·krafts′mən, -kräfts′-) *n. pl.* **·men** (-mən) An artisan; mechanic.

Hand·ie-Talk·ie *Trademark* (han′dē·tô′kē) *n. Telecom.* A portable radio transmitter-receiver small enough to be carried in the hand.

hand·i·ly (han′də·lē) *adv.* **1** In a handy manner; dexterously. **2** Conveniently.

hand·i·ness (han′dē·nis) *n.* **1** Skilfulness with the hands; dexterity. **2** Convenience.

hand-in-glove (hand′in·gluv′) *adj.* In close collaboration or intimacy.

hand-in-hand (hand′in·hand′) *adj.* With hands joined. *—adv.* Together; cooperatively.

hand·i·work (han′dē·wûrk′) *n.* Work done by the hands. [OE *handgeweorc*]

hand·ker·chief (hang′kər·chif) *n.* **1** A kerchief for wiping the face or nose. **2** A neckerchief.

hand·knit (hand′nit′) *adj.* Knitted by hand: also **hand′-knit′ted.**

han·dle (han′dəl) *v.* **han·dled, han·dling** *v.t.* **1** To touch, feel, etc., with the hands; use the hands upon. **2** To manage or use with the hands; manipulate: to *handle* a rifle. **3** To manage or direct; control. **4** To deal or treat with: to *handle* a disagreement. **5** To trade or deal in; buy and sell: to *handle* cotton. **6** To act toward; treat: They *handled* the matter shamefully. *—v.i.* **7** To submit or respond to handling: The horse *handles* well. **—to handle with (kid) gloves on** To deal with very carefully and tactfully. *—n.* That part of an object intended to be grasped with the hand in lifting or using, as a haft, helve, hilt, crank, bail, or knob. **—to fly off the handle** To be suddenly and unreasonably angry; make an emotional scene. [OE *handlian* < *hand* hand]

han·dle·bar (han′dəl·bär′) *n.* **1** A handle or handles in the form of a bar; specifically, the steering bar of a bicycle, motorcycle, or similar vehicle. **2** *pl. U.S. Colloq.* A long mustache curved like a handlebar.

han·dler (hand′lər) *n.* **1** One who or that which handles; specifically, one who trains, breaks in, or manages certain animals, as dogs, colts, fighting cocks, etc. **2** The trainer of a pugilist.

hand·less (hand′lis) *adj.* **1** Without hands. **2** Awkward; clumsy.

hand level A telescopic hand instrument used in surveying to find approximate elevations.

han·dling (hand′ling) *n.* **1** The act of touching or turning with the hands. **2** Manner of treatment, as in writing, drawing, arguing, etc.

hand-made (hand′mād′) *adj.* Made by hand or by hand tools.

hand·maid (hand′mād′) *n.* A female servant or attendant. Also **hand′maid′en.**

hand-me-down (hand′mē·doun′) *n. U.S. Colloq.* **1** A garment which has been outgrown and is passed to a smaller person. **2** A shabby or second-hand garment. **3** A cheap, ready-made garment. **—hand′-me-down′** *adj.*

hand organ A musical instrument consisting of a boxed revolving cylinder turned by a hand crank; a portable barrel organ.

hand-out (hand′out′) *n. U.S. Colloq.* **1** Anything given to a beggar, especially food. **2** A printed or mimeographed press release usually distributed at a press conference.

hand-pick (hand′pik′) *v.t.* **1** To pick by hand. **2** To select with care. **3** To choose for an ulterior purpose: to *hand-pick* a candidate.

hand pump Any pump worked by hand; especially, an auxiliary fuel pump used to start an engine or for emergency: also called *wobble pump.*

hand rail A rail that can be grasped by the hand, as at the edge of a gallery or along the outer edge of a stairway.

hand saw A saw made to be used with one hand.

hand's breadth See HANDBREADTH.

hand·sel (hand′səl, han′-) *n.* **1** A gift as a token of good will or to secure good luck. **2** Earnest money on a contract. **3** A bridegroom's gift to a bride. **4** Money given as a gift at New Year's. *—v.t.* **·seled** or **·selled, ·sel·ing** or **·sel·ling 1** To give handsel to. **2** To do or use for the first time. **3** To inaugurate, as with a ceremony. Also spelled *hansel.* [OE *handselen* < *hand* hand + *selen* gift]

hand·set (hand′set′) *n.* An apparatus, device, or instrument, especially a telephone, designed to be held in or operated by one hand.

hand·shake (hand′shāk′) *n.* A clasping and shaking of a person's hand, as in greeting, agreement, parting, etc.

hand·some (han′səm) *adj.* **1** Agreeable to the eye or to good taste; of pleasing aspect. **2** Of liberal dimensions or proportions. **3** Marked by magnanimity, generosity, or liberality. **4** Marked by propriety. **5** *Obs.* Handy; convenient; dexterous. See synonyms under BEAUTIFUL, FINE. ◆ Homophone: *hansom.* [< HAND + -SOME, orig. with sense "easy to handle"] **—hand′some·ness** *n.*

hand·some·ly (han′səm·lē) *adv.* **1** Becomingly; liberally; generously. **2** Cleverly; neatly.

hands-on (handz′on′; -ôn′) *adj.* Designating an action that requires active participation; *hands-on techniques.*

hand·spike (hand′spīk′) *n.* A bar used as a lever.

hand·spring (hand′spring′) *n.* A somersault in which only the hands, when the feet are in the air, touch the ground.

hand-to-hand (hand′tə·hand′) *adj.* At close quarters: a *hand-to-hand* fight.

hand-to-mouth (hand′tə·mouth′) *adj.* Spending as fast as one earns; improvident.

hand·work (hand′wûrk′) *n.* Work done by hand, not by machine.

hand·writ·ing (hand′rī′ting) *n.* **1** The form of writing peculiar to a given person. **2** Penmanship. **3** Written matter.

hand·y (han′dē) *adj.* **hand·i·er, hand·i·est 1** Ready at hand or convenient for use; nearby. **2** Skilful with the hands. **3** Easy to handle: said of a ship or a tool. See synonyms under CONVENIENT, SKILFUL.

handy man One good at odd jobs; a jack-of-all-trades.

Ha·ne·da (hä·nē·dä) The airport of Tokyo, on central Honshu island, Japan.

hang (hang) *v.* **hung** or (*esp. for v. defs.* **3** *and* **9**) **hanged, hang·ing** *v.t.* **1** To fasten or attach to something above; suspend. **2** To attach, as upon hinges, so as to allow some motion. **3** To put (someone) to death by suspending from a gallows, cross, etc.; execute on a gallows. **4** To ornament, cover, or furnish by or as by something suspended: to *hang* walls with tapestry. **5** To fasten in position or at the correct angle: to *hang* a scythe.

6 *U.S.* To cause, as a jury, to come to or remain in deadlock, as one juror by refusing to vote with the rest. —*v.i.* 7 To be suspended; swing; dangle. 8 To be suspended without visible support; float, as in the air. 9 To be put to death on the gallows. 10 To project out; overhang. 11 To droop; incline downward. 12 To be imminent or impending: War *hangs* over the world. 13 To be dependent or contingent, as on a decision. 14 To be uncertain or in doubt. 15 To watch or attend closely: to *hang* on someone's words. 16 *U.S.* To be or remain in deadlock, as a jury. **—to hang around** (or **about**) 1 To linger or loiter. 2 To group around. **—to hang back** To be reluctant or unwilling. **—to hang fire** 1 To fail to fire promptly, as a firearm. 2 To be delayed, as an event. 3 To be undecided, as a business agreement. **—to hang in** *Slang* To stay; persevere; hold on. **—to hang out** 1 To lean out. 2 To suspend out in the open: to *hang out* the wash. 3 *Slang* To reside or spend one's time: usually with *at* or *in.* **—to hang together** 1 To stay together. 2 To be coherent or consistent, as an explanation. **—to hang up** 1 To place on hooks or hangers. 2 To place a telephone receiver on the hook and thus break off communication. **—to let it all hang out** *Slang* 1 To make no effort to conceal one's motives, fears, desires, etc. 2 To be altogether free of restraint or inhibition. —*n.* 1 The way a thing hangs: the *hang* of a drape. 2 *U.S. Colloq.* Familiar knowledge or wont; knack. 3 A bit: I don't give a *hang*: euphemism for *damn.* 4 Rake, as of a mast. **—to get the hang of** *U.S. Colloq.* To come to understand or be able to do. [Fusion of ME *hangen* (OE *hangian* hang down), OE *hon* suspend, and ME *henge* cause or condemn to hang (< ON *hengjan*)]

han·gar (hang′ər, -gär) *n.* A shelter or shed, especially one for the maintenance and storage of aircraft. [< F]

Hang·chow (hang′chou′, *Chinese* häng′jō′) A port in eastern China, capital of Chekiang province, at the head of **Hangchow Bay,** an inlet of the East China Sea.

hang·dog (hang′dôg′, -dog′) *adj.* Of mean, sneaking, or abject character or appearance. —*n.* A skulking person; sneak.

hang·er (hang′ər) *n.* 1 One who hangs, as a hangman. 2 A device on which something is hung. 3 A shaped frame on which a garment is suspended or draped.

hang·er-on (hang′ər·on′) *n. pl.* **hang·ers-on** A self-attached dependent; parasite.

hang glider A kitelike metal and cloth frame to which a person is harnessed while soaring through the air.

hang·ing (hang′ing) *adj.* 1 Suspended from something; dangling. 2 Involving or suggesting death on the gallows. 3 Lying on a steep slope: a *hanging* garden. 4 Drooping and dejected: said of the countenance. 5 Held in abeyance. —*n.* 1 The act of suspending. 2 Execution on the gallows. 3 *pl.* Drapery for a room, as tapestry.

hanging wall *Geol.* The layer of an inclined fault plane which overlies the footwall.

hang·man (hang′mən) *n. pl.* **·men** (-mən) A public executioner.

hang·nail (hang′nāl′) *n.* Skin partially torn loose at the side or root of a fingernail. [Alter. of AGNAIL; infl. by HANG]

hang-nest (hang′nest′) *n.* A hangbird's nest.

Hang·ö (häng′œ) A port on the Baltic in SW Finland. *Finnish* **Han·ko** (häng′kô).

hang-out (hang′out′) *n. Slang* A habitual meeting place or resort.

hang-o·ver (hang′ō′vər) *n. U.S. Colloq.* 1 A person or thing remaining from something that is past; a survival, as of a tradition. 2 The aftereffects of alcoholic dissipation, as headache and nausea.

hang-up (hang′up′) *n. Slang* 1 A psychological difficulty; especially, a neurotic preoccupation or obsession. 2 Anything blocking a natural or normal process.

hank (hangk) *n.* 1 A bundle of two or more skeins of yarn tied together; also, a single skein. 2 A measure of yarn varying for different materials: a hank of No. 1 cotton is 840 yards long and weighs 1 pound; a hank of woolen yarn is 560 yards long. 3 *Naut.* **a** A rope, string, coil, or tie. **b** Any fastening; specifically, a ring of rope or iron on the edge of a jib or staysail, used for fastening it. [ME < Scand. Cf. Icel. *hankar,* genitive of *hönk* a skein, coil.]

Han·ka (hang′kə) See KHANKA, LAKE.

han·ker (hang′kər) *v.i.* To yearn; have desire: with *after, for,* or an infinitive. [Cf. Flemish *hankeren* long for] **—han′ker·er** *n.* **—han′ker·ing** *n.*

Han·kow (hang′kou′, *Chinese* häng′jō′) A city in east central China on the Yangtze.

han·ky-pan·ky (hang′kē·pang′kē) *n. Slang* 1 Trickery. 2 Jugglery; sleight-of-hand. [An arbitrary formation, ? < HAND]

Han·na (hän′ə) Dutch form of JOAN.

Han·na (han′ə), **Marcus Alonzo,** 1837–1904, U.S. financier and politician: known as *Mark Hanna.*

Han·nah (han′ə) A feminine personal name. [< Hebrew, grace]
—Hannah A Jewish prophetess; mother of the prophet Samuel. 1 *Sam.* i 2.

Han·ni·bal (han′ə·bəl) A masculine personal name. [< Phoenician, grace of Baal]
— Hannibal, 247–183 B.C., Carthaginian general who invaded Italy by crossing the Alps; son of Hamilcar Barca.

Han·no (han′ō), third century B.C. Carthaginian leader.

Ha·noi (hä·noi′) A city in North Vietnam, capital of the Democratic Republic of Vietnam (Vietminh).

Ha·no·taux (á·nô·tō′), **Albert Auguste Gabriel,** 1853–1944, French statesman and author.

Han·o·ver (han′ō·vər) A former Prussian province included since 1945 in the state of Lower Saxony, Germany. *German* **Han·no·ver** (hä·nō′vər). **—Han·o·ve·ri·an** (han′ō·vir′ē·ən) *adj.* & *n.*

Hanoverian dynasty A reigning family of Great Britain, founded by George I, who was elector of Hanover, and ending with Victoria: also called **House of Hanover.**

Hans (häns) Dutch, German, and Swedish diminutive form of JOHANNES.

Han·sard (han′sərd) *n.* The printed record of the proceedings of the British Parliament. [after Luke *Hansard,* 1752–1828, its first publisher]

hanse (hans) *n.* 1 A guild of medieval merchants. 2 An entrance fee; especially, one paid by merchants not members of a guild. [< OF < OHG *hansa* band]

Hanse (hans) *n.* The Hanseatic League.

Han·se·at·ic (han′sē·at′ik) *adj.* Pertaining to the Hanse towns of Germany.

Hanseatic League A league of about 85 towns and cities in northern Germany and neighboring countries, called **Hanse towns,** which banded together in the Middle Ages (about 1241–1669) for mutual protection and trade advantages. Hamburg, Lübeck, and Bremen are still called Hanse towns.

han·sel (han′səl) See HANDSEL.

Han·sen's disease (han′sənz) Leprosy.

han·som (han′səm) *n.* A low, two-wheeled, one-horse cab, with the driver mounted back of the top: also **hansom cab.** ◆ Homophone: *handsome.* [after J. A. *Hansom,* 1803–82, English inventor]

HANSOM

Hants (hants) Hampshire: a shortened form of *Hantesshire,* the Middle English spelling.

Ha·nuk·kah (khä′nōō·kə) A Jewish festival lasting eight days from Kislew 25th (early December), in memory of the rededication of the temple at Jerusalem under the Maccabees in 164 B.C. It is also known, usually by Christians, as the *Feast of Dedication.* Also **Ha′nu·kah:** also spelled *Chanuca.* [< Hebrew *hanukkah* dedication]

han·u·man (hän′ōō·mən) *n.* The entellus monkey. [< Hind., lit., the one with a jaw]

Han·u·man (hän′ōō·mən) In Hindu mythology, a monkey god.

Han·yang (hän′yäng′) A city on the Yangtse in east central China.

hap (hap) *Archaic n.* 1 A casual occurrence; happening; chance. 2 Luck; good fortune. See synonyms under ACCIDENT. —*v.i.* **happed, hap·ping** To happen; chance. [< ON *happ*]

ha·pax le·go·me·non (hā′paks lə·gom′ə·non) *Greek* Occurring but once: said in reference to rare or nonce words or phrases.

hap·haz·ard (hap′haz′ərd) *adj.* Accidental; happening by chance. —*n.* Mere chance; hazard. —*adv.* By chance; at random. [< HAP + HAZARD] **—hap′haz′ard·ly** *adv.*

haph·e·pho·bi·a (haf′ə·fō′bē·ə) See HAPTEPHOBIA.

haph·ta·rah (häf′tä·rä′, -tô′rô) *n. pl.* **·roth** (-rōth′, -rōth) The selection from the prophets read in the synagog service after each lesson from the law. See PARASHAH. [< Hebrew *haphṭārāh* conclusion]

hap·less (hap′lis) *adj.* Having no luck; unfortunate; unlucky. **—hap′less·ly** *adv.* **—hap′less·ness** *n.*

hap·lite (hap′līt) *n.* A fine-grained, acid granite, composed mostly of quartz and feldspar and occurring in dikes. Its micaceous constituent, when present, is usually muscovite. Also called *aplite.* [< HAPL(O)- + -ITE[1]] **—hap·lit·ic** (hap·lit′ik) *adj.*

haplo- *combining form* Simple; single. Also, before vowels, **hapl-.** [< Gk. *haploos* simple]

hap·loid (hap′loid) *adj. Biol.* Having the character of gametes with a reduced number of chromosomes, in contradistinction to the diploid with the doubled number found in somatic cells. Also **hap·loid′ic.**

hap·lo·sis (hap·lō′sis) *n. Biol.* The halving of the chromosome number during meiosis.

hap·ly (hap′lē) *adv.* By chance.

hap·pen (hap′ən) *v.i.* 1 To take place or occur; come to pass. 2 To come about or occur by chance or without expectation or design. 3 To chance; have the fortune: We *happened* to be there. 4 To come by chance: to *happen* upon the answer. 5 To come or go by chance: with *in, along, by,* etc. **—to happen to** 1 To befall. 2 To become of: What *happened to* your old friend? [< HAP]

Synonyms: bechance, betide, chance, fall, occur, supervene. A thing is said to *happen* when no design is manifest or thought of; it is said to *chance* when it appears to be the result of accident (compare synonyms for ACCIDENT). An incident *happens* or *occurs;* something external or actual *happens* to one; a thought or fancy *occurs* to him. *Befall* and *betide* are transitive; *happen* is intransitive; something *befalls* or *betides* a person or *happens* to him. *Betide* is especially used for anticipated evil, thought of as waiting and coming at its appointed time; as, Woe *betide* him. One event *supervenes* upon another event, one disease upon another, etc.

hap·pen·ing (hap′ən·ing) *n.* 1 Something that happens; an event. See synonyms under ACCIDENT. 2 A staged but usually partly improvised event, often bizarre or spectacular, intended to engage the attention or elicit a response through shock or novelty.

hap·pen·stance (hap′ən·stans, -stəns) *n. U.S. Colloq.* A chance occurrence. [< HAPPEN + (CIRCUM)STANCE]

hap·per (hap′ər) *n. Scot.* The hopper of a mill.

hap·pi·ly (hap′ə·lē) *adv.* 1 In a happy manner; cheerfully. 2 Fortunately; luckily. 3 Felicitously. 4 *Obs.* Haply; by chance.

hap·pi·ness (hap′ē·nis) *n.* 1 The state or quality of being happy; the pleasurable experience that springs from possession of good or the gratification of desires; enjoyment; blessedness. 2 Good fortune; luck; prosperity. 3 Unstudied grace; aptness or felicitousness, as of a remark or turn of phrase.

Synonyms: blessedness, bliss, cheer, comfort, contentment, delight, ecstasy, enjoyment, felicity, gaiety, gladness, gratification, joy, merriment, mirth, pleasure, rapture, rejoicing, satisfaction, triumph. *Comfort* may be almost wholly negative, being found in security or relief from that which pains or annoys. *Enjoyment* is more positive and *pleasure* still more vivid; *satisfaction* is more tranquil than *pleasure;* when a worthy *pleasure* is past, a worthy *satisfaction* remains. *Happiness* is more complete than *comfort, enjoyment,* or *satisfaction,* more serene and rational than *pleasure. Felicity* is a colder and more formal term than *happiness. Gladness* is *happiness* that overflows. *Joy* is more intense than *happiness,* deeper than *gladness,* to which it is akin, nobler and more enduring than *pleasure. Bliss* is ecstatic, perfected *happiness.* See RAPTURE.

hap·py (hap′ē) *adj.* **·pi·er, ·pi·est 1** Enjoying, giving or indicating pleasure; joyous; blessed. **2** Dexterously or fortunately effective; opportune; felicitous. **3** Yielding or marked by happiness: *happy* moments. [<HAP]

Synonyms: blessed, blissful, blithe, blithesome, bright, buoyant, cheerful, cheering, cheery, delighted, delightful, dexterous, felicitous, fortunate, gay, glad, jocund, jolly, joyful, joyous, lucky, merry, mirthful, pleased, prosperous, rapturous, rejoiced, rejoicing, smiling, sprightly, successful, sunny. *Happy* primarily refers to something that comes "by good hap," a chance that brings prosperity, benefit, or success. In its most frequent present use, *happy* is applied to the state of one enjoying happiness, or to that by which happiness is expressed; as, a *happy* heart, *happy* laughter. (Compare synonyms for HAPPINESS.) *Cheerful* applies to the possession or expression of a moderate and tranquil happiness. A *cheery* word spontaneously gives cheer to others; a *cheering* word is more distinctly planned to cheer and encourage. *Gay* applies to an effusive and superficial happiness perhaps resulting largely from abundant animal spirits. A *buoyant* spirit is, as it were, borne up by joy and hope. A *sunny* disposition has a tranquil brightness that irradiates all who come within its influence. See AUSPICIOUS, CHEERFUL, CLEVER, FORTUNATE, SKILFUL, WELL. *Antonyms*: despondent, gloomy, melancholy, miserable, mournful, regretful, sad, sorrowful, woeful, wretched.

hap·py-go-luck·y (hap′ē·gō·luk′ē) *adj.* Trusting easily to luck; improvident; haphazard. —*adv.* As one pleases; anyhow; at will.

Haps·burg (haps′bûrg, *Ger.* häps′bo͝orkh) An ancient German family from which were descended rulers of Austria, Hungary and Bohemia, the Holy Roman Empire, and Spain; the male line ended 1740: also called **House of Hapsburg.** Also spelled *Habsburg.*

Haps·burg-Lor·raine (haps′bûrg·lə·rān′, *Ger.* häps′bo͝orkh·lō·rān′) The royal house of Austria, 1740–1918.

hap·shack·le (hap′shak′əl) See HAMSHACKLE.

hap·tene (hap′tēn) *n. Biochem.* A partial antigen: a substance which, when combined with certain proteins, has the power of conferring on them specific antigenic properties. Also **hap′ten** (-ten). [<Gk. *haptein* touch + -ENE]

hap·te·pho·bi·a (hap′tə·fō′bē·ə) *n.* A morbid fear of being touched: also called *haphephobia.* [<Gk. *haptein* touch + -PHOBIA] —**hap′te·pho′bic** *adj.*

hap·ter·on (hap′tər·on) *n. pl.* **·ter·a** (-tər·ə) *Bot.* A special organ of attachment developed by many aquatic plants, or marine algae, by which they anchor themselves to rocks. Also **hap′tere** (-tir). [<NL <Gk. *haptein* touch]

hap·to·phore (hap′tə·fôr, -fōr) *n. Biochem.* The thermostable portion of a toxin molecule which combines with an antitoxin cell to neutralize the toxic thermolabile portion. [<Gk. *haptein* touch + -PHORE]

hap·tot·ro·pism (hap·tot′rə·piz′əm) *n. Bot.* A one-sided growth in plants, induced by pressure or other stimuli. [<Gk. *haptein* + -TROPISM] —**hap′to·trop′ic** (-trop′ik, -trō′pik) *adj.*

ha·ra-ki·ri (hä′rä·kē′rē) *n.* Suicide by disembowelment: traditional form of suicide practiced by the Japanese samurai when disgraced or in lieu of execution: also *hari-kari.* Also **ha′ra-ka′ri** (-kä′rē). [<Japanese *hara* belly + *kiri* cut]

ha·rangue (hə·rang′) *n.* An oration; especially, a loud and vehement speech. —*v.* **·rangued, ·rangu·ing** *v.t.* To address in a harangue. —*v.i.* To deliver a harangue. See synonyms under SPEECH. [<F <Med. L *harenga* <OHG *hari* host + *hringa* ring] —**ha·rangu′er** *n.*

Ha·rar (hä′rər) A town in east central Ethiopia: formerly *Harrar.*

har·ass (har′əs, hə·ras′) *v.t.* **1** To trouble or worry persistently with cares, annoyances, etc.; torment. **2** *Mil.* To worry (an enemy) by raids and small attacks. **3** *Obs.* To ravage; raid. See synonyms under PERSECUTE, PERPLEX, TIRE[1]. [<OF *harasser* <*harer* set dogs on, prob. <OHG *haren* cry out] —**har′ass·er** *n.* —**har′ass·ment** *n.*

Har·bin (här′bin) A port on the Sungari, capital of Sungkiang province, NE Manchuria.

har·bin·ger (här′bin·jər) *n.* **1** One who or that which foreruns and announces the coming of something. **2** Formerly, a courier who rode in advance of a party to arrange for their lodging and entertainment. See synonyms under HERALD. —*v.t.* To act as a harbinger to; presage. [<OF *herbergeor* provider of shelter <*herberge* shelter <Gmc.]

har·bor (här′bər) *n.* **1** A port or haven so protected, naturally or artificially, as to provide shelter for ships. **2** Any place of refuge or rest. See synonyms under REFUGE, SHELTER. —*v.t.* **1** To give refuge to; shelter; protect. **2** To entertain in the mind; cherish, as a grudge. —*v.i.* **3** To take shelter in or as in a harbor. See synonyms under CHERISH, SHELTER. Also, *Brit.,* **har′bour.** [ME *herberwe* <OE *here* army + *beorg* refuge] —**har′bor·er** *n.*

har·bor·age (här bər·ij) *n.* **1** A port or place of shelter for ships. **2** Shelter; entertainment.

har·bor·mas·ter (här′bər·mas′tər, -mäs′-) *n.* **1** An officer who inspects vessels in harbor to see that they are properly berthed and moored. **2** The chief of the harbor police.

hard (härd) *adj.* **1** Solid and firm in substance and consistency; not easily receiving indentation or impression: opposed to *soft.* **2** Capable of endurance; hardy. **3** Difficult of accomplishment, management, or solution; troublesome: opposed to *easy.* **4** Obdurate or callous in character or demeanor; hard-hearted. **5** Harsh or cruel: He was too *hard* on her; *hard* words. **6** Shrewd and obstinate. **7** Oppressive; difficult to endure: a *hard* life; *hard* times. **8** Strict or exacting in terms: a *hard* bargain. **9** Vigorous; persistent; energetic: *hard* study; a *hard* worker. **10** Sound; trustworthy. **11** Esthetically harsh or unpleasant: a *hard* face. **12** Stormy; inclement; rigorous: a *hard* winter. **13** Indisputable; definite: *hard* facts. **14** Strictly factual: *hard* news. **15** In specie; metallic: said of money. **16** Containing certain mineral salts in solution which interfere with the cleansing action of soap: said of water. **17** Containing much alcohol; strong: said of liquor. **18** Addictive: said of drugs. **19** *Agric.* High in gluten content: said of wheat. **20** Denoting *c* or *g* when articulated as a stop, as in *cod* and *god,* rather than as a fricative or an affricate. —*adv.* **1** With great energy or force; vigorously: to work *hard;* to rain *hard.* **2** Intently; earnestly: to look *hard* for something. **3** Harshly or severely. **4** With effort or difficulty. **5** Securely; tightly: to hold on *hard.* **6** So as to become hard: It was frozen *hard.* **7** In close proximity; near: often with *after, by,* or *upon.* [OE *heard*]

Synonyms (*adj.*): arduous, austere, bad, callous, compact, cruel, dense, difficult, distressing, exacting, firm, flinty, grievous, hardened, harsh, impenetrable, obdurate, oppressive, rigid, severe, solid, stern, stubborn, unfeeling, unforgiving, unrelenting, unyielding. See ARDUOUS, AUSTERE, BAD, COMPACT, DIFFICULT, FIRM, IMPENETRABLE, TROUBLESOME. *Antonyms*: easy, facile, fluid, genial, gentle, intelligible, kind, lenient, meek, mild, penetrable, soft, submissive, tender, yielding.

hard-and-fast (härd′ən·fast′, -fäst′) *adj.* Absolutely binding; fixed and unalterable.

hard·back (härd′bak′) *adj.* Hard-cover. —*n.* A hard-cover book.

hard·ball (härd′bol′) *n.* **1** A baseball. —*adj. U.S. Colloq.* Tough; intense: a *hardball* confrontation.

hard-bit·ten (härd′bit′n) *adj.* Tough; unyielding.

hard·board (härd′bôrd′, -bōrd′) *n.* A material composed of fibers from wood chips pressed into sheets.

hard-boiled (härd′boild′) *adj.* **1** Boiled until cooked through; said of an egg. **2** *Colloq.* Hardened or unyielding in character; tough.

hard·bound (härd′bound′) *adj.* Hard-cover.

hard by *Archaic* or *Dial.* Close by.

hard cash Actual money as distinguished from debts or claims to be collected or settled.

hard coal Anthracite.

hard-core (härd′kôr′) *adj.* **1** Thoroughly dedicated, determined, loyal, etc., to a cause or movement: *hard-core* radicals. **2** Extremely explicit: *hard-core* pornography. **3** Of or pertaining to the hard core.

hard core 1 The basic, central, or most important part; nucleus. **2** Unemployed or underemployed people not trained for any job.

hard-cov·er (härd′kuv′ər) *adj.* Designating a book having rigid sides, as of cardboard bound in cloth or another material: contrasted to *soft-cover.*

hard-earned (härd′ûrnd′) *adj.* Earned or gained with difficulty; obtained by hard work.

Har·de·ca·nute (här′də·kə·no͞ot′, -nyo͞ot′), 1019?–42, king of England and Denmark 1040–42; son of Canute.

hard·en (här′dən) *v.t.* **1** To make hard or harder; make solid. **2** To make unyielding, pitiless, or indifferent. **3** To strengthen or make firm in any element of character, disposition, etc. **4** To make tough, strong, or hardy; inure. —*v.i.* **5** To become hard. **6** In commerce: **a** To become higher, as prices. **b** To become stable. [<ON *harthna*]

hard·en·ing (här′dən·ing) *n.* Any substance or material that hardens another; specifically, any metal added to iron to make steel.

hard-fea·tured (härd′fē′chərd) *adj.* Stern or forbidding in countenance or aspect.

hard-fist·ed (härd′fis′tid) *adj.* **1** Of an avaricious or miserly disposition. **2** Having hard, horny, or strong hands. —**hard′-fist′ed·ness** *n.*

hard·hack (härd′hak′) *n.* The steeplebush.

hard-hand·ed (hard′han′did) *adj.* **1** Having hard or horny hands. **2** Governing with severity or cruelty; despotic; tyrannical.

hard-hat (härd′hat′) *n. U.S. Colloq.* A construction worker.

hard hat 1 Any of various helmets worn for protection, as by construction workers, motorcyclists, etc. **2** *Brit.* Any hat having a hard crown, as a derby or bowler.

hard·head (härd′hed′) *n. pl.* **·heads** *for defs.* **1, 2; ·head** or **·heads** *for defs.* **3, 4. 1** A shrewd, tough-minded person. **2** An obstinate or stupid person. **3** The menhaden. **4** The alewife.

hard-head·ed (härd′hed′id) *adj.* **1** Possessing shrewdness and a practical turn. **2** Inclined to obstinacy; stubborn. —**hard′-head′ed·ness** *n.*

hard-heart·ed (härd′här′tid) *adj.* Lacking pity or sympathy; unfeeling; obdurate. —**hard′-heart′ed·ly** *adv.* —**hard′-heart′ed·ness** *n.*

har·di·hood (här′dē·hood) *n.* **1** Sturdy courage. **2** Rash or foolish daring; presumptuous boldness; audacity; effrontery. **3** The quality of being hardy; physical endurance. See synonyms under COURAGE, EFFRONTERY, TEMERITY.

har·di·ly (här′də·lē) *adv.* With hardihood; boldly.

har·di·ness (här′dē·nis) *n.* **1** The state of being hardy or physically strong. **2** Stout-heartedness; intrepidity.

Har·ding (här′ding), **Warren Gamaliel,** 1865–1923, president of the United States 1921–23.

hard labor Heavy labor, such as stone-breaking, etc., imposed as a form of punishment upon imprisoned convicts.

hard line An unyielding position, as in negotiation. —**hard′-line′** *adj.* —**hard′-lin′er** *n.*

hard-look·ing (härd′lo͝ok′ing) *adj.* Appearing hard; tough-looking.

hard·ly (härd′lē) *adv.* **1** Scarcely; not quite: She was *hardly* aware of what she was doing. **2** With difficulty or great pains. **3** Improbably. **4** Rigorously; harshly; severely.

hard maple Sugar maple.

hard-mouthed (härd′mouthd′, -moutht′) *adj.* Having a hard mouth, as a horse; hence, not easily guided or controlled.

hard·ness (härd′nis) *n.* **1** The state of being hard. **2** Unyieldingness of spirit; insensitivity; callousness. **3** A property of water that contains mineral salts. **4** *Med.* Tension: said of the pulse. **5** In art, harsh effect or treatment. **6** That quality of a mineral that resists scratching: see MOHS SCALE. **7** The toughness of a metal or alloy: see BRINELL HARDNESS. **8** *Physics* A high-penetrating

power of X-rays or other forms of radiant energy.
hard-nosed (härd′nōzd′) *adj. Slang* Hard-bitten, unyielding, or firmly businesslike: a *hard-nosed* approach to government spending. Also **hard-nose** (härd′nōz′).
hard of hearing Deaf or partially deaf.
hard·pan (härd′pan′) *n.* **1** A layer of firm detritus under soft soil. **2** A firm foundation; solid basis.
hard rubber Vulcanite.
hard sauce Butter, sugar, and flavorings creamed together and used as a sauce with puddings, etc.
hard sell *U.S. Colloq.* The use of aggressive methods of salesmanship.
hard-set (härd′set′) *adj.* **1** In a difficult situation; beset. **2** Firmly resolved; obstinate.
hard·shell (härd′shel′) *adj.* **1** Having a hard shell, as a lobster or crab, previous to shedding the carapace. **2** Stubbornly devoted to one's principles; uncompromising; inflexible.
Hardshell Baptist A Primitive or Old School Baptist.
hard-shell clam (härd′shel′) The quahaug.
hard-shell crab A crab, particularly the blue crab (*Callinectes sapidus*) of North America, before it has molted: after it has molted it is known as a *soft-shell crab.*
hard·ship (härd′ship) *n.* **1** Something hard to endure, as injustice. **2** *Obs.* Rigor; severity. See synonyms under MISFORTUNE.
hard-spun (härd′spun′) *adj.* Spun with a fine twist.
hard·stand (härd′stand′) *n. Aeron.* A paved, hard-surfaced area adjacent to a runway, for the parking of aircraft and ground vehicles.
hard·tack (härd′tak′) *n.* Large, unsalted, crackerlike, hard-baked biscuit for army and navy use: also called *ship biscuit.*
hard·top (härd′top′) *adj.* Describing an automobile with the body design of a convertible, but with a rigid top. —*n.* Such a car.
hard up **1** In need or want, as of money. **2** Having a meager choice.
hard·ware (härd′wâr′) *n.* **1** Manufactured articles of metal, as utensils or tools. **2** Weapons: military *hardware.* **3** Mechanical, electronic, or other devices or materials, as distinguished from people, planning, operational procedures, etc. **4** Any of the machinery that makes up a computer installation: distinguished from *software.*
hard·wood (härd′wŏŏd′) *n.* **1** Wood from broad-leaved deciduous trees as distinguished from the wood of coniferous or needle-leaved trees. **2** Any such tree.
har·dy[1] (här′dē) *adj.* **·di·er, ·di·est** **1** Inured to hardship; robust. **2** Showing hardihood; bold; audacious; strenuous. **3** Able to survive the winter in the open air; perennial: said of plants. **4** Rigid; strong; durable. See synonyms under STRONG. [<OF *hardi,* pp. of *hardir* embolden <OHG *hartjan* make hard]
har·dy[2] (har′dē) *n. pl.* **·dies** A square-shanked chisel or fuller for insertion in a hardy-hole. [<HARD + -Y[1]]
Har·dy (här′dē), **Thomas,** 1840–1928, English novelist and poet.
har·dy-hole (här′dē·hōl′) *n.* A hole in a blacksmith's anvil in which a hardy or other tool may be placed.
hare (hâr) *n. pl.* **hares** or **hare** **1** A rodent (genus *Lepus*) with cleft upper lip, long ears, and long hind legs: proverbial for its timidity and swiftness. **2** The common American rabbit. ◆ Collateral adjective: *leporine.* ◆ Homophone: *hair.* [OE *hara*]
hare-and-hounds (hâr′ən·houndz′) *n.* An outdoor sport in which some players (*hounds*) pursue others (*hares*) who have scattered scraps of paper as "scent" behind them.
hare·bell (hâr′bel′) *n.* **1** A perennial Scottish herb (*Campanula rotundifolia*) with blue, bell-shaped flowers. **2** Any of several related plants, as the western harebell of the U.S. (*C. petiolata*). Also called *bluebell.*
hare·brained (hâr′brānd′) *adj.* Foolish; flighty; giddy.
Ha·re Krish·na (hä′rā krish′nə) The name of a U.S. cult, adopted from the title of a Buddhist love chant dedicated to the Hindu god Krishna.
hare·lip (hâr′lip′) *n.* A congenital fissure of the upper lip a short distance from the median line.
har·em (hâr′əm, har′-) *n.* **1** The apartments of a Moslem household reserved for females. **2** The wives, concubines, etc., occupying the harem. **3** A Moslem holy place forbidden to all but the faithful. Also **ha·reem** (hä·rēm′). [<Arabic *harim* (something) forbidden, sacred <*ḥarama* forbid]
hare's-eye (hârz′ī′) *n.* Lagophthalmos.
Har·fleur (är·flœr′) A port on the Seine near Le Havre, northern France.
Har·gei·sa (här·gā′sə) A city in NW Somalia, capital of the former British Somaliland.
Har·greaves (här′grēvz), **James,** died 1778, English weaver; inventor of the spinning jenny.
har·i·cot (har′ə·kō) *n.* **1** A stew of meat, especially mutton, and vegetables. **2** The ripe seeds or green pods of the kidney bean and other string beans; also, the kidney bean. [<F <Nahuatl *ayecotl*]
ha·ri-ka·ri (hä′rē·kä′rē) See HARA-KIRI.
Har·ing·ton (har′ing·tən), **Sir John,** 1561–1622, English writer and translator: also *Harrington.*
hark (härk) *v.i.* To listen; harken: usually in the imperative. —*v.t. Archaic* To hear; listen to. —**to hark back** **1** In hunting, to retrace the trail so as to find again a lost scent: said of hounds. **2** To return to some previous point, as after a digression. —*n.* The cry "hark" as used to urge on or guide hounds in the chase. [ME *herkien*]
hark·en (här′kən) *v.t. Archaic* To hear; listen to; heed. —*v.i. Poetic* To listen; give heed. Also spelled *hearken.* See synonyms under LISTEN. [OE *heorcnian*]
hark·er (här′kər) *n. Scot.* A listener.
harl[1] (härl) *v.t. & v.i. Scot. & Brit. Dial.* To drag or be dragged; scrape. Also **harle.**
harl[2] (härl) *n.* **1** Filaments of flax or hemp drawn out or hackled; hence, any fibrous substance. **2** A barb of a large feather, as from a peacock: used for making artificial flies in angling. [Prob. <MLG *herle*]
Har·lan (här′lən), **John Marshall,** 1899–1971, U.S. jurist; associate justice of the Supreme Court 1954–1971.
Har·le·ian (här′lē·ən) *adj.* Belonging to or connected with **Robert Har·ley** (här′lē), 1661–1724, and his son **Edward,** 1689–1741, earls of Oxford and Mortimer and founders of the Harleian collection of books and manuscripts in the British Museum.
Har·lem (här′ləm) **1** A former village of NE Manhattan Island; now a section of New York City with a large Negro population. **2** Haarlem.
Harlem River A navigable tidal stream forming the northern boundary of Manhattan Island, connected with the Hudson River by a ship canal.
har·le·quin (här′lə·kwin, -kin) *n.* A buffoon. —*adj.* **1** Comic; buffoonlike. **2** Parti-colored, like the dress of a Harlequin. —*v.i. Rare* To play the harlequin. —**har′le·quin·esque′** (-esk′) *adj.*
Har·le·quin (här′lə·kwin, -kin) A traditional pantomine character, originally from old Italian comedy, the lover of Columbine, traditionally dressed in parti-colored tights, with shaved head, masked face, and bearing a light wooden sword.
har·le·quin·ade (här′lə·kwin·ād′, -kin-) *n.* **1** That part of a pantomime in which the harlequin and clown play the principal parts: hence, pantomime. **2** Fantastic antics or show; buffoonery.
harlequin brant The laughing goose.
harlequin bug A shiny, black or blue bug with red or red and yellow spots (*Murgantia histrionica*) which feeds on cabbage and related plants: also called *cabbage bug, fire bug.*
harlequin duck A northern sea duck (*Histrionicus histrionicus*) the male of which is brilliantly and variously colored.
harlequin snake One of the coral snakes.
Har·ley Street (här′lē) A street in the West End of London, occupied chiefly by specialists in medicine and surgery.
har·lot (här′lət) *n.* **1** A lewd woman; prostitute. **2** *Obs.* A knave or vagabond. [<OF *herlot* fellow, rogue]
har·lot·ry (här′lət·rē) *n.* The trade of a harlot; habitual lewdness.
harm (härm) *n.* **1** That which inflicts injury or loss. **2** The injury inflicted; hurt. **3** Offense against right or morality; wrong. See synonyms under INJURY, MISFORTUNE. —*v.t.* To do harm to; damage; hurt. See synonyms under ABUSE, HURT. [OE *hearm* insult]
har·mat·tan (här′mə·tan′) *n.* A dry, sandy wind of the west coast of Africa, blowing from the interior during December, January, and February. [<Sp. *harmatán* <native name]
H-ar·ma·ture (āch′är′mə·chər, -chŏŏr) *n. Electr.* An early form of armature having a section shaped like an H: also called *shuttle armature.*
harm·ful (härm′fəl) *adj.* Having power to injure; noxious. See synonyms under INIMICAL, NOISOME, PERNICIOUS. —**harm′ful·ly** *adv.* —**harm′ful·ness** *n.*
har·mine (här′mēn, -min) *n.* Banisterine. Also **har′min** (-min). [<Gk. *harmala* wild rue + -INE[2]]
harm·less (härm′lis) *adj.* **1** Not harmful; innoxious. **2** Without hurt, loss, or liability. See synonyms under INNOCENT. —**harm′less·ly** *adv.* —**harm′less·ness** *n.*
har·mon·ic (här·mon′ik) *adj.* **1** Producing, characterized by, or pertaining to harmony; consonant; harmonious. **2** *Music* **a** Pertaining to harmony, as distinguished from melody or rhythm. **b** Pertaining to a tone whose rate of vibration is an exact multiple of a given primary tone. **3** *Math.* Derived from or originally suggested by the numerical relations between the vibrations of the musical harmonics or overtones of the same fundamental tone: *harmonic* functions. —*n.* **1** An attendant or secondary tone, produced by the vibration in aliquot parts of the same body or string which gives, by its complete simultaneous vibration, the primary or fundamental tone; overtone. **2** *Music* A note on a stringed instrument produced by stopping a string at a specific point. **3** *Physics* Any component of a periodic quantity which is an integral multiple of the fundamental frequency. Also **har·mon′i·cal.** [<L *harmonicus* <Gk. *harmonikos* <*harmonia* harmony] —**har·mon′i·cal·ly** *adv.*
har·mon·i·ca (här·mon′i·kə) *n.* **1** A musical instrument consisting of small metal reeds fixed within a series of slots in a narrow case, and played by blowing through the slots. **2** An instrument composed of a series of glass tubes, goblets, or the like, graduated to a musical scale and played by rubbing the rims. **3** An instrument composed of glass or metal strips struck by hammers. [<L, fem. of *harmonicus* harmonic]
harmonic analyzer *Physics* An instrument which separates the components of a complex sound wave into the corresponding sine waves.
harmonic distortion *Physics* A wave form distortion which contains both fundamental and harmonic frequencies.
har·mon·i·con (här·mon′i·kən) *n.* **1** An orchestrion. **2** A mouth organ; harmonica. [<Gk. *harmonikon,* neuter of *harmonikos* harmonic]
har·mon·ics (här·mon′iks) *n. pl.* **1** That branch of acoustics dealing with musical sounds: construed as singular. **2** The overtones or partials of a fundamental: construed as plural.
har·mo·ni·ous (här·mō′nē·əs) *adj.* **1** Characterized by harmony or agreement; free from discord. **2** Having the parts related in pleasing combination; symmetrical; congruous. **3** Melodious; pleasing to the ear.
har·mo·nist (här′mə·nist) *n.* **1** A master of the principles of musical harmony. **2** A student or expounder of the harmony of different writings, as of the Christian Gospels. **3** A musician. **4** A harmonizer.
har·mo·nis·tic (här′mə·nis′tik) *adj.* Pertaining or relating to harmony, specifically to the work of literary harmonists.
har·mo·ni·um (här·mō′nē·əm) *n.* A reed organ. [<F <L *harmonia*]
har·mo·nize (här′mə·nīz) *v.t. & v.i.* **·nized, ·niz·ing** **1** To make or become harmonious or suitable. **2** To arrange or sing in musical

harmony. Also, *Brit.*, **har′mo·nise.** See synonyms under ACCOMMODATE, ADAPT, AGREE. — **har′mo·ni·za′tion** *n.* — **har′mo·niz′er** *n.*

har·mo·ny (här′mə·nē) *n. pl.* **·nies 1** Accord or agreement in feeling, manner, or action: the *harmony* of a loving family. **2** A state of order, agreement, or completeness in the relations of things or of parts of a whole to each other. **3** Pleasing sounds; music. **4** *Music* **a** Any agreeable combination of simultaneous tones. **b** The science or study of the relations of combinations of tones or chords, their progressions, resolutions, modulations, etc., as distinguished from melody and rhythm. **5** A literary work to display the agreement of different books: a *harmony* of the Gospels. [<OF *armonie* <L *harmonia* <Gk. < *harmos* joint < *harmozein* join]

Synonyms: accord, accordance, agreement, amity, concord, concurrence, conformity, congruity, consent, consistency, consonance, symmetry, unanimity, uniformity, union, unison, unity. When tones, thoughts, or feelings, individually different, combine to form a consistent and pleasing whole, there is *harmony. Harmony* is deeper and more essential than *agreement. Concord* implies more volition than *accord. Conformity* is submission to authority or necessity. *Congruity* involves the element of suitableness; *consent* and *concurrence* refer to decision or action, but *consent* is more passive than *concurrence.* See MELODY, TUNE, SYMMETRY. *Antonyms*: antagonism, conflict, controversy, disagreement, discord, disproportion, dissension, disunion, hostility, incongruity, inconsistency, opposition, schism, variance.

har·mo·tome (här′mə·tōm) *n.* A vitreous hydrous silicate of potassium, barium, and aluminum, crystallizing in the monoclinic system, and forming characteristic cross-shaped crystals. [<Gk. *harmos* joint + -TOME]

harn (härn) *n. Scot.* A very coarse linen.

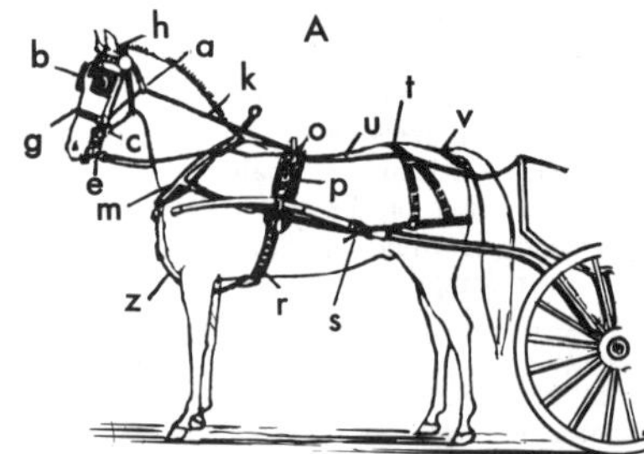

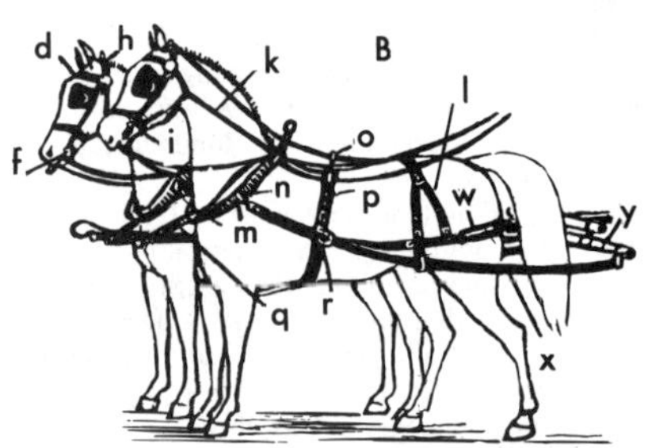

NOMENCLATURE OF HARNESS
A. Single harness. *B.* Double harness.

a.	Runner.	*o.*	Terrets.
b.	Blinder.	*p.*	Saddle.
c.	Throatlatch.	*q.*	Pole chain.
d.	Browband or front piece.	*r.*	Bellyband strap.
e.	Bit.	*s.*	Breeching strap.
f.	Curb bit.	*t.*	Hipstrap.
g.	Nose piece.	*u.*	Backstrap.
h.	Crownpiece.	*v.*	Crupper.
i.	Curb chain.	*w.*	Breeching.
k.	Checkrein.	*x.*	Traces.
l.	Breech stay.	*y.*	Whiffletree or swingletree.
m.	Hame.	*z.*	Martingale.
n.	Collar showing afterwale.		

har·ness (här′nis) *n.* **1** The combination of traces, straps, and other pieces forming the gear of a draft animal and used to attach it for work to a wheeled vehicle or plow. **2** *Archaic* The defensive armor of a soldier or of his horse. **3** Any arrangement of straps, cords, etc., as for lifting or performing some mechanical operation. **4** A device on a loom comprising the heddles which shift the sets of warp threads alternately. **5** The routine or obligations of work or business. — *v.t.* **1** To put harness on, as a horse. **2** To make use of the power or potential of: to *harness* a waterfall. **3** *Archaic* To dress in or equip with armor. [<OF *harneis*; ult. origin unknown] — **har′ness·er** *n.*

harnessed antelope Any of several African antelopes with harnesslike markings, especially the bushbuck.

harness race A race for pacers or trotters harnessed to sulkies.

Har·ney Peak (här′nē) A mountain in the Black Hills, the highest point in South Dakota; 7,242 feet.

Har·old (har′əld, *Fr.* à·rôld′) A masculine personal name; also, the name of several kings of England, Norway, and Denmark. Also *Lat.* **Ha·rol·dus** (hä·rōl′dəs), *Dan.* **Ha·rald** (hä′räld). [<Gmc., chief of the army] — **Harold I,** died 1040, king of England 1035–1040: called "Harold Harefoot."
— **Harold II,** 1022?–66, king of England Jan.–Oct. 1066; killed at battle of Hastings.
— **Harold III,** 1015–66, king of Norway; killed at battle of Stamford Bridge, where he was defeated by Harold II of England: known as *Harald Haardraade.*

harp (härp) *n.* **1** A stringed musical instrument, nearly triangular in modern form, played with the fingers. **2** One of several old Irish coins of various values. **3** A harplike part in a mechanism. — *v.i.* **1** To play on a harp. **2** To speak or write persistently; dwell tediously: with *on* or *upon.* — *v.t.* **3** *Archaic* To give utterance to; express. **4** *Poetic* To affect in some way by playing the harp: to *harp* one to sleep. [OE *hearpe*]

Harp (härp) The constellation Lyra.

harp·er (här′pər) *n.* One who plays the harp; a harpist.

Harpers Ferry A town in NE West Virginia; scene of John Brown's raid and arrest.

harp·ings (här′pingz) *n. pl. Naut.* **1** The foreparts of the wales surrounding the bow of a ship. **2** Extensions of the ribbands. Also **harp′ins.** [Prob. <F *harper* grip]

harp·ist (här′pist) *n.* One who plays the harp: a minstrel.

TOGGLED HAND HARPOON

har·poon (här·pōōn′) *n.* A barbed missile weapon, carrying a long cord, for striking whales or large fish. — *v.t.* To strike, take, or kill with a harpoon. [<F *harpon* grappling iron < *harper* grip < *harpe* claw] — **har·poon′er, har′poon·eer′** (-ir′) *n.*

harpoon gun A small cannon which fires a harpoon: used in whaling.

HARPSICHORD

harp·si·chord (härp′sə·kôrd) *n.* A keyboard instrument in wide-spread use from the 16th to the 18th century, and revived in the 20th, precursor of the piano, but having the strings plucked by quills instead of struck. [<MF *harpechorde* <Ital. *arpicordo* <LL *harpa* harp + L *chorda* string <Gk. *chordē*]

har·py (här′pē) *n. pl.* **·pies 1** Any rapacious person; a plunderer; extortioner. **2** A very large, crested, voracious tropical American eagle, the **harpy eagle** (*Thrasaetus harpyia*): also called *winged wolf.* [<HARPY]

Har·py (här′pē) *n.* In Greek mythology, a filthy, winged monster with the head of a woman and the tail, legs, and talons of a bird; usually three (the **Harpies**), Aello, Celaeno, and Ocypete, who fouled or seized the food of their victims, carried off the souls of the dead, etc. [<F *Harpie* <L *Harpyia* <Gk. < *harpazein* seize]

har·que·bus (här′kwə·bəs) *n.* **1** An ancient hand firearm, the predecessor of the musket. **2** A number of soldiers armed with harquebuses. Also spelled *arquebus.* Also **har′que·buse, har′que·buss.** [<F *harquebuse* <MLG *hakebusse* hook-gun]

HARQUEBUS

har·que·bus·ier (här′kwə·bəs·ir′) *n.* One armed with a harquebus.

Har·rar (hä′rər) A former spelling of HARAR.

har·ri·dan (har′ə·dən) *n.* A vixenish old woman; a hag. [<OF *haridelle* jade]

har·ri·er[1] (har′ē·ər) *n.* **1** One who or that which harries. **2** The marsh hawk.

har·ri·er[2] (har′ē·ər) *n.* **1** A small hound used for hunting hares. **2** *Brit.* A member of a hare-and-hounds team. [<HARE + -IER]

Har·ri·et (har′ē·ət) A feminine personal name. Also **Har′ri·ot, Har′ri·ott.** [<Gmc., home-ruler]

Har·ring·ton (har′ing·tən), **Sir John** See HARINGTON.

Har·ris (har′is), **Joel Chandler,** 1848–1908, U. S. writer. — **Roy,** born 1898, U. S. composer.

Har·ris·burg (har′is·bûrg) The capital of Pennsylvania, on the Susquehanna River.

Har·ri·son (har′ə·sən) Name of a prominent American political family including: **Benjamin,** 1726?–91, signer of the Declaration of Independence; his son **William Henry,** 1773–1841, U. S. general, president of the United States March 4–April 4, 1841; **Benjamin,** 1833–1901, president of the United States 1889–93, grandson of William Henry Harrison.

Har·ro·gate (har′ə·git, -gāt) A municipal borough in central Yorkshire, England.

Har·ro·vi·an (ha·rō′vē·ən, hə-) *adj.* Of or pertaining to the school at Harrow-on-the-Hill, England. — *n.* A student at or alumnus of Harrow.

har·row (har′ō) *n.* A farm implement, commonly a frame set with spikes or teeth, or disks, for leveling plowed ground, breaking clods, etc. — *v.t.* **1** To draw a harrow over (a field, etc.). **2** To disturb the mind or feelings of painfully; distress. — *v.i.* **3** To undergo harrowing. [ME *harwe,* prob. <Scand. Cf. ON *herfi.*] — **har′row·er** *n.*

har·row·ing (har′ō·ing) *adj.* Lacerating or tormenting to the feelings. — **har′row·ing·ly** *adv.*

Harrowing of Hell The descent of Christ into hell between his crucifixion and resurrection, when he is supposed to have brought salvation to the souls of the dead; a frequent subject in literature and art.

Har·row-on-the-Hill (har′ō·on·thə·hil′) An urban district in Middlesex NW of London; seat of Harrow, a public school founded 1571. Also **Har′row.**

har·ry (har′ē) *v.* **har·ried, har·ry·ing** *v.t.* **1** To lay waste, as in war or invasion; pillage; sack. **2** To harass in any way. **3** *Scot.* To carry off in a raid; seize. — *v.i.* **4** To make raids for plunder. Also *Obs.* **har·row.** See synonyms under PERSECUTE. [OE *hergian* ravage]

Har·ry (har′ē) Diminutive of HAROLD or HENRY.

har·ry-soph (har′i·sof′) *n. Brit.* At Cambridge University, a student with a B.A. degree who is a candidate for a medical or law degree. [<*Harry,* a nickname for Henry VIII + SOPHISTER]

harsh (härsh) *adj.* **1** Grating or rough to any of the senses; violently disagreeable; discordant; rasping; irritating. 2 Irritating to the mind; offensive. 3 Rigorous; severe; also, unfeeling: a *harsh* judge, a *harsh* sentence. See synonyms under ARBITRARY, AUSTERE, BITTER, HARD, ROUGH. [ME *harsk*, prob. < Scand. Cf. Sw. *härsk*, Dan. *harsk* rancid.] —**harsh′ly** *adv.* —**harsh′ness** *n.*

harsh·en (här′shən) *v.t.* To make harsh, rough, or severe.

hars·let (härs′lit) See HASLET.

hart (härt) *n.* The male of the red deer, especially after it has passed its fifth year. ◆ Homophone: *heart.* [OE *heort*]

Hart (härt), **Moss,** 1904–1961, U.S. playwright and librettist.

har·tal (här·täl′) *n.* In India, a suspension or stopping of business, as a form of mourning or passive protest against a political measure or situation. [<Hind. *hartāl* <*hat* shop + *tala* lock]

Harte (härt), **(Francis) Bret,** 1836–1902, U.S. novelist and story writer.

harte·beest (härt′bēst, här′tə-) *n.* 1 A large antelope of Africa (genera *Bubalis* and *Alcelaphus*), grayish-brown above and whitish below. 2 The bontebok. Also **hart′beest.** [< Afrikaans <Du. *hert* hart + *beest* beast]

Hart·ford (härt′fərd) The capital of Connecticut, on the Connecticut River.

harts·horn (härts′hôrn′) *n.* 1 A volatile preparation of ammonia, used as smelling salts, formerly distilled from deer horns. 2 Sal volatile. 3 The antler of a hart.

hart's–tongue (härts′tung′) *n.* A fern *(Phyllitis scolopendrium)* having bright green fronds, found throughout the temperate zone.

har·um–scar·um (hâr′əm·skâr′əm) *adj.* Reckless; irresponsible. —*n.* A wild, reckless, or thoughtless person. [<obs. *hare* frighten + SCARE]

Ha·run al–Ra·shid (hä·ro͞on′ äl′rə·shēd′) 766?–809, caliph of Bagdad; hero of the *Arabian Nights.*

ha·rus·pex (hə·rus′peks, har′əs·peks) *n. pl.* **ha·rus·pi·ces** (hə·rus′pə·sēz) A soothsayer or diviner of ancient Rome who interpreted the will of the gods from inspection of the entrails of sacrificed animals: also spelled *aruspex.* [< L] —**ha·rus′pi·cal** (-kəl) *adj.* —**ha·rus·pi·ca·tion** (hə·rus′pə·kā′shən) *n.* —**ha·rus·pi·cy** (hə·rus′pə·sē) *n.*

Har·vard (här′vərd), **John,** 1607–1638, English nonconformist clergyman, who emigrated to America; endowed Harvard College, 1636.

har·vest (här′vist) *n.* 1 A crop, as of grain, gathered or ready for gathering. 2 The time of gathering. 3 The product of any toil or effort. —*v.t. & v.i.* 1 To gather (a crop). 2 To gather the crop of (a field, etc.). [OE *hærfest* autumn, harvest]

Synonyms (noun): crop, fruit, growth, harvesting, harvest time, increase, ingathering, proceeds, produce, product, reaping, result, return, yield. *Harvest* is the generic word; *crop* is the common and commercial expression; we say a man sells his *crop,* but we should not speak of his selling his *harvest;* we speak of an ample or abundant *harvest,* a good *crop. Harvest* is applied almost wholly to grain; *crop* applies to almost anything that is gathered in; we speak of the potato *crop,* not the potato *harvest;* we may say either the wheat *crop* or the wheat *harvest.* We speak of *produce* collectively, but of a *product* or various *products;* vegetables, fruits, eggs, butter, etc., may be termed farm *produce,* or the *products* of the farm. *Product* is a word of wider application than *produce;* we speak of the *products* of manufacturing, the *product* obtained by multiplying one number by another, etc. The word *proceeds* is chiefly used of the *return* from an investment; we speak of the *produce* of a farm, but of the *proceeds* of the money invested in farming. The *yield* is what the land gives up to the farmer's demand, as the *yield* of corn or oats. *Harvest* has also a figurative use; as, The result of lax enforcement of law is a *harvest* of crime. See INCREASE, PRODUCT.

harvest bug 1 The harvest tick. 2 A harvest fly.

har·vest·er (här′vis·tər) *n.* 1 One who harvests 2 A reaping machine.

harvest feast A feast after the harvest has been gathered or the season in which it occurs: also called **harvest festival.**

harvest fly A large cicada *(Tibicen linnei)* of North America, noted for its shrill, noisy cry.

harvest home 1 An Old English festival held at the bringing home of the harvest. 2 The song sung at such festivals. 3 The season for garnering the harvest.

har·vest·man (här′vist·mən) *n. pl.* **·men** (-mən) 1 One who labors in the harvest. 2 An arachnid of the order *Phalangida;* a daddy-long-legs.

harvest moon The full moon that occurs near the autumnal equinox.

harvest tick An acaridan mite (genus *Trombicula*), mostly red, that attaches itself to the skin, being especially abundant about harvest time; a chigger.

Har·vey (här′vē) A masculine personal name. [<Gmc., army battle]

Har·vey (här′vē), **William,** 1578–1657, English physician; discovered the circulation of the blood.

Har·wich (har′ij, -ich) A port in NE Essex, England.

Harz Mountains (härts) A mountain range between the Elbe and Weser rivers, central Germany; highest peak, 3,747 feet. Also **Hartz.**

has (haz) Present indicative, third person singular, of HAVE.

Ha·sa (hä′sə, has′ə), A province and eastern dependency of Nejd, Saudi Arabia, on the Persian Gulf; capital, Hofuf: also *Al Ahsa.*

has–been (haz′bin′) *n. Colloq.* A person or thing no longer popular or effective.

Has·dru·bal (haz′dro͝o·bəl, haz·dro͞o′bəl) Name of several Carthaginian generals, especially Hannibal's brother; killed 207 B.C.

ha·sen·pfef·fer (hä′zən·fef′ər) *n.* A stew made with marinated rabbit meat. [G]

hash (hash) *n.* 1 A dish of chopped and cooked meat and vegetables, usually sautéed. 2 A mess; a jumble. 3 A rehash; any old thing brought forth in new form. 4 *Scot.* A wasteful or slovenly person; blockhead; dunce. —**to make a hash of** *Colloq.* To bungle; spoil. —**to settle (one's) hash** *Colloq.* To silence, finish off, or put down (a person). —*v.t.* 1 To cut or chop into small pieces; mince. 2 *U.S. Colloq.* To make a mess of; bungle. —**to hash over** *U.S. Colloq.* To talk or think about carefully; mull. [<OF *hacher* chop. See HATCH[3].]

Hash·e·mite Kingdom of the Jordan (hash′ə·mīt) See JORDAN, HASHEMITE KINGDOM OF THE.

hash house *U.S. Slang* A cheap restaurant.

hash·ish (häsh′ēsh, -ish) *n.* 1 The tops and sprouts of Indian hemp, used as a narcotic and intoxicant. 2 An intoxicating preparation of this plant. Also **hash′eesh.** [<Arabic *hashish* hemp]

hash mark *Mil. Slang* A service stripe worn on the uniform sleeve.

hash–sling·er (hash′sling′ər) *n. U.S. Slang* A waiter or waitress in a cheap restaurant.

Has·i·dim (has′i·dim, *Hebrew* khä·sē′dim) See CHASSIDIM.

has·let (häs′lit, häz′-) *n.* The heart, liver, etc., especially of a hog, used as food: also spelled *harslet.* [<OF *hastelet* broiled meat <*haste* spit <L *hasta* spear]

has·lock (has′lok′) *n.* The fine short wool on the throat of a sheep. [<HALSE + LOCK[3]]

Has·mo·ne·an (haz′mə·nē′ən) *n.* One of the Jewish family to which the Maccabees belonged, noted for its leadership and patriotism.—*adj.* Of or pertaining to the Hasmoneans. Also **Has′mo·nae′an.**

has·n't (haz′ənt) Contraction of HAS NOT.

hasp (hasp, häsp) *n.* A fastening passing over a staple and secured as by a padlock. See synonyms under LOCK. —*v.t.* To shut or fasten with or as with a hasp. [OE *hæpse*]

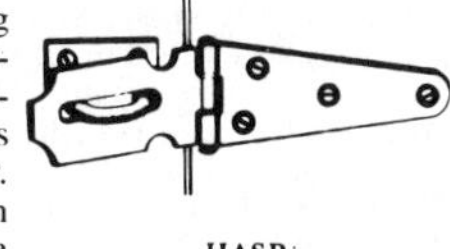
HASP

Has·sam (has′əm), **Childe,** 1859–1935, U.S. painter and etcher.

Has·selt (häs′əlt) The capital of Limburg province, Belgium.

has·sle (has′əl) *Slang n.* An argument; squabble. —*v.i.* **·sled, ·sling** To argue. Also **has′sel.** [? <HAGGLE + TUSSLE]

has·sock (has′ək) *n.* 1 An upholstered footstool. 2 A rank tuft of coarse or boggy grass. 3 *Scot.* A shock of hair. [OE *hassuc* coarse grass <Celtic]

hast (hast) Have: archaic or poetic second person singular, present tense,of HAVE: used with *thou.*

has·tate (has′tāt) *adj. Bot.* Triangular or halberd-shaped, with the base diverging on each side into an acute lobe: said of plant leaves. Also **has′tat·ed.** [<L *hasta* spear]

haste (hāst) *n.* 1 Celerity of movement or action; speed; dispatch. 2 Necessity for speed; urgency. 3 Hurry; precipitancy; unpremeditated or impulsive action. —*v.t. & v.i.* **hast·ed, hast·ing** *Poetic* To hasten. [<OF <Gmc.]

hast·en (hā′sən) *v.t.* To cause to hurry or move quickly; expedite. —*v.i.* To move with speed or haste; be quick; hurry. See synonyms under FLY, PUSH, QUICKEN. —**hast′en·er** *n.*

Has·tings (hās′tingz) A county borough on the coast of SE Sussex, England; scene of **Battle of Hastings,** 1066, fought at Senlac Hill, where William of Normandy defeated Harold II of England.

Has·tings (hās′tingz), **Warren,** 1732–1818, first British governor general of India.

hast·y (hās′tē) *adj.* **hast·i·er, hast·i·est** 1 Acting with, or done with haste. 2 Acting or done without due consideration; rash. 3 Quick-tempered; impetuous; irascible. 4 *Obs.* Eager; in a hurry. See synonyms under IMPETUOUS, SWIFT. —**hast′i·ly** *adv.* —**hast′i·ness** *n.*

hasty pudding 1 Pudding made of meal, seasoning, and boiling water or milk. 2 *U.S.* Cornmeal mush.

hat (hat) *n.* 1 A covering for the head, generally with a crown and brim; also, any piece of millinery worn for a hat. 2 A cardinal's red hat; hence, the rank or dignity of a cardinal. —**to pass the hat** To take up a collection. —**to talk through one's hat** *Colloq.* To talk nonsense; also, to bluff. —**under one's hat** *Colloq.* Secret; private: Keep it *under your hat.* [OE *hæt.* Akin to HOOD.]

Hat may appear as a combining form in hyphemes or solidemes, or as the first element in two-word phrases; as in:

hat brim	**hatmaking**	**hat–shaped**
hat brush	**hat peg**	**hat shop**
hatful	**hatpin**	**hat–sizing**
hatless	**hatrack**	**hat–tipping**
hatmaker	**hatrail**	**hat–wearing**

hat·band (hat′band′) *n.* A narrow ribbon or other band of silk or cloth surrounding a hat just above the brim.

hat·box (hat′boks′) *n.* A case, often of leather, for a hat; also, a small compartment in a trunk for a hat.

hatch[1] (hach) *n.* 1 *Naut.* **a** An opening in the deck of a vessel affording passage to the hold, as for cargo, etc.: also called *hatchway.* **b** The cover over a hatch. 2 Any similar opening in the floor or roof of a warehouse or other building, or the cover or grating for such an opening. 3 A door or gate with an opening above; a divided door; wicket. 4 A sluice gate. [OE *hæcc* grating]

hatch[2] (hach) *v.t.* 1 To bring forth (young) from the egg by incubation. 2 To bring forth young from (the egg). 3 To devise, as a plan; contrive secretly, as a plot. —*v.i.* 4 To emerge from the egg. 5 To produce young. —*n.* 1 The act of hatching. 2 The brood hatched at one time. 3 The result or outcome of any plan. [ME *hacchen;* origin uncertain]

hatch[3] (hach) *v.t.* To mark with hatchings. —*n.* A shade line in drawing or engraving. [< OF *hacher* chop <*hache* an ax <Gmc.]

hatch·back (hach′bak′) *n.* An automobile having a hatch or door at the back of the sloping roof.

hatch·el (hach′əl) *n.* An implement for cleaning flax or hemp, consisting of a set of teeth fastened in a board: also *hackle.* —*v.t.* **hatch·eled** or **·elled, hatch·el·ing** or **·el·ling** 1 To comb or clean with a hatchel, as flax or hemp: also *hackle.* 2 *Rare* To irritate; heckle. [ME *hechele*] —**hatch′el·er, hatch′el·ler** *n.*

hatch·er (hach′ər) *n.* **1** A bird that incubates; also, an incubator. **2** One who hatches or contrives.

hatch·er·y (hach′ər·ē) *n.* *pl.* **·er·ies** A place where eggs are hatched; especially, a place for producing poultry on a large scale, or a place for hatching fish to restock streams.

hatch·et (hach′it) *n.* A small short-handled ax, for use with one hand. **—to bury the hatchet** To cease from hostilities; forget injuries; make peace. [<F *hachette,* dim. of *hache* an ax <Gmc.]

hatch·et·face (hach′it·fās′) *n.* A thin sharp-featured face. **—hatch′et·faced′** *adj.*

hatch·ing (hach′ing) *n.* In drawing or engraving, the marking with fine parallel lines for shading; also, the result of such lines or shading.

hatch·ment (hach′mənt) *n.* *Her.* The armorial bearings of a deceased person, so blazoned as to indicate the rank, sex, etc.: usually in a lozenge-shaped panel, as over a tomb. [Alter. of ACHIEVEMENT]

HATCHETS
a. Broad.
b. Lathing.
c. Half.
d. Claw.

hatch·way (hach′wā′) See HATCH[1].

hate (hāt) *v.* **hat·ed, hat·ing** *v.t.* **1** To regard with extreme aversion; have great dislike for; detest. **2** To be unwilling; dislike: with a clause or an infinitive as object: I *hate* doing that. —*v.i.* **3** To feel hatred. See synonyms under ABHOR. —*n.* **1** Intense aversion; animosity; malignity. **2** A person or thing detested. See synonyms under HATRED. [OE *hatian*] **—hat′a·ble** *adj.* **—hat′er** *n.*

hate·ful (hāt′fəl) *adj.* **1** Exciting strong aversion; odious. **2** Feeling or manifesting hatred. **—hate′ful·ly** *adv.* **—hate′ful·ness** *n.*

hath (hath) Has: archaic or poetic third person singular, present tense, of HAVE.

Hath·a·way (hath′ə·wā), **Anne,** 1557?–1623, wife of Shakespeare.

Ha·thor (hä′thôr) The Egyptian goddess of love and joy: identified with the Greek *Aphrodite*: represented as having a cow's head.

Ha·thor·ic (hə·thôr′ik, -thor′-) *adj.* *Archit.* Denoting columns with sculptures on the capitals representing the head of Hathor.

ha·tred (hā′trid) *n.* Bitter dislike or aversion; antipathy; animosity; enmity.

Synonyms: abhorrence, anger, animosity, antipathy, aversion, detestation, dislike, enmity, grudge, hate, hostility, malevolence, malice, malignity, odium, rancor, repugnance, resentment, revenge, spite. *Repugnance* applies to that which one feels when summoned or impelled to do or to endure something from which he instinctively draws back. *Aversion* is the turning away of the mind or feelings from some person or thing, or from some course of action, etc. *Hate,* or *hatred,* as applied to persons, is intense and continued *aversion,* usually with disposition to injure; *anger* is sudden and brief, *hatred* is lingering and enduring. As applied to things, *hatred* is intense *aversion,* with desire to destroy or remove; *hatred* of evil is a righteous passion, akin to *abhorrence,* but more vehement. *Malice* involves the active intent to injure; *malignity* is deep, lingering, and venomous, while often impotent to act; *rancor* (akin to *rancid*) is cherished *malignity* that has soured and festered and is virulent and implacable. *Spite* is petty *malice* that delights to inflict stinging pain; *grudge* is deeper than *spite*; it is sinister and bitter; *resentment* always holds itself to be justifiable, but looks less certainly to action than *grudge* or *revenge.* Compare ABOMINATION, ANGER, ANTIPATHY, ENMITY, REVENGE. *Antonyms*: see synonyms for FRIENDSHIP, LOVE.

Ha·tshep·sut (ha·chep′sŏŏt) Queen of Egypt 1501?–1481? B.C.

hat·ter (hat′ər) *n.* **1** One who makes or deals in hats. **2** *Austral.* A person who lives alone, especially in a remote area.

Hat·ter·as (hat′ər·əs), **Cape** A promontory on SE **Hatteras Island,** a narrow barrier beach between the Atlantic and Pamlico Sound off North Carolina.

hat·te·ri·a (ha·tir′ē·ə) *n.* The sphenodon. [Origin uncertain]

hat-tree (hat′trē′) *n.* A frame with hooks or pegs on which to hang hats.

hau·berk (hô′bûrk) *n.* A coat of chain mail. [<OF *hauberc* <OHG *halsberc* neck-protector]

haugh·ty (hô′tē) *adj.* **·ti·er, ·ti·est** **1** Proud and disdainful; arrogant. **2** *Obs.* Lofty; bold. [<OF *haut* high] **—haugh′ti·ly** *adv.* **—haugh′·ti·ness** *n.*

Synonyms: austere, churlish, cold, contemptuous, disdainful, distant, high, insolent, proud, reserved, stately, supercilious, surly, unapproachable, uncivil, unsociable. Compare ABSOLUTE, ARROGANT, IMPERIOUS, PROUD.

haul (hôl) *v.t.* **1** To pull or draw with force; drag. **2** To transport as if by pulling, as in a truck or cart. **3** *Naut.* To shift the course of (a ship), especially so as to sail nearer the wind. —*v.i.* **4** To drag or pull. **5** To shift in direction: said of the wind. **6** To change one's views or course of action. **7** *Naut.* To change course, especially so as to sail nearer the wind. See synonyms under DRAW. **—to haul off** **1** To draw back the arm so as to deliver a blow. **2** *Naut.* To change course so as to move further away from an object. **—to haul up** **1** To come to a stop. **2** *Naut.* To sail nearer the wind. —*n.* **1** A pulling with force. **2** That which is obtained by hauling. **3** The drawing of a fish net. **4** The amount of fish caught in a single drawing of a net. **5** The distance over which anything is hauled. ◆ Homophone: *hall.* [<OF *haler* <Gmc.]

haul·age (hô′lij) *n.* **1** The act, process, or operation of hauling. **2** A charge for hauling. **3** The charge made by a railroad company for the use of a line or track.

haul·er (hô′lər) *n.* **1** One who or that which hauls; specifically a carter: also *Brit.* **haul·ier** (hôl′yər). **2** A fish-hauling apparatus.

haulm (hôm) *n.* **1** The stalks or stems of any of the grains, or of hops, beans, etc. **2** Any plant stem. Also spelled *halm.* [OE *healm*] **—haulm′y** *adj.*

haul·yard (hôl′yərd) See HALYARD.

haun (hôn) *n.* *Scot.* A hand.

haunch (hônch, hänch) *n.* **1** The fleshy part of the hip and buttock; the hip or a hindquarter: a *haunch* of venison. **2** *Archit.* The part of an arch on either side of its crown: also spelled *hanch.* [<OF *hanche* <Gmc.] **—haunched** *adj.*

haunch bone The innominate bone.

haunt (hônt, hänt) *v.t.* **1** To visit frequently or customarily in disembodied form; appear to as a ghost or other spirit. **2** To recur persistently to the mind or memory of: The face *haunts* me. **3** To visit often; frequent, as a saloon. —*v.i.* **4** To make ghostly appearances. **5** *Rare* To be present often. —*n.* **1** A place often visited; specifically, a place where wild animals come habitually to feed. **2** *Dial.* A ghost. [<OF *hanter*]

haunt·ed (hôn′tid, hän′-) *adj.* Frequently visited or resorted to, especially by ghosts or apparitions.

haunt·ing (hôn′ting, hän′-) *adj.* Difficult to forget; frequently occurring to memory: a *haunting* melody. **—haunt′ing·ly** *adv.*

Haupt·mann (houpt′män), **Gerhart,** 1862–1946, German poet and dramatist.

Hau·ra·ki Gulf (hou·rä′kē, -rak′ē) An inlet of the South Pacific in northern North Island, New Zealand.

Hau·sa (hou′sə) *n.* **1** A Negroid people occupying a tract of central Sudan north of the confluence of the Niger and Benue rivers. **2** The language of these people, bearing some resemblance to the Sudanic family, and much used as a medium of commerce. Also **Haus′sa.**

hause (hôs) *n.* *Scot.* The throat; halse.

hau·sen (hô′zən, *Ger.* hou′zən) *n.* The Russian sturgeon (genus *Acipenser*). [<G]

Haus·frau (hous′frou′) *n.* *German* Housewife.

Haus·ho·fer (hous′hō·fər), **Karl,** 1869–1946, German general and exponent of geopolitics.

haus·mann·ite (hous′mən·īt) *n.* A submetallic brownish-black manganese oxide, Mn_3O_4, crystallizing in the tetragonal system. [after J. F. L. *Hausmann,* 1782–1859, German metallurgist]

Hauss·mann (ōs·män′), **Baron Georges,** 1809–1891, French administrator; redesigned Paris streets and public buildings.

haus·tel·lum (hôs·tel′əm) *n.* *pl.* **·tel·la** (-tel′ə) *Zool.* The proboscis or sucking organ of certain insects and crustaceans. [<NL, dim of L *haustrum* water-drawing machine <*haurire* draw]

haus·to·ri·um (hôs·tôr′ē·əm, -tō′rē-) *n.* *pl.* **·to·ri·a** (-tôr′ē·ə, -tō′rē·ə) *Bot.* A root or sucker found in certain fungi and parasitic plants by which they absorb nutriment without damage to the host. [<NL <L *haustor* drainer < *haurire* draw]

haut·boy (hō′boi, ō′-) *n.* A woodwind instrument; oboe. [<F *hautbois* <*haut* high (in tone) + *bois* wood]

haute cou·ture (ōt kōō·tür′) *French* High fashion, represented especially by the leading designers of stylish apparel.

haute cui·sine (ōt kwē·zēn′) *French* An elaborate or elegant cuisine.

Haute-Ga·ronne (ōt·gȧ·rôn′) A department in SW France; 2,457 square miles; capital, Toulouse.

Haute-Marne (ōt·mȧrn′) A department in NE France; 2,416 square miles; capital, Chaumont.

Haute-Saône (ōt·sōn′) A department in E France; 2,074 square miles; capital, Vesoul.

Haute-Sa·voie (ōt·sȧ·vwȧ′) A department in E France; 1,774 square miles; capital, Annecy.

hau·teur (hō·tûr′, *Fr.* ō·tœr′) *n.* Haughty manner or spirit; haughtiness. [<F]

Haute-Vol·ta (ōt·vôl·tȧ′) The French name for UPPER VOLTA.

haut monde (ō môṅd′) *French* The upper class; high society.

Haut-Rhin (ō·raṅ′) A department of eastern France; 1,354 square miles; capital, Colmar.

Ha·van·a (hə·van′ə) **1** A province of western Cuba; 3,174 square miles. **2** Its capital, the largest port of the West Indies and capital of Cuba: Spanish *La Habana.* **—Hav·a·nese** (hav′ə·nēz′, -nēs′) *adj.* & *n.*

Ha·vas (ȧ·vȧ′) A French news agency.

have (hav) *v.t.* Present indicative: I, you, we, they **have** (*Archaic* **thou hast**), he, she, it **has** (*Archaic* **hath**); past indicative **had** (*Archaic* **thou hadst**); present subjunctive **have**; past subjunctive **had**; *pp.* **had**; *ppr.* **hav·ing** **1** To hold as a possession; own. **2** To possess as a characteristic, attribute, etc.: He *has* only one leg; The very walls *have* ears. **3** To receive; get: I *had* a letter this morning. **4** To hold in the mind; entertain, as an opinion or a doubt. **5** To manifest or exercise: *Have* patience! **6** To experience; undergo: to *have* an operation. **7** To be affected with: to *have* a cold. **8** To carry on; engage in: to *have* a party. **9** To cause to be: to *have* someone shot; *Have* him leave. **10** To allow or permit; tolerate: I will *have* no interference. **11** To possess a certain relation to: to *have* the wind at one's back. **12** To be in relationship to or association with: to *have* three children. **13** To bring forth or beget (young): to *have* a baby. **14** To maintain or declare: so rumor *has* it. **15** *Colloq.* To gain or possess an advantage over; baffle: He *had* me there. **16** *Colloq.* To trick; cheat: I've been *had!* **17** To engage in sexual intercourse with. —*auxiliary* As an auxiliary *have* is used: **a** With past participles to form perfect tenses expressing completed action: often with the addition of other auxiliary verbs: I *have* gone; I *have* been given; I shall *have* gone. **b** With the infinitive to express obligation or compulsion: I *have* to go. **—to have at** To attack. **—to have done** To stop; desist. **—to have it in for** *Colloq.* To hold a grudge against. **—to have it out** To continue a fight or discussion to a final settlement. **—to have on** To be wearing; be clothed in. ◆ *Have* is used in the form *had* (early *hadde,* past subjunctive) in certain phrases of preference: you *had better* hurry = You would be wiser to hurry; I *had rather* (or *liefer*) die = I would prefer to die. —*n.* A person or country possessing relatively much wealth. [OE *habban*]

Synonyms: hold, occupy, own, possess. *Have* is applied to whatever belongs to or is connected with one; a man may be said to *have* what is his own, what he has borrowed, what has been entrusted to him, or what he has stolen. To *possess* a thing is to *have* the ownership with control and enjoyment of it. To *hold* is to *have* in one's hand, or securely in one's control; a man *holds* his friend's coat for a moment, or he *holds* a struggling horse; he *holds* a promissory note, or *holds* an office.

To *own* is to *have* the right of property in; to *possess* is to *have* that right in actual exercise; to *occupy* is to *have* possession and use with or without ownership. A man *occupies* his own house or a room in a hotel; he may *own* a farm of which he is not in possession because a tenant *occupies* it and is determined to *hold* it. To be in possession differs from *possess* in that to *possess* denotes both right and fact, while to be in possession denotes simply the fact with no affirmation as to the right. To *have* reason is to be endowed with the faculty; to be in possession of one's reason denotes that the faculty is in actual present exercise.

Ha·vel (hä′fəl) A river in NE East Germany, flowing 215 miles south to the Elbe.

have·lock (hav′lok) *n.* A cover for a military cap, made with a long rear flap, as a protection from the sun. [after Sir Henry *Havelock,* 1795–1857, British general]

ha·ven (hā′vən) *n.* **1** A place of anchorage for ships; a harbor; port. **2** A refuge; shelter. See synonyms under SHELTER. —*v.t.* To shelter (a vessel, etc.) in or as in a haven. [OE *hæfen*]

have–not (hav′not′) *n.* A person or country relatively lacking in wealth: the haves and *have-nots.*

have·n't (hav′ənt) Contraction of HAVE NOT.

hav·er[1] (hav′ər, häv′-, av′-, äv′-) *n. Scot.* Oats.

ha·ver[2] (hā′vər) *v.i. Scot.* To babble.

ha·ver·el (hā′vər·əl, ā′-) *adj.* Half–witted; silly. Also **hav·rel** (hav′rəl).

hav·er·meal (hav′ər·mēl′, häv′-, av′-, äv′) *n. Scot.* Oatmeal.

ha·vers (hā′vərz) *n. Scot.* Foolish talk.

hav·er·sack (hav′ər·sak) *n.* A bag, slung from the shoulder, for a soldier's rations. [<F *havresac* <G *habersack* oat sack]

Ha·ver·sian canals (hə·vûr′shən) *Anat.* The numerous channels for capillary blood vessels in bone substance. [after Clopton *Havers,* 1650–1702, English anatomist]

hav·er·sine (hav′ər·sīn) *n. Trig.* Half of a versed sine.

haves and have–nots The rich and the poor; of nations, those possessing and those lacking the raw materials for autarchy.

hav·ing (hav′ing) *n. Scot.* Good behavior or breeding; good manners.

hav·iour (hāv′yər) *n. Obs.* Behavior. Also **hav′·ior.**

hav·oc (hav′ək) *n.* **1** General carnage or destruction; ruin. **2** Tumultuous disorder, confusion, or uproar. See synonyms under MASSACRE —**to cry havoc** To give a signal for pillage and destruction. —*v.t.* **hav·ocked, hav·ock·ing** *Rare* To lay waste; destroy. [<OF *havot* plunder<Gmc.]

Ha·vre (hä′vər, -vrə; *Fr.* äv′r′), **Le** A port of NW France on the English Channel. Founded as **Ha–vre–de–Grâce** (äv′r′·də·gräs′).

haw[1] (hô) *interj.* A meaningless utterance occurring in hesitating or drawling speech. —*v.i.* To hesitate in speaking.

haw[2] (hô) *n.* The fruit of the hawthorn. [OE *haga*]

haw[3] (hô) *n.* **1** The nictitating membrane or third eyelid of certain animals. **2** *pl.* A disease of this membrane. [Origin uncertain]

haw[4] (hô) *n. & interj.* An order to turn to the left or near side in driving, usually to a yoked team without reins: opposed to *gee.* —*v.t. & v.i.* To turn to the left. [Origin uncertain]

Ha·wai·i (hə·wä′ē, hə·wī′yə) **1** A State of the United States comprising the Hawaiian Islands; 6,435 square miles; capital, Honolulu; entered the Union Aug. 21, 1959: nickname, *Aloha State*: Abbr. HI **2** The largest of the Hawaiian Islands; 4,030 square miles; chief town, Hilo.

Ha·wai·ian (hə·wī′yən) *adj.* Of or pertaining to Hawaii or its inhabitants. —*n.* **1** A native or naturalized inhabitant of Hawaii. **2** The Polynesian language of the aboriginal inhabitants of Hawaii.

Hawaiian Islands A group of islands in the North Pacific constituting the State of Hawaii: formerly *Sandwich Islands.*

Hawaii National Park Two volcanic areas containing the active volcanoes Mauna Loa and Kilauea on the island of Hawaii and the extinct crater of Haleakala on Maui Island; 276 square miles; established 1916.

Ha·wash (hä′wäsh) A former name for AWASH.

haw·finch (hô′finch′) *n.* The European grosbeak (genus *Coccothraustes*), having a very large beak.

haw–haw[1] (hô′hô′) *n.* A loud coarse laugh.

haw–haw[2] (hô′hô′) See HA-HA.

Haw–Haw, (hô′hô′), Lord Sobriquet of William Joyce, 1906–46, born in the United States, propagandist for Germany in World War II, executed as a British traitor.

hawk[1] (hôk) *n.* **1** A diurnal bird of prey (family *Accipitridae*) with relatively short rounded wings, a hooked beak, and strong claws; including the North American species, Cooper's hawk *(Accipiter cooperi)* and the sharp–shinned hawk *(A. velox).* **2** The goshawk (genus *Astur*) and the red–tailed hawk (genus *Buteo*). **3** Any falconine bird except a vulture or an eagle, as a falcon, buzzard, or kite. **4** One who seeks to resolve a war primarily by means of military force: opposed to *dove*[1] (def. 4). —*v.i.* **1** To hunt game with hawks; practice falconry. **2** To fly in search of prey; soar, as a hawk. [OE *hafoc, hafuc*]

AMERICAN ROUGH–LEGGED HAWK
(About 20 to 23 inches)

hawk[2] (hôk) *v.t. & v.i.* To cry (goods) for sale in the streets or in public places; peddle. [Back formation <HAWKER[2]]

hawk[3] (hôk) *v.t.* To cough up (phlegm). —*v.i.* To clear the throat with a coughing sound. —*n.* A forcible effort to raise phlegm from the throat; also, the sound of this. [Imit.]

hawk[4] (hôk) *n.* A small square board with a handle underneath, used to hold plaster or mortar. [Origin uncertain]

hawk·bill (hôk′bil′) *n.* A small tropical marine turtle *(Eretmochelys imbricata)* which furnishes the best grade of tortoise shell used in commerce: also **hawk's–bill.**

hawk·er[1] (hô′kər) *n.* One who hunts with hawks; a falconer.

hawk·er[2] (hô′kər) *n.* A street peddler; one who cries goods for sale in the streets. [< MLG *hoker* a peddler, huckster]

Hawk·eye (hôk′ī′) *n.* A native or inhabitant of Iowa.

Hawk·eye (hôk′ī′) In Cooper's *Last of the Mohicans,* a sobriquet of Leatherstocking or Natty Bumppo.

hawk·eyed (hôk′īd′) *adj.* Having keen, piercing eyes; keen–sighted.

Hawkeye State Nickname of IOWA.

hawk·ing (hô′king) *n.* The sport of hunting small game with hawks or falcons; falconry.

Haw·kins (hô′kinz), **Sir John,** 1532–1595, English admiral; aided defeat of Spanish Armada. Also **Haw′kyns.** —**Sir Anthony Hope,** 1863–1933, English novelist; wrote under the name *Anthony Hope.*

hawk·ish (hôk′ish) *adj.* Disposed to rely on military force to resolve a war: opposed to *dovish.*

hawk moth A large stout–bodied moth (family *Sphingidae*) which flies by twilight and sucks the nectar from flowers: also called *humming-bird moth.*

hawk's–beard (hôks′bird′) *n.* Any species of a genus *(Crepis)* of European herbs: so called from the long bristly pappus.

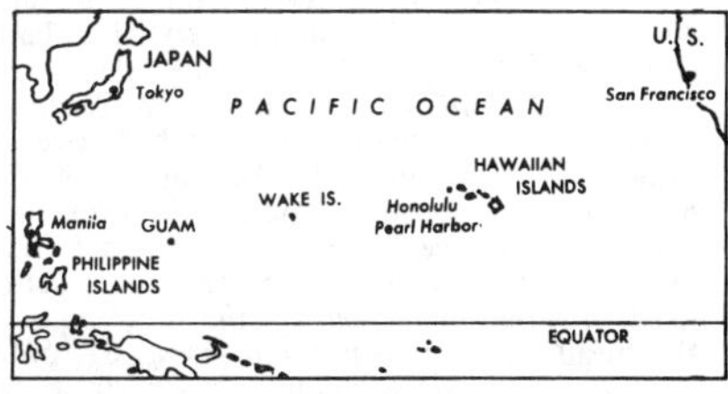

hawks·beak (hôks′bēk) *n. Archit.* A compound molding, often ornamented with a Doric leaf pattern.

hawk's–bill turtle (hôks′bil′) See HAWKBILL.

hawk's–eye (hôks′ī′) *n.* **1** The American golden plover *(Pluvialis dominica).* **2** The tiger–eye.

hawk·shaw (hôk′shô) *n. Colloq.* A detective: a humorous term. [after a character in *The Ticket of Leave Man* by Tom Taylor, 1817–1880, English novelist]

hawk·weed (hôk′wēd′) *n.* Any species of a genus *(Hieracium)* of weedy perennial herbs of the composite family having small yellow or orange flowers.

Ha·worth (hā′wûrth), **Sir Walter Norman,** 1883–1950, English chemist.

hawse (hôz) *n. Naut.* **1** The part of a vessel's bow having openings, usually steel–lined, for the passage of cables. **2** A hawsehole. **3** The situation of the cables that lead from a moored vessel to her anchors. **4** The horizontal distance between the vessel and her anchors. [<ON *hals* neck, bow of a ship]

hawse·hole (hôz′hōl′) *n. Naut.* A hole in the bow of a vessel for the passage of a cable or hawser.

haw·ser (hô′zər) *n. Naut.* A large rope or cable used in mooring, towing, etc. [<OF *haucier* lift]

haw·ser–laid (hô′zər·lād′) *adj.* Made of three small ropes laid up into one; cable–laid.

haw·thorn (hô′thôrn) *n.* A thorny, spring–flowering, ornamental shrub or small tree of the rose family (genus *Crataegus*) with white or pink flowers and small pome fruits called *haws.* The American **downy hawthorn** is the State flower of Missouri. [OE *haguthorn*]

Haw·thorne (hô′thôrn), **Nathaniel,** 1804–1864, U.S. novelist.

hay[1] (hā) *n.* Grass, clover, or the like, cut and dried for fodder. —**to hit the hay** *U.S. Slang* To go to bed. —**to make hay while the sun shines** To take full advantage of an opportunity. —*v.t.* **1** To make, as clover, into hay. **2** To feed with hay. **3** To plant (land) with hay. —*v.i.* **4** To make hay. [OE *hēg*]

hay[2] (hā) *n. Obs.* A net or snare, especially a net enclosing the burrow, hole, or haunt of an animal. [<AF *haie;* ult. origin uncertain]

hay[3] (hā) *n. Obs.* A hedge, palisade, or fence; also, a place enclosed by such. [OE *hege*]

hay[4] (hā) *n.* A country dance with a winding in–and–out movement. [<MF *haye*]

Hay (hā), **John,** 1838–1905, U.S. statesman, diplomat, author, and poet.

hay·cock (hā′kok′) *n.* A dome–shaped pile of hay in the field

Hay·dn (hīd′n), **Franz Joseph,** 1732–1809, Austrian composer.

Hayes (hāz), **Helen,** born 1900, U.S. actress: married name Mrs. Charles MacArthur.
—**Roland,** born 1887, U.S. Negro tenor.
—**Rutherford Birchard,** 1822–93, president of the United States 1877–81.

hay fever *Pathol.* An annually recurring catarrhal affection of the mucous membranes of the eyes and air passages, caused chiefly by the pollen of certain plants.

hay foot One of the alternate marching steps in military drill, as in the phrase *hayfoot, straw foot*: from the alleged use of hay and straw to help country recruits tell the difference between right and left.

hay·fork (hā′fôrk′) *n.* **1** A long–handled fork for turning or pitching hay by hand. **2** A large power–driven fork for moving hay.

hay·ing (hā′ing) *n.* The act or process of cutting, curing, and storing hay.

hay·loft (hā′lôft′, -loft′) *n.* A loft in a barn or stable for storing hay.

hay·mak·er (hā′mā′kər) *n.* **1** One who makes hay, especially, one who spreads it to dry. **2** A haytedder. **3** A rustic dance. **4** *Colloq.* A wide, swinging blow of the fist; in boxing, a knockout punch.

Hay·mar·ket (hā′mär′kit) **1** A street in London between Piccadilly Circus and Pall Mall; site of many theaters. **2** A square in Chicago; site of a riot for better labor conditions, 1886.

hay·mow (hā′mou′) *n.* **1** A mass of hay; especially, one stored in a loft or bay. **2** A hayloft.

Haynes (hānz), **Elwood,** 1857–1925, U.S. inventor; pioneer automobile designer.

hay·rack (hā′rak′) *n.* **1** A broad, long, open frame or rack mounted on wheels or placed on a wagon body, in which hay, straw, etc., are hauled. 2 A framework for holding hay to feed cattle, horses, etc.

hay ride A pleasure ride in a wagon or hayrack half full of hay or straw.

Hays (hāz), **Will H.,** 1879–1954, U.S. politician; first president of the Motion Picture Producers and Distributors of America.

hay seed Grass seed; also, the mingled seeds, chaff, etc., that fall from hay, as on a barn floor.

hay·seed (hā′sēd′) *n. U.S. Slang* A country person; a rustic.

hay·stack (hā′stak′) *n.* A conical pile of hay, stacked in the open air, and sometimes covered. Also **hay′rick′.**

hay·ted·der (hā′ted′ər) *n.* One who or that which teds hay; especially, a wheeled farm implement for stirring and spreading newly cut hay.

Hay·ti·an (hā′tē·ən, -shən) See HAITIAN.

hay·ward (hā′wôrd′, -wərd) *n. Obs.* An officer of a parish, township, or manor charged with inspecting fences and enclosures for cattle or impounding strays. [<HAY[3] + WARD]

hay·wire (hā′wīr′) *n.* Wire for baling hay. *—adj. U.S. Slang* 1 Confused; mixed up; scrambled. 2 Crazy: to go *haywire.* [Slang sense < *haywire outfit,* loggers' term for a camp with poor or broken equipment which had to be mended with haywire]

Ha·za (hä′zä), **El** See HASA, EL.

haz·ard (haz′ərd) *n.* 1 Exposure to the chance of loss or injury; risk; peril. 2 A chance or fortuitous event or consequence, as the result of dice; a chance. 3 That which is hazarded, risked, or staked; the stake in gambling. 4 A gambling game played with a dice box and two dice by any number of players. 5 An obstacle on a golf course, such as a bunker, water (except casual water), sand trap, path, etc. 6 In English billiards, the pocketing of a ball, or the stroke that puts a ball into a pocket. When the object ball is forced into a pocket the stroke is called a **winning hazard;** when the striker's ball falls into a pocket after contact with the object ball it is a **losing hazard.** 7 In court tennis, a stroke in which the server drives the ball, either direct from the racket or on the first bound, into the grille or the winning gallery. **—moral hazard** The element of personal character of a property-owner as it affects the willingness of an insurance company to insure his property. *—v.t.* 1 To put to hazard; imperil. 2 To venture; to take the risk involved in; risk. [<OF *hasard* <Arabic *al-zahr* the die]

Synonyms (noun): accident, casualty, chance, contingency, danger, fortuity, jeopardy, peril, risk, venture. *Hazard* is the incurring of the possibility of loss or harm for the possibility of gain; *danger* may have no compensating alternative. In *hazard* the possibilities of gain or loss are nearly balanced; in *risk* the possibility of loss is the chief thought; in *chance* and *venture* the hope of good predominates; we speak of a merchant's *venture,* but of an insurance company's *risk;* one may be driven by circumstances to run a *risk;* he freely seeks a *venture;* we speak of the *chance* of winning, the *hazard* or *risk* of losing. A *contingency* is simply an indeterminable future event, which may or may not be attended with *danger* or *risk.* See ACCIDENT, DANGER. *Antonyms*: assurance, certainty, necessity, plan, protection, safeguard, safety, security, surety.

haz·ard·ous (haz′ər·dəs) *adj.* 1 Exposed to, exposing to, or involving danger of risk or loss. 2 Dependent on chance; fortuitous. See synonyms under PRECARIOUS. **—haz′ard·ous·ly** *adv.* **—haz′ard·ous·ness** *n.*

haze[1] (hāz) *n.* 1 Very fine suspended particles in the air, often with little or no moisture. 2 Dimness, as of perception or knowledge. [? Back formation <HAZY]

haze[2] (hāz) *v.t.* **hazed, haz·ing** 1 *U.S.* To subject (new students) to pranks and humiliating horseplay. 2 *Naut.* To punish or harass by the imposition of heavy or disagreeable tasks. [<OF *haser* irritate] **—haz′er** *n.*

ha·zel (hā′zəl) *n.* 1 A bushy shrub or small tree of the birch family (genus *Corylus*) yielding a hard-shelled edible nut enclosed in a leafy involucre. 2 The wood or nut of the hazel. 3 The color of the hazelnut shell, a medium yellowish-brown. *—adj.* 1 Made of hazel wood. 2 Of the color of hazel. [OE *hæsel*] **—ha′zel·ly** *adj.*

Ha·zel (hā′zəl) A feminine personal name. [<Hebrew, God sees]

ha·zel·nut (hā′zəl·nut′) *n.* 1 The nut of the hazel: also called *filbert.* 2 The hazel shrub or tree.

haz·ing (hā′zing) *n.* 1 Imposition of heavy or disagreeable tasks. 2 *U.S.* The subjection (of new students or initiates) to pranks and humiliating ordeals. 3 A thorough beating.

Haz·litt (haz′lit), **William,** 1778–1830, English essayist.

haz·y (hā′zē) *adj.* **haz·i·er, haz·i·est** 1 Obscured with haze. 2 Figuratively, lacking clearness; dim; obscure. See synonyms under THICK. [Cf. OE *hasu* gray] **—haz′i·ly** *adv.* **—haz′i·ness** *n.*

haz·zan (khä·zän′, khä′zən) *n.* A cantor of a synagog: also spelled *chazan, khazen.* [<Hebrew *hazzan* prefect]

H-beam (āch′bēm′) *n.* A structural member having a cross-section resembling an H: also called *H-girder.*

H-bomb (āch′bom′) *n.* The hydrogen bomb.

he[1] (hē) *pron.* 1 The male person or being previously mentioned or understood, in the nominative case. 2 Anyone; any man: *He* who hesitates is lost. *—n.* A male, as a man, boy, bull, etc. [OE]

he[2] (hā) *n.* The fifth Hebrew letter. See ALPHABET.

He *Chem.* Helium (symbol He).

he- *combining form* Male; masculine: in hyphenated compounds: *he-goat.* [<HE]

head (hed) *n.* 1 The part of the body of an animal that contains the brain and the organs of special sense, the ears, eyes, mouth, and nose. ◆ Collateral adjective: *cephalic.* 2 Something having the shape or position of a head, or being in some way analogous to a head, as a barrel top. 3 The length of the head: taller by a *head.* 4 Mind; intelligence: He used his *head.* 5 Mental aptitude: a good *head* for mathematics. 6 Mental poise; self-possession: He kept his *head.* 7 A person: crowned *heads;* learned *heads.* 8 An individual or single entity, considered as a unit of counting: a price of two dollars a *head.* In this sense *head* may appear as a plural: six *head* of cattle. 9 The end regarded as the uppermost or higher part of something: the *head* of a valley, bed, table, etc. 10 The source, as of a river. 11 The fore or forward part of anything: the *head* of a column of troops. 12 The bow of a ship. 13 A headland; cape: chiefly in place names: Beachy *Head.* 14 A leader; chief; director. 15 The position or rank of a leader: the *head* of one's profession. 16 The top or summit of something: the *head* of the stairs; the *head* of a page. 17 The heading of a book, composition, chapter, etc. 18 The headlines of a single newspaper item. 19 A division of a subject, discourse, composition, or the like: He had little to say on that *head.* 20 Culmination: climax: to come to a *head.* 21 The maturated part of a boil or abscess before breaking. 22 Advance in the face of opposition: to make *head* against the storm. 23 A compact cluster of leaves or leaf stalks, as a *head* of cabbage, lettuce, or celery. 24 A rounded, compact bud, as a *head* of cauliflower. 25 A capitulum. 26 A cluster of cereal grain at the top of a stem. 27 The foam that rises to the surface of a fermenting liquid, as of beer or ale. 28 The measure of stored-up force or capacity, as of steam. 29 The height of a column or body of fluid above a certain point, considered as causing pressure: a *head* of water driving a turbine. 30 The striking or pounding part of a hammer, ax, golf club, etc. 31 The obverse of a coin. 32 *Mining* A heading. 33 *Naut.* A toilet. 34 The membrane stretched over a drum or tambourine. 35 The part of a violin, lute, etc., above the neck. 36 *Gram.* The part of an endocentric construction that functions in the same manner as the construction itself. In *the man holding the flag, man* is the head: also called *head word.* 37 *Slang* One who uses or is addicted to a drug. See synonyms under CHIEF, MASTER. *—v.t.* 1 To be first or most prominent on: to *head* the list. 2 To be chief or leader of; command. 3 To furnish with a head. 4 To cut off the head or top of, as a person or tree. 5 To turn or direct the course of: to *head* a vessel toward shore. 6 To pass around the head of: to *head* a stream. 7 To excel; beat, as in sports. 8 In soccer, to bunt (the ball) with the head. *—v.i.* 9 To move in a specified direction or toward a specified point. 10 To come to or form a head. 11 To originate; rise: said of rivers and streams. **—to head off** To intercept the course of: We'll *head* him *off* at the pass. **—to head up** *Colloq.* To be the leader or manager of; command. See synonyms under LEAD, PRECEDE. *—adj.* 1 Principal; chief. 2 Situated at the top or front. 3 Bearing against the front: a *head* wind. [OE *hēafod*]

-head *suffix* Condition, state, totality: *godhead.* [ME *-hede*]

head·ache (hed′āk′) *n.* 1 A pain in the head. 2 *Colloq.* A source of vexation or trouble. **—head′a′chy** (-ā′kē) *adj.*

head·band (hed′band′) *n.* 1 A band worn on the head. 2 A decorative terminal cord or roll forming the end of the inner back of a book. 3 A decorative band at the head of a page or chapter in a printed book.

head·board (hed′bôrd′, -bōrd′) *n.* A board placed at or forming the head, as of a bed.

head·cheese (hed′chēz′) *n.* A pressed and jellied cheeselike mass made of small pieces of the head and feet of a hog or calf.

head·dress (hed′dres′) *n.* 1 A covering or ornament for the head. 2 The style in which the hair is arranged; coiffure.

head·ed (hed′id) *adj.* 1 Furnished with a head. 2 Formed or grown into a head, as cabbage. 3 Furnished with a heading.

-headed *combining form* Having a (specified number or kind of) head: clear-*headed.*

head·er (hed′ər) *n.* 1 A person who makes or puts on heads, as in barrelmaking. 2 *Colloq.* A plunge or fall headforemost, as diving. 3 One of various machines or tools for making, attaching, or removing heads; especially, a kind of harvesting machine that cuts the ripe heads off grain in the field. 4 A brick or stone placed with its end toward the face of a wall. 5 In building, a timber resting in trimmers and carrying the ends or heads of the tail beams. 6 A pipe, duct, channel, or conduit which serves as a central distributing point of a fluid flow to auxiliary branches.

head·first (hed′fûrst′) *adv.* With the head first; precipitately. Also **head′fore′most′** (-fôr′mōst′, -məst, -fōr′-).

head gate The upstream gate of a canal lock; a watergate or floodgate of any race or sluice.

head·gear (hed′gir′) *n.* 1 A headdress or the like. 2 That part of the hoisting apparatus at the top of a mine shaft. 3 The parts of the harness that belong about the horse's head. 4 *Naut.* The running rigging of headsails.

head·hunt·ing (hed′hun′ting) *n.* Among certain savage tribes, the custom of decapitating slain enemies and preserving the heads as trophies. **—head′-hunt′er** *n.*

head·ing (hed′ing) *n.* 1 Something located at the head, as a title. 2 *Mining* A driftway in the line of a tunnel; also, any place where work is done in driving a horizontal passage. 3 The action of providing with a head. 4 Boards or other material from which the heads of casks, barrels, etc., are made. 5 A strip along the edge of a piece of lace; also, the part of a ruffle above the gathering line.

head·ker·chief (hed′kûr′chif) *n.* A kerchief for the head.

head·land (hed′lənd *for def. 1;* hed′land′ *for def. 2*) *n.* 1 A cliff projecting into the sea. 2 A strip of unplowed land at the ends of furrows or near a fence.

head·less (hed′lis) *adj.* 1 Without a head; decapitated. 2 Without a leader. 3 Stupid; erratic; brainless.

head·light (hed′līt′) *n.* A powerful light, as at the front of a locomotive, motor vehicle, or street car.

head·line (hed′līn′) *n.* 1 A word or words set in bold type at the head of a newspaper column or news story, indicating or summarizing the content, especially the heading of the main front-page story. 2 A line at the head of a page, containing title, page number, etc. 3 A line inside a hat where the brim joins the crown. 4 A rope attached to an animal's head. 5 *Naut.* A rope used to fasten the bow of a vessel to a pier or shore.

head·lin·er (hed′lī′nər) *n.* The main attraction at a theatrical performance; the actor or performer whose name appears in large letters.

head·lock (hed′lok′) *n.* A wrestling grip in which the head is held between the opponent's arm and body.

head·long (hed′lông′, -long′) *adv.* **1** Headfirst. **2** Without deliberation; rashly; recklessly. **3** With unbridled speed or force. —*adj.* Precipitate; impetuous; rash.

head man 1 A leader or person of authority in a community. **2** A North American Indian chief. **3** A workman in charge of other workers.

head·mas·ter (hed′mas′tər, -mäs′-) *n.* The principal of a school. —**head′mas′ter·ly** *adj.* —**head′mas′ter·ship** *n.*

head·mis·tress (hed′mis′tris) *n. fem.* The female principal of a school. —**head′mis′tress·ship** *n.*

head money 1 Prize money per head for prisoners captured in war, or for the apprehension of outlaws. **2** A per capita tax; a poll tax.

head·most (hed′mōst′) *adj.* Most advanced; foremost.

head-on (hed′on′, -ôn′) *adj.* & *adv.* Front end to front end; a *head-on* collision.

head over heels 1 Somersaulting or tumbling heels over head. **2** Completely: *head over heels* in love. **3** Rashly; impetuously.

head·phone (hed′fōn′) *n.* A device for telephone or radio reception, single or paired, usually attached by a band passing over the head.

head·piece (hed′pēs′) *n.* **1** A piece of armor to protect the head. **2** A decorative design at the top of a printed page. **3** The head; hence, the wits.

head·pin (hed′pin′) *n.* In tenpins, a kingpin.

head·quar·ters (hed′kwôr′tərz) *n. sing.* & *pl.* **1** The quarters or operating base of an officer in command, as of an army unit, police force, etc. **2** Any center of operations.

head·race (hed′rās′) *n.* The channel by which water is led to a water wheel, or to any machinery. [<HEAD + RACE[2]]

head resistance *Aeron.* Parasite drag.

head·rest (hed′rest′) *n.* Any device to support the head.

head·right (hed′rīt′) *n.* **1** The right of ownership to a piece of public land granted by a government to a head of a family settling on it; also, the land so granted. **2** In the State of Texas, a similar grant; also, the land so granted, usually 640 acres. **3** The right of a North American Indian to a share of the tribal property.

head·sail (hed′sāl′, -səl) *n. Naut.* A sail set forward of the foremast, as a jib; also, one set on the foremast.

head·set (hed′set′) *n.* A radio or telephone headphone.

head·ship (hed′ship) *n.* The office of a chief; chief authority.

heads·man (hedz′mən) *n. pl.* **·men** (-mən) A public executioner.

head·spin (hed′spin′) *n.* A wrestling movement used to break away from a half-nelson.

head·spring (hed′spring′) *n.* **1** The fountainhead; source. **2** A gymnastic feat in which the performer springs, without using his hands and using his head as lever, from a supine position to his feet.

head·stall (hed′stôl′) *n.* The part of a bridle that fits over the horse's head.

head·stand (hed′stand′) *n.* The act of holding one's body upside-down in a vertical position, with one's weight resting on one's head and, usually, on one's hands or arms.

head start An advance start; an advantage in time or distance, as in a handicap race.

head·stock (hed′stok′) *n. Mech.* One of various devices supporting the end or head of a part or member, as the live spindle of a lathe.

head·stone (hed′stōn′) *n.* **1** The stone at the head of a grave. **2** The cornerstone or keystone of a structure: also **head stone.**

head·strong (hed′strông′, -strong′) *adj.* **1** Stubbornly bent on having one's own way; obstinate; determined. **2** Involving or proceeding from wilfulness or obstinacy. —**head′strong′ly** *adv.* —**head′strong′ness** *n.*

head waiter An employee, as of a restaurant, who supervises the seating of guests, the serving of food and drink, etc.

head·wa·ters (hed′wô′tərz, -wot′ərz) *n. pl.* The waters at or near the source of any stream, river, or the like: sometimes in the singular.

head·way (hed′wā′) *n.* **1** Forward motion; momentum; progress. **2** The interval of time between consecutive trains, etc. **3** The clear distance under a girder arch, etc.

head wind A wind from ahead, blowing directly opposite to the course of a ship, airplane, etc.

head word 1 A word or expression that introduces or begins, as a chapter. **2** *Gram.* A head (def. 36).

head·work (hed′wûrk′) *n.* Mental labor. —**head′work′er** *n.* —**head′work′ing** *n.*

head·y (hed′ē) *adj.* **head·i·er, head·i·est 1** Headstrong. **2** Tending to affect the head, as liquor. —**head′i·ly** *adv.* —**head′i·ness** *n.*

heal (hēl) *v.t.* **1** To restore to health or soundness; make healthy again; cure. **2** To bring about the remedy or cure of, as a wound or disease. **3** To remedy, repair, or counteract, as a quarrel, breach, etc. **4** To free from sin, grief, worry, etc.; purify: to *heal* the spirit. —*v.i.* **5** To become well or sound. **6** To perform a cure or cures. See synonyms under RECOVER. ◆Homophone: *heel.* [OE *halan*] —**heal′a·ble** *adj.* —**heal′ing** *adj.* & *n.* —**heal′ing·ly** *adv.*

heal-all (hēl′ôl′) *n.* **1** A catholicon; remedy for all diseases. **2** The allheal.

heald (held) *n.* In weaving, a device for holding and guiding the heddles in a loom. [OE *hefeld*]

heal·er (hē′lər) *n.* **1** Someone or something that heals. **2** One who undertakes to heal through prayer and faith.

heal·some (hēl′səm) *adj. Scot.* Wholesome. —**heal′some·ness** *n.*

health (helth) *n.* **1** Soundness of any living organism. **2** General condition of body or mind, as to vigor and soundness. **3** A toast wishing health. —*adj.* **1** Pertaining to, connected with, or engaged in public-health work: *health* education, *health* inspector. **2** Conducive to good health: a *health* food. [OE *hœlth* <*hāl* whole]

Health, Education, and Welfare, Department of An executive department of the U.S. government (established in 1953), headed by the Secretary of Health, Education, and Welfare, which administers Federal services relating to health, education, and social security.

health food Any food believed to have special health-giving benefits.

health·ful (helth′fəl) *adj.* **1** Promoting health; salubrious. **2** Being in health: properly *healthy.* See synonyms under HEALTHY. —**health′ful·ly** *adv.* —**health′ful·ness** *n.*

health officer A quarantine officer; an officer of a health board.

health·y (hel′thē) *adj.* **health·i·er, health·i·est 1** Having good health; sound; well. **2** Conducive to health; salutary: *healthy* recreation. **3** Indicative or characteristic of sound health: a *healthy* complexion. —**health′i·ly** *adv.* —**health′i·ness** *n.*

Synonyms: hale, healthful, hearty, hygienic, salubrious, salutary, sanitary, sound, strong, vigorous, well, wholesome. *Healthy* is correctly used to signify possessing or enjoying health or its results; as, a *healthy* person, a *healthy* condition. *Healthful* signifies promotive of health, tending or adapted to confer, preserve, or promote health; as, a *healthful* climate, a *healthful* diet. *Salubrious* is always used in the physical sense, and is chiefly applied to air or climate. *Salutary* is now chiefly used in the moral sense; as, a *salutary* lesson. See SANE. *Antonyms*: delicate, diseased, emaciated, exhausted, failing, fainting, fragile, frail, ill, sick, unhealthy, unsound, wasted, weak, worn.

heap (hēp) *n.* **1** A collection of things piled up; a pile; mass. **2** A large number; lot. **3** A crowd. **4** *Slang* An old, broken-down automobile. —*v.t.* **1** To pile into a heap; make a mound or mass of. **2** To fill or pile (a container) full or more than full. **3** To strew with heaps: to *heap* a field with bodies. **4** To give or bestow in great quantities: to *heap* insults on someone. **5** To give or bestow great quantities upon: to *heap* someone with riches. —*v.i.* **6** To form or rise in a heap or pile. —*adv.* Very; very much: North American Indian term. [OE *hēap* a crowd]

Synonyms (*noun*): accumulation, agglomeration, aggregate, aggregation, collection, drift, hoard, mass, pile, store. See COLLECTION, MASS.

heaped measure A measure in which the contents more than fill the container, rising in a mound above its rim. See STRUCK MEASURE.

heap·ing (hē′ping) *adj.* Having the contents raised above the top; heaped.

hear (hir) *v.* **heard** (hûrd), **hear·ing** *v.t.* **1** To perceive by means of the ear. **2** To listen to; give audience to: *Hear* what I say! **3** To attend as part of the audience: to *hear* a concert. **4** To learn or be informed of: I *hear* you are leaving town. **5** To listen to officially, judicially, or by way of examination: to *hear* a case in court; to *hear* a lesson. **6** To respond or accede to; grant: to *hear* a prayer. —*v.i.* **7** To perceive or be capable of perceiving sound by means of the ear. **8** To be informed or made aware; receive information: with *of, about,* or *from.* See synonyms under LISTEN. —**hear! hear!** *Brit.* Listen! An expression of approval accorded a public speaker. —**to hear of** To approve of: usually in the negative: He will not *hear of* it. [OE *hēran*] —**hear′er** *n.*

hear·ing (hir′ing) *n.* **1** The capacity to hear. **2** The special sense by which sounds are perceived. **3** An opportunity to be heard; audience. **4** The distance or space within which sound may be heard. **5** The examination of a person charged with an offense, and of the witnesses; a judicial trial, especially without a jury, as in an equity suit.

hearing aid Any of various portable instruments for the improvement of hearing, especially those which amplify sound waves by the use of microphones connected with transistors or vacuum tubes operated by small batteries.

hear·ing-loss (hir′ing·lôs′) *n.* A measure of defective hearing, expressed as a percentage of the tones normally audible under standard conditions: determined by audiograms.

heark·en (här′kən) See HARKEN.

Hearn (hûrn), **Lafcadio,** 1850–1904, U.S. writer born in Europe, who became a Japanese citizen under the name of Yakumo Koizumi.

hear·say (hir′sā′) *n.* Information received indirectly; common talk; report; rumor; also, hearsay evidence.

hearsay evidence Evidence, oral or written, derived from something the witness has heard others say; any evidence depending upon the credibility and competency of some person other than the witness: generally excluded but admissible in some litigations.

hearse (hûrs) *n.* **1** A vehicle for carrying the dead to the grave. **2** A symbolical triangular frame set with spikes, resembling teeth of a harrow, on which lighted candles are placed during the singing of Tenebrae in Holy Week. —*v.t.* **hearsed, hears·ing 1** To put in or on a hearse. **2** To bury. [<F *herse* a harrow <L *hirpex, -icis;* so called because the frame for candles about a coffin resembled a harrow]

Hearst (hûrst), **William Randolph,** 1863–1951, U.S. publisher.

heart (härt) *n.* **1** The central organ of the vascular system of animals; a hollow muscular structure which maintains the circulation of

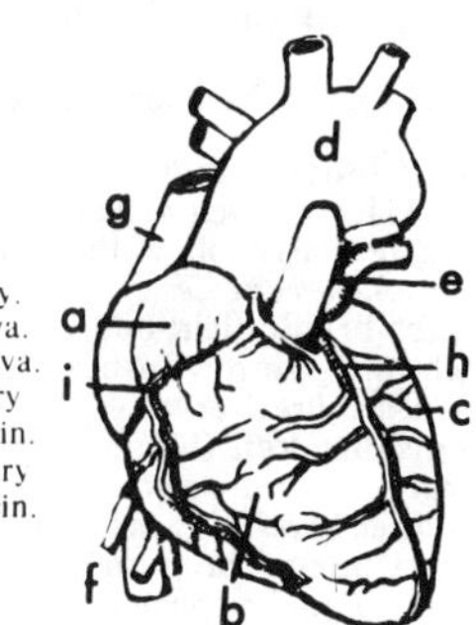

HEART
a. Right atrium.
b. Right ventricle.
c. Left ventricle.
d. Aorta.
e. Pulmonary artery.
f. Inferior vena cava.
g. Superior vena cava.
h. Anterior coronary artery, with vein.
i. Posterior coronary artery, with vein.

the blood by alternate contraction (systole) and dilatation (diastole). ◆ Collateral adjective: *cardiac.* 2 The breast regarded as the seat of the heart. 3 The seat of the affections and emotions, as distinguished from the head as the center of intellect and will. 4 One's inmost thoughts or feelings: to pour out one's *heart.* 5 Affection; love: to win one's *heart.* 6 Tenderness; capacity for sympathy: to have no *heart.* 7 Courage; resolution; firmness of will: The men lost *heart.* 8 Ardor; enthusiasm; energy: He put his whole *heart* into the task. 9 Mood; spirit: a heavy *heart.* 10 A person, especially a dear or courageous one: a brave *heart.* 11 The central part of anything; the core: the *heart* of the city. 12 The inner part or core of a tree, plant, vegetable, etc. 13 The vital or essential part; the essence: the *heart* of the matter. 14 Anything represented as or shaped like a heart; especially the conventional roundish figure with a point opposite two lobes. 15 A playing card bearing red, heart-shaped spots or pips. 16 *pl.* The suit of such playing cards. 17 *pl.* A game of cards played with a full pack, in which the object is to take no hearts. —**after one's own heart** Suiting one perfectly; conforming to one's ideas; to one's taste: a man *after one's own heart.* —**at heart** At the center or bottom; essentially; substantially; in fact. —**athletic heart** Enlargement of the heart induced by excessive participation in athletic sports. —**by heart** By rote, so as to be memorized perfectly: said of recitations. —**from one's heart** With all sincerity. —**to have at heart** To cherish; be concerned for earnestly. —**to have one's heart in one's mouth** To be excessively excited or frightened. —**to have the heart** To be callous or cruel enough. —**to take to heart** To consider seriously. —**to wear one's heart on one's sleeve** To show one's feelings plainly. —**with all one's heart** Intensely; thoroughly; completely; wholly. —*v.t. Rare* 1 To hearten. 2 To place in the heart. —*v.i.* 3 To form a heart. ◆ Homophone: *hart.* [OE *heorte*]

Heart may appear as a combining form (in hyphemes or solidemes) or as the first element in two-word phrases; as in:

heart action	**heart murmur**
heart-affecting	**heart-purifying**
heart-angry	**heart-ravishing**
heart-bred	**heart-robbing**
heart-burdened	**heart-shaking**
heart-cheering	**heartsickening**
heart-chilling	**heartsickness**
heart complaint	**heart-sorrowing**
heart-corroding	**heart-stimulant**
heart-dulling	**heart strain**
heart-fashioned	**heart-swelling**
heart-freezing	**heart-swollen**
heart-fretting	**heart-tearing**
heart-gnawing	**heart-thrilling**
heart-gripping	**heart-throb**
heart-happy	**heart-throbbing**
heart-hardened	**heart-tickling**
heart-hardening	**heart-warm**
heartheaviness	**heart-warming**
heartheavy	**heart-weariness**
heart-ill	**heart-weary**
heart-melting	**heart-wounded**
heart-moving	**heart-wringing**

heart·ache (härt′āk′) *n.* Mental anguish; grief; sorrow.

heart and soul Entirely; wholly; enthusiastically.

heart·beat (härt′bēt′) *n.* A pulsation of the heart.

heart·block (härt′blok′) *n. Pathol.* A condition in which the ventricular beats of the heart do not regularly follow the atrial also called *Adams-Stokes disease.*

heart-break (härt′brāk′) *n.* Deep grief; overwhelming sorrow. —**heart′-break′ing** *adj.* & *n.* —**heart′-break′er** *n.*

heart-bro·ken (härt′brō′kən) *adj.* Overwhelmingly grieved: also *heart-stricken.* —**heart′-bro′ken·ly** *adv.* —**heart′-bro′ken·ness** *n.*

heart-burn (härt′bûrn′) *n.* 1 A burning sensation in the esophagus, due to acidity of the stomach. 2 Discontent; jealousy.

heart-burn·ing (härt′bûr′ning) *n.* Gnawing discontent or rancor, as from envy or jealousy. —*adj.* Deeply felt; distressful.

heart cherry A variety of cherry having heart-shaped fruit.

heart disease Any morbid condition of the heart, whether organic or functional.

heart·ed (här′tid) *adj.* 1 Having a heart of a specified kind: used in combination: kind-*hearted.* 2 Heart-shaped: a *hearted* shield.

heart·en (här′tən) *v.t.* To give heart or courage to; strengthen. See synonyms under ENCOURAGE.

heart failure 1 Inability of the heart to pump enough blood to maintain normal circulation. 2 Sudden and fatal stoppage of the action of the heart.

heart-felt (härt′felt′) *adj.* Deeply felt; most sincere.

heart-free (härt′frē′) *adj.* Having the affections disengaged.

hearth (härth) *n.* 1 The floor of a fireplace, furnace, or the like. 2 The fireside; home. 3 *Metall.* That part of a reverberatory furnace upon which the ore is laid to be subjected to the action of fire; in a blast furnace, the lowest part, through which the melted metal flows. 4 A bloomery. See synonyms under HOME. [OE *heorth*]

hearth money 1 Peter's pence (def. 2). 2 In English law (1662–1689), a tax of two shillings laid on hearths in houses paying church and poor rates: also called *chimney money.*

hearth·stone (härth′stōn′) *n.* 1 A stone forming a hearth. 2 Figuratively, a fireside. 3 A soft stone used for scouring floors, doorsteps, etc. See synonyms under HOME.

heart·i·ly (här′tə·lē) *adv.* 1 With sincerity or cordiality. 2 Earnestly; enthusiastically. 3 Abundantly and with good appetite: to eat *heartily.* 4 Completely; thoroughly: to be *heartily* beaten.

heart·i·ness (här′tē·nis) *n.* The state or quality of being hearty.

heart·land (härt′land′) *n.* 1 That portion of a country essential to the maintenance of its defensive and offensive strength in wartime. 2 The interior of a country as distinguished from its more exposed peripheral areas. 3 Any large geographic area supposed to give the nation controlling it decisive strategic advantage in any struggle for world domination: compare GEOPOLITICS.

heart·less (härt′lis) *adj.* 1 Without sympathy or affection; hard-hearted; pitiless. 2 Without courage; cowardly; craven. —**heart′less·ly** *adv.* —**heart′less·ness** *n.*

heart-rend·ing (härt′ren′ding) *adj.* Extremely distressing; causing anguish.

hearts·ease (härts′ēz′) *n.* 1 The pansy or violet. 2 Freedom from sorrow or care. Also **heart's′-ease′.**

heart·seed (härt′sēd′) *n.* Balloonvine, an ornamental climbing vine.

heart-shaped (härt′shāpt′) *adj.* Shaped like a heart; oval, with one end obtusely pointed and the other notched.

heart·sick (härt′sik′) *adj.* Deeply disappointed or despondent. Also **heart′sore′** (-sôr′, -sōr′).

heart·some (härt′səm) *adj.* Cheerful or animated; lively; merry; gay. —**heart′some·ly** *adv.*

heart-strick·en (härt′strik′ən) *adj.* Overwhelmed with grief or fear.

heart·strings (härt′stringz′) *n. pl.* The strongest feelings or affections.

heart-struck (härt′struk′) *adj.* 1 Heart-stricken. 2 Ineradicable.

heart-to-heart (härt′tə·härt′) *adj.* Marked by frankness, intimacy, and sincerity.

heart·wa·ter (härt′wô′tər, -wot′ər) *n.* A disease of cattle, sheep, and goats due to the destruction of blood corpuscles by a filtrable virus.

heart·whole (härt′hōl′) *adj.* 1 Having the affections free; not in love. 2 Undaunted; sincere. —**heart′whole′ness** *n.*

heart·wood (härt′wo͝od′) *n.* The older, nonfunctioning xylem in the central part of a woody stem, usually denser and darker than the surrounding sapwood. Also called *duramen.*

heart·worm (härt′wûrm′) *n.* A nematode worm (genus *Filaria*) parasitic in the heart and blood stream of dogs, occasionally of cats and other animals.

heart-worn (härt′wôrn′) *adj.* Worn with care and trouble.

heart·y (här′tē) *adj.* **heart·i·er, heart·i·est** 1 Full of affection or cordiality; genial. 2 Strongly felt; vigorous: a *hearty* dislike. 3 Healthy and strong. 4 Supplying abundant nourishment: a *hearty* meal. 5 Enjoying or requiring abundant nourishment: a *hearty* appetite. 6 Fertile: said of land. —*n. pl.* **heart·ies** A hearty fellow or sailor.

heat (hēt) *n.* 1 That which raises the temperature of a body or substance or any material system; also the rise itself, however produced. 2 *Physics* A form of energy directly associated with and proportional to the random molecular motions of a substance or body; it may be variously generated (as by combustion, friction, chemical action, radiation, etc.), converted by suitable processes into other forms of energy, and its total absence corresponds with that complete cessation of all translational molecular motion known as absolute zero. ◆ Collateral adjective: *thermal.* 3 The sensation produced by a rise in temperature. 4 The state of being hot; a temperature high as compared with a mean, standard, or normal temperature: summer *heat.* 5 Color, appearance, or condition indicating high temperature; high color; redness; flush. 6 *Metall.* A single heating, melting, or smelting operation, as in working iron or steel; also, the material heated, melted, etc., at one time: The foundry runs three *heats* a day. 7 A single effort or action, or one of an interrupted series of such efforts; especially, a single course or division of a race: to run several *heats.* 8 Greatest vehemence or fury; excitement or agitation; unusual animation; ardor; fervency: the *heat* of battle. 9 Sexual excitement in animals, especially in females; estrus. 10 *Physiol.* The sensation of warmth experienced when certain receptors in the skin are stimulated. 11 A fundamental quality of elements, humors, and bodies in general: opposed to *cold.* See synonyms under WARMTH. —*v.t.* & *v.i.* 1 To make or become hot or warm. 2 To excite or become excited; arouse. See synonyms under INCENSE. [OE *hatu*] —**heat′ed** *adj.* —**heat′ed·ly** *adv.*

heat-bal·ance (hēt′bal′əns) *n. Physics* A method of accounting for all the heat units supplied, transferred, and consumed in a given process, as in a diesel engine, steam turbine, furnace, refrigerating system, etc.

heat capacity The amount of heat required to raise the temperature of a given mass of a substance or material by one degree.

heat content Enthalpy.

heat death *Physics* The state of complete thermodynamic equilibrium in a material system; maximum entropy.

heat engine Any engine for the conversion of heat into mechanical energy, as a steam or diesel engine.

heat·er (hē′tər) *n.* 1 Any device, apparatus, or contrivance designed to generate, impart, transmit, or conserve heat, as a stove, radiator, etc. 2 One who attends to the heating of something: often in combination: a rivet *heater.* 3 *Electronics* An element which supplies current for heating the cathode of a vacuum tube. 4 *Colloq.* A pistol or revolver.

heath (hēth) *n.* 1 A low, hardy, evergreen shrub of a large genus *(Erica)* with narrow, usually whorled leaves and small tubular or globose, rose, white, or yellow flowers. Two of the most durable species are the fine-leaved heath *(E. cinerea)* and the cross-leaved heath *(E. tetralix).* 2 The common heather. 3 *Brit.* An area of open land overgrown with heath or with coarse herbage. 4 In Coverdale's and later versions of the Old Testament, a desert plant; identified both as tamarisk and savin. *Jer.* xvii 6; xlviii 6. [OE *hath*]

heath aster A common aster of the eastern United States *(Aster ericoides),* having thick clusters of small white or pink flowers.

heath·ber·ry (hēth′ber′ē, -bər·ē) *n. pl.* **·ries** The crowberry.

heath bird The heath grouse. Also **heath cock.**

hea·then (hē′thən) *n. pl.* **·thens** or **·then** 1 One who is not a believer in the God of the Bible; one who is neither Christian, Jew, nor Mohammedan; a pagan; Gentile; idolater. 2 Any irreligious, rude, or uncultured person. —*adj.* 1 Unbelieving; Gentile; pagan. 2 Irreligious; uncultured. 3 Of or pertaining to the heathen or their customs. [OE *haethen.* Akin to HEATH.]

hea·then·dom (hē′thən·dəm) *n.* 1 Heathenism. 2 The regions of the world, collectively, inhabited by heathen peoples. 3 Heathen peoples collectively.

hea·then·ish (hē′thən·ish) *adj.* Pertaining to, characteristic of, or resembling heathen; hence, irreligious; rude; barbarous; cruel. — **hea′then·ish·ly** *adv.* — **hea′then·ish·ness** *n.*

hea·then·ism (hē′thən·iz′əm) *n.* **1** Paganism; idolatry. **2** The condition, manners, or morals of heathen ignorance; barbarism. Also **hea′then·ry** (-rē).

hea·then·ize (hē′thən·īz) *v.t.* & *v.i.* **·ized, ·iz·ing** To make or become heathenish or heathen.

hea·then·ness (hē′thən·is) *n.* **1** The state of being heathen. **2** The regions inhabited by the heathen.

heath·er (heth′ər) *n.* **1** A hardy evergreen shrub related to the heath; especially, the true heather of Scotland *(Calluna vulgaris)*, with minute leaves and close, one-sided, spikelike racemes of pinkish-lavender flowers. **2** The heath. **3** A dull, grayish-red color. [ME *hadder*; origin unknown; infl. in form by HEATH]

heath·er-bleat (heth′ər·blēt′) *n.* The snipe. Also **heath′er-bleat′er, heath′er-bluit′er** (-blōōt′·ər, -blüt′ər), **heath′er-blut′ter.**

heather mixture A combination of colored fibers giving a flecked appearance suggesting heather fields: used chiefly in tweeds or other woolen fabrics.

heath·er·y (heth′ər·ē) *adj.* **1** Resembling heather. **2** Abounding in heather.

heath grass A perennial grass *(Sieglingia decumbens)* found growing on heaths and moors in Europe. Also **heather grass.**

heath grouse A European grouse *(Tetrao tetrix)* found in the heath country of Great Britain, the male of which is mostly black, with a lyre-shaped tail: also called *heath bird.*

heath hen An American grouse *(Tympanuchus cupido cupido)* related to the prairie chicken of western North America: now extinct.

heath·y (hē′thē) *adj.* **heath·i·er, heath·i·est** **1** Of, pertaining to, or resembling heath. **2** Covered by or abounding in heath.

heat index An index expressing the heating value of an oil, determined by the rise in temperature from mixing 50 cc. of a specified oil with 10 cc. of concentrated sulfuric acid. Also **heat number.**

heat lightning A fitful play of lightning unattended by thunder, usually seen near the horizon at the close of a hot day, due to the reflection from distant clouds of far-off flashes, causing a diffused glow.

heat of formation The quantity of heat absorbed or evolved in the formation of a gram-molecule of a compound from its constituents at constant volume. Also **heat of combination.**

heat of fusion The quantity of heat required to convert into the liquid state a given mass of a solid which has already been brought to the melting point.

heat of vaporization The latent heat required to vaporize one gram of a liquid.

hea·tron·ic (hē·tron′ik) *adj.* Of or pertaining to the subjection of a material to a required uniform temperature through the application of high-frequency radio waves: applied in the rapid and accurate molding of plastics. [<HEAT + (ELECT)RONIC]

heat stroke The state of exhaustion and collapse caused by prolonged exposure to heat, as in furnace rooms, foundries, or from the sun's rays. Also **heat prostration.**

heat treatment *Metall.* The application of heat to metals and alloys under such conditions of temperature, time, range of variation, etc., as will give the desired properties, as hardness, to the product.

heaume (hōm) *n.* In medieval armor, a large supplemental helmet fitting over an inner helmet and resting on the shoulders; a casque. [<F <OF *helme.* Related to HELM[2].]

heave (hēv) *v.* **heaved** or **hove, heav·ing** *v.t.* **1** To raise with effort; lift; hoist. **2** To lift and throw, especially with effort; hurl. **3** To cause to swell, rise, or bulge out, as the chest in breathing. **4** To cause to rise and fall repeatedly: The waves *heaved* the ship up and down. **5** To emit or bring forth (a sigh, groan, etc.) as with effort or pain. **6** *Naut.* **a** To raise or haul up (the anchor); pull on (a cable, etc.). **b** To cause (a ship) to move in a specified direction by or as by hauling on cables or ropes. **7** *Geol.* To fracture and displace (a vein or stratum). — *v.i.* **8** To rise or swell up; bulge. **9** To rise and fall repeatedly. **10** To breathe with effort; gasp; pant. **11** To vomit or make an effort to vomit; retch. **12** *Naut.* **a** To move or proceed: said of ships. **b** To haul or pull, as on a rope; push, as on a capstan. — **heave, ho!** *Naut.* Pull (or push) hard together! — **to heave in** (or **into**) **sight** To come into view, as a ship at sea. — **to heave to** *Naut.* **1** To bring (a ship) to a standstill by heading into the wind with one or more sails aback. **2** To cause a ship to lie to, as in a storm. — *n.* **1** An upward and onward throw; an effort to lift or raise. **2** A rising or an upward movement. **3** A swell or an expansion, as of sea waves, or the earth in an earthquake. **4** *Geol.* The amount of actual displacement of the parts of a fractured mineral vein or stratum, vertically or horizontally or in both directions combined. [OE *hebban* lift]

heav·en (hev′ən) *n.* **1** *Theol.* The abode of God and of blest spirits; the dwelling place or state of existence of righteous souls after their life on earth. **2** *Usually pl.* The region or regions surrounding the earth; especially, the domelike expanse over the earth; the sky; firmament. **3** Any place or condition of supreme happiness; a state of bliss. **4** In Christian Science, harmony; the atmosphere of Soul. **5** Climate, especially as regards the sky of a particular place. [OE *heofon*] — **heav′en·li·ness** *n.* — **heav′en·ward** *adj.* & *adv.* — **heav′en·wards** *adv.*

Heav·en (hev′ən) God, or the Supreme Being; Providence: *Heaven* keep thee.

heav·en·ly (hev′ən·lē) *adj.* **1** Of or belonging to the heaven of God. **2** Of or pertaining to the natural sky: chiefly in the phrase, *heavenly* bodies. **3** Having excellence or beauty or giving pleasure that belongs to heaven: often, in colloquial usage, a general expression of approval.

heave offering An offering of the Jewish service: so called because heaved or lifted up.

heav·er (hē′vər) *n.* **1** One who heaves or lifts. **2** A short bar or stick used as a lever for twisting rope; handspike.

heaves (hēvz) *n. pl.* An asthmatic disease of horses; quick, labored breathing; broken wind. [Plural of HEAVE]

heav·i·er-than-air (hev′ē·ər·thən·âr′) *adj.* Describing any aircraft whose weight is greater than that of the air it displaces. See AERODYNE.

heav·i·ly (hev′ə·lē) *adv.* **1** With great weight or burden; oppressively; also, densely. **2** With depressing affliction or misfortune; grievously; tediously.

heav·i·ness (hev′ē·nis) *n.* **1** The quality of being heavy; ponderousness. **2** Despondency; grief. See synonyms under WEIGHT.

Heav·i·side (hev′ē·sīd), **Oliver,** 1850–1925, English physicist.

Heaviside layer A layer of the ionosphere which begins at about 65 miles above the earth and acts as a reflector of radio waves: also called *E-layer, Kennelly-Heaviside layer.*

heav·y (hev′ē) *adj.* **heav·i·er, heav·i·est** **1** Hard to lift or carry; weighty: opposed to *light.* **2** Having great specific gravity; hence, of dense or concentrated weight: *heavy* as lead. **3** Over the usual weight: *heavy* luggage; *heavy* woolens. **4** Of great quantity or amount; abundant: a *heavy* crop; a *heavy* vote. **5** Dealing in large amounts: *heavy* trade; a *heavy* investor. **6** Laden or weighted: an atmosphere *heavy* with moisture. **7** Permeating; diffuse: a *heavy* odor. **8** Forceful; powerful: *heavy* gunfire; a *heavy* blow. **9** Tempestuous; violent: a *heavy* sea, storm, etc. **10** *Mil.* **a** Of large size: said of weapons. **b** Heavily armed: *heavy* infantry. **11** Clayey; cloggy: said of soils, roads, etc. **12** Doughy; dense and compact: said of bread, pastries, etc. **13** Not easily digested: *heavy* food. **14** Thick; massive; coarse: *heavy* lines, features, etc. **15** Slow and cumbrous: a *heavy* step. **16** Loud and intense: *heavy* applause. **17** Hard to do or accomplish; laborious: *heavy* work. **18** Hard to bear or suffer; oppressive: *heavy* taxes; *heavy* sorrow. **19** Weary; sleepy. **20** Tedious; dull: a *heavy* style. **21** Profound; intense: a *heavy* silence. **22** Gloomy; overcast: a *heavy* sky. **23** Feeling or expressing sorrow or grief; sad; despondent: a *heavy* heart. **24** Serious; grave: a *heavy* role; a *heavy* offense. **25** Pregnant. **26** Steep: a *heavy* grade. — *adv.* Heavily. — *n. pl.* **heav·ies** **1** A serious role in a play, representing dignity or self-importance in middle life or vigorous age; often the villain. **2** An actor who interprets such a role. [OE *hefig*]

Synonyms (adj.): burdensome, crushing, cumbrous, dull, grievous, inert, oppressive, ponderous, slow, sluggish, stolid, stupid, weighty. See DROWSY, SAD. *Antonyms*: airy, buoyant, ethereal, light, lively, subtile, trifling, trivial, volatile.

heav·y-dut·y (hev′ē·dōō′tē, -dyōō′-) *adj.* Stoutly constructed so as to bear up under severe or long strain, usage, etc.

heavy earth Baryta.

heav·y-foot·ed (hev′ē·fŏŏt′id) *adj.* Clumsy or plodding in gait. — **heav′y-foot′ed·ly** *adv.* — **heav′y-foot′ed·ness** *n.*

heav·y-hand·ed (hev′ē·han′did) *adj.* **1** Lacking lightness of touch; clumsy. **2** Oppressive; overbearing; dogmatic. — **heav′y-hand′ed·ly** *adv.* — **heav′y-hand′ed·ness** *n.*

heav·y-heart·ed (hev′ē·här′tid) *adj.* Sad; melancholy. — **heav′y-heart′ed·ly** *adv.* — **heav′y-heart′ed·ness** *n.*

heavy hydrogen Deuterium.

heav·y-lad·en (hev′ē·lād′n) *adj.* **1** Bearing a heavy burden. **2** Troubled; oppressed.

heavy metal Any metal with a specific gravity greater than 4.

heavy spar Barite.

heavy timber **1** Dense, unbroken forest; thick woods. **2** Big trees. **3** Big logs.

heavy water Deuterium oxide, D_2O, the compound of oxygen and the heavy isotope of hydrogen.

heav·y·weight (hev′ē·wāt′) *n.* A person of more than average weight; specifically, a boxer or wrestler over 175 pounds in weight. — *adj.* Of more than average weight or thickness.

Heb·bel (heb′əl), **Friedrich,** 1813–63, German dramatist.

heb·do·mad (heb′də·mad) *n.* The number seven; any seven things; especially, a period of seven days; a week. [<L *hebdomas, -adis* <Gk. *hebdomas* < *hepta* seven]

heb·dom·a·dal (heb·dom′ə·dəl) *adj.* **1** Composed of seven days. **2** Occurring weekly. — **heb·dom′a·dal·ly** *adv.*

heb·dom·a·dar·y (heb·dom′ə·der′ē) *n. pl.* **·dar·ies** *Eccl.* A member of a chapter or monastic choir who presides over the recitation of the breviary for the week.

He·be (hē′bē) In Greek mythology, the daughter of Zeus and Hera, goddess of youth and, before she was replaced by Ganymede, the cupbearer of the gods.

he·be·phre·ni·a (hē′bə·frē′nē·ə) *n. Psychiatry* A type of dementia precox occurring at puberty. [<NL <Gk. *hēbē* youth + *phrēn* mind] — **he′be·phre′nic** (-frē′nik, -fren′ik) *adj.*

He·ber (hē′bər), **Reginald,** 1783–1826, English bishop and hymn writer.

He·ber·to (ā·ber′tō) Spanish form of HERBERT.

heb·e·tate (heb′ə·tāt) *v.i.* & *v.t.* **·tat·ed, ·tat·ing** To make or become blunt or dull. — *adj.* **1** *Bot.* Having a blunt, soft point, as certain plants. **2** Stupid; dull. [<L *hebetatus,* pp. of *hebetare* be dull < *hebes* dull] — **heb′e·ta′tion** *n.* — **heb′e·ta′tive** *adj.*

he·bet·ic (hə·bet′ik) *adj.* Of or pertaining to the period of puberty.

heb·e·tude (heb′ə·tōōd, -tyōōd) *n.* Stupidity and dulness of the senses, especially as noted in grave fevers. [<LL *hebetudo* <*hebes, -etis* dull]

He·bra·ic (hi·brā′ik) *adj.* Relating to or characteristic of the Hebrews. Also **He·bra′i·cal.** [<LL *Hebraicus* <Gk. *Hebraikos* < *Hebraios* a Hebrew] — **He·bra′i·cal·ly** *adv.*

He·bra·ism (hē′brā·iz′əm, -brə-) *n.* **1** A distinctive characteristic of the Hebrews. **2** A Hebrew idiom. **3** The religion of the Hebrews; Judaism.

He·bra·ist (hē′brā·ist, -brə-) *n.* **1** One proficient in or a student of Hebrew. **2** One who conforms to Hebraic thought and traditions. **3** Among the early Jews, one who upheld the Hebrew language and traditions in opposition to the Hellenists. Also **He'brew·ist.**

He·bra·is·tic (hē'brā·is'tik, -brə-) *adj.* Belonging to or resembling the Hebrew language, thought, or manners. Also **He'bra·is'ti·cal.**

He·bra·ize (hē'brā·īz, -brə-) *v.* **·ized, ·iz·ing** *v.t.* To make Hebrew. —*v.i.* To adopt Hebrew customs, language, etc.

He·brew (hē'brōō) *n.* **1** A member of one of a group of Semitic tribes; especially, an Israelite. **2** The Semitic language of the ancient Hebrews, used in the Old Testament: retained as a scholarly and religious language after its decline as a vernacular about the fourth century B.C. **3** The modern descendant of ancient Hebrew, the official language of the republic of Israel. —**Epistle to the Hebrews** A New Testament book of uncertain authorship, addressed to Hebrew Christians: also **Hebrews.** —*adj.* Relating or belonging to the Hebrews; Hebraic. [<OF *Hebreu* <L *Hebraeus* <Gk. *Hebraios* <Hebrew *'ibhri,* lit., one from beyond (Jordan)]

Hebrew calendar See under CALENDAR.

Heb·ri·des (heb'rə·dēz) The islands off the western coast of Scotland, divided into two groups, the *Inner Hebrides* and the *Outer Hebrides;* total, 2,900 square miles: also *Western Islands.* —**Heb'ri·de'an** (-dē'ən) or **He·brid·i·an** (hə·brid'ē·ən) *adj.* & *n.*

He·bron (hē'brən) A town in Palestine SW of Jerusalem: ancient *Kirjath-Arba*: Arabic *El Khalil.*

Hec·a·te (hek'ə·tē) In Greek mythology, a goddess of earth, moon, and underworld: later associated with sorcery: also *Hekate.*

Hec·a·te Strait (hek'ə·tē) A channel separating Queen Charlotte Islands from western British Columbia.

hec·a·tomb (hek'ə·tōm, -tōōm) *n.* A great sacrifice, originally of a hundred oxen. [<L *hecatombe* <Gk. *hecatombē* < *hekaton* a hundred + *bous* an ox]

Hec·a·ton·chei·res (hek'ə·tən·kī'rēz) In Greek mythology, the three hundred-handed, fifty-headed giants, sons of Uranus and Gaea: Briareus, Cottus, and Gyes: identified with the Roman *Centimanus.* [<Gk. < *hekaton* a hundred + *cheir* hand]

hec·is·to·ther·mic (hek'is·tə·thûr'mik) See HEKISTOTHERMIC.

heck (hek) *interj. Slang* An exclamation: euphemism for hell.

heck·le (hek'əl) *v.t.* **heck·led, heck·ling 1** To try to confuse or annoy (a speaker) with taunts, questions, etc. **2** To hackle (flax, etc.). —*n.* A hackle or hatchel. [ME *hechelen* < *hechele* a hatchel] —**heck'ler** *n.*

Hec·la (hek'lə) See HEKLA.

hec·tare (hek'târ) *n.* A unit of area in the metric system; 100 ares; equal to 10,000 square meters, or 2.471 acres: also spelled *hektare.* See METRIC SYSTEM. [<F <Gk. *hekaton* a hundred + F *are* ARE[2]]

hec·tic (hek'tik) *adj.* **1** Characterized by intense excitement or wild feeling. **2** Characterized by or denoting a wasting habit or condition of body. **3** Pertaining to or affected with hectic fever; consumptive. Also **hec'ti·cal.** [<F *hectique* <LL *hecticus* <Gk. *hektikos* consumptive < *hexis* state of the body < *echein* have] —**hec'ti·cal·ly** *adv.*

hectic fever *Pathol.* A fever connected with some organic disease, as pulmonary tuberculosis.

hectic flush A flush on the cheek in hectic fever.

hecto- *combining form* A hundred: *hectogram.* Also, before vowels, **hect-.** For words beginning thus see below or under METRIC SYSTEM. [<F <Gk. *hekaton* a hundred]

hec·to·cot·y·lus (hek'tə·kot'ə·ləs) *n. pl.* **·li** (-lī) *Zool.* One of the arms in male cephalopods that is modified to serve a reproductive function. [<HECTO- + Gk. *kotylē* cup]

hec·to·gram (hek'tə·gram) *n.* A measure of weight equal to 100 grams or 3.527 ounces avoirdupois: also spelled *hektogram.* See METRIC SYSTEM. Also **hec'to·gramme.**

hec·to·graph (hek'tə·graf, -gräf) *n.* A gelatin pad for making multiple copies of a writing or drawing. —*v.t.* To copy by hectograph. —**hec'to·graph'ic** *adj.*

hec·to·li·ter (hek'tə·lē'tər) *n.* A measure of capacity equal to 100 liters or 2.838 U.S. bushels. See METRIC SYSTEM. Also **hec'to·li'tre.**

hec·to·me·ter (hek'tə·mē'tər, hek·tom'ə·tər) *n.* A measure of length equal to 100 meters or 328.08 feet. See METRIC SYSTEM. Also **hec'to·me'tre.**

hec·tor (hek'tər) *v.t.* & *v.i.* **1** To bully; bluster. **2** To tease; torment. [< *n.*] —*n.* A quarrelsome, domineering fellow; bully. [after HECTOR]

Hec·tor (hek'tər) In the *Iliad,* a Trojan hero, son of Priam and Hecuba: killed by Achilles to avenge the death of Patroclus.

hec·to·stere (hek'tə·stir) *n.* A measure of volume equal to 100 steres.

Hec·u·ba (hek'yōō·bə) In the *Iliad,* the wife of Priam and mother of Hector, Troilus, Paris, and Cassandra.

he'd (hēd) **1** He had. **2** He would.

hed·dle (hed'l) *n.* In weaving, the parallel vertical cords or wires of a loom through which the warp is threaded: used to separate, raise, or lower the warp. See illustration under LOOM. [OE *hefeld* thread for weaving]

hedge (hej) *n.* **1** A fence or barrier formed by bushes set close together. **2** Any barrier or boundary. **3** The act of hedging. —*v.* **hedged, hedg·ing** *v.t.* **1** To surround or border with a hedge; separate with a hedge. **2** To surround, guard, or hem in with or as with obstructions or barriers: usually with *in.* **3** To try to compensate for possible loss from (a bet, investment, etc.) by making offsetting bets or investments. —*v.i.* **4** To hide, as in or behind a hedge; skulk. **5** To make offsetting bets, investments, etc. **6** To avoid definite statement or involvement; refuse to commit oneself. [OE *hegg*] —**hedg'er** *n.* —**hedg'y** *adj.*

hedge apple The Osage orange.

hedge bill A tool used in pruning hedges; billhook. Also **hedging bill.**

hedge garlic A tall hedge weed (*Sisymbrium alliaria*) of the mustard family, with heart-shaped leaves, white flowers, erect pods, and a garlicky odor.

hedge·hog (hej'hôg', -hog') *n.* **1** A small, nocturnal, insectivorous mammal of the Old World (family *Erinaceidae*), having the back and sides covered with stout spines; also **hedge'pig'.** **2** The porcupine. **3** *Mil.* **a** One of a chain of strongly fortified villages. **b** A wooden rack or frame, on which barbed wire is strung: used in trench warfare.

EUROPEAN HEDGEHOG (Average length: 10 inches)

hedge·hop (hej'hop') *v.i.* **·hopped, ·hop·ping** To fly close to the ground in an airplane, rising over houses, trees, etc., as in spraying insecticide or strafing enemy positions. —**hedge'hop'per** *n.* —**hedge'hop'ping** *n.* & *adj.*

hedge hyssop 1 A European perennial herb (*Gratiola officinalis*) of the figwort family, once used medicinally as an emetic and purgative. **2** The skullcap (genus *Scutellaria*).

hedge marriage *Brit.* A marriage performed by a hedge parson, a clandestine marriage.

hedge parson *Brit.* Formerly, one of a class of vagabond and illiterate clergy. Also **hedge priest.**

hedge·row (hej'rō') *n.* A row of shrubs, planted as a hedge.

hedge school *Brit.* Formerly, a school kept in the open air; a makeshift school.

hedge sparrow A small brownish European warbler (*Prunella modularis*) that frequents hedges.

He·din (he·dēn'), **Sven Anders,** 1865–1952, Swedish explorer.

He·djaz (hē·jaz', he-) See HEJAZ.

he·don·ic (hē·don'ik) *adj.* **1** Pertaining to or of the nature of pleasure. **2** Of or pertaining to hedonism or hedonics. [<Gk. *hēdonikos* < *hēdonē* pleasure < *hēdys* sweet]

he·don·ics (hē·don'iks) *n. pl.* (*construed as singular*) **1** The science of pleasure or positive enjoyment: as a branch of ethics it treats of pleasure in its relation to duty. **2** That branch of psychology which considers pleasurable sensations in their bearing on life.

he·don·ism (hē'dən·iz'əm) *n.* **1** The doctrine of certain Greek philosophers (Aristippus and the Cyrenaics) that pleasure, of whatever kind, is the only good. **2** In ethics, gross self-interest; self-indulgence. **3** A tendency to exaggerate and dwell upon pleasurable sensations. —**he'don·ist** *n.* —**he'don·is'tic** *adj.* —**he'don·is'ti·cal·ly** *adv.*

-hedral *combining form* Having a (given) form or number of sides: *octahedral*: used in adjectives corresponding to nouns in *-hedron.* [<-HEDR(ON) + -AL]

-hedron *combining form Geom.* & *Mineral.* A figure or crystal having a (given) form or a (specific) number of surfaces: *octahedron.* [<Gk. *hedra* side, surface]

hee·bie-jee·bies (hē'bē·jē'bēz) *n. pl. U.S. Slang* A fit of nervousness. [Coined by Billy de Beck, U.S. comic cartoonist, died 1942]

heed (hēd) *v.t.* To take notice of; pay attention to. —*v.i.* To pay attention. See synonyms under CARE, FOLLOW, LISTEN. —*n.* Careful attention or consideration. [OE *hēdan*] —**heed'er** *n.*

heed·ful (hēd'fəl) *adj.* Attentive. See synonyms under THOUGHTFUL. —**heed'ful·ly** *adv.* —**heed'ful·ness** *n.*

heed·less (hēd'lis) *adj.* Careless, thoughtless. See synonyms under IMPRUDENT, INATTENTIVE. —**heed'less·ly** *adv.* —**heed'less·ness** *n.*

hee-haw (hē'hô') *n.* **1** The braying sound of an ass. **2** Loud, rude laughter. —*v.i.* **1** To bray, as an ass. **2** To laugh in a loud, rude manner. [Imit.]

heel[1] (hēl) *n.* **1** In man, the rounded posterior part of the foot; the calcaneum with its associated structures. **2** The corresponding part of the foot or tarsus in any other animal. **3** The part of a shoe, or other foot covering, that surrounds or lies just beneath or around this part of the foot; in a boot or shoe, the built-up portion on which the rear of the foot rests; in hosiery, the separately knitted rear part of the foot. **4** The whole foot, as seen from the rear; sometimes, *pl.,* the hind feet of an animal. **5** Something resembling a heel or located like a heel, as cyma reversa, a form of molding; the lower end of a stud or rafter. **6** *Naut.* **a** The hindmost part of a vessel's keel. **b** The lower end of a mast. **7** That part of the head of a golf club that is nearest to the neck; also, that part of a tool that is nearest to the handle. **8** The last part or remainder: the *heel* of tobacco in a pipe. **9** *Colloq.* A cad. —**down at the heel** Presenting a seedy or slovenly appearance. —**to be at, on,** or **upon the heels of** To follow closely. —**to heel** To a position close behind a master: said of dogs. —*v.t.* **1** To supply with a heel. **2** To follow at the heels of; pursue closely. **3** To touch or strike with the heel. **4** To arm (a fighting cock) with steel spurs. **5** In golf, to strike (the ball) with the heel of the club. **6** *Slang* To supply with money, etc. —*v.i.* **7** To follow at the heels of someone. **8** To touch the ground with or move the heels, as in dancing. ◆ Homophone: *heal.* [OE *hela*] —**heel'less** *adj.*

heel[2] (hēl) *v.t.* & *v.i. Naut.* To lean or cause to lean to one side; cant, as a ship. —*n.* The act of heeling or inclining laterally from an upright position; a cant; list: also **heel'ing.** ◆ Homophone: *heal.* [Earlier *heeld,* OE *hieldan*]

heel-and-toe (hēl'ən·tō') *adj.* Designating a manner of walking in which the heel of one foot touches the ground before the toes of the other foot leave it.

heel bone The calcaneum.

heeled (hēld) *adj.* **1** Having heels; fitted with heels. **2** *Slang* **a** Supplied with money. **b** Armed, as with a gun.

heel·er (hē'lər) *n.* **1** *U.S. Slang* A disreputable political retainer: often called **ward heeler.** **2** One who heels shoes.

heel·piece (hēl'pēs') *n.* **1** That part of a stocking which encloses the heel. **2** One thickness of leather in making the heel of a shoe. **3** The bar of iron which connects the soft iron cores in an electromagnet.

heel·post (hēl'pōst') *n.* The post in a doorframe to which the door is hinged.

heel·tap (hēl'tap') *n.* **1** A thickness of leather on the heel of a shoe. **2** A small quantity of liquor left in a glass.

Heep (hēp), **Uriah** In Dickens' *David Copperfield,* an obsequious, dishonest, and hypocritical clerk.

Heer·len (hār'lən) A city of SE Netherlands.

heeze (hēz) *v.t. Scot.* To hoist.

Hef·ner lamp (hef'nər) See STANDARD LAMP.

heft[1] (heft) *v.t. Colloq.* **1** To test the weight of by lifting. **2** To lift up; heave. —*v.i.*

3 *Colloq.* To weigh. —*n.* *U.S. Colloq.* **1** The bulk or gist of a thing; major part. **2** Weight. [Related to HEAVE]

heft² (heft) See HAFT.

heft·y (hef′tē) *adj.* **heft·i·er, heft·i·est** *Colloq.* **1** Heavy; weighty. **2** Big and powerful; muscular.

He·gel (hā′gəl), **Georg Wilhelm Friedrich,** 1770–1831, German philosopher.

He·ge·li·an (hā·gā′lē·ən, hə·jēl′yən) *adj.* According with or pertaining to the philosophical system of Hegel. —*n.* An adherent of this system.

He·ge·li·an·ism (hā·gā′lē·ən·iz′əm, hə·jēl′yən-) *n.* The philosophical system of Hegel. Its controlling assumption was the so-called Hegelian *dialectic,* or principle which enables reflective thinking to arrange all the categories, or necessary conceptions of reason, in an order of development that corresponds to the actual order, in development, of all reality. The system is customarily characterized as *absolute idealism.* Also **He·gel·ism** (hā′gəl·iz′əm).

he·gem·o·ny (hə·jem′ə·nē, hej′ə·mō′nē, hē′jə-) *n.* *pl.* **·nies 1** Predominant influence of one state over others as in a league or alliance. **2** Leadership, or supreme command. [< Gk. *hēgemonia* < *hēgeesthai* lead] —**heg·e·mon·ic** (hej′ə·mon′ik) *adj.*

he·gi·ra (hə·jī′rə, hej′ə·rə) *n.* Any precipitate flight or departure: also spelled *hejira.* [< Med. L < Arabic *hijrah* departure < *hajara* go away]

He·gi·ra (hi·jī′rə, hej′ə·rə) *n.* **1** The flight of Mohammed from Mecca to Medina in 622; now taken as the beginning of the Mohammedan era. **2** The Mohammedan era. Also spelled *Hejira.*

he·gu·men (hə·gyōō′men) *n.* In the Eastern Church, the head of a body of monks: an office of dignity rather than jurisdiction. See ARCHIMANDRITE. Also **he·gu′me·nos** (-nos), **he·gou′me·nos.** [< Med. L *hegumenus* < Gk. *hēgoumenos,* var. of *hēgeomenos,* ppr. of *hēgeesthai* lead]

he·gu·me·ne (hə·gyōō′mə·nē) *n.* In the Eastern Church, the head of a nunnery: similar to an abbess in the Western Church. [< Gk. *hēgoumenē,* fem. var. of *hēgeomenos.* See HEGUMEN.]

he·gu·me·ny (hə·gyōō′mə·nē) *n. pl.* **·nies** The office or position of a hegumen.

Hei·del·berg (hī′dəl·bûrg, *Ger.* hī′dəl·berkh) A city in Baden-Württemberg, Germany.

Heidelberg man A primitive human type *(Homo heidelbergensis)* reconstructed from a massive lower jaw with teeth which was discovered in 1907 in a sandpit near Heidelberg: considered by some authorities to form a single genus with Sinanthropus and Pithecanthropus.

heif·er (hef′ər) *n.* A young cow. [OE *heahfore*]

Hei·fetz (hī′fits), **Ja·scha** (yä′shə), born 1901, U.S. violinist born in Lithuania.

heigh (hā, hī) *interj.* An exclamation to attract attention, or to encourage, as a race horse.

heigh-ho (hī′hō′, hā′-) *interj.* An exclamation of varying significance, as of weariness, disappointment, surprise, etc.

height (hīt) *n.* **1** Distance above a base; altitude; highness. **2** An eminence. **3** The acme; culmination. [OE *hiehthо*]

Synonyms: acclivity, altitude, elevation, eminence, exaltation, loftiness. See SUMMIT. Compare HIGH. *Antonyms*: depression, depth, descent, lowliness, lowness.

height·en (hīt′n) *v.t. & v.i.* **1** To make or become high or higher; raise or lift. **2** To make or become more in degree, amount, size, etc.; intensify. —**height′en·er** *n.*

Synonyms: elevate, enhance, exalt, lift, raise, uplift. See AGGRAVATE, INCREASE. *Antonyms*: abase, debase, depress, deteriorate, diminish, lower, reduce.

height-find·er (hīt′fīn′dər) *n.* *Aeron.* An optical instrument used to determine the height of aircraft.

height-to-pa·per (hīt′tə·pā′pər) *n.* *Printing* The standard height of type: in the United States, 0.9186 inch; in England, 0.9175 inch. Compare TYPE-HIGH.

heil (hīl) *German interj.* Hail! —*v.t.* To salute with "heil."

Heil·bronn (hīl′brôn) A city in Baden-Württemberg, Germany.

Hei·lung·kiang (hā′lōōng·jyäng′) A province of north central Manchuria; 130,000 square miles; capital, Tsitsihar. Also **Hei-lung-chiang.**

Heim·dall (hām′däl) In Norse mythology, the guardian of Bifröst, the rainbow bridge that leads to Asgard. Also **Heim′dal, Heim′dallr** (-däl·r′).

Heim·lich maneuver (hīm′lik) A life-saving method of preventing a person's choking on food lodged in the windpipe by firmly grasping the victim around the midsection from behind, and pressing a fist hard against the diaphragm to produce a burst of air up through the throat.

Hei·ne (hī′nə), **Heinrich,** 1797–1856, German poet.

hei·nie (hī′nē) *n. Slang* A German soldier: a term of contempt. [< G *Heine,* dim. of *Heinrich*]

hei·nous (hā′nəs) *adj.* Extremely wicked; atrocious; odiously sinful. See synonyms under FLAGRANT, INFAMOUS. [< OF *haïnos* < *haine* hatred < *haïr* hate] —**hei′nous·ly** *adv.* —**hei′nous·ness** *n.*

heir (âr) *n.* **1** *Law* One who on the death of another becomes entitled by operation of law to succeed to the deceased person's estate, as an estate of inheritance: also **heir at law. 2** In states and countries which have adopted the civil law, all persons called to the succession. **3** Anyone inheriting from a deceased person. **4** One who or that which succeeds to any qualities of another by reason of community of origin, or inherits anything by transmission. **5** *Obs.* Offspring. ◆ Homophone: *air.* [< OF < L *heres*] —**heir′ess** *n. fem.* —**heir′less** *adj.*

heir apparent One who must by course of law become the heir if he survives his ancestor.

heir·loom (âr′lōōm) *n.* **1** Any movable chattel that descends to an heir; especially, something that has been handed down for generations. **2** Any personal quality, endowment, or family characteristic inherited from ancestors. [< HEIR + LOOM, in obs. sense "tool"]

heir presumptive One who is at present heir to another but whose claims may become void by birth of a nearer relative.

heir·ship (âr′ship) *n.* **1** The state or condition of an heir. **2** Succession by inheritance. Also **heir′dom** (-dəm).

Hei·sen·berg (hī′zən·berkh), **Werner,** 1901–76, German physicist.

heist (hīst) *v.t. Slang* To steal. [Var. of HOIST]

He·jaz (hē·jaz′, he-) A viceroyalty of Saudi Arabia extending along the Red Sea; 150,000 square miles; capital, Mecca: also *Hedjaz.*

he·ji·ra (hə·jī′rə, hej′ə·rə) See HEGIRA.

Hek·a·te (hek′ə·tē) See HECATE.

hek·is·to·ther·mic (hek′is·tə·thûr′mik) *adj.* *Ecol.* Of or designating plants adapted for living beyond the limits of tree growth and in the prolonged absence of light and warmth. Also spelled *hecistothermic.* [< Gk. *hēkistos* least + *thermē* heat]

Hek·la (hek′lə) An active volcano in SW Iceland; 4,747 feet: also *Hecla.*

hek·tare (hek′târ), **hek·to·gram** (hek′tə·gram), etc. See HECTARE, etc.

Hel (hel) In Norse mythology: **1** The daughter of Loki, goddess of those who died of old age or disease. **2** The kingdom of the dead not killed in battle: see VALHALLA.

hel·co·sis (hel·kō′sis) *n.* *Pathol.* The development of an ulcer. [< Gk. *helkos* an ulcer + -OSIS] —**hel·cot′ic** (-kot′ik) *adj.*

held (held) Past tense of HOLD.

Hel·der (hel′dər) A port of NW Netherlands. Also **Den Helder** (den).

Hel·en (hel′ən) A feminine personal name. Also **Hel·e·na** (hel′ə·nə), *Dan., Du.* **He·le·na** (hā·lā′nä), *Fr.* **Hé·lène** (ā·len′), **He·le·ne** (*Ger.* hā·lā′nə, *Greek* hā·lā′nā). [< Gk., a torch]

—**Helen of Troy** In Greek mythology, the most beautiful woman in the world, daughter of Zeus and Leda and wife of Menelaus; awarded as a prize to Paris by Aphrodite, she eloped with him to Troy, thus causing the Trojan War.

Hel·e·na (hel′ə·nə) The capital of Montana.

Hel·e·na (hel′ə·nə), **Saint,** 247?–327?, mother of Constantine the Great.

Hel·e·nus (hel′ə·nəs) In Greek legend, a son of Priam and Hecuba, endowed like his twin sister Cassandra with the gift of prophecy: captured by the Greeks, he was forced to reveal how Troy could be taken. *Greek* **Hel′e·nos.**

Hel·go·land (hel′gō·länt) A small island in the North Sea off NW Germany; formerly a resort and German naval base: English *Heligoland.*

he·li·a·cal (hi·lī′ə·kəl) *adj.* *Astron.* **1** Pertaining to the sun. **2** Designating those risings and settings of the stars that take place as near the sun as they can be observed. Also **he·li·ac** (hē′lē·ak). [< LL *heliacus* < Gk. *hēliakos* < *hēlios* the sun] —**he·li′a·cal·ly** *adv.*

He·li·an·thus (hē′lē·an′thəs) *n.* A large genus of mainly North American annual or perennial plants of the composite family, the sunflowers, with usually opposite leaves and large heads of yellow flowers. [< NL < Gk. *hēlios* sun + *anthos* a flower]

he·li·ast (hē′lē·ast) *n.* A dicast. [< Gk. *heliastēs* < *heliazesthai* sit in court]

hel·i·cal (hel′i·kəl) *adj.* Pertaining to or shaped like a helix. —**hel′i·cal·ly** *adv.*

helical gear *Mech.* A gear wheel whose teeth are cut across the face at an angle with the axis.

hel·i·cline (hel′ə·klīn) *n.* A ramp with a curving or spiral passageway. [< HELI(X) + (IN)-CLINE]

helico- *combining form* Spiral; helical: *helicodromic.* Also, before vowels, **helic-.** [< Gk. *helix* a spiral]

hel·i·co·dro·mic (hel′i·kō·drō′mik, -drom′ik) *adj.* Having a flight path curving like a corkscrew or a bent skew spiral: said of guided missiles. [< HELICO- + -DROM(OUS) + -IC]

hel·i·coid (hel′ə·koid) *adj.* Coiled spirally, as certain univalve shells: also **hel′i·coi′dal.** —*n.* A geometrical surface resembling that of a screw. —**hel′i·coi′dal·ly** *adv.*

hel·i·con (hel′i·kon, -kən) *n.* A horn-shaped bass or contrabass tuba. [< L < Gk. *Helikōn,* the mountain of the Muses; infl. by HELIX]

Hel·i·con (hel′i·kon, -kən) A mountain range in Boeotia, east central Greece; highest point, 5,736 feet; legendary home of the Muses; site of the fountains of Aganippe and Hippocrene. —**Hel·i·co·ni·an** (hel′i·kō′nē·ən) *adj.*

hel·i·cop·ter (hel′ə·kop′tər, hē′lə-) *n.* *Aeron.* A type of aircraft whose aerodynamic support is obtained from propellers rotating on a vertical axis and which is capable of rising and descending vertically. [< F *hélicoptère* < Gk. *helix, -ikos* a spiral + *pteron* a wing]

FOUR-PASSENGER HELICOPTER
A. Pitch control mechanism. *B.* Torque control rotor.

hel·i·co·tre·ma (hel′ə·kō·trē′mə) *n.* *Anat.* The opening in the inner ear which connects the inner and outer spiral canals at the apex of the cochlea. [< NL < Gk. *helix, -ikos* a spiral + *trēma* hole]

Hel·i·go·land (hel′ə·go·land′) See HELGOLAND.

Heligoland Bight An arm of the North Sea between Helgoland and the German mainland; scene of a British naval victory in World War I, August 28, 1914. *German* **Hel·go·län·der Bucht** (hel′gō·len′dər bōōkht′).

he·li·o (hē′lē·ō) *n. pl.* **·os** *Colloq.* A heliograph.

helio- *combining form* Sun; of the sun: *heliotropic.* [< Gk. *hēlios* the sun]

he·li·o·cen·tric (hē′lē·ə·sen′trik) *adj.* Having reference to the sun as a center: a *heliocentric* system. Also **he′li·o·cen′tri·cal.**

he·li·o·chrome (hē′lē·ə·krōm′) *n.* A photograph in natural colors. —**he′li·o·chro′mic** *adj.*

He·li·o·gab·a·lus (hē′lē·ə·gab′ə·ləs), 204–222, emperor of Rome 218–222, under name of Marcus Aurelius Antoninus: also spelled *Elagabalus.*

he·li·o·gram (hē′lē·ə·gram′) *n.* A message sent by means of a heliograph.

he·li·o·graph (hē′lē·ə·graf′, -gräf′) *n.* **1** An instrument for taking photographs of the sun. **2** A photograph taken by sunlight. **3** A mirror for signaling by flashes of light. —*v.t. & v.i.* To signal with a heliograph. —**he·li·og·ra·pher** (hē′·lē·og′rə·fər) *n.* —**he′li·o·graph′ic** *adj.* —**he′li·og′ra·phy** *n.*

he·li·o·gra·vure (hē′lē·ō·grə·vyŏŏr′) *n.* Photo engraving, or a print or plate produced by it. See PHOTOGRAVURE.

he·li·ol·a·try (hē′lē·ol′ə·trē) *n.* Worship of the sun. —**he′li·ol′a·ter** *n.* —**he′li·ol′a·trous** *adj.*

he·li·o·lith·ic (hē′lē·ə·lith′ik) *adj.* Denoting a culture characterized by sun-worship and megaliths. [< HELIO- + (MEGA)LITHIC]

he·li·ol·o·gy (hē′lē·ol′ə·jē) *n. Obs.* The science of the sun's energy and action. —**he′li·ol′o·gist** *n.*

he·li·om·e·ter (hē′lē·om′ə·tər) *n. Astron.* An instrument for the accurate measurement of small angles in the heavens. —**he·li·o·met·ric** (hē′lē·ə·met′rik) or **·ri·cal** *adj.* —**he′li·om′e·try** *n.*

he·li·oph·i·lous (hē′lē·of′ə·ləs) *adj. Bot.* Fond of or turning toward the sun, as the sunflower. [< HELIO- + Gk. *philos* loving]

he·li·o·pho·bi·a (hē′lē·ə·fō′bē·ə) *n.* Morbid aversion to sunlight.

he·li·o·phyte (hē′lē·ə·fīt′) *n. Bot.* A plant growing in the light.

He·li·op·o·lis (hē′lē·op′ə·lis) **1** An ancient city at the apex of the Nile delta in lower Egypt: Egyptian *On.* **2** The Greek name for BAALBEK.

He·li·os (hē′lē·os) In Greek mythology, the sun god, son of Hyperion: also called *Hyperion.*

he·li·o·scope (hē′lē·ə·skōp′) *n. Astron.* A telescope in which the eyes are protected during observations of the sun.

he·li·o·stat (hē′lē·ə·stat′) *n. Astron.* An instrument consisting of a mirror moved by clockwork so that the rays of the sun shall be reflected from it in a fixed direction.

he·li·o·tax·is (hē′lē·ə·tak′sis) *n.* Phototaxis resulting from the effect of the sun's rays. [< HELIO- + (PHOTO)TAXIS] —**he′li·o·tac′tic** (-tak′tik) *adj.*

he·li·o·ther·a·py (hē′lē·ō·ther′ə·pē) *n. Med.* Exposure to the sun for remedial purposes.

he·li·o·trope (hē′lē·ə·trōp′, hēl′yə-) *n.* **1** An herb (genus *Heliotropium*) with small white or purplish fragrant flowers. **2** Any plant which turns toward the sun. **3** The garden heliotrope or common valerian *(Valeriana officinalis)*; also, the winter heliotrope or butterburr *(Petasites fragrans).* **4** A variety of quartz, the bloodstone. **5** A soft rosy-purple, the color of flowers of *Heliotropium arborescens.* [< F *héliotrope* < L *heliotropium* < Gk. *hēliotropion* < *hēlios* sun + *trepein* turn]

he·li·o·trop·ic (hē′lē·ə·trop′ik, -trō′pik, hēl′yə-) *adj.* Characterized by or pertaining to heliotropism. —**he′li·o·trop′i·cal·ly** *adv.*

he·li·ot·ro·pism (hē′lē·ot′rə·piz′əm) *n. Biol.* That property of an organism by virtue of which it tends, when not symmetrically illuminated on all sides, to move either toward or away from the source of light. Also **he′li·ot′ro·py.**

he·li·o·type (hē′lē·ə·tīp′) *n.* A photoengraving from which impressions can be taken by a printing press; an impression so taken. —*adj.* Of or pertaining to such photoengravings, or to the process of making them. Also **he′li·o·typ′ic** (-tip′ik). —**he′li·o·ty′py** (-tī′pē) *n.*

He·li·o·zo·a (hē′lē·ə·zō′ə) *n. pl.* An order of protozoan aquatic organisms with filamentous pseudopodia radiating from a spherical body. [< NL < Gk. *hēlios* sun + *zōon* animal]

hel·i·port (hel′ə·pôrt′, -pōrt′, hē′lə-) *n.* An airport for helicopters. [< HELI(COPTER) + PORT[1] a harbor]

hel·i·spher·ic (hel′ə·sfer′ik) *adj.* Turning spirally on a sphere. See HELIX, SPHERIC. Also **hel′i·spher′i·cal.** [< Gk. *helix* a spiral + SPHERE]

he·li·um (hē′lē·əm) *n.* A chemically inert, odorless, colorless, gaseous element (symbol He, atomic number 2) having a boiling point near absolute zero, found in natural gas deposits and comprising only about 5 parts per million of the atmosphere but the second most abundant element, after hydrogen, in the universe. See PERIODIC TABLE. [< NL < Gk. *hēlios* sun]

he·lix (hē′liks) *n. pl.* **he·lix·es** or **hel·i·ces** (hel′·ə·sēz) **1** *Geom.* A line, thread, wire, or the like, curved into a shape such as it would assume if wound in a single layer round a cylinder; a form like a screw thread. **2** Any spiral. **3** *Anat.* The recurved border of the external ear. **4** *Archit.* A small volute. [< L, a spiral < Gk.]

hell (hel) *n.* **1** The abode of evil spirits; infernal regions; place of eternal punishment, of extreme torment, etc. See GEHENNA, INFERNO, TARTARUS. **2** Any condition of extreme physical or mental suffering. **3** In ancient times, the place of departed spirits; called by the Greeks *Hades,* by the Hebrews *Sheol,* and by the Scandinavians *Hel.* **4** A place of evil, as a gambling house; also, a place for rejected things or refuse. **5** In Christian Science, mortal belief; error; lust; remorse; hatred; revenge; sin. **6** Hellbox. [OE *hel*]

he'll (hēl) Contraction of HE WILL.

Hel·lad·ic (he·lad′ik) *adj.* Of or pertaining to the pre-Greek civilization of the Aegean.

Hel·las (hel′əs) **1** Originally, a small district and town in Thessaly; later, by extension, all lands inhabited by Greek-speaking peoples. **2** The Greek name as well as a poetic and literary usage for GREECE.

hell·bend·er (hel′ben′dər) *n.* **1** A large and voracious amphibian *(Cryptobranchus allegheniensis)* common in the valley of the Ohio River, and very tenacious of life. **2** *U.S. Slang* A drunken debauch; also, a debauchee.

hell-bent (hel′bent′) *adj. U.S. Slang* Determined; recklessly eager: *hell-bent* for election.

hell·box (hel′boks′) *n. Printing* A receptacle for broken and battered type.

hell·broth (hel′brôth′, -broth′) *n.* A magical mixture prepared for malignant purposes.

hell·cat (hel′kat′) *n.* **1** A furious or spiteful woman. **2** A witch; hag.

hell·div·er (hel′dī′vər) *n.* The dabchick.

Hel·le (hel′ē) In Greek legend, the daughter of Nephele and Athamas who, fleeing with her brother Phrixus on a ram with golden fleece, fell off and was drowned in the strait thenceforth called *Hellespont,* or "sea of Helle."

hel·le·bo·ras·ter (hel′ə·bə·ras′tər) *n.* An English species of hellebore *(Helleborus foetidus)* with numerous globular flowers, often cultivated for ornament: also called *bear's-foot, stinking* or *fetid hellebore.*

hel·le·bore (hel′ə·bôr, -bōr) *n.* **1** A perennial herb (genus *Helleborus*) of the crowfoot family having serrated leaves and large flowers. Cultivated species are, in the United States, the green hellebore *(H. viridis),* and in Europe, the black hellebore or *Christmas rose (H. niger),* the black roots of which are a powerful cathartic. **2** Any of certain herbs (genus *Veratrum*) of the lily family whose dried rootstocks yield poisonous alkaloids of use in medicine and as insecticides; especially the American or green hellebore *(V. viride)* and the European white hellebore *(V. album)*: also called *false hellebore.* **3** The powdered root of the American hellebore, used to destroy plant vermin. [< L *helleborus* < Gk. *helleboros*]

hel·le·bo·re·in (hel′ə·bôr′ē·in, -bō′rē-) *n. Chem.* A toxic glucoside, $C_{37}H_{56}O_{18}$, from the rhizome of *Helleborus niger* and *H. viridis*: a powerful cardiac stimulant.

hel·leb·o·rin (hə·leb′ə·rin, hel′ə·bôr′in, -bō′rin) *n. Chem.* A colorless crystalline glucoside, $C_{28}H_{36}O_6$, from the same sources as helleborein: a powerful cathartic and emmenagog.

Hel·len (hel′ən) In Greek legend, son of Deucalion and Pyrrha and progenitor, through his sons Aeolus, Dorus, and Xuthus, of the Greek race.

Hel·lene (hel′ēn) *n.* A Greek. Also **Hel·le′ni·an.** [< Gk. *Hellēn*]

Hel·len·ic (he·len′ik, -lē′nik) *adj.* Greek; Grecian. —*n.* A subfamily of the Indo-European languages, consisting of the Greek language and its dialects, ancient and modern. See GREEK.

Hel·le·nism (hel′ə·niz′əm) *n.* **1** Ancient Greek character, ideals, or civilization. **2** A Greek idiom or phrase. **3** Assimilation of Greek speech, manners, and culture, as by the Romans or the Jews of the Diaspora.

Hel·le·nist (hel′ə·nist) *n.* **1** An adopter of Greek customs, language, and usages; especially, a Grecizing Jew in the time of the Apostles or in the Alexandrian church: called in the English versions of the New Testament *Grecian Jew* or *Grecian.* **2** A Greek scholar; a specialist in Greek. **3** One of the Byzantine Greeks who contributed to the revival of classical learning in Europe in the 15th century.

Hel·le·nis·tic (hel′ə·nis′tik) *adj.* **1** Of or pertaining to Hellenists. **2** Resembling, representing, or akin to the Greek in thought or style; especially, Greek with an admixture of foreign elements. **3** Of or pertaining to the Hellenistic Age. Also **Hel′le·nis′ti·cal.**

Hellenistic Age The period which began with the conquests of Alexander the Great and ended about 300 years later: characterized by the spread of Greek language and culture throughout the Near East.

Hellenistic Greek See KOINÉ.

Hel·le·nize (hel′ə·nīz) *v.t. & v.i.* **·nized, ·niz·ing** To make or become Greek or Hellenic; adopt or imbue with Greek language or customs; Grecize. —**Hel·le·ni·za·tion** (hel′ə·nə·zā′shən, -nī·zā′-) *n.* —**Hel′le·niz′er** *n.*

hel·ler (hel′ər) *n.* Any one of several small silver or copper coins formerly current in Germany, Switzerland, and Austria. [< G, from *Hall,* a Swabian town where first minted]

Hel·les (hel′əs), **Cape** The southern extremity of Gallipoli Peninsula, European Turkey.

Hel·les·pont (hel′əs·pont) The ancient Greek name for the DARDANELLES. See HELLE.

hell·fire (hel′fīr′) *n.* One of the torments of the damned; the flames of hell.

Hell Gate A narrow channel of the East River in New York City.

hell·gram·mite (hel′grə·mīt) *n.* The large aquatic larva of a megalopterous insect, the four-winged dobson fly, much used as a bait for black bass and other fish: also called *dobson.* See DOBSON FLY. [Origin unknown]

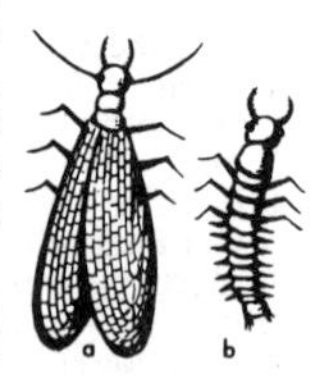

HELLGRAMMITE
Dobson fly *(a)* and larva *(b).*

hell·hound (hel′hound′) *n.* A hound of hell; a fierce and cruel pursuer.

hel·lion (hel′yən) *n. Colloq.* A mischievous person; one given to wild and unpredictable actions. Also called *hallion.* [< HELL]

hell·ish (hel′ish) *adj.* Of or like hell; diabolical; also, wicked; malignant; horrible. See synonyms under INFERNAL. —**hell′ish·ly** *adv.* —**hell′ish·ness** *n.*

hell·kite (hel′kīt′) *n.* **1** A fierce bird of prey. **2** A wantonly malignant or cruel person.

hel·lo (hə·lō′) *interj.* **1** An exclamation used in calling the attention and in greeting, especially over the telephone. **2** An exclamation of surpise. —*n. pl.* **hel·loes** The call "hello." —*v.t. & v.i.* **·loed, ·lo·ing** To call "hello" to.

Hells Canyon A canyon of the Snake River on the Idaho-Oregon border; maximum depth, 7,900 feet.

helm[1] (helm) *n.* **1** *Naut.* The steering apparatus of a vessel, especially the tiller. **2** Metaphorically, any place of control or responsibility; administration. —*v.t.* To manage the helm of; steer; direct. [OE *helma* rudder]

helm[2] (helm) *n. Archaic & Poetic* A helmet; covering. —*v.t.* To cover or supply with a helmet. [OE *helm* covering]

Hel·mand (hel′mənd) A river in Afghanistan, flowing 700 miles SW to the Seistan depression. Also **Hil·mand** (hil′mənd).

hel·met (hel′mit) *n.* **1** A covering of defensive or protective armor for the head, made of metal, as worn by soldiers of all times, or of leather, as worn by football players. **2** Something resembling head armor in shape, position, or function: as, protective headgear, etc.; the metal head covering of a diving suit, or the wire-mesh headguard worn by fencers. [<OF, dim. of *helme* a helmet <Gmc.] — **hel′met·ed** *adj.*

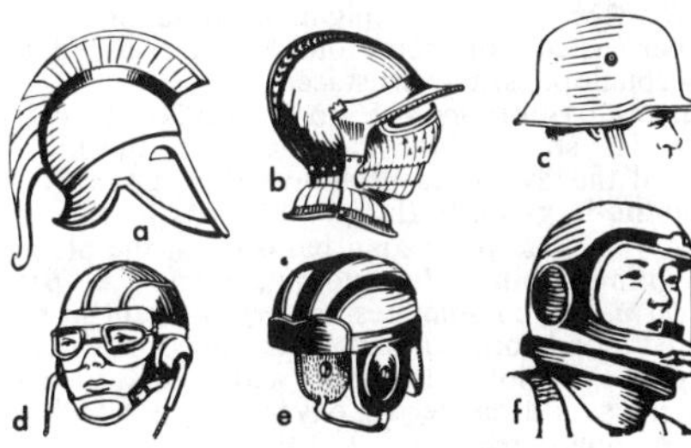

TYPES OF HELMETS
a. Helmet of Grecian warrior.
b. Casque, 16th century knight.
c. German, World War II.
d. Aviator's with headphone.
e. Football player.
f. Space pilot.

Helm·holtz (helm′hōlts), **Baron von,** 1821–1894, Hermann Ludwig Ferdinand, German physiologist and physicist.

hel·minth (hel′minth) *n.* A worm; specifically, a parasitic intestinal worm. [<Gk. *helmins, -inthos* a worm]

hel·min·thi·a·sis (hel′min·thī′ə·sis) *n. Pathol.* Any disorder caused by infestation with worms. [<Gk. *helmins, -inthos* a worm + -IASIS]

hel·min·thic (hel·min′thik) *adj.* **1** Worm-expelling. **2** Pertaining to helminths. — *n.* A vermifuge; an anthelmintic.

hel·min·thol·o·gy (hel′min·thol′ə·jē) *n.* **1** The study of intestinal worms and their effects. **2** The branch of zoology that treats of worms, especially of parasitic worms. [<Gk. *helmins, -inthos* a worm + -LOGY]

helms·man (helmz′mən) *n. pl.* **·men** (-mən) A steersman; one who guides a ship.

helm roof *Archit.* A pointed roof with four inclined faces, gabled at the apex.

Helm·stedt (helm′shtet) A city in Lower Saxony, Germany. Formerly **Helm′städt** (-shtet).

He·lo·der·ma (hē′lə·dûr′mə) *n.* A genus of American lizards, including the Gila monster. [<NL <Gk. *hēlos* a nail + *derma* skin] — **he′lo·der′ma·toid** (-toid) *adj.* & *n.* — **he′lo·der′mid** (-mid) *n.* — **he′lo·der′moid** (-moid) *adj.* & *n.*

Hé·lo·ïse (ā·lō·ēz′) French form of LOUISE. — **Héloïse,** 1101–64, French abbess; pupil and mistress of Abélard and, later, his wife.

he·lo·phyte (hē′lə·fīt) *n. Bot.* A plant growing in marshes and adapted to an amphibious life. [<Gk. *helos* marsh + -PHYTE]

hel·o·plank·ton (hel′ə·plangk′tən) See HELEOPLANKTON.

hel·ot (hel′ət, hē′lət) *n.* **1** One of a class of serfs of ancient Sparta, bound to the soil, and in most cases descended from prisoners of war. **2** Any slave. [<L *helotes* <Gk. *heilōs, heilōtos*; appar. from *Helos,* a Laconian town enslaved by Sparta]

hel·ot·ism (hel′ət·iz′əm, hē′lət-) *n.* **1** Serfdom, as that of ancient Sparta. **2** *Bot.* A type of symbiosis, especially the relation between algae and fungi in forming lichens.

hel·ot·ry (hel′ət·rē, hē′lət-) *n.* **1** Serfdom. **2** Helots as a class.

help (help) *v.t.* **1** To give or provide assistance to; aid. **2** To assist in some action, motion, etc.: with *on, into, out of, up, down,* etc. **3** To rescue, as from death or danger. **4** To give relief to; ease; comfort: to *help* a cold. **5** To be responsible for: He can't *help* it if he's lame. **6** To avoid; refrain from: I couldn't *help* seeing her. **7** To serve; wait on as a waiter, clerk, etc. — *v.i.* **8** To give assistance; be of service. — *n.* **1** Assistance afforded toward the promotion of an object or the attainment of an end. **2** Remedy or relief. **3** Rescue or succor. **4** One who or that which aids; a helper. **5** *U.S.* A hired servant; domestic: often used collectively: The *help* are on strike. **6** *Dial.* A portion of food. [OE *helpan*] — **help′er** *n.*

Synonyms (verb): abet, aid, assist, befriend, cooperate, encourage, foster, relieve, second, succor, support, sustain, uphold. *Help* expresses greater dependence and deeper need than *aid.* In extremity we say "God *help* me" rather than "God *aid* me." In time of danger we cry *"Help! Help!"* rather than *"Aid! Aid!"* To *aid* is to *second* another's own exertions. We speak of *helping* the helpless, rather than of *aiding* them. *Help* includes *aid,* but *aid* may fall short of the meaning of *help.* In law to *aid* or *abet* makes one a principal. (Compare synonyms for ACCESSORY.) To *cooperate* is to *aid* as an equal; to *assist* implies a subordinate and secondary relation. One *assists* a fallen friend to rise; he *cooperates* with him in helping others. *Encourage,* and usually *uphold,* refer to mental *aid*; *succor* and *support,* oftenest to material assistance. We *encourage* the timid or despondent, *succor* the endangered, *support* the weak, *uphold* those who else might be shaken or cast down. Compare ABET, AID, PROMOTE, SERVE. *Antonyms*: see synonyms for HINDER.

help·ful (help′fəl) *adj.* Affording aid; beneficial. — **help′ful·ly** *adv.* — **help′ful·ness** *n.*

help·ing (hel′ping) *n.* **1** A giving of aid. **2** A portion of food.

helping verb An auxiliary verb. See *auxiliary* (*n.,* def. 2a).

help·less (help′lis) *adj.* **1** Unable to help oneself; feeble. **2** Incompetent; incapable. **3** Destitute of help.

help·mate (help′māt) *n.* **1** A helper; partner. **2** A wife. See synonyms under ASSOCIATE.

help·meet (help′mēt) *n.* A helpmate.

Hel·sing·ør (hel′sing·œr′) The Danish name for ELSINORE.

Hel·sin·ki (hel′sing·kē) The capital of Finland, on the Gulf of Finland. *Swedish* **Hel·sing·fors** (hel′sing·fôrz).

hel·ter-skel·ter (hel′tər·skel′tər) *adv.* In a hurried and confused manner. — *adj.* Hurried and confused. — *n.* Disorderly hurry; confused and hasty action. [Imit.]

helve (helv) *n.* The handle, as of an ax or hatchet. [OE *helfe*]

Hel·ve·tia (hel·vē′shə) The Latin name for SWITZERLAND. — **Hel·ve′tian** *adj.* & *n.*

Hel·vet·ic (hel·vet′ik) *adj.* Pertaining to the people of Helvetia (Switzerland); Swiss. — *n.* An adherent of Zwingli and the other Swiss reformers; a Swiss Protestant.

Hel·ve·ti·i (hel·vē′shē·ī) *n. pl.* The members of an ancient Germano-Celtic tribe, originally living in the region bounded by the Black Forest, the Main, and the Rhine; also, in the time of Julius Caesar, in western Switzerland.

Hel·vé·tius (hel·vē′shəs, *Fr.* el·vā·syüs′), **Claude,** 1715–71, French philosopher.

hem[1] (hem) *n.* A finished edge made on a fabric by turning over the raw edge (usually twice) and sewing down the first fold: done to prevent raveling or as an ornament. — *v.t.* **hemmed, hem·ming 1** To make a hem on; border; edge. **2** To shut in; enclose; restrict: usually with *in, about,* etc. [OE] — **hem′mer** *n.*

hem[2] (hem) *n.* & *interj.* A sound made as in clearing the throat; ahem. — *v.i.* **hemmed, hem·ming 1** To make the sound "hem." **2** To hesitate in speaking. [Imit.]

hem- See also words beginning HAEM-.

hem- Var. of HEMO-.

hema- *combining form* Blood: *hemapoiesis.* Also spelled *haema-.* [<Gk. *haima* blood]

he·ma·ba·rom·e·ter (hē′mə·bə·rom′ə·tər, hem′ə-) *n. Med.* An instrument for determining the specific gravity of the blood.

he·ma·chrome (hē′mə·krōm, hem′ə-) *n. Biochem.* The red coloring matter of the blood.

he·ma·cy·tom·e·ter (hē′mə·sī·tom′ə·tər, hem′ə-) *n.* An instrument used in counting blood cells and micro-organisms. — **he′ma·cy·tom′e·try** *n.*

he·ma·gog (hē′mə·gôg, -gog, hem′ə-) *n. Med.* An agent which promotes or favors the discharge of blood. Also **he′ma·gogue.** [<HEM- + -AGOG] — **he′ma·gog′ic** (-goj′ik) *adj.*

he·mal (hē′məl) *adj.* **1** Pertaining to blood or the vascular system; of the nature of blood. **2** Pertaining to or situated on the side of the body that contains the heart. Also spelled *haemal.* [<Gk. *haima* blood + -AL]

he-man (hē′man′) *n. pl.* **·men** (-men′) *Slang* A virile, muscular man.

Hem·ans (hem′ənz, hē′mənz), **Felicia Dorothea,** 1793–1835, *née* Browne, English poet.

he·ma·pho·bi·a (hē′mə·fō′bē·ə, hem′ə-) See HEMOPHOBIA.

he·ma·poi·e·sis (hē′mə·poi·ē′sis, hem′ə-) *n.* The promotion or production of blood. Also called *hematopoiesis.* [<HEMA- + Gk. *poiēsis* a making <*poieein* make] — **he′ma·poi·et′ic** (-poi·et′ik) *adj.*

hemat- Var. of HEMATO-.

he·ma·tal (hē′mə·təl, hem′ə-) *adj.* Of, relating to, or associated with the blood or blood vessels.

he·ma·tal·los·co·py (hē′mə·təl·os′kə·pē, hem′ə-) *n.* The scientific analysis of blood to determine the blood type to which it belongs. [HEMAT- + ALLO- (def. 3) + -SCOPY]

he·ma·te·in (hē′mə·tē′in, hem′ə-) *n. Chem.* A reddish-brown, crystalline substance, $C_{16}H_{12}O_6$, extracted from logwood, and used as an indicator and stain. [<HEMAT- + -EIN]

he·ma·tem·e·sis (hē′mə·tem′ə·sis, hem′ə-) *n. Pathol.* Vomiting of blood; gastric hemorrhage.

he·ma·ther·mal (hē′mə·thûr′məl, hem′ə-) See HEMATOTHERMAL.

he·mat·ic (hi·mat′ik) *adj.* **1** Of, pertaining to, or contained in blood. **2** Effecting a change in the blood. — *n.* A medicine that produces a change in the blood.

hem·a·tin (hem′ə·tin, hē′mə-) *n.* A brownish-black, iron-containing powder formed from hemoglobin by treatment with acid.

hem·a·tin·ic (hem′ə·tin′ik, hē′mə-) *n. Med.* Any agent which increases the number of red corpuscles in the blood. — *adj.* Of or pertaining to hematin.

hem·a·tite (hem′ə·tīt, hē′mə-) *n.* Red ferric oxide, Fe_2O_3, one of the important ores of iron, occurring in columnar, granular, or other forms, and crystallizing in the hexagonal system. Also spelled *haematite.* [<L *haematites* <Gk. *haimatitēs* bloodlike < *haima* blood] — **hem·a·tit·ic** (hem′ə·tit′ik, hē′mə-) *adj.*

hemato- *combining form* Blood: *hematoblast*: also, before vowels, *hemat-.* Also spelled *haemato-.* [<Gk. *haima, haimatos* blood]

hem·a·to·blast (hem′ə·tō·blast′, hē′mə-) *n. Biol.* A cell in the bone marrow or liver which produces the red corpuscles of the blood; a blood platelet.

hem·a·to·cele (hem′ə·tō·sēl′, hē′mə-) *n. Pathol.* A tumor containing blood.

hem·a·to·crit (hem′ə·tō·krit′, hē′mə-) *n.* An instrument which, by centrifugal action, separates the corpuscles and the serum in blood in order to determine the relative amounts. Also spelled *haematokrit.* [<HEMATO- + Gk. *kritēs* a judge < *krinein* judge]

hem·a·toc·ry·al (hem′ə·tok′rē·əl, hē′mə-) *adj. Zool.* Cold-blooded, as fishes and reptiles: also spelled *haematocryal.* [<HEMATO- + Gk. *kryos* cold]

hem·a·to·gen·e·sis (hem′ə·tō·jen′ə·sis, hē′mə-) *n.* The formation of blood. — **hem·a·to·gen′ic** or **hem′a·to·ge·net′ic** (-jə·net′ik) *adj.*

he·ma·toid (hē′mə·toid, hem′ə-) *adj.* Bloody, or resembling blood.

he·ma·tol·o·gy (hē′mə·tol′ə·jē, hem′ə-) *n.* The branch of medical science that treats of the blood, its formation, functions, and diseases: also spelled *haematology.* Also **he′ma·to·lo′·gi·a** (-tə·lō′jē·ə).

he·ma·tol·y·sis (hē′mə·tol′ə·sis, hem′ə-), **he·ma·to·lyt·ic** (hē′mə·tō·lit′ik, hem′ə-) See HEMOLYSIS, etc.

he·ma·to·ma (hē′mə·tō′mə, hem′ə-) *n. pl.* **·to·ma·ta** (-tō′mə·tə) *Pathol.* A blood tumor. [<HEMAT- + -OMA]

he·ma·tom·e·ter (hē′mə·tom′ə·tər, hem′ə-) *n.* An instrument for determining the number of corpuscles in a given quantity of blood. — **he′ma·tom′e·try** *n.*

he·ma·to·pho·bi·a (hē′mə·tō·fō′bē·ə, hem′ə-) See HEMOPHOBIA.

he·ma·to·poi·e·sis (hē′mə·tō′poi·ē′sis, hem′ə-), **he·ma·to·poi·et·ic** (hē′mə·tō′poi·et′ik, hem′ə-) See HEMAPOIESIS, etc.

he·ma·tose (hē′mə·tōs, hem′ə-) *adj.* Fully or abnormally charged with blood.

he·ma·to·sis (hē′mə·tō′sis, hem′ə-) *n. Physiol.* The formation of blood; conversion of chyle or venous blood into arterial blood. [<NL

<Gk. *haimatōsis* <*haimatoein* make into blood]

he·ma·to·ther·a·py (hē′mə·tō·ther′ə·pē, hem′ə-) See HEMOTHERAPY.

he·ma·to·ther·mal (hē′mə·tō·thûr′məl, hem′ə-) *adj. Zool.* Warm-blooded, as mammals and birds: also spelled *haematothermal.*

hem·a·tox·y·lin (hem′ə·tok′sə·lin, hē′mə-) *n. Chem.* A colorless crystalline compound, $C_{16}H_{14}O_6 \cdot 3H_2O$, containing the coloring matter of logwood: used as a dye and indicator. [<HEMATO- + XYL- + -IN]

hem·a·to·zo·on (hem′ə·tō·zō′on, hē′mə-) *n. pl.* **·zo·a** (-zō′ə) An animal parasite living in the blood. [<HEMATO- + Gk. *zōon* animal]

hem·a·tu·ri·a (hem′ə·tŏŏr′ē·ə, -tyŏŏr′-, hē′mə-) *n. Pathol.* Bloody urine. [<HEMAT- + -URIA]

hem·el·y·tron (hem·el′ə·tron) *n. pl.* **·tra** (-trə) *Entomol.* One of the partially thickened and hardened forewings of certain insects: also called *hemielytron.* Also **hem·el′y·trum** (-trəm). [<HEMI-, + ELYTRON] —**hem·el′y·tral** *adj.*

hem·er·a·lo·pi·a (hem′ər·ə·lō′pē·ə) *n. Pathol.* Day blindness, in which sight is less distinct by daylight than by night or by artificial light. See NYCTALOPIA. [<NL <Gk. *hēmera* day + *alaos* blind + *ōps* eye] —**hem′er·a·lo′·pic** *adj.*

Hem·er·o·bap·tist (hem′ər·ə·bap′tist) *n.* **1** A member of an ancient Jewish sect practicing daily ceremonial ablution. **2** One of an early Christian sect holding to daily baptism. [<Med. L *Hemerobaptista* <Gk. *Hēmerobaptistēs* <*hēmera* day + *baptistēs* baptizer]

hem·er·o·phyte (hem′ər·ə·fīt′) *n. Bot.* A plant introduced through the agency of man. [<Gk. *hēmeros* cultivated + -PHYTE]

hemi- *prefix* Half: *hemisphere.* [<Gk., half]

-hemia See -EMIA.

hem·i·al·gi·a (hem′ē·al′jē·ə) *n. Pathol.* Pain, especially in the head, confined to one side; unilateral pain. [<HEMI- on one side + -ALGIA]

hem·i·a·nop·si·a (hem′ē·ə·nop′sē·ə) *n. Pathol.* A paralysis, partial or total, of some of the fibers of the optic nerve, with the result that part of the field of vision is obscured or obliterated in one or both eyes. Also **hem′i·a·no′pi·a** (-nō′pē·ə). [<NL <Gk. *hēmi-* half + *an-* without + *ōps* eye] —**hem′i·a·nop′tic** (-nop′tik) *adj.*

hem·i·at·ro·phy (hem′ē·at′rə·fē) *n. Pathol.* The wasting away of one side, as of the face.

he·mic (hē′mik, hem′ik) *adj.* Pertaining or relating to blood: *hemic* diseases. Also spelled *haemic.*

hem·i·cel·lu·lose (hem′i·sel′yə·lōs) *n. Biochem.* Any of a class of polysaccharide carbohydrates more readily hydrolyzed than cellulose; they occur widely in plants.

hem·i·chor·date (hem′i·kôr′dāt) *adj.* Of, pertaining to or belonging to a division of chordates *(Hemichordata)* characterized by paired gill slits and a primitive notochord including many small marine forms. —*n.* A member of this division; a tongue worm. [<NL <Gk. *hēmi-* half + *chordata* chordate]

hem·i·cra·ny (hem′i·krā′nē) *n. Pathol.* Migraine, or nervous headache. Also **hem′i·cra′·ni·a** (-nē·ə). [<F *hemicraine* <LL *hemicrania* <Gk. *hemikrania* <*hēmi-* half + *kranion* skull]

hem·i·cy·cle (hem′i·sī′kəl) *n.* **1** A semicircular arena, as in a theater. **2** A semicircle, or objects arranged in a semicircle. —**hem′i·cy′·clic** (-sī′klik, -sik′lik) *adj.*

hem·i·dem·i·sem·i·qua·ver (hem′ē·dem′ē·sem′·ē·kwā′vər) *n. Music* A sixty-fourth note.

hem·i·dome (hem′i·dōm) *n. Mineral.* That form in a crystal composed of two parallel domed planes in the triclinic, or of two parallel orthodomic planes in the monoclinic system of crystallization.

hem·i·el·y·tron (hem′ē·el′ə·tron) See HEMELYTRON, etc.

he·mig·na·thous (hə·mig′nə·thəs) *adj.* Having one jaw shorter than the other, as in certain birds. [<HEMI- + Gk. *gnathos* jaw]

hem·i·he·dral (hem′i·hē′drəl) *adj. Mineral.* Pertaining to crystal forms that possess only one half as many planes as are required for complete symmetry in the class to which they belong. [<HEMI- + Gk. *hedra* seat, surface] —**hem′i·he′dral·ly** *adv.*

hem·i·he·dron (hem′i·hē′drən) *n. pl.* **·dra** (-drə) A hemihedral crystal form.

hem·i·met·a·bol·ic (hem′i·met′ə·bol′ik) *adj. Entomol.* Designating those insects whose larvae have an incomplete metamorphosis, developing gradually into the adult stage: opposed to *holometabolic.* Also **hem·i·me·tab·o·lous** (hem′i·mə·tab′ə·ləs). —**hem′i·me·tab′o·lism** (-tab′ə·liz′əm) *n.*

hem·i·mor·phic (hem′i·môr′fik) *adj. Mineral.* **1** Pertaining to crystals that are unsymmetric with reference to the opposite ends of a symmetry axis. **2** Pertaining to a class in the monoclinic system. —**hem′i·mor′phism** (-fiz·əm) *n.*

hem·i·mor·phite (hem′i·môr′fīt) *n.* A white to yellowish or brown orthorhombic hydrous zinc silicate, $Zn_2SiO_4 \cdot H_2O$, pyroelectric and sometimes called *electric calamine*: an important ore of zinc.

he·min (hē′min) *n. Biochem.* A brownish-red, crystalline compound, $C_{34}H_{32}O_4N_4FeCl$, formed by the action of glacial acetic or hydrochloric acid on hemoglobin; hematin hydrochloride: also spelled *haemin.* [<Gk. *haima* blood]

Hem·ing·way (hem′ing·wā), **Ernest,** 1899–1961, U.S. novelist.

hem·i·par·a·site (hem′i·par′ə·sīt) *n. Bot.* A plant partly parasitic, as the mistletoe. —**hem′i·par′a·sit′ic** (-par′ə·sit′ik) *adj.*

hem·i·ple·gi·a (hem′i·plē′jē·ə) *n. Pathol.* Paralysis of one side of the body. Also **hem′i·ple′gy.** —**hem′i·ple′gic** (-plē′jik, -plej′ik) *adj.*

He·mip·ter·a (hi·mip′tər·ə) *n. pl.* An order of insects generally with suctorial mouth parts, and usually with four wings thick at the base and membranous at the free end, including the true bugs, cicadas, crickets, plant lice, etc. [<NL <Gk. *hēmi-* half + *pteron* wing] —**he·mip′ter** *n.* —**he·mip′ter·al** or **he·mip′·ter·ous** *adj.* —**he·mip′ter·an** *adj.* & *n.*

hem·i·sphere (hem′ə·sfir) *n.* **1** A half-sphere, formed by a plane passing through the center of the sphere. **2** A half of the terrestrial or of the celestial globe, or a map or projection of the half of either on a plane surface. The world is usually considered as divided either at the equator into the *northern* and *southern* hemispheres, or at some meridian between Europe and America into the *eastern* and *western*, usually at the twentieth meridian west of Greenwich. **3** *Anat.* One of two large convoluted, semiovoid masses forming the bulk of the cerebrum. [<F *hémisphère* <L *hemisphaerium* <Gk. *hēmisphairion* <*hēmi-* half + *sphaira* a sphere] —**hem·i·spher·ic** (hem′ə·sfer′ik) or **·i·cal** *adj.*

hem·i·sphe·roid (hem′ə·sfir′oid) *n.* A half of a spheroid. —**hem′i·sphe·roi′dal** (-sfi·roid′l) *adj.*

hem·i·stich (hem′i·stik) *n.* A half of a poetic line; an incomplete poetic line. [<LL *hemistichium* <Gk. *hēmistichion* <*hēmi-* half + *stichos* a row, line of poetry]

hem·i·sys·to·le (hem′i·sis′tə·lē) *n. Med.* Contraction of only one of the heart ventricles, producing only one pulse beat for every two heartbeats.

hem·i·ter·pene (hem′i·tûr′pēn) *n. Chem.* Any of a group of isomeric hydrocarbons related to the terpenes, and having the general formula C_5H_8.

hem·i·trope (hem′i·trōp) *n.* A twin crystal. —*adj.* **1** Having one part in reverse position with reference to the other: said of a crystal form. **2** Half inverted. Also **hem′i·trop′ic** (-trop′ik, -trō′pik) *adj.* [<F *hémitrope* <Gk. *hēmi-* half + *tropē* a turning <*trepein* turn]

he·mit·ro·pous (hə·mit′rə·pəs) *adj.* **1** *Bot.* Half anatropous: said of a half-inverted ovule. **2** *Entomol.* Adapted for pollinating certain kinds of flowers: said of bees, etc.

hem·line (hem′līn′) *n.* The line formed by the lower edge of a garment, as a dress.

hem·lock (hem′lok) *n.* **1** An evergreen tree (genus *Tsuga*) of North America and Asia. **2** The wood of this tree. **3** The hemlock spruce. **4** The spotted hemlock *(Conium maculatum)*, a large biennial herb of the parsley or carrot family, yielding coniine: also **poison hemlock.** **5** A poison made from the unripe dried fruit of this herb: Socrates drank the *hemlock.* **6** Any of several related herbs, as the water hemlock *(Cicuta maculata).* [OE *hymlice*]

hemlock spruce A North American coniferous tree of the pine family *(Tsuga canadense)*, having a coarse non-resinous wood used for paper pulp and packing boxes, and a bark which yields an important tanning material.

hemo- *combining form* Blood: *hemoglobin*: also, before vowels, *hem-*. Also spelled *haemo-*. [<Gk. *haima* blood]

he·mo·cy·a·nin (hē′mə·sī′ə·nin, hem′ə-) *n. Biochem.* A protein pigment containing copper instead of iron, found in the blood of cephalopods and crustacea.

he·mo·dy·nam·ics (hē′mō·dī·nam′iks, hem′ō-) *n.* The study of the movements of the blood and the dynamics of blood pressure.

he·mo·flag·el·late (hē′mə·flaj′ə·lāt, hem′ə-) *n.* A flagellate protozoan parasitic in the blood.

he·mo·glo·bin (hē′mə·glō′bin, hem′ə-) *n. Biochem.* The complex respiratory pigment in the red blood corpuscles of vertebrates. It is composed of globin in union with hematin, and serves as a carrier of oxygen, with which it combines freely.

he·mo·hy·per·ox·i·a (hē′mō·hī′pər·ok′sē·ə, hem′ō-) *n. Med.* Hyperoxia of the blood.

he·mo·hy·pox·i·a (hē′mō·hī·pok′sē·ə, hem′ō-) *n. Med.* Hypoxia of the blood.

he·moid (hē′moid) *adj.* Resembling blood; hematoid: also spelled *haemoid.*

he·mo·leu·ko·cyte (hē′mə·lōō′kə·sīt, hem′ə-) *n.* A white blood corpuscle. Also **he′mo·leu′·co·cyte.**

he·mo·ly·sin (hē′mə·lī′sin, hem′ə-, hi·mol′ə·sin) *n. Biochem.* A substance contained or formed in the blood and having the power to liberate hemoglobin from the red blood corpuscles.

he·mol·y·sis (hi·mol′ə·sis) *n.* Dissolution or breakdown of red blood corpuscles with liberation of their contained hemoglobin: also called *hematolysis.* —**he·mo·lyt·ic** (hē′·mə·lit′ik, hem′ə-) *adj.*

Hé·mon (ā·môn′), **Louis,** 1880–1913, French novelist.

he·mo·phil·i·a (hē′mə·fil′ē·ə, -fil′yə, hem′ə-) *n. Pathol.* A disorder characterized by profuse and excessive bleeding even from slight injuries: typically affecting only males, who inherit it as a sex-linked genetic factor transmitted through the mother; the bleeder's disease. Also spelled *haemophilia.* [<NL <Gk. *haima* blood + *philia* fondness]

he·mo·phil·i·ac (hē′mə·fil′ē·ak, hem′ə-) *n.* One afflicted with hemophilia; a bleeder. Also **he′mo·phile** (-fīl).

he·mo·phil·ic (hē′mə·fil′ik, hem′ə-) *adj.* **1** Pertaining to hemophilia. **2** Thriving in blood, as certain bacteria.

he·mo·pho·bi·a (hē′mə·fō′bē·ə, hem′ə-) *n.* A morbid fear of blood: also *hemaphobia, hematophobia.* —**he′mo·pho′bic** *adj.*

he·mo·ple·o·nex·i·a (hē′mə·plē′ə·nek′sē·ə, hem′ə-) *n.* Pleonexia.

hem·op·ty·sis (hem·op′tə·sis) *n. Pathol.* Bleeding from the lungs or bronchial tubes. [<HEMO- + *ptysis* spitting <Gk. *ptyein* spit]

hem·or·rhage (hem′ər·ij, hem′rij) *n.* Discharge of blood from a ruptured blood vessel. —*v.i.* **hem·or·rhaged, hem·or·rhag·ing** To bleed copiously. Also spelled *haemorrhage.* [<L *haemorrhagia* <Gk. *haimorrhagia* <*haima* blood + *-rhagia* <*rhēgnynai* burst] —**hem·or·rhag·ic** (hem′ə·raj′ik) *adj.*

hem·or·rhoid (hem′ə·roid) *n. Often pl.* A swollen mass of varicose veins in the rectal mucous membrane: also called (in the plural) *piles.* Also spelled *haemorrhoid.* [<F <L <Gk. *haimorrhoides (phlebes)* bleeding (veins) <*haima* blood + *rheein* flow] —**hem·or·rhoi·dal** (hem′ə·roid′l) *adj.*

he·mo·spa·sia (hē′mə·spā′zhə, -zhē·ə, hem′ə-) *n.* The drawing of blood to a given part of the body by means of a suction cup. [<HEMO- + Gk. *spasis* suction <*spaein* draw]

he·mo·sta·sia (hē′mə·stā′zhə, -zhē·ə, hem′ə-) *n.* **1** Congestion of blood in a part. **2** The checking of hemorrhage. Also **he·mos·ta·sis** (hi·mos′tə·sis). [<NL <Gk. *haima* blood + *stasis* a standing]

he·mo·stat (hē′mə·stat, hem′ə-) *n. Med.* A device or drug for checking the flow of blood.

he·mo·stat·ic (hē′mə·stat′ik, hem′ə-) *adj. Med.* **1** Stopping the flow of blood. **2** Preventive of bleeding. —*n.* A hemostat.

he·mo·ther·a·py (hē′mə·ther′ə·pē, hem′ə-) *n. Med.* The treatment of disease by the administration of blood or blood preparations: also called *hematotherapy.*

he·mo·tho·rax (hē′mə·thôr′aks, -thō′raks, hem′ə-) *n.* Effusion of blood into the chest.

he·mo·thy·mi·a (hē′mə·thī′mē·ə, hem′ə-) *n. Psychiatry* A morbid craving for blood; impulse to murder. [<NL <Gk. *haima* blood + *thymos* passion <*thyein* rage] **—he'mo·thy'mic** *adj.*

hemp (hemp) *n.* **1** A tall, annual Asian herb *(Cannabis sativa)* of the mulberry family, with small green flowers and a tough bark; Indian hemp. **2** The tough and strong fiber obtained from this plant, used for cloth and cordage. **3** A narcotic prepared from the plant, as bhang or hashish. **4** *Colloq.* The hangman's rope. **—Bengal, Bombay, Madras,** or **sunn hemp** See SUNN. [OE *henep*]

HEMP (Plant 4 to 8 feet tall)

hemp agrimony A coarse European herb *(Eupatorium cannabinum)* resembling the boneset of the United States.

hemp dogbane See INDIAN HEMP (def. 2).

hemp·en (hem'pən) *adj.* **1** Made of hemp. **2** Of or pertaining to hemp.

hemp nettle A common weed *(Galeopsis tetrahit)* of the mint family, having stems covered with prickly deflexed bristles and leaves hairy on both sides.

hemp·seed (hemp'sēd') *n.* The seed of hemp.

hemp·y (hem'pē) *adj.* **hemp·i·er, hemp·i·est 1** Hempen. **2** *Scot.* & *Brit. Dial.* Worthy of hanging: used humorously. Also **hemp'ie.**

hem·stitch (hem'stich') *n.* The ornamental finishing of the inner edge of a hem, made by pulling out several threads adjoining it and drawing the cross-threads together in groups by successive stitches. —*v.t.* To embroider with a hemstitch. **—hem'stitch'er** *n.*

A B C

HEMSTITCH
A. Threads pulled.
B. Cross-threads drawn together at one edge.
C. Cross-threads drawn together at both edges.

hen (hen) *n.* **1** The mature female of the common domestic fowl. **2** Any female bird. **3** The female of the lobster and certain fishes. [OE *henn*]

hen-and-chickens (hen'ən·chik'ənz) *n.* A plant which propagates by means of offshoots, runners, and other ground parts, as the ground ivy and the European houseleek.

hen·bane (hen'bān') *n.* A poisonous, Old World herb *(Hyoscyamus niger)* of the nightshade family, with sticky, malodorous foliage and reddish-brown flowers: the source of hyoscyamine.

hen·bit (hen'bit') *n.* **1** A low herb *(Lamium amplexicaule)* of the mint family; deadnettle. **2** The ivy-leaved speedwell *(Veronica hederaefolia).* [Trans. of MLG *hoenderbeet*]

hence (hens) *adv.* **1** Away from this place. **2** In the future. **3** From this cause or source; consequently; therefore. See synonyms under THEREFORE. —*interj.* Depart! [ME *hennes* <*henne* (OE *heonan* from here) + *-s,* adverbial suffix]

hence·forth (hens'fôrth', -fōrth', hens'fôrth', -fōrth') *adv.* From this time on. Also **hence'for'ward** (-fôr'wərd).

hench·man (hench'mən) *n. pl.* **·men** (-mən) **1** A servile assistant. **2** A faithful follower. **3** A male servant. See synonyms under ACCESSORY. [ME *henxstman* <OE *hengst* horse + *man* a groom]

hen·coop (hen'ko͞op', -ko͝op') *n.* A cage or crib for confining poultry.

hen·dec·a·gon (hen·dek'ə·gon) *n.* A plane figure, with eleven sides and eleven angles: also spelled *endecagon.* [<Gk. *hendeka* eleven + -GON] **—hen·de·cag·o·nal** (hen'də·kag'ə·nəl) *adj.*

hen·dec·a·syl·lab·ic (hen'dek·ə·si·lab'ik) *adj.* Containing eleven syllables. —*n.* A metrical line containing eleven syllables: also **hen'dec·a·syl'la·ble.** [<L *hendecasyllabus* <Gk. *hendekasyllabos* + -IC]

hen·di·a·dys (hen·dī'ə·dis) *n.* In rhetoric, the use of two words connected by a conjunction to express the same idea as a single word with a qualifier; as, with *might and main* instead of by *main strength.* [<LL <Gk. *hen dia dyoin* one through two]

Hen·don (hen'dən) A municipal borough of Middlesex, England; site of Royal Air Force airfield and scene of annual air show.

hen·e·quen (hen'ə·kin) *n.* **1** A tough fiber obtained from the leaves of the Mexican plant *Agave fourcroydes,* or from the related *A. sisalana;* Mexican sisal. **2** The plant from which this fiber is obtained. Also **hen'e·quin.** [<Sp. <Taino]

Hen·gist (heng'gist, hen'jist), died 488, and his brother **Hor·sa** (hôr'sə), died 455, leaders of the Jutish invaders of Kent, England.

Heng·yang (hung'yäng') A city of SE central China. Formerly **Heng·chow** (hung'jō').

Hen·ley (hen'lē) A municipal borough of Oxfordshire, England; site of an annual rowing regatta since 1839. Also **Hen'ley-on-Thames'** (-temz').

Hen·ley (hen'lē), **William Ernest,** 1849–1903, English journalist, poet, and author.

Hen·lo·pen (hen·lō'pən), **Cape** A cape in Delaware opposite Cape May, New Jersey, at the entrance to Delaware Bay.

hen·na (hen'ə) *n.* **1** An Oriental shrub or small tree *(Lawsonia inermis)* with lance-shaped, entire leaves. **2** A cosmetic preparation from the leaves of this plant: used for dyeing the fingernails, hair, etc. **3** The color of this dye, varying from reddish-orange to coppery-brown. [<Arabic *henna*]

Hen·ne·pin (hen'ə·pin, *Fr.* en·pan'), **Louis,** 1640–1708?, Flemish Franciscan missionary to Canada.

hen·ner·y (hen'ər·ē) *n. pl.* **·ner·ies** A place where hens are kept.

hen·o·the·ism (hen'ō·thē·iz'əm) *n.* The doctrine that ascribes supreme power to some one of several gods in turn; also, the belief in a special supreme god for each region, race, or nation. [<Gk. *hen* one + THEISM] **—hen'o·the'ist** *n.* **—hen'o·the·is'tic** *adj.*

hen·peck (hen'pek') *v.t.* To harass or domineer over (the husband): said of wives.

Hen·ri (hen'rī), **Robert,** 1865–1929, U.S. painter.

Hen·ri·et·ta (hen'rē·et'ə, *Du., Sw.* hen'rē·et'ä) A feminine personal name. Also **Hen·ri·et·te** (*Dan.* hen'rē·et'ä; *Ger.* hen'rē·et'ə), *Fr.* **Hen·ri·ette** (äṅ·rē·et'), *Pg.* **Hen·ri·que·ta** (eṅ·rē·kā'tä). [<Gmc., ruler of the home]

hen·roost (hen'ro͞ost') *n.* A place where poultry roost.

hen·ry (hen'rē) *n. Electr.* The practical unit of inductance; the inductance of a circuit in which the variation of the current at the rate of one ampere per second induces an electromotive force of one volt. [after Joseph *Henry*]

Hen·ry (hen'rē) A masculine personal name; also, the name of many European monarchs. Also *Du., Dan.* **Hen·drik** (hen'drik), *Fr.* **Hen·ri** (äṅ·rē'), *Latin* **Hen·ri·cus** (hen·rē'kəs), *Sw.* **Hen·rik** (hen'rik), *Pg.* **Hen·ri·que** (eṅ·rē'kä). [<Gmc., ruler of the home]

—Henry I, 1068–1135, king of England 1100–1135; son of William the Conqueror, conquered Normandy: called "Beauclerc."

—Henry II, 1133–89, king of England 1154–1189, first Plantagenet king.

—Henry III, 1207–72, king of England 1216–1272; barons rebelled against his rule under leadership of Simon de Montfort.

—Henry III, 1551–89, king of France 1574–1589; with his mother, Catherine de' Medici, plotted the Massacre of St. Bartholomew's, 1572.

—Henry IV, 1050–1106, Holy Roman Emperor 1056–1106; excommunicated by Pope Gregory VII.

—Henry IV, 1367–1413, king of England 1399–1413; first Lancastrian king: called "Bolingbroke."

—Henry IV, 1553–1610, king of France 1589–1610; first Bourbon king: also known as **Henry of Navarre.**

—Henry V, 1387–1422, king of England 1413–22; conquered France.

—Henry VI, 1421–71, king of England 1422–1461 and 1470–71.

—Henry VII, 1457–1509, king of England 1485–1509; first Tudor king.

—Henry VIII, 1491–1547, king of England 1509–47; threw off papal authority.

—Henry the Navigator, 1394–1460, prince of Portugal; patron of voyagers and explorers.

Henry, Cape A cape in southern Virginia at the southern entrance of Chesapeake Bay.

Hen·ry (hen'rē), **Joseph,** 1797–1878, U.S. physicist. **—O.** See O. HENRY. **—Patrick,** 1736–99, U.S. statesman and orator.

Hens·lowe (henz'lō), **Philip,** died 1616, English theatrical manager.

hent (hent) *v.t. Archaic* To seize; catch. —*n. Obs.* A catch or grasp. [OE *hentan*]

hep (hep) *adj. U.S. Slang* Aware; informed; cognizant: often with *to.* [? Alter. of STEP, as pronounced in counting time for marching]

he·par (hē'pär) *n. Med.* A liver-brown alkaline sulfide formed by fusing an alkaline carbonate, as potash, with sulfur: used as an antacid and alterative: also called *liver of sulfur.* [<Med. L <Gk. *hēpar* the liver]

hep·a·rin (hep'ə·rin) *n. Biochem.* A polysaccharide found in liver and other animal tissues and having the power to prevent the coagulation of blood: used in medicine and surgery. [<Gk. *hēpar* liver + -IN]

he·pat·ic (hi·pat'ik) *adj.* **1** Of, pertaining to, or resembling the liver. **2** Occurring in, affecting, or acting upon the liver. **3** *Bot.* Pertaining to or resembling a class of plants, the liverworts. **4** Liver-colored. —*n.* **1** A drug acting on the liver. **2** A liverwort. Also **he·pat'i·cal.** [<L *hepaticus* <Gk. *hēpatikos* <*hēpar* the liver]

he·pat·i·ca (hi·pat'ə·kə) *n. pl.* **·cas** or **·cae** (-sē) Any of a genus *(Hepatica)* of small perennial herbs of the crowfoot family, with three-lobed leaves and delicate, variously colored flowers; the liverleaf. [<NL <L *hepaticus* of the liver]

hepatic cells The functional cells of the liver.

hep·a·ti·tis (hep'ə·tī'tis) *n. Pathol.* Inflammation of the liver.

hep·a·ti·za·tion (hep'ə·tə·zā'shən, -tī·zā'-) *n.* The conversion of any tissue into a substance resembling liver. Also *Brit.* **hep'a·ti·sa'tion.**

hepato- *combining form* Pertaining to the liver: *hepatogenic.* Also, before vowels, **hepat-.** [<Gk. *hēpar, hēpatos* the liver]

hep·a·to·gen·ic (hep'ə·tō·jen'ik) *adj.* Produced by or proceeding from the liver. Also **hep·a·tog·e·nous** (hep'ə·toj'ə·nəs).

hep·a·to·pan·cre·as (hep'ə·tō·pan'krē·əs) *n. Zool.* A glandular organ of many invertebrates, supposed to have the function of the liver and the pancreas.

hep·a·tos·co·py (hep'ə·tos'kə·pē) *n.* **1** Divination by inspecting the livers of animals. **2** Inspection of the liver.

hep·cat (hep'kat') *n. Slang* A jazz expert or enthusiast. [<HEP + CAT (def. 11)]

He·phaes·tus (hi·fes'təs) In Greek mythology, the ugly, lame god of fire and of metallurgy; son of Zeus and Hera, and, in the *Odyssey,* the husband of Aphrodite: identified with the Roman *Vulcan*: also called the *Lemnian smith. Greek* **He·phais'tos.** Also **He·phæs'tus.**

Hep·ple·white (hep'əl·hwīt) *adj.* Denoting an English style of furniture characterized by graceful curves and light, slender woodwork: developed in the reign of George III. [after G. *Hepplewhite,* died 1786, the designer]

HEPPLEWHITE CHAIR

hepta- *combining form* Seven: *heptachord.* Also, before vowels, **hept-.** [<Gk. *hepta-* <*hepta* seven]

hep·ta·chlor (hep'tə·klôr, -klōr) *n.* A chlorinated hydrocarbon, $C_{10}H_7Cl_7$, toxic to humans and used as an insecticide.

hep·ta·chord (hep'tə·kôrd) *n. Music* **1** A diatonic octave considered without the upper note. **2** An instrument with seven strings. **3** The interval of the major seventh. [<Gk.

heptachordos < *hepta-* seven + *chordē* a string]

hep·tad (hep′tad) *adj.* Having a combining power of seven; of or belonging to a heptad. — *n.* **1** A collection of seven things. **2** *Chem.* An atom, radical, or element that has a valence of seven. [<Gk. *heptas, -ados* a group of seven]

hep·ta·glot (hep′tə·glot) *adj.* Written in seven languages. — *n.* A book in seven languages.

hep·ta·gon (hep′tə·gon) *n.* A plane figure having seven sides and seven angles. — **hep·tag·o·nal** (hep·tag′ə·nəl) *adj.*

HEPTAGON

hep·ta·he·dron (hep′tə·hē′·drən) *n.* A solid bounded by seven plane faces. — **hep′ta·he′dral** (-drəl) *adj.*

hep·tam·er·ous (hep·tam′ər·əs) *adj.* **1** Having seven parts. **2** *Bot.* Having seven members in each whorl: said of flowers. [<HEPTA- + -MEROUS]

hep·tam·e·ter (hep·tam′ə·tər) *n.* A verse of seven feet or measures.

hep·tane (hep′tān) *n.* A colorless, inflammable, liquid hydrocarbon of the methane series, C_7H_{16}: used as a solvent and in the determination of the octane number of motor fuels. [<HEPT(A)- + -ANE[2]]

hep·tan·gu·lar (hep·tang′gyə·lər) *adj.* Having seven angles.

hep·tar·chy (hep′tär·kē) *n. pl.* **·chies 1** A group of seven kingdoms or governments; specifically, the seven Saxon kingdoms in England (fifth to ninth century). **2** Government by seven persons.

hep·ta·stich (hep′tə·stik) *n.* A heptameter.

Hep·ta·teuch (hep′tə·to͞ok, -tyo͞ok) *n.* The first seven books of the Old Testament. [<HEPTA- + Gk. *teuchos* book]

hep·tode (hep′tōd) *n. Electronics* A seven-electrode vacuum tube containing an anode, cathode, control electrode, and four additional electrodes ordinarily acting as grids. [<HEPT(A)- + -ODE[1]]

her (hûr) *pron.* The objective case of *she.* — *pronominal adj.* Belonging or pertaining to a female person, animal, etc.: the form of the possessive case of the pronoun *she* when used attributively: *her* garden. [OE *hire*]

He·ra (hir′ə) In Greek mythology, the queen of the gods and goddess of women and marriage, sister and wife of Zeus: identified with the Roman *Juno.* Also spelled *Here.*

Her·a·cle·a (her′ə·klē′ə) An ancient city of southern Italy; scene of a Roman defeat by Pyrrhus of Epirus, 280 B.C.

Her·a·cles (her′ə·klēz) Hercules. Also **Her′a·kles.** — **Her·a·cle·an** (her′ə·klē′ən) *adj.*

Her·a·clid (her′ə·klid) *n. pl.* **Her·a·cli·dae** (her′ə·klī′dē) A descendant of Hercules; one of the ancient Spartan royalty, who claimed such descent. [<Gk. *Herakleidēs*] — **Her·a·cli·dan** (her′ə·klī′dən) *adj.*

Her·a·cli·tus (her′ə·klī′təs), 535?–475? B.C., Greek philosopher.

He·rak·lei·on (hə·rak′lē·ən, her′ə·klī′ən) The Greek name for CANDIA. Also **I·rá·kli·on** (i·räk′lē·ôn).

her·ald (her′əld) *n.* **1** Formerly, an officer whose business it was to bear messages, challenges, etc., from a sovereign or from the commander of an army. **2** *Brit.* An official whose duty and profession it is to grant or record arms, trace and record genealogies, record the creation of peers, etc. **3** An official bearer of important tidings; hence, any bearer of news. **4** A precursor; harbinger. — *v.t.* To announce publicly; usher in; proclaim. See synonyms under ANNOUNCE, PRECEDE. [<OF *heralt,* ? <OHG *heren* call] — **he·ral·dic** (hi·ral′dik) *adj.*

Synonyms (noun): ambassador, courier, forerunner, harbinger, pioneer, precursor.

her·ald·ry (her′əl·drē) *n.* **1** The science that treats of blazoning or describing armorial bearings, etc. **2** An emblazonment. **3** The symbolism of heraldic bearings. **4** The ceremony attendant upon heraldry.

Heralds' College In England, a corporate body of officials, instituted in 1484 to determine all questions concerning heraldry, the use of heraldic devices, the rights of those privileged to use them, etc.

her·ald·ship (her′əld·ship) *n.* The office or rank of a herald.

Her·at (he·rät′) A province of NW Afghanistan; 50,000 square miles; capital, Herat.

herb (ûrb, hûrb) *n.* **1** A seed plant devoid of woody tissue which dies completely, or down to the ground, after flowering. **2** A herbaceous plant valued for its medicinal qualities or for its smell or taste. **3** *Rare* Herbage. [<L *herba* grass, herbage]

her·ba·ceous (hûr·bā′shəs) *adj.* **1** Pertaining to, having the character of, or similar to herbs. **2** Having the semblance, color, or structure of an ordinary leaf.

herb·age (ûr′bij, hûr′-) *n.* **1** Herbs collectively. **2** Pasturage. **3** The leaves, stems, and other succulent parts of herbaceous plants.

herb·al (hûr′bəl, ûr′-) *adj.* Of or pertaining to herbs. — *n.* **1** A book containing classifications and descriptions of herbs or plants. **2** A herbarium.

herb·al·ist (hûr′bəl·ist, ûr′-) *n.* **1** A dealer in herbs, especially medicinal herbs. **2** Formerly, one skilled in the study of herbs or plants. Also **herb′ist.**

her·bar·i·um (hûr·bâr′ē·əm) *n. pl.* **·bar·i·ums** or **·bar·i·a** (-bâr′ē·ə) **1** A collection of dried plants scientifically arranged. **2** A room or building containing such a collection. [<LL <L *herba* grass]

Her·bart (hûr′bärt, *Ger.* her′bärt), **Johann Friedrich,** 1776–1841, German philosopher. — **Her·bar·ti·an** (hûr·bär′tē·ən) *adj.* — **Her·bar′ti·an·ism** *n.*

herb·a·ry (hûr′bə·rē) *n. pl.* **·ries** A garden containing only herbs or vegetables.

herb-ben·net (ûrb′ben′it, hûrb′-) *n.* A European herb of the rose family (*Geum urbanum*); avens. [<OF *herbe beneite* <Med. L *herba benedicta,* lit., blessed herb]

Her·bert (hûr′bərt, *Ger., Sw.* her′bərt; *Fr.* er·bâr′) A masculine personal name. Also *Lat.* **Her·ber·tus** (hər·bûr′təs), *Pg.* **Her·ber·to** (er·ber′to͞o). [<Gmc., bright warrior]

Herbert (hûr′bərt), **George,** 1593–1633, English clergyman and poet. — **Victor,** 1859–1924, U.S. composer born in Ireland.

her·bes·cent (hûr·bes′ənt) *adj.* **1** Herblike. **2** Tending to become herbaceous.

her·bi·cide (hûr′bə·sīd) *n.* A weed-killer.

her·bif·er·ous (hûr·bif′ər·əs) *adj.* Producing herbs or vegetation. [<L *herbifer* < *herba* grass + *ferre* bear]

her·bi·vore (hûr′bə·vôr, -vōr) *n.* A herbivorous animal.

her·biv·o·rous (hûr·biv′ər·əs) *adj.* **1** Feeding on vegetable matter. **2** Belonging to a group or division (*Herbivora*) of mammals (now generally called *Ungulata*) that feed mainly on herbage, as cows, horses, camels, etc. [<L *herba* grass + -VOROUS]

herb-Par·is (ûrb′par′is, hûrb′-) *n.* A European herb of the lily family (*Paris quadrifolia*) closely allied to the wakerobin: also called *paris.*

herb-rob·ert (ûrb′rob′ərt, hûrb′-) *n.* A species of cranebill or geranium (*Geranium robertianum*).

herb·y (ûr′bē, hûr′-) *adj.* **1** Of the nature of herbs. **2** Relating to or abounding with herbs.

Her·ce·go·vi·na (hûr′tsə·gô·vē′nə, *Serbian* her′·tsə·gō′vi·nä) The Serbo-Croatian spelling of HERZEGOVINA.

Her·cu·la·ne·um (hûr′kyə·lā′nē·əm) A Roman city near Naples, buried by an eruption of Vesuvius in A.D. 79.

her·cu·le·an (hûr·kyo͞o′lē·ən, hûr′kyə·lē′ən) *adj.* Possessing or requiring great strength; laborious; mighty.

Her·cu·le·an (hûr·kyo͞o′lē·ən, hûr′kyə·lē′ən) *adj.* Like or pertaining to Hercules (Heracles), the ancient hero.

Her·cu·les (hûr′kyə·lēz) **1** In Greek mythology, the son of Alcmene and Zeus, renowned for his strength and endurance: also spelled *Heracles.* **2** Any man of great size and strength. **3** A large northern constellation. See CONSTELLATION. — **labors of Hercules** A series of twelve great tasks imposed by Eurystheus upon Hercules, because of the hostility of Hera: the killing of the Nemean lion; the killing of the Hydra of Lerna; the capture of the Erymanthian boar; the capture of the stag of Ceryneia; the killing of the man-eating birds of Stymphalus; the cleansing of the stables of Augeas; the capture of the Cretan bull; the capture of the horses of Diomedes; the theft of the girdle of Hippolyta; the capture of the cattle of Geryon; the theft of the apples of the Hesperides; and the capture of Cerberus from Hades.

Her·cu·les-club (hûr′kyə·lēz·klub′) *n.* **1** One of several small trees or shrubs, as the prickly ash, the spikenard, etc.: also called *angelica-tree.* **2** A large variety of the common gourd.

her·cy·nite (hûr′sə·nīt) *n.* A vitreous, black iron spinel, $FeAl_2O_4$, crystallizing in the isometric system. [<L *Hercynia (silva)* the Bohemian (forest) + -ITE[1]]

herd[1] (hûrd) *n.* **1** A number of animals feeding or traveling together. **2** A large crowd; especially, the common people; rabble. — *v.t.* & *v.i.* To bring or group together in or as in a herd. [OE *heord*]

herd[2] (hûrd) *n. Scot.* & *Brit. Dial.* A herdsman; shepherd. — *v.t.* To care for or drive (sheep, cattle, etc.).

-herd *combining form* Herdsman: *swineherd, cowherd,* etc. [OE *hirde* herdsman]

herd·book (hûrd′bo͝ok′) *n.* A record of the pedigrees of cattle in important herds.

Her·der (hûr′dər, *Ger.* her′dər), **Johann Gottfried von,** 1744–1803, German poet, theologian, and philosopher.

herd·er (hûr′dər) *n.* **1** A herdsman. **2** *U.S.* One who looks after a herd of cattle or a flock of sheep.

her·dic (hûr′dik) *n.* A carriage, usually two-wheeled, with low-hung body, back entrance, and side seats. [after Peter *Herdic,* 1824–88, its inventor]

herd's-grass (hûrdz′gras′, -gräs′) *n.* **1** Redtop. **2** Timothy. Also **herd′-grass′.** [after John *Herd,* early New Hampshire farmer]

herds·man (hûrdz′mən) *n. pl.* **·men** (-mən) *Brit.* One who owns or tends a herd. Also **herd′man.**

here (hir) *adv.* **1** In or at this place. **2** To this place; hither. **3** At this point of time or stage of proceedings; now. **4** At a place indicated. **5** In the present life. ◆ Homophone: *hear.* [OE *hēr*]

He·re (hir′ē) See HERA.

here·a·bout (hir′ə·bout′) *adv.* About this place; in this vicinity. Also **here′a·bouts′.**

here·af·ter (hir·af′tər, -äf′-) *adj.* **1** At some future time. **2** From this time forth. **3** In the state of life after death; after the present life. — *n.* A future state or existence. [OE *hēræfter*]

here and there In one place and another; so as to be irregularly scattered. — **neither here nor there** Foreign to the subject under discussion; unimportant; irrelevant.

here·at (hir·at′) *adv.* **1** At this time. **2** By reason of this; because of this.

here·by (hir·bī′) *adv.* **1** By means or by virtue of this. **2** Near this.

He·re·dia (ā·rā′thyä), **José Maria de,** 1842–1905, French poet born in Cuba.

he·red·i·ta·bil·i·ty (hə·red′i·tə·bil′ə·tē), **he·red·i·ta·ble** (hə·red′i·tə·bəl), etc. See HERITABILITY, etc.

her·e·dit·a·ment (her′ə·dit′ə·mənt) *n. Law* That capable of being inherited. — **corporeal hereditament** Property of such a nature as to be cognizable by the senses and in any way connected with land. — **incorporeal hereditament** An inheritable right issuing out of and annexed to some corporeal inheritance, as the right of way over another's land, or the right to the use of running water. [<Med. L *hereditamentum* <L *heres, -edis* an heir]

he·red·i·tar·y (hə·red′ə·ter′ē) *adj.* **1** *Law* Passing, capable of passing, or that must necessarily pass by inheritance, or from an ancestor, to an heir; deriving by inheritance. **2** Passing naturally from parent to child. **3** *Biol.* Transmitted or transmissible directly from a plant or animal to its offspring: distinguished from *congenital.* **4** Endowed with certain qualities derived from an ancestor. **5** Of or pertaining to heredity or inheritance. [<L *hereditārius* < *hereditas.* See HEREDITY.] — **he·red′i·tar′i·ly** *adv.* — **he·red′i·tar′i·ness** *n.*

he·red·i·tist (hə·red′ə·tist) *n.* An adherent of the theory that individuality is determined by heredity.

he·red·i·ty (hə·red′ə·tē) *n. pl.* **·ties 1** Transmission of physical characteristics, mental traits, tendency to disease, etc., from parents to offspring. **2** *Biol.* The tendency manifested by an organism to develop in the likeness of a progenitor, because of the transmission of genetic factors in the reproductive process. **3** The sum total of an individual's inherited

characteristics. [<F *hérédité* <L *hereditas, -tatis* an inheritance <*heres, -edis* an heir]
Her·e·ford (her'ə·fərd) *n.* One of a breed of cattle, commonly red with a white face and markings. [from HEREFORD]
Her·e·ford (her'ə·fərd) A county in western England; 842 square miles; county seat, Hereford. Also **Her'e·ford·shire** (-shir', -shər).
her·e·geld (her'ə·geld) *n.* In Old Scots law, a due analogous to the English heriot. Also **her'e·gild** (-gild). [OE *heregield* <*here* army + *gield* tribute]
here·in (hir·in') *adv.* In this; in this place, circumstance, etc. [OE *hērinne*]
here·in·af·ter (hir'in·af'tər, -äf'-) *adv.* In a subsequent part of this (document).
here·in·be·fore (hir'in·bi·fôr', -fōr') *adv.* In a preceding part of this (document).
here·in·to (hir·in'tōō) *adv.* Into this.
here·of (hir·uv') *adv.* 1 Of this; about this. 2 From this; because of this.
here·on (hir·on', -ôn') *adv.* On this; hereupon.
he·res (hir'ēz) *n. pl.* **he·re·des** (hi·rē'dēz) *Law* An heir. Also spelled *haeres.* [<L]
he·re·si·arch (hi·rē'sē·ärk, her'ə·sē·ärk') *n.* The chief exponent of a heresy. See synonyms under HERETIC. [<LL *haeresiarcha* <Gk. *hairesiarchēs* <*hairesis* a sect + *archēs* leader <*archein* rule]
her·e·sy (her'ə·sē) *n. pl.* **·sies** 1 A doctrinal view or belief at variance with the recognized tenets of a system, church, school, or party. 2 The maintenance of such a doctrinal view or tenet. 3 *Obs.* Any course of conduct or instruction tending to produce dissension and schism in the church. [<OF *heresie,* ult. <Gk. *hairesis* a sect, lit., a choosing <*haireesthai* choose]
her·e·tic (her'ə·tik) *n.* 1 One who holds a heresy. 2 An actual or former member of a church, or one whose allegiance is claimed by it, who holds religious opinions contrary to the fundamental doctrines and tenets of that church. [<MF *hérétique* <LL *haereticus* <Gk. *hairetikos* able to choose <*haireesthai* choose] —**he·ret·i·cal** (hə·ret'i·kəl) *adj.* —**he·ret'i·cal·ly** *adv.*
Synonyms: dissenter, heresiarch, nonconformist, schismatic. Etymologically, a *heretic* is one who takes or chooses his own belief, instead of the belief of his church; a *schismatic* is primarily one who produces a split or rent in the church. A *heretic* differs in doctrine from the religious body with which he is connected; a *schismatic* differs in doctrine or practice, or in both. A *heretic* may be reticent, or even silent; a *schismatic* introduces divisions. A *heresiarch* is the author of a heresy or the leader of a heretical party, and is thus at once a *heretic* and a *schismatic.* With advancing ideas of religious liberty, the odious sense once attached to these words is largely modified, and *heretic* is often used playfully. *Dissenter* and *nonconformist* are terms specifically applied to English subjects who hold themselves aloof from the Church of England.
here·to (hir·tōō') *adv.* To this time, place, or end.
here·to·fore (hir'tə·fôr', -fōr') *adv.* Previously; hitherto.
here·un·to (hir'un·tōō') *adv.* To this; hereto; up to this point, or to this end or result.
here·up·on (hir'ə·pon', -pôn') *adv.* Upon this; following immediately after this.
here·with (hir·with', -wiṯh') *adv.* Along with this.
Her·ges·hei·mer (hûr'gəs·hī'mər), **Joseph,** 1880–1954, U. S. novelist.
Her·ing window (her'ing) *Optics* An apparatus for demonstrating color contrast by means of a shutter whose two openings contain samples of the desired colors. [after Ewald *Hering,* 1834–1918, German psychologist]
her·i·ot (her'ē·ət) *n.* In feudal law, a tribute or contribution to the lord of the manor from the heir of a tenant upon succeeding his father. [OE *heregeatwa* <*here* army + *geatwa* equipment]
her·i·ta·ble (her'ə·tə·bəl) *adj.* 1 That can be inherited. 2 Capable of inheriting. [<OF <*heriter* inherit] —**her'i·ta·bil'i·ty** *n.* —**her'i·ta·bly** *adv.*
her·i·tage (her'ə·tij) *n.* 1 Property that is or can be inherited. 2 Any condition or culture which is allotted or handed down to one, as by ancestors. 3 The chosen people of God, as the Israelites or the Christian elect. [<OF <*heriter* inherit <L *hereditare* <*heres, -edis* an heir]
her·i·tor (her'ə·tər) *n.* An inheritor. [<AF *heriter,* OF *heritier* <L *hereditarius.* See HEREDITARY.] —**her'i·trix** (-triks) *n. fem.*
Her·ki·mer (hûr'kə·mər), **Nicholas,** 1728–77, American general in the Revolutionary War.
herl (hûrl) *n.* 1 A barb of a feather, used in making artificial flies for angling. 2 A fly so made. [Cf. MLG *herle* a fiber]
her·ma (hûr'mə) *n. pl.* **·mae** (-mē) or **·mai** (-mī) In ancient Greece, a rough square stone, broader at the base than above, with a sculptured head of Hermes or some other deity on the top, placed in front of houses and to mark boundaries of estates, streets, etc.; also, such a stone with the head of a mortal. [<L <Gk. *Hermēs* Hermes]
Her·ma·ic (hûr·mā'ik) *adj.* Pertaining to or characteristic of the Greek god Hermes (Mercury), or the Egyptian Thoth (Hermes Trismegistus).
Her·man (hûr'mən, *Du., Sw.* her'män) A masculine personal name. Also *Ger.* **Her·mann** (her'män), *Fr.* **Ar·mand** (är·mäṅ'), *Ital.* **Er·man·no** (er·män'nō), *Lat.* **Ar·min·i·us** (är·min'ē·əs). [<Gmc., man of the army]
Her·mann·stadt (her'män·shtät) The German name for SIBIU.
her·maph·ro·dite (hûr·maf'rə·dīt) *adj.* 1 Having the characteristics of both sexes; bisexual. 2 *Naut.* Denoting a type of ship which is square-rigged forward and schooner-rigged aft. 3 *Bot.* Monoclinous. —*n.* 1 *Biol.* A plant or animal organism that combines the characteristics of both sexes. 2 *Naut.* A hermaphrodite brig. [<L *hermaphroditus* <Gk. *hermaphroditos,* after *Hermaphroditos* HERMAPHRODITUS] —**her·maph'ro·dit'ic** (-dit'ik) or **·i·cal** *adj.* —**her·maph'ro·dit'i·cal·ly** *adv.* —**her·maph'ro·dit·ism, her·maph'ro·dism** *n.*
hermaphrodite brig A brigantine.
Her·maph·ro·di·tus (hûr·maf'rə·dī'təs) In Greek mythology, the son of Hermes and Aphrodite, who, after loving the nymph Salmacis, became united with her in a single body combining both sexes.
her·me·neu·tics (hûr'mə·nōō'tiks, -nyōō'-) *n.* The science or art of interpretation, especially of the Scriptures. [<Gk. *hermēneutikē (technē)* interpretive (art) <*hermēneutēs* an interpreter] —**her'me·neu'tic** or **·ti·cal** *adj.* —**her'me·neu'ti·cal·ly** *adv.*
Her·mes (hûr'mēz) In Greek mythology, the son of Zeus and Maia, messenger and herald of the gods, god of science, eloquence, and cunning, patron of thieves, travelers, and commerce, protector of boundaries, and guide of souls on their way to Hades: identified with the Roman *Mercury.*
Hermes Tris·me·gis·tus (tris'mə·jis'təs) The Greek name for the Egyptian god Thoth, regarded as the founder of alchemy and other occult sciences: partially identified with *Hermes.*
her·met·ic (hûr·met'ik) *adj.* Made airtight; impervious to air and liquids, as by fusion. Also **her·met'i·cal.** [<Med. L *hermeticus* <*Hermes (Trismegistus)*; with ref. to alchemy]
Her·met·ic (hûr·met'ik) *adj.* Belonging or relating to Hermes, or to Hermes Trismegistus. —**Her·met'i·cal·ly** *adv.*
her·met·i·cal·ly (hûr·met'ik·lē) *adv.* So as to be airtight or impervious.
hermetic art Alchemy.
Her·mi·o·ne (hûr·mī'ə·nē) In Greek legend, the daughter of Menelaus and Helen, wife of Neoptolemus and later of Orestes.
her·mit (hûr'mit) *n.* 1 A person who abandons society and lives alone, especially for religious contemplation; an anchorite. 2 A molasses cooky containing spice and sometimes raisins. 3 *Obs.* A beadsman. Also *Obs. ermyte.* [<OF *hermite* <L *eremita* <Gk. *erēmitēs* <*erēmia* a desert <*erēmos* solitary] —**her·mit'ic** or **·i·cal** *adj.* —**her·mit'i·cal·ly** *adv.* —**her'mit·like'** *adj.*
her·mit·age (hûr'mə·tij) *n.* The retreat or cell of a hermit. See synonyms under CLOISTER.
hermit crab A decapod crustacean (genus *Pagurus*) usually having a soft abdomen which for protection is thrust into the empty shell of a univalve mollusk.
hermit thrush A thrush (*Hylocichla guttata*) of eastern North America, having a spotted breast and reddish tail.
hermit warbler A brilliantly colored songbird (*Dendroica occidentalis*) of the Sierra Nevadas.
Her·mod (hûr'məd) In Norse mythology, the son of Odin, and messenger of the gods, who went to Hel to bring back Balder. Also **Her'modr.**
Her·mon (hûr'mən), **Mount** A mountain on the Syria–Lebanon border; the highest peak in ancient Palestine; 9,232 feet.
hern (hûrn) *n. Archaic* The heron. [OE *hyrne*]
Her·nan·do (er·nän'dō) Spanish form of FERDINAND.
Her·ne (her'nə) A city in North Rhine–Westphalia, Germany.
her·ni·a (hûr'nē·ə) *n. Pathol.* Protrusion, as of an intestine or other organ from its normal position; rupture. [<L] —**her'ni·al** *adj.*
hernio– *combining form* Hernia: *hernioplasty.* [<L *hernia*]
her·ni·o·plas·ty (hûr'nē·ə·plas'tē) *n. Surg.* An operation for the radical cure of hernia. —**her'ni·o·plas'tic** *adj.*
her·ni·ot·o·my (hûr'nē·ot'ə·mē) *n. pl.* **·mies** *Surg.* The operation of cutting down to and severing the constricting part in strangulated hernia.
hern·shaw (hûrn'shô) *n.* 1 A heron. 2 *Her.* The representation of a heron or similar bird. [Var. of HERONSEW]
he·ro (hir'ō) *n. pl.* **·roes** 1 A person distinguished for valor, fortitude, or bold enterprise; anyone regarded as having displayed great courage or exceptionally noble qualities. 2 In classical mythology, the son of a god or goddess and a mortal: the eponymous founder of a city or family, as Cadmus, was sometimes locally worshiped as a hero. 3 The central male figure of a poem, play, romance, or the like; in modern fiction, the male character in whom the principal interest centers. [<L *heros* <Gk. *hērōs*]
He·ro (hir'ō) In Greek legend, a priestess of Aphrodite at Sestos, for whom Leander, her lover, swam the Hellespont from Abydos every night: when he drowned one night, Hero cast herself into the sea.
Her·od (her'əd), 73?–4 B.C., king of Judea 37–4 B.C.: known as **Herod the Great.**
—**Herod Agrippa I,** 10? B.C.–A.D. 44, king of Judea 41–44.
—**Herod Antipas,** 4 B.C.–A.D. 39, tetrarch of Galilee; son of Herod the Great. —**He·ro·di·an** (hi·rō'dē·ən) *adj.* & *n.*
He·ro·di·as (hi·rō'dē·əs) Second wife of Herod Antipas. *Mark* vi 17–28.
He·rod·o·tus (hi·rod'ə·təs), 484?–424? B.C., Greek historian: called the "Father of History."
he·ro·ic (hi·rō'ik) *adj.* 1 Characteristic of a hero; brave; noble: *heroic* courage; a *heroic* death. 2 Of or involving the heroes of antiquity: a *heroic* age. 3 Describing heroes and their deeds: a *heroic* poem. 4 Like heroic poetry in style; magniloquent; high-flown: *heroic* language. 5 Bold; daring; extreme: a *heroic* attempt. 6 In art and sculpture, larger than life and smaller than colossal. Also **he·ro'i·cal.** —*n.* 1 *pl.* Heroic verse. 2 *pl.* High-flown or extravagant language, sentiments, or actions: Cut out the *heroics.* —**he·ro'i·cal·ly** *adv.*
heroic age The mythical age when heroes and demigods lived on earth.
heroic couplet An English verse form consisting of two riming lines of iambic pentameter, often epigrammatic in character.
heroic poetry Epic poetry, especially as dealing with heroes and demigods.
heroic verse A verse form adapted to heroic or lofty themes, and used especially in epic and dramatic poetry, as the hexameter in Greek and Latin, the hendecasyllabic ottava rima in Italian, the Alexandrine in French drama, and the heroic couplet and blank verse, with various other combinations of iambic verse, in English.
her·o·in (her'ō·in) *n.* Diacetylmorphine, $C_{21}H_{23}O_5N$, a white, odorless, crystalline

derivative of morphine with a bitter taste: a powerful, habit-forming narcotic of which the manufacture is prohibited in the United States. [<G]

her·o·ine (her′ō·in) *n. fem.* **1** A woman of heroic character. **2** The chief female character in a story, play, or the like. [<L *heroina* <Gk. *hērōinē*, fem. of *hērōs* a hero]

her·o·ism (her′ō·iz′əm) *n.* **1** Heroic character or qualities. **2** A heroic act. See synonyms under FORTITUDE, PROWESS.

He·rold (he′rōlt) Dutch form of HAROLD.

her·on (her′ən) *n.* A long-necked and long-legged wading bird; specifically, one of a family *(Ardeidae)* of birds with 12 stiff tail feathers and the outer toe as long as or longer than the inner. See EGRET. — **great blue heron** A large, bluish-gray American heron *(Ardea herodias)*. [<OF *hairon*, ult. <Gmc.]

GREAT BLUE HERON (About 4 feet tall)

her·on·bill (her′ən·bil′) *n.* Any of a genus *(Erodium)* of annual or perennial herbs with toothed leaves, widely distributed in temperate regions. Also **her′on's-bill′, her′ons·bill′.**

her·on·ry (her′ən·rē) *n. pl.* **·ries** A place where herons congregate and breed.

he·ro-wor·ship (hir′ō·wûr′ship) *n.* Enthusiastic or extravagant admiration for heroes or other distinguished personages.

her·pes (hûr′pēz) *n. Pathol.* An inflammatory eruption on the skin, forming groups of small blisters which tend to spread. [<L <Gk. *herpēs* < *herpein* creep]

herpes sim·plex (sim′pleks) Cold sore.

herpes zos·ter (zos′tər) Shingles.

her·pet·ic (hûr·pet′ik) *adj.* Relating to or like herpes. Also **her·pet′i·cal.** — **her·pe·tism** (hûr′pə·tiz′əm) *n.*

her·pe·tol·o·gy (hûr′pə·tol′ə·jē) *n.* The branch of zoology that treats of reptiles and amphibians. [<Gk. *herpeton* a reptile <*herpein* creep + -LOGY] — **her·pe·to·log·i·cal** (hûr′pə·tə·loj′i·kəl) *adj.* — **her′pe·tol′o·gist** *n.*

Herr (her) *n. pl.* **Her·ren** (her′ən) *German* A title of respectful address, equivalent to the English *mister.*

Herr·en·volk (her′ən·fôlk′) *n. German* The master race.

Her·re·ra (er·rā′rä), **Francisco de,** 1576–1656, Spanish painter.

Her·rick (her′ik), **Robert,** 1591–1674, English poet.

her·ring (her′ing) *n. pl.* **·rings** or **·ring** **1** A small food fish *(Clupea harengus)* frequenting moderate depths of the North Atlantic in great numbers. The young are canned as sardines and the adults are smoked or salted. **2** A fish allied to the herring (family *Clupeidae)*, especially *Clupea cacruteus* of Pacific waters and the pilchard or sardine. [OE *hǣring*]

her·ring·bone (her′ing·bōn′) *adj.* Similar to the spinal structure of a herring; especially, laid out, arranged, woven, or stitched in rows of parallel lines with the lines of adjoining rows slanting in opposite directions: said of masonry, textiles, etc. — *n.* Anything made or arranged in such a pattern. — *v.t.* & *v.i.* **·boned, ·bon·ing** **1** To ornament with or arrange in herringbone stitches, patterns, etc. **2** To walk on skis (up an incline) with the toes pointed out: so called from the herringbone tracks made by the skis.

her·ring·bone-work (her′ing·bōn′wûrk′) *n.* **1** Masonry in which the stones are laid slanting in opposite directions alternately. **2** A cross-stitch made of rows of diagonal stitches.

herring gull A small American gull *(Larus argentatus smithsonianus)* of the Atlantic coast that feeds on herring.

Her·riot (e·ryō′), **Édouard,** 1872–1957, French statesman; premier 1924–25, 1932.

her·ry (her′ē) *v.t. Scot.* To harry. — **her′ri·ment** (-mənt) or **her′ry·ment** *n.*

hers (hûrz) *pron.* **1** Belonging or pertaining to her: the form of the possessive case of *she* when used in predicative position, without a following noun, or after *of*: That book is *hers*; those eyes of *hers.* **2** The things or persons belonging to or relating to her: John's story is funnier than *hers*; She provides for herself and *hers.* [OE *hire* + *-s* (after *his*)]

Her·schel (hûr′shəl), **Sir John Frederick William,** 1792–1871, English astronomer. — **Sir William,** 1738–1822, English astronomer of German birth: original name *Friedrich Wilhelm Herschel*; father of the preceding.

her·self (hər·self′) *pron.* **1** Reflexive form of *her.* **2** Emphatic or intensive form of *she.*

Herst·mon·ceux (hûrst′mən·sōō, hûrs′-) A village of SE Sussex, England: the British meteorological station and time clocks were moved here from Greenwich in 1946: also *Hurstmonceux.*

Hert·ford (här′fərd, härt′-) A county in SE England; 633 square miles; county seat, Hertford. Also **Hert′ford·shire** (-shir, -shər). Shortened form **Herts** (härts, hûrts).

Her·to·gen·bosch, 's (ser′tō·khən·bôs′) See 's HERTOGENBOSCH.

hertz (hûrts) *n. Physics* A unit of electromagnetic wave frequency, equal to one cycle per second. [after Heinrich *Hertz*]

Hertz (herts), **Gustav,** born 1887, German physicist. — **Heinrich,** 1857–94, German physicist. — **Hertz′i·an** *adj.*

Hertzian wave One of the electromagnetic waves; a radio wave: also **Hertzian radiation.** [after Heinrich *Hertz*]

Hertz·sprung-Rus·sell diagram (hert′sprung′·rus′əl) *Astron.* A classification of stars plotted on a chart in which the luminosity increases on a vertical scale from bottom to top and the color or spectral type changes from blue or white to red on a horizontal scale from left to right: also called *Russell diagram.* See MAIN SEQUENCE. [after Ejnar *Hertzsprung*, born 1873, Dutch astronomer, and Henry Norris *Russell*, 1877–1957, U.S. astronomer]

Her·ze·go·vi·na (hûr′tsə·gō·vē′nə) See BOSNIA AND HERZEGOVINA: Serbo-Croatian *Hercegovina.* — **Her′ze·go·vin′i·an** (-vin′ē·ən) *adj.* & *n.*

Her·zl (her′tsəl), **Theodor,** 1860–1904, Hungarian journalist; founder of the Zionist movement. See ZIONISM.

he's (hēz) **1** He is. **2** He has.

He·se·ki·el (hā·zā′kē·el) German form of EZEKIEL.

Hesh·wan (hesh′van, *Hebrew* khesh′vän) A Hebrew month: also called *Marchesvan* or *Bul.* Also spelled *Hesvan.* Also **Hesh′van.** See CALENDAR (Hebrew).

He·si·od (hē′sē·əd, hes′ē·əd) Greek poet of the eighth century B.C. — **He·si·od·ic** (hē′sē·od′ik, hes′ē-) *adj.*

He·si·o·ne (hi·sī′ə·nē) In Greek legend, the daughter of Laomedon, who was rescued from a monster by Hercules.

hes·i·tan·cy (hez′ə·tən·sē) *n. pl.* **·cies** **1** The act or manner of one who falters or is uncertain; hesitation; vacillation. **2** A faltering in speech. Also **hes′i·tance.** See synonyms under DOUBT.

hes·i·tant (hez′ə·tənt) *adj.* Hesitating; uncertain. [<L *haesitans, -antis*, ppr. of *haestare.* See HESITATE.] — **hes′i·tant·ly** *adv.*

hes·i·tate (hez′ə·tāt) *v.i.* **·tat·ed, ·tat·ing** **1** To be uncertain as to decision or action; waver. **2** To pause. **3** To be slow or faltering in speech. [<L *haesitatus*, pp. of *haesitare*, freq. of *haerere* stick] — **hes′i·ta′tive** *adj.* — **hes′i·ta′tive·ly** *adv.*

hes·i·ta·tion (hez′ə·tā′shən) *n.* **1** The act of hesitating; a delay caused by indecision or uncertainty. **2** A state of uncertainty; doubt. **3** A pause or faltering in speech.

hesp (hesp) *n. Scot.* & *Brit. Dial.* **1** A hasp. **2** The length of two linen-thread hanks.

Hes·per·es·thu·sa (hes′pər·əs·thōō′zə) One of the Hesperides.

Hes·pe·ri·a (hes·pir′ē·ə) Land of the West: the ancient Greek name for Italy and the Latin name for the Iberian Peninsula.

Hes·pe·ri·an (hes·pir′ē·ən) *adj.* **1** *Poetic* In or of the west; western. **2** Of or pertaining to the Hesperides. [<L *hesperius* <Gk. *hesperios* western]

Hes·per·id (hes′pər·id) Any of the Hesperides.

Hes·per·i·des (hes·per′ə·dēz) In Greek mythology, the daughters of Atlas (Aegle, Erytheia, and Hesperesthusa), who with the dragon, Ladon, guarded the golden apples given to Hera by Gaea and later stolen by Hercules: also called *Atlantides.* [<Gk. *hesperis* western] — **Hes·per·id·i·an** (hes′pə·rid′ē·ən) or **·e·an** *adj.*

hes·per·i·din (hes·per′ə·din) *n.* A glycoside, $C_{28}H_{34}O_{15}$, obtained from citrus fruits as a white, tasteless, odorless, crystalline powder. [<HESPERIDIUM + -IN]

hes·per·id·i·um (hes′pə·rid′ē·əm) *n. pl.* **·i·a** (-ē·ə) *Bot.* An indehiscent, many-celled, fleshy fruit with a spongy or leathery rind; a berry with a hard rind, as the lemon. [<NL <Gk. *Hesperides* the Hesperides; with ref. to the golden apples]

Hes·per·or·nis (hes′pər·ôr′nis) *n.* One of a genus *(Hesperornis)* of extinct swimming birds from the Cretaceous of Kansas with pointed teeth and serpentlike jaws. The type species was six feet long. [<NL <Gk. *hesperos* western + *ornis* a bird]

Hes·pe·rus (hes′pər·əs) The evening star, especially Venus. Also **Hes′per.** [<L <Gk. *Hesperos*]

Hess (hess), **Myra,** born 1890, English pianist. — **Rudolf,** born 1894, German Nazi leader; sentenced to life imprisonment in 1946.

Hes·se (hes′ə), **Hermann,** 1877–1962, German novelist.

Hesse (hes) A state of western Germany; 8,153 square miles; capital, Wiesbaden. *German* **Hes′sen** (hes′ən).

Hesse-Cas·sel (hes′kas′əl) A former landgravate of Germany; incorporated into Prussia, 1866: also **Electoral Hesse, Hesse′-Kas′·sel.** *German* **Hes·sen-Kas·sel** (hes′ən·käs′əl).

Hesse-Darm·stadt (hes′därm′shtät) A former grand duchy of Germany. *German* **Hes′sen-Darm′stadt.**

Hesse-Nas·sau (hes′nas′ô) A former province of Prussia in western Germany. *German* **Hes·sen-Nas·sau** (hes′ən·näs′ou).

hes·sian (hesh′ən) *n.* A strong coarse hempen cloth. [from *Hesse*]

Hes·sian (hesh′ən) *n.* **1** A native or citizen of Hesse. **2** A soldier from Hesse hired by the British to fight in the American Revolution. **3** *pl.* Hessian boots. — *adj.* Of or pertaining to Hesse or its inhabitants.

Hessian boots High boots, reaching to the knees, worn early in the 19th century.

Hessian fly A small blackish fly or midge *(Mayetiola* or *Phytophaga destructor)* with red lines on the upper surface, very destructive to wheat, barley, and rye: supposedly introduced into America by the Hessian troops during the Revolutionary War.

hess·ite (hes′īt) *n.* A metallic, lead-gray, silver telluride, Ag_2Te, crystallizing in the isometric system. [after G. H. *Hess*, 1802–50, Swiss chemist]

hes·son·ite (hes′ən·īt) See ESSONITE.

hest (hest) *n. Archaic* Behest.

Hes·ter (hes′tər) See ESTHER. Also **Hes′ther.**

Hes·ti·a (hes′tē·ə) In Greek mythology, the eldest daughter of Kronos and Rhea, and goddess of the hearth: identified with the Roman *Vesta.*

Hes·van (hes′van) See HESHWAN.

Hes·y·chast (hes′i·kast) *n.* A quietist; especially, one of a mystic and quietistic sect that originated in the Greek Church among the monks of Mt. Athos in the 14th century. See ILLUMINATI. [<Med. L *hesychasta* <Gk. *hēsychastēs* < *hēsychazein* be still < *hēsychos* quiet] — **hes′y·chas′tic** *adj.*

het (het) Dialectal past tense and past participle of HEAT. — **to get het up** *Dial.* To become angry, disturbed, or excited.

he·tae·ra (hi·tir′ə) *n. pl.* **·tae·rae** (-tir′ē) In ancient Greece, one of a class of professional entertainers or courtesans: composed of slaves, freedwomen, and foreigners. Also **he·tai·ra** (hi·tī′rə). [<Gk. *hetaira*, fem. of *hetairos* a companion]

he·tae·rism (hi·tir′iz·əm) *n.* **1** Promiscuous concubinage. **2** The theory that this condition characterized all primitive society. Also **he·tai·rism** (hi·tī′riz·əm).

hetero- *combining form* Other; different: *heterogeneous*: opposed to *homo-*. Also, before vowels, **heter-**. [<Gk. *hetero-* < *heteros* other]

het·er·o·cer·cy (het′ər·ə·sûr′sē) *n. Zool.* Inequality of the caudal fin of a fish produced by the extension of the vertebral column upward and consequent enlargement of one of the lobes, as in sharks, sturgeons, etc. [<HETERO- + Gk. *kerkos* tail] — **het′er·o·cer′cal** (-sûr′kəl) *adj.*

het·er·o·chro·mat·ic (het′ər·ə·krō·mat′ik) *adj.* Of, pertaining to, characterized by, or designating an array or pattern of different colors. Also **het′er·o·chrome′** (-krōm′), **het′er·o·chro′·mous** (-krō′məs).

het·er·o·chro·ma·tin (het′ər·ə·krō′mə·tin) *n. Biol.* An inert fraction of chromatin, unchanged during mitosis.

het·er·o·chro·mo·some (het′ər·ə·krō′mə·sōm) *n.* 1 Sex chromosome. 2 Any aberrant chromosome.

het·er·o·chron·ic (het′ər·ə·kron′ik) *adj. Med.* Occurring at irregular or abnormal times: said of an illness. Also **het·er·och·ro·nous** (het′ər·ok′·rə·nəs).

het·er·och·tho·nous (het′ər·ok′thə·nəs) *adj.* Foreign; not indigenous or native. [< HETERO- + Gk. *chthōn* land, country]

het·er·o·clite (het′ər·ə·klīt′) *n.* 1 *Gram.* A word that varies or is irregular in inflection; particularly, a noun inflected from more than one stem, as Latin *domus.* 2 A person or thing deviating from the ordinary or correct form. —*adj.* 1 Anomalous. 2 *Gram.* With an irregular inflection: also **het′er·o·clit′ic** (-klit′ik) or **·i·cal.** [< F *hétéroclite* < L *heteroclitus* < Gk. *heteroklitos* irregular < *hetero-* other + *klinein* bend]

het·er·o·cy·clic (het′ər·ə·sī′klik, -sik′lik) *adj. Chem.* Pertaining to or designating an organic ring compound containing one or more types of atoms other than carbon: opposed to *homocyclic.*

het·er·o·cyst (het′ər·ə·sist′) *n. Bot.* A cell of doubtful function, larger than its neighbors, developed in some blue-green algae.

het·er·o·dox (het′ər·ə·doks′) *adj.* 1 At variance with a commonly accepted doctrine in religion. 2 In general, at variance with any commonly accepted doctrine or opinion: opposed to *orthodox.* [< Gk. *heterodoxos* < *hetero-* other + *doxa* opinion]

het·er·o·dox·y (het′ər·ə·dok′sē) *n. pl.* **·dox·ies** 1 The character of being heterodox. 2 A heterodox doctrine or opinion. See synonyms under SECT.

het·er·o·dyne (het′ər·ə·dīn′) *adj. Telecom.* Describing the manner by which oscillations of a frequency almost equal to that of the transmitted waves are developed in a separate tube of a radio receiving set, the two oscillations forming beats. —*v.t.* **·dyned, ·dyn·ing** To effect such oscillations.

het·er·oe·cism (het′ə·rē′siz·əm) *n. Bot.* A type of parasitism associated with certain fungi and characterized by the development of different stages of the parasite on different hosts: also called *metoxeny.* [< HETER(O)- + Gk. *oikos* house] —**het′er·oe′cious** (-shəs) *adj.*

het·er·o·gam·ete (het′ər·ə·gam′ēt, -gə·mēt′) *n. Biol.* A gamete sexually or otherwise differentiated: also called *anisogamete.*

het·er·og·a·mous (het′ər·og′ə·məs) *adj.* 1 *Bot.* Bearing flowers that are sexually of two kinds: opposed to *homogamous.* 2 *Biol.* Having unlike gametes: opposed to *isogamous.*

het·er·og·a·my (het′ər·og′ə·mē) *n.* The character or condition of being heterogamous. — **het·er·o·gam·ic** (het′ər·ə·gam′ik) *adj.*

het·er·o·ge·ne·ous (het′ər·ə·jē′nē·əs) *adj.* Consisting of dissimilar elements or ingredients. [< Med. L *heterogeneus* < Gk. *heterogenēs* < *hetero-* other + *genos* kind] —**het·er·o·ge·ne·i·ty** (het′ər·ə·jə·nē′ə·tē) *n.* —**het′er·o·ge′ne·ous·ly** *adv.*

Synonyms: confused, conglomerate, discordant, dissimilar, mingled, miscellaneous, mixed, nonhomogeneous, unhomogeneous, unlike, variant, various. Substances quite *unlike* are *heterogeneous* as regards each other. A *heterogeneous* mixture is one whose constituents are not only *unlike* in kind, but unevenly distributed; cement is composed of substances such as lime, sand, and clay, which are *heterogeneous* as regards each other, but the cement is said to be homogeneous if the different constituents are evenly *mixed* throughout, so that any one portion of the mixture is exactly like any other. A substance may fail of being homogeneous and yet not be *heterogeneous,* in which case it is said to be *nonhomogeneous* or *unhomogeneous;* a bar of iron that contains flaws, air bubbles, etc., or for any reason is not of uniform structure and density throughout, even if no foreign substance be *mixed* with the iron, is said to be *non-homogeneous.* A *miscellaneous* mixture may or may not be *heterogeneous;* if the objects are alike in kind, but different in size, form, quality, use, etc., and without special order or relation, the collection is *miscellaneous;* if the objects differ in kind, such a mixture is also, and more strictly, *heterogeneous.* See COMPLEX. *Antonyms*: alike, homogeneous, identical, like, pure, same, similar, uniform.

het·er·o·gen·e·sis (het′ər·ə·jen′ə·sis) *n. Biol.* 1 Asexual generation. 2 Metagenesis. —**het·er·o·ge·net·ic** (het′ər·ə·jə·net′ik) *adj.*

het·er·og·o·ny (het′ər·og′ə·nē) *n.* 1 *Bot.* The state of having flowers differing in kind, length of stamens and styles: opposed to *homogony.* 2 Metagenesis. —**het′er·og′o·nous** *adj.* —**het′·er·og′o·nous·ly** *adv.*

het·er·o·grade (het′ər·ə·grād′) *adj. Stat.* Having or denoting a variable magnitude, grade, or intensity. Compare HOMOGRADE.

het·er·og·ra·phy (het′ə·rog′rə·fē) *n.* 1 Orthography in which the same letter represents different sounds in different words or syllables, as *c* in *camp* and *cent.* 2 Spelling varying from the standard everyday usage. —**het·er·o·graph·ic** (het′ər·ə·graf′ik) or **·i·cal** *adj.*

het·er·og·y·nous (het′ə·roj′ə·nəs) *adj. Biol.* Having the females differentiated into sexual and neuter forms, as a bee or an ant.

het·er·o·ki·ne·sis (het′ər·ə·ki·nē′sis, -kī-) *n. Biol.* A differential distribution of the sex chromosomes in meiosis. —**het′er·o·ki·net′ic** (-net′ik) *adj.*

het·er·ol·o·gy (het′ə·rol′ə·jē) *n. Biol.* 1 Difference of structure as compared with a type; lack of homology; abnormality. 2 Analogy between unrelated organisms: contrasted with *homology* between related organisms. —**het′er·ol′ogous** (-gəs) *adj.*

het·er·ol·y·sis (het′ə·rol′ə·sis) *n. Biochem.* Dissolution effected by an outside agent; specifically, the destruction of a cell by external enzymes or lysins: opposed to *autolysis.* — **het·er·o·lyt·ic** (het′ər·ə·lit′ik) *adj.*

het·er·om·er·ous (het′ə·rom′ər·əs) *adj. Bot.* Possessing parts that differ in number, form, or composition, as the whorls of a flower: opposed to *isomerous.*

het·er·o·mor·phic (het′ər·ə·môr′fik) *adj. Biol.* 1 Deviating from the normal form or standard type. 2 Undergoing complete metamorphosis, as certain insects. Also **het′er·o·mor′phous** (-fəs). —**het′er·o·mor′phism** (-fiz·əm) *n.*

het·er·on·o·mous (het′ə·ron′ə·məs) *adj.* 1 *Biol.* Divergent or differing from the common type: said of one of a series of related things, as the somites of an arthropod. 2 Subject to the law or rule of another. [< HETERO- + Gk. *nomos* law, rule] —**het′er·on′o·my** *n.*

het·er·o·nym (het′ər·ə·nim′) *n.* 1 A word spelled like another, but having a different sound and meaning, as *bass* (a male voice) and *bass* (a fish). 2 Another name for the same thing; especially, one of two precisely equivalent terms in different languages: "Water" is a *heteronym* of the French word "eau." Compare HOMONYM. [< HETER(O)- + Gk. *onyma,* var. of *onoma* name; on analogy with *synonym*]

het·er·on·y·mous het′ə·ron′ə·məs) *adj.* 1 Relating to, having the nature of, or containing a heteronym. 2 *Optics* Appearing on the side opposite to that of the eye that produced it: said of double images of an object when the image seen by the right eye is on the left side and vice versa.

Het·er·o·ou·si·an (het′ər·ō·ōō′sē·ən, -ou′sē-), etc. See HETEROUSIAN, etc.

het·er·o·pha·sia (het′ər·ə·fā′zhə, -zhē·ə) *n. Psychiatry* A form of aphasia in which the patient says or writes one thing when he means another. [< NL < Gk. *hetero-* other + *-phasia* < *phanai* speak]

het·er·o·phyl·lous (het′ər·ə·fil′əs) *adj. Bot.* Having leaves that differ, as in size, form, or function, on the same plant. —**het′er·o·phyl′ly** (-fil′ē) *n.*

het·er·o·pla·sia (het′ər·ə·plā′zhə, -zhē·ə) *n. Pathol.* The development of abnormal tissue by diseased action where the cells of the abnormal tissues differ from the normal ones. [< NL]

het·er·o·plas·ty (het′ər·ə·plas′tē) *n. Surg.* A plastic operation in which the portion grafted is taken from an organism or person other than the patient.

het·er·o·po·lar (het′ər·ə·pō′lər) *adj. Electr.* Designating an unequal distribution of an electric charge: opposed to *homopolar.*

Het·er·op·ter·a (het′ə·rop′tər·ə) *n. pl.* A suborder of the *Hemiptera* that includes many of the true bugs. [< NL < Gk. *hetero-* other + *pteron* wing] —**het′er·op′ter·ous** *adj.*

het·er·o·sex·u·al (het′ər·ə·sek′shōō·əl) *adj.* 1 Pertaining to or characterized by sexual attraction toward a person of the opposite sex. 2 *Biol.* Pertaining to different sexes. —*n.* A heterosexual person. Compare BISEXUAL, HOMOSEXUAL. — **het′er·o·sex′u·al′i·ty** (-sek′shōō·al′ə·tē) *n.*

het·er·o·sis (het′ə·rō′sis) *n. Biol.* Exceptional vigor of plant and animal organisms through crossbreeding between two different types; hybrid vigor. [< NL < Gk. *heterosis* alteration < *heteros* other]

het·er·os·po·rous (het′ə·ros′pər·əs, het′ər·ə·spôr′əs, -spō′rəs) *adj. Bot.* 1 Producing both large and small spores. 2 Producing spores of more than one sex. Also **het·er·o·spor·ic** (het′ər·ə·spôr′ik, -spor′ik).

het·er·o·stat·ic (het′ər·ə·stat′ik) *adj. Electr.* Measuring by the aid of a charge other than the one to be measured: applied to an electrometer, thus distinguishing it from an *idiostatic* one.

het·er·o·sty·ly (het′ər·ə·stī′lē) *n. Bot.* A difference in the length of the styles in flowers of the same species, whereby certain plants insure cross-pollination. Also **het′er·o·sty′lism** (-stī′·liz·əm). [< HETERO- + STYLE[2]]

het·er·o·tax·is (het′ər·ə·tak′sis) *n.* 1 *Pathol.* A malformation caused by displacement or lateral transposition of organs. 2 Any irregular or abnormal arrangement of parts, as of rock strata, geographic features, etc.: opposed to *homotaxis.* Also **het′er·o·tax′i·a** (-tak′sē·ə), **het′er·o·tax′y** (-tak′sē). [< NL < Gk. *hetero-* other + *taxis* arrangement] —**het′er·o·tac′tic** (-tak′tik), **het′er·o·tax′ic** (-tak′sik) *adj.*

het·er·o·thal·lism (het′ər·ə·thal′iz·əm) *n. Bot.* A form of sexual differentiation in certain fungi, as the bread mold (*Rhizopus nigricans*), characterized by the possession of two types of mycelia whose hyphae conjugate to produce zygotes. [< HETERO- + Gk. *thallos* sprout] — **het′er·o·thal′lic** *adj.*

het·er·o·to·pi·a (het′ər·ə·tō′pē·ə) *n. Pathol.* A misplacement of an organ, or a growth abnormally situated in the body. Also **het′er·ot′o·py** (-ot′ə·pē). [< NL < Gk. *hetero-* other + *topos* place] —**het′er·o·top′ic** (-top′ik), **het′er·ot′o·pous** (-ot′ə·pəs) *adj.*

het·er·ot·ri·chous (het′ə·rot′rə·kəs) *adj.* 1 Having unlike cilia. 2 Of or pertaining to an order (*Heterotrichida*) of ciliate infusorians. [< HETERO- + Gk. *trichos* hair]

het·er·ot·ro·phy (het′ə·rot′rə·fē) *n.* 1 Any disorder of nutrition. 2 *Bot.* An abnormal manner of obtaining nourishment: applied to certain plants having no true root hairs, and obtaining all nourishment by a fungus, the hyphae of which closely invest the roots and take the place of root hairs. [< HETERO- + Gk. *trophē* nurture < *trephein* feed] —**het′er·o·troph′ic** (-ə·trof′ik, -trō′fik) *adj.*

het·er·o·tro·pi·a (het′ər·ə·trō′pē·ə) *n. Pathol.* A deviation of the eyes in which the two visual lines so diverge that binocular vision is impaired; a form of strabismus. [< HETERO- + -TROP(E) + -IA]

het·er·o·typ·ic (het′ər·ə·tip′ik) *adj. Biol.* Denoting a form of meiosis in which the chromosomes split at an early period, the halves remaining united at the ends and opening out into rings, each of which represents two chromosomes: contrasted with *homeotypic.* Also **het′er·o·typ′i·cal.**

het·er·ou·si·a (het′ə·rōō′sē·ə, -rou′sē-) *n.* Difference in substance or essence: a theological term. [< LGk. *heterousia* < *heterousios* of different essence < *heteros* other + *ousia* being] — **het er·ou′si·ous, het er·ou′si·an** *adj.*

Het·er·ou·si·an (het′ə·rōō′sē·ən, -rou′sē-) *n.* One of a party in the early Christian church that affirmed that the substance of the Son is essentially different from that of the Father; an Arian: distinguished from *Homoousian*:

Also **Het'er·ou'si·ast** (-ast). *—adj.* Pertaining to the Heterousians or their belief.

het·er·o·zy·go·sis (het'ər·ə·zī·gō'sis, -zi-) *n. Biol.* The descent of an organism from two different races, species, or varieties; hybridism. [< NL]

het·er·o·zy·gote (het'ər·ə·zī'gōt, -zig'ōt) *n. Biol.* A hybrid resulting from the fusion of two gametes that bear different allelomorphs of the same character and which in consequence does not breed true; a heterozygous individual: contrasted with *homozygote.*

het·er·o·zy·gous (het'ər·ə·zī'gəs) *adj. Biol.* Designating that condition of an individual in which any given genetic factor has been derived from only one of the two generating gametes.

heth (kheth) *n.* The eighth Hebrew letter: also spelled *cheth.* See ALPHABET

het·man (het'mən) *n. pl.* **·mans** (-mənz) The chieftain of the Cossacks. See ATAMAN [< Polish < G. *hauptmann* head man, captain]

heugh (hyōōkh) *n. Scot.* **1** A precipice; a crag. **2** A ravine with steep sides. **3** A coalpit. Also **heuch.**

heu·land·ite (hyōō'lən·dīt) *n.* A pearly, variously colored, transparent, hydrous silicate of aluminum and calcium, belonging to the group of zeolites. [after H. *Heuland,* 19th c. English mineralogist]

heu·ris·tic (hyōō·ris'tik) *adj.* **1** Aiding or guiding in discovery. **2** Inciting to find out. [< Gk. *heuriskein* find out]

hew (hyōō) *v.* **hewed, hewn** or **hewed, hew·ing** *v.t.* **1** To make or shape with or as with blows of an ax: often with *out.* **2** To cut with blows of an ax, sword, etc.; chop; hack. **3** To bring down or fell with or as with blows of an ax: usually with *down.* *—v.i.* **4** To make cutting and repeated blows, as with an ax or sword. ◆ Homophone: *hue.* [OE *hēawan*] **—hew'er** *n.*

Hew·lett (hyōō'lit), **Maurice Henry,** 1861–1923, English novelist and essayist.

hex (heks) *U.S. Colloq. v.t.* To bewitch; enchant. *—n.* **1** A witch; sorceress; specifically, a witch doctor. **2** A bewitchment; enchantment: to put a *hex* on one. [< G *hexe* witch]

hexa- *combining form* Six: *hexagon.* Also, before vowels, **hex-.** [< Gk. *hexa-* < *hex* six]

hex·a·ba·sic (hek'sə·bā'sik) *adj. Chem.* **1** Denoting an acid in which six hydrogen atoms can be replaced by a basic radical. **2** Any compound containing six atoms of a univalent metal or their equivalent.

hex·a·chlo·ro·eth·ane (hek'sə·klôr'ō·eth'ān, -klō'rō-) *n. Chem.* A white crystalline trichloride of carbon, C_2Cl_6, used in the manufacture of explosives, dyestuffs, disinfectants, and smoke screens.

hex·a·chlo·ro·phene (hek'sə·klôr'ə·fēn) *n.* An antibacterial agent used in some soaps.

hex·a·chord (hek'sə·kôrd) *n. Music* A series of six tones with a half-step between the third and fourth tones, and whole steps between the others.

hex·ad (hek'sad) *n.* **1** The number six. **2** A group or series of six. [< LL *hexas, hexadis* the number six < Gk. *hexas, hexados*]

hex·ad·ic (hek·sad'ik) *adj.* **1** Of the nature of a hexad. **2** Arranged in groups of six. **3** Based on the number six.

hex·a·em·er·on (hek'sə·em'ər·on) *n.* **1** A period of six days, usually applied specifically to those of the creation. **2** An account of the creation. Also **hex'a·hem'er·on** (-hem'-). [< LL < Gk. *hexaēmeros* the six days' work, lit., of six days < *hex* six + *hēmera* day] **—hex'a·em'er·ic, hex'a·hem'er·ic** *adj.*

hex·a·gon (hek'sə·gon) *n.* A figure with six sides and six angles. [< L *hexagonum* < Gk. *hexagonos* six-cornered < *hex* six + *gōnia* angle]

HEXAGON

hex·ag·o·nal (hek·sag'ə·nəl) *adj.* **1** Having the form of a hexagon. **2** Having its section a hexagon; six-sided. **—hex·ag'o·nal·ly** *adv.*

hexagonal system A crystal system having three equal axes intersecting in one plane at 60°, and one of different length intersecting the others at right angles. See CRYSTAL.

hex·a·gram (hek'sə·gram) *n.* One of various figures formed by six intersecting lines, especially one made by completing the equilateral triangles based on the sides of a regular hexagon.

hex·a·he·dron (hek'sə·hē'drən) *n. pl.* **·drons** or **·dra** (-drə) A solid bounded by six plane faces. [< NL] **—hex'a·he'dral** *adj.*

hex·a·hy·drate (hek'sə·hī'drāt) *n. Chem.* A hydrate with six molecules of water.

hex·a·hy·dric (hek'sə·hī'drik) *adj. Chem.* Composed of six hydroxyl groups.

hex·am·er·ous (hek·sam'ər·əs) *adj.* **1** *Bot.* Having a six-parted floral whorl: generally written 6-*merous.* **2** *Zool.* Having six parts or divisions; arranged in sixes or multiples of sixes, as in corals. Also **hex·am'er·al.** [< HEXA- + -MEROUS]

hex·am·e·ter (hek·sam'ə·tər) *n.* A verse of six feet or measures, especially the dactylic verse of the Greek and Latin epics. *—adj.* Having six metrical feet in a verse. [< L < Gk. *hexametros*] **—hex·a·met·ric** (hek'sə·met'rik), **hex·am'e·tral** (-ə·trəl), **hex'a·met'ri·cal** *adj.*

hex·a·meth·yl·ene·tet·ra·mine (hek'sə·meth'·ə·lēn·tet'rə·mēn) See METHENAMINE.

hex·ane (hek'sān) *n. Chem.* One of five isomers, C_6H_{14}, of the methane series of saturated hydrocarbon compounds; especially, a volatile colorless oil contained in petroleum. [< HEX(A)- + -ANE]

hex·an·gu·lar (hek·sang'gyə·lər) *adj.* Having six angles.

Hex·a·pla (hek'sə·plə) *n. pl.* An edition of the Holy Scriptures containing six versions in parallel columns; especially, a collection of Hebrew and Greek versions of the Old Testament thus arranged, published by Origen in the third century: construed as singular. [< Gk., pl. of *hexaploos* < *hex* six + *-ploos* -fold] **—hex'a·plar** *adj.*

hex·a·pod (hek'sə·pod) *adj.* Having six feet. *—n.* One of the true or six-legged insects *(Hexapoda).* [< Gk. *hexapous, hexapodos* six-footed] **—hex·ap·o·dous** (hek·sap'ə·dəs) *adj.*

hex·ap·o·dy (hek·sap'ə·dē) *n. pl.* **·dies** Six metrical feet taken together, or a verse or line consisting of six feet.

hex·arch·y (hek'sär·kē) *n. pl.* **·arch·ies 1** A group of six states. **2** Government by six persons.

hex·a·stich (hek'sə·stik) *n.* In Greek or Latin prosody, a section or stanza of six lines. Also **hex·as·ti·chon** (heks·as'tə·kon). [< L *hexastichus* < Gk. *hexastichos* < *hex* six + *stichos* line] **—hex'a·stich'ic** *adj.*

hex·a·style (hek'sə·stīl) *adj. Archit.* Having a front with six columns, as a temple. [< L *hexastylus* < Gk. *hexastylos* having six columns in front < *hex* six + *stylos* column] **—hex'a·sty'los** (-stī'ləs) *n.*

Hex·a·teuch (hek'sə·tōōk, -tyōōk) *n.* The first six books of the Bible considered as constituting one series. [< HEXA- + Gk. *teuchos* tool, book] **—Hex'a·teu'chal** *adj.*

hex·en·be·sen (hek'sən·bā'zən) *n.* A compact broomlike growth of various trees; witches'-broom. [< G, witches'-broom]

hex·oc·ta·he·dron (heks·ok'tə·hē'drən) *n.* A form of the isometric crystal system consisting of 48 similar triangular planes. [< HEX- + OCTA- + -HEDRON] **—hex·oc'ta·he'dral** (-drəl) *adj.*

hex·one (hek'sōn) *n. Chem.* A colorless liquid ketone compound, $C_6H_{12}O$, used as a solvent for gums and resins.

hex·o·san (hek'sə·san) *n. Biochem.* Any of a group of polysaccharides which hydrolyze to a hexose. [< HEXOSE + -AN]

hex·ose (hek'sōs) *n. Biochem.* Any simple sugar containing six oxygen atoms to the molecule.

hex·tet·ra·he·dron (heks·tet'rə·hē'drən) *n.* A variety of crystal in the isometric system consisting of 24 similar triangular faces. **—hex·tet'ra·he'dral** (-drəl) *adj.*

hex·yl (hek'səl) *n. Chem.* The univalent hydrocarbon radical, C_6H_{13}, of hexane and its derivatives.

hex·yl·re·sor·ci·nol (hek'səl·rə·zôr'sə·nōl) *n.* A yellowish-white compound, $C_{12}H_{18}O_2$, with a pungent odor and astringent taste, used as a germicide and antiseptic.

hey (hā) *interj.* An exclamation of surprise, pleasure, inquiry, incitement, etc., or calling for attention. [Imit.]

hey·day[1] (hā'dā') *n.* **1** The time of greatest vitality and vigor. **2** Exuberant spirits; wildness. [Prob. < HIGH DAY]

hey·day[2] (hā'dā') *interj.* An exclamation of surprise, joy, etc. [< Du. *heida!* hey there!]

Hey·drich (hī'drikh), **Reinhard,** 1904–42, German Nazi politician; assassinated.

Hey·duck (hī'dōōk) See HAIDUK

Hey·mans (hī'mäns), **Corneille,** born 1892, Belgian physiologist.

Hey·se (hī'zə), **Paul von,** 1830–1914, German dramatist and novelist.

Hey·ward (hā'wərd), **Du·Bose** (də·bōz'), 1885–1940, U.S. novelist and playwright.

Hey·wood (hā'wōōd), **John,** 1497?–1580?, English writer of interludes. **—Thomas,** 1575?–1641?, English playwright and actor.

Hez·e·ki·ah (hez'ə·kī'ə) A masculine personal name. [< Hebrew, Jehovah is strength]

—Hezekiah Twelfth king of Judah; son of Ahaz; reigned 726–715 B.C. II *Kings* xviii 1. Also *Ezechias.*

Hg *Chem.* Mercury (symbol Hg). [L *hydrargyrum*]

H-hinge (āch'hinj') *n.* A hinge with long, narrow leaves, which, when open, resembles the letter H. See illustration under HINGE.

H-hour (āch'our') *n.* The hour appointed for a military operation to begin: also called *zero hour.*

hi (hī) *interj. Colloq.* Hello: an exclamation of greeting. [Contraction of *how are you?*]

Hi·a·le·ah (hī'ə·lē'ə) A city in SE Florida, just NW of Miami; noted for its race track.

hi·a·tus (hī·ā'təs) *n. pl.* **·tus·es** or **·tus 1** A gap or opening; break, with a part missing; lacuna; interruption. **2** A pause or break due to the concurrence of two separate vowels without an intervening consonant.

Hi·a·wath·a (hī'ə·woth'ə, -wôth'ə, hē'ə-) Mohawk chief and venerated counselor of the League of the Iroquois, shortly before the advent of the Europeans: name used by Longfellow for the hero of his poem *Hiawatha.*

hi·ba·chi (hi·bä'chē) *n. pl.* **·chis** A charcoal-burning brazier, used for cooking food, etc. [< Jap. *hi* fire + *bachi* bowl]

hi·ber·nac·le (hī'bər·nak'əl) *n.* Hibernaculum (def. 3). [< L *hibernaculum* < *hibernare* pass the winter + -CULUM, dim. suffix]

hi·ber·nac·u·lum (hī'bər·nak'yə·ləm) *n. pl.* **·la** (-lə) *Biol.* **1** An encysted winter polyzoon bud capable of germinating in the spring. **2** A hibernating case constructed of foreign materials by certain insects. A den or shelter occupied by a hibernating animal. [< NL]

hi·ber·nal (hī·bûr'nəl) *adj.* Pertaining to winter; wintry. [< L *hibernalis* < *hibernus* wintry]

hi·ber·nate (hī'bər·nāt) *v.i.* **·nat·ed, ·nat·ing 1** To pass the winter, especially in a torpid state, as certain animals. **2** To pass the time in seclusion. [< L *hibernatus,* pp. of *hibernare* < *hiems* winter] **—hi'ber·na'tion** *n.*

Hi·ber·ni·a (hī·bûr'nē·ə) The Latin and poetic name for Ireland. [< L, alter. of *Iverna* < Celtic. Related to ERIN.]

Hi·ber·ni·an (hī·bûr'nē·ən) *adj.* Pertaining to Hibernia or Ireland, or its people; Irish. *—n.* A native or naturalized inhabitant of Ireland.

Hi·ber·ni·an·ism (hī·bûr'nē·ən·iz'əm) *n.* An Irish idiom or peculiarity of speech. Also **Hi·ber'ni·cism** (-nə·siz'əm).

Hi·ber·ni·cize (hī·bûr'nə·sīz) *v.t.* **·cized, ·ciz·ing** To make Irish. **—Hi·ber'ni·ci·za'tion** *n.*

hi·bis·cus (hī·bis'kəs, hi-) *n.* Any of various malvaceous herbs, shrubs and trees of the genus *Hibiscus,* having large, showy flowers of various colors. [< L < Gk. *hibiskos* mallow]

Hi·bok·hi·bok (hē'bôk·hē'bôk) A volcano on Camiguin island, Philippines; erupted 1948; 4,370 feet: also *Mount Camiguin.*

hic·cup (hik'əp) *n.* A short, catching sound, caused by spasmodic contraction of the diaphragm and windpipe. *—v.i.* **1** To have the hiccups; make a hiccup. *—v.t.* **2** To utter with hiccups. Also **hic·cough** (hik'əp): also spelled *hickup.* [Imit.]

hic et u·bi·que (hik et yōō·bī'kwē) *Latin* Here and everywhere.

hic ja·cet (hik jā'set) *Latin* Here lies: often inscribed on tombstones.

hick (hik) *n. Slang* One characterized by countrified manners, speech, or dress. [Alter. of RICHARD]

hick·ey (hik'ē) *n. pl.* **·eys 1** *Mech.* A T-shaped device of iron pipe used for bending a conduit. **2** *Electr.* A small fitting employed to secure an electric fixture to an outlet box. [Origin unknown]

Hick·ok (hik'ok), **James Butler,** 1837–76, U.S. frontier scout: called "Wild Bill Hickok."

hick·o·ry (hik'ər·ē) *n. pl.* **·ries 1** An American tree of the walnut family (genus *Carya*), yielding an edible nut and having hard, tough, heavy wood: also called *shellbark.* **2** Something made of this wood, as a walking stick or a switch. **3** A strong cotton fabric, usually twilled: used for men's trousers and shirts. **— Old Hickory** Andrew Jackson: so nicknamed for his tough unyielding character. — *adj.* **1** Having a growth of hickory trees. **2** Made of hickory. **3** Tough, like hickory wood. **4** Pertaining to a hickory switch, used in punishment: *hickory* discipline. [<Algonquian *pawcohiccoro*]

hick·up (hik′əp) See HICCUP.

hick·wall (hik′wôl′) *n.* The green woodpecker. [ME *hyghwhele*; prob. imit.]

Hic·po·chee (hik′pə·chē), **Lake** A lake of central Florida, comprising a link of the Cross-Florida Waterway.

hic se·pul·tus (hik sə·pul′təs) *Latin* Here (is) buried.

hid (hid) Past tense and alternative past participle of HIDE. — *adj.* Hidden.

hi·dal·go (hi·dal′gō, *Sp.* ē·thäl′gō) *n.* *pl.* **·gos** (-gōz, *Sp.* -gōs) A Spanish nobleman of the lower rank. [<Sp. < *hijo de algo* son of something] **— hi·dal′ga** (-gä) *n. fem.*

Hi·dal·go (hi·dal′gō, *Sp.* ē·thäl′gō) A state in central Mexico; 8,057 square miles; capital, Pachuca.

Hid·de·kel (hid′i·kəl) The Biblical name for the TIGRIS.

hid·den (hid′n) Past participle of HIDE. — *adj.* Put out of sight; secreted; not known; unseen: also *hid.* See synonyms under SECRET.

hid·den·ite (hid′ən·it) *n.* A transparent, yellow to green variety of spodumene found in Alexander County, N.C.: used as a gemstone. [after W. E. *Hidden,* 1853–1918, U.S. mineralogist]

hide[1] (hīd) *v.* **hid, hid·den** or **hid, hid·ing** *v.t.* **1** To put or keep out of sight; conceal. **2** To keep secret; withhold from knowledge: to *hide* one's fears. **3** To block or obstruct the sight of; keep from view: The smoke *hid* the buildings. **4** To turn away, as from shame or so as to ignore: *Hide* not thy face from me. — *v.i.* **5** To keep oneself out of sight; remain concealed. **— to hide out** To go into hiding. [OE *hȳdan*] **— hid′er** *n.*

Synonyms: bury, cloak, conceal, cover, disguise, dissemble, entomb, inter, mask, overwhelm, screen, secrete, suppress, veil. *Hide* is the general term, including all the rest, signifying to put out of sight or beyond ready observation or approach; a thing may be *hidden* by intention, by accident, or by the imperfection of the faculties of the one from whom it is *hidden.* As an act of persons, to *conceal* is always intentional; one may *hide* his face in anger, grief, or abstraction; he *conceals* his face when he fears recognition. A house is *hidden* by foliage; the bird's nest is artfully *concealed.* A thing is *covered* by putting something over or around it, by accident or design; it is *screened* by putting something before it, always for protection from observation, inconvenience, attack, censure, etc. In the figurative use, a person may *hide* honorable feelings; he *conceals* an evil or hostile intent. Compare BURY, MASK, PALLIATE. *Antonyms*: admit, advertise, avow, betray, confess, disclose, discover, disinter, divulge, exhibit, exhume, expose, manifest, promulgate, publish, raise, reveal, show, tell, uncover, unmask, unveil.

hide[2] (hīd) *n.* **1** The skin of a large animal, as an ox, especially as material for leather. **2** The human skin: humorously or with contempt. — *v.t.* **hid·ed, hid·ing** **1** To whip; flog severely. **2** To remove the hide from. [OE *hȳd* skin]

hide[3] (hīd) *n.* In Old English law, a measure of land, originally about 120 acres, considered enough to support a family. [OE *hīd, hīgid*]

hide-and-seek (hīd′ən·sēk′) *n.* A children's game in which those who hide are sought by one who is "it." Also **hide′-and-go-seek′.**

hide·bound (hīd′bound′) *adj.* **1** Obstinately fixed in opinion; narrow-minded; bigoted. **2** Having the bark so closely adherent that it impedes growth: said of trees.

hid·e·ous (hid′ē·əs) *adj.* Shocking or dreadful, especially in looks; ghastly; revolting. See synonyms under FRIGHTFUL, GHASTLY, GRIM. [<AF *hidous,* OF *hideus* < *hisde, hide* fright; ult. origin unknown] **— hid′e·ous·ly** *adv.* **— hid′e·ous·ness** *n.*

hide-out (hīd′out′) *n.* A place of concealment and safety; hiding place.

hid·ing[1] (hī′ding) *n.* The act of secreting, or the state of being secreted; concealment.

hid·ing[2] (hī′ding) *n. Colloq.* A flogging.

hiding power **1** The opacity of a paint. **2** The ability of a paint to reduce the contrast of a black-and-white surface.

hi·dro·sis (hi·drō′sis) *n.* **1** *Med.* The formation and excretion of sweat. **2** *Pathol.* **a** Any skin disease characterized by sweating. **b** Profuse sweating. [<NL <Gk. *hidroein* sweat < *hidrōs* sweat]

hi·drot·ic (hi·drot′ik) *n.* A drug or other substance to promote sweating; a sudorific. [<Med. L *hidroticus* <Gk. *hidrōtikos*]

hie (hī) *v.t.* & *v.i.* **hied, hie·ing** or **hy·ing** To hasten; hurry: often reflexive. [OE *hīgian*]

hie·la·man (hē′lə·mən) *n.* A shield of wood or bark about 3 feet long and 4 inches wide, used by Australian aborigines. [<native word]

hi·e·mal (hī′ə·məl) *adj.* Hibernal. [<L *hiemalis* < *hiems* winter]

hi·er·a·co·sphinx (hī′ər·ā′kō·sfingks) *n.* In ancient Egyptian art, a hawk-headed sphinx. See SPHINX. [<Gk. *hierax* hawk + SPHINX]

hi·er·arch (hī′ər·ärk) *n.* **1** An ecclesiastical chief ruler. **2** An official of ancient Greece who had charge of the votive offerings in a temple. [<Med. L *hierarcha* < *hierarchēs* < *hieros* sacred + *archos* ruler < *archein* rule]

hi·er·ar·chism (hī′ər·är′kiz·əm) *n.* The principles, character, and rule of a hierarchy. **— hi′er·ar′chist** *n.*

hi·er·ar·chy (hī′ər·är′kē) *n.* *pl.* **·chies** **1** A body of persons, especially ecclesiastics, ranked according to successive orders or classes. **2** Government or rule by a body of ecclesiastics organized in ranks or orders. **3** *Theol.* **a** Any of three ranks of angels. See ANGEL. **b** The body of angels collectively. **4** In science and logic, a series of systematic groups, as kingdoms, classes, orders, families, genera, and species. [<LL *hierarchia* <Gk. *hierarchia* rule of a *hierarch*] **— hi′er·ar′chic, hi′er·ar′chi·cal, hi′er·ar′chal** *adj.*

hi·er·at·ic (hī′ə·rat′ik) *adj.* **1** Of or pertaining to priests; devoted to sacred uses; sacerdotal; consecrated. **2** Of or pertaining to a cursive form of ancient Egyptian hieroglyphs, more complex than the demotic or popular cursive: employed for state papers, rituals, etc. Also **hi′er·at′i·cal.** [<L *hieraticus* <Gk. *hieratikos* of a priest's office < *hieros* sacred]

hi·er·at·i·ca (hī′ə·rat′i·kə) *n.* A fine grade of papyrus.

hiero- *combining form* Sacred; divine. [<Gk. *hieros* sacred]

Hi·er·o I (hī′ər·ō), died 467 B.C., tyrant of Syracuse 478–467 B.C.; patron of literature. Also **Hi′er·on** (-on).

hi·er·oc·ra·cy (hī′ə·rok′rə·sē) *n.* *pl.* **·cies** Ecclesiastical rule or supremacy. [<HIERO- + -CRACY] **— hi·er·o·crat·ic** (hī′ər·ə·krat′ik) or **·i·cal** *adj.*

hi·er·o·dule (hī′ər·ə·dyōōl) *n.* In ancient Greece, a temple slave, or one set apart as the property of some deity. [<Gk. *hierodoulos* < *hieron* temple + *doulos* slave]

hi·er·o·glyph (hī′ər·ə·glif′, hī′rə·glif) *n.* **1** Picture writing, especially of the ancient Egyptians: usually in the plural. **2** A character or word supposed to convey a hidden meaning. **3** *pl.* Humorously, illegible handwriting; unintelligible scribbling. Also **hi′er·o·glyph′ic.** [<LL *hieroglyphicus* <Gk. *hieroglyphikos* hieroglyphic < *hieros* sacred + *glyphein* carve] **— hi′er·o·glyph′ic** or **·i·cal** *adj.* **— hi′er·o·glyph′i·cal·ly** *adv.*

HIEROGLYPHS (*n. def. 1*)

hi·er·og·ly·phist (hī′ər·og′lə·fist, hī·rog′-) *n.* One skilled in the art of reading hieroglyphs.

hi·er·o·gram (hī′ər·ə·gram′, hī′rə-) *n.* **1** A sacred writing. **2** A character or symbol of sacred significance.

hi·er·ol·o·gy (hī′ə·rol′ə·jē, hī·rol′-) *n.* **1** The science of or a treatise on ancient Egyptian writings and inscriptions. **2** The scientific study and comparison of religions. [<HIERO- + -LOGY] **— hi·er·o·log·ic** (hī′ər·ə·loj′ik, hī′rə-) or **·i·cal** *adj.* **— hi′er·ol′o·gist** *n.*

hi·er·o·man·cy (hī′ər·ə·man′sē, hī′rə-) *n.* The act of divining by observing things offered in sacrifice.

Hi·er·on·y·mite (hī′ə·ron′ə·mīt) *n.* A follower of St. Jerome (Hieronymus); also, a member of one of the several monastic orders named after him. [<Med. L *Hieronymita* <LL *Hieronymus* Jerome. See HIERONYMUS.]

Hi·er·on·y·mus (hī′ə·ron′ə·məs, *Du., Ger., Sw.* ē·ā·rō′ni·mōōs) Latin form of JEROME. Also *Pg.* **Hi·e·ro·ni·mo** (ē·ā·rō′ni·mō). [<L <Gk. *hieronymos* having a sacred name < *hieros* sacred + *onyma, onoma* name]

hi·er·o·phant (hī′ər·ə·fant′, hī·er′-) *n.* **1** In ancient Greece, an official expounder of religious mysteries or rites. **2** One who expounds any esoteric cult or doctrine. [<LL *hierophanta* <Gk. *hierophantēs* < *hieros* sacred + *phainein* show] **— hi′er·o·phan′tic** *adj.*

hi·er·o·pho·bi·a (hī′ər·ə·fō′bē·ə) *n.* Morbid fear of sacred and religious things.

Hier·ro (yer′rō) The westernmost of the Canary Islands; 106 square miles: formerly *Ferro.*

Hi·er·o·sol·y·ma (hī′ər·ə·sol′i·mə) The ancient name for JERUSALEM.

hi·er·o·ther·a·py (hī′ər·ə·ther′ə·pē) *n.* Treatment of disease by religious symbolism and exercises. **— hi′er·o·ther′a·pist** *n.*

hi-fi (hī′fī′) *adj.* High-fidelity. — *n.* A radio receiver or phonograph capable of reproducing high-fidelity sound.

hig·gle (hig′əl) *v.i.* **hig·gled, hig·gling** To dispute about terms; haggle; chaffer. [Var. of HAGGLE] **— hig′gler** *n.*

hig·gle·dy-pig·gle·dy (hig′əl·dē·pig′əl·dē) *adj.* In a disordered state; jumbled; muddled. — *n.* Great confusion; a jumble. — *adv.* In a confused manner. [< obs. *higle-pigle,* a varied reduplication, ? < *pig*]

high (hī) *adj.* **1** Greatly elevated; lofty. **2** Having a (specified) elevation: an inch *high.* **3** Of or pertaining to an elevated, or inland, district: *High* German. **4** Extending to or performed from a height: *high* jump; *high* dive. **5** *Geog.* Far from the equator: said of latitudes. **6** Remote; old: *high* antiquity. **7** Of exalted rank or estimation: *high* heaven. **8** Of superior character or kind: *high* art. **9** Important; serious: *high* crimes. **10** Expensive; costly: Rent is *high.* **11** Intensified; of great degree, measure, force, etc.: *high* wind; *high* explosives. **12** Fully advanced or culminated: *high* noon. **13** Haughty; arrogant: *high* words. **14** Strict, as in opinion or doctrine: *high* Tory. **15** Elated; merry: *high* spirits. **16** Complex: usually in the comparative degree: *higher* mathematics, *higher* mammals. **17** Slightly tainted: said of meat. **18** *Music* Acute in pitch; shrill. **19** *Phonet.* Produced with the tongue raised close to the roof of the mouth; close: said of vowel sounds, as the (ē) in *bead*: opposed to *low.* **20** *Mech.* Designating a step-up gear mechanism operating at its greatest speed transmission. **21** *Colloq.* Feeling the effects of liquor, drugs, etc.; intoxicated. — *adv.* **1** To or at a high level, position, degree, etc. **2** In a high manner. **3** At a high pitch. — *n.* **1** A high level, position, etc. **2** *Meteorol.* An anti-cyclone. **3** *Mech.* An arrangement of gears for the greatest speed transmission. **— on high** **1** High above. **2** In heaven. [OE *hēah*] **— high′ly** *adv.* **— high′ness** *n.*

Synonyms (adj.): elevated, eminent, exalted, lofty, noble, proud, steep, tall, towering, uplifted. *Deep,* while an antonym of *high* in usage, may apply to the very same distance simply measured in an opposite direction, *high* applying to vertical distance measured from below upward, and *deep* to vertical distance measured from above downward; as, a *deep* valley nestling between *high* mountains. *High* is a relative term signifying greatly raised above any object, base, or surface, in comparison with what is usual, or with some standard; a table is *high* if it exceeds thirty inches; a hill is not *high* at a hundred feet. That is *tall* whose height is greatly in excess of its breadth or diameter, and whose actual height is great for an object of its kind; as, a *tall* tree; a *tall* man; *tall* grass. That is *lofty* which is imposing or majestic in height; we term a spire *tall* with reference to its altitude, or *lofty* with reference to its majestic appearance. That is *elevated* which is raised somewhat above its surroundings; that is *eminent* which is far above them; as, an *elevated* platform; an *eminent* promontory. In the figurative sense, *elevated* is less than *eminent,* and this less than *exalted;* we speak of *high, lofty,* or *elevated* thoughts, aims, etc., in the good sense, but sometimes of *high* feelings, looks, words, etc., in the invidious sense of haughty or arrogant. A *high* ambition may be merely selfish; a *lofty* ambition is worthy and *noble.* Compare HAUGHTY, STEEP[1]. *Antonyms*: base, deep, degraded, depressed, dwarfed, inferior, low, mean, short, stunted.

high and dry **1** On shore above the reach of water. **2** Stranded; helpless.

high and low Everywhere.

high and mighty Haughty; imperious.

high·ball[1] (hī′bôl′) *n.* An alcoholic drink, consisting of whisky to which is added soda water, mineral water, or ginger ale, served with ice in a tall glass. [Prob. <HIGH + *ball* whisky glass (in bartender's slang)]

high·ball[2] (hī′bôl′) *n.* A railroad signal meaning to "go ahead." —*v.i. U.S. Slang* To go at great speed. [From a large ball that could be raised or lowered, once used as a semaphore]

high-bind·er (hī′bīn′dər) *n. U.S. Slang* **1** A member of a Chinese secret society of blackmailers. **2** A ruffian; a tough. [? <HELLBENDER]

high-born (hī′bôrn′) *adj.* Of noble birth or extraction.

high·boy (hī′boi′) *n.* A tall chest of drawers usually in two sections, the lower a tablelike structure: called *tallboy* in England. See LOWBOY. [Origin unknown]

HIGHBOY

high-bred (hī′bred′) *adj.* **1** Of a fine pedigree. **2** Characterized by fine manners or good breeding.

high·brow (hī′brou′) *Colloq. n.* A person of cultivated or intellectual tastes: sometimes a term of derision. —*adj.* Of or suitable for such a person: also **high′browed′.** —**high′brow′ism** *n.*

high·chair (hī′châr′) *n.* A baby's chair provided with an eating tray and standing on tall legs.

High Church The group in the Anglican Church that exalts the authority of the church and emphasizes the value of ritual. See LOW CHURCH. —**High′-Church′man** *n.*

high-class (hī′klas′, -kläs′) *adj. Colloq.* Superior; of high quality.

high comedy Comedy presenting the world of polite society and relying chiefly on witty dialog.

high day A holiday; feast day.

higher criticism The scientific and historical study of literature, especially the Bible. Compare LOWER CRITICISM.

higher education **1** College education. **2** Any education beyond secondary schooling, giving advanced opportunities in general or special fields of learning.

Higher Thought New Thought.

high·er-up (hī′ər·up′) *n. Colloq.* A person of superior rank or position.

high explosive **1** A bursting charge that explodes by detonation and with extreme rapidity. **2** A shell charged with high explosive.

high·fa·lu·tin (hī′fə·lōōt′n) *Colloq. adj.* High-flown in manner or speech. —*n.* High-sounding language or writing; pompous speech. Also **high′fa·lu′ting.** [? <HIGH-FLOWN]

high-fi·del·i·ty (hī′fi·del′ə·tē) *adj. Electronics* Capable of reproducing sound with a minimum of distortion: said of certain radio and phonographic equipment: also *hi-fi.*

high-fli·er (hī′flī′ər) *n.* **1** One who or that which flies high. **2** One who goes to extremes or lives extravagantly. Also **high′-fly′er.**

high-flown (hī′flōn′) *adj.* **1** Pretentious. **2** Extravagant in style.

high-fly·ing (hī′flī′ing) *adj.* **1** That flies high, as a bird or airplane. **2** Having pretentious ideas and aims; extravagant in claims or opinions.

high-fre·quen·cy (hī′frē′kwən·sē) *adj. Physics* Of or pertaining to a band of wave frequencies, usually from 3 to 30 megacycles.

High German See under GERMAN.

high-grade (hī′grād′) *adj.* Of superior quality.

high-hand·ed (hī′han′did) *adj.* Carried on in an overbearing manner.

high-hat (hī′hat′) *Colloq. n.* One who wears a top hat; hence, an aristocrat; snob. —*adj.* Aristocratic; snobbish. —*v.t.* To snub; treat snobbishly.

high-hole (hī′hōl′) *n.* A bird, the flicker. Also **high′-hold′er.**

high-jinks (hī′jingks′) *n.* **1** An old Scottish game of forfeits, in which one was chosen by lot to perform a task. **2** *Colloq.* Rough sports or jollification. [Origin uncertain]

high jump An athletic event in which the contestants jump for height over a horizontal bar.

high-keyed (hī′kēd′) *adj.* **1** With high musical pitch. **2** Sensitive; spirited.

high·land (hī′lənd) *n.* An elevation of land.

high·land·er (hī′lən·dər) *n.* A mountaineer. Also **high′land·man** (-mən).

High·land·er (hī′lən·dər) *n.* A native of the Scottish Highlands; a Gael.

Highland fling A lively Scotch dance.

High·lands (hī′ləndz) *n. pl.* The mountainous part of northern and western Scotland in and north of the Grampians.

Highlands of the Hudson A mountainous region in SE New York; intersected by the Hudson River.

high life The life of fashionable society.

high·light (hī′līt′) *n.* **1** *pl.* The white or bright spots in a photograph or picture; conversely, the dark spots on the negative of a photograph. **2** A part or detail of special importance or vividness: That touchdown was the *highlight* of the game. —*v.t.* To give special emphasis to; feature.

high living A luxurious manner of life, as in diet.

high mass In the Roman Catholic Church, a mass that is sung and accompanied by full ceremonial.

high-mind·ed (hī′mīn′did) *adj.* **1** Showing an elevated mind; with lofty ethics or feelings. **2** Haughty; arrogant. —**high′-mind′ed·ly** *adv.* —**high′-mind′ed·ness** *n.*

high-muck-a-muck (hī′muk′ə·muk) *n. U.S. Colloq.* A person of importance, real or pretended. [<HIGH + reduplication of MUCKLE]

High·ness (hī′nis) *n.* A title of honor belonging to persons of royal rank: with *His, Her,* or *Your.*

high-oc·tane (hī′ok′tān) *adj.* Having a high octane number, indicating superior antiknock properties.

high-pitched (hī′picht′) *adj.* **1** Shrill. **2** Having a steep slope: said of roofs.

high place Among Semitic peoples, an altar or place of worship, generally on a bare, lofty hill or mountain. —**high′-placed′** *adj.*

high-pres·sure (hī′presh′ər) *adj.* **1** Having or using a high steam pressure: said of steam engines. **2** Exerting vigorous tactics, pressing; urgent: *high-pressure* salesmanship. —*v.t.* **·sured, ·sur·ing** To persuade or influence by such methods.

high priest A chief priest.

high-proof (hī′prōōf′) *adj.* Containing a high percentage of alcohol: *high-proof* whisky.

high relief Alto-relievo.

high-rise (hī′rīz′) *adj.* Describing a relatively tall building or structure. —*n.* A tall building, as a many-storied apartment house: also **high rise.**

high·road (hī′rōd′) *n.* **1** A main road. **2** A common or easy method or course. See synonyms under WAY.

high school See under SCHOOL. —**high′-school′** *adj.*

high seas The unenclosed waters of the ocean or sea, especially those beyond the territorial jurisdiction of any one country or nation.

high-sea·soned (hī′sē′zənd) *adj.* **1** Made rich in flavor, as by the addition of spices. **2** Racy; sparkling; lively.

High Sierras The highest portion of the Sierra Nevada, south of Lake Tahoe.

high·sign (hī′sīn′) *n. Colloq.* An informing or warning gesture or grimace.

high-sound·ing (hī′soun′ding) *adj.* Ostentatious or imposing in sound or import.

high-spir·it·ed (hī′spir′ə·tid) *adj.* Full of spirit; not brooking restraint.

high-strung (hī′strung′) *adj.* Strung to a high pitch; strained; highly sensitive.

hight[1] (hīt) *adj. Archaic* Called or named. [OE *heht,* pt. of *hātan* call]

hight[2] (hīt) See HEIGHT. Also *Obs.* **highth** (hītth, hīth).

high·tail (hī′tāl′) *v.i. U.S. Slang* To depart hastily, especially in fright.

high tea A substantial afternoon or early evening meal at which meat is served.

high-ten·sion (hī′ten′shən) *adj. Electr.* Pertaining to, characterized by, or operating under very high voltage, usually in excess of 1,000 volts.

high-test (hī′test′) *adj.* **1** Designating a material or substance which has passed severe tests of fitness. **2** Denoting a grade of gasoline with a low boiling-point range.

high tide **1** The maximum tidal elevation of the water at any point; also, the time of its occurrence. **2** Any culminating point in a series of events. Also **high water.**

high time **1** About time; past the proper time. **2** *Slang* An occasion of revelry and excitement.

high-toned (hī′tōnd′) *adj.* **1** Of high principles; honorable. **2** Having a high pitch. **3** *U.S. Colloq.* Aristocratic; fashionable.

high treason Treason against the sovereign or state.

high·ty-tigh·ty (hī′tē·tī′tē) *adj.* & *interj.* Hoity-toity.

high-up (hī′up′) *adj.* In a high or superior position.

High Veld (velt) See NORTHERN KARROO.

high-water (hī′wô′tər, -wot′ər) *adj.* Pertaining to high tide or to its time or highest elevation.

high·way (hī′wā′) *n.* **1** A public thoroughfare; specified line of travel. **2** A common or open way or course. See synonyms under ROAD, WAY.

high·way·man (hī′wā′mən) *n. pl.* **·men** (-mən) One who practices robbery on the highway. See synonyms under ROBBER.

high wine Grain spirits distilled to a high percentage of alcohol; usually in the plural.

high-wrought (hī′rôt′) *adj.* **1** Skilfully or finely wrought. **2** Highly agitated; impassioned.

Hii·u·maa (hē′ōō·mä) See KHIUMA.

hi·jack (hī′jak′) *v.t. U.S. Colloq.* **1** To steal a shipment of (goods, bootleg liquor, etc.) by force. **2** To rob or steal (a truck, etc., carrying such goods). **3** To seize control of (an aircraft) while in flight by the threat or use of force and redirect it to a different destination; skyjack. **4** To rob, swindle, etc., by force or coercion. [Origin unknown] —**hi′jack′er** *n.*

hike (hīk) *v.* **hiked, hik·ing** *v.i.* To go on foot, as for pleasure or on a military march; tramp. —*v.t.* To raise or lift: usually with *up* —*n.* **1** A weary journey on foot; a long walk. **2** *Colloq.* An increase: a price *hike.* [? Var. of HITCH]

hi·lar·i·ous (hi·lâr′ē·əs, hī-) *adj.* Boisterously merry; romping. See synonyms under MERRY. —**hi·lar′i·ous·ly** *adv.*

hi·lar·i·ty (hi·lar′ə·tē, hī-) *n.* Boisterous mirth. See synonyms under LAUGHTER. [<OF *hilarité* <L *hilaritas, -tatis* <*hilaris* <Gk. *hilaros* cheerful]

Hil·a·ry (hil′ər·ē) A masculine personal name. Also **Hi·la·ri·us** (*Dan., Du., Ger., Sw.* hē·lä′·rē·ōōs; *Lat.* hi·lā′rē·əs), *Fr.* **Hi·laire** (ē·lâr′), *Sp.* **Hi·la·ri·o** (ē·lä′rē·ō). [<L, joyful] —**Hilary, Saint,** 300?–367?, anti-Arian bishop of Poitiers.

Hilary term or **sitting** One of the four terms recognized in English courts of law, lasting from Jan. 11 to March 23: so called from the festival of St. Hilary (Jan. 13).

Hil·da (hil′də) A feminine personal name. [<Gmc., war]

Hil·de·brand (hil′də·brand) Personal name of

Gregory VII. —**Hil′de·bran·dine** (-din, -dīn) *adj.*

Hil·des·heim (hil′dəs·hīm) A city in SW Lower Saxony, north central West Germany.

hill (hil) *n.* **1** A conspicuous natural elevation rising above the earth's surface and smaller than a mountain. **2** A heap or pile: a *mole-hill.* **3** A small mound of earth placed over or around certain plants and tubers. **4** The plants and tubers so surrounded. —**the Hill** Capitol Hill. —*v.t.* **1** To surround or cover with hills, as potatoes. **2** To form a hill or heap of. —*adj.* Living in, or coming from, a hilly country: *hill* folk, *hill* songs; also, having many hills: *hill* country. [OE *hyll*]

Hill (hil), **Ambrose Powell,** 1825–65, American Confederate general. —**Archibald Vivian,** born 1886, English physiologist. —**James Jerome,** 1838–1916, U. S. railroad promoter; financier.

Hil·la (hil′ə) A town in central Iraq on the Euphrates, near the ruins of Babylon. Also **Hil′lah.**

hill-and-dale (hil′ən·dāl′) *adj.* Designating a method of phonograph recording by making the cuts perpendicular to the surface of the disk, the varying depth corresponding with the sound values. Compare LATERAL-CUT.

Hil·lar·y (hil′ər·ē), **Sir Edmond,** born 1919, New Zealand apiarist; scaled Mt. Everest 1953 with Tensing Norkay of Nepal.

hill·bil·ly (hil′bil′ē) *n. pl.* **·lies** *Colloq.* A person inhabiting or from the mountains or a backwoods area, especially of the southern United States: originally a derogatory term. —*adj. Colloq.* Of or characteristic of hillbillies: *hillbilly* music. [<HILL + BILLY[2]]

hill·er (hil′ər) *n.* **1** One who makes hills about seeding plants. **2** A mechanical appliance for this purpose.

hill·man (hil′man′) *n. pl.* **·men** (-men′) **1** A dweller in a hilly country; highlander; especially, a member of any hill tribe of India. **2** A climber of hills. **3** A Cameronian. **4** A fairy; troll.

Hill·man (hil′mən), **Sidney,** 1887–1946, U. S. labor leader.

hill mi·na (mī′nə) An East Indian starling-like bird *(Eulabes religiosa)* that can be taught to speak. Also **hill my′na.**

hil·lo (hil′ō, hi·lō′), **hil·loa** See HALLOO.

hill·ock (hil′ək) *n.* A small hill; a mound. —**hill′ock·y** *adj.*

Hill·quit (hil′kwit), **Morris,** 1869–1933, U. S. lawyer and socialist born in Latvia.

hill·side (hil′sīd′) *n.* The side of a hill; a slope or rise of ground.

hill·top (hil′top′) *n.* The summit of a hill.

hill·y (hil′ē) *adj.* **hill·i·er, hill·i·est** **1** Full of hills; swelling; rounded. **2** Like a hill; steep. —**hill′i·ness** *n.*

Hi·lo (hē′lō) A port, the chief city on the island of Hawaii.

hilt (hilt) *n.* The handle and guard of a sword or dagger. —**to the hilt** Thoroughly; completely. —*v.t.* To provide with a hilt. [OE]

hi·lum (hī′ləm) *n. pl.* **·la** (-lə) **1** *Bot.* The scar on a seed indicating its point of attachment; also, the nucleus of a starch grain or the eye of a bean. **2** *Anat.* The fissurelike interval where ducts, vessels, and nerves enter and leave an organ. Also **hi′lus** (-ləs). [<L, a trifle]

Hil·ver·sum (hil′vər·sum) A city in west central Netherlands.

him (him) *pron.* The objective case of *he.* [OE]

Hi·ma·chal Pra·desh (hi·mä′chəl prə·dāsh′) A Union Territory of NE central India, bordering on Tibet; it contains twenty-two former princely states, of which nineteen, before 1936, were grouped in the Punjab Hill States agency, and the rest, 1921–36, in the Punjab States agency; 10,904 square miles; capital, Simla.

Hi·ma·la·yas (hi·mäl′yəz, -mä′lə·yəz, him′ə·lā′əz) A mountain chain between Tibet and India and in Nepal; highest point, 29,002 feet, world's highest point. Also **the Hi·ma′·la·ya.** —**Hi·ma′la·yan** *adj.*

hi·mat·i·on (hi·mat′ē·on) *n. pl.* **·i·a** (-ē·ə) A large square or oblong piece of cloth worn as a mantle by ancient Greeks. [<Gk.]

Hi·me·ji (hē·me·jē) A city on southern Honshu island, Japan.

Himm·ler (him′lər), **Heinrich,** 1900–45, German Nazi official; head of the Gestapo, 1936–45.

him·self (him·self′) *pron.* **1** A reflexive and usually intensive or emphatic form of the third-person pronoun, masculine gender. **2** One's normal physical or mental condition; one's consciousness; one's individuality: He stumbled, but soon recovered *himself.* **3** *Dial.* He: used as nominative alone without noun or pronoun: The dagger which *himself* gave Edith was lost; *himself* has said so.

Him·yar·ite (him′yə·rīt) *n.* **1** One of an ancient tribe of SW Arabia and the opposite African mainland. **2** An Arab of a group of ancient kindred tribes, or of their descendants, inhabiting southern Arabia. [after Arabic *Himyar* a legendary king of Yemen + -ITE[1]] —**Him·yar·it·ic** (him′yə·rit′ik) *adj.*

hind[1] (hīnd) *adj.* **hind·er, hind·most** or **hind·er·most** Belonging to the rear. [OE *hindan* behind]

hind[2] (hīnd) *n.* The female of the red deer or stag. [OE]

hind[3] (hīnd) *n. Archaic* A farm laborer; also, a peasant. [OE *hīna, hīgna,* genitive pl. of *hīgan* domestics]

hind·brain (hīnd′brān′) *n. Anat.* That part of the brain which develops from the posterior or third embryonic vesicle, including the cerebellum and pons, the medulla oblongata and its membranous roof, or the epencephalon, metencephalon, etc.

Hin·de·mith (hin′də·mit), **Paul,** 1895–1963, German composer active in the United States.

Hin·den·burg (hin′dən·bûrg, *Ger.* hin′dən·bŏŏrkh) The German name for ZABRZE.

Hin·den·burg (hin′dən·bûrg, *Ger.* hin′dən·bŏŏrkh), **Paul von Beneckendorff und von,** 1847–1934, German general and statesman; president of the German Republic 1925–34.

Hindenburg line A strongly fortified line of defense in World War I, established by the Germans in 1916, and running through Saint Laurent, Cambrai, Canal du Nord, Saint Quentin, and La Fère; abandoned in October, 1918. [after Paul von *Hindenburg*]

hin·der[1] (hin′dər) *v.t.* **1** To keep back or delay; check. **2** To prevent; obstruct. —*v.i.* **3** To be an obstruction or obstacle. [OE *hindrian* <*hinder* behind] —**hin′der·er** *n.*

Synonyms: baffle, balk, bar, block, check, clog, counteract, delay, embarrass, encumber, foil, frustrate, hamper, impede, obstruct, prevent, resist, retard, stay, stop, thwart. A railroad train may be *hindered* by a snowstorm from arriving on time; it may by special order be *prevented* from starting. To *retard* is simply to make slow by any means whatever. To *obstruct* is to *hinder*, or possibly to *prevent* advance or passage by putting something in the way; to *oppose* or *resist* is to *hinder*, or possibly to *prevent*, by directly contrary or hostile action, *resist* being the stronger term and having more suggestion of physical force; *obstructed* roads *hinder* the march of an enemy, though there may be no force strong enough to *oppose* it. Compare EMBARRASS, IMPEDE, LIMIT, PROHIBIT, RESTRAIN, SUSPEND. *Antonyms*: see synonyms for HELP, QUICKEN.

hind·er[2] (hīn′dər) *adj.* Pertaining to or constituting the rear. [OE]

hind·gut (hīnd′gut′) *n. Anat.* The embryonic structure from which the colon develops.

Hin·di (hin′dē) *n.* The principal language of northern India, belonging to the Indic branch of the Indo-Iranian languages. It includes **Western Hindi,** of which Hindustani is the major dialect, and **Eastern Hindi.** [<Hind. *hindī* <*Hind* India <Persian <OPersian *Hindu* land on the Indus <Skt. *sindhu* river, the Indus]

hind·most (hīnd′mōst′) *adj.* Situated in the extreme rear. Also **hind′er·most′** (hīn′dər-).

Hin·doo (hin′dōō), **Hin·doo·ism** (-iz′əm), etc. See HINDU, etc.

hind·quar·ter (hīnd′kwôr′tər) *n.* One of the two back parts into which the sagittal half of a carcass of a quadruped is usually divided, including a hind leg.

hin·drance (hin′drəns) *n.* **1** The act of hindering. **2** An obstacle or check. See synonyms under IMPEDIMENT.

hind·sight (hīnd′sīt′, hīn′sīt′) *n.* **1** Insight into the nature and difficulties of a situation after the event or after the difficulties have been resolved. **2** The rear sight of a gun or rifle.

Hin·du (hin′dōō) *n.* **1** A member of the native Aryan race of India. **2** Any native of India who professes Hinduism. —*adj.* Of or pertaining to the people or religion of India. Also *Hindoo.* [<Persian *Hindū* < *Hind.* See HINDI.]

Hin·du·ism (hin′dōō·iz′əm) *n.* The popular religion of India, consisting of the ancient religion of the Brahmans, with an admixture of Buddhism and other philosophies: its supreme deities are the triad of Brahma, Vishnu, and Siva, while numberless inferior divinities and natural objects, as trees, serpents, etc., are objects of worship. Also *Hindooism.*

Hin·du·ize (hin′dōō·īz) *v.t.* **·ized, ·iz·ing** To make Hindu in customs, speech, etc.

Hindu Kush (kōōsh) A mountain range in central Asia, on the Afghanistan-Pakistan border; highest point, 25,263 feet: ancient *Caucasus Indicus.*

Hin·du·stan (hin′dōō·stan′, -stän′) **1** The Persian name for the land east of the Indus. **2** The region of the Ganges plain where Hindi is largely spoken. **3** The Republic of India as opposed to Pakistan. Also **Hin′do·stan′** (-dō-).

Hin·du·sta·ni (hin′dōō·stä′nē, -stan′ē) *n.* The principal dialect of Western Hindi: the official language and general medium of communication in India. See URDU. —*adj.* Of or pertaining to Hindustan, its people, or to Hindustani. Abbr. *Hind.*

hing (hing) *v.t.* & *v.i. Scot.* To hang.

hinge (hinj) *n.* **1** A device allowing one part to turn upon another: the hook or joint on which a door or shutter swings or turns.

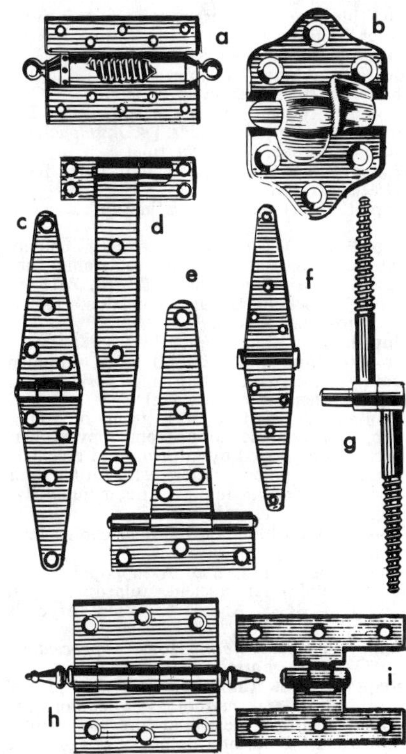

HINGES

a. Spring hinge. *b.* Blind hinge. *c.* Strap hinge. *d.* Plate hinge. *e.* T-hinge. *f.* Link hinge. *g.* Gate hinge. *h.* Butt hinge. *i.* H-hinge.

2 A device consisting of two metal plates joined by a rod, used as to connect a lid to a box. **3** A natural articulation; a joint, as in the shell of an oyster. **4** A pivotal point on which anything depends for its effect or course. —*v.* **hinged, hing·ing** *v.i.* **1** To have one's course determined by an action or eventuality; be dependent: with *on* or *upon*: The deal *hinged* on his acceptance of the offer. —*v.t.* 2 To attach by or equip with a hinge or hinges. [ME *hengen*, prob. <ON *hengja* hang. Related to HANG.]

hinge joint *Anat.* A joint in which angular motion occurs in but one plane, as the elbow joint.

hin·ny[1] (hin′ē) *n. pl.* **·nies** The offspring of a stallion and a she-ass. [<L *hinnus* <Gk. *ginnos*]

hin·ny[2] (hin′ē) *v.i.* **·nied, ·ny·ing** To whinny; neigh. [Var. of WHINNY]

hint (hint) *n.* 1 An indirect suggestion or implication in avoidance of or allusion to a direct statement. 2 A small amount or part: a *hint* of rain. 3 *Obs.* An opportunity; occasion. See synonyms under SUGGESTION. —*v.t.* To suggest indirectly; imply. —*v.i.* To make hints: often with *at*. See synonyms under ALLUDE. [OE *hentan* seize, grasp]

hin·ter·land (hin′tər·land′) *n.* 1 The region lying behind the district along a seacoast or riverside. 2 The region remote from urban areas; the back country. [<G]

Hi·ob (hē′ōp) German form of JOB.

hip[1] (hip) *n.* 1 The lateral part of the body between the brim of the pelvis and the free part of the thigh. ◆ Collateral adjective: *coxal.* 2 The hip joint. 3 The coxa in insects. 4 *Archit.* The external angle in which adjacent roof slopes meet each other. —**on** (or **upon**) **the hip** In a position prejudicial to success: in allusion to a wrestler's trick. —*v.t.* **hipped, hip·ping** 1 To fracture or sprain the hip of (an animal). 2 *Archit.* To build with a hip or hips, as a roof. [OE *hype*]

hip[2] (hip) *n.* The fruit of a rose, especially of the dogrose. [OE *hēope*]

hip[3] (hip) *interj.* An exclamation used to introduce a hurrah, or to give the signal for it. [Origin unknown]

hip[4] (hip) *adj. U.S. Slang* Aware; informed: often followed by *to*. [? Alter. of HEP]

hip bone The innominate bone.

hip joint *Anat.* The joint between the hip bone and the thigh bone or femur.

hip·parch (hip′ärk) *n.* In ancient Greek history, a cavalry commander. [<Gk. *hipparchos* <*hippos* horse + *archein* rule]

Hip·par·chus (hi·pär′kəs), 160?–125? B.C., Greek astronomer.

hipped[1] (hipt) *adj.* Having hips of a stated kind: heavy-*hipped.*

hipped[2] (hipt) *adj.* 1 *U.S. Slang* Unduly interested or engrossed by something; obsessed: *hipped* on socialism. 2 *Brit.* Affected with hypochondria or depression. [<HY-P(OCHONDRIA) + -ED]

hipped roof A hip roof.

hip·pet·y-hop (hip′ə·tē·hop′) *n.* A hopping gait. —*adv.* With a hop and a skip: also **hip′pet·y-hop·pet·y** (-hop′ə·tē).

hip·pie (hip′ē) *n.* One of a group of young people whose alienation from conventional society is expressed by informal and eccentric clothing, a preoccupation with drugs and mysticism, and an interest in communal living. [Var. of HIPSTER]

hip·pish (hip′ish) *adj. Brit.* Melancholic; low-spirited.

hip·po (hip′ō) *n. Colloq.* A hippopotamus.

Hip·po (hip′ō) An ancient, ruined city just south of Bône, Algeria: a center of early Christianity: also *Hippo Regius.*

hippo– *combining form* Horse: *hippocentaur.* [<Gk. *hippos* horse]

hip·po·cam·pus (hip′ə·kam′pəs) *n. pl.* **·pi** (-pī) 1 In Greek mythology, a fabulous sea monster with the head and forequarters of a horse and the tail of a dolphin. 2 *Anat.* One of two eminences found on the floor of the lateral ventricles of the brain. The larger, **hippocampus major,** is in the descending or temporal cornu of the ventricle; the smaller, **hippocampus minor,** is in the occipital cornu. 3 The sea horse. [<L <Gk. *hippos* horse + *kampos* sea monster] —**hip′po·cam′pal** *adj.*

hip·po·cen·taur (hip′ə·sen′tôr) *n.* A centaur.

hip·po·cras (hip′ə·kras) *n.* A cordial made of spiced wine, lemon, etc.: used for medicinal purposes: popular in the Middle Ages. [<OF *ypocras*, after *Hippocrates*]

Hip·poc·ra·tes (hi·pok′rə·tēz), 460?–377 B.C., Greek physician: called the "Father of Medicine."

Hip·po·crat·ic (hip′ə·krat′ik) *adj.* Of or pertaining to Hippocrates.

Hippocratic oath An oath administered to those entering the practice of medicine in early days and credited to Hippocrates, and still administered to graduates about to receive a medical degree.

Hip·po·crene (hip′ə·krēn, hip′ə·krē′nē) A fountain on Mount Helicon, Greece, traditionally sacred to the Muses. [<L <Gk. *hippokrēnē* <*hippos* horse + *krēnē* fountain]

Hip·po·da·mi·a (hip′ō·dā′mē·ə) In Greek legend, the wife of Pirithous, abused at a banquet by centaurs: the subject of the Parthenon metopes.

hip·po·drome (hip′ə·drōm) *n.* 1 An arena, stadium, or large structure for equestrian exhibitions, circuses, etc. 2 In ancient Greece and Rome, a course or track for horse races and chariot races. [<F <L *hippodromos* < Gk. <*hippos* horse + *dromos* running, course <*dramein* run]

hip·po·griff (hip′ə·grif) *n.* A mythological beast with the wings, head, and claws of a griffin, and the hoofs and tail of a horse. Also **hip′po·gryph.** [<F *hippogriffe* < Ital. *ippogrifo* <Gk. *hippos* horse + LL *gryphus* GRIFFIN]

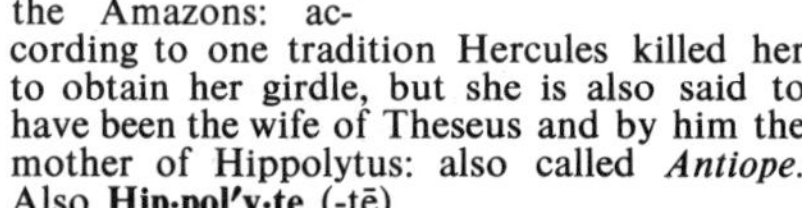

HIPPOGRIFF

Hip·pol·y·ta (hi·pol′·ə·tə) In Greek mythology, a queen of the Amazons: according to one tradition Hercules killed her to obtain her girdle, but she is also said to have been the wife of Theseus and by him the mother of Hippolytus: also called *Antiope.* Also **Hip·pol′y·te** (-tē).

Hip·pol·y·tus (hi·pol′ə·təs) In Greek mythology, the son of Theseus and Hippolyta, who spurned the love of his stepmother Phaedra and was killed by Poseidon at his father's request after Phaedra had turned Theseus against him.

Hip·pom·e·don (hi·pom′ə·don) See SEVEN AGAINST THEBES.

Hip·pom·e·nes (hi·pom′ə·nēz) In Greek mythology, the man who won Atalanta by beating her in a race.

hip·poph·a·gist (hi·pof′ə·jist) *n.* An eater of horseflesh. Also **hip·poph′a·gus** (-ə·gəs). [< HIPPO- + Gk. *phagein* eat] —**hip·poph′a·gous** (-gəs) *adj.*

hip·poph·a·gy (hi·pof′ə·jē) *n.* The act or habit of eating horseflesh. [<HIPPO- + -PHAGY]

hip·po·pot·a·mus (hip′ə·pot′ə·məs) *n. pl.* **·mus·es** or **·mi** (-mī) A large, amphibious, short-legged, thick-skinned African pachyderm related to the pigs *(Hippopotamus amphibius),* having a massive body and very broad obtuse muzzle; river horse. Among living quadrupeds it ranks next to the elephant in size. [<L <Gk. *hippopotamos* <*hippos* horse + *potamos* river]

HIPPOPOTAMUS
(From 4 1/2 to 5 feet at shoulder; length about 12 feet)

Hip·po Re·gi·us (hip′ō rē′jē·əs) See HIPPO.

Hippo Za·ry·tus (zə·rī′təs) An ancient name for BIZERTE.

hip·pus (hip′əs) *n. Pathol.* A disorder of the eyes characterized by rapid, spasmodic changes in size of the pupil when exposed to light. [<NL <Gk. *hippos* horse; from the movement of the eye]

-hippus *combining form Paleontol.* Horse: *Eohippus.* [<Gk. *hippos* horse]

hip roof *Archit.* 1 A roof rising directly from the wall plate on all sides, and thus having no gable. 2 A short portion of a roof over a truncated gable. Also called *hipped roof.*

hip–shot (hip′shot′) *adj.* 1 Having the hip joint dislocated. 2 Lame; awkward.

hip·ster (hip′stər) *n. U.S. Slang* One who is hip, as one versed in jazz. [<HIP[4] + -STER]

Hi·ram (hī′rəm) A masculine personal name. [<Hebrew, nobly born]
—**Hiram,** 980?–936 B.C., king of Tyre who helped to build Solomon's temple. I *Kings* v.

hi·ran (hī′ran) *n. Telecom.* A form of radar designed for operations requiring extreme precision and accuracy in the location of positions. [<HI(GH PRECISION SHO)RAN]

hir·cine (hûr′sin, -sīn) *adj.* Like a goat; especially, having a goatlike smell. [<L *hircinus* <*hircus* goat]

hire (hīr) *v.t.* **hired, hir·ing** 1 To obtain the services of (a person) or the use of (a thing) for a compensation; employ; rent. 2 To grant the use of (a thing) or the services of (a person) for a compensation; let: often with *out.* See synonyms under EMPLOY, RETAIN. —**to hire out** To give one's services for a compensation. —*n.* 1 Compensation for labor, services, etc. 2 The act of hiring. See synonyms under SALARY. —**for hire** Offered for use or rent for a compensation. [OE *hȳr*] —**hir′a·ble, hire′a·ble** *adj.* —**hir′er** *n.*

hired girl A woman hired to do household or farm chores.

hired hand A person employed on a farm.

hired man A man hired to do odd jobs, especially about a farm.

hire·ling (hīr′ling) *adj.* Serving for hire; venal. See synonyms under VENAL. —*n.* One who serves for or only for hire.

Hi·ro·hi·to (hir·ō·hē·tō), born 1901, emperor of Japan 1926–.

Hi·ro·shi·ge (hir·ō·shē·ge), **Ando,** 1797–1858, Japanese painter and printmaker.

Hi·ro·shi·ma (hir′ō·shē′mä, hē·rō′shē·mä) A port in SW Honshu island, Japan; devastated by first atomic bomb used in warfare, August 6, 1945.

hir·sel[1] (hûr′səl) *Scot. v.t.* To arrange in flocks, as sheep. —*n.* A flock of sheep. Also *hissel.*

hir·sel[2] (hûr′səl) *v.i. Scot. & Brit. Dial.* To move along with friction or with a rustling effect. Also **hir′sle.**

hir·sute (hûr′sōōt, hûr·sōōt′) *adj.* 1 Having a hairy covering; set with bristles; shaggy. 2 Covered with coarse hairs or hairlike processes. 3 Covered with fine hairlike feathers, as the feet of certain birds. [<L *hirsutus* rough] —**hir′sute·ness** *n.*

Hir·u·din·e·a (hir′ə·din′ē·ə) *n. pl.* A class of annelids which includes the leeches. [<NL <L *hirudo, -inis* leech]

hi·ru·di·noid (hi·rōō′də·noid) *adj.* Pertaining to or resembling a leech.

hi·run·dine (hi·run′din, -dīn) *adj.* Of, pertaining to, or resembling the swallow; swallowlike. [<L *hirundo, -dinis* a swallow]

his (hiz) *pron.* 1 Belonging or pertaining to him: the possessive case of *he* used predicatively or after *of*: This room is *his*; that laugh of *his.* 2 The things, persons, etc., belonging or pertaining to him: Her book is better than *his*; He protects himself and *his.* —*pronominal adj.* Belonging or relating to him: the possessive case of *he* used attributively: *his* book. [OE]

His·ki·a (his·kē′ä) Dutch form of HEZEKIAH.

his'n (hiz′ən) *pron. Archaic* or *Dial.* His. Also **hisn.**

His·pan·ic (his·pan′ik) *adj.* Of or pertaining to the countries or people of Spain, Portugal, and Latin America, or to their languages, customs, or culture. —*n. U.S.* A native or inhabitant of Spanish America; Spanish American.

Hispanic America See SPANISH AMERICA.

His·pan·i·cism (his·pan′ə·siz′əm) *n.* A turn of phrase peculiar to the Spanish.

His·pa·nio·la (his′pə·nyō′lə) An island of the West Indies; 30,000 square miles; formerly *Haiti*; divided into Haiti and the Dominican Republic. *Spanish* **Es·pa·ño·la** (es′pä·nyō′lä).

His·pa·no-Mo·resque (his·pä′nō·mô·resk′) *adj.* Pertaining to or naming the art of Spain having Moorish characteristics.

his·pid (his′pid) *adj. Biol.* Rough with stiff hairs or bristles; bristly. [<L *hispidus* hairy] —**his·pid·i·ty** (his·pid′ə·tē) *n.*

hiss (his) *n.* 1 The prolonged sound of *s*, as that made by escaping air. 2 Such a sound made to express disapproval, hatred, etc. —*v.i.* 1 To make or emit a hiss or hisses. 2 To express disapproval or hatred by hissing. —*v.t.* 3 To express disapproval or hatred of by hissing. 4 To express by means of a hiss or hisses. 5 To pursue, drive off, silence, etc., by hissing: usually with *off, down,* etc. [OE *hyscan* jeer at]

His·sar·lik (hi·sär·lik′) The site of ancient Troy in NW Turkey in Asia.

his·sel (his′əl) *Scot.* See HIRSEL[1].

hiss·ing (his′ing) *n.* 1 The act of uttering a

hiss. 2 *Archaic* An object of scorn or contempt.

hist (hist) *interj.* Be silent! hush! hark! —*v.t. Poetic* To urge on or signal by making a hissing sound. [Imit.]

his·tam·i·nase (his·tam′ə·nās) *n. Biochem.* An enzyme capable of inactivating histamine: used in the treatment of allergic conditions. [< HISTAMINE + -ASE]

his·ta·mine (his′tə·mēn, -min) *n. Biochem.* A white crystalline substance, $C_5H_9N_3$, found in plant and animal tissues and as a decomposition product of histidine. It stimulates gastric secretion, reduces blood pressure, and has a contracting action on the uterus. [< HIST(IDINE)+ AMINE]

his·ti·dine (his′tə·dēn, -din) *n.* A basic amino acid, $C_6H_9N_2O_3$, obtained upon hydrolysis of most proteins. [< Gk. *histion* tissue + -IDE(E) + -INE[2]]

his·ti·o·cyte (his′tē·ə·sīt) *n.* A macrophage that functions in connective tissue. Also **his·to·cyte.** —**his·ti·o·cyt·ic** (his′tē·ə·sit′ik) *adj.*

his·ti·oid (his′tē·oid) *adj.* Appearing like a normal tissue. Also **his·toid** (his′toid). [< Gk. *histos* web + -OID]

histo- *combining form* Tissue: *histology.* Also, before vowels, **hist-.** [< Gk. *histos* a web]

his·to·blast (his′tə·blast) *n.* A tissue-forming cell

his·to·chem·is·try (his′tə·kem′is·trē) *n.* The chemistry of tissue structures in organisms.

his·to·gen·e·sis (his′tə·jen′ə·sis) *n.* The formation and development of tissues. Also **his·tog·e·ny** (his·toj′ə·nē). —**his′to·gen′ic** *adj.*

his·to·gram (his′tə·gram) *n. Stat.* A graph of frequency distribution in the form of a series of rectangles whose width and area correspond to the range of the class interval and the quantities represented. See HISTORIGRAM.

his·tol·o·gy (his·tol′ə·jē) *n.* 1 The branch of biology treating of the structure of the tissues of organized bodies; microscopic anatomy. 2 The tissue structure of a plant or animal organism. [< HISTO- + -LOGY] —**his·to·log·i·cal** (his′tə·loj′i·kəl) *adj.* —**his·tol′o·gist** *n.*

his·tol·y·sis (his·tol′ə·sis) *n.* 1 *Biol.* The degeneration and dissolution of the organic tissue. 2 *Entomol.* The process by which the larval organs of many insects dissolve into a creamy consistency during the pupa stage, save for certain cell groups which develop into the organs of the future imago. [< HISTO- + -LYSIS]

his·tone (his′tōn) *n. Biochem.* One of a group of simple proteins which yield amino acids on hydrolysis: occurs frequently with nucleic acid and hematin. Also **his′ton** (-ton). [< HIST(O)- + -ONE]

his·to·plas·mo·sis (his′tə·plaz·mō′sis) *n. Pathol.* A serious fungous disease that may infect the lymph nodes and the lungs.

his·to·ri·an (his·tôr′ē·ən, -tō′rē-) *n.* 1 One who writes a history; a chronicler. 2 One versed in history.

his·to·ri·at·ed (his·tôr′ē·ā′tid, -tō′rē-) *adj.* Adorned with figures or designs, especially human or animal figures, as the illuminated manuscripts and capitals of columns of the Middle Ages. [< LL *historiatus,* pp. of *historiare* relate a history < *historia* a history]

his·tor·ic (his·tôr′ik, -tor′-) *adj.* 1 Mentioned or celebrated in history; notable. 2 Historical.

his·tor·i·cal (his·tôr′i·kəl, -tor′-) *adj.* 1 Belonging or relating to history or historians; containing the record or representation of facts. 2 Relating to the past. 3 Pertaining to things as known by testimony, or purely as matters of fact: Memory is the *historical* faculty. 4 Phylogenetic. 5 Historic. —**his·tor′i·cal·ly** *adv.* —**his·tor′i·cal·ness** *n.*

historical geology That branch of geology which treats of the chronological succession of earth events, including past forms of plant and animal life as revealed in fossils, etc.

historical linguistics See under LINGUISTICS.

historical method The method which would found conclusions on a detailed and critical study of the history of the development of the object under consideration.

historical present *Gram.* The present tense used to narrate a past event as if it were happening contemporaneously with the narrative.

historical school Followers of and believers in the historical method.

his·tor·i·cism (his·tôr′ə·siz′əm, -tor′ə-) *n.* The conception that the history of anything sufficiently accounts for its nature or values. —**his·tor′i·cist** *n.*

his·to·ric·i·ty (his′tə·ris′ə·tē) *n.* Historical authenticity.

his·to·ried (his′tə·rēd) *adj. Rare* Rich in historic deeds or events; storied.

his·tor·i·fy (his·tôr′ə·fī, -tor′-) **·fied, ·fy·ing** To write the history of; chronicle.

his·tor·i·gram (his·tôr′ə·gram, -tor′-) *n. Stat.* A graph illustrating the changes of a given variable as a function of the time: distinguished from *histogram.* [< HISTORY + -GRAM]

his·to·ri·og·ra·pher (his·tôr′ē·og′rə·fər, -tō′rē-) *n.* One who writes history, especially in an official capacity.

his·to·ri·og·ra·phy (his·tôr′ē·og′rə·fē, -tō′rē-) *n.* 1 The writing of history. 2 History that is written. —**his·to·ri·o·graph·ic** (his·tôr′ē·ə·graf′ik, -tō′rē-) or **·i·cal** *adj.* —**his·to′ri·o·graph′i·cal·ly** *adv.*

his·to·ry (his′tə·rē, his′trē) *n. pl.* **·ries** 1 A recorded narrative of past events, especially those concerning a particular period, nation, individual, etc. 2 The branch of knowledge dealing with the records of the past, especially those involving human affairs. 3 The aggregate of events concerning a given subject, recorded or unrecorded. 4 Past events in general: in the course of *history.* 5 A past worthy of notice; an eventful career. 6 Something in the past: This is all *history* now. 7 *Med.* The facts received from a patient concerning his health, past and present, together with current symptoms: in full, **medical history.** 8 A historical drama. [< L *historia* < Gk., knowledge, narrative < *histōr* knowing. Doublet of STORY.]

Synonyms: account, annals, archives, autobiography, biography, chronicle, memoir, memorial, muniment, narration, narrative, recital, record, register, story. *History* is a systematic *record* of past events. *Annals* and *chronicles* relate events with little regard to their relative importance, and with complete subserviency to their succession in time. *Annals* (L *annus,* year) are yearly records; *chronicles* (Gk. *chronos,* time) follow the order of time. Both necessarily lack emphasis, selection, and perspective. *Archives* are public *records,* which may be *annals,* or *chronicles,* or deeds of property, etc. *Memoirs* generally record the lives of individuals or facts pertaining to individual lives. A *biography* is distinctively a written *account* of one person's life and actions; an *autobiography* is a *biography* written by the person whose life it records. *Annals, archives, chronicles, biographies,* and *memoirs* and other *records* furnish the materials of *history. History* recounts events with careful attention to their importance, their mutual relations, their causes and consequences, selecting and grouping events on the ground of interest or importance. *History* is usually applied to such an *account* of events affecting communities and nations, yet sometimes we speak of the *history* of a single eminent life. Compare RECORD. *Antonyms*: see synonyms for FICTION.

his·tri·on·ic (his′trē·on′ik) *adj.* 1 Pertaining to the stage; theatrical. 2 Having a theatrical manner; artificial; affected. Also **his′tri·on′i·cal.** [< L *histrionicus* < *histrio* actor] —**his′·tri·on′i·cal·ly** *adv.*

his·tri·on·ics (his′trē·on′iks) *n. pl.* 1 The art of dramatic representation. 2 Theatrical affectations.

his·tri·on·i·cism (his′trē·on′ə·siz′əm) *n.* A use of histrionic art; stage effect.

hit (hit) *v.* **hit, hit·ting** *v.t.* 1 To come against or in contact with, usually with impact or force. 2 To inflict (a blow, etc.). 3 To strike with a blow: She *hit* him too hard. 4 To strike with or as with a missile: He *hit* the robber in the leg. 5 To move or propel by striking: He *hit* the ball over the fence. 6 To arrive at or achieve, as after effort or search: often with *upon*: to *hit* upon the right answer. 7 To suit; be in accordance with: The idea *hit* her fancy. 8 To affect the emotion, well-being, etc., of: His father's death *hit* him hard. 9 *Colloq.* To go at vigorously or to excess: to *hit* the bottle. 10 In baseball, to make a (specified base) hit: to *hit* a triple. —*v.i.* 11 To deliver a blow or blows: often with *out.* 12 To strike with force; bump: often with *against.* 13 To fire the cylinder charges of an internal-combustion engine: The car was *hitting* on all eight cylinders. See synonyms under REACH. —**to hit it off** *Colloq.* To take pleasure in one another's company; be congenial. —**to hit off** 1 To imitate. 2 To express or describe exactly. —*n.* 1 A striking against something; a stroke; blow. 2 A stroke of wit or sarcasm; repartee. 3 A stroke of luck; success. 4 Anything enjoying quick public acclaim: The play was a *hit.* 5 In baseball, a base hit. 6 In backgammon, a move that throws one of the opponent's men back to the entering point, or a game won after one or more men are thrown off by the opponent. See synonyms under BLOW. —**clean hit** In baseball, a hit which drives the ball so that it cannot be fielded in time to prevent the earning of a base. [OE *hittan* < ON *hitta* come upon]

hit-and-run (hit′ən·run′) *adj.* 1 Designating an automobile operator who hits a pedestrian and drives away without stopping. 2 Describing the tactics of a military force which makes small harassing attacks on a larger force without venturing a major engagement. 3 In baseball, describing a maneuver in which the batter and the base runners work together by a prearranged plan.

hitch (hich) *n.* 1 A stop or sudden halt; obstruction; hence, an obstacle to an enterprise. 2 The act of catching or fastening, as by a rope, hook, etc.; also a connection so made. 3 *Naut.* Any of various knots made with

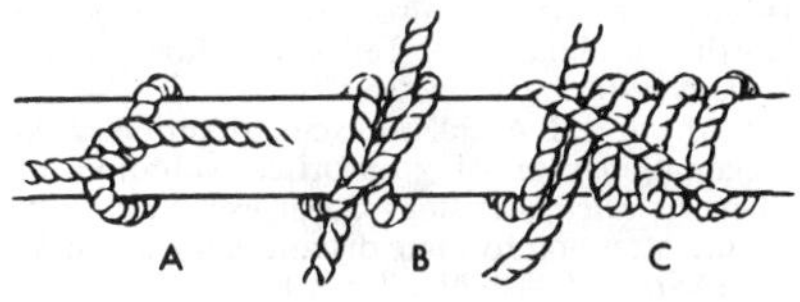

HITCHES
A. Half hitch. *B.* Clove hitch. *C.* Rolling hitch.

rope, rigging, etc. 4 A quick or sudden push or pull; a jerk. 5 A limp; halt; hobble. 6 *U.S. Colloq.* A period of enlistment in military service, especially in the U.S. Navy. —*v.t.* 1 To fasten or tie, especially temporarily, with a knot, rope, strap, etc. 2 To harness to a vehicle: often with *up*: to *hitch* a horse to a buggy. 3 To move or shift with a jerk or jerks: He *hitched* himself around in his chair. 4 To marry: often with *up.* 5 *U.S. Slang* To obtain (a ride) by hitchhiking. —*v.i.* 6 To move with jerks: to *hitch* forward. 7 To become caught or entangled. 8 To strike the feet together, as in trotting: said of horses. 9 *U.S. Colloq.* To get on together; agree: He and I don't *hitch.* 10 *U.S. Slang* To travel by hitchhiking. [ME *hicchen;* origin uncertain]

Hitch·cock (hich′kok), **Alfred,** 1900-1980, English motion-picture director active in the United States. —**Edward,** 1793–1864, U.S. geologist.

hitch·hike (hich′hīk′) *v.i. U.S. Colloq.* To travel on foot and by asking rides from passing vehicles. —**hitch′hik′er** *n.*

hitching post A post having iron loops or rings to which a horse, team, etc., may be hitched.

hith·er (hith′ər) *adj.* Near to or toward the person speaking: opposed to *farther.* —*adv.* In this direction; toward this place. [OE *hider*]

hith·er·most (hith′ər·mōst′) *adj.* Nearest.

hith·er·to (hith′ər·tōō′, hith′ər·tōō′) *adv.* 1 Till now. 2 *Archaic* Thus far. See synonyms under YET.

hith·er·ward (hith′ər·wərd) *adv.* Hither. Also **hith′er·wards.**

Hit·ler (hit′lər), **Adolf,** 1889–1945, head of the Nazi party and dictator, officially chancellor, of Germany 1933–45; born in Austria: called "der Führer." —**Hit'ler·ism** (hit·lir'ē·ən) *adj.* —**Hit'ler·ism** *n.*

hit-or-miss (hit'ər·mis') *adj.* **1** Heedless; haphazard: to live a *hit-or-miss* life. **2** Varicolored. —*adv.* Haphazardly.

hit·ter (hit'ər) *n.* One who strikes or hits.

Hit·tite (hit'īt) *n.* **1** One of an ancient people who established a powerful empire in Asia Minor and Northern Syria about 2000–1200 B.C. **2** The language of the Hittites, known from cuneiform inscriptions discovered in Asia Minor which date from about 1400 B.C. **(Cuneiform Hittite).** Hieroglyphic inscriptions from about 1000 B.C., found in Asia Minor and Northern Syria, have also been attributed to the Hittites **(Hieroglyphic Hittite).** Although Hittite has been established as having a definite connection with Indo-European, it exhibits characteristics which distinguish it so markedly from the rest of the Indo-European family that the exact nature of the relationship remains uncertain. See INDO-HITTITE. —*adj.* Of or relating to the Hittites or their language. [< Hebrew *hittīm*]

Hit·torf (hit'ôrf), **Johann Wilhelm,** 1824–1914, German physicist.

Hittorf tube Physics **1** A glass tube having metallic electrodes almost touching, so as to show the insulating effects of a vacuum. **2** A Crookes tube. [after J. W. *Hittorf*]

Hi·va O·a (hē'və ō'ə) The second largest of the Marquesas Islands; capital, Atuona.

hive (hīv) *n.* **1** A structure in which bees may dwell. **2** A colony of bees. **3** A place full of activity. —*v.* **hived, hiv·ing** *v.t.* **1** To cause (bees) to enter a hive; gather into a hive. **2** To store (honey) in a hive. **3** To store (anything) for future use. —*v.i.* **4** To enter or dwell in or as in a hive. [OE *hȳf*]

hives (hīvz) *n.* Any of various skin diseases, especially urticaria. [Origin unknown]

Hi·was·see River (hī·wos'ē) A river in Georgia, North Carolina, and Tennessee, flowing 132 miles NW to the Tennessee River.

ho (hō) *interj.* **1** A call to excite attention. **2** An exclamation expressing surprise, exultation, or, when repeated, derision. **3** An exclamation directing attention to some distant point: Land *ho!* Westward *ho!* Also **hoa.** [Imit.]

Ho *Chem.* Holmium (symbol Ho).

ho·ac·tzin (hō·ak'tsin) See HOATZIN.

Hoang Ho (hwäng' hō') See HWANG HO.

hoar (hôr, hōr) *adj.* **1** White or gray with age; hoary. **2** White or grayish-white in color. **3** Ancient. **4** *Obs.* Musty; moldy. —*n.* **1** Hoarfrost. **2** The condition of being white with age or frost; hoariness. ◆ Homophone: *whore.* [OE *hār* gray-haired]

hoard (hôrd, hōrd) *n.* An accumulation stored away for safeguarding or for future use. See synonyms under HEAP, STOCK. —*v.t.* To gather and store away or hide for future use. —*v.i.* To gather and store away food, jewels, etc. ◆ Homophone: *horde.* [OE *hord* treasure] —**hoard'er** *n.*

hoard·ing[1] (hôr'ding, hōr'-) *n.* **1** The act of accumulating a hoard. **2** *pl.* Treasure laid by; savings.

hoard·ing[2] (hôr'ding, hōr'-) *n. Brit.* **1** A fence, as about a place where building is in progress. **2** A billboard. [< OF *hourd* palisade < Gmc.]

hoar·frost (hôr'frôst', -frost', hōr'-) *n.* Frost having the form of silvery ice needles. [ME *horfrost*]

hoar·hound (hôr'hound', hōr'-) *n.* Horehound.

hoarse (hôrs, hōrs) *adj.* **1** Harsh and rough in sound. **2** Having the voice harsh and rough. [OE *hā(r)s*] —**hoarse'ly** *adv.* —**hoarse'ness** *n.*

hoars·en (hôr'sən, hōr'-) *v.t.* & *v.i.* To make or become hoarse or harsh.

hoar·y (hôr'ē, hō'rē) *adj.* **hoar·i·er, hoar·i·est 1** White, as from age. **2** Ancient. **3** Covered with short and dense grayish-white hairs, as certain animals. See synonyms under ANCIENT. —**hoar'i·ness** *n.*

hoast (hōst) *Scot.* & *Brit. Dial.* *v.i.* To cough. —*n.* A cough; hoarseness.

ho·at·zin (hō·at'sin) *n.* A South American bird (genus *Opisthocomus*) resembling the curassow in appearance, prevailingly olive, with a yellowish crest and a pair of hooked claws on each wing: also called *hoactzin.* Also **ho·az'in.** [< Sp. Am. < Nahuatl *uatzin*]

hoax (hōks) *v.t.* To deceive by a trick. —*n.* **1** A deception practiced for sport. **2** A practical joke or fraud. [< HOCUS(-POCUS)] —**hoax'er** *n.*

hob[1] (hob) *n.* **1** A projection on the side of a fireplace; also, its top, serving as a shelf. **2** The nave of a wheel. **3** A hardened fluted steel mandrel for cutting screw threads. **4** A steel punch with a design in relief. **5** A game in which quoits or other objects are tossed at a stake; also, the stake. [? Var. of HUB]

hob[2] (hob) *n.* A fairy; hobgoblin; elf. —**to play hob with** To throw into confusion; upset; ruin. [Orig., a nickname for ROBERT, ROBIN]

Ho·bart (hō'bərt, -bärt) The capital of Tasmania, on the Derwent river.

Hob·be·ma (hob'ə·mä), **Meindert,** 1638–1709, Dutch painter.

Hobbes (hobz), **Thomas,** 1588–1679, English philosopher.

Hobb·ism (hob'iz·əm) *n.* The philosophy of Thomas Hobbes; especially his theory that an absolute monarch is necessary to control the antagonisms of individual interests. Also **Hob·bi·an·ism** (hob'ē·ən·iz'əm). —**Hobbes·i·an** (hobz'ē·ən), **Hob·bi·an** (hob'ē·ən) *adj.* —**Hob·bist** (hob'ist) *n.*

hob·bit (hob'it) *n.* One of a fictitious race of amiable, elflike creatures with furry feet, created by the British author John Ronald Reuel Tolkien (1882–1973).

hob·ble (hob'əl) *v.* **hob·bled, hob·bling** *v.i.* **1** walk with or as with a limp; go lamely or on crutches. **2** To move or proceed in an irregular or clumsy manner. —*v.t.* **3** To hamper the free movement of (a horse, etc.), as by tying the legs together. **4** To cause to move lamely or awkwardly. —*n.* **1** A limping gait. **2** A fetter for the legs; specifically, a rope, strap, or pair of linked rings used to fetter the forelegs of an animal. **3** An embarrassment; difficulty. [? Freq. of HOP. Cf. G *hoppeln* hobble.] —**hob'bler** *n.*

hob·ble-bush (hob'əl·bŏŏsh') *n.* A straggling shrub *(Viburnum alnifolium)* of the honeysuckle family, having flowers resembling those of hydrangea, and the fruit coral-red drupes.

hob·ble·de·hoy (hob'əl·dē·hoi') *n.* **1** An awkward youth. **2** An adolescent boy. Also **hob'be·de·hoy'** (hob'ə·dē-). [Origin uncertain]

hob·ble·show (hob'əl·shō) See HUBBLESHOW.

hobble skirt A narrow skirt, formerly worn by women, so made below the knee as to permit the wearer to take only short steps.

hob·by (hob'ē) *n. pl.* **·bies 1** A subject or pursuit in which one takes absorbing interest. **2** A hobbyhorse. **3** An ambling nag. **4** A small falcon *(Falco subbuteo)* with long wings. [from *Robin,* a personal name]

hob·by·horse (hob'ē·hôrs') *n.* **1** A rocking-horse; also, a toy consisting of a stick with a wooden horse's head attached. **2** The figure of a horse attached to a person's waist so that he appears to be riding it: used in morris dances, pantomimes, etc.

hob·gob·lin (hob'gob'lin) *n.* **1** A mischievous imp. **2** Anything that causes superstitious terror, particularly anything imagined. See synonyms under SCARECROW. [< HOB[2] + GOBLIN]

hob·nail (hob'nāl') *n.* A nail for studding the soles of heavy shoes.

hob·nailed (hob'nāld') *adj.* **1** Provided or armed with hobnails. **2** Wearing hobnailed boots or shoes; clownish. **3** Ornamented with knobs, as glassware.

hobnail liver The liver in an advanced stage of cirrhosis, characterized by warty surface projections resembling hobnails.

hob·nob (hob'nob) *v.i.* **·nobbed, ·nob·bing 1** To drink together familiarly and convivially. **2** To be on familiar terms; chat socially. —*n.* A friendly talk. Also **hob-or-nob** (hob'ər·nob'). [OE *habban* have + *nabban* have not]

ho·bo (hō'bō) *n. pl.* **·boes** or **·bos** *U.S.* **1** A migratory, unskilled workman. **2** A professional idler; a tramp. —*v.i.* To live or wander as a hobo. [< *Hey, Bo,* a vagrant's greeting] —**ho'bo·ism** *n.*

Ho·bo·ken (hō'bō·kən) A port of entry in NE New Jersey on the Hudson River.

Hob·son-Job·son (hob'sən·job'sən) *n.* Anglo-Indian (*n.* def. 3).

Hob·son's choice (hob'sənz) This or nothing; a choice with no alternative: in allusion to the practice of Thomas Hobson, 1544–1631, English liveryman, who required each customer to take the horse nearest the door.

Hoc·cleve (hok'lēv), **Thomas,** 1370–1450, English poet.

Ho Chi Minh (hō' chē' min'), 1890?–1969, leader of the Viet Minh; president of North Vietnam 1945–1969.

Ho Chi Minh City A city in S Vietnam; formerly called *Saigon* and formerly capital of South Vietnam.

hock[1] (hok) *n.* **1** The joint of the hind leg in digitigrade mammals, as the horse and ox, corresponding to the ankle in man. **2** The knee joint of a fowl. **3** In man, the back part of the knee joint. —*v.t.* To disable by cutting the tendons of the hock; hamstring. [OE *hōh* heel]

hock[2] (hok) *n.* Any white Rhine wine; originally, that known as *Hochheimer.* [Contraction of *hockamore* < G *Hochheimer* < *Hochheim,* a German town where it was first produced]

hock[3] (hok) *v.t.* & *n.* *U.S. Slang* Pawn. —**in hock** *Slang* **1** In pawn. **2** In prison. [Du. *hok* prison, debt]

hock·ey (hok'ē) *n.* **1** A game played either on a field or on ice, in which opposing players, equipped with curved or hooked sticks, try to drive a small block (puck) or ball into or past the opposite goals. **2** A hockey stick. [< *hock* bent stick, var. of HOOK]

hockey stick The curved stick used to hit the ball or puck in hockey.

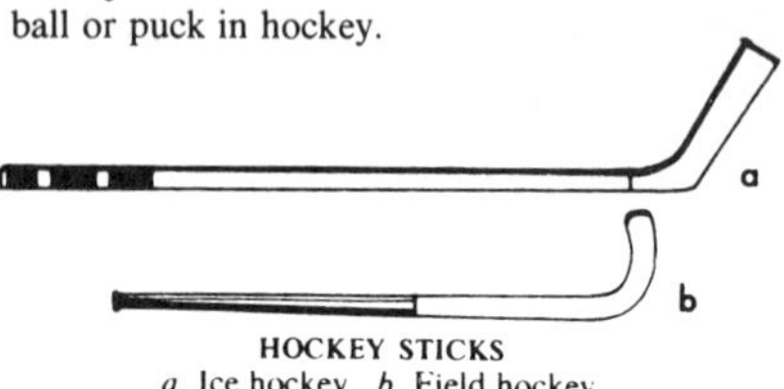

HOCKEY STICKS
a. Ice hockey. *b.* Field hockey.

hock·shop (hok'shop') *n.* *U.S. Slang* A pawnshop.

ho·cus (hō'kəs) *v.t.* **·cused** or **·cussed, ·cus·ing** or **·cus·sing 1** To deceive by a trick; impose upon. **2** To drug. **3** To add drugs to, as a drink. [Abbreviation of HOCUS-POCUS]

ho·cus-po·cus (hō'kəs·pō'kəs) *n.* **1** A verbal formula used in conjuring or juggling. **2** A conjurer's trick, or deception wrought as if by the conjurer's art. —*v.t.* & *v.i.* To cheat; trick. [A sham Latin phrase, ? alter. of *hoc est corpus* this is my body, a eucharistic formula]

hod (hod) *n.* **1** A long-handled receptacle for holding bricks and mortar, carried on the shoulder. **2** A coal scuttle or a box for coals. [< obs. *hot* < OF *hotte* pannier < Gmc. Cf. MDu. *hodde.*]

hod-car·ri·er (hod'kar'ē·ər) *n.* A man who carries a hod. Also **hod'man** (-mən).

hod·den gray (hod'n) A coarse cloth having the natural color of the wool: formerly worn in northern England and Scotland.

Ho·dei·da (hō·dā'də, -dī'-) A port on the Red Sea in western Yemen. Also *Hudaida.*

Hö·der (hœ'thər) In Norse mythology, a blind son of Odin, slayer of Balder: also spelled *Hoth, Höthr.* Also **Ho'dur.**

Hodge (hoj) *Brit.* A nickname for an agricultural laborer. [from ROGER, a personal name]

Hodg·en·ville (hoj'ən·vil) A town in central Kentucky. See ABRAHAM LINCOLN NATIONAL PARK.

hodge-podge (hoj'poj') *n.* **1** A stew of mixed meats and vegetables. **2** A jumbled mixture; conglomeration. Also *hotch-potch.* [Var. of HOTCH-POTCH]

Hodg·kin's disease (hoj'kinz) *Pathol.* A progressive and fatal enlargement of the lymph nodes, lymphoid tissue, and spleen; a form of granuloma. [after Dr. Thomas *Hodgkin,* 1798–1866, English physician, who first described it]

ho·di·er·nal (hō'di·ûr'nəl) *adj.* Of or pertaining to the present day. [< L *hodiernus* < *hoc die* (on) this day]

Hód·me·zö·vá·sár·hely (hōd'me·zœ·vä'shär·hey') A city in southern Hungary.

ho·do·graph (hō'də·graf, -gräf) *n. Math.* The curve traced by the terminal point of a vector drawn from a fixed origin and representing the acceleration of a particle moving at a known velocity along any given path. [<Gk. *hodos* way + GRAPH]

ho·dom·e·ter (hō·dom′ə·tər) *n.* An odometer.

ho·do·scope (hō′də·skōp) *n. Physics* A device for indicating the path of cosmic rays, consisting of a series of Geiger counters connected with a neon lamp to record the passage of the separate particles. [<Gk. *hodos* way + -SCOPE]

hoe (hō) *n.* A flat-bladed implement for digging, scraping, and tilling, having in the simplest form a flat and thin blade set nearly at

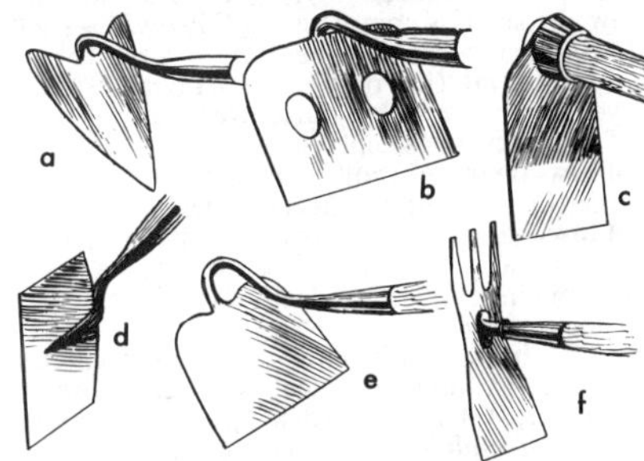

TYPES OF HOES
a. Warren hoe. *c.* Grub hoe. *e.* Garden hoe.
b. Mortar hoe. *d.* Scuffle hoe. *f.* Weeding hoe.

a right angle to a long handle. —*v.t.* & *v.i.* **hoed, hoe·ing** To dig, scrape, or till with a hoe. [<OF *houe* <OHG *houwa* < *houwan* cut] —**ho′er** *n.*

Hoe (hō) Name of a family identified with the manufacture and improvement of the printing press in America: especially, **Robert,** 1784–1833; his son, **Richard March,** 1812–86, and grandson, **Robert,** 1839–1909.

hoe·cake (hō′kāk′) *n. U.S.* A thin cake of Indian meal: originally baked on a hoe.

hoe-down (hō′doun′) *n. U.S.* **1** A lively, shuffling dance: originally Southern. **2** The music for such a dance. [Origin uncertain]

Hoek van Hol·land (hœk van hôl′änt) The Dutch name for HOOK OF HOLLAND.

Hœ·nir (hœ′nir) In Norse mythology, one of the creators of Ask, the first man, and Embla, the first woman.

Hof (hōf) A city in Franconia, West Germany.

Ho·fer (hō′fər), **Andreas,** 1767–1810, Tirolese patriot.

Hoff·man (hof′mən), **Malvina,** 1887–1966, U. S. sculptor.

Hoff·mann (hôf′män), **Ernst Theodor Amadeus,** 1776–1822, German writer and composer.

Hof·mann (hôf′män), **August Wilhelm von,** 1818–92, German chemist. —**Josef,** 1876–1957, Polish pianist and composer.

Hof·mans·thal (hôf′mäns·täl), **Hugo von,** 1874–1929, Austrian poet and dramatist.

Ho·fuf (hŏŏ·fōōf′) The capital of El Hasa, Saudi Arabia. Also *Hufuf.*

hog (hôg, hog) *n.* **1** An omnivorous ungulate having a long mobile snout with flat, expanded end containing the nostrils; especially, any domestic variety of the wild boar (family *Suidae*) bred and raised for its meat, called *pork.* **2** Some animal like the foregoing, as the peccary, warthog, etc. **3** *Colloq.* A filthy, gluttonous person. **4** A stirrer in a paper-pulp vat. —*v.* **hogged, hog·ging** *v.t.* **1** *U.S. Slang* To take more than one's share of; grab selfishly. **2** To arch (the back) upward like a hog's. **3** To cut short, as a horse's mane. —*v.i.* **4** To sag at both ends: said of ships. [OE *hogg*]

ho·gan (hō′gən) *n.* The rude hut of the Navaho and other roving tribes of the SW United States. [<Navaho *qoghan* house]

Ho·garth (hō′gärth), **William,** 1697–1764, English painter and engraver.

Hogarth line A serpentine curve drawn by William Hogarth and later explained, in his *Analysis of Beauty* (1753), as the most perfect figure that man can devise.

hog·back (hôg′bak′, hog′-) *n.* **1** A back humped like that of certain hogs. **2** A sandy or rocky ridge caused by unequal erosion or the outcropping edge of tilted strata. Also called *hog's-back.*

hog-backed (hôg′bakt′, hog′-) *adj.* Elevated toward the middle, like the back of a hog.

Hog·ben (hog′bən), **Lancelot,** born 1895, English biologist and writer.

hog·chain (hôg′chān′, hog′-) *n. Naut.* A tension chain passing from bow to stern of a vessel and fastened to posts amidships: used to prevent the ends from sagging.

hog cholera A highly infectious and contagious disease of swine caused by a filtrable virus, characterized by loss of appetite, fever, exhaustion, and high mortality.

hog·fish (hôg′fish′, hog′-) *n. pl.* **·fish** or **·fish·es** **1** A labroid fish (*Lachnolaemus maximus*) of Florida and the West Indies, with the first three dorsal spines filamentous. **2** A grunt or pigfish; especially, the sailor's-choice.

HOGFISH
(About 14 inches long)

Hogg (hog), **James,** 1770–1835, Scottish poet: called "the Ettrick Shepherd."

hog·gish (hôg′ish, hog′-) *adj.* Like a hog. —**hog′gish·ly** *adv.* —**hog′gish·ness** *n.*

hog·ma·nay (hog′mə·nā′) *n. Scot.* & *Brit. Dial.* The day before New Year's, when gifts or refreshments are sought and bestowed. Also **hog′me·nay′.**

hog·nose (hôg′nōz′, hog′-) *n.* Any North American non-venomous colubrine snake (genus *Heterodon*) with a flattened head and prominent snout, known for its formidable appearance and contorted movements when disturbed. Also **hog′-nosed′ snake.**

hog-nosed skunk (hôg′nōzd′, hog′-) See under CONEPATE.

hog·nut (hôg′nut′, hog′-) *n.* **1** The nut of the pignut hickory. **2** *Brit.* The earth chestnut.

hog peanut A slender vine (*Amphicarpa bracteata*) of the bean family bearing usually a one-seeded pod: also called *earth pea.*

hog pen A pigsty.

hog's-back (hôgz′bak′, hogz′-) *n.* A hogback.

hog·score (hôg′skôr′, -skōr′, hog′-) *n.* A line drawn across the rink in curling, one sixth of the way from each tee to the other.

hogs·head (hôgz′hed′, hogz′-) *n.* **1** A large cask. **2** A liquid measure of varying capacity: in the United States and Great Britain ordinarily 63 gallons, or 0.238 cubic meter, or 52 1/2 imperial gallons.

hog-shou·ther (hôg′shōōth′ər, hog′-) *v.i. Scot.* To jostle with the shoulder.

hog's-pud·ding (hôgz′pŏŏd′ing, hogz′-) *n. Brit. Dial.* A pudding of flour, with currants, etc., stuffed into a hog's entrail like a sausage.

hog·suck·er (hôg′suk′ər, hog′-) *n.* A fresh-water fish (*Catostomus nigricans*) of central United States.

hog-tie (hôg′tī′, hog′-) *v.t.* **·tied, ·ty·ing** or **·tie·ing** **1** To tie all four feet or the hands and feet of. **2** *Colloq.* To bind fast; keep from taking action.

hog·tight (hôg′tīt′, hog′-) *adj.* Strong enough to keep swine in or out: said of a fence.

Hog·town (hôg′toun′, hog′-) *Canadian Slang* Toronto. —**Hog′town′er**

Hogue (ôg), **La** A roadstead off the coast of NW France; scene of French naval defeat, 1692.

hog·wal·low (hôg′wol′ō, hog′-) *n.* **1** A damp, muddy place in which hogs wallow. **2** A depression in a prairie that remains damp and grassy.

hog·wash (hôg′wosh′, -wôsh′, hog′-) *n.* **1** Kitchen refuse, swill, etc., fed to hogs. **2** Any worthless rubbish; nonsense; foolishness.

hog·weed (hôg′wēd′, hog′-) *n.* Any of numerous coarse weeds of persistent growth, including the ragweeds, knotweed, dogfennel, etc.

hog wild *U. S. Slang* Wildly excited.

Ho·hen·lin·den (hō′ən·lin′dən) A village east of Munich; scene of French victory over the Austrians, 1800.

Ho·hen·lo·he (hō′ən·lō′ə) A family of German princes.

Ho·hen·stau·fen (hō′ən·shtou′fən) A German princely family, prominent especially in the 12th and 13th centuries.

Ho·hen·zol·lern (hō′ən·tsôl′ərn) A family of Prussian kings of the 18th and 19th centuries and German emperors, 1871–1918.

Ho·hen·zol·lern (hō′ən·tsôl′ərn) A former Prussian province in southern Germany.

hoick (hoik) *Aeron. v.t.* To throw (an aircraft) into sharp, sudden changes of direction, as in making a steep climb. —*v.i.* To engage in this kind of maneuver or operation: usually with *about* or *around.* [Origin unknown]

hoicks (hoiks) *interj.* A cry used to stir up the hounds in hunting. Also *yoicks.*

hoi·den (hoid′n) *n.* See HOYDEN.

hoigh (hoi) See HOY[2].

hoi pol·loi (hoi′ pə·loi′) The common people; the masses; the herd: usually used contemptuously, and preceded by a redundant *the.* [<Gk., the many]

hoist (hoist) *v.t.* To raise to a higher position; lift or heave up, especially by some mechanical means. —*n.* **1** A hoisting machine; lift. **2** The act of hoisting; a boost. **3** The vertical dimension of a flag or the like, measured along the pole or halyard: distinguished from the *fly.* **4** *Naut.* **a** The length of a sail between the boom and the peak or the jaws of the gaff. **b** The midship depth of a square sail set by hoisting the yard. [? <Du. *hijschen*] —**hoist′er** *n.*

hoi·ty-toi·ty (hoi′tē·toi′tē) *interj.* Think of that! what now! —*adj.* **1** Self-important; putting on airs. **2** Flighty; giddy. **3** Petulant; huffy. Also spelled *highty-tighty.* [Reduplication of obs. *hoit* romp; infl. in meaning by HIGH]

ho·key-po·key (hō′kē·pō′kē) *n.* **1** Ice-cream sold by street peddlers in small quantities: also **ho′ky-po′ky.** **2** Hocus-pocus.

Hok·kai·do (hôk·kī·dō) A northern island of Japan; 29,600 square miles: formerly *Yezo.* Also **Ho·ku·shu** (hō·kōō·shōō).

hok·ku (hôk·kōō) See HAIKU.

ho·kum (hō′kəm) *n. Slang* **1** A phrase or device deliberately used by an actor, writer, or speaker to win a laugh or catch attention. **2** Contrived sentimental or pathetic effects in a play or story. **3** Nonsense; bunk. [Alter. of HOCUS]

Ho·ku·sai (hō·kōō·sī), **Katsuhika,** 1760–1849, Japanese painter and engraver.

hol- Var. of HOLO-.

Hol·arc·tic (hol·ärk′tik, -är′tik, hōl-) *adj.* Pertaining to or designating a zoogeographical region of the world, including the Nearctic and Palearctic realms. See ZOOGEOGRAPHIC REALM.

ho·lard (hō′lərd) *n.* The total quantity of water found in the soil. See CHRESARD, ECHARD. [<HOL- + Gk. *ardeia* irrigation]

Hol·bein (hōl′bīn, *Ger.* hôl′bīn), **Hans,** 1465?–1524, German painter: called "the Elder." —**Hans,** 1497?–1543, German painter, son of the preceding: called "the Younger."

hol·co·dont (hol′kə·dont) *adj. Zool.* Having teeth set in a continuous groove. [<Gk. *holkos* furrow + *odous, odontos* tooth]

hold[1] (hōld) *v.* **held, held** or *in legal use* **hold·en, hold·ing** *v.t.* **1** To take and keep in the hand; retain. **2** To prevent the movement or escape of: He *held* her so that she could not move. **3** To restrain from acting or speaking: *Hold* your tongue! **4** To keep in a specified state: to *hold* one a prisoner. **5** To regard in a specified manner; consider: to *hold* someone dear. **6** To require to fulfil, as the conditions of a contract; obligate. **7** To support or keep in position: Ropes *held* the tower in position. **8** To be capable of enclosing or containing: The barrel *holds* ten gallons. **9** To maintain in the mind; believe: to *hold* an opinion or a grudge. **10** To conduct or engage in; carry on: to *hold* court or services. **11** To have and retain ownership or control of; keep as one's own; occupy: to *hold* the chair. **12** To retain possession or control of, as against an enemy: They *held* the town against the enemy. —*v.i.* **13** To maintain a grip or grasp. **14** To remain firm or unbroken: if the rope *holds*; He *held* to his purpose. **15** To remain or continue unchanged: The breeze *held* all day. **16** To be relevant; remain true, correct, etc.: This decision *holds* for all such cases. **17** To check or restrain oneself; forbear: usually used in the imperative. See synonyms under AR-

REST, EMBRAGE, ESTEEM, GRASP, HAVE, INTEREST, KEEP, OCCUPY, RESTRAIN, RETAIN. **— to hold back** 1 To prevent from acting or doing. 2 To refrain. 3 To keep apart or aside; retain, as for an undisclosed purpose. **— to hold down** 1 To suppress; keep under control. 2 *Colloq.* To occupy (a job, etc.) successfully. **— to hold forth** To harangue; preach or speak at length. **— to hold in** To keep in check; restrain. **— to hold off** 1 To keep at a distance. 2 To refrain. **— to hold on** 1 To maintain a grip or hold. 2 To persist; continue. 3 *Colloq.* To stop or wait: used in the imperative. **— to hold one's own** To maintain one's position, as in a contest; lose no ground. **— to hold out** 1 To stretch forth; offer. 2 To last to the end: Our supplies *held out.* 3 To continue resistance; endure; persist. 4 *U.S. Slang* To keep back part or all of (something). **— to hold out for** *Colloq.* To insist upon as a condition of an agreement: He *held out for* a higher salary. **— to hold over** 1 To put off to a later date; delay. 2 To remain beyond the expected time or limit; extend. **— to hold up** 1 To support; prop. 2 To exhibit to view. 3 *Colloq.* To last; endure. 4 To delay; stop. 5 *Colloq.* To stop and rob; also, to rob. **—** *n.* 1 The act of holding, as with the hands; a seizure; figuratively, a controlling force or influence; restraint. 2 A place to grasp. 3 A place of security; a fortified place; stronghold; refuge. 4 The state of being held; possession. 5 *Law* A holding or tenure: in composition: *copyhold, freehold.* 6 *Music* A character (𝄐) indicating the sustention of a tone. 7 A cell in jail. 8 Something to hold articles; a receptacle. 9 A lock or latch. [OE *haldan*]

hold[2] (hōld) *n. Naut.* The space below the decks of a vessel where cargo is stowed. [<HOLE or <MDu. *hol*]

Hol·da (hôl′dä) In German folklore, the feminine spirit who leads the souls of the dead in their aerial flight. She was associated as well with fruitfulness and the hearth, and was also called "Frau Holle."

hold–all (hōld′ôl′) *n.* A general receptacle; especially, a sort of bag used by travelers.

hold·back (hōld′bak′) *n.* 1 That which keeps back; a check. 2 A strap passing from the shafts of a horse–drawn vehicle and through the breeching harness, permitting the horse to hold back the vehicle or to push it back.

hold·en (hōld′n) Alternative past participle of HOLD, obsolete except in legal use.

hold·er (hōl′dər) *n.* 1 One who or that which holds. 2 An owner; possessor: chiefly in compounds: *householder.* 3 *Law* One who has legal possession of a bill of exchange, check, or promissory note for which he is entitled to receive payment.

hold·fast (hōld′fast′, -fäst′) *n.* 1 That by which something is held securely in place. 2 Something to cling to; a support. 3 A firm grasp. 4 *Bot.* A specialized organ of attachment at the base of certain algae: also **holdfast cell.**

hold·ing (hōl′ding) *n.* 1 The action of someone or something that holds. 2 A tenure or right of possession. 3 *Often pl.* Property held by legal right, especially stocks or bonds. 4 In football, basketball, etc., the act of obstructing an opponent, as with the arms or hands, contrary to the rules of the game.

holding company A company that holds stock in one or more companies for investment or operating purposes, or both.

hold·o·ver (hōld′ō′vər) *n.* 1 Something remaining from a previous time or situation. 2 A place of detention for prisoners awaiting trial. 3 One who continues in office after his term has expired, or after a change of administration. 4 One who is kept on from one engagement to another.

hold–up (hōld′up′) *n.* 1 Stoppage, delay, or obstruction of some activity. 2 A forcible stoppage to commit robbery, especially of a traveler, a train, etc. 3 An overcharge, extortion.

hole (hōl) *n.* 1 A cavity extending into any solid body; a pit; hollow; cave. 2 An opening running or made through a body; aperture or orifice; perforation. 3 An animal's burrow or den. 4 Hence, a vile place; also, a place of hiding. 5 In golf, a cavity in a putting green into which the ball must be played; the distance within bounds between the teeing ground and the flag marking the hole toward which the play is moving; also, one of the points in the game of golf scored by the player who holes out, hole by hole, in the fewest strokes. 6 In various other games, a cavity into which a ball is played, or a point thus scored. 7 *Colloq.* A dilemma. 8 A fault; defect: to expose the *holes* in an argument. **— in the hole** *Colloq.* In debt. **—** *v.* **holed, hol·ing** *v.t.* 1 To make a hole or holes in; perforate. 2 To drive or put into a hole, as in billiards or golf. 3 To dig (a shaft, tunnel, etc.). **—** *v.i.* 4 To make a hole or holes. **— to hole out** In golf, to hit the ball into a hole. **— to hole up** 1 To hibernate. 2 To take refuge in hiding. ◆ Homophone: *whole.* [OE *hol.* Appar. related to HOLLOW.]

Synonyms (noun): aperture, bore, breach, cave, cavern, cavity, chasm, concavity, den, dent, dungeon, excavation, gap, hollow, indentation, kennel, lair, notch, opening, orifice, perforation, rent, A *hole* is an *opening* in a solid body; it may extend entirely through it, forming a passageway or vent, or only partly through it, forming a *cavity,* and may be of any shape, provided the axes are not greatly unequal. An *opening* very long in proportion to its width is more commonly called a crack, fissure, slit, etc., or on the surface of the earth such an opening is designated as a *chasm,* gorge, or ravine; a *rent* in a garment is made by tearing, a slit by cutting. An *orifice* is the mouth of a *hole* or tube. *Aperture* is a very general word; the crack of a partly opened door is an *aperture,* but not a *hole.* The noun *hollow* denotes a shallow *concavity* on the outer surface of a solid, usually round or oval. A *dent* is a depression on the surface of a solid, usually sharp or angular, as if beaten in. A *breach* is roughly broken, generally from the top or edge down through a wall or other object; a *gap* may be between portions that never were joined. See BREACH, BREAK.

hole in one In golf, the act of sinking the ball into a hole in one drive.

hole·y (hō′lē) *adj.* Having holes.

hol·i·but (hol′ə·bət) See HALIBUT.

hol·i·day (hol′ə·dā) *n.* 1 A day appointed by law or custom for the suspension of general business, usually in commemoration of some person or event. 2 Any day of rest or exemption from work. ◆ Collateral adjective: *ferial.* 3 A period of festivity or leisure; a vacation. 4 *Archaic* A day for special religious observance: now usually spelled *holy day.* **—** *adj.* Suitable for a holiday; festive. **—** *v.i.* To vacation. [OE *hālig dæg* holy day]

ho·li·er–than–thou (hō′lē·ər·thən·thou′) *adj.* Affecting an attitude of superior goodness or virtue; sanctimonious.

ho·li·ly (hō′lə·lē) *adv.* In a holy manner; piously; sacredly.

ho·li·ness (hō′lē·nis) *n.* 1 The state of being holy; piety. 2 *Theol.* Completeness of moral and spiritual purity. 3 The state of anything hallowed or consecrated to God. See synonyms under SANCTITY. **— His** (or **Your**) **Holiness** A title of the pope.

Hol·ins·hed (hol′inz·hed, -in·shed), **Raphael,** died 1580?, English chronicler. Also **Hollingshed** (hol′ingz·hed).

ho·lism (hō′liz·əm, hol′iz-) *n. Philos.* The theory that nature tends to synthesize units into organized wholes. [<HOL- + -ISM] **— ho·lis·tic** (hō·lis′tik) *adj.* **— ho·lis′ti·cal·ly** *adv.*

holk (hōk) See HOWK.

hol·la (hol′ə, hə·lä′), **hol·lo** (hol′ō, hə·lō′), **hol·loa** (hol′ō, hə·lō′) See HALLOO.

hol·land (hol′ənd) *n.* 1 Unbleached linen, glazed or unglazed: used sometimes in the plural, but construed as a singular. 2 In dressmaking, a form–fitting foundation used as a guide to size. 3 *pl.* Spirit flavored with juniper alone, especially that made in the Netherlands; gin: also **Holland gin** or **Hollands.** [from HOLLAND, where first made]

Hol·land (hol′ənd) See NETHERLANDS.

hol·lan·daise sauce (hol′ən·dāz′) A creamy sauce made of butter, yolks of eggs, lemon juice or vinegar, and seasoning. [<F, fem. of *hollandais* of Holland]

Hol·land·er (hol′ən·dər) *n.* A native of the Netherlands; a Dutchman.

Hol·lan·di·a (hô·län′dē·ä) The former name of KOTABARU.

hol·ler (hol′ər) *v.t.* & *v.i.* To call out loudly; shout; yell. **—** *n.* A loud shout; yell. [Imit.]

hol·low (hol′ō) *adj.* 1 Having a cavity or depression scooped out; not solid: a *hollow* tree. 2 Sunken; fallen: *hollow* cheeks. 3 Empty; vacant; hence, worthless; fruitless; insincere. 4 Sounding like the reverberation from an empty vessel or cavity; deep; murmuring. **—** *n.* 1 Any depression in a body; a cavity. 2 A valley. 3 A concave tool for making grooves and moldings. See synonyms under HOLE. **—** *v.t.* & *v.i.* To make or become hollow: usually with *out.* **—** *adv. Colloq.* Completely; thoroughly. **— to beat all hollow** To surpass completely. [OE *holh*] **— hol′low·ly** *adv.* **— hol′low·ness** *n.*

hol·low–eyed (hol′ō·īd′) *adj.* Having sunken eyes surrounded by dark areas, as a result of sickness or sleeplessness.

hol·low–heart·ed (hol′ō·här′tid) *adj.* Insincere; deceitful. **— hol′low–heart′ed·ness** *n.*

hol·low·ware (hol′ō·wâr′) *n.* Silver serving dishes that are more or less hollow, as bowls and pitchers, taken collectively: distinguished from *flatware.*

hol·lus·chick (hol′əs·chik) *n. pl.* **·chick·ie** (-chik′ē) A male fur seal six years old or younger; a bachelor (def. 5). [? <Russian *golyshka* childless <*golyĭ* naked]

hol·ly (hol′ē) *n. pl.* **·lies** 1 A tree or shrub (genus *Ilex*) with alternate leaves, white flowers, and the fruit a red berry. 2 The holm oak: also **holly oak.** [OE *holen*]

hol·ly·hock (hol′ē·hok) *n.* A tall biennial herb *(Althaea rosea)* of the mallow family, with large flowers of numerous shades. It was originally a native of China. [ME *holihoc* <*holi* holy + *hoc* mallow]

HOLLYHOCK
a. Single.
b. Double.

Hol·ly·wood (hol′ē·wo͝od) *n.* The American motion–picture industry, its character, life, etc. **—** *adj.* Of, pertaining to, or characteristic of Hollywood.

Hol·ly·wood (hol′ē·wo͝od) A NW section of Los Angeles, California, considered the center of the motion–picture industry.

holm[1] (hōm) *n.* 1 An island in a river. 2 *Brit.* Low–lying land by a stream. [OE; infl. in meaning by ON *holmr* land by water, island]

holm[2] (hōm) *n.* A European evergreen oak *(Quercus ilex).* Also **holly oak, holm oak.** [OE *holen* holly. Doublet of HOLLY.]

Hol·man–Hunt (hōl′mən·hunt′), **William,** 1827–1910, English painter.

Holmes (hōmz), **Oliver Wendell,** 1809–94, U. S. physician, poet, and humorist. **— Oliver Wendell,** 1841–1935, U. S. jurist, associate justice of the Supreme Court 1902–32; son of preceding.

— Sherlock See SHERLOCK HOLMES.

hol·mi·a (hōl′mē·ə) *n. Chem.* The oxide of holmium. [<NL <HOLMIUM] **— hol′mic** *adj.*

hol·mi·um (hōl′mē·əm) *n.* A metallic element (symbol Ho) of the lanthanide series found in gadolinite. See ELEMENT. [from *Holmia,* Latinized name of Stockholm, Sweden]

holo– *combining form* Whole; wholly: *holograph.* Also, before vowels, *hol–.* [<Gk. *holos* whole]

hol·o·ax·i·al (hol′ō·ak′sē·əl) *adj.* Designating a crystal having all the possible axes of symmetry but without symmetrical planes.

hol·o·blas·tic (hol′ə·blas′tik) *adj. Biol.* 1 Undergoing segmentation throughout the entire mass; wholly germinal, as the ova of all mammals except the monotremes. 2 Of or pertaining to such ova: opposed to *meroblastic.*

Hol·o·caine (hol′ə·kān) *n.* Proprietary name for a brand of phenacaine.

hol·o·caust (hol′ə·kôst) *n.* 1 A sacrifice wholly consumed by fire. 2 Wholesale destruction or loss of life by fire, war, etc. [<F *holocauste* <LL *holocaustum* <Gk. *holokauston,* neut. of *holokaustos* <*holos* whole + *kaustos* burnt] **— hol′o·caus′tal, hol′o·caus′tic** *adj.*

Hol·o·cene (hol′ə·sēn) *Geol. n.* The epoch following the Pleistocene and extending to the present time. **—** *adj.* Pertaining to the epoch

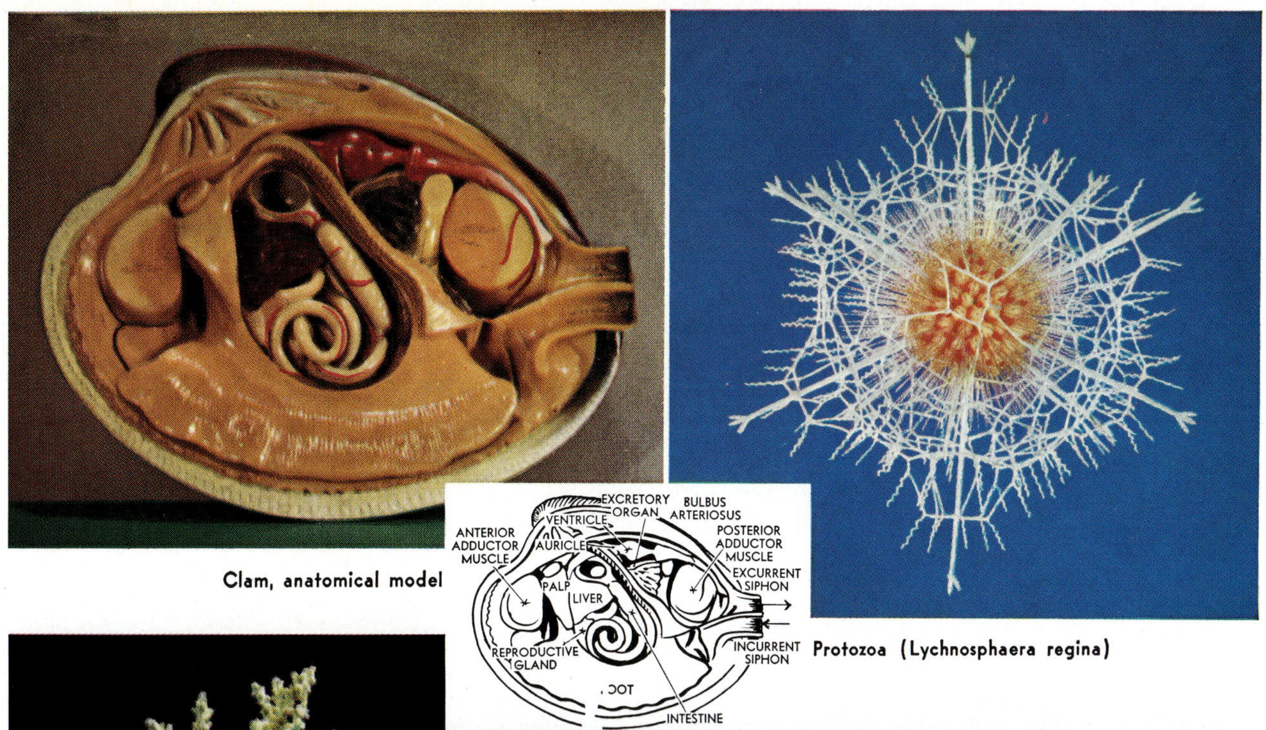

Clam, anatomical model

Protozoa (Lychnosphaera regina)

Tridacna shell with coral growth

Sea Anemone

Sponge

Stalk Medusa (Halyclistis auricula)

INVERTEBRATES (Glass Models)

Courtesy The American Museum of Natural History

Ancient Monuments

Historic statues on Easter Island in the South Pacific (© Bob Skelly/Image Finders)

The Collosseum, Rome, Italy (Roloc Color Slides)

The monument at Stonehenge in Wiltshire, England (© Bob Skelly/Image Finders)

Statue of Ramses guarding the Abu Simbel Temple above the Nile River (Roloc Color Slides)

The Parthenon on the Acropolis in Athens (Roloc Color Slides)

PARTHENON, Doric style building on the Acropolis, Athens, Greece. —Greek Line

ERECHTHEUM, Ionic style building on the Acropolis, Athens, erected as a temple of the Gods.

—American Export Lines

PONT DU GARD, an aqueduct over the river Gard in the south of France constructed by the Romans. —California-Texas Oil Co. Ltd.

COLOSSEUM at Rome which to a large degree still stands. The work of Vespasian and Titus in the first century after the birth of Christ.

—Italian Consulate

POMPEII —American Export Lines

AMPHITHEATRE at Delphi

ARCHAEOLOGY

Thailand Dancers
—American President Lines

Festive peasant costumes of the Lake Constance region of Germany
—German Tourist

Prayer before a Buddhist statue in India
—California Texas Oil Co

Dancing the Tarantella in Sicily
—Sheridan H. Garth

Women and children in the Belgian Congo, Africa

A procession of virgins in Bali
—Sheridan H. Gar

A spring festival in Nidwalden, Switzerland, when the cows are driven to upper Alpine pastures.
—Swiss Tourist

Croatian women of Yugoslavia dressed for church in em broidered peasant costumes.
—Sheridan H. Gar

COSTUMES

NE-O-MON-NI,
AN IOWAY CHIEF

MON-KA-USH-KA,
A SIOUX CHIEF

AHYOUWAIGHS,
CHIEF OF THE SIX NATIONS

WA-PEL-LA,
A MUSQUAKEE CHIEF

KISH-KE-KOSH,
A FOX BRAVE

WESH-CUBB,
A CHIPPEWAY CHIEF

MAR-KO-ME-TE,
A MENOMINIE BRAVE

WA-KAUN-HA-KA,
A WINNEBAGO CHIEF

CHITTEE-YOHOLO,
A SEMINOLE CHIEF

LE-SOLDAT-DU-CHENE,
AN OSAGE CHIEF

THAYENDANEGEA,
GREAT CAPTAIN OF THE SIX NATIONS

KA-TA-WA-BE-DA,
A CHIPPEWAY CHIEF

WA-KAWN,
WINNEBAGO CHIEF

PEAH-MUS-KA,
A MUSQUAKEE CHIEF

KEE-SHE-WAA,
A FOX WARRIOR

TAH-RO-HON,
AN IOWAY WARRIOR

CHIEFS OF NORTH AMERICAN INDIAN TRIBES IN CEREMONIAL DRESS

These portraits were painted during visits to Washington in the administration of President Andrew Jackson when the Chiefs of many tribes were called for the purpose of enacting treaties with the United States government.

U.S. National Parks

Bryce Canyon National Park, Utah (© Bob & Ira Spring)

Grand Canyon National Park, Arizona (© Jeff Apoian/Nawrocki Stock Photo)

Glacier National Park, Montana (© Bob & Ira Spring)

Badlands National Park, South Dakota (© Kirkendall/Spring)

Yosemite National Park, California (© Bob & Ira Spring)

Zion National Park, Utah (© Bob & Ira Spring)

Grand Teton National Park, Wyoming (© Bob & Ira Spring)

Mesa Verde National Park, Colorado (© Bob & Ira Spring)

U.S. National Monuments and Memorials

Washington Monument, Washington, D.C. ulik/Photri)

The Lincoln Memorial, close-up of Abraham Lincoln (© Eugene L. Drifmeyer/Photri)

The Lincoln Memorial, Washington, D.C. (Photri)

Mount Rushmore National Memorial, South Dakota (© Kirkendall/Spring)

The Vietnam Nam War Memorial, Washington, D.C. (Roloc Color Slides)

The Statue of Liberty National Monument, Liberty Island, New York (© 1986 Peter B. Kaplan)

Jefferson Memorial, Washington, D.C. (Photri)

Architecture

"Falling Waters," Bear Run, Pennsylvania, Frank L. Wright
(Shostal Associates)

Woolworth Building (interior, New York City, Cass Gilbert
(Shostal Associates)

Holy Family Cathedral, Barcelona, Spain, Antonio Gaudi,
(© Robert Frerck/Odyssey Productions, Chicago)

333 West Wacker Drive, Chicago, Illinois, Kohn, Pederson Fox Associates/Perkins & Will (© Gregory Murphey/Journalism Services)

Railway Exchange Building, Chicago, Illinois, D.H. Burnham & Company (© Gregory Murphey/Journalism Services)

Carson Pirie Scott & Company, Chicago, Illinois, Louis H. Sullivan
(© Gregory Murphey/Journalism Services)

THE TOWER BRIDGE OVER THE RIVER THAMES IN LONDON
(A Bascule Bridge)

THE QUEBEC BRIDGE
(A Cantilever Bridge)

—Photo Courtesy of W. B. Edwards

THE GOLDEN GATE BRIDGE, SAN FRANCISCO
(A Suspension Bridge)

FAMOUS BRIDGES

The Coming of the Horse—1539

The Indian Canoe—1607

The Boston Post Road—1763

The Wilderness Road—1774

The Lancaster Pike—1795

The Santa Fe Trail—1822

The Erie Canal—1825

The Iron Horse Wins—1830

The Oregon Trail—1843

The Pony Express—1860

The Meeting of Rails—1869

The Horseless Carriage—1900

Mud at the State Line—1916

Roads to Serve the Land—1933

The Modern Expressway—1959

HIGHWAYS OF HISTORY

CANALS

A merchant ship in the Suez Canal—Picture Post Library

Manchester Ship Canal—Aerofilms Ltd.

Gatun Locks, Panama Canal—U.S. Information Service

t. Lawrence Canal, oulanges section, ear Quebec border. —Aerofilms Ltd.

EOHIPPUS — Eocene — Europe, North America. Size: from fox terrier to collie. Four toes on fore feet, 3 on hind feet.

HYPOHIPPUS — Middle Miocene — Asia, Europe, North America. Size: Shetland pony. Broad, hoofed middle toe with 2 side toes.

MESOHIPPUS — Oligocene — North America. Size: from coyote to sheep. Large middle toe with 2 slender side toes.

HIPPARION — Upper Miocene and Pliocene — Asia, Europe, North Africa, North America. Size: antelope.

EQUUS SCOTTI — Pleistocene — Asia, Africa, Europe, North America. Size: modern horse.

PLIOHIPPUS — Pliocene — North America. Size: nearly that of the modern horse. One-toed hoofed feet with vestigial side toes.

AMERICAN SADDLE HORSES

THE ENGLISH THOROUGHBRED

HORSES AND RELATED ANIMALS IN THE EVOLUTION OF THE HORSE

Paintings by Charles R. Knight

Courtesy The American Museum of Natural History

Dryptosaurus

Agathaumus-Monoclonius

Allosaurus

Brontosaurus

Stegosaurus

Trachodon

DINOSAURS

Courtesy The American Museum of Natural History. Paintings (except Stegosaurus) by Charles R. Knight

Sailfish
Swordfish
Tarpon
Yellowfin Tuna
Salmon
Muskellunge
Largemouthed Black Bass
Brook Trout
Great Northern Pike
Rock Bass
Walleyed Pike
Yellow Perch
Lake Trout
Catfish

GAME FISH

Altocumulus with outstanding wave cloud

Altocumulus

Mammato-Cumulus during thunderstorm preceding warm front in Aberdeen, South Dakota

Cumulus with shower in progress outside Manila, Republic of Philippines

Cumulo-nimbus just grown from cumulus at Mount Wilson, California.

Cumulus associated with fracto cumulus Monroe County, West Virginia.

Cumulus and altocumulus hovering over Florida Island off Guadalcanal.
Official U. S. Navy Photo

Cumulus over harbor in moonlight

Orographic formation of cumulus and cirrus off Greenland

Altocumulus inactive

Cumulus

Lower scattered cumulus

Tornado

CLOUD FORMATIONS

Courtesy U. S. Weather Bureau

"Chariotter of Delphi" (left), Greece, 460-475 B.C.; "David" (right) by Michelangelo Buonarroti (Scala/Art Resource)

"Romulus and Remus" (Scala/Art Resource)

"Pieta" by Michelangelo Buonarroti (Scala/Art Resourc

"Bronco Buster" by Frederic Remington (Thomas Gilcrease Institute, Tulsa, Oklahoma)

"Reclining Figure" No. 4 by Henry Moore (Scala/Art Resource)

"Chicago Picasso" by Pablo Picasso (© Janet Davis/Nawrocki Stock Photo) following the Pleistocene. [<HOLO- + Gk. *kainos* recent]

Hol·o·fer·nes (hol′ə·fûr′nēz) In the book of Judith in the Apocrypha, an Assyrian general slain by Judith.

hol·o·gram (hol′ə·gram) *n.* Photosensitive film containing a three–dimensional image produced by holography. [<HOLO- + -GRAM[1]]

hol·o·graph (hol′ə·graf, -gräf) *adj.* Denoting a document wholly in the handwriting of the person whose signature it bears. — *n.* A document so written. [<F *holographe* <Gk. *holographos* < *holos* entire + *graphein* write]

hol·o·graph·ic (hol′ə·graf′ik, -gräf′-) *adj.* 1 Holograph. 2 Of or pertaining to holography. Also **hol′o·graph′i·cal.**

ho·log·ra·phy (hə·log′rə·fē) *n.* A photographic process utilizing a split beam of laser light to produce on a photographic plate, without the use of a lens, the interference pattern of light waves, thus recording a three–dimensional image that can be reconstructed and viewed. [<HOLO- + -GRAPHY]

hol·o·he·dron (hol′ə·hē′drən) *n.* A crystal form having the full number of symmetrically arranged planes crystallographically possible. — **hol′o·he′dral** (-drəl) *adj.*

hol·o·me·tab·o·lism (hol′ə·mə·tab′ə·liz′əm) *n. Entomol.* The condition of having a complete metamorphosis, with a larval and pupal stage preceding the adult: opposed to *hemimetabolism.* — **hol′o·met′a·bol′ic** (-met′ə·bol′·ik), **hol′o·me·tab′o·lous** *adj.*

hol·o·mor·phic (hol′ə·môr′fik) *adj.* Denoting likeness of form at the ends, as of crystals.

hol·o·phote (hol′ə·fōt) *n.* A lamp for a lighthouse, etc., so arranged that all light is utilized and thrown in the desired direction by reflectors, refracting lenses, or both. [<HOLO- + Gk. *phos, phōtos* light] — **hol′o·pho′tal** *adj.*

ho·loph·ra·sis (hə·lof′rə·sis) *n.* Expression of a sentence or a complex idea in the form of a single word, as in some American Indian languages. [<HOLO- + Gk. *phrasis* phrase] — **hol·o·phras·tic** (hol′ə·fras′tik) *adj.*

hol·o·phyte (hol′ə·fīt) *n. Bot.* A plant possessing chlorophyll, and therefore capable of manufacturing its own food. — **hol·o·phyt·ic** (hol′ə·fit′ik) *adj.*

hol·o·sym·met·ric (hol′ə·si·met′rik) *adj.* Wholly symmetrical. — **hol′o·sym′me·try** (-sim′ə·trē) *n.*

hol·o·thu·ri·an (hol′ə·thŏŏr′ē·ən) *n.* Any of a class (*Holothurioidea*) of echinoderms with generally wormlike shape, skinlike integument, and tentacles about the mouth: including trepangs, sea cucumbers, sea slugs, etc. [<L *holothurium,* a kind of zoophyte <Gk. *holothurion*]

Hol·o·trich·i·da (hol′ə·trik′ə·də) *n.* An order of ciliate infusorians with cilia nearly uniformly disposed over the surface of the body. [<NL <HOLO- + Gk. *trix, trichos* hair] — **ho·lot·ri·chal** (hə·lot′ri·kəl), **ho·lot′ri·chous** *adj.*

hol·o·type (hol′ə·tīp) *n.* In taxonomy, the single specimen of a plant or animal which is taken as representative of a new species.

hol·o·zo·ic (hol′ə·zō′ik) *adj.* Wholly like an animal: distinguished from *holophytic.*

holp (hōlp), **holp·en** (hōl′pən) Obsolete forms of past tense and past participle of HELP.

Hol·stein (hōl′stīn, -stēn) *n.* One of a breed of cattle originally developed in the Netherlands province of Friesland and adjoining German provinces: valued for both beef and milk: also **Hol′stein–Frie′sian** (-frē′zhən).

Hol·stein (hōl′stīn, *Ger.* hōl′shtīn) A former Danish duchy, now part of Schleswig–Holstein, northern West Germany.

hol·ster (hōl′stər) *n.* A pistol case. [<Du.]

Hol·ston River (hōl′stən) A river in NE Tennessee, flowing 110 miles SW to the Tennessee River.

holt (hōlt) *n. Archaic* 1 A wooded hill. 2 A wood. [OE]

ho·lus–bo·lus (hō′ləs·bō′ləs) *n.* The whole lot or quantity. — *adv.* All together; at a gulp. [Dog Latin <WHOLE + BOLUS]

ho·ly (hō′lē) *adj.* **·li·er, ·li·est** 1 Devoted to religious or sacred use; consecrated; hallowed. 2 Of highest spiritual purity; saintly: a *holy* martyr. 3 Befitting a saintly character; devout: *holy* fear. 4 Of divine nature or origin. 5 Worthy of veneration because associated with something divine. — *n. pl.* **ho·lies** A holy thing or quality [OE *hālig*]

Synonyms (adj.): blessed, consecrated, devoted, devout, divine, hallowed, sacred, saintly. *Sacred* is applied to that which is to be regarded as inviolable on any account, and so is not restricted to divine things; therefore in its lower applications it is less than *holy.* That which is *sacred* may be made so by institution, decree, or association; that which is *holy* is so by its own nature, possessing intrinsic moral purity, and, in the highest sense, absolute moral perfection. God is *holy*; his commands are *sacred. Holy* may be applied also to that which is *hallowed*; as, "the place whereon thou standest is *holy* ground," *Ex.* iii 5. In such use *holy* is more than *sacred,* as if the very qualities of a spiritual or divine presence were imparted to the place or object. *Divine* has been used with great looseness, denoting goodness or power in eloquence, music, etc., but the tendency is to restrict its use to attributes of the Divine Being. See PERFECT, PURE. *Antonyms*: abominable, common, cursed, impure, polluted, secular, unconsecrated, unhallowed, unholy, unsanctified, wicked, worldly.

Holy Alliance A treaty concluded by Russia, Austria, and Prussia at Paris, France, in 1815, binding the sovereign rulers in brotherhood and proclaiming Christianity the foundation of government.

Holy City A city considered sacred by the believers in a religion, as Jerusalem or Mecca.

Holy Communion The Eucharist or Lord's Supper.

Holy Cross, Mount of the A peak of the Sawatch Range in Colorado; 13,986 feet.

holy day A sacred day, as the Sabbath, or one set apart for religious uses.

Holy Father A title of the pope.

Holy Ghost See HOLY SPIRIT.

Holy Grail See GRAIL.

Hol·y·head (hol′i·hed) An island and its chief port in NW Wales. *Welsh* **Caer Gy·bi** (kīr gē′bē).

Holy Land Palestine.

Holy Mother The Virgin Mary.

Holy Office See CONGREGATION OF THE HOLY OFFICE.

holy of holies The innermost and most sacred shrine of the Jewish tabernacle.

Hol·yoke (hōl′yōk) A city in west central Massachusetts.

holy orders The state of being ordained to the ministry of a church: a term used chiefly in the Anglican, Eastern, and Roman Catholic churches. See also under ORDER.

Holy Roller One belonging to a Protestant sect whose members express religious emotion by violent bodily movements and shouting: a humorous or derogatory term.

Holy Roman Empire An empire in central and western Europe, established in 962 and lasting until 1806: regarded as an extension of the Western Roman Empire and as the temporal form of the dominion of which the pope was spiritual head: sometimes considered as established with the crowning of Charlemagne. See map below: extent in 11th cent.

holy rood The cross over the entrance to the chancel of many churches and cathedrals.

Holy Rood The cross on which Jesus was crucified.

Holy Saturday The Saturday before Easter.

Holy See See under SEE[2].

Holy Sepulcher See under SEPULCHER.

Holy Spirit The third person of the Trinity: also called *Holy Ghost.*

ho·ly·stone (hō′lē·stōn′) *n.* A flat piece of soft sandstone used for cleaning the wood decks of a vessel. — *v.t.* **·stoned, ·ston·ing** To scrub with a holystone. [Said to be so called because used to clean decks for Sunday]

Holy Synod The supreme governing body in any of the Greek Catholic churches.

Holy Thursday 1 In the Roman Catholic Church, the Thursday of Holy Week, or Maundy Thursday. 2 *Rare* In the Anglican Church, Ascension Day.

ho·ly·tide (hō′lē·tīd′) *n.* A holy season.

holy water Water regarded as sacred; especially, in the Eastern and Roman Catholic churches, water blessed by a priest.

Holy Week In the Christian church, the week before Easter.

Holy Writ The Scriptures.

hom·age (hom′ij, om′-) *n.* 1 Reverential regard or worship; deference. 2 In feudal law, formal acknowledgment of tenure by a tenant to his lord. 3 An act evincing deference or vassalage. See synonyms under ALLEGIANCE, REVERENCE. — *v.t. Obs.* **·aged, ·ag·ing** To pay respect or allegiance to. [<OF <LL *hominaticum* < *homo, -inis* vassal, client, man]

hom·ag·er (hom′ə·jər, om′-) *n.* One who does homage or holds land under tenure of homage.

hom·bre (ôm′brā, om′brē) *n. U.S. Slang* A man. [<Sp.]

Hom·burg (hom′bûrg) *n.* 1 A man's hat of soft felt with slightly rolled–up brim and crown dented lengthwise: so called because originally worn by men in Homburg, Germany. 2 A woman's hat styled after this.

home (hōm) *n.* 1 One's fixed place of abode; the family residence. 2 A family circle; household: a happy *home.* 3 The place of abode of one's affections, peace, or rest: He found a *home* in the church. 4 One's native place or country. 5 The seat or habitat of something; the place of origin: New Orleans is the *home* of jazz. 6 An establishment for the shelter and care of the needy or infirm. 7 In some games, the goal that must be reached in order to win or score. — **at home** 1 In one's own house, place, or country. 2 At ease, as if in familiar surroundings. 3 Prepared to receive callers. — *adj.* 1 Of or pertaining to one's home or country. 2 At the place regarded as the base of operations: the *home* office; a *home* game. 3 Going to the point; effective: a *home* thrust. — *adv.* 1 To or at home. 2 To the place or point intended: to thrust the dagger *home.* 3 Deeply and intimately; to the heart: Her words struck *home.* — *v.* **homed, hom·ing** *v.t.* 1 To carry or send to a home. 2 To furnish with a home. — *v.i.* 3 To go to a home; fly home, as homing pigeons. 4 To have residence. — **to home on** (or **in on**) 1 *Mil.* To direct toward, seek, or find the target, as a guided missile. 2 *Aeron.* To direct (an aircraft) to or toward a given spot by radio or other signals. [OE *hām*]

Synonyms (noun): abode, domicile, dwelling, fireside, habitation, hearth, hearthstone, house, ingleside, residence. See HOUSE.

Home may appear as a combining form in hyphemes or solidemes, or as the first element in two–word phrases, with the following meanings:

1 Of or pertaining to one's home or country:

home address	**homekeeper**	**homemaking**
home base	**homekeeping**	**home–owner**
home–builder	**home lot**	**home–owning**
home–defense	**home–lover**	**home–seeker**
home–folks	**home–loving**	**home site**
home island	**homemaker**	**home worship**

2 At or in the home:

home-abiding	**homelife**
home-baked	**home-raised**
home-built	**home-reared**
home-cooked	**home-sheltered**
home-fed	**home-staying**
home-grown	**home-woven**

3 To or toward the home:

home-bound	**home letter**
homecomer	**home-longing**
home correspondent	**home-wind**

4 Relating to, produced or carried on in, one's home or country; domestic; hence, also, belonging to headdquarters:

home affairs	**home market**
home farm	**home office**
home manufacture	**home trade**

Home (hyo͞om), **Earl of** See DOUGLAS-HOME.

home•bod•y (hōm′bod′ē) *n. pl.* **•bod•ies** A person who habitually stays at home.

home-born (hōm′bôrn′) *adj.* Native to the home; derived through the home.

home-bred (hōm′bred′) *adj.* **1** Bred at home; native; domestic. **2**Uncultivated.

home-brew (hōm′bro͞o′) *n.* Spirituous or malt liquor distilled or brewed at home. **—home′-brewed′** *adj.*

home•com•ing (hōm′kum′ing) *n.* **1** A return home. **2** *U.S.* In colleges, an annual celebration for visiting alumni.

home economics The science that treats of the economic and social interests and activities of the home: food, clothing, hygiene, heating and ventilation, thrifty management, etc.

home guard Local volunteers organized to defend the home region or country when the standing army is afield.

home•land (hōm′land′) *n.* The country of one's birth or allegiance.

home•less (hōm′lis) *adj.* Having no home. **—home′less•ness** *n.*

home•like (hōm′līk′) *adj.* Like home; reminding of home. **—home′like′ness** *n.*

home•ly (hōm′lē) *adj.* **•li•er, •li•est 1** Having a familiar everyday character; unpretentious. **2** *U.S.* Having plain features; not good-looking. **3** Domestic. **—home′li•ness** *n.*

home-made (hōm′mād′) *adj.* **1** Of household or domestic manufacture, as distinguished from factory or foreign make. **2** Simple; homely.

homeo- *combining form* Like; similar: *homeothermal: also spelled homoeo-.* Also, before vowels, **home-.** [<**Gk.** *homoios* similar]

Home Office In the British government, the department handling domestic affairs, particularly supervision of the police, elections, and naturalization.

ho•me•o•mor•phism (hō′mē•ə•môr′fiz•əm, hom′ē-) *n.* A close similarity in the crystalline forms of unlike chemical compounds. **—ho′me•o•mor′phous** *adj.*

ho•me•o•path•ic (hō′mēə•path′ik, hom′ē-) *adj.* **1** Relating to homeopathy. **2** Diluted in nature. Also spelled *homeopathic.*

ho•me•op•a•thist (hō′mē•op′ə•thist, hom′ē-) *n.* One who advocates or practices homeopathy. Also **ho•me•o• path** (hō′mē•ə•path′, hom′ē-).

ho•me•op•a•thy (hō′mē•op′ə•thē, hom′ē-) *n.* A system of medicine formulated by Dr. Samuel Hahnemann, 1755–1843. It is founded on the principle that "like cures like," and prescribes minute doses of such medicines as would produce in a healty person the symptoms of the disease treated. Also spelled *homoeopathy.* [< HOMEO- + -PATHY]

ho•me•o•pla•sia (hō′mē• ə•plā′zhə, -zhē•ə, hom′•ē-) *n. Med.* The formation of tissue similar in appearance to the adjacent tissue. **—ho′me•o•plas′tic** (-plas′tik) *adj.*

ho•me•o•sta•sis (hō′mē•ə•stā′sis, hom′ē-) *n.* The tendency of an organism to maintain a uniform and beneficial physiological stability within and between its parts; organic equilibrium. **—ho′me•o•stat′ic** (-stat′ik) *adj.*

ho•me•o•typ•ic (hō′mē•ə•tip′ik, hom′ē-) *adj. Biol.* Of or pertaining to the second meiotic division in cells, more nearly resembling typical cell mitosis: contrasted with *heterotypic.* Also **ho′me•o•typ′i•cal.**

home plate In baseball, the base at which the batter stands when batting: a run is scored when the batter touches first, second, and third base, and home plate consecutively without being retired. See illustration under BASEBALL.

hom•er¹ (hē′mər) *n. U.S. Colloq.* A home run.

ho•mer² (hō′mər) *n.* **1** In Jewish antiquity, a liquid measure of 10 baths. See BATH². **2** A dry measure of 10 ephahs. [<Hebrew *hōmer* <*hāmar* swell up]

Ho•mer (hō′mər) A masculine personal name. Also *Du., Ger.* **Ho•me•rus** (hō•mā′ro͞os), *Fr.* **Ho•mère** (ō•mâr′), *Gk.* **Ho•me•ros** (hō•me′•rōs). [<Gk. (Cumaean), blind] **—Homer** A Greek epic poet of about the ninth century B.C.; traditional author of the *Iliad* and *Odyssey.*

Ho•mer (hō′mər), **Winslow,** 1836–1910, U.S. painter.

Ho•mer•ic (hō•mer′ik) *adj.* Of or pertaining to Homer or his age or writings. Also **Ho•me•ri•an** (hō•mir′ē•ən), **Ho•mer′i•cal.**

Homeric laughter Loud and irrepressible laughter.

home•room (hōm′ro͞om′, -ro͝om′) *n.* The schoolroom in which a class meets daily for attendance check, hearing of bulletins, guidance, etc.

home rule 1 Self-government in local affairs within the framework of state or national laws. **2** A political movement, begun about 1870, to gain autonomy for Ireland.

home-rul•er (hōm′ro͞o′lər) *n.* One who favors home rule.

home run In baseball, a base hit in which the ball is driven beyond reach of the opposing fielders, thus allowing the batter to touch all bases and score a run.

home•sick (hōm′sik′) *adj.* Suffering because of absence from home; ill in mind or body through longing for home; nostalgic. **—home′•sick′ness** *n.*

home•spun (hōm′spun′) *adj.* **1** Of domestic manufacture. **2**Plain and homely in character. *—n.* **1** Fabric woven at home. **2** A loose, rough fabric having the appearance of tweed.

home•stake (hōm′stāk′) *n.* Enough money to get back home.

home•stead (hōm′sted) *n.* **1** The place of a home; the house, subsidiary buildings, and adjacent land occupied as a home. **2** *U.S.* A tract of land occupied by a settler under the Homestead Act (1862) or its revisions. *—v.i. U.S.* To become a settler on a homestead under the Homestead Act. *—v.t. U.S.* To settle on land under the Homestead Act.

Homestead Act A Congressional enactment of 1862, later revised and extended, which enables a settler to acquire 160 acres of free public land providing he reside on, cultivate, and improve his land for five years (in 1912, reduced to three years), after which time he may obtain full title and unrestricted ownership. In less fertile areas, 320 or even 640 acres were later allowed.

home•stead•er (hōm′sted′ər) *n.* **1** One who has a homestead. **2** One who holds lands acquired under the Homestead Act of Congress.

homestead law *U.S.* A law in many States exempting a homestead from seizure or sale to satisfy general debts of a certain amount. Also **homestead exemption law.**

home•stretch (hōm′strech′) *n.* **1** The last part of a racecourse before the winning post is reached; the last part of a horse race. **2** The last part of any journey or endeavor.

home•ward (hōm′wərd) *adj.* Directed toward home. *—adv.* Toward home. Also **home′•wards.**

home•work (hōm′wûrk′) *n.* Work performed or assigned for performance at home; work done at home by wage-earners, or lessons assigned to students for home study.

home•y (hō′mē) *adj.* **•hom•i•er, hom•i•est** *Colloq.* Reminding of home; homelike: also spelled *homy.* **—home′y•ness, hom′i•ness** *n.*

hom•i•cide (hom′ə•sīd, hō ′mə-) *n.* **1** The killing of one human being by another. **2** A person who has killed another. [<F <L *homicidium* <*homicida* murderer <*homo* man + *-cidere* <*caedere* cut, kill] **—hom′i•ci′dal** *adj.* **—hom′i•ci′dal•ly** *adv.*

hom•i•let•ics (hom′ə•let′ iks) *n.* The branch of rhetoric that treats of the composition and delivery of sermons. [<Gk. *homilētikos* sociable <*homileein* be in company with <*homilos* assembly]

hom•i•list (hom′ə•list) *n.* **1** A writer of homilies. **2** One who delivers homilies or preaches to a congregation.

hom•i•ly (hom′ə•lē) *n. pl.* **•lies 1** A didactic sermon on some text or topic from the Bible. **2** A serious admonition, especially upon morals or conduct. **3** A tedious, moralizing discourse. [<OF *omelie* <LL *homilia* <Gk. *homilia* <*homilos* assembly < *homos* the same + *ilē* crowd] **—hom′i•let′ic** or **•i•cal** *adj.*

hom•i•nal (hom′ə•nəl) *adj.* Pertaining to man. [<L *homo, hominis* man]

hom•ing (hō′ming) *adj.* **1** Readily finding the way home, returning home. **2** Pertaining to any of various methods and devices for directing an aircraft or guided missile to a specified spot: a *homing* beacon. *—n.* The act of heading for or reaching home.

homing pigeon A pigeon with remarkable capability of making its way home from great distances: used for conveying messages. Also called *carrier pigeon.*

hom•i•nid (hom′ə•nid, hō′mə-) *n. Zool.* A member of the family *Hominidae* of the primate order, now represented by only one living species, *Homo sapiens.* *—adj.* Of or pertaining to any member of this group. [<NL <L *homo, hominis* man]

hom•i•noid (hom′ə•noid, hō′mə-) *adj.* **1** Manlike. **2** *Zool.* Pertaining to or describing any member of the superfamily or group *Hominoidea* of the primate order, including the large tailless apes, as the gibbons, orangutans, gorillas, and chimpanzees, and the genus *Homo* as its most advanced form. *—n.* **1** An animal resembling man. **2** Any primate of the superfamily *Hominoidea.* [<NL <L *homo, hominis* man]

hom•i•ny (hom′ə•nē) *n.* Hulled corn (maize), broken up or coarsely ground, boiled in water or milk for food. Also (**hominy grits.** [< Algonquian *rockahominie* parched corn]

Ho•mo (hō′mō) *n.* **1** Man. **2** *Zool.* Generic name of various species of erect, large-brained anthropoids belonging to the family *Hominidae* of the primate order of vertebrates, now represented only by *Homo sapiens.* [<L]

homo- *combining form* Same; similar; equal: *homogeneous* : opposed to *hetero-.* [<Gk. *homo-* <*homos* same]

ho•mo•cen•tric (hō′mə•sen′trik, hom′ə-) *adj.* Having a common center. Also **ho′mo•cen′•tri•cal.**

ho•mo•cer•cal (hō′mə•sûr′kəl, hom′ə-) *adj.* Zool. Characterized by a similarity of the upper and lower halves of the caudal fin in fishes, due to the straight, central position of the caudal verdtebrae. [<HOMO- + Gk. *kerkos* tail] **—ho′mo•cer′cy** (-sûr′sē) *n.*

ho•mo•chro•mat•ic (hō′mə•krō•mat′ik, hom′ə-) *adj.* Pertaining to or consisting of one color; monochromatic. Also **ho•mo•chrome** (hō′mə•krōm, hom′ə-). **—ho•mo•chro•ma•tism** (hō′mə•krō′mə•tiz′əm, hom′ə-) *n.*

ho•mo•chro•mous (hō′mə•krō′məs, hom′ə-) *adj. Bot.* Of one color, as a flower head with similar florets. [< HOMO- + Gk. *chrōma* color]

ho•mo•cy•clic (hō′mə•sī′klik, -sik′lik, hom′ə-) *adj. Chem.* Pertaining to or designating an organic compound of the closed-chain or ring type, as benzene: opposed to *heterocyclic.*

ho•mo•dyne (hō′mə•dīn, hom′ə-) *adj.* Electronics Pertaining to or designating a system of radio reception by the aid of a locally generated voltage of carrier frequency; zero-beat in reception. Compare HETERODYNE. [<HOMO- + Gk. *dynamos* power]

homoeo- See HOMEO-.

ho•mo•er•o•tism (hō′mō•er′ə•tiz′əm) *n.* Sexual attraction to members of the same sex, normally well sublimated. Also **ho•mo•e•rot•i•cism** (hō′mō•i•rot′ə•siz′əm). **—ho′mo•e•rot′ic** *adj.*

ho•mog•a•mous (hō•mog′ə•məs) *adj. Bot.* **1** Having but one kind of flowers; opposed to *heterogamous.* **2** Having pistils and stamens which ripen at the same time: opposed to *dichogamous.* Also **ho•mo•gam•ic** (hō′mə•gam′•ik). [<HOMO- + -GAMOUS]

ho•mog•a•my (hō•mog′ə•mē) *n.* **1** *Bot.* **a** The simultaneous maturity of stamens and pistils in a flower: distinguished from *dichogamy.* **b** The condition of having all flowers alike: distinguished from *heterogamy.* **2** *Biol.* Interbreeding among an isolated group of individuals having similar characters, or characters different from those from which they are isolated. [<HOMO- + -GAMY]

ho•mo•ge•ne•i•ty (hō′mə•jə•nē′ə•tē, hom′ə-) *n.*

Identity or similarity of kind or structure.

ho·mo·ge·ne·ous (hō′mə·jē′nē·əs, hom′ə-) *adj.* **1** Of the same composition or character throughout. **2** Of the same kind, nature, etc. (with another); like; similar: opposed to *heterogeneous.* **3** *Math.* Having all its terms of the same degree, as an algebraic equation. Also **ho·mo·gene** (ho′mə·jēn), **ho′mo·ge′ne·al.** See synonyms under ALIKE. [< Med. L *homogeneus* < Gk. *homogenēs* of the same race < *homos* the same + *genos* race] —**ho′mo·ge′ne·ous·ly** *adv.* —**ho′mo·ge′ne·ous·ness** *n.*

ho·mo·gen·e·sis (hō′mə·jen′ə·sis, hom′ə-) *n. Biol.* **1** A mode of reproduction in which the offspring are like the parent and have the same cycle of existence: opposed to *heterogenesis.* **2** Homogeny.

ho·mog·en·ize (hə·moj′ə·nīz, hō′mə·jə·nīz′) *v.t.* **·ized, ·iz·ing 1** To make or render homogeneous. **2** To process, as milk, by subjecting to high temperature and pressure so as to break up fat globules and disperse them uniformly throughout; emulsify. —**ho·mog′en·ized** *adj.* —**ho·mog′en·i·za′tion** *n.* —**ho·mog′en·iz′er** *n.*

ho·mog·e·nous (hə·moj′ə·nəs) *adj. Biol.* Having a similarity in structure due to descent from a common ancestor or development from a common stock.

ho·mog·e·ny (hə·moj′ə·nē) *n. Biol.* Homology of structures genetically related through a common ancestor: opposed to *homoplasy.* [< Gk. *homogeneia* community of birth < *homos* the same + *genos* race]

ho·mog·o·ny (hə·mog′ə·nē) *n. Bot.* The condition of having stamens and pistils of uniform respective length in all flowers of the same species; opposed to *heterogony.* [< HOMO- + -GONY] —**ho·mog′o·nous** *adj.* —**ho·mog′o·nous·ly** *adv.*

ho·mo·grade (hō′mə·grād) *adj. Stat.* Expressed in one or the other of two contrasting categories, as male or female. Compare HETEROGRADE.

hom·o·graph (hom′ə·graf, -gräf, hō′mə-) *n.* A word identical with another in spelling, but differing from it in origin and meaning, and sometimes in pronunciation, as *bass,* a fish, and *bass,* a male voice: also called *homonym.* ◆ See note under HOMONYM. [< Gk. *homographos* having the same letters < *homos* same + *graphein* to write] —**hom′o·graph′ic** *adj.*

homoio- *combining form* Homeo-. [< Gk. *homoios* similar]

ho·moi·o·ther·mal (hə·moi′ə·thûr′məl) *adj.* Preserving a uniform temperature, as warm-blooded animals: opposed to *poikilothermal.* Also **homothermal.**

ho·moi·ou·sian (hō′moi·o͞o′sē·ən, -ou′sē-) *adj.* Alike in nature or characteristics. Also **ho′moi·ou′si·ous.**

Ho·moi·ou·si·an (hō′moi·o͞o′sē·ən, -ou′sē-) *n.* One of the Arian sectaries of the fourth century who held that Christ was of a similar nature but not of the same nature with the Father: opposed to *Homoousian.* —*adj.* Of or pertaining to the Homoiousians or their beliefs: also **Ho′moi·ou′si·ous.** [< Gk. *homoios* like + *ousia* being] —**Ho′moi·ou′si·an·ism** *n.*

hom·o·log (hom′ə·lôg, -log) *n.* **1** Something that answers in position, proportion, or type to, or has structural affinity with, something else; a member or form of a homologous series: Ethane is a *homolog* of methane. **2** *Biol.* A structure or part of an organism showing homology: The wing of a bat is the *homolog* of the arm of a man: distinguished from *analog.* Also **hom′o·logue.**

ho·mol·o·gate (hō·mol′ə·gāt) *v.* **·gat·ed, ·gat·ing** *v.t.* **1** To acknowledge; express approval of. **2** In Scots law, to make valid; ratify. —*v.i.* **3** To agree; to express assent. [< Med. L *homologatus,* pp. of *homologare* < Gk. *homologein* agree]

ho·mo·log·ic (hō′mə·loj′ik, hom′ə-) *adj.* **1** *Geom.* Designating two figures so related that either may be the projection of the other upon a plane. **2** Relating to or governed by homology; corresponding in structure; homologous. Also **ho·mo·log′i·cal.** —**ho·mo·log′i·cal·ly** *adv.*

ho·mol·o·gize (hō·mol′ə·jīz) *v.* **·gized, ·giz·ing** *v.t.* **1** To make homologous. **2** To demonstrate the homologies of. —*v.i.* **3** To be homologous; correspond in structure or value.

ho·mol·o·gous (hō·mol′ə·gəs) *adj.* **1** Having a similar structure, proportion, value, or position. **2** Proportional to each other. **3** Identical in nature, relation, or the like. **4** *Biol.* Denoting either of a pair of sexually differentiated chromosomes which unite at meiosis. **5** *Med.* Pertaining to or designating a serum protecting against the same bacterium from which it was prepared. [< Gk. *homologos* agreeing < *homos* the same + *logos* speech < *legein* speak]

hom·o·lo·graph·ic (hom′ə·lə·graf′ik) *adj.* Pertaining to homolography.

homolographic projection A method of map drawing by which the relative areas of different countries are accurately indicated.

homo·log·ra·phy (hom′ə·log′rə·fē) *n.* The study or presentation of proportions, anatomical or geodetic. [< Gk. *homalos* even + *graphein* write]

ho·mol·o·gy (hō·mol′ə·jē) *n.* **1** The state or quality of being homologous; correspondence in structure and properties. **2** *Biol.* The correspondence of a part or organ of one animal with a similar part or organ of another, determined by agreement in derivation and development from a like primitive origin, as the foreleg of a quadruped, the wing of a bird, and the pectoral fin of a fish: distinguished from *analogy* and contrasted with *heterology.* **3** *Chem.* A similarity in compounds having the same fundamental structure but differing in constituents by a regular succession of changes, as the alcohols. **4** *Bacteriol.* A relationship between a bacterium and the serum obtained from it. [< HOMO- + -LOGY]

ho·mol·o·sine (hə·mol′ə·sin, -sīn) *adj.* Designating a world map combining two homolographic projections so as to portray continents with the least distortion possible. [< Gk. *homalas* even + L *sinus* curve]

ho·mo·mor·phism (hō′mə·môr′fiz·əm, hom′ə-) *n.* **1** *Biol.* Resemblance in form, as among the members of a zoophytic colony. **2** *Entomol.* The exhibition of imperfect metamorphosis in insects; resemblance of larva to adult. **3** *Bot.* The possession of perfect flowers of only one form or kind. Compare HETEROMORPHISM. —**ho′mo·mor′phic, ho′mo·mor′phous** *adj.*

ho·mo·mor·phy (hō′mə·môr′fē, hom′ə-) *n. Biol.* Imitative resemblance between unrelated organisms; adaptive mimicry without structural similarity.

hom·o·nym (hom′ə·nim, hō′mə-) *n.* **1** A word identical with another in pronunciation, but differing from it in spelling and meaning, as *fair* and *fare, read* and *reed* : also called *homophone.* **2** A homograph. **3** A word identical with another in spelling and pronunciation, but differing from it in origin and meaning, as *butter,* the food, and *butter,* one who butts. **4** One who has the same name as another; namesake. **5** *Biol.* A generic or specific name rejected because of previous application to another animal or plant. [< Gk. *homos* same + *onyma* name] —**hom·o·nym·ic** (hom′ə·nim′ik, hō′mə-) or **·i·cal** *adj.*

◆*Homonym* is used with a variety of meanings, the most common sense being that of definition 1 above. Although *homophone* is etymologically more precise and is unambiguous in meaning, *homonym* is nevertheless the more commonly used form in this sense. *Homonym* is also, but less commonly, used interchangeably with *homograph.*

ho·mon·y·mous (hō·mon′ə·məs) *adj.* **1** Of the nature of a homonym; ambiguous. **2** Indicated by the same name because occupying the same relation.

ho·mon·y·my (hō·mon′ə·mē) *n.* Identity of sound or name with diversity of sense; ambiguity.

ho·mo·ou·si·an (hō′mō·o͞o′sē·ən, -ou′sē-, hom′·ō-) *adj.* Identical in nature. Also **ho′mo·ou′·si·ous.**

Ho·mo·ou·si·an (hō′mō·o͞o′sē·ən, -ou′sē-, hom′ō-) *n.* One of the Christians, who, in the great controversy of the fourth century about the nature of Christ, maintained that it was identical with that of the Father, instead of similar, or different, as maintained by the less strict and more rigid Arians respectively: distinguished from *Homoiousian* and *Heterousian.* —*adj.* Of or pertaining to the Homoousians or their beliefs: also **Ho′·mo·ou′si·ous.** [< Gk. *homos* the same + *ousia* being] —**Ho′mo·ou′si·an·ism** *n.*

ho·mo·phile (hō′mō·fīl) *n.* A homosexual.

ho·mo·pho·bi·a (hō′mō·fō′bē·ə) *n.* Extreme hatred or fear of either homosexuals or of homosexuality.

hom·o·phone (hom′ə·fōn, hō′mə-) *n.* A homonym (def. 1). ◆See note under HOMONYM. [< Gk. *homophōnos* of the same sound < *homos* same + *phōnē* sound]

hom·o·phon·ic (hom′ə·fon′ik, hō′mə-) *adj.* **1** *Music* **a** Consisting of sounds having the same pitch; in unison: said of ancient music. **b** Having one predominant part carrying the melody, with the other parts used for harmonic rather than for contrapuntal effect: opposed to *polyphonic.* **2** Of or pertaining to homophones; having the same sound. Also **ho·moph·o·nous** (hō·mof′ə·nəs).

ho·moph·o·ny (hō·mof′ə·nē) *n.* **1** Identity of sound, with difference of meaning. **2** *Music* The condition or quality of being homophonic.

ho·mo·plas·tic (hō′mə·plas′tik, hom′ə-) *adj. Biol.* Pertaining to a resemblance (in forms or organs) not traceable to homogeny: opposed to *homogenous.*

ho·mo·po·lar (hō′mə·pō′lər) *adj. Chem.* Having uniform distribution of an electric charge, as in compounds linked by a covalent bond: opposed to *heteropolar.*

Ho·mop·ter·a (hō·mop′tər·ə) *n. pl.* A suborder of hemipterous insects with sucking mouth parts and usually two pairs of wings, including the cicadas, aphids, etc. [< NL < Gk. *homos* same + *pteron* wing] —**ho·mop′ter·an** *adj. & n.*

ho·mop·ter·ous (hō·mop′tər·əs) *adj.* Of, pertaining to, or belonging to the suborder *Homoptera.*

ho·mor·gan·ic (hō′môr·gan′ik) *adj. Phonet.* Describing speech sounds which are produced in a similar position in the mouth, as (p) and (b).

Homo sa·pi·ens (sā′pē·enz) See HOMO.

ho·mo·sex·u·al (hō′mə·sek′sho͞o·əl, hom′ə-) *adj.* Pertaining to or characterized by homosexuality. —*n.* A homosexual person. Compare BISEXUAL, HETEROSEXUAL.

ho·mo·sex·u·al·i·ty (hō′mə·sek′sho͞o·al′ə·tē, hom′ə-) *n.* **1** Sexual attraction toward a person of the same sex. **2** Sexual relations between persons of the same sex.

ho·mos·po·rous (hō·mos′pər·əs, hō′mə·spôr′·əs, -spō′rəs) *adj. Bot.* Having or producing asexual spores of one kind only. —**ho·mos′·po·ry** (hō·mos′pər·ē, hō′mə·spôr′ē, -spō′rē) *n.*

ho·mo·tax·is (hō′mə·tak′sis, hom′ə-) *n.* **1** Classification in the same category. **2** *Geol.* The assignment to the same period in the life history of the earth of those groups of strata exhibiting the same general faunal characteristics, however widely separated from one another geographically; similarity of fossil formations. —**ho′mo·tax′i·al, ho′·mo·tax′ic** *adj.* —**ho′mo·tax′i·al·ly** *adv.*

ho·mo·thal·lic (hō′mə·thal′ik, hom′ə-) *adj. Bot.* Designating that condition of the mold fungi in which the sexual gametes which conjugate arise from the same mycelium: opposed to *heterothallic.* [< Gk. *homos* same + *thallos* branch]

ho·mo·ther·mal (hō′mə·thûr′məl, hom′ə-) *adj.* Homoiothermal.

ho·mo·type (hō′mə·tīp) *n. Biol.* A part or organ similar to a preceeding, succeeding, or opposite one in the same animal, as one of the legs or arms. —**ho′mo·typ′ic** (-tip′ik) or **·i·cal** *adj.*

ho·mo·ty·py (hō′mə·tī′pē) *n. Biol.* The correspondence of a part or organ of one region with that of another in the same animal.

homo vul·ga·is (vul·gā′ris) *n. Latin* The average or common man.

ho·mo·zy·go·sis (hō′mə·zī·gō′sis, -zi-, hom′ə-) *n. Biol.* The formation of a homozygote by the union of gametes.

ho·mo·zy·gote (hō′mə·zī′gōt, -zig′ōt, hom′ə-) *n. Biol.* A zygote formed by the conjugation of two gametes having the same genetic factors; a homozygous individual. See HETEROZYGOTE.

ho·mo·zy·gous (hō′mə·zī′gəs, hom′ə-) *adj. Biol.* Designating that condition of an individual in which any given genetic factor is doubly present, due usually to conjugating gametes which were alike in respect to this factor. [<HOMO- + Gk. *zygōsis* joining < *zygon* a yoke]

Homs (hôms) A city on the Orontes in western Syria: ancient *Emesa.*

ho·mun·cu·lus (hō·mung′kyə·ləs) *n. pl.* **·li** (-lī) **1** According to Paracelsus, a tiny man produced artificially and endowed with magic power. **2** An undersized man; dwarf; manikin. **3** The human fetus. [<L, dim. of *homo* man] —**ho·mun′cu·lar** *adj.*

ho·my (hō′mē) See HOMEY.

Ho·nan (hō′nän′) *n.* A fine Chinese silk, sometimes distinguished by blue edges.

Ho·nan (hō′nän′) A province of north central China; 55,000 square miles; capital, Kaifeng.

Hon·do (hon·dō) See HONSHU.

Hon·du·ran (hon·dŏŏr′ən, -dyŏŏr′-) *adj.* Of or relating to Honduras. —*n.* A native or inhabitant of Honduras.

Hon·du·ras (hon·dŏŏr′əs, -dyŏŏr′-) A republic of NE Central America; 43,278 square miles; capital, Tegucigalpa.

Honduras, British See BRITISH HONDURAS.

Honduras, Gulf of An inlet of the Caribbean Sea in Honduras, British Honduras, and Guatemala. Also **Bay of Honduras.**

hone[1] (hōn) *n.* A block of fine compact stone for sharpening edged tools, razors, etc. —*v.t.* **honed, hon·ing** To sharpen, as a razor, on a hone. [OE *hān* stone]

hone[2] (hōn) *v.i.* **honed, hon·ing** *Dial.* **1** To pine; long for. **2** To moan; grumble. [<F *hogner* mutter]

Ho·neg·ger (hō′neg·ər, *Fr.* ô·ne·gâr′), **Arthur,** 1892–1955, French composer.

hon·est (on′ist) *adj.* **1** Fair and candid in dealing with others; true; just; upright; trustworthy. **2** Chaste; virtuous. **3** Free from fraud; equitable; fair. **4** Of respectable quality or appearance; creditable; unimpeached. **5** Characterized by openness or sincerity; frank. [<OF *honeste* <L *honestus* <*honos* honor] —**hon′est·ly** *adv.*

Synonyms: candid, equitable, fair, faithful, frank, genuine, good, honorable, ingenuous, just, sincere, straightforward, true, trustworthy, trusty, upright. One who is *honest* in the ordinary sense is disposed to act with regard for the rights of others, especially in matters of business or property; one who is *honorable* scrupulously observes the dictates of a personal honor that is higher than any demands of mercantile law or public opinion. Compare CANDID, JUST, MORAL, RIGHT, VIRTUOUS. *Antonyms*: deceitful, dishonest, disingenuous, faithless, false, fraudulent, hypocritical, lying, mendacious, perfidious, traitorous, treacherous, unfaithful, unscrupulous, untrue.

hone·stone (hōn′stōn′) *n.* **1** Any fine-grained stone from which hones are made, as novaculite. **2** A hone.

hon·es·ty (on′is·tē) *n.* **1** The character or quality of being honest; uprightness of conduct in general; justice; fairness. **2** Chastity; virtue. **3** An ornamental garden plant (*Lundria annua*) of the mustard family.

hone·wort (hōn′wûrt′) *n.* Any of a number of plants formerly believed to have medicinal properties, as the stone parsley, goldenrod, etc.

hon·ey (hun′ē) *n.* **1** A sweet, sirupy secretion, deposited by bees and derived chiefly from the nectaries of flowers. **2** Sweetness or lusciousness in general. **3** Sweet one: a pet name. —*v.* **hon·eyed** or **hon·ied, hon·ey·ing** —*v.t.* **1** To talk in an endearing or flattering manner to. **2** To sweeten. —*v.i.* **3** To talk fondly or in a coaxing manner. —*adj.* Honey-like; sweet. [OE *hunig*]

honey ant A small ant of the SW United States (genus *Myrmecocystus*), having one form of worker which receives and stores in its abdomen the honey gathered by the other workers.

honey bag The receptacle or dilatation of the esophagus in which the bee carries honey. Also **honey sac.**

hon·ey-balls (hun′ē·bôlz′) *n. pl. U.S. Dial.* The spherical, white flower heads of the buttonbush.

honey bee A bee that collects honey; specifically, the common hive bee (*Apis mellifera*).

hon·ey·comb (hun′ē·kōm′) *n.* **1** A structure of hexagonal waxen cells, made by bees to contain honey, eggs, etc. **2** Anything full of small holes or cells. —*v.t.* **1** To fill with small holes or passages. **2** To pervade; corrupt. —*v.i.* **3** To become full of holes or passages. [OE *hunigcamb*] —**hon′ey·combed′** *adj.*

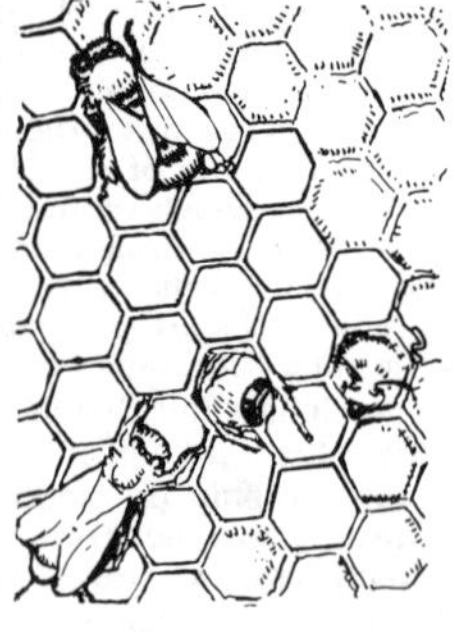

HONEYCOMB

honeycomb moth A moth (*Galleria mellonella*) that infests beehives; bee moth. Also called *waxworm.*

honey creeper A small, brightly colored bird (family *Coeribidae*) of the warmer parts of America; the guitguit.

hon·ey·dew (hun′ē·dōō′, -dyōō′) *n.* **1** A sweet secretion of plants or insects, as of aphids. **2** A honeydew melon. **3** A light pinkish orange. —**hon′ey·dewed′** *adj.*

honeydew melon A variety of muskmelon with a smooth white skin and sweet pulp.

hon·ey-eat·er (hun′ē·ē′tər) *n.* One of several Australian oscine birds (family *Meliphagidae*) which extract honey from flowers.

hon·eyed (hun′ēd) *adj.* **1** Covered with or full of honey. **2** Sweet; hence, soothing; agreeable; sweetly flattering. Also spelled *honied.* —**hon′eyed·ly** *adv.* —**hon′eyed·ness** *n.*

honey guide A small plain-colored bird of Africa, Asia, and the East Indies (genera *Indicator* and *Prodotiscus*) said to lead persons to the nests of wild bees.

honey locust A large, thorny North American tree (*Gleditsia triacanthos*) of the bean family, bearing long pods with a sweet pulp between the seeds.

honey lotus See under MELILOT.

honey mesquite See under MESQUITE.

hon·ey·moon (hun′ē·mōōn) *n.* **1** A wedding trip. **2** The first month or so after marriage.

honey mouse A small marsupial of southern Australia (family *Phalangeridae*) with a long, pointed nose and extensible tongue. It feeds on nectar and small insects.

hon·ey·pot (hun′ē·pot′) *n.* A receptacle, of wax or other substance, made by many species of wild bees to store their honey.

honey shucks The beans of the honey locust.

hon·ey·stone (hun′ē·stōn′) *n.* A soft, yellowish or reddish aluminum mineral having a resinous appearance and crystallizing in the octahedral system: also called *mellite.*

hon·ey·suck·er (hun′ē·suk′ər) See HONEY-EATER.

hon·ey·suck·le (hun′ē·suk′əl) *n.* **1** Any of a genus (*Lonicera*) of ornamental erect or climbing shrubs having tubular white, buff, or crimson flowers. **2** Any one of a number of other plants, as the bush honeysuckle. [OE *hunisūce*]

honeysuckle pattern The anthemion.

honey tree **1** A honey locust. **2** A hollow tree in which wild bees have stored honey.

honey yellow A soft yellow, as of honey.

Hon·fleur (ôn·flœr′) A port of the Seine estuary opposite Le Havre, NW France.

hong (hong, hông) *n.* **1** A mercantile warehouse in China, comprising a number of connecting rooms; also, a connected row of warehouses. **2** A foreign trading establishment in China. [<Chinese *hang* row of houses, mercantile association]

Hong Kong (hong′kong′, hông′ kông′) A British crown colony in SE China; 391 square miles, comprising **Hong Kong Island** (32 square miles), Kowloon peninsula, and the New Territories; capital, Victoria on Hong Kong Island; under Japanese occupation, 1941–45.

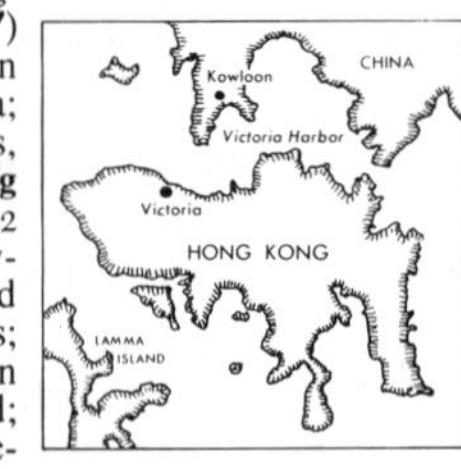

Ho·ni·a·ra (hō′nē·ä′rä) A coast town of NW Guadalcanal, capital of the British Solomon Islands protectorate.

hon·ied (hun′ēd) See HONEYED.

ho·ni soit qui mal y pense (ô·nē swà′ kē màl ē päṅs′) *French* Evil be to him who evil thinks: motto of the Order of the Garter.

honk (hôngk, hongk) *n.* The cry of a wild goose or a sound imitating it, as that of an automobile horn. —*v.i.* To utter or make a honk or honks. —*v.t.* To cause to emit a honk or honks, as an automobile horn. [Imit.]

honk·er (hông′kər, hong′-) *n.* **1** A wild goose. **2** One who honks.

hon·ky (hông′kē, hungk′ē) *n. pl.* **·kies** *U.S. Slang* A white man: an offensive term. Also **hon′kie.** [? <HUNKY. See BOHUNK.]

hon·ky-tonk (hông′kē·tôngk′, hong′kē·tongk′) *n. Slang* A noisy, low-class barroom or night club. [Prob. imit.]

Hon·o·lu·lu (hon′ə·lōō′lōō) A port on SE Oahu; capital of Hawaii.

hon·or (on′ər) *n.* **1** Consideration due or paid, as to worth; respectful regard. **2** Any outward token of such feeling, such as college distinctions. **3** A nice sense of what is right. **4** That to which respect is due; a cause of esteem. **5** A title used in addressing judges, mayors, etc.: used with a possessive pronoun: *his honor,* the mayor. **6** In whist, one of the four highest trump cards; in bridge, one of the five highest cards of the trump suit, or one of the four aces when there are no trumps. **7** In golf, the privilege of playing first from the tee. See synonyms under FAME, JUSTICE, REVERENCE, VIRTUE. —**to do the honors** To act as host. —*v.t.* **1** To regard with honor or respect; treat with courtesy or respect. **2** To worship. **3** To do honor to; dignify; ennoble. **4** To accept or pay, as a check or draft. See synonyms under ADMIRE, VENERATE, WORSHIP. —*adj.* Having received recognition for outstanding academic work: an *honor* student. Also, *Brit.,* **hon′our.** [<OF <L] —**hon′or·er** *n.*

Ho·no·ra (ə·nôr′ə, ə·nō′rə) A feminine personal name. Also **Ho·no·ri·a** (ə·nôr′ē·ə, ə·nō′·rē·ə). [<L, honor]

hon·or·a·ble (on′ər·ə·bəl) *adj.* **1** Worthy of honor, in any degree from simple respectability to eminence; creditable; estimable; illustrious. **2** Conferring honor. **3** Consistent with or acting in accordance with principles of honor; conforming to a code of honor. **4** Betokening honor; accompanied by marks or testimonials of honor: *honorable* burial. **5** Entitled to honor: formal epithet of respect prefixed to the names of persons holding important offices. See synonyms under GOOD, HONEST, ILLUSTRIOUS, JUST, MORAL. Also *Brit.* **hon′our·a·ble.** —**hon′or·a·ble·ness** *n.* —**hon′·or·a·bly** *adv.*

hon·o·rar·i·um (on′ə·râr′ē·əm) *n. pl.* **·i·ums** or **·i·a** A gratuity given, as to a professional man, for services rendered when law, custom, or propriety forbids a set fee. See synonyms under SALARY. [<L *honorarium (donum)* honorary (gift), neut. of *honorarius* honorary]

hon·or·ar·y (on′ə·rer′ē) *adj.* **1** Done, conferred, or held merely as an honor. **2** Designating an office or title bestowed as a sign of honor, without emoluments or without powers or duties. **3** Depending solely on one's honor: said of a debt or other obligation not legally binding. [<L *honorarius*]

Ho·no·ré (ô·nô·rā′) A French masculine personal name. [<F, honored]

hon·or·if·ic (on′ə·rif′ik) *adj.* **1** Conferring or implying honor or respect. **2** Denoting certain phrases, words, or word elements, as in Oriental languages, used in respectful address. —*n.* Any honorific title, word, phrase, etc. [<L *honorificus* <*honor* + *facere* make] —**hon′or·if′i·cal·ly** *adv.*

Ho·no·ri·us (hə·nôr′ē·əs, -nō′rē-), **Flavius Augustus,** 384–423, emperor of the Western (Roman) Empire 395–423.

honor point *Her.* The point just above the fess point. See illustration under ESCUTCHEON.

honors of war Marks of respect or honorable terms granted to a capitulating force.

honors system In some colleges and universities, a plan of advanced study for selected students, in which the student is excused from classroom routine to undertake individual, specialized work.

honor system A system of administering examinations and schoolwork without supervision and relying upon the honor of the students not to cheat.

Hon·shu (hon·shōō) The largest island of Japan; 88,745 square miles, including outlying islands; capital, Tokyo: also *Hondo.*

hooch (hōōch) *n. U.S. Slang* Intoxicating liquor. Also spelled *hootch.* [< *hoochinoo,* alter. of *Hutanuwu,* name of Alaskan Indian tribe that made liquor]

Hooch (hōkh), **Pieter de,** 1629–77?, Dutch painter.

hood[1] (hŏŏd) *n.* **1** A soft or flexible covering for the head and the back of the neck. **2** Anything of similar form or character. **3** A monk's cowl. **4** An ornamental fold attached to the back of an academic gown. **5** In falconry, a cover for the entire head of a hawk. **6** A projecting cover to a hearth, forge, or ventilator. **7** The movable cover of a machine, as of the engine of an automobile. **8** *Biol.* A concave expansion of any organ, resembling a hood; a crest. — *v.t.* To cover or furnish with or as with a hood. [OE *hōd*]

hood[2] (hŏŏd) *n. U.S. Slang* A hoodlum. [< HOODLUM]

-hood *suffix of nouns* **1** Condition of; state of being: *babyhood, falsehood.* **2** Class or totality of those having a certain character: *priesthood.* [OE *had* state, condition]

Hood (hŏŏd), **John Bell,** 1831–79, American Confederate general. — **Samuel,** 1724–1816, first Viscount Hood, English admiral. — **Thomas,** 1799–1845, English poet and humorist. — **Robin** See ROBIN HOOD.

Hood (hŏŏd), **Mount** A volcanic peak in the Cascade Range, NW Oregon; 11,245 feet.

hood·ed (hŏŏd′id) *adj.* **1** Wearing or having a hood. **2** Shaped like a hood. **3** Having a hoodlike part. **4** *Ornithol.* A conspicuous patch of feathers on the head of a bird. **5** *Zool.* The folds of skin near the head of certain animals and capable of voluntary expansion, as in the cobra and certain other snakes.

hooded seal One of the more abundant seals of the North Atlantic *(Cystophora cristata).* The males have an inflatable bag on the top of the head.

hood·er (hŏŏd′ər) *n. Brit.* The top sheaf of a shock of grain; hence, a finishing touch.

hood·ie (hŏŏd′ē) *n. Scot.* The hooded crow of Europe *(Corvus cornix).*

hood·lum (hŏŏd′ləm) *n. U.S.* One of a class of street rowdies; any ruffian or rowdy. [? < dial. G *hodalum* a rowdy] — **hood′lum·ism** *n.*

hood·man (hŏŏd′mən) *n. pl.* **·men** (-mən) The person blindfolded in the game of **hoodman-blind,** an old form of blindman's-buff.

hoo·doo (hōō′dōō) *n.* **1** Voodoo. **2** *Colloq.* A person or thing that brings bad luck; a jinx. — *v.t. Colloq.* To bring bad luck to; bewitch. [Var. of VOODOO] — **hoo′doo·ism** *n.*

Hood River A city on the Columbia River in northern Oregon.

hood·wink (hŏŏd′wingk′) *v.t.* **1** To deceive as if by blinding; impose upon; delude. **2** To blindfold. **3** *Obs.* To cover; conceal. [<HOOD + WINK] — **hood′wink′er** *n.*

hoo·ey (hōō′ē) *n.* & *interj. U.S. Slang* Nonsense.

hoof (hŏŏf, hōōf) *n. pl.* **hoofs** (*Rare* **hooves**) **1** The horny sheath incasing the ends of the digits or foot in various mammals. ◆ Collateral adjective: *ungular.* **2** An animal with hoofs. — **cloven hoof** The sign of Satan. — **on the hoof** Alive; not butchered: said of cattle. — *v.t.* & *v.i.* **1** To trample with the hoofs. **2** *Colloq.* To walk or dance: usually with *it.* [OE *hōf*] — **hoofed** (hŏŏft, hōōft) *adj.*

hoof-and-mouth disease (hŏŏf′ən·mouth′) See FOOT-AND-MOUTH DISEASE.

hoof-bound (hŏŏf′bound′, hōōf′-) *adj.* Having a contraction of the hoof, causing pain and lameness.

hoof·er (hŏŏf′ər, hōōf′-) *n. U.S. Slang* A professional dancer, especially a tap dancer.

hoof·print (hŏŏf′print′, hōōf′-) *n.* The print left by a hoof on the ground; a track.

hook (hŏŏk) *n.* **1** A curved or bent piece serving to catch or hold another object. **2** A tool in hooked form; especially, a sickle. **3** *Music* The flag-shaped projection from the stem of an eighth note, or one of still shorter duration. **4** A hook-shaped part, as of a written character. **5** The act of hooking. **6** Something that catches or snares; a trap. **7** In golf, a shot in which the ball deviates to the side on which the player stands. **8** In baseball, a sharp-breaking curve. **9** In boxing, a short blow delivered in a swinging manner crosswise and with the elbow bent and rigid. **10** A bend in a river; a point of land; a cape: Sandy *Hook.* See synonyms under LOCK. — **by hook or by crook** In one way or another. — **on one's own hook** **1** By oneself. **2** On one's own authority. — *v.t.* **1** To fasten, attach, or take hold of with or as with a hook. **2** To catch on or with a hook, as fish. **3** To trick; take in: I've been *hooked.* **4** To make or bend in the shape of a hook; crook. **5** To catch on or toss with the horns: said of bulls, etc. **6** To make, as a rug, by looping thread, yarn, etc., through burlap with a hook. **7** *Slang* To steal; pilfer. **8** In baseball, to throw (a ball) with a hook. **9** In boxing, to strike with a hook. **10** In golf, to drive (the ball) in a hook. — *v.i.* **11** To curve like a hook; bend. **12** To be fastened with a hook. — **to hook up** **1** To fasten or attach with hooks. **2** To put together, as the parts of a machine. — **to hook up to** To connect (apparatus) to a source of power: The trailer was *hooked up to* the car. — **to hook up with** *Colloq.* To join; become a companion or adherent of. [OE *hōc*]

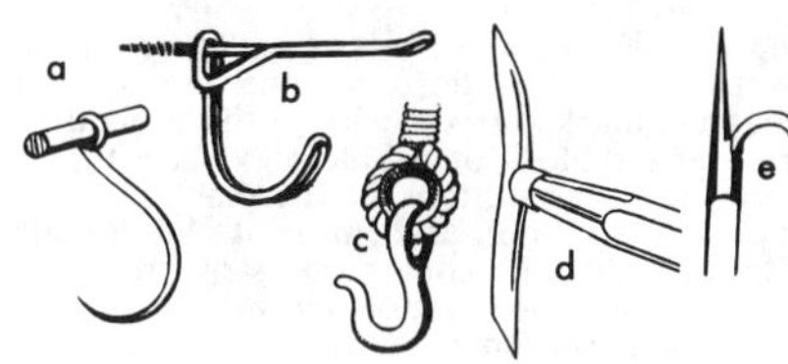

HOOKS
a. Box hook. *b.* Coat hook. *c.* Eyehook. *d.* Ice hook. *e.* Boat hook.

hook·ah (hŏŏk′ə) *n.* In India and Iran, a form of tobacco pipe by which the smoke is drawn through water; a narghile. Also **hook′a.** [< Arabic *ḥuqqah*]

hook-and-lad·der (hŏŏk′ən·lad′ər) *n.* A vehicle, equipped with ladders for effecting rescues, and hooks, axes, etc., for tearing down walls, used by fire departments. Also **hook-and-ladder truck.**

Hooke (hŏŏk), **Robert,** 1635–1703, English physicist.

hooked (hŏŏkt) *adj.* **1** Curved like a hook. **2** Supplied with a hook. **3** Made with a hook. — **hook·ed·ness** (hŏŏk′id·nis) *n.*

hook·er[1] (hŏŏk′ər) *n.* **1** A two-masted Dutch vessel. **2** A fishing boat used on the English and Irish coasts. **3** An old or clumsy craft. [<Du. *hoeker* <*hoek* hook]

hook·er[2] (hŏŏk′ər) *n. Slang* A drink, especially an alcoholic one. [<HOOK, prob. with ref. to the bend of the arm in drinking]

hook·er[3] (hŏŏk′ər) *n. Slang* A prostitute. [from Corlears *Hook,* formerly a notorious waterfront district in Manhattan]

Hook·er (hŏŏk′ər), **Joseph,** 1814–79, Union general in the American Civil War. — **Sir Joseph Dalton,** 1817–1911, English botanist. — **Richard,** 1554?–1600, English theologian. — **Thomas,** 1586?–1647, English clergyman, one of the founders of Connecticut. — **Sir William Jackson,** 1785–1865, English botanist; father of Sir J. D. Hooker.

Hooker's green A green pigment composed of Prussian blue and gamboge.

Hooke's law (hŏŏks) *Physics* The law that the elastic distortion of a body under stress is proportional to the stress producing the distortion. [after Robert *Hooke*]

hook, line, and sinker Completely; without question or reservation.

hook-nose (hŏŏk′nōz′) *n.* An aquiline nose, or a person having such a nose. — **hook′-nosed′** *adj.*

Hook of Holland A headland and harbor of SW Netherlands: Dutch *Hoek van Holland.*

hook·up (hŏŏk′up′) *n.* **1** *Telecom.* **a** The assembled apparatus for a radio broadcast or other electrical transmission. **b** The diagram giving the connections for such transmission. **2** A mechanical connection, as of gas or water lines. **3** *Colloq.* An alliance or pact between governments, organizations, etc.

hook·worm (hŏŏk′wûrm′) *n.* Any of various nematode worms of the genera *Ancylostoma, Necator,* etc., infesting man and several animals, such as sheep, dogs, cattle, etc.

hookworm disease Ancylostomiasis.

hook·y[1] (hŏŏk′ē) *adj.* Full of hooks, pertaining to hooks, or like a hook.

hook·y[2] (hŏŏk′ē) *n. U.S. Colloq.* The condition of being illegitimately absent, truant, etc.: used only in the phrase **to play hooky,** to be a truant. [<HOOK, in dial. sense of "make off"]

hoo·li·gan (hōō′lə·gən) *n.* A hoodlum; a gangster. [after *Hooligan,* name of an Irish family in London] — **hoo′li·gan·ism** *n.*

hoop[1] (hōōp, hŏŏp) *n.* **1** A circular band of stiff material, especially one used to confine the staves of a barrel, cask, etc. **2** A child's toy in the shape of a large circular ring of metal or wood that is trundled along the ground. **3** A large ring of flexible material used for expanding a woman's skirt. **4** The band of a finger ring. **5** An arched wicket in croquet. **6** Anything shaped like a ring or band. — *v.t.* **1** To surround or fasten with hoops, as a cask. **2** To encircle. [OE *hōp*]

hoop[2] (hōōp) *n.* **1** A whoop; shout. **2** The sound made in whooping cough. — *v.t.* & *v.i.* To whoop. [Var. of WHOOP]

hoop·er (hōō′pər, hŏŏp′ər) *n.* One who hoops casks or tubs; a cooper.

Hoop·er·at·ing (hōō′pə·rā′ting) *n.* A rating of the popularity of television or radio programs or performers by means of telephone interviews with a sample poll of listeners taken during the performance: given in terms of millions of estimated listeners. Also **Hoop·er rating** (hōō′pər). [after Claude E. *Hooper,* 1898–1954, U. S. statistician]

hoop·ing (hōō′ping, hŏŏp′ing) *n.* **1** Material from which to make hoops; also, hoops in general. **2** A system of hoops, as on some breechloading guns.

hoop·la (hōōp′lä) *n. U.S. Slang* Excitement; fervor. [Orig., a coach driver's exclamation]

hoop·le (hōō′pəl) *n.* A child's hoop.

hoo·poe (hōō′pōō) *n.* An Old World bird (family *Upupidae*), having a long, pointed, curved bill and an erectile crest. Also **hoo′poo.** [<F *huppe* <L *upupa*]

HOOPOE
(About 12 inches long; bill: 2 1/2 inches)

hoop skirt A framework of hoops or crinoline for expanding a skirt; also, the skirt itself.

hoop snake A harmless snake of the southern United States *(Abastor erythrogrammus)*: formerly believed to take its tail in its mouth and roll like a hoop.

hoo·ray (hōō·rā′, hə-, hōō-) See HURRAH.

hoord (hōrd) *v.t.* & *v.i. Scot.* To hoard. — **hoord′et** (-it) *adj.*

Hoo·sac Range (hōō′sək) A spur of the Green Mountains in western Massachusetts; highest point, 3,000 feet; pierced by the **Hoosac Tunnel,** a railway tunnel 25,000 feet long.

hoose (hōōs) *n. Scot.* A house.

hoose·gow (hōōs′gou) *n. U.S. Slang* Jail or prison. Also **hoos′gow.** [<Sp. *juzgado* tribunal]

Hoo·sier (hōō′zhər) *n. U.S.* A native or citizen of the **Hoosier State,** a nickname for Indiana. [Prob. <dial. *hoosier* mountaineer, in ref. to Kentucky settlers in southern part of the State]

hoot (hōōt) *v.i.* **1** To jeer or call out, as in contempt or disapproval. **2** To utter the low, hollow cry of an owl. — *v.t.* **3** To jeer at or mock with hooting cries. **4** To drive off with shouts of contempt, disapproval, etc. **5** To express by hooting. — *n.* **1** A cry uttered in derision. **2** The cry of an owl. **3** *Slang* A whit: not worth a *hoot.* [<Scand. Cf. Sw. *huta.*]

hootch (hōōch) See HOOCH.

hoot·chy-koot·chy (ho͞o′chē·ko͞o′chē) *n. U.S. Slang* A suggestive dance involving much hip and abdominal movement. [Origin unknown]

hoot·en·an·ny (ho͞ot′n·an′ē) *n. Slang* A gathering of folk singers. [Origin unknown]

hoot owl An owl that hoots, especially the American northern barred owl (*Strix varia*).

Hoo·ver (ho͞o′vər), **Herbert Clark,** 1874–1964, president of the United States 1929–33. — **J(ohn) Edgar,** 1895–1972, U.S. criminologist; director of the Federal Bureau of Investigation 1924–1972.

Hoover Dam A dam in the Colorado River on the Arizona–Nevada border, forming Lake Mead; 727 feet high; 1,282 feet long: formerly *Boulder Dam.*

Hoo·ver·ville (ho͞o′vər·vil) *n.* Any group of ramshackle huts, usually on the outskirts of a town, in which the jobless camped during the depression of the early 1930's. [after Herbert *Hoover* + *-ville* city, town]

hooves (ho͞ovz, ho͝ovz) Alternative plural of HOOF.

hooy (hoi) See HOY[2].

hop[1] (hop) *v.* **hopped, hop·ping** *v.i.* **1** To move in short leaps with the feet off the ground. **2** To jump about on one foot. — *v.t.* **3** To jump over, as a fence. **4** To board or catch; get on: to *hop* a train. See synonyms under LEAP. — *n.* **1** The act or result of hopping. **2** *Colloq.* A dance or dancing party. **3** *Colloq.* An ascent, flight, or trip in an airplane. [OE *hoppian*]

hop[2] (hop) *n.* **1** A perennial climbing herb (*Humulus lupulus*) with opposite lobed leaves and scaly fruit. **2** *pl.* The ripe and carefully dried multiple fruit of this plant: used in the brewing of beer and in medicine as an aromatic bitter stomachic. [<MDu. *hoppe*]

hop·cal·ite (hop′kəl·īt) *n.* A granular mixture of the oxides of copper, cobalt, manganese, and silver: effective as a catalyzing material to protect against carbon monoxide. [< (*Johns*) *Hop*(*kins University*) + (*University of*) *Cal*(*ifornia*) + -ITE[1]]

hop clover Yellow clover (*Trifolium procumbens*) whose dried flowers resemble hops.

hope (hōp) *v.* **hoped, hop·ing** *v.t.* **1** To desire with expectation of fulfilment: I *hope* to be able to join you. **2** To wish; want: I *hope* that you will be happy. — *v.i.* **3** To have desire or expectation: usually with *for*: to *hope* for the best. See synonyms under ANTICIPATE, TRUST. — *n.* **1** Desire accompanied by expectation. **2** The cause of hopeful expectation. **3** The thing confidently desired or hoped for. — **in hopes** Having hope. See synonyms under TRUST. [OE *hopa*]

Hope (hōp), **Anthony** See HAWKINS, ANTHONY HOPE.

hope chest A box or chest used by young women to hold linen, clothing, etc., in anticipation of marriage.

hope·ful (hōp′fəl) *adj.* **1** Full of hope; promising. **2** Having qualities that excite hope. See synonyms under AUSPICIOUS, SANGUINE. — *n.* A young person who seems likely to succeed in life: a humorous or ironic use. — **hope′ful·ness** *n.*

hope·ful·ly (hōp′fə·lē) *adv.* **1** In a hopeful manner. **2** It is hoped; one hopes: *Hopefully,* a strike can be averted.

Ho·peh (hō′pā′) A province in NE China; 50,000 square miles; capital, Paoting: formerly *Chihli.* Also **Ho′pei′.**

hope·less (hōp′lis) *adj.* **1** Without hope; despairing. **2** Affording no ground of hope. — **hope′less·ly** *adv.* — **hope′less·ness** *n.*

hope·sick (hōp′sik′) *adj.* Sick at heart with unfulfilled hope or ungratified longing.

Ho·pi (hō′pē) *n.* **1** One of a group of North American Pueblo Indians of Shoshonean linguistic stock: now on a reservation in NE Arizona: also called *Moqui* or *Moki.* **2** Their Shoshonean language. [<Hopi *hópitu,* lit., peaceful ones]

Hop·kins (hop′kinz), **Sir Frederick Gowland,** 1861–1947, English biochemist. — **Gerard Manley,** 1844–89, English poet. — **Harry Lloyd,** 1890–1946, U. S. statesman; advisor to President F. D. Roosevelt. — **Johns,** 1795–1873, U. S. financier and philanthropist. — **Mark,** 1802–87, U. S. educator.

Hop·kin·son (hop′kin·sən), **Francis,** 1737–91, American writer; signed the Declaration of Independence.

hop·lite (hop′līt) *n.* In ancient Greece, a heavily armed foot soldier. [<Gk. *hoplitēs* <*hoplon* a shield]

hop-o'-my-thumb (hop′ə·mī·thum′) *n.* A very small person. [after *Hop-o'-my-thumb,* tiny hero of a fairy tale by Perrault]

hopped-up (hopt′up′) *adj. U.S. Slang* **1** Stimulated by a narcotic drug. **2** Excited; exhilarated. **3** Supercharged for high speed: said of an automobile. [? <HOP[2]]

hop·per (hop′ər) *n.* **1** One who or that which hops. **2** A saltatorial insect or larva, as a grasshopper or the larva of a fly that infests cheese. **3** A shaking or conveying receiver, funnel, or trough in which something is placed to be passed or fed, as to a mill. **4** A funnel-shaped spout or tank with a movable bottom or no bottom, as for conveying grain to cars. **5** A tilting, dumping, or discharging bottom or receptacle, as in a car or boat. **6** A tank or boxlike receptacle for holding water, grain, sugar, etc., which may be emptied by opening its bottom.

hopper car A car for coal, gravel, etc., with an opening to discharge the contents.

hop·ple (hop′əl) *v.t.* **·pled, ·pling** To hamper; hobble. — *n.* A fetter for the legs of a horse, etc. [Var. of HOBBLE]

hop·sack·ing (hop′sak′ing) *n.* A coarse fabric with rough surface: used for dresses, etc. [<HOP[2] + SACK]

hop·scotch (hop′skoch′) *n.* A child's game in which the player hops on one foot over a diagram marked (scotched) on the ground to recover the block or pebble previously tossed into successive sections of the diagram.

hop, skip (or **step**), **and jump** **1** An athletic feat in which the contestants strive to cover as much distance as possible in a successive hop, step, and jump. **2** A short distance or interval.

hop trefoil **1** Hop clover. **2** Black medic.

Hor (hôr), **Mount** A mountain in SW Jordan; 4,430 feet.

Hor·ace (hôr′is, hor′-) A masculine personal name: see HORATIO. Also *Fr.* **Ho·race** (ô·räs′), **Ho·ra·ci·o** (*Pg.* ô·rä′sē·o͞o, *Sp.* ō·rä′thē·ō). [<L, light of the sun, keeper of the hours] — **Horace** Anglicized name of *Quintus Horatius Flaccus,* 65–8 B.C., Roman poet. — **Ho·ra·tian** (hə·rā′shən) *adj.*

Ho·rae (hō′rē) In Greek mythology, the three goddesses of natural order and the seasons.

ho·ral (hō′rəl) *adj.* Pertaining to an hour; hourly. [<L *hora* hour]

ho·rar·i·ous (hō·râr′ē·əs) *adj. Bot.* Lasting but one or two hours: said of flowers. [<L *hor*(*a*) hour + -ARIOUS]

ho·ra·ry (hō′rə·rē) *adj.* **1** Pertaining to an hour; designating the hours. **2** Continuing only an hour; occurring hourly. **3** In astrology, referring to propitious or specific times. [<L *hora* hour]

Ho·ra·ti·i (hə·rā′shē·ī) In Roman legend, three Roman brothers who fought and killed the Curiatii, three brothers from Alba Longa.

Ho·ra·ti·o (hə·rā′shē·ō, -shō) A masculine personal name. Also **Ho·ra·ti·us** (*Du.* hô·rä′sē·o͞os, *Ger.* hô·rä′tsē·o͞os, *Lat.* hô·rā′shē·əs), *Dan.* **Ho·rats** (hô·räts′). [See HORACE] — **Horatio** In Shakespeare's *Hamlet,* the close friend of Hamlet.

Ho·ra·tius Co·cles (hə·rā′shəs kō′klēz) In Roman legend, a hero who with two comrades held the bridge over the Tiber against the Etruscan army.

horde (hôrd, hōrd) *n.* **1** A clan or tribe of Mongolian, especially Tatar, nomads; hence, any nomadic group. **2** A multitude; a pack or swarm, as of men, animals, or insects. — **Golden Horde** A fierce and powerful Mongol horde, named from the golden tent of Batu Khan, under whose lead they laid waste eastern Europe in the 13th century; the Kipchaks. — *v.i.* **hord·ed, hord·ing** To gather in a horde. ◆ Homophone: *hoard.* [<F <G <Polish *horda* <Turkish *ordū* camp. Related to URDU.]

hor·de·in (hôr′dē·in, hōr′-) *n. Biochem.* An alcohol-soluble protein from barley: of the prolamine group of simple proteins. [<L *hordeum* barley]

hor·de·nine (hôr′də·nēn, -nin, hōr′-) *n.* A white, crystalline, almost tasteless alkaloid, $C_{10}H_{15}ON$, obtained from malt sprouts: its sulfate is used in the treatment of diarrhea and as a heart stimulant. [<L *hordeum* barley + -INE[2]]

Hor·de·um (hôr′dē·əm, hōr′-) *n.* A genus of true grasses, one species of which is the cultivated barley. [<L]

hore (hôr, hōr) *Obs.* See HOAR.

Ho·reb (hō′reb) The mountain where the law was given to Moses; generally identified with Mount Sinai. *Ex.* iii 1.

hore·hound (hôr′hound′, hōr′-) *n.* **1** A whitish, bitter, perennial herb of the mint family (genus *Marrubium*): used as a remedy for colds. **2** A candy flavored with an extract of this herb. **3** One of various allied plants. Also spelled *hoarhound.* [OE *harhune*]

Hor·i·con (hôr′i·kon, hor′-), **Lake** Lake George in the novels of J. Fenimore Cooper.

ho·ri·zon (hə·rī′zən) *n.* **1** The line of the apparent meeting of earth or sea and sky: called the **local** or **visible horizon. 2** The bounds of observation or experience. **3** *Astron.* **a** The plane passing through a position on the earth's surface at right angles to the line of gravity: called the **sensible horizon. b** The great circle in which the sensible horizon cuts the celestial sphere: called the **celestial, geometric, rational,** or **true horizon. 4** *Geol.* **a** A definite position in the stratigraphic column, or in the scheme of classification of strata according to age. **b** A bed or limited number of beds characterized by one or more distinctive fossils; a zone. **5** One of the layers in a cross-section of soil. **6** The imaginary line, taking the place of the natural horizon, in a picture of a landscape, on which is projected the point of sight of the viewer. See PERSPECTIVE. [<OF *orizonte* <L *horizon* <Gk. *horizōn* (*kyklos*) bounding (circle), ppr. of *horizein* bound <*horos* limit, bound]

horizon blue A soft gray-blue.

hor·i·zon·tal (hôr′ə·zon′təl, hor′-) *adj.* **1** Parallel to the horizon; on a level. **2** Included or measured in a plane of the horizon. **3** Of, pertaining to, on, or close to the horizon. **4** Equal and uniform: a *horizontal* tariff. **5** Made up of similar units: a *horizontal* trust. — *n.* A line or plane assumed, for the purpose of measurement or description, to be parallel with the horizon. — **hor′i·zon′tal·ly** *adv.*

Synonyms (*adj.*): flat, level, plain, plane. For practical purposes *level* and *horizontal* are identical, but *level* is more loosely used of that which has no especially noticeable elevations or inequalities; as, a *level* road. *Flat* applies to a surface only, and, in the first, most usual sense, to a surface that is *horizontal* or *level* in all directions; *flat* is also applied to any *plane* surface without irregularities or elevations, as a picture may be painted on the *flat* surface of a perpendicular wall. *Plane* applies only to a surface, and is used with more mathematical exactness than *flat. Plain,* originally the same word as *plane,* is now rarely used except in senses pertaining to *level* ground. We speak of a *horizontal* line, a *flat* morass, a *level* road, a *plain* country, a *plane* surface (especially in the scientific sense). See FLAT, LEVEL. *Antonyms*: broken, hilly, inclined, irregular, rolling, rough, rugged, slanting, sloping, uneven.

hor·i·zon·tal·ism (hôr′ə·zon′təl·iz′əm, hor′-) *n.* The character of being horizontal; horizontal extension. — **hor′i·zon·tal′i·ty** (-zon·tal′ə·tē) *n.*

hor·mone (hôr′mōn) *n. Physiol.* An internal secretion, produced in and by one of the endocrine glands; specifically, one of a group of complex chemical compounds evolved in one part of an organism and carried thence by the blood stream or body fluids to other parts, on which it exercises a specific physiological action. Many important hormones are now made synthetically. Compare COLYONE. See ENDOCRINE. [<Gk. *hormōn,* ppr. of *hormaein* excite] — **hor·mo·nal** (hôr·mō′nəl), **hor·mon·ic** (hôr·mon′ik) *adj.*

Hor·muz (hôr′muz) A small island of SE Iran in the **Strait of Hormuz,** a channel connecting the Persian Gulf and the Gulf of Oman: also *Ormuz.*

horn (hôrn) *n.* **1** A hard bonelike growth projecting from the head of various hoofed mammals, as oxen, sheep, cattle, etc.; also, the antler of a deer, shed annually. **2** Any hardened and thickened outgrowth of epidermal tissue, as a feeler, antenna, tentacle, etc. **3** A feather tuft, as on the head of some birds. **4** The appendage like an animal's horn attributed to demons, deities, etc. **5** An imaginary projection from the forehead of a cuckold. **6** The substance of which animal horn consists, as keratin, calcium phosphate, etc. **7** A vessel or implement formed from or shaped like a horn: a powder *horn.* **8** A wind instrument, made formerly of animal horn, now of brass, in the shape of a long tube constricted at one end and widening out to a large bell at the other. **9** *Slang* A trumpet. **10** Any pointed or tapering projection. **11** One of the extremities of a crescent moon. **12** One of the branches forming the delta of a stream. **13** A cape or peninsula. **14** The pommel of a saddle. **15** The point of an anvil. **16** *Aeron.* The lever which operates the wire connecting with the rudder, aileron, or elevator of an aircraft. **17** A hollow conical device with a bell-shaped aperture, for collecting sound waves, as in a sound locator. **18** A device for sounding warning signals: an automobile *horn.* **— on the horns of a dilemma** Forced to choose between two painful alternatives. **— to haul** (or **pull** or **draw**) **in one's horns** To check one's anger, zeal, pretensions, etc. — *adj.* Of horn or horns. — *v.t.* **1** To provide with horns. **2** To shape like a horn. **3** To attack with the horns; gore. **4** *Obs.* To cuckold. **— to horn in** To enter without invitation. [OE. Akin to CORN[2].] **— horn'less** *adj.* **— horn'like'** *adj.*

Horn, Cape The southern extremity of South America, on the last island of the Fuegian archipelago. Also **the Horn.**

horn angle *Geom.* The angle formed by two curved lines tangent to each other at one point.

horn·beam (hôrn'bēm') *n.* A small tree of the birch family (genus *Carpinus*), resembling the beech, with white, hard wood.

horn·bill (hôrn'bil') *n.* A large bird of tropical Asia and Africa, related to the kingfishers (family *Bucerotidae*) and having a large bill surmounted by a hornlike extension.

horn·blende (hôrn'blend) *n.* A common mineral, greenish-black or black, containing iron and silicate of magnesium, calcium, and aluminum. **— horn'blend'ic** *adj.*

hornblende schist A schistose rock consisting essentially of hornblende in parallel layers.

horn·book (hôrn'bo͝ok') *n.* **1** A leaf or page containing a printed alphabet, etc., covered with transparent horn and framed: formerly used in teaching reading to children. **2** A primer or book of rudimentary knowledge.

horn bug The stag beetle.

Horn·church (hôrn'chûrch) An urban district of SW Essex, England.

horned (hôrnd, *Poetic* hôr'nid) *adj.* Having a horn or horns.

horned horse The gnu.

horned owl Any of various American owls with conspicuous ear tufts; especially, the great horned owl or the screech owl.

horned pout A fresh-water catfish of North America (*Ameiurus nebulosus*); one of the bullheads. Also **horn pout.**

horned toad A harmless, flat-bodied, spiny lizard (*Phrynosoma cornutum*) with a very short tail and toad-like appearance: common in semi-arid regions of the western part of the United States: also *horn toad.*

HORNED TOAD
(From 3 to 7 inches long)

horned viper A venomous African or Indian viper (*Cerastes cornutus*) with a horn over each eye.

hor·net (hôr'nit) *n.* Any of various strong-bodied social wasps (family *Vespidae*) capable of inflicting a severe sting; especially, the American bald-faced hornet (*Dolichovespula maculata*) and the European giant hornet (*Vespa crabo*). [OE *hyrnet*]

hornets' nest A nest of hornets; hence, a troubled, angry, and dangerous situation. **— to stir up a hornets' nest** To bring about an angry and dangerous situation, often inadvertently.

horn·fels (hôrn'fels') *n.* A speckled, fine-grained rock produced by the intrusion of granite into slate. [<G, horn rock]

horn fly A small black fly (*Siphona irritans*) that attacks cattle, clustering about their horns, and seriously affects vitality and milk production.

Horn·ie (hôr'nē) See HORNY.

horn·ing (hôr'ning) *n.* **1** *U.S. Dial.* A charivari. **2** The act of one who or that which horns.

hor·ni·to (hôr·nē'tō, *Sp.* ôr·nē'tō) *n. pl.* **·tos** (-tōz, *Sp.* -tōs) A low, oven-shaped fumarole, common in South American volcanic regions. Also **hor'nite** (-nīt). [<Sp., lit., little oven]

horn-mad (hôrn'mad') *adj.* **1** Mad enough to gore: said of a bull. **2** Crazy; insane; wild. **— horn'-mad'ness** *n.*

horn of plenty **1** In Greek mythology, the horn of Amalthea. **2** A symbol of abundance in general, represented in art as a curved horn filled with fruit, etc.: also called *cornucopia.*

horn·pipe (hôrn'pīp') *n.* **1** A lively English country dance. **2** The music of such a dance, or similar music. **3** A musical instrument resembling the clarinet formerly used in England and Wales.

horn-rimmed (hôrn'rimd') *adj.* Having frames of horn or of dark-colored plastic, often relatively thick and heavy: said of spectacles or eyeglasses.

horn silver **1** Fused silver chloride. **2** Cerargyrite.

horn spoon A scoop made of cow horn: used by miners for testing washings.

horn·stone (hôrn'stōn') *n.* Chert.

horn·swog·gle (hôrn'swog'əl) *v.t.* **·gled, ·gling** *Slang* To deceive; bamboozle; cheat.

horn·tail (hôrn'tāl') *n.* A large type of sawfly (family *Siricidae*) with a horn at the end of the abdomen. The larva is a wood borer. For illustration see under INSECT (injurious).

horn toad The horned toad.

horn·work (hôrn'wûrk') *n.* **1** The art of working horn. **2** Objects collectively that are made of horn. **3** *Mil.* A fortification outwork made up of two half bastions connected by a curtain.

horn·worm (hôrn'wûrm') *n.* A caterpillar with a hornlike hind appendage: the larva of a hawk moth.

horn·wort (hôrn'wûrt') *n.* An aquatic herb (*Ceratophyllum demersum*) widely distributed in lakes, ponds, and slow streams.

horn·y (hôr'nē) *adj.* **horn·i·er, horn·i·est** **1** Resembling horn; callous. **2** Made of horn. **3** Having horns. **4** *Slang* Lustful; lecherous.

Horn·y (hôr'nē) *n. Scot.* & *Brit. Dial.* The devil: also spelled *Hornie.*

horn·y-hand·ed (hôr'nē·han'did) *adj.* Having hard or calloused hands.

hor·o·loge (hôr'ə·lōj, hor'-) *n.* **1** A timepiece. **2** A clock tower. [<OF *horloge* <L *horologium* <Gk. *hōrologion* <*hōra* time + *legein* tell]

ho·rol·o·ger (hō·rol'ə·jər, hō-) *n.* One skilled in horology; also, one who makes or sells timepieces. Also **ho·rol'o·gist.**

hor·o·log·ic (hôr'ə·loj'ik, hor'-) *adj.* **1** Pertaining to horology or to a horologe. **2** *Bot.* Opening and closing at certain hours, as some flowers. Also **hor'o·log'i·cal.**

Hor·o·lo·gi·um (hôr'ə·lō'jē·əm, hor'-) A southern constellation, the Clock. See CONSTELLATION.

ho·rol·o·gy (hô·rol'ə·jē, hō-) *n.* The science of time-measurement or of the construction of timepieces.

hor·o·scope (hôr'ə·skōp, hor'-) *n.* **1** In astrology, the aspect of the heavens, with special reference to the positions of the planets at any instant. **2** A figure or statement showing such aspect, from which astrologers profess to foretell the future of an individual. **3** The diagram of the twelve divisions or houses of the heavens, used by astrologers in predicting the future. [<L *horoscopus* <Gk. *hōroskopos* observer of hour of nativity <*hōra* hour + *skopos* watcher <*skopeein* watch]

ho·ros·co·py (hô·ros'kə·pē, hō-) *n.* **1** The art of casting horoscopes or of determining the future from the positions of the heavenly bodies. **2** In astrology, the situation of the heavenly bodies at the time of a person's birth; a horoscope.

Ho·ro·witz (hôr'ə·wits, hor'-; *Russian* hôr'ə·vits), **Vladimir,** born 1904, U. S. pianist born in Russia.

hor·ren·dous (hô·ren'dəs, ho-) *adj.* Frightful; fearful. [<L *horrendus,* gerundive of *horrere* bristle] **— hor·ren'dous·ly** *adv.*

hor·rent (hôr'ənt, hor'-) *adj.* **1** Standing erect like bristles; bristling. **2** Causing terror and abhorrence. **3** Feeling or expressing horror. [<L *horrens, -entis,* ppr. of *horrere* bristle]

hor·ri·bi·le dic·tu (hō·rē'bə·lā dik'to͞o) *Latin* Horrible to be told.

hor·ri·ble (hôr'ə·bəl, hor'-) *adj.* Exciting abhorrence; terrible. See synonyms under AWFUL, FRIGHTFUL. [<F <L *horribilis* <*horrere* bristle] **— hor'ri·ble·ness** *n.* **— hor'ri·bly** *adj.*

hor·rid (hôr'id, hor'-) *adj.* **1** Fitted to inspire horror; dreadful. **2** *Colloq.* Highly obnoxious; outrageous. See synonyms under FRIGHTFUL. [<L *horridus* bristling <*horrere* bristle] **— hor'rid·ly** *adv.* **— hor'rid·ness** *n.*

hor·rif·ic (hô·rif'ik, ho-) *adj.* Causing horror.

hor·ri·fy (hôr'ə·fī, hor'-) *v.t.* **·fied, ·fy·ing** To affect or fill with horror. **— hor'ri·fi·ca'tion** *n.*

hor·rip·i·la·tion (hô·rip'ə·lā'shən, ho-) *n.* A chilliness accompanied by the appearance of goose-pimples and bristling of the hair over the body, preceding fever; goose-flesh. [<L *horripilatio, -onis* <*horripilare* <*horrere* bristle + *pilus* hair]

hor·ror (hôr'ər, hor'-) *n.* **1** The painful emotion of extreme fear or abhorrence; dread. **2** Extreme repugnance. **3** That which excites fear or dread; especially, some great accident or calamity. **4** *Obs.* The shivering fit that precedes a fever. See synonyms under ABOMINATION, FEAR, FRIGHT. **— the horrors** *Colloq.* **1** The blues. **2** Delirium tremens. [<L]

Hor·sa (hôr'sə) See HENGIST.

hors de com·bat (ôr də kôṅ·bȧ') *French* Out of the fight.

hors de sai·son (ôr də se·zôṅ') *French* Out of season.

hors d'oeuvre (ôr dûrv', *Fr.* ôr dœ'vr') An appetizer served before a meal. ◆ This form is both singular and plural in French. An English plural, **hors d'oeuvres,** is also seen. [<F]

horse (hôrs) *n. pl.* **hors·es** or **horse** **1** A large, solid-hoofed quadruped (*Equus caballus*) with coarse mane and tail: commonly, in the domestic state, employed as a beast of draught and burden and especially for riding upon.

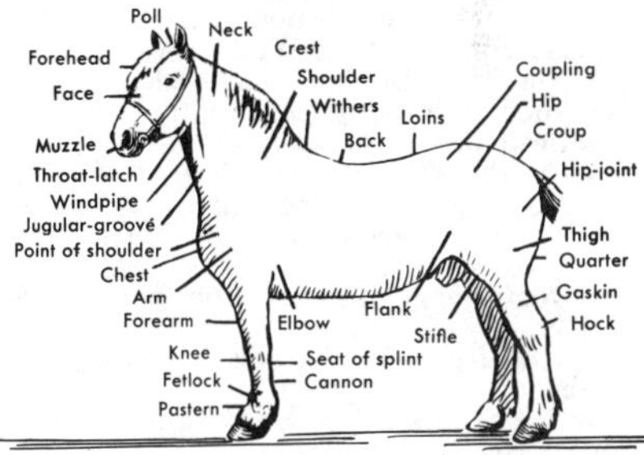

HORSE
Nomenclature for anatomical parts.

◆ Collateral adjective: *equine.* **2** Any of various extinct mammals related to or supposed to be of the ancestral line of the horse, as the eohippus. **3** A male horse, especially when castrated; a gelding. **4** Cavalry: a regiment of *horse.* **5** A device used to support anything or suggesting the uses of a horse: usually used in combination: a *clotheshorse.* **6** *Mining* A mass of rock, similar to the wall rock, found in a vein of ore. **7** *U.S. Slang* A translation or other similar aid used by pupils in working out lessons; pony; crib. **8** A man: a friendly, joking, or opprobrious term. **9** *U.S. Slang* Horseplay; foolery. **10** *Colloq.* In chess, a knight. **11** In gymnastics, a wooden block on four legs used for vaulting and other exercises. **— a horse of another** (or **different**) **color** A completely different matter. **— to hold one's horses** To be patient; curb one's impetuosity; wait; take things easy. **— to horse** **1** The bugle call summoning mounted troops to saddle and stand equipped at their horses' heads. **2** A signal to mount. **— *v.* horsed, hors·ing** *v.t.* **1** To furnish with horses; mount. **2** To put on another's back or on a sawhorse for flogging. **3** To flog. **4** *Aeron.* To jerk violently at (the controls of an aircraft). **5** *U.S. Slang* To subject to pranks or horseplay. **—** *v.i.* **6** To mount or ride on a horse. **7** *U.S. Slang* To engage in horseplay: usually with *around.* **—** *adj.* Coarse; large for its kind: *horse* chestnut, *horselaugh* [OE *hors*]

horse·back (hôrs′bak′) *n.* **1** A horse's back. **2** An object shaped like a horse's back. **—** *adv.* On a horse's back.

horse balm Richweed.

horse·block (hôrs′blok′) *n.* **1** A block or platform used in mounting a horse. **2** A frame of boards used as a support.

horse·boat (hôrs′bōt′) *n.* **1** A boat moved by horsepower. **2** A boat for carrying horses.

horse·boot (hôrs′bōōt′) *n.* A leather covering to protect a horse's pastern against injury.

horse·bot (hôrs′bot′) *n.* A botfly or its larva that infests the stomach and intestines of the horse.

horse·boy (hôrs′boi′) *n.* A stableboy.

horse·break·er (hôrs′brā′kər) *n.* One who trains horses to work in harness or under the saddle.

horse·brush (hôrs′brush′) *n.* Any of a genus *(Tetradymia)* of low, tough, hoary, sometimes spiny shrubs of the western United States, especially the little-leaf horsebrush *(T. glabrata)*, considered poisonous to sheep.

horse car **1** A car drawn by horses; tramcar. **2** A car for transporting horses by rail.

horse chestnut **1** A tree *(Aesculus hippocastanum)* of Asian origin, having digitate leaves, clusters of flowers, and large chestnutlike fruits: in the United States some species are known as *buckeyes.* **2** The fruit of this tree.

horse·cloth (hôrs′klôth′, -kloth′) *n.* A cloth to cover a horse.

horse collar A stuffed collar for a horse's neck, used to support the hames of a draft harness and to ease the pressure on the shoulders in drawing.

horse·drench (hôrs′drench′) *n.* A medicinal dose for a horse, or the instrument with which it is administered.

horse·fish (hôrs′fish′) *n.* *pl.* **·fish** or **·fish·es** The moonfish.

horse·flesh (hôrs′flesh′) *n.* **1** The flesh of a horse. **2** Horses, considered collectively. **3** The lustrous brown wood of the sabicu tree (genus *Lysiloma*) of the West Indies and Central America: also **horseflesh mahogany.** **4** The wood of the bullytree; also, the tree itself.

horseflesh ore Bornite.

horse·fly (hôrs′flī′) *n.* *pl.* **·flies** **1** A large bloodsucking fly of the family *Tabanidae,* especially of the genus *Tabanus.* **2** The forest fly. **3** A botfly.

horse·foot (hôrs′fōōt′) *n.* **1** Coltsfoot. **2** The king crab.

horse furniture The harness or housing of a horse.

horse-gear (hôrs′gir′) *n.* Horse furniture; also, horsepower.

horse gentian A perennial weedy herb (genus *Triosteum*) of the honeysuckle family, especially the feverwort.

Horse Guards **1** In the British Army, a body of cavalry serving as guards, especially the **Royal Horse Guards** (2nd Regiment) forming the personal escort of the sovereign. **2** A building in Whitehall, London, the headquarters of the Horse Guards and offices for some departments of the War Office. **3** The chief military officials of the British Army, as distinguished from civilian officials.

horse·hair (hôrs′hâr′) *n.* **1** The hair of horses, especially of their manes and tails. **2** Haircloth.

horse·hair-snake (hôrs′hâr′snāk′) *n.* A hairworm.

horse·head (hôrs′hed′) *n.* A tropical American moonfish *(Selene vomer).*

horse·hide (hôrs′hīd′) *n.* **1** The hide of a horse. **2** Leather made from a horse's hide.

horse latitudes *Naut.* A belt of high pressure at about 35° north or south latitude, characterized by calms and light variable winds, with diminishing to prevailing westerlies toward the poles and trade winds toward the equator.

horse·laugh (hôrs′laf′, -läf′) *n.* A loud, boisterous laugh.

horse·leech (hôrs′lēch′) *n.* **1** A large leech (genus *Haemopis*), said to enter the nostrils of cattle, horses, etc., when they are drinking. **2** One who is perpetually begging or teasing: *Prov.* xxx 15: also **horse′leach′.**

horse·less (hôrs′lis) *adj.* Not possessing, using, or requiring a horse: usually in such phrases as *horseless* carriage.

horse mackerel **1** A carangoid fish of Pacific waters *(Trachurus symmetricus).* **2** The tunny.

horse·man (hôrs′mən) *n.* *pl.* **·men** (-mən) **1** One who rides a horse. **2** A cavalryman. **3** A man who is skilled in riding or managing horses.

horse·man·ship (hôrs′mən·ship) *n.* Equestrian skill.

horse marine **1** A member of an imaginary corps of mounted marines. **2** One who is as awkward and out of place as a mounted marine would be aboard ship. **3** A mounted marine or sailor on duty ashore.

horse·mint (hôrs′mint′) *n.* **1** An erect American herb *(Monarda punctata)* of the mint family; wild bergamot. **2** Either of two European woodland mints *(Mentha longifolia* and *M. aquatica),* both naturalized in the United States.

horse·net·tle (hôrs′net′l) *n.* A rough roadside weed *(Solanum carolinense)* with straw-colored prickles, white flowers, and yellow berries, found in the central and southern United States.

horse opera *U.S. Slang* A motion picture dealing with ranch life in the western United States.

horse pistol A large pistol formerly carried in a holster by horsemen.

horse·play (hôrs′plā′) *n.* Rough, boisterous play.

horse·pond (hôrs′pond′) *n.* A pond for watering horses.

horse-post (hôrs′pōst′) *n.* A system of sending mail by a carrier on horseback; also, the carrier. See PONY EXPRESS.

horse post A hitching post.

horse·pow·er (hôrs′pou′ər) *n.* **1** The force exerted by, or rate of work maintained by, an average dray horse. **2** *Mech.* The standard theoretical unit of the rate of work, equal to 33,000 pounds lifted one foot in one minute, or 550 foot-pounds per second. **3** A mechanical arrangement for utilizing a horse's power.

horse·pow·er-hour (hôrs′pou′ər·our′) *n.* A measure of work performed at the rate of one horsepower in one hour. Expressed in foot-pounds it is equal to 33,000 × 60, or 1,980,000 foot-pounds.

horse race A race by horses. **— horse′-rac′er** *n.* **— horse′-rac′ing** *n.*

horse rack A long pole supported by posts to which horses are hitched.

horse·rad·ish (hôrs′rad′ish) *n.* **1** A coarse, tall, common garden herb *(Armoracia lapathifolia)* of the mustard family. **2** Its pungent root, used as a condiment.

horse·rake (hôrs′rāk′) *n.* A large mechanical rake worked by horsepower.

horse sense *Colloq.* Innate practical intelligence; common sense; shrewdness.

horse·shoe (hôr′shōō′, hôrs′-) *n.* **1** A metal shoe for a horse, U-shaped like the edge of a horse's hoof, to which it is nailed. **2** Something roughly U-shaped, especially if the opening is narrower than the sweep of the curve. **3** The horseshoe crab. **—** *v.t.* **·shoed, ·shoe·ing** To furnish with horseshoes.

horseshoe crab A king crab.

horse·shoes (hôr′shōōz′, hôrs′-) *n.* A game, similar to quoits, originally played with discarded horseshoes, now often with new or imitation horseshoes.

horse sugar The sweetleaf, a shrub *(Symplocos tinctoria)* of the southern United States: eaten by cattle and horses.

horse·tail (hôrs′tāl′) *n.* **1** The tail of a horse, especially when severed from the body and used as a distinction of rank or as a standard. In Turkey the two ranks of pashas were distinguished by two and three horsetails. **2** A perennial, hollow-stemmed, pteridophytic plant (genus *Equisetum*); the scouring rush.

horse-tam·er (hôrs′tā′mər) *n.* A horsebreaker.

horse tick The forest fly.

horse·weed (hôrs′wēd′) *n.* **1** A common weed *(Erigeron canadensis)* of the composite family, found in most parts of North America. **2** The wild lettuce. **3** The great ragweed.

horse·whip (hôrs′hwip′) *n.* A whip for driving or managing horses. **—** *v.t.* **·whipped, ·whip·ping** To chastise with a horsewhip.

horse·wom·an (hôrs′wōōm′ən) *n.* *pl.* **·wom·en** (-wim′in) **1** A woman who rides on horseback. **2** A woman who is skilled in riding or managing horses.

horst (hôrst) *n.* *Geol.* A portion of the earth's crust slightly elevated from the surrounding tracts by faults. Also **horste.** [<G]

hors·y (hôr′sē) *adj.* **hors·i·er, hors·i·est** **1** Pertaining to or suggestive of horses. **2** Devoted to horses or horse-racing. **3** *Slang* Coarse or gross in appearance. Also **hors′ey. — hors′i·ly** *adv.* **— hors′i·ness** *n.*

Hor·ta (hôr′tə, *Pg.* ôr′tə) Westernmost of the three districts of the Azores, comprising Pico, Fayal, Flores, and Corvo islands; total, 294 square miles; capital, Horta, on Fayal.

hor·ta·tive (hôr′tə·tiv) *adj.* Hortatory. [<L *hortativus* < *hortari* urge] **— hor′ta·tive·ly** *adv.*

hor·ta·to·ry (hôr′tə·tôr′ē, -tō′rē) *adj.* **1** Giving exhortation. **2** *Ling.* Pertaining to a mood used in some languages to express exhortation, encouragement, etc., or to the imperative or subjunctive moods when used in this manner. [<L *hortatorius*]

Hor·tense (hôr′tens, *Fr.* ôr·täṅs′) A feminine personal name. Also **Hor·ten·si·a** (*Ger.* hôr·ten′sē·ä, *Lat.* hôr·ten′shē·ə). [<F <L, gardener]

Hor·thy (hôr′tē), **Nicholas von,** 1868–1957, Hungarian admiral and statesman; regent of Hungary 1920–44: also known as *Miklos von Horthy.*

hor·ti·cul·ture (hôr′tə·kul′chər) *n.* **1** The cultivation of a garden, or the mode of cultivation employed in a garden. **2** That department of the science of agriculture which relates to the cultivation of gardens or orchards, including the growing of vegetables, fruits, flowers, and ornamental shrubs and trees. See synonyms under AGRICULTURE. [<L *hortus* garden + *cultura* cultivation] **— hor′ti·cul′tor** (-kul′tər) *n.* **— hor′ti·cul′tur·al** *adj.* **— hor′ti·cul′tur·ist, hor′ti·cul′tist, hor′ti·cul′tur·al·ist** *n.*

hor·tus sic·cus (hôr′təs sik′əs) *Latin* Literally, a dry garden; a herbarium.

Ho·rus (hō′rəs) In Egyptian mythology, the hawk-headed god of the sun.

HORUS
In legend, the son of Isis and Osiris.

ho·san·na (hō·zan′ə) *interj.* An exclamation of praise to God. **—** *n.* A cry of hosanna; hence, any exultant acclamation in praise of the Almighty. [<LL < Gk. *hōsanna* <Hebrew *hōshī'āhnnā* save, I pray]

hose (hōz) *n.* *pl.* **hose** (*Archaic* **hos·en**) **1** *Usually pl.* Formerly, a garment worn by men, covering the legs and the lower part of the body, like very tight trousers. **2** *pl.* Stockings; socks. **3** *pl.* **hos·es** A flexible tube or pipe, of leather, rubber, cotton, etc., for conveying water and other fluids. **—** *v.t.* **hosed, hos·ing** To drench or douse with a hose. [OE *hosa*]

Ho·se·a (hō·zē′ə, -zā′ə) A masculine personal name. [<Hebrew *Hōshēa',* lit., salvation < *yasha* save]

— Hosea One of the Hebrew minor prophets, eighth century B.C.; also, the Old Testament book bearing his name.

hose company A group of men who convey and man the hose for extinguishing fires.

ho·sier (hō′zhər) *n.* A dealer in hose, etc.

ho·sier·y (hō′zhər·ē) *n.* Hosiers' wares; stockings; hose; the hosier's business.

Hos·kins (hos′kinz), **Roy Graham,** 1880–1964, U.S. physiologist.

hos·pice (hos′pis) *n.* A place of entertainment or shelter, as a monastery in an Alpine pass. [<F <L *hospitium* inn, hospitality < *hospes* host, guest]

hos·pi·ta·ble (hos′pi·tə·bəl, hos·pit′ə·bəl) *adj.* 1 Disposed to behave in a warm manner or to entertain with generous kindness. 2 Characterized by hospitality. 3 Figuratively, very receptive. [<OF <L *hospitare* entertain] — **hos′pi·ta·ble·ness** *n.* — **hos′pi·ta·bly** *adv.*

hos·pi·tal (hos′pi·təl) *n.* 1 An institution for the reception, care, and medical treatment of the sick or wounded; also, the building used for that purpose. 2 *Obs.* An inn or hospice. 3 Formerly, a place of hospitality for those in need of shelter and maintenance: foundling *hospital,* Greenwich *Hospital* (a home for retired seamen in London). [<OF <L *hospitalis* of a guest <*hospes* guest. Doublet of HOTEL, HOSTEL.]

hos·pi·tal·er (hos′pi·təl·ər) *n.* 1 One cared for or supported in a hospital. 2 The title of the chief resident official in certain London hospitals which were originally religious foundations. See HOSTELER (def. 2). Also **hos′pi·tal·ler.**

Hos·pi·tal·er (hos′pi·təl·ər) *n.* A member of one of various charitable brotherhoods or military orders of the Middle Ages, of which the best known is the **Knights Hospitalers of St. John of Jerusalem,** which originated during the crusades in a hospital built at Jerusalem by merchants of Amalfi and dedicated to St. John the Baptist. When the order had to move its seat elsewhere, it was known as *Knights of Malta* and *Knights of Rhodes.*

hos·pi·tal·i·ty (hos′pə·tal′ə·tē) *n. pl.* **·ties** The spirit, practice, or act of being hospitable. ◆ Collateral adjective: *xenial.*

hos·pi·tal·ize (hos′pi·təl·īz′) *v.t.* **·ized, ·iz·ing** To put in a hospital for treatment. — **hos′pi·tal·i·za′tion** *n.*

hos·pi·ti·um (hos·pish′ē·əm) *n. pl.* **·ti·a** (-ē·ə) *Archaic* 1 A monastic inn. 2 An inn; hostel. [<L <*hospes* guest]

hos·po·dar (hos′pə·där) *n.* A title of dignity formerly borne by the princes of Lithuania and the kings of Poland, later by the princes or governors of Moldavia and Wallachia and the emperor of Russia. [<Rumanian, ult. <Slavic]

host[1] (hōst) *n.* 1 One who entertains guests in private life. 2 The landlord of a hotel. 3 *Biol.* Any living plant or animal that harbors another as a parasite. — *v.t. Colloq.* To conduct or entertain in the role of a host. [<OF *hoste* <L *hospes* guest, host. Akin to GUEST, HOST[2].]

host[2] (hōst) *n.* 1 An army. 2 A large body of men; a multitude. See synonyms under ARMY, ASSEMBLY, COMPANY, THRONG. [<OF <L *hostis* enemy. Akin to GUEST, HOST[1].]

host[3] (hōst) *n.* 1 *Usually cap.* In the Roman Catholic, Greek, Lutheran, and some other churches, the eucharistic bread or wafer before or after consecration. 2 *Obs.* An offering; sacrifice. [<OF *hoiste* <L *hostia* sacrificial victim]

hos·tage (hos′tij) *n.* 1 A person held as a pledge, as in war, for the performance of some stipulation. 2 Hence, anything given as a pledge. [<OF]

hos·tel (hos′təl) *n.* An inn; a lodging house; especially, a **youth hostel,** a supervised shelter for the use of young people on walking trips. Also **hos′tel·ry** (-təl·rē), **hos·tler·y** (hos′·lər·ē). [<OF <LL *hospitale* inn <*hospes* guest. Doublet of HOTEL, HOSPITAL.]

hos·tel·er (hos′təl·ər) *n.* 1 A student living in a hostel. 2 The monk who acted as host in a monastery. 3 *Archaic* An innkeeper. Also **hos′tel·ler.**

host·ess (hōs′tis) *n.* A female host.

hos·tile (hos′təl, *esp. Brit.* hos′tīl) *adj.* 1 Having a spirit of enmity. 2 Pertaining to an enemy. See synonyms under ALIEN, MALICIOUS. — *n.* An enemy; antagonist. [<F <L *hostilis*] — **hos′tile·ly** *adv.*

hos·til·i·ty (hos·til′ə·tē) *n. pl.* **·ties** 1 The state of being hostile. 2 *Obs.* Hostile action. 3 *pl.* Warlike measures. See synonyms under ANTIPATHY, ENMITY, FEUD, HATRED.

host·ing (hōs′ting) *n. Obs.* 1 The gathering of an armed host; a muster. 2 An encounter.

hos·tler (hos′lər, os′-) *n.* 1 A stableman; groom: also spelled *ostler.* 2 A man who prepares locomotives for their succeeding trips. [<OF *hostelier* innkeeper]

hot (hot) *adj.* **hot·ter, hot·test** 1 Having or giving heat; of high temperature: opposed to *cold* and exceeding *warm* in degree. 2 Producing a burning or biting sensation to the taste or touch: *hot* pepper; *hot* acid. 3 Marked by passion or zeal; fiery; fervent: *hot* words. 4 *Slang* Excited with sexual desire. 5 Violent; intense; raging: a *hot* battle. 6 *Slang* So new as not to have lost its freshness, currency, excitement, etc. 7 *Slang* Recently stolen or smuggled: *hot* goods. 8 *Music Slang* **a** In jazz, characterized by fervent and exciting rhythm and spirit, a lively tempo, and improvised variations on the original score. **b** Performing such music. 9 Following very closely: in *hot* pursuit. 10 In games, near to the subject or solution sought. 11 In hunting, distinct; strong: said of a scent. 12 Having an electrical charge, especially of high voltage: a *hot* wire. 13 Dangerously radioactive, as the fall-out of an atomic bomb. — **to make it hot for** *Slang* To make the situation extremely uncomfortable for. — *adv.* In a hot manner. [OE *hāt*] — **hot′ly** *adv.* — **hot′ness** *n.*

Synonyms: burning, choleric, fervent, fervid, fiery, glowing, heated, irascible, passionate, peppery, pungent, stinging, vehement, violent. See ARDENT, EAGER[1]. *Antonyms*: arctic, bleak, boreal, chill, chilly, cold, cool, freezing, frigid, frosty, frozen, gelid, icy, polar, wintry.

hot–air (hot′âr′) *adj.* 1 Heating by means of hot air: a *hot-air* furnace. 2 Inflated with hot air: a *hot–air* balloon.

hot air 1 Heated air. 2 *Slang* Empty or pretentious talk; humbug.

hot·bed (hot′bed′) *n.* 1 A bed of rich earth, protected by glass, and warmed for promoting the growth of plants. 2 A place or condition favoring rapid growth or heated activity.

hot blast A blast of hot air blown into a smelting furnace. — **hot′–blast′** *adj.*

hot–blood·ed (hot′blud′id) *adj.* Being of hot blood; passionate; amorous.

hot·box (hot′boks′) *n.* The overheated journal box of a railroad car or other fast-moving wheeled vehicle: caused by friction.

hot cake A pancake or fritter.

hotch (hoch) *v.t.* & *v.i. Scot.* & *Brit. Dial.* To shake; jiggle or fidget.

hotch·pot (hoch′pot) *n. Law* A commixture of property made in order to secure an equable division. [<OF *hochepot* <MDu. *hutspot*]

hotch–potch (hoch′poch) *n.* 1 A hodgepodge. 2 *Law* A hotchpot. [Var. of HOTCHPOT]

hot cross bun A circular cake or bun marked with a cross of frosting, eaten especially during Lent.

hot dog *Colloq.* A cooked frankfurter, usually grilled and served in a split roll.

ho·tel (hō·tel′) *n.* 1 An establishment or building providing lodging, food, etc., for travelers and others; an inn. 2 In French usage: **a** An official residence or private dwelling in a city or town. **b** A building for the transaction of public business in a city or town. [<F *hôtel* <OF *hostel* inn. Doublet of HOSTEL, HOSPITAL.]

Hô·tel des In·va·lides (ô·tel′ dā·zaṅ·vȧ·lēd′) An institution in Paris, originally founded in 1607 for disabled veterans, now a military museum containing the tomb of Napoleon.

hô·tel de ville (ô·tel′ də vēl′) *French* A town hall.

hô·tel Dieu (ô·tel′ dyœ′) *French* A hospital.

ho·tel·ier (hō′təl·ir′) *n.* A hotel-keeper; hotelman. [<F]

hot·foot (hot′fŏŏt′) *v.i. Colloq.* To hurry; go hastily. — *adv. Colloq.* In all haste; hastily. — *n. Slang* The prank of furtively wedging a match between the upper and sole of a victim's shoe, lighting it, and letting it burn down.

Hoth (hoth) Höder. Also **Höthr** (hœ′thər).

hot·head (hot′hed′) *n.* A hasty, impetuous, or quick-tempered person. — **hot′–head′ed** *adj.* — **hot′–head′ed·ly** *adv.* — **hot′–head′ed·ness** *n.*

hot·house (hot′hous′) *n.* 1 A structure kept warm artificially, as for the forced growth of flowers, etc. 2 *Obs.* A brothel.

Ho·tien (hō′tyen′) The Chinese name for KHOTAN.

hot line A direct means of communication; specifically, a telephone line for emergency use by heads of state of nuclear powers, or for immediate communication between an official and his chief subordinates.

hot plate 1 A heated metal plate for maintaining at a uniform temperature anything set upon it. 2 A small portable gas or electric stove.

hot·pot (hot′pot′) *n.* A dish of meat stewed with potatoes in a covered pot.

hot·press (hot′pres′) *v.t.* To subject to heat and mechanical pressure, as for calendering or to extract oil. — *n.* A machine for hot-pressing. — **hot′pressed′** *adj.* — **hot′press′er** *n.* — **hot′press′ing** *n.*

hot rod *Slang* An automobile, popularly a jalopy, with a motor modified for speed.

hot seat *U.S. Slang* The electric chair.

hot spring A natural spring, the waters of which issue forth at 98° F. or above.

Hot Springs A resort in western Virginia.

Hot Springs National Park A resort area in central Arkansas containing mineral-bearing thermal springs; established 1921.

hot·spur (hot′spûr′) *n.* A person who pushes on, heedless of advice or warning; a hot-headed person. — *adj.* Impetuous; reckless: also **hot′spurred′.**

Hot·ten·tot (hot′ən·tot) *n.* 1 One of a yellowish-brown South African people believed to be related to both the Bantus and Bushmen. 2 The agglutinative language of these people, forming a subfamily of the Khoisan family of African languages: related to and having some of the clicks of Bushman.

Hottentot bread A plant, the elephant foot. Also **Hottentot's bread.**

hou·dah (hou′də) See HOWDAH.

Hou·dan (hōō′dan) *n.* A breed of domestic fowls having black-and-white coloring, flesh-colored and blue legs, and V-shaped comb. [from *Houdan,* a town in France]

Hou·di·ni (hōō·dē′nē), **Harry,** 1874–1926, U.S. magician and author: real name *Erich Weiss.*

Hou·don (ōō·dôṅ′), **Jean Antoine,** 1741?–1828, French sculptor.

Hou·ma·youn (hōō·mä′yōōn) See HUMAYUN.

hound (hound) *n.* 1 A hunting dog which hunts by scent; specifically, in Great Britain, a foxhound. 2 A dastardly fellow. 3 In the game of hare-and-hounds, one who acts the part of a hound. 4 *pl. Naut.* Projections at the head of a mast which support the top trestletrees and the lower rigging. 5 *Mech.* A brace to strengthen the running gear of a vehicle: if between the reach and hinder axle, called **hind hound;** if between the tongue and forward axle, **fore hound.** — *v.t.* 1 To hunt with or as with hounds; nag persistently. 2 To incite to pursue; set on the chase. [OE *hund* dog]

hound's–tongue (houndz′tung′) *n.* 1 A coarse hairy weed (*Cynoglossum officinale*) found in pastures and waste grounds, with tongue-shaped leaves, dull-red flowers, and prickly nutlets. 2 The vanilla plant.

hound's–tooth check (houndz′tōōth′) A design of small broken checks in cloth.

hour (our) *n.* 1 A space of time equal to one twenty-fourth of a day; sixty minutes; before the general use of timepieces, one twelfth of the interval from sunrise to sunset (called *hour of the day*), or one twelfth that from sunset to sunrise (called *hour of the night*). 2 A measure of time as indicated by the sun in relation to the horizon: the sun was two *hours* high. 3 The point of time indicated by a chronometer, watch, or clock; the time of day. 4 A set, appointed, or definite time; specifically, the time of death. 5 *pl.* Prayers to be repeated at stated times of the day; also, the time for these devotions, or the book containing them. 6 An hour's journey: commonly a league or three miles. 7 A sidereal hour. See SIDEREAL (def. 2). 8 *Astron.* An angular measure of right ascension or longitude, being 15 degrees or the 24th part of a great circle of the sphere. — **after hours** After the prescribed hours for school, business, etc. — **the small hours** The early morning hours. ◆ Collateral adjective: *horal.* [<L *hora* <Gk. *hōra* time, period]

hour angle *Astron.* The angle subtended by a place on the celestial sphere between the meridian and the hour circle passing through the object: used in determining time.

hour circle *Astron.* A great circle which passes through the celestial pole: used in the determination of the hour angle.

hour·glass (our′glas′, -gläs′) *n.* A glass vessel having two globular parts connected by a narrow neck: used for measuring time by the running of sand from the upper into the lower compartment, the passage taking a full hour.

HOURGLASS

hou·ri (hōō′rē) *n.* A nymph of the Moslem Paradise. [<F <Persian *ḥūri* <Arabic *ḥūrīyah* black-eyed woman]

hour·ly (our′lē) *adj.* Happening every hour. —*adv.* At intervals of an hour.

Hours (ourz) *n. pl.* The Horae.

house (hous) *n.* **1** A building intended for human habitation, especially one used as the residence of a family or single tenant. **2** A household; family. **3** A building used for any purpose: a coffee *house*; a *house* of worship. **4** The abode of a fraternity, order, etc.: a sorority *house.* **5** A dormitory or residence hall in a college or university; also, its resident students, collectively. **6** *Brit.* A college in a university; also, its member students, collectively. **7** A legislative body; also, the chamber it occupies. **8** *Eccl.* The deliberative body of a congregation or convocation. **9** A place of business. **10** A business firm: the *house* of Morgan. **11** A theater. **12** An audience at a public entertainment or service: to speak to a full *house.* **13** A line of ancestors and descendants regarded as forming a single family: the *House* of Tudor. **14** In astrology, one of the twelve divisions of the heavens, made by projecting great circles through the north and south points of the horizon. Each division, having special significance, is used in casting horoscopes. See ZODIAC. **15** A sign of the zodiac considered as the seat of greatest influence of a particular planet. —**on the house** At the expense of the proprietor; gratis. —**to bring down the house** To receive loud and enthusiastic applause. —**to clean house** *Colloq.* To get rid of undesirable conditions or persons in an organization. —**to keep house** To manage the affairs or work of a home. —*v.* (houz) **housed, hous·ing** *v.t.* **1** To take or put into a house; furnish with a house; lodge. **2** To store in a house or building. **3** To fit into a mortise, joint, etc. **4** *Naut.* To place in a secure or safe position, as in time of storms. —*v.i.* **5** To take shelter or lodgings; dwell. [OE *hūs*] —**house′ful** *n.*

Synonyms (noun): abode, building, cabin, cot, cottage, domicile, dwelling, dwelling place, edifice, habitation, hall, home, hovel, hut, manor, mansion, palace, residence, shanty, villa. See EDIFICE, HOME.

House (hous), **Edward Mandell,** 1858–1938, U. S. diplomat; adviser to President Wilson: known as *Colonel House.*

house arrest Detention in one's own house by authority of law.

house-boat (hous′bōt′) *n.* A boat or barge fitted out as a dwelling.

house·boy (hous′boi′) *n.* A houseman.

house·break·er (hous′brā′kər) *n.* One who breaks into a house to rob. —**house′break′·ing** *n.*

house·bro·ken (hous′brō′kən) *adj.* Trained to live cleanly in a house: said of animals.

house·carl (hous′kärl) *n.* A member of the bodyguard or household troops of a Danish or early English king or noble.

house coat A long, loose-skirted garment designed for informal indoor wear.

house·fly (hous′flī′) *n. pl.* **·flies** The common fly (*Musca domestica*), found in nearly all parts of the world: an agent in transmitting certain diseases. For illustration see under INSECTS (injurious).

house guest A guest invited to stay one or more nights.

house·hold (hous′hōld) *n.* A number of persons dwelling under the same roof. —*adj.* Domestic. [<HOUSE + HOLD, *n.*]

household arts See under ART.

house·hold·er (hous′hōl′dər) *n.* The head of a family; specifically, in England, one who inhabits a dwelling or tenement of such a nature as to qualify him for the exercise of the franchise.

household goods The furniture, utensils, and supplies necessary for keeping house.

household linen See FLATWORK.

household troops A special body of soldiers detailed for the protection of a sovereign, his family, and residence.

house·keep·er (hous′kē′pər) *n.* One who directs the affairs or work of a household either as mistress or as an upper servant. —**house′keep′ing** *n.*

hou·sel (hou′zəl) *n. Obs.* The Eucharist. [OE *hūsel*]

house·leek (hous′lēk′) *n.* An Old World garden plant (*Sempervivum tectorum*) of the orpine family, with pink flowers and thick fleshy leaves that grow on walls and roofs.

house·line (hous′līn′) *n. Naut.* A small three-stranded line of fine-dressed hemp, used for seizings, etc.: sometimes called *housing.* Also spelled *houslin.*

house·maid (hous′mād′) *n.* A girl employed to do housework.

housemaid's knee *Pathol.* A chronic inflammation of the bursa in front of the knee, afflicting housemaids and others who kneel in working.

house·man (hous′mən) *n.* A handy man employed to do heavy work about a house, hotel, etc.: also called *houseboy.*

house·mas·ter (hous′mas′tər, -mäs′-) *n.* The master having charge of a school residence, specifically in a British school.

House of Burgesses In colonial times, the lower house of the legislature of Virginia.

house of cards Any weak, unstable organization, plan, etc.

House of Commons The lower house of the British Parliament.

house of correction An institution for minor criminals; reform school.

House of Delegates The lower house of the legislature in Maryland, Virginia, and West Virginia.

House of Keys The lower house of the legislature of the Isle of Man. See KEYS.

House of Lords The upper house of the British Parliament.

House of Peers The upper chamber of the Japanese Diet.

House of Representatives 1 The lower, larger branch of the United States Congress, and of many State legislatures, composed of members elected popularly on the basis of population. **2** A similar legislative body, as in Australia, Japan, or Mexico.

House of Saxe-Coburg-Gotha See under WINDSOR.

house organ A publication issued by a commercial enterprise to promote the interest of customers in its products, or to maintain efficiency among its employees.

house party An entertainment of guests for several days, usually in a country house or a college fraternity; also, the guests.

house physician A physician resident by appointment in a hospital or other institution.

house·room (hous′rōōm;, -rŏŏm′) *n.* Room or lodging in a house or hotel; accommodation.

house snake A harmless snake (*Lampropeltis triangulum*) of the northern United States that frequents houses and preys on rats and mice: also called *milk snake* and *spotted adder.*

house sparrow See under SPARROW (def. 1).

house·top (hous′top′) *n.* **1** The top or roof of a house. **2** Figuratively, an exposed or public place: to cry it from the *housetops.*

house·ware (hous′wâr′) *n.* Kitchen equipment and other wares used in a home.

house·warm·ing (hous′wôr′ming) *n.* A festivity on entering a new home.

house·wife (hous′wīf′) *n. pl.* **·wives** (-wīvz′) **1** A married woman who manages the affairs of her own household as a full-time occupation. **2** (hous′wīf′ *esp. Brit.* huz′if) A receptable for small articles required in sewing. —**house′wife′ly** *adj. & adv.* —**house′·wife′li·ness** *n.*

house·wife·ry (hous′wīf′rē) *n.* The part of household management under a woman's direction; housekeeping processes. Also **house′·wife′ship** (-ship).

house·work (hous′wûrk′) *n.* Work in keeping house, especially the more menial tasks.

house wren See under WREN.

hous·ie (hōō′sē) *n. Scot.* A small house.

hous·ing[1] (hou′zing) *n.* **1** The act of providing with a house or shelter. **2** The act of bringing into a house, or putting under cover. **3** Shelter from the weather. **4** *Mech.* **a** A hollow made in one member of an engine or machine to receive a portion of another member. **b** That part of a frame of a machine which sustains a journal box; a jaw. **c** The casing containing either the differential gear or a set of ball bearings in the transmission of an automobile. **5** A niche for a statue. **6** *Naut.* **a** A houseline. **b** A hoarding to protect a ship's deck when in repair dock. **c** That part of a mast or bowsprit below the deck or abaft the knightheads. **7** A mortise in a timber, for receiving the end of another timber.

hous·ing[2] (hou′zing) *n.* The ornamental trappings of a horse, especially the saddlecloth: usually in the plural. See synonyms under CAPARISON. [<OF *houce*; of uncertain origin]

hous·lin (hous′lin) See HOUSELINE.

Hous·man (hous′mən), **Alfred Edward,** 1859–1936, English poet and classical scholar.

Hous·say (ou′sī), **Bernardo Alberto,** born 1887, Argentine physiologist.

Hous·ton (hyōōs′tən), **Sam,** 1793–1863, U.S. statesman and general; president of the Republic of Texas 1836–38, 1841–44.

Hous·ton (hyōōs′tən) A city in SE Texas.

Hous·to·ni·a (hōōs·tō′nē·ə) *n.* A genus of low, slender North American plants of the madder family, including the bluet. [after Dr. William *Houston,* 1695–1733, English naturalist]

Hou·yhn·hnm (hōō·in′əm, hwin′əm) In Swift's *Gulliver's Travels,* one of a race of horses having reason and all the noble qualities of ideal man: contrasted with the apelike *Yahoo,* having all the vices of man. [Imit. of the whinny of a horse]

hove[1] (hōv) *v.t. & v.i. Obs.* **1** To raise or move upward. **2** To inflate. [<HEAVE]

hove[2] (hōv) Past tense of HEAVE.

hov·el (huv′əl, hov′-) *n.* **1** A wretched dwelling; hut. **2** An open shed for sheltering cattle, tools, or produce. See synonyms under HOUSE, HUT. —*v.t.* **hov·eled** or **hov·elled, hov·el·ing** or **hov·el·ling 1** To shelter in a hovel. **2** To build like a hovel. [? Dim. of OE *hof* building]

hov·er (huv′ər, hov′-) *v.i.* **1** To remain suspended in or near one place in the air, as by fluttering the wings. **2** To linger; be nearby, as if waiting or watching: with *around, near,* etc. **3** To remain in an uncertain or irresolute state: with *between.* —*n.* **1** A shelter or retreat. **2** The act of hovering. [< obs. *hove* float] —**hov′er·er** *n.*

Hov·er·craft (huv′ər·kraft′, hov′-, -kräft′) *n.* A vehicle traveling on a thin cushion of air produced by fans directed downward: a trade name. Also **hov′er·craft′.**

how[1] (hou) *adv.* **1** In what way or manner: I knew *how* it was done. **2** To what degree, extent, or amount; in what proportion: showing *how* great was the concentration of ions. **3** In what state or condition: Let me see *how* the account stands. **4** For what reason or purpose: I can't see *how* he came to do it. **5** For what price; at what sum: I inquired *how* the stock sold. **6** By what name or designation: We know *how* he is called among his own people. **7** To what effect; with what meaning: *How* do you intend that remark to be taken? **8** *Colloq.* What? —*n.* Way of doing or becoming; means: Teach me the *how* of it. [OE *hū*]

how[2] (hou) *adj. Scot.* Hollow or deep; also, hollow in sound. —*n.* A valley; glen. Also spelled *howe.*

how[3] (hou) *interj.* An expression of greeting attributed to and used humorously in imitation of American Indians.

How·ard (hou′ərd) A masculine personal name. [<Gmc., hedge guard]

How·ard (hou′ərd), **Catherine,** 1522?–42, fifth wife of Henry VIII of England; executed.

how·be·it (hou·bē′it) *adv.* Nevertheless. —*conj. Obs.* Although; be that as it may. See synonyms under NOTWITHSTANDING.

how·dah (hou′də) *n.* A railed or canopied seat on the back of an elephant: also spelled *houdah.* [<Hind. *haudah*]

how·die (hou′dē, ou′-, hō′, ō′-) *n. Scot.* A midwife.

how-do-you-do (hou′də·yə·dōō′) *n. Colloq.* An awkward situation or occasion: usually preceded by an intensive *fine, pretty, nice,* etc. Also **how-d'ye-do** (hou′dyə·dōō′).

How do you do? What is the state of your health?: a phrase often used as a greeting when being introduced to or meeting a person.

how·dy (hou′dē) *interj. Colloq.* An expression of greeting. [Contraction of HOW DO YOU (DO)?]

howe (hō) See HOW².

Howe (hou), **Elias,** 1819–67, U.S. inventor of the sewing machine. —**Julia Ward,** 1819–1910, U.S. author. —**Richard,** 1725–99, Earl Howe, English admiral in the American Revolution. —**William,** 1729–1814, fifth Viscount Howe, English general; commander in chief during American Revolution; brother of the preceding.

how·el (hou′əl) *n.* A cooper's plane for smoothing the inside of casks. —*v.t.* To make smooth with a howel. [<MLG *hövel*]

How·ells (hou′əlz), **William Dean,** 1837–1920, U.S. novelist and editor.

how·ev·er (hou·ev′ər) *adv.* **1** In whatever manner; by whatever means. **2** To whatever degree or extent: Spend *however* much it costs. **3** How; in what manner: *However* did it happen? —*conj.* Notwithstanding; still; yet. See synonyms under BUT, NOTWITHSTANDING. Also **how·e'er′** (-âr′).

how·it·zer (hou′it·sər) *n.* A piece of artillery having a barrel longer than a mortar's, and firing at angles up to 65° with medium muzzle velocity. [Appar. <Du. *houwitzer,* ult. <Czech *houfnice* catapult]

HOWITZER—BRITISH ARMY, 1914

howk (hōk) *v.t.* & *v.i. Brit. Dial.* To dig; burrow: also spelled *holk.* —**howk′it** (-it) *adj.*

howl (houl) *v.i.* **1** To utter the loud, mournful wail of a wolf or dog. **2** To utter such a cry in rage, grief, etc. **3** To make such a sound: The storm *howled.* —*v.i.* **4** To utter or express with a howl or howls. **5** To drive or effect with a howl or howls. —*n.* **1** The cry of a wolf or dog. **2** Any resonant cry expressive of grief or rage. **3** An undesirable sound distortion in radio reception, due to acoustic or electrical feedback. [Imit.]

How·land Island (hou′lənd) A United States possession in the mid-Pacific near the equator.

howl·er (hou′lər) *n.* **1** One who or that which howls. **2** A siren for signaling, or, when attached to a military airplane, for creating confusion or panic among the enemy. **3** A tropical American monkey having a long, prehensile tail and great vocal power: the ursine *howler* (*Alouatta ursinus*): also **howling monkey. 4** *Colloq.* Gross exaggeration; also, an absurd mistake or blunder.

how·let (hou′lit) *n. Obs.* An owl; owlet. [<F *hulotte*]

howl·ing (hou′ling) *adj.* **1** Filled with or abounding in howls; dismal: the *howling* wilderness. **2** *Slang* Prodigious; tremendous; enormous: a *howling* success, a *howling* lie.

How·rah (hou′rə) A city on the Hooghly opposite Calcutta, NE India.

how·so·ev·er (hou′sō·ev′ər) *adv.* In whatever manner; to whatever extent.

hoy¹ (hoi) *n.* **1** A barge used to convey bulky cargo to ships in port. **2** A single-masted, heavy, coastwise vessel or tender of obsolete type. [<MDu. *hoei*]

hoy² (hoi) *interj.* Ho; hallo: a cry to attract attention. Compare AHOY. Also spelled *hoigh, hooy.* [Imit. Cf. Du. *hui!*]

hoy·den (hoid′n) *n.* A romping or bold girl; tomboy. —*adj.* Inelegant or unseemly; bold. —*v.i.* To romp rudely or indecently. Also spelled *hoiden.* [? <obs. *hoit* romp] —**hoy′·den·ish** *adj.*

Hoyle (hoil) *n.* A book or rules and instructions for indoor games, especially for card games: so called from the original author, **Edmund Hoyle,** 1672–1769, English writer on card games. —**according to Hoyle** Following the rules laid down in Hoyle; hence, sportsmanlike; acting fairly in a game or sport, or in any matter.

hoyte (hoit) *v.i. Scot.* To walk or run awkwardly; limp.

Hra·dec Krá·lo·vé (hrä′dets krä′lô·ve) A city in NE Bohemia, Czechoslovakia: German *Königgrätz.*

Hr·dlič·ka (hûrd′lich·kə), **A·leš** (ä′lesh), 1869–1943, U.S. anthropologist born in Czechoslovakia.

hsien (shyen) *n.* A subprefecture of Chinese provincial administration.

Hsin·chu (shin′chōō′) A city in NW Taiwan.

Hsin·king (shin′jing′) A former name for CHANGCHUN. Also **Hsin′ching′.**

Hual·la·ga (wä·yä′gä) A river in central and northern Peru, flowing 700 miles NE to the Amazon basin.

Huam·bo (wäm′bō) The former name of NOVA LISBOA.

hua·na·co (wä·nä′kō) See GUANACO.

hua·ra·che (wä·rä′chā) *n.* A Mexican sandal woven of strips of leather and having leather heel straps. Also **hua·ra′cho** (-chō). [<Am. Sp. <Quechua *huaraca* leather thong]

Huás·car (wäs′kär) An Inca ruler of Peru, 1495–1532, who was put to death by his brother Atahualpa.

Huas·ca·rán (wäs′kä·rän′) An extinct Andean volcano; the highest point in Peru; 22,205 feet.

hub (hub) *n.* **1** The central part of a wheel. **2** Anything central; a center of traffic. —**the Hub** Boston, Massachusetts. [Prob. var. of HOB]

hub·ba hub·ba (hub′ə hub′ə) *Colloq.* An exclamation expressing emphatic approval. [Imit.]

Hub·bard (hub′ərd), **Elbert Green,** 1856–1915, U.S. writer and publisher.

hub·ble (hub′əl) *n.* A small protuberance or lump, as in a road; roughness. [Dim. of HUB] —**hub′bly** (-lē) *adj.*

hub·ble-bub·ble (hub′əl·bub′əl) *n.* **1** A continuous bubbling or gurgling sound. **2** A hookah or water pipe. [Reduplication of BUBBLE]

hub·ble·show (hub′əl·shō′) *n. Brit. Dial.* Uproar; confusion.

hub·bub (hub′ub) *n.* A confused noise; uproar. See synonyms under NOISE, TUMULT. [Said to be an Irish cry]

Hu·ber·tus·burg (hōō·ber′təs·bōōrkh) A town in former Saxony, East Germany, east of Leipzig: scene of the signing of the treaty ending the Seven Years War, 1763.

hu·bris (hyōō′bris) *n.* Wanton arrogance. [<Gk.]

huck·a·back (huk′ə·bak) *n.* A coarse, durable linen or cotton cloth used for towels. Also **huck, huck′a·buck** (-buk). [Origin uncertain]

huck·le (huk′əl) *n.* The hip; also, a hump or projection resembling the hip. [Dim. of obs. *huck* hip; ult. origin unknown]

huck·le·ber·ry (huk′əl·ber′ē) *n. pl.* **·ries 1** The edible black or dark-blue berry of a species of heath (genus *Gaylussacia*), often confused with the blueberry. **2** The European whortleberry. **3** The shrub producing either of these berries. Also called *hurtleberry, whortleberry.* [Prob. alter. of HURTLEBERRY]

Huck·le·ber·ry Finn (huk′əl·ber′ē fin′) The title character of Mark Twain's novel *The Adventures of Huckleberry Finn.*

huckle bone The innominate bone; hip bone.

huck·ster (huk′stər) *n.* **1** One who retails small wares, provisions, or the like; a peddler; hawker; especially, one who raises and sells garden products. **2** A mean, venal fellow; a petty jobber or trickster. **3** *U.S. Slang* An advertising man. —*v.t.* **1** To put up for sale; peddle. **2** To haggle over. —*v.i.* **3** To haggle. [<MDu. *hoekster* <*heuken* retail] —**huck′ster·ism** *n.*

Hu·dai·da (hō·dā′də, -dī′-) See HODEIDA.

Hud·ders·field (hud′ərz·fēld) A county borough of SW Yorkshire, England.

hud·dle (hud′l) *v.* **hud·dled, hud·dling** *v.i.* **1** To crowd closely together, as from fear or for warmth. **2** To draw or hunch oneself together, as from cold. **3** In football, to gather in a huddle. —*v.t.* **4** To bring together in a group or mass. **5** To draw or hunch (oneself) together. **6** To make or do hurriedly or carelessly. **7** To push or put hastily or confusedly. —*n.* **1** A confused crowd or collection. **2** In football, the grouping of a team before each play, in which signals and instructions are given. **3** Any small, intimate conference. [Origin uncertain]

Hu·di·bras (hyōō′di·bras) Hero of Samuel Butler's *Hudibras,* a mock-heroic poem caricaturing the Puritans.

Hu·di·bras·tic (hyōō′di·bras′tik) *adj.* Pertaining to or in the style or meter of *Hudibras;* in tetrameter couplets, with elaborate, often comical, rimes.

Hud·son (hud′sən), **Henry,** died 1611?, English navigator in the service of Dutch merchants; explored the Hudson River, 1609; discovered Hudson Bay, 1611. —**William Henry,** 1841–1922, English author and naturalist.

Hudson Bay An inland sea in northern Canada; 850 miles long; 600 miles wide.

Hudson River A river in eastern New York State, flowing 306 miles south to New York Bay.

Hudson's Bay Company 1 A British joint-stock association chartered in 1670 to conduct the fur trade in lands beyond the Hudson Strait. **2** A large private corporation in Canada.

Hudson seal Muskrat fur dyed and trimmed to resemble Alaskan sealskin.

Hudson Strait The strait connecting Hudson Bay with the Atlantic Ocean; 450 miles long.

hue¹ (hyōō) *n.* **1** The particular shade of a color; that in which one color or shade differs from another; color; tint. **2** That attribute of a chromatic color, as red, green, blue, which determines the character of its difference from the nearest achromatic color. Compare BRIGHTNESS, LIGHTNESS, SATURATION. See COLOR. **3** A compound color, especially one in which one or more of the primary colors is predominant. **4** *Obs.* Appearance; form. ◆ Homophone: *hew.* [OE *heow* appearance]

hue² (hyōō) *n.* A vociferous cry; shouting. ◆ Homophone: *hew.* [<OF *hu* cry <*huer*]

Hué (hwā, hyōō·ā′) A port, capital of Central Vietnam.

hue and cry 1 A great stir and clamor about any matter. **2** Formerly, the common-law process of pursuing felons by shouts and cries until taken.

hued (hyōōd) *adj.* Having a hue or color: usually in combination: dark-*hued.*

Huel·va (wel′vä) A province of SW Spain; 3,894 square miles; capital, Huelva.

Hues·ca (wes′kä) **1** A province of NE Spain; 6,054 square miles. **2** Its capital, the former residence of the kings of Aragon.

huff (huf) *v.t.* **1** To offend; make angry. **2** To treat insolently or arrogantly; bully; hector. **3** *Obs.* To cause to swell; blow up. **4** In checkers, to remove (an opponent's piece) from the board as a forfeit for neglecting to capture an opposing piece. —*v.i.* **5** To be offended. **6** To puff; blow. **7** *Obs.* To puff or swell with anger or pride; bluster. —*n.* **1** Offense suddenly taken. **2** In checkers, the act of huffing. [Imit.]

huff·ish (huf′ish) *adj.* Petulant; irascible. —**huff′ish·ly** *adv.* —**huff′ish·ness** *n.*

huff·y (huf′ē) *adj.* **huff·i·er, huff·i·est 1** Easily offended. **2** Puffed up. —**huff′i·ly** *adv.* —**huff′i·ness** *n.*

Hu·fuf (hōō·fōōf′) See HOFUF.

hug (hug) *v.* **hugged, hug·ging** *v.t.* **1** To clasp tightly within the arms, as from affection. **2** To keep fondly in the mind; cherish, as a belief or opinion. **3** To keep close to, as a shore. —*v.i.* 4 To lie close; nestle. See synonyms under EMBRACE. —*n.* A close embrace. [Prob. <ON *hugga* console]

huge (hyo͞oj) *adj.* Having great bulk; vast. See synonyms under IMMENSE, LARGE. Also *Colloq.* **huge′ous.** [<OF *ahuge* high] —**huge′ly** *adv.* —**huge′ness** *n.*

hug·ger-mug·ger (hug′ər·mug′ər) *n.* 1 Secrecy; privacy. 2 Confusion and disorder. —*adj.* 1 Secret; sly. 2 Slovenly. [<obs. *hoker-moker*, prob. reduplication of ME *mokern* conceal]

Hug·gins (hug′inz), **Sir William,** 1824–1910, English astronomer.

Hugh (hyo͞o) A masculine personal name. Also **Hu·go** (hyo͞o′gō; *Dan., Du., Ger., Sw.* ho͞o′gō; *Pg., Sp.* o͞o′gō), *Fr.* **Hugues** (üg). [<Gmc., intelligent]
—**Hugh Ca·pet** (kā′pit, kap′it; *Fr.* kȧ·pe′), 940?–996, king of France 987–996, founder of the Capetian dynasty.

Hughes (hyo͞oz), **Charles Evans,** 1862–1948, U.S. jurist and statesman; chief justice, U.S. Supreme Court 1930–41. —**(James) Langston,** 1902–1967, U.S. poet and author. —**Thomas,** 1822–96, English author.

hug-me-tight (hug′mē·tīt′) *n.* A short, close-fitting jacket, usually knitted.

Hu·go (hyo͞o′gō, *Fr.* ü·gō′), **Victor (Marie),** 1802–85, French poet, novelist, and dramatist.

Hu·gue·not (hyo͞o′gə·not) *n.* A French Protestant of the 16th and 17th centuries: persecuted during the religious wars of the time. [<F <G *Eidgenoss* confederate] —**Hu′gue·not′ic** *adj.*

Hu·gue·not·ism (hyo͞o′gə·not′iz·əm) *n.* The doctrines of the Huguenots; French Protestantism.

huh (hu) *interj.* An exclamation of inquiry, surprise, contempt, etc. [Imit.]

Hui·la (wē′lä), **Ne·va·do del** (nā·vä′thō thel) A volcanic peak in south central Colombia; 18,865 feet.

hu·la (ho͞o′lə) *n.* A native Hawaiian dance performed by women, with intricate arm movements that tell a story in pantomime. Also **hu′la-hu′la.** [<Hawaiian]

Hu·la (ho͞o′lä), **Lake** An expansion of the Jordan headwaters in NE Israel near the Syrian border: also *Waters of Merom.* Also **Hu′le** (-le).

hulk (hulk) *n.* 1 The body of a ship or decked vessel, especially of an old, unseaworthy vessel, or of one wrecked. 2 An old ship used for a prison or for purposes other than seagoing. 3 Any bulky or unwieldy object or person. 4 A heavy, clumsy ship. —*v.i.* 1 To rise or loom bulkily: usually with *up.* 2 *Brit. Dial.* To lounge or slouch in a lazy, clumsy manner. [OE *hulc* ship, prob. < Med. L *hulcus* <Gk. *holkas* towed vessel <*hélkein* drag]

hulk·ing (hul′king) *adj.* Bulky; unwieldy. Also **hulk′y.**

hull (hul) *n.* 1 The outer covering, as of a kernel of grain or of a nut; husk; pod; also, any outer covering; specifically, in the plural, garments, clothes. 2 *Naut.* The body of a ship, exclusive of the masts, sails, yards, and rigging. 3 *Aeron.* The main covered structure of a rigid airship; also, that part of a flying boat which rests upon the water. —*v.t.* 1 To shell; free from the hull. 2 To strike or pierce the hull of (a vessel). [OE *hulu* a covering] —**hull′er** *n.*

Hull (hul), **Cordell,** 1871–1955, U.S. secretary of state 1933–44. —**Isaac,** 1773–1843, American commodore.

Hull (hul) A port in SE Yorkshire, England: officially *Kingston-upon-Hull.*

hul·la·ba·loo (hul′ə·bə·lo͞o′) *n.* A loud and confused noise; uproar; tumult. Also **hul′la·bal·loo′.** [Imit. reduplication of HULLO]

hull down *Naut.* So far away as to have the hull hidden by the curvature of the earth.

hul·lo (hə·lō′) See HALLOO.

hum[1] (hum) *v.* **hummed, hum·ming** *v.i.* 1 To make a low, continuous, buzzing sound, as a bee. 2 To sing with the lips closed, not articulating the words. 3 To give forth a confused, indistinct sound, as of mingled voices. 4 To pause in speaking, as from confusion; hem. 5 *Colloq.* To be busily active: The office *hummed.* —*v.t.* 6 To sing, as a tune, with the lips closed. 7 To put into a specified state or condition by humming: to *hum* someone to sleep. See synonyms under SING. —*n.* A low, monotonous, or inarticulate sound (as of *h'm*). —*interj.* A sound as of *h'm* or *hem.* [Imit.] —**hum′mer** *n.*

hu·man (hyo͞o′mən) *adj.* 1 Pertaining to or characterizing man or mankind. See synonyms under HUMANE. 2 Possessed by or suitable for man. —*n. Colloq.* One of the human race; a human being. [<OF *humain* <L *humanus*] —**hu′man·ness** *n.*

hu·mane (hyo͞o·mān′) *adj.* 1 Having or showing kindness and tenderness; compassionate. 2 Tending to refine; polite; elegant. [Var. of HUMAN] —**hu·mane′ly** *adv.* —**hu·mane′ness** *n.*

Synonyms: benevolent, benignant, charitable, clement, compassionate, forgiving, gentle, gracious, human, kind, kind-hearted, merciful, pitying, sympathetic, tender, tender-hearted. *Human* denotes what pertains to mankind, with no suggestion as to its being good or evil. *Humane* denotes what may rightly be expected of mankind at its best in the treatment of sentient beings; a *humane* enterprise or endeavor is one that is intended to prevent or relieve suffering. The *humane* man will not needlessly inflict pain upon the meanest thing that lives; a *merciful* man is disposed to withhold or mitigate the suffering even of the guilty. The *compassionate* man sympathizes with and desires to relieve actual suffering, while one who is *humane* would forestall and prevent the suffering which he sees to be possible. Compare GOOD, PITIFUL. *Antonyms*: barbarous, brutal, cruel, fierce, ferocious, inhuman, merciless, pitiless, ruthless, savage, selfish, unmerciful, unpitying.

hu·man·ism (hyo͞o′mən·iz′əm) *n.* 1 Culture derived from classical training; polite learning. 2 A system of thinking in which man, his interests and development are made central and dominant, tending to exalt the cultural and practical rather than the scientific and speculative. 3 Humanity.

Hu·man·ism (hyo͞o′mən·iz′əm) *n.* The intellectual, scientific, and literary movement of the 14th to 16th centuries which exalted Greek and Roman culture and learning: opposed to *Scholasticism.*

hu·man·ist (hyo͞o′mən·ist) *n.* 1 One versed in the study of humanities; a classical scholar. 2 One who is versed in human nature. —**hu′·man·is′tic** *adj.* —**hu′man·is′ti·cal·ly** *adv.*

hu·man·i·tar·i·an (hyo͞o·man′ə·târ′ē·ən) *n.* 1 One who is broadly philanthropic and humane: a philanthropist. 2 One who seeks to forward the welfare of humanity by ameliorating pain and suffering in any of their manifestations. 3 One who believes that Christ was a mere man; an anti-Trinitarian. 4 One who holds that the perfectibility of the human race is attainable without superhuman aid. —*adj.* Of or pertaining to humanitarianism or the humanitarians.

hu·man·i·tar·i·an·ism (hyo͞o·man′ə·târ′ē·ən·iz′·əm) *n.* 1 The doctrines, principles, or practices of humanitarians, in any sense. 2 In Comtism, the theory that humanity is the ultimate reality.

hu·man·i·ty (hyo͞o·man′ə·tē) *n.* *pl.* **·ties** 1 Mankind collectively. 2 Human nature. 3 The state or quality of being human. 4 The state or quality of being humane; also, a humane act. 5 *pl.* The branches of learning including literature, language, and philosophy, especially as distinguished from the natural and social sciences. [<OF *humanité* <L *humanitas, -tatis* <*humanus* human]

Synonyms: civilization, culture, refinement; (*pl.* the humanities) belles-lettres. See BENEVOLENCE, MANKIND. *Antonyms*: barbarism, boorishness, coarseness, rudeness.

hu·man·ize (hyo͞o′mən·īz) *v.t.* & *v.i.* **·ized, ·iz·ing** To make or become humane or human. Also *Brit.* **hu′man·ise.** —**hu′man·i·za′tion** (-ə·zā′shən, -ī·zā′-) *n.*

hu·man·kind (hyo͞o′mən·kīnd′) *n.* The human race. See synonyms under MANKIND.

hu·man·ly (hyo͞o′mən·lē) *adv.* 1 In accordance with man's nature. 2 Within human power or experience. 3 In a humane or kindly manner.

hu·ma·noid (hyo͞o′mə·noid) *adj.* 1 Resembling a human being in structure, function, and general appearance. 2 Imperfectly or deceptively human. —*n.* An imaginary creature having some resemblance to a human being.

hu·ma·num est er·ra·re (hyo͞o·mā′nəm est e·rā′rē) *Latin* To err is human.

Hu·ma·yun (ho͞o·mä′yo͞on), 1508–56, Mogul emperor of India: also *Houmayoun.*

Hum·ber (hum′bər) An estuary of the Ouse and Trent rivers, flowing into the North Sea from the NE English coast.

Hum·bert (hum′bərt) A masculine personal name. [<Gmc., bright giant]
—**Humbert I,** 1844–1900, king of Italy 1878–1900; assassinated. —**Humbert II,** born 1904, Prince of Piedmont, king of Italy May to June 1946; abdicated.

hum·ble (hum′bəl) *adj.* **·bler, ·blest** 1 Having or expressing a sense of inferiority, dependence, or unworthiness; meek. 2 Lowly in condition; unpretending; obscure. 3 Lowly in feeling or manner; submissive; deferential. —*v.t.* **hum·bled, hum·bling** 1 To reduce the pride of; make meek; humiliate. 2 To lower in rank or dignity; abase. [<F <L *humilis* low <*humus* ground] —**hum′ble·ness** *n.* —**hum′bler** *n.* —**hum′bling** *adj.* —**hum′bling·ly** *adv.* —**hum′bly** *adv.*

Synonyms (adj.): low, lowly, meek, modest, obscure, poor, submissive, unassuming, unobtrusive, unpretending, unpretentious. See MODEST. *Antonyms*: arrogant, boastful, exalted, haughty, high, lofty, presuming, pretentious, proud.

hum·ble·bee (hum′bəl·bē′) *n.* A bumblebee. [ME *humbylbee* <*humbler,* freq. of HUM + BEE]

humble pie A pie made of the humbles of a deer, formerly served to the huntsmen and servants at hunting feasts. —**to eat humble pie** To make humble apologies; be humiliated: also **to eat umble pie.**

hum·bles (hum′bəlz) *n. pl.* The entrails, etc., of a deer. [<OF *numbles* <L *lumbulus,* dim. of *lumbus* loin]

Hum·boldt (hum′bōlt, *Ger.* ho͝om′bōlt), **Baron (Friedrich Heinrich) Alexander von,** 1769–1859, German naturalist and explorer. —**Baron (Karl) Wilhelm von,** 1767–1835, German philologist, statesman, and poet.

Hum·boldt Bay (hum′bōlt) A Pacific inlet on the coast of NW California.

Humboldt River A river in northern Nevada, flowing 300 miles SW to the **Humboldt Sink,** a lake in west central Nevada.

hum·bug (hum′bug) *n.* 1 Anything intended or calculated to deceive; a sham. 2 An impostor. 3 The spirit or practice of deception; sham. See synonyms under QUACK[2]. —*v.* **·bugged, ·bug·ging** *v.t.* To impose upon; deceive. —*v.i.* To practice deceit. [Origin unknown] —**hum′bug·ger** *n.* —**hum′bug·ger·y** *n.*

hum·ding·er (hum·ding′ər) *n. Slang* One who or that which excels.

hum·drum (hum′drum′) *adj.* Without interest; tedious. —*n.* 1 Monotonous existence; tedious talk; anything tiresome. 2 A dull or tedious fellow; bore. [<HUM + DRUM]

Hume (hyo͞om), **David,** 1711–76, Scottish historian and philosopher.

hu·mec·tant (hyo͞o·mek′tənt) *adj.* Moistening. —*n.* A moistening preparation or drug; a diluent. [<L *humectans, -antis,* ppr. of *humectare* moisten]

hu·mer·al (hyo͞o′mər·əl) *adj.* 1 Of or pertaining to the humerus. 2 Of or pertaining to the shoulder. [<L *humerus* shoulder]

humeral veil *Eccl.* A veil or scarf worn round the shoulders by the subdeacon at high mass from the offertory to the paternoster, and also by the officiating priest in processions and benediction of the sacrament.

hu·mer·us (hyo͞o′mər·əs) *n.* *pl.* **·mer·i** (-mər·ī) 1 *Anat.* The bone of the upper part of the arm or forelimb; also, the upper arm or brachium. 2 *Entomol.* **a** The front upper corner or angle of the thorax of a wing cover or elytron. **b** The subcostal nervure in the forewings of certain *Hymenoptera,* or femur of a foreleg in *Orthoptera.* ◆ Homophone: *humorous.* [<L, shoulder]

HUMERUS

Hum·fried (ho͝om′frēt) Dutch and German form of HUMPHREY. Also *Sw.* **Hum′frid.**

hu·mic (hyo͞o′mik) *adj.* Of, pertaining to, or derived from humus. [<L *humus* ground, soil]

hu·mic·o·lous (hyo͞o·mik′ə·ləs) *adj. Bot.* Of or pertaining to plants growing on medium-dry soil. [<L *humus* soil + *colere* dwell]

hu·mid (hyōō′mid) *adj.* Containing sensible moisture; damp. [<L *humidus* <*humere, umere* be moist] —**hu′mid·ly** *adv.*

hu·mid·i·fy (hyōō·mid′ə·fī) *v.t.* **·fied, ·fy·ing** To make moist or humid, as the atmosphere of a room. —**hu·mid′i·fi·ca′tion** *n.*

hu·mid·i·stat (hyōō·mid′ə·stat) *n.* A device for measuring the relative humidity of air.

hu·mid·i·ty (hyōō·mid′ə·tē) *n.* **1** Moisture; dampness. **2** *Meteorol.* The percentage of water vapor in the air to the total amount possible at the same temperature (**relative humidity**). The actual amount of water vapor per unit of volume is known as **absolute humidity.** Also **hu′mid·ness.** [<OF *humidité* <L *humiditas* <*humidus* humid]

hu·mi·dor (hyōō′mə·dôr) *n.* **1** A place for storing cigars or tobacco where the percentage of moisture is regulated; also, a small box fitted for the same purpose. **2** *Printing* A cabinet in which mats are stored to keep them sufficiently moist for proper impression by type.

hu·mil·i·ate (hyōō·mil′ē·āt) *v.t.* **·at·ed, ·at·ing** To lower or offend the pride or self–respect of. See synonyms under ABASE, ABASH. [<L *humiliatus,* pp. of *humiliare* <*humilis* lowly] —**hu·mil′i·at′ing, hu·mil′i·a·to′ry** (-tôr′ē, -tō′·rē) *adj.*

hu·mil·i·a·tion (hyōō·mil′ē·ā′shən) *n.* The act of humiliating, or the state of being humiliated; abasement; mortification; also, that which humiliates. See synonyms under CHAGRIN.

hu·mil·i·ty (hyōō·mil′ə·tē) *n. pl.* **·ties 1** The quality of being humble. **2** Deference; courtesy; kindness. **3** An act of submission or of humbleness. [<L *humilitas, -tatis* lowness]

hu·mit (hyōō′mit) *n.* One degree in the measurement of humiture.

hu·mi·ture (hyōō′mə·chər) *n.* The combined effect of humidity and temperature: expressed quantitatively by adding the values of the relative humidity and the temperature and dividing by 2. [<HUMI(DITY) + (TEMPERA)TURE; coined (1937) by O. F. Hevener, U.S. banker]

hum·mel (hum′əl) *Scot. n.* **1** A cow or other animal with its horns broken off. **2** Grain with the awns broken off. —*adj.* **1** Without horns. **2** Without awns. —*v.t.* **·meled** or **·melled, ·mel·ing** or **·mel·ling** To remove the horns or awns of.

hum·ming (hum′ing) *adj.* **1** Making a low murmuring or buzzing. **2** Lively; frothing; hence, strong or stimulating. **3** *Colloq.* Speedy; spirited. —**hum′ming·ly** *adv.*

hum·ming·bird (hum′ing·bûrd′) *n.* A small, brilliantly colored bird of the New World (family *Trochilidae*), mostly tropical, related to the swifts. They feed chiefly upon insects and the sweets of flowers, and are named from the humming sound produced by the rapid motion of their wings as they hover over the flowers. The common hummingbird of the eastern United States is known as the *rubythroat.*

hummingbird moth The hawk moth.

hum·mock (hum′ək) *n.* **1** A small elevation; hillock. See HAMMOCK[2]. **2** A pile or ridge of ice on an ice field. [Origin unknown] — **hum′mock·y** *adj.*

hu·mor (hyōō′mər, yōō′-) *n.* **1** Disposition of mind or feeling; caprice; freak; whim. **2** A facetious turn of thought; playful fancy; jocularity; drollery. **3** The capacity to perceive, appreciate, or express what is funny, amusing, incongruous, ludicrous, etc.; also, the capacity to make something seem funny, amusing, ludicrous, etc.; specifically in literature, the expression of this in speech or action. **4** Moisture; specifically, an animal fluid: the serous *humor.* In medieval times, the humors, consisting of blood, phlegm, yellow bile, and black bile, were supposed to give rise to the sanguine, phlegmatic, choleric, and melancholic temperaments, respectively. **5** *Pathol.* Any chronic cutaneous eruption supposed to be due to disorder of the blood. See synonyms under FANCY, TEMPER, WHIM, WIT. —**out of humor** Irritated; annoyed. —*v.t.* **1** To comply with the moods or caprices of. **2** To accommodate or adapt oneself to. See synonyms under INDULGE. Also *Brit.* **hu′·mour.** [<OF <L *umor* <*umere* be moist]

hu·mor·al (hyōō′mər·əl, yōō′-) *adj.* Relating to or arising from the humors of the body.

hu·mor·esque (hyōō′mə·resk′) *n. Music* A lively or fanciful instrumental composition. [<G *humoreske*]

hu·mor·ism (hyōō′mər·iz′əm, yōō′-) *n.* **1** The theory that disease proceeds from vitiated humors in the body. **2** The spirit of a humorist. Also **hu·mor·al·ism** (hyōō′mər·əl·iz′əm)

hu·mor·ist (hyōō′mər·ist, yōō′-) *n.* **1** One who displays or exercises humor; a wag. **2** A professional writer or entertainer whose work is humorous. —**hu′mor·is′tic** *adj.*

hu·mor·ous (hyōō′mər·əs, yōō′-) *adj.* **1** Adapted to excite merriment; amusing. **2** Moved by caprice; whimsical; also, irritable; peevish. **3** *Obs.* Humid; watery; moist. ◆ Homophone: *humerus.* —**hu′mor·ous·ly** *adv.* —**hu′mor·ous·ness** *n.*

Synonyms: amusing, comic, comical, droll, facetious, funny, jocose, jocular, ludicrous, sportive, witty. See JOCOSE. *Antonyms*: dreary, dull, grave, melancholy, mournful, sad, serious, sober, solemn.

hu·mor·some (hyōō′mər·səm, yōō′-) *adj.* **1** Full of humor or whims. **2** Characterized by humor; droll. —**hu′mor·some·ly** *adv.* —**hu′·mor·some·ness** *n.*

hu·mous (hyōō′məs) *adj.* Relating to or derived from the ground or humus. [<HUMUS]

hump (hump) *n.* **1** A protuberance, especially that formed by a curved spine or a fleshy growth on the back: the *hump* of a camel or bison. **2** A mound in a railroad switchyard up one side of which cars are taken by an engine and then allowed to coast down the other; hence, any obstacle. **3** *Brit. Slang* An attack of ill temper; blues. **4** *Colloq.* A long tramp or hike, especially with a load on the back. —**over the hump** Beyond the point where force or effort is needed; at the point where all is easy going. —**The Hump** The Himalayas: name applied by aviators in World War II. —*v.t.* **1** To bend or round (the back) in a hump; hunch. **2** *U.S. Slang* To put forth great effort: used reflexively: *Hump* yourself. **3** *Austral. Slang* To carry on the shoulders or back; also, to carry. [Origin uncertain]

hump·back (hump′bak′) *n.* **1** A crooked back. **2** A hunchback. **3** A whalebone whale (genus *Megaptera*) with a low humplike dorsal fin. —**hump′backed′** *adj.*

Hum·per·dinck (hōōm′pər·dingk), **Engelbert,** 1854–1921, German composer.

humph (humf) *interj.* An exclamation of doubt or dissatisfaction.[<HUM[1]]

Hum·phrey (hum′frē) A masculine personal name. Also *Lat.* **Hum·phre·dus** (hum·frē′dəs). [<Gmc., peaceful giant]

—**Humphrey,** 1391–1447, Duke of Gloucester, son of Henry IV of England; Protector during minority of Henry VI: called "the Good Duke."

—**Humphrey, Hubert Horatio,** 1911–1978, American politician, vice president of the United States, 1965–69.

Hum·phrey Island (hum′frē) See MANIHIKI.

Hump·ty Dump·ty (hump′tē dump′tē) A personified egg in English and European nursery rhyme; an important character in Lewis Carroll's *Through the Looking–Glass.*

hump·y[1] (hum′pē) *adj.* **hump·i·er, hump·i·est** Marked by or covered with humps.

hump·y[2] (hum′pē) *n. Austral.* Any small hut or shack. [<native Australian]

hu·mus (hyōō′məs) *n.* The organic matter of the soil, usually leaf mold and other materials, in which decomposition is well advanced. [< L, ground]

Hun (hun) *n.* **1** One of a barbarous nomadic Asian people which invaded Europe in the fourth and fifth centuries. See ATTILA. **2** Any barbarous or destructive warrior; a vandal. [OE *Hune* <LL *Hunnus*]—**Hun′nish** *adj.* —**Hun′nish·ness** *n.*

Hu·nan (hōō′nän′) A province in south central China; 80,000 square miles; capital, Changsha.

hunch (hunch) *n.* **1** A hump. **2** A lump or hunk. **3** A sudden shove. **4** *U.S. Colloq.* A premonition: from the belief that good luck attends the touching of a hunchback's hunch. —*v.t.* **1** To bend, as the back, so as to form a hump; arch. **2** *Obs.* To push or jostle. —*v.i.* **3** To move or thrust oneself forward. [Origin uncertain]

hunch·back (hunch′bak′) *n.* A person having a crooked or deformed back. —**hunch′backed′** *adj.*

hun·der (hun′dər) *adj. & n. Scot.* Hundred.

hun·dred (hun′drid) *adj.* Being one more than ninety–nine; ten times ten. —*n.* **1** The product of ten multiplied by ten; the number following ninety–nine; also, the symbols (100, c, C) representing it. ◆ Collateral adjective: *cental.* **2** An ancient subdivision of a county, common in England and Ireland and still used in the State of Delaware. [OE]

Hundred Days, the The period from March 20 to June 28, 1815, between Napoleon's arrival in Paris after his escape from Elba and the restoration of Louis XVIII after Waterloo.

hun·dred·fold (hun′drid·fōld′) *n.* An amount or number a hundred times as great as a given unit. —*adj.* Indicating a hundred times as much or as many; centuplicate. —*adv.* By a hundred: now always used with *a* (in British usage, with *an*).

hun·dred–per·cent·er (hun′drid·pər·sen′tər) *n. Colloq.* An overpatriotic person; a Jingo.

hun·dredth (hun′dridth) *n.* **1** The last in a series of a hundred. **2** One of a hundred equal parts of anything; the quotient of a unit divided by one hundred. —*adj.* **1** Being the tenth group of ten in order after the ninetieth: the ordinal of *one hundred.* **2** Being one of a hundred equal parts.

hun·dred·weight (hun′drid·wāt′) *n.* A weight commonly reckoned in the United States at 100 pounds avoirdupois, in England at 112 pounds. Abbreviated *cwt.*

Hundred Years' War See table under WAR.

Hun·e·ker (hun′ə·kər), **James Gibbons,** 1860–1921, U.S. author and critic.

hung (hung) Past tense and past participle of HANG.

Hun·gar·i·an (hung·gâr′ē·ən) *adj.* Of or pertaining to Hungary, its people, or their language. —*n.* **1** A native or citizen of Hungary; one of a people formerly Magyar, Ruthenian, Slovak, Serbo–Croatian, German, etc., existing side by side: now dominantly Magyar; hence, a Magyar. **2** The Finno–Ugric language of the Hungarians: also called *Magyar.* [<Med. L *Hungarus*]

Hun·ga·ry (hung′gə·rē) A state in central Europe; 35,902 square miles; capital, Budapest: Hungarian *Magyarország.* Officially **Hungarian People's Republic.**

hun·ger (hung′gər) *n.* **1** Craving for food; also, the weakness caused by the lack of it. **2** Any strong desire. —*v.i.* **1** To feel hunger; be hungry. **2** To have a craving or desire: with *for* or *after.* —*v.t.* **3** To starve; famish. [OE]

hun·ger–strike (hung′gər·strīk′) *n.* Persistent abstention from food in order to obtain concessions from authority: sometimes practiced by prisoners with the object of securing release or a melioration of punishment.

Hung·nam (hōōng·näm) A city of North Korea. *Japanese* **Ko·nan** (kō·nän).

hun·gry (hung′grē) *adj.* **·gri·er, ·gri·est 1** Having a keen appetite; suffering from want of food. **2** Eagerly desiring; craving. **3** Indicating hunger. **4** Poor or barren. See synonyms under GAUNT. [OE *hungrig* <*hunger*] —**hun′·gri·ly** *adv.* —**hun′gri·ness** *n.*

Hung·shui (hōōng′shwā′) A river in southern China, flowing 900 miles to the West River.

hung up *Slang* **1** Psychologically disturbed; especially, preoccupied or obsessed. **2** Sidetracked or impeded, as from a natural or normal process: *hung up* on legal technicalities.

hunk (hungk) *n. Colloq.* A large piece; lump. [Prob. <Flemish *hunke*]

hun·ker (hung′kər) *v.i.* To squat or stoop so that the body rests on the calves of the legs. —*n. pl.* The buttocks resting on the calves of the legs. —**on one's hunkers** In a stooping or squatting position.

Hun·ker (hung′kər) *n.* **1** A member of one of the conservative factions of the Democratic party in New York State in 1842: opposed to the *Barnburners.* **2** Hence, one opposed to political progress; old fogy. [? <Du. *honk* home, goal]

hun·ker·ish (hung′kər·ish) *adj.* Extremely conservative. —**hun′ker·ism** *n.*
hunks (hungks) *n. sing.* & *pl.* A niggardly fellow; miser. [Origin unknown]
hunk·y (hung′kē) See BOHUNK.
hun·ky–do·ry (hung′kē·dôr′ē, -dō′rē) *adj. U.S. Slang* Done satisfactorily or in a satisfactory condition; all right. Also **hunk′y.** [Fanciful extension of slang *hunky* safe, satisfactory]
hunt (hunt) *v.t.* **1** To pursue (game or other wild animals) for the purpose of killing or catching. **2 a** To search (a region) for game. **b** To search (a place): to *hunt* a room. **3** To search for diligently; look for. **4** To manage or use in hunting: to *hunt* a pack of hounds. **5** To chase or drive away; pursue. **6** To persecute; harass. —*v.i.* **7** To pursue game or other wild animals; follow the chase. **8** To make a search; seek. **9** *Aeron.* To make weaving motions about its normal flight path, as an aircraft or guided missile. **10** *Mech.* To run alternately fast and slow owing to unsteady action in the governor: said of stationary engines, etc. —**to hunt down 1** To pursue until caught or killed. **2** To search for until found. —**to hunt up 1** To search for until found. **2** To go in search of. —*n.* **1** The act of hunting game; chase. **2** A search. **3** An association of huntsmen; the participants in a hunt. **4** A district hunted over. —**still hunt 1** A hunting for game in quiet manner. **2** Any quiet and cautious hunt for something. [OE *huntian*]
Synonyms (noun): chase, hunting, inquisition, pursuit, search. A *hunt* may be either the act of pursuing or the act of seeking, or a combination of the two. A *chase* or *pursuit* is after that which is fleeing or departing; a *search* is for that which is hidden; a *hunt* may be for that which is either hidden or fleeing; a *search* is a minute and careful seeking, and is especially applied to a locality; we make a *search* of or through a house, for an object, in which connection it would be colloquial to say a *hunt. Hunt* never quite loses its association with field sports, where it includes both *search* and *chase*; the *search* till the game is hunted out, and the *chase* till it is hunted down. Figuratively, we speak of literary *pursuits*, or of the *pursuit* of knowledge; a *search* for reasons; the *chase* of fame or honor; *hunt*, in figurative use, inclines to the unfavorable sense of *inquisition*, but with aggressiveness; as, a *hunt* for heresy.
Hunt (hunt), **(James Henry) Leigh,** 1784–1859, English poet and essayist. —**William Holman** See HOLMAN-HUNT.
hunt·er (hun′tər) *n.* **1** A person who hunts in any way; especially, one who hunts game. **2** A horse or dog used in hunting. **3** A hunting watch.
Hunt·er (hun′tər), **John,** 1728–93, Scottish surgeon and anatomist.
Hun·ter River (hun′tər) A river in eastern New South Wales, Australia, flowing 287 miles SW to the Pacific.
hunt·er's–green (hun′tərz·grēn′) *n.* A dark, dull-green color formerly used for hunting costume. Also **hunt′er–green′.**
hunt·ing (hun′ting) *n.* The act of pursuing, as game.
hunting bit Snafflebit.
hunting case The case of a hunting watch, designed with a hinged cover for the crystal.
Hunt·ing·don (hun′ting·dən) A county in east central England; 366 square miles; county seat, Huntingdon. Also **Hunt′ing·don·shire** (-shir). Shortened form **Hunts.**
hunting knife A long, sharp, single- or double-edged knife used by hunters and campers.
Hunt·ing·ton (hun′ting·tən), **Collis Potter,** 1821–1900, U.S. railroad builder. —**Ellsworth,** 1876–1947, U.S. geographer and explorer. —**Samuel,** 1731–96, Connecticut patriot; signer of the Declaration of Independence.
Hunt·ing·ton (hun′ting·tən) A city on the Ohio River in western West Virginia.
hunting watch A watch having the dial side as well as the reverse protected by a metal cap or lid.
hunt·ress (hun′tris) *n.* A woman who hunts.
hunts·man (hunts′mən) *n. pl.* ·**men** (-mən) **1** One who practices hunting. **2** The attendant who has charge of the pack of hounds in a hunt.
hunts·man's–cup (hunts′mənz·kup′) *n.* The common American pitcherplant.
hunt's–up (hunts′up′) *n.* A tune played on a horn to awaken huntsmen in the morning; hence, anything that awakens.
Hun·ya·dy (hōōn′yô·dē), **Já·nos** (yä′nôsh), 1385?–1456, Hungarian general and national hero; checked the Moslem advance in SE Europe. Also **Hun′ya·di.**
Hu·on de Bor·deaux (ü·ôṅ′ də bôr·dō′) The hero of a 13th century French *chanson de geste* belonging to the Charlemagne cycle.
Hu·on pine (hyōō′on) A large evergreen tree *(Dacrydium franklini)* growing in Tasmania. [from *Huon* River, Tasmania]
Hu·peh (hōō′pe′) A province in east central China; 70,000 square miles; capital, Wuchang. Also **Hu′pei′.**
hur·cheon (hûr′chən) *n. Brit. Dial.* **1** An urchin. **2** A hedgehog.
hur·dle (hûr′dəl) *n.* **1** A movable framework wattled together and used for making fences, etc. **2** A framework to be leaped over in racing. **3** Formerly, a sledge for conveying criminals to execution. **4** *pl.* A race over hurdles. —*v.* ·**dled,** ·**dling** *v.t.* **1** To leap over, as an obstacle in a race. **2** To make, cover, or enclose with hurdles. **3** To surmount (a difficulty, etc.). —*v.i.* **4** To leap over hurdles, obstacles, etc. [OE *hyrdel*] —**hur′dler** *n.*

HURDLE *(def. 2)*

hur·dles (hûr′dəlz) *n. pl. Scot.* The loins; buttocks.
hurds (hûrdz) See HARDS.
hur·dy–gur·dy (hûr′dē·gûr′dē) *n. pl.* ·**dies** One of various musical instruments played by turning a crank; specifically, a hand organ played by street musicians. [Appar. imit. of the instrument]
hurl (hûrl) *v.t.* **1** To throw with violence; fling. **2** To throw down; overthrow. **3** To utter with vehemence. —*v.i.* **4** *Rare* To throw a missile. **5** In baseball, to pitch. See synonyms under SEND. —*n.* The act of throwing with violence; a cast. [ME *hurlen,* ? <Scand. Cf. Dan. *hurle* whirr, Norw. *hurla* buzz.]
hurl·bar·row (hûrl′bar′ō) *n. Scot.* A wheelbarrow.
hur·ley (hûr′lē) *n. Irish* The game of hurling.
hur·ley–hack·et (hûr′lē·hak′it) *n.* A small trough or sledge for sliding down a steep hill or an inclined plane. [Origin uncertain]
hurl·ing (hûr′ling) *n.* **1** A former game similar to football. **2** In Ireland, the game of hockey. [<HURL]
hur·ly (hûr′lē) *n. pl.* ·**lies** Confusion; noise; uproar.
hur·ly–bur·ly (hûr′lē·bûr′lē) *n. pl.* ·**lies** Tumult; uproar. See synonyms under TUMULT. [Origin uncertain]
Hu·ron (hyŏŏr′on) *n.* A member of any one of four confederated tribes of North American Indians of Iroquoian stock, originally occupying the territory between Lakes Huron and Ontario: destroyed or dispersed by Iroquois tribes to the south of them, 1648–50. [<F, ruffian]
Hu·ron (hyŏŏr′ən), **Lake** The second largest of the Great Lakes of North America, between Michigan and Ontario; 23,200 square miles.
hur·rah (hōō·rô′, hə·rä′) *interj.* An exclamation expressing triumph or joy. —*n.* A shout of triumph. —*v.t.* To cheer, as a speaker, with hurrahs. —*v.i.* To shout a hurrah or hurrahs: sometimes spelled *hooray.* Also **hur·ra′.** [Imit. Cf. Sw., Dan. *hurra!* and Du. *hoera!*]
hur·rah's–nest (hōō·rôz′nest′, hə·räz′-) *n.* A disorderly, untidy mess; wild confusion. [Origin unknown]
hur·ri·cane (hûr′ə·kān) *n. Meteorol.* **1** A tropical cyclone, especially one originating in the West Indies. **2** In the Beaufort scale, a wind force of the 12th or highest degree, moving at more than 75 miles an hour. Also *Obs.* **hur′ri·ca′no** (-kā′nō). See synonyms under CYCLONE. [<Sp. *huracán* <Cariban]
hurricane deck *Naut.* The upper deck of a passenger steamer, as those on the larger rivers of the United States.
hur·ry (hûr′ē) *v.* **hur·ried, hur·ry·ing** *v.i.* **1** To act or move rapidly or in haste; hasten. —*v.t.* **2** To cause or urge to act or move more rapidly: often with *up.* **3** To cause to act or move too hastily: I was *hurried* into it. **4** To hasten the progress, completion, etc., of, often unduly: to *hurry* a decision. See synonyms under HUSTLE, QUICKEN. —*n. pl.* **hur·ries 1** Haste; precipitation. **2** The act of hurrying. [Origin uncertain] —**hur′ried** *adj.* —**hur′·ried·ly** *adv.* —**hur′ried·ness** *n.*
hur·ry–scur·ry (hûr′ē·skûr′ē) *v.i.* To rush in haste and confusion; act hurriedly. —*adj.* Hurried; confused. —*n.* Hasty, confused, or disorderly movement; bustling haste. —*adv.* With disorderly haste; pell-mell; confusedly.
Hurst·mon·ceux (hûrst′mən·sōō′, hûrs′-) See HERSTMONCEUX.
hurt (hûrt) *v.* **hurt, hurt·ing** *v.t.* **1** To cause physical harm or suffering to; injure. **2** To cause material damage to; mark; score. **3** To have a bad effect on; do harm to: Another drink won't *hurt* you. **4** To cause mental suffering to; grieve; worry. —*v.i.* **5** To cause suffering: My feet *hurt.* **6** To cause damage, hurt, etc. —*n.* **1** An injury, especially one causing pain, as a bruise. **2** Damage; detriment. **3** An injury to the feelings; a slight. [<OF *hurter* hit] —**hurt′er** *n.*
Synonyms (verb): afflict, damage, grieve, harm, impair, injure, mar, pain, wound. See VIOLATE. *Antonyms*: benefit, comfort, console, delight, heal, help, please, profit, rejoice, relieve, repair, soothe.
hur·ter (hûr′tər) *n.* **1** The shoulder of the axle of a vehicle, or a reenforcing piece thereon. **2** A buffer, to check the motion of a gun carriage. [<F *heurtoir* knocker]
hurt·ful (hûrt′fəl) *adj.* Causing hurt. See synonyms under BAD, INIMICAL, NOISOME, PERNICIOUS. —**hurt′ful·ly** *adv.* —**hurt′ful·ness** *n.*
Hürt·gen (hürt′gən) A village in North Rhine-Westphalia, Germany, near **Hürtgen Forest,** scene of heavy fighting (November, 1944) in World War II.
hur·tle (hûr′təl) *v.* **hur·tled, hur·tling** *v.i.* **1** To come with violence or noise; crash: with *against* or *together.* **2** To make a crashing, rushing sound; move with noisy speed: The shell *hurtled* through the air. **3** To move or rush headlong or impetuously: He *hurtled* from the room. —*v.t.* **4** To drive, shoot, or throw violently. **5** *Archaic* To strike against; collide with. [Freq. of ME *hurten* hit, hurt]
hur·tle·ber·ry (hûr′təl·ber′ē) *n. pl.* ·**ries** The huckleberry. [Appar. <dial. *hurt,* OE *horta* a hurtleberry + BERRY]
hurt·less (hûrt′lis) *adj.* **1** Harmless. **2** Unharmed.
Hus (hus, *Czech* hōōs), **Jan** See HUSS, JOHN.
hus·band (huz′bənd) *n.* **1** A married man; man with a wife. **2** *Obs.* A thrifty manager. **3** *Obs.* A husbandman. —*v.t.* **1** To use or spend wisely; economize on; conserve. **2** To be a husband to; marry. **3** *Archaic* To provide with a husband. **4** *Archaic* To till; cultivate. [OE *hūsbonda* <*hūs* house + *bonda* freeholder] —**hus′band·less** *adj.* —**hus′band·like′** *adj.* —**hus′band·ly** *adj.*
hus·band·man (huz′bənd·mən) *n. pl.* ·**men** (-mən) A farmer.
hus·band·ry (huz′bən·drē) *n.* **1** Agriculture. **2** Economical management; also, any management, good or bad. See synonyms under AGRICULTURE. —**Patrons of Husbandry** See GRANGE.
Hu·sein ibn–A·li (hōō·sīn′ ib′n·ä′lē), 1856–1931, first king of Hejaz 1916–24.
hush (hush) *v.t.* **1** To make silent; repress the noise of. **2** To suppress mention of; keep from being public. **3** To soothe; allay, as fears. —*v.i.* **4** To be or become silent or still. [<*adj.*] —*n.* Deep silence; stillness; quiet. —*adj. Obs.* Quiet; still; silent. —*interj.* Be still; calm yourself. [ME *hussht* quiet]
hush·a·by (hush′ə·bī) *interj.* Hush: an expression used to lull a child to sleep.
hush–hush (hush′hush′) *adj. Colloq.* Secret.
Hu Shih (hōō′ shir′), 1891–1962, Chinese philosopher and author; invented modern simplified Chinese.
hush·ion (hush′ən) *n. Scot.* A footless stocking.
hush money A bribe to secure silence or secrecy.

hush·pup·py (hush′pup′ē) *n. pl.* **·pies** *U.S.* In the South, a fried ball of cornmeal dough.

husk (husk) *n.* **1** The outer covering of certain fruits or seeds; rind; hull; especially, that of an ear of maize or Indian corn. **2** The carob pod. *Luke* xv 16. **3** Any covering, especially when comparatively worthless. — *v.t.* To remove the husk of. [ME *huske,* ? OE *hosu* husk] — **husk′er** *n.*

husk·ing (hus′king) *n.* **1** The act of stripping off husks, as from maize. **2** A gathering of friends to aid in husking corn: also **husking bee.**

husk·y[1] (hus′kē) *adj.* **husk·i·er, husk·i·est** **1** Abounding in husks; like husks. **2** Dry as a husk; hoarse: said of the voice. [<HUSK] — **husk′i·ly** *adv.* — **husk′i·ness** *n.*

husk·y[2] (hus′kē) *U.S. Colloq. adj.* **husk·i·er, husk·i·est** Strong; burly. — *n.* A strong or powerfully built person. [Special use of HUSKY[1], with ref. to toughness of husks]

Husk·y (hus′kē) *n. pl.* **Husk·ies** A heavy-furred Eskimo dog. See SIBERIAN HUSKY. Also **husk′y.** [? Alter. of ESKIMO]

Huss (hus), **John,** 1369–1415, Bohemian religious reformer; burned as a heretic: also *Jan Hus.*

hus·sar (hŏŏ·zär′) *n.* Originally, a light-armed horse trooper of the Hungarian army; later, a member of any light-armed cavalry regiment in other European armies, usually with brilliant dress uniforms. [<Hungarian *huszár* <Serbian *gusar* <Ital. *corsaro* <Med. L *corsarius.* Doublet of CORSAIR.]

Hus·serl (hŏŏs′ərl), **Edmund,** 1859–1938, German philosopher.

Huss·ite (hus′īt) *n.* A follower of John Huss. — **Huss·it·ism** (hus′īt·iz′əm) *n.*

hus·sy (huz′ē, hus′ē) *n. pl.* **·sies** **1** A pert or forward girl; jade: in reproach or playfully. Also *huzzy.* **2** A case or bag. See HOUSEWIFE (def. 2). [Alter. of HOUSEWIFE]

hust·ing (hus′ting) *n.* **1** A British court formerly held in the larger cities (and still in existence in London): now more commonly in the plural. **2** *pl.* The temporary platform on which the nomination of parliamentary candidates was made prior to the Ballot Act of 1872; hence, the proceedings at an election; now, any platform or place where political speeches are made; hence, a political campaign. [OE *hūsting* council <ON *hūsthing* < *hūs* house + *thing* assembly]

hus·tle (hus′əl) *v.* **hus·tled, hus·tling** *v.t.* **1** To push or knock about roughly or rudely; jostle. **2** To force or impel roughly and hurriedly: to *hustle* a man from a room. **3** *U.S. Colloq.* To hurry; cause to proceed rapidly. **4** *U.S. Slang* **a** To sell aggressively, as for quick profit. **b** To obtain by aggressive action. **c** To dupe; victimize. — *v.i.* **5** To push one's way; shove; elbow. **6** *U.S. Colloq.* To act or work with energy and speed. **7** *U.S. Slang* To be a prostitute. **8** *U.S. Slang* To live by one's wits, as by gambling, petty thievery, etc. **9** In sports, to put forth extra effort. — *n.* **1** The act of hustling. **2** *Colloq.* Energetic activity; push. **3** *U.S. Slang* A way of getting money illegitimately, as by fraud or thievery; a racket. [<Du *hutselen* shake, toss]

Synonyms (verb): crowd, elbow, hasten, hurry, jam, jostle, push, rush, shove. *Antonyms*: dally, dawdle, delay, hold back, loaf.

hus·tler (hus′lər, hus′əl·ər) *n.* **1** *U.S. Colloq.* An aggressive, energetic person; go-getter. **2** *U.S. Slang* A prostitute. **3** *U.S. Slang* One who lives by his wits, as a gambler, confidence man, petty thief, etc.

hus·wife (huz′if) *n. Obs.* **1** A housewife. **2** A hussy. [Var. of HOUSEWIFE]

hut (hut) *n.* A small rude dwelling. — *v.t.* & *v.i.* **hut·ted, hut·ting** To shelter or live in a hut. [<OF *hutte* <OHG *huttā*]

Synonyms (noun): cabin, cot, cottage, hovel, shanty, shed. See HOUSE. *Antonyms*: castle, hall, mansion, palace.

hutch (huch) *n.* **1** A place for storing anything. **2** A small or dark room. **3** A coop or pen for rabbits, etc. **4** A chest or locker. **5** A measure; also, a basket. — *v.t.* To store up or hoard. [<F *huche* <LL *hutica*]

Hutch·ins (huch′inz), **Robert Maynard,** born 1899, U.S. educator; president of the University of Chicago 1929–45; chancellor 1945–51.

Hutchinson's teeth *Pathol.* The notched permanent incisor teeth sometimes associated with congenital syphilis. [after Sir Jonathan *Hutchinson,* 1828–1913, English physician]

hut·ment (hut′mənt) *n.* **1** A group of huts, as in an encampment. **2** The housing of people in huts.

Hux·ley (huks′lē) Name of an English family distinguished in science and literature: especially **Thomas Henry,** 1825–95, biologist and author; upheld Darwin's views on evolution; **Sir Julian Sorell,** 1887–1975, biologist; grandson of Thomas Henry; **Aldous Leonard,** 1894–1963, novelist; brother of the preceding.

Huy·gens (hī′gənz), **Christian,** 1629–95, Dutch mathematician, physicist, and astronomer. Also **Huy·ghens.**

Huys·mans (wēs·mäns′), **Joris Karl,** 1848–1907, French novelist.

huz·za (hə·zä′) *n.* & *interj.* Hurrah: a shout of joy. Also **huz·zah′, huz·zay′** (-zā′). [Imit.]

huz·zy (huz′ē) See HUSSY.

Hwai (hwī) A river in east central China, flowing 600 miles NE.

Hwai·ning (hwī′ning′) A former name of ANKING.

Hwang Hai (hwäng′ hī′) The Chinese name for the YELLOW SEA.

Hwang Ho (hwäng′ hō′) The second-longest river of China, flowing 2,900 miles east from the Tibetan highlands across northern China to the Gulf of Chihli: also *Yellow River, Hoang Ho.*

Hwang·poo (hwäng′pōō′) A river in eastern China, flowing 100 miles north to the Yangtse: also *Whangpoo.*

hy·a·cinth (hī′ə·sinth) *n.* **1** A bulbous plant of the lily family (genus *Hyacinthus*) cultivated for its spikelike cluster of flowers. **2** The bulb or flower of this plant. **3** A gem, anciently bluish-violet, probably the sapphire, now a brownish, reddish, or orange zircon. **4** A plant frequently alluded to by the Greek poets, fabled to have sprung from the blood of Hyacinthus, beloved of Apollo, and to have borne on its petals the words of grief, *Ai, Ai*: sometimes identified as the iris, larkspur, or gladiolus. [Var. of older *jacynth* <OF *jacincte* <L *hyacinthus* <Gk. *hyakinthos.* Doublet of JACINTH.]

HYACINTH *(def. 1)*

hyacinth blue A medium purplish-blue, the color of certain hyacinths.

hy·a·cin·thine (hī′ə·sin′thin, -thīn) *adj.* Pertaining to or like the hyacinth.

Hy·a·cin·thus (hī′ə·sin′thəs) In Greek mythology, a youth loved and accidentally killed by Apollo who caused a flower to spring from his blood.

Hy·a·des (hī′ə·dēz) **1** In Greek mythology, five daughters of Atlas whom Zeus set among the stars. **2** *Astron.* A cluster of five stars in Taurus, including Aldebaran, shaped like the letter V: when they rose with the sun they were considered to be a sign of rain by ancient astronomers. [<L <Gk., ? < *hyein* rain] Also **Hy·ads** (hī′adz).

hy·ae·na (hī·ē′nə) See HYENA.

hy·a·line (hī′ə·lin, -līn) *n.* **1** A glassy surface, as of the sea; something transparent. **2** *Biochem.* A nitrogenous compound, related to chitin, the chief constituent of hydatid cysts, which on decomposition yields a reducing sugar. **3** *Anat.* The hyaloid membrane. Also **hy′a·lin** (-lin). — *adj.* Consisting of or resembling glass; transparent: the *hyaline* substance of a cell. [<L *hyalinus* <Gk. *hyalos* glass]

hyaline cartilage *Anat.* That form of cartilage in which the cells are embedded in a homogeneous translucent matrix.

hy·a·lite (hī′ə·līt) *n.* A pellucid glassy variety of opal.

hyalo– *combining form* Glass; of or resembling glass: *hyaloplasm.* Also, before vowels, **hyal–.** [<Gk. *hyalos* glass]

hy·al·o·gen (hī·al′ə·jən) *n. Biochem.* Any of various insoluble substances found in animal tissues and related to mucin; it yields hyaline on hydrolysis.

hy·a·loid (hī′ə·loid) *adj.* Like glass; pellucid: the *hyaloid* membrane. [<Gk. *hyaloeidēs* glassy]

hyaloid membrane *Anat.* A delicate membrane enveloping the vitreous humor of the eye.

hy·a·lo·plasm (hī′ə·lō·plaz′əm) *n. Biol.* The clear, fluid or semifluid ground substance of protoplasm, as distinguished from the granular substance. Also **hy′a·lo·plas′ma** (-plaz′·mə). — **hy′a·lo·plas′mic** *adj.*

Hy·bla (hī′blə) An ancient town in Sicily on the site of modern Paternò. Also **Hybla Major.**

Hy·blae·an (hī·blē′ən) *adj.* Of or relating to Hybla or the famous honey produced there in ancient times; hence, smoothly flowing. Also **Hy·blæ′an, Hy·ble′an.**

hy·brid (hī′brid) *adj.* **1** Produced by inter-breeding or cross-fertilization. **2** Derived from incongruous sources; mixed. — *n.* **1** An animal or plant of mixed parentage; a mongrel. **2** Anything of heterogeneous origin or incongruous parts. **3** *Ling.* A word composed of elements from more than one language, as *genocide.* [<L *hybrida* offspring of tame sow and wild boar]

hy·brid·ism (hī′brid·iz′əm) *n.* **1** The state of being hybrid: also **hy·brid·i·ty** (hī·brid′ə·tē). **2** The act of interbreeding, or of inducing hybridization. **3** *Ling.* The mingling in one word of elements from more than one language.

hy·brid·ize (hī′brid·īz) *v.t.* & *v.i.* **·ized, ·iz·ing** To produce or cause to produce hybrids; crossbreed. Also *Brit.* **hy′brid·ise.** — **hy·brid·i·za·tion** (hī′brid·ə·zā′shən, -ī·zā′-) *n.* — **hy′·brid·iz′er** *n.* — **hy′brid·ous** *adj.*

hybrid vigor Heterosis.

hy·dan·to·in (hī·dan′tō·in) *n.* A white crystalline derivative of allantoin, C_3H_4ON. [<Gk. *hydōr, hydatos* water + (ALL)ANTOIN]

Hy·das·pes (hi·das′pēz) The ancient name for the JHELUM.

hy·da·thode (hī′də·thōd) *n. Bot.* An epidermal cellular structure, as a gland, that exudes water: found in plants. [<Gk. *hydōr, hydatos* water + *hodos* way]

hy·da·tid (hī′də·tid) *n.* **1** An encysted vesicle containing an aqueous fluid. **2** An encysted larval stage of a tapeworm. — *adj.* Of or pertaining to a water-containing cyst. [<Gk. *hydatis* drop of water]

hy·da·to·gen·e·sis (hī′də·tō·jen′ə·sis) *n.* Formation of water, as in the tissues and cavities of the body. [<Gk. *hydōr, hydatos* water + GENESIS]

Hyde (hīd), **Douglas,** 1860–1949, Irish Gaelic scholar; president of Ireland 1938–45. — **Edward,** 1609–74, first Earl of Clarendon, English historian and statesman.

Hyde (hīd), **Mr.** See JEKYLL.

Hyde Park **1** A public park in the West End of London, England; noted as a meeting place of soapbox orators. **2** A village on the Hudson in southern New York; site of the estate and burial place of Franklin Roosevelt.

Hy·der·a·bad (hī′dər·ə·bad′, -bäd′) **1** A former State of south central India on the Deccan Plateau, merged, November 1, 1956, into the States of Andhra Pradesh, Bombay, and Mysore; 82,698 square miles; former capital, Hyderabad: formerly *Nizam's Dominions*: also *Haidarabad.* **2** A Commissioners' Division of SE West Pakistan, formerly a district of the former province of Sind; 35,998 square miles. **3** A city on the Indus, SE West Pakistan, formerly capital of the former province of Sind. **4** A city on the Deccan Plateau, south central India, capital of Andhra Pradesh State; formerly capital of the former State of Hyderabad.

Hy·der A·li (hī′dər ä′lē), 1728–82, regent of Mysore who fought against the British; father of Tipu Sahib.

hyd·no·car·pate (hid′nə·kär′pāt) *n. Chem.* A salt or ester of hydnocarpic acid, especially the sodium salt or ethyl ester, used in the treatment of leprosy.

hyd·no·car·pic (hid′nə·kär′pik) *adj. Chem.* Denoting an acid, $C_{16}H_{28}O_2$, extracted from the seeds and oil of the chaulmoogra tree, and used in the treatment of leprosy. [<Gk. *hydnon* truffle + *karpos* fruit]

hydr– Var. of HYDRO–.

hy·dra (hī′drə) *n.* *pl.* **·dras** or **·drae** (-drē) **1** Any evil having many forms. **2** A fresh-water polyp (genus *Hydra*). [<Gk. *hydra* water serpent]

Hy·dra (hī′drə) **1** In Greek mythology, the nine-headed serpent of Lerna, which grew two heads for each one that was cut off: slain by Hercules with a firebrand. **2** *Astron.* A southern constellation. See CONSTELLATION.

hy·drac·id (hī·dras′id) *n.* *Chem.* An acid that contains no oxygen, as hydrochloric acid: contrasted with *oxyacid.*

hy·dra·gog (hī′drə·gôg, -gog) *n.* Any medicine that causes abundant watery evacuations. Also **hy′dra·gogue.** [<F <L *hydragogus* <Gk. *hydragōgos* < *hydōr* water + *agein* lead]

hy·dra–head·ed (hī′drə·hed′id) *adj.* Having many heads; hard to destroy.

hy·dran·ge·a (hī·drān′jē·ə, -jə) *n.* A plant of a genus *(Hydrangea)* of trees and shrubs of the saxifrage family, with opposite, usually serrate, leaves and cymose clusters of large, showy flowers. [<NL <Gk. *hydōr* water + *angeion* vessel]

hy·drant (hī′drənt) *n.* A valved discharge pipe connected with a water main; a plug. [<Gk. *hydōr* water]

hy·dranth (hī′dranth) *n.* *Zool.* A nutritive zooid in a hydroid colony, or the part with the mouth and digestive cavity. [<HYDRA + Gk. *anthos* flower]

Hy·dra·o·tes (hī′drā·ō′tēz) The ancient name for the RAVI.

hy·drar·gyr·ic (hī′drär·jir′ik) *adj.* Of, pertaining to, or containing mercury.

hy·drar·gy·rism (hī·drär′jə·riz′əm) *n.* Mercury poisoning; mercurialism.

hy·drar·gy·rum (hī·drär′jə·rəm) *n.* Mercury: especially so called in pharmacy. [<NL <L *hydrargyrus* <Gk. *hydrargyros* < *hydōr* water + *argyros* silver]

hy·dras·tine (hī·dras′tēn, -tin) *n.* *Chem.* A bitter, crystalline alkaloid, $C_{21}H_{21}NO_6$, contained in the roots of goldenseal, having tonic and febrifuge properties. [<NL *Hydrastis* botanical genus name <Gk. *hydōr* water]

hy·drate (hī′drāt) *n.* *Chem.* Any of a class of compounds formed by the union of molecules of water with other molecules or atoms. — *v.t.* **·drat·ed, ·drat·ing** To combine with water or its elements to form a hydrate. [<HYDR- + -ATE[3]] — **hy′drat·ed** *adj.* — **hy·dra·tion** (hī·drā′shən) *n.*

hy·drau·lic (hī·drô′lik) *adj.* **1** Pertaining to hydraulics, involving the moving of water, or force exerted by water: *hydraulic* engineering, mining, etc. **2** Denoting any of various machines and structures operating by means of water or other liquid under pressure: a *hydraulic* elevator, crane, ram, press, etc. **3** Hardening under water: *hydraulic* cement. Also **hy·drau′li·cal.** [<L *hydraulicus* <Gk. *hydraulikos* of a water organ < *hydraulos* water organ < *hydōr* water + *aulos* pipe] — **hy·drau′li·cal·ly** *adv.*

hydraulic brake A brake actuated by fluids under pressure in cylinders and tubular connecting lines.

hydraulic press A machine which operates by means of fluid under pressure to exert a large force over an extended area: used in forming steel dies, in baling, etc.

hydraulic ram An automatic device by which the fall of a comparatively large quantity of water furnishes the power to raise a smaller quantity to a height above that of the source.

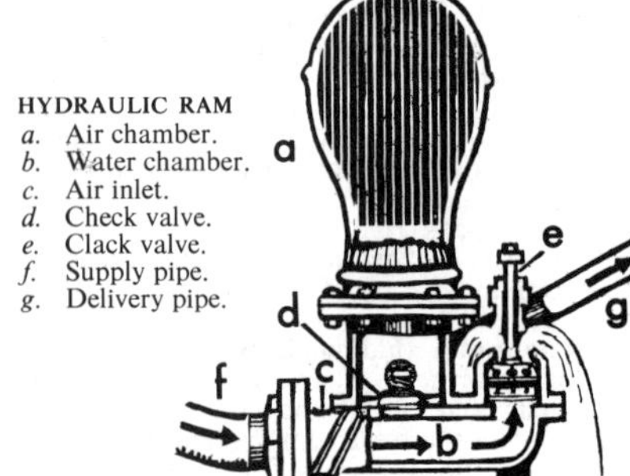

HYDRAULIC RAM
a. Air chamber.
b. Water chamber.
c. Air inlet.
d. Check valve.
e. Clack valve.
f. Supply pipe.
g. Delivery pipe.

hy·drau·lics (hī·drô′liks) *n.* *pl.* *(construed as singular)* The science of the laws of motion of water and other liquids and of their practical applications.

hydraulic transmission See FLUID DRIVE.

hy·dra·zine (hī′drə·zēn, -zin) *n.* *Chem.* **1** A colorless fuming liquid, N_2H_4, derived from diazoacetic acid: used as a reducing agent in organic synthesis and as a fuel in jet engines. **2** One of a group of compounds derived from the foregoing by replacement of one or more hydrogen atoms by another radical: phenyl *hydrazine.* [<HYDR- + AZ(O) + -INE[2]]

hy·dra·zo·ic (hī′drə·zō′ik) *adj.* *Chem.* Of or pertaining to a colorless, very toxic acid, HN_3, obtained from hydrazine by various methods; its salts, **hy·dra·zo·ates** (hī′drə·zō′·āts), explode with great violence when heated.

hy·dric (hī′drik) *adj.* Of or pertaining to hydrogen in combination.

hy·dride (hī′drīd, -drid) *n.* *Chem.* **1** A compound of hydrogen with another element or a radical acting as an element. **2** A hydroxide. Also **hy′drid** (-drid).

hy·dri·od·ic (hī′drē·od′ik) *adj.* *Chem.* Pertaining to or designating a dense, colorless, suffocating acid, HI, soluble in water, formed by the union of hydrogen and iodine.

hydro– *combining form* **1** Water; of, related to, or resembling water: *hydrophone.* **2** *Chem.* Denoting a compound of hydrogen: *hydrochloric.* Also, before vowels, *hydr–.* [<Gk. *hydro-* < *hydōr* water]

hy·dro·air·plane (hī′drō·âr′plān′) See HYDROPLANE (def. 1).

hy·dro·bro·mic (hī′drə·brō′mik) *adj.* *Chem.* Designating a colorless, pungent acid, HBr, formed by the union of hydrogen and bromine.

hy·dro·car·bon (hī′drə·kär′bən) *n.* *Chem.* One of a large and important group of compounds that contain hydrogen and carbon only. There are many types and classes, including the aliphatic, aromatic, saturated, and unsaturated hydrocarbons.

hy·dro·cele (hī′drə·sēl) *n.* *Pathol.* A localized accumulation of fluid surrounding the testicles or along the spermatic cord. [<L <Gk. *hydrokēlē* < *hydōr* water + *kēlē* tumor]

hy·dro·ceph·a·lus (hī′drə·sef′ə·ləs) *n.* *Pathol.* An accumulation of watery fluid within the ventricles or between the membranes of the brain. [<HYDRO- + Gk. *kephalē* head] — **hy′dro·ceph′a·loid** (-loid), **hy′dro·ceph′a·lous** *adj.*

hy·dro·chlo·ric (hī′drə·klôr′ik, -klō′rik) *adj.* *Chem.* Pertaining to or designating a colorless, corrosive, fuming acid, HCl, exceedingly soluble in water, in which form it is largely used in manufactures and sometimes called *muriatic acid.*

hy·dro·chlo·ride (hī′drə·klôr′īd, -klō′rīd) *n.* *Chem.* A compound produced by the union of hydrochloric acid with an element or radical.

hy·dro·cy·an·ic (hī′drō·sī·an′ik) *adj.* *Chem.* Of, pertaining to, or designating an unstable, volatile, colorless, and extremely poisonous acid, HCN, formed by decomposing metallic cyanides with hydrochloric acid. It is only slightly dissociated in water, and has a characteristic odor resembling that of bitter almonds: also called *prussic acid.*

hy·dro·dy·nam·ic (hī′drō·dī·nam′ik) *adj.* Of or pertaining to the force or pressure of water or other fluids. Also **hy′dro·dy·nam′i·cal.**

hy·dro·dy·nam·ics (hī′drō·dī·nam′iks) *n.* *pl.* *(construed as singular)* The branch of mechanics that treats of the dynamics of fluids, chiefly water and other liquids.

hy·dro·e·lec·tric (hī′drō·i·lek′trik) *adj.* Of or pertaining to electricity developed by water power, or by the escape of steam under high pressure, etc. — **hy·dro·e·lec·tric·i·ty** (hī′drō·i·lek·tris′ə·tē) *n.*

hy·dro·flu·or·ic (hī′drō·flo͞o·ôr′ik, -or′-) *adj.* *Chem.* Pertaining to or designating a volatile, colorless, hygroscopic, corrosive acid, HF, formed by decomposing metallic fluorides. It readily attacks silica, hence is used for etching on glass.

hy·dro·foil (hī′drə·foil) *n.* A streamlined surface designed to provide support in or obtain a reaction from the water through which it moves, as an attachment to a boat, submarine, or hydroplane.

hy·dro·gel (hī′drə·jel) *n.* *Chem.* A colloid which has assumed a jellylike form in the presence of water.

hy·dro·gen (hī′drə·jən) *n.* The lightest of the elements (symbol H) occurring chiefly in combination with oxygen as water, and in hydrocarbons and other organic compounds. When isolated it is usually a colorless, odorless, tasteless, inflammable gas, lighter than air and liquefying under great pressure and low temperature. — **heavy hydrogen** See DEUTERIUM. [<F *hydrogène* <Gk. *hydōr* water + *gen-*, stem of *gignesthai* be born; so called with ref. to the water formed by its combustion] — **hy·drog·e·nous** (hī·droj′ə·nəs) *adj.*

hy·dro·gen·ate (hī′drə·jə·nāt′) *v.t.* **·at·ed, ·at·ing** *Chem.* **1** To cause to combine with hydrogen. **2** To expose to hydrogen, or to effect chemical action of by the use of or by exposure to hydrogen: to *hydrogenate* fats and oils. Also **hy′dro·gen·ize′** (-īz′).

hy·dro·gen·a·tion (hī′drə·jə·nā′shən) *n.* *Chem.* The act or process of subjecting to the action of hydrogen, usually in the presence of a catalyst: the *hydrogenation* of coal to form liquid hydrocarbons.

hydrogen bomb A bomb of great destructive power, releasing enormous quantities of energy by the fusion, under extremely high temperatures, of deuterium or tritium atoms, with the formation of helium.

hydrogen cyanide Hydrocyanic acid.

hydrogen ion *Chem.* The positively charged hydrogen ion (H^+) present in all acids. The number of hydrogen ions per unit volume of an aqueous solution is known as the **hydrogen ion concentration,** or *p*H value.

hydrogen peroxide *Chem.* A sirupy liquid, H_2O_2, whose aqueous solutions are important as antiseptics and bleaching agents, the usual solution being a slightly acid one containing about 3 percent by weight of pure hydrogen peroxide. Also called *peroxide.*

hydrogen sulfide *Chem.* A colorless, gaseous compound, H_2S, having a characteristic odor of rotten eggs, made by decomposing certain metallic sulfides, chiefly iron, by means of acids. It is poisonous and is a valuable laboratory reagent.

hy·dro·glid·er (hī′drə·glī′dər) *n.* A glider with floats attached to permit it to land on or take off from water.

Hy·dro·graph·ic Office (hī′drə·graf′ik) A bureau of the U. S. Navy Department in charge of the charting of navigable waters and the studying of oceanography.

hy·drog·ra·phy (hī·drog′rə·fē) *n.* The science of determining and making known the conditions of navigable waters, charting rivers, coasts, etc. — **hy·drog′ra·pher** *n.* — **hy′dro·graph′ic** or **·i·cal** *adj.*

hy·droid (hī′droid) *adj.* **1** Of or pertaining to a class *(Hydrozoa)* of mostly marine coelenterates resembling the hydra; like a polyp. **2** Designating a reproductive phase in the development of certain hydrozoans characterized by the formation of colonies. — *n.* A hydrozoan.

hy·dro·ki·net·ic (hī′drō·ki·net′ik) *adj.* Relating to the motion and kinetic energy of fluids. Also **hy′dro·ki·net′i·cal.**

hy·dro·ki·net·ics (hī′drō·ki·net′iks) *n.* *pl.* *(construed as singular)* The branch of hydrodynamics that treats of fluids in motion.

hy·drol·o·gy (hī·drol′ə·jē) *n.* The branch of physical geography that treats of the waters of the earth, their distribution, characteristics, and effects. [<HYDRO- + -LOGY] — **hy·dro·log·ic** (hī′drə·loj′ik) or **·i·cal** *adj.* — **hy′dro·log′i·cal·ly** *adv.* — **hy·drol′o·gist** *n.*

hy·drol·y·sis (hī·drol′ə·sis) *n.* *Chem.* Any decomposition involving the addition of water; specifically, a double decomposition reaction between water and some other compound, as phosphorus trichloride. [< HYDRO- + -LYSIS] — **hy·dro·lyt·ic** (hī′drə·lit′ik) *adj.*

hy·dro·lyte (hī′drə·līt) *n.* Any substance affected by hydrolysis.

hy·dro·lyze (hī′drə·līz) *v.t.* & *v.i.* **·lyzed, ·lyz·ing** To undergo or cause to undergo the process of hydrolysis. — **hy′dro·lyz′a·ble** *adj.* — **hy·dro·ly·za·tion** (hī′drə·lə·zā′shən, -lī·zā′-) *n.*

hy·dro·man·cy (hī′drə·man′sē) *n.* Divination by means of water. — **hy′dro·manc′er** *n.* — **hy′dro·man′tic** (-tik) *adj.*

hy·dro·me·chan·ics (hī′drō·mə·kan′iks) *n.* The mechanics of fluids, including hydrostatics, hydrodynamics, hydrokinetics, and pneumatics. — **hy′dro·me·chan′i·cal** *adj.*

hy·dro·me·du·sa (hī′drō·mə·do͞o′sə, -dyo͞o′-) *n.* *pl.* **·sae** (-sē) A type of coelenterate produced by budding from an individual, as the jellyfish and medusa.

hy·dro·mel (hī′drə·mel) *n.* A liquor, usually unfermented, consisting of honey diluted with water; when fermented, it is called *mead.* [<L <Gk. *hydromeli* <*hydōr* water + *meli* honey]

hy·dro·met·al·lur·gy (hī′drō·met′əl·ûr′jē) *n.* The process of assaying or reducing ore by means of liquid reagents. — **hy′dro·met′al·lur′gi·cal** *adj.*

hy·dro·me·te·or (hī′drō·mē′tē·ər) *n. Meteorol.* A watery or aqueous meteor; any of the conditions or effects produced by water, as rain, snow, hail, etc.

hy·dro·me·te·or·ol·o·gy (hī′drō·mē′tē·ə·rol′ə·jē) *n.* The branch of meteorology that treats of hydrometeors or of water in the atmosphere.

hy·drom·e·ter (hī·drom′ə·tər) *n.* 1 A calibrated sealed tube weighted at one end for determining the density or specific gravity, especially of liquids and solutions: also called *densimeter.* 2 A current gage. — **hy·dro·met·ric** (hī′drə·met′rik) or **·ri·cal** *adj.* — **hy·drom′e·try** *n.*

hy·drop·a·thy (hī·drop′ə·thē) *n.* The treatment of diseases by the use of water; water cure. — **hy·dro·path·ic** (hī′drə·path′ik) or **·i·cal** *adj.* — **hy·drop′a·thist, hy′dro·path** *n.*

hy·dro·phane (hī′drə·fān) *n.* A whitish or light-colored opal, opaque when dry, but translucent when wet. — **hy·droph·a·nous** (hī·drof′ə·nəs) *adj.*

hy·droph·i·lous (hī·drof′ə·ləs) *adj. Bot.* Having the flowers pollinated by the agency of water: said of certain higher plants. [<HYDRO- + Gk. *philos* loving]

hy·dro·pho·bi·a (hī′drə·fō′bē·ə) *n.* 1 Rabies. 2 Any morbid dread of water. [<L <Gk., <*hydōr* water + *phobos* fear] — **hy′dro·pho′bic** *adj.*

hy·dro·phone (hī′drə·fōn) *n.* 1 An electrical instrument for detecting underwater sounds, especially of enemy submarines. 2 A device used for the purpose of detecting leaks in water pipes.

hy·dro·phyte (hī′drə·fīt) *n. Bot.* A plant living in water or in wet ground. — **hy·dro·phyt·ic** (hī′drə·fit′ik) *adj.*

hy·drop·ic (hī·drop′ik) *adj.* Dropsical; affected with dropsy. Also **hy·drop′i·cal.** [<OF *idropique* <L *hydropicus* <Gk. *hydrōpikos* <*hydrōps* dropsy <*hydōr* water] — **hy·drop′i·cal·ly** *adv.*

hy·dro·plane (hī′drə·plān) *n.* 1 An airplane constructed for alighting upon or rising from the water: also called *hydroairplane.* 2 A motorboat of extremely light construction driven either by submerged screws or by aerial propellers. 3 A hydrofoil. — *v.i.* **·planed, ·plan·ing** 1 To move on water at a speed sufficient to give support through hydrodynamic and aerodynamic forces alone. 2 To drive or ride in a hydroplane.

hy·dro·pon·ics (hī′drə·pon′iks) *n. pl.* (*construed as singular*) Soilless agriculture; the raising of plants in nutrient mineral solutions without earth around the roots: also called *water culture, tank farming.* [<HYDRO- + Gk. *ponos* labor] — **hy′dro·pon′ic** *adj.*

hy·drop·sy (hī′drop′sē) *n.* Dropsy. Also **hy′·drops, hy·drop′si·a.**

hy·dro·qui·none (hī′drō·kwi·nōn′) *n. Chem.* A white crystalline compound, $C_6H_4(OH)_2$, derived from quinone: used in medicine as an antiseptic and antipyretic, and in photography as a developing agent. Also **hy′dro·quin′ol** (-kwin′ōl, -ol).

hy·dro·scope (hī′drə·skōp) *n.* 1 An instrument for detecting moisture, especially in the air. 2 An instrument for seeing through considerable depths of water. — **hy′dro·scop′ic** (-skop′ik) or **·i·cal** *adj.*

hy·dro·sere (hī′drə·sir) *n. Ecol.* In plant succession, the series of changes in vegetation which take place in the water. [<HYDRO- + SERE[2]]

hy·dro·sol (hī′drə·sol, -sōl) *n. Chem.* A water solution of a colloid. [<HYDRO- + SOL(UTION)]

hy·dro·some (hī′drə·sōm) *n. Zool.* A hydroid colony as a whole. Also **hy′dro·so′ma** (-sō′mə). [<HYDRO- + -SOME[2]]

hy·dro·sphere (hī′drə·sfir) *n.* 1 The total water surrounding the earth. 2 The atmospheric moisture enveloping the globe, in distinction from the atmosphere itself.

hy·dro·stat (hī′drə·stat) *n.* 1 A contrivance for preventing the explosion of steam boilers. 2 An electrical device for making known the presence of water, as a protection against leakage, overflow, etc.

hy·dro·stat·ic (hī′drə·stat′ik) *adj.* Pertaining to hydrostatics. Also **hy′dro·stat′i·cal.**

hy·dro·stat·ics (hī′drə·stat′iks) *n. pl.* (*construed as singular*) The science of the pressure and equilibrium of fluids, as water.

hy·dro·sul·fate (hī′drə·sul′fāt) *n. Chem.* A compound of sulfuric acid and an alkaloid or other organic base.

hy·dro·sul·fide (hī′drə·sul′fīd) *n. Chem.* A compound derived from hydrogen sulfide, by replacing one of the hydrogen atoms with a basic radical or a base.

hy·dro·sul·fite (hī′drə·sul′fīt) *n.* Sodium hydrosulfite.

hy·dro·sul·fu·rous (hī′drō·sul·fyŏŏr′əs, hī′drə·sul′fər·əs) See HYPOSULFUROUS.

hy·dro·tax·is (hī′drə·tak′sis) *n. Biol.* 1 The irritable response or turning of organisms under the influence of humidity or water. 2 The action of moisture in determining the direction of motion, as in protoplasm. — **hy′dro·tac′tic** (-tak′tik) *adj.*

hy·dro·the·ca (hī′drə·thē′kə) *n.* A calicle. [<NL <Gk. *hydōr* water + *thēkē* case]

hy·dro·ther·a·peu·tics (hī′drō·ther′ə·pyōō′tiks) *n.* Hydropathy. Also **hy′dro·ther′a·py** (-ther′ə·pē). — **hy′dro·ther′a·peu′tic** *adj.*

hy·dro·ther·mal (hī′drə·thûr′məl) *adj. Geol.* Of, pertaining to, or produced by action of heated or superheated water, especially the action of such water in dissolving, transporting, and redepositing mineral matter.

hy·dro·tho·rax (hī′drə·thôr′aks, -thō′raks) *n. Pathol.* An accumulation of fluid in the pleural cavity; dropsy of the chest. —**hy·dro·tho·rac·ic** (hī′drō·thə·ras′ik) *adj.*

hy·drot·ro·pism (hī·drot′rə·piz′əm) *n. Bot.* The phenomena of curvature induced in a growing plant organ by the stimulation of moisture. — **hy·dro·trop·ic** (hī′drə·trop′ik) *adj.*

hy·drous (hī′drəs) *adj. Chem.* 1 Watery; containing water of crystallization or hydration. 2 Containing hydrogen.

Hy·dro·vize (hī′drə·vīz) *v.t.* **·vized, ·viz·ing** To make (a textile fabric) rainproof and resistant to stains, winds, and perspiration by the application to its surface of a water repellent: a trade name.

hy·drox·ide (hī·drok′sīd) *n. Chem.* A compound containing hydroxyl.

hy·drox·y (hī·drok′sē) *adj. Chem.* Any of a class of compounds containing the hydroxyl radical: a *hydroxy* acid.

hy·drox·yl (hī·drok′sil) *n. Chem.* The univalent radical OH, consisting of one atom of oxygen and one of hydrogen. It occurs in alcohols, most acids, and many organic compounds. [<HYDR- + OX(YGEN) + -YL]

hy·drox·yl·a·mine (hī·drok′sil·ə·mēn′, -am′in) *n. Chem.* A colorless crystalline organic base, NH_2OH, formed by the partial reduction of nitric acid, but usually obtained as an unstable solution in water. In chemical behavior it is similar to ammonia.

Hy·dro·zo·a (hī′drə·zō′ə) *n. pl.* A class of coelenterates, mostly marine, including jellyfishes, polyps, etc. — **hy′dro·zo′an** *adj.* & *n.*

Hy·drus (hī′drəs) A southern constellation. [<Gk. *hydros* water snake]

hy·e·na (hī·ē′nə) *n.* A catlike carnivorous mammal of Africa and Asia (family *Hyaenidae*) with very strong, large teeth, striped or spotted body, and skulking habits, as the African laughing hyena (*Hyaena brunnea*) and the spotted hyena (*Crocuta crocuta*): also spelled *hyaena.* [<L *hyaena* <Gk. *hyaina* <*hys* pig]

HYENA
(About 2 feet high at the shoulder)

Hyères (yâr′) A port and resort in SE France.

hy·e·tal (hī′ə·təl) *adj. Meteorol.* 1 Of or pertaining to rain or the amount of the rainfall at different places and seasons. 2 Rainy.

hyeto– *combining form* Rain: *hyetograph.* Also, before vowels, **hyet–.** [<Gk. *hyetos* rain <*hyein* rain]

hy·e·to·graph (hī′i·tə·graf′, -gräf′) *n. Meteorol.* A chart showing the distribution of rainfall over the earth, or over any part of it.

hy·e·to·graph·ic (hī′i·tə·graf′ik) *adj. Meteorol.* Relating to or showing the amount of rainfall: a *hyetographic* map. Also **hy′e·to·graph′i·cal.**

hy·e·tog·ra·phy (hī′i·tog′rə·fē) *n.* The branch of meteorology that treats of the distribution of rainfall, and of the exhibition of it graphically in charts, maps, etc.

hy·e·tol·o·gy (hī′i·tol′ə·jē) *n.* That branch of meteorology which treats of precipitation. [<HYETO- + -LOGY] — **hy·e·to·log·i·cal** (hī′i·tə·loj′i·kəl) *adj.*

Hy·ge·ia (hī·jē′ə) In Greek mythology, the goddess of health; daughter of Aesculapius, the god of medicine: identified with the Roman *Salus.* Also **Hy·ge′a, Hy·gi′a** (-jī′ə). [<Gk. *hygeia* health] — **Hy·ge′ian** *adj.*

hy·giene (hī′jēn, -ji·ēn) *n.* The branch of medical science that relates to the preservation of health; sanitary science. [<F *hygiène* <Gk. *hygienios* healthful]

hy·gi·en·ic (hī′jē·en′ik, hī·jē′nik) *adj.* Pertaining to hygiene; sanitary. See synonyms under HEALTHY. — **hy′gi·en′i·cal·ly** *adv.*

hy·gi·en·ics (hī′jē·en′iks, hī·jē′niks) *n.* The science of preserving and promoting health.

hy·gi·en·ist (hī′jē·ən·ist) *n.* One who studies or is versed in the principles of hygiene. Also **hy′ge·ist** (-jē·ist), **hy′gie·ist.**

hygro– *combining form* Wet; denoting relation to moisture. [<Gk. *hygros* wet]

hy·gro·graph (hī′grə·graf, -gräf) *n.* A recording hygrometer.

hy·grom·e·ter (hī·grom′ə·tər) *n.* An instrument for ascertaining the humidity or degree of moisture in the atmosphere. [<HYGRO- + -METER]

hy·gro·met·ric (hī′grə·met′rik) *adj.* 1 Pertaining to hygrometry or the state of the atmosphere as to moisture. 2 Readily absorbing and retaining moisture. Also **hy′gro·met′ri·cal.**

hy·grom·e·try (hī·grom′ə·trē) *n.* The branch of physics that treats of the measurement of degrees of moisture, especially the moisture of the air.

hy·gro·scope (hī′grə·skōp) *n.* A device for approximating the humidity of the air.

hy·gro·scop·ic (hī′grə·skop′ik) *adj.* 1 Pertaining to the hygroscope, or capable of being detected only by it. 2 Able to absorb or condense moisture from the atmosphere, as glycerol. 3 Expanding or shrinking according to the amount of moisture: said of plants.

Hyk·sos (hik′sōs, -sos) A dynasty of kings of Egypt, probably of Syro-Semitic origin, who ruled at Memphis 1685–1580 B.C.: often called *Shepherd Kings.*

hy·la (hī′lə) *n.* The tree frog (genus *Hyla*). [<NL <Gk. *hylē* wood]

Hy·las (hī′ləs) In Greek mythology, a beautiful youth, loved by Hercules, whose companion he was on the cruise of the Argonauts; he was stolen by Naiads while bathing in a spring at Mysia.

hy·lic (hī′lik) *adj.* Relating to or of the nature of matter; material. — **hy′li·cism** (-lə·siz′əm) *n.*

hy·li·cist (hī′lə·sist) *n.* A believer or teacher of materialism; specifically, one of the early Ionic philosophers.

hy·lism (hī′liz·əm) *n.* 1 Materialism. 2 The theory that matter is the principle or source of evil.

hylo– *combining form* Related to matter; material: *hylotropic.* Also, before vowels, **hyl–.** [<Gk. *hylē* wood]

hy·lo·the·ism (hī′lə·thē′iz·əm) *n.* The doctrine of belief that the material universe is God; pantheism.

hy·lo·trop·ic (hī′lə·trop′ik, -trō′pik) *adj.* Having the capacity to change in form without a change in composition; as ice, water, and steam.

hy·lo·zo·ism (hī′lə·zō′iz·əm) *n.* The doctrine that life and matter are inseparable. [<HYLO- + Gk. *zōē* life] — **hy′lo·zo′ic** *adj.* — **hy′lo·zo′ist** *n.* — **hy′lo·zo·is′tic** *adj.*

hy·men (hī′mən) *n.* 1 *Anat.* A thin mucous membrane partially covering the entrance of the vagina; the virginal membrane or maidenhead. 2 The wedded state; marriage. [<Gk. *hymēn* membrane]

Hy·men (hī′mən) In Greek mythology, the god of marriage and of the wedding feast. Also **Hy′me·nae′us** (-nē′əs).

hy·me·ne·al (hī′mə·nē′əl) *adj.* Pertaining to marriage: also **hy′me·ne′an.** See synonyms under MATRIMONIAL. —*n.* A wedding song.

hy·me·ni·um (hī·mē′nē·əm) *n. pl.* **·ni·a** (-nē·ə) or **·ni·ums** *Bot.* The fruit-bearing surface or stratum in the higher fungi of the *Ascomycetes* or *Basidiomycetes,* as the two vertical faces on the gills of the common mushroom. It consists of a collection of basidia, sometimes interspersed with sterile cells in a layer or stratum. [<NL <Gk. *hymenion,* dim. of *hymen* membrane]

hymeno– *combining form* Membrane: *hymenophore.* Also, before vowels, **hymen–.** [<Gk. *hymēn* skin, membrane]

Hy·men·o·my·ce·tes (hī′mən·ō·mī·sē′tēz) *n. pl.* A subgroup of fleshy, leathery, or woody fungi, having an exposed hymenium, including the common edible mushroom, *Agaricus campestris.* —**hy′men·o·my·ce′tal** or **·tous** *adj.*

hy·men·o·phore (hī′mən·ə·fôr′, -fōr′) *n. Bot.* The stem and pileus of a hymenomycetous fungus; more specifically, that part of the sporophore which bears the hymenium. Also **hy·men·i·o·phore** (hī·men′ē·ə·fôr′, -fōr′), **hy′·men·o·pho′rum** (-fôr′əm, -fō′rəm).

Hy·men·op·ter·a (hī′mən·op′tər·ə) *n. pl.* An extensive and highly developed order of insects typically having four membranous wings, of which the front pair are larger, and mostly a wormlike larva and inactive pupa, including bees, wasps, sawflies, ants, etc. [<NL <Gk. *hymen* membrane + *ptera,* pl. of *pteron* a wing] —**hy′men·op′ter** *n.* —**hy′men·op′ter·an** *adj.* & *n.* —**hy′men·op′ter·ous** *adj.*

Hy·met·tus (hī·met′əs) A mountain range in east central Greece; highest point, 3,367 feet. *Greek* **Hy·met′tos.**

hymn (him) *n.* A song expressive of praise, adoration, or elevated emotion; specifically, a metrical composition, divided into stanzas or verses, intended to be sung in religious worship; also, a religious or patriotic ode, song, lyric, or other poem. —*v.* **hymned, hymn·ing** *v.t.* 1 To praise or worship in hymns. 2 To express by singing: to *hymn* praises. —*v.i.* 3 To sing hymns or praises. See synonyms under SONG. [Fusion of OE *hymen* and OF *ymne,* both <LL *ymnus, hymnus* <Gk. *hymnos* a song, ode] —**hym′nic** (-nik) *adj.*

hym·nal (him′nəl) *n.* A book of hymns: also **hymn book.** —*adj.* Of or concerning a hymn or hymns.

hymnal stanza Common measure.

hym·nist (him′nist) *n.* A writer of hymns. Also **hym′no·dist** (-nə·dist).

hym·no·dy (him′nə·dē) *n. pl.* **·dies** 1 Hymns collectively; hymnology. 2 The practice of singing hymns. [<LL *hymnodia* <Gk. *hymnōidia* <*hymnos* hymn + *ōidē* singing]

hym·nog·ra·phy (him·nog′rə·fē) *n.* The art of composing hymns.

hym·nol·o·gy (him·nol′ə·jē) *n.* 1 The study or science of hymns, including their history, use, and classification. 2 A treatise on hymns, or hymns collectively. [<HYMN + -(O)LOGY] —**hym·no·log·ic** (him′nə·loj′ik) or **·i·cal** *adj.* —**hym·nol′o·gist** *n.*

hy·oid (hī′oid) *n. Anat.* A U-shaped bone at the base of the tongue, for the attachment of the muscles of deglutition: also **hyoid bone.** —*adj.* 1 Pertaining to the hyoid bone. 2 Having the form of the Greek letter upsilon (Υ, υ). [<F *hyoïde* <Gk. *hyoeidēs* <Υ upsilon + *eidos* form]

hy·os·cine (hī′ə·sēn) *n.* Scopolamine. [<HYOS-C(YAMUS) + -INE]

hy·os·cy·a·mine (hī′ə·sī′ə·mēn, -min) *n. Chem.* A white, crystalline, poisonous alkaloid, $C_{17}H_{23}NO_3$, contained in henbane, thorn apple, deadly nightshade, and other plants: used medicinally. Also **hy′os·cy′a·min** (-min).

hy·os·cy·a·mus (hī′ə·sī′ə·məs) *n.* The henbane, containing alkaloids used for their anodyne and antispasmodic properties. [<Gk. *hyoskyamos* henbane <*hys* hog + *kyamos* bean]

hyp– Var. of HYPO–.

hyp·a·bys·sal (hip′ə·bis′əl) *adj. Geol.* Pertaining to or designating igneous rocks which form minor intrusions, such as dikes and sills; also, the intrusions themselves. [<HYP- + ABYSSAL]

hyp·aes·the·si·a (hip′əs·thē′zhē·ə, -zhə), **hy·pae·thral** (hi·pē′thrəl), etc. See HYPESTHESIA, etc.

Hy·pa·tia (hī·pā′shə, -shē·ə) A Greek philosopher celebrated for her beauty, killed by a mob A.D. 415.

hype (hīp) *Slang v.t.* **hyped, hyp·ing** 1 To deceive; fool. 2 To stimulate with or as with drugs: with *up.* —*n.* 1 A deception; fraud. 2 A promotional talk or message. [<HYPODERMIC, with ref. to the injection of drugs]

hyper– *prefix* 1 Over; above; excessive: *hypertension*: opposed to *hypo–.* 2 *Chem.* Denoting the highest in a series of compounds: now generally replaced by *per–.* [<Gk. *hyper-* <*hyper* above]

In the following self-explanatory compounds, *hyper–* appears in sense 1:

hyperabsorption
hyperaccurate
hyperacoustics
hyperaction
hyperactive
hyperacuity
hyperacute
hyperacuteness
hyperaltruism
hyperanarchy
hyperangelical
hyperbarbarous
hyperbrutal
hypercarnal
hypercatharsis
hypercathartic
hypercivilization
hypercivilized
hyperclassical
hyperclimax
hyperconcentration
hyperconfident
hyperconformist
hyperconscientious
hyperconscious
hyperconservatism
hyperconstitutional
hyperdelicacy
hyperdelicate
hyperdemocratic
hyperdiabolical
hyperdistention
hyper–Dorian
hyperelegant
hyperemphasize
hyperenthusiasm
hyperethical
hyperexaltation
hyperexcitability
hyperexcitable
hyperexcitement
hyperfastidious
hypergenesis
hypergrammatical
hyperhilarious
hyperhypocrisy
hyperidealistic
hyperimmune
hyperimmunity
hyperingenuity
hyperintellectual
hyperintelligence
hyperlogical
hyperlustrous
hypermagical
hypermedication
hypermetaphorical
hypermetaphysical
hypermiraculous
hypermodest
hypermoral
hypermotile
hypermotility
hypermystical
hypernatural
hyperneurotic
hypernormal
hypernote
hypernutrition
hyperobtrusive
hyperorganic
hyperorthodox
hyperorthodoxy
hyperpanegyric
hyperparoxysm
hyperpathetic
hyperpatriotic
hyperpersonal
hyperpigmentation
hyperplagiarism
hyperpolysyllabic
hyperproduction
hyperprophetical
hyperpure
hyperpurist
hyperrational
hyperreactive
hyperrealize
hyperresonance
hyperresonant
hyperreverential
hyperridiculous
hyperritualism
hyper–Romantic
hypersaintly
hyperscholastic
hyperscrupulosity
hypersecretion
hypersensitization
hypersensual
hypersensualism
hypersensuous
hypersentimental
hyperskeptical
hypersophisticated
hyperspeculative
hyperspiritualizing
hyperstoic
hypersubtlety
hypersuggestibility
hypersuperlative
hypertechnical
hypertense
hypertorrid
hypertoxic
hypertragical
hypertragically
hypertropical
hypervigilant
hypervitalize

hy·per·ac·id (hī′pər·as′id) *adj.* Excessively acid. —**hy′per·a·cid′i·ty** (-ə·sid′ə·tē) *n.*

hy·per·a·cu·si·a (hī′pər·ə·kyōō′zhē·ə) *n. Pathol.* Morbid acuteness of hearing. Also **hy′per·a·cu′sis** (-sis). [<HYPER- + Gk. *akousis* hearing]

hy·per·a·dre·ni·a (hī′pər·ə·drē′nē·ə) *n. Pathol.* A disorder caused by excessive secretory activity of the adrenal glands, and characterized by sudden increases in blood pressure. Also **hy·per·ad·re·nal·ism** (hī′pər·ə·drē′nəl·iz′·əm).

hy·per·ae·mi·a (hī′pər·ē′mē·ə), **hy·per·aes·the·si·a** (hī′pər·es·thē′zhē·ə, -zhə) See HYPEREMIA, etc.

hy·per·al·ge·si·a (hī′pər·al·jē′zē·ə, -sē·ə) *n. Pathol.* Excessive sensitiveness to pain. Also **hy′per·al·ge′sis.** [<HYPER- + Gk. *algēsis* sense of pain <*algos* pain] —**hy′per·al·ge′sic** (-zik, -sik) *adj.*

hy·per·bar·ic (hī′pər·bar′ik) *adj. Med.* 1 Of, pertaining to, or affected by hyperbarism. 2 Designating a spinal anesthetic solution having a density greater than that of the spinal fluid.

hy·per·bar·ism (hī·per′bə·riz′əm) *n. Med.* A disturbed condition caused by an atmospheric pressure which is greater than the pressure within the tissues, fluids, or cavities of the body: occurs in a sudden descent from a high to a low altitude. Opposed to *hypobarism.* [<HYPER- + Gk. *baros* weight]

hy·per·bo·la (hī·pûr′bə·lə) *n. Math.* A curve traced by a point moving so that the difference between its distances from two fixed points, or foci, remains constant; the curves traced by the edges where a plane intersects the nappes of a right circular cone. [<NL <Gk. *hyperbolē* a throwing beyond, excess. See HYPERBOLE.]

hy·per·bo·le (hī·pûr′bə·lē) *n.* Poetic or rhetorical overstatement; exaggeration. [<L <Gk. *hyperbolē* a throwing beyond, excess <*hyper-* over + *ballein* throw]

hy·per·bol·ic (hī′pər·bol′ik) *adj.* 1 Relating to or containing hyperbole; exaggerating. 2 Of, pertaining to, or having the shape of a hyperbola. Also **hy′per·bol′i·cal.** —**hy′per·bol′i·cal·ly** *adv.*

hyperbolic paraboloid *Math.* A quadric surface generated in such a way that, parallel to one plane, its sections are hyperbolas, and, parallel to the other planes, all sections are parabolas.

hyperbolic sine curve *Math.* A sine curve with hyperbolic convolutions.

hyperbolic spiral *Math.* A polar curve traced by a point moving so that its distance from the pole varies inversely as its polar angle: it is asymptotic to a line parallel to the polar axis.

hy·per·bo·lize (hī·pûr′bə·līz) *v.t.* & *v.i.* **·lized, ·liz·ing** To express in or use hyperbole; exaggerate. Also *Brit.* **hy·per′bo·lise.** —**hy·per′·bo·lism** (-liz′əm) *n.*

hy·per·bo·loid (hī·pûr′bə·loid) *n. Math.* A quadratic surface generated by a hyperbola revolving about a fixed line: also called a **hyperboloid of one sheet.** A **hyperboloid of two sheets** is a quadratic surface generated by an ellipse moving so as to remain parallel to a common transverse axis, and varying so that the ends of its axes coincide with given hyperbolas having the same transverse axis.

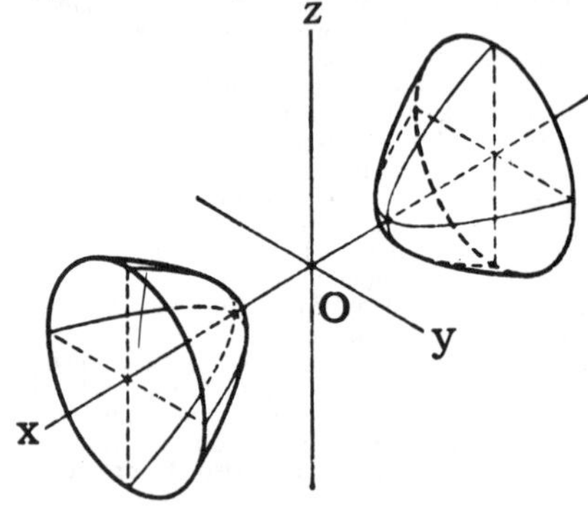

HYPERBOLOID OF TWO SHEETS
O. Origin. *x.* Transverse axis. *y, z.* Coordinate axes.

hy·per·bo·re·an (hī′pər·bôr′ē·ən, -bō′rē-) *adj.* Of the far north; frigid.

Hy·per·bo·re·an (hī′pər·bôr′ē·ən, -bō′rē-) *n.* One of a people supposed by the ancient Greeks to dwell in a blessed land lying beyond the north wind and inaccessible by land or sea. —*adj.* Pertaining to the Hyperboreans. [<L *hyperboreus* <Gk. *hyperboreos* <*hyper-* beyond + *Boreas* north wind]

hy·per·cat·a·lec·tic (hī′pər·kat′ə·lek′tik) *adj.* Having one or two syllables beyond the final regular measure: said of a line of poetry; hypermetric. [<L *hypercatalecticus* <Gk. *hyperkatalēktikos* <*hyper-* beyond + *katalēktikos* CATALECTIC] —**hy′per·cat′a·lex′is** (-lek′·sis) *n.*

hy·per·crit·ic (hī′pər·krit′ik) *n.* A very severe critic.

hy·per·crit·i·cal (hī′pər·krit′i·kəl) *adj.* 1

Given to strained or captious criticism. 2 Excessively exact or precise. See synonyms under CAPTIOUS. —**hy'per·crit'i·cal·ly** *adv.* —**hy'per·crit'i·cism** (-siz'əm) *n.*

hy·per·cube (hī'pər·kyōōb) *n.* A tesseract.

hy·per·du·li·a (hī'pər·dōō'lē·ə, -dyōō'-) *n. Eccl.* Worship given to the Virgin Mary as the most sacred of mortal creatures: superior to *dulia.* Compare LATRIA. [<Med. L <*hyper-* beyond + *dulia* service]

hy·per·e·mi·a (hī'pər·ē'mē·ə) *n. Pathol.* Abnormal accumulation of the blood in any part of the body: also spelled *hyperaemia.* —**hy'·per·e'mic** *adj.*

hy·per·es·the·si·a (hī'pər·es·thē'zhē·ə, -zhə) *n.* Exaggerated sensitiveness to touch, heat, pain, etc.: also spelled *hyperaesthesia.*

hy·per·es·thet·ic (hī'pər·es·thet'ik) *adj.* 1 Morbidly sensitive. 2 Immoderately esthetic. Also spelled *hyperaesthetic.*

hy·per·eu·tec·tic (hī'pər·yōō·tek'tik) *adj.* Having the minor component in a proportion greater than that of the corresponding eutectic mixture: said of a mineral, alloy, or solution.

hy·per·ex·ten·sion (hī'pər·ik·sten'shən) *n. Physiol.* The maximum extension of an arm or leg beyond the plane of the body.

hy·per·fine (hī'pər·fīn') *adj. Physics* Of, pertaining to, or characterized by very closely spaced lines, as in the spectra of certain elements and isotopes.

hy·per·fo·cal (hī'pər·fō'kəl) *adj. Phot.* Designating that distance in front of a given camera lens under specified conditions, at and beyond which all objects are in substantially clear focus.

hy·per·gol·ic (hī'pər·gol'ik) *adj.* Pertaining to or describing a type of rocket propellant that ignites spontaneously on contact with an oxidizer. [HYPER- + G *gola* a code word used in German rocketry]

hy·per·hi·dro·sis (hī'pər·hi·drō'sis) *n.* Abnormal sweating. Also **hy'per·i·dro'sis** (-ī·drō'sis).

Hy·pe·ri·on (hī·pir'ē·ən) 1 In Greek mythology, a Titan, the son of Uranus and Gaea and father of Helios, Selene, and Eos. 2 Helios.

hy·per·ki·ne·si·a (hī'pər·ki·nē'zhē·ə, -zhə) *n. Pathol.* Exaggerated muscular action; spasm. Also **hy'per·ki·ne'sis** (-nē'sis). —**hy'per·ki·net'·ic** (-net'ik) *adj.*

hy·per·me·ter (hī·pûr'mə·tər) *n.* A hypercatalectic line; also, a period containing a redundant syllable. —**hy·per·met·ric** (hī'pər·met'·rik) or **·ri·cal** *adj.*

hy·per·me·tro·pi·a (hī'pər·mə·trō'pē·ə) *n. Pathol.* An abnormal condition of the eye in which objects at a distance are seen more plainly than those near at hand; far-sightedness. Also **hy'per·met'ro·py** (-met'rə·pē), **hy'·per·o'pi·a** (-ō'pē·ə). [<NL <Gk. *hypermetros* excessive + *ōps* eye] —**hy'per·me·trop'ic** (-mə·trop'ik, -trō'pik) *adj.*

hy·perm·ne·si·a (hī'pərm·nē'zhē·ə, -zhə) *n.* A condition marked by an abnormal retentivity and acuteness of memory; total recall: distinguished from *amnesia.* Also **hy'perm·ne'sis** (-nē'sis). [<HYPER- + Gk. *mnesis* remembrance]

Hy·perm·nes·tra (hī'pərm·nes'trə) In Greek mythology, the only one of the Danaides who did not kill her husband on her wedding night.

hy·per·on (hī'pər·on) *n. Physics* Any of a class of atomic particles having a mass intermediate between that of a neutron and a deuteron. Symbol, Λ (lambda), followed by an identifying superscript. Also called *V-particle.* [< NL <Gk. *hyper-* above, more]

hy·per·o·pi·a (hī'pər·ō'pē·ə) *n.* Hypermetropia.

hy·per·os·mi·a (hī'pər·oz'mē·ə) *n.* Morbid sensitiveness to odors. [<HYPER- + Gk. *osmē* smell]

hy·per·os·to·sis (hī'pər·os·tō'sis) *n. pl.* **·ses** (-sēz) *Pathol.* An abnormal increase in or thickening of bony tissue.

hy·per·ox·i·a (hī'pər·ok'sē·ə) *n. Med.* An excess of oxygen in the atmosphere or in an animal body. [<NL <HYPER- + OX(Y)- + -IA]

hy·per·par·a·site (hī'pər·par'ə·sīt) *n.* An organism parasitic on another parasite. —**hy'per·par'a·sit'ic** (-sit'ik) *adj.* —**hy'per·par'a·sit·ism** (-ə·sit·iz'əm) *n.*

hy·per·phe·nom·e·nal (hī'pər·fə·nom'ə·nəl) *adj.* Transcending phenomena; real.

hy·per·phys·i·cal (hī'pər·fiz'i·kəl) *adj.* 1 Independent of the physical. 2 Supernatural. —**hy'per·phys'i·cal·ly** *adv.*

hy·per·pi·e·si·a (hī'pər·pī·ē'zhē·ə, -zhə) *n. Pathol.* Abnormally high blood pressure. Also **hy'per·pi·e'sis** (-sis). [<NL <Gk. *hyper-* beyond + *piesis* pressure <*piezein* press]

hy·per·pi·tu·i·ta·rism (hī'pər·pi·tōō'i·tə·riz'əm, -tyōō'-) *n. Pathol.* Abnormal functioning of the pituitary gland; also, the disorders resulting from it.

hy·per·pla·si·a (hī'pər·plā'zhē·ə, -zhə) *n. Pathol.* Excessive production of cells in a part; enlargement from quantitative increase produced by cell division: distinguished from *hypertrophy.* —**hy'per·plas'ic** (-plas'ik), **hy'·per·plas'tic** (-plas'tik) *adj.*

hy·per·ploid (hī'pər·ploid) *adj. Biol.* Pertaining to or designating a chromosome number greater than the normal number but not an exact multiple of it. —**hy'per·ploid'y** *n.*

hy·perp·ne·a (hī'pərp·nē'ə) *n. Pathol.* Violent or labored breathing caused by a deficiency of oxygen in the blood. Also **hy'perp·noe'a.** [<NL <Gk. *hyper-* above + *pnoē* breathing <*pneein* breathe]

hy·per·pro·sex·i·a (hī'pər·prō·sek'sē·ə) *n. Psychiatry* An inordinate and exaggerated attention to certain things, as the symptoms of an illness or mental disorder. [<HYPER- + Gk. *prosexis* attention]

hy·per·py·rex·i·a (hī'pər·pī·rek'sē·ə) *n. Pathol.* Very high fever. —**hy'per·py·ret'ic** (-ret'ik), **hy'per·py·rex'i·al** *adj.*

hy·per·sen·si·tive (hī'pər·sen'sə·tiv) *adj.* 1 Excessively sensitive. 2 Allergic. —**hy'per·sen'·si·tive·ness, hy'per·sen'si·tiv'i·ty** (-sen'sə·tiv'ə·tē) *n.*

hy·per·sen·si·tize (hī'pər·sen'sə·tīz) *v.t.* **·tized, ·tiz·ing** *Phot.* To increase the sensitiveness or speed of, as a plate or film, usually by immersion in a suitable solution or by exposure to mercury vapor. —**hy'per·sen'si·tiz'ing** *n.*

hy·per·son·ic (hī'pər·son'ik) *adj.* Of, pertaining to, or characterized by supersonic speeds of mach 5 or greater.

hy·per·son·ics (hī'pər·son'iks) *n. pl. (construed as singular)* That branch of dynamics which studies the design, characteristics, and performance of objects moving at supersonic speeds of mach 5 or greater: applied especially to jet planes, guided missiles, rockets, and the like.

hy·per·space (hī'pər·spās') *n.* Space regarded as having more than three dimensions.

hy·per·sthene (hī'pər·sthēn) *n.* A pearly, dark-colored, ferrous magnesium-pyroxene mineral found in igneous rocks. [<HYPER- + Gk. *sthenos* strength]

hy·per·sthe·ni·a (hī'pər·sthē'nē·ə) *n.* Excessive physical vigor and tone. [<HYPER- + Gk. *sthenos* strength] —**hy'per·sthen'ic** (-sthen'ik) *adj.*

hy·per·ten·sion (hī'pər·ten'shən) *n. Pathol.* 1 Excessively high blood pressure. 2 A disease of the arteries caused by or associated with such pressure.

Hy·per·therm (hī'pər·thûrm) *n.* An apparatus for producing hyperthermia: a trade name.

hy·per·ther·mi·a (hī'pər·thûr'mē·ə) *n. Med.* 1 An abnormally high temperature. 2 Therapeutic treatment by means of artifically induced fever. Also **hy'per·ther'my.** [<HYPER- + Gk. *thermē* heat] —**hy'per·ther'mal** *adj.*

hy·per·thy·mic (hī'pər·thī'mik) *adj.* 1 *Psychiatry* Denoting a state of morbidly exaggerated activity of mind or body. 2 Designating a constitutional type associated with persistent overdevelopment of the thymus gland. [<HYPER- + Gk. *thymos* spirit, passion]

hy·per·thy·roid (hī'pər·thī'roid) *adj.* Marked by hyperthyroidism. —*n.* One affected by hyperthyroidism.

hy·per·thy·roid·ism (hī'pər·thī'roid·iz'əm) *n. Pathol.* 1 Abnormal activity of the thyroid gland. 2 Any disorder caused by such activity: opposed to *hypothyroidism.*

hy·per·ton·ic (hī'pər·ton'ik) *adj. Pathol.* Pertaining to or designating a higher osmotic pressure than the normal, as of blood: opposed to *isotonic.* —**hy'per·to·nic'i·ty** (-tō·nis'ə·tē) *n.*

hy·per·tro·phy (hī·pûr'trə·fē) *n. Pathol.* 1 The excessive development of an organ or part. 2 The morbid enlargement of a part from increased nutrition without increase of waste: opposed to *atrophy.* —*v.i.* **·phied, ·phy·ing** To grow excessively; develop abnormally. —**hy·per·troph·ic** (hī'pər·trof'ik, -trō'fik) or **·i·cal** *adj.*

hy·per·ven·ti·la·tion (hī'pər·ven'tə·lā'shən) *n.* 1 An excess supply of air to the lungs, as when airplane pilots resort to deep and rapid breathing to ensure adequate oxygen: often resulting in lowering carbon dioxide content of the blood. 2 Physical therapy by exposure of the body to drafts of air.

hy·per·vi·ta·mi·no·sis (hī'pər·vī'tə·mi·nō'sis) *n. Pathol.* A condition due to an excess of vitamins, either in the diet or in prepared form: opposed to *avitaminosis.*

hyp·es·the·si·a (hip'əs·thē'zhē·ə, -zhə) *n. Pathol.* Diminished sensitiveness; partial loss of capacity for sensation: also spelled *hypaesthesia.* —**hyp'es·the'sic** (-sik) or **·thet'ic** (-thet'ik) *adj.*

hy·pe·thral (hi·pē'thrəl, hī-) *adj.* Roofless, as a building open to the sky: said of a building whose roof has been destroyed or never completed, or of a sanctuary, etc., never intended to be roofed. Also spelled *hypaethral.* [<L *hypaethrus* <Gk. *hypaithros* <*hypo-* under + *aithēr* ether, clear sky]

hy·pha (hī'fə) *n. pl.* **·phae** (-fē) *Bot.* A long, threadlike, usually branching body in the thallus of a fungus: the vegetative hyphae, as opposed to the reproductive ones, constitute the mycelium of fungi. [<NL <Gk. *hyphē* web] —**hy'phal** *adj.*

hy·pheme (hī'fēm) *n.* A hyphened compound word. Compare SOLIDEME. [<HYPH(EN) + (PHON)EME]

hy·phe·mi·a (hī·fē'mē·ə) *n. Pathol.* 1 Deficiency of blood, or a lack of supply of the red corpuscles in the blood. 2 Extravasation of the blood into a surrounding tissue, especially in the eye. Also **hy·phae'mi·a.** [< HYPO- + -HEMIA]

hy·phen (hī'fən) *n.* A mark (- or - or ⸗) indicating connection: used to connect the elements of certain compound words, to show division of a word at the end of a line, and to indicate a unit modifier: a *hit-and-run* driver. —*v.t.* To hyphenate. [<LL <Gk. *hyph' hen* under one, together <*hypo-* under + *hen* one]

hy·phen·ate (hī'fən·āt) *v.t.* **·at·ed, ·at·ing** 1 To connect by a hyphen. 2 To print or write with a hyphen. Also **hy'phen·ize.** —**hy'phen·a'tion, hy'phen·i·za'tion** (-ə·zā'shən, -ī·zā'-) *n.*

hy·phen·at·ed (hī'fən·ā'tid) *adj.* Implying or relating to a naturalized person of foreign birth, especially to one whose sympathies are with the land of his birth.

hyp·na·gog·ic (hip'nə·goj'ik) *adj.* 1 Inducing or promoting sleep, as by a drug or by hypnosis. 2 Of or pertaining to the mental condition occurring just before sleep; dreamlike; visionary. [<HYPN(O)- + -AGOG]

hyp·na·pa·gog·ic (hip'nə·pə·goj'ik) *adj.* Preventing or inhibiting sleep. [<HYPN(O)- + AP(O)- + -AGOG]

hyp·nic (hip'nik) *adj.* Calculated to induce sleep; pertaining to sleep. —*n.* A soporific.

hypno- *combining form* Sleep; of or related to sleep: *hypnology.* Also, before vowels, **hypn-.** [<Gk. *hypnos* sleep]

hyp·no·a·nal·y·sis (hip'nō·ə·nal'ə·sis) *n.* A psychoanalytic technique which utilizes data obtained by or under the conditions resulting from hypnosis. —**hyp'no·an'a·lyt'ic** (-an'ə·lit'ik) *adj.*

hyp·no·gen·e·sis (hip'nō·jen'ə·sis) *n.* The production of hypnotic sleep. —**hyp'no·ge·net'ic** (-jə·net'ik), **hyp'no·ge·net'i·cal, hyp·nog·e·nous** (hip·noj'ə·nəs) *adj.*

hyp·noid·al (hip·noid'l) *adj. Psychiatry* Characterizing a condition of the nervous organization resembling slight hypnosis, with heightened suggestibility, partial anesthesia, etc.

hyp·nol·o·gy (hip·nol'ə·jē) *n.* The science of the phenomena of sleep. —**hyp·no·log·ic** (hip'nə·loj'ik) or **·i·cal** *adj.* —**hyp·nol'o·gist** *n.*

hyp·no·pae·di·a (hip'nə·pē'dē·ə) *n.* Training and instruction during sleep: a word used by Aldous Huxley in his novel *Brave New World* (1932), now applied to a technique in actual use. [<HYPNO- + Gk. *paideia* education] — **hyp'no·pae'dic** (-pē'dik) *adj.*

hyp·no·pho·bi·a (hip'nə·fō'bē·ə) *n.* A morbid fear of sleep or of falling asleep. — **hyp'no·pho'bic** *adj.*

hyp·no·pom·pic (hip'nə·pom'pik) *adj. Psychol.* Persisting after or emerging from sleep: describing the semiconscious state between sleep and waking often marked by visions and fantasies. [<HYPNO- + Gk. *pompaios* accompanying]

Hyp·nos (hip'nos) In Greek mythology, the god of sleep: identified with the Roman *Somnus.* Also **Hyp'nus** (-nəs).

hyp·no·sis (hip·nō'sis) *n. pl.* **·ses** (-sēz) *Psychol.* **1** A trancelike condition that may be psychically induced by another person, characterized by loss of consciousness and a greater or lesser degree of responsiveness to the suggestions of the hypnotist. **2** The causing of such a condition.

hyp·no·ther·a·py (hip'nə·ther'ə·pē) *n. Med.* The use of hypnotism in treating disease.

hyp·not·ic (hip·not'ik) *adj.* **1** Pertaining to hypnotism or tending to produce hypnosis. **2** Tending to produce sleep. — *n.* **1** An agent efficacious in producing sleep. **2** A hypnotized person. [<Gk. *hypnōtikos* <*hypnos* sleep] — **hyp·not'i·cal·ly** *adv.*

hyp·no·tism (hip'nə·tiz'əm) *n.* The theory and practice of hypnosis. — **hyp'no·tist, hyp'no·tiz'er** *n.*

hyp·no·tize (hip'nə·tīz) *v.t.* **·tized, ·tiz·ing** **1** To produce hypnosis in. **2** *Colloq.* To fascinate; entrance. Also *Brit.* **hyp'no·tise.** — **hyp'·no·tiz'a·ble** *adj.* — **hyp'no·ti·za'tion** (-tə·zā'·shən, -tī·zā'-) *n.*

hy·po (hī'pō) *n.* **1** *Chem.* Sodium thiosulfate. **2** *Slang* Hypochondria; also, a hypochondriac. **3** *Colloq.* A hypodermic injection or needle.

hypo– *prefix* **1** Under; beneath; less than: *hypodermic*: opposed to *hyper–.* **2** *Chem.* Indicating the lowest member in a series of compounds, that is, the lowest degree of oxidation: *hypophosphate.* **3** *Med.* Denoting a lack of or deficiency in: *hypofunction.* Also, before vowels, **hyp–.** [<Gk. *hypo-* <*hypo* under]

hy·po·a·cid·i·ty (hī'pō·ə·sid'ə·tē) *n. Med.* Deficient or subnormal acidity, as of the gastric juices.

hy·po·bar·ic (hī'pə·bar'ik) *adj. Med.* **1** Pertaining to or affected by hypobarism. **2** Denoting a spinal anesthetic solution whose density is less than that of the spinal fluid. Opposed to *hyperbaric.*

hy·po·bar·ism (hī'pə·bär'iz·əm) *n. Med.* A condition brought about when the pressure of the gases within the body is in excess of the atmospheric pressure: opposed to *hyperbarism.* Compare *aeroembolism.* [<HYPO- + Gk. *baros* weight]

hy·po·blast (hī'pə·blast) *n. Biol.* The innermost of the blastodermic membranes, from which is derived the epithelium of the digestive tract and its annexes. — **hy'po·blas'·tic** *adj.*

hy·po·bran·chi·al (hī'pə·brang'kē·əl) *adj. Zool.* Of or pertaining to the lower segment of the branchial arch in animals.

hy·po·cap·ni·a (hī'pə·kap'nē·ə) *n. Med.* A deficiency of carbon dioxide in the blood, often due to hyperventilation. [<HYPO- + Gk. *kapnos* smoke] — **hy'po·cap'nic** *adj.*

hy·po·caust (hī'pə·kôst) *n.* In ancient Roman houses, a hollow space for the accumulation of heat under the floor. [<L *hypocaustum* <Gk. *hypokauston* <*hypo* beneath + *kaiein* burn]

hy·po·cen·ter (hī'pə·sen'tər) *n.* That point on the earth's surface directly beneath or above the burst of an atomic or thermonuclear bomb; ground zero.

hy·po·chlo·rite (hī'pə·klôr'īt, -klō'rīt) *n. Chem.* A salt of hypochlorous acid.

hy·po·chlo·rous (hī'pə·klôr'əs, -klō'rəs) *adj. Chem.* Denoting an acid, HClO, obtained by the action of chlorine on mercurous oxide and water, and in other ways. It acts as an oxidizing and bleaching agent.

hy·po·chon·dri·a (hī'pə·kon'drē·ə, hip'ə-) *n. Psychiatry* **1** A morbid melancholy and depression of mind or spirits. **2** A morbidly extreme anxiety about one's health, usually associated with one or another part of the body, and accompanied by imagined symptoms of illness. Also **hy·po·chon·dri·a·sis** (hī'·pō·kən·drī'ə·sis). [<L, abdomen (once taken to be the seat of this condition) <Gk. *hypochondria,* neut. pl. from *hypochondrios* under the cartilage <*hypo-* under + *chondros* cartilage]

hy·po·chon·dri·ac (hī'pə·kon'drē·ak, hip'ə-) *adj.* **1** Pertaining to or affected by hypochondria. **2** Of, pertaining to, or situated in the hypochondrium. Also **hy·po·chon·dri·a·cal** (hī'pō·kən·drī'ə·kəl). — *n.* A person subject to or afflicted by hypochondria. — **hy'po·chon·dri'a·cal·ly** *adv.*

hy·po·chon·dri·um (hī'pə·kon'drē·əm, hip'ə-) *n. pl.* **·dri·a** (-drē·ə) *Anat.* That region of the abdomen situated on either side under the costal cartilages and short ribs. [<NL <Gk. *hypochondrion.* See HYPOCHONDRIA.]

hy·po·co·ris·tic (hī'pō·kə·ris'tik) *adj.* Of or pertaining to an endearing diminutive or pet name. [<Gk. *hypokoristikos* <*hypo-* under + *korizesthai* caress <*koros* child]

hy·po·cot·yl (hī'pə·kot'l) *n. Bot.* That part of the seedling axis of a plant below the seed leaves or cotyledons. [<HYPO- + COTYL(EDON)] — **hy'po·cot'y·lous** *adj.*

hy·poc·ri·sy (hi·pok'rə·sē) *n. pl.* **·sies** The feigning to be what one is not; extreme insincerity; dissimulation. [<OF *ypocrisie* <L *hypocrisis* <Gk. *hypokrisis* acting a part, feigning <*hypo-* under + *krinein* decide]

Synonyms: affectation, cant, dissimulation, formalism, pharisaism, pietism, pretense, sanctimoniousness, sanctimony, sham. *Pretense* (L. *praetendo*) primarily signifies the holding something forward as having certain rights or claims, whether truly or falsely; in the good sense, it is now rarely used except with a negative; as, There can be no *pretense* that this is due; a false *pretense* implies the possibility of a true *pretense*; but, alone and unlimited, *pretense* commonly signifies the offering of something for what it is not. *Hypocrisy* is the false *pretense* of moral excellence, either as a cover for actual wrong, or for the sake of the credit and advantage attaching to virtue. *Cant* (L. *cantus,* a song), primarily the singsong iteration of the language of any party, school, or sect, denotes the mechanical and pretentious use of religious phraseology, without corresponding feeling or character; *sanctimoniousness* is the assumption of a saintly manner without a saintly character. *Affectation* is in matters of intellect, taste, etc., much what *hypocrisy* is in morals and religion: *affectation* might be termed petty *hypocrisy.* Compare DECEPTION. *Antonyms*: candor, frankness, genuineness, honesty, ingenuousness, openness, sincerity, transparency, truth, truthfulness.

hyp·o·crite (hip'ə·krit) *n.* One who acts a false part or makes false professions. [<Gk. *hypokritēs* an actor. See HYPOCRISY.] — **hyp'o·crit'i·cal** *adj.* — **hyp'o·crit'i·cal·ly** *adv.*

Synonyms: cheat, deceiver, dissembler, impostor, pretender. A *hypocrite* is one who acts a false part, or assumes a character other than the real. The *deceiver* seeks to give false impressions of any matter where he has an end to gain; the *dissembler* or *hypocrite* seeks to give false impressions in regard to himself. The *dissembler* is content if he can keep some base conduct or evil purpose from being discovered; the *hypocrite* seeks not merely to cover his vices, but to gain credit for virtue. The *cheat* and *impostor* endeavor to make something out of those whom they may deceive. The *cheat* is the inferior and more mercenary, as the thimblerig gambler; the *impostor* may aspire to a fortune or a throne. Compare HYPOCRISY.

hy·po·cy·cloid (hī'pə·sī'kloid, hip'ə-) *n. Math.* A curve generated by a point on the circumference of a circle which rolls, without slipping, on the inside of another circle.

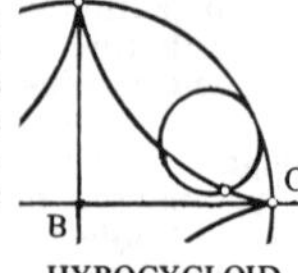

HYPOCYCLOID
B. Center of circle.
AC. Arc on which circle rolls.

hy·po·derm (hī'pə·dûrm) *n. Zool.* The cellular layer between the cuticle and the basal membrane of an arthropod. Also **hy'po·der'·mis.**

hy·po·der·ma (hī'pə·dûr'mə) *n.* **1** *Bot.* The distinct sheath of strengthening tissue beneath the epidermis of stems in plants. **2** The hypoderm. **3** Any of a genus *(Hypoderma)* of dipterous insects, the botflies. [<NL <Gk. *hypo-* under + *derma* skin]

hy·po·der·mal (hī'pə·dûr'məl) *adj.* **1** Pertaining to the hypoderma; situated below the epidermis. **2** Hypodermic.

hy·po·der·mic (hī'pə·dûr'mik) *adj.* **1** Of or pertaining to the area under the skin. **2** Of or pertaining to the hypoderma. — *n.* A hypodermic injection or syringe.

hypodermic injection An injection under the skin.

hypodermic medication Medical treatment by subcutaneous means, as by hypodermic injection.

hypodermic needle The needle of a hypodermic syringe.

hypodermic syringe A syringe having a sharp, hollow needle for injection of substances beneath the skin.

hy·po·der·mis (hī'pə·dûr'məs) *n.* The hypoderm. [<NL]

hy·po·eu·tec·tic (hī'pō·yōō·tek'tik, hip'ō-) *adj.* Having the minor component in a proportion less than that in the corresponding eutectic mixture: said of a mineral, alloy, or solution.

hy·po·gas·tri·um (hī'pə·gas'trē·əm) *n. pl.* **·tri·a** (-trē·ə) *Anat.* The region at the lower part of the abdomen on the middle line. [<NL <Gk. *hypogastrion* <*hypo-* below + *gastēr* belly] — **hy'po·gas'tric** *adj.*

hy·po·ge·al (hī'pə·jē'əl, hip'ə-) *adj.* **1** *Geol.* Situated beneath the surface of the earth, or underlying the superficial outcropping strata. **2** Hypogeous. [<HYPO- + Gk. *gē* earth]

hyp·o·gene (hip'ə·jēn) *adj. Geol.* **1** Formed beneath the earth's surface, as granite. **2** Pertaining to or caused by subterranean agencies; plutonic: contrasted with *epigene* and *volcanic.*

hy·pog·e·nous (hī·poj'ə·nəs, hi-) *adj. Bot.* Growing beneath, as fungi on the under surface of a leaf. Compare EPIGENOUS. [<HYPO- + -GENOUS]

hyp·o·ge·ous (hip'ə·jē'əs, hī'pə-) *adj.* **1** Underground. **2** *Bot.* Growing or fruiting underground, as truffles and other fungi. [<L *hypogeus* <Gk. *hypogeios* <*hypo-* under + *gē* earth]

hyp·o·ge·um (hip'ə·jē'əm, hī'pə-) *n. pl.* **·ge·a** (-jē'ə) **1** *Archit.* The part of a building below the ground. **2** Any underground structure; an artificial cave. [<L <Gk. *hypogeios* subterranean]

hy·po·glos·sal (hī'pə·glos'əl, hip'ə-) *adj. Biol.* Of or pertaining to a nerve situated under the tongue in birds, reptiles, and mammals; underneath the tongue. — *n.* A hypoglossal nerve. [<HYPO- + Gk. *glōssa* tongue]

hy·pog·y·nous (hī·poj'ə·nəs, hi-) *adj. Bot.* Situated on or growing from the receptacle of the flower beneath the ovary or pistil. [<HYPO- + GYNOUS] — **hy·pog'y·ny** *n.*

hy·po·ma·ni·a (hī'pə·mā'nē·ə, -mān'yə, hip'ə-) *n.* A mild form of mania; a condition of moderate elation and overactivity.

hyp·o·nas·ty (hip'ə·nas'tē, hī'pə-) *n. Bot.* A state of curvature induced in an extending plant organ by the excessively active growth of its lower side, causing it to bend downward. Compare EPINASTY. [<HYPO- + Gk. *nastos* compact] — **hyp'o·nas'tic** *adj.* — **hyp'o·nas'ti·cal·ly** *adv.*

hy·po·ni·trous (hī'pə·nī'trəs) *adj. Chem.* Designating an unstable white crystalline nitrogenous acid, $(HNO)_2$, formed by the union of hydroxylamine and nitrous acid, and in other ways. Its salts are known as **hy'po·ni'trites** (-trīts).

hy·po·phos·phate (hī'pə·fos'fāt) *n. Chem.* A salt of hypophosphoric acid.

hy·po·phos·phite (hī'pə·fos'fīt) *n. Chem.* A salt of hypophosphorous acid.

hy·po·phos·phor·ic (hī'pō·fos·fôr'ik, -for'ik) *adj. Chem.* Denoting a crystalline tetrabasic acid, $H_4P_2O_6$, formed from moist phosphorus by oxidation.

hy·po·phos·pho·rous (hī'pə·fos'fər·əs) *adj. Chem.* Denoting a monobasic acid derived from phosphorus, H_3PO_2, a powerful reducing agent.

hy·poph·y·ge (hī·pof'ə·jē, hi-) *n. Archit.* A horizontal rounded groove under a structural member, as in the case of archaic Doric capitals. [<Gk. *hypophygē* refuge, recess <*hypo-* under + *pheugein* flee]

hy·poph·y·sis (hī·pof'ə·sis, hi-) *n. pl.* **·ses** (-sēz) *Anat.* A process or outgrowth. [<NL <Gk.,

an undergrowth <*hypo-* under + *physis* nature <*phyein* grow]

hypophysis cer·e·bri (ser'ə·brī) *Anat.* The pituitary gland. [<NL, outgrowth of the brain]

hy·po·pi·tu·i·ta·rism (hī'pō·pi·tōō'i·tə·riz'əm, -tyōō'-) *n. Pathol.* **1** Diminished activity of the pituitary gland. **2** Any condition produced by this, marked by excessive fat and by adolescent traits.

hy·po·pla·si·a (hī'pə·plā'zhē·ə, -zhə, hip'ə-) *n. Pathol.* The condition of arrested development. —**hy'po·plas'tic** (-plas'tik) *adj.*

hy·po·ploid (hī'pə·ploid, hip'ə-) *adj. Biol.* Denoting a chromosome number less than the basic number. —**hy'po·ploid'y** *n.*

hy·po·pne·a (hī'pə·nē'ə, hip'ə-) *n. Med.* Abnormal rapidity and shallowness of breathing, as from hypoventilation. Also **hy'po·pnoe'a.** [<NL <Gk. *hypo-* under + *pnoē* breathing <*pneein* breathe]

hy·po·po·di·um (hī'pə·pō'dē·əm, hip'ə-) *n. pl.* **·di·a** (-dē·ə) *Bot.* The basal portion of a leaf, including the stalk; a supporting structure in plants. [<NL <Gk. *hypo-* under + *podion,* dim. of *pous, podos* a foot]

hy·po·py·on (hī·pō'pē·on, hi-) *n. Pathol.* An accumulation of pus in the cavity of the eye which contains the aqueous humor. [<NL <Gk., a kind of ulcer <*hypo-* under + *pyon* pus]

hy·po·scope (hī'pə·skōp) *n.* A form of altiscope for military use, as a sighting attachment to a rifle, etc.

hy·pos·ta·sis (hī·pos'tə·sis, hi-) *n.* **1** That which forms, either in fact or hypothesis, a groundwork or support for anything; a basis. **2** *Philos.* A distinct individual subsistence; also, a logical substance. **3** *Theol.* Any one of the persons of the Trinity; also, the separate personal subsistence of each of the three persons of the Trinity in one divine substance. **4** *Med.* A settling down of a fluid of the body. **5** *Pathol.* A morbid deposition of sedimentary matter within the body. [<L <Gk. *hypostasis* substance, subsistence < *hypo-* under + *histhastai* stand, middle voice of *histanai* cause to stand]

hy·po·stat·ic (hī'pə·stat'ik, hip'ə-) *adj.* **1** Of, pertaining to, or constituting a distinct personality or substance; distinctly personal. **2** Of, relating to, or proceeding from hypostasis; elemental. **3** *Med.* Resulting from downward pressure or deposition of sediment in the body: *hypostatic* congestion. **4** *Genetics* Denoting a factor hidden or masked by another which is not an allelomorph. Also **hy'po·stat'i·cal.** [<Gk. *hypostatikos*] —**hy'po·stat'i·cal·ly** *adv.*

hypostatic union *Theol.* The union of two natures in the one person or hypostasis of Christ.

hy·pos·ta·tize (hī·pos'tə·tīz, hi-) *v.t.* **·tized, ·tiz·ing** To treat as real; ascribe substantial or distinct existence to. —**hy·pos'ta·ti·za'tion** (-tə·ti·zā'shən, -tə·tī·zā'-) *n.*

hy·po·sthe·ni·a (hī'pə·sthē'nē·ə) *n. Pathol.* Deficient vitality. Compare HYPERSTHENIA. [< HYPO- + Gk. *sthenos* strength] —**hy'po·sthen'ic** (-sthen'ik) *adj.*

hy·pos·to·ma (hī·pos'tə·mə, hi-) *n. pl.* **hy·po·sto·ma·ta** (hī'pə·stō'mə·tə) *Zool.* A part or organ lying below the mouth, as in certain crustaceans and coelenterates. Also **hyp·o·stome** (hip'ə·stōm). [<NL <Gk. *hypo-* under + *stoma* mouth] —**hy'po·sto'mi·al** *adj.*

hyp·o·style (hip'ə·stīl, hī'pə-) *n. Archit.* **1** Any structure having a ceiling resting upon columns; a pillared hall. **2** One of the halls with huge pillars characteristic of Egyptian architecture. —*adj.* Of, similar to, or pertaining to such a structure. [<HYPO- + Gk. *stylos* pillar]

HYPOSTYLE

hy·po·sul·fite (hī'po·sul'fīt) *n. Chem.* **1** Sodium thiosulfate. **2** A salt of hyposulfurous acid.

hy·po·sul·fur·ic (hī'pō·sul·fyōōr'ik, hī'pə·sul'fər·ik) *adj. Chem.* Of or pertaining to an unstable, colorless acid, $H_2S_2O_6$, having no odor and forming soluble salts with certain bases: also *dithionic.*

hy·po·sul·fu·rous (hī'pō·sul·fyōōr'əs, hī'pə·sul'·fər·əs) *adj. Chem.* Pertaining to or designating an unstable acid, $H_2S_2O_4$, of strong reducing and bleaching properties: also *hydrosulfurous.*

hy·po·tax·is (hī'pə·tak'sis, hip'ə-) *n. Gram.* Subordinate or dependent arrangement of clauses, phrases, etc.: opposed to *parataxis.* —**hy'po·tac'tic** (-tak'tik) or **·ti·cal** *adj.* —**hy'·po·tac'ti·cal·ly** *adv.*

hy·pot·e·nuse (hī·pot'ə·nōōs, -nyōōs, hi-) *n. Geom.* The side of a right-angled triangle opposite the right angle. Also **hy·poth'e·nuse** (-poth'-). [<L *hypotenusa* <Gk. *hypoteinousa (grammē)* a subtending (line) <*hypo-* under + *teinein* stretch]

hy·po·thal·a·mus (hī'pə·thal'ə·məs, hip'ə-) *n. Anat.* The region below the thalamus, controlling visceral activities. —**hy·po·tha·lam·ic** (hī'pə·thə·lam'ik) *adj.*

hy·po·thal·lus (hī'pə·thal'əs, hip'ə-) *n. pl.* **·li** (-ī) *Bot.* **1** The delicate hyphal filaments upon which a lichen thallus is first developed; a mycelial or hyphal outgrowth from the margin of the thallus of a crustaceous lichen. **2** In fungi, an under thallus on which spore cases are produced. [<HYPO- + Gk. *thallos* young shoot] —**hy'po·thal'line** (-ēn, -in) *adj.*

hy·poth·ec (hī·poth'ik, hi-) *n.* A pledge or mortgage of either lands or goods as security for debt where the property pledged remains in possession of the debtor. [<F *hypothèque* <LL *hypotheca* <Gk. *hypothēkē* pledge < *hypotithenai* deposit as a pledge <*hypo-* under + *tithenai* put] —**hy·poth'e·car'y** (-ə·ker'ē) *adj.*

hy·poth·e·cate (hī·poth'ə·kāt, hi-) *v.t.* **·cat·ed, ·cat·ing** To give (personal property) in pledge as security for debt. [<Med. L *hypothecatus,* pp. of *hypothecare* <LL *hypotheca* pledge] —**hy·poth'e·ca'tion** *n.* —**hy·poth'e·ca'tor** *n.*

hy·poth·e·nar (hī·poth'ə·nər, hi-) *n. Biol.* The ridge on the palm at the base of the little finger, or at a corresponding part in the forefoot of a quadruped. [<HYPO- + Gk. *thenar* palm]

hy·po·ther·mal (hī'pō·thûr'məl, hip'ō-) *adj.* Tepid; moderately warm.

hy·po·ther·mi·a (hī'pō·thûr'mē·ə, hip'ō-) *n. Med.* **1** An abnormally low temperature. **2** Therapeutic anesthesia produced by gradually reducing body temperature to as low as 75° F.; frozen sleep. Also **hy'po·ther'my.** [<HYPO- + Gk. *thermē* heat] —**hy'po·ther'·mal** *adj.*

hy·poth·e·sis (hī·poth'ə·sis, hi-) *n. pl.* **·ses** (-sēz) **1** A set of assumptions provisionally accepted as a basis of reasoning, experiment, or investigation. **2** An unsupported or ill-supported theory. [<NL <Gk., foundation, supposition <*hypotithenai* put under <*hypo-* under + *tithenai* put]

Synonyms: conjecture, guess, scheme, speculation, supposition, surmise, system, theory. A *hypothesis* is a statement of what is deemed possibly true, assumed and reasoned upon as if certainly true, with a view of reaching truth not yet surely known; especially, in the sciences, a *hypothesis* is a comprehensive tentative explanation of certain phenomena, which is meant to include all other facts of the same class, and which is assumed as true till there has been opportunity to bring all related facts into comparison; if the *hypothesis* explains all the facts, it is regarded as verified; till then it is regarded as a working *hypothesis,* that is, one that may answer for present practical purposes. A *hypothesis* may be termed a comprehensive *guess.* Compare GUESS, SYSTEM, THEORY. *Antonyms:* certainty, demonstration, discovery, evidence, fact, proof.

hy·poth·e·size (hī·poth'ə·sīz, hi-) *v.* **·sized, ·siz·ing** *v.t.* To make a hypothesis of. —*v.i.* To conceive or suggest hypotheses.

hy·po·thet·ic (hī'pə·thet'ik) *adj.* **1** Having the nature of or based on hypothesis; assumed conditionally or tentatively as a basis for argument or investigation; also, involving a formal hypothesis. **2** Given to using hypotheses. Also **hy'po·thet'i·cal.** See synonyms under IMAGINARY. [<L *hypotheticus* <Gk. *hypothetikos*] —**hy'po·thet'i·cal·ly** *adv.*

hy·po·thy·roid (hī'pō·thī'roid) *adj.* Manifesting hypothyroidism. —*n.* One affected by hypothyroidism.

hy·po·thy·roid·ism (hī'pō·thī'roid·iz'əm) *n. Pathol.* **1** Deficient functioning of the thyroid gland. **2** The resulting psychosomatic disorders: sometimes called *cretinism,* and opposed to *hyperthyroidism.*

hy·po·ton·ic (hī'po·ton'ik) *adj.* **1** Deficient in body tone. **2** Below the osmotic pressure of an isotonic fluid. —**hy'po·to·nic'i·ty** (-tō·nis'ə·tē) *n.*

hy·po·tro·choid (hī'pə·trō'koid) *n. Math.* The curve traced by a point inside a circle, or on its extended radius, as the circle rolls, without slipping, on the inside of another given, fixed circle.

hy·po·tro·phy (hī'pə·trō'fē) *n. Med.* Abiotrophy.

hy·po·ven·ti·la·tion (hī'pō·ven'tə·lā'shən) *n.* Deficient or inadequate ventilation.

hy·po·xan·thine (hī'pə·zan'thēn, -thin) *n. Biochem.* A crystalline alkaloid, $C_5H_4N_4O$, found in various organs, and especially in the muscular tissue of animals, also in certain seeds. Also **hy'po·xan'thin** (-thin). [<Gk. *hypoxanthos* yellowish-brown <*hypo-* under + *xanthos* yellow] —**hy'po·xan'thic** *adj.*

hy·po·xe·mi·a (hī'pok·sē'mē·ə) *n. Med.* Deficient oxygenation of the blood, as from hypoxia. [<HYP- + OX(Y)- + -EMIA]

hy·pox·i·a (hī·pok'sē·ə) *n. Med.* Low oxygen intake by the body, especially as resulting from decreased pressure at high altitudes. [<HYP- + OX(Y)- + -IA]

hypped (hipt), **hyp·pish** (hip'ish) See HIPPED[2], etc.

hypso– *combining form* Height: *hypsometer.* Also, before vowels, **hyps–.** [<Gk. *hypsos* height]

hyp·sog·ra·phy (hip·sog'rə·fē) *n.* **1** The science of observing or describing the topographical features of the earth's surface above sea level. **2** Topographic relief. [<HYPSO- + -GRAPHY] —**hyp·so·graph·ic** (hip'sə·graf'ik) or **·i·cal** *adj.*

hyp·som·e·ter (hip·som'ə·tər) *n.* An instrument for the measurement of heights above sea level by determining the atmospheric pressure through observation of the boiling point of water. [<HYPSO- + -METER]

hyp·som·e·try (hip·som'ə·trē) *n.* The art of measuring, by any method, the heights of points upon the earth's surface above sea level. —**hyp·so·met·ric** (hip'sə·met'rik) or **·ri·cal** *adj.* —**hyp'so·met'ri·cal·ly** *adv.* —**hyp·som'e·trist** *n.*

hyp·so·phyl·lum (hip'sə·fil'əm) *n. Bot.* A bract, or the like, in plant inflorescence. Also **hyp'·so·phyl, hyp'so·phyll.** [<HYPSO- + Gk. *phyllon* leaf]

hy·ra·coid (hī'rə·koid) *n.* A hyrax. —*adj.* Of or pertaining to a hyrax. Also **hy'ra·coi'de·an.** [<NL *Hyracoidea,* genus name]

hy·rax (hī'raks) *n. pl.* **·rax·es** or **·ra·ces** (-rə·sēz) A small, harelike ungulate mammal (order *Hyracoidea*) of Africa and SW Asia; the cony of the Bible; the rock hyrax (genus *Procavia*) shelters in crevices and the tree hyrax (genus *Dendrohyrax*) is arboreal. [< Gk., shrewmouse]

Hyr·ca·ni·a (hûr·kā'nē·ə) A province of the ancient Persian Empire, on the SE shore of the Caspian Sea. —**Hyr·ca'ni·an** *adj.* & *n.*

hy·son (hī'sən) *n.* A grade of green tea from China. The early crop is known as **young hyson.** [<Chinese *hsi-ch'un,* lit., blooming spring]

hys·sop (his'əp) *n.* **1** A bushy, medicinal herb *(Hyssopus officinalis)* of the mint family, about 2 feet high, with small clusters of blue flowers. **2** An unidentified plant furnishing the twigs used in the Mosaic purificatory and sacrificial rites, etc. **3** One of various other plants, as the **giant hyssop** (genus *Agastache*). [OE *ysope* <OF <L *hyssopus* <Gk. *hyssōpos* <Hebrew *ēzōb*]

hys·ter·ec·to·my (his'tə·rek'tə·mē) *n. Surg.* Complete removal of the uterus by excision.

hys·ter·e·sis (his'tə·rē'sis) *n.* **1** *Physics* **a** The tendency of a magnetic substance to persist in any state of magnetization; that property of a medium by virtue of which work is done in changing the direction or intensity of magnetic force among its parts. **b** Some analogous phenomenon, as in dielectrics. When there has been a decrease in magnetization it is called *hysteretic loss,* and the hysteretic loss in ergs per cubic centimeter per cycle is called the *hysteretic constant.* 2 *Biochem.* The influence of the past history of a colloid upon its present condition and behavior. 3 Any state of a material or substance which can be adequately described only in terms of its previous history. [<Gk. *hysterēsis* deficiency <*hystereein* lag] —**hys·ter·et·ic** (his′tə·ret′ik) *adj.*

hys·te·ri·a (his·tir′ē·ə, -ter′-) *n.* 1 *Psychiatry* A psychoneurotic condition characterized by violent emotional paroxysms, anxiety, and morbid effects, as of the sensory and motor functions. 2 Abnormal excitement; morbid emotionalism, as in wild outbursts of alternate laughing and crying. Also **hys·ter·ics** (his·ter′iks). [<NL <Gk. *hystera* the womb; because the condition was thought to affect women more than men] —**hys·ter·i·cal** (his·ter′i·kəl), **hys·ter′ic** *adj.* —**hys·ter′i·cal·ly** *adv.*

hys·ter·i·tis (his′tə·rī′tis) *n. Pathol.* Inflammation of the womb.

hystero– *combining form* 1 The womb; uterine: *hysteropexy.* 2 Hysteria; hysteric: *hysterogenic.* Also, before vowels, **hyster–.** [< Gk. *hystera* the womb]

hys·ter·o·gen·ic (his′tər·ə·jen′ik) *adj.* Producing or concerned in the production of hysteria.

hys·ter·oid (his′tər·oid) *adj.* Resembling hysteria.

hys·ter·on prot·er·on (his′tər·on prot′ər·on) 1 A figure of speech that reverses the natural order of words or clauses. Example: "Is your father well? is he yet alive?" 2 That form of fallacy in which one asserts a consequent and then infers the antecedent. [<LL <Gk., the latter (put) first]

hys·ter·o·pex·y (his′tər·ə·pek′sē) *n. Surg.* The operation of fixing the uterus to the abdominal wall to relieve prolapsus. [<HYSTERO- + Gk. *pēxis* fixing]

hys·ter·o·phyte (his′tər·ə·fīt′) *n.* A plant included in an obsolete group *(Hysterophyta)* embracing fungi. —**hys′ter·o·phyt′ic** (-fit′ik) *adj.*

hys·ter·ot·o·my (his′tə·rot′ə·mē) *n. Surg.* 1 The operation of cutting into the womb. 2 Caesarean section. [<HYSTERO- + -TOMY]

hys·tri·co mor·phic (his′tri·kō·môr′fik) *adj.* Of or pertaining to a division *(Hystricomorpha)* of rodents, including porcupines, cavies, etc. [<Gk. *hystrix* porcupine + -MORPHIC]

hyte (hīt) *adj. Scot.* Crazy; mad.

hy·ther (hī′thər) *n. Biol.* The combined effect of moisture and heat on an organism. [<Gk. *hy(dōr)* water + *ther(mē)* heat]

hy·zone (hī′zōn) *n.* Tritium. [<HY(DROGEN) + Gk. *ozein* smell; with ref. to its strong odor]

I

i, I (ī) *n. pl.* **i's, I's** or **Is, eyes** (īz) 1 The ninth letter of the English alphabet: from Phoenician *yod,* Greek *iota,* Roman *I.* 2 Any sound of the letter *i.* See ALPHABET. —*symbol* 1 The Roman numeral one: written I or i. See under NUMERAL. 2 *Chem.* Iodine (symbol I).

I[1] (ī) *pron.* The person speaking or writing, as he denotes himself in the nominative case. —*n.* 1 The self; the pronoun *I* employed as a noun. 2 *Philos.* The ego. [OE *ic*]

I[2] (ī) *adj.* Shaped like the letter I: an *I*–beam, *I*–rail.

I[3] (ī) *interj. Obs.* See AYE or AY.

i' (i) *prep. Scot.* In.

i–[1] Reduced var. of IN–[1].

i–[2] See Y–.

–ia[1] *suffix of nouns* Used in: 1 *Geog.* Names of countries: *Australia.* 2 *Pathol.* Names of diseases and related terms: *hysteria.* 3 *Bot.* Names of genera: *Lobelia.* 4 *Chem.* Names of alkaloids: *morphia.* 5 Words borrowed directly from Greek and Latin: *militia.* [<L and Gk. *-ia,* suffix of fem. nouns]

–ia[2] *suffix of nouns* Used in: 1 *Biol.* Names of classes: *Mammalia.* 2 Names of classical festivals: *Bacchanalia.* 3 Words, usually collectives, borrowed from Latin or Greek: *regalia.* [<L and Gk. *-ia,* plural suffix of neut. nouns]

I·a·go (ē·ä′gō) The perfidious adviser of Othello.

Ia·ko·bos (yä′kə·bôs) Greek form of JAMES.

–ial *suffix of adjectives* Of, pertaining to, or like the first element of the word: *nuptial, filial.* [Var. of -AL[1], with connective *-i*]

i·am·bic (ī·am′bik) *adj.* 1 Pertaining to or employing the iambus: *iambic* poetry. 2 Having characteristics of iambics. —*n.* 1 An iambus. 2 A verse, line, or stanza composed of iambic feet. 3 A satire or invective poem in iambic verse. [<L *iambicus* <Gk. *iambikos*]

i·am·bus (ī·am′bəs) *n. pl.* **·bi** (-bī) A foot of two syllables, a short or unaccented followed by a long or accented one. Also **i·amb** (ī′amb). [<L <Gk. *iambos* < *iambein* assail verbally; because orig. utilized by satiric poets]

–ian *suffix* Of, pertaining to, from, or like the proper name appearing in the stem: *Baconian, Bostonian,* etc. [Var. of -AN, with connective *-i*]

–iana See –ANA.

–iasis *suffix Med.* Denoting a process and its results, especially in diseased conditions: *psoriasis.* [Var. of -OSIS]

Ia·sy (yä′shē, yäsh) See JASSY.

i·at·ric (ī·at′rik) *adj.* Relating to physicians and the healing art; medical. Also **i·at′ri·cal.** [<Gk. *iatrikos* healing < *iatros* physician < *iasthai* heal]

–iatrics *combining form* Denoting treatment of disease: *pediatrics.* [<Gk. *iatrikos* pertaining to the art of healing]

iatro– *combining form* Signifying a connection with or relation to medicine: *iatrochemistry, iatrophysics,* etc. [<Gk. *iatros* physician]

i·at·ro·gen·ic (ī·at′rə·jen′ik) *adj. Med.* Generated or induced by the physician; said especially of disorders resulting from autosuggestion based on the physician's manner of handling or discussing a case.

–iatry *combining form* Medical or curative treatment: *psychiatry.* [<Gk. *iatreia* healing]

I·ba·dan (ē·bä′dän) A city in SW Nigeria.

I·ba·ñez (ē·vä′nyeth) See BLASCO Y IBAÑEZ.

I–beam (ī′bēm′) *n.* A beam or joist having a cross–section in the shape of an I.

I·be·ri·a (ī·bir′ē·ə) 1 The part of SW Europe comprising Spain and Portugal: also **Iberian Peninsula.** 2 An ancient country between the Caucasus and Armenia, corresponding to modern Georgia.

I·be·ri·an (ī·bir′ē·ən) *adj.* 1 Of or pertaining to ancient Iberia in Asia, now Transcaucasian Georgia. 2 Of or pertaining to the Iberian Peninsula, including Spain and Portugal, or relating to the people of this region. —*n.* 1 One of the inhabitants of ancient Iberia in Asia, conquered by the Arabs in the seventh century. 2 A member of the oldest ethnological group of Europe, which existed on the Iberian Peninsula as early as the Neolithic era. 3 The unclassified language of the ancient inhabitants of the Iberian Peninsula, of which Basque may be a modern survivor: known only through some proper names and about 150 inscriptions. [<L *Iberus* <Gk. *Iberes* Spaniards]

I·ber·ville (dē′bər·vil, *Fr.* dē·ber·vēl′), **Sieur d',** 1661–1706, Pierre Lemoyne (or Le Moyne), French–Canadian explorer; colonized Louisiana.

i·bex (ī′beks) *n. pl.* **i·bex·es** or **i·bi·ces** (ī′bə·sēz, ib′ə-) One of various wild goats of Europe and Asia, with long, recurved horns, especially the Alpine ibex *(Capra ibex)* and the Cretan ibex *(C. hircus).* [<L]

IBEX
(Species vary from 2 1/2 to 3 1/2 feet tall)

I·bi·cuí (ē·bē·kwē′) A river in southern Brazil, flowing 300 miles west to the Uruguay.

i·bi·dem (i·bī′dem) *adv. Latin* In the same place. Abbr. *ibid.*

i·bis (ī′bis) *n. pl.* **i·bis·es** or **i·bis** 1 A wading bird related to the heron (family *Threskiornithidae*), with cylindrical bill bent downward; especially the sacred ibis *(Threskiornis aethiopica),* venerated among the ancient Egyptians. 2 The wood ibis. [<L <Gk. <Egyptian *hab*]

-ible See –ABLE.

Ib·lees (ib′lēs). See EBLIS.

Ibn Sa·ud (ib′n sä·ōōd′), **Abdul Aziz,** 1880–1953, king of Saudi Arabia 1932–53. See SAUD.

I·bo (ē′bō) *n. pl.* **I·bo** 1 A member of a group of Negro tribes of western Africa. 2 The Sudanic language of these tribes. [< the native name]

i·bo·ga (i·bō′gə) *n.* A cultivated shrub (genus *Tabernaemontana,* formerly *Tabernanthe iboga)* of the dogbane family, of central Africa. [< native name]

i·bo·gaine (i·bō′gān, -gə·ēn) *n. Chem.* A poisonous alkaloid, $C_{52}H_{66}O_2N_6$, from the root, bark, and leaves of the iboga: similar in action to cocaine.

Ib·ra·him Pa·sha (ib·rä·hēm′ pä′shə), 1789–1848, Egyptian commander and viceroy.

Ib·sen (ib′sən), **Henrik,** 1828–1906, Norwegian dramatist and poet.

Ib·sen·ism (ib′sən·iz′əm) *n.* A theory or doctrine concerning Ibsen's plays, which were conceived by his imitators and critics, though not by Ibsen himself, as problem plays in which social conventions and attitudes were criticized.

–ic *suffix* Of adjectives: 1 Of or pertaining to: *volcanic.* 2 Like; resembling; characteristic of: *angelic.* 3 Consisting of; containing: *alcoholic.* 4 Produced or caused by: *Homeric.* 5 Related to; connected with: *domestic.* 6 *Chem.* Having a higher valence than that indicated by *–ous*: said of elements in compounds: *cupric* oxide, *sulfuric* acid. —Of nouns: 1 By the conversion of adjectives in any of the above senses: *Stoic, public.* 2 The art or knowledge of: *rhetoric, music.* [<F *-ique* <L *-icus* <Gk. *-ikos*]

◆ **–ic, –icly** A few adjectives in *–ic* form adverbs in *–icly,* as, *publicly,* but the adverb is usually formed by adding *–ally*: *musically, rhythmically, volcanically.* See also note under –ICAL, –ICS.

I·çá (ē·sä′) The Putumayo in its lower courses in Brazil.

–ical *suffix* 1 Like; pertaining to: *ethical*: used in adjectives derived from nouns in *–ic, –ics.* 2 With the same general meaning as *–ic*: *comical*; sometimes with extended or special meaning: *economical.* [<LL *-icalis* < *-icus* -IC + < *-alis* -AL]

◆ **–ic, –ical** In cases where both forms exist and do not differ greatly in meaning, there is no set rule governing usage. Euphony and past usage alone generally determine the choice of one form over the other.

I·car·i·a (i·kâr′ē·ə, ī-) A Greek Aegean island SW of Samos; 99 square miles: formerly *Nicaria*: also *Ikaria.*

I·car·i·an (i·kâr′ē·ən, ī-) *adj.* Of or pertaining to Icarus, son of Daedalus; hence, high-flying; rash or adventurous; presumptuous. [<L *Icarus* <Gk. *Ikarios*]

Icarian Sea The Aegean Sea off the coast of Asia Minor, where Icarus was supposed to have fallen after his flight.

Ic·a·rus (ik′ə·rəs, ī′kə-) In Greek mythology, the son of Daedalus, who, escaping with his father from Crete, flew too near the sun so that the wax that fastened his artificial wings melted and he fell into the sea and drowned.

ICBM The intercontinental ballistic missile, having a range of at least 5,000 miles. Compare *IRBM*.

ice (īs) *n.* **1** Congealed or frozen water; the solid condition assumed by water at or below 32° F. or 0° C. ◆ Collateral adjective: *glacial*. **2** A frozen dessert made without cream, as a sherbet, water ice, or frappé. **3** Something resembling ice in appearance: camphor *ice*. **4** Frosting or icing for cake. **5** Chilly reserve; a very formal or dignified attitude. **6** *Slang* A diamond; also, diamonds collectively. —**to break the ice** To break through reserve or formality. —**to cut no ice** *U.S. Slang* To have no importance. —**on ice** *U.S. Slang* **1** Set aside or reserved for future action. **2** In prison. **3** Sure; already determined. —*v.* **iced, ic·ing** *v.t.* **1** To cause to freeze; congeal into ice. **2** To cover with ice. **3** To chill with or as with ice. **4** To frost, as cake, with icing. —*v.i.* **5** To freeze; congeal into ice. —*adj.* Made of ice; to be used on ice: *ice* skates. [OE *īs*]

-ice *suffix of nouns* Condition, quality, or state of: *justice*. [<OF *-ice* <L *-itius, -itia, -itium*]

ice age The glacial epoch.

ice anchor See ICE HOOK (def. 2).

ice ax An ax used by mountaineers for cutting steps in the ice: usually equipped with a spiked butt.

ice·berg (īs′bûrg′) *n.* **1** A thick mass of ice found floating in the sea at high latitudes; a portion of a glacier discharged into the sea: distinguished from *field ice*. **2** A cold, unemotional person. [<Du. *ijsberg*]

ice·blink (īs′blingk′) *n.* A shining whiteness on the horizon produced by the reflection of distant masses of ice. [Cf. Du. *ijsblin*, Dan. *iisblink*]

ice·boat (īs′bōt′) *n.* **1** A framework with skatelike runners and sails for sailing over ice. **2** An icebreaker (def. 2).

ICEBOAT

ice·bone (īs′bōn′) *n.* The aitchbone. [Prob. <L *ischium* ischium + BONE. Cf. MDu. *yschbeen*.]

ice boulder A boulder transported and deposited through glacial action.

ice·bound (īs′bound′) *adj.* Surrounded, beset, or obstructed by ice; frozen in: an *icebound* ship, an *icebound* harbor.

ice·box (īs′boks′) *n.* A refrigerator. Also **ice′-chest′** (-chest′).

ice·break·er (īs′brā′kər) *n.* **1** A structure for deflecting ice from a bridge pier or the like: also **ice′-a′pron** (-ā′prən). **2** A specially constructed ship having a strong prow and powerful engines, used to break up ice in navigable channels of icebound waters and harbors.

ice cap An extensive covering of ice and snow permanently overlying a tract of land and moving in all directions from a center. See ICE SHEET.

ice-cream (īs′krēm′) *n.* A mixture of cream or butterfat, flavoring, sweetening, and often eggs, beaten to a uniform consistency and frozen. Also **ice cream.** [Orig., *iced cream*]

iced (īst) *adj.* **1** Coated or covered with ice or sleet. **2** Made cold with ice. **3** Covered with icing, as cake.

ice·fall (īs′fôl′) *n.* The steepest part or the precipice of a glacier, resembling a frozen waterfall.

ice field A large field of floating ice. Also **ice float, ice floe.**

ice fishing Fishing through holes cut in the ice.

ice-foot (īs′fo͝ot′) *n.* A wall of ice formed by sea water and snow frozen along the shore in polar regions. [Trans. of Dan. *isfod*]

ice hook **1** A hook attached to a pole: used in handling large blocks of ice. See illustration under HOOK. **2** An S-shaped iron bar sharpened at one point: used with a hawser to secure a vessel to ice: also *ice anchor*.

ice·house (īs′hous′) *n.* A building for storing ice.

I·çel (ē·chel′) A city in southern Turkey: also *Mersin*. *Turkish* **İ·çel′**

Ice·land (īs′lənd) The westernmost state of Europe, comprising an independent island republic in the North Atlantic; 39,709 square miles; capital, Reykjavik; a Danish possession until 1944. *Icelandic* **Ís·land** (ēs′länt).

Ice·land·er (īs′lan′dər) *n.* A native or naturalized inhabitant of Iceland.

Ice·land·ic (īs·lan′dik) *adj.* Of or pertaining to Iceland. —*n.* The North Germanic language of Iceland; strictly, this language since the 16th century. —**Old Icelandic** The language of Iceland before the 16th century, exemplified in the Eddas: the best literary representative of Old Norse, and sometimes used synonymously for it.

Iceland moss An edible and medicinal lichen (*Cetraria islandica*) of the arctic regions.

Iceland poppy See under POPPY.

ice·man (īs′man′, -mən) *n.* *pl.* **·men** (-men′, -mən) **1** One who gathers and stores or deals in ice; also, one who carts and delivers ice to consumers. **2** One skilled in traveling upon ice or navigating among masses of ice.

ice needle *Meteorol.* A thin crystal of ice, so light that it floats suspended in the air.

I·ce·ni (ī·sē′nī) *n. pl.* An ancient British tribe, led by its queen, Boadicea, against the Romans; defeated by Suetonius Paulinus, A.D. 61. [<L]

ice pack **1** A large tract of floating ice cakes closely compacted and held together. **2** A container for cracked ice, used for medical applications.

ice pick An awl-like tool for breaking ice into small pieces.

ice plant A fig marigold of southern Africa, the Mediterranean region, and southern California (*Mesembryanthemum crystallinum*) having leaves covered with glistening frost-like protuberances.

ice point *Physics* The melting point of ice at standard atmospheric pressure, 0.0° C: one of the fixed points of the international temperature scale.

ice·quake (īs′kwāk′) *n.* The disturbance attending the rupture of masses of ice.

ice rain **1** A rain that congeals quickly in a deposit of glaze. **2** Falling pellets of clear ice; sleet.

ice sheet A large ice cap; a continental glacier.

ice-skate (īs′skāt′) *v.i.* **-skat·ed, -skat·ing** To skate on ice.

ice skate A skate with a metal runner for skating on ice.

ice-up (īs′up′) *n.* *Aeron.* The formation of ice on the leading edges or other exposed surfaces of airplanes when passing through moist air at low temperatures. Also **ic′ing.**

ice water **1** Water chilled by ice. **2** Melted ice.

Ich·a·bod (ik′ə·bod) A grandson of Eli. 1 *Sam.* iv 21. [<Hebrew, ? inglorious]

Ich·a·bod Crane (ik′ə·bod krān′) A Yankee schoolteacher in Irving's *Legend of Sleepy Hollow*.

I·chang (ē′chäng′) A port on the Yangtze, south central China.

ich dien (ikh dēn) *German* I serve: motto of the Prince of Wales.

ich·neu·mon (ik·no͞o′mən, -nyo͞o′-) *n.* **1** An Old World civetlike carnivore of somewhat weasel-like aspect (genus *Herpestes*), as the mongoose, feeding on mice, eggs, snakes, etc. **2** An ichneumon fly. [<L <Gk. *ichneumōn*, lit., tracker < *ichneuein* track down < *ichnos* footstep, trace; because it was believed to track down and eat crocodiles' eggs]

ichneumon fly A hymenopterous insect (family *Ichneumonidae*) that deposits its eggs upon or in other insects which its larvae will feed upon. For illustration see under INSECT (beneficial).

ich·nite (ik′nīt) *n.* *Paleontol.* A fossil footprint. Also **ich′no·lite** (-nə·līt). [<Gk. *ichnos* footprint]

ich·no·graph (ik′nə·graf, -gräf) *n.* A ground plan.

ich·nog·ra·phy (ik·nog′rə·fē) *n.* **1** The art of drawing by means of compass and rule, or of tracing plans, etc. **2** The plan drawn. [<LL *ichnografia* <Gk. < *ichnos* trace + *graphein* write] —**ich·no·graph·ic** (ik′nə·graf′ik) or **·i·cal** *adj.*

i·chor (ī′kôr, ī′kər) *n.* **1** In classical mythology, the ethereal fluid supposed to flow in the veins of the gods. **2** A watery acrid humor discharged from sores. [<Gk. *ichōr*]

i·chor·ous (ī′kər·əs) *adj.* Full of, mingled with, or like ichor.

ich·thy·ic (ik′thē·ik) *adj.* Fishlike.

ichthyo- *combining form* Fish: *ichthyology*. Also, before vowels, **ichthy-**. [<Gk. *ichthys* fish]

ich·thy·o·cen·taur (ik′thē·ə·sen′tôr) *n.* A fabulous monster, combining the form of man and fish.

ich·thy·oid (ik′thē·oid) *adj.* Of or like a fish: also **ich′thy·oi′dal.** —*n.* A fishlike vertebrate.

Ich·thy·ol (ik′thē·ōl, -ol) *n.* Proprietary name for a compound of sulfonated hydrocarbons obtained by the distillation of certain shales: used mainly in skin diseases.

ich·thy·o·lite (ik′thē·ə·līt′) *n.* *Paleontol.* A fossil fish.

ich·thy·ol·o·gy (ik′thē·ol′ə·jē) *n.* The branch of zoology that treats of fishes. [<ICHTHYO- + -LOGY] —**ich·thy·o·log·ic** (ik′thē·ə·loj′ik) *adj.* —**ich′thy·ol′o·gist** *n.*

ich·thy·oph·a·gist (ik′thē·of′ə·jist) *n.* One who feeds on fish.

ich·thy·oph·a·gous (ik′thē·of′ə·gəs) *adj.* Fish-eating.

ich·thy·oph·a·gy (ik′thē·of′ə·jē) *n.* The practice of feeding on fish.

ich·thy·or·nis (ik′thē·ôr′nis) *n.* *Paleontol.* One of a genus (*Ichthyornis*) of extinct toothed birds of the Cretaceous having fishlike vertebrae. [<ICHTHY- + Gk. *ornis* bird]

ich·thy·o·sau·rus (ik′thē·ə·sôr′əs) *n.* *pl.* **·sau·ri** (-sôr′ī) *Paleontol.* Any of an order (*Ichthyosauria*) of extinct marine reptiles of the Mesozoic era, having a porpoise-like form with four paddlelike limbs, a large, elongated head, long tail, and broad vertebrae resembling those of fishes. Also **ich′thy·o·saur′**. [<ICHTHYO- + Gk. *sauros* lizard]

ICHTHYOSAURUS
(The largest are thought to have been about 30 feet long)

ich·thy·o·sis (ik′thē·ō′sis) *n.* *Pathol.* A congenital skin disease characterized by dry, scaly or horny formations. —**ich′thy·ot′ic** (-ot′ik) *adj.*

-ician *suffix of nouns* One skilled in, or engaged in, the field of: *logician, mathematician*: originally used with names of arts and sciences ending in *-ic* or *-ics*, but now, by analogy, with any stem, as in *beautician, mortician*. [<F *-icien*]

i·ci·cle (ī′si·kəl) *n.* A pendent, tapering mass or rod of ice formed by the freezing of drops of dripping water. [OE *īsgicel* < *īs* ice + *gicel* piece of ice, icicle] —**i′ci·cled** *adj.*

i·ci·ly (ī′sə·lē) *adv.* In an icy manner; frigidly; frostily.

ic·ing (ī′sing) *n.* A glazing or coating of sugar, usually mixed with white of egg or cream, for a cake; frosting.

i·ci on parle fran·çais (ē·sē′ ôn pårl′ fräṅ·se′) *French* French is spoken here.

ick·er (ik′ər) *n.* *Scot.* A head of grain; an ear of corn.

Ick·es (ik′əs, -ēz), **Harold,** 1874–1952, U.S. public administrator and writer.

Ic·olm·kill (ik′əlm·kil) See IONA.

i·con (ī′kon) *n.* *pl.* **i·cons** or **i·con·es** (ī′kə·nēz) **1** An image or likeness. **2** In the Greek Church, a holy picture, mosaic, etc.: also spelled *ikon.* **3** Formerly, any book illustration. Also called *eikon.* See synonyms under IMAGE. [<Gk. *eikōn* image]

i·con·ic (ī·kon′ik) *adj.* **1** Relating to or of the nature of an icon. **2** Relating to portraiture. **3** Customary or conventional, in art: applied originally to the portraits or statues of athletes who had been victorious in the contests, and later to memorial busts, etc., made after conventional types. Also **i·con′i·cal.**

I·co·ni·um (ī·kō′nē·əm) The ancient name for KONYA.

icono– *combining form* Image; of or related to images: *iconography.* Also, before vowels, **icon–.** [<Gk. *eikōn* image]

i·con·o·clast (ī·kon′ə·klast) *n.* **1** An image breaker. **2** One of certain religious parties devoted to the destruction of images that were venerated or worshiped. **3** One who assails traditional beliefs. [<LL *iconoclastes* <Gk. *eikonoklastēs* <*eikōn* image + *-klastēs* breaker <*klaein* break, destroy] **—i·con′o·clas′tic** *adj.*

i·con·o·ge·net·ic (ī·kon′ə·jə·net′ik) *adj.* **1** Image–forming. **2** *Biol.* Capable of gathering visual information about external objects, as the eyes of animals.

i·co·nog·ra·phy (ī′kə·nog′rə·fē) *n. pl.* **·phies** **1** The science of the description and study of paintings, sculptures, portraits, busts, statues, emblems, and symbolism: Christian *iconography.* **2** The art of illustration by figures; pictorial representation. **3** *Obs.* A picture or other representation, or a collection of representations. [<Med. L *iconografia* <Gk. *eikonografia* <*eikōn* icon + *graphein* write] **—i·con·o·graph·ic** (ī·kon′ə·graf′ik) or **·i·cal** *adj.*

i·co·nol·a·ter (ī′kə·nol′ə·tər) *n.* A worshiper of images; an idolater. [<ICONO-+ -LATRY] **—i′co·nol′a·try** *n.*

i·co·nol·o·gy (ī′kə·nol′ə·jē) *n. pl.* **·gies** **1** The science of pictorial or emblematic representation. **2** A study or description of works of art, emblematic figures, and particularly the attributes of religious, mythological and historical personages. [<ICONO- + -LOGY] **—i·con·o·log·i·cal** (ī·kon′ə·loj′i·kəl) *adj.*

i·con·o·ma·ni·a (ī·kon′ə·mā′nē·ə, -mān′yə) *n.* A morbid interest in, or obsession with, images, fancied or real.

i·con·o·scope (ī·kon′ə·skōp) *n. Telecom.* A scanning device used in television, consisting of an evacuated glass bulb containing a photosensitive screen from whose surface the image is picked up by a narrow, intense, swiftly moving beam of electrons.

i·co·nos·ta·sis (ī′kə·nos′tə·sis) *n. pl.* **·ses** (-sēz) In the Eastern Church, the screen separating the sacristy, bema, and chapel of prothesis from the rest of the church. Also **i·con·o·stas** (ī·kon′ə·stas). [<NL <NGk. *eikonostasis* < *eikōn* icon + *stasis* standing]

i·co·sa·he·dron (ī′kō·sə·hē′drən) *n. pl.* **·dra** (-drə) *Geom.* A solid bounded by 20 plane faces. [<Gk. *eikosaedron*] **—i′co·sa·he′dral** (-drəl) *adj.*

icosi– *combining form* Twenty. Also, before vowels, **icos–.** [<Gk. *eikosi* twenty]

–ics *suffix of nouns* **1** Art, science, or field of study of: *mathematics.* **2** Methods, practices, or activities of: *athletics.* [See -IC]

◆ **–ic, –ics** Adjectives in Greek, ending in *–ikē* (feminine singular) and *–ika* (neuter plural) were often used as nouns to indicate the names of arts or the various departments of life and knowledge. These words were borrowed, through Latin *–ica,* as singular nouns in the Romance languages and later into English. After the 16th century, it became customary to use the plural form in *–ics,* on analogy with Greek *–ika*: *optics, logistics, acoustics.* Nouns ending in *–ics* are construed as singular when they strictly denote an art, science, or system (as, mathematics is difficult; politics offers an uncertain future); they are construed as plural if they denote personal attributes (as, his mathematics are poor; his politics are suspect), if they denote inherent qualities (as, the acoustics are bad) or specific activities (as, athletics are compulsory; hysterics are unseemly; our tactics are superior to the enemy's).

ic·ter·ic (ik·ter′ik) *adj. Pathol.* Affected with jaundice. Also **ic·ter′i·cal.** [<Gk. *ikterikos*]

ic·ter·us (ik′tər·əs) *n.* **1** *Pathol.* Jaundice. **2** *Bot.* Yellowness in the leaves of plants, caused by protracted wet or cold weather. [<LL <Gk. *ikteros* jaundice]

Ic·ti·nus (ik·tī′nəs) Fifth century B.C. Greek architect; designed the Parthenon.

ic·tus (ik′təs) *n. pl.* **·tus·es** or **·tus** **1** *Pathol.* **a** A stroke or blow. **b** A sudden attack or fit. **2** The sting of an insect. **3** A metrical stress or a syllable. [<L, pp. of *icere* strike]

i·cy (ī′sē) *adj.* **i·ci·er, i·ci·est** **1** Pertaining to ice; frigid; as cold as ice; full of or like ice. **2** Marked by coldness of manner, aspect, etc.; chilling. [OE *isig*] **—i′ci·ness, i′cy·ness** *n.*

id (id) *n.* **1** *Biol.* In Weismann's theory of heredity, a unit of germ plasm representing the characteristics of an ancestral member of the species: supposedly composed of determinants, which are made up of biophores. **2** *Psychoanal.* The concealed, inaccessible part of the psyche, seated in the unconscious, independent of a sense of reality, logic, and morality, but actuated by fundamental impulses towards fulfilling instinctual needs; the reservoir of psychic energy or libido. [Def. 1, short for IDIOPLASM; def. 2, <NL <L *id* it, trans. of G *es*]

I'd (īd) **1** I would. **2** I had.

–id[1] *suffix* **1** *Zool.* **a** A member of a family: *leporid.* **b** A member of a class: *arachnid.* **2** *Astron.* A meteor from: used to denote meteors which seem to radiate from certain constellations: *Perseid.* **3** An epic about: *Aeneid.* **4** Son or daughter of: often used in personal names from classical myth or legend: *Danaid.* [<L - *is, -idis* <Gk.*-is, -idos,* suffix of patronymics]

–id[2] *suffix of adjectives* Having a particular quality, or in a specified state: *fluid, vivid.* [< F *-ide* <L *-idus;* or directly <L]

I·da (ī′də, *Du., Ger., Ital.* ē′dä; *Fr.* ē·dȧ′) A feminine personal name. [<Gmc., happy]

I·da (ī′də) **1** A mountain range in NW Asia Minor near the site of ancient Troy; highest peak, 5,797 feet: *Turkish* **Kaz Da·gi** (käz′dä·ē′). **2** The highest mountain in Crete; 8,058 feet: also *Psiloriti*: *Greek* **I·dhi** (ē′thi).

–idae *suffix Zool.* Used to form the names of families of animals when added to the stem of the name of the type genus: *Canidae.* [<NL *-idae* <L <Gk. *-idai,* plural patronymic suffix]

I·dae·an (ī·dē′ən) *adj.* Of or pertaining to Mount Ida.

I·da·ho (ī′də·hō) A NW State of the United States; 83,557 square miles; capital, Boise; entered the Union July 3, 1890; nickname, *Gem State*: abbr. ID **—I′da·ho′an** *adj. & n.*

–ide *suffix Chem.* Used in the names of compounds, usually binary, and attached to the electronegative or non–metallic element or radical: sodium *chloride.* Also **–id.** [<F *-ide.* See -ID[2].]

i·de·a (ī·dē′ə) *n.* **1** Any notion or thought: the *idea* of a horse or of happiness. **2** The result of thinking; a definitely formulated thought; an opinion: a clear *idea* of social justice. **3** A plan or project: to have an *idea* of going into business. **4** A concept; a mental representation of something perceived through the senses. **5** A vague thought or fancy; supposition: I had no *idea* you'd come. **6** *Colloq.* Meaning; aim: What's the *idea*? **7** In Platonic philosophy, the archetype or external pattern of which all existing things are imperfect representations. **8** *Obs.* The embodiment of a conception, belief, or view. [<L <Gk. < *idein* see]

Synonyms: apprehension, archetype, belief, conceit, concept, conception, design, fancy, fantasy, ideal, image, imagination, impression, judgment, model, notion, opinion, pattern, plan, purpose, sentiment, supposition, theory, thought. *Idea* is in Greek a *form* or an *image.* The sense implied by early Platonic philosophy has nearly disappeared and has been largely appropriated by *ideal,* but something of the original meaning still appears when in theological or philosophical language we speak of the *ideas* of God. The present popular use of *idea* makes it signify any product of mental *apprehension* or activity, considered as an object of knowledge or thought; this coincides with the primitive sense at but a single point—that an *idea* is mental as opposed to anything substantial or physical; thus, almost any mental product, as a *belief, conception, design, opinion,* etc., may now be called an *idea.* Compare FANCY, IDEAL, IMAGF THOUGHT[1]. *Antonyms*: actuality, fact, reality, substance.

i·de·al (ī·dē′əl, ī·dēl′) *adj.* **1** Pertaining to or existing in ideas; conceptional. **2** Of or pertaining to an ideal or perfection. **3** Conceived as perfect, supremely excellent, or very desirable. **4** Existing only in imagination or notion; of such perfection as to be practically unattainable. **5** In philosophy, existing as an archetypal idea or pattern. —*n.* **1** That which is taken as a standard of excellence or beauty; an ultimate object of attainment; model; type. **2** That which exists only in imagination. [<L *idealis*]

Synonyms (adj.): fancied, fanciful, imaginary, unreal, visionary. Compare IMAGINARY, ROMANTIC. See also PERFECT. *Antonyms*: actual, material, palpable, physical, real, substantial, tangible, visible.

Synonyms (noun): archetype, idea, model, original, pattern, prototype, standard. An *ideal* is that which is conceived or taken as the highest type of excellence or ultimate object of attainment. The *archetype* is the primal form, actual or imaginary, according to which any existing thing is constructed; the *prototype* has or has had actual existence; in the derived sense, as in metrology, a *prototype* may not be the original form, but one having equal authority with that as a standard. An *ideal* may be primal, or may be slowly developed even from failures and by negations; an *ideal* is meant to be perfect, the best conceivable thing that could by possibility be attained. The artist's *ideal* is his own mental image, of which his finished work is but an imperfect expression. The *original* is the first specimen, good or bad; the *original* of a master is superior to all copies. The *standard* may be below the *ideal.* The *ideal* is ordinarily unattainable; the *standard* is concrete, and ordinarily attainable, being a measure to which all else of its kind must conform; as, the *standard* of weights and measures, of corn, or of cotton. The *idea* of virtue is the mental concept or image of virtue in general: the *ideal* of virtue is the mental concept or image of virtue in its highest conceivable perfection. Compare EXAMPLE, IDEA. *Antonyms*: accomplishment, achievement, act, action, attainment, development, doing, embodiment, execution, fact, incarnation, performance, practice, reality, realization.

i·de·al·ism (ī·dē′əl·iz′əm) *n.* **1** Any of several philosophical theories that there is no reality, no world of objects or "thing–in–itself" apart from a reacting mind or consciousness; that only the mental is knowable, and therefore that reality is essentially spiritual or mental: variously developed by Berkeley, Kant, Hegel. **2** In literature, the development of subject matter following an imaginative or preconceived idea of perfection instead of adhering strictly to facts: opposed to *realism.* **3** The quest of the ideal; the habit of forming ideals and of striving after their realization; by extension, that which is so realized; the attainment of an ideal. **4** In art, the endeavor to attain perfection by improving and uniting in one form all the best qualities to be found in different individual forms. *Idealism* creates in conformity with a preconceived ideal; *realism* restricts the imaginative faculty.

i·de·al·ist (ī·dē′əl·ist) *n.* **1** One who idealizes, or seeks an ideal or ideal conditions; a visionary; a romantic. **2** An exponent of idealism in art or literature. **3** One who holds the doctrines of any philosophic idealism. **—i·de′·al·is′tic** or **·ti·cal** *adj.***—i·de′al·is′ti·cal·ly** *adv.*

i·de·al·i·ty (ī′dē·al′ə·tē) *n. pl.* **·ties** **1** The condition or character of being ideal; existence only in the mind **2** The power or tendency to form ideals; imagination.

i·de·al·ize (ī·dē′əl·īz) *v.* **·ized, ·iz·ing** *v.t.* To represent or think of as conforming to some standard of perfection or beauty; make ideal; exalt. —*v.i.* To form an ideal or ideals. **—i·de·al·i·za·tion** (ī·dē′əl·ə·zā′shən, -ī·zā′-) *n.* **—i·de′al·iz′er** *n.*

i·de·al·ly (ī·dē′əl·ē) *adv.* **1** Conforming to an ideal. **2** In idea or imagination; mentally; intellectually.

i·de·ate (ī·dē′āt) *v.* **·at·ed, ·at·ing** *v.t.* To form an idea of; frame in the mind; conceive. —*v.i.* To form ideas; think. —*n. Philos.* The object corresponding to an idea: so distinguished by those who regard the object not simply as perceived, but as the product of perception: also **i·de·a·tum** (ī′dē·ā′təm).

i·de·a·tion (ī′dē·ā′shən) *n.* 1 The mental power to form ideas. 2 The mental process of forming and using ideas. — **i′de·a′tion·al** *adj.*

i·dée fixe (ē·dā′ fēks′) *French pl.* **idées fixes** (ē·dā′ fēks′) A fixed idea; obsession.

i·dem (ī′dem) *n.* & *adj. Latin* The same: often as referring to what was previously mentioned.

i·den·tic (ī·den′tik) *adj.* 1 Identical. 2 In diplomatic correspondence, identical in form: said of notes sent by two governments dealing with a third.

i·den·ti·cal (ī·den′ti·kəl) *adj.* 1 Absolutely the same; the very same. 2 Uniform with something else in quality, condition, execution, appearance, etc. [<Med. L *identicus* < *idem* the same] — **i·den′ti·cal·ly** *adv.* — **i·den′ti·cal·ness** *n.*

Synonyms: alike, equivalent, interchangeable, same, selfsame. Strictly, no two persons or things can be *identical* or the *same*. In looser usage, two volumes may be said to be *identical* or the *same* in contents; a carbon copy is *identical* in substance with the original, but it is not the *same* document. Two synonyms, as "begin" and "commence," may be in most cases *equivalent* and *interchangeable*, but one is not the *same* as the other, and at some point they will be found to draw apart, either in meaning or use. A check may be *equivalent* to the money specified, but it is not the *same* as cash. When a person or thing is surely recognized as the very one referred to, and no other, we say, "This is the *identical* man, the *identical* document," or "the *same* man, document." See SYNONYMOUS. *Antonyms*: contrary, different, dissimilar, distinct, unlike.

identical twin *Genetics* One of a pair of human offspring which develop from a division of a single fertilized egg cell. They are invariably of the same sex and exhibit similarities due to participation in the same genetic factors: distinguished from *fraternal twin.*

i·den·ti·fi·ca·tion (ī·den′tə·fə·kā′shən) *n.* 1 The act or process of showing to be the same. 2 The state of being shown or proved to be identical. 3 Anything by which identity can be established. 4 *Psychoanal.* A process by which an individual, usually subconsciously, behaves or imagines himself behaving as if he were a person with whom he has formed an emotional tie. 5 The act or state of feeling sympathy for a fictitious or dramatic character, sometimes extending to projection of the image of the self into the character. See EMPATHY.

identification tag 1 *Mil.* Either of two metal disks worn by a soldier, and bearing his name, serial number, and other personal data: popularly called *dog tag.* 2 Any tag affixed, as to a suitcase or trunk, for purpose of identification.

i·den·ti·fy (ī·den′tə·fī) *v.t.* **·fied, ·fy·ing** 1 To determine or establish as a particular person or thing; ascertain the nature or supposed identity of. 2 To consider or treat as the same; make the same or identical: He *identifies* money with happiness. 3 To serve as a means of recognition or identification of: The teeth *identified* the skull. 4 To join or associate in interest, action, etc.: usually with *with*: He *identified* his name with a well-known charity. 5 *Biol.* To determine the proper genus, order, etc., of. 6 *Psychoanal.* To make identification of (oneself) with someone else. [<LL *identificare*] — **i·den′ti·fi′a·ble** *adj.* — **i·den′ti·fi′er** *n.*

i·den·ti·ty (ī·den′tə·tē) *n. pl.* **·ties** 1 The state of being identical or absolutely the same; selfsameness. 2 Sameness of character or quality. Identity may be of two sorts: *absolute*, which involves exact equality with itself, or selfsameness, as the equation $a = a$; and *relative*, a less rigid sense, which implies a close material resemblance or similarity, as that of the green of two leaves. 3 The distinctive character belonging to an individual; personality; individuality. 4 The state of being what is asserted or described. [<LL *identitas, -tatis* < *idem* the same]

ideo– *combining form* Idea; of or pertaining to ideas: *ideograph.* [<Gk. *idea* a form, idea]

i·de·o·graph (ī′dē ə·graf′, -gräf′, id′ē-) *n.* 1 A picture symbol or sign of an object, or the graphic representation of a thought, as distinguished from a representation of the sound of a word in the given language. 2 A symbol, as +, =, ¶, $, etc. Also **i′de·o·gram′** (-gram′). — **i′de·o·graph′ic** or **·i·cal** *adj.* — **i′de·o·graph′i·cal·ly** *adv.*

i·de·og·ra·phy (ī′dē·og′rə·fē, id′ē-) *n.* The graphic representation of ideas by symbolic characters: use of ideographs. [<IDEO- + -GRAPHY]

i·de·ol·o·gist (ī′dē·ol′ə·jist, id′ē-) *n.* 1 One who formulates or is expert in an ideology. 2 A visionary.

i·de·ol·o·gize (ī′dē·ol′ə·jīz, id′ē-) *v.t.* To imbue, as a person, group, or nation, with a certain ideology; to indoctrinate.

i·de·o·logue (ī′dē·ə·lôg, -log, id′ē-) *n.* One who is committed to an ideology. [<F]

i·de·ol·o·gy (ī′dē·ol′ə·jē, id′ē-) *n.* 1 The ideas or kind of thinking characteristic of an individual or group; specifically, the ideas and objectives that influence a whole group or national culture, shaping especially their political and social procedure: German *ideology.* 2 The science that treats of the evolution of human ideas. [<IDEO- + -LOGY] — **i·de·o·log·ic** (ī′dē·ə·loj′ik, id′ē-) or **·i·cal** *adj.*

i·de·o·mo·tor (ī′dē·ə·mō′tər, id′ē-) *adj. Psychol.* Of or pertaining to involuntary muscular or other movements induced by a dominant idea. Compare SENSORIMOTOR. — **i′de·o·mo′·tion** (-mō′shən) *n.*

i·de·o·phone (ī′dē·ə·fōn′, id′ē-) *n.* A sound or combination of sounds representing a thought or an idea; an uttered word or phrase.

ides (īdz) *n. pl.* In the ancient Roman calendar, the 15th of March, May, July, and October, and the 13th of the other months. [<L *idus*]

id est (id est) *Latin* That is. Abbr. *i.e.*

Id·fu (id′fōō) See EDFU.

idio– *combining form* One's own, individual, peculiar: *idiosyncratic.* [<Gk. *idios* own, private, peculiar]

id·i·o·blast (id′ē·ə·blast′) *n. Biol.* One of the hypothetical structural units that are thought to make up animal and vegetable cells.

id·i·o·chro·mat·ic (id′ē·ō·krō·mat′ik) *adj. Mineral.* Pertaining to or designating a crystal whose color and optical properties are due to the material of the pure crystal itself and not to any foreign substance.

id·i·oc·ra·sy (id′ē·ok′rə·sē) *n. pl.* **·sies** Idiosyncrasy. [<Gk. *idiokrasia* < *idios* one's own + *krasis* mixture]

id·i·o·cy (id′ē·ə·sē) *n. pl.* **·cies** 1 The condition of being an idiot; mental deficiency amounting almost to total absence of understanding, caused by non-development or abnormality of the brain tissue. 2 *Psychiatry* The lowest grade of mental capacity and intelligence, often accompanied by physical abnormalities. 3 An idiotic utterance or act. [<IDIOT]

Synonyms: fatuity, folly, foolishness, imbecility, incapacity, senselessness, stupidity. *Idiocy* is a state of mental deficiency amounting almost or quite to total absence of understanding. *Imbecility* is a condition of mental weakness, which incapacitates for the serious duties of life. *Incapacity*, or lack of legal qualification for certain acts, necessarily results from *imbecility*, but may also result from other causes, as from insanity or from age, sex, etc.; as, the *incapacity* of a minor to make a contract. *Idiocy* or *imbecility* is deficiency of mind, while insanity is disorder or abnormal action of the brain. *Folly* and *foolishness* denote a want of mental and often of moral balance. *Fatuity* is sometimes used as equivalent to *idiocy*, but more frequently signifies conceited and excessive *folly. Stupidity* is dulness and slowness of mental action which may range all the way from lack of normal readiness to absolute *imbecility.* Compare INSANITY.

id·i·o·e·lec·tric (id′ē·ō·i·lek′trik) *adj.* Electric by virtue of inherent properties: formerly said of bodies readily electrified by friction: distinguished from *anelectric.* Also **id′i·o·e·lec′·tri·cal.**

id·i·o·glos·si·a (id′ē·ō·glos′ē·ə, -glôs′-) *n. Psychiatry* Defective speech, characterized by a succession of meaningless sounds. [<IDIO- + Gk. *glōssa* tongue]

id·i·o·graph (id′ē·ə·graf′, -gräf′) *n.* One's private mark or signature; a trademark. — **id′i·o·graph′ic** or **·i·cal** *adj.*

id·i·om (id′ē·əm) *n.* 1 An expression peculiar to a language, not readily analyzable from its grammatical construction or from the meaning of its component parts, as *to put up with* (tolerate, endure). 2 A speech pattern, dialect, or language characteristic of a certain group, class, trade, region, etc.: legal *idiom.* 3 The peculiar genius or spirit of a language. 4 Specific character, peculiarity, or style, as in art or literature. See synonyms under LANGUAGE. [<L *idioma* <Gk. *idiōma* peculiarity, property < *idioein* appropriate < *idios* one's own]

id·i·o·mat·ic (id′ē·ə·mat′ik) *adj.* 1 Full of idiom; vernacular. 2 Peculiar to or characteristic of a certain language or dialect. Also **id′i·o·mat′i·cal.** [<Gk. *idiōmatikos* characteristic <*idiōma.* See IDIOM.] — **id′i·o·mat′·i·cal·ly** *adv.*

id·i·o·mor·phic (id′ē·ō·môr′fik) *adj.* 1 *Mineral.* Possessing its characteristic crystallographic faces: said of one of the constituent minerals of a rock. 2 Having its own peculiar form. — **id′i·o·mor′phi·cal·ly** *adv.*

id·i·op·a·thy (id′ē·op′ə·thē) *n. pl.* **·thies** *Pathol.* 1 A disease of unknown or indeterminate origin. 2 A disease generated by an allergy or by some forms of eczema and gastro-intestinal disorder. [<IDIO- + -PATHY] — **id·i·o·path·ic** (id′ē·ō·path′ik) or **·i·cal** *adj.*

id·i·o·plasm (id′ē·ō·plaz′əm) *n. Biol.* The portion of a cell derived from the parent organism, in distinction from that which is the product of the growth of the individual; germ plasm. — **id′i·o·plas·mat′ic** (-plaz·mat′ik) *adj.*

id·i·o·stat·ic (id′ē·ō·stat′ik) *adj. Electr.* Effecting measurement by repulsion of charges instead of by attraction: said of electrometry: distinguished from *heterostatic.*

id·i·o·syn·cra·sy (id′ē·ō·sing′krə·sē) *n. pl.* **·sies** 1 A constitutional peculiarity, as of susceptibility or aversion. 2 Any quality, characteristic, tendency, or mode of expression peculiar to an individual; quirk. [<Gk. *idiosynkrasia* <*idios* peculiar + *synkrasis* a mixing together < *syn* together + *krasis* mixing] — **id′i·o·syn·crat′ic** (-sin·krat′ik) *adj.* — **id′i·o·syn·crat′i·cal·ly** *adv.*

id·i·ot (id′ē·ət) *n.* 1 A human being conspicuously deficient in mental powers and in the capacity for self-protection. 2 *Psychiatry* A person exhibiting the lowest grade of mental development. 3 A foolish fellow; a simpleton. [<OF *idiot* <L *idiota* <Gk. *idiōtēs* private person < *idios* one's own]

id·i·ot·ic (id′ē·ot′ik) *adj.* Like or pertaining to an idiot; senseless; stupid. Also **id′i·ot′i·cal.** — **id′i·ot′i·cal·ly** *adv.*

id·i·ot·ism (id′ē·ət·iz′əm) *n.* 1 Excessive stupidity; a senseless course of action. 2 Idiocy. 3 *Obs.* An idiom. [<F *idiotisme*]

i·dle (īd′l) *adj.* 1 Not occupied; doing nothing. 2 Averse to labor; lazy. 3 Affording leisure. 4 Without effect; useless; unavailing: *idle* talk, *idle* rage. — *v.* **i·dled, i·dling** *v.i.* 1 To spend time in idleness. 2 To saunter or move idly; loaf. 3 *Mech.* To operate without transmitting power, usually at reduced speed: said of motors and machines. — *v.t.* 4 To pass in idleness; waste, as a day. 5 To cause to be idle, as a person or an industry. ◆ Homophones: *idol, idyl.* [OE *īdel* empty, useless]

Synonyms (adj.): inactive, indolent, inert, lazy, slothful, sluggish, trifling, unemployed, unoccupied, vacant. *Idle* etymologically denotes not the absence of action, but vain, useless action—the absence of useful, effective action; the *idle* schoolboy may be very actively whittling his desk or tormenting his neighbors. Doing nothing whatever is the secondary meaning of *idle.* A *lazy* person may chance to be employed in useful work, but he acts without energy or impetus. We speak figuratively of a *lazy* stream. *Slothful* belongs in the moral realm, denoting a self-indulgent aversion to exertion. *Indolent* is a milder term for the same quality. See INSIGNIFICANT. *Antonyms*: active, busy, diligent, employed, industrious, occupied, working.

i·dle·ness (īd′l·nis) *n.* The state of being idle in any sense; slothfulness; inactivity. [OE *īdelnes*]

idle pulley *Mech.* A pulley to guide a driving belt, increase its tension, or increase its arc of contact on one of the working pulleys.

i·dler (īd′lər) *n.* **1** One who idles; a lazy person; a loafer. **2** An idle wheel. **3** One of a ship's crew who stands no night watches, having special day duties.

i·dlesse (īd′les) *n.* *Archaic* Idleness. [A pseudo-antique formation]

idle wheel *Mech.* **1** A gear wheel to convey motion from one wheel to another, all three being upon different axes. **2** An idle pulley. Also *idler.*

IDLE WHEEL

I·dle·wild (īd′l·wīld) A locality in Queens borough, New York City: site of New York International Airport.

i·dly (īd′lē) *adv.* **1** In an idle manner. **2** Uselessly; vainly; without effect.

I·do (ē′dō) *n.* An artificial language, a simplification of the principles of Esperanto: developed in 1907. [<Esperanto, offspring]

id·o·crase (id′ō·krās, ī′dō-) *n.* Vesuvianite. [<IDIO- + Gk. *krasis* mixture]

i·dol (īd′l) *n.* **1** An image of a god or saint, or an object to which or through which worship is offered. **2** The image of a heathen god. **3** That on which the affections are passionately set. **4** A source of error; a fallacy. **5** An unsubstantial apparition; a phantom due to reflection, as in a mirror. **6** *Obs.* An impostor; counterfeit. See synonyms under IMAGE. ◆ Homophones: *idle, idyl.* [<OF *idele* <L *idolum* <Gk. *eidōlon* image, phantom < *eidos* form, shape]

i·dol·a·ter (ī·dol′ə·tər) *n.* **1** An adorer of images. **2** One who is inordinately fond of some person or thing. [<OF *idolatre* <LL *idololatres* <Gk. *eidōlolatrēs* < *eidōlon* an idol + *latreuein* worship] —**i·dol′a·tress** *n. fem.*

i·dol·a·trize (ī·dol′ə·trīz) *v.* **·trized, ·triz·ing** *v.t.* To make an idol of; idolize. —*v.i.* To practice idolatry.

i·dol·a·trous (ī·dol′ə·trəs) *adj.* **1** Pertaining to idolatry. **2** Extravagant in admiration. —**i·dol′a·trous·ly** *adv.* —**i·dol′a·trous·ness** *n.*

i·dol·a·try (ī·dol′ə·trē) *n.* *pl.* **·tries** **1** The worship of idols. **2** Idolatrous admiration. [<OF *idolatrie* <LL *idololatria* <Gk. *eidōlolatreia* < *eidolon* an idol + *latreuein* worship]

i·dol·ism (ī′dəl·iz′əm) *n.* **1** A fanciful or false notion. **2** Idol-worship.

i·dol·ize (ī′dəl·īz) *v.* **·ized, ·iz·ing** *v.t.* **1** To have inordinate love for; adore. **2** To worship as an idol. —*v.i.* **3** To worship idols. Also *Brit.* **i′dol·ise.** See synonyms under WORSHIP. —**i·dol·i·za·tion** (ī′dəl·ə·zā′shən, -ī·zā′-) *n.* —**i′dol·iz′er** *n.*

i·dol·o·clast (ī·dol′ə·klast) *n.* A breaker of images. [<IDOL + (ICON)OCLAST]

i·dol·o·clas·tic (ī·dol′ə·klas′tik) *adj.* Of or pertaining to the breaking of images.

I·dom·e·neus (ī·dom′ə·nōōs, -nyōōs) In Greek legend, a king of Crete who fought on the Greek side in the Trojan War.

i·do·ne·ous (ī·dō′nē·əs) *adj.* Proper; suitable; proportionate. [<L *idoneus* fitting]

I·du·mae·a (ī′dyōō·mē′ə, id′yōō-) An ancient country SE of Palestine: also *Edom.* Also **I′du·me′a, I′du·mæ′a.** —**I′du·mae′an** *adj.*

i·dyl (īd′l) *n.* **1** A short poem or prose piece depicting simple scenes of pastoral, domestic, or country life; also, a more extended descriptive or narrative poem. **2** Any event, scene, or circumstance of a kind suitable for such a work. **3** *Music* A composition of simple or pastoral character. Also **i′dyll.** ◆ Homophones: *idle, idol.* [<L *idyllium* <Gk. *eidyllion,* dim. of *eidos* form] —**i′dyl·ist, i′dyl·list** *n.*

i·dyl·lic (ī·dil′ik) *adj.* Of or pertaining to the idyl; having the essential qualities of an idyl or pastoral poem. Also **i·dyl′li·cal.** —**i·dyl′li·cal·ly** *adv.*

-ie *suffix* Little; dear: *birdie*: often used in nicknames or affectionately, as in *Annie.* [Var. of -Y³]

-ier *suffix of nouns* One who is concerned with or works with: *cashier.* Also, after vowels and *w, -yer,* as in *lawyer.* [<F. See -EER]

If (ēf) An islet SW of Marseilles, France: site of the **Château d'If,** formerly a state prison.

if (if) *conj.* **1** On the supposition or condition that: We'll go by plane *if* the weather permits. **2** Allowing that; although: *If* he was there, I didn't see him. **3** Whether: I am not sure *if* he is at home. ◆ *If* is also used in exclamatory clauses to introduce (a) a wish or determination: *If* I had only thought of that!; and (b) surprise or irritation: Well, *if* he hasn't run away again! —*n.* **1** The word *if* itself. **2** A condition; supposition. [OE *gif*]

if·fy (if′ē) *adj.* *Colloq.* Conditional; hypothetical. [<IF]

If·ni (ēf′nē) A Spanish territory comprising an enclave on the west coast of Morocco; 741 square miles; capital, Sidi Ifni.

Ig·dra·sil (ig′drə·sil) See YGDRASIL.

ig·loo (ig′lōō) *n.* *pl.* **·loos** **1** An Eskimo house, dome-shaped and usually built of blocks of packed snow. **2** A conical mound, for protecting munitions, made of earth and concrete. Also **ig′lu.** [<Eskimo *igdlu*]

ig·na·ti·a (ig·nā′shē·ə, -shə) *n.* The dried seed of a small tree *(Strychnos ignatia)* native to the Philippines: used like nux vomica. [<NL *(faba) ignatia* (bean) of Ignatius]

Ig·na·ti·us (ig·nā′shē·əs, -shəs; *Du.* ig·nä′sē·ōōs; *Ger.* ig·nä′tsē·ōōs) A masculine personal name. Also *Fr.* **I·gnace** (ē·nyȧs′), *Ger.* **Ig·naz** (ig·näts′), *Ital.* **I·gna·zi·o** (ē·nyä′tsē·ō) or **I·gna·ci·o** (ē·nyä′chē·ō, *Pg.* ig·nä′sē·ōō, *Sp.* ig·nä′·thē·ō), *Polish* **Ig·na·cy** (ēg·nä′tsē). [<L, fiery]

—**Ignatius, Saint,** 67?–107?, bishop of Antioch: called "Theophorus."

—**Ignatius, Saint,** 798?–878, patriarch of Constantinople.

—**Ignatius of Loyola** See LOYOLA.

ig·ne·ous (ig′nē·əs) *adj.* **1** Pertaining to or resembling fire. **2** *Geol.* Formed by the action of a fusing heat within the earth: said especially of rocks consolidated from a molten state: distinguished from *sedimentary.* [<L *igneus* < *ignis* fire]

ig·nes·cent (ig·nes′ənt) *adj.* **1** Emitting sparks of fire when struck with steel or iron. **2** Coruscating. [<L *ignescere* burn < *ignis* fire]

igni- *combining form* Fire: *ignify.* [<L *ignis* fire]

ig·ni·fy (ig′nə·fī) *v.t.* **·fied, ·fy·ing** *Rare* **1** To set on fire; burn. **2** To fuse or melt. [Cf. LL *ignifacere* set on fire]

ig·nis fat·u·us (ig′nis fach′ōō·əs) *pl.* **ig·nes fat·u·i** (ig′nēz fach′ōō·ī) **1** A phosphorescent light seen in the air over marshy places; jack-o'-lantern; will-o'-the-wisp. **2** Figuratively, a delusion; deceptive attraction. [<Med. L, foolish fire]

ig·nite (ig·nīt′) *v.* **ig·nit·ed, ig·nit·ing** *v.t.* **1** To set on fire; cause to burn. **2** To cause to glow with intense heat; make incandescent. **3** *Chem.* To bring to the point of combustion. —*v.i.* **4** To take fire; start burning. See synonyms under BURN. [<L *ignitus,* pp. of *ignire* set on fire] —**ig·nit′i·ble, ig·nit′a·ble** *adj.* —**ig·nit′i·bil′i·ty, ig·nit′a·bil′i·ty** *n.*

ig·nit·er (ig·nī′tər) *n.* **1** One who or that which ignites. **2** A device for exploding a shell or torpedo, for setting off a blasting charge, etc. **3** An ignitor.

ig·ni·tion (ig·nish′ən) *n.* **1** The act of, or system employed in, igniting. **2** The act of exploding the charge of gases in the cylinder of an internal-combustion engine. **3** The electrical apparatus that fires these gases. [<Med. L *ignitio, -onis* burning < *ignire* burn]

ig·ni·tor (ig·nī′tər) *n.* *Electronics* A silicon carbide electrode used to initiate the action of an Ignitron. Also spelled *igniter.*

Ig·ni·tron (ig·nī′trən, ig′nə·tron) *n.* *Electronics* A gas-discharge rectifier tube with a mercury electrode and an ignitor: used to control the starting of a unidirectional current flow: a trade name.

ig·no·ble (ig·nō′bəl) *adj.* **1** Unworthy or degraded in character. **2** *Rare* Low-born. **3** Of inferior kind; specifically, in falconry, said of the short-winged hawks, which chase their prey, as distinguished from the *noble* falcons which attack by a single swoop. See synonyms under BASE, VULGAR. [<F <L *ignobilis* < *in-* not + *gnobilis* noble, known] —**ig·no·bil·i·ty** (ig′nə·bil′ə·tē), **ig·no′ble·ness** *n.* —**ig·no′bly** *adv.*

ig·no·min·i·ous (ig′nə·min′ē·əs) *adj.* **1** Entailing or implying dishonor or disgrace. **2** Deserving ignominy; despicable. **3** Abasing; humiliating. See synonyms under INFAMOUS. [<L *ignominiosus* < *ignominia* IGNOMINY] —**ig′no·min′i·ous·ly** *adv.* —**ig′no·min′i·ous·ness** *n.*

ig·no·min·y (ig′nə·min′ē) *n.* *pl.* **·min·ies** **1** Disgrace or dishonor. **2** That which causes disgrace; disgraceful action or conduct. [<L *ignominia* < *in-* not + *nomen* name, reputation]

ig·no·ra·mus (ig′nə·rā′məs, -ram′əs) *n.* An ignorant pretender to knowledge. [<L, we do not know]

ig·no·rance (ig′nər·əns) *n.* **1** The state of being ignorant; the condition of not being informed; lack of knowledge. **2** An act, offense, or sin due to ignorance. [<F <L *ignorantia*]

ig·no·rant (ig′nər·ənt) *adj.* **1** Destitute of education or knowledge. **2** Unacquainted; unaware. **3** Manifesting or characterized by ignorance. [<OF <L *ignorans, -antis,* ppr. of *ignorare* not to know. See IGNORE.] —**ig′no·rant·ly** *adv.*

Synonyms (adj.): ill-informed, illiterate, uneducated, unenlightened, uninformed, uninstructed, unlearned, unlettered, unskilled, untaught, untutored. *Ignorant* signifies destitute of education or knowledge, or lacking knowledge or information; it is thus a relative term. The most learned man is still *ignorant* of many things; persons are spoken of as *ignorant* who have not the knowledge that has become generally diffused in the world; the *ignorant* savage may be well-instructed in matters of the field and the chase, and is thus more properly *untutored* than *ignorant. Illiterate* is without letters and the knowledge that comes through reading. *Unlettered* is similar in meaning to *illiterate,* but less absolute; the *unlettered* man may have acquired the art of reading and writing and some elementary knowledge; the *uneducated* man has never taken any systematic course of mental training. *Ignorance* is relative; *illiteracy* is absolute; we have statistics of *illiteracy*; no statistics of *ignorance* are possible. See BRUTISH. *Antonyms*: educated, instructed, learned, sage, skilled, trained, well-informed, wise.

ig·nore (ig·nôr′, -nōr′) *v.t.* **·nored, ·nor·ing** **1** To refuse to notice or recognize; disregard intentionally. **2** *Law* To reject (a bill of indictment) for insufficient evidence. [<F *ignorer* <L *ignorare* < *in-* not + *gno-,* stem of *gnoscere* know] —**ig·nor′er** *n.*

I·go·rot (ē′gə·rōt′, ig′ə-) *n.* *pl.* **·rot** or **·rots** **1** One belonging to a group of Malay tribes of northern Luzon, Philippines, some of whom are head-hunters. **2** The Indonesian language of these tribes. Also **I·gor·ro·te** (ē′gôr·rō′tā). [<Sp. *Igorrote,* prob. <Tagalog]

I·graine (i·grān′) In Arthurian legend, the mother of King Arthur: also *Ygerne.*

i·gua·na (i·gwä′nə) *n.* **1** An edible, tropical American lizard (family *Iguanidae*); especially *Iguana iguana,* which sometimes attains a length of 6 feet: it is partly arboreal, partly herbivorous, and, unless attacked, is harmless. **2** Any one of several lizards related to the iguana. [<Sp. <Cariban]

COMMON IGUANA
Grass-green in color with black and white markings; the dewlap and spiny crest are characteristic of the true iguana.

i·guan·o·don (i·gwan′ə·don) *n.* A large, powerfully built, herbivorous, bipedal dinosaur (order *Ornithischia*), associated with the Lower Cretaceous period in Belgium. [<NL < IGUANA + Gk. *odōn* tooth]

I·guas·sú (ē′gwä·sōō′) A river in SE Brazil, flowing about 820 miles west to the Paraná; 14 miles above its mouth are the **Iguassú Falls,** 210 feet high and almost a mile wide. Also **I′gua·çu′.** *Spanish* **I′gua·zú′.**

ih·ram (ē·räm′) *n.* **1** A two-piece, white cotton dress worn by the Moslem pilgrims to Mecca, of which one piece is girded round the waist and the other is worn over the left shoulder. **2** A pilgrim who has assumed this garb. **3** The regulations that he must observe. [<Arabic *iḥram* interdiction < *ḥarama* forbid]

IHS, ihs A monogram of the name Jesus, derived from the Greek IH(ΣΟΥ)Σ, Jesus.

Ijs·sel (ī′səl) A branch of the lower Rhine in the Netherlands, flowing 72 miles north to Lake Ijssel: also *Yssel. Dutch* **IJs′sel.**

Ijs·sel (ī′səl), **Lake** A fresh-water lake enclosed by a dam from the Zuyder Zee, central Netherlands. *Dutch* **IJs′sel·meer′**(-mär′).

I·ka·ri·a (ē′kä·rē′ə) See ICARIA.

Ikh·na·ton (ik·nä′tən) Egyptian king 1375–1358 B.C.; monotheist religious reformer: also known as *Amenhotep IV.* Also spelled *Akhnaton.*

i·kon (ī′kon) See ICON (def. 2).

i·lang–i·lang (ē′läng·ē′lang) See YLANG-YLANG.

I·la·ri·o (ē·lä′rē·ō) Italian form of HILARY.

Il·de·fon·so (ēl′dā·fōn′sō) Spanish form of ALPHONSO.

–ile *suffix* Of, like, pertaining to; capable of; suited to: *docile, mobile.* Also, sometimes, **–il,** as in *civil, fossil.* [<F *-il, -ile* <L *-ilis,* suffix of adjectives; or directly <L]

il·e·ac (il′ē·ak) *adj.* Of or pertaining to the ileum. Also **il′e·al.** [A refashioning of ILIAC]

Île de France (ēl də fräns′) A region and former province of north central France at the center of the Paris Basin.

Île du Dia·ble (ēl dü dyá′bl′) The French name for DEVIL'S ISLAND.

il·e·i·tis (il′ē·ī′tis) *n. Pathol.* Inflammation of the ileum.

ileo– *combining form* Of or pertaining to the ileum: *ileostomy.* Also, before vowels, **ile–.** [< L *ileum* the ileum]

il·e·os·to·my (il′ē·os′tə·mē) *n. Surg.* The operation of forming an artificial opening into the ileum. [<ILEO- + -STOMY]

I·ler·da (i·lûr′də) The ancient name for LÉRIDA.

il·e·um (il′ē·əm) *n. Anat.* The lower three fifths of the small intestine from the jejunum to the cecum, excluding the duodenum. [<L <Gk. *eilein* roll, twist]

il·e·us (il′ē·əs) *n. Pathol.* An obstruction of the intestines, variously caused and resulting in severe colic. [<L <Gk. *eileos* colic <*eilein* twist]

i·lex (ī′leks) *n.* **1** A tree or shrub (genus *Ilex*) of the holly family. **2** The holm oak. **3** The holly. [<L, holm oak]

Il·ford (il′fərd) A municipal borough in SW Essex, England.

I·li (ē′lē) A river flowing 590 miles west from Sinkiang province, China, to Lake Balkash in the S.R.

il·i·ac (il′ē·ak) *adj.* Pertaining to or near the ilium. [<LL *iliacus* suffering from colic <*ileus* colic]

Il·i·ac (il′ē·ak) *adj.* Pertaining to ancient Ilium or Troy; also, pertaining to the Trojan War. Also **Il′i·an.**

Il·i·ad (il′ē·əd) **1** An ancient Greek epic poem in 24 books on the siege of Ilium (Troy), traditionally ascribed to Homer. **2** Any similar long narrative poem. **3** A tale of many sorrows or miseries. [<L *Ilias, -adis* <Gk. *Ilias, -ados* <*Ilios, Ilion* Ilium (Troy)]

il·i·um (il′ē·əm) *n. pl.* **·i·a** (-ē·ə) *Anat.* The large upper portion of the innominate bone. [<L, flank]

Il·i·um (il′ē·əm) See TROY (def. 1). Also **Il′i·on** (-ən).

ilk[1] (ilk) *adj. & n. Obs.* Same. **—of that ilk 1** Of that same: a phrase denoting that a person's surname and the name of his estate are the same: Kent *of that ilk*—that is, Kent of Kent. **2** Of that race, class, or kind. [OE *ilka* the same]

ilk[2] (ilk) *adj. Scot. & Dial.* **1** Each; every. **2** Ordinary; common. Also **il′ka** (-kə). [Var. of EACH]

ill (il) *adj.* **1** Disordered in physical condition; diseased; unwell; sick. **2** Evil in effect or tendency; baneful; harmful; unjust; unkind. **3** Of inferior quality; wretched. **4** Lacking skill; ineffective. **5** Evil; malevolent; wrong: *ill* wind, *ill* repute. **6** *Scot.* Difficult; also, grieved; afflicted with sorrow. See synonyms under BAD[1], SICKLY.—*n.* Anything that prevents or impairs what is good or desirable, as sickness, misfortune, or bad luck. See synonyms under MISFORTUNE. —*adv.* **1** Not well. **2** With difficulty; hardly. **3** Badly; unfavorably. **—ill at ease** Uneasy; uncomfortable. [<ON *illr*]

Ill may appear as a combining form in hyphemes, as in:

ill–accoutered	**ill–disposed**	**ill–matched**
ill–accustomed	**ill–doing**	**ill–mated**
ill–advised	**ill–equipped**	**ill–minded**
ill–affected	**ill–fated**	**ill–omened**
ill–afford	**ill–health**	**ill–placed**
ill–assorted	**ill–housed**	**ill–pleased**
ill–breeding	**ill–informed**	**ill–seeming**
ill–concealed	**ill–judged**	**ill–timed**
ill–conceived	**ill–judging**	**ill–tongued**
ill–considered	**ill–kept**	**ill–trained**
ill–contrived	**ill–luck**	**ill–wisher**
ill–defined	**ill–mannered**	**ill–wishing**

I'll (īl) **1** I will. **2** I shall.

Il·lam·pu (ē·yäm′pōō) A peak in western Bolivia; 21,490 feet: also *Sorata.*

il·la·tion (i·lā′shən) *n.* **1** The act of inferring. **2** That which is inferred; deduction. [<L *illatio, -onis* <*illatus,* pp. of *inferre* bring in, infer]

il·la·tive (il′ə·tiv) *adj.* Pertaining to, denoting, or derived by inference, especially legitimate inference. —*n.* A word denoting an inference, as *therefore.* **—il′la·tive·ly** *adv.*

il·laud·a·ble (i·lô′də·bəl) *adj.* Blameworthy.

ill–be·ing (il′bē′ing) *n.* The condition of being ill or evil: opposed to *well-being.*

ill–bod·ing (il′bō′ding) *adj.* Ill-omened; inauspicious.

ill–bred (il′bred′) *adj.* Badly taught, reared, or trained; rude.

il·le·gal (i·lē′gəl) *adj.* Contrary to the law; not legal. See synonyms under CRIMINAL. **—il·le′·gal·ly** *adv.*

il·le·gal·i·ty (il′ē·gal′ə·tē) *n. pl.* **·ties 1** The state of being illegal. **2** Something unlawful.

il·le·gal·ize (i·lē′gəl·īz) *v.t.* **·ized, ·iz·ing** To make illegal or unlawful.

il·leg·i·ble (i·lej′ə·bəl) *adj.* Not legible; undecipherable. **—il·leg′i·bil′i·ty, il·leg′i·ble·ness** *n.* **—il·leg′i·bly** *adv.*

il·le·git·i·ma·cy (il′i·jit′ə·mə·sē) *n. pl.* **·cies 1** The character or condition of being born out of lawful wedlock; bastardy. **2** Unsoundness, spuriousness, or irregularity, as of an argument; illogicality.

il·le·git·i·mate (il′i·jit′ə·mit) *adj.* **1** Not legitimate; contrary to law. **2** Born out of wedlock. **3** Illogical; unsound. **4** Contrary to good usage; irregular. [<L *illegitimus* < *in-* not + *legitimus.* See LEGITIMATE.] **—il′le·git′i·ma′tion** *n.* **—il′le·git′i·mate·ly** *adv.*

ill fame Bad repute.

ill–fa·vored (il′fā′vərd) *adj.* **1** Repulsive; ugly. **2** Objectionable. Also *Brit.* **ill′–fa′voured.**

ill–got·ten (il′got′n) *adj.* Obtained dishonestly.

ill–hu·mor (il′hyōō′mər) *n.* A morose, disagreeable, or choleric state of mind; sullenness. **—ill′–hu′mored** *adj.*

il·lib·er·al (i·lib′ər·əl) *adj.* **1** Not liberal; not generous in giving; parsimonious. **2** Narrow-minded. **3** Lacking breadth of culture; vulgar. **—il·lib′er·al·ism** (-iz′əm) *n.* **—il·lib′er·al′·i·ty** (-al′ə·tē) *n.* **—il·lib′er·al·ly** *adv.* **—il·lib′er·al·ness** *n.*

il·lic·it (i·lis′it) *adj.* **1** Not permitted; unlawful. **2** Having to do with unlawful things or actions. [<F *illicite* <L *illicitus* <*in-* not + *licitus.* See LICIT.] **—il·lic′it·ly** *adv.* **—il·lic′it·ness** *n.*

Il·li·ma·ni (ē′yē·mä′nē) A peak in western Bolivia; 21,185 feet.

il·lim·it·a·ble (i·lim′i·tə·bəl) *adj.* That can not be limited; boundless. See synonyms under INFINITE.**—il·lim′it·a·bil′i·ty, il·lim′it·a·ble·ness, il·lim′i·ta′tion** (-ə·tā′shən) *n.* **—il·lim′it·a·bly** *adv.*

il·lin·i·um (i·lin′ē·əm) *n.* A former name for PROMETHEUM. [<NL, from *Illinois*]

Il·li·nois (il′ə·noi′, -noiz′) *n. pl.* **·nois** A North American Indian belonging to any one of the Algonquian tribes of the Illinois Confederacy. [<F <N. Am. Ind.]

Il·li·nois (il′ə·noi′, -noiz′) A north central State of the United States; 56,400 square miles; capital, Springfield; entered the Union Dec. 3, 1818; nickname, *Prairie State*: abbr. IL **—Il′li·nois′an (-noi′ən, -noi′zən)** *adj. & n.*

Illinois Confederacy A confederacy of Algonquian tribes of North American Indians whose territory included Illinois and parts of Wisconsin and Iowa.

Illinois River A river in Illinois, flowing 273 miles west and SW to the Mississippi.

il·liq·uid (i·lik′wid) *adj. Law* Not clearly manifest or proved: said of a debt, right, or claim which has no legal standing. [<IL- + LIQUID]

il·lit·er·a·cy (i·lit′ər·ə·sē) *n. pl.* **·cies 1** The state of being illiterate or untaught; lack of culture; ignorance of letters; especially, as in census statistics, inability to read or to read and write. **2** A literary blunder or series of such blunders.

il·lit·er·ate (i·lit′ər·it) *adj.* **1** Unable to read or write. **2** Ignorant of letters; not literate; manifesting want of culture; uneducated. See synonyms under IGNORANT. —*n.* An illiterate person; especially, one who cannot read or write. [<L *illiteratus* <*in-* not + *literatus.* See LITERATE.] **—il·lit′er·ate·ly** *adv.* **—il·lit′·er·ate·ness** *n.*

ill–look·ing (il′look′ing) *adj.* Looking ill; homely; uncomely.

ill nature Peevishness; surliness; sullenness.

ill–na·tured (il′nā′chərd) *adj.* Surly; cross. See synonyms under MALICIOUS, MOROSE. **—ill′–na′tured·ly** *adv.* **—ill′–na′tured·ness** *n.*

ill·ness (il′nis) *n.* **1** The state of being out of health. **2** An ailment; sickness. **3** *Obs.* Badness; evil.

Synonyms: ailment, complaint, disease, disorder, distemper, indisposition, infirmity, sickness. See DISEASE. *Antonyms*: health, soundness, strength, vigor.

il·lo·cal (i·lō′kəl) *adj.* Having no location in space; without place. [<LL *illocalis* <*in-* not + *localis.* See LOCAL.] **—il·lo·cal·i·ty** (il′ō·kal′ə·tē) *n.*

il·log·ic (i·loj′ik) *n.* That which is not logical.

il·log·i·cal (i·loj′i·kəl) *adj.* Not logical; contrary to or neglectful of the rules of logic; not reasonable. **—il·log′i·cal′i·ty, il·log′i·cal·ness** *n.* **—il·log′i·cal·ly** *adv.*

ill–set (il′set′) *adj.* Incorrectly or improperly set.

ill–sort·ed (il′sôr′tid) *adj.* Not well sorted; unharmonious; unsuitably matched.

ill–starred (il′stärd′) *adj.* Unfortunate; as if under an evil star.

ill temper Irritability; moroseness.

ill–tem·pered (il′tem′pərd) *adj.* **1** Characterized by bad temper. **2** *Obs.* In an unhealthy condition.

ill–treat (il′trēt′) *v.t.* To treat badly; maltreat. See synonyms under ABUSE. **—ill′–treat′ment** *n.*

ill turn An act of unkindness or hostility.

il·lude (i·lōōd′) *v.t. Obs.* To trick; cheat. [<L *illudere* make sport of <*in-* toward, against + *ludere* play]

il·lume (i·lōōm′) *v.t.* **·lumed, ·lum·ing** *Poetic* To illumine; illuminate. [<ILLUMINE, prob. influenced in form by F *rallumer* light]

il·lu·min·ance (i·lōō′mə·nəns) *n. Physics* The luminous flux per unit area of a uniformly illuminated surface.

il·lu·mi·nant (i·lōō′mə·nənt) *adj.* Giving light; illuminating. —*n.* Any material used for illuminating. [<L *illuminans, -antis,* ppr. of *illuminare* give light]

il·lu·mi·nate (i·lōō′mə·nāt) *v.* **·nat·ed, ·nat·ing** *v.t.* **1** To give light to; light up. **2** To explain; make clear. **3** To enlighten, as the mind. **4** To make illustrious or resplendent. **5** To decorate with lights. **6** To decorate (a manuscript, letter, etc.) with ornamental borders, figures, etc., of gold or other colors. —*v.i.* **7** To light up. —*adj.* **1** Lighted up. **2** *Obs.* Enlightened. —*n.* One of the illuminati. [<L *illuminatus,* pp. of *illuminare* < *in-* thoroughly + *luminare* light <*lumen* light]

il·lu·mi·na·ti (i·lōō′mə·nä′tī, -nä′tē) *n. pl. sing.* **·na·to** (-nä′tō, -nä′tō) **1** Those who have or profess to have remarkable discernment or spiritual enlightenment. **2** In early church usage, baptized persons, to whom in the ceremony a lighted taper was given as a symbol of spiritual enlightenment. [<L, pl. of *illuminatus,* pp of *illuminare* light up]

Il·lu·mi·na·ti (i·lōō′mə·nä′tī, -nä′tē) *n. pl.* **1** Any of various European religious sects which claimed to have received a special religious enlightenment. **2** A select, secret, deistic and republican society founded by Adam Weishaupt at Ingolstadt, Bavaria, in 1776, aiming at emancipation from despotism: also called *Perfectibilists.*

add,āce,câre,pälm; end,ēven; it,īce; odd,ōpen,ôrder; tŏŏk,pōōl; up,bûrn; ə = a in *above,* e in *sicken,* i in *clarity,* o in *melon,* u in *focus;* yōō = u in *fuse;* oi,oil; ou,pout; ch,check; g,go; ng,ring; th,thin; th,this; zh,vision. Foreign sounds à,œ,ü,kh,ń; and ◆: see page xx. <from; + plus; ? possibly.

il·lu·mi·nat·ing gas (i·lo͞o′mə·nā′ting) Gas consisting of hydrogen mixed with carbon monoxide, methane, ethylene, and other hydrocarbons (as well as impurities such as carbon dioxide, nitrogen, etc.): used for lighting purposes.

il·lu·mi·na·tion (i·lo͞o′mə·nā′shən) *n.* **1** The act of illuminating. **2** The fact or state of being illuminated. **3** A lighting up, especially for festal purposes. **4** Illuminance. **5** Mental enlightenment; imparted light; spiritual enlightenment. **6** *Often cap.* The specific doctrines held by the Illuminati. **7** Embellishment of manuscript, with colors and gold, or a particular figure or design in such ornamentation. See synonyms under LIGHT. [<L *illuminatio, -onis*]

il·lu·mi·na·tive (i·lo͞o′mə·nā′tiv) *adj.* **1** Having power or tending to illuminate; illustrative. **2** Relating to adornment or decoration of books or manuscripts.

il·lu·mi·na·tor (i·lo͞o′mə·nā′tər) *n.* **1** One who or that which gives light. **2** A lamp, lens, etc., for throwing light on particular objects or places. **3** One who executes illuminations on manuscripts. [<L *illuminator*]

il·lu·mine (i·lo͞o′min) *v.t.* & *v.i.* **·mined, ·min·ing** To illuminate or be illuminated. [<F *illuminer* <L *illuminare* illuminate. Related to LIMN.] **— il·lu′mi·na·ble** *adj.*

Il·lu·mi·nism (i·lo͞o′mə·niz′əm) *n.* The principles of the Illuminati.

il·lu·mi·nist (i·lo͞o′mə·nist) *n.* **1** One aspiring to or claiming high spiritual enlightenment. **2** One who professionally illuminates manuscripts, etc.; an illuminator.

Il·lu·mi·nist (i·lo͞o′mə·nist) *n.* One of the Illuminati.

ill–use (il′yo͞oz′) *v.t.* **·used, ·us·ing** To treat roughly, cruelly, or unjustly; misuse; abuse. **—** *n.* (-yo͞os′) Bad treatment; misuse. **— ill′–us′age** (-yo͞o′sij, -yo͞o′zij) *n.*

il·lu·sion (i·lo͞o′zhən) *n.* **1** An unreal image seemingly presented to the senses; any misleading appearance; a false show. **2** *Psychol.* A sensory impression which misrepresents the true character of the object perceived; false perception. See HALLUCINATION. **3** The act of deceiving or misleading by a false appearance. **4** The state of being deceived; delusion; false impression. **5** A thin material resembling tulle, usually of silk: used for veils and garments. **6** An artistic effect giving the appearance of reality to a painting. See synonyms under DELUSION, DREAM. [<OF <L *illusio, -onis* mocking, deceit < *illudere* make sport of. See ILLUDE.] **— il·lu′sion·al** *adj.*

il·lu·sion·ism (i·lo͞o′zhən·iz′əm) *n.* Any doctrine that treats the material world as an illusion of the senses.

il·lu·sion·ist (i·lo͞o′zhən·ist) *n.* **1** One given to illusions; a visionary; a dreamer. **2** One who creates illusions; a sleight–of–hand performer. **3** A believer in illusionism.

il·lu·sive (i·lo͞o′siv) *adj.* Misleading; deceptive; unreal. Also **il·lu′so·ry** (-sər·ē). See synonyms under DECEPTIVE, IMAGINARY. **— il·lu′sive·ly** *adv.* **— il·lu′sive·ness** *n.*

il·lus·trate (il′əs·trāt, i·lus′trāt) *v.t.* **·trat·ed, ·trat·ing 1** To explain or make clear by means of figures, examples, etc.; exemplify. **2** To furnish with drawings, pictures, etc., for decoration or explanation, as a book or article. **3** *Obs.* To make luminous or bright. **4** *Obs.* To make illustrious. See synonyms under ADORN. [<L *illustratus,* pp. of *illustrare* light up < *in-* thoroughly + *lustrare* illuminate] **— il′lus·tra′tor** *n.*

il·lus·tra·tive (i·lus′trə·tiv, il′əs·trā′tiv) *adj.* Serving to illustrate or exemplify. **— il·lus′tra·tive·ly** *adv.*

il·lus·tra·tion (il′əs·trā′shən) *n.* **1** That which illustrates, as an example, comparison, anecdote, etc., by which a subject or statement is elucidated or explained. **2** A print, drawing, or picture of any kind inserted in written or printed text to elucidate or adorn it. **3** The act or art of illustrating. See synonyms under ALLEGORY, SAMPLE, SIMILE. [<L *illustratio, -onis*]

il·lus·tri·ous (i·lus′trē·əs) *adj.* **1** Greatly distinguished; renowned. **2** Conferring luster. **3** *Obs.* Luminous; bright. [<L *illustris* < *in-* in + *lustrum* light] **— il·lus′tri·ous·ly** *adv.* **— il·lus′tri·ous·ness** *n.*

Synonyms: celebrated, distinguished, eminent, famed, famous, glorious, honorable, honored, noble, noted, renowned. See GRAND. *Antonyms*: base, besmirched, degraded, despised, disgraced, dishonored, disreputable, ignominious, infamous, inglorious, notorious, stained, sullied, unhonored, unknown.

ill will Enmity; malevolence.

il·ly (il′lē) *adv.* In an ill or evil manner; not well; ill. ◆ While *illy* is regularly formed from the adjective *ill,* discriminating writers prefer to use *ill* as the adverb as well.

Il·lyr·i·a (i·lir′ē·ə) An ancient country north and east of the Adriatic.

Il·lyr·i·an (i·lir′ē·ən) *n.* **1** One of the inhabitants of ancient Illyria. **2** The Indo–European language of the Illyrians, of which few traces remain: regarded by some as the ancestor of modern Albanian. **—** *adj.* Of or pertaining to ancient Illyria, its inhabitants, or their language.

Il·lyr·i·cum (i·lir′i·kəm) One of the earliest of the ancient Roman colonies, established in Illyria.

Il·men (il′mən), **Lake** A lake south of Novgorod, Russian S.F.S.R.; 850 square miles.

il·men·ite (il′mən·īt) *n.* An iron–black, opaque titanium–iron oxide, $FeTiO_3$, crystallizing in the hexagonal system. [from Lake *Ilmen*]

I·lo·ca·no (ē′lō·kä′nō) *n.* **1** A member of one of the most highly developed peoples of the Philippines, inhabiting western and NW Luzon. **2** The Indonesian language of these peoples. Also **I′lo·ka′no.** [<Philippine Sp. *Ilocano,* lit., river man <Tagalog *ilog* river]

I·lo·i·lo (ē′lō·ē′lō) A port and chief city on Panay island, Philippines.

Il Pen·se·ro·so (il pen′sə·rō′sō) The pensive man: title of a poem by Milton. [<Ital.]

I·lus (ī′ləs) In Greek mythology, the father of Laomedon and grandfather of Priam; founder of Troy (Ilium). [<Gk. *Ilos*]

im–[1] See also words beginning with **em–**.

im–[2] Assimilated var. of IN–[1] and IN–[2].

I'm (īm) I am.

im·age (im′ij) *n.* **1** A visible representation of something; a statue, picture, idol, etc. **2** *Optics* The picture or counterpart of an object produced by reflection or refraction, or the passage of rays through a small aperture. If such an image can be actually thrown on a surface as in a camera, it is a **real image;** but if it is visible only as in a mirror, it is a **virtual image. 3** A natural resemblance; also, that which resembles something; counterpart. **4** A representation in the mind of something not perceived at the moment through the senses; a product of the reproductive imagination or memory, of things seen, heard, touched, etc., including the accompanying emotion. **5** A mental picture or idea: a false *image* of oneself. **6** The way in which a person or thing is popularly perceived or regarded, especially through the agency of the mass media, as television, magazines, etc.; public impression: a politician striving to improve his *image*; a distorted *image* of the U.S. **7** A metaphor or a simile that reproduces or suggests in words the form, color, aspect, or semblance of an object. **6** A symbol of anything; embodiment; type. **7** *Telecom.* The optical replica of a scene produced by a television camera. **8** *Obs.* An apparition. **—** *v.t.* **·aged, ·ag·ing 1** To form a mental picture of; imagine. **2** To make a visible representation of; portray; delineate. **3** To mirror; reflect. **4** To describe vividly in speech or writing, as with images, figures of speech, etc. **5** To symbolize. [<OF <L *imago* <the base of *imitari* imitate]

Synonyms (noun): conception, copy, effigy, emblem, figure, icon, idea, idol, likeness, picture, representation, semblance, similitude, shadow, statue. See FANCY, FIGURE, IDEA, MODEL, PICTURE, SIMILE.

image point The point whose depth below ground zero is equal to the height of an exploding atomic or hydrogen bomb: it is considered as a source of radiating reflected shock.

im·age·ry (im′ij·rē) *n. pl.* **·ries 1** The act of forming images; images collectively. **2** Figurative description in speech or writing. See synonyms under SIMILE.

im·ag·i·na·ble (i·maj′ə·nə·bəl) *adj.* Conceivable. [<LL *imaginabilis*] **— im·ag′i·na·bly** *adv.*

im·ag·i·nal (i·maj′ə·nəl) *adj. Entomol.* Of or pertaining to the imago, or complete adult stage of an insect.

im·ag·i·nar·y (i·maj′ə·ner′ē) *adj.* Existing only in imagination; unreal. **—** *n. Math.* An algebraic quantity or value that involves the square root of a negative quantity. **— im·ag′i·nar′i·ly** *adv.* **— im·ag′i·nar′i·ness** *n.*

Synonyms (adj.): airy, chimerical, dreamy, fancied, fanciful, hypothetical, ideal, illusive, illusory, quixotic, shadowy, utopian, visionary. See IDEAL. *Antonyms*: actual, material, palpable, physical, real, realized, substantial, tangible, visible.

im·ag·i·na·tion (i·maj′ə·nā′shən) *n.* **1** The picturing power or act of the mind. **2** *Psychol.* The constructive or creative faculty, expressed in terms of images which either reproduce past experiences or recombine them in ideal or creative forms. **3** That which is imagined; a mental image; a fantasy. **4** An irrational notion or belief. **5** *Archaic* Planning, plotting, or scheming, as involving mental construction. [<L *imaginatio, -onis* < *imaginatus,* pp. of *imaginari* IMAGINE]

Synonyms: fancy, fantasy. *Fancy* and *imagination* both belong to the productive or, more properly, the constructive faculty. Both recombine and modify mental images; the one great distinction between them is that *fancy* is superficial, while *imagination* is deep, essential, spiritual. *Fantasy* in ordinary usage simply denotes capricious or erratic *fancy,* as appears in the adjective *fantastic.* Compare FANCY, IDEA, THOUGHT[1].

im·ag·i·na·tion·al (i·maj′ə·nā′shən·əl) *adj.* Pertaining to, resulting from, or affected by the imagination.

im·ag·i·na·tive (i·maj′ə·nə·tiv, -nā′tiv) *adj.* **1** Creative or constructive; having capacity for imagining. **2** Characterized by or proceeding from imagination. See synonyms under FANCIFUL, ROMANTIC. [<L *imaginatus,* pp. of *imaginari* IMAGINE] **— im·ag′i·na·tive·ly** *adv.* **— im·ag′i·na·tive·ness** *n.*

im·ag·ine (i·maj′in) *v.* **·ined, ·in·ing** *v.t.* **1** To form a mental image of; conceive or create in the mind. **2** To suppose or conjecture; think. **—** *v.i.* **3** To use the imagination. **4** To make conjectures; suppose. See synonyms under GUESS, SUPPOSE. [<L *imaginari* imagine < *imago* image]

im·a·gism (im′ə·jiz′əm) *n.* A movement in modern poetry, originating around 1910 and characterized by the use of precise, concrete images and freedom from convention in versification and form. [<F *Des Imagistes,* the title of the first anthology of imagist poetry] **— im′a·gist** (-jist) *n.* **— im′a·gis′tic** *adj.*

i·ma·go (i·mā′gō) *n. pl.* **i·ma·goes** or **i·mag·i·nes** (i·maj′ə·nēz) **1** *Entomol.* An adult, sexually matured insect. **2** *Psychoanal.* The infantile, subconscious idea of the parent or other loved one persisting in the adult. [<L]

i·mam (i·mäm′) *n.* A Moslem priest, who recites prayers and leads devotions. Also **i·maum** (i·mäm′, i·môm′). [<Arabic *imām* leader < *amma* lead]

I·mam (i·mäm′) *n.* **1** A title of Mohammed and his four immediate successors: so called because they conducted the devotions of the faithful. **2** A title of a Moslem religious leader or chief. **3** The title of the leaders of the Shiahs, or heterodox Persian sect of Moslems; Ali and his ten successors: ascribed also to the Mahdi. Compare MAHDI. Also **I·maum** (i·mäm′, i·môm′).

i·mam·ate (i·mäm′āt) *n.* The office or jurisdiction of an imam.

i·ma·ret (i·mä′ret) *n.* In Turkey, an inn or hotel. [<Turkish *'imāret* <Arabic *'imārah* building]

im·bal·ance (im·bal′əns) *n.* **1** A lack of balance. **2** Inability to maintain an erect position. **3** Defective coordination of the eye muscles, endocrine glands, etc.

im·balm (im·bäm′) See EMBALM.

im·be·cile (im′bə·sil) *adj.* **1** Having the mental faculties feeble or defective; feeble–minded. **2** Characterized by stupidity. **—** *n. Psychiatry* A person of feeble mind; one intermediate between an idiot and a moron. See IDIOT. [<F *imbécile* <L *imbecillus* weak]

im·be·cil·i·ty (im′bə·sil′ə·tē) *n. pl.* **·ties 1** The condition or quality of being imbecile or impotent; feebleness, especially of the mind. **2** *Psychiatry* The next to the lowest grade of mental capacity and intelligence. See IDIOCY. **3** Any expression of character or opinion that indicates mental feebleness. **4** Incompetency;

inability. 5 Absurdity; folly; silliness. [<MF *imbécillité* <L *imbecillitas* feebleness]

im·bibe (im·bīb′) *v.* **·bibed, ·bib·ing** *v.t.* 1 To drink in; drink. 2 To take in as if drinking; absorb. 3 To receive into the mind or character: to *imbibe* good principles. 4 *Obs.* To saturate; imbue. —*v.i.* 5 To drink. See synonyms under ABSORB. [<F *imbiber* <L *imbibere* < *in-* in + *bibere* drink] —**im·bib′er** *n.*

im·bi·bi·tion (im′bi·bish′ən) *n.* 1 The act or process of imbibing, drinking in, or absorbing. 2 The absorption of moisture by any porous body.

im·bri·cate (im′brə·kāt) *v.* **·cat·ed, ·cat·ing** *v.t.* To lay or arrange regularly so as to overlap, as tiles on a roof. —*v.i.* To overlap. —*adj.* (-brə·kit) 1 Lying regularly over one another like shingles or slates, so as to break joints. 2 *Biol.* Overlapping with the extremities or margins, as the scales of fishes, the feathers of birds, or flower petals in the bud. 3 Decorated with overlapping scales, or so as to represent a surface of overlapping scales or tiles. Also **im′bri·cat′ed, im′bri·ca′tive.** [<L *imbricatus,* pp. of *imbricare* cover with gutter tiles < *imbrex* gutter tile < *imber* rain] —**im′bri·ca′tive·ly** *adv.*

im·bri·ca·tion (im′brə·kā′shən) *n.* 1 The condition of being imbricate: especially applied to shingles or tiles. 2 An imbricated organ, part, or structure.

im·bro·glio (im·brōl′yō) *n. pl.* **·glios** 1 A troublesome complication of affairs; a misunderstanding attended by ill feeling, perplexity, or strife; an entanglement. 2 An intricate plot, as of a tale or drama. [<Ital.]

Im·bros (im′brəs) The largest Turkish island in the Aegean, west of the mouth of the Dardanelles: Turkish *Imroz.*

im·brue (im·brōō′) *v.t.* **·brued, ·bru·ing** To stain or wet; moisten, especially with blood. [<OF *embreuver* <L *imbibere* drink]

im·brute (im·brōōt′) *v.t. & v.i.* **·brut·ed, ·brut·ing** To make or become brutal or brutish; brutalize.

im·bue (im·byōō′) *v.t.* **·bued, ·bu·ing** 1 To wet thoroughly; saturate. 2 To impregnate with color; dye; imbrue. 3 To impregnate or fill, as the mind, with emotions, principles, etc. [<OF *imbuer* <L *imbuere* wet, soak]

im·id·az·ole (im′id·az′ōl, -ə·zōl′) *n. Chem.* A white, crystalline, monacid base, $C_3H_4N_2$, isomeric with pyrazole: also called *glyoxaline.* [<IMID(O)- + AZOLE]

im·ide (im′īd, -id) *n. Chem.* A compound containing the bivalent radical NH united to a bivalent acid radical. Also **im′id** (-id). [< AMIDE]

imido– *combining form Chem.* 1 Used to indicate the presence of an imide in a compound. 2 Loosely, imino–. Also, before vowels, **imid–.** [<IMIDE]

i·mine (i·mēn′, im′in) *n. Chem.* An organic compound in which a non-acid radical is united with the NH radical. [<AMINE]

imino– *combining form Chem.* Used to indicate the presence of an imine in a compound. Also, before vowels, **imin–.** [<IMINE]

im·i·tate (im′ə·tāt) *v.t.* **·tat·ed, ·tat·ing** 1 To do or try to do after the manner of; try to be the same as. 2 To mimic; counterfeit, as a tone of voice. 3 To make a copy or reproduction of; duplicate. 4 To use as a pattern or model. 5 To assume the appearance of; look like: lead painted to *imitate* gold. See IMITATION. [<L *imitatus,* pp. of *imitari* imitate] —**im·i·ta·ble** (im′ə·tə·bəl) *adj.* —**im′·i·ta·bil′i·ty** *n.* —**im′i·ta′tor** *n.*

Synonyms: ape, copy, counterfeit, duplicate, follow, impersonate, mimic, mock, pattern, personate, portray, repeat, represent, resemble, simulate. See FOLLOW. *Antonyms*: alter, change, differentiate, distort, misrepresent, modify, pervert, remodel, transform, vary.

im·i·ta·tion (im′ə·tā′shən) *n.* 1 The act of imitating. 2 Something done or made in resemblance of something else; a likeness; also, a counterfeit: *imitation* of money. 3 *Music* The repetition of a phrase or subject in another voice or a different key. 4 *Biol.* Mimicry of environment or of another animal, plant, etc., for concealment or protection. See synonyms under CARICATURE, DUPLICATE, MODEL. —*adj.* Counterfeit; imitating something genuine or superior: *imitation* diamonds. [<L *imitatio, -onis*]

im·i·ta·tive (im′ə·tā′tiv) *adj.* 1 Inclined to imitate; given to or characterized by imitation. 2 Formed after a copy or model; resembling an original. 3 Fictitious; counterfeit. 4 *Ling.* Designating a word that approximates a natural sound, as *buzz, clink, swish.* Abbr. *imit.* —**im′i·ta′tive·ly** *adv.* —**im′i·ta′·tive·ness** *n.*

im·mac·u·late (i·mak′yə·lit) *adj.* 1 Without spot or blemish; pure; without taint of evil or sin. 2 Faultless; flawless. 3 Of one color; not spotted. See synonyms under GOOD, INNOCENT, PERFECT, PURE. [<L *immaculatus* < *in-* not + *maculatus* spotted] —**im·mac′u·late·ly** *adv.* —**im·mac′u·late·ness** *n.*

Immaculate Conception In the Roman Catholic Church, the doctrine that the Virgin Mary was conceived in her mother's womb without the stain of original sin: distinguished from *Virgin Birth.*

im·man·a·cle (i·man′ə·kəl) *v.t. Rare* To put manacles on; fetter.

im·mane (i·mān′) *adj. Archaic* Of vast size; gigantic; cruel. [<L *immanis*]

im·ma·nence (im′ə·nəns) *n.* 1 A permanent abiding within; an indwelling. 2 The doctrine that the ultimate principle of the universe is not to be distinguished from the universe itself, that God dwells in all things and permeates the spirit of man. Also **im′ma·nen·cy.**

im·ma·nent (im′ə·nənt) *adj.* 1 Remaining within; indwelling; inherent: opposed to *transeunt, transcendent.* 2 Pertaining to the philosophical or the theological doctrine of immanence. See synonyms under INHERENT. [<L *immanens, -entis,* ppr. of *immanere* remain in < *in-* in + *manere* stay] —**im′ma·nent·ly** *adv.*

Im·man·u·el (i·man′yōō·əl, *Ger.* i·mä′nōō·el) A masculine personal name. See EMMANUEL. [<Hebrew, God with us]

—**Immanuel** A name of the Messiah. *Isa.* vii 14; *Matt.* i 23.

im·ma·te·ri·al (im′ə·tir′ē·əl) *adj.* 1 Not material; incorporeal: opposed to corporeal. 2 Unimportant. See synonyms under INSIGNIFICANT. [<Med. L *immaterialis*] —**im′ma·te′ri·al·ly** *adv.* —**im′ma·te′ri·al·ness** *n.*

im·ma·te·ri·al·ism (im′ə·tir′ē·əl·iz′əm) *n.* The doctrine that the objective world has no existence apart from perception by the consciousness; specifically, the idealism of Berkeley. —**im′ma·te′ri·al·ist** *n.*

im·ma·te·ri·al·i·ty (im′ə·tir′ē·al′ə·tē) *n. pl.* **·ties** 1 The state or quality of being immaterial. 2 That which has no material existence or essence.

im·ma·te·ri·al·ize (im′ə·tir′ē·əl·īz) *v.t.* **·ized, ·iz·ing** To make immaterial or incorporeal.

im·ma·ture (im′ə·chŏŏr′, -tyŏŏr′, -tŏŏr′) *adj.* 1 Not mature or ripe; not full-grown; undeveloped. 2 Not brought to a complete state; imperfect. 3 In physical geography, not in accordance with or thoroughly adapted to surrounding or local conditions, particularly of base level: *immature* topography. 4 *Obs.* Too early; premature. [<L *immaturus*] —**im′·ma·ture′ly** *adv.* —**im′ma·tur′i·ty, im′ma·ture′·ness** *n.*

im·meas·ur·a·ble (i·mezh′ər·ə·bəl) *adj.* Not capable of being measured; indefinitely extensive; boundless. See synonyms under INFINITE. —**im·meas′ur·a·ble·ness, im·meas′ur·a·bil′i·ty** *n.* —**im·meas′ur·a·bly** *adv.*

im·me·di·a·cy (i·mē′dē·ə·sē) *n.* 1 The state or quality of being immediate; freedom from the intervention of any intermediate person or thing. 2 In the feudal system, the condition of being next in rank to the suzerain. 3 *Philos.* **a** Independent or non-relative existence or being. **b** Consciousness or direct awareness, apart from memory or reasoning. **c** Intuitive knowledge as distinguished from that arrived at by proof or reasoning.

im·me·di·ate (i·mē′dē·it) *adj.* 1 Without delay; instant. 2 Separated by no appreciable space; nearly related; close. 3 Acting without the intervention of anything; direct: opposed to *mediate.* 4 Pertaining to a direct perception; intuitive. 5 Directly concerning; having a direct bearing. [<Med. L *immediatus*] —**im·me′di·ate·ness** *n.*

Synonyms: close, contiguous, direct, instant, intimate, next, present, proximate. *Antonyms*: distant, far, future, remote.

im·me·di·ate·ly (i·mē′dē·it·lē) *adv.* 1 In an immediate manner; without lapse of time; instantly; at once. 2 Without the intervention of anything; directly. —*conj.* As soon as.

Synonyms (adv.): directly, forthwith, instanter, instantly, now, presently, straightway. *Immediately* primarily signifies without the intervention of anything as a medium, hence without the intervention of any, even the briefest, interval or lapse of time. *Directly,* which once meant with no intervening time, now means after some little while; *presently* no longer means in this very present, but before very long. Even *immediately* is sliding from its instantaneousness, so that we are fain to substitute *at once, instantly,* etc., when we would make promptness emphatic.

im·med·i·ca·ble (i·med′i·kə·bəl) *adj.* Incurable. [<L *immedicabilis* < *in-* not + *medicabilis* curable]

Im·mel·mann turn (im′əl·män, -mən) *Aeron.* An airplane maneuver consisting of a partial loop followed by a half-roll on the longitudinal axis: used to gain altitude while simultaneously reversing the direction of flight. [after Max *Immelmann,* 1890–1916, German aviator]

im·me·mo·ri·al (im′ə·môr′ē·əl, -mō′rē-) *adj.* Reaching back beyond memory; having its origin in the indefinite past. See synonyms under PRIMEVAL. [<Med. L *immemorialis*] —**im′me·mo′ri·al·ly** *adv.*

im·mense (i·mens′) *adj.* 1 Very great in degree or size; vast; huge. 2 Infinite. —*n.* The limitless void; infinity. [<F <L *immensus* < *in-* not + *mensus,* pp. of *metiri* measure] —**im·mense′ly** *adj.*

Synonyms (adj.): colossal, enormous, gigantic, huge, prodigious, stupendous, vast. See LARGE.

im·men·si·ty (i·men′sə·tē) *n. pl.* **·ties** 1 The state or quality of being immense; vastness. 2 Boundless space. See synonyms under MAGNITUDE. Also **im·mense′ness.** [<MF *immensité* <L *immensitas* < *immensus* IMMENSE]

im·men·sur·a·ble (i·men′shŏŏr·ə·bəl) *adj.* Immeasurable. [<MF <L *immensurabilis* < *in-* not + *mensurabilis* MENSURABLE] —**im·men′sur·a·bil′i·ty** *n.*

im·merge (i·mûrj′) *v.* **·merged, ·merg·ing** *v.t.* To immerse. —*v.i.* To plunge, as into a liquid; sink. [<L *immergere* < *in-* in + *mergere* dip] —**im·mer′gence** *n.*

im·merse (i·mûrs′) *v.t.* **·mersed, ·mers·ing** 1 To plunge or dip entirely in water or other fluid. 2 To involve deeply; engross: He *immersed* himself in study. 3 To baptize by immersion. [<L *immersus,* pp. of *immergere* dip]

Synonyms: bury, dip, douse, duck, immerge, plunge, sink, submerge. *Dip* is a native word, while *immerse* is a Latin borrowing; *dip* is accordingly the more popular and commonplace, *immerse* the more elegant and dignified expression in many cases. To speak of baptism by immersion as *dipping* now seems rude, but was entirely proper and usual in early English. Baptists now universally use the word *immerse.* To *dip* and to *immerse* alike signify to *bury* or *submerge* some object in a liquid; but *dip* implies that the object *dipped* is at once removed from the liquid. *Immerse* suggests more absolute completeness of the action; one may *dip* his sleeve or *dip* a sponge in a liquid, if he but touches the edge; if he *immerses* it, he completely *sinks* it under, and covers it with the liquid. *Submerge* implies that the object cannot readily be removed, if at all; as, a *submerged* wreck. To *plunge* is to *immerse* suddenly and violently, for which *douse* and *duck* are colloquial terms. *Dip* is used, also, unlike the other words, to denote the putting of a hollow vessel into a liquid in order to remove a portion of it; in this sense we say *dip up, dip out.* Compare synonyms for BURY[1].

im·mer·sion (i·mûr′zhən, -shən) *n.* 1 The act of immersing or the state of being immersed; specifically, baptism by submersion in water. 2 The state of being overwhelmed or deeply engaged; absorption: *immersion* in business. 3 *Astron.* The disappearance of a heavenly body, either by passing behind another or by entering into the light of the sun or the shadow of the earth. [<L *immersio, -onis*]

im·mer·sion·ism (i·mûr′zhən·iz′əm, -shən-) *n.* **1** The theological doctrine of immersion. **2** The custom of baptizing by immersion.

im·mesh (i·mesh′) See ENMESH.

im·mew (i-myōō′) *v.t. Obs.* To coop up; imprison. [See MEW¹.]

im·mi·grant (im′ə·grənt) *n.* **1** One who or that which immigrates. **2** A foreigner who enters a country to settle there. Compare EMIGRANT. —*adj.* Immigrating.

im·mi·grate (im′ə·grāt) *v.* **·grat·ed, ·grat·ing** *v.i.* To come into a new country or region for the purpose of settling there. —*v.t.* To bring in as an immigrant or settler. See synonyms under EMIGRATE. [< L *immigratus,* pp. of *immigrare* go into < *in-* in + *migrare* migrate] —**im′mi·gra·to′ry** (-tôr′ē, -tō′rē) *adj.*

im·mi·gra·tion (im′ə·grā′shən) *n.* **1** The act of immigrating; entrance of a settler or settlers from a foreign country. **2** The total number of aliens entering a country for permanent residence during a stated period. **3** Immigrants collectively.

im·mi·nence (im′ə·nəns) *n.* **1** The state or quality of being imminent. **2** Impending evil. Also **im′mi·nen·cy.** [< LL *imminentia*]

im·mi·nent (im′ə·nənt) *adj.* **1** About to happen; impending; said especially of danger or evil. **2** Overhanging as if about to fall. [< L *imminens, -entis* < *imminere* lean over, impend < *in-* on + *-minere* project]—**im′mi·nent·ly** *adv.*

Synonyms : impending, threatening. *Imminent,* from the Latin, with the sense of projecting over, signifies liable to happen at once, as some calamity, dangerous and close at hand. *Impending,* also from the Latin, with the sense of hanging over, is closely akin to *imminent,* but somewhat less emphatic. *Imminent* is more immediate, *impending* more remote, *threatening* more contingent. An *impending* evil is almost sure to happen at some uncertain time, near or remote; an *imminent* peril is one liable to befall very speedily; a *threatening* peril may be near or remote, but always with hope that it may be averted. *Antonyms* : chimerical, contingent, doubtful, improbable, problematical, unexpected, unlikely.

im·min·gle (i·ming′gəl) *v.t.* & *v.i.* **·gled, ·gling** To mix thoroughly; mingle.

im·mis·ci·ble (i·mis′ə·bəl) *adj.* Not capable of mixing, as oil and water. Also **im·mix′a·ble** (-mik′sə-). [? < L *immiscibilis* < *in-* not + *miscere* mix] —**im·mis′ci·bil′i·ty** *n.*

im·mit (i·mit′) *v.t. Obs.* To send in; inject. [< L *immittere* < *in-* in + *mittere* send] —**im·mis·sion** (i·mish′ən) *n.*

im·mit·i·ga·ble (i·mit′ə·gə·bəl) *adj.* That cannot be mitigated. [< L *immitigabilis*] —**im·mit′·i·ga·bly** *adv.*

im·mix (i·miks′) *v.t.* To mingle; mix in. [< L *immixtus,* pp. of *immiscere* < *in-* in + *miscere* mix]

im·mix·ture (i·miks′chər) *n.* An intermingling; association with; commingling.

im·mo·bile (i·mō′bəl, -bēl) *adj.* **1** Unmovable; stable. **2** Not to be touched through the emotions. [< OF < L *immobilis*]

im·mo·bil·i·ty (im′ō·bil′ə·tē) *n.* The condition of being immovable or immobile; fixedness. See synonyms under APATHY.

im·mo·bi·lize (i·mō′bə·līz) *v.t.* **·lized, ·liz·ing 1** To make immovable; fix in place, as a limb by splints or bandages. **2** To make unable to move or mobilize, as a fleet or body of troops. **3** To withdraw (specie) from circulation and hold as security for banknotes. [< F *immobiliser*] —**im·mo′bi·li·za′tion** (-lə·zā′shən, -lī·zā′-) *n.*

im·mod·er·ate (i·mod′ər·it) *adj.* Not moderate; exceeding reasonable bounds. [< L *immoderatus*] —**im·mod′er·ate·ly** *adv.* —**im·mod′er·ate·ness** *n.*

Synonyms : excessive, exorbitant, extravagant, inordinate, intemperate, unreasonable, violent. Compare IRREGULAR, VIOLENT. *Antonyms*: see synonyms for MODERATE.

im·mod·er·a·tion (i·mod′ə·rā′shən) *n.* Want of moderation; excess. Also **im·mod′er·a·cy** (-ə·sē). [< L *immoderatio, -onis*]

im·mod·est (i·mod′ist) *adj.* **1** Wanting in modesty; indelicate or indecent. **2** Impudent; bold. [< L *immodestus*] —**im·mod′est·ly** *adv.* —**im·mod′es·ty** *n.*

Synonyms : bold, brazen, coarse, forward, gross, impure, indecent, indecorous, indelicate, lewd, obscene, shameless, unchaste, wanton. Compare synonyms for IMPUDENT. *Antonyms* : see synonyms for PURE.

im·mo·late (im′ə·lāt) *v.t.* **·lat·ed, ·lat·ing** To sacrifice; especially, to kill as a sacrifice. [< L *immolatus,* pp. of *immolare* sprinkle with sacrificial meal < *in-* on + *mola* meal] **im′mo·la′tor** *n.*

im·mo·la·tion (im′ə·lā′shən) *n.* **1** The act of immolating. **2** The state of being immolated. **3** That which is immolated or sacrificed. [< L *immolatio, -onis*]

im·mor·al (i·môr′əl, i·mor′-) *adj.* **1** Violating the moral law; contrary to rectitude or public morality. **2** Habitually licentious. —**im·mor′al·ly** *adv.*

Synonyms : bad, corrupt, criminal, depraved, dishonest, dissolute, evil, loose, profligate, sinful, unprincipled, vicious, vile, wicked, wrong. See BAD¹, CRIMINAL, SINFUL. *Antonyms* : chaste, devout, dutiful, godly, good, just, moral, pious, pure, religious, righteous, upright, virtuous, worthy.

im·mo·ral·i·ty (im′ə·ral′ə·tē) *n. pl.* **·ties 1** The quality or condition of being immoral; vice; wickedness; licentiousness. **2** An act of licentiousness. **3** An immoral act. See synonyms under SIN.

im·mor·tal (i·môr′təl) *adj.* Having unending existence; deathless; enduring. —*n.* **1** A person considered worthy of immortality. **2** In mythology, a god. —**the Immortals 1** The members of the French Academy, forty in number: also called **the Forty Immortals. 2** The royal guard of ancient Persia; hence, any band or group that has conducted itself with marked gallantry in the face of extraordinary perils (especially of war). [< L *immortalis*] —**im·mor′tal·ly** *adv.*

Synonyms (adj.): deathless, endless, eternal, everlasting, imperishable, incorruptible, indestructible, indissoluble, never-dying, never-fading, never-failing, sempiternal, undying, unfading, unfailing. See ETERNAL. *Antonyms* : dying, ephemeral, fading, failing, fleeting, mortal, perishable, perishing, transient, transitory.

im·mor·tal·i·ty (im′ôr·tal′ə·tē) *n.* **1** Exemption from death or oblivion; eternal life. **2** Eternal fame. [< OF *immortalité* < L *immortalitas*]

im·mor·tal·ize (i·môr′təl·īz) *v.t.* **·ized, ·iz·ing** To make immortal; give perpetual fame or life to.

im·mor·telle (im′ôr·tel′) *n.* **1** A flower (genus *Xeranthemum*) of the composite family that retains its form and color for a long time after being gathered. **2** The everlasting. [< F]

im·mo·tile (i·mō′til) *adj.* Not motile; stationary.

im·mov·a·ble (i·mōō′və·bəl) *adj.* **1** That cannot be moved or stirred from its place; fixed: an *immovable* foundation. **2** Steadfast; unchangeable: an *immovable* purpose. **3** Not having the feelings easily roused; impassive. **4** *Law* Not liable to be removed; permanent in place: *immovable* property. See synonyms under FIRM, INFLEXIBLE, OBSTINATE. —*n.* **1** That which cannot be moved. **2** *Law* Any piece of land, together with trees, buildings, etc., strictly appertaining to it, either naturally or otherwise, so as not to be movable: opposed to *movable.* —**im·mov′a·bil′i·ty, im·mov′a·ble·ness** *n.* —**im·mov′a·bly** *adv.*

im·mune (i·myōōn′) *adj.* **1** Exempt, as from taxation. **2** *Med.* Protected from disease by inoculation. —*n.* A person not susceptible to some particular disease. [< F < L *immunis*]

im·mu·ni·ty (i·myōō′nə·tē) *n. pl.* **·ties 1** Freedom or exemption, as from a penalty, burden, duty, or evil, such as the exemption of ecclesiastical persons and places from duties and burdens thought unbecoming their sacred character: followed by *from.* **2** *Med.* Exemption from contagion or infection or from liability to suffer from epidemic or endemic disease. It may be *active* through the formation of specific antibodies in the organism, or *passive* through the effect of a serum injected from another organism. See synonyms under RIGHT. [< OF *immunité* < L *immunitas* < *immunis* exempt < *in-* not + *munis* serviceable < *munus* service, duty]

im·mu·nize (im′yə·nīz) *v.t.* **·nized, ·niz·ing** To make immune; protect, as from infection. —**im·mu·ni·za·tion** (im′yə·nə·zā′shən, -nī·zā′-) *n.*

immuno- *combining form* Immune; immunity: *immunology.* [< IMMUNE]

im·mu·no·gen·ic (i·myōō′nō·jen′ik) *adj. Med.* Producing or conferring immunity to a specified disease.

im·mu·no·ge·net·ics (i·myōō′nō·jə·net′iks) *n.* The study of immunity to disease as conditioned by and associated with the transmission of specific genetic factors.

im·mu·nol·o·gy (im′yə·nol′ə·jē) *n.* The science which treats of the phenomena and techniques of immunity from disease. [< IMMUNO- + -LOGY] —**im·mu·no·log·i·cal** (i·myōō′nə·loj′i·kəl) *adj.*

im·mu·no·re·ac·tion (i·myōō′nō·rē·ak′shən) *n. Med.* The reaction which takes place between an antigen and its antibody, as in the blood.

im·mu·no·sup·pres·sive (i·myōō′nō·sə·pres′iv) *adj.* Preventing the action of an antibody in order to permit an organism to accept foreign material, such as an organ transplant.

im·mure (i·myōōr′) *v.t.* **·mured, ·mur·ing** To shut up within or as within walls; imprison. [< Med. L *immurare* < *in-* in + LL *murare* wall < *murus* wall] —**im·mure′ment** *n.*

im·mu·si·cal (i·myōō′zi·kəl) *adj.* Unmusical.

im·mu·ta·bil·i·ty (i·myōō′tə·bil′ə·tē) *n.* The state or quality of being immutable or unchangeable. Also **im·mu′ta·ble·ness.** [< L *immutabilitas, -tatis*]

im·mu·ta·ble (i·myōō′tə·bəl) *adj.* Not mutable; unchangeable. See synonyms under FIRM, PERMANENT. [< L *immutabilis*] —**im·mu′ta·bly** *adv.*

Im·o·gen (im′ə·jən) In Shakespeare's *Cymbeline,* the heroine, a model of conjugal fidelity.

imp (imp) *n.* **1** An evil spirit; a little devil; a child of the devil. **2** A mischievous or malicious person: especially applied to a child. **3** *Obs.* Progeny; offspring. —*v.t.* **1** To mend or repair by something inserted or added. **2** To furnish with wings. **3** In falconry, to repair or improve powers of flight by grafting feathers to (a falcon, a falcon's wing, tail, etc.); to graft (a feather or feathers). **4** *Obs.* To graft; implant [OE *impa* a graft < *impian* ingraft < LL *impotus* a shoot < Gk. *emphytos* < *emphyein* implant < *en-* in + *phyein* produce]

im·pact (im·pakt′) *v.t.* To press or drive firmly together; pack; wedge. —*n.* (im′pakt) **1** The act of striking; collision. **2** The forcible momentary contact of a moving body with another either moving or at rest: the *impact* of a bullet against a target. **3** A continuing, powerful influence: the *impact* of science on culture. See synonyms under COLLISION. [< L *impactus,* pp. of *impingere.* See IMPINGE]

im·pact·ed (im·pak′tid) *adj.* **1** Packed firmly. **2** *Dent.* Denoting a tooth wedged between the jawbone and another tooth in such a way as to prevent its emergence through the gums.

im·pac·tion (im·pak′shən) *n.* **1** An overloading of an organ, as of the intestine. **2** A wedging of one part into another. **3** *Dent.* An impacted tooth. [< L *impactio, -onis* a striking]

im·pair (im·pâr′) *v.t.* To diminish in quality, strength, or value; injure. [< OF *empeirer* < LL *in-* thoroughly + *pejorare* make worse < L *pejor* worse]

Synonyms : debase, decrease, deteriorate, diminish, enervate, enfeeble, lessen, reduce, weaken. See HURT, WEAKEN, WEAR. *Antonyms* : see synonyms for AMEND, INCREASE.

im·pair·ment (im·pâr′mənt) *n.* **1** The act of impairing. **2** The state of being impaired. **3** Deterioration; injury. [< OF *empeirement*]

im·pa·la (im·pä′lə) *n.* A South African antelope (*Aepyceros melampus*), dark red fading into clear white below, with the spreading horns in the male: also called *pallah.* [< native name]

im·pale (im·pāl′) *v.t.* **·paled, ·pal·ing 1** To fix upon a pale or sharp stake. **2** To torture or put to death by thrusting a sharp stake through the body. **3** To make helpless as if by fixing upon a stake; transfix: to *impale* someone with a glance. **4** *Her.* To place (two coats of arms) side by side on an escutcheon. Also spelled *empale.* [< OF *empaler* < LL *impalare* < *in-* in + *palus* a stake]

im·pale·ment (im·pāl′mənt) *n.* **1** The act of impaling. **2** That which impales, or the space impaled; an enclosure. **3** The displaying of two coats of arms side by side on one escutcheon. Also spelled *empalement.*

im·pal·pa·ble (im·pal′pə·bəl) *adj.* **1** Imperceptible to the touch; specifically, ground so fine that no grit can be felt. **2** Intangible unreal. **3** Immaterial: incorporeal. [< Med. L *impalpabilis*] — **im·pal′pa·bil′i·ty** *n.* — **im·pal′·pa·bly** *adv.*

im·pal·u·dism (im·pal′yə·diz′əm) *n. Pathol.* Chronic malarial infection: often called *marsh poisoning.* [<L *in-* in + *palus, paludis* swamp]

im·pa·na·tion (im′pə·nā′shən) *n.* The doctrine that the body and blood of Christ are united into one substance with the consecrated bread and wine: distinguished from *transubstantiation.* [<Med. L *impanatus,* pp. of *impanare* embody in bread <*in-* in + *panis* bread] — **im·pa·nate** (im·pā′nit, -nāt), **im·pa·nat·ed** (im·pā′nā·tid) *adj.*

im·pan·el (im·pan′əl) *v.t.* **·eled** or **·elled, ·el·ing** or **·el·ling** 1 To enrol upon a panel or list, as for jury duty. 2 To draw from such a list, as a jury. Also spelled *empanel.* — **im·pan′el·ment** *n.*

im·par (im·pär′) *adj.* Odd or unequal; without a corresponding part; not paired. [<L <*in-* not + *par* equal]

im·par·a·dise (im·par′ə·dīs) *v.t.* **·dised, ·dis·ing** To place in or as in paradise; make supremely happy.

im·par·i·pin·nate (im·par′ə·pin′āt) *adj. Bot.* Pinnate with an odd terminal leaflet; odd-pinnate. [<L *impar* unequal + PINNATE]

im·par·i·ty (im·par′ə·tē) *n. pl.* **·ties** Lack of correspondence; inequality; diversity. [<LL *imparitas, -tatis*]

im·park (im·pärk′) *v.t.* 1 To enclose (land) as a park. 2 To place (animals) in or as in a park or enclosure. [<AF *enparker,* OF *emparquer*] — **im·par·ka·tion** (im′pär·kā′shən) *n.*

im·part (im·pärt′) *v.t.* 1 To make known; tell; communicate. 2 To give a portion of; give. — *v.i.* 3 To give a part; share. See synonyms under GIVE, INFORM, PUBLISH. [<OF *empartir* <L *impartire* <*in-* on + *partire* share <*pars, partis* part, share] — **im·part′er** *n.*

im·par·ta·tion (im′pär·tā′shən) *n.* The act of imparting, as knowledge. Also **im·part′ment.**

im·par·tial (im·pär′shəl) *adj.* Not partial; unbiased; just. See synonyms under CANDID, JUST. — **im·par′tial·ly** *adv.*

im·par·ti·al·i·ty (im′pär·shē·al′ə·tē, im·pär′-) *n.* The quality or character of being impartial; fairness. Also **im·par′tial·ness.**

im·part·i·ble[1] (im·pär′tə·bəl) *adj.* Not subject to partition; not dividable. [<LL *impartibilis*] — **im·part′i·bil′i·ty** *n.* — **im·part′i·bly** *adv.*

im·part·i·ble[2] (im·pär′tə·bəl) *adj. Obs.* Capable of being imparted, shared, or made known.

im·pass·a·ble (im·pas′ə·bəl, -päs′-) *adj.* Not passable. See synonyms under IMPENETRABLE. — **im·pass′a·bil′i·ty, im·pass′a·ble·ness** *n.* — **im·pass′a·bly** *adv.*

im·passe (im′pas, im·pas′; *Fr.* aṅ·päs′) *n.* 1 A blind alley, or passage open only at one end; cul-de-sac. 2 Any serious and insurmountable obstacle or problem. [<F]

im·pas·si·bil·i·ty (im·pas′ə·bil′ə·tē) *n.* 1 Essential incapacity for suffering. 2 The state of being unfeeling or apathetic. Also **im·pas′si·ble·ness.** [<OF *impassibilité* <L *impassibilitas* <*impassibilis* impassible]

im·pas·si·ble (im·pas′ə·bəl) *adj.* 1 Incapable of suffering or sympathizing. 2 Not affected by feeling; apathetic. [<OF *impassible* <Med. L *impassibilis* <*in-* not + *passibilis.* See PASSIBLE.] — **im·pas′si·bly** *adv.*

im·pas·sion (im·pash′ən) *v.t.* To affect with passion; inflame. [<Ital. *impassionare*]

im·pas·sion·ate (im·pash′ən·it) *adj.* Without passion: dispassionate.

im·pas·sioned (im·pash′ənd) *adj.* Fervent; stirring. See synonyms under ARDENT.

im·pas·sive (im·pas′iv) *adj.* 1 Insensible to or unaffected by suffering or pain; unimpressionable. 2 Unmoved by or not exhibiting feeling; apathetic. 3 Not susceptible of injury. 4 Lifeless; insensible; also, unconscious. — **im·pas′sive·ly** *adv.* — **im·pas′sive·ness, im·pas·siv·i·ty** (im′pa·siv′ə·tē) *n.*

im·paste (im·pāst′) *v.t.* **·past·ed, ·past·ing** 1 To encrust with or as with paste. 2 To make into a paste or crust. 3 To apply paint thickly to; employ the technique of impasto on. [<Ital. *impastare*] — **im·pas·ta·tion** (im′pās·tā′shən) *n.*

im·pas·to (im·päs′tō) *n.* 1 A technique of painting in which thick pigment is applied to a surface to give relief or force. 2 The pigment so applied. [<Ital.]

im·pa·tience (im·pā′shəns) *n.* 1 Lack of patience; unwillingness to brook delay. 2 Intolerance of opposition or control. [<OF *impacience* <L *impatientia*]

Synonyms: fretfulness, irritation, peevishness, pettishness, petulance, vexation. These words express the slighter forms of anger. *Irritation, petulance,* and *vexation* are temporary and for immediate cause. *Fretfulness, pettishness,* and *peevishness* are chronic states finding in any petty matter an occasion for their exercise. Compare ACRIMONY, ANGER. *Antonyms*: amiability, benignity, forbearance, gentleness, leniency, lenity, long-suffering, mildness, patience, peace, peaceableness, peacefulness, self-control, self-restraint.

im·pa·ti·ens (im·pā′shē·enz) *n.* Any of a large genus (*Impatiens*) of herbs with stems enlarged at the joints, opposite leaves, and irregular flowers, as the *jewelweed, snapweed,* or *touch-me-not.* The ripe elastic seed vessels, when touched, burst open and scatter the seeds. [<L]

im·pa·tient (im·pā′shənt) *adj.* 1 Not possessed of or not exercising patience; intolerant; disturbed by or complaining about pain, delay, strain, etc. 2 Exhibiting or expressing impatience. See synonyms under EAGER, FRETFUL, RESTIVE. [<OF *impacient* <L *impatiens, -entis* <*in-* not + *patiens.* See PATIENT.] — **im·pa′tient·ly** *adv.*

im·pav·id (im·pav′id) *adj.* Without fear; intrepid; bold. [<L *impavidus* <*in-* not + *pavidus* timid] — **im·pa·vid·i·ty** (im′pə·vid′ə·tē) *n.* — **im·pav′id·ly** *adv.*

im·pawn (im·pôn′) *v.t.* To pledge as security; pawn.

im·peach (im·pēch′) *v.t.* 1 To bring discredit upon; challenge: to *impeach* one's honesty. 2 To charge with crime or misdemeanor in office; arraign (a public official) before a competent tribunal on such a charge. See synonyms under ARRAIGN. [<OF *empescher* hinder <LL *impedicare* entangle <*in-* in + *pedica* fetter <*pes, pedis* foot] — **im·peach′er** *n.*

im·peach·a·ble (im·pē′chə·bəl) *adj.* Liable to be impeached; censurable. — **im·peach′a·bil′·i·ty** *n.*

im·peach·ment (im·pēch′mənt) *n.* 1 A discrediting. 2 The act of impeaching; especially the arraignment of a high civil officer. [<OF *empeschement* obstruction]

im·pearl (im·pûrl′) *v.t.* 1 To form into pearl-like drops. 2 To make pearl-like. 3 To adorn with or as with pearls. [<F *emperler*]

im·pec·ca·ble (im·pek′ə·bəl) *adj.* 1 Not liable to commit sin or wrong. 2 Faultless. — *n.* An impeccable person. [<LL *impeccabilis* <*in-* not + *peccare* sin] — **im·pec′ca·bil′i·ty** *n.* — **im·pec′ca·bly** *adv.*

im·pec·cant (im·pek′ənt) *adj.* Free from sin or error; blameless. — **im·pec′cance, im·pec′·can·cy** *n.*

im·pe·cu·ni·ar·y (im′pə·kyōō′nē·er′ē) *adj.* Impecunious.

im·pe·cu·ni·ous (im′pə·kyōō′nē·əs) *adj.* Having no money; habitually poor. [<F *impécunieux*] — **im′pe·cu′ni·os′i·ty** (-kyōō′nē·os′ə·tē) *n.* — **im′pe·cu′ni·ous·ly** *adv.* — **im′pe·cu′ni·ous·ness** *n.*

im·pe·dance (im·pēd′ns) *n.* 1 *Electr.* **a** The resistance met by an alternating current on passing through a conductor. **b** The ratio of the effective electromotive force to the effective current of an alternating-current circuit. 2 *Physics* In a sound-transmitting medium, the ratio of the force per unit area to the volume velocity of a given surface.

impede (im·pēd′) *v.t.* **·ped·ed, ·ped·ing** To retard or hinder in progress or action; obstruct. See synonyms under EMBARRASS, HINDER[1], LIMIT, OBSTRUCT. [<L *impedire,* lit., shackle the feet <*in-* in + *pes, pedis* foot] — **im·ped′er** *n.*

im·pe·di·ent (im·pē′dē·ənt) *adj.* That impedes. — *n.* That which impedes. [<L *impediens, -ientis,* ppr. of *impedire.* See IMPEDE.]

im·ped·i·ment (im·ped′ə·mənt) *n.* 1 That which hinders or impedes; an obstruction. 2 An organic hindrance to easy speech; a stammer. 3 *Law* Anything that prevents the contraction of a valid marriage. — **absolute impediment** *Law* A condition which makes it impossible for a person to contract a valid marriage. — **prohibitive impediment** *Law* A condition under which persons who have contracted marriage are subject to punishment for having done so. — **relative impediment** *Law* A state of facts which bars only people of a certain degree of consanguinity from contracting marriage with each other, as a brother with a sister. See also DIRIMENT IMPEDIMENT OF MARRIAGE. [<L *impedimentum*]

Synonyms: bar, barrier, clog, difficulty, encumbrance, hindrance, obstacle, obstruction. *Difficulty* makes an undertaking not easy. That which rests upon one as a burden is an *encumbrance.* A *hindrance* (kindred with *hind, behind*) is anything that makes one come behind or short of his purpose. An *impediment* (literally, that which checks the foot) may be either what one finds in his way or what he carries with him; *impedimenta* was the Latin name for the baggage of a soldier or of an army. The tendency is to view an *impediment* as something constant or, at least for a time, continuous; as, an *impediment* in one's speech. A *difficulty* or a *hindrance* may be either within one or without; a speaker may find *difficulty* in expressing himself, or *difficulty* in holding the attention of restless children. An *encumbrance* is always what one carries with him; an *obstacle* or an *obstruction* is always without. To an infantryman the steepness of a mountain path is a *difficulty,* loose stones are *impediments,* a fence is an *obstruction,* a cliff or a boulder across the way is an *obstacle,* a bedroll is an *encumbrance. Antonyms*: advantage, aid, assistance, benefit, help, relief, succor.

im·ped·i·men·ta (im·ped′ə·men′tə) *n. pl.* 1 Baggage or other supplies of an army. 2 *Law* Impediments. 3 Any drawbacks or burdens. [<L]

im·ped·i·tive (im·ped′ə·tiv) *adj.* Causing hindrance: obstructive.

im·pel (im·pel′) *v.t.* **·pelled, ·pel·ling** 1 To drive or push (something) forward or onward. 2 To urge or force (someone) to an action, course, etc.; incite; compel. See synonyms under ACTUATE, DRIVE, ENCOURAGE, INFLUENCE, PERSUADE, PUSH, SEND[1], SPUR. [<L *impellere* <*in-* on + *pellere* drive]

im·pel·lent (im·pel′ənt) *adj.* Tending to impel. — *n.* An impelling person, thing, or force. [<L *impellens, -entis,* ppr. of *impellere.* See IMPEL.]

im·pel·ler (im·pel′ər) *n.* 1 One who or that which impels. 2 *Mech.* The rotor of a pump or blower.

im·pend (im·pend′) *v.i.* 1 To be imminent; threaten, as something evil or destructive. 2 To be suspended; hang: with *over.* [<L *impendere* overhang <*in-* on + *pendere* hang] — **im·pen′dence, im·pen′den·cy** *n.*

im·pen·dent (im·pen′dənt) *adj.* Imminent; threatening. [<L *impendens, -entis,* ppr. of *impendere.* See IMPEND.]

im·pend·ing (im·pen′ding) *adj.* Hanging over; threatening; about to happen. See synonyms under IMMINENT.

im·pen·e·tra·bil·i·ty (im·pen′ə·trə·bil′ə·tē) *n.* 1 The quality of being impenetrable. 2 *Physics* The property of matter which prevents two bodies from occupying the same space at the same time. Also **im·pen′e·tra·ble·ness.**

im·pen·e·tra·ble (im·pen′ə·trə·bəl) *adj.* 1 That cannot be penetrated or pierced: said of material things. 2 That cannot be penetrated by the eye or mind; abstruse; dense: an *impenetrable* darkness or mystery. 3 Not to be affected by moral considerations: an *impenetrable* conscience. 4 Possessing the property of impenetrability. [<OF *impenetrable* <L *impenetrabilis*] — **im·pen′e·tra·bly** *adv.*

Synonyms: close, dense, hard, impassable, impermeable, impervious, solid. See HARD. *Antonyms*: fluid, loose, open, penetrable, pervious, soft, yielding.

im·pen·i·tence (im·pen′ə·təns) *n.* Want of penitence or repentance; hardness of heart. Also **im·pen′i·ten·cy.** [<LL *impaenitentia*]

im·pen·i·tent (im·pen′ə·tənt) *adj.* Not penitent; hardened; obdurate. [<LL *impaenitens, -entis* <*in-* not + *paenitens.* See PENITENT.] — **im·pen′i·tent·ly** *adv.* — **im·pen′i·tent·ness** *n.*

im·pen·nate (im·pen′āt) *adj. Ornithol.* Having short wings with scalelike feathers, as a penguin.

im·per·a·tive (im·per′ə·tiv) *adj.* 1 Expressive of or containing positive, as distinguished from advisory or discretionary, command; authoritative; peremptory. 2 *Gram.* Designating that mood of the verb which expresses command, entreaty, or exhortation. 3 Not to be evaded or avoided; obligatory. — *n.* 1 That which is imperative. 2 *Gram.* The mood of the verb which expresses command; also, a verb in this mood. [<L *imperativus* <*imperare* command] — **im·per′a·tive·ly** *adv.* — **im·per′a·tive·ness** *n.*

im·pe·ra·tor (im′pə·rā′tər, -tôr) *n.* 1 The official designation of the Roman emperors; originally a commander in chief. 2 Any emperor or absolute ruler.

im·per·a·to·ri·al (im·per′ə·tôr′ē·əl, -tō′rē·əl) *adj.* Of or pertaining to the title or office of imperator. [<L *imperatorius*] — **im·per′a·to′ri·al·ly** *adv.*

im·pe·ra·trice (im′pə·rā′tris) *n. Obs.* An empress. Also **im′pe·ra′trix** (-triks). [<F *impératrice* <L *imperatrix, -icis*]

im·per·cep·ti·ble (im′pər·sep′tə·bəl) *adj.* That cannot be perceived, as by reason of smallness, extreme tenuity or delicacy, distance or gradual progress; inappreciable by the mind or sense; undiscernible: an *imperceptible* change. [<F <L *imperceptibilis*] — **im′per·cep′ti·ble·ness, im′per·cep′ti·bil′i·ty** *n.* — **im′·per·cep′ti·bly** *adv.*

im·per·cep·tive (im′pər·sep′tiv) *adj.* Not perceptive; deficient in perception. — **im·per·cep·tiv·i·ty** (im′pər·sep·tiv′ə·tē), **im′per·cep′tive·ness** *n.*

im·per·fect (im·pûr′fikt) *adj.* 1 Not perfect; incomplete; defective. 2 *Gram.* Pertaining to a tense of the verb that indicates past action as uncompleted, continuous, or synchronous with some other action. 3 *Law* Without binding force; not enforceable by law. 4 *Music* Diminished: an *imperfect* interval. 5 *Bot.* Lacking certain parts normally present; diclinous. See synonyms under BAD[1]. — *n. Gram.* The imperfect tense, or a verb or verbal form expressing this tense. [<OF *imparfait* <L *imperfectus*; refashioned after L] — **im·per′fect·ly** *adv.* — **im·per′fect·ness** *n.*

imperfect flower *Bot.* A flower which lacks some essential part or member.

im·per·fec·tion (im′pər·fek′shən) *n.* 1 Lack of perfection: also **im·per′fect·ness.** 2 A defect. See synonyms under BLEMISH, FOIBLE. [<OF *imperfection* <LL *imperfectio, -onis* <L *imperfectus* incomplete]

im·per·fec·tive (im′pər·fek′tiv) *Gram. adj.* Of or pertaining to an aspect of the verb which expresses continuing action or repetition; durative. — *n.* The imperfective aspect, or a verb in this aspect. — **im′per·fec′tive·ly** *adv.*

im·per·fo·ra·ble (im·pûr′fər·ə·bəl) *adj.* That cannot be perforated.

im·per·fo·rate (im·pûr′fər·it) *adj.* 1 Without perforations; not perforated. 2 Not separated by a line of perforations, as stamps. Also **im·per′fo·rat′ed** (-rā′tid). — *n.* An unperforated stamp.

im·per·fo·ra·tion (im·pûr′fə·rā′shən) *n.* The state of being imperforate.

im·pe·ri·al (im·pir′ē·əl) *adj.* 1 Of or pertaining to an empire, or to an emperor or an empress. 2 Designating the legal weights and measures of the United Kingdom. 3 Of or pertaining to a state as supreme over colonies or the like. 4 Possessing commanding power or dignity; predominant. 5 Superior in size or quality. — *n.* 1 A pointed tuft of hair on the chin: from the emperor Napoleon III, who wore such a beard. 2 Anything of more than usual size of the class to which it belongs, or of superior excellence. 3 A size of paper: in the United States, 23 in. × 31 in.; in Great Britain, 22 in. × 30 in. 4 A size of slate 24 inches wide and from 12 to 30 inches long. 5 A former Russian gold coin worth 15 rubles. 6 The top of a carriage, as of a diligence. [<OF <L *imperialis* <*imperium* rule] — **im·pe′ri·al·ly** *adv.*

Synonyms (adj.): exalted, grand, kingly, magnificent, majestic, noble, queenly, regal, royal, sovereign, supreme. *Antonyms*: base, beggarly, cowering, cringing, ignoble, inferior, mean, paltry, poor, servile, slavish.

Im·pe·ri·al (im·pir′ē·əl) *n.* An adherent or soldier of the Holy Roman Empire.

Imperial City 1 The capital city of an empire. 2 Specifically, Rome, Italy, in the ancient Roman or Holy Roman empires.

imperial eagle See under EAGLE.

imperial gallon See under GALLON.

im·pe·ri·al·ism (im·pir′ē·əl·iz′əm) *n.* 1 A policy that aims at creating, maintaining, or extending an empire or superstate, comprising many nations and areas, all controlled by a central government. 2 A governmental policy of developing foreign trade and exploiting the raw materials of backward countries through the use of political and military pressures, without necessarily assuming direct political control of the nations affected. 3 A system of imperial government. 4 Imperial character, authority, or spirit.

im·pe·ri·al·ist (im·pir′ē·əl·ist) *n.* 1 One who advocates or upholds imperialism. 2 A partisan or supporter of an emperor. — *adj.* Imperialistic.

im·pe·ri·al·is·tic (im·pir′ē·əl·is′tik) *adj.* 1 Of, pertaining to, or characteristic of imperialism. 2 Favoring imperialism or government by an emperor. — **im·pe′ri·al·is′ti·cal·ly** *adv.*

imperial jade A green-tinted aventurine quartz: used as a gem.

imperial moth A beautiful, large American moth (*Eacles* or *Basilona imperialis*) having yellow wings sprinkled and barred with lavender, with wing spread often of 5 inches.

IMPERIAL MOTH
Showing the character of the markings.

imperial quart One fourth of an imperial gallon.

Imperial Valley A region of SE California, mostly below sea level, reclaimed from the Colorado Desert.

im·per·il (im·per′il) *v.t.* **·iled** or **·illed, ·il·ing** or **·il·ling** To place in peril; endanger.

im·pe·ri·ous (im·pir′ē·əs) *adj.* 1 Assuming and determined to command; domineering; arrogant. 2 Urgent; imperative. 3 *Obs.* Imperial; lordly. [<L *imperiosus*] — **im·pe′ri·ous·ly** *adv.* — **im·pe′ri·ous·ness** *n.*

Synonyms: arbitrary, arrogant, authoritative, commanding, controlling, despotic, dictatorial, dogmatic, domineering, exacting, haughty, imperative, irresistible, lordly, overbearing. An *imperious* demand or requirement may have in it nothing offensive; it is simply one that resolutely insists upon compliance, and will not brook refusal; an *arrogant* demand is offensive by its tone of superiority, an *arbitrary* demand by its unreasonableness; an *imperious* disposition is liable to become *arbitrary* and *arrogant.* A person of an independent spirit is inclined to resent an *imperious* manner in anyone, especially in one whose superiority or authority is not clearly recognized. *Commanding* is always used in a good sense; as, a *commanding* appearance; a *commanding* eminence. See ARBITRARY, DOGMATIC. *Antonyms*: complaisant, compliant, docile, ductile, gentle, humble, lenient, lowly, meek, mild, submissive.

im·per·ish·a·ble (im·per′ish·ə·bəl) *adj.* Not perishable or subject to decay. See synonyms under ETERNAL, IMMORTAL. — **im·per′ish·a·bil′i·ty, im·per′ish·a·ble·ness** *n.* — **im·per′ish·a·bly** *adv.*

im·pe·ri·um (im·pir′ē·əm) *n. pl.* **·ri·a** (-ē·ə) 1 Command not subject to definition or limitation of function; absolute command. 2 *Law* The right to command, which includes authority to use the force of the state to enforce its laws. [<L. See EMPIRE.]

im·per·ma·nence (im·pûr′mə·nəns) *n.* The state or quality of being impermanent; also, something impermanent. Also **im·per′ma·nen·cy.**

im·per·ma·nent (im·pûr′mə·nənt) *adj.* Not permanent.

im·per·me·a·ble (im·pûr′mē·ə·bəl) *adj.* 1 Not permeable. 2 Impervious to moisture. See synonyms under IMPENETRABLE. [<LL *impermeabilis*] — **im·per′me·a·bil′i·ty** *n.* — **im·per′me·a·bly** *adv.*

im·per·son·al (im·pûr′sən·əl) *adj.* 1 Not having personality: an *impersonal* deity. 2 Not relating to a particular person or thing: an *impersonal* statement. 3 *Gram.* Having or containing an indeterminate subject: an *impersonal* verb. In English the subject of an impersonal verb is usually the pronoun *it,* as *it thunders*: often in apposition with a following clause or phrase, as *it is fun to swim.* — *n.* That which lacks personality; especially, an impersonal verb. [<LL *impersonalis*] — **im·per′son·al′i·ty** (-al′ə·tē) *n.* — **im·per′son·al·ly** *adv.*

im·per·son·al·ize (im·pûr′sən·əl·īz′) *v.t.* **·ized, ·iz·ing** To render impersonal.

im·per·son·ate (im·pûr′sən·āt) *v.t.* **·at·ed, ·at·ing** 1 To adopt or mimic the appearance, mannerisms, etc., of. 2 To act or play the part of. 3 To represent in human form; personify: He *impersonates* the quality of virtue. See synonyms under IMITATE. — *adj.* (-it) Embodied in a person; having personality.

im·per·son·a·tion (im·pûr′sən·ā′shən) *n.* 1 The act of impersonating. 2 Personification.

im·per·son·a·tor (im·pûr′sən·ā′tər) *n.* One who impersonates or plays a character part.

im·per·ti·nence (im·pûr′tə·nəns) *n.* 1 The state, quality, or instance of being impertinent. 2 Improper intrusion: rudeness. 3 Irrelevancy; inappropriateness. Also **im·per′·ti·nen·cy.**

im·per·ti·nent (im·pûr′tə·nənt) *adj.* 1 Rude; impudent. 2 Irrelevant; not to the point. 3 Not suitable or fitting. See synonyms under IMPUDENT, MEDDLESOME. [<F <L *impertinens, -entis* <*in-* not + *pertinens.* See PERTINENT.] — **im·per′ti·nent·ly** *adv.*

im·per·turb·a·ble (im′pər·tûr′bə·bəl) *adj.* Incapable of being agitated. See synonyms under CALM. [<LL *imperturbabilis*] — **im′per·turb′a·bil′i·ty, im′per·turb′a·ble·ness** *n.* — **im′·per·turb′a·bly** *adv.*

im·per·tur·ba·tion (im·pûr′tər·bā′shən) *n.* Freedom from agitation; calmness.

im·per·turbed (im′pər·tûrbd′) *adj.* Not perturbed or agitated.

im·per·vi·a·ble (im·pûr′vē·ə·bəl) *adj.* Impervious.

im·per·vi·ous (im·pûr′vē·əs) *adj.* 1 Permitting no passage into or through; impenetrable; impermeable. 2 Not permeable by fluids, light rays, etc. 3 Not capable of being influenced by; deaf to: a mind *impervious* to reason. See synonyms under IMPENETRABLE. [<L *impervius* <*in-* not + *per-* through + *via* way, road] — **im·per′vi·ous·ly** *adv.* — **im·per′vi·ous·ness** *n.*

im·pe·ti·go (im′pə·tī′gō) *n. Pathol.* A contagious skin disease characterized by pustular eruptions. [<L <*impetere* attack. See IMPETUS.] — **im·pe·tig·i·nous** (im′pə·tij′ə·nəs) *adj.*

im·pe·trate (im′pə·trāt) *v.t.* **·trat·ed, ·trat·ing** 1 To obtain by request or entreaty. 2 *Rare* To importune; beseech. [<L *impetratus,* pp. of *impetrare* obtain by request <*in-* to + *patrare* bring to pass] — **im′pe·tra′tion** *n.* — **im′pe·tra′tor** *n.*

im·pe·tra·tive (im′pə·trā′tiv) *adj.* Using prayer or entreaty, or tending to obtain by entreaty. [<L *impetrativus*]

im·pet·u·ous (im·pech′ōō·əs) *adj.* 1 Characterized by impetus, energy, or violent force: *impetuous* haste. 2 Characterized by spontaneous or vehement impulse of action or emotion: *impetuous* affection. [<MF *impétueux* <L *impetuosus*] — **im·pet′u·os′i·ty** (-os′·ə·tē) *n.* — **im·pet′u·ous·ly** *adv.* — **im·pet′u·ous·ness** *n.*

Synonyms: excitable, fiery, hasty, headlong, impulsive, passionate, precipitate, quick, rash, sudden, swift. See EAGER, FIERCE, VIOLENT. *Antonyms*: calm, careful, cautious, circumspect, considerate, deliberate, lazy, leisurely, slow, sluggish, steady.

im·pe·tus (im′pə·təs) *n.* 1 The energy with which anything moves or is driven. 2 Momentum. 3 Any impulse or incentive. See synonyms under IMPULSE. [<L <*impetere* rush upon <*in-* upon + *petere* seek]

Imp·hal (imp′hul) The capital of Manipur, India.

im·phee (im′fē) *n.* An African cereal grass (*Sorghum vulgare*) which yields a sirup: also used for fodder and grain. [<Zulu *imfe*]

im·pi (im′pē) *n. pl.* A body of armed Zulus or other native warriors. [<Zulu]

im·pi·e·ty (im·pī′ə·tē) *n. pl.* **·ties** 1 Ungodliness; irreverence. 2 An impious act. 3 Want of natural dutifulness toward parents. [<OF *impieté* <L *impietas, -tatis*]

imp·ing (im′ping) *n.* The process of grafting;

a graft, as of feathers on a hawk's wing. [OE *impian* graft. See IMP.]

im·pinge (im·pinj′) *v.i.* **·pinged, ·ping·ing** 1 To come into contact; strike; collide, especially sharply: with *on, upon,* or *against.* 2 To encroach; infringe: with *on* or *upon.* [<L *impingere* < *in-* against + *pangere* strike] — **im·pinge′ment** *n.* — **im·ping′er** *n.*

im·pi·ous (im′pē·əs) *adj.* 1 Destitute of reverence for the divine character or will; ungodly; wicked. 2 Characterized by irreverence; blasphemous. 3 Unfilial; lacking reverence, especially to one's parents. See synonyms under PROFANE. [<L *impius* < *in-* not + *pius* reverent] — **im′pi·ous·ly** *adv.* — **im′pi·ous·ness** *n.*

imp·ish (im′pish) *adj.* Implike. — **imp′ish·ly** *adv.* — **imp·ish·ness** *n.*

im·pla·ca·ble (im·plā′kə·bəl, -plak′ə-) *adj.* That cannot be placated; inexorable. [<F <L *implacabilis* < *in-* not + *placere* please] — **im·pla′ca·bil′i·ty, im·pla′ca·ble·ness** *n.* — **im·pla′ca·bly** *adv.*

Synonyms: cruel, inexorable, irreconcilable, merciless, pitiless, relentless, severe, unappeasable, unforgiving, unrelenting. *Antonyms*: forgiving, gentle, mild, placable, tender, yielding.

im·pla·cen·tal (im′plə·sen′təl) *adj. Zool.* 1 Having no placenta. 2 Of or pertaining to a former division of mammals (*Implacentalia*), including the monotremes and marsupials, having no placenta. — *n.* An implacental mammal. Also **im′pla·cen′tate** (-tāt).

im·plant (im·plant′, -plänt′) *v.t.* 1 To insert or graft, as living tissue. 2 To inculcate or instil, as principles. 3 To plant, as seeds. — *n.* (im′plant′, -plänt′) *Med.* 1 A tissue implanted in the body. 2 A small tube containing radon or other radioactive material, embedded in tissue for therapeutic or remedial purposes. [<F *implanter*] — **im·plant′er** *n.*

im·plan·ta·tion (im′plan·tā′shən) *n.* 1 The act of implanting. 2 The introduction of a solid drug under the skin. 3 The subcutaneous injection of a drug: called **hypodermic implantation.** 4 Skin- or tissue-grafting. 5 The self-planting of body cells, especially tumor cells, in a new part of the body; spontaneous metastasis. 6 The setting of a new tooth in a jaw. [<F]

im·plau·si·ble (im·plô′zə·bəl) *adj.* Not plausible. — **im·plau′si·bly** *adv.*

im·plead (im·plēd′) *v.t. Law* 1 To sue in a court of justice. 2 To accuse; arraign. 3 To plead, as a cause. — *v.i.* 4 To bring a suit at law. [<AF *empleder,* OF *empleidier*] — **im·plead′a·ble** *adj.*

im·plead·er (im·plē′dər) *n.* A complainant or prosecutor.

im·pledge (im·plej′) *v.t.* **·pledged, ·pledg·ing** To put in pledge; pawn.

im·ple·ment (im′plə·mənt) *n.* 1 A thing used in work, especially in manual work; a utensil; tool. 2 Originally, that which supplies a want; any means or agent for the accomplishment of a purpose. See synonyms under TOOL. — *v.t.* (-ment) 1 To carry into effect; fulfil; accomplish. 2 To provide what is needed for; supplement. 3 To furnish with implements. [<L *implementum* a filling up < *implere* fill up < *in-* in + *plere* fill] — **im′ple·men′tal** *adj.*

im·ple·men·ta·tion (im′plə·men·tā′shən) *n.* A putting into effect, fulfilment, or carrying through, as of ideas, a program, etc.

im·ple·tion (im·plē′shən) *n.* The act of filling, or the state of being full; also, that which fills. [<LL *impletio, -onis* < *implere.* See IMPLEMENT.]

im·pli·cate (im′plə·kāt) *v.t.* **·cat·ed, ·cat·ing** 1 To show to be involved or concerned, as in a plot or crime. 2 To imply. 3 To fold or twist together; entangle; intertwine. See synonyms under INVOLVE. [<L *implicatus,* pp. of *implicare* involve < *in-* in + *plicare* fold]

im·pli·ca·tion (im′plə·kā′shən) *n.* 1 The act of implying; something implied; especially, something that leads to a deduction. 2 An entanglement. — **im′pli·ca′tion·al** *adj.*

im·pli·ca·tive (im′plə·kā′tiv) *adj.* Tending to imply or to implicate. Also **im·pli·ca·to·ry** (im′pli·kə·tôr′ē, -tō′rē). — **im′pli·ca′tive·ly** *adv.*

im·plic·it (im·plis′it) *adj.* 1 Fairly to be understood, but not specifically stated; implied. 2 Arising from thorough confidence in another; unquestioning: *implicit* trust. 3 Virtually contained in; essential, though not apparent; potential: The man is *implicit* in the child. 4 *Obs.* Infolded; entangled. [<F *implicite* <L *implicitus,* later form of *implicatus,* pp. of *implicare* involve. See IMPLICATE.] — **im·plic′it·ly** *adv.* — **im·plic′it·ness** *n.*

Synonyms: absolute, blind, complete, firm, full, perfect, steadfast, submissive, undoubting, unhesitating, unquestioning, unreserved, unshaken. *Implicit* primarily signifies "implied." *Implicit* faith assumes all reasons for belief or action to be "implied" in the fact that a statement, for instance, comes from some trusted source, as the Scriptures or the church; *implicit* obedience assumes that all reasons for action are "implied" in the mere command given by adequate authority. As contrasted with *explicit, implicit* belief is given to an *explicit* statement, *implicit* obedience rendered to an *explicit* command. Compare EXPLICIT; see, also, TACIT.

im·plied (im·plīd′) *adj.* Contained or included, but not directly stated. See synonyms under TACIT. — **im·pli·ed·ly** (im·plī′id·lē) *adv.*

implied powers *U.S.* Powers not expressly granted by the Constitution to the Federal government but inferred because of their necessary relation to powers which are expressly granted.

im·plode (im·plōd′) *v.t.* & *v.i.* **·plod·ed, ·plod·ing** 1 To burst inward. 2 *Phonet.* To pronounce by implosion. [<IM- + (EX)PLODE]

im·plo·ra·tion (im′plə·rā′shən) *n.* The act of imploring; entreaty. [<F *imploratio, -onis*]

im·plore (im·plôr′, -plōr′) *v.* **·plored, ·plor·ing** *v.t.* 1 To call upon in supplication; beseech; entreat. 2 To beg for urgently; pray for. — *v.i.* 3 To make urgent supplication. See synonyms under ASK, PLEAD, PRAY. [<L *implorare* < *in-* thoroughly + *plorare* cry out]

im·plor·er (im·plôr′ər, -plō′rər) *n.* One who implores; a suppliant.

im·plor·ing (im·plôr′ing, -plō′ring) *adj.* That implores; beseeching. — **im·plor′ing·ly** *adv.* — **im·plor′ing·ness** *n.*

im·plo·sion (im·plō′zhən) *n.* 1 A bursting inward; sudden collapse: opposed to *explosion.* 2 *Phonet.* The initial, sudden blockage of the breath stream in the production of a stop consonant: opposed to *plosion.* [<IMPLODE, on analogy with *explosion*] — **im·plo′sive** (-siv) *adj.*

im·plu·vi·um (im·plo͞o′vē·əm) *n. pl.* **·vi·a** (-vē·ə) A basin in the floor of the atrium of an ancient Roman house to receive the rain that fell through the compluvium. [<L < *impluere* rain into < *in-* in + *pluere* rain]

im·ply (im·plī′) *v.t.* **·plied, ·ply·ing** 1 To involve necessarily as a circumstance, condition, effect, etc.: An action *implies* an agent. 2 To indicate (a meaning not expressed); hint at; intimate. 3 *Obs.* To entangle; infold. See synonyms under ALLUDE, IMPORT, INVOLVE. [<OF *emplier* <L *implicare* involve < *in-* in + *plicare* fold. Doublet of EMPLOY.]

im·pol·i·cy (im·pol′ə·sē) *n.* Unsuitableness to the end proposed; inexpediency. [<IMPOLITIC, on analogy with *policy*]

im·po·lite (im′pə·līt′) *adj.* Lacking in politeness; rude. See synonyms under BLUFF. [<L *impolitus* < *in-* not + *politus.* See POLITE.] — **im′po·lite′ly** *adv.* — **im′po·lite′ness** *n.*

im·pol·i·tic (im·pol′ə·tik) *adj.* 1 Pursuing unwise measures. 2 Adapted to injure the interests involved; inexpedient; injudicious. See synonyms under IMPRUDENT. Also **im·po·lit·i·cal** (im′pə·lit′i·kəl). — **im·pol′i·tic·ly, im′po·lit′i·cal·ly** *adv.*

im·pon·der·a·ble (im·pon′dər·ə·bəl) *adj.* 1 Without weight. 2 Impossible of reckoning. — *n.* A factor in a situation which cannot be definitely foreseen. — **im·pon′der·a·bil′i·ty, im·pon′der·a·ble·ness** *n.* — **im·pon′der·a·bly** *adv.*

impone (im·pōn′) *v.t. Obs.* To wager; stake. [<L *imponere* place upon < *in-* on + *ponere* place]

im·po·rous (im·pôr′əs, -pō′rəs) *adj.* Very close or compact in texture; without pores; solid. — **im·po·ros·i·ty** (im′pə·ros′ə·tē) *n.*

im·port (im·pôrt′, -pōrt′, im′pôrt, -pōrt) *v.t.* 1 To bring (goods) into one country from a foreign country in commerce: opposed to *export.* 2 To bring in; introduce: to *import* acrimony into a debate. 3 To mean; signify: His expression *imports* no good for me. 4 To be of importance or significance to; concern. — *v.i.* 5 To be of importance or significance; matter: The argument does not *import.* — *n.* (im′pôrt, -pōrt) 1 That which is implied; meaning; significance. 2 That which is brought from one country into another. 3 Importance. See synonyms under WEIGHT. [<F *importer* <L *importare* bring in < *in-* in + *portare* carry; prob. infl. in meaning by L *oportet* it is necessary] — **im·port′a·ble** *adj.*

Synonyms (verb): betoken, denote, imply, mean, purport, signify, suggest. See INTEREST.

im·por·tance (im·pôr′təns) *n.* 1 The quality of being important or momentous. 2 Weight or consequence, as in public estimation or in self-esteem. 3 Consequential manner; pretentiousness. 4 *Obs.* Significance; meaning; also, urgency. Also *Obs.* **im·por′tan·cy.** [<Med. L *importantia*]

im·por·tant (im·pôr′tənt) *adj.* 1 Of great import, consequence, prominence, or value. 2 Mattering greatly: with *to*: evidence *important* to the case. 3 Pompous; pretentious. 4 *Obs.* Importunate; urgent. [<F <L *importans, -antis,* ppr. of *importare.* See IMPORT.] — **im·por′tant·ly** *adv.*

Synonyms: grave, influential, material, momentous, prominent, serious, significant, valuable, weighty. See SERIOUS. *Antonyms*: empty, idle, inconsiderable, irrelevant, mean, petty, slight, trifling, trivial, unimportant, useless, worthless.

im·por·ta·tion (im′pôr·tā′shən, -pōr-) *n.* 1 The act of importing, or bringing from one country into another merchandise for sale, processing, etc. 2 That which is imported.

im·port·er (im·pôr′tər, -pōr′-) *n.* One who imports or brings in goods from a foreign country.

im·por·tu·nate (im·pôr′chə·nit) *adj.* 1 Urgent in character, request, or demand; insistent; pertinacious. 2 *Obs.* Vexatious. See synonyms under EAGER[1], TROUBLESOME, URGENT. [<Med. L *importunatus,* pp. of *importunari.* See IMPORTUNE.] — **im·por′tu·nate·ly** *adv.* — **im·por′tu·nate·ness** *n.*

im·por·tune (im′pôr·to͞on′, -tyo͞on′, im·pôr′·chən) *v.* **·tuned, ·tun·ing** *v.t.* 1 To beset with persistent requests or demands. 2 To ask for persistently or urgently. 3 *Obs.* To annoy. 4 *Obs.* To impel; urge. — *v.i.* 5 To make persistent requests or demands. — *adj.* Persistent; importunate. [<F *importuner* < Med. L *importunari* be troublesome <L *importunus* having no access, vexatious < *in-* without + *portus* a port] — **im′por·tune′ly** *adv.* — **im′por·tun′er** *n.*

im·por·tu·ni·ty (im′pôr·to͞o′nə·tē, -tyo͞o′-) *n. pl.* **·ties** 1 The act of importuning. 2 The state of being importunate. 3 *pl.* Importunate demands. Also **im·por·tu·na·cy** (im·pôr′chə·nə·sē). [<L *importunitas, -tatis*]

im·pose (im·pōz′) *v.t.* **·posed, ·pos·ing** 1 To place or lay by authority, as something to be borne, endured, or obeyed: to *impose* a tax or penalty. 2 To place by or as by force: to *impose* opinions on another. 3 To obtrude or force (oneself, one's presence, etc.) upon others. 4 To palm off (something) as true or genuine; foist. 5 *Printing* To arrange in a form, as pages of type. 6 *Eccl.* To lay on (hands), as in confirmation or ordination. 7 *Obs.* To lay down; deposit. — **to impose on** (or **upon**) 1 To take advantage of; presume. 2 To cheat or deceive by trickery or false representation. 3 To make an impression; influence. — *n. Obs.* An injunction; command. [<F *imposer* < *im-* on + *poser.* See POSE[1].] — **im·pos′a·ble** *adj.* — **im·pos′er** *n.*

im·pos·ing (im·pō′zing) *adj.* Adapted to make an impression; grand; elegant.

imposing stone A flat, level slab, on which printers impose forms of type. Also **imposing table.**

im·po·si·tion (im′pə·zish′ən) *n.* 1 The act of imposing, in any sense of the word. 2 An unjust requirement. 3 A trick of deception; imposture. 4 *Printing* The arrangement of pages of type or plates, in the right order for printing. 5 The act of laying on hands, as in confirmation or ordination. 6 A tax, toll, or duty. See synonyms under DECEPTION, FRAUD. [<L *impositio, -onis* < *impositus*. See IMPOST.]

im·pos·si·bil·i·ty (im·pos′ə·bil′ə·tē) *n. pl.* **·ties** 1 The fact or state of being impossible. 2 That which is impossible; something that cannot exist or be done. [<L *impossibilitas, -tatis*]

im·pos·si·ble (im·pos′ə·bəl) *adj.* 1 Not possible. 2 *Law* Impracticable in the nature of the case. 3 Unimaginable; hopelessly objectionable; intolerable; absurd. See synonyms under IMPRACTICABLE. [<F] —**im·pos′·si·bly** *adv.*

im·post (im′pōst) *n.* 1 That which is imposed; specifically, a customs duty. 2 *Archit.* A projecting band or block placed at the top of a column or pier, and from which an arch springs. See illustration under ARCH. 3 A weight carried by a horse in a handicap race. See synonyms under TAX. —*v.t.* To classify so as to fix the customs duty: said of imported goods. [<OF <Med. L *impostum* <L *impositus*, pp. of *imponere* lay on < *in-* on + *ponere* lay, place]

im·pos·tor (im·pos′tər) *n.* One who deceives by false pretenses, especially under an assumed name or character. See synonyms under HYPOCRITE, QUACK[2]. [<F *imposteur* <LL *impostor* < *impositus*, pp. of *imponere* lay on, impose]

im·pos·tu·mate (im·pos′chə·māt) *v.t.* & *v.i. Obs.* To affect with an abscess; become abscessed or ulcerous. Also **im·pos′thu·mate.** [<IMPOSTUME] —**im·pos′tu·ma′tion** *n.*

im·pos·tume (im·pos′chōōm, -tyōōm) *n. Rare* An abscess. Also **im·pos′thume.** [Alter. of APOSTEME]

im·pos·ture (im·pos′chər) *n.* Deception by means of false pretenses. See synonyms under ARTIFICE, FRAUD. [<F <LL *impostura*]

im·po·tence (im′pə·təns) *n.* 1 The state or quality of being impotent; feebleness. 2 Loss or lack of capacity for sexual intercourse: said of men. Compare FRIGIDITY. Also **im′·po·ten·cy.** [<OF <L *impotentia*]

im·po·tent (im′pə·tənt) *adj.* 1 Destitute of or lacking in power, physical, moral, or intellectual; not potent; weak; feeble. 2 Destitute of sexual power: said usually of the male; also, occasionally, barren; sterile. 3 Lacking in self-control. [<OF <L *impotens, -entis* < *in-* not + *potens*. See POTENT.] —**im′po·tent·ly** *adv.*

im·pound (im·pound′) *v.t.* 1 To shut up in a pound, as a stray dog. 2 To place in custody of a court of law. 3 To collect (water) in a pond, reservoir, etc., as for irrigation. —**im·pound′age** (-poun′dij) *n.* —**im·pound′er** *n.*

im·pov·er·ish (im·pov′ər·ish) *v.t.* 1 To reduce to poverty. 2 To exhaust the fertility or quality of, as soil; deteriorate. Also spelled EMPOVERISH. [<OF *empovrir* < *em-* thoroughly + L *pauperare* impoverish < *pauper* poor]

im·pov·er·ish·ment (im·pov′ər·ish·mənt) *n.* The act of impoverishing, or the state of being impoverished.

im·prac·ti·ca·ble (im·prak′ti·kə·bəl) *adj.* 1 Impossible or unreasonably difficult of performance. 2 Unserviceable. 3 Hard to get on with; unreasonable; intractable: said of persons. —**im·prac′ti·ca·bil′i·ty, im·prac′ti·ca·ble·ness** *n.* —**im·prac′ti·ca·bly** *adv.*

Synonyms: impossible, impractical, intractable. That which is *impossible* cannot be done at all; that which is *impracticable* is theoretically possible, but cannot be done under existing conditions. *Impractical*, which strictly means not practical, is coming into frequent popular use as the equivalent of *impracticable*, but the difference should be maintained; an *impractical* man lacks practical judgment or efficiency; an *impracticable* man is difficult to deal with (compare OBSTINATE, PERVERSE); an *impractical* scheme lacks practical fitness, is theoretic or visionary; an *impracticable* scheme has some inherent difficulties that would insure its failure in action. *Antonyms*: easy, feasible, possible, practicable.

im·prac·ti·cal (im·prak′ti·kəl) *adj.* Not practical; unpractical. See synonyms under IMPRACTICABLE. —**im·prac′ti·cal′i·ty** (-kal′ə·tē) *n.*

im·pre·cate (im′prə·kāt) *v.t.* **·cat·ed, ·cat·ing** To invoke or call down, as a judgment, calamity, or curse. [<L *imprecatus*, pp. of *imprecare* pray to < *in-* to + *precari* pray < *prex, precis* prayer] —**im′pre·ca′tor** *n.* —**im′pre·ca·to′ry** (-kə·tôr′ē, -tō′rē) *adj.*

im·pre·ca·tion (im′prə·kā′shən) *n.* A malediction; curse. [<L *imprecatio, -onis*]

Synonyms: anathema, curse, execration, malediction. See OATH. *Antonyms*: benediction, benison, blessing, praise.

im·pre·ci·sion (im′pri·sizh′ən) *n.* Want of precision.

im·preg (im′preg) *n.* A tough, durable, weather-resistant plywood whose layers are impregnated with an aqueous solution of resin-forming chemicals, then dried, cured, and bonded with resin glue. [Short for IMPREGNATED]

im·pregn (im·prēn′) *v.t. Obs.* To impregnate. [<LL *impraegnare* make pregnant]

im·preg·na·ble (im·preg′nə·bəl) *adj.* 1 Proof against attack; that cannot be taken. 2 Not to be overcome by temptation. See synonyms under INCONTESTABLE, SECURE. [<OF *imprenable* < *im-* not (<L *in-*) + *prenable* pregnable < *prendre* take <L *prehendere*] —**im·preg′na·bil′i·ty** *n.* —**im·preg′na·bly** *adv.*

im·preg·nate (im·preg′nāt) *v.t.* **·nat·ed, ·nat·ing** 1 To make pregnant; get with child. 2 To fertilize. 3 To saturate or permeate with another substance. 4 To fill or imbue with emotion, ideas, principles, etc.: to *impregnate* a book with religious feeling. —*adj.* Made pregnant. [<LL *impraegnatus*, pp. of *impraegnare* impregnate < *in-* in + *praegnans* pregnant] —**im·preg′na·ble** (-nə·bəl) *adj.* —**im·preg′na·tor** *n.*

im·preg·na·tion (im′preg·nā′shən) *n.* 1 The act of impregnating. 2 The state of being impregnated. 3 That with which anything is impregnated.

im·pre·sa·ri·o (im′prə·sä′rē·ō) *n. pl.* **·sa·ri·os** One who organizes, manages, or is responsible for an opera company or public musical performance. [<Ital. < *impresa* undertaking < *imprendere* undertake <L *in-* on + *prehendere* take]

im·pre·scrip·ti·ble (im′pri·skrip′tə·bəl) *adj.* 1 Incapable of being either lost or acquired by usage or prescription. 2 Inalienable. [<F] —**im′pre·scrip′ti·bil′i·ty** *n.* —**im′pre·scrip′·ti·bly** *adv.*

im·prese (im·prēz′) *n. Obs.* A heraldic device or emblematic design. Also **im·pre·sa** (im·prä′zä). [<F <Ital. *impresa* undertaking]

im·press[1] (im·pres′) *v.t.* 1 To produce a marked effect upon, as the mind; influence: His proposal *impressed* me. 2 To fix firmly in the mind, as ideas, beliefs, etc.: to *impress* a fact on the memory. 3 To form or make (an imprint or mark) by pressure; stamp: to *impress* a design on metal. 4 To form or make an imprint or mark upon. 5 To apply with pressure; press: to *impress* one's hand into the mud. 6 *Electr.* To create or establish (a difference of potential) in a conductor by means of a dynamo, battery, or other source of electrical energy. —*n.* (im′pres) 1 A mark or indentation produced by pressure. 2 The effect of a force. 3 The act or process of making an impression. 4 Peculiar character or form; stamp. [<L *impressus*, pp. of *imprimere* impress < *in-* on + *premere* press]

Synonyms (verb): imprint, inculcate, press, print, stamp. *Antonyms*: see synonyms for CANCEL.

im·press[2] (im·pres′) *v.t.* 1 To compel to enter public service: to *impress* seamen. 2 To seize (property) for public use. —*n.* Impressment. [<IM- in + PRESS[1]] —**im·press′er** *n.*

im·press·i·ble (im·pres′ə·bəl) *adj.* Capable of being impressed or of receiving an impression; sensitive; susceptible. —**im·press′i·bil′i·ty, im·press′i·ble·ness** *n.* —**im·press′i·bly** *adv.*

im·pres·sion (im·presh′ən) *n.* 1 The act of impressing or imprinting; the imparting of a distinguishing mark, form, or character. 2 The result of exterior influence, as impressment; a stamp, mark, or figure made by pressure. 3 An effect produced on the senses, the mind, the feelings, or the conscience. 4 A slight or indistinct remembrance; a notion or belief held by the mind without adequate grounds. 5 An effect left upon the mind, which resembles in any way, or bears the marks of, some past experience; specifically, any mental effect regarded as the resultant of a previous experience. 6 *Printing* **a** The imprint of types, illustrations, etc., on a page or sheet. **b** All the copies of a book printed at one time: especially, an unaltered reprint from standing type or from plates, as distinguished from *edition*. **c** One copy of a book, engraving, etching, etc. See synonyms under FEELING, IDEA, MARK[1]. [<OF <L *impressio, -onis*] —**im·pres′sion·al** *adj.*

im·pres·sion·a·ble (im·presh′ən·ə·bəl) *adj.* Subject to or susceptible of impression; easily molded; plastic. [<F] —**im·pres′sion·a·bil′·i·ty, im·pres′sion·a·ble·ness** *n.*

im·pres·sion·ism (im·presh′ən·iz′əm) *n.* 1 In painting, a theory and school of art, developed in the third quarter of the 19th century, which attempted to produce, with the vividness and immediacy of nature and particularly of light itself, the impressions made by the subject on the artist. See IMPRESSIONIST SCHOOL. 2 In literature, a theory and practice of presenting the most immediate and arresting aspects of character, emotion, scene, or situation with relatively little study of explicit realistic detail. 3 *Music* A theory and school of composition, developed in the late 19th and early 20th centuries, as by Debussy and Ravel, striving to create impressions, moods, and atmospheric qualities by new tonal effects and other characteristic devices. —**im·pres′·sion·ist** *adj.* & *n.* —**im·pres′sion·is′tic** *adj.*

Impressionist School A group of French painters of the later 19th century who developed the doctrines and style of impressionism, including Manet, Monet, Pissarro, Sisley, Renoir, Degas, and others.

im·pres·sive (im·pres′iv) *adj.* Producing or tending to produce an impression; holding the attention; exciting emotion or admiration. See synonyms under GRAND. [<IMPRESS[1]] —**im·pres′sive·ly** *adv.* —**im·pres′sive·ness** *n.*

im·press·ment (im·pres′mənt) *n.* 1 The act of impressing into the public service, or of seizing property for public use. 2 The seizure of civilians for service in the navy or the seizure of members of a ship's crew by a foreign vessel.

im·pres·sure (im·presh′ər) *n.* An impression.

im·prest (im·prest′) *adj. Obs.* Given as a loan in advance: said of money given, as to soldiers, sailors, or government employees. —*n.* A prepayment of money, especially to carry on some public service. [< *in prest* on loan, after Ital. *impresto* loan. See PREST.]

im·pri·ma·tur (im′pri·mā′tər, -prī-) *n.* 1 Literally, let it be printed: an official formula of license to print or publish, affixed by a censor or board of censors to a book or pamphlet. 2 License or approval in general; sanction. [<L, let it be printed < *imprimere* impress]

im·pri·mis (im·prī′mis) *adv.* In the first place; first in order. [<L]

im·print (im·print′) *v.t.* 1 To produce or reproduce (a figure, mark, etc.) by pressure: to *imprint* a design on wax. 2 To mark (something), as with a stamp or seal. 3 To fix firmly in the heart, mind, etc. See synonyms under IMPRESS[1], INSCRIBE. —*n.* (im′print) 1 A mark or character made by printing, stamping, or pressing. 2 The effect left by impression. 3 A publisher's or printer's name, place of publication, date, etc., printed in a book or other publication. 4 An impression, as of a medal, etc. [<OF *empreinte*, pp. of *empreinter* <L *imprimere* < *in-* in + *premere* press]

im·pris·on (im·priz′ən) *v.t.* 1 To put into or keep in a prison. 2 To confine or restrain in any way. See synonyms under SHUT. [<OF *emprisoner* < *en-* in + *prison*. See PRISON.]

im·pris·on·ment (im·priz′ən·mənt) *n.* 1 The act of imprisoning. 2 Confinement in, or as in a prison.

im·prob·a·ble (im·prob′ə·bəl) *adj.* Not likely to be true; not reasonably to be expected. [<L *improbabilis*] —**im·prob·a·bil·i·ty** (im′·prob·ə·bil′ə·tē, im·prob′-), **im·prob′a·ble·ness** *n.* —**im·prob′a·bly** *adv.*

im·pro·bi·ty (im·prō′bə·tē) *n. pl.* **·ties** Want of probity; dishonesty. [<L *improbitas, -tatis* < *improbus* wicked < *in-* not + *probus* honest]

im·promp·tu (im·promp′tōō, -tyōō) *adj.* Made, done, or uttered on the spur of the moment; extempore; offhand. See synonyms under EXTEMPORANEOUS. —*n.* Anything done on the impulse of the moment. —*adv.* Without preparation. [<F <L *in promptu* in readiness]

im·prop·er (im·prop′ər) *adj.* 1 Not proper;

not strictly belonging or appropriate; inapplicable. **2** Not in accord with the proprieties of speech, manners, or conduct; indecorous. **3** Unsuitable; inappropriate. **4** Irregular or abnormal. [<OF *impropre* <L *improprius*] —**im·prop′er·ly** *adv.*

improper fraction See under FRACTION.

im·pro·pri·ate (im·prō′prē·āt) *v.t.* **·at·ed, ·at·ing** To transfer (ecclesiastical property or revenues) to laymen. —*adj.* (-prē·it) Vested or placed in the hands of a layman; impropriated. [<Med. L *impropriatus,* pp. of *impropriare* take as one's own <L *in-* on + *proprius* one's own] —**im·pro′pri·a′tion** *n.* —**im·pro′·pri·a′tor** *n.*

im·pro·pri·e·ty (im′prə·prī′ə·tē) *n. pl.* **·ties** **1** The state or quality of being improper. **2** Anything that is improper, as an act. **3** A violation of good usage in speech or writing. See synonyms under INDECENCY. [<L *improprietas, -tatis*]

im·prove (im·pro͞ov′) *v.* **·proved, ·prov·ing** *v.t.* **1** To make better the quality, condition, etc., of. **2** To use to good advantage; utilize: to *improve* one's opportunities. **3** *U.S.* To increase the value or profit of, as land by cultivation or lots by construction of buildings. —*v.i.* **4** To become better. **5** To make improvements: with *on* or *upon.* See synonyms under AMEND. [<AF *emprower* <OF *en-* into + *prou* profit] —**im·prov′a·bil′i·ty, im·prov′a·ble·ness** *n.* —**im·prov′a·ble** *adj.* —**im·prov′a·bly** *adv.* —**im·prov′er** *n.*

im·prove·ment (im·pro͞ov′mənt) *n.* **1** The act or process of improving; betterment; amelioration. **2** Something that is better than (something previous): Diesel power is an *improvement* over steam. **3** A beneficial change or addition; an advance. **4** *U.S.* A tract of land developed by cultivation, buildings, enclosures, etc. **5** *pl. U.S.* The enclosures, buildings, clearings, etc., produced on a piece of land. See synonyms under INCREASE, PROFIT, PROGRESS.

im·prov·i·dent (im·prov′ə·dənt) *adj.* **1** Lacking foresight; incautious. **2** Taking no thought for future needs. —**im·prov′i·dence** *n.* —**im·prov′i·dent·ly** *adv.*

Synonyms: careless, imprudent, prodigal, reckless, shiftless, thoughtless, thriftless, unthrifty. See IMPRUDENT. *Antonyms*: careful, economical, provident, prudent, saving, thoughtful, thrifty.

im·pro·vise (im′prə·vīz) *v.t. & v.i.* **·vised, ·vis·ing** **1** To compose, recite, sing, etc., without previous preparation; extemporize. **2** To make or devise on the spur of the moment, especially from what is at hand: to *improvise* a raft from driftwood. Also **im·prov′i·sate** (im·prov′ə·zāt). [<F *improviser* <Ital. *improvvisare* < *improvviso* unforeseen <L *improvisus* < *in-* not + *provisus* foreseen] —**im·prov·i·sa·tion** (im·prov′ə·zā′shən, im′prə·vī·zā′shən) *n.* —**im′pro·vis′er, im·prov′i·sa′tor** *n.* —**im·prov·i·sa·to·ri·al** (im·prov′ə·zə·tôr′ē·əl, -tō′rē·əl), **im·prov′i·sa·to′ry** (-tôr′ē, -tō′rē) *adj.*

im·prov·vi·sa·to·re (ēm′prôv·vē·zä·tō′rā) *n. pl.* **·ri** (-rē) *Italian* An improviser, especially of poems and songs.

im·pru·dent (im·pro͞o′dənt) *adj.* Not prudent; lacking discretion. [<L *imprudens, -entis* < *in-* not + *prudens* PRUDENT] —**im·pru′dent·ly** *adv.* —**im·pru′dence** *n.*

Synonyms: careless, foolhardy, heedless, ill-advised, ill-judged, impolitic, improvident, incautious, inconsiderate, indiscreet, injudicious, rash, reckless, short-sighted, thoughtless, thriftless, unthinking, unthrifty, venturesome, venturous. *Improvident* is chiefly used of lack of provision for future need, supply, support, etc.; *imprudent,* of a lack of provision against future danger, loss, or harm. Each word has also acquired a positive meaning: *improvident* referring to *careless* or *reckless* waste of present resources without thought of future need; *imprudent,* to *thoughtless* or *reckless* disregard of possible or probable future dangers. See IMPROVIDENT. *Antonyms*: see synonyms for ASTUTE.

im·pu·dence (im′pyə·dəns) *n.* **1** Effrontery; insolence. **2** Insolent language or behavior. **3** *Obs.* Shamelessness; immodesty. Also **im′·pu·den·cy.** [<OF <L *impudentia*]

Synonyms: assurance, boldness, effrontery, forwardness, impertinence, incivility, insolence, intrusiveness, officiousness, pertness, presumption, rudeness, sauciness. *Impertinence* primarily denotes what does not pertain or belong to the occasion or the person, and hence comes to signify interference by word or act not consistent with the age, position, or relation of the person interfered with or of the one who interferes; especially, forward, presumptuous, or meddlesome speech. *Impudence* is shameless *impertinence.* What would be arrogance in a superior becomes *impertinence* or *impudence* in an inferior. *Impertinence* has less of intent and determination than *impudence.* We speak of thoughtless *impertinence,* shameless *impudence. Insolence* is literally that which is against custom, that is, the violation of customary respect and courtesy. *Officiousness* is thrusting upon others unasked and undesired service, and is often as well-meant as it is annoying. *Rudeness* is the behavior that might be expected from a thoroughly uncultured person, and may be either deliberate and insulting or unintentional and even unconscious. Compare ARROGANCE, ASSURANCE, EFFRONTERY. *Antonyms*: bashfulness, coyness, diffidence, humility, lowliness, meekness, modesty, submissiveness.

im·pu·dent (im′pyə·dənt) *adj.* **1** Offensively bold; insolently assured. **2** *Obs.* Immodest; shameless. [<OF <L *impudens* < *in-* not + *pudens* modest, orig. ppr. of *pudere* feel shame] —**im′pu·dent·ly** *adv.*

Synonyms: bold, bold-faced, brazen, brazen-faced, forward, immodest, impertinent, insolent, pert, rude, saucy, shameless. Compare synonyms for IMPUDENCE. *Antonyms*: bashful, deferential, diffident, modest, obsequious, retiring, shrinking, shy, timid.

im·pu·dic·i·ty (im′pyə·dis′ə·tē) *n.* Immodesty; shamelessness. [<F *impudicité* <L *impudicitia* < *impudicus* shameless < *in-* not + *pudicus* modest < *pudor* shame]

im·pugn (im·pyo͞on′) *v.t.* To assail by words or arguments; attack as false or untrustworthy; challenge. [<OF *impugner* <L *impugnare* < *in-* against + *pugnare* fight < *pugna* battle < *pugnus* fist] —**im·pugn′a·ble** *adj.* —**im·pug·na·tion** (im′pəg·nā′shən) *n.* —**im·pugn′er** *n.* —**im·pugn′ment** *n.*

im·pu·is·sance (im·pyo͞o′ə·səns) *n.* Want of power or ability; impotence. [<F] —**im·pu′·is·sant** *adj.*

im·pulse (im′puls) *n.* **1** An impelling force, especially one that acts suddenly and produces motion; impulsion. **2** The motion produced by a sudden impelling force; impetus. **3** A sudden or transient mental urge resulting in undeliberated action, caused by the feelings or by some objective stimulus. **4** Any natural, unreasoned motive or tendency to act: a kind *impulse.* **5** An instinctive or reactive craving for action; a desire to act resulting from instantaneous judgments as to how to meet an emergency. **6** *Physiol.* A stimulus. **7** *Mech.* A great force acting for a very short time; also, the momentum due to a force. **8** *Electr.* A surge of current flowing in one direction. [<L *impulsus,* pp. of *impellere.* See IMPEL.]

Synonyms: feeling, force, impetus, incentive, incitement, influence, instigation, motive. See INFLUENCE.

impulse excitation See SHOCK EXCITATION.

im·pul·sion (im·pul′shən) *n.* **1** The act of impelling. **2** The state of being impelled. **3** An impulse or motion suddenly communicated; impetus. **4** That which impels, whether a force or motive. **5** Mental impetus. **6** Incitement; instigation. [<OF <L *impulsio, -onis*]

im·pul·sive (im·pul′siv) *adj.* **1** Actuated by impulse. **2** Having the power of impelling. **3** Acting by instantaneous or intermittent force or impulse. See synonyms under IMPETUOUS. [<OF *impulsif* <Med. L *impulsivus*] —**im·pul′sive·ly** *adv.* —**im·pul′sive·ness** *n.*

im·pu·ni·ty (im·pyo͞o′nə·tē) *n. pl.* **·ties** Freedom from punishment or from injurious consequences. [<L *impunitas, -tatis* < *impunis* unpunished < *in-* not + *poena* punishment]

im·pure (im·pyo͝or′) *adj.* **1** Not pure; containing some foreign substance; adulterated. **2** Unchaste. **3** Containing foreign idioms or grammatical blemishes. **4** Unfit for religious use; unhallowed. **5** Mixed with or having a tendency toward extraneous, corporeal, or foreign matter. See synonyms under FOUL, IMMODEST. [<L *impurus*] —**im·pure′ly** *adv.* —**im·pure′ness** *n.*

im·pu·ri·ty (im·pyo͝or′ə·tē) *n. pl.* **·ties** **1** The state of being impure. **2** Adulteration. **3** Moral pollution. **4** That which is impure or polluting. See synonyms under INDECENCY. [<OF *impurité* <L *impuritas, -tatis* < *in-* not + *purus* pure]

im·pur·ple (im·pûr′pəl) See EMPURPLE.

im·pu·ta·tion (im′pyo͞o·tā′shən) *n.* **1** The act of imputing. **2** Whatever is ascribed or charged; especially, censure or reproach. [<LL *imputatio, -onis*]

im·pu·ta·tive (im·pyo͞o′tə·tiv) *adj.* **1** Transferred or transmitted by imputation; imputed. **2** Addicted to making imputations. [<LL *imputativus*] —**im·pu′ta·tive·ly** *adv.*

im·pute (im·pyo͞ot′) *v.t.* **·put·ed, ·put·ing** **1** To attribute, as a fault or crime, to a person; ascribe. **2** *Theol.* To attribute, as righteousness or guilt, vicariously. See synonyms under ATTRIBUTE. [<OF *emputer* <L *imputare* enter into the account < *in-* in + *putare* reckon, think] —**im·put′a·bil′i·ty, im·put′a·ble·ness** *n.* —**im·put′a·ble** *adj.* —**im·put′er** *n.*

im·pu·tres·ci·ble (im′pyo͞o·tres′ə·bəl) *adj.* Not subject to corruption.

Im·roz (ēm·rôs′) The Turkish name for IMBROS.

in (in) *prep.* **1** Within the bounds of; contained or included within: six rooms *in* the house. **2** Amidst; surrounded by: *in* the rain; buried *in* sand. **3** Within the class or group of; being a worker at, investor *in,* etc.: a man *in* a thousand; He is *in* munitions. **4** Occupied or concerned with: *in* search of truth. **5** Wearing, decorated with, etc.: that girl *in* blue; a room *in* green. **6** Made out of: I can show you this watch *in* gold. **7** So as to form or constitute: ornaments arranged *in* a spiral. **8** So as to enter into or remain within: sinking *in* the mud; putting his hands *in* his pockets. **9** As a part or function of; belonging to: We knew you had it *in* you. **10** According to or within the scope or range of: *In* my opinion you're mistaken; to come *in* hearing. **11** During; throughout the course of: a concert given *in* the evening. **12** At or before the end or expiration of: the note due *in* three days; I'll be there *in* no time. **13** With regard or respect to: Students vary *in* talent. **14** Affected by; under the influence of: *in* doubt as to the outcome. **15** By means of; with the use of: speaking *in* whispers; painted *in* water colors. **16** For the purpose of: to run *in* pursuit. **17** By reason or as a result of: to run *in* fear. —*adv.* **1** To or toward the interior or inside from the exterior or outside: Please come *in.* **2** So as to be part of, contained by, or included with: to join *in;* to stir *in* flour. —**all in** *Colloq.* Exhausted; worn out. —**in that** Because; since: *In that* you're here already, you might as well stay. —**in with** In association or friendship with. —**to be in for** *Colloq.* To have the certain expectation of receiving (usually something unpleasant). —**to have it in for** *Colloq.* To resent; bear ill will toward. —*adj.* **1** That is successful; having control or authority. **2** On the inside; inner. **3** Leading or going in: the *in* train. **4** *Colloq.* **a** Privileged in status. **b** Much publicized and often admired. **5** *Colloq.* Understandable only to a select few: *in* jokes. —*n.* **1** A member of a party in office or power, a team at bat, etc. **2** *Colloq.* A door or other means of entrance or access. **3** *Colloq.* Favored position or influence: an *in* with the boss. **4** A nook or corner. —**ins and outs** **1** All the twists and turns, nooks and corners, etc. **2** The full complexities, details, etc.: the *ins and outs* of a question. —*v.t.* **inned, in·ning** **1** To gather, as hay. **2** *Dial.* To enclose, as land. [OE]

in-[1] *prefix* Not; without; un-; non-. Also: *i-* before *gn,* as in *ignore; il-* before *l,* as in *illiterate; im-* before *b, m, p,* as in *imbalance, immiscible, impecunious; ir-* before *r,* as in *irrefragable.* [<L]

There follows a list of self-defining words with this prefix, most of them being variants of words beginning with *un–*. *In–* as here used has the meaning of "want or lack of," "not" (as *incivility*, lack of civility; *indevout*, not devout). See the foot of this page, etc.

in–[2] *prefix* In; into; on; within; toward: *include, incur, invade*: also used intensively, as in *inflame*, or without perceptible force. Also *il–* before *l*, as in *illuminate*; *im–* before *b, m, p*, as in *imbibe, immigrate, impress*; ir– before *r*, as in *irradiate*. The form generally remains unassimilated in words formed in English, as in *inbreed*. [Fusion of IN, *prep. & adv.* + L *in–*]

in–[3] *prefix* In, into; within: *inlet*. [OE]

–in *suffix Chem.* Used generally to denote neutral compounds, as fats, proteins, and glycerides: *stearin*: sometimes spelled *–ine*. Also *–ein*. [Var. of -INE[2]]

in·a·bil·i·ty (in′ə·bil′ə·tē) *n.* The state of being unable; lack of necessary power.

in ab·sen·ti·a (in ab·sen′shē·ə, -shə) *Latin* In absence (of the person concerned).

in ab·strac·to (ab·strak′tō) *Latin* In the abstract.

in·ac·ces·si·ble (in′ak·ses′ə·bəl) *adj.* Not accessible; incapable of being reached. — **in′ac·ces′si·bil′i·ty** *n.*

in·ac·cu·ra·cy (in·ak′yər·ə·sē) *n. pl.* **·cies** 1 The state or condition of being inaccurate. 2 Something which is inaccurate.

in·ac·cu·rate (in·ak′yər·it) *adj.* Wanting in accuracy. — **in·ac′cu·rate·ly** *adv.* — **in·ac′cu·rate·ness** *n.*

In·a·chus (in′ə·kəs) In Greek mythology, a river god and the first king of Argos; son of Oceanus and Tethys and father of Io.

in·ac·tion (in·ak′shən) *n.* A state of inactivity; forbearance from action; idleness.

in·ac·ti·vate (in·ak′tə·vāt) *v.t.* **·vat·ed, ·vat·ing** 1 To render inactive. 2 *Med.* To stop the activity of (a serum or its complement) by heat or other means. — **in·ac′ti·va′tion** *n.*

in·ac·tive (in·ak′tiv) *adj.* 1 Characterized by inaction; not making special exertion or effort. 2 Marked by absence of effort or desire for action; indolent. 3 Without power to act. 4 *Physics* Having no effect or action upon polarized light. See synonyms under IDLE, PASSIVE, SLOW. — **in·ac′tive·ly** *adv.* — **in·ac·tiv·i·ty** (in′ak·tiv′ə·tē), **in·ac′tive·ness** *n.*

in ac·tu (ak′to͞o) *Latin* In reality.

in·ad·e·quate (in·ad′ə·kwit) *adj.* Not equal to that which is required; inapt; insufficient; imperfect. — **in·ad′e·qua·cy, in·ad′e·quate·ness** *n.* — **in·ad′e·quate·ly** *adv.*

in·ad·ver·tence (in′əd·vûr′təns) *n.* 1 The quality of being inadvertent; want of care or circumspection. 2 An effect of inattention; oversight: This error was a mere *inadvertence*. Also **in′ad·ver′ten·cy**. [<Med. L *inadvertentia*]

in·ad·ver·tent (in′əd·vûr′tənt) *adj.* 1 Done without consideration. 2 Habitually heedless. 3 Unintentional. — **in′ad·ver′tent·ly** *adv.*

in·ad·vis·a·ble (in′əd·vī′zə·bəl) *adj.* Not advisable. — **in′ad·vis′a·bil′i·ty** *n.*

–inae *suffix Zool.* Used in the names of subfamilies: *Cervinae* (see CERVINE). [<NL <L, fem. pl. of *-inus* -INE[1]]

in ae·ter·num (ē·tûr′nəm) *Latin* Forever.

in·af·fa·ble (in·af′ə·bəl) *adj.* Not affable; austere; disagreeable.

in·al·ien·a·ble (in·āl′yən·ə·bəl) *adj.* Not transferable; that cannot be rightfully taken away. — **in·al′ien·a·bil′i·ty, in·al′ien·a·ble·ness** *n.* — **in·al′ien·a·bly** *adv.*

in·al·ter·a·ble (in·ôl′tər·ə·bəl) *adj.* That cannot be altered; unalterable. — **in·al′ter·a·bil′i·ty, in·al′ter·a·ble·ness** *n.* — **in·al′ter·a·bly** *adv.*

in·am·o·ra·ta (in·am′ə·rä′tə, in′am-) *n.* A woman with whom one is enamored; sweetheart. [<Ital. *innamorata*, fem. pp. of *innamorare* enamor] — **in·am′o·ra′to** (-tō) *n. masc.*

in–and–in (in′ənd·in′) *adj. & adv.* 1 From animals of the same or closely related parentage: breeding *in–and–in*. 2 Figuratively, with continuous reciprocal action.

in·ane (in·ān′) *adj.* 1 Wanting in understanding; silly. 2 Having no substance or contents; vacant. — *n.* That which is void; any vacuity; infinite space. [<L *inanis* empty]

in·an·i·mate (in·an′ə·mit) *adj.* Wanting in life and animation; not animate: opposed to *sentient*. [<LL *inanimatus*] — **in·an′i·mate·ly** *adv.* — **in·an′i·mate·ness** *n.*

in·a·ni·tion (in′ə·nish′ən) *n.* 1 The state of being void or empty. 2 Exhaustion from lack of nourishment. [<F <LL *inanitio, -onis* < *inanitus*, pp. of *inanire* empty < *inanis* empty]

in·an·i·ty (in·an′ə·tē) *n. pl.* **·ties** 1 The condition of being inane or empty; inanition; lack of sense. 2 A frivolous or silly thing. 3 A stupid or trite remark. [<OF *inanité* <L *inanitas* < *inanis* empty]

in·ap·peas·a·ble (in′ə·pē′zə·bəl) *adj.* That cannot be appeased; not to be appeased.

in·ap·pe·tence (in·ap′ə·təns) *n.* A lack of appetite or desire. Also **in·ap′pe·ten·cy**. — **in·ap′pe·tent** *adj.*

in·ap·pro·pri·ate (in′ə·prō′prē·it) *adj.* Not appropriate; unsuitable; unfitting.

in·arch (in·ärch′) *v.t. Bot.* To graft by attaching (a branch) without severing it from the parent stock until it has become united with the new stock; graft by approach. [<IN-[2] + ARCH]

in·arm (in·ärm′) *v.t.* To encircle with or as with the arms; embrace.

In·ar·tic·u·la·ta (in′är·tik′yə·lā′tə) See ECARDINES.

in·ar·tic·u·late (in′är·tik′yə·lit) *adj.* 1 Indistinctly or unintelligibly uttered by the speech organs. 2 Incapable of speech; dumb. 3 Unable to speak coherently or to express oneself fully. 4 Unspoken; unexpressed. 5 *Anat.* Not jointed or segmented, as certain worms; also, not hinged. — **in′ar·tic′u·late·ly** *adv.* — **in′ar·tic′u·late·ness** *n.*

in ar·ti·cu·lo mor·tis (in är·tik′yə·lō môr′tis) *Latin* At the moment of death.

in·as·much as (in′əz·much′ az′) 1 Since; because; seeing that. 2 *Archaic* In the measure that; to the degree that.

in·at·ten·tion (in′ə·ten′shən) *n.* Lack of or failure to give attention; heedlessness; negligence; disregard.

in·at·ten·tive (in′ə·ten′tiv) *adj.* Neglecting or failing to pay attention; careless. — **in′at·ten′tive·ly** *adv.* — **in′at·ten′tive·ness** *n.*

Synonyms: absent, absent–minded, careless, heedless, inconsiderate, listless, neglectful, negligent, regardless, remiss, restless, unmindful, unobservant. See ABSTRACTED. *Antonyms*: attentive, careful, considerate, heedful, listening, noticing, noting, observing, regardful, studious, thoughtful, watchful.

in·au·di·ble (in·ô′də·bəl) *adj.* That cannot be heard; beyond the range of hearing. — **in·au′di·bil′i·ty** *n.* — **in·au′di·bly** *adv.*

in·au·gu·rate (in·ô′gyə·rāt) *v.t.* **·rat·ed, ·rat·ing** 1 To induct into office with formal ceremony; invest. 2 To begin or commence upon formally; initiate: to *inaugurate* a reform. 3 To celebrate the public opening or first use of: to *inaugurate* a bridge. See synonyms under INSTALL. [<L *inauguratus*, pp. of *inaugurare* take omens, consecrate, install. See AUGUR.] — **in·au′gu·ral** (-rəl) *adj.* — **in·au′gu·ra′tor** *n.* — **in·au′gu·ra·to′ry** (-tôr′ē, -tō′rē) *adj.*

in·au·gu·ra·tion (in·ô′gyə·rā′shən) *n.* The act or ceremony of inaugurating. See synonyms under ACCESSION, BEGINNING. [<L *inauguratio, -onis*]

Inauguration Day The day for the inauguration of a president of the United States following his election: January 20. Prior to the inauguration of 1937 the date was March 4.

in·be·ing (in′bē′ing) *n.* 1 Inherent existence. 2 Essential nature; what a thing is in itself.

in·board (in′bôrd′, -bōrd′) *adj.* 1 *Naut.* Inside the hull or bulwarks of a ship: used also adverbially. 2 *Mech.* Toward the inside.

inboard brakes In automobiles, brake assemblies mounted within the chassis rather than on the wheels, the object being to reduce unsprung weight.

in·born (in′bôrn′) *adj.* Implanted by nature; innate. See synonyms under INHERENT.

in·bound (in′bound′) *adj.* Bound inward: an *inbound* ship.

in·breathe (in·brēth′) *v.t.* **·breathed, ·breath·ing** 1 To draw in, as breath; inhale. 2 To inspire.

in·bred (in′bred′) *adj.* 1 Bred within; innate. 2 Bred from closely related parents. See synonyms under INHERENT.

in·breed (in′brēd′, in′brēd′) *v.t.* **·bred, ·breed·ing** 1 To develop or produce within. 2 To breed by continual mating of closely related stock.

in·burst (in′bûrst′) *n.* 1 A bursting from without inward. 2 That which bursts in: an *inburst* of water.

in·by (in′bī′) *Scot. adv.* Inward; toward the interior or center. — *adj.* Located nearby.

In·ca (ing′kə) *n.* 1 An emperor or chief of Peru or one of its divisions, at the time of the Spanish conquest. 2 One of the native Quechuan Indians formerly dominant in Peru. [<Sp. <Quechua *Ynca* royal prince]

in·cage (in·kāj′) *v.t.* To encage.

in·cal·cu·la·ble (in·kal′kyə·lə·bəl) *adj.* 1 That cannot be counted or calculated. 2 Uncertain. 3 Not foreseeable. — **in·cal′cu·la·bil′i·ty** *n.* — **in·cal′cu·la·bly** *adv.*

in·ca·les·cent (in′kə·les′ənt) *adj.* Growing warm; increasing in heat. [<L *incalescens, -entis*, ppr. of *incalescere* grow hot < *in-* thoroughly + *calescens*. See CALESCENT.] — **in′ca·les′cence** *n.*

in cam·er·a (in kam′ər·ə) 1 In secret; privately. 2 *Law* In chambers. [<L, in a room]

In·can (ing′kən) *n.* 1 A member of the Inca empire. 2 Quechua. — *adj.* Of or pertaining to the Inca empire, its culture, or to its people.

in·can·desce (in′kən·des′) *v.t. & v.i.* **·desced, ·desc·ing** To be or become, or cause to become luminous with heat. [<L *incandescere*] — **in′can·des′cence, in′can·des′cen·cy** *n.*

in·can·des·cent (in′kən·des′ənt) *adj.* 1 Made luminous by heat; white or glowing with heat. 2 Of or pertaining to a lamp the light of which is derived from incandescing material, such as the filament in an electric lamp or the mantle in a Welsbach burner. [<L *incandescens, -entis*, ppr. of *incandescere* grow hot < *in-* in + *candescere*, inceptive of *candere* glow white] — **in′can·des′cent·ly** *adv.*

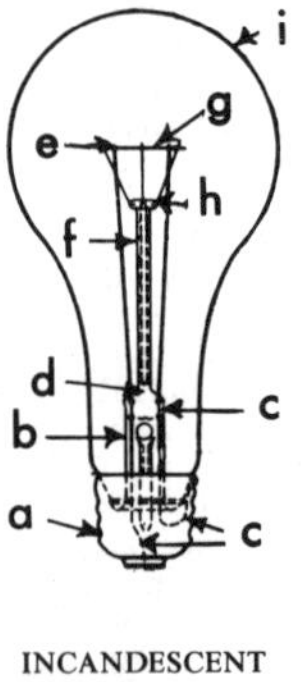

INCANDESCENT LIGHT BULB
a. Base.
b. Stem.
c. Leading–in wires.
d. Stem seal.
e, h. Anchors.
f. Hub.
g. Filament.
i. Bulb.

in·can·ta·tion (in′kan·tā′shən) 1 The utterance of magical words for enchantment or exorcism. 2 The formula so used. 3 Any magic or sorcery. See synonyms under SORCERY. [<F <L *incantatio, -onis* < *incantare* make an incantation. See ENCHANT.] — **in′can·ta′tor** *n.* — **in·can·ta·to·ry** (in·kan′tə·tôr′ē, -tō′rē) *adj.*

in·ca·pa·ble (in·kā′pə·bəl) *adj.* 1 Not capable; lacking power, capacity or ability: with *of*; incompetent. 2 Without legal qualifications or eligibility. — *n.* A totally incompetent person. — **in·ca′pa·bil′i·ty, in·ca′pa·ble·ness** *n.* — **in·ca′pa·bly** *adv.*

in·ca·pac·i·tate (in′kə·pas′ə·tāt) *v.t.* **·tat·ed, ·tat·ing** 1 To make incapable or unfit; deprive of capacity; disable. 2 *Law* To deprive of legal or political capacity; disqualify. — **in′ca·pac′i·ta′tion** *n.*

in·ca·pac·i·ty (in′kə·pas′ə·tē) *n. pl.* **·ties** 1 Lack of capacity; incapability. 2 *Law* Want of competency. See synonyms under IDIOCY.

in·cap·su·late (in·kap′sə·lāt, -syo͞o-) *v.t.* **·lat·ed, ·lat·ing** To enclose as in a capsule. [<IN- + CAPSUL(E) + -ATE[1]]

in·car·cer·ate (in·kär′sər·āt) *v.t.* **·at·ed, ·at·ing** 1 To imprison; put in jail. 2 To confine; enclose. — *adj.* Imprisoned. [<Med. L *incarceratus*, pp. of *incarcerare* imprison < *in-* in + *carcer* jail] — **in·car′cer·a′tion** *n.* — **in·car′cer·a′tor** *n.*

in·car·di·nate (in·kär′də·nāt) *v.t.* **·nat·ed, ·nat·ing** In the Roman Catholic Church: 1 To establish in a particular church, diocese, or place as principal priest, deacon, etc. 2 To

inacceptable
inaccordance
inaccordancy
inacquaintance
inacquiescent
inadept
inadmissibility
inadmissible
inaffability
inaidable
inappealable
inapplicability
inapplicable
inapplication
inapposite
inappreciable
inappreciative
inapprehensible
inapprehension
inapprehensive
inapproachability
inapproachable
inapt
inaptitude
inaqueous
inarable
inartificial
inartistic
inartistical
inassignable
inassimilate
inauspicious
inauthentic
incapacious
incaution

make a cardinal. [<Med. L *incardinatus*, pp. of *incardinare* install a priest < *in-* in + *cardinalis* a chief priest] — **in·car'di·na'tion** *n.*

in·car·na·dine (in·kär'nə·dīn, -din) *v.t.* **·dined, ·din·ing** To dye or stain red or flesh-color. — *adj.* Of pale-red. pink, flesh- or blood-color. [<F *incarnadin* <Ital. *incarnatino*, dim. of *incarnato* flesh-colored, pp. of *incarnare* INCARNATE]

in·car·nant (in·kär'nənt) *adj. Med.* Promoting the granulation of wounds. — *n.* An agent that promotes the healing of wounds. Also **in·car'na·tive.** [< earlier *incarn* cover with flesh, heal over <LL *incarnare* INCARNATE]

in·car·nate (in·kär'nāt) *v.t.* **·nat·ed, ·nat·ing** **1** To embody in flesh; give bodily form to. **2** To give concrete shape or form to; actualize: a doctrine *incarnated* in institutions. **3** To be the embodiment of; typify: The warrior *incarnates* the spirit of battle. — *adj.* (-nit) **1** Invested with flesh. **2** Embodied in human form: a fiend *incarnate*. **3** Personified or epitomized: savagery *incarnate*. **4** Flesh colored; roseate. [<LL *incarnatus*, pp. of *incarnare* embody in flesh < *in-* in + *caro, carnis* flesh]

in·car·na·tion (in'kär·nā'shən) *n.* **1** The act of becoming incarnate. **2** *Often cap.* The assumption of the human nature by Jesus Christ as the second person of the Trinity. **3** That which is personified by, or embodied in or as in human form; personification; embodiment of a quality, idea, principle, etc.; specifically, an avatar. [<AF *incarnaciun* < LL *incarnatio, -onis*]

in·case (in·kās') *v.t.* **·cased, ·cas·ing** To place or enclose in or as in a case or cases: often spelled *encase*.

in·case·ment (in·kās'mənt) *n.* **1** The act of incasing, or the state of being incased. **2** That which incases. — **theory of incasement** *Biol.* An old theory of reproduction that assumes each ovum to contain a fully formed organism in miniature; preformation.

in·ca·va·tion (in'kə·vā'shən) *n.* **1** The act of making hollow. **2** The hollow itself. [<L *incavatus*, pp. of *incavare* < *in-* in + *cavare* make hollow < *cavus* hollow]

in·cen·di·ar·y (in·sen'dē·er'ē) *adj.* **1** Pertaining to malicious setting on fire. **2** Tending to inflame passion. **3** Capable of generating intense heat, as any of various substances such as magnesium, thermit, or white phosphorus. **4** Pertaining to or containing such a substance: an *incendiary* bomb. — *n. pl.* **·ries** **1** One who maliciously sets a building on fire; one who commits arson. **2** One who excites to sedition, inflames evil passions, or the like. **3** An incendiary bomb or shell. [<L *incendiarius* < *incendium* a fire < *incendere* set on fire] — **in·cen'di·a·rism** (-ə·riz'əm) *n.*

incendiary bomb See under BOMB.

in·cense[1] (in·sens') *v.t.* **·censed, ·cens·ing** To excite or arouse the wrath of; inflame to anger; enrage. [<OF *incenser* <L *incendere* set on fire < *in-* in + *candere* glow] — **in·cense'ment** *n.* — **in·cen'sor** *n.*

Synonyms: anger, chafe, enrage, exasperate, fire, gall, goad, heat, inflame, irritate, provoke, sting. *Antonyms*: allay, appease, conciliate, mollify, pacify, placate, soothe.

in·cense[2] (in'sens) *n.* **1** An aromatic substance that exhales perfume during combustion, as certain gums and spices. **2** The odor or fumes of spices, etc., burnt as an act of worship. **3** Any agreeable perfume. **4** Figuratively, pleasing attention; praise. — *v.* **·censed, ·cens·ing** *v.t.* **1** To perfume with incense. **2** To burn incense to. — *v.i.* **3** To burn incense. [<OF *encens* <L *incensus*, pp. of *incendere* set on fire]

in·cen·tive (in·sen'tiv) *adj.* Encouraging or impelling. — *n.* That which incites, or tends to incite, to action. See synonyms under IMPULSE, MOTIVE. [<L *incentivus* < *incentus*, pp. of *incinere* set the tune < *in-* in + *canere* sing] — **in·cen'tive·ly** *adv.*

in·cept (in·sept') *v.t.* **1** *Biol.* To take in, as a cell or organism. **2** *Obs.* To begin; undertake. [<L *inceptus*, pp. of *incipere* begin < *in-* on + *capere* take]

in·cep·tion (in·sep'shən) *n.* **1** The act of beginning. **2** The state of being begun. **3** The initial period, as of an undertaking. See synonyms under BEGINNING. [<L *inceptio, -onis* < *inceptus*, pp. of *incipere*. See INCEPT.]

in·cep·tive (in·sep'tiv) *adj.* **1** Noting the beginning or commencement of an action or occurrence; initial. **2** *Gram.* Referring to a class of verbs or to the aspect of a verb denoting the commencement of an action; inchoative; ingressive. In Latin, for example, such verbs are formed by the addition of *-scere* to the present stem, as *cale(scere)*, to grow warm, from *cale(re)*, to be hot. — *n.* **1** That which tends to commence, as an inceptive word or construction. **2** *Gram.* An inceptive word or construction. [<OF *inceptif* <L *inceptus*, pp. of *incipere*. See INCEPT.] — **in·cep'tive·ly** *adv.*

in·cer·ti·tude (in·sûr'tə·to͞od, -tyo͞od) *n.* **1** The state of being uncertain; uncertainty; doubtfulness. **2** Insecurity. [<F <Med. L *incertitudo* <L *incertus* uncertain]

in·ces·sant (in·ses'ənt) *adj.* Continued or repeated without cessation. See synonyms under CONTINUAL, PERPETUAL. [<F <LL *incessans, -antis* < *in-* not + *cessare* cease] — **in·ces'san·cy** (-ən·sē) *n.* — **in·ces'sant·ly** *adv.*

in·cest (in'sest) *n.* **1** Sexual intercourse between persons too closely related for legal marriage. **2** *Theol.* Spiritual incest. [<L *incestum* < *incestus* unchaste < *in-* not + *castus* chaste]

in·ces·tu·ous (in·ses'cho͞o·əs) *adj.* **1** Guilty of incest. **2** Of the nature of incest. [<L *incestuosus*] — **in·ces'tu·ous·ly** *adv.*

inch[1] (inch) *n.* **1** A linear measure: the twelfth part of a foot or 2.54 centimeters. **2** *Meteorol.* The amount of snow or rain which would cover a surface to the depth of an inch. **3** *Physics* The unit of pressure equivalent to the weight of a fluid column, as of mercury, having a height of one inch. **4** An exceedingly small distance, amount of time, or quantity of material. — **by inches** Gradually; very slowly. — *v.t.* & *v.i.* To move by inches or small degrees. [OE *ynce* <L *uncia* the twelfth part, inch, ounce. Doublet of OUNCE.]

inch[2] (inch) *n. Scot.* An island: often used in combination in Scottish local names.

inch·meal (inch'mēl') *adv.* Inch by inch; piecemeal. — *n.* A fragment an inch long; a little piece. [<INCH + -MEAL]

in·cho·ate (in·kō'it, in'kō·āt) *adj.* Existing in its elements only; begun or entered upon, but not in full existence or operation; incipient. — *v.t.* & *v.i.* (in'kō·āt) **·at·ed, ·at·ing** *Rare* To begin. [<L *inchoatus, incohatus*, pp. of *incohare* begin] — **in·cho'ate·ly** *adv.* — **in'cho·a'tion, in·cho'ate·ness** *n.*

in·cho·a·tive (in·kō'ə·tiv) *adj.* **1** *Gram.* Inceptive. **2** *Rare* Inchoate; incipient. — *n.* That which begins or expresses beginning; an inceptive; especially, an inceptive verb.

In·chon (in·chon) A port on the Yellow Sea in central Korea: also *Chemulpo. Japanese* **Jin·sen** (jin·sen).

inch·worm (inch'wûrm') *n.* A measuring worm. See under GEOMETRID.

in·ci·dence (in'sə·dəns) *n.* **1** A falling, or the direction or manner of falling. **2** *Physics* The angle which the path of a body or of any form of radiant energy makes with the perpendicular of a surface at the point of impact. **3** The fact or the manner of being incident. **4** The degree of occurrence or effect of something: a high *incidence* of typhus. **5** *Geom.* Partial coincidence in the position of two figures, as a line and a point on it.

in·ci·dent (in'sə·dənt) *n.* **1** Anything that takes place as part of an action or in connection with an event; a subordinate or concomitant event or act. **2** A happening in general, especially one of little importance; any event; an occurrence. **3** Something characteristically, naturally, or legally depending upon, connected with, or contained in another thing as its principal. See synonyms under ACCIDENT, CIRCUMSTANCE, EVENT, SCENE, STORY. — *adj.* **1** Falling or striking upon; impinging from without: *incident* rays. **2** Likely to befall; naturally or usually appertaining or attending: danger *incident* to travel. **3** Of the nature of an incident or concomitant; belonging subsidiarily; appurtenant: The right of alienation is *incident* to a title in fee simple. **4** *Obs.* Incidental. [<F <L *incidens, -entis*, ppr. of *incidere* fall upon < *in-* on + *cadere* fall]

in·ci·den·tal (in'sə·den'təl) *adj.* **1** Occurring in the course of something else; contingent. **2** Happening without regularity or design; casual. — *n.* **1** Something that is incidental, contingent, or fortuitous; a subordinate or minor occurrence, circumstance, or result. **2** *Music* In the tonic sol-fa system, a tone foreign to a chord. **3** *Usually pl.* Minor or casual expenses or items. — **in'ci·den'tal·ly** *adv.*

Synonyms (adj.): accessory, accidental, casual, chance, collateral, concomitant, concurrent, contingent, fortuitous, occasional. That is *incidental* which comes in the regular course of things, but is not viewed as primary or important; as, an *incidental* allusion, reference, or mention. That which is *incidental* is subordinate to the main design; that which is *accidental* occurs without design. Compare ACCIDENT. *Antonyms*: essential, fundamental, independent, inherent, invariable, regular, systematic, underlying.

in·cin·er·ate (in·sin'ər·āt) *v.t.* **·at·ed, ·at·ing** To consume with fire; reduce to ashes; cremate. See synonyms under BURN. [<Med. L *incineratus*, pp. of *incinerare* < *in-* in + *cinis, cineris* ashes]

in·cin·er·a·tion (in·sin'ə·rā'shən) *n.* The act or state of cremation. [<F]

in·cin·er·a·tor (in·sin'ə·rā'tər) *n.* **1** One who or that which incinerates. **2** A furnace or apparatus for reducing any substance to ashes, as for consuming refuse or for cremating.

in·cip·i·ence (in·sip'ē·əns) *n.* Inception; the state of being incipient. Also **in·cip'i·en·cy.** ◆ Homophone: *insipience*.

in·cip·i·ent (in·sip'ē·ənt) *adj.* Belonging to the first stages. [<L *incipiens, -entis*, ppr. of *incipere*. See INCEPT.] — **in·cip'i·ent·ly** *adv.*

in·ci·pit (in'si·pit) *Latin* Here begins: a term often found at the beginning of medieval manuscripts.

in·cise (in·sīz') *v.t.* **·cised, ·cis·ing** **1** To cut into with a sharp instrument; gash. **2** To make (designs, marks, etc.) by cutting; engrave; carve. [<MF *inciser* <L *incidere* cut into < *in-* in + *caedere* cut]

in·cised (in·sīzd') *adj.* **1** Cut in; engraved. **2** Notched irregularly but sharply, as a leaf or an insect's wing.

in·ci·sion (in·sizh'ən) *n.* **1** The act of incising. **2** An opening made with a cutting instrument: a cut; gash. **3** *Surg.* A division of soft parts with a cutting instrument, as in an operation. **4** Sharpness; incisiveness; trenchancy. **5** A slit or notch, having the appearance of a cut, as in the margin of a leaf, a butterfly's wing, etc. [<OF <L *incisio, -onis*]

in·ci·sive (in·sī'siv) *adj.* **1** Having the power of incising. **2** Cutting; trenchant; acute: *incisive* wit. **3** Pertaining to an incisor. Also **in·ci'so·ry** (-sər·ē). [<Med. L *incisivus*] — **in·ci'sive·ly** *adv.* — **in·ci'sive·ness** *n.*

in·ci·sor (in·sī'zər) *adj.* Adapted for cutting. — *n.* A front or cutting tooth; in man, one of eight such teeth, four in each jaw. [<NL]

in·ci·sure (in·sizh'ər) *n.* An incision; cut. [<L *incisura*]

in·ci·tant (in·sī'tənt) *adj.* Inciting; instigating. — *n.* One who or that which incites. [<L *incitans, -antis*, ppr. of *incitare*. See INCITE.]

in·ci·ta·tion (in'sī·tā'shən) *n.* **1** Incitement. **2** An incentive. [<OF <L *incitatio, -onis*]

in·cite (in·sīt') *v.t.* **·cit·ed, ·cit·ing** To urge to a particular action; instigate; stir up. See synonyms under ABET, ACTUATE, INFLUENCE, PERSUADE, SPUR, STIR. [<OF *inciter* <L *incitare*

incautious	**incognoscible**	**incompact**	**incompressibility**	**incondensability**	**inconsiderable**	**incontrollable**
incelebrity	**incoherentness**	**incompassionate**	**incompressible**	**incondensable**	**inconsolable**	**incontrovertibility**
incertain	**incohesive**	**incompliance**	**incomputable**	**inconducive**	**inconsonance**	**incontrovertible**
incircumspect	**incommutability**	**incompliant**	**inconcealable**	**inconformity**	**inconsonant**	**inconversant**
incogent	**incommutable**	**incomposite**	**inconcrete**	**inconsecutive**	**inconsumable**	**inconversion**

< *in-* thoroughly + *citare* rouse, freq. of *ciere* set in motion] — **in·ci′ta·tive** (-tə·tiv) *adj.* — **in·cit′er** *n.*

in·cite·ment (in·sīt′mənt) *n.* **1** The act of inciting. **2** That which incites; incentive; motive. See synonyms under IMPULSE.

in·ci·vil·i·ty (in′sə·vil′ə·tē) *n. pl.* **·ties 1** The state of being uncivil; discourteous manner. **2** An uncivil or rude act.

in·clasp (in·klasp′, -kläsp′) *v.t.* To enclasp.

in·clem·ent (in·klem′ənt) *adj.* Not clement; harsh; severe; rigorous, as weather; unpropitious or untoward. [<L *inclemens, -entis*] — **in·clem′en·cy** *n.*

in·cli·na·tion (in′klə·nā′shən) *n.* **1** Deviation from a given direction, especially from the vertical or horizontal. **2** The act of inclining or state of being inclined. **3** A slope or declivity. **4** A mental bent or tendency; predilection. **5** *Geom.* The angle between two lines, planes, etc. **6** *Astron.* The angle formed between the orbital plane of a planet and the ecliptic. [<F <L *inclinatio, -onis*] — **in·cli·na·to·ry** (in·klī′nə·tôr′ē, -tō′rē) *adj.*

Synonyms: appetite, attraction, bent, bias, desire, direction, disposition, drift, fancy, predilection, prepossession, proclivity, proneness, propensity, tendency. See AIM, APPETITE, ATTACHMENT, DESIRE, DIRECTION, FANCY, RELISH, WILL. *Antonyms*: aversion, disinclination, dislike, opposition, repulsion, resistance.

in·cline (in·klīn′) *v.* **·clined, ·clin·ing** *v.i.* **1** To deviate from the horizontal or vertical; slant; slope. **2** To have a tendency or disposition of the mind; be disposed or biased. **3** To tend in some quality or degree: purple *inclining* toward blue. **4** To bow or bend the head or body, as in courtesy. — *v.t.* **5** To cause to bend, lean, or slope. **6** To give a tendency or leaning to; influence. **7** To bow, as the head. See synonyms under ACTUATE, DRAW, INFLUENCE, LEAN[1], PERSUADE, TIP. — **to incline one's ear** To hear with favor; heed. — *n.* (in′klīn, in·klīn′) That which inclines from the horizontal; a gradient; slope. [<OF *encliner* <L *inclinare* < *in-* on + *clinare* lean] — **in·clin′a·ble** *adj.* — **in·clin′er** *n.*

in·clined (in·klīnd′) *adj.* **1** Bent out of line, or making an angle with some standard. **2** Having a tendency in some (specified) direction. **3** *Bot.* Bent out of the perpendicular, or with convex side up. **4** Toward the horizontal.

inclined plane A plane forming any but a right angle with a horizontal plane.

INCLINED PLANE
ab. Base.
bc. Height.
ac. Inclined plane.
bac. Angle formed by plane.

in·cli·nom·e·ter (in′klə·nom′ə·tər) *n.* **1** *Aeron.* An instrument for measuring inclination or slope of an aircraft with relation to the horizontal. **2** A magnetic needle pivoted to swing vertically in order to indicate the inclination of the earth's magnetic field; a dip needle. [<INCLIN(E) + -(O)METER]

in·close (in·klōz′), **in·clo·sure** (in·klō′zhər) See ENCLOSE, etc.

in·clude (in·klo͞od′) *v.t.* **·clud·ed, clud·ing 1** To have as a component part; contain. **2** To have or involve as a subordinate part, quality, element, etc.; imply: Religion *includes* morality. **3** To place in a general category, aggregate, etc. **4** To enclose within; confine. [<L *includere* < *in-* in + *claudere* shut] — **in·clud′a·ble, in·clud′i·ble** *adj.*

in·clud·ed (in·klo͞o′did) *adj. Bot.* Designating stamens or style not projecting above the corolla.

in·clu·sion (in·klo͞o′zhən) *n.* **1** The act of including. **2** That which is included. **3** *Mineral.* A substance either gaseous (as air), liquid (as water), or solid (as crystal), enclosed in a mineral, usually in a crystal. **4** *Biol.* Any inactive particle lodged in a living cell. [<L *inclusio, -onis* < *includere.* See INCLUDE.]

in·clu·sive (in·klo͞o′siv) *adj.* **1** Including the things, times, places, limits, or extremes mentioned: from A to Z *inclusive.* **2** Including within; surrounding: often with *of*: The list is *inclusive of* all the items. [<Med. L *inclusivus*] — **in·clu′sive·ly** *adv.* — **in·clu′sive·ness** *n.*

in·co·er·ci·ble (in′kō·ûr′sə·bəl) *adj.* **1** That cannot be coerced. **2** *Physics* Resistant to forces tending to change the form or properties of a substance or material.

in·cog·i·ta·ble (in·koj′ə·tə·bəl) *adj.* Not capable of being thought of; inconceivable. [<LL *incogitabilis*] — **in·cog′i·ta·bil′i·ty** *n.*

in·cog·i·tant (in·koj′ə·tənt) *adj.* Unthinking; thoughtless. [<L *incogitans, -antis*]

in·cog·ni·to (in·kog′nə·tō, in′kəg·nē′tō) *adj.* & *adv.* Unknown; under an assumed name, so as to avoid notice or ceremony. — *n. pl.* **·tos** (-tōz) **1** The state of being incognito. **2** One who passes under an assumed name. **3** The assumed name. [<Ital. <L *incognitus* unknown < *in-* not + *cognitus,* pp. of *cognoscere* know] — **in·cog′ni·ta** (-tə) *n.* & *adj. fem.*

in·co·her·ence (in′kō·hir′əns) *n.* **1** Want of coherence. **2** Looseness or separateness of material particles. **3** That which is incoherent. Also **in′co·her′en·cy.**

in·co·her·ent (in′kō·hir′ənt) *adj.* **1** Having little or no coherence; incongruous; unconnected. **2** Manifesting incoherence in thought, speech, or action. **3** Without physical coherence of parts. — **in′co·her′ent·ly** *adv.*

in·com·bus·ti·ble (in·kəm·bus′tə·bəl) *adj.* Incapable of burning or of being burned. — *n.* That which does not burn; an incombustible substance or material. — **in′com·bus′ti·bil′i·ty, in′com·bus′ti·ble·ness** *n.* — **in′com·bus′ti·bly** *adv.*

in·come (in′kum) *n.* **1** Money, or other benefit, periodically received; the amount so received. **2** The gain derived from capital, or labor, or both, inclusive of profit gained through the sale or conversion of capital assets. **3** *Obs.* The act of coming in; an incoming; specifically, the influx of divine grace into the soul. — **earned income** Income from labor, professional work, or business. — **unearned income** Income from capital investments, etc.

in·com·er (in′kum′ər) *n.* **1** One who or that which comes in. **2** One who follows or succeeds another.

income tax See under TAX.

in·com·ing (in′kum′ing) *adj.* Coming in or about to come in: an *incoming* tenant, *incoming* profits. — *n.* The act of coming in; entrance or arrival.

in·com·men·su·ra·ble (in′kə·men′shər·ə·bəl, -sər·ə-) *adj.* **1** Lacking a common measure or standard of comparison. **2** *Math.* Not expressible in terms of a common measure or unit: *incommensurable* numbers. **3** Conspicuously disproportionate. — *n.* That which is incommensurable. — **in′com·men′su·ra·bil′i·ty, in′com·men′su·ra·ble·ness** *n.* — **in′com·men′su·ra·bly** *adv.*

in·com·men·su·rate (in′kə·men′shər·it) *adj.* **1** Incommensurable. **2** Inadequate; disproportionate. — **in′com·men′su·rate·ly** *adv.* — **in′·com·men′su·rate·ness** *n.*

in·com·mode (in′kə·mōd′) *v.t.* **·mod·ed, ·mod·ing** To cause inconvenience to; disturb. [<F *incommoder* <L *incommodare* < *incommodus* inconvenient < *in-* not + *commodus* proper measure]

in·com·mo·di·ous (in′kə·mō′dē·əs) *adj.* Not commodious; not affording sufficient accommodation; inconvenient. — **in′com·mo′di·ous·ly** *adv.* — **in′com·mo′di·ous·ness** *n.* — **in′com·mod′i·ty** (-mod′ə·tē) *n.*

in·com·mu·ni·ca·ble (in′kə·myo͞o′nə·kə·bəl) *adj.* **1** Not capable of being communicated or imparted. **2** Incommunicative. — **in′com·mu′·ni·ca·bil′i·ty** *n.*

in·com·mu·ni·ca·do (in′kə·myo͞o′nə·kä′dō) *adj.* & *adv.* Confined without the opportunity to communicate, as a prisoner. [<Sp.]

in·com·mu·ni·ca·tive (in′kə·myo͞o′nə·kā′tiv, -kə·tiv) *adj.* Reserved; guarded in speech and manner. — **in′com·mu′ni·ca′tive·ly** *adv.* — **in′·com·mu′ni·ca′tive·ness** *n.*

in·com·pa·ra·ble (in·kom′pər·ə·bəl) *adj.* **1** Not admitting of comparison, as being inapproachable; peerless. **2** Unsuitable for comparison. See synonyms under RARE[1]. [<F] — **in·com′pa·ra·bil′i·ty, in·com′pa·ra·ble·ness** *n.* — **in·com′pa·ra·bly** *adv.*

in·com·pat·i·ble (in′kəm·pat′ə·bəl) *adj.* **1** Not compatible; incapable of existing together in agreement or harmony; discordant. **2** Incapable of coexisting. **3** *Med.* **a** Incapable of use in combination, as certain drugs. **b** Mutually antagonistic, as different blood types. **4** *Logic* Incapable of being true simultaneously: said of two or more propositions. — *n. Usually pl.* Incompatible persons or things. See synonyms under CONTRARY, INCONGRUOUS. — **in′·com·pat′i·bly** *adv.*

in·com·pat·i·bil·i·ty (in′kəm·pat′ə·bil′ə·tē) *n. pl.* **·ties 1** The quality of being incompatible: also **in′com·pat′i·ble·ness. 2** That which is incompatible. [<F *incompatibilité*]

in·com·pe·tent (in·kom′pə·tənt) *adj.* **1** Not competent; unable to do what is required. **2** Not legally qualified. See synonyms under BAD. — *n.* An incompetent person. [<F *incompétent*] — **in·com′pe·tence, in·com′pe·ten·cy** *n.* — **in·com′pe·tent·ly** *adv.*

in·com·plete (in′kəm·plēt′) *adj.* **1** Not complete; imperfect. **2** Lacking in certain parts, as some flowers. — **in′com·plete′ly** *adv.* — **in′·com·plete′ness** *n.* — **in′com·ple′tion** *n.*

in·com·pre·hen·si·ble (in′kom·pri·hen′sə·bəl, in·kom′-) *adj.* **1** Not comprehensible; not understandable; inconceivable. **2** *Archaic* That cannot be included or confined within limits. See synonyms under MYSTERIOUS. [<L *incomprehensibilis*] — **in·com′pre·hen·si·bil′i·ty, in·com′pre·hen′si·ble·ness** *n.* — **in·com′pre·hen′·si·bly** *adv.*

in·com·pre·hen·sion (in′kom·pri·hen′shən, in·kom′-) *n.* Lack of understanding.

in·com·pre·hen·sive (in′kom·pri·hen′siv, in·kom′-) *adj.* Not comprehensive; limited.

in·com·put·a·bil·i·ty (in′kəm·pyo͞o′tə·bil′ə·tē) *n.* That which is not computable.

in·con·ceiv·a·ble (in′kən·sē′və·bəl) *adj.* **1** That cannot be conceived; incomprehensible. **2** Incredible; impossible. **3** *Philos.* Involving a contradiction in terms; inherently contradictory. — **in′con·ceiv′a·ble·ness, in′con·ceiv′a·bil′i·ty** *n.* — **in′con·ceiv′a·bly** *adv.*

in·con·clu·sive (in′kən·klo͞o′siv) *adj.* **1** Not leading to an ultimate conclusion; indecisive. **2** Not achieving a definite result; ineffective: *inconclusive* efforts.

in·con·dite (in·kon′dit) *adj.* Badly constructed; irregular. [<L *inconditus* < *in-* not + *conditus,* pp. of *condere* put together]

in·con·gru·ent (in·kong′gro͞o·ənt) *adj.* Incongruous. — **in·con′gru·ence** *n.* — **in·con′gru·ent·ly** *adv.*

in·con·gru·i·ty (in′kən·gro͞o′ə·tē) *n. pl.* **·ties 1** The state of being incongruous; lack of harmony or suitableness. **2** That which is incongruous. [<Med. L *incongruitas, -tatis*]

in·con·gru·ous (in·kong′gro͞o·əs) *adj.* **1** Not congruous. **2** Composed of inharmonious elements. — **in·con′gru·ous·ly** *adv.* — **in·con′gru·ous·ness** *n.*

Synonyms: absurd, conflicting, contradictory, contrary, discordant, discrepant, ill-matched, inapposite, inappropriate, incommensurable, incompatible, inconsistent, inharmonious, irreconcilable, mismatched, mismated, repugnant, unsuitable. Two or more things that do not fit well together, or are not adapted to each other, are said to be *incongruous*; a thing is said to be *incongruous* that is not adapted to the time, place, or occasion; the term is also applied to a thing made up of ill-assorted parts or *inharmonious* elements. *Discordant* is applied to all things that jar like musical notes that are not in accord; *inharmonious* has the same original sense, but is a milder term. Things are *incompatible* which cannot exist together in harmonious relations, and whose action when associated tends to ultimate extinction of one by the other. *Inconsistent* applies to things that cannot be made to agree in thought with each other, or with some standard of truth or right; slavery and freedom are *inconsistent* with each other in theory, and *incompatible* in fact. *Incongruous*

inconvincibility
inconvincible
incoordinate
incorresponding
incorrodible
increate
incurability
incurable
incuriosity
incurious
indecipherability
indecipherable
indeclinable
indecorous
indecorum
indefensibility
indeficiency
indefinitive
indemonstrability
indemonstrable
indescribable
indestructibility
indestructible
indestructibleness
indetectable
indevotion
indevout
indiscernible
indiscoverable
indiscussible
indisposable
indistinguishable
indivertible
individable
indivinity

applies to relations, *unsuitable* to purpose or use; two colors are *incongruous* which cannot be agreeably associated: either may be *unsuitable* for a person, a room, or an occasion. *Incommensurable* is a mathematical term, applying to two or more quantities that have no common measure or aliquot part. See CONTRARY. *Antonyms*: accordant, agreeing, compatible, consistent, harmonious, suitable.

in·con·se·quent (in·kon′sə·kwənt) *adj.* 1 Contrary to reasonable inference. 2 Not according to sequence; hence, irrelevant. 3 Illogical in thought or action; eccentric. —**in·con′se·quence** *n.* —**in·con′se·quent·ly** *adv.*

inconsequent drainage In physical geography, drainage established prior to the deformation of the drained section, and continuing after such a change in the earth's surface.

in·con·se·quen·tial (in′kon·sə·kwen′shəl, in·kon′-) *adj.* 1 Of little consequence; trivial. 2 Irrelevant. —**in·con′se·quen′ti·al′i·ty** (-kwen′·shē·al′ə·tē) *n.* —**in·con′se·quen′tial·ly** *adv.*

in·con·sid·er·ate (in′kən·sid′ər·it) *adj.* 1 Not considerate; thoughtless. 2 Showing want of consideration. See synonyms under BLUFF, IMPRUDENT, INATTENTIVE. —**in′con·sid′er·ate·ly** *adv.* —**in′con·sid′er·ate·ness** *n.* —**in′con·sid′·er·a′tion** *n.*

in·con·sis·ten·cy (in′kən·sis′tən·sē) *n. pl.* **·cies** 1 The state or quality of being inconsistent; logical incompatibility; lack of uniformity or coherence in thought or conduct. 2 That which is inconsistent. Also **in′con·sis′tence.**

in·con·sis·tent (in′kən·sis′tənt) *adj.* 1 Logically incompatible. 2 Self-contradictory. 3 Not consistent; capricious. See synonyms under CONTRARY, INCONGRUOUS. —**in′con·sis′tent·ly** *adv.*

in·con·spic·u·ous (in′kən·spik′yōō·əs) *adj.* 1 Not conspicuous; not prominent. 2 Not attracting attention to oneself.

in·con·stant (in·kon′stənt) *adj.* Not constant; fickle; variable. See synonyms under FICKLE, VAIN. [<F <L *inconstans, -antis*] —**in·con′·stan·cy** *n.* —**in·con′stant·ly** *adv.*

in·con·test·a·ble (in′kən·tes′tə·bəl) *adj.* Not admitting of controversy. [<F]

Synonyms: certain, impregnable, incontrovertible, indisputable, indubitable, irrefragable, unassailable, undeniable, undoubted, unquestionable. *Antonyms*: apocryphal, doubtful, dubious, fictitious, hypothetical, problematical, questionable, uncertain, unsustained, unverified.

in·con·ti·nent (in·kon′tə·nənt) *adj.* 1 Not continent; exercising no control over the appetites, especially sexual passion; unchaste. 2 Unrestrained: an *incontinent* passion. 3 *Pathol.* Unable to hold back bodily discharges or evacuations. 4 *Obs.* Immediate. —*adv. Archaic* Immediately. [<OF <L *incontinens, -entis*. See IN-[1], CONTINENT.] —**in·con′ti·nence, in·con′ti·nen·cy** *n.* —**in·con′ti·nent·ly** *adv.*

in·con·ven·ience (in′kən·vēn′yəns) *n.* 1 The state of being inconvenient. 2 A disadvantage; embarrassment. Also **in′con·ven′ien·cy.** —*v.t.* **·ienced, ·ienc·ing** To cause inconvenience to; incommode; trouble. [<OF]

in·con·ven·ient (in′kən·vēn′yənt) *adj.* 1 Not convenient; incommodious; embarrassing. 2 Not expedient; unsuitable. [<OF *inconvenient* <L *inconveniens, -entis*. See IN-[1], CONVENIENT.] —**in′con·ven′ient·ly** *adv.*

in·con·vert·i·ble (in′kən·vûr′tə·bəl) *adj.* Not interchangeable, as paper money into specie. —**in′con·vert′i·bil′i·ty** *n.*

in·co·or·di·na·tion (in′kō·ôr′də·nā′shən) *n.* 1 Lack of coordination. 2 *Physiol.* **a** Lack of balance or harmony between moving parts. **b** Inability to effect voluntary muscular actions in proper order and at adequate speed.

in·cor·po·rate[1] (in·kôr′pə·rāt) *v.* **·rat·ed, ·rat·ing** *v.t.* 1 To take into or include as part of a mass or whole: His philosophy *incorporates* the ideas of Hegel. 2 To form into a legal corporation. 3 To combine or unite into one body or whole; blend; mix. 4 *Rare* To give material form to; embody. —*v.i.* 5 To become combined or united as one body or whole. 6 To form a legal corporation. See synonyms under ENROL, MIX, UNITE. —*adj.* (-pər·it) 1 Joined, or intimately associated. 2 Incorporated. [<LL *incorporatus*, pp. of *incorporare* embody <*in-* in + *corporare*. See CORPORATE.] —**in·cor′po·ra′tive** *adj.*

in·cor·po·rate[2] (in·kôr′pər·it) *adj.* 1 Not consisting of matter; incorporeal. 2 Not formed into a corporation. [<L *incorporatus*]

in·cor·po·rat·ed (in·kôr′pə·rā′tid) *adj.* 1 Constituting a legal corporation. 2 Combined.

in·cor·po·ra·tion (in·kôr′pə·rā′shən) *n.* 1 The act of incorporating. 2 A corporation. 3 The combining of elements.

in·cor·po·ra·tor (in·kôr′pə·rā′tər) *n.* 1 One who forms a corporation. 2 One of the members of a corporation named in the incorporating charter.

in·cor·po·re·al (in′kôr·pôr′ē·əl, -pō′rē-) *adj.* 1 Not consisting of matter; immaterial. 2 Pertaining to the immaterial world. 3 Not appreciable by the senses. 4 *Law* Having no material existence, but regarded as existing by the law; intangible: *incorporeal* rights. Also *Obs.* **in·cor′po·ral** (in·kôr′pər·əl). [<L *incorporeus*] —**in′cor·po′re·al·ism** *n.* —**in′cor·po′re·al·ly** *adv.*

in·cor·po·re·i·ty (in′kôr·pə·rē′ə·tē) *n. pl.* **·ties** 1 The quality of being not material. 2 An incorporeal entity.

in·corpse (in·kôrps′) *v.t. Obs.* To incorporate.

in·cor·rect (in′kə·rekt′) *adj.* 1 Inaccurate or untrue. 2 Not proper; unsuitable. 3 Erroneous; faulty. —**in′cor·rect′ly** *adv.*

in·cor·ri·gi·ble (in·kôr′ə·jə·bəl, -kor′-) *adj.* 1 That cannot be corrected. 2 Depraved beyond reform. —*n.* One who is beyond correction. [<MF <*in-* not + *corrigible*. See CORRIGIBLE.] —**in·cor′ri·gi·ble·ness, in·cor′ri·gi·bil′i·ty** *n.* —**in·cor′ri·gi·bly** *adv.*

in·cor·rupt (in′kə·rupt′) *adj.* 1 Not depraved nor defiled morally; above the power of bribes; pure. 2 Not marred in physical substance; not acted upon by decay. 3 Not tainted by other idioms: free from error, as a language. 4 Unchanged; unaltered, as a text. Also **in′cor·rupt′ed.** [<L *incorruptus* <*in-* not + *corruptus*. See CORRUPT.] —**in′cor·rupt′ly** *adv.* —**in′cor·rupt′ness** *n.* —**in′cor·rup′tion** (-rup′shən) *n.* —**in′cor·rup′tive** *adj.*

in·cor·rupt·i·ble (in′kə·rup′tə·bəl) *adj.* Incapable of corruption; especially, not accessible to bribery. See synonyms under FAITHFUL, IMMORTAL, JUST, MORAL. —**in′cor·rupt′i·bil′i·ty, in′cor·rupt′i·ble·ness** *n.* —**in′cor·rupt′i·bly** *adv.*

in·cras·sate (in·kras′āt) *v.t.* & *v.i.* **·sat·ed, ·sat·ing** 1 To make or become thick or thicker. 2 To thicken (a fluid), as by mixing or evaporation. —*adj. Biol.* Thickened, as the antennae or femora of certain insects: also **in·cras′sat·ed.** [<L *incrassatus*, pp. of *incrassare* <*in-* very + *crassus* thick]

in·cras·sa·tion (in′kra·sā′shən) *n.* 1 The act or process of thickening. 2 A thickening or swelling. —**in·cras·sa·tive** (in·kras′ə·tiv) *adj.*

in·crease (in·krēs′) *v.* **·creased, ·creas·ing** *v.i.* 1 To become greater, as in amount, size, degree, etc.; grow. 2 To grow in numbers, especially by reproduction: May your tribe *increase*. —*v.t.* 3 To make greater, as in amount, size, degree, etc.; augment; enlarge. —*n.* (in′krēs) 1 The act or process of growing larger, as in quantity, size, degree, etc.; augmentation; enlargement; extension. 2 An added or increased amount; increment: an *increase* in pay. 3 A production of offspring; propagation: blessed with a large *increase*. 4 Offspring; progeny. 5 *Archaic.* Crops of the earth. [<OF *encreistre* <L *increscere* <*in-* in + *crescere* grow <*creare* create] —**in·creas′a·ble** *adj.* —**in·creas′ing·ly** *adv.*

Synonyms (verb): advance, aggravate, augment, enhance, enlarge, exaggerate, extend, heighten, intensify, magnify, prolong, raise. See ADD, AGGRAVATE, AMPLIFY, FLOURISH, PROPAGATE, SWELL. *Antonyms*: abbreviate, abridge, contract, curtail, decrease, diminish.

Synonyms (noun): access, accession, accretion, addendum, addition, aggravation, amplification, appendage, augmentation, complement, enhancement, enlargement, expansion, extension, growth, harvest, improvement, increment, product, reenforcement, return. See ACCESSION, HARVEST, PROGRESS. *Antonyms*: abbreviation, contraction, deduction, diminution, expenditure, loss, subtraction, waste.

in·creas·er (in·krē′sər) *n.* 1 One who or that which increases. 2 A breeder; grower. 3 A pipefitting for joining the female end of a small pipe to the male end of a large one. 4 *Obs.* One who advances or promotes.

in·cred·i·bil·i·ty (in·kred′ə·bil′ə·tē) *n. pl.* **·ties** 1 The state or quality of being unbelievable or hard to believe. 2 An unbelievable thing.

in·cred·i·ble (in·kred′ə·bəl) *adj.* 1 Seeming too far-fetched or extraordinary to be possible. 2 Beyond or difficult of belief. —**in·cred′i·ble·ness** *n.* —**in·cred′i·bly** *adv.*

in·cre·du·li·ty (in′krə·dōō′lə·tē, -dyōō′-) *n.* Indisposition or refusal to believe. See synonyms under DOUBT. Also **in·cred·u·lous·ness** (in·krej′ə·ləs·nis). [<OF *incredulité*]

in·cred·u·lous (in·krej′ə·ləs) *adj.* 1 Refusing belief; skeptical. 2 Characterized by, caused by, or manifesting doubt. 3 *Obs.* Incredible. [<L *incredulus* <*in-* not + *credulus*. See CREDULOUS.] —**in·cred′u·lous·ly** *adv.*

in·cre·mate (in′krə·māt) *v.t. Obs.* **·mat·ed, ·mat·ing** To cremate.

in·cre·ment (in′krə·mənt) *n.* 1 The act of increasing; enlargement. 2 That which is added; increase: opposed to *decrement*. 3 *Math.* The amount by which a varying quantity increases between two of its stages. 4 *Mil.* The quantity of powder added to, or subtracted from, the propelling charge of separate loaded artillery ammunition to compensate for differences in range. See synonyms under INCREASE. —**unearned increment** Any increase of value produced by forces independent of the person who receives it; specifically, increase of value in land that springs from the increase of population or other cause independent of the land itself and of its owner. [<L *incrementum* <*increscere* INCREASE] —**in′cre·men′tal** (-men′·təl) *adj.*

in·cres·cent (in·kres′ənt) *adj.* Characterized by increase; growing: said especially of the moon. [<L *increscens, -entis*, ppr. *of increscere* INCREASE]

in·cre·tion (in·krē′shən) *n.* Internal secretion or its product; a hormone. [<IN-[2] + (SE)CRETION]

in·crim·i·nate (in·krim′ə·nāt) *v.t.* **·nat·ed, ·nat·ing** 1 To charge with a crime or fault; accuse. 2 To show or appear to show the guilt or error of. [<Med. L *incriminatus*, pp. of *incriminare* <*in-* in + *criminare* accuse one of a crime] —**in·crim′i·na′tion** *n.* —**in·crim′i·na·to′ry** (-nə·tôr′ē, -tō′rē) *adj.*

in·croy·a·ble (aṅ·krwä·yá′bl′) *n. French* A member of the Royalist party in France who affected extravagance and foppery in dress and language during the French Directorate (1795–99). [<F, lit., incredible]

in·crust (in·krust′) *v.t.* 1 To cover with a crust or hard coat. 2 To decorate, as with jewels. Also spelled *encrust*. [<OF *encrouster* <L *incrustare* <*in-* on + *crustare* form a crust]

in·crus·ta·tion (in′krus·tā′shən) *n.* 1 The act of incrusting, or the state of being incrusted. 2 A crust, coating, or scale on the surface of a body.

in·cu·bate (in′kyə·bāt, ing′-) *v.* **·bat·ed, ·bat·ing** *v.t.* 1 To sit upon (eggs) in order to hatch; brood. 2 To hatch (eggs) in this manner or by artificial heat. 3 To maintain under conditions favoring optimum growth or development, as bacterial cultures. —*v.i.* 4 To sit on eggs; brood. 5 To undergo incubation. [<L *incubatus*, pp. of *incubare* <*in-* on + *cubare* lie] —**in′cu·ba′tive** *adj.*

in·cu·ba·tion (in′kyə·bā′shən, ing′-) *n.* 1 The act of hatching. 2 State of being hatched.

indivision	**inductile**	**ineffaceable**	**inelegance**	**inenergetic**	**inerrability**	**inevident**
indocibility	**inductility**	**inefficacious**	**inelegancy**	**inequable**	**inerrable**	**inexcitable**
indocible	**indurable**	**inefficacy**	**ineloquence**	**inequitable**	**inerratic**	**inexcusability**
indocile	**ineconomic**	**ineffulgent**	**ineloquent**	**ineradicable**	**inerroneous**	**inexecution**
indocility	**ineffaceability**	**inelaborate**	**ineludible**	**inerasable**	**inerudite**	**inexertion**

3 A planning or producing. 4 Figuratively, a brooding upon, especially that of the Spirit of God over chaos at the Creation (*Gen.* i 2). 5 *Med.* The period between the time of exposure to an infectious disease and its development. [<L *incubatio, -onis*]

in·cu·ba·tor (in′kyə·bā′tər, ing′-) *n.* 1 An apparatus kept at a uniform warmth, as by a lamp, for artificial hatching of eggs. 2 *Bacteriol.* An apparatus for artificial development of micro-organisms, as bacteria, especially one in which the temperature may be regulated. 3 An appliance for keeping warm a prematurely born child. 4 One who or that which incubates. [<L, a hatcher]

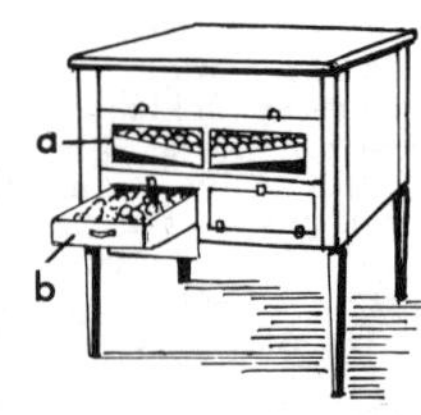

INCUBATOR
a. Egg tray.
b. Nursery drawer.
Incubators are variously heated by attached gas- or oil-fired heating units or by electrical units.

in·cu·bus (in′kyə·bəs, ing′-) *n. pl.* **·bus·es** or **·bi** (-bī) 1 Anything that tends to weigh down or discourage. 2 A nightmare. 3 A demon supposed to descend upon sleeping persons with whom it sought to have sexual intercourse. Compare SUCCUBUS. See synonyms under LOAD. [<Med. L, a demon that causes nightmare <LL, nightmare <L *incubare* lie on]

in·cu·des (in·kyōō′dēz) Plural of INCUS.

in·cul·cate (in·kul′kāt, in′kul-) *v.t.* **·cat·ed, ·cat·ing** To impress upon the mind by frequent and emphatic repetition; instil. See synonyms under IMPRESS. [<L *inculcatus*, pp. of *inculcare* tread on < *in-* on + *calcare* tread < *calx, calcis* heel] — **in·cul·ca·tion** (in′kul·kā′shən) *n.* — **in′cul·ca′tor** *n.*

in·cul·pa·ble (in·kul′pə·bəl) *adj.* Not culpable.

in·cul·pate (in·kul′pāt, in′kul-) *v.t.* **·pat·ed, ·pat·ing** 1 To charge with fault; blame. 2 To involve in guilt; implicate. [<Med. L *inculpatus*, pp. of *inculpare* blame < *in-* in + *culpa* fault] — **in′cul·pa′tion** *n.* — **in·cul′pa·to′ry** (-pə·tôr′ē, -tō′rē) *adj.*

in·cult (in·kult′) *adj. Obs.* 1 Uncultivated; unpolished. 2 Wanting in refinement. [<L < *in-* not + *cultus*, pp. of *colere* cultivate]

in·cum·ben·cy (in·kum′bən·sē) *n. pl.* **·cies** 1 The state of holding an office or discharging its duties or functions. 2 The period during which an office is held. 3 The state of being incumbent, or that which is incumbent, as a mental or physical burden. 4 *Rare* An obligation.

in·cum·bent (in·kum′bənt) *adj.* 1 Resting upon one as a moral obligation, or as necessary under the circumstances; obligatory. 2 Resting, leaning, or weighing wholly or partly upon something. — *n.* One who holds an office or performs official duties. [<L *incumbens, -entis*, ppr. of *incumbere* recline < *in-* on + *cubare* lie down]

in·cum·ber (in·kum′bər), **in·cum·brance** (in·kum′brəns), etc. See ENCUMBER, etc.

in·cu·nab·u·la (in′kyōō·nab′yə·lə) *n. pl. of* **in·cu·nab·u·lum** (-ləm) The beginnings or the earliest monuments of an art, race, or development; cradle; birthplace; specifically, specimens of printing and block engraving that appeared before A.D. 1500. [<L < *in-* in + *cunabula*, dim. of *cunae* a cradle] — **in′·cu·nab′u·lar** *adj.*

in·cur (in·kûr′) *v.t.* **·curred, ·cur·ring** To meet with or become subject to, as unpleasant consequences, especially through one's own action; bring upon oneself. [<L *incurrere* run into < *in-* in + *currere* run]

in cu·ri·a (in kyōōr′ē·ə) *Latin* In court.

in·cur·rent (in·kûr′ənt) *adj.* Having or characterized by an inward-flowing current. [<L *incurrens, -entis*, ppr. of *incurrere* INCUR]

in·cur·sion (in·kûr′zhən, -shən) *n.* A hostile entrance into a territory; a temporary invasion; raid. See synonyms under AGGRESSION, ATTACK, INVASION. [<L *incursio, -onis* < *incurrere* INCUR] — **in·cur′sive** *adj.*

in·cur·vate (in·kûr′vāt) *v.t.* & *v.i.* **·vat·ed, ·vat·ing** To curve; bend, especially inwards. — *adj.* Curved. [<L *incurvatus*, pp. of *incurvare* curve inward < *in-* in + *curvare* curve]

in·cur·va·tion (in′kər·vā′shən) *n.* 1 The state of being curved or bent. 2 The act of bending. 3 The growing inward of the nails. 4 An ingrowing nail.

in·curve (in·kûrv′) *v.t.* & *v.i.* To curve inward. — *n.* (in′kûrv′) In baseball, a pitched ball that curves inward toward the batter.

in·cus (ing′kəs) *n. pl.* **in·cu·des** (in·kyōō′dēz) 1 *Anat.* The central one of three small bones in the tympanum or middle ear; so called from its fancied resemblance to an anvil. See illustration under EAR. 2 *Meteorol.* The anvil-shaped upper part of a cumulonimbus cloud; an anviltop. [<L, anvil] — **in′cu·dal** *adj.*

in·cuse (in·kyōōz′) *adj.* Formed by hammering or stamping. — *n.* An impression made by striking a coin with or against a die. [<L *incusus*, pp. of *incudere* forge with a hammer < *in-* on + *cudere* beat]

Ind (ind) 1 *Poetic* India. 2 *Obs.* The Indies.

In·da (in′də) See INDRA.

in·da·ba (in·dä′bä) *n.* A great meeting of South African natives; parliament; council. [<Zulu *in-daba* subject, matter]

in·da·gate (in′də·gāt) *v.t. Obs.* **·gat·ed, ·gat·ing** To investigate. [<L *indagatus*, pp. of *indagare* investigate] — **in′da·ga′tion** *n.* — **in′da·ga′tor** *n.*

in·da·mine (in′də·mēn, -min) *Chem.* Any of a class of weak, unstable, organic bases derived from anilines which form bluish and greenish salts: also called *phenylene blue.* Also **in′da·min** (-min). [<IND(IGO) + AMINE]

in·debt·ed (in·det′id) *adj.* 1 Having contracted a debt. 2 Owing gratitude; beholden. [<OF *endetté*, pp. of *endetter* < *en-* on + *dette* debt. See DEBT.]

in·debt·ed·ness (in·det′id·nis) *n.* 1 The state of being indebted. 2 The amount of one's debts.

in·de·cen·cy (in·dē′sən·sē) *n. pl.* **·cies** 1 The condition of being indecent; especially, vulgarity or immorality in actions, spoken or printed words, pictures, etc. 2 An indecent act. 3 Obscenity.

Synonyms: coarseness, filthiness, foulness, grossness, immodesty, impropriety, impurity, indecorum, indelicacy, obscenity, offensiveness, uncleanness, unseemliness, vileness. See OUTRAGE. *Antonyms*: delicacy, modesty, nicety, propriety, purity, refinement.

in·de·cent (in·dē′sənt) *adj.* 1 Offensive to decency or propriety; immodest; gross. 2 Contrary to what is fit and proper. See synonyms under IMMODEST. — **in·de′cent·ly** *adv.*

in·de·cid·u·ate (in′də·sij′ōō·it) *adj.* Without a decidua.

in·de·cid·u·ous (in′də·sij′ōō·əs) *adj. Bot.* Not dropping off at maturity; evergreen.

in·de·ci·sive (in′də·sī′siv) *adj.* 1 Not decisive. 2 Hesitant; irresolute. — **in′de·ci′sive·ly** *adv.* — **in′de·ci′sion** *n.*

in·deed (in·dēd′) *adv.* In fact; in truth: used to emphasize an affirmation, to mark a qualifying word or clause, to denote a concession, or interrogatively for the purpose of drawing forth confirmation of a fact stated. — *interj.* An exclamation of surprise, irony, incredulity, etc. [<IN + DEED]

in·de·fat·i·ga·ble (in′də·fat′ə·gə·bəl) *adj.* Not yielding readily to fatigue; tireless; unflagging. [<MF *indéfatigable* <L *indefatigabilis* < *in-* not + *defatigare* tire out] — **in′de·fat′i·ga·bil′·i·ty, in′de·fat′i·ga·ble·ness** *n.* — **in′de·fat′i·ga·bly** *adv.*

Synonyms: assiduous, indomitable, industrious, never-failing, never-tiring, persevering, persistent, tireless, unfailing, unfaltering, unflagging, untiring, unwearied. *Antonyms*: defeated, despondent, discouraged, fainting, faltering, flagging, indolent, negligent, remiss, wearied.

in·de·fea·si·ble (in′də·fē′zə·bəl) *adj.* Not defeasible; incapable of being annulled, set aside, or made void. — **in′de·fea′si·bil′i·ty** *n.* — **in′de·fea′si·bly** *adv.*

in·de·fen·si·ble (in′di·fen′sə·bəl) *adj.* 1 Incapable of being justified, excused, etc. 2 Incapable of being defended.

in·de·fin·a·ble (in′di·fī′nə·bəl) *adj.* That cannot be defined or described; vague; subtle. — **in′·de·fin′a·ble·ness** *n.* — **in′de·fin′a·bly** *adv.*

in·def·i·nite (in·def′ə·nit) *adj.* 1 Not definite or precise. 2 Indeterminate; without fixed boundaries; incapable of measurement. 3 So large as to have no definite or particular limit; also, infinite. 4 *Bot.* Uncertain: said of stamens when too many to be counted easily, and of inflorescence when not terminated absolutely by a flower. 5 *Gram.* Not defining or determining; tending to generalize, as the *indefinite* articles *a* and *an.* See synonyms under EQUIVOCAL, VAGUE. — **in·def′i·nite·ly** *adv.* — **in·def′i·nite·ness** *n.*

indefinite pronoun See under PRONOUN.

in·de·his·cent (in′də·his′ənt) *adj. Bot.* Not opening spontaneously or naturally when ripe: said of certain grains and fruits. — **in′de·his′·cence** *n.*

in·del·i·ble (in·del′ə·bəl) *adj.* That cannot be blotted out; ineffaceable. [<L *indelibilis* < *in-* not + *delibilis* perishable < *delere* destroy] — **in·del′i·bil′i·ty, in·del′i·ble·ness** *n.* — **in·del′i·bly** *adv.*

in·del·i·ca·cy (in·del′ə·kə·sē) *n. pl.* **·cies** 1 The quality of being indelicate; coarseness. 2 An act offensive to propriety or refined feeling.

in·del·i·cate (in·del′ə·kit) *adj.* Not delicate; offensive to propriety; immodest. See synonyms under IMMODEST. — **in·del′i·cate·ly** *adv.*

in·dem·ni·fy (in·dem′nə·fī) *v.t.* **·fied, ·fy·ing** 1 To compensate for loss or damage sustained. 2 To make good (a loss). 3 To give security against future loss or punishment to. See synonyms under PAY. [<L *indemnis* unhurt (< *in-* not + *damnum* harm) + -FY] — **in·dem′ni·fi·ca′tion** *n.* — **in·dem′ni·tor** (-nə·tər) *n.*

in·dem·ni·ty (in·dem′nə·tē) *n. pl.* **·ties** 1 That which is given as compensation for a loss or for damage. 2 An undertaking to remunerate another for loss or to protect him against liability. 3 Exemption from penalties or liabilities incurred. See synonyms under RECOMPENSE, RESTITUTION, SUBSIDY. [<F *indemnité* <L *indemnitas* < *indemnis.* See INDEMNIFY.]

indemnity bond See under BOND.

in·dene (in′dēn) *n. Chem.* A colorless, oily hydrocarbon, C_9H_8, obtained from coal tar by fractional distillation. [<IND(OLE) + -ENE]

in·dent (in·dent′) *v.t.* 1 To set, as the first line of a paragraph, in from the margin. 2 To cut or mark the edge of with toothlike hollows or notches; serrate. 3 To make an order for goods upon. 4 To make an order for (goods). 5 To cut or tear (a document drawn in duplicate) along an irregular line in order to identify the halves when fitted together. 6 To cut or tear the edge or top of (a document) in an irregular line. 7 To indenture, as an apprentice. — *v.i.* 8 To be notched or cut; form a recess. 9 To set a line, etc., in from the margin. 10 To make out an order in duplicate; make a requisition. 11 *Archaic* To enter into a bargain or covenant. — *n.* (in′dent, in·dent′) 1 A cut or notch in the edge of anything; an opening like a notch; an indentation or impression. 2 An indented contract; indenture. 3 An indented certificate issued by the United States government at the close of the American Revolution, for principal or interest due on the public debt. 4 An official order for supplies. 5 In commerce, a foreign order for goods, with or without specified particulars as to quality, price, mode of shipment, etc. 6 An indention. [<OF *endenter* <Med. L *indentare* < *in-* in + *dens, dentis* tooth]

in·den·ta·tion (in′den·tā′shən) *n.* 1 The act of denting. 2 A cut or notch in an edge or border. 3 An indention. See synonyms under HOLE.

in·dent·ed (in·den′tid) *adj.* 1 *Archit.* **a** Notched or serrated. **b** Formed into several angles: said of a parapet. 2 *Her.* Toothed like a saw. 3 In printing or typewriting, set in from the margin. 4 Indentured.

in·den·tion (in·den′shən) *n.* 1 A dent. 2 *Printing* **a** The setting in of a line or body of type at the left side. **b** The space thus left blank.

inexhausted
inexhaustibility
inexistence
inexistency
inexistent
inexpectant
inexpedience
inexpediency
inexpedient
inexperience
inexpert
inexpiable
inexplainable
inexplicability
inexplicit
inexplosive
inexpressive
inextensibility
inextensible
inextension
inextinguishable
infeasible
infecund
infecundity
infelonious
infeminine
infrequence
infrugal
inhomogeneity
inhomogeneous
inirritability
inobservable
inobtrusive
inoppressive
inoppugnable

—hanging indention *Printing* Equal indention of all lines of a paragraph except the first, which is not indented.

in·den·ture (in·den′chər) *n.* **1** *Law* An instrument of contract under seal; an instrument in duplicate between parties, each party keeping a counterpart. **2** *Often pl.* A legal instrument for binding an apprentice or a servant to his master. **3** The act of indenting, or the state of being indented. —*v.t.* **·tured, ·tur·ing 1** To bind by indenture, as an apprentice. **2** To indent; furrow. [<OF *endenture* <Med. L *indentare.* See INDENT.]

in·de·pen·dence (in′di·pen′dəns) *n.* **1** Freedom from dependence upon others, as for government or financial support. **2** A competency. **3** A spirit of self–reliance. See synonyms under LIBERTY, WEALTH. See DECLARATION OF INDEPENDENCE.

Independence Day The Fourth of July: so called in the United States in commemoration of the Declaration of Independence, adopted July 4, 1776.

in·de·pen·den·cy (in′di·pen′dən·sē) *n. pl.* **·cies 1** Independence. **2** An independent state or territory.

In·de·pen·den·cy (in′di·pen′dən·sē) *n. Eccl.* The doctrine that each congregation of the Christian church is an entity independent of central ecclesiastical control.

in·de·pen·dent (in′di·pen′dənt) *adj.* **1** Not subordinate or subject to nor dependent for support upon another government, person, or thing. **2** Affording means of independence or freedom of action. **3** Indicating self–reliance; resentful of, or uninfluenced by, advice or assistance. **4** Separate or disconnected. **5** Pertaining to the Independents or Congregationalists. **6** Not identified with any political party. **7** Possessing sufficient means to live without labor. **8** *Math.* **a** Capable of taking any value without regard to the variation of other quantities. **b** Denoting two or more quantities such that the value of none of them depends upon that of the others. —*n.* **1** One who exercises his own will or judgment without the guidance or control of others. **2** *Often cap.* One who is not an adherent of any political party. **—in′de·pen′·dent·ly** *adv.*

In·de·pen·dent (in′di·pen′dənt) *n.* **1** A believer in Independency. **2** In England, a Congregationalist.

independent clause *Gram.* A clause capable of constituting a sentence.

in–depth (in′depth′) *adj.* Extensive and thorough; not superficial; penetrating or profound: an *in–depth* study of world–wide intelligence operations.

in·de·ter·mi·na·ble (in′di·tûr′mi·nə·bəl) *adj.* **1** Not capable of exact determination or measurement. **2** Not decided or clearly established. **—in′de·ter′mi·na·bly** *adv.*

in·de·ter·mi·na·cy (in′di·tûr′mə·nə·sē) *n.* The state of being indefinite or undetermined; lack of certainty.

indeterminacy principle The uncertainty principle.

in·de·ter·mi·nate (in′di·tûr′mə·nit) *adj.* **1** Not definite in extent, amount, or nature. **2** Not clear or precise; vague. **3** Not decided; unsettled. **4** *Bot.* Not definitely terminated, as a raceme. **5** *Math.* Designating any of a class of undefined expressions, as infinity minus infinity, zero divided by infinity, zero to the zero power, etc. **—in′de·ter′mi·nate·ly** *adv.* **—in′de·ter′mi·nate·ness** *n.*

in·de·ter·mi·na·tion (in′di·tûr′mə·nā′shən) *n.* **1** Lack of determination. **2** The state of being indeterminate.

in·de·ter·min·ism (in′di·tûr′mə·niz′əm) *n.* The doctrine that the will, while influenced, is not absolutely determined by motives or environment. **—in′de·ter′min·ist** *n.*

in·dex (in′deks) *n. pl.* **·dex·es** or **·di·ces** (-də·sēz) **1** Anything used to indicate, point out, or guide, as the index finger, or forefinger, the hand of a clock, a pointer, etc. **2** Anything that manifests or denotes: an *index* of character. **3** An alphabetic list of matters or references, as in a book. **4** *Math.* An exponent. **5** A mark [☞] employed to direct attention. **6** A numerical expression of the ratio between one dimension or magnitude and another with which it is regarded as comparable: the cephalic *index.* **7** *Obs.* A prolog; prelude. —*v.t.* **1** To provide with an index. **2** To enter in an index. **3** To indicate; mark. [<L. See INDICATE.] **—in′dex·er** *n.* **—in·dex′i·cal** *adj.*

In·dex (in′deks) *n.* A list of interdicted books prepared by the Holy Office of the Roman Catholic Church. The *Index Expurgatorius,* no longer officially prepared, indicated those books which, with certain expurgations, might be read; the *Index Librorum Prohibitorum,* those which are forbidden.

index finger The forefinger: so called from its universal use as a pointer or indicator.

index number *Stat.* Any of a series of numbers indicating the quantitative time changes in a given statistical aggregate, as prices, costs, etc., with reference to an arbitrary base (usually 100) which represents the status of the aggregate at a specified previous time or period.

index of refraction *Optics* The ratio of the sine of the angle of incidence to that of the angle of refraction when light enters a transparent substance.

In·di·a (in′dē·ə) The central peninsula of southern Asia, south of the Himalayas; 1,581,000 square miles: ancient *Bharat;* divided into: (1) the **Republic of India,** a self–governing member of the Commonwealth of Nations; 1,138,814 square miles; capital, New Delhi; (2) Pakistan; (3) several smaller states unaffiliated with the Commonwealth.

India ink 1 A black pigment composed of a mixture of lampblack or burnt cork with gelatin and water, originally made in India, China, and Japan and molded in sticks or cakes. **2** A liquid ink made from this pigment. **3** Any of various heavy drawing inks in different colors, especially one containing sepia. Also called *Chinese ink.*

In·di·a·man (in′dē·ə·mən) *n. pl.* **·men** (-mən) A large merchant ship in the India trade, especially one in the service of the East India Company.

In·di·an (in′dē·ən) *adj.* **1** Pertaining to India or the East Indies or to Indians. **2** Pertaining to the American aboriginal race or to the West Indies. **3** Made from maize. —*n.* **1** A native of India or of the East Indies. **2** A member of the aboriginal race of America (American Indian) or of the West Indies. **3** Loosely, any of the languages of the American Indians. [<L *India* <Gk. <*Indos* the Indus river <OPersian *Hindu* India <Skt. *sindhu* river. Cf. HINDI.

In·di·an·a (in′dē·an′ə) A north central State of the United States; 36,291 square miles; capital, Indianapolis; entered the Union Dec. 11, 1816; nickname, *Hoosier State*: abbr. IN **—In′·di·an′i·an** *adj. & n.*

Indian agent *U.S. & Canadian* A federal representative in Indian affairs, often on a reservation.

In·di·an·ap·o·lis (in′dē·ə·nap′ə·lis) The capital of Indiana.

Indian bean The catalpa tree *(Catalpa bignoniodes)* of China, the West Indies, and the United States: it yields a fine, durable wood adapted for cabinetwork.

Indian bread Tuckahoe.

Indian clubs See under CLUB[1].

Indian corn Maize.

Indian Desert See THAR DESERT.

Indian field *U.S.* A clearing in a forest, known or believed to have once been cultivated by Indians.

Indian file Single file: the usual order of the American Indians when walking a trail.

Indian giver *U.S. Colloq.* One who gives a present and then wants it back.

Indian hemp 1 The common Asian hemp *(Cannabis sativa).* **2** A perennial American herb *(Apocynum cannabinum)* of the dogbane family, with a tough bark, greenish–white flowers, and a milky juice: its dried roots have medicinal properties: also called *Canada hemp, hemp dogbane, Indian physic.*

Indian licorice Jequirity.

Indian mallow A tall weed *(Abutilon incanum)* with large velvety leaves and small yellow flowers.

Indian meal Cornmeal.

Indian millet The tall grass *(Sorghum vulgare)* of which sorgo, broomcorn, and durra are varieties.

Indian mulberry The aal.

Indian Mutiny An uprising in India (1857–1858) occasioned by native resentment against British colonial policies: also called *Sepoy Mutiny.*

Indian Ocean The smallest of the three great oceans of the world, bounded by Africa, Asia, Australia, and Antarctica; 28,357,000 square miles.

Indian paintbrush A flower, the painted cup.

Indian physic 1 Either of two perennial herbs (genus *Gillenia*) common in the woods of the United States, and reputed to be emetic, cathartic, or tonic, according to the dose. **2** Indian hemp (def. 2).

Indian pipe A low, smooth, waxy–white, one–flowered, saprophytic, somewhat pipe–shaped herb *(Monotropa uniflora)* common in moist woodlands of Asia and North America.

Indian pudding A pudding made with cornmeal, milk, and molasses.

Indian red 1 A pure native iron oxide found in India and used as a pigment. **2** A red earth used by the American Indian and by early American painters.

Indian rice See WILD RICE.

Indian River A lagoon of eastern Florida, extending 120 miles between the mainland and a coastal strip.

Indian States Formerly, the 560 semi–independent states of British India ruled by native princes: also *Native States.*

Indian summer See under SUMMER.

Indian Territory Formerly, a Territory of the United States: now a part of Oklahoma.

Indian tobacco An erect, hairy, branched herb *(Lobelia inflata)* with ovate, obtusely toothed leaves and small, pale–blue flowers. Compare LOBELINE.

Indian turnip Jack–in–the–pulpit.

In·di·an–wres·tle (in′dē·ən·res′əl) *v.i.* **·tled, ·tling** To engage in any of various contests of strength and agility in which two people grasp hands, lock legs, etc., and attempt to force each other into an inferior position.

India paper 1 A thin, yellowish, absorbent printing paper, made in China and Japan from vegetable fiber, and used in taking the finest proofs from engraved plates. **2** A thin, tough, and opaque printing paper, originally from the Orient, used for Bibles, etc.

India print Lightweight cotton fabric, usually handblocked in Oriental patterns and rich colors.

India proof A proof taken on India paper.

India rubber A soft and elastic substance derived from the sap of various tropical plants and having many uses in industry and the arts; caoutchouc. See RUBBER.

In·dic (in′dik) *adj.* Pertaining to India, its peoples, languages, and culture; Indian. —*n.* A branch of the Indo–Iranian subfamily of Indo–European languages, including many of the ancient and modern languages of India, as Sanskrit, Gujarati, Hindi, Bengali, Romany, etc. [<L *Indicus* <Gk. *Indikos* <*India* INDIA]

in·di·can (in′də·kən) *n.* **1** *Chem.* A colorless, crystalline, toxic glycoside, $C_{14}H_{17}O_6N$, contained in several species of indigo plants. **2** *Biochem.* Potassium indoxyl sulfate, $C_8H_6NSO_4K$, contained in the urine and other body fluids of certain animals, including man:

inopulent	**insapient**	**insonorous**	**intranquility**	**intranslatable**	**inurbanity**	**inverity**
inostensible	**insaturable**	**insubduable**	**intranscalent**	**intransmissible**	**inutilized**	**invirile**
insagacity	**insensuous**	**insubmergible**	**intransferable**	**intransmutable**	**inutterable**	**invirility**
insalutary	**inseverable**	**insubmissible**	**intransformable**	**intransparent**	**invalorous**	**inviscid**
insalvable	**insolidity**	**insubvertible**	**intransfusible**	**inurbane**	**inverisimilitude**	**invital**

add,āce,câre,pälm; end,ēven; it,īce; odd,ōpen,ôrder; to͝ok,po͞ol; up,bûrn; ə = a in *above,* e in *sicken,* i in *clarity,* o in *melon,* u in *focus;* yo͞o = u in *fuse;* oi,oil; ou,pout; ch,check; g,go; ng,ring; th,thin; th,this; zh,vision. Foreign sounds à,œ,ü,kh,ṅ; and ◆: see page xx. <from; + plus; ? possibly.

also called *uroxanthin.* [<L *indicum* INDIGO + -AN]

in·di·cant (in′də·kənt) *adj.* Indicating. — *n.* An indicator.

in·di·cate (in′də·kāt) *v.t.* **·cat·ed, ·cat·ing 1** To be or give a sign of; betoken: Those clouds *indicate* rain. **2** To point out; direct attention to: to *indicate* the correct page. **3** To express or make known, especially briefly or indirectly: His smile *indicates* his approval. **4** *Med.* To show or suggest, as a disease or its remedy: said of symptoms, etc. [<L *indicatus,* pp. of *indicare* < *in-* in + *dicare* point out, proclaim] — **in′di·ca·to′ry** (-kə·tôr′ē, -tō′rē) *adj.*

in·di·ca·tion (in′də·kā′shən) *n.* **1** The act of indicating, in any sense; manifestation; prediction. **2** That which indicates or suggests; a token; sign; symptom. **3** *Med.* The manifestation afforded by the symptoms of a disease as to the course of treatment. See synonyms under CHARACTERISTIC, MARK[1], SIGN. [<F]

in·dic·a·tive (in·dik′ə·tiv) *adj.* **1** Suggestive; giving intimation. **2** *Gram.* Of or pertaining to a mood in which an act or condition is stated or questioned as an actual fact, rather than as a potentiality or an unrealized condition. — *n. Gram.* The indicative mood, or a verb in this mood. — **in·dic′a·tive·ly** *adv.*

in·di·ca·tor (in′də·kā′tər) *n.* **1** One who or that which indicates or points out. **2** Any contrivance or apparatus, automatic or otherwise, which makes a mark, record, or sign to indicate the condition or position of something: a water gage; a speed indicator; a dial showing the position of elevators, cages, etc.; a device for recording the arrival and departure of trains, the number of fares collected in street cars, etc. **3** An instrument attached to a steam engine which, by the action of the steam itself, draws an **indicator-diagram** from which may be ascertained the gross power, the correct adjustment of the distribution valves, the ratio of the pressure in the cylinder to the boiler pressure, etc. **4** *Chem.* A substance, as litmus, potassium permanganate, etc., which colors a solution and by its disappearance, reappearance, or change of color when a reagent is added, indicates alkalinity, acidity, etc. **5** *Ecol.* A type of vegetation or plant growth serving to indicate the general character of a habitat. [<LL]

in·di·ca·tor-reg·u·la·tor (in′də·kā′tər·reg′yə·lā′·tər) *n. Mil.* A device which supplies data on the various elements, as timing, elevation, etc., required for accurate firing of a gun.

in·di·ces (in′də·sēz) Plural of INDEX: used especially in mathematical or other abstract works.

in·di·cia (in·dish′ə) *n. pl. sing.,* **·di·cium** (-dish′·əm) Discriminating marks; indications; badges; tokens; symptoms. [<L, pl. of *indicium* sign]

in·dict (in·dīt′) *v.t.* **1** *Law* To prefer an indictment against: said of the action of grand juries. **2** To charge with a crime. See synonyms under ARRAIGN. ◆ Homophone: *indite.* [<AF *enditer* make known, inform; later infl. in form by Med. L *dictare* accuse. Related to INDITE.] — **in·dict′a·ble** *adj.* — **in·dict·ee** (in·dī·tē′) *n.* — **indict′er, in·dict′or** *n.*

in·dic·tion (in·dik′shən) *n.* **1** A cycle of fifteen years, introduced by Constantine as a fiscal term, and adopted by the popes as part of their chronological system. **2** The number of one of these cycles, or that of any particular year in its cycle. [<OF <L *indictio, -onis* < *indicere* announce < *in-* in + *dicere* say, tell]

in·dict·ment (in·dīt′mənt) *n.* **1** The act of indicting, or the state of being indicted; formal charge or accusation in general. **2** A formal written charge of crime, preferred at the suit of the government and presented by a grand jury on oath to the court in which it is impaneled, as the basis for trial of the accused; the legal document itself. [<AF *enditement*]

In·dies (in′dēz) **1** The East Indies. **2** The East Indies, India, and Indochina. **3** The West Indies.

in·dif·fer·ence (in·dif′ər·əns) *n.* **1** The state of being unconcerned or indifferent; lack of interest or feeling; apathy; freedom from prejudice or bias. **2** The quality of not arousing interest or approval; a low degree of excellence; immateriality; slight importance. See synonyms under APATHY, NEGLECT. Also **in·dif′fer·en·cy.**

in·dif·fer·ent (in·dif′ər·ənt) *adj.* **1** Having no inclination or interest; apathetic. **2** Only passably or tolerably good or large; mediocre; ordinary. **3** Awakening no concern or preference; unimportant. **4** Unprejudiced; with no predominating tendency; impartial. **5** *Biol.* **a** Undifferentiated; not specialized, as plant or animal tissue. **b** Denoting a species of plants or animals found in diversified habitats. **6** Not active; neutral: said of chemical compounds, parts of magnets, etc. — *n.* **1** An apathetic person. **2** An object of indifference. — *adv. Obs.* Tolerably. [<OF *indifferent* <L *indifferens.* See IN-[1], DIFFERENT.] — **in·dif′fer·ent·ly** *adv.*

in·dif·fer·ent·ism (in·dif′ər·ən·tiz′əm) *n.* **1** The doctrine that the differences in religious faiths are of no importance. **2** The doctrine that to be in thought and in reality are one and the same thing; the doctrine of absolute identity. **3** Habitual or systematic indifference. — **in·dif′fer·ent·ist** *n.*

in·di·gen (in′də·jən) *n.* A person, animal, or thing native to the soil; aboriginal; autochthon: distinguished from *cultigen.* Also **in′de·gene** (-jēn). [<F *indigène*]

in·dig·e·nous (in·dij′ə·nəs) *adj.* **1** Originating in a (specified) place or country; not exotic; native. **2** Innate; inherent. See synonyms under NATIVE, PRIMEVAL. Also **in·dig′e·nal.** [<LL *indigenus* <L *indigena* native < *indu-* within + *gen-,* root of *gignere* beget] — **in·dig′e·nous·ly** *adv.* — **in·dig′e·nous·ness** *n.*

in·di·gent (in′də·jənt) *adj.* Destitute of property; poor. [<F <L *indigens, -entis,* ppr. of *indigere* lack, want < *indu-* within + *egere* need] — **in′di·gence, in′di·gen·cy** *n.*

in·di·gest (in′də·jest′) *Obs. adj.* Undigested; confused. — *n.* A disordered mass. [<L *indigestus*] — **in′di·gest′ed** *adj.*

in·di·gest·i·ble (in′də·jes′tə·bəl) *adj.* Not digestible; difficult to digest. — **in′di·gest′i·bil′·i·ty, in′di·gest′i·ble·ness** *n.* — **in′di·gest′i·bly** *adv.*

in·di·ges·tion (in′də·jes′chən) *n.* Defective digestion; dyspepsia. [<F]

In·di·gir·ka (in′di·gir′kə) A river in NE Siberia, flowing 1,113 miles north to the Siberian Sea.

in·dign (in·dīn′) *adj. Obs.* Unworthy. [<MF *indigne* <L *indignus*]

in·dig·nant (in·dig′nənt) *adj.* **1** Having just anger and scorn. **2** Manifesting or provoked by such a feeling. [<L *indignans, -antis,* ppr. of *indignari* regard as unworthy < *indignus* unworthy] — **in·dig′nant·ly** *adv.*

in·dig·na·tion (in′dig·nā′shən) *n.* Just resentment. See synonyms under ANGER. [<OF < *indignatio, -onis* < *indignari* think unworthy]

in·dig·ni·ty (in·dig′nə·tē) *n. pl.* **·ties 1** An act tending to degrade or mortify; an insult; affront. **2** *Obs.* Base character or conduct; also, anger aroused thereby. See synonyms under OFFENSE, OUTRAGE. [<L *indignitas, -tatis* < *indignus*]

in·di·go (in′də·gō) *n.* **1** A blue coloring substance, $C_{16}H_{10}N_2O_2$, obtained by the decomposition of indican, contained in the indigo plant and now synthetically produced from various aromatic hydrocarbons. Mixed with oil, it forms a paint of great body, but one easily decomposed by impure air. **2** A deep violet blue: often used adjectivally. **3** The indigo plant. [<Sp. <L *indicum* <Gk. *Indikon (pharmakon)* Indian (dye), neut. of *Indikos* Indian]

indigo blue 1 The blue coloring substance of crude indigo; indigotin. **2** Any similar dark-blue color.

indigo bunting A North American finch (*Passerina cyanea*), the male of brilliant indigo-blue color and the female brownish: often called *lazuli finch.* Also **indigo bird.**

in·di·goid (in′də·goid) *adj.* Pertaining to or designating a class of vat dyes resembling indigo.

indigo plant Any of several plants yielding indigo, especially the tropical shrub *Indigofera tinctoria,* and woad.

indigo snake The gopher snake.

in·dig·o·tin (in·dig′ə·tin, in′də·gō′tin) *n.* Pure indigo: it occurs as a dark-blue crystalline compound, $C_{16}H_{10}N_2O_2$, extracted from indican and made synthetically. Also **indigo blue.** [<INDIGO + *-t-* + -IN]

in·di·rect (in′də·rekt′) *adj.* **1** Deviating from a direct line in space. **2** Not in the direct line of derivation or succession: *indirect* descent. **3** Not in direct relation; not tending to a result by the shortest or plainest course; inferential. **4** Designating gunfire aimed at a target which cannot be seen by sighting at a known aiming point. **5** Not morally direct; tending to mislead or deceive: *indirect* conduct. **6** Not in the exact words of the speaker. — **in′di·rect′ly** *adv.* — **in′di·rect′ness** *n.*

indirect discourse See under DISCOURSE.

in·di·rec·tion (in′də·rek′shən) *n.* **1** Indirect course of practice. **2** Dishonest means; deceit.

indirect lighting Lighting that is reflected, as from a white ceiling, or diffused to give a minimum of glare and shadow.

indirect object See under OBJECT.

in·dis·creet (in′dis·krēt′) *adj.* Lacking discretion; imprudent. See synonyms under IMPRUDENT. — **in′dis·creet′ly** *adv.* — **in′dis·creet′·ness** *n.*

in·dis·cre·tion (in′dis·kresh′ən) *n.* **1** The state of being indiscreet. **2** An indiscreet act.

in·dis·crim·i·nate (in′dis·krim′ə·nit) *adj.* **1** Showing no discrimination. **2** Mingled in confusion. — **in′dis·crim′i·nate·ly** *adv.* — **in′·dis·crim′i·nate·ness** *n.* — **in′dis·crim′i·nat′ing** *adj.* — **in′dis·crim′i·na′tion** *n.*

in·dis·pen·sa·ble (in′dis·pen′sə·bəl) *adj.* Not to be dispensed with; necessary or requisite for a purpose. See synonyms under INHERENT, NECESSARY. — *n.* An indispensable person or thing. — **in′dis·pen′sa·bil′i·ty, in′dis·pen′sa·ble·ness** *n.* — **in′dis·pen′sa·bly** *adv.*

in·dis·pose (in′dis·pōz′) *v.t.* **·posed, ·pos·ing 1** To render unwilling or averse; disincline. **2** To render unfit; disqualify. **3** To make ill or ailing.

in·dis·posed (in′dis·pōzd′) *adj.* **1** Ill; unwell. **2** Disinclined. See synonyms under RELUCTANT. — **in′dis·posed′ness** (-pōzd′-, -pō′zid-) *n.*

in·dis·po·si·tion (in′dis·pə·zish′ən) *n.* **1** Slight illness. **2** The state of being mentally disinclined. See synonyms under ILLNESS.

in·dis·put·a·ble (in′dis·pyōō′tə·bəl, in·dis′pyōō·tə·bəl) *adj.* Incapable of being disputed; unquestionable. See synonyms under INCONTESTABLE, SURE. [<LL *indisputabilis*] — **in′·dis·put′a·bil′i·ty, in′dis·put′a·ble·ness** *n.* — **in′·dis·put′a·bly** *adv.*

in·dis·sol·u·ble (in′di·sol′yə·bəl, in·dis′ə·lyə·bəl) *adj.* **1** That cannot be dissolved, liquefied, or melted. **2** Perpetually binding. Also **in·dis·solv·a·ble** (in′di·zol′və·bəl). See synonyms under IMMORTAL. [<L *indissolubilis*] — **in′dis·sol′u·bil′i·ty, in′dis·sol′u·ble·ness** *n.* — **in′dis·sol′u·bly** *adv.*

in·dis·tinct (in′dis·tingkt′) *adj.* **1** Not clearly distinguishable or separable by senses or intellect; not distinct; confused; dim; vague; obscure. **2** Not presenting clear and well-defined images or impressions; obscured. **3** Indiscriminate. See synonyms under EQUIVOCAL, OBSCURE. [<L *indistinctus*] — **in′dis·tinct′ly** *adv.*

in·dis·tinc·tion (in′dis·tingk′shən) *n.* **1** Want of distinction; indiscrimination; confusion. **2** Equality of rank or condition. **3** Indistinctness.

in·dis·tinc·tive (in′dis·tingk′tiv) *adj.* **1** Having no distinguishing quality. **2** Incapable of distinguishing. — **in′dis·tinc′tive·ly** *adv.* — **in′·dis·tinc′tive·ness** *n.*

in·dis·tinct·ness (in′dis·tingkt′nis) *n.* **1** Lack of distinctness; obscurity; faintness. **2** Lack of mental qualities necessary for the purpose of making a clear distinction; indistinguishableness.

in·dite (in·dīt′) *v.t.* **·dit·ed, ·dit·ing 1** To put into words or writing; write; compose. **2** *Obs.* To dictate. ◆ Homophone: *indict.* [<AF *enditer* make known, inform <L *in-* in + *dictare* declare. Related to INDICT.] — **in·dite′·ment** *n.* — **in·dit′er** *n.*

in·di·um (in′dē·əm) *n.* A soft malleable silver-white metallic element (symbol In), found in very small quantities in sphalerite and many other ores. See ELEMENT. [<NL < *indicum* indigo + -IUM; with ref. to its spectrum color]

in·di·vid·u·al (in′də·vij′ōō·əl) *adj.* **1** Existing as an entity; single; particular. **2** Not divisible; not capable of actual division without loss of something essential to its existence. **3** Pertaining, belonging, or peculiar to one particular person or thing. **4** Differentiated from others by peculiar or distinctive characteristics: an *individual* style. See synonyms under PARTICULAR. — *n.* **1** A single person, animal, or thing; especially, a human being;

a person with distinctive or marked peculiarities. 2 Anything that cannot be divided or separated into parts without losing its identity. [<Med. L *individualis* <L *individuus* indivisible < *in-* not + *dividuus* divisible] —**in'di·vid'u·al·ly** *adv.*

in·di·vid·u·al·ism (in'də·vij'ōō·əl·iz'əm) *n.* 1 The quality of being separate. 2 Personal independence in action, character, or interest. 3 A personal peculiarity; idiosyncrasy. 4 A tendency or attitude, in religion, ethics, or politics, favoring the liberty of the individual: opposed to *socialism, totalitarianism,* etc. 5 Excessive self–interest; selfishness. 6 *Philos.* Egoism. —**in'di·vid'u·al·ist** *n.* —**in'di·vid'u·al·is'tic** *adj.*

in·di·vid·u·al·i·ty (in'də·vij'ōō·al'ə·tē) *n. pl.* **·ties** 1 Something that distinguishes one person or thing from others. 2 Distinctive character or personality. 3 The quality or state of existing separately. 4 An individual; a personality. 5 *Archaic* State or quality of inseparability; indivisibility.

in·di·vid·u·al·ize (in'də·vij'ōō·əl·īz') *v.t.* **·ized, ·iz·ing** 1 To make individual; give individual characteristics to; distinguish. 2 To treat, mention, or consider individually; particularize. —**in'di·vid'u·al·i·za'tion** (-ə·zā'shən, -ī·zā'-) *n.*

in·di·vid·u·ate (in'də·vij'ōō·āt) *v.t.* **·at·ed, ·at·ting** 1 To distinguish from others; individualize. 2 To bring into existence as an individual. [<Med. L *individuatus,* pp. of *individuare* < *individuus* individual]

in·di·vid·u·a·tion (in'də·vij'ōō·ā'shən) *n.* 1 The action or process of rendering individual. 2 State of being individualized. 3 Personal identity; individuality. 4 *Zool.* The development of separate units in a colony of protozoans. 5 *Philos.* The differentiation of the individual from the species and from every other individual. [<Med. L *individuatio, -onis*]

in·di·vis·i·ble (in'də·viz'ə·bəl) *adj.* Not divisible; incapable of being divided. —**in'di·vis'i·bil'i·ty** *n.* —**in'di·vis'i·bly** *adv.*

Indo- *combining form* Indian: *Indonesia.* [< Gk. *Indos* Indian]

In·do–Af·ri·can (in'dō·af'ri·kən) *adj.* Of or pertaining to both India and Africa.

In·do–Ar·y·an (in'dō·âr'ē·ən) *adj.* Of the Indic branch of the Indo–Iranian subfamily. —*n.* An Aryan of India. See ARYAN.

In·do·chi·na (in'dō·chī'nə) 1 The SE peninsula of Asia, comprising the Union of Burma, Cambodia, Laos, the Federation of Malaya, Thailand, North Vietnam and South Vietnam: sometimes *Farther India.* 2 The states of Cambodia, Laos, North Vietnam and South Vietnam: formerly *French Indochina.* Also **Indo–China.**

In·do·chi·nese (in'dō·chī·nēz', -nēs') *adj.* Of or pertaining to Indochina or its inhabitants. —*n.* 1 A member of one of the native Mongoloid races inhabiting Indochina. 2 The Sino–Tibetan family of languages.

in·doc·tri·nate (in·dok'trə·nāt) *v.t.* **·nat·ed, ·nat·ing** 1 To instruct in doctrines, principles, etc. 2 To instruct; teach. See synonyms under TEACH. [<Med. L *in-* into + *doctrinare* teach < *doctrina* teaching < *doctor* a teacher < *docere* teach] —**in·doc'tri·na'tion** *n.*

In·do–Eu·ro·pe·an (in'dō·yŏŏr'ə·pē'ən) *n.* 1 The largest family of languages in the world, assumed to have descended from an unrecorded common ancestor and comprising most of the languages of Europe and many languages of India and SW Asia. These languages are conventionally divided into two classifications, *centum* and *satem* (from the Latin and Avestan words for 'hundred'), primarily according to the representation of the proto–Indo–European palatalized velar (k) as velar stops in the *centum* (mainly western) division, and as sibilants in the *satem* (mainly eastern) division. The principal *centum* subfamilies are Hellenic, Italic, Celtic, and Germanic. The principal *satem* subfamilies are Indo–Iranian, Armenian, Albanian, and Balto–Slavic. Among the lesser–known, extinct languages which have been established as belonging to the Indo–European family are Hittite and Tocharian. Cuneiform Hittite is grouped with the *centum* languages, while Hieroglyphic Hittite is thought by some to be a *satem* language. Tocharian is generally classed with the *centum* languages. See also THRACIAN, PHRYGIAN, LIGURIAN, SICEL, ILLYRIAN, MESSAPIAN, and VENETIC. 2 The assumed prehistoric parent language of this family of languages: now fairly well reconstructed by linguists. —*adj.* Of or pertaining to the Indo–European family of languages, or to the peoples speaking them. Also *Aryan, Indo–Germanic.*

In·do–French (in'dō·french') *adj.* Pertaining to both India and France.

In·do–Ger·man·ic (in'dō·jər·man'ik) *n., adj.* Indo–European: the German term.

In·do–Hit·tite (in'dō·hit'īt) *n.* A language hypothesized by some as the parent of both the Indo–European and Anatolian families. According to this theory, Hittite is a sister language to Indo–European, rather than an offspring of it.

In·do–I·ra·ni·an (in'dō·ī·rā'nē·ən) *n.* A subfamily of the Indo–European family of languages, consisting of Indic and Iranian branches. —*adj.* Of or pertaining to this subfamily. Also *Aryan.*

in·dole (in'dōl) *n. Chem.* A white, crystalline, malodorous compound, C_8H_7N, formed by the reduction of indigo, and also from putrefactive animal proteins and certain albuminous compounds by fermentation. Highly diluted, it is used in perfumery. Also **in'dol** (-dōl, -dol). [<IND(IGO) + -OLE]

in·do·lence (in'də·ləns) *n.* Habitual idleness; laziness. Also **in'do·len·cy.** [<L *indolentia* freedom from pain]

in·do·lent (in'də·lənt) *adj.* 1 Averse to exertion; habitually inactive or idle. 2 Without pain; sluggish. See synonyms under IDLE. [<LL *indolens, -entis* < *in-* not + *dolens,* ppr. of *dolere* feel pain] —**in'do·lent·ly** *adv.*

in·dom·i·ta·ble (in·dom'i·tə·bəl) *adj.* Not to be subdued. See synonyms under INDEFATIGABLE, OBSTINATE. [<LL *indomitabilis* <L *indomitus* untamed < *in-* not + *domitus* tamed, pp. of *domitare,* intens. of *domare* subdue] —**in·dom'i·ta·bly** *adv.*

In·do·ne·sia (in'dō·nē'zhə, -shə) Since 1950 a republic, the **Republic of Indonesia,** comprising Java, Sumatra, most of Borneo, half of Timor, Celebes, the Moluccas, and other islands of the Malay Archipelago: 575,893 square miles; capital, Jakarta: formerly *Netherlands East Indies.*

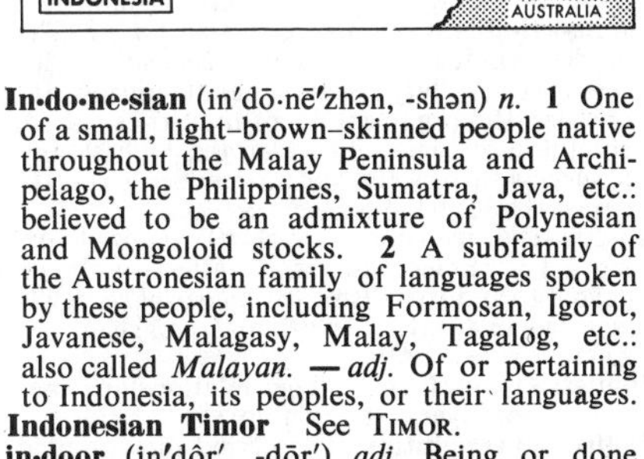

INDONESIA

In·do·ne·sian (in'dō·nē'zhən, -shən) *n.* 1 One of a small, light–brown–skinned people native throughout the Malay Peninsula and Archipelago, the Philippines, Sumatra, Java, etc.: believed to be an admixture of Polynesian and Mongoloid stocks. 2 A subfamily of the Austronesian family of languages spoken by these people, including Formosan, Igorot, Javanese, Malagasy, Malay, Tagalog, etc.: also called *Malayan.* —*adj.* Of or pertaining to Indonesia, its peoples, or their languages.

Indonesian Timor See TIMOR.

in·door (in'dôr', -dōr') *adj.* Being or done within doors; pertaining to the interior of a building.

in·doors (in'dôrz', -dōrz') *adv.* Inside or toward the inside of a building.

in·do·phe·nol (in'dō·fē'nōl, -nol) *n. Chem.* One of a series of synthetic quinonimine coloring compounds resembling indigo: used for dyeing cotton and wool blue. [<IND(IG)O + PHENOL]

In·dore (in·dôr', -dōr') 1 A former princely state in west central India; 9,934 square miles. 2 Its former capital, since 1948 the summer capital of Madhya Bharat.

in·dorse (in·dôrs'), **in·dorse·ment** (in·dôrs'·mənt) See ENDORSE, ENDORSEMENT.

in·dor·see (in'dôr·sē', in·dôr'sē) See ENDORSEE.

in·dow (in·dou'), **in·dow·ment** (in·dou'mənt) See ENDOW, etc.

in·dox·yl (in·dok'sil) *n. Chem.* A crystalline compound, C_8H_7NO, formed from indole and used as an intermediate in the synthesis of indigo. [<IND(IGO) + (HYDR)OXYL]

In·dra (in'drə) In early Hindu mythology, the god of the firmament and of rain. In the Vedas he is a god of the first rank: in later mythology he falls to a second rank.

INDRA
Drawn from an early Indian sculpture of the Vedic period. Indra was the god of the east in Hindu legend.

in·draft (in'draft', -dräft') *n.* The act of drawing in or that which is drawn in; an inward flow. Also **in'draught'.**

In·dra·pu·ra (in'drə·pŏŏr'ə) See KERINCHI.

in·drawn (in'drôn') *adj.* 1 Drawn in; uttered with suppressed breath. 2 Abstracted; preoccupied.

in·dri (in'drē) *n.* A lemur of Madagascar; especially, a species (*Indris brevicaudata*) about two feet long, with exserted ears, rudimentary tail, and usually prevailingly black in color. [<F <Malagasy *indry lo,* there he goes: mistaken for the name of the animal]

in·du·bi·ta·ble (in·dōō'bə·tə·bəl, -dyōō'-) *adj.* Not open to doubt or question; unquestionable; certain. See synonyms under EVIDENT, INCONTESTABLE, MANIFEST. [<F] —**in·du'bi·ta·ble·ness** *n.* —**in·du'bi·ta·bly** *adv.*

in·duce (in·dōōs', -dyōōs') *v.t.* **·duced, ·duc·ing** 1 To lead on to a specific action, belief, etc., by persuasion or influence; prevail on. 2 To bring on; produce; cause: a sickness *induced* by fatigue. 3 *Physics* To produce, as by exposure to electric, magnetic, or radioactive influences. 4 To reach as a conclusion by an inductive process of reasoning. 5 *Obs.* To lead in; introduce. [<L *inducere* introduce < *in-* in + *ducere* lead] —**in·duc'er** *n.* —**in·duc'i·ble** *adj.*

induced drag *Aeron.* That portion of the drag of an aircraft induced by the lift. Compare PARASITE DRAG, PROFILE DRAG.

in·duce·ment (in·dōōs'mənt, -dyōōs'-) *n.* 1 An incentive; motive. 2 The act of inducing. 3 *Law* In pleading, the preamble, or explanatory introduction to the particular charges and allegations.

in·duct (in·dukt') *v.t.* 1 To bring into or install in an office, benefice, etc., especially with formal ceremony. 2 To bring or lead in; introduce; initiate. 3 *U.S.* To bring (one who has been conscripted) into a military service. [<L *inductus,* pp. of *inducere.* See INDUCE.]

in·duc·tance (in·duk'təns) *n. Electr.* 1 The capacity of an electric circuit for responding to a magnetoelectrically induced current. 2 Self–induction in an electrical circuit or its equivalent, for purposes of measurement in terms of henries.

in·duc·tee (in'duk·tē') *n.* One inducted into military service.

in·duc·tion (in·duk'shən) *n.* 1 The process of causing an event or bringing about a conclusion by some particular path or course of reasoning. 2 *Logic* The process of inferring or aiming at the general from observation of the particular; specifically, the inference of a specific law of causational connection from the observation and analysis of some particular instance or instances. 3 Any conclusion reached by inductive reasoning. 4 In

English ecclesiastical law, the formal installation of a person into an office or church living. **5** An introduction; especially, a preamble, prolog, or prelude foreshadowing the argument or character of a literary work. **6** The bringing forward of separate facts as evidence in order to prove a general statement. **7** *Electr.* The production of magnetization or electrification in a body by the mere proximity of a magnetic field or electric charge, or of an electric current in a conductor by the variation of the magnetic field in its vicinity. **8** *Physiol.* The stimulating effect of one tissue upon the growth or alteration of another. **9** The act or process of inducting, as for military service; initiation; installation. **10** *Obs.* A beginning or introduction to anything; that which leads to or induces a thing. — **magnetic induction** The magnetization of iron, steel, etc., by its introduction into a magnetic field. [<OF <L *inductio, -onis*] — **in·duc′tion·al** *adj.*

Synonyms: deduction, inference. *Deduction* is reasoning from the general to the particular; *induction* is reasoning from the particular to the general. In *deduction,* if the general rule is true, and the special case falls under the rule, the conclusion is certain; *induction* can ordinarily give no more than a probable conclusion, because we can never be sure that we have collated all instances. An *induction* is of the nature of an *inference,* but while an *inference* may be partial and hasty, an *induction* is careful, and aims to be complete. Compare DEMONSTRATION, INFERENCE.

induction coil *Electr.* An apparatus for generating currents by electromagnetic induction, consisting usually of two concentric coils of insulated wire enclosing an iron core. One of the coils, called the *primary,* is usually short and of thick wire, and the *secondary* long and of thin wire. An alternating current of high tension is induced in the secondary coil by rapid automatic making and breaking of the circuit in the primary.

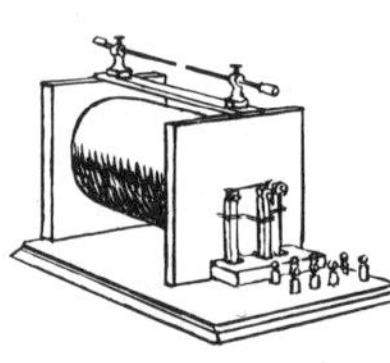

INDUCTION COIL

in·duc·tive (in·duk′tiv) *adj.* **1** Pertaining to or proceeding by induction. **2** Produced by induction. **3** Introductory. [<LL *inductivus*] — **in·duc′tive·ly** *adv.* — **in·duc′tive·ness** *n.*

in·duc·tiv·i·ty (in′duk·tiv′ə·tē) *n. Electr.* Specific capacity for induction.

in·duc·tor (in·duk′tər) *n.* **1** One who or that which inducts. **2** *Electr.* Any part of an electrical apparatus which acts inductively upon another. [<L]

in·due (in·dōō′, -dyōō′) *v.t.* **·dued, ·du·ing** To endue. [See ENDUE]

in·dulge (in·dulj′) *v.* **·dulged, ·dulg·ing** *v.t.* **1** To yield to or gratify, as desires or whims. **2** To yield to or gratify the desires, whims, etc., of. **3** *Eccl.* To grant a dispensation or indulgence to. **4** *Obs.* To grant as a privilege or favor. **5** In business: **a** To grant more time to (someone) to meet a bill. **b** To grant more time for (a bill) to be met. — *v.i.* **6** To yield to or gratify desires; indulge oneself; with *in.* [<L *indulgere* be kind to, concede] — **in·dulg′er** *n.*

Synonyms: content, favor, gratify, humor, pamper, please, satisfy, spoil. See PAMPER. *Antonyms*: check, contradict, control, deny, disappoint, discipline, displease, oppose, refuse, thwart.

in·dul·gence (in·dul′jəns) *n.* **1** The act of indulging; hence, excess; self-gratification. **2** That with which a person is indulged or indulges himself; an act of compliance, grace, or favor. **3** Permission to defer payment, as of a note. **4** In the Roman Catholic Church, remission, by those authorized, of the temporal punishment still due to sin after sacramental absolution, either in this world or in purgatory; also, a relaxation, in a person's favor, of a particular rule of ecclesiastical law: properly called *dispensation.* **5** The granting of special favors by the Declaration of Indulgence. Also **in·dul′gen·cy.** — **Declaration of Indulgence** In English history, a royal proclamation granting a larger measure of religious freedom to nonconformists: especially those of Charles II, 1671, and James II, 1687. [<OF <L *indulgentia*]

in·dul·gent (in·dul′jənt) *adj.* Prone to indulge; lenient. See synonyms under CHARITABLE. [<L *indulgens, -entis,* ppr. of *indulgere* concede] — **in·dul′gent·ly** *adv.*

in·dul·gen·tial (in′dul·jen′shəl) *adj.* Pertaining to ecclesiastical indulgences.

in·du·line (in′dyə·lēn, -lin) *n. Chem.* Any one of an extensive group of coal-tar dyestuffs yielding a violet to intense blue color. Also **in′du·lin** (-lin). [<IND(IGO) + -UL(E) + -INE[2]]

in·dult (in·dult′) *n.* **1** An indulgence or privilege granted by the pope, to bishops and others, as exemption from some canonical or ecclesiastical duty. **2** In Spain, an import duty: also **in·dul′to** (-dul′tō). [<LL *indultum* < *indultus,* pp. of *indulgere* concede]

in·du·na (in·dōō′nə) *n.* Among the Zulus, an officer serving under the king or chief. [< Zulu *in-duna*]

in·du·pli·cate (in·dōō′plə·kit, -dyōō′-) *adj. Bot.* Having the edges turned or folded inward: said of calyx or corolla in estivation, or of leaves in vernation. Also **in·du′pli·ca′tive.** — **in·du′pli·ca′tion** *n.*

in·du·rate (in′dōō·rāt, -dyōō-) *v.t.* & *v.i.* **·rat·ed, ·rat·ing** To make or become hard, hardy, or callous; harden; inure. — *adj.* (-rit) Hard or hardened: also **in′du·rat′ed.** [<L *induratus,* pp. of *indurare* make hard. See ENDURE.] — **in′du·ra′tive** *adj.*

in·du·ra·tion (in′dōō·rā′shən, -dyōō-) *n.* **1** The act or process of indurating, or the state of being indurated. **2** Hardening of the heart; obduracy. **3** An indurated part. [<OF < Med. L *induratio, -onis*]

In·dus (in′dəs) A river in western Tibet and NW India, flowing over 1,900 miles NW to the Arabian Sea.

In·dus (in′dəs) A southern constellation, the Indian. See CONSTELLATION. [<L, an Indian]

in·du·si·um (in·dōō′zē·əm, -zhē-, -dyōō′-) *n. pl.* **·si·a** (-zē·ə, -zhē·ə) **1** *Bot.* **a** An outgrowth of a fern leaf covering the immature sori or fruit clusters. **b** A hairy cup surrounding the stigma in a flower. **2** *Biol.* **a** The larval case of an insect. **b** Any similar membranous envelope, as the amnion. [<L, a tunic < *induere* put on; infl. in form by Gk. *endysis* dress, garment < *endyein* put on] — **in·du′si·al** *adj.*

in·dus·tri·al (in·dus′trē·əl) *adj.* **1** Pertaining to or engaged in industry. **2** Denoting the processes or products of manufacture. — *n.* **1** One engaged in industry. **2** A stock or security based upon an established manufacture. [<F *industriel* and Med. L *industrialis*] — **in·dus′tri·al·ly** *adv.*

industrial arts See under ART[1].

industrial democracy **1** Control, or equal participation in the control, of an industry by the workers in that industry. **2** Nondiscrimination among employees in an industry, as for race or religion.

industrial insurance Insurance for small amounts, usually for low-income groups, the premium being paid in weekly instalments.

in·dus·tri·al·ism (in·dus′trē·əl·iz′əm) *n.* **1** The modern industrial system, especially with reference to large-scale manufacturing industries; the organization of industries. **2** A condition of society in which the highest aim is success in peaceful industries. See CAPITALISM. — **in·dus′tri·al·ist** *adj.* & *n.*

in·dus·tri·al·ize (in·dus′trē·əl·īz′) *v.t.* **·ized, ·iz·ing** To render industrial; affect with or devote to industrialism: to *industrialize* a village. — **in·dus′tri·al·i·za′tion** (-ə·zā′shən, -ī·zā′-) *n.*

industrial relations The relationships between employers and employees.

industrial revolution The period of economic transition from hand industry to the application of power-driven machinery which began in England in the second half of the 18th century.

industrial union A labor union in which membership is open to all workers in a particular industry. Compare CRAFT UNION.

Industrial Workers of the World A syndicalist labor organization founded at Chicago in 1905 and flourishing through the early 1920's. *Abbr. IWW.* See WOBBLY.

in·dus·tri·ous (in·dus′trē·əs) *adj.* **1** Assiduously or habitually occupied in any work, business, or pursuit. **2** Indicating diligence. **3** Industrial. [<F *industrieux* <L *industriosus*] — **in·dus′tri·ous·ly** *adv.* — **in·dus′tri·ous·ness** *n.*

Synonyms: active, assiduous, busy, diligent, employed, engaged, occupied, sedulous. *Industrious* signifies zealously or habitually applying oneself to any work or business. *Busy* applies to an activity which may be temporary, *industrious* to a habit of life. We say a man is *busy* just now; that is, *occupied* at the moment with something that takes his full attention. It would be ridiculous or satirical to say, He is *industrious* just now. But *busy* can be used in the sense of *industrious,* as when we say he is a *busy* man. *Diligent* indicates also a disposition, which is ordinarily habitual, and suggests more of heartiness and volition than *industrious.* We say one is a *diligent,* rather than an *industrious,* reader of the Bible. Compare ACTIVE, BUSY, INDEFATIGABLE.

in·dus·try (in′dəs·trē) *n. pl.* **·tries** **1** Earnest or constant application to work or business. **2** Useful labor in general. **3** A special branch of productive work, or the capital or workers employed in it: the steel *industry,* the farming *industry.* **4** The mechanical and manufacturing branches of productive activity, as distinguished from agricultural. **5** *Obs.* Skill, dexterity; also, a clever device or contrivance. [<F *industrie* <L *industria* diligence < *industrius* diligent]

Synonyms: application, assiduity, attention, constancy, diligence, effort, exertion, intentness, labor, pains, patience, perseverance, persistence, sedulousness. *Industry* is the quality, action, or habit of earnest, steady, and continued attention or devotion to any useful or productive work or task, manual or mental. *Assiduity* (L *ad,* to, and *sedere,* sit), as the etymology suggests, sits down to a task until it is done. *Diligence* (L *diligere,* love, choose) invests more effort and exertion, with love of the work or deep interest in its accomplishment; *application* (L *ad,* to, and *plicare,* fold) bends to its work and concentrates all one's powers upon it with utmost intensity; hence, *application* can hardly be as unremitting as *assiduity. Constancy* is a steady devotion of heart and principle. *Patience* works on in spite of annoyances; *perseverance* overcomes hindrances and difficulties; *persistence* strives relentlessly against opposition; *persistence* has very frequently an unfavorable meaning, implying that one persists in spite of considerations that should induce him to desist. *Industry* is *diligence* applied to some vocation, business, or profession; hence, by derived use, the occupation itself. *Labor* and *pains* refer to the *exertions* of the worker and the tax upon him, while *assiduity, perseverance,* etc., refer to his continuance in the work. See BUSINESS. *Antonyms*: idleness, inattention, inconstancy, indolence, neglect, negligence, remissness, sloth.

in·dwell (in′dwel′) *v.* **·dwelt, ·dwell·ing** *v.t.* To dwell in; inhabit. — *v.i.* To dwell; abide: with *in.* — **in′dwell′er** *n.* — **in′dwell′ing** *n.*

In·dy (dan·dē′), **Vincent d',** 1851–1931, French composer.

-ine[1] *suffix of adjectives* Like; pertaining to; of the nature of: *marine, canine.* [<F *-in, -ine* <L *-inus,* adj. suffix]

-ine[2] *suffix* **1** *Chem.* **a** Used in the names of halogens: *bromine, fluorine.* **b** Used to indicate an alkaloid or basic substance: *morphine, amine.* **c** Var. of -IN. **2** Used in names of commercial products: *gasoline, brilliantine.* [Special use of -INE[1]]

-ine[3] *suffix* Used to form feminine words, names, and titles: *heroine, Josephine.* [<F <L *-ina,* suffix of fem. nouns <Gk. *-inē*; or directly <L or <Gk.]

-ine[4] *suffix* Like; resembling: *crystalline.* [<L *-inus* <Gk. *-inos*]

in·earth (in·ûrth′) *v.t. Poetic* To place in the earth; bury.

in·e·bri·ant (in·ē′brē·ənt) *adj.* Intoxicating. — *n.* Anything that intoxicates.

in·e·bri·ate (in·ē′brē·āt) *v.t.* **·at·ed, ·at·ing** **1** To make drunk; intoxicate. **2** To exhilarate; excite. — *n.* (-it, -āt) A habitual drunkard. — *adj.* (-it, -āt) Intoxicated: also **in·e′bri·at′ed.** [<L *inebriatus,* pp. of *inebriare* intoxicate < *in-* thoroughly + *ebriare* make drunk < *ebrius* drunk]

in·e·bri·a·tion (in·ē′brē·ā′shən) *n.* 1 Drunkenness; habitual intoxication. 2 Exhilaration. Also **in·e·bri·e·ty** (in′ē·brī′ə·tē).

in·ed·i·ble (in·ed′ə·bəl) *adj.* Not edible; not fit to eat. —**in·ed′i·bil′i·ty** *n.*

in·ef·fa·ble (in·ef′ə·bəl) *adj.* 1 That cannot be expressed in speech. 2 That must not be spoken; too lofty or sacred for expression. [<F <L *ineffabilis* < *in-* not + *effabilis* utterable < *effari* speak < *ex-* out + *fari* speak] —**in·ef′fa·bil′i·ty** *n.* —**in·ef′fa·bly** *adv.*

in·ef·fec·tive (in′i·fek′tiv) *adj.* 1 Not effective; not producing the effect expected. 2 Incompetent. —**in′ef·fec′tive·ly** *adv.* —**in′ef·fec′tive·ness** *n.*

in·ef·fec·tu·al (in′i·fek′cho͞o·əl) *adj.* 1 Not effectual; not able to produce an intended effect. 2 Unsuccessful; fruitless. —**in′ef·fec′tu·al·ly** *adv.*

in·ef·fi·cient (in′i·fish′ənt) *adj.* 1 Not efficient; uneconomical or wasteful. 2 Not capable; incompetent. —**in′ef·fi′cien·cy** *n.* —**in′ef·fi′cient·ly** *adv.*

in·e·las·tic (in′i·las′tik) *adj.* Not elastic; inflexible; unyielding; unadaptable. —**in·e·las·tic·i·ty** (in′i·las′tis′ə·tē) *n.*

in·el·e·gant (in·el′ə·gənt) *adj.* 1 Not elegant; lacking in beauty, polish, grace, refinement, good taste, or the like. 2 Coarse; crude.

in·el·i·gi·ble (in·el′ə·jə·bəl) *adj.* Not eligible; disqualified; unsuitable; inexpedient. —**in·el′i·gi·bil′i·ty** *n.* —**in·el′i·gi·bly** *adv.*

in·e·luc·ta·ble (in′i·luk′tə·bəl) *adj.* Not to be escaped; impossible to struggle against; irresistible. [<L *ineluctabilis* < *in-* not + *eluctabilis* surmountable < *eluctari* surmount] —**in′e·luc′ta·bil′i·ty** *n.* —**in′e·luc′ta·bly** *adv.*

in·ept (in·ept′) *adj.* 1 Not suitable or qualified; out of place. 2 Absurd; foolish. 3 Clumsy; awkward. [<L *ineptus* < *in-* not + *aptus* fit] —**in·ep′ti·tude** *n.* —**in·ept′ly** *adv.* —**in·ept′ness** *n.*

in·e·qual·i·ty (in′i·kwol′ə·tē) *n. pl.* **·ties** 1 The condition of being unequal; disparity. 2 Lack of evenness or proportion; variableness: *inequalities* of surface; *inequalities* of climate. 3 Inadequacy; incompetency. 4 *Math.* A statement that two quantities are not equal, made by placing the sign ≠ between them; or by the sign < or >, the angle being toward the symbol of smaller quantity. 5 The daily variation in rise of the tides due to varying lunar influences. See synonyms under DIFFERENCE.

in·eq·ui·ty (in·ek′wə·tē) *n. pl.* **·ties** 1 Want of equity; injustice. 2 An unfair act.

in·er·ran·cy (in·er′ən·sē, -ûr′-) *n.* 1 The state of being free from error. 2 As applied to Scripture, plenary inspiration.

in·ert (in·ûrt′) *adj.* 1 Destitute of inherent power to move; possessing inertia; inactive. 2 Sluggish. 3 *Chem.* Devoid of active properties; incapable of or resisting combination: the *inert* gases. See synonyms under HEAVY, IDLE, LIFELESS, PASSIVE, SLOW. [<L *iners, inertis* < *in-* not + *ars* art] —**in·ert′ly** *adv.* —**in·ert′ness** *n.* —**in·er′tion** (-ûr′shən) *n.*

in·er·tia (in·ûr′shə) *n.* 1 The state of being inert; sluggishness. 2 *Physics* **a** That property of matter by virtue of which any physical body persists in its state of rest or of uniform motion until acted upon by some external force; its quantitative expression is *mass.* **b** A similar property noted in certain forms of energy, as electricity and quanta. [<L, idleness] —**in·er′tial** *adj.*

inertial guidance *Aeron.* The control of the flight path of aircraft and guided missiles by built-in gyroscopic mechanisms which automatically compensate for the action of inertial forces tending to change the direction of a predetermined course.

in·es·cap·a·ble (in′ə·skā′pə·bəl) *adj.* Inevitable; unavoidable. —**in′es·cap′a·bly** *adv.*

in es·se (in es′ē) *Latin* In being; actually existing. Compare IN POSSE.

in·es·sen·tial (in′i·sen′shəl) *adj.* 1 Unessential; not essential. 2 Immaterial. —**in′es·sen′ti·al′i·ty** *n.*

in·es·ti·ma·ble (in·es′tə·mə·bəl) *adj.* Above price; very valuable. —**in·es′ti·ma·bly** *adv.*

in·ev·i·ta·ble (in·ev′ə·tə·bəl) *adj.* 1 That cannot be prevented; unavoidable. 2 Hence, customary; usual: a humorous usage. See synonyms under NECESSARY. [<L *inevitabilis* < *in-* not + *evitare* avoid < *ex-* completely + *vitare* avoid] —**in·ev′i·ta·ble·ness, in·ev′i·ta·bil′i·ty** *n.* —**in·ev′i·ta·bly** *adv.*

inevitable accident See FORCE MAJEURE.

in·ex·act (in′ig·zakt′) *adj.* Not exact, accurate, or true. —**in′ex·act′ly** *adv.* —**in′ex·act′ness, in′ex·act′i·tude** *n.*

in·ex·cus·a·ble (in′ik·skyo͞o′zə·bəl) *adj.* Not excusable; impossible to excuse or justify. —**in′·ex·cus′a·bly** *adv.*

in·ex·haust·i·ble (in′ig·zôs′tə·bəl) *adj.* 1 Incapable of being exhausted or used up. 2 Incapable of fatigue; tireless.

in·ex·o·ra·ble (in·ek′sər·ə·bəl) *adj.* Not to be moved by entreaty; unyielding. See synonyms under IMPLACABLE, INFLEXIBLE. [<L *inexorabilis.* See IN-^{2}, EXORABLE.] —**in·ex′o·ra·bil′i·ty, in·ex′o·ra·ble·ness** *n.* —**in·ex′o·ra·bly** *adv.*

in·ex·pen·sive (in′ik·spen′siv) *adj.* Not expensive; costing little.

in·ex·pe·ri·enced (in′ik·spir′ē·ənst) *adj.* Not experienced; lacking in the skill and knowledge derived from experience.

in·ex·plic·a·ble (in·eks′pli·kə·bəl, in′iks·plik′ə·bəl) *adj.* Not explicable; impossible to explain; inexplainable. —**in·ex′pli·ca·bil′i·ty, in′ex·plic′a·ble·ness** *n.* —**in·ex′pli·ca·bly** *adv.*

in·ex·press·i·ble (in′iks·pres′ə·bəl) *adj.* Incapable of being expressed; especially, that cannot be expressed in words; unutterable: often used loosely for *great.* —**in′ex·press′i·bil′i·ty, in′ex·press′i·ble·ness** *n.* —**in′ex·press′i·bly** *adv.*

in·ex·pug·na·ble (in′iks·pug′nə·bəl) *adj.* Impregnable; unconquerable. [<F <L *inexpugnabilis* < *in-* not + *ex-* out + *pugnare* fight] —**in′ex·pug′na·bil′i·ty, in′ex·pug′na·ble·ness** *n.* —**in′ex·pug′na·bly** *adv.*

in ex·ten·so (in ik·sten′sō) *Latin* At full length.

in ex·tre·mis (in iks·trē′mis) *Latin* At the point of death; at the last gasp.

in·ex·tri·ca·ble (in·eks′tri·kə·bəl) *adj.* So involved that extrication is impossible. [<L *inextricabilis* <*in-* not + *extricare.* See EXTRICATE.] —**in·ex′tri·ca·bil′i·ty, in·ex′tri·ca·ble·ness** *n.* —**in·ex′tri·ca·bly** *adv.*

I·nez (ī′nez′) Portuguese form of AGNES. Also *Sp.* **I·nés** (ē·nās′).

in·fal·li·ble (in·fal′ə·bəl) *adj.* 1 Exempt from fallacy or error of judgment. 2 Exempt from uncertainty or liability to error. 3 In Roman Catholic theology, insusceptible of error in matters relating to faith and morals: said of the pope speaking *ex cathedra.* —*n.* One who or that which is infallible. —**in·fal′li·bil′i·ty, in·fal′li·ble·ness** *n.* —**in·fal′li·bly** *adv.*

in·fa·mous (in′fə·məs) *adj.* 1 Having an odious reputation; notorious. 2 Involving infamy. 3 *Law* Convicted of infamy. [< Med. L *infamosus* <L *infamis* < *in-* not + *fama* fame < *fari* speak] —**in′fa·mous·ly** *adv.* —**in′fa·mous·ness** *n.*

Synonyms: atrocious, base, detestable, disgraceful, dishonorable, disreputable, heinous, ignominious, ill-famed, nefarious, odious, outrageous, scandalous, shameful, shameless, vile, villainous, wicked. See BASE.

in·fa·my (in′fə·mē) *n. pl.* **·mies** 1 Total lack of honor or reputation. 2 That which is odious; depravity; an infamous act. 3 *Law* The legal status of a person convicted of serious crimes which, in the United States, disqualify him as a witness or juror. [<F *infamie* <L *infamia* < *infamis.* See INFAMOUS.]

in·fan·cy (in′fən·sē) *n. pl.* **·cies** 1 The state of being an infant. 2 *Law* Minority. 3 The earliest period in the history of a thing.

in·fant (in′fənt) *n.* 1 A baby; a child under seven years of age. 2 *Law* A minor; in most States of the United States, a person under 21 years of age. —*adj.* 1 Babyish; infantile. 2 *Law* Minor; not yet of age. [<OF *enfant* <L *infans, -antis* not speaking < *in-* not + *fans, fantis,* ppr. of *fari* talk]

in·fan·ta (in·fan′tə) *n.* A daughter of a Spanish or Portuguese king. [<Sp., infant]

in·fan·te (in·fan′tā) *n.* A son, except the eldest, of a Spanish or Portuguese king. [<Sp., infant]

in·fan·ti·cide (in·fan′tə·sīd) *n.* 1 Child murder. 2 One who murders a child. [<F <LL *infanticidium* <L *infans, -antis* child + *caedere* kill; def. 2 <L *infanticida*]

in·fan·tile (in′fən·tīl, -til) *adj.* 1 Pertaining to or characteristic of infants or infancy. 2 *Geol.* In an early period of development succeeding an upheaval of the earth's crust or other change affecting basic level. See synonyms under CHILDISH. Also **in′an·tine** (-tīn, -tin).

infantile paralysis Poliomyelitis.

infantile scurvy *Pathol.* A disease of young children characterized by foul breath, diarrhea, anemia, hemorrhages, etc.: also called *Barlow's disease.*

in·fan·til·ism (in′fən·təl·iz′əm) *n.* 1 Abnormal prolonging of an infantile condition as to sex and body in adults. 2 Backwardness in physical and mental development.

in·fan·try (in′fən·trē) *n. pl.* **·tries** Soldiers or units of an army that fight on foot and are equipped with small arms. [<F *infanterie* < Ital. *infanteria* < *infante* boy, page, foot soldier <L *infans, infantis* child]

in·fan·try·man (in′fən·trē·mən) *n. pl.* **·men** (-mən) A foot soldier.

in·farct (in·färkt′) *n. Pathol.* A portion of tissue congested because of an embolus and undergoing necrosis. [<Med. L *infarctus* <L *infartus,* pp. of *infarcire* < *in-* in + *farcire* stuff] —**in·farc′tion** *n.*

in·fat·u·ate (in·fach′o͞o·āt) *v.t.* **·at·ed, ·at·ing** 1 To make foolish or fatuous; deprive of sound judgment. 2 To inspire with foolish and unreasoning passion. [<L *infatuatus,* pp. of *infatuare* make a fool of < *in-* very + *fatuus* foolish] —**in·fat′u·at′ed** *adj.* —**in·fat′u·a′tion** *n.*

in·fect (in·fekt′) *v.t.* 1 To introduce pathogenic micro-organisms into, as a wound; communicate disease to, as a person, etc. 2 To contaminate, as a scalpel, with disease-bearing matter. 3 To affect or influence, as with emotion, beliefs, etc., especially harmfully; taint. 4 *Law* To taint with illegality; render subject to seizure or penalty. See synonyms under DEFILE, POLLUTE. [<L *infectus,* pp. of *inficere* dip into, stain < *in-* in + *facere* do, make] —**in·fect′er, in·fec′tor** *n.*

in·fec·tion (in·fek′shən) *n.* 1 The act of infecting, as with disease, attitude, mood, ideas, etc. 2 Communication of disease, as by entrance of pathogenic germs into an organism in any manner. 3 Any diseased condition so produced. 4 The instilation of a quality, usually evil, by influence or communication. 5 *Law* Taint of illegality. 6 That which infects; especially, infectious morbific matter. 7 *Rare* Liking; affection: in humorous use. See synonyms under CONTAGION. [<F] —**focal infection** A bacterial infection localized in certain body tissues, as the tonsils or a tooth, from which toxins are sent to other areas.

in·fec·tious (in·fek′shəs) *adj.* 1 That may be communicated by infection. 2 Able to communicate infection. 3 *Law* Tainting with illegality. 4 Having the quality of being transmitted from one to another: *infectious* laughter. 5 *Obs.* Infected. —**in·fec′tious·ly** *adv.* —**in·fec′tious·ness** *n.*

infectious disease Any disease due to the entrance into and growth in the body of micro-organisms.

infectious mononucleosis *Pathol.* An acute communicable disease marked by fever, sore throat, a swelling of the lymph nodes, especially in the cervical region, and an increase in abnormal mononuclear cells: also called *glandular fever.*

in·fec·tive (in·fek′tiv) *adj.* Infectious.

in·fe·lic·i·tous (in′fə·lis′ə·təs) *adj.* Not felicitous, happy, or suitable in application, condition, or result. —**in′fe·lic′i·tous·ly** *adv.* —**in′·fe·lic′i·tous·ness** *n.*

in·fe·lic·i·ty (in′fə·lis′ə·tē) *n. pl.* **·ties** 1 The state of being infelicitous; unhappiness. 2 That which is infelicitous; an inappropriate or inapt remark, act, etc. [<L *infelicitas, -tatis*]

in·felt (in′felt′) *adj.* Felt inwardly or deeply.

in·feoff (in·fēf′), **in·feoff·ment** (in·fēf′mənt) See ENFEOFF, etc.

in·fer (in·fûr′) *v.* **·ferred, ·fer·ring** *v.t.* 1 To derive by reasoning; conclude or accept from evidence or premises; deduce. Compare POSIT. 2 To involve or imply as a conclusion; give evidence of: said of facts, statements, etc.: His actions *infer* a motive. 3 Loosely, to imply; hint. 4 *Obs.* To bring in; advance; also, to cause. —*v.i.* 5 To draw inferences.

[<L *inferre* bring into <*in-* in + *ferre* bring, carry] **—in·fer′a·ble, in·fer′ri·ble** *adj.*

in·fer·ence (in′fər·əns) *n.* 1 The act of inferring. 2 That which is inferred; a deduction or conclusion. 3 Loosely, a conjecture. [< Med. L *inferentia* <L *inferens, -entis,* ppr. of *inferre.* See INFER.]

Synonyms: conclusion, consequence, deduction, demonstration, induction. A *conclusion* is the absolute and necessary result of the admission of certain premises; an *inference* is a probable *conclusion*, toward which known facts, statements, or admissions point, but which they do not absolutely establish; sound premises together with their necessary *conclusion* constitute a *demonstration.* See DEMONSTRATION, INDUCTION.

in·fer·en·tial (in′fə·ren′shəl) *adj.* Deducible by inference. **—in′fer·en′tial·ly** *adv.*

in·fe·ri·or (in·fir′ē·ər) *adj.* 1 Lower in quality, merit, importance, or rank. 2 *Biol.* Situated or placed lower, as certain parts of the body relative to others; in animals, situated on or pertaining to the lower or ventral side. 3 Later in point of time: the *inferior* limit of a year. 4 In music, having a lower pitch. 5 *Bot.* Below some other organ; in a blossom, anterior. 6 *Astron.* **a** Between the earth and the sun: an *inferior* planet. **b** Below the horizon; below the celestial pole. 7 *Printing* Set below the level of the line, as small characters without a shoulder below, used in chemical formulas. See synonyms under BAD[1]. —*n.* One who or that which is classed lower than others; a subordinate. [<L, lower, compar. of *inferus* low]

in·fe·ri·or·i·ty (in·fir′ē·ôr′ə·tē, -or′-) *n.* The state of being inferior; low condition.

inferiority complex *Psychol.* An emotional trend or state of mind characterized by a morbidly exaggerated sense of one's own limitations and incapacities, and sometimes compensated for by aggressive behavior.

in·fer·nal (in·fûr′nəl) *adj.* 1 Belonging to hell; diabolical: often used colloquially to express indignation or emphasis: an *infernal* rascal. 2 Pertaining to Tartarus. [<OF <L *infernalis* <*infernus* situated below <*inferus* below] **—in·fer′nal·ly** *adv.*

Synonyms: demoniac, demoniacal, devilish, diabolic, diabolical, fiendish, hellish, satanic.

infernal machine Any device for doing unusual damage by explosion.

in·fer·no (in·fûr′nō) *n. pl.* **·nos** 1 The infernal regions; hell. 2 Any place comparable to hell; especially, a hot or fiery place. [<Ital.]

In·fer·no (in·fûr′nō) The first of the three parts of the *Divina Commedia* of Dante, describing the poet's journey through Hell, under the guidance of Vergil.

infero– *combining form Anat. & Zool.* On the under side; below. [<L *inferus* low]

in·fer·o·lat·er·al (in′fər·ō·lat′ər·əl) *adj.* Below and on one side.

in·fer·tile (in·fûr′til) *adj.* Not fertile or productive; sterile; barren. **—in′fer·til′i·ty** *n.*

in·fest (in·fest′) *v.t.* To overrun or haunt in large numbers, especially so as to render unpleasant or unsafe: The barn is *infested* with rats. [<MF *infester* <L *infestare* assail <*infestus* hostile] **—in·fest′er** *n.*

in·fes·ta·tion (in′fes·tā′shən) *n.* 1 The act of infesting. 2 The state of being infested, as with parasites or vermin. [<LL *infestatio, -onis*]

in·feu·da·tion (in′fyōō·dā′shən) *n.* 1 In feudal law, the granting or the putting in possession of an estate in fee; also, the feudal relation. 2 The granting of tithes to laymen. [<Med. L *infeudatio, -onis* <*infeudare* enfeoff <*in-* in + *feudum* FEUD[2]]

in·fi·del (in′fi·dəl) *n.* 1 One who denies the existence of God. 2 An unbeliever, as viewed from the standpoint of a believer in any particular religion or belief. See synonyms under SKEPTIC. —*adj.* 1 Lacking the true faith; especially, rejecting the Christian religion. 2 Faithless; recreant. 3 Of, relating to, or characteristic of infidels or infidelity. [<OF *infidèle* <L *infidelis* unfaithful <*in-* not + *fidelis* faithful]

in·fi·del·i·ty (in′fi·del′ə·tē) *n. pl.* **·ties** 1 The state of being an infidel; lack of belief. 2 Lack of fidelity; specifically, violation of the marriage vow by adultery.

in·field (in′fēld′) *n.* 1 **a** The space thirty yards square enclosed within the base lines of a baseball field: distinguished from *outfield.* **b** The infielders collectively. See illustration under BASEBALL. 2 Land under tillage; distinguished from *outfield.*

in·field·er (in′fēl′dər) *n.* In baseball, a defensive player in the infield: the first, second, and third basemen, the shortstop, and, when fielding the ball, the pitcher and catcher: distinguished from *outfielder.*

in·fil·ter (in·fil′tər) *v.t.* & *v.i.* To enter by infiltration.

in·fil·trate (in·fil′trāt; *esp. for v. defs. 2, 3* in′fil·trāt) *v.* **·trat·ed, ·trat·ing** *v.t.* 1 To cause (a liquid or gas) to pass into or through pores or interstices. 2 To filter through or into; permeate. 3 *Mil.* To pass through, as enemy lines, singly or in small groups so as to attack from the rear or on the flanks. —*v.i.* 4 To pass into or through a substance, as in filtering. —*n.* 1 That which infiltrates or has infiltrated. 2 Any morbid substance that passes into the tissues of the body.

in·fil·tra·tion (in′fil·trā′shən) *n.* 1 The act or process of infiltrating. 2 That which infiltrates. **—in·fil·tra·tive** (in·fil′trə·tiv) *adj.*

in·fin·i·tate (in·fin′ə·tāt) *v.t.* **·tat·ed, ·tat·ing** *Logic* To make (a positive concept or proposition) infinite or indefinite by adding a negative prefix to one of its terms; also, to make (a negative concept or proposition) positive by the reverse of this method: "Tigers are not herbivorous" when *infinitated* becomes "Tigers are non-herbivorous." [<Med. L *infinitatus,* pp. of *infinitare* render infinite <*infinitus* infinite] **—in·fin′i·ta′tion** *n.*

in·fi·nite (in′fə·nit) *adj.* 1 So great as to be immeasurable and unbounded; limitless: *infinite* power or space. 2 All-embracing; perfect; absolute: the *infinite* God. 3 *Math.* **a** Of, pertaining to, or designating a quantity conceived as always increasing so as to exceed any other assignable quantity in value. **b** Consisting of as many elements as a proper part of a total assemblage. 4 In music, composed so that it can be repeated over and over, without finale. 5 Very numerous; very great: to take *infinite* pains. —*n.* That which is infinite; an infinite quantity or magnitude; infinity. **—the Infinite** God; Eternity; the Absolute. [<L *infinitus* unlimited <*in-* not + *finitus* finite <*finis* limit] **—in′fi·nite·ly** *adv.* **—in′fi·nite·ness** *n.*

Synonyms: absolute, boundless, countless, eternal, illimitable, immeasurable, innumerable, interminable, limitless, measureless, numberless, unbounded, unconditioned, unfathomable, unlimited, unmeasured. *Infinite* signifies without bounds or limits in any way, and may be applied to space, time, quantity, or number. *Countless, innumerable,* and *numberless,* which should be the same as *infinite,* are in common usage vaguely employed to denote what it is difficult or practically impossible to count or number, but still perhaps falling far short of *infinite*; as, *countless* leaves, the *countless* sands on the seashore, *numberless* battles, *innumerable* delays. So, too, *boundless, illimitable, limitless, measureless,* and *unlimited* are loosely used in reference to what has no apparent or readily determinable limits in space or time; as, we speak of the *boundless* ocean. *Infinite* space is without bounds, not only in fact, but in thought; *infinite* time is truly *eternal.* Compare ETERNAL, PERFECT. *Antonyms*: bounded, brief, circumscribed, evanescent, finite, limited, little, measurable, moderate, narrow, restricted, shallow, short, small, transient, transitory.

in·fin·i·tes·i·mal (in′fin·ə·tes′ə·məl) *adj.* 1 Infinitely small. 2 So small as to be incalculable and insignificant for all practical purposes. 3 *Math.* Denoting a quantity conceived as continually diminishing toward zero as a limit. —*n.* An infinitesimal quantity. [<NL *infinitesimus* <*infinitus* infinite + *-esimus* (after *centesimus* hundredth)] **—in′fin·i·tes′i·mal·ly** *adv.*

infinitesimal calculus 1 Differential and integral calculus taken together. See under CALCULUS. 2 A branch of calculus which deals with differentials and the sums of infinitesimals.

in·fin·i·ti·val (in·fin′ə·tī′vəl) *adj. Gram.* Of or pertaining to the infinitive mood of the verb. **—in·fin′i·ti′val·ly** *adv.*

in·fin·i·tive (in·fin′ə·tiv) *Gram. adj.* 1 Without limitation of person or number: opposed to *finite.* 2 Of, pertaining to, or using the infinitive mood. —*n.* In many languages, a mood of the verb expressing action or condition without the limitation of person or number, as *to run.* In English, its sign *to* is omitted after the auxiliaries *can, could, do, may, might, must, shall, should, will, would,* and after such phrases as *had better, had rather,* and is used optionally after *bid, dare, help, let, make, need, please, see,* etc. The infinitive may also function as a noun while retaining the ability of the verb to take objects and adverbial modifiers. Example: *To ride* horses was his favorite sport. Also **infinitive mood. —split infinitive** An expression in which the sign of the infinitive "to" is separated from its verb by an intervening word, usually an adverb, as in the phrase "to quickly return." Although the construction is often condemned, it is sometimes justified to escape ambiguity. [<LL *infinitivus*]

in·fin·i·tude (in·fin′ə·tōōd, -tyōōd) *n.* 1 The quality of being infinite or boundless. 2 An infinite or unlimited quantity.

in·fin·i·ty (in·fin′ə·tē) *n. pl.* **·ties** 1 The quality or state of being infinite; boundlessness; perfection. 2 Something, as space, regarded as boundless. 3 The portion of space that lies at an infinite distance. 4 *Math.* **a** An infinite number or quantity: denoted by ∞. **b** The point or series of points in space that by supposition lie at an infinite distance from the definite point in question. [<OF *infinité* <L *infinitas, -tatis* <*infinitus* INFINITE]

in·firm (in·fûrm′) *adj.* 1 Feeble or weak from age. 2 Lacking soundness, resolution, stability, or firmness. 3 Not legally secure; voidable. See synonyms under FRAGILE, SICKLY. [<OF *enferm* <L *infirmus*] **—in·firm′ly** *adv.* **—in·firm′ness** *n.*

in·fir·mar·i·an (in′fər·mâr′ē·ən) *n.* A person having charge of a hospital, especially in a monastery, or who is delegated to perform hospital service.

in·fir·ma·ry (in·fûr′mər·ē) *n. pl.* **·ries** 1 A place for the treatment of the sick; a dispensary. 2 A small hospital. [<Med. L *infirmaria* <*infirmus* infirm]

in·fir·mi·ty (in·fûr′mə·tē) *n. pl.* **·ties** 1 A physical, mental, or moral weakness or flaw. 2 Infirm condition. See synonyms under DISEASE, FOIBLE, ILLNESS.

in·fix (in·fiks′) *v.t.* 1 To fix or drive in, as by thrusting. 2 To implant firmly; instil; inculcate. 3 *Gram.* To insert (an infix) within a word. —*n.* (in′fiks) *Gram.* A modifying addition inserted in the body of a word. Compare PREFIX, SUFFIX. **—in·fix′ion** *n.*

in fla·gran·te de·lic·to (in flə·gran′tē di·lik′·tō) *Latin* In the very act of committing a crime: literally, while the crime is blazing.

in·flame (in·flām′) *v.* **·flamed, ·flam·ing** *v.t.* 1 To set on fire; kindle. 2 To excite to violent emotion or activity; arouse the fury of. 3 To excite or make more intense, as anger or lust. 4 To make red or florid, as with rage. 5 To cause inflammation in; heat morbidly. —*v.i.* 6 To catch fire; burst into flame. 7 To become excited or aroused. 8 To become inflamed by infection, etc. See synonyms under INCENSE[1]. [<OF *enflammer* <L *inflammare* <*in-* in + *flammare* flame <*flamma* flame] **—in·flam′er** *n.*

in·flam·ma·ble (in·flam′ə·bəl) *adj.* 1 Readily set on fire; combustible: also *flammable.* 2 Easily excited or roused to passion. —*n.* A combustible substance or material. See synonyms under ARDENT. [<F] **—in·flam′ma·bil′·i·ty, in·flam′ma·ble·ness** *n.* **—in·flam′ma·bly** *adv.*

in·flam·ma·tion (in′flə·mā′shən) *n.* 1 *Pathol.* A morbid process in some tissue, organ, or part of the body characterized by heat, redness, swelling, and pain. 2 The act of inflaming.

in·flam·ma·to·ry (in·flam′ə·tôr′ē, -tō′rē) *adj.* 1 Tending to produce heat or excitement. 2 Calculated to arouse evil passions, riot, etc.; seditious. 3 Characterized by or pertaining to inflammation. 4 Inducing or provoking inflammation.

in·flate (in·flāt′) *v.* **·flat·ed, ·flat·ing** *v.t.* 1 To fill with gas or air so as to distend or expand; blow up; dilate. 2 To increase the proportions of; puff up: to *inflate* one's pride. 3 To increase unduly, especially so that the nominal value exceeds the real: to *inflate* currency or prices. —*v.i.* **4** To become distended or inflated. See synonyms under PUFF, SWELL. [<L *inflatus*, pp. of *inflare* blow into <*in-* in + *flare* blow] — **in·flat'a·ble** *adj.*

in·flat·ed (in·flā'tid) *adj.* **1** Puffed out; distended; swollen, as by air or gas. **2** Hollowed or puffed out, as a plant stem or capsule; bulbous; dilated. **3** Overloaded with figures of speech and high-sounding words; pompous; bombastic; magniloquent. **4** Enhanced

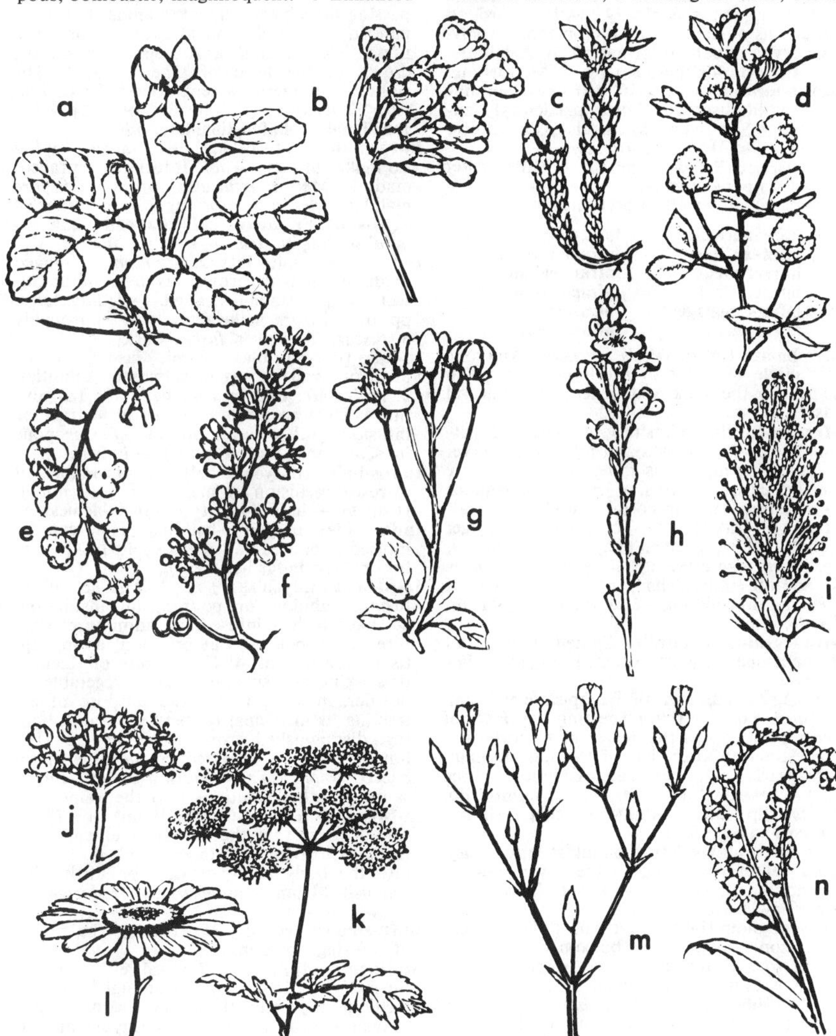

INFLORESCENCE

a. Uniflorous (violet).
b. Many-flowered (primrose).
c. Terminal (sedum).
d. Axillary (black medic).
e. Ordinary (grape currant).
f. Variegate (grapevine).
g. Clustered (cherry tree).
h. Corymb (verbena).
i. Catkin (willow).
j. Simple umbel (ivy).
k. Compound umbel (parsnips).
l. Capitulum (large marguerite).
m. Cyme: biparous or dichotomous (chickweed).
n. Cyme: uniparous or scorpion's-tail (forget-me-not).

or swollen abnormally or improperly; increased unjustifiably: *inflated* values. **5** Puffed up with conceit.

in·flat·er (in·flā'tər) *n.* One who or that which inflates; especially, any mechanical device, as an air pump, for inflating. Also **in·fla'tor.**

in·fla·tion (in·flā'shən) *n.* **1** The act of inflating, or the state of being inflated; distention: the *inflation* of a bubble or a balloon. **2** Bombast; conceit. **3** Expansion or extension beyond natural or proper limits or so as to exceed normal or just value; specifically, overissue of currency, or the state resulting therefrom; also, increase in price levels arising from mounting effective demand without corresponding increase in commodity supply. **4** That which is inflated or puffed up. — **in·fla'·tion·ar'y** *adj.*

in·fla·tion·ist (in·flā'shən·ist) *n.* An advocate of or believer in the issuing of an abnormally large amount of currency.

in·flect (in·flekt') *v.t.* **1** *Gram.* To give or recite the inflections of (a word); conjugate; decline. **2** To modulate, as the voice. **3** To turn inward or aside; deflect; curve. —*v.i.* **4** To take grammatical inflection. [<L *inflectere* <*in-* in + *flectere* bend]

in·flec·tion (in·flek'shən) *n.* **1** The act of inflecting, the state of being inflected, or that which is inflected; a bending or bend; curvature; angle. **2** *Gram.* **a** A pattern of change undergone by words to express grammatical and syntactical relations, as of case, number, gender, person, tense, etc. The inflection of nouns, pronouns and adjectives is called *declension*; that of verbs, *conjugation.* **b** An element denoting the grammatical function of a word, as the use of *'s* to signify possession in *boy's.* **c** An inflected form. **3** Modulation or change of pitch in the voice. **4** *Geom.* A change in the nature of a curve, as from convex to concave. Also *Brit.* **in·flex'ion**: sometimes called *flection.*

◆ The few inflections surviving in English include: *s* for the regular plural of nouns, and for the third person singular present indicative of verbs; *'s* for the possessive: *-er* for the comparative, and *-est* for the superlative, of many adjectives and adverbs; *-ed* for the past and past participle of regular (or weak) verbs, and *-ing* for the present participle.

in·flec·tion·al (in·flek'shən·əl) *adj. Ling.* **1** Belonging to, relating to, or showing grammatical inflection. **2** Designating a language, such as Latin, that expresses grammatical relationships by means of inflections, rather than by auxiliary words; synthetic: opposed to *analytic.* Also *Brit.* **in·flex'ion·al.** — **in·flec'·tion·al·ly** *adv.*

in·flexed (in·flekst') *adj. Bot.* Abruptly turned or bent inward, as the petals of a flower.

in·flex·i·ble (in·flek'sə·bəl) *adj.* **1** Not to be turned from a purpose; unyielding; firm; inexorable: *inflexible* resolves, an *inflexible* will. **2** Incapable of being physically bent; unbending; rigid; not flexible. **3** That cannot be altered or varied: the *inflexible* laws of nature. [<L *inflexibilis*] — **in·flex'i·bil'i·ty, in·flex'i·ble·ness** *n.* — **in·flex'i·bly** *adv.*

Synonyms: immovable, inexorable, obstinate, persistent, pertinacious, resolute, rigid, steadfast, stiff, stubborn, unbending, unrelenting, unyielding. See OBSTINATE. *Antonyms*: ductile, elastic, flexible, indulgent, lithe, pliable, pliant, supple, yielding.

in·flict (in·flikt') *v.t.* **1** To cause another to suffer or endure, as a blow or wound. **2** To impose, as punishment. **3** To impose as if by force or against opposition: to *inflict* one's views on the public. [<L *inflictus*, pp. of *infligere* strike on <*in-* on + *fligere* strike] — **in·flict'er, in·flic'tor** *n.* — **in·flic'tive** *adj.*

in·flic·tion (in·flik'shən) *n.* **1** The act or process of inflicting or imposing: the *infliction* of a penalty. **2** That which is inflicted, as pain or punishment.

in·flo·res·cence (in'flə·res'əns) *n. Bot.* **1** The act of flowering; the expanding of blossoms. **2** The mode of disposition of flowers: racemose and cymose *inflorescence.* **3** Flowers collectively: said of certain plants or of a tree or a group of trees: the *inflorescence* of the horse chestnut. **4** An axis along which all the buds are flower buds. [<NL *inflorescentia* <LL *inflorescens*, ppr. of *inflorescere* come into flower. See IN-², FLORESCENCE.] — **in'flo·res'cent** *adj.*

in·flow (in'flō') *n.* The act of flowing in, or that which flows in.

in·flu·ence (in'flo͞o·əns) *n.* **1** The power or process of producing an effect upon a person, by imperceptible or intangible means. **2** Power arising from social, financial, moral, or similar authority. **3** A person, group, or the like possessing such power. **4** *Electr.* Electrostatic induction. **5** In astrology, originally, an ethereal fluid flowing from the stars and affecting the character and actions of men; later, an occult force of the stars exercising a similar control. See synonyms under IMPULSE, OPERATION. —*v.t.* **·enced, ·enc·ing 1** To exert mental or moral influence upon or over; sway; persuade. **2** To act upon physically; affect the nature or condition of; modify: Fatigue often *influences* the eyesight. [<F <LL *influentia* <*influens, -entis*, ppr. of *influere* <*in-* in + *fluere* flow. Doublet of INFLUENZA.] — **in'flu·enc'er** *n.*

Synonyms (verb): activate, actuate, affect, command, compel, dispose, draw, drive, excite, impel, incite, incline, induce, instigate, lead, mold, move, persuade, prompt, stir, sway, urge. To *influence* is to affect, modify, or act upon by physical, mental, or moral power, especially in some gentle, subtle, and gradual way; as, Vegetation is *influenced* by light; Everyone is *influenced* to some extent by public opinion; *influence* is chiefly used of power acting from without, but it may be used of motives regarded as forces acting upon the will. *Activate* means to put or go into action, to make capable of acting. *Actuate* refers to that which initiates the action of a mechanism or apparatus, as well as to mental or moral power *impelling* one from within. One may *influence,* but cannot directly *actuate* another; but one may be *actuated* to cruelty by hatred. *Prompt* and *stir* are words of mere suggestion toward some course of action; *dispose, draw, incline, influence,* and *lead* refer to the use of mild means to awaken in another a purpose or disposition to act. To *excite* is to arouse one from lethargy or indifference to action. *Incite* and *instigate,* to spur or goad to action, differ in the fact that *incite* may be good, while *instigate* is usually to evil (compare ABET). To *urge* and *impel* signify to produce strong excitation toward some act. *Drive* and *compel* imply irresistible influence accomplishing its object. One may be *driven* either by his own passions or by external force or urgency; one is *compelled* only by some external power; as, The owner was *compelled* by his misfortunes to sell his estate. Compare ACTUATE, BEND, COMPEL, DRIVE, GOVERN, PERSUADE. *Antonyms*: deter, discourage, dissuade, hinder, impede, inhibit, prevent, restrain, retard.

influence fuze A proximity fuze.

in·flu·ent (in′flōō·ənt) *adj.* **1** Flowing in. **2** Relating to a channel through which either air or any fluid passes into a receptacle. — *n.* An inflow; a tributary stream or river; affluent. [<L *influens, -entis,* ppr. of *influere.* See INFLUENCE.]

in·flu·en·tial (in′flōō·en′shəl) *adj.* **1** Having or exercising influence. **2** Having or exercising a great influence or power; effective. — **in′flu·en′tial·ly** *adv.*

in·flu·en·za (in′flōō·en′zə) *n.* **1** *Pathol.* A contagious, infective, sometimes epidemic disease generally caused by a filtrable virus and commonly characterized by inflammation of the upper air passages, attended by fever and nervous and muscular prostration. **2** A contagious disease common among horses: characterized by its attack upon the mucous membranes of the throat and eyelids. [<Ital. < *influire* influence <L *influere* flow in. Doublet of INFLUENCE.] — **in′flu·en′zal** *adj.* — **in′flu·en′za·like′** *adj.*

in·flux (in′fluks′) *n.* **1** The act of flowing in; a continuous flowing in. **2** A pouring in or instilling. **3** The mouth of a river. **4** The place or point at which one stream flows into another. See synonyms under ACCESSION. [<F <LL *influxus,* pp. of *influere* flow in]

in·fold (in·fōld′) *v.t.* **1** To wrap in folds; enclose. **2** To embrace in or as in the arms; contain. **3** To turn or fold inward; make a fold in. Also *enfold.* — **in·fold′er** *n.*

in·form[1] (in·fôrm′) *v.t.* **1** To tell (someone) facts or information previously unknown; make something known to; notify: He *informed* me of the outcome. **2** To give character to; inspire; animate. **3** *Obs.* To give form or vitality to; shape. **4** *Rare* To teach; instruct. — *v.i.* **5** To give information, especially concerning infractions of the law: with *on* or *against.* [<OF *enformer* <L *informare* give form to, describe < *in-* in + *forma* form]

Synonyms: advertise, advise, apprise, communicate, disclose, divulge, impart, instruct, intimate, mention, notify, reveal, teach, tell. See LEARN, TEACH.

in·form[2] (in·fôrm′) *adj.* **1** Shapeless; unformed. **2** Deformed. [<F *informe* <L *informis* < *in-* not + *forma* form]

in·for·mal (in·fôr′məl) *adj.* **1** Not in the usual or prescribed form; unofficial: an *informal* truce. **2** Without ceremony or formality: an *informal* dinner. **3** Describing a manner of speech or writing characteristic of familiar conversation; colloquial. — **in·for′mal·ly** *adv.*

in·for·mal·i·ty (in′fôr·mal′ə·tē) *n. pl.* **·ties** **1** Absence of regular form; the state of being informal. **2** An informal act or proceeding.

in·form·ant (in·fôr′mənt) *n.* **1** One who imparts information. **2** *Ling.* A native speaker of a language whose speech is used by linguists in recording and studying linguistic forms, sounds, etc.

in for·ma pau·pe·ris (in fôr′mə pô′pər·is) *Latin* In the character or condition of a pauper; hence, in a lawsuit, free from costs.

in·for·ma·tion (in′fər·mā′shən) *n.* **1** Knowledge acquired or derived. **2** Timely or specific knowledge. **3** *Law* An accusation or complaint made without the intervention of a grand jury. **4** The act of informing. **5** Any distinct signal element forming part of a message or communication, especially one assembled and made available for use by automatic machines, as a digital computer: usually measured in bits. [<OF *enformacion*] — **in′for·ma′tion·al** *adj.* See synonyms under EDUCATION, KNOWLEDGE, TIDINGS, WISDOM.

information theory The scientific study of the characteristics, properties, and functions of any signal system designed to transmit information, with special emphasis on the number of bits that can be sent on a given power in a given time over a communication system operating under given conditions: also called *communication theory.*

in·form·a·tive (in·fôr′mə·tiv) *adj.* Instructive; affording information. Also **in·form′a·to′ry.** [<L *informatus,* pp. of *informare* describe]

in·formed (in·fôrmd′) *adj.* Having a high degree of knowledge, information, or education.

in·form·er (in·fôr′mər) *n.* **1** One who informs against others; specifically, with regard to infractions of the law; a stool pigeon; a spy. **2** One who imparts information. **3** A telltale.

in·for·tune (in·fôr′chən) *n. Obs.* **1** Misfortune: also **in′for·tu′ni·ty.** **2** In astrology, an unlucky or ill-disposed planet: particularly applicable to Saturn and Mars; also, sometimes, Mercury. [<OF <L *infortunium*]

infra– *prefix* Below; beneath; on the lower part. Compare SUPRA–.

Infra– may appear as a prefix, as in:

infra–auricular	**inframarginal**
infra–axillary	**inframolecular**
infraclavicle	**inframundane**
infracortical	**infraposition**
infra–esophageal	**infraspinal**
infrahuman	**infraspinous**

in·fra·ba·sal (in′frə·bā′səl) *n. Zool.* Any one of a circle of plates of a crinoid cup which lie next to the stalk and beneath the natural basal plates.

in·fra·cos·tal (in′frə·kos′təl) *adj. Anat.* **1** Situated below a rib (costa): an *infracostal* nerve. **2** Indicating numerous minor muscles below the surface of the ribs. — *n. pl.* **·kos·ta·les** (-kos·tā′lēz) An infracostal muscle.

in·fract (in·frakt′) *v.t.* To break; infringe; violate (a law, pledge, etc.). [<L *infractus,* pp. of *infringere* INFRINGE] — **in·frac′tor** *n.*

in·frac·tion (in·frak′shən) *n.* **1** The act of breaking or violating. **2** A fracture. [<L *infractio, -onis*]

in·fra dig·ni·ta·tem (in′frə dig′nə·tā′təm) *Latin* Beneath one's dignity: often abridged to **in′·fra dig.**

in·fra·lap·sar·i·an·ism (in′frə·lap·sâr′ē·ən·iz′əm) *n. Theol.* The doctrine respecting the order of decrees that places the decree of election and predestination after that of the fall of man; sublapsarianism; moderate Calvinism. See SUPRALAPSARIAN. [<INFRA- + L *lapsus,* pp. of *labi* slip, fall + -ARIAN + -ISM] — **in′fra·lap·sar′i·an** *adj.* & *n.*

in·fra·max·il·lar·y (in′frə·mak′sə·ler′ē) *adj. Anat.* Of or pertaining to the lower jaw or inferior maxillary bone. — *n. pl.* **·lar·ies** The lower jaw bone.

in·fra·me·di·an (in′frə·mē′dē·ən) *n.* That interval or zone along the sea bottom which is between 50 and 100 fathoms in depth. — *adj.* Of or pertaining to this zone.

in·fran·gi·ble (in·fran′jə·bəl) *adj.* **1** Not breakable or capable of being broken into parts. **2** Inviolable. — **in·fran′gi·bil′i·ty, in·fran′gi·ble·ness** *n.* — **in·fran′gi·bly** *adv.*

in·fra–o·ral (in′frə·ôr′əl, -ō′rəl) *adj. Anat.* Placed beneath the mouth.

in·fra–or·bit·al (in′frə·ôr′bit·əl) *adj. Anat.* Situated below the orbit of the eye.

in·fra·red (in′frə·red′) *adj. Physics* **1** Situated beyond the red end of the visible spectrum, as certain heat rays. **2** Designating radiations of wavelength in excess of about 7,600 angstroms but less than radio waves.

in·fra·son·ic (in′frə·son′ik) *adj.* Of, pertaining to, or characterized by a sound frequency below the range of audibility: also called *subsonic.* Compare ULTRASONIC.

in·fra·struc·ture (in′frə·struk′chər) *n.* The permanent foundation or essential elements of a structure, system, plan of operations, etc.; especially, the essential installations of a community, as schools, hospitals, transportation facilities, power plants, etc.

in·fre·quent (in·frē′kwənt) *adj.* Occurring at widely separate intervals; uncommon. — **in·fre′quent·ly** *adv.* — **in·fre′quen·cy** *n.*

in·fringe (in·frinj′) *v.t.* **·fringed, ·fring·ing** To break or disregard the terms or requirements of, as an oath or law; violate. — **to infringe on** (or **upon**) To transgress or trespass on rights or privileges; encroach: to *infringe on* a liberty or a patent. [<L *infringere* < *in-* in + *frangere* break] — **in·fring′er** *n.*

in·fringe·ment (in·frinj′mənt) *n.* **1** The act of infringing. **2** Any breaking in upon or violation of a right, privilege, regulation, law, contract, etc. **3** The wrongful use of trademarks or trade names.

in·fun·dib·u·li·form (in′fən·dib′yə·lə·fôrm′) *adj.* **1** Funnel–shaped. **2** *Bot.* Having a tube below and gradually enlarged above.

in·fun·dib·u·lum (in′fən·dib′yə·ləm) *n. pl.* **·la** (-lə) **1** *Anat.* **a** A structure or conduit shaped like a funnel, as that connecting the third ventricle of the brain with the pituitary body, passing through the hypothalamus. **b** An expanded end of a bronchial tubule or of a ureter, etc. **2** *Biol.* **a** A depression on the crown of the head of tapeworms. **b** The siphon or funnel of a cephalopod. [<L, funnel < *infundere* pour into. See INFUSE.] — **in′·fun·dib′u·lar, in′fun·dib′u·late** *adj.*

in·fu·ri·ate (in·fyŏŏr′ē·āt) *v.t.* **·at·ed, ·at·ing** To make furious. — *adj.* Infuriated; enraged; mad. [<Med. L *infuriatus,* pp. of *infuriare* madden < *in-* in + *furia* rage] — **in·fu′ri·at′ed** *adj.* — **in·fu′ri·ate·ly, in·fu′ri·at′ed·ly** *adv.* — **in·fu′ri·at′ing·ly** *adv.* — **in·fu′ri·a′tion** *n.*

in·fus·cate (in·fus′kit) *adj. Entomol.* Tinged or darkened with brown, as part of an insect's wing. Also **in·fus′cat·ed.** [<L *infuscatus,* pp. of *infuscare* make dark < *in-* thoroughly + *fuscare* darken <*fuscus* dark]

in·fuse (in·fyōōz′) *v.t.* **·fused, ·fus·ing** **1** To instil or inculcate, as principles or qualities. **2** To inspire; imbue: with *with.* **3** To pour in. **4** To steep, so as to make an extract or infusion. [<L *infusus,* pp. of *infunder* pour in < *in-* in + *fundere* pour] — **in·fus′er** *n.*

in·fus·i·ble[1] (in·fyōō′zə·bəl) *adj.* Incapable of or resisting fusion or melting. [<IN-[1] not + FUSIBLE] — **in·fus′i·bil′i·ty, in·fus′i·ble·ness** *n.*

in·fus·i·ble[2] (in·fyōō′zə·bəl) *adj.* That can be infused or poured in. [<INFUSE + -IBLE] — **in·fus′i·bil′i·ty, in·fus′i·ble·ness** *n.*

in·fu·sion (in·fyōō′zhən) *n.* **1** The act of infusing, imbuing, or pouring in; instilation. **2** That which is infused; an admixture; tincture. **3** A pouring out or upon, as in baptism; an affusion. **4** The process of steeping or soaking any substance, as a vegetable or powder, in a liquid for the purpose of extracting its medicinal properties without boiling: distinguished from *decoction.* **5** The liquid extract so obtained: an *infusion* of tobacco. **6** *Med.* The operation of introducing saline or other solutions into the veins.

in·fu·sion·ism (in·fyōō′zhən·iz′əm) *n. Theol.* The doctrine that the human soul emanates from the divine substance, and is infused into the body at conception or birth: distinguished from *creationism* and *traducianism.* — **in·fu′sion·ist** *n.*

in·fu·sive (in·fyōō′siv) *adj.* Having the power of infusing; inspiring.

In·fu·so·ri·a (in′fyōō·sôr′ē·ə, -sō′rē·ə) *n. pl.* **1** Formerly, a division of the animal kingdom, including especially those microscopic protozoans found in infusions of decaying matter. **2** A class of the phylum *Protozoa,* characterized by ciliated bodies and free–living aquatic habits, including *Paramecium* and *Stentor*: also called *Ciliata.* — **in′fu·so′ri·an** *adj.* & *n.* [<NL *infusus,* pp. of *infundere* pour into]

in·fu·so·ri·al (in′fyōō·sôr′ē·əl, -sō′rē-) *adj.* **1** Of or pertaining to infusorians. **2** Containing or composed of infusorians.

infusorial earth Kieselguhr.

in fu·tu·ro (in fyōō·tyŏŏr′ō) *Latin* In the future.

–ing[1] *suffix* **1** The act or art of doing the action expressed in the root verb: *hunting.* **2** The product or result of an action: a *painting,* a *building.* **3** Material for: *flooring.* **4** That which performs the action of the root verb: a *covering.* [OE *-ung, -ing*]

–ing[2] *suffix* Used in the present participle of verbs and in participial adjectives: He is *talking*; an *eating* apple. [ME *-inde* <OE *-ende*; infl. by ME *-inge* -ING[1]]

–ing[3] *suffix of nouns* **1** Related or belonging to; having the quality of: *farthing.* **2** Descendant of: *Browning.* **3** Small; little: *atheling.* [OE]

in·gath·er (in·gath′ər) *v.t.* & *v.i.* To gather in; harvest; assemble. — **in·gath′er·er** *n.*

in·gath·er·ing (in·gath′ər·ing) *n.* The act or occupation of gathering in, specifically, of a harvest. See synonyms under HARVEST.

Inge (ing), **William Ralph,** 1860–1954, English

churchman and author; dean of St. Paul's, London, 1911–34.

In·ge·low (in′jə·lō), **Jean,** 1820–97, English author.

in·gem·i·nate (in·jem′ə·nāt) *v.t.* **·nat·ed, ·nat·ing** To repeat or redouble; reiterate. —*adj.* (-it) Repeated; redoubled. [<L *ingeminatus,* pp. of *ingeminare* double. See IN-[1], GERMINATE.] —**in·gem′i·na′tion** *n.*

in·gen·er·ate[1] (in·jen′ər·āt) *v.t.* **·at·ed, ·at·ing** To generate or produce within. —*adj.* (-it) Inborn. [<L *ingeneratus,* pp. of *ingenerare* ENGENDER] —**in·gen′er·a′tion** *n.*

in·gen·er·ate[2] (in·jen′ər·it) *adj.* Not brought into being by generation. [<LL *ingeneratus* self-existent]

in·gen·ious (in·jēn′yəs) *adj.* **1** Possessed of or manifesting inventive faculty. **2** Characterized by ingenuity; well conceived; apt. **3** *Obs.* Of clever mind or genius, or displaying exceptional mental qualities. See synonyms under CLEVER. [<MF *ingénieux* <L *ingeniosus* talented < *ingenium* natural quality, ability < *in-* in + *gignere* beget] —**in·gen′ious·ly** *adv.* —**in·gen′ious·ness** *n.*

in·gen·i·tal (in·jen′ə·təl) *adj. Obs.* That is natural to one; inherent. [<L *ingenitus,* pp. of *ingignere* implant, beget]

in·gé·nue (an′zhə·no͞o′, *Fr.* aṅ·zhā·nü′) *n. pl.* **·nues** (-no͞oz′, *Fr.* ·nü′) **1** A young woman or girl who is artless, ingenuous, or innocent. **2** An actress who fills such a role; also, the role. [<F, fem. of *ingénu* <L *ingenuus* INGENUOUS]

in·ge·nu·i·ty (in′jə·no͞o′ə·tē, -nyo͞o′-) *n.* **1** The quality of having inventive power; cleverness in contriving or originating. **2** Ingeniousness of execution or design. **3** *Obs.* Ingenuousness; candor.

Synonyms: acuteness, cleverness, cunning, dexterity, genius, ingeniousness, invention, inventiveness, readiness, skill. *Ingenuity* is inferior to *genius,* being rather mechanical than creative, and is shown in devising expedients, overcoming difficulties, inventing appliances, adapting means to ends. *Dexterity* is chiefly of the hand; *cleverness* may be either of the hand or of the mind, but chiefly of the latter. See ADDRESS. *Antonyms*: awkwardness, clumsiness, dulness, stupidity, unskilfulness.

in·gen·u·ous (in·jen′yo͞o·əs) *adj.* **1** Free from disguise or dissimulation; frank; artless. **2** High-minded; sincere. **3** Ingenious: an incorrect use. See synonyms under CANDID, HONEST. [<L *ingenuus* inborn, natural, frank < *in-gignere* beget, engender] —**in·gen′u·ous·ly** *adv.* —**in·gen′u·ous·ness** *n.*

In·ger·soll (ing′gər·səl, -sôl), **Robert Green,** 1833–99, U.S. lawyer, agnostic, and writer.

in·gest (in·jest′) *v.t.* To take in (food) for digestion. [<L *ingestus,* pp. of *ingere* carry in < *in-* in + *gerere* carry] —**in·ges′tion** *n.* —**in·ges′tive** *adj.*

in·ges·ta (in·jes′tə) *n. pl.* **1** Things introduced or taken into a living body, as food: opposed to *egesta.* **2** Anything incorporated. [<NL, neut. pl. of *ingestus,* pp. of *ingerere* carry in]

in·gine (in·jīn′) *n. Scot.* Natural ability; a gifted person.

in·gle (ing′gəl) *n. Scot.* A fire or fireplace.

in·gle·nook (ing′gəl·no͝ok′) *n.* A corner by the fire.

in·gle·side (ing′gəl·sīd′) *n. Scot.* The fireside. Also **in′gle–cheek′** (-chēk).

in·glo·ri·ous (in·glôr′ē·əs, -glō′rē-) *adj.* **1** Characterized by failure or disgrace. **2** Without glory; obscure; humble. [<L *ingloriosus*] —**in·glo′ri·ous·ly** *adv.* —**in·glo′ri·ous·ness** *n.*

in·go·ing (in′gō′ing) *adj.* Entering; going in.

In·golds·by (ing′gəldz·bē), **Thomas** See BARHAM.

In·gol·stadt (ing′ôl·shtät) A city on the Danube in Upper Bavaria, West Germany.

in·got (ing′gət) *n.* **1** A mass of cast metal from the crucible, as a bar of gold. **2** *Obs.* A mold in which an ingot may be cast. [<IN-[2] + OE *goten,* pp. of *geoton* pour]

in·graft (in·graft′, -gräft′) See ENGRAFT.

in·grain (in·grān′) *v.t.* **1** To fix deeply; impress indelibly upon the mind or character. **2** To dye before weaving; dye with "grain" or scarlet. Also spelled *engrain.* —*n.* (in′grān′) A carpet made of ingrained worsted; also, the ingrained wool or other material of which it is made. —*adj.* (in′grān′) Dyed in the yarn before manufacture; hence, thoroughly inwrought. [Var. of ENGRAIN]

in·grained (in·grānd′) *adj.* **1** Dyed in the wool; deeply rooted or worked in. **2** Thorough; inveterate.

in·grate (in′grāt) *adj. Obs.* Ungrateful. Also **in·grate′ful.** —*n.* One who is ungrateful. [<OF *ingrat* <L *ingratus* unpleasant, ungrateful < *in-* not + *gratus* pleasing]

in·gra·ti·ate (in·grā′shē·āt) *v.t.* **·at·ed, ·at·ing** To bring (oneself) into the favor or confidence of others. —**in·gra′ti·at′ing·ly** *adv.* —**in·gra′ti·a′tion** *n.* —**in·gra′ti·a·to′ry** (-ə·tôr′ē, -tō′rē) *adj.* [<Ital. *ingraziare* <L *in gratiam* in favor]

in·grat·i·tude (in·grat′ə·to͞od, -tyo͞od) *n.* Lack of gratitude; insensibility to kindness; thanklessness.

in·gra·ves·cent (in′grə·ves′ənt) *adj. Pathol.* Increasing in severity or gravity, as a disease. [<L *ingravescens, -entis,* ppr. of *ingravescere* grow heavier, worse < *in-* in + *gravis* heavy] —**in′gra·ves′cence** *n.*

in·gre·di·ent (in·grē′dē·ənt) *n.* **1** That which enters into the composition of a mixture: usually distinguished from the *constituent* of a chemical compound. **2** A component part of anything. See synonyms under PART. [<F *ingrédient* <L *ingrediens, -entis,* ppr. of *ingredi* entering into < *in-* in + *gradi* walk]

In·gres (aṅ′gr′), **Jean Auguste Dominique,** 1780–1867, French painter.

in·gress (in′gres) *n.* **1** Means or power of effecting entrance. **2** A place of entrance. **3** The act of entering. See synonyms under ENTRANCE[1]. [<L *ingressus,* pp. of *ingredi* enter]

in·gres·sion (in·gresh′ən) *n.* The act of entering, or an entrance into something.

in·gres·sive (in·gres′iv) *adj.* **1** Pertaining to entrance; entering. **2** *Gram.* Inceptive. —**in·gres′sive·ness** *n.*

in–group (in′gro͞op′) *n. Sociol.* Any group considered by any of its members to have a certain exclusiveness: contrasted with *out-group.*

in·grown (in′grōn′) *adj.* **1** Grown into the flesh, as a toe nail. **2** Growing inward or within. —**in′grow′ing** *adj.*

in·growth (in′grōth′) *n.* An inward growth, or a thing that grows inward.

in·gui·nal (ing′gwə·nəl) *adj.* Of, pertaining to, or near the groin. See illustration under ABDOMINAL. [<L *inguinalis*]

inguino– *combining form* In, affecting, or related to the groin. Also, before vowels, **inguin–.** [<L *inguen, -inis* the groin]

in·gui·no–ab·dom·i·nal (ing′gwə·nō·ab·dom′ə·nəl) *adj.* Related to the groin and the abdomen.

in·gulf (in·gulf′) *v.t.* To engulf. —**in·gulf′·ment** *n.*

in·gur·gi·tate (in·gûr′jə·tāt) *v.t.* & *v.i.* **·tat·ed, ·tat·ing** To eat or drink greedily or to excess; gorge; swill. [<L *ingurgitatus,* pp. of *ingurgitare* pour in, gorge oneself < *in-* in + *gurges, -ites* whirlpool] —**in·gur′gi·ta′tion** *n.*

in·hab·it (in·hab′it) *v.t.* To live or dwell in; occupy as a home. —*v.i. Archaic* To dwell; abide. [<OF *enhabiter* <L *inhabitare* < *in-* in + *habitare* dwell, freq. of *habere* have] —**in·hab′it·a·bil′i·ty** *n.* —**in·hab′it·a·ble** *adj.* —**in·hab′it·er** *n.* —**in·hab′i·ta′tion** *n.*

in·hab·i·tance (in·hab′ə·təns) *n.* **1** The act of dwelling; state of being inhabited; residence, as distinguished from sojourn. **2** A habitation; abode. Also **in·hab′i·tan·cy.**

in·hab·i·tant (in·hab′ə·tənt) *n.* One making his home or dwelling permanently in a place, as distinguished from a lodger or visitor; a resident. [<AF <L *inhabitans -antis,* pp. of *inhabitare*]

in·hab·it·ed (in·hab′ə·tid) *adj.* **1** Having inhabitants; populated. **2** *Obs.* Lodged.

in·ha·lant (in·hā′lənt) *adj.* **1** That inhales or draws in. **2** Used for inhaling. —*n.* **1** An apparatus used for inhaling. **2** That which is to be inhaled. Also **in·ha′lent.**

in·ha·la·tion (in′hə·lā′shən) *n,* **1** The act of inhaling. **2** That which is inhaled; an inhalant.

in·hale (in·hāl′) *v.* **·haled, ·hal·ing** *v.t.* To draw into the lungs, as breath or tobacco smoke; breathe in. —*v.i.* To draw breath, tobacco smoke, etc., into the lungs. Opposed to *exhale.* [<L *inhalare* < *in-* in + *halare* breathe]

in·hal·er (in·hā′lər) *n.* **1** One who inhales. **2** Something from or through which one inhales; specifically an appliance or apparatus enabling one to inhale air, medicinal vapors, anesthetics, etc.

in·har·mo·ni·ous (in′här·mō′nē·əs) *adj.* Lacking in, or not in, harmony; discordant. Also **in′har·mon′ic** (-mon′ik), **in′har·mon′i·cal.** See synonyms under INCONGRUOUS. —**in′har·mo′·ni·ous·ly** *adv.* —**in′har·mo′ni·ous·ness** *n.*

in·haul (in′hôl′) *n. Naut.* A rope or rigging for bringing in a sail or spar, as the jib boom. Also **in′haul′er.**

in·here (in·hir′) *v.i.* **·hered, ·her·ing** To be a permanent or essential part: with *in.* [<L *inhaerere* < *in-* in + *haerere* stick] —**in·her′ence, in·her′en·cy** *n.*

in·her·ent (in·hir′ənt, -her′-) *adj.* **1** Permanently united; intrinsic; innate; essential. **2** Pertaining as a property or attribute. Also **in·he·ren·tial** (in′hi·ren′shəl). [<L *inhaerens, -entis,* ppr. of *inhaerere* INHERE] —**in·her′ent·ly** *adv.*

Synonyms: congenital, essential, immanent, inborn, inbred, indispensable, indwelling, infixed, ingrained, innate, inseparable, internal, intrinsic, inwrought, native, natural, subjective. *Immanent* is a philosophic word, to denote that which dwells in or pervades any substance or spirit without necessarily being a part of it. That which is *inherent* is an *inseparable* part of that in which it inheres, and is usually thought of with reference to some outworking or effect; as, an *inherent* difficulty. God is said to be *immanent* (not *inherent*) in the universe. Frequently *intrinsic* and *inherent* can be interchanged, but *inherent* applies to qualities, while *intrinsic* applies to essence, so that to speak of *intrinsic* excellence conveys higher praise than if we say *inherent* excellence. *Inherent* and *intrinsic* may be said of persons or things; *congenital, inborn, inbred, innate,* apply to living beings. *Congenital* is frequent in medical and legal use with special application to defects; as, *congenital* idiocy. *Innate* and *inborn* are almost identical, but *innate* is preferred in philosophic use, as when we speak of *innate* ideas; that which is *inborn, congenital,* or *innate* may be original with the individual, but that which is *inbred* is inherited. *Ingrained* signifies dyed in the grain, and denotes that which is deeply wrought into substance or character. See NATURAL. *Antonyms*: accidental, casual, external, extrinsic, fortuitous, incidental, outward, subsidiary, superadded, superficial, superfluous, superimposed, supplemental, transient, unconnected.

in·her·it (in·her′it) *v.t.* **1** To receive, as property or a title, by succession or will; fall heir to. **2** To receive (traits, qualities, etc.) as if by succession or will; have as hereditary traits. **3** *Obs.* To make heir; place (an heir) in possession: usually with *of.* —*v.i.* **4** To come into or possess an inheritance. **5** To receive traits, qualities, etc.: with *from.* [<OF *enheriter* <LL *inhereditare* inherit < *in-* in + *heres* heir]

in·her·it·a·ble (in·her′ə·tə·bəl) *adj.* **1** Transmissible by descent; descendible to an heir by mere operation of law. **2** Capacitated or qualified to take by inheritance: having *inheritable* blood. **3** That may be transmitted by ancestors; heritable. [<AF *enheritable*] —**in·her′it·a·bil′i·ty, in·her′it·a·ble·ness** *n.* —**in·her′it·a·bly** *adv.*

in·her·i·tance (in·her′ə·təns) *n.* **1** Anything acquired or possessed by descent or succession; something which is or can be inherited, as property or title acquired by an heir at the owner's death. **2** A heritage, especially in the sense of mental, cultural or spiritual legacies left by past generations to succeeding generations. **3** Physical or mental characteristics derived from ancestry. **4** Act or fact of inheriting.

inheritance tax A tax imposed on an inherited estate.

inherited character *Genetics* A modification of an organism considered as having been transmitted by inheritance: distinguished from *acquired character.*

in·her·i·tor (in·her′ə·tər) *n.* An heir. —**in·her′i·tress** (-tris), **in·her′i·trix** (-triks) *n. fem.*

in·he·sion (in·hē′zhən) *n.* The condition of inhering or being fixed in something; inherence. [<LL *inhaesio, -onis* < *inhaerere.* See INHERE.]

in·hib·it (in·hib′it) *v.t.* **1** To hold back; restrain, as an impulse. **2** To forbid (a cleric) to perform religious functions. **3** To check or block (one mental or nervous process) by another, nearly simultaneous, opposed process. See synonyms under PROHIBIT. [<L *inhibitus,* pp. of *inhibere* check < *in-* in + *habere* have, hold] — **in·hib′it·er, in·hib′i·tor** *n.* — **in·hib′it·a·ble** *adj.* — **in·hib′i·tive, in·hib′i·to′ry** (-tôr′ē, -tō′rē) *adj.*

in·hi·bi·tion (in′hi·bish′ən, in′i-) *n.* **1** The act of inhibiting or the state of being inhibited; restriction; repression; embargo; ban. **2** *Physiol.* **a** The checking of one stimulus or reflex by another acting in opposition. **b** A state of diminished activity at the synapses of the nerves. **3** *Psychol.* **a** The blocking of one mental impulse or process by another. **b** The restraint of will over the impulsive tendencies to habitual or strongly stimulated reactions. **c** Any mental or emotional block.

in·hib·i·tor (in·hib′ə·tər) *n.* **1** That which causes inhibitory action; especially, an inhibitory nerve. **2** A medicinal agent that tends or operates to check organic activity.

in hoc sig·no vin·ces (in hok sig′nō vin′sēz) *Latin* By this sign (i.e., of the cross) thou wilt conquer: motto of the emperor Constantine.

in·hos·pi·ta·ble (in·hos′pi·tə·bəl, in′hos·pit′ə·bəl) *adj.* **1** Not hospitable. **2** Barren; wild; cheerless; affording no shelter or subsistence. — **in·hos′pi·ta·ble·ness** *n.* — **in·hos′pi·ta·bly** *adv.* — **in·hos′pi·tal′i·ty** (-tal′ə·tē) *n.*

in·hu·man (in·hyōō′mən) *adj.* **1** Not possessed of human qualities; cruel; savage; barbarous. **2** Characterized by cruelty; manifesting lack of humanity. **3** Not of the ordinary human type. See synonyms under BARBAROUS, SANGUINARY. [<F *inhumain* <L *inhumanus*] — **in·hu′man·ly** *adv.* — **in·hu′man·ness** *n.*

in·hu·mane (in′hyōō·mān′) *adj.* Not humane; not kind; inhuman. — **in′hu·mane′ly** *adv.*

in·hu·man·i·ty (in′hyōō·man′ə·tē) *n. pl.* **·ties** The state of lacking human or humane qualities; cruelty; also, a cruel act, word, etc. [<F *inhumanité* <L *inhumanitas*]

in·hu·ma·tion (in′hyōō·mā′shən) *n.* Burial.

in·hume (in·hyōōm′) *v.t.* **·humed, ·hum·ing** To place in the earth, as a dead body; bury; inter. [<L *inhumare* < *in-* in + *humus* soil, earth] — **in·hum′er** *n.*

In·i·go (in′i·gō) A masculine personal name. [<Sp., fiery (lit., igneous)]

in·im·i·cal (in·im′i·kəl) *adj.* **1** Of a character regarded as hurtful in tendency or opposed in influence; antagonistic. **2** Unfriendly; hostile. [<LL *inimicalis* < *inimicus* unfriendly < *in-* not + *amicus* friend] — **in·im′i·cal′i·ty** (-kal′ə·tē) *n.* — **in·im′i·cal·ly** *adv.*

Synonyms: adverse, antagonistic, averse, contradictory, contrary, disaffected, harmful, hurtful, noxious, opposed, pernicious, repugnant, unfriendly, unwilling.

in·im·i·ta·ble (in·im′ə·tə·bəl) *adj.* That cannot be imitated; matchless; incomparable. [<L *inimitabilis*] — **in·im′i·ta·bil′i·ty, in·im′i·ta·ble·ness** *n.* — **in·im′i·ta·bly** *adv.*

I·ni·ni (ē·nē·nē′) A dependency of southern French Guiana bordering on Brazil; 30,300 square miles.

in·i·on (in′ē·ən) *n. pl.* **in·i·a** (in′ē·ə) *Anat.* The occipital protuberance on the exterior of the skull. [<NL <Gk., nape of the neck < *is, inos* muscle]

in·iq·ui·tous (in·ik′wə·təs) *adj.* Wicked; unjust. See synonyms under CRIMINAL, SINFUL. — **in·iq′ui·tous·ly** *adv.* — **in·iq′ui·tous·ness** *n.*

in·iq·ui·ty (in·ik′wə·tē) *n. pl.* **·ties** **1** Deviation from right; wickedness; gross injustice. **2** A wrongful act; unjust thing or deed. See synonyms under ABOMINATION, INJUSTICE, SIN. [<OF *iniquité* <L *iniquitas* < *iniquus* unequal < *in-* not + *aequus* equal]

in·i·tial (in·ish′əl) *adj.* **1** Standing at the beginning or head. **2** Pertaining to the first stage. — *n.* **1** The first letter of a word, name, etc. **2** In a book or manuscript, the first letter of a chapter, division of a chapter, or verse: often elaborately painted and gilded. — *v.t.* **·tialed** or **·tialled, ·tial·ing** or **·tial·ling** To mark or sign with initials. [<F <L *initialis* < *initium* beginning < *initus,* pp. of *inire* go into, enter upon < *in-* in + *ire* go] — **in·i′tial·ly** *adv.*

initial meridian axis *Math.* The vertical, fixed plane passing through the polar axis of a sphere in the spherical coordinate system.

Initial Teaching Alphabet An alphabet of 43 characters representing the sounds of English, used in teaching children to read: also called *Augmented Roman.* Abbr. *I.T.A.*

in·i·ti·ate (in·ish′ē·āt) *v.t.* **·at·ed, ·at·ing** **1** To begin; originate. **2** To introduce, as into a position or club, usually with rites or ceremony. **3** To instruct in fundamentals or principles. See synonyms under ENROL, INSTALL, TEACH. — *adj.* (-it, -āt) **1** Instructed in the rudiments or secrets; initiated; newly admitted, as into a secret society. **2** Initial; begun; commenced; new. **3** Characteristic of an inexperienced person or of one newly initiated. — *n.* (-it, -āt) One who has been initiated; also, a beginner. [<L *initiatus,* pp. of *initiare* enter upon < *initium* beginning. See INITIAL.] — **in·i′ti·a′tor** *n.*

in·i·ti·a·tion (in·ish′ē·ā′shən) *n.* **1** The act of initiating. **2** Ceremonial admission, as into a society; the rites or ceremonies which have to be undergone. See synonyms under BEGINNING.

in·i·ti·a·tive (in·ish′ē·ə·tiv) *n.* **1** A first move. **2** The power of initiating; ability for original conception and independent action. **3** The process by which the electorate initiates or enacts legislation. See REFERENDUM. — *adj.* Pertaining to initiation; serving to initiate; preliminary. — **in·i′ti·a·tive·ly** *adv.*

in·i·ti·a·to·ry (in·ish′ē·ə·tôr′ē, -tō′rē) *adj.* **1** Introductory. **2** Serving to initiate.

in·ject (in·jekt′) *v.t.* **1** To drive or force in: to *inject* gas into a carburetor. **2** To force a fluid into, as for anesthetizing, preserving, etc., especially by means of a syringe or hypodermic needle. **3** To introduce (something new or lacking): with *into*: to *inject* life into a play. **4** To throw in or interject, as a remark or comment, usually by way of interruption. [<L *injectus,* pp. of *inicere, injicere* throw, cast in < *in-* in + *jacere* throw]

in·jec·tion (in·jek′shən) *n.* **1** The act of injecting, the state of being injected, or that which is injected. **2** *Med.* The introduction by instruments of a fluid into some cavity or tissue of the body. **3** The similar introduction of a substance into a cadaver to facilitate dissection or anatomical demonstration. **4** Any liquid or substance so introduced. **5** An enema. **6** The state of being hyperemic.

in·jec·tor (in·jek′tər) *n.* **1** One who or that which injects. **2** An apparatus by which steam carries and delivers water to a boiler that is supplying steam.

in·ju·di·cious (in′jōō·dish′əs) *adj.* **1** Not judicious; indiscreet; ill-advised. **2** Wanting in judgment. See synonyms under IMPRUDENT. — **in′ju·di′cious·ly** *adv.* — **in′ju·di′cious·ness** *n.*

in·junc·tion (in·jungk′shən) *n.* **1** The act of enjoining. **2** An admonition or order given with authority. **3** *Law* A judicial order requiring the party enjoined to take or (usually) to refrain from some specified action. See synonyms under ORDER. [<LL *injunctio, -onis* < *injunctum,* pp. of *injungere* join to, enjoin. See IN-[2], JUNCTION.]

in·jure (in′jər) *v.t.* **·jured, ·jur·ing** **1** To do harm or hurt to; wound; damage; impair. **2** To do wrong to; treat with injustice. See synonyms under ABUSE, HURT, VIOLATE. [<F *injurier* <L *injurari* < *injuria* INJURY] — **in′jur·er** *n.*

in·ju·ri·ous (in·jōōr′ē·əs) *adj.* **1** Hurtful, deleterious, or detrimental in any way. **2** *Obs.* Disposed to inflict injury; inimical. **3** Slanderous; abusive. See synonyms under BAD, PERNICIOUS. Compare INJURY. [<F *injurieux* <L *injuriosus*] — **in·ju′ri·ous·ly** *adv.* — **in·ju′ri·ous·ness** *n.*

in·ju·ry (in′jər·ē) *n. pl.* **·ries** **1** Any wrong, damage, or mischief done or suffered. **2** A source of harm. **3** A wrong or damage done to another; the unlawful infringement or privation of rights. **4** *Obs.* Abuse; insult. [<AF *injurie* <L *injuria* < *injurius* injust < *in-* not + *jus, juris* right, law]

Synonyms: blemish, damage, detriment, disadvantage, evil, harm, hurt, impairment, injustice, loss, mischief, outrage, prejudice, wrong. *Injury* is the general term including all the rest. Whatever reduces the value, utility, beauty, or desirableness of anything is an *injury* to that thing; of persons, whatever is so done as to operate adversely to one in his person, rights, property, or reputation is an *injury. Damage* (L *damnum,* loss) is that which occasions *loss* to the possessor; hence, *damage* reduces value, utility, or beauty; *detriment* (L *deterere,* to rub or wear away) is similar in meaning, but far milder. As a rule, the slightest use of an article by a purchaser operates to its *detriment* if again offered for sale, even when the article may not have received the slightest *damage. Damage* is partial; *loss* is properly absolute as far as it is predicted at all; the *loss* of a ship implies that it is gone beyond recovery; the *loss* of the rudder is a *damage* to the ship; but since the *loss* of a part still leaves a part, we may speak of a partial or total *loss. Evil* commonly suggests suffering or sin, or both; as, the *evils* of poverty, the social *evil. Harm* is closely synonymous with *injury*; it may apply to body, mind, or estate, but always affects real worth, while *injury* may concern only estimated value. A *hurt* is an *injury* that causes pain, physical or mental; a slight *hurt* may be no real *harm. Mischief* is disarrangement, trouble, or *harm* usually caused by some voluntary agent, with or without injurious intent; a child's thoughtless sport may do great *mischief*; *wrong* is *harm* done with evil intent. An *outrage* combines insult and *injury.* Compare synonyms for BLEMISH, INJUSTICE, LOSS, OUTRAGE, VIOLENCE. *Antonyms*: advantage, amelioration, benefit, blessing, boon, help, improvement, remedy, service, utility.

in·jus·tice (in·jus′tis) *n.* **1** The violation or denial of justice. **2** An unjust act; a wrong. [<OF <L *injustitia*]

Synonyms: grievance, inequity, iniquity, injury, unfairness, unrighteousness, wrong. *Injustice* is a violation or denial of justice, an act or omission that is contrary to equity or justice; as, the *injustice* of unequal taxes. In legal usage a *wrong* involves *injury* to person, property, or reputation, as the result of evil intent; *injustice* applies to civil damage or loss, not necessarily involving *injury* to person or property, as by misrepresentation of goods which does not amount to a legal warranty. In popular usage, *injustice* may involve no direct *injury* to person, property, interest, or character, and no harmful intent, while *wrong* always involves both; one who attributes another's truly generous act to a selfish motive does him an *injustice.* Compare synonyms for INJURY, SIN. *Antonyms*: equity, fairness, faithfulness, honesty, honor, impartiality, integrity, justice, lawfulness, rectitude, right, righteousness, uprightness.

ink (ingk) *n.* **1** A colored liquid or viscous substance, used in writing, printing, etc. ◆ Collateral adjective: *atramental.* **2** The dark fluid secreted by a cuttlefish and ejected so as to color the water and thus assist in escaping an enemy. — *v.t.* To spread ink upon; mark or color with ink. [<OF *enque* <LL *encaustum* purple ink used by the Caesars <Gk. *enkauston,* neut. of *enkaustos* burned out. See ENCAUSTIC.] — **ink′er** *n.*

ink·ber·ry (ingk′ber′ē) *n. pl.* **·ries** **1** A small shrub *(Ilex glabra)* of the holly family, with oblong leaves and roundish, black, shining berries. **2** One of its berries. **3** Pokeweed.

Ink·er·man (ing′kər·mən, *Russian* in·ker·män′) An eastern suburb of Sevastopol: site of the Russian defeat in the Crimean War, 1854.

ink·horn (ingk′hôrn′) *n.* An inkholder: so called because formerly made of horn.

inkhorn term A bookish word. Also **ink′·horn′ism.**

in·kle (ing′kəl) *n.* **1** A broad linen tape; the thread or yarn from which it is made. **2** Formerly, a braid trimming.

ink·ling (ingk′ling) *n.* A slight intimation; a faint notion; hint. [ME *inkle* hint, ? <OE *inca* suspicion]

ink-sac (ingk′sak′) *n. Zool.* A pear-shaped glandular organ in the mantle cavity of cuttlefish from which a black substance is ejected as a protective screen.

ink·stand (ingk′stand′) *n.* A vessel to hold ink for writing: often combined with a rack for pens, etc. Also **ink′well′** (-wel′).

ink·wood (ingk′wood′) *n.* An evergreen pinnate-leaved tree *(Exothea paniculata)* found in southern Florida, the West Indies, and Guatemala, and yielding a reddish-brown, hard, heavy wood: also called *butterbough.*

ink·y (ing′kē) *adj.* **ink·i·er, ink·i·est 1** Consisting of, stained with, like, or containing ink **2** Black. **—ink′i·ness** *n.*

ink·y–cap (ing′kē·kap′) *n.* A mushroom (genus *Coprinus*) whose gills dissolve into a black, inky liquid after the spores have matured.

in·lace (in·lās′) See ENLACE.

in·laid (in′lād′, in·lād′) *adj.* **1** Decorated by the insertion of wood, ivory, or other material. **2** Inserted to form such decoration. See INLAY.

in·land (in′lənd) *adj.* **1** Remote from the sea. **2** Located in or limited to the interior of a country. **3** Not foreign; domestic. **—***n.* (in′·lənd, -land′) The interior of a country. **—***adv.* (in′lənd, -land′) Toward the interior of a land.

Inland Empire A region of the Columbia River basin in eastern Washington, northern Oregon, and northern Idaho.

in·land·er (in′lən·dər, -lan′dər) *n.* One living inland or from inland.

Inland Sea An arm of the Philippine Sea between Honshu and Shikoku and Kyushu islands, Japan. *Japanese* **Se·to–nai·kai** (se·tō·nī·kī).

in·law (in·lô′) *v.t.* In old English law, to free from outlawry; replace under protection of law; restore to civil rights. [OE *inlagian*]

in–law (in′lô′) *n. Colloq.* A member of the family of one's husband or wife, or the spouse of one's child.

in·law·ry (in′lô′rē) *n. pl.* **·ries** In old English law, annulment of outlawry; restoration to the protection of the law.

in·lay (in·lā′, in′lā′) *v.t.* **in·laid, in·lay·ing 1** To set decorative patterns or designs of (ivory, gold, etc.) into the surface of an object. **2** To decorate, as a piece of furniture, by inserting such patterns or designs. **3** To attach (a page, illustration, etc.) in a place cut for it in a larger or heavier sheet, either for framing or enlarging the margin. **—***n.* (in′lā) **1** That which is inlaid. **2** A pattern or design so produced. **3** *Dent.* A filling for a tooth, of gold, porcelain, etc., cemented into a cavity so as to be even with the surface. **4** An inlay graft. **—in′lay′er** *n.*

inlay graft *Bot.* A cion inserted at a place in the stock from which a closely matching piece of bark has been removed.

in·let (in·let′) *v.t.* **·let, ·let·ting 1** To insert; inlay. **2** *Obs.* To admit. **—***n.* (in′lit) **1** A small body of water leading into a larger, as a small bay or creek or a tributary of a lake. **2** An entrance, as to a culvert. **3** Something inserted. **4** *Obs.* The act of admitting. See synonyms under ENTRANCE[1].

in·li·er (in′lī′ər) *n. Geol.* An underlying uneroded formation of rock imbedded in a later deposit: opposed to *outlier.*

in lo·co (in lō′kō) *Latin* In the place; in the right or proper spot.

in lo·co pa·ren·tis (in lō′kō pə·ren′tis) *Latin* In the place of a parent.

in·ly (in′lē) *adv. Poetic* **1** In the inner parts; inwardly. **2** Intimately. **—***adj. Obs.* Inward. [OE *inlīce*]

in·mate (in′māt′) *n.* **1** One who lives in a place with others; an associate or mate in occupancy. **2** One who is kept or confined in a prison, asylum, or similar institution. **3** *Obs.* An alien; a stranger; one not properly belonging to the place where he dwells. [? <INN + MATE]

in me·di·as res (in mē′dē·əs rēz′) *Latin* In the midst of things; into the heart of the matter.

in me·mo·ri·am (in mə·môr′ē·əm, -mō′rē-) *Latin* In memory (of); as a memorial (to).

in·mesh (in·mesh′) See ENMESH.

in–mi·grant (in′mī′grənt) *n.* A person who has moved from one locality to another in the same country. **—in′–mi·gra′tion** (-grā′·shən) *n.*

in·most (in′mōst′, -məst) *adj.* **1** Farthest from the exterior. **2** Figuratively, deepest, most secret, or most intimate. [OE *innemest,* a double superlative of *inne* in]

inn (in) *n.* **1** A public house for the entertainment of travelers; a place where meals and lodging are obtainable; hostelry; tavern. **2** *Brit.* A house of residence for students: now only in the names of such residences, as *Inns* of Court. **3** *Obs.* A dwelling place; abode. [OE < *inn* in]

Inn (in) A river of eastern Switzerland, western Austria, and southern Bavaria, flowing 320 miles NE to the Danube.

in·nards (in′ərdz) *n.pl. Dial.* or *Colloq.* Inner or interior parts or organs; the insides. [<INWARDS, *n.*]

in·nate (in′āt, i·nāt′) *adj.* **1** Native to or original with the individual; inborn; natural. **2** Immediately in or from the mind or intellect rather than acquired by experience; intuitive: *innate* truths. **3** *Bot.* Attached by its base to the apex of a filament: said of an anther. **4** Endogenous. Compare ADNATE. See synonyms under INHERENT, NATIVE, RADICAL. [<L *innatus,* pp. of *innasci* be born in < *in-* in + *nasci* be born] **—in′nate·ly** *adv.* **—in′nate·ness** *n.*

in·ner (in′ər) *adj.* **1** At a point farther in or inward; interior; nearer a center. **2** Pertaining to that which is within; specifically, denoting the spiritual or immaterial. **3** Not easily discerned or understood; esoteric; hidden. **—***n.* **1** The inside of something. **2** The section of a target between the center and the outer. **3** A shot striking this section. [OE *innerra,* compar. of *inne* in]

inner city A central part of a large city, usually characterized by poverty and often populated by minority groups. **—in′ner–cit′y** *adj.*

Inner Hebrides See HEBRIDES.

Inner Light The presence of God in man, giving guidance and enlightenment: a doctrine of Quakerism. Also **Inner Word.**

Inner Mongolia See MONGOLIA.

in·ner·most (in′ər·mōst′) *adj.* Inmost; farthest within. **—***n.* The inmost part, thing, or place.

in·ner·sole (in′ər·sōl′) *n.* A continuous piece of leather or other material cut to the contour of a shoe last and placed inside to give a smooth surface.

Inner Temple See INNS OF COURT.

inner tube A flexible, inflatable tube, usually of rubber, which together with an outer casing comprises a pneumatic tire.

in·ner·vate (i·nûr′vāt, in′ər·vāt) *v.t.* **·vat·ed, ·vat·ing** *Physiol.* **1** To supply with nerves or nervous filaments. **2** To give stimulus to (a nerve); innerve. [<INNERVE]

in·ner·va·tion (in′ər·vā′shən) *n.* **1** *Physiol.* The act of innervating. **2** *Anat.* The arrangement of nervous filaments in any part of the body.

in·nerve (i·nûrv′) *v.t.* **·nerved, ·nerv·ing** To impart nervous energy to; invigorate; animate; stimulate. [<IN-[2] + NERVE]

In·ness (in′is), **George,** 1825–94, U.S. painter.

in·ning (in′ing) *n.* **1** The period during which a party or person is in power, control, or action. **2** In baseball and other games, a turn at the bat; the period during which one side is at the bat, or the period when each side takes one turn at the bat. **3** *pl.* In cricket, the play of, or score made by, either side while batting or by any one batsman during his turn: construed in the singular. **4** Reclamation (of marsh or swamp land). **5** *pl.* Lands reclaimed from the sea. **6** An ingathering, as of grain into a barn; a harvest. [OE *innung,* gerund of *innian* get it, put in]

inn·keep·er (in′kē′pər) *n.* The proprietor or keeper of an inn. Also **inn′hold′er** (-hōl′dər).

in·no·cence (in′ə·səns) *n.* **1** The state of being innocent; the condition of being free from evil or guile, or from that which corrupts or vitiates; purity of heart; freedom from taint. **2** Freedom from guilt, as of some specific crime or charge; absence of legal guilt. **3** Freedom from harmful or noxious qualities; harmlessness; innocuousness. **4** Simplicity or ignorance through lack of intellect or imperfect development; hence, weak-mindedness. **5** Freedom from illegal taint, as violation of an embargo or blockade by conveying goods to a belligerent. **6** A bluet. **7** A slender-stemmed, erect herb (*Collinsia verna*) with a blue and white corolla; also a related California herb (*C. bicolor*). [<OF <L *innocentia*]

Synonyms: blamelessness, goodness, guilelessness, guiltlessness, harmlessness, innocuousness, inoffensiveness, purity, simplicity, sincerity, sinlessness, stainlessness, virtue. *Innocence,* which is *goodness* without temptation or trial, or perhaps without knowledge of evil, is less than *virtue* which is *goodness* that resists and overcomes temptation. Compare synonyms for INNOCENT. *Antonyms*: contamination, corruption, crime, criminality, evil, fault, guile, guilt, harm, harmfulness, hurt, hurtfulness, impurity, ruin, sin, sinfulness, stain, wrong.

in·no·cen·cy (in′ə·sən·sē) *n. pl.* **·cies** Innocence; also, an instance of innocence.

in·no·cent (in′ə·sənt) *adj.* **1** Not tainted with sin; pure; ignorant of evil; blameless: an *innocent* babe. **2** Free from the guilt of a particular evil action or crime. **3** Free from qualities that can harm or injure; innocuous; harmless. **4** Of artless or ingenuous disposition; naive. **5** Not maliciously intended: an *innocent* lie, an *innocent* remark. **6** Free from liability to forfeiture; not contraband; lawful; permitted. **7** Lacking in knowledge or sense; simple or ignorant; imbecile. **8** Lacking in worldly knowledge: an *innocent* girl. **9** Entirely lacking; devoid: with *of*: *innocent* of grammar. **—***n.* **1** One unstained by sin. **2** A young child. **3** A simpleton. **4** The bluet. **—the Innocents** The children put to death by Herod: commemorated Dec. 28. Matt. *ii* 16. [<OF <L *innocens, -entis* < *in-* not + *nocens,* ppr. of *nocere* harm] **—in′no·cent·ly** *adv.*

Synonyms (adj.): blameless, clean, clear, faultless, guileless, guiltless, harmless, immaculate, innocuous, innoxious, inoffensive, pure, right, righteous, sinless, spotless, stainless, upright, virtuous. *Innocent,* in the full sense, signifies not tainted with sin; not having done wrong or violated legal or moral precept or duty; as, an *innocent* babe. *Innocent* is a negative word, expressing less than *righteous, upright,* or *virtuous,* which imply knowledge of good and evil, with free choice of the good. A little child or a lamb is *innocent*; a tried and faithful man is *righteous, upright, virtuous. Immaculate, pure,* and *sinless* may be used either of one who has never known the possibility of evil or of one who has perfectly and triumphantly resisted it. *Innocent,* in a specific case, signifies free from the guilt of a particular act, even when the total character may be very evil; as, The thief was found to be *innocent* of the murder. See CANDID, PURE. *Antonyms*: compare synonyms for CRIMINAL.

In·no·cent (in′ə·sənt, *Fr.* ē·nō·sän′) A masculine personal name; also, the appellation of 13 popes. Also *Lat.* **In·no·cen·tius** (in′ə·sen′·shəs, *Du.* in′ə·sen′sē·o͝os; *Ger.* in′ə·tsen′tsē·o͝os), *Ger.* **In·no·cenz** (in′ə·tsents), *Ital.* **In·no·cen·te** (ēn′nō·chen′tā) or **In·no·cen·zio** (ēn′nō·chen′·dzyō), *Sp.* **I·no·cen·ci·o** (ē′nō·then′thē·ō). [<L, blameless]

—Innocent I, died 417, pope 402–17, condemned Pelagianism: canonized *Saint Innocent.*

—Innocent II, died 1143, pope 1130–43, condemned Abelard: real name Gregorio Papareschi.

—Innocent III, 1161–1216, pope 1198–1216; raised the papal power to the highest point: real name Lotario de' Conti.

—Innocent IV, died 1254, pope 1243–54; proclaimed a crusade against Frederick II: real name Sinibaldo de' Freschi.

—Innocent XI, 1611–89, pope 1676–89; quarreled with Louis XIV on the limitation of papal powers in France (see GALLICANISM): real name Benedetto Odescalchi.

in·noc·u·ous (i·nok′yo͞o·əs) *adj.* **1** Having no harmful qualities. **2** Non-poisonous: said of plants and animals, especially snakes. See synonyms under INNOCENT. [<L *innocuus* < *in-* not + *nocuus* harmful < *nocere* harm] **—in·noc′u·ous·ly** *adv.* **—in·noc′u·ous·ness** *n.*

in·nom·i·nate (i·nom′ə·nit) *adj.* **1** Without specific name. **2** Anonymous. [<LL *innominatus* < *in-* not + *nominatus,* pp. of *nominare* name. See NOMINATE.]

innominate artery *Anat.* A large but short trunk springing from the arch of the aorta near the heart.

innominate bone *Anat.* A large, irregular bone resulting from the consolidation of the ilium, ischium, and pubis to form one of the sides of the pelvis in adult mammals; the hip bone; haunch bone; huckle bone: also called *os innominatum.*

in no·mi·ne Do·mi·ni (in nom′ə·nē dom′ə·nī) *Latin* In the name of the Lord.

in·no·vate (in′ə·vāt) *v.* **·vat·ed, ·vat·ing** *v.i.* To make changes or alterations in anything established; bring in new ideas, methods, etc.: often with *in, on,* or *upon.* —*v.t. Obs.* To bring in as an innovation. [<L *innovatus,* pp. of *innovare* renew < *in-* in + *novare* make new, alter < *novus* new] —**in′no·va′tor** *n.*

in·no·va·tion (in′ə·vā′shən) *n.* **1** The making of a change in something established. **2** A novelty. See synonyms under CHANGE. [<LL *innovatio, -onis*]

in·no·va·tive (in′ə·vā′tiv) *adj.* Characterized by or tending to introduce innovations.

in·no·va·to·ry (in′ə·vā′tər·ē) *adj.* Having the character of innovation.

in·nox·ious (i·nok′shəs) *adj.* Free from harmful qualities; not noxious. [<L *innoxius* < *in-* not + *noxius* NOXIOUS. Related to INNOCENT, INNOCUOUS.]

Inns·bruck (inz′brŏŏk, *Ger.* ins′brŏŏk) The capital of Tirol in Austria, on the Inn.

Inns of Chancery **1** Formerly, in London, residences in which students for the Chancery bar began their law studies; later occupied as offices by attorneys, solicitors, etc. **2** The law societies occupying these buildings.

Inns of Court The sets of buildings occupied by the four legal societies of London, the Inner Temple, Middle Temple, Lincoln's Inn, and Gray's Inn, that exercise the exclusive right of calling law students to the bar; hence, the societies themselves.

in·nu·en·do (in′yōō·en′dō) *n. pl.* **·dos** or **·does** **1** A suggestion or hint about some person or thing; an indirect aspersion; insinuation: usually in derogation. **2** *Law* In pleading, an explanatory phrase employed to make a previous phrase more explicit, as in saying "the perjured villain, meaning the plaintiff," in which the phrase "meaning the plaintiff" is an innuendo. Also spelled *inuendo.* See synonyms under SUGGESTION. [<L, by nodding at, intimating, ablative gerund of *innuere* nod to, signify < *in-* to + *-nuere* nod]

In·nu·it (in′yōō·it) *n. sing. & pl.* An Eskimo of Alaska: distinguished from the *Yuit,* or Asian Eskimos; also, Arctic Eskimos as distinct from the Aleuts. Compare YUIT. [<Eskimo]

in·nu·mer·a·ble (i·nōō′mər·ə·bəl, i·nyōō′-) *adj.* Too numerous to be counted; very numerous; countless. Also **in·nu′mer·ous.** See synonyms under INFINITE. [<L *innumerabilis*] —**in·nu′·mer·a·bil′i·ty, in·nu′mer·a·ble·ness** *n.* —**in·nu′·mer·a·bly** *adv.*

in·nu·tri·tion (in′nōō·trish′ən, -yōō-) *n.* Lack of nutrition; failure of nourishment. —**in′nu·tri′·tious** *adj.*

in·ob·serv·ance (in′əb·zûr′vəns) *n.* Non-observance; inattention.

in·oc·u·la·ble (in·ok′yə·lə·bəl) *adj.* That can be inoculated or communicated by inoculation. —**in·oc′u·la·bil′i·ty** *n.* —**in·oc′u·la′tor** (-lā′tər) *n.*

in·oc·u·late (in·ok′yə·lāt) *v.t.* **·lat·ed, ·lat·ing** **1** To communicate a disease to (a person or animal) by inoculation. **2** To inject an immunizing serum into. **3** To implant ideas, opinions, etc., in the mind of. **4** *Bot.* To insert a bud in, as a tree, for propagation. [<L *inoculatus,* pp. of *inoculare* engraft an eye or bud < *in-* in + *oculus* bud, eye]

in·oc·u·la·tion (in·ok′yə·lā′shən) *n.* **1** *Med.* The introduction of specific disease organisms into the living tissues of animals and man, as a means of securing immunity through inducing a mild form of the disease. Inoculation may be *curative,* when an antitoxin is injected as a remedy, or *protective,* when the substance injected aims to secure immunity from disease. **2** *Bot.* The operation of inserting a bud in a tree for propagation. **3** Contamination; infection: the *inoculation* of vice. **4** The improvement of soils by introducing special micro-organisms: practiced especially in the cultivation of leguminous crops.

in·oc·u·lum (in·ok′yə·ləm) *n.* The prepared material, as bacteria, viruses, spores, etc., used in making an inoculation. [<NL <INOCULATE]

in·o·dor·ous (in·ō′dər·əs) *adj.* Having no odor; emitting no scent.

in·of·fen·sive (in′ə·fen′siv) *adj.* Giving no offense; unobjectionable; causing nothing displeasing, disturbing, or harmful. See synonyms under INNOCENT. —**in′of·fen′sive·ly** *adv.* —**in′of·fen′sive·ness** *n.*

in·of·fi·cious (in′ə·fish′əs) *adj.* **1** *Law* Without consideration of duty or natural obligation; regardless of office or duty: An *inofficious* will neglects to provide for those naturally dependent on the testator. **2** Without office; inoperative. **3** *Obs.* Not civil or attentive. [<L *inofficiosus*] —**in′of·fi′cious·ly** *adv.*

in om·ni·a pa·ra·tus (in om′nē·ə pə·rā′təs) *Latin* Prepared for anything.

I·nö·nü (e′nœ·nü), **Ismet,** 1884–1973, president of Turkey 1938–50.

in·op·er·a·ble (in·op′ər·ə·bəl) *adj.* **1** *Surg.* Not suitable for operative procedures without undue risk: an *inoperable* cancer. **2** Not practicable.

in·op·er·a·tive (in·op′ər·ə·tiv) *adj.* Not operative; having no effect or result; ineffectual. —**in·op′er·a·tive·ness** *n.*

in·op·por·tune (in·op′ər·tōōn′, -tyōōn′) *adj.* Unseasonable or inappropriate; unsuitable or inconvenient, especially as to time; not opportune. [<L *inopportunus*] —**in·op′por·tune′ly** *adv.* —**in·op′por·tune′ness** *n.*

in·or·di·nate (in·ôr′də·nit) *adj.* Not restrained by prescribed rules or bounds; immoderate; excessive. See synonyms under IMMODERATE, IRREGULAR. —**in·or′di·na·cy** (-nə·sē), **in·or′di·nate·ness** *n.* —**in·or′di·nate·ly** *adv.*

in·or·gan·ic (in′ôr·gan′ik) *adj.* **1** Devoid of organized vital structure; not organic; not being animal or vegetable; inanimate. **2** Not the result of living or organic processes. **3** Of, pertaining to, or designating the branch of chemistry that treats of substances lacking carbon, but including the carbonates and cyanides. **4** *Ling.* Not belonging to the normal development of a word; extraneous, as the final *t* in *against.* —**in′or·gan′i·cal·ly** *adv.*

in·os·cu·late (in·os′kyə·lāt) *v.t. & v.i.* **·lat·ed, ·lat·ing** **1** To unite by contact of openings, as two blood vessels. **2** To unite or join together, as in continuity.

in·os·cu·la·tion (in·os′kyə·lā′shən) *n.* **1** Union by tubelike passages; intercommunication. **2** A union that implies continuity.

in·o·si·tol (in·ō′sə·tōl, -tol) *n. Biochem.* An efflorescent, crystalline, water-soluble, polyhydric alcohol, $C_6H_6(OH)_6$, regarded as the anti-alopecia factor of the vitamin B complex. It is widely distributed in plant and animal tissue and also made synthetically. Also called *muscle sugar.* Also **in·o·site** (in′ə·sīt). [<Gk. *is, inos* muscle + -IT(E)[1] + -OL[1]]

in·ot·ro·pism (in·ot′rə·piz′əm, ī·not′-) *n. Med.* Any interference with the contractility of muscle. —**in·o·trop·ic** (in′ō·trop′ik, -trō′pik, ī′nō-) *adj.* [<Gk. *is, inos* muscle + -TROPISM]

in·ox·i·dize (in·ok′sə·dīz) *v.t.* **·dized, ·diz·ing** To render incapable of oxidation.

in pa·ce (in pā′sē, pä′kā) *Latin* In peace.

in·pa·tient (in′pā′shənt) *n.* A patient who is lodged, fed, and receives treatment in a hospital or the like: distinguished from *outpatient.*

in per·pet·u·um (in pər·pech′ōō·əm) *Latin* Forever; perpetually.

in per·so·nam (in pər·sō′nəm) *Latin* Against the person, rather than against specific things: used in certain legal proceedings.

in pet·to (ēn pet′tō) *Italian* In the breast; secretly: said of Roman Catholic cardinals appointed in consistory as "reserves," but not officially announced.

in·phase (in′fāz′) *adj. Electr.* Being of the same phase: said of currents. See PHASE.

in pos·se (in pos′ē) *Latin* Having a possible but not an actual existence; potential. Compare IN ESSE.

in pro·pri·a per·so·na (in prō′prē·ə pər·sō′nə) *Latin* In one's own person.

in·put (in′pŏŏt′) *n.* **1** Something put into a system or device, as energy into a machine, food into the body, data into a computer, or a signal into an electronic device. **2** A place or point of introduction, as of data into a computer. **3** An effect or influence resulting from contributing opinions, information, suggestions, etc.: The staff had real *input* in the directive.

in·quest (in′kwest) *n.* **1** A judicial inquiry, aided by a jury, into a special matter, as a sudden death. **2** The body of men making such inquiry. **3** Inquiry; investigation. [<OF *enqueste* <L *inquisita (res)* (thing) inquired (into), fem. of *inquisitus, inquestus,* pp. of *inquirere* INQUIRE]

in·qui·e·tude (in·kwī′ə·tōōd, -tyōōd) *n.* **1** A state of restlessness; uneasiness. **2** *pl.* Anxieties; disquieting thoughts. [<F *inquiétude* <LL *inquietudo*] —**in·qui′et** *adj.* —**in·qui′et·ly** *adv.*

in·qui·line (in′kwə·līn, -lin) *adj. Zool.* Living in the abode of another, as an insect in a gall made by another: also **in·quil·i·nous** (in·kwil′ə·nəs). —*n.* An animal that lives in the abode of another; a commensal. [<L *inquilinus* lodger < *in-* in + *colere* dwell]

in·qui·nate (in′kwə·nāt) *v.t.* **·nat·ed, ·nat·ing** To pollute; corrupt. [<L *inquinatus,* pp. of *inquinare* pollute < *in-* in + *cunire* void excrement]

in·qui·na·tion (in′kwə·nā′shən) *n.* **1** The state of being defiled; corruption. **2** Pollution; infection. [<L *inquinatio, -onis*]

in·quire (in·kwīr′) *v.* **·quired, ·quir·ing** *v.t.* **1** To ask information about: They *inquired* the way. —*v.i.* **2** To seek information by asking questions: to *inquire* about one's health. **3** To make investigation, search, or inquiry: with *into.* Also spelled *enquire.* [<L *inquirere* inquire into < *in-* into + *quaerere* seek] —**in·quir′a·ble** *adj.* —**in·quir′er** *n.* —**in·quir′ing** *adj.* —**in·quir′ing·ly** *adv.*

Synonyms: ask, examine, interrogate, query, question. One may either *ask* or *inquire* one's way. In this sense *ask* and *inquire* are nearly interchangeable, chiefly differing in the fact that *ask* is the popular and *inquire* the more formal word, although *ask* has place in the best literary use. Also, *ask* has more reference to the presence of a second person; the solitary investigator *inquires* rather than *asks* the cause of some phenomenon: in this sense *ask* is often used reflexively; as, "I *asked* myself why this happened." *Inquire into* thus becomes a natural synonym for *examine, investigate,* etc. Compare ASK, EXAMINE, QUESTION.

in·quir·y (in·kwīr′ē, in′kwə·rē) *n. pl.* **·quir·ies** **1** The act of inquiring. **2** Investigation; research; search for knowledge. **3** A query. [ME *enquere*]

Synonyms: examination, interrogation, investigation, query, question, research, scrutiny, study. See QUESTION. *Antonyms*: see synonyms for ANSWER.

in·qui·si·tion (in′kwə·zish′ən) *n.* **1** The proceedings and findings of a jury of inquest. **2** The jury or other body making judicial inquiry into some particular matter. **3** Investigation. See synonyms under HUNT, QUESTION. [<OF <L *inquisitio, -onis* < *inquisitus.* See INQUIRE.]

In·qui·si·tion (in′kwə·zish′ən) *n.* **1** A court or tribunal of the Roman Catholic Church for the discovery, examination, and punishment of heretics; specifically, the ecclesiastical tribunal for the discovery and punishment of heretics, active in central and southern Europe in the 13th century; also, the **Spanish Inquisition** (1237–1834), the notoriously severe tribunal which continued its persecutions through the 16th century: put under state control 1480; abolished 1834: also called *Holy Office.* **2** The Congregation of the Holy Office. —**In′qui·si′tion·ist, In·quis·i·tor** (in·kwiz′ə·tər) *n.*

in·qui·si·tion·al (in′kwə·zish′ən·əl) *adj.* Of or pertaining to the Inquisition; characterized by searching investigation, or by severities like those of the Inquisition. —**in′qui·si′tion·al·ly** *adv.*

in·qui·si·tion·ist (in′kwə·zish′ən·ist) *n.* One who practices the methods of the Inquisition; an inquisitor.

in·quis·i·tive (in·kwiz′ə·tiv) *adj.* **1** Given to questioning, especially for the gratification of curiosity; prying: an *inquisitive* busybody. **2** Inclined to the pursuit of knowledge. [<L *inquisitus*] —**in·quis′i·tive·ly** *adv.* —**in·quis′i·tive·ness** *n.*

Synonyms: curious, inquiring, intrusive, meddlesome, meddling, peeping, prying, scrutinizing, searching. An *inquisitive* person is one who is bent on finding out all that can be found out by inquiry, especially of little and personal matters, and hence is generally *meddlesome* and *prying. Inquisitive* may be used in a good sense, but in such connection *inquiring* is to be preferred; as, an *inquiring* mind. As applied to a state of mind, *curious* denotes a keen and rather pleasurable desire to know fully something to which one's attention has been called, but without the active tendency that *inquisitive* implies; a well-bred person may be *curious* to know, but will not be *inquisitive* in trying to ascertain what is of interest in the affairs of another. *Antonyms*:

apathetic, careless, heedless, inattentive, indifferent, unconcerned, uninterested.

in·quis·i·tor (in·kwiz′ə·tər) *n.* **1** One who inquires or investigates; specifically, an official whose duty it is to investigate or examine. **2** A member of the Inquisition. [<OF *inquisiteur* <L *inquisitor*]

in·quis·i·to·ri·al (in·kwiz′ə·tôr′ē·əl, -tō′rē-, in′·kwiz-) *adj.* **1** After the manner of an inquisitor; disposed to ask cruel and offensive questions. **2** Pertaining to a court of inquisition or to an inquisitor or his duties. **3** *Law* Pertaining to a system of criminal procedure in which the proceedings are conducted secretly and the judge acts also as prosecutor. Compare ACCUSATORY, ACCUSATORIAL. **—in·quis′i·to′ri·al·ly** *adv.* **—in·quis′i·to′ri·al·ness** *n.*

in re (in rē′) *Law Latin* In the case or matter of; concerning: *in re* Smith vs. Jones.

in rem (in rem′) *Law Latin* Against the thing: designating a proceeding instituted for the disposition of property and not directed against any specific person.

in·ro (in′rō′) *n.* A set or nest of small lacquered boxes worn at the girdle by Japanese, designed to contain small articles of convenience, as medicines, a seal, and sealing wax. [<Japanese *in* seal + *ro* wax]

in·road (in′rōd′) *n.* **1** A hostile entrance into a country; raid; any forcible encroachment. **2** Any illegal, destructive, or wasteful encroachment: *inroads* upon one's health, time, savings, etc. See synonyms under INVASION. [<IN-[3] + obs. *road* riding]

in·rush (in′rush′) *n.* A sudden rushing in; invasion.

in·sal·i·vate (in·sal′ə·vāt) *v.t.* **·vat·ed, ·vat·ing** To mix with saliva, as food, in eating. **—in·sal′i·va′tion** *n.*

in·sa·lu·bri·ous (in′sə·lōō′brē·əs) *adj.* Not wholesome; not healthful. [<L *insalubris*] **—in′sa·lu′bri·ous·ly** *adv.* **—in′sa·lu′bri·ty** *n.*

ins and outs Minute details; particulars; ramifications.

in·sane (in·sān′) *adj.* **1** Not sane; mentally deranged or unsound; crazy; irrational. **2** Set apart for or used by the insane. **3** Characteristic of those who are mentally deranged; insensate. **4** Foolish, extravagant, or impractical: *insane* hopes. [<L *insanus* < *in-* not + *sanus* whole] **—in·sane′ly** *adv.* **—in·sane′ness** *n.*

Synonyms: absurd, cracked, crazed, crazy, delirious, demented, deranged, distracted, frantic, frenzied, irrational, lunatic, mad, maniac, maniacal, monomaniac, wandering, wild. *Antonyms*: clear, collected, level-headed, sage, sane, sensible, sober, sound, wise.

in·san·i·ty (in·san′ə·tē) *n.* **1** Any mental disorder characterized by temporary or permanent irrational or violent deviations from normal thinking, feeling, and behavior: not a technical term in medicine or psychiatry. **2** *Law* Any degree of mental unsoundness resulting in inability to distinguish between right and wrong, to control the will, foresee the consequences of an act, make a valid contract, or manage one's own affairs. **3** Lack of sound sense; extreme folly.

Synonyms: alienation, craziness, delirium, dementia, derangement, frenzy, lunacy, madness, mania, monomania. Of these terms *insanity* is the most comprehensive, including in a loose sense all morbid conditions of mind due to diseased action of the brain or nervous system. *Craziness* is a vague popular term for any sort of disordered mental action, or for conduct suggesting it. *Lunacy* originally denoted intermittent *insanity*, supposed to be dependent on the changes of the moon (L *luna*). *Madness* is the old popular term, now suggesting excitement akin to *mania*. *Derangement* is a common euphemism for *insanity*. *Delirium* is always temporary, and is specifically the *insanity* of disease, as in acute fevers. *Dementia* is a general weakening of the mental powers: the word is specifically applied to the mental incapacities of senility. *Monomania* is mental *derangement* as to one subject or object. *Frenzy* and *mania* are forms of raving and furious *insanity*. Compare DELUSION, FRENZY, IDIOCY. *Antonyms*: clearness, lucidity, rationality, sanity.

in·sa·tia·ble (in·sā′shə·bəl, -shē·ə·bəl) *adj.* Not satiable; not to be sated or satisfied; unappeasable. Also **in·sa′ti·ate** (-it). See synonyms under GREEDY. [<OF *insaciable*] **—in·sa′ti·a·bil′i·ty, in·sa′tia·ble·ness** *n.* **—in·sa′tia·bly, in·sa′ti·ate·ly** *adv.* **—in·sa′ti·ate·ness** *n.*

in·sa·ti·e·ty (in′sə·tī′ə·tē) *n.* Lack of satiety or surfeit; unsatisfied wish or appetite. [<L *insatietas, -tatis*]

in·scribe (in·skrīb′) *v.t.* **·scribed, ·scrib·ing** **1** To write or engrave (signs, words, names, etc.). **2** To mark the surface of with engraved or written characters, especially in a durable or conspicuous way. **3** To dedicate, as a book, usually by an informal, written note. **4** To enter the name of on a list; enrol. **5** *Brit.* To register or record the names of holders of (stocks, securities, etc.). **6** *Geom.* To draw (one figure) in another so that the latter circumscribes the former. [<L *inscribere* < *in-* on, in + *scribere* write] **—in·scrib′er** *n.*

Synonyms: address, dedicate, engrave, impress, imprint, mark, stamp, write.

in·scrip·tion (in·skrip′shən) *n.* **1** The act or operation of inscribing, or that which is inscribed. **2** Incised or relief lettering; any legend or record marked in lasting characters on a solid and durable object. **3** Entry in a roll or the like. **4** *Brit.* A registry, as of securities. **5** The lettering on a print or similar work. **6** An address in a book; a dedication. See synonyms under RECORD, SUPERSCRIPTION. [<L *inscriptio, -onis* < *inscriptus*, pp. of *inscribere* INSCRIBE] **—in·scrip′tion·al, in·scrip′tive** *adj.*

in·scru·ta·ble (in·skrōō′tə·bəl) *adj.* That cannot be searched into; incomprehensible; unfathomable; impenetrable. See synonyms under MYSTERIOUS. [<LL *inscrutabilis* < *in-* not + *scrutare* look at] **—in·scru′ta·bil′i·ty, in·scru′·ta·ble·ness** *n.* **—in·scru′ta·bly** *adv.*

in·sect (in′sekt) *n.* **1** A minute invertebrate animal; one of the class *Insecta*. The true insects or hexapods have the body divided into a head, a thorax of 3 segments, each of which bears a pair of legs, and an abdomen of 7 to 11 segments, and in development usually pass through a metamorphosis. There are usually 2 pairs of wings, sometimes one pair or none. **2** Loosely, any small, air-breathing invertebrate resembling or suggesting an insect, as spiders, centipedes, ticks, etc. See illustrations of INSECTS (injurious, beneficial) on pages 656 and 657. [<L *(animal) insectum* (animal) notched or cut into < *insectus*, pp. of *insecare* cut into, notch] **—in·sec′te·an** (-sek′tē·ən) *adj.* **—in′sect·like′** *adj.*

In·sec·ta (in·sek′tə) *n. pl.* A class of six-legged arthropods, including and restricted to the true insects or hexapods. [<NL]

in·sec·tar·i·um (in′sek·târ′ē·əm) *n. pl.* **·i·ums** or **·i·a** (-ē·ə) A place for keeping and breeding insects, as for the purpose of studying economic entomology. Also **in·sec·tar·y** (in′·sek·ter′ē). [<NL]

in·sec·ti·cide (in·sek′tə·sīd) *n.* A substance which kills insects, usually in powder, paste, or liquid form. [<INSECT + -CIDE]

in·sec·tion (in·sek′shən) *n.* A cutting into; incision. [<L *insectus*, pp. of *insecare* cut up]

in·sec·ti·val (in′sek·tī′vəl, in·sek′tə-) *adj.* Pertaining to, or like, insects.

in·sec·ti·vore (in·sek′tə·vôr, -vōr) *n.* **1** Any of an order *(Insectivora)* of insect-eating mammals, as shrews, moles, and hedgehogs. **2** An insectivorous animal or plant. [<F <L *insectum* insect + *-vorus* devouring < *vorare* devour]

in·sec·tiv·o·rous (in′sek·tiv′ər·əs) *adj.* **1** Feeding upon or subsisting upon insects. **2** Pertaining to the *Insectivora*.

in·sec·to·cu·tion (in·sek′tə·kyōō′shən) *n.* The destruction of insect pests by electric shock, with the use of electrified wire screens, grids, etc. [<INSECT (ELECTR)OCUTION] **—in·sec′·to·cu′tor** *n.*

insect wax Chinese wax.

in·se·cure (in′sə·kyŏŏr′) *adj.* **1** Not secure or safe; in danger of breaking or failing; infirm. **2** Not assured of safety; liable to suffer loss or harm. **—in′se·cure′ly** *adv.* **—in′·se·cure′ness** *n.*

in·se·cu·ri·ty (in′sə·kyŏŏr′ə·tē) *n.* The condition of being unsafe; liability to injury, loss or failure; uncertainty; instability.

in·sem·i·nate (in·sem′ə·nāt) *v.t.* **·nat·ed, ·nat·ing** **1** To impregnate; make pregnant. **2** To sow seed in, as soil. [<L *inseminatus*, pp. of *inseminare* sow < *in-* in + *seminare* sow < *semen* seed] **—in·sem′i·na′tion** *n.*

in·se·nes·cence (in′sə·nes′əns) *n.* The process of becoming old, especially in a normal manner and without undue loss of vigor. [<IN-[2] + SENESCENCE] **—in′se·nes′cent** *adj.*

in·sen·sate (in·sen′sāt, -sit) *adj.* **1** Manifesting or marked by a lack of sense or reason; brutish; mad. **2** Destitute of sensibility. **3** Inanimate. [<LL *insensatus*] **—in·sen′sate·ly** *adv.* **—in·sen′sate·ness** *n.*

in·sen·si·ble (in·sen′sə·bəl) *adj.* **1** That is not or cannot be felt or perceived by the sense; an *insensible* motion or change. **2** Blunted in feeling or perception: to be *insensible* to pity. **3** Deprived of sensation or perception; senseless. **4** Insensate; inanimate: *insensible* earth. **5** *Obs.* Without intelligent meaning; senseless. **6** Devoid of passion, emotion, or sensitiveness; apathetic; unaware. See synonyms under BRUTISH, NUMB. [<L *insensibilis*] **—in·sen′si·bil′i·ty, in·sen′si·ble·ness** *n.* **—in·sen′si·bly** *adv.*

in·sen·si·tive (in·sen′sə·tiv) *adj.* Not sensitive to impressions, whether physical, mental, or emotional. **—in·sen′si·tiv′i·ty, in·sen′si·tive·ness** *n.*

in·sen·ti·ent (in·sen′shē·ənt, -shənt) *adj.* Inanimate. **—in·sen′ti·ence, in·sen′ti·en·cy** *n.*

in·sep·a·ra·ble (in·sep′ər·ə·bəl) *adj.* Incapable of being separated or disjoined: *inseparable* friends. **—in·sep′a·ra·ble·ness** *n.* **—in·sep′a·ra·bly** *adv.*

in·sert (in·sûrt′) *v.t.* To put or place into something else; put between or among other things; introduce. **—*n.*** (in′sûrt) That which is inserted; an addition made by insertion; specifically, in bookbinding, an inset; also, a circular or the like placed within a newspaper or book for mailing. [<L *insertus*, pp. of *inserere* < *in-* in + *serere* place, join] **—in·sert′er** *n.*

in·sert·ed (in·sûr′tid) *adj.* **1** *Anat.* Attached to, as the tendon of a muscle to a bone. **2** *Bot.* Growing from a part, as stamens on the corolla of a flower.

in·ser·tion (in·sûr′shən) *n.* **1** The act of inserting, or the state of being inserted. **2** That which is inserted, as lace or embroidery placed between pieces of plain fabric. **3** *Bot.* Place or mode of attachment, as of a leaf to a branch. **4** *Anat.* The end of a muscle that is attached to the bone or part which it moves. **5** A word, paragraph, or written material inserted in a written or printed page; also, an advertisement in a newspaper. See INSERT.

in·ses·so·ri·al (in′sə·sôr′ē·əl, -sō′rē-) *adj.* **1** Of or pertaining to a former order or class *(Insessores)* of perching birds. **2** Perching or fitted for perching, as a bird's foot. [<L *insessor* a sitter < *insessum*, pp. of *insidere* sit on < *in-* on + *sedere* sit]

in·set (in·set′) *v.t.* To set in; implant; insert. **—*n.*** (in′set′) **1** A leaf or leaves inserted, as in a book or newspaper. **2** A small diagram, map, etc., inserted in the border of a larger one. **3** A piece of material let or set into a garment. **4** Influx, as of the tide.

in·sheathe (in·shēth′) *v.t.* **·sheathed, ·sheath·ing** To place or enclose in or as in a sheath.

in·shore (in′shôr′, -shōr′, in′shôr′, -shōr′) *adj.* **1** Being or occurring near the shore: *inshore* fishing. **2** Coming toward the shore: an *inshore* wind. **—*adv.*** Toward the shore.

in·shrine (in·shrīn′) *v.t.* To enshrine.

in·side (in′sīd′, -sīd′) *n.* **1** The side, surface, or part that is within; interior. **2** That which is contained; contents. **3** Inner thoughts or feelings: One cannot know the *inside* of a man's mind. **4** *pl. Colloq.* Inner organs; entrails. **5** *Printing* **a** *pl.* Sheets of paper that do not include any of the outer or soiled sheets of a ream or package. **b** The side of a sheet containing the second page. **6** An inside passenger or place for a passenger, as in a vehicle. **—*adj.*** **1** Situated or occurring on or in the inside; internal. **2** Suited for or pertaining to the inside. **3** For use indoors: *inside* paint. **4** Private; confidential; known only within a certain group or organization:

inside reports. —*adv.* (in′sīd′) **1** In or into the interior; within. **2** Indoors. —**inside out** Reversed so that the inside is exposed. —*prep.* (in′sīd′) In or into the interior of; within. —**inside of** *Colloq.* Within the time or distance of: a house *inside of* a mile away.

in·sid·er (in′sī′dər) *n.* One who is inside; hence, one who has special information or advantages.

inside track The inner and shorter way around a race track; hence, a position of advantage; the favored position.

in·sid·i·ous (in·sid′ē·əs) *adj.* **1** Designed to entrap; full of wiles. **2** Doing or contriving harm. **3** Awaiting a chance to harm. **4** Causing harm by slow, stealthy, usually imperceptible means: an *insidious* disease. [<L *insidiosus* <*insidiae* ambush <*insidere* sit in, lie in wait] —**in·sid′i·ous·ly** *adv.* —**in·sid′·i·ous·ness** *n.*

Synonyms: artful, crafty, cunning, deceitful, designing, guileful, intriguing, sly, subtle, treacherous, tricky, wily.

in·sight (in′sīt′) *n.* **1** Intellectual discernment. **2** A perception of the inner nature of a thing; intuition. See synonyms under ACUMEN, WISDOM.

in·sig·ni·a (in·sig′nē·ə) *n. pl. of* **in·sig·ne** (in·sig′nē) **1** Badges, emblems, etc., used as marks of office or distinction. **2** Things significant or indicative of a calling. See illustration under SHOULDER PATCH. [<L, neut pl. of *insignis* eminent <*in-* in + *signum* sign, emblem, badge]

in·sig·nif·i·cance (in′sig·nif′ə·kəns) *n.* The state of being insignificant; lack of import or of importance; triviality. Also **in′sig·nif′·i·can·cy.**

in·sig·nif·i·cant (in′sig·nif′ə·kənt) *adj.* **1** Not significant; without import, meaning, or bearing; without importance; trivial. **2** Small, little. —**in′sig·nif′i·cant·ly** *adv.*

Synonyms: idle, immaterial, irrelevant, little, mean, meaningless, paltry, petty, slight, small, trifling, trivial. See LITTLE. *Antonyms*: considerable, essential, grand, grave, great, immense, influential, large, mighty, significant.

in·sin·cere (in′sin·sir′) *adj.* Not sincere, honest, or genuine; hypocritical. —**in′sin·cere′ly** *adv.* —**in′sin·cer′i·ty** (-ser′ə·tē) *n.*

in·sin·u·ate (in·sin′yōō·āt) *v.t.* **·at·ed, ·at·ing** **1** To indicate slyly or deviously; imply; intimate. **2** To infuse or instil gradually or subtly into the mind: to *insinuate* distrust. **3** To introduce (someone) gradually or artfully into a position or relation: to *insinuate* oneself into another's confidence. See synonyms under ALLUDE. [<L *insinuatus*, pp. of *insinuare* curve <*in-* in + *sinus* bosom, curved surface]

in·sin·u·at·ing (in·sin′yōō·ā′ting) *adj.* Characterized by insinuation; winding, or creeping in; insensibly or subtly winning favor and confidence; ingratiating.

in·sin·u·a·tion (in·sin′yōō·ā′shən) *n.* **1** The act of insinuating; indirect suggestion; implication; specifically, an injurious suggestion. **2** That which is insinuated; hint; a subtly ingratiating act, remark, etc. **3** Gradual or sly introduction. **4** Power or faculty of gaining affection, favor, or confidence. See synonyms under SUGGESTION.

in·sin·u·a·tive (in·sin′yōō·ā′tiv) *adj.* **1** Making use of insinuation, as to gain favor or confidence. **2** Tending to instil into the mind. **3** Characterized by or necessitating insinuation; suggestive.

in·sin·u·a·tor (in·sin′yōō·ā·tər) *n.* **1** One who worms his way into favor. **2** One who subtly hints or intimates (something usually malicious).

in·sip·id (in·sip′id) *adj.* **1** Without flavor; unsavory; tasteless. **2** Not qualified to interest; vapid; lacking in energy or ambition; dull. See synonyms under FLAT. [<F *insipide* <LL *insipidus* <*in-* not + *sapidus* savory <*sapere* savor, taste] —**in·si·pid·i·ty** (in′si·pid′ə·tē), **in·sip′id·ness** *n.* —**in·sip′id·ly** *adv.*

in·sip·i·ence (in·sip′ē·əns) *n.* Lack of wisdom; foolishness. ◆ Homophone: *incipience.* [<OF <L *insipientia* <*insipiens, -entis* unwise]

in·sip·i·ent (in·sip′i·ənt) *adj.* Foolish; unwise.

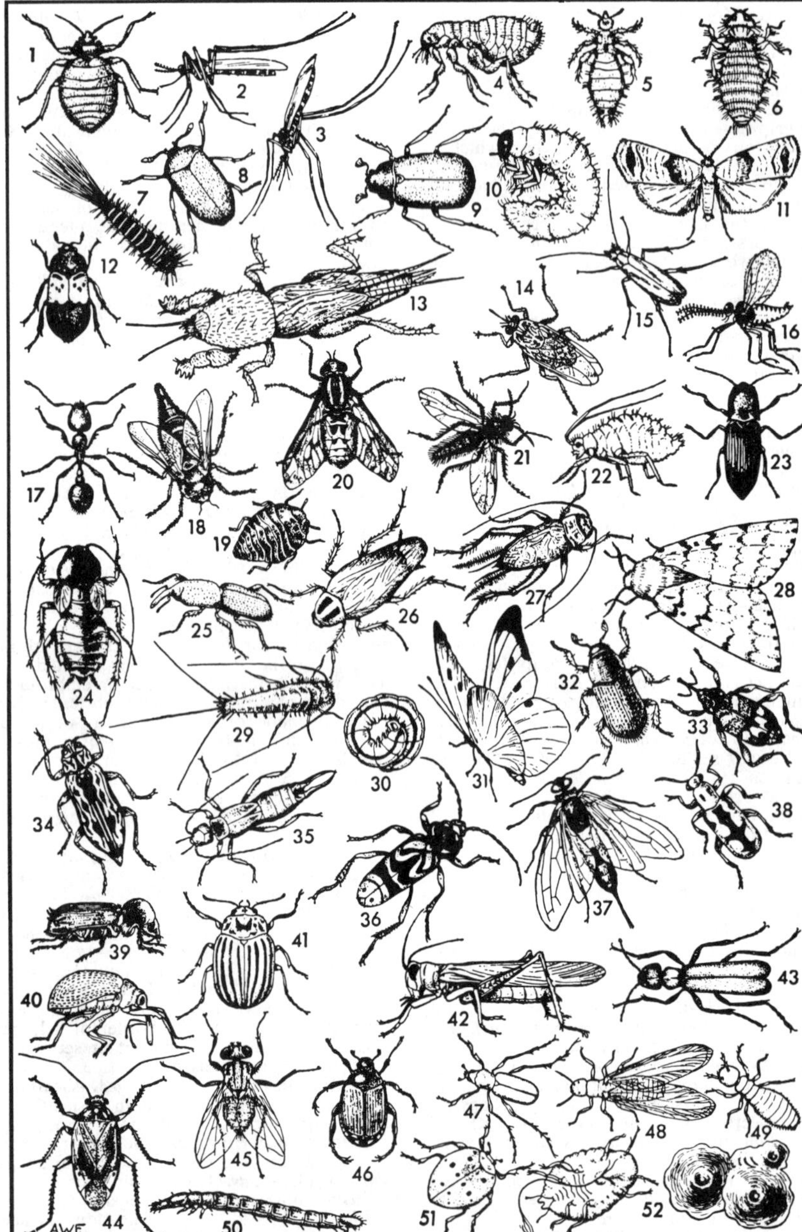

INJURIOUS INSECTS

1. Bedbug, *Cimex lectularius.*
2. Mosquito, genus *Culex.*
3. Mosquito, genus *Anopheles.*
4. Flea, *Pulex irritans.*
5. Body louse, *Pediculus humanus.*
6. Chicken louse, genus *Mallophaga.*
7. Carpet beetle larva.
8. Carpet beetle, *Attagenus piceus.*
9. June beetle, genus *Scarabaeidae.*
10. June beetle grub.
11. Codling moth, *Carpocapsa pomonella.*
12. Larder beetle, *Dermestes lardarius.*
13. Mole cricket, genus *Gryllotalpa.*
14. Tsetse fly, genus *Glossina.*
15. Clothes moth, *Tineola bisselliella.*
16. Gall midge, family *Cecidomyidae.*
17. Ant, family *Formicidae.*
18. Botfly, genus *Gasterophilus.*
19. Phylloxera, *Dactylosphaera vitifoliae.*
20. Deer fly, *Chrysops discalis.*
21. Midge, genus *Culicoides.*
22. Plant louse or aphid, family *Aphididae.*
23. Click beetle, family *Elateridae.*
24. Oriental roach, *Blatta orientalis.*
25. Rice weevil, genus *Sitophilus.*
26. Cockroach, *Blatella germanica.*
27. Cricket, *Gryllus domesticus.*
28. Gipsy moth, *Lymantria dispar.*
29. Firebrat, genus *Thermobia.*
30. Cutworm larva, family *Noctuidae.*
31. Cabbage butterfly, *Pieris rapae.*
32. Bark beetle, family *Scolytidae.*
33. White pine weevil, genus *Pissodes.*
34. Metallic wood borer, family *Buprestidae.*
35. Earwig, *Forficula auricularia.*
36. Maple borer, family *Cerambycidae.*
37. Horntail, genus *Urocerus.*
38. Asparagus beetle, *Crioceris asparagi.*
39. Palm borer, family *Bostrichidae.*
40. Cotton boll weevil, *Anthonomus grandis.*
41. Potato beetle, *Leptinotarsus decemlineata.*
42. Grasshopper, family *Acrididae.*
43. Blister beetle, *Epicauta pennsylvanicus.*
44. Tarnished plant bug, *Lygus pratensis.*
45. House fly, *Musca domestica.*
46. Japanese beetle, *Popillia japonica.*
47. Rose chafer, *Macrodactylus subspinosus.*
48. Termite, genus *Kalotermes*, winged form.
49. Termite, wingless form.
50. Wireworm (larva of click beetle).
51. Mexican bean beetle, *Epilachna varivestris.*
52. San José scale, *Quadriaspidiotus perniciosus*, showing scales.

in·sist (in·sist′) *v.i.* To make emphatic or repeated assertion, demand, or request: often with *on* or *upon*: He *insisted* on the correctness of his theory. —*v.t.* To state or demand emphatically: with a clause as object: He *insisted* that he was right. [<F *insister* <L *insistere* dwell upon, persist <*in-* on + *sistere* stand] —**in·sis′tence, in·sis′ten·cy** *n.*

Synonyms: persevere, persist. *Insist* implies some alleged authority or right; *persist* implies simply determination of will; we *insist* upon the action of others; we *persist* in our own. *Insist* is used of any urgency, good or bad, but largely in the good sense; *persist* is used chiefly in a bad sense, *persevere* being preferred for the better meaning. See PERSIST.

in·sis·tent (in·sis′tənt) *adj.* **1** Insisting; persistent; urgent. **2** Standing out prominently; conspicuous: *insistent* colors. **— in·sis′tent·ly** *adv.*

in si·tu (in sī′tyōō) *Latin* In its original site or position.

in·snare (in·snâr′) See ENSNARE.

in·so·bri·e·ty (in′sə·brī′ə·tē) *n.* Lack of moderation; intemperance, especially in drinking.

in·so·far as (in′sō·fär′ az′) To the extent that; in such measure as. Also **in so far as.**

in·so·late (in′sō·lāt) *v.t.* **·lat·ed, ·lat·ing** To expose to the rays of the sun, as for bleaching, drying, maturing, etc. [<L *insolatus,* pp. of *insolare* expose to the sun < *in-* in + *sol* sun]

in·so·la·tion (in′sō·lā′shən) *n.* **1** The act of insolating; exposure to the rays of the sun. **2** Sunstroke. **3** A method of treating disease by exposure to the rays of the sun. **4** A disease in plants caused by exposure to the sun. **5** *Meteorol.* **a** Solar radiation received by the earth or other planets. **b** The rate of delivery of such radiant energy per unit of horizontal surface.

in·sole (in′sōl′) *n.* **1** The fixed inner sole of a boot or shoe. **2** A removable inner sole placed within a shoe to improve its fit or as a protection against dampness.

in·so·lence (in′sə·ləns) *n.* **1** The quality of being insolent; pride or haughtiness exhibited in contemptuous and overbearing treatment of others; offensive impertinence. **2** An insult. See synonyms under ARROGANCE, IMPUDENCE. [<OF <L *insolentia* < *insolens, -entis* unwonted]

in·so·lent (in′sə·lənt) *adj.* **1** Presumptuously or defiantly offensive in language or manner; impudent. **2** Grossly disrespectful; characterized by insolence. See synonyms under HAUGHTY, IMPUDENT. [<L *insolens, -entis* unusual, haughty, insolent < *in-* not + *solens, -entis,* ppr. of *solere* be wont, accustomed] **— in′so·lent·ly** *adv.*

in·sol·u·ble (in·sol′yə·bəl) *adj.* **1** Not capable of being dissolved, as in a liquid; not soluble. **2** That cannot be explained or solved; insolvable. **3** Impossible to pay or discharge, as a debt or obligation. [<OF <L *insolubilis*] **— in·sol′u·bil′i·ty, in·sol′u·ble·ness** *n.* **— in·sol′u·bly** *adv.*

in·solv·a·ble (in·sol′və·bəl) *adj.* **1** Not admitting of explanation; insoluble. **2** *Obs.* That cannot be untied or loosened.

in·sol·ven·cy (in·sol′vən·sē) *n.* *pl.* **·cies** Bankruptcy.

in·sol·vent (in·sol′vənt) *adj.* **1** Unable to meet the claims of creditors; not solvent; bankrupt. **2** Inadequate for the payment of debts. **3** Pertaining to insolvency. **—** *n.* A debtor who is not solvent; a bankrupt; specifically, a debtor whose property is taken to be divided among his creditors by a court under the operation of bankruptcy law.

in·som·ni·a (in·som′nē·ə) *n.* Chronic inability to sleep. [<L < *insomnis* sleepless]

in·som·ni·ac (in·som′nē·ak) *n.* One who suffers from sleeplessness.

in·som·ni·ous (in·som′nē·əs) *adj.* Affected with insomnia; sleepless.

in·som·no·lence (in·som′nə·ləns) *n.* Sleeplessness.

in·so·much (in′sō·much′) *adv.* **1** To such a degree or extent: with *that* or *as.* **2** Inasmuch: with *as.*

in·so·nate (in′sə·nāt) *v.t.* **·nat·ed, ·nat·ing** To expose or subject to the action of sound waves, especially those of very high frequency. [<IN-[2] + L *sonatus,* pp. of *sonare* sound] **— in′so·na′tion** *n.*

in·sou·ci·ance (in·sōō′sē·əns, *Fr.* aṅ·sōō·syäṅs′) *n.* Careless unconcern; indifference; heedlessness. [<F]

in·sou·ci·ant (in·sōō′sē·ənt, *Fr.* aṅ·sōō·syäṅ′) *adj.* Without concern or care; heedless; unmindful. [<F < *in-* not + *souciant,* ppr. of *soucier* care <OF *solcier* <L *sollicitare* disturb] **— in·sou·ci·ant·ly** (in·sōō′sē·ənt·lē) *adv.*

in·soul (in·sōl′) See ENSOUL.

in·span (in·span′) *v.t.* & *v.i.* **·spanned, ·span·ning** To harness or yoke (animals) to a vehicle. [<Afrikaans <Du. *inspannen*]

in·spect (in·spekt′) *v.t.* **1** To look at or examine carefully and critically. **2** To examine or review officially and with ceremony, as troops. See synonyms under EXAMINE, LOOK. [<L *inspectus,* pp. of *inspicere* look into < *in-* into + *specere* look]

in·spec·tion (in·spek′shən) *n.* Critical viewing or investigation; especially, an official examination. See synonyms under OVERSIGHT. [<OF <L *inspectio, -onis*] **— in·spec′tion·al** *adj.*

in·spec·tive (in·spek′tiv) *adj.* Of or pertaining to inspection; tending to inspect, or that may be inspected.

in·spec·tor (in·spek′tər) *n.* **1** One who inspects. **2** An official designated to carry out inspection; a supervisor. **3** An officer of police usually ranking next below the superintendent. See synonyms under SUPERINTENDENT. [<L]

in·spec·tor·ate (in·spek′tər·it) *n.* The office or district of an inspector. Also **in·spec′tor·ship** (-ship).

Inspector General A military, air, or naval officer responsible for the conduct of inspec-

BENEFICIAL INSECTS

1. Tiger beetle, genus *Cicindella.*
2. Fiery hunter, *Calosoma calidus.*
3. Praying mantis nymph.
4. Ground beetle larva.
5. Syrphus or hover fly, genus *Syrphus.*
6. Tachina fly, genus *Winthemia.*
7. Praying mantis, *Paratenodera sinensis.*
8. Syrphus fly larva.
9. Ichneumon fly, genus *Ephialtes.*
10. Tachina fly, *Alophora diversa.*
11. Darning needle, *Anax junius.*
12. Dragon fly, *Libellula semifasciata.*
13. Scorpion fly, *Panorpa rufescens.*
14. Assassin fly, genus *Erax.*
15. Ichneumon fly, genus *Amblyteles.*
16. Big-headed fly, genus *Pipunculus.*
17. Bee fly, *Villa alternata.*
18. Spanish fly, *Lytta vesicatoria.*
19. Damsel fly, genus *Agrion.*
20. Dance fly, genus *Empis.*
21. Ladybird, *Adalia bipunctata.*
22. Digger wasp, genus *Ammophila.*
23. Ant lion, *Hesperoleon abdominalis.*
24. Ant lion larva and pit.
25. Lacewing, genus *Chrysopa,* with eggs.
26. Digger wasp, *Bembidula quadrifasciatus.*
27. Rove beetle, genus *Staphylinus.*
28. Assassin bug, *Sinea diadema.*
29. Mud dauber, genus *Scleripheron.*
30. Potter wasp, genus *Eumenes.*
31. Ground beetle, genus *Pterosticus.*
32. Caterpillar hunter, *Calosoma scrutator.*
33. Cicada killer, *Sphecius speciosus.*

tions and investigations of the economy, discipline, and efficiency of the branch of the armed forces in which he serves; also an officer of his department serving on the staff of a division or higher unit.

in·sphere (in·sfir′) *v.t.* To ensphere.

in·spir·a·ble (in·spīr′ə·bəl) *adj.* **1** That can be breathed; inhalable. **2** Capable of being inspired. **— in·spir′a·bil′i·ty** *n.*

in·spi·ra·tion (in′spə·rā′shən) *n.* **1** The infusion or imparting of an idea, an emotion, or a mental or spiritual influence. **2** That which is so infused or imparted. **3** An actuating or exalting influence; a stimulus to creativity in thought or action. **4** State of being inspired. **5** Divine or supernatural influence considered as exerted upon men so that their writings have divine authority; attributed by the Society of Friends to the direct teaching of the mind of man by the Holy Spirit. **6** A person or thing that inspires. **7** The act of drawing air into the lungs, inbreathing, or inspiring; inhalation: opposite of *expiration.* See synonyms under ENTHUSIASM. [<OF <LL *inspiratio, -onis*]

in·spi·ra·tion·al (in′spə·rā′shən·əl) *adj.* Of or pertaining to inspiration; bestowing or influenced by inspiration; inspiring. **— in′spi·ra′·tion·al·ly** *adv.*

in·spi·ra·tion·al·ist (in′spə·rā′shən·əl·ist) *n.* One who inspires others, whether by speech, writing, or conduct.

in·spir·a·to·ry (in·spīr′ə·tôr′ē, -tō′rē) *adj.* Of or pertaining to inspiration or inhalation. [<L *inspiratus* + -ORY]

in·spire (in·spīr′) *v.* **·spired, ·spir·ing** *v.t.* **1** To stir or affect by some mental or spiritual influence; stimulate; animate: A brave leader *inspires* his followers. **2** To affect or imbue with a specified idea or feeling: to *inspire* survivors with hope. **3** To arouse or give rise to; generate: Fear *inspires* hatred. **4** To motivate or cause by supernatural influence or guidance. **5** To draw into the lungs; inhale. **6** To prompt the saying or writing of indirectly so as to avoid responsibility: This rumor was *inspired* by my enemies. **7** *Obs.* To blow or breathe into or upon. **—** *v.i.* **8** To draw in breath; inhale. **9** To give or provide inspiration. See synonyms under ENCOURAGE. [<OF *enspirer* <L *inspirare* breathe into <*in-* into + *spirare* breathe] **— in·spir′er** *n.*

in·spired (in·spīrd′) *adj.* **1** Communicated, imparted, or guided by inspiration: the *inspired* writings (Scriptures). **2** Prompted or kindled by ideas, emotions, etc.: an *inspired* speech. **3** Officially motivated or shaped: an *inspired* editorial. **— in·spir·ed·ly** (in·spīr′·id·lē, -spīrd′lē) *adv.*

in·spir·it (in·spir′it) *v.t.* To fill with spirit or life; animate; exhilarate; enliven. See synonyms under ENCOURAGE. **— in·spir′it·ing·ly** *adv.*

in·spis·sate (in·spis′āt) *v.t.* & *v.i.* **·sat·ed, ·sat·ing** To thicken, as by evaporation. **—** *adj.* Thickened; inspissated. See synonyms under THICK. [<LL *inspissatus,* pp. of *inspissare* thicken <*in-* thoroughly + *spissare* thicken <*spissus* thick] **— in·spis·sa·tion** (in′spi·sā′·shən) *n.* **— in′spis·sa′tor** *n.*

in·sta·bil·i·ty (in′stə·bil′ə·tē) *n. pl.* **·ties** **1** Lack of stability or firmness. **2** Mutability of opinion or conduct; inconstancy; changeableness. **3** Flimsiness of construction; liability to give way; insecurity: the *instability* of a bridge.

Synonyms: changeableness, fickleness, flightiness, inconstancy, mutability, unstableness, unsteadiness. *Antonyms*: certainty, constancy, firmness, persistence, stability, steadiness.

in·sta·ble (in·stā′bəl) *adj.* Unstable.

in·stall (in·stôl′) *v.t.* **1** To place in office, etc., with formal ceremony. **2** To establish in a place or position. **3** To place in position for service or use: to *install* a hot-water system. [<F *installer* <Med. L *installare* <*in-* in + *stallare* seat <OHG *stal* a seat] **— in·stall′er** *n.*

Synonyms: inaugurate, induct, initiate, ordain. *Antonyms*: break, cashier, depose, dismiss.

in·stal·la·tion (in′stə·lā′shən) *n.* **1** The act or ceremony of inducting into an office or place of honor. **2** An installing or being installed; especially, the introduction of apparatus or machines for use. **3** Such a machine or apparatus fixed for use: a ventilating *installation.* **4** Any large, fixed base of the armed service.

in·stal·ment (in·stôl′mənt) *n.* **1** A partial payment of a price due; a payment on account. **2** One of several parts of anything furnished at different times; especially a section of a novel or other writing running serially in a magazine, newspaper, etc. **3** The act of installing. Also **in·stall′ment.** [<obs. *estall* arrange payments <OF *estaler* stop <OHG *stal* seat, place]

instalment plan The purchase of goods or services by means of deferred payments at regular intervals.

in·stance (in′stəns) *n.* **1** Something offered or occurring as an exemplification. **2** A case. **3** Illustration, evidence, or proof: an *instance* of her forthrightness. **4** *Archaic* Urgency. **5** The act of asking, soliciting, suggesting or urging: They took action at the *instance* of aroused taxpayers. **6** *Obs.* An impelling motive. **7** A step in proceeding: in the first *instance.* **8** *Law* The institution of a process or suit. **— for instance** For example. **—** *v.t.* **·stanced, ·stanc·ing** **1** To refer to as illustration or example. **2** *Rare* To manifest or show. **3** *Rare* To cite an instance, or as an instance. [<OF <L *instantia* a standing near, urgent supplication <*instans, -antis* standing. See INSTANT.]

in·stan·cy (in′stən·sē) *n.* **1** Urgency; solicitation. **2** Immediateness.

in·stant (in′stənt) *adj.* **1** Immediately impending. **2** Now passing; current; present: the 10th *instant* (the 10th day of the month now passing). See PROXIMO, ULTIMO. **3** Direct; immediate. **4** Eager and active; urgent; importunate. See synonyms under IMMEDIATE. **—** *n.* **1** A particular point of time; the moment which in passing may be called now. **2** A very brief portion of time; moment. **—** *adv. Poetic* Instantaneously; instantly. [<OF <L *instans, -antis,* ppr. of *instare* stand near, urge <*in-* upon + *stare* stand]

in·stan·ta·ne·ous (in′stən·tā′nē·əs) *adj.* **1** Acting or done instantly. **2** Relating to a particular instant. [<INSTANT, on analogy with *simultaneous*] **— in′stan·ta′ne·ous·ly** *adv.* **— in′·stan·ta′ne·ous·ness** *n.*

in·stan·ter (in·stan′tər) *adj.* Without an instant of delay. See synonyms under IMMEDIATELY. [<L]

in·stant·ly (in′stənt·lē) *adv.* **1** On the instant; at once. **2** *Archaic* With urgency; insistently. **—** *conj.* As soon as. See synonyms under IMMEDIATELY.

in·star[1] (in·stär′) *v.t.* **·starred, ·star·ring** **1** To adorn or stud with or as with stars. **2** To set as a star; make a star of.

in·star[2] (in′stär′) *n. Entomol.* **1** Any stage in the metamorphosis of an insect or other arthropod between successive molts: the pupal *instar* of a butterfly. **2** The insect or arthropod while undergoing any of these stages. [<L, form, likeness]

in·state (in·stāt′) *v.t.* **·stat·ed, ·stat·ing** **1** To place or establish in a certain office or rank; induct. **2** *Obs.* To endow.

in sta·tu quo (in stā′tyōō kwō′, stach′ōō) *Latin* **1** In the present condition. **2** In the original state.

in·stau·rate (in·stôr′āt) *v.t.* **·rat·ed, ·rat·ing** *Rare* To renew; renovate; restore. [<L *instauratus,* pp. of *instaurare* renew] **— in·stau·ra·tion** (in′stô·rā′shən) *n.*

in·stead (in·sted′) *adv.* **1** In place or room; in lieu: with *of*: a friend *instead* of an enemy. **2** In one's (its, their, etc.) stead or place: They went prospecting for silver and found gold *instead.*

in·step (in′step′) *n.* **1** *Anat.* The arched upper part of the human foot, extending from the toes to the ankle. ◆ Collateral adjective: *tarsal.* **2** The front part of the hind leg of a horse, extending from the ham, or hock, to the pastern joint. **3** That part of a shoe or of a stocking that covers the instep.

in·sti·gate (in′stə·gāt) *v.t.* **·gat·ed, ·gat·ing** **1** To bring about by inciting; foment. **2** To urge or incite to an action or course: to *instigate* someone to treason. See synonyms under ABET, ENCOURAGE, INFLUENCE, SPUR, STIR. [<L *instigatus,* pp. of *instigare* <*in-* against + the root *-stig-* prick, goad] **— in′sti·ga′tive** *adj.* **— in′sti·ga′tor** *n.*

in·sti·ga·tion (in′stə·gā′shən) *n.* **1** The act of instigating, inciting, or urging, especially to evil. **2** That in which instigating is embodied; an incitement; stimulus.

in·stil (in·stil′) *v.t.* **·stilled, ·stil·ling** **1** To put into the mind gradually, as if drop by drop. **2** To pour in by drops. Also **in·still′.** [<L *instillare* drop, drip <*in-* in + *stillare* drop <*stilla* a drop] **— in·stil·a·tion** (in′stə·lā′shən) or **in′stil·la′tion, in·stil′ment** or **in·still′ment** *n.* **— in·still′er** *n.*

in·stinct (in′stingkt) *n.* **1** A natural impulse or innate propensity that incites animals (including man) to the actions that are essential to their existence, preservation, and development; animal intuition. **2** *Psychol.* **a** A strong, innate tendency to certain actions and forms of behavior, often accompanied by emotional excitement. **b** A complex, unlearned, adaptive response to some situation or experience. **3** A natural aptitude. **—** *adj.* (in·stingkt′) Animated from within; moved by or imbued with inward impulse; filled; alive: usually with *with.* [<L *instinctus,* pp. of *instinguere* impel]

in·stinc·tive (in·stingk′tiv) *adj.* Of the nature of, or prompted by, instinct; spontaneous; innate. Also **in·stinc′tu·al** (-chōō·əl). See synonyms under SPONTANEOUS. **— in·stinc′tive·ly, in·stinct′ly** *adv.*

in·sti·tute (in′stə·tōōt, -tyōōt) *v.t.* **·tut·ed, ·tut·ing** **1** To set up or establish; found. **2** To set in operation; initiate. **3** To appoint to an office, position, etc.; place in a benefice. **4** *Law* To nominate as heir or executor. **—** *n.* **1** An established organization or society pledged to some special purpose and work, or the building devoted to its use; an institution. **2** *pl.* Fundamental principles of law, or a digest of them, as for beginners. **3** An established principle, rule, or order. **— farmers' institute** An organization of farmers addressed by experts in agriculture for the purpose of disseminating knowledge in farming. **— naval institute** A society having as its object the development of naval knowledge. **— teachers' institute** A meeting of the schoolteachers of a state or county for the discussion of methods of teaching and problems which arise within a certain period. [<L *institutus,* pp. of *instituere* erect, establish <*in-* in, on + *statuere* set up, stand]

Synonyms (verb): appoint, begin, commence, erect, establish, found, ordain, organize, originate, start. *Antonyms*: see synonyms for ABOLISH.

Institute of France A national society established in 1795 to promote science, literature, and art, composed of a union of five academies: The French Academy; the Academy of Inscriptions and Belles-lettres; the Academy of Sciences; the Academy of Fine Arts; the Academy of Political and Moral Sciences. Also **the Institute.**

in·sti·tu·tion (in′stə·tōō′shən, -tyōō′-) *n.* **1** That which is instituted or established; an established order, principle, law, or usage as an element of organized society or of civilization: the *institution* of chivalry. **2** A corporate body or establishment instituted and organized for an educational, medical, charitable, or similar purpose, or the building occupied by such a corporate body: the Smithsonian *Institution.* **3** The act of instituting, establishing, or setting on foot: *institution* of an investigation. **4** *Eccl.* **a** The investment of a clergyman by a competent authority with the spiritualities of his office: contrasted with *induction,* which confers the temporalities. **b** The establishment of a sacrament, especially of the Eucharist. **c** That part of the ritual in baptism or the Eucharist at which the words used by Christ in establishing the sacrament are recited. **5** *Law* The formal designation by one person of another to be his heir. **6** *Colloq.* A well-established custom, object, or person: The postman was one of the *institutions* of the place. **7** *Obs.* Instruction, or a book of instruction. [<OF <L *institutio, -onis*]

in·sti·tu·tion·al (in′stə·tōō′shən·əl, -tyōō′-) *adj.* **1** Pertaining to or enjoined by institutions: *institutional* principles. **2** Relating to first principles or elements; rudimentary: *institutional* instruction. **3** Pertaining to investiture in office. **4** Designating a form of advertising intended to promote good will and prestige, as for an institution, rather than to get immediate sales. **— in′sti·tu′tion·al·ly** *adv.*

in·sti·tu·tion·al·ism (in′stə·tōō′shən·əl·iz′əm, -tyōō′-) *n.* 1 The system of institutions. 2 Belief in and support of the usefulness and authority of institutions. 3 The spirit that exalts established institutions, especially in religion: opposed to *individualism.*

in·sti·tu·tion·al·ize (in′stə·tōō′shen·əl·īz′, -tyōō′-) *v.t.* **·ized, ·iz·ing** 1 To make institutional. 2 To turn into or regard as an institution. 3 *U.S. Colloq.* To put (someone) in an institution (def. 2).

in·sti·tu·tion·ar·y (in′stə·tōō′shən·er′ē, -tyōō′-) *adj.* Of or pertaining to legal or ecclesiastical institutions or to institutions of learning.

in·sti·tu·tive (in′stə·tōō′tiv, -tyōō′-) *adj.* 1 Tending or intended to institute or establish; having power to ordain. 2 Established by authority; instituted. — **in′sti·tu′tive·ly** *adv.*

in·sti·tu·tor (in′stə·tōō′tər, -tyōō′-) *n.* 1 One who establishes, organizes, or sets in operation; a founder. 2 *U.S.* In the Protestant Episcopal Church, one who institutes a clergyman into a church or parish. 3 *Obs.* An educator. Also **in′sti·tut′er.** [<L]

in·stroke (in′strōk′) *n.* 1 An inwardly directed stroke. 2 *Mech.* The thrust of an engine's piston away from the crankshaft. Compare OUTSTROKE.

in·struct (in·strukt′) *v.t.* 1 To impart knowledge or skill to, especially by systematic method; educate; teach. 2 To give specific orders or directions to; order: He *instructed* his men to break camp. 3 To give information or explanation to; inform. See synonyms under INFORM[1], LEARN, TEACH. [<L *instructus,* pp. of *instruere* <*in-* in + *struere* build]

in·struc·tion (in·struk′shən) *n.* 1 The act of instructing; teaching. 2 Imparted knowledge; precept. 3 The act of giving specific directions or commands. 4 The directions given. 5 *pl.* In English law, directions given to a solicitor or counsel. See synonyms under EDUCATION, LEARNING, NURTURE, ORDER. [< OF *enstruccion* <L *instructio, -onis*]

in·struc·tion·al (in·struk′shən·əl) *adj.* Pertaining or relating to instruction; educational; containing information.

in·struc·tive (in·struk′tiv) *adj.* Serving to instruct; conveying knowledge. — **in·struc′tive·ly** *adv.* — **in·struc′tive·ness** *n.*

in·struc·tor (in·struk′tər) *n.* 1 One who instructs; a teacher. 2 *U.S.* A college teacher of lower rank than the lowest professorial grade. Also **in·struct′er.** [<L]

in·struc·tor·ship (in·struk′tər·ship) *n.* The position or office of an instructor.

in·stru·ment (in′strə·mənt) *n.* 1 A means by which work is done; an implement or tool, especially a device or mechanism for scientific or professional purposes, as distinguished from an apparatus, tool, or machine for industrial use. 2 Any means of accomplishment: The hands are *instruments* of the will. 3 A mechanical or other contrivance for the production of musical sounds. 4 A person doing the will of another. 5 *Law* A formal document, as a contract, deed, etc. See synonyms under AGENT, RECORD, TOOL. — *v.t.* 1 *Law* To draw up an instrument. 2 *Music* To orchestrate. [<L *instrumentum* <*instruere* fit out, INSTRUCT]

in·stru·men·tal (in′strə·men′təl) *adj.* 1 Serving as a means or instrument; serviceable. 2 Fitted for or produced by musical instruments. 3 Traceable to a mechanical instrument, as errors in observation or measurement. 4 *Gram.* Pertaining to a case of the noun, as in Sanskrit, indicating the means or instrument by or with which something is done. — *n. Gram.* 1 The instrumental case. 2 A word in this case.

in·stru·men·tal·ism (in′strə·men′təl·iz′əm) *n.* *Philos.* The doctrine that experience (or use) determines the value of anything; hence, the doctrine that ideas are true or valid according to their usefulness; pragmatism.

in·stru·men·tal·ist (in′strə·men′təl·ist) *n.* 1 *Music* One who plays an instrument, as distinguished from a vocalist. 2 A believer in instrumentalism.

in·stru·men·tal·i·ty (in′strə·men·tal′ə·tē) *n. pl.* **·ties** 1 The condition of being instrumental; subordinate agency. 2 That which is instrumental; means.

in·stru·men·tal·ly (in′strə·men′təl·ē) *adv.* 1 By means of an instrument or agency; not directly. 2 With musical instruments.

in·stru·men·ta·tion (in′strə·men·tā′shən) *n.* 1 *Music* **a** The act or art of arranging compositions for performance by instruments; orchestration. **b** The use of an instrument, as for producing special or peculiar effects. 2 The art and technique of using instruments of precision. 3 Instrumentality; agency.

instrument board The panel containing the gages and other indicators of performance in an automobile, airplane, or other complex apparatus. Also **instrument panel.**

instrument flight *Aeron.* Control of the course of an aircraft by reference to instruments within the craft rather than by observation of landmarks: contrasted to *contact flight.*

in·sub·or·di·nate (in′sə·bôr′də·nit) *adj.* 1 Not subordinate or obedient; not submitting to authority; rebellious; mutinous. 2 Not lower or inferior in height: an *insubordinate* hill. — *n.* A disobedient or unsubmissive person. — **in′sub·or′di·nate·ly** *adv.*

in·sub·or·di·na·tion (in′sə·bôr′də·nā′shən) *n.* The state of being insubordinate; disobedience to constituted authorities; unruliness.

in·sub·stan·tial (in′səb·stan′shəl) *adj.* Unsubstantial; not material; illusive. — **in′sub·stan′·ti·al′i·ty** (-shē·al′ə·tē) *n.*

in·suf·fer·a·ble (in·suf′ər·ə·bəl) *adj.* Not to be endured; intolerable. — **in·suf′fer·a·ble·ness** *n.* — **in·suf′fer·a·bly** *adv.*

in·suf·fi·cien·cy (in′sə·fish′ən·sē) *n. pl.* **·cies** 1 Lack of sufficiency; inadequacy in amount, value, power, fitness, etc.; deficiency; also, mental inability. 2 Anything that is not enough. [<F *insuffisance* <LL *insufficientia*]

in·suf·fi·cient (in′sə·fish′ənt) *adj.* 1 Inadequate for some need, purpose, or use. 2 Mentally or physically unfit. — **in′suf·fi′cient·ly** *adv.*

in·suf·flate (in·suf′lāt, in′sə·flāt) *v.t.* **·flat·ed, ·flat·ing** 1 To blow or breathe into or upon. 2 To blow a substance into: to *insufflate* a room with disinfectant. 3 *Med.* **a** To blow (air, medicinal gas, etc.) into an opening or upon some part of the body. **b** To treat by insufflation, as an asphyxiated person. 4 *Eccl.* To breathe upon, as at baptism. [<L *insufflatus,* pp. of *insufflare* <*in-* in + *sufflare* <blow from below <*sub-* under + *flare* blow] — **in·suf′fla·tor** *n.*

in·suf·fla·tion (in′sə·flā′shən) *n.* 1 The act or process of blowing or breathing upon or into. 2 *Eccl.* A breathing upon a person or thing as symbolic of the operation and entrance of the Holy Spirit, or the casting out of unclean spirits, as in some churches in the ordinance of baptism for the purification of catechumens. 3 *Med.* A forcible blowing, as of air into the lungs, or of a gas, vapor, or powder into some opening or cavity of the body. [<LL *insufflatio, -onis*]

in·su·la (in′sə·lə) *n. pl.* **·lae** (-lē) 1 *Anat.* Any detached or isolated area in an organ of the body, as the central lobe of the cerebral cortex. 2 In ancient Rome, a block of houses. [<L, island]

in·su·lar (in′sə·lər) *adj.* 1 Of or pertaining to, like, living on or characteristic of an island. 2 Standing alone; isolated. 3 *Biol.* Having an island as its habitat. 4 Of or pertaining to people inhabiting an island or otherwise isolated, or to their customs, opinions, etc. 5 Not broad, liberal, nor cosmopolitan; narrow: *insular* ideas or prejudices. 6 *Med.* **a** Breaking out or appearing sporadically in spots, as a rash on the body. **b** Characterized by spots appearing singly here and there. 7 *Anat.* Pertaining to an insula or to the islands of Langerhans in the pancreas. [<L *insularis* <*insula* island]

in·su·lar·i·ty (in′sə·lar′ə·tē) *n.* 1 The state or quality of being insular or belonging to an island. 2 Insular position, character, or condition. 3 Narrowness or illiberality. Compare PENINSULARITY. Also **in′su·lar·ism.**

in·su·late (in′sə·lāt) *v.t.* **·lat·ed, ·lat·ing** 1 To place in a detached state or situation; isolate. 2 To change into an island; surround by water. 3 *Physics* To separate from conducting bodies, as by a covering or support of a non-conducting substance, usually in order to prevent or lessen the leakage of an electric current, heat, sound, radiation, etc. [<L *insulatus* formed like an island <*insula* island]

in·su·la·tion (in′sə·lā′shən) *n.* 1 The act of insulating; isolation. 2 The act of surrounding a body with non-conductors. 3 Material used in insulating.

in·su·la·tor (in′sə·lā′tər) *n.* 1 One who or that which insulates. 2 *Electr.* A dielectric substance or material, as glass or porcelain, adapted to minimize leakage from a charged conductor which it supports.

in·su·lin (in′sə·lin) *n.* A protein hormone secreted by and obtained from the pancreas: used in the form of a standardized aqueous solution, it checks the accumulation of glucose in the blood and promotes the utilization of sugar in the treatment of diabetes. [<L *insula* island (of Langerhans) + -IN]

in·su·lize (in′sə·līz) *v.t.* **·lized, ·liz·ing** To inject insulin into; treat with insulin.

in·sult (in·sult′) *v.t.* 1 To treat with insolence or contempt; affront. 2 *Obs.* To attack suddenly; assault. — *v.i.* 3 *Obs.* To exult or behave insolently. See synonyms under AFFRONT, MOCK, OUTRAGE. — *n.* (in′sult) 1 Something offensive said or done; an indignity or affront. 2 Contumelious treatment; abuse; outrage. 3 *Obs.* A sudden attack or assault. See synonyms under OFFENSE. [<F *insulter* <L *insultare* leap at, insult, freq. of *insilire* leap upon <*in-* on + *salire* leap] — **in·sult′er** *n.*

in·sult·ing (in·sul′ting) *adj.* Conveying or intending to insult. — **in·sult′ing·ly** *adv.*

in·su·per·a·ble (in·sōō′pər·ə·bəl) *adj.* Not to be surmounted or overcome; insurmountable. [<L *insuperabilis*] — **in·su′per·a·bil′i·ty, in·su′per·a·ble·ness** *n.* — **in·su′per·a·bly** *adv.*

in·sup·port·a·ble (in′sə·pôr′tə·bəl, -pōr′-) *adj.* 1 Intolerable; insufferable. 2 Without grounds; unjustifiable. — **in′sup·port′a·bly** *adv.*

in·sup·press·i·ble (in′sə·pres′ə·bəl) *adj.* Incapable of being suppressed or concealed; irrepressible. Also **in′sup·pres′sive** (-pres′iv).

in·sur·ance (in·shŏŏr′əns) *n.* 1 An act, business, or system by which pecuniary indemnity is guaranteed by one party (as a company) to another party in certain contingencies, as of death, accident, damage, disaster, injury, loss, old age, risk, sickness, unemployment, etc., upon specified terms: in Great Britain, often *assurance.* 2 A contract made under such a system. 3 The consideration paid for insuring; premium. 4 The sum that the insurer has agreed to pay in case of the occurrence of the specified contingency. 5 The act of making safe or secure. 6 Something that provides protection or security.

— **accident insurance** A form of insurance covering loss due to accidental personal injury.

— **casualty insurance** Insurance of property against loss from accidental causes.

— **endowment insurance** A form of life insurance in which the whole amount agreed upon is paid to the insured if he survives beyond a specified date, or to some designated person or his heirs if he dies before that time.

— **fire insurance** Insurance covering loss or damage to property by fire or from the efforts to extinguish fire.

— **life insurance** Insurance on the life of oneself or another. The first life insurance company established in Great Britain was the "Amicable" in 1706, and the first in America was introduced from England in 1759 as the Presbyterian Ministers' Fund, and established in Philadelphia.

— **marine insurance** Insurance which covers loss on ships, cargo, and freight by shipwreck or disaster at sea.

— **unemployment insurance** A form of government insurance in which a worker is paid, during an extended period of involuntary unemployment, from a fund contributed to by employers and employees.

in·sur·ant (in·shŏŏr′ənt) *n.* One to whom an insurance policy is issued; also, the beneficiary.

in·sure (in·shŏŏr′) *v.* **·sured, ·sur·ing** *v.t.* 1 To contract to pay or be paid an indemnity in the event of harm to or the loss or death of; issue or take out a policy of insurance on. 2 To make safe; guard or protect: with *against* or *from*: Only vigilance *insures* freedom against tyranny. 3 To make sure or certain; guarantee: His researches *insure* the accuracy of the report. — *v.i.* **4** To issue or take out a policy of insurance. Also spelled *ensure.* [<OF *enseurer* make sure <*en-* in + *seur* sure] — **in·sur'a·bil'i·ty** *n.* — **in·sur'a·ble** *adj.*

in·sured (in·shŏŏrd') *n.* **1** The person or persons to whom insurance (as fire or marine) is to be paid after loss or damage. **2** The person or persons upon whose death or disability insurance (life or accident) becomes due.

in·sur·er (in·shŏŏr'ər) *n.* One who or that which insures; especially, a company or individual that undertakes, for compensation, to guarantee against loss; an underwriter.

in·sur·gence (in·sûr'jəns) *n.* The act of rising in insurrection; insurrection; uprising.

in·sur·gen·cy (in·sûr'jən·sē) *n.* **1** The state of being insurgent. **2** In international law, any uprising against a government of less gravity than a revolution.

in·sur·gent (in·sûr'jənt) *adj.* Rebellious; rising in rebellion against an existing government. See synonyms under TURBULENT. — *n.* One who takes part in active and forcible opposition or resistance to the constituted authorities; also, a rebel to whom belligerent rights have not been accorded. [<L *insurgens, -entis,* ppr. of *insurgere* rise up against <*in-* against + *surgere* rise]

in·sur·mount·a·ble (in'sər·moun'tə·bəl) *adj.* That cannot be surmounted, passed over, or overcome; insuperable. — **in'sur·mount'a·bly** *adv.*

in·sur·rec·tion (in'sə·rek'shən) *n.* An organized resistance to established government. See synonyms under REVOLUTION. [<F <LL *insurrectio, -onis* <*insurrectus,* pp. of *insurgere* rise up against. See INSURGENT.] — **in'sur·rec'tion·al** *adj.* — **in'sur·rec'tion·ar'y** *adj.* & *n.* — **in'sur·rec'tion·ism** *n.* — **in'sur·rec'tion·ist** *n.*

in·sus·cep·ti·ble (in'sə·sep'tə·bəl) *adj.* Not susceptible; incapable of being moved or impressed. — **in'sus·cep'ti·bil'i·ty** *n.*

in·swathe (in·swāth') See ENSWATHE.

in·swept (in'swept') *adj.* Narrowed or tapering in front, as an airplane wing.

in·tact (in·takt') *adj.* Left complete or unimpaired. [<L *intactus* untouched <*in-* not + *tactus,* pp. of *tangere* touch] — **in·tact'ness** *n.*

in·ta·glio (in·tal'yō, *Ital.* in·tä'lyō) *n.* *pl.* **·glios** or **·gli** (-lyē) **1** Incised carving; a sunken design: compare RILIEVO. **2** The art of making such designs. **3** A work, especially a gem, with incised carving: compare CAMEO. **4** A countersunk die for producing a relief design. — *v.t.* **1** To engrave with a sunken design. **2** To execute or represent in intaglio. [<Ital. <*intagliare* engrave <*in-* in + *tagliare* cut]

intaglio printing A method of printing from sunken or incised plates: also called *copperplate* or *steel-die printing.*

in·take (in'tāk') *n.* **1** That which is taken in; also, a taking in. **2** A point at which a knit or woven article is narrowed. **3** The area in which a water supply is formed. **4** The point at which a fluid is taken into a pipe or channel, as distinguished from the outlet. **5** The current flowing in such a pipe. **6** The amount so taken in. **7** The amount of energy or power taken into a machine or system.

in·tan·gi·ble (in·tan'jə·bəl) *adj.* **1** Not capable of being touched; not tangible; impalpable. **2** Not directly appreciable by the mind; unfathomable — *n.* Something intangible but often noteworthy or influential nevertheless. [<Med. L *intangibilis*] — **in·tan'gi·bil'i·ty, in·tan'gi·ble·ness** *n.* — **in·tan'gi·bly** *adv.*

in·tar·si·a (in·tär'sē·ə) *n.* Mosaic woodwork of tinted and natural woods. [<Ital. *intarsio* < *intarsiare* inlay, encrust <*in-* in + Arabic *tarsi* incrustation]

in·te·ger (in'tə·jər) *n.* **1** A whole. **2** A number that is not a fraction; a whole number. [<L <*in-* not + root *tag-,* of *tangere.* Doublet of ENTIRE.]

in·te·ger vi·tae (in'tə·jər vī'tē) *Latin* Innocent; pure: literally, blameless in life.

in·te·gra·ble (in'tə·grə·bəl) *adj.* Capable of being integrated.

in·te·gral (in'tə·grəl) *adj.* **1** Constituting a completed whole. **2** Constituting an essential part of a whole necessary for completeness; intrinsic. **3** *Math.* **a** Pertaining to an integer. **b** Produced by integration. — *n.* **1** An entire thing; a whole. **2** *Math.* The result of integration. [<LL *integralis*] — **in'te·gral'i·ty** (-gral'ə·tē) *n.* — **in'te·gral·ly** *adv.*

integral calculus See under CALCULUS.

in·te·grand (in'tə·grand) *n.* *Math.* An expression to be integrated, or whose integration is indicated. [<L *integrandus,* gerundive of *integrare* make whole]

in·te·grant (in'tə·grənt) *adj.* Contributing or essential to the making up of a whole; integral. — *n.* A component. [<L *integrans, -antis,* ppr. of *integrare* make whole]

in·te·grate (in'tə·grāt) *v.* **·grat·ed, ·grat·ing** *v.t.* **1** To make whole by the bringing together or addition of parts. **2** To give the sum total or mean value of. **3** *Math.* To find the integral of. **4** *U.S.* **a** To make (schools, housing, public facilities, etc.) available to people of all races and ethnic groups on an equal basis. **b** To remove any barriers imposing segregation upon (religious, racial, or other groups). — *v.i.* **5** To become integrated. [<L *integratus,* pp. of *integrare* make whole, renew <*integer* whole, intact] — **in'te·gra'tive** (-grā'tiv) *adj.*

in·te·grat·ed (in'tə·grā'tid) *adj.* **1** Made whole by combining in systematic order or arrangement the component parts or factors: an *integrated* curriculum. **2** Well adjusted: an *integrated* personality. **3** *Econ.* Organized and equipped to produce all materials (usually excluding the raw materials) and components required by a manufacturing process without recourse to independent suppliers; a fully *integrated* plant. **4** *U.S.* Made up of individuals or groups of various cultural, economic, racial, etc., backgrounds functioning as a unit: an *integrated* school.

in·te·gra·tion (in'tə·grā'shən) *n.* **1** The act or operation of integrating; the bringing together of parts into a whole. **2** *Math.* The process of determining a function from its derivative; the inverse of *differentiation.* **3** *Physiol.* The combination of different nervous processes or reflexes so that they cooperate in a larger activity and thus unify the bodily functions. **4** *Psychol.* The orderly arrangement of the physical, emotional, and mental components of the personality into a more or less stable and harmonious pattern of behavior. **5** *U.S.* The act or process of integrating, especially racially, an institution, place, or group. — **in'te·gra'tion·ist** (*especially for def. 5*) *n.* [<L *integratio, -onis*]

in·te·gra·tor (in'tə·grā'tər) *n.* **1** One who or that which integrates. **2** Any mechanical device for obtaining the numerical value of an integral, especially the area of an irregular figure. **3** An integrating instrument, as a planimeter.

in·teg·ri·ty (in·teg'rə·tē) *n.* **1** Uprightness of character; probity; honesty. **2** Unimpaired state; soundness. **3** Undivided or unbroken state; completeness. See synonyms under FIDELITY, JUSTICE, VIRTUE, WORTH. [<L *integritas, -tatis* <*integer* whole]

in·teg·u·ment (in·teg'yə·mənt) *n.* **1** A covering; coating; investment. **2** *Biol.* Any natural outer covering or envelope, as the skin of an animal, coat of a seed, etc. [<L *integumentum* covering <*integere* cover <*in-* thoroughly + *tegere* cover] — **in·teg·u·men·ta·ry** (in·teg'yə·men'tə·rē) *adj.*

in·tel·lect (in'tə·lekt) *n.* **1** The faculty or power of perception or thought; intelligence; mind; sometimes, the higher thinking powers, as distinguished from the senses and memory: *Intellect* distinguishes man from brutes. **2** Intelligent people collectively: The *intellect* of the age is enlisted in these inquiries. **3** The faculty or power of understanding, whether of the objects immediately presented in sense perception, or of those known by processes of reasoning. **4** Formerly, in the archaic threefold division of psychology, the faculty of knowing, as distinguished from sensibility and will. **5** The power to perceive things in a rational way, as involving a more than ordinary comprehension of their relations, laws, and profounder meanings; the scientific or philosophical mind: Aristotle was a man of mighty *intellect.* **6** The sum of the mental powers by which knowledge is acquired, retained, and extended, as distinguished from the senses; the understanding. [<L *intellectus* perception, understanding, sense <*intelligere* understand. See INTELLIGENT.]

Synonyms: intelligence, reason, reasoning, understanding. According to the long-established division of the mental powers into the *intellect,* the sensibilities, and the will, the *intellect* is that assemblage of faculties which is concerned with knowledge, as distinguished from emotion and volition. *Understanding* is the Saxon word of the same general import, but is chiefly used of the reasoning powers. See MIND, UNDERSTANDING. *Antonyms*: body, matter, passion, sensation, sense.

in·tel·lec·tion (in'tə·lek'shən) *n.* Exercise of the intellect; thought. [<Med. L *intellectio, -onis*]

in·tel·lec·tive (in'tə·lek'tiv) *adj.* Of or pertaining to the intellect; intelligent. [<OF *intellectif* <LL *intellectivus*] — **in'tel·lec'tive·ly** *adv.*

in·tel·lec·tu·al (in'tə·lek'chōō·əl) *adj.* **1** Pertaining to the intellect; bringing into action the intellect or higher capacities; mental. **2** Possessing intellect or intelligence; characterized by a high degree of intelligence. **3** Requiring intelligence or study: *intellectual* pursuits. See synonyms under CLEVER, WISE. — *n.* **1** An intellectual person. **2** *pl.* *Archaic* The mental faculties; intellect: often in the plural. [<L *intellectualis*] — **in'tel·lec'tu·al·ly** *adv.*

in·tel·lec·tu·al·ism (in'tə·lek'chōō·əl·iz'əm) *n.* **1** Intellectual quality or power; intellectuality. **2** Devotion to intellectual occupation. **3** Belief in the supremacy of the intellect among human faculties. **4** The doctrine that the ultimate principle of all reality is intellect or reason. — **in'tel·lec'tu·al·ist** *n.* — **in'tel·lec'tu·al·is'tic** *adj.*

in·tel·lec·tu·al·i·ty (in'tə·lek'chōō·al'ə·tē) *n.* The quality or state of being intellectual; possession of intellectual force or endowment.

in·tel·lec·tu·al·ize (in'tə·lek'chōō·əl·īz') *v.t.* & *v.i.* **·ized, ·iz·ing** To make or become intellectual.

in·tel·li·gence (in·tel'ə·jəns) *n.* **1** The quality, exercise, or product of active intellect; intellect; knowledge; ability to exercise the higher mental functions; readiness of comprehension. **2** The capacity to meet situations, especially if new or unforeseen, by a rapid and effective adjustment of behavior; also, the native ability to grasp the significant factors of a complex problem or situation. **3** Information acquired or communicated; notification; news; especially, secret information, political, military, etc. **4** Mutual understanding; interchange of information or thought: to exchange a look of *intelligence.* **5** An intelligent being; especially, a spirit not embodied: the Supreme *Intelligence.* See synonyms under INTELLECT, KNOWLEDGE, MIND, TIDINGS, UNDERSTANDING. [<OF <L *intelligentia* <*intelligens, -entis,* ppr. of *intelligere* understand]

intelligence department A department charged with getting information for a government, an army, or a navy, as by means of spies.

intelligence office **1** An office where information may be obtained. **2** *U.S.* Formerly, an employment bureau, especially for servants.

intelligence officer An officer in the service of an intelligence department.

intelligence quotient *Psychol.* A numerical quotient obtained by multiplying the mental age of a person by 100, and dividing the result by his chronological age. Abbr. *I.Q.* or *IQ.*

in·tel·li·genc·er (in·tel'ə·jən·sər) *n.* A sender or conveyor of intelligence or news; a messenger; spy.

intelligence test *Psychol.* Any test designed to show the relative mental capacity of a person.

in·tel·li·gent (in·tel'ə·jənt) *adj.* **1** Distinguished for intelligence; of active mind; discerning; acute: an *intelligent* reader. **2** Marked by intelligence: an *intelligent* reply. **3** Endowed with intellect; reasoning: Man is an *intelligent* animal. **4** *Archaic* Informed; cognizant: with *of.* **5** *Obs.* Communicating information. [<L *intelligens, -entis,* ppr. of *intelligere* understand, perceive <*inter-* between + *legere* choose, pick] — **in·tel'li·gent·ly** *adv.*

Synonyms: acute, astute, bright, clear-headed, clear-sighted, clever, discerning, educated, instructed, keen, keen-sighted, knowing, long-headed, quick-sighted, sensible, sharp-sighted, sharp-witted, shrewd, well-informed. *Antonyms*: see synonyms for IGNORANT.

in·tel·li·gen·tial (in·tel'ə·jen'shəl) *adj.* **1** Exercising or characterized by intelligence; rational. **2** Conveying intelligence.

in·tel·li·gent·si·a (in·tel′ə·jent′sē·ə, -gent′-) *n. pl.* Intellectual or learned people, collectively; especially those capable of thinking for themselves: sometimes used derisively: a term adopted during the Russian Revolution to differentiate the intellectual classes as such from the bourgeoisie and proletariat. Also **in·tel′li·gent′zi·a.** [<Russian *intelligentsiya* < Ital. *intelligenza* intelligence <L *intelligentia*]

in·tel·li·gi·bil·i·ty (in·tel′ə·jə·bil′ə·tē) *n. pl.* **·ties 1** Clearness; understandableness. **2** That which is intelligible.

in·tel·li·gi·ble (in·tel′ə·jə·bəl) *adj.* **1** Capable of being understood. **2** *Philos.* Capable of being apprehended only by the intellect, not by the senses. Compare SENSIBLE. See synonyms under CLEAR, PLAIN. [<L *intelligibilis*] **— in·tel′li·gi·bly** *adv.*

in·tem·er·ate (in·tem′ər·it) *adj.* Undefiled; pure. [<L *intemeratus* <*in-* not + *temeratus,* pp. of *temerare* violate < *temere* rashly, by chance]

in·tem·per·ance (in·tem′pər·əns) *n.* **1** Lack of moderation or due restraint. **2** Excess in speech or action, especially in the use of alcoholic drinks. **3** An intemperate act. See synonyms under EXCESS. [<OF <L *intemperantia*]

in·tem·per·ate (in·tem′pər·it) *adj.* **1** Characterized by lack of moderation, as in speech or action; unrestrained, as in indulgence or exertion. **2** Given to or characterized by excessive use of alcoholic drinks: *intemperate* habits. **3** Excessive in character or degree: inordinate; inclement: *intemperate* weather. **—in·tem′per·ate·ly** *adv.* **—in·tem′per·ate·ness** *n.*

in·tend (in·tend′) *v.t.* **1** To have in mind to accomplish or do; purpose: He *intends* to go. **2** To make or destine for a purpose, use, etc.: Was that gift *intended* for me? **3** To have the purpose of meaning or expressing; mean: She *intended* nothing by the remark. **4** *Obs.* To direct, as one's course or thoughts. — *v.i.* **5** *Rare* To have intention; mean: to *intend* well. **6** *Obs.* To tend; incline. See synonyms under PURPOSE. [<OF *entendre* <L *intendere* stretch out (for) < *in-* in, at + *tendere* stretch] **— in·tend′er** *n.*

in·ten·dance (in·ten′dəns) *n.* **1** Business management or superintendence. **2** An intendancy. [<F]

in·ten·dan·cy (in·ten′dən·sē) *n. pl.* **·cies 1** The office or work of an intendant; intendants collectively. **2** An administrative district in Spanish America. Also **in·ten′den·cy.**

in·ten·dant (in·ten′dənt) *n.* **1** A superintendent; provincial administrator, as under the Bourbons in France. **2** A Spanish or Mexican district administrator or treasurer. Also **in·ten′dent,** *Spanish* **in·ten·den·te** (ēn′ten·den′·tā). See synonyms under SUPERINTENDENT. [<F]

in·tend·ed (in·ten′did) *adj.* **1** Made the object of design or intent; designed. **2** Betrothed. — *n. Colloq.* One who is betrothed.

in·tend·ment (in·tend′mənt) *n.* **1** The true intent or meaning, or correct understanding, of the law, or of a legal instrument; also, a general presumption of law. **2** *Obs.* Intention; object, as of an action; purpose; design. [<OF *entendement*]

in·ten·er·ate (in·ten′ər·āt) *v.t.* **·at·ed, ·at·ing** *Rare* To make tender; soften. [<L *in-* very + *tener* tender + -ATE¹] **— in·ten′er·a′tion** *n.*

in·tense (in·tens′) *adj.* **in·tens·er, in·tens·est 1** Strained or exerted to a high degree; ardent; unremitting; fervid: *intense* study. **2** Extreme in degree; very deep or strong; severe; violent; excessive: *intense* light or pain. **3** Putting forth strenuous effort; intent. **4** Susceptible to or exhibiting deep emotion, earnestness, or application: said of a person. **5** *Phot.* Having strength or marked contrast; dense: said of a negative. See synonyms under ARDENT, EAGER, VIOLENT, VIVID. [<OF <L *intensus,* pp. of *intendere* stretch out] **— in·tense′ly** *adv.* **— in·tense′ness** *n.*

in·ten·si·fi·ca·tion (in·ten′sə·fə·kā′shən) *n.* **1** The act or result of intensifying or of making intense. **2** *Phot.* The process of increasing the density of a negative.

in·ten·si·fi·er (in·ten′sə·fī′ər) *n.* **1** One who or that which intensifies. **2** *Phot.* A chemical solution used to effect intensification. **3** A device by which fluid pressure is intensified.

in·ten·si·fy (in·ten′sə·fī) *v.* **·fied, ·fy·ing** *v.t.* **1** To make intense; increase in intensity. **2** *Phot.* To increase the density of (a film) so as to obtain stronger contrast between light and shadow. — *v.i.* **3** To become intense or more intense. See synonyms under AGGRAVATE, INCREASE.

in·ten·sion (in·ten′shən) *n.* **1** The act of straining or stretching, or state of being strained or made tense; tension. **2** Increase of energy or power; intensification. **3** *Logic* All the implications in a concept or term; connotation: distinguished from *extension.* **4** Intensity; degree. **5** Intense exertion of the mind or the will. [<L *intensio, -onis*]

in·ten·si·ty (in·ten′sə·tē) *n. pl.* **·ties 1** The state or quality of being intense; relative strength or degree of a quality or force; intenseness. **2** *Physics* The force, energy, or quantity of action of any physical agent, generally estimated by its ratio to the space within which it acts, or to the quantity of matter on which it acts: the *intensity* of pressure of a fluid, the *intensity* of gravity. **3** *Electr.* **a** The strength of an electric or magnetic field as measured by the number of force lines that pass through unit area of cross-section. **b** Current strength or density. **c** Potential or electromotive force. **4** *Phot.* Strong contrast between light and shade in a negative; density; also, opacity. See synonyms under ENTHUSIASM, VIOLENCE, WARMTH.

in·ten·sive (in·ten′siv) *adj.* **1** Serving or tending to intensify. **2** Admitting of increase of force or degree; capable of being intensified. **3** Thorough, as contrasted with extensive. **4** *Logic* Relating to intension or content. See CONTENT. **5** *Agric.* Of or pertaining to the tillage of land by the application of much labor and costly fertilization to a given area (usually small) which is thereby brought to a high degree of productiveness. **6** Of or relating to a way of making any industry more lucrative by perfecting methods and appliances without enlarging the scale of operations. **7** *Med.* **a** Characterizing a method of inoculation wherein the injections are successively increased in strength. **b** A method of administering increasingly strong remedies or doses. **8** *Gram.* Adding emphasis or force. **9** Intense; assiduous; concentrated: *intensive* research; *intensive* warfare. **10** Characterized by a relatively heavy investment in (something specified) as compared with other factors: used in combination: an *energy-intensive* method of heating; a *labor-intensive* industry. — *n.* **1** Whatever gives intensity or emphasis. **2** *Gram.* An intensive particle, word, or phrase. [<F *intensif*] **— in·ten′sive·ly** *adv.* **— in·ten′sive·ness** *n.*

intensive particle A particle or prefix expressing heightened meaning: as *be-* in *besmirch*; *for-* in *forlorn*; *de-* in *desiccate*; *per-* in *perjure.* Also **intensive prefix.**

in·tent (in·tent′) *adj.* **1** Having the mind earnestly bent or fixed; attentive; earnest. **2** Firmly, constantly, or assiduously directed. See synonyms under EAGER. — *n.* **1** That which is designed; intention; meaning; connotation; aim; purpose. **2** *Law* The state of mind in which or the purpose with which one does an act; also, the character that the law imputes to an act. See synonyms under DESIGN, PURPOSE. [<OF *entent, entente* <L *intentus,* pp. of *intendere* stretch out, endeavor] **— in·tent′ly** *adv.* **— in·tent′ness** *n.*

in·ten·tion (in·ten′shən) *n.* **1** A settled direction of the mind toward the doing of a certain act. **2** That upon which the mind is set or which it wishes to express or achieve; meaning; purpose conceived. **3** *pl. Colloq.* Purpose with regard to marriage. **4** *Law* An intelligent purpose to do a criminal act; intent; purpose: an essential element in a criminal offense. **5** *Med.* Natural course, operation, or process, as in the healing of a wound. **6** *Logic* In scholasticism: **a** First intention, a general concept of an object, kind of object, or notion formed from something outside the mind, as *man, house, integrity, word, to run.* **b** Second intention, a general concept formed from or extended to abstractions of other concepts of objects and their relationships, as *genus* and *species, property, ethics, language* and *meaning, physiological functions.* Compare CONSTRUCT *n.* (def. 2). **7** *Eccl.* **a** The inward intent or purpose on the part of the minister of a sacrament to do what the church requires to be done: considered essential to the validity of a sacrament. **b** The purpose for which a person offers up prayers or other devotions: often with *special* or *particular.* **8** Earnest attention; application. See synonyms under AIM, DESIGN, PURPOSE. [<OF *entencion* <L *intentio, -onis*]

in·ten·tion·al (in·ten′shən·əl) *adj.* Done with intention; designed. [<Med. L *intentionalis*] **— in·ten′tion·al·ly** *adv.*

in·ten·tioned (in·ten′shənd) *adj.* Having designs or intentions: used in composition with a qualifying adverb: well-*intentioned.*

in·ter (in·tûr′) *v.t.* **·terred, ·ter·ring** To place in a grave or tomb; bury. See synonyms under BURY, HIDE. [<OF *enterrer* <LL *interrare* < *in-* in + *terra* earth]

inter- *prefix* **1** With each other; together: *interwind.* **2** Mutual; mutually: *intercommunion.* **3** Between (the units signified): *intercollegiate, intertribal.* **4** Occurring or situated between; intermediate: *intermural, interpolar.* [<L *inter-* < *inter* between, among]

A large number of words beginning with *inter-* are self-explaining or readily understood, as in the following list; those that require special definition will be found in their proper alphabetical place.

interagency
inter-American
interanimate
interblend
interbrachial
intercarotid
intercarpal
interchain
intercirculate
interclasp
intercolonial
intercommunion
intercomplexity
intercontinental
interconversion
interconvertible
intercross
interdenominational
interdepartmental
interdependence
interdependency
interdependent
interdiffuse
interdiffusion
interdigital
interfibrous
interfold
interfriction
interfulgent
interfuse
interfusion
interglandular
interglobular
intergovernmental
intergrowth
interisland
interjoin
interjunction
interknit
interknot
interlay
interligamentous
interlocate
intermigration
intermolecular
intermundane
intermural
inter-oceanic
inter-ocular
interplace
interplanetary
interpolar
interracial
interreceive
interregional
interrule
interscapular
interscene
interscholastic
interseptal
intersocial
intersonant
interspeech
interstellar
interstratification
interstratify
intertangle
interterritorial
intertraffic
intertribal
intertropical
intertubular
intertwist
inter-union
inter-university
interwind
interwork
interwreathe

in·ter·act (in′tər·akt′) *v.i.* To act on each other. **— in′ter·ac′tive** *adj.*

in·ter·ac·tion (in′tər·ak′shən) *n.* Reciprocal action or influence: the *interaction* between the executive and legislative branches of government. **— in′ter·ac′tion·al** *adj.*

in·ter·ac·tion·ism (in′tər·ak′shən·iz′əm) *n. Psychol.* The theory that physical occurrences are the causes of mental modifications and that mental modifications give rise to physical changes.

in·ter a·li·a (in′tər ā′lē·ə) *Latin* Among other things.

in·ter a·li·os (in′tər ā′lē·ōs) *Latin* Among other persons.

in·ter·bed·ded (in′tər·bed′id) *adj. Geol.* Occurring between beds, said of rocks.

in·ter·bor·ough (in′tər·bûr′ō) *adj.* Pertaining to, situated in, or running in two or more boroughs: an *interborough* railroad.

in·ter·brain (in′tər·brān′) *n. Anat.* The portion

of the brain that is derived from the second cerebral vesicle; the diencephalon.

in·ter·breed (in'tər·brēd') *v.* **·bred, ·breed·ing** *v.t.* **1** To breed by crossing different stocks, varieties, etc.; crossbreed. **2** To cause (animals or plants) to breed by crossing. —*v.i.* **3** To breed with another: said of different varieties, stocks, etc.

in·ter·ca·lar·y (in·tûr'kə·ler'ē) *adj.* **1** Added to the calendar. **2** Containing an added day. **3** Interposed; inserted. [<L *intercalarius*]

in·ter·ca·late (in·tûr'kə·lāt) *v.t.* **·lat·ed, ·lat·ing 1** To insert or interpolate. **2** To insert, as an additional day or month, into the calendar. [<L *intercalatus,* pp. of *intercalare* insert <*inter-* between +*calare* proclaim, call]

in·ter·ca·la·tion (in·tûr'kə·lā'shən) *n.* **1** The insertion of one thing between other things, especially in an irregular manner. **2** An insertion of a day or days in the calendar. —**in·ter'ca·la'tive** *adj.*

in·ter·car·di·nal (in'tər·kär'də·nəl) *adj. Naut.* Between the cardinal points of the compass, as northeast, southwest, etc. —*n.* One of the intercardinal points of the compass.

in·ter·cede (in'tər·sēd') *v.i.* **·ced·ed, ·ced·ing 1** To plead in behalf of another; make intercession. **2** To interpose a veto: said of the ancient Roman tribunes. See synonyms under INTERPOSE. [<L *intercedere* come between <*inter-* between +*cedere* pass, go]—**in'·ter·ced'er** *n.*

in·ter·cel·lu·lar (in'tər·sel'yə·lər) *adj. Biol.* Situated between or among cells: the *intercellular* substance or matrix of cartilage.

intercellular spaces *Bot.* The spaces or passages filled with air between or among the cells of plant tissues.

in·ter·cept (in'tər·sept') *v.t.* **1** To seize or stop on the way to a destination; arrest in passage: to *intercept* a messenger. **2** To stop, interrupt, or prevent: to *intercept* the flow of water. **3** To cut off from connection, sight, etc. **4** *Math.* To contain or include between two points of a curve. See synonyms under INTERPOSE, SHUT. —*n.* (in'tər·sept) **1** That which is cut off or intercepted. **2** *Math.* The part of a curve contained between two points of intersection with other curves. [<L *interceptus,* pp. of *intercipere* <*inter-* between +*capere* seize]—**in'ter·cep'tion** *n.* —**in'ter·cep'tive** *adj.*

in·ter·cep·tor (in'tər·sep'tər) *n.* **1** One who or that which intercepts. **2** *Aeron.* **a** A lateral control device in an airplane. **b** An airplane adapted to the pursuit and interception of enemy aircraft. Also **in'ter·cept'er.** [<L]

in·ter·ces·sion (in'tər·sesh'ən) *n.* **1** The act of interceding between persons; entreaty in behalf of others. **2** A prayer, or series of prayers. [<L *intercessio, -onis* <*intercessus,* pp. of *intercedere* INTERCEDE]—**in'ter·ces'·sion·al** *adj.*

in·ter·ces·sor (in'tər·ses'ər) *n.* One who intercedes; a mediator. [<L]—**in'ter·ces'so·ry** *adj.*

in·ter·change (in'tər·chānj') *v.* **·changed, ·chang·ing** *v.t.* **1** To put each of (two things) in the place of the other. **2** To give and receive in return, as gifts; exchange. **3** To alternate: to *interchange* work and rest. —*v.i.* **4** To make an interchange. —*n.* (in'tər·chānj') **1** Exchange. **2** Alternation. See synonyms under INTERCOURSE. [<OF *entrechangier* <*entre-* between (<L *inter-*) +*changier* <LL *cambiare* exchange]—**in'ter·chang'er** *n.*

in·ter·change·a·ble (in'tər·chān'jə·bəl) *adj.* Capable of being interchanged or substituted one for the other; permitting transposition. [<OF *entrechangeable*]—**in'ter·change'a·ble·ness, in'ter·change'a·bil'i·ty** *n.* —**in'ter·change'·a·bly** *adv.*

in·ter·cip·i·ent (in'tər·sip'ē·ənt) *adj.* Intercepting; stopping. —*n.* One who or that which intercepts. [<L *intercipiens, -entis,* ppr. of *intercipere.* See INTERCEPT.]

in·ter·clav·i·cle (in'tər·klav'i·kəl) *n. Anat.* The median ventral bone between the clavicles. —**in'ter·cla·vic'u·lar** (-klə·vik'yə·lər) *adj.*

in·ter·clude (in'tər·klōōd') *v.t.* **·clud·ed, ·clud·ing** *Obs.* To shut out; cut off; intercept. [<L *intercludere* <*inter-* between +*claudere* close]—**in'ter·clu'sion** (-zhən) *n.*

in·ter·col·le·giate (in'tər·kə·lē'jit, -jē·it) *adj.* Existing, representing, or conducted between, two or more colleges: an *intercollegiate* committee, *intercollegiate* rules, games, etc.

in·ter·co·lum·ni·a·tion (in'tər·kə·lum'nē·ā'shən) *n. Archit.* **1** The space or method of spacing between columns. **2** The space between two consecutive columns. [<L *intercolumnium* space between columns +-ATION]—**in'·ter·co·lum'nar** *adj.*

in·ter·com (in'tər·kom) *n. Colloq.* A system for intercommunication.

in·ter·com·mon (in'tər·kom'ən) *v.i. Brit. Law* To share the use of a common with a nearby town, village, etc. [<AF *entrecomuner* <*entre-* between (<L *inter-*) +*comuner* share <L *communis* common]

in·ter·com·mu·ni·cate (in'tər·kə·myōō'nə·kāt) *v.t.* **·cat·ed, ·cat·ing** To communicate mutually, as between individuals, rooms, different units of an organization, factory, etc. —**in'ter·com·mu'ni·ca'tion** *n.* —**in'ter·com·mu'ni·ca'tive** *adj.*

in·ter·com·mu·ni·ty (in'tər·kə·myōō'nə·tē) *n.* Mutual community or participation.

in·ter·con·nect (in'tər·kə·nekt') *v.t. & v.i.* To connect with one another.

in·ter·con·nect·ed (in'tər·kə·nek'tid) *adj.* So joined as to move in unison; geared: said of mechanical parts. —**in'ter·con·nec'tion** *n.*

in·ter·con·ti·nen·tal (in'tər·kon'tə·nen'təl) *adj.* Being or operating between continents: an *intercontinental* ballistic missile.

in·ter·cos·tal (in'tər·kos'təl) *adj. Anat.* Being or occurring between the ribs. —*n.* An intercostal muscle. [<NL *intercostalis* <L *inter-* between +*costa* rib]—**in'ter·cos'tal·ly** *adv.*

in·ter·course (in'tər·kôrs, -kōrs) *n.* **1** Mutual exchange; commerce; communication. **2** The interchange of ideas. **3** Sexual connection; coitus. [<OF *entrecours* <L *intercursus,* pp. of *intercurrere* run between <*inter-* between +*currere* run]

Synonyms: association, commerce, communication, communion, connection, conversation, converse, correspondence, dealing, exchange, fellowship, interchange, intercommunication, intercommunion, reciprocation, reciprocity. See CONVERSATION. *Antonyms*: alienation, avoidance, boycotting, estrangement, ostracism, reserve, reticence, silence.

in·ter·crop (in'tər·krop') *Agric. v.t. & v.i.* **·cropped, ·crop·ping 1** To raise (one crop) between the rows of another. **2** To raise (a quick-growing crop) between the harvesting and planting of the regular crops. —*n.* (in'·tər·krop') **1** A crop cultivated between the rows of another crop. **2** A quickly maturing crop raised when ground is unoccupied by the crops grown in regular rotation.

in·ter·cur·rent (in'tər·kûr'ənt) *adj. Med.* Coming or taking place between: an *intercurrent* disease. [<L *intercurrens, -entis,* ppr. of *intercurrere* run between]

in·ter·den·tal (in'tər·den'təl) *adj.* **1** Situated between the teeth. **2** *Phonet.* Produced with the tip of the tongue between the teeth, as *th* in *thin*: also *dentilingual, linguadental.* —*n. Phonet.* An interdental consonant.

in·ter·dict (in'tər·dikt') *v.t.* **1** To prohibit or restrain authoritatively. **2** *Eccl.* To exclude from religious privileges. —*n.* **1** A prohibitive order; ban. **2** A ban formerly declared by the pope, forbidding the clergy to perform religious services or administer the sacraments under certain circumstances. **3** In ancient Roman law, an interlocutory edict of the pretor, in matters affecting right of possession. **4** In Scots law, a judicial injunction. See synonyms under PROHIBIT. [<OF *entredit* <L *interdictum,* pp. of *interdicere* forbid <*inter-* between +*dicere* say; refashioned after L]—**in'ter·dic'tion** *n.* —**in'ter·dic'tive** *adj.* —**in'·ter·dic'tive·ly** *adv.* —**in'ter·dic'tor** *n.* —**in'ter·dic'to·ry** *adj.*

in·ter·est (in'tər·ist, -trist) *n.* **1** Attention with a sense of concern; lively sympathy or curiosity; also, the power to excite or hold such attention. **2** That which is of advantage or profit; benefit; also, selfish or private advantage. **3** Payment for the use of money, or money so paid; an agreed or statutory compensation accruing to a creditor during the time that a loan or debt remains unpaid, reckoned usually as a yearly percentage of the sum owed. **4** Something added in making a return; something more than is due. **5** Proprietary right or share; part ownership; participation in profit: sometimes used in the plural. **6** The persons interested in some department of work or business. **7** Power to procure favorable regard; influence. —*v.t.* (*also* in'tə·rest) **1** To excite or hold the curiosity or attention of. **2** To cause to have a share or interest in; induce to participate. **3** *Obs.* To relate to; affect; concern. [<OF <L *interest* it is of concern or advantage; 3rd person sing. of *interesse* lie between, be important <*inter-* between +*esse* be]

Synonyms (verb): amuse, attract, concern, engage, entertain, excite, hold, import, matter, occupy. *Interest* is used absolutely without a preposition, and with or without other qualification; *import* is now commonly used with a preposition and with some word or phrase indicating measure or estimate of value; as, It *imports* much *to* me. A matter may *interest* one financially or intellectually; in this sense the noun is commonly used; as, It is of *interest* to me. See AMUSE, CONCERN, ENTERTAIN. *Antonyms*: bore, disturb, fatigue, tire, weary, worry.

in·ter·est·ed (in'tər·is·tid, -tris-, -tə·res'-) *adj.* **1** Having the attention attracted or the feelings engaged. **2** Biased; not impartial. **3** Being a part owner. —**in'ter·est·ed·ly** *adv.* —**in'ter·est·ed·ness** *n.*

in·ter·est·ing (in'tər·is·ting, -tris-, -tə·res'-) *adj.* Possessing or exciting interest; attractive. —**in'ter·est·ing·ly** *adv.* —**in'ter·est·ing·ness** *n.*

in·ter·face (in'tər·fās) *n.* A surface, usually a plane surface, forming the boundary between adjacent solids, spaces, or immiscible liquids.

in·ter·fa·cial (in'tər·fā'shəl) *adj.* **1** Of or pertaining to an interface. **2** Denoting the surface tension between two adjacent bodies, as dissimilar fluids which do not mix.

in·ter·fas·cic·u·lar (in'tər·fə·sik'yə·lər) *adj.* **1** *Bot.* Situated between fascicles, as the cambium between the fibrovascular bundles in the stems of dicotyledons and gymnosperms. **2** *Anat.* Pertaining to or situated between fasciculi.

in·ter·fere (in'tər·fir') *v.i.* **·fered, ·fer·ing 1** To come into mutual conflict or opposition; clash. **2** To get in the way; be an obstacle or obstruction; intervene: The noise *interferes* with concentration. **3** To enter into or take part unasked in the concerns of others; meddle. **4** To strike one foot against the opposite foot or fetlock in walking or running: said of horses. **5** *Physics* To counteract one another, as waves of light, sound, or electricity. **6** In sports, to obstruct the actions of an opponent in an illegal manner. **7** In patent law, to claim priority for an invention: distinguished from *infringe.* See synonyms under INTERPOSE. [<OF *(s')entreferir* strike each other <L *inter-* between +*ferire* strike]—**in'ter·fer'er** *n.* —**in'ter·fer'ing·ly** *adv.*

in·ter·fer·ence (in'tər·fir'əns) *n.* **1** The act of interfering; conflict; collision. **2** *Physics* The action of two or more wave trains, as of light, sound, electricity, radiation, etc., which on meeting tend to neutralize or to augment each other by a combination of dissimilar or like phases. With light rays, interference may produce alternate dark and bright bands; with sound, intervals of silence, or increased volume; in radio, a disturbance in reception due to conflict of signals, etc. **3** *Aeron.* The aerodynamic influence of two or more bodies on one another. **4** In patent law, the conflict created by an application for a patent, covering, wholly or partly, any pending application or unexpired patent. **5** In sports, obstruction of the actions of an opponent in an illegal manner. **6** In football: **a** The pro-

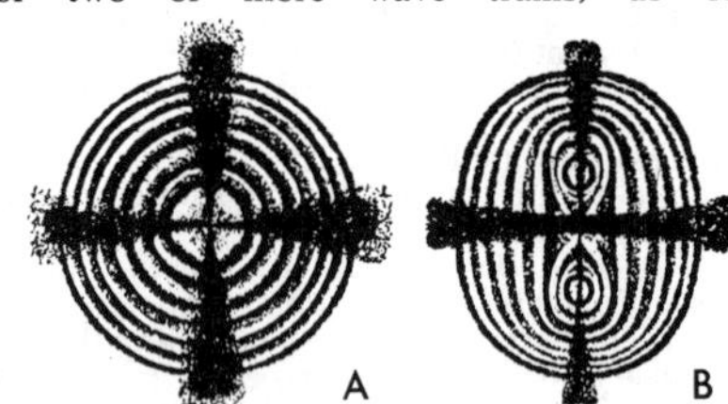

PATTERNS OF LIGHT INTERFERENCE
A. Interference pattern of a uniaxial crystal. *B.* Interference patterns of a biaxial crystal when the axes of the polarizer and analyzer are at right angles to each other.

tecting of the ball carrier from opposing tacklers. **b** The players providing this protection. See synonyms under FRICTION.

in·ter·fe·ren·tial (in′tər·fə·ren′shəl) *adj.* Of or pertaining to interference.

in·ter·fe·rom·e·ter (in′tər·fə·rom′ə·tər) *n. Physics* An instrument which utilizes the interference of light rays for the comparison of wavelengths and the measurement of very small distances: largely developed by A. A. Michelson, of Chicago. [<INTERFER(E) + -(O)METER] — **in′ter·fe·rom′e·try** *n.*

in·ter·fer·on (in′tər·fir′on) *n. Biochem.* A protein produced by virus-infected cells that halts the multiplication of the virus.

in·ter·fer·tile (in′tər·fûr′til) *adj. Biol.* Having the power to interbreed, as individuals of the same species.

in·ter·flu·ent (in·tûr′flo͞o·ənt) *adj.* **1** Flowing between. **2** Flowing together; blending. Also **in·ter′flu·ous** (-əs). [<L *interfluens, -entis,* ppr. of *interfluere* flow between] — **in·ter′·flu·ence** *n.*

in·ter·fluve (in′tər·flo͞ov) *n. Geog.* The area between two neighboring rivers or river valleys. [<INTER- + L *fluvius* stream]

in·ter·ga·lac·tic (in′tər·gə·lak′tik) *adj. Astron.* Between or among the galaxies: *intergalactic* space.

in·ter·gla·cial (in′tər·glā′shəl) *adj. Geol.* Pertaining to, or occurring in, the interval between periods of continental glaciation.

In·ter·glos·sa (in′tər·glôs′ə, -glos′ə) *n.* An international language based chiefly on Greek and Latin roots and having few grammatical inflections. [<INTER- + Gk. *glōssa* tongue]

in·ter·gra·da·tion (in′tər·grā·dā′shən) *n. Biol.* A stage or grade between two types, varieties, genetic characters, or the like.

in·ter·grade (in′tər·grād′) *v.i.* **·grad·ed, ·grad·ing** To merge gradually with each other, as two varieties. —*n.* (in′tər·grād′) A form transitional or intermediate between others in a graded series. — **in′ter·gra′di·ent** (-grā′dē·ənt) *adj.*

in·ter·im (in′tər·im) *n.* **1** An intermediate season; time between periods or events. **2** An interval of time; the meantime. — *adj.* For or during an intervening period of time; temporary: an *interim* appointment. [<L, meanwhile]

in·te·ri·or (in·tir′ē·ər) *adj.* **1** Existing, pertaining to, or occurring within something or between limits; internal; inner: opposed to *exterior.* **2** Inland. **3** Of a private or confidential nature. **4** Of or pertaining to spiritual matters; not worldly. **5** *Astron.* Having an orbit within the earth's, as Mercury and Venus. — *n.* **1** The internal part; inside. **2** The inland or central region of a country. **3** A painted scene or drop representing the inside of a dwelling, etc. **4** The domestic affairs of a country; home ministry. **5** The spiritual nature or basic character. — **Department of the Interior** An executive department of the U.S. government (established in 1849), headed by the Secretary of the Interior, dealing with mines, government lands, parks and reservations, Indian affairs, wildlife, geological survey, etc. [<OF *interieur* <L *interior,* compar. of *inter* within] — **in·te′ri·or′i·ty** (-ôr′·ə·tē, -or′-) *n.* — **in·te′ri·or·ly** *adv.*

interior angle See under ANGLE.

interior decorator One whose occupation is the furnishing and decorating of interiors of houses, offices, etc.

interior drainage Drainage whose waters are confined to and evaporate within a land area not connected with the ocean.

in·ter·ja·cent (in′tər·jā′sənt) *adj.* Situated between; intermediate. [<L *interjacens, -entis* lying between, pp. of *interjacere* <*inter-* between + *jacere* lie]

in·ter·ject (in′tər·jekt′) *v.t.* To throw between other things; introduce abruptly; insert; interpose. [<L *interjectus,* pp. of *interjicere* < *inter-* between + *jacere* throw]

in·ter·jec·tion (in′tər·jek′shən) *n.* **1** *Gram.* A word expressing emotion or simple exclamation, as *oh! alas! look!*: one of the eight traditional parts of speech. **2** The act of ejaculating. **3** A sudden interposition. [<OF <L *interjectio, -onis*] — **in′ter·jec′tion·al** *adj.* — **in′·ter·jec′tion·al·ly** *adv.*

in·ter·jec·to·ry (in′tər·jek′tər·ē) *adj.* Full of interjections; also, interposed. — **in′ter·jec′·to·ri·ly** *adv.*

in·ter·ki·ne·sis (in′tər·ki·nē′sis) *n. Biol.* The pause or interval of relative quiescence between two meiotic divisions of the cell: applied particularly to the vegetative stage of the nucleus. — **in′ter·ki·net′ic** (-net′ik) *adj.*

in·ter·lace (in′tər·lās′) *v.* **·laced, ·lac·ing** *v.t.* **1** To pass (branches, strips, etc.) over and under one another; interlock; lace; weave. **2** To blend; combine. **3** To mingle or cross; intersperse. — *v.i.* **4** To pass over and under one another. [<OF *entrelacier*] — **in′ter·lace′·ment** *n.*

In·ter·la·ken (in′tər·lä′kən) A resort town in central Switzerland between the Lake of Brienz and the Lake of Thun.

in·ter·lam·i·nate (in′tər·lam′ə·nāt) *v.t.* **·nat·ed, ·nat·ing** To lay or insert between laminae; arrange in layers. — **in′ter·lam′i·na′tion** *n.* — **in′ter·lam′i·nar** (-nər) *adj.*

in·ter·lard (in′tər·lärd′) *v.t.* **1** To scatter throughout with something different from or irrelevant to the subject or material: to *interlard* a conversation with sarcasms. **2** To insert fat, bacon, etc., into (meat) for cooking. [<MF *entrelarder*]

in·ter·leaf (in′tər·lēf′) *n. pl.* **·leaves** (-lēvz′) A blank leaf inserted or bound between others; also, the printed or written matter on a leaf so inserted.

in·ter·leave (in′tər·lēv′) *v.t.* **·leaved, ·leav·ing** **1** To insert interleaves into (a book). **2** To insert an interleaf or interleaves between (printed leaves).

in·ter·line[1] (in′tər·līn′) *v.t.* **·lined, ·lin·ing** **1** To write or print between the lines of. **2** To insert between lines. [OF *entreligner* < Med. L *interlineare* <L *inter-* between + *linea* line] — **in′ter·lin′er** *n.*

in·ter·line[2] (in′tər·līn′) *v.t.* **·lined, ·lin·ing** To put a lining between the usual lining and the outer fabric of (a garment).

in·ter·lin·e·al (in′tər·lin′ē·əl) *adj.* **1** Interlinear. **2** Arranged in alternate lines. — **in′·ter·lin′e·al·ly** *adv.*

in·ter·lin·e·ar (in′tər·lin′ē·ər) *adj.* **1** Situated or occurring between lines: *interlinear* annotations. **2** Having translations or glosses inserted between the lines of the text. [<Med. L *interlinearis*]

in·ter·lin·e·ate (in′tər·lin′ē·āt) *v.t.* **·at·ed, ·at·ing** To interline (a book, etc.). [<Med. L *interlineatus,* pp. of *interlineare.* See INTERLINE[1].]

in·ter·lin·e·a·tion (in′tər·lin′ē·ā′shən) *n.* **1** The act or process of interlining. **2** An interpolation between lines.

In·ter·lin·gua (in′tər·ling′gwə) *n.* An international auxiliary language, published in the United States in 1951, based primarily on English and the Romance languages. [<L *inter-* between + *lingua* tongue, language]

in·ter·lin·ing (in′tər·lī′ning) *n.* **1** Interlineation. **2** An intermediate lining in a garment; also, the material of which it is made.

in·ter·lock (in′tər·lok′) *v.t.* & *v.i.* **1** To join together; link with one another. **2** *Mech.* To connect or engage so that the operation of any part of a machine, apparatus, or system is interrelated with the operation of one or more other parts. — *n.* (in′tər·lok′) The action of interlocking, or the state of being interlocked.

interlocking directorates *Econ.* Boards of directors which, through shared membership, assume dominant control of and responsibility for the operation of many separately organized and legally distinct corporations, especially when in related fields of activity.

in·ter·lo·cu·tion (in′tər·lō·kyo͞o′shən) *n.* Interchange of speech; dialog. [<L *interlocutio, -onis* < *interlocutus,* pp. of *interloqui* speak between <*inter-* between + *loqui* speak]

in·ter·loc·u·tor (in′tər·lok′yə·tər) *n.* **1** One who takes part in a conversation; an interpreter; questioner. **2** The center man in a minstrel troupe. [<L *interlocutus,* pp. of *interloqui* speak between, converse] — **in′ter·loc′u·tress** (-tris) *n. fem.*

in·ter·loc·u·to·ry (in′tər·lok′yə·tôr′ē, -tō′rē) *adj.* **1** Consisting of or pertaining to dialog; conversational. **2** Interposed, as in a narrative. **3** *Law* Done during pendency of a lawsuit, but not final.

in·ter·lope (in′tər·lōp′) *v.i.* **·loped, ·lop·ing** **1** Originally, to engage in a commerce, trade, etc., legally belonging to others. **2** To intrude in the affairs of others. [<INTER- + *lope,* Du. *loopen* run]

in·ter·lop·er (in′tər·lō′pər) *n.* **1** One who thrusts himself into a place without right. **2** One who traffics in a trade legally belonging to others.

in·ter·lude (in′tər·lo͞od) *n.* **1** An action or event considered as coming between others of greater length or importance; a differing and intervening time or space. **2** A song of the chorus in Greek drama without dialog **3** An independent performance, usually light or humorous, introduced between the acts of a play or the parts of a performance. **4** A short passage of music played to bridge a transition; an intermezzo; also, an instrumental passage between stanzas of a hymn, between portions of a formal church service, between the acts of a play or opera, or the like. **5** Anything introduced or inserted, breaking the regular order or aspect; any intervening time or act. [<Med. L *interludium* <L *inter-* between + *ludus* a game, play <*ludere* play]

in·ter·lu·nar (in′tər·lo͞o′nər) *adj. Astron.* Pertaining to the period, generally about four days, between old and new moon, during which the moon is invisible, owing to its proximity to the sun. Also **in′ter·lu′na·ry.** [<L *interlunium* period between old and new moon]

in·ter·mar·riage (in′tər·mar′ij) *n.* **1** Marriage between persons of different families, races, etc. **2** Marriage between blood kindred.

in·ter·mar·ry (in′tər·mar′ē) *v.i.* **·ried, ·ry·ing** **1** To become connected by marriage: said of different clans, families, etc. **2** To marry each other: said of members of the same clan, family, etc.

in·ter·max·il·lar·y (in′tər·mak′sə·ler′ē) *adj.* **1** *Anat.* **a** Situated between the two maxillae or bones of the upper jaw. **b** Of or pertaining to one of two or more bones at the anterior and median part of the upper jaw, carrying the incisor teeth. **2** *Zool.* Situated between the maxillary lobes, as in crustaceans.

in·ter·med·dle (in′tər·med′l) *v.i.* **·dled ·dling** To interfere unduly in the affairs of others; meddle. See synonyms under INTERPOSE. [<AF *entremedler*] — **in′ter·med′dler** *n.*

in·ter·me·di·a·cy (in′tər·mē′dē·ə·sē) *n.* The state or character of being intermediate; intermediate action or agency.

in·ter·me·di·ar·y (in′tər·mē′dē·er′ē) *adj.* **1** Situated, acting, or coming between; having an intermediate function. **2** Acting as a mediator; mediatory. — *n.* **1** An intermediate agent or medium. **2** A form, stage, or product intermediate between others. [<F *intermédiaire*]

in·ter·me·di·ate (in′tər·mē′dē·it) *adj.* **1** Being in a middle place or degree. **2** Situated or occurring between limits or extremes. — *n.* (-it) **1** An intermediator; adjuster. **2** Something intermediate. **3** A substance formed at a state between the raw material and the finished product. **4** *Chem.* An organic compound derived from coal tar or petroleum crude oil and used as a starting point in the manufacture of a wide range of drugs, cosmetics, plastics, and dyestuffs. — *v.i.* (-āt) **·at·ed, ·at·ing** To act as an intermediary; mediate. [<Med. L *intermediatus* <*intermedius*] — **in′ter·me′di·ate·ly** *adv.* — **in′ter·me′di·ate·ness** *n.*

in·ter·me·di·a·tion (in′tər·mē′dē·ā′shən) *n.* The act of intermediating; intervention.

in·ter·me·di·a·tor (in′tər·mē′dē·ā′tər) *n.* One who adjusts differences; a mediator; also, an intervening agent; intermediary. — **in′ter·me′di·a·to′ry** (-tôr′ē, -tō′rē) *adj.*

in·ter·ment (in·tûr′mənt) *n.* The act of interring; burial.

in·ter·mez·zo (in′tər·met′sō, -med′zō) *n. pl.* **·zos** or **·zi** (-sē, -zē) **1** A song, chorus, or short ballet given between the acts of a play or opera. **2** A short light movement connecting the main divisions of a large musical composition; also, a short piece of instrumental music composed in this style to be played independently. [<Ital. <L *intermedius* intermediate]

in·ter·mi·na·ble (in·tûr′mə·nə·bəl) *adj.* Having no limit or end; continuing for a very long time; endless. See synonyms under ETERNAL, INFINITE, PERPETUAL. [<OF] —**in·ter′mi·na·bly** *adv.*

in·ter·min·gle (in′tər·ming′gəl) *v.t.* & *v.i.* **·gled, ·gling** To mingle together; mix.

in·ter·mis·sion (in′tər·mish′ən) *n.* **1** Temporary cessation; interruption. **2** A recess; interval, as between acts in the theater; entr'acte. [<L *intermissio, -onis* < *intermissus,* pp. of *intermittere.* See INTERMIT.] —**in′ter·mis′sive** *adj.*

in·ter·mit (in′tər·mit′) *v.t.* & *v.i.* **·mit·ted, ·mit·ting** To stop temporarily or at intervals; cease or interrupt; pause. See synonyms under CEASE, SUSPEND. [<L *intermittere* < *inter-* between + *mittere* send, put] —**in′ter·mit′tence** *n.*

in·ter·mit·tent (in′tər·mit′ənt) *adj.* **1** Having periods of intermission. **2** Alternately ceasing and beginning: an *intermittent* fever. —**in′ter·mit′tent·ly** *adv.*

intermittent current *Electr.* An interrupted current flowing in one direction.

intermittent fever *Pathol.* A fever in which the paroxysms occur at regular intervals, as in malaria. See AGUE.

in·ter·mix (in′tər·miks′) *v.t.* & *v.i.* To mix together; intermingle.

in·ter·mix·ture (in′tər·miks′chər) *n.* **1** The act of mixing together, or the state of being so mixed. **2** A mass of mixed ingredients. **3** An additional ingredient; admixture.

in·ter·mod·u·late (in′tər·moj′ŏŏ·lāt) *v.t.* & *v.i.* **·lat·ed, ·lat·ing** *Electronics* To cause a reciprocal modulation of (the components of a complex wave), with the production of new waves having frequencies equal to the sums and differences of integral multiples of the original complex wave. —**in′ter·mod′u·la′tion** *n.*

in·ter·mon·tane (in′tər·mon′tān) *adj.* Situated between mountains: *intermontane* silt. Also **in′ter·moun′tain** (-moun′tən). [<INTER- + L *montanus* mountainous <*mons, montis* mountain]

in·tern (in·tûrn′) *v.t.* To confine or detain within the limits of a country or area, as enemy aliens, or, in neutral countries, soldiers, ships, etc., of warring countries. —*v.i.* To undergo resident training in medicine or surgery in a hospital; be an intern. —*adj. Archaic* Internal. —*n.* (in′tûrn) **1** An advanced medical student or graduate undergoing resident training in a hospital: opposed to *extern.* **2** A person confined and segregated in wartime as a prisoner of war or enemy alien. Also **in′terne.** [<F *interne* resident within <L *internus* internal] —**in′tern·ship** (-ship) *n.*

in·ter·nal (in·tûr′nəl) *adj.* **1** Situated in or applicable to the inside; interior: opposed to *external.* **2** Pertaining to or derived from the inside; based on the thing itself; inherent. **3** Pertaining to the inner self or the mind; subjective. **4** Pertaining to the domestic affairs of a country: opposed to *external* or *foreign.* **5** *Anat.* **a** Situated relatively nearer to the median plane of the body or farther from the surface. **b** Supplying the interior of an organ or region. See synonyms under INHERENT. —*n.* **1** A remedy to be taken internally. **2** *pl.* The internal bodily organs; entrails. **3** *pl.* The essential qualities of anything. [<LL *internalis* < *internus* < *in* in]

in·ter·nal-com·bus·tion (in·tûr′nəl·kəm·bus′chən) *adj.* Designating a type of engine in which the energy is produced by burning or exploding a mixture of compressed air and fuel, as gasoline, in one or more of its cylinders.

in·ter·nal·i·ty (in′tər·nal′ə·tē) *n.* The quality or state of lying within; inwardness; interiority.

in·ter·nal·ly (in·tûr′nəl·ē) *adv.* **1** As to the interior or inner part; interiorly: cold on the surface but hot *internally.* **2** Mentally or spiritually: *internally* content. **3** In respect to internal affairs.

internal medicine The branch of medicine which is concerned with diagnosis and treatment of internal diseases.

internal revenue See under REVENUE.

internal rime The riming of a word or group of syllables in a line of verse, as the word before the caesura, with a word or group of syllables at the end of the line or another line: also called *leonine rime.*

internal secretion *Physiol.* **1** A secretion of any one of the endocrine glands. **2** A hormone.

in·ter·na·sal (in′tər·nā′zəl) *n. Zool.* One of a pair of dermal scutes of some reptiles lying between the nasals.

in·ter·na·tion·al (in′tər·nash′ən·əl) *adj.* Pertaining to two or more nations; affecting nations generally. —*n.* A person who is a citizen of more than one nation. —**in′ter·na′tion·al·ly** *adv.*

In·ter·na·tion·al (in′tər·nash′ən·əl) *n.* **1** One of several international organizations of socialist workers. **2** A society formed in London in 1864 for the international political organization of workingmen, in the socialistic conflict with capital, of which Karl Marx was the dominant spirit; its full title was the **International Workingmen's Association:** last convention in Philadelphia, 1876. **3** See INTERNATIONALE. —**Second International** An organization, formed in 1889, to replace the First International, from which the Third International seceded: also called **Socialist International.** —**Third** or **Red International** A socialist workers' organization proclaimed in Russia March 5, 1919, representing twelve countries: dissolved in 1943: also called *Comintern.*

international candle A candela.

In·ter·na·tio·nale (in′tər·nash′ən·əl, *Fr.* an·ter·nà·syô·nàl′) A French song written by Eugene Pottier in 1871 and adopted as a revolutionary hymn by French Socialists and those of other European countries: the national anthem of Soviet Russia until 1944, and still popular as a workers' song: usually written *L'Internationale.* [<F]

in·ter·na·tion·al·ism (in′tər·nash′ən·əl·iz′əm) *n.* **1** The character of being related to more nations than one or to nations generally. **2** The doctrine that common interest, mutual understanding, and friendly dependence among nations can be the foundation of world-wide equality, justice, and peace: opposed to *nationalism.* **3** The doctrine of a workers' international socialist organization for the betterment of workers throughout the world. —**in′ter·na′tion·al·ist** *n.* —**in′ter·na′tion·al′i·ty** *n.*

in·ter·na·tion·al·ize (in′tər·nash′ən·əl·īz′) *v.t.* **·ized, ·iz·ing** To make international, as in character or administration. —**in′ter·na′tion·al·i·za′tion** *n.*

International Labor Organization A permanent administrative association of 77 nations including the United States, constituting a specialized agency of the United Nations, with tripartite representation of workers, employers, and governments, working for the improvement of labor conditions in member nations, and functioning through the **International Labor Conference** and the **International Labor Office.** Commonly known as the **ILO.**

International Morse code A variation, differing in eleven letters, of the telegraphic code devised by S. F. B. Morse: also called **continental Morse code.**

International News Service An organization for collecting news and distributing it to member newspapers. Abbr. *INS, I.N.S.*

International Phonetic Alphabet The alphabet of the International Phonetic Association (a society founded in 1886), in which the speech sounds of a language can be transcribed. Each of the symbols of this alphabet represents a specific sound, distinguished as to place and manner of articulation, regardless of the language being recorded. Abbr. *IPA.* See chart on page 665.

in·terne (in′tûrn) *n.* **1** Intern. **2** The inner nature: poetical usage. [<F]

in·ter·ne·cine (in′tər·nē′sin, -sīn) *adj.* Involving mutual slaughter; sanguinary. [<L *internecinus* < *internecare* kill, slaughter < *inter-* among + *necare* kill]

in·tern·ee (in′tûr·nē′) *n.* An interned person. [<INTERN + -EE]

in·ter·nist (in·tûr′nist) *n.* A specialist in internal medicine. [<INTERN(AL) + -IST]

in·tern·ment (in·tûrn′mənt) *n.* The act of interning; the state of being interned.

internment camp A military station for the detention of prisoners of war and enemy aliens.

in·ter·no·dal (in′tər·nōd′l) *adj.* **1** Of or pertaining to an internode. **2** Situated between two nodes or joints. —*n.* An internodal joint.

in·ter·node (in′tər·nōd′) *n.* **1** *Anat.* A part situated between two joints or nodes, as a phalanx or other segment of a limb. **2** *Bot.* The part of a plant stem between the nodes or places from which the leaves grow. **3** *Ornithol.* In a feather, the contracted part between the roots of the barbs. **4** The part of a vibrating string between two nodes. [<L *internodium* < *inter-* between + *nodus* node]

in·ter nos (in′tər nōs′) *Latin* Between ourselves.

in·ter·nun·ci·o (in′tər·nun′shē·ō) *n. pl.* **·ci·os** **1** A diplomatic representative of the pope in countries not represented by a papal nuncio. **2** A go-between; messenger between two parties. [<Ital. <L *inter-* between + *nuntius* messenger] —**in′ter·nun′cial** (-shəl) *adj.*

in·ter·o·cep·tor (in′tər·ə·sep′tər) *n. Physiol.* A peripheral sense organ excited by internal stimuli arising chiefly within the viscera: also spelled *enteroceptor.* Compare EXTEROCEPTOR. [< *intero-* <INTERNAL + (RE)CEPTOR] —**in′ter·o·cep′tive** *adj.*

in·ter·or·bi·tal (in′tər·ôr′bə·təl) *adj. Anat.* Situated between the orbits of the eyes.

in·ter·os·cu·late (in′tər·os′kyə·lāt) *v.i.* **1** To form a connecting link, as between objects, genera, etc.; osculate. **2** To inosculate with each other; interpenetrate. —**in′ter·os′cu·la′tion** *n.*

in·ter·os·se·ous (in′tər·os′ē·əs) *adj. Anat.* Pertaining to structures situated between bones: an *interosseous* membrane.

in·ter·pel·lant (in′tər·pel′ənt) *adj.* Causing interpellation. —*n.* One who interpellates: also **in·ter·pel·la·tor** (in′tər·pə·lā′tər, in·tûr′pə·lā′tər). [<L *interpellans, -antis,* ppr. of *interpellare.* See INTERPELLATE.]

in·ter·pel·late (in′tər·pel′āt, in·tûr′pə·lāt) *v.t.* **·lat·ed, ·lat·ing** To subject to an interpellation. [<L *interpellatus,* pp. of *interpellare* interrupt by speaking < *inter-* between + *pellere* drive]

in·ter·pel·la·tion (in′tər·pə·lā′shən, in·tûr′-) *n.* A formal demand upon a member of a government to explain an official action or policy. [<L *interpellatio, -onis*]

in·ter·pen·e·trate (in′tər·pen′ə·trāt) *v.* **·trat·ed, ·trat·ing** *v.t.* **1** To penetrate thoroughly; pervade; permeate. **2** To penetrate mutually. —*v.i.* **3** To penetrate each other. **4** To penetrate between or among parts or things. —**in′ter·pen′e·tra′tion** *n.*

in·ter·per·son·al (in′tər·pûr′sən·əl) *adj.* Existing between people: *interpersonal* relations.

in·ter·phone (in′tər·fōn′) *n.* A telephone for use exclusively within a building, office, ship, airplane, etc.

in·ter·plane (in′tər·plān′) *adj. Aeron.* Situated or placed between the wings of an airplane.

in·ter·plan·e·tary (in′tər·plan′ə·ter′ē) *adj.* Between or among planets: *interplanetary* travel.

in·ter·play (in′tər·plā′) *n.* Action or movement between parts of something, as parts of a machine; mutual or reciprocal action or influence. —*v.i.* (in′tər·plā′) To exert influence reciprocally.

in·ter·plead (in′tər·plēd′) *v.i. Law* To litigate adverse claims by bill of interpleader. [<AF *entrepleder*]

in·ter·plead·er (in′tər·plē′dər) *n. Law* A proceeding in which one who has money or goods claimed by two or more persons may ask that the claimants be required to litigate the title between themselves.

in·ter·po·late (in·tûr′pə·lāt) *v.* **·lat·ed, ·lat·ing** *v.t.* **1** To alter, as a manuscript, by the insertion of new or unauthorized matter; corrupt. **2** To insert (such matter). **3** To put (something different or irrelevant) between other things; intercalate; interpose. **4** *Math.* **a** To compute intermediate values of a quantity between a series of given values: distinguished from *extrapolate.* **b** To insert (an intermediate term or terms) in a series. —*v.i.* **5** To make interpolations. [<L *interpolatus,* pp. of *interpolare* polish, form anew < *interpolis* refurbished, vamped up < *inter-* between + root of *polire* polish] —**in·ter′po·la′tion** *n.* —**in·ter′po·la′tive** *adj.* —**in·ter′po·la′tor, in·ter′po·lat′er** *n.*

in·ter·pose (in′tər·pōz′) *v.* **·posed, ·pos·ing** *v.t.* **1** To place between other things; insert. **2** To put forward or introduce by way of intervention or interference: He *interposed* his authority. **3** To put in or inject, as a remark, into a conversation, argument, etc. —*v.i.* **4** To come between; intervene. **5** To put in a remark; interrupt. [<F *interposer* place between < *inter-* between (<L) + *poser.* See

POSE[1].] —**in′ter·po′sal** *n.* —**in′ter·pos′er** *n.* —**in′ter·pos′ing·ly** *adv.*

Synonyms: arbitrate, intercede, intercept, interfere, intermeddle, interrupt, meddle, mediate. To *interpose* is to place or come between other things or persons, usually as a means of obstruction or prevention of some effect or result that might otherwise occur. *Intercede* and *interpose* are used in a good sense; *intermeddle* always in a bad sense, and *interfere* frequently so. To *intercede* is to come between persons who are at variance, and plead with the stronger in behalf of the weaker. To *intermeddle* is to thrust oneself into the concerns of others with officiousness; *meddling* commonly arises from idle curiosity. To *interfere* is to intrude into others' affairs with more serious purpose, with or without acknowledged right or propriety. *Intercept* is applied to an object that may be seized or stopped while in transit; as, to *intercept* a letter or a messenger; *interrupt* is applied to an action which might or should be continuous, but is broken in upon (L *rumpere* to break) by some disturbing power. One who *arbitrates* or *mediates* must do so by the request or at least with the consent of the contending parties; the other words of the group imply that he steps in of his own accord. *Antonyms*: avoid, retire, withdraw.

in·ter·po·si·tion (in′tər·pə·zish′ən) *n.* **1** The act of interposing. **2** That which is interposed. **3** In U. S. political theory, the doctrine and practice of interposing the sovereign powers of a State between the people of that State and the enforcement of a Federal statute or judicial ruling that is deemed by the State government to infringe upon its sovereignty and the autonomy of its institutions. [<OF]

in·ter·pret (in·tûr′prit) *v.t.* **1** To give the meaning of; explain or make clear; elucidate: to *interpret* Scripture. **2** To derive a particular understanding of; give a certain explanation to; construe: We *interpreted* his silence as pride. **3** To bring out the meaning of by artistic representation or performance. **4** To translate. —*v.i.* **5** To act as interpreter. **6** To explain. [<F *interpréter* <L *interpretatus*, pp. of *interpretari* < *interpres* agent, interpreter] —**in·ter′pret·a·ble** *adj.* —**in·ter′pret·a·bil′i·ty, in·ter′pret·a·ble·ness** *n.*

Synonyms: construe, decipher, define, elucidate, explain, explicate, expound, render, translate, unfold, unravel. See synonyms for DEFINITION, SOLVE. *Antonyms*: confound, confuse, darken, distort, falsify, involve, jumble, mingle, misinterpret, misread, misrepresent, mistake, misunderstand, mix, perplex.

in·ter·pre·ta·tion (in·tûr′prə·tā′shən) *n.* **1** The act of interpreting. **2** The sense given by an interpreter or an expositor; meaning. **3** Histrionic or artistic representation. See synonyms under DEFINITION. —**authentic interpretation** *Law* An interpretation made by the author himself. —**close interpretation** *Law* One in which the words are taken in their narrowest meaning. —**extravagant interpretation** *Law* One which substitutes a broader meaning for the true one. —**free interpretation** *Law* One made in good faith but uncontrolled by any specific principle. —**judicial interpretation** *Law* Judge-made rulings construing the meaning and purport of a statute; the act of making such rulings. [<F] —**in·ter′pre·ta′tion·al** *adj.*

in·ter·pre·ta·tive (in·tûr′prə·tā′tiv) *adj.* **1** Designed or fitted to interpret; explanatory; defining. **2** Containing an interpretation; embodying ideas or facts; significative. **3** Admitting of interpretation; constructive. Also **in·ter′pre·tive.** —**in·ter′pre·ta′tive·ly** *adv.*

in·ter·pret·er (in·tûr′prit·ər) *n.* One who interprets or translates; specifically, one who serves as oral translator between people speaking different languages. [<OF *interpreteur* <LL *interpretor*]

in·ter·ra·di·al (in′tər·rā′dē·əl) *adj.* Between rays or radii.

in·ter·reg·num (in′tər·reg′nəm) *n.* **1** The time during which a throne is vacant. **2** A suspension of executive authority through a change of government. **3** Any period of abeyance or derangement. **4** In Roman history, the interval filled by an interrex. [<L *interregnum* < *inter-* between + *regnum* reign]

in·ter·re·late (in′tər·ri·lāt′) *v.t.* & *v.i.* **·lat·ed ·lat·ing** To bring or come into reciprocal relation.

in·ter·re·lat·ed (in′tər·ri·lā′tid) *adj.* Reciprocally related.

in·ter·re·la·tion (in′tər·ri·lā′shən) *n.* Mutual or reciprocal relation. —**in′ter·re·la′tion·ship** *n.*

in·ter·rex (in′tər·reks) *n.* *pl.* **in·ter·re·ges** (in′·tər·rē′jēz) One who governs during an interregnum; specifically, in Roman history, one of the magistrates appointed to govern during a vacancy on the throne or in the consulate. [<L *interrex* < *inter-* between + *rex* king]

in·ter·ro·gate (in·ter′ə·gāt) *v.* **·gat·ed, ·gat·ing** *v.t.* To put questions to; question. —*v.i.* To ask

THE INTERNATIONAL PHONETIC ALPHABET.

(Revised to 1951.)

		Bi-labial	Labio-dental	Dental and Alveolar	Retroflex	Palato-alveolar	Alveolo-palatal	Palatal	Velar	Uvular	Pharyngal	Glottal
CONSONANTS	Plosive	p b		t d	ʈ ɖ			c ɟ	k g	q ɢ		ʔ
	Nasal	m	ɱ	n	ɳ			ɲ	ŋ	ɴ		
	Lateral Fricative			ɬ ɮ								
	Lateral Non-fricative			l	ɭ			ʎ				
	Rolled			r						ʀ		
	Flapped			ɾ	ɽ					ʀ		
	Fricative	ɸ β	f v	θ ð | s z | ɹ	ʂ ʐ	ʃ ʒ	ɕ ʑ	ç ʝ	x ɣ	χ ʁ	ħ ʕ	h ɦ
	Frictionless Continuants and Semi-vowels	w | ɥ	ʋ	ɹ				j (ɥ)	(w)	ʁ		
VOWELS								Front Central	Back			
	Close	(y ʉ u)						i y ɨ ʉ	ɯ u			
	Half-close	(ø o)						e ø	ɤ o ə			
	Half-open	(œ ɔ)						ɛ œ æ	ʌ ɔ ɐ			
	Open	(ɒ)						a	ɑ ɒ			

(Secondary articulations are shown by symbols in brackets.)

OTHER SOUNDS.—Palatalized consonants: ƫ, ȡ, etc.; palatalized ʃ, ʒ : ʆ, ʓ. Velarized or pharyngalized consonants: ɫ, ᵭ, ᵶ, etc. Ejective consonants (with simultaneous glottal stop): p', t', etc. Implosive voiced consonants: ɓ, ɗ, etc. ɼ fricative trill. σ, ϱ (labialized θ, ð, or s, z). ʅ, ʓ (labialized ʃ, ʒ). ʇ, ʗ, ʖ (clicks, Zulu *c*, *q*, *x*). ɺ (a sound between r and l). ɳ Japanese syllabic nasal. ɧ (combination of x and ʃ). ʍ (voiceless w). ɩ, ʏ, ɷ (lowered varieties of i, y, u). ɜ (a variety of ə). ɵ (a vowel between ø and o).

Affricates are normally represented by groups of two consonants (ts, tʃ, dʒ, etc.), but, when necessary, ligatures are used (ʦ, ʧ, ʤ, etc.), or the marks ⁀ or ‿ (t͡s or t͜s, etc.). ⁀ ‿ also denote synchronic articulation (m͡ŋ = simultaneous m and ŋ). c, ɟ may occasionally be used in place of tʃ, dʒ, and ƺ, ƻ for ts, dz. Aspirated plosives: ph, th, etc. r-coloured vowels: eɹ, aɹ, ɔɹ, etc., or eʴ. aʴ, ɔʴ, etc., or ᶒ, ᶏ, ᶗ, etc.; r-coloured ə : əɹ or əʴ or ɹ or ɚ or ɚ.

LENGTH, STRESS, PITCH.— ː (full length). ˑ (half length). ˈ (stress, placed at beginning of the stressed syllable). ˌ (secondary stress). ˉ (high level pitch); ˍ (low level); ˊ (high rising); ˏ (low rising); ˋ (high falling); ˎ (low falling); ^ (rise-fall); ˇ (fall-rise)

MODIFIERS.— ˜ nasality. ̥ breath (l̥ = breathed l). ̬ voice (s̬ = z). ʻ slight aspiration following p, t, etc. ̫ labialization (n̫ = labialized n). ̪ dental articulation (t̪ = dental t). ˙ palatalization (ż = ʓ). ̣ specially close vowel (ẹ = a very close e). ̨ specially open vowel (ę = a rather open e). ˔ tongue raised (e˔ or e̝ = ẹ). ˕ tongue lowered (e˕ or e̞ = ę). ˖ tongue advanced (u˖ or u̟ = an advanced u, t̟ = t̪). ˗ or ˗ tongue retracted (i˗ or i̠ = ɨ˖, t̠ = alveolar t). ˒ lips more rounded. ˓ lips more spread. Central vowels: ï (= ɨ), ü (= ʉ), ë (= ə˔), ö (= ɵ), ɛ̈, ɔ̈. ̩ (e.g. n̩) syllabic consonant. ˘ consonantal vowel. ʃˢ variety of ʃ resembling s, etc.

Courtesy, Association Phonétique Internationale

questions. See synonyms under EXAMINE, INQUIRE, QUESTION. [<L *interrogatus,* pp. of *interrogare* < *inter-* between + *rogare* ask]

in·ter·ro·ga·tion (in·ter′ə·gā′shən) *n.* **1** The act of interrogating. **2** A question; query. **3** An interrogation point. **4** *Telecom.* The transmission of a signal pulse or combination of such pulses by an interrogator. See synonyms under INQUIRY, QUESTION.

interrogation point A mark of punctuation (?) indicating that the foregoing sentence asks a direct question: sometimes called *question mark.* Also **interrogation mark.**

in·ter·rog·a·tive (in′tə·rog′ə·tiv) *adj.* **1** Denoting inquiry; questioning. **2** *Gram.* Of or pertaining to a word, phrase, or sentence which asks a question. — *n. Gram.* A word, phrase, or sentence used to ask a question, as *who, whose book, Who is there?* [<L *interrogativus*] — **in′ter·rog′a·tive·ly** *adv.*

interrogative pronoun See under PRONOUN.

in·ter·ro·ga·tor (in·ter′ə·gā′tər) *n.* **1** One who or that which interrogates. **2** *Telecom.* A device for transmitting pulses of challenge or inquiry to a transponder: usually connected with a responser for receiving and displaying the return pulses.

in·ter·rog·a·to·ry (in′tə·rog′ə·tôr′ē, -tō′rē) *adj.* Pertaining to, expressing, or implying a question; interrogative. — *n.* A question; interrogation. See synonyms under INQUIRY, QUESTION. — **in′ter·rog′a·to′ri·ly** (-tôr′ə·lē, -tō′rə-) *adv.*

in·ter·rupt (in′tə·rupt′) *v.t.* **1** To cause a delay or break in: to *interrupt* service; hinder the doing or completion of: to *interrupt* a speech. **2** To break the continuity, course, or sameness of: to *interrupt* work or a speech. **3** To break in on (someone) talking, working, etc. — *v.i.* **4** To break in upon an action or speech. See synonyms under HINDER[1], INTERPOSE, OBSTRUCT, SUSPEND. [<L *interruptus,* pp. of *interrumpere* < *inter-* between + *rumpere* break]

in·ter·rupt·ed (in′tə·rup′tid) *adj.* **1** Broken in upon; irregular; intermittent. **2** *Bot.* Suddenly or abruptly stopped. — **in′ter·rupt′ed·ly** *adv.*

interrupted screw *Mil.* A screw placed in the breech of certain guns, permitting the block to be engaged or released by turning through a small arc.

in·ter·rupt·er (in′tə·rup′tər) *n.* **1** One who or that which interrupts. **2** *Electr.* A device, usually automatic, for rapidly breaking and making an electric circuit, as in an induction coil. **3** *Mil.* An electrical device, in connection with a chronoscope, for causing a pencil to register the exact time of passage of a projectile through a wire screen. **4** *Mil.* An automatic device that interrupts the firing of a flexibly mounted gun, as in a turret, when structural parts of the craft or vehicle in which it is mounted come within the field of fire. Also **in′ter·rup′tor.**

in·ter·rup·tion (in′tə·rup′shən) *n.* **1** The act of interrupting. **2** The state of being interrupted; breach in continuity; an interval. **3** Obstruction caused by breaking in upon any course, progress, or motion; hindrance; stop; check. **4** In Scots law, the legal step necessary to terminate a period of prescription; exception or reply against prescription. **5** An intermission; a temporary cessation.

in·ter·rup·tive (in′tə·rup′tiv) *adj.* Tending to interrupt; interrupting. — **in′ter·rup′tive·ly** *adv.*

in·ter se (in′tər sē′) *Latin* Between (or among) themselves.

in·ter·sect (in′tər·sekt′) *v.t.* To pass across; cut through or into so as to divide. — *v.i.* To cross each other. [<L *intersectus,* pp. of *intersecare* < *inter-* between + *secare* cut]

in·ter·sec·tion (in′tər·sek′shən) *n.* **1** The act of intersecting. **2** A place of crossing. [<L *intersectio, -onis*]

in·ter·sex (in′tər·seks′) *n. Biol.* An individual, usually sterile, showing biological characteristics of both sexes. — **in′ter·sex′u·al** *adj.* — **in′ter·sex′u·al′i·ty** *n.*

in·ter·space (in′tər·spās′) *v.t.* **·spaced, ·spac·ing** **1** To make spaces between. **2** To occupy spaces between. — *n.* (in′tər·spās′) Intervening room; space between.

in·ter·sperse (in′tər·spûrs′) *v.t.* **·spersed, ·spers·ing** **1** To scatter among other things; set here and there. **2** To diversify or adorn with other things scattered here and there. [<L *interspersus,* pp. of *interspergere* < *inter-* among + *spargere* scatter] — **in′ter·spers′ed·ly** *adv.* — **in′ter·sper′sion** (-spûr′zhən) *n.*

in·ter·state (in′tər·stāt′) *adj.* Between different States, as of the United States, or their citizens: *interstate* commerce.

Interstate Commerce Act An act passed by Congress, and approved February 4, 1887, which established a commission of five (since increased to eleven) members to regulate commerce between States when carried by common carriers, as by railroad, vessel, motor vehicle, and pipeline (except water pipes). The **Interstate Commerce Commission** executes and enforces the act in the public interest, promotes safe service and conditions, prevents unjust rates and discriminatory practice, etc.

in·ter·stice (in·tûr′stis) *n.* **1** An opening in anything. **2** A narrow space between adjoining parts or things. **3** A crack; crevice; chink; cranny. **4** An interval of time; specifically, the interval that canon law requires between promotions from one order to another in the Roman Catholic Church. [<F <L *interstitium* < *interstitus,* pp. of *intersistere* stand between < *inter-* between + *sistere* cause to stand < *stare* stand]

in·ter·sti·tial (in′tər·stish′əl) *adj.* **1** Pertaining to, existing in, or forming an interstice. **2** *Biol.* Situated within the tissues of an organ or part; *interstitial* cells. [<L *interstitus*] — **in′ter·sti′tial·ly** *adv.*

in·ter·tex·ture (in′tər·teks′chər) *n.* **1** The act of interweaving. **2** The web or tissue interwoven.

in·ter·twine (in′tər·twīn′) *v.t.* & *v.i.* **·twined, ·twin·ing** To unite by twisting or interlacing.

in·ter·ur·ban (in′tər·ûr′bən) *adj.* Between cities.

in·ter·val (in′tər·vəl) *n.* **1** An open space between two objects; distance between points; intervening room. **2** The degree of difference between objects. **3** The time that intervenes between two events or periods or between a state or condition and its recurrence. **4** *U.S.* & *Can.* Intervale. **5** *Music* **a** The difference in pitch between two tones sounded in succession.

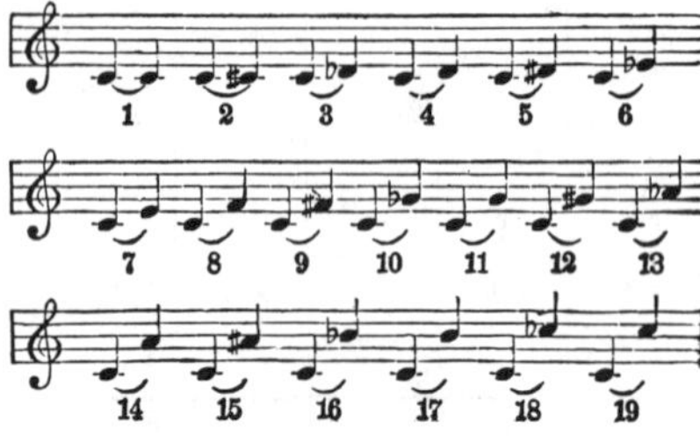

MUSICAL INTERVALS

1. Prime or unison. 2. Augmented prime. 3. Minor second. 4. Major second. 5. Augmented second. 6. Minor third. 7. Major third. 8. Perfect fourth. 9. Augmented fourth. 10. Diminished fifth. 11. Perfect fifth. 12. Augmented fifth. 13. Minor sixth. 14. Major sixth. 15. Augmented sixth. 16. Minor seventh. 17. Major seventh. 18. Diminished octave. 19. Octave. On a keyboard instrument where mechanical limitations make it necessary to make one tone serve for two slightly different ones, some of the intervals above appear identical, as 5 and 6.

b The difference in pitch of tones sounded at or near the same time. — **augmented interval** A musical interval longer than the indicated standard by a half-step or semitone. — **diminished interval** An interval that is a half-step shorter than the perfect or minor interval indicated. — **harmonic interval** An interval in which the tones are simultaneous. — **inverted interval** A simple interval in which the lower tone is transposed an octave upward, or the upper tone an octave downward. — **melodic interval** An interval in which the tones are successive. — **perfect interval.** An interval admitting of no change without destroying the consonance, as the prime, fourth, fifth, and octave. [<OF *entreval, intervalle* <L *intervallum* between the ramparts < *inter-* between + *vallum* rampart]

in·ter·vale (in′tər·vāl′) *n. U.S.* & *Can.* A low tract of land between hills, especially along a river; interval. [Fusion of INTERVAL + VALE[1]]

in·ter·va·ri·e·tal (in′tər·və·rī′ə·təl) *adj. Biol.* Pertaining to or designating a cross between two varieties, strains, or breeds of the same species.

in·ter·vein (in′tər·vān′) *v.t.* **1** To intersect with or as if with veins. **2** To set in alternate veins.

in·ter·vene (in′tər·vēn′) *v.i.* **·vened, ·ven·ing** **1** To come between by action or authority; interfere or mediate: The king *intervened* in the quarrel. **2** To occur, as something irrelevant or unexpected, so as to influence or modify an action, result, etc.: I will come if nothing *intervenes.* **3** To be located between; lie between. **4** To take place between other events or times; happen in the meantime: Many years *intervened.* **5** *Law* To interpose in a lawsuit so as to become a party to it. [<L *intervenire* < *inter-* between + *venire* come] — **in′ter·ven′er** *n.* — **in′ter·ven′ient** (-vēn′yənt) *adj.*

in·ter·ven·tion (in′tər·ven′shən) *n.* **1** The act of intervening or coming between. **2** Interference with the acts of others. **3** *Law* The becoming or applying to become a party to a suit in which the applicant has an interest. **4** In international law, interference in the affairs of one country by another by force or threat of force. **5** An intervening time, event, or thing. [<LL *interventio, -onis* < *interventus,* pp. of *intervenire* intervene] — **in′ter·ven′tion·al** *adj.*

in·ter·ven·tion·ist (in′tər·ven′shən·ist) *n.* One who advocates intervention, as in the affairs of another state.

in·ter·view (in′tər·vyōō) *n.* **1** A meeting of two persons, as by appointment. **2** Specifically, in journalism, a colloquy with one whose views are sought for publication. **3** The report of such a colloquy. — *v.t.* To have an interview with. [<MF *entrevu,* pp. of *entrevoir* glimpse, *s'entrevoir* see each other <L *inter-* between + *videre* see] — **in′ter·view′er** *n.*

in·ter·volve (in′tər·volv′) *v.t.* & *v.i.* **·volved, ·volv·ing** To wind or coil one within another; involve or be involved with each other. [<INTER- + L *volvere* roll]

in·ter·weave (in′tər·wēv′) *v.t.* & *v.i.* **·wove** or **·weaved, ·wo·ven** (*Obs.* **·wove**), **·weav·ing** To weave together; intermingle or connect closely; interlace; blend.

in·tes·ta·ble (in·tes′tə·bəl) *adj.* Legally disqualified from making a will, as a lunatic. [<LL *intestabilis.* See INTESTATE.]

in·tes·ta·cy (in·tes′tə·sē) The condition resulting from one's dying intestate: opposed to *testacy.*

in·tes·tate (in·tes′tāt) *adj.* **1** Not having made a valid will. **2** Not legally devised or disposed of by will. — *n.* A person who dies intestate. [<L *intestatus* < *in-* not + *testatus,* pp. of *testari* make a will < *testis* witness]

in·tes·ta·tion (in′tes·tā′shən) *n. Law* **1** Testamentary incapacity. **2** Withdrawal of the right to make a will.

in·tes·tine (in·tes′·tin) *n. Anat.* That part of the alimentary canal between the pylorus and the anus; bowel. In man the small intestine, divided into *duodenum, jejunum,* and *ileum,* is the upper part, and is much convoluted; the large intestine is of greater caliber, and is divided into *cecum, colon,* and *rectum.*

HUMAN INTESTINES
a. Duodenum. *b.* Small intestine. *c.* Colon. *d.* Vermiform appendix.

◆ Collateral adjective: *alvine.* — *adj.* **1** Internal with regard to state or community; domestic; civil. **2** Pertaining to the interior. [<L *intestinus* internal < *intus* within < *in* in] — **in·tes′ti·nal** *adj.*

in·thral (in·thrôl′), **in·throne** (in·thrōn′), etc. See ENTHRAL, etc.

in·ti·ma (in′tə·mə) *n. pl.* **·mae** (-mē) **1** *Anat.* The internal coat of a part or organ, as of a lymphatic, blood vessel, intestine, or artery. **2** *Entomol.* The lining membrane of the trachea of an insect. [<NL <L *intimus* innermost. See INTIMATE[1].] — **in′ti·mal** *adj.*

in·ti·ma·cy (in′tə·mə·sē) *n. pl.* **·cies** **1** Close or confidential friendship. **2** An intimate act;

especially, illicit sexual connection: a euphemistic use. See synonyms under ACQUAINTANCE.

in·ti·mate[1] (in'tə·mit) *adj.* 1 Closely connected by friendship or association; personal; confidential. 2 Pertaining to the inmost being; innermost; indwelling; *intimate* knowledge. 3 Adhering closely; close: *intimate* union. 4 Proceeding from within; inward; internal: an *intimate* impulse. 5 Having illicit sexual relations (with): a euphemism. —*n.* A close or confidential friend. [<F *intime* <L *intimus,* superl. of *intus* within] —**in'ti·mate·ly** *adv.*

in·ti·mate[2] (in'tə·māt) *v.t.* **·mat·ed, ·mat·ing** 1 To make known without direct statement; hint; imply. 2 *Rare* To make known formally; declare. [<L *intimatus,* pp. of *intimare* announce < *intimus,* superl. of *intus* within]

in·ti·ma·tion (in'tə·mā'shən) *n.* 1 Information communicated indirectly; a hint. 2 A declaration or notification. See synonyms under SUGGESTION. [<F]

in·tim·i·date (in·tim'ə·dāt) *v.t.* **·dat·ed, ·dat·ing** 1 To make timid; cause fear in; cow. 2 To force or restrain by threats or violence. See synonyms under FRIGHTEN. [<Med. L *intimidatus,* pp. of *intimidare* <L *in-* very + *timidus* afraid] —**in·tim'i·da'tor** *n.*

in·tim·i·da·tion (in·tim'ə·dā'shən) *n.* 1 The use of violence or threats to influence the conduct of another. 2 The state of being intimidated.

in·tinc·tion (in·tingk'shən) *n. Eccl.* A method of administering both elements of the Eucharist at once, by dipping the bread into the wine. [<LL *intinctio, -onis* < *intinctus,* pp. of *intingere* dip in < *in-* in + *tingere* tinge]

in·tine (in'tin, -tīn) *n. Bot.* The inner coating of the wall of a pollen grain. [<L *intus* within]

in·ti·tle (in·tīt'l) See ENTITLE.

in·tit·ule (in·tit'yōōl) *v.t.* **·uled, ·ul·ing** To give a title or designation to. [<F *intituler* <LL *intitulare* <L *in-* in, on + *titulus* title]

in·to (in'tōō) *prep.* 1 To or toward the inside of; penetrating or entering within: Come *into* the house. 2 Extending within (a period of time): talking well *into* the night. 3 So as to become: Boiling changes water *into* steam. 4 *Math.* Dividing: Two *into* six is three. 5 As an addition to: *into* the bargain. 6 In the direction of: *into* the northwest. 7 To the practice or study of: to go *into* medicine. 8 *Slang* Actively engaged or involved with, as an interest or enthusiasm: He's *into* oriental religion. [OE]

Synonyms: in, to. *Into* is the preposition of tendency, direction, destination, etc.; *in* is that of condition, state, position, or situation. *Into* should be used and not *in,* when entrance or insertion is intended; *into* indicates motion, change, entrance, in a more marked degree than *in.* "I throw the stone *into* the water, and it lies *in* the water." Used adverbially *in* follows verbs of motion, as *come, go, walk,* and such use has established certain phrases as idioms. One says, "Come *in* the house" but the preferred expression is "Come *into* the house." Where no object is expressed, we say "come *in,*" "go *in.*" *Antonyms*: beyond, by, from, out, past, through.

in·tol·er·a·ble (in·tol'ər·ə·bəl) *adj.* Not tolerable; that cannot be borne or endured; insufferable. —*adv. Obs.* Intolerably. —**in·tol'er·a·bil'i·ty, in·tol'er·a·ble·ness** *n.* —**in·tol'er·a·bly** *adv.*

in·tol·er·ance (in·tol'ər·əns) *n.* 1 Refusal to tolerate opposing beliefs; bigotry. 2 Incapacity or unwillingness to bear or endure. Also **in·tol'·er·an·cy.** See synonyms under FANATICISM.

in·tol·er·ant (in·tol'ər·ənt) *adj.* 1 Not disposed to tolerate contrary beliefs or opinions; bigoted. 2 Unable or unwilling to bear or endure: with *of*: *intolerant* of opposition. —**in·tol'er·ant·ly** *adv.*

in·tomb (in·tōōm'), **in·tomb·ment** (in·tōōm'·mənt), etc. See ENTOMB, etc.

in·to·nate (in'tō·nāt) *v.t.* **·nat·ed, ·nat·ing** 1 To intone. 2 To sound the tones of the musical scale, as in sol-faing. [<Med. L *intonatus,* pp. of *intonare* intone, thunder < *in-* in + L *tonus* tone]

in·to·na·tion (in'tō·nā'shən) *n.* 1 The modulation of the voice in speaking: distinguished from *articulation*: Her *intonation* is soft and sweet. 2 The act of intoning, as of the church service by a priest. 3 *Music* Production of tones, as by the voice, especially in regard to precision of tone. 4 In plain song, the notes leading up to the reciting tone: commonly sung by a single voice.

in·tone (in·tōn') *v.* **·toned, ·ton·ing** *v.t.* 1 To utter or recite in a musical monotone: chant. 2 To give particular tones or intonation to. —*v.i.* 3 To utter a musical monotone; chant. [<MF *entonner* < Med. L *intonare.* See INTONATE.] —**in·ton'er** *n.*

in to·to (in tō'tō) *Latin* In the whole; altogether; entirely.

in·tox·i·cate (in·tok'sə·kāt) *v.t.* **·cat·ed, ·cat·ing** 1 To make drunk; inebriate. 2 To elate or excite to a degree of frenzy. 3 To poison, as by bacterial toxins, serum injections, drugs, alcohol, etc. —*adj.* (-kit) Drunk; intoxicated. [<Med. L *intoxicatus,* pp. of *intoxicare* poison, drug <L *toxicum* poison] —**in·tox'i·cant** *adj.* & *n.* —**in·tox'i·ca'tion** *n.* —**in·tox'i·ca'·tive** *adj.*

intra- *prefix* Within; inside of. [<L *intra-* < *intra* within]

Intra- may appear as a prefix in hyphemes or solidemes, with the meaning *situated* or *occurring within*; as in:

intra-abdominal
intra-abdominally
intra-acinous
intra-alveolar
intra-appendicular
intra-arachnoid
intra-arterial
intra-articular
intra-aural
intra-auricular
intrabranchial
intrabronchial
intrabuccal
intracanalicular
intracapsular
intracardiac
intracarpal
intracarpellary
intracartilaginous
intracellular
intracephalic
intracerebellar
intracerebral
intracervical
intracloacal
intracolic
intracollegiate
intracontinental
intracorporeal
intracorpuscular
intracortical
intracostal
intracranial
intracutaneous
intracystic
intradermal
intradermic
intradivisional
intraduodenal
intraecclesiastical
intraepiphyseal
intraepithelial
intrafilamentary
intrafistular
intragastric
intraglandular
intraglobular
intragyral
intrahepatic
intrahyoid
intra-imperial
intrajugular
intralamellar
intralaryngeal
intraligamentary
intraligamentous
intralingual
intralobar
intralobular
intralocular
intralumbar
intramammary
intramandibular
intramarginal
intramastoid
intramedullary
intramembranous
intrameningeal
intrametropolitan
intramontane
intramundane
intramuscularly
intramyocardial
intranarial
intranasal
intraneural
intra-ocular
intra-oral
intra-orbital
intra-osseous
intra-osteal
intra-ovarian
intra-ovular
intraparasitic
intraparenchymatous
intraparochial
intrapelvic
intrapericardiac
intrapericardial
intraperineal
intraperiosteal
intraperitoneal
intraphilosophic
intraplacental
intrapleural
intrapolar
intrapontine
intraprostatic
intrapulmonary
intrarectal
intrarenal
intraretinal
intrascrotal
intrasegmental
intraseptal
intraserous
intraspinal
intraspinally
intrastation
intrasynovial
intratarsal
intraterritorial
intrathecal
intrathoracic
intratrabecular
intratracheal
intratropical
intratubal
intratubular
intratympanic
intra-umbilical
intra-urban
intra-urethral
intra-uterine
intravalvular
intravascular
intraventricular
intraverbal
intravertebral
intravesical

in·tra-a·tom·ic (in'trə·ə·tom'ik) *adj. Physics* Within an atom or atoms; pertaining to atomic structure.

in·trac·ta·ble (in·trak'tə·bəl) *adj.* 1 Not tractable; refractory; unruly. 2 Lacking plastic quality; difficult to treat or work. See synonyms under IMPRACTICABLE, OBSTINATE, PERVERSE, REBELLIOUS, RESTIVE. —**in·trac'ta·bil'i·ty, in·trac'ta·ble·ness** *n.* —**in·trac'ta·bly** *adv.*

in·tra·dos (in·trā'dos) *n. Archit.* The interior or lower surface of an arch or vault. See illustration under ARCH. [<F *intrados* <L *intra-* within + F *dos* back <L *dorsum*]

in·tra·mo·lec·u·lar (in'trə·mə·lek'yə·lər) *adj. Chem.* Pertaining to or occurring in the interior of a molecule.

in·tra·mu·ral (in'trə·myŏŏr'əl) *adj.* 1 Situated within the walls of a city. 2 *Anat.* Situated within the walls of a hollow organ. 3 Taking place within the confines of an educational institution: *intramural* football: opposed to *extramural.*

in·tra mu·ros (in'trə myŏŏr'ōs) *Latin* Within the walls.

in·tra·mus·cu·lar (in'trə·mus'kyə·lər) *adj. Anat.* Within a muscle or muscular tissue, as an injection.

in·tra·na·tion·al (in'trə·nash'ən·əl) *adj.* Situated within or relating to matters within a nation: opposed to *international.*

in·tran·si·gent (in·tran'sə·jənt) *adj.* Refusing to agree or compromise; irreconcilable. —*n.* One who is intransigent; a radical or revolutionary: also **in·tran'si·gent·ist.** Also *French* **in·tran·si·geant** (aṅ·träṅ·sē·zhäṅ'). [<F *intransigeant* <Sp. *intransigente* <L *in-* not + *transigens, -entis,* ppr. of *transigere* agree. See TRANSACT.] —**in·tran'si·gence** *n.*

in·tran·si·tive (in·tran'sə·tiv) *Gram. adj.* 1 Not taking or requiring an object, as certain verbs. 2 Of or pertaining to such verbs. —*n.* An intransitive verb. —**in·tran'si·tive·ly** *adv.*

intransitive verb A verb whose action is not transferred to an object but terminates in the subject or doer. *Waits, sleeps, dreams, grows,* are intransitive in the following: the man waits, he sleeps, he dreams, the grass grows. Intransitive verbs become transitive only with a cognate object: I dreamed a dream; to sleep the sleep of the just; to die a soldier's death.

in tran·si·tu (in tran'sə·tyōō) *Latin* In transit; during transmission.

in·trant (in'trənt) *adj.* Entering. —*n.* An entrant; especially, one entering an association or institution. [<L *intrans, -antis,* ppr. of *intrare* enter. See ENTER.]

in·tra·nu·cle·ar (in'trə·nōō'klē·ər, -nyōō'-) *adj.* Within the nucleus, as of an atom or a cell.

in·tra·state (in'trə·stāt') *adj.* Confined within or pertaining to a single state.

in·tra·tel·lu·ric (in'trə·tə·lŏŏr'ik) *adj. Geol.* 1 Formed or occurring within the earth. 2 Pertaining to the constituents of an effusive rock formed prior to their appearance on the surface, or to the period of their formation.

in·tra·ve·nous (in'trə·vē'nəs) *adj. Med.* Into or within a vein: an *intravenous* injection. —**in'tra·ve'nous·ly** *adv.*

in·tra·vi·tel·line (in'trə·vi·tel'in, -vī-) *adj. Biol.* Within the yolk of an egg.

in·trench (in·trench'), **in·trench·ment** (in·trench'mənt) See ENTRENCH, etc.

in·trench·ant (in·tren'chənt) *adj. Obs.* Indivisible.

in·trep·id (in·trep'id) *adj.* Unshaken in the presence of danger; dauntless. See synonyms under BRAVE. [<L *intrepidus* < *in-* not + *trepidus* agitated] —**in·tre·pid·i·ty** (in'trə·pid'ə·tē) *n.* —**in·trep'id·ly** *adv.*

in·tri·ca·cy (in'tri·kə·sē) *n. pl.* **·cies** 1 The quality of being complicated or entangled. 2 A complication; complexity.

in·tri·cate (in'tri·kit) *adj.* 1 Exceedingly or perplexingly entangled, complicated, or involved. 2 Difficult to follow or understand. See synonyms under COMPLEX. [<L *intricatus,* pp. of *intricare* entangle < *in-* in + *tricae* difficulties] —**in'tri·cate·ly** *adv.* —**in'tri·cate·ness** *n.*

in·tri·gant (in'trə·gənt, *Fr.* aṅ·trē·gäṅ') *n. pl.* **·gants** (-gənts, *Fr.* -gäṅ') One given to intrigue. [<F <Ital. *intrigante,* ppr. of *intrigare* intrigue <L *intricare* entangle. See INTRICATE.]

— **in·tri·gante** (in′trə·gant′, -gänt′; *Fr.* aṅ·trē·gäṅt′) *n. fem.*

in·trigue (in·trēg′, in′trēg) *n.* 1 The working for an end by secret or underhand means; a plot or scheme. 2 A clandestine and illicit love affair; liaison. 3 The plot of a play, poem, or story, or the complications in which the characters are involved. — *v.* **·trigued, ·tri·guing** *v.t.* 1 To arouse and hold the interest or curiosity of; beguile; allure. 2 To plot for; bring on or get by secret or underhand means. 3 *Rare* To puzzle; perplex. —*v.i.* 4 To use secret or underhand means; make plots. 5 To carry on a secret or illicit love affair. [<F *intriguer* <Ital. *intrigare* <L *intricare.* See INTRICATE.] — **in·tri′guer** *n.*

in·trinse (in·trins′) *adj. Obs.* Tightly drawn; intricate; entangled. [Short for obs. *intrinsecate* <Ital. *intrinsecato* familiar, confused in sense with *intricate* intricate]

in·trin·sic (in·trin′sik) *adj.* 1 Pertaining to the nature of a thing or person; inherent; real; true: opposed to *extrinsic.* 2 Contained or being within. 3 *Anat.* Contained within a certain portion of the body as nerves or muscles. Also **in·trin′si·cal.** See synonyms under INHERENT. [<OF *intrinseque* <Med. L <L *intrinsecus* internally] — **in·trin′si·cal·ly** *adv.*

intro– *prefix* In; into; within: *introvert.* [<L *intro-* < *intro* inwardly]

in·tro·cep·tion (in′trə·sep′shən) *n. Psychol.* The thorough acceptance by an individual of the fundamental moral standards and conventions of society; social conformity in motives and purpose. [<INTRO- + (RE)CEPTION]

in·tro·duce (in′trə·dōōs′, -dyōōs′) *v.t.* **·duced, ·duc·ing** 1 To bring (someone) to acquaintance with another; cause to become acquainted: He *introduced* me to his cousin; He *introduced* the women to each other. 2 To present formally: to *introduce* one to society. 3 To bring (someone) to acquaintance with or knowledge of something: with *to*: to *introduce* someone to gambling. 4 To bring into notice, use, or practice: to *introduce* a new fashion. 5 To bring, lead, or put into; insert: to *introduce* a probe into a wound. 6 To bring forward for notice or consideration: to *introduce* a resolution. 7 To begin; start: to *introduce* a new line of questioning. See synonyms under ALLEGE. [<L *introducere* < *in-* within + *ducere* lead] — **in′tro·duc′er** *n.* — **in′·tro·duc′i·ble** *adj.*

in·tro·duc·tion (in′trə·duk′shən) *n.* 1 The act of introducing, as inserting, bringing into notice or use, or making acquainted. 2 The means of introducing one person to another, as by letter, card, etc. 3 Something that leads up to and tends to explain something else; specifically, a preliminary statement made by an author or speaker in explanation of the subject or design of his writing or discourse. 4 Hence, an elementary treatise in any branch of study: an *introduction* to chemistry. 5 *Music* A preparatory movement intended to foreshadow or lead up to the theme. See synonyms under ENTRANCE. [<OF] — **in′tro·duc′tor** *n.*

in·tro·duc·to·ry (in′trə·duk′tər·ē) *adj.* Serving as an introduction; prefatory; preliminary. Also **in′tro·duc′tive.** [<LL *introductorius*] — **in′tro·duc′to·ri·ly** *adv.*

in·tro·fac·tion (in′trə·fak′shən) *n. Chem.* A change in the wetting properties and fluidity of an impregnating substance when acted upon by an introfier. [<INTRO- + *-faction* doing <L *factus,* pp. of *facere* do]

in·tro·fi·er (in′trə·fī′ər) *n. Chem.* A substance which speeds up the impregnating capacity of fluids, as naphthalene or its derivatives when acting on molten sulfur. [<INTRO- + -FY]

in·tro·it (in·trō′it) *n.* 1 An antiphon said or chanted at the beginning of the Eucharist, as the priest enters the sanctuary. 2 In the Anglican Church, an anthem or hymn sung at the beginning of public worship. [<F <L *introitus* an entrance < *introire* < *intro-* in + *ire* go]

in·tro·ject (in′trə·jekt′) *v.t. Psychoanal.* To transform external realities, as persons and objects, into mental replicas or images with which one may enter into direct emotional relations. [<INTRO- + (PRO)JECT]

in·tro·jec·tion (in′trə·jek′shən) *n.* 1 *Psychoanal.* The incorporation into the ego of mental images of persons and objects to the extent of being emotionally affected by them: compare PROJECTION. 2 *Psychol.* The attribution of sentient qualities to inanimate objects; personification. [<intro- + (PRO)JECTION]

in·tro·mit (in′trə·mit′) *v.t.* **·mit·ted, ·mit·ting** 1 To send or place in; insert. 2 To permit to enter; admit. [<L *intromittere* < *intro-* within + *mittere* send] — **in′tro·mis′sion** (-mish′ən) *n.* — **in′tro·mis′sive** (-mis′iv), **in′tro·mit′tent** *adj.*

in·trorse (in·trôrs′) *adj. Bot.* Turned inward or toward the axis, as an anther that faces the axis of a flower. Compare EXTRORSE. [<L *introrsus* inward, contraction of *introversus* < *intro-* within + *versus* turned] — **in·trorse′ly** *adv.*

in·tro·spect (in′trə·spekt′) *v.t.* To look into; examine the interior of. — *v.i. Psychol.* To examine and analyze one's own thoughts and emotions; practice self–examination. [<L *introspectus,* pp. of *introspicere* < *intro-* within + *specere* look] — **in′tro·spec′tive** *adj.* — **in′·tro·spec′tive·ly** *adv.* — **in′tro·spec′tive·ness** *n.*

in·tro·spec·tion (in′trə·spek′shən) *n.* 1 The act of looking within. 2 *Psychol.* The contemplation of one's own mental processes and emotional states; self–examination.

in·tro·sus·cept (in′trə·sə·sept′) See INTUSSUSCEPT.

in·tro·ver·sion (in′trə·vûr′zhən, -shən) *n.* 1 The act or process of introverting. 2 *Psychol.* The direction or concentration of one's interest upon oneself. 3 *Psychoanal.* The concentration of the libido upon inwardly derived activities or satisfactions. Compare EXTROVERSION. [<NL *introversio, -onis* <L *intro-* within + *versio, -onis* a turning] — **in′tro·ver′sive** (-vûr′siv) *adj.*

in·tro·vert (in′trə·vûrt) *n.* 1 *Psychol.* An individual with strongly self–centered patterns of emotion, fantasy, and thought: opposed to *extrovert.* 2 *Biol.* An organ capable of being turned inward, as the eye tentacle of a land snail or the proboscis of a gastropod. — *v.t.* 1 To turn within; cause to take an inward direction, as the mind or one's thoughts. 2 *Biol.* To turn (an organ) inward upon itself. — *adj.* Characterized by or tending to introversion: *introvert* habits. [<INTRO- + L *vertere* turn]

in·trude (in·trōōd′) *v.* **·trud·ed, ·trud·ing** *v.t.* 1 To thrust or force in without leave or excuse: to *intrude* one's views. 2 *Geol.* To cause to enter by intrusion. — *v.i.* 3 To come in without leave or invitation; thrust oneself in. [<L *intrudere* < *in-* in + *trudere* thrust] — **in·trud′er** *n.*

in·tru·sion (in·trōō′zhən) *n.* 1 The act of intruding; encroachment. 2 *Geol.* **a** The thrusting of molten rock within an earlier formation. **b** An intrusive rock.

in·tru·sive (in·trōō′siv) *adj* 1 Coming without warrant; intruding; obtrusive; prone to intrude. 2 *Geol.* Formed by solidification before reaching the surface of the earth, as certain igneous rocks; plutonic. 3 *Phonet.* Referring to speech sounds in a word which do not have etymological basis, but result from the adjustment of the vocal organs to the sounds preceding and following, as the *d* in *spindle* (Old English *spinel*). —**intrusive r** An *r* sound sometimes heard between a word ending in a vowel and a following word beginning with a vowel, as in law*r* office. [<L *intrusus,* pp. of *intrudere.* See INTRUDE.] — **in·tru′sive·ly** *adv.* — **in·tru′sive·ness** *n.*

in·trust (in·trust′) See ENTRUST.

in·tu·bate (in′tyōō·bāt, -tōō-) *v.t.* **·bat·ed, ·bat·ing** *Med.* To treat by intubation. [<IN- + L *tuba* tube + -ATE[2]]

in·tu·ba·tion (in′tyōō·bā′shən, -tōō-) *n. Med.* The insertion of a tube in an orifice, as in the larynx in cases of diphtheria.

in·tu·it (in′tyōō·it, in·tōō′it) *v.t.* & *v.i.* To know by intuition. [<L *intuitus,* pp. of *intueri* look upon < *in-* on + *tueri* look]

in·tu·i·tion (in′tōō·ish′ən, -tyōō-) *n.* 1 Quick perception of truth without conscious attention or reasoning. 2 Knowledge from within; instinctive knowledge or feeling. 3 *Philos.* **a** An immediate knowledge, or envisagement, of an object, truth, or principle, whether of a physical, rational, artistic, or ethical nature: a conception derived by analogy from the act and result of clear and concentrated vision. **b** That which is known intuitively; truth obtained by internal apprehension without the aid of perception or the reasoning powers. See synonyms under KNOWLEDGE. [<Med. L *intuitio, -onis* < *intuitus,* pp. of *intueri* look upon. See INTUIT.] — **in′tu·i′tion·al** *adj.* — **in′·tu·i′tion·al·ly** *adv.*

intuitional ethics The teaching of that school of ethics which holds that man has an intuitive apprehension and intrinsically valid judgment of moral values.

in·tu·i·tion·al·ism (in′tōō·ish′ən·əl·iz′əm, -tyōō-) *n.* The doctrine that certain truths are immediately, and without discursive argument, cognized as fundamental and incontestable and are the foundation of all knowledge. Also **in′tu·i′tion·ism.** — **in′tu·i′tion·al·ist, in′tu·i′·tion·ist** *n.*

in·tu·i·tive (in·tōō′ə·tiv, -tyōō′-) *adj.* 1 Perceived by the mind without the intervention of any process of thought: *intuitive* evidence. 2 Discovering truth or reaching a just conclusion without resort to the powers of reason: the *intuitive* faculty. — **in·tu′i·tive·ly** *adv.* — **in·tu′i·tive·ness** *n.*

in·tu·i·tiv·ism (in·tōō′ə·tiv·iz′əm, -tyōō′-) *n.* 1 The doctrine that all ethical principles are intuitive. 2 Intuitive faculty; insight; instinct. — **in·tu′i·tiv·ist** *n.*

in·tu·mesce (in′tōō·mes′, -tyōō-) *v.i.* **·mesced, ·mesc·ing** 1 To enlarge or expand, as from heat or congestion. 2 To swell or bubble up; become tumid. [<L *intumescere,* intens. of *tumescere,* inceptive of *tumere* swell]

in·tu·mes·cence (in′tōō·mes′əns, -tyōō-) *n.* 1 A tumid state or process. 2 A tumid growth; a swelling. 3 The bubbling up of a molten mass. 4 Excited feeling or language. Also **in′tu·mes′cen·cy.** — **in′tu·mes′cent** *adj.*

in·turn (in′tûrn′) *n.* 1 The act of turning inward, or the state of being so turned, as of the toes. 2 A dancing step. Also **in′turn′ing.**

in·tus·sus·cept (in′təs·sə·sept′) *v.t.* To receive within itself or within something else; invaginate: also *introsuscept.* [<L *intus* within + *susceptus,* pp. of *suscipere* take up < *sub-* under + *capere* take] — **in′tus·sus·cep′tive** *adj.*

in·tus·sus·cep·tion (in′təs·sə·sep′shən) *n.* 1 A receiving within. 2 The state of being received within. 3 *Pathol.* The introversion of a portion of an intestine or other tube into the portion adjoining it. 4 *Physiol.* The reception into an organ of foreign matter, as food, and its conversion into living tissue; interstitial growth. 5 *Bot.* The interposition of new molecules between the molecules of the original material, as in the cell walls of plants or grains of starch.

in·twine (in·twīn′), **in·twist** (in·twist′), etc. See ENTWINE, etc.

in·u·en·do (in′yōō·en′dō) See INNUENDO.

in·u·lase (in′yə·lās) *n. Biochem.* An enzyme arising from the action of certain species of fungi on inulin, which it converts into levulose. [<INUL(IN) + -ASE]

in·u·lin (in′yə·lin) *n. Biochem.* A white, amorphous, soluble polysaccharide, $C_6H_{10}O_5$, isomeric with starch, and occurring in the underground parts of some composite plants such as the dahlia, the dandelion, and the elecampane: it yields a fructose on hydrolysis. [<L *inula* elecampane + -IN]

in·unc·tion (in·ungk′shən) *n.* 1 The act of anointing. 2 *Med.* The process of rubbing into the skin, as an ointment or liniment. [<L *inunctio, -onis* < *inunctus,* pp. of *inungere* anoint]

in·un·dant (in·un′dənt) *adj.* Inundating; overflowing.

in·un·date (in′un·dāt) *v.t.* **·dat·ed, ·dat·ing** To cover by overflowing; flood; fill to overflowing. [<L *inundatus,* pp. of *inundare* < *in-* in, on + *undare* overflow < *unda* wave] — **in′un·da′tor** *n.* — **in·un·da·to·ry** (in·un′də·tôr′ē, -tō′·rē) *adj.*

Synonyms: deluge, flood, overflow, overwhelm, submerge. *Antonyms*: drain, dry, parch, scorch.

in·un·da·tion (in′un·dā′shən) *n.* 1 A flood. 2 A condition of superabundance.

in·ure (in·yōōr′) *v.* **·ured, ·ur·ing** *v.t.* To harden or toughen by use or exercise; accustom; habituate. — *v.i.* To have or take effect; be applied. Also spelled *enure.* [<IN[2] + obs. *ure* work, use <OF *eure* <L *opera* work] — **in·ure′ment** *n.*

in·urn (in·ûrn′) *v.t.* To put into a cinerary urn; bury; entomb.

in·u·tile (in·yōō′til) *adj.* Useless. [<F <L *inutilis*] — **in·u′tile·ly** *adv.* — **in′u·til′i·ty** *n.*

in va·cu·o (in vak′yōō·ō) *Latin* In a vacuum.

in·vade (in·vād′) *v.* **·vad·ed, ·vad·ing** *v.t.* **1** To enter with or as with hostile intent, as for conquering or plundering. **2** To encroach upon; trespass on: to *invade* privacy. **3** To spread over or penetrate injuriously: Disease *invaded* the lungs. —*v.i.* **4** To make an invasion. [<L *invadere* <*in-* in + *vadere* go] —**in·vad′er** *n.*

in·vag·i·nate (in·vaj′ə·nāt) *v.* **·nat·ed, ·nat·ing** *v.t.* **1** To put or receive into a sheath. **2** To turn back within itself, as a tubular organ or part. —*v.i.* **3** To undergo invagination. [<L *in-* in + *vagina* sheath + -ATE[2]] —**in·vag′i·nat′ed** *adj.*

in·vag·i·na·tion (in·vaj′ə·nā′shən) *n.* **1** The act of invaginating, or the state of being invaginated; intussusception. **2** *Biol.* **a** The differentiation of the germinal layers by a pushing in of the wall of the blastula to form the gastrula, or by the growth of the epiblast cells as a thin layer over the hypoblast. **b** That which is invaginated; specifically, a pouch formed by an infolding of a membrane: the buccal *invagination.*

in·va·lid[1] (in′və·lid) *n.* A sickly person, or one disabled, as by wounds, disease, etc. —*adj.* **1** Enfeebled by ill health. **2** Pertaining to or for the use of sick persons. —*v.t.* **1** To cause to become an invalid; disable. **2** To classify, or release (a soldier, sailor, etc.) from active service as an invalid. —*v.i.* **3** To become an invalid. **4** To retire from active service because of ill health: said of soldiers, sailors, etc. [<F *invalide* <L *invalidus* not strong] —**in′va·lid·ism** *n.*

in·val·id[2] (in·val′id) *adj.* Having no force, weight, or cogency; null; void. [<L *invalidus*] —**in·va·lid·i·ty** (in′və·lid′ə·tē) *n.* —**in·val′id·ly** *adv.*

in·val·i·date (in·val′ə·dāt) *v.t.* **·dat·ed, ·dat·ing** To weaken or destroy the force or validity of; render invalid; annul. [<INVALID[2] + -ATE[1]] —**in·val′i·da′tion** *n.* —**in·val′i·da′tor** *n.*

in·val·u·a·ble (in·val′yōō·ə·bəl, -yōō·bəl) *adj.* Of a value beyond estimation; very precious. —**in·val′u·a·bly** *adv.*

In·var (in·vär′) *n.* An alloy of nickel and steel, containing 36 percent of nickel, employed in the manufacture of instruments of precision and of standard measures, because it is practically free from expansion or contraction by heat or cold: a trade name. [<INVAR(IABLE)]

in·var·i·a·ble (in·vâr′ē·ə·bəl) *adj.* That does not or can not vary or be varied; always uniform. See synonyms under CONTINUAL, PERMANENT. —**in·var′i·a·bil′i·ty, in·var′i·a·ble·ness** *n.* —**in·var′i·a·bly** *adv.*

in·var·iance (in·vâr′ē·əns) *n.* The property or condition of being invariant.

in·var·i·ant (in·vâr′ē·ənt) *adj.* Constant; not subject to variation. —*n. Math.* A quantity which remains unchanged; a constant.

in·va·sion (in·vā′zhən) *n.* **1** The act of invading; a military inroad or incursion for conquest, reconquest, or plunder. **2** Hence, any attack with harmful intent or result: an *invasion* of disease. **3** Encroachment, as by an act of intrusion or trespass: the *invasion* of privacy. [<LL *invasio, -onis* < *invasum,* pp. of *invadere.* See INVADE.]

Synonyms: aggression, encroachment, foray, incursion, inroad, irruption, raid. See AGGRESSION, ATTACK.

in·va·sive (in·vā′siv) *adj.* Having the character or effect of an invasion; encroaching; aggressive.

in·vect·ed (in·vek′tid) *adj. Archit.* **1** Having a border line consisting of a series of convex arcs or scallops. **2** Consisting of such arcs, as a line, the edge of a molding, etc.: opposed to *engrailed.* [<L *invectus,* pp. of *invehere.* See INVEIGH.]

in·vec·tive (in·vek′tiv) *n.* Railing accusation; vituperation; abuse. —*adj.* Using or characterized by vituperation or abuse. [<OF *invectif* <LL *invectivus* <L *invectus,* pp. of *invehere.* See INVEIGH.] —**in·vec′tive·ly** *adv.* —**in·vec′tive·ness** *n.*

in·veigh (in·vā′) *v.i.* To utter vehement censure or invective: with *against.* [<L *invehere* carry into <*in-* into + *vehere* carry] —**in·veigh′er** *n.*

in·vei·gle (in·vē′gəl, -vā′-) *v.t.* **·gled, ·gling** **1** To lead on, as by trickery or flattery; draw; entice. **2** To win over or seduce; captivate. See synonyms under ALLURE. [<F *aveugler* blind, deceive <*aveugle* blind, ult. <L *ab-* without + *oculus* eye] —**in·vei′gle·ment** *n.* —**in·vei′gler** *n.*

in·veil (in·vāl′) *v.t. Obs.* To cover with a veil.

in·vent (in·vent′) *v.t.* **1** To create the idea, form, or existence of by original thought or effort; devise: to *invent* a better mousetrap. **2** To fabricate in the mind; make up, as something untrue or contrary to fact: He *invented* an excuse. **3** *Obs.* To come or chance upon; find. See synonyms under DISCOVER, PLAN. [<L *inventus,* pp. of *invenire* come upon, discover <*in-* on + *venire* come] —**in·vent′i·ble** *adj.*

in·ven·tion (in·ven′shən) *n.* **1** The act or process of inventing. **2** That which is invented: a useful *invention.* **3** Skill or ingenuity in contriving. **4** Mental fabrication or concoction. **5** In literature or art, creation by the exercise of imaginative powers: poetic *invention.* **6** In rhetoric, the finding out or selection of topics to be treated, or arguments to be used. **7** *Archaic* A finding; discovery. **8** *Law* **a** The process of devising and producing by independent investigation and experiment something not previously known or existing. **b** The article, device, or composition thus created. See synonyms under ARTIFICE, FICTION, INGENUITY, PROJECT. [<OF *invencion*]

in·ven·tive (in·ven′tiv) *adj.* Able to invent; quick at contrivance. —**in·ven′tive·ly** *adv.* —**in·ven′tive·ness** *n.*

in·ven·tor (in·ven′tər) *n.* One who invents; especially, one who has originated some method, process, or mechanical device, or who devotes his time to invention. Also **in·vent′er.** [<L]

in·ven·to·ry (in′vən·tôr′ē, -tō′rē) *n. pl.* **·ries** **1** An itemized list of articles, with the number and value of each. **2** The items so listed or to be listed, as the stock of goods of a business. **3** The process of listing articles, supplies, or materials with the description, quantity, and value of each. **4** The value of the goods or stock of a business. **5** A detailed account of the property of a deceased person. **6** A list of articles, with valuations, covered by an insurance policy. See synonyms under RECORD. —*v.t.* **·ried, ·ry·ing** **1** To make an inventory of; to list in detail. **2** To insert in an inventory. **3** To take stock of; appraise. [<Med. L *inventarium,* L *inventorium.* See INVENT.] —**in′ven·to′ri·al** (-tôr′ē·əl, -tō′rē-) *adj.* —**in′ven·to′ri·al·ly** *adv.*

in·ve·rac·i·ty (in′və·ras′ə·tē) *n. pl.* **·ties** **1** Lack of veracity; untruthfulness. **2** An untruth; lie.

In·ver·chap·el (in′vər·chap′əl) See KERR.

in·ver·ness (in′vər·nes′) *n.* A sleeveless, cloaklike garment. Also **Inverness cape.** [from *Inverness,* Scotland]

In·ver·ness (in′vər·nes′) A maritime county in NW Scotland; 4,211 square miles; county seat, Inverness. Also **In′ver·ness′shire** (-shir).

in·verse (in·vûrs′, in′vûrs) *adj.* Opposite in order or effect; inverted; reciprocal. —*n.* That which is inverted. —**in·verse′ly** *adv.*

in·ver·sion (in·vûr′zhən, -shən) *n.* **1** The act of inverting. **2** The state of being inverted; a reversal of the natural order of things. **3** In rhetoric: **a** A reversal of the natural order of words. **b** A form of discussion that makes use of a speaker's own argument against himself. **4** *Music* The alteration of a harmony or melody by inverting the relations of its intervals; also, the arrangement resulting from such change. **5** In marching, a reversal of the order of companies in line, so as to bring the left to the right, and vice versa. **6** *Chem.* A rearrangement of the molecular structure of compounds, with the forming of two new compounds whose effects on the plane of polarization are opposed to each other: Sucrose, by acid hydrolysis, is an *inversion* of glucose and fructose. **7** *Meteorol.* An increase of temperature with elevation often noted in anticyclones. **8** *Phonet.* A tongue position in which the tip is turned up and back. **9** Homosexuality. [<L *inversio, -onis* <*inversus,* pp. of *invertere.* See INVERT.] —**in·ver′sive** *adj.*

in·vert (in·vûrt′) *v.t.* **1** To turn upside down or inside out. **2** To reverse the position, order, or sequence of; turn in the opposite direction. **3** To change to the opposite: to *invert* a meaning. **4** *Music* To transpose, as an interval, phrase, or vocal part. **5** *Chem.* To alter, as a compound, by inversion. **6** *Phonet.* To articulate with inversion of the tongue. —*v.i.* **7** To undergo inversion. —*adj.* (in′vûrt) Inverted. —*n.* (in′vûrt) A homosexual. [<L *invertere* <*in-* in + *vertere* turn] —**in·vert′i·ble** *adj.* —**in·ver′tor** *n.*

in·ver·tase (in·vûr′tās) *n. Biochem.* An enzyme capable of splitting sucrose and related sugars into glucose and fructose, found in certain plants and the intestines of animals; specifically, a ferment which inverts cane sugar into fructose and glucose. Also **in·ver′tin** (-tin). [<INVERT + -ASE]

In·ver·te·bra·ta (in·vûr′tə·brā′tə) *n. pl.* A former name for a section of the animal kingdom including all animals without a spinal column: opposed to *Vertebrata.* [<NL]

in·ver·te·brate (in·vûr′tə·brit, -brāt) *adj.* **1** Destitute of a backbone; not vertebrate. **2** Of or pertaining to the *Invertebrata.* **3** Lacking force or firmness; irresolute: also **in·ver′te·bral.** —*n.* **1** An invertebrate animal; one of the *Invertebrata.* **2** One who lacks resolution.

in·vert·ed (in·vûr′tid) *adj.* **1** Turned in a contrary direction, or turned upside down; reversed in order or position. **2** Having a position the opposite of the usual or normal one: an *inverted* ovule in plants, *inverted* commas, etc. **3** *Phonet.* Cacuminal. —**in·vert′ed·ly** *adv.*

inverted arch *Archit.* An arch having its crown downward: used in foundations.

inverted commas *Brit.* Quotation marks.

inverted mordent See under MORDENT.

in·vert·er (in·vûr′tər) *n. Electr.* A device for converting direct current into alternating current; a converter.

invert soap A synthetic detergent with strong disinfectant qualities due to the presence of positive ions in its molecular structure causing its resistance to the action of acids and alkalis.

invert sugar A mixture of fructose and glucose occurring in some fruits and artificially produced by the hydrolysis of cane sugar.

in·vest (in·vest′) *v.t.* **1** To use (money or capital) for the purchase of property, stocks, securities, etc., with the expectation of future profit or income. **2** To place in office formally; install. **3** To give power, authority, or rank to. **4** To cover or surround as if with a garment: Mystery *invested* the whole affair. **5** To surround or hem in; lay siege to. **6** *Rare* To confer or settle (a right, power, etc.): with *in.* **7** *Obs.* To clothe; also, to don. —*v.i.* **8** To make an investment or investments. [<L *investire* clothe, enshroud <*in-* on + *vestire* clothe <*vestis* clothing; infl. in meaning by Ital. *investire* invest] —**in·ves′tor** *n.*

in·ves·ti·gate (in·ves′tə·gāt) *v.* **·gat·ed, ·gat·ing** To search or inquire into; examine in detail. —*v.i.* To make an investigation. See synonyms under EXAMINE, QUESTION. [<L *investigatus,* pp. of *investigare* <*in-* in + *vestigare* track, trace <*vestigium* track] —**in·ves′ti·ga·ble** (-tə·gə·bəl) *adj.* —**in·ves′ti·ga′tive** *adj.* —**in·ves′ti·ga′tor** *n.*

in·ves·ti·ga·tion (in·ves′tə·gā′shən) *n.* **1** The act of investigating; careful inquiry or research. **2** An inquiry by authority, as by a legislative committee, into certain facts. **3** A systematic examination of some scientific question, whether by experiment or mathematical treatment. [<F]

in·ves·ti·tive (in·ves′tə·tiv) *adj.* **1** Of or pertaining to investiture. **2** Having the function of investing; serving to invest. [<L *investitus,* pp. of *investire.* See INVEST.]

in·ves·ti·ture (in·ves′tə·chər) *n.* **1** The act or ceremony of investing with something, as robes of office. **2** That which invests or clothes. **3** In feudal law, the delivery of possession of lands in the presence of witnesses. **4** *Eccl.* The ceremony of inducting an abbot or bishop into his office by placing the symbols of the office in his hands and receiving his oath of fealty. **5** *Obs.* Clothing. [<Med. L *investitura.*]

in·vest·ment (in·vest′mənt) *n.* **1** The placing of money, capital, or other resources to gain a profit, as in interest. **2** That which is invested. **3** That in which one invests. **4** Investiture. **5** *Biol.* An outer covering. **6** *Archaic* Clothing; a garment. **7** *Mil.* The surrounding of a fort or town by an enemy force to create a state of siege; a blockade.

investment trust A company that invests its capital in other companies.

in·vet·er·a·cy (in·vet′ər·ə·sē) *n. pl.* **·cies** **1** Persistence from habit; habitual nature or character. **2** Deep-rooted hostility.

in·vet·er·ate (in·vet′ər·it) *adj.* **1** Firmly established by long continuance; deep-rooted. **2** Confirmed in a particular character or habit. **3** *Obs.* Characteristic of long enmity; bitter; malignant; also, ancient. [<L *inveteratus,* pp. of *inveterare* make old < *in-* very + *vetus* old] —**in·vet′er·ate·ly** *adv.* —**in·vet′·er·ate·ness** *n.*

in·vid·i·ous (in·vid′ē·əs) *adj.* **1** Expressing, prompted by, or provoking envy or ill will; unjustly discriminating; hence, displeasing. **2** *Obs.* Showing envy. See synonyms under MALICIOUS. [<L *invidiosus* < *invidia* envy. Doublet of ENVIOUS.] —**in·vid′i·ous·ly** *adv.* —**in·vid′i·ous·ness** *n.*

in·vig·i·late (in·vij′ə·lāt) *v.t.* **·lat·ed, ·lat·ing** **1** *Brit.* To keep watch over or proctor students at examination. **2** *Obs.* To watch carefully. [<L *invigilatus,* pp. of *invigilare* <*in-* thoroughly + *vigilare* watch < *vigilia* watch < *vigil* awake < *vigere* be vigorous] —**in·vig′i·la′tion** *n.* —**in·vig′i·la′tor** *n.*

in·vig·or·ate (in·vig′ər·āt) *v.t.* **·at·ed, ·at·ing** To give vigor and energy to; animate. [<L *in-* in + *vigor* vigor + -ATE[2]] —**in·vig′or·at′ing·ly** *adv.* —**in·vig′or·a′tion** *n.*

in·vin·ci·ble (in·vin′sə·bəl) *adj.* Not to be overcome; unconquerable. [<F <L *invincibilis.* See IN-[1], VINCIBLE.] —**in·vin′ci·bil′i·ty, in·vin′·ci·ble·ness** *n.* —**in·vin′ci·bly** *adv.*

in vi·no ver·i·tas (in vī′nō ver′i·tas) *Latin* In wine (there is) truth.

in·vi·o·la·ble (in·vī′ə·lə·bəl) *adj.* That must not or can not be violated. [<L *inviolabilis*] —**in·vi′o·la·bil′i·ty, in·vi′o·la·ble·ness** *n.* —**in·vi′·o·la·bly** *adv.*

in·vi·o·la·cy (in·vī′ə·lə·sē) *n.* The state of being inviolate.

in·vi·o·late (in·vī′ə·lit) *adj.* **1** Not violated; unprofaned; pure; unbroken. **2** Inviolable; not to be violated. —**in·vi′o·late·ly** *adv.* —**in·vi′o·late·ness** *n.*

in·vis·i·ble (in·viz′ə·bəl) *adj.* **1** Not visible; not capable of being seen. **2** Not in sight; concealed. **3** *Econ.* Referring to resources or reserves that do not appear in regular processes or in financial statements: *invisible* products, *invisible* revenue, *invisible* assets. —*n.* **1** One who or that which is invisible. **2** *Often cap.* One of a sect of Protestants in the 16th century who denied the visibility of the church. **3** A Rosicrucian, as belonging to a secret fraternity. —**the Invisible** The Supreme Being; God. [<OF] —**in·vis′i·bil′i·ty, in·vis′i·ble·ness** *n.* —**in·vis′i·bly** *adv.*

invisible ink Sympathetic ink.

in·vi·ta·tion (in′və·tā′shən) *n.* **1** The act of inviting; courteous solicitation to come to some place or to do some act; especially, a requesting of another's company: a standing *invitation* to dinner. **2** The means of inviting; the words by which one is invited: a written *invitation.* **3** The act of alluring; incitement; attraction. **4** In the Anglican Church, the hortatory introduction preceding the confession in the communion office; the invitatory. [<L *invitatio, -onis*]

in·vi·ta·to·ry (in·vī′tə·tôr′ē, -tō′rē) *Eccl. adj.* Using or containing invitation: the *invitatory* psalm, "O come let us sing," *Ps.* xcv. —*n. pl.* **·ries** One of several forms of invitation to worship; especially, the antiphon to the Venite. [<Med. L *invitatorius*]

in·vite (in·vīt′) *v.* **·vit·ed, ·vit·ing** *v.t.* **1** To ask (someone) politely or graciously to be present in some place, to attend some event, or to perform some action. **2** To make formal or polite request for: to *invite* suggestions. **3** To present opportunity or inducement for; attract: The situation *invites* criticism. **4** To tempt; entice. —*v.i.* **5** To give invitation; entice. —*n.* (in′vīt) *Slang* An invitation. [<F *inviter* <L *invitare* entertain] —**in·vit′er** *n.*

in·vit·ing (in·vī′ting) *adj.* That invites or allures. —**in·vit′ing·ly** *adv.* —**in·vit′ing·ness** *n.*

in vi·tro (in vī′trō) *Latin* Within glass: said especially of experiments carried on in test tubes or outside of the living organisms.

in vi·vo (in vī′vō) *Latin* Within the living organism: opposed to *in vitro.*

in·vo·ca·tion (in′vō·kā′shən) *n.* **1** The act of invoking. **2** A judicial order. **3** *Eccl.* A form of prayer, as at the opening of a service. **4** An appeal invoking the Muses or some divine being, at the beginning of an epic or other work. **5** The act of conjuring an evil spirit. **6** The formula or incantation thus used. See synonyms under PRAYER. [<OF <L *invocatio, -onis* < *invocare.* See INVOKE.]

in·voc·a·to·ry (in·vok′ə·tôr′ē, -tō′rē) *adj.* Having the nature of, expressive of, or employed in invocation.

in·voice (in′vois) *n.* **1** A list sent to a purchaser, etc., containing the items and charges of merchandise. **2** The goods so listed. —*v.t.* **·voiced, ·voic·ing** To itemize; make an invoice of. [<F *envois,* pl. of *envoi* a thing sent < *envoyer* send. See ENVOY[1].]

in·voke (in·vōk′) *v.t.* **·voked, ·vok·ing** **1** To call on for aid, protection, etc.; address, as in prayer. **2** To call for, as in supplication: to *invoke* a blessing. **3** To summon or conjure by incantation, as evil spirits. **4** To appeal to for confirmation; quote as an authority. See synonyms under PRAY. [<F *invoquer* <L *invocare* call upon < *in-* on + *vocare* call] —**in·vok′er** *n.*

in·vol·u·cel (in·vol′yə·sel) *n. Bot.* **1** A secondary involucre. **2** A rosette of bracts beneath a calyx. Also **in·vol′u·cel′lum.** [<NL *involucellum,* dim. of L *involucrum* covering]

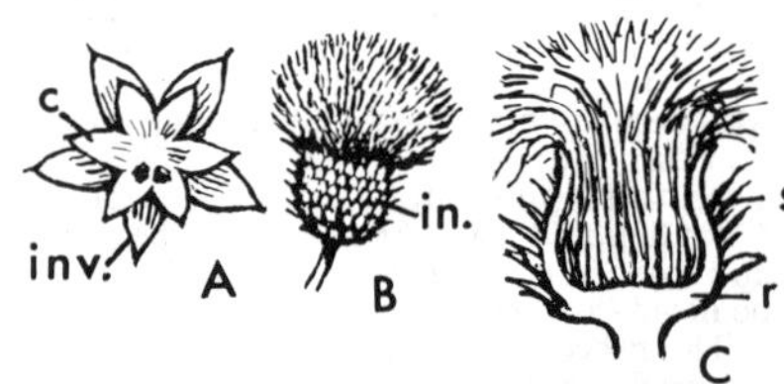

INVOLUCEL AND INVOLUCRE
A. Involucel of hollyhock; *c,* calyx; *inv.,* involucel.
B. Head of thistle; *in.,* involucre.
C. Section of thistle, showing arrangement of the scales *(s)* of the involucre, and the receptacle *(r).*

in·vo·lu·cral (in′və·lōō′krəl) *adj.* Pertaining to, resembling, or provided with an involucre.

in·vo·lu·crate (in′və·lōō′krit, -krāt) *adj.* Provided with or forming an involucre. Also **in′·vo·lu′crat·ed.**

in·vo·lu·cre (in′və·lōō′kər) *n.* **1** An enveloping membrane or wrapper. **2** *Bot.* A ring or rosette of bracts surrounding the base of a flower cluster. In many flowers the subtending involucres resemble calyxes and all composites are involucrate. [<F <L *involucrum* covering < *involvere.* See INVOLVE.]

in·vo·lu·crum (in′və·lōō′krəm) *n. pl.* **·cra** (-krə) **1** An involucre. **2** *Zool.* The sheath at the base of a nematocyst. [<L]

in·vol·un·tar·y (in·vol′ən·ter′ē) *adj.* **1** Contrary to one's will or wish. **2** Not under the control of the will. **3** Unintentional. **4** *Physiol.* Describing those muscles, glands, and other bodily organs which act independently of conscious control. See synonyms under SPONTANEOUS. —**in·vol′un·tar′i·ly** *adv.* —**in·vol′un·tar′i·ness** *n.*

in·vo·lute (in′və·lōōt) *adj.* **1** Complicated by reason of the intertwinings or the interrelation of parts or elements. **2** *Bot.* Having the edges rolled inward, as a leaf. **3** *Zool.* Having the whorls nearly or quite concealing the axis, as a shell; also, coiled spirally, as certain antennae. Also **in′vo·lut′ed.** —*n. Geom.* The curve traced by a point on a line as the line unrolls from a fixed curve. [<L *involutus,* pp. of *involvere* involve]

in·vo·lu·tion (in′və·lōō′shən) *n.* **1** The act of involving, infolding, or rolling up, or the state of being involved or rolled up; complication; entanglement. **2** Something involved, rolled up, or entangled. **3** *Physiol.* **a** The return of an organ to its normal condition after a physiological increase in its size and structure: the *involution* of the womb after childbirth. **b** Retrograde development; the physiological decline preceding and accompanying old age. **4** *Math.* The multiplication of a quantity by itself any number of times; the raising of a quantity to any power. **5** In rhetoric, complicated or cumbrous arrangement of words, clauses, or phrases, caused by the insertion of qualifying or modifying phrases between words that belong together. **6** *Biol.* Degeneration; retrograde evolution.

in·volve (in·volv′) *v.t.* **·volved, ·volv·ing** **1** To have as a necessary circumstance, condition, or implication. **2** To have effect on; affect: The law will *involve* many people. **3** To draw within itself; swallow up; overwhelm: The whirlpool *involved* ten persons. **4** To draw into entanglement, trouble, etc.; implicate; entangle. **5** To make intricate or difficult; complicate. **6** To hold the attention of; engross: He was *involved* in his work. **7** To wrap up or infold; cover or conceal; envelop: to *involve* a place in darkness. **8** To wind in spirals or curves; coil, especially intricately. **9** *Math.* To raise (a number) to a given power. [<L *involvere* roll into or up < *in-* in + *volvere* roll] —**in·volve′ment** *n.*

Synonyms: complicate, embarrass, embroil, entangle, implicate, imply, include, overwhelm. To *involve* is to roll or wind up with or in, so as to combine inextricably or very nearly inseparably; as, The nation is *involved* in war; The bookkeeper's accounts, or the writer's sentences, are *involved. Involve* is a stronger word than *implicate,* denoting more complete entanglement. As applied to persons, *implicate* applies only to that which is wrong, while *involve* is more commonly used of that which is unfortunate; one is *implicated* in a crime, *involved* in embarrassments, misfortunes, or perplexities. One is *embroiled* in a serious conflict, *entangled* in a conspiracy, which, once the situation is *complicated* by treachery, may *overwhelm* the participants who are *involved.* As regards logical connection, that which is *included* is usually expressly stated; that which is *implied* is not stated, but is naturally to be inferred; that which is *involved* is necessarily to be inferred, as, a slate roof is *included* in the contract; that the roof shall be watertight is *implied*; the contrary supposition *involves* an absurdity. Compare COMPLEX, PERPLEX. *Antonyms*: disconnect, disentangle, distinguish, explicate, extricate, remove, separate.

in·volved (in·volvd′) *adj.* Intricate; complicated; not easily comprehended. —**in·volv·ed·ness** (in·vol′vid·nis) *n.*

in·vul·ner·a·ble (in·vul′nər·ə·bəl) *adj.* Not capable of being wounded; not to be overcome; having no weak point; unconquerable. —**in·vul′ner·a·bil′i·ty, in·vul′ner·a·ble·ness** *n.* —**in·vul′ner·a·bly** *adv.*

in·wall (in′wôl′) *n.* An inner wall or lining wall, particularly of a blast furnace. —*v.t.* (in·wôl′) To wall in; fortify with a wall.

in·ward (in′wərd) *adv.* **1** Toward the inside, center, or interior. **2** In or on the inside. **3** Into the spirit or mind. Also *inwards.* —*adj.* **1** Situated within, especially with reference to the body; inner: opposed to *outward.* **2** Pertaining to the mind or spirit: an *inward* light. **3** Muffled; low, as the voice. **4** Proceeding toward the inside. **5** Inland. **6** Inherent; intrinsic. —*n. Obs.* An intimate. [OE *inweard*]

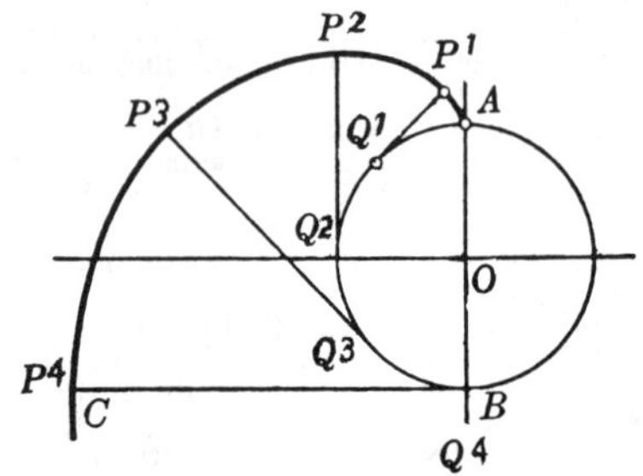

INVOLUTE
Involute *AC* is formed by the locus of point *P* (at P^1, P^2, P^3, P^4) as line *BC* unrolls from curve *BA*. Length of the tangent to the curve (P^1 Q^1, P^2 Q^2, etc.) from any point on the involute *AC* is equal to the length of the curve to the point of tangency ($AQ^1 = P^1Q^1$; $AQ^2 = P^2Q^2$; etc.).

in·ward·ly (in′wərd·lē) *adv.* **1** In an inward manner; especially, in one's thoughts and feelings; with no outward manifestation; secretly. 2 *Rare* Toward the center or interior; inward: to turn *inwardly.* 3 Essentially; inherently; intrinsically. [OE *inweardlīce*]

in·ward·ness (in′wərd·nis) *n.* 1 The inner quality or meaning; true nature or import. 2 The state of being inward or internal, mentally or physically, actually or figuratively. 3 Collectively, the ideas and interests which belong to the life of the mind or spirit, and to its true development. 4 *Obs.* Intimacy.

in·wards (in′wərdz) *adv.* 1 Inward. 2 With respect to taxable imports: duties paid *inwards.* —*n. pl.* Inner or interior parts.

in·weave (in·wēv′) *v.t.* **·wove** or **·weaved, ·woven** (*Obs.* **·wove**), **·weav·ing** To weave in or together; introduce into a fabric as a component part.

in·wind (in·wīnd′) *v.t.* **·wound, ·wind·ing** To wind in or around; entwine.

in·wo·ven (in·wō′vən) *adj.* Woven in; entwined.

in·wrap (in·rap′) See ENWRAP.

in·wreathe (in·rēth′) See ENWREATHE.

in·wrought (in·rôt′) *adj.* Worked into, as a fabric or metalwork, so as to form part of it. See synonyms under INHERENT.

i·o (ē′ō) *interj.* An exclamation expressive of gladness or exultation. [<L <Gk. *iō*]

I·o (ī′ō) In Greek mythology, the daughter of Inachus, who was loved by Zeus and changed by him into a heifer to escape the jealous wrath of Hera, who set hundred-eyed Argus to watch her; when Argus was killed by Hermes on Zeus's orders, Hera sent a gadfly which drove Io to Egypt where she regained her human form.

Io·an·ni·na (yô·ä′nē·nä) A city of NW Greece: also *Janina, Yanina.*

iod– Var. of IODO–.

i·o·date (ī′ə·dāt) *v.t.* **·dat·ed, ·dat·ing** To iodize. —*n. Chem.* A salt of iodic acid. [<IOD- + -ATE[3]] —**i′o·da′tion** *n.*

i·od·ic (ī·od′ik) *adj. Chem.* 1 Of, pertaining to, or containing iodine. 2 Designating a white crystalline acid, HIO_3, used as an oxidizing agent.

i·o·dide (ī′ə·dīd) *n. Chem.* 1 A binary compound of iodine. 2 A salt or compound in which iodine is the acid radical. 3 A salt of hydriodic acid: potassium *iodide.* Also **i′o·did** (-did). [<IOD- + -IDE]

i·o·dim·e·try (ī′ə·dim′ə·trē) *n.* Iodometry. [< *iodi-*, var. of IODO- + -METRY]

i·o·dine (ī′ə·dīn, -din, -dēn) *n.* A bluish-black crystalline element (symbol I) of the halogen group, having a metallic luster and yielding, when heated, corrosive fumes of a rich violet color. It is valuable for its powerful antiseptic properties, and is applied externally as a counterirritant. It is also extensively used in photography and organic synthesis. See ELEMENT. Also **i·o·din** (ī′ə·din). [<F *iode* <Gk. *iōdēs* violetlike (<*ion* a violet + *eidos* form) + -INE[2] (as in *chlorine*); from its violet-colored vapor]

iodine number *Biochem.* The number of milligrams of iodine absorbed from an iodine solution by 100 grams of fat.

i·o·dize (ī′ə·dīz) *v.t.* **·dized, ·diz·ing** 1 To treat with or bring under the influence of iodine. 2 To add iodine to: to *iodize* collodion. 3 To expose to the vapor of iodine. [<IOD- + -IZE] —**i′o·diz′er** *n.* —**i′o·di·za′tion** *n.*

iodo– *combining form* Denoting the presence of, or relation to, iodine: *iodoform.* Also, before vowels, *iod–.*

I·o·do·bis·mi·tol (ī′ə·dō·biz′mə·tol, ·tol) *n.* Proprietary name for a bismuth sodium iodide solution in ethylene glycol with acetic acid: used by intramuscular injection in the treatment of syphilis. [<IODO-+ BISMUTH (arbitrarily altered) + -OL]

i·o·do·form (ī·ō′də·fôrm) *n. Chem.* A light-yellow crystalline compound, CHI_3, formed by the action of iodine on alcohol in a alkaline solution: used in medicine as an antiseptic. [<IODO- + FORM(YL)]

i·o·dol (ī′ə·dōl, -dol) *n. Chem.* A yellowish-brown crystalline compound, C_4I_4NH: used as a substitute for iodoform. [<IOD- + -OL]

i·o·dom·e·try (ī′ə·dom′ə·trē) *n. Chem.* 1 The determination of iodine by volumetric methods. 2 The art of making quantitative determination by the use of standard solutions of iodine, or by the liberation of iodine from an iodide. Also *iodimetry.*[<IODO- + -METRY] —**i·o·do·met·ric** (ī′ə·dō·met′rik) or **·ri·cal** *adj.*

i·o·dous (ī′ə·dəs) *adj. Chem.* 1 Of, pertaining to, or like iodine. 2 Containing iodine in its lower valency. [<IOD- + -OUS]

I·ol·cus (ī·ol′kəs) In classical geography, a city at the foot of Mount Pelion in Thessaly, NE Greece, near modern Volos; traditionally the home of Jason.

i·o·lite (ī′ə·līt) *n.* Cordierite. [<Gk. *ion* violet + -LITE]

i·o moth (ī′ō) A large American moth *(Automeris io)* having conspicuous eyelike spots on the hind wings. The caterpillar has stinging spines. [See IO]

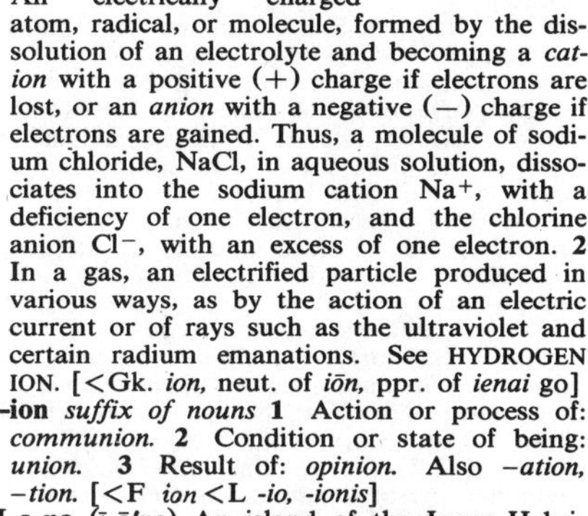

IO MOTH

i·on (ī′ən, ī′on) *n. Physics* 1 An electrically charged atom, radical, or molecule, formed by the dissolution of an electrolyte and becoming a *cation* with a positive (+) charge if electrons are lost, or an *anion* with a negative (−) charge if electrons are gained. Thus, a molecule of sodium chloride, NaCl, in aqueous solution, dissociates into the sodium cation Na^+, with a deficiency of one electron, and the chlorine anion Cl^-, with an excess of one electron. 2 In a gas, an electrified particle produced in various ways, as by the action of an electric current or of rays such as the ultraviolet and certain radium emanations. See HYDROGEN ION. [<Gk. *ion,* neut. of *iōn,* ppr. of *ienai* go]

–ion *suffix of nouns* 1 Action or process of: *communion.* 2 Condition or state of being: *union.* 3 Result of: *opinion.* Also *–ation, –tion.* [<F *ion* <L *-io, -ionis*]

I·o·na (ī·ō′nə) An island of the Inner Hebrides, Scotland; 1½ by 3½ miles; site of monastery established by St. Columba in 563: also *Icolmkill.*

ion engine A reaction engine producing a small but sustained thrust by emission of positive ions accelerated in an electrical field. Compare PLASMA ENGINE.

ion exchange *Chem.* 1 A process whereby ions may be reversibly interchanged at the boundary of a liquid and solid in contact, the composition of the solid not being altered: used especially in water softening with zeolites and in the purification of solutions. 2 A similar process occurring between immiscible electrolytes.

ion exchange resin *Chem.* Any of a class of substances which yield cations and anions in the ion-exchange process.

I·o·ni·a (ī·ō′nē·ə) The coastal region and adjacent islands of western Asia Minor, anciently colonized by Greeks.

I·o·ni·an (ī·ō′nē·ən) *adj.* Pertaining to Ionia, its people, or their culture. —*n.* A member of one of the four major tribes of ancient Greece. The Ionians settled eastern Greece and Ionia about 1100 B.C.

Ionian Islands An island group in the Ionian Sea off the western coast of Greece; 963 square miles.

Ionian Sea A part of the Mediterranean between Greece and Sicily and the foot of the Italian peninsula.

i·on·ic (ī·on′ik) *adj. Chem.* 1 Of, pertaining to, or containing ions. 2 Designating the theory of electrolytic dissociation, according to which the molecules of all acids, bases, and salts dissociate in varying degrees when they are dissolved in water and certain other solvents.

I·on·ic (ī·on′ik) *adj.* 1 Ionian. 2 *Archit.* Of or pertaining to an order of Greek architecture characterized by scroll-like ornaments of the capital. See illustration under CAPITAL. 3 In prosody, designating a metrical foot, consisting either of two long and two short syllables (- - ⏑ ⏑) and called **greater Ionic,** or *Ionic a majore,* or of two short and two long (⏑ ⏑ - -), when it is called **lesser Ionic** or *Ionic a minore.* —*n.* 1 In prosody, an Ionic foot; also, a verse composed of Ionic feet. 2 A dialect of ancient Greek spoken in Ionia and in most of the Aegean Islands, divided into **Old Ionic** or **Epic,** the language of the Homeric poems, and **New Ionic,** of the fifth century B.C., used by Herodotus and Hippocrates. 3 *Printing* A style of type with a large, heavy roman face. [<L *Ionicus* <Gk. *Iōnikos*]

ionic crystal *Physics* A crystal formed chiefly of ions held together by electrostatic attraction.

i·o·ni·um (ī·ō′nē·əm) *n. Physics* The immediate precursor of radium in the radioactive disintegration of uranium: it is an isotope of thorium, of mass 230 and a half-life of about 80,000 years.[<ION + (URAN)IUM; from its ionizing action]

i·on·i·za·tion (ī′ən·ə·zā′shən, -ī·zā′-) *n.* 1 *Chem.* The breaking apart of electrolytes into anions and cations, by solution or other process, mechanical or chemical; electrolytic dissociation. 2 *Physics* The generation of ions by radioactivity. —**degree of ionization** The fraction of the molecules of an electrolyte dissociated or ionized at a given temperature and concentration of solution, usually expressed as a percentage.

ionization chamber *Physics* An enclosed cylinder containing two oppositely charged electrodes and air or other gas: used to determine the intensity of an X-ray beam by its ionizing effect upon the gas.

ionization potential *Physics* The energy, expressed in electron volts, required to remove an electron from an atom by impact: 5.13 is the *ionization potential* for sodium.

i·on·ize (ī′ən·īz) *v.t.* **·ized, ·iz·ing** 1 To convert, totally or in part, into ions. 2 To divide into ions. —**i′on·iz′a·ble** *adj.* —**i′on·iz′er** *n.*

i·on·o·gen·ic (ī′ən·ə·jen′ik) *adj. Chem.* Forming or supplying ions, as an electrolyte.

i·o·none (ī′ə·nōn) *n. Chem.* Either of two isomeric compounds, $C_{13}H_{20}O$, related to the terpenes and containing the aromatic principle of violet and orrisroot. [<Gk. *ion* violet + -ONE]

i·on·o·pause (ī·on′ə·pôz) *n.* The zone of transition between the ionosphere and the exosphere, beginning at a height of about 400 miles beyond the earth's surface. [<IONO- (< ION)+ PAUSE]

i·on·o·sphere (ī·on′ə·sfir) *n.* An upper layer of the earth's atmosphere above the mesosphere consisting of several layers subject to ionization, with seasonal variations: it is a part of the Heaviside layer responsible for the reflection of radio waves [<IONO- (<ION) + SPHERE]

i·on·to·pho·re·sis (ī·on′to·fə·rē′sis) *n. Med.* Treatment by the introduction of ions into the body; therapeutic ionization of affected organs and tissues. Also **i·on·o·ther·a·py** (ī′ən·ō·ther′·ə·pē). [<*ionto-*, combining form of ION + PHORESIS]

i·o·pho·bi·a (ī′ə·fō′bē·ə) *n.* Toxicophobia. [< Gk. *ios* venom + -PHOBIA]

I·os (ē′os) An Aegean island in the Cyclades; 43 square miles: also *Nios.*

Iosh·kar–O·la (yosh·kär′o·lä′) The capital of Mari Autonomous S.S.R.

i·o·ta (ī·ō′tə) *n.* 1 The ninth letter and fourth vowel in the Greek alphabet (Ι, ι): corresponding to English I, i. As a numeral it denotes 10. 2 A small or insignificant mark or part. See synonyms under PARTICLE. [<L < Gk. *iōta.* Doublet of JOT.]

i·o·ta·cism (ī·ō′tə·siz′əm) *n.* Over-frequent use of the letter iota (Ι) or of its sound, also, the practice in modern Greek of giving the pronunciation of iota (ē) to certain diphthongs and long vowels. [<LL *iotacismus* <Gk. *iōtakismos*]

I O U 1 A paper having on it these letters (meaning *I owe you*) followed by a named sum and duly signed. 2 A symbol and acknowledgment of indebtedness. Also **I.O.U.**

I·o·wa (ī′ə·wə) *n. pl.* **·was** or **·wa** 1 One of a North American tribe of Siouan Indians, formerly living in Minnesota, and now on reservations in Oklahoma and Kansas. 2 The Siouan language of this tribe.

I·o·wa (ī′ə·wə, ī′ə·wā) A north central State of the United States; 56,280 square miles; capital, Des Moines; entered the Union Dec. 28, 1846; nickname *Hawkeye State*: abbr. IA —**I′o·wan** *adj. & n.*

Iowa River A river in Iowa, flowing 329 miles SE to the Mississippi.

ip·e·cac (ip′ə·kak) *n.* 1 A South American creeping or shrubby plant *(Cephaelis ipecacuanha)* of the madder family, yielding the medicinal alkaloids emetine and cephaeline. **2** An extract or tincture of the root of this plant, generally used as an emetic, but also having cathartic properties; also, the root itself. Also **ip·e·cac·u·an·ha** (ip′ə·kak′yōō·ä′nə). [<Pg. *ipecacuanha* <Tupian *ipi–kaa–guéne* < *ipe* little + *kaa* tree, herb + *guéne* causing sickness]

ipecacuanha wine Wine in which ipecac has been steeped: used medicinally.

Iph·i·cles (if′ə·klēz) In Greek legend, the son of Amphitryon and Alcmene; twin brother of Hercules.

Iph·i·ge·ni·a (if′ə·jə·nī′ə) In Greek legend, the daughter of Agamemnon and Clytemnestra, sacrificed by her father at Aulis to Artemis, who rescued her and made her a priestess in Tauris: here she later rescued her brother Orestes and fled with him to Greece.

I·pin (ē′pin′) A city on the Yangtze in south central China: formerly *Suchow.*

I·poh (ē′pō) The capital of Perak State, Malaya.

ip·o·moe·a (ip′ə·mē′ə) *n.* Any of a large genus *(Ipomoea)* of mainly tropical herbs, or, rarely, shrubs or trees, of the convolvulus family, with trumpet–shaped flowers, including the morning–glory and sweet potato. Also **ip′o·me′a.** [<NL <Gk. *ips, ipos* sort of horn + *homoios* like]

IPOMOEA

Ip·po·li·tov–I·va·nov (ē·pô·lē′tôf·ē·vä′nôf), **Mik·hail,** 1859–1935, Russian composer.

Ip·sam·bul (ip·säm·bōōl′) See Abu Simbel.

ip·se dix·it (ip′sē dik′sit) *Latin* Literally, he himself has said; hence, a dogmatic assertion; dictum. [<L]

ip·sis·si·ma ver·ba (ip·sis′ə·mə vûr′bə) *Latin* The very words; the exact language. In a different grammatical case, **ipsissimis verbis,** the phrase means "in the very words."

ip·so fac·to (ip′sō fak′tō) *Latin* By the fact itself, or in and by the very fact or act: *ipso facto* outlawed. [<L]

ip·so ju·re (ip′sō jōōr′ē) *Latin* By the law itself.

Ip·sus (ip′səs) An ancient town in southern Phrygia, Asia Minor; scene of a victory of Lysimachus, 301 B.C.

Ips·wich (ips′wich) The county town of Suffolk, SE England.

I·qui·que (ē·kē′kā) A port in northern Chile.

I·qui·tos (ē·kē′tōs) A port on the upper Amazon, NE Peru.

ir– Assimilated var. of in–[1] and in–[2].

i·ra·cund (ī′rə·kund) *adj.* Angry, or easily angered; choleric; passionate. [<L *iracundus* < *ira* anger] **—i′ra·cun′di·ty** *n.*

i·ra·de (i·rä′dē) *n.* A decree of the Sublime Porte or of any Moslem ruler. Also **i·ra′deh.** [<Turkish <Arabic *irādah* will, desire]

I·ran (i·ran′, ē·rän′) A kingdom of SW Asia; 630,000 square miles; capital, Teheran: officially called *Persia* until March, 1935.

I·ra·ni·an (ī·rā′nē·ən) *adj.* Belonging or relating to Iran or Persia. **—***n.* **1** A modern Persian. **2** A member of the ancient Persian or Iranian race. **3** A branch of the Indo–Iranian subfamily of Indo–European languages, embracing Afghan or Pushtu in the east and, in the west, Avestan, Old Persian, Middle Persian, Scythian, etc., modern Persian, Kurdish, and other ancient and modern tongues of Persia, Caucasia, etc. **—I·ran·ic** (ī·ran′ik) *adj.*

Iranian Plateau The upland, mostly in Iran, extending from the Tigris to the Indus.

I·raq (i·rak′, ē·räk′) A kingdom approximately coextensive with ancient Mesopotamia in SW Asia; 168,040 square miles; capital, Baghdad; with Jordan, formed the Arab Federation, 1958. Also **I·rak′.**

I·ra·qi (ē·rä′kē) *adj.* Of or pertaining to Iraq, its inhabitants, or their language. **—***n.* **1** A native or inhabitant of the kingdom of Iraq. **2** The dialect of Arabic spoken in Iraq.

i·ras·ci·ble (i·ras′ə·bəl, ī–) *adj.* **1** Prone to anger; choleric. **2** Caused by anger. See synonyms under hot. [<F <LL *irascibilis* < *irasci* be angry < *ira* anger] **—i·ras′ci·bil′i·ty, i·ras′·ci·ble·ness** *n.* **—i·ras′ci·bly** *adv.*

i·ra·ta·men·te (ē·rä′tä·men′tā) *adv. Music* Angrily; indignantly; passionately: a direction as to the style of playing a composition or passage. [<Ital.]

i·rate (ī′rāt, ī·rāt′) *adj.* Moved to anger; wrathful. See synonyms under bitter. [<L *iratus*, pp. of *irasci* be angry] **—i′rate·ly** *adv.*

I·ra·zú (ē·rä·zōō′) A volcano in central Costa Rica; 11,260 feet.

IRBM The intermediate range ballistic missile, having a range of 1500 miles. Compare *ICBM.*

ire (īr) *n.* Strong resentment; wrath; anger. See synonyms under anger. [<OF <L *ira* . anger]

ire·ful (īr′fəl) *adj.* Full of ire; wrathful; angry. **—ire′ful·ly** *adv.* **—ire′ful·ness** *n.*

Ire·land (īr′lənd) The westernmost and second largest of the British Isles; 31,838 square miles; divided into: **1 Northern Ireland,** a part of the United Kingdom comprising six counties and two boroughs of the former province of Ulster in the north; 5,237 square miles; capital, Belfast; and **2** the **Republic of Ireland,** independent (1949) of the Commonwealth of Nations and comprising 26 southern counties; 26,600 square miles; capital, Dublin: formerly *Irish Free State* (Irish *Saorstat Eireann*), 1922–37; *Eire,* 1937–49.

I·re·nae·us (ī′rə·nē′əs), **Saint** Greek church father of the second century; bishop of Lyons.

I·rene (ī·rēn′; *Ger.* ē·rā′nə, *Ital.* ē·rā′nā) A feminine personal name. Also *Fr.* **I·rène** (ē·ren′). [<Gk., peace]

—Irene In Greek mythology, the goddess of peace, daughter of Zeus and Themis: identified with the Roman *Pax.*

—Irene, 752–803, Byzantine empress, wife of Leo IV, East Roman emperor.

i·ren·ic (ī·ren′ik) *adj.* Tending to promote peace; conciliatory. Also **i·ren′i·cal.** [<Gk. *eirēnikos* < *eirēnē* peace]

i·ren·ics (ī·ren′iks) *n.* Irenical theology; theology concerned with promoting Christian unity.

Ire·ton (īr′tən), **Henry,** 1611–51, English parliamentary general.

i·ri·da·ceous (ī′rə·dā′shəs, ir′ə–) *adj.* Relating to a family *(Iridaceae)* of perennial herbs, the iris family. [<Gk. *iris, iridos* iris + -aceous]

ir·i·dec·to·my (ir′ə·dek′tə·mē, ī′rə–) *n. Surg.* The operation of removing a part of the iris. [<irid(o)- + -ectomy]

ir·i·des·cence (ir′ə·des′əns) *n. Optics* The many–colored appearance caused by the interference effect of light rays striking the outer and inner surface layers of various bodies, as clouds, mother–of–pearl, oil films, etc. [< iridescent <Gk. *iris, iridos* rainbow + -escence] **—ir′i·des′cent** *adj.* **—ir′i·des′cent·ly** *adv.*

i·rid·ic (i·rid′ik, ī–) *adj. Chem.* Of, pertaining to, or containing iridium in its higher valence: *iridic* bromide, $IrBr_4$. [<irid(ium) + -ic]

i·rid·i·um (i·rid′ē·əm, ī–) *n.* A brittle, silver–gray, metallic element (symbol Ir) of extreme hardness belonging to the platinum group: discovered by William Tennant in 1904. It is used in certain alloys, for penpoints, jewelry, etc. [<NL <L *iris, iridis* rainbow <Gk. *Iris* goddess of the rainbow + -ium; from the iridescence of some of its salts]

irido– *combining form Med.* Iris of the eye: *iridotomy.* Also, before vowels, **irid–.** [<Gk. *iris, iridos* the iris]

i·rid·o·cyte (i·rid′ə·sīt, ī–) *n. Biol.* A cell having the power to produce color in an organism, especially a cell containing guanine and located in the integument of the cuttlefish. [<L *iris, iridos* rainbow <Gk. *iris* + -cyte]

ir·i·do·ple·gi·a (ir′ə·do·plē′jē·ə, ī′rə–) *n. Pathol.* Paralysis of the sphincter of the iris, resulting in an inability of the pupil to contract. **—ir′i·do·pleg′ic** (-plej′ik, -plē′jik) *adj.*

ir·i·dos·mi·um (ir′ə·doz′mē·əm, -dos′-, ī′rə–) *n.* Osmiridium. Also **ir·i·dos·mine** (ir′ə·doz′·min, -dos′-, ī′rə–). [<irid(ium) + osmium]

ir·i·dot·o·my (ir′ə·dot′ə·mē, ī′rə–) *n. pl.* **·mies** *Surg.* Any incision into the iris. [<irido- + -tomy]

I·ri·go·yen (ē·rē·gō′yen), **Hipólito,** 1852–1933, president of Argentina 1916–22, and 1928–30.

i·ris (ī′ris) *n. pl.* **i·ris·es** or **ir·i·des** (ir′·ə·dēz, ī′rə–) **1** *Anat.* The colored circular, contractile membrane between the cornea and the lens of the eye, whose central perforation is occupied by the pupil. See illustration under eye. **2** *Bot.* Any one of a notable genus *(Iris)* of plants with sword–shaped leaves and large handsome flowers: the cultivated varieties are also known as *fleur–de–lis.* **3** The orris. **4** The rainbow; any similar iridescent appearance. **5** Rainbow quartz. [<L *iris* rainbow, iris <Gk. *iris*]

IRIS
a. Bearded iris.
b. Japanese iris.
c. Siberian iris.

I·ris (ī′ris) In Greek mythology the goddess of the rainbow, attendant of Zeus and Hera; in Homer's *Illiad,* the messenger of the gods.

I·ris (ī′ris) The ancient name for the Yesil Irmak, Turkey.

i·ris·at·ed (ī′rə·sā′tid) *adj.* Iridescent. **—i′ris·a′tion** *n.*

iris diaphragm An adjustable diaphragm, like the iris of the eye, designed for regulating the size of an aperture, as in a camera lens.

i·rised (ī′rist) *adj.* Having colors like those of the rainbow.

I·rish (ī′rish) *adj.* Pertaining to Ireland, its people, or their language. **—***n.* **1** The people of Ireland collectively: with *the.* **2** The ancient or modern language of Ireland, belonging to the Goidelic branch of the Celtic languages; Irish Gaelic: sometimes called *Erse.* Historically, the language is divided into **Old Irish,** from approximately 700 to 1100; **Middle Irish,** from 1100 to 1600; and **Modern Irish,** after 1600. **3** The dialect of English spoken in Ireland; Irish English. **4** *Colloq.* Temper: He got his *Irish* up. [ME *Irisc,* OE *Īras* <ON *Īrar* the Irish <OIrish *Ēriu* Ireland. Cf. Eire.]

Irish bridge *Engin.* A surface of reinforced concrete laid on the bed of a river, over which flood waters may run without causing damage.

Irish English See Irish (def. 3).

I·rish·er (ī′rish·ər) *n. U.S. Slang* An Irish settler in the United States.

Irish Free State A former name for the Republic of Ireland. See under Ireland.

Irish Gaelic See Irish (def 2).

I·rish·ism (ī′rish·iz′əm) *n.* **1** An expression or idiom characteristic of the Irish; Hibernianism. **2** Irish character or traits collectively.

I·rish·man (ī′rish·mən) *n. pl.* **·men** (-mən) A man of Irish birth or race.

Irish moss A seaweed *(Chondrus crispus)* found off the coasts of Ireland and North America: used as a food, especially in blanc–mange, and in medicine and industry; carrageen.

Irish potato The common or white potato *(Solanum tuberosum),* as distinguished from the sweet potato.

Irish Republican Army An anti–British secret organization originally organized in behalf of Irish independence and outlawed by the Irish government in 1936, but continuing terrorist activities to force annexation of Northern Ireland.

I·rish·ry (ī′rish·rē) *n. pl.* **·ries 1** The Irish collectively, or a company of Irish. **2** Irishism.

Irish Sea The arm of the Atlantic separating Ireland from England, Scotland, and Wales; 130 miles long, 130 miles wide.

Irish setter See under setter.

Irish stew A stew made originally with mutton, potatoes, and onions; now with almost any meat and vegetables.

Irish terrier See under terrier.

Irish water spaniel See under SPANIEL.

Irish wolfhound A large, powerful dog of an ancient breed used in hunting wolf and elk; characterized by straight, heavy forelegs and a hard, rough coat, usually gray, brindle, black, fawn, or white in color.

IRISH WOLFHOUND (From 30 to 38 inches high at the shoulder)

I·rish·wom·an (ī′·rish·wo͝om′ən) *n. pl.* **·wom·en** (-wim′in) A woman of Irish birth or race.

i·ri·tis (ī·rī′tis) *n. Pathol.* Inflammation of the iris. Also **i·ri·si·tis** (ī′rə·sī′tis). [<NL <L *iris* iris + -ITIS] — **i·rit·ic** (ī·rit′ik) *adj.*

irk (ûrk) *v.t.* To annoy or weary; irritate; disgust; vex. [ME *irken*; origin uncertain]

irk·some (ûrk′səm) *adj.* Troublesome or tiresome; tedious. See synonyms under TEDIOUS, TROUBLESOME, WEARISOME. — **irk′some·ly** *adv.* — **irk′some·ness** *n.*

Ir·kutsk 1 A region (oblast) in southern Siberia, Russia, near Lake Baikal in central Asia. 2 The chief city of this region, pop. 640,000.

i·ron (ī′ərn) *n.* 1 A tough, abundant, malleable, ductile, and strongly magnetic metallic element (symbol Fe). Easily oxidized in moist air and attacked by many reagents, iron is seldom obtained in its pure, silver-white form, but occurs widely in both ferrous and ferric compounds, and combines in varying proportions with carbon, phosphorus, silicon, sulfur, etc. Typical commercial varieties are: cast iron, pig iron, steel, and wrought iron. 2 An iron tool, weapon, utensil, or anything composed of iron. 3 *pl.* Fetters, especially shackles for the feet. 4 A metal-headed golf club with the face slightly laid back. 5 In the leather industry, a unit of thickness, equal to one forty-eighth of an inch. 6 A flatiron. — **in irons** 1 Fettered. 2 *Naut.* Unable to cast away on either side; in stays: said of a vessel coming about into the wind. — *adj.* 1 Made of iron. 2 Resembling iron; hard; rude; heavy; also, firm; unyielding: an *iron* will. 3 Of or pertaining to the Iron Age. — *v.t.* 1 To smooth or press with an iron implement, as cloth or clothing. 2 To fetter. 3 To furnish or arm with iron. — *v.i.* 4 To smooth or press cloth, clothing, etc., with an iron implement. — **to iron out** To smooth out; remove. [OE *īren, īsen, īsern*] — **i′ron·er** *n.*

Iron Age *Archeol.* The last and most advanced of the three roughly classified prehistoric stages of human progress, preceded by the Stone Age and Bronze Age.

i·ron·bark (ī′ərn·bärk′) *n.* Any one of a genus (*Eucalyptus*) of large, valuable Australian timber trees having a solid rather than a fibrous, stringy, or scaly bark.

iron black Finely divided antimony.

i·ron·bound (ī′ərn·bound′) *adj.* 1 Bound with iron. 2 Faced or surrounded with rocks; rugged. 3 Hard to change; unyielding.

i·ron·clad (ī′ərn·klad′) *adj.* 1 Protected by iron or steel armor, as warships. 2 Not to be evaded; rigorous. 3 Strong. — *n.* A warship sheathed with armor: a term not common since the Spanish-American War.

iron curtain An impenetrable barrier of secrecy and censorship: a term made current by Winston Churchill in a speech in Fulton, Missouri (1946), to describe the dividing line between Western Europe and the Soviet sphere of influence.

i·rone (ī·rōn′) *n. Chem.* A colorless, volatile, aromatic oil, $C_{14}H_{22}O$, extracted from orrisroot and used in perfumery. [<IR(IS) + -ONE]

iron froth A spongy variety of hematite.

Iron Gate A narrow pass in the valley of the Danube, SW Rumania, on the Yugoslav border: German *Eisernes Tor. Rumanian* **Por·ți·le de Fier** (pôr·tsē′le de fyer′). Also **Iron Gates.**

iron glance A crystallized variety of hematite.

iron gray The color of freshly cut or broken iron. Also **iron grey.** — **i′ron-gray′** *adj.*

i·ron-hand·ed (ī′ərn·han′did) *adj.* Severe and rigorous; despotic.

iron hat See GOSSAN.

iron horse A railroad engine.

i·ron·ic (ī·ron′ik) *adj.* 1 Conveying a meaning that contradicts the literal sense of the words used: an *ironic* comment. 2 Being the reverse of what was expected: an *ironic* event. 3 Of the nature of or given to the use of irony. Also **i·ron′i·cal** (-i·kəl). — **i·ron′i·cal·ly** *adv.* — **i·ron′·i·cal·ness** *n.*

i·ron·ing (ī′ər·ning) *n.* The process of pressing and smoothing with flatirons.

iron lung A cabinetlike enclosure used in the treatment of pulmonary disorders, fitted with automatically operated bellows, in order to promote the rhythmic action of the impaired lungs and thus maintain respiration in the patient who lies within it, his head only exposed: also called *Drinker respirator.*

i·ron·mas·ter (ī′ərn·mas′ter, -mäs′-) *n.* A manufacturer of iron.

i·ron·mon·ger (ī′ərn·mung′gər, -mong′-) *n.* A dealer in iron articles.

i·ron·mon·ger·y (ī′ərn·mung′gər·ē, -mong′-) *n. pl.* **·ger·ies** 1 Iron articles collectively; hardware. 2 Trade in such articles. 3 An ironmonger's place of business. 4 Humorously, firearms.

iron putty See under PUTTY.

iron pyrites 1 Ordinary pyrites; fool's-gold. 2 Marcasite. 3 Pyrrhotite.

i·ron·side (ī′ərn·sīd′) *n.* A person or thing of tremendous strength or endurance.

I·ron·sides (ī′ərn·sīdz′) *n. pl.* 1 Nickname of Edmund II of England. 2 Nickname of Oliver Cromwell. 3 One of Cromwell's soldiers. — **Old Ironsides** See CONSTITUTION.

i·ron·smith (ī′ərn·smith′) *n.* A worker in iron; a blacksmith.

i·ron·stone (ī′ərn·stōn′) *n.* Any mineral or rock containing iron; iron ore.

i·ron·ware (ī′ərn·wâr′) *n.* Hardware; iron utensils.

i·ron·weed (ī′ərn·wēd′) *n.* An herb or shrub (genus *Vernonia*) of the composite family, from three to six feet high, with alternate leaves, and heads of perfect, tubular, mostly purple or reddish flowers.

i·ron·wood (ī′ərn·wo͝od′) *n.* Any of various trees of unusually hard, heavy, or strong wood; especially, the Catalina ironwood (*Lyonothamnus floribundus*) of southern California and the hop hornbeam (*Ostrya virginiana*) of the eastern United States.

i·ron·work (ī′ərn·wûrk′) *n.* Anything made of iron, as parts of a building. — **i′ron·work′er** *n.*

i·ron·works (ī′ərn·wûrks′) *n. sing. & pl.* An establishment for the manufacture of iron or of heavy ironwork.

i·ron·wort (ī′ərn·wûrt′) *n.* Any of various plants of the mint family, especially the red hemp nettle.

i·ro·ny[1] (ī′rə·nē) *n. pl.* **·nies** 1 The use of words to signify the opposite of what they usually express; ridicule disguised as praise or compliment; covert sarcasm or satire. 2 The feigning of ignorance, as in the Socratic method of questions and answers: hence **Socratic irony.** 3 A condition of affairs or events exactly the reverse of what was expected: the *irony* of fate. [<L *ironia* <Gk. *eirōneia* < *eirōn* dissembler < *erein* question, ask]

i·ron·y[2] (ī′ər·nē) *adj.* Of or like iron.

Ir·o·quoi·an (ir′ə·kwoi′ən) *n.* 1 A large North American Indian linguistic stock including the Cayuga, Cherokee, Conestoga, Erie, Mohawk, Oneida, Onondaga, Seneca, Tuscarora, Wyandot, and certain other tribes. 2 A member of any of the Iroquoian tribes. — *adj.* Of or pertaining to the Iroquois Indians, or to any of their languages.

Ir·o·quois (ir′ə·kwoi, -kwoiz) *n. pl.* **·quois** 1 A member of any of the powerful North American Indian tribes comprising the confederacy known as the Five Nations. See FIVE NATIONS. 2 A member of any tribe belonging to the Iroquoian linguistic stock. [<F <Algonquian *Irinakoiw*, lit., real adders]

ir·ra·di·ant (i·rā′dē·ənt) *adj.* Sending out rays of light. [<L *irradians, -antis*, ppr. of *irradiare* shine] — **ir·ra′di·ance, ir·ra′di·an·cy** *n.*

ir·ra·di·ate (i·rā′dē·āt) *v.* **·at·ed, ·at·ing** *v.t.* 1 To direct light upon; light up; illuminate. 2 To make clear or understandable; enlighten. 3 To send forth in or as in rays of light; diffuse; radiate. 4 To treat with or subject to X-rays, ultraviolet light, or other radiant energy. 5 To heat with radiant energy. — *v.i.* 6 To emit rays; shine. 7 To become radiant. [<L *irradiatus*, pp. of *irradiare* < *in-* thoroughly + *radiare* shine < *radius* ray] — **ir·ra′·di·a′tive** *adj.* — **ir·ra′di·a′tor** *n.*

ir·ra·di·a·tion (i·rā′dē·ā′shən) *n.* 1 The act of irradiating. 2 The state of being irradiated. 3 Rays emitted: the *irradiation* of a candle. 4 *Optics* An apparent enlargement of a bright object, when seen against a dark background, due to the fact that the rays of light do not converge accurately to a focus upon the retina. 5 The application, to a person, substance, or object, of any form of radiant energy, for therapeutic, preservative, or other purposes. 6 The amount or intensity of radiation falling on a surface in a given time. 7 *Physiol.* A diffusion or branching out of afferent nerve impulses or of conditioned reflexes.

ir·ra·tion·al (i·rash′ən·əl) *adj.* 1 Not possessed of or not exercising reasoning powers. 2 *Math.* a Pertaining to an irrational number. b Denoting an algebraic expression containing variables that are irreducible, as $\sqrt{-1}, \sqrt[3]{x^2}$. Compare RATIONAL. 3 Contrary to reason; absurd. 4 In Greek and Latin prosody, not keeping the proper ratio between thesis and arsis, as a long syllable used in place of a short one. See synonyms under ABSURD, INSANE. [<L *irrationalis*] — **ir·ra′tion·al·ly** *adv.*

ir·ra·tion·al·ism (i·rash′ən·əl·iz′əm) *n.* A belief or philosophy that is not grounded in reason.

ir·ra·tion·al·i·ty (i·rash′ə·nal′ə·tē) *n. pl.* **·ties** 1 The state of lacking reason or understanding. 2 Something irrational or absurd. Also **ir·ra′tion·al·ness.**

irrational number See under NUMBER.

Ir·ra·wad·dy (ir′ə·wä′dē) A river rising in Tibet and flowing 1,000 miles south through Burma to the Bay of Bengal.

ir·re·cip·ro·cal (ir′i·sip′rə·kəl) *adj.* 1 Not reciprocal; wanting in mutual interaction, assistance, or exchange. 2 Designating a type of colony or group whose members do not contribute equally to the general welfare.

ir·re·claim·a·ble (ir′i·klā′mə·bəl) *adj.* That cannot be reclaimed or redeemed. — **ir′re·claim′a·bil′i·ty, ir′re·claim′a·ble·ness** *n.* — **ir′·re·claim′a·bly** *adv.*

ir·rec·on·cil·a·ble (i·rek′ən·sī′lə·bəl, i·rek′ən·sī′lə·bəl) *adj.* That cannot be reconciled: *irreconcilable* enemies. — *n.* One who will not agree or become reconciled: said especially of political factionists. — **ir·rec′on·cil′a·bil′i·ty, ir·rec′on·cil′a·ble·ness** *n.* — **ir·rec′on·cil′a·bly** *adv.*

ir·re·cov·er·a·ble (ir′i·kuv′er·ə·bəl) *adj.* That cannot be recovered or regained; irredeemable; lost beyond recall. — **ir′re·cov′er·a·ble·ness** *n.* — **ir′re·cov′er·a·bly** *adv.*

ir·re·cu·sa·ble (ir′i·kyo͞o′zə·bəl) *adj.* That cannot be rejected. [<F *irrécusable* <LL *irrecusabilis* < *in-* not + *recusabilis* that should be rejected < *recusare* reject] — **ir′re·cu′sa·bly** *adv.*

ir·re·deem·a·ble (ir′i·dē′mə·bəl) *adj.* 1 Not to be redeemed or replaced by an equivalent. 2 That cannot be reclaimed; not to be atoned for or escaped from: an *irredeemable* scoundrel, crime, or slavery. 3 Not ended by payment of principal: an *irredeemable* annuity. — **ir′re·deem′a·bly** *adv.*

ir·re·den·ta (ir′rā·den′tä) *adj. Italian* Unredeemed: said of a separated territory whose reunion with the mother country is sought.

Ir·re·den·tist (ir′i·den′tist) *n.* 1 One of a party formed in Italy about 1878 to secure the incorporation with that country of regions Italian in speech and race, but subject to other governments. 2 Any person or party that advocates the reunion with the "mother country" of a separate or separated national group or region. — *adj.* Of or pertaining to the Irredentists or their policies. [<Ital. *irredentista* <(*Italia*) *irredenta* unredeemed (Italy), fem. of *irredento* <L *in-* not + *redemptus* redeemed. See REDEEM.] — **Ir′re·den′·tism** *n.*

ir·re·duc·i·ble (ir′i·do͞o′sə·bəl, -dyo͞o′-) *adj.* Not reducible.

ir·ref·ra·ga·ble (i·ref′rə·gə·bəl) *adj.* That cannot be refuted or disproved. [<LL *irrefragabilis* < *in-* not + *refragari* oppose] — **ir·ref′·ra·ga·bil′i·ty, ir·ref′ra·ga·ble·ness** *n.* — **ir·ref′ra·ga·bly** *adv.*

ir·re·fran·gi·ble (ir′i·fran′jə·bəl) *adj.* **1** That cannot be broken or violated: an *irrefrangible* law. **2** Not susceptible of refraction: said of light rays. — **ir′re·fran′gi·bly** *adv.*

ir·ref·u·ta·ble (i·ref′yə·tə·bəl, ir′i·fyo͞o′tə·bəl) *adj.* Not refutable; that cannot be disproved; irrefragable, as an argument. — **ir·ref′u·ta·bil′i·ty** *n.* — **ir·ref′u·ta·bly** *adv.*

ir·re·gard·less (ir′i·gärd′lis) *adj.* & *adv. Illit.* Regardless: an incorrect or humorous usage.

ir·reg·u·lar (i·reg′yə·lər) *adj.* **1** Not regular; departing from or being out of the usual or proper form, order, course, method, proportion, etc. **2** Not conforming in action or character to rule, duty, discipline, etc.; lawless: *irregular* habits. **3** *Bot.* Exhibiting a want of symmetry in form and size: said of flowers in which the members of the various whorls differ from one another in size or shape. **4** Laboring under an ecclesiastical irregularity. See IRREGULARITY (def. 2). **5** Not belonging to a regular military force: *irregular* troops. **6** *Gram.* Not inflected or conjugated according to the most prevalent pattern: *irregular* verbs. See STRONG (def. 28). **7** *Law* Not according to rule; improper; not complying with legal formalities. —*n.* A person exercising a calling or profession without belonging to its regular organization or conforming to its regulations, as a soldier not in a regular military force. [<OF *irreguler* <Med. L *irregularis*] — **ir·reg′u·lar·ly** *adv.*

Synonyms (adj.): abnormal, anomalous, confused, crooked, desultory, devious, disorderly, dissolute, eccentric, erratic, exceptional, fitful, immoderate, inordinate, uneven, unnatural, unsettled, unsymmetrical, unsystematic, unusual, variable, vicious, wandering, wild. *Antonyms*: common, constant, established, fixed, formal, methodical, natural, normal, orderly, ordinary, periodical, punctual, regular, stated, steady, systematic, uniform, universal, unvarying, usual.

ir·reg·u·lar·i·ty (i·reg′yə·lar′ə·tē) *n. pl.* **·ties** **1** The condition of being irregular; an aberration, inconsistency, etc. **2** In the Roman Catholic and Anglican churches, an impediment to the taking or performing the functions of orders. See synonyms under DISORDER.

ir·rel·a·tive (i·rel′ə·tiv) *adj.* **1** Not relative; unconnected. **2** *Music* Having no common tone. — **ir·rel′a·tive·ly** *adv.* — **ir·rel′a·tive·ness** *n.*

ir·rel·e·vant (i·rel′ə·vənt) *adj.* Not relevant; not apposite; impertinent. See synonyms under ALIEN, INSIGNIFICANT. — **ir·rel′e·vance, ir·rel′e·van·cy** *n.* — **ir·rel′e·vant·ly** *adv.*

ir·re·liev·a·ble (ir′i·lē′və·bəl) *adj.* That cannot be relieved.

ir·re·lig·ion (ir′i·lij′ən) *n.* The state of being without or opposed to religion; unbelief; ungodliness. [<F *irréligion*] — **ir′re·lig′ion·ist** *n.*

ir·re·lig·ious (ir′i·lij′əs) *adj.* **1** Not religious; indifferent or hostile to religion. **2** Profane or sinful; ungodly. — **ir′re·lig′ious·ly** *adv.* — **ir′·re·lig′ious·ness** *n.*

ir·rem·e·a·ble (i·rem′ē·ə·bəl, i·rē′mē-) *adj.* Admitting no return, irretraceable. [<L *irremeabilis* < *in-* not + *remeabilis* returning < *remeare* return < *re-* back + *meare* go] — **ir·rem′e·a·bly** *adv.*

ir·re·me·di·a·ble (ir′i·mē′dē·ə·bəl) *adj.* Not to be remedied; incurable; irreparable. [<L *irremediabilis*] — **ir′re·me′di·a·ble·ness** *n.* — **ir′re·me′di·a·bly** *adv.*

ir·re·mis·si·bil·i·ty (ir′i·mis′ə·bil′ə·tē) *n.* Impossibility of being forgiven; the state of being without remission. — **ir′re·mis′si·ble** *adj.* — **ir′re·mis′si·ble·ness** *n.* — **ir′re·mis′si·bly** *adv.*

ir·re·mov·a·bil·i·ty (ir′i·mo͞o′və·bil′ə·tē) *n.* **1** Perpetuity. **2** The quality of certain offices implying that the incumbent's appointment is for the term of his natural life.

ir·re·mov·a·ble (ir′i·mo͞o′və·bəl) *adj.* Not removable; permanent. — **ir′re·mov′a·bly** *adv.*

ir·rep·a·ra·ble (i·rep′ər·ə·bəl) *adj.* That cannot be repaired, rectified, or made amends for. — **ir·rep′a·ra·bil′i·ty, ir·rep′a·ra·ble·ness** *n.* — **ir·rep′a·ra·bly** *adv.*

ir·re·peal·a·ble (ir′i·pē′lə·bəl) *adj.* Not repealable.

ir·re·place·a·ble (ir′i·plā′sə·bəl) *adj.* Not capable of being replaced.

ir·re·plev·i·sa·ble (ir′i·plev′ə·sə·bəl) *adj. Law* That cannot be replevied. Also **ir′re·plev′i·a·ble** (-plev′ē·ə·bəl). [<IR- + AF *replevisable* repleviable <OF *replevir* replevy. See REPLEVIN.]

ir·re·pres·si·ble (ir′i·pres′ə·bəl) *adj.* Not repressible; that cannot be restrained. — **ir′re·pres′si·ble·ness, ir′re·pres′si·bil′i·ty** *n.* — **ir′re·pres′si·bly** *adv.*

ir·re·proach·a·ble (ir′i·prō′chə·bəl) *adj.* Not reproachable; blameless. [<F *irréprochable*] — **ir′re·proach′a·ble·ness** *n.* — **ir′re·proach′a·bly** *adv.*

ir·re·sis·ti·ble (ir′i·zis′tə·bəl) *adj.* Not resistible; that cannot be successfully withstood or opposed. — **ir′re·sis′ti·bil′i·ty, ir′re·sis′ti·ble·ness** *n.* — **ir′re·sis′ti·bly** *adv.*

ir·res·o·lu·ble (i·rez′ə·lo͝o·bəl) *adj.* **1** Not resoluble. **2** Not to be relieved; beyond help. **3** Not solvable; insoluble.

ir·res·o·lute (i·rez′ə·lo͞ot) *adj.* Not resolute or resolved; wavering; hesitating. — **ir·res′o·lute′·ly** *adv.* — **ir·res′o·lute′ness, ir·res′o·lu′tion** *n.*

Synonyms: capricious, doubtful, faint-hearted, faltering, fickle, fitful, half-hearted, hesitant, hesitating, indecisive, undecided, vacillating, wavering. Indecision denotes lack of intellectual conviction; irresolution denotes defect of volition, weakness of will. A thoughtful man may be *undecided* as to the course to take in perplexing circumstances; yet when decided he may act with promptness; an *irresolute* man lacks the nerve to act. Indecision commonly denotes a temporary state or condition, irresolution a trait of character. See FAINT, FICKLE. *Antonyms*: decided, determined, firm, persistent, resolute, resolved.

ir·re·solv·a·ble (ir′i·zol′və·bəl) *adj.* Not separable into parts; incapable of being resolved; not analyzable.

ir·re·spec·tive (ir′i·spek′tiv) *adj.* Lacking respect or relation; regardless: now used mostly with *of*, often adverbially. — **ir′re·spec′tive·ly** *adv.*

ir·re·spir·a·ble (ir′i·spīr′ə·bəl, ir·res′pi·rə·bəl) *adv.* Not respirable; not fit to be breathed. — **ir′re·spir′a·ble·ness** *n.*

ir·re·spon·si·ble (ir′i·spon′sə·bəl) *adj.* **1** Not accountable or amenable; not of sound mind. **2** Careless of responsibilities; unreliable. See synonyms under ARBITRARY. —*n.* A person who is irresponsible. — **ir′re·spon′si·bil′i·ty, ir′re·spon′si·ble·ness** *n.* — **ir′re·spon′si·bly** *adv.* — **ir′re·spon′sive** *adj.* — **ir′re·spon′sive·ness** *n.*

ir·re·ten·tion (ir′i·ten′shən) *n.* Lack of power of retaining. — **ir′re·ten′tive** *adj.* — **ir′re·ten′·tive·ness** *n.*

ir·re·trace·a·ble (ir′i·trā′sə·bəl) *adj.* Not retraceable.

ir·re·triev·a·ble (ir′i·trē′və·bəl) *adj.* Not retrievable; irreparable. — **ir′re·triev′a·ble·ness, ir′re·triev′a·bil′i·ty** *n.* — **ir′re·triev′a·bly** *adv.*

ir·rev·er·ence (i·rev′ər·əns) *n.* **1** The quality or condition of being irreverent. **2** The condition of not being reverenced; lack of honor.

ir·rev·er·ent (i·rev′ər·ənt) *adj.* Lacking in proper reverence; without deep respect or veneration. — **ir·rev′er·ent·ly** *adv.*

ir·re·vers·i·ble (ir′i·vûr′sə·bəl) *adj.* **1** That cannot be reversed or inverted. **2** Of, pertaining to, or designating a chemical or biological process which can continue only in one direction, as the coagulation of the white of a raw egg by heat, a degenerative disease, or the path of a stimulus along the nerves. — **ir′re·vers′i·bil′i·ty, ir′re·vers′i·ble·ness** *n.* — **ir′re·vers′i·bly** *adv.*

ir·rev·o·ca·ble (i·rev′ə·kə·bəl) *adj.* Incapable of being revoked or repealed; unalterable. — **ir·rev′o·ca·bil′i·ty, ir·rev′o·ca·ble·ness** *n.* — **ir·rev′o·ca·bly** *adv.*

ir·ri·gate (ir′ə·gāt) *v.t.* **gat·ed, ·gat·ing** **1** To supply (land) with water by means of ditches or other artificial channels. **2** *Med.* To moisten, as a wound, with dropping water, or spray, jet, etc. **3** *Rare* To moisten; wet. [<L *irrigatus*, pp. of *irrigare* bring water to < *in-* to + *rigare* water] — **ir′ri·ga·ble** (ir′ə·gə·bəl) *adj.* — **ir′ri·ga′tor** *n.*

ir·ri·ga·tion (ir′ə·gā′shən) *n.* **1** The artificial watering of land. **2** The conditon of being irrigated. **3** *Med.* The steady maintenance of a flow of water over an affected part, for cleansing or therapeutic purposes. — **ir′ri·ga′·tion·al** *adj.*

ir·ri·ga·tion·ist (ir′ə·gā′shən·ist) *n.* One who conducts or is an authority on irrigation.

ir·ri·ga·tive (ir′ə·gā′tiv) *adj.* **1** Of or pertaining to irrigation. **2** Designed for irrigation.

ir·rig·u·ous (i·rig′yo͞o·əs) *adj.* **1** Watered or watery. **2** Supplying water. [<L *irriguus* < *in-* very + *riguus* watered < *rigare* wet, water]

ir·ri·ta·bil·i·ty (ir′ə·tə·bil′ə·tē) *n. pl.* **·ties** **1** The state of being irritable. **2** Susceptibility to anger or impatience. **3** *Biol.* **a** The responsiveness of living matter or protoplasm in general to changes in external conditions, manifested by motion, change of form, and in other ways; specifically, the response to stimuli characterizing certain tissues or organs of plants and animals. Compare STIMULUS. **b** A morbid condition of an organ, manifested by undue excitability under the action of a stimulant. Also **ir′ri·ta·ble·ness.**

ir·ri·ta·ble (ir′ə·tə·bəl) *adj.* **1** Showing impatience or ill temper on little provocation; irascible; petulant. **2** *Biol.* Responding easily to the action of external stimuli. **3** *Pathol.* Influenced to an abnormal degree by the action of stimulants or irritants. See synonyms under FRETFUL. [<L *irritabilis* < *irritare*] — **ir′ri·ta·bly** *adv.*

ir·ri·tant (ir′ə·tənt) *adj.* **1** Causing irritation. **2** *Med.* Irritating the eyes, nose, or digestive system: an *irritant* gas or smoke. —*n.* **1** *Pathol.* An agent of inflammation, pain, etc. **2** A provocation; spur. [<L *irritans, -antis*, ppr. of *irritare*] — **ir′ri·tan·cy** *n.*

ir·ri·tate (ir′ə·tāt) *v.t.* **·tat·ed, ·tat·ing** **1** To excite ill temper or impatience in; fret; exasperate. **2** To make sore or inflamed. **3** *Biol.* To excite, as organic tissue, to a characteristic function or action. See synonyms under AFFRONT, INCENSE[1], PIQUE[1]. [<L *irritatus*, pp. of *irritare* irritate]

ir·ri·ta·tion (ir′ə·tā′shən) *n.* **1** The act of irritating. **2** The state of being irritated. **3** *Pathol.* A condition of morbid irritability in an organ or part of the body.

ir·ri·ta·tive (ir′ə·tā′tiv) *adj.* **1** Serving to produce irritation. **2** Accompanied by irritation.

ir·ro·ta·tion·al (ir′rō·tā′shən·əl) *adj.* Without rotatory motion.

ir·rup·tion (i·rup′shən) *n.* **1** A breaking or rushing in. **2** A violent incursion. See synonyms under INVASION. [<L *irruptio, -onis* < *irruptus*, pp. of *irrumpere* burst in < *in-* in + *rumpere* break] — **ir·rup′tive** *adj.*

Ir·tish (ir·tish′) A river in western Siberian Russian S.F.S.R., flowing 1,844 miles west and NW to the Ob. Also **Ir·tysh′.**

Ir·ving (ûr′ving) A masculine personal name. [from a place name in Scotland]

Ir·ving (ûr′ving), **Sir Henry,** 1838–1905, English actor: original name *John Henry Brodribb.* — **Washington,** 1783–1859, U. S. author, historian, and humorist.

Ir·win (ûr′win) A masculine personal name. [Appar. var. of IRVING]

is (iz) Present tense, third person singular of BE. [OE]

is– Var. of ISO-.

I·saac (ī′zek, *Fr.* ē·zȧk′) A masculine personal name. Also *Ger.* **I·saak** (ē′zäk), *Latin* **I·sa·a·cus** (ī·sā′ə·kəs), *Ital.* **I·sac·co** (ē·zäk′kō), *Dan., Sw.* **I·sak** (ē′säk). [<Hebrew, laughter] — **Isaac** A Hebrew patriarch; son of Abraham and Sarah, and father of Esau and Jacob. *Gen.* xxi 3.

I·saacs (ī′zəks), **Rufus Daniel** See READING, MARQUIS OF.

Is·a·bel (iz′ə·bel, *Pg., Sp.* ē′sä·bel′) A feminine personal name. Also **Is·a·bel·la** (iz′ə·bel′ə, *Du.* iz′ä·bel′ä, *Ital.* ē′zä·bel′lä), **Is·a·belle** (iz′ə·bel, *Fr.* ē·zä·bel′, *Ger.* ē′zä·bel′ə), *Fr.* **I·sa·beau** (ē·zä·bō′). [<Hebrew, oath of Baal]

Is·a·bel (iz′ə·bel) See SANTA ISABEL (def. 2).

Is·a·bel·la I (iz′ə·bel′ə), 1451–1504, queen of Castile and León, wife of Ferdinand V of Aragon, with whom she unified Spain and subdued Granada; aided Columbus: known as Isabel la Católica.

i·sa·cous·tic (ī′sə·ko͞os′tik, -kous′-) *adj. Physics* **1** Of or pertaining to equality in the clearness or intensity of sound. **2** Denoting a line, curve, or surface connecting all points within an enclosed space having the same acoustic characteristics. [<IS- + ACOUSTIC]

I·sae·us (ī·sē′əs), 420–348 B.C., Attic orator and rhetorician; reputed teacher of Demosthenes.

i·sa·go·ge (ī′sə·gō′jē) *n.* An introduction, as to a work of scholarship. [<L <Gk. *eisagōgē* < *eisagein* introduce < *eis-* into + *agein* lead] — **i′sa·gog′ic** (-goj′ik) *adj.*

i·sa·gog·ics (ī′sə·goj′iks) *n. pl.* (*construed as sing.*) That part of exegetical theology which has to do with the literary history of the books of the Bible, their inspiration, authorship, genuineness, and time and place of composition; Biblical introduction.

I·sa·iah (ī·zā′ə, ī·zī′ə) A masculine personal name. Also *Fr.* **I·sa·ie** (ē·zä·ē′), *Ital.* **I·sai·a** (ē·zī′ä), *Pg., Sp.* **I·sa·i·as** (ē′sä·ē′äs). [<Hebrew *yĕsha′ yah* salvation]
— **Isaiah** A major Hebrew prophet of the eighth century B.C.; also, a book of the Old Testament attributed wholly or in part to him. See DEUTERO-ISAIAH. Also **I·sai′as** (-əs).

I·sa·ian (ī·zā′ən, ī·zī′-) *adj.* Pertaining or relating to Isaiah. Also **I·sa·ian·ic** (ī′zā·an′ik).

i·sal·lo·bar (ī·sal′ə·bär) *n. Meteorol.* A contour line on a chart connecting places which show equal changes in barometric pressure over a specified interval. [<IS- + ALLO- + Gk. *baros* weight] — **i·sal′lo·bar′ic** *adj.*

i·san·drous (ī·san′drəs) *adj. Bot.* Having the stamens all similar and of the same number as the petals. [<IS- + -ANDROUS]

i·sa·nom·al (ī′sə·nom′əl) *n. Meteorol.* A line on a map or chart, connecting all those places which exhibit the same types or degrees of meteorological anomaly, as of pressure, temperature, wind, etc. [<IS- + ANOM(ALOUS)] — **i′sa·nom′a·lous** *adj.*

i·san·ther·ous (ī·san′thər·əs) *adj. Bot.* Having equal anthers. [<IS- + Gk. *antheros* flowery < *anthos* flower]

i·san·thous (ī·san′thəs) *adj. Bot.* Having regular flowers. [<IS- + Gk. *anthos* flower]

I·sar (ē′zär) A river in the Tirol, Austria, and Bavaria, SW West Germany, flowing 163 miles NE to the Danube.

i·sa·tin (ī′sə·tin) *n. Chem.* A yellowish or brownish-red crystalline compound with a bitter taste, $C_8H_5NO_2$, obtained by oxidizing indigo: used as a reagent and in the manufacture of vat dyes. Also **i′sa·tine** (-tēn, -tin). [<L *isatis* woad <Gk. + -IN] — **i′sa·tin′ic** *adj.*

I·sau·ri·a (ī·sô′rē·ə) An ancient district of SE Asia Minor between Cilicia and Pisidia. — **I·sau′ri·an** *adj. & n.*

is·ba (ēs′bä) *n. Russian* A log cabin.

ISBA

Is·car·i·ot (is·kar′ē·ət) See JUDAS ISCARIOT.

is·che·mi·a (is·kē′mē·ə) *n. Pathol.* A localized deficiency of blood, as from a contracted blood vessel. Also **is·chae′mi·a.** [<NL <Gk. *ischein* hold, check + -EMIA] — **is·che′mic** *adj.*

Is·chia (ēs′kyä) An island in the Tyrrhenian Sea near Naples; 18 square miles.

is·chi·um (is′kē·əm) *n. pl.* **·chi·a** (-kē·ə) **1** *Anat.* The posterior part of the pelvic arch; in man, the part of the hip bone on which the body rests when sitting. **2** *Zool.* The third joint of any limb or lateral appendage in crustaceans. **3** *Entomol.* A side of the thorax in insects. Also **is·chi·on** (is′kē·ən). [<L <Gk. *ischion* hip, hip joint < *ischys* strong] — **is·chi·at·ic** (is′kē·at′ik) or **·ad·ic** (-ad′ik), **is′chi·ac** (-ak) or **is′ki·al** (-əl) *adj.*

I′se (īz) *Scot.* Contraction of *I shall.*

-ise Var. of -IZE.

I·se Bay (ē·se) An inlet of the Philippine Sea in central Honshu, Japan.

is·en·trop·ic (īs′en·trop′ik, -trō′pik) *adj. Physics* Without change in entropy.

I·ser (ē′zər) The German name for the JIZERA.

I·sère (ē·zâr′) A river in SE France, flowing 150 miles SW to the Rhone.

I·seult (i·soo͞lt′) In medieval romance, either of two princesses: Iseult of the White Hand of Britanny, married to Tristan, or Iseult the Beautiful of Ireland, married to King Mark. See TRISTAN. Also spelled *Isolde, Isolt, Isoud, Yseult.*

Is·fa·han (is·fə·hän′) A city in west central Iran: formerly *Ispahan*: also *Esfahan.*

-ish[1] *suffix* **1** Of or belonging to (a national group): *Polish*; *Danish.* **2** Of the nature of; like: *boyish*; *clownish.* **3** Verging toward the character of: *feverish*; *bookish.* **4** Somewhat; rather: *bluish*; *tallish.* **5** *Colloq.* Approximately: *fortyish.* [OE *-isc,* adjectival suffix]

-ish[2] *suffix of verbs* Found in verbs of French origin: *brandish, demolish.* [<F *-iss-*, stem ending of *-ir* verbs <L *-isc-*, stem ending of inceptives]

I·shim (ē·shem′) A river in Russian S.F.S.R., flowing 1,123 miles NW to the Irtish.

Ish·ma·el (ish′mā·əl) **1** The son of Abraham and Hagar; exiled with the latter. **2** An outcast. [<Hebrew, God hears]

Ish·ma·el·ite (ish′mē·əl·īt′) *n.* **1** A traditional descendant of Ishmael; an Arab. *Gen.* xxi 9–21. **2** One having the character of Ishmael. *Gen.* xxi 9–21. **3** Any wanderer; outcast. — **Ish′ma·el·it′ic** (-īt′ik), **Ish·ma·el·it′ish** (-ī′·tish) *adj.* — **Ish′ma·el·it′ism** *n.*

Ish·tar (ish′tär) In Babylonian and Assyrian mythology, the wife of Tammuz and goddess of love and fertility.

I·si·ac (ī′sē·ak) *adj.* Belonging or relating to the goddess Isis: the *Isiac* tablet. [<L *Isiacus* <Gk. *Isiakos* <*Isis* Isis]

Is·i·dore (iz′ə·dôr, -dōr; *Fr.* ē·zē·dôr′) A masculine personal name. Also *Ital.* **I·si·do·ro** (ē′zē·dō′rō), *Latin* **Is·i·do·rus** (is′ə·dô′rəs). [<Gk., gift of Isis]
— **Isidore, Saint,** 560?–636, Spanish theologian and scholar; archbishop of Seville.

i·sin·glass (ē′zing·glas, -gläs, ī′zən-) *n.* **1** A preparation of nearly pure gelatin made from the swim bladders of certain fishes, as sturgeons, cod, and carp. **2** Mica, chiefly in the form of thin sheets. [<MDu. *huysenblas* sturgeon bladder < *huysen* sturgeon + *blase* bladder; infl. in form by GLASS]

I·sis (ī′sis) In Egyptian mythology, the goddess of fertility, sister and wife of Osiris.

Is·ken·de·run (ēs·ken′de·roo͞n′) A port of southern Turkey at the NE Mediterranean: formerly *Alexandretta.* Also **Is·kan′de·run.**

Is·lam (is′ləm, iz′-, is·läm′) *n.* **1** The religion of the Muslims, which maintains that there is but one God, Allah, and that Mohammed is his prophet; Mohammedanism. **2** The body of Muslim believers, their culture, and the countries they inhabit. [<Arabic *islām* submission < *salama* to be resigned]

Is·lam·a·bad (iz·läm′ə·bäd) The capital of Pakistan.

Is·lam·ic (is·lam′ik, -läm′-, iz-) *adj.* Muslim.

Is·lam·ism (is′ləm·iz′əm, iz′-) *n.* Islam. — **Is′·lam·is′tic, Is′lam·it′ic** *adj.*

Is·lam·ite (is′ləm·īt, iz′-) *n.* A Muslim; Mussulman.

Is·lam·ize (is′ləm·īz, iz′-) *v.t. & v.i.* **·ized, ·iz·ing** To convert or conform to Islam.

is·land (ī′lənd) *n.* **1** A tract of land, usually of moderate extent, surrounded by water. **2** Anything isolated or like an island; anything set distinctly apart from its surroundings, as a piece of elevated woodland surrounded by prairie. **3** A patch of land differentiated from the surrounding area by a certain kind of vegetation: They walked to the oak *island.* **4** A cultivated or settled spot, especially a big farm in the woods or other unsettled area: often used as a place name. **5** *Anat.* Any of various isolated structures of the body; an insula. —*v.t.* **1** To make into an island or islands; insulate. **2** To isolate; set apart. **3** To intersperse with or as with islands. [OE *īgland,* lit., island land < *īg, īeg* isle + *land*; the *s* was added to the spelling in the 16th c. on a mistaken association from *isle*]

is·land·er (ī′lən·dər) *n.* An inhabitant of an island. Also **isles·man** (īlz′mən).

islands of Lang·er·hans (läng′ər·häns) *Anat.* Clusters of cells dispersed within the tissues of the pancreas and involved in the secretion of insulin. [after E. R. *Langerhans,* 1847–1888, German histologist]

Islands of the Blessed In Greek mythology, islands in the Western Ocean where the favorites of the gods lived after death.

island universe *Astron.* A galaxy.

isle (īl) *n.* **1** A small island. **2** *Poetic* An island. — *v.* **isled, isl·ing** *v.t.* To make into or place on an isle or island. — *v.i.* To live on an isle or island. ◆ Homophone: *aisle.* [<OF <L *insula* island]

Isle of Ely See ELY.

Isle of Man See MAN, ISLE OF.

Isle of Pines **1** A Cuban island SW of Havana; 1,182 square miles; chief town, Nueva Gerona. *Spanish* **Is·la de Pi·nos** (ēs′lä thā pē′·nōs). **2** A dependency of New Caledonia off its southern tip; 58 square miles: also *Kunie. French* **Ile des Pins** (ēl dā paṅ′).

Isle of Sheppey See SHEPPEY, ISLE OF.

Isle of Thanet See THANET, ISLE OF.

Isle of Wight See WIGHT, ISLE OF.

Isle Roy·ale (roi′əl, *Fr.* ēl rwȧ·yȧl′) An island in Lake Superior, within Michigan; 209 square miles: site of **Isle Royale National Park,** established 1940.

is·let (ī′lit) *n.* A little island. [<OF *islette,* dim. of *isle*]

Is·ling·ton (iz′ling·tən) A metropolitan borough of London north of the Thames.

ism (iz′əm) *n.* A doctrine or system: often applied satirically or with derogatory force. [<-ISM]

-ism *suffix of nouns* **1** The act, process, or result of: *ostracism.* **2** The condition of being: *skepticism.* **3** The characteristic action or behavior of: *heroism.* **4** The beliefs, teachings, or system of: *Calvinism.* **5** Devotion to; adherence to the teachings of: *nationalism.* **6** A characteristic or peculiarity of: said of language or idiom: *Americanism.* **7** *Med.* An abnormal condition resulting from an excess of: *alcoholism.* [<L *-ismus* <Gk. *-ismos*]

Is·ma·el·ite (is′mē·əl·īt′) *n.* **1** An Ishmaelite. **2** An Ismailian.

Is·ma·i·li·a (is′mä·ē′lē·ə) A town in NE Egypt at the mid-point of the Suez Canal. Also **Is′ma·i′li·ya.**

Is·ma·i·li·an (is′mä·ē′lē·ən) *n.* A member of a sect of the Shiah branch of Islam. Also **Is′ma·el′i·an.** [after *Ismail,* son of the sixth imam of the Moslems]

Is·ma·il Pa·sha (is′mä·ēl′ pä′shə), 1830–95, khedive of Egypt 1863–79.

Is·nik (ēz·nēk′) See IZNIK.

is·n't (iz′ənt) Is not: a contraction.

iso- *combining form* **1** Equal; the same; identical. **2** *Chem.* Isomeric with, or an isomer of (the compound named): *isoprene.* Also, before vowels, *is-*. [<Gk. *isos* equal]

i·so·ag·glu·ti·na·tion (ī′sō·ə·gloo͞′tə·nā′shən) *n. Med.* The agglutination of the red blood corpuscles of an animal by a serum taken from another individual of the same species.

i·so·ag·glu·tin·in (ī′sō·ə·gloo͞′tə·nin) *n. Physiol.* An agglutinin having the power to agglutinate the red blood corpuscles of another individual of the same species.

i·so·am·yl (ī′sō·am′il) *n. Chem.* The univalent radical C_5H_{11} which enters into many organic compounds: *isoamyl* acetate (pear oil), *isoamyl* alcohol (fusel oil), etc.

i·so·bar (ī′sə·bär) *n.* **1** *Meteorol.* A line on a chart or diagram connecting places on the earth's surface having the same barometric pressure for a specified time or period. **2** *Physics* Any of two or more atoms having the same atomic weights but different atomic numbers and chemical properties. [<ISO- + Gk. *baros* weight] — **i′so·bar′ic** (-bar′ik) *adj.* — **i′so·bar′o·met′ric** (-bar′ə·met′rik) *adj.*

i·so·bath (ī′sə·bath) *n.* A contour line connecting points of equal depth beneath the earth or along the ocean floor. [<ISO- + Gk. *bathys* deep]

i·so·bront (ī′sə·bront) *n. Meteorol.* A line joining points at which any specified phase of a thunderstorm occurs at the same time. [<ISO- + Gk. *brontē* thunder]

i·so·can·dle (ī′sə·kan′dəl) *adj. Physics* **1** Designating a curve drawn through those points about a source of light at which the candlepower is the same. **2** Denoting a diagram comprising several sets of such curves.

i·so·chasm (ī′sə·kaz′əm) *n.* An isogram indicating the same average frequency of auroral displays. [<ISO- + Gk. *chasma* gap]

i·so·cheim (ī′sə·kīm) *n. Meteorol.* A line joining points on the earth's surface which have the same mean winter temperature. Also **i′so·chime.** [<ISO- + Gk. *cheima* winter] — **i′so·chei′mal** *adj.*

i·so·chore (ī′sə·kôr) *n. Physics* An isogram for

which volume is the constant quantity. Also **i′so·chor.** [<ISO- + Gk. *chōra* space] — **i′so·chor′ic** *adj.*

i·so·chro·mat·ic (ī′sō·krō·mat′ik) *adj.* **1** *Optics* Having or denoting identity of color. **2** Orthochromatic.

i·so·chron (ī′sə·kron) *n. Biol.* In studies of growth, a mathematical function equal to one percent of the time required to attain maturity. Also **i′so·chrone** (-krōn). [<ISO- + Gk. *chronos* time]

i·soch·ro·nal (ī·sok′rə·nəl) *adj.* Relating to or characterized by equal intervals of time, as a pendulum that always vibrates in the same period. Also **i·so·chron·ic** (ī′sə·kron′ik), **i·soch′·ro·nous.** — **i·soch′ro·nous·ly** *adv.*

i·soch·ro·nize (ī·sok′rə·nīz) *v.t.* **·nized, ·niz·ing** To make isochronal. — **i·soch′ro·nism** *n.*

i·soch·ro·ous (ī·sok′rō·əs) *adj.* Having the same color or tint throughout. [<ISO- + -CHROOUS]

i·so·cli·nal (ī′sə·klī′nəl) *adj.* **1** Dipping at the same angle and in the same direction. **2** Designating a line projected on the earth's surface connecting places that have the same inclination to the earth's magnetic field. **3** *Geol.* Pertaining to an isocline. — *n.* An isoclinal line.

i·so·cline (ī′sə·klīn) *n. Geol.* A rock fold in which the strata are so closely appressed that the sides are parallel. [<ISO- + Gk. *klinein* bend] — **i′so·clin′ic** (-klin′ik) *adj.*

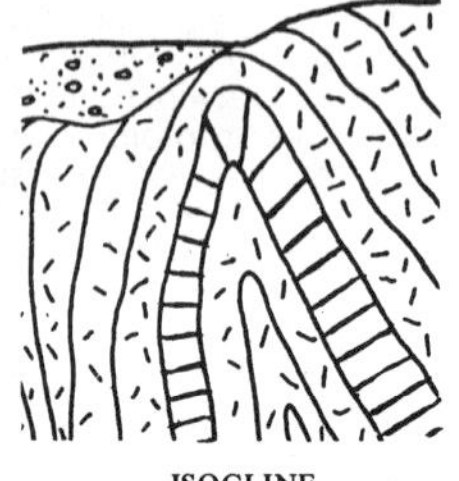

ISOCLINE
Vertical isoclinal folds.

i·so·cosm (ī′sə·koz′·əm) *n. Physics* A line connecting points on the earth's surface showing an equal cosmic ray intensity. [<ISO- + Gk. *kosmos* world]

i·soc·ra·cy (ī·sok′rə·sē) *n. pl.* **·cies** Equality in government; government in which all have equal power. [<Gk. *isokratia* < *iso-* same + *-kratia* rule < *kratos* power] — **i·so·crat** (ī′sə·krat) *n.* — **i′so·crat′ic** *adj.*

I·soc·ra·tes (ī·sok′rə·tēz), 436–338 B.C., Athenian orator.

i·so·cy·a·nine (ī′sō·sī′ə·nēn, -nin) *n. Chem.* Any of a group of quinoline dyes used in sensitizing photographic plates. Also **i′so·cy′a·nin** (-nin).

i·so·cy·clic (ī′sō·sī′klik, -sik′lik) *adj.* **1** *Chem.* Pertaining to or designating any of two or more closed-chain hydrocarbon compounds containing the same number of atoms. **2** *Bot.* Denoting a flower whose whorls have an equal number of parts.

i·so·def (ī′sə·def) *n.* An isogram joining points that show an equal percentage deviation from the mean of some specified phenomenon or characteristic. [<ISO- + DEF(ICIENCY)]

i·so·des·mic (ī′sō·dez′mik) *adj. Physics* Pertaining to or denoting an ionic crystal structure in which all the bonds are of equal strength. [<ISO- + Gk. *desmos* chain]

i·so·di·a·met·ric (ī′sō·dī′ə·met′rik) *adj.* **1** Equal in the three dimensions. **2** Having only the lateral axes equal, as crystals of the tetragonal and hexagonal systems.

i·so·di·mor·phism (ī′sō·dī·môr′fiz·əm) *n.* The phenomenon in which two or more similar crystals are at the same time isomorphous and dimorphous. — **i′so·di·mor′phous** *adj.*

i·so·dose (ī′sə·dōs) *n.* The same or an equal dose, as of drugs, X-rays or other forms of radioactivity.

i·so·dy·nam·ic (ī′sō·dī·nam′ik) *adj.* **1** Relating to or characterized by equality of force. **2** Designating any line on the earth's surface at all points of which the intensity of terrestrial magnetism is the same. Also **i′so·dy·nam′i·cal.**

i·so·e·lec·tric (ī′sō·i·lek′trik) *adj.* **1** Exhibiting the same electric potential. **2** *Chem.* Designating the *p*H value at which a colloidal suspension is electrically neutral with respect to the surrounding medium. [<ISO- + ELECTRIC]

i·so·e·lec·tron·ic (ī′sō·i·lek·tron′ik) *adj. Physics* Pertaining to or denoting atoms having the same number of valence electrons and similar physical properties.

i·so·eu·ge·nol (ī′sō·yōō′jə·nōl, -nol) *n. Chem.* A colorless oily liquid, $C_{10}H_{12}O_2$, derived from ylang-ylang and used in the manufacture of vanillin. [<ISO- + EUGENOL]

i·so·gam·ete (ī′sō·gam′ēt, -gə·mēt′) *n. Biol.* One of a pair of uniting gametes similar in size, form, and structure: opposed to *heterogamete.*

i·sog·a·my (ī·sog′ə·mē) *n. Biol.* That form of sexual reproduction in which there is a union of two similarly formed sexual cells, or gametes. Compare OOGAMY. [<ISO- + -GAMY] — **i·sog′a·mous** *adj.*

i·sog·e·nous (ī·soj′ə·nəs) *adj.* **1** Having a similarity of origin. **2** *Biol.* Developed from the same cells or tissues. [<ISO- + -GENOUS] — **i·so·gen·e·sis** (ī′sō·jen′ə·sis), **i·sog′e·ny** *n.*

i·so·ge·o·therm (ī′sō·jē′ə·thərm) *n. Geol.* A line or surface along which the earth, below its surface, has the same temperature. [<ISO- + GEO- + Gk. *thermē* heat] — **i′so·ge′o·ther′mal, i′so·ge′o·ther′mic** *adj.*

i·so·gloss (ī′sə·glôs, -glos) *n. Ling.* A line on a map in a dialect atlas delimiting areas within which certain linguistic features, as pronunciation, vocabulary, etc., are exhibited in common.

i·so·gon (ī′sə·gon) *n.* A polygon whose angles are all equal. [<ISOGONIC]

i·so·gon·ic (ī′sə·gon′ik) *adj.* **1** Having equal angles. **2** Denoting an isogonic line. Also **i·sog·o·nal** (ī·sog′ə·nəl). — *n.* An isogonic line. [<Gk. *isogōnios*]

isogonic line A line connecting points on the earth's surface having equal magnetic declination.

i·so·gram (ī′sə·gram) *n.* A line connecting points on a chart, map, or diagram which have equal values in relation to specified geographic features, physical conditions, or meteorological phenomena.

i·so·griv (ī′sə·griv) *n. Nav.* A line connecting points of equal grid variation. [<ISO- + GRIV(ATION)]

i·so·hel (ī′sə·hel) *n. Meteorol.* An isogram showing places of equal sunshine. [<ISO- + Gk. *hēlios* sun]

i·so·hy·dric (ī′sə·hī′drik) *adj. Chem.* Pertaining to or designating a chemical neutralization in which the *p*H value remains constant.

i·so·hy·et (ī′sə·hī′ət) *n. Meteorol.* A curve joining places of equal rainfall. [<ISO- + Gk. *hyetos* rain]

i·so·late (ī′sə·lāt, is′ə-) *v.t.* **·lat·ed, ·lat·ing** **1** To place in a detached or separate situation; set apart. **2** *Electr.* To insulate. **3** *Chem.* To obtain in a free or uncombined state, as an element or compound. **4** *Med.* To set apart from others, as a person with a communicable disease. **5** *Bacteriol.* To obtain a pure bacterial culture of (a specified disease or bacterium). — *n.* **1** A definite constituent or factor of some natural phenomenon, or aspect of experience, set apart from the whole for purposes of study, experiment, and analysis. **2** *Chem.* A pure compound, as one derived from an essential oil. [Back formation of ISOLATED <Ital. *isolato,* pp. of *isolare* isolate < *isola* island <L *insula* island] — **i′so·la′tor** *n.*

i·so·lat·ing (ī′sə·lā′ting, is′ə-) *adj. Ling.* Describing a language, such as Chinese, in which there is no distinction in form between the parts of speech, with meaning being determined primarily by word order.

i·so·la·tion·ism (ī′sə·lā′shən·iz′əm) *n.* The advocacy of national self-sufficiency and freedom from foreign political and economic alliances. — **i′so·la′tion·ist** *n.*

I·solde (i·sōld′, *Ger.* i·zôl′də) See ISEULT. Also **I·solt′.**

i·so·lead (ī′sə·lēd) *n. Mil.* A curved line drawn on a chart which indicates instantly the required lead of a gun in relation to a moving target. Also **isolead curve.**

i·so·lec·i·thal (ī′sō·les′ə·thəl) *adj. Biol.* Having the yolk evenly distributed through the protoplasm of an egg. [<ISO- + Gk. *lekithos* yolk of an egg]

I·so·le E·o·lie (ē′zō·lā ē·ō′lyā) An Italian name for the LIPARI ISLANDS.

i·so·leu·cine (ī′sə·lōō′sēn) *n. Biochem.* An amino acid, $C_6H_{13}NO_2$, found in body tissues and believed to be essential in nutrition.

i·so·log (ī′sə·lôg, -log) *n. Chem.* An isologous compound. Also **i′so·logue.** [<ISOLOGOUS]

i·sol·o·gous (ī·sol′ə·gəs) *adj. Chem.* Having similar molecular structure but different atoms of the same valency: applied especially to those groups of hydrocarbon compounds that have a constant difference of two hydrogen atoms in their composition. [<ISO- + Gk. *logos* proportion]

i·so·lux (ī′sə·luks) *n. Optics* **1** A line plotted on an appropriate set of coordinates to connect points of equal illumination. **2** A diagram containing sets of such lines. [<ISO- + L *lux* light]

i·so·mag·net·ic (ī′sō·mag·net′ik) *adj.* Relating to or designating lines connecting points of equal magnetic force. — *n.* An isomagnetic line.

i·so·mer (ī′sə·mər) *n. Chem.* A compound having the same molecular weight and formula as another but with a different spatial arrangement of its atoms, resulting in different properties. [<Gk. *isomerēs* equally divided < *isos* equal + *meros* part] — **i′so·mer′ic** (-mer′ik) *adj.*

i·som·er·ism (ī·som′ər·iz′əm) *n. Chem.* The condition of having different chemical or physical properties, or both, but identical molecular composition.

i·som·er·ous (ī·som′ər·əs) *adj.* **1** *Bot.* Equal in number, as the members of the successive circles or whorls of a flower: opposed to *heteromerous.* **2** *Entomol.* Having an equal number of tarsal joints on all feet: said of certain coleopterous insects. **3** Isomeric.

i·so·met·ric (ī′sō·met′rik) *adj.* **1** Having equality in dimensions or measurements. **2** Pertaining to that system of crystallization in which the three axes are equal in length and at right angles to each other. **3** *Physics* Indicating or maintaining the same proportions, measure, dimensions, etc., as a constant volume in a gas. Also **i′so·met′ri·cal.** **4** Based upon the forceful contraction of muscles against immovable resistance without shortening muscle fibers, a means of strengthening muscles: *isometric* exercises. — *n.* An isometric line. [<Gk. *isometros* < *isos* equal + *metron* measure] — **i′so·met′·ri·cal·ly** *adv.*

i·so·me·tro·pi·a (ī′sō·mə·trō′pē·ə) *n. Optics* Equality of the focal length of the two eyes. [<ISO- + Gk. *metron* measure + -OPIA]

i·som·e·try (ī·som′ə·trē) *n.* **1** Equality in measured parts or proportions. **2** *Geog.* Equality of elevation, as of mountain peaks. [<Gk. *isometria* equality of measure < *isos* same + *metros* measure]

i·so·morph (ī′sə·môrf) *n.* An organism or crystal superficially like another but morphologically different. [<ISO- + Gk. *morphē* form] — **i′so·mor′phic** *adj.*

i·so·mor·phism (ī′sə·môr′fiz·əm) *n.* **1** The property shown by two substances of analogous chemical composition that crystallize in identical or nearly identical forms. **2** *Biol.* The possession of like characters by organisms of different groups, resulting usually from like environmental influences. — **i′so·mor′phous** *adj.*

i·so·neph (ī′sə·nef) *n. Meteorol.* An isogram showing places of equal degrees of cloudiness. [<ISO- + Gk. *nephos* cloud]

i·son·o·my (ī·son′ə·mē) *n.* **1** Equality of civil rights. **2** Equality in rank, kind, or grade, in classification. [<Gk. *isonomia* < *isos* same + *nomos* law] — **i·so·nom·ic** (ī′sō·nom′ik) *adj.*

I·son·zo (ē·zôn′tsō) A river in NW Yugoslavia and NE Italy, flowing 84 miles south to the Gulf of Trieste.

i·so·oc·tane (ī′sō·ok′tān) *n. Chem.* Trimethylpentane.

i·sop·a·thy (ī·sop′ə·thē) *n. Med.* **1** The theory that a contagious disease contains in its own causative agent the means for its cure. **2** Treatment by the application or use of diseased matter. — **i·so·path·ic** (ī′sə·path′ik) *adj.*

i·so·phene (ī′sə·fēn) *n.* **1** *Ecol.* A contour line on a map indicating areas of equal frequency of a given plant or animal. **2** A line joining all places within a given area or region of the earth along which seasonal phenomena take place at the same time. [<ISO- + Gk. *phainein* reveal]

i·so·phot·ic (ī′sō·fot′ik) *adj. Bot.* Equally illuminated: said of leaves and other organs.

i·so·phyl·ly (ī′sō·fil′ē) *n. Bot.* The condition in which a plant bears only one kind of leaf. [<ISO- + Gk. *phyllon* leaf] — **i′so·phyl′·lous** *adj.*

i·so·pi·es·tic (ī′sō·pī·es′tik) *adj.* Showing equal

pressure; isobaric. — *n.* An isobar. [<ISO- + Gk. *piezein* press]

i·so·pleth (ī′sə·pleth) *n.* **1** *Meteorol.* A graph showing the variations of a specified climatic element with respect to two coordinates, temporal and spatial, the latter generally being an altitude factor. **2** An isogram. **3** A nomograph. [<Gk. *isoplēthēs* equal in number or quantity < *iso-* equal + *plēthos* number, quantity]

i·so·pod (ī′sə·pod) *n.* Any of a large and varied order *(Isopoda)* of terrestrial and aquatic crustaceans, having sessile eyes, flattened bodies lacking a carapace, and seven free thoracic segments, of which each carries a pair of closely similar legs. — *adj.* Of or pertaining to the *Isopoda.* [<NL <Gk. *isos* equal + *pous, podos* foot] — **i·sop·o·dan** (ī·sop′ə·dən) *adj.*

i·so·pol·i·ty (ī′sō·pol′ə·tē) *n.* Reciprocity of civil rights.

i·so·por (ī′sə·pôr, -pōr) *n.* An isogram indicating an equal rate of change in any element of the earth's magnetic field. [<ISO- + Gk. *poros* passage] — **i′so·por′ic** *adj.*

i·so·pract (ī′sə·prakt) *n.* A boundary enclosing areas of equal frequency or value of specified physical conditions, as population, snowfall, etc. [<ISO- + Gk. *praktikos* of action]

i·so·prene (ī′sə·prēn) *n.* *Chem.* A volatile liquid hydrocarbon of the terpene group, C_5H_8, obtained when caoutchouc and gutta-percha are subjected to dry distillation. [Appar. an arbitrary coinage]

i·so·pro·pyl (ī′sə·prō′pil) *n.* *Chem.* The univalent radical $(CH_3)_2CH$, an important constituent of many organic compounds, as isopropyl alcohol, $(CH_3)_2CHOH$, used as a solvent and in perfumery. Also called **i′so·pro′pa·nol** (-pə·nōl, -nol).

i·sop·ter·ous (ī·sop′tər·əs) *adj.* Of or pertaining to an order *(Isoptera)* of small and medium-sized social insects having soft bodies, strong mandibles, and well-developed claws, the workers and soldiers being wingless and sterile. See WHITE ANT. [<ISO- + -PTEROUS]

i·so·pyc·nic (ī′sə·pik′nik) *adj.* Of, pertaining to, or having equal density, as sea water or air masses. — *n.* A line connecting points of equal density. [<ISO- + Gk. *pyknos* thick, dense]

i·so·pyre (ī′sə·pīr) *n.* A variety of impure opal.

i·sos·ce·les (ī·sos′ə·lēz) *adj.* *Geom.* Pertaining to or designating a triangle having two sides of equal length. [<LL <Gk. *isoskelēs* equal-legged < *iso-* equal + *skelos* leg]

B A C

ISOSCELES TRIANGLE
AB, CB are of equal length.

i·so·seis·mal (ī′sə·sīz′məl, -sīs′-) See COSEISMAL.

i·so·seis·mic (ī′sə·sīz′mik, -sīs′-) *adj.* Pertaining to or designating equal intensities of earthquake shocks. — *n.* A coseismal.

i·sos·mot·ic (ī′sos·mot′ik) Isotonic. [<ISO- + (O)SMOTIC]

i·sos·po·ry (ī·sos′pər·ē) *n.* *Bot.* The condition of having only one kind of spore, as in the true ferns and club mosses. Also **i·so·spore** (ī′sə·spôr, -spōr). [<ISO- + SPOR(E) + -Y[1]] — **i·sos′po·rous** *adj.*

i·sos·ta·sy (ī·sos′tə·sē) *n.* **1** *Geol.* The theoretical condition of equilibrium which the earth's surface tends to assume under the action of terrestrial gravitation, as affected by the transference of material from regions of denudation to those of deposition, and by differences in density in various portions of the earth's mass near the surface. **2** Equilibrium resulting from equal pressure on all sides. [<ISO- + Gk. *stasis* a standing still] — **i·so·stat·ic** (ī′sə·stat′ik) *adj.*

i·so·stem·o·nous (ī′sə·stem′ə·nəs) *adj.* *Bot.* Having the stamens in a single series and of the same number as the petals and sepals. [<ISO- + Gk. *stēmōn* thread + -OUS] — **i′so·stem′o·ny** *n.*

i·so·stere (ī′sə·stir) *n.* **1** *Meteorol.* A line connecting points of equal atmospheric density. **2** *Chem.* A compound or radical which exhibits isosterism. [<ISO- + Gk. *stereos* solid]

i·sos·ter·ism (ī·sos′tər·iz′əm) *n.* *Chem.* A similarity in the physical properties of certain compounds, radicals, and elements, due to their having the same number and arrangement of electrons. — **i·so·ster·ic** (ī′sə·ster′ik) *adj.*

i·so·there (ī′sə·thir) *n.* *Meteorol.* An isogram indicating places having the same mean summer temperature. [<ISO- + Gk. *theros* summer] — **i·soth·er·al** (ī·soth′ər·əl) *adj.* & *n.*

i·so·therm (ī′sə·thûrm) *n.* *Meteorol.* A line passing through points on the earth's surface which have the same temperature at a given time or over the same period. [<ISO- + Gk. *thermē* heat]

i·so·ther·mal (ī′sə·thûr′məl) *adj.* **1** Having the same temperature. **2** Designating a layer of the atmosphere lying above the region of convection: also called *stratospheric.* **3** Of or pertaining to an isotherm. — *n.* An isotherm.

i·so·tone (ī′sə·tōn) *n.* *Physics* One of two or more atomic nuclei having the same number of neutrons. [<ISOTONIC]

i·so·ton·ic (ī′sə·ton′ik) *adj.* **1** Having the same tonicity. **2** *Physiol.* **a** Having the same osmotic pressure on opposite sides of a membrane: said of solutions, especially blood or plasma: distinguished from *hypertonic*: also *isosmotic.* **b** Denoting a muscle which contracts against a small but uniform tension or the curve of such a contraction. **3** *Music* Pertaining to, characterized by, or having equal tones. [<Gk. *isotonos* having equal accent or tone < *iso-* equal + *tonos* accent, tone] — **i·so·to·nic·i·ty** (ī′sə·tō·nis′ə·tē) *n.*

i·so·tope (ī′sə·tōp) *n.* *Physics* Any of two or more forms of an element having the same atomic number and similar chemical properties but differing in atomic weight and radioactive behavior. The accepted atomic weight of an element is the average of the nuclear masses of all the isotopes it may contain. [<ISO- + Gk. *topos* place] — **i·so·top·ic** (ī′sə·top′ik, -tō′pik) *adj.* — **i·sot·o·py** (ī·sot′ə·pē) *n.*

i·so·tron (ī′sə·tron) *n.* An apparatus for the electromagnetic separation of uranium isotopes, especially in the generation of atomic energy. [<ISO(TOPE) + (ELEC)TRON]

i·so·trop·ic (ī′sə·trop′ik, -trō′pik) *adj.* **1** *Physics* Exhibiting the same physical properties in every direction. **2** *Biol.* Having indifferent structure, as various eggs. Also **i′so·trope, i·sot·ro·pous** (ī·sot′rə·pəs).

i·sot·ro·pism (ī·sot′rə·piz′əm) *n.* **1** The quality of being isotropic. **2** *Biol.* An ability in an unsegmented egg to develop an embryo from any part. Also **i·sot·ro·py** (ī·sot′rə·pē). [<ISO- + -TROPISM]

I·soud (i·sōōd′) See ISEULT.

Is·pa·han (is′pä·hän′) A former spelling of ISFAHAN.

Is·ra·el (iz′rē·əl) A masculine personal name. [<Hebrew, contender with God] — **Israel** The patriarch Jacob. *Gen.* xxxii 28.

Is·ra·el (iz′rē·əl) *n.* **1** The Jewish people, traditionally regarded as descended from Israel (Jacob). **2** The kingdom in the northern part of ancient Palestine formed by the ten tribes of Israel.

Is·ra·el (iz′rē·əl) A republic comprising parts of Palestine, proclaimed as a Jewish national state in May, 1948; 8,040 square miles; capital, Jerusalem. — **Is·rae·li** (iz·rā′lē) *adj.* & *n.*

Is·ra·el·ite (iz′rē·əl·īt′) *n.* **1** Any of the people of Israel or their descendants; a Hebrew; a Jew. **2** One of God's chosen people. — **Is′ra·el·it′ish** (-ī′tish), **Is′ra·el·it′ic** (-it′ik) *adj.*

Is·ra·fel (iz′rə·fel) In Moslem mythology, the one of the four archangels who is to sound the resurrection trumpet. Also **Is′ra·feel, Is′ra·fil** (-fēl).

Is·sa·char (is′ə·kär) The ninth son of Jacob. *Gen.* xxx 18.

Is·sei (ēs·sā) *n.* *pl.* **·seis** or **·sei** A Japanese who emigrated to the United States after the Oriental exclusion proclamation of 1907, and is not legally eligible to become an American citizen. Compare NISEI, KIBEI. [<Japanese *is* first + *sei* generation]

is·su·a·ble (ish′ōō·ə·bəl, -yōō-) *adj.* **1** That can issue or be issued. **2** *Law* Tending to an issue. — **is′su·a·bly** *adv.*

is·su·ance (ish′ōō·əns, -yōō-) *n.* The act of putting, sending, or giving out; promulgation; distribution.

is·su·ant (ish′ōō·ənt, -yōō-) *adj.* **1** Issuing or emerging. **2** *Her.* Denoting a beast of which the upper half only is seen.

is·sue (ish′ōō, -yōō) *v.* **·sued, ·su·ing** *v.t.* **1** To give out or deliver in a public or official manner; put into circulation; publish: to *issue* a new stamp; to *issue* a magazine. **2** To deal out or distribute: to *issue* ammunition. **3** To send forth or emit; let out; discharge. — *v.i.* **4** To come forth or flow out; emerge: Water *issued* from the pipe. **5** To come as a result or consequence; proceed: His charity *issues* from his good character. **6** To come to a specified end: with *in*: The argument *issued* in a duel. **7** To be given out or published; appear. **8** To come as profit or revenue; accrue: with *out of.* **9** *Rare* or *Law* To be born or descended. — *n.* **1** The act of going out; outflow. **2** A place or way of egress. **3** Result; outcome; upshot. **4** The action of giving out or supplying officially or publicly. **5** An item or amount which is issued. **6** Offspring; progeny. **7** Profits; proceeds. **8** *Med.* **a** A suppurating sore, produced and maintained by artificial means. **b** A discharge, as of blood. **9** *Law* The point in question between parties to an action. **10** A subject of discussion or interest. See synonyms under CONSEQUENCE, END, EVENT, TOPIC. [<F *issue* < *issir, eissir* <L *exire* < *ex-* out of + *ire* go] — **at issue** Under dispute; in question. — **to take issue** To disagree. — **is′su·er** *n.*

Is·sus (is′əs) An ancient port in Cilicia, NE Asia Minor; scene of the victory of Alexander the Great over Darius III, 333 B.C.

Is·syk Kul (ē′sik kōōl′) The second largest mountain lake in the world, in eastern Kirghiz S.S.R.; 2,395 square miles.

-ist *suffix of nouns* **1** One who or that which does or has to do with: often used with verbs in *-ize*: *catechist.* **2** One whose profession is; one who practices: *pharmacist.* **3** A student or devotee of: *genealogist.* **4** One who advocates or adheres to: in extension from nouns ending in *-ism*: *socialist.* [<L *-ista* <Gk. *-istēs*]

Is·tan·bul (is′tan·bōōl′, -tän-, *Turkish* is·täm′·bōōl) The largest city of Turkey, a port on both sides of the Bosporus at its entrance into the Sea of Marmara: formerly *Byzantium* and, as *Constantinople,* capital of Turkey until 1923: also *Stambul.* Also **Is′tan·boul′.**

isth·mi·an (is′mē·ən, *rarely* isth′-) *adj.* Of or pertaining to an isthmus. — *n.* An inhabitant of an isthmus.

Isthmian Canal The Panama Canal.

Isthmian games The Pan-Hellenic festival, celebrated every two years in ancient Greece on the Isthmus of Corinth.

isth·mus (is′məs, *rarely* isth′-) *n.* *pl.* **·mus·es** or **·mi** (-mī) **1** A narrow body of land connecting two larger bodies. **2** *Anat.* A contracted passage or portion of an organ between two larger cavities or parts: the portion of the brain which joins the pons Varolii with the interbrain and hemisphere. **3** *Bot.* The constricted or contracted part of the cells of desmids connecting the two hemicells. [<L <Gk. *isthmos* narrow passage]

is·tle (ist′lē) *n.* **1** A fiber derived principally from a tropical American agave plant *(Agave fourcroydes* or *A. lophantha)*: used for carpets, belting, cordage, etc.: also called *pita, Tampico fiber.* **2** A similar fiber obtained from certain plants of the pineapple family (genus *Bromelia*). Also spelled *ixtle.* [<Am. Sp. *ixtle* <Nahuatl *ichtli*]

Is·tri·a (is′trē·ə) A peninsula, mostly in Yugoslavia, in the north Adriatic Sea; 1,908 square miles. *Serbo-Croatian* **Is·tra** (ēs′trä). Also **Istrian Peninsula.** — **Is′tri·an** *adj.* & *n.*

Ist·van (ēst·vän′) Hungarian form of STEPHEN.

it (it) *pron.* The neuter pronoun, nominative (pl. *they*) and objective (pl. *them*), of the third person singular, used: **1** As a substitute for things or for infants and animals when the sex is unspecified. **2** As the subject of an impersonal verb: *It* rained. **3** As the subject or object of a clause regarding a general condition or state of affairs: How was *it? It* was warm. **4** As the subject or predicate nominative of a verb whose logical subject is anticipated: Who was *it? It* was John. **5** As the indefinite subject of a verb introducing a clause or phrase: *It* seems that he knew. **6** *Colloq.* As the indefinite object after certain verbs in idiomatic expressions: to lord *it* over; to face *it.* — *n.* In certain children's games, the player required to perform some specified act. [OE *hit*]

I.T.A. Initial Teaching Alphabet.

I·ta·bi·ra (ē'tə·vir'ə) A town in SE Brazil.

i·tab·i·rite (i·tab'ə·rīt) *n.* A schist containing hematite in grains or scales. Also **i·tab'i·ryte.** [from *Itabira,* Brazil]

it·a·col·u·mite (it'ə·kol'yə·mīt) *n.* A laminated, granular, friable sandstone which is flexible in thin slabs. [from *Itacolumi,* mountain in eastern Brazil]

I·tal·ian (i·tal'yən) *adj.* Pertaining to Italy, its people, culture or language. — *n.* **1** A native or naturalized inhabitant of Italy. **2** The Romance language of modern Italy. [<L *Italianus* < *Italia* Italy]

I·tal·ian·ate (i·tal'yən·āt, -it) *adj.* Italian in nature or characteristics. — *v.t.* (-āt) **·at·ed, ·at·ing** To Italianize. [< earlier *Italianated* <Ital. *italianato* made Italian] — **I·tal'ian·a'·tion** *n.*

Italian East Africa A former Italian colony, comprising Eritrea, Italian Somaliland, and Ethiopia.

Italian hand The flowing script, developing from the 15th century, used in documents and forming the basis for modern English handwriting. Compare COURT HAND. — **fine Italian hand** Subtle cunning: The scheme showed her *fine Italian hand.*

I·tal·ian·ism (i·tal'yən·iz'əm) *n.* **1** An Italian idiom or expression; a custom or fashion peculiar to Italy. **2** The spirit, manner, or taste of the Italians. **3** A preference for or sympathy with Italy or things Italian.

I·tal·ian·ize (i·tal'yən·īz) *v.t.* & *v.i.* **·ized, ·iz·ing** To make or become Italian in manner, customs, language, etc. — **I·tal'ian·i·za'tion** *n.*

Italian millet See under MILLET.

Italian poplar The Lombardy poplar.

Italian Somaliland See SOMALILAND.

Italian squash Zucchini.

Italian sonnet See under SONNET.

i·tal·ic (i·tal'ik) *Printing n.* A style of type in which the letters slope, as *these*: also **i·tal'ics.** — *adj.* Designating, or printed in, italic. Compare ROMAN.

I·tal·ic (i·tal'ik) *adj.* Relating to any of the peoples of ancient Italy. — *n.* A subfamily of the Indo-European languages, comprising three branches—Falisco-Latinian (including Latin and the Romance languages), Osco-Umbrian, and Sabellian. [<L *Italicus*]

i·tal·i·cize (i·tal'ə·sīz) *v.t.* & *v.i.* **·cized, ·ciz·ing** **1** To print in italics. **2** To underscore (written words or phrases) with a single line to indicate italics. Also *Brit.* **i·tal'i·cise.**

I·tal·i·ote (i·tal'ē·ōt) *n.* One of the Greek inhabitants of Italy. Also **I·tal'i·ot** (-ot). [<Gk. *Italiōtēs* <*Italia* Italy]

It·a·ly (it'ə·lē) A republic in southern Europe; 116,224 square miles; capital, Rome. *Italian* **I·ta·lia** (ē·tä'lyä).

I·tas·ca (ī·tas'kə), **Lake** A lake in northern Minnesota, considered to be the source of the Mississippi.

itch (ich) *v.i.* **1** To feel a peculiar irritation of the skin which inclines one to scratch the part affected. **2** To have a desire or longing; crave. — *n.* **1** Any of various usually contagious skin diseases accompanied by itching, as scabies. **2** An itching of the skin. **3** A restless desire or yearning. [OE *giccan*] — **itch'i·ness** *n.* — **itch'ing** *n.* — **itch'y** *adj.*

itch mite A mite *(Sarcoptes scabiei)*, the female of which burrows and lays eggs under the scarfskin, causing inflammation and intense itching.

-ite[1] *suffix of nouns* **1** A native of: *Brooklynite.* **2** An adherent of: *Darwinite.* **3** A descendant of: *Israelite.* **4** *Mineral.* A rock or mineral: *graphite.* **5** *Zool.* A part of the body or of an organ: *somite.* **6** *Paleontol.* A fossil: *ammonite.* **7** Like; resembling; related to: often used in the names of commercial products: *dynamite.* [<F *-ite* <L *-ita* <Gk. *-itēs*]

-ite[2] *suffix Chem.* A salt or ester of an acid whose name ends in *-ous: sulfite.* [<F *-ite*; arbitrarily coined (1787) from *-ate* -ATE[3]]

-ite[3] *suffix* Used in adjectives and verbs formed on the past participial stems of Latin verbs in the second, third, and fourth conjugations: *finite, unite.* [<L *-itus*]

i·tem (ī'təm) *n.* **1** A separate article or entry in an account, etc. **2** A newspaper paragraph. **3** *Obs.* An admonition; hint; especially, a maxim or saying, formerly introduced by the word *item.* See synonyms under CIRCUMSTANCE. — *v.t.* **1** To set down by items. **2** To make a note or memorandum of. — *adv.* Likewise. [<L, likewise]

i·tem·ize (ī'təm·īz) *v.t.* **·ized, ·iz·ing** To set down or specify by items. — **i'tem·iz'er** *n.* — **i'tem·i·za'tion** *n.*

item veto The power of a government executive to veto parts of a bill without vetoing the entire bill.

I·té·nez (ē·tā'nes) See GUAPORÉ.

it·er·ate (it'ə·rāt) *v.t.* **·at·ed, ·at·ing** **1** To utter or do again. **2** To utter or do repeatedly. [<L *iteratus,* pp. of *iterare* repeat < *iterum* again] — **it'er·a·ble** (it'ər·ə·bəl) *adj.* — **it'er·ant** *adj.* — **it'er·ance, it'er·a'tion** *n.*

it·er·a·tive (it'ə·rā'tiv, it'ər·ə·tiv) *adj.* **1** Characterized by repetition; repetitious. **2** *Gram.* Frequentative.

i·te·rum (it'ər·əm) *adv. Latin* Again; once more.

Ith·a·ca (ith'ə·kə) **1** A Greek island of the Ionian group; 36 square miles; legendary home of Odysseus. *Modern Greek* **I·thá·ki** (ē·thä'kē). **2** A city in south central New York. — **Ith'a·can** *adj.* & *n.*

ith·er (ith'ər) *adj.* & *pron. Scot.* Other.

I·thunn (ē'thōōn) In Norse mythology, keeper of the golden apples of youth; wife of Bragi. Also **I'thun.**

I·thu·ri·el (i·thyōōr'ē·əl) In Milton's *Paradise Lost,* an angel sent by Gabriel to search for Satan. [<Hebrew *Yithūrī'ēl* the superiority of God]

ith·y·phal·lic (ith'ə·fal'ik) *adj.* **1** Relating to the phallus used in the festivals of Bacchus; hence, obscene; lewd. **2** In classical prosody, describing a trochaic tripody: used in verse sung in the phallic processions. [<L *ithyphallicus* <Gk. *ithyphallikos* < *ithyphallos* < *ithys* erect, rigid + *phallos* a phallus]

i·tin·er·a·cy (ī·tin'ər·ə·sē, i·tin'-) *n.* A passing from place to place in circuit, as in the discharge of ministerial duties. Also **i·tin'er·an·cy.**

i·tin·er·ant (ī·tin'ər·ənt, i·tin'-) *adj.* Going from place to place. — *n.* One who travels from place to place, as a minister serving a circuit of churches. [<LL *itinerans, -antis,* ppr. of *itinerari* make a journey < *iter, itineris* journey] — **i·tin'er·ant·ly** *adv.*

i·tin·er·ar·y (ī·tin'ə·rer'ē, i·tin'-) *n. pl.* **·ar·ies** **1** A detailed account or diary of a journey. **2** A plan of a proposed tour. **3** An exploring tour, or its record. **4** A route pursued in traveling. **5** Originally, a book or chart giving the roads, places, and distances of a region or along a route. **6** A guidebook. **7** In the Roman Catholic Church, a form of prayer for clergy departing on a journey. — *adj.* **1** Pertaining to or done on a journey. **2** Itinerant. [<LL *itinerarium,* neut. of *itinerarius* pertaining to a journey < *iter, itineris* journey, route]

i·tin·er·ate (ī·tin'ər·āt, i·tin'-) *v.i.* **·at·ed, ·at·ing** To journey from place to place or on circuit; to roam; wander. [<LL *itineratus,* pp. of *itinerari* make a journey. See ITINERANT.] — **i·tin'er·a'tion** *n.*

-itis *suffix* Inflammation of: *peritonitis, laryngitis.* [<Gk.]

it'll (it'l) **1** It will. **2** It shall.

its (its) *pronominal adj.* (possessive case of the pronoun *it*) Belonging or pertaining to it: *its* color. [<IT + *'s,* possessive case ending; written *it's* until the 19th century]

it's (its) **1** It is. **2** It has.

it·self (it·self') *pron.* It: an intensive or reflexive use. Also *Scot.* **it·sel'.**

it's me See note under ME.

I·tur·bi (ē·tōōr'bē), **José,** born 1895, U.S. pianist and conductor born in Spain.

-ity *suffix of nouns* The state or condition of being: *probity.* [<F *-ité* <L *-itas*]

I·tys (ī'tis) In Greek mythology, the son of Tereus, who was killed by his mother and aunt. See PHILOMELA.

I·u·lus (ī·yōō'ləs) See ASCANIUS.

I·van (ī'vən, *Russian* i·vän') Russian form of JOHN.
— **Ivan III,** 1440–1505, grand duke of Muscovy from 1462; founded the Russian Empire: known as *Ivan the Great.*
— **Ivan IV,** 1530–84, first czar of Russia 1547–1584: known as *Ivan the Terrible.*

I·van·hoe (ī'vən·hō) A historical romance by Sir Walter Scott based on the Norman-Saxon conflict in England at the time of Richard I.

I·va·no·vo (ē·vä'nô·vô) A city in Russian S.F.S.R. NE of Moscow. Formerly **Ivanovo-Voz·ne·sensk** (vôz·nye·syensk').

I've (īv) I have.

-ive *suffix of adjectives* **1** Having a tendency or predisposition to: *disruptive.* **2** Having the nature, character, or quality of: *massive.* Also *-ative.* [<F *-if* <L *-ivus,* suffix of adjectives]

Ives (īvz), **Charles,** 1874–1954, U.S. composer. — **Frederick Eugene,** 1856–1937, U.S. inventor, pioneer in photography. — **James Merritt** See CURRIER AND IVES.

i·vied (ī'vēd) *adj.* Covered or overgrown with ivy.

I·vi·za (ē·vē'thä) Third largest of the Balearic Islands; 230 square miles; capital, Iviza. *Spanish* **I·bi·za** (ē·vē'thä).

i·vo·ry (ī'vər·ē) *n. pl.* **·ries** **1** The hard, creamy-white, fine-grained, opaque dentine that constitutes the greater part of the tusks of certain animals, as the elephant, walrus, etc. ◆ Collateral adjective: *eburnean.* **2** Any form of dentine. **3** Some ivorylike substance. **4** *pl.* Things made of, consisting of, or similar to ivory; especially, in slang use, the teeth, billiard balls, dice, keys of a piano. **5** The ivory nut. **6** The color of ivory. — *adj.* Made of or resembling ivory. [<OF *ivurie* <L *eboreus* of ivory < *ebur* ivory]

i·vo·ry·bill (ī'vər·ē·bil') *n.* A large North American woodpecker *(Campephilus principalis),* now rare, having a white or ivorylike bill.

ivory black A deep-black pigment made by charring bones or ivory scraps; carbon black.

Ivory Coast The coastal region of western Africa along the Gulf of Guinea.

Ivory Coast Republic An independent republic of the French Community in western Africa; 127,520 miles; capital, Abidjan.

ivory gull The white arctic gull *(Pagophila alba).*

ivory nut The hard, ivorylike seed of the ivory palm, used for small carvings, buttons, etc.; vegetable ivory.

ivory palm The South American palm *(Phytelephas macrocarpa)* that bears ivory nuts.

ivory tower A place or condition of seclusion from the world and worldly attitudes, reality, action, etc.

i·vo·ry·type (ī'vər·ē·tīp') *n. Phot.* A picture made by fixing a translucent photograph over another.

I·vry-la-Ba·tail·le (ē·vrē'là·bà·tä'y') A town in NW France; scene of a Huguenot victory under Henri of Navarre over the Catholic league, 1590.

i·vy (ī'vē) *n. pl.* **i·vies** **1** A European, evergreen, climbing or creeping shrub *(Hedera helix)* of the ginseng or ivy family, bearing glossy leaves, small yellowish flowers, and black berries: also called **English ivy.** **2** One of various other climbing plants, as the **Japanese** or **Boston ivy** *(Parthenocissus tricuspidata)* and the **ground ivy** *(Nepeta hederacea).* [OE *īfig*]

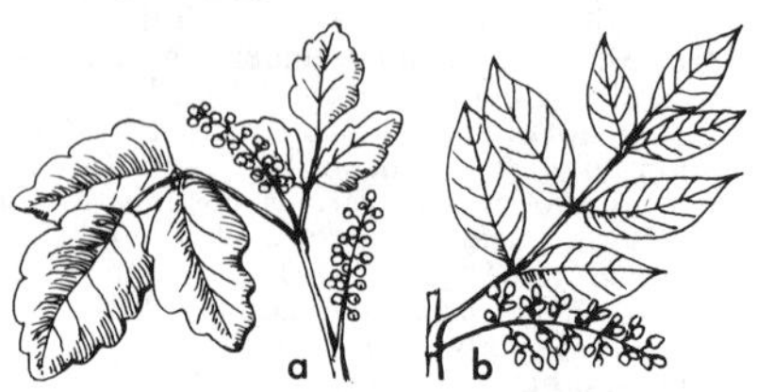

IVY
a. Poison ivy (*Rhus radicans*).
b. Poison sumac (*Rhus vernix*).

i·vy·ber·ry (ī'vē·ber'ē) *n. pl.* **·ries** Wintergreen.

Ivy League An association, primarily athletic, of colleges in the NE United States, comprising Brown, Columbia, Cornell, Dartmouth, Harvard, Princeton, the University of

Pennsylvania, and Yale: often used attributively to denote the fashions or manners characteristic of students in these colleges: *Ivy League* clothes.

ivy tod An ivy plant.

ivy vine **1** An American vitaceous plant *(Ampelopsis cordata)* with cordate leaves. **2** The Virginia creeper.

i·wis (i·wis′) *adv. Archaic* Certainly; surely; to wit: in later use written mistakenly *I wis*, through confusion with the verb *wit*. Also spelled *ywis*. [OE *gewis*]

I·wo Ji·ma (ē′wō jē′mä, ē′wə jē′mə) The largest of the Volcano Islands in the North Pacific; taken after severe fighting (1945) by American forces in World War II.

Ix·elles (ēk·sel′) A suburb SE of Brussels. *Flemish* **El·se·ne** (el′sə·nə).

ix·i·a (ik′sē·ə) *n.* Any of a genus *(Ixia)* of South African bulbous plants of the iris family, with narrow sword-shaped leaves, and spikes of large, showy, ornamental flowers. [<NL <Gk. *ixos* birdlime; from their viscid nature]

Ix·i·on (ik·sī′ən) In Greek mythology, a Thessalian king and father of the Centaurs, who was punished by Zeus for his love for Hera by being tied to a perpetually revolving wheel in Hades. [<Gk. *Ixiōn*]

ix·o·di·a·sis (ik′sə·dī′ə·sis) *n. Pathol.* Skin disease caused by ticks of the genus *Ixodes*; tick fever. [<NL *Ixodes*, genus of ticks + -IASIS]

Ix·ta·ci·hau·tl (ēs′tä·sē′wät·l) A dormant volcano in central Mexico; 17,342 feet; last eruption, 1868. Also **Iz·tac·ci·hua·tl** (ēs′täk·sē′wät·l).

ix·tle (iks′tlē, is′tlē) See ISTLE.

I·ye·ya·su (ē·yā·yä·sōō), 1543–1616, Japanese shogun, general, and statesman; founder of the Tokugawa shogunate.

Iy·yar (ē′yär) A Hebrew month. Also **I′yar.** See CALENDAR (Hebrew).

I·zaak (ē′zäk) Dutch and Polish form of ISAAC. Also *Hungarian* **I·zsák** (ē′zäk).

I·za·bal (ē·sä·bäl′), **Lake** A lake in eastern Guatemala.

iz·ar (iz′ər) *n. Arabic* A piece of white cotton fabric worn as the chief outer garment of Moslem women.

-ization *suffix* State or process of: used to form nouns from verbs in *-ize*: *oxidization*. [<-IZE + -ATION]

-ize *suffix of verbs* **1** To make; cause to become or resemble: *Christianize, concretize, Americanize.* **2** Subject to the action of; affect with: *oxidize.* **3** Change into; become: *mineralize.* **4** To act in the manner of; to practice: *sympathize.* Also *-ise*. [<F *-iser* <L *-izare* <Gk. *-izein*]

I·zhevsk (ē·zhefsk′) The capital of the Udmurt Autonomous S.S.R.

Iz·ma·il (ēz·mä·ēl′) A city on the Danube in Ukrainian S.S.R.

Iz·mir (ēz·mir′) The Turkish name for SMYRNA.

Iz·nik (ēz·nēk′) A village of NW Turkey on the site of ancient Nicaea. Also **Is·nik′.**

iz·zard (iz′ərd) *n. Colloq.* The letter Z. **— from A to izzard** From beginning to end. [Earlier *ezed*, var. of ZED]

J

j, J (jā) *n. pl.* **j's, J's** or **js, Js, jays** (jāz) **1** The tenth letter of the English alphabet: originally identical with Roman *I*. In the 17th century, the calligraphic practice of carrying initial *I* (which usually had consonant value) both above and below the line gradually developed into a graphic distinction between *i* the vowel and *i* or *j* the consonant. **2** A sound of the letter *j*, usually a voiced affricate, as in *judge* (juj); in borrowings from Modern French, often a voiced, alveolar fricative, as in *jabot*. See ALPHABET. **—** *symbol* **1** In Roman numerals, one: used as a variant of i at the end of a number, as *vij*, especially in medical prescriptions. **2** Anything shaped like a J, as a bolt or hook.

ja (yä) *interj. & adv. German* Yes.

jab (jab) *v.t. & v.i.* **jabbed, jab·bing** **1** To poke or thrust sharply, as with the point of something. **2** To punch or strike with sharp blows. **—** *n.* A sharp thrust or poke: punch. [Var. of JOB[2]]

Jab·al·pur (jub′əl·pôr, -pōr) The Hindi name for JUBBULPORE.

jab·ber (jab′ər) *v.t. & v.i.* To speak rapidly or unintelligibly; chatter. See synonyms under BABBLE. **—** *n.* Rapid or unintelligible talk; chatter. [Prob. imit.] **— jab′ber·er** *n.*

Ja·bez (jā′biz) A masculine personal name. [<Hebrew, sorrow]

jab·i·ru (jab′ə·rōō) *n.* A large tropical American wading bird *(Jabiru mycteria)* of the stork family, with white plumage and a scarlet inflatable pouch. [<Tupian]

jab·o·ran·di (jab′ə·ran′dē) *n.* **1** Any of a genus *(Pilocarpus)* of numerous South American shrubs of the rue family, especially *P. jaborandi*. **2** The dried leaves of this and allied plants, which yield pilocarpine and other medicinal alkaloids. [<Tupian]

ja·bot (zha·bō′, jab′ō; *Fr.* zhà·bō′) *n. pl.* **·bots** (-bōz′, *Fr.* -bō′) A lace frill worn by women on the bodice; formerly, a ruffle on a man's shirt bosom. [<F, lit., a gizzard]

ja·bot·i·ca·ba (jə·bot′ə·kä′bə) *n.* A semitropical evergreen tree *(Myrciaria cauliflora)* of the myrtle family, with edible, grapelike fruit: cultivated in Florida and California. [< Tupian *jabuti* a tortoise + *caba* fat]

jab·o·ty (jab′ə·tē) *n.* **1** An oil-bearing seed from a tropical American tree (genus *Erisma*). **2** The oil from this seed, sometimes used as a substitute for cocoa butter. [<Tupian]

ja·cal (hä·käl′) *n. pl.* **·ca·les** (-kä′lās) A one-room Mexican hut built of upright poles laced together with wicker and plastered with mud or adobe. [<Sp. <Nahuatl]

jac·a·mar (jak′ə·mär) *n.* A tropical American insectivorous bird (family *Galbulidae*) of various genera, having golden-green or coppery plumage. [<F <Tupian *jacamaciri*]

ja·ça·na (zhä′sə·nä′) Any of a family *(Jacanidae)* of small tropical wading birds with long, straight claws by which they walk over the floating leaves of aquatic plants. [<Pg. <Tupian]

jac·a·ran·da (jak′ə·ran′də) *n.* **1** Any of a genus *(Jacaranda)* of tropical American trees and shrubs of the bignonia family, with a hard, fine-textured wood: some species, as *J. caroba*, are used in medicine. **2** Brazilian rosewood *(Dalbergia nigra)*: used for making tool handles, radio cabinets, etc. [<Tupian]

Já·chy·mov (yä′khi·môv) A town in western Czechoslovakia, in the former province of Bohemia: German *Joachimsthal*.

ja·cinth (jā′sinth, jas′inth) *n.* **1** A reddish-orange variety of zircon: used as a gemstone. **2** *Obs.* A hyacinth. [<OF *iacinte* <L *hyacinthus*. Doublet of HYACINTH.]

jack[1] (jak) *n.* **1** *Mech.* **a** A device, appliance, or part of a machine: so called from its serving to supply the place of an assistant. **b** A portable device, operating by lever, screw, or other mechanical principle, for exerting considerable energy through a short distance: used in raising weights. **2** The male of the ass or of certain other animals. **3** A flag showing the canton or union of the national ensign without the fly, as of the United States or of Great Britain. See UNION JACK. **4** A playing card; in most games, the lowest of the face cards; a knave. **5** *U.S. Slang* Money. **6** *Electr.* A spring clip to which the wires of a circuit may be attached and which is arranged for the insertion of a plug. **7** A bootjack. **8** A jacklight. **9** A device to prevent back draft in a chimney or vent pipe. **10** *Naut.* An iron crosstree at the topgallant-masthead: also **jack crosstree.** **11** An automatic figure of a man which strikes the time bell of a clock. **12** A small white ball used as the object played for in the game of bowls. **13** The hopper of a pianoforte; in a harpsichord, the piece of wood holding the quill which strikes the string. **14** One of various fishes, as a pike or pickerel. **15** *pl.* The game played with jackstones. **— hydraulic jack** A device for lifting heavy weights or exerting great force by fluid pressure from a hand pump connected with a large-bore cylinder and a piston: also **hydrostatic jack.** **—** *v.t.* **1** To raise or lift with or as with a jack. **2** *Colloq.* To advance, as a price or charge: often with *up*. **3** *U.S.* To jack-light. [from *Jack*, a personal name]

jack[2] (jak) *n.* **1** A cultivated tree *(Artocarpus heterophyllus)* of SE Asia, resembling the breadfruit tree. **2** Its yellow wood, furnishing valuable lumber. **3** The large fruit, resembling the breadfruit, produced by this tree. [<Pg. *jaca* <Malayalam *chakka*]

jack[3] (jak) *n.* A medieval coat of mail made of two thicknesses of leather or cloth and padded; a gambeson. [<OF *jacque* <Sp. *jaco*, ? <Arabic *shakk*]

Jack (jak) **1** A nickname for JOHN; earlier, for JAMES, as derived from JACOB. **2** Hence, from its frequency, a man; fellow; especially, a sailor; also, a handy man for odd jobs: in these senses usually **jack.** [<OF *Jacques* Jacob]

jack-a-dan·dy (jak′ə·dan′dē) *n. pl.* **·dies** A ridiculous fop.

jack·al (jak′ôl, -əl) *n.* **1** One of various dog-like carnivorous mammals (family *Canidae*), smaller than the wolf, with a long bushy tail, feeding on small animals and on carrion. **2** One who does base work to serve another's purpose: from the erroneous notion that the jackal finds prey for the lion. Also **jack′all.** **—** *v.i.* To do menial work. [<Turkish *chakal* <Persian *shaghal*]

Jack-a-Lent (jak′ə·lent′) See JACK-O'-LENT.

jack-a-napes (jak′ə·nāps) *n.* An impertinent fellow; an upstart. [<*Jack Napes*, nickname of William de la Pole, 15th c. Duke of Suffolk]

Jack and Jill In an old English nursery rime, a boy and girl who "went up a hill to fetch a pail of water." Hence, any man and his sweetheart or wife.

jack·ass (jak′as′) *n.* **1** The male ass. **2** A foolish person; blockhead.

jackass brig A brigantine.

jack bean A three-leaved climber of the bean family *(Canavalia ensiformis)* having purple flowers in auxiliary racemes and long pods: grown for stock feed in the southern United States: also called *overlook*.

jack·boots (jak′bōōts′) *n. pl.* Heavy topboots reaching above the knees.

jack box A unit for plugging a loudspeaker or individual headphone into a radio receiving system: used in airplanes, etc.

jack·daw (jak′dô′) *n.* **1** A small, glossy-black, crowlike bird *(Corvus monedual)* of Europe, often tamed as a pet. **2** Any of various American grackles, especially the boat-tailed grackle *(Cassidix mexicanus)*.

jack·er (jak′ər) *n.* One who or that which jacks.

jack·e·roo (jak′ə·roo′) *n. Austral. Colloq.* A station employee who is being trained for managerial status. Also **jack′a·roo′.** [<JACK[1] + (KANGA)ROO]

jack·et (jak′it) *n.* **1** A short coat, usually not extending below the hips. **2** Anything resembling a jacket. **3** A covering for a steam cylinder, to prevent radiation of heat. **4** A removable paper wrapper or cover for a bound book. **5** An open envelope or folder, used for filing letters, documents, papers, etc. **6** A covering of hard metal on a bullet or shell. **7** The skin of a potato. — *v.t.* To cover with a jacket. [<OF *jaquette*, dim. of *jaque* a coat] — **jack′et·ed** *adj.*

jack·ey (jak′ē), **jack·ie** See JACKY.

Jack Frost A personification of wintry or frosty weather.

jack·ham·mer (jak′ham′ər) A rock drill operated by compressed air.

jack-in-a-box (jak′in·ə·boks′) *n.* **1** A toy consisting of a grotesque figure in a box, springing up when the lid is unfastened. **2** A tropical tree *(Hernandia sonora)* yielding a fruit that when shaken makes a rattling sound. **3** A rogue; swindler. Also **jack′-in-the-box′.**

jack-in-the-pul·pit (jak′in·thə·po͝ol′pit) *n.* A common American herb *(Arisaema triphyllum)* of the arum family, growing from a turnip-shaped bulb, with an intensely acrid juice and a curious spike of flowers enclosed in a greenish-purple spathe: also called *Indian turnip.*

JACK-IN-THE-PULPIT
Fruit and flower.

Jack Ketch (kech) A public executioner or hangman. [after *John Ketch,* died 1686, executioner under James II]

jack·knife (jak′nīf′) *n. pl.* **·knives** (-nīvz) **1** A large pocket knife with recessed handle into which the blade is folded. **2** A dive during which the body is doubled from the hips with the hands touching the ankles, and then straightened before entering the water.

jack·leg (jak′leg′) *n.* One who professes more knowledge, skill, or standing than he has; especially, an unprincipled lawyer; a shyster. — *adj.* Untrained; incompetent; unprincipled.

jack·light (jak′līt′) *n. U.S.* A torch or light used in hunting or fishing at night to attract and dazzle game or fish.

jack-light (jak′līt′) *v.t.* & *v.i.* To seek (game or fish) with a jacklight.

jack·o (jak′ō) *n. pl.* **jack·os** An ape; jocko.

jack oak A black-barked oak of the eastern United States *(Quercus marilandica).*

jack-of-all-trades (jak′əv·ôl′trādz) *n.* One who is able to do many kinds of work.

jack-o′-lan·tern (jak′ə·lan′tərn) *n.* **1** A will-o′-the-wisp; ignis fatuus. **2** A lantern made of a pumpkin hollowed and carved into a grotesque face, or an imitation of this. Also **jack′-a-lan′tern.**

Jack-o′-Lent (jak′ə·lent′) *n.* An effigy of Judas Iscariot, formerly carried in processions and pelted in Lent; hence, a target for criticism; butt. Also spelled *Jack-a-lent.*

jack pine The gray pine *(Pinus banksiana),* growing chiefly on barren tracts of North America.

jack·plane (jak′plān′) *n.* A carpenter's roughing plane.

jack·pot (jak′pot′) *n.* **1** In poker, a pot that must accumulate till one of the players gets a pair of jacks or cards of higher value on the deal; also, a game or part of it in which this rule is observed. **2** Hence, any pot or pool in which contributions accumulate. — **to hit the jackpot** *U.S. Colloq.* To win the biggest possible prize; to achieve a major success.

jack rabbit One of a genus *(Lepus)* of large American hares with long hind legs and long ears.

jack·screw (jak′skro͞o′) *n.* A mechanical jack in which pressure is transmitted by the action of a screw.

jack·shaft (jak′shaft′, -shäft′) *n.* **1** A shaft sunk in a mine. **2** A bar or crosspiece for supporting a mechanical drill, held in place by jackscrews.

jack snipe **1** A small European snipe. **2** The pectoral sandpiper.

Jack·son (jak′sən) The capital of Mississippi.

Jack·son (jak′sən), **Andrew,** 1767–1845, president of the United States 1829–37: called "Old Hickory." — **Chevalier,** born 1865, U. S. laryngologist. — **Helen Hunt,** 1831–85, *née* Maria Fiske, U. S. novelist. — **Thomas Jonathan,** 1824–63, Confederate general: known as *Stonewall Jackson* from the firm stand of his command at the first battle of Bull Run, 1861.

Jackson Day An anniversary celebration of Andrew Jackson's victory at New Orleans on January 8, 1815: often commemorated by a Democratic party dinner.

Jack·so·ni·an (jak·sō′nē·ən) *adj.* Of, pertaining to, or brought into notice by a person named Jackson; specifically, relating to Andrew Jackson, seventh president of the United States. — *n.* An advocate of the political principles of Andrew Jackson.

Jacksonian epilepsy *Pathol.* A form of epilepsy characterized by local spasms which tend to spread gradually outward from the focal point, usually without loss of consciousness. Also called *focal epilepsy.* [after John Hughlings *Jackson,* 1834–1911, English physician]

Jack·son·ville (jak′sən·vil) A port near the mouth of the St. Johns River in northern Florida.

Jack Sprat A character in an English nursery rime.

jack·stay (jak′stā′) *n. Naut.* **1** A rope or rod along the upper surface of a yard, to which to fasten a sail. **2** A rope or rod running up and down on the forward side of a mast, on which a yard travels; a traveler.

jack·stone (jak′stōn′) *n.* **1** One of a set of stones or knobbed metal pieces used in a child's game: also **jack.** **2** *pl.* The game so played; jacks.

jack·straw (jak′strô′) *n.* **1** A straw effigy; man of straw. **2** One of a set of straws or thin strips of wood, bone, etc., used in playing a child's game. **3** *pl.* The game played with them.

jack·tar (jak′tär′) *n. Colloq.* A sailor. Also spelled **jack′-tar′, jack tar, Jack Tar.**

jack towel A long coarse towel hanging on a roller.

jack·y (jak′ē) *n. pl.* **jack·ies** **1** A sailor. **2** *Brit. Slang* Gin. Also spelled *jackey, jackie.* [Dim. of JACK]

Ja·co (yä′ko͞o) An island dependency of Portuguese Timor; 5 square miles: also *Yako.*

Ja·cob (jā′kəb, *Du., Ger.* yä′kôp) A masculine personal name. Also *Fr.* **Ja·cob** (zhà·kôb′), *Sp.* **Ja·co·bo** (hä·kō′bō), *Lat.* **Ja·co·bus** (jə·kō′bəs). [<Hebrew, supplanter]

— **Jacob** A Hebrew patriarch; second son of Isaac and father of the founders of the twelve tribes of Israel: also called *Israel. Gen* xxv 26.

Ja·cob (jā′kəb), **Arthur,** 1790–1874, Irish physician.

Jac·o·be·an (jak′ə·bē′ən) *adj.* **1** Of or pertaining to the time of James I of England and sometimes of James II; specifically, of or pertaining to an English architectural and furniture style of the early 17th century, representing the merging of English Tudor forms into to those of the Renaissance, and sometimes, by extension, the architecture of the entire Stuart period and of the Commonwealth. **2** Of or pertaining to the apostle St. James the Less or the epistle ascribed to him. — *n.* A Jacobean writer or politician. Also **Jac′o·bae′an.** [<LL *Jacobaeus* <*Jacobus* James]

jac·o·bin (jak′ə·bin) *n.* A pigeon with neck feathers ruffed so as to form a hood.

Jac·o·bin (jak′ə·bin) *n,* **1** A member of a French revolutionary society that inaugurated the Reign of Terror, 1793; dissolved, 1799. **2** Hence, an extreme revolutionist. **3** *pl.* Dominican friars before the French Revolution. [<F *Jacobin* of St. James <Med. L *Jacobinus* <LL *Jacobus* James; with ref. to the church of St. James, in Paris, where they first met]

Jac·o·bin·i·cal (jak′ə·bin′i·kəl) *adj.* **1** Belonging to the French Jacobins. **2** Turbulently democratic; revolutionary; radical. Also **Jac′·o·bin′ic.** — **Jac′o·bin′i·cal·ly** *adv.*

Jac·o·bin·ism (jak′ə·bin·iz′əm) *n.* **1** Unreasonable or violent opposition to legitimate government; popular turbulence. **2** A Jacobinical characteristic or idea.

Jac·o·bin·ize (jak′ə·bin·īz′) *v.t.* **·ized, ·iz·ing** To affect with or convert to Jacobinism.

Jac·o·bite (jak′ə·bīt) *n.* **1** An adherent of James II of England after his abdication in 1688, or of his royal line. **2** An adherent of the Jacobite Church. — *adj.* Of or pertaining to the Jacobites: also **Jac·o·bit·ic** (jak′ə·bit′ik), **Jac′o·bit′i·cal.** [<L *Jacobus* James + -ITE[1]]

Jacobite Church A Monophysitic sect of Syria, Mesopotamia, and Kurdistan, founded by Jacobus Baradaeus, died 578, a Greek monk of Constantinople: regarded as heretical by the Greek Church.

Jac·o·bit·ism (jak′ə·bīt′iz·əm) *n.* The tenets of the English Jacobites, or of the Syrian sect of Jacobites.

Jacob's ladder **1** A ladder from earth to heaven that Jacob saw in a dream. *Gen.* xxviii 12. **2** *Naut.* A rope ladder, often with wooden steps.

Ja·cob's-lad·der (ja′kəbz·lad′ər) *n.* **1** A common European ornamental herb *(Polemonium caeruleum),* having an arrangement of its leaves and leaflets suggestive of a ladder: often called *makebate.* **2** Any of several related species found in America.

ja·co·bus (jə·kō′bəs) *n.* An English gold coin of the reign of James I, varying in value from 20 to 22 shillings. [<L *Jacobus* James]

jac·o·net (jak′ə·net) *n.* **1** A soft, thin, white cotton cloth. **2** A cotton fabric with one side glazed. [from *Jagganath* (now Puri) in India, where first made]

Jac·quard (jə·kärd′, *Fr.* zhà·kàr′) *adj.* Invented by or pertaining to J. M. Jacquard, 1752–1834, a French weaver who invented the **Jacquard loom,** used in weaving figured materials.

Jacque·mi·not (jak′mi·nō, *Fr.* zhàk·mē·nō′) *n.* A deep-red, hybrid perpetual rose. Also **General Jacqueminot.** [after J. F. *Jacqueminot,* 1787–1865, French general]

Jacque·rie (zhàk·rē′) *n.* The peasant insurrection in France in 1358: so called from the scornful nickname *Jacques Bonhomme* given by the nobles to the peasantry; hence, any revolt of peasants.

Jacques (zhàk) The French form of JAMES.

jac·ta a·le·a est (jak′tə ā′lē·ə est) *Latin* The die has been cast.

jac·ta·tion (jak·tā′shən) *n.* **1** The act of throwing. **2** Jactitation (def. 2). **3** Exercise, as in riding. **4** Boasting. [<L *jactatio, -onis* <*jactare,* freq. of *jacere* throw]

jac·ti·ta·tion (jak′tə·tā′shən) *n.* **1** A public boasting; bragging. **2** *Pathol.* A morbid restlessness, as in acute disease. **3** *Law* A false assertion, as of marriage, repeated to the injury of another; an action to enjoin such false pretension. [<Med. L *jactitatio, -onis* <L *jactitare* say publicly, freq. of *jactare* hurl]

Ja·cuí (zhə·kwē′) A river in central Río Grande do Sul state, Brazil, flowing 280 miles south and east to the Lagoa dos Patos.

jac·u·late (jak′yə·lāt) *v.t.* **·lat·ed, ·lat·ing** *Rare* To hurl, as a dart. [<L *jaculatus,* pp. of *jaculare* throw] — **jac′u·la′tion** *n.*

jac·u·la·to·ry (jak′yə·lə·tôr′ē, -tō′rē) *adj.* Darting or thrown out suddenly.

jade[1] (jād) *n.* **1** A hard, tough, greenish or white silicate, used for making ornaments and including chiefly two species: jadeite and nephrite. **2** The greenish color of jade; jade green. [<F *jade,* var. of *ejade* <Sp. *(piedra de) ijada* (stone for) colic, lit., the side, ribs]

jade[2] (jād) *n.* **1** An old, worn-out horse. **2** A worthless person; specifically, a hussy. **3** A woman: ironical usage. — *v.t.* & *v.i.* **jad·ed, jad·ing** To weary or become weary by hard service; tire. See synonyms under TIRE[1]. [Origin uncertain]

jad·ed (jā′did) *adj.* **1** Worn-out; exhausted. **2** Satiated; sated, as from overindulgence. — **jad′ed·ly** *adv.* — **jad′ed·ness** *n.*

jade green Any of several shades of green characteristic of jade.

jade·ite (jā′dīt) *n.* A translucent sodium-aluminum silicate of the pyroxene group. [<JADE[1] + -ITE[1]]

jad·ish (jā′dish) *adj.* **1** Vicious: said of a horse. **2** Unchaste or wanton: said of a woman. Also **jad′y.** — **jad′ish·ly** *adv.* — **jad′ish·ness** *n.*

jae·ger (yā′gər) *n.* **1** (*also* jā′gər) Any of a genus *(Stercorarius)* of sea birds which pursue and harass gulls and terns until they drop or disgorge their prey. **2** A huntsman or hunting attendant. **3** *Obs.* A soldier of the German or Austrian army especially trained in scouting, sharpshooting, and forestry: hired by England during the American Revolution. Also spelled *yager*. Also **jä'ger.** [<G, hunter <*jagen* hunt]

Ja·el (jā'əl) In the Bible, an Israelite heroine who killed Sisera. *Judges* iv 17.

Ja·én (hä·än') A province of southern Spain; 5,205 square miles; capital Jaén.

Jaf·fa (jaf'ə, yaf'ə) A port in western Israel; included in Tel Aviv since 1950: Old Testament *Joppa*. *Hebrew* **Ya·fo** (yä·fō').

Jaff·na (jäf'nə) A port on **Jaffna Peninsula,** the northernmost part of Ceylon.

jag[1] (jag) *n.* **1** A projecting point; notch; tooth. **2** A bolt with barbed point. **3** *Brit. Dial.* A stab or jab, as of a dirk. —*v.t.* **jagged, jag·ging 1** To cut notches or jags in. **2** To cut unevenly or with slashing strokes, as a garment. Also **jagg.** [ME *jagge*; origin unknown]

jag[2] (jag) *n.* **1** A load for one horse; small load. **2** *Slang* Enough liquor to intoxicate; also, intoxication: to have a *jag* on. Also **jagg.** [Origin unknown]

Jag·a·nath (jug'ə·nät, -nôt), **Jag·a·na·tha** (jug'ə·nä'tə), **Jag·gur·nath** (jug'ər·nät) See JUGGERNAUT.

jag·ged (jag'id) *adj.* Having jags or notches. Also *jaggy*. See synonyms under ROUGH. —**jag'ged·ly** *adv.* —**jag'ged·ness** *n.*

jag·ger·y (jag'ər·ē) *n.* **1** A coarse sugar made in the East Indies from the sap of the date palm or from sugarcane. **2** A wine made from the coconut palm. Also **jag'gar·y, jag'gher·y, jag·ra** (jag'rə). [<Hind. *jāgrī* <Skt. *çarkara* sugar]

jag·gy (jag'ē) *adj.* **·gi·er, ·gi·est** Having notches; jagged.

ja·ghir (jä·gɪr') *n. Anglo-Indian* The government revenues of a tract of land assigned with the power to collect and administer. Also **ja·gheer', ja·ghire'.** [<Persian *jā* place + *gīr* holding]

jag·uar (jag'wär, jag'yoo·är) *n.* A large, tawny, spotted feline (*Panthera onca*) of tropical America. [<Tupian *jaguara*]

JAGUAR
(Up to 9 feet in length; tail: about 2 1/2 feet)

ja·gua·run·di (jä'gwə·run'dē) *n.* A carnivorous, weasel-like wildcat (genus *Felis*) of tropical America, having grayish-brown fur: also called *yaguarundi*. Also **ja'gua·ron'di.** [<Tupian]

Jah (jä, yä) *Hebrew* Jehovah. *Psalms* lxviii 4.

Jah·veh, Jah·we (yä've), **Jah·vism, Jah·wism** (yä'viz·əm), etc. See YAHWEH, etc.

jai a·lai (hī ə·lī') A Spanish game, popular in Latin America, played by two opposed couples in a court called a *frontón*: the ball is served against a wall, and each player wears a gauntlet from which projects a long, curved wicker racket, called the *cesta*, in which he alternately receives the ball and hurls it back against the wall. The first to miss loses the point. Compare *pelota*. [<Sp. <Basque, jolly festival]

Jai·hun (jī·hoon') The Arabic name for the AMU DARYA.

jail (jāl) *n.* A building or place for the confinement of arrested persons or those guilty of minor offenses. —*v.t.* To put or hold in jail; imprison. Also, *Brit.*, *gaol*. [<OF *jaiole*, ult. <L *cavea* cave]

jail·bird (jāl'bûrd') *n. Colloq.* **1** One sentenced to or confined in prison. **2** A habitual lawbreaker; one often confined in jail. Also, *Brit.*, *gaolbird*.

jail–de·liv·er·y (jāl'di·liv'ər·ē) *n.* **1** *Law* The legal disposal, as by trial and condemnation or acquittal, of the cases of all prisoners awaiting trial. **2** The escape or forcible liberation of prisoners from jail.

jail·er (jā'lər) *n.* The officer in charge of a jail: also, *Brit.*, *gaoler*. Also **jail'or.**

Jai·lo·lo (jī·lō'lō) See HALMAHERA.

Jai·me (hī'mā) A Spanish form of JAMES.

Jain (jīn) *n.* An adherent of Jainism. —*adj.* Of or pertaining to Jainism. Also **Jai·na** (jī'nə). [<Hind. *Jaina* <*jina* victorious]

Jain·ism (jī'niz·əm) *n.* A Hindu religious system, founded about 500 B.C., which combines certain elements of Brahmanism and Buddhism, its principal distinctive features being the worship of sages or saints, known as *jinas*, and the great respect for the lives of animals.

Jai·pur (jī·poor') **1** A former princely state in the Rajputana States, India. **2** The capital of Rajasthan, formerly the capital of Jaipur.

Ja·kar·ta (jä·kär'tä) A port of NW Java, capital of the Republic of Indonesia: formerly *Batavia*: also *Djakarta*.

jake (jāk) *adj. Slang* All right; fine.

Jake (jāk) Diminutive of JACOB.

jakes (jāks) *n. Archaic* or *Dial.* A privy. [? from *Jake*, a personal name]

Ja·kob (yä'kôb) Danish, Polish, Swedish, and German form of JACOB.

jal·ap (jal'əp) *n.* **1** The dried root of any of several Mexican plants of the morning-glory family (especially *Exogonium purga*), used in medicine as a hydragog. **2** Any allied plant yielding a similar drug. Also *Obs.* **jal'op.** [<Sp. (*purga de*) *Jalapa* (medicine from) Jalapa] —**ja·lap·ic** (jə·lap'ik) *adj.*

Ja·la·pa (hä·lä'pä) The capital of Veracruz state, eastern Mexico. Officially **Ja·la'pa En·rí·quez** (en·rē'kās).

jal·a·pin (jal'ə·pin) *n.* A resinous glycoside contained in several convolvulaceous plants: used in medicine as a cathartic. [<JALAP + -IN]

Ja·lis·co (hä·lēs'kō) A state in west central Mexico, 31,152 square miles; capital, Guadalajara.

ja·lop·y (jə·lop'ē) *n. pl.* **·lop·ies** *U.S. Colloq.* A decrepit automobile. [Origin uncertain]

ja·lou·sie (jal'oo·sē, zhal'oo·zē') *n.* A Venetian blind. [<F, lit., jealousy]

Jal·u·it (jal'oo·it) The largest atoll and administrative center of the Marshall Islands; 4 square miles.

jam[1] (jam) *v.* **jammed, jam·ming** *v.t.* **1** To press or force into a tight place or position; wedge or squeeze in. **2** To fill and block up by crowding: to *jam* a corridor. **3** To bruise or crush by violent pressure. **4** To cause (a machine, part, etc.) to become wedged or stuck fast so that it cannot work. **5** In radio, to interfere with (a broadcast, station, etc.) by transmitting on the same wavelength. —*v.i.* **6** To become wedged; stick fast. **7** To press or wedge; push: The crowd *jammed* into the room. **8** In jazz music, to improvise; also, to take part in a jam session. —*n.* **1** A number of people or objects closely crowded; a crush; the act of jamming. **2** A mass of logs, ice, etc., blocked in a stream. See synonyms under THRONG. —*adv.* Completely: *jam* full. ◆ Homophone: *jamb*. [Related to CHAMP[1]]

Synonyms (verb): crowd, crush, force, pack, press, push, squeeze, throng. See HUSTLE. *Antonyms*: ease, free, liberate, loosen, release, relieve.

jam[2] (jam) *n.* A pulpy, sweet conserve of fruit boiled with sugar: distinguished from *jelly*. ◆ Homophone: *jamb*. [? <JAM[1], *v.*]

Ja·mai·ca (jə·mā'kə) *n.* Rum produced in Jamaica.

Ja·mai·ca (jə·mā'kə) An independent member of the Commonwealth of nations comprising the island of Jamaica, SE of Cuba; 4,411 square miles; capital, Kingston; and its dependencies, the Cayman Islands and Turks and Caicos Islands; total, 4,705 square miles. —**Ja·mai'can** *adj.* & *n.*

jamb (jam) *n.* **1** A side post or side of a doorway, window, etc. **2** A jambeau. ◆ Homophone: *jam*. [<OF *jambe* leg, support <LL *gamba* hoof, leg <Celtic]

jam·ba·la·ya (jam'bə·lä'yə, zham'-) *n.* A traditional Creole dish of rice cooked with seafood and fowl. [<Provençal *jambalaia*]

jam·beau (jam·bō') *n. pl.* **·beaux** (-bōz') A piece of armor for the leg. Also **jambe** (jam). [<OF *jambe* a leg]

Jam·bol (yäm'bôl) See YAMBOL.

jam·bo·ree (jam'bə·rē') *n.* **1** *Colloq.* A boisterous frolic or spree. **2** A large, especially international, assembly of Boy Scouts. **3** In euchre, a lone hand consisting of the five highest cards. [<JAM[1]; on analogy with *corroboree, chivaree*]

James (jāmz) A masculine personal name. [<Sp. *Jaime*, var. of *Jacobo* JACOB]

—**James** One of the brothers of Jesus: identified by some with James the Less. *Mark* vi 3.

—**James I,** 1394–1437, king of Scotland 1406–1437: educated in England; author of *The Kingis Quair*.

—**James III,** 1451–88, king of Scotland 1460–1488, defeated at Bannockburn; murdered.

—**James IV,** 1473–1513, king of Scotland 1488–1513; defeated and killed at Flodden Field.

—**James I,** 1566–1625, first Stuart king of England 1603–25; as **James VI,** king of Scotland 1567–1625. See under BIBLE.

—**James II,** 1633–1701, king of England 1685–88; deposed.

—**James Edward** See STUART, JAMES EDWARD.

—**James the Greater** One of the Twelve Apostles; son of Zebedee, brother of John.

—**James the Less** One of the Twelve Apostles; son of Alphaeus.

James (jāmz), **Henry,** 1843–1916, U.S. novelist and critic active in England. —**Jesse (Woodson),** 1847–82, U.S. outlaw. —**William,** 1842–1910, U.S. psychologist; brother of Henry James.

James Bay The southern projection of Hudson Bay, Canada.

Jame·son (jām'sən), **Sir Leander Starr,** 1853–1917, administrator in South Africa; leader of the unsuccessful **Jameson's raid** into the Transvaal, Dec. 29, 1895.

James River 1 A river in Virginia, flowing 340 miles to Hampton Roads. **2** A river in North and South Dakota, flowing 710 miles SE to the Missouri: also *Dakota River*.

James·town (jāmz'toun) **1** A restored village in eastern Virginia: the first permanent English settlement within the limits of the United States, 1607. **2** A port and the capital of St. Helena.

Jamestown weed See JIMSONWEED.

jammed on the wind *Naut.* Sailing close-hauled.

Jam·mu (jum'oo) **1** A province of Jammu and Kashmir; 12,378 square miles. **2** A city in SW Jammu and Kashmir, India, capital of Jammu province, and former winter capital of Jammu and Kashmir.

Jammu and Kashmir A constituent State of India, 1957; an independent republic, 1952–57; a princely state within the Dominion of India, 1947–52, and in British India, 1846–1947; an object of contention between India and Pakistan since 1947; 92,780 square miles in all, 85,861 square miles under Indian control, the rest under Pakistani occupation though claimed by both countries; capital, Srinigar. Formerly **Kashmir and Jammu.**

jam–packed (jam'pakt') *adj. Colloq.* Crowded to capacity; as tightly packed as possible.

jam session An informal gathering of jazz musicians performing improvisations on various themes, each exploring the possibilities of his instrument while following no set musical form other than a motif mutually evolved.

Jam·shed·pur (jäm'shed·poor') A city in SE Bihar, India.

Jam·shid (jam'shid) In Iranian mythology, an early king, said to have reigned 700 years. Also **Jam'shyd.**

Jan (yän) Dutch and Polish form of JOHN.

Ja·ná·ček (yä'nä·chek), **Leoš,** 1854–1928, Czech composer.

Jane (jān) A feminine personal name; variant form of JOAN.

Janes·ville (jānz'vil) A city in southern Wisconsin, near Beloit; pop. 35,164.

Jan·et (jan'it, jə·net') A feminine personal name. [See JOAN]

Ja·net (zhà·ne'), **Pierre Marie Félix,** 1859–1947, French psychologist and neurologist.

jan·gle (jang'gəl) *v.* **·gled, ·gling** *v.i.* **1** To make harsh, unmusical sounds. **2** To wrangle, bicker. —*v.t.* **3** To cause to sound discordantly. —*n.* Discordant sound; wrangling. See synonyms under NOISE, QUARREL. [<OF *jangler*] —**jan'gler** *n.* —**jan'gling** *n.*

Ja·nic·u·lum (jə·nik'yə·ləm) A hill in Rome on the Tiber, opposite the original seven.

Ja·ni·na (yä'nē·nä) See IOANNINA.

jan·i·tor (jan′i·tər) *n.* **1** One who has the care of a building, offices, etc. **2** A doorkeeper; porter. [<L <*janua* door]

jan·i·zar·y (jan′ə·zer′ē) *n. pl.* **·zar·ies** One of the former bodyguards of the Turkish sultans, originally composed of young prisoners trained to arms: suppressed in 1826; also, sometimes, any Turkish soldier. Also **jan′i·sar·y, jan′is·sar·y.** [<F *janissaire* <Turkish *yenicheri* new army]

Jan May·en (yän′ mī′ən) A Norwegian island in the Arctic Ocean between Norway and Greenland; 144 square miles.

jan·nock (jan′ok) *n. Scot.* Oaten bread; a cake.

Já·nos (ya′nôsh) Hungarian form of JOHN.

Jan·sen (jan′sən, *Du.* yän′sən), **Cornelis,** 1585–1638, Roman Catholic theologian; bishop of Ypres in Flanders. Also **Jan·se·ni·us** (jan·sē′·nē·əs).

Jan·sen·ism (jan′sən·iz′əm) *n. Theol.* The doctrines taught by Cornelis Jansen, emphasizing predestination and the irresistibility of God's grace, and denying free will. **—Jan′·sen·ist** *n.* **—Jan′sen·is′tic** or **·ti·cal** *adj.*

jant·y (jan′tē) See JAUNTY.

Jan·u·ar·y (jan′yōō·er′ē) The first month of the year, containing 31 days. [<L *Januarius* < *Janus* Janus]

Ja·nus (jā′nəs) In Roman mythology, the god of portals and beginnings, having two faces, one on each side of his head.

JANUS

Ja·nus-faced (jā′·nəs·fāst′) *adj.* Two-faced; looking both ways; deceitful.

Jap (jap) *adj.* & *n. Slang* Japanese: an opprobrious usage.

jap·a·con·i·tine (jap′·ə·kon′ə·tēn) *n. Chem.* A white, crystalline, extremely poisonous alkaloid, $C_{24}H_{47}O_{11}N$, from the root of the Japanese aconite (*Aconitum japonicum*). [<JAP(ANESE) + ACONIT(E) + -INE[2]]

ja·pan (jə·pan′) *n.* **1** A varnish used as a medium in which to grind colors, and as a drier for pigments. **2** A hard jet-black lacquer for coating sheet metal; Brunswick-black. **—** *adj.* Pertaining to or lacquered with japan. **—** *v.t.* **·panned, ·pan·ning** To lacquer with or as with japan. [from JAPAN] **—ja·pan′ner** *n.*

Ja·pan (jə·pan′) A constitutional empire of eastern Asia, comprising the four main islands of Honshu, Hokkaido, Kyushu, and Shikoku with many adjacent smaller islands; 147,692 square miles; capital, Tokyo: also *Nihon, Nippon, Dai Nippon.*

MANCHUKUO
U.S.S.R.
HOKKAIDO
Sea of Japan
Seoul
KOREA
HONSHU
JAPAN
Tokyo
Yokohama
Hiroshima
Nagasaki
KYUSHU
PACIFIC OCEAN

Japan, Sea of The arm of the Pacific Ocean lying between the islands of Japan and the Asian mainland.

japan black See JAPAN (lacquer): also called *black-japan.*

Japan clover A perennial, cloverlike herb (*Lespedeza striata*) of the bean family, from eastern Asia, naturalized in the United States and used for feeding horses and cattle. Also **Japanese clover.**

Jap·a·nese (jap′ə·nēz′, -nēs′) *adj.* Belonging or relating to Japan, its language, or its people. **—** *n.* **1** A native of Japan. **2** The agglutinative language of Japan, showing a slight similarity to Korean, but generally considered to be unrelated to any language: see KANA.

Japanese barberry A dwarfed variety of barberry (*Berberis thunbergi*): used for hedges, etc.

Japanese beetle A small green and brown beetle (*Popillia japonica*) with a metallic luster introduced into this country from Japan and first noted in 1916. The adults eat the leaves and fruits of various plants; the larvae feed on grass roots. See illustration under INSECT (injurious).

Japanese ivy A climbing shrub (*Parthenocissus tricuspidata*) closely related to the Virginia creeper.

Japanese persimmon Kaki.

Japanese river fever Tsutsugamushi disease.

Japanese spaniel See under SPANIEL.

Japanese tissue A fine silky paper, originally made from the bark of the paper mulberry.

Japanese vellum A smooth, creamy, handmade paper of exceptional strength, originally made from the paper mulberry.

Jap·a·nesque (jap′ə·nesk′) *adj.* In the style of Japanese art or industry. **—** *n.* An article made in such style. **—Jap′a·nesque′ly** *adv.* **—Jap′a·nesque′ry** *n.*

Japan rose Any of several true roses native to Japan; specifically, *Rosa multiflora* and *Rosa rugosa,* both widely cultivated garden plants in the United States.

Japan Stream See under CURRENT.

Japan wax A vegetable fat containing palmitic acid and extracted from the berries of certain species of sumac (genus *Rhus*): used largely for adulterating beeswax: also called *Japan tallow.*

jape (jāp) *v.* **japed, jap·ing** *v.i. Archaic* To joke; make jests. **—** *v.t. Obs.* To mock; jibe at. **—** *n.* A jest; jibe. [ME *jappen*; origin uncertain] **—jap′er** *n.* **—jap′er·y** *n.*

Ja·pheth (jā′fith) A masculine proper name. Also **Ja′phet** (-fit). [<Hebrew, the extender] **—Japheth** Third son of Noah. *Gen.* v 32.

Ja·phet·ic (jə·fet′ik) *adj.* **1** Belonging to or descended from Japheth, Noah's son: distinguished from Hamitic and Semitic. **2** *Obs.* Indo-European.

Ja·pon·ic (jə·pon′ik) *adj.* Of, pertaining to, or from Japan. [<*Japon,* obs. var. of *Japan* + -IC]

ja·pon·i·ca (jə·pon′i·kə) *n.* **1** An eastern-Asian shrub (*Chaenomeles lagenaria*) with toothed leaves and bright scarlet flowers; the Japanese quince. **2** The camellia (*Camellia japonica*). [<NL, Japanese]

Jap·o·nism (jap′ə·niz′əm) *n.* A Japanese characteristic, as in art.

Ja·pu·rá (zhä′pōō·rä′) A river rising in the Andes of SW Colombia and flowing 1,150 miles SE to the Amazon in NE Brazil: also *Yapurá.*

Ja·ques (jā′kwēz, -kwiz) In Shakespeare's *As You Like It,* a lord, melancholy and cynical, attending on the banished duke.

jar[1] (jär) *n.* **1** A deep, wide-mouthed vessel of earthenware or glass. **2** The quantity which a jar contains; jarful. [<F *jarre* < Arabic *jarrah*]

jar[2] (jär) *v.* **jarred, jar·ring** *v.i.* **1** To shake or rattle, as from a shock or blow. **2** To make a harsh, discordant sound. **3** To have an unpleasant or painful effect: Her manner *jarred* on my nerves. **4** To disagree or conflict; quarrel. **—** *v.t.* **5** To cause to shake or rattle, as by a shock or blow. **6** To affect unpleasantly or painfully, as one's nerves or feelings; shock. **7** To cause to make a harsh, discordant sound. See synonyms under SHAKE. **—** *n.* **1** A shaking, as from a sudden shock. **2** A discordant sound. **3** Discord; strife. See synonyms under QUARREL. [Imit.]

jar[3] (jär) *n.* A swinging, as of a door on its hinges: used only in the phrases **on a jar** and **on the jar,** meaning slightly opened. [OE *cerr.* See AJAR[1].]

ja·ra·be (hä·rä′bā) *n.* A Mexican dance. [<Sp., lit., sirup]

Ja·ra·bub (jä′rä·bōōb′) An oasis in eastern Cyrenaica, Libya: Italian *Giarabub.*

jar·di·nière (jär′də·nir′, *Fr.* zhär·dē·nyâr′) *n.* An ornamental pot or stand, as of porcelain, for flowers or plants. [<F, fem. of *jardinier* a gardener]

jar·fly (jär′flī′) *n. pl.* **·flies** A cicada or harvest fly: so called because of the jarring noise it makes.

jar·gon[1] (jär′gən) *n.* **1** Confused, unintelligible speech; gibberish. **2** Any language thought to be meaningless or excessively confused. **3** The technical or specialized language characteristic of a particular sect, profession, or similarly restrictive group; cant; lingo: the *jargon* of the law courts. **4** A mixture of two or more dissimilar languages, often used as a lingua franca, as the Chinook *jargon*; pidgin. See synonyms under SLANG. **—** *v.i.* To talk in jargon; gabble. [<OF]

jar·gon[2] (jär′gon) *n.* A transparent, adamantine, colorless, yellowish, leaf-green, or smoky zircon found in Ceylon. Also **jar·goon′** (-gōōn′). [<F, ult. <Persian *zargūn* gold-colored]

jar·go·nelle (jär′gə·nel′) *n.* An early variety of pear. Also **jar′go·nel′, jar′gon·nelle′.** [<F, dim. of *jargon* JARGON[2]]

jar·gon·ize (jär′gən·īz) *v.* **·ized, ·iz·ing** *v.t.* To translate into jargon. **—** *v.i.* To speak in jargon.

ja·ri·na (jə·rē′nə) *n.* The ivory nut.

jarl (yärl) *n.* Formerly, a Scandinavian nobleman or chieftain; an earl. [<ON. Akin to EARL.]

jar·o·site (jar′ə·sīt, jə·rō′-) *n.* A hydrous sulfate of iron and potassium, occurring massive or in brown or yellow crystals. [from Barranco *Jarosa,* in Spain]

Jar·row (jar′ō) A port on the Tyne in NE Durham, England.

jar·vey (jär′vē) *n. Brit. Colloq.* The driver of a hackney coach; also, the driver of a jaunting car. [from *Jarvis,* a personal name]

Jar·vis Island (jär′vis) A United States possession (1936) in the central Pacific near the equator; 1 1/2 square miles.

jas·mine (jas′min, jaz′-) *n.* **1** An ornamental plant of the olive family (genus *Jasminum*) with fragrant, generally white, flowers. **2** One of various other plants, as the **Cape Jasmine** (*Gardenia jasminoides*), the **Carolina** or **yellow jasmine** (*Gelsemium sempervirens*), etc. **3** Frangipani. **4** Papaw. Also spelled *jessamine.* [<F *jasmin* <Persian *yāsmin*]

Ja·son (jā′sən) A masculine personal name. **—Jason** In Greek legend, a prince of Iolcus who led the Argonauts in search of the Golden Fleece which he obtained with the help of Medea. [<Gk., healer]

jas·pé (zhas·pā′) *adj.* Veined or clouded on the surface in imitation of jasper; streaked. **—** *n.* A variety of plain-weave shaded cloth, usually printed or embroidered. [<F, like jasper]

jas·per (jas′pər) *n.* **1** An impure, opaque, usually red, brown, or yellow variety of quartz, admitting of a high polish and used for vases and other articles: also **jas′per·ite.** **2** A stone in the breastplate of the high priest. *Exod.* xxviii 20. [<MF *jaspre,* var. of *jaspe* <L *jaspis* <Gk. <Semitic. Cf. Hebrew *yashpeh.*]

Jas·per (jas′pər, *Du.* yäs′pər) A masculine personal name. Also *Dan.* **Jes·per** (yes′pər). [<Persian, bearer of treasure]

jas·per·ize (jas′pər·īz) *v.t.* **·ized, ·iz·ing** To convert into jasper: the *jasperized* wood of Arizona.

Jasper National Park A park on the eastern slope of the Rockies, western Alberta, Canada; 4,200 square miles.

Jas·pers (yäs′pərz), **Karl,** 1883–1969, German philosopher.

jas·pid·e·an (jas·pid′ē·ən) *adj.* Consisting of or containing jasper; like jasper. Also **jas·pid′e·ous.** [<L *jaspideus* <*jaspis, -idos* jasper]

Jas·sy (yä′sē) A city in NE Rumania: also *Iasi.*

Jas·trow (jas′trō), **Joseph,** 1863–1944, U. S. psychologist born in Poland.

Jat (jät, jôt) *n. Hindi* One of an important Indian race or caste in the Punjab, Rajputana, and the United Provinces, numbering over 8,000,000.

JA·TO (jā′tō) *n. Aeron.* A jet-propulsion unit attached to airplanes to facilitate quick take-off. Also **jato.** [<J(ET) A(SSISTED) T(AKE)-O(FF)]

Jat·ro·pha (jat′rə·fə) *n.* A genus of tropical American herbs, shrubs, and trees of the spurge family, the seeds of which yield alkaloids having medicinal properties. [<NL < Gk. *iatros* physician + *trophē* food]

jaud (jäd, jôd) *n. Scot.* A jade.

jauk (jäk, jôk) *v.i. Scot.* To trifle; idle.

jaun·der (jän′dər, jôn′-) *v.i. Scot.* To talk idly. Also **jaun·er** (jä′nər, jô′-).

jaun·dice (jôn′dis, jän′-) *n.* 1 *Pathol.* A morbid condition due to excretion of bile pigments in the blood, characterized by yellowness of the skin, lassitude, and anorexia; icterus. 2 A mental condition, as in jealousy or prejudice, in which the judgment is warped. —*v.t.* **·diced, ·dic·ing** 1 To affect with jaundice. 2 To affect with prejudice or envy. [<OF *jaunisse* <*jaune* yellow <L *galbinus* yellowish <*galbus* yellow]

jaun·diced (jôn′dist, jän′-) *adj.* 1 Affected with jaundice. 2 Yellow-colored. 3 Prejudiced because of envy or jealousy.

jaunt (jônt, jänt) *n.* 1 A short journey; pleasure trip; excursion. 2 A tiresome journey. 3 *Obs.* A jolting; jounce. —*v.i.* To make a short trip, especially for pleasure. [Cf. obs. *jaunce* prance]

jaunting car In Ireland, a horse-drawn, two-wheeled vehicle having seats placed lengthwise over the wheels, back to back or face to face: also called *sidecar.* Also **jaunty car.**

JAUNTING CAR

jaunt·y (jôn′tē, jän′-) *adj.* **jaunt·i·er, jaunt·i·est** 1 Affecting a careless ease or self-satisfaction; sprightly. 2 *Obs.* Genteel. Also spelled *janty.* [<F *gentil* GENTLE] —**jaunt′i·ly** *adv.* —**jaunt′i·ness** *n.*

Jau·rès (zhô·res′), **Jean Léon,** 1859–1914, French socialist; assassinated.

Ja·va (jä′və, jav′ə) *n.* 1 A type of coffee. 2 Coffee: a cup of *Java.* 3 A domestic fowl. [from *Java,* where first grown]

Ja·va (jä′və, jav′ə) An Indonesian island SE of Sumatra; with Madura and adjacent islands, 51,032 square miles; capital, Jakarta.

Java man Pithecanthropus.

Jav·a·nese (jav′ə·nēz′, -nēs′) *adj.* Of or pertaining to Java, its language, or its people. —*n. pl.* **·nese** 1 A native or naturalized inhabitant of Java. 2 The Indonesian language of central Java, closely related to Malay, and containing some elements of Sanskrit.

Ja·va·ri (zhä′vä·rē′) A river forming about one-half the boundary of Brazil and Peru and flowing 600 miles NE to the Amazon: also *Yavari.* Also **Ja′va·ry′.**

Java Sea The part of the Pacific between Borneo and Java.

Java sparrow A seed-eating bird (*Munia oryzivora*) of Java: a common cage bird.

jave·lin (jav′lin, jav′ə·lin) *n.* 1 A short, light spear, used as a missile weapon for hunting or in war. 2 A long spear with wooden shaft, thrown for distance in an athletic contest. [<F, prob. <Celtic]

Ja·velle water (zhə·vel′) A solution of chlorinated potash or of sodium hypochlorite, used as an antiseptic and as a bleaching agent. Also **Ja·vel′ water.**

jaw (jô) *n.* 1 *Anat.* One of the two bony structures forming the framework of the mouth; a maxilla or a mandible. 2 The mouth. 3 Anything like or suggesting a jaw, as one of the gripping parts of a vise: often used figuratively: the *jaws* of death. 4 *Slang* Needless talk; scolding; abuse. —*v.i. Slang* 1 To talk; jabber. 2 To scold. —*v.t.* 3 *Slang* To scold. [Earlier *jowe, chawe.* ? Akin to *chew,* infl. by F *joue* cheek.]

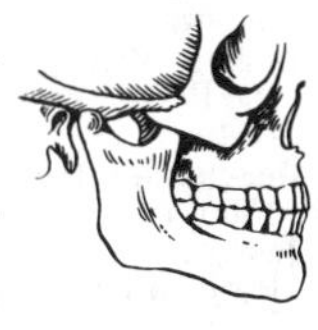
HUMAN JAW

jaw·bone (jô′bōn′) *n.* One of the bones of the jaw; especially, the mandible. —*v.t.* **·boned, ·bon·ing** *U.S. Slang* 1 To urge vigorously; especially, to urge to abide voluntarily by price or wage guidelines fixed by government. —*v.i.* 2 To argue vigorously. —*adj. U.S. Slang* Based on voluntary compliance.

jaw·break·er (jô′brā′kər) *n.* 1 Very hard candy. 2 A machine that crushes ore: also **jaw′crush′er.** 3 A word hard to pronounce.

Jax·ar·tes (jak·sär′tēz) The ancient name for the SYR DARYA.

Jay (jā), **John,** 1745–1829, American statesman; first chief justice of the United States, 1789–95.

jay (jā) *n.* 1 A small crowlike bird, usually of brilliant coloring, as the **European jay** (*Garrulus glandarius*), the **blue jay** (*Cyanocitta cristata*), the **Canada jay** (*Perisoreus canadensis*), etc. 2 *Slang* A poor actor; also, a country bumpkin; greenhorn. 3 An unscrupulous chatterbox. 4 *Obs.* A coarse or loud woman. [<OF; ult. origin unknown]

jay·hawk·er (jā′hô′kər) *n.* 1 A freebooting guerrilla; especially, one of the border ruffians who, in the Free-soil conflict in Kansas and during the Civil War, combined pillage with guerilla fighting in Missouri and the neighboring states. 2 Any freebooter or robber. 3 A native of Kansas. 4 A tarantula. [Origin uncertain]

jay·hawk·ing (jā′hô′king) *n.* Stealing; raiding.

Jay·me (zhä′me) Portuguese form of JAMES.

jay·walk (jā′wôk′) *v.i. Colloq.* To cross a street without observing the traffic regulations. [<JAY (def. 2) + WALK] —**jay′walk′er** *n.* —**jay′walk′ing** *n.*

jaz·er·ant (jaz′ər·ənt) *n.* Armor made of small overlapping metal plates quilted into a cloth or velvet jacket: also *jesseraunte, jesseraunce.* [<OF (*hauberc*) *jazerant* Algerian (mail) <Sp. *jazarino* <Arabic *Al-jaza′ir* Algiers]

jazz (jaz) *n.* 1 A kind of music, generally improvised but sometimes arranged, achieving its effects by syncopation, heavily accented rhythms, dissonance, melodic variation, and particular tonal qualities of the saxophone, trumpet, clarinet, and other instruments. It was originated by New Orleans Negro musicians. 2 Popular dance music. 3 *Slang* Nonsense; claptrap. —*adj.* Of or pertaining to jazz. —*v.t.* To play or arrange (music) as jazz. —*v.i.* To dance to or play jazz. —**to jazz up** *Slang* To make exciting or more exciting. [< Creole *jass* coition; from its origin in the brothels of New Orleans]

jazz age *U. S.* The 1920's regarded as a period of relaxed morality and gay, irresponsible behavior.

jazz·y (jaz′ē) *adj.* **jazz·i·er, jazz·i·est** 1 Resembling or characteristic of jazz. 2 *Slang* Showy or loud, as clothes; also, lively or swinging. —**jazz′i·ly** *adv.*

jeal·ous (jel′əs) *adj.* 1 Apprehensive of being displaced by a rival in affection or favor; revengeful on account of fickle treatment or the like. 2 Earnestly and anxiously suspicious; vigilant in guarding; watchful. 3 Demanding exclusive worship and love: applied to God. *Ex.* xx 5. 4 *Obs.* Zealous. 5 *Obs.* Fearful; doubtful. See synonyms under ENVIOUS. [<OF *gelos* <Med. L *zelosus* <LL *zelus* <Gk. *zēlos* zeal. Doublet of ZEALOUS.] —**jeal′ous·ly** *adv.* —**jeal′ous·ness** *n.*

jeal·ous·y (jel′əs·ē) *n. pl.* **·ous·ies** The state or quality of being jealous in any sense.

jean (jēn) *n.* 1 A sturdy, twilled cotton cloth, used especially in work clothes or for casual wear. 2 *pl.* Trousers made of jean, denim, or a similar fabric. 3 *pl. U.S. Colloq.* Trousers. [Orig. *jene fustian* <ME *Jene, Gene* Genoa, where it was made]

Jean (jēn) Scottish form of JOAN.

Jean (zhän) French form of JOHN.

Jeanne (jēn, *Fr.* zhän) See JOAN. —**Jeanne d'Arc** (dárk) See JOAN OF ARC.

Jean·nette (jə·net′) Diminutive of JANE.

Jean Paul (zhän pôl) Pseudonym of *J. P. F. Richter.*

Jeans (jēnz), **Sir James Hopwood,** 1877–1946, English astronomer and physicist.

Jebb (jeb), **Sir Richard Claverhouse,** 1841–1905, Scottish classical scholar.

jeb·el (jeb′əl) *n. Arabic* A mountain: used in geographical names of North Africa and Arabia: also French *djebel.*

Jeb·el Druze (jeb′əl drōōz′) A province of southern Syria; 2,584 square miles. Also **Jebel ed Druz** (ed drōōz′).

Jeb·el Mu·sa (jeb′əl mōō′sə) A mountain in northern Spanish Morocco on the Strait of Gibraltar: identified with one of the *Pillars of Hercules*; 2,790 feet.

Jed·burgh (jed′bûrg) The county town of Roxburghshire, Scotland.

Jed·da (jed′ə) See JIDDA.

Jed·dart (jed′ərt) *adj. Scot.* Of or pertaining to Jedburgh, Scotland. Also **Jed′wood** (-wŏŏd).

Jeddart justice *Scot.* Hanging a suspected criminal and holding the trial afterward. Also **Jedburgh** (or **Jedwood**) **justice.**

Jeddart staff *Scot.* A kind of battle-ax. Also **Jedburgh** (or **Jedwood**) **ax.**

jee (jē) See GEE[2].

Jeep (jēp) *n.* A military motor vehicle with four-wheel drive and a carrying capacity of one quarter of a ton, used for reconnaissance and for the transportation of passengers and light cargo: a trade name. [Alter. of *G.P.,* for *General Purpose* Vehicle, its military designation]

jeep·a·ble (jē′pə·bəl) *adj.* Traversable by jeep.

jeer[1] (jir) *v.i.* To speak or shout in a derisive, mocking manner; scoff. —*v.t.* To treat with derision or mockery; scoff at. See synonyms under MOCK, SCOFF. —*n.* A derisive and flouting word or speech. See synonyms under SNEER. [? OE *cēir* clamor] —**jeer′er** *n.* —**jeer′ing·ly** *adv.*

jeer[2] (jir) *n. Naut.* A tackle for raising or lowering a lower yard of a sailing ship. [? <GEE[2] + -ER[1]]

je·fe (hā′fā) *n. Spanish* Chief; leader; head.

Jef·fers (jef′ərz), **(John) Robinson,** 1887–1961, U. S. poet.

Jef·fer·son (jef′ər·sən), **Joseph,** 1829–1905, U. S. actor. —**Thomas,** 1743–1826, American statesman: drafted the Declaration of Independence; president of the United States 1801–1809.

Jefferson (jef′ər·sən), **Mount** 1 A peak in the Cascade Range, NW central Oregon; 10,495 feet. 2 A peak in the White Mountains, New Hampshire, 5,725 feet.

Jefferson City The capital of Missouri, on the Missouri River.

Jefferson Day The anniversary of Thomas Jefferson's birthday, April 13th: often commemorated by a Democratic party dinner.

Jef·fer·so·ni·an (jef′ər·sō′nē·ən) *adj.* Of or relating to Thomas Jefferson or his political opinions; democratic. —**Jef′fer·so′ni·an·ism** *n.*

Jef·frey (jef′rē), **Francis,** 1773–1850, editor and Scottish jurist: as lord advocate known as *Lord Jeffrey.*

Jef·freys (jef′rēz), **George,** 1648–89, first Baron Jeffreys of Wem, English judge.

je·had (ji·häd′) See JIHAD.

Jeh·lam (jā′lum) See JHELUM.

Je·ho·ash (jə·hō′ash) Same as JOASH.

Je·hol (jə·hol′, hōl′; *Chinese* ru′hu′) A province of SW Manchuria; 40,000 square miles; capital Chengteh.

Je·hosh·a·phat (ji·hosh′ə·fat, -hos′-) King of Judah about 873–848 B.C. I *Kings* xxii 41.

Je·ho·vah (ji·hō′və) In the Old Testament, God; the Lord: the common transliteration of the Tetragrammaton. See YAHWEH. [<Hebrew *JHVH* Yahweh, with the substitution of vowels from *'adhonay* my Lord] —**Je·ho′vi·an, Je·ho′vic** *adj.*

Jehovah's Witnesses A Christian sect, originally known as the International Bible Students' Association, strongly opposed to war and denying the authority of the government in matters of conscience.

Je·ho·vist (ji·hō′vist) *n.* 1 One who maintains that the vowel points of the word *Jehovah* as found in the Hebrew text of the Bible properly belong to it, and are not merely those of *Adonai*: opposed to *Adonist.* 2 Yahwist. —**Je·ho′vism** *n.*

Je·ho·vis·tic (jē′hō·vis′tik) *adj.* Yahwistic.

je·hu (jē′hyōō) *n.* 1 A fast or furious driver. 2 A coachman or driver. [after JEHU]

Je·hu (jē′hyōō) The tenth king of Israel, reigned at the beginning of the ninth century B.C. II *Kings* ix 20. [<Hebrew, the Lord is He]

je·june (jə·jōōn′) *adj.* 1 Lifeless; dry; dull. 2 Wanting in substance; barren. 3 Not mature; puerile; childish. See synonyms under MEAGER. [<L *jejunus* hungry] —**je·june′ly** *adv.* —**je·june′ness** *n.*

je·ju·num (jə·jōō′nəm) *n. pl.* **·na** (-nə) *Anat.* That portion of the small intestine that extends from the duodenum to the ileum. [<NL <L *jejunus* hungry, empty]

Je·kyll (jē′kəl, jek′əl), **Doctor** In Robert Louis Stevenson's *Strange Case of Doctor Jekyll and Mr. Hyde,* one half of the dual personality

consisting of a kindly physician (Jekyll) and a criminal ruffian (Hyde).
Jel·ga·va (yel′gä·vä) A city in west central Latvia: German *Mitau*: also *Yelgava.*
jel·ick (jel′ik) *n.* A long coat, open at the sides from the hip down, worn by Turkish women. [<Turkish *yelek*]
jell (jel) *v.i.* & *v.t.* **1** To jelly. **2** To assume or cause to assume definite form. [Back formation <JELLY]
Jel·li·coe (jel′i·kō), **John Rushworth,** 1859–1935, Earl Jellicoe, British admiral; governor general of New Zealand 1920–24.
jel·lied (jel′ēd) *adj.* Brought to a jelly.
jel·li·fy (jel′ə·fī) *v.t.* & *v.i.* **·fied, ·fy·ing** To make or turn into jelly. **—jel′li·fi·ca′tion** *n.*
jel·lo (jel′ō) *n.* A fruit-flavored gelatin dessert. [<*Jell-O,* a trade name]
jel·ly (jel′ē) *n. pl.* **·lies 1** Any semisolid gelatinous substance that will quiver when shaken, but will not flow, as fruit juice boiled with sugar or meat juice boiled down. **2** Any food preparation having the consistency of jelly. **3** A gelatin filter placed in front of electric lamps to change their color values; used with motion-picture cameras. **—***v.t.* & *v.i.* **·lied, ·ly·ing** To bring or turn to jelly. [<OF *gelee* <L *gelata,* orig. pp. fem. of *gelare* freeze]
jel·ly·bean (jel′ē·bēn′) *n.* A bean-shaped candy consisting of a hard, often colored coating over a gelatinous center.
jel·ly·fish (jel′ē·fish′) *n. pl.* **·fish** or **·fish·es 1** Any of a number of marine coelenterates (classes *Hydrozoa* and *Scyphozoa*) of jellylike appearance, and usually umbrella-shaped bodies with trailing tentacles, as the medusa and the Portuguese man-of-war. **2** *Colloq.* A person without energy, determination, or stamina.
je·lu·tong (zhə·lo͞o·tong′) *n.* **1** The milky resinous exudate from a Malayan tree (*Dyera costulata*), resembling chicle and also used as a substitute for rubber. **2** The tree itself, or its soft, corklike timber. [<Malay]
Jem (jem), **Jem·my** (jem′ē) Diminutives of JAMES.
jem·a·dar (jem′ə·där′) *n. Anglo-Indian* **1** A native lieutenant in the army next in rank below a subahdar. **2** A head servant or employee in a household or other establishment; sometimes, a police or customs officer of the military caste. Also **jem′i·dar′.**
Je·mappes (zhə·màp′) A town in SW Belgium; scene of the first battle of the French Revolutionary War, in which the French defeated the Austrians, 1792.
Je·mi·ma (jə·mī′mə) A feminine personal name. Also **Je·mi′mah.** [<Hebrew, a dove]
jem·my (jem′ē) *n. pl.* **·mies** *Brit.* **1** A short crowbar; a jimmy. **2** A baked sheep's head. **3** *Obs.* A type of riding boot. **4** *Dial.* A greatcoat. [Var. of JIMMY]
Je·na (yā′nə) A city in the former state of Thuringia, East Germany; site of Napoleon's defeat of the Prussians, 1806.
je ne sais quoi (zhə nə se kwà′) *French* I know not what; an indefinable something.
Jen·ghiz Khan (jeng′giz kän′) See GENGHIS KHAN.
Jen·ner (jen′ər), **Edward,** 1749–1823, English physician; introduced vaccination. **—Sir William,** 1815–98, English physician and pathologist.
jen·net (jen′it) *n.* **1** A small Spanish horse, a cross of Arabian and native stock. **2** A female donkey: also spelled *genet.* [<OF *genet* <Sp. *jinete* a light horseman <Arabic *Zenāta,* a Barbary tribe]
jen·net·ing (jen′it·ing) *n. Brit.* A variety of early apple, ripening about St. John's Day (June 24). [<F *Jeannet,* dim. of *Jean* John]
Jen·nings (jen′ingz), **Herbert Spencer,** 1868–1947, U.S. naturalist and geneticist.
jen·ny (jen′ē) *n. pl.* **·nies 1** Short for spinning jenny. **2** A female: also used in combination or alone for a female bird or animal, as *jenny* wren, *jenny* ass. **3** A traveling crane. **4** A portable electric generator for use on a motion-picture set. **5** A man who interests himself or interferes in feminine matters: also called *betty.* **6** A jinny. Also spelled *jinny.* [from *Jenny,* a personal name]
Jen·ny (jen′ē) Diminutive of JANE. Also **Jen′nie.**
jeof·ail (jef′āl) *n. Law* An oversight; a mistake; the acknowledgement of an error in pleading. Also **jeof′aile.** [<AF *jeo fail* I am wrong]
jeop·ard·ize (jep′ər·dīz) *v.t.* **·ized, ·iz·ing** To put in jeopardy; expose to loss or injury; imperil. Also **jeop′ard.**
jeop·ard·y (jep′ər·dē) *n.* **1** Exposure to or danger of death, loss, or injury; danger; peril. **2** The peril in which a defendant is put when placed on trial for a crime. See synonyms under DANGER, HAZARD. [<OF *jeu parti* even chance]
Jeph·thah (jef′thə, jep′-) A judge in Israel; sacrificed his daughter. *Judges* xi 34–40.
je·quir·i·ty (ji·kwir′ə·tē) *n.* **1** A twining, tropical shrub (*Abrus praecatorius*), the Indian or wild licorice. **2** One of the handsome, poisonous seeds, **jequirity beans,** of this plant used in India as weights, ornaments, and in medicine: often called *jumble-beads.* Also **je·quer′·i·ty.** [<F *jéquirity* <Tupian]
Je·qui·ti·nho·nha (zhə·kē′ti·nyō′nyə) A river in eastern Brazil, flowing 500 miles NE to the Atlantic.
Je·rah·me·el (jə·rā′mē·əl) One of the seven archangels of Hebrew and Christian legend.
jer·bo·a (jər·bō′ə) *n.* An Old World, nocturnal, social rodent (family *Dipodidae*) with the hind legs much elongated for jumping, especially *Jaculus jaculus* of North Africa. [<NL <Arabic *yarbu'*]

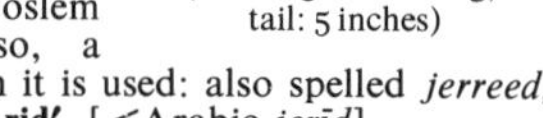

JERBOA
Can make a jump of 6 feet. (About 3 inches long; tail: 5 inches)

je·reed (je·rēd′) *n.* A javelin of Moslem countries; also, a game in which it is used: also spelled *jerreed, jerrid.* Also **je·rid′.** [<Arabic *jerīd*]
jer·e·mi·ad (jer′ə·mī′ad) *n.* A lament; tale of woe; a denunciation of existing conditions. [<F *jérémiade* <*Jérémie* Jeremiah]
Jer·e·mi·ah (jer′ə·mī′ə) A masculine personal name. Also **Jer·e·my** (jer′ə·mē), **Jer·e·ma·i** (jer′ə·mä′ē), *Dan., Du., Ger., Sw.* **Je·re·mi·as** (yā·rə·mē′äs), *Fr.* **Jé·ré·mie** (zhā·rā·mē′).
—Jeremiah A major Hebrew prophet who flourished in the seventh century B.C.; also, an Old Testament book containing his prophecies. Also **Jer′e·mi′as.** [<Hebrew, exalted of the Lord]
Je·rez (hā·rāth′, -rās′) A town in SW Spain: formerly *Xeres.* Also **Je·rez de la Fron·te·ra** (tha lä frōn·tā′rä).
Jer·i·cho (jer′i·kō) A village in western Jordan, north of the Dead Sea; site of an ancient city of the same name (*Num.* xxii 1).
Jericho rose See ROSE OF JERICHO.
Jer·it·za (yer′it·sä), **Maria,** born 1887, Austrian soprano active in the United States.
jerk[1] (jûrk) *v.t.* **1** To give a sharp, sudden pull, tug, or twist to. **2** To throw or move with a sharp, suddenly arrested motion. **3** To utter in broken or abrupt manner. **—***v.i.* **4** To give a jerk or jerks. **5** To move with sharp, sudden motions; twitch. **—***n.* **1** A short, sharp pull, twitch, or fling. **2** *Physiol.* An involuntary contraction of some muscle, due to the reflex action of nerves; specifically, an involuntary muscular spasm or twitching caused by religious excitement. **3** *Slang* A railroad local branch line. **4** *Slang* A stupid or unsophisticated person. [Prob. imit.] **—jerk′y** *adj.* **—jerk′i·ly** *adv.* **—jerk′i·ness** *n.*
jerk[2] (jûrk) *v.t.* To cure (meat) by cutting into strips and drying. **—***n.* Jerky[2]. [Alter. of Sp. *charquear* < *charqui.* See CHARQUI.]
jer·kin (jûr′kin) *n.* A waistcoat; short coat; jacket; doublet: often made of leather. **—buff jerkin** A jerkin of buff leather or, later, of buff-colored cloth. [Origin unknown]
jerk·wa·ter (jûrk′wô′tər, -wot′ər) *adj. U.S. Colloq.* **1** Not on the main line: a *jerkwater* train or station. **2** Insignificant; small: a *jerkwater* college. **—***n.* A train serving a branch line. [<JERK[1], *v.* + WATER]
jerk·y[1] (jûr′kē) *n.* A springless wagon or carriage: also spelled *jirky.* [<JERK[1], *n.* + -Y[1]]
jerk·y[2] (jûr′kē) *n.* Jerked meat: also called *charqui.* Also **jerked beef.** [Alter. of CHARQUI]
jer·o·bo·am (jer′ə·bō′əm) *n.* **1** An oversized champagne bottle holding about four quarts. **2** A drinking cup of great size. [after JEROBOAM]
Jer·o·bo·am (jer′ə·bō′əm) A Jewish leader who led the revolt of the ten tribes against Rehoboam and became first king of Israel, as distinguished from Judah; introduced idolatry. I *Kings* xi, xii.
—Jeroboam A king of Israel; son of Joash: reigned 790–749? B.C. II *Kings* xiv.
Je·rome (jə·rōm′, *Brit.* jer′əm) A masculine personal name. Also *Fr.* **Jé·rôme** (zhā·rôm′), *Dan.* **Je·ro·ny·mus** (ye·rō′ni·məs), *Pg., Sp.* **Je·ro·ni·mo** (*Pg.* zhe·rō′ni·mo͞o, *Sp.* hā·rō′nē·mō). [<Gk., holy name]
—Jerome, Saint, 340?–420, one of the four great Latin church fathers; prepared the Vulgate.
Je·rome (jə·rōm′, *Brit.* jer′əm), **Jerome K(lapka),** 1859–1927, English humorist.
jer·reed (je·rēd′), **jer·rid** See JEREED.
jer·ry[1] (jer′ē) *n. pl.* **·ries 1** One who erects buildings or does work in an unsubstantial and mean manner: also **jer′ry·build′er** (-bil′·dər). **2** Work that is inferior or fraudulent in material or construction. **—***adj.* Cheaply and fraudulently constructed; flimsy. [Origin unknown]
jer·ry[2] (jer′ē) *n. pl.* **·ries** *Slang* A German; especially, a German soldier. [Alter. of GERMAN]
Jer·ry (jer′ē) Popular form of JEREMIAH, JEREMY, GERALD, etc.
jer·ry·build (jer′ē·bild′) *v.t.* **·built, ·build·ing** To build flimsily and of inferior materials. **—jer′ry·build′ing** *n.* **—jer′ry·built′** *adj.*
jer·sey (jûr′zē) *n.* **1** A plain-knitted, elastic, ribbed fabric of wool, cotton, rayon, etc. **2** A close-fitting knit shirt as worn by athletes; hence, any close-fitting upper garment of knitted material. **3** Fine woolen yarn, or fine-combed wool, as spun in the island of Jersey. [from *Jersey*]
Jer·sey (jûr′zē) *n.* One of a breed of cattle, usually fawn-colored, originating in the island of Jersey or the Channel Islands, noted for milk rich in butterfat content. **—***adj.* Of or pertaining to the island of Jersey or to the State of New Jersey.
Jer·sey (jûr′zē) The largest of the Channel Islands; 45 square miles; capital, St. Hélier.
Jersey City A port on the Hudson River in NE New Jersey.
Je·ru·sa·lem (ji·ro͞o′sə·ləm, -lem) A holy city of Judaism and Christianity in central Palestine, partly in Israel (of which it is the capital) and partly in Jordan: identified with the Old Testament *Salem.* Ancient *Hierosolyma. Arabic* **El Quds esh She·rif** (al ko͝ots′ ash sha·rēf′).
Jerusalem artichoke A tall sunflower (*Helianthus tuberosus*) of the composite family of NE North America having an edible tuber. [Alter. of Ital. *girasole* sunflower + ARTICHOKE]
Jerusalem cherry A small, evergreen shrub (*Solanum pseudocapsicum*) of the nightshade family, from Mauritius. It has white flowers succeeded by scarlet or yellow, cherrylike berries.
Jerusalem cross See under CROSS.
Jerusalem oak See under OAK.
jer·vine (jûr′vēn) *n. Chem.* A white, crystalline, toxic alkaloid, $C_{26}H_{37}O_3N$, obtained from the rhizome of the white hellebore (*Veratrum album*). [<Sp. *yerva,* the root of the hellebore + -INE[2]]
Jer·vis Bay (jûr′vis, *Brit.* jär′vis) An inlet of the Pacific in eastern New South Wales, Australia.
Jes·per·sen (yes′pər·sən), **(Jens) Otto (Harry),** 1860–1943, Danish philologist.
jess (jes) *n.* **1** A short strap fastened to the leg of a hawk: used in falconry. **2** A ribbon hanging from a garland or crown. [<OF *ges* <L *jactus* a throw <*jacere* throw] **—jessed** *adj.*
jes·sa·mine (jes′ə·min) *n.* The jasmine: a popular name. [Var. of JASMINE]
jes·sant (jes′ənt) *adj. Her.* **1** Shooting forth as a plant. **2** Issuing, as an animal, from the middle of an ordinary. Compare ISSUANT. [<OF *issant,* ppr. of *isser* spring forth]
Jes·se (jes′ē) A masculine personal name. [<Hebrew, the Lord is]
—Jesse The father of David. I *Sam.* xvi 1.
Jes·sel·ton (jes′əl·tən) A port on the South China Sea, capital of Sabah.
jes·ser·aunte (jes′ər·ônt) See JAZERANT. Also **jes′ser·aunce.**
Jes·si·ca (jes′i·kə) A feminine personal name. [<Hebrew, the Lord's grace]
—Jessica In Shakespeare's *Merchant of Venice,* the daughter of Shylock, who elopes with Lorenzo.
Jes·sie (jes′ē) A feminine personal name.

jest (jest) *n.* **1** Something said or done in joke, plesantary, or raillery; a joke. **2** The object of laughter, sport, or raillery; a laughingstock. **3** *Obs.* An exploit, tale of exploits; a masquerade; pageant. See synonyms under WIT. —*v.i.* **1** To speak or act an a playful or trifling manner. **2** To scoff; jeer. —*v.t.* **3** To scoff at; ridicule. [< OF *geste, jeste* < L *gesta* deeds < *gerere* do]

jest·er (jest′ər) *n.* **1** One who jests; specifically. a medieval cort fool. **2** *Archaic* In the Middle Ages, a professional teller of romances.

jest·ing (jes′ting) *n.* The action of one who jokes; fun; raillery; —*adj.* Of the nature of a jest; prone to humor; mirthful; jocose. —**jest′ing·ly** *adv.*

Je·su (jē′zōō, -sōō) Jesus: used poetically, especially in the vocative.

Jes·u·ate (jezh′ōō·āt, jez′yōō-) *n. pl.* **Jes·u·ates** or **Jes·u·a·ti** (jezh′ōō·ä′tī, jez′yōō-) One of the order or congregation of *Jesuati,* founded by St. John Colombini of Siena in the 14th century, and suppressed by Pope Clement IX in 1688. Their chief occupation was care of the sick, especially the plague–stricken. Also **Jes′u·et.** [< Ital. *Gesuato* < *Gesú* Jesus]

Jes·u·it (jezh′ōō·at, jez′yōō-) *n.* **1** A member of the Society of Jesus, a Roman Catholic religious order founded in 1534 by Ignatious Loyola to combat the Reformation and propagate the faith among the heathen. Abbr. *S.J.* [< NL *Jesuita* < L *Jesus* Jesus]

Jes·u·it·ic (jezh′ōō·it′ik, jez′yōō-) *adj.* **1** Of, pertaining to, or like the Jesuits, or their principles, methods, or practices. **2** Using crafty or insidious arts or methods; designing; crafty; a derogatory use. Also **Jes′u·it′i·cal.** —**Jes′u·it′i·cal·ly** *adv.*

Jes·u·it·ism (jezh′ōō·it·iz′əm, jez′yōō-) *n.* **1** The doctrines, system, principles, and methods of the Jesuits. **2** Practices such as those attributed to the Jesuits. **3** Deceptive practices, subtle distinctions, or political duplicity: a derogatory use.

Jes·u·it·ize (jezh′ōō·it·īz′, jez′yōō-) *v.t. & v.i.* **·ized, ·iz·ing** To be or make Jesuitic.

Jes·u·i·try (jezh′ōō·t·trē, jer′yōō-) *n.* The methods or principles professed by or ascribed to the Jesuits.

Jesuits' bark **1** Peruvian bark, a species of cinchona, yielding quinine. **2** The marsh elder.

Je·sus (jē′zəs) A masculine personal name. [< Hebrew, the Lord is salvation]
—**Jesus** The source of Christianity; probably living from 6 B.C. to A.D. 29 or 30; son of Mary; regarded in all Christian faiths as Christ, the Messiah. Hence, also **Jesus Christ.** —**Jesus** The son of Sirach; lived about the third or fourth century B.C.; author of *Ecclesiasticus.*

jet[1] (jet) *n.* **1** A rich black variety of lignite, used for ornaments. **2** The color of jet; a deep, glossy black. **3** *Obs.* Black marble. —*adj.* Made of or having the appearance of jet. [< OF *jaiet* < L *gagates* < Gk. *gagatēs,* from *Gagai,* a Lycian town where it was mined]—**jet′–black′** (-blak′) *adj. & n.*

jet[2] (jet) *n.* **1** That which spurts out from a narrow orifice; a gushing flow. **2** A spout or nozzle. **3** A projecting or overhanging course of bricks or the like; jut. **3** A jet plane. [< *v.*]—*v.t. & v.i.* **jet·ted, jet·ting** To spurt forth or emit in a stream; spout. [< F *jeter* throw, ult. < L *jactare,* freq. of *jacere* throw]
Jet. meaning operating by, of, or relating to jet propulsion, may appear as a combining form in hyphemes or solidemes or as the first element in two–word phrases; as in:

jet aircraft	**jet bomber**	**jet pilot**
jet airplane	**jet fighter**	**jet plane**
jet aviation	**jetliner**	**jet–propelled**

jet d'eau (zhe dō′) *n. pl.* **jets d'eau** (zhe dō′) *French* A jet of water; fountain. Also **jet·teau** (je·tō′), **jette d'eau** (jet dō′), **jet·to** (jet′ō).

jet deflection The directional control of the blast in a jet engine in order to change the speed or direction of a jet–propelled aircraft without loss of stability.

je·té (zhə·tā′) *n.* In ballet, a wide leap with one leg forward and the other back. [< F, p.p. of *jeter,* to jump]

jet engine An engine that takes in outside air to oxidize fuel which is coverted into the energy of a powerful jet of heated gas expelled to the rear under high pressure: a special form of reaction engine.

Jeth·ro (jeth′rō) Moses' father–in–law. *Exod.* xviii.

jet lag A disruption of the body's accustomed rhythms of sleep, hunger, etc. owing to the change of time zones when traveling long distances by jet aircraft.

jet·lin·er (jet′lī′nər) *n.* A large, commercial jet aircraft.

jet·port (jet′pôrt′, -pōrt′) *n.* An airport designed to accomodate jet aircraft.

jet propulsion **1** Propulsion by meams of a jet of gas or other fluid. **2** *Aeron.* Aircraft propulsion by means of jet engines. —**jet′–pro·pul′sion** *adj.*

jet rotor The rotor unit of a helicopter powererd by jet engines mounted on the blades.

jet·sam (jet′səm) *n.* **1** Unbuoyed goods cast from a vessel in peril, and which sink: distinguished from *flotsam* and *lagan.* **2** Jettison [Earlier *jetson,* short for JETTISON]

jet set A group of wealthy, international celebrities who frequently travel long distances, as by jet aircraft, for social events, etc. —**jet–set·ter** (jet′set′ər) *n.*

jet stream **1** The strong flow of gas or other fluid expelled from a jet engine, rocket motor, and the like. **2** *Meteorol.* A high–velocity circumpolar wind circulating, usually from west to east, near the base of the stratosphere.

jet·ti·son (jet′ə·sən) *n.* **1** The throwing overboard of goods, or cargo, especially from a ship in danger of foundering. **2** Jetsam. —*v.t.* **1** To throw overboard, as goods or cargo. **2** Hence, to discard or abandon something that hampers. [< AF *getteson* < L *jactatio, -onis* a throwing < *jactare.* See JET[2].]

jet·ton (jet′ən) *n.* A counter or token. Also **jet′on.** [< MF *jeton* < *jeter* throw. See JET[2].]

jet·ty[1] (jet′ē) *n. pl.* **·ties** **1** A structure in a body of water serving to control or divert a current, protect a harbor or the like, or as a wharf or pier. **2** A part of a building projecting or overhanging. Also, *Obs. jutty.* [< OF *jetee,* jetee, orig. pp. of *jeter* throw. See JET[2].]

jet·ty[2] (jet′ē) *adj.* Like or made of jet; black as jet. —**jet′ti·ness** *n.*

jet vane A fixed or adjustable vane of heat–resistant material placed in a jet stream for purposes of stability and control.

jet wash *Aeron.* The backwash caused by a jet engine, rocket, guided missle, and the like.

jeu (zhœ) *n. pl.* **jeux** (zhœ) *French* Play; pastime; game.

jeu de mots (zhœ də mō′) *French* Play on words; pun or quibble.

jeu d'es·prit (zhœ des·prē′) A play of fancy; witticism. [< F]

jeune fille (zhœn fēy′) *French* Young girl.

jeu·nesse do·rée (zhə·nes′ do·rā′) Any group of wealthy and fashionable young persons. [F, lit., gilded youth]

Jev·ons (jev′ənz), **William Stanley,** 1835–82, English logician and economist.

Jew (jōō) *n.* **1** A member of the ancient Near Eastern Hebrew people, the Israelites, or one tracing descent from them by genealogy or conversion. **2** Any person professing Judaism. **3** Originally, a member of the tribe or the kingdom of Judah. —**Wandering Jew** The shoemaker Ahasuerus, fabled to be condemned to wander perpetually for driving Christ from his door; hence, a restless wanderer. —*adj.* Jewish; relating to Jews. [OF *gui, jueu* < L *Judaeus* < Gk. *Ioudaios* < Hebrew *y'hudi* descendant of Judah.

Jew–bait·ing (jōō′bā′ting) *n. Slang (an offensive usage)* The act of harassing, harrying, or otherwise persecuting the Jews. —**Jew′–bait′er** *n.*

jew·el (jōō′əl) *n.* **1** A precious stone; gem, especially one set in precious metal. **2** Anything or rare excellence or special value. **3** A bit of precious stone, crystal, or glass used to form a durable bearing, as for a watch pivot. **4** One dearly beloved. —*v.t.* **·eled** or **·elled, ·el·ling** or **·el·ling** To adorn with jewels; set jewels in. [< OF *jouel,* ult. < L *jocus* a joke, sport]

jew·el·er (jōō′əl·ər) *n.* A dealer or maker of jewelry. Also **jew′el·ler.**

jew·el·ry (jōō′əl·rē) *n.* **1** Jewels collectively. **2** The art of mounting precious stones; trade of a jeweler. Also *Brit.* **jew′el·ler·y.**

jew·el·weed (jōō′əl·wēd′) *n.* Either of two American plants of the genus *Impatiens,* the touch–me–nots *(I. biflora* or *I. pallida).*

Jew·ett (jōō′it), **Frank Baldwin,** 1879–1949. U.S. electrical engineer. —**Sarah Orne,** 1849–1909, U.S. novelist.

jew·fish (jōō′fish′) *n. pl.* **·fish** or **·fishes** **1** One of various large groupers of American waters, especially *Stereolepis gigas* of the California coast. **2** The giant grouper *(Promicrops itaiara)* of the Florida coast. **3** The tarpon.

Jew·ish (jōō′ish) *Adj.* Belonging to, like, or characteristic of the Jews, their customs, religion, etc.; Hebrew. —**Jew′ish·ness** *n.*

Jewish Autonomous Oblast See BIRDOBIDZHAN.

Jewish calendar The Hebrew calendar. See under CALENDAR.

Jewish holidays See HANUKKAH, PESACH, ROSH HASHANA, SUKKOTH, and YOM KIPPUR for the principal holidays of Judaism.

Jew·ry (jōō′rē) *n.* **1** The country of the Jews; Judea. **2** The Jewish people or race.

jew's–harp (jōōz′härp′) *n.* **1** A small musical instrument with a lyre–shaped metal frame and a bent metallic tounge. **2** *Naut.* The shackle that connects the chain cable with the anchor ring.

JEW'S–HARP
Held against the teeth and struck with the hand.

Jew's–pitch (jōōz′pich′) *n.* Bitumen. Also **Jew's′–pitch′.**

Jew's–thorn (jōōz′thôrn′) *n.* Christ's–thorn.

je·zail (jə·zīl′) *n. Afghan* A long and heavy Afghan musket.

Je·za·jas (yā·zä′yäs) Dutch form of ISAIAH.

Jez·e·bel (jez′ə·bel) The wife of Ahab, notorious for her evil life (I *Kings* xvi 31); hence, a bold, vicious or cruel woman.

Jez·re·el (jer′rē·əl, jez·rēl′), **Plain of** A plain in northern Israel between the Jordan valley and Mount Carmel. *Judith* iii 9. Also *Esdraelon.*

Jhe·lum (jā′ləm) A river in Kashmir and West Pakistan, flowing 480 miles to the Chenab: ancient *Hydaspes:* also *Jehlem.*

jhong (jông) *n.* In India, a musical instrument resembling cymbals, used to accompany native folk music.

JHVH *Alt. of* YHWH.

jib[1] (jib) *n.* **1** *Naut.* A triangular sail, set on a stay and extending from the foretopmast head to the jib boom or the bowspirit. **2** The swinging boom of a crane or derrick. —**flying jib** A jib set out beyond the standing jib, or an extended boom, called the **flying–jib boom.** —**the cut of one's jib** One's appearance. —*v.t. & v.i.* **jibbed. jib·bing** *Naut.* To shift or swing; jibe. Also **jibb.** [? Short for GIBBET]

jib[2] (jib) *v.t.* **jibbed, jib·bing** **1** To move restively sidewise and backward; refuse to go forward, as a horse. **2** To refuse to do something; balk. —*n.* A horse that jibs; also **jib′ber** [Cf. OF *giber* kick]

jib·ba (jib′ə) *n. Arabic* A shirt, especially a patched shirt adopted as a uniform by followers of the Mahdi. Compare to JUBHA. Also **jib′bah, jib′beh.**

jib boom *Naut.* A spar forming a continuation of the bowsprit.

jib crane A crane having a swinging boom.

jibe[1] (jīb) *v.* **jibed, jib·ing** *v.t.* **1** *Naut.* To swing from one side of a vessel to the other; said of a fore–and–aft sail or its boom. **2** To change course so that the sails shift in this manner. —*v.t.* **3** To cause to swing from one side of a vessel to the other. Also spelled *gibe, gybe, jib.* [< Du. *gijben*]

jibe[2] (jīb) See GIBE[1].

jibe[3] (jīb) *v.i.* **jibed, jib·bing** *U.S. Colloq.* To agree; be in accordance. [Origin uncertain]

Ji·bu·ti (ji·bōō′tē) See DJIBOUTI.

ji·ca·ma (hē′·kə·mə) *n.* A tropical plant with edible tuberous roots and with seeds that yield rotenone and oils [< Nahuatl *xicama*]

Jid·da (jid′ə) The port for Mecca, Saudi Arabia, on the Red Sea: also *Jedda.* Also **Jid′dah.**

jif·fy (jif′ē) *n. pl.* **·fies** *Colloq.* An instant; moment. Also **jiff.** [Origin unknown]

jig (jig) *n.* **1** A light, gay dance to a rapid tune, usually in triple time, or the music for it. **2** A practical joke. **3** *Mech.* A tool or fixture used to guide cutting tools. **4** A fish hook having a loaded shank. **5** *Mining* A wire sieve or system of sieves used in separating ore by vibration. —**the jig is up** *Colloq.* All is over and done. —*v.* **jigged, jig·ging** *v.i.* **1** To dance or play a jig. **2** To move with quick, jerky motions. **3** To fish with a jig. **4** *Mech.* To use a jig. —*v.t.* **5** To sing or play to the time of a jig. **6** To dance, as a jig. **7** To jerk up and down or to and fro. **8** To catch (fish) by hooking through the body with a jig. **9** *Mech.* To form or produce with the aid of jigs. [Cf. OF *gigue* a fiddle]

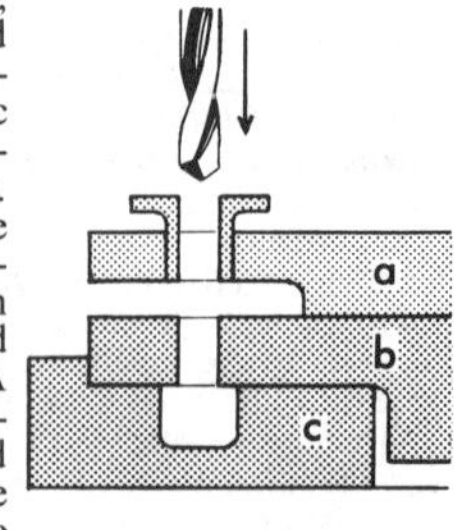

JIG
a. A drill jig.
b. Matter to be drilled.
c. Support block.

jig·ger¹ (jig′ər) *n.* **1** One who or that which jigs. **2** One of various jolting mechanisms: an apparatus for separating ores by jolting in sieves in water. **3** A potter's wheel. **4** *Naut.* A small spanker sail set on a short mast in the stern of a canoe; also, a small smacklike boat carrying such a sail. **5** Jiggermast. **6** A short, lofting, iron-headed golf club used for approaching. **7** A support for a billiard cue when about to strike a ball in an awkward position; a bridge. **8** A small glass or cup for measuring liquor, holding about one ounce; also, the amount of liquor so measured. **9** *Colloq.* Any small indefinite device.

jig·ger² (jig′ər) *n.* **1** A chigger or chigoe: also **jigger flea.** **2** Some other insect of similar habits to the chigoe, as a harvest tick. [Alter. of CHIGGER]

jig·ger·mast (jig′ər·mast′, -mäst′) *n. Naut.* The aftermast in a yawl or a four-masted vessel.

jig·gle (jig′əl) *v.t.* & *v.i.* **·gled, ·gling** To move with slight, quick jerks. —*n.* An up-and-down unsteady movement. [Freq. of JIG, *v.*]

jig·saw (jig′sô′) *n.* A fine, narrow saw set vertically in a frame, so as to be moved rapidly up and down.

jigsaw puzzle A puzzle, the object of which is to reassemble into the original pattern a mounted picture which has been cut by a jigsaw into numerous irregularly shaped, and often interlocking pieces.

ji·had (ji·häd′) *n.* **1** A religious war of Moslems against the enemies of their faith. **2** Any war for a faith. Also spelled *jehad.* [<Arabic *jihād*]

jill¹ (jil) *n.* See GILL².

jill² (jil) *n.* **1** A young woman; sweetheart. **2** A female ferret. **3** A cup. [<from *Jill,* a personal name]

jil·let (jil′it) *n. Scot.* A sportive or wanton girl or woman; a flirt or jilt.

jill-flirt (jil′flûrt′) *n.* A wanton or depraved woman; gill-flirt.

Ji·lo·lo (ji·lō′lō) See HALMAHERA.

jilt (jilt) *v.t.* To cast off or discard (a previously favored lover or sweetheart); deceive in love. —*n.* One who capriciously discards a lover. [Cf. dial. E (Scottish) *jillet* a giddy girl] —**jilt′er** *n.*

Jim (jim), **Jim·my** (jim′ē) Diminutives of JAMES.

jim-crow (jim′krō′) *U.S. Colloq. adj.* Segregating Negroes: *jim-crow* buses; *jim-crow* laws. —*v.t.* To subject to Negro segregation. Also **Jim′-Crow′.**

Jim Crow *U.S. Colloq.* **1** A Negro: a term of contempt, from a Negro character in an old Negro song. **2** The segregation of Negroes. —**Jim-Crow·ism** (jim′krō′iz·əm) *n.*

Ji·mé·nez de Cis·ne·ros (hē·mā′nāth thā thēs·nā′rōs), **Francisco,** 1436–1517, Spanish cardinal and statesman.

jim-jams (jim′jamz′) *n. Slang* **1** Delirium tremens. **2** Extreme nervousness; the jitters.

jim·my (jim′ē) *n. pl.* **·mies** A burglar's crowbar: sometimes made in sections. —*v.t.* **·mied, ·my·ing** To break or pry open with a jimmy. Also, *Brit., jemmy.* [from *Jimmy,* dim. of *James,* a personal name]

Jim·my Wood·ser (jim′ē wood′zər) *Austral. Slang* **1** A solitary drinker. **2** A solitary drink.

jimp (jimp) *Scot. adj.* **1** Natty. **2** Scanty; scarce. Also **jimp′y.** —*adv.* **1** Neatly. **2** Barely; scarcely. Also **jimp′ly, jimp′y.**

jim·son·weed (jim′sən·wēd′) *n.* **1** A tall, coarse, evil-smelling, very poisonous annual weed of the nightshade family (*Datura stramonium*): it yields several important alkaloids, as atropine and scopolamine. **2** Apple of Peru. Also **jimp·son weed** (jimp′sən). [Alter. of *Jamestown weed,* so called because first observed in Jamestown, Va.]

ji·na (jī′nə) See JAINISM.

jin·gal (jing′gôl) *n.* A heavy musket mounted on a swivel rest, formerly used in China and Burma: often spelled *gingal, gingall.* Also **jin′·gall.** [<Hind. *jangāl* large musket]

jing·ko (jing′kō) See GINKGO.

jin·gle (jing′gəl) *v.* **·gled, ·gling** *v.i.* **1** To make light, ringing sounds, as keys striking together. **2** To sound regularly or pleasingly on the ear, as verse, tunes, etc. —*v.t.* **3** To cause to jingle. —*n.* **1** A tinkling or clinking sound; also, that which produces it. **2** Any pleasing succession of rhythmical sounds in a verse; also, such a verse. **3** A one-horse, two-wheeled carriage or car, once used in Ireland and Australia. [Imit.] —**jin′gly** *adj.*

jin·glet (jing′glit) *n.* **1** A small, free, metallic ball used as the clapper of a globular sleigh bell. **2** Any small jingling appendage.

Jin·go (jing′gō) *n. pl.* **·goes** **1** One who boasts of his patriotism and favors an aggressive foreign policy. **2** *Brit.* Originally, one of a party supporting Disraeli's Near Eastern policy. —**by Jingo!** A meaningless oath or ejaculation expressing strong conviction, surprise, etc. —*adj.* Of, pertaining to, or characteristic of the Jingoes. [Origin uncertain] —**Jin′go·ish** *adj.* —**Jin′go·ism** *n.* —**Jin′go·ist** *n.* —**Jin′go·is′tic** *adj.*

jink (jingk) *v.i. Scot.* To move quickly; dodge. —*n.* **1** *pl.* Frolics; pranks: high *jinks.* **2** *Scot.* A dodging turn; dodge. —**jink′er** *n.*

Jin·nah (jin′ə), **Mohammed Ali,** 1876–1948, Moslem leader; first governor general of Pakistan 1947–48.

jin·ni (ji·nē′) *n. pl.* **jinn** In Moslem mythology, an order of supernatural beings able to assume animal or human form, and often at the call and service of men through some magical controlling object: the plural form is often erroneously used as a singular: sometimes spelled *djinni, genie.* Also **jin·nee′.** [<Arabic *jinnī*]

jin·ny (jin′ē) *n. pl.* **·nies** **1** An incline in a mine, upon which loaded cars descend by gravity: also **jinny road.** **2** *Mech.* The traveler on the arm of a crane: also *jenny.* [Cf. JENNY]

Jin·ny (jin′ē) See JENNY.

jin·rik·sha (jin·rik′·shə, -shô) *n.* A small, two-wheeled passenger carriage drawn by one man. Also **jin·rick′sha, jin·rik′i·sha.** [<Japanese *jin* man + *riki* power + *sha* carriage]

JINRIKSHA

Jin·sen (jin·sen) The Japanese name for INCHON.

jinx (jingks) *n.* A person or thing supposed to bring bad luck; a hoodoo. —*v.t.* To bring bad luck to. [<Earlier *jynx* <Gk. *iynx* the wryneck (a bird anciently used in witchcraft)]

ji·pi·ja·pa (hē′pē·hä′pä) *n.* A shrubby, stemless, palmlike plant (*Carludovica palmata*), native to South America; the fan-shaped leaves provide the fiber of which Panama hats are made. [from *Jipijapa,* town in Ecuador]

jirk·y (jûr′kē) See JERKY (def. 1).

jit·ney (jit′nē) *n. U.S. Colloq.* **1** A small coin; a nickel. **2** A motor vehicle that carries passengers for a small fare. [Cf. F *jeton* JETTON]

jit·ter (jit′ər) *v.i. Colloq.* To talk or act nervously. [Var. of CHITTER]

jit·ter·bug (jit′ər·bug′) *U.S. Slang n.* A person who responds to swing or jazz music by dancing in a fast, violent manner. —*v.i.* **·bugged, ·bug·ging** To dance to swing or jazz music in a fast, violent manner.

jit·ters (jit′ərz) *n. pl. Colloq.* Intense nervousness or a spell of nerves. —**jit′ter·y** *adj.*

jiu·jit·su (jōō·jit′sōō) *n.* A Japanese system of unarmed self-defense in which one's opponent is compelled to use his strength to his own disadvantage: also spelled *jujitsu, jujutsu.* Also **jiu·jut·su** (jōō·jit′sōō, -jōōt′sōō). Compare JUDO. [<Japanese *jiu, ju* gentle, pliant + *jitsu* art]

jive (jīv) *n. Slang* **1** The jargon of jazz music and musicians. **2** Jazz music. [Origin uncertain]

Jiz·er·a (yiz′ər·ä) A river in northern Bohemia, Czechoslovakia, flowing 100 miles SW to the Elbe: German *Iser.*

jo (jō) *n. Scot.* A sweetheart of either sex. Also **joe.**

Jo·ab (jō′ab) A masculine personal name. [<Hebrew, the Lord is father]
—**Joab** David's nephew, commander of the Hebrew army. II *Sam.* xviii 2.

Jo·a·chim (jō′ə·kim; *Du.* yō′ä·kim, *Fr.* zhō·ä·kaṅ′, *Ger.* yō′ä·khim) A masculine personal name. Also *Ital.* **Joa·chi·no** (jä·kē′nō) or **Joa·chi·mo** (jä·kē′mō), *Sp.* **Joa·quin** (hwä·kēn′) or **Joa·quim** (hwä·kēm′). [<Hebrew, the Lord will judge]

Jo·a·chim (yō′ə·kim), **Joseph,** 1831–1907, Hungarian violinist.

Jo·a·chims·thal (yō′ä·khims·täl′) A German name for JACHYMOV.

joad (jōd) *n.* A migratory worker. [after the *Joad* family in John Steinbeck's *Grapes of Wrath*]

Joan (jōn) A feminine personal name. Also **Jo·an·na** (jō·an′ə), **Jo·a·net·ta** (jō′ə·net′ə). [<Hebrew, the Lord's grace]
—**Joan of Arc,** 1412–31, a French heroine and martyr who compelled the English to raise the siege of Orléans; captured; burned as a sorceress and heretic: called the "Maid of Orleans"; beatified 1909; canonized 1920. Also French *Jeanne d'Arc.*
—**Joan, Pope** See POPE JOAN.

jo·an·nes (jō·an′əs) See JOHANNES.

Jo·an·nes (jō·an′ēz) Latin form of JOHN.

João (zhwouṅ) Portuguese form of JOHN.

João Pes·so·a (zhwouṅ pe·sō′ə) A city in NE Brazil, capital of Paraíba state: formerly *Parahiba.*

Jo·ash (jō′ash) Name of two Jewish kings: Joash, king of Judah 837–797 B.C., and Joash, king of Israel 800–785 B.C. Also called *Jehoash.*

job¹ (job) *n.* **1** A piece of work of a definite extent or character, especially one done in the course of one's profession or occupation. **2** A specific piece of work done for a certain fee. **3** Anything to be done. **4** *Colloq.* A situation or position of employment. **5** A material thing to be worked on. **6** A public service or transaction done ostensibly for the public good but actually for private or partisan gain. **7** *Colloq.* An affair; circumstance: to make the best of a bad *job.* **8** *Slang* A theft; robbery. **9** *Printing* The printing of small or miscellaneous circulars, cards, posters, etc. See synonyms under BUSINESS, TASK. —*v.* **jobbed, job·bing** *v.i.* **1** To work by the job or piece. **2** To be a jobber. **3** To turn a position of public trust improperly to private advantage. —*v.t.* **4** To buy in bulk from the importers or manufacturers and resell in lots to dealers. **5** To sublet (work) among separate contractors. —*adj.* That may be bought, sold, or used by the job: a *job* lot. [Origin unknown]

job² (job) *v.t.* & *v.i.* **jobbed, job·bing** To jab. —*n.* The act of thrusting, poking, or stabbing suddenly; a jab. [ME *jobben*]

Job (jōb; *Fr.* zhōb, *Sw.* yōb) A masculine personal name. Also *Lat.* **Jo·bus** (jō′bəs). [<Hebrew, persecuted]
—**Job** The chief personage of the Old Testament book of Job: often referred to as the symbol of patience on account of his many afflictions; also this book itself.

job·ber (job′ər) *n.* **1** One who buys goods in bulk from the manufacturer or importer and sells to the retailer. **2** *Brit.* A middleman, as among stockbrokers. **3** An intriguer, as in politics. **4** One who works by the job, or on small jobs.

job·ber·y (job′ər·ē) *n. pl.* **·ber·ies** Corrupt use

of a public office or trust for private or partisan gain.

job·less (job′lis) *adj.* 1 Without a job. 2 Of or pertaining to those without a job. **—job′·less·ness** *n.*

job lot A collection of miscellaneous goods sold as a lot.

job printer One who does miscellaneous printing. **—job printing.**

Job's comforter One who, like the friends of Job, professes to console or comfort, but actually increases one's wretchedness.

Job's-tears (jōbz′tirz′) *n.* 1 A hardy, annual, tropical grass *(Coix lacryma-jobi).* 2 The white, pearly seeds of this plant, sometimes used as beads.

Jo·cas·ta (jō·kas′tə) In Greek legend, the wife of Laius, who unwittingly married her own son Oedipus and killed herself when she discovered it.

jock[1] (jok) *n.* 1 *Colloq.* A jockstrap. 2 *Slang* An athlete. [<JOCK(STRAP)]

jock[2] (jok) *n.* Colloq. 1 A jockey. 2 A disc jockey.

Jock (jok) *n.* Scot. 1 A nickname for the personal name JOHN. 2 A nickname for any Scotsman.

jock·ey (jok′ē) *n.* 1 One employed to ride horses, especially at races. 2 One who takes undue advantage in trade. 3 *Obs.* A strolling minstrel. 4 *Obs.* A lad; boy. 5 *Obs.* A horse dealer. — *v.* **·eyed, ·ey·ing** *v.i.* 1 To maneuver for an advantage: to *jockey* for position. 2 To be tricky; cheat. 3 To ride as a jockey. —*v.t.* 4 To put or guide by skilful handling or control. 5 To trick; cheat. 6 To ride (a horse) in a race. [Dim. of JOCK]

jock·o (jok′ō) *n.* 1 A chimpanzee. 2 Any ape or monkey. Also called *jacko.*

jock·strap (jok′strap′) *n.* An elastic support for the genitals worn by male athletes. [< cant *jock* the male genitals + STRAP]

jo·cose (jō·kōs′) *adj.* Of the nature of a joke; jocular. [<L *jocosus* < *jocus* joke] **—jo·cose′ly** *adv.* **—jo·cose′ness** *n.*

Synonyms : droll, facetious, funny, humorous, jocular, merry, sportive, waggish. See HUMOROUS, MERRY, VIVACIOUS. *Antonyms*: care-worn, cheerless, doleful, dreary, dull, grave, lugubrious, melancholy, miserable, mordant, mournful, rueful, sad, serious, solemn, sorrowful, woeful.

jo·cos·i·ty (jō·kos′ə·tē) *n. pl.* **·ties** 1 Jocularity; jocoseness; mirthfulness. 2 A joke.

joc·u·lar (jok′yə·lər) *adj.* 1 Being in a joking mood; making jokes. 2 Having the nature of, intended as, or appropriate to a joke or joking; comic; funny. Also **joc′u·la·to′ry** (-tôr′ē, -tō′·rē). See synonyms under HUMOROUS, JOCOSE. [<L *jocularis* < *joculus,* dim. of *jocus* a joke] **—joc′u·lar′i·ty** (-lar′ə·tē) *n.* **—joc′u·lar·ly** *adv.*

joc·und (jok′ənd, jō′kənd) *adj.* Having a blithe or gay disposition or appearance; jovial; sportive. [<OF *jocund* <LL *jocundus,* alter. of L *jucundus* pleasant < *juvare* delight] **—joc′und·ly** *adv.* **—joc′und·ness** *n.*

jo·cun·di·ty (jō·kun′də·tē) *n. pl.* **·ties** The state or quality of being jocund; sportiveness; mirth.

Jodh·pur (jōd·poor′, jōd′ poor) 1 A former princely state in the Rajputana States, India: also *Marwar.* 2 A city in central Rajasthan; formerly the capital of Jodhpur state.

jodh·pur boots (jod′pər) Riding shoes that end just above the ankle, buckled on the sides.

jodh·purs (jod′pərz) *n. pl.* Wide riding breeches, close-fitting from knee to ankle, designed to be worn with jodhpur boots. Also **jodhpur breeches.** [from *Jodhpur,* India]

Joe (jō) 1 Diminutive of JOSEPH. 2 *U.S. Slang* A person: a good *Joe.* **—G.I. Joe** *U.S. Slang* 1 An enlisted man in the U.S. Army. 2 An enlisted man in any of the U.S. armed services.

Jo·el (jō′əl) A masculine personal name. [<Hebrew, the Lord is God]

—Joel A prophet, son of Pethuel; also, the Old Testament book by this prophet. *Joel* i 1.

joe-pye weed (jō′pī′) Either of two tall American herbs. *Eupatorium purpureum* or *E. maculatum,* with pale-purple flowers.

jo·ey (jō′ē) *n. Austral.* The young of an animal, especially a young kangaroo.

Jof·fre (zhôf′r'), **Joseph Jacques Césaire,** 1852–1931. French marshal; commander in chief of French army in World War I.

jog (jog) *v.* **jogged, jog·ging** *v.t.* 1 To push or touch with a slight jar; shake. 2 To nudge; arouse the attention of. 3 To give a slight reminder to; stimulate: to *jog* the memory. —*v.i.* 4 To move with a slow, jolting pace or trot. 5 To proceed slowly or monotonously: with *on* or *along.* —*n.* 1 A slight push, as with the elbow; any slight incentive. 2 A slow, jolting motion or pace. 3 Any angle or break in a line or surface. 4 In the theater, a narrow flat used with other scenery to form a corner or projection in the stage set. [Prob. imit. Akin to SHOG.] **—jog′ger** *n.*

jog·ging (jog′ing) *n.* The exercise of running at a slow, regular pace, often alternately with walking.

jog·gle (jog′əl) *v.* **·gled, ·gling** *v.t.* 1 To shake slightly; jog; jolt. 2 To fasten or join together by a joggle or joggles. —*v.i.* 3 To have an irregular or jolting motion; shake. See synonyms under SHAKE. —*n.* 1 An irregular shake; jog; jolt. 2 A joint by means of which a piece, as of stone, is fitted to another. 3 A dowel. 4 A shoulder to receive the thrust of a brace or strut. [Freq. of JOG, *v.*]

joggle post 1 A post having shoulders to receive the feet of struts; kingpost. 2 A post built of timbers joggled together.

Jog·ja·kar·ta (jog′yə·kär′tə) A town in southern Java; formerly capital of the Republic of Indonesia: also *Djokjakarta, Jokjakarta.*

jog trot 1 A slow, easy trot, as of a horse. 2 A slow, humdrum habit of living or doing the daily tasks.

Jo·hann (yō′hän) Dutch, German, and Swedish form of JOHN. Also **Jo·han·nes** (*Ger.* yō·hän′·əs, *Lat.* jō·an′ēz).

Jo·han·na (jō·hän′ə, *Ger. Sw.* yō·hän′ə) German and Swedish form of JOAN. Also *Dan.* **Jo·han·ne** (yō·hän′ə).

jo·han·nes (jō·han′ēz) *n.* A former gold coin of Portugal: also *joannes.* [after *Joannes V* of Portugal]

Jo·han·nes·burg (jō·han′is·bûrg, yō·hän′is-) A city in Gauteng, Republic of South Africa.

Jo·hann·sen (yō·hän′sən), **Wilhelm Ludwig,** 1857–1927, Danish botanist and geneticist.

Jo·hans·son gage (yō·hän′ sən) One of a series of metallurgically perfect, flat, steel blocks with parallel surfaces: used in precision measurements. [after C.E. *Johansson,* Swedish engineer]

john (jon) *n.* Slang 1 A toilet. 2 A man who patronizes a prostitute.

John (jon) A masculine personal name: often used, especially in phrases or compounds, to denote a man or boy in general. [<Hebrew, the grace of the Lord]

—John One of the twelve apostles, son of Zebedee and brother of James: also, the Gospel according to this apostle, or one of the three Epistles written by him: also called "Saint John the Evangelist."

—John Son of Zacharias; the forerunner of Jesus; beheaded by Herod Antipas: known as *John the Baptist.*

—John, 1166?–1216, king of England 1199–1216; signed Magna Carta, 1215: called "John Lackland."

—John I, 1357–1433, king of Portugal 1385–1433; made treaty alliance with England, 1386: called "John the Great."

—John II, 1319– 64, king of France 1350–64; defeated at Poitiers, imprisoned in England: called "John the Good."

—John III, 1624–96, king of Poland 1674–96; fought against the Turks: real name *John Sobieski.*

—John IV, 1605–56, king of Portugal 1640–1656; founder of the Braganza dynasty: called "John the Fortunate."

—John XXIII, 1881–1963, real name Angelo Giuseppe Roncalli; pope 1958–63.

—John Chrysostom, Saint, 347?–407, one of the four Greek Christian fathers; patriarch of Constantinople.

—John of Austria, Don, 1547–78, natural son of Emperor Charles V; defeated Turks at Lepanto, 1571.

—John of Damascus, Saint, 700?–754?, Greek theologian: also called "John Damascene."

—John of Gaunt, 1340–99, duke of Lancaster, son of Edward III of England; patron of Chaucer and Wyclif.

—John of Leiden, 1500?–36, Dutch Anabaptist leader.

—John of Salisbury, died 1180, English churchman.

—John of the Cross, Saint, 1542–91, Spanish mystic: also Spanish *San Juan de la Cruz.*

John (jon), **Augustus Edwin,** 1878–1961, English portrait painter.

John apple *Obs.* See APPLEJOHN.

John Bull The Englishman personified: a nickname; hence, the English people. Also *Johnny Bull.* [after a character in a satire (1712) by John Arbuthnot] **—John-Bul·lism** (jon′bo͝ol′iz·əm) *n.*

John Doe (dō) A name commonly used to designate a fictitious or real personage: from the fictitious plaintiff in the action at common law for ejectment, the fictitious defendant being *Richard Roe.*

john do·ry (dôr′ē dō′rē) A small food fish (family *Zeidae*) of the Atlantic coast of Europe, the Mediterranean and Australian seas: of compressed form and a prevailing golden-yellow. Also **John Do′ry, John Do′ree:** also called *dory.*

John Hancock *U.S. Colloq.* A person's autograph. [after *John Hancock,* whose large signature is the first on the Declaration of Independence]

John·ny (jon′ē) *n. pl.* **·nies** A Confederate soldier. Also **Johnny Reb.**

Johnny Appleseed See APPLESEED, J OHNNY.

john·ny·cake (jon′ē·kāk′) *n.* A flat cake of Indian meal, baked on a griddle; also, cornbread: often spelled *johnnycake.* [? < obs. *jonikin,* a type of bread (<N. Am. Ind.) + CAKE]

John·ny-come-late·ly (jon′ē·kum′·lāt′lē) *n. Colloq.* A person who has recently arrived on the scene.

john·ny-jump-up (jon′ē·jump′up′) *n.* 1 A naturalized variety of the pansy *(Viola kitaibeliana).* 2 The bird's-foot violet. 3 The wild pansy. Also **john′ny-jump′er.**

Johnny on the spot *Colloq.* One who is always on hand and ready for anything. **—John· ny-on-the-spot** (jon′ē·on·thə·spot′) *adj.*

Johnny red *Pathol.* kwashiorkor.

John o' Groat's (ə grōts′) A locality of northern Scotland, often erroneously regarded as the northernmost point of Britain. Also **John o' Groat's House.**

John Paul Appellation of two popes.

— John Paul I, 1912–1978, real name Albino Luciani; pope 1978.

—John Paul II, born 1920, real name Karol Wojtyla, pope 1978–.

John·son (jon′sən), **Andrew,** 1808–75, president of the United States 1865–69. **— James Weldon,** 1871–1938, U.S. lawyer and author.

—Lyndon Baines, 1908–1973, 36th president of the United States 1963–1969. **—Samuel,** 1709–84, English author, critic, and lexicographer: known as *Doctor Johnson.* **—Sir William,** 1715–74, English official in the American colonies.

John·son·ese (jon′sən·ēz′, -ēs′) *n.* 1 Ponderous, oracular, and elaborate style attempting to imitate that of Dr. Samuel Johnson. 2 Johnsonian, in a derogatory sense.

Johnson grass A perennial pasture grass *(Sorghum halepense)* also valued for hay, but considered a weed in cultivated land: also called *Arabian millet.* [after Wm. *Johnson,* Alabama planter]

John·so·ni·an (jon·sō′nē ·ən) *adj.* Having the characteristics of the style of Dr. Samuel Johnson: precise, often sesquipedalian, carefully elaborated, judicious, and final. See JOHNSONESE. —*n.* One who follows or copies the style of Dr. Johnson. **—John·so′ni·an·ism, John′son·ism** *n.*

John·ston (jon′stən), **Albert Sidney,** 1803–62, American Confederate general; killed at Shiloh. **—Joseph Eggleston,** 1807–91, American Confederate general.

Johnston Island A small island in the central Pacific 700 miles SW of Honolulu, under jurisdiction of the United States Navy.

Jo·hore (jə·hôr′, -hōr′) The southernmost State of Malaya; 7,330 square miles: capital, Johore Bahru.

joie de vi·vre (zhwà də vēv′r') *French* Joy of living.

join (join) *v.t.* 1 To set or bring together; connect; combine: to *join* girders. 2 To come to a junction with; become part of: The path *joins* the road here. 3 To become a member of, as a club. 4 To unite in act or purpose: to *join* forces. 5 To come to as a companion or participant; meet and accompany: When will you *join* us? 6 To unite in marriage. 7 To engage in (battle, etc.). 8 *Colloq.* To adjoin. 9 *Geom.* To draw a straight line or curve between. —*v.i.* 10 To come together; connect; unite: The roads *joined.* 11 To enter into association or agreement. 12 To take part: usually with *in.* —**to join up** To enlist in a military service. —*n.* A place of junction or contact; joint. [<OF *joign-*, stem of *joindre* <L *jungere*]

join·der (join′dər) *n.* 1 The act of joining. 2 *Law* A joining of causes of action or defense; a joining of parties in an action; also, the acceptance of an issue tendered. [<F *joindre* join]

join·er (joi′nər) 1 One who or that which joins. 2 An artisan who finishes woodwork in houses; also, loosely, any mechanic who puts together pieces of wood.

join·er·y (joi′nər·ē) *n.* 1 The art or work of a joiner. 2 The articles constructed by a joiner.

joint (joint) *n.* 1 The place, point, line, or surface where two or more things are joined together; a junction or mode of junction; hinge. 2 An articulation or place of natural or easy separation between two parts, as of a machine, animal, or plant; a node; also, an internode or portion between two nodes or joints. 3 *Anat.* A place of union of two bones or separate parts of the skeleton; an articulation. 4 *Geol.* One of a series of approximately parallel divisional planes occurring in many rocks. 5 One of the pieces into which a carcass is divided by the butcher. 6 *U.S. Slang* A marihuana cigarette. 7 *U.S. Slang* A place of low resort, as for gambling. 8 *U.S. Slang* Any place of dwelling or gathering. —**out of joint** 1 Not fitted at the joint; dislocated. 2 Disordered; disorganized. —*adj.* 1 Produced by combined action. 2 Sharing together. 3 Participated in or used by two or more; held or shared in common. 4 *Law* Joined together in unity of interest or of liability: opposed to *several.* 5 Of or relating to both branches of a legislature: a *joint* session. See synonyms under MUTUAL. —*v.t.* 1 To fasten by means of a joint or joints. 2 To form or shape with a joint or joints, as a board. 3 To separate into joints, as meat. [<OF <L *junctus*, pp. of *jungere* join] —**joint′less** *adj.*

joint account An account in the name of two or more persons.

joint committee A committee of representatives from both houses of a legislative body.

joint convention 1 A session of both houses of a legislature. 2 An assembly of delegates representing two or more political parties. Also **joint session.**

joint·ed (join′tid) *adj.* Having joints, knots, or nodes; articulated.

joint·er (join′tər) *n.* 1 One who or that which joints; especially, one of several instruments for constructing joints. 2 An edged part, triangular in shape, attached to the beam of a plow. 3 A trying plane.

joint evil *Pathol.* A form of leprosy which is anesthetic in its later stages, especially as known in the West Indies.

joint fir Any of a genus of shrubs *(Ephedra)* growing in dry or desert regions, with jointed green branches and red berries; especially, ma huang.

joint·grass (joint′gras′, -gräs′) *n.* A creeping grass *(Paspalum distichum)* of the southern United States, which roots at the joints: used as fodder.

joint·ly (joint′lē) *adv.* In a joint manner; unitedly.

joint·mouse (joint′mous′) *n.* A movable cartilage, calculus, or other foreign body in a joint.

joint·ress (join′tris) *n.* 1 A woman who has a jointure: also **join·tur·ess** (join′chər·is). 2 A woman who is a joint ruler or owner.

joint snake The glass snake.

joint stock Capital or stock that is held jointly.

joint-stock company (joint′stok′) A company or partnership whose capital is divided into shares (usually transferable), some of which are held by each of the members. Also **joint′-stock′ association.**

join·ture (join′chər) *n.* 1 *Law* A settlement, as of land, made to a woman in place of dower. 2 *Obs.* A joining together. —*v.t.* **join·tured, join·tur·ing** To settle a jointure on. [<F <L *junctura* <*jungere* join]

join·ture·less (join′chər·lis) *adj.* Having no jointure.

joint·weed (joint′wēd′) *n.* A slender, erect American annual herb *(Polygonella articulata)* with small, white flowers on jointed stems.

joint·worm (joint′wûrm′) *n.* The larva of a plant-feeding chalcidid hymenopterous fly (genus *Harmolita*), especially *H. tritici,* that does great damage to wheat, barley, etc., by causing a gall-like excrescence at the joints of the stalk.

Join·ville (zhwan·vēl′), **Jean de,** 1224–1317, French crusader and chronicler.

joist (joist) *n.* A horizontal timber in a floor or ceiling. See synonyms under STICK. —*v.t.* To furnish with joists. [<OF *giste* <*gesir* lie <L *jacere*]

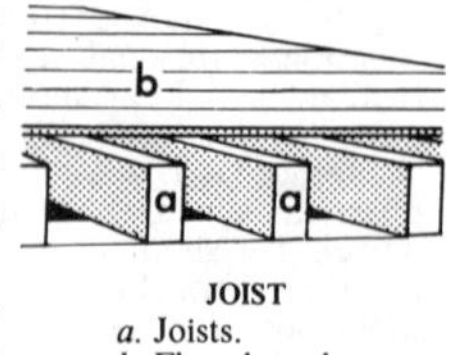

JOIST
a. Joists.
b. Floor boards.

Jó·kai (yō′koi), **Mau·rus,** 1825–1904, Hungarian novelist.

joke (jōk) *n.* 1 Something said or done for the purpose of creating amusement; a jest. 2 A subject of merriment. 3 Something not said or done in earnest; sport. See synonyms under WIT. —*v.* **joked, jok·ing** *v.t.* To make merry with. —*v.i.* To make jokes; jest. [<L *jocus*] —**jok′ing·ly** *adv.*

jok·er (jō′kər) *n.* 1 One who jokes. 2 In certain card games, as euchre, an extra card that counts as the highest trump, or, in poker, as any card the holder names. 3 *U.S.* An ambiguous or inconspicuous clause, inserted in a legislative bill to render it ineffectual or cause it to serve some purpose other than the original intention of the bill. 4 Any hidden device or ruse used for purposes of trickery or deception.

Jok·ja·kar·ta (jōk′yə·kär′tə) See JOGJAKARTA.

jole (jōl) See JOWL.

Jo·li·et (jō′lē·et, jō′lē·et′; *Fr.* zhô·lye′), **Louis,** 1645–1700, French-Canadian explorer. Also **Jol·liet** (jol′ē·et, *Fr.* zhô·lye′).

Jo·liot-Cu·rie (zhô·lyō′kü·rē′), **Frédéric,** 1900–1958, and his wife **Irène,** 1897–1956, daughter of Marie and Pierre Curie, French physicists.

jol·li·fi·ca·tion (jol′ə·fə·kā′shən) *n.* An act or occasion of festivity; a merrymaking.

jol·li·fy (jol′ə·fī) *v.t.* & *v.i.* **·fied, ·fy·ing** To be or cause to be merry or jolly.

jol·li·ness (jol′ē·nis) *n.* The state or quality of being jolly; gaiety. Also **jol·li·ty** (jol′ə·tē).

jol·ly (jol′ē) *adj.* **·li·er, ·li·est** 1 Full of life and mirth; jovial. 2 Expressing, inspiring, or characterized by mirth; exciting gaiety. 3 *Obs.* Exhilarated. See synonyms under HAPPY, MERRY. —*adv. Brit. Colloq.* Extremely; very: a *jolly* good time. —*n. pl.* **·lies** 1 Fun; banter; flattery. 2 *Brit. Slang* A British marine. 3 *Brit. Colloq.* A merry or festive gathering. —*v.t.* **·lied, ·ly·ing** *Colloq.* 1 To attempt to put or keep in good humor by agreeable or flattering attentions: often with *along* or *up.* 2 To make fun of; joke; rally. [<OF *joli*] —**jol′li·er** *n.* —**jol′li·ly** *adv.*

Jolly balance A spring balance used in the determination of specific gravities. [after Philip von *Jolly*, 1809–84, German physicist]

jol·ly·boat (jol′ē·bōt′) *n.* A small boat belonging to a ship. [<Dan. *jolle* yawl + BOAT]

Jolly Roger See BLACK FLAG under FLAG[1].

Jo·lo (hō′lō, hō·lō′) 1 The chief island in the Sulu archipelago, Philippines; 345 square miles. 2 Its chief city, capital of Sulu province.

jolt (jōlt) *v.t.* 1 To strike or knock against with a jarring shock. 2 To shake about with such shock. —*v.i.* 3 To move with jolts or bumps, as over a rough road. See synonyms under SHAKE. —*n.* A sudden, slight shock. [? Blend of ME *jot* bump and *joll* bump] —**jolt′er** *n.* —**jolt′y** *adj.*

Jo·ma·da (jō·mä′dä) The name of two Mohammedan months. See under CALENDAR (Mohammedan). Also spelled *Jumada.*

Jon (jon) An old form of JOHN.

Jo·nah (jō′nə) A masculine personal name. Also **Jo·nas** (jō′nəs; *Fr.* zhô·näs′, *Ger.* yō′näs). [<Hebrew, dove]

—**Jonah** 1 A Hebrew prophet of the eighth or ninth century B.C., who was cast overboard during a tempest sent because he had defied God: he was swallowed by a large fish, lived in its belly for three days, and was vomited up on shore alive. 2 The minor book of the Old Testament named for him and telling his story. 3 Any person or thing regarded as bringing bad luck: in allusion to the bad luck brought upon the sailors of the vessel the prophet traveled on. *Jonah* i 13–17. Also **Jo·nas** (jō′nəs).

Jon·a·than (jon′ə·thən) A masculine personal name. [<Hebrew, gift of the Lord]

—**Jonathan** Son of Saul and close friend of David. I *Sam.* xiv 1.

—**Jonathan** See BROTHER JONATHAN.

Jon·a·than (jon′ə·thən) *n.* A yellowish-red variety of late autumn apple.

Jones (jōnz), **Casey** See CASEY JONES. —**Daniel,** born 1881, English phonetician. —**Ernest,** 1879–1958, English psychologist and biographer of Sigmund Freud. —**Henry Arthur,** 1851–1929, English playwright. —**In·i·go** (in′i·gō), 1573–1652, English architect and stage designer. —**John Paul,** 1747–92, American naval commander born in Scotland. —**Rufus Matthew,** 1863–1948, U.S. Quaker leader, philosopher, and writer; co-founder of the American Friends Service Committee.

Jones Sound An arm of Baffin Bay between Ellesmere and Devon islands, Northwest Territories, Canada.

jon·gler·y (jong′glə·rē) *n. Archaic* Juggling; trickery. [<F *jonglerie* <*jongleur* a juggler]

jon·gleur (jong′glər, *Fr.* zhôn·glœr′) *n.* A medieval minstrel; also, later, a storyteller or buffoon. See JUGGLER. [<OF]

jon·ny·cake (jon′ē·kāk′) See JOHNNYCAKE.

jon·quil (jon′kwil, jong′-) *n.* 1 An ornamental bulbous plant *(Narcissus jonquilla)* related to the daffodil, having long, linear leaves and fragrant, white or yellow flowers. 2 The bulb or flower of this plant. 3 One of several other species of *Narcissus.* 4 A light-yellow color used in staining porcelains. Also **jon′quille.** [<F *jonquille,* ult. <L *juncus* a rush]

Jon·son (jon′sən), **Ben(jamin),** 1573–1637, English poet and dramatist.

Jop·pa (jop′ə) The Old Testament name for JAFFA. II *Chron.* ii 16.

Jor·daens (yôr′däns), **Jacob,** 1593–1678, Flemish painter.

jor·dan (jôr′dən) *n. Brit. Slang* A chamber pot.

Jor·dan (jôr′dən) The chief river of Palestine, flowing over 200 miles south to the Dead Sea.

Jor·dan (jôr′dən), **David Starr,** 1851–1931, U.S. zoologist and educator.

Jordan, Hashemite Kingdom of the A constitutional monarchy comprising the territories of Trans-Jordan and Arab Palestine; formed, with Iraq, The Arab Federation, 1958, but remains a sovereign state; 37,758 square miles: capital, Amman. *Arabic* **Al Ur·du·ni·yah** (al ŏŏr·dōō·nē′yä). Also **Jordan.** —**Jor·da·ni·an** (jôr·dā′nē·ən) *adj.* & *n.*

Jordan almond A large Spanish almond, frequently sugar-coated as a confection.

Jor·ge (*Sp.* hôr′hā, *Pg.* zhôr′zhe) Spanish and Portuguese form of GEORGE.

jor·na·da (hôr·nä′thä) *n. SW U.S.* A stretch of desert land that can be crossed in a day's journey. [<Sp., ult. <L *diurnus* of a day]

jo·rum (jôr′əm, jō′rəm) *n.* A drinking bowl or its contents. Also **jo′ram.** [? after *Joram,* a Biblical character who brought vessels of silver and gold to David]

jo·seph (jō′zef) *n.* A long coat formerly worn by men; also, a similar garment formerly worn as a riding habit by women. [In allusion to the coat of *Joseph* (*Gen.* xxxvii 3)]

Jo·seph (jō′zəf, *Fr.* zhō·zef′; *Ger.* yō′zef) A masculine personal name. Also *Lat.* **Jo·se·phus** (jō·sē′fəs), *Pg., Sp.* **Jo·sé** (*Pg.* zhōō·ze′, *Sp.* hō·sā′). [<Hebrew, addition]

—**Joseph** Hebrew patriarch; son of Jacob and Rachel: sold into slavery in Egypt by his brothers. *Gen.* xxx 24–5.

—**Joseph** Husband of Mary, the mother of Jesus. *Matt.* i 18.

—**Joseph II,** 1741–90; Holy Roman Emperor 1765–90.

—**Joseph of Arimathea** A wealthy Israelite who believed in Christ and provided a tomb for his burial. Compare GRAIL.

Joseph flower See GOATBEARD (def. 1). Also **Joseph's flower.**

Jo·se·phine (jō′zə·fēn, *Ger.* yō′zə·fē′nə) Feminine form of JOSEPH. Also *Fr.* **Jo·sé·phine**

(zhō·zā·fēn′) or **Jo·sèphe** (zho·zef′) *Ger.* **Jo·seph·e** (yō·zef′ə), *Lat.* **Jo·se·pha** (jō·sē′fə), *Pg.* **Jo·se·phi·na** (zhō′zə·fē′nə), *Sp.* **Jo·se·fi·na** (hō′·sā·fē′nä).
— **Josephine,** 1763–1814, Marie Joséphine-Rose Tascher de la Pagerie, widow of Viscount Beauharnais; married Napoleon I 1796; divorced 1809.
Jo·seph·ite (jō′zəf·īt) *n.* A member of the Reorganized church of Jesus Christ of Latter-day Saints (the Mormon Church), established about 1860 by the followers of Joseph Smith.
Jo·se·phus (jō·sē′fəs), **Flavius,** A.D. 37–96?, Jewish historian.
josh (josh) *U.S. Slang v.t. & v.i.* To make good-humored fun of (someone); tease; banter. — *n.* A hoax; a good-natured joke. [Blend of JOKE and BOSH] —**josh′er** *n.*
Josh Bil·lings (josh bil′ingz) Pseudonym of Henry Wheeler Shaw.
Josh·u·a (josh′ōō·ə) A masculine personal name. Also *Lat.* **Jos·u·a** (jos′ōō·ə; *Du., Sw.* yō′sōō·ä, *Ger.* yō′zōō·ə), *Fr.* **Jo·sué** (zhō·zwā′). [<Hebrew, the Lord is salvation]
— **Joshua** Son of Nun and successor of Moses as leader of the Israelites; also, the book of the Old Testament ascribed to him.
Joshua tree A tall, treelike desert plant (*Yucca brevifolia*) with forking branches that end in a cluster of leaves.
Jo·si·ah (jō·sī′ə) A masculine personal name. Also *Lat.* **Jo·si·as** (jō·sī′əs, *Dan.* yō·zī′äs; *Fr.* zhō·zē·äs′), *Du.* **Jo·zi·as** (yō·zē′äs). [<Hebrew, given to the Lord]
— **Josiah** A king of Judah in the seventh century B.C. II *Kings* xxii 1.
jos·kin (jos′kin) *n. Brit. Dial.* An awkward rustic; a boor.
Jos·quin des Prés (zhôs·kaṅ′ dā prā′), 1445?–1521, Flemish composer.
joss (jos) *n.* A Chinese god. [Pidgin English <Pg. *deos* God]
joss house A Chinese temple or place for idols.
joss paper Gold or silver paper burnt by the Chinese at funerals, etc.
joss stick A stick of perfumed paste burnt as incense.
jos·tle (jos′əl) *v.t. & v.i.* **·tled, ·tling** To push or crowd; elbow; hustle; bump. See synonyms under HUSTLE. — *n.* A collision, bumping against, or slight shaking. Also spelled *justle.* [Freq. of JOUST] —**jos′tler** *n.*
jot (jot) *v.t.* **jot·ted, jot·ting** To make a hasty note of: usually with *down.* — *n.* The least bit; an iota. See synonyms under PARTICLE. [<IOTA]
jo·ta (hō′tä) *n.* A lively Spanish dance in 3/4 time danced by a man and a woman with castanets.
Jo·tham (jō′thəm) A masculine personal name. [<Hebrew, the Lord is perfect]
— **Jotham** A son of Gideon, who survived the murder of his brothers. *Judges* ix 5–16.
jot·tings (jot′ingz) *n. pl.* Items of news, or memoranda.
Jö·tun (yœ′tōōn) In Norse mythology, one of the giants personifying the hostile powers of nature. Also **Jo·tun** (yô′tōōn, yō′-), **Jo′tunn.**
Jö·tunn·heim (yœ′tōōn·hām) See UTGARD. Also **Jo′tun·heim** (yô′-, yō′-).
Jou·bert (zhōō·bâr′), **Joseph,** 1754–1824, French moralist. — **Petrus Jacobus,** 1831–1900, Boer general.
jougs (jōōgz) *n. pl.* An old Scottish instrument of punishment, consisting of an iron yoke by which the culprit was fastened to a wall or post. [<OF *joug* yoke <L *jugum* yoke]
jouk (jōōk) *v.i. Scot.* To dodge; also, to bow.
joule (joul, jōōl) *n. Physics* The mks unit of work or energy: equivalent to the work done, or heat generated, in one second by an electric current of one ampere against a resistance of one ohm, or in raising the potential of one coulomb by one volt: equal to 10,000,000 ergs or .737324 foot-pounds. [after James Prescott *Joule*]
Joule (joul, jōōl), **James Prescott,** 1818–89, English physicist.
jounce (jouns) *v.t. & v.i.* **jounced, jounc·ing** To shake or move roughly up and down; bounce; jolt. — *n.* A shake; a bump. [? Blend of GEE[2] and BOUNCE]
jour (zhōōr) *n. French* Day; daylight; dawn.
Jour·dan (zhōōr·däṅ′), **Comte Jean Baptiste,** 1762–1833, French marshal.
jour de fête (də fet′) *French* A feast day; festival.
jour·nal (jûr′nəl) *n.* 1 A record of daily occurrences of personal interest; a diary. 2 An official record of the daily proceedings of a legislature or other deliberative body. 3 A periodical recording news or other events of current interest. 4 A daily chronicle of a voyage. 5 *Naut.* A log or logbook. 6 In bookkeeping: **a** A daybook. **b** In double entry, a book in which transactions of the day are entered in systematic form, either as original entries or as transfers from the daybook, in order to facilitate later posting in the ledger. 7 *Mech.* That part of a shaft or axle which rotates in or against a bearing. [<OF <L *diurnalis.* Doublet of DIURNAL.]

JOURNAL (*def. 7*)
a. Journal. *b.* Bearing.

journal box *Mech.* The box or bearing for a rotating axle or shaft.
jour·nal·ese (jûr′nəl·ēz′, -ēs′) *n.* A style of writing supposedly characteristic of newspapers; facile and sensational writing, hackneyed phrases and effects, etc.
jour·nal in·time (zhōōr·nȧl′ aṅ·tēm′) *French* Private diary.
jour·nal·ism (jûr′nəl·iz′əm) *n.* 1 The occupation of a journalist; the writing, editing, or publishing of newspapers or other periodicals. 2 Newspapers collectively.
jour·nal·ist (jûr′nəl·ist) *n.* One who manages, edits, or writes for a journal or newspaper.
jour·nal·is·tic (jûr′nəl·is′tik) *adj.* Pertaining to journalists or journalism. —**jour′nal·is′ti·cal·ly** *adv.*
jour·nal·ize (jûr′nəl·īz) *v.* **·ized, ·iz·ing** *v.t.* 1 To enter in a journal. 2 To write or describe in a journal. — *v.i.* 3 To keep a journal or diary. Also *Brit.* **jour′nal·ise.**
jour·ney (jûr′nē) *n.* 1 Passage from one place to another, especially by land: sometimes applied figuratively to the passage through life. 2 The distance traversed, or traversable, in a specified time: a week's *journey* away. 3 In glassmaking, the round of work or the time taken in making raw material into glass. — *v.i.* To travel; go on a journey. [<OF *journee* a day's travel <L *diurnum,* orig. neut. sing. of *diurnus* daily < *dies* a day] —**jour′ney·er** *n.*
Synonyms (noun): excursion, expedition, pilgrimage, tour, transit, travel, trip, voyage. A *journey* is a direct going from a starting point to a destination, ordinarily over a considerable distance; we speak of a day's *journey,* or the *journey* of life. *Travel* is a passing from place to place, not necessarily in a direct line or with a fixed destination. A *voyage,* which was formerly a *journey* of any kind, is now a going to a considerable distance by water, especially by sea. A *trip* is a short and direct *journey.* A *tour* is a *journey* that returns to the starting point, generally over a considerable distance; as, a bridal *tour,* or business *tour.* An *excursion* is a brief *tour* or *journey* taken for pleasure, often by many persons at once; as, an *excursion* to West Point. *Passage* is a general word for a *journey* by any conveyance, especially by water; as, rough *passage* across the Atlantic. *Transit,* literally the act of passing over or through, is used specifically of the conveyance of passengers or merchandise; rapid *transit* is demanded for surburban residents or perishable goods. *Pilgrimage,* once always of a sacred character, retains in derived uses something of that sense; as, a *pilgrimage* to Monticello.
jour·ney·man (jûr′nē·mən) *n. pl.* **·men** (-mən) A mechanic who has learned his trade and who works at it for another.
jour·ney·work (jûr′nē·wûrk′) *n.* Work done by a journeyman.
joust (just, joust, jōōst) *n.* A tilting match between mounted knights, usually with blunt lances and in single combat. — *v.i.* To engage in a joust. Also spelled *just.* [<OF *jouste* <*jouster* <LL *juxtare* approach <*juxta* nearby] —**joust′er** *n.*
Jo·van·na (zhō·vä′nə) Portuguese form of JOAN.
Jove (jōv) Jupiter. —**by Jove!** A mild oath expressing surprise, emphasis, etc.
jo·vi·al (jō′vē·əl) *adj.* Possessing or expressive of good-natured mirth or gaiety; jolly. See synonyms under MERRY. [<F <LL *Jovialis* born under the influence of Jupiter] —**jo′vi·al·ly** *adv.* —**jo′vi·al·ness** *n.*
Jo·vi·al (jō′vē·əl) *adj.* 1 In astrology, pertaining to the influence of the planet Jupiter; favorable; benignant. 2 *Obs.* Of or pertaining to the god Jupiter; Jovelike; majestic.
jo·vi·al·i·ty (jō′vē·al′ə·tē) *n.* 1 The quality of being jovial. 2 Merriment; conviviality; mirth. Also **jo·vi·al·ty** (jō′vē·əl·tē). See synonyms under SPORT.
jo·vi·al·ize (jō′vē·əl·īz′) *v.t.* **·ized, ·iz·ing** To make jovial.
Jo·vi·an (jō′vē·ən) *adj.* Of or pertaining to Jove or Jupiter.
Jo·vi·a·nus (jō′vē·ā′nəs), **Flavius Claudius,** 331?–364, Roman emperor 363–364. Also **Jo′vi·an** (-ən).
jow (jou, jō) *Scot. v.t. & v.i.* To ring; toll. — *n.* The stroke or sound of a bell.
Jow·ett (jou′it), **Benjamin,** 1817–93, English classical scholar.
jowl[1] (joul, jōl) *n.* 1 The fleshy part of the lower jaw, especially when fat and pendulous. 2 The wattle of fowls. 3 The dewlap of cattle. Also spelled *jole.* [ME *cholle,* ? OE *coelur* throat]
jowl[2] (joul, jōl) *n.* The cheek or jaw. Also spelled *jole.* [OE *ceafl*] —**jowled** *adj.*
jowl·er (jou′lər) *n.* A heavy-jawed hound.
joy (joi) *n.* 1 A lively emotion of happiness; gladness. 2 Anything which causes delight. 3 An expression or manifestation of this. 4 *Obs.* Festivity. See synonyms under HAPPINESS, RAPTURE. — *v.i.* To be glad; rejoice. — *v.t. Obs.* To gladden. See synonyms under REJOICE. [<OF *joie* <L *gaudium* < *gaudere* rejoice]
joy·ance (joi′əns) *n.* 1 *Poetic* Delight; enjoyment. 2 *Archaic* Gaiety; festivity.
Joyce (jois), **James,** 1882–1941, Irish novelist and poet. — **William** See HAW-HAW, LORD.
joy·ful (joi′fəl) *adj.* 1 Full of joy. 2 Manifesting or causing joy. See synonyms under HAPPY. —**joy′ful·ly** *adv.* —**joy′ful·ness** *n.*
joy·less (joi′lis) *adj.* Destitute of joy; having or causing no joy. —**joy′less·ly** *adv.* —**joy′less·ness** *n.*
joy·ous (joi′əs) *adj.* Joyful. See synonyms under AIRY, CHEERFUL, HAPPY, MERRY. —**joy′ous·ly** *adv.* —**joy′ous·ness** *n.*
joy-ride (joi′rīd′) *n. Colloq.* An automobile ride taken exclusively for pleasure: often with the idea of reckless driving in a stolen car. —**joy′-rid′er** *n.* —**joy′-rid′ing** *n.*
joy-stick (joi′stik′) *n. Slang* The control stick in an airplane.
Jo·zsef (*Hungarian* yō′sef, *Polish* yôsh′if) Hungarian and Polish form of JOSEPH.
Juan (hwän) Spanish form of JOHN. See also DON JUAN.
Jua·na (hwä′nä) Spanish form of JOAN.
Juan de Fu·ca Strait (hwän′ də fōō′kə) An arm of the Pacific Ocean between Vancouver Island and the Washington mainland.
Ju·an Fer·nan·dez (jōō′ən fər·nan′dēz, *Sp.* hwän fer·nän′dās) A group of Chilean islands lying 425 miles west of central Chile: total land area, 70 square miles. See SELKIRK, ALEXANDER.
Juá·rez (hwä′rās), **Benito Pablo,** 1806–72, Mexican patriot who opposed Maximilian; president of Mexico 1858–63, 1867–72.
Juárez, Ciudad See CIUDAD JUÁREZ.
ju·ba (jōō′bə) *n.* A lively Southern Negro dance. — **to pat juba** To keep time to the juba by patting with the hands and feet. [Of African origin]
Ju·ba (jōō′bä) A river in southern Italian Somaliland, flowing 548 miles south to the Indian Ocean: Italian *Giuba.*
Ju·bal (jōō′bəl) A descendant of Cain; a musician or inventor of musical instruments. *Gen.* iv 21.
ju·bate (jōō′bāt) *adj.* Having a manelike growth. [<L *jubatus* <*juba* a mane]
Jub·bul·pore (jub′əl·pôr′) A city in northern Madhya Pradesh, central India: also *Jabalpur.*
ju·be (jōō′bē) *n.* 1 *Archit.* A rood loft or screen and gallery at the entrance of the choir of a church. 2 *Obs.* An ambo. [<L *jube,* imperative of *jubere* bid; from the first word of a prayer anciently recited from this gallery]

jubh·a (jōōb′ə) *n.* A long, loose outer garment, worn in Moslem countries. Also **jub′·bah.** See JIBBA. [<Arabic *jubbah*]

ju·bi·lance (jōō′bə·ləns) *n.* Jubilation. Also **ju′bi·lan·cy.**

ju·bi·lant (jōō′bə·lənt) *adj.* **1** Manifesting great joy; exultingly glad. **2** Expressing triumph. [<L *jubilans, -antis,* ppr. of *jubilare* exult] **—ju′bi·lant·ly** *adv.*

ju·bi·late (jōō′bə·lāt) *v.t.* & *v.i.* **·lat·ed, ·lat·ing** To rejoice; exult. [<L *jubilatus,* pp. of *jubilare* exult]

Ju·bi·la·te (jōō′bə·lā′tē, -lä′-) *n.* **1** The 100th (in the Vulgate and Douai versions, the 99th) Psalm, or the music to which it may be set: from its opening word in the Latin version. **2** The third Sunday after Easter, whose introit begins *Jubilate.* [<L, imperative of *jubilare* exult, be joyful]

Ju·bi·la·te De·o (jōō′bə·lā′tē dē′ō, jōō′bə·lä′tē dā′ō) *Latin* Be joyful in the Lord.

ju·bi·la·tion (jōō′bə·lā′shən) *n.* Rejoicing; exultation.

ju·bi·lee (jōō′bə·lē) *n.* **1** In Jewish history, every fiftieth year, from the entrance of the Hebrews into Canaan. At its recurrence, all Hebrew slaves were emancipated and all alienated lands reverted to their former owners or their heirs. **2** In the Roman Catholic Church, a year of special indulgence, appointed by the Pope, during which compliance with certain conditions of confession, communion, good works, etc., will secure remission from the penal consequences of sin: also called *Annus Sanctus.* **3** The fiftieth or the twenty-fifth anniversary of an event; also, the celebration of this. **4** Any season of rejoicing or festivity. **5** *Obs.* A state or manifestation of exultation or delight. Also **ju′bi·le.** [<OF *jubile* <LL *jubilaeus* (infl. by *jubilum* a shout of joy) <Gk. *iōbēlaios* <Hebrew *yōbēl* ram's horn, trumpet]

jubilee singer One, especially a Negro, who sings jubilee songs.

jubilee song A Negro folk song or spiritual; originally, one of rejoicing over emancipation from slavery.

Ju·by (jōō′bē), **Cape** A headland of Spanish West Africa opposite the Canary Islands: also *Cape Yubi.*

Jú·car (hōō′kär) A river in eastern Spain, rising in NE Cuenca province and flowing 310 miles south and east to the Mediterranean.

ju chin (jōō′ chin′) **1** A creamy gold emulsion made by rubbing gold leaf under water with a circular motion of the fingers: used in Chinese and Japanese painting to outline rocks in landscapes, to impart bright highlights to birds and flowers, and to decorate the garments in Buddhistic portraits. **2** A brush technique for applying this emulsion. [<Chinese, lit., milk gold]

Ju·dae·a (jōō·dē′ə), **Ju·dae·an** (jōō·dē′ən) See JUDEA, etc.

Ju·dah (jōō′də) A masculine personal name. Also *Lat.* **Ju·das** (jōō′dəs, *Ger., Polish, Sw.* yōō′däs), **Jude** (jōōd, *Fr.* zhüd), *Fr.* **Ju·da** (zhü·dà′). [<Hebrew, praise]
—Judah The fourth son of Jacob and Leah, or the tribe descended from him; also, the kingdom, comprising the tribes of Judah and Benjamin, ruled over by the descendants of Solomon. I *Kings* xi–xii.

Ju·dah (jōō′də) An ancient kingdom of the Jews in southern Palestine.

Ju·da·ic (jōō·dā′ik) *adj.* Pertaining to the Jews. Also **Ju·da′i·cal.** [<L *Judaicus* <Gk. *Ioudaikos* <*Ioudaios.* See JEW.] **—Ju·da′i·cal·ly** *adv.*

Ju·da·ism (jōō′dē·iz′əm) *n.* **1** The religious beliefs or practices of the Jews. **2** The acceptance of Jewish rites or doctrines. **—Ju′da·ist** *n.* **—Ju′da·is′tic** *adj.*

Ju·da·ize (jōō′dē·īz) *v.t.* & *v.i.* **·ized, ·iz·ing** To bring over to or accept Judaism. Also *Brit.* **Ju′da·ise.**

Ju·da·iz·er (jōō′dē·ī′zər) *n.* **1** One who accepts or advocates Judaism. **2** In apostolic times, a Jew converted to Christianity who clung to the Mosaic ritual. Also *Brit.* **Ju′da·is′er.**

Ju·das (jōō′dəs) See JUDAH.
—Judas The disciple of Jesus who betrayed him with a kiss, thus identifying him to the Roman captors; hence, one who betrays another under the guise of friendship: also **Judas Iscariot.**
—Judas A brother of Jesus. *Matt.* xiii 55.
—Judas Maccabeus See under MACCABEUS.

Judas kiss A treacherous kiss or other gesture simulating friendliness.

Judas tree Any of a genus *(Cercis)* of trees, as *C. siliquastrum,* a European species, or the redbud *(C. canadensis)* with profuse, reddish-purple flowers, of the central and western United States. [From a tradition that Judas hanged himself upon a tree of this kind]

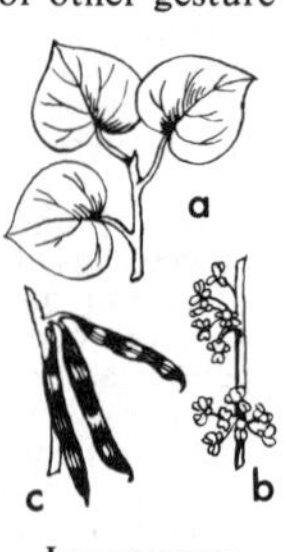

JUDAS TREE
a. Leaves.
b. Blossom.
c. Fruit.

Jude (jōōd) See JUDAH. **—Jude** One of the apostles, the brother of James, and possibly of Jesus: sometimes identified with Thaddeus (*Luke* vi 16); also, a New Testament epistle attributed to him.

Ju·de·a (jōō·dē′ə) The southern part of ancient Palestine under Persian, Greek, and Roman dominion: also *Judaea.*

Ju·de·an (jōō·dē′ən) *adj.* Of or pertaining to Judea. **—***n.* A native of Judea. Also spelled *Judaean.*

judge (juj) *n.* **1** An officer invested with authority to administer justice. **2** One who decides upon the merits of things, as in contests. **3** One who is competent to decide upon the merits of persons, animals, things, etc.; a connoisseur. **4** In Jewish history, one of the Israelitish rulers from the death of Joshua to the anointing of Saul. **—***v.* **judged, judg·ing** *v.t.* **1** To hear and decide in an official capacity the merits of (a case) or the guilt of (a person); examine and pass judgment on; try. **2** To form an opinion or judgment concerning; evaluate; estimate: to *judge* a painting. **3** To hold as judgment or opinion; consider; suppose: We *judged* it the proper time. **4** To govern: said of the ancient Hebrew judges. **—***v.i.* **5** To act as a judge; sit in judgment. **6** To form a judgment or estimate. **7** To make a judgment or decision. [<OF *juge* <L *judex, -icis* <*ius* right + *dic-,* root of *dicere* speak] **—judg′er** *n.*
Synonyms (noun): arbiter, arbitrator, justice, referee, umpire. A *judge,* in the legal sense, is a judicial officer appointed or elected to preside in courts of law, and to decide legal questions duly brought before him; the name is sometimes given to other legally constituted officers; as, the *judges* of election; in other relations, any person duly appointed to pass upon the merits of contestants or of competing articles may be called a *judge.* In various sports the *judge* is called an *umpire* or in some cases the *referee,* as, the *umpire* of a ball game. In law, a *referee* is appointed by a court to decide disputed matters between litigants; an *arbitrator* is chosen by the contending parties to decide matters in dispute without action by a court. In certain cases, an *umpire* is appointed by a court to decide where *arbitrators* disagree. *Arbiter,* with its suggestion of final and absolute decision, has come to be used only in a high or sacred sense; as, war must now be the *arbiter*; the Supreme *Arbiter* of our destinies. The *judges* of certain courts, as the United States Supreme Court, are technically known as *justices.*

judge advocate *Mil.* **1** A commissioned officer of the U. S. Army belonging to the Judge Advocate General's Department. **2** The legal staff officer for a commander. **3** The prosecutor in a general or special court martial.

Judge Advocate General A major general in the U. S. Army serving as head of the Judge Advocate General's Department.

judge-made (juj′mād′) *adj.* Created or constituted by judges or judicial decision: frequently used in an opprobrious sense.

Judg·es (juj′iz) The seventh book of the Old Testament.

judge·ship (juj′ship) *n.* The office, or period in office, of a judge.

judg·mat·ic (juj·mat′ik) *adj. Colloq.* Evincing good judgment; skilful. Also **judg·mat′i·cal.** [<*judge*; on analogy with *dogmatic*] **—judg·mat′i·cal·ly** *adv.*

judg·ment (juj′mənt) *n.* **1** The act or faculty of affirming or denying a conclusion, whether as based upon a direct comparison of objects or ideas, or derived by a process of reasoning. **2** The result of judging; the decision or conclusion reached, as after consideration or deliberation. **3** *Law* The sentence or final order of a court in a civil or criminal proceeding; the sentence of the law; the final determination or adjudication of the rights of the parties to an action; decision; award; also, the obligation or debt created by the decision or verdict of a court, or the official certificate or record of such decision, which constitutes a lien on leviable property. **4** A disaster or affliction regarded as inflicted by God as a punishment for sin. **5** *Theol.* The final award or sentence of the human race; also, the time of this: also **Judgment** or **Last Judgment. 6** *Psychol.* The mental act or attitude of decision with which the process of observation, comparison, or ratiocination is terminated; also, loosely, the rational faculty; thought. **7** *Logic* That form of thought in which two terms are compared and their fitness to be joined under a given relation is affirmed or denied; also, the result of judging, the verbal expression of which is called an assertion or proposition. **8** *Obs.* Uprightness; rectitude. Also *Brit.* **judge′ment.** See synonyms under IDEA, PRUDENCE, THOUGHT[1], UNDERSTANDING, WISDOM. **—general judgment** *Theol.* The final judgment of all men after the dissolution of the world. **—particular judgment** *Theol.* The judgment of the soul immediately after death.

Judgment Day *Theol.* The day or time of the Last Judgment.

judgment debtor *Law* A debtor against whom judgment of indebtedness has been recorded.

judgment of God Trial by single combat or by ordeal or the like, supposed to be under direct divine control.

judgment seat A judges' bench or a place where judgment is delivered.

ju·di·ca·ble (jōō′də·kə·bəl) *adj.* That can be tried or judged. Also **ju·di·ci·a·ble** (jōō·dish′·ē·ə·bəl).

ju·di·ca·tive (jōō′də·kā′tiv, -kə-) *adj.* Competent to judge; judicial. [<L *judicatus,* pp. of *judicare* judge]

ju·di·ca·tor (jōō′də·kā′tər) *n.* One who performs the office of a judge.

ju·di·ca·to·ry (jōō′də·kə·tôr′ē, -tō′rē) *adj.* Pertaining to the administration of justice. **—***n. pl.* **·ries 1** A tribunal. **2** The judiciary. **3** *Obs.* Judicial power; justice.

ju·di·ca·ture (jōō′də·kə·chōōr) *n.* **1** The power of administering justice. **2** The jurisdiction of a court. **3** A court of justice; also, judges collectively. **4** *Obs.* Established right; legality; lawfulness.

ju·di·cial (jōō·dish′əl) *adj.* **1** Pertaining to the administration of justice. **2** Of, pertaining to, or connected with a court or judge. **3** Discriminating; impartial. **4** Serving to decide or determine; judging: *judicial* duels. **5** *Obs.* Established by formal enactment or positive law. [<L *judicialis* <*judex, -icis* a judge] **—ju·di′cial·ly** *adv.*

ju·di·ci·ar·y (jōō·dish′ē·er′ē, -dish′ə·rē) *adj.* Pertaining to courts of justice or to a judge. **—***n. pl.* **·ar·ies 1** That department of government which administers the law. **2** The judges of the courts considered collectively.

ju·di·cious (jōō·dish′əs) *adj.* **1** Having or acting on sound judgment; proceeding with discretion; manifesting forethought and sense; wise; prudent. **2** Done with sound judgment; well-calculated; planned or arranged with discretion. See synonyms under POLITIC, SAGACIOUS, WISE[1]. [<F *judicieux* <L *judicium* a judgment] **—ju·di′cious·ly** *adv.* **—ju·di′cious·ness** *n.*

Ju·dith (jōō′dith; *Fr.* zhü·dēt′, *Ger.* yōō′dēt) A feminine personal name. Also *Lat.* **Ju·di·tha** (jōō′di·tə). [<Hebrew, praise]
—Judith A Jewish woman, heroine of a book in the Apocrypha of the same name, who rescued her countrymen by slaying the Assyrian general, Holofernes.

ju·do (jōō′dō) *n.* A Japanese system of mental and physical conditioning based upon jiujitsu and often practiced as a sport. Compare JIUJITSU. [<Japanese *ju* gentle, pliant + *do* way of life]

Ju·dy (jōō′dē) **1** Diminutive of JUDITH. **2** The wife of Punch.

jug[1] (jug) *n.* **1** A narrow-necked, stout, bulging vessel with a cork, for keeping or carrying liquids. **2** A deep vessel for holding or serving liquids; a drinking vessel; pitcher. **3** A pint of ale or beer. **4** *Slang* A prison; jail. **—***v.t.* **jugged, jug·ging 1** To put into a jug. 2 To cook in a jug. 3 *Slang* To imprison; jail. [from *Jug,* a nickname for *Joan*]

jug[2] (jug) *v.i.* **jugged, jug·ging** To utter a cry like that of the nightingale, as some birds. — *n.* The note of some birds, as the nightingale. [Imit.]

jug[3] (jug) *v.i.* **jugged, jug·ging** To collect together and nestle in a flock or covey: said of partridges. [Cf. OF *jouquier* be at rest]

jug[4] (jug) *n.* An act of worship by which Brahmans are said to acquire preternatural power. Also **jug′gul** (-gəl). [<Hind. *jag* <Skt. *jagata* the world]

ju·gal (jōō′gəl) *adj. Anat.* Of or pertaining to a bone of the zygomatic arch or malar bone. [<L *jugalis* <*jugum* a yoke]

ju·gate (jōō′git, -gāt) *adj.* 1 Occurring in pairs. 2 *Bot.* Having paired leaves, as certain plants. [<L *jugatus,* pp. of *jugare* bind together <*jugum* a yoke]

jug·ger·naut (jug′ər·nôt) *n.* 1 Anything to which one makes unquestioning sacrifices. 2 Any irresistible force. [after JUGGERNAUT]

Jug·ger·naut (jug′ər·nôt) The eighth avatar of Vishnu whose idol at Puri, India, was drawn on a heavy car under the wheels of which devotees were said to have thrown themselves to be crushed. Also spelled *Jaganath, Jaganatha, Jaggurnath.* [<Hind. *jagannāth* lord of the universe]

jug·gle (jug′əl) *v.* **·gled, ·gling** *v.t.* 1 To toss (a number of balls, plates, etc.) into the air, keeping them in continuous motion by successively catching and tossing them up again. 2 To perform tricks of sleight of hand with. 3 To manipulate for the purpose of deception or trickery: to *juggle* financial accounts. — *v.i.* 4 To perform as a juggler. 5 To practice deception or trickery. — *n.* 1 A feat of legerdemain. 2 A trick or deception. [<OF *jogler* <L *joculari* jest]

jug·gler (jug′lər) *n.* 1 One who juggles; a prestidigitator. 2 One who deceives by cheating; an impostor. [<OF *joglere* <L *joculator* jester]

jug·gler·y (jug′lər·ē) *n. pl.* **·gler·ies** 1 The art of a juggler; legerdemain. 2 Deception; trickery.

jug·gling (jug′ling) *adj.* Deceiving; cheating; relating to tricks of magic. — *n.* Jugglery.

jug-han·dled (jug′han′dəld) *adj.* One-sided; partial; hence, unjust.

jug·head (jug′hed′) *n. U.S. Slang* 1 A slow-witted horse. 2 A slow or stupid person.

ju·glan·da·ceous (jōō′glan·dā′shəs) *adj.* Designating a family *(Juglandaceae)* of trees with odd-pinnate leaves and monoecious flowers, including the walnut and hickory. [<NL *Juglandaceae,* the walnut family <L *juglans* a walnut]

ju·glone (jōō′glōn) *n.* A brownish-red crystalline compound, $C_{10}H_6O_3$, extracted from the bark or unripe fruit of the walnut tree *(Juglans cinerea).* [<L *juglans* walnut + -ONE]

Ju·go·slav (yōō′gō·släv′, -slav′), **Ju·go·sla·vi·a** (yōō′gō·slä′vē·ə) See YUGOSLAV, YUGOSLAVIA.

jug·u·lar (jug′yə·lər, jōō′gyə-) *adj.* 1 *Anat.* Pertaining to the throat or to the jugular vein. 2 *Biol.* **a** Situated in front of the pectoral fins. **b** Having the ventral fins at the throat, as a fish. — *n.* One of the jugular veins. [<NL *jugularis* <L *jugulum* a collar bone]

jugular vein *Anat.* One of the large veins on either side of the neck that returns blood from the brain, face, and neck.

ju·gu·late (jōō′gyə·lāt) *v.t.* **·lat·ed, ·lat·ing** 1 *Med.* To arrest the course of (a disease) by drastic therapeutic measures. 2 *Obs.* To cut the throat of. [<L *jugulatus,* pp. of *jugulare* slay, cut the throat of <*jugulum* a collar bone] — **ju′gu·la′tion** *n.*

Ju·gur·tha (jōō·gûr′thə), died 104 B.C., Numidian king.

juice (jōōs) *n.* 1 The fluid part of vegetable or animal matter; especially, the expressible watery matter in fruits, containing usually the characteristic flavor. 2 *Usually pl.* The fluids of the body. 3 The essence of anything. 4 *Slang* Electric current, or other means of generating power, as oil, gasoline, etc. 5 The liquid extracted from anything. [<OF *jus* <L] — **juice′less** *adj.*

juiced rehearsal (jōōst) In television, a final or dress rehearsal, for which the mechanical equipment is used exactly as in the actual telecast.

juic·y (jōō′sē) *adj.* **juic·i·er, juic·i·est** 1 Abounding with juice; moist. 2 Full of interest; colorful; spicy. — **juic′i·ly** *adv.* — **juic′i·ness** *n.*

Juiz de Fo·ra (zhwēzh thə fô′rə) A city in southern Minas Gerais state, Brazil.

ju·jit·su (jōō·jit′sōō), **ju·jut·su** (jōō·jit′sōō, -jōōt′-) See JIUJITSU.

ju·ju (jōō′jōō) *n.* An African fetish or talisman; an object of religious veneration or awe; hence, anything inexplicable, mysterious, or magical; also, the charm said to be worked by a juju. [< native West African name, ? ult. <F *joujou* a toy] — **ju′ju·ism** *n.*

ju·jube (jōō′jōōb) *n.* 1 Any of a genus *(Zizyphus)* of several Old World trees or shrubs of the buckthorn family; especially, the common jujube *(Z. jujuba),* the lotus tree. 2 Its edible fruit. 3 A lozenge. [<F <Med. L *jujuba,* alter. of L *zizyphum* <Gk. *zizyphon* <Persian *zīzafūn*]

Ju·juy (hōō·hwē′) A province of NW Argentina; 22,952 square miles; capital, Jujuy.

juke box A large automatic phonograph, usually coin-operated and permitting selection of the records to be played.

juke joint *U.S. Slang* A roadhouse or barroom for drinking and dancing. [<Gullah *juke,* orig. a brothel (of West African origin) + JOINT (*n.* def. 6)]

Jukes, the A pseudonym used for the members of an actual New York family whose history, as investigated over several generations by 19th century sociologists, showed abnormal incidence of crime, disease, and pauperism. See KALLIKAK.

ju·lep (jōō′lip) *n.* 1 A drink composed usually of brandy or whisky, sugar, cracked ice, and some flavoring, commonly fresh green mint: also **mint julep.** 2 A subacid, mucilaginous, sweetened drink, often used as a vehicle for the administration of medicine. 3 A cool drink made with herbs. Also **ju′lap.** [<MF <Persian *gulāb* rose-water]

Jul·ia (jōōl′yə; *Du.* yōō′lē·ə, *Pg.* zhōō′lē·ə, *Sp.* hōō′lē·ä) A feminine personal name. Also **Ju·lie** (jōō′lē; *Fr.* zhü·lē′, *Ger.* yōō′lē·ä). [<L, fem. of *Julius* JULIUS]

Jul·ian (jōōl′yən; *Ger. Sw.* yōō′lē·än, *Sp.* hōō′lē·än′) A masculine personal name. Also *Lat.* **Ju·li·a·nus** (jōō′lē·ā′nəs, *Du.* yōō′lē·ä′nōōs), *Sp.* **Ju·li·a·no** (hōō′lē·ä′nō), *Fr.* **Ju·lien** (zhü·lyaṅ′), *Pg.* **Ju·li·ão** (zhōō·lē·ouṅ′). [<L, of Julius]

— **Julian the Apostate,** 331–363, Flavius Claudius Julianus, Roman emperor 361–63; renounced Christianity and revived paganism.

Jul·ian (jōōl′yən) *adj.* Of, pertaining to, or named after, Julius Caesar.

Ju·li·an·a (jōō′lē·an′ə; *Du., Sw.* yōō′lē·ä′nä, *Pg.* zhōō′lē·ä′nə, *Sp.* hōō′lē·ä′nä) A feminine personal name. Also *Ger.* **Ju·li·a·ne** (yōō′lē·ä′nə), *Fr.* **Ju·li·enne** (zhü·lē·en′). [<L, fem. of *Julianus* JULIAN]

— **Juliana Louise Emma Marie Wilhelmina,** born 1909, queen of the Netherlands 1948–.

Julian Alps A division of the eastern Alps in NW Yugoslavia and eastern Italy; highest peak, 9,394 feet.

Julian calendar. See under CALENDAR.

Ju·li·a·ne·haab (yōō′lē·ä′nə·hôp) A port in SW Greenland.

ju·li·enne (jōō′lē·en′) *n.* A clear meat soup containing vegetables chopped or cut into thin strips. — *adj.* Cut into thin strips: *julienne* potatoes. [<F, from *Julienne,* a personal name]

Ju·li·et (jōō′lē·et, jōōl′yit) A feminine personal name: diminutive of JULIA.

— **Juliet** The heroine of Shakespeare's *Romeo and Juliet.*

Jul·ius (jōōl′yəs; *Du., Ger.* yōō′lē·ōōs) A masculine personal name; also the name of three popes. *Fr.* **Jules** (zhül), *Pg., Sp.* **Ju·lio** (*Pg.* zhōō′lyō, *Sp.* hōō′lyō). [<L, downy beard]

— **Julius II,** 1443–1513, pope 1503–13; patron of the arts: real name Giuliano della Rovere.

— **Julius Caesar** See under CAESAR.

Jul·lun·der (jul′ən·dər) A city of central Punjab, India.

Ju·ly (jōō·lī′, jōō-) The seventh month of the calendar year, having 31 days. [<OF *Julie* <L *(mensis) Julius* (month) of Julius; because inserted in the calendar by Julius Caesar]

Ju·ma·da (jōō·mä′də) See JOMADA.

jum·ble (jum′bəl) *v.* **·bled, ·bling** *v.t.* 1 To mix in a confused mass; put or throw together without order. 2 To confuse in the mind. — *v.i.* 3 To meet or unite confusedly. See synonyms under DISPLACE. — *n.* 1 A confused mixture or collection: also **jum′ble·ment.** 2 A thin sweet cake. [Origin uncertain]

jum·ble-beads (jum′bəl·bēdz′) *n. pl.* The seeds of the jequirity.

jum·bo (jum′bō) *n. pl.* **·bos** A very large person, animal, or thing. — *adj.* Very large; especially, larger than usual. [after JUMBO]

Jum·bo (jum′bō) An elephant exhibited by P. T. Barnum: the largest ever captured; killed by accident, 1885.

jum·buck (jum′buk′) *n. Austral.* A sheep. [?< native Australian *jimbuc* small kangaroo]

Jum·na (jum′nə) A river in northern India, flowing 860 miles SW to the Ganges.

jump (jump) *v.i.* 1 To spring from the ground, floor, etc., by the action of the muscles of the feet and legs. 2 To move abruptly as by bounds or leaps. 3 To rise abruptly: The temperature *jumped.* 4 In checkers, to capture an opponent's piece by passing a man over it to a vacant square beyond. — *v.t.* 5 To leap over. 6 To cause to leap: to *jump* a horse over a barrier. 7 To cause to rise, as prices. 8 To pass over; leave out: to *jump* a stage in explaining a process. 9 To leave or move from abruptly: to *jump* the track. 10 To take possession of illegally: to *jump* a claim. 11 *U.S. Colloq.* To get on or off (a train, etc.) by or as by jumping. 12 *Colloq.* To assault; attack. 13 *Slang* To leave or quit abruptly or secretly: to *jump* town. 14 In checkers, to capture (an opponent's piece) by passing a man over it. 15 In bridge, to raise (the bid) in a partner's suit more than necessary, as in indicating a strong hand. 16 In hunting, to cause (game) to leave cover; start; flush. — **to jump at** 1 To accept quickly or eagerly. 2 To reach (a conclusion) hastily and illogically. — **to jump bail** *U.S. Slang* To forfeit by violating the terms of. — **to jump on** To scold; castigate. — **to jump ship** To desert a ship. — **to jump the gun** *Colloq.* 1 To begin before the starting signal is given. 2 To begin prematurely. — *n.* 1 The act of jumping; a leap; spring. 2 The length or height of a leap; also, that which is jumped over. 3 *Colloq.* A head start; advantage: He has the *jump* on me. 4 An involuntary twitch or movement, as when startled. 5 *pl.* Convulsive starts, as in delirium tremens. 6 *Mining* A fault or dislocation, as of a vein. 7 An abrupt break in a level course of masonry. 8 *Obs.* An effort; attempt. — **on the jump** *Colloq.* Hurrying from one thing to another; on the go; working hard and fast. [Origin uncertain]

jump area *Mil.* A locality, usually behind enemy lines, assigned for the landing of parachute troops: also called *landing area.*

jump ball In basketball, a ball tossed between two opposing players by the referee, as in beginning or resuming play.

jump bid In bridge, a bid higher than needed to beat or raise a previous declaration.

jump·er[1] (jum′pər) *n.* 1 One who or that which jumps. 2 The larva of a cheese fly. 3 A piece of mechanism or a tool having a jumping motion. 4 A rude sled. 5 *Electr.* A wire used to cut out part of a circuit, or to close a temporary gap in it.

jum·per[2] (jum′pər) *n.* 1 *Chiefly Brit.* A loose outer jacket, often of coarse cloth, worn over or instead of other clothes, as to protect them from getting soiled. 2 A hooded fur jacket used by Eskimos and Arctic explorers. 3 A one-piece, sleeveless dress, usually worn with a blouse or sweater by women and children: also **jumper dress.** [Prob. alter. of OF *juppe*

JUMPER DRESS
(def. 3)

a jacket, ult. <Arabic *jubbah* a short coat]

jumping bean The seed of certain tropical shrubs (genera *Sebastiania* and *Sapium*) of the spurge family, which jumps about owing to the movements of the larva of a small moth *(Carpocapsa saltitans)* inside.

jump·ing-jack (jum′ping·jak′) *n.* A toy figure of a man, whose jointed limbs are moved by strings.

jumping mouse A small, hibernating mouse of North America *(Zapus hudsonius)* having long hind legs and tail: able to leap 9 to 15 feet.

jump·ing-off place (jum′ping·ôf′, -of′) **1** The end of a journey. **2** The utmost limit of settlement or civilization; a deserted, depressing place. **3** The edge of the world; the end of life. **4** The end or limit of one's resources.

jump-off (jump′ôf′, -of′) *n.* The commencement of a planned attack by ground forces.

jump seat An extra seat that folds up, as in the rear of a limousine or taxi.

jump shot In basketball, a shot attempted at the height of a leap.

jump spark A spark produced by electricity jumping across a fixed gap.

jump suit **1** A one-piece garment consisting of pants with a blouse or shirt attached. **2** A kind of coverall worn by parachutists, mechanics, etc.

jump weld A weld of metal effected by hammering together the butt ends of two pieces heated to the welding point.

jump·y (jum′pē) *adj.* **jump·i·er, jump·i·est** **1** Subject to sudden changes; fluctuating. **2** Characterized by nervous, spasmodic movements; apprehensive. **—jump′i·ness** *n.*

jun·ca·ceous (jung·kā′shəs) *adj. Bot.* Pertaining or belonging to a family *(Juncaceae)* of widely distributed grasslike plants, the rush family, mostly growing in moist places. [<NL *Juncaceae,* the rush family <L *juncus* bulrush]

jun·co (jung′kō) *n. pl.* **·cos** Any of a genus *(Junco)* of North American finches, mainly gray with white underparts: also called *snowbird.* [<Sp., a rush]

junc·tion (jungk′shən) *n.* **1** The act of joining, or condition of being joined. **2** A place of union or meeting, as of railroads. See synonyms under UNION. [<L *junctio, -onis* <*jungere* join] **—junc′tion·al** *adj.*

junc·ture (jungk′chər) *n.* **1** An act of joining; junction. **2** A point or line of junction, as of two bodies; an articulation, joint, or seam. **3** A coincidence of two chains of events; a crisis, exigency. See synonyms under UNION. [<L *junctura* <*jungere* join]

June (jo͞on) The sixth month of the calendar year, having 30 days. [<OF *Juin* <L *(mensis) Junius* (month) of the Junii, a Roman gens]

Ju·neau (jo͞o′nō) The capital of Alaska, a port on the SE coast.

June beetle **1** A large, brightly colored scarabaeid beetle (genus *Polyphylla*) that begins to fly early in June: often called *Maybug.* Also **June bug.** For illustrations see under INSECT (injurious). **2** The fig-eater of the southern United States.

June·ber·ry (jo͞on′ber′ē) *n. pl.* **·ries** **1** A small tree *(Amelanchier canadensis)* bearing racemes of white flowers followed by purple edible berries. **2** One of the berries. Also called *shadbush, serviceberry, service tree.*

June·teenth (jo͞on′tēnth′) *n.* June 19, a holiday observed especially in Texas by Negroes in commemoration of the freeing of Texas slaves on June 19, 1865.

Jung (yo͝ong), **Carl Gustav,** 1875–1961, Swiss psychologist and psychiatrist.

Jung·frau (yo͝ong′frou) A mountain peak in the Bernese Alps, Switzerland; 13,653 feet.

jun·gle (jung′gəl) *n.* **1** A dense tropical thicket of high grass, reeds, vines, brush, or trees choked with undergrowth; hence, any similar tangled growth. **2** *U.S. Slang* A gathering place for hoboes and tramps. [<Hind. *jangal* a desert, forest <Skt. *jangala* dry, desert] **—jun′gly** *adj.*

jungle fever **1** A malarial or intermittent fever characteristic of the jungles of the East Indies. **2** Yellow fever.

jungle fowl One of a genus *(Gallus)* of East Indian gallinaceous birds: one species *(G. gallus)* resembles a black-breasted red game fowl and is held to be the original of the domestic fowl.

Ju·ni·at·a River (jo͞o′nē·at′ə) A river in central Pennsylvania, flowing about 150 miles east to the Susquehanna.

Ju·nín (ho͞o·nēn′) A city of central Peru; scene of Bolívar's defeat of the Spanish in 1824.

jun·ior (jo͞on′yər) *adj.* **1** Younger in years or lower in rank. **2** Denoting the younger of two: opposed to *senior* and distinguishing a father from a son, usually abbreviated *Jr.* **3** Belonging to youth or earlier life. **4** Later in point of existence or occurrence: *junior* securities. **5** Pertaining to the third year of a high-school or collegiate course of four years. **—*n.*** **1** The younger of two; one later or lower in service or standing; a younger person. **2** A student in the third or junior year of a high-school, college, or university course. [<L *junior,* comp. of *juvenis* young]

junior college A college giving academic courses up to and including the sophomore year.

junior high school See under SCHOOL.

jun·ior·i·ty (jo͞on·yôr′ə·tē, -yor′-) *n.* The state or rank of being a junior.

Junior League Any of the various local branches of the Association of the Junior Leagues of America, Inc., composed of young society women engaged in volunteer welfare work.

ju·ni·per (jo͞o′nə·pər) *n.* **1** Any of a genus *(Juniperus)* of evergreen pinaceous shrubs; especially the common juniper *(J. communis)* of Europe and America. It has dark-blue berries of a pungent taste, which are used in making gin. **2** The dried berries of the juniper plant. **3** A leafless shrub *(Retama)* mentioned in the Old Testament. **4** Loosely, the American larch or tamarack. [<L *juniperus*]

Jun·ius (jo͞on′yəs, jo͞o′nē·əs) A masculine personal name. [<L, name of Roman gens] **—Junius** Pseudonym of an unknown English political writer from 1769?–72.

junk[1] (jungk) *n.* **1** A sea term for discarded cable or cordage. **2** Salt meat supplied to ships. **3** Cast-off materials of little or no value. **4** A chunk; small mass. **5** *Surg.* A type of cushion used in dressing wounds. **—*v.t. Colloq.*** To scrap; to demolish or cast aside. [<OF *jonc* <L *juncus* rush]

junk[2] (jungk) *n.* A large Chinese vessel with high poop, prominent stem, full stern and lug sails. [<Sp. and Pg. *junco* <Malay *djong* a ship]

CHINESE JUNK

Jun·ker (yo͝ong′kər) *n.* **1** A younger member of a German noble family. **2** One of the reactionary aristocracy of Prussia seeking to maintain social and political supremacy. [<G <*jung* young + *herr* master] **—Jun′ker·dom** *n.* **—Jun′ker·ism** *n.*

Jun·kers (yo͝ong′kərs), **Hugo,** 1859–1935, German airplane engineer and builder.

jun·ket (jung′kit) *n.* **1** A feast, banquet, picnic, or pleasure trip. **2** A trip taken with all expenses paid, usually from public funds: also **jun′ket·ing.** **3** A delicacy made of curds or of sweetened milk and rennet. **—*v.i.*** **1** To have a feast; banquet. **2** To go on a pleasure trip, especially at public expense. **—*v.t.*** **3** To entertain by feasting; regale. [<AF *jonquette* rush basket <L *juncus* rush]

junk·ie (jung′kē) *n. Slang* One addicted to narcotic drugs, especially to heroin.

junk·man (jungk′man′) *n. pl.* **·men** (-men′) One who purchases, collects, and sells junk.

junk·yard (jungk′yärd′) *n.* A place where junk is thrown or collected.

Ju·no (jo͞o′nō) In Roman mythology, the wife of Jupiter, queen of the gods and goddess of marriage: identified with the Greek *Hera.*

Ju·no·esque (jo͞o′nō·esk′) *adj.* Resembling the stately beauty of Juno.

Ju·not (zhü·nō′), **Andoche,** 1771–1813, Duc d'Abrantès, French marshal.

jun·ta (jun′tə) *n.* **1** A Central or South American legislative council. **2** A junto. [<Sp. <L *juncta,* pp. fem. of *jungere* join]

jun·to (jun′tō) *n. pl.* **·tos** A faction; a cabal. See synonyms under CABAL. [<JUNTA]

jupe (jo͞op) *n. Scot.* A jupon.

Ju·pi·ter (jo͞o′pə·tər) **1** In Roman mythology, the god ruling over all the other gods and all men: identified with the Greek *Zeus*: also called *Jove.* **2** *Astron.* The fifth planet from the sun; its mean diameter is 87,000 miles, and it revolves around the sun in about 11 7/8 years at a mean distance of 483,000,000 miles. See PLANET.

Ju·pi·ter-Am·mon (jo͞o′pə·tər·am′ən) A Roman name for the Egyptian god AMMON. Also **Ju′pi·ter-A′men** or **Ju′pi·ter-A′mon** (ä′mən).

Ju·pi·ter Plu·vi·us (jo͞o′pə·tər plo͞o′vē·əs) *Latin* Jupiter considered as the giver of rain.

ju·pon (jo͞o′pon, jo͞o·pon′) **1** A petticoat. **2** A medieval doublet or tunic. [<OF <*juppe.* See JUMPER[2].]

ju·ra (jo͝or′ə) Plural of JUS.

Ju·ra (jo͝or′ə, *Fr.* zhü·rà′) **1** A mountain range in eastern France and western Switzerland; highest peak, 5,652 feet. **2** One of the Inner Hebrides; 146 square miles.

ju·ral (jo͝or′əl) *adj.* Relating to rights and obligations as subjects of jurisprudence. [<L *jus, juris* law]

Ju·ras·sic (jo͝o·ras′ik) *adj. Geol.* Of or pertaining to a period of the Mesozoic era succeeding the Triassic and followed by the Cretaceous: it was characterized by the dominance of dinosaurian reptiles and the earliest bird forms. **—*n.*** The Jurassic period or corresponding rock system. [<F *jurassique,* from *Jura*]

ju·rat (jo͝or′at) *n.* **1** One sworn to the faithful performance of a duty, as a magistrate or juror. **2** An officer with duties similar to those of an alderman, as in the English Cinque Ports. **3** A magistrate in the Channel Islands. **4** *Law* The clause in an official certificate testifying that the deposition has been duly sworn to at a stated time before a competent authority. [<L *juratus,* pp. of *jurare* swear]

ju·ra·to·ry (jo͝or′ə·tôr′ē, -tō′rē) *adj. Law* Pertaining to an oath.

ju·re di·vi·no (jo͞o′rē di·vī′nō) *Latin* By divine law.

ju·re hu·ma·no (jo͞o′rē hyo͞o·man′ō) *Latin* By human law.

ju·rel (ho͞o·rel′) *n. Spanish* One of various carangoid fishes (genus *Caranx*), especially *C. crysos* and *C. latus,* found along the southern Atlantic coast of the United States.

ju·rid·i·cal (jo͝o·rid′i·kəl) *adj.* **1** Relating to law and judicial proceedings. **2** Pertaining to the judicial office, or to jurisprudence. Also **ju·rid′ic.** [<L *juridicus* <*jus, juris* law + *dicere* declare] **—ju·rid′i·cal·ly** *adv.*

ju·ris·con·sult (jo͝or′is·kən·sult′, -kon′sult) *n.* One learned in the law; a jurist. [<L *jurisconsultus* <*jus, juris* law + *consultus* skilled]

ju·ris·dic·tion (jo͝or′is·dik′shən) *n.* **1** Lawful right to exercise official authority, whether executive, legislative, or judicial. **2** The territory within or the matter over which such authority may be lawfully exercised. **3** A judicature; a court, or series of courts, of justice. **4** Power of those in authority; control. [<OF *juridiction* <L *jurisdictio, -onis* <*jus, juris* law + *dicere* declare] **—ju′ris·dic′tion·al** *adj.* **—ju′ris·dic′tion·al·ly** *adv.*

ju·ris·pru·dence (jo͝or′is·pro͞od′ns) *n.* **1** The philosophy of positive law and its administration; the science of law. **2** A system of laws, as of a particular country. See synonyms under LEGISLATION. **—analytical jurisprudence** Jurisprudence formed by analysis and comparison of legal conceptions. **—comparative jurisprudence** The analytical comparison of systems of law prevailing in different countries and nations, ancient and modern. **—medical jurisprudence** The branch of jurisprudence that pertains to questions involving wounds, poisons, insanity, and presumption of survivorship. [<L *jurisprudentia* <*jus, juris* law + *prudentia* knowledge]

ju·ris·pru·dent (jŏŏr′is·prōōd′nt) *adj.* Skilled in jurisprudence. — *n.* A person learned in the law. — **ju′ris·pru·den′tial** (-prōō·den′shəl) *adj.*

ju·rist (jŏŏr′ist) *n.* One versed in the science of laws. [<F *juriste* <Med. L *jurista* <L *jus, juris* law]

ju·ris·tic (jŏŏ·ris′tik) *adj.* Of or pertaining to a jurist or the profession of law. Also **ju·ris′ti·cal.** — **ju·ris′ti·cal·ly** *adv.*

juristic act A proceeding intended to have a legal result and having the necessary qualifications.

ju·ror (jŏŏr′ər) *n.* One who serves on a jury or is sworn in for jury duty. [<AF *jurour* <L *jurator* <*jurare* swear]

Ju·ruá (zhōō·rwä′) A river flowing 1,200 miles NW across Brazil to the Amazon from the mountains of Peru.

Ju·rue·na (zhōō·rwā′nə) A river in northern Mato Grosso, Brazil, flowing 500 miles north to the Tapajós.

ju·ry[1] (jŏŏr′ē) *n. pl.* **·ries 1** A body of persons (usually twelve) legally qualified and summoned to serve on a judicial tribunal, there sworn to try well and truly a cause and give a true verdict according to the evidence. **2** A committee of award in a competition. — **coroner's jury** A body of persons selected to attend a coroner's investigation and determine the causes of deaths not obviously due to natural causes. — **grand jury** A jury called to hear complaints of the commission of offenses and to ascertain whether there is prima-facie ground for a criminal accusation. — **petit jury** The jury that sits at a trial in civil and criminal cases: also **petty jury.** [<AF *juree* an oath <Med. L *jurata,* orig. pp. of L *jurare* swear <*jus, juris* law]

ju·ry[2] (jŏŏr′ē) *adj. Naut.* Rigged up temporarily, for relief, replacement, or emergency use: a *jury* mast. [Prob. <OF *ajurie* aid <L *adjutare* help]

ju·ry·man (jŏŏr′ē·mən) *n. pl.* **·men** (-mən) A juror.

jury mast 1 *Naut.* A temporary mast. **2** *Med.* An iron rod used for supporting the weight of the head in spinal disease or injury.

jus (jus) *n. pl.* **ju·ra** (jŏŏr′ə) **1** Law in its abstract sense distinguished from statute law; right; justice. **2** Any right that is enforceable by law. [<L, law]

jus ca·no·ni·cum (jus kə·non′i·kəm) *Latin* The canon law.

jus ci·vi·le (jus si·vī′lē) *Latin* Civil law.

jus di·vi·num (jus di·vī′nəm) *Latin* Divine law.

jus gen·ti·um (jus jen′shē·əm) *Latin* The law of nations.

jus na·tu·ra·le (jus nach′ə·rā′lē) *Latin* Natural law; the law of nature. Also **jus na·tu·rae** (nə·tyōō′rē).

Jus·se·rand (zhüs·räṅ′), **Jean Adrien Antoine Jules,** 1855–1932, French diplomat and author.

jus·sive (jus′iv) *adj. Gram.* In Semitic languages, denoting a mood expressing mild command. — *n.* A jussive mood, word, or construction. [<L *jussus,* pp. of *jubere* order]

jussive subjunctive *Gram.* The subjunctive used to express mild command, as in Latin *dicat,* let him speak: usually restricted to the second and third persons.

just[1] (just) *adj.* **1** Actuated by or doing justice; righteous; upright; honest: *just* to all concerned. **2** Based on or conforming to the principles of justice; impartial; legitimate. **3** Agreeing with a required standard; true. **4** Consistent with what is proper or reasonable: *just* in one's dealings. **5** Morally pure; perfect; righteous before God. **6** *Obs.* Faithful; true; exact. — *adv.* **1** To the exact point, instant, or degree; without lack, excess, or variation; exactly; precisely. **2** But now; this moment. **3** A moment ago; very lately: He has *just* left. **4** By very little; barely; only. **5** *Colloq.* Actually; positively: That gift is *just* wonderful. [<L *justus* <*jus* law] — **just′ly** *adv.*

Synonyms (adj.): equitable, even, exact, fair, fitting, honest, honorable, impartial, incorrupt, incorruptible, lawful, reasonable, right, righteous, rightful, square, straightforward, true, trusty, upright, virtuous. See HONEST, MORAL, RIGHT, VIRTUOUS. Compare synonyms for JUSTICE. *Antonyms*: corrupt, dishonest, dishonorable, faithless, false, inequitable, one-sided, partial, perfidious, treacherous, unfair, unfaithful, unjust, unreasonable, unrighteous, venal.

just[2] (just), **just·er** (jus′tər) See JOUST, etc.

juste mi·lieu (zhüst mē·lyœ′) *French* Golden mean.

jus·tice (jus′tis) *n.* **1** Conformity in conduct or practice to the principles of right or of positive law; regard for or fulfilment of obligations; rectitude; honesty. **2** The moral principle by which actions are determined as just or unjust. **3** Adherence to truth of fact; impartiality. **4** The rendering of what is due or merited; that which is due or merited; just requital or consideration. **5** The quality of being just or reasonable; rightness; equitableness. **6** A judge, as of the U.S. Supreme Court, etc. **7** Administration of law; the forms and processes by which it is made effective. **8** Right of authority; also, formerly, jurisdiction. **9** *Theol.* One of God's attributes, by virtue of which he wills equal laws and makes just awards. **10** *Obs.* Exactness or precision; justness. — **bed of justice** The seat occupied by the French king when attending the deliberations of the parliament; also, the session itself. — **Department of Justice** An executive department of the U. S. government (established in 1870) under the direction of the Attorney General: it supervises enforcement of Federal laws, directs the activities of U. S. judicial districts, and represents the government in legal matters generally. Also **Justice Department.** [<OF <L *justitia* < *justus* JUST]

Synonyms: equity, fairness, faithfulness, honor, impartiality, integrity, justness, law, lawfulness, legality, propriety, rectitude, right, righteousness, rightfulness, truth, uprightness, virtue. In its governmental relations, *justice* is the giving to every person exactly what he deserves, not necessarily involving any consideration of what any other may deserve; *equity* (the quality of being equal) is giving every one as much advantage, privilege, or consideration as is given to any other; it is that which is equally right or just to all concerned; *equity* is a close synonym for *fairness* and *impartiality,* but it has a legal precision that those words have not. In legal proceedings, the system of *equity,* devised to supply the insufficiencies of *law,* deals with cases to which the *law* by reason of its universality cannot apply. *Integrity, rectitude, right, righteousness,* and *virtue* denote conformity of personal conduct to the moral law, and thus necessarily include *justice,* which is giving others that which is their due. *Lawfulness* is an ambiguous word, meaning in its narrower sense mere *legality,* which may be far from *justice,* but in its higher sense signifying accordance with the supreme *law* or *right,* and thus including perfect *justice. Justness* refers rather to logical relations than to practical matters; as, we speak of the *justness* of a statement or of a criticism. See JUDGE, VIRTUE. *Antonyms*: dishonesty, inequity, injustice, partiality, unfairness, unlawfulness, unreasonableness, untruth, wrong.

justice of the peace An inferior magistrate elected or appointed to prevent breaches of the peace within a county or township, to punish violators of the law, and to discharge various other local magisterial duties.

jus·tic·er (jus′tis·ər) *n. Obs.* A magistrate; justice of the peace.

jus·tice·ship (jus′tis·ship) *n.* A justice's office or dignity.

jus·ti·ci·a·ble (jus·tish′ə·bəl) *adj.* Proper to be examined in a court of justice. — *n.* A person subject to the jurisdiction of another. [<AF <*justicier* try in court]

jus·ti·ci·ar (jus·tish′ē·ər) *n.* A justiciary (def. 2). Also **jus·ti′ci·er.**

jus·ti·ci·ar·y (jus·tish′ē·er′ē) *adj.* Pertaining to law or the administration of justice. — *n. pl.* **·ar·ies 1** A high judicial officer; a judge. **2** In medieval England, a high officer, or king's deputy, who, during the time of the Norman kings, exercised both administrative and judicial powers. [<Med. L *justiciarius* a judge <*justicia* JUSTICE]

jus·ti·fi·a·ble (jus′tə·fī′ə·bəl) *adj.* Capable of being justified. — **jus′ti·fi′a·bil′i·ty, jus′ti·fi·a·ble·ness** *n.* — **jus′ti·fi′a·bly** *adv.*

jus·ti·fi·ca·tion (jus′tə·fə·kā′shən) *n.* **1** The state of being justified. **2** The ground of justifying, or that which justifies. **3** *Theol.* The forensic, juridical, or gracious act of God by which the sinner is declared righteous, or justly free from obligation to penalty, and fully restored to divine favor. **4** *Printing* The even spacing of type within a fixed measure. **5** *Law* A plea in bar to a plaintiff's action alleging and showing the rightfulness or lawfulness of the act complained of and sued for: in slander, to plead the truth of the words spoken in *justification* of the speaking. See synonyms under APOLOGY, DEFENSE. [<LL *justificatio, -onis* <*justificare* JUSTIFY]

jus·ti·fi·ca·tive (jus′tə·fə·kā′tiv) *adj.* Tending to justify, or capable of justifying; vindicatory. Also, **jus·tif·i·ca·tor·y** (jus·tif′ə·kə·tôr′ē, -tō′rē).

jus·ti·fi·er (jus′tə·fī′ər) *n.* One who justifies. Also **jus′ti·fi·ca′tor.**

jus·ti·fy (jus′tə·fī) *v.* **·fied, ·fy·ing** *v.t.* **1** To show to be just, right, or proper. **2** To declare or prove guiltless or blameless; exonerate; acquit. **3** *Law* To show sufficient reason for (something done). **4** *Printing* To adjust (lines) to the proper length by spacing. — *v.i.* **5** *Law* **a** To show sufficient reason for something done. **b** To qualify as a bondsman. **6** *Printing* To be properly spaced; fit. [<OF *justifier* <LL *justificare* pardon <*justus* just + *facere* make]

Synonyms: absolve, acquit, approve, authorize, clear, defend, endorse, exculpate, excuse, exonerate, maintain, sustain, uphold, vindicate, warrant. That may sometimes be *excused* which cannot be *justified*; that which can be *justified* does not need to be *excused.* See RATIFY. *Antonyms*: arraign, blame, censure, chide, condemn, convict, criminate, denounce, reprehend, reprobate, reprove.

Jus·tin (jus′tin; *Fr.* zhüs·taṅ′; *Ger.* yōōs′tēn) A masculine personal name. Also *Lat.* **Jus·ti·nus** (jus·tī′nəs), *Sp.* **Jus·ti·no** (hōōs·tē′nō). [<L, just]

— **Justin Martyr,** 100?–165?, a Greek father of the church; probably beheaded in Rome under Marcus Aurelius.

Jus·ti·na (jus·tī′nə, *Sp.* hōōs·tē′nä) A feminine personal name. Also *Fr., Ger.* **Jus·tine** (*Fr.* zhüs·tēn′, *Ger.* yōōs·tē′nä). [<L, fem. of *Justinus* JUSTIN]

Jus·tin·i·an (jus·tin′ē·ən) *adj.* Of or pertaining to Justinian. Also **Jus·tin′i·a′ni·an** (-ā′nē·ən).

Jus·tin·i·an (jus·tin′ē·ən), 483–565, Roman emperor of the East 527–565; codified the Roman laws.

Justinian Code The body of Roman law as codified by Justinian.

jus·ti·ti·a om·ni·bus (jus·tish′e·ə om′nə·bəs) *Latin* Justice for all: motto of the District of Columbia.

jus·tle (jus′əl) See JOSTLE.

just·ness (just′nis) *n.* The quality of being just; justice. See synonyms under JUSTICE.

just now Scarcely a moment ago.

Jus·tus (jus′təs, *Ger.* yōōs′tōōs) A masculine personal name. Also *Fr.* **Juste** (zhüst), *Ger.* **Just** (yōōst), *Sp.* **Jus·to** (hōōs′tō). [<L, just]

jut (jut) *v.i.* **jut·ted, jut·ting** To extend beyond the main portion; project: often with *out.* — *n.* Anything that juts; a projection. [Var. of JET[2]]

jute (jōōt) *n.* **1** A tall annual Asian herb (*Corchorus capsularis* or *C. olitorius*) of the linden family. **2** The soft, lustrous fiber obtained from the inner bark of this plant, used for bags, cordage, etc. [<Bengali *jhuṭo* <Skt. *jūṭa* a braid of hair]

Jute (jōōt) *n.* A member of a Germanic tribe from Jutland that invaded Britain in the fifth century. [<LL *Jutae* the Jutes <OE *Iōtas*] — **Jut′ish** *adj.*

Jut·land (jut′lənd) A peninsula of northern Europe comprising continental Denmark and Germany north of the Eider; 11,411 square miles; Battle of Jutland, only major engagement of British and German fleets, was fought 70 miles to the west in 1916: also *Cimbrian Chersonese*: Danish *Jylland.*

jut·ty (jut′ē) See JETTY.

ju·ve·nal (jōō′və·nəl) *n.* **1** *Obs.* A youth;

young man. 2 *Ornithol.* The plumage acquired by a bird subsequent to leaving the nest. [<L *juvenalis* young]

Ju·ve·nal (jo͞o′və·nəl), **60?–140?,** Roman poet: full name, Decimus Junius Juvenalis.

ju·ve·nes·cent (to͞o′və·nəs′nt), *adj.* Becoming young; also, rejuvenating. [<L *juvenescens, -entis,* ppr. of *juvenescere* grow younger] **—ju′ve·nes′cence** *n.*

ju·ve·nile (jo͞o′vənil, -nīl) *adj.* 1 Characteristic of youth; young. 2 Adapted to youth. *—n.* 1 A young person; a youth. 2 An actor who interprets youthful roles. 3 A book for children or youth. See synonyms under YOUTHFUL. [<L *juvenilis* <*juvenis* young]

juvenile court See under COURT.

ju·ve·nil·i·a (jo͞o′və·,-nil′yə) *n. pl.* Youthful writings. [<L, orig. neut. of *juvenalis* young]

ju·ve·nil·i·ty (jo͞o′və·nil′ə·tē) *n. pl.* **ties** 1 A youthful act or character; juvenile character or manner. 2 Youthfulness; youth; the state of being juvenile. Also **ju′ve·nile·ness.**

juxta- *prefix* Near; next to: *juxtamarine,* bordering on the sea. [<L *juxta* near]

jux·ta·pose (juks′tə·pōz) *v.t* **posed, ·posing** To place close together; put side by side. [<F *juxtaposer* <L *juxta* near + *poser.* See POSE[1].]

jux·ta·po·si·tion (juks′tə·pə·zish′ən) *n* A placing close together or side by side; contiguity.

Jyl·land (yūl′lān) The Danish name for JUTLAND.

K

k, K (kā) *n. pl.* **k's, K's** or **ks, Ks** or **kays** (kāz) 1 The eleventh letter of the English alphabet: from Phoenician *kaph,* Greek *kappa,* Roman *K.* 2 The sound of the letter *k,* a voiceless plosive which varies from velar to alveolar position according to the place of articulation of the accompanying vowel, as in *coop* and *keep.* It is normally not pronounced when initial before *n,* as in *knee, knight, know,* etc. See ALPHABET. *—symbol Chem.* Potassium (K for *kalium*).

K2 (kā′to͞o′) The world's second highest mountain peak, in the Karakoram range, northern Kashmir, India; 28,250 feet: also *Dapsang, Godwin Austen.*

ka (kä) *n.* In Egyptian religion, the genius or spiritual self: believed to dwell in man and images and to survive in the tomb. [<Egyptian]

Ka·a·ba (kä′ə·bə, kä′bə) *n.* The Moslem shrine at Mecca enclosing a sacred black stone, supposedly given to Abraham by the angel Gabriel, toward which worshipers face when praying: also spelled *Caaba.*

kaas (käs) See KAS.

kab (kab) See CAB.[2]

kab·a·la (kab′ə·lə, kə·bä′lə), **kab·ba·la,** etc. See CABALA, etc.

ka·bar (kä′bär) See CABER.

ka·ba·ra·go·ya (kä·bä′rä·gō′yä) See MONITOR (def. 5).

Ka·bar·din·i·an Autonomous Soviet Socialist Republic (kä′bər·din′ē·ən) An autonomous republic in southern European Russian S.F.S.R.; 4,550 square miles; capital, Nalchik. *Russian* **Kab·ar·din·ska·ya Av·to·no·mna·ya S.S.R.** (kab′är·dyēn′skä·ya äf·tô′no·mnä′yä).

ka·bob (kə·bob′) *n.* 1 A dish of small pieces of meat roasted or broiled on skewers and served with various condiments. 2 In India, any roast meat. Also **ka·bab′:** sometimes spelled *cabob.* [<Arabic *kabāb*]

ka·bu·ki (kä·bo͝o·kē) *n.* A kind of Japanese play on popular or comic themes, employing elaborate costume, stylized gesture, music, and dancing. Compare NO[2]. [<Japanese]

Ka·bul (kÅU/′bəl) 1 A river in eastern Afghanistan and western Pakistan, flowing 320 miles east to the Indus 2 A city on the Kabul river, capital of Afghanistan.

Ka·byle (kə·bīl′) *n.* 1 One of the Berbers living in Algeria or Tunisia. 2 The Berber dialect spoken by these people.

Ka·chin State (kə·chin′) A constituent unit of the Union of Burma in NW Upper Burma: 33,871 square miles; capital, Myitkyina.

kad·dish (kä′dish) *n. Often cap.* In Judaism, a daily prayer recited in the synagogue service, in one form used by mourners. [<Aramaic *qaddish* holy]

ka·di (kä′dē) See CADI.

Ka·di·ak (kä′dē·ak, *Russian* kə·dyäk′) See KODIAK ISLAND.

Kadiak bear A very large brown bear (*Ursus middendorffi*) found on Kodiak and adjacent islands off the Alaskan coast: also *Kodiak bear.*

kaf·fee·klatsch (kôf′ē·klach′, -kläch′, kof′-) *n.* A social gathering for conversation while coffee and refreshments are served. [<G, lit., coffee + gossip]

Kae·song (kā′sông′) A city in central Korea, NW of Seoul; an ancient capital of Korea. *Japanese* **Kai·jo** (kī·jō).

kaf·fir (kaf′ər) *n.* A variety of sorghum grown in dry regions as a grain and forage plant; East Indian millet. Also **kaf′ir:** erroneously **kaffir corn.** [after the *Kaffirs*]

Kaf·fir (kaf′ər) *n.* 1 A member of a group of southern African Bantu-speaking peoples. 2 An offensive and vulgar term of contempt for a black African, especially of the Republic of South Africa. A non-Moslem: term used contemptuously by Arab Moslems. Also **Kaf′ir:** sometimes spelled *Caffer, Caffre.* [<Arabic *kāfir* unbeliever]

kaf·fi·yeh (kə·fē′ye) *n. Arabic* A large, square kerchief worn by Arabs over the head and shoulders and held in place by an agal. Also **kef·fi′yeh.** [<Arabic *kafiyah, ?* <LL *cuphia, cofia.* See COIF.]

Kaf·fra·ri·a (Kə·frā′rē·ə) A region in Eastern Cape Province, Republic of South Africa.

Ka·fir (kä′fər, kaf′ər) *n.* One of the people of Kafiristan. Also **Kaf′fir.**

Ka·fi·ri (kä·fir′ē) *n.* The Indic language spoken by the Kafirs of Kafiristan.

Ka·fi·ri·stan (kä′fi·ri·stän′) A former name for NURISTAN.

Kaf·ka (käf′kä), **Franz,** 1883–1924, Austrian novelist and writer of short stories.

Kaf·ka·esque (käf′kə·esk′) *adj.* Characteristic of the novels of Franz Kafka; especially, bizarre or absurd, and often marked by the ineffectuality of the individual.

kaf·tan (kaf′tən, käf·tän′) See CAFTAN.

Ka·fu·e (kä·fo͞o′ā) A river in central Zambia, flowing 600 miles NE through **Kafue Gorge** to the Zambesi.

Ka·ga·wa (kä·gȧ·wä), **Toyohiko,** 1888–1960, Japanese Christian social reformer.

Ka·ge·ra (kä·gā′rä) A river in east central Africa, flowing 250 miles NE to Lake Victoria: also *Alexandra Nile.*

ka·go (kä′gō) *n.* A form of palanquin. [<Japanese *kango]*

Ka·go·shi·ma (kä·gō·shē·mÅU/) A port on southern Kyushu island, Japan. Also **Ka·go·si·ma.**

Ka·hoo·la·we (kä′ho͞o·lÅU/′we) An island in the south central Hawaiian Islands; 45 square miles. Also **Ka′hu·la′we.**

Kai Islands (kī) See KEI ISLANDS.

kai·ak (kī′ak) See KAYAK.

Ka·e·teur Falls (kī′ə·tr′) A waterfall in central British Guiana in the Potaro River; 741 feet.

Kai·feng (kī′fung′) A city in east central China, capital of Honan province.

kail (kāl), **kail·yard** (kāl′yärd′) See KALE, KALEYARD.

kain (kān) *n.* Rental or tax paid in land produce, livestock, eggs, etc.: also spelled *cain, kane.* [<OIrish *cāin* law]

kai·nite (kī′nīt, kaā′ə·nīt) *n.* A colorless to dark flesh-red hydrous sulfate of potassium and magnesium and magnesium chloride, crystallizing in the monoclinic system: used as a fertilizer. [<G *kainit* <Gk. *kainos* recent]

Kair·ouan (kīr·wän′, *Fr.* ker·wän′) A city in NE Tunisia; holy city of the Moslems: also *Qairwan.* Also **Kair·wan′.**

kai·ser (kī′zər) *n.* Emperor: the German title applied to the emperors of the Holy Roman Empire, as successors to those of the old Roman Empire. [<G <L *Caesar* Caesar]

Kaiser Title of the German emperors, 1871–1918.

Kaiser (kī′zər), **Henry J.,** 1882–1967, U.S. industrialist.

Kai·sers·lau·tern (kī′zərs·lou′tərn) A city in Rhineland-Palatinate. SW West Germany.

Kai·ser-Wil·helm's Land (kī′zər·vil′helms) A former German territory in NE New Guinea, part of the Territory of New Guinea.

kaj·e·put (kaj′ə·pət) See CAJUPUT.

ka·ka (kä′kə) *n.* A New Zealand parrot (genus *Nestor*), typically with olive-green body, gray crown, ad crimson-red on the rump and abdomen. [<Maori]

ka·ka·po (kä′kə·pō′) *n.* A nocturnal, flightless, greenish-brown New Zealand parrot (*Strigops habroptilus*). [<Maori *kaka* a parrot + *po* night]

ka·ke·mo·no (kä′ke·mō′nAM/) *n.* A picture on paper or silk attached to a roller and used as a wall hanging. [<Japanese <*kake* hang + *mono* thing]

ka·ki (kä′kē) *n.* An Asian tree (*Diospyros kaki*) of the ebony family, with yellowish-white flowers and an edible orange or yellow fruit; cultivated in southern and western Untied States; also called *Japanese persimmoh.* [<Japanese, persimmon]

ka·la-a·zar (kä′lä·zī′, -az′ər) *n. Pathol.* An infectious fever of India, China, and Egypt characterized by enlarged spleen, anemia, and emaciation: caused by a protozoan parasite (*Leishmania donovani*). [<Hind. *kālā-āzār* black disease]

Ka·la·ha·ri Desert (kä′lä·hä′rē) An arid plateau region in Namibia, Botswana, and the Republic of South Africa.

Ka·lakh (kä′läkh) An ancient city of Assyria, south of Nineveh on the site of modern, *Nimrud:* Biblical *Calah.*

Ka·la·ma·ta (kä′lä·mä′tä) A port of southern Greece; capital of Messenia. Also **Ka·la·mai** (kä·lä′me).

Kal·a·ma·zoo (kal′ə·mə·zo͞o′) A city in SW Michigan.

ka·lam·ka·ri (kä′läm·kä′rē) *n.* An East Indian cotton fabric having designs that are drawn and colored by hand [<Hind.]

Ka·lat (kə·lät′) A princely state of eastern Baluchistan. West Pakistan; 30,799 square miles; capital, Kalat: also *Khelat.*

Kalb (kalb, *Ger.* kälp), **Johann,** 1721–80, German general in the American Revolution; known as *Baron de Kalb.*

kale (kāl) *n.* 1 A variety of headless cabbage yielding curled leaves. 2 *Scot.* Cabbage of any kind; also, broth of kale; broth. 3 *U.S. Slang* Money. Also spelled *kail.* [Var. of COLE]

ka·lei·do·scope (kə·lī′də·skōp) *n.* An instrument which, by means of mirrors, presents bits of colored glass, viewed through it, in ever-changing symmetrical patterns, as the tube is rotated. [<Gk. *kalos* beautiful + *eidos* form + -SCOPE]

ka·lei·do·scop·ic (kə·lī′də·skop′ik) *adj.* Pertaining to a kaleidoscope; picturesquely diversified. Also **ka·lei′do·scop′i·cal. —ka·lei′do·scop′·i·cal·ly** *adv.*

kal·ends (kal′əndz) See CALENDS.

kale runt *Scot.* A cabbage stem. Also **kale stock.**

Ka·le·va·la (kä′lə·vä′lä) The national epic of Finland: a collection of ancient poems embodying the myths and hero legends of Finland: compiled by Elias Lönnrott, 1849. [<Finnish, land of heroes]

kale•wife (kal′wīf′) *n. pl.* **•wives** (-wīvz′) *Scot.* A woman who sells vegetables.

kale•yard (kal′yärd′) *n.* **1** *Scot.* A cabbage garden. **2** A kitchen garden. Also spelled *kailyard.*

kaleyard school A late 19th century school of fiction writers, including J. M. Barrie and Ian Maclaren, who described Scottish life with much use of dialect. Also *kailyard school.*

Kal•gan (käl′gän′) The capital of Chahar province, China.

kal•i (kal′ē, kā′lē) *n.* The common saltwort. [<Arabic *qalī.* See ALKALI.]

Ka•li (kä′lē) In Hindu mythology, the goddess of destruction and wife of Siva: worshiped with bloody sacrifices.

kal•ian (käl•yän′) *n.* The hookah of Persia. [< Persian *kaliān*]

Ka•li•da•sa (kä′lē•dä′sä) Indian poet and dramatist, who lived about the fifth century.

ka•lif (kā′lif, kal′if) See CALIPH.

Ka•li•nin (kä•lē′nin) A city in western Russian S.F.S.R. on the Volga: formerly *Tver.*

Ka•li•nin (kä•lē′nin), **Mikhail Ivanovich,** 1875–1946, president of the U.S.S.R. 1923–46.

Ka•li•nin•grad (kä•lē′nin•grät′) A port on the Pregel River in Russian S.F.S.R.; formerly, as German *Königsberg,* the capital of East Prussia.

Ka•lisz (kä′lēsh) A city in west central Poland: German **Ka•lisch** (kä′lish).

ka•li•um (kā′lē•əm) *n.* Potassium: from this name, used by pharmacists and German chemists, its symbol K is derived. [<KALI]

Kal•li•kak (kal′ə•kak) A pseudonym used for the members of an actual New Jersey family whose history, as investigated by H. H. Goddard, in 1912, showed abnormal incidence of crime, disease, and pauperism. Compare JUKES. [<Gk. *kalli-* beautiful + *kakos* evil]

kal•li•type (kal′ə•tīp) *n.* A photoprinting process by which ferric salts are reduced to ferrous salts, which in turn act upon soluble silver salts. [<Gk. *kalli-* beautiful + TYPE]

Kal•mar (käl′mär) A port in SE Sweden on **Kalmar Sound,** an arm of the Baltic between Sweden and Öland Island.

kal•mi•a (kal′mē•ə) Any plant of a genus *(Kalmia)* of North American shrubs of the heath family, with evergreen leaves and umbellate clusters of rose, purple, or white flowers. [<NL, after Peter *Kalm,* 1716–79, Swedish botanist]

Kal•muck (kal′muk) *n.* **1** A member of one of the western Buddhistic Mongol tribes extending from western China to the valley of the Volga river. **2** The Mongolian language of these tribes. Also **Kal′muk.**

Kal•myk Autonomous Soviet Socialist Republic (kal′mik) A former administrative division of SE European Russian S.F.S.R. Also **Kal•muck Autonomous S.S.R.** (kal′muk).

ka•long (kä′lông) *n.* A fruit-eating bat (family *Pteropodidae*) of Africa, Asia, and Australia. [<Malay *kālong*]

kal•pac (kal′pak) See CALPAC.

kal•so•mine (kal′sə•mīn) See CALCIMINE.

Ka•lu•ga (kä•lo͞o′gä) A city in western Russian S.F.S.R. on the Oka river.

ka•lyp•tra (kə•lip′trə) *n.* A thin veil worn by women of ancient Greece over the face and as a headdress. [<Gk. <*kalyptein* hide]

Ka•ma (kä′mä) A river in eastern European Russian S.F.S.R., flowing 1,262 miles from the Urals to the Volga.

kam•a•cite (kam′ə•sīt) *n.* A variety of meteoric iron containing nickel and showing, when polished, a fine network of bands. [<G *kamacit* <Gk. *kamax, -akos* a vine pole]

Ka•ma•ku•ra (kä•mä•ko͝o•rä) A city on Honshu island, Japan; site of a 42-foot, 13th century bronze image of Buddha.

ka•ma•la (kə•mā′lə, kam′ə-) *n.* **1** An Indian tree *(Mallotus philippinensis)* of the spurge family. **2** The fine orange-red powder from its capsular fruit, used as a purgative and in dyeing. [<Skt.]

Kam•chat•ka (kam•chat′kə, *Russian* käm•chät′•kä) A peninsula at the eastern end of U.S.S.R. extending 750 miles southward between the Bering and Okhotsk Seas; 104,200 square miles.

kame[1] (kām) *n. Scot.* Comb.

kame[2] (kām) *n. Geol.* A conical hill or short ridge of stratified sand and gravel formed by glacier deposition. [See COOMB]

Ka•me•ha•me•ha I (kä•mā′hä•mā′hä), 1753?–1819, first king of Hawaii; known as *Kamehameha the Great.*

Ka•me•rad (kä′mə•rät′) *n. pl.* **•rad•en** (-rä′dən) *German* Comrade: used by German soldiers to indicate readiness to surrender.

Kam•er•lingh On•nes (kä′mər•ling ôn′əs), **Heike,** 1853–1926, Dutch physicist.

Ka•me•run (kä′mə•ro͞on) The German name for CAMEROONS.

kame•ster (kām′stər) *n. Scot.* A woolcomber.

Ka•met (kä′met) A mountain on the Tibetan border of Uttar Pradesh State, India; 25,447 feet.

ka•mi (kä•mē) *n. Japanese* **1** The gods collectively of the first and second mythological dynasties of Japan; also, their descendants, the mikados. **2** The deified spirits of the heroes and famous men of Japan.

ka•mi•ka•ze (kä′mi•kä′zē) *n.* In World War II, a Japanese pilot pledged to die in crashing his bomb-laden plane against the target; also, the airplane itself on such a mission. [<Japanese, divine wind<*kami* a god + *kaze* the wind]

Kam•pa•la (käm•pä′lä) The capital of Uganda, in the southern part.

kam•pong (käm•pong′, käm′pong) *n.* An enclosed space; a compound. [<Malay]

kam•sin (kam′sin) See KHAMSIN.

Kan (gän) The chief river of Kiangsi province, China, flowing 540 miles north to Poyang Lake.

ka•na (kä′nə) *n.* Japanese syllabic writing: a system of 46 phonetic symbols normally used for foreign words, and used collaterally with Chinese ideographs to indicate Japanese grammatical inflections. [<Japanese]

Ka•nak•a (kə•nak′ə, kan′ə•kə) *n.* **1** A native of Hawaii. **2** Any South Sea Islander. [< Polynesian, man]

Ka•na•ra (kä′nə•rə, kə•nä′rə) **1** A region of the southern Deccan Plateau, India; 60,000 square miles: *Canarese* **Kar′na•tak. 2** A district of southern Bombay State, India, on the western edge of the Deccan Plateau; 3,961 square miles: also **North Kanara:** formerly *Canara.*

Ka•na•rese (kä′nə•rēz′, -rēs′) *adj.* Of or pertaining to Kanara. —*n.* **1** A native or naturalized inhabitant of Kanara. **2** The Dravidian language of Kanara. Also spelled *Canarese.*

Ka•na•wha River (kə•nô′wə) A river in SW West Virginia, flowing 97 miles NW to the Ohio.

Ka•na•za•wa (kä•nä•zä•wä) A port of western Honshu island, Japan.

Kan•chen•jun•ga (kun′chən•jo͝ong′gə) The third highest mountain in the world, in the eastern Nepal Himalayas; 28,146 feet: formerly *Kinchi*

Kan•da•har (kän′dä•här′) A city in southern Afghanistan: also *Qandahar.*

Kan•din•ski (kan•din′skē, *Russian* kän•dyēn′•ski) **Vasili,** 1866–1946, Russian painter.

Kan•dy (kan′dē, kän′dē) A city in central Sri Lanka: formerly *Candy.*

kane (kān) See KAIN.

Kane (kān), **Elisha Kent,** 1820–57, U.S. arctic explorer.

Ka•nem (kä′nem) An administrative region of western Chad territory, French Equatorial Africa; formerly a state; 56,000 square miles.

Kan•gar (käng•gär′) Capital of Perlis state, Federation of Malaya.

kan•ga•roo (kang′gə•ro͞o′) *n.* Any of a large family *(Macropodidae)* of herbivorous marsupials of the Australian region, having weak forelimbs and strong hind limbs, with stout tail, moving by leaping bounds, and ranging in size from nine feet long to about the size of a rat. [Australian]

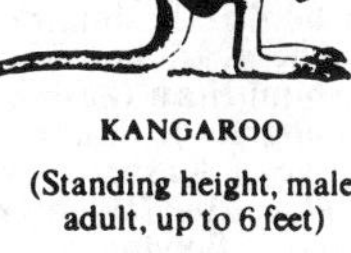

KANGAROO
(Standing height, male adult, up to 6 feet)

kangaroo court 1 An unofficial court in which the law is disregarded or wilfully misinterpreted. **2** A mock court or trial. **3** A frontier or backwoods court.

kangaroo rat 1 One of various pouched rodents *(Dipodomys agilis)* of the SW United States and Mexico, with elongated hind limbs and tail. **2** Any of several Australian rodents (genus *Notomys*) noted for their leaping habits.

K′ang-hsi (käng′shē′), 1654–1722, also called Sheng-tsu. First Manchu emperor of China, 1662–1722; annexed Tibet and made the first Chinese treaty with a European power (Russia, 1689).

Kang Te (käng′ tā′) Emperor of Manchukuo, 1934–45. See PU-YI.

Kang•ting (käng′ting′) A city in SW China.

Kan•ka•kee (kang′kə•kē′) A river in Indiana and Illinois, flowing 135 miles to the Illinois River.

Ka•no (kä′nō) A city in northern Nigeria.

ka•noon (kə•no͞on′) A kind of dulcimer having fifty or sixty strings and played with the fingers. Also **ka•nun′.** [<Persian *qānūn*]

Kan•pur (kän′po͝or) A city on the Ganges in Uttar Pradesh, India: formerly *Cawnpore.*

Kan•sas (kan′zəs) A north central State of the United States; 82,276 square miles; capital, Topeka; entered the Union Jan. 29, 1861: nickname, *Sunflower State.* Abbr. KS —**Kan′•san** (-zən) *adj. & n.*

Kansas City 1 A city on the Missouri River in NE Kansas. **2** A city on the Missouri River in western Missouri.

Kansas River A river in NE Kansas, flowing 200 miles east to the Missouri: also *Kaw.*

Kan•su (kän′so͞o′, *Chinese* gän′so͞o′) A province in NW China; 150,000 square miles; capital, Lanchow.

Kant (kant, *Ger.* känt), **Immanuel,** 1724–1804, German philosopher; author of *Critique of Pure Reason* (1781).

kan•tar (kän•tär′) See CANTAR.

Kant•i•an (kan′tē•ən) *adj.* Of or pertaining to Kant or his philosophy. —*n.* A follower of Kantianism.

Kant•i•an•ism (kan′tē•ən•iz′əm) *n.* The critical philosophy of Immanuel Kant that sets forth the doctrine of a priori knowledge: man experiences the material world through sense perception, but its form is determined by the mind alone. Also **Kant′ism.**

Kao•hsiung (gou′shyo͝ong′) A port in SW Taiwan.

Kao•lan (gou′län′) A former name for LANCHOW.

ka•o•li•ang (kä′ō•lē•ang′) *n. Chinese* Any of a variety of sorghums of eastern Asia, some introduced into the United States.

ka•o•lin (kā′ə•lin) *n.* A claylike, friable, hydrous aluminum silicate used in making porcelain. Also **ka′o•line.** [from Chinese *Kao Ling* High Ridge, a mountain range where first mined]

ka•o•lin•ite (kā′ə•lin•īt′) *n.* A highly purified form of kaolin.

kap•a (kap′ə) *n. pl.* **kap•a-kap•a** Tapa cloth. [<Hawaiian]

Ka•pell•meis•ter (kä•pel′mīs′tər) *n.* The musical director of a choir, orchestra, etc.: also called *chapelmaster.* [<G, bandmaster]

Kap•e•naar (kap′ə•nar′) *Afrikaans* A white person born in the Cape of Good Hope province.

kaph (käf) *n.* The eleventh Hebrew letter: also spelled *caph.* See ALPHABET.

Ka•pi•da•ği Peninsula (kä′pi•dä•gē′) An extension of NW Turkey into the Sea of Marmara: ancient *Cyzicus.* Also **Ka•pu Dagh** (kä′po͞o däg).

ka•pok (kā′pok) *n.* A cottony or silky fiber covering the seeds of a tropical tree *(Ceiba pentandra)* of the silk-cotton family: used for mattresses, life-savers, insulation material, etc. [<Malay *kāpoq*]

kap•pa (kap′ə) *n. Greek* The tenth letter in the Greek alphabet (Κ, κ), equivalent to English *k.* See under ALPHABET.

kappa curve *Math.* A plane, kappa-shaped curve, symmetrical with respect to the coordinate axes and the origin, and having two cusps at the origin.

Ka•pu•as (kä′po͞o•äs) A river in central Borneo, flowing 710 miles SW to the South China Sea. Also **Ka′poe•as.**

ka•put (kä•po͝ot′) *adj. Slang* Ruined; done for; finished. [<G]

Ka•ra (kä′rə) A river in northern European

Russian S.F.S.R., flowing 130 miles north from the northern Urals.

kar·a·bi·ner (kar′ə·bē′nər) *n.* An article of mountaineering equipment: a steel loop or ring snapped into a piton, through which a rope may be passed, to hold climbers. [Short for G *karabinerhaken* carbine snap]

a b

KARABINER
a. Closed.
b. Open.

Ka·ra·chi (kə·rä′chē) A port on the Arabian Sea NW of the Indus delta.

Ka·ra·fu·to (kä·rä·fōō·tō) The Japanese name for the southern part of SAKHALIN.

Ka·ra·gan·da (kä′rä·gän·dä′) A city in central Kazakh S.S.R.

Kar·a·george (kar′ə·jôrj′), 1776–1817, Serbian leader and patriot: real name *George Petrovich.*

Ka·ra-Kal.pak Autonomous S.S.R. The former name of **Karakalpakstan,** the territory in NW Uzbekistan along the Amu Darya; 61,000 square miles; capital Nukus.

Kar·a·ko·ram (kar′ə·kôr′əm, -kō′rəm) A mountain range in NE Kashmir; highest peak, 28,250 feet: traversed by **Karakoram Pass** at 18,550 feet on the China–Kashmir trade route: also *Mustagh.* Also **Kar′a·ko′rum.**

kar·a·kul (kar′ə·kəl) *n.* **1** A breed of sheep of Bokhara. **2** Astrakhan of the best quality, obtained from the black, lustrous, tightly curled coat of young lambs of the karakul sheep. Also spelled *caracul.* [from *Kara Kul,* lake in central Siberia]

Ka·ra Kum (kä′rä kōōm′) A desert in central Turkmen S.S.R., extending from the Caspian Sea to Amu Darya.

Ka·ra Sea (kä′rə) An arm of the Arctic Ocean between Novaya Zemlya and northern U.S.S.R.

kar·at (kar′ət) *n.* The twenty-fourth part by weight of gold in an article; thus, 18-karat gold means an article 18/24 or 3/4 gold by weight: distinguished from *carat.* [Var. of CARAT]

ka·ra·te (kä·rä′tā, -tē) *n.* An Oriental style of hand-to-hand fighting using sudden forceful blows, as with the side of the hand or with the fingertips. [<Japanese]

Kar·ba·la (kär′bə·lə) A city and Moslem pilgrimage center in central Iraq. Also **Kar′be·la.**

Ka·re·li·a (kə·rē′lē·ə, -rēl′yə) **1** A former autonomous republic of NW Russian S.F.S.R.; included since 1940 in Karelo-Finnish S.S.R. **2** Karelo-Finnish S.S.R.

Ka·re·li·an Isthmus (kə·rē′lē·ən, -rēl′yən) A glacial land bridge between the Gulf of Finland and Lake Ladoga in Russia.

Ka·re·lo-Fin·nish S.S.R. A former constituent republic of NW U.S.S.R., now a republic of Russia; 66,000 square miles; capital, Petrozavodsk; comprising territory ceded by Finland in March 1940, and joined with Karelia: also Karelia.

Ka·ren State A constituent unit of the Union of Myanmar; 11,700 square miles; capital, Pa-an.

Ka·ri·kal (kä′rē·käl′) A free city and former French settlement in southern Madras, India; 52 square miles. Formerly **Ca′ri·cal′.**

Kar·kheh (kär′ke) A river in SW Iran, flowing 350 miles SE to the Tigris: ancient *Choaspes*: also *Kerkheh.*

Karl (kärl) The German and alternate Scandinavian form of CHARLES.

Kar·lov·ei A village on the Danube in Croatia: by a treaty signed here in 1699, Turkey ceded most of her European territories to Poland, Venice, and Austria.

Kar·lo·vy Va·ry (kär′lô·vē vä′rē) A town in NW Bohemia, Czech republic. *German* **Karlsbad:** also *Carlsbad.*

Karls·kro·na (kärls·krōō′nä) A city in southern Sweden, site of the chief Swedish naval base.

Karls·ruh·e A city in SW Germany, in the state of Baden-Wurttemberg: also Carlsruhe.

kar·ma (kär′mə, kûr′-) *n.* The effect of any act, religious or otherwise; the law of cause and effect regulating one's future life; inevitable retribution: a Brahmanic idea developed by the Buddhists. [<Sanskrit, action]

karn (kärn) *n. Brit.* A cairn.

Kar·nak (kär′nak) A village on the Nile in Upper Egypt, on the northern part of the site of ancient Thebes.

Kärn·ten (kern′tən) The German name for CARINTHIA.

Ká·rol·yi (kä′rō·yē), **Count Mihály,** 1875–1955, Hungarian politician.

ka·ross (kə·ros′) *n. Afrikaans* **1** A native garment made of skins sewed together in the form of a square. **2** A rug made of skins.

Kar·pa·thos (kär′pə·thos) The third largest island of the Dodecanese group in the Aegean; 111 square miles: Italian *Scarpanto.*

Kar·rer (kär′ər), **Paul,** 1889–1971, Swiss chemist.

kar·roo (kə·rōō′, ka-) *n. pl.* **·roos** A dry plateau or tableland of South Africa. Also **ka·roo′.** See GREAT KARROO, SOUTHERN KARROO, NORTHERN KARROO. [<Hottentot]

Kar·roo (kə·rōō′, ka-) *adj. Geol.* Belonging to or designating a period or rock system of the Paleozoic and Mesozoic eras, developed in South Africa. Also **Ka·roo′.**

Kars (kärs) A city in NE Turkey in Asia.

Karst (kärst) The German name for CARSO.

kart (kärt) *n.* A small, low, motorized vehicle for one person, used especially in racing. [Var. of CART] — **kart′ing** *n.*

Ka·run (kä·rōōn′) A river in SW Iran, flowing SE, west and NW 500 miles from NE Khuzistan to the Shatt el Arab.

karyo- *combining form Biol.* Nucleus: *karyoplasm.* Also, before vowels, **kary-**: also spelled *caryo-.* [<Gk. *karyon* a nut]

kar·y·og·a·my (kar′ē·og′ə·mē) *n. Biol.* The merging or close union of the nuclei of two gametes to form the primary nucleus of the embryo. [<KARYO- + -GAMY]

kar·y·o·ki·ne·sis (kar′ē·ō·ki·nē′sis) *n. Biol.* **1** The series of changes which the nucleus goes through in indirect or mitotic cell division. **2** Such cell division; mitosis. Also spelled *caryokinesis.* [<KARYO- + Gk. *kinēsis* movement] — **kar·y·o·ki·net′ic** (-net′ik) *adj.*

kar·y·o·lymph (kar′ē·ə·limf′) *n. Biol.* The clear protoplasmic fluid surrounding the structures of the cell nucleus.

kar·y·o·mere (kar′ē·ə·mir′) *n. Biol.* One of the small vesicles formed in chromosomes in certain types of mitosis. Also **kar′y·om′er·ite** (-om′ər·īt).

kar·y·o·plasm (kar′ē·ə·plaz′əm) *n. Biol.* The protoplasm of the nucleus of a cell: also called *nucleoplasm.* — **kar′y·o·plas′mic** *adj.*

kar·y·o·some (kar′ē·ə·sōm′) *n. Biol.* **1** A chromosome. **2** A mass of chromatin in the resting nucleus of the cell. **3** The cell nucleus itself. Also **kar′y·o·so′ma** (-sō′mə).

kar·y·o·tin (kar′ē·ō′tin) *n. Biol.* The stainable, usually reticulated substance of the cell nucleus; chromatin: also spelled *caryotin.* [<KARYO- + (CHROMA)TIN]

kar·y·o·type (kar′ē·ə·tīp′) *n. Genetics* The particular chromosome number and gene arrangement in the gametes of any given species, type, or strain of organism.

Ka·sai (kä·sī′) A river in southern central Africa, flowing 1,100 miles east and north to the Congo.

Kas·bah (käz′bä) See CASBAH.

Ka·schau (kä′shou) The German name for KOŠICE.

Ka·shan (kä·shän′) A city in north central Iran.

ka·sher (kä′shər) *v.t.* To make or pronounce kosher. —*adj.* & *n.* See KOSHER.

Kash·gar (käsh′gär′) A town in western Sinkiang province, China: Chinese *Shufu.*

Kash·mir (kash·mir′, kash′mir) **1** See JAMMU AND KASHMIR. **2** A province of Jammu and Kashmir; 8,539 square miles; capital, Srinagar; containing the **Vale of Kashmir,** a valley in the Himalayas in western Kashmir province. Formerly *Cashmere.*

Kash·mi·ri (kash·mir′ē) *n.* The Indic language of the Kashmirians.

Kash·mi·ri·an (kash·mir′ē·ən) *adj.* Of or pertaining to Kashmir or its people. —*n.* A native of Kashmir. Also spelled *Cashmerian.*

Kas·kas·ki·a River (kas·kas′kē·ə) A river in Illinois, flowing 320 miles SW to the Mississippi.

Kas·par (käs′pär) German form of JASPAR and GASPAR. Also *Sw.* **Kas′per** (käs′pər).

Kas·sa (kôsh′shô) The Hungarian name for KOŠICE.

Kas·sa·la (kas′ə·lə) A city in NE Sudan.

Kas·sel (käs′əl) A city in Hesse, eastern West Germany: also *Cassel.*

Kas·tel·lo·ri·zo (käs′te·lô′ri·zô) The easternmost island of the Dodecanese group in the Aegean: Italian *Castelrosso.*

Kas·tro (käs′trô) A former name of MYTILINE. Also **Kas′tron** (-trən).

kata- See CATA-.

ka·tab·a·sis (kə·tab′ə·sis) *n.* **1** The march back to the sea of the Greek mercenaries who followed Cyrus against Artaxerxes. See ANABASIS. **2** Any retreat. [<Gk., a going down]

kat·a·bat·ic (kat′ə·bat′ik) *adj. Meteorol.* Pertaining to or designating a down-flowing wind cooled by radiation, as one reaching a valley from high ground.

kat·a·bol·ic (kat′ə·bol′ik), **ka·tab·o·lism** (kə·tab′ə·liz′əm), etc. See CATABOLIC, etc.

Ka·tah·din (kə·tä′din), **Mount** A peak in central Maine; 5,268 feet.

ka·tal·y·sis (kə·tal′ə·sis), **kat·a·lyt·ic** (kat′ə·lit′ik), etc. See CATALYSIS, etc.

kat·a·mor·phism (kat′ə·môr′fiz·əm) *n.* Metamorphism.

Ka·tan·ga (kə·tang′gə) A SE province of the Republic of the Congo; 191,827 square miles; capital, Elisabethville.

Ka·ta·ri·na (kä′tä·rē′nä) Swedish form of CATHERINE.

Kate (kāt) Diminutive of CATHERINE.

Kath·a·rine (kath′ə·rin, kath′rin), **Kath·e·rine** See CATHERINE.

ka·thar·sis (kə·thär′sis), **ka·thar·tic** (kə·thär′·tik) See CATHARSIS, etc.

Kath·er·i·na (kath′ə·rē′nə), **Ge·bel** (jeb′əl) A mountain in NE Egypt, highest peak in the Sinai Peninsula and in Egypt; 8,651 feet: also *Mount Catherine.*

Ka·thi·a·war (kä′tē·ə·wär′) A peninsula of western India extending into the Arabian Sea between the Gulfs of Cambay and Cutch.

Kath·leen (kath′lēn, kath·lēn′) See CATHERINE.

kath·ode (kath′ōd), etc. See CATHODE, etc.

kat·i·on (kat′ī′ən) See CATION.

Kat·mai National Monument (kat′mī) A region of the NE Alaska Peninsula, southern Alaska; 14,214 square miles; contains **Katmai Volcano;** 7,000 feet; last eruption, 1912; and the Valley of the Ten Thousand Smokes.

Kat·man·du (kät′män·dōō′) The capital of Nepal. Also **Kath′man·du′.**

Ka·to·wi·ce (kä′tô·vē′tse) A city in southern Poland: *German* **Kat·to·witz** (kät′ō·vits).

Kat·rine (kat′rin), **Loch** A lake in SW Perthshire, Scotland.

Kat·te·gat (kat′ə·gat) An arm of the North Sea, between Sweden and Jutland: also *Cattegat.* Also **Kat·te·gott** (kät′ə·got).

ka·ty·did (kā′tē·did) *n.* An arboreal, green, long-horned insect allied to the grasshoppers and crickets (family *Tettigonidae*): named from the sound produced by the stridulating organs at the base of the wing covers in the male.

Kau·ai (kou′ī) The fourth largest of the Hawaiian Islands; 555 square miles.

Kauf·man (kôf′mən), **George S.,** 1889–1961, U. S. playwright.

Kau·nas (kou′näs) A city on the Nemen river in south central Lithuania: Russian *Kovno.*

kau·ri (kou′rē) *n.* **1** A large timber tree (*Agathis australis*) of New Zealand. **2** The wood of this tree. **3** Any other species of the genus *Agathis.* **4** Kauri gum. Also **kau′ry.** [<Maori]

kauri gum A colorless to amber or brown resinous exudation of the kauri tree, used in varnishes, for oilcloth, linoleum, etc. Also **kauri copal, kauri resin.**

ka·va (kä′vä) *n.* **1** A shrub (*Piper methysticum*) of the pepper family. **2** An intoxicating and narcotic beverage made from the roots of this plant by the Polynesians: also **ka′va-ka′va.** [<Maori *kawa* bitter]

Ka·val·la (kä·vä′lä) A port of NE Greece.

ka·vass (kə·väs′) *n.* A guard or military courier attending Turkish dignitaries; also, a Turkish police officer. [<Turkish *qawwās* a maker of bows < *qaws* a bow]

Ka·ver·i (kô′vər·ē) A river in southern India, flowing 475 miles NE to the Bay of Bengal: also *Cauvery.*

Ka·vi (kä′vē) *n.* The extinct language of Java from which modern Javanese developed: preserved in ancient Buddhist writings.

Ka·vi·eng (kä′vē·eng′) A port and the chief city of northern New Ireland, Bismarck Archipelago.

Ka·vir (kä·vir′) See DASHT-I-KAVIR.
Kaw (kô) *n.* A Kansas Indian.
Ka·wa·gu·chi (kä·wä·goo·chē) A city of central Honshu island, Japan.
Ka·wa·sa·ki (kä·wä·sä·kē) A city of central Honshu island on Tokyo Bay.
Kaw River See KANSAS RIVER.
Ka·wu·la (kä·woo′lä) See LOMBLEM. Also **Ka·woe′la.**
kay (kā) See KEY[2].
Kay (kā), **Sir** A braggart and spiteful knight of the Round Table; foster brother and seneschal of King Arthur. Also spelled *Kai* and, in French romances, *Queux.*
kay·ak (kī′ak) *n.* The hunting canoe of arctic America, made of sealskins stretched over a pointed frame, leaving a hole amidships where the navigator sits, excluding the water by fastening the deck covering around him. Also spelled *kaiak.* [<Eskimo]

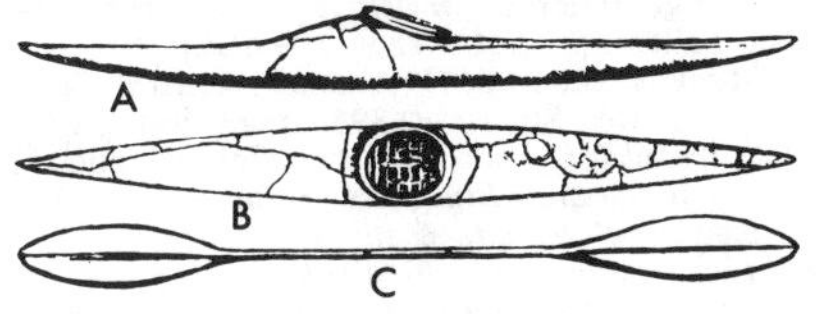

KAYAK
A. Side view. *B.* Top view. *C.* Paddle.

Kaye-Smith (kā′smith′), **Sheila,** 1889–1956, English novelist.
kayles (kālz) *n. pl. Brit. Dial.* **1** A game of ninepins or skittles. **2** The pins used in the game.
kay·o (kā′ō) *Slang v.t.* **kay·oed, kay·o·ing** In boxing, to knock out. —*n.* A knockout (def. 1). Also *KO.* [<*k(nock) o(ut)*]
Kay·se·ri (kī′sə·rē′) A city in central Turkey in Asia: ancient *Caesarea Mazaca.*
Ka·zakh *n.* **1** One of a Turkic people, formerly largely nomadic, dwelling in Kazakhstan. **2** A long-piled rug, usually in geometrical patterns, made by the Kazakhs.
Kazakhstan A republic in central Asia; pop. 17,000,000, 1,050,000 square miles; capital, Alma-Ata; formerly **Kazakh Soviet Socialist Republic** (1936–1991).
Ka·zan A city in west central Russia; capital of Tatarstan republic.
Ka·zan River (kə·zan′) A river in Northwest Territories, Canada, flowing 455 miles NE from SE Mackenzie to a lake in central Keewatin which drains into Hudson Bay.
ka·zoo (kə·zoo′) *n.* A toy musical instrument: a wooden or metal tube to which is attached a piece of stretched catgut or paper which vibrates when the tube is sung or hummed into. [Origin uncertain]
Kaz·vin (käz·vēn′) A city in NW Iran: also *Qazvin.*
ke·a (kā′ə, kē′ə) *n.* A large New Zealand parrot (*Nestor notabilis*), olive-brown variegated with blue and green, which feeds on carrion in addition to fruits, etc., and even attacks live sheep. [Maori]
Ke·a (kā′ä) See KEOS.
Kean (kēn), **Edmund,** 1787–1833, English actor.
Kear·ny (kär′nē), **Philip,** 1815?–62, U. S. general; served in Mexican and Civil wars.
keat (kēt) *n.* A young guinea fowl.
Keats (kēts), **John,** 1795–1821, English poet.
ke·bar (kē′bär) See CABER.
keb·bie (keb′ē) *n. Scot.* A cudgel, or rude walking stick.
keb·boc (keb′ək) *n. Scot.* A cheese. Also **keb′·buck.**
Ke·ble (kē′bəl), **John,** 1792–1866, English divine and poet; one of the founders of the Oxford movement.
Kech·ua (kech′wä), **Kech·uan** (kech′wən) See QUECHUA, QUECHUAN.
keck[1] (kek) *v.i.* **1** To heave as in vomiting; retch. **2** To show or feel great disgust. —*n.* Nausea. [Prob. imit.]
keck[2] (kek) *n.* A hollow stalk of a plant. [Back formation <KEX, mistaken as a plural]
keck·le[1] (kek′əl) *v.t.* **keck·led, keck·ling** *Naut.* To wrap or serve, as a cable, with canvas, rope, etc., as a protection from chafing. [Origin unknown]
keck·le[2] (kek′əl) *Scot. v.i.* **keck·led, keck·ling** To cackle; chuckle. —*n.* A chuckle or giggle.
Kecs·ke·mét (kech′kə·māt) A city in central Hungary.
Ke·dah (kā′dä) One of the States of Malaya, in the NW part; 3,660 square miles; capital, Alor Star.
Ke·dar (kē′dər) A son of Ishmael; also, a tribe or confederacy of Arabian tent-dwellers descending from him. —**Ke′dar·ite** *adj.*
ked·dah (ked′ə) *n.* An enclosure or corral for the capture of wild elephants: also spelled *khedah.* [<Hind. *khedā*]
kedge (kej) *Naut. n.* A light anchor used in warping, freeing a vessel from shoals, etc.: also **kedge anchor.** —*v.i.* **1** To move a vessel by hauling up to a kedge anchor placed at a distance. **2** To be moved in this way. —*v.t.* **3** To move (a vessel) in this way. [<*kedge (anchor)* <CADGE]
Ke·dron (kē′drən) A valley east of Jerusalem. *John* xviii 1. Also *Kidron.*
ke·ef (kē·ef′) See KEF.
keek (kēk) *Scot.* To peep; pry. —*n.* A peep.
keek·ing-glass (kē′king·glas′, -gläs′) *n. Scot.* A looking-glass.
keel[1] (kēl) *n.* **1** *Naut.* The lowest lengthwise member of the framework of a vessel, serving to stiffen it and, when it projects below the planking or plating, as is usually the case, giving it stability. **2** Figuratively, a ship. **3** *Aeron.* **a** A vertical fin which extends longitudinally for a considerable length at the bottom of an airship. **b** The center bottom of an airplane fuselage. **4** Any keel-shaped part or object. **5** *Ornithol.* A median longitudinal ridge or process, as of the breast bone of a fowl. —**fin keel** An extension of a yacht's keel downward, suggesting the back fin of a fish: commonly of metal, and serving to ballast and prevent lateral drifting. —*v.t.* & *v.i.* To turn over with the keel uppermost; capsize. —**to keel over 1** To turn bottom up; capsize. **2** To fall over or be felled, as from an injury. [<ON *kjölr* keel]
keel[2] (kēl) *n.* **1** A coal barge used on the Tyne in England. **2** The quantity of coal in a barge load. **3** A former British unit of weight for coal, equal to 21.54 metric tons. [<MDu. *kiel* ship]
keel[3] (kēl) *v.t. Obs.* To cool. [OE *cēlan*]
keel[4] (kēl) *n. Scot.* Red chalk or ocher; ruddle.
keel·age (kē′lij) *n. Naut.* The sum paid for anchoring a vessel in a harbor.
keel·boat (kēl′bōt′) *n.* A covered freight boat of shallow draft having a keel but no sails, usually propelled by poles or the current: used on rivers in the western United States.
keel·er (kē′lər) *n.* **1** A shallow tub. **2** A box used to hold salt in salting fish. [<KEEL[3]]
Kee·ley cure (kē′lē) A proprietary system for the treatment of drug addiction and alcoholism by the administration of gold chloride. [after Leslie J. *Keeley,* 1832–1900, American physician]
keel·haul (kēl′hôl′) *v.t.* **1** *Naut.* To haul (a man) through the water under a ship from one side to the other or from stem to stern: a former punishment. **2** To reprove severely; castigate. Also **keel·hale** (kēl′hāl′).
Kee·ling Islands (kē′ling) See COCOS ISLANDS.
keel·son (kēl′sən) *n.* **1** *Naut.* A beam running lengthwise above the keel of a ship. **2** A similar structural member running above the keel of a flying boat. Also spelled *kelson.* [Related to KEEL[1]]
Kee·lung (kē′loong′) A port of northern Taiwan: also *Kilung, Chilung.*
keen[1] (kēn) *adj.* **1** Very sharp, as a knife. **2** Cutting; piercing, as wit. **3** Vivid; pungent. **4** Having or exhibiting sharpness or penetration; shrewd. **5** Acute: *keen* sight. **6** Exceptionally intelligent. **7** Characterized by intensity, force, or zest: a *keen* appetite. See synonyms under ACUTE, ARDENT, ASTUTE, CLEVER, EAGER[1], FINE[1], KNOWING, SAGACIOUS, SHARP, VIVID. [OE *cēne*] —**keen′ly** *adv.* —**keen′ness** *n.*
keen[2] (kēn) *n.* A wailing cry; dirge. —*v.i.* To wail loudly over the dead. [<Irish *caoine* < *caoinim* I wail] —**keen′er** *n.*
keep (kēp) *v.* **kept, keep·ing** *v.t.* **1** To have and retain possession or control of; hold. **2** To withhold knowledge of, as a secret. **3** To manage or conduct: to *keep* a shop. **4** To have charge of; tend: to *keep* bar. **5** To care for; guard or defend from harm: May God *keep* you. **6** To be faithful to the conditions of; fulfil, as a promise or contract. **7** To maintain by action or conduct: to *keep* silence. **8** To cause to continue in some condition or state; preserve unchanged: *Keep* the home fires burning. **9** To make regular entries in: to *keep* a diary. **10** To set down in writing; maintain a written record of: to *keep* accounts. **11** To have regularly for sale: to *keep* groceries. **12** To provide for or maintain, as with food or lodging. **13** To have in one's employ or for one's use or pleasure. **14** To celebrate or observe, especially with rites or ceremony, as a holiday. **15** To conduct, as a meeting. **16** To detain or restrain; prevent: What *kept* you? **17** To hold prisoner; confine. **18** To remain; hold to: *Keep* your present course. **19** To hold or maintain in the same position or state as before: *Keep* your seat. —*v.i.* **20** To continue in a condition, place, or action: They *kept* firing; *Keep* to the right-hand side. **21** To remain; stay: often with *up, down, in, out, off, away,* etc. **22** To remain sound, fresh, etc.: This fruit *keeps* till spring. **23** *Colloq.* To be in session: School *keeps* till three o'clock. —**to keep back 1** To restrain. **2** To withhold. —**to keep in with** *Colloq.* To remain in the good graces of. —**to keep on** To continue; persist. —**to keep time 1** To indicate time correctly, as a clock. **2** To make movements in unison or concord with others. **3** To count or observe rhythmic accents. —**to keep track of** (or **tabs on**) To continue to be informed about. —**to keep up 1** To keep pace with; not fall behind. **2** To maintain in good condition or repair. **3** To continue; go on with. **4** To maintain and renew knowledge or information concerning: usually with *with* or *on.* **5** To cause to stay awake or out of bed. —*n.* **1** Means of subsistence; livelihood. **2** The donjon of a medieval castle; hence, a castle; fortress. **3** That in which something is kept. —**for keeps** *Colloq.* For permanent keeping; for good; for ever. [OE *cēpan* observe]

Synonyms (verb): carry, celebrate, conduct, continue, defend, detain, fulfil, guard, hold, maintain, obey, observe, preserve, protect, refrain, restrain, retain, support, sustain, withhold. *Keep,* signifying generally to have and *retain* in possession, is the terse, strong Old English term for many acts which are more exactly discriminated by other words. We *keep, observe,* or *celebrate* a festival; we *keep* or *hold* a prisoner in custody; we *keep* or *preserve* silence, *keep* the peace, *preserve* order—*preserve* being the more formal word; we *keep* or *maintain* a horse, a servant, etc.; a man *supports* his family; we *keep* or *obey* a commandment, *keep* or *fulfil* a promise. In the expressions to *keep* a secret, *keep* one's own counsel, *keep* faith or *keep* the faith, such words as *preserve* or *maintain* could not be substituted without loss. A person *keeps* a shop or store, *conducts* or carries on a business; he *keeps* or *carries* a certain line of goods; we may *keep* or *restrain* one from folly, crime, or violence; we *keep* from or *refrain* from evil, ourselves. *Keep* in the sense of *guard* or *defend* implies that the defense is effectual. Compare CELEBRATE, OCCUPY, PRESERVE, RESTRAIN, RETAIN. *Antonyms:* see synonyms for ABANDON.
keep·er (kē′pər) *n.* **1** One who or that which keeps; specifically, the overseer of a prison; the guardian of an insane person; the caretaker of a wild animal; any guardian. **2** A device for keeping something in place, as the socket into which a bolt slides. **3** One who observes or obeys: a *keeper* of promises. **4** That which keeps well, without spoiling, as fruit. **5** The armature of a magnet; also, the soft iron bar placed across the poles of a horseshoe magnet to prevent loss of magnetism.
keep·ing (kē′ping) *n.* **1** Custody, charge, or possession. **2** Right relation or proportion;

harmony; congruity: The act was in *keeping* with his mood. 3 Maintenance; support.
keep•sake (kēp′sāk′) *n.* Anything kept, or given to be kept, for the sake of the giver; a memento.
kees•hond (kās′hond, kēs′-) *n. pl.* **•hond•en** (-hon′dən) A breed of dog of Arctic or sub-Arctic origin, long popular in Holland, ash-gray in color and having a short, closely knit body, straight legs, wedge-shaped head, thick feathery coat, and curly tail. [<Du. *Kees,* a nickname for Cornelius + *hond* a dog; so called from the first breeder]

KEESHOND
(About 20 inches high at the shoulder)

keeve (kēv) *n.* A large vat. [OE *cȳf*]
Kee•wa•tin (kē·wä′tin) A district of the Northwest Territories, Canada; 228,160 square miles.
kef (kāf) *n.* 1 A condition marked by voluptuous and dreamy repose and the passive enjoyment of languor. 2 Indian hemp, smoked to produce this condition: also spelled *keef, kief.* [<Arabic *kaif* good humor]
kef•ir (kef′ər) *n.* A kind of fermented milk resembling kumiss: used in the Caucasus. Also spelled *kephir.* [<Caucasian]
keg (keg) *n.* A small, strong barrel, usually of 5- to 10-gallon capacity. [<earlier *cag* <ON *kaggi*]
keg•ler (keg′lər) *n. Colloq.* One who bowls; a bowler. [<G *kegel* ninepin]
Keigh•ley (kēth′lē) A municipal borough in western Yorkshire, England.
Kei Islands (kā) An Indonesian island group between Ceram and the Aru Islands; total 555 square miles: also *Kai Islands.*
Kei•jo (kā·jō) The Japanese name for SEOUL.
keir (kir) See KIER.
keist•er (kēs′tər) *n. U.S. Slang* A box, trunk, suitcase, or the like: also spelled *keyster, kiester.* Also **keest′er.** [? <Yiddish <G *kiste* a box]
Kei•tel (kīt′l), **Wilhelm,** 1882–1946, German marshal in World War II.
Keith (kēth), **Sir Arthur,** 1866–1955, English anthropologist.
keit•lo•a (kīt′lō·ə, kāt′-) *n.* A South African two-horned rhinoceros. [<native name]
Ke•ku•lé von Stra•do•nitz (kā′kōō·lā fôn shträ′dō·nits), **Friedrich August,** 1829–96, German chemist.
Ke•lan•tan (kə·län·tän′) One of the States of Malaya, in the northern part; 5,746 square miles; capital, Kota Bharu.
Kel•lar (kel′ər), **Harry,** 1849–1922, U.S. magician.
Kel•ler (kel′ər), **Helen Adams,** 1880–1968, U.S. writer and lecturer; blind and deaf from infancy.
Kel•ly (kel′ē), **Howard Atwood,** 1858–1943, U.S. gynecological surgeon.
ke•loid (kē′loid) *n. Pathol.* A fibrous tumor in the connective tissue of the skin, of various shapes and sizes, and usually caused by injury: also spelled *cheloid.* [<Gk. *kēlē* tumor + -OID]
kelp (kelp) *n.* 1 Any large coarse seaweed (family *Laminariaceae*); specifically, the California sea palm *(Postelsia palmaeformis).* 2 The ashes of seaweeds: formerly the source of soda as used in glassmaking and soapmaking, now a source chiefly of iodine. **—giant kelp** A very large, tough, and massive seaweed *(Macrocystis pyrifera),* belonging to the brown algae: it is found mainly on the Pacific coast of the United States, and has been known to reach a length of 700 feet. [ME *culp*; origin uncertain]
kel•pie (kel′pē) *n. Scot.* A malevolent water sprite, supposed to haunt fords in the form of a horse. Also **kel′py.**
kel•son (kel′sən) See KEELSON.
kelt (kelt) *n. Scot.* Undyed cloth of black and white wool mixed.
Kelt (kelt), **Kelt•ic** (kel′tik) See CELT, etc.
kel•ter (kel′tər) *n. Brit. Dial.* Working order; kilter.
Kel•vin scale (kel′vin) *Physics* The absolute scale of temperature, based on the average kinetic energy per molecule of a perfect gas. Zero is equal to −273° Celsius or −459.4° Fahrenheit. [after William Thompson, 1824–1907, Lord *Kelvin,* English physicist]
Ke•mal A•ta•türk (ke·mäl′ ä·tä·türk′), 1881–1938, Turkish general; president 1923–38: known as *Mustapha Kemal.*
Kem•ble (kem′bəl), **Frances Anne,** 1809–93, English actress: called "Fanny Kemble." — **John Philip,** 1757–1823, English tragedian; uncle of the preceding.
Kem•pis (kem′pis), **Thomas à,** 1380–1471, German mystic, reputed author of the *Imitation of Christ.*
ken (ken) *v.* **kenned** or **kent, ken•ning** *v.t.* 1 *Scot.* To know; have knowledge of. 2 *Scot. Law* To recognize as heir. 3 *Obs.* To see. — *v.i.* 4 *Scot. & Brit. Dial.* To have understanding. —*n.* Reach of sight or knowledge; cognizance.
Ke•nai Peninsula (kē′nī) An extension of southern Alaska into the Gulf of Alaska; 150 miles long.
kench (kench) *n.* A bin for salting fish or skins. —*v.t. Dial.* To place in a salting bin. [Var. of dial. E *canch* a trench]
Ken•dal (ken′dəl) *n.* A coarse woolen cloth of green color made at Kendal, England; also, the color of this cloth. Also **Kendal green.**
Keng•tung (keng′tŏŏng) The easternmost and largest of the Shan States, Upper Burma; 12,405 square miles; capital, Kengtung.
Ken•il•worth (ken′əl·wûrth) An urban district in central Warwickshire, England; site of the ruins of **Kenilworth Castle** where Leicester entertained Queen Elizabeth I, 1575.
Kenilworth ivy A scrophulariaceous herb *(Cymbalaria muralis)* of delicate growth.
Ké•ni•tra (kā·nē·trä′) The former name of Port-Lyautey.
Ken•nan (ken′ən), **George Frost,** born 1904, U.S. diplomat; writer on Russian affairs.
Ken•ne•bec (ken′ə·bek) A river in central Maine, flowing about 150 miles SW to the Atlantic.
Ken•ne•dy (ken′ə·de), **John Fitzgerald,** 1917–1963, 35th president of the United States, 1961–63; assassinated. **—Robert Francis,** 1925–68, U.S. Senator; assassinated.
Kennedy, Cape A cape of eastern Florida, site of a rocket and missile launching installation: formerly *Cape Canaveral.*
ken•nel[1] (ken′əl) *n.* 1 A house for a dog or for a pack of hounds; also, the pack. 2 *pl.* A professional establishment where dogs are bred, raised, boarded, trained, etc. 3 The hole or lair of a fox or like beast. 4 A vile lodging. —*v.* **•neled** or **•nelled, •nel•ing** or **•nel•ling** *v.t.* To keep or confine in or as in a kennel. —*v.i.* To lodge or take shelter in a kennel. [<F *chenil* <L *canis* a dog; formed on analogy with *ovile* a sheepfold <*ovis* a sheep]
ken•nel[2] (ken′əl) *n.* The gutter of a street; channel. [Var. of obs. *cannel* a channel]
ken•nel[3] (ken′əl) See CANNEL.
Ken•nel•ly (ken′əl·ē), **Arthur Edwin,** 1861–1939, U.S. electrical engineer.
Ken•nel•ly–Heav•i•side layer (ken′əl·ē·hev′ē·sīd) See HEAVISIDE LAYER.
Ken•ne•saw Mountain (ken′ə·sô) A national monument in NW Georgia; scene of a decisive Union victory in the Civil War, 1864.
Ken•neth (ken′əth) A masculine personal name. [<Celtic, handsome]
ken•ning[1] (ken′ing) *n. Scot.* 1 The smallest recognizable portion. 2 Recognition.
ken•ning[2] (ken′ing) *n.* In early Germanic and Scandinavian literature, a poetical periphrasis used instead of a simple name of a thing, as "oar-steed" for "ship." [<ON *kennungar* symbols]
Ken•ny (ken′ē), **Elizabeth,** 1886–1952, Australian nurse; developed a physiotherapy for poliomyelitis: known as *Sister Kenny.*
ke•no (kē′nō) *n.* A game of chance played by drawing numbers from a container and covering with counters the corresponding numbers on cards. The player who first covers a row of five numbers is the winner. Also called *bingo, lotto.* [<F *quine* five winners]
ken•o•gen•e•sis (ken′ə·jen′ə·sis, kē′nə-) See CENOGENESIS.
Ke•no•sha (kə·nō′shə) A city on Lake Michigan in SE Wisconsin.
ke•no•sis (ki·nō′sis) *n. Theol.* Christ's action in putting aside his divinity during the Incarnation, *Phil.* ii 5–8. [<Gk. *kenōsis* an emptying <*kenoein* empty]
ke•not•ic (ki·not′ik) *adj.* Of or pertaining to the doctrine of kenosis. —*n.* One who believes in the doctrine of kenosis.
ken•o•tron (ken′ə·tron) *n.* A unidirectional, two-electrode thermionic tube, which acts as a rectifier of high-voltage alternating currents. [<Gk. *kenōsis* emptying +(ELEC)TRON]
Ken•sing•ton (ken′zing·tən) A metropolitan borough of western London.
kent[1] (kent) *Scot.* Past tense and past participle of KEN. Also **kend** (kend).
Kent (kent) A county in SE England; 1,525 square miles; county town, Maidstone.
Kent (kent), **James,** 1763–1847, U.S. jurist. — **Rockwell,** 1882–1971, U.S. artist.
Kent•ish (ken′tish) *adj.* Of or pertaining to Kent. —*n.* The Old English and Middle English dialects of Kent.
kent•ledge (kent′lej) *n. Naut.* Permanent pig-iron ballast. [? <QUINTAL + -AGE]
Ken•tuck•y (kən·tuk′ē) A south central State of the United States; 40,395 square miles; capital, Frankfort; entered the Union June 1, 1792: nickname *Bluegrass State.* Abbr. KY —**Ken•tuck′i•an** *adj. & n.*
Kentucky bluegrass A grass *(Poa pratensis)* common in temperate and cold regions: valuable for forage.
Kentucky boat A large flat-bottomed river boat, usually towed or propelled by oars, formerly used for transporting freight. Also **Kentucky ark, Kentucky flat.**
Kentucky coffee tree A tall leguminous tree *(Gymnocladus dioicus)* having seeds, called **Kentucky coffee beans,** often used as a substitute for coffee.
Kentucky Derby A famous American horse race, run at Churchill Downs, Louisville, Ky., since 1875.
Kentucky River A river in Kentucky, flowing 259 miles NW to the Ohio River.
Ken•ya (kēn′yə, ken′-) A republic of the Commonwealth of Nations in eastern Africa; 224,960 square miles; capital, Nairobi: formerly *East African Protectorate.*
Kenya, Mount An extinct volcanic cone in central Kenya, the second highest mountain in Africa; 17,040 feet.
Ken•yat•ta (ken·yä′tə), **Jomo,** 1893?–1978, black African leader; prime minister of Kenya 1963–64; president 1964–78.
Ke•o•kuk (kē′ə·kuk) A city in SE Iowa on the Mississippi.
Ke•os (kē′os) A Greek island in the Cyclades: ancient *Ceos*: medieval *Zea*: also *Kea.*
kep (kep) *v.t. Scot.* To catch; stop.
keph•a•lin (kef′ə·lin) See CEPHALIN.
Ke•phal•le•ni•a (ke′fä·lə·nē′ə) See CEPHALONIA.
keph•ir (kef′ər) See KEFIR.
kep•i (kep′ē) *n.* A flat-topped military cap with vizor. [<F *képi* <dial. G *käppi,* dim. of *kappe* a cap]
Kep•ler (kep′lər), **Johannes,** 1571–1630, German astronomer; formulated **Kepler's laws,** relative to the motions of planets.
kept (kept) Past tense and past participle of KEEP.
ker (kûr) *n.* 1 In Greek religion, a spirit or soul of one dead; sometimes, a malignant spirit. 2 The personification of fate. [<Gk. *Kēr*]
Ker•ak (ker′äk) A town of south central Jordan, near the Dead Sea.
Ke•ra•la (kā′ru·lu) A constituent State of extreme SW India on the Malabar Coast, consisting of most of the former State of Travencore-Cochin and of the Malabar district and other former sections of Madras State; 15,035 square miles; capital, Trivandrum.
ke•ram•ic (kə·ram′ik), **ke•ram•ics** See CERAMIC, etc.
ker•a•tin (ker′ə·tin) *n. Biochem.* A highly insoluble albuminous compound containing sulfur that forms the essential ingredient of horny tissue, as of horns, claws, nails, etc. — **ke•rat•i•nous** (kə·rat′ə·nəs) *adj.*
ker•a•ti•tis (ker′ə·tī′tis) *n. Pathol.* Inflammation of the cornea.
kerato- *combining form* 1 Horn: *keratogenous.* 2 Cornea of the eye: *keratoplasty.* Also, before vowels, **kerat-.** [<Gk. *keras, keratos* horn]
ker•a•to•con•junc•ti•vi•tis (ker′ə·tō·kən·jungk′·tə·vī′tis) *n. Pathol.* Inflammation of the cornea and conjunctiva; shipyard eye.

ker·a·tog·e·nous (ker′ə·toj′ə·nəs) *adj.* Promoting the growth of horn.
ker·a·toid (ker′ə·toid) *adj.* Resembling keratin or horn; horny.
Ker·a·tol (ker′ə·tōl, -tol) *n.* A pyroxylin-coated waterproof cloth resembling leather: a trade name.
ker·a·to·plas·ty (ker′ə·tō·plas′tē) *n. Surg.* The operation of transplanting corneal tissue; plastic surgery of the cornea. — **ker′a·to·plas′tic** *adj.*
ker·a·tose (ker′ə·tōs) *adj.* Pertaining to or characterized by horny tissue, as certain sponges.
kerb (kûrb), **kerb·stone** (-stōn) See CURB, etc.
Kerch (kûrch) A port in the Crimea at the end of **Kerch Peninsula,** an eastern extension of the Crimea on **Kerch Strait** which connects the Sea of Azov with the Black Sea.
ker·chief (kûr′chif) *n.* A square of linen, silk, or other fabric used to cover the head or neck, or as a handkerchief. [ME *keverchef, kerchef* <OF *couvrechef* < *covrir* cover + *chef* head] — **ker′chiefed** *adj.*
Ke·ren·sky (kə·ren′skē, *Russian* kyer′in·skē), **Alexander Feodorovich,** 1881–1970, Russian revolutionary leader; prime minister, July–Nov. 1917; removed by Bolsheviks.
kerf (kûrf) *n.* **1** The channel made by a saw, or the width of such a channel. **2** A cut of a cloth-shearing machine. **3** The act or process of cutting. [OE *cyrf* a cutting]
Ker·gue·len Islands (kûr′gə·lən) An archipelago in the southern Indian Ocean, comprising a dependency of Madagascar; 2,700 square miles; the chief island, **Kerguelen** (1,318 square miles), is also called *Desolation Island.*
Ke·rin·chi (kə·rin′chē), **Mount** A peak of western Sumatra; 12,467 feet: also *Indrapura.*
Ker·kheh (kär′khe) See KARKHEH.
Ker·ky·ra (ker′kē·rä) The Greek name for CORFU.
Ker·mad·ec Islands (kər·mad′ek) An island group NE of New Zealand, comprising a dependency of New Zealand; 13 square miles.
Ker·man (kûr′män, ker′-) **1** A former province of SE Iran: ancient *Carmania.* **2** A city in SE Iran; former capital of Kerman: also *Kirman.*
Ker·man·sha (ker′män·shä′) A city in western Iran. Also **Ker′man·sha·han′** (-hän′).
ker·mes (kûr′mēz) *n.* The dried bodies of the females of a cochineal-like scale insect (genus *Kermes*), used as a red dyestuff. [<Arabic *qirmiz.* Related to CRIMSON.]
kermes oak A small evergreen oak (*Quercus coccifera*) of the Mediterranean region, infested by the kermes insect. Also **ker′mes.**
ker·mess (kûr′mis) *n.* **1** In Flanders, etc., a periodical outdoor festival. **2** An indoor or outdoor festival imitative of the Flemish. Often spelled *kirmess.* Also **ker′mis.** [<Du. *kermis* < *kerk misse* church mass]
kern[1] (kûrn) *n.* **1** *Archaic* An Irish irregular, light-armed foot soldier. **2** *Archaic* A body of such soldiers. **3** A peasant; churl. Also **kerne.** [<Irish *ceithern* a band of soldiers]
kern[2] (kûrn) *n. Printing* That part of a type which overhangs the shaft or shank, as of an italic *f.* — *v.t.* To make (type) with a kern. [<F *carne* projecting angle]
Kern (kûrn), **Jerome David,** 1885–1945, U.S. composer.
ker·nel (kûr′nəl) *n.* **1** A grain or seed; the edible part of a nut. **2** A hard concretion of flesh. **3** The central part of anything; nucleus; gist. — *v.i.* To envelop as a kernel. ◆ Homophone: *colonel.* [OE *cyrnel,* dim. of *corn* a seed]
Kern River (kûrn) A river in southern central California, flowing 155 miles SW from the Sierra Nevada.
ker·o·sene (ker′ə·sēn) *n.* A mixture of hydrocarbons distilled from crude petroleum and used for burning in lamps: also called *coal oil.* [<Gk. *kēros* wax + -ENE]
Kerr (kär), **Archibald John,** 1882–1951, Baron Inverchapel, British diplomat.
Ker·ry (ker′ē) A county of SW Munster, Ireland; 1,815 square miles; county town, Tralee.
Ker·ry (ker′ē) *n. pl.* **·ries** One of an Irish breed of cattle raised in County Kerry.
Kerry blue terrier See under TERRIER.
ker·sey (kûr′zē) *n.* **1** A smooth, lightweight, ribbed woolen cloth. **2** *pl.* Kinds of kersey; also trousers of kersey. [from *Kersey,* village in England]
ker·sey·mere (kûr′zē·mir) *n.* Cassimere.
kes·trel (kes′trəl) *n.* A European falcon (*Falco tinnunculus*), resembling the American sparrow hawk and noted for its hovering habits. [Var. of ME *castrel* <OF *cresserelle*]
ketch[1] (kech) *n.* A fore-and-aft rigged, two-masted vessel: similar to a yawl but having the mizzen- or jiggermast forward of the rudder post. [Earlier *cache.* Related to CATCH, *v.*]

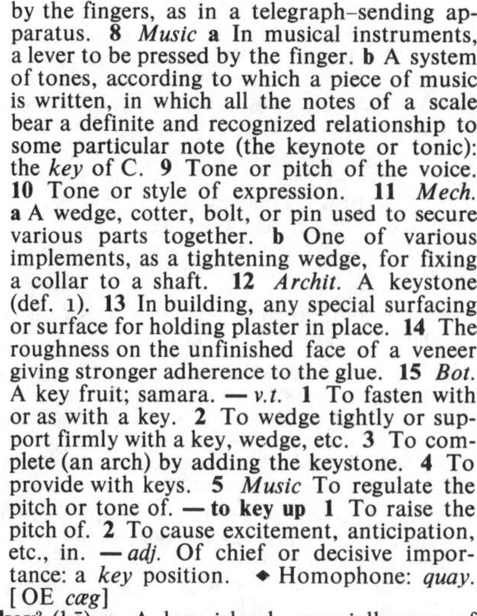
GAFF-RIGGED KETCH

ketch[2] (kech) *n.* A hangman. [after Jack *Ketch*]
Ketch·i·kan (kech′i·kan) A port of entry in SE Alaska.
ketch·up (kech′əp) *n.* A spiced condiment for meats: also spelled *catchup, catsup.* [Appar. <Chinese *ke-tsiap* brine of pickled fish]
ke·tene (kē′tēn) *n. Chem.* **1** A pungent, colorless gas, H_2C:CO, obtained by decomposing acetone, ethyl acetate, or acetic anhydride with intense heat. **2** Any of a group of organic compounds of the form R_2C:CO. [<KET(ONE) + -ENE]
keto- *combining form Chem.* Ketone; related to ketone bodies. Also, before vowels, **ket-,** as in *ketosis.* [<KETONE]
ke·to-e·nol tautomerism (kē′tō·ē′nôl) *Chem.* Tautomerism in which certain organic compounds may occur in both the keto and enol forms.
ke·tone (kē′tōn) *n. Chem.* One of a class of reactive organic compounds in which the carbonyl group unites with two hydrocarbon radicals, a single bivalent radical, or derivatives. The simplest member of the class is acetic ketone or acetone. [<G *keton* <F *acétone* acetone] — **ke·ton·ic** (ki·ton′ik) *adj.*
ke·tose (kē′tōs) *n. Chem.* Any of a class of monosaccharides containing a ketone group.
ke·to·sis (kē·tō′sis) *n. Pathol.* Excessive formation or secretion of ketones in the body, as in acidosis, diabetes, etc.
Ket·ter·ing (ket′ər·ing), **Charles Franklin,** 1876–1958, U.S. electrical engineer and inventor.
ket·tle (ket′l) *n.* **1** A metallic vessel for stewing or boiling; a teakettle. **2** A tin pail. **3** A hole in the bottom of a stream or pond where carp lie in winter. **4** A kettle-shaped cavity, as in rock or glacial drift: also **kettle hole.** **5** A kettledrum. [OE *cetel*]
ket·tle·drum (ket′l·drum′) *n.* **1** A drum having a brass hemispherical shell and parchment head, and sounded by soft-headed elastic drumsticks. **2** An informal afternoon party.
Keu·ka Lake (kyōō′kə, kə·yōō′-) One of the Finger Lakes in west central New York.
kev·el (kev′əl) *n. Naut.* A belaying cleat or peg: usually in pairs. [<AF *keville* a pin, peg <LL *clavicula* bar of a door, orig. dim. of L *clavis* a key]
Kew (kyōō) A borough of Richmond and suburb of London, in Surrey, England.
Ke·wee·naw Peninsula (kē′wə·nô) A Michigan headland extending 60 miles NE into Lake Superior to form **Keweenaw Bay.**
Kew·pie (kyōō′pē) *n.* A chubby, cherubic doll, made of chalkstone or plastic: a trade name.
kex (keks) *n.* A hollow stalk; a weed. [Origin unknown]
key[1] (kē) *n.* **1** A detachable instrument for turning the catch or bolt of a lock forwards or backwards in order to lock or unlock. **2** An instrument for holding and turning a screw, nut, valve, or the like, as for winding a clock. **3** Anything serving to disclose, open, or solve something. **4** Something that opens or prepares a way. **5** A gloss, table, or group of notes interpreting certain symbols, ciphers, problems, etc. **6** Any one of the finger levers in typewriters, typesetting machines, etc. **7** *Electr.* A circuit-breaker or -opener operated by the fingers, as in a telegraph-sending apparatus. **8** *Music* **a** In musical instruments, a lever to be pressed by the finger. **b** A system of tones, according to which a piece of music is written, in which all the notes of a scale bear a definite and recognized relationship to some particular note (the keynote or tonic): the *key* of C. **9** Tone or pitch of the voice. **10** Tone or style of expression. **11** *Mech.* **a** A wedge, cotter, bolt, or pin used to secure various parts together. **b** One of various implements, as a tightening wedge, for fixing a collar to a shaft. **12** *Archit.* A keystone (def. 1). **13** In building, any special surfacing or surface for holding plaster in place. **14** The roughness on the unfinished face of a veneer giving stronger adherence to the glue. **15** *Bot.* A key fruit; samara. — *v.t.* **1** To fasten with or as with a key. **2** To wedge tightly or support firmly with a key, wedge, etc. **3** To complete (an arch) by adding the keystone. **4** To provide with keys. **5** *Music* To regulate the pitch or tone of. — **to key up** **1** To raise the pitch of. **2** To cause excitement, anticipation, etc., in. — *adj.* Of chief or decisive importance: a *key* position. ◆ Homophone: *quay.* [OE *cæg*]
key[2] (kē) *n.* A low island, especially one of coral, along a coast: usually *cay* in the Gulf of Mexico and the West Indies: rarely *kay.* ◆ Homophone: *quay.* [Var. of CAY]
Key (kē), **Francis Scott,** 1780?–1843, American lawyer; wrote *The Star-Spangled Banner.*
key·board (kē′bōrd′, -bōrd′) *n.* A row of keys as in a piano or typewriter; also, the range or arrangement of the keys, as of an organ, piano, etc.
key bugle A bugle having keys, and a compass of two octaves including semitones.
keyed (kēd) *adj.* **1** Having keys: said of musical instruments, etc. **2** Brought to a tension, as a musical string. **3** Tuned, as a musical instrument. **4** Secured by a keystone or key.
key fruit *Bot.* A dry, indehiscent, winged fruit, as that of the ash or elm; a samara.
key·hole (kē′hōl′) *n.* A hole for a key, as in a door or lock.
Key Lar·go (kē lär′gō) The largest island of the Florida Keys; 28 miles long.
key log The log caught or wedged in a log jam that must be released to break the jam.
key man **1** A person without whose work or direction something could not go on; an indispensable person. **2** A telegraph operator.
Keynes (kānz), **John Maynard,** 1883–1946, English economist.
key·note (kē′nōt′) *n.* **1** *Music* The tonic of a key, from which it is named: also **key tone.** **2** A basic idea, fact, principle, or sentiment. — *v.t.* **·not·ed, ·not·ing** **1** To sound the keynote of. **2** To give the essential points of, as a political platform.
key·not·er (kē′nō′tər) *n.* The person selected to present the basic issues, especially of a political platform.
key-plug (kē′plug′) *n.* That part of a cylinder lock which receives the key, permitting it to turn when all the tumblers are in the release position. See illustration under LOCK.
Keys (kēz) *n. pl.* The 24 members of the House of Keys, the elective branch of the legislature of the Isle of Man.
Key·ser·ling (kī′zər·ling), **Count Hermann Alexander,** 1880–1946, German social philosopher and writer.
key signature *Music* The number of sharps or flats following the clef sign at the beginning of each staff, to indicate in what key the music is to be played.
keyst·er (kēs′tər) See KEISTER.
key·stone (kē′stōn′) *n.* **1** *Archit.* The uppermost and last-set stone of an arch, which completes it and locks its members together. **2** The fundamental element, as of a science or doctrine.

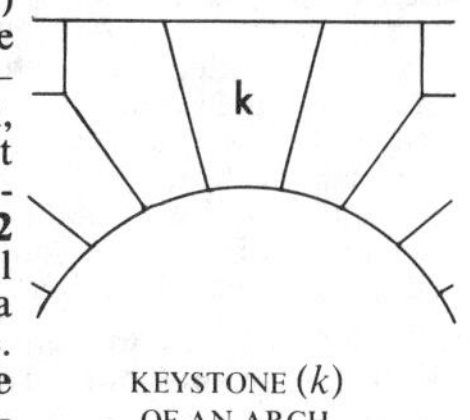

KEYSTONE (*k*) OF AN ARCH

Keystone State Nickname of PENNSYLVANIA.

key·way (kē′wā′) *n. Mech.* **1** The groove or recess in a shaft or wheel hub for the insertion of key: also called **key bed.** **2** The opening in a cylinder lock to receive the key.

Key West A port on **Key West Island,** westernmost of the Florida Keys.

K.G.B. In the former Soviet Union, a division of the Ministry of State Security. The K.G.B. was created in 1954 for internal and external espionage and policing, renowned for its meticulous and far-reaching methods of information-gathering. There were 17 divisions within the K.G.B., including the border guard, counterintelligence, and the secret police. [*Russian* K(omitet) G(osudarstvennoy) B(ezopasnosti)]

Kha·ba·rovsk **1** A mountainous territory (kray) in southeastern Russia, bordering the Sea of Okhotsk, and the territory of Amur; 965,400 square miles. **2** The capital of the Khabarovsk region; pop. 615,000, on the southwestern edge of the territory, near the disputed border with China.

khad·dar (kud′ər) *n.* Homespun cotton cloth made in India: also **khadi** (kä′dē). [< Hind. *khādar*]

Kha·kas·sia A republic within Russia, in the south central region of Siberia; capital, Abakan; 24,000 square miles, pop. 600,000. Formerly **the Khakass Autonomous Region** of the Soviet Union.

khak·i (kak′ē, kä′kē) *adj.* Of the color of dust; having a neutral tannish-brown or olive-drab color. —*n.* A light olive-drab or brownish cotton cloth. [< Hind. *khākī* dusty]

kha·lif (kä′lif, kal′if) See CALIPH.

Kha·lil (khä·lēl′), **El** The Arabic name for HEBRON.

Khal·kis (khäl·kēs′) The Greek name for CHALCIS.

kham·sin (kam′sin, kam·sēn′) *n. Meteorol.* A hot wind from the Sahara that prevails in Egypt before the vernal equinox; simoom. Also **kam·sean′**: sometimes spelled *kamsin.* [< Arabic *khamsīn* < *khamsūn* fifty; so called because it occurs for a period of 50 days]

khan[1] (kän, kan) *n.* An Oriental inn surrounding a courtyard. [< Arabic *khān* an inn]

khan[2] (kän, kan) *n.* In various Oriental countries, a ruler, chief, etc.; now a title of respect for any dignitary. See CHAM. [< Persian *khān* prince]

khan·ate (kän′āt, kan′-) *n.* The jurisdiction of a khan; a principality.

Kha·nia (khä·nyä′) The Greek name for CANEA.

khan·jar (khän′jär) See CANJIAR.

Khan·ka, Lake A lake on the China-Russian border, 1,700 square miles; in the territory (okrug) of Primor′ye. The country borders bisect the lake.

Khan·ty-Man·si An autonomous region (okrug) in Russia; capital, Khanty-Mansiysk; 200,000 square miles; pop. 1,300,000.

Khar·kiv **1** An eastern province in the Ukraine; 12,100 square miles, pop. 3,200,000. **2** The capital of the province of Kharkiv, pop. 1,700,000.

Khar·toum (kär·to͞om′) A city near the confluence of the Blue Nile with the White Nile; capital of Sudan. Also **Khar·tum′.**

Kha·si (kä′sē) **and Jain·ti·a** (jīn′tē·ə) **Hills** An autonomous district of western Assam, India; 6,141 square miles; capital, Shillong.

Kha·tan·ga Gulf A gulf on the western coast of the Laptev Sea, north of Siberia, Russia.

Khay·yám (kī·äm′), **Omar** See OMAR KHAYYAM.

khed·ah (ked′ə) See KEDDAH.

khe·dive (kə·dēv′) *n.* The title of the Turkish viceroy of Egypt from 1867 to 1914. [< Persian *khidīv* king]

Khe·lat (kə·lät′) See KALAT.

khen·em stone (ken′əm) In ancient Egyptian practice, the inscribed amulet placed on the body of the deceased, while passages were recited from the Book of the Dead.

Kher·son **1** A province in the Ukraine bordering the Black Sea, 11,000 square miles; pop. 1,300,000. **2** The capital of the Kherson province in the Ukraine; a port on the Dnieper near the opening to the Black Sea.

khid·mut·gar (kid′mət·gär) *n. Hindi* A male waiter. Also **khid′mat·gar.**

Khing·an Mountains A range of mountains in northeastern China, bordering Mongolia and China. The range is divided into the **Great Khingan Mountains** to the west and the **Little Khingan Mountains** to the east.

Khi·u·ma The former name of the island province of Hiiumaa, Estonia; 14 miles from the mainland in the Baltic Sea; 395 square miles; pop. 11,500.

Khi·va A city in Uzbekistan; former capital of an independent khanate.

Khmer *n.* **1** One of the ethnic groups of Cambodia, accounting for 95 percent of the population of the country. The other ethnic groups in Cambodia are the Chinese, Cham, and other Asian nationalities. **2** The traditional language of the Khmer population and the official language of Cambodia.

Khmer Republic The former name of Cambodia (1970–1975) a republic in SW Indochina; 53,668 square miles; capital, Phnom Penh; Also **the State of Kampuchia.**

Khnum (khno͞om) The ram-headed god associated with ancient Elephantine in Egypt; in early Egypt, the ram and other animals were considered as actual gods associated with particular cities.

Khoi·san (koi′sän) *n.* A family of languages spoken by Negroid tribes in SW Africa, including Bushman and Hottentot.

Kholm (khôlm) The Russian name for CHELM.

Khond (kond) *n.* **1** A member of an aboriginal hill people of India, of Dravidian stock. **2** Their Dravidian language.

Kho·ra·san (khō′rä·sän′) A province of NE Iran. Also **Khu′ra·san′**(kho͞o′-).

Khor·ram·shahr (kho͞or′räm·shär′) A port on the Shatt al Arab in SW Iran.

Kho·tan (kō′tän′) A town and oasis in SW Sinkiang province, China: Chinese *Hotien.*

Khrush·chev (khro͞osh′chef), **Nikita,** 1894–1971, U.S.S.R. official; first secretary of the Communist Party 1953–1964; chairman of the Council of Ministers (premier) 1958–1964.

Khu·fu (ko͞o′fo͞o) See CHEOPS.

Khu·zi·stan (kho͞o′zē·stän′) A province of SW Iran, corresponding to ancient Elam: formerly *Arabistan.*

Khy·ber Pass (kī′bər) A mountain pass on the India-Pakistan border; over 30 miles long: also *Khaiber Pass.*

Kia·mu·sze A city in the province of Manchuria, China; also **Chiamussu.**

Ki·an (kē·än′) A city in western Kiansi province, China.

Kiang·ling (jyäng′ling′) A city on the Yangtze in southern Hupeh province, China: formerly *Kingchow.*

Kiang·si (jyäng′shē′) A province in SE China; 65,000 square miles; capital, Nanchang.

Kiang·su (jyäng′sō′) A province in eastern China; 35,000 square miles; since 1949 divided administratively into **North Kiangsu;** 24,000 square miles; capital, Yangchow; and **South Kiangsu;** 11,000 square miles; capital, Wusih.

Kiao·chow (jyou′chou′) A former German leased territory on the SE coast of Shantung, China; 400 square miles.

kiaugh (kyäkh) *n. Scot.* Trouble; toil; worry.

Kia·yi (jyä′yē) See CHIAYI.

kib·blings (kib′lingz) *n. pl.* Small bits or strips cut from fish, used as bait by Newfoundland fishermen. [Cf. dial. E *kibble* grind coarsely]

kib·butz (ki·bo͞ots) *n. pl.* **·butz·im** (·bo͞o tsēm′) An Israeli collective or communal settlement, esp. a cooperative farm.

kibe (kīb) *n.* **1** A chap or crack in the flesh; an ulcerated chilblain. **2** A sore on the hoof of a sheep. [Cf. Welsh *cibi* a chilblain]

Ki·bei (kē′bā′) *n. pl.* **·bei** A citizen or citizens of the United States of Japanese parentage, born in America but educated in Japan. Compare ISSEI, NISEI. [< Japanese]

kib·itz (kib′its) *v.i. Colloq.* To act as a kibitzer. [Back formation < KIBITZER]

kib·itz·er (kib′it·sər) *n. Colloq.* One who meddles with other persons' affairs; specifically, a person who, although not a player, makes suggestions and gives gratuitous advice to card-players. [< Yiddish]

kib·lah (kib′lä) *n.* The direction toward which Moslems kneel and bow in prayer indicated by a niche on the wall in each mosque in Islam. See KAABA. [Arabic *qiblah* something placed opposite < *qabala* be opposite]

ki·bosh (kī′bosh) *n. Slang* Nonsense or humbug. **—to put the kibosh on** To put a stop to; do for. [Prob. < Yiddish]

kick (kik) *v.i.* **1** To strike out with the foot or feet; give a blow with the foot, as in swimming, propelling the ball in football, etc. **2** To strike out with the foot habitually: This horse *kicks.* **3** To recoil, as a firearm. **4** *Colloq.* To object; complain. —*v.t.* **5** To strike with the foot. **6** To drive or impel by striking with the foot. **7** To strike in recoiling. **8** In football, to score (a goal) by a kick. **—to kick about** (or **around**) **1** To abuse; neglect. **2** *Colloq.* To roam from place to place. **3** To be neglected; go unnoticed. **4** *Colloq.* To give thought or consideration to; discuss. **—to kick back** **1** To recoil violently or unexpectedly, as a gun. **2** *Colloq.* To pay (part of a commission, salary, etc.) to someone in a position to grant privilege, power, etc., usually as a bribe. **—to kick in** **1** *Colloq.* To contribute or participate by contributing. **2** *Slang* To die. **—to kick off** **1** In football, to put the ball in play by kicking it toward the opposing team. **2** *Slang* To die. **—to kick oneself** To have remorse or regret. **—to kick out** *Colloq.* To exclude or eject violently or suddenly, as with a kick. **—to kick the bucket** *Slang* To die. **—to kick up** *Slang* To make or stir up (trouble, confusion, etc.). **—to kick upstairs** To give an apparent promotion to (someone) in order to remove from a position of actual power. —*n.* **1** A blow with the foot; also, ability or power to kick. **2** The recoil of a firearm. **3** In football, one who kicks; also, a turn at kicking. **4** *Slang* An act of violent opposition or objection. **5** Something that stimulates or excites, as the alcoholic content of drink. **6** Effective action or power; energy; vim; pep. **7** *Slang* Stimulation; pleasure; thrill. **8** The depression in the bottom of a molded bottle. **9** *Slang* A pocket. **—on a kick** *Slang* Intensely but temporarily interested in a particular subject or activity; He's on a silent-movie *kick.* [ME *kike;* origin unknown]

Kick·a·poo (kik′ə·po͞o) *n.* One of a tribe of Algonquian Indians, formerly of northern Illinois: now on reservations in Kansas, Oklahoma, and Mexico.

kick·back (kik′bak′) *n.* **1** A recoil; repercussion; any reaction to something said or done. **2** Money comprising part of a commission, fee, etc., returned by prior agreement or coercion, often illegal or unethical.

kick·er (kik′ər) *n.* **1** One who or that which kicks. **2** *Slang* A surprising element or turn of events.

kick-off (kik′ôf′, -of′) *n.* **1** In football, the kick with which a game or half is begun. **2** Any beginning.

kick plate A metal plate affixed to the bottom portion of a door to protect its surface. Also **kicking plate.**

kick·shaw (kik′shô) *n.* **1** Something fantastic or trifling; a nameless trifle. **2** Any unsubstantial, fancy, or unrecognizable dish of food. Also **kick′shaws.** [Alter. of F *quelque chose* something]

kick·y (kik′ē) *adj.* **kick·i·er, kick·i·est** *Slang* Stimulating; exciting.

kid[1] (kid) *n.* **1** A young goat. **2** Leather, or, in the plural, gloves or shoes made from goatskin. **3** The meat of a young goat. **4** *Colloq.* A child or infant; youngster. **5** Formerly, a white servant in the American colonies indentured for four or five years. —*adj.* **1** Made of kidskin. **2** *Colloq.* Younger: my *kid* brother. —*v.t. & v.i.* **kid·ded, kid·ding** **1** To give birth to (young): said of goats. **2** *Slang* To make fun of (someone); tease jokingly. **3** *Slang* To deceive or try to deceive (someone); humbug. [< ON *kidh*] —**kid′der** *n.*

kid[2] (kid) *n.* **1** A small tub for sailors' rations. **2** On fishing vessels, a small wooden tub to hold fish when caught. [? Var. of KIT[1]]

Kidd (kid), **William,** 1650?–1701, British sea captain and pirate; hanged: called "Captain Kidd."

Kid·der·min·ster (kid′ər·min′stər) *n.* A two-ply ingrain carpet, showing warp and filling on each side. [from *Kidderminster,* England, where first made]

kid·dy (kid′ē) *n. pl.* **kid·dies** *Slang* A small child.

kid glove A glove made of kidskin or similar material. **—with kid gloves** In a tactful or gingerly manner.

kid-glove (kid′gluv′) *adj.* **1** Wearing or requiring kid gloves; hence, socially formal. **2** Over-nice; too fastidious to use the hands for work.

kid·nap (kid′nap) *v.t.* **·naped** or **·napped, ·nap·ing** or **·nap·ping** **1** To seize and carry off (someone) by force or fraud, usually so as to demand a ransom. 2 To steal (a child). [<KID[1] (def. 4) + *nap,* dial. var. of NAB] **—kid′·nap′er, kid′nap·per** *n.*

kid·ney (kid′nē) *n.* 1 *Biol.* One of a pair of bean-shaped glandular organs situated at the back of the abdominal cavity, close to the spinal column in man and other vertebrates. The kidneys serve in the excretion of waste products through a fine network of tubules to the ureters and thence to the bladder. ◆ Collateral adjective: *renal.* 2 Temperament. [Origin uncertain]

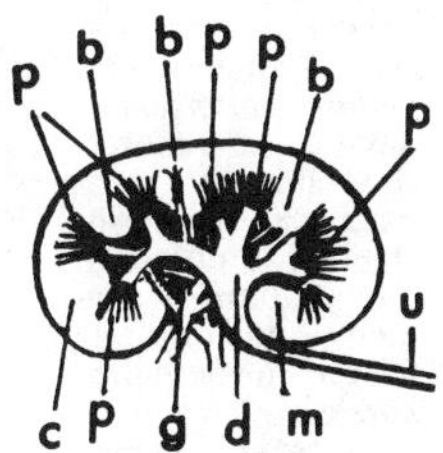

HUMAN KIDNEY
Longitudinal Section
p. Pyramids. *u.* Ureter. *g.* Papillae. *d.* Pelvis. *c.* Cortical portion. *b.* Bertin's columns.

kidney bean 1 The kidney-shaped seed of a plant of the bean family *(Phaseolus vulgaris);* French bean; haricot. 2 The plant itself. 3 The scarlet runner.

kidney ore A variety of hematite found in compact, kidney-shaped masses.

kidney stone 1 Nephrite. 2 A hard mineral formed in the kidney or bladder.

kidney vetch A European herb *(Anthyllis vulneraria)* having cloverlike flower heads, commonly yellow: once reputed useful in kidney troubles and for stanching wounds.

Ki·dron (kē′drən, kid′rən) See KEDRON.

kid·skin (kid′skin′) *n.* 1 Leather tanned from the skin of a young goat, used for gloves, shoes, etc. 2 The fur, used for coats.

kief (kēf) See KEF.

Kiel (kēl) A port in NW Germany, capital of Schleswig-Holstein, on the **Kiel Canal,** extending 61 miles from the Baltic Sea to the North Sea.

Kiel·ce (kyel′tse) A city in SE central Poland. *Russian* **Kel·tsy** (kel′tsi).

Kien (jyen) The chief river of Kweichow province, China, flowing 700 miles east to the Yangtze.

kier (kir) *n.* A cylindrical tank or vat in which fabric materials are boiled, cleaned, and bleached: also spelled *keir.* [Prob. <ON *ker* tub]

Kier·ke·gaard (kir′kə·gôr), **Sören Aabye,** 1813–55, Danish philosopher and theologian.

kie·sel·guhr (kē′zəl·gŏŏr) *n.* A fine, variously colored earth, derived from the accumulated deposits of the cell walls of diatoms, used as an absorbent for dynamite, as a polishing powder, etc.; diatomite. [<G *kiesel* flint + *guhr* sediment]

kie·ser·ite (kē′zər·īt) *n.* A white, friable, slightly soluble hydrous magnesium sulfate, $MgSO_4{\cdot}H_2O$. [after D. G. *Kieser,* German mineralogist]

kiest·er (kēs′tər) See KEISTER.

Ki·ev (kē·ev′, kē′ev; *Russian* kē′yef) A city on the Dnieper; of the Ukraine, historical capital of the princes of Kiev.

kike (kīk) *n. Slang* A Jew: a vulgar and offensive term of contempt. [Origin uncertain]

Ki·ku·yu (kē·kōō′yōō) *n. pl.* **·yu** 1 One of a Bantu tribe of British East Africa in the area of Mount Kenya. 2 The Bantu language of this tribe.

Ki·lau·e·a (kē′lou·ā′ə) An active crater on Mauna Loa volcano, Hawaii Island.

Kil·dare (kil·dâr′) A county in central Leinster province, eastern Ireland; 654 square miles; county town, Kildare.

kil·der·kin (kil′dər·kin) *n.* 1 A cask with the capacity of half a barrel. 2 An old English measure of 18 gallons. [<MDu. *kinderkin* little child]

ki·lim (ki·lēm′) *n.* A tapestry-woven type of rug or spread made in the Caucasus, Turkey, and other parts of the Near East. [<Turkish *kilīm* <Persian]

Kil·i·man·ja·ro (kil′i·män·jä′rō) The highest mountain of Africa, in NE Tanganyika; 19,565 feet.

Kil·ken·ny (kil·ken′ē) A county of southern Leinster province, Ireland; 796 square miles; county town, Kilkenny.

Kilkenny cats In Irish legend, two cats said to have fought till only their tails remained: supposed to refer to a contest between Kilkenny and Irishtown.

kill[1] (kil) *v.t.* 1 To deprive of life; cause the death of; slay. 2 To slaughter for food; butcher. 3 To destroy; put an end to: to *kill* love with hatred. 4 To destroy the active qualities of; neutralize: to *kill* lye. 5 To spoil the effect of; offset, as a color. 6 To cancel; cross out: to *kill* a paragraph. 7 To stop, as an engine or electric current. 8 To pass (time) aimlessly. 9 *Colloq.* To overwhelm with strong emotion, laughter, etc. 10 In tennis, to strike (the ball) to the opponent's court with such force that it cannot be returned. *—v.i.* 11 To slay or murder. 12 To suffer or undergo death; die: These plants *kill* easily. *—n.* 1 An animal killed as prey. 2 The act of killing, especially in hunting. **—in at the kill** Present at the climax of a chase or other undertaking. [ME *cullen, killen;* origin uncertain]

Synonyms (verb) : assassinate, butcher, destroy, dispatch, execute, massacre, murder, slaughter, slay. To *kill* is simply to *destroy* life, whether human, animal, or vegetable, with no suggestion of how or why. *Assassinate, execute, murder,* apply only to the taking of human life; to *murder* is to *kill* with premeditation and malicious intent; to *execute* is to *kill* in fulfilment of a legal sentence; to *assassinate* is to *kill* by assault; this word is chiefly applied to the *killing* of public or eminent persons through political motives, whether secretly or openly. To *slay* is to *kill* by a blow, or by a weapon. *Butcher* and *slaughter* apply primarily to the *killing* of cattle; to *butcher* when the *killing* is especially brutal; soldiers mown down in a hopeless charge are said to be *slaughtered* when no brutality on the enemy's part is implied. To *dispatch* is to *kill* swiftly and in general quietly, always with intention, with or without right.

kill[2] (kil) *n.* A creek, stream, or channel: an element in many U.S. geographical names: *Schuylkill.* [<Du. *kil*]

Kil·lar·ney (ki·lär′nē) An urban district of central County Kerry in SW Ireland near the three **Lakes of Killarney.**

kill·deer (kil′dir) *n. pl.* **·deers** or **·deer** A North American ring plover *(Oxyechus vociferus),* common in the Mississippi Valley. Also **kill′dee** (-dē). [Imit.; from its cry]

kill·er (kil′ər) *n.* 1 A destroyer of life; a slayer. 2 A murderer or an assassin. 3 A delphinoid cetacean of the genus *Orcinus* ; the **killer whale** of northern seas, especially *Orcinus orca* of the North Atlantic.

Kil·lie·cran·kie (kil′ē·krang′kē) A pass in the Grampians, Scotland; scene of Scottish victory over British forces, 1689.

kil·li·fish (kil′i·fish′) *n. pl.* **·fish** or **·fish·es** One of a family *(Cyprinodontidae)* of widely distributed small fishes *(Fundulus* and related genera), found in fresh or brackish waters. [Appar. KILL[2] + FISH]

kil·li·ki·nick (kil′ē·ki·nik′) See KINNIKINIC.

kill·ing (kil′ing) *n.* 1 The act of taking life; murder. 2 *Colloq.* A phenomenal profit resulting from bold speculation; a financial coup. 3 Any great success. *—adj.* 1 Slaying; that kills. 2 *Slang* Very amusing.

kill·kid (kil′kid′) *n.* Lambkill.

kill·joy (kil′joi′) *n.* One who spoils pleasure; a gloomy person.

kil·lock (kil′ək) *n. Naut.* A small anchor; specifically, a heavy stone in a wooden frame used as an anchor by small boats. Also **kil′lick.** [Origin unknown]

Kil·mar·nock (kil·mär′nək) A burgh in northern Ayrshire, Scotland.

Kil·mer (kil′mər), **Joyce,** 1886–1918, U.S. poet and editor; killed in World War I.

kiln (kil, kiln) *n.* An oven or furnace for baking, burning, or drying industrial products, as for burning bricks. [OE *cylne* <L *culina* kitchen]

kiln-dry (kil′drī′, kiln′-) *v.t.* **·dried, ·dry·ing** To dry in a kiln.

kil·o (kil′ō, kē′lō) *n. pl.* **kil·os** Kilogram: an abbreviated form.

kilo- *prefix* One thousand (times a given unit): used chiefly in the metric system of weights and measures: *kilogram, kilocalorie.* [<F <Gk. *chilioi* a thousand]

kil·o·cal·o·rie (kil′ə·kal′ə·rē) *n.* A great calorie: equal to one thousand calories.

kil·o·gram (kil′ə·gram) *n.* A measure of weight equal to 1,000 grams. See METRIC SYSTEM. Also **kil′o·gramme.**

kil·o·gram-me·ter (kil′ə·gram·mē′tər) *n.* A unit of work, the equivalent of the force expended in raising one kilogram one meter vertically: about 7.2 foot-pounds. Also **kil′o·gram-me′·tre.**

kil·o·hertz (kil′ə·hûrts) *n.* The unit of electrical frequency equal to one thousand cycles per second: formerly called *kilocycle.*

kil·o·li·ter (kil′ə·lē′tər) *n.* A measure of capacity equal to 1,000 liters. See METRIC SYSTEM. Also **kil′o·li′tre.**

kil·o·me·ter (kil′ə·mē′ tər, ki·lom′ə·tar) *n.* A measure of length equal to 1,000 meters. See METRIC SYSTEM. Also **kil′o·me′tre.**

kil·o·met·ric (kil′ə·met′rik) *adj.* Of, pertaining to, or expressed in terms of kilometers. Also **kil′o·met′ri·cal.**

kil·o·ton (kil′ə·tun) *n.* 1 A weight of 1,000 tons. 2 A unit equivalent to the explosive power of 1,000 tons of TNT; used in expressing the energy of atomic and thermonuclear weapons.

kil·o·watt (kil′ə·wät) *n.* One thousand watts: a unit of electrical power.

kil·o·watt-hour (kil′ə·wät·our′) *n.* The work done or the energy resulting from one kilowatt acting for one hour: equal to approximately 1.34 horsepower-hours.

Kil·pat·rick (kil·pat′rik), **Hugh Judson,** 1836–1881, U.S. general.

kilt (kilt) *n.* A short pleated skirt worn by Scottish Highland men. *—v.* 1 To make broad, vertical pleats in; pleat. 2 *Scot.* To tuck up, as the skirts of a dress. [Prob. <Scand. Cf. Dan. *kilte* tuck up.] **—kilt′ing** *n.*

KILT
a. Tartan. *b.* Kilt. *c.* Sporran.

kilt·ed (kil′tid) *adj.* 1 Attired in a kilt. 2 Made with pleats, as a dress. 3 Tucked up, as a skirt.

kil·ter (kil′tər) *n.* U.S. Dial. Proper or working order: My radio is out of *kilter.* Also, *Brit. Dial., kelter.*

kilt·ie (kil′tē) *n.* Scot. 1 One wearing a kilt. 2 A Highland soldier. Also **kilt′y.**

kilt·ing (kil′ting) *n.* A series of flat pleats, each of which partly overlaps the preceding one.

Ki·lung (kē′lŏŏng′) See KEELUNG.

Kim·ber·ley (kim′bər·lē) Capital city in Northern Cape Province, Republic of South Africa.

kim·ber·lite (kim′bər·līt) *n.* A biotite-bearing, commonly porphyritic, variety of peridotite. The residual clay resulting from its decomposition is the diamond-bearing "blue ground" of Kimberley.

kim·mer (kim′ər) *n.* Scot. 1 A gossip. 2 A young girl.

ki·mo·no (kə·mō′nə, ki·mō′nō) *n. pl.* **·nos** A Japanese loose robe fastened with a sash: imitated as an Occidental woman's negligée. [<Japanese]

kin (kin) *n.* 1 Relationship; consanguinity. 2 Collectively, relatives by blood. 3 *Obs.* A group of persons having a common ancestor; clan; tribe. *—adj.* Of the same blood or ancestry; hence, related; kindred. [OE *cyn.* Akin to KIND[2].

Synonyms (noun): affinity, alliance, birth, blood, consanguinity, descent, family, kind, kindred, race, relationship. *Kind* is broader than *kin,* denoting the most general *relationship,* as the whole human species in *mankind, humankind,* etc; *kin* denotes direct *relationship* that can be traced through either blood or marriage, preferably the former; either of these words may signify collectively all persons of the same blood or members of the same family, relatives, or relations. *Affinity* denotes *relationship* by marriage, *consanguinity* denotes *relationship* by blood. There are no true antonyms of *kin* or *kindred,* except those by negatives, since strangers, aliens, foreigners, and foes may still be *kin* or *kindred.* See KINDRED.

-kin *suffix* Little; small: *lambkin.* [<MDu. *-kijn, -ken*]

Kin·a·ba·lu (kin'ə·bə·lo͞o') The highest mountain in Borneo, in British North Borneo; 13,455 feet.

kin·aes·the·sia (kin'is·thē'zhə, -zhē·ə), **kin·aes·the·sis** (kin'is·thē'sis) See KINESTHESIA, etc.

kin·ase (kin'ās, kī'nās) *n. Biochem.* A ferment capable of activating another ferment, as zymogen. [<KIN(ETIC) + -ASE]

Kin·caid (kin·kād') An archeological site in southern Illinois where ceremonial temple mounds are found, thought to date from 1300 to 1700 B.C.

Kin·car·dine (kin·kär'din) A county in eastern Scotland on the North Sea; 383 square miles; county town, Stonehaven: also *The Mearus.* Also **Kin·car'dine·shire** (-shir).

Kin·chin·jun·ga (kin'chin·jung'gə) A former name for KANCHENJUNGA.

Kin·chow (kin'chou', *Chinese* jin'jō') See CHINCHOW.

kind[1] (kīnd) *adj.* **1** Having gentleness, tenderness, or goodness of heart; humane; kindly; also, proceeding from or expressing good-heartedness: *kind* words. **2** Gentle or tractable, as an animal. **3** *Archaic* Affectionate; loving. **4** *Obs.* Characteristic; native. See synonyms under AMIABLE, AMICABLE, CHARITABLE, FRIENDLY, GOOD, HUMANE, PLEASANT, PROPITIOUS. [OE *gecynde*]

kind[2] (kīnd) *n.* **1** Essential or distinguishing quality; sort. **2** A number of persons or things of the same character; a class. **3** A modification or variety of a given sort of thing; a species. **4** *Obs.* Nature in general, or natural disposition. See synonyms under AFFINITY, KIN, SORT. —**in kind 1** With something of the same sort: to repay a blow *in kind.* **2** Specifically, in produce instead of money: to pay taxes *in kind.* —**of a kind 1** Of the same sort or variety. **2** Of imperfect quality; of sorts; poetry *of a kind.* [OE *cynd.* Akin to KIN.]

kin·der·gar·ten (kin'dər·gär'tən) *n.* A school for little children in which instructive diversions, object lessons, and healthful games are prominent features. [<G <*kinder* children + *garten* garden]

kin·der·gart·ner (kin'dər·gärt'nər) *n.* A kindergarten teacher or pupil. Also **kin'der·gar'·ten·er** (-gär'tən·ər)· [<G]

kin·der·spiel (kin'dər·shpēl') *n. German* A dramatic piece or entertainment performed by children.

kind-heart·ed (kīnd'här'tid) *adj.* Having a kind and sympathetic nature. —**kind'-heart'·ed·ly** *adv.* —**kind'-heart'ed·ness** *n.*

kin·dle[1] (kin'dəl) *v.* **·dled, ·dling** *v.t.* **1** To cause (a flame, fire, etc.) to burn; light. **2** To set fire to; ignite. **3** To excite or inflame, as the feelings or passions. **4** To make bright or glowing as if with flame. —*v.i.* **5** To take fire; start burning. **6** To become excited or inflamed. **7** To become bright or glowing. See synonyms under BURN[1]. [ON *kynda*]

kin·dle[2] (kin'dəl) *v.t.* & *v.i.* **·dled, ·dling** To give birth to (young). —*n. Dial.* Progeny. [ME *kindlen.* Akin to KIND[2].]

kin·dler (kind'lər) *n.* **1** One who or that which kindles, illumines, or animates. **2** A piece of light wood or artificial composition used in kindling fires.

kind·less (kīnd'lis) *adj.* **1** *Poetic* Heartless; unkind. **2** *Obs.* Unnatural. —**kind'less·ly** *adv.*

kin·dling (kind'ling) *n.* **1** Material with which a fire is started or kindled. **2** The act of starting a fire or causing to burn. **3** The act of arousing emotion, ambition, etc.

kind·ly (kīnd'lē) *adj.* **·li·er, ·li·est 1** Having or manifesting kindness; sympathetic. **2** Having a favorable or grateful effect; beneficial. **3** *Obs.* Proper to its kind; natural; native; akin. —*adv.* **1** In a kind manner or spirit; good-naturedly. **2** *Obs.* By nature; naturally. See synonyms under FRIENDLY, PLEASANT, PROPITIOUS. —**kind'li·ness** *n.*

kind·ness (kīnd'nis) *n.* **1** The quality of being kind; good will; kindly disposition. **2** A kind act; a favor. **3** A kindly feeling. See synonyms under BENEVOLENCE, MERCY.

kind of Somewhat.

kin·dred (kin'drid) *adj.* **1** Of the same family; related by blood; akin. **2** Of a like nature or character; congenial. —*n.* **1** Relationship; consanguinity. **2** Collectively: relatives by blood; kind. **3** Affinity. [Earlier *kynred* <OE *cyn* family + *-rœden* state]

Synonyms (noun): kin, kinfolk, kinsmen, relations, relatives. *Kin* and *kindred* are used to denote both relationship and the persons related. See AFFINITY, KIN. Compare FAMILY.

kine (kīn) *n. Archaic* Cattle: plural of COW[1].

kin·e·mat·ics (kin'ə·mat'iks) *n. pl. (construed as singular)* That branch of mechanics treating of the motion of bodies in the abstract and without reference to the action of forces. [<Gk. *kinēma, -atos* movement <*kineein* move] —**kin'e·mat'ic** or **·i·cal** *adj.* —**kin'e·mat'i·cal·ly** *adv.*

kin·e·mat·o·graph (kin'ə·mat'ə·graf, -gräf) See CINEMATOGRAPH.

kin·e·phan·tom (kin'ə·fan'təm) *n.* The illusion of reversed motion in a fast-moving object, as the spokes of a wheel in a motion picture. [<KINE(MATOGRAPH) + PHANTOM]

kin·e·scope (kin'ə·skōp) *n.* **1** A vacuum tube attached to a prepared screen against which a beam of electrons reproduces the images sent out from a television transmitter. **2** A filmed record of a television program made with such a device: also **kin·e** (kin'ē). [<KINE(MATOGRAPH) + -SCOPE]

ki·ne·si·at·rics (ki·nē'sē·at'riks) *n.* The treatment of disease by muscular movement or exercise. [<Gk. *kinēsis* motion + -IATRICS]

ki·ne·sim·e·ter (ki·nə·sim'ə·tər) *n.* An instrument for measuring the motion of a part. Also **ki·ne·si·om·e·ter** (ki·nē'sē·om'ə·tər).

ki·ne·si·ther·a·py (ki·nē'si·ther'ə·pē) *n. Med.* A mode of treating disease by muscular movements. [<Gk. *kinēsis* motion + THERAPY]

kin·es·the·si·a (kin'is·thē'zhə, -zhē·ə) *n. Psychol.* The perception or consciousness of one's own muscular movements: often spelled *kinaesthesia.* Also **kin'es·the'sis** (-thē'sis). [<NL <Gk. *kineein* move + *aisthēsis* perception] —**kin'es·thet'ic** (-thet'ik) *adj.*

ki·net·ic (ki·net'ik) *adj.* **1** Producing motion; motor. **2** Consisting in or depending upon motion; active: distinguished from *potential*: *kinetic* energy. [<Gk. *kinētikos* <*kineein* move]

kinetic lead *Mil.* In gunnery, the correction made for the relative motion of a target when the lead angle is computed.

ki·net·ics (ki·net'iks) *n. pl. (construed as singular)* That branch of dynamics treating of the production or modification of motion in bodies.

kinetic theory *Physics* Any theory of the constitution of bodies which explains their properties by the motion of their particles, especially that according to which the elasticity of gases is due to the rapid motion of their molecules, which dart about in straight lines with an average velocity that increases with the temperature, until deflected by encounters with one another or with the walls of the containing vessel. This theory has been found capable of explaining nearly all the phenomena of gases, and is now generally accepted.

kin·folk (kin'fōk') *n. pl.* Relatives collectively; kin. Also **kin'folks**: also *kinsfolk, kinspeople.* See synonyms under KINDRED.

king (king) *n.* **1** The sovereign male ruler of a kingdom. ◆ Collateral adjective: *regal.* **2** One who or that which is preeminent among others of the same kind or class; a leader; chief; head. **3** A person or thing of great importance, position, or power: a *king* of finance. **4** A playing card bearing the semblance of a king. **5** In chess, the principal piece; in checkers, a piece that has reached the adversary's king row, and may then be moved in any direction. [OE *cyng*]

King (king), **Charles Glen,** 1878–1956, U.S. chemist. —**Ernest Joseph,** 1878–1956, U.S. admiral; Chief of Naval Operations in World War II. —**Martin Luther, Jr.,** 1929–1968, U.S. leader of nonviolent civil rights movement for Negroes; winner of Nobel peace prize in 1964; assassinated. —**Rufus,** 1775–1827, U.S. statesman and diplomat. —**William Lyon Mackenzie,** 1874–1950, Canadian premier, 1921–26, 1926–1930, 1935–48.

king apple A kind of winter apple.

King Arthur See ARTHUR.

king·bird (king'bûrd') *n.* An American tyrant flycatcher (genus *Tyrannus*).

king·bolt (king'bōlt') *n.* A vertical central bolt attaching the body of a vehicle to the fore axle and serving as a pivot in turning.

King Charles spaniel See under SPANIEL.

King·chow (king'jō') A former name for KIANGLING.

king crab A large marine arachnid *(Limulus polyphemus)* having a horseshoe-shaped carapace, a posterior shield composed of the abdominal segments, and a long telson: also called *horseshoe crab.*

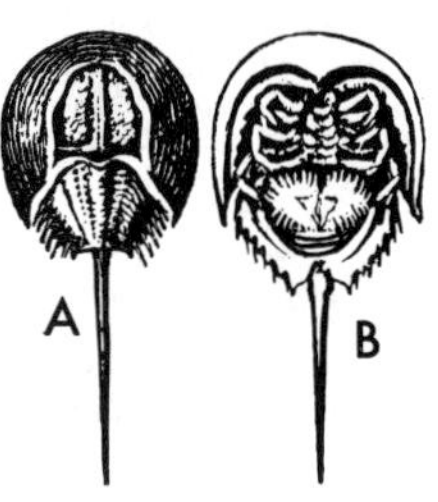

KING CRAB
A. Shell, or carapace, seen from above.
B. Under side, showing legs and telson.

king·craft (king'kraft', -kräft') *n.* The craft or calling of kings; kingly statesmanship.

king·cup (king'kup') *n.* **1** Any of several buttercups, especially the bulbous buttercup *(Ranunculus bulbosus)* and the creeping buttercup *(R. repens).* **2** The common marsh marigold.

king·dom (king'dəm) *n.* **1** The territory, people, state, or realm ruled by a king or a queen; a monarchy. **2** The spiritual dominion of God on earth. **3** Any separate field of independent authority, action, or influence; sphere. **4** One of the three primary divisions of natural objects known as the *animal, vegetable,* and *mineral kingdoms.*

king·fish (king'fish') *n. pl.* **·fish** or **·fish·es 1** One of various American food fishes (genus *Menticirrhus*), especially *M. saxatilis,* common on the northern Atlantic coast. **2** The opah. **3** The cero. **4** *U.S. Slang* A vainglorious person.

king·fish·er (king'fish'ər) *n.* Any of several non-passerine birds (family *Alcedinidae*), generally crested, with straight, deeply cleft bill, which feed on fish; especially, the **eastern belted kingfisher** of the United States *(Megaceryle alcyon).*

King George's Falls See AUGHRABIES FALLS.

King Horn In certain medieval English and French romances, an exiled prince who falls in love and after many hardships wins his bride.

King James Bible See under BIBLE.

King Lear See LEAR.

king·let (king'lit) *n.* **1** A little or unimportant king. **2** Any of several small birds, resembling the warblers, especially the American **golden-crowned kinglet** *(Regulus satrapa)* and the **ruby-crowned kinglet** *(Regulus calendula).*

king·ly (king'lē) *adj.* **·li·er, ·li·est** Pertaining to or worthy of a king; regal; kinglike. —*adv.* In a regal or kingly way; royally. —**king'li·ness** *n.*

Synonyms (adj.): august, kinglike, majestic, princely, regal, royal. *Royal* denotes that which actually belongs or pertains to a monarch; *regal* denotes that which in outward state is appropriate for a king; a subject may assume *regal* magnificence in residence, dress, and equipage. *Kingly* denotes that which is worthy of a king in personal qualities, especially of character and conduct; *princely* is especially used of treasure, expenditure, gifts, etc., as *princely* munificence, a *princely* fortune, where *royal* would change the sense. See IMPERIAL. *Antonyms*: beggarly, contemptible, inferior, mean, poor, servile, slavish, vile.

King·man Reef (king'mən) The northernmost atoll of the Line Islands, administered (1934) by the United States Navy.

king-of-arms (king'uv·ärmz') *n.* In Great Britain, one of a body of officials instituted in 1484 to examine and inquire concerning rights and titles in heraldry.

king·palm (king'päm') *n.* Any of a genus *(Archontophoenix)* of tropical and subtropical forest feather palms.

king·pin (king'pin') *n.* **1** A kingbolt. **2** In tenpins, the foremost pin of a set arranged in order for playing: also called *headpin.* **3** In ninepins, the center pin. **4** *Slang* A person of first importance.

king·post (king'pōst') *n.* A single vertical strut supporting the apex of a triangular truss and resting on a crossbeam. Also **king post.**

king row In checkers, the row of squares nearest to either of the players.

Kings (kingz) Either of two books of the Old Testament chronicling the history of the Jewish kings.

king salmon The quinnat, or North Pacific salmon.

king's bench See under COURT.

Kings Canyon National Park A mountainous region in the Sierra Nevada, east central California; 708 square miles; noted for its giant sequoia trees; established 1940.

king's counsel In the British Empire, barristers who are designated as counsel of the crown and cannot afterward plead against the crown without permission: also *queen's counsel.*

king's English See under ENGLISH.

king's evidence See STATE'S EVIDENCE.

king's evil Scrofula: once supposed to be curable by a monarch's touch.

king•ship (king′ship) *n.* **1** Royal state; kinghood. **2** Government by a king **3** The person of a king.

Kings•ley (kingz′lē), **Charles,** 1819–75, English novelist. **—Henry,** 1830–76, novelist; brother of Charles. **—Sidney,** born 1906, U.S. playwright.

King's Lynn A municipal borough of western Norfolk, England: also *Lynn, Lynn Regis.*

Kings Mountain A ridge in NW South Carolina; scene of an American victory in the Revolutionary War, 1780.

king snake A large harmless colubrine snake *(Lampropeltis getulus)* of the southern United States that kills other snakes and feeds largely on rats and mice.

king's silver A soft, very pure silver formerly used for costly dishes and plate.

King•ston (king′stən, kingz′tən) **1** A port, capital of Jamaica, British West Indies. **2** A city on the Hudson River in SE New York. **3** A city in SE Ontario, Canada.

King•ston–on–Thames (king′stən·on′temz′, kingz′tən) A municipal borough in NE Surrey, England; site of the King's Stone on which the West Saxon kings were crowned and of the last battle of the Civil War, 1648. Also **King′ston–up•on′–Thames′.**

King•ston–up•on–Hull (king′stən·ə·pon′hul′, kingz′tən-) See HULL.

Kings•town (king′stən, kingz′toun) Capital of St. Vincent in the Windward Islands.

king's yellow A vivid yellow pigment, formerly obtained from orpiment, now also made synthetically from arsenic trisulfide: also called *Chinese yellow.*

King•teh•chen (jing′du′jun′) The former name of FOWLIANG.

king•truss (king′trus′) *n.* A truss, as in roofing, having a kingpost.

king•wood (king′wo͝od′) *n.* **1** A Brazilian tree *(Dalbergia cearensis)* prized for its wood of fine texture having handsome dark–violet stripings. **2** The wood of this tree.

kink[1] (kingk) *n.* **1** An abrupt bend, twist, loop, or tangle, as in a wire rope. **2** A tightly twisted curl, as in hair or wool. **3** A mental quirk or prejudice. **4** An original, novel, or clever way of doing something. **5** A fashion or fad. **6** A hindrance, obstruction, or difficulty. **7** A crick; cramp. See synonyms under WHIM. **—***v.t. & v.i.* To form or cause to form a kink or kinks. [<Du., twist, curl]

kink[2] (kingk) *n. Scot.* **1** A violent or convulsive laughing fit. **2** The whoop in whooping cough. **—***v.i.* **1** To laugh violently or convulsively. **2** To gasp, as in laughing or coughing.

kink•a•jou (king′kə·jo͞o) *n.* A nocturnal, arboreal, raccoon-like carnivore (genus *Potos,* family *Procyonidae*) of the warmer parts of South and Central America, having large eyes, soft woolly fur, and a long prehensile tail. [<F *quincajou* < Tupian]

KINKAJOU
(Up to 3 feet long including the tail)

kink•y (king′kē) *adj.* **kink•i•er, kink•i•est 1** Full of kinks; snarled. **2** Closely or tightly curled, as hair. **3** *Slang* Odd; queer; eccentric. **4** *Slang* Involving or appealing to unconventional or perverted sexual tastes. **5** *Slang* Unconventional in a sophisticated way. **—kink′i•ly** *adv.* **—kink′i•ness** *n.*

kin•ni•ki•nic (kin′ē·kə·nik′) *n.* **1** The leaves or bark of certain plants, as the willow and sumac, prepared for smoking. **2** Any plant so used. Also **kin′ni•kin•nic′, kin′ni•kin•nick′:** sometimes *killikinnick.* [<Algonquian, that which is mixed]

Kin•ross (kin·rôs′), A county of east central Scotland; 82 square miles; county town, Kinross. Also **Kin•ross•shire** (-shir).

Kin•sey (kin′zē), **Alfred,** 1894–1956, U.S. zoologist; especially known for his statistical reports on sexual behavior in the United States.

kins•folk (kinz′fōk′), **kins•peo•ple** (kinz′pē′pəl) See KINFOLK.

Kin•sha•sa (kēn·shä′sä) The capital of Zaire.

kin•ship (kin′ship) *n.* Relationship, especially by blood.

kins•man (kinz′mən) *n. pl.* **•men** (-mən) A blood relation. **—kins′wom′an** (-wo͝om′ən) *n. fem.*

Synonyms: connection, relative, relation. *Kinsman* is preferred in certain cases, on the ground of greater clearness, to *relative, relation, connection.* A man's *relative* or *relation* is one who is related to him, either by blood, as a brother (a *kinsman*), or by law, as a brother–in–law (not a *kinsman*), or, loosely, by some other bond. *Connection* is still more vague and unsatisfactory. The same applies to *kinswoman.* See KINDRED.

Kio•ga (kyō′gə) See KYOGA, LAKE

ki•osk (kē·osk′, kē′osk, kī′-) *n.* An open ornamental summerhouse in Turkey now imitated in other countries and modified to serve as a booth, news–stand, bandstand, or the like. [< Turkish *kiūshk*]

Kio•to (kyō′tō) See KYOTO.

Ki•o•wa (kī′ə·wä, -wə) *n.* One of a fierce tribe of Plains Indians of the Kiowan linguistic stock, formerly inhabiting parts of Nebraska and Wyoming. Also **Ki′o•way** (-wā).

Ki•o•wan (kī′ə·wən) *n.* A North American Indian linguistic stock consisting of the Kiowas.

kip[1] (kip) *n.* **1** The untanned skin of a calf. **2** The untanned skin of an adult of any small breed of cattle. **3** A collection of such skins composed of a specific number. Also **kip′•skin′** (-skin′). [Origin uncertain]

kip[2] (kip) *n. Slang* **1** A lodging house. **2** A bed there. **3** *Obs.* A brothel. [Cf. Dan. *horekippe* brothel]

Kip•chak (kip·chäk′) *n.* **1** One of the Mongol Tatars of the Golden Horde, who established a kingdom in Europe and Asia in the 13th century, with its capital Sarai on the lower Volga. **2** One of a group of tribes inhabiting Turkestan. **3** The Turkic language of the Kipchaks.

Kip•ling (kip′ling), **Rudyard,** 1865–1936, English author and poet.

kip•per (kip′ər) *n.* **1** A salmon or herring cured by kippering. **2** The male salmon during the spawning season. **—***v.t.* To cure, as fish, by splitting, salting, and drying or smoking. [? OE *cypera* spawning salmon]

Kirch•hoff (kirkh′hôf), **Gustav Robert,** 1824–1887, German physicist.

Kir•ghiz *n. pl.* **-ghiz** or **-ghiz•es** (also **Kyr•gyz**) **1** One of a Turkic people of Mongolian descent, dwelling in the Asian region, south of Kazakhstan. **2** The Turkic language of the Kirghiz.

Kir•ghiz•stan (also Kyr•gyz•stan; the Kyrgyz Republic) A republic in central Asia, a member of the Commonwealth of Independent States; 76,042 square miles; capital, Bishkek (formerly Frunze); pop. 4,500,000; formerly the **Kirghiz Soviet Socialist Republic** (1936–1991).

Kirghiz Range A vast mountain range bordering south Kazakhstan and covering Kirghizstan.

Ki•rin (kē′rin′) A province of east central Manchuria; 45,000 square miles.

Kir•jath–Ar•ba (kûr′jath·är′bə) The ancient name for HEBRON.

kirk (kûrk) *n.* **1** *Scot.* A church or the church. **2** The established Presbyterian Church of Scotland, as distinguished from the Roman Catholic Church, the Church of England, or the Episcopal Church.

Kirk•cal•dy (kər·kôl′dē, -kô′dē) A port on the Firth of Forth in southern Fifeshire, Scotland.

Kirk•cud•bright (kər·ko͞o′brē) A county in SW Scotland; 899 square miles; capital, Kircudbright. Also **Kirk•cud′bright•shire** (-shir).

Kirk•la•re•li (kərk·lä′rə·lē) A town in northern Turkey in Europe: scene of a Bulgarian victory over the Turks, 1912. Formerly **Kirk–ki•lis•sa** (kirk′kē·lē·sä′).

Kirk•man (kûrk′mən) *n. pl.* **•men** (-mən) A member of the Church of Scotland.

Kir•kuk (kir·kook′) A city in NE Iraq.

Kirk•wall (kûrk′wôl, -wəl) A port, county seat of Orkney county, Scotland.

Kir•man (kir·män′) *n.* A type of Persian rug having naturalistic floral patterns and soft, rich coloring. [from *Kerman,* Iran, where originally made]

Kir•man (kir·män′) See KERMAN.

kir•mess (kûr′mis) See KERMESS.

kirn[1] (kûrn, kirn) *n. Scot.* The last sheaf of the harvest; hence, a harvest celebration. [Origin obscure]

kirn[2] (kûrn, kirn) *n. Scot.* Churn.

kirn•milk (kûrn′milk′, kirn′-) *n. Scot.* Buttermilk.

Ki•rov 1 A city on the Vyatka river in west central Russia. **2** The territory (oblast) around the Vyatka river and Severnyye Uvaly (the northern hills).

Ki•ro•va•bad (also **Gyandzha, Gäncä**) The second largest city in Azerbaijan, in the Caucasus region; formerly (1830–1920) Elisavetpol, (1921–1935) Gandzha.

Kirsch (kirsh) *n.* A brandy distilled from the fermented juice of cherries and their pits, originally from Germany and Alsace. Also **Kirsch′•was′ser** (-väs′ər).

kirs•ten (kûr′sən) *v.t. Scot.* To christen. Also **kir′sen. —kirs′ten•ing** *adj.*

kir•tle (kûrt′l) *n.* A garment with a skirt; a frock or mantle. [OE *cyrtel,* prob. ult. <L *curtus* short] **—kir′tled** *adj.*

kish (kish) *n.* Graphite which forms on the top of molten iron high in carbon. [<G *kies* gravel, pyrites]

Ki•shi•nev (kish′i·nef, *Russian* kē·shē·nyôf′) The capital of the Moldavian S.S.R.: Rumanian *Chișinău.*

Kis•ka (kis′kə) An island in the Rat Island group of the Aleutian Islands, SW Alaska.

Kis•lew (kis′lef) *n.* A Hebrew month: also called *Chisleu.* Also **Kish′lev, Kis′lev.** See CALENDAR (*Hebrew*).

kis•met (kiz′met, kis′-) *n.* Appointed lot; fate. [<Turkish <Arabic *qisma* <*qasama* divide]

Kis•pest (kish′pesht) A city in north central Hungary SE of Budapest.

kiss (kis) *n.* **1** An affectionate salutation by contact of the lips. **2** A gentle touch. **3** One of various forms of confectionery. [<*v.*] **—***v.t. & v.i.* **1** To touch with the lips, as in greeting or love. **2** To touch slightly. **3** *Printing* To touch: said of printed characters. See synonyms under CARESS. [OE *cyssan* kiss] **—kiss′er** *n.*

kissing bug 1 A hemipterous insect *(Reduvius personatus)* which occasionally bites man on the lips or cheeks: also called *masked hunter.* **2** One of several other bloodsucking insects, as the sharp–beaked *Melanolestes picipes.*

kist (kist) *n. Scot.* A chest, box, or coffin. **—kist′ful** *n.*

Kist•na (kist′nə) A river in southern India, flowing 800 miles across the Deccan: also *Krishna.*

kist•vaen (kist′vīn) *n.* An ancient, box–shaped sepulchral chamber smaller than a dolmen, made of flat stones: sometimes spelled *cistvaen.* Also **kist.** [Welsh *cist faen* <*cist* coffin + *faen* stone]

kit[1] (kit) *n.* **1** A tub, pail, or box for packing. **2** A small pail. **3** A collection of articles and appliances for any special purpose; an outfit; also, a group of persons; especially, a political constituency. **4** A collection of persons or things; the whole lot: the whole *kit* and caboodle of them. Compare CABOODLE. [<MDu. *kitte*]

kit[2] (kit) *n.* A kitten.

kit[3] (kit) *n.* A small, three-stringed violin, used from the 16th to the 18th century: also *kit violin.* [Origin unknown]
Kit (kit) Diminutive of CATHERINE, CHRISTOPHER.
Ki·ta·za·to (kē·tä·zä·tō), **Shibamiro,** 1852–1931, Japanese bacteriologist and pathologist; discoverer of the bacilli of bubonic plague and of dysentery. Also **Ki·ta·sa·to.**
kitch·en (kich′ən) *n.* **1** A room specially set apart and containing the necessary utensils for cooking food. **2** A culinary department. [OE *cycene,* ult. <L *coquina* < *coquere* cook]
kitch·en·er (kich′ən·ər) *n.* **1** *Brit.* A cookstove. **2** A kitchen employee; also, one who has charge of a kitchen; chef.
Kitch·en·er (kich′ən·ər), **Horatio Herbert,** 1850–1916, first Earl of Khartoum; English statesman and field marshal.
kitch·en·ette (kich′ən·et′) *n.* A small kitchen.
kitchen garden A garden in which vegetables and, sometimes, fruits are grown for home use.
kitchen midden *Anthropol.* A mound composed of shells, bones, rude stone implements, and other refuse of primitive or prehistoric dwellings. [Trans. of Dan. *kökkenmödding*]
kitchen police *Mil.* Enlisted men detailed to perform routine kitchen chores; also, such duty. Abbr. *K.P.*
kitch·en·ware (kich′ən·wâr′) *n.* Kitchen utensils.
kite (kīt) **1** Any of certain birds of prey of the hawk family *(Falconidae),* having long, pointed wings and a forked tail. Some species are scavengers, as the **pariah kite** (genus *Milvus*) of India. **2** A light frame, usually of wood, covered with paper or some light fabric, to be flown in the air at the end of a long string. **3** *Naut.* One of several light

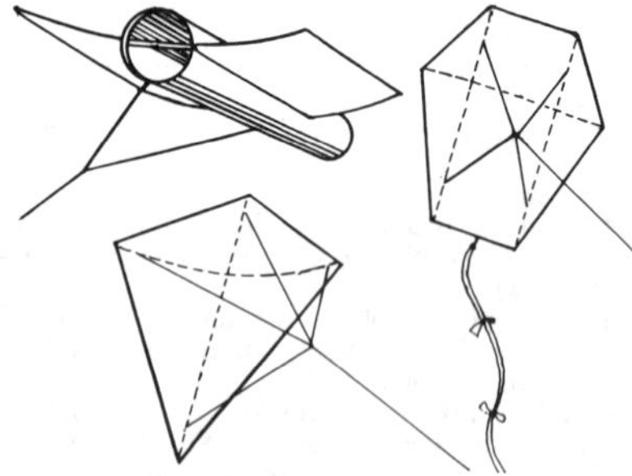

TYPES OF KITES *(def. 2)*

sails for use in a very light wind, as skysails. **4** In commerce, any negotiable paper not representing a genuine transaction but so employed as to obtain money, sustain credit, etc.; also, a bank check which is drawn with insufficient funds on deposit to secure the advantage of the time period prior to collection: considered to be a malpractice. **5** A shrewd and greedy bargainer; a sharper. **— to fly one's own kite** To tend to one's own affairs. **—** *v.* **kit·ed, kit·ing** *v.i.* **1** To soar or fly like a kite; move along swiftly. **2** In commerce, to obtain money or credit by the use of kites. **—** *v.t.* **3** In commerce, to issue as a kite. [OE *cȳta*]
kite balloon See under BALLOON.
kith (kith) *n. Scot. & Brit. Dial.* One's friends, acquaintances, or associates.
kith and kin Friends and relatives.
Ki·thai·ron (kē′the·rôn′) The Greek name for CITHAERON.
kith·a·ra (kith′ə·rə) *n.* A cithara.
kithe (kīth) *v.i. & v.t. Scot.* To recognize; show; make or become known: also spelled *kythe.*
kit·ling (kit′ling) *n. Scot.* A young cat; kitten.
kitsch (kich) *n.* Art or literary works, etc., having broad popular appeal and little aesthetic merit. [<G]
kit·tel (kit′l) *n.* A white cotton gown worn by orthodox Jews for solemn occasions and as a burial garment. [<G, a smock]
kit·ten (kit′n) *n.* A young cat or other feline animal. **—** *v.t. & v.i.* **·tened, ·ten·ing** To give birth to (kittens). [<OF *chitoun,* dim. of *chat* a cat]
kit·ten·ish (kit′ən·ish) · *adj.* Playfully coy. **— kit′ten·ish·ly** *adv.* **— kit′ten·ish·ness** *n.*
kit·ti·wake (kit′ē·wāk) *n.* A gull of northern seas (genus *Rissa*), having the hind toe rudimentary. [Imit.]
kit·tle (kit′l) *adj. Scot.* Skittish; ticklish.
kit·tool (ki·to͞ol′) *n.* A stiff, elastic fiber from the leaves of the fishtail palm *(Caryota urens)* of Ceylon and India: used for machine brushes. Also **kit·tul′.** [<Singhalese *kitūl* <Skt. *hintāla* marshy date tree]
Kitt·redge (kit′rij), **George Lyman,** 1860–1941, U.S. educator, author, editor, and scholar.
kit·ty[1] (kit′ē) *n. pl.* **·ties 1** In certain card games, the pool to which each player contributes a percentage of his winnings, used to cover expenses, the cost of refreshments, etc.: also called *widow.* **2** Hence, money pooled for any specific purpose. **3** In certain card games, a hand or part of a hand left over after a deal, which may be used by the highest bidder. [Cf. obs. *kidcote* a prison]
kit·ty[2] (kit′ē) *n. pl.* **·ties 1** A kitten. **2** A pet name for a cat.
Kit·ty (kit′ē) Diminutive of CATHERINE.
kit·ty-cor·nered (kit′ē·kôr′nərd) See CATER-CORNERED.
Kitty Hawk A village on Albermarle Sound, North Carolina: here Wilbur and Orville Wright made the first sustained airplane flight in the United States, December, 1903.
kit violin See KIT[3].
Kiung·shan (kyo͝ong′shän′, *Chinese* jyo͝ong′·shän′) A city in northern Hainan, Kwangtung province, China. Former name: **Kiung′chow′** (-chou′, *Chinese* -jō′).
Kiu·shu (kyo͞o·sho͞o) See KYUSHU.
ki·va (kē′və) *n.* A room built in a Pueblo dwelling or beneath it, devoted to secret religious ceremonies, tribal councils, etc., entered by an opening in the roof. [<Hopi]
kiv·er[1] (kiv′ər) *v.t. & n. Scot.* Cover; shelter.
kiv·er[2] (kiv′ər) *n.* A shallow keeve.
Ki·vu (kē′vo͞o), **Lake** A lake in east central Africa on the Belgian Congo border; 1,110 square miles.
Ki·wa·ni·an (kə·wä′nē·ən, -wô′-) *n.* A member of a Kiwanis Club.
Ki·wa·nis Clubs (kə·wä′nis, -wô′-) A chain of clubs of businessmen in the United States and Canada, having the slogan "Service": originated, 1914; organized, 1915. [<N. Am. Ind. *keewanis* make oneself known]
ki·wi (kē′wē) *n.* **1** A flightless bird of New Zealand, the apteryx: named from its cry. **2** *Mil. Slang* An air force officer who does not make flights. **3** *Austral.* A New Zealander. [Imit.]
Kiz·il-Ir·mak (ki·zil′ir·mäk′) A river in central Asia Minor, flowing 715 miles SW to the Black Sea: ancient *Halys.*
Ki·zil Kum (ki·zil′ ko͞om′) See KYZYL KUM.
Kjö·len (khœ′lən) A range of mountains between Norway and Sweden; highest point about 6,900 feet.
Kla·gen·furt (klä′gən·fo͝ort) A city in southern Austria, capital of Carinthia.
Klai·pe·da (klī′pe·dä) The Lithuanian name for MEMEL.
Klam·ath (klam′əth) *n.* **1** One of a tribe of North American Indians of Lutuamian linguistic stock, formerly occupying the Klamath Lake and River region in Oregon, now on Klamath reservation, Oregon. **2** The language of the Klamath Indians: term usually extended also to the Modoc dialect.
Klam·ath River (klam′əth) A river in southern Oregon and NW California, flowing 263 miles from **Upper Klamath Lake** to the Pacific.
Klan (klan) See KU KLUX.
Klans·man (klanz′mən) *n. pl.* **·men** (-mən) A member of the Ku Klux Klan.
Kla·ra (klä′rä) German and Swedish form of CLARA.
Klau·sen·burg (klou′zen·bo͝orkh) The German name for CLUJ.
klax·on (klak′sən) *n.* **1** An early type of automobile horn. **2** A low horn, especially one used on shipboard for sounding an alarm. Also **klaxon horn.** [<Gk. *klazein* make a harsh sound]
Klea·gle (klē′gəl) *n.* An organizer of Ku Klux Klans.
Klé·ber (klā·bâr′), **Jean Baptiste,** 1753–1800, French general.
Klebs-Löff·ler bacillus (klebz′lœf′lər) The diphtheria bacillus. [after Edwin *Klebs,* 1834–1913, and Friedrich August Johannes *Löffler,* 1852–1915, German bacteriologists]
Klee (klā, klē), **Paul,** 1879–1940, Swiss painter.
Kleen·ex (klē′neks) *n.* A soft paper tissue, used as a handkerchief, etc.: a trade name.
Klein (klīn), **Felix,** 1849–1925, German mathematician.
Klein bottle *Math.* A surface having only one side and no edges, constructed by inserting the smaller end of a tapering tube through one side of its larger end, then spreading the smaller end to join and coincide with the larger. [after Felix *Klein*]
Kleist (klīst), **Heinrich von,** 1777–1811, German dramatist.
klepht (kleft) *n.* One of a group of patriotic Greek mountaineers who organized into brigand bands and carried out robberies to aid the cause of Greek independence from Turkish rule. [<Gk. *kleptēs* a thief < *kleptein* steal]
klep·to·ma·ni·a (klep′tə·mā′nē·ə) *n.* An uncontrollable, morbid propensity to steal: also spelled *cleptomania.* [<Gk. *kleptein* steal + -MANIA] **— klep′to·ma′ni·ac** (-mā′nē·ak) *n.*
klet·ter·schuh·e (klet′ər·sho͞o′ə) *n. pl. German* Rope-soled shoes used in mountaineering.
Kle·ve (klā′və) The German name for CLEVES.
klieg light (klēg) A powerful incandescent floodlight, rich in actinic rays: used in making motion pictures. [after A. *Kliegl,* 1872–1927, and his brother John, 1869–1959, U.S. stage-lighting pioneers born in Germany]
Kling·sor (kling′zôr, -zōr) In Wagner's *Parsifal,* a magician who in revenge for his exclusion from the knighthood of the Grail attempts to corrupt the knights by his arts, and, after failing to tempt Parsifal, is destroyed.
klip·spring·er (klip′spring·ər) *n.* A small, agile African antelope *(Oreotragus oreotragus)* inhabiting mountainous regions from Ethiopia to the Cape of Good Hope. [<Du., lit., cliff-springer]
Klon·dike (klon′dīk) A region in NW Canada in the basin of the **Klondike River,** a tributary of the Yukon River, flowing 100 miles west.
kloof (klo͞of) *n. Afrikaans* A mountain pass or cleft; a gorge or narrow valley.
Klop·stock (klôp′shtôk), **Friedrich Gottlieb,** 1724–1803, German poet.
Klu·ane (klo͞o·ān′), **Lake** A lake in SW Yukon near the Alaska border; 184 square miles.
Kluck (klo͝ok), **Alexander von,** 1846–1934, German general.
klys·tron (klis′tron, -trən, klī′stron, -strən) *n.* A vacuum tube for generating a powerful, high-frequency radio beam by means of a flow of electrons rhythmically accelerated and retarded between cavities within which electrical oscillations are produced. [<Gk. *kleistos* closed + (ELEC)TRON]
knack (nak) *n.* **1** The trick of doing a thing readily and well. **2** Cleverness; adroitness. **3** A clever device. **—** *v.t. & v.i. Rare* To strike sharply. [Cf. ME *knack* a sharp blow]
knack·er (nak′ər) *n. Brit.* A dealer in, and slaughterer of, old horses. [Origin uncertain]
knack·wurst (näk′wûrst) *n.* A short, thick sausage, often highly seasoned: also *knockwurst.* [<G < *knacken* sputter, crackle + *wurst* sausage]
knag (nag) *n. Scot.* A knot or knob.
knag·gy (nag′ē) *adj.* **·gi·er, ·gi·est** Full of knots; rough.
knap[1] (nap) *v.t. & v.i.* **knapped, knap·ping 1** *Archaic* To break in pieces; snap. **2** *Rare* To bite sharply; nibble. **—** *n.* A sharp cracking noise. [Imit.]
knap[2] (nap) *n. Scot.* A knob or mound.
knapping hammer A long-handled steel hammer for breaking stones.
knap·sack (nap′sak) *n.* A case or bag of leather or canvas worn strapped across the shoulders, for carrying equipment or supplies; especially, a soldier's traveling case. [<Du. *knapzak* < *knappen* bite + *zak* a sack]
knap·weed (nap′wēd′) *n.* **1** A common European meadow plant *(Centaurea nigra)* naturalized in the United States, with heads of purple flowers: also called *bullweed.* **2** Any of various other species of *Centaurea.* [Earlier *knopweed* <obs. *knop* a knob + WEED]
knar (när) *n.* A knot on a tree or in wood. [Akin to Du. *knar* stump, knot] **— knarred, knar′ry** *adj.*
knave (nāv) *n.* **1** A dishonest person; rogue. **2** A playing card, the jack. **3** *Archaic* A male servant. ◆ Homophone: *nave.* [OE *cnafa* servant]

knav•er•y (nā′vər•ē) *n. pl.* **•er•ies** 1 Deceitfulness; trickery. 2 An instance of this; knavish action or behavior. 3 *Archaic* Mischievous quality; roguery.

knav•ish (nā′vish) *adj.* Of, pertaining to, or characteristic of a knave. —**knav′ish•ly** *adv.*

knead (nēd) *v.t.* 1 To mix and work, as dough or clay, into a uniform mass, usually by pressing, turning, etc., with the hands. 2 To work upon by thumps or squeezes of the hands; massage. 3 To make by or as by kneading. ◆ Homophone: *need.* [OE *cnedan*]—**knead′•er** *n.*

knee (nē) *n.* 1 *Anat.* The joint, or the region about the joint of the human leg, midway between the hip joint and the ankle. 2 A region considered similar to the knee of man: in the hind leg of horses, dogs, and similar animals, the stifle joint; in the foreleg, the carpal joint at the top of the cannon bone: said of hoofed beasts. 3 In birds, the joint at the top of the tarsus. 4 A plate, usually triangular, for connecting or joining structural members. 5 Anything like or suggesting a knee; also, in clothing, the part covering the knee. 6 Any of the upward projections, spurlike or angular, from the roots of swamp trees, especially the bald cypress. —*v.t.* To touch or strike with the knee. —*v.i. Obs.* To kneel. [OE *cnēow*]

KNEE JOINT
c.Crucial ligament.
f.Femur.
lp.Ligamentum patellae.
p.Patellae.
pl.Posterior ligament.
t.Tibia

knee action A method of suspending the front wheels of an automotive vehicle so that each wheel can move up and down independently of the other.

knee breeches Breeches extending from the waist to a point just below the knee. Also **knee-smalls** (nē′smôlz′).

knee•cap (nē′kap′) *n.* 1 The patella. 2 A protective covering or padding for the knee: also **knee′pad′.**

knee-deep (nē′dēp′) *adj.* 1 Rising to the knee. 2 Sunk to the knee.

knee-high (nē′hī′) *adj.* Reaching as high as the knees.

knee•hole (nē′hōl′) *adj.* Having a recessed space for the knees: a *kneehole* desk.

knee-jerk (nē′jûrk′) *adj. Colloq.* Acting in a way that displays unthinking acceptance of preconceived ideas or stereotypes: *knee-jerk* liberals.

knee jerk A reflex action of the lower leg caused by a sudden, brisk tapping of the tendon just below the kneecap.

knee joint 1 *Anat.* The articulation between the femur and the tibia, which includes the patella. 2 A joint made or stiffened by a knee, as in shipbuilding. 3 A toggle joint.

kneel (nēl) *v.i.* **knelt** or **kneeled, kneeling** To fall or rest on the bent knee or knees. [OE *cnēowlian*]—**kneel′er** *n.*

knee-pad (nē′pad′) *n.* A protective covering for the knee or for the stocking at the knee.

knee•pan (nē′pan′) *n.* The patella; the kneecap.

knee•piece (nē′pēs′) *n.* In medieval armor, a covering strapped to the leg as protection for the knee and adjacent parts.

knell (nel) *n.* 1 The tolling of a bell, as in announcing a death. 2 An omen of death, rain, or failure. —*v.i.* 1 To sound a knell; toll, as mourning. 2 To give a sad or warning sound. —**v.t.** 3 To summon or proclaim by or as by a knell. [OE *cnyll* <*cnyllan* knock]

Knel•ler (nel′ər), **Sir Godfrey,** 1646–1723, English painter born in Germany; original name *Gottfried Kneller.*

knelt (nelt) Past tense and past participle of KNEEL.

Knes•set (knes′et) *n.* The single-chamber Constituent Assembly or Parliament of the Republic of Israel *(Knesseth Israel),* established by the Constitution of December, 1948. [<Hebrew]

knew (no͞o, nyo͞o) Past tense of KNOW.

knibb•lack (nib′lak) *n. Scot.* A small round stone; a lump; knob. Also **knibb′loch** (-lôkh).

Knick•er•bock•er (nik′ər•bok′ər) *n.* 1 A descendant of one of the early Dutch settlers in New York State. 2 A New Yorker. [after Diedrich, *Knickerbocker,* typical Dutch character, fictitious author of Irving's *History of New York*]

knick•er•bock•ers (nik′ər•bok′ərz) *n. pl.* Wide short breeches gathered below the knee; knickers.

knick•ers (nik′ərz) *n. pl.* 1 Knickerbockers. 2 A woman's or girl's undergarment, similar to bloomers.

knick-knack (nik′nak) *n.* A trifling article; trinket; trifle: also spelled *nick-nack.* [Varied reduplication of KNACK]

knife (nīf) *n. pl.* **knives** (nīvz) 1 A cutting instrument with one or more sharp-edged, often pointed, blades, commonly set in a handle. 2 An edged blade forming a part of an implement or machine. 3 A weapon such as a cutlas or sword. —*v.t.* **knifed, knif•ing** 1 To stab or cut with a knife. 2 *U.S. Slang* To work against with underhand methods. [OE cnīf]

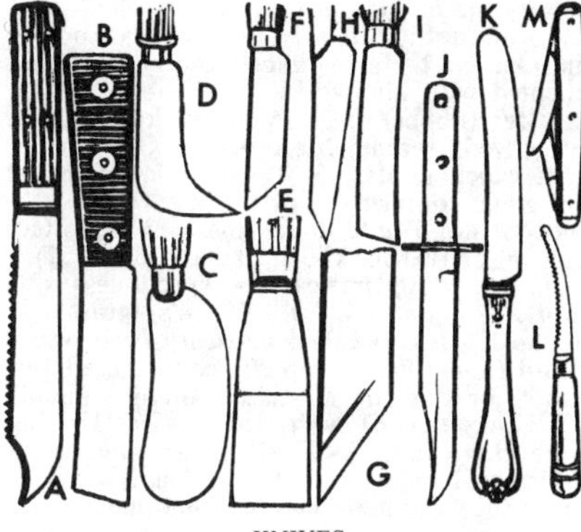

KNIVES

A. saw—back fish knife.	*G.* Blade of mat—knife.
B. Hacking knife.	*H.* Felt knife.
C. Paperhanger's knife.	*I.* Paring knife.
D. Oilcloth knife.	*J.* Hunting knife.
E. Putty knife.	*K.* Table knife.
F. Woodcarver's knife.	*L.* Paring or fruit knife.

M. Folding pocket knife or penknife.

knife-edge (nīf′ej′) *n.* 1 An edge sharpened like that of a knife. 2 A wedge of steel with a fine edge, serving as a fulcrum, as for a balance beam or a pendulum. 3 The girdle of a gem.

knife pleat A very narrow pleat, pressed to sharpness; usually in the plural.

knife switch *Electr.* A switch consisting of one or more knifelike blades which make contact between flat springs.

knight (nīt) *n.* 1 In medieval times, a gentleman bred to the profession of arms, and admitted with special ceremonies to honorable military rank. 2 *Brit.* The holder of a title next below that of baronet, entitling him to use *Sir* before his given name. 3 A champion or devoted follower, as of a cause; any man devoted to the service of a woman, principle, etc. 4 A member of any society in which the official title of knight obtains. 5 A chessman bearing a horse's head and moving one square in any direction, then one diagonally, without regard to intervening pieces. —*v.t.* To make (someone) a knight. ◆ Homophone: *night.* [OE *cniht* boy, servant] —**knight′age** *n.* ◆ Such terms as *knight banneret, knight baronet, knight companion,* and *Knight Templar* are each two nouns in apposition. In the plural each word often takes the inflection: *Knight Templars,* etc.

knight bachelor *pl.* **knights bachelors** In England, a member of the most ancient but lowest order of knighthood.

knight errant *pl.* **knights errant** A medieval knight who went forth to redress wrongs or seek adventures.

knight-er•rant•ry (nīt′er′ən•trē) *n. pl.* **•ries** 1 The customs and practices of the knights errant; chivalry. 2 Quixotic behavior.

knight•head (nīt′hed′) *n. Naut.* One of two timbers rising from the keel of a vessel and supporting the bowsprit between them.

knight•hood (nīt′ho͝od) *n.* 1 The character, dignity, rank, or vocation of a knight. 2Knights collectively. 3 Chivalry.

knight•ly (nīt′lē) *adj.* 1 Pertaining to a knight; chivalrous. 2 Composed of knights: a *knightly* order. —**knight′li•ness** *n.*

Knights Hospitalers of St. John of Jerusalem See HOSPITALER.

Knights of Columbus A fraternal and benevolent society of American Roman Catholic men: founded 1882.

Knights of Labor A national organization of laboring men in the United States, active between 1869 and 1917.

Knights of Malta, Knights of Rhodes See HOSPITALER.

Knights of the Round Table The body of knights comprising King Arthur's court. See ROUND TABLE.

Knights of the White Camelia One of various local, secret organizations of the southern United States that rose after the Civil War, dedicated to maintain white supremacy.

Knight Templar *pl.* **Knights Templars** *for def.* 1; **Knights Templar** *for def.* **2.** 1 A member of a great military order founded in 1119 for the defense of the Latin kingdom of Jerusalem and for the protection of pilgrims, and known as the **Knights of the Temple,** or **Knights Templars,** from the fact that their headquarters was once next to the so-called Temple of Solomon in Jerusalem. 2 A Free-mason of an order claiming descent from the medieval order of Knights Templars.

knish (kə•nish′) *n.* A small square or round of dough filled with potatoes, meat, kasha, etc., and baked or fried. [<Yiddish]

knit (nit) *v.* **knit** or **knit•ted, knit•ting** *v.t.* 1 To form (a fabric or garment) by interlocking loops of a single yarn or thread by means of needles. 2 To fasten or unite closely and firmly. 3 To draw (the brows) together into wrinkles; contract. —*v.i.* 4 To make a fabric by interweaving a yarn or thread. 5 To become closely and firmly united; grow together, as broken bones. 6 To come together in wrinkles; contract. [OE *cnyttan.* Akin to KNOT.]

knit•ter (nit′ər) *n.* 1 One who knits. 2 A knitting machine.

knit•ting (nit′ing) *n.* 1 The act of one who or that which knits. 2 The fabric produced by knitting.

knitting needle A straight, slender rod, pointed at one or both ends, used in hand knitting.

knives (nīvz) Plural of KNIFE.

knob (nob) *n.* 1 A rounded protuberance, bunch, or boss. 2 A rounded handle, as of a door. 3 A rounded mountain; knoll. [ME *knobbe,* prob. <MLG. Cf. Flemish *knobbe.*] —**knobbed** (nobd) *adj.* —**knob′like′** *adj.*

knob•by (nob′ē) *adj.* **•bi•er, •bi•est** Full of knobs; also, knoblike. —**knob′bi•ness** *n.*

knob•ker•rie (nob′ker•ē) *n.* A round-headed stick used as a club and a missile in southern Africa. [<Afrikaans *knopkirie*]

knock (nok) *v.t.* 1 To give a heavy blow to; hit. 2 To strike (one thing) against another; bring into collision. 3 To drive or impel by striking: to *knock* a ball over a fence. 4 To make or cause by striking: to *knock* a hole in a wall. 5 *U.S. Slang* To find fault with; carp at. —*v.i.* 6 To strike a blow or blows, as with the fist or a club. 7 To come into collision; bump. 8 To make a pounding or clanking noise, as an engine. 9 *U.S. Slang* To find fault; carp. —**to knock about** (or **around**) 1 To strike repeatedly; hit from side to side. 2 To wander from place to place. 3 To treat neglectfully; abuse. —**to knock down** 1 To take apart for convenience in shipping or storing. 2 In auctions, to sell to the highest bidder. 3 *U.S. Slang* To embezzle a part of money passing through one's hands. —**to knock off** 1 To leave off; stop, as work, talking, etc. **2** To deduct. **3** To do or make quickly or easily. **4** *U.S. Slang* To kill; also, to overwhelm or defeat. **— to knock out 1** In boxing, to defeat (an opponent) by striking him to the ground for a count of ten. **2** To render unconscious or exhausted. **— to knock out of the box** In baseball, to hit the pitches of (an opposing pitcher) so often as to cause his removal from the game. **— to knock together** To build or make roughly or hurriedly. **— to knock up 1** *Brit.* To rouse, as by knocking on the door. **2** *Brit. Colloq.* To tire out; exhaust. **3** *U.S. Slang* To make pregnant. **—** *n.* **1** A sharp blow; a rap; also, a knocking. **2** *Mech.* **a** The noise produced in machinery or in engines when the operating parts are defective, badly worn, or poorly adjusted. **b** In an internal-combustion engine, the metallic explosive sounds due to uneven or improperly timed combustion. **3** *U.S. Colloq.* Hostile criticism; an adverse comment. [OE *cnocian*]

knock-a·bout (nok'ə·bout') *adj.* **1** Characterized by knocking about, noisiness, or roughness. **2** Adapted for or suitable to any kind of rough usage. **3** Adaptable to all kinds of labor. **—** *n. Naut.* A small, partially decked yacht, carrying a mainsail and jib rigged fore-and-aft. Compare RACE-ABOUT.

knock·down (nok'doun') *adj.* **1** Having sufficient force to fell or overthrow. **2** Constructed so as to be easily taken down, or apart, or so that the parts can be readily put together. **—** *n.* **1** A blow that fells; also, the act of felling. **2** Any prefabricated unassembled article.

knocked-on-at·om (nokt'on'at'əm) *n. Physics* An atom in a solid substance which recoils after the impact of a high-energy particle, often with sufficient energy to displace other atoms.

knock·er (nok'ər) *n.* **1** One who knocks. **2** A hinged metal hammer fastened to a door as a means of signaling for admittance.

knock-knee (nok'nē') *n.* **1** An inward curvature of the legs that causes the knees to knock together in walking. **2** *pl.* Such knees. **— knock'-kneed'** *adj.*

knock-off hub (nok'ôf', -of') In automobiles, the system by which a wheel is affixed to an axle by an eared screw cap, enabling rapid removal and replacement of the wheel.

knock·out (nok'out') *adj.* Rendering insensible, as a blow at the angle of the jaw; overpowering. **—** *n.* **1** A knockout blow; also, a prizefight that has been ended by such a blow. **2** *Slang.* An overwhelmingly attractive or successful person or thing.

knockout drops Drops of some powerful narcotic, as chloral hydrate, used to produce unconsciousness, often for criminal purposes.

knock·wurst (näk'wûrst) See KNACKWURST.

knoll[1] (nōl) *n.* A small round hill; a mound; also, a hilltop. [OE *cnoll* hill]

knoll[2] (nōl) *Archaic v.t.* **1** To proclaim or call by ringing a bell. **2** To sound, as a knell. **—** *v.i.* **3** To sound a knell; toll. **—** *n.* The tolling of a bell; knell. [Var. of KNELL]

knop (nop) *n.* A knob; an ornamental boss or stud. [Prob. var. of KNOB]

knosp (nosp) *n. Archit.* A flower bud, or a budlike ornament. [<MHG *knospe* bud]

Knos·sos (nos'əs) See CNOSSUS.

knot[1] (not) *n.* **1** An intertwining of the parts of one or more ropes, cords, etc., so that they will not slip. **2** An ornamental bow of silk, lace, etc. **3** Anything that resembles a knot. **4** A hard, gnarled portion of the trunk of a tree at the insertion of a branch; especially, such a gnarled knob of a pine tree, used for kindling or firewood. **5** *Bot.* **a** A node or joint in a stem; also, a protuberance or swelling. **b** *pl.* Any of several diseases of trees, characterized by such swellings. **6** A cluster or group, as of persons. **7** *Naut.* **a** A division of a log line, marked by pieces of cloth or knotted string at equal distances, and used to determine the rate of a ship's motion. **b** A speed of a nautical mile in an hour. **c** A nautical mile. **8** A knob. **9** A bond or association or union. **10** Something not easily solved; a difficulty; problem. **11** An enlargement of a muscle or of the bone beneath it; a swollen gland or nerve. **12** The red-breasted sandpiper. See REDBREAST. **— French knot** A decorative knot made by twisting or winding a thread several times around a needle and then pushing the latter through the coil. **—** *v.* **knot·ted, knot·ting** *v.t.* **1** To tie in a knot; form a knot or knots in. **2** To secure or fasten by a knot. **3** To form knobs, bosses, etc., in. **—** *v.i.* **4** To form a knot or knots. **5** To tie knots for fringe. [OE *cnotta*]

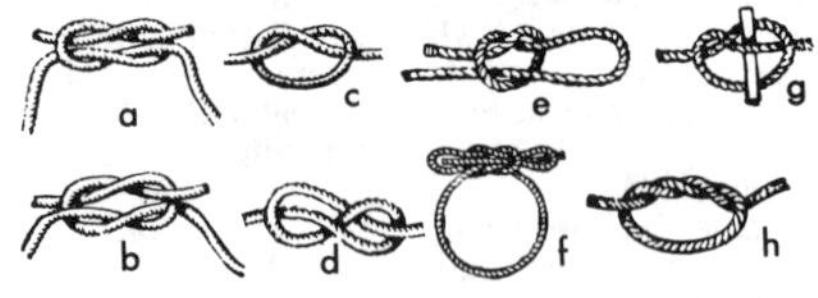

KNOTS

a. Square or reef knot. *e.* Single bowknot.
b. Granny knot. *f.* Double bowknot.
c. Overhand knot. *g.* Boat knot.
d. Figure-8 knot. *h.* Surgeon's knot.

knot[2] (not) *n.* A migratory sandpiper *(Calidris Canutis)* breeding in Arctic regions. [Origin unknown]

knot·grass (not'gras', -gräs') *n.* **1** A widely distributed polygonaceous herb *(Polygonum aviculare)* with jointed stems and small greenish flowers. **2** Any of several other grasses, as the wild oat *(Avena fatua).* Also called *birdgrass.*

knot·hole (not'hōl') *n.* A hole, as in a plank, left by the falling out of a knot.

knot·ted (not'id) *adj.* **1** Tied with a knot or into knots. **2** Having knots; knotty. **3** Ornamented with knotwork.

knot·ter (not'ər) *n.* **1** A person or machine employed for removing knots. **2** One who or that which knots. **3** Tangled; intricate. **4** Puzzling; confusing.

knot·ty (not'ē) *adj.* **·ti·er, ·ti·est 1** Knotted; full of, or tied in, knots; like a knot. **2** Difficult; puzzling; intricate. **— knot'ti·ness** *n.*

knot·weed (not'wēd') *n.* **1** Knotgrass. **2** Knapweed. Also called *persicary, smartweed.*

knout (nout) *n.* A whip or scourge used formerly for flogging in Russia: often a bundle of thongs twisted with wire. **—** *v.t.* To flog with the knout. [<F <Russian *knut* knot, whip, prob. <Scand. Cf. Sw. *knut.*]

know (nō) *v.* **knew, known, know·ing** *v.t.* **1** To perceive or understand clearly or with certainty; apprehend as objectively true: to *know* the truth. **2** To have information or intelligence of: to *know* the enemy's plans. **3** To be acquainted with; have experience of or familiarity with: Do you *know* each other? **4** To recognize; identify; also, to distinguish between: to *know* peas from beans. **5** To have practical skill in or knowledge of: often with *how*: Do you *know* how to ski? **6** *Archaic* To have sexual intercourse with. **—** *v.i.* **7** To have knowledge: often with *of*: Do you *know* of any better reason? **8** To be or become aware or cognizant. **—** *n.* The fact or condition of knowing; knowledge. **— in the know** *Colloq.* Having full, or more than usual, information. [OE *cnāwan*] **— know'a·ble** *adj.* & *n.* **— know'er** *n.*

Synonyms (verb): apprehend, ascertain, cognize, comprehend, discern, discover, discriminate, distinguish, experience, learn, perceive, realize, recognize, understand. See LEARN. Compare synonyms for KNOWLEDGE. *Antonyms*: Compare synonyms for IGNORANT.

know-how (nō'hou') *n. Colloq.* Knowledge of how to perform a complicated operation or procedure; technical skill.

know·ing (nō'ing) *adj.* **1** Perceptive; astute; shrewd; also, possessing sly, covert, or secret knowledge: a *knowing* look. **2** Conscious; intentional. **3** Having knowledge or information. **— know'ing·ness** *n.*

Synonyms: acute, astute, clever, cunning, discerning, intelligent, keen, penetrating, sagacious, sharp, shrewd. A *knowing* look, air, etc., indicates the possession of reserved knowledge which the person could impart if he chose. *Knowing* has often a slightly invidious sense. We speak of a *knowing* rascal, meaning *cunning* or *shrewd* within a narrow range, but a *knowing* child has more knowledge than would be looked for at his years, perhaps more than is quite desirable, although to speak of a child as *intelligent* is altogether complimentary. See ASTUTE, CLEVER, INTELLIGENT, WISE[2]. *Antonyms*: dull, gullible, senseless, silly, simple, stolid, stupid, undiscerning, unintelligent.

know·ing·ly (nō'ing·lē) *adv.* **1** With knowledge. **2** Shrewdly; slyly. **3** Intentionally; on purpose: Who would *knowingly* commit a crime?

know-it-all (nō'it·ôl') *n. Colloq.* A person affecting knowledge in almost all subjects. Also **know'-all'.**

knowl·edge (nol'ij) *n.* **1** A result or product of knowing; information or understanding acquired through experience; practical ability or skill. **2** Information; learning; specifically, the cumulative culture of the human race. **3** The clear and certain apprehension of truth; assured rational conviction. **4** The act, process, or state of knowing; cognition. **5** Any object of knowing or mental apprehension; that which is or may be known; the knowable; also actual or possible range of information. **6** Specific information; notification; notice. **7** *Archaic* Sexual intercourse. [OE *cnawlæc* < *cnāwan* know]

Synonyms: acquaintance, apprehension, cognition, cognizance, comprehension, erudition, experience, information, intelligence, intuition, learning, light, lore, perception, recognition, scholarship, science, wisdom. *Knowledge* is all that the mind knows, from whatever source derived or obtained, or by whatever process; the aggregate facts, truths, or principles acquired or retained by the mind, including alike the *intuitions* native to the mind and all that has been learned respecting phenomena, causes, laws, principles, literature, etc. We say of a studious man that he has a great store of *knowledge,* or of an intelligent man of the world, that he has a fund of varied *information.* We speak of *perception* of external objects, *apprehension* of intellectual truth. Simple *perception* gives a limited *knowledge* of external objects, merely as such; the *cognition* of the same objects is a *knowledge* of them in some relation; *cognizance* is the formal or official *recognition* of something as an object of *knowledge*; we take *cognizance* of it. *Intuition* is primary *knowledge* antecedent to all teaching or reasoning; *experience* is *knowledge* that has entered directly into one's own life; as, a child's *experience* that fire will burn. See ACQUAINTANCE, EDUCATION, LEARNING, SCIENCE, WISDOM. *Antonyms*: ignorance, illiteracy, inexperience, misapprehension, misconception, misunderstanding, rudeness, unfamiliarity.

knowl·edge·a·ble (nol'ij·ə·bəl) *adj. Colloq.* Having knowledge; knowing; shrewd.

known (nōn) Past participle of KNOW. **—** *adj.* Apprehended mentally; recognized; understood; especially, recognized by all as the truth.

know-noth·ing (nō'nuth'ing) *n.* An uneducated or ignorant person; an ignoramus.

Know-noth·ing (nō'nuth'ing) *n.* A member of a party in U. S. politics (1853–56), which aimed at excluding foreign-born persons from the government, and at making it difficult for them to become citizens: so called because, in its original form as a secret society, its members professed to "know nothing" about it when questioned. **— Know'-noth'ing·ism** *n.*

known quantity *Math.* A quantity whose value is stated: generally denoted by one of the earlier letters of the alphabet, *a, b, c,* etc.

Knox (noks), **Henry,** 1750–1806, American Revolutionary general. **— John,** 1505?–72, Scottish Protestant reformer, theologian, and historian. **— (William) Frank(lin),** 1874–1944, U. S. publisher; secretary of the navy, 1940–1944.

Knox·ville (noks'vil) A city on the Tennessee River in eastern Tennessee.

knub·bly (nub'lē) *adj.* Having protuberances; gnarled. [< *knubble,* dim. of *knub,* var. of KNOB]

knuck·le (nuk'əl) *n.* **1** One of the joints of the fingers, or the region about it; especially, one of the joints connecting the fingers to the rest of the hand. **2** The knee or ankle joint of certain animals, used as foods. **3** The central tubular projection of a hinge through which the pin passes. **4** In shipbuilding, an angular fitting of timbers. **5** *pl. U.S.* A children's game of marbles. **— brass knuckles** A device of metal, fitting over the knuckles, used as a protection for them in striking and to add force to the blow; also **knuck'le-dust'er.** **—** *v.i.* **knuck·led, knuck·ling** To hold the knuckles on the ground in shooting a marble. **—to knuckle down 1** To apply oneself seriously and assiduously. **2** To yield; submit; give in: also **knuckle under.** [ME *knokel* <LG. Cf. G *knöchel,* dim. of *knochen* bone.]

knuckle bone 1 A huckle bone, as of a sheep; also, in man, one of the bones of the fingers. **2** *pl.* A children's game.

knuck·led (nuk′əld) *adj.* Jointed.

knuckle joint 1 The joint formed at a knuckle. **2** A hinge joint in which a projection in one part lies between two projections of the other part.

knur (nûr) *n.* A knot or knob. [ME *knorre, knurre* <MDu. knorre]

knurl (nûrl) *n.* **1** A hard substance or protuberance; knot; lump. **2** One of a series of small ridges on the edge of a thumbscrew to facilitate manual turning. **3** *Scot.* A hunchbacked dwarf. [? Dim. of KNUR] **— knurled, knurl′y** *adj.*

KOALA
(About 2 feet 9 inches in length)

Knut (kno͞ot) See CANUTE.

KO (kā′ō′) See KAYO.

ko·a·la (kō·ä′lə) *n.* An arboreal marsupial of Australia (*Phascolarctos cinereus*), having cheek pouches, large ears, gray woolly fur, and no external tail. It feeds on the leaves and buds of the eucalyptus, but descends at night to dig up and eat roots. [<native Australian name]

kob (kob, kōb) *n.* **1** A large antelope (genus *Kobus* or *Adenota*), with elongated horns, ringed at the base, and a long tufted tail, as the waterbuck. **2** Any of the several smaller related antelopes, as a reedbuck: all natives of southern Africa. Also **ko·ba** (kō′bə). [<Senegalese]

KOB (*Kobus kob*)
(About 3 feet high at the shoulder)

Ko·be (kō·be) A port in southern Honshu, Japan.

Kö·ben·havn (kœ′·pən·houn′) Danish name for COPENHAGEN.

Ko·blenz (kō′blents) See COBLENZ.

ko·bold (kō′bold, -bōld) *n.* In German folklore, an underground being inhabiting mines and caves; goblin; gnome. [<G; ult. origin unknown]

Ko·burg (kō′bo͝orkh) See COBURG.

Koch (kôkh), **Robert,** 1843–1910, German physician and bacteriologist; discovered pathogenic bacteria of tuberculosis and cholera.

Koch·er (kôkh′ər), **Emil Theodor,** 1841–1917, Swiss physician and surgeon.

Ko·chi (kō·chē) A city in central Shikoku, Japan.

Kock (kôk), **Paul de,** 1794–1871, French novelist and dramatist.

Ko·da·chrome (kō′də·krōm) *n.* A full-color photographic film: a trade name.

Ko·dak (kō′dak) *n.* A small portable camera carrying a roll of sensitized film upon which a series of negatives can be quickly made: a trade name. **—** *v.t.* & *v.i.* To photograph with a Kodak.

Ko·di·ak bear (kō′dē·ak) See KADIAK BEAR.

Ko·di·ak Island (kō′dē·ak) An island in the Gulf of Alaska off Alaska Peninsula; over 5,000 square miles: also *Kadiak.*

Ko·dok (kō′dok) The modern name for FASHODA.

ko·el (kō′əl) *n.* A cuckoo (genus *Eudanamys*) native to Australia, India, and the East Indies; the coee bird. [<Hind. <Skt. *kokila*]

Koen·raad (kœn′rät) Dutch form of CONRAD.

Koff·ka (kôf′kä), **Kurt,** 1886–1941, U. S. psychologist born in Germany.

Ko·fu (kō·fo͞o) A city on central Honshu island, Japan.

Ko·hel·eth (kō·hel′ith) **1** The preacher: often identified with Solomon. *Eccles.* i 1–2. **2** The book of Ecclesiastes. [<Hebrew *qōheleth*]

Koh·i·nor (kō′i·no͝or′) A famous Indian diamond, weight (cut) about 106 carats; one of the British crown jewels since the annexation of Punjab, 1849. Also **Koh′i·noor′, Koh′i·nur′.** [<Persian *kōhinūr* mountain of light]

kohl (kōl) *n.* In Eastern countries, a powder of antimony used to darken the edges of the eyes. [<Arabic *kuhl.* Akin to ALCOHOL.]

Köh·ler (kœ′lər), **Wolfgang,** 1887–1959, U. S. psychologist born in Germany.

kohl·ra·bi (kōl′rä·bē, kōl·rä′-) *n. pl.* **·bies** A variety of cabbage with an edible turnip-shaped stem. [<G <Ital. *cavoli rope (pl.)* <L *caulis* cabbage + *rapa* turnip]

Koi·ne (koi·nā′) *n.* **1** The common form of Greek, an outgrowth of the Attic dialect with many Ionic elements, used throughout the Greek world from the time of the conquests of Alexander to the sixth century A.D. Koine was the literary language of Aristotle and Plutarch, and was used in the Septuagint and the New Testament; in its spoken form it became the basis of virtually all modern Greek dialects. **2** Any mixed language that becomes the lingua franca of a region: also *koine.* [<Gk. *koinē (dialektos)* common (language)]

Ko·kand (kô·känt′) A city in eastern Uzbek S.S.R.

Ko·ko·mo (kō′kə·mō) A city in north central Indiana.

Ko·ko Nor (kō′kō′ nôr′) A salt lake in NE Tsinghai province, China; 2,300 square miles: also *Kuku Nor.*

kok-sa·ghyz (kōk′sa·gēz′) *n.* A dandelionlike plant (*Taraxacum kok-saghyz*) native to Turkestan, the roots of which yield latex and inulin: cultivated as a source of rubber. [<Russian <Turkish *kök* a root + *sagïz* rubber]

Ko·ku·ra (kō·ko͞o·rä) A port in northern Kyushu island, Japan.

ko·la (kō′lə), **ko·la·nut** (-nut′) See COLA, etc.

Ko·la Peninsula (kō′lə) A projection of NW U.S.S.R. between the Barents Sea and the White Sea; 50,000 square miles; 250 miles long.

Ko·lar Gold Fields (kō·lär′) A city of eastern Mysore State, India.

Kol·ha·pur (kōl′hä·po͝or′) **1** A former Deccan State in Bombay State, India. **2** A city in southern Bombay State, formerly the capital of Kolhapur.

Kolhapur and the Deccan States A former (1933–1947) political agency of princely states in western India.

ko·lin·sky (kə·lin′skē, kō-) *n.* Any of several minks of northern China and Russia; especially, *Mustela siberica,* the Siberian mink; also, the fur of any of these: sometimes called *Tartar Sable.* [<Russian *kolinski* of Kola, a peninsula abounding in minks]

kol·khoz (kôl·khôz′) *n.* A collective farm in the U.S.S.R. [<Russian *kol(lektivnoe)* collective + *khoz(aĭstvo)* farm, household]

Kol·lon·tai (ko·lon·tī′), **Aleksandra,** 1872–1952, U.S.S.R. revolutionary and diplomat; also **Kol·lon·tay′.**

Koll·witz (kôl′vits), **Käthe,** 1867–1945, German painter, etcher, and lithographer.

Köln (kœln) The German name for COLOGNE.

Ko·lozs·vár (kō′lōzh·vär) The Hungarian name for CLUJ.

Ko·lusch·an (kə·lush′ən) *n.* A linguistic stock of North American Indians of SE Alaska, consisting of the 18 Tlingit tribes. Also **Ko·lush′.** [<Russian *kalyuschka* piece of wood (inserted in the nether lip)]

Kol·y·ma (kol·ē·mä′) A river in NE Yakut Autonomous S.S.R., flowing 1,335 miles north to the East Siberian Sea. Also **Kol·i·ma′.**

Kolyma Range A mountain system in northern Khabarovsk territory; highest point, over 6,000 feet.

Kom·an·dor·ski Islands (kom′än·dôr′skē) An island group in the SW Bering Sea: also *Commander Islands.*

Ko·ma·ti (kə·mä′tē) A river in southern Africa, flowing 500 miles NE to the Indian Ocean.

ko·mat·ik (kō·mad′ik) *n. Canadian* An Eskimo sled: also spelled *comatik.* [<Eskimo]

Ko·men·ský (kô′men·skē) See COMENIUS.

Ko·mi Autonomous S.S.R. (kō′mē) An administrative division of NE European Russian S.F.S.R.; 156,000 square miles; capital, Syktyvkar: formerly *Zyrian Autonomous Region.*

Kom·in·tern (kom′in·tûrn) See COMINTERN.

ko·mon·dor (kō′mon·dôr) *n.* A breed of working dog used in Hungary for ten centuries; tall, sturdy, and having a wide muzzle and long, thick, white coat. [<Magyar]

Kom·so·molsk (kom′so·môlsk′) A city in eastern European Russian S.F.S.R. on the Amur.

Kon·a·kri (kon′ə·krē) See CONAKRY.

Kon·go (kong′gō) The German name for the CONGO.

Kö·nig·grätz (kœ′nik·grets) The German name for HRADEC KRÁLOVÉ.

Kö·nigs·berg (kœ′nikhs·berkh) The former German name for KALININGRAD.

ko·ni·ol·o·gy (kō′nē·ol′ə·jē) See CONIOLOGY.

Kon·stan·tin (kōn′stän·tēn′) German form of CONSTANTINE.

Kon·stanz (kōn′stänts) German form of CONSTANT.

Kon·stanz (kōn′stänts) The German name for CONSTANCE.

Kon·stan·ze (kōn·stän′tsə) German form of CONSTANCE.

Kon·ya (kôn′yä) A city in SW central Turkey in Asia: ancient *Iconium.* Also **Kon′ia.**

Koo (ko͞o), **V. K. Wellington,** born 1887, Chinese statesman and diplomat; original name *Ku Wei-chün.*

Kooch Behar (ko͞och′ bi·här′) A former name for COOCH BEHAR.

koo·doo (ko͞o′do͞o) *n.* A large, striped African antelope (genus *Strepsiceros*), grayish-brown in color: also spelled *kudu.* [<Hottentot *kudu*]

GREATER KOODOO
(Up to 5 feet high at the shoulder)

kook (ko͞ok) *n. Slang* An unconventional, eccentric, or unbalanced person. [? <CUCKOO] **— kook′i·ness** *n.* **— kook′y** *adj.*

kook·a·bur·ra (ko͝ok′ə·bûr′ə) *n.* A large, insectivorous Australian kingfisher; the laughing jackass. [< native Australian]

koo·ra·jong (ko͞o′rə·jong) See KURRAJONG.

Koo·te·nay (ko͞o′tə·nā) A river rising in **Kootenay National Park** in SE British Columbia; 543 square miles; established 1920; flowing through northern Montana and Idaho, thence through **Kootenay Lake,** a lake 75 miles long in SE British Columbia, to the Columbia River; total length 450 miles, of which 276 are in Canada. Also, in the United States, **Koo′te·nai.**

kop (kop) *n.* In South Africa, a hill; headland. [<Afrikaans <Du., a head]

ko·peck (kō′pek) *n.* A small copper coin of Russia; one one-hundredth of a ruble: also spelled *copeck.* Also **ko′pek.** [<Russian *kopeĭka* < *kopye* lance]

koph (kôf) *n.* The nineteenth Hebrew letter. See ALPHABET. [<Hebrew *qoph*]

kop·je (kop′ē) *n.* In South Africa, a hillock. [<Afrikaans *kopje,* dim. of *kop* kop]

kor (kôr, kōr) See HOMER[2]. [<Hebrew *kōr,* lit., round vessel]

Ko·ran (kō·rän′, -ran′) *n.* The Moslem sacred scripture, written in Arabic and professing to record the revelations of Allah (God) to Mohammed: also *Alcoran, Alkoran.* [<Arabic *Qur'ān,* lit., book < *quar'a* read]

Kor·do·fan (kôr′dō·fän′) A province of central Sudan; 146,930 square miles; capital, El Obeid.

Ko·re·a (kô·rē′ə, kō-) A peninsula of eastern Asia; 85,228 square miles; 1910–45 Japanese *Chosen*; divided (1948) into: **1** the **Republic of Korea (South Korea)**; 36,760 square miles; capital, Seoul; and **2** the **Democratic People's Republic of Korea (North Korea)**; 46,968 square miles; capital, Pyongyang.

Korea Bay An arm of the Yellow Sea between the Liaotung Peninsula, NE China, and the western coast of North Korea. Also **East Korea Bay.** Formerly **Bay of Chosen.**

Ko·re·an (kô·rē′ən, kō-) *adj.* Belonging or relating to Korea (Chosen) or its inhabitants. —*n.* **1** An inhabitant or a native of Korea. **2** The agglutinative language of Korea, somewhat similar to Japanese.

Korea Strait The passage from the Sea of Japan to the East China Sea between Korea and Japan.

Ko·rit·sa (kô·r·6ē·tsä′) A city in SE Albania. *Albanian* **Kor·çë** (Kô′chə).

Kor·ne·lis (kôr·nā′lis) Dutch form of CORNELIUS.

Korn·gold (kôrn′gōlt), **Erich Wolfgang,** 1897–41957, U.S. composer born in Austria.

Kor·o·len·ko (k336 r′ē·leng′kō, *Russian* Kô·rô·lyen′kə), **Vladimir Galaktionovich,** 1853-1921, Russian novelist.

ko·ru·na (kô·rōō′nä) *n.* The monetary unit of Czechoslovakia. See CROWN (money). [<Czech <L *corona* crown]

Ko·rze·niow·ski (kô′zhe·nyôfa′skē), **Teodor Józef Konrad** See CONRAD, JOSEPH.

Kor·zyb·ski (kôr·zib′skē), **Alfred Habdank,** 1879–1950, U.S. scientist and originator of general semantics; born in Poland.

kos (kos) *n.* A Hebrew measure of capacity of about four cubic inches. [<Hebrew, cup]

Kos (kos, kôs) The second largest island of the Dodecanese group; 114 square miles: Italian *Coo*: also *Cos*.

Kos·ci·us·ko (kos′ē·us′kō), **Thaddeus,** 1746–1817, Polish patriot in the American Revolution. Also Polish **Tadeusz Koś·ciusz·ko** (kosh·chōōsh′kō).

Kos·ci·us·ko (kos′ē·us′kō), **Mount** A mountain in SE New South Wales; highest peak in Australia; 7,316 feet.

ko·sher (kō′shər) *adj.* **1** Permitted by the Jewish ceremonial law; clean; pure: said usually of food. **2** *Slang* All right; good; legitimate. —*n.* A kosher shop, also, the food sold there. —*v.t.* (kosh′ər) To make kosher. Also spelled *kasher.* [<Hebrew *kāshēr* fit, proper]

Ko·ši·ce (kô′shē·tse) A city in SE Slovakia, Czechoslovakia: German *Kaschau,* Hungarian *Kassa.*

Kos·so·vo (kô′sô·vô) A region of southern Serbia, Yugoslavia; scene of Turkish victories over the Serbs, 1389, and Hungarians, 1448. Also **Ko′so·vo.**

Kos·suth (kos′ōōth, ko·sōōth′; *Hungarian* kô′·shōōt), **Ferenc,** 1841–1914, Hungarian politician; son of Louis. —**Louis,** 1802–94, Hungarian patriot: led insurrection, 1848.

Kos·tro·ma A region (okrug) in north central European Russia bordering the Volga river.

Ko·sy·gin (ko·sig′in) **Alexei Nikolayevich,** born 1904–1980, Soviet statesman; chairman of the Council of Ministers (premier) 1964–.

Ko·ta·ba·ru (kō′tə·bä ′rōō) The capital of West Irian, a port in the NE part: formerly *Hollandia.*

Ko·ta Bha·ru The capital of Kelantan, Malaysia. Also **Kota Ba′roe** or **Ba′ru.**

Kot·ka (kôt′kä) A port in SE Finland, on the Gulf of Finland.

ko·to (kō′tō) *n.* A Japanese musical instrument with 13 strings, plucked with 3 plectra fastened to the thumb, index, and middle finger of the right hand, while the left adjusts the strings. [<Japanese]

Ko·tor (kô′tôr) A port in western Montenegro, Yugoslavia, on the **Gulf of Kotor,** an inlet of the Adriatic in SW Yugoslavia: Italian *Cattaro.*

Kot·ze·bue (kôt′sə·bōō), **August Friedrich Ferdinand von,** 1761–1819, German dramatist.

Kot·ze·bue Sound (kot′sə·byōō) An inlet of the Chukchi Sea in NW Alaska.

kou·miss (kōō′mis), **kou·mys** See KUMISS.

Kous·se·vitz·ky (kōō′sə·vit′skē), **Serge,** 1874–1951, Russian orchestral conductor active in the United States.

kous·so (kōōs′ō) See CUSSO.

Kov·no (kôv′nō) The Russian name for KAUNAS.

Ko·weit (kō·wāt′) See KUWAIT.

Kow·loon (kou′lōōn′) The chief port of Hong Kong on **Kowloon Peninsula** (3 square miles) NE of Hong Kong Island.

kow·tow (kou′tou′, kō′-) *n.* A Chinese form of obeisance: kneeling and touching the forehead to the ground before a superior. —*v.i.* **1** To make such obeisance. **2** To act in an obsequious or servile manner. Also **ko·tow** (kō′tou′). [<Chinese *k'o-t'ou,* lit., knock the head]

Kra (krä), **Isthmus of** A neck of land in SE Asia, 40 miles wide at its narrowest point, connecting the Malay Peninsula with Burma and Thailand.

kraal (kräl) *n.* **1** A village or group of native huts in South Africa, usually surrounded by a stockade. **2** The social unit such a community represents. **3** An enclosure for cattle. Also spelled *craal.* [<Afrikaans, village, pen <Pg. *curral* pen for cattle. Related to CORRAL.]

Krae·pe·lin (krā′pə·lin), **Emil,** 1856–1926, German psychiatrist.

Krafft-E·bing (kräft′ā′bing), **Baron Richard von,** 1840–1902, German neurologist and psychiatrist.

kraft (kraft, kräft) *n.* A tough, usually dark-brown paper, made from high-grade sulfate wood pulp. [<G, strength]

Krag (krag) *n.* A bolt-action repeating rifle formerly used in the U.S. Army: in full, **Krag-Jör·gen·sen rifle** (-jûr′gən·sən). [after O. *Krag* and E. *Jörgensen,* Norwegian inventors]

krait (krīt) *n.* An extremely venomous dull-bluish snake (genus *Bungarus*), especially the **banded krait** *(B. fasciatus)*of the Malay Peninisula, India, and Borneo. [<Hind. *karait*]

Kra·ka·to·a (krä′kə·tō ′ä) A volcanic island in the Strait of Sunda, between Java and Sumatra, Malay Archipelago; major eruption, 1883. Also **Kra′ka·tau′** (-tou′).

kra·ken (krä′kən, krā′-P) *n.* A fabulous sea monster of Norwegian seas. [<Norw.]

Kra·ków (krä′kōōf) The Polish name for CRACOW. *Russian* **Kra·kov** (krä′kôf).

kra·ko·wi·ak (krə·kō′vē ·ak) See CRACOVIENNE.

Kras·no·dar 1 A territory of southern European Russia on the Sea of Azov and the Black Sea; 32,800 square miles. **2** The capital of the Krasnodar okrug; formerly Ekaterinodar.

Kras·no·yarsk 1 A territory of central Siberian Russia; 928,000 square miles. **2** Its capital, a city on the Yenisei, pop. 900,000.

K-ra·tion (kā′rash′ən, -rā′shən) *n.* A highly condensed emergency ration provided for soldiers of the U.S. Army.

Kre·feld (krā′felt) A city on the Rhine in North Rhine–Westphalia, West Germany.

Kreh·biel (krā′bēl), **Henry,** 1854–1923, U.S. music critic, author, and editor.

Kreis·ler (krīs′lər), **Fritz,** 1875–1962, U.S. violinist and composer born in Austria.

Kre·men·chug (kre′min·chōōk′) A city in central Ukrainian S.S.R. on the Dnieper river.

krem·lin (krem′lin) *n.* The citadel of a Russian town. [<F <Russian *kreml'* citadel]

Krem·lin (krem′lin) **1** The citadel of Moscow, enclosing the former palace of the Czar. **2** The government of the U.S.S.R.

Krem·nitz white (krem′nits) See CREMNITZ WHITE.

kreu·zer (kroit′sər) *n.* Any of several former small silver or copper coins of Austria and Germany. Also **kreut′zer.** [<G <*kreuz* cross]

Krieg (krēg) *n.* German War.

krieg·spiel (krēg′spēl) *n.* A game in which figures representing troops, guns, etc., are moved about a model of the terrain in simulation of actual military maneuvers: used in the instruction or practice of military tactics. [<G *kriegspiel,* lit., war game]

Kriem·hild (krēm′hild, *Ger.* krēm′hilt) In the *Nibelungenlied,* the wife of Siegfried and sister of King Gunther; rival of Brunhild. Also **Kriem·hil·de** (krēm·hil′dē).

krim·mer (krim′ər) *n.* A fur resembling Persian lamb prepared from fleece of lambs raised mostly in the Crimean Peninsula. [<G *krimmer* <*Krim* Crimea]

kris (krēs) *n.* A dagger with a wavy blade used in Malaysia: also spelled *crease, creese, cris.* [<Malay]

KRIS WITH SHEATH

Krish·na (krish′nə) **1** A celebrated Hindu deity, an incarnation of Vishnu. **2** See KISTNA. —**Krish′na·ism** *n.*

Kris·pin (kris·pēn′) Swedish form of CRISPIN. Also *Dutch* **Kris·pijn** (krēs′pīn).

Kriss Krin·gle (kris kring′gəl) St. Nicholas; Santa Claus. [<G *Christkindl,* dim. of *Christkind* Christ child]

Kris·ti·a·ni·a (kris′chē·a′nē·ə) The former name of OSLO.

Kris·tian·sand (kris′chən·sand, *Norwegian* kris·tyän·sän′) A port on the Skagerrak, SW Norway.

Kris·to·fer (kris′tə·fer) Swedish form of CHRISTOPHER.

Kri·voi Rog (krē·voi′ rôk′) A city in SE Ukrainian S.S.R.

Krk (kûrk) The largest of the Yugoslav islands in the northern Adriatic; 165 square miles: Italian *Veglia.*

Krogh (krôg), **August,** 1874–1946, Danish physiologist.

Kró·lew·ska Hu·ta (krōō·lef′skähōō′tä) A former name of CHORZOW.

kro·na (krō′nə, *Sw.* krōō′nə) *n. pl.* **kro·nor** (krō′nôr) The Swedish monetary unit, equivalent to 100 öre. [<Sw.]

kro·ne (krō′nə) *n.* **1** *pl.* **kro·ner** (krō′nər) A gold coin, the monetary unit of Norway and Denmark, equivalent to 100 öre: also called *crown.* **2** *pl.* **kro·nen** (krō′nən) Any of several former European gold coins, equivalent in Germany to 10 marks, in Austria-Hungary to 100 heller. [<Dan.]

Kro·nos (krō′nos) In Greek mythology, the youngest of the Titans, son of Uranus and Gaea, who deposed his father, married his sister, Rhea, and was himself deposed by his son Zeus, who threw him into Tartarus with the other Titans: identified with the Roman *Saturn* : also spelled *Cronus.*

Kron·stadt (krōn′shtät) **1** A Russian port and naval base on an island in the Gulf of Finland, 14 miles west of Leningrad. *Russian* **Kron′·shtadt. 2** The German name for STALIN.

kroon (krōōn) *n. pl.* **kroons** or **kroo·ni** (krōō′nē) The monetary unit of Estonia. [<Estonian *kron*]

Kro·pot·kin (krə·pot′kin, *Russian* krô·pōt′·kēn), **Prince Peter Alexeivich,** 1842–1921, Russian geographer, anarchist, and author.

kru·bi (krōō′bē) *n.* A giant plant *(Amorphophallus titanum)* of the arum family native in Sumatra, with tuberous roots and a malodorous vaselike spathe that may grow to a diameter of 8 feet and a height of 12 feet or more: regarded as the largest flower in the world: also called *grubi.* Also **kru′but** (-but). [<native name]

Kru·ger (krōō′gər, *Afrikaans* krü′gər), **Stephanus Johannes Paulus,** 1825–1904, Boer statesman; president of the South African Republic, 1883–1900: called "Oom Paul."

Kruger National Park A game preserve lying in Eastern and Northern Transvaal provinces, Republic of South Africa; about 8,650 square miles; established 1926.

Kru·gers·dorp (krōō′gərz·dôrp, *Afrikaans* krü′·gərs·dôrp) A town, in Gauteng, Republic of South Africa.

krul·ler (krul′ər) See CRULLER.

Krupp (krup, *Ger.* krōōp) A German family of steel and munition manufacturers at Essen, Germany, notably **Alfred,** 1812–87; his son **Friedrich Alfred,** 1854–1902; and **Bertha,** 1886–1957, daughter of the preceding.

kry·o·lite (krī′ə·līt), **kry·o·lith** (-lith) See CRYOLITE.

kryp·ton (krip′ton) *n.* A colorless, insert, gaseous element (symbol Kr) of the zero group in the periodic table, isolated by Ramsay in 1898. See ELEMENT. [<NL <Gk. *krypton,* neut. of *kryptos* hidden]

K-se·ries (kā′sir′ē) *Physics* The group of shorter wavelengths in the typical X-ray spectrum of an element, believed to be caused by the transition of electrons to the quantum number of one.

Kshat·ri·ya (kshat′rē·yə) *n.* The warrior caste of the Aryan Hindus; a member of the caste. Also **Kshat′ru·ya** (-rōō-). [<Skt. *kṣatriya* <*kṣatra* rule]

Kua·la Be·lait A city in Brunei, capital of the district of Belait.

Kua·la Lum·pur A city in the SW part of Malaysia, capital of Malaysia, and a federal territory in Malaysia; pop. 1,300,000.

Kua·la Treng·ga·nu A city on the South China Sea, capital of Trengganu, a State of Malaysia; pop. 750,000.

Kuan Yin (kwän yin) A Chinese Buddhistic goddess: often called the Goddess of Mercy: also spelled *Kwan Yin*, or, in Japanese, *Kwannon.*

Ku·ban (kōō·bän′) A river in Georgian S.S.R., flowing 584 miles north to the Black Sea.

Ku·blai Khan (kōō′blī kän′), 1214–94, founder of the Mongol dynasty of China. Also *Kubla Khan.*

ku·chen (kōō′khən) *n.* A yeast dough coffee cake. [<G]

Ku·ching (kōō′ching) The capital of Sarawak, Malaysia.

ku·dos (kyoo′dos) *n.* Glory; credit; praise. [<Gk. *kydos* glory]

ku·du (kōō′dōō) See KOODOO.

Ku·dus (kōō′dōōs) A town of central Java. *Dutch* **Koe′does.**

kud·zu-vine (kōōd′zōō·vīn′) *n.* A hairy, fragrant climbing vine of China and Japan *(Pueraria thunbergiana).* A fiber from the inner bark is used by the Japanese for fabrics and cordage. [<Japanese]

Kuen·lun (kōōn′lōōn′) See KUNLUN.

Ku·fic (kyōō′fik) *adj.* Relating to Kufa, an ancient Arabian city on the Euphrates, or to the primitive Arabic characters used by its writers, and in which the Koran was originally written. — *n.* The Arabic alphabet, as written at Kufa. Also spelled *Cufic.*

Ku·fra (kōō′frä) A group of oases in the center of the Libyan Desert, southern Cyrenaica, Libya. *Italian* **Cu′fra.**

Kuhn (kōōn), **Richard,** 1900–1967, Austrian chemist.

Kui·by·shev (kwē′bi·shef) A city on the Volga river in SW Russian S.F.S.R.: formerly *Samara.*

Ku·ke·naam (kōō′kə·näm) A mountain (8,620 feet) and waterfall (dropping 2,000 feet) on the British Guiana–Venezuela boundary: also *Cuquenán.*

Ku Klux Klan (kyōō′ kluks′ klan′) *n.* **1** A secret society in the southern United States after the Civil War, aiming to prevent Negro ascendency. **2** A modern secret society, founded in 1915 at Atlanta, Ga., aiming at arbitrary regulation of life by white Protestants: also **Ku-Klux Klan. 3** A member of either society. [Alter. of Gk. *kyklos* a circle] — **Ku′ Klux′ Klan′ner.**

Ku·ku Nor (kōō′kōō′ nôr′) See KOKO NOR.

Ku·la Gulf (kōō′lə) A section of the SW Pacific in the Solomon Islands off New Georgia.

ku·lak (kōō′lak, kyōō′-, kōō·lak′, kyōō-) *n.* A well-to-do Russian peasant employing hired labor: the object of particular liquidation by the Soviet government after the Bolshevik revolution. [<Russian, lit., fist, tight-fisted man <Estonian]

Kul·tur (kōōl·tōōr′) *n.* Progress, achievement, and efficiency, in all phases, practical or theoretical, of political, economic, social, scientific, or artistic life. [<G]

Kul·tur·kampf (kōōl·tōōr′kämpf) *n.* The abortive political struggle initiated by Bismarck in 1872, between the German imperial government and the Roman Catholic Church, which had for its main issue the control by the state of educational and ecclesiastical appointments. [<G, culture-conflict]

Ku·lun (kōō′lōōn′) The Chinese name for ULAN BATOR.

Ku·ma·mo·to (kōō·mä·mō·tō) A port on the west coast of Kyushu island, Japan.

Ku·ma·si (kōō·mä′sē) A city in south central Ghana, the former capital of Ashanti: formerly *Coomassie.*

Kum·chon (kōōm·chon) A city of South Korea. *Japanese* **Kin·sen** (kin·sen).

ku·miss (kōō′mis) *n.* Fermented mare's milk, used by the Tatar tribes of central Asia, or a drink made in imitation of it: often spelled *koumiss, koumys.* Also **ku′mys.** [<Russian *kumys* <Tatar *kumix*]

küm·mel (kim′əl, *Ger.* kü′məl) *n.* A German or Russian liqueur flavored with aniseed, cumin, or caraway. [<G, caraway seed <L *cuminum*]

kum·mer·bund (kum′ər·bund) See CUMMERBUND.

kum·quat (kum′kwot) *n.* **1** A small citrus tree (genus *Fortunella*) cultivated in China, Japan, and the United States. **2** Its acid, plumlike, orange-colored fruit. Also spelled *cumquat.* [Cantonese alter. of Mandarin *chin-chü*, lit., golden orange]

Kun (kōōn), **Béla,** 1886–1938?, Hungarian Communist leader; premier 1919.

Kun·dry (kōōn′drē) In Wagner's *Parsifal,* a beautiful woman, slave of Klingsor, doomed to eternal penitence for having laughed at Christ while he carried the cross. She is redeemed from sin by Parsifal.

Ku·ne·ne (kōō·nā′nə) See CUNENE.

Ku·ners·dorf (kōō′nərs·dôrf) A village in western Poland, 4 miles east of Frankfort on the Oder; scene of a decisive defeat of Frederick the Great 1759. *Polish* **Ku·no·wi·ce** (kōō′nô·vē′·tse).

Kung (kōōng), **Hsiang-hsi,** born 1881, Chinese statesman.

K'ung Fu-tse (kōōng′ fōō′tse′) See CONFUCIUS.

Ku·nie (kōō′nye) See ISLE OF PINES, New Caledonia.

Ku·ni·yo·shi (kōō·nē·yō·shē), **Yasuo,** 1893–1953, U. S. painter born in Japan.

Kun·lun (kōōn′lōōn′) A series of mountain ranges in northern Tibet and southern Sinkiang; highest altitude, 25,340 feet: also *Kuenlun.*

Kun·ming (kōōn′ming′) The capital of Yunnan province, China: formerly *Yunnan.*

Kun·san (kōōn·sän) A port of South Korea. *Japanese* **Gun·zan** (gōōn·zän).

kunz·ite (kōōnts′īt) *n.* A lilac-colored variety of spodumene, used as a gemstone: found at Pala, California. [after G. F. *Kunz,* 1856–1932, U. S. mineralogist]

Kuo·min·tang (kwō′min′tang′) *n.* The nationalist party of China, founded in 1912 by Sun Yat-sen and led since 1927 by Chiang Kai-shek; defeated and ousted by the Chinese Communists following the Chinese civil war (1945–49). It retains control of Taiwan. [< Chinese *kuo* nationalist + *min* people's + *tang* party]

Ku·pang (kōō·päng′) A port of SW Timor, capital of Indonesian Timor.

Ku·pre·a·nof (kōō′prē·ä′nôf) An island in the Alexander Archipelago, SE Alaska.

Ku·ra (kōō′rä) A river in Transcaucasia, flowing 940 miles NE to the Caspian Sea: ancient *Cyrus.* Also **Kur** (kōōr).

kur·bash (kōōr′bash) *n.* A whip of heavy hide, used as an instrument of torture by the Turks. [<Turkish *qirbāch*]

Kurd (kûrd, kōōrd) *n.* One of a Moslem people dwelling chiefly in Kurdistan.

Kurd·ish (kûr′dish, kōōr′-) *adj.* Of or pertaining to the Kurds, their culture, or language. — *n.* The Iranian language of the Kurds.

Kur·di·stan (kûr′di·stan, kōōr′di·stän) A region in NW Iran, NE Iraq, and SE Turkey in Asia.

Ku·re (kōō·re) A city in SW Hondo island, Japan.

Kurg (kōōrg) See COORG.

Ku·ri·a Mu·ri·a Islands (kōō′rē·ə mōō′rē·ə) A group of five islands off the SE Oman coast in the Arabian Sea, considered part of Aden Colony; 28 square miles.

Ku·rile Islands (kōō·rēl′, kōō′ril) A chain of Russian islands between the southern tip of Kamchatka and the main islands of Japan; 5,700 square miles: Japanese *Chishima Retto.* Also **Ku′ril Islands, Ku′riles.**

Ku·ril·i·an (kōō·ril′ē·ən) *adj.* Of or pertaining to the Kurile Islands or their inhabitants. — *n.* A native of the Kurile Islands.

Kur·land (kōōr′lənd) See COURLAND.

Ku·ro·shi·wo (kōō·rō·shē·wō) See JAPAN CURRENT under CURRENT.

kur·ra·jong (kûr′ə·jong) *n.* Any of various Australian trees of the families *Sterculiaceae* and *Malvaceae* whose leaves are valued as fodder; especially, the **black kurrajong** *(Brachychiton populneum),* whose bark yields a durable, tough fiber: also spelled *currajong, koorajong.* [< native name]

Kursk (kōōrsk) A city in SW Russian S.F.S.R.

kur·to·sis (kər·tō′sis) *n. Stat.* The relative degree of curvature near the mode of a frequency curve, as compared with that of a normal curve of the same variance. [<Gk. *kyrtos* curved + -OSIS]

Ku·ru·su (kōō·rōō·sōō), **Saburo,** 1883–1954, Japanese diplomat.

Kush (kush), **Kush·it·ic** (kōōsh·it′ik) See CUSH, etc.

Kus·ko·kwim River (kus′kə·kwim) A river in western Alaska, flowing 600 miles SW to **Kuskokwim Bay,** an inlet of the Bering Sea.

kus·so (kus′ō) See CUSSO.

Kutch (kōōch, kuch) See CUTCH.

Kut-el-A·ma·ra (kōōt′el·ə·mä′rə) A city on the Tigris in eastern Iraq. Also **Kut** (kōōt), **Kut-al-I·ma·ra** (kōōt′äl·i·mä′rə).

Ku·tu·zov (kōō·tōō′zôf), **Mikhail Ilarionovich,** 1745–1813, Russian field marshal; defeated Napoleon at Smolensk (1812).

ku·vasz (kōō′väsh) *n.* A breed of large, powerful working dog with a thick, white coat. [<Magyar]

Ku·wait (kōō·wīt′) A sheikdom in NE Arabia; 1,930 square miles; capital, Kuwait: also *Koweit.* — **Ku·wait′i** *n.* & *adj.*

Kux·ha·ven (kōōks′hä·fən) See CUXHAVEN.

Kuyp (koip) See CUYP.

Kuz·netsk Basin (kōōz·nyetsk′) The richest coal basin in the U.S.S.R., comprising a region along the Tom in the south central Russian S.F.S.R. in Asia. Shortened form **Kuz·bas** (kōōz·bäs′).

kvass (kväs, kvas) *n.* A Russian fermented drink resembling sour beer, made from rye, barley, etc. [<Russian *kvas*]

Kwa·ja·lein (kwä′jə·lān) An atoll in the Marshall Islands; 6 square miles. Also **Kwa′ja·long** (-lông).

Kwang·chow (kwäng′chō′, *Chinese* gwäng′·jō′) The Chinese name for CANTON.

Kwang·cho·wan (kwäng′chō′wän′, *Chinese* gwäng′jō′wän′) The French name for CHANKIANG.

Kwang·si (kwang′sē′, *Chinese* gwäng′sē′) A province of SE China; 85,000 square miles; capital, Kweilin.

Kwang·tung (kwang′tōōng′, *Chinese* gwän′·dōōng′) A province in SE China; 85,000 square miles; capital, Canton.

Kwan·non (kwän·nōn) See KUAN YIN. Also **Kwan Yin** (kwän yin).

Kwan·tung Leased Territory (kwan′tōōng′, *Chinese* gwän′dōōng′) A region on the southern tip of Liaotung Peninsula, SE Manchuria, leased, 1905–1945, by Japan; 1,337 square miles. *Japanese* **Kan·to** (kän·tō).

kwash·i·or·kor (kwäsh′ē·ôr′kôr) *n. Pathol.* A nutritional disease prevalent among children in South Africa and elsewhere, characterized by swelling of the hands, feet, and face and the appearance of discolored blotches on the body. It is associated with a carbohydrate diet low in proteins and amino acids. Also called *Johnny red.* [< native name]

Kwei·chow (kwā′chou′, *Chinese* gwā′jō′) A province in southern China; 65,000 square miles; capital, Kweiyang.

Kwei·lin (kwā′lin′, *Chinese* gwā′lin′) The capital of Kwangsi province, China.

Kwei·sui (kwā′swā′, *Chinese* gwā′swā′) The capital of Suiyuan province, northern China.

Kwei·yang (kwā′yang′, *Chinese* gwā′yäng′) The capital of Kweichow province, China.

ky·a·nite (kī′ə·nīt) See CYANITE.

ky·an·ize (kī′ən·īz) *v.t.* **·ized, ·iz·ing** To impregnate, as wood, with mercuric chloride so as to prevent decay. Also, *Brit.* **ky′an·ise.** [<after J. H. *Kyan,* 1774–1850, Irish inventor] — **ky′an·i·za′tion** (-ə·zā′shən, -ī·zā′-) *n.*

kyar (kyär) See COIR.

Kyd (kid), **Thomas,** 1558–94, English dramatist.

kye (kī) *n. pl. Scot.* Kine.

Ky·klops (kī′klops) See CYCLOPS.

ky·lix (kī′liks) *n. pl.* **ky·li·kes** (kī′li·kēz) A shallow, circular, earthenware drinking cup, having small handles at the sides and resting on a slender, moderately high foot: used chiefly at banquets in ancient Greece: also spelled *cylix.* [<Gk., cup]

KYLIX

ky·mo·graph (kī′mə·graf, -gräf) *n.* **1** *Med.* An instrument for recording wavelike oscillations, composed of a revolving tambour on which a stylus records pulse waves, muscular contractions, respiratory

add,āce,câre,pälm; end,ēven; it,īce; odd,ōpen,ôrder; tōōk,pōōl; up,bûrn; ə = a in *above,* e in *sicken,* i in *clarity,* o in *melon,* u in *focus;* yōō = u in *fuse;* oi,oil; ou,pout; ch,check; g,go; ng,ring; th,thin; th,this; zh,vision. Foreign sounds à,œ,ü,kh,ṅ; and ◆: see page xx. < from; + plus; ? possibly.

movements, and the like. 2 *Aeron.* A device for recording the oscillations of an aircraft in flight. Also **ky′mo·graph′i·on** (-ē·on): sometimes spelled *cymograph.* [<Gk. *kyma* wave + -GRAPH] —**ky′mo·graph′ic** *adj.*

Kym·ric (kim′rik), **Kym·ry** (kim′rē) See CYMRIC, etc.

Kyn·e·wulf (kin′ə·wo͝olf, kün′-) See CYNEWULF.

Kyo·ga (kyō′gə), **Lake** A lake in central Uganda in the middle course of the Victoria Nile: also *Kioga.*

Kyong·song (kyông·sông) See SEOUL.

Kyo·to (kyō·tō) A city on SW Honshu island, Japan; the third largest city and the capital of the Japanese Empire until 1868: also *Kioto.*

ky·pho·sis (kī·fō′sis) *n. Pathol.* Backward curvature of the spine; humpback. [<NL <Gk. *kyphōsis* <*kyphos* humpbacked] —**ky·phot·ic** (kī·fot′ik) *adj.*

Kyr·i·e e·le·i·son (kir′i·ē i·lā′i·sən) *Eccl.* 1 An ancient petition used in eucharistic rites and other offices: **a** In the Greek Church, a response made by the people to prayers said in the liturgy. **b** In the Roman Catholic Church, a part of a short litany said or chanted immediately after the introit of the mass. 2 In the Anglican Church, a translation of this, said or chanted during the Eucharist. 3 A musical setting for this petition. [<LL <Gk. *Kyrie eleēson* Lord, have mercy]

kyr·i·o·log·ic (kir′ē·ə·loj′ik) See CURIOLOGIC.

kyte (kīt) *n. Scot.* The belly.

kythe (kīth) See KITHE.

Ky·the·ra (kē′thē·rä) A Greek island south of the Peloponnesus; 108 square miles: Latin *Cythera,* Italian *Cerigo.*

Kyu·shu (kyo͞o·sho͞o) The southernmost of the five principal islands of Japan; 16,247 square miles: also *Kiushu.*

Ky·zyl Kum (ki·zil′ ko͞om′) A desert area in Kazakh and Uzbek S.S.R., extending SE from the Aral Sea: also *Kizil Kum.*

L

l, L (el) *n. pl.* **l's, L's** or **ls, Ls** or **ells** (elz) 1 The 12th letter of the English alphabet: from Phoenician *lamed,* Greek *lambda,* Roman *L.* 2 The sound of the letter *l,* normally a voiced alveolar continuant. See ALPHABET. —*symbol* 1 The Roman numeral 50: see under NUMERAL. 2 *Chem.* Lithium (L). 3 Anything shaped like an L.

la[1] (lä) *n. Music* The sixth tone of the diatonic scale. [<Ital. <Med. L. See GAMUT.]

la[2] (lä, lô) *interj.* Look! O!: an exclamation expressing surprise, emphasis, etc. Also spelled *law.* [OE *lā.* Doublet of LO.]

L.A. (el′ā′) *Colloq.* Los Angeles.

laa·ger (lä′gər) *n.* A defensive enclosure formed by wagons or otherwise; camp. —*v.t.* & *v.i.* To camp in or form into a laager. Also spelled *lager.* [<Afrikaans <Du. *leger* a camp]

Laa·land (lô′län) A Danish island in the Baltic Sea; 479 square miles; chief city, Maribo: also *Lolland.*

lab·an (lab′ən) See LEBEN.

La·ban (lā′bən) Brother of Rebecca; father of Rachel and Leah. *Gen.* xxix 10–30.

lab·a·rum (lab′ə·rəm) *n. pl.* **·ra** (-rə) 1 The form of the Roman military standard adopted by Constantine, bearing the cross and the monogram of Christ. 2 An ecclesiastical banner borne in processions. [<LL <Gk. *labaron;* ult. origin unknown]

lab·da·num (lab′də·nəm) See LADANUM.

lab·e·fac·tion (lab′ə·fak′shən) *n.* The act of making or becoming weak or tottering; decay; downfall. Also *Archaic* **lab′e·fac·ta′tion** (-fak·tā′shən). [<L *labefactus,* pp. of *labefacere* cause to totter <*labare* totter, fall to pieces + *facere* make]

la·bel (lā′bəl) *n.* 1 A slip, as of paper, affixed to something and bearing an inscription to indicate its character, ownership, etc. 2 *Archit.* A projecting molding or dripstone over a wall opening. —*v.t.* **·beled** or **·belled, ·bel·ing** or **·bel·ling** 1 To mark with a label; attach a label to. 2 To classify; designate. [<OF, a ribbon, ? <OHG *lappa* a rag] —**la′·bel·er** or **la′bel·ler** *n.*

la·bel·lum (lə·bel′əm) *n. pl.* **·la** (-ə) 1 *Bot.* The lip or lower petal of an orchid, often enlarged or variously shaped. 2 *Entomol.* Part of the proboscis of a dipterous insect. [<NL <L, dim. of *labrum* a lip]

la·bi·a (lā′bē·ə) Plural of LABIUM.

la·bi·al (lā′bē·əl) *adj.* 1 Of or pertaining to the lips: a *labial* vein. 2 *Phonet.* Formed, articulated, or modified by the lips, as (p), (b), (m), (w), or the rounded vowels (ō) and (o͞o). 3 Having edges or lips, as an organ pipe. 4 Pertaining to the labia. —*n.* 1 *Phonet.* A labial sound. 2 An appliance designed to correct stammering. 3 An organ pipe with lips. [<Med. L *labialis* <L *labium* a lip]

la·bi·al·ize (lā′bē·əl·īz′) *v.t.* **·ized, ·iz·ing** *Phonet.* 1 To make labial; give a labial sound to. 2 To modify (a vowel) by rounding the lips; round. —**la′bi·al·ism, la′bi·al·i·za′tion** *n.*

la·bi·a ma·jo·ra (lā′bē·ə mə·jō′rə) *Anat.* The external mucous folds of the vulva. [<NL <L, lit., the larger lips]

labia mi·no·ra (mi·nō′rə) *Anat.* The inner mucous folds of the vulva. [<NL <L, lit., the smaller lips]

La·bi·a·tae (lā′bē·ā′tē) *n. pl.* A family of widely distributed herbs and shrubs with characteristically square stems, opposite leaves, and whorled flowers: it includes mint, hyssop, thyme, and many other aromatic and medicinal plants. [<NL <*labiatus* LABIATE]

la·bi·ate (lā′bē·āt, -it) *adj. Bot.* 1 Having lips or liplike parts, as a calyx or corolla. 2 Belonging to the *Labiatae.* Also **la′bi·at′ed.** [<NL *labiatus* <L *labium* a lip]

La·biche (là·bēsh′), **Eugène Marin,** 1815–88, French dramatist.

la·bile (lā′bil) *adj.* 1 Prone to undergo chemical change or alteration of atomic structure; unstable. 2 Having a tendency to glide from place to place; smoothly flowing or passing along. 3 Liable to err, slip, or fall. 4 Being free and uncontrolled: said of the emotions. [<L *labilis* <*labi* slip, fall] —**la·bil′i·ty** *n.*

labio- *combining form* Related to, or formed by the lips and (another organ): *labiodental.* [<L *labium* a lip]

la·bi·o·den·tal (lā′bē·ō·den′təl) *Phonet. adj.* Formed with the lower lip and the upper front teeth, as *f* and *v* in English. —*n.* A sound so formed. Also *dentilabial.*

la·bi·o·na·sal (lā′bē·ō·nā′zəl) *Phonet. adj.* Produced with the lips closed and the voiced breath passing through the nose, as *m.* —*n.* A sound so formed.

la·bi·o·ve·lar (lā′bē·ō·vē′lər) *Phonet. adj.* Produced with the lips rounded and partially closed and the back of the tongue near or against the velum, as *w.* —*n.* A sound so formed.

la·bi·um (lā′bē·əm) *n. pl.* **·bi·a** (-bē·ə) 1 A lip or liplike organ or part. 2 *pl.* The folds of the external genitals of the mammalian female. 3 *Entomol.* A movable sclerite between the maxillae of an insect, forming the lower surface of the mouth; the lower lip. [<L, a lip]

la·bor (lā′bər) *n.* 1 Physical or mental exertion, particularly for some useful or desired end; toil; work. 2 That which requires exertion or effort; a task. 3 The working class collectively. 4 Parturition; travail. 5 Any stress or difficulty. 6 *Naut.* Heavy rolling and pitching of a vessel. —**Department of Labor** An executive department of the U. S. government, since 1913 (from 1903 to 1913 part of the Department of Commerce and Labor) headed by the Secretary of Labor and charged with matters pertaining to the welfare of wage earners, especially in regard to wages, working conditions, and opportunities for employment. Also **Labor Department.** See synonyms under BUSINESS, INDUSTRY, TASK, TOIL[1], WORK. —*v.i.* 1 To do work; toil; strive to accomplish a work or purpose. 2 To move with difficulty or painful exertion. 3 To roll or pitch, as a ship in a heavy sea. 4 To be hindered, burdened, or oppressed: to *labor* under a misapprehension. 5 To suffer the pains of childbirth; be in travail. —*v.t.* 6 To work at laboriously; develop in great detail: to *labor* a point. 7 *Archaic* or *Poetic* To till; cultivate. Also, *Brit.,* *labour.* [<OF *labor, labour* <L *labor, -oris* toil, distress]

lab·o·ra·to·ry (lab′rə·tôr′ē, -tō′rē; *Brit.* lə·bor′ə·trē) *n. pl.* **·ries** 1 A building or room fitted up for conducting scientific experiments, analyses, or similar work. 2 A department, as in a factory, for research, testing, and experimental technical work. [<Med. L *laboratorium* <L *laborare* labor <*labor, -oris* labor]

Labor Day In most States of the United States, a legal holiday, usually the first Monday in September, originally set aside as a holiday in honor of labor.

la·bored (lā′bərd) *adj.* Performed laboriously; elaborate; strained: a *labored* joke.

la·bor·er (lā′bər·ər) *n.* One who performs physical or manual, especially unskilled, labor.

la·bo·ri·ous (lə·bôr′ē·əs, -bō′rē-) *adj.* 1 Requiring much labor; toilsome. 2 Diligent; industrious. See synonyms under ARDUOUS, DIFFICULT, WEARISOME. —**la·bo′ri·ous·ly** *adv.* —**la·bo′ri·ous·ness** *n.* [<OF *laborios* <L *laboriosus* <*labor* labor]

la·bor·ite (lā′bər·īt) *n.* One who supports labor interests, especially in politics. Also *Brit.* **la′bour·ite.**

la·bor om·ni·a vin·cit (lā′bôr om′nē·ə vin′sit) *Latin* Labor conquers all things.

la·bor-sav·ing (lā′bər·sā′ving) *adj.* Doing away with, or diminishing the need for, manual work.

labor union A union of workers organized to better working conditions and advance mutual interests; a trade union.

la·bour (lā′bər), **la·bour·er** (lā′bər·ər), etc. British spelling of LABOR, etc.

La·bour·ite (lā′bər·īt) *n.* A member of a Labour party in Great Britain or the Commonwealth.

Labour Party 1 In Great Britain, a political party drawing its chief support from the working class and committed to socialistic reform. Organized in the later 19th century, by the 1920's it had supplanted the Liberal Party as the chief opposition to the Conservative Party. 2 A similar party in other members of the Commonwealth.

Lab·ra·dor (lab′rə·dôr) 1 A territory of eastern Canada, comprising a dependency of Newfoundland; 110,000 square miles; capital, Battle Harbor. 2 The peninsula of NE North America between the Saint Lawrence River and Hudson Bay; 530,000 square miles.

Labrador auk See PUFFIN.

lab·ra·dor·ite (lab′rə·dôr′īt) *n.* A triclinic lime-soda feldspar exhibiting a brilliant play of colors. [from *Labrador,* where originally found + -ITE[1]]

Labrador Sea A part of the North Atlantic between Labrador and SW Greenland.

Labrador tea An evergreen shrub (*Ledum groenlandicum*) of the northern regions, having white flowers and rust-colored leaves used for tea.

la·bret (lā′bret) *n.* A stud or plug of hard material, as stone, worn as an ornament in a hole pierced in the lip by various primitive peoples. [Dim. of LABRUM]

la·broid (lā′broid) *adj.* Of or pertaining to a family (*Labridae*) of fishes including the wrasses, tautog, etc. —*n.* A labroid fish. [< NL *Labroidea* <*Labrus* a genus of the family

Labridae <L *labrus* a kind of fish < *labrum* a lip]

la·brum (lā′brəm, lab′rəm) *n. pl.* **·bra** (-brə) **1** A lip (especially an outer lip) or a liplike part. **2** *Entomol.* A usually movable sclerite situated between the mandibles of an insect; the upper lip. **3** *Zool.* The outer lip of a univalve shell. [<L, a lip]

La Bru·yère (lä brü·yâr′), **Jean de,** 1645–96, French writer and moralist.

La·bu·an (lä′bo͞o·än′) An island off the NW coast of Borneo, a part of Sabah; 30 square miles; chief town, Victoria.

la·bur·num (lə·bûr′nəm) *n.* Any of a genus *(Laburnum)* of deciduous Old World trees, especially the **golden-chain laburnum** *(L. anagyroides),* having pendulous racemes of yellow flowers and hard, dark wood: it yields a poisonous alkaloid used in medicine as a purgative and emetic. [<NL <L; ult. origin unknown]

lab·y·rinth (lab′ə·rinth) *n.* **1** A confusing network of passages, as in a building; a maze of intricate paths, as in a park or garden. **2** Hence, any perplexing combination. **3** *Anat.* The winding passages of the internal ear. [<LABYRINTH] — **lab′y·rin′·thine** (-thin, -thēn) or **thi·an** or **·thic** or **·thi·cal** *adj.* — **lab′y·rin′·thi·cal·ly** *adv.*

THE LABYRINTH OF MINOS

Lab·y·rinth (lab′ə·rinth) In Greek mythology, the maze used to confine the Minotaur, constructed by Daedalus for Minos of Crete. [<L *labyrinthus* <Gk. *labyrinthos*; ult. origin unknown]

lac[1] (lak) *n.* **1** A resinous substance exuded from an East Indian lac insect *(Tachardia lacca)* and used in making varnishes, etc. Compare SHELLAC. **2** The sap of certain trees or plants used for varnish. **3** Lacquer. [< Hind. *lākh* <Prakrit *lakkha* <Skt. *lākshā*]

lac[2] (lak) See LAKH.

lac[3] (lak) *n.* Milk. [<NL <L]

Lac·ca·dive Islands (lak′ə·dīv) A group of 14 coral reefs and islands in the SE Arabian Sea off the Malabar Coast, comprising a Union Territory of India; total, long thought to be about 80 square miles; the Indian government figure is 10 square miles; headquarters at Kozhikode in Kerala, India.

lac·case (lak′ās) *n.* A copper-protein enzyme which oxidizes phenols, found in the lacquer tree and other plants. [<NL *lacc(a)* lacquer + -ASE]

lac·cate (lak′āt) *adj. Bot.* Having a varnished appearance, as the leaves of certain plants. [<NL *lacc(a)* lacquer + -ATE[1]]

lac·co·lith (lak′ə·lith) *n. Geol.* A mass of intrusive lava spreading out between strata and lifting the overlying rocks into domes. Also **lac′co·lite** (-līt). [<Gk. *lakkos* a reservoir + -LITH[1]] — **lac′co·lith′ic, lac′co·lit′ic** (-lit′ik) *adj.*

lace (lās) *n.* **1** A cord or string for fastening together the parts of a shoe, a corset, etc.; any string. **2** A delicate network of threads of linen, silk, cotton, etc., arranged in figures or patterns; also, any ornamental cord or braid. **3** A dash of spirits, as in tea or coffee. — *v.* **laced, lac·ing** *v.t.* **1** To fasten or draw together by tying the lace or laces of. **2** To pass (a cord or string) through hooks, eyelets, etc., as a lace. **3** To trim with or as with lace. **4** To compress the waist of (a person) by tightening laces, as of a corset. **5** To intertwine or interlace. **6** To streak, as with color. **7** To add a dash of spirits to. **8** *Colloq.* To beat; thrash. — *v.i.* **9** To be fastened by means of a lace. — **to lace into** To strike or attack with or as with a heavy blow or blows. [<OF *laz, las* orig. a noose <L *laqueus* a noose, trap. Akin to LASH, LATCH.]

TYPES OF LACE
Alencon Battenberg Blonde Pointe
Mechlin Honiton d'Angleterre

Lac·e·dae·mon (las′ə·dē′mən) See SPARTA.

Lac·e·dae·mo·ni·an (las′ə·di·mō′nē·ən) *adj.* & *n.* Spartan; Laconian.

lace·ground (lās′ground′) *n.* A foundation of lacelike net; a réseau.

lac·er (lā′sər) *n.* **1** One who laces. **2** A dash of spirits added to a beverage.

lac·er·ate (las′ər·āt) *v.t.* **·at·ed, ·at·ing** **1** To tear raggedly, as the flesh. **2** To hurt; injure, as the feelings. See synonyms under REND. — *adj.* Rent; jagged; torn. [<L *laceratus,* pp. of *lacerare* tear < *lacer* mangled] — **lac′·er·a·ble** *adj.* — **lac′er·a′tion** *n.* — **lac′er·a′tive** *adj.*

La·cer·ta (lə·sûr′tə) *n.* **1** *Astron.* A northern constellation near Cepheus. See CONSTELLATION. **2** *Zool.* A genus of Old World lizards typical of the family *Lacertidae,* especially the common green lizard *(L. viridis)* of southern Europe. [<L, a lizard]

lac·er·til·i·an (las′ər·til′ē·ən) *n.* One of a suborder of reptiles *(Lacertilia)* which includes lizards, chameleons, and related limbless forms. — *adj.* Of or pertaining to the *Lacertilia*: also **la·cer·ti·an** (lə·sûr′shē·ən, -shən). [<NL *Lacertilia* <L *lacertus, lacerta* a lizard]

lace·wing (lās′wing′) *n.* Any of certain insects (order *Neuroptera)* having four lacy wings and shiny eyes, especially the green lacewing (genus *Chrysopa)* or the brown lacewing (genus *Hemerobius*), the larvae of which destroy insects. For illustration see INSECT (beneficial).

lace·wood (lās′wo͝od′) *n.* **1** The American sycamore. **2** The silky oak *(Cardwellia sublimis)* of Queensland, Australia. **3** The wood of either of these trees, used for furniture, cabinetwork, and veneering.

lace·work (lās′wûrk′) *n.* **1** Lace. **2** Any openwork resembling lace.

lach·es (lach′iz) *n. Law* Inexcusable delay in asserting a right. [<AF *laches, lachesse,* OF *laschesse* < *lasche* negligent < *laschier* slacken <L *laxare* < *laxus* lax]

Lach·e·sis (lak′ə·sis) One of the three Fates. [<L <Gk., lit., a lot < *lanchanein* obtain by lot or fate]

La·chish (lā′kish) A Bibical locality south of Jerusalem, a Canaanite capital, II *Kings* xiv 19.

Lach·lan River (läk′lən) A river in south central New South Wales, Australia, flowing 922 miles SW to the Murrumbidgee River.

lach·ry·mal (lak′rə·məl), **lach·ry·ma·tor** (lak′·rə·mā′tər), etc. See LACRIMAL, etc.

lac·ing (lā′sing) *n.* **1** The act of fastening, as with a lace. **2** Lace (def. 1). **3** A connecting or strengthening member; crosspiece. **4** *Colloq.* A thrashing. **5** Any ornamental braid, as of gold or silver.

lacing course A band of dressed stone inset into a rough-hewn stone wall to form a horizontal line in an otherwise unrelieved design.

la·cin·i·ate (lə·sin′ē·āt, -it) *adj.* **1** Bordered with fringe; fringed. **2** *Bot.* Slashed or cut irregularly into narrow lobes or segments; fringed; incised, as flower petals. Also **la·cin′i·at′ed, la·cin′i·ose** (-ōs). [<NL *lacinia* a slash in a leaf or petal (<L, a flap) + -ATE[1]]

lack (lak) *v.t.* **1** To be without; have none or too little of. **2** To be short by; require: It *lacks* two months till summer. — *v.i.* **3** To be wanting or deficient; be missing. — *n.* **1** The state of being needy. **2** Want; deficiency; failure. [ME *lac,* prob. <MLG *lak* deficiency]

lack·a·dai·si·cal (lak′ə·dā′zi·kəl) *adj.* Affectedly sentimental; languishing; listless. Also **lack′a·dai′sy** (-dā′zē). [< *lackadaisy,* alter. of LACKADAY. — **lack′a·dai′si·cal·ly** *adv.* — **lack′a·dai′si·cal·ness** *n.*

lack·a·day (lak′ə·dā′) *interj. Archaic* Alack!: an exclamation expressing grief or regret. [Aphetic var. of ALACKADAY. See ALACK.]

lack·ey (lak′ē) *n.* **1** A male servant; a footman; menial. **2** Any servile attendant or follower. — *v.t.* & *v.i.* To attend or act as a lackey. Also LACQUEY. [<OF *laquay* <Sp. *lacayo,* ? <Arabic *luka'* servile]

lack·lus·ter (lak′lus′tər) *adj.* Wanting luster; dim. — *n.* A lack of luster; dullness; also, that which wants luster. Also *Brit.* **lack′lus′tre.**

lac·mus (lak′məs) See LITMUS.

La·co·ni·a (lə·kō′nē·ə) A region and ancient country in the SE Peloponnesus, Greece; 1,500 square miles; capital, Sparta: Modern Greek *Lakonía.* Also **La·con·i·ca** (lə·kon′i·kə). — **La·co′ni·an** *adj.* & *n.*

la·con·ic (lə·kon′ik) *adj.* Using or consisting of few words; short and forceful; concise; pithy. Also **la·con′i·cal.** See synonyms under TERSE. [<L *Laconicus* <Gk. *Lakonikos* <*Lakōn* a Spartan; with ref. to the habitual terseness of Spartan speech] — **la·con′i·cal·ly** *adv.*

lac·o·nism (lak′ə·niz′əm) *n.* **1** A brief and sententious manner of expression. **2** A terse, pointed phrase; laconic expression. Also **la·con·i·cism** (lə·kon′ə·siz′əm).

La Co·ru·ña (lä kō·ro͞o′nyä) See CORUÑA, LA.

lac·quer (lak′ər) *n.* **1** A quick-drying varnish made from pyroxylin or other resin, nitrocellulose, and sometimes a pigment, dissolved in a volatile solvent. **2** Varnished woodwork, often inlaid: Chinese *lacquer,* Japanese *lacquer*: also **lac′quer·work′.** **3** A resinous varnish susceptible of a fine polish, obtained from the lacquer tree *(Toxicodendron verniciflnum)* of China and Japan. **4** Decorative work, as on leather lacquered in imitation of enamel. — *v.t.* To coat or varnish with lacquer. Also **lack′er.** [<MF *lacre* a kind of sealing wax <Pg. < *lacca* gum lac <Hind. *lākh* LAC[1]; infl. in form by F *lacque* LAC[1]] — **lac′quer·er** *n.*

lacquer red Any of various shades of vermilion characteristic of Chinese lacquer.

lac·ri·mal (lak′rə·məl) *adj.* **1** Of or pertaining to tears. **2** Pertaining to or related to tear-producing organs. — *n.* A lacrimatory. Also spelled *lachrymal.* [<Med. L *lacrimalis, lacrymalis* <L *lacrima* a tear]

lac·ri·mar·y (lak′rə·mer′ē) *adj.* Pertaining to, containing, or meant to contain tears: also *lacrimatory.* Also spelled *lachrymary.* [<L *lacrima*]

lac·ri·ma·tion (lak′rə·mā′shən) *n.* **1** The act of shedding tears. **2** The secretion of tears. [<L *lacrimatio, -onis* < *lacrimatus,* pp. of *lacrimare* shed tears < *lacrima* a tear]

lac·ri·ma·tor (lak′rə·mā′tər) *n.* Any of various chemicals which, on being released from shells, bombs, or other containers, provoke a copious flow of tears, with irritation of the eyes: also called *tear gas.* [<L *lacrima* a tear + -ATOR]

lac·ri·ma·to·ry (lak′rə·mə·tôr′ē, -tō′rē) *n. pl.* **·ries** A small, narrow-necked glass bottle of a type found in ancient tombs, formerly supposed to have contained the tears of mourners. — *adj.* Lacrimary. Also spelled *lachrymatory.* [<Med. L *lacrimatorium* <L, neut. of *lacrimatorius* of tears < *lacrima* a tear]

LACRIMATORY

lac·ri·mose (lak′rə·mōs) *adj.* Shedding, or given to shedding, tears; tearful: also spelled *lachrymose.* [<L *lacrimosus* < *lacrima* a tear] — **lac′ri·mose′ly** *adv.*

la·crosse (lə·krôs′, -kros′) *n.* A ball game of American Indian origin, played by two teams of ten men each: the object of each side is to advance the ball across the field with a long, racketlike implement (the *crosse*) between the opponents' goal posts. [<F *la crosse,* lit., the crozier, hooked stick]

La Crosse (lə krôs′, -kros′) A city on the Mississippi in western Wisconsin.

lac·tal·bu·min (lak′təl·byo͞o′min) *n. Biochem.* A water-soluble protein found in milk. [<LACT- + ALBUMIN]

lac·tam (lak′tam) *n. Chem.* Any of a series of organic ring compounds containing the CO·NH group and formed by the elimination of water from the carboxyl and amino groups. [<LACT- + AM(INO)]

Lac·tan·tius (lak·tan′shəs), **Lucius Caecilius,**

Latin Christian author of the fourth century.

lac·ta·ry (lak′tər·ē) *adj.* Of or pertaining to milk. [<*lactarius* <*lac, lactis* milk]

lac·tase (lak′tās) *n. Biochem.* An enzyme present in the digestive juices, in certain yeasts, etc., and capable of changing lactose into glucose and galactose.

lac·tate (lak′tāt) *v.i.* **·tat·ed, ·tat·ing 1** To form or secrete milk. **2** To suckle young. —*n.* A salt or ester of lactic acid. —**lac·ta′·tion** *n.*

lac·te·al (lak′tē·əl) *adj.* Pertaining to or like milk; conveying a milklike fluid: also **lac′te·an, lac′te·ous.** —*n. Anat.* One of the lymphatic vessels that take up and convey the chyle. [<L *lacteus* <*lac, lactis* milk]

lac·tes·cence (lak·tes′əns) *n.* The quality of being milklike; milkiness. Also **lac·tes′cen·cy.**

lac·tes·cent (lak·tes′ənt) *adj.* **1** Milklike; becoming milky. **2** Having or secreting a milky juice. [<L *lactescens, -entis,* ppr. of *lactescere,* inceptive of *lactere* be milky <*lac, lactis* milk]

lac·tic (lak′tik) *adj.* **1** Of, pertaining to, or derived from milk. **2** *Chem.* Designating a limpid sirupy acid, **lactic acid,** $C_3H_6O_3$, with a very bitter taste, contained in sour milk, and the result of lactic fermentation in many compounds.

lac·tif·er·ous (lak·tif′ər·əs) *adj.* **1** Conveying or containing milk or milky fluid; lacteal. **2** Yielding a milky juice, as certain plants. [<LL *lactifer* milk-bearing <L *lac, lactis* milk + *-fer* -FEROUS]

lacto- *combining form* Milk: *lactogenic.* Also before vowels, **lact-.** [<L *lac, lactis* milk]

lac·to·ba·cil·lus (lac′tō·bə·sil′əs) *n. pl.* **·cil·li** (-sil′ī) Any aerobic, rod-shaped bacterium of a genus *(Lactobacillus)* which forms lactic acid, especially *L. acidophilus,* used in the dairy industry and in fermentation processes. [<NL <L *lac, lactis* milk + BACILLUS]

lac·to·fla·vin (lak′tō·flā′vin) See RIBOFLAVIN.

lac·to·gen·ic (lak′tō·jen′ik) *adj.* **1** Stimulating the milk glands. **2** Designating a hormone, as prolactin, which stimulates the secretion of milk.

lac·to·glob·u·lin (lak′tō·glob′yə·lin) *n.* A globulin of milk.

lac·tom·e·ter (lak·tom′ə·tər) *n.* A hydrometer for determining the density or richness of milk.

lac·tone (lak′tōn) *n. Chem.* One of a class of organic anhydrides in which the molecule of water is derived from hydroxyl and carboxyl, both contained in the same radical, with the etherification in the same radical, with the etherification of the acid part by the alcoholic part. [<LACT- + -ONE] —**lac·ton·ic** (lak·ton′ik) *adj.*

lac·to·pro·te·in (lak′tō·prō′tē·in, -tēn) *n.* A protein derived from milk.

lac·to·scope (lak′tə·skōp) *n.* An instrument for determining the purity or richness of milk.

lac·tose (lak′tōs) *n. Biochem.* A white, odorless, cyrstalline disaccharide, $C_{12}H_{22}O_{11}·H_2O$, present in milk; milk sugar. [<LACT(O)- + -OSE[2]]

lac·tu·ca·ri·um (lak′tŏŏ·kâr′ē·əm) *n.* The wild lettuce *(Lactuca virosa)* or its inspissated milky juice, used as a sedative. [<NL <L *lactuca* lettuce]

La Cum·bre (lä kŏŏm′brā) See USPALLATA.

la·cu·na (lə·kyŏŏ′nə) *n. pl.* **·nas** or **·nae** (-nē) **1** A space from which something is wanting or has been omitted; hiatus; gap. **2** A small pit, hollow, or depression; a gap or small opening. **3** *Anat.* One of the cavities in which lie the osteoblasts of bone. Also **la·cune′** (-kyŏŏn′). [<L, a hole, pool <*lacus* a basin, pond]

la·cu·nar (lə·kyŏŏ′nər) *adj.* **1** Of or pertaining to a lacuna. **2** Containing or having lacunae: also **la·cu′nal.** —*n. pl.* **la·cu·nars** or **lac·u·nar·i·a (lak′yōō·nâr′ē·ə)** *Archit.* **1** A sunken panel or coffer in a ceiling or a soffit. **2** A ceiling or a soffit having sunken panels or compartments. —**lac·u·nar·y** (lak′yōō·ner′ē) *adj.*

la·cu·nose (lə·kyŏŏ′nōs) *adj.* Marked by shallow depressions. [<L *lacunosus* <*lacuna.* See LACUNA.]

la·cus·trine (lə·kus′trin) *adj.* **1** Of or pertaining to a lake. **2** Found in or growing in lakes, as certain plants. **3** Formed in or near lakes, as geological deposits. Also **la·cus′tral, la·cus′tri·an.** [<L *lacus* a lake]

lac·y (lā′sē) *adj.* **lac·i·er, lac·i·est 1** Lacelike. **2** Of lace. —**lac′i·ly** *adv.* —**lac′i·ness** *n.*

lad (lad) *n.* A boy or youth; companion; fellow. Also **lad′die.** [<ME *ladde,* ? ult. <ON]

La·dakh (lə·däkh′) A district of eastern Kashmir; 45,762 square miles; capital, Leh

lad·a·num (lad′ə·nəm) *n.* A dark-colored, brittle, bitter resin from various species of the rockrose (genus *Cistus*): often spelled *labdanum.* See LAUDANUM. [<L *ladanum, ledanum* <Gk. *ladanon, lēdanon* <*lēdon* mastic]

lad·der (lad′ər) *n.* **1** A device of wood, rope, etc., for climbing and descending: usually a series of rounds, supported at their ends by long sidepieces; also, any means of ascending. **2** A run in a stocking or other knit fabric. **3** *Mil.* A three-round burst fired rapidly from a gun pointing in the same direction but with the second and third rounds at a decreased range. [OE *hlædder*]

lad·der-back (lad′ər·bak′) *n.* A chair back constructed with two posts connected by horizontal slats; also, a chair having such a back.

ladder stitch An embroidery stitch giving a ladder effect.

lade (lād) *v.* **lad·ed, lad·ed** or **lad·en, lad·ing** *v.t.* **1** To load with a burden or cargo; also, to load as a cargo. **2** To weight down; burden; oppress. **3** To dip or lift (a liquid) in or out with a ladle or dipper. —*v.i* **4** To receive cargo. **5** To dip or lift a liquid. See synonyms under LOAD. [OE *hladan* load]

lad·en[1] (lād′n) Alternative past participate of LADE. —*adj.* Burdened: *laden* with care.

lad·en[2] (lād′n) *v.t.* & *v.i.* **lad·ened, lad·en·ing** To lade. [Var. of LADE]

La·dies' Aid Society (lā′dēz) **1** A women's organization founded during the Civil War to make and send clothing, bandages, etc., to the soldiers. **2** Any of various women's societies engaged in raising money for church purposes.

ladies' room In a public building, a room or rooms provided with toilet facilities for women.

la·dies-tress·es (lā′dēz·tres′iz) See LADY-TRESSES.

La·din lə·dēn′) *n.* **1** A Rhaeto-Romanic dialect spoken in the Engadine and Friuli regions of Switzerland and northern Italy. **2** One who speaks Ladin. [<L *Latinus* Latin]

la·ding (lā′ding) *n.* **1** The act of loading. **2** A load or cargo.

la·di·no (lə·dē′nō *n. SW U.S.* A horse that is cunning as well as vicious and unmanageable. [<Sp., cunning, crafty]

La·di·no lä·dē′nō *n.* **1** A Spanish dialect, with many Hebrew elements, spoken by Turkish and other Sephardic Jews. **2** In Latin America, a mestizo. [<Sp., wise, learned, <L *Latinus* Latin]

Lad·is·laus (lad′is·lôs) A masculine personal name. Also **Lad′is·las** (-läs). [<Slavic, ruling with fame]

—**Ladislaus I** —**Ladislaus I,** 1040?–95, king of Hungary 1077–95; canonized, 1192.

la·dle (lād′l) *n.* **1** A cup-shaped vessel, with a long handle, for dipping or conveying liquids. **2** A milwheel float. —*v.t.* **·dled, ·dling** To dip up and carry in a ladle. [OE *hlædel* <*hladan* lade] —**la′dler** *n.*

La·do·ga (lä′dô·gä), **Lake** The largest lake in Europe, in NW European U.S.S.R.; 7,100 square miles. *Finnish* **Laa·tok·ka** (lä′tôk·kä).

La·don (lā′dən) In Greek mythology, the never-sleeping dragon guarding the golden apples of the Hesperides.

la·drone (lə·drōn′) *n.* A mercenary soldier; robber; rascal. [<Sp. *ladrón,* <L *latro, -onis* a robber]

La·drone Islands (lə·drōn′) See MARIANAS ISLANDS. Also **La·drones′.**

la·dro·nism (lə·drō′niz·əm) *n.* **1** Brigandage; plunder. **2** Resistance by ladrones.

la·dy (lā′dē) *n. pl.* **·dies 1** A refined and well-bred woman; a gentlewoman. **2** A woman of superior position in society; a woman of good family and recognized social standing. **3** Any woman: in the plural, used as a form of address. **4** The woman who is at the head of or has authority over a household or an estate: the *lady* of the house; the mistress of a family or manor. **5** A sweetheart; ladylove. **6** *Colloq.* Wife: the colonel's *lady.* —*adj.* **1** Of or like a lady; becoming to a lady. **2** Female: a *lady* doctor. ◆ *Lady* is here a genteelism, as it is in such compounds as *saleslady. Woman* is the more appropriate word to indicate the feminine gender of these occupational terms: a *woman* doctor, a *saleswoman,* etc. [OE *hlǣfdīge,* lit., bread-kneader <*hlāf* bread, loaf + *-dige,* a stem akin to *dāh* dough]

La·dy (lā′dē) *n.* **1** In Great Britain, the title belonging to the wife of any peer below the rank of duke; also given by courtesy to the daughters of dukes, marquises, and earls, and to the wives of lords, baronets, and knights: correlative to *Lord* or *Sir.* **2** The Virgin Mary: usually with *Our.*

la·dy·bell (lā′dē·bel′) *n.* An Erect perennial herb (genus *Adenophora)* having fleshy roots and bell-shaped, usually violet, flowers: often confused with the bellflower.

la·dy·bird (lā′dē·bûrd′) *n.* A small, convex, brightly-colored beetle *(Adalia bipunctata),* usually red spotted with black, or black spotted with red. It feeds on aphids and other small insects. Also **lady beetle, la′dy·bug′** (-bug′). For illustration see INSECT (beneficial).

Lady Day A day observed in honor of the Virgin Mary; specifically, the feast of the Annunciation, March 25: one of the quarter days in England.

la·dy·fin·ger (lā′dē·fing′gər) *n.* **1** A small sponge cake: so called from its shape. **2** A very small firecracker.

la·dy-in-wait·ing (lā′dē·in·wā′ting) *n. pl.* **la·dies-in-wait·ing** A lady of the British royal household in attendance at court.

la·dy-kill·er (lā′dē·kil′ər) *n. Colloq.* A man supposed to be peculiarly fascinating to women. —**la′dy-kill′ing** *adj.* & *n.*

la·dy·kin (lā′di·kin) *n.* A little lady. [Dim. of LADY]

la·dy·like (lā′dē·līk′) *adj.* **1** Like or suitable to a lady; gentle; delicate. **2** Effeminate.

la·dy·love (lā′dē·luv′) *n.* A woman who is beloved; sweetheart.

Lady of the Lake See VIVIEN.

la·dy·palm (lā′dē·päm′) *n.* A low, reedlike fan palm (genus *Rhaphis*) with broad leaves and yellowish flowers, native to southern China.

la·dy·ship (lā′dē·ship) *n.* The rank or condition of a lady: used as a title, with *her* or *your.*

la·dy·slip·per (lā′dē·slip′ər) *n.* **1** Any of a genus *(Cypripedium)* of orchids resembling a slipper; especially, in the United States, the common wild species. *C. calceolus pubescens* and *C. parviflorum.* **2** The moccasin flower. Also **la′dy's-slip′per.**

SHOWY LADYSLIPPER (Up to 2 feet tall)

lady's man A man fond of the company of women and attentive to them. Also **ladies' man.**

La·dy·smith (lā′dē·smith) A town in Kwa Zulu/Natal province, Republic of South Africa; besieged by Boers 1899–1900.

la·dy-smock (lā′dē·smok′) *n.* The cuckoo flower. Also **la′dy's-smock′.**

la·dy's-thumb (lā′dēz·thum′) *n.* Persicary.

la·dy-tress·es (lā′dē·tres′iz) *n.* A hardy terrestrial orchid (genus *Spiranthes*) of wide distribution, having slender stems and small flowers in more or less twisted spikes: also spelled *ladies-tresses.* Also **la′dy's-tress′es.**

La·e (lä′ā) A port, chief city of the Territory of New Guinea.

Laën·nec (lā·nek′), **René Théophile Hyacinthe,** 1781–1826, French physician; invented the stethoscope.

La·er·tes (lā·ûr′tēz) **1** In the *Odyssey,* a king of Ithaca; father of Odysseus. **2** In Shakespeare's *Hamlet,* brother of Ophelia and son of Polonius.

Lae·ta·re Sunday (lē·târ′ē) *n.* The fourth Sunday in Lent: Mid-Lent Sunday: so called from the first word in the introit of the mass of that day. [<L. imperative sing. of *laetari* rejoice <*laetus* joyful]

laevo- See LEVO-.

La Farge (Lə färj′), John, 1835–1910, U.S. painter.

La·fay·ette (lä′fē·et′, laf′ē·et′; *Fr.* lä·fä·yet′), **Marquis de,** 1757–1834, Marie Joseph Paul Yves Roch Gilbert Motier, French general and patriot; served in the American Revolutionary army. Also **La Fay·ette′.**

La Fol·lette (lə fol′it), Robert Marion, 1855–

1925, U.S. political leader; U.S. senator 1906–1925.

La Fon·taine (lä fon·tān′, *Fr.* là fôn·ten′), **Jean de,** 1621–95, French fabulist and poet.

lag[1] (lag) *v.i.* **lagged, lag·ging** **1** To move slowly; stay or fall behind; loiter. **2** In billiards, to shoot one's cue ball to the end rail so that it will rebound to the head rail, the player whose ball stops nearest the end rail winning first place in the order of play. **3** In marbles, to throw one's taw as near as possible to a line on the ground in order to decide the order of play. See synonyms under LINGER. — *n.* **1** Retardation of movement for any cause. **2** The retardation of magnetization in respect of a magnetizing force. **3** In billiards and marbles, an act of lagging. [? Var. of LACK]

lag[2] (lag) *n.* **1** A stave of a barrel, cask, drum, etc. **2** A piece forming part of a lagging. — *v.t.* **lagged, lag·ging** To provide or cover with lags or lagging. [Prob. <ON *lögg* rim of a barrel]

lag[3] (lag) *v.t.* **lagged, lag·ging** *Slang* **1** To arrest. **2** To send to penal servitude. — *n.* *Slang* **1** A convict. **2** A period of penal servitude. [Prob. <LEG, with ref. to fetters]

lag·an (lag′ən) *n.* In maritime law, goods cast from a vessel in peril, but to which a buoy or float is attached as evidence of ownership: also spelled *ligan.* Compare FLOTSAM, JETSAM. [<AF <Gmc.: prob. akin to ON *lögn* a net laid in the sea]

La·gash (lā′gash) An ancient Sumerian city in southern Babylonia: also *Shirpula.*

Lag b'O·mer (läg′ bō′mər) A Jewish festival, the 18th day of Iyyar. [<Hebrew, lit., 33rd (day) of the omer (the 49 days from the second day of Passover to the first of Shabuoth)]

la·ger (lä′gər) *n.* **1** Beer containing few hops, and stored for several months before use: also **lager beer. 2** Laager. [<G *lager-bier,* lit., store beer, < *lager* a storehouse + *bier* beer]

La·ger·kvist (lä′yər·kvist), **Pär,** born 1891, Swedish novelist and dramatist.

La·ger·lof (lä′yər·lœf), **Selma,** 1858–1940, Swedish novelist.

lag·gard (lag′ərd) *n.* One who lags; a loiterer. — *adj.* Falling behind; loitering; slow; tardy. [<LAG[1] + -ARD] — **lag′gard·ly** *adv.* — **lag′·gard·ness** *n.*

lag·gen (lag′ən) *n.* *Dial. & Scot.* **1** The angle formed by the bottom and side of a wooden dish. **2** The bottom hoop, as of a cask. **3** *pl.* Barrel staves. Also **lag′gin.** [<ON *lögg;* infl. in form by LAGGING]

lag·ger (lag′ər) *n.* **1** One who lags. **2** *Slang* A convict serving or having served a term of penal servitude.

lag·ging (lag′ing) *n.* **1** Strips of wood used for various purposes, as to form a jacketing for a steam cylinder, to support an arch of masonry while in construction, to brace the beams of a floor, etc. **2** The action of covering. [<LAG[2]]

La Gio·con·da (lä jō·kôn′dä) See MONA LISA.

la·gniappe (lan·yap′, lan′yap) *n.* *Dial.* A small present given to the purchaser of an article by a merchant or storekeeper; a gratuity: also spelled *lanyappe.* Also **la·gnappe′.** [<dial. F (Creole) <F *la* the + Sp. *ñapa* a lagniappe <Quechua *yapa*]

La·go·a dos Pa·tos (lə·gō′ə thōosh pä′tōos) See PATOS, LAGOA DOS.

La·go di Gar·da (lä′gō dē gär′dä) See GARDA.

Lag·o·mor·pha (lag′ə·môr′fə) *n. pl.* An order of gnawing mammals regarded as differing from the rodents in dentition and in structure of the jaws, including rabbits, hares, and pikas. [<NL <Gk. *lagōs* a hare + *morphē* form]

la·goon (lə·gōon′) *n.* *Geog.* **1** A body of shallow salt water, as a bay or inlet, separated from but connecting with the sea. **2** A body of shallow fresh water, as a pond or lake, usually connecting with a river or lake. **3** A depression in high tablelands of the western United States. Also **la·gune′.** [<F *lagune* <Ital. *laguna* <L *lacuna.* See LACUNA.]

Lagoon Islands A former name for the ELLICE ISLANDS.

lag·oph·thal·mos (lag′əf·thal′məs) *n.* *Pathol.* A morbid condition in which the eyes cannot be completely closed; also called *hare's-eye.* [<NL <Gk. *lagōphthalmos* hare-eyed, unable to close the eyes < *lagōs* a hare + *ophthalmos* an eye] — **lag′oph·thal′mic** *adj.*

La·gos (lä′gōs, lā′gos) **1** A port on the Gulf of Guinea, capital of Nigeria. **2** A former British colony, amalgamated with Nigeria since 1906.

La·grange (lə·grānj′, *Fr.* là·gräṅzh′), **Joseph Louis,** 1736–1813, French mathematician and astronomer.

La Gran·ja (lä gräng′hä) See SAN ILDEFONSO.

Lag·ting (läg′ting) *n.* The upper house of the Norwegian parliament. [<Norw. *lag* society, law + *ting* parliament]

La Guai·ra (lä gwī′rä) The port of Caracas in northern Venezuela. Also **La Guay′ra.**

La Guar·di·a (lə gwär′dē·ə), **Fiorello,** 1882–1947, U.S. politician and mayor of New York 1934–45.

La Hague (lə hāg′, *Fr.* là àg′) See HAGUE, LA.

La Hogue (là ōg′) See SAINT-VAAST-LA-HOGUE.

La·hore (lə·hōr′) **1** A commissioner's division of West Pakistan; 9,119 square miles. **2** The leading city of this division, capital of the province of West Pakistan; capital of the former province of the Punjab, Pakistan, 1947–55; capital of the former province of the Punjab, British India, 1849–1947.

Lai·bach (lī′bäkh) The German name for LJUBLJANA.

la·ic (lā′ik) *adj.* Pertaining to the laity: also **la′i·cal.** — *n.* A layman. [<LL *laicus* <Gk. *laikos* < *laos* the people] — **la′i·cal·ly** *adv.*

la·i·cize (lā′ə·sīz) *v.t.* **·cized, ·ciz·ing** To secularize. — **la′i·ci·za′tion** *n.*

laid (lād) Past tense and past participle of LAY[1]. — *adj.* Covered with close, fine, parallel watermarked lines: *laid* paper.

laigh (lākh) *Scot. adj.* Low. — *n.* A hollow. Also **laich.**

l'Ai·glon (lā·glôṅ′) Son of Napoleon I. [<F, lit., the eaglet]

Lai·ka (lī′kə) *n.* **1** A breed of dog of Siberian Arctic origin, of medium size and white or gray coloring, noted for its sturdiness and intelligence. **2** The name of a dog of this breed sent aloft in the second U.S.S.R. artificial earth satellite in November, 1957.

lain (lān) Past participle of LIE[1].

lair[1] (lâr) *n.* **1** The resting place or den of a wild animal. **2** *Scot.* Any place for resting; a bed. **3** A burial plot. — *v.i.* **1** To rest in a lair; make a lair. — *v.t.* **2** To place in a lair. **3** To serve as a lair for. [OE *leger* bed. Akin to LIE[1].]

lair[2] (lâr) *n.* *Scot.* Lore; learning.

laird (lârd) *n.* *Scot.* A lord; also, the proprietor of a landed estate; occasionally, merely a landlord. — **laird′ly** *adj.* — **laird′ship** *n.*

lais·sez-faire (les′ā·fâr′) *n.* **1** The let-alone principle; in economics, absolutely uncontrolled industrial and commercial competition; non-interference. **2** Indifference. Also **lais′ser-faire′.** [<F, lit., let do <*laissez,* imperative of *laisser* let + *faire* do, make]

lais·sez-pas·ser (les′ā pä·sā′) *n.* A permit. [<F, lit., let pass <*laissez,* imperative of *laisser* let + *passer* pass]

laith (lāth) *Scot.* Loath; reluctant. — **laith′·ly** *adv.*

la·i·ty (lā′ə·tē) *n. pl.* **·ties** **1** The people as distinguished from the clergy. **2** Those outside a certain profession. [<LAY[2] + -ITY]

La·ius (lā′yəs) In Greek legend, a king of Thebes, husband of Jocasta, who was unwittingly killed by his son Oedipus. He is said to have introduced homosexual love into Greece.

lake[1] (lāk) *n.* **1** A considerable inland body of water or natural enclosed basin serving to drain the surrounding country. ◆ Collateral adjective: *lacustrine.* **2** A small artificial pond; also, a pool of any liquid: a *lake* of wine. [Fusion of OE *lac* a stream, pool and OF *lac* a basin, pond, lake <L *lacus.* Akin to LEACH, LEAK.]

lake[2] (lāk) *n.* **1** A deep red pigment made by combining some animal (as cochineal) or vegetable (as madder) coloring matter with a metallic oxide, usually that of aluminum or tin. **2** The color of this pigment. **3** Any insoluble metallic compound yielding variously colored pigments by the chemical interaction of mordant and dye. [Var. of LAC[1]]

lake[3] (lāk) *v.t.* **laked, lak·ing** **1** To separate the hemoglobin from the red corpuscles of (blood). **2** To make red in color, as the blood. [<LAKE[2] (from the red color of the corpuscles)] — **lak′ing** *n.*

Lake (lāk), **Simon,** 1866–1945, U. S. engineer, naval architect and submarine builder.

Lake District A region in Cumberland, Lancashire, and Westmoreland counties, England, containing the principal English lakes. Also **Lake Country, Lake Land.**

lake dweller An inhabitant of a lake dwelling; a lacustrian.

lake dwelling A habitation erected on piles over the waters of a lake, as in prehistoric Switzerland.

lake herring A herringlike whitefish or cisco (genus *Leucichthys*) of the Great Lakes.

Lake of Geneva See GENEVA, LAKE OF.

Lake of the Woods A lake between the northern part of Minnesota and Manitoba and Ontario provinces, Canada; 1,485 square miles.

Lake Poets The English poets Coleridge, Wordsworth, and Southey, who lived for a while in the English Lake District.

lak·er (lā′kər) *n.* **1** A lake fish; especially, the lake trout of America. **2** One connected with a lake, or lakes, as a visitor to a lake, or a vessel engaged in lake trade. [<LAKE[1]]

Lake Success A village in SE New York on Long Island; headquarters of the United Nations Security Council, 1946–50.

lake trout Any of various salmonoid fishes, especially, in North America, the namaycush. Also **lake salmon.**

lakh (lak) *n.* The sum of 100,000; 100,000 rupees; a great number: also spelled *lac.* [<Hind. *lākh* <Skt. *laksha* 100,000]

La·ko·ní·a (lä′kô·nyē′ä) The modern Greek name for LACONIA.

lak·y[1] (lā′kē) *adj.* Like a lake. [<LAKE[1]]

lak·y[2] (lā′kē) *adj.* Of or pertaining to the pigment lake. [<LAKE[2]]

lak·y[3] (lā′kē) *adj.* Transparent: said of blood in which the red corpuscles have been made colorless. [<LAKE[3]]

la·li·a·try (lə·lī′ə·trē) *n.* The branch of medicine which studies disorders of speech. [<NL <Gk. *lalia* speech + -IATRY]

La Lí·ne·a (lä lē′nā·ä) A port of southern Spain. Also **La Lí′ne·a de la Con·cep·ción** (thā lä kōn′·thep·thyōn′).

Lal·lan (lal′ən) *Scot. adj.* Of or pertaining to the Lowlands of Scotland; Lowland. — *n.* The Lowland Scottish dialect. Also **Lal′land.**

lal·la·tion (la·lā′shən) *n.* An imperfect pronunciation of *r* which makes it sound like *l*; lambdacism; babbling speech. [<L *lallatus,* pp. of *lallare* sing "la la" or a lullaby]

l'Al·le·gro (lä·lā′grō) *Italian* The merry or cheerful one; the joyous man: title of a poem by Milton.

La·lo (là·lō′), **Édouard Victor Antoine,** 1823–1892, French composer.

lal·o·neu·ro·sis (lal′ō·nōo·rō′sis, -nyōo-) *n.* *Psychiatry* A nervous disorder affecting speech. [<NL <Gk. *laleein* talk, chatter + NEUROSIS]

lal·o·pa·thol·o·gy (lal′ō·pa·thol′ə·jē) *n.* The branch of medicine which deals with speech disorders. [<Gk. *laleein* talk, chatter + PATHOLOGY]

lal·o·pho·bi·a (lal′ō·fō′bē·ə) *n.* A morbid fear of speaking. [<NL <Gk. *laleein* talk, chatter + -PHOBIA]

lam[1] (lam) *v.t.* **lammed, lam·ming** *Slang* To beat; thrash; punish. [? <ON *lamdha,* pt. of *lemja* thrash. Akin to LAME.]

lam[2] (lam) *Slang v.i.* **lammed, lam·ming** To run away; flee hastily. — *n.* Sudden flight. — **on the lam** In flight; fleeing. — **to take it on the lam** To flee hastily; run away. [Prob. < *lammas,* alter. of *nammus,* ? alter. of Sp. *vamos* let us be off, infl. in form by G *nehmen* take]

la·ma[1] (lä′mə) *n.* **1** A priest or monk of Lamaism ranking high in the hierarchy. **2** A title of courtesy given to all monks of Lamaism. See DALAI LAMA. [<Tibetan *blama* < *bla* above]

la·ma[2] (lä′mə) See LLAMA: an erroneous use.

La·ma·ism (lä′mə·iz′əm) *n.* The religious system of Tibet and Mongolia, a variety of Northern Buddhism, introduced into Tibet in the 7th century, and essentially modified by Sivaism and native Shamanistic beliefs and practices. [<LAMA[1] + -ISM] —**La'ma·ist** *n.* —**La'ma·is'tic** *adj.*

La Man·cha (lä män'chä) A generally arid region of south central Spain.

La Manche (là mänsh) The French name for the ENGLISH CHANNEL.

La·marck (là·märk'), **Chevalier de,** 1744–1829, Jean Baptiste Pierre Antoine de Monet, French naturalist; pioneer of the theory of evolution of species by adaptation to environments and by the inheritance of acquired characteristics.

La·marck·i·an (lə·märk'ē·ən) *adj.* Of or pertaining to Jean de Lamarck, or to Lamarckism. —*n.* A believer in Lamarckism.

La·marck·ism (lə·märk'iz·əm) *n. Biol.* The theory of descent or evolution propounded by Lamarck, which assumes that species have become developed by the efforts of an organism to adapt itself to new conditions, and by the inheritance of the changes thus produced: often applied to belief in the inheritability of acquired characteristics.

La·mar·tine (là·màr·tēn'), **Alphonse Marie Louis de Prat de,** 1790–1869, French poet.

la·ma·ser·y (lä'mə·ser'ē) *n. pl.* **·ser·ies** A Buddhist monastery or convent of Tibet or Mongolia. [<F *lamaserie* < *lama* a lama]

lamb (lam) *n.* **1** A young sheep; also, its flesh. **2** Any gentle or innocent person. **3** An unsophisticated person; simpleton. **4** An inexperienced and gullible speculator in stocks. —**the Lamb** Christ. —*v.i.* To give birth: said of sheep. [OE] —**lamb'like', lamb'ish** *adj.*

Lamb (lam), **Charles,** 1775–1834, English essayist and critic: pen name *Elia.* —**Mary,** 1764–1847, sister of Charles; co-author with him of *Tales from Shakespeare.* —**William** See MELBOURNE, VISCOUNT.

lam·baste (lam·bāst') *v.t.* **·bast·ed, ·bast·ing** *Slang* **1** To beat or thrash. **2** To scold; castigate. [<LAM[1] + BASTE[3]] —**lam·bast'ing** *n.*

lamb·da (lam'də) *n.* The eleventh letter and seventh consonant of the Greek alphabet (Λ, λ). See ALPHABET. [<Phoenician *lamed*]

lamb·da·cism (lam'də·siz'əm) *n.* A disorder of speech in which the sufferer cannot pronounce the letter *l* correctly. See LALLATION. [<L *lambdacismus* <Gk. *lambdakismos* < *lambdakizein* pronounce lambda imperfectly < *lambda* LAMBDA]

lamb·doid (lam'doid) *adj.* Resembling in form the Greek letter lambda (Λ): said of the suture between the occipital and the two parietal bones of the skull. Also **lamb·doi'dal.**

lam·bent (lam'bənt) *adj.* **1** Playing with a soft, undulatory movement; gliding; flickering. **2** Softly radiant. **3** Touching lightly but brilliantly: *lambent* wit. [<L *lambens, -entis,* ppr. of *lambere* lick] —**lam'ben·cy, lam'bent·ness** *n.* —**lam'bent·ly** *adv.*

lam·bert (lam'bərt) *n. Physics* The cgs unit of brightness; the uniform brightness of a perfect diffusing surface emitting or reflecting light at the rate of one lumen per square centimeter. [after J. H. *Lambert,* 1728–1777, German physicist]

Lam·beth (lam'bəth) A metropolitan borough of SW London.

Lambeth Palace The official London residence of the archbishop of Canterbury.

lamb·kill (lam'kil') *n.* A North American shrub (*Kalmia angustifolia*) with deep-pink flowers and narrow leaves said to be poisonous to animals: also called *killikid, sheep laurel.*

lamb·kin (lam'kin) *n.* A little lamb; figuratively, a cherished child. Also **lamb'ie.** [Dim. of LAMB]

lamb lettuce Corn salad.

Lamb of God Christ, by analogy with the paschal lamb. *John* i 29.

lam·boys (lam'boiz) *n. pl.* Flexible steel plates worn skirtlike from the waist of 15th century armor. [? Alter. of JAMBEAUX]

lam·bre·quin (lam'bər·kin, -brə-) *n.* **1** A draped strip, as of cloth or leather, hanging from the casing above a window, doorway, etc. **2** An ornamental covering for a helmet. [<F <Du. *lamperkin,* dim. of *lamper* a veil]

LAMBREQUIN (*def. 1*)

lamb·skin (lam'skin') *n.* A lamb's skin, especially when dressed, as for glovemaking.

lamb's wool The wool of lambs used in the manufacture of various textile fabrics.

lamb's-wool (lamz'wŏŏl) *n.* A drink made of hot ale with sugar, nutmeg, and roasted apples.

lam·dan (läm'dən) *n.* A person learned in Jewish lore. [<Hebrew]

lame[1] (lām) *adj.* **1** Crippled or disabled, especially in the legs. **2** Hence, inefficient; halting. **3** Sore; painful: a *lame* back. —*v.t.* **lamed, lam·ing** To make lame; cripple. [OE *lama.* Akin to LAM[1].] —**lame'ly** *adv.* —**lame'·ness** *n.*

lame[2] (lām) *n.* A thin plate of metal; specifically one used in making armor. [<F <L *lamina* a lamina]

la·mé (la·mā') *n.* A fabric woven of flat gold or silver thread, often brocaded, sometimes mixed with silk or other fiber. [<F, orig. pp. of *lamer* laminate < *lame* a lame[2]]

la·med (lä'med) The twelfth Hebrew letter. Also **la'medh.** See ALPHABET. [<Hebrew, lit., a whip, club]

lame duck *Colloq.* **1** A helpless or disabled person. **2** On the stock exchange, one who cannot fulfil his contracts. **3** *U.S.* A member of a legislature, especially of Congress, whose term continues some time after his defeat for reelection.

la·mel·la (lə·mel'ə) *n. pl.* **·lae** (-ē) **1** A thin plate, scale, or lamina, as in the gills of bivalves, or in bone. **2** *Bot.* A gill of a mushroom, one of the thin plates attached to the under side of the cap. [<NL <L, dim. of *lamina* a lamina]

lam·el·lar (lə·mel'ər, lam'ə·lər) *adj.* Scalelike; composed of thin layers or scales. Also **lam·el·late** (lam'ə·lāt, lə·mel'āt), **lam'el·lat'ed.** —**lam'el·la'tion** *n.*

la·mel·li·branch (lə·mel'i·brangk) *n.* One of a class (*Pelecypoda,* formerly *Lamellibranchiata*) of mollusks, having bivalve shells enclosing a mantle within which is the compressed body of the organism, including clams, mussels, and oysters. —*adj.* Of or pertaining to this class. [<NL *lamellibranchia,* name of this class <L *lamella* LAMELLA + Gk. *branchia* gills, pl. of *branchion* a fin] —**la·mel'li·bran'·chi·ate** (-brang'kē·āt, -it) *adj.* & *n.*

la·mel·li·corn (lə·mel'i·kôrn) *adj. Entomol.* **1** Terminating in leaflike joints, as the antennae of certain beetles. **2** Having such antennae. **3** Of or pertaining to a division of beetles (*Lamellicornia*) having a lateral leaflike expansion on each of the terminal antennal segments, as the scarab beetle. —*n.* One of the lamellicorn beetles. [<NL *lamellicornis* <L *lamella* LAMELLA + *cornu* a horn]

la·mel·li·form (lə·mel'i·fôrm) *adj.* Having the form of a thin plate, scale, or lamella; scalelike; lamellar.

la·mel·li·ros·tral (lə·mel'i·ros'trəl) *adj. Ornithol.* Of or pertaining to a group of birds having lamellar ridges on the inner edges of the bills, as ducks, swans, and geese. Also **la·mel'li·ros'trate** (-trāt). [<NL *lamellirostris* <L *lamella* LAMELLA + *rostrum* a beak]

lamelli- *combining form* Lamellae; resembling lamellae: *lamellibranch.* [<L *lamella* a plate]

la·mel·loid (lə·mel'oid, lam'ə·loid) *adj.* Of or resembling a plate or lamella. [<LAMELL(A) + -OID]

la·mel·lose (lə·mel'ōs, lam'ə·lōs) *adj.* Composed of or full of thin plates, scales, or lamellae; lamelliform. [<LAMELL(A) + -OSE[1]]

la·ment (lə·ment') *v.t.* To feel or express sorrow for; bewail. —*v.i.* To feel or express sorrow; mourn; grieve. —*n.* **1** The expression of grief; lamentation. **2** A plaintive song or melody. See synonyms under MOURN. [<L *lamentari* < *lamentum* a wailing, weeping] —**la·ment'er** *n.*

lam·en·ta·ble (lam'ən·tə·bəl) *adj.* **1** Expressing sorrow; mournful: a *lamentable* cry. **2** Exciting regret or dissatisfaction; despicable; deplorable: a *lamentable* failure. See synonyms under PITIFUL. —**lam'en·ta·bly** *adv.*

lam·en·ta·tion (lam'ən·tā'shən) *n.* The act of lamenting or bewailing; utterance of profound regret or grief; a wailing cry.

Lam·en·ta·tions (lam'ən·tā'shəns) A lyrical poetic book of the Old Testament, attributed to Jeremiah the prophet; also, the music to which a portion of it is sung in the Roman Catholic Church at Tenebrae.

la·mi·a (lā'mē·ə) *n.* A female demon or vampire; witch. [<L, a witch sucking children's blood <Gk., a fabulous monster]

La·mi·a (lā'mē·ə) In Greek mythology, a queen of Libya, beloved of Zeus, who was robbed of her children by Hera and took revenge by killing the children of others.

lam·i·na (lam'ə·nə) *n. pl.* **·nae** (-nē) or **·nas** **1** A thin scale or sheet. **2** A layer or coat lying over another, as in bone, minerals, armor, etc. **3** *Bot.* The blade or flat expanded portion of a leaf, or the blade of a petal. [<L]

lam·i·nar·i·a (lam'ə·nâr'ē·ə) *n.* Any member of a genus (*Laminaria*) of brown algae, especially the giant kelp. [<NL <L *lamina* a leaf] —**lam·i·nar·i·a·ceous** (lam'ə·nâr'ē·ā'shəs) *adj.*

lam·i·nate (lam'ə·nāt) *v.* **·nat·ed, ·nat·ing** *v.t.* **1** To beat, roll, or press, as metal, into thin sheets. **2** To cut or separate into thin sheets. **3** To make, as plastic materials or plywood, of layers united by the action of heat and pressure. **4** To cover with thin sheets or laminae. —*v.i.* **5** To become separated into sheets or laminae. —*adj.* Consisting of or disposed in laminae: also **lam'i·nal, lam'i·nar, lam'i·nar'y, lam'i·nat'ed.** [<NL *laminatus* laminated <L *lamina* a leaf] —**lam'·i·na·ble** *adj.* —**lam'i·na'tion** *n.*

lam·i·nif·er·ous (lam'ə·nif'ər·əs) *adj.* Bearing or composed of laminae.

lam·i·ni·tis (lam'ə·nī'tis) *n.* Inflammation of the laminae of a horse's hoof; founder. [<NL <L *lamina* a leaf, layer + *-itis* -ITIS]

lam·i·nose (lam'ə·nōs) *adj.* Laminate. Also **lam'i·nous** (-nəs). [<LAMIN(A) + -OSE[1]]

Lam·mas (lam'əs) *n.* **1** A Roman Catholic festival celebrated on August 1; the feast of Peter's Chains. **2** Quarter day in Scotland, and half-quarter day in England, falling on August 1. Also **Lammas day.** [OE *hlāfmæsse* bread feast < *hlāf* bread, loaf + *mæsse* a mass]

Lam·mas·tide (lam'əs·tīd') *n.* The season of Lammas. [<LAMMAS + TIDE[1] (def. 4)]

lam·mer·gei·er (lam'ər·gī'ər) *n.* The great bearded vulture (*Gypaëtus barbatus*), native to the mountains of Asia, southern Europe, and North Africa. Also **lam'mer·geir** (-gīr), **lam'mer·gey'er.** [<G *lämmergeier,* lit., lamb-vulture < *lämmer,* pl. of *lamm* a lamb + *geier* a vulture]

Lam·mer·muir Hills (lam'ər·mŏŏr', lam'ər·mŏŏr) A range of low hills in SE Scotland; highest point, 1,733 feet. Also **Lam'mer·moor' Hills.**

lam·my (lam'ē) *n. pl.* **·mies** A sailor's quilted woolen jumper. Also **lam'mie.** [? < *lammy,* var. of *lambie,* affectionate dim. of LAMB]

La·mont (lə·mont'), **Thomas William,** 1870–1948, U. S. banker.

La·motte-Fou·qué (là·môt'fōō·kā') See FOUQUÉ.

lamp (lamp) *n.* **1** A vessel in which oil is burnt through a wick; hence, any device employing a flame, incandescent wire, or the like, for furnishing an artificial light, or a similar device for heating. ◆ Collateral adjective: *lucernal.* **2** Anything that gives out light, actually or metaphorically. **3** A flash, as of lightning. **4** A heavenly body. **5** A torch. **6** *pl. Slang* The eyes. —*v.t. Slang* To look at. [<OF *lampe* <L *lampas* <Gk. < *lampein* shine]

lam·pad (lam'pad) *n.* A lamp or torch; candlestick. [<Gk. *lampas, lampados* < *lampein* shine]

lam·pas[1] (lam'pəs) *n.* Inflammation and swelling of the fleshy bars in the roof of a horse's mouth. Also **lam'pers** (-pərs). [<F <OF, throat]

lam·pas[2] (lam'pəs) *n.* Any elaborately patterned fabric; specifically, a fabric similar to damask, but in many colors, used as furniture covering. [<F; origin uncertain]

lamp·black (lamp'blak') *n.* Fine carbon deposited from smoke or smoky flame: used as a pigment, in printer's ink, etc.: also called *carbon black.*

Lam·pe·du·sa (läm'pe·dōō'zä) The largest of the Pelagie Islands between Malta and Tunisia: ancient *Lopadusa.*

lam·per-eel (lam'pər·ēl') *n.* **1** A lamprey: also **lam'preel** (-prēl). **2** An eelpout or mutton fish. [? < *lampre,* var. of LAMPREY + EEL]

lam·pi·on (lam'pē·ən) *n.* A small lamp. [<F <Ital. *lampione* a carriage or street lamp, aug. of *lampa* <L *lampas* LAMP]

lamp·light (lamp′līt′) *n.* Light emitted by lamps; artificial light.

lamp·light·er (lamp′lī′tər) *n.* **1** A person who lights lamps, especially gas street lamps. **2** That by which a lamp is lighted, as a torch, or an electric device.

lam·poon (lam·po͞on′) *n.* A written satire designed to bring a person into ridicule or contempt; a pasquinade. See synonyms under RIDICULE. —*v.t.* To abuse or satirize in a lampoon. [< MF *lampon* < *lampons* let's drink (a drinking-song refrain) < *lamper* guzzle] —**lam·poon′er, lam·poon′ist** *n.* —**lam·poon′er·y** *n.*

lamp·post (lamp′pōst′) *n.* A post supporting a lamp in a street, park, etc.

lam·prey (lam′prē) *n.* An eel-like carnivorous cyclostome (*Petromyzon* and related genera) having in the adult stages a circular suctorial mouth, with sharp rasping teeth on its inner surface, and well-developed eyes. [< OF *lampreie* < Med. L. *lampreda, lampetra* < L *lambere* lick + *petra* rock < Gk.; supposedly so called because they cling to rocks with their mouths]

lamp shell *Zool.* A brachiopod: so called from its resemblance to an old Roman oil lamp.

lamp·wick (lamp′wik′) *n.* A wick for a lamp.

lam·yik (läm′yik) *n.* A piece of parchment issued by the Dalai Lama of Tibet to serve as a passport permitting a Westerner to enter the Forbidden City of Lhasa: also called *red arrow letter.* [< Tibetan]

lan′ (lan) *n. Scot.* Land.

la·na·i (lä·nä′ē) *n. Hawaiian* A veranda or porch.

La·na·i (lä·nä′ē) An island in the central Hawaiian Islands; 156 square miles.

Lan·ark (lan′ərk) A county in south central Scotland; 853 square miles; capital, Lanark. Also **Lan′ark·shire** (-shir).

la·na·ry (lā′nə·rē) *n. pl.* **·ries** A place for storing wool. [< L *lanaria,* fem. of *lanarius* of wool < *lana* wool]

la·nate (lā′nāt) *adj.* **1** Woolly. **2** *Bot.* Provided or covered with long, fine, wool-like hairs. Also **la′nat·ed.** [< L *lanatus* < *lana* wool]

Lan·ca·shire (lang′kə·shir) A county in NW England; 1,875 square miles; capital, Lancaster. Also **Lan·cas·ter** (lang′kəs·tər).

Lan·cas·ter (lang′kəs·tər) A royal house of England, reigning from 1399 to 1461, and descended from John of Gaunt, fourth son of Edward III. The three Lancastrian kings were Henry IV, Henry V, and Henry VI. See YORK, and WARS OF THE ROSES in table under WAR.

Lan·cas·te·ri·an (lang′kəs·tir′ē·ən) *adj.* Pertaining to the system introduced in primary schools by Joseph Lancaster, 1778–1838, of England, in which advanced pupils taught those below them.

Lan·cas·tri·an (lang·kas′trē·ən) *adj.* Belonging or relating to the House of Lancaster. —*n.* **1** An adherent of the House of Lancaster, as opposed to the Yorkists, especially in the Wars of the Roses. **2** A native or inhabitant of Lancashire.

lance (lans, läns) *n.* **1** A long shaft with a spearhead, used as a thrusting weapon; any long, slender spear, or something resembling one. **2** A lancet. **3** A thrust with a lance or lancet. **4** One who uses a lance; lancer. **5** In pyrotechnics, a small paper case for white or colored fire. **6** A whaler's spear for killing the whale after its capture with the harpoon and line. —*v.t.* **lanced, lanc·ing 1** To pierce with a lance. **2** To cut or open with a lancet. [< OF < L *lancea* a light spear < Celtic]

lance corporal See under CORPORAL².

lance·let (lans′lit, läns′-) *n.* Any of several species of small fishlike translucent animals (genus *Branchiostoma*) having a notochord and other vertebrate characteristics, which burrow in the sand of warm sea beaches; an amphioxus. [Dim. of LANCE]

Lan·ce·lot (lan′sə·lot, län′-; *Fr.* län·slō′) A masculine personal name: often spelled *Launcelot.* Also *Pg.* **Lan·ce·lo·te** (län·sə·lō′tē).
—**Lancelot of the Lake** In Arthurian romance, the bravest and ablest of the knights of the Round Table; lover of Guinevere; father of Galahad. Also **Lancelot du Lac.** [< F, servant]

lan·ce·o·late (lan′sē·ə·lit, -lāt) *adj.* **1** Shaped like the head of a lance or spear. **2** *Bot.* Tapering, as some leaves. Also **lan′ce·o·lar** (-lər), **lan′ce·o·lat′ed.** [< LL *lanceolatus* < *lanceola* a small lance, dim. of *lancea* LANCE]

lanc·er (lan′sər, län′-) **1** One who lances; a cavalry soldier armed with a lance. **2** *pl.* A quadrille, or square dance for eight or sixteen couples; also, the music for it: also **lan′ciers** (-sərz).

lance sergeant See under SERGEANT.

lan·cet (lan′sit, län′-) *n.* **1** A surgeon's two-edged cutting or bloodletting instrument with one or more small blades. **2** *Archit.* **a** A lancet-shaped or acutely pointed window: also **lancet window. b** An acutely pointed arch: also **lancet arch. 3** A small lance. [< F *lancette,* dim. of *lance* < OF, LANCE]

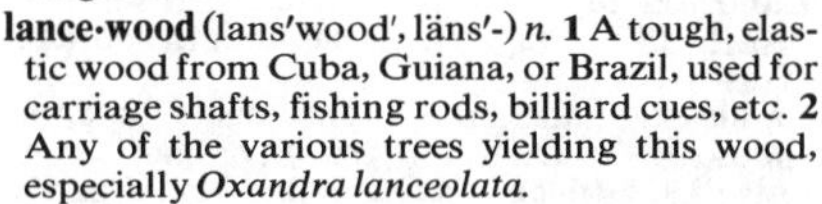
LANCET WINDOWS

lan·cet·ed (lan′sit·id, län′-) *adj.* Having lancet windows or arches.

lancet fish 1 An ocean fish (genus *Alepisaurus*) with large, lancetlike teeth. **2** A surgeon fish.

lance·wood (lans′wood′, läns′-) *n.* **1** A tough, elastic wood from Cuba, Guiana, or Brazil, used for carriage shafts, fishing rods, billiard cues, etc. **2** Any of the various trees yielding this wood, especially *Oxandra lanceolata.*

Lan·chow (lan′chou′, *Chinese* län′jō′) Capital of Kansu province, NW China: formerly *Kaolan.*

Lan·ci·lot·to (län′chē·lôt′tō) Italian form of LANCELOT.

lan·ci·nate (lan′sə·nāt) *v.t.* **·nat·ed, ·nat·ing** To strike through; pierce, as with pain. [< L *lancinatus,* pp. of *lancinare* tear to pieces]

lan·ci·na·tion (lan′sə·nā′shən) *n.* **1** Shooting or acute pain. **2** A tearing away; laceration.

land (land) *n.* **1** The solid substance composing the material part of the earth, considered in its entirety. **2** A country or district, large or small, especially considered as a place of human habitation, or as distinguished by events or facts of interest. **3** Ground or soil considered with reference to its use, value, condition, etc.: real estate: farm *land* ; coal *land.* **4** *Law* Any tract of ground whatever, together with all its appurtenances; also, a share or interest in land, tenements, or any hereditament, both corporeal and incorporeal. ◆ Collateral adjective: *predial.* **5** Any unindented space in a surface marked with indentations, as a level space between the furrows of millstone, or a space on the bore of a rifle between two grooves. **6** In economic discussion, those resources which are supplied by nature, as distinguished from the developments and improvements resulting from human labor. —*v.t.* **1** To put ashore; transfer from a vessel to the shore. **2** To bring to rest on land or water: He *landed* the plane at Washington. **3** To bring to some point, condition, or state: His words *landed* him in trouble. **4** In fishing, to bring (a fish) from the water or into a net, boat, etc.; catch. **5** *Colloq.* To obtain or secure; win, as a position. **6** *Colloq.* To deliver, as a blow. —*v.i.* **7** To go or come ashore, as from a boat. **8** To touch at a port; come to land: said of ships. **9** To descend and come to rest, as after flight; come down: The bird *landed* in the tree. **10** To come to some place, condition, or state; arrive; end: The swindlers soon *landed* in jail. See synonyms under ARRIVE, REACH. [OE]

Synonyms (noun) : continent, country, district, earth, ground, region, shore, soil. *Antonyms* : deep, flood, ocean, sea, surge, water, wave.

-land *combining form* **1** A region of a certain kind: *woodland.* **2** The country of: *Scotland.* **3** A specified place or realm: *cloudland.* An inhabitant of any of these places is denoted by the combining form **-lander.** [< LAND]

land agent 1 A real-estate agent. **2** One who helps settlers get title to their claims.

lan·dau (lan′dô, -dou) *n.* **1** A type of closed automobile body the rear top of which may be raised or lowered. **2** A four-wheeled covered carriage with a double top that can be removed or folded back. [from *Landau,* a Bavarian city where it was first made]

TWO TYPES OF THE LANDAU
a. Closed top.
b. Open top.

lan·dau·let (lan′dô·let′) *n.* **1** An automobile body with rear section enclosed and the top collapsible. **2** A small landau. Also **lan′dau·lette′.** [Dim. of *landau*]

land bank 1 A bank taking mortgages on land in exchange for currency notes; especially, the **Massachusetts Land Bank** of 1740. **2** One of twelve U.S. government banks organized in 1916 to make mortgage loans on land.

land claim 1 A claim to a piece of land based on conformity to the legal requirements for settlement and title. **2** The land claimed, and the paper entitling the claimant to the land.

lande (land) *n.* A level sandy region unfit for cultivation and covered with heath or broom, as along the seacoast in SW France. [< F < OF *launde* < Breton *lann* < Celtic. Doublet of LAWN.]

land·ed (lan′did) *adj.* **1** Having an estate in land. **2** Consisting in land.

land·fall (land′fôl′) *n.* **1** Property in land immediately transferred by the death of its owner. **2** A landslide. **3** A sighting of or coming to land.

land·fill (land′fil′) *n.* **1** The disposal of garbage, trash, excavated earth, etc., by depositing in a site, often used to build up swampy or shoreline areas. **2** Materials so used. **3** A site where such deposits are made.

land·form (land fôrm′) *n.* A physical feature of the earth's surface, such as a plateau, an isthmus, a mountain, etc.

land-grant (land′grant′, -gränt′) *n.* Government land granted to a railroad, educational institution, etc.

land·grave (land′grāv′) *n.* A title of superior distinction borne by certain German counts or Grafen. [< MHG *lantgrave* < *lant, land* land + *grave, graf* a count]

land·gra·vi·ate (land·grā′vē·it, -āt) *n.* The territory, office, authority, or jurisdiction of a landgrave. Also **land′gra·vate** (-grā·vāt). [< Med. L *landgraviatus* < *landgravio* a count < MLG *landgrave* LANDGRAVE]

land·hold·er (land′hōl′dər) *n.* A landowner.

land·ing (lan′ding) *n.* **1** The act of going or placing ashore from any kind of craft or vessel: the *landing* of passengers; also, the act of coming or falling to earth, as of an airplane. **2** The place where any kind of craft lands; a wharf; pier. **3** *Archit.* The place at the head of a staircase, or a platform interrupting a flight of stairs.

landing area 1 A landing field. **2** A jump area.

landing beam *Aeron.* A short-wave radio beam transmitted from a landing field to an aircraft pilot in order to facilitate safe landing.

landing craft One of several types of military vessels especially designed for the landing of men and materiel upon a hostile shore.

landing field A tract of ground properly surfaced for the landing and take-off of aircraft.

landing gear *Aeron.* The under-structure of an aircraft designed to carry the load when resting or running on the surface of land or water, and also to buffer the shock of landing.

landing ramp A broad gangplank to permit the rapid landing of men and supplies from a landing craft.

landing strip A narrow, surfaced runway for the landing and take-off of aircraft.

Lan·dis (lan′dis), **Kenesaw Mountain,** 1866–1944, U.S. jurist and baseball commissioner.
land·la·dy (land′lā′dē) *n. pl.* **·dies** A woman who keeps an inn or boarding house, or who lets her property; also, the wife of a landlord.
länd·ler (lent′lər) *n.* An Austrian country dance in slow triple time, probably the precursor of the waltz; also, music for this dance: also called *Tyrolienne.* [<G < dial. G *Landl* upper Austria, dim. of *land* land]
land·less (land′lis) *adj.* Destitute of property in lands.
land·locked (land′lokt′) *adj.* **1** Surrounded and protected by land. **2** Living in or confined to landlocked water: said especially of a normally anadromous fish: *landlocked* salmon.
land·lop·er (land′lō′pər) *n.* A tramp; vagabond. Also **land′loup′er** (-lou′pər,-lōō′-). [<Du. *landlooper* < *land* land + *loopen* run]
land·lord (land′lôrd′) *n.* **1** A man who keeps an inn or hotel. **2** A man who owns and lets real estate. **3** In England, the lord of a manor. [OE *landhlāford* < *land* land + *hlāford* lord]
land·lord·ism (land′lord′iz·əm) *n.* **1** Action, conduct, or opinions peculiar to a landlord; a landlord's authority, or the view that landed interests should be paramount. **2** The system under which land is owned by persons to whom tenants pay a fixed rent.
land·lub·ber (land′lub′ər) *n.* An awkward or inexperienced person on board a ship; a raw sailor. [<LAND + LUBBER]
land·man (land′mən) *n. pl.* **·men** (-mən) One who lives or serves on land.
land·mark (land′märk′) *n.* **1** A fixed object serving as a boundary mark to a tract of land, or as a guide to seamen, etc. **2** A prominent or memorable object in the landscape. **3** A distinguishing fact, event, etc. See synonyms under BOUNDARY. [OE *landmearc* < *land* land + *mearc* boundary]
landmark beacon A beacon light, other than an airport or airway beacon, that serves to indicate a definite geographical location.
land mine See under MINE[1].
land office A U.S. government office of the Department of the Interior for the transaction of business pertaining to the public lands. Officially, **General Land Office.**
land-of·fice business (land′ô′fis,-of′is) *U.S. Colloq.* A flourishing business conducted at a rapid pace.
Land of Nod (nod) See NOD, LAND OF.
Land of Promise **1** Canaan, promised to Abraham by God. *Gen.* xv 18. **2** Any longed-for place of happiness or improvement.
Land of the Midnight Sun Norway.
Land of the Rising Sun Japan.
Lan·dor (lan′dər, -dôr), **Walter Savage,** 1775–1864, English poet and prose writer.
land·own·er (land′ō′nər) *n.* One who owns real estate. **— land′own′er·ship** *n.* **— land′·own′ing** *n.* & *adj.*
land pike *U.S.* **1** The hellbender (def. 1). **2** An inferior breed of hog.
land·plane (land′plān′) *n. Aeron.* An airplane designed to rise from and alight on land.
land-poor (land′po͝or′) *adj.* Owning much land which yields an income insufficient to meet its expenses.
land power A nation having military strength on land: opposed to *sea power.*
land·scape (land′skāp) *n.* **1** A stretch of country as seen from a single point. **2** A picture representing natural scenery. Also *Obs.* **land′skip** (-skip). — *v.* **·scaped, ·scap·ing** *v.t.* To improve or change the natural features or appearance of, as a park or garden. — *v.i.* To be a landscape gardener. [<Du. *landschap* < *land* land + *-schap* -SHIP]
landscape architect One who draws up, coordinates, and supervises the execution of plans for converting a given area of land into a unified ornamental development.
landscape gardener One who plans, executes, and supervises operations for the horticultural improvement of private or public grounds.
land·scap·ist (land′skā·pist) *n.* **1** A painter of landscapes. **2** A landscape gardener.
land scrip *U.S.* **1** A landholding certificate issued to a person or company. **2** In connection with land grants made for higher education, a certificate granted to a State having insufficient public lands, entitling it to its share of such lands in other States.
Land·seer (land′sir), **Sir Edwin Henry,** 1802–1873, English painter.
Land's End A cape on the SW coast of Cornwall, the westernmost point of England. Also **Lands End.**
land side The side, as of a seashore house, toward the land.
land·side (land′sīd′) *n.* The flat side of a plowshare, away from the furrow.
land·slide (land′slīd′) *n.* **1** The slipping of a mass of land from a higher to a lower level. **2** The land that has slipped down: also **land′slip′.** **3** *Colloq.* An overwhelming plurality of votes for one political party or candidate in an election.
Lands·mål (läns′mōl) *n.* One of the two official forms of Norwegian, based on an arbitrary consolidation of Norwegian dialects: also called *New Norwegian.* Compare RIKSMÅL. [<Norw., lit., country's language < *land* country + *mål* language]
lands·man (landz′mən) *n. pl.* **·men** (-mən) **1** One who lives on the land. **2** *Naut.* An inexperienced sailor, as one on his first voyage or one rated below an ordinary seaman: opposed to *seaman.*
land speculator One who buys and sells land; specifically, one who profits illegally in the buying and selling of unsettled government lands.
Land·stei·ner (land′stī·nər, *Ger.* länt′shtī·nər), **Karl,** 1868–1943, U.S. pathologist born in Austria.
Lands·ting (läns′ting) *n.* The senate or upper house of the Danish Rigsdag, or parliament. Also **Lands′thing.** [<Dan., lit., land's parliament < *land* land + *t(h)ing* parliament]
Land·sturm (länt′shto͝orm) *n.* **1** A general levy in time of war, as made in various European countries. **2** The final reserve forces of a nation, called out in cases of great emergency or for home-defense. [<G, lit., land-storm < dial. G (Swiss), trans. of F *levée en masse,* general levy of troops]
Land·tag (länt′täkh) *n.* The general legislative assembly in a German state. [<G <MHG *lanttac,* lit., land-day < *land, lant* land + *tag, tac* day]
land·ward (land′wərd) *adj.* & *adv.* Being, facing, or going toward the land. Also **land′·wards.**
Land·wehr (länt′vār) *n.* An emergency military force of various European countries. [<G < *land* land + *wehr* defense < *wehren* defend]
lane[1] (lān) *n.* **1** A narrow way or path, confined between fences, walls, hedges, or similar boundaries: distinguished from an *alley,* which is ordinarily between buildings and in city or town, while the *lane* is rural. **2** Any narrow way, passage, or similar course; a prescribed route or passage, as for steamers: a shipping *lane.* See synonyms under ROAD. [OE *lanu* lane]
lane[2] (lān) *adj. Scot.* Alone. **— his lane, my lane, their lane,** etc. Himself alone, myself alone, themselves alone, etc.
lane·ly (lān′lē) *adj. Scot.* Lonely.
lane route One of the routes prescribed for trans-Atlantic steamers in northern waters, being different for eastward- and westward-bound vessels to avoid collisions: also called *ocean-lane route.*
Lan·franc (lan′frangk), 1005–89, Benedictine prior; archbishop of Canterbury.
lang (lang) *adj. Scot.* Long.
Lang (lang), **Andrew,** 1844–1912, Scottish critic, essayist, historian, poet, and translator. **— Cosmo Gordon,** 1864–1945, English prelate; archbishop of Canterbury, 1928–42.
Lang·er·hans (läng′ər·häns), **Islands of** See ISLANDS OF LANGERHANS.
Lang·land (lang′lənd), **William,** 1330?–1400?, English poet. Also **Lang′ley** (-lē).
lang·lauf (läng′louf) *n.* A cross-country run, especially in skiing. [<G < *lang* long + *lauf* a course < *laufen* run]
lang·läuf·er (läng′loi·fər) *n.* A cross-country skier. [<G < *langlauf* LANGLAUF]
lang·ley (lang′lē) *n.* A unit of solar radiation, equal to 1 small calorie per square centimeter of surface per unit of time. [after S. P. *Langley*]
Lang·ley (lang′lē), **Samuel Pierpont,** 1834–1906, U.S. astronomer, scientist, inventor; student of mechanical flight.
Lang·muir (lang′myo͝or), **Irving,** 1881–1957, U.S. chemist.
Lan·go·bar·di (lang′gō·bär′dē) *n. pl.* The Lombards. [<L, prob. <OHG *lang* long + *bart* beard] **— Lan′go·bar′dic** *adj.*
Lan·gre·o (läng·grā′ō) A mining region of NW Spain.
lang·shan (lang′shan) *n.* A breed of large domestic fowl introduced from China. [< Chinese, from *Langshan,* lit., wolf hill, a town near Shanghai]
lang·syne (lang′sīn′, -zīn′) *adv. Scot.* Long since; long ago: used also as a noun. See AULD LANG SYNE.
Lang·ton (lang′tən), **Stephen,** died 1228, English patriot and archbishop of Canterbury.
Lang·try (lang′trē), **Lily,** 1852–1929, *née* Emily Charlotte Le Breton, English actress: called the "Jersey Lily."
lan·guage (lang′gwij) *n.* **1** The expression and communication of emotions or ideas between human beings by means of speech and hearing, the sounds spoken or heard being systematized and confirmed by usage among a given people over a period of time. **2** Transmission of emotions or ideas between any living creatures by any means. **3** The words forming the means of communication among members of a single nation or group at a given period; tongue: the French *language.* **4** The impulses, capacities, and powers which induce and make possible the creation and use of all forms of human communication by speech and hearing. **5** The vocabulary or technical expressions used in a specific business, science, etc.: the *language* of mathematics. **6** One's characteristic manner of expression or use of speech. [<OF *langage* < *langue* tongue <L *lingua* tongue, language. Akin to TONGUE.]

Synonyms: barbarism, dialect, diction, expression, gibberish, idiom, patois, speech, tongue, vernacular. *Language* originally signified only the *expression* of thought by spoken words; it has now acquired the broader interpretation of the *expression* of thought by any means. *Speech* denotes the power of articulate utterance; we can speak of the *language* of animals, but not of their *speech.* A *tongue* is the *speech* or *language* of some one people, country, or race. A *dialect* is a special mode of speaking a *language* peculiar to some locality or class; a *barbarism* is a usage that is felt to be substandard. *Idiom* refers to the construction of phrases and sentences, and the way of forming or using words; it is the peculiar mold in which each *language* casts its thought. The great difficulty of translation lies in giving the thought expressed in one *language* in the *idiom* of another. A *dialect* may be used by the highest as well as the lowest within its range; a *patois* is usually illiterate, belonging to the lower classes; those who speak a *patois* understand the cultured form of their own *language,* but speak only their own form; often a *patois* is a kind of linguistic enclave, as the dialect of the French-Canadians in rural Quebec, or the speech of the Cajuns in Louisiana.
language arts Those elementary-school subjects, especially, reading, spelling, literature, and composition, both written and oral, that deal with the acquisition of facility in one's native language.
Langue·doc (läṅg·dôk′) A region and former province in southern France, between the Loire and the Pyrenees.
langue d'oc (läṅg dôk′) The form of Old French spoken south of the Loire in the Middle Ages, surviving in modern Provençal: so called from the use of the word *oc* for "yes." [<OF, lit., language of *oc* <Provençal: *oc* yes <L *hoc* this (thing)]
langue d'o·ïl (läṅg dō·ēl′) The form of Old French spoken north of the Loire during the Middle Ages, from which modern French developed: so called from the use of the word *oui* or *oïl* for "yes". [<OF, lit., language of *oïl* <L *hoc illi* this for that < *hoc this* + *ille* that]
lan·guet (lang′gwet) *n.* A little tongue or something resembling a tongue in structure or function. Also **lan′guette.** [<F *languette,* dim. of *langue* tongue. See LANGUAGE.]
lan·guid (lang′gwid) *adj.* **1** Indisposed to physical exertion; affected by weakness or fatigue. **2** Wanting in interest or animation;

listless. 3 Lacking in force or quickness of movement. See synonyms under FAINT, SICKLY. [<L *languidus* faint, weak <*languere* languish] — **lan′guid·ly** *adv.* —**lan′guid·ness** *n.*

lan·guish (lang′gwish) *v.i.* **1** To become weak or feeble; be or grow faint or listless. **2** To live or be in unfavorable circumstances so as to be weakened by them: to *languish* in a dungeon. **3** To affect a look of sentimental longing or melancholy. **4** To pine with love or desire. —*n.* **1** A tender look. **2** The act or state of languishing. [<OF *languiss-*, stem of *languir* <L *languescere*, inceptive of *languere* be weary, languish] —**lan′guish·er** *n.*

lan·guish·ing (lang′gwish·ing) *adj.* **1** Lacking interest or force. **2** Sentimentally pensive. **3** Becoming weak or listless. —**lan′guish·ing·ly** *adv.*

lan·guish·ment (lang′gwish·mənt) *n.* **1** The state of being languid. **2** Sentimental languor or tenderness.

lan·guor (lang′gər) *n.* **1** Lassitude of body or depression of mind, as from exertion; weakness. **2** An atonic debility or prostration. **3** Amorous dreaminess. **4** The absence of activity; dulness. **5** A state of premature decay in plants. [<OF <L *languor, languoris* <*languere* languish] — **lan′·guor·ous** *adj.* —**lan′guor·ous·ly** *adv.* — **lan′·guor·ous·ness** *n.*

lan·gur (lung·go͞or′) *n.* A long-tailed Asian monkey (genus *Presbytis*), noted for its remarkable leaping power; as, the common langur or hanuman and the Himalayan langur. [<Hind. *langūr* <Skt. *lāṅgūlin*, lit., having a tail]

lan·iard (lan′yərd) See LANYARD.

la·ni·ar·y (lā′nē·er′ē, lan′ē-) *adj.* Adapted for tearing, as the canine teeth. —*n. pl.* **·ar·ies** A canine tooth. [<L *laniarius* pertaining to a butcher <*lanius* a butcher <*laniare* tear]

La·nier (lə·nir′), **Sidney,** 1842–81, U.S. poet.

la·nif·er·ous (lə·nif′ər·əs) *adj.* Bearing wool: often **la·nig′er·ous** (-nij′-). [<L *lanifer* <*lana* wool + *-fer* -FEROUS]

lan·i·tal (lan′ə·tal) *n.* A substance originally produced in Italy from casein, similar to wool in chemical composition and use. [<Ital. *lan(a)* wool + *Ital(ia)* Italy]

lank (langk) *adj.* **1** Lean; shrunken. **2** Long, straight, and thin: *lank* hair. **3** *Obs.* Languid. See synonyms under GAUNT, MEAGER. [OE *hlanc* flexible] —**lank′ly** *adv.* —**lank′ness** *n.*

Lan·kes·ter (lang′kəs·tər), **Sir Edwin Ray,** 1847–1929, English zoologist and comparative anatomist.

lank·y (lang′kē) *adj.* **lank·i·er, lank·i·est** Tall; thin; shrunken. [<LANK + -Y] —**lank′i·ly** *adv.* —**lank′i·ness** *n.*

lan·ner (lan′ər) *n.* **1** A falcon of southern Europe and Asia, especially *Falco biarmicus.* **2** In falconry, the female of this falcon. [<OF *lanier*, ? ult. <L *laniarius.* See LANIARY.]

lan·ner·et (lan′ər·et) *n.* In falconry, the male of the lanner. [<OF *laneret*, dim. of *lanier* LANNER]

lan·o·lin (lan′ə·lin) *n.* An unctuous fatty mixture of the ethers of cholesterin with fatty acids, obtained from various keratin tissues, as the wool of sheep, valuable in pharmacy as a vehicle for substances intended to be applied to the skin: also called *wool fat.* Also **lan′o·line** (-lin, -lēn). [<L *lan(a)* wool + *ol(eum)* oil + -IN]

la·nose (lā′nōs) *adj.* Woolly; resembling wool. [<L *lanosus* <*lana* wool]

lans·downe (lanz′doun) *n.* A material made of silk or similar fiber and wool mixed. [? from *Lansdown*, a town in England]

Lan·sing (lan′sing) The capital of Michigan.

lans·que·net (lans′kə·net) *n.* A card game for any number of players, in which all bets are made on single cards and must be covered by the banker. [<F <G *landsknecht* a (mercenary) foot soldier <*land* country + *knecht* servant]

lant (lant) *n.* Urine, particularly if stale: used as a detergent in wool-scouring. [OE *hland* urine]

lan·ta·na (lan·tā′nə, -tä′-) *n.* Any of a genus *(Lantana)* of mainly tropical American shrubs of the verbena family bearing spikes or umbels of red, orange, lilac, or white flowers. [<NL, viburnum]

lan·tern (lan′tərn) *n.* **1** A transparent case, as on a lamp post or of portable character, for enclosing and protecting a light. **2** *Archit.* A tower or the like, as on a roof or dome, open below and admitting light from the sides; also, a small tower, pavilion, or pinnacle placed on the apex of a dome or crowning another tower. **3** One of various mechanisms likened to a lantern. **4** A lighthouse. **5** A magic lantern. **6** One of the street lamps of Paris, used as gallows during the French Revolution. Also *Obs.* **lant·horn** (lant′hôrn′, lan′tərn). [<F *lanterne* <L *lanterna* <Gk. *lamptēr* <*lampein* shine]

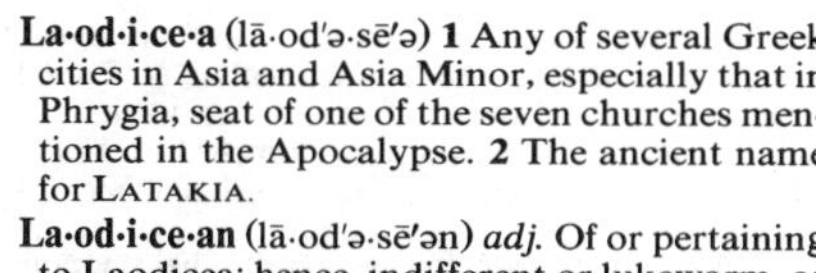
LANTERN ON CHURCH TOWER

lantern fish Any of various small, large-eyed marine fishes bearing rows of phosphorescent organs along the under parts of their bodies.

lantern fly A homopterous insect (family *Fulgoridae*) formerly supposed to produce light from a large protuberant snout.

lan·tern-jawed (lan′tərn·jôd′) *adj.* Having long, thin jaws; hence, having a thin visage.

lantern wheel *Mech.* A lantern-shaped device performing the work of a pinion, in which a circle of bars between two heads takes the place of pinion teeth: sometimes called *trundle.* Also **lantern pinion.**

lan·tha·nide series (lan′thə·nīd) *Physics* The group of rare-earth elements beginning with lanthanum and ending with lutetium, atomic numbers 57 to 71, characterized by closely related properties and great difficulty of separation. [<LANTHAN(UM) + *-ide*, var. of -ID[2]]

lan·tha·num (lan′thə·nəm) *n.* A dark lead-gray metallic element (symbol La) of the lanthanide series. See ELEMENT. [<NL <Gk. *lanthanein* lie concealed]

lan·tho·pine (lan′thə·pēn) *n.* A white crystalline alkaloid, $C_{23}H_{25}O_4N$, obtained from opium. [<Gk. *lanth(anein)* lie hidden + OP(IUM) + -INE[2]]

Lan·tsang (län′tsäng′) The Chinese name for the MEKONG.

la·nu·gi·nous (lə·no͞o′jə·nəs, -nyo͞o′-) *adj.* Woolly or downy. Also **la·nu′gi·nose** (-nōs). [<L *lanuginosus* <*lanugo, -inis* down <*lana* wool]

la·nu·go (lə·no͞o′gō, -nyo͞o′-) *n. Biol.* A downy growth; specifically, the soft, rudimentary hair found on the body of a child at birth. [<L, down <*lana* wool]

lan·yappe (lan·yap′) See LAGNIAPPE.

lan·yard (lan′yərd) *n.* **1** *Naut.* A small rope used on a ship, especially, a four-stranded hemp rope, especially one rove through deadeyes and used in setting up riggings. **2** A cord used in firing certain kinds of cannon. **3** A stout cord worn around the neck, especially by sailors, and used for attaching a knife: called a **knife lanyard.** Also spelled *laniard.* [Alter. of obs. *lanyer* <OF *lasniere* a thong <*lasne* a noose; infl. in form by *yard* [1] a spar]

Lan·za·ro·te (län′thä·rō′tā) Northeasternmost of the Canary Islands; 310 square miles.

Lan·ze·lot (län′tsə·lôt) German form of LANCELOT.

La·o (lä′ō) *n.* **1** A Buddhistic people living in Laos and northern and eastern Thailand. **2** Their Thai language.

La·oag (lä·wäg′) A port in NW Luzon, Philippines.

La·oc·o·on (lā·ok′ə·won, -ō·won) In Greek legend, a priest of Apollo who warned the Trojans against the wooden horse of the Greeks, and was destroyed with his two sons by two serpents sent by Athena or Apollo.

La·od·a·mi·a (lā·od′ə·mī′ə) In the *Iliad*, the wife of Protesilaus, the first Greek killed at Troy, who died from grief at his loss, after persuading the gods to grant him three more hours of life in which to be with her. Also **La·o·da·mei·a** (lā′ə·də·mī′ə).

La·od·i·ce·a (lā·od′ə·sē′ə) **1** Any of several Greek cities in Asia and Asia Minor, especially that in Phrygia, seat of one of the seven churches mentioned in the Apocalypse. **2** The ancient name for LATAKIA.

La·od·i·ce·an (lā·od′ə·sē′ən) *adj.* Of or pertaining to Laodicea; hence, indifferent or lukewarm, as in religion *Rev.* iii 14–22. —*n.* **1** An inhabitant of one of the eight Greek cities named Laodicea. **2** An indifferent or lukewarm Christian; hence, any indifferent or lukewarm person.

La·oighis (lā′ish) A county of western Leinster province, Ireland; 664 square miles; county town, Maryborough: also *Leix.*

La·om·e·don (lā·om′ə·don) In Greek legend, the founder of Troy and father of Priam.

Laon (län) A city in northern France.

La·os (lā′os, lä′ōs) A constitutional monarchy in NW Indochina; 91,400 square miles; capital, Vientiane; royal residence, Luang Prabang.

Lao-tse (lou′dzu′), 604?–531? B.C., Chinese philosopher and mystic, founder of Taoism; also **Lao-tze** and **Lao-tzu.**

lap [1] (lap) *n.* **1** That part of the body below the waist on which, when in a sitting posture, one may conveniently support anything; the upper and front surface of the thighs or knees: to hold a child on one's *lap.* **2** The clothing that covers the front of the thighs when one sits down. **3** By extension, a place for supporting or fostering: fortune's *lap.* **4** A loose fold or flap of a garment; a skirt. **5** That part of a substance which extends over another; also, the length of such extension: the *lap* of a shingle. **6** One course around a race track, usually an even fraction of a mile. **7** A piece of soft metal, wood, or leather, usually in the form of a rotating disk, used in cutting gems and polishing hard metal. **8** The state of overlapping. —*v.* **lapped, lap·ping** *v.t.* **1** To fold and lay over; wrap around something. **2** To lay (one thing) partly over or beyond another: to *lap* weatherboards. **3** To reach or extend partly over or beyond; overlap: These doors *lap* each other. **4** To take upon or as upon the lap; surround with love, care, etc.: *lapped* in idleness and luxury. **5** To grind or polish (a gem) with a lap. **6** To get one or more laps ahead of (an opponent) in a race. —*v.i.* **7** To be folded; wrap. **8** To lie partly upon or beside something else; overlap. **9** To lie beyond or into something else: One wall *laps* into the other. [OE *læpa, lappa* a fold or hanging part of a garment]

lap [2] (lap) *v.t.* & *v.i.* **lapped, lap·ping 1** To take (a liquid) into the mouth with the tongue: said of animals. **2** To wash against (the shore, etc.) with a slight, rippling sound: said of water. —*n.* **1** The act of lapping, as with the tongue; a lick. **2** The sound of lapping, or a similar sound. **3** *Colloq.* That which is licked up, as pap or a drink, especially a weak or diluted drink. [Prob. fusion of OE *lapian* lap and OF *laper* lick <Gmc.] —**lap′per** *n.*

La Pal·ma (lä päl′mä) See PALMA (sense 2).

La Pam·pa (lä päm′pä) An interior province of central Argentina; 55,103 square miles; capital, Santa Rosa.

laparo- *combining form Med.* The flanks or loins; the wall of the abdomen. Also, before vowels, **lapar-.** [<Gk. *lapara* flank]

lap·a·ros·co·py (lap′ə·ros′kə·pē) *n. Surg.* The examination of the abdominal cavity by means of a narrow instrument inserted through an incision.

lap·a·rot·o·my (lap′ə·rot′ə·mē) *n. Surg.* The operation of opening the abdomen by incision in the loin. [<LAPARO- + -TOMY]

La Paz (lä päz′, *Sp.* lä päs′) A city in western Bolivia; the de facto capital, although Sucre is nominally the capital.

lap·board (lap′bôrd′, -bōrd′) *n.* A flat wide board sometimes having a cavity on one edge hollowed out to fit the waist: used especially by tailors, etc., or over the arms of a chair, as a table.

lap·dis·solve (lap′di·zolv′) *n.* In motion pictures, the gradual change of one scene into another, as by lapping two exposures on the same strip of film.

lap dog A dog small enough to be held on the lap.

la·pel (lə·pel′) *n.* The part of the front of a coat, attached to the collar, which is folded back: usually plural. [Dim. of LAP[1]]

La Pé·rouse (lȧ pā·ro͞oz′), **Comte de,** 1741–1788?, Jean François de Galaup, French navigator.

La Pé·rouse Strait (lȧ pā·ro͞oz′) The passage from the Sea of Okhotsk to the Sea of Japan between Sakhalin and Hokkaido.

lap·ful (lap′fo͝ol′) *n.* As much as the lap can hold.

lap·i·dar·i·an (lap′ə·dâr′ē·ən) *adj.* Of or relating to stones; written on stones: a *lapidarian* inscription. [<L *lapidarius* <*lapis, -idis* a stone]

lap·i·dar·y (lap′ə·der′ē) *adj.* **1** Pertaining to stones or the art of working in precious stones. **2** Inscribed upon or cut in stone. —*n. pl.* **·dar·ies 1** One who cuts, engraves, and sets precious stones. **2** A connoisseur in lapidary work or gems; lapidist. [<L *lapidarius* LAPIDARIAN]

lap·i·date (lap′ə·dāt) *v.t.* **·dat·ed, ·dat·ing 1** To hurl stones at. **2** To stone to death. [<L *lapidatus,* pp. of *lapidare* <*lapis, -idis* a stone] —**lap′i·da′tion** *n.*

la·pid·i·fy (lə·pid′ə·fī) *v.t.* & *v.i.* **·fied, ·fy·ing** To turn to stone; petrify. [<F *lapidifier* <Med. L *lapidificare* <L *lapis, -idis* a stone + *facere* make] —**lap·i·dif·ic** (lap′ə·dif′ik) or **·i·cal** *adj.* —**la·pid′i·fi·ca′tion** *n.*

la·pil·lus (lə·pil′əs) *n. pl.* **·li** (-ī) A small fragment of lava ejected from a volcano. [<L, dim. of *lapis* a stone]

lap·in (lap′in, *Fr.* lȧ·paṅ′) *n.* A rabbit; also, its fur. [<F]

la·pis (lā′pis, lap′is) *n. pl.* **lap·i·des** (lap′ə·dēz) A stone: used in Latin phrases. [<L]

lap·is laz·u·li (lap′is laz′yo͝o·lī) **1** A rich blue complex mixture of minerals, originally used to produce ultramarine and by the ancients for decoration, and believed to be their sapphire. **2** The color of this substance. [<NL <L *lapis* a stone + Med. L *lazuli,* genitive of *lazulus* azure <Arabic *lāzaward.* See AZURE.]

Lap·i·thae (lap′ə·thē) *n. pl. of* **Lap·ith** (lap′·ith) In Greek mythology, a wild tribe of Thessaly who, at the wedding of their king Pirithous, fought and overcame the centaurs, after the latter had attempted to carry off the bride and other women present at the feast. Also **Lap′i·thæ.**

lap–joint (lap′joint′) *v.t.* To join together by a lap joint.

lap joint A joint in which a layer of material laps over another, as in shingling. —**lap–joint·ed** (lap′join′tid) *adj.*

La·place (lȧ·plȧs′), **Marquis de,** 1749–1827, Pierre Simon, French astronomer and mathematician. —**La·pla′ci·an** *adj.*

Lap·land (lap′land) A region of northern Europe on the Barents Sea, largely within the Arctic Circle. See LAPP. —**Lap′land·er** *n.*

La Pla·ta (lä plä′tä) A port in eastern Argentina, capital of Buenos Aires province. See also PLATA, RÍO DE LA.

Lapp (lap) *n.* **1** One of a Mongoloid people inhabiting Lapland, of short stature, and markedly brachycephalic: also called *Saami.* Formerly nomadic and dependent upon reindeer herds for food and clothing, the Lapps are now settled largely in Sweden and Norway. Also **Lap′land′er. 2** The Finno-Ugric language of the Lapps. [<Sw.]

lap·per[1] (lap′ər) *n.* **1** One who laps or folds. **2** One who polishes with a lap. **3** A lapping machine.

lap·per[2] (lap′ər) See LOPPER.

lap·pet (lap′it) *n.* **1** A small lap or flap used for ornamenting a garment, etc. **2** *Ornithol.* A fleshy process pendent from the head of a bird; a wattle. **3** A lobe, as of the ear. **4** A portion of anything that hangs loose. **5** The guard of a keyhole. [Dim. of LAP[1]]

lap·sa·tion (lap·sā′shən) *n.* In insurance, a lapsing.

lapse (laps) *v.i.* **lapsed, laps·ing 1** To pass slowly or by degrees; slip; sink: to *lapse* into a coma. **2** To deviate from virtue or truth; fail in duty or accuracy. **3** To pass or elapse, as time. **4** To become void, usually by disuse or neglect: The agreement *lapsed.* **5** *Law* To pass or be forfeited to another because of the negligence, failure, or death of the holder. See synonyms under FALL. —*n.* **1** An insensible or gradual slipping, gliding, or passing away; imperceptible movement onward or downward: the *lapse* of ages. **2** A fall to a lower form or state; a falling into decay or ruin, as a building: used also figuratively. **3** A slight deviation from what is right, proper, or just; a slip or mistake through lack of care or attention: a *lapse* in conduct; *lapse* of the pen. **4** Failure or miscarriage, as through fault or negligence: a *lapse* of justice. **5** *Law* The defeat of a right or privilege through fault, failure, or neglect, as, to perform certain conditions of a testamentary bequest. **6** Apostasy. [<L *lapsus* a slip <*labi* glide, slip] —**laps′a·ble, laps′i·ble** *adj.* —**laps′er** *n.*

lapse rate *Meteorol.* The rate of decrease of temperature with vertical height above the earth.

lap·si (lap′sī) *n. pl. Latin* Apostates among the early Christians.

lap·stone (lap′stōn′) *n.* A stone, held in the lap, on which a shoemaker hammers leather.

lap·strake (lap′·strāk′) *adj.* Built with planks overlapping and riveted together; clinker-built, as a boat. —*n.* A boat so built. Also **lap′streak′** (-strēk′). [<LAP[1] + STRAKE]

LAPSTRAKE
Flat-bottom rowboat.

lap·sus (lap′səs) *n. Latin* A slip; a mistake.

lap·sus cal·a·mi (lap′səs kal′ə·mī) *Latin* A slip of the pen.

lap·sus lin·guae (lap′səs ling′gwē) *Latin* A slip of the tongue.

lap·sus me·mo·ri·ae (lap′səs mə·mō′ri·ē) *Latin* A slip of the memory.

Lap·tev Sea (läp′tyif) An arm of the Arctic Ocean north of the Yakut S.S.R.: formerly *Nordenskjöld Sea. Russian* **More Lap·te·vykh** (läp′tyə·vēk).

La·pu·ta (lə·pyo͞o′tə) In Swift's *Gulliver's Travels,* a flying island peopled by philosophers.

lap·wing (lap′wing′) *n.* A ploverlike bird (*Vanellus vanellus*) having the plumage of the upper parts lustrous or metallic and the head crested. Its flight is heavy and flopping; its shrill note resembles the sound *pee-weet.* [OE *hlēapwince* <*hleapan* leap + *wince,* prob. <*wincan* totter; so called from its awkward manner of flight; infl. in form by LAP[1] and WING]

Lar (lär) The singular of LARES.

La·rache (lä·räsh′) A port in western Spanish Morocco: Arabic *El Araish.*

Lar·a·mie (lar′ə·mē) A city in SE Wyoming on the **Laramie River,** a river flowing 216 miles NE to the North Platte through northern Colorado and SE Wyoming.

lar·board (lär′bərd, -bôrd′, -bōrd′) *adj* & *adv. Naut.* Being or going on or toward the left side of a ship as one faces the bow. —*n.* The left-hand side of a ship: now replaced by *port.* [ME *laddebord,* lit., prob., lading side <OE *hladan* lade + *bord* side; infl. in form by STARBOARD]

lar·ce·ner (lär′sə·nər) *n.* A thief; one who commits larceny. Also **lar′ce·nist.**

lar·ce·ny (lär′sə·nē) *n. pl.* **·nies** *Law* The unlawful abstraction, without claim of right, of the personal goods of another with intent to defraud the owner; theft. The distinction between **grand larceny** and **petit** (or **petty**) **larceny,** based on the value of the stolen property, has been abolished in England and most of the United States. [<AF *larcin,* OF *larrecin* <L *latrocinium* theft <*latrocinari* rob <*latro* robber] —**lar′ce·nous** *adj.* —**lar′·ce·nous·ly** *adv.*

larch (lärch) *n.* **1** Any one of several cone-bearing, deciduous trees of the pine family (genus *Larix*). **2** The strong, durable wood of this tree. [<G *lärche* <MHG *lerche* <L *larix, laricis*]

lard (lärd) *n.* The semisolid oil of hog's fat after rendering. —*v.t.* **1** To prepare lean meat or poultry by inserting strips of bacon or fat before cooking. **2** To cover or smear with lard or grease. **3** To mix with something so as to enrich or improve; interlard. [<OF, bacon <L *lardum* lard] —**lard′y** *adj.*

lar·da·ce·in (lär·dā′sē·in, -sēn) *n.* A fatty protein compound produced in waxy or albuminoid degeneration. [<LARD + -ACE(OUS) + -IN]

lar·da·ceous (lär·dā′shəs) *adj.* **1** Of the nature of lard. **2** Pertaining to or indicative of lardacein; fatty or waxy.

lar·der (lär′dər) *n.* A room where articles of food are kept before cooking; pantry; hence, the provisions of a household. [<AF *larder,* OF *lardier* <Med. L *lardarium,* orig., a storehouse for bacon <L *lardum* lard]

larder beetle A small, blackish-and-gray beetle (*Dermestes lardarius*) about 1/3 inch long, whose larva feeds on dried meats, etc. For illustration see INSECT (injurious).

Lard·ner (lärd′nər), **Ring(gold) (Wilmer),** 1885–1933, U. S. author.

lard oil A heavy oil expressed from lard.

lar·don (lär′dən) *n.* A thin slice of bacon or pork for larding meat. Also **lar·doon** (lär·do͞on′). [<F <*lard.* See LARD.]

Lar·es (lâr′ēz, lā′rēz) *n. pl. of* **Lar** (lär) Tutelary deities of ancient Rome, adopted from the Etruscans, and worshiped as spirits of departed ancestors presiding over the households of their descendants: associated with the *Penates.*

lares and pe·na·tes (pə·nā′tēz) The household gods; hence, one's home and cherished belongings.

large (lärj) *adj.* **larg·er, larg·est 1** Absolutely or relatively great or ample as regards size, dimensions, quantity, number, extent, range, etc.; big; great; spacious; ample; extensive: opposed to *little* or *small.* **2** Having unusual breadth of sympathy or comprehension: a *large* heart or mind. **3** Favorable in direction; fair: said of a wind when it is abeam. **4** Characterized by fullness: said of the pulse. **5** *Obs.* Prodigal of words, gifts, or money; lavish. **6** *Obs.* Unrestrained in liberty or morals. **7** *Obs.* Complete; full. —**at large** (Formerly with the possessive pronoun: *at his large.*) **1** To the fullest extent; in full. **2** Free or unrestrained in movement; at liberty: The thief is still *at large.* **3** Not included within particular limitations; in general; for all. **4** Elected from a State as a whole rather than from a particular congressional or electoral district: a congressman *at large.* —*adv.* **1** *Naut.* Before the wind, or with the wind on the quarter. **2** *Colloq.* Boastfully. [<OF <L *larga,* fem. of *largus* abundant] —**large′·ness** *n.*

Synonyms (*adj.*): abundant, ample, big, broad, bulky, capacious, coarse, colossal, commodious, considerable, enormous, extensive, gigantic, grand, great, huge, immense, long, massive, spacious, vast, wide. *Large* denotes extension in more than one direction, and beyond the average of the class to which the object belongs; we speak of a *large* surface or a *large* solid, but of a *long* line. A *large* man is a man of more than ordinary size; a *great* man is a man of remarkable ability. *Big* is a more emphatic word than *large,* but ordinarily less elegant. *Antonyms*: diminutive, inconsiderable, infinitesimal, insignificant, limited, little, mean, microscopic, minute, narrow, paltry, petty, scanty, slender, slight, small, tiny, trifling, trivial.

large–heart·ed (lärj′här′tid) *adj.* Generous. —**large′–heart′ed·ness** *n.*

large·ly (lärj′lē) *adv.* **1** In a large manner. **2** To a great extent; generally. **3** Generously; abundantly; copiously. **4** Pompously.

large–mind·ed (lärj′mīn′did) *adj.* Liberal in ideas; not narrow-minded. —**large′–mind′ed·ness** *n.*

large–scale (lärj′skāl′) *adj.* Of large size or scope.

lar·gess (lär′jis, -jes) *n.* **1** A gift; gratuity. **2** Liberality; bounty. Also **lar′gesse.** See synonyms under GIFT. [<F *largesse* <L *largus* abundant]

lar·ghet·to (lär·get′ō) *Music adj.* Slow; in a time not quite so slow as *largo*: a direction to the performer. —*n.* A musical movement requiring moderately slow time. [<Ital., dim. of *largo* LARGO]

lar·ghis·si·mo (lär·gis′i·mō) *adj. Music* Very slow. [<Ital., superl. of *largo* LARGO]

larg·ish (lär′jish) *adj.* Somewhat large.

lar·go (lär′gō) *adj.* & *adv. Music* Slow; broad; majestic. —*n. pl.* **·gos** A movement in slow time. [<Ital., slow, large <L *largus* abundant]

lar·i·at (lar′ē·ət) *n.* **1** A rope, especially of horsehair, for tethering animals. **2** A lasso. —*v.t.* To fasten or catch with a lariat. [<Sp. *la reata* <*la* the + *reata* rope]

lar·ine (lar′in, lā′rīn) *n.* One of a subfamily

(Larinae) of longipennate birds, having the upper mandible as long as the lower and with a single sheath; a gull or tern. —*adj.* Of or pertaining to the *Larinae.* [<NL <LL *larus* a gull <Gk. *laros*]

La Rio·ja (lä ryō′hä) A province of western Argentina; 35,691 square miles; capital, La Rioja.

La·ri·sa (lä′rē·sä) The chief city of Thessaly, Greece. Also **La·ris·sa** (lə·ris′ə).

la·rith·mics (lə·rith′miks) *n.* The scientific study and analysis of human populations in their quantitative aspects: distinguished from *eugenics.* [<Gk. *laos* people + *arithmos* a number] —**la·rith′mic** *adj.*

lark[1] (lärk) *n.* **1** Any of numerous small singing birds (family *Alaudidae*), as the European skylark *(Alauda arvensis).* **2** One of various other birds, as a titlark or meadowlark. [OE *lāferce, lǣwerce*]

lark[2] (lärk) *n.* A hilarious time; frolic; humorous adventure. —*v.i.* To play pranks; frolic. [<dial. E (Northern) *lake* play, fusion of ON *leika* leap and OE *lācan* frolic; infl. in form by LARK[1]] —**lark′er** *n.* —**lark′some** *adj.*

lark·spur (lärk′spûr) *n.* Any of several showy herbs of the crowfoot family (genus *Delphinium*) with alternate, palmately divided leaves, and loose, terminal clusters of irregular, spurred, white, pink, lavender, or blue flowers. —**scarlet larkspur** A species of larkspur *(Delphinium cardinale)* that grows wild in California. [<LARK[1] + SPUR]

larkspur blue A light, bright blue, the color of some larkspurs.

lark·y (lär′kē) *adj.* **lark·i·er, lark·i·est** *Colloq.* High-spirited and carefree; frolicsome: a *larky* adventure.

La Roche·fou·cauld (lå rôsh·fōō·kō′), **Duc François de,** 1613–80, Prince de Marcillac, French writer and politician.

La Ro·chelle (lå rō·shel′) A port city of western France on the Bay of Biscay; Huguenot stronghold, besieged and taken by Cardinal Richelieu, 1627–28.

La·rousse (lå·rōōs′), **Pierre Athanase,** 1817–1875, French grammarian and encyclopedist.

lar·ri·gan (lar′ə·gən) *n.* A moccasin made of prepared oiled leather: used chiefly by lumbermen. [<dial. E (Canadian); origin unknown]

lar·ri·kin (lar′ə·kin) *Chiefly Austral. adj.* Boisterously rude; rowdyish. —*n.* A rough, disorderly fellow; rowdy. [<dial. E (Australian), prob. <*Larry,* nickname for LAWRENCE]

lar·rup (lar′əp) *Colloq. v.t.* To beat; thrash. —*n.* A blow. [<dial. E (East Anglian), ? <Du. *larpen* thrash]

Lar·ry (lar′ē) Diminutive of LAWRENCE.

Lars (lärs) Swedish form of LAWRENCE.

lar·um (lar′əm) *Archaic* An alarm. [Aphetic var. of ALARUM]

lar·va (lär′və) *n. pl.* **·vae** (-vē) **1** *Biol.* The early form of any animal when it is unlike the parent, or undergoes a metamorphosis. **2** *Entomol.* The first stage of an insect after leaving the egg, preceding the pupa, as a caterpillar, a grub, or a maggot. **3** In ancient Roman superstition, an evil spirit. [<L, a ghost, a mask] —**lar′val** *adj.*

lar·vate (lär′vāt, -vit) *adj.* Clothed or concealed as if with a mask: said of certain diseases. Also **lar′vat·ed.** [<L *larvatus* <*larva* a mask]

lar·vi·pos·i·tor (lär′və·poz′ə·tər) *n. Entomol.* In certain dipterous insects, the modified ovipositor. [<LARVA + L *positor* a placer <*positus,* pp. of *ponere* put, place]

la·ryn·gal (lə·ring′gəl) *adj.* Originating in the larynx.

la·ryn·ga·phone (lə·ring′gə·fōn) *n.* A type of microphone which picks up and transmits voice vibrations by direct contact with the throat of the speaker: used to minimize interference by external sounds. [<*larynga-,* var. of LARYNGO- + -PHONE]

la·ryn·ge·al (lə·rin′je·əl, -jəl) *adj.* **1** Of, pertaining to, or near the larynx: also **la·ryn′·ge·an. 2** Attacking the larynx, as a disease. **3** Adapted or used for treating the larynx, as an instrument. [<NL *laryngeus* <Gk. *larynx, laryngos* larynx]

lar·yn·gis·mus (lar′ən·jiz′məs) *n.* **1** *Pathol.* Spasm of the muscles of the glottis. **2** A disease of horses caused by paralysis of muscles of the larynx; roaring. [<NL <Gk. *laryngismos* shouting <*laryngizein* shout <*larynx, laryngos* larynx] —**lar′yn·gis′mal** *adj.*

laryngismus strid·u·lus (strid′yə·ləs) *Pathol.* A disease of children marked by laryngeal spasms and a strident breathing; false or spasmodic croup. [<NL, lit., rattling laryngismus]

lar·yn·gi·tis (lar′ən·jī′tis) *n. Pathol.* Inflammation of the larynx. —**lar′yn·git′ic** (-jit′ik) *adj.*

laryngo– *combining form* The larynx; pertaining to the larynx: *laryngoscope.* Also, before vowels, **laryng–.** [<Gk. *larynx, laryngos* the larynx]

lar·yn·gol·o·gy (lar′ing·gol′ə·jē) *n.* Scientific knowledge of the larynx, its functions and diseases. —**la·ryn·go·log·i·cal** (lə·ring′gō·loj′i·kəl) *adj.* —**lar′yn·gol′o·gist** *n.*

la·ryn·go·scope (lə·ring′gə·skōp) *n.* An instrument for inspecting the larynx. —**la·ryn′go·scop′ic** (-skop′ik) *adj.*

lar·yn·gos·co·py (lar′ing·gos′kə·pē) *n.* Examination by means of the laryngoscope.

lar·yn·got·o·my (lar′ing·got′ə·mē) *n. Surg.* The operation of cutting into the larynx. [<Gk. *laryngotomia* <*larynx, laryngos* the larynx + *tomē* a cutting <*temnein* cut]

lar·ynx (lar′ingks) *n. pl.* **la·ryn·ges** (lə·rin′jēz) or **lar·ynx·es** *Anat.* The organ of voice in mammals and most other vertebrates, situated at the upper part of the trachea, consisting of a cartilaginous box across which are stretched the vocal cords whose vibrations produce sound. [<Gk. *larynx, laryngos* the larynx]

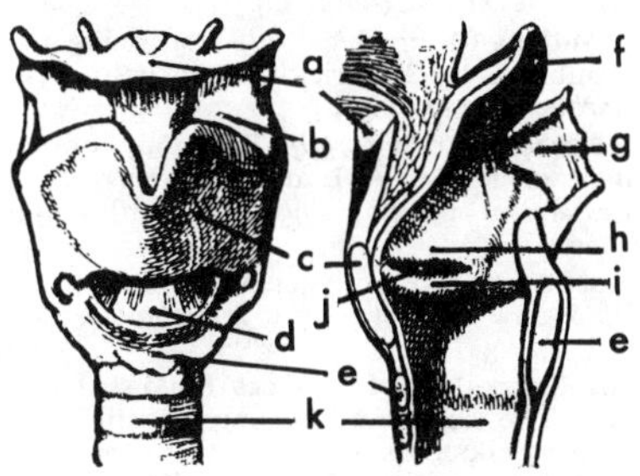

HUMAN LARYNX

Left: front view.	Right: side view.
a. Hyoid bone.	*f.* Epiglottis.
b. Thyrohyoid ligament.	*g.* Thyrohyoid membrane.
c. Thyroid cartilage.	*h.* Vocal chord.
d. Cricothyroid ligament.	*i.* Vocal chord.
e. Cricoid cartilage.	*j.* Laryngeal ventricle.

k. Trachea.

La·sa (lä′sä′) The Chinese name for LHASA.

La Salle (lå sål′), **Sieur Robert Cavelier de,** 1643–87, French explorer.

Las Be·la (lus bā′lə) A princely state of SE Baluchistan, West Pakistan; 7,043 square miles; capital, Bela.

las·car (las′kər) *n.* An East Indian native, serving as a sailor. [<Hind. *lashkar* army (used for *lashkari* belonging to the army, a soldier) <Persian <Arabic *al-'askar* the army]

Las Ca·sas (läs kä′säs), **Bartolomé de,** 1474–1566, Spanish historian and missionary to the American Indians: called "Apostle of the Indies."

las·civ·i·ous (lə·siv′ē·əs) *adj.* **1** Having wanton desires; lustful; lewd. **2** Tending to produce sensual desires. See synonyms under BRUTISH. [<LL *lasciviosus* <L *lascivia* wantonness < *lascivus* sportive, lustful] —**las·civ′i·ous·ly** *adv.* —**las·civ′i·ous·ness** *n.*

la·ser (lā′zər) *n.* An optical maser.

lash (lash) *n.* **1** A thong on a whip handle; a whip. **2** A stroke with or as with a whip. **3** A sharp, sarcastic remark. **4** An eyelash. **5** Any heavy blow, as of waves beating the shore. —*v.t.* **1** To strike, punish, or urge forward with or as with a whip. **2** To throw or move quickly or suddenly, as from side to side: to *lash* the tail. **3** To beat or dash against with force or violence: The waves *lashed* the pier. **4** To attack or criticize severely; berate. **5** To arouse the emotions of, as with words. **6** To bind or tie with or as with a lashing. —*v.i.* **7** To move quickly or violently; dash. —**to lash out 1** To strike out violently or wildly. **2** To break into angry or vehement speech. [<Prob. fusion of MLG *lasch* a flap and OF *laz* a cord; infl. in form and sense by OF *lachier* fasten. Akin to LACE, LATCH.]

lash·er[1] (lash′ər) *n.* One who or that which lashes.

lash·er[2] (lash′ər) *n.* **1** Slack water, as above a weir. **2** The weir itself. [<LASH (*v.* def. 7) + -ER[1]]

lash·ing (lash′ing) *n.* **1** A fastening made by passing a rope, cord, or the like, around two or more objects. **2** The rope used to do this. **3** A whipping.

Lash·io (läsh′yō) The capital of Shan State and Northern Shan States, Upper Burma.

Lash·kar (lush′kər) The winter capital of Madhya Bharat State, India.

lash–up (lash′up′) *n. Colloq.* A temporary connection or contrivance.

Las·ki (las′kē), **Harold J(oseph),** 1893–1950, English political scientist.

La Sou·fri·ère (lå sōō·frē·âr′) A volcano on St. Vincent, Windward Islands, The West Indies; 4,048 feet; dormant since 1903: also *Soufrière.* Also **La Grande Soufrière.**

Las Pal·mas (läs päl′mäs) See PALMAS, LAS.

La Spe·zia (lä spā′tsyä) A port on the Gulf of Spezia: also *Spezia.*

lass (las) *n.* **1** A young woman; girl. **2** A sweetheart. **3** *Scot.* A servant-girl; maid. [<Scand. Cf. OSw. *lösk kona* an unmarried woman.]

Las·salle (lä·säl′), **Ferdinand Johann Gottlieb,** 1825–64, German socialist.

Las·sen Volcanic National Park (las′ən) An area of lava formations in northern California containing **Lassen Peak** (10,453 feet), the only active volcano in the United States; 161 square miles; established, 1916.

las·sie (las′ē) *n.* A little girl; a lass. Also **las′·sock** (-ək). [Dim. of LASS]

las·si·tude (las′ə·tōōd, -tyōōd) *n.* A state of disinclination to exertion; languor; weariness; debility. [<F <L *lassitudo* <*lassus* faint]

las·so (las′ō) *n. pl.* **·sos** or **·soes** A long rope or leather thong, with a running noose, for catching horses and cattle. —*v.t.* To catch with a lasso. [<Sp. *lazo* <L *laqueus* a snare] —**las′so·er** *n.*

lasso cell A nematocyst.

last[1] (last, läst) *adj.* **1** Being at the end; latest; hindmost; final. **2** Next before the present; most recent. **3** Least fit or likely; most remote. **4** Beyond or above all others; utmost. **5** Beneath all others. —*adv.* **1** After all others in time or order. **2** At a time next preceding the present: He was *last* seen heading west. **3** In conclusion; finally. —*n.* **1** The end; conclusion. **2** The final appearance, experience, or mention: We'll never hear the *last* of this. —**at last** At length; at the end; finally. [OE *latost,* superl. of *læt* late, slow] —**last′ly** *adv.*

last[2] (last, läst) *v.i.* **1** To remain in existence; continue to be; endure. **2** To continue unchanged or unaltered; persevere. **3** To be as much as or more than needed; hold out: Will our supplies *last* through the winter? —*n.* Ability to endure; stamina. [OE *lǣsten* follow a track, continue, accomplish. Akin to LAST[3].] —**last′er** *n.*

last[3] (last, läst) *n.* A shaped form, usually of wood, on which to make a boot or shoe. —*v.t.* To fit to or form on a last. [OE *læst* a boot, shoemaker's last <*last* a footstep, track. Akin to LAST[2].] —**last′er** *n.*

last[4] (last, läst) *n.* **1** A weight or measure varying for different articles, but often reckoned as 80 bushels. **2** One or two tons, usually 4,000 pounds: a unit in estimating ship capacity. [OE *hlæst* a load <*hladan* lade]

Las·tex (las′teks) *n.* A fine, round, rubber thread, manufactured in strands and wound with rayon, cotton, silk, or wool: a trade name. [<(E)LAS(TIC) + TEX(TILE)]

last·ing[1] (las′ting, läs′-) *adj.* Continuing; durable; permanent. See synonyms under PERMANENT, PERPETUAL. —*n.* Endurance; continuance. [<LAST[2]] —**last′ing·ly** *adv.* —**last′ing·ness** *n.*

last·ing[2] (las′ting, läs′-) *n.* **1** A fabric used for the uppers of shoes, etc. **2** The operation of stretching an upper on a shoemaker's last. [< LAST[3]]

Last Judgment See under JUDGMENT

Last Supper The last meal of Jesus Christ with his disciples before the Crucifixion.

last word 1 The final say, as in a dispute. **2** The latest or most modern fashion, style, advancement, etc.

Las Ve·gas (läs vā′gəs) The second largest city of Nevada, in the SE part; famous for its gambling casinos.

Lász·ló (läs′lō) Hungarian form of LADISLAUS.

lat (lät) *n. pl.* **lats** or **la·tu** (lä′to͞o) The monetary unit of Latvia. [< Lettish *lats* < *Latvia* Latvia]

Lat·a·ki·a (lat′ə·kē′ə) *n.* A fine grade of tobacco developed in Turkey. [from *Latakia;* so called because produced near there]

La·ta·ki·a (lä′tä·kē′ä) **1** A province of western Syria, on the Mediterranean; 2,433 square miles. **2** Its capital, the chief Syrian port: ancient *Laodicea*: French *Lattaquié*.

la·ta·ni·a (lə·tä′nē·ə) *n.* The palmetto or cabbage palm of the southern United States. [< NL < F *lattanier* < Cariban *aláttani*]

latch[1] (lach) *n.* A catch for fastening a door, lid, shutter, etc., commonly not requiring any special key. See synonyms under LOCK[1] **—** *v.t.* & *v.i.* To fasten by means of a latch; close. **—to latch on to** *Slang* **1** To fasten (oneself) to. **2** To obtain; get. [OE *laeccan, laeccean* seize. Akin to LACE, LASH.]

latch[2] (lach) *v.t.* See LEACH.

latch·et (lach′it) *n.* A lace, thong, or strap that fastens a shoe or sandal. Also **shoe latchet.** [< OF *lachet,* dial. var. of *lacet,* dim. of *las, laz.* See LACE.]

latch·key (lach′kē′) *n.* A key for releasing a latch, especially on an outside or front door.

latchkey child A child who comes home after school to an empty house, the parent or parents being still at work.

latch·string (lach′string′) *n.* A string fastened to a latch and passed through a hole above it to the outside: used for lifting a latch.

late (lāt) *adj.* **lat·er** or **lat·ter, lat·est** or **last 1** Coming after the appointed time; tardy. **2** Far advanced toward the end or close; at or continuing to an advanced hour. **3** Recent or comparatively recent: often implying a subsequent change. **4** Deceased, especially recently deceased. **—***adv.* **1** After or beyond the usual proper or appointed time; after delay; at or until an advanced hour. **2** Not long ago; recently. **3** After a while; in course of time: contrasted with *soon* or *early* : We rue our follies soon or *late* : more frequently used in the comparative degree. **—of late** In time not long past or near present; recently. [OE *lœt* late, slow] **—late′ness** *n.*

lat·ed (lā′tid) *adj.* Belated.

la·teen (la·tēn′) *adj. Naut.* Designating a rig common in the Mediterranean, having a triangular sail (**lateen sail**) suspended from a long yard set obliquely to the mast. [< F *(voile) latine* Latin (sail), fem. of *latin* < L *Latinus*]

la·teen-rigged (la·tēn′rigd′) *adj. Naut.* Having a lateen sail or sails.

LATEEN SAIL
Shown on a dhow.

Late Greek See under GREEK.

Late Latin See under LATIN.

late·ly (lāt′lē) *adv.* Not long ago; recently.

la·ten·si·fi·ca·tion (lə·ten′sə·fə·kā′·shən) *n. Phot.* The technique of making a fogging exposure after the initial exposure, in order to bring out shadow details and increase the effective emulsion speed of some negative materials. [< LATEN(CY) + (INTEN)SIFICATION]

la·tent (lā′tənt) *adj.* **1** Not visible or apparent; hidden; dormant. **2** *Psychol.* Potentially capable of being expressed, as an emotion or attitude. **3** *Bot.* Undeveloped, as a concealed bud. [< L *latens, -entis,* ppr. of *latere* be hidden] **—la′ten·cy** *n.* **—la′tent·ly** *adv.*

latent heat *Physics* The amount of heat required to change the state of a unit mass of a body, either from solid to liquid or from liquid to vapor, without changing the temperature of the body.

latent image *Phot.* The invisible image produced by the action of light on the silver halide or other grains of a photographic emulsion before development of the film.

latent period 1 *Pathol.* The interval between the incubation period of a disease and its outbreak. **2** *Physiol.* Elapsed time between a stimulus and its response.

lat·er (lā′tər) *adv.* At a subsequent time; hereafter.

lat·er·al (lat′ər·əl) *adj.* **1** Pertaining to, proceeding from, or directed toward the side. **2** *Biol.* Situated on one or both sides of the median plane of a body, limb, or organ: opposed to *medial.* [< L *lateralis* < *latus, lateris* a side] **—lat′er·al·ly** *adv.*

lat·er·al-cut (lat′ər·əl·kut′) *adj.* Having sound-producing lines indented in a horizontal plane by the recording instrument of a phonograph: said of a recording: distinguished from *hill-and-dale.*

lateral pass See under PASS.

Lat·er·an (lat′ər·ən) **1** The basilica of St. John Lateran, the cathedral church of the pope as bishop of Rome, ranking above all other churches in the Roman Catholic world. **2** The palace, formerly a papal residence and now a museum, adjacent to the basilica. [< L *Lateranus,* name of a Roman family]

lat·er·ite (lat′ər·īt) *n.* A red, ferruginous, porous clay of tropical regions. [< L *later* a brick + -ITE[1]] **—lat′er·it′ic** (-it′ik) *adj.*

lat·er·i·tious (lat′ər·ish′əs) *adj.* Pertaining to or resembling brick; brick-red in color. [< L *lateritius* < *later* a brick]

la·tes·cent (lə·tes′ənt) *adj.* Becoming obscure, latent, or hidden. [< L *latescens, -entis,* ppr. of *latescere,* inceptive of *latere* be hidden] **—la·tes′cence** *n.*

lat·est (lā′tist) Alternative superlative of LATE. **—** *adj.* & *adv.* **1** Most recent. **2** *Archaic* & *Poetic* Last.

la·tex (lā′teks) *n. pl.* **lat·i·ces** (lat′ə·sēz) or **la·tex·es** The viscid, milky, complex emulsion of proteins, alkaloids, starches, resins, and other substances secreted by the cells of certain plants, as the milkweed, rubber tree, poppy, dandelion, etc. [< L, a liquid]

lath (lath, läth) *n.* **1** A thin strip of wood or metal, as one of a number nailed to studs or beams and serving to support a coat of plaster, or on rafters to support shingles or slates. **2** An angle-iron forming the support for an iron roof. **3** Laths taken collectively; lathwork. **4** Figuratively, a thin, slender, or delicate person or thing. **—***v.t.* To cover or line with laths. [Prob. fusion of OE *lætt* and OE *læth* (assumed); ? infl. in form by Welsh *llath*] **—lath′er** *n.*

lathe[1] (lāth) *n.* **1** A machine for shaping articles in which an object is mounted and rotated, while a tool is thrust against the work, shaping it down, usually to some circular form. **2** In a loom, the swinging beam which beats up the weft. **3** A potter's wheel. **—***v.t.* **lathed, lath·ing** To form or shape on a lathe. [Prob. < MDu. *lade*]

lathe[2] (lāth) *n.* An English administrative district, now existing only in Kent, composed of several hundreds. [OE *læth*]

lath·er (lath′ər) *n.* **1** Foam or froth of soapsuds. **2** Foam of profuse sweating, as of a horse. **—in a lather** *Colloq.* In a state of intense excitement or agitation. **—***v.t.* **1** To cover with lather. **2** *Colloq.* To flog; thrash. **—***v.i.* **3** To become covered with lather. **4** To form lather. [OE *lēathor* washing soda, soap. Akin to LAVE.] **—lath′er·er** *n.* **—lath′·er·y** *adj.*

lath·ing (lath′ing, läth′-) *n.* **1** The act or process of covering with laths. **2** The foundation of laths on which plaster may be laid; the material for such foundation. **3** Any work with laths or like material.

lathing hatchet A hatchet with a narrow blade, for cutting and attaching wooden laths. See illustration under HATCHET.

lath·work (lath′wûrk′, läth′-) *n.* Lathing.

lath·y (lath′ē, läth′ē) *adj.* **lath·i·er, lath·i·est** Like a lath; long and slender.

La·tian (lā′shən) *adj.* Of or pertaining to ancient Latium in Italy; Latin.

lat·i·ces (lat′ə·sēz) Plural of LATEX.

lat·i·cif·er·ous (lat′ə·sif′ər·əs) *adj.* Containing or conveying latex. [< L *latex, laticis* a liquid + -FEROUS]

lat·i·clave (lat′ə·klāv) *n.* **1** A broad vertical purple stripe down the tunics of ancient Romans of senatorial rank. **2** A tunic thus marked. [< LL *laticlavium, laticlavus* < *latus* broad + *clavus* a purple stripe]

lat·i·fo·li·ate (lat′ə·fō′lē·it, -āt) *adj. Bot.* Having broad leaves. Also **lat′i·fo′li·ous.** [< NL *latifoliatus* < L *latus* broad + *folia* a leaf]

lat·i·fun·di·um (lat′ə·fun′dē·əm) *n. pl.* **·di·a**(-dē·ə) A large landed property. [< L < *latus* wide + *fundus* an estate]

Lat·i·mer (lat′ə·mər), **Hugh,** 1485?–1555, English Protestant churchman; burned at the stake.

Lat·in (lat′n) *adj.* **1** Pertaining to ancient Latium, its inhabitants, their culture, or language. **2** Pertaining to or denoting the peoples or countries, as France, Italy, and Spain, whose languages and cultures are derived from the ancient Roman civilization. **3** Of or belonging to the Western or, since the Reformation, the Roman Catholic Church, as distinguished from the Greek Church. **—***n.* **1** One of the people of ancient Latium. **2** A member of any of the modern Latin peoples. **3** A member of the Western or Roman Catholic Church: used especially in the Greek Church. **4** The Indo-European, Italic language of ancient Latium and Rome: extensively used in western Europe until modern times as a language of learning, and still retained as the official language of the Roman Catholic Church. **— Old Latin,** the language before the first century B.C., as preserved in early inscriptions and the comedies of Plautus. **—Classical Latin,** the literary language of the period 80 B.C. to A.D. 200, standardized by such writers as Cicero, Caesar, Livy, Vergil, Tacitus, and Juvenal. Abbr. *L* **—Late Latin,** the language from 200–600, including the patristic writings. Abbr. *LL* **—Low Latin,** the language of any period after the classical, as Medieval Latin, especially as influenced and modified by other continental languages. **—Medieval Latin,** the language used by the writers of the Middle Ages, from 600–1500: also called *Middle Latin.* Abbr. *Med. L* **—New Latin,** a form of the language, based on Latin and Greek elements, developed since the Renaissance and used chiefly in scientific and taxonomic terms. Abbr. *NL* **—Vulgar Latin,** the popular speech of the Romans in all stages of the language from about A.D. 200 through the medieval period: the chief source of the Romance languages. [< L *Latinus* of Latium, Latin]

Latin alphabet A set of letters containing, originally, 20 characters derived from the Western Greek alphabet (in turn, developed from the Phoenician) with the later addition of G, Y, and Z. The English alphabet, descendent from the Latin, has the added characters J, U, and W. Also called *Roman alphabet.*

Latin America Those countries of the western hemisphere south of the Rio Grande, in which the official languages are derived from Latin. See SPANISH AMERICA. **—Lat′in-A·mer′·i·can** *adj.*

Latin American A native or inhabitant of Latin America.

Lat·in·ate (lat′ən·āt) *adj.* Resembling or derived from Latin.

Latin Church That part of the Catholic Church which accepts the pope as supreme authority on earth, and uses Latin for the liturgy of the mass. Compare UNIAT.

Latin cross See under CROSS.

La·tin·ic (lə·tin′ik) *adj.* Of Latin.

Lat·in·ism (lat′ən·iz′əm) *n.* An idiom peculiar to or imitating Latin. **—Lat′in·is′tic** *adj.*

Lat·in·ist (lat′ən·ist) *n.* One versed in Latin.

La·tin·i·ty (lə·tin′ə·tē) *n.* Latin style or idiom.

Lat·in·ize (lat′ən·īz) *v.* **·ized, ·iz·ing** *v.t.* **1** To translate into Latin. **2** To make Latin in customs, thought, etc. **3** To cause to resemble the Roman Catholic Church, as in dogma or ritual. **4** To transliterate into Latin characters, as a Greek word. **—***v.i.* **5** To use Latin words, forms, etc. [< L *latinizare* < *Latinus* Latin] **—Lat′in·i·za′tion** *n.* **—Lat′in·iz′er** *n.*

la·ti·no (la·tē′nō) *n. pl.* **·nos** *Often cap.* A Latin American. [< Am. Sp. < Sp., L]

Latin Quarter A section of Paris on the left (south) bank of the Seine, known for the large number of artists and students who live there.

lat·i·ros·tral (lat′ə·ros′trəl) *adj. Ornithol.* Having a broad beak, as certain birds. [<NL *Latirostres,* former group name for the swallows <L *latus* broad + *rostrum* a beak]

lat·ish (lā′tish) *adj.* Rather late.

lat·i·tude (lat′ə·tōōd, -tyōōd) *n.* **1** *Geog.* Distance on the earth's surface northward or southward from the equator measured in degrees of the meridian; angular distance reckoned on a meridian. **2** *Astron.* The angular distance of a heavenly body above the plane of the ecliptic, as viewed from some point. **3** A region or place with reference to its distance north or south of the equator. **4** Figuratively, one's proper place or environment. **5** Extent of deviation from what is regular or customary; independence or liberty of action or conduct. **6** Laxity. **7** Strength of application; range or scope. [<L *latitudo* breadth <*latus* broad] —**lat′i·tu′di·nal** *adj.*

lat·i·tu·di·nar·i·an (lat′ə·tōō′də·nâr′ē·ən,-tyōō′-) *adj.* Broad, tolerant, or lax in religious principles. —*n.* **1** One who is extremely tolerant or lax in religious principles; a freethinker; liberal. **2** One who departs from the strict standards of orthodoxy. [<L *latitudo, -inis* LATITUDE + -ARIAN] —**lat′i·tu′di·nar′i·an·ism** *n.*

Lat·i·tu·di·nar·i·an (lat′ə·tōō′də·nâr′ē·ən, -tyōō′-) *n.* One of a party of English churchmen of the 17th century who advocated the union of the dissenters with the established church.

La·ti·um (lā′shē·əm) A region and ancient country in central Italy; original home of the Latins. *Italian* **La·zio** (lä′tsyō).

La·to·na (lə·tō′nə) In Roman mythology, the mother of Diana and Apollo: identified with the Greek *Leto.*

la·tri·a (lə·trī′ə) *n.* In the Roman Catholic Church, that supreme worship which can be lawfully given to God only: distinguished from *dulia* and *hyperdulia.* [<LL *latria* <Gk. *latreia* service, worship <*latreuein* work for hire, worship <*latris* a hired servant]

la·trine (lə·trēn′) *n.* A privy, especially in a camp, barracks, hospital, etc. [<F <L *latrina* a bath, a privy <*lavatrina* <*lavare* wash]

La·trobe (lə·trōb′), **Benjamin Henry,** 1764–1820, American architect born in England.

-latry *combining form* Worship of; excessive devotion to: *idolatry.* [<Gk. *latreia* worship]

Lat·ta·quié (là·tà·kyā′) The French name for LATAKIA.

lat·ten (lat′n) *n.* Metal in thin sheets, especially (and originally) brass. [<OF *laton, leiton,* prob. <MHG *latta* a thin plate, a lath. Akin to LATH.]

lat·ter (lat′ər) *adj.* **1** Of more recent date; modern. **2** *Obs.* Latest or last. —**the latter** The second of two mentioned persons or things: opposed to *the former.* [OE *lætra,* compar. of *læt* late] —**lat′ter·ly** *adv.*

lat·ter-day (lat′ər·dā′) *adj.* Belonging to the present; recent; modern.

Latter-day Saint A Mormon.

lat·ter·most (lat′ər·mōst′) *adj.* Last; latest.

lat·tice (lat′is) *n.* **1** Open-work of metal or wood, formed by crossing or interlacing strips or bars; also, anything made of such work, as a window, a blind, or a screen: also called *latticework.* **2** That which resembles a lattice: a *lattice* of branches. **3** *Her.* A bearing of vertical and horizontal bars crossing one another. **4** *Physics* A space lattice. **5** *Telecom.* A network of lines indicating fixed positions in a radio or radar system. —*v.t.* **lat·ticed, lat·tic·ing** **1** To furnish or enclose with a lattice. **2** To arrange or interlace like latticework. [<OF *lattis* <*latte* a lath <MHG. Akin to LATH.]

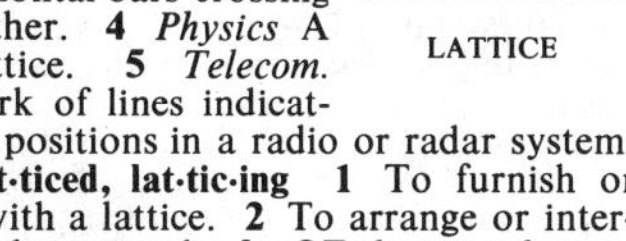

LATTICE

lat·tice·work (lat′is·wûrk′) *n.* **1** Lattice (def. 1). **2** In embroidery, stitching in an outline resembling a lattice: done on solid material, and used as a background.

lat·tic·ing (lat′is·ing) *n.* **1** The act of making or furnishing with lattice. **2** In bridge-building, a system of timbers or bars crossing in such a manner as to connect and strengthen the two channels of a strut and cause them to act as one construction.

la·tus rec·tum (lā′təs rek′təm) *Math.* The chord drawn through a focus of a plane curve perpendicular to its major axis. [<NL, a

Lat·vi·a A republic on the Baltic Sea in NE Europe; 24,900 square miles; capital, Riga; pop. 2,700,000. Formerly the **Latvian Soviet Socialist Republic** (1940–1991).

Lat·vi·an (lat′vē·ən) *adj.* Of or pertaining to Latvia, its inhabitants, or their language. —*n.* **1** A Lett. **2** The Lettish language.

laud (lôd) *n.* **1** Praise or commendation; extolment. **2** The part of divine worship that consists chiefly of praise; also, a song of praise or honor. **3** *pl.* A religious service consisting of the psalms immediately following matins, and constituting with the latter the first of the seven canonical hours: sometimes **Lauds.** See synonyms under PRAISE. —v.t. To praise; extol. [<OF *laude* <L *laus, laudis* praise] —**laud′er** *n.*

Laud (lôd), **William,** 1573–1645, archbishop of Canterbury; supporter of Charles I; impeached and beheaded.

laud·a·ble (lô′də·bəl) *adj.* **1** Worthy of approval; praiseworthy. **2** Healthy or promotive of health or healing; salubrious; normal: said of pus or bodily juices. —**laud′a·ble·ness, laud′a·bil′i·ty** *n.* —**laud′a·bly** *adv.*

lau·da·nine (lô′də·nēn) *n. Chem.* A white, crystalline alkaloid from opium, $C_{20}H_{25}O_4N$, belonging pharmacologically to the codeine group. [<LAUDAN(UM) + -INE[2]]

lau·da·num (lô′də·nəm) *n.* **1** Tincture of opium. **2** Formerly, a preparation in which opium predominated. [<NL <Med. L, var. of L *ladanum* LADANUM]

lau·da·tion (lô·dā′shən) *n.* The act of praising; praise.

laud·a·to·ry (lô′də·tôr′ē, -tō′rē) *adj.* Eulogizing; praising: also **laud′a·tive.** —*n.* *pl.* **·ries** A panegyric. [<L *laudatorius* <L *laudare* praise, celebrate]

Lau·der (lô′dər), **Sir Harry,** 1870–1950, Scottish singer and comedian.

Lau·e (lou′ə), **Max von,** 1879–1960, German physicist.

laugh (laf, läf) *v.i.* **1** To express amusement, hilarity, derision, etc., by expressions of the face and by a series of explosive sounds made in the chest and throat. **2** To be or appear gay or lively. —*v.t.* **3** To express by laughter. **4** To move or influence by laughter or ridicule: He *laughed* himself out of his worries. —**to laugh at** **1** To express amusement concerning. **2** To make light of; belittle. —**to laugh away** To drive off or away by laughter. —**to laugh in** (or **up**) **one's sleeve** To be secretly amused although outwardly serious. —**to laugh off** To dismiss with a laugh; treat lightly or scornfully. —**to laugh on** (or **out of**) **the other** (or **wrong**) **side of the mouth** To feel sudden disappointment or annoyance after mirth or supposed triumph. —*n.* **1** The act or sound of laughter. **2** *Colloq.* Anything provoking or producing laughter. [OE *hlæhhan*] —**laugh′er** *n.*

laugh·a·ble (laf′ə·bəl, läf′-) *adj.* Ridiculous; exciting laughter; humorous; ludicrous. —**laugh′a·ble·ness** *n.* —**laugh′a·bly** *adv.*

laugh·ing (laf′ing, läf′-) *adj.* Fit to be laughed at: a *laughing* matter.

laughing gas Nitrous oxide, N_2O, an anesthetic with exhilarating effect when inhaled: used in dental surgery.

laughing goose The white-fronted goose *(Anser albifrons)* of western North America: also called *harlequin brant.*

laughing gull The black-headed gull *(Larus atricilla)* of the Atlantic coast of North America.

laughing jackass The kookaburra.

laugh·ing·ly (laf′ing·lē, läf′-) *adv.* With a laugh, laughter, or merriment.

laugh·ing·stock (laf′ing·stok′, läf′-) *n.* A butt for ridicule.

laugh·ter (laf′tər, läf′-) *n.* **1** The sound or action of laughing. **2** Any exclamation or expression indicating merriment or derision. ◆ Collateral adjective; *risible.* [OE *hleahtor* <root of *hlæhhan* laugh]

Synonyms: cachinnation, fun, giggling, glee, hilarity, jollity, merriment, mirth, rejoicing, snickering, tittering. *Antonyms*: distress, frowning, gloom, glowering, groaning, lowering, mourning, sadness, sorrow, tears, wailing, weeping.

launce (lôns) *n.* The sand eel: also spelled *lance.*

Laun·ce·lot (lôn′sə·lot, län′-) See LANCELOT.

launch[1] (lônch, länch) *v.t.* **1** To cause to move from land into water for the first time, as a ship on completion of its hull. **2** To put into the water; set afloat, as a boat or log. **3** To make a beginning of; set in motion: to *launch* an enterprise. **4** To start (someone) on a career, course, etc. **5** To give a start to the flight or course of, as a rocket, torpedo, or airplane. **6** To hurl or throw, as a spear. —*v.i.* **7** To put or go to sea: usually with *out* or *forth.* **8** To start on a career, course, etc. **9** To begin something with vehemence or urgency; plunge: He *launched* into a tirade. —**to launch out** **1** To strike out suddenly or wildly. **2** To be vehement or reckless. **3** To start; commence. —*n.* **1** The act of launching. **2** The movement of a ship, boat, etc., from the land into the water; especially, the sliding over ways of a newly built vessel from the stocks into the water; also, the spot where a ship is built, and the tackle used in launching it. **3** The start of a bird for flight. [<AF *lancher,* OF *lancier* <*lance* LANCE]

launch[2] (lônch, länch) *n.* **1** The largest of the boats carried by a warship, used for transporting men and supplies. **2** A large, open boat, propelled by steam or electricity, and used as a pleasure craft. [<Sp. *lancha,* prob. <Malay *lanca* a three-masted boat <*lancār* speedy]

launch·er (lôn′chər, län′-) *n.* **1** One who or that which launches. **2** Any mechanical device or installation for launching rockets, guided missiles, satellites, etc.

launching pad The platform from which a rocket or guided missile is fired.

laun·der (lôn′dər, län′-) *v.t.* **1** To wash and iron, as clothing. —*v.i.* **2** To wash and iron laundry. **3** To undergo washing and ironing. —*n.* A trough or gutter, as of wood, for conveying water. [Contraction of ME *lavender* a laundress <OF *lavendier* a washerwoman <LL *lavandarius,* ult. <L *lavare* wash] —**laun′der·er** *n.*

laun·dress (lôn′dris, län′-) *n.* A woman who works in a laundry; washerwoman.

laun·dro·mat (lôn′drə·mat, län-) *n. U. S.* A commercial establishment where the customer brings laundry to be washed and dried in coin-operated automatic machines. [<*Laundromat,* a trade name]

laun·dry (lôn′drē, län′-) *n.* *pl.* **·dries** **1** A place for washing and ironing clothes. **2** Articles sent to a laundry for washing and ironing. **3** *Obs.* A laundress. [Alter. of obs. *lavendry* <OF *lavenderie* <*lavendier.* See LAUNDER.] —**laun′dry·man** (-mən) *n.* —**laun′dry·wom′an** (-wōōm′ən) *n. fem.*

Laun·fal (lôn′fəl), **Sir** In romances by Thomas Chestre and James Russell Lowell, a knight of the Round Table.

Lau·ra (lô′rə, *Ger., Ital.* lou′rä) A feminine personal name. Also *French* **Laure** (lōr). [<L *laurus* the laurel]
—**Laura** The idealized lady to whom Petrarch's sonnets were addressed: identified with **Laura de Noves,** 1307–48, wife of Hugues de Sade of Avignon.

lau·ra·ceous (lô·rā′shəs) *adj.* Belonging to a family *(Lauraceae)* of aromatic and medicinal trees and shrubs, the laurels, which includes sassafras and cinnamon, mostly natives of warm climates. [<NL <L *laurus* the laurel]

lau·re·ate (lô′rē·it) *adj.* **1** Crowned or decked with laurel, as a mark of distinction or honor. **2** Deserving of distinction; preeminent, especially as a poet; also, relating to or distinctive of poets. **3** Made of laurel or in imitation of laurel. —*n.* **1** In England, the poet officially invested with the title of poet laureate by the crown. **2** In former times, a poet publicly crowned with laurel in recognition of his merit. See under POET. —*v.t.* (-rē·āt) **·at·ed, ·at·ing** **1** To crown with a laurel wreath. **2** To make poet laureate. [<L *laureatus* crowned with laurel < *laurea* a laurel tree or crown, orig. fem. of *laureus* made of laurel < *laurus* laurel] **—lau′re·ate·ship′** *n.* **—lau′re·a′tion** *n.*

lau·rel (lôr′əl, lor′-) *n.* **1** An evergreen shrub *(Laurus nobilis)* of the Mediterranean area, with aromatic, lance-shaped leaves, yellowish flowers, and succulent, cherrylike fruit: also called **bay laurel, Grecian laurel, noble laurel:** also called *bay.* **2** Any other species of the genus *Laurus.* **3** An American evergreen shrub of either of two genera, as the mountain laurel *(Kalmia latifolia)* or the great laurel *(Rhododendron maximum).* **4** In England, a species of evergreen cherry tree (genus *Prunus*) with flowers in racemes and inedible fruit. **5** *pl.* A crown or wreath of laurel, indicating honor or high merit; hence, honor or distinction. **6** A salmon that has passed the summer in fresh water. **—to rest on one's laurels** To be content with what one has already achieved or accomplished. **—***v.t.* **·reled** or **·relled, ·rel·ing** or **·rel·ling 1** To wreathe or crown with laurel. **2** To honor. [<OF *laurier, lorier* < *lor* <L *laurus* a laurel]

Lau·rence (lôr′əns, lor′-) See LAWRENCE. Also *Du.* **Lau·rens** (lou′rens), *Fr.* **Lau·rent** (lō·räṅ′), *Ger.* **Lau·renz** (lou′rents), *Lat.* **Lau·ren·tius** (lô·ren′shəs).

Lau·ren·cin (lô·räṅ·saṅ′), **Marie,** 1885–1956, French painter.

Lau·ren·tian (lô·ren′shən) *adj.* **1** Of or pertaining to the St. Lawrence River. **2** *Geol.* Pertaining to the ancient Archean rocks underlying the Algonquian rocks of North America.

Laurentian Mountains A crescent-shaped range extending from the Saint Lawrence River to the Arctic Ocean and forming the watershed between Hudson Bay and the Saint Lawrence; highest peak, 3,905 feet. Also **Lau·ren·tides** (lô·räṅ·tēd′).

Laurentian Plateau See CANADIAN SHIELD.

lau·ric (lô′rik) *adj. Biochem.* Designating a fatty acid, $C_{11}H_{23}COOH$, found as a glyceride in spermaceti, laurel oil, etc. [<L *laurus* laurel + -IC]

Lau·rie (lô′rē) Diminutive of LAURA, LAURENCE.

Lau·rier (lô·ryā′), **Sir Wilfred,** 1841–1919, French-Canadian statesman.

Lau·rin·da (lô·rin′də) Latin form of LAURA.

Lau·rus (lô′rəs) *n.* A genus of evergreen trees of the family *Lauraceae.* [<L, laurel tree]

lau·rus·tine (lô′rəs·tin) *n.* A southern European shrub *(Viburnum tinus)* having oblong leaves hairy on the underside and fragrant white or pink flowers appearing in winter. Also **lau·rus·ti·nus** (lô′rəs·tī′nəs). [<NL *laurustinus* <L *laurus tinus* < *laurus* laurel + *tinus* a plant]

Lau·sanne (lō·zàn′) A Swiss city on the northern shore of Lake Geneva, capital of Vaud canton.

laus De·o (lôs dē′ō) *Latin* Praise be to God.

la·va (lä′və, lav′ə) *n.* **1** Melted rock, issuing from a volcanic crater or a fissure in the earth's surface. **2** Such rock when solidified. [<Ital., orig. a stream of rain < *lavare* wash <L]

la·va·bo (lə·vä′bō) *n. pl.* **·boes 1** In the Anglican and Roman Catholic churches, the washing of the hands by the celebrant after the offertory, during the Eucharist. **2** That part of Psalm xxvi which is recited by the priest while washing the hands: from the opening word. **3** A small linen towel used to wipe the priest's hands in this rite. **4** A stationary washbowl or lavatory with running water; also, in monasteries, the room in which this is placed. [<L, I shall wash, 1st person sing. future of *lavare* wash]

lav·age (lav′ij, *Fr.* là·vàzh′) *n. Med.* A cleansing, especially the washing out or irrigation of an organ, as the stomach. [<F < *laver* wash <L *lavare*]

La·val (là·vàl′), **Pierre,** 1883–1945, premier of France 1931–32, 1935–36; premier of Vichy government 1942–44; executed for treason.

la·va-la·va (lä′və·lä′və) *n.* A loincloth or waistcloth of printed calico worn by natives of Samoa and other islands of the Pacific. [<Samoan]

lav·a·liere (lav′ə·lir′) *n.* A piece of jewelry, consisting of a necklace and pendant. Also **lav′a·lier′.** [<F *la vallière* a sort of necktie, ? after Louise de *La Vallière,* 1644–1710, mistress of Louis XIV]

La·va·ter (lä′vä·tər, lä·vä′-), **Johann Kaspar,** 1741–1801, Swiss poet, theologian, and physiognomist.

la·va·tion (la·vā′shən) *n.* A washing. Also **lave·ment** (lāv′mənt). [<L *lavatio, -onis* < *lavare* wash]

lav·a·to·ry (lav′ə·tôr′ē, -tō′rē) *n. pl.* **·ries 1** An apartment for washing; a place where anything is washed; specifically, a room in a public or semipublic place, as in a school or hotel, provided with appliances for washing and usually with urinals and toilets. **2** *Med.* A wash for a diseased part; lotion. **3** *Eccl.* A piscina; also, a water drain in a sacristy where the priest washes his hands before vesting. **—***adj.* Washing. [<LL *lavatorium* a place for washing < *lavare* wash]

lave[1] (lāv) *v.t.* & *v.i.* **laved, lav·ing 1** To wash; bathe. **2** To flow along or against as if washing. [Fusion of OE *lafian* wash, pour and OF *laver* wash, both <L *lavare* wash. Akin to LATHER.]

lave[2] (lāv) *n. Scot.* The rest; remainder. [OE *laf*]

lav·en·der (lav′ən·dər) *n.* **1** An aromatic shrub (genus *Lavandula*) of the mint family, especially the Old World **spike lavender** *(L. officinalis),* the source of oil of lavender. **2** Its characteristic perfume. **3** The dried flowers and leaves of this plant, used to scent linen, etc. **4** The color of lavender flowers, a pale lilac. **—***adj.* Of, pertaining to, or like lavender. [<AF *lavendre* <Med. L *lavendula, livendula,* ? <L *livere* be bluish < *lividus* blue; infl. in form by *lavare* wash, because used as a perfume in baths]

SPIKE LAVENDER
(Plant from 2 to 3 feet tall)

la·ver[1] (lā′vər) *n.* **1** A large basin or other receptacle to wash in; specifically, in Solomon's temple and the ancient Jewish tabernacle, a large vessel of bronze at which the priests washed their hands and feet before sacrifices. **2** That which laves. [<LAVE[1]]

la·ver[2] (lā′vər) *n.* Any edible purple seaweed (genus *Porphyra*) or a dish prepared from it. Also **red laver.** [<L, a water plant]

La·ve·ran (là·vräṅ′), **Charles Louis Alphonse,** 1845–1922, French pathologist; discovered the plasmodium that causes malarial fever.

lav·er·ock (lav′ər·ək, lāv′rək) *n. Scot.* The lark. Also **lav·rock** (lav′rək).

La·ver·y (lā′vər·ē, lav′ər·ē), **Sir John,** 1856–1941, English painter.

La·vin·i·um (lə·vin′ē·əm) In classical geography, a city in Latium founded by Aeneas.

lav·ish (lav′ish) *adj.* **1** Bestowed, expended, or existing in profusion; superabundant. **2** Spending extravagantly; prodigal. **3** Wild or unrestrained. **—***v.t.* To give or bestow profusely or generously; squander. See synonyms under SQUANDER. [<OF *lavasse, lavache* a downpour of rain <Provençal *lavaci* <L *lavatio* a lavation] **—lav′ish·er** *n.* **—lav′ish·ly** *adv.* **—lav′ish·ness** *n.*

lav·ish·ment (lav′ish·mənt) *n.* A lavishing prodigality.

La·voi·sier (là·vwà·zyā′), **Antoine Laurent,** 1743–94, French chemist; identified and named oxygen; guillotined.

la·vol·ta (lə·vol′tə) *n.* An old dance for two persons consisting of lively, bounding steps. Also **la·volt′, la·vol′to.** [<Ital. < *la* the + *volta* a turn <L *volutus,* pp. of *volvere* turn]

La·von·gai (lä·vông′gī) An island in the Bismarck Archipelago; 460 square miles: formerly *New Hanover.*

law[1] (lô) *n.* **1** A rule of conduct, recognized by custom or by formal enactment, which a community considers as binding upon its members. **2** A system or body of such rules. **3** The condition of society when such rules are observed: to establish *law* and order. **4** The body of rules relating to a specified subject: criminal *law;* statute *law.* **5** Statute and common law, as opposed to equity. **6** An enactment of a legislature, as opposed to a constitution. **7** Remedial justice as administered by the courts: to resort to the *law.* **8** The branch of knowledge concerned with jurisprudence: to study *law.* **9** The vocation of an attorney, solicitor, etc.: to practice *law.* **10** The legal profession as a whole. **11** The Mosaic system of rules recorded in the Pentateuch. **12** A rule of conduct having divine origin; also such rules, collectively. **13** An imperative rule or command: His word is *law.* **14** Any rule of conduct or procedure: the *laws* of hospitality; the *laws* of poetry. **15** In science and philosophy, a statement of the manner or order in which a defined group of natural phenomena occur under certain conditions: also called *law of nature.* **16** *Math.* The rule or formula by which certain functions vary or according to which certain operations are performed. **17** An allowance made or a start given to a competitor in a race or to a hunted animal. **—the law** The police, personifying legal force. **—***v.t.* & *v.i.* To proceed against (someone) at law. **—***adj.* Of or pertaining to law or the law. [OE *lagu* <ON *lag* something laid or fixed, in pl., law. Akin to LAY[1].]

Synonyms (noun): canon, code, command, commandment, decree, edict, enactment, formula, mandate, order, ordinance, principle, regulation, rule, statute. *Law* in its ideal is the statement of a *principle* of right in mandatory form, by competent authority, with adequate penalty for disobedience; in common use the term is applied to any legislative act, however imperfect or unjust. *Command* and *commandment* are personal and particular; as, the *commands* of a parent; the Ten *Commandments.* An *edict* is the act of an absolute sovereign or other authority; we speak of the *edict* of an emperor, the *decree* of a court. A *mandate* is specific for an occasion or a purpose; a superior court issues its *mandate* to an inferior court to send up its records (see MANDATE). *Statute* is the recognized legal term for a specific *law; enactment* is the more vague and general expression. We speak of algebraic or chemical *formulas,* municipal *ordinances,* military *orders,* army *regulations,* ecclesiastical *canons,* the *rules* of a business house. *Law* is often used, also, for a recognized *principle,* whose violation is attended with injury or loss that acts like a penalty; as, the *laws* of business; the *laws* of nature. In more strictly scientific use, a natural *law* is simply a recognized system of sequences or relations; as Kepler's *laws* of planetary distances. See JUSTICE, LEGISLATION.

—canon law See CANON LAW.

—ceremonial law Law pertaining to the religious ceremonies of the Jews, as given in the Old Testament.

—civil law 1 The body or system of jurisprudence which the people of a state or nation establish for their government as citizens. **2** The body of Roman law, received by the governments of continental Europe as the foundation of their jurisprudence; also so received in the State of Louisiana.

—common law A system of jurisprudence originating in custom or usage, as distinguished from statutory law: the *common law* of England.

—criminal law The branch or department of jurisprudence which relates to crimes, their repression and punishment.

—international law The rules of conduct generally recognized by civilized states as binding them in their conduct toward each other: also LAW OF NATIONS.

—maritime law The body of principles and usages recognized by commercial nations as just and equitable in regulating affairs on the sea.

—moral law The divinely prescribed law regarding moral conduct; the law of right; especially, the Decalog.

—Mosaic law The Law of Moses.

—natural law 1 The rule of civil conduct deducible from the common reason and conscience of mankind: the *natural law* of self-defense. **2** A law of nature. See LAW (def. 15).

—organic law The fundamental law of a state; a constitution.

—parliamentary law The body of rules recognized or ordained for preserving order and regulating the modes of procedure and course of debate in legislative or deliberative bodies.

—Roman Law See CIVIL LAW.

law[2] (lô) *adj. Scot.* Low.

law[3] (lô) *interj.* An exclamation expressing

astonishment, admiration, etc. [Fusion of *law*, var. of LA[2] and *law*, alter. of LORD, used as an exclamation]

Law (lô), **(Andrew) Bonar,** 1858–1923, English statesman. —**John,** 1671–1729, Scottish financier. —**William,** 1686–1761, English devotional writer.

law–a·bid·ing (lô′ə·bī′ding) *adj.* Obedient to or abiding by the law.

law–break·er (lô′brā′kər) *n.* One who violates the law; a criminal. —**law′–break′ing** *n.* & *adj.*

Lawes (lôz), **Henry,** 1596–1662, English composer. —**Lewis Edward,** 1883–1947, U.S. penologist.

law·ful (lô′fəl) *adj.* **1** Permitted or not forbidden by law; legitimate: *lawful* acts. **2** Constituted by law; enforceable at law: *lawful* claims. **3** Valid, or regarded as valid: said of a marriage; also, born of such a marriage: said of offspring. **4** Having full legal rights. See synonyms under JUST, RIGHT. —**law′ful·ly** *adv.* —**law′ful·ness** *n.*

law·giv·er (lô′giv′ər) *n.* One who makes or enacts a law or laws; a legislator. —**law′giv′·ing** *adj.* & *n.*

law–hand (lô′hand′) *n.* The handwriting used in or characteristic of old legal documents; also, manuscripts written in this hand.

la·wi·ne (lä·vē′nə) *n.* *pl.* **·nen** (-nən) An avalanche. Also *lauwine.* [<G <LL *labina.* See AVALANCHE.]

law·less (lô′lis) *adj.* **1** Not subject or obedient to law of any sort; unruly; disobedient. **2** Without the sanction or authority of law; contrary to law: *lawless* measures. **3** Not formed or constructed according to law or rule; irregular: *lawless* verses. **4** Beyond the reach, or not within the province, of law. **5** Without the protection of law; outlawed: a *lawless* fugitive. —**law′less·ly** *adv.* —**law′less·ness** *n.*

law·mak·ing (lô′mā′king) *n.* The enacting of laws; legislation. —**law′mak′er** *n.*

Law·man (lô′mən) See LAYAMON.

law merchant **1** The body of commercial usages or rules recognized by civilized nations as regulating the rights of persons engaged in trade. **2** Commercial and mercantile law.

lawn[1] (lôn) *n.* **1** A piece of ground with grass kept closely mown. **2** A glade between woods. [Var. of LAUNDE] —**lawn′y** *adj.*

lawn[2] (lôn) *n.* **1** Fine thin linen or cotton fabric. **2** A fine clay sieve. [Earlier *laune (lynen)* Laon (linen) <*Laon* Laon, where it was formerly made]

lawn bowling See BOWLS.

lawn·mow·er (lôn′mō′ər) *n.* A machine for clipping the grass of lawns, either power-driven or propelled by hand, and equipped with spiral blades rotating against a horizontal bar, or rotary cutting blades.

lawn tennis See TENNIS.

Law of Moses The Pentateuch; Mosaic law.

law of nations International law.

law of parsimony *Philos.* A regulative principle in the interpretation of scientific data, requiring that of several equiprobable assumptions, hypotheses, or theories regarding a given phenomenon or group of phenomena, the simplest and least cumbersome is to be preferred. Also called *Ockham's razor.*

Law·rence (lôr′əns, lor′-) A masculine personal name. [<L, prob. a laurel]

—**Lawrence, Saint** Christian martyr of the third century.

Law·rence (lôr′əns, lor′-) A city on the Merrimac River in NE Massachusetts.

Law·rence (lôr′əns, lor′-), **D(avid) H(erbert),** 1885–1930, English novelist and poet. —**Ernest Orlando,** 1901–58, U.S. physicist. —**Sir Thomas,** 1769–1835, English painter. —**T(homas) E(dward),** 1888–1935, English soldier, archeologist, adventurer, and writer: known as *Lawrence of Arabia*: changed his surname to *Shaw* after 1927.

law·ren·ci·um (lô·ren′sē·əm) *n.* A very short-lived radioactive element (symbol Lw), originally produced by bombarding californium with the nuclei of a boron isotope.

law·sone (lô′sōn) *n.* The red coloring matter extracted from the leaves and twigs of the henna plant: used as a hair dye and as a constituent of henna. [after Dr. John *Lawson,* died about 1712, Scottish naturalist]

law·suit (lô′sōōt′) *n.* A proceeding in a court of law for redress of wrongs, or for enforcement of right.

law·yer (lô′yər) *n.* **1** One who practices law; an attorney or solicitor. **2** A member of any branch of the legal profession. **3** In the New Testament, an expositor of the Mosaic law. **4** *U.S.* The black-necked stilt (*Himantopus mexicanus*): also called *longshanks.* **5** The American burbot. **6** The bowfin: also called *mudfish* and *grindle.* **7** *Brit. Dial.* A long briar or bramble. [<LAW[1] + -YER]

lax (laks) *adj.* **1** Lacking tenseness or firmness; slack; yielding. **2** Not stringent or energetic; remiss; weak in control. **3** Wanting exactness of meaning or application. **4** *Med.* Loose: said of the bowels. **5** *Bot.* Not having the parts close together: a *lax* flower cluster. **6** *Phonet.* Formed with a relatively relaxed tongue and jaw, as (i) and (ŏŏ); wide: opposed to *tense.* See synonyms under VAGUE. [<L *laxus* loose] —**lax′i·ty, lax′ness** *n.* —**lax′ly** *adv.*

lax·a·tion (lak·sā′shən) *n.* The act of loosening, or the state of being loosed; relaxation.

lax·a·tive (lak′sə·tiv) *n. Med.* A gentle purgative. —*adj. Med.* **1** Having power to open or loosen the bowels, as a medicine; gently purgative. **2** Subject to or characterized by diarrhea: *laxative* bowels, a *laxative* disease. [<F, fem. of *laxatif* <L *laxativus* < *laxare.* See LAXATION.]

lay[1] (lā) *v.* **laid, lay·ing** *v.t.* **1** To cause to lie; place prostrate or at length; deposit. **2** To put or place: Don't *lay* a hand on me. **3** To strike or beat down; overthrow; destroy: to *lay* a city in ashes. **4** To cause to settle or subside, as dust, a storm, etc. **5** To calm or allay, as doubts. **6** To place in regular order or proper position: to *lay* title. **7** To think out; devise; arrange: to *lay* plans. **8** To attribute or ascribe: to *lay* blame. **9** To give importance to; put: to *lay* emphasis on something. **10** To bring forward; advance, as a claim. **11** To bring forth from the body and deposit, as an egg. **12** To construct; build, as a foundation. **13** To make (a table) ready for a meal. **14** To bury; inter. **15** To impose, as taxes, punishment, etc.; assess. **16** To spread over a surface: to *lay* a fixative. **17** To strike with or apply, as in punishment: He *laid* the whip across the culprit's back. **18** To locate: The scene is *laid* in the boudoir. **19** To set or prepare, as a trap. **20** To place as a wager or bet. **21** To twist strands so as to form (rope). **22** *Mil.* To aim (a cannon). **23** *U.S. Slang* To have sexual intercourse with; seduce. —*v.i.* **24** To bring forth and deposit eggs. **25** To make a bet or bets. **26** *Naut.* To go to a specified position: *Lay* aloft to hand sail! **27** To lie; recline: an incorrect use. See synonyms under PUT[1]. —**to lay about one** **1** To deal blows on all sides. **2** To exert oneself to the utmost. —**to lay away** **1** To store up; save. **2** To bury. —**to lay before** To put forward or present, as a report. —**to lay by** To lay away (def. 1). —**to lay down** **1** To give up or relinquish; sacrifice. **2** To state or proclaim: to *lay down* the law. **3** To bet. —**to lay for** To wait to attack or harm. —**to lay hold of** To seize or grasp. —**to lay in** To procure and store. —**to lay into** To attack vigorously. —**to lay it on** *Colloq.* To be extravagant or exorbitant, as in praise or demands. —**to lay off** **1** To take off and put aside, as clothes. **2** To survey; mark off. **3** *U.S. Colloq.* To dismiss from a job, usually temporarily. **4** *U.S. Colloq.* To take a rest; stop working. **5** *U.S. Slang* To stop annoying, teasing, etc. —**to lay on** **1** To put on; apply, as color. **2** To beat or strike; attack. —**to lay out** **1** To spend. **2** To prepare for burial. **3** *Slang* To strike prostrate or unconscious. **4** To set forth the details of: to *lay out* the plot of a novel. —**to lay over** To stop, as for a rest, on a journey. —**to lay siege to** To besiege. —**to lay up** **1** To make a store of. **2** To confine, as by illness or injury. —*n.* **1** The manner in which something lies or is placed; relative arrangement: the *lay* of the land. **2** *Slang* A line of work; particular business or field of activity. **3** A definite quantity of yarn or thread. **4** The swinging beam or batten of a loom. **5** The direction or amount of twist given to the strands of a rope. **6** A profit or share of profits; a price; specifically, a share of the profits of a whaling or sealing voyage, according to an arrangement made before sailing. [OE *lecgan* make lie < pt. of *licgan* lie[1]. Akin to LAW[1].]

lay[2] (lā) *adj.* Pertaining to the laity; non-professional; inexperienced. [<OF *lai* <Med. L *laicus* <Gk. *laïkos* < *laos* the people]

lay[3] (lā) Past tense of LIE[1].

lay[4] (lā) *n.* A song, ballad, or narrative poem; also, any melody or melodious utterance. [<OF *lai,* prob. <Gmc.]

lay·a·bout (lā′ə·bout′) *n. Chiefly Brit.* A lazy, idle person; a good-for-nothing.

Lay·a·mon (lā′ə·mən, lä′yə-) English priest and poet chronicler of the 13th century; author of *Brut,* a long, Middle English history of Britain from the legendary Brutus to Cadwallader, A.D. 689. Also *Lawman.*

Lay·ard (lā′yərd, lârd), **Sir Austen Henry,** 1817–94, English diplomat and archeologist.

lay·a·way (lā′ə·wā′) *n.* An agreement to make a series of payments to buy merchandise that is delivered when fully paid for. Also **lay-away plan.**

lay brother **1** A layman. **2** A brother in a monastery, serving under vows and wearing the dress of the order, but not in holy orders.

lay–by (lā′bī′) *n.* *pl.* **–bys** **1** *Brit.* A roadside area where vehicles may turn off, as for repairs or parking. **2** In New Zealand, a layaway.

lay communion **1** The communion of the laity at the Lord's table. **2** The condition of being in communion with the church as a layman only.

lay–days (lā′dāz′) *n. pl.* **1** In commerce, the days allowed a ship's lessee for loading and discharging cargo. **2** In marine insurance, the days (usually not beyond 30) while a ship lies idle in port without fires, for which return of insurance premium may be demanded. [<LAY[1] + pl. of DAY]

lay·er (lā′ər) *n.* **1** One who or that which lays. **2** A single horizontal thickness of a course, stratum, or coat. **3** *Bot.* A shoot or twig laid in the ground to take root without being detached from the parent plant. **4** In leatherwork, a welt. **5** In tanning, a pit in which hides are soaked in layers. **6** An artificial oyster bed. —*v.t. Bot.* To propagate by layers. [<LAY[1] + -ER[1]] —**lay′·er·ing** *n.*

LAYER (*def. 3*)
A method of securing new plants from old stock.

lay·er·age (lā′ər·ij) *n. Bot.* The propagation of plants by rooting parts of them.

layer cake A cake made in layers, having a sweetened filling or icing between layers, and usually frosted.

lay·ered (lā′ərd) *adj.* Having or covered with layers; arranged in layers.

lay·ette (lā·et′) *n.* A full equipment of clothes, bedding, etc., for a newly born child. [<F, dim. of *laie* a packing box, drawer <Flemish *laeye* <MDu. *lade* a chest, trunk. Akin to LADE.]

lay figure **1** A jointed model of the human body that can be arranged, as by artists, to hang drapery upon. **2** A mere puppet; a tool of others. [<Earlier *layman* (<Du. *leeman* < *led* a limb + *man* man) + FIGURE]

lay·man (lā′mən) *n.* *pl.* **·men** (-mən) One of the laity; a man not belonging to the clergy or other profession or body of experts. —**lay′·wom′an** (-wŏŏm′ən) *n. fem.* [<LAY[2] + MAN]

lay–off (lā′ôf′, -of′) *n.* The act of discharging or firing workmen or employees; also, a discontinuance, as of work.

lay–out (lā′out′) *n.* **1** *Slang* That which is laid out; a set of articles set out or provided; an outfit; a spread. **2** The space dragged over by a seine in fishing. **3** A laying out or planning, as of a piece of work, a campaign, etc.; a design; an arrangement. **4** In faro, the thirteen cards of a suit laid face upward at the beginning of the game. **5** The make-up of a book, magazine, etc. Also **lay·out.**

lay-o·ver (lā′ō′vər) *n.* A stopover.

la·zar (lā′zər, laz′ər) *n.* One afflicted with a loathsome disease; a leper. [<Med. L *lazarus,* after LAZARUS (*Luke* xiv 20)]

laz·a·ret·to (laz′ə·ret′ō) *n. pl.* **·tos** **1** A pest-house or pest ship; also, a hospital. **2** A quarantine building. **3** A storeroom near a vessel's stern. Also **laz′a·ret′, laz′a·rette′, la·zar·house** (lā′zər·hous′, laz′ər-). [<Ital. *lazzaretto* < dial. Ital. (Venetian) *lazareto, nazareto* < (Santa Madonna di) *Nazaret,* a Venetian church used as a plague hospital in the 15th c.; infl. in form by *lazzaro* a leper <Med. L *lazarus.* See LAZAR.]

Laz·a·rist (laz′ə·rist) *n.* A member of a Roman Catholic order founded in 1624 by St. Vincent de Paul for rural mission work in France. Called *Vincentian* in the United States. Also **Laz′a·rite** (-rit). [<F *lazariste,* from *(Collège de St.) Lazare,* a school at Paris, where the order was established <L *Lazarus* Lazarus]

la·zar·like (lā′zər·līk′, laz′ər-) *adj.* Covered with sores; leprous. Also **la′zar·ly.**

Laz·a·rus (laz′ə·rəs) A masculine personal name. Also *Fr.* **La·zare** (là·zàr′), *Ital.* **Laz·za·ro** (läd′dzä·rō). [<Hebrew, God has helped]

—**Lazarus** A brother of Martha and Mary, raised from the dead by Christ. *John* xi 1.

—**Lazarus** A sick beggar in the parable of the rich and the poor man. *Luke* xvi 20.

Laz·a·rus (laz′ə·rəs), **Emma,** 1849–87, U.S. poet and philanthropist.

laze (lāz) *v.* **lazed, laz·ing** *v.i.* To be lazy; loaf; idle. —*v.t.* To pass (time) in idleness. —*n.* Idleness; laziness. [Back formation <LAZY]

laz·u·li (laz′yōō·lī) See LAPIS LAZULI.

lazuli finch The indigo bunting.

laz·u·lite (laz′yōō·līt) *n.* A vitreous, azure-blue, brittle phosphate of aluminum and magnesium, crystallizing in the monoclinic system. [<Med. L *lazulus* lazuli + -ITE[1]]

laz·u·rite (laz′yōō·rīt) *n. Mineral.* A silicate of sodium and aluminum containing sulfur and occurring in deep-blue crystals: the principal constituent of lapis lazuli. [<Med. L *lazur* azure + -ITE[1]]

la·zy (lā′zē) *adj.* **·zi·er, ·zi·est** **1** Indisposed to exertion; indolent; slothful. **2** Moving or acting slowly or heavily; sluggish. See synonyms under IDLE. [Prob. <MLG *lasich* loose, feeble] —**la′zi·ly** *adv.* —**la′zi·ness** *n.*

la·zy·bones (lā′zē·bōnz′) *n. Colloq.* A lazy person; an idler.

La·zy-Su·san (lā′zē·sōō′zən) *n.* A revolving stand for condiments, bread, butter, etc., usually placed in the center of the table.

la·zy-tongs (lā′zē·tongz′) *n. pl.* Tongs consisting of a series of diagonal levers pivoted together in the middle and at the ends, by which device the tongs can be extended by a simple movement of scissorslike handles so as to pick up objects at a distance.

LAZY-TONGS

laz·za·ro·ne (laz′ə·rō′nā, *Ital.* läd′dzä·rō′nā) *n. pl.* **·ro·ni** (-rō′nē, *Ital.* -rō′nē) A Neapolitan beggar. [<Ital., aug. of *lazzaro* a leper <Med. L *lazarus* a lazar]

L-bar (el′bär′) *n.* A steel bar shaped like an L.

-le *suffix* Repeatedly: used to form frequentative verbs, but often without appreciable force: *sparkle, haggle.* [OE *-lian*]

lea[1] (lē) *n.* A grassy field or plain. ◆ Homophone: *lee.* [OE *lēah,* orig. open ground in a wood]

lea[2] (lē) *n.* A varying measure of yarn: 80 yards in worsted, 120 yards in cotton and silk, and 300 yards in linen: also spelled *lay.* ◆ Homophone: *lee.* [Back formation <earlier *leas,* taken as pl., prob. <F *lier* <L *ligare* bind]

leach (lēch) *v.t.* **1** To cause (a liquid) to percolate through something. **2** To percolate a liquid through (ashes, etc.) so as to remove the soluble portions. **3** To remove (soluble portions) by means of a percolating liquid. **4** *Metall.* To dissolve (metals or minerals) out of ore by cyanide or chlorine solutions, acids, etc. —*v.i.* **5** To lose soluble matter by percolation. **6** To be removed by percolations. —*n.* **1** Wood ashes, through which water is passed to carry away the soluble portions. **2** The vessel in which ashes, etc., are leached: also **leach tub.** **3** The act or process of leaching. **4** The solution obtained by leaching. Also spelled *latch.* ◆ Homophone: *leech.* [OE *leccan* wet, irrigate. Akin to LAKE[1], LEAK.] —**leach′er** *n.*

leach·y (lē′chē) *adj.* **leach·i·er, leach·i·est** Pervious; porous.

Lea·cock (lē′kok), **Stephen Butler,** 1869–1944, Canadian economist and humorist.

lead[1] (lēd) *v.* **led, lead·ing** *v.t.* **1** To go with or ahead of so as to show the way; guide. **2** To draw along; guide by or as by pulling: to *lead* a person by the hand. **3** To serve as a direction or route for: The path *led* them to a valley. **4** To cause to go in a certain course of direction, as wire, water, etc. **5** **a** To direct the affairs or actions of; be the leader of, as an army or expedition. **b** To direct the playing or performance of: to *lead* an orchestra. **6** To have the first or foremost place among: He *led* the field by ten feet. **7** To influence or control the opinions, thoughts, actions, etc., of; induce: His experiments *led* him to these conclusions. **8** To live or experience; pass: to *lead* a happy life. **9** To begin or open: to *lead* a discussion. **10** In card games, to begin a round of play with: He *led* the ace. **11** In hunting, to aim a weapon or missile ahead of (a moving target). —*v.i.* **12** To act as guide; conduct. **13** To have leadership or command; be in control. **14** To be guided: The horse *leads* easily. **15** To be first or in advance. **16** To afford a way or passage; reach or extend: The road *led* into a swamp. **17** In card games, to make the first play. **18** In boxing, to strike at an opponent, especially in testing his defense: to *lead* with a left. —**to lead off** To make a beginning; start. —**to lead on** To entice or tempt, especially to extravagance or error. —**to lead one a merry chase** (or **dance**) To cause someone trouble or confusion by unpredictable actions. —**to lead the way** **1** To act as guide. **2** To take the initiative. —**to lead to** To result in; cause: His carelessness *led to* his downfall. —**to lead with one's chin** *U.S. Slang* To expose oneself to unnecessary harm. —*n.* **1** Position in advance or at the head; priority. **2** The distance, time, etc., by which anything precedes. **3** The act of leading or conducting; guidance: to give a novice a *lead* in hunting; a clue or hint. **4** In cards, etc., the right to play first in a round; the card, piece, or suit played first. **5** A way or passage; especially, an open channel or passage through ice. **6** A lode or vein of ore; also, an old river bed where gold has been found. **7** In drama, the principal part; the actor who performs in such a part. **8** *Naut.* The course of a rope. **9** *Electr.* A main electrical conductor. **10** In shooting a gun, the act of aiming ahead of a moving target. **11** In baseball, the distance from base of a runner ready to run to the next base. **12** A leash for leading a dog. **13** In journalism, the opening of a news story with a summary of its contents. —*adj.* Acting as leader: the *lead* dog. [OE *lædan* cause to go]

Synonyms (verb): conduct, convey, direct, escort, excel, guide, head, outstrip, precede, surpass. See ACTUATE, DRAW, INFLUENCE, PERSUADE, PRECEDE. *Antonyms*: ape, chase, copy, follow, imitate, obey, pursue, succeed.

lead[2] (led) *n.* **1** A soft, heavy, inelastic, malleable, ductile, bluish-gray metallic element (symbol Pb) in the fourth group of the periodic table, most commonly occurring in the sulfide mineral, galena. **2** Any one of various articles made of lead or its alloys. **3** *Printing* A thin strip of type metal or brass used in composition. **4** *Naut.* A weight of lead used in sounding at sea. **5** Leaden sheets or plates used for covering roofs. **6** One of the cames in a diamond-paned window. **7** Graphite: also called **black lead.** **8** A mixture of lead carbonate and hydrated lead oxide: also called **white lead.** **9** *Colloq.* Projectiles from firearms; bullets. —*v.t.* **1** To cover, weight, fasten, treat, or fill with lead. **2** To glaze, as porcelain, with powdered metallic ore. **3** *Printing* To separate (lines of type) with leads. **4** To construct (a window) with leaden cames. —*v.i.* **5** To become filled or clogged with lead: said of rifle grooves. [OE *lēad,* prob. <Celtic] —**lead′y** *adj.*

lead acetate *Chem.* A white, soluble, crystalline salt, $Pb(C_2H_3O_2)_2 \cdot 3H_2O$, made by the action of acetic acid on litharge. From the sweet taste of the solution it is named *sugar of lead.*

lead arsenate *Chem.* A white, heavy, poisonous crystalline compound, $Pb_3(AsO_4)_2$: used as a constituent of insecticides.

lead azide *Chem.* A white to brownish crystalline compound, PbN_6: used as a substitute for mercury fulminate in explosives.

Lead·beat·er's possum (led′bē′tərz) An arboreal marsupial *(Gymnobelideus leadbeateri)* of Australia, related to the flying phalangers; thought to be extinct until rediscovered in 1961.

lead carbonate Cerusite.

lead chromate Chrome yellow.

lead dioxide *Chem.* The compound PbO_2 prepared as a dark-brown, amorphous powder: used in the manufacture of storage batteries.

lead·en (led′n) *adj.* **1** Made of lead; also, of the dull-gray color of lead. **2** Heavy; dull or sluggish; also, base in quality. —**lead′en·ly** *adv.* —**lead′en·ness** *n.*

lead·er (lē′dər) *n.* **1** One who leads or conducts; a guide; commander. **2** *Music* A director or conductor of an orchestra; also, the player of the first or principal instrument in an orchestra or band; in an orchestra, usually the head of the first violins. **3** That which leads, or occupies a chief place, as the foremost horse of a team, etc. **4** A tendon or sinew. **5** In journalism, the chief editorial article of a newspaper. **6** An article of merchandise offered at a special price to attract customers. **7** *Printing* A horizontal row of printed dots or hyphens, or a dot or hyphen of such a row, used to guide the eye, as from one side of a page to the other. **8** In fishing, a short line of gut, nylon, etc., attaching the hook or lure to the line. **9** A pipe to carry water from the roof or upper part of a building to the ground. See synonyms under CHIEF, MASTER.

lead·er·ship (lē′dər·ship) *n.* The office or position of a leader; guidance. See synonyms under PRECEDENCE.

lead glass (led) Flint glass. See under GLASS.

lead-in (lēd′in′) *n.* A wire connecting the antenna of a radio with the receiving set: also, *Brit., down-lead.*

lead·ing (lē′ding) *adj.* **1** Having priority or influence; chief. **2** Attention-getting, as, a *leading* display. **3** Furnishing a lead or precedence. See synonyms under FIRST. —*n.* A directing or guiding influence; specifically, spiritual guidance. —**lead′ing·ly** *adv.*

leading article **1** An editorial; also, the first article, as in a magazine. **2** Leader (def. 6).

leading edge *Aeron.* The forward edge of an airfoil or propeller blade.

leading strings **1** Strings to support children learning to walk. **2** Guidance or restraint.

lead line (led) A line for taking soundings.

lead-off (lēd′ôf′, -of′) *n.* **1** A beginning; the first of a succession or series. **2** The opening or attacking movement in any bout of skill or strength, competitive game, etc. **3** The player who leads off.

lead pencil (led) A pencil, usually of graphite mixed with clay for hardness, and incased in wood, paper, or the like.

lead plant (led) A low shrub *(Amorpha canescens)* of the southern and southwestern United States, with lead-gray leaves and twigs.

lead poisoning (led) *Pathol.* Poisoning caused by the slow, continuous absorption of lead by the tissues of the body: marked by nutritional disturbances, anemia, paralysis, and cerebral disorders: also called *plumbism.*

leads·man (ledz′mən) *n. pl.* **·men** (-mən) *Naut.* A sailor who heaves the lead.

lead tetraethyl *Chem.* A colorless, heavy, inflammable, extremely poisonous, liquid hydrocarbon, $Pb(C_2H_5)_4$, prepared by the action of ethyl chloride on a lead sodium alloy: used as an anti-knock agent in internal-combustion engines.

lead time (lēd) **1** *Mil.* **a** The time required to move from the planning and development stage of a new aircraft, ship, weapon, etc., to active production for use. **b** The calculation based on target distance and speed that determines the point of aim of a projectile or missile. **2** The interval between one stage in a sequence of industrial operations or commercial procedures and a subsequent one.

lead·wort (led′wûrt′) *n.* Plumbago.

leaf (lēf) *n.* *pl.* **leaves** (lēvz) **1** A lateral photosynthetic appendage of the stem of a plant, commonly broad, flat, thin, and of a green color. ◆ Collateral adjective: *foliar.* **2** Foliage collectively; leafage; specifically, the leaves of the tobacco or the tea plant when gathered for curing or sale. **3** A single division of a folded sheet of paper or the like, as in a book, or a single unfolded piece; also, what is written or printed on a leaf. **4** A hinged, folding, sliding, or removable part or section, as of a table, door, gate, screen, or folding fan. **5** A very thin sheet or plate of metal, as gold; also, one of marble, horn, etc. **6** A layer or fold of fat, especially over the kidneys of a hog. **7** One of the thin, flat strips of metal composing a spring of an automobile. **8** A petal: incorrect, but popularly used. **— to turn over a new leaf** To change one's ways or conduct, especially for the better. *— adj.* Of, pertaining to, suggestive of, or occurring in, a leaf or leaves. *— v.i.* To put forth or produce leaves. *— v.t.* To turn or run through the pages of a book: often with *through.* ◆ Homophone: *lief.* [OE *lēaf*]

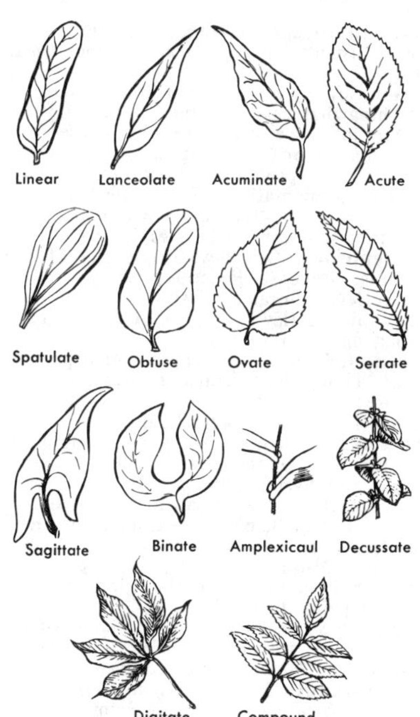

TYPES OF TREE LEAVES

leaf·age (lē′fij) *n.* Leaves collectively; foliage.

leaf beet Chard (def. 2).

leaf beetle Any of a family *(Chrysomelidae)* of usually small, bright-colored beetles which are found, both in the larval and the adult stages, on leaves.

leaf blight Any of various plant diseases, chiefly of fungous origin, having a conspicuously damaging effect on leaves, especially those affecting pome fruits.

leaf bud A bud that develops into a leafy branch without flowers.

leaf curl A destructive plant disease caused by various fungi of the family *Exoascaceae,* which attack certain forest and fruit trees, as the oak, poplar, and peach, with serious deformation of the leaves: also called *witch broom.* Also **leaf blister.**

leaf fat **1** A layer of fat about the kidneys of swine, from which is obtained leaf lard. **2** Folds of fat over the kidneys of other animals.

leaf·hop·per (lēf′hop′ər) *n.* Any of a family *(Cicadellidae)* of homopterous leaping insects which suck the juices of various plants.

leaf insect Phyllium.

leaf lard Lard made from leaf fat; also, the leaves themselves.

leaf·less (lēf′lis) *adj.* Having or bearing no leaves.

leaf·let (lēf′lit) *n.* **1** A little leaf. **2** *Bot.* One of the separate divisions of a compound leaf. **3** A small printed leaf; a tract; also, a folding circular having several unsewed or unstitched pages in one strip; a folder. **4** A leaflike part. [Dim. of LEAF]

leaf miner The larva of a tineid moth, or of a beetle, fly, or other insect, which feeds on the leaves of plants and trees.

leaf roll **1** A virus disease of the potato, characterized by a pronounced upward curling of the leaves and by a reduction in the size of the tubers. **2** Any of various other plant diseases having a similar effect upon the leaves.

leaf roller The larva of certain small moths, especially of the family *Tortricidae,* that rolls itself up in the leaves of the plant it attacks.

leaf spot A disease of apples, pears, quinces, and other fruits, caused by a sac fungus *(Physalospora malorum)* and resulting in widespread damage: also called *black rot, fruit rot.*

leaf spring *Mech.* A spring made of one or more flat plates or strips: distinguished from a spiral spring.

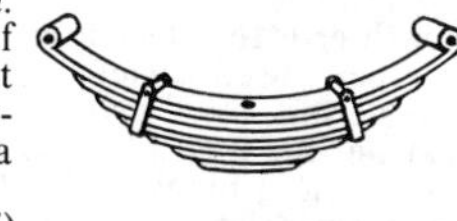

LEAF SPRING

leaf·stalk (lēf′stôk′) *n.* A petiole.

leaf·y (lē′fē) *adj.* **leaf·i·er, leaf·i·est** **1** Having or full of leaves; consisting of or characterized by leaves. **2** Producing broad leaves. **3** Like a leaf or leaves. **4** Existing in thin sheets or layers; laminate.

league[1] (lēg) *n.* **1** A measure of distance, varying from about 2.42 to 4.6 English statute miles. The English **land league** contains approximately 3 statute miles, or 4.82 kilometers; the **marine league** in common use equals 3 geographic miles, or 5.56 kilometers. **2** In Texas, an old Spanish land measure equaling about 4,438 acres; a square league. [<OF *legue* <LL *leuga, leuca* a Gaulish mile <Celtic]

league[2] (lēg) *n.* **1** An alliance of persons or states for mutual support in a common cause. **2** Any close connection or union; as, a commercial *league.* **3** An association of baseball, football, basketball, or other teams which play among themselves. See synonyms under ALLIANCE. *— v.t. & v.i.* **leagued, lea·guing** To join in a league; combine. [<OF *ligue* <Ital. *liga, lega* < *legare* bind <L *ligare*] **— lea·guer** (lē′gər) *n.*

League of Nations An international organization established January 10, 1920, primarily for the preservation of peace under the Covenant of the League in the Treaty of Versailles; formally dissolved April 18, 1946, when its functions, library, and buildings were turned over to the United Nations.

lea·guer (lē′gər) *Archaic n.* **1** A siege. **2** The camp of a besieging force; also, any military camp. *— v.t.* To beleaguer; besiege. [<Du. *leger* a camp]

Le·ah (lē′ə) A feminine personal name. [<Hebrew, weary]

— Leah The elder daughter of Laban; one of the wives of Jacob. *Gen.* xxix 16.

Lea·hy (lā′hē), **William Daniel,** 1875–1959, U. S. admiral of the fleet 1944–48.

leak (lēk) *n.* **1** An opening, mechanical or otherwise, that permits the unintended entrance or escape of a fluid, of electric current, etc. **2** Hence, anything which permits the unintentional loss or accrual of something: a *leak* in the espionage system. **3** Leakage. **— to spring a leak** To spring open, part, or crack, so as to let a fluid in or out. *— v.i.* **1** To let a liquid, etc., enter or escape undesignedly, as through a hole or crack. **2** To pass in or out accidentally: often with *in* or *out.* **3** To become known despite efforts at secrecy: usually with *out*: Our plans *leaked* out. *— v.t.* **4** To let (a liquid, etc.) enter or escape undesignedly. **5** To disclose (information, etc.) without authorization. ◆ Homophone: *leek.* [<ON *leka* drip. Akin to LEACH, LAKE[1].] **— leak′y** *adj.*

leak·age (lē′kij) *n.* **1** The act of leaking. **2** The quantity that leaks. **3** An allowance for loss by leaking.

leakage current *Electr.* A stray current, generally weak, which escapes through inadequate or defective insulation.

leal (lēl) *adj. Scot.* **1** True-hearted; loyal; faithful. **2** True; actual. **— leal′ly** *adv.* **— le·al·ty** (lē′əl·tē) *n.*

lean[1] (lēn) *v.* **leaned** or **leant, lean·ing** *v.i.* **1** To incline from an erect position: The tower is *leaning.* **2** To incline against or rest on something for support: to *lean* against a tree. **3** To depend or rely: with *on* or *upon*: to *lean* on friendship. **4** To have a mental tendency or inclination: to *lean* toward an opinion. *— v.t.* **5** To cause to incline from an erect position. **6** To place (one thing) against another for support: to *lean* a ladder against a house. *— n.* A leaning; inclination. ◆ Homophone: *lien.* [Fusion of OE *hleonian* lean and OE *hlænen* cause to lean]

Synonyms (verb): bear, confide, depend, recline, rely, repose, rest, trust. See REST[1].

lean[2] (lēn) *adj.* **1** Free from or lacking fat; lank; thin. **2** Lacking in richness, productiveness, or other desirable qualities: *lean* ore, a *lean* harvest. **3** Manifesting thinness, or attended by want. See synonyms under MEAGER. *— n.* Flesh or muscle without fat: *lean* meat. ◆ Homophone: *lien.* [OE *hlæne* thin] **— lean′ly** *adv.* **— lean′ness** *n.*

Le·an·der (lē·an′dər) **1** A masculine personal name. Also *Fr.* **Lé·an·dre** (lā·äṅ′dr′), *Ital., Sp.* **Le·an·dro** (*Ital.* lā·än′drō, *Sp.* -thrō). **2** In Greek legend, the lover of Hero. [<Gk., lion man]

lean·ing (lē′ning) *adj.* Inclining from the vertical: a *leaning* tower. *— n.* An inclination; bias; tendency.

Le·a·nor (lā′ä·nôr′) Spanish form of ELEANOR.

leant (lent) Alternative past tense and past participle of LEAN.

lean-to (lēn′tōō′) *n.* *pl.* **-tos** (-tōōz′) **1** A building having a single-pitched roof with its apex against an adjoining wall. **2** A rude shelter consisting of branches or planks which slope from a crossbar to the ground. *— adj.* Having rafters, as a roof, which slope in only one direction.

leap (lēp) *v.* **leaped** or **leapt, leap·ing** *v.i.* **1** To jump from the ground with the feet in the air, as from one place or position to another. **2** To move suddenly by or as by jumps or jumping: to *leap* aboard; to *leap* to a conclusion. *— v.t.* **3** To clear by jumping over: to *leap* a barrier. **4** To cause to leap: to *leap* a horse over a hedge. *— n.* **1** The act of leaping; a bound. **2** The space passed over in leaping. [OE *hlēapan*] **— leap′er** *n.*

Synonyms (verb): bounce, bound, caper, dance, frisk, gambol, hop, jump, skip, spring, vault.

leap·frog (lēp′frôg′, -frog′) *n.* A game in which one player puts his hands on the back of another, who is stooping over, and leaps over him. *— v.* **·frogged, ·frog·ging** *v.t.* **1** To jump over as in the game of leapfrog. **2** *Mil.* To bypass (an enemy position), the capture of which is considered strategically unnecessary. *— v.i.* **3** To jump as in the game of leapfrog.

leaping evil Louping ill.

leapt (lept, lēpt) Alternative past tense and past participle of LEAP.

leap year In the Julian and Gregorian calendars, a year of 366 days, an additional day being added to February to allow for the difference in length between the common and the astronomical years. Every year exactly divisible by four, or, in centesimal years, exactly divisible by 400, is a leap year.

lear[1] (lir) *n. Scot.* Learning; lore; also, a lesson.

lear[2] (lir) See LEER[2].

lear[3] (lir) See LEER[3].

Lear (lir) Legendary king of Britain mentioned by Geoffrey of Monmouth, Layamon, Holinshed, etc.; hero of Shakespeare's *King Lear.*

Lear (lir), **Edward,** 1812–88, English humorist.

lea-rig (lē'rig', lā'-) *n. Scot.* A grassy ridge, particularly on the outskirts of a plowed field.

learn (lûrn) *v.* **learned** or **learnt, learn·ing** *v.t.* **1** To acquire knowledge of or skill in by observation, study, instruction, etc. **2** To find out; gain acquaintance with; ascertain: to *learn* the facts. **3** To fix in the mind; memorize. **4** To become practiced in: to *learn* bad habits. —*v.i.* **5** To gain knowledge; acquire skill. **6** To be informed; hear. [OE *leornian.* Akin to LORE[1].] —**learn'er** *n.*

Synonyms: acquire, commit, get, inform, instruct, know, master, memorize, perceive, teach, train. *Learn* refers to the process of getting knowledge, *know* to the result. What we once thoroughly *learn* we *know.* See ACQUIRE, GAIN, KNOW. Compare KNOWLEDGE. *Antonyms:* forget, lose, miss, pass.

learn·ed (lûr'nid) *adj.* Possessed of learning; erudite. —**learn'ed·ly** *adv.*

learn·ing (lûr'ning) *n.* **1** Knowledge obtained by study or from instruction; scholarship; erudition. **2** The act of acquiring knowledge or skill. **3** *Psychol.* The modification of behavior following upon and induced by interaction with the environment and as a result of experiences leading to the establishment of new patterns of response to external stimuli.

Synonyms: education, erudition, instruction, knowledge, lore, scholarship, study, training, tuition. *Learning* may be acquired by one's unaided industry, but any full *education* must be the result in great part of *instruction, training,* and personal association. *Study* is emphatically what one does for himself, and in which *instruction* and *tuition* can only point the way. *Lore* is used only in poetic style, for accumulated *knowledge,* as of a people or age, or in a general sense for *learning* or *erudition. Information* is *knowledge* of fact, real or supposed, derived from persons, books, or observation; it is regarded as casual and haphazard. *Learning* is much higher, being wide and systematic *knowledge,* the result of long, assiduous *study; erudition* is recondite *learning* secured only by extraordinary industry, opportunity, and ability. See EDUCATION, KNOWLEDGE, SCIENCE, WISDOM. *Antonyms:* ignorance, illiteracy. See synonyms for IGNORANT.

lease[1] (lēs) *n.* The system of crossing warp threads during weaving. [Appar. var. of LEASH, in this sense]

lease[2] (lēs) *v.t.* **leased, leas·ing** **1** To grant the temporary possession and profits of, as lands or tenements, usually for a specified rent; let. **2** To take possession of or hold under a lease. —*n.* **1** A contract for the letting of land, etc., for rent; also, such letting. **2** Any tenure by permission, or its duration. [<AF *les,* OF *lais* a letting <*laissier* let, leave <L *laxare* loosen <*laxus* loose] —**leas'a·ble** *adj.*

lease·back (lēs'bak') *n.* The sale of real property to a buyer who as part of the same transaction leases it to the seller: short for *sale and lease back.*

lease·hold (lēs'hōld') *adj.* Held by lease. —*n.* A tenure held by a lease. —**lease'hold'er** *n.*

leash (lēsh) *n.* **1** A line or thong, as for holding a dog, etc. **2** A brace and a half; three creatures of like kind, as greyhounds; three in general. —*v.t.* To hold or secure by a leash. [<OF *lesse, laisse* <L *laxa,* fem. of *laxus* loose]

leas·ing (lē'sing) *n. Brit. Dial.* Lying or a lie; falsehood. [OE *lēasung* <*lēasian* tell lies <*lēas* destitute of, false]

least (lēst) *adj.* Smallest in size, value, etc.; minimal. —*n.* That which is least. —*adv.* In the lowest or smallest degree. [OE *lǣst, lǣsest,* superl. of *lǣssa* less]

least action *Physics* That property of a dynamic system having a constant total energy whereby any change in its configuration will take place with a minimum of action among and between its constituent particles.

least common denominator See under DENOMINATOR.

least energy *Physics* The tendency of a dynamic system to remain in stable equilibrium only under those conditions for which the potential energy of the system is at a minimum.

least flycatcher See under FLYCATCHER.

least sandpiper See under SANDPIPER.

least squares *Math.* A method of deducing the most probable value of a quantity from a set of observations or measurements, in accordance with the principle that the sum of the squares of all the errors is at a minimum.

least·wise (lēst'wīz') *adv. Colloq.* At least. Also **least'ways'** (-wāz').

leath·er (leth'ər) *n.* **1** The skin or hide of an animal, when tanned or dressed for use. **2** A piece, part, or article consisting or made of leather, as a football. —*v.t.* **1** To cover or furnish with leather. **2** *Colloq.* To beat or flog with or as with a leather strap. [OE *lether*] —**leath'er·y** *adj.* —**leath'er·i·ness** *n.*

leath·er·back (leth'ər·bak') *n.* The soft-shelled turtle (*Dermochelys coriacea*) living in warm seas, and notable for its flexible, leathery carapace. It sometimes exceeds 1,000 pounds in weight.

leath·er·board (leth'ər·bôrd', -bōrd') *n.* An imitation leather sole made from scraps of leather assembled and pressed into sheets: also called *fiber leather.*

leath·er·coat (leth'ər·kōt') *n.* A russet apple.

leath·er·craft (leth'ər·kraft', -kräft') *n.* The handicraft of designing and making things of leather.

Leath·er·ette (leth'ər·et') *n.* An imitation leather, used chiefly in bookbinding, upholstering, etc.: a trade name.

leath·er·head (leth'ər·hed') *n.* **1** *Slang* A stupid person; blockhead. **2** The friarbird.

leath·ern (leth'ərn) *adj.* Made of leather. [OE *letheren* <*lether* leather]

leath·er·neck (leth'ər·nek') *n. Slang* A member of the U.S. Marine Corps.

leath·er·oid (leth'ər·oid) *n.* A material with leatherlike qualities, made by treating vegetable fiber with certain chemicals.

leath·er·stock·ing (leth'ər·stok'ing) *n.* A person who wears leather stockings; hence, a frontiersman. —*adj.* Characteristic of, or about, pioneers and pioneer life: *leatherstocking* customs or stories.

Leath·er·stock·ing (leth'ər·stok'ing) Natty Bumppo, the hero of J. F. Cooper's *Leather-stocking Tales.*

leath·er·wood (leth'ər·wo͝od') *n.* A low, thymelaeaceous, North American shrub or bush (*Dirca palustris*) with white, soft wood, tough, fibrous bark, and small, yellow flowers: also called *moosewood.*

leath·er·work (leth'ər·wûrk') *n.* **1** The process of preparing or tooling leather. **2** An ornamental pattern tooled in leather.

leath·er·work·er (leth'ər·wûr'kər) *n.* One who prepares or ornaments leather. —**leath'er·work'ing** *n.*

leave[1] (lēv) *v.* **left, leav·ing** *v.t.* **1** To go or depart from; quit. **2** To allow to remain behind or continue as specified; abandon: to *leave* work undone; to *leave* a plow in a field. **3** To place or deposit so as to allow to remain behind: to *leave* word. **4** To cause to remain after departure, cessation, healing, etc.: The war *left* its mark. **5** To refer or entrust to another for doing, deciding, etc.: I *leave* the matter to you. **6** To sever or terminate connection, employment, etc., with: to *leave* a job. **7** To have as a remainder: Three minus two *leaves* one. **8** To have remaining after death: to *leave* a large family. **9** To give by will; bequeath. **10** To desist from; stop: usually with *off.* —*v.i.* **11** To depart or go away; set out. **12** To desist; cease: with *off:* He *left* off where I began. See synonyms under ABANDON. —**to leave out** To omit from consideration; fail to include. [OE *lǣfan,* lit., let remain] —**leav'er** *n.*

◆ **leave, let** *Leave* and *let,* often confused, are not synonyms. *Leave* means to go away or depart, *let* to permit. Perhaps because the noun *leave* has "permission" as one of its meanings, popular usage endows the verb *leave* with the sense "permit," and tries to make it interchangeable with *let* in such expressions as *Let me go.* But the substitution of *leave* for *let* violates established idiom, for while *let* can be followed by the infinitive without "to," *leave* cannot: *Leave it to him to decide* or *Leave the decision to him,* but never *Leave him decide. Leave me go* is readily recognized as violating both sense and idiom, and is hence considered illiterate. So with *Leave me be.* This last is synonymous with *Leave me alone,* widespread in children's speech as a replacement for the standard English *Let me alone,* which has the idiomatic meaning "Don't bother me" or "Stop bothering me." In this case, and in this case only, *Leave it alone* may be regarded as having acquired fair colloquial standing, with two reservations. It is only in the imperative that *leave* is here admissible as a substitute for *let;* in declined forms, the idiomatic sense does not carry over. *They left him alone* does not mean *They let him alone.* The second reservation follows from this. In formal English, *Leave me alone* means "Go away so that I may be alone." Solitude may insure freedom from annoyance, but asking *to be left alone* is not the same as demanding *to be let alone.*

leave[2] (lēv) *n.* **1** Permission given to do something otherwise forbidden or unlawful. **2** Liberty to go or to be absent. **3** A departure; parting. **4** Permission granted an officer of a military service or to enlisted naval personnel to be absent from duty: also **leave of absence.** See synonyms under PERMISSION. —**to take leave** **1** To depart; go away. **2** To abandon; quit: with *of:* He *took leave* of his senses. [OE *lēaf* permission]

leave[3] (lēv) *v.i.* **leaved, leav·ing** To put forth leaves.

leaved (lēvd) *adj.* Having a leaf, leaves, or folds: usually in composition: *four-leaved* clover.

leav·en (lev'ən) *n.* **1** Fermenting dough, or anything that causes fermentation, as yeast. **2** Any influence or addition that causes general change or modification of the whole. —*v.t.* **1** To produce fermentation in; make light by fermentation. **2** To affect in character; imbue. [<OF *levain* <L *levamen* alleviation <*levare* raise] —**leav'en·ing** *n.*

Leav·en·worth (lev'ən·wûrth) A city of NE Kansas; site of a Federal prison.

leaves (lēvz) Plural of LEAF.

leave-tak·ing (lēv'tā'king) *n.* A taking leave; a parting; a farewell.

leav·ing (lē'ving) *n.* **1** The act of departure. **2** *pl.* Things left; scraps; refuse; offal. See synonyms under WASTE.

leav·y (lē'vē) *adj. Poetic* Leafy.

Leb·a·non (leb'ə·nən) An Arab republic on the east coast of the Mediterranean, between Israel and Syria; 3,880 square miles; capital, Beirut; formerly a French mandate. *French* **Li·ban** (lē·bäṅ'). —**Leb'a·nese'** (-nēz', -nēs') *adj. & n.*

Lebanon Mountains A range extending through Lebanon along the Mediterranean; highest peak, 10,131 feet.

leb·en (leb'ən) *n.* An Arabian beverage of fermented milk, similar to the Turkish matzoon: also spelled *laban.* [<Arabic *laban*]

Le·bens·raum (lā'bəns·roum) *n. German* Territory into which a nation claims it must expand to fulfill its economic needs. A term of Nazi ideology; literally, space for living. See GEOPOLITICS.

Le Bour·get (lə bo͞or·zhe') A suburb of NE Paris; site of an important airport.

Le·brun (lə·brœṅ'), **Charles,** 1619–90, French historical painter. Also **Le Brun.**

Lec·ce (let'chā) A city in Apulia, SE Italy.

Lech (lekh) A river in Austria and Germany, flowing 175 miles NE to the Danube.

lech·er (lech'ər) *n.* A habitually lewd or excessively sensual man. [<OF *lecheor* <*lechier* live in debauchery, lick <OHG *leccōn* lick]

lech·er·ous (lech'ər·əs) *adj.* Given to or characterized by lewdness or lust. —**lech'er·ous·ly** *adv.* —**lech'er·ous·ness** *n.*

lech·er·y (lech'ər·ē) *n.* **1** Free indulgence in lust; gross sensuality. **2** Selfish pleasure. [<OF *lecherie, licherie* <*lecheor* LECHER]

lec·i·thin (les'ə·thin) *n. Biochem.* A brownish-yellow, waxy, phosphorized fat contained in the cell tissue of many plants and animals, especially the brain, nerves, egg yolk, and protoplasm: used in medicine as a tonic and nutrient. [<Gk. *lekithos* an egg's yolk + -IN]

lec·i·thin·ase (les'ə·thin·ās') *n.* Any of several enzymes capable of hydrolyzing lecithin. [< LECITHIN + -ASE]

Leck·y (lek'ē), **William Edward Hartpole,** 1838–1903, English historian.

Le·conte de Lisle (lə·kôṅt' də lēl'), **Charles Marie René,** 1818–94, French poet.

Le Cor·bu·sier (lə kôr·bü·zyā′) Pseudonym of *Charles Edouard Jeanneret,* 1887–1965, Swiss architect, painter, and writer.

Le Creu·sot (lə krœ·zō′) A town in east central France.

lec·tern (lek′tərn) *n.* **1** A reading desk, in some churches, from which various services are chanted or read. **2** A reading stand, as on a rostrum. [<OF *lettrun* <LL *lectrum* <L *lectus,* pp. of *legere* read]

lec·tion (lek′shən) *n.* **1** A lesson appointed to be read in church service. **2** A variation in the text of an author. [<OF *lectiun* <L *lectio, -onis* < *lectus,* pp. of *legere* read]

lec·tion·ar·y (lek′shən·er′ē) *n. pl.* **·ar·ies** A book or a table of lessons for church service. [<Med. L *lectionarium* <L *lectio* LECTION]

lec·tor (lek′tər) *n.* A reader; specifically, one who reads lessons in a church or lectures in a university. [<L, a reader < *lectus,* pp. of *legere* read]

lec·tu·al (lek′chōō·əl) *adj.* **1** Of or pertaining to a bed or couch. **2** Confining one to his bed: a *lectual* disease. [<LL *lectualis* <L *lectus* a bed, couch]

lec·ture (lek′chər) *n.* **1** A discourse delivered aloud for instruction or entertainment. **2** A formal reproof; reprimand. — *v.* **·tured, ·tur·ing** *v.t.* **1** To deliver lectures to; instruct by lecturing. **2** To rebuke or castigate authoritatively or at length. — *v.i.* **3** To give a lecture. [<L *lectura* an act of reading < *lectus,* pp. of *legere* read] — **lec′tur·er** *n.*

lec·ture·ship (lek′chər·ship) *n.* The office or rank of lecturer.

led (led) Past tense and past participle of LEAD[1].

Le·da (lē′də) In Greek mythology, the wife of Tyndareus and by him mother of Clytemnestra; by Zeus, who appeared to her in the form of a swan, she was the mother of Helen and of Castor and Pollux.

ledge (lej) *n.* **1** A shelf upon which articles can be laid. **2** Something resembling a shelf, as a shelflike ridge of rock, or a shelflike projection from a building. **3** A rocky outcrop or reef. **4** A metal-bearing rock stratum; a lode or vein. [ME *legge,* prob. < root of *leggen* LAY[1]] — **ledg′y** *adj.*

ledg·er[1] (lej′ər) *n.* **1** The principal book of accounts of a business establishment, in which all the transactions of each day are entered under appropriate heads so as to show the debits and credits of each account. **2** A bar, stone, or the like, that is made to lie flat or stay in a fixed position. **3** A horizontal piece fastened to a timber scaffolding to sustain the putlogs. **4** A horizontal stone slab over a grave. **5** Ledger tackle or ledger bait: also spelled *leger.* [ME *legger,* prob. < *leggen* LAY[1]; infl. by MDu. *legger* lay]

ledg·er[2] (lej′ər) *adj.* Remaining or lying in a place: *ledger* bait. Also *leger.* [See LEDGER[1]]

ledger bait A fishing bait lying at the bottom of the water: also spelled *leger bait.*

ledger board The horizontal board forming the top rail of a fence, the handrail of a stairway, etc.

ledger tackle Any form of floating tackle the lower portion of which lies on the bottom: also *leger line, leger tackle.* Also **ledger line.**

lee[1] (lē) *n.* **1** The direction opposite that from which the wind comes; the side sheltered, or that shelters, from wind. **2** A shelter afforded by any object in a wind. — *adj.* Pertaining to the side opposite to that from which the wind comes: a *lee* shore. ◆ Homophone: *lea.* [OE *hlēo* a shelter]

lee[2] (lē) *n. Scot.* A falsehood; lie. ◆ Homophone: *lea.*

Lee (lē) A Virginia family prominent in American history, including **Richard Henry,** 1732–1794, his brother **Francis Lightfoot,** 1734–97, Revolutionary statesmen and signers of the Declaration of Independence; **Henry,** 1756–1818, Revolutionary soldier and statesman: known as *Light-Horse Harry Lee*; his son **Robert Edward,** 1807–70, commander in chief of the Confederate army; **Fitzhugh,** 1835–1905, Confederate general, nephew of Robert Edward Lee.

— **Charles,** 1731–82, American Revolutionary general; court-martialed and dismissed.

— **Sir Sidney,** 1859–1926, English editor and scholar.

Lee (lē), **T(sung) D(ao),** born 1926, U.S. physicist born in China.

lee·an·gle (lē′ang′gəl) *n. Austral.* A heavy war club, with the head bent to a shape much like a miners' pick: also spelled *liangle.*

lee·board (lē′bôrd′, -bōrd′) *n. Naut.* A board lowered on the lee side of a vessel and acting as a keel or centerboard to keep it from drifting to leeward.

leech[1] (lēch) *n.* **1** Any one of a class *(Hirudinea)* of carnivorous, aquatic, bloodsucking annelid worms; especially, the **medicinal leech** *(Hirudo medicinalis),* formerly used for drawing blood, which can ingest three times its weight in blood. **2** Hence, one who appropriates or filches the substance or wealth of others. **3** *Archaic* A physician; doctor. **4** A blood-drawing apparatus: also **artificial leech.** — *v.t.* **1** To bleed with leeches. **2** *Obs.* To treat with medicine; heal. ◆ Homophone: *leach.* [OE *lǣce,* orig. a physician] — **leech′er** *n.*

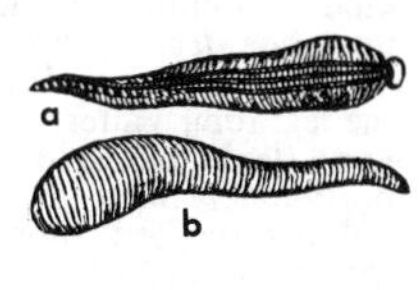

LEECH
a. Common. *b.* Medicinal. (Vary in size from 1 to 18 inches)

leech[2] (lēch) *n. Naut.* **1** The edge of a square sail. **2** The after edge of a fore-and-aft sail. ◆ Homophone: *leach.* [ME *lich,* ? <Scand. Cf. ON *lik* a boltrope.]

Leeds (lēdz) A city and county borough in central Yorkshire, England.

leek (lēk) *n.* A culinary herb *(Allium porrum)* of the lily family, closely allied to the onion. ◆ Homophone: *leak.* [OE *lēac*]

leer[1] (lir) *n.* A sly look or glance expressing immodest desire, malicious intent, etc. — *v.i.* To look with a leer. [OE *hlēor* a cheek, face; hence "a glance over one's cheek"]

leer[2] (lir) *n.* An oven for annealing glass: also spelled *lear, lehr.* [Origin unknown]

leer[3] (lir) *adj. Brit. Dial.* Empty: also spelled *lear.* [OE *lǣre* (assumed from *lǣrnes* emptiness)]

leer·ing·ly (lir′ing·lē) *adv.* With a leer. [< LEER[1]]

leer·y (lir′ē) *adj. Slang* Shrewd and sly; suspicious; wary. [<LEER[1] + -Y]

lees (lēz) *n. pl.* The settlings of liquor; sediment; dregs. [Pl. of obs. *lee* <OF *lie* < Med. L *lia,* prob. <Celtic]

lee shore The shore on the lee side of a ship, toward which the wind blows the ship. — **on a lee shore** In danger or difficulties.

lee·some (lē′səm) *adj. Scot.* Pleasant; agreeable.

leet (lēt) *n.* In England, a former court of jurisdiction for petty offenses: also called *courtleet.* [<AF *lete*; ult. origin uncertain]

lee tide A tide running with the wind

Leeu·war·den (lā′vär·dən) A city in northern Netherlands, capital of Friesland province.

Leeu·wen·hoek (lā′vən·hōōk), **Anton van,** 1632–1723, Dutch naturalist and microscopist; discovered the red blood corpuscles and the capillary circulation of blood.

lee·ward (lē′wərd, lōō′ərd) *adj. Naut.* Pertaining to the direction in which the wind blows. — *n.* The direction toward which the wind blows: opposed to *windward.* — *adv.* Toward the lee: also **lee′ward·ly.**

Lee·ward Islands (lē′wərd) **1** A northern group of West Indian islands in the Lesser Antilles, extending SE from Puerto Rico to the Windward Islands. **2** A former British colony in this group, divided into the four colonies (former federated presidencies) of (1) Antigua, (2) St. Christopher, Nevis and Anguilla, (3) Montserrat, these three being members of The West Indies, and (4) the British Virgin Islands; 422.5 square miles; former capital, St. John's, on Antigua. **3** See SOCIETY ISLANDS.

lee·way (lē′wā′) *n.* **1** *Naut.* The lateral drift of a vessel to leeward. **2** The falling behind or away from a set course. **3** *Colloq.* Extra margin, space, time, money, etc.

left[1] (left) Past tense and past participle of LEAVE[1].

left[2] (left) *adj.* **1** Pertaining to that side of the body which is toward the north when one faces the rising sun: opposite to *right.* **2** Situated on the left-hand side; sinistral. **3** Designating that side or bank of a river which is on the left facing the direction of flow. — *n.* **1** The left side. **2** Anything on or toward that side of the human body which normally contains the lower portion of the heart. **3** In European countries, the more radical political parties, seated to the left of the presiding officer in a deliberative assembly: also **The Left.** — *adv.* On or to the left. [OE (Kentish), weak, worthless, as in *lyftādl* paralysis]

Left Bank A district of Paris along the left (south) bank of the Seine, famous for its many artist and student inhabitants.

left-hand (left′hand′) *adj.* **1** Situated on the left side; sinistral. **2** Turning, opening, or swinging to the left.

left-hand·ed (left′han′did) *adj.* **1** Having the left hand or arm stronger or more dexterous than the right. **2** Done with the left hand; turning or moving from right to left or oppositely to the motion of the hands of a clock: a *left-handed* screw. **3** Adapted for use by the left hand, as a tool. **4** Clumsy; awkward. **5** Without sincerity; indirect: a *left-handed* compliment. **6** Morganatic: from the giving to the bride of the left hand instead of the right by the bridegroom in a morganatic marriage. — **left′-hand′ed·ly** *adv.* — **left′-hand′·ed·ness** *n.*

left-hand·er (left′han′dər) *n.* **1** One who is left-handed. **2** A left-handed blow.

left·ism (lef′tiz·əm) *n.* The advocacy of radical or ultraliberal policies. — **left′ist** *n.* & *adj.*

left·o·ver (left′ō′vər) *n.* A part not used or consumed. — *adj.* Remaining unconsumed.

left wing **1** A political party or group advocating radical or liberal politics. **2** That part of any group advocating radical liberal policies. Also **Left Wing.** — **left′-wing′** *adj.* — **left′-wing′er** *n.*

left·y (lef′tē) *n. Slang* A left-handed person: especially applied to a baseball pitcher or batter.

leg (leg) *n.* **1** A limb of an animal used for supporting the body and for walking; especially, in man, the part of the lower limb between knee and ankle. ◆ Collateral adjective: *crural.* **2** Something that resembles a leg: the *leg* of a table, etc. **3** Hence, anything that gives support. **4** That portion of a garment or stocking which covers the leg. **5** *Naut.* The distance run by a vessel on one tack. **6** Any appreciable section of a journey. **7** That portion of a cricket field which would be included between an imaginary line drawn at right angles from the batsman's left leg to the boundary and a line drawn from the batsman's middle wicket to the boundary. **8** *Archaic* An obeisance. — **a leg to stand on** A tenable or logical basis for argument. — **to pull one's leg** *Slang* To fool or make fun of someone. — **on one's last legs** On the verge of death or collapse. — **to shake a leg** *Slang* To make haste; hurry. — *v.i.* **legged, leg·ging** *Colloq.* To walk; run: often with *it.* [<ON *leggr*]

leg·a·cy (leg′ə·sē) *n. pl.* **·cies** **1** Something left by will; a bequest. **2** Hence, anything, as a characteristic, derived from an ancestor. [<OF *legacie,* orig. a legateship <Med. L *legatia* the district of a legate <L *legatus.* See LEGATE.]

le·gal (lē′gəl) *adj.* **1** Created or permitted by law. **2** Of, pertaining to, or connected with law: the *legal* mind. **3** In conformity with law; lawful: a *legal* rate of interest. **4** Capable of being remedied by a resort to law, as distinguished from equity. **5** Characteristic of those who practice law: He has a *legal* approach to all situations. **6** *Theol.* **a** Relating to or founded upon the Mosaic law. **b** Pertaining to the doctrine of salvation by works rather than by grace. — *n. pl.* Investments legally open to trustees, fiduciaries, etc. [< OF *legal* <L *legalis* < *lex, legis* law. Doublet of LOYAL.]

legal cap Ruled writing paper, about 8 1/2 x 13 inches, made up in pads gummed at the top for lawyers' use.

le·ga·lis ho·mo (li·gā′lis hō′mō) *Latin* A lawful or legal person.

le·gal·ism (lē′gəl·iz′əm) *n.* **1** Close adherence to law; strict conformity to law. **2** *Theol.* The doctrine of salvation by works, as distinguished from that by grace. **3** The tendency to observe the letter rather than the spirit of the law. — **le′gal·ist** *n.* — **le′gal·is′tic** *adj.*

le·gal·i·ty (li·gal′ə·tē) *n. pl.* **·ties 1** The condition of being legal. **2** The distinctive spirit of the legal profession. **3** Adherence or conformity to law.

le·gal·ize (lē′gəl·īz) *v.t.* **·ized, ·iz·ing** To make legal; sanction. Also *Brit.* **le′gal·ise.** — **le′gal·i·za′tion** (-ə·zā′shən, -ī·sā′-) *n.*

Le Gal·lienne (lə gal′yən, gal·yen′), **Richard,** 1866–1947, English poet and journalist. — **Eva,** born 1899, U. S. actress; daughter of the preceding.

legal memory *Law* The period through which things past are accepted in law as definitely affecting present rights or principles.

legal separation *Law* See A MENSA ET THORO.

legal tender Coin or other money that may legally be offered in payment of a debt, and that may not be refused by a creditor.

leg·ate (leg′it) *n.* **1** A person accredited by one state or nation as its diplomatic representative to the court or government of another state or nation; an ambassador; envoy. **2** A representative of the pope in various functions, political or ecclesiastical. **3** In ancient Roman history: **a** An ambassador sent from ancient Rome to a foreign nation, or one sent by a foreign nation to Rome. **b** A person accompanying a Roman general into the field as adviser, or a subordinate in command. **c** A governor of a province **4** A district governed by a legate; specifically, formerly one of the six provinces of the Romagna. See synonyms under DELEGATE. [<OF *legat* <L *legatus,* pp. of *legare* send as a deputy, bequeath] — **leg′ate·ship** *n.* — **leg′a·tine** (-tin, -tīn), **leg·an·tine** (-ən·tin, -tīn) *adj.*

leg·a·tee (leg′ə·tē′) *n.* The recipient of a legacy. [< *legate, v.* bequeath <L *legatus,* pp. of *legare* bequeath]

le·ga·tion (li·gā′shən) *n.* **1** The act of deputing or delegating. **2** A diplomatic mission, or the persons composing it. **3** The official residence or place of business of the chief of a diplomatic mission. **4** The office or rank of a legate. [<L *legatio, -onis* < *legare* send]

le·ga·to (li·gä′tō) *adj.* & *adv. Music* In a smooth, connected manner: opposed to *staccato.* [<Ital., lit., bound, pp. of *legare* bind <L *ligare*]

le·ga·tor (li·gā′tər, leg′ə·tôr′) *n.* One who makes a will; a testator. [<L < *legatus,* pp. of *legare* bequeath]

leg–by (leg′bī′) *n.* In cricket, a run made upon a ball which glances off the batsman's body (exclusive of the hand or wrist). Also **leg′–bye′.**

leg·end (lej′ənd) *n.* **1** An unauthenticated story from early times, preserved by tradition and popularly thought to be historical. **2** Such narratives, collectively. **3** A chronicle of the life of a saint, originally to be read aloud in religious services or at meals. **4** Loosely, the fame of a person or place: the Woodrow Wilson *legend.* **5** An inscription or motto on a coin or monument. **6** A caption for an illustration; an explanatory description or key to a map or chart. **7** *Music* A composition intended to describe or relate a story, without words. See synonyms under FICTION.— **local legend** A story, current in a definite region, which explains some local custom, geographical feature, name, etc., as of lovers' leaps, outlaws, haunted places, buried treasure, etc. [<OF *legende* <Med. L *legenda* things read, neut. pl. of L *legendus* to be read, gerundive of *legere* read]

leg·en·dar·y (lej′ən·der′ē) *adj.* **1** Of or pertaining to a legend. **2** Quasi–historical or traditional. **3** Celebrated in or known from legends.

Le·gen·da Au·re·a (li·jen′də ô′rē·ə) The Golden Legend.

Le·gen·dre (lə·zhäṅ′dr′), **Adrien Marie,** 1752–1833, French mathematician.

leg·er (lej′ər) See LEDGER[2].

Lé·ger (lā·zhā′), **Fernand,** 1881–1955, French painter.

leger bait, etc. See LEDGER BAIT, etc.

leg·er·de·main (lej′ər·də·mān′) *n.* **1** Sleight of hand. **2** Any deceptive adroitness; any artful trick. [<F *léger de main,* lit., light of hand < *léger* light (<L *levis*) + *de* of (<L, from) + *main* hand <L *manus*] — **leg′er·de·main′ist** *n.*

leger lines Short lines added above or below a musical staff to increase its range. [< *leger,* var. of LEDGER[1] + *lines,* pl. of LINE]

le·ges (lē′jēz) Plural of LEX.

leg·ged (leg′id, legd) *adj.* Having a specified kind or number of legs: usually in combination: *bow–legged, two–legged,* etc.

leg·ging (leg′ing) *n. Usually pl.* A covering for the leg; long gaiter.

leg·gy (leg′ē) *adj.* **·gi·er, ·gi·est** Having disproportionately long or conspicuous legs.

leg·horn[1] (leg′ərn, -hôrn) *n.* **1** A fine plait of leghorn straw, used for making bonnets and hats. **2** A bonnet or hat made of this plait. — *adj.* Made of leghorn straw. [from *Leghorn*]

leg·horn[2] (leg′hôrn, leg′ərn) *n.* A hardy Mediterranean breed of domestic fowls. [from *Leghorn*]

Leg·horn (leg′hôrn) A port on the Ligurian Sea, central Italy: Italian *Livorno.*

leghorn straw The straw of a variety of wheat (*Triticum aestivum*) or of spelt.

leg·i·ble (lej′ə·bəl) *adj.* **1** That can be deciphered or read with ease. **2** That can be discovered or discerned from evident indications. [<LL *legibilis* <L *legere* read] — **leg′i·bil′i·ty, leg′i·ble·ness** *n.* — **leg′i·bly** *adv.*

le·gion (lē′jən) *n.* **1** A division of the ancient Roman army, consisting of ten cohorts of infantry, with an auxiliary force of 300 cavalry: altogether between 4,200 and 6,000 men. **2** One of various other military organizations of other countries. **3** *pl.* Military force. **4** A great number; multitude. **5** *Zool.* A taxonomic category, no longer used. [<OF *legiun* <L *legio -onis* < *legere* choose, levy an army]

le·gion·ar·y (lē′jən·er′ē) *adj.* **1** Pertaining to a legion. **2** Innumerable. — *n. pl.* **·ar·ies** A soldier of a legion.

legionary ant See DRIVER ANT.

le·gion·naire (lē′jən·âr′) *n.* **1** A legionary. **2** A member of the American Legion. Also *Fr.* **lé·gion·naire** (lā·zhə·nâr′). [<F *légionnaire* < *légion* (<OF *legiun* LEGION) + *-aire* -ARY]

Legion of Honor An order of merit instituted by Napoleon in 1802 as a reward for civil and military services.

Legion of Merit A decoration established in 1942 and awarded to personnel of the armed forces of the United States and its allies who have distinguished themselves by exceptionally meritorious conduct and fidelity.

leg·is·late (lej′is·lāt) *v.* **·lat·ed, ·lat·ing** *v.i.* To make a law or laws. — *v.t.* To bring about or effect by legislation. [Back formation < LEGISLATOR]

leg·is·la·tion (lej′is·lā′shən) *n.* **1** Enactment of laws, or business incidental thereto. **2** The laws enacted by a legislative power. [<LL *legislatio, -onis* < *legis,* genitive of *lex* a law + *latio, -onis* a bringing, proposing < *latus,* pp. to *ferre* bring]

Synonyms: code, economy, jurisprudence, law, polity. A *code* is a system of *laws*; *jurisprudence* is the science of *law,* or a system of *laws* scientifically considered, classed, and interpreted; *legislation,* primarily the act of legislating, denotes also the body of statutes enacted by a legislative body; an *economy* is a body of *laws* and regulations, with the entire system, political or religious, especially the latter, of which they form a part; as, the *code* of Draco, Roman *jurisprudence,* British *legislation,* the Mosaic *economy.* The Mosaic *economy* is known also as the Mosaic *law,* and we speak of the English common *law,* or the *law* of nations. *Polity* differs from *economy* as applying to the system itself, while *economy* applies to the method of administration or to the system as administered. See LAW[1].

leg·is·la·tive (lej′is·lā′tiv) *adj.* **1** Having the power to legislate; that makes or enacts laws: distinguished from *administrative* and *judicial.* **2** Of, pertaining to, or suitable to legislation. **3** Of or pertaining to a legislature. — *n.* The law–making power in government. — **leg′is·la′tive·ly** *adv.*

leg·is·la·tor (lej′is·lā′tər) *n.* **1** One who legislates; a lawgiver. **2** A member of a legislature. [L, proposer of a law < *lex, legis* a law + *lator* < *latus,* pp. to *ferre* bring] — **leg·is·la·to·ri·al** (lej′is·lə·tôr′ē·əl, -tō′rē-) *adj.* — **leg′is·la′tress** (-tris), **leg′is·la′trix** (-triks) *n. fem.*

leg·is·la·ture (lej′is·lā′chər) *n.* A body of men empowered to make laws for a country or state; the legislative body of a state or territory. See CONGRESS.

le·git·i·mate (lə·jit′ə·mit) *adj.* **1** Having the sanction of law or custom; authorized; lawful; also, genuine. **2** Born in wedlock. **3** Based strictly on hereditary rights or sovereignty. **4** Following in regular or natural sequence; logically deduced. See synonyms under AUTHENTIC. — *v.t.* (lə·jit′ə·māt) **·mat·ed, ·mat·ing 1** To make legitimate. **2** To justify. [<Med. L *legitimatus,* pp. of *legitimare* declare to be lawful <L *legitimus* lawful < *lex, legis* a law] — **le·git′i·ma·cy, le·git′i·mate·ness** *n.* — **le·git′i·mate·ly** *adv.* — **le·git′i·ma′tion** *n.*

legitimate drama 1 Any drama spoken and acted on the stage: opposed to motion pictures, television, etc. **2** Formerly, drama conforming to certain literary and dramatic principles; not burlesque or melodrama.

le·git·i·mist (lə·jit′ə·mist) *n.* One who supports legitimate authority or supports a certain authority as legitimate; specifically, in France, a supporter of the claims of the elder branch of the Bourbon family. Also **le·git′i·ma·tist.** [<F *légitimiste* < *légitime* legitimate <L *legitimus.* See LEGITIMATE.] — **le·git′i·mism** *n.*

le·git·i·mize (lə·jit′ə·mīz) *v.t.* **·mized, ·miz·ing 1** To make legitimate. **2** To make acceptable or tolerable: to assert that some TV programs *legitimize* violence. Also **le·git′i·ma·tize.** — **le·git′i·mi·za′tion** *n.*

leg·len (leg′lən) *n. Scot.* A milk pail.

leg·less (leg′lis) *adj.* Having no legs.

leg·man (leg′man′) *n. pl.* **·men** (-men′) **1** A reporter who collects data for a news story outside the editorial offices, as from interviews, obtaining official statements and documents, etc. **2** An office assistant or subordinate employed to do various errands.

leg–of–mut·ton (leg′ə·mut′n) *adj.* Shaped like a leg of mutton, as a sail or sleeve.

Le·gree (lə·grē′), **Simon** See SIMON LEGREE.

leg·ume (leg′yo͞om, lə·gyo͞om′) *n.* **1** The fruit or seed of any leguminous plant, as peas and beans. **2** A one–celled, two–valved seed vessel formed of a single dehiscent carpel having the seeds arranged along the inner or ventral suture. [<F *légume* <L *legumen,* lit., a gatherable thing < *legere* gather]

le·gu·min (lə·gyo͞o′min) *n. Biochem.* A globulin present in peas and other leguminous seeds. [<LEGUM(E) + -IN]

le·gu·mi·nous (lə·gyo͞o′mə·nəs) *adj.* **1** Of or pertaining to legumes, or to a large, widely distributed family (*Leguminosae*) of plants, the pea or bean family, bearing legumes. **2** Producing legumes. Also **le·gu′mi·nose** (-nōs). [<L *legumen, -inis* a legume + -OUS]

leg·work (leg′wûrk′) *n. Colloq.* The physical activity incidental to doing research.

Leh (lā) The capital of Ladakh, Kashmir.

Le Ha·vre (lə ä′vr′) See HAVRE, LE.

Le·hár (lā′här), **Franz,** 1870–1948, Austrian composer of operettas.

Le·high River (lē′hī) A river in eastern Pennsylvania, flowing 100 miles south and east to the Delaware River.

Leh·man (lē′mən, lā′-), **Herbert Henry,** 1878–1963, U.S. banker and statesman.

Leh·man Caves National Monument (lē′·mən) An area of subterranean chambers and tunnels in the Snake Mountains, eastern Nevada; 640 acres; established as a national monument in 1922.

Leh·mann (lā′mən, *Ger.* lā′män), **Lotte,** born 1888, German soprano. — **Rosamond,** born 1904?, English novelist.

Lehm·bruck (lām′bro͝ok), **Wilhelm,** 1881–1919, German sculptor.

lehr (lâr) See LEER[2].

le·hu·a (lā·ho͞o′ä) *n.* **1** A tree (*Metrosideros tremuloides*) of the myrtle family, native in the Pacific Islands, having vivid red flowers and a hard wood. **2** The blossom of this tree. **3** Its wood. [<Hawaiian]

lei[1] (lā, lā′ē) *n.* In the Hawaiian Islands, a garland or wreath of showy flowers and leaves, as hibiscus blossoms, or of feathers: usually worn around the neck or as an ornamental headdress. [<Hawaiian]

lei[2] (lā) Plural of LEU.

Leib·nitz (līp′nits), **Baron Gottfried Wilhelm von,** 1646–1716, German philosopher and mathematician. Also **Leib′niz.** —**Leib·nitz′·i·an** *adj.* & *n.*

Leices·ter (les′tər) *n.* A variety of long-wooled sheep originally developed in Leicester.

Leices·ter (les′tər) A county in central England; 832 square miles: county town, Leicester. Also **Leices′ter·shire** (-shir).

Leices·ter (les′tər), **Earl of,** 1533–88, Robert Dudley, politician and general; favorite of Queen Elizabeth I.

Lei·den (līd′n) See LEYDEN.

Leif Ericson See ERICSON.

Leigh·ton (lā′tən), **Lord Frederick,** 1830–96, English painter.

Lein·ster (len′stər) A province of SE Ireland on the Irish Sea; 7,580 square miles.

lei·ot·ri·chous (lī·ot′rə·kəs) *adj.* Lissotrichous. [<NL *Leiotrichi* the smooth-haired (division of mankind) <Gk. *leios* smooth + *thrix, trichos* hair]

Leip·zig (līp′sik, -sig; *Ger.* līp′tsikh) A city in the former state of Saxony, southern East Germany.

leish·man·i·a·sis (līsh′mən·ī′ə·sis) *n. Pathol.* Any disease caused by parasitic protozoans of the genus *Leishmania,* especially the tropical disease kala-azar. Also **leish′man·i′o·sis.** [after Sir William B. *Leishman,* 1865–1926, English army surgeon]

leis·ter (lēs′tər) *n.* A three-pronged fishing spear. —*v.t.* To spear with a leister. [<ON *liōstr* < *liōsta* strike] —**leis′ter·er** *n.*

lei·sure (lē′zhər, lezh′ər) *n.* **1** Freedom from the demands of work or duty. **2** Spare time; time available for some particular purpose. —*adj.* **1** Free or unoccupied. **2** Having leisure: the *leisure* class. [<OF *leisir* be permitted <L *licere*]

lei·sure·ly (lē′zhər·lē, lezh′ər-) *adj.* Done at leisure; deliberate; slow. —*adv.* At leisure; deliberately. —**lei′sure·li·ness** *n.*

Leith (lēth) A port on the Firth of Forth in SE Scotland; incorporated since 1920 in the city of Edinburgh.

Leith·a (lī′tä) A river in eastern Austria and NW Hungary, flowing 112 miles north and east to the Danube.

leit·mo·tif (līt′mō·tēf′) *n. Music* A representative theme used to indicate a certain person, attribute, or idea, in an opera or other composition. Also **leit′mo·tiv** (-tēf′). [<G *leitmotiv* < *leiten* lead + *motiv* <Med. L *motivus.* See MOTIVE.]

Lei·trim (lē′trim) A county of NE Connacht province, Ireland; 589 square miles; county town Carrick-on-Shannon.

Leix (lāks) See LAOIGHIS.

Lek (lek) The northern branch of the Rhine delta in central Netherlands.

Le·ly (lē′lē), **Sir Peter,** 1618–80, Dutch painter born in Germany and active in England.

Le·maî·tre (lə·me′tr′), **François Élie Jules,** 1853–1914, French critic. —**Abbé Georges Edouard,** born 1894, Belgian physicist and astronomer.

lem·an (lem′ən, lē′mən) *n. Archaic* A sweetheart of either sex; especially, a mistress. Also **lem′man.** [ME *lemman, leofmon* <OE *leof* beloved + *mann* a man]

Le·man (lē′mən), **Lake** The Lake of Geneva. *French* **Lac Le·man** (läk lä·män′).

Le Mans (lə mäṅ′) A city in NW France.

Le Mans start In automobile racing, a method of starting contestants by lining the cars diagonally on one side of the track, the drivers standing on the other; at a signal the drivers run to their cars, start them, and proceed onto the track. [from *Le Mans;* because traditionally used at an annual automobile race held there]

Lem·berg (lem′berkh) The German name for Lvov.

lem·ma[1] (lem′ə) *n. pl.* **lem·mas** or **lem·ma·ta** (lem′ə·tə) **1** A subject or theme assumed for treatment, as in verse. **2** *Logic* **a** A subsidiary proposition employed as auxiliary in demonstrating another one. **b** A proposition assumed to be true. [<L <Gk. *lēmma* something taken, a premise < *lēmm-,* stem of *lambanein* take]

lem·ma[2] (lem′ə) *n. Bot.* A small, chaffy bract inside and above the glumes in a spikelet of grass. [<Gk. *lemma* a husk < *lepein* peel]

lem·ming (lem′ing) *n.* Any of several small arctic rodents (genera *Lemmus, Dicrostonyx,* and *Myopus*) with a short tail and furry feet. One European species is noted for recurrent migrations in vast numbers, often terminated by drowning in the ocean. [<Norw.]

LEMMING
(About 4 inches long)

Lem·ni·an (lem′nē·ən) *adj.* Of or pertaining to Lemnos. —*n.* A native or inhabitant of Lemnos.

Lemnian bole A white or grayish-yellow variety of aluminous earth. Also **Lemnian earth.**

Lemnian smith Hephaestus, whose forge was said to be in the volcanic regions of Lemnos.

Lem·nos (lem′nəs) A Greek island in the NE Aegean Sea; 184 square miles: also *Limnos.*

lem·nis·cate (lem′nis·kāt, -kit) *n. Math.* The plane curve in the shape of a figure eight traced by the foot of a perpendicular drawn from the origin to a tangent to a rectangular hyperbola: the locus of the vertex of a triangle when the product of the two adjacent sides is maintained equal to 1/4 of the fixed, opposite side. Also called **Bernoulli's lemniscate.** [<NL *lemniscata,* orig. fem. of L *lemniscatus* adorned with ribbons < *lemniscus.* See LEMNISCUS.]

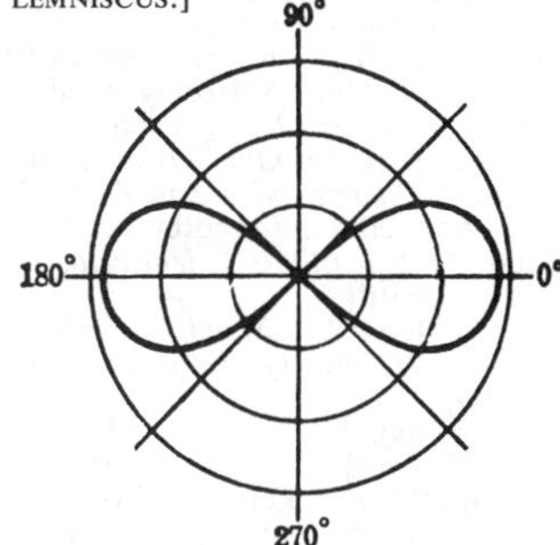

LEMNISCATE
A symmetrical tracing in polar coordinates.

lem·nis·cus (lem·nis′kəs) *n. pl.* **·nis·ci** (-nis′ī) **1** *Anat.* A bundle or fillet of nerve fibers in the medulla and pons. **2** *Zool.* One of a pair of club-shaped organs at the base of the proboscis of certain parasitic worms (class *Acanthocephala*). [<NL <L, a ribbon <Gk. *lēmniskos*]

lem·on (lem′ən) *n.* **1** An oval citrus fruit with a bright-yellow skin containing the essential **oil of lemon,** and very acid pulp and juice. **2** The small or medium-sized evergreen tree (*Citrus medica* and *C. lemon*) of the rue family that produces this fruit. **3** The color of the rind of lemon; bright yellow. **4** *U. S. Slang* Something disappointing, worthless. or unpleasant. —*adj.* **1** Flavored with or containing lemon: *lemon* pie. **2** Lemon-colored. [<OF *limon* <Sp. *limón* <Arabic *laimūn* <Persian *līmūn.* Related to LIME[2].]

lem·on·ade (lem′ən·ād′) *n.* A drink made of lemon juice, water, and sugar. [<F *limonade* < *limon* LEMON]

lemon geranium A common garden flower (*Pelargonium limoneum*) related to the geranium, having the odor of lemons.

lemon grass An Old World tropical grass (*Cymbopogon citratus*) whose leaves yield an oil used as a flavoring and in perfumery.

lemon squash *Brit.* Lemonade.

lemon verbena A tropical American shrub (*Lippia citriodora*) with white flowers and lanceolate leaves having an odor of lemon.

lem·on·wood (lem′ən·wŏŏd′) *n.* **1** The yellowish-white, tough, flexible wood of a Central American tree (*Calycophyllum candidissimum*), used for fishing rods, bow staves, etc. **2** The tree itself. Also called *degame.*

lemon yellow **1** A pigment consisting of a mixture of barium and chromic acid ground in water or oil. **2** Lead chromate.

lem·pi·ra (lem·pē′rä) *n.* The gold monetary unit of Honduras. [<Am. Sp., after *Lempira,* an Indian chief who fought the Spanish]

Lem·u·el (lem′yŏŏ·əl) A masculine personal name. [<Hebrew, belonging to God]

le·mur (lē′mər) *n.* A small, arboreal, mostly nocturnal mammal with fox-like face and soft fur, found chiefly in Madagascar, related to the monkeys, and belonging to a class or sub-order (*Lemuroidea*) which, with the *Tarsioidea,* is believed to represent the ancestral primate form. [<NL <L *lemures* ghosts; with ref. to their nocturnal habits]

RING-TAILED LEMUR
(About 2 feet long; tail: 2 feet)

lem·u·res (lem′yŏŏ·rēz) *n. pl.* In Roman religion, the shades or spirits of the dead; ghosts; specters. On the ninth of May a festival, the **Le·mu·ri·a** (lə·myŏŏr′ē·ə), was held to appease these departed spirits. [<L]

Le·mu·ri·a (lə·myŏŏr′ē·ə) A hypothetical continent, supposedly submerged beneath the Indian Ocean, thought by E. Haeckel to be the original home of lemuroid primates.

lem·u·roid (lem′yŏŏ·roid) *adj.* Of or pertaining to the lemurs. —*n.* A lemur. Also **lem′u·rine** (-rīn, -rin).

Le·na (lē′nə) Diminutive of HELEN and of MAGDALENE.

Le·na (lē′nə, *Russian* lyā′nə) The easternmost and longest river of Siberian Russian S.F.S.R., flowing 2,648 miles north to the Laptev Sea.

Len·a·pe (len′ə·pē) *n.* The generic name of the Algonquian tribes in Pennsylvania, New Jersey, and vicinity; the Delawares: also called *Leni-Lenape, Lenni-Lenape.* [Short for Algonquian (Lenape) *Leni-lenape,* lit., a real man < *leni* real + *lenape* a man]

Le·nard rays (lā′närt) *Physics* Cathode rays that stream into the atmosphere through a metallic window of a vacuum tube known as a **Lenard tube** or a Coolidge cathode-ray tube. [after Philipp von *Lenard,* 1862–1947, German physicist]

Le·nau (lā′nou), **Nikolaus,** 1802–1850, pseudonym of *Nikolaus Niembsch von Strehlenau,* Austrian lyric poet.

Len·clos (läṅ·klō′), **Ninon de,** 1620–1705, French beauty and wit: real name *Anne L'Enclos.*

lend (lend) *v.* **lent, lend·ing** *v.t.* **1** To grant the temporary use of without further compensation than the understanding that the thing or its equivalent will be returned. **2** To grant the temporary use of, as money, for a compensation. **3** To impart; furnish: The thought *lends* beauty to the poem. **4** To accommodate (oneself or itself): The statement *lends* itself to interpretation. —*v.i.* **5** To make a loan or loans. —**to lend a hand** To give assistance. —**to lend an ear** To hearken. [OE *lǣnan* < *lǣn* a loan. Akin to LOAN.] —**lend′er** *n.*

lend-lease (lend′lēs′) *n.* In World War II, the furnishing of goods and services to any country whose defense was deemed vital to the defense of the United States, under the terms of the **Lend-Lease Act** passed by Congress March 11, 1941.

le·net·ic (lə·net′ik) *adj. Ecol.* Of, pertaining to, or designating plant or animal communities inhabiting still waters. Also **le·nit′ic** (-nit′-). [<L *lenis* smooth]

L'En·fant (läṅ·fäṅ′), **Pierre Charles,** 1754–1825, French architect; planned the city of Washington, D.C.

length (lengkth) *n.* **1** Extension from end to end; hence, usually, the greatest dimension of a surface or body, as distinguished from *breadth* or *width.* **2** Distance measured along a line from end to end. **3** The state of being long. **4** Extent in point of time. **5** A specific or understood distance; a thing of known extent: a boat's *length.* **6** Power of extension; reach; extent; the distance reached or that may be reached. **7** In classical prosody, quantity. **8** *Phonet.* **a** The period required for the pronunciation of a vowel. **b** The quality of a vowel. —**at length** **1** After an interval of expectation; finally; at last. **2** At full length; without omission or contraction. [OE *lengthu* < *lang* long]

length·en (lengk′thən) *v.t.* & *v.i.* To make or become longer. See synonyms under PROTRACT, STRETCH.

length·wise (lengkth′wīz′) *adv.* In a longitudinal direction. Also **length′ways′** (-wāz′).

length·y (lengk′thē) *adj.* **length·i·er, length·i·est** Having length; unduly long. —**length′i·ly** *adv.* —**length′i·ness** *n.*

le·ni·ent (lē′nē·ənt, lēn′yənt) *adj.* **1** Of merciful disposition; gentle; mild; indulgent. **2** *Archaic* Soothing; emollient. See synonyms under CHARITABLE. [<L *leniens, -entis,* ppr. of *lenire* soothe < *lenis* soft, mild] —**le′ni·en·cy, le′ni·ence** *n.* —**le′ni·ent·ly** *adv.*

Len·i–Len·a·pe (len′ē·len′ə·pē), **Len·ni–Len·a·pe** See LENAPE.

Le·nin (len′in, *Russian* lye′nyin), **Nikolai,** 1870–1924, Russian revolutionary; leader of Bolshevik party; chief leader of the Russian Revolution and head of the Soviet government 1917–24: real name *Vladimir Ilyich Ulianov.*

Le·ni·na·kan The former name of Gyumri, a city in NW Armenia; pop. 163,00; formerly **Aleksandropol.**

Le·nin·grad The former name of Saint Petersburg, a city in NW Russia on the Gulf of Finland; capital of the Russian Empire, 1712–1917; the name has been changed through history: **Saint Petersburg** (1703–1914; 1993–), **Petrograd** (1914–1924). **Leningrad** (1924–1993).

Lenin Peak A mountain on the Kirghiz–Tadzhik border, the second highest in the Soviet Union; 23,382 feet.

le·nis (lē′nis) *adj. Phonet.* Weakly articulated, with little or no aspiration: said especially of stop consonants, and opposed to *fortis.* —*n. pl.* **le·nes** (lē′nēz) **1** A lenis consonant. **2** In Greek grammar, the smooth breathing *(spiritus lenis).* Also **le·ne** (lē′nē). [<L, smooth, soft]

len·i·tive (len′ə·tiv) *adj.* Having the power or tendency to allay pain or mitigate suffering. —*n.* That which soothes or mitigates; an aperient medicine; a laxative. [<Med. L *lenitivus* <L *lenitus,* pp. of *lenire* soothe]

len·i·ty (len′ə·tē) *n.* The state or quality of being lenient. [<OF *lenité* <L *lenitas, -tatis* softness < *lenis* soft]

le·no (lē′nō) *n.* **1** A type of weave with paired and twisted warp yarns. **2** A loose, open fabric of such a weave. [<F *linon* < *lin* flax]

Le·no·ra (lə·nôr′ə, -nō′rə) See ELEANOR. Also *Ger.* **Le·no·re** (lā·nō′rə), *Fr.* **Le·noir** (lə·nwär′).

Le·nor·mant (lə·nôr·mäṅ′), **François,** 1837–1883, French scholar and archeologist.

lens (lenz) *n.* **1** A piece of glass or other transparent substance, bounded by two surfaces, of different curvature, generally spherical, or by one spherical or curved, and one plane surface, by which rays of light may be made to converge or to diverge. ◆ Collateral adjective: *lenticular.* **2** Any device for concentrating or dispersing radiation by refraction. **3** A biconvex transparent body situated behind the iris of the eye. See illustration under EYE. —**crown lens** The convex portion in an achromatic lens. [<L *lens, lentis* a lentil; so called from the similarity in form]

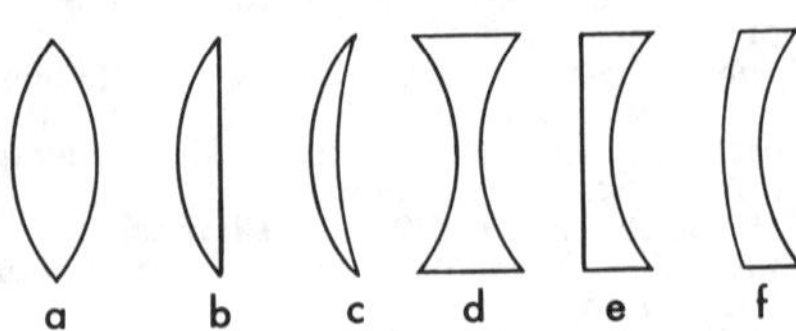

LENS

a. Convexo–convex. *d.* Concavo–concave.
b. Plano–convex. *e.* Plano–concave.
c. Convexo–concave. *f.* Concavo–convex.

lent (lent) Past tense and past participle of LEND.

Lent (lent) *n.* **1** *Eccl.* A fast of forty days (excluding Sundays), observed annually from Ash Wednesday till Easter as a season of penitence and self–denial. **2** *Obs.* In the Middle Ages, a period of fasting at any time of the year: St. Martin's *Lent,* observed from Martinmas (November 11) till Christmas. [Short for *Lenten,* OE *lencten, lengten* the spring] —**Lent′en** *adj.*

len·ta·men·te (len′tä·men′tā) *adv. Music* Slowly. [<Ital. < *lento* LENTO]

len·tan·do (len·tän′dō) *adj.* & *adv. Music* Becoming slower by degrees; rallentando. [<Ital., ppr. of *lentare* become slow < *lento* LENTO]

lent·en (len′tən) *adj.* **1** Plain; spare; meager. **2** Cold or chary. [OE *lencten* spring, Lent; with ref. to the traditional meagerness of Lenten fare]

len·ti·cel (len′tə·sel) *n. Bot.* A loose, lens–shaped mass of cells belonging to the corky layer of plants, constituting a break in the continuity of the epidermis and permitting an interchange between gases within the plant and the external air. [<F *lenticelle* <NL *lenticella,* dim. of L *lens, lentis* a lentil]

len·tic·u·lar (len·tik′yə·lər) *adj.* **1** Resembling a double–convex lens; lens–shaped. **2** Of or pertaining to a lens. **3** *Meteorol.* Designating an ovoid–shaped cloud with usually clean edges, found at all levels and characterized by a tendency to remain stationary for long intervals, despite constant evaporation. [<LL *lenticularis* < *lenticula,* dim. of L *lens, lentis* a lentil. See LENS.]

len·ti·form (len′tə·fôrm) *adj.* Lens–shaped. [<L *lens, lentis* a lentil + -FORM. See LENS.]

len·tig·i·nose (len·tij′ə·nōs) *adj.* Pertaining to lentigo; freckled; dusty. Also **len·tig′i·nous** (-nəs). [<LL *lentiginosus* <L *lentigo, -ginis* a freckle < *lens, lentis* a lentil]

len·ti·go (len·tī′gō) *n. pl.* **·tig·i·nes** (-tij′ə·nēz) **1** A freckle. **2** *Med.* A freckly condition of the skin. [<L < *lens, lentis* a lentil]

len·til (len′təl) *n.* **1** An Old World leguminous plant *(Lens culinaris)* with pale–blue flowers and broad pods containing edible seeds. **2** The seed itself. [<F *lentille* <L *lenticula,* dim. of *lens, lentis* a lentil]

len·tis·si·mo (len·tis′i·mō) *adj.* & *adv. Music* Very slow; very slowly. [<Ital., superl. of *lento* LENTO]

len·to (len′tō) *adj.* & *adv. Music* Slow; slowly. [<Ital. <L *lentus*]

len·toid (len′toid) *adj.* Lens–shaped; lenticular. [<L *lens, lentis* a lentil + -OID. See LENS.]

len·tor (len′tôr) *n.* Extreme slowness of movement or function; sluggishness: heart *lentor.* [<F *lenteur* <L *lentor* < *lentus* slow]

l'en·voi (len′voi, *Fr.* läṅ·vwȧ′) See ENVOY. Also **l'en′voy.**

Le·o (lē′ō) A masculine personal name; the appellation of thirteen popes, and six Byzantine emperors. [<L, a lion]
—**Leo I,** 390?–461, pope 440–461; defended Rome against Attila: called "Leo the Great."
—**Leo III,** 675?–741; emperor of Byzantium 717–741: called "The Isaurian."
—**Leo III,** 750?–816, pope 795–816; crowned Charlemagne as emperor; canonized.
—**Leo X,** 1475–1521, pope 1513–21: real name Giovanni de' Medici.
—**Leo XIII,** 1810–1903, pope 1878–1903: real name Gioacchino Pecci.

Le·o (lē′ō) **1** The fifth sign of the zodiac, which the sun enters about July 21. **2** A constellation containing the Sickle and the bright star Regulus. See CONSTELLATION. [<NL <L, a lion]

Le·on (lē′on) A masculine personal name. [<L, a lion]

Le·ón (lā·ôn′) **1** A region and former kingdom in NW Spain, part of an ancient kingdom; 20,504 square miles. **2** A province of NW Spain; 5,432 square miles; capital, León. **3** A city in Guanajuato state, central Mexico: officially **León de los Al·da·mas** (thā lōs äl·thä′mäs). **4** The second largest city and former capital of Nicaragua.

Leon·ard (len′ərd, *Du.* lā′ō·närt) A masculine personal name. Also *Fr.* **Lé·o·nard** (lā·ō·nȧr′), *Ital., Sp.* **Le·o·nar·do** (lā′ō·när′dō, *Sp.* -thō), *Ger.* **Le·on·hard** (lā′ōn·härt), *Lat.* **Le·o·nar·dus** (lē′ə·när′dəs). [<Gmc., strong as a lion]

Le·o·nar·desque (lē′ə·när·desk′) *adj.* Resembling or pertaining to the style of Leonardo da Vinci.

Le·o·nar·do da Vin·ci (lā′ō·när′dō dä vēn′·chē), 1452–1519, Italian painter, sculptor, architect, engineer, musician, scientist, and natural philosopher.

Le·on·ca·val·lo (lā·ôn′kä·väl′lō), **Ruggiero,** 1858–1919, Italian composer.

Le·o·nid (lē′ə·nid) *n.* One of the meteors that form a shower about November 14 in a modified form every year, but especially brilliant at intervals of approximately 33 years: their radiant point is in the constellation Leo. [<F <NL *Leo, Leonis* the constellation LEO + *-id* -ID[1]]

Le·on·i·das (lē·on′ə·dəs) A masculine personal name. [<Gk., lionlike]
—**Leonidas I,** died 480 B.C., king of Sparta, killed at Thermopylae.

le·o·nine (lē′ə·nīn, -nin) *adj.* Pertaining to or like a lion; fierce; powerful; majestic. [<OF *leonin* <L *leoninus* < *leo, leonis* a lion]

Le·o·nine (lē′ə·nīn, -nin) *adj.* **1** Belonging or relating to any of the thirteen popes named Leo. **2** Designating a medieval Latin verse, or an English verse resembling it, in which the final syllable of a line rimes with the one in the middle: so called after Leo of St. Victor, a medieval monk who used such rimes in his verse. [<L *leoninus*]

Le·o·no·ra (lē′ə·nôr′ə, -nō′rə; *Ital.* lā′ō·nō′rä) See ELEANOR. Also **Le·o·nore** (lē′ə·nôr, -nōr; *Ger.* lā′ō·nō′rə).

le·on·ti·a·sis (lē′on·tī′ə·sis) *n. Pathol.* A morbid thickening of the facial bones, giving a leonine appearance: seen in leprosy, elephantiasis, and certain other diseases. [<NL <Gk. < *leōn, leontos* a lion + -IASIS]

leop·ard (lep′ərd) *n.* **1** A ferocious, carnivorous mammal of the cat family *(Felis* or *Panthera pardus)* of Asia and Africa, of a pale fawn color, spotted with dark brown or black. A black variety, but having detectable spots, is often called a *panther.* **2** Any similar cat, such as the **American leopard** or jaguar, the **hunting leopard** or cheetah, the **snow leopard** or ounce. **3** *Her.* A lion passant gardant. **4** *Brit.* A gold coin of the reign of Edward III; a half–florin. [<OF <LL *leopardus* <Gk. *leopardos* < *leōn* a lion + *pardos* a panther] —**leop′ard·ess** *n. fem.*

LEOPARD
(About 2 1/2 feet high at the shoulder; length: 7 feet over–all)

leopard cat The American ocelot *(Felis pardalis).*

Le·o·par·di (lā′ō·pär′dē), **Count Giacomo,** 1798–1837, Italian poet.

leopard moth A European moth *(Zeuzera pyrina)* introduced into the United States; its larvae are destructive borers in trees and shrubs.

Le·o·pold (lē′ə·pōld, *Ger.* lā′ō·pōlt) A masculine personal name. Also *Fr.* **Lé·o·pold** (lā·ō·pôld′), *Ital., Sp.* **Le·o·pol·do** (*Ital.* lā′ō·pōl′dō, *Sp.* -thō), *Lat.* **Le·o·pol·dus** (lē′ə·pōl′dəs). [<Gmc., bold for the people]
—**Leopold I,** 1640–1705, Holy Roman Emperor 1658–1705.
—**Leopold I,** 1790–1865, king of the Belgians 1831–65.
—**Leopold II,** 1747–92, Holy Roman Emperor 1790–92.
—**Leopold II,** 1835–1909, king of the Belgians, 1865–1909; exploiter of the Belgian Congo.
—**Leopold III,** born 1901, king of the Belgians 1934–51; German prisoner of war 1944; exiled 1945.

Leopold II, Lake A lake in the western Belgian Congo; 900 square miles.

Le·o·pold·ville (lē′ə·pōld·vil′) A former name for KINSHASA.

le·o·tard (lē′ə·tärd) *n.* **1** A short, close–fitting, sleeveless garment, low at the neck, and fitted between the legs: worn by acrobats, etc. **2** A modern adaptation of this, having a high neck and covering the body to the wrist and ankle: used by dancers as practice clothes. [after *Léotard,* 19th c. French aerialist]

Le·pan·to (le·pän′tō) The Italian name for NAUPAKTOS; scene of a European naval victory over the Turks, 1571.

Lepanto, Gulf of The Italian name for the GULF OF CORINTH.

Lepanto, Straits of The former name for RION STRAIT.

Le·pa·ya (lye′pə·yə) See LIEPAJA.

lep·er (lep′ər) *n.* One afflicted with leprosy. [< obs. *leper* leprosy <OF *lepre, liepre* <L *lepra* <Gk., orig. fem. of *lepros* scaly < *lepos* a scale < *lepein* peel]

lepido– *combining form* Scale or flake: *lepidolite.* Also, before vowels, **lepid–.** [<Gk. *lepis, lepidos* a scale]

le·pid·o·lite (li·pid′ə·līt, lep′ə·dō·līt′) *n.* A lithium-bearing variety of mica. [<Gk. *lepis, -idos* a scale + -LITE]

lep·i·dop·ter·an (lep′ə·dop′tər·ən) *n.* Any of an order *(Lepidoptera)* of insects having four wings covered with minute scales, and undergoing a complete metamorphosis through the egg, caterpillar, pupa, and imago stages; butterflies and moths. — *adj.* Of or pertaining to the *Lepidoptera.* [<NL, order name < *lepidopteron* LEPIDOPTERON] — **lep′i·dop′ter·al, lep′i·dop′ter·ous** *adj.*

lep·i·dop·ter·on (lep′ə·dop′tər·on) *n. pl.* **·ter·a** (-tər·ə) Any lepidopterous insect; a moth or butterfly. [<NL <Gk. *lepis, -idos* a scale + *pteron* a wing]

lep·i·do·si·ren (lep′ə·dō·sī′rən) *n.* One of a genus *(Lepidosiren)* of primitive, eel-like lungfishes, as *L. paradoxa* of South America. [<LEPIDO- + SIREN (def. 3)]

lep·i·dote (lep′ə·dōt) *adj. Bot.* Scurfy with minute scales. [<NL *lepidotus* <Gk. *lepidōtos* < *lepis, lepidos* a scale]

Lep·i·dus (lep′ə·dəs), **Marcus Aemilius,** died 13 B.C., Roman triumvir with Antony and Octavian (Augustus).

Le·pon·tine Alps (li·pon′tin) The central part of the Alps between southern Switzerland and northern Italy.

lep·o·rid (lep′ə·rid) *n.* One of a family *(Leporidae)* of gnawing mammals belonging to the order *Lagomorpha* or suborder *Duplicidentata*; a rabbit or hare. — *adj.* Of or pertaining to the *Leporidae.* [<NL *Leporidae,* family name <L *lepus, leporis* a hare]

lep·o·ride (lep′ə·rid) *n.* The hybrid offspring of the European hare and rabbit; a Belgian hare. [<F *léporide* <L *lepus, leporis* a hare]

lep·o·rine (lep′ə·rīn, -rin) *adj.* Like or pertaining to hares. [<L *leporinus* < *lepus, leporis* a hare]

lep·re·chaun (lep′rə·kôn) *n.* In Irish folklore, a fairy cobbler who, if caught and held, must reveal the location of treasure. [<Irish *lupracān* <OIrish *luchorpan* < *lu* little + *corpān,* dim. of *corp* body <L *corpus, -oris*]

lep·ro·sar·i·um (lep′rə·sâr′ē·əm) *n.* A leper colony or hospital. [<NL <LEPROS(Y) + (SANIT)ARIUM]

lep·rose (lep′rōs) *adj. Bot.* Having a scurfy appearance; scalelike; leprous: usually said of crustaceous lichens. [<L *leprosus* < *lepra.* See LEPER.]

lep·ro·sy (lep′rə·sē) *n. Pathol.* A chronic, endemic, communicable disease characterized by nodular skin lesions, nerve paralysis, and physical mutilation: caused by the microorganism *Mycobacterium* or *Bacillus leprae.* Also *Hansen's disease.* [<OF *leprosie,* prob. <LL *leprosus* <L *lepra.* See LEPER.]

lep·rous (lep′rəs) *adj.* **1** Affected with leprosy; unclean. **2** Scalelike; scurfy; covered with scales; leprose. Also **lep′er·ous** (-ər·əs). [<OF *lepros, leprous* <LL *leprosus* <L *lepra.* See LEPER.] — **lep′rous·ly** *adv.* — **lep′rous·ness** *n.*

-lepsy *combining form* Seizure; attack: *catalepsy.* Also **–lepsia.** [<Gk. *lepsis* a seizure < *lambanein* seize]

lepto– *combining form Biol.* Fine; slender; small: *leptorrhine.* Also, before vowels, **lept–.** [<Gk. *leptos* slender]

lep·tome (lep′tōm) *n.* Phloem. [<Gk. *leptos* fine, delicate]

lep·ton[1] (lep′ton) *n. pl.* **·ta** (-tə) A coin of modern Greece, valued at 1/100 drachma. [<Gk. *lepton (nomisma),* lit., a small coin, neut. of *leptos* small, fine]

lep·ton[2] (lep′ton) *n. Physics* An atomic particle of very small mass as the electron, positron, neutrino, or antineutron. [<Gk., neut. of *leptos* fine]

lep·tor·rhine (lep′tə·rīn, -rin) *adj.* Having a narrow or slender nose. [<LEPTO- + Gk. *rhis, rhinos* nose]

lep·to·so·mat·ic (lep′tə·sō·mat′ik) *adj.* Denoting a person having a light, lean, narrow body.

lep·to·tene (lep′tə·tēn) *adj. Biol.* Designating a stage in cell meiosis in which the nuclear substance assumes the form of delicate threads. [<LEPTO- + Gk. *tainia* a ribbon]

Le·pus (lē′pəs) *n.* **1** The genus of mammals (family *Leporidae*) which includes most of the hares and rabbits. **2** A southern constellation, the Hare. See CONSTELLATION. [<L, a hare]

Lé·ri·da (lā′rē·thä) A city in NE Spain: ancient *Ilerda.*

Ler·mon·tov (lyer′mən·tôf), **Mikhail Yurevich,** 1814–41, Russian poet.

Ler·na (lûr′nə) A marshy district in the NE Peloponnesus.

Le·sage (lə·sȧzh′), **Alain René,** 1668–1747, French novelist and dramatist.

Les·bi·an (lez′bē·ən) *n.* **1** A native or inhabitant of Lesbos. **2** A homosexual woman: so called from the alleged homosexuality of Sappho and her followers. — *adj.* **1** Of or pertaining to Lesbos or to Lesbians. **2** *Rare* Erotic. [<L *Lesbius* <Gk. *Lesbios* <*Lesbos* Lesbos, the home of Sappho]

Les·bi·an·ism (lez′bē·ən·iz′əm) *n.* Homosexuality among women.

Les·bos (lez′bəs, -bos) A Greek island off NW Turkey; 623 square miles: also *Mytilene.*

Les Cayes (lā kā′) A port of SW Haiti: also *Aux Cayes, Cayes.*

Les·caze (les·käz′), **William,** born 1896, U.S. architect born in Switzerland.

Le·sche·tiz·ky (le′shə·tit′skē), **Teodor,** 1830–1915, Polish pianist, teacher, and composer.

lèse–ma·jes·té (lez′mȧ·zhes·tā′) *n.* In some European countries, an offense against the sovereign power; treason. In England, the term **lese–maj·es·ty** (lēz′maj′is·tē) has been replaced by *treason.* [<F <L *laesa majestas* < *laesa,* fem. of *laesus,* pp. of *laedere* injure + *majestas* MAJESTY]

Les·ghi·an (lez′gē·ən) *n.* One of a group of mountain people of Dagestan, U.S.S.R. Also spelled *Lezghian.*

le·sion (lē′zhən) *n.* **1** A hurt; loss; injury. **2** *Pathol.* Any morbid change in function or structure of an organ or tissue. [<F *lésion* <L *laesio, -onis* < *laesus,* pp. of *laedere* injure]

Le·so·tho (le·sōō′tōō, -sō′thō) An independent member of the Commonwealth of Nations consisting of an enclave in the eastern part of South Africa; 11,716 sq. mi.; capital, Maseru: formerly *Basutoland.*

less (les) Comparative of LITTLE. — *adj.* **1** Smaller; not as large or much. **2** Of slighter consequence; inferior in age, rank, etc. **3** Fewer: used with collective nouns. *Less* refers to quantity, measure, or degree; *fewer* refers to number. — *n.* **1** A smaller part or quantity. **2** The smaller (of things compared); the younger (of persons). — *adv.* In an inferior degree; not as much. — *prep.* Minus; by the subtraction or omission of: a year *less* a month, nine *less* six. [OE *lǣssa*]

-less *suffix* **1** Deprived or destitute of; without: *harmless.* **2** Beyond the range of (the action of the main element): *countless.* [OE *-leas* < *leas* free from]

Les Saintes (lā saṅt′) An island group comprising a dependency of Guadeloupe; 5 1/2 sq. mi. *French* **Îles des Saintes** (ēl dā saṅt′).

les·see (les·ē′) *n.* One to whom a lease is made; one holding property by lease. [<AF *lessee,* OF *lessé,* pp. of *lesser, laissier.* See LEASE[2].]

less·en[1] (les′ən) *v.t.* **1** To make less; decrease. **2** To make little of; disparage. — *v.i.* **3** To become less. ◆ Homophone: *lesson.* See synonyms under ABATE, ALLAY, ALLEVIATE, IMPAIR. — **less′en·er** *n.* — **less′en·ing** *adj.* & *n.*

less·en[2] (les′ən) *conj. Dial.* Unless.

Les·seps (les′əps, *Fr.* le·seps′), **Count Ferdinand de,** 1805–94, French engineer; built the Suez Canal.

less·er (les′ər) *adj.* Less; smaller; inferior.

Lesser Antilles See ANTILLES.

Lesser Bear The constellation Ursa Minor.

Lesser Dog The constellation Canis Minor.

lesser doxology See DOXOLOGY, GLORIA.

Lesser Slave Lake A lake in central Alberta, Canada; 461 square miles.

Lesser Sunda Islands An island group in the Malay Archipelago, including Bali, Lombok, Sumbawa, Sumba, Flores, Timor, and the Solor Islands, together with adjacent smaller islands, and comprising the province of Nusa Tenggara, Indonesia and Portuguese Timor; about 28,600 square miles.

Lesser Wallachia See OLTENIA.

Les·sing (les′ing), **Gotthold Ephraim,** 1729–1781, German dramatist and critic.

les·son (les′ən) *n.* **1** A specific exercise to be learned or recited at one time; task assigned by a teacher. **2** Instruction; an instance of instruction. **3** *pl.* A course of instruction. **4** A set portion of any work or writing suitable for reading at one time; a reading; specifically, a portion of Scripture read or appointed to be read in divine service. **5** Knowledge gained by experience. **6** A reprimand; lecture. See synonyms under TASK. — *v.t.* **1** To give a lesson or lessons to. **2** To rebuke; scold. ◆ Homophone: *lessen.* [<OF *lecon* <L *lectio, -onis* a reading. Doublet of LECTION.]

les·sor (les′ôr, les·ôr′) *n.* One who grants a lease or demises a property. [<AF < *lesser, laissier.* See LESSEE.]

lest (lest) *conj.* **1** In order that . . . not; so that . . . not; for fear that: We hid it *lest* he should see it. **2** That: following expressions indicating alarm or anxiety: We were worried *lest* the money run out. [OE *(thy) læs the* (by the) less that]

let[1] (let) *v.* **let, let·ting** *v.t.* **1** To allow; permit: He won't *let* her do it. **2** To allow to go, come, or pass: They would not *let* us on board. **3** To cause; make: She disliked him and *let* him know it. **4** To cause to escape or be released: to *let* blood. **5** To grant the temporary possession or occupancy of, as a room or house, for rent or other compensation: often with *out.* **6** To assign, as a contract, for performance. **7** As an auxiliary verb, *let* is used to express command or suggestion: *Let* him come. — *v.i.* **8** To be rented or leased. — **to let alone** (or **be**) To refrain from disturbing, bothering, or tampering with. See note under LEAVE. — **to let down 1** To allow to descend; lower. **2** To relax; reduce effort or concentration. **3** *Colloq.* To disappoint. — **to let fly** To hurl, as a missile. — **to let loose 1** To free; liberate. **2** *Colloq.* To act unrestrainedly. — **to let off 1** To discharge or reduce, as pressure. **2** *Colloq.* To excuse from an engagement, duty, or penalty; dismiss. — **to let on** *Colloq.* **1** To pretend. **2** To reveal; allow to be known. — **to let out 1** To release; allow to go, escape, etc. **2** To reveal; divulge. **3** To make larger by releasing a part previously fastened: to *let out* a seam. **4** *Colloq.* To dismiss or be dismissed, as a school. — **to let up** To slacken; abate. — **to let up on** *Colloq.* To reduce or cease applying pressure or harsh measures to. — **to let well enough alone** To refrain from tampering with what is regarded as unfavorable to change or already satisfactory. [OE *lætan*]

let[2] (let) *n.* **1** Anything that obstructs or hinders; an obstacle; impediment: usually in the phrase "without *let* or hindrance." **2** In tennis, rackets, fives, ping-pong, etc., a served ball which touches the net in passing over. — *v.t. Archaic* **let** or **let·ted, let·ting** To hinder or impede; obstruct. [OE *lettan,* lit., make late]

-let *suffix of nouns* **1** Small; little: *kinglet.* **2** A band or small article for: *bracelet.* [<OF *-let, -lette* < *-el* (<L *-ellus*) + *-et,* dim. suffixes]

let alone Without mentioning; to say nothing of: He can't even float, *let alone* swim.

let–down (let′doun′) *n.* **1** Abatement or slackening; decrease, as of speed or energy. **2** *Colloq.* Disillusionment; disappointment.

le·thal (lē′thəl) *adj.* **1** Causing death; deadly; fatal. **2** Pertaining to death. [<L *lethalis* < *lethum, letum* death] — **le′thal·ly** *adv.*

le·thal·i·ty (lē·thal′ə·tē) *n.* **1** The quality of being lethal. **2** The degree of destructiveness produced by the action of a bomb, warhead, or similar weapon.

le·thar·gic (li·thär′jik) *adj.* Pertaining to, resembling, or affected by lethargy; drowsy; apathetic; dull; sleepy. Also **le·thar′gi·cal.** — **le·thar′gi·cal·ly** *adv.*

leth·ar·gize (leth′ər·jīz) *v.t.* **·gized, ·giz·ing** To make lethargic.

leth·ar·gy (leth′ər·jē) *n. pl.* **·gies 1** *Pathol.* A state of morbid and prolonged sleep; stupor. **2** A state of inaction, indifference, or dulness; apathy. See synonyms under

APATHY, STUPOR. [<OF *lethargie* <LL *lethargia* <Gk. *lēthargia* < *lēthargos* forgetful < *lēthē* oblivion]

Le·the (lē′thē) **1** In Greek and Roman mythology, the river of forgetfulness, one of the five rivers surrounding Hades. **2** Oblivion; forgetfulness. [<Gk. *lēthē* oblivion] — **Le·the·an** (li·thē′ən) *adj.*

le·thif·er·ous (li·thif′ər·əs) *adj.* Deadly; lethal; fatal. [<L *lethifer* < *lethum, letum* death + *ferre* carry]

Le·ti·cia (lā·tē′syä) A town in extreme SE Colombia; capital of Amazonas commissionary; claimed by Peru but awarded to Colombia in 1934.

Le·ti·ti·a (li·tish′ē·ə, -tish′ə) A feminine personal name. Also *Ital.* **Le·ti·zi·a** (lā·tēt′sē·ä), *Lat.* **Lae·ti·ti·a** (lē·tish′ē·ə). [<L, joy]

Le·to (lē′tō) In Greek mythology, the mother by Zeus of Apollo and Artemis: identified with the Roman *Latona.*

Lett (let) *n.* **1** One of a people inhabiting Latvia and adjacent Baltic regions. **2** Lettish.

let·ter (let′ər) *n.* **1** A mark or character used to represent a sound or articulation of human speech; a character of the alphabet; a primary element of written speech; also, a type bearing such a character, or, collectively, printer's type or a style of type. **2** A school insigne of cloth to be worn on a sweater, customarily awarded by a school or college to its distinguished athletes. **3** A written or printed communication from one person to another; especially, a missive longer than a note; an epistle. **4** A document certifying a grant of authority, right, privilege, or the like, made to the person named therein: often in the plural: *letters* dimissory, *letters* patent. **5** The literal or exact meaning or requirement of the words used: the *letter* of the law. **6** *pl.* Literary culture; learning; knowledge; erudition; also, literature in the aggregate or in general: the domain of *letters.* **7** *Music* A tone, note, key, or degree designated or symbolized by a letter of the alphabet. — **man of letters** A man who follows literature as a profession; also, a man of learning; a scholar. — *v.t.* To inscribe or write with letters. [<OF *lettre* <L *littera* a letter of the alphabet, in pl., an epistle] — **let′ter·er** *n.*
Synonyms (noun): character, emblem, mark, sign, symbol, type.

let·ter·box (let′ər·boks′) *n.* A receptacle for posting letters.

let·ter–car·ri·er (let′ər·kar′ē·ər) *n.* A postman; one who carries and delivers letters.

let·ter–drop (let′ər·drop′) *n.* A small opening in a mailbox, post office, etc., through which letters are dropped.

let·tered (let′ərd) *adj.* **1** Versed in letters; learned; literary; educated. **2** Inscribed or marked with letters.

let·ter·gram (let′ər·gram) *n.* A telegraphic communication, slower than a regular telegram and sent at a reduced rate. See DAY LETTER, NIGHT LETTER. [<LETTER + (TELE)GRAM]

let·ter·head (let′ər·hed′) *n.* A printed heading at the top of a sheet of letter paper, or a sheet that bears such a heading.

let·ter–high (let′ər·hī′) *adj.* Type-high.

let·ter·ing (let′ər·ing) *n.* **1** The act, process, or business of marking or stamping with letters or of making letters. **2** Letters collectively; an inscription.

let·ter·man (let′ər·man′) *n.* *pl.* **·men** (-men′) *U.S.* An athlete to whom a letter has been awarded.

letter of advice A letter giving special information, as from a consignor to a consignee, from an agent to a principal, or from drawer to drawee of a bill of exchange.

letter of credence The document accrediting an envoy to a foreign power.

letter of credit A commercial instrument issued by a merchant or banker authorizing the bearer to draw money or obtain goods up to a certain amount from other bankers or merchants.

letter of marque A commission issued by a government authorizing a private person to take the property of a foreign state; especially, a document licensing an individual to arm a vessel and prey upon enemy merchant shipping. Also **letter of marque and reprisal.**

letter paper Paper for business or personal correspondence, usually a size of writing paper 8 1/2 x 11 or 8 x 10 inches.

let·ter–per·fect (let′ər·pûr′fikt) *adj.* **1** Having thoroughly memorized (something, as a speech, dramatic role, etc.); knowing by heart. **2** Accurate as to spelling, etc.: said of a manuscript, proof, etc.

let·ter·press (let′ər·pres′) *n.* Letters and words printed; the printed text of a book. — *adj.* Printed from type or plates with a raised surface, as distinguished from matter printed by lithography, gravure, and offset printing.

let·ter·shop (let′ər·shop′) *n.* An establishment that furnishes a service for duplicating, addressing, or mailing letters in quantity.

letters of administration *Law* A document issued by a court authorizing a certain person named therein to administer or settle the estate of one who has died without making a will.

letters patent An open document, under seal of the government, granting some special right, authority, privilege, or property, or conferring some title; especially, a document giving to the person named the exclusive right to use, make, or sell some invention.

letters testamentary *Law* A document issued to an executor of a will authorizing him to be executor.

Let·tic (let′ik) *adj.* Of or pertaining to the language of the Letts. — *n.* Lettish.

Let·tish (let′ish) *adj.* Of or pertaining to the Letts or their language. — *n.* The language of the Letts, belonging to the Baltic branch of the Balto-Slavic languages; Latvian: spoken in Latvia, Lithuania, and East Prussia.

let·tre de ca·chet (let′r′ də kȧ·she′) *French* In French history, a sealed, secret, royal letter ordering arrest and imprisonment without trial.

let·tuce (let′is) *n.* **1** A garden herb *(Lactuca sativa)* whose crisp, edible leaves are used as a salad. **2** Any of several similar plants. [<OF *laitues,* pl. of *laitue* <L *lactuca* < *lac, lactis* milk; with ref. to its milky juice]

let–up (let′up′) *n.* *Colloq.* Abatement; cessation; intermission.

le·u (lā′ōō) *n.* *pl.* **lei** (lā) A silver coin, the monetary unit of Rumania, equivalent to 100 bani. Also **ley.** [<Rumanian, lit., a lion <L *leo*]

Leu·cas (lōō′kəs) The Latin name for LEVKAS. Also **Leu·ca′di·a** (lōō·kā′dē·ə).

leu·cine (lōō′sin, -sēn) *n.* *Biochem.* A white, crystalline amino acid, $C_6H_{13}NO_2$, produced in the decomposition of proteins during pancreatic digestion. Also **leu′cin** (-sin). [<Gk. *leukos* white + -INE[2]]

leu·cite (lōō′sīt) *n.* A white potassium-aluminum silicate found in igneous rocks. [<Gk. *leukos* white + -ITE[1]]

leuco– See LEUKO-.

leu·co·crat·ic (lōō′kō·krat′ik) *adj.* *Geol.* Characterized by the predominance of light-colored minerals, as certain igneous rocks: opposed to *melanocratic.* [<LEUCO- + Gk. *krat(eein)* rule + -IC]

leu·co·cyte (lōō′kə·sīt) *n.* *Biol.* The most commonly occurring type of the white or colorless blood corpuscle: a large, nucleated ameboid cell formed in red bone marrow, constituting an important agent in protection against infectious diseases. Also *leukocyte.* [<LEUCO- + -CYTE] — **leu′co·cyt′ic** (-sit′ik) *adj.*

leu·co·ma·ine (lōō·kō′mə·ēn, -in) *n.* *Biochem.* One of various nitrogen compounds normally present in animal tissues as products of metabolism: related to uric acid and creatine, and sometimes toxic. [<LEUCO- + (PTO)MAINE]

leu·co·mel·a·nous (lōō′kō·mel′ə·nəs) *adj.* Having a light or fair complexion, with dark eyes and hair. Also **leu′co·me·lan′ic** (-mə·lan′ik). [<LEUCO- + Gk. *melas, melanos* black]

leu·co·plas·tid (lōō′kō·plas′tid) *n.* *Bot.* One of the colorless granules embedded in the protoplasmic mass of active vegetable cells, forming points about which the starch accumulates. Also **leu′co·plast.**

leu·co·poi·e·sis (lōō′kō·poi·ē′sis) *n.* *Physiol.* The production of leucocytes. [<NL <LEUCO(CYTE) + Gk. *poiēsis* a making < *poieein* make] — **leu′co·poi·et′ic** (-et′ik) *adj.*

leu·co·sin (lōō′kə·sin) *n.* *Biochem.* A simple protein found in wheat. [<Gk. *leukos* white + -IN]

leu·co·stic·te (lōō′kō·stik′tē) *n.* A fringilline bird *(Leucosticte tephrocotis littoralis),* the rosy finch of the NW United States. [<NL *Leucosticte,* genus name <Gk. *leukos* white + *stiktos* pricked]

Leuc·tra (lōōk′trə) An ancient city of Boeotia, Greece, SW of Thebes; scene of the Theban defeat of the Spartans, 371 B.C.

leud (lōōd) *n.* *pl.* **leuds** or **leu·des** (lōō′dēz) A feudal vassal in the Frankish kingdoms. [<Med. L *leudes* <OHG *liudi, liuti*]

leuk (lōōk) *v.t.* & *v.i.* *Scot.* To look.

leu·ke·mi·a (lōō·kē′mē·ə) *n.* *Pathol.* A disordered and generally fatal condition of the blood and bloodmaking tissues, characterized by a marked and persistent excess in the number of leucocytes, accompanied by hyperactivity of the lymph glands, internal hemorrhage, anemia, and exhaustion. Also **leu·kae′mi·a.** — **leu·ke′mic** *adj.*

leuko– *combining form* Whiteness; lack of color: *leukoderma*: also spelled *leuco-*. Also, before vowels, **leuk–.** [<Gk. *leukos* white]
◆ *Leuko-,* though used interchangeably with *leuco-,* is preferred for most medical and many biological terms.

leu·ko·cyte (lōō′kə·sīt) See LEUCOCYTE.

leu·ko·cy·the·mi·a (lōō′kō·sī·thē′mē·ə) *n.* Leukemia. [<NL <Gk. *leukos* white + *kytos* vessel + *haima* blood]

leu·ko·cy·to·sis (lōō′kō·sī·tō′sis) *n.* *Pathol.* An abnormal increase in the number of leucocytes in the blood. — **leu′ko·cy·tot′ic** (-tot′ik) *adj.*

leu·ko·der·ma (lōō′kō·dûr′mə) *n.* *Pathol.* Defective pigmentation of the skin, occurring in white patches. [<LEUKO- + Gk. *derma* skin] — **leu′ko·der′mic** *adj.*

leu·ko·ma (lōō·kō′mə) *n.* *Pathol.* An opaque and whitish condition of the cornea. [<NL <Gk. *leukōma* < *leukos* white]

leu·ko·pe·ni·a (lōō′kō·pē′nē·ə) *n.* *Pathol.* An abnormal reduction in the number of white blood corpuscles in the blood. [<NL <Gk. *leukos* white + *penia* poverty < *penesthai* be poor] — **leu′ko·pe′nic** *adj.*

leu·kor·rhe·a (lōō′kə·rē′ə) *n.* *Pathol.* A whitish morbid discharge from the vagina. Also **leu′cor·rhe′a, leu′cor·rhoe′a.** [<NL <Gk. *leukos* white + *rheein* flow]

Leu·pold (loi′pōlt) German form of LEOPOLD.

Leu·tze (loit′sə), **Emanuel,** 1816–68, American historical painter born in Germany.

lev (lef) *n.* *pl.* **lev·a** (lev′ə) A copper coin, the monetary unit of Bulgaria, equivalent to 100 stotinki. [<Bulgarian, lit., a lion <OSlavic *livu,* ult. <Gk. *leōn, -ontos*]

Lev·al·loi·si·an (lev′ə·loi′zē·ən) *adj.* *Anthropol.* Denoting a culture stage of the Lower Paleolithic following the Acheulean and merging with the Mousterian. [after the *Levallois* flake, a type of flint tool first found near Levallois-Perret]

Le·val·lois–Per·ret (lə·vȧ·lwȧ′pe·re′) A NW suburb of Paris, France.

le·vant[1] (lə·vant′) *n.* **1** Morocco leather from the Levant: also **Levant morocco. 2** Levanter. — *adj.* Made of Levant morocco.

le·vant[2] (lə·vant′) *v.i.* *Brit.* To decamp; abscond. [<Sp. *levantar* lift < *levar* <L *levare* raise] — **le·vant′er** *n.*

Le·vant (lə·vant′) **1** The coast of the eastern Mediterranean from western Greece to western Egypt. **2** The non-European coastlands along the eastern shore of the Mediterranean. [<F <Ital. *levante* <L *levans, -antis,* pp. of *levare* raise]

Levant dollar See under DOLLAR.

le·vant·er (lə·van′tər) *n.* An easterly gale in the Mediterranean: also called *levant.*

le·van·tine (lə·van′tin, lev′ən·tīn, -tēn) *n.* A stout, closely woven, reversible silk fabric.

Le·van·tine (lə·van′tin, lev′ən·tīn, -tēn) *adj.* **1** Pertaining to the Levant; eastern; Oriental. **2** Pertaining to the descendants of Europeans in the East. — *n.* A native or naturalized inhabitant of the Levant, especially one of European descent.

Levant States The parts of Syria under French mandate, 1920–44, comprising Syria, Lebanon, Latakia, and Jebel ed Druz.

le·va·tor (lə·vā′tər) *n.* *pl.* **le·va·to·res** (lev′ə·tôr′ēz, -tō′rēz) or **le·va·tors** **1** *Anat.* A muscle that raises an organ or part. **2** *Surg.* An instrument for lifting up the depressed part in a fracture of the skull or in trephining. [<LL, a raiser <L *levare* raise]

lev·ee[1] (lev′ē) *n.* **1** An embankment beside

a stream, to prevent overflow. 2 A steep natural bank. — *v.t.* To furnish with a levee or levees; embank. [<F *levée,* pp. fem. of *lever* raise <L *levare*]

lev·ee[2] (lev′ē, lə·vē′) *n.* 1 A morning reception or assembly at the house of a sovereign or great personage. 2 In Great Britain, a formal reception held shortly after midday by the sovereign at which only men are received. 3 A reception or promiscuous assembly of callers or guests; especially, a reception given by the president of the United States. [<F *levé,* an arising, var. of *lever* < *se lever* arise <L *levare* raise]

lev·el (lev′əl) *adj.* 1 Having a flat and even surface; without inequalities; strictly conforming to the surface of a body of still water; also, approximately flat. 2 Conforming to a horizontal plane; not sloping. 3 Being in the same line or plane with something else. 4 Equal to something or someone else in importance, rank, or degree. 5 Aimed or moving in a direct line; hence, straightforward; honest. 6 Well-balanced; having good judgment. 7 Even in tone, color, etc. 8 Denoting a surface everywhere at right angles to the line in which a force acts, so that motion upon it causes no gain or loss of energy. — **one's level best** *Colloq.* One's very best. — *n.* 1 A line or surface wholly at right angles to the vertical. 2 A horizontal line, surface, plane, or position; also, an approximately horizontal surface, as a plain. 3 The mean altitude of something: sea *level.* 4 Degree of moral, intellectual, or social elevation; rank; specifically, an equal rank: The men were on a *level* mentally. 5 The line in which anything is aimed. 6 A device for ascertaining, or for adjusting something to, a horizontal line or plane by noting the position of a bubble contained within a sealed tube of alcohol or other liquid: used by builders and surveyors, with or without a microscope. 7 Differences in altitude thus measured. 8 A section of a canal from one lock to another. — **on the level** *U.S. Colloq.* Without equivocation; in a fair, honest manner. — *v.* **lev·eled** or **lev·elled, lev·el·ing** or **lev·el·ling** *v.t.* 1 To make flat; give a flat or horizontal surface to: often with *off.* 2 To reduce to the ground; demolish; raze. 3 To bring or reduce to a common condition, state, etc. 4 To make horizontal, as with a level (def. 6). 5 To aim or direct, as a rifle, the eyes, etc. 6 To make even and uniform, as colors. 7 In surveying, to ascertain the vertical contours of (ground). — *v.i.* 8 To aim a weapon directly at a mark or target. 9 To bring persons or things to a common state or condition. — **to level off** *Aeron.* To fly a plane parallel with the ground, as before landing. — *adv.* 1 In a right or level line; direct; straight. 2 In an even manner; steadily. [<OF *livel, nivel* <L *libella,* dim. of *libra,* balance] — **lev′el·ly** *adv.* — **lev′el·ness** *n.*

Synonyms (adj.): even, flat, horizontal, plain, plane, smooth. We speak of a *horizontal* line, a *flat* morass, a *level* road, a *plain* country, a *plane* surface (especially in the scientific sense). That which is *level* may not be *even,* and that which is *even* may not be *level*; a *level* road may be very rough; a slope may be *even.* See FLAT, HORIZONTAL, SMOOTH. *Antonyms*: broken, hilly, inclined, irregular, rolling, rugged, slanting, sloping, uneven.

lev·el·er (lev′əl·ər) *n.* 1 One who or that which levels. 2 One who would destroy social distinctions; specifically, **Leveler,** a member of an English political body during the rule of Oliver Cromwell. 3 A scraping implement used in grading, or a device for leveling. Also **lev′el·ler.**

lev·el-head·ed (lev′əl·hed′id) *adj.* 1 Having sound common sense; not flighty or impulsive. 2 Steady, reliable: said of a horse. — **lev′el-head′ed·ness** *n.*

lev·el·ing (lev′əl·ing) *n.* 1 The reduction of uneven surfaces to a level. 2 The reduction of unequal ranks or conditions to a common level. 3 In surveying, the operation of ascertaining the comparative levels of different points of land, so as to lay out a grade. Also **lev′el·ling.**

leveling rod A graduated pole bearing a marker: used by surveyors to mark a level, being sighted through a leveling instrument. Also **levelling rod.**

Le·ven (lē′vən), **Loch** A lake in Kinross County, east central Scotland; 8 square miles; on an island are the ruins of **Lochleven Castle,** where Mary Queen of Scots was imprisoned.

lev·er (lev′ər, lē′vər) *n.* 1 A mechanical device, consisting of a rigid structure, often a straight bar, turning freely on a fixed point or fulcrum, and serving to impart pressure or motion from a source of power to a resistance; one of the six so-called mechanical powers. 2 Any one of various tools on the principle defined above, as a starting bar for a marine engine. 3 Any means of exerting effective power. — *v.t.* & *v.i.* To move with or use a lever. [<OF *leveour,* lit., a lifter < *lever* raise <L *levare*]

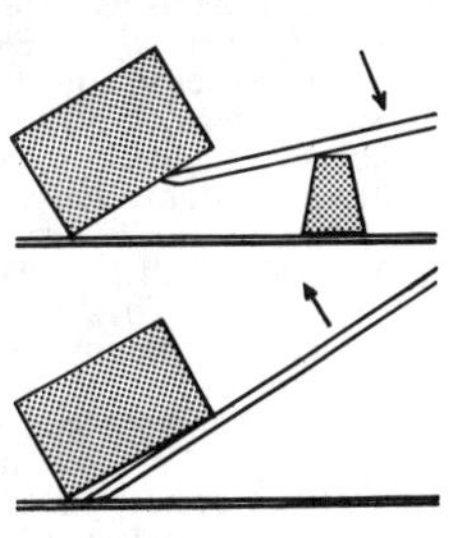

TWO PRINCIPAL TYPES OF LEVERS
Above: First class.
Below: Second class.

Le·ver (lē′vər), **Charles James,** 1806–72, Irish novelist.

lev·er·age (lev′ər·ij, lē′vər-) *n.* 1 The mechanical advantage gained by use of a lever. 2 Increased power or advantage. 3 The arrangement by which the power of a lever is controlled.

lev·er·et (lev′ər·it) *n.* A young hare; a hare less than a year old. [<AF, OF *levrete,* dim. of *levre* a hare <L *lepus, leporis*]

Le·ver·ku·sen (lā′vər·kōō′zən) A town in North Rhine–Westphalia, West Germany.

Le·ver·rier (lə·ve·ryā′), **Urbain Jean Joseph,** 1811–77, French astronomer.

Le·vi (lē′vī) A masculine personal name. — **Levi** The third son of Jacob, or the tribe descended from him. [<Hebrew, joining]

lev·i·a·ble (lev′ē·ə·bəl) *adj.* That may be levied or levied upon or seized. [<LEVY[1] + -ABLE]

le·vi·a·than (lə·vī′ə·thən) *n.* 1 A large aquatic but unidentified animal mentioned in the Scriptures: possibly a crocodile or other large reptile (*Job* xli 1), a serpent (*Isa.* xxvii 1), or a whale (*Ps.* civ 26). 2 Hence, any large animal, as a whale. 3 By extension, something huge and colossal, as a ship of unusual size. [<LL <Hebrew *liwyāthān*]

Le·vi·a·than (lə·vī′ə·thən) The title of a work by Thomas Hobbes which develops the analogy between the human body and human society and expounds the monarchic principle; hence, the political organism; the state.

lev·i·gate (lev′ə·gāt) *v.t.* **·gat·ed, ·gat·ing** 1 To reduce to a fine powder, as by grinding between hard surfaces. 2 To make a smooth paste of. — *adj.* Made smooth; polished. [<L *levigatus,* pp. of *levigare* polish < *levis* smooth + *agere* make] — **lev′i·ga′tion** *n.* — **lev′i·ga′·tor** *n.*

lev·in (lev′in) *n. Archaic* Lightning. [ME *levene,* prob. <Gmc.]

lev·i·rate (lev′ə·rāt, lē′və·rit) *n.* The ancient custom of marriage between a man and the widow of his brother, required by the Mosaic law when there was no male issue and when the two brothers had been residing on the same family estate. [<L *levir* a husband's brother + -ATE[1]] — **lev′i·rat′i·cal** (-rat′i·kəl) *adj.*

Le·vis (lē′vīz) *n. pl.* Tight-fitting, heavy denim trousers, with narrow legs and with rivets inserted at points of greatest strain: a trade name. Also **Levi Strauss·es** (strou′siz). [after *Levi* Strauss, U. S. manufacturer]

lev·i·tate (lev′ə·tāt) *v.* **·tat·ed, ·tat·ing** *v.i.* To rise and float in the air, as from lightness or buoyancy. — *v.t.* To cause to rise and float in the air. [<L *levis* light, on analogy with *gravitate*] — **lev′i·ta′tor** *n.*

lev·i·ta·tion (lev′ə·tā′shən) *n.* 1 The act of making light, or the state of being light; buoyancy, whether physical or spiritual. 2 The illusion of suspending heavy objects or the human body in the air without support.

Le·vite (lē′vīt) *n.* One of the tribe or family of Levi, especially a descendant of Levi, acting as assistant to the priests of the tribe in the services of the sanctuary. *Num.* xviii 6.

Le·vit·i·cal (lə·vit′i·kəl) *adj.* Pertaining to the Levites, to the law, or the book of Leviticus. Also **Le·vit′ic.**

Le·vit·i·cus (lə·vit′i·kəs) The third book of the Old Testament, containing ceremonial laws. [<L *Leviticus (liber)* <Gk. *Leuitikon (biblion),* lit., the Levitical (book)]

lev·i·ty (lev′ə·tē) *n.* 1 Lightness of humor or temperament; lack of mental gravity; want of seriousness or earnestness. 2 Frivolity; volatility; also, fickleness. 3 The state or quality of being light; especially, the quality of relative lightness. 4 A supposed tendency to rise in spite of gravity. [<L *levitas, -tatis* < *levis* light]

Synonyms: flightiness, frivolity, giddiness, inconstancy, lightness, thoughtlessness, vanity. *Antonyms*: earnestness, gravity, seriousness, sobriety, steadiness, thoughtfulness.

Lev·kas (lef·käs′) A Greek island, northernmost of the Ionian chain and often identified with the Homeric Ithaca; 114 square miles: Italian *Santa Maura*: Latin *Leucadia, Leucas.*

levo- *combining form* Turned or turning to the left: used especially in chemistry and physics: *levorotatory.* Also spelled *laevo-.* [<L *laevus* left]

le·vo·duc·tion (lē′vō·duk′shən) *n.* Movement toward the left: said of the eye. [<LEVO- + L *ductus,* pp. of *ducere* lead]

le·vo·ro·ta·to·ry (lē′vō·rō′tə·tôr′ē, -tō′rē) *adj. Physics* Rotating the plane of polarization from right to left: opposed to *dextrorotatory*: also called **le′vo·gy′rate** (-jī′rāt). — **le′vo·ro·ta′tion** *n.*

lev·u·lin (lev′yə·lin) *n. Biochem.* A colorless amorphous compound resembling starch. It readily decomposes into levulose. [<LEVUL-(OSE) + -IN]

lev·u·lin·ic (lev′yə·lin′ik) *adj. Chem.* Denoting an odorless, colorless acid, $C_5H_8O_3$, extracted from the nucleic acid of the thymus gland and also obtained synthetically by heating levulose and certain other sugars with concentrated hydrochloric acid.

lev·u·lose (lev′yə·lōs) *n.* Fructose. [<L *laevus* left + -UL(E) + -OSE[2]]

lev·y[1] (lev′ē) *v.* **lev·ied, lev·y·ing** *v.t.* 1 To impose and collect by authority or force, as a tax, fine, etc. 2 To enlist or call up (troops, etc.) for military service. 3 To prepare for, begin, or wage (war). — *v.i.* 4 To make a levy. 5 *Law* To seize property by judicial writ in order to fulfil a judgment: usually with *on.* — *n. pl.* **lev·ies** 1 The act of exacting or collecting by compulsion. 2 That which is levied, as money or troops. [<OF *levée,* pp. fem. of *lever* raise <L *levare*] — **lev′i·er** *n.*

lev·y[2] (lev′ē) *n. pl.* **lev·ies** The Spanish real, equal to 12 1/2 cents: once current in the United States as *elevenpence.* [Short for ELEVENPENCE]

levy in mass A levy of all men capable of military service and within the control of the power making the levy.

lev·y·ist (lev′ē·ist) *n.* One who advocates a levy on capital.

lewd (lōōd) *adj.* 1 Characterized by lust; lustful; carnal; licentious. 2 Morally depraved; vicious; wicked. 3 *Obs.* Low; unlearned. See synonyms under IMMODEST. [OE *lǣwede* lay, unlearned, ? fusion of L *laicus* LAY[2] and OE *lǣwan* betray] — **lewd′ly** *adv.* — **lewd′·ness** *n.*

Lew·es (lōō′is) The county town of East Sussex; scene of Simon de Montfort's victory over Henry III, 1264.

Lew·es (lōō′is), **George Henry,** 1817–78, English philosopher and critic.

Lew·es River (lōō′is) The upper course of the Yukon River in southern Yukon, Canada, flowing 338 miles north.

lew·is (lōō′is) *n.* A dovetailed tenon made in several parts and inserted into a corresponding mortise in a heavy stone, for the purpose of attaching a hoisting gear. Also **lew′is·son** (-ən). [? <LEWIS, proper name]

Lew·is (lōō′is) See LOUIS.

Lew·is (lōō′is), **Cecil Day,** 1904–1972, English poet. **—G(ilbert) N(ewton),** 1875–1946, U.S. chemist. **—John L(lewellyn),** 1880–1969, U.S. labor leader. **—Matthew Gregory,** 1775–1818, English novelist and dramatist: known as *Monk Lewis.* **—Meriwether,** 1774–1809, U.S. explorer. See CLARK, WILLIAM. **—(Percy) Wyndham,** 1884–1957, British painter and writer. **—Sinclair,** 1885–1951, U.S. novelist.

Lewis gun A small automatic machine-gun. [after Col. Isaac N. *Lewis,* 1858–1931, U.S. inventor]

lew·is·ite (lōō′is·īt) *n. Chem.* An oily, colorless to light-amber liquid, $C_2H_2Cl_3As$, having a faint odor of geraniums. Used in chemical warfare it combines the vesicant effects of mustard gas with the toxic action of arsenic. Also called *chlorvinylchlorarsine.* [after W. L. *Lewis,* 1878–1943, U.S. chemist]

Lew·i·sohn (lōō′ə·sən), **Adolph,** 1849–1938, U.S. philanthropist born in Germany. **— Ludwig,** 1883–1955, U.S. novelist and critic.

Lew·is·ton (lōō′is·tən) A city on the Androscoggin River in SW Maine.

Lew·is-with-Har·ris (lōō′is·with·har′is) An island, the largest and northernmost of the Outer Hebrides, Scotland; 825 square miles.

lex (leks) *n. pl.* **le·ges** (lē′jēz) Law: used in numerous Latin phrases. [<L]

lex·i·cal (lek′si·kəl) *adj.* **1** *Ling.* Relating to the meaning of the words of a language, as distinguished from their syntactical function. **2** Pertaining to a lexicon or to lexicography. [<Gk. *lexikos* pertaining to words <*lexikon* LEXICON]

lex·i·cog·ra·phy (lek′sə·kog′rə·fē) *n.* The art or process of compiling lexicons or dictionaries. [<NL *lexicografia* <Gk. *lexikographos* one who writes a lexicon <*lexikon* lexicon + *graphein* write] **—lex′i·cog′ra·pher** *n.* **—lex′i·co·graph′ic** (-kō·graf′ik) or **·i·cal** *adj.*

lex·i·con (lek′sə·kon) *n.* **1** An alphabetically arranged book setting forth the meanings and etymology of the words of a language; a dictionary: specifically applied to dictionaries of Latin, Greek, or Hebrew. **2** All the morphemes in any language. [<Gk. *lexikon,* neut. of *lexikos* pertaining to words <*lexis* way of speaking <*legein* say, speak]

Lex·ing·ton (lek′sing·tən) **1** A city in NE central Kentucky. **2** A town in eastern Massachusetts; scene of the first battle of the Revolutionary War, April 19, 1775.

lex lo·ci (leks′ lō′sī) *Latin* The law of the place.

lex non scrip·ta (leks′ non skrip′tə) *Latin* Unwritten law; the common law.

lex scrip·ta (leks′ skrip′tə) *Latin* The written or statute law.

lex ta·li·o·nis (leks′ tal′ē·ō′nis) *Latin* The law of retaliation.

Ley·den (lī′dən) A city in SW Netherlands: also *Leiden.*

Leyden jar *Electr.* A condenser for static electricity, consisting of a glass jar coated inside and out with tinfoil nearly to the top. Also **Leyden vial.** [from *Leyden,* where it was invented]

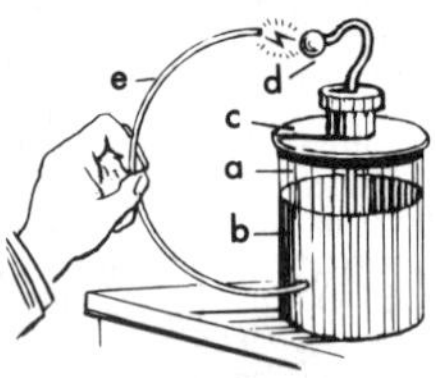

LEYDEN JAR
a. Glass jar.
b. Tinfoil.
c. Ebonite stopper.
d. Brass rod and ball.
e. Discharging wire.

Ley·te (lā′tā) An island in the Visayan Islands, Philippines; 2,785 square miles.

Leyte Gulf An inlet of the Pacific in the eastern Philippines between Leyte and Samar; scene of a United States naval victory over Japanese forces in World War II, October, 1944.

Ley·ton (lāt′n) A municipal borough in SW Essex county, England.

Lez·ghi·an (lez′gē·ən) See LESGHIAN.

Lha·sa (lä′sä) The capital of Tibet, near the southern border; seat of the Dalai Lama: Chinese *Lasa.* Also **Lhas′sa.**

Lhasa ap·so (äp′sō) A small, long-haired, ancient breed of dog, native to Tibet, used as watchdogs in lamaseries: also called *Tibetan lion dog.* [<LHASA + Tibetan *abso seng kye* bark lion sentinel dog]

Lhé·vinne (lā·vēn′), **Josef,** 1874–1944, Russian pianist.

li (lē) *n.* A Chinese unit of length, approximately one-third of a mile. [<Chinese *li*]

li·a·bil·i·ty (lī′ə·bil′ə·tē) *n. pl.* **·ties** **1** The state of being liable, or exposed to some accidental or incidental result or occurrence: *liability* to disease. **2** The condition of being responsible for a possible or actual loss, penalty, evil, expense, or burden: *liability* for damages. **3** That for which one is liable; in the plural, debts as opposed to *assets.*

li·a·ble (lī′ə·bəl) *adj.* **1** Exposed, as to damage, penalty, expense, burden, etc.: with *to.* **2** Justly or legally responsible. **3** Having a tendency, inclination, or likelihood; likely: with unfavorable sense. See synonyms under APT, LIKELY. [<F *lier* <L *ligare* bind]

li·aise (lē·āz′) *v.i.* **·aised, ·ais·ing** *Chiefly Brit. Colloq.* To act as an agent or intermediary; communicate. [Back formation <LIAISON]

li·ai·son (lē′ā·zon′, lē·ā′zon, lē′ə·zon; *Fr.* lē·ā·zôṅ′) *n.* **1** An illicit intimacy between two persons of opposite sex; intrigue. **2** A bond or union: a *liaison* of the intellect. **3** In cookery, a thickening used in sauces, soups, etc., as yolks of eggs beaten with cream. **4** In speaking or reading French, the carrying over in pronunciation of a final consonant to a succeeding word beginning with a vowel or silent *h,* as in *Est-il un homme?* Applied also to such sound-unions in certain other languages. **5** Unity of action, as between distant fighting forces or between an executive officer and his subordinates, maintained by various forms of contact and communication. *—adj.* Pertaining to one who or that which serves to maintain unity of action, as between an executive officer and his subordinates, or between parts of an army, etc.: a *liaison* officer. [<F <L *ligatio* <*ligare* bind]

Liá·kou·ra (lyä′kōō·rä) The former name for PARNASSUS.

li·an·a (lē·an′ə, -ä′nə) *n.* A twining or climbing plant of tropical forests, with ropelike, woody stems. Also **li·ane** (lē·än′). [<F *liane,* earlier *viorne* <L *viburnum* viburnum; infl. in F by *lier* bind <L *ligare*]

Liao (lyou) A river flowing 900 miles south through southern Manchuria to the Gulf of Liaotung. *Chinese* **Liao Ho.**

Liao·ning (lyou′ning′) Formerly, the southernmost of the three original provinces of Manchuria; divided, 1934, 1949: formerly *Shengking.*

Liao·noing (lyou′noing′) A province of southern Manchuria, NE China; 65,000 square miles; capital, Shenyang.

Liao·si (lyou′shē′) A former province of SW Manchuria, NE China; 21.676 square miles; capital, Chinchow.

Liao·tung (lyou′dōōng′) A former province of southern Manchuria, NE China; 39,758 square miles; capital, Antung; extending south as **Liaotung Peninsula,** dividing the northern Yellow Sea into the Bay of Chosen and the **Gulf of Liaotung.** See KWANTUNG.

Liao·yang (lyou′yäng′) A city in western Liaoning province, NE China.

li·ar (lī′ər) *n.* One who intentionally utters falsehood, or is given to lying. [OE *leogere*]

Li·ard (lē′ärd) A river of SE Yukon Territory, NE British Columbia, and SW Northwest Territories, Canada, flowing about 550 miles north to the Mackenzie River.

Li·as (lī′əs) *n. Geol.* The lowest of the rock series comprised in the Jurassic system of Europe. [<F *liais,* kind of limestone; ult. origin unknown] **—Li·as·sic** (lī·as′ik) *adj.* & *n.*

lib (lib) *n. Slang* Liberation (def. 2). **—lib′ber** *n.*

li·ba·tion (lī·bā′shən) *n.* **1** Liquid poured out, as in honor of a deity; also, the act of so pouring liquid. **2** Humorously, a drinking; potation. [<F <L *libatio, -onis* <*libare* pour out (as an offering)]

Li·bau (lē′bou) The German name for LIEPAJA. *Russian* **Li·ba·va** (lē·bä′və).

Lib·by (lib′ē) Diminutive of ELIZABETH.

li·bec·cio (lē·bet′chō) *n.* A Mediterranean wind blowing from the southwest. Also *Obs.* **li·bec′·chio** (-bek′yō). [<Ital. <L *Libs, Libis* <Gk. *Lips, Libos* southwest wind]

li·bel (lī′bəl) *n.* **1** Anything tending to degrade or asperse character or reputation. **2** *Law* Slander written and published; the act or crime of publishing it; also, a false publication damaging to property or business. **3** *Law* The written allegation of the plaintiff in a suit before a court of admiralty or an ecclesiastical court. **4** Any publicly circulated slanderous document. *—v.t.* **·beled** or **·belled, ·bel·ing** or **·bel·ling** **1** To publish a libel concerning; defame. **2** In admiralty law, to bring suit against, as a ship or cargo. See synonyms under ASPERSE. [<OF <L *libellus,* dim. of *liber* book] **—li′bel·er** or **li′bel·ler, li′bel·ist** or **li′bel·list** *n.*

li·bel·ant (lī′bəl·ənt) *n.* One who institutes a libel or suit in admiralty. Also **li′bel·lant.** [<F *libellant,* ppr. of *libeller* institute a suit]

li·bel·ee (lī′bəl·ē′) *n.* The party against whom a suit in admiralty is filed. Also **li′bel·lee′.**

li·bel·lu·la (lī·bel′yōō·lə) *n.* Any of a genus (*Libellula*) of typical dragonflies. [<NL <L *libellulus,* reduplicated dim. of *liber* book; from its resemblance to a book when in flight]

li·bel·ous (lī′bəl·əs) *adj.* Containing that which defames or libels; defamatory; slanderous. Also **li′bel·lous.**

li·ber (lī′bər) *n. pl.* **li·bri** (lī′brī) **1** A book, as a volume of public records of deeds, mortgages, etc. **2** *Bot.* The bast or inner bark of exogenous plants. [<L, book, inner bark (which was once used to write upon)]

lib·er·al (lib′ər·əl, lib′rəl) *adj.* **1** Possessing or manifesting a free and generous heart; bountiful. **2** Appropriate or fitting for a broad and enlightened mind: a *liberal* education; *liberal* arts. **3** Free from narrowness, bigotry, or bondage to authority or creed, as in religion; inclined to democratic or republican ideas, as opposed to monarchical or aristocratic, as in politics; broad; popular; progressive. **4** Bestowed without stint; abundant. **5** Not restricted to the literal meaning: a *liberal* construction. **6** Free by or from birth; hence, of high character; refined; independent. **7** *Obs.* Unduly free; licentious. See synonyms under AMPLE, CHARITABLE, GENEROUS. *—n.* Any person who advocates liberty of thought, speech, or action; one who is opposed to conservatism: distinguished from *radical.* Also **lib′er·al·ist.** [<OF <L *liberalis* pertaining to a freeman <*liber* free] **—lib′er·al·is′tic** *adj.* **—lib′er·al·ly** *adv.*

Lib·er·al (lib′ər·əl, lib′rəl) *n.* A member of the Liberal Party in Great Britain, Canada, or Australia.

liberal arts See under ART[1].

lib·er·al·ism (lib′ər·əl·iz′əm) *n.* **1** An attitude toward social, economic, political, and ecclesiastical policies, favoring gradual reform and ordered change rather than reaction or revolution and opposed equally to arbitrary censorship and undue license in dealing with ideas. **2** A doctrine often equated with laissez-faire economics, holding to free trade and to minimum interference by the state with economic activities: contrasted to SOCIALISM, SYNDICALISM, and COMMUNISM. **3** In political theory, adherence to policies of gradual reform through parliamentary procedure, the upholding of civil liberties as central in a free society, and a belief in the doctrine of progress: opposed to *conservatism.* **4** *Eccl.* **a** In 19th century Roman Catholic church polity, a movement opposed to ultramontanism, and favoring the formulation of doctrines and practices governing the relation of theology to social ethics; opposing promulgation of the infallibility doctrine with broad participation by laity, clergy, and prelacy in formulating the social and economic policies of the state. **b** In Protestant church bodies, an attitude favoring the use of the methods of historical criticism on the Bible, wide leeway for individual interpretation of creeds, doctrines, and ritual, and latitude as to methods of church government and congregational organization: opposed to *fundamentalism.* **5** Loosely, general opposition to conservatism and reaction in any field.

lib·er·al·i·ty (lib′ə·ral′ə·tē) *n. pl.* **·ties** **1** The quality of being liberal or generous. **2** A gift; donation. See synonyms under BENEVOLENCE.

lib·er·al·ize (lib′ər·əl·īz′) *v.t.* & *v.i.* **·ized, ·iz·ing** To make or become liberal. **—lib′er·al·i·za′·tion** (lib′ər·əl·ə·zā′shən, -ī·zā′, lib′rəl-) *n.* **—lib′er·al·iz′er** *n.*

Liberal Party **1** In Great Britain, the political party formed by the coalition of Whigs and Radicals about 1832 and opposed to the Conservative Party. Since 1918 its power declined with the rise of the Labour Party. 2 One of the principal political parties of Canada. 3 One of the principal political parties of Australia.

lib·er·ate (lib′ə·rāt) *v.t.* **·at·ed, ·at·ing** 1 To set free; release from bondage. 2 To release from chemical combination. 3 *Colloq.* To free from oppression or from conventions considered oppressive. [<L *liberatus,* pp. of *liberare* free <*liber* free] — **lib′er·a′tor** *n.*

lib·er·a·tion (lib′ər·ā′shən) *n.* 1 The act of liberating, or the state of being liberated. 2 A political and social movement formed to promote the interests of a group regarded as the object of unfair discrimination or bias: women's *liberation.* — **lib′·er·a′tion·ist** *n.*

Li·be·rec (lē′be·rets) A city in northern Bohemia, Czechoslovakia: German *Reichenberg.*

Li·be·ri·a (lī·bir′ē·ə) A republic on the west coast of Africa; 43,000 square miles; capital, Monrovia. — **Li·be′ri·an** *adj.* & *n.*

lib·er·tar·i·an (lib′ər·târ′ē·ən) *n.* 1 One who believes in the freedom of the will. 2 One who maintains the principles and doctrines of liberty, particularly in thought and conduct. 3 An adherent of libertarianism. — *adj.* Of or pertaining to the doctrine of the libertarians.

lib·er·tar·i·an·ism (lib′ər·târ′ē·ən·iz′əm) *n.* A theory of government which holds that the state is subordinate to the individual. It may range from anarchism to democracy.

lib·er·tine (lib′ər·tēn) *n.* 1 One who does not restrain his desires or appetites; a debauchee. 2 In ancient Rome, a manumitted slave, a freedman, or the child of such a person. — *adj.* 1 Dissolute; licentious. 2 Freed from slavery; manumitted. [<L *libertinus* <*libertus* freedman <*liber* free]

lib·er·tin·ism (lib′ər·tēn·iz′əm) *n.* 1 Unrestrained indulgence in licentious practices. 2 An extreme exercise of freedom in thought or opinion, especially on religious subjects. Also **lib′er·tin·age** (-ij).

lib·er·ty (lib′ər·tē) *n. pl.* **·ties** 1 The state of being exempt from the domination of others or from restricting circumstances; freedom. 2 A special exemption; franchise; privilege; in the U. S. Navy, permission to be absent from one's ship or station for a short period. 3 Unusual or undue freedom or familiarity. 4 The possession and exercise of the right of self-government. 5 The power of voluntary choice; freedom from necessity. 6 A place or district within which certain immunities or privileges are enjoyed; specifically, in England, a district within a county, exempt from the jurisdiction of the sheriff. — **at liberty** Free; unconfined; having permission (to do something). — **civil liberty** Freedom of the individual citizen from government control, restraint of, or interference with, his property, opinions, or affairs, except as the public good may require. — **individual liberty** Freedom from restraint in the performance of rights outside of government control. — **political liberty** The right to participate in the election of rulers and the making and administration of laws. [<F *liberté* <L *libertas, -tatis* <*liber* free]

Synonyms: emancipation, freedom, independence, license. In general terms, it may be said that *freedom* is absolute, *liberty* relative; *freedom* is the absence of restraint, *liberty* is the removal or avoidance of restraint. The two words are constantly interchanged; the slave is set at *liberty*, or gains his *freedom. Independence* is said of states or nations, *freedom* and *liberty* of individuals. *Liberty* keeps strictly to the thought of being clear from restraint or compulsion; *freedom* takes a wider range, applying to other oppressive influences; we speak of *freedom* from annoyance or intrusion. *License* is a permission or privilege granted by adequate authority, a bounded *liberty*; in the wider sense, *license* is an ignoring and defiance of all that should restrain. See PERMISSION, RIGHT. *Antonyms*: captivity, compulsion, constraint, imprisonment, necessity, obligation, oppression, serfdom, servitude, slavery, superstition.

Liberty Bell The bell in Independence Hall, Philadelphia, rung July 4, 1776, when the Declaration of Independence was adopted; cracked 1835.

liberty cap A close-fitting, soft cap, with elongated crown, usually folded over: originally worn by freedmen in ancient Rome, and adopted as a symbol of liberty in the French Revolution: also called *Phrygian cap.*

Liberty Island A small island off the southern tip of Manhattan, New York; site of the Statue of Liberty: formerly *Bedloe's Island.*

Liberty Ship A U. S. merchant ship of about 10,000 tons displacement: designed for rapid manufacture and built in large numbers during World War II.

Lib·i·a (lib′ē·ə) See LIBYA.

li·bid·i·nous (li·bid′ə·nəs) *adj.* Lustful; lewd. [<F *libidineux* <L *libidinosus* <*libido, -inis* lust <*libet, lubet* it pleases] — **li·bid′i·nous·ly** *adv.* — **li·bid′i·nous·ness** *n.*

li·bi·do (li·bī′dō, -bē′-) *n. Psychoanal.* 1 The instinctual craving or drive behind all human activities, the repression of which leads to psychoneuroses. 2 Psychic energy, especially that associated with sexual instinct. [<L, lust] — **li·bid′i·nal** (-bid′ə·nəl) *adj.*

li·bra (lī′brə *for def. 1,* lē′brä *for defs. 2 and 3*) *n.* 1 The Roman pound, equivalent to 327 grams. 2 The Spanish and Portuguese pound of sixteen ounces. 3 A gold coin of Peru, equal to ten soles. [<L, pound]

Li·bra (lī′brə) 1 The Balance, the seventh sign of the zodiac which the sun enters about Sept. 21. 2 *Astron.* A zodiacal constellation. See CONSTELLATION. [<L, a balance]

li·brar·i·an (lī·brâr′ē·ən) *n.* 1 A person in charge of a library. 2 A person qualified by training for library service. — **li·brar′i·an·ship′** *n.*

li·brar·y (lī′brer·ē, -brə·rē) *n. pl.* **·brar·ies** 1 A collection of books, pamphlets, etc., kept for reading and consultation; especially, such a collection arranged to facilitate reference, as by classification and indexing. 2 A building, an apartment, or a series of apartments containing such a collection: the *Library* of Congress. 3 A series of books having some characteristic in common issued by the same publisher. 4 A collection of books for recreation or study belonging to a private individual: a doctor's *library.* 5 A commercial establishment for selling or hiring out books. — **circulating library** A library from which books can be taken away under certain restrictions: also **lending library:** distinguished from a **reference library,** where books may be consulted but not carried away. [<OF *librarie* <L *librarium* <*liber, libri* book]

Library of Congress The national library of the United States in Washington, D.C.; established 1800.

li·brate (lī′brāt) *v.i.* **li·brat·ed, li·brat·ing** 1 To move back and forth, as a balance before coming to rest; oscillate. 2 To be poised; hover. [<L *libratus,* ppr. of *librare* balance <*libra* balance] — **li′bra·to′ry** (-brə·tôr′ē, -tō′rē) *adj.*

li·bra·tion (lī·brā′shən) *n.* 1 The act of balancing or librating; balance; equipoise. 2 *Astron.* An apparent slow swinging motion of a body on each side of its mean position, as in the *libration* of the moon.

li·bret·tist (li·bret′ist) *n.* A writer of librettos.

li·bret·to (li·bret′ō) *n. pl.* **·tos** or **·ti** (-ē) A book containing the words of an opera, or the words themselves. [<Ital., little book, dim. of *libro* <L *liber*]

Li·bre·ville (lē′brə·vēl) A port on the west coast of equatorial Africa, capital of Gabon Republic.

li·bri·form (lī′brə·fôrm) *adj. Bot.* Having the form of liber or bast. [<L *liber, libri* liber (def. 2) + -FORM]

Lib·y·a (lib′ē·ə) 1 The ancient Greek and Roman name for all of North Africa except Egypt. 2 A constitutional monarchy (1951) in North Africa on the Mediterranean; formerly an Italian colony; 679,358 square miles; capitals, Tripoli and Bengasi. *Italian* **Lib′i·a.**

Lib·y·an (lib′ē·ən) *adj.* Pertaining to Libya, its inhabitants, or their language. — *n.* 1 A native or inhabitant of Libya. 2 The extinct Hamitic language spoken in ancient Libya, including the Numidian and Mauretanian dialects.

Libyan Desert A part of the Sahara Desert extending through eastern Libya, western Egypt, and NW Sudan.

Lib·y·co-Ber·ber (lib′i·kō·bûr′bər) *n.* A branch of the Hamitic subfamily of the Hamito-Semitic language family, consisting of ancient Libyan and the modern Berber dialects.

lice (līs) Plural of LOUSE.

li·cense (lī′səns) *n.* 1 Authority or liberty granted to do or omit an act; specifically, in law, a permission, as for manufacturing a patented article or for the sale of intoxicants. 2 A written or printed certificate of a legal permit. 3 Unrestrained liberty of action; abuse of privilege; disregard of propriety. 4 Allowable deviation from established rule; variation from a standard for a purpose: poetic *license.* See synonyms under LIBERTY, PERMISSION, RIGHT. — *v.t.* **·censed, ·cens·ing** To grant a license to or for; give permission to; authorize. See synonyms under PERMIT. Also **li′cence.** [<OF *licence* <L *licentia* <*licens, licentis,* ppr. of *licere* be permitted] — **li′cens·a·ble** *adj.* — **li′cens·er** or **li′cenc·er** or *Law* **li′cen·sor** *n.*

li·cen·see (lī′sən·sē′) *n.* One to whom a license is granted. Also **li′cen·cee′.**

li·cen·ti·ate (lī·sen′shē·it, -āt) *n.* 1 A person licensed, as by a university, to practice a certain profession: a *licentiate* in dental surgery. 2 In some Continental universities, a person holding a degree intermediate between bachelor and doctor. [<Med. L *licentiatus,* pp. of *licentiare* allow, license <L *licentia* LICENSE]

li·cen·tious (lī·sen′shəs) *adj.* 1 Exceeding the limits of propriety; wanton; lewd. 2 Careless of rule and accuracy, especially in literary matters. [<F *licentieux* <L *licentiosus*] — **li·cen′tious·ly** *adv.* — **li·cen′tious·ness** *n.*

li·chee (lē′chē) See LITCHI.

li·chen (lī′kən) *n.* 1 A flowerless plant (class or group *Lichenes*) commonly growing flat upon a surface, as of a rock, and composed of loose cellular tissue, a slender white-celled epiphytic ascomycetous or (rarely) basidiomycetous fungus, and a number of globular greenish or bluish algal cells upon which the fungal cells prey. 2 *Pathol.* Any of several papular skin diseases. — *v.t.* To cover with lichens. [<L <Gk. *leichēn,* prob. <*leichein* lick] — **li′chen·a′ceous** (-ā′shəs), **li′chen·ous, li′chen·ose** (-ōs) *adj.*

li·chen·in (lī′kən·in) *n. Biochem.* A white gelatinous carbohydrate, $C_6H_{10}O_5$, obtained from Iceland moss; moss starch. [<LICHEN + -IN]

li·chen·ol·o·gy (lī′kən·ol′ə·jē) *n.* The science or study of lichens. — **li′chen·ol′o·gist** *n.*

Lich·field (lich′fēld) A city in SE Staffordshire, England; birthplace of Samuel Johnson.

lich·gate (lich′gāt′) *n.* A churchyard gate covered with a roof under which a bier may stand. [OE *lic* corpse + GATE]

LICHGATE
Little Church Around the Corner, New York.

licht (likht) *n., adj., v.t.* & *v.i. Scot.* Light (in all senses).

lic·it (lis′it) *adj.* Lawful. [<L *licitus* <*licere* be allowed] — **lic′it·ly** *adv.*

lick (lik) *v.t.* 1 To pass the tongue over the surface of. 2 To bring to a specified state or condition by passing the tongue over: to *lick* a surface clean. 3 To take in by the tongue; lap up. 4 To move or pass lightly over or about: The waves *licked* the base of the cliff. 5 *Colloq.* **a** To defeat; overcome. **b** To thrash; beat. — *v.i.* 6 To move quickly or lightly: The flame *licked* up in the grate. — **to lick into shape** *Colloq.* To put in proper form or condition. — **to lick one's chops** To show pleased anticipation. — **to lick up** To consume or devour entirely. — *n.* 1 A stroke of the tongue in licking. 2 The application of something, as if by a stroke of the tongue, or something so applied: a *lick* of paint. 3 As much as can be taken up by the tongue at one stroke or lap. 4 A deposit of salt frequented by animals that lick it. 5 A camping place along a trail near a pond, pool, or creek. 6 *Colloq.* A stroke, blow, or whack: a *lick* on the ear; also, in the plural, in baseball, an inning at bat. 7 *Slang* A spurt of speed or energy; exertion. [OE *liccian* lick]

lick·er·ish (lik′ə·rish) *adj.* 1 *Archaic* Tempting or enticing the appetite. 2 Eager to taste or enjoy. 3 Lustful. Also spelled *liquorish.* [Var. of LECHEROUS] —**lick′er·ish·ly** *adv.* —**lick′er·ish·ness** *n.*

lick·e·ty-split (lik′ə·tē·split′) *adv. Slang* At full speed. Also **lick′e·ty-cut′** (-kut′).

lick·ing (lik′ing) *n.* 1 A lapping with the tongue. 2 *Colloq.* A whipping; castigation; also, a defeat.

Lick·ing River (lik′ing) A river in eastern Kentucky, flowing 320 miles NW to the Ohio River.

lick·spit·tle (lik′spit′l) *n.* A servile flatterer.

lic·o·rice (lik′ə·ris, -rish) *n.* 1 A perennial leguminous herb *(Glycyrrhiza glabra)* of southern and central Europe. 2 Its root, used in medicine and confection. 3 The inspissated juice of the root. Also spelled *liquorice.* [<AF *licorys,* OF *licoresse* <LL *liquiritia,* alter. of Gk. *glycyrrhiza* <*glykys* sweet + *rhiza* root]

lic·tor (lik′tər) *n.* One of the officers or guards attending the chief Roman magistrates: they bore the fasces as a symbol of office. [<L, prob. <*ligare* tie]

ROMAN LICTOR

lid (lid) *n.* 1 A cover closing an aperture, as of a receptacle, movable to afford access to the inside. 2 An eyelid. 3 *Bot.* A top, as that of a pyxis or the capsule of a moss, which separates by a transverse dividing line; an operculum. 4 *Slang* A hat. [OE *hlid*] —**lid′ded** *adj.*

Lid·dell Hart (lid′əl härt′), **Basil Henry,** born 1895, English military authority.

Li·di·a (lē′dē·ä) Italian form of LYDIA.

Li·di·ce (lē′di·tse) A village in west central Bohemia, Czechoslovakia, destroyed 1942 by the Germans in World War II.

lid·less (lid′lis) *adj.* 1 Having no lid, as a pot or kettle. 2 Without eyelids; hence, watchful; sleepless.

Li·do (lē′dō) An Italian island on the Adriatic, separating the Lagoon of Venice from the Gulf of Venice; fashionable bathing resort.

lie[1] (lī) *v.i.* **lay, lain, ly·ing** 1 To rest or place oneself prone or at full length, as on a bed: often with *down*: He is *lying* down. 2 To be on or rest against a surface: The sign is *lying* next to the wall. 3 To be or continue in or as in a specified condition or position: to *lie* in ambush: to *lie* at a disadvantage. 4 To be situated: Rome *lies* in a plain of central Italy. 5 To extend in some direction: Our route *lies* northward. 6 To have source or cause; exist: usually with *in*: His trouble *lies* in his carelessness. 7 To be buried, as in a tomb. 8 *Law* To be maintainable, as a criminal charge. —**to lie** (or **lay**) **down on the job** *U.S. Colloq.* To loaf; do something in a desultory manner. —**to lie in** To be in childbed. —**to lie in wait (for)** To wait in ambush (for). —**to lie low** *Slang* To go into hiding. —**to lie to** *Naut.* To remain nearly stationary with the bow as near the wind as possible. —**to lie with** *Archaic* To have sexual intercourse with. —*n.* 1 The position or arrangement in which a thing lies; manner of lying; lay. 2 The lair of an animal. [OE *licgan*]

lie[2] (lī) *n.* 1 An untruth; falsehood. 2 Anything that deceives or creates a false impression. 3 An accusation of lying: to give him the *lie.* —**white lie** An untruth uttered or implied in deference to conventionality, expediency, or courtesy; a fib. —**to give the lie to** 1 To accuse of lying. 2 To expose as false; belie. —*v.* **lied, ly·ing** *v.i.* 1 To make untrue statements knowingly, especially with intent to deceive. 2 To give an erroneous or misleading impression: Figures do not *lie.* —*v.t.* 3 To bring or obtain by lying: He *lied* his way out of trouble. [OE *lyge*]

Synonyms (noun): deceit, deception, fabrication, falsehood, untruth. A *lie* is the uttering of what one knows to be false with intent to deceive. The novel or drama is not a *lie,* because not meant to deceive; the ancient teaching that the earth was flat was not a *lie,* because not then known to be false. *Untruth* is more than lack of accuracy, implying always lack of veracity; but it is a somewhat milder and more dignified word than *lie.* See DECEPTION, FRAUD. *Antonyms*: fact, truth, veracity.

Lie (lē), **Jonas Lauritz,** 1833–1908, Norwegian novelist. —**Jonas,** 1880–1940, U. S. painter, born in Norway. —**Trygve,** 1896–1968, Norwegian statesman; first secretary general of the United Nations.

Lie·big (lē′bikh), **Baron Justus von,** 1803–73, German chemist; founded agricultural chemistry

Lieb·knecht (lēp′knekht), **Karl,** 1871–1919, German journalist and socialist leader; shot by the monarchists.

Liech·ten·stein (lik′tən·stīn, *Ger.* lēkh′tən·shtīn) A sovereign principality of central Europe between Switzerland and Austria; 62 square miles; capital, Vaduz.

Lied (lēd, *Ger.* lēt) *n. pl.* **Lied·er** (lē′dər) *German* A reflective lyric poem or ballad set to music, expressing a single sentiment or emotion in a series of stanzas.

Lie·der·kranz (lē′dər·kränts) *n.* 1 A singing society. 2 A group of songs. 3 A soft cheese with a strong flavor and odor: a trade name. [<G, lit., garland of songs]

lie detector A psychogalvanometer or similar instrument whose records are assumed to indicate the guilt or innocence of the person under questioning to whom it is applied.

lief (lēf) *adv.* Willingly; freely; as willingly as not: I had as *lief* stay as go: often used to imply preference: as *lief* die as live dishonored. —*adj. Archaic* 1 Dear; dearly loved; pleasing. 2 Willing; glad. ◆ Homophone: *leaf.* [OE *lēof* dear]

lief·er (lē′fər) *adv.* More gladly or willingly; rather.

liege (lēj) *adj.* 1 Bound in vassalage to a lord. 2 Having the right to the service and allegiance of a vassal; sovereign; supreme. 3 Faithful; loyal. —*n.* 1 A vassal; also, a citizen. 2 A liege lord; a feudal sovereign or superior. [<OF <Med. L *ligius* free <*laeticus* free <*letus* freedman <OHG *ledig* free]

Liége (lyezh) A city in eastern Belgium. *Flemish* **Luik** (loik).

liege·man (lēj′mən) *n. pl.* **·men** (-mən) A feudal vassal; a loyal servitor.

Lieg·nitz (lēg′nits) A city in SW Poland, formerly in Lower Silesia, Germany. *Polish* **Leg·ni·ca** (leg·nē′tsä).

lien (lēn, lē′ən) *n.* A legal claim on property, as security for a debt. ◆ Homophone: *lean.* [<F, band <L *ligamen* <*ligare* tie]

li·e·nal (lī·ē′nəl) *adj.* Of or pertaining to the spleen. [<L *lien* spleen]

li·en·ter·y (lī′ən·ter′ē) *n. Pathol.* Diarrhea characterized by the discharge of undigested food. [<Med. L *lienteria* <Gk. *leienteria* <*leios* smooth + *enteron* intestine] —**li′en·ter′ic** *adj.*

Lie·pa·ja (lye′pä·yä) The second largest city of Latvia: German *Libau*: also *Lepaya.*

li·erne (lē·ûrn′) *n. Archit.* A crossrib or a branch rib in Gothic vaulting. [<F]

lieu (lo͞o) *n.* Place; stead: in the phrase *in lieu of.* [<F <L *locus.* Doublet of LOCUS.]

lieu·ten·ant (lo͞o·ten′ənt, *Brit. Army* lef·ten′·ənt) *n.* 1 An officer who fills the place of a superior in the latter's absence or acts for him under his direction; deputy. 2 In the U. S. Army, Air Force, and Marine Corps, a commissioned officer holding either of two ranks, **first** or **second lieutenant,** the former ranking next below a captain. 3 In the U. S. Navy and Coast Guard, a commissioned officer holding either of two ranks, **lieutenant** or **lieutenant (junior grade),** the former ranking next below a lieutenant commander and the latter next above an ensign. 4 A police officer next above a sergeant and below a captain. [<F *lieutenant* <*lieu* place + *tenant,* ppr. of *tenir* hold] —**lieu·ten′an·cy** *n.*

lieutenant colonel, lieutenant commander, lieutenant general See under COLONEL, etc.

lieutenant governor 1 An officer authorized to perform the duties of a governor during his absence or disability, or to take his place in case of death or resignation. 2 Occasionally, in the British Empire, a subordinate governor, who is acting governor of a territory under a governor general. —**lieu·ten′·ant-gov′er·nor·ship′** *n.*

life (līf) *n. pl.* **lives** (līvz) 1 That state in which animals and plants exist which distinguishes them from inorganic substances and from dead organisms: characterized by metabolism and growth, reproduction, and internally initiated adaptations to the environment. 2 That vital existence, the loss of which means death: to give one's *life.* 3 The period of animate existence from birth until death, or a part of it. 4 Any conscious and intelligent existence: the *life* here and hereafter. 5 Energy and animation; spirit; vivacity: to put *life* into an enterprise. 6 A source of liveliness, animation, etc.: to be the *life* of the party. 7 That which keeps something alive; the source or essence of existence. 8 A living being; a person: Many *lives* were lost. 9 Living things in the aggregate: plant *life.* 10 In art, a living figure or semblance: a picture drawn from *life.* 11 The course of active human existence; human affairs: daily *life* in the city. 12 A certain manner or way of living: the *life* of a recluse. 13 *Theol.* A state of spiritual attainment or awareness following conversion. 14 A biography. 15 The duration of efficiency or usefulness of anything: the *life* of a machine. —**for life** For the remainder of one's existence, until death: to hold office *for life.* —*adj.* 1 Of or pertaining to life or a life. 2 Lasting for a lifetime, or from a given point until death: a *life* sentence. 3 In art, studying from a living model: a *life* class. [OE *līf*]

Synonym: vitality. *Life* is the state of actual living; *vitality* is the power of living or the capacity of maintaining *life*; as, Reptiles have remarkable *vitality. Life* may also be used for the vital principle; as, the *life* of a seed. See WARMTH. *Antonyms*: death, decease, dissolution.

life belt *n.* A life preserver in the form of a belt.

life·blood (līf′blud′) *n.* 1 The blood necessary to life; vital blood. 2 Anything giving strength or energy or as indispensable as blood.

life·boat (līf′bōt′) *n.* A strong, buoyant boat used in abandoning ship, saving castaways, etc.

life·buoy (līf′boi′, -bo͞o′ē) *n.* A life preserver, usually in the shape of a ring: also *life ring.*

life class A class in which artists draw from living models.

life cycle The entire series of processes comprehended in the life of an organism from the ovum.

life expectancy The probable length of life of a person, varying according to age, sex, physical condition, occupation, and prevailing environmental factors. Compare LIFE SPAN.

life·ful (līf′fo͝ol) *adj.* Full of vitality; outgoing. —**life′ful·ly** *adv.* —**life′ful·ness** *n.*

life·guard (līf′gärd′) *n.* An expert swimmer hired by a bathing resort, pool, etc., to protect the safety of bathers.

Life Guards *Brit.* The two cavalry regiments serving to protect the lives of the British sovereigns.

life history *Biol.* The complete train of phenomena characterizing the existence and growth of an organism from its inception to its decease.

life insurance Insurance on the life of oneself or of another. Also **life assurance.** See under INSURANCE.

life jacket A life preserver in the form of a jacket.

life·less (līf′lis) *adj.* 1 Destitute of life, either naturally or by deprivation; dead; inanimate. 2 Wanting in energy, power, vigor, or spirit; torpid; dull. 3 Exhibiting none of the signs of life; apparently dead: She fell *lifeless* at his feet. 4 Uninhabited by men or animals. —**life′less·ly** *adv.* —**life′less·ness** *n.*

Synonyms: dead, deceased, defunct, dull, extinct, inanimate, inert, spiritless, torpid. *Dead* primarily applies to a once-living organism from which life has departed: this original meaning controls the derived senses; *inanimate* primarily applies to that which never had life. *Lifeless* may be used in either connection, and may be also used of that which exhibits none of the signs of life. The derived meanings of these words are many. A picture, a statue, a poem, an actor's rendering of his part may be spoken of as *lifeless*; we speak of a *dead* book, *dead* capital, a *dead* wall, and even of a *dead* (that is, a dull or non-resonant) sound. *Deceased* is in formal and approved use as a euphemism for *dead*; *defunct* is used to mean finished or *extinct* as well as *dead*. *Extinct* implies cessation of vitality or force: an *extinct* volcano. See DEAD, FLAT. *Antonyms*: active, alive, animated, live, living, stirring, vigorous.

life·like (līf′līk′) *adj.* Resembling that which is living; true to life; realistic. —**life′like′·ness** *n.*

life line 1 A rope shot to a wrecked ship by which a heavier line for a breeches buoy may be rigged. 2 A line attached to a buoy, mast, etc., which may be clung to, as by bathers, sailors in stormy weather, etc. 3 A line for raising and lowering a diver. 4 Any route for transporting vital supplies. 5 In palmistry, a line about the base of the thumb which allegedly foretells facts of a person's life.

life·long (līf′lông′, -long′) *adj.* Lasting or continuing through life.

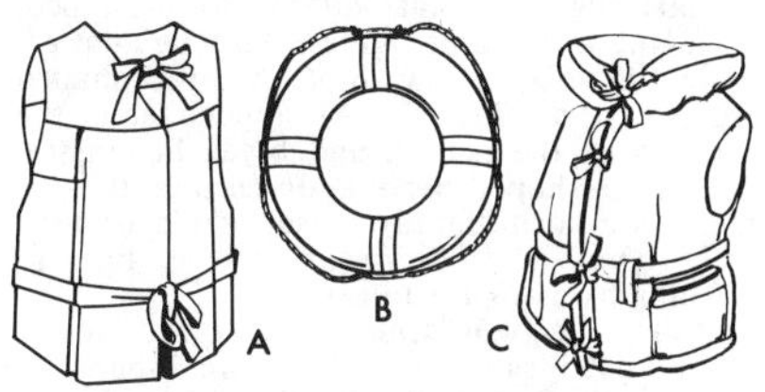

LIFE PRESERVERS
A. Solid block cork. *B.* Cork ring buoy. *C.* Collar-type life jacket.

life peer *Brit.* A peer whose rank and title expire at his death.

life preserver 1 A buoyant device, often inflatable, in the form of a belt, jacket, ring, etc., used to keep a person afloat in water. 2 *Brit.* A loaded cane or other weapon for self-defense.

lif·er (lī′fər) *n. Slang* 1 One serving a prison sentence for life. 2 The life sentence.

life raft A raftlike structure for saving life in time of shipwreck; especially, a collapsible rubber boat equipped with oars and an apparatus permitting rapid inflation.

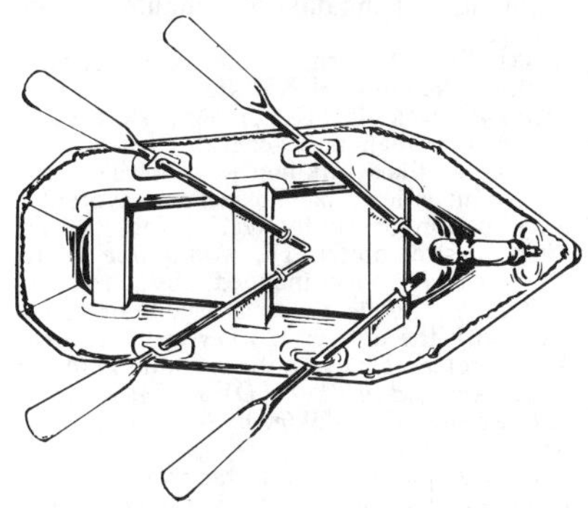

INFLATABLE LIFE RAFT
Capacity, 7 men; weight, 50 pounds.

life ring A lifebuoy.

Life-Sav·ing Service (līf′sā′ving) A former U. S. government service in charge of life-saving stations: since 1915 its activities have been performed by the U. S. Coast Guard.

life-sav·er (līf′sā′vər) *n.* 1 One who saves a life; especially, a trained person stationed at a bathing beach, or the like, to prevent loss of life by drowning. 2 A life preserver. —**life′-sav′ing** *n.* & *adj.*

life-saving station One of a system of U. S. Coast Guard stations or headquarters along the coasts and lakeshores, equipped to rescue shipwrecked or drowning persons.

life-size (līf′sīz′) *adj.* Of natural size; of the size of the object portrayed. Also **life′-sized′**.

life span The extreme length of life regarded as biologically possible in any plant or animal, or in the species to which it belongs. Compare LIFE EXPECTANCY.

life style Style (def. 6).

life table A statistical table arranged to show the number of people in a population who will survive to a given age and the probable life expectancy of a person at that or any other age: also called *mortality table.*

life·time (līf′tīm′) *n.* The whole period of a life. —*adj.* Lasting for the duration of a life: a *lifetime* job.

life·work (līf′wûrk′) *n.* The work of a lifetime; the work to which one is devoted.

Lif·fey (lif′ē) A river in eastern Ireland, flowing 50 miles through Dublin to Dublin Bay.

lift[1] (lift) *v.t.* 1 To raise from a lower to a higher position or place; hoist; elevate. 2 To hold up; support or display in the air. 3 To raise to a higher degree or condition; exalt. 4 To make clearly audible; shout: to *lift* a cry. 5 To subject (the face) to plastic surgery, usually so as to impart beauty or restore an appearance of youth: She had her face *lifted.* 6 *Colloq.* To take surreptitiously; steal; plagiarize. 7 *U. S.* To pay off, as a mortgage. 8 In golf, to pick up (the ball), as from an unfavorable position, and concede the prescribed penalty. —*v.i.* 9 To put forth effort in order to raise something: All together now, *lift*! 10 To rise; yield to upward pressure. 11 To rise or disperse; dissipate: The fog *lifted.* —*n.* 1 The act of lifting or raising. 2 The distance through which something rises or is raised. 3 The amount of weight lifted. 4 Exaltation or stimulation of the mind or feelings. 5 A rise in condition; promotion. 6 Elevated carriage or position: the *lift* of her chin. 7 Assistance by lifting or raising. 8 A ride in a vehicle offered to a pedestrian, taking him part or all of the way to his destination. 9 A machine, device, or the like that lifts or assists in lifting, as a hoisting machine. 10 *Brit.* An elevator in a building. 11 *Mining* **a** A set of pumps. **b** A vertical slice of ore removed in one series of operations. **c** The difference in height between one level and another. 12 In shoemaking, any layer of leather or other material forming the heel. 13 *Aeron.* The vertical component of the aerodynamic pressure upon an aircraft. 14 An elevation of ground. [<ON *lypta* raise in the air. Akin to LOFT.] —**lift′·er** *n.*

lift[2] (lift) *n. Brit. Dial.* The sky.

lift·off (lift′ôf′, -of′) *n. Aerospace* The vertical ascent of a rocket or spacecraft from its launching pad.

lift pump A pump for lifting a liquid to its own level: distinguished from *force pump.*

lig·a·ment (lig′ə·mənt) *n.* 1 *Anat.* A band or sheet of firm, compact, fibrous tissue, closely binding related structures, as bones, etc., together; especially one connecting or investing the opposed surfaces of a joint. 2 A band or connecting tie; that which binds together. [<L *ligamentum* band < *ligare* bind] —**lig′a·men′tous, lig′a·men′tal, lig′a·men′ta·ry** *adj.*

li·gan (lī′gən) See LAGAN.

li·gate (lī′gāt) *v.t.* **·gat·ed, ·gat·ing** To bind with a ligature; bandage. [<L *ligatus,* pp. of *ligare* bind, tie]

li·ga·tion (lī·gā′shən) *n.* 1 The act of tying or binding up, especially an artery; also, the condition of being bound. 2 Something used in tying; bandage.

lig·a·ture (lig′ə·chər) *n.* 1 Anything that constricts, or serves for binding or tying. 2 *Surg.* A thread or wire tied around a blood vessel to arrest bleeding or used for removing a tumor. 3 A ligation; the act of binding. 4 *Printing* Two or more connected letters, as *fi, ffi, æ*; also, in writing, the character used to indicate the connection (⌒). Compare DIGRAPH. 5 *Music* A slur; notes joined by a slur. —*v.t.* **·tured, ·tur·ing** To bind or compress with a ligature. [<F <L *ligatura* < *ligatus,* pp. of *ligare* bind]

li·geance (lī′jəns, lē′-) *n.* 1 *Law* The jurisdiction or territory of a sovereign. 2 *Obs.* Allegiance. [<OF *ligeance* < *lige* liege; infl. by L *ligare* bind]

light[1] (līt) *n.* 1 *Physics* **a** That form of radiant energy that stimulates the organs of sight, having wavelengths ranging from about 3900 to 7700 angstrom units and propagated at a speed of about 186,300 miles a second. **b** Ultraviolet or infrared light. Also called *luminous energy.* 2 The natural condition or medium that permits vision; luminosity: opposed to *darkness.* 3 The sensation produced by exciting the organs of vision, as the eye, optical nerves, and visual centers of the brain. 4 Mental or spiritual illumination. 5 A source of light, as the sun, moon, a flame, lamp, beacon, etc.; also, an emission of light. 6 That which admits light; a window or pane. 7 The state of being visible, known, or exposed: to come to *light.* 8 Daytime; daylight; dawn. 9 The point of view from which, or circumstances in which, a thing is seen or considered; aspect. 10 A part of a picture representing an illuminated object. 11 The power of vision; perception by eyesight. 12 Something with which to enkindle or make a blaze or light: a *light* for a pipe. 13 One who is noteworthy or eminent; a model. —**accidental light** In art, light coming from some other source than that of the chief light; a cross light. —**in the light of** In view of; considering. —**pick-up light** An anti-aircraft searchlight working alone or in coordination with a locator system to spot aircraft targets. —*adj.* 1 Full of light; not dark; bright. 2 Of a faint or pale color. —*v.* **light·ed** or **lit, light·ing** *v.t.* 1 To set burning, as wood, a lamp, etc.; ignite; kindle, as a fire. 2 To make light; illuminate. 3 To brighten or animate. 4 To guide or conduct with light: The fires *lighted* him home. —*v.i.* 5 To take fire; start burning. 6 To become bright or luminous: usually with *up.* [OE *lēoht*] —**light′er** *n.* —**light′less** *adj.*

◆ **lighted, lit** Either form is acceptable as the past tense and past participle of *light,* but *lighted* is probably more common as the past participle and is the usual form for the attributive adjective: The moon *lighted* (or *lit*) my path; I have already *lighted* (or *lit*) the oven; a *lighted* cigarette. In figurative use, the more common form is *lit*: Her face was *lit* with joy.

Synonyms (noun): blaze, flame, flare flash, flicker, glare, gleam, glimmer, glisten, glistening, glitter, glow, illumination, incandescence, scintillation, sheen, shimmer, shine, shining, sparkle, twinkle, twinkling. A *flame* is both hot and luminous; if it contains few solid particles it will yield little *light,* but it may afford intense heat, as in the case of a hydrogen *flame.* A *blaze* is an extensive, brilliant *flame. Light* is the general term for any luminous effect discernible by the eye, from the faintest phosphorescence to the *blaze* of the sun. A *flare* is a wavering *flame* or *blaze,* a *flash* is a *light* that appears and disappears in an instant. The *glare* and *glow* are steady, the *glare* painfully bright, the *glow* subdued. *Shine* and *shining* refer to a steady or continuous emission of *light*; *sheen* is faint *shining,* usually by reflection. *Glimmer, glitter,* and *shimmer* denote wavering *light.* A *gleam* is not wavering, but transient or intermittent; a *glitter* is a hard *light*: the *glitter* of burnished arms. A *sparkle* is a sudden *light,* as of sparks thrown out; *scintillation* is the more exact and scientific term for the actual emission of sparks, also the figurative term for what suggests such emission: *scintillations* of wit or of genius. *Illumination* is wide-spread, brilliant *light,* as when all the windows of a house are lighted. The *light* of *incandescence* is intense and white like that from metal at a white heat. See KNOWLEDGE. *Antonyms*: blackness, dark, darkness, dimness, dusk, gloom, gloominess, obscurity, shade, shadow.

light[2] (līt) *adj.* 1 Having little weight; of small weight by comparison; not heavy: *light* as air. 2 Easy to carry, handle, move, etc.; not taxing to the muscles or digestive organs; not burdensome: a *light* task; *light* food. 3 Free from that which encumbers; not heavily loaded: *light* troops. 4 Of no great consequence; lacking gravity; trivial. 5 Lacking in intensity or effect; moderate. 6 Free from anxiety, trouble or distress; cheerful. 7 Not in full possession of the senses; flighty; delirious: *light* in the head. 8 Below the proper or usual weight: *light* coin. 9 Well-leavened and raised; not soggy: *light* bread. 10 Loose or sandy: a *light* soil. 11 Characterized by levity; without dignity or substantial character; also, loose in morals. 12 Handling or touching with slight force; hence, easy; graceful; active; nimble: a *light* touch; a *light* style. 13 Suitable for easy work. 14 Free from clumsiness or heaviness in appearance or construction: *light* tracery. **15** Having no metrical stress: said of a syllable or vowel. **16** In Sanskrit grammar, having a short vowel: said of a syllable. **17** *Meteorol.* Designating air (No. 1) or a breeze (No. 2) on the Beaufort scale. — **to make light of** To treat or consider as trifling. — *v.i.* **light·ed** or **lit, light·ing 1** To descend and settle down after flight, as a bird; land. **2** To happen or come, as by chance or accident: with *on* or *upon.* **3** To get down, as from a horse or carriage; dismount. **4** To fall; strike, as a blow. — **to light into** *Slang* **1** To attack; assail. **2** To scold; castigate. — **to light out** *U.S. Slang* To depart in haste. — *adv.* Lightly; cheaply; easily. [OE *lēoht, līht*] — **light′ly** *adv.*

light·en[1] (līt′n) *v.t.* **1** To make light or more light. **2** To enlighten, as the mind. **3** *Rare* To send forth like lightning. — *v.i.* **4** To become light or more light. **5** To flash or shine. **6** To flash lightning.

light·en[2] (līt′n) *v.t.* **1** To make less heavy. **2** To reduce the load of: to *lighten* ship. **3** To make less burdensome or oppressive. **4** To relieve from distress; gladden. — *v.i.* **5** To become less heavy. See synonyms under ALLAY, ALLEVIATE.

light·er[1] (lī′tər) *n.* A device for lighting a cigarette, cigar, or pipe.

light·er[2] (lī′tər) *n.* A bargelike vessel used in loading or unloading ships lying at a distance from a wharf, or in transporting goods in bulk for short distances. — *v.t.* & *v.i.* To transport (goods) by lighter. [<Du. *lichter* < *lichten* make light, unload < *licht* light]

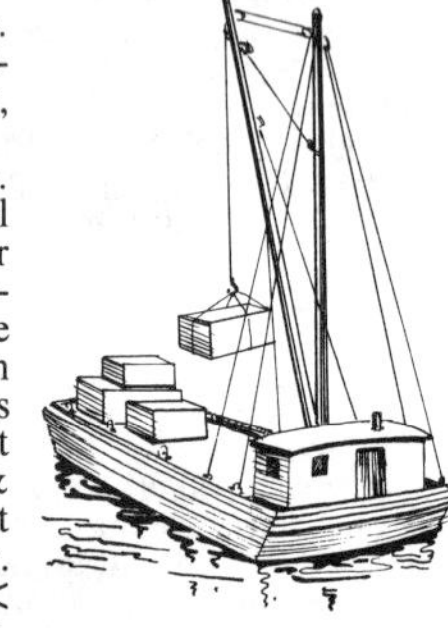
LIGHTER

light·er·age (lī′tər·ij) *n.* **1** The price for unloading a ship by lighters, or for the use of lighters. **2** The removal or conveying of a cargo by lighters.

light·er-than-air (lī′tər·thən·âr′) *adj. Aeron.* Having a specific gravity less than that of air: said especially of aircraft of the aerostat type, as a balloon or dirigible.

light·face (līt′fās′) *n. Printing* Type having light, thin lines.

light-fin·gered (līt′fing′gərd) *adj.* Addicted to petty theft; thievish; pilfering.

light-fog (līt′fôg′, -fog′) *n. Phot.* A blur of light, by accident or design, fogging a negative.

light-foot·ed (līt′fŏŏt′id) *adj.* Nimble in running or dancing; having a light step. — **light′-foot′ed·ly** *adv.*

light-head·ed (līt′hed′id) *adj.* **1** Silly; frivolous. **2** Dizzy; delirious. — **light′-head′ed·ly** *adv.* — **light′-head′ed·ness** *n.*

light-heart·ed (līt′här′tid) *adj.* Free from care; gay. See synonyms under MERRY. — **light′-heart′ed·ly** *adv.* — **light′-heart′ed·ness** *n.*

light heavyweight A boxer or wrestler weighing between 161 and 175 pounds.

light·horse·man (līt′hôrs′mən) *n. pl.* **·men** (-mən) A cavalryman bearing light arms and equipment.

light·house (līt′hous′) *n.* A tower equipped with high-powered lamps, erected at a point of danger to guide seamen by night.

LIGHTHOUSE
a. Stone and steel construction.
b. Screwpile ocean lighthouse.

light·ing (lī′ting) *n.* **1** Illumination. **2** A distribution of light, as on a face or in a picture. **3** An arrangement of lights, especially on a stage.

light·ly (līt′lē) *adv.* **1** With little weight, force, pressure, or effect. **2** Without heaviness of spirit; airily; cheerily. **3** With levity; carelessly; heedlessly; also, frivolously, wantonly, or irreverently. **4** In a slight degree; slightly; mildly. **5** For slight reasons. **6** Nimbly; with light or swift step or motion. **7** Easily; readily. — *v.t. Scot.* To make light of; slight.

light-mind·ed (līt′mīn′did) *adj.* Lacking seriousness or strength of mind; foolish. — **light′-mind′ed·ly** *adv.* — **light′-mind′ed·ness** *n.*

light·ness (līt′nis) *n.* **1** The state, quality, or condition of being light. **2** That attribute of a color which identifies it as equivalent to some member of the series of grays between black and white: also called *brilliance.* Compare BRIGHTNESS, HUE, SATURATION. See COLOR.

light·ning (līt′ning) *n.* **1** A sudden flash of light caused by the discharge of electricity between two electrified regions of cloud, or between a cloud and the earth. **2** The discharge itself. — **ball lightning** A luminous, electrically charged sphere, usually less than a foot across, which sometimes appears during a thunderstorm, moving slowly and generally discharging on contact. — **chain lightning** Lightning discharged in swift, long strokes, forked or jagged in appearance. — *adj.* Fast; rapid: a *lightning* movement. [Earlier *lightening* < *lighten* flash]

lightning arrester A device for preventing damage to electrical equipment by carrying off excess voltage due to lightning or other electric disturbance.

lightning bug A firefly.

lightning rod A sharp-pointed metallic conductor used to protect buildings from lightning by carrying an electric current harmlessly to the ground. Also **lightning conductor.**

light-o'-love (līt′ə·luv′) *n.* **1** An old dance tune. **2** A coquettish or wanton woman.

light ratio *Astron.* The constant numerical factor 2.512 by which stars of successive apparent magnitudes differ from each other in brightness.

light red High-quality burnt ocher, used as a permanent pigment; loosely, any calcined ocher or certain iron oxides. — **light-red** *adj.*

lights (līts) *n. pl.* Lungs, especially of mammals. [ME *lihtes*; so called from their light weight]

light·ship (līt′ship′) *n.* A vessel, having warning lights, signals, etc., moored in dangerous waters as a guide to ships.

light·some[1] (līt′səm) *adj.* **1** Light; playful. **2** Graceful. **3** Nimble. **4** Frivolous. — **light′·some·ly** *adv.* — **light′some·ness** *n.*

light·some[2] (līt′səm) *adj.* Full of light; luminous. — **light′some·ly** *adv.* — **light′some·ness** *n.*

light·stand (līt′stand′) *n.* A small table on which to set a light.

light·struck (līt′struk′) *adj.* Exhibiting a light-fog.

light·weight (līt′wāt′) *n.* **1** A boxer or wrestler weighing between 127 and 135 pounds. **2** *Slang* An unimportant, incompetent, or stupid person. — *adj.* **1** Having little weight; trivial. **2** Pertaining to lightweights.

light·wood (līt′wŏŏd′) *n.* **1** Resinous pine, commonly the heart of the yellow pine. **2** The resinous knots of pine used for kindling.

light-year (līt′yir′) *n. Astron.* The distance that light traverses in one year, approximately six trillion miles: used as a unit in measuring the distance of stars. Compare PARSEC.

lign·al·oes (līn·al′ōz, lig·nal′-) *n.* **1** A fragrant, resinous Oriental wood (*Aquilaria agallocha*); aloe weed. **2** Aloes, the drug. [<OF <L *lignum aloes* wood of aloes]

lig·ne·ous (lig′nē·əs) *adj.* Composed of or like wood; woody. [<L *ligneus* < *lignum* wood]

ligni- *combining form* Wood: *lignivorous.* Also, before vowels, **lign-.** Also **ligno-.** [<L *lignum* wood]

lig·ni·form (lig′nə·fôrm) *adj.* Having the form or appearance of wood.

lig·ni·fy (lig′nə·fī) *v.t.* & *v.i.* **·fied, ·fy·ing** To convert into or become wood. [<LIGNI- + -FY] — **lig′ni·fi·ca′tion** *n.*

lig·nin (lig′nin) *n. Bot.* An organic substance which, with cellulose, forms the chief part of woody tissue. Also **lig′nose** (-nōs). [<LIGN(I)- + -IN]

lig·nite (lig′nīt) *n.* A compact, carbonized vegetable substance often retaining fibrous structure, forming an imperfect fuel intermediate between peat and true coal; brown coal. [<F] — **lig·nit′ic** (-nit′ik) *adj.*

lig·niv·o·rous (lig·niv′ə·rəs) *adj.* Wood-eating, as certain insects. [<LIGNI- + -VOROUS]

lig·no·cel·lu·lose (lig′nō·sel′yə·lōs) *n. Bot.* The substance making up the woody and fibrous parts of plants, consisting of lignin combined with cellulose.

lig·nose (lig′nōs) *n.* One of the constituents of lignin. [<L *lignosus* < *lignum* wood]

lig·num·vi·tae (lig′nəm·vī′tē) *n.* **1** A small tropical American tree (*Guaiacum officinale*). **2** Its greenish-brown, hard, heavy wood. **3** Any of certain related American trees, as the **bastard lignumvitae** (*G. sanctum*). [<NL <L, wood of life]

Li·gny (lē·nyē′) A village in central Belgium; scene of a French victory over the Prussians two days before Waterloo, 1815.

lig·ro·in (lig′rō·in) *n. Chem.* A distillate of petroleum used as a solvent and illuminant; petroleum naphtha. Also **lig′ro·ine.** [Origin unknown]

lig·u·late (lig′yə·lit, -lāt) *adj.* **1** Strap-shaped. **2** Having a ligule or ligules. Also **lig′u·lat′ed.**

lig·ule (lig′yŏŏl) *n.* **1** *Biol.* A strap-shaped organ or part. **2** *Bot.* **a** An appendage at the junction of the petiole and blade in grasses. **b** A strap-shaped corolla of certain flowers in the composite family. Also **lig′u·la** (-yə·lə). [<L *ligula,* dim. of *lingua* tongue; infl. in meaning by L *ligare* bind]

Li·guo·rist (lē·gwôr′ist) *n.* **1** *Theol.* A follower of the doctrines of St. Alfonso de Liguori; a probabilist. **2** A Redemptorist. Also **Li·guo′·ri·an.**

lig·ure (lig′yŏŏr) *n.* A precious stone, possibly the jacinth, worn by the high priest of ancient Israel. *Exod.* xxviii 19. [<LL *ligurius* <Gk. *ligyrion* <Hebrew *leshem*]

Li·gu·ri·a (li·gyŏŏr′ē·ə) A region of northern Italy on the Mediterranean; 2,098 square miles.

Li·gu·ri·an (li·gyŏŏr′ē·ən) *n.* **1** A member of a tribe who, in ancient times, inhabited central and northern Italy and parts of Switzerland, France, and Spain. **2** The extinct, primarily Indo-European language of the Ligurians, probably closely related to Italic and Celtic. **3** An inhabitant of modern Liguria. **4** The dialect of Italian spoken in modern Liguria. — *adj.* Of or pertaining to ancient or modern Liguria, its inhabitants, its culture, or its language.

Ligurian Sea An arm of the Mediterranean Sea along the coast of NW Italy.

Li Hung-Chang (lē hŏŏng′jäng′), 1823–1901, Chinese statesman and general.

like[1] (līk) *v.* **liked, lik·ing** *v.t.* **1** To take pleasure in; enjoy. **2** To regard favorably; have affection or kindly feeling for. **3** To wish or desire; prefer: He would *like* us to do it. — *v.i.* **4** To feel inclined; choose: Do as you *like*! **5** *Archaic* To be agreeable or pleasing to: with the dative: It *likes* me not. — *n.* Liking; preference; inclination: common in the phrase *likes and dislikes.* [OE *līcian*] — **lik′a·ble, like′a·ble** *adj.* — **lik′er** *n.* — **lik′a·ble·ness, like′a·ble·ness** *n.*

Synonyms (verb): affect, approve, enjoy, esteem, fancy, love, relish. See LOVE. *Antonyms*: see synonyms under ABHOR.

like[2] (līk) *adj.* **1** Resembling; similar in qualities, appearance, etc. **2** Bearing a close or faithful resemblance, as a portrait. **3** *Math.* Identical: *like* angles. **4** Nearly identical; equivalent: Take a *like* amount of plaster. **5** In golf, having played the same number of strokes: said of competing players. **6** *Dial.* Likely to; expected: We are *like* to meet no more. **7** *Dial.* On the point or verge of; about to: I am *like* to cry when I think of her. — **like . . . , like . . .** As the one is, so the other will be: *like* father, *like* son. — *adv.* **1** In the manner of; as if: To run *like* mad. **2** *Colloq.* Likely: *Like* as not we'll meet again. — *prep.* **1** Similar to; resembling: You look *like* your father. **2** Characteristic of; expected from: That's just *like* your impudence! **3** In the mood or frame of mind for: to feel *like* sleeping. **4** So as to indicate, promise, or presage: to look *like* rain. — **like anything** (or **blazes, the devil,** etc.) *Colloq.* With great speed, force, violence, or vehemence. — *n.* That which is similar or equivalent to, or of the same nature as, something else. — **the like** (or **likes**) of: *Colloq.* Any thing or person like. — *v.i. Dial.* To come near or be on the point of: used in the past and past perfect tenses with the perfect infinitive: He *liked* (or *had liked*) to have died. — *conj.* **1** *Colloq.* As; in the manner that: It all happened *like* you said. 2 *Colloq.* As if: It looks *like* he's going to fall. [OE *gelīc*]

◆ **like, as, as if** *Like* is unacceptable as a conjunction at the formal level of writing, where factual clauses of comparison are introduced by *as,* contrary-to-fact ones by *as if* with the subjunctive. At the informal level, because it signals a coming comparison much more strongly than the rather neutral *as, like* is in widespread use. It has good colloquial standing, except with die-hard sticklers for correctness, in idiomatic expressions where it serves both as an adverb to round out a phrasal verb, and as a conjunction governing a finite verb: It looks *like* we're in for trouble; It sounds *like* a train's coming, and I'll have to run for it. In the last, the almost imperceptible gradation from the formally correct *That sounds like a train coming* to the informal *It sounds like a train's coming* shows why any ironclad prohibition of *like* as a conjunction at the informal level is ill-advised. The effort to ban it has frightened the timid into substituting *as* for *like* in adjectival or prepositional uses where *like* is idiomatic. Nor has the attempted ban deterred novelists and playwrights, whose trade demands a good ear for the way people actually speak, from representing their literate characters as making rather free use in dialog of *like* as a conjunction, usually, however, with a regard for idiom.

-like *suffix of adjectives* Resembling or similar to: *childlike, wavelike.* [<LIKE]

◆ Compounds containing *-like* are usually written solid, but hyphenated when three *l*'s occur together, as in *shell-like,* or when two *l*'s occur in a confusing sequence of letters, as in *eel-like.*

like·li·hood (līk′lē·ho͝od) *n.* 1 The character of being likely. 2 Probability or a probability: There is some *likelihood* of his coming. Also **like′li·ness.** See synonyms under PROBABILITY.

like·ly (līk′lē) *adj.* **·li·er, ·li·est** 1 Apparently true or real; plausible; probable. 2 Reasonably to be expected; liable. 3 Apt to please; promising. 4 Well adapted for the purpose. —*adv.* Probably.

Synonyms: *(adj.)*: apt, credible, liable, presumable, probable, reasonable. *Apt* implies a natural fitness or tendency: An impetuous person is *apt* to speak hastily. *Liable* refers to a contingency regarded as unfavorable: The ship was *liable* to founder at any moment. *Likely* refers to a contingent event regarded as very probable: An industrious worker is *likely* to succeed. *Credible* signifies readily to be believed: a *credible* narrative; *likely* in such connection is used ironically to signify the reverse: a *likely* story! A thing is *presumable* which, from what is known, may be taken for granted in advance of proof. *Reasonable* in this connection signifies such as the reason can be satisfied with, independently of external grounds for belief or disbelief. Compare APPARENT, PROBABLE. *Antonyms*: doubtful, dubious, improbable, incredible, questionable, unlikely.

like-mind·ed (līk′mīn′did) *adj.* Similarly disposed in opinion or tastes.

lik·en (lī′kən) *v.t.* To represent as similar; compare. See synonyms under COMPARE.

like·ness (līk′nis) *n.* 1 The state or quality of being like; a resemblance. 2 A portrait; representation. 3 Counterfeit form; guise. See synonyms under ANALOGY, APPROXIMATION, DUPLICATE, IMAGE, PICTURE.

like·wise (līk′wīz′) *adv.* 1 In like manner. 2 Also; moreover.

li·kin (lē′kēn′) *n.* A Chinese provincial transit duty. [<Chinese *li-chin*]

lik·ing (lī′king) *n.* Inclination due to some attraction; preference.

li·lac (lī′lak, -lək) *n.* 1 An ornamental flowering shrub (genus *Syringa*) having fragrant purplish or white flowers. The species best known in America are the **common lilac** *(S. vulgaris),* which has light rosy-purple flowers and is the State flower of New Hampshire, and the **Persian lilac** *(S. persica),* a smaller shrub with white or purplish flowers. 2 The light rosy-purple color of the common lilac flower. [<Sp. <Arabic *līlak, laylak* <Persian *līlak* bluish, var. of *nīlak,* dim. of *nīl* blue]

lil·i·a·ceous (lil′ē·ā′shəs) *adj.* Of or pertaining to a large, widely distributed family *(Liliaceae)* of monocotyledonous, mostly perennial herbs and shrubs, characterized by radially symmetrical flowers and bulbous rootstocks; designating the lily family. [<LL *liliaceus* <L *lilium* lily]

Lil·i·an (lil′ē·ən) A feminine personal name. Also **Lil′li·an.** [<L, lily]

lil·ied (lil′ēd) *adj.* 1 Like lilies. 2 Covered or decorated with, or abounding in, lilies.

Lil·i·en·thal (lil′ē·ən·thôl′), **David Eli,** born 1899, U. S. civil administrator.

Lil·ith (lil′ith) 1 In Babylonian legend, a female demon who inhabited ruins. 2 In Hebrew folklore, Adam's first wife. 3 In medieval folklore, a famous witch. [<Hebrew *Līlīth* <Assyrian-Babylonian *līlītu* of the night]

Li·li·u·o·ka·la·ni (lē·lē′o͞o·ō·kä·lä′nē), **Lydia Kamehameha,** 1838–1917, queen of the Hawaiian Islands 1891–93.

Lille (lēl) A city in northern France: formerly *Lisle.*

Lil·li·bul·le·ro (lil′ē·bə·lâr′ō) *n.* An English revolutionary song ridiculing the appointment of Talbot of Tyrconnell as lieutenant of Ireland in 1686. It helped foment the revolution of 1688. [An arbitrary formation]

Lil·li·put (lil′i·put, -pət) In Swift's *Gulliver's Travels,* a country inhabited by a race of diminutive people.

Lil·li·pu·tian (lil′i·pyo͞o′shən) *adj.* Pertaining to the fictitious kingdom of Lilliput or to its inhabitants; very small. —*n.* 1 An inhabitant of Lilliput. 2 A very small person, especially, a self-important one.

lilt (lilt) *n.* 1 A brisk, merry song. 2 Rhythmic movement or flow. 3 A buoyant manner of walking. —*v.t.* & *v.i.* To sing or speak in a light, rhythmic manner. [ME *lulte.* Cf. Du. *lul* pipe.]

lil·y (lil′ē) *n. pl.* **lil·ies** 1 Any of numerous ornamental liliaceous plants (genus *Lilium*) having a bulbous root, erect stem, and large, showy, erect or nodding flowers; especially, the **madonna lily** *(L. candidum)* and the **gold-band lily** *(L. auratum).* 2 A fleur-de-lis. 3 Any of numerous plants resembling the true lilies: *waterlily; daylily.* —*adj.* White and soft; pale and delicate, like a lily. [OE *lilie* <L *lilium,* prob. <Gk. *leirion*]

lily iron A harpoon with a detachable head.

lil·y-liv·ered (lil′ē·liv′ərd) *adj.* Cowardly.

lil·y-of-the-Nile (lil′ē·uv·thə·nīl′) *n.* 1 The calla. 2 The African lily.

lil·y-of-the-val·ley (lil′ē·uv·thə·val′ē) *n. pl.* **lil·ies-of-the-val·ley** A low, smooth, stemless lilywort *(Convallaria majalis)* with two oblong leaves and nodding, fragrant, cup-shaped flowers.

lil·y-white (lil′ē·hwīt′) *adj.* 1 White as a lily. 2 Pure; unsullied: often used ironically: hard to believe in her *lily-white* innocence. 3 Composed of or admitting white people only: a *lily-white* country club.

lil·y·wort (lil′ē·wûrt′) *n.* Any plant of the lily family.

Li·ma (lē′mə) 1 A department in west central Peru; 15,048 square miles. 2 Its capital, the capital and largest city of Peru.

Li·ma bean (lī′mə) 1 A variety of climbing bean *(Phaseolus limensis).* 2 Its large flat seeds, a common article of food. [after *Lima,* Peru]

lim·a·cine (lim′ə·sīn, -sin) *adj.* 1 Of or pertaining to a family *(Limacidae)* of gastropods; the slug family. 2 Sluglike. [<L *limax, limacis* slug]

li·ma·çon (lim′ə·son) *n. Math.* The curve traced by a point fixed on a secant of a fixed circle, the circumference of which touches the origin, as the secant revolves about the origin. Also called **Pascal's limaçon.**

limb[1] (lim) *n.* 1 One of the jointed parts of the animal body, as a leg, arm, or wing. 2 A branch of a tree. 3 A person or thing forming a part of something else; an arm or branch of anything; member: *limb* of the law. 4 *Colloq.* A roguish young person; a mischievous child. —**out on a limb** *Colloq.* At a great disadvantage. —*v.t.* To dismember. ◆ Homophone: *limn.* [OE *lim*] —**limb′less** *adj.*

limb[2] (lim) *n.* 1 An edge or part, as of a disk; specifically, the edge of the disk of the moon or other heavenly body. 2 The graduated portion of a leveling rod or instrument for determining angles. ◆ Homophone: *limn.* [<F *limbe* <L *limbus* edge]

lim·bate (lim′bāt) *adj. Bot.* Bordered, as a leaf or flower having the margin of a different color from the rest. [<LL *limbatus* <L *limbus* border]

limbed (limd) *adj.* Possessing limbs: often used in compounds: strong-*limbed.*

lim·ber[1] (lim′bər) *adj.* 1 Easily bent; pliant; flexible. 2 Lithe and agile; nimble; supple: said of persons or their movements. See synonyms under SUPPLE. —*v.t.* & *v.i.* To make or become limber: often with *up.* [Origin uncertain] —**lim′ber·ly** *adv.* —**lim′ber·ness** *n.*

lim·ber[2] (lim′bər) *n.* 1 *Mil.* A two-wheeled, detachable vehicle at the forepart of a gun carriage, used to transport ammunition. 2 *Naut.* A lengthwise gutter on each side of the keelson to permit water to pass into the pump well. —*v.t.* & *v.i.* To attach a limber to (a gun): often with *up.* [Origin uncertain. Cf. F *limonière* <*limon* shaft.]

GUN LIMBER

lim·bic (lim′bik) *adj.* Of, pertaining to, or forming a border. [<LIMBUS]

lim·bo (lim′bō) *n.* 1 *Theol.* A region on the edge of hell to which are consigned the souls of the righteous who died before the coming of Christ (**limbo patrum,** or **limbo of the fathers**) and the souls of infants who died before baptism (**limbo infantum,** or **limbo of the infants**). 2 A place of neglect or oblivion to which unwanted or worthless persons or things are relegated and forgotten. 3 A place of confinement; a prison. [<L *limbus* border, *in limbo* on the border]

Lim·burg (lim′bûrg, *Du., Flemish* lim′bœrkh) 1 A province of NE Belgium; 930 square miles; capital, Hasselt. Also **Lim·bourg** (laṅ·bo͞or′). 2 A province of SE Netherlands; 839 square miles; capital, Maastricht.

Lim·burg·er cheese (lim′bûr·gər) A soft, white cheese with a strong odor, originally made at Limburg, Belgium. Also **Lim′burg cheese, Lim′burg·er.**

lim·bus (lim′bəs) *n.* A border or interface, especially if marked by a difference in color or structure between the adjoining parts. [<L, border]

lime[1] (līm) *n.* A white, earthlike calcium oxide, CaO. It is produced artificially by calcining calcium carbonate, as limestone, marble, or seashells, yielding the anhydrous calcium-oxide quicklime, which with water forms **slaked lime.** It also readily absorbs moisture from the air, forming **air-slaked lime.** —*v.t.* **limed, lim·ing** 1 To apply lime to. 2 To catch with or as with birdlime; ensnare. 3 To cement. [OE *līm*]

lime[2] (līm) *n.* 1 A small tree *(Citrus aurantifolia)* of the rue family, native in tropical regions. 2 Its small, green, lemonlike, acid fruit. [<F <Sp. *lima* <Arabic *limah.* Related to LEMON.]

lime·ade (līm·ād′) *n.* A drink made of lime juice, water, and sugar.

Lime·house (līm′hous′) A district of Stepney, east London, on the Thames, largely inhabited by sailors and dock workers.

lime·kiln (līm′kil′, -kiln′) *n.* A kiln for burning lime from limestone or seashells. Also **lime kiln.**

lime·light (līm′līt′) *n.* 1 A powerful light originally produced by burning lime, now often replaced by the electric spotlight: thrown on the stage to make actors more prominent. 2 That part of a theater stage illuminated by a limelight or spotlight. 3 Publicity; notoriety.

li·men (lī′mən) *n. pl.* **li·mens** or **lim·i·na** (lim′·ə·nə) A threshold (def. 3). [<L, threshold]

lim•er•ick (lim′ər•ik) *n.* A humorous verse of five anapestic lines, of which the first, second, and fifth lines are three-stress and rime, and the third and fourth lines are two-stress and rime. [after LIMERICK]

Lim•er•ick (lim′ər•ik) **1** A county in central Munster province, Ireland; 1,037 square miles. **2** Its capital, a port on the Shannon River. Irish Gaelic *Luimneach.*

Li•mes (lī′mēz) *n.* **1** A system of fortifications built by the Romans under Vespasian and Trajan to protect the provinces of southern Germany and Rhaetia against the Germans: about 336 miles long. Also **Li′mes Ger•man•i•cus** (jər•man•i•kəs). **2** (*Ger.* lē′mes) An elaborate series of fortifications built by Germany in 1938–39, opposing the French Maginot line and extending from the Swiss border along the French, Belgian, and Dutch frontiers: also *Siegfried Line, Westwall.* [<L *limes* border]

lime•stone (līm′stōn′) *n.* A rock composed wholly or in part of calcium carbonate. When containing magnesium carbonate, it is *dolomitic* or *magnesian* ; when clayey, *argillaceous*; when sandy or quartzose, *siliceous.* Crystalline limestone is called *marble.*

lime tree 1 The linden. **2** The tupelo or sour-gum tree *(Nyssa ogeche)* of Florida and Texas. [Earlier *line* <OE *lind* linden]

lime twig A twig on which birdlime has been smeared; hence, a snare; a trick.

lime•wa•ter (līm′wô′tər, -wot′ər) *n.* **1** A saturated solution of lime in water. **2** Water in which slaked lime has been dissolved. Also **lime water.**

lime•y (lī′mē) *n.* Slang **1** A British sailor: from the former practice of averting scurvy on long voyages by eating limes. Also **lime′ juic′er. 2** Any Englishman, sometimes taken to be offensive.

li•mic•o•line (lī•mik′ə•līn) *adj.* Shore-dwelling: said of certain wading birds, as plovers and snipes. Also **li•mic′o•lous.** [<LL *limicola* dweller in mud <*limus* mud + *colere* dwell]

lim•i•nal (lim′ə•nəl) *adj.* Relating to or at the threshold, entrance, or beginning. [<L *limen* threshold]

lim•it (lim′it) *n.* **1** A line, point, or boundary beyond which something ceases to extend, operate, avail, etc. **2** That which is limited or has bounds; ;a district; period. **3** That which impedes or hinders; a check. **4** *Math.* A definite quantity or value which a series is conceived or proved to approach but never reach. **5** In certain games, as of cards, the largest amount which may be wagered at one time: used with the definite article, especially in poker. See synonyms under BOUNDARY, END, MARGIN. **—off limits** A locality or area forbidden to military personnel except on official business. **—three-mile limit** A distance of three geographic miles from the shore line seaward, allowed by international law for territorial jurisdiction. —*v.t.* To set a bound or bounds to; keep within a limit; restrict. [<L *limes, limites*] **—lim′it•a•ble** *adj.* **—lim•i•ta•tive** (lim′ə•tā′tiv) *adj.* **—lim′it•er** *n.* **—lim′it•less** *adj.*

Synonyms (verb) : bound, check, circumscribe, confine, define, hinder, impede, repress, restrain, restrict. See CIRCUMSCRIBE, SCRIMP.

lim•i•tar•y (lim′ə•ter′ē) *adj.* **1** Forming or marking a limit or boundary; limiting. **2** Limited.

lim•i•ta•tion (lim′ə•tā′shən) *n.* **1** The act of limiting. **2** Restriction; circumscription. **3** *Law* A restrictive condition or stipulation; also, a period of time fixed by law within which certain acts are to be performed to render them valid. [<L *limitatio, -onis*]

lim•it•ed (lim′it•id) *adj.* **1** Confined to certain limits; in law, restricted within prescribed limits. **2** Circumscribed, as a government, a monarchy, etc.; held in check by a constitution. **3** Making only a few specific stops, carrying only a certain +number of passengers, and usually charging extra fare: a *limited* train. **4** Restricted to use on or within certain dates: a *limited* ticket. **5** *Brit.* Restricted in liability to the amount invested in stock of a business: a *limited* company.

lim•it•ed-slip differential (lim′it•id•slip′) An automobile differential-gear system so designed that in the event of one driving wheel losing its traction, the power is transmitted to the other wheel.

limit load *Engin.* The load which may safely be carried by a given structure under normal conditions.

limn (lim) *v.t.* **1** To draw or paint; delineate. **2** To describe in words. **3** To decorate, as manuscripts; illuminate. ◆ Homophone: *limb.* [ME *limnen* <*luminen* <OF *enluminer* <L *illuminare.* Doublet of ILLUMINATE.] **—lim•ner** (lim•nər) *n.* **—lim•ning** (lim′ning) *n.*

lim•net•ic (lim•net′ik) *adj. Ecol.* Pertaining to or dwelling in lakes, as certain plants and animals. Also **lim•nic•o•lous** (lim•nik′ ə•ləs). [<Gk. *limnētēs* marsh-dwelling <*limnē* pool]

lim•nol•o•gy (lim•nol′ə•jē) *n.* The scientific study of bodies of fresh water in all their aspects, with special reference to plant and animal life. [<Gk. *limnē* pool + -LOGY]

Lim•nos (lēm′nôs) See LEMNOS.

Li•moges (lē•mōzh′, *Fr.* lē•môzh′) A city in west central France.

Limoges ware A type of fine porcelain manufactured at Limoges, France.

lim•o•nene (lim′ə•nēn) *n. Chem.* One of three isomeric terpenes, $C_{10}H_{16}$, occurring in various essential oils, and having a lemonlike odor. [<NL *Limonum* lemon + -ENE]

li•mo•nite (lī′mə•nīt) *n.* A stalactitic, fibrous, silky, brown or yellow ferric hydroxide; bog ore. [<Gk. *leimōn* meadow + -ITE[2]] **—li′mo•nit′ic** (-nit′ik) *adj.*

Li•mou•sin (lē•mo͞o•zaṅ′) A region and former province of central France.

lim•ou•sine (lim′ə•zēn′, lim′ə•zēn) *n.* A large automobile, originally with a closed compartment for three to five passengers, and the roof projecting over the driver's seat; later, with each compartment separately enclosed. [<F, from *Limousin*]

limp[1] (limp) *v.i.* **1** To walk with a halting or irregular gait, as in favoring an injured leg or foot. **2** To proceed in a defective or irregular manner: His logic *limps.* —*n.* The step of a lame person; a halt. [Prob. OE *limpan* occur, walk lamely. Cf. OE *lempheallt* lame.] **—limp′er** *n.*

limp[2] (limp) *adj.* **1** Lacking stiffness; limber. **2** Lacking positiveness or firmness. [Origin uncertain. Cf. ON *limpa* indisposition, weakness.] **—limp′ly** *adv.* **—limp′ness** *n.*

lim•pet (lim′pit) *n.* A small, edible gastropod with a spirally coiled shell, found clinging to rocks. [OE *lempedu* <LL *lampreda* lamprey]

lim•pid (lim′pid) *adj.* Characterized by liquid clearness; transparent; lucid; clear. See synonyms under CLEAR, TRANSPARENT. [<L *limpidus* clear] **—lim•pid•i•ty** (lim•pid′ə•tē), **lim′•+pid•ness** *n.* **—lim′pid•ly** *adv.*

limp•kin (limp′kin) *n.* A courlan of Florida and tropical America. [<LIMP[1] + -KIN; from its walk]

Lim•po•po (lim•pō′pō) A river forming northern border of the Republic of South Africa's North West and Northern Transvaal provinces, flowing 995 miles partially through Mozambique into the Indian Ocean.

limp•sy (limp′sē) *adj.* **•si•er, •si•est** Limp; flimsy.

lim•u•loid (lim′yə•loid) *adj.* Pertaining to or resembling the king crab. —*n.* A king crab. [<LIMULUS]

lim•u•lus (lim′yə•ləs) *n. pl.* **L•li** A king crab. [<L, dim. of *limus* sidelong, askance]

lim•y (lī′mē) *adj.* **lim•i•er, lim•i•est 1** Containing or covered with lime. **2** Resembling lime. **3** Smeared with birdlime.

lin (lin) *n.* Scot. **1** A waterfall. **2** A precipice or ravine. Also spelled *lyn.* [OE *hlynn* torrent]

Li•na (lē′nə, lī′nə) Diminutive of CAROLINE.

lin•age (lī′nij) *n.* **1** The number of printed lines, as of text or advertising matter, contained in a book or magazine. **2** Alinement. Also spelled *lineage.*

lin•al•o•ol (lin•al′ō•ōl, lin′ə•lo͞ol′) *n. Chem.* An unsaturated, open-chain alcohol, $C_{10}H_{17}OH$, found in the essential oils of certain plants, as the bergamot. [<*linaloa,* a scented Mexican wood <Sp. *linaloe.* Cf. LIGNALOES.]

Li•na•res (lē•nä′rās) A city in southern Spain.

linch•pin (linch′pin′) *n.* A pin through the end of an axle, to keep a wheel in place. [OE *lynis* linchpin + PIN]

Lin•coln (ling′kən), **Abraham,** 1809–1865, 16th president of the United States during the Civil War, 1861–65; issued Proclamation of Emancipation; assassinated. **—Benjamin,** 1733–1810, American Revolutionary general and statesman.

Lin•coln (ling′kən) **1** A maritime county in eastern England; 2,664 square miles; county seat, Lincoln. Also **Lin′coln•shire** (-shir); shortened form **Lincs** (lingks). **2** The capital of Nebraska.

Lincoln's Birthday The anniversary of Abraham Lincoln's birth, February 12: a legal holiday in many States of the United States.

Lincoln's Inn See INNS OF COURT.

l'in•con•nu (laṅ•kô•nü′) *French* The unknown.

Lind (lind), **Jenny,** 1820–87, Swedish coloratura soprano: called "the Swedish Nightingale."

Lind•bergh (lind′bûrg), **Charles Augustus,** 1902–74, U.S. aviator; made the first nonstop solo flight from New York to Paris, 1927.

lin•den (lin′dən) *n.* A tree (genus *Tilia*) with soft white wood, cordate leaves, and cream-colored flowers; especially, the **American linden** *(T. Yamericana),* used for making furniture. Also called *basswood, lime tree.* [OE, orig. adj. < *lind* linden, lime tree]

Lin•des•nes (lin′dəs•nes) See NAZE, THE.

Lind•say (lin′zē), **Sir David,** 1490–1555, Scottish poet: also spelled *Lyndsay.* **—(Nicholas) Vachel,** 1879–1931, U.S. poet.

Lind•sey (lin′zē), **Benjamin Barr,** 1869–1943, U.S. jurist and reformer.

line[1] (līn) *n.* **1** A string or cord. **2** *Naut.* A rope, cord, or wire used for a specific purpose. **3** A wire or cable conducting power or telecommunication signals between two stations. **4** A fishing line. **5** Any slender mark or stroke, as drawn with a pen, pencil, tool, etc. **6** Something resembling the long mark or trace made by a pen or tool; band; seam; furrow. **7** In art: **a** The representation of form by the use of strokes, instead of by shading or coloring. **b** *pl.* The distinguishing features of the composition of a painting or drawing. **8** *Music* One of the parallel horizontal strokes that form a musical staff. **9** In various games, as football, baseball, tennis, etc., a mark of division or outline on the field, diamond, court, etc. **10** In television, one horizontal trace of the electron beam across the screen. **11** A thin furrow or wrinkle on the face or hands. **12** *Geom.* The trace, straight or curved, made by a moving point; an extent of length conceived without breadth or thickness. **13** A boundary or limit: the Mason-Dixon *Line.* **14** Contour; outline: the broken *line* of the shore. **15** *Geog.* **a** The equator. **b** Any circle, arc, or boundary conceived for purposes of plotting the earth's surface: the date *line.* **16** A row of persons or things: The people stood in *line.* **17** Agreement; accord: to bring all the factions into *line.* **18** A course of action, thought, procedure, etc.: a *line* of argument; the *line* of duty. **19** Plan of construction or procedure: an argument based on political *lines. P* **20** A course of movement; route: the *line* of march. **21** A branch of activity; a business or vocation: the advertising *line.* **22** The compass of one's ability, talent, etc.: Such jokes are not in his *line.* **23** A series of persons each of whom is the next descendant or heir of the one preceding. **24** A row of printed or written words bounded by the margins of a page or column. **25** A short letter; a note. **26** A verse (def. 1). **27** *pl.:* The words of a play or of an actor's part. **28** In advertising, a measure of column space equaling 1/14 inch. **29** A railroad track or roadbed. **30** Any system of public transportation: a steamship *line.* **31** A pipe or system of pipes conveying a fluid: a gas *line.* **32** *Mil.* **a** A series of fortifications presenting an extended front: Maginot *line.* **b** A trench or rampart. **c** A row of soldiers standing abreast, as distinguished from *column.* **33** *Naut.* An arrangement of ships in a certain order. **34** *Mil.* The combatant forces, as distinguished from the special services and the staff. **35** *Nav.* The class of officers having command of combat operations. **36** In football: **a** The linemen, collectively. **b** The line of scrimmage: see LINE OF SCRIMMAGE under SCRIMMAGE. **37** A variety of goods of a certain class or type, carried by a store or offered by an advertiser. **38** *pl. Colloq.* Marriage-lines. **39** *Colloq.* **a** A glib manner of speech. **b** A few words or a speech intended to sway or influence. See synonyms under BOUNDARY, MARK. — **in line for** In succession for; ready for. — **in line with** In accord with. — *v.* **lined, lin·ing** *v.t.* **1** To mark with lines; put lines upon. **2** To place in a line; bring into alinement or conformity: often with *up.* **3** To form a line along: Police *lined* the side of the road. **4** To place something in a line along: to *line* a wall with archers. **5** In baseball, to bat (the ball) in a line drive. — *v.i.* **6** To form a line; assume position or place: usually with *up.* — **to line out** In baseball: **a** To be retired by batting a line drive to a fielder. **b** To get (a hit) by batting a line drive which is not caught or fielded. — **to line up 1** To form a line. **2** To bring into line. **3** To organize for or against some activity, issue, etc. [OE *līne* cord; infl. by F *ligne* <L *linea* linen thread < *linum* flax]

line[2] (līn) *v.t.* **lined, lin·ing 1** To apply a covering or layer, usually of different material, to the inside surface of. **2** To serve as an inner covering or layer for: Lockers *lined* the wall. **3** To fill or supply: to *line* one's pockets with bribes. — *n.* **1** The fiber of flax. **2** Linen. [OE *līn* flax]

lin·e·age[1] (lin′ē·ij) *n.* Ancestral line of consanguinity; pedigree; family. [<OF *lignage* <L *linea* line]

line·age[2] (lī′nij) See LINAGE.

lin·e·al (lin′ē·əl) *adj.* **1** Of the nature of an ancestral line or lineage; ascending or descending in a direct line: distinguished from *collateral.* **2** Made with lines. [<L *linealis* < *linea* line] — **lin′e·al·ly** *adv.*

lin·e·a·ment (lin′ē·ə·mənt) *n.* A distinguishing line or mark; a feature. [<L *lineamentum* < *linea* line]

lin·e·ar (lin′ē·ər) *adj.* **1** Pertaining to or composed of lines. **2** Very narrow and elongate: a *linear* leaf. **3** Denoting a measurement in one dimension. **4** *Math.* Pertaining to an equation of the first degree. [<L *linearis*]

linear measure Measurement by length; a unit or system of units for measuring length, as in the following table of the principal customary standards. See also METRIC SYSTEM.

1 mil	=	0.001 inch (in.)
12 inches	=	1 foot (ft.)
3 feet	=	1 yard (yd., yds.)
6 feet	=	1 fathom (fath.)
5.5 yards	=	1 rod (rd.)
40 rods	=	1 furlong (fur.)
5280 feet	=	1 mile (mi.)
1760 yards	=	1 mile

lin·e·ate (lin′ē·it, -āt) *adj.* Marked with lines. Also **lin′e·at′ed.** [<L *lineatus*]

lin·e·a·tion (lin′ē·ā′shən) *n.* **1** A drawing of lines; delineation. **2** A contour or outline.

line·back·er (līn′bak′ər) *n.* In football, a defensive player whose normal position is just behind the line of scrimmage.

line-breed (līn′brēd′) *v.t. Genetics* To interbreed (successive generations) to one ancestor of a given line in order to develop selected characteristics. — **line′-breed′ing** *n.*

line drive In baseball, a ball batted with such force as to travel almost parallel to the ground.

Line Islands (līn) A Pacific island group south of Hawaii, divided between the United States and Great Britain; 112 square miles: also *Equatorial Islands.*

line·man (līn′mən) *n. pl.* **·men** (-mən) **1** In surveying, a man who carries the tape, line, or chain. **2** A man employed about the line of a railway, telegraph, or telephone, especially in making repairs. **3** In football, one of the players stationed along the line of scrimmage, consisting of the center and the right and left guards, tackles, and ends.

lin·en (lin′in) *n.* **1** A fabric woven from the fibers of flax. **2** Articles made of linen, or made formerly of linen but now often of cotton: bed *linen,* table *linen,* body *linen.* — *adj.* Made of the textile fiber of flax: *linen* cloth. [OE *līnen* made of flax < *līn* flax]

line of force *Physics* A line in a field of force every point on which coincides with the field intensity.

line of scrimmage See under SCRIMMAGE.

line of sight The straight line joining the eye of an observer and a target or other observed object.

line of vision The straight line joining the central fovea of the retina and the point to which vision is directed.

lin·e·o·late (lin′ē·ə·lāt′) *adj.* Minutely lineate. Also **lin′e·o·lat′ed.** [<L *lineola,* dim. of *linea* line + -ATE[1]]

lin·er[1] (lī′nər) *n.* **1** A ship, aircraft, etc., operated commercially by a specific line. **2** A person or thing that marks or traces lines. **3** In baseball, a line drive.

lin·er[2] (lī′nər) *n.* **1** One who makes linings. **2** A lining, or a piece used in forming a lining.

line-rid·er (līn′rī′dər) See FENCE-RIDER.

lines·man (līnz′mən) *n. pl.* **·men** (-mən) **1** In many games, as in tennis, the official watching the lines of the court. **2** In football, the official supervising the sidelines and marking the distances gained or lost in each play.

line squall *Meteorol.* A squall or series of squalls occurring along a squall line and usually marked by sudden changes in wind direction.

line storm *Dial.* An equinoctial.

line-up (līn′up′) *n.* **1** The formation of players in any game, such as football, hockey, etc., when drawn up for action. **2** An array of people united by some aim. **3** A mustering of criminal suspects by police for identification and questioning.

lin·ey (lī′nē) See LINY.

ling[1] (ling) *n.* **1** A codlike food fish (*Molva molva*) of the North Atlantic. **2** The Lake Ontario burbot (*Lota maculosa*). [? <Du. *leng* or OE *lengu* length]

ling[2] (ling) *n.* The heath or heather. [<ON *lyng*]

-ling[1] *suffix of nouns* **1** Little; young; petty: *duckling*: often used contemptuously: *princeling.* **2** A person or thing related to or characterized by: *worldling.* [OE]

-ling[2] *suffix* Forming adverbs: **1** (from nouns) Toward: *sideling.* **2** (from adjectives) Being; becoming: *darkling.* Also **-lings.** [OE *-ling, -linga*]

lin·ga (ling′gə) *n.* A phallus or phallic symbol, used extensively in the cult worship of Siva. Also **lin′gam** (-gəm). [<Skt. *lingam,* lit., symbol]

Lin·ga·yen Gulf (ling′gä·yen′) An inlet of the South China Sea in western Luzon, Philippines.

lin·ger (ling′gər) *v.i.* **1** To stay on as if reluctant to leave; delay going. **2** To move slowly; saunter; loiter: to *linger* on the way. **3** To dwell upon, as from enjoyment or persistence. **4** To continue in life or existence; endure: often with *on*: The sound *lingers* on in my memory. — *v.t.* **5** To protract; drag out. **6** To pass (time) in lingering: with *away* or *out.* [Earlier *lenger,* freq. of OE *lengen* delay. Akin to LONG.] — **lin′ger·er** *n.*

Synonyms: crawl, creep, dawdle, delay, drag, flag, halt, hesitate, lag, loiter, saunter, wait. *Antonyms*: see synonyms for ACCELERATE.

lin·ge·rie (län′zhə·rē, *Fr.* lan·zhrē′) *n.* Women's underwear: originally of laced linen, now of silk, rayon, nylon, etc. [<F *lingerie,* collective noun formed from *linge* linen]

lin·ger·ing (ling′gər·ing) *adj.* Protracted; slow; dilatory.

Ling·ga Archipelago (ling′gə) An Indonesian island group, including **Lingga Island** (319 square miles) off the east coast of Sumatra; 842 square miles.

lin·go (ling′gō) *n. pl.* **lin·goes 1** Language, especially if strange or unintelligible. **2** The specialized vocabulary and idiom of a profession, class, etc.: medical *lingo.* See synonyms under SLANG. [<Pg. <L *lingua* tongue]

lin·gua (ling′gwə) *n. pl.* **·guae** (-gwē) **1** The tongue. **2** A language. [<L]

lin·gua·den·tal (ling′gwə·den′təl) *adj.* & *n.* *Phonet.* Interdental. Also **lin·gui·den·tal** (ling′·gwi·den′təl).

lin·gua fran·ca (ling′gwə frang′kə) **1** A mixture of French, Spanish, Italian, Greek, and Arabic, spoken in the Mediterranean ports: often called *Sabir.* **2** Any mixed jargon used as a commercial or trade language, such as pidgin English, Chinook jargon, etc. [<Ital., lit., language of the Franks; prob. infl. by *franco* rough and ready]

lin·gual (ling′gwəl) *adj.* Pertaining to the tongue or the use of the tongue in utterance. — *n. Phonet.* A sound pronounced chiefly with the tongue, as (t), (d), and (l). [<Med. L *lingualis*]

Lin·guet·ta (lēng·gwet′tä), **Cape** The Italian name for CAPE GLOSSA.

lin·gui·form (ling′gwi·fôrm) *adj.* Tongue-shaped. [<L *lingua* + -FORM]

lin·guist (ling′gwist) *n.* **1** One who knows many languages. **2** An authority in linguistics. [<L *lingua* + -IST]

lin·guis·tic (ling·gwis′tik) *adj.* **1** Of or pertaining to language. **2** Pertaining to linguistics. Also **lin·guis′ti·cal.** — **lin·guis′ti·cal·ly** *adv.*

linguistic atlas Dialect atlas.

linguistic form Any unit of speech that has meaning, as a sentence, phrase, word, combining form, affix, etc.

lin·guis·tics (ling·gwis′tiks) *n.* The science of language, its origin, structure, modifications, etc., including among its studies the fields of phonetics, phonemics, morphology, syntax, and semantics: usually divided into **historical** (or *diachronic*) **linguistics,** the study of the evolution of languages and linguistic phenomena; **descriptive** (or *synchronic*) **linguistics,** the study of a language or languages at a given stage of development; **comparative linguistics,** the comparison and contrast of related languages; **geographical linguistics** (or **linguistic geography**), the classification of the distribution of languages and dialects on a regional basis.

linguistic stock 1 An original language and all the languages and dialects derived from it. **2** All the people speaking languages or dialects derived from one original: The Shawnee Indians belong to the Algonquian *linguistic stock.*

lin·gu·late (ling′gyə·lāt) *adj.* Having the shape of a tongue; linguiform; ligulate. [<L *lingula,* dim. of *lingua* tongue]

ling·y (ling′ē) *adj.* Covered with ling or heather.

lin·i·ment (lin′ə·mənt) *n.* A liquid preparation for external use, for bruises, inflammation, etc. [<LL *linimentum* <L *linire* anoint]

li·nin (lī′nin) *n.* **1** *Chem.* A white, bitter, crystalline compound, $C_{23}H_{22}O_9$, found in the purging flax (*Linum catharticum*). **2** *Biol.* A fiber of the nuclear reticulum of the cell that has little affinity for dyes; an achromatic thread of the nucleus: contrasted with *chromatin.* [<L *linum* + -IN]

lin·ing (lī′ning) *n.* **1** The act of one who lines. **2** A covering of the inner surface of a thing; also, material suitable for such use. **3** Contents.

link[1] (lingk) *n.* **1** One of the loops of which a chain is made; hence, something which connects separate things; a tie. **2** A hinge. **3** A single constituent part of a continuous series. **4** *Mech.* A connecting rod which transmits power from one part of a machine to another. **5** A length of 7.92 inches, or 20.11 centimeters, used in surveying. **6** *Colloq.* A section of a chain of sausages. **7** One of the component parts of a mechanical device formed of a number of identical or similar units. **8** *Chem.* A bond. **9** Links (def. 2). — *v.t.* & *v.i.* To join or connect by or as by links; unite. See synonyms under UNITE. [ME *linke* <Scand.; cf. Icel. *hlekkr,* Sw. *länk* a link. Akin to OE *hlencan* twist.]

link[2] (lingk) *n.* A torch. [Origin uncertain]

link[3] (lingk) *v.i. Scot.* & *Brit. Dial.* To walk lightly and quickly; trip.

link·age (ling′kij) *n.* **1** The act of linking, or the state of being linked. **2** *Mech.* A series or system of links and connecting rods for transmitting power, especially as used in automotive vehicles. **3** *Electr.* A relation between a magnetic line of force and the conductive coil that forms its vehicle. **4** *Biol.* Inheritance of the kind in which the genes, usually in the same chromosome, tend to act together as a unit or **linkage group** in the general process of segregation. **5** A pantograph.

link block *Mech.* The block sliding in or on a link, actuated thereby, and operating on the valve stem in link motion, either directly or through other members.

link·boy (lingk′boi′) *n.* A boy or man employed to light the way, by means of a link or torch, for pedestrians on dark streets. Also **link, link′man** (-mən).

linked (lingkt) *adj.* **1** Joined together. **2** *Biol.* Exhibiting linkage.

link hinge *Mech.* A hinge having the two leaves permanently attached to a link permitting free rotation. See illustration under HINGE.

link motion *Mech.* An assemblage of parts for operating the valves of locomotive and similar engines, its essential feature being a slotted bar, which is driven by one or two eccentrics.

Lin·kö·ping (lin′chœ·ping) A city of SE Sweden.

links (lingks) *n. pl.* **1** Flat or undulating land. **2** A golf course: sometimes construed as singular. [OE *hlinc* slope]

Link trainer *Aeron.* A ground device equipped to train airplane pilots for instrument flight: a trade name.

link·up (lingk′up′) *n.* **1** A linking together; contact: the *linkup* of space vehicles. **2** A pooling or combining, as of resources or efforts.

link·work (lingk′wûrk′) *n.* A fabric consisting of links joined together; a chain.

Lin·lith·gow (lin·lith′gō) A burgh in east central Scotland, county town of West Lothian.

Lin·lith·gow·shire (lin·lith′gō·shir) A former name for WEST LOTHIAN.

linn (lin) *n.* The linden tree. [<LINDEN]

Lin·nae·us (li·nē′əs), **Carolus,** 1707–78, Swedish naturalist and taxonomist; Latinized form of **Karl von Lin·né** (lē·nā′).

Lin·ne·an (li·nē′ən) *adj.* Pertaining to Linnaeus, especially to his binomial system of classifying plants and animals according to genus and species. Also **Lin·nae′an.**

lin·net (lin′it) *n.* **1** One of various singing birds, as the common European **gray** or **gorse linnet** (genus *Carduelis*), the male of which in summer has the breast and crown bright crimson. **2** The house finch (*Carpodacus mexicana*) of the western United States. [<OF *linette* <L *linum* flax; from its feeding on flax seeds]

Lin·nhe (lin′ē), **Loch** An inlet on the west coast of Scotland between Inverness and Argyll.

lin·o·le·ic (lin′ə·lē′ik, li·nō′lē·ik) *adj. Chem.* Of or denoting a colorless to yellow, oily, fatty acid, $C_{18}H_{32}O_2$, found in linseed oil, cottonseed oil, and other vegetable oils. [< LINOLEUM]

li·no·le·um (li·nō′lē·əm) *n.* A preparation of linseed oil hardened by oxidizing. When mixed with ground cork and pressed upon canvas or burlap, it is used as a floor covering. [<L *linum* flax + *oleum* oil]

Li·no·type (lī′nə·tīp) *n.* A machine which casts a complete line of type on a single body: a trade name. **— li′no·typ′er, li′no·typ′·ist** *n.*

lin·sang (lin′sang) *n.* A long-tailed, East Indian viverrine mammal (genus *Prionodon*) related to but smaller than the genet. [< Javanese *linsang*]

lin·seed (lin′sēd′) *n.* Flaxseed. [OE *līnsǣd*]

linseed oil A yellowish drying oil made from flaxseed.

lin·sey-wool·sey (lin′zē·wŏŏl′zē) *n.* **1** A cloth made of linen and wool or cotton and wool mixed. **2** *Obs.* Nonsense; jargon. **—** *adj.* Made of linen and wool. [ME *lynsy-wolsye* < *lynsy* (? < *lin* linen + *saye* cloth) + WOOL]

lin·stock (lin′stok) *n.* Formerly, an iron-shod pike with a crotch designed to hold a rope match for firing a gun. [<Du. *lontstok* < *lont* match + *stok* stick]

lint (lint) *n.* **1** The soft down of raveled or scraped linen; also, downy feathers. **2** A net; netting. **3** Cotton fiber. [<L *linteum* linen cloth < *linum* flax] **— lint′y** *adj.*

lin·tel (lin′təl) *n.* A horizontal top piece, as of a doorway or window opening. [<OF <LL *lintellus, limitellus,* dim. of *limes, limites* limit]

lint·er (lin′tər) *n.* A machine for removing linters from cotton seeds after they have been ginned.

lint·ers (lin′tərz) *n. pl.* A mixture of cotton fuzz and fibers left behind on the cotton gin: used as batting, for stuffing upholstery, and in the manufacture of rayon.

lint·white (lint′hwīt′) *n.* The European gray linnet. [OE *līnetwige,* lit., flax-plucker]

lin·y (lī′nē) *adj.* **lin·i·er, lin·i·est** **1** Like a line. **2** Full of, or marked with, lines or streaks. Also spelled *liney.*

Lin Yu·tang (lin′yōō′täng′), born 1895, Chinese writer and philologist active in the United States.

Linz (lints) A city on the Danube, the capital of Upper Austria.

li·on (lī′ən) *n.* **1** A large, yellowish-brown or tawny, carnivorous mammal (*Panthera leo*) of the cat family, native to Africa and SW Asia, the adult male having a long mane. **2** Figuratively, a man of conspicuous courage; one of leonine character or mien. **3** An object of peculiar interest and curiosity; a prominent or notable person. **4** A former gold coin of Scotland. **— mountain lion** The puma. **— to twist the lion's tail** To make anti-British statements: from the lion on the heraldic shield of England. [<F <L *leo* <Gk. *leōn*]

LION
(About 3 feet high at the shoulder; length: 10 feet over-all)

Li·on (lī′ən) The zodiacal sign or the constellation Leo. See CONSTELLATION.

Lion, Gulf of the A wide bay of the Mediterranean Sea in the southern coast of France. *French* **Golfe du Lion** (lē·ôn′).

lion dog **1** In Chinese and Japanese art and sculpture, a stylized lion, distorted so that the body resembles that of a dog, used as a symbol of good luck: also *Foo dog.* **2** Any of several breeds of small dog, as the Lhasa apso or Pekingese, having a leonine head.

li·on·ess (lī′ən·is) *n.* A female lion. [<OF *lionnesse*]

li·on·et (lī′ən·et) *n.* A small or young lion; a lion cub. [<OF]

li·on·heart (lī′ən·härt′) *n.* A person of exceptional bravery; especially, **Lionheart,** as a nickname of Richard I of England. See COEUR DE LION. **— lion′heart′ed** *adj.*

li·on·ize (lī′ən·īz) *v.t.* **·ized, ·iz·ing** To treat or regard as a celebrity. **— li′on·i·za′tion** *n.*

lip (lip) *n.* **1** One of the two folds of flesh that bound the mouth and cover the teeth. ◆ Collateral adjective: *labial.* **2** Hence, from the use of these organs in speaking, speech; especially, impertinent speech; sauciness. **3** Anything having the appearance or purpose of a lip, as of a cup, bell, crater, wound, etc. **4** An embouchure. **5** Any structure that bounds an orifice, slit, or groove. **6** *Bot.* Either of the two large lobes of a bilabiate corolla or calyx; also, in orchids, a labium. **— to keep a stiff upper lip** To keep up one's courage; be stoical. **—** *v.* **lipped, lip·ping** *v.t.* **1** To touch with the lips; apply the lips to. **2** *Archaic* To utter with the lips; whisper. **3** In golf, to hit the ball so that it strikes the edge of (the cup) without dropping in. **—** *v.i.* **4** To adjust the lips to the mouthpiece of a wind instrument for playing. **—** *adj.* **1** Of or pertaining to the lips or a lip. **2** Characterized by or made with the lips. **3** Made with the lips only; superficial; insincere: *lip* service. [OE *lippa*]

Lip·a·ri Islands (lip′ə·rē, *Ital.* lē′pä·rē) A group of volcanic islands off the NE coast of Sicily; 45 square miles. Italian *Isole Eolie*: also *Aeolian Islands.*

lip·a·roid (lip′ə·roid) *adj.* Fatty; resembling fat. [<Gk. *liparos* fat, greasy + -OID]

lip·ase (lip′ās, lī′pās) *n.* A fat-splitting enzyme.

li·pec·to·my (li·pek′tə·mē) *n. Surg.* An operation for the removal of excess fatty tissue. [<LIP(O)- + -ECTOMY]

lip·id (lip′id, lī′pid) *n. Biochem.* Any of a large class of organic substances which include the true fats and certain related compounds, as waxes and sterols. They are insoluble in water and have a typical greasy feel. Also **lip·ide** (lip′īd, lī′pīd).

Li Po (lē′ bō′), 700?–762, Chinese poet: also *Li T'ai-po.*

lipo- *combining form* **1** Fat; fatty: *lipotropic.* **2** A lipid: *lipoprotein.* Also, before vowels, **lip-.** [<Gk. *lipos* fat]

lip·o·ca·ic (lip′ō·kā′ik) *n. Biochem.* A hormonelike substance extracted from raw pancreas and having the power to regulate the fat metabolism of the liver. [<LIPO- + Gk. *kaiein* burn]

lip·o·chrome (lip′ō·krōm) *n. Biochem.* Any of a class of pigments, including the carotenoids, found in natural fats, as butter or egg yolk.

lip·o·cyte (lip′ō·sīt) *n. Biol.* A fat-bearing cell.

lip·oid (lip′oid) *n. Biochem.* A fat that is not decomposed by alkalis, as cholesterol.

li·pol·y·sis (li·pol′ə·sis) *n.* The breakdown and decomposition of fat. [<LIPO- + -LYSIS] **— lip·o·lyt·ic** (lip′ō·lit′ik) *adj.*

li·po·ma (li·pō′mə) *n. Pathol.* A tumor, generally painless and benign, made up of fat cells. [<LIP(O)- + -OMA] **— li·pom·a·tous** (li·pom′ə·təs) *adj.*

lip·o·pro·te·in (lip′ō·prō′tē·in, -tēn) *n. Biochem.* Any of a class of proteins found in combination with lipids, as in blood, egg yolk, milk, etc.

li·pot·ro·py (li·pot′rə·pē) *n.* An affinity for fats or oils or for fatty tissue. Also **li·pot′ro·pism. — lip·o·trop·ic** (lip′ō·trop′ik) *adj.*

Lip·pe (lip′ə) A former state of NW Germany, now included in North Rhine-Westphalia; 469 square miles; capital, Detmold.

lipped (lipt) *adj.* **1** Having a lip, lips, or a structure resembling lips. **2** *Bot.* Labiate.

lip·pen (lip′ən) *v.t.* & *v.i. Scot.* To trust.

Lip·pi (lip′ē, *Ital.* lēp′pē), **Filippo,** 1406?–69, Florentine painter and monk: known as *Fra Lippo Lippi.* **— Filippino,** 1457?–1504, Florentine painter; son of the preceding.

Lip·pi·zan·er (lip′it·sä′nər) *n.* One of a breed of generally white horses developed in Austria and often ridden in dressage exhibitions.

Lipp·mann (lēp·mån′), **Gabriel,** 1845–1921, French physicist.

Lipp·mann (lip′mən), **Walter,** 1889–1974, U.S. journalist and author.

lip-read (lip′rēd′) *v.t. & v.i.* **-read, -read·ing** To interpret (speech) from the position assumed by the lips and mouth for each word.

lip-read·ing (lip′rē′ding) *n.* Interpretation of speech from the position of the lips and mouth of the speaker: practiced especially by the deaf. **— lip′-read′er** *n.*

lip service Service that is professed but not intended or performed.

lip·stick (lip′stik′) *n.* A small, colored cosmetic stick of creamy texture, used to tint lips.

Lip·ton (lip′tən), **Sir Thomas Johnston,** 1850–1931, English merchant and yachtsman.

li·quate (lī′kwāt) *v.t.* **·quat·ed, ·quat·ing** **1** To liquefy; melt. **2** *Metall.* To separate (a metal) from its impurities by the application of heat. [<L *liquatus,* pp. of *liquare* melt] **— li·qua·tion** (lī·kwā′shən) *n.*

liq·ue·fac·tion (lik′wə·fak′shən) *n.* **1** The operation of liquefying. **2** The state of being liquefied. **— liq′ue·fa′cient** (-fā′shənt) *adj.* & *n.*

liq·ue·fi·er (lik′wə·fī′ər) *n.* An apparatus devised for the liquefaction of gases.

liq·ue·fy (lik′wə·fī) *v.t.* & *v.i.* **·fied, ·fy·ing** To convert into or become liquid; melt. See synonyms under MELT. [<L *liquefacere* < *liquere* be liquid + *facere* make] **— liq′ue·fi′a·ble** *adj.*

li·ques·cent (li·kwes′ənt) *adj.* **1** Melting. **2** Having a tendency to melt or to become liquid. [<L *liquescens, -entis,* ppr. of *liquescere,* incept. of *liquere* become liquid] **— li·ques′cence, li·ques′cen·cy** *n.*

li·queur (li·kûr′) *n.* A sweetened alcoholic beverage, usually served after dinner, made by flavoring a spirit with aromatic ingredients, such as fruit, seeds, or herbs, before the distillation process; a cordial. [<F <OF *licur.* Doublet of LIQUOR.]

liq·uid (lik′wid) *adj.* **1** Flowing, or capable of flowing; being a liquid. **2** Limpid; clear. **3** *Physics* Composed of molecules having free movement among themselves, but without a separative tendency like that of gases. **4** Flowing smoothly; mellifluous: *liquid* tones. **5** Containing or suggesting liquid; watery. **6** *Phonet.* Pronounced with a smoothly flowing sound; vowel-like, as (l) and (r). **7** Easily or quickly converted into cash: *liquid* assets. See synonyms for FLUID. **—** *n.* **1** *Physics* A substance in that state in which the particles move freely among themselves and remain in one mass; a fluid which differs from a gas in not diffusing through the entire volume of a containing vessel. **2** *Phonet.* The consonants (l) and (r). [<F *liquide* <L *liquidus* < *liquere* be liquid] **— li·quid·i·ty** (li·kwid′·ə·tē), **liq′uid·ness** *n.* **— liq′uid·ly** *adv.*

liquid air An intensely cold mixture of nitrogen and oxygen, existing only at temperatures below the boiling point of its components, and brought to a liquid condition by a reduction of temperature and an increase of pressure: chiefly used as a refrigerant.

liq·uid·am·bar (lik′wid·am′bər) *n.* **1** Any of a genus *(Liquidambar)* of balsamiferous trees of eastern Asia and Atlantic North America; especially, the American sweetgum. **2** The balsam yielded by such trees: used in medicine and the arts; copalm. [<NL]

liq·ui·date (lik′wə·dāt) *v.* **·dat·ed, ·dat·ing** *v.t.* **1** *Law* **a** To determine and settle the liabilities of (an estate, firm, etc.) and apportion the assets. **b** To determine and settle the amount of, as indebtedness or damages. **2** To pay or settle, as a debt. **3** To convert into cash. **4** To destroy or annihilate; do away with. **5** *Slang* To murder. — *v.i.* **6** To settle one's debts; go into liquidation. [< Med. L *liquidatus,* pp. of *liquidare* make liquid or clear <L *liquidus* liquid] — **liq′ui·da′·tor** *n.*

liq·ui·da·tion (lik′wə·dā′shən) *n.* The act of liquidating or the state of being liquidated. — **to go into liquidation** To cease from transacting business and gather in assets, settle debts, and divide surpluses, if any.

liquid crystal *Chem.* A substance intermediate in state between liquid and solid, having the fluidity of a liquid and the optical anisotropy of a crystalline solid.

liquid fire Burning oil or other inflammable chemicals: used in warfare, as from flame-throwers.

liquid measure A unit or system of units for measuring liquids, as in the following table of principal customary standards. See also METRIC SYSTEM.

4 gills	=	1 pint (pt., pts.)
2 pints	=	1 quart (qt., qts.)
4 quarts	=	1 gallon (gal., gals.)
60 minims (min., ♏)	=	1 fluid dram (fl. dr., ʒ)
8 fluid drams	=	1 fluid ounce (fl. oz., ℥)
16 fluid ounces	=	1 pint

liq·uo·crys·tal·line (lik′wō·kris′tə·lin, -līn) *adj.* Designating that state of a liquid which exhibits properties similar to those of a crystal; mesomorphic.

liq·uor (lik′ər) *n.* **1** Any alcoholic or intoxicating liquid; especially, one that is distilled. **2** One of various solutions; specifically, an aqueous solution of a non-volatile substance: distinguished from a sirup, infusion, or decoction. **3** A liquid of any sort, as blood, milk, etc. — *v.t.* **1** To treat with liquor (def. 2). **2** *Slang* To supply or ply with alcoholic liquor: often with *up.* — *v.i.* **3** *Slang* To drink alcoholic liquor, especially in quantity: usually with *up.* [<OF *licor, licur* <L *liquor.* Doublet of LIQUEUR.]

liq·uo·rice (lik′ə·ris, -rish) See LICORICE.

liq·uor·ish (lik′ə·rish) See LICKERISH.

li·ra (lir′ə, *Ital.* lē′rä) *n. pl.* **li·re** (lir′ə, *Ital.* lē′rā) **1** The monetary unit of Italy, a small coin equivalent to 100 centesimi. **2** A gold coin of Turkey equivalent to 100 piasters: also called *Turkish pound.* [<Ital. <L *libra* pound]

Li·ri (lē′rē) A river in south central Italy, flowing 98 miles south to the Gulf of Gaeta. Ancient **Li·ris** (lir′is).

lir·i·o·den·dron (lir′ē·ō·den′drən) *n. pl.* **·dra** (-drə) Any of a genus *(Liriodendron)* of Asian and North American trees of the magnolia family; especially, the tuliptree of the United States. [<NL <Gk. *leirion* lily + *dendron* tree]

lir·i·pipe (lir′ə·pīp) *n.* In medieval dress, the long tail of a clerical tippet; hence, any long scarf or streamer attached to a headdress. Also **lir′i·poop** (-po͞op). [<Med. L *liripipium;* ult. origin uncertain]

LIRIPIPE

Li·sa (lē′sə, -zə, lī′-) Diminutive of ELIZABETH. Also **Li′za.**

Lis·bon (liz′bən) A port on the Tagus, capital of Portugal. *Portuguese* **Lis·bo·a** (lēzh·bō′ə).

Li·sette (lē·zet′) French diminutive of ELIZABETH.

lisle (līl) *n.* **1** A fine, hard-twisted cotton thread, formerly linen: used in knitting gloves, stockings, etc. **2** Any fabric made of lisle thread. [from *Lisle,* now Lille, France]

Lisle (lēl) A former spelling of LILLE.

lisp (lisp) *n.* **1** A speech defect or affectation in which the sibilants (s) and (z) are pronounced with the tongue between the teeth so that the sounds produced are like (th) in *thank* and (t͟h) in *this.* **2** The act or habit of speaking with a lisp. **3** The sound of a lisp. — *v.t.* & *v.i.* **1** To pronounce or speak with a lisp. **2** To speak imperfectly or in a childlike manner. [OE *wlispian*] — **lisp′er** *n.*

lis pen·dens (lis pen′denz) *Law Latin* A suit pending; during the pendency of a suit: Land bought of a defendant *lis pendens* is taken subject to the judgment afterward rendered.

lis·some (lis′əm) *adj.* Lithesome. Also **lis′som.** See synonyms under SUPPLE. [Alter. of LITHESOME] — **lis′some·ness** *n.*

lis·sot·ri·chous (li·sot′rə·kəs) *adj.* Having straight hair. [<Gk. *lissos* smooth + *thrix, trichos* hair]

list[1] (list) *n.* A series of words, numbers, names, etc., as on a strip of paper; a roll or catalog. — *v.t.* To place on or in a list or catalog, especially in alphabetical or numerical order. [<OF *liste* <OHG *līsta*]

list[2] (list) *n.* **1** The selvage or edge of a woven textile fabric. **2** Selvages, collectively. **3** A strip of fabric. **4** A colored stripe. **5** A narrow strip of wood cut from a plank. **6** *Agric.* A ridge or furrow made with a lister in cultivating corn. **7** *pl.* The palisades bounding a piece of ground used as a jousting field; hence, the field itself. — **to enter the lists** To accept a challenge; enter a contest or discussion. — *v.t.* **1** To cover with lists of cloth. **2** To sew or arrange in strips or stripes. **3** *Agric.* **a** To plow by means of a lister. **b** To plant by means of a lister. **4** In carpentry, to remove the rough edge of, as a board. [OE *līste*]

list[3] (list) *v.t.* & *v.i.* **1** To lean or incline to one side; careen, as a ship. **2** *Archaic* To wish or choose; please. — *n.* **1** A careening; leaning or inclination of a ship to one side. **2** *Archaic* Desire; wish. [OE *lystan* < *lust* desire]

list[4] (list) *v.t.* & *v.i. Poetic* To listen to or listen. See synonyms under LISTEN. [OE *hlystan* < *hlyst* hearing]

List (list), **Siegmund Wilhelm Walther,** born 1880, German field marshal in World War II.

listed security A stock or bond that has been admitted to the roster of approved securities by a stock exchange, thus becoming available for trading on the exchange.

lis·tel (lis′təl) *n. Archit.* A small square molding; a list. [<F <Ital. *listello,* dim. of *lista* list[2]]

lis·ten (lis′ən) *v.i.* **1** To make an effort to hear; give ear. **2** To pay attention; give heed or compliance, as to warning or advice. — *n.* The act of listening. [OE *hlysnan*] — **lis′·ten·er** *n.*

Synonyms (verb): attend, hark, harken, hear, heed, list[4]. To *hear* is simply to become conscious of sound, to *listen* is to make a conscious effort to *hear.* We may *hear* without *listening,* as words suddenly uttered in an adjoining room; or we may *listen* without *hearing,* as to a distant speaker. In *listening* the ear is intent upon the sound; in *attending* the mind is intent upon the thought, but *listening* implies some attention to the meaning or import of the sound. To *heed* is not only to *attend,* but to remember and observe. *Harken* is nearly obsolete. *Antonyms:* ignore, neglect, scorn, slight.

listening post **1** A concealed position near enemy lines from which an observer may transmit to his own forces information or warning of hostile action. **2** A station equipped with sound-locating devices for warning against the approach of enemy aircraft or sea vessels. **3** A radio station equipped to pick up short-wave messages from different countries.

list·er[1] (lis′tər) *n. Agric.* A double-moldboard plow for throwing up ridges, as in beet- or corn-culture: it simultaneously throws a deep furrow, plants the seed, and covers it with earth. Also called *middle-breaker.* [<LIST[2] + -ER[1]]

list·er[2] (lis′tər) *n.* One who makes a list or lists; specifically, a tax appraiser.

Lis·ter (lis′tər), **Joseph,** 1827–1912, Baron Lister of Lyme Regis, English surgeon; founder of antiseptic surgery.

Lister bag See LYSTER BAG.

Lis·ter·ine (lis′tə·rēn′, lis′tə·rēn) *n.* Proprietary name for a weak antiseptic solution. [after Sir Joseph *Lister*]

list·ing (lis′ting) *n.* **1** The compiling of a list. **2** A place on a list.

list·less (list′lis) *adj.* Inattentive; heedless of what is passing; indifferent; languid; lacking energy. See synonyms under FAINT, INATTENTIVE. [OE *lust* desire + -LESS] — **list′·less·ly** *adv.* — **list′less·ness** *n.*

list mill A power-driven wheel covered with cloth on which gemstones are buffed or polished.

list price The price of goods as published in price lists or catalogs.

Liszt (list), **Franz,** 1811–86, Hungarian composer and pianist.

lit[1] (lit) Alternative past tense and past participle of LIGHT[1] and LIGHT[2].

lit[2] (lit) *n.* The gold monetary unit of Lithuania. Also *Lithuanian* **li·tas** (lē′täs).

lit·a·ny (lit′ə·nē) *n. pl.* **·nies** **1** *Eccl.* A liturgical form of prayer, consisting of a series of different supplications said by the clergy, to which the choir or people repeat the same response. **2** Any solemn prayer. See synonyms under prayer. — **the Litany** In the Book of Common Prayer, a general supplication in this form. [<OF *letanie* <LL *litania* <Gk. *litaneia* < *litaneuein* pray]

li·tchi (lē′chē) *n.* **1** A Chinese tree *(Litchi chinensis)* of the soapberry family, producing small, thin-shelled, edible fruits called **litchi nuts. 2** The fruit of this tree. Also spelled *lichee, lychee.* [<Chinese *li-chih*]

lit de ju·stice (lē də zhü·stēs′) *French* Literally, bed of justice; the seat which the king of France occupied when holding a formal session of the parliament; hence, the session itself.

-lite *combining form Mineral.* Stone; stonelike: *cryolite.* Also spelled *-lyte.* [<F, var. of *-lithe* <Gk. *lithos* stone]

li·te pen·den·te (lī′tē pen·den′tē) *Latin* During the trial.

li·ter (lē′tər) *n.* A measure of capacity in the metric system, equal to the volume of one kilogram of water at 4° C. and 760 mm. atmospheric pressure, or to 1.0567 liquid quarts. See METRIC SYSTEM. Also *litre.* [<F *litre* <Gk. *litra* pound]

lit·er·a·cy (lit′ər·ə·sē) *n.* The state or condition of being literate.

lit·er·al (lit′ər·əl) *adj.* **1** According to the letter or verbal statement; not figurative or metaphorical. **2** Following the exact words or construction: a *literal* translation. **3** Consisting of or expressed by letters. **4** Matter-of-fact; unimaginative: said of persons. **5** Exact as to fact or detail; not exaggerated. See synonyms under VERBAL. ◆ Homophone: *littoral.* [<OF <LL *literalis, litteralis* < *littera* letter]

lit·er·al·ism (lit′ər·əl·iz′əm) *n.* **1** Close adherence to the exact word or sense, often to the point of unimaginativeness. **2** In the fine arts, a tendency to represent without idealizing; realistic representation or depiction. — **lit′er·al·ist** *n.*

lit·er·al·ize (lit′ər·əl·īz′) *v.t.* **·ized, ·iz·ing** To make literal; interpret or accept literally.

lit·er·al·ly (lit′ər·ə·lē) *adv.* **1** In a literal manner. **2** *Colloq.* In a manner of speaking; figuratively: used for emphasis: He was *literally* green with envy.

lit·er·ar·y (lit′ə·rer′ē) *adj.* **1** Of or pertaining to letters or used in literature. **2** Versed in or devoted to literature. **3** Engaged or occupied in the field of literature: a *literary* man. [<L *litterarius*]

lit·er·ate (lit′ər·it) *adj.* **1** Able to read and write. **2** Having a knowledge of letters or literature; educated. **3** Literary. — *n.* **1** Anyone able to read and write. **2** One versed in letters or literature. [<L *litteratus* < *littera* letter]

lit·e·ra·ti (lit′ə·rä′tē, -rā′tī) *n. pl.* Men of letters; scholars. [<L]

lit·e·ra·tim (lit′ə·rā′tim, -rä′-) *adv.* Letter for letter; with exact literalness; literally. [<L]

lit·er·a·tor (lit′ə·rā′tər) *n.* A literary man. [<L]

lit·er·a·ture (lit′ər·ə·cho͝or, lit′rə·chər) *n.* **1** The written or printed productions of the human mind collectively. **2** Written works which deal with themes of permanent and universal interest, characterized by creativeness and grace of expression, as poetry, fiction, essays, etc.: distinguished from works of scientific, technical, or journalistic nature; belles-lettres. **3** The writings that pertain to a particular epoch, country, language, subject, or branch of learning: ancient *literature*; the *literature* of chemistry. **4** The act or occupation of a literary man; literary work. **5** Acquaintance with letters or books; learning. **6** *Music* The total number of compositions for a particular instrument or ensemble. **7** Any printed matter used or distributed for advertising or political purposes, etc.: campaign *literature.* [<L *litteratura* < *littera* letter]

Synonyms: belles-lettres, books, publications, writings. *Literature* is collective, referring to all that has been written in some land or age, or in some department of human knowledge: the *literature* of Greece; the *literature* of art. *Literature,* used absolutely, denotes *belles-lettres, i.e.,* the works collectively that embody taste, feeling, loftiness of thought, and purity and beauty of style, as poetry, history, fiction, and dramatic compositions. In the broad sense we speak of the *literature* of science; in the narrower sense, we speak of *literature* and science as distinct departments of knowledge. *Literature* is also used to signify literary pursuits or occupations: to devote one's life to *literature.* Compare KNOWLEDGE.

lith (lith) *n. Archaic* A limb; joint; segment: usually in the phrase **lith and limb.** [OE]

-lith *combining form* Stone; rock: *monolith.* [<Gk. *lithos* a stone]

lith·arge (lith′ärj, li·thärj′) *n.* Yellow lead monoxide, PbO, made by heating lead in a current of air: used in glassmaking, as a pigment, cement, etc. [<F *litarge* <L *lithargyrus* <Gk. *lithargyros* silver scum < *lithos* stone + *argyros* silver]

lithe (līth) *adj.* Bending easily or gracefully; supple. See synonyms under SUPPLE. [OE, soft] **— lithe′ly** *adv.* **— lithe′ness** *n.*

li·the·mi·a (li·thē′mē·ə) *n. Pathol.* An excess of urates and uric acid in the blood. Also **li·thae·mi·a.** [<LITH(O)- + -EMIA] **— li·the′mic** *adj.*

lithe·some (līth′səm) *adj.* Lithe; nimble; lissome.

lith·i·a (lith′ē·ə) *n.* A white, caustic compound, Li_2O, that dissolves slowly in water to form lithium hydrate; lithium oxide. [<NL <Gk. *lithos* stone]

li·thi·a·sis (li·thī′ə·sis) *n. Pathol.* The formation of stones or calculi in the body. [<NL <Gk. < *lithos* stone]

lithia water A natural mineral water containing lithium salts.

lith·ic (lith′ik) *adj.* **1** Of, pertaining to, or having calculus or stone in the bladder. **2** Of or pertaining to stone. **3** *Chem.* Of or pertaining to lithium. [<Gk. *lithikos* of stone]

lith·i·um (lith′ē·əm) *n.* A soft, silver-white, metallic element (symbol Li) belonging to the first group of the periodic table. It is the lightest of the metals and is found only in combination. See ELEMENT. [<NL <Gk. *lithos* stone]

litho- *combining form* Stone; related to stone: *lithophilous.* Also, before vowels, **lith-.** [<Gk. *lithos* stone]

lith·o·graph (lith′ə·graf, -gräf) *v.t.* To produce or reproduce by lithography. **—** *n.* A lithographic print. [<LITHO- + -GRAPH] **— li·thog·ra·pher** (li·thog′rə·fər) *n.* **— lith′o·graph′ic** or **·i·cal** *adj.* **— lith′o·graph′i·cal·ly** *adv.*

li·thog·ra·phy (li·thog′rə·fē) *n.* The art of producing printed matter from a stone or stones on which the design or matter to be printed has been made in a soapy ink, grease pencil, or other suitable material. Zinc and aluminum are now widely substituted for stone.

lithographic stone A yellowish, compact, fine-grained, slaty limestone used in lithography. Also **lithographic slate.**

lith·oid (lith′oid) *adj.* Of or resembling stone; having stony structure or texture. Also **li·thoi·dal** (li·thoid′l).

li·thol·o·gy (li·thol′ə·jē) *n.* **1** The science that treats of rocks as mineral masses, especially with reference to their structure. **2** The branch of medicine which treats of calculi in the body. [<LITHO- + -LOGY] **— lith·o·log·ic** (lith′ə·loj′ik) or **·i·cal** *adj.* **— li·thol′o·gist** *n.*

lith·o·marge (lith′ə·märj) *n.* A mixture of hydrous aluminum silicates, related to kaolin. [<LITHO- + L *marga* marl]

lith·o·phane (lith′ə·fān) *n.* Ornamentation impressed in porcelain or glass, as in a lampshade, made visible by light passing through it. [<LITHO- +Gk. *-phaneia, phainein* appear]

li·thoph·i·lous (li·thof′ə·ləs) *adj.* **1** Stone-loving. **2** *Ecol.* Living among, beneath, or on stones: said of insects and plants preferring a stony habitat. [<LITHO- + -PHILOUS]

lith·o·phyte (lith′ə·fīt) *n.* **1** *Zool.* A calcareous or stony polyp or plantlike organism, as a coral. **2** *Bot.* A plant that lives on stony or rocky surfaces in air or under water. **— lith′o·phyt′ic** (-fit′ik) *adj.*

lith·o·pone (lith′ə·pōn) *n.* A mixture of barium sulfate and zinc sulfide, used as a white paint and in the manufacture of rubber tires, linoleums, etc. [<LITHO- + L *ponere* place]

lith·o·sphere (lith′ə·sfir) *n.* The rigid crust of rock surrounding the inner viscous material of the earth and similar bodies in the solar system.

li·thot·o·my (li·thot′ə·mē) *n. Surg.* The operation of removing stones from the bladder by incision into the organ. [<LL *lithotomia* <Gk. < *lithos* stone + *temnein* cut] **— lith·o·tom·ic** (lith′-ə·tom′ik) or **·i·cal** *adj.* **— li·thot′o·mist** *n.*

lith·o·tint (lith′ə·tint) *n.* **1** The art of producing pictures in color tints from lithographic stones. **2** A picture so produced.

li·thot·ri·ty (li·thot′rə·tē) *n. Surg.* The operation of reducing stone in the bladder to fine, easily voided fragments. Also **li·thot′rip·sy** (-rip·sē). [<LITHO- + L *tritus,* pp. of *terere* rub, grind]

Lith·u·a·ni·a (lith′o͞o·ā′nē·ə) Southernmost of the Baltic States of NE Europe; since 1940 formally **Lithuanian Soviet Socialist Republic,** a constituent republic of the U.S.S.R.; 25,200 square miles; capital, Vilna. *Lithuanian* **Lie·tu·va** (lye·to͞o′vä).

Lith·u·a·ni·an (lith′o͞o·ā′nē·ən) *adj.* Of or pertaining to Lithuania, its people, or their language. **—** *n.* **1** A native or inhabitant of Lithuania. **2** The Balto-Slavic language of the Lithuanians, belonging to the Baltic branch.

lith·y (lī′thē) *adj.* **lith·i·er, lith·i·est** *Archaic* Lithe; flexible; willowy.

lit·i·gant (lit′ə·gənt) *adj.* Disposed to litigate; engaged in litigation. **—** *n.* A party to a lawsuit. [<F]

lit·i·gate (lit′ə·gāt) *v.* **·gat·ed, ·gat·ing** *v.t.* To bring before a court of law for decision or settlement; contest at law. **—** *v.i.* To carry on a lawsuit. [<L *litigatus,* pp. of *litigare* < *lis, litis* lawsuit + *agere* do, act] **— lit′i·ga·ble** (-gə·bəl) *adj.* **— lit′i·ga′tor** *n.*

lit·i·ga·tion (lit′ə·gā′shən) *n.* The act of carrying on a suit in a law court; a judicial contest; hence, any controversy that must be decided upon evidence.

li·tig·ious (li·tij′əs) *adj.* **1** Inclined to litigation; hence, quarrelsome. **2** Subject to litigation or contention; controvertible; disputable: a *litigious* right. **3** Of or pertaining to litigation: *litigious* form. [<F *litigieux* <L *litigiosus* < *litigium* litigation] **— li·tig′ious·ly** *adv.* **— li·tig′ious·ness** *n.*

lit·mus (lit′məs) *n.* A blue dyestuff made by fermenting certain coarsely powdered lichens. It is turned red by acids and remains blue when treated with an alkali. Also called *lacmus.* [<AF *lytemoise* <ON *litmose* lichen used in dyeing < *litr* color + *mosi* moss]

litmus paper Unsized paper dipped into a solution of litmus, and used to test solutions for acidity.

lit·o·ral (lit′ər·əl) See LITTORAL.

li·to·tes (lī′tə·tēz, -tō-, lit′ə-) *n.* A rhetorical figure in which an assertion is made by means of negation or understatement; ironic understatement. Example: a fact of no small importance (*i.e.,* of very great importance). See MEIOSIS. [<NL <Gk. *litotēs* < *litos* simple, spare]

li·tre (lē′tər) See LITER.

lit·ter (lit′ər) *n.* **1** The offspring borne at one time by a cat, sow, or other multiparous animal. **2** A stretcher used for conveying sick or wounded. **3** A couch carried on shafts protruding at each end, and used for the transportation of people of wealth or importance. **4** Straw, hay, or other similar material, used as bedding for horses, cattle, etc. **5** Waste materials, shreds, and fragments scattered about; a clutter; a state of disorder. **6** The upper part of a forest floor which is not in an advanced state of decomposition. See synonyms under FLOCK. **—** *v.t.* **1** To bring forth young: said of animals. **2** To furnish, as cattle, with litter. **3** To cover or strew with or as with litter: often with *up*: to *litter* a room with toys. **4** To throw or spread about carelessly. **—** *v.i.* **5** To give birth to a litter of young. [<OF *litiere* < Med. L *lectaria* <L *lectus* bed] **— lit′ter·y** *adj.*

LITTER
Late Roman period.

lit·te·rae hu·ma·ni·o·res (lit′ə·rē hyo͞o·mā′nē·ō′rēz) *Latin* Humanistic studies; classical literature, history, and philosophy.

lit·ter·a·teur (lit′ər·ə·tûr′) *n.* One who is by profession engaged in literature. [<F]

lit·ter·bug (lit′ər·bug′) *n. Colloq.* A person who is careless in disposing of garbage, waste, and litter; one who violates or ignores street-cleaning regulations.

lit·tle (lit′l) *adj.* **less** or *Colloq.* **lit·tler, least** or *Colloq.* **lit·tlest 1** Of a size, amount, quantity, etc., below the ordinary; diminutive; small. **2** Below the usual amount; restricted. **3** Below the normal distance or time; short; brief. **4** Below the standard in respect to dignity or consequence; insignificant; petty; hence, mean; narrow: a *little* quarrel, a *little* nature. **5** Lacking in ability, efficiency, or force; weak. **6** Smaller than other like things. **7** Being in the early years of life: when I was *little.* **—** *n.* A small quantity, space, time, degree, etc. **—** *adv.* **less, least 1** In a small degree; slightly. **2** Not at all: used before a verb: She *little* knows how much I care. [OE *lȳtel* < *lȳt* small] **— lit′tle·ness** *n.*

Synonyms (adj.): brief, contemptible, diminutive, feeble, inconsiderable, insignificant, mean, microscopic, minute, narrow, paltry, petty, short, slender, slight, small, tiny, trifling, trivial, unimportant. See INSIGNIFICANT, MINUTE², SMALL.

Little America An Antarctic base for exploring expeditions, on the Ross Shelf Ice south of the Bay of Wales; established by Admiral Byrd, 1929.

Lit·tle (lit′l), **Malcolm** See MALCOLM X.

Little Armenia See CILICIA.

Little Bear See under BEAR.

Little Big·horn River (big′hôrn′) A river in Wyoming and Montana, flowing 90 miles north to the Bighorn River; scene of Custer's defeat by Indians, 1876.

little boy A young boy, usually one between the ages of two and ten or eleven.

Little Colorado River A river flowing 315 miles north through Arizona to the Colorado River in the Grand Canyon.

Little Dipper See URSA MINOR.

Lit·tle-end·i·an (lit′l·en′dē·ən) *n.* One who disputes about trifles: from Swift's *Gulliver's Travels,* in which a religious party of this name in Lilliput maintained that eggs should be broken at the little end. See BIG-ENDIAN.

Lit·tle-Eng·land·er (lit′l·ing′glən·dər) *n.* In the 19th century, one of those opposed to the territorial expansion of the British Empire and to imperial federation.

Little Fox The northern constellation, Vulpecula.

little girl A young girl, usually one between the ages of two and ten or eleven.

Little Go The preliminary examination for the B.A. degree at Cambridge University, England: also called *Previous Examination.*

little hours In the Roman Catholic Church,

the offices of prime, tierce, sext, and nones.
Little John One of Robin Hood's lieutenants.
Little Kar·roo (kə·ro͞o′) See SOUTHERN KARROO.
Little Missouri River A river in the NW United States, flowing 560 miles NE to the Missouri.
lit·tle·neck clam (lit′l·nek′) The young of the hardshell clam or quahaug: much esteemed as a food. Also **lit′tle·neck′**. [from *Little Neck*, Long Island]
Little Office In the Roman Catholic Church, an office of lessons and hymns in honor of the Virgin Mary.
Little Rho·dy (rō′dē) Nickname of RHODE ISLAND.
Little Rock The capital of Arkansas.
Little Russia A name formerly applied to the Ukraine region, and often extended to include adjacent areas in Poland and Rumania.
Little Russian See under RUSSIAN.
Little St. Bernard Pass See under ST. BERNARD.
little theater A small theater, usually composed of an artists' group, college students, etc., producing plays which are often experimental and innovative: often used attributively to denote a movement in the 1920's involving the growth of these theaters.
Lit·tle·ton (lit′əl·tən), **Sir Thomas**, 1407?–81, English jurist; author of earliest printed treatise on English law.
lit·to·ral (lit′ər·əl) *n.* A shore and the country contiguous to it. —*adj.* Pertaining to the shore. Also spelled *litoral*. ◆ Homophone: *literal*. [<L *littoralis* < *litus, -oris* +6 seashore]
li·tur·gics (li·tûr′jiks) *n.* The doctrine, history, or science of liturgies.
lit·ur·gist (lit′ər·jist) *n.* **1** One who uses or advocates liturgical forms of worship. **2** One versed in liturgics. **3** One who leads in reciting the liturgy.
lit·ur·gy (lit′ər·jē) *n. pl.* **·gies 1** A collection of prescribed forms for public worship; a ritual; specifically, in the Roman Catholic Church, the mass. **2** In the Greek Church, the Eucharist: also **Divine Liturgy.** [<F *liturgie* <Med. L *liturgia* <Gk. *leitourgia* public duty, ult. <*laos* people + *ergon* work] —**li·tur·gic** (li·tûr′jik) or **·gi·cal** *adj.* —**li·tur′·gi·cal·ly** *adv.*
lit·u·us (lit′yo͞o·əs) *n. pl.* **lit·u·i** (lit′yo͞o·ī) *Math.* A polar curve traced by a point moving so that the square of its distance from the pole varies inversely as its polar angle: it is trumpet-shaped, asymptotic to the polar axis, and approaches the pole as a limit. [<L, crooked staff, curved trumpet]

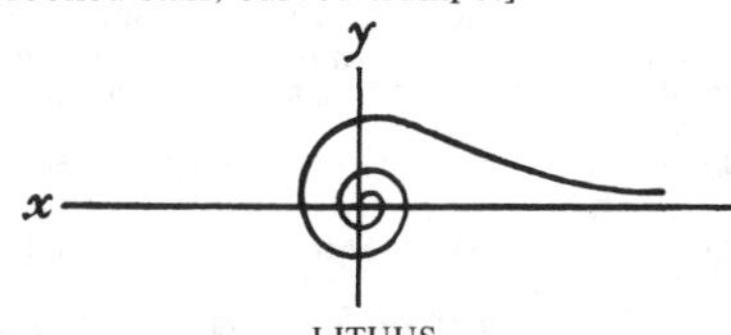

LITUUS

Lit·vi·nov (lit·vē′nôf), **Maxim**, 1876–1951, Soviet Russian statesman and diplomat.
Liu Shao-chi (lyo͞o′ shou′chē′), 1898?-1973, Chinese Communist leader, chairman of the People's Republic of China 1959–1973.
Li·ut·prand (lē′o͞ot·pränd), 922?–972?, Lombard prelate, diplomat, and historian: also *Luitprand*.
liv·a·ble (liv′ə·bəl) *adj.* **1** Worth living; fit to be lived. **2** Agreeable or fit for living in or with. Also **live′a·ble.**
live (liv) *v.* **lived, liv·ing** *v.i.* **1** To be alive; have life. **2** To continue in life; remain alive: As long as you *live*. **3** To endure or persist; last: This day will *live* in infamy. **4** To maintain life; subsist: to *live* on a pittance. **5** To depend for food; feed: with *on* or *upon* : to *live* on carrion. **6** To dwell; abide. **7** To pass life in a specified manner: to *live* frugally. **8** To enjoy a varied and active life. **9** To escape destruction; stay afloat: No boat can *live* in that surf. —*v.t.* **10** To pass: to *live* the life of a saint. **11** To manifest or practice in one's life: to *live* a lie. —**to live down** To live in such a manner as to expiate (a crime), forget or cause to be forgotten (shame),or mature beyond (folly). —**to live high** To live luxuriously. —**to live in** To reside at one's place of employment. —**to live on** To depend on parasitically, as for one's maintenance. —**to live out** To reside away from one's place of employment. —**to live through** To have experience of and survive. —**to live up to** To fulfil the hopes, terms, or character of. —**to live well 1** To live luxuriously. **2** To live virtuously. —**to live with 1** To dwell with as a lodger or companion. **2** To cohabit with: also **to live together.** —*adj.* (līv) **1** Possessing life; living; alive; quick: opposed to *dead* and *inanimate;* hence, ready for use; operative; effective. **2** Burning or glowing; a *live* coal. **3** Of present interest and importance; vital: a *live* book or topic. **4** Possessing liveliness, interest, or animation; alert; energetic: a *live* man of business. **5** *Printing* Ready for printing; kept for use: *live* copy. **6** Of or pertaining to living beings. **7** Containing an unexploded charge: said of munitions, etc.: a *live* shell. **8** Swarming with, or caused by a great number of living creatures. **9** Charged with electricity; carrying a current: a *live* wire. **10** Unwrought; pure; vivid: *live* rock or color. **11** Having motion or power to impart motion, as a part of a machine. See synonyms under ALIVE. [OE *lifian* live]
Synonyms (verb): continue, endure, exist, feed (with *on* or *upon*), subsist, survive. See ABIDE. *Antonyms*: see synonyms for DIE.
-lived *combining form* Having a (specified kind of) life or life span or (a given number of) lives: long-*lived*, nine-*lived*. [<LIFE]
live-for·ev·er (liv′fər·ev′ ər) *n.* A garden herb *(Sedum telephium)* of the orpine family, with greenish-white or purple flowers: naturalized in the United States.
live–in (liv′in″) *adj.* Living at the home or other place where one works: a *live-in* housekeeper.
live·li·hood (līv′lē·ho͝od) *n.* Means of subsistence; regular maintenance; employment; living.
live·long (liv′lông′, -long′) *adj.* That lives long or is tediously slow in passing; whole; entire: the *livelong* day. [ME *lefe longe*, lit., lief long; *lief*, here orig. intens., was later confused with *live*]
live·ly (līv′lē) *adj.* **·li·er, ·li·est 1** Full of energy or of animation; stimulating; brisk; vivacious. **2** Intensely alive or active in the mind; animated; also, enlivening. **3** Striking to the senses; forcible; vivid. **4** In games, reactive; responsive to impact; rebounding: said of a ball: opposed to *dead*. **5** *Obs.* Lifelike. See synonyms under ACTIVE, AIRY, ALIVE, CHEERFUL, GOOD, MERRY, NIMBLE, RACY, SPRIGHTLY, VIVACIOUS, VIVID . —*adv.* Briskly. [OE *līflīce*] —live′li·ly *adv.* —**live′li·ness** *n.*
li·ven (lī′vən) *v.t.* & *v.i.* To make or become lively or cheerful: often with *up*.
Liv·ens projector (liv′ənz) A type of mortar for the discharge of gas-containing projectiles: usually employed in large numbers to give a high concentration of gas. [after Capt. W. H. *Livens*, born 1889, British army officer]
live oak 1 One of several evergreen trees of the oak family native in the United States, especially *Quercus virginiana*. **2** The hard, durable wood of this tree.
liv·er[1] (liv′ər) *n.* **1** The largest glandular organ of vertebrates, in man situated just under the diaphragm and on the right side: it secretes bile, and is of great importance in metabolism. ◆ Collateral adjective: *hepatic*. **2** A digestive gland in invertebrates usually functioning as a pancreas, and consisting of cecal tubes. **3** The liver of certain animals, used as food. [OE *lifer*]
liv·er[2] (liv′ər) *n.* One who lives; a dweller.
liver extract A concentrated extract of mammalian liver, used in the treatment of anemia.
liver fluke Any of various trematode worms parasitic in the bile ducts of sheep, cows, pigs, and sometimes man, especially *Fasciola hepatica*, associated with the black disease of sheep.
liv·er·ied (liv′ər·ēd) *adj.* Dressed in livery, as a servant.
liv·er·ish (liv′ər·ish) *adj.* Feeling or exhibiting symptoms of disordered liver.
liv·er·leaf (liv′ər·lēf′) *n.* Hepatica.
liver of sulfur See HEPAR.
liver ore 1 A variety of cinnabar. **2** A brownish variety of cuprite.
Liv·er·pool (liv′ər·po͞ol) A port and county borough of SW Lancashire, England, on the Mersey estuary. —**Liv·er·pud·li·an** (liv′ər·pud′·lē·ən) *adj.* & *n.*
liv·er·stone (liv′ər·stōn′) *n.* A form of barite which yields an unpleasant odor when heated or rubbed.
liv·er·wort (liv′ər·wûrt′) *n.* Any mosslike plant belonging to the family *Hepaticae*, but differing from true mosses in always having bilateral stems, vertically ranked leaves, and a capsule which opens by two or four valves.
liv·er·wurst (liv′ər·wûrst′) *n.* A sausage made of or containing ground liver. [<G *leberwurst*]
liv·er·y (liv′ər·ē) *n. pl.* **·er·ies 1** A particular dress or uniform worn by servants. **2** The distinguishing dress of any association or organization. **3** Formerly, the dress or badge peculiar to a retainer of a feudal baron or knight. **4** Any characteristic dress, covering or outward appearance: trees in the *livery* of spring. **5** The stabling and care of horses for compensation, as at a boarding stable. **6** *Law* Delivery, as of lands. **7** *U.S.* A livery stable. [<OF *livree* gift of clothes by a master to a servant <*livrer* deliver, free <L *liberare* free <*liber* free]
livery cupboard A cupboard or stand formerly used in a dining-room to hold the liveries or rations.
liv·er·y·man (liv′ər·ē·mən) *n. pl.* **·men** (-mən) **1** A man who keeps a livery stable. **2** A freeman of the City companies or guilds of London, England.
livery stable A stable where horses and vehicles are kept for hire.
lives (līvz) Plural of LIFE.
live steam Steam supplied direct from a boiler, before doing or while doing its work in a cylinder: distinguished from *exhaust steam*.
live·stock (līv′stok′) *n.* Domestic animals kept for farm purposes, especially marketable animals, as cattle, horses, and sheep.
live wire 1 A wire carrying an electric current. **2** *Colloq.* An energetic person; a hustler.
liv·id (liv′id) *adj.* Black-and-blue, as contused flesh; lead-colored; ashy-pale. [<F *livide* <L *lividus* <*livere* be livid] —**liv′id·ly** *adv.* —**liv′·id·ness, li·vid·i·ty** (li·vid′ə·tē) *n.*
liv·ing (liv′ing) *adj.* **1** Having life or vitality; live: opposed to *dead;* pertaining to the living. **2** Actually operative or efficient; also, quickening or vivifying. **3** Flowing, as water: distinguished from *stagnant*. **4** Ignited; flaming: said of coal, etc. **5** Filled with or true to life; vivacious; lively; animated. **6** Enough to sustain life or live on: a *living* wage. See synonyms under ALIVE. —*n.* **1** Livelihood. **2** In the Church of England, a benefice, or the revenue derived from it. **3** Manner of life. **4** Those who live; formerly, also, he who lives: with the definite article. **5** The fact of existing, or of dwelling in a certain place. **6** The action of existing or of passing one's life in a specified manner. **7** *Obs.* An estate; property; possessions.
living death A condition so wretched as scarcely to deserve the name of life.
living picture A tableau vivant.
liv·ing-room (liv′ing·ro͞om′, -ro͝om′) *n.* A room designed and furnished for the general occupancy of a family.
living space Lebensraum.
Liv·ing·ston (liv′ing·stən), **Robert R.**, 1746–1813, American Revolutionary statesman: helped draw up the Declaration of Independence.
Liv·ing·stone (liv′ing·stən), **David**,1813–73, Scottish explorer and missionary in Africa.
Liv·ing·stone (liv′ing·stən) A town on the Zambezi, the former capital of Northern Rhodesia; now in Zambia.
living wage A wage that will enable a person to support himself and his family in reasonable security.
Li·vo·ni·a (li·vō′nē·ə) A region and former province of Russia in NE Europe, divided in 1918 between Latvia and Estonia. —**Li·vo′·ni·an** *adj.* & *n.*

Li·vor·no (li·vôr′nō) The Italian name for LEGHORN.

li·vre (lē′vər) *n.* An old French money of account, originally equal in value to a pound of silver. [<F <L *libra* pound]

Liv·y (liv′ē) Anglicized name of Titus Livius, 59 B.C.–A.D. 17, Roman historian.

lix·iv·i·ate (lik·siv′ē·āt) *v.t.* **·at·ed, ·at·ing** To leach. [<L *lixivius* made into lye < *lix* ashes, lye] — **lix·iv′i·al** *adj.*

lix·iv·i·a·tion (lik·siv′ē·ā′shən) *n.* The process of extracting a soluble alkali or saline compound from a mixture by washing; leaching.

lix·iv·i·um (lik·siv′ē·əm) *n.* **1** A solution of alkaline salts, as lye. **2** A solution obtained by leaching. [<L < *lix* ashes, lye]

liz·ard (liz′ərd) *n.* **1** Any of various reptiles (suborder *Sauria*), as an agama, basilisk, chameleon, gecko, glass snake, horned toad, iguana, monitor, or skink. Lizards commonly have an elongate, scaly body, a long tail, and four legs, but the latter may be reduced to two or may be rudimentary or absent. **2** Any four-legged reptile of similar form. **3** A kind of low sledge for hauling logs, stones, etc. [<OF *laisard* <L *lacerta*]

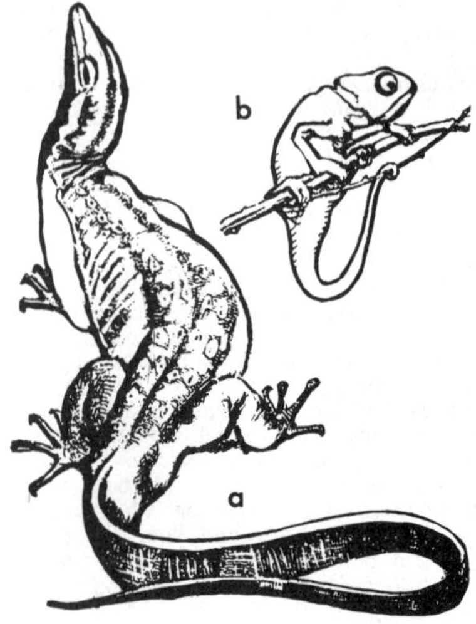

LIZARD
a. Varanus (from 4 to 12 feet in length).
b. Chameleon (up to 18 inches in length).

Lizard, The A promontory in SW Cornwall, England; its extremity, **Lizard Head** or **Lizard Point,** is the southernmost point of Great Britain.

lizard fish 1 An elongate marine fish (family *Synodontidae*), having a lizardlike head. **2** The saury.

Liz·zie (liz′ē) Diminutive of ELIZABETH.

Lju·blja·na (lyōō′blyä·nä) A city in NW Yugoslavia, capital of Slovenia: German *Laibach.*

lla·ma (lä′mə, *Sp.* lyä′mä) *n.* A South American woolly-haired, humpless, cameloid ruminant (genus *Auchenia* or *Lama*), usually white or spotted with brown or black; the guanaco: used as a beast of burden in the Andes. [<Sp. <Quechua]

LLAMA
(From 3 1/2 to 4 feet at the shoulder)

Llan·daff (lan′daf, lan·daf′) A suburb of Cardiff in SE Glamorganshire, Wales; site of a 12th century cathedral.

Llan·dud·no (lan·dud′nō, -did′-) A resort town in NE Carnarvonshire, Wales.

Lla·nel·ly (la·nel′ē) A port in SE Carmarthenshire, Wales.

lla·no (lä′nō, *Sp.* lyä′nō) *n. pl.* **·nos** A flat, treeless plain, as the wide, grassy tracts of northern South America. [<Sp., plain, flat <L *planus*]

Lla·no Es·ta·ca·do (lä′nō es′tə·kä′dō, *Sp.* lyä′·nō es′tä·kä′dō) A barren plateau region in western Texas and SE New Mexico south of the Great Plains: also *Staked Plain.* [<Sp., staked plain]

Llew·el·lyn (lōō·el′ən) A masculine personal name. [<Celtic, lightning]

Lloyd (loid) A masculine personal name. [<Celtic, gray]

Lloyd George (loid jôrj), **David,** 1863–1945, Earl of Dwyfor, British statesman; prime minister 1916–22.

Lloyd's (loidz) *n.* A corporation of English underwriters of marine insurance for the collection and distribution of maritime intelligence and the protection of their common interests and credit: started in 1688 in a London coffee house by Edward Lloyd.

Lloyd's Register An annual list of the seagoing vessels of all nations, their age, tonnage, etc., classified according to seaworthiness.

lo (lō) *interj.* Behold! observe!: used mainly in the phrase *Lo and behold!* [OE *lā*]

loach (lōch) *n.* A small, fresh-water, cyprinoid fish of the Old World (family *Cobitidae*), related to the minnow. [<F *loche*]

load (lōd) *n.* **1** That which is laid upon anything for conveyance; a burden; specifically, as much as can be carried, or as is customarily carried. **2** That which is borne with difficulty; hence, figuratively, a grievous mental burden. **3** The charge of a firearm. **4** A weight of various amounts. **5** The resistance overcome by a motor or engine in driving machinery. **6** Downward pressure on a structure: when caused by gravity alone, it is called **dead load**; when caused by gravity increased by the stresses of transverse motion, it is called **live load. 7** The power delivered by a machine or apparatus, especially an electric generator. **8** *Slang* An excess of alcoholic liquor. **9** *pl. Colloq.* A great plenty; abundance: *loads* of time. — **to get a load of** *U.S. Slang* To listen to or look at. — *v.t.* **1** To put something on or into to be carried. **2** To place (a load) in or on a carrier. **3** To supply with something excessively or in abundance: to *load* one with honors. **4** To weigh down or oppress; burden. **5** To charge (a firearm) with ammunition. **6** To take on (a load, cargo, etc.). **7** To make heavy on one side or end by adding extra weight: to *load* dice or a whip. **8** To add a substance to for the purpose of falsifying; adulterate; doctor: to *load* silk with gum. **9** In insurance, to increase (a premium) by the addition of loading. See LOADING (def. 4). — *v.i.* **10** To take on or put on a load or cargo. **11** To charge a firearm with ammunition. **12** To be charged with ammunition: The new gun *loads* through the breech. ◆ Homophone: *lode.* [OE *lād* way, journey, act of carrying goods. Doublet of LODE.] — **load′er** *n.*

Synonyms (noun): burden, cargo, charge, clog, encumbrance, freight, incubus, pack, weight. A *burden* is what one has to bear, and is used chiefly of that which is borne by a living agent. A *load* is what is laid upon a person, animal, or conveyance, or what is customarily so imposed: as, a *load* of coal. *Weight* measures the pressure due to gravity. A ship's *load* is called distinctively a *cargo*, or it may be known as *freight* or *lading. Freight* denotes merchandise in or for transportation. A *load* to be fastened upon a horse or mule is called a *pack.* See WEIGHT. *Synonyms (verb)*: burden, charge, cumber, lade, oppress.

load displacement *Naut.* A ship's displacement when fully loaded.

load·ed (lō′did) *adj.* **1** Filled or laden. **2** Weighted, as fraudulent dice. **3** Charged with ammunition. **4** Charged with special implication: a *loaded* question. **5** *Slang* Intoxicated. **6** *Slang* Wealthy.

load factor *Electr.* The ratio of the average load of a generating station to the maximum or peak load.

load·ing (lō′ding) *adj.* Arranged so that it may be loaded (in a specified way): used in compounds: a *breechloading* cannon. — *n.* **1** Anything added to a substance for the purpose of giving it weight or body. **2** In art, a heavy charge of opaque color. **3** A load or burden; lading. **4** In insurance, an addition to the premium to cover expenses, fluctuations in the death rate, etc. **5** The act or operation of furnishing with a load.

loading coil *Electr.* An inductance coil connected in a circuit to increase its period of oscillation.

load line *Naut.* **1** A line drawn on the plan of a ship to indicate the maximum mean draft to which it may be submerged by the weight of its cargo or under various conditions. **2** The Plimsoll mark. **3** The line of intersection of the surface of the water with a ship's side under any given load.

load·star (lōd′stär′), **load·stone** (lōd′stōn′) See LODESTAR, LODESTONE.

loaf[1] (lōf) *v.i.* **1** To hang about or saunter lazily or aimlessly; idle time away. **2** To neglect one's work. — *v.t.* **3** To spend (time) idly: with *away.* [Back formation <LOAFER]

loaf[2] (lōf) *n. pl.* **loaves** (lōvz) A shaped mass, as of bread, cake, etc., intended to be cut. [OE *hlāf* bread]

loaf·er (lō′fər) *n.* **1** One who loafs; an idler. **2** A casual shoe resembling a moccasin. [Cf. G *landläufer* an idler, loiterer, Du. *landloper* a vagrant]

loam (lōm) *n.* **1** A non-coherent mixture of sand and clay, containing organic matter. **2** A mixture of sand and clay, usually with straw or the like: used in foundry work to make molds, in plastering walls, plugging holes, etc. **3** *Archaic* Any soil; especially, fertile earth. — *v.t.* To coat or fill with loam. [OE *lām*] — **loam′y** *adj.*

loan (lōn) *n.* **1** Something lent, especially a sum of money lent at interest. **2** The act of lending; a lending. **3** Permission to use: a *loan* of credit. — *v.t.* & *v.i.* To lend. ◆ Homophone: *lone.* [OE *lān*]

Lo·an·da (lō·än′dä) A former spelling of LUANDA.

Loan·gwa (lwäng′gwä) See LUANGWA.

loan·ing (lō′ning) *n. Scot.* **1** A lane. **2** A milking place. Also **loan, loan′in.**

loan office 1 A pawnshop. **2** An office where loans are arranged, the accounts kept, and interest paid to lenders. **3** Formerly, an office set up in certain states by the Revolutionary Continental government to handle subscriptions to government loans.

loan-shark (lōn′shärk′) *U.S. Colloq.* One who lends money at a usurious or illegal rate of interest.

loan word A word adopted from another language and partly or completely naturalized phonetically or morphologically, as the English word *chauffeur*, taken from the French.

lo·a·sis (lō′ə·sis) *n. Pathol.* A species of filariasis common in West Africa, caused by a wandering parasitic roundworm (*Loa loa*) which often invades the orbit and conjunctiva of the eye: also called *loiasis.* [<NL < *loa* a trematode worm <African native name + -(O)SIS]

loath (lōth) *adj.* Strongly disinclined; reluctant; averse: often with *to.* Also spelled *loth.* See synonyms under RELUCTANT. [OE *lāth* hateful] — **loath′ness** *n.*

loathe (lōth) *v.t.* **loathed, loath·ing** To feel great hatred or disgust for; abhor; detest. See synonyms under ABHOR. [OE *lāthian* be hateful] — **loath′er** *n.*

loath·ful (lōth′fəl) *adj.* Exciting abhorrence; hateful; detestable. — **loath′ful·ly** *adv.* — **loath′·ful·ness** *n.*

loath·ing (lō′thing) *n.* Extreme dislike or disgust; aversion. See synonyms under ANTIPATHY.

loath·ly (lōth′lē) *adj.* Loathsome; repulsive. — *adv.* With reluctance; not willingly. [OE *lāthlice*] — **loath′li·ness** *n.*

loath·some (lōth′səm) *adj.* Exciting revulsion or disgust. — **loath′some·ly** *adv.* — **loath′some·ness** *n.*

loaves (lōvz) Plural of LOAF.

lob (lob) *v.* **lobbed, lob·bing** *v.t.* **1** To pitch or strike (a ball, etc.) in a high, arching curve, as in tennis or cricket. — *v.i.* **2** To move clumsily or heavily. **3** To lob a ball. — *n.* **1** In tennis, a stroke that sends the ball high into the air. **2** In cricket, a slow, underhand ball. **3** A soft, thick, lumpy mixture. **4** A worm for bait. [? Imit.] — **lob′ber** *n.*

Lo·ba·chev·ski (lō·bä·chef′skē), **Nikolai,** 1793–1856, Russian mathematician.

lo·bar (lō′bər, -bär) *adj.* **1** Of a lobe or lobes. **2** *Pathol.* Of, pertaining to, or describing acute febrile pneumonia affecting one or more lobes of the lungs. [<NL *lobaris*]

lo·bate (lō'bāt) *adj.* Composed of lobes; lobe-like. Also **lo'bat·ed.** [<NL *lobatus*] **—lo'bate·ly** *adv.* **—lo·ba'tion** *n.*

lob·by (lob'ē) *n. pl.* **·bies 1** A hall, vestibule, or corridor on the main floor of a large public building, as a theater or hotel; a lounge; foyer. **2** The part of an assembly-room of a legislative or deliberative body not appropriated to the official use of members, and to which outsiders have free entry. **3** *U. S.* The persons or groups of persons who accost or solicit legislators in order to influence the action of a legislative body in the interest of a special group, industry, etc.: so called because supposed to frequent lobbies. **4** A cold-storage chamber for the temporary storage of ice. **—***v.* **·bied, ·by·ing** *v.i.* To attempt to influence a legislator or legislators in favor of one's own interests. **—***v.t.* To attempt to obtain passage or defeat of (a bill, etc.) by such means. [<Med. L *lobia.* Doublet of LODGE, *n.*, LOGE, LOGGIA.]

lob·by·ism (lob'ē·iz'əm) *n. U. S.* The practice of lobbying. **—lob'by·ist** *n.*

lobe (lōb) *n.* **1** A protuberance, especially globular, as of an organ or part. **2** The soft lower extension of the external ear. **3** A principal division of a molar tooth. [<F <Gk. *lobos*]

lo·bec·to·my (lō·bek'tə·mē) *n. Surg.* The operation of removing a lobe, as of the brain, lung, etc. [<LOBE + -ECTOMY]

lobed (lōbd) *adj.* **1** Lobate; having lobes. **2** *Bot.* Having divisions that extend not more than half-way from the margin to the center and rounded lobes or sinuses: said of leaves, petals, etc.

lo·be·li·a (lō·bē'lē·ə, -bēl'yə) *n.* Any of a large genus *(Lobelia)* of herbaceous plants with showy flowers either axillary or in bracted racemes. [<NL, after Matthias de *Lobel,* 1538–1616, Flemish botanist]

lo·be·line (lō'bə·lēn) *n. Chem.* A white, crystalline alkaloid, $C_{22}H_{27}O_2N$, from the seeds of Indian tobacco. Its hydrochloride is used as a respiratory stimulant. [<LOBEL(IA) + -INE[2]]

Lo·ben·gu·la (lō'beng·gyōō'lə, lō·beng'gyə·lə), 1833–94, king of the Matabele.

lob·lol·ly (lob'lol·ē) *n. pl.* **·lies** *U. S.* **1** *Colloq.* A mudhole; oozy mire. **2** A loblolly bay or pine. [< dial. E *lob* bubble + *lolly* broth]

loblolly bay A tree *(Gordonia lasianthus)* with smooth, shining, lanceolate leaves and showy white flowers, growing in southern U. S. coastal swamps.

loblolly boy *Obs.* A ship's surgeon's assistant and dispenser. [obs. nautical slang *loblolly* medicine + boy]

loblolly pine See under PINE.

lo·bo (lō'bō) *n. pl.* **·bos** The timber wolf *(Canis nubilus),* of the western United States. [<Sp., wolf]

lo·bot·o·my (lō·bot'ə·mē) *n. Surg.* The operation of cutting into or across a lobe, especially of the brain. [<Gk. *lobos* a lobe + -TOMY]

lob·scouse (lob'skous) *n.* A dish consisting of salt meat, vegetables, and biscuit. Also **lob·scourse** (-skōrs, -skôrs). [Origin unknown]

lob·ster (lob'stər) *n.* **1** A marine crustacean (genus *Homarus*) much used as food, having a large first pair of ambulatory legs, which form the claws, and compound eyes carried on flexible stalks. **2** One of various other long-tailed crustaceans, as a spiny lobster or crayfish. [OE *loppestre* lobster, grasshopper <L *locusta* lobster, locust; infl. in form by *loppe* spider. Doublet of LOCUST.]

lobster pot A trap consisting of a cage with netting at the ends for catching lobsters.

lobster shift A work shift during the latter part of the night; a graveyard shift.

lob·ule (lob'yōōl) *n.* A small lobe, or lobe made small by separation from a larger lobe. [<NL *lobulus,* dim. of *lobus* a lobe] **—lob'u·lar, lob'u·late** (-lit, -lāt) *adj.*

lob·worm (lob'wûrm') See LUGWORM.

lo·cal (lō'kəl) *adj.* **1** Pertaining to a prescribed place or a limited portion of space. **2** Restricted to or characteristic of a particular place. **3** Pertaining to place in general. **4** *Med.* Relating to or affecting a specific part or organ of the body: said of a disease or injury, or of the remedies used. **5** Relating to a locus. **—***n.* **1** A subway or suburban train that stops at all the stations. **2** A local branch or unit of a trade union or fraternal organization. **3** An item of local interest in a newspaper. [<F <L *localis* < *locus* place] **—lo'cal·ly** *adv.*

local anesthesia Anesthesia restricted in action to a specific part of the body.

local color In literature and art, the presentation of the characteristic manners, speech, dress, scenery, etc., of a certain period or region so as to achieve a sense of realism.

lo·cale (lō·kal', -käl') *n.* Locality; specifically, a spot considered with reference to surrounding features or circumstances. [<F]

local government 1 Independent government in local affairs by the small political entity of a limited region. **2** The governing head or body of such a locality.

lo·cal·ism (lō'kəl·iz'əm) *n.* **1** A manner of acting or speaking particular to a place; local custom or idiom. **2** A word, a meaning of a word, a pronunciation, etc., peculiar to a locality, rather than in general usage. **3** Provincialism. **4** The state or condition of being local; influence exerted by a particular place.

lo·cal·i·ty (lō·kal'ə·tē) *n. pl.* **·ties 1** A definite region in any part of space; geographical position. **2** Restriction to a particular place. See synonyms under NEIGHBORHOOD, PLACE. [<F *localité* <LL *localitas, -tatis*]

lo·cal·ize (lō'kəl·īz) *v.t.* **·ized, ·iz·ing 1** To make local; limit or assign to a specific area or locality. **2** To determine the place of origin of. Also *Brit.* **lo'cal·ise. —lo'cal·i·za'·tion** *n.*

local option The privilege granted to a political division, as a county or town, of determining whether something, especially the sale of intoxicants, shall be permitted within its limits.

local time See under TIME.

Lo·car·no (lō·kär'nō) A town on Lago Maggiore in SE central Switzerland; scene of an international conference on political problems following World War I, 1925.

lo·cate (lō'kāt, lō·kāt') *v.* **·cat·ed, ·cat·ing** *v.t.* **1** To discover the position or source of; find. **2** To assign place or locality to: to *locate* a scene in a valley. **3** *U. S.* To establish in a place; situate: My office is *located* in Portland. **4** *U. S.* To survey, set, or designate the site or boundaries of, as a mining claim. **—***v.i.* **5** *Colloq.* To establish oneself or take up residence; settle. See synonyms under SET. [<L *locatus,* pp. of *locare* < *locus* place]

lo·ca·tion (lō·kā'shən) *n.* **1** The act of locating, or the state of being located. **2** The exact position in space; place. **3** A plot of ground defined by boundaries; a mining claim. **4** *Law* A renting or letting for hire; also, the establishment or fixing of the boundaries of a tract of land. **5** A site selected for staging a scene in a motion picture. **6** Any one of five minor civil divisions in New Hampshire. See synonyms under PLACE. [<L *locatio, -onis*]

loc·a·tive (lok'ə·tiv) *adj.* **1** *Gram.* In certain inflected languages, as Latin, Greek, and Sanskrit, designating the case of the noun denoting place where or at which. **2** *Anat.* & *Zool.* Indicating relative position in a series. **—***n. Gram.* **1** The locative case. **2** A word in this case. [<L *locatus,* pp. of *locare* locate; on analogy with L *vocativus* vocative]

lo·ca·tor (lō'kā·tər) *n.* **1** One who or that which locates. **2** One who locates land under the land laws, or is entitled to locate it. **3** *Law* One who lets a thing or services for hire. [<L]

locator card 1 A card bearing all essential facts about a person, especially an enlisted man or officer. **2** A similar card describing an article in a military depot.

loch (lokh, lok) *n. Scot.* **1** A lake. **2** A bay, or arm of the sea.

loch·an (lokh'ən) *n. Scot.* A little loch; pond.

lo·chi·a (lō'kē·ə, lok'ē·ə) *n. pl. Med.* The discharges from the vaginal passages after childbirth, continuing from two to three weeks. [<NL <Gk. *lochia,* neut. pl. of *lochios* pertaining to childbirth < *lochos* childbirth] **—lo'chi·al** *adj.*

Loch·in·var (lok'in·vär, lokh'-) The young hero of a ballad in Scott's *Marmion* who abducts his sweetheart just before she is to be wedded to another.

lo·ci (lō'sī) Plural of LOCUS.

lock[1] (lok) *n.* **1** A device to fasten an object; specifically, one for securing a door, drawer, or the like, as to prevent its being opened, except by a special key or combination. **2** A spring mechanism for exploding the charge of a firearm. **3** A section of a canal, etc., enclosed by gates at either end, within which the water level may be varied to raise or lower vessels from one level to another. **4** An intermingling or fastening together; hence, a hold, hug, or grapple in wrestling. **5** A lockup. **6** One of various mechanical devices for fixing something so that it may remain in place. **7** An airlock. **8** A device to prevent a carriage wheel from turning, as in descending a hill. **9** The oblique position of the fore axle with relation to the hind axle of a vehicle when turning or swerving. **—combination lock** A lock which can be opened only by combining its dial-operated tumblers in a certain sequence. **—cylinder lock** A lock fitted with a cylinder having a control element which can be actuated only by a key whose particularly shaped surface engages with the tumblers and sets them to the exact position for unlocking. **—***v.t.* **1** To secure or fasten by means of a lock. **2** To shut, confine, or exclude by means of a lock: with *in, up,* or *out.* **3** To join or unite securely; interlock; link: to *lock* arms. **4** To make immovable, as by jamming or by a lock. **5** To provide (a canal, etc.) with a lock or locks. **6** To move (a ship) through a waterway by means of locks. **—***v.i.* **7** To become locked or fastened. **8** To become joined or linked. **9** To become jammed immovably. **10** To proceed by means of locks: said of ships. **11** To turn (wheels) under a carriage body. [OE *loc* fastening, enclosure]

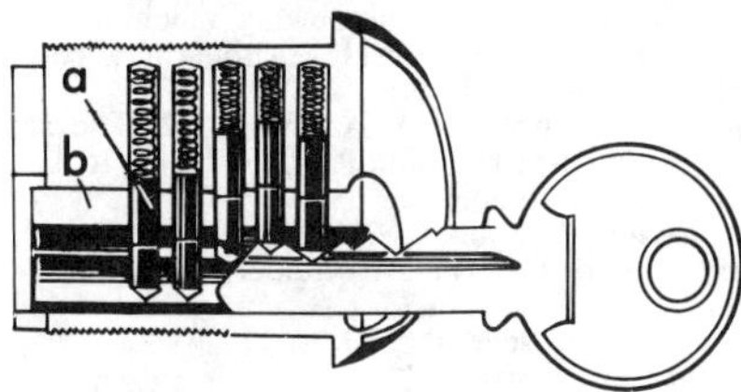

CYLINDER LOCK
Insertion of the proper key raises all the tumblers *(a)* to the exact position required to release the key-plug *(b),* thus permitting the key to turn (here partly inserted).

Synonyms (noun): bar, bolt, catch, clasp, fastening, hasp, hook, latch. A *bar* is a piece of wood or metal, usually of considerable size, by which an opening is obstructed, a door held fast, etc. A *bar* may be movable or permanent; a *bolt* is a movable rod or pin of metal sliding in a socket, and adapted for securing a door or window. A *lock* is an arrangement by which an enclosed *bolt* is shot forward or backward by a key, or other device; the *bolt* is the essential part of the *lock.* A *latch* or *catch* is an accessible *fastening* designed to be easily movable, and simply to secure against accidental opening of the door, cover, etc. A *hasp* is a metallic strap that fits over a staple, calculated to be secured by a padlock; a simple *hook* that fits into a staple is also called a *hasp.* A *clasp* is a *fastening* that can be sprung into place, to draw and hold the parts of some object firmly together, as the *clasp* of a book.

lock[2] (lok) *n.* **1** A tuft of hair; ringlet; tress. **2** *pl.* A head of hair. **3** A small quantity of hay, wool, etc. [OE *locc*]

lock·age (lok'ij) *n.* **1** Material going to form the lock of a canal. **2** The difference in level between the locks of a canal. **3** The toll levied for passing through a lock.

Locke (lok), **David Ross,** 1833–88, U. S. political satirist; pseudonym *Petroleum V. Nasby.* **—John,** 1632–1704, English philosopher and essayist.

lock·er (lok'ər) *n.* **1** One who or that which

locks. 2 A closet or receptacle fastened with a lock.
lock·et (lok'it) *n.* A small case, suspended on a necklace or chain, often holding a portrait. [<OF *locquet,* dim. of *loc* latch <Gmc.]
lock·fast (lok'fast', -fäst') *adj.* Securely held by some locked contrivance.
Lock·hart (lok'ərt, -härt), **John Gibson,** 1794–1854, Scottish writer and biographer.
lock·jaw (lok'jô') *n. Pathol.* A spasmodic contraction of the muscles of the lower jaw; trismus. See TETANUS.
lock nut *Mech.* 1 An auxiliary nut used to prevent the loosening of another. 2 A nut that automatically locks when screwed tight.
lock-out (lok'out') *n.* The closing of a factory or other place of business by employers to bring employees on strike to terms. Also **lock'out'.** Compare STRIKE.
lock·ram (lok'rəm) *n.* A coarse, cheap linen. [after *Locronan,* a village in Brittany]
locks·man (loks'mən) *n. pl.* **·men** (-mən) A warden; turnkey.
lock·smith (lok'smith') *n.* A maker or repairer of locks. **— lock'smith'er·y, lock'smith'ing** *n.*
lock step A marching step in which each marcher follows as closely as possible the one in front of him.
lock stitch A stitch made by two interlocking threads, as on some sewing machines.
lock, stock, and barrel Altogether; completely; in its entirety.
lock·up (lok'up') *n.* 1 A prison. 2 The act of locking up; the condition of being locked up; imprisonment.
Lock·yer (lok'yər), **Sir Joseph Norman,** 1836–1920, English astronomer.
loco (lō'kō) *n.* 1 Any one of several plants of the bean family (genera *Astragalus* and *Oxytropis*), often poisonous to livestock, and found in the western and SW United States: also called *crazyweed.* 2 Loco disease. — *adj. Slang* Crazy; insane. — *v.t.* 1 To poison with locoweed. 2 *U.S. Slang* To render insane. [<Sp., insane]

LOCO
(About 12 inches tall)

lo·co ci·ta·to (lō'kō sī·tā'tō) *Latin* In the place cited. Abbr. *loc. cit.*
loco disease An ailment attacking horses or other animals that have eaten the loco. It affects the brain, causing slowness of gait, loss of flesh, defective vision, delirium, and eventually, death: generally curable by careful and prolonged dieting.
Lo·co·fo·co (lō'kō·fō'kō) *n. pl.* **·cos** 1 The extreme section of the Democratic party of 1835, known as the Equal Rights party. 2 Any adherent of that party. [after *Locofoco,* trade name for a friction match; from the use of these matches to light the candles at one of their early meetings]
lo·co·mo·bile (lō'kə·mō'bil) *adj.* Self-propelling.
lo·co·mo·tion (lō'kə·mō'shən) *n.* The act or power of moving from one place to another. [<L *loco* from a place + *motio, -onis* movement]
lo·co·mo·tive (lō'kə·mō'tiv) *adj.* 1 Pertaining to locomotion. 2 Moving from one place to another. 3 Possessed of the power of moving. — *n.* A self-propelling electric, diesel, or steam engine on wheels, especially one for use on a railway.
lo·co·mo·tor (lō'kə·mō'tər) *adj.* Of or pertaining to locomotion. — *n.* One who or that which has the power of locomotion.
locomotor ataxia *Pathol.* A disease of the spinal cord, characterized by unsteadiness and inability to coordinate locomotor and other voluntary movements; tabes dorsalis.
lo·co·weed (lō'kō·wēd') *n.* Loco (def. 1).
Lo·cri (lō'krī, lok'rī) *n. pl.* The people of Locris.
Lo·cris (lō'kris, lok'ris) An ancient state of eastern and central Greece, divided into **Eastern Locris,** NW of Boeotia, and **Western Locris,** north of the Gulf of Corinth. **— Lo'cri·an** *adj.*
loc·u·lus (lok'yə·ləs) *n. pl.* **·li** (-lī) A small cavity or chamber; a cell. [<L, dim. of *locus* place] **— loc'u·lar, loc'u·late** (-lāt, -lit), **loc'u·lat'ed** *adj.*
lo·cum te·nens (lō'kəm tē'nenz) *Chiefly Brit.* A temporary representative or substitute. [<L, holding the place < *locus* place + *tenens,* ppr. of *tenere* hold]
lo·cus (lō'kəs) *n. pl.* **·ci** (-sī) 1 A place; locality; area. 2 *Math.* A surface or curve regarded as traced by a line or point moving under specified conditions; any figure made up wholly of points or lines that satisfy given conditions. 3 A figure formed by the foci of a series of pencils of light. 4 A passage in a writing. 5 *pl.* A series of passages, as from the Scriptures, classified for reading or study; any book containing such passages. 6 *Genetics* The linear position of a gene on a chromosome. [<L. Doublet of LIEU.]
lo·cus clas·si·cus (lō'kəs klas'ə·kəs) *Latin* An illustrative or authoritative passage from a standard work.
lo·cus si·gil·li (lō'kəs si·jil'ī) *Latin* The place of the seal; abbreviated in legal documents, *L. S.*
lo·cust[1] (lō'kəst) *n.* 1 Any of a family (*Locustidae*) of widely distributed orthopterous insects resembling grasshoppers but having short antennae, especially those of migratory habits (*Locusta, Pachytylus, Melanoplus,* and related genera), which are destructive of grain and vegetation in many parts of the world. 2 A cicada or harvest fly. [<OF *locuste* <L *locusta.* Doublet of LOBSTER.]
lo·cust[2] (lō'kəst) *n.* 1 A North American tree (*Robinia pseudoacacia*) of the bean family, with a rough bark, odd-pinnate leaves, and loose, slender racemes of fragrant, white flowers; also, its wood. 2 Any of several other trees with similar pods, as the carob tree. 3 The honey locust. [<NL *locusta;* orig. applied to the carob pod from its fancied resemblance to the insect]
lo·cus·ta (lō·kus'tə) *n. Bot.* A spikelet in grasses. [<NL. See LOCUST[2].]
lo·cu·tion (lō·kyōō'shən) *n.* 1 A mode of speech. 2 An idiom; phrase. [<L *locutio, -onis* a speaking < *loqui* speak]
loc·u·to·ry (lok'yə·tôr'ē, -tō'rē) *n. pl.* **·ries** A place for conversation; specifically, a reception room in a monastery or convent. [<Med. L *locutorium* <L *locutor* speaker < *loqui* talk]
lode (lōd) *n.* 1 A somewhat continuous, unstratified, metal-bearing vein. 2 A tabular deposit of valuable mineral between definite boundaries of associated rock. 3 A reach of water, as in a canal. ◆ Homophone: *load.* [OE *lād* way, journey. Doublet of LOAD.]
lode·star (lōd'stär') *n.* A guiding star; the polestar: also spelled *loadstar.*
lode·stone (lōd'stōn') *n.* A variety of magnetite that shows polarity and acts like a magnet when freely suspended: also spelled *loadstone.*
Lo·de·wijk (lō'də·vīk) Dutch form of LOUIS. Also *Ital.* **Lo·do·vi·co** (lō'dō·vē'kō).
lodge (loj) *v.* **lodged, lodg·ing** *v.t.* 1 To furnish with temporary living quarters; house. 2 To rent a room or rooms to; take as a paying guest. 3 To serve as a shelter or dwelling for. 4 To deposit for safekeeping or storage. 5 To place or implant, as by throwing, thrusting, etc.: I *lodged* an arrow in the tree. 6 To place (a complaint, information, etc.) before proper authority. 7 To confer or invest (power, etc.). 8 To beat down (crops): said of rain, storms, etc. — *v.i.* 9 To take temporary shelter or quarters; pass the night. 10 To live in a rented room or rooms. 11 To become fixed in some place or position: The bullet *lodged* in his leg. See synonyms under ABIDE, ACCOMMODATE. — *n.* 1 A small house affording temporary accommodations; a hut. 2 A small dwelling appurtenant to a manor house, park, or the like. 3 The lair of a wild animal, especially of a group of beavers; also, collectively, the beavers themselves. 4 A local subdivision of a secret society, or its meeting place. 5 *U. S.* Among the American Indians, a small hut or tepee of skins, bark, and poles; also, its inhabitants. [<OF *logier* < *loge* <Med. L *lobia, laubia* porch, gallery <OHG *louba* < *loub* foliage; *n.,* doublet of LOBBY, LOGE, LOGGIA]
Lodge (loj), **Henry Cabot,** 1850–1924, U. S. politician and historian. **— Sir Oliver (Joseph),** 1851–1940, English physicist, author, and investigator of psychic phenomena. **— Thomas,** 1558?–1625, English dramatist and novelist.
lodge pole A pole used in building an American Indian lodge.
lodge-pole pine (loj'pōl') A tall, slender tree (*Pinus contorta latifolia*) of the western United States.
lodg·er (loj'ər) *n.* Something or someone that lodges; especially, one who occupies a rented room or rooms in the house of another.
lodg·ing (loj'ing) *n.* 1 A place of temporary abode. 2 *pl.* A room or rooms hired as a place of residence in the house of another. 3 Accommodation, as a room: to include board and *lodging.*
lodging house A house other than a hotel where lodgings are let.
lodg·ment (loj'mənt) *n.* 1 The act of lodging or the state of being lodged. 2 A foothold gained in some place. 3 Lodgings; accommodation; a lodging house. Also **lodge'ment.**
Lo·di (lō'dē) A city in northern Italy; scene of Napoleon's defeat of the Austrians, 1796.
Łódź (wōōj) A city in central Poland. *Russian* **Lodz** (lôts'y').
lo'e (lōō) *v.* & *n. Scot.* Love. Also spelled *loo.*
Loeb (lōb, *Ger.* lœp), **Jacques,** 1859–1924, U. S. physiologist born in Germany. — **James,** 1867–1933, U. S. philanthropist and banker, born in Germany; endowed the publication of the Loeb Classical Library.
loess (lō'is, lœs) *n. Geol.* A pale, yellowish clay or loam forming deposits along river valleys, etc., in Asia, Europe, and North America. [<G < *lösen* pour, dissolve]
Loe·wi (lœ'vē), **Otto,** 1873–1961, U. S. pharmacologist born in Germany.
Lo·fo·ten Islands (lō·fō'tən) A group of islands off the NW coast of Norway; 550 square miles.
loft (lôft, loft) *n.* 1 A low story directly under a roof. 2 A large storeroom. 3 An elevated floor or gallery within a large building, as a church or barn. 4 An incline on the face of a golf club tending to cause elevation in the trajectory of the ball; also, a stroke which lifts the ball high in the air. 5 A place for keeping pigeons; hence, a flock of pigeons. — *v.t.* 1 To provide with a loft. 2 In golf: **a** To give loft to (a club). **b** To strike (a ball) so that it rises or travels in a high arc. — *v.i.* 3 In golf, to strike the ball so that it rises in a high arc. [OE <ON, upper room, air, sky. Akin to LIFT.]
loft·er (lôf'tər, lof'-) *n.* In golf, an iron club used for lofting the ball. Also **lofting iron.**
loft·y (lôf'tē, lof'-) *adj.* **loft·i·er, loft·i·est** Elevated, as in position, character, language, or quality; exalted; haughty; stately. See synonyms under EMINENT, GRAND, HIGH, SUBLIME. **— loft'i·ly** *adj.* **— loft'i·ness** *n.*
log (lôg, log) *n.* 1 A bulky piece of timber cut down and cleared of branches. 2 Figuratively, a dull, stupid person. 3 *Naut.* A device for showing the speed of a vessel, consisting of a triangular board, the **log chip** or **ship,** weighted on one edge and attached to a line, the **log line,** that runs out from a reel, the **log reel,** on shipboard. 4 A record of the daily progress of a vessel and of the events of a voyage. 5 Any record of performance, as of an engine, oil well, aircraft, etc. — *v.* **logged, log·ging** *v.t.* 1 To cut (trees) into logs. 2 To cut down the trees of (a region) for timber. 3 *Naut.* **a** To enter in a logbook. **b** To travel (a specified distance) as shown by a log. **c** To travel at (a specified speed). — *v.i.* 4 To cut down trees and transport logs for sawing into lumber. [ME *logge,* prob. <Scand. Cf. ON *lāg,* Dan. *laag* felled tree.]
log- Var. of LOGO-.
Lo·gan (lō'gən), **Mount** A peak in SW Yukon Territory, Canada, the second highest in North America; 19,850 feet.
lo·ga·ni·a·ceous (lō·gā'nē·ā'shəs) *adj.* Designating or pertaining to a family (*Loganiaceae*) of poisonous herbs, shrubs, and trees, with opposite, entire, stipulate leaves and a cymose inflorescence of regular, perfect, four- or five-parted flowers. [<NL, after James *Logan,* 1674–1751, Irish botanist]
lo·gan·ber·ry (lō'gən·ber'ē) *n. pl.* **·ries** 1 A hybrid plant (*Rubus loganobaccus*) obtained by crossing the red raspberry with the blackberry: cultivated for its edible fruit. 2 The

fruit itself. [after J. H. *Logan* of California, the originator]

log·a·oe·dic (lôg′ə·ē′dik, log′-) *adj.* Prose–poetic; partaking of the nature of prose and poetry: applied to a meter composed of cyclic dactyls and trochees. — *n.* A logaoedic verse. [<LL *logaoedicus* <Gk. *logaoidikos* < *logos* speech + *aoidē* song]

log·a·pha·si·a (lôg′ə·fā′zhē·ə, -zhə, log′-) *n. Psychiatry* Inability to communicate ideas in speech. [<Gk. *logos* speech + APHASIA]

log·a·rithm (lôg′ə·rith′əm, log′-) *n. Math.* **1** The exponent of the power to which a fixed number, called the base, must be raised in order to produce a given number. For example, in decimal logarithms the base is 10 and the logarithm of 100 is 2 because 10 raised to the second power is 100; the logarithm of 1000 is 3 because 10 raised to the third power is 1000, and so on. **2** In a former and broader sense, one of any series of numbers whose members correspond, each to each, with the natural numbers, but are in arithmetical progression when the latter are in geometrical, so that, if the products of two sets of numbers are equal, the sums of the corresponding logarithms are also equal. [<NL <Gk. *logos* word, ratio + *arithmos* number] — **log′a·rith′mic** or **·mi·cal** *adj.* — **log′a·rith′mi·cal·ly** *adv.*

logarithmic curve *Math.* A curve traced by a point with ordinates increasing arithmetically and abscissas increasing geometrically. It is asymptotic to the negative axis of the dependent variable and passes through the coordinate (1,0) or (0,1) depending on which coordinate is assumed as the variable.

logarithmic spiral *Math.* The polar curve traced by a point moving so that the angle subtended between its radius vector and a tangent to the curve is equal to the modulus; a polar curve traced by a point with a polar angle proportional to the logarithm of the distance from the point to the pole: also called *equiangular spiral, logistic spiral.*

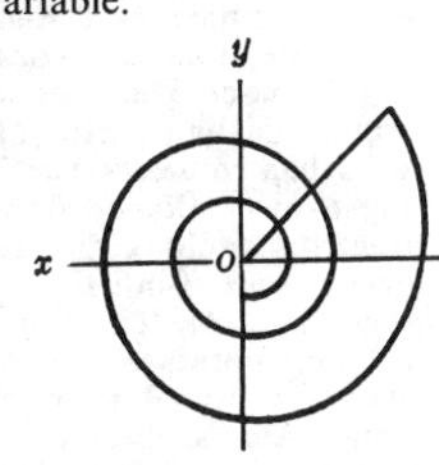

LOGARITHMIC SPIRAL
*o.*Origin.
x.,y. x–axis,*y*–axis.

log·book (lôg′bŏŏk′, log′-) *n.* The book in which the official record of a ship or aircraft is entered; also, a book containing a similar record of performance of a small military unit. Also **log book.**

log cabin A small, rough house built of logs. Also **log house, log hut.**

log carriage The carriage in a sawing machine that moves the log back and forth before the saw.

loge (lōzh) *n.* A box in a theater; booth; stall. [<F <OF. Doublet of LOBBY, LODGE, *n.*, LOGGIA.]

log·gan (lôg′ən, log′-) *n.* A large boulder so balanced as to rock easily; a rocking stone. Also **lo·gan** (lō′gən), **loggan stone.** [<dial. E rock, move to and fro]

log·ger (lôg′ər, log′-) *n.* **1** A person engaged in logging; a lumberjack. **2** A machine used for loading logs on flat cars.

log·ger·head (lôg′ər·hed′, log′-) *n.* **1** A blockhead; dunce. **2** A large marine turtle (*genus Caretta*) of tropical Atlantic waters. **3** The loggerhead shrike. See under SHRIKE. **4** A post on the gunwale of a whaleboat around which the line is turned to retard the motion of a harpooned whale. — **at loggerheads** Engaged in a quarrel; unable to agree. [<dial. E *logger* log tied to a horse's leg to impede movement + HEAD]

log·gi·a (loj′ē·ə, lô′jə; *Ital.* lôd′jä) *n.* A covered gallery or portico having a colonnade on one or more sides, open to the air: compare PORCH, VERANDA. [<Ital. <OF *loge.* Doublet of LOBBY, LODGE, *n.*, LOGE.]

log·ging (lôg′ing, log′-) *n.* The business or occupation of felling timber and transporting logs to a mill or market.

log·i·a (log′ē·ə) *n. pl.* of **log·i·on** (log′ē·on) Collections of sayings attributed to a religious leader; especially, **Logia,** the maxims, doctrines, or truths ascribed to Jesus in the four Gospels; also, the agrapha, or collection of sayings ascribed to Jesus, but not found in the Bible. [<Gk., pl. of *logos* word]

log·ic (loj′ik) *n.* **1** The normative science which investigates the principles of valid reasoning and correct inference, either from the general to the particular, **deductive logic;** or from the particular to the general, **inductive logic.** Compare FORMAL LOGIC, SYMBOLIC LOGIC. **2** The basic principles of reasoning developed by and applicable to any field of knowledge: the *logic* of science. **3** Effective or convincing force: The *logic* of his argument is unassailable. **4** The system of thought or ideas governing conduct, belief, behavior, etc.: the *logic* of business enterprise. [<F *logique* <L *logica* <Gk. *logikē (technē)* logical (art) < *logikos* of speaking or reason < *logos* word, speech, thought]

log·i·cal (loj′i·kəl) *adj.* **1** Relating to or of the nature of logic. **2** Conformed to the laws of logic; consistent in point of reasoning: a *logical* conclusion. **3** Capable of or characterized by clear reasoning; versed in the principles of logic: a *logical* writer. — **log′i·cal·ly** *adv.* — **log′i·cal′i·ty** (-kal′ə·tē), **log′i·cal·ness** *n.*

-logical *combining form* Of or related to a (specified) science or study: *biological, geological, zoological.* [<-LOG(Y) + -ICAL]

logical positivism A movement in philosophy devoted to unifying the sciences, chiefly by creation of a unified terminology in which the statements of any science are expressible. Also called **logical empiricism.**

lo·gi·cian (lō·jish′ən) *n.* One versed in logic.

lo·gis·tic (lō·jis′tik) *adj.* **1** Of, pertaining to, or skilled in calculation. **2** Of or pertaining to proportion. **3** Sexagesimal. **4** Of or pertaining to logistics. Also **lo·gis′ti·cal.** — *n.* **1** The art of calculation; common practical arithmetic. **2** Sexagesimal arithmetic. [< Med. L *logisticus* <Gk. *logistikos* < *logizesthai* reckon < *logos* word, calculation]

lo·gis·tics (lō·jis′tiks) *n. pl. (construed as singular)* **1** The branch of military science that embraces the details of moving, evacuating, and supplying armies. **2** Logistic. [<F *logistique* < *logis* quarters, lodging < *loger* quarter <OF *logier.* See LODGE.]

logistic spiral Logarithmic spiral.

log jam A mass of logs that have become jammed in their course down a stream.

logo– *combining form* Word; speech: *logomachy.* Also, before vowels, *log–.* [<Gk. *logos* word, speech]

log·o·gram (lôg′ə·gram, log′-) *n.* **1** An abbreviation or other sign representing a word, as $ for *dollar.* **2** A form of versified word puzzle. — **log′o·gram·mat′ic** *adj.*

log·o·graph (lôg′ə·graf, -gräf, log′-) *n.* **1** A character, or combination of characters, used to represent a word; logogram. **2** A logotype. — **log′o·graph′ic** or **·i·cal** *adj.*

lo·gog·ra·phy (lō·gog′rə·fē) *n.* **1** *Printing* The use of logotypes. **2** The art of reporting speeches in longhand by several reporters, each taking down a few words in succession.

log·o·griph (lôg′ə·grif, log′-) *n.* **1** A word riddle, in which it is required to discover some word by a recombination of the letters or elements of various given words or by guessing and combining other words which (when correctly arranged) form the word to be guessed. **2** Any anagram or puzzle which involves an anagram. [<LOGO- + Gk. *griphos* riddle] — **log′o·griph′ic** *adj.*

lo·gom·a·chy (lō·gom′ə·kē) *n. pl.* **·chies** **1** Strife over mere words; verbal contention. **2** Any of various games in which letters are arranged into words. [<Gk. *logomachia* < *logos* word + *machē* a battle] — **lo·gom′a·chist** *n.*

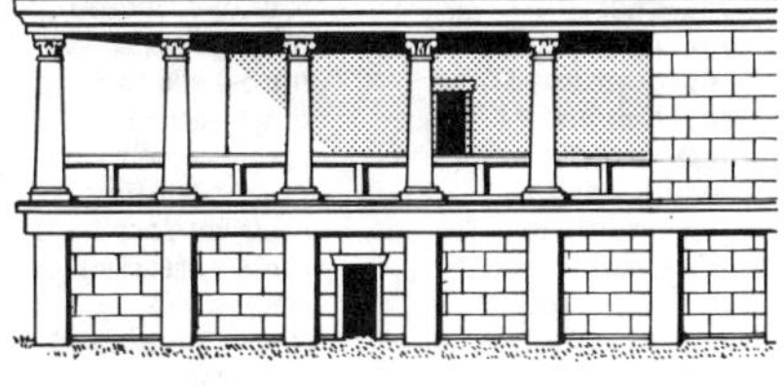

LOGGIA

log·on (lôg′ən, log′-) *n.* An elementary tone signal, of whatever frequency and intensity, distinguishable as such by the human ear: used especially in the quantitative study and analysis of auditory capacity. [<Gk. *logon,* accusative of *logos* word, utterance]

lo·gop·a·thy (lō·gop′ə·thē) *n. Pathol.* Any disorder affecting the speech. [<LOGO- + -PATHY]

Log·os (log′os, lôg′-) *n.* **1** In classical Greek and neo–Platonic philosophy, the cosmic reason giving order, purpose, and intelligibility to the world. **2** The creative Word of God, the second person of the Trinity, incarnate as Jesus Christ, identified with the cosmic reason. *John* i 1–14. [<Gk., word]

lo·go·tech·nics (lō′gō·tek′niks) *n.* The theory, art, and practice of forming new words, especially with reference to specific requirements in science, technology, medicine, etc. [<Gk. *logotechnēs* an artificer of words + -ICS; coined (1954) by R. W. Brown, U. S. geologist] — **lo′go·tech′ni·cal** *adj.*

log·o·thete (lôg′ə·thēt, log′-) *n.* In Byzantine history, any one of several officials, especially, the imperial auditor or accountant. [<Med. L *logotheta* <Gk. *logothetēs* < *logos* word, account + *tithenai* set]

log·o·type (lôg′ə·tīp, log′-) *n. Printing* A type bearing a syllable, a word, or words. Compare LIGATURE (def. 4).

log·o·typ·y (lôg′ə·tī′pē, log′-) *n.* The use of logotypes.

log-roll (lôg′rōl′, log′-) *v.t.* To obtain passage of (a bill) by log–rolling. — *v.i.* To engage in log–rolling. Also **log′roll.** [Back formation <LOG–ROLLING]

log-rolling (lôg′rō′ling, log′-) *n.* **1** Handling and removing of logs, as in clearing land. **2** *U.S.* A combining of politicians for mutual assistance on their separate projects. **3** Birling. — **log′–roll′er** *n.*

Lo·gro·ño (lō·grō′nyō) A city on the Ebro in northern Spain.

log scale A table showing the amount of lumber in board measure one inch thick contained in a round log of given length and diameter.

-logue *combining form* Speech; recitation; discourse: *monologue.* Also **–log.** [<Gk. *logos* word, speech]

log·way (lôg′wā′, log′-) *n.* **1** An inclined chute or slide up which logs are moved from the water to the sawmill: also called *gangway.* **2** A corduroy road.

log·wood (lôg′wŏŏd′, log′-) *n.* **1** A Central American tree (*Haematoxylon campechianum*). **2** Its heavy, reddish wood: used as a dyestuff.

log·work (lôg′wûrk′, log′-) *n.* **1** The service of keeping a ship's log. **2** A structure of logs.

lo·gy (lō′gē) *adj.* **·gi·er, ·gi·est** *U.S. Colloq.* Dull; heavy; lethargic. [? <Du. *log* heavy]

-logy *combining form* **1** The science or study of: *biology, conchology.* **2** A list or compilation of: *anthology, martyrology.* [<Gk. *-logia* < *logos* word, study < *legein* speak]

Lo·hen·grin (lō′ən·grin) In German medieval romances, son of Parsifal and a knight of the Grail: first mentioned in Wolfram von Eschenbach's *Parzival*; subject of an opera by Wagner.

loi·a·sis (loi′ə·sis) See LOASIS.

Loi·kaw (loi′kô′) The capital of Karenni State, Upper Burma.

loin (loin) *n.* **1** The part of the body between the lower rib and hip bone. ◆ Collateral adjective: *lumbar.* **2** The forepart of the hindquarters of beef, lamb, veal, etc., with the flank removed. — **to gird one's loins** To prepare for action. [<OF *loigne, logne* <L *lumbus*]

loin·cloth (loin′klôth′, -kloth′) *n.* A piece or strip of cloth worn about the loins and hips; a waistcloth; breechcloth.

loir (lwär) *n.* A large European dormouse (*Glis glis*). [<F <L *glis, gliris*]

Loire (lwȧr) The longest river in France, flowing 620 miles NW from the Cévennes to the Bay of Biscay.

loi·ter (loi′tər) *v.i.* **1** To remain or pause idly or aimlessly; loaf. **2** To travel in a leisurely manner and with frequent pauses; linger on the way; dawdle. — *v.t.* **3** To pass (time) idly:

with *away.* [<Du. *leuteren* shake, totter, dawdle]—**loi'ter·er** *n.* —**loi'ter·ing** *adj. & n.*

Lo·ki (lō'kē) In Norse mythology, a god who created disorder and mischief: he appears occasionally as a helper but mostly as an enemy of the gods. [<ON]

loll (lol) *v.i.* **1** To lie or lean in a relaxed or languid manner; lounge. **2** To hang loosely; droop. —*v.t.* **3** To permit to droop or hang, as the tongue. —*n.* **1** The act of lolling. **2** An indolent person. [Cf. MDu. *lollen* sleep] —**loll'er** *n.*

Loll·and (lôl'än) See LAALAND.

Lol·lard (lol'ərd) *n.* The name applied to a follower of John Wyclif, an English religious reformer and precursor of Protestantism. Also **Lol'ler.** [<MDu. *lollaerd,* lit., grumbler, mumbler (of prayers) <*lollen* mumble, doze]

lol·li·pop (lol'ē·pop) *n.* A lump or piece of hard candy attached to the end of a stick. Also **lol'ly·pop.** [Prob.<dial. E *lolly* tongue + POP[1]]

lol·lop (lol'əp) *v.i. Colloq.* **1** To lounge; sprawl. **2** To move with leaps or jumps. [< LOLL]

lol·ly (lol'ē) *n. pl.* **·lies** *Brit.* **1** A piece of candy, especially hard candy. **2** *Colloq.* Ice cream, flavored ices, etc., frozen on a stick. **3** *Slang* Money. [Short for LOLLIPOP]

Lo·ma·mi (lō·mä'mē) A tributary of the Congo in SE and central Zaïre, flowing 900 miles north.

Lo·mas de Za·mo·ra (lō'mäs thā sä·mō'rä) A city in greater Buenos Aires, Argentina.

Lo·max (lō'maks), **Alan,** born 1915, U.S. folklorist. —**John Avery,** 1872?–1948, U.S. folklorist, father of the preceding.

Lombard (lom'bərd, -bärd, lum'-) *n.* **1** One of a Germanic tribe that established a kingdom, the modern Lombardy, in northern Italy, 568–774. **2** A native or inhabitant of Lombardy. [< OF <Ital. *Lombardo* <LL *Longobardus,* ? < OHG *lang* long +*bart* beard] —**Lom·bar'dic** *adj.*

Lom·bard (lom'bärd, -bərd, lum'-), **Peter,** 1100?–60, Italian theologian.

Lombard Street 1 A street in London where many banks and financial offices are located. **2** Figuratively, the world of London finance and financiers.

Lom·bar·dy (lom'bər·dē, lum'-) A region of northern Italy; 9,190 square miles; capital, Milan; formerly an independent kingdom. *Italian* **Lom·bar·di·a** (lôm·bär'dē·ä).

Lombardy poplar See under POPLAR.

Lom·blem (lom·blem') One of the Lesser Sunda Islands east of Alor, the largest of the Solor group; 499 square miles; also *Kawula.*

Lom·bok (lom·bok') One of the Lesser Sunda Islands east of Bali; 1,825 square miles; capital, Mataram.

Lombok Strait A channel connecting the Indian Ocean with the Java Sea between Bali and Lombok.

Lom·bro·so (lôm·brō'sō), **Cesare,** 1836–1909, Italian criminologist.

Lo·mé (lô·mā') A port on the Gulf of Guinea, capital of Togo.

lo·ment (lō'ment) *n. Bot.* An indehiscent legume with constrictions or transverse articulations between the seeds, as a peanut. Also **lo·men·tum** (lō·men'təm). [<L *lomentum* bean meal <*lotum,* pp. of *lavare* wash; because used as a cosmetic wash in antiquity] —**lo'men·ta'ceous** (-tā'shəs) *adj.*

Lo·mond (lō'mənd), **Loch** The largest lake of Scotland, in Dumbarton and Stirling counties; 23 miles long.

Lon·don (lun'dən), **Jack,** 1876–1916, U.S. author.

Lon·don (lun'dən) **1** A city and administrative county near the mouth of the Thames, England, capital of the United Kingdom and chief city of the British Empire. The **City of London** represents London within its ancient boundaries and is the business and financial center: often called *the City;* 1 square mile. The **County of London** comprises the cities of London and Westminster and 28 metropolitan boroughs; administered by the **London County Council;** 117 square miles. **Greater London,** embracing the City and Metropolitan Police Districts, comprises the County of London, County of Middlesex, and parts of Surrey, Hertford, Essex, and Kent, an area roughly within a radius of 15 miles from Charing Cross; 693 square miles. *Ancient* **Lon·din·i·um** (lən·din'ē·əm). **2** A city on the Thames in SW Ontario, Canada.

Lon·don·der·ry (lun'dən·der'ē) A county of Ulster, Northern Ireland; 801 square miles; county town, Londonderry: also *Derry.*

lone (lōn) *adj.* **1** Standing by itself; isolated. **2** Unaccompanied; solitary. **3** Single; unmarried; widowed. **4** Lonesome. **5** Lonely; unfrequented. ◆ Homophone: *loan.* [Aphetic var. of ALONE] —**lone'ness** *n.*

lone hand *n.* In some card games, a person playing without aid from a partner; also, the hand he plays.

lone·ly (lōn'lē) *adj.* **·li·er, ·li·est 1** Deserted or unfrequented by human beings; sequestered: a *lonely* dell or gorge. **2** Solitary or addicted to solitude; living in seclusion. **3** Sad from lack of sympathy or friendship; lonesome; forlorn. See synonyms under SOLITARY. —**lone'li·ly** *adv.* —**lone'li·ness** *n.*

lon·er (lō'nər) n. *U.S. Colloq.* One who prefers to live or work alone.

lone·some (lōn'səm) *adj.* **1** Depressed or sad because of loneliness. **2** Lonely or secluded; so sequestered as to cause uneasiness: a *lonesome* forest. See synonyms under SOLITARY. —**lone'some·ly** *adv.* —**lone'some·ness** *n.*

Lone Star State Nickname of TEXAS.

long[1] (lông, long) *adj.* **1** Having relatively great linear extension; not short: opposed to *short,* and distinguished from *broad* and *wide.* **2** Having relatively great extension in time; lasting. **3** Extended either in space or time to a specified degree: an hour *long,* a foot *long.* **4** Continued in a series to a great extent: a *long* list of grievances. **5** Delayed unexpectedly or unduly; dilatory. **6** Far–reaching; extending far in prospect or into the future; far away in time. **7** Holding for a rise, as stocks. **8** Denoting measure, weight, quantity, etc., in excess of a standard: a *long* five minutes. **9** *Phonet.* **a** Relatively more prolonged in sound: The sound (ē) is *longer* in *seed* than in *seat.* **b** Conventionally, indicating the sounds of *a, e, i, o, u* as they are pronounced in *mate, scene, nice, dote, fuse* (in diacritical systems, often written with a macron), as opposed to the "short" sounds of *bat, fed, pit, rot, cup*: in the early Old English period, each of these letters indicated a long or a short vowel sound of similar quality but different duration; this distinction no longer exists and the designation is now an arbitrary one. **10** In classical prosody, requiring relatively more time to pronounce: said of syllables containing a long vowel (*eta, omega,* etc.), a diphthong, or a vowel followed by two consonants or a double consonant. **11** In English prosody, accented. —*n.* **1** The whole extent of a thing; something that is characterized by length: used elliptically. **2** In medieval music, a note equal to four or sometimes six whole notes. **3** A long syllable. **4** *pl.* Those who have purchased securities or commodities and are holding them for an advance in price: opposed to *shorts.* —**the long and the short** The whole; the entire sum and substance. —*adv.* **1** To or at a great extent or period. **2** For a length of time. **3** Through the whole extent or duration. **4** At a point of duration far distant: *long* before or after. —**as** (or **so**) **long as** Under condition that; since. —**before long** Soon. —**for long** For a long time. —**so long** *Colloq.* Good–by. [OE *lang, long*]

Long, meaning "for a long time," may appear as a combining form in hyphemes:

long–accustomed
long–agitated
long–awaited
long–borne
long–breathed
long–buried
long–cherished
long–contended
long–continued
long–delayed
long–deserted
long–desired
long–enduring
long–established
long–expected
long–experienced
long–felt
long–forgotten
long–hidden
long–kept
long–lasting
long–living
long–lost
long–neglected
long–past
long–planned
long–possessed
long–projected
long–protracted
long–resounding
long–settled
long–sought
long–standing
long–suffered
long–suffering
long–term
long–threatened
long–time
long–wandering
long–wedded
long–wished
long–withheld

long[2] (lông, long) *v.i.* To have a strong or yearning desire; wish earnestly. [OE *langian* grow long]

long[3] (lông, long) *v.i. Obs.* **1** To be fitting or proper. **2** To belong. [Aphetic form of OE *gelang* dependent on]

Long (lông, long), **Crawford Williamson,** 1815–78, U.S. surgeon; pioneer in use of ether anesthesia in surgery. —**Huey,** 1893–1935, U.S. lawyer and politician.

lon·gan (long'gən) *n.* **1** A Chinese and East Indian tree *(Euphoria longan)* of the soapberry family. **2** Its small, edible fruit, resembling the litchi. [<NL *longanum* <Chinese *lung–yen* dragon's–eye]

lon·ga·nim·i·ty (long'gə·nim'ə·tē) *n.* Disposition to endure patiently. [<LL *longanimitas* <*longus* long + *animus* mind]

long·boat (lông'bōt', long'-) *n. Naut.* The largest boat carried on a sailing vessel.

long·bow (lông'bō', long'-) *n.* A bow of great length drawn and discharged by hand: distinguished from the *crossbow.*—**to draw, use,** or **pull the longbow** To overstate; exaggerate.

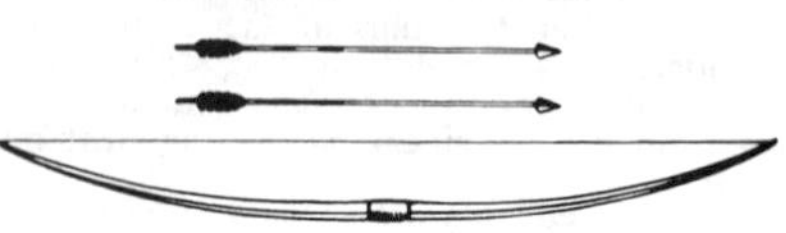

LONGBOW AND ARROWS

long·cloth (lông'klôth', long'kloth) *n.* A fine, soft, cotton cloth garment.

long–dis·tance (lông'dis'təns, long'-) *adj. & adv.* **1** Connecting distant places: a *long–distance* telephone. **2** To or from a distant place.

long distance The telephone exchange or operator dealing with other than local or suburban connections.

long–drawn (lông'drôn', long'-) *adj.* Protracted; prolonged; tedious. Also **long'–drawn'–out'** (-out').

longe (lunj, *Fr.* lōṅzh) *n.* A long rein used in training horses. —*v.t.* **longed, longe·ing** To cause (a horse) to circle at the end of a longe. Also spelled *lunge.* [<F]

long–eared owl (lông'ird', long'-) See under OWL.

lon·ge·ron (lon'jər·ən, *Fr.* lôṅzh·rôṅ) *n. Aeron.* A main longitudinal member of the body of an airplane. [<F]

lon·gev·i·ty (lon·jev'ə·tē) *n.* **1** Great age, or length of life. **2** The tendency to live long. [<L *longaevitas, -tatis* < *longaevus* long–lived < *longus* long + *aevum* age]

longevity pay Additional pay for long service given to members of the U.S. armed forces. Also called *fogy pay.*

long face An expression of the face indicating exaggerated sadness. —**long–faced** (lông'fāst', long'-) *adj.*

Long·fel·low (lông'fel·ō, long'-), **Henry Wadsworth,** 1807–82, U.S. poet.

Long·ford (lông'fərd, long'-) A county in NW Leinster Province, Ireland; 403 square miles; county town, Longford.

long green *U.S. Slang* Paper money.

long·hair (lông'hâr', long'-) *n. U.S. Slang* **1** A person interested in classical rather than popular music. **2** A man or boy with long hair, esp. a hippie. —*adj.* Of or pertaining to classical rather than popular music. —**long'hair, long'haired** *adj.*

long·hand (lông'hand', long'-) *n.* Ordinary handwriting with the words spelled in full: distinguished from *shorthand.*

long·head (lông'hed', long'-) *n.* A dolichocephalic person. —**long'head'ed** *adj.* —**long'·head'ed·ly** *adv.* —**long'head'ed·ness** *n.*

long head *Colloq.* Shrewdness; foresight; common sense. —**long'–head'ed** *adj.*

long·horn (lông'·hôrn', long'-) *n.* **1** One of a breed of domestic cattle with long horns: also **Texas longhorn. 2** *Entomol.* A longicorn beetle. **3** In the western United States, a seasoned inhabitant who knows the ways and cannot be tricked: opposed to *tenderfoot.*

TEXAS LONGHORN

long house Among North American Indians, especially the Iroquois, a council house or community dwelling sometimes 100 to 200 feet long.

longi– *combining form* Long: *longipennate.* [<L *longus* long]

lon·gi·corn (lon′ji·kôrn) *n. adj.* **1** Having long antennae. **2** Of or pertaining to a family of beetles *(Cerambycidae)*, usually with long, filiform antennae: the larvae are woodborers. [<LONGI- + L *cornu* horn]

lon·gi·lin·e·al (lon′ji·lin′ē·əl) *adj. Anthropol.* Designating a physical type characterized by length and relative slenderness of body; dolichomorphic: opposed to *brevilineal.*

long·ing (lông′ing, long′-) *n.* An eager, strong, or earnest craving. See synonyms under APPETITE, DESIRE. —**long′ing·ly** *adv.*

Lon·gi·nus (lon·jī′nəs), **Dionysius Cassius,** 213?–273, Greek Platonic philosopher.

lon·gi·pen·nate (lon′ji·pen′āt) *adj. Ornithol.* Having long wings or feathers, as certain birds. Also **lon′gi·pen′nine** (-pen′ēn, -īn).

lon·gi·ros·tral (lon′ji·ros′trəl) *adj. Ornithol.* Having a long bill, as the ibis and related birds. Also **lon′gi·ros′trate** (-trāt, -trit).

long·ish (lông′ish, long′-) *adj.* Rather long.

Long Island An island of SE New York just east of the mouth of the Hudson; 1,723 square miles; separated from Connecticut by **Long Island Sound,** a sheltered arm of the Atlantic 90 miles long.

lon·gi·tude (lon′ji·tōōd, -tyōōd) *n.* **1** *Geog.* Distance east or west on the earth's surface, measured by the angle which the meridian through a place makes with some standard meridian, as that of Greenwich or Paris. Longitude may be expressed either in time (**longitude in time**) or in degrees (**longitude in arc**). **2** *Astron.* The angular distance from the vernal equinox to the intersection with the ecliptic of the perpendicular from a heavenly body: usually termed **celestial longitude,** and distinguished as *geocentric* when the earth's center is assumed as the central point, and *heliocentric* when the sun's center is taken as the central point. **3** *Math.* The angle the radius vector makes with the initial meridian axis in the spherical coordinate system. [<F <L *longitudo* <*longus* long]

lon·gi·tu·di·nal (lon′ji·tōō′də·nəl, -tyōō′-) *adj.* **1** Pertaining to longitude or length. **2** Running lengthwise. **3** *Biol.* Of, pertaining to, or extending along the cephalocaudal axis. —**lon′gi·tu′di·nal·ly** *adv.*

long johns (jonz) *Slang* Ankle-length, fitted underdrawers of knitted fabric.

long jump In sports, the broad jump.

long·leaf pine (lông′lēf′, long′-) The southern yellow or Georgia pine *(Pinus palustris)*, important as a source of turpentine.

long·lin·er (lông′lī′nər) *n. Canadian* A type of fishing vessel using a long line with many baited hooks.

long·lin·er·man (lông′lī′nər·mən, long′-) *n. Canadian* A fisherman on a longliner.

long–lived (lông′līvd′, -livd′, long′-) *adj.* Having a long life. —**long′–lived′ness** *n.*

long measure Linear measure.

long moss Spanish moss.

long·neck (lông′nek′, long′-) *n.* The pintail duck.

Lon·go·bar·di (long′gō·bär′dē) *n. pl.* The Lombards (def. 1). [<LL] —**Lon′go·bar′di·an, Lon′go·bard** *adj.*

long pig Human flesh, as prepared for a cannibal feast: Maori and Polynesian term.

long–range (lông′rānj′, long′-) *adj.* **1** Designed to shoot or move over distances: a *long-range* projectile. **2** Taking account of, or extending over, a long span of future time: *long–range* plans.

long run An extended series of occurrences. —**in the long run** After the whole course of events; eventually.

long·shanks (lông′shangks′, long′-) *n.* The black-necked stilt *(Himantopus mexicanus).*

long·shore (lông′shôr′, -shōr′, long′-) *adj.* Belonging, living, or working along a shore or waterside. [Aphetic var. of ALONGSHORE]

long·shore·man (lông′shôr′mən, -shōr′-, long′-) *n. pl.* **·men** (-mən) One who loads and unloads vessels; a stevedore.

long shot *Colloq.* **1** A bet made with little chance of winning and hence at great odds. **2** Something backed at great odds, as a horse. —**not by a long shot** Decidedly not; not at all.

long–sight·ed (lông′sī′tid, long′-) *adj.* **1** Seeing far or to a great distance; sagacious. **2** Far-sighted; hypermetropic. —**long′–sight′·ed·ness** *n.*

long·some (lông′səm, long′-) *adj.* Very long; hence, irksome; tedious. [OE *langsum*]

Longs Peak (lôngz, longz) A mountain in Rocky Mountain National Park, north central Colorado; 14,255 feet.

long·spur (lông′spûr′, long′-) *n.* A fringilline bird (genera *Calcarius* and *Rhynchophanes*) with elongated hind claws, found in the arctic regions and Great Plains of North America.

long–sta·ple (lông′stā′pəl, long′-) *adj.* Having a long fiber: said of cotton.

Long·street (lông′strēt, long′-), **James,** 1821–1904, American Confederate general.

long–suf·fer·ing (lông′suf′ər·ing, long′-) *adj.* Enduring injuries for a long time; patient; forbearing. —*n.* Patient and forbearing endurance of injuries or offense: also **long′–suf′fer·ance.**

long–tom (lông′tom′, long′-) *n.* A cradle used by miners for washing gold-bearing dirt.

Long Tom **1** A long swivel gun mounted on the decks of old sailing vessels. **2** A long-range coastal gun. **3** *Slang* Any large cannon having a long range. [<*long Tom Turk*; 19th century naval slang]

long–wind·ed (lông′win′did, long′-) *adj.* Continuing for a long time in speaking or writing; hence, tedious; lacking conciseness. —**long′wind′ed·ly** *adv.* —**long′wind′ed·ness** *n.*

long·wise (lông′wīz′, long′-) *adv.* Lengthwise. Also **long′ways′** (-wāz′).

Long·xu·yen (loung′swē′un) A city in southern Vietnam.

loo[1] (lōō) *n.* **1** A game of cards resembling euchre, played by several persons with three or five cards apiece. **2** The deposit made in the pool in the game of loo. **3** The fact of failing to take a trick at loo. —*v.t.* To subject to a forfeit at loo. [Short for *lanterloo* <F *lanturelu,* name of the game; orig. a vaudeville refrain]

loo[2] (lōō) See LO'E.

loo·by (lōō′bē) *n. pl.* **·bies** *Colloq.* **1** A lubber; a lout. **2** The ruddy duck. [? Akin to LUBBER]

loof[1] (lōōf) See LUFF.

loof[2] (lōōf) *n. Scot.* The palm of the hand.

loo·fah (lōō′fə) *n.* **1** Any of a genus *(Luffa)* of Old World, tropical, cucurbitaceous herbs with the male flowers in racemes and the female solitary. **2** The ovate or oblong fruit of this herb, fibrous within, and often used to filter oil and grease from condensed steam, as well as for cleaning and scrubbing. Also **loo′fa.** Also called *dishcloth gourd, vegetable sponge, luffa.* [<Arabic *lūfah*]

look (lōōk) *v.i.* **1** To direct the eyes toward something in order to see. **2** To direct or turn one's attention or consideration. **3** To search; make examination or inquiry: to *look* through a desk. **4** To appear to be; seem: He *looks* trustworthy. **5** To have a specified direction or view; front: This house *looks* over the park. **6** To expect: with an infinitive: I didn't *look* to find you home. —*v.t.* **7** To turn or direct the eyes upon: He *looked* her up and down. **8** To express by looks: to *look* one's hatred. **9** To give the appearance of being (a specified age). **10** To influence by looks: to *look* someone into silence. —**to look after** To take care of. —**to look daggers (at)** To scowl; glare (at). —**to look down on** To regard condescendingly or contemptuously. —**to look for** **1** To search for. **2** To expect. —**to look forward to** To anticipate pleasurably. —**to look in** (or **in on**) To make a short visit to. —**to look into** To examine; make inquiry. —**to look like** **1** To have the appearance of being; resemble. **2** To indicate the probability of: It *looks like* rain. —**to look on** **1** To be a spectator. **2** To consider; regard. —**to look out** To be on the watch; take care. —**to look over** To examine; scrutinize. —**to look to** **1** To attend to. **2** To turn to, as for help, advice, etc. —**to look up** **1** To search for and find, as in a file, dictionary, etc. **2** *Colloq.* To discover the whereabouts of and make a visit to. **3** *Colloq.* To improve; become better. —**to look up to** To have respect for. —*n.* **1** The act of looking or seeing with voluntary attention: I will take a *look* at it. **2** *pl.* The appearance of the face or figure; cast of countenance. **3** Aspect; expression. **4** Appearance in general, either to the eye or understanding: I do not like the *look* of the thing. See synonyms under AIR, MANNER. [OE *locian*]

Synonyms (verb): behold, contemplate, descry, discern, gaze, glance, inspect, regard, scan, see, stare, survey, view, watch. To *see* is simply to become conscious of an object of vision; to *look* is to make a conscious and direct endeavor to *see.* To *behold* is to fix the sight and the mind with distinctness and consideration upon something that has come to be clearly before the eyes. We may *look* without *seeing,* as in darkness, and we may *see* without *looking,* as in the case of a flash of lightning. To *gaze* is to *look* intently, long, and steadily. To *glance* is to *look* casually or momentarily. To *stare* is to *look* with a fixed intensity. To *scan* is to *look* at minutely, to note every visible feature. To *inspect* is to go below the surface, study item by item. *View* and *survey* are comprehensive, *survey* expressing the greater exactness of measurement. *Watch* brings in the element of time; we *watch* for a movement or change.

look·er (lōōk′ər) *n.* **1** One who looks or watches. **2** *U.S. Slang* A handsome or good-looking person.

look·er–on (lōōk′ər·on′) *n. pl.* **look·ers–on** A spectator; onlooker.

look–in (lōōk′in′) *n. Slang* **1** A hasty, casual glance or visit. **2** *U.S. Colloq.* A chance: If he fights the champion, he hasn't a *look-in.*

look·ing–glass (lōōk′ing·glas′, -gläs′) *n.* A mirror.

look–out (lōōk′out′) *n.* **1** The act of watching or looking out; especially, careful or alert watchfulness. **2** A post of observation; also, the person or the group on watch in or at such a post. **3** One engaged in the U.S. Forest Service to detect fires. **4** One assigned to watch for enemy aircraft, tanks, or troop movements. **5** Prospect; outlook; chances of good or bad to come: a good *look-out* ahead. **6** *Colloq.* Concern; care: It's your own *look-out.*

Look·out Mountain (lōōk′out′) A ridge in SE Tennessee, near Chattanooga; scene of a Civil War battle, 1863.

look–see (lōōk′sē′) *n. Slang* An inspection or survey: Have a *look-see.* [Orig. Pidgin English]

loom[1] (lōōm) *v.i.* **1** To appear or come into view indistinctly, as from below the horizon or through a mist, especially so as to seem large or ominous. **2** To appear to the mind as threatening or portentous: Great difficulties *loom* ahead. **3** To shine. —*n.* A gradual, vague appearance of something, as of a ship in the fog. [Origin uncertain. Cf. Sw. *loma* move slowly (toward).]

loom[2] (lōōm) *n.* **1** A machine in which yarn or thread is woven into a fabric, by the crossing of threads called chain or warp, running lengthwise, with others called weft, woof, or filling. See illustration on page following. **2** The art or technique of working with a loom; the occupation of a weaver; weaving. **3** *Naut.* **a** The shaft of an oar, as distinguished from the blade. **b** That part of an oar between the rowlock and the handle. [OE *gelōma* tool]

loom[3] (lōōm) *n.* **1** A guillemot. **2** A loon (def. 1). [<ON *lomr*]

loom·ing (lōō′ming) *n.* A mirage that elevates and elongates a figure, especially when viewed across the water.

loon[1] (lōōn) *n.* **1** A diving, fish-eating waterfowl (genus *Gavia*), with short tail feathers and webbed feet. **2** A guillemot. —**common loon** The great northern diver *(Gavia immer)*. [See LOOM[3]]

LOON
(Length 31 to 36 inches)

loon[2] (lōōn) *n.* **1** A worthless, demented, or

stupid person; a lout; dolt. **2** A rogue; scamp. **3** *Obs.* A menial. Also *Obs.* & *Scot. loun, lown.* [Cf. Du. *loen* stupid fellow G *lümmel* lout]

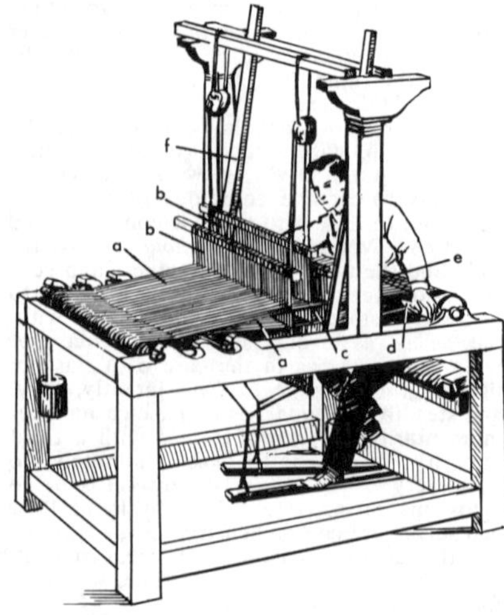

HAND LOOM

The two sets of warp threads *(a, a),* alternately raised and lowered by the heddle *(b, b),* form between them a tunnel of threads called the shed *(c).* Through this shed the shuttle *(d)* is passed, carrying across the weft thread *(e),* which is beaten against the finished fabric by the movable comblike frame or reed *(f).* When the heddle is shifted, the two sets of warp reverse position, binding the weft into the fabric and opening another shed.

loon·y (lōō′nē) *Slang. adj.* **1** Lunatic or demented. **2** Foolish; somewhat crazy; erratic; silly. —*n. pl.* **loon·ies** A demented or daft person. Also spelled *luny.* [<LUNATIC]

loop[1] (lōōp) *n.* **1** A fold or doubling, as of a string or rope, so as to form an eye or a bend through which something may be passed; a noose; bight; hence, a curve or bend of any kind. **2** A stitch used in crocheting and knitting. **3** *Electr.* A complete magnetic or electrical circuit. **4** A curve in a railroad, carried completely around to reach a different level; also, a branch from the main line, returning to it after making a detour. **5** One of the basic patterns by which fingerprints are classified and identified, consisting of one or more ridges whose terminal points are on or toward the same side of the design. **6** *Aeron.* A complete, vertical, circular turn made by an airplane in flight. **7** *Physics* The part of a vibrating string, column of air, or standing wave system which is between two nodes; an antinode. —**to loop the loop** To make a vertical, circular turn, as an airplane in flight. —*v.t.* **1** To form a loop or loops in or of. **2** To fasten, connect, or encircle by means of a loop or loops. **3** *Aeron.* To fly (an aircraft) in a loop or loops. —*v.i.* **4** To make a loop or loops. **5** To move by forming loops, as a measuring worm. [Cf. Irish *lub* loop]

loop[2] (lōōp) *n.* Iron of pasty consistency ready for rolling. [<F *loupe*]

loop[3] (lōōp) *n.* Any small window or aperture; a loophole. [Cf. MDu. *lupen* lie in wait, peer]

Loop, The The principal business, financial, hotel, and theatrical district of downtown Chicago, near the lake front.

loop buttonhole A loop of crochet, cord, or fabric serving as a buttonhole.

loop·er (lōō′pər) *n.* **1** A bodkinlike instrument for making loops. **2** A measuring worm.

loop·hole (lōōp′hōl′) *n.* **1** A narrow opening through which small arms are fired. **2** A means of escape, or place of observation. —*v.t.* **·holed, ·hol·ing** To furnish with loopholes. [<LOOP[2] + HOLE]

loop stitch A stitch composed of a series of loops, the last one finished with a knot; also called *picot stitch.*

loop·y (lōō′pē) *adj.* **1** Having or full of loops. **2** *Slang* Crazy. **3** *Scot.* Shrewd; sly.

loose (lōōs) *adj.* **loos·er, loos·est 1** Not fastened or confined; not bound or attached; unbound or untied; freed from normal bonds or restraint: *loose* tresses; to be *loose* from old habits. **2** Lax in power, character, quality, principle, or conduct; careless; slovenly; slack; relaxed; wanton; dissolute: *loose* bond; *loose* conduct. **3** Not precise or exact; vague; indefinite; rambling; unconnected: *loose* reasoning; a *loose* style. **4** Not close, compact, dense, tight, or crowded; lacking union of parts; slackly joined or tied; not compact in frame: a *loose* knot or bond; a *loose* array; a fabric of *loose* texture; a man of *loose* build. **5** Not tight; open: said of a cough when expectoration is without difficulty, or of an abnormal laxity of the bowels. **6** Designating a stable or stall in which the animals are kept untied. See synonyms under IMMORAL, VAGUE, VULGAR, WANTON. —**on the loose** At liberty; at large; unconfined. —*adv.* In a loose manner: to play fast and *loose.* —*v.* **loosed, loos·ing** *v.t.* **1** To set free, as from bondage, penalty, etc. **2** To untie or undo, as a knot or rope. **3** To make less tight; loosen; slacken. **4** *Naut.* To cast off; release, as a boat from its moorings. **5** To let fly; shoot or discharge, as arrows. —*v.i.* **6** To become loose. **7** To loose something. [<ON *lauss*] —**loose′ly** *adv.* —**loose′ness** *n.*

loose-joint·ed (lōōs′join′tid) *adj.* **1** Having joints not tightly articulated; hence, able to move with more than ordinary freedom. **2** Ungainly.

loose-leaf (lōōs′lēf′) *adj.* Designed for the easy insertion and removal of pages: a *loose-leaf* notebook.

loos·en (lōō′sən) *v.t.* **1** To untie or undo, as bonds or chains. **2** To set free; release. **3** To make less tight, firm, or compact: to *loosen* the stones of a wall. **4** To effect laxity in the action of (the bowels). **5** To relax the strictness of, as discipline. —*v.i.* **6** To become loose or looser. See synonyms under RELAX. —**loos′en·er** *n.*

loose sentence A sentence that is grammatically complete before its end: All compound sentences are *loose sentences.*

loose·strife (lōōs′strīf′) *n.* **1** Any one of various plants, mostly with four-cornered branches and regular or irregular flowers, as the **common loosestrife** *(Lysimachia vulgaris)* of the primrose family or the **purple loosestrife** *(Lythrum salicaria)* of the family *Lythraceae.* **2** Any plant of the loosestrife family. [<LOOSE + STRIFE; direct trans. of L *lysimachia* <Gk. *lysimachion* <*lyein* loose + *machē* battle]

loo·some (lōō′səm) *adj. Scot.* Lovable.

loot[1] (lōōt) *v.t.* **1** To plunder, as a conquered city; pillage. **2** To carry off as plunder. —*v.i.* **3** To engage in plundering. —*n.* **1** Booty taken from a sacked city by a victorious army; plunder. **2** Anything unlawfully taken, as by one in an official position. [<Hind. *lūt* <Skt. *lunt*] —**loot′er** *n.*

loot[2] (lōōt) *Scot.* Past tense of LET[1].

looves (lōōvz) Plural of LOOF.

lop[1] (lop) *v.t.* **lopped, lop·ping 1** To cut or trim the branches, twigs, etc., from, as a tree. **2** To cut off, as branches or twigs. —*n.* A cutting from a tree; specifically, the trimmings or small twigs and branches not measured as timber; fagot. [Origin unknown] —**lop′per** *n.*

lop[2] (lop) *v.* **lopped, lop·ping** *v.i.* **1** To droop or hang down. **2** To hang or move about in an awkward or slouching manner. —*v.t.* **3** To permit to droop or hang down. —*adj.* Drooping. [Origin unknown]

Lo·pa·du·sa (lō′pə·dōō′sə, -dyōō′-) An ancient name for LAMPEDUSA.

lope (lōp) *v.t.* & *v.i.* **loped, lop·ing** To run or cause to run with a steady, swinging stride. —*n.* A slow, easy gallop. [<ON *hlaupa* leap, run] —**lop′er** *n.*

lop-eared (lop′ird′) *adj.* Having drooping or pendulous ears.

Lo·pe de Ve·ga (lō′pā thā vā′gä) See VEGA, LOPE DE.

lopho- *combining form* Crest; crested. Also, before vowels, **loph-.** [<Gk. *lophos* crest]

lo·pho·branch (lō′fō·brangk, lof′ō-) *adj.* Of or pertaining to a division of teleost fishes *(Lophobranchii),* especially an order with imperfect branchial arches and tuftlike gill elements, including pipefishes and sea horses. —*n.* One of the *Lophobranchii.* [<LOPHO- + Gk. *branchion* gill] —**lo′pho·bran′chi·ate** (-kē·it, -āt) *adj.* & *n.*

lo·phot·ri·chous (lō·fot′ri·kəs) *adj. Zool.* Having a tuft of cilia at one pole of the cell: characteristic of some micro-organisms. Also **lo·pho·trich·ic** (lō′fō·trik′ik, lof′ō-). [<LOPHO- + Gk. *thrix, trichos* hair]

lop·per (lop′ər) *v.t.* & *v.i. Scot.* To curdle: also spelled *lapper.*

lop·py (lop′ē) *adj.* **·pi·er, ·pi·est 1** Limp; pendulous; hanging down. **2** Choppy: said of water.

lop-sid·ed (lop′sī′did) *adj.* Heavy or hanging down on one side; lacking in symmetry. —**lop′-sid′ed·ly** *adv.* —**lop′-sid′ed·ness** *n.*

lo·qua·cious (lō·kwā′shəs) *adj.* Given to continual talking; chattering. See synonyms under GARRULOUS. [<L *loquax, loquacis* <*loqui* talk] —**lo·qua′cious·ly** *adv.* —**lo·qua′cious·ness, lo·quac·i·ty** (lō·kwas′ə·tē) *n.*

lo·quat (lō′kwot, -kwat) *n.* **1** A low-growing, pomaceous tree *(Eriobotrya japonica),* cultivated for its fruit, a small, yellow pome. **2** This fruit. [Cantonese alter. of Chinese *lu-chü* rush orange]

lo·qui·tur (lok′wi·tər) *Latin* He or she speaks.

lo·ran (lôr′an, lō′ran) *n.* A navigation system by which a ship or an aircraft may accurately determine its position by noting the time intervals between radio pulse signals transmitted from a network of ground stations and recorded on an oscilloscope. [<LO(NG) RA(NGE) N(AVIGATION)]

Lor·ca (lôr′kä) A city in Murcia, SE Spain.

Lor·ca (lôr′kä), **Federico García** See *García Lorca, Federico.*

lord (lôrd) *n.* **1** One possessing supreme power and authority; a ruler. **2** A title of respect, formerly given to any superior, as by a wife to a husband: still sometimes humorously so used. **3** In feudal law, the owner of a manor under grant from the crown; a landlord. **4** A title of honor or nobility in Great Britain, given generally to men noble by birth or ennobled by patent. This includes **lords spiritual** (archbishops and bishops), who are members of the House of Lords, and also **lords temporal**: marquises, earls, viscounts, and barons. The formal titles are as follows: *Baron* X, the *Marquis* of X, the *Earl* of X, *Viscount* X; informally all are addressed *Lord* X. The given name is mentioned only to distinguish holders of the same title at different periods. Where the names are homonymous, the locality of the peerage is stated, as *Viscount Grey of Fallodon,* who was spoken of as *Lord Grey.* The title is given by courtesy to the eldest sons of dukes, marquises, and earls, who each take by courtesy also an inferior title held by the father, frequently the second title, and to the younger sons of dukes and marquises, prefixed to their Christian name and surname; in these cases the Christian names must always be mentioned, coming after "Lord," to distinguish among brothers: *Lord* Robert Cecil. It is also a title of office, such as the *Lord* Lieutenant, the *Lord* Chancellor, *Lord* Privy Seal, *Lords* of the Treasury, Admiralty, Bedchamber. **5** In astrology, a controlling planet. —*v.t.* To invest with the title of lord. —**to lord it** (**over**) To act in a domineering or arrogant manner. [OE *hlāford, hlāfweard,* lit., bread keeper <*hlāf* loaf + *weard* keeper, ward] —**lord′less** *adj.* —**lord′like** *adj.*

Lord (lôrd) **1** God. **2** Jesus Christ. Also *Our Lord.*

Lord Advocate The principal public prosecutor in Scotland.

lord-and-la·dy (lord′ənd·lā′dē) *n. pl.* **lord-and-la·dies** The harlequin duck.

Lord Howe Island (hou) An Australian dependency NE of Sydney; 5 square miles.

lord·ing (lôr′ding) *n.* **1** A lordling. **2** *Obs.* Lord; master.

lord lieutenant 1 The chief executive officer of a county in England. **2** Until 1922, the English viceroy in Ireland.

lord·ling (lôrd′ling) *n.* A little lord; petty chieftain: generally used contemptuously.

lord·ly (lôrd′lē) *adj.* **·li·er, ·li·est 1** Of, pertaining to, or like a lord; becoming a lord; lofty; noble; insisting on compliance: a *lordly* presence. **2** Characterized by undue loftiness; insolent: a *lordly* air or demeanor. See synonyms under IMPERIOUS. —*adv.* In a lordly manner. —**lord′li·ness** *n.*

Lord of Hosts Jehovah; God.

Lord of Misrule Formerly, a person chosen to preside over the revels, festivities, and sports in English royal or aristocratic households.

lor·do·sis (lôr·dō′sis) *n. Pathol.* Inward curvature of a bone; specifically, curvature of the spine with the convexity forward. Also **lor·do′ma** (-mə). [<NL <Gk. *lordōsis* <*lordos* bent backward] — **lor·dot′ic** (-dot′ik) *adj.*

lords–and–la·dies (lôrdz′ənd·lā′dēz) *n.* **1** The cuckoo pint or wakerobin. **2** The jack–in–the–pulpit.

Lord's Day Sunday; the Sabbath. [Trans. of L *dies dominica*]

lord·ship (lôrd′ship) *n.* **1** The state or quality of a lord; hence, the title by which noblemen (excluding dukes), bishops, and judges in England are addressed or spoken of, preceded by *your* or *his.* **2** The jurisdiction of a lord; seigniory; domain; manor. **3** The dominion, power, or authority of a lord; hence, sovereignty in general; supremacy. [OE *hlafordscipe.* See LORD.]

Lord's Prayer The prayer taught by Jesus to his disciples. *Matt.* vi 9–13.

Lord's Supper *Eccl.* **1** The Eucharist; the Holy Communion. **2** The Last Supper.

Lord's Table The altar or table on which the elements of the Eucharist are laid during and after consecration.

lore[1] (lôr, lōr) *n.* **1** The body of traditional, popular, often anecdotal knowledge about a particular subject. **2** Learning or erudition. **3** *Archaic* Any special instruction; also, a lesson or the act of teaching. See synonyms under LEARNING, WISDOM. [OE *lar*]

lore[2] (lôr, lōr) *n.* **1** *Ornithol.* The side of a bird's head between the eye and the beak. **2** *Zool.* A corresponding part in fishes and reptiles. [<L *lorum* strap, thong]

Lo·re·lei (lôr′ə·lī, *Ger.* lō′rə·lī) In German folklore, a siren on a rock in the Rhine, who lured boatmen to shipwreck by her singing: also called *Lurlei.* [<G]

Lo·ren·gau (lō′rən·gou) A port on Manus island, chief city of the Admiralty Islands.

Lo·rentz (lō′rents), **Hendrik Antoon,** 1853–1928, Dutch physicist.

Lo·renz (lō·rents′) Danish and German form of LAWRENCE. Also **Lo·ren·zo** (lə·ren′zō; *Ital.* lō·ren′tsō, *Sp.* lō·ren′thō).

Lo·renz (lō′rents), **Adolf,** 1854–1946, Austrian orthopedic surgeon.

lor·gnette (lôr·nyet′) *n.* **1** A pair of eyeglasses with an ornamental handle into which they may be folded when not in use. **2** A long–handled opera glass. [<F <*lorgner* spy, peer <OF *lorgne* squinting]

lor·gnon (lôr·nyôn′) *n. French* **1** A monocle. **2** A lorgnette.

lo·ri·ca (lō·rī′kə) *n. pl.* **·cae** (-kē) **1** An ancient Roman cuirass or corselet. **2** *Zool.* A protective covering or shell, as in infusorians or rotifers. [<L <*lorum* thong]

lor·i·cate (lôr′ə·kāt, lor′-) *v.t.* **·cat·ed, ·cat·ing** To cover with a protective coating. — *adj.* Covered with a lorica or shell. [<L *loricatus,* pp. of *loricare* clothe in mail, harness <*lorica* corselet] — **lor′i·ca′tion** *n.*

Lo·rient (lô·ryän′) A port of NW France on the Bay of Biscay.

lor·i·keet (lôr′ə·kēt, lor′-) *n.* Any of certain small Polynesian parrots resembling the lory. [<LORY + (PARA)KEET]

Lo·rin·da (lô·rin′də, lə-) See LAURA.

lo·ris (lôr′is, lō′ris) *n.* A small, arboreal, nocturnal, Asian lemur (genera *Loris* and *Nycticebus*), having the index finger small. *Loris gracilis* is the **slender loris** of southern India and Ceylon; *Nycticebus tardigradus* is the slow lemur or **East Indian loris.** [<F <Flemish *lorrias* lazy, the sloth]

lorn (lôrn) *adj.* **1** *Archaic* Without kindred or friends; forlorn. **2** *Obs.* Lost. [OE *loren,* pp. of *lēosan* lose. Akin to FORLORN.]

Lorne (lôrn), **Firth of** An arm of the Atlantic separating Mull island from the Scottish mainland.

Lor·rain (lô·rañ′), **Claude** Pseudonym of *Claude Gelée,* 1600–82, French painter.

Lor·raine (lô·rān′, lō-, lə-; *Fr.* lô·ren′) A region and former province of eastern France; after the Franco–Prussian War part of Alsace–Lorraine; restored to France, 1919: German *Lothringen.* See ALSACE–LORRAINE.

lor·ry (lôr′ē, lor′ē) *n. pl.* **·ries** **1** A low, four-wheeled, platform wagon. **2** *Brit.* A similar motor vehicle for carrying heavy loads; a truck. [Prob. dial. E *lurry* pull, tug]

lo·ry (lō′rē, lôr′ē) *n. pl.* **·ries** Any of certain parrots of Australasia (genera *Lorius, Apnosmictus,* and others) with brilliant, scarlet plumage, long bill, and tongue ending in a form of brush. [<Malay *lūrī*]

Los An·ge·les (lôs an′jə·lēz, ang′gə·ləs, los) A port in southern California, the fourth largest city in the United States: also *Colloq. L.A.* A native of Los Angeles is known as an *Angeleno.*

Lo·schmidt number (lō′shmit) *Physics* **1** The number of molecules in 1 cubic centimeter of an ideal gas at 0° C. and normal atmospheric pressure, equal to 2.687 x 10^{19}. **2** The Avogadro number. [after Joseph *Loschmidt,* 1821–95, Austrian physicist]

lose (lo͞oz) *v.* **lost, los·ing** *v.t.* **1** To part with, as by accident or negligence, and be unable to find; mislay. **2** To fail to keep, control, or maintain: to *lose* one's footing; to *lose* one's mind. **3** To be deprived of; suffer the loss of, as by accident, death, removal, etc.: to *lose* a leg. **4** To fail to gain or win: to *lose* a prize; to *lose* a battle. **5** To fail to utilize or take advantage of; miss: to *lose* a chance. **6** To fail to see or hear; miss: I *lost* not a word of the speech. **7** To fail to keep in sight, memory, etc.: We *lost* him in the crowd. **8** To cease to have: to *lose* one's sense of duty. **9** To squander; waste, as time. **10** To wander from so as to be unable to find: to *lose* the path. **11** To outdistance or elude, as runners or pursuers. **12** To cause the loss of: His rashness *lost* him his opportunity. **13** To bring to destruction or death; ruin: usually in the passive: All hands were *lost.* — *v.i.* **14** To suffer loss. **15** To be defeated. — **to lose heart** To become discouraged. — **to lose oneself** **1** To lose one's way, as in a wood. **2** To disappear or hide: The thief *lost himself* in the crowd. **3** To become engrossed. **4** To become confused or bewildered. — **to lose one's heart (to)** To fall in love (with). — **to lose out** *U.S. Colloq.* To fail or be defeated. — **to lose sight of** **1** To fail to keep in sight. **2** To take no notice of; ignore or forget. [Fusion of OE *losian* be lost and *lēosan* lose] — **los′a·ble** *adj.*

lo·sel (lō′zəl, lo͞o′zəl, loz′əl) *adj.* Inclined to idleness and waste. — *n.* A worthless fellow. [OE *losen,* pp. of *losian* be lost]

los·er (lo͞o′zər) *n.* One who loses or fails to win in any transaction; a defeated contestant.

losh (losh) *interj. Scot.* An exclamation of surprise or deprecation. [Euphemistic alter. of LORD; cf. GOSH]

los·ing (lo͞o′zing) *n.* **1** The act or fact of letting go, missing, lacking, or being deprived. **2** *pl.* Money lost, especially in gambling. — *adj.* **1** That incurs loss: a *losing* business. **2** Not winning; defeated: the *losing* team.

loss (lôs, los) *n.* **1** The act or state of losing; failure to keep or win; privation: *loss* of fortune or friends. **2** *Usually pl.* That which is lost, or its amount: His *losses* were great; The *losses* of the army were severe. **3** The state of being lost, or of having suffered destruction: the *loss* of a ship at sea. **4** Useless application; futile expenditure; waste. **5** Injury or diminution of value within the limits provided in an insurance policy, or the sum payable on that account. **6** *Physics* That part of electrical or mechanical energy which is expended in overcoming friction, etc., and from which no productive work is obtained. — **at a loss** **1** At so low a price as to result in a loss. **2** In confusion or doubt; perplexed. — **dead loss** An irremediable loss; one without hope of salvage, insurance, or any mitigation. — **to bear a loss** **1** To sustain a loss bravely. **2** To make good a loss. [OE *los*]

Synonyms: damage, defeat, deprivation, destruction, detriment, disadvantage, failure, forfeiture, injury, misfortune, privation, waste. See INJURY.

lost (lôst, lost) *adj.* **1** Not to be found or recovered; parted with; missing; left, as by accident, in a forgotten place: *lost* goods or friends. **2** Not won, gained, used, or enjoyed; missed; wasted: *lost* opportunity. **3** Ruined physically, morally, or spiritually; damned; destroyed. **4** Having wandered from the way; also, abstracted: *lost* in thought; bewildered; perplexed. **5** No longer known or used: a *lost* art. — **to be lost upon** (or **on**) To have no effect upon (a person).

lost cause Any cause that cannot possibly succeed; specifically, in American history, the cause of the Confederate States.

lost motion Slackness in a mechanical connection resulting in an appreciable difference between the travel of the driving and the driven elements.

lost tribes Those members of the ten northern, or Israelitish, Hebrew tribes that were taken into Assyrian captivity (II *Kings* xvii 6), believed never to have returned.

lot (lot) *n.* **1** Anything, as a die or piece of paper, used in determining something by chance; also, the fact or process of deciding something in such manner. **2** The share that comes to one as the result of drawing lots. **3** The part in life that comes to one without his planning; chance; fate. **4** A collection or parcel of things separated from others: The auctioneer sold the goods in ten *lots.* **5** A parcel or quantity of land, as surveyed and apportioned for sale or other special purpose: a city *lot,* a wood *lot.* **6** *Colloq.* A kind of person: He is a bad *lot.* **7** *Often pl. Colloq.* A great quantity or amount; a number of things, collectively: a *lot* of money, *lots* of trouble. ◆ *Lot* or *lots* is construed as a singular if attributed to a singular word, plural if to a plural word: A *lot* of money was hidden, but, A *lot* of diamonds were hidden. **8** A proportion of taxes allotted to one. **9** A motion–picture studio and the space it uses. See synonyms under FLOCK. — *adv.* Very much: a *lot* worse. — *v.* **lot·ted, lot·ting** *v.t.* **1** To divide, as land, into lots. **2** To apportion by lots; allot. — *v.i.* **3** To cast lots. [OE *hlot*]

Lot (lot) A nephew of Abraham, who with his wife and daughters escaped the destruction of Sodom. His wife, disobeying a warning, looked back at the city and became a pillar of salt. *Gen.* xi 27, xix.

Lot (lôt) A river in south central France, flowing 300 miles west from the Cévennes to the Garonne: ancient *Oltis.*

lo·tah (lō′tə) *n. Anglo–Indian* A small, round pot, usually of brass or copper, used in India for drinking and ablution. Also **lo′ta.**

lote (lōt) *n.* The lotus. [<LOTUS]

loth (lōth) *adj.* Loath.

Lo·thair (lō·thâr′, *Fr.* lō·târ′) A masculine personal name. Also *Ger.* **Lo·thar** (lō·tär′), *Ital.* **Lo·tha·rio** (lō·tä′ryō). [<Gmc., famous warrior]

— **Lothair I,** 795–855, Holy Roman Emperor 840–55.

— **Lothair the Saxon,** 1060?–1137, Holy Roman Emperor 1133–37.

Lo·thar·i·o (lō·thâr′ē·ō) In Nicholas Rowe's *The Fair Penitent,* a young Genoese nobleman and gay rake; hence, a seducer.

Lo·thi·ans (lō′thē·ənz), **The** A division of SE Scotland including East Lothian, Midlothian, and West Lothian.

Loth·ring·en (lōt′ring·ən) The German name for LORRAINE.

Lo·ti (lō·tē′), **Pierre** Pseudonym of *Louis Marie Julien Viaud,* 1850–1923, French novelist.

lo·tion (lō′shən) *n.* **1** A medicated liquid for the skin, eyes, or any diseased or bruised part, for cleansing or healing. **2** *Archaic* A bathing or washing. [<L *lotio, -onis* washing <*lavare* wash]

Lo·toph·a·gi (lō·tof′ə·jī) *n. pl.* In the *Odyssey,* a people living on the northern coast of Africa who lived a life of indolence and forgetfulness induced by eating the fruit of the lotus: some of Odysseus' followers ate with them, and forgot their friends, homes, and native land. [<Gk. *lōtophagoi* <*lōtos* lotus + *phagein* eat]

Lot·ta (lot′ə), **Lot·tie** (lot′ē), **Lot·ty** Diminutives of CHARLOTTE.

lot·ter·y (lot′ər·ē) *n. pl.* **·ter·ies** A distribution of, or scheme for distributing, prizes as determined by chance or lot, especially where such chances are allotted by sale of tickets; hence, any chance disposition of any matter. [<Ital. *lotteria* <*lotto* lottery, lot <F *lot* <Gmc.]

lot·to (lot′ō) *n.* A game of chance played with cards and disks: also called *keno.* Also **lo·to** (lō′tō). [<Ital. See LOTTERY.]

Lot·to (lôt′tō), **Lorenzo,** 1480?–1556, Venetian painter.

lo·tus (lō′təs) *n.* **1** One of various Old World plants of the waterlily family, noted for their large floating leaves and showy flowers; especially, the **white** and **blue lotus** of the Nile (respectively *Nymphaea lotus,* and *N. caerulea*); also, the **sacred lotus** of India *Nelumbium nelumbo)* with fragrant pink or rose flowers. **2** The lotus tree. **3** Any of a genus *(Lotus)* of herbs or shrubs of the bean family. **4** *Archit.* A representation or conventionalization of the lotus flower, bud, or leaves. Also **lo′tos.** [<L <Gk. *lōtos*]

LOTUS
a. Bud and leaf.
b. Blossom and leaf.
c. Stylized lotus in Egyptian architecture and ornament.

lo·tus-eat·er (lō′təs·ē′tər) *n.* In the *Odyssey,* one who lives in irresponsible enjoyment from eating the fruit of the lotus tree; hence, a voluptuary. See LOTOPHAGI.

lotus tree The common jujube.

Loua·la·ba (lwà·là·bà′) The French spelling of LUALABA.

loud (loud) *adj.* **1** Striking the auditory nerves with great force; having great volume or intensity of sound; noisy. **2** Making a great noise. **3** Pressing or urgent; clamorous: a *loud* demand. **4** Conspicuous or ostentatious without taste or refinement; vulgarly showy; flashy. —*adv.* With loudness; loudly. [OE *hlūd*] —**loud′ly** *adv.* —**loud′ness** *n.*

loud·en (loud′n) *v.t. & v.i.* To make or become louder.

loud-mouthed (loud′mouthd, -moutht′) *adj.* Possessed of a loud voice; offensively clamorous or talkative.

loud·speak·er (loud′spē′kər) *n.* An electromagnetic device for amplifying the sounds transmitted by radio, public-address system, or the like.

lough (lokh) *n. Irish* **1** A loch; lake or pool. **2** A partially landlocked arm of the sea.

lou·is (lōō′ē) *n.* **1** A French gold coin worth twenty francs. **2** An old French gold coin worth about twenty-three francs, used through the reigns of Louis XIII–Louis XVI. Also *louis d'or.* [<F, after *Louis* XIII]

Lou·is (lōō′is, *Fr.* lōō·ē′) A masculine personal name. Also spelled *Lewis.* [<Gmc., famed warrior]

—**Louis I,** 778–840, Holy Roman Emperor 814–840; son and successor of Charlemagne: called "le Débonnaire."

—**Louis VIII,** 1187–1226, king of France 1223–26.

—**Louis IX,** 1214–70; king of France 1226–70; defeated and captured by the Saracens at Mansûra 1249; canonized 1297 as *Saint Louis.*

—**Louis XI,** 1423–83, king of France 1461–1483; made the power of the throne paramount.

—**Louis XIII,** 1601–43, king of France 1610–1643; son of Henry IV.

—**Louis XIV,** 1638–1715, king of France 1643–1715; son of the preceding: called "Le Grand Monarque," "le roi soleil."

—**Louis XV,** 1710–74, king of France 1715–1774; great-grandson of the preceding; ceded Canada to Great Britain.

—**Louis XVI,** 1754–93, king of France 1774–1792; grandson of Louis XV; dethroned by the revolution and guillotined.

—**Louis XVIII,** 1755–1824, brother of Louis XVI; king of France April, 1814–March, 1815, and June, 1815–24.

—**Louis Napoleon** See NAPOLEON III.

—**Louis Philippe,** 1773–1850, king of France 1830–48; abdicated: known as *The Citizen King.*

Lou·is (lōō′is), **Joe,** born 1914, U.S. heavyweight boxing champion 1937–49; real name *Joseph Louis Barrow.*

Lou·i·sa (lōō·ē′zə) A feminine personal name. Also **Lou·ise** (lōō·ēz′). [See LOUIS]

Lou·is·burg (lōō′is·bûrg) A town on the eastern coast of Cape Breton Island, Canada; captured from the French by British forces in 1745 and 1758. Also **Lou′is·bourg.**

lou·is d'or (lōō′ē dôr) A louis. [<F, gold louis]

Lou·ise (lōō·ēz′), **Lake** A lake in Banff National Park, SW Alberta, Canada.

Lou·i·si·ade Archipelago (lōō·ē′zē·äd′) A Papuan island group SE of New Guinea; 980 square miles.

Lou·i·si·an·a (lōō·ē′zē·an′ə) One of the United States, fronting south on the Gulf of Mexico; 48,523 square miles; capital, Baton Rouge; comprised of portions of West Florida and of the Louisiana Purchase of 1803, it entered the Union April 8, 1812; nickname, *Pelican State* or *Creole State*: abbr. LA —**Lou·i′si·an′i·an, Lou·i′si·an′an** *adj. & n.*

Louisiana Purchase The French colonial territory in west central North America, purchased from France by the United States in 1803 for $15,000,000: the land between the Mississippi River and the Rocky Mountains, the Gulf of Mexico and Canada.

Lou·is-Qua·torze (lōō′ē·kà·tôrz′) *adj.* Designating the style of architecture, interior decoration, and furniture which characterized the period of Louis XIV in France (1643–1715), marked by baroque architectural forms and ornate and grandiose decorative treatment employing animal and mythological forms richly carved. [<F]

Lou·is-Quinze (lōō′ē·kaṅz′) *adj.* Designating the style of architecture, decoration, and furniture characteristic of the period of Louis XV (1715–74), marked by the culmination of the rococo as expressed in flowing lines, rounded forms, and graceful shell, flower, and other ornaments. [<F]

Lou·is-Seize (lōō′ē·sez′) *adj.* Designating the style of architecture, decoration, and furniture which characterized the period of Louis XVI (1774–93): a reaction against the Louis-Quinze period, marked by simple, rectilinear forms, and using symmetrical Greco-Roman wreaths, birds, etc., as ornaments, or Greek egg-and-anchor or leaf motifs, achieving a plain internal decoration. [<F]

Lou·is-Treize (lōō′ē·trez′) *adj.* Designating the style of architecture, decoration, and furniture which characterized the period of Louis XIII (1610–43), marked by Renaissance forms, rich inlaid ornaments, geometric panels and deep moldings, and carving in the Flemish style. [<F]

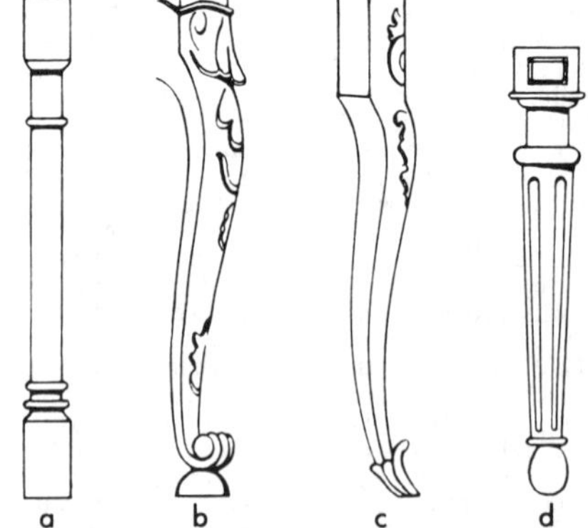

PERIOD STYLES ILLUSTRATED BY CHAIR LEGS
a. Louis XIII. *b.* Louis XIV. *c.* Louis XV. *d.* Louis XVI.

Lou·is·ville (lōō′ē·vil) A city on the Ohio River in Kentucky.

loun (loun) *adj. Scot.* Lown.

lounge (lounj) *v.* **lounged, loung·ing** *v.i.* **1** To lie, lean, move, etc., in an idle or lazy manner. **2** To pass time indolently. —*v.t.* **3** To spend or pass indolently, as time. —*n.* **1** act of lounging. **2** A room in a hotel, club, etc., for lounging. **3** A couch with little or no back; any sofa. [Origin unknown]

loung·er (loun′jər) *n.* One who lounges; an idler.

loup[1] (loup, lōōp) *v.t. & v.i.* **lap** or **loup·en, loup·ing** *Scot. & Brit. Dial.* To leap. [<ON *hlaupa*]

loup[2] (lōō) *n.* A light mask or half-mask made of silk: worn at masquerades. [<F]

loup-cer·vier (lōō·ser·vyā′) *n. French* The Canada lynx *(Lynx canadensis).* [<L *lupus cervarius* lynx <*lupus* wolf + *cervarius* stag-hunting <*cervus* stag]

loupe (lōōp) *n.* A small magnifying glass; a lens, especially one adapted for the use of jewelers and watchmakers. [<F]

loup-ga·rou (lōō·gà·rōō′) *n. pl.* **loups-ga·rous** (lōō·gà·rōō′) A werewolf. [<F *loup* wolf (<L *lupus*) + *garou* werewolf <Gmc.]

LOUPE
Made to be used as an eyepiece.

loup·ing ill (lou′ping, lō′-) *Scot.* An infectious virus disease of sheep; leaping evil. Also **loup ill.**

Loup River (lōōp) A river in east central Nebraska, flowing 300 miles east to the Platte River.

lour (lour), **lour·ing** (lour′ing), **lour·y** (lour′ē) See LOWER[1], etc.

Lourdes (lōōrd) A town in SW France; shrine and grotto of the Virgin *(Our Lady of Lourdes).*

Lou·ren·ço Mar·ques (lō·ren′sō mär′kəs, *Pg.* lō·rāṅ′sōō mär′kish) A port on Delagoa Bay, capital of Mozambique.

louse (lous) *n. pl.* **lice** (līs) **1** A small, flat-bodied, wingless insect (order *Anoplura*) living as an external parasite on birds or mammals, especially the crab louse *(Phthirus pubis)* and the human body louse (genus *Pediculus*). **2** One of various other insects parasitic on other animals or plants, as the biting bird louse (order *Mallophaga*) and the plant louse. For illustrations see under INSECTS (injurious). **3** *Slang* A contemptible person. —*v.t. & v.i. U.S. Slang* To ruin; bungle: with *up.* [OE *lūs*]

louse·wort (lous′wûrt′) *n.* Any one of a genus *(Pedicularis)* of scrophulariaceous woodland herbs; wood betony.

lous·y (lou′zē) *adj.* **lous·i·er, lous·i·est** **1** Infested with lice; pedicular. **2** *Slang* Dirty. **3** *Slang* Contemptible; foul; mean. **4** *Slang* Having plenty (of): usually with *with*: *lousy* with money.

lout[1] (lout) *n.* An awkward fellow; clown; boor. [? <ON *lutr* bent, stooped]

lout[2] (lout) *v.i. Obs.* To bow or curtsy; bend; stoop. [OE *lūtan* bow]

Louth (louth) A county of NE Leinster province, Ireland; 317 square miles; county town, Drogheda.

lou·ther (lōō′thər) *v.i. Scot.* To plod, as in mire or wet snow.

lout·ish (lou′tish) *adj.* Clumsy; awkward; boorish. —**lout′ish·ly** *adv.* —**lout′ish·ness** *n.*

Lou·vain (lōō·vān′, *Fr.* lōō·vaṅ′) A city in central Belgium. *Flemish* **Leu·ven** (lœ′vən, -və).

lou·ver (lōō′vər) *n.* **1** A window, as in a belfry tower, designed for ventilation and having slats **(louver boards)** sloped to keep out the rain: also **lou′ver-win′dow** (-win′dō). **2** A lantern-like cupola or turret on the roof of a medieval dwelling. **3** Any of several narrow openings, or the slatted piece having these, serving as outlets for heated air. [<OF *lover*]

LOUVER
a. Construction set in gable *(b).*

Lou·vre (lōō′vr′) An ancient royal palace in Paris, made a museum in the 18th century.

Lou·ÿs (lōō·ē′, *Fr.* lwē), **Pierre,** 1870–1925, French writer.

lov·a·ble (luv′ə·bəl) *adj.* Worthy of love; amiable; also, evoking love. See synonyms under AMIABLE, LOVELY. Also **love′a·ble.** —**lov′a·bil′i·ty, lov′a·ble·ness** *n.* —**lov′a·bly** *adv.*

lov·age (luv′ij) *n.* A European herb *(Levisticum officinale)* of the parsley family: used sometimes as a domestic remedy. [<OF *luvesche* <LL *levisticum,* alter. of L *ligusticum,* neut. of *ligusticus* Ligurian]

love (luv) *n.* **1** A strong, complex emotion or feeling causing one to appreciate, delight in, and crave the presence or possession of another and to please or promote the welfare of the other; devoted affection or attachment. 2 Specifically, such feeling between husband and wife or lover and sweetheart. 3 One who is beloved; a sweetheart. 4 Sexual passion, or the gratification of it. 5 A very great interest or fondness: *love* of learning. 6 In tennis, a score of nothing. **— for the love of** For the sake of; in loving remembrance of: used in adjurations, solemn oaths, etc. **— for love or money** For any consideration; under any circumstances. **— in love** Experiencing love; enamored. **— no love lost between** No affection or liking between. **— v. loved, lov·ing** *v.t.* 1 To feel love or affection for. 2 To take pleasure or delight in; like very much. 3 To caress. **—** *v.i.* 4 To feel love, especially for one of the opposite sex; be in love. See synonyms under ADMIRE, LIKE. [OE *lufu*]

Synonyms (noun): affection, attachment, attraction, charity, devotion, esteem, feeling, fondness, friendship, liking, passion, regard, tenderness. *Affection* is kindly feeling, deep, tender, and constant, going out to some person or object, being less fervent and ardent than *love*. *Love* is the yearning or outgoing of soul toward something that is regarded as excellent, beautiful, or desirable; *love* may be briefly defined as strong and absorbing *affection* for and *attraction* toward a person or object. *Love* is more intense, absorbing, and tender than *friendship*, more intense, impulsive, and perhaps passionate than *affection*; we speak of fervent *love*, but of deep or tender *affection*, or of close, firm, strong *friendship*. *Love* is used specifically for personal *affection* between the sexes, and can never properly denote mere animal passion, which is expressed by such words as appetite, desire, lust. One may have *love* for animals, inanimate objects, or for abstract qualities that enlist the affections, as we speak of *love* for a horse or a dog, for mountains, woods, ocean, or of *love* of nature, and *love* of virtue. *Love* of articles of food is better expressed by *liking*, as *love*, in its full sense, denotes something spiritual and reciprocal, such as can have no place in connection with objects that minister merely to the senses. See ATTACHMENT, FRIENDSHIP. *Antonyms*: see synonyms for ANTIPATHY, ENMITY, HATRED.

Love (luv) A personification of love; Cupid or Eros.

love affair A romantic attachment between two people not married to each other.

love apple The tomato.

love·bird (luv′bûrd′) *n.* One of several small parrots (genera *Agapornis* and *Psitta*) often kept as cage birds: so called from the affection they appear to show for their mates.

love feast 1 A common devotional meal partaken of by early Christians, originally culminating in the Eucharist; agape. 2 A somewhat similar celebration observed in some modern churches, as the Methodist and Moravian. 3 A banquet held in common rejoicing over something.

love game In tennis, a game in which the winner has lost no point.

love-in-a-mist (luv′in·ə·mist′) *n.* A European ranunculaceous garden plant (*Nigella damascena*) with blue flowers.

love-in-i·dle·ness (luv′in·ī′dəl·nis) *n.* The pansy.

love·knot (luv′not′) *n.* A knot tied in pledge of love and constancy, or representation of it, as in jewelry.

Love·lace (luv′lās), **Richard,** 1618–58, English poet.

love·less (luv′lis) *adj.* Having no love; unloving; also, not lovable. **— love′less·ly** *adv.* **— love′less·ness** *n.*

love-lies-bleed·ing (luv′līz′blē′ding) *n.* Any of several species of amaranth.

love·lock (luv′lok′) *n.* A separate lock of hair worn curled and tied with ribbons; especially such a lock as worn formerly by courtiers.

love·lorn (luv′lôrn) *adj.* Forsaken by or pining for a lover.

love·ly (luv′lē) *adj.* **·li·er, ·li·est** 1 Possessing mental or physical qualities that inspire admiration and love; charming. 2 Beautiful. 3 Attractive; inviting. 4 *Colloq.* Delightful; pleasing: We had a *lovely* visit with them. 5 *Obs.* Affectionate; loving. [OE *luflic*] **— love′·li·ness** *n.*

Synonyms: amiable, beautiful, charming, delectable, delightful, enchanting, lovable, pleasing, sweet, winning, winsome. See AMIABLE, BEAUTIFUL.

love·mak·ing (luv′mā′king) *n.* The act of making love; wooing; courtship.

love potion A magic draft or drink designed to arouse love toward a certain person in the one who drinks.

lov·er (luv′ər) *n.* 1 One who loves; a warm admirer; devoted friend. 2 One who is in love; specifically, a paramour: in the singular now used only of the man. 3 One who enjoys or is strongly attracted by some object or diversion. **— lov′er·ly** *adj.* & *adv.*

Lov·er (luv′ər), **Samuel,** 1797–1868, Irish novelist.

love seat A double chair or small sofa for two persons in Queen Anne and later styles.

love set In tennis, a set in which the winner has not lost a game.

love·sick (luv′sik′) *adj.* 1 Languishing with love. 2 Indicating or expressing such a condition: a *lovesick* serenade. **— love′sick′ness** *n.*

love·some (luv′səm) *adj. Obs.* 1 Inspiring love; lovable. 2 Expressing love; loving.

love·vine (luv′vīn′) *n.* The dodder.

lov·ing (luv′ing) *adj.* 1 Affectionate; devoted; kind: *loving* friends or brothers. 2 Indicative of love or kind feeling: *loving* looks and words. See synonyms under AMIABLE, CHARITABLE. **— lov′ing·ly** *adv.* **— lov′ing·ness** *n.*

loving cup 1 A wine cup, usually with two or more handles, meant to be passed from hand to hand around a circle of friends; a parting cup. 2 A trophy presented to the winner of an athletic or other kind of contest.

lov·ing-kind·ness (luv′ing·kīnd′nis) *n.* Kindness that comes from personal attachment; specifically, the loving care of God for his people.

low[1] (lō) *adj.* 1 Having relatively little upward extension; not high or tall. 2 Having relatively little elevation; raised only slightly above a recognized level: a *low* bridge; near the horizon: a *low* moon. 3 Situated below a recognized level; deep; depressed. 4 Having less than the normal or regular height, or less height than something taken as a standard; descending from the usual level. 5 Cut so as to expose the neck; décolleté. 6 Of sounds having depth of pitch; deep; also, having little volume or strength; soft. 7 Being less than the usual rate, amount, or reckoning; scant: *low* wages or interest. 8 Being little in degree, number, grade, station, quality, character, etc.; humble; moderate. 9 Being below the proper standard in refinement, moral character, principle, or condition; lacking pride, principle, force, dignity, or worth; vulgar; weak: *low* spirits; *low* standards of morality. 10 Dead; prostrate: He lies *low*. 11 *Phonet.* Pronounced with the tongue low and flat; open: said of vowels: opposed to *high*. 12 Little advanced in civilization or organic evolution. 13 Badly nourished; lacking in vigor; also, not nourishing; plain: a *low* diet. 14 *Mech.* Giving the least speed: *low* gear. 15 *Geog.* Pertaining to latitudes near the equator. 16 *Eccl.* **a** Pertaining to broad evangelical doctrine. **b** Denoting a service shorn of elaborate ritual: a *low* mass. 17 *Bot.* Growing close to the ground: a *low* herb. See synonyms under BASE, COMMON, HUMBLE, VULGAR. **—** *adv.* 1 In a low way; in or to a low position; not on high. 2 At a low price; cheap. 3 In a humble rank or degraded condition. 4 So as not to be loud in sound; softly; also, at a low pitch. 5 In such a path that the declination or the altitude is small; near the equator or the horizon. **— to lie low** 1 To be dead or prostrate. 2 To be or remain in hiding. 3 To hold one's tongue till the proper moment; wait. **—** *n.* 1 A low area. 2 The first gear or speed of an automobile: Put it in *low*. [OE *lah* <ON *lagr*] **— low′·ness** *n.*

low[2] (lō) *n.* The moo or bellow of cattle: also **low′ing.** **—** *v.i.* To bellow, as cattle; moo. **—** *v.t.* To utter by lowing. [OE *hlowan*]

low[3] (lō) *n. Scot.* A glowing fire; blaze. Also **lowe.**

Low (lō), **David,** 1891–1963, English cartoonist.

Low Archipelago See TUAMOTU ARCHIPELAGO.

low area *Meteorol.* A region of low atmospheric pressure.

low-ar·e·a storm (lō′âr′ē·ə) A cyclone.

low-born (lō′bôrn′) *adj.* Of humble birth.

low·boy (lō′boi′) *n.* A table, often a dressing table, with drawers, similar to the lower part of a highboy.

low-bred (lō′bred′) *adj.* Vulgar; ill-bred.

low·brow (lō′brou′) *Colloq. n.* A person of uncultivated tastes; a non-intellectual: an uncomplimentary term. **—** *adj.* Of or suitable for such a person: also **low′browed′.** **— low′brow′·ism** *n.*

Low-Church (lō′chûrch′) *adj.* Of or belonging to a group (**Low Church**) in the Anglican Church which stresses evangelical doctrine and is, in general, opposed to extreme ritualism. **— Low-Church·man** (lō′chûrch′·mən) *n.*

low comedy Comedy in which both subject matter and presentation are in the broad style of farce or burlesque; comedy characterized by slapstick and lively physical action rather than by witty dialog.

Low Countries The region of NW Europe comprising the Netherlands, Belgium, and Luxemburg.

low-down[1] (lō′doun′) *n. Slang* Inside or secret information; the truth of a matter.

low-down[2] (lō′doun′) *adj. Colloq.* Degraded; mean.

low-down·er (lō′dou′nər) *n. Dial.* A poor white.

Low·ell (lō′əl) A distinguished Massachusetts family, descendants of **John,** 1743–1802, jurist, including **James Russell,** 1819–91, poet, essayist, editor, and diplomat; **Percival,** 1855–1916, astronomer; **Abbott Lawrence,** 1856–1943, educator; president of Harvard University 1909–33; brother of Percival; **Amy,** 1874–1925, poet and critic; sister of Percival.

Low·ell (lō′əl) A city on the Merrimac River in NE Massachusetts.

low·er[1] (lou′ər) *v.i.* 1 To look angry or sullen; scowl. 2 To appear dark and threatening, as the weather. **—** *n.* A scowl; a gloomy aspect. Also spelled *lour.* [Cf. G *lauern* lurk]

low·er[2] (lō′ər) Comparative of LOW. **—** *adj.* 1 Inferior in position, in value or rank; situated below something else: a *lower* berth. 2 *Geol.* Older; designating strata normally beneath the newer (and upper) rock formations. **—** *n.* That which is beneath something above; specifically, a lower berth. **—** *v.t.* 1 To bring to a lower position or level; let down, as a window. 2 To reduce in degree, quality, amount, etc.: to *lower* prices. 3 To bring down in estimation, rank, etc.; humble or degrade. 4 To change, as a sound, to a lower pitch or volume. **—** *v.i.* 5 To become lower; sink; decrease. See synonyms under ABASE, ABATE, DISPARAGE, WEAKEN.

Lower Austria An autonomous province of NE Austria; 7,097 square miles; capital, Vienna. *German* **Nie·der·ös·ter·reich** (nē′dər·œs′tə·rīkh).

Lower Burma See BURMA, UNION OF.

Lower California A peninsula of NW Mexico separating the Gulf of California from the Pacific; about 760 miles long; 55,634 square miles: divided into **Northern Territory;** 27,655 square miles; capital, Mexicali; and **Southern Territory;** 27,979 square miles; capital, La Paz. Spanish *Baja California.*

Lower Canada A former name for the province of QUEBEC.

low·er-case (lō′ər·kās′) *adj. Printing* Describing the small letters of a font of type which are kept in the low case (see CASE); small letters. **—** *v.t.* **-cased, -cas·ing** To set as or change to lower-case letters. [From their being kept in the lower two cases of type]

lower class The socially or economically inferior group in society. **— low·er-class** (lō′ər·klas′, -kläs′) *adj.*

low·er-class·man (lō′ər·klas′mən, -kläs′-) *n. pl.* **·men** (-mən) A freshman or a sophomore.

Lower Cretaceous *Geol.* The older part of the

Cretaceous period, or its representative rocks or fossils. See CRETACEOUS.

lower criticism The method of critical investigation which seeks to determine the original wording of a text: also called *textual criticism.* Compare HIGHER CRITICISM.

Lower Franconia An administrative division of NW Bavaria, West Germany; 3,277 square miles; capital, Würzburg: formerly *Mainfranken. German* **Un·ter·fran·ken** (o͝on′tər·fräng′kən).

Lower House The popular division of a legislative body; in the United States, the House of Representatives, as opposed to the Upper House or Senate; in Great Britain, the House of Commons, as opposed to the House of Lords.

low·er·ing (lou′ər·ing) *adj.* **1** Overcast with clouds; gloomy; threatening. **2** Frowning or sullen. Also spelled *louring.* **—low′er·ing·ly** *adv.* **—low′er·ing·ness** *n.*

low·er·most (lō′ər·mōst′) *adj.* Lowest.

Lower Saxony A state of north central West Germany; 18,279 square miles; capital, Hanover. *German* **Nie·der·sach·sen** (nē′dər·zäk′sən).

Lower Silurian *Geol.* The former name for ORDOVICIAN.

lower world 1 The abode of the dead; hell; Hades. Also **lower regions. 2** The earth.

low·er·y (lou′ər·ē) *adj.* Cloudy; threatening storm: also spelled *loury.*

Lowes (lōz), **John Livingston,** –1945, U.S. scholar, critic, and educator.

lowest common multiple See under MULTIPLE.

Lowes·toft (lōs′tôft, -təft) *n.* A variety of porcelain originally made at Lowestoft, England.

Lowes·toft (lōs′tôft, -təft) A municipal borough and port in eastern Suffolk, England.

Low German See under GERMAN.

low–key (lō′kē′) *adj.* Having a low degree of intensity; relatively pale or quiet; understated. Also **low–keyed** (lō′kēd′).

low·land (lō′lənd) *adj.* Pertaining to or characteristic of a low or level country. —*n.* (*also* lō′land′) *Usually pl.* Land lower than the adjacent country; level land. **—The Lowlands** The less elevated districts lying in the south and west of Scotland. **—Low′land′er** *n.*

Low·land (lō′lənd) *adj.* Pertaining to or belonging to The Lowlands. —*n.* (*also* lō′land′) The speech or dialect of the Scotch Lowlands.

Low Latin See under LATIN.

low·ly (lō′lē) *adj.* **·li·er, ·li·est 1** Situated or lying low, as land. **2** Having low rank or importance; unpretending; humble. See synonyms under HUMBLE. —*adv.* **1** In a manner appropriate to humble life; rudely; meanly. **2** In a meek or modest manner. **—low′li·ness** *n.*

low mass The ordinary form of mass without music.

low–mind·ed (lō′mīn′did) *adj.* Having low or mean thoughts, sentiments, or motives; base.

lown[1] (loun) *adj. Scot.* Sheltered; tranquil. **—lown′ly** *adv.*

lown[2] (lo͞on) See LOON[2].

low–necked (lō′nekt′) *adj.* Cut low in the neck; décolleté: said of a garment.

low–pitched (lō′picht′) *adj.* **1** Low in tone, key, or range of tone, as a voice. **2** Having little angular elevation: said of a roof.

low–pres·sure (lō′presh′ər) *adj.* **1** Requiring a low degree of pressure. **2** Having a condenser, as an engine. **3** *Meteorol.* Designating an atmospheric pressure below that which is normal at sea level.

low relief Bas-relief.

low–spir·it·ed (lō′spir′it·id) *adj.* Lacking spirit or animation; despondent; melancholy. **—low′–spir′it·ed·ly** *adv.* **—low′–spir′it·ed·ness** *n.*

Low Sunday The Sunday following Easter.

low–ten·sion (lō′ten′shən) *adj. Electr.* Having or characterized by a low electric potential, as a battery, magneto, or vacuum tube.

low–test (lō′test′) *adj.* Possessing a relatively high boiling point, as gasoline.

low tide The furthest recession of the tide at any point; also, the time of its occurrence. Also **low water.**

low–wa·ter (lō′wô′tər, -wot′ər) *adj.* Pertaining to low tide or its time or measure of recession.

lox[1] (loks) *n.* Smoked salmon. [<Yiddish <G *lachs* salmon]

lox[2], **LOKS** (loks) *n.* Liquid oxygen.

lox·o·drom·ic (lok′sə·drom′ik) *adj.* Pertaining to oblique sailing on the rhumb line. Also **lox′o·drom′i·cal.** [<Gk. *loxos* oblique + *dromos* a running]

lox·o·drom·ics (lok′sə·drom′iks) *n. pl.* (construed as singular) The art of oblique sailing. Also **lox·od·ro·my** (lok·sod′rə·mē).

loy·al (loi′əl) *adj.* **1** Constant and faithful in any relation implying trust or confidence; bearing true allegiance to constituted authority. **2** Professing or indicative of faithful devotion. **3** *Obs.* Legitimate. See synonyms under FAITHFUL. [<OF *loial, leial* <L *legalis.* Doublet of LEGAL.] **—loy′al·ism** *n.* **—loy′al·ly** *adv.*

loy·al·ist (loi′əl·ist) *n.* One who adheres to and defends his sovereign or state.

Loy·al·ist (loi′əl·ist) *n.* **1** One who was loyal to the British crown during the American Revolution. **2** One who was loyal to the Union during the Civil War. **3** One who was loyal to the Republican Constitution during the Spanish Civil War.

loy·al·ty (loi′əl·tē) *n. pl.* **·ties** Devoted allegiance. See synonyms under ALLEGIANCE, FIDELITY. [<OF *loialte*]

Loyalty Islands A dependency of New Caledonia; total, 740 square miles. *French* **Îles Loy·au·té** (ēllwȧ·yō·tā′).

Lo·yo·la (loi·ō′lə, *Sp.* lō·yō′lä), **Ignatius of,** 1491–1556, Spanish soldier and priest; founder, with Francisco Xavier, of the Society of Jesus (the Jesuits); canonized in 1622: original name *Iñigo de Oñez y Loyola.* **—Loy·o·lism** (loi′ə·liz′əm) *n.*

loz·enge (loz′inj) *n.* **1** *Math.* A rhombus with all sides equal, having two acute and two obtuse angles. **2** A small medicated or sweetened tablet, originally diamond-shaped. [<OF *losenge,?* <L *lapis, -idis* stone]

LP (el′pē′) *adj.* Designating a phonograph record pressed with microgrooves and played at a speed of 33⅓ revolutions per minute. —*n.* A long-playing phonograph record: a trade name. [< *l(ong)-p(laying)*]

LSD (el′es′dē′) *n.* A drug that produces states similar to those of schizophrenia, used in medicine and illicitly as a hallucinogen. See LYCSERGIC ACID. Also **LSD–25.** [<*l(y)s(ergic acid) d(iethylamide)*]

Lu·a·la·ba (lo͞o′ä·lä′bä) The upper course of the Congo, flowing 400 miles north: French *Loualaba.*

Lu·an·da (lo͞o·än′də) A port, capital of Angola: formerly *Loanda, São Paulo de Loanda.*

Luang Pra·bang (lwäng prä·bäng′) A city of north central Laos; royal residence.

Luang·wa (lwäng′gwä) A river in eastern Zambia, flowing 500 miles SW to the Zambesi: formerly *Loangwa.*

lu·au (lo͞o′ou) *n.* A Hawaiian outdoor feast, esp. one that features roast pig. [< Hawaiian *lu′au*]

Lu·bang Islands (lo͞o·bäng′) A Philippine island group off NE Mindoro; 88 square miles.

lub·ber (lub′ər) *n.* An awkward, ungainly fellow; specifically, a landsman on shipboard. [Origin uncertain. Cf. ON *lubba* short.] **—lub′·ber·li·ness** *n.* **—lub′ ber·ly** *adj.* & *adv.*

lubber line *Aeron.* A fixed line in an aircraft compass, gyro, direction finder, or similar instrument, parallel to the longitudinal axis of the aircraft and used as a base line.

lubber's hole *Naut.* A hole through the floor of a platform or top at the head of a lower mast by which sailors can go aloft without climbing over the rim by the futtock shrouds.

Lü·beck (lo͞o′bek, *Ger.* lü′bek) A city in northern West Germany.

Lu·blin (lo͞o′blin, *Polish* lyo͞o′blēn) A city in eastern Poland Russian *Lyublin.*

lu·bra (lo͞o′brə) *n. Austral.* A young aboriginal female. [<native Australian]

lu·bric (lo͞o′brik) *adj. Obs.* Lubricous. Also **lu′·bri·cal.** [<L *lubricus* slippery]

lu·bri·cant (lo͞o′brə·kənt) *adj.* Lubricating. —*n.* Anything that lubricates, as grease.

lu·bri·cate (lo͞o′brə·kāt) *v.t.* **·cat·ed, ·cat·ing 1** To apply grease, oil, or other lubricant to so as to reduce friction and wear. **2** To make slippery or smooth. [<L *lubricatus,* pp. of *lubricare* make slippery <*lubricus* slippery] **—lu′bri·ca′tion** *n.* **—lu′bri·ca′tive** *adj.*

lu·bri·ca·tor (lo͞o′brə·kā′tər) *n.* **1** One who or that which lubricates. **2** A device, as an oil cup, by which a lubricant is fed or applied to a bearing surface.

lu·bric·i·ty (lo͞o·bris′ə·tē) *n.* **1** The state of being slippery; hence, shiftiness; instability; evanescence. **2** Lewdness. **3** Power for lubrication. [<F *lubricité* <L *lubricitas* <*lubricus* slippery]

lu·bri·cous (lo͞o′brə·kəs) *adj.* **1** Smooth and slippery. **2** Elusive; unstable. **3** Lascivious; lewd; wanton. Also **lu·bri·cious** (lo͞o·brish′əs). [<L *lubricus*]

lu·bri·fac·tion (lo͞o′brə·fak′shən) *n.* The act or process of lubricating or making slippery or smooth. [<L *lubricus* smooth + *factus,* pp. of *facere* make]

Lu·bum·ba·shi (lo͞o·bo͞om′bä·shē) The capital of Katanga province, Republic of the Congo.

Luc (lük) French form of LUKE. Also *Ital.* **Lu·ca** (lo͞o′kä), **Lu·cas** (*Dan., Du., Ger., Sw.* lo͞o′·käs; *Lat.* lo͞o′kəs), *Hungarian* **Lu·cáts** (lo͞o′·käch). [<L, light]

Lu·can (lo͞o′kən), 39–65, Roman poet: full name *Marcus Annaeus Lucanus.*

Lu·ca·ni·a (lo͞o·kā′nē·ə) The ancient name for BASILICATA.

lu·carne (lo͞o·kärn′) *n.* A dormer or garret window; also, a small window or light in a spire. [<F; ult. origin uncertain. Cf. OHG *lukka* opening.]

Luc·ca (look′kä) A city in Tuscany, north central Italy.

luce (lo͞os) *n.* A fish, the pike, especially when fully grown. [<OF *lus* <L *lucius*]

Luce (lüs) French form of LUCIUS.

Luce (lo͞os), **Clare Boothe,** born 1903, U.S. dramatist and diplomat; wife of Henry R. **—Henry Robinson,** 1898–1967, U.S. editor and publisher.

lu·cent (lo͞o′sənt) *adj.* Showing radiance or brilliance; shining; luminous. [<L *lucens, -entis,* ppr. of *lucere* shine] **—lu′cen·cy** *n.*

lu·cer·nal (lo͞o·sûr′nəl) *adj.* Relating to a lamp or to any artificial light. [<L *lucerna* lamp <*lux* light]

lu·cerne (lo͞o·sûrn′) *n.* A tall, cloverlike herb of the pea family *(Medicago sativa),* used for forage: now commonly called *alfalfa, purple medic.* Also **lu·cern′.** [<F *luzerne*; ult. origin unknown]

Lu·cerne (lo͞o·sûrn′, *Fr.* lü·sern′) A canton of central Switzerland; 580 square miles; capital, Lucerne (German *Luzern*) on **Lake of Lucerne,** a lake in north central Switzerland; 44 square miles: also **Lake of the Four Forest Cantons** (German *Vierwaldstättersee*).

lu·ces (lo͞o′sēz) Plural of LUX.

Lu·cia (lo͞o′shə; *Ger.* lo͞o′tsē·ə, *Ital.* lo͞o·chē′ä, *Lat.* lo͞o′shē·ə, *Pg.* lo͞o′sē·ə, *Sp.* lo͞o·thē′ä) A feminine personal name: also *Lucy.* Also *Fr.* **Lu·cie** (lü·sē′, *Du.* lo͞ov′sē·ä). [<L, light]

Lu·cian (lo͞o′shən), 125?–210?, Greek satirist. Also **Lu·ci·a·nus** (lo͞o′shē·ā′·nəs).

lu·cid (lo͞o′sid) *adj.* **1** Intellectually bright and clear; mentally sound; sane. **2** Easily understood; perspicuous; clear. **3** Giving forth light; shining. **4** Translucent; pellucid. **5** Smooth and shining. See synonyms under CLEAR, SANE, TRANSPARENT. [<L *lucidus* <*lucere* shine] **—lu·cid·i·ty** (lo͞o·sid′ə·tē), **lu′·cid·ness** *n.* **—lu′cid·ly** *adv.*

lu·ci·fer (lo͞o′sə·fər) *n.* A friction match. —*adj.* Emitting light. [after *Lucifer*]

Lu·ci·fer (lo͞o′sə·fər) **1** The planet Venus as the morning star. **2** Satan, especially as the leader of the revolt of the angels before his fall from heaven. [<L, light-bearer <*lux, lucis* light + *ferre* bear] **—Lu·cif·er·ous** (lo͞o·sif′ər·əs) *adj.*

lu·cif·er·ase (lo͞o·sif′ə·rās) *n.* Biochem. An enzyme present in fireflies and in certain other luminous organisms: it oxidizes luciferin to produce light. [<L *lucifer* light-bearing + -ASE]

lu·cif·er·in (lo͞o·sif′ər·in) *n.* Biochem. A water-soluble, heat-stable protein which produces heatless light, as in fireflies. [<L *lucifer* light-bearing + -IN]

lu·cif·er·ous (lo͞o·sif′ər·əs) *adj.* Emitting light. [<L *lucifer* light-bearing + -OUS]

lu·ci·form (lo͞o′sə·fôrm) *adj.* Having the nature or appearance of light. [< L *lux, lucis* light + -FORM]

Lu·ci·na (lo͞o·sī′nə) In Roman mythology, the goddess presiding over childbirth. [< L *lucina,* fem. of *lucinus* bringing to the light <*lux, lucis* light]

Lu·cin·da (lo͞o·sin′də) See LUCY.

Lu·cite (lo͞o′sīt) *n.* A thermoplastic, transparent acrylic resin, easily machined into various shapes and having the property of transmitting light around curves and corners: a trade name.

Lu·cius (lo͞o′shəs; *Ger.* lo͞o′tsē·o͞os, *Fr.* lü·sē·üs′) A masculine personal name. Also *Ital.*

Lucio (lo͞o′chō, *Pg.* lo͞o′sy;oo *Sp.* lo͞o′thyō). [<L, light]

lu·ci·vee (lo͞o′sə·vē) *n.* The loup-cervier. Also **lu′ci·fee** (-fē). [Alter. of LOUP-CERVIER]

luck (luk) *n.* **1** That which happens by chance; fortune or lot. **2** Happy chance; good fortune; success. [Prob. <MDu. *luk, geluk*]

luck·less (luk′lis) *adj.* Having no luck. —**luck′·less·ly** *adv.*

Luck·ner (luk′nər, *Ger.* lo͝ok′nər), **Count Felix von,** 1881–1966, German naval officer: known as the *Sea Devil.*

Luck·now (luk′nou) A city in central Uttar Pradesh, India; the capital of the State; British forces were besieged here during the Sepoy Rebellion, 1857.

luck·y[1] (luk′ē) *adj.* **luck·i·er, luck·i·est 1** Favored by fortune; fortunate; successful. **2** Productive of luck; auspicious; favorable: said of events and things: a *lucky* penny or circumstance. See synonyms under AUSPICIOUS, FORTUNATE, HAPPY, WELL. —**luck′i·ly** *adv.* —**luck′i·ness** *n.*

luck·y[2] (luk′ē) *n. pl.* **luck·ies** *Scot.* A grandam or aged woman; goody; sometimes part of a person's name: *Lucky* Macpherson. Also **luck′ie.**

luck·y[3] (luk′ē) *adv. Scot.* More than sufficiently: *lucky* hot.

lu·cra·tive (lo͞o′krə·tiv) *adj.* Productive of wealth; highly profitable. See synonyms under PROFITABLE [<L *lucrativus* <*lucratus,* pp. of *lucrari* gain <*lucrum* wealth] —**lu′cra·tive·ly** *adv.* —**lu′cra·tive·ness** *n.*

lu·cre (o͞o′kər) *n.* Money, especially as the object of greed; gain. See synonyms under WEALTH. [<F <L *lucrum* gain]

Lu·cre·tia (lo͞o·krē′shə, *Ger.* lo͞o·krā′tsē·ə) A feminine personal name. Also *Fr.* **Lu·crèce** (lü·kres′), *Ital.* **Lu·cre·zi·a**, **Sp.* **Lu·cre·ci·a** (lo͞o·krā′thē·ä). [<L, wealth] —**Lucretia** In Roman legend, the wife of Collatinus who killed herself after she had been violated by Sextus Tarquinius; subject of a poem by Shakespeare.

Lu·cre·tius (lo͞o·krē′shəs, -shē·əs), 96?–55 B.C. Roman poet and philosopher: full name *Titus Lucretius Carus.*

lu·cu·brate (lo͞o′kyo͞o·brāt) *v.i.* **·brat·ed, ·brat·ing 1** To study or write laboriously, as at night. **2** To write in a learned manner. [<L *lucubratus,* pp. of *lucubrare* work by artificial light <*lux, lucis* light]

lu·cu·bra·tion (lo͞o′ky·brā′shən) *n.* **1** Close and earnest meditation or study. **2** The product of deep meditation or earnest study; a literary composition; often, a pedantic or overelaborated work. [<L *lucubratio, -onis*] —**lu′cu·bra′tor** *n.* —**lu′cu·bra·to′ry** (-brətôr′ē, -tō′rē) *adj.*

lu·cu·lent (lo͞o′kyo͞o·lənt) *adj.* **1** Full of light; brilliant. **2** Clearly evident; lucid. [<L *luculentus*]

Lu·cul·lus (lo͞o·kul′əs), **Lucius Licinius,** 110?–57? B.C., Roman consul, proverbial for his wealth and luxury. —**Lu·cul′lan, Lu·cul·le·an** (lo͞o′kə·lē′ən), **Lu·cul′li·an** *adj.*

lu·cus a non lu·cen·do (lo͞o′kəs ā non lo͞o·sen′·dō) *Latin* Literally, a grove because it is *not* light: in allusion to an ancient absurd derivation of *lucus,* grove, from *lucere,* be light. Hence, something absurdly reasoned out.

Lu·cy (lo͞o′sē) Variant of LUCIA.

Lucy Sto·ner (stō′nər) An advocate of women's rights; especially one advocating the retention of maiden names by married women. [after *Lucy Stone,* 1818–93, U.S. woman suffragist].

Lud·dite (lud′it) *n.* One of a band of workmen who joined in riots (1811–16) for the destruction of machinery, under the belief that its introduction reduced wages and increased unemployment: called who after Ned Lud, a feeble-witted mechanic who destroyed several stocking-frames: in English industrial history.

Lu·dcn·dorff (lo͞o′dən·dôrf), **Erich von,** 1865–1937, German general in World War I.

Lü·der·itz (lü′dər·its) A port in SW Namibia: formerly *Angra Pequeña.*

Lu·dhi·a·na (lo͞o′dē·ä′nə) A city in central Punjab, India.

lu·di·crous (lo͞o′də·krəs) *adj.* Calculated to excite laughter; incongruous; droll; ridiculous. See synonyms under ABSURD, HUMOROUS, QUEER, RIDICULOUS. <L *ludicrus* <*ludere* play] —**lu′di·crous·ly** *adv.* —**lu′di·crous·ness** *n.*

Lu·do·vi·ka (lo͞o′dō·vē′kä) German and Swedish form of LOUISE.

Lud·wig (*Ger.* lo͞ot′vikh, *Sw.* lo͝od′vig) German and Swedish form of LOUIS. Also *Latin* **Lu·do·vi·cus** (lo͞o′dō·vē′kəs). —**Ludwig II,** 1845–86, king of Bavaria, 1864–1886; patron of the arts; declared insane; committed suicide.

Lud·wigs·ha·fen (lo͞ot′viks·hä·fən) A city in the Rhineland Palatinate, West Germany. Also **Lud′wigs·ha′fen-am-Rhein** (-äm·rīn′).

lu·es (lo͞o′ēz) *n.* **1**Formerly, an infectious or pestilential disease. **2** Plague. **3** Syphilis. [<L, plague, discharge <*luere* flow] —**lu·et·ic** (lo͞o·et′ik) *adj.*

luff (luf) *n. Naut.* **1** The sailing of a ship close to the wind. **2** The rounded part of a vessel's bow. **3** The foremost edge of a fore-and-aft sail. —*v.i. Naut.* **1** To bring the head of a vessel nearer the wind; sail near the wind. **2** To bring the head of a vessel into the wind, with the sails shaking. Also spelled *loof.*

luf·fa (luf′ə) See LOOFAH.

Luft·waf·fe (lo͞oft′väf′ə) *n. German* The German air force, as organized by the Nazi regime in 1939. [<G, lit., air weapon]

lug[1] (lug) *n.* **1** The lobe of the ear; the ear. **2** Hence, an earlike projection such as an ear or handle for carrying or supporting, or for insertion of a handle, ring, pole, etc.; the *lugs* of a kettle. **3** The loop at the side of the saddle of a harness which holds the shaft. [Origin uncertain. Cf. Sw. *lugg* foreclock.]

lug[2] (lug) *n.* **1** The act or exertion of lugging; anything that is moved with slowness and difficulty. **2** A shallow box or container, 13 ½ by 16 inches inside dimensions, for carrying fruit or vegetables. **3** *Naut.* A square sail bet to a yard and having no boom: also *lugsail.* **4** *Slang* An exaction, especially of money for political uses. —*v.t.* **lugged, lug·ging 1** To carry or pull with effort; drag. **2** *Colloq.* To bring, as irrelevant topics, into a conversation, discussion, etc.; introduce unreasonably. [Prob. <Scand. CF. Sw. *lugga* pull by the hair.]

lug[3] (lug) *n.* A lugworm. [Origin uncertain. Cf. LG *lug* slow, heavy.]

Lug (lo͞o) In old Irish mythology, one of the Tuatha De Danann, the god of light and sun, patron of the arts; father of Cuchulain. Also transliterated **Lugh.** [<Irish **Lugh,** lit., swift, active]

Lug·aid (lo͞o′ē) In Old Irish mythology, a king of Munster who joined forces with Maeve, Queen of Connacht, in the Cattle Raid of Cuailgne; also, his son, who later slew Cuchulain.

Lu·gansk (lo͞o·gänsk′) An industrial city of eastern Ukrainian S.S.R.: formerly (1935–58) called *Voroshilovgrad.*

luge (lo͞oj) *n.* A short, stout sled; also called *toboggan.* [<F <dial. F]

Lu·ger (lo͞o′gər) *n.* A German automatic pistol widely used in Europe as a military sidearm: manufactured in various calibers, most commonly 7.65 mm, and 9 mm.: also called *Parabellum* in Europe. [after Georg *Luger,* 19th c. German engineer]

lug·gage (lug′ij) *n.* **1** Anything burdensome or heavy to carry. **2** Baggage. [<LUG[2]]

lugged (lugd) *adj. Scot.* Having ears or earlike appendages.

lug·ger (lug′ər) *n.* A one-, two-, or three-masted vessel having lugsails only. [<LUG(SAIL) + -ER[2]]

LUGGER

lug·gie (lug′ē, lo͝og′ē, lo͞o′gē) *n. Scot.* A small wooden dish with lugs or ears.

Lu·go lo͞o′gō) A city in Galicia, NW Spain.

lug·sail (lug′səl, -sāl′) *n.* Lug[2] (def. 3).

lu·gu·bri·ous (loo·go͞o′brē·əs, -gyo͞o′-) *adj.* **1** Exhibiting or producing sadness; doleful. **2** Exaggeratedly solemn or sad. See synonyms under SAD. [<L *lugubris* <*lugere* mourn] —**lu·gu′·bri·ous·ly** *adv.* —**lu·gu′bri·ous·ness** *n.*

lug·worm (lug′wûrm′) *n.* An annelid worm (genus *Arenicola*) with two rows of tufted gills on the back, living in the sand of seashores; much used for bait: also called *lobworm.*

Lu·i·gi (lo͞o′ē′jē) Italian form of LOUIS. Also *Sp.* **Lu·is** (lo͞o·ēs′), *Pg.* **Luis** (lo͞o·ēs′)

Lu·i·gia (lo͞o·ē′jä) Italian form of LOUISA.

Luim·neach (lim′nəkh) The Gaelic name for LIMERICK.

Lu·i·ni (lo͞o·ē′nē), **Bernardino,** 1470?–1530?, Italian painter.

Lu·i·sa (lo͞o·ē′sä) Italian and Spanish form of LOUISA. Also *Ger.* **Lu·i·se** (lo͞o·ē′zə), *Pg.* **Lu·i·za** (lo͞o·ēzə).

Lu·it·pold (lo͞o′it·pōlt) Old German form of LEOPOLD.

Luke lo͝ok A masculine personal name. [<L, light] —**Luke, Saint** Physician and companion of St. Paul; traditionally thought to be author of the third gospel and of *The Acts of the Apostles.*

luke·warm (lo͝ok′wôrm′) *adj.* **1** Moderately warm; tepid. **2** Hence, not ardent or hearty; indifferent. [Prob. OE *hlēow* warm. Cf. LG *luk* tepid.] —**luke′warm′ly** *adv.* —**luke′warm′·ness** *n.*

Lü·le·bur·gaz (lü′lə·bo͝or·gäz′, -gaž′) A town in central Turkey in Europe; scene of a battle of the First Balkan War, 1912. Also **Lu′le Bur·gas′.**

lull (lul) *v.t.* **1** To soothe or quiet; put to sleep. **2** To calm; allay, as suspicions. —*v.i.* **3** To become calm. —*n.* **1** An abatement of noise or violence; an interval of calm or quiet. **2** That which lulls or soothes. See synonyms under TRANQUILIZE. [Pro. <Sw. *lulla* sing to sleep; ult. imit.]

lull·a·by (lul′ə·bī) *n. pl.* **·bies 1** A song to lull a child to sleep; a cradlesong; also, the music for such a song. **2** *Obs.* A goodnight or farewell. [<LULL]

Lul·ly (lü·lē′), **Jean Baptiste,** 1633?–87, French composer born in Italy. Also **Lul·li′.** —**Lul·ly** (lul′ē), **Raymond,** 1235?–1315, Spanish ecclesiastic and philosopher.

lu·lu (lo͞o′lo͞o) *n. Slang* Anything of an exceptional or outstanding nature, as a difficult examination, a beautiful person, etc. [Prob. reduplication of *Lou,* the familiar form of LOUISE]

lum (lum) *n. Brit. Dial. & Scot.* A chimney.

lu·ma·chelle (lo͞o′mə·kel) *n.* A variety of limestone containing fragments of shells, fossils, etc., sometimes brilliantly iridescent. Also **lu′ma·chel, lu′ma·chel′la** (-kel′ə). [<Ital. *lumachella,* dim. of *lumaca* snail <L *limax, limacis*]

lum·ba·go (lum·bā′gō) *n. Pathol.* Rheumatic pain in the lumbar region of the back; backache. [<L <*lumbus* loin]

lum·bar (lum′bər, -bär) *adj.* Pertaining to or situated near the loins. —*n.* A lumbar vertebra or nerve. [<NL *lumbaris* <L *lumbus loin*]

lum·ber[1] (lum′bər) *n.* **1** *U.S. & Can.* Timber sawed into board, planks, etc. **2** Disused articles laid aside. **3** Hence, rubbish. *adj.* Made of, pertaining to, or dealing in, lumber. — *v.t.* **1** *U.S. & Can.* To cut down (timber); also, to cut down the timber of (an area). **2** To fill or obstruct with useless articles. **3** To heap in disorder. —*v.i.* **4** *U.S. & Can.* To cut down or saw timber for marketing. [Var. of *Lombard* in obs. sense of "money-lender, pawnshop"; hence, stored articles] —**lum′ber·er** *n.*

lum·ber[2] (lum′bər) *v.i.* **1** To move or proceed in a heavy or awkward manner. **2** To move with a rumbling noise. —*n.* A rumbling noise. [Origin uncertain. Cf. Sw. *lomra* resound, *loma* walk heavily.]

lum·bered (lum′bərd) *adj.* Having the timber cut off: said of land.

lum·ber·ing[1] (lum′bər·ing) *n.* The business of felling and shaping timber into logs, boards, etc.

lum·ber·ing[2] (lum′bər·ing) *adj.* Clumsily huge and heavy; moving heavily; rumbling. —**lum′ber·ing·ly** *adv.* —**lum′ber·ing·ness** *n.*

lum·ber·jack (lum′bər·jak) *n.* **1** A lumberman.

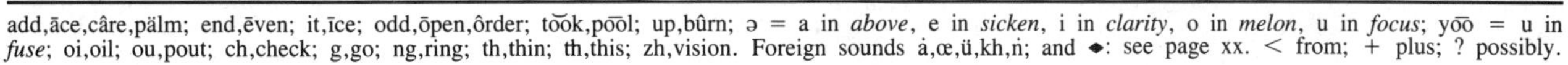

2 A boy's or man's short, straight jacket of heavy warm material: originally made in imitation of coats worn by lumbermen: also **lum'ber·jack'et** (-jak'it). [<LUMBER[1] + *jack* man, boy]
lum·ber·man (lum'bər·mən) *n. pl.* **·men** (-mən) A person engaged in the business of lumbering.
lum·ber-room (lum'bər·rōōm', -rōōm') *n.* A room for lumber or useless articles.
lum·ber·some (lum'bər·səm) *adj.* Cumbersome.
lum·ber·yard (lum'bər·yärd') *n.* A yard for the storage or sale of lumber.
lum·bri·ca·lis (lum'brə·kā'lis) *n. pl.* **·les** (-lēz) *Anat.* 1 One of the four vermiform muscles in the palm of the hand. 2 One of four similar muscles in the sole of the foot. [<NL <L *lumbricus* worm] — **lum'bri·cal** *adj.*
lum·bri·coid (lum'brə·koid) *adj.* 1 Of or pertaining to the common earthworm (genus *Lumbricus*). 2 Pertaining to or designating a roundworm (*Ascaris lumbricoides*) parasitic in the intestines of man. — *n.* The roundworm. [<L *lumbricus* earthworm + -OID]
lu·men (lōō'mən) *n. pl.* **·mens** or **·mi·na** (-mə·nə) 1 A passageway or opening. 2 *Biol.* The inner cavity of a cell or tubular organ, as a gland. 3 *Physics* A unit for measuring luminous flux, equal to the flow through a steradian from a uniform point source of one international candle. [<L, light]
lum·head (lum'hed') *n. Scot.* A chimney top.
Lu·mi·nal (lōō'mə·nəl, -nôl) Proprietary name for a brand of phenobarbital.
lu·mi·nance (lōō'mə·nəns) See BRIGHTNESS (def. 2).
lu·mi·nar·y (lōō'mə·ner'ē) *n. pl.* **·nar·ies** 1 Any body that gives light; specifically, one of the heavenly bodies as a source of light. 2 One who enlightens men or makes clear any subject. 3 Any light or source of illumination. [<OF *luminaire* <LL *luminarium* candle, torch < *lumen* light]
lu·mi·nesce (lōō'mə·nes') *v.i.* **·nesced, ·nesc·ing** To become luminescent. [Back formation <LUMINESCENT]
lu·mi·nes·cence (lōō'mə·nes'əns) *n.* A light-emission not directly attributable to the heat that produces incandescence, as *bioluminescence.*
lu·mi·nes·cent (lōō'mə·nes'ənt) *adj.* Emitting or capable of emitting light apart from incandescence or high temperature. [<L *lumen* light + -ESCENT]
lu·mi·nif·er·ous (lōō'mə·nif'ər·əs) *adj.* Producing or conveying light. [<L *lumen* light + -FEROUS]
lu·mi·nos·i·ty (lōō'mə·nos'ə·tē) *n. pl.* **·ties** 1 The quality of being luminous. 2 Something luminous. 3 *Physics* The ratio of the luminous flux of an object to the corresponding radiant flux, expressed in lumens per watt.
lu·mi·nous (lōō'mə·nəs) *adj.* 1 Giving or emitting light; shining. 2 Full of light; well lighted; bright. 3 Perspicuous; lucid. See synonyms under BRIGHT, VIVID. [<L *luminosus* <*lumen* light] — **lu'mi·nous·ly** *adv.* — **lu'mi·nous·ness** *n.*
luminous energy Light.
luminous flux *Physics* The time rate of the flow of visible light, expressed in lumens.
luminous intensity *Physics* The luminous flux emitted from a point source of light per spheradian.
lu·mis·ter·ol (lōō·mis'tər·ōl) *n.* A sterol, $C_{28}H_{44}O$, resulting from the ultraviolet irradiation of ergosterol. [< *lumi-* (<L *lumen* light) + (ERGO)STEROL]
lum·mox (lum'əks) *n. U. S. Colloq.* A stupid, heavy, clumsy person. [Cf. G *lümmel* lout]
lump[1] (lump) *n.* 1 A shapeless mass of inert matter, especially a small mass. 2 A mass of things thrown together. 3 A protuberance. 4 A stupid person. 5 A heavy, ungainly person. See synonyms under MASS. — **in a** (or **the**) **lump** All together; with no distinction. — *v.t.* 1 To put together in one mass, group, etc. 2 To consider or treat collectively: to *lump* facts. 3 To make lumps in or on. — *v.i.* 4 To become lumpy; raise in lumps. 5 To move or fall heavily. [<ME, prob. <Scand. Cf. Dan. *lumpe* a lump.]
lump[2] (lump) *v.t. Colloq.* To put up with; endure (something disagreeable): You may like it or *lump* it. [Origin uncertain]
lump·er (lum'pər) *n.* 1 One who lumps. 2 A stevedore.
lump·fish (lump'fish') *n. pl.* **·fish** or **·fish·es** A fish of northern seas (*Cyclopterus lumpus*), oval in shape and with the skin studded with three lateral rows of tubercles. Also **lump'suck'·er** (-suk'ər). [So called from its bulk]
lump·ish (lum'pish) *adj.* Like a lump; stupid. — **lump'ish·ly** *adv.* — **lump'ish·ness** *n.*
lump sum A full and single sum.
lump·y (lum'pē) *adj.* **lump·i·er, lump·i·est** 1 Full of lumps. 2 Lumpish or gross. 3 Running in confused, pounding waves that do not break: a *lumpy* sea. — **lump'i·ly** *adv.* — **lump'i·ness** *n.*
lumpy jaw Actinomycosis.
lu·na (lōō'nə) *n.* In alchemy, silver. [<L, the moon]
Lu·na (lōō'nə) In Roman mythology, the goddess of the moon and of months: identified with the Greek *Selene.* [<L]
lu·na·cy (lōō'nə·sē) *n. pl.* **·cies** 1 An intermittent form of insanity: formerly supposed to depend on the changes of the moon. 2 In forensic psychiatry and law, mental unsoundness to the point of irresponsibility. 3 Wild foolishness; wanton and senseless conduct. See synonyms under INSANITY. [<LUNATIC]
Luna moth A large North American moth (*Tropaea luna*), having light-green wings with long tails and lunate spots. [So called from the crescent-shaped spots on its wings]

LUNA MOTH
(Wingspread from 4 1/2 to 6 inches)

lu·nar (lōō'nər) *adj.* 1 Of or pertaining to the moon; crescented or orbed; like the moon. 2 Measured by revolutions of the moon. 3 In alchemy and medicine, of or pertaining to silver. [<L *lunaris* < *luna* the moon]
lunar caustic *Chem.* Silver nitrate formed into pencils and used for cauterizing. [<LUNA]
lunar day The period of the moon's rotation on its axis.
lu·nar·i·an (lōō·nâr'ē·ən) *adj.* Pertaining to the moon. — *n.* 1 A supposed inhabitant of the moon. 2 An investigator of the moon. [<L *lunaris*]
lunar module *Aerospace* A part of a space vehicle designed to land astronauts on the moon and lift them off to link up with the command module. Also **lunar excursion module.**
lunar month See under MONTH.
lu·na·ry (lōō'nər·ē) *adj.* Connected with the moon; lunar. — *n.* A fern, the moonwort. [<L *lunaris*]
lunar year Twelve lunar months.
lu·nate (lōō'nāt) *adj.* Crescent-shaped. Also **lu'nat·ed.** [<L *lunatus*]
lu·na·tic (lōō'nə·tik) *adj.* 1 Affected with lunacy. 2 Characteristic of or resembling lunacy; crazy; insane. Also **lu·nat·i·cal** (lōō·nat'i·kəl). See synonyms under INSANE. — *n.* An insane person. [<LL *lunaticus* <L *luna* moon]
lu·na·tion (lōō·nā'shən) *n. Astron.* The interval between two returns of the new moon, averaging 29.53059 days. [<Med. L *lunatio, -onis* <L *luna* the moon]
lunch (lunch) *n.* 1 A light meal between other meals, as between breakfast and dinner. 2 Food provided for a lunch. — *v.i.* To eat lunch. — *v.t.* To furnish lunch for. [Short for LUNCHEON] — **lunch'er** *n.*
lunch·eon (lun'chən) *n.* 1 A bit of food taken between meals. 2 A lunch. [? Blend of dial. E *lunch* a lump of food + obs. *nuncheon* afternoon snack]
lunch·eon·ette (lun'chən·et') *n.* A place or counter where light lunches can be obtained.
lunch·room (lunch'rōōm', -rōōm') *n.* A restaurant serving light meals and refreshments.
Lun·dy's Lane (lun'dēz) A region near Niagara Falls, Ontario; scene of a battle (1814) in the War of 1812.
lune[1] (lōōn) *n.* 1 *Geom.* A figure bounded by two arcs of circles. 2 The moon. ◆ Homophone: *loon.* [<F <L *luna* the moon]
lune[2] (lōōn) *n.* A leash used in hawking. ◆ Homophone: *loon.* [<OF *loigne* leash < Med. L *longea* <L *longus* long]
Lü·ne·burg (lü'nə·bōōrkh) A city in Lower Saxony, West Germany.
Lü·nen (lü'nən) A city in North Rhine-Westphalia, West Germany.
lunes (lōōnz) *n. pl. Archaic* Outbreaks of lunacy; mad freaks. [<Med. L *luna* moon, fit of lunacy]
lu·nette (lōō·net') *n.* 1 Something shaped like a half-moon. 2 *Mil.* A fieldwork or a detached work formed by two parallel flanks, two faces meeting in a salient angle, with an open gorge. 3 *Archit.* An arched opening in the side of a long vault formed by the intersection with it of a smaller vault, as for a window. 4 A ring on the tongue or trail plate of a vehicle, for attaching to a limber, motor truck, or other towing vehicle. Also **lu·net** (lōō'nit). [<F, dim. of *lune* moon]
Lu·né·ville (lü·nā·vēl') A town in NE France; the Treaty of Lunéville, effecting peace between Austria and France, was signed here in 1801.
lung (lung) *n. Anat.* 1 Either of the two saclike organs of respiration in air-breathing vertebrates. ◆ Collateral adjective: *pulmonary.* 2 An analogous organ in invertebrates. [OE *lungen*]
lunge[1] (lunj) *n.* 1 A sudden pass or thrust; specifically, a long thrust with a sword or a bayonet. 2 A sudden forward lurch; plunge. — *v.* **lunged, lung·ing** — *v.i.* 1 To make a lunge or pass; thrust. 2 To move with a lunge. — *v.t.* 3 To thrust with or as with a lunge. [Aphetic var. of obs. *allonge* <F *allonger* prolong <L *ad* to + *longus* long]
lunge[2] (lunj) See LONGE.
lung·er (lung'ər) *n. Slang* A person having tuberculosis of the lungs.
lung·fish (lung'fish') *n. pl.* **·fish** or **·fish·es** A dipnoan.
lun·gi (lung'gē) *n.* 1 In India, a loincloth. 2 The material from which it is made: also used for scarfs and turbans. Also **lun'gee.** [<Hind.]
Lung·ki (lōōng'kē') A port of southern Fukien province, China: formerly *Changchow.*
lung·worm (lung'wûrm') *n.* Any of several nematode worms parasitic in the lungs of animals, especially the common lungworm (genus *Dictyocaulus*) of horses, cattle, and sheep.
lung·wort (lung'wûrt') *n.* 1 A European herb (genus *Pulmonaria*) of the borage family, having white blotches on the leaves. 2 The Virginia cowslip.
luni- *combining form* Of or pertaining to the moon; lunar. [<L *luna* moon]
lu·ni·so·lar (lōō'ni·sō'lər) *adj.* Of or resulting from the combined action of the sun and moon.
lu·ni·ti·dal (lōō'ni·tīd'l) *adj.* Relating to the tides as produced by the moon's attraction.
lunitidal interval The interval between the moon's passage of the meridian and lunar high tide.
lunk·head (lungk'hed') *n. Slang* A slow-witted person. [Prob. alter. of LUMP + HEAD] — **lunk'head'ed** *adj.*
lunt (lunt, lōōnt) *n. Scot.* 1 A whiff of smoke. 2 A slow-burning match or torch.
Lunt (lunt), **Alfred,** born 1893, U. S. actor.
lu·nu·la (lōō'nyə·lə) *n. pl.* **·lae** (-lē) 1 A crescentic structure or appearance. 2 The whitish area at the base of the nails: also **lu'nule** (-nyōōl). 3 A lune (arc). [<L, diminutive of *luna* the moon]
lu·nu·lar (lōō'nyə·lər) *adj.* Having the form of a small crescent. [<LUNULA]
lu·nu·late (lōō'nyə·lāt, -lit) *adj.* 1 Having or approaching a crescent form. 2 Having crescentic markings. Also **lu'nu·lat'ed.**
lu·ny (lōō'nē) See LOONY.
Lu·per·ca·li·a (lōō'pər·kā'lē·ə, -kāl'yə) *n. pl.* A Roman festival celebrated on February 15, in honor of a rustic deity, **Lu·per·cus** (lōō·pûr'·kəs) or *Faunus,* at which after various ceremonies the priests ran half-clothed through the streets. Also **Lu'per·cal** (-kal). [<L, neut. pl. of *Lupercalis* of Lupercus <*Lupercus* Faunus < *lupus* wolf]
Lu·per·ci (lōō'pər·sī) *n. pl.* The priests of Lupercus or Faunus. [<L]
lu·pine[1] (lōō'pīn) *adj.* 1 Of or pertaining to a wolf; like a wolf; wolfish. 2 Pertaining to the group of canines that includes dogs and wolves. [<L *lupinus* < *lupus* wolf]
lu·pine[2] (lōō'pin) *n.* A plant of the bean family (genus *Lupinus*) bearing terminal racemes of mostly blue or purple flowers, as the **white lupine** of the Old World (*L. albus*) whose seeds are edible. Also **lu'pin** (-pin). [<F *lupin*

<L *lupinus* wolflike: reason for the name unknown]

lu·pu·lin (lo͞o′pyə·lin) *n.* **1** A brittle crystalline compound forming the active principle of hops. **2** A yellow aromatic powder contained in the fruit of hops, and used medicinally as a sedative. [<NL *lupulus* the hop, dim. of L *lupus*]

lu·pus (lo͞o′pəs) *n. Pathol.* A chronic tuberculous skin disease with warty nodules, generally about the nose. Also **lupus vul·ga·ris** (vul·gar′is). [<L, wolf]

Lu·pus (lo͞o′pəs) The Wolf, a constellation. See CONSTELLATION. [<L]

lurch[1] (lûrch) *v.i.* **1** To roll suddenly to one side, as a ship at sea. **2** To move unsteadily; stagger. —*n.* A sudden swaying or rolling to one side: hence; any sudden swinging movement. [Origin uncertain]

lurch[2] (lûrch) *n.* In cribbage, the state of a player who has made 30 holes or less while his opponent has won with 61; also a game thus won. —**to leave in the lurch** To leave in an embarrassing position. —*v.i.* In cribbage, piquet, and similar games, to win a double game. [<F *lourche,* name of a game <*lourche* deceived <Gmc. Cf. MDu. *lurz* left-handed, unlucky.]

lurch[3] (lûrch) *v.t.* & *v.i. Obs.* To swindle; cheat. [Var. of LURK]

lurch·er (lûr′chər) *n.* **1** One who lies in wait or lurks: a lurking thief; poacher. **2** A crossbred dog that hunts by scent and in silence.

lur·dan (lûr′dən) *Archaic adj.* Stupid: incapable. —*n.* A stupid person; blockhead. Also **lur′dane.** [<OF *lourdin* <*lourd* heavy]

lure (lo͝or) *n.* **1** A device resembling a bird and sometimes baited with food: fastened to a falconer's wrist and used to recall the hawk. **2** In angling, an artificial bait; also, a decoy for animals. **3** Anything that invites by the prospect of advantage or pleasure. —*v.t.* **lured, lur·ing** **1** To attract or entice; allure. **2** To recall (a hawk) with a lure. See synonyms under ALLURE, DRAW. [<OF *leurre* <MHG *louder* bait] —**lur′er** *n.*

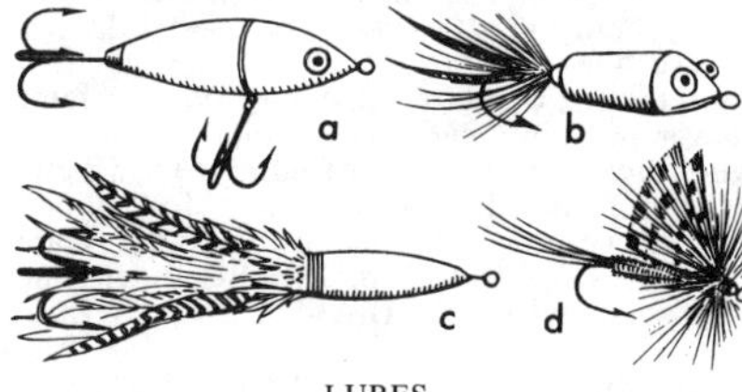

LURES
a. Wood or plastic lure. *c.* Feather lure.
b. Floating cork lure. *d.* Dry fly.

lu·rid (lo͝or′id) *adj.* **1** Giving a ghastly or dull-red light: dismal. **2** Of a dingy, dirty-brown color. **3** Violent; terrible; sensational: a *lurid* crime. **4** Pale; wan; sallow; ghastly. [<L *luridus* sallow] —**lu′rid·ly** *adv.* —**lu′rid·ness** *n.*

lurk (lûrk) *v.i.* **1** To lie hidden, as in ambush. **2** To exist unnoticed or unsuspected. **3** To move secretly or furtively; slink. —*n. Austral. Slang* A dodge: scheme; racket. [Origin uncertain. Cf. Norw. *lurka* sneak off.] —**lurk′er** *n.* —**lurk′ing·ly** *adv.*

Lur·lei (lo͝or′lī) See LORELEI.

Lu·sa·ka (lo͞o·sä′kə) The capital of Zambia.

Lu·sa·tia (lo͞o·sā′shə) A region of SE Germany and SW Poland between the Elbe and the Oder. *German* **Lau·sitz** (lou′zits).

lus·cious (lush′əs) *adj.* **1** Very grateful to the sense of taste; rich, sweet, and delicious; pleasing to any sense or to the mind. **2** Sweet and rich to excess. See synonyms under DELICIOUS, SWEET. [? blend of LUSH and DELICIOUS] —**lus′cious·ly** *adv.* —**lus′cious·ness** *n.*

lush[1] lush *adj.* **1** Full of juice or succulence; fresh and luxuriant: also, having abundant growth. **2** Easily plowed and mellow, as ground. [? Var. of dial. E *lash* soft and watery <OF *lasche* <L *laxus* loose] —**lush′ness** *n.*

lush[2] (lush) *Slang n.* **1** Intoxicating, or strong alcoholic beverage. **2** A drunken man: also **lush′er.** —*v.t.* & *v.i.* To drink (alcoholic liquor). [Origin unknown]

Lu·shun (lü′sho͞on′) The Chinese name for PORT ARTHUR.

lush·y (lush′ē) *adj. Slang* Drunk.

Lu·si·ta·ni·a (lo͞o′sə·tā′nē·ə) An ancient name for PORTUGAL.

Lu·si·ta·ni·a (lo͞o′sə·tā′nē·ə) *n.* A British passenger ship torpedoed and sunk by a German submarine off the coast of Ireland May 7, 1915, with loss of 1,198 lives including 128 Americans.

Lu·si·ta·ni·an (lo͞o′sə·tā′nē·ən) *adj.* Of or pertaining to Lusitania. —*n.* A native or inhabitant of Lusitania.

lust (lust) *n.* **1** Vehement or longing affection or desire. **2** Inordinate desire for carnal pleasure. **3** *Obs.* Pleasure; inclination. See synonyms under APPETITE. —*v.i.* To have passionate or inordinate desire, especially sexual desire. [OE, pleasure]

lus·ter (lus′tər) *n.* **1** Natural or artificial brilliancy or sheen; refulgence; gloss. **2** Brilliancy of beauty, of character, or of achievements; splendor. **3** A glaze, varnish, or enamel applied to porcelain in a thin layer, and giving it a smooth, glistening surface: common in the phrase *metallic luster.* **4** A dress material having a highly finished surface. **5** A source or center of light; specifically, a branched candelabrum, chandelier, or the like. **6** *Mineral.* The quality of the surface of a mineral as regards the kind and intensity of the light it reflects. —*v.* **·tered** or **·tred, ·ter·ing** or **·tring** *v.t.* To give a luster or gloss to. —*v.i.* To be or become lustrous. Also **lus′tre.** [<F *lustre* <Ital. *lustro* <*lustrare* shine <L <*lustrum* purification]

lus·ter·ware (lus′tər·wâr′) *n.* Pottery treated with metallic luster.

lust·ful (lust′fəl) *adj.* **1** Having carnal or sensual desire. **2** *Archaic* Vigorous; lusty. —**lust′ful·ly** *adv.* —**lust′ful·ness** *n.*

lust·i·hood (lus′tē·ho͝od) *n. Archaic* Vigor of body; brawny strength. Also **lust′i·head** (-hed).

lus·tral (lus′trəl) *adj.* **1** Pertaining to or used in purification. **2** Pertaining to a lustrum. [<L *lustralis* <*lustrum* purification]

lus·trate (lus′trāt) *v.t.* **·trat·ed, ·trat·ing** To make pure by propitiatory offering or ceremony. [<L *lustratus,* pp. of *lustrare* purify by propitiatory offerings <*lustrum* purification]

lus·tra·tion (lus·trā′shən) *n.* The ancient rite of purification and expiation. [<L *lustratio, -onis*]

lust·trous (lus′trəs) *adj.* Having luster; shining; also, illustrious. See synonyms under BRIGHT. —**lus′trous·ly** *adv.* —**lus′trous·ness** *n.*

lus·trum (lus′trəm) *n.* **1** A lustration or purification; the solemn ceremony of purification of the entire Roman people made every five years. **2** A period of five years. [<L, ? <*luere* wash]

lust·y (lus′tē) *adj.* **lust·i·er, lust·i·est** **1** Full of vigor and health; able-bodied; robust. **2** *Obs.* Jolly; merry. **3** *Obs.* Agreeable; delightful. **4** *Obs.* Lustful. —**lust′i·ly** *adv.* —**lust′i·ness** *n.*

lu·sus na·tu·rae (lo͞osəs nə·to͝or′ē, -tyo͝or′ē) A strange and abnormal natural production; a freak or sport of nature: also **lu′sus.** [<L, joke of nature]

Lut (lo͞ot) See DASHT-I-LUT.

lu·ta·nist (lo͞o′tə·nist) *n.* One who plays the lute. Also **lu′te·nist.**

lute[1] (lo͞ot) *n.* A stringed musical instrument having a large, pear-shaped body like a mandolin, played by plucking the strings with the fingers. —*v.t.* & *v.i.* To play on the lute. [<OF *leüt* <Pg. *laut* <Arabic *al'ūd* the piece of wood]

LUTE

lute[2] (lo͞ot) *n.* **1** A cementlike composition used to exclude air, as around pipe joints. **2** In brick-making, a scraper having a cutting edge to smooth the surface of a drying yard. Also **lut′ing.** —*v.t.* **lut·ed, lut·ing** To seal with lute. [<OF *lut* <L *lutum* mud] —**lu·ta′tion** *n.*

lu·te·al (lo͞o′tē·əl) *adj. Anat.* Pertaining to or similar to the cells of the corpus luteum. [<L *luteus* yellow]

lu·te·in (lo͞o′tē·in, -tēn) *n. Biochem.* A yellow pigment, $C_{48}H_{56}O_2$, found in egg yolks, fat cells, and in the corpus luteum. [<L *luteum* egg yolk <*luteus* yellow] —**lu′te·in′ic** *adj.*

lu·te·o·lin (lo͞o′tē·ə·lin) *n. Chem.* A yellow crystalline compound, $C_{15}H_{10}O_6$, obtained from dyer's-broom, and used as a dyestuff. [<F *lutéoline* <NL *(Reseda) luteola* dyer's weed <L *luteolus* yellowish <*luteus* yellow]

lu·te·ous (lo͞o′tē·əs) *adj.* Of golden-yellowish color. [<L *luteus* <*lutum* weed used by dyers]

Lu·te·tia (lo͞o·tē′shə) Ancient name for PARIS. Also **Lu·te′tia Pa·ri·si·o·rum** (pa·rē′sē·ō′rəm).

lu·te·tium (lo͞o·tē′shəm) *n.* A metallic element (symbol Lu) of the lanthanide series, isolated from ytterbium. See ELEMENT. [from LUTETIA]

lu·te·um (lo͞o′tē·əm) See CORPUS LUTEUM.

Lu·ther (lo͞o′thər, *Ger.* lo͞o′tər) A masculine personal name. Also *Latin* **Lu·ther·us** (lo͞o′·tə r·əs). [<Gmc., famous warrior]

Lu·ther (lo͞o′thər), **Martin,** 1483–1546, German monk, theologian, and leader of the Reformation; excommunicated in 1520 by Pope Leo X; composed many Lutheran hymns and translated the Bible into German.

Lu·ther·an (lo͞o′thər·ən) *n.* A follower or disciple of Luther; a member of the Lutheran Church. —*adj..* **1** Pertaining to or believing in Martin Luther or his doctrines. **2** Pertaining to the Lutheran Church or its doctrines. —**Lu′ther·an·ism** *n.*

Lutheran Church A Protestant denomination founded in Germany by Martin Luther in the 16th century. Its chief doctrine is justification by faith alone. The Lutheran churches in America are grouped in three principal bodies: the **American Lutheran Church, Evangelical Lutheran Synodical Conference of North America,** and **United Lutheran Church in America.** See also MISSOURI SYNOD.

lu·thern (lo͞o′thərn) *n.* A lucarne. [? Alter. of LUCARNE]

Lu·ton (lo͞o′tən) A municipal borough of southern Bedford, England.

Lu·tu·a·mi·an (lo͞o′to͞o·ä′mē·ən) *n.* An independent linguistic stock of North American Indians, having two divisions, Klamath and Modoc, formerly dwelling in California and Oregon: now inhabiting reservations in Oregon and Oklahoma. Both dialects were most commonly known as *Klamath.*

Lüt·zen (lü′tsən) A town in the former state of Saxony-Anhalt, East Germany; scene of battles in the Thirty Years' War (1632) and the Nopoleonic Wars (1813).

Lu·wi·an (lo͞o′ē·ən) *n.* An extinct language of Asia Minor of which few inscriptions remain: considered to be closely related to Hittite. —*adj.* Of this language. Also **Lu·vi·an** (lo͞o′·vē·ən).

lux (luks) *n. pl.* **lux·es** or **lu·ces** (lo͞o′sēz) *Physics* The unit of illumination in the metric system, equivalent to the illumination on a surface of one square meter on which there is a uniformly distributed flux of one lumen. [<L, light]

lux·ate (luk′sāt) *v.t.* **·at·ed, ·at·ing** To put out of joint; dislocate. [<L *luxatus,* pp. of *luxare* dislocate <*luxus* dislocated] —**lux·a′tion** *n.*

luxe (lo͝oks. luks; *Fr.* lüks) *n.* Superfline quality; luxury: usually with *de:* edition *de luxe.* [<F <L *luxus* extravagance]

Lux·em·burg (luk′səm·bûrg, *Fr.* lük·säṅ·bo͞or′) **1** A constitutional grand duchy between Belgium, France, and Germany; 999 square miles; capital, Luxemburg. **2** A province of SE Belgium; 1,795 square miles; capital, Arlon. Also **Lux′em·bourg.**

Lux·em·burg (lo͝ok′səm·bo͝orkh), **Rosa,** 1870–1919, German socialist leader.

lux·me·ter (luks′mē′tər) *n.* An instrument that measures illumination in terms of luxes.

lux mun·di (luks mun′dī) *Latin* Light of the world.

Lux·or (luk′sôr, lo͝ok′-) A city on the Nile in Upper Egypt on the southern part of the site of ancient Thebes. *Arabic* **El Uk·sor** (al ŏŏk′sŏŏr).

lux·u·ri·ance (lug·zhŏŏr′ē·əns, luk·shŏŏr′-) *n.* Excessive growth; exuberance; lushness. Also **lux·u′ri·an·cy.**

lux·u·ri·ant (lug·zhŏŏr′ē·ənt, luk·shŏŏr′-) *adj.* **1** Exhibiting or characterized by luxuriance in growth; also, fertile, as soil. **2** Exuberant in fancy, invention, etc.; abundant, extravagant, or excessive in action or speech; ornate, florid, or rich in design. See synonyms under FERTILE. [<L *luxurians, -antis,* ppr. of *luxuriare.* See LUXURIATE.] — **lux·u′ri·ant·ly** *adv.*

lux·u·ri·ate (lug·zhŏŏr′ē·āt, luk·shŏŏr′-) *v.i.* **·at·ed, ·at·ing 1** To take great pleasure; indulge oneself fully. **2** To live sumptuously. **3** To grow profusely. [<L *luxuriatus,* pp. of *luxuriare* be fruitful, abound < *luxuria.* See LUXURY.] — **lux·u′ri·a′tion** *n.*

lux·u·ri·ous (lug·zhŏŏr′ē·əs, luk·shŏŏr′-) *adj.* **1** Pertaining or administering to luxury; voluptuous. **2** Supplied with luxuries. [<L *luxuriosus*] — **lux·u′ri·ous·ly** *adv.* — **lux·u′ri·ous·ness** *n.*

lux·u·ry (luk′shər·ē, *occasionally* lug′zhər·ē) *n. pl.* **·ries 1** A free indulgence in the pleasures that gratify the senses. **2** Anything that ministers to comfort or pleasure that is expensive or rare, but is not necessary to life, health, subsistence, etc.; a delicacy. [<OF *luxurie* <L *luxuria* < *luxus* extravagance]

Lu·zern (lōō·tsern′) The German name for LUCERNE.

Lu·zon (lōō·zon′, *Sp.* lōō·sōn′) The largest of the Philippines; 40,420 square miles; capital, Manila.

Luzon Strait The channel connecting the Pacific and the South China Sea: divided into the Bashi, Balintang, and Babuyan Channels.

Lvov (lvôf) A city in Ukrainian S.S.R.: German *Lemberg. Polish* **Lwów** (lvŏŏf).

-ly[1] *suffix of adjectives* Like; characteristic of; pertaining to: *manly, godly.* Compare -LIKE. [OE *-lic*]

-ly[2] *suffix of adverbs* **1** In a (specified) manner: used to form adverbs from adjectives, or (rarely) from nouns: *brightly, busily.* **2** Occurring every (specified interval): *hourly, yearly.* [OE *-lice* < *-lic* -LY[1]]

◆ In cases where an adjective already ends in *-ly,* the forms of the adjective and adverb are often identical: He spoke *kindly.* Occasionally, *-ly* is added to *-ly* (which is then changed to *-li*), as in *surlily,* but this is generally avoided as awkward. In the case of words derived from French adjectives in *-le,* the ending is dropped before adding *-ly,* as in *nobly, possibly.*

Lya·khov Islands (lyä′khôf) A southern group of the New Siberian Islands in Yakut Autonomous S.S.R.; total, 2,660 square miles.

Ly·all·pur (lī′əl·pŏŏr) A city in Punjab, West Pakistan.

ly·ard (lī′ərd) *adj. Scot.* Silver–gray or streaked with gray. Also **ly′art** (-ərt). [<OF *liart*]

Lyau·tey (lyō·tā′), **Louis Hubert,** 1854–1934, French marshal and colonial administrator.

Lyau·tey (lyō·tā′), **Port** See PORT-LYAUTEY.

ly·can·thrope (lī′kən·thrōp, lī·kan′thrōp) *n.* **1** A werewolf. **2** One afflicted with lycanthropy. [<Gk. *lykanthrōpos* < *lykos* wolf + *anthrōpos* a man]

ly·can·thro·py (lī·kan′thrə·pē) *n.* **1** The supposed power of turning a human being into a wolf or of becoming a wolf, by magic or witchcraft. **2** Belief in werewolves. **3** *Psychiatry* A mania in which the patient imagines himself to be a wolf or some other wild animal. [<Gk. *lykanthrōpia*] — **ly′can·throp′ic** (-throp′ik) *adj.*

Ly·ca·on (lī·kā′on) In Greek mythology, a king of Arcadia and father of Callisto, who, when Zeus sought his hospitality disguised as a poor man, tested the god's divinity by offering him human flesh as food: Zeus transformed him into a wolf. [<Gk. *Lykaōn* < *lykos* wolf]

Ly·ca·o·ni·a (lī′kā·ō′nē·ə, lik′ə-) An ancient district in the SE part of Phrygia, Asia Minor.

ly·cée (lē·sā′) *n. French* A public classical secondary school in France qualifying its students for a university; a lyceum. [<F <L *lyceum.* See LYCEUM.]

ly·ce·um (lī·sē′əm) *n. pl.* **·ce·ums** or **·ce·a** (-sē′ə) **1** An association for popular instruction by lectures, a library, debates, etc.; also, its building or hall. **2** An intermediate classical school. [<LYCEUM]

Ly·ce·um (lī·sē′əm) A grove near Athens in which Aristotle taught. [<L <Gk. *Lykeion* < *lykeios,* ? wolf–slaying, epithet of Apollo (whose temple was near this grove)]

ly·chee (lē′chē) See LITCHI.

lych·nis (lik′nis) *n.* Any plant of the genus *Lychnis* of erect ornamental herbs. *L. chalcedonica* is the scarlet lychnis, and *L. coronaria* the rose campion. [<L <Gk.]

Lyc·i·a (sis′ē·ə, lish′ə) An ancient country on the SW coast of Asia Minor; a Roman province.

Lyc·i·an (lish′ē·ən, lish′ən) *adj.* Belonging or relating to ancient Lycia. — *n.* **1** A member of the people that inhabited Lycia. **2** Their language, believed to be related to Hittite.

Lyc·i·das (lis′ə·dəs) **1** In Virgil's *Eclogue* iii, a shepherd. **2** Subject of an elegy (1637) by Milton.

Ly·co·me·des (lī′kə·mē′dēz) In Greek legend, a king of Scyros; son of Apollo and guardian of Achilles.

ly·co·pod (lī′kə·pod) *n.* A plant of the club-moss family. [<Gk. *lykos* wolf + -POD; after the resemblance of the root to a claw]

ly·co·po·di·um (lī′kə·pō′dē·əm) *n.* **1** A plant (genus *Lycopodium*) of erect or creeping evergreen pteridophytes, the clubmosses. **2** An inflammable fine yellow powder, the spores of clubmosses. [<NL]

Ly·cur·gus (lī·kûr′gəs) A traditional Spartan lawgiver of the ninth century B.C.

Lyd·da (lid′ə) A town and site of Israel's chief airport in central Israel. *Arabic* **Ludd** (lŏŏd). *Hebrew* **Lud** (lŏŏd).

lyd·dite (lid′īt) *n.* A high explosive, chiefly of picric acid: used for torpedo and other shells which on explosion kill by shock or suffocation from its deadly fumes. [from *Lydd,* town in England, where first manufactured]

Lyd·gate (lid′gāt, -git), **John,** 1370?–1451?, English poet.

Lyd·i·a (lid′ē·ə; *Dan., Du.* lē′dē·ä, *Greek* lē·dē′ä) A feminine personal name. Also *Fr.* **Ly·die** (lē·dē′). [<Gk., Lydian girl]

Lyd·i·a (lid′ē·ə) An ancient country of western Asia Minor on the Aegean.

Lyd·i·an (lid′ē·ən) *adj.* **1** Belonging or relating to ancient Lydia in Asia Minor, famous for wealth, luxury and music; also, pertaining to its inhabitants. **2** By extension, effeminate; gentle: in reference to Lydian accomplishments and culture; also, sensuous or voluptuous. — *n.* **1** One of the people of ancient Lydia. **2** Their language, probably related to Hittite. **3** One of the modes in early music.

lye (lī) *n.* **1** A solution leached from ashes, or derived from a substance containing alkali: used in making soap, preparing hominy, etc. **2** A lixivium. [OE *lēah*]

Ly·ell (lī′əl), **Sir Charles,** 1797–1875, English geologist.

ly·ing[1] (lī′ing) *n.* The practice of telling lies; untruthfulness. See synonyms under DECEPTION. — *adj.* Addicted to, conveying, or constituting falsehood; mendacious; false. — **ly′·ing·ly** *adv.*

ly·ing[2] (lī′ing) Present participle of LIE[1]. — *adj.* Being in a horizontal position; prostrate.

ly·ing–in (lī′ing·in′) *n.* The confinement of women during childbirth; parturition. — *adj.* Of or pertaining to childbirth: a *lying–in* home or hospital.

Lyl·y (lil′ē), **John,** 1554–1606, English dramatist and novelist. See EUPHUISM.

lymph (limf) *n.* **1** A transparent, colorless, alkaline fluid which circulates in the lymph vessels of vertebrates. It consists of a plasma resembling that of the blood and of corpuscles like the white blood corpuscles. **2** The coagulable exudation from the blood vessels in inflammation. **3** The virus, or a culture of the virus, of a disease, used in vaccination or similar treatment. **4** *Obs.* A spring; water. [<L *lympha,* var. of *limpa* water, ? <Gk. *nymphē* nymph, goddess of moisture]

lym·phad·e·ni·tis (lim·fad′ə·nī′tis, lim′fə·də-) *n. Pathol.* Inflammation of the lymphatic glands. [<NL <LYMPH(O)- + ADEN(O)- + -ITIS]

lym·phan·gi·al (lim·fan′jē·əl) *adj.* Of or pertaining to the lymphatic vessels; lymphatic. [<LYMPH(O)- + ANGI(O)- + -AL[1]]

lym·phat·ic (lim·fat′ik) *adj.* **1** Pertaining to, containing, or conveying lymph. **2** Caused by or affecting the lymphatic glands. **3** Having a phlegmatic temperament. — *n.* A vessel that conveys lymph into the veins; an absorbent vessel. [<NL <L *lymphaticus* frantic, frenzied, trans. of Gk. *nympholēptos* caught by nymphs]

lym·pha·tism (lim′fə·tiz′əm) *n.* **1** Lymphatic temperament. **2** *Pathol.* An unhealthy condition due to an excess of lymphatic tissue. [<LYMPHATIC]

lym·pha·ti·tis (lim′fə·tī′tis) *n. Pathol.* Inflammation in any part of the lymphatic system. [<LYMPHAT(O)- + -ITIS]

lymphato– *combining form* Lymphatic. Also, before vowels, **lymphat–.**

lym·pha·tol·y·sis (lim′fə·tol′ə·sis) *n. Pathol.* Dissolution or breakdown of lymphatic tissue. [<LYMPHATO- + -LYSIS] — **lym·pha·to·lyt·ic** (lim′fə·tō·lit′ik) *adj.*

lymph cell A lymphocyte.

lymph gland *Anat.* One of the nodular bodies about the size of a pea, found in the course of the lymphatic vessels, composed of a reticulum containing lymphoid cells.

lympho– *combining form* Lymph; of or pertaining to lymph or the lymphatic system: *lymphocyte.* Also, before vowels, **lymph–.** [See LYMPH]

lym·pho·cyte (lim′fə·sīt) *n. Anat.* A variety of nucleated, colorless leucocyte in the lymphatic glands of all vertebrate animals, resembling a small white blood corpuscle.

lym·pho·cy·to·sis (lim′fə·sī·tō′sis) *n. Pathol.* An excess of lymphocytes in the blood. — **lym′pho·cy·tot′ic** (-tot′ik) *adj.*

lym·phoid (lim′foid) *adj.* Of, pertaining to, or resembling lymph or a lymphatic gland. [< LYMPH + -OID]

lymphoid tissue Tissue constituting the lymph glands; adenoid tissue.

lym·phor·rhe·a (lim′fə·rē′ə) *n. Pathol.* A flow of lymph from ruptured lymph vessels.

lyn (lin) See LIN.

lyn·ce·an (lin·sē′ən) *adj.* **1** Pertaining to or characteristic of the lynx. **2** Lynx–eyed; sharp–sighted. [<L *lynceus* <Gk. *lynkeios* < *lynx* lynx]

lynch (linch) *v.t.* To kill by mob action, as by hanging or burning. — *adj.* Of or relating to lynching. [<LYNCH LAW] — **lynch′er** *n.* — **lynch′ing** *n.*

Lynch·burg (linch′bûrg) A city on the James River in south central Virginia.

lynch law The practice of administering punishment, usually by hanging, for alleged crimes without trial by law. [? after Capt. Wm. *Lynch,* 1742–1820, Virginia magistrate]

Lynd·say (lin′zē), **Sir David** See under LINDSAY.

Lynn (lin) **1** An industrial city in eastern Massachusetts. **2** See KING'S LYNN.

Lynn Canal A fiord in the mainland of SE Alaska near Alexander Archipelago.

Lynn Re·gis (rē′jis) See KING'S LYNN.

lynx (lingks) *n.* Any of several wildcats (genus *Lynx*) of Europe and North America, with short tails, tufted ears, and relatively long limbs; especially, the Canadian lynx *(L. canadensis)* and the North American bay lynx *(L. rufus).* [<L *lynx, lyncis* <Gk. *lynx*]

Lynx (lingks) A northern constellation. See CONSTELLATION.

lynx–eyed (lingks′īd′) *adj.* Having acute sight.

lyo– *combining form* A loosening; dissolution: *lyophilic.* Also, before vowels, **ly–.** [<Gk. *lyein* loosen]

Ly·on (lī′ən), **Mary,** 1797–1849, U. S. educator; founder of Mt. Holyoke College.

Ly·on·nais (lē·ô·nā′) A region and former province of east central France. Also **Ly·o·nais′.**

ly·on·naise (lī′ə·nāz′, *Fr.* lē·ô·nez′) *adj.* Made with finely sliced onions; especially, designating a method of preparing potatoes with fried onions. [<F, fem. of *lyonnais* of Lyon]

Ly·on·nesse (lī′ə·nes′) In Arthurian legend, a region lying between Cornwall and the Scilly Islands, supposed to have sunk into the sea.

Ly·ons (lī′ənz, *Fr.* lē·ôN′) A city of east central France at the confluence of the Rhône and the Saône; the third largest city of France. Also **Ly·on′.** — **Ly·on·nais′** *adj.*

ly·o·phil·ic (lī′ə·fil′ik) *adj. Chem.* Pertaining to or designating a colloidal system either phase of which is more or less freely soluble

in the other. [<LYO- + Gk. *philos* loving]
ly·o·pho·bic (lī'ə·fō'bik) *adj. Chem.* Resisting solution: said of colloidal systems neither phase of which will freely dissolve in the other. [<LYO- + Gk. *phobos* fear]
ly·o·sorp·tion (lī'ə·sôrp'shən) *n. Chem.* The adsorption of a solvent film upon the surface of suspended particles. [<LYO- + (AD)SORPTION]
ly·o·trop·ic (lī'ə·trop'ik, -trō'pik) *adj. Chem.* **1** Designating a series of ions, radicals, or salts arranged according to their influence on certain colloidal, physiological, or catalytic phenomena. **2** Having an affinity for entering into solution.
Ly·ra (lī'rə) An ancient constellation representing the lyre of Hermes or of Orpheus; the Harp. It contains the bright star Vega. See CONSTELLATION. [<L <Gk.]
ly·rate (lī'rāt) *adj. Bot.* Lyre-shaped, as a pinnatifid leaf having its upper lobes largest. Also **ly'rat·ed.** [<NL *lyratus*] **— ly'rate·ly** *adv.*
lyre (līr) *n.* An ancient harplike stringed instrument, having a hollow body and two horns bearing a crosspiece between which and the body were stretched the strings, generally seven. [<L *lyra* <Gk.]

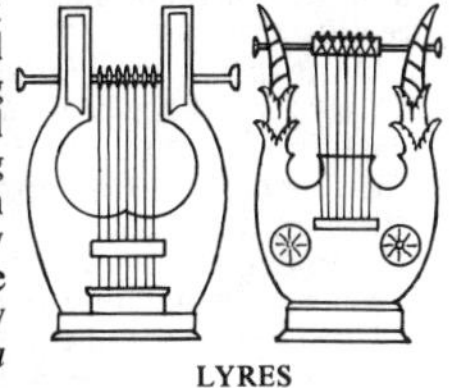
LYRES

Lyre (līr) The constellation Lyra.
lyre·bird (līr'bûrd') *n.* An Australian passerine bird (genera *Menura* and *Harriwhitea*) having the tail feathers of the males arranged in lyre shape.
lyr·ic (lir'ik) *adj.* **1** Originally, belonging to a lyre; hence, adapted for singing to a lyre. **2** Characterizing verse expressing the poet's personal emotions or sentiments; songlike: distinguished from *epic, dramatic.* **3** Pertaining to the writing of such verse; having written lyric poetry. **4** Musical; singing or to be sung. **5** *Music* Light, graceful, and having a flexible quality: opposed to *dramatic*: said of the voice in singing. Also **lyr'i·cal.** — *n.* **1** A lyric poem; a song. **2** *Usually pl.* The words of a song, especially as distinguished from the music. [<L *lyricus* <Gk. *lyrikos* <*lyra* a lyre] **— lyr'i·cal·ly** *adv.*
lyr·i·cism (lir'ə·siz'əm) *n.* **1** Lyrical quality; a lyric composition. **2** Emotional expression, as of enthusiasm.
lyr·i·cist (lir'ə·sist) *n.* **1** One who writes the words of a song or the lyrics for a musical play. **2** A lyric poet.
lyric poetry Any form of poetry giving expression to the poet's personal emotions or sentiments. It includes the *sonnet,* the *elegy, ode, song, psalm, hymn,* etc.
ly·ri·form (lī'rə·fôrm) *adj.* Shaped like a lyre.
lyr·ism (lir'iz·əm) *n.* **1** Lyre-playing; hence, the singing of lyrics, or music in general. **2** Lyricism. [<F *lyrisme*]
lyr·ist (lir'ist) *n.* **1** One who plays the lyre. **2** A lyric poet. [<L *lyristes* <Gk. *lyristēs* <*lyrixein* play on a lyre]
Lys (lēs) A river in northern France and western Belgium, flowing 130 miles NE to the Scheldt. *Flemish* **Lei'e** (lī'ə).
Ly·san·der (lī·san'dər), died 395 B.C., Spartan general.
lyse (līs) *v.t. & v.i.* **lysed, lys·ing** To undergo or cause to undergo lysis. [<Gk. *lysis* loosening]
Ly·sen·ko (li·seng'kō, *Russian* lē'sin·kə), **Trofim,** born 1898, U.S.S.R. biologist and agronomist: also *Lisenko.*
Ly·sen·ko·ism (li·seng'kō·iz'əm) *n.* The theory regarding the nature and processes of inheritance which challenges the formal genetics of Mendel, Weismann, and Morgan, claiming especially that the genes may be permanently modified by somatic influences, thus permitting a selective inheritance of acquired characteristics. [after T. *Lysenko*]
ly·ser·gic acid (lī·sûr'jik) *n. Biochem.* A crystalline alkaloid, $C_{16}H_{16}N_2O_2$, derived from ergot, of which it is the chief toxic principle, and forming the base of **lysergic acid di·eth·yl·am·ide-25** (dī'eth·əl·am'īd), or LSD. [< LYS- + *erg(ot)* + -IC]
lysi- *combining form* A loosening: *lysigenetic.* Also, before vowels, **lys-.** [<Gk. *lysis* a loosening]
Lys·i·as (lis'ē·əs), 458?–378? B.C., Athenian orator.
ly·si·ge·net·ic (lī'sə·jə·net'ik) *adj. Biol.* Produced or producing by the breakdown or absorption of intermediate or contiguous cells: said of certain intercellular spaces or of their mode of formation. Also **ly'si·gen'ic, ly·sig·e·nous** (lī·sij'ə·nəs). **— ly'si·ge·net'i·cal·ly** *adv.*
Ly·sim·a·chus (lī·sim'ə·kəs), 361?–281 B.C., Macedonian general under Alexander the Great; king of Thrace.
ly·sim·e·ter (lī·sim'ə·tər) *n.* An instrument for determining the solubility of substances.
ly·sin (lī'sin) *n.* A substance capable of destroying bacteria, blood corpuscles, etc. [< LYS(I)- + -IN]
ly·sine (lī'sēn, -sin) *n. Biochem.* An important amino acid, $C_6H_{14}O_2N_2$, produced on the hydrolysis of various proteins. Also **ly'sin.** [<LYS(I)- + -INE[2]]
Ly·sip·pus (lī·sip'əs) Greek sculptor of the fourth century B.C. **— Ly·sip'pan** *adj.*
ly·sis (lī'sis) *n.* **1** *Pathol.* The gradual disappearing of a disease. Compare CRISIS. **2** *Biochem.* The process of disintegration or destruction of cells. [<NL <Gk., loosening <*lyein* loose, dissolve]
-lysis *combining form* A loosing, dissolving, etc.: *hydrolysis, paralysis.* [<Gk., loosening]
lys·sa (lis'ə) *n.* Hydrophobia; rabies. [<Gk., frenzy, madness]
lys·so·pho·bi·a (lis'ə·fō'bē·ə) *n. Psychiatry* A morbid fear of insanity. [<Gk. *lyssa* madness + -PHOBIA] **— lys'so·pho'bic** *adj.*
Lys·ter bag (lis'tər) A portable, waterproof bag for supplying disinfected drinking water to troops: also spelled *Lister bag.* [after W.J.L. *Lyster,* 1869–1947, U. S. Army surgeon]
Lys·tra (lis'trə) An ancient town of Lycaonia.
-lyte[1] *combining form* A substance decomposed by a (specified) process: *electrolyte.* [<Gk. *lytos* loosened, dissolved <*lyein* loosen]
-lyte[2] See -LITE.
-lytic *combining form* Loosing; dissolving: used in adjectives corresponding to nouns in *-lysis*: *hydrolytic paralytic.* [<Gk. *lytikos* loosing <*lysis* a loosening]
lyt·ta (lit'ə) *n. pl.* **lyt·tae** (lit'ē) *Anat.* A vermiform cartilage or fibrous band on the under surface of the tongue in carnivores, as the dog. [<L, a worm said to grow under a dog's tongue and cause madness <Gk., madness]
Lyt·ton (lit'ən), **Earl of,** 1831–91, Edward Robert Bulwer-Lytton, son of Lord Lytton; English poet and diplomat; pseudonym *Owen Meredith.* **— Lord,** 1803–73, Edward George Earle Lytton Bulwer-Lytton, first Baron Lytton, English novelist.
Lyu·blin (lyōō'blin) The Russian name for LUBLIN.

M

m, M (em) *n. pl.* **m's, M's** or **ms, Ms** or **ems** (emz) **1** The 13th letter of the English alphabet: from Phoenician *mem,* Greek *mu,* Roman *M.* **2** The sound of the letter *m,* usually a voiced, bilabial nasal. See ALPHABET. — *symbol* **1** The Roman numeral 1,000. See under NUMERAL. **2** *Printing* An em.
ma (mä, mô) *n.* Mama; mother. [Short for MAMA]
ma'am (mam, mäm, *unstressed* məm) *n.* **1** A respectful address to women, corresponding to *sir* in the case of men. **2** A dame; mistress: used in combination: a *schoolma'am.* **3** *Brit.* A term of respectful address used to the queen or to a royal princess. [Contraction of MADAM]
Maar·tens (mär'tənz), **Maarten** Pen name of Joost Marius Willem Van der Poorten-Schwartz, 1858–1915, Dutch novelist; wrote in English.
Maas (mäs) The Dutch name for the MEUSE.
Maas·tricht (mäs'trikht, mäs·trikht') See MAESTRICHT.
Mab (mab), **Queen** In English folklore, the queen of the fairies.
Ma·bel (mā'bəl) A feminine personal name. Also *Irish* **Mab,** *Fr.* **Ma·belle** (må·bel'), *Lat.* **Ma·bil·i·a** (mə·bil'ē·ə). [Short for AMABEL]
Mab·i·no·gi·on (mab'ə·nō'gē·ən) *n.* A collection of eleven medieval Welsh romances translated by Lady Charlotte Guest in 1838–1849. [<Welsh *mabinogion,* pl. of *mabinogi* bardic instructional material <*mabinog* a bard's apprentice]
Mac- *prefix* In Scottish and Irish names, son of: *MacDougal,* son of Dougal: abbr. *Mc, M^c,* or *M'.* See also MC-. [<Scottish Gaelic and Irish, son]
ma·ca·bre (mə·kä'brə, -bər) *adj.* Suggestive of death; gruesome; frightful. Also **ma·ca'ber.** [<F <OF *(danse) macabré* (dance) of death, prob. alter. of *Macabé* <LL *Maccabaeus,* ? a character in a morality play]
ma·ca·co (mə·kā'kō) *n. pl.* **·cos** Any one of various lemurs, especially the black lemur of Madagascar *(Lemur macaco).* [<Pg. < Tupian *macaco, macaca* a monkey]
mac·ad·am (mə·kad'əm) *n.* **1** Broken stone for macadamizing a road. **2** A macadamized road. [after John L. *McAdam,* 1756–1836, British engineer]
mac·ad·am·ize (mə·kad'ə·mīz) *v.t.* **·ized, ·iz·ing** To pave with small consolidated broken stone on a soft or hard, but drained and convex, substratum. **— mac·ad'am·i·za'tion** *n.* **— mac·ad'am·iz'er** *n.*
Ma·cao (mə·kou', -kä'ō) A Portuguese overseas province at the mouth of the Canton River, comprising a peninsula of an island in the delta (often called **Macao Island**) and three small offshore islands, the **Tai·pa Islands** (tī'pä') and **Co·lo·a·ne** (kŏŏ·lō'ə·nē); total, 6 square miles; capital, Macao, on Macao Island. *Portuguese* **Ma·cáu** (mə·kou').
ma·caque (mə·käk') *n.* An Old World monkey (genus *Macaca*) with stout body, short tail, cheek pouches, and pronounced muzzle. [<F <Pg. *macaco.* See MACACO.]

MACAQUE
(Body length: 2 to 3 feet, depending on species)

mac·a·ro·ni (mak'ə·rō'nē) *n. pl.* **·nis** or **·nies** **1** An edible paste of wheat flour made into slender tubes. Compare SPAGHETTI, VERMICELLI. **2** A medley. **3** One of a body of Revolutionary soldiers from Maryland who wore a showy uniform. **4** An English dandy of the 18th century who affected the tastes and fashions prevalent in Continental society; a fop. Also **mac'ca·ro'ni.** [<

Ital. *maccaroni, maccheroni,* pl. of *macherone* groats <LGk. *makaria* a broth with barley groats <Gk., blessedness <*makar* blessed]

mac·a·ron·ic (mak′ə·ron′ik) *adj.* **1** Consisting of a burlesque medley of real or coined words from various languages; hence, jumbled; mixed. **2** Pertaining to or like macaroni. Also **mac′a·ron′i·cal.** [<NL *macaronicus* <Ital. *maccheronico* <*maccheroni* MACARONI]

mac·a·roon (mak′ə·ro͞on′) *n.* A small cooky of ground almonds or almond paste, white of egg, and sugar; also, an imitation of this made with coconut. [<MF *macaron* <Ital. *maccarone,* var. of *macherone* MACARONI]

Mac·Ar·thur (mək·är′thər), **Douglas,** 1880–1964, U. S. general in World War II; commander in chief in the Pacific and in Japan.

Ma·cas·sar (mə·kas′ər) A port and the largest city of Celebes, on **Macassar Strait,** a channel between Borneo and Celebes: also *Makassar.*

Ma·cas·sar oil (mə·kas′ər) **1** A volatile oil distilled from the flowers of ylang-ylang, and originally obtained from Macassar. **2** A substitute made from perfumed castor oil, etc.: used as a hair dressing.

Ma·cau·lay (mə·kô′lē), **Thomas Babington,** first Baron Macaulay of Rothley, 1800–59, English historian, essayist, statesman.

ma·caw (mə·kô′) *n.* A large tropical American parrot (genus *Ara*), with a long tail, harsh voice, and brilliant plumage. [<Pg. *macao,* prob. <Tupian *maca(vuana)*]

Mac·beth (mək·beth′), died 1057, king of Scotland; hero of Shakespeare's tragedy of the same name.

Mac·ca·bees (mak′ə·bēz) A family of Jewish patriots who, beginning in the reign of Antiochus IV (175–164 B.C.), led a revolt against Syrian religious oppression, which resulted in the deliverance and freedom of Judea; also, four books written in Hebrew and translated into Greek, treating of Jewish oppression and persecution from 222 to 135 B.C. The first two books are regarded as canonical by Roman Catholics, but all as apocryphal by Protestants. [<LL *Machabaei,* pl. of *Machabaeus* <Gk. *Makkabaios,* prob. < Aramaic *maggābā* a hammer]

Mac·ca·be·us (mak′ə·bē′əs), **Judas,** died 160? B.C., Jewish patriot; leader against the Seleucids. **— Mac′ca·be′an** *adj.*

mac·chia (mak′yə) See MAQUIS.

Mac·don·ald (mək·don′əld), **George,** 1824–1905, Scottish novelist and poet. **— James Ramsay,** 1866–1937, English labor leader and statesman; prime minister 1924, 1929–35.

Mac·Don·ough (mək·don′ō), **Thomas,** 1783–1825, U. S. naval officer in the War of 1812.

Mac·Dow·ell (mək·dou′əl), **Edward Alexander,** 1861–1908, U. S. composer.

Mac·Duff (mək·duf′) A character in Shakespeare's *Macbeth,* who kills Macbeth.

mace[1] (mās) *n.* **1** A club-shaped staff of office borne before officials or displayed on the table of a legislative body. **2** A medieval steel war club, often with spiked metal head, for use against armor. **3** A person who carries a mace, as in a ceremony. **4** A curriers' knobbed mallet for softening hides. **5** A flat-headed form of billiard cue, formerly used on pocket tables. [<OF *masse, mace.* Cf. LL *matteola* a mallet.]

mace[2] (mās) *n.* An aromatic spice made from the covering of nutmeg seed. [<OF *macis* <L *macir* <Gk. *maker* a spicy bark from India]

MACES

Mace (mās) *n.* A chemical solution similar to tear gas that temporarily blinds or incapacitates one when sprayed in the face, used as a weapon. — *v.t.* **Maced, Mac·ing** To spray with Mace. [<Chemical *Mace,* a trade name]

mace·bear·er (mās′bâr′ər) *n.* An official who carries a mace, as in a procession.

mac·é·doine (mas′i·dwän′, *Fr.* mà·sā·dwàn′) *n.* A dish of mixed vegetables or fruits, served as a salad or dessert; also, any mixture; medley; olio. [<F, a type of parsley <OF *(perresel) macedoine* Macedonian (parsley)]

Mac·e·do·ni·a (mas′ə·dō′nē·ə) A region of SE Europe in the southern Balkan peninsula on the Aegean, divided among Bulgaria, Greece, and Yugoslavia; the ancient Greek kingdom of **Mac·e·don** (mas′ə·don) under Alexander the Great became a leading world power in the fourth century B.C. **— Mac′e·do′ni·an** *adj.* & *n.*

Ma·cei·ó (mä′sā·ô′) A port on the Atlantic, capital of Alagoas state, eastern Brazil.

mac·er (mā′sər) *n.* **1** A macebearer. **2** In Scotland, an officer who attends the courts and executes their orders. [<OF *maissier* <*masse, mace* mace]

mac·er·ate (mas′ə·rāt) *v.* **·at·ed, ·at·ing** *v.t.* **1 a** To reduce to a soft mass by soaking. **b** To separate the soft parts of by soaking; digest. **2** To make thin; emaciate. — *v.i.* **3** To undergo maceration. [<L *maceratus,* pp. of *macerare* make soft, knead] **— mac′er·at′er, mac′·er·a′tor** *n.*

mac·er·a·tion (mas′ə·rā′shən) *n.* The process or action of steeping a solid material in liquid so as to soften it or break down its structure; digestion.

mach (mak, mäk) See MACH NUMBER.

Ma·cha·do y Mo·ra·les (mä·chä′thō ē mō·rä′·läs), **Gerardo,** 1871–1939, president of Cuba 1925–33.

mach effect (mak, mäk) *Physics* **1** Any effect produced by an object moving at transonic or supersonic speeds, as a shock wave. **2** The aggregate of such effects.

ma chère (mà shâr′) *French fem.* My dear.

ma·chet·e (mə·shet′ē, mə·shet′; *Sp.* mä·chā′tā) *n.* A heavy knife or cutlas used both as an implement and as a weapon by the natives of tropical America. [<Sp., dim. of *macho* an ax, a hammer <L *marculus,* dim. of *marcus* a hammer]

SPANISH MACHETES

Mach·i·a·vel·li (mäk′ē·ə·vel′ē, *Ital.* mä′kyä·vel′·lē), **Niccolò,** 1469–1527, Florentine statesman and writer on government.

Mach·i·a·vel·li·an (mak′ē·ə·vel′ē·ən) *adj.* Of or pertaining to Niccolò Machiavelli, or to the unscrupulous doctrines of political opportunism associated with his name. — *n.* A follower of Machiavelli.

Mach·i·a·vel·li·an·ism (mak′ē·ə·vel′ē·ən·iz′əm) *n.* The theory and practice of power politics elaborated from Machiavelli's *The Prince:* envisaging (1) seizure, maintenance, and extension of absolute power by the nicely graduated use of guile, fraud, force, and terror; (2) control by the ruler of all avenues of communication, thus facilitating the deliberate molding of public opinion; (3) the employment for surveillance and terrorist activities of subordinates who can be disowned and liquidated by the ruler, who thus escapes the blame for their atrocities.

ma·chic·o·late (mə·chik′ə·lāt) *v.t.* **·lat·ed, ·lat·ing** To furnish with machicolations. [<Med. L *machicolatus,* pp. of *machicolare*]

ma·chic·o·la·tion (mə·chik′ə·lā′shən) *n.* **1** *Archit.* An opening between a wall and a parapet, to permit missiles or boiling liquids to be dropped upon an assailing enemy. **2** The act of showering missiles on an attacking party through such openings.

ma·chin·a·ble (mə·shē′nə·bəl) *adj. Metall.* Capable of being shaped, cut, or polished by high-speed machine tools, as certain metals and alloys. **— ma·chin′a·bil′i·ty** *n.*

mach·i·nate (mak′ə·nāt) *v.t.* & *v.i.* **·nat·ed, ·nat·ing** To plan or devise; scheme, especially with evil intent. [<L *machinatus,* pp. of *machinari* contrive <*machina* MACHINE]

mach·i·na·tion (mak′ə·nā′shən) *n.* The act of contriving a secret or hostile plan; also, such a plan; plot. See synonyms under ARTIFICE. **— mach′i·na′tor** *n.*

ma·chine (mə·shēn′) *n.* **1** Any combination of mechanisms for utilizing, modifying, applying, or transmitting energy, whether simple, as a lever and fulcrum, pulley, etc., or complex, as a Fourdrinier papermaking apparatus. **2** An automobile; also, any other mechanical vehicle, as a bicycle, airplane, etc. **3** In many trades or vocations, the construction principally used or typical of the trade. **4** One who acts in a mechanical manner; a robot. **5** An ancient theatrical contrivance, originating in Greece, for the creation of stage effects: also applied to such portions of the plot of a work of fiction as are introduced for the sake of effect. **6** The organization of the powers of any complex body: the *machine* of government; specifically, an organization within a political party, controlled by practical politicians, in which discipline and subordination are maintained chiefly by the use of patronage, as in the distribution of offices and contracts. **7** Formerly, a military engine. — *adj.* **1** Pertaining to, for, produced by, or producing a machine or machinery: *machine* knitting, *machine* shop, etc. **2** Typified by the application or predominance of machines: *machine* age. **3** Mechanical; lacking in originality or uniqueness. — *v.t.* **·chined, ·chin·ing** To shape, mill, make, etc., by machinery. [<F <L *machina* <Gk. *mēchanē* <*mēchos* a contrivance] **— ma·chin′al** *adj.*

machine element One of various simple mechanisms, as the lever, pulley, cam, gearwheel, etc., which, alone or in combination, facilitate conversion of energy to useful work. See illustration, page 763. Also **simple machine.**

ma·chine–gun (mə·shēn′gun′) *n.* An automatic gun that discharges small-arms ammunition in a rapid, continuous fire: also **machine gun.** — *v.t.* **-gunned, -gun·ning** To fire at or shoot with a machine-gun. **— ma·chine′-gun′ner** *n.*

ma·chin·er·y (mə·shē′nər·ē) *n. pl.* **·er·ies** **1** The parts of a machine or a number of machines and kindred appliances collectively. **2** Any combination of means working together; a complex system of appliances; the arrangements for effecting a specific end. **3** The supernatural or other means by which the catastrophe of a classical drama was brought about; hence, the incidents and events introduced to build up the plot in a work of fiction.

machine shop A workshop for making or repairing machines.

machine tool A power-driven tool, partly or wholly automatic in action, as a lathe, used for cutting and shaping the parts of a machine.

ma·chin·ist (mə·shē′nist) *n.* A maker or repairer of machines; one expert in their design or construction, or in using metalworking tools.

ma·chis·mo (mä·chēz′mō, -chiz′-) *n.* Maleness or masculinity, especially when associated with strong or exaggerated pride in or a conspicuous display of the qualities, attitudes, etc., considered characteristically masculine. [<Sp. <*macho* male]

mach·me·ter (mak′mē′tər, mäk′-) *n. Aeron.* An instrument for determining the speed of airplanes, especially with reference to the mach number. [<MACH (NUMBER) + -METER]

mach number (mak, mäk) A number expressing the speed of an object moving through a fluid medium in relation to the speed of sound in the same medium: in aeronautics it is the ratio of the air speed to the speed of sound in the undisturbed medium, a mach number of 1 indicating a speed equal to the speed of sound. Also *mach.* [after Ernst *Mach,* 1838–1916, Austrian physicist]

ma·cho (mä′chō) *n. pl.* **·chos** (-chōs) A virile man, especially one who takes excessive pride in his virility. — *adj.* Of or characteristic of a macho. [<Sp., male]

ma·chree (mə·krē′) *n.* My heart; my love: a term of endearment. [<Irish <*mo* my + *croidhe* heart <OIrish *cride*]

Ma·chu·pic·chu (mä′cho͞o·pēk′cho͞o) A ruined pre-Incan city in south central Peru. Also **Machu Picchu.**

-machy *combining form* A fight between, or by means of: *logomachy.* [<Gk. *-machia* <*machē* a battle]

Ma·cie (mā′sē), **James Lewis** See SMITHSON, JAMES.

mac·in·tosh (mak′ən·tosh) See MACKINTOSH.

Mack·en·sen (mäk′ən·zən), **August von,** 1849–1945, German field marshal in World War I.

Mac·Ken·zie (mə·ken′zē) **1** A district in the Northwest Territories, Canada; 527,490 square miles. **2** A river in NW Canada, flowing generally north 2,514 miles to the Beaufort Sea.

Mac·Ken·zie (mə·ken′zē), **Sir Alexander,** 1755–1820, Scottish explorer in North America.

mack·er·el (mak′ər·əl) *n.* **1** An Atlantic food fish *(Scomber scombrus),* steel-blue above with blackish bars, and silvery beneath. **2** Some scombroid fish resembling it, as the

Spanish mackerel (*Scomberomorus maculatus*). [<OF *makerel*; ult. origin unknown]

mackerel gull The common tern.

mackerel sky *Meteorol.* A cloud formation with numerous detached cloudlets resembling the markings on a mackerel's back.

Mack·i·nac (mak'ə·nô), **Straits of** A channel between Lake Michigan and Lake Huron; 4 miles wide at the narrowest point.

Mack·i·nac Island (mak'ə·nô) A resort city on the southern end of Mackinac Island in the Straits of Mackinac. Also **Mackinac.**

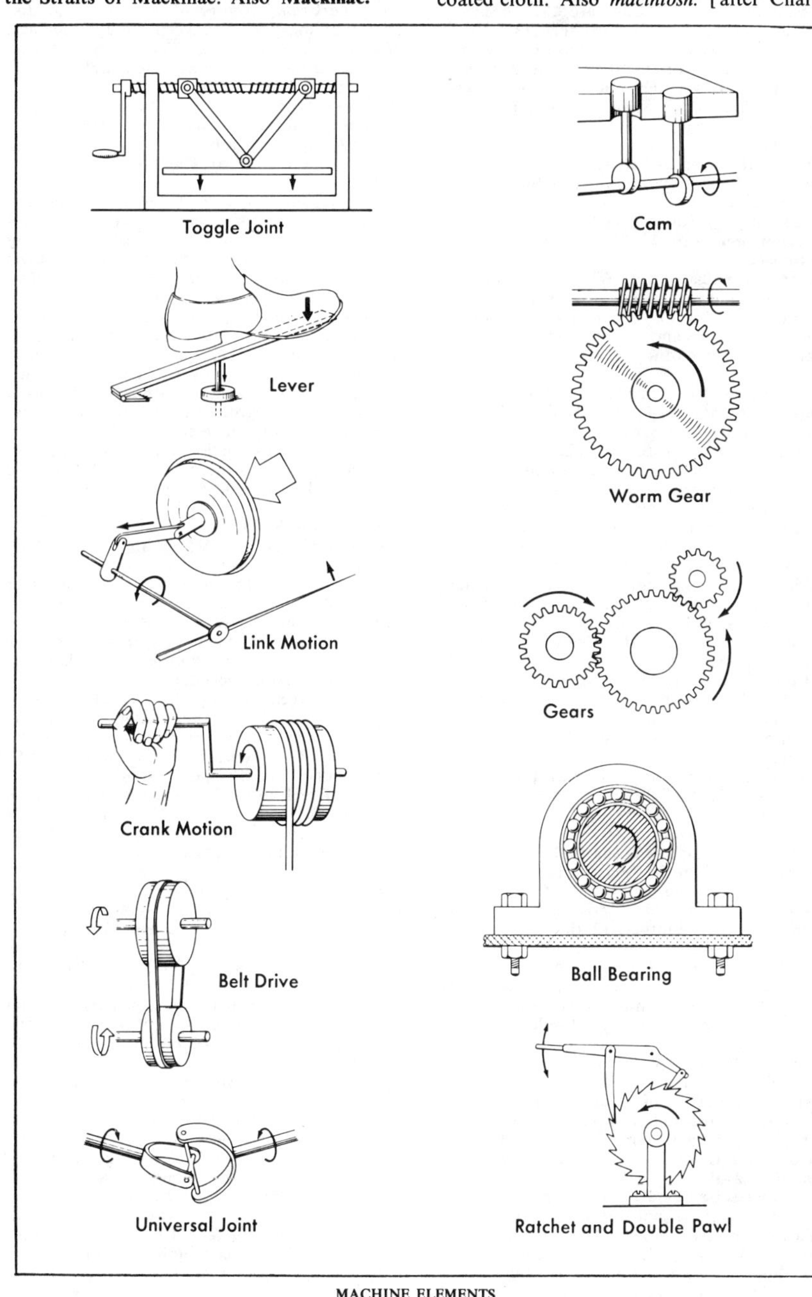

MACHINE ELEMENTS

mack·i·naw (mak'ə·nô) A shortened form of MACKINAW BLANKET, MACKINAW BOAT, MACKINAW COAT. [<dial. F (Canadian) *Mackinac* <*Michilimackinac* Mackinac Island <Algonquian (Ojibwa) *mitchimakinak* a large turtle]

Mackinaw blanket A thick, heavy blanket formerly used by Indians and traders of the western United States.

Mackinaw boat A large, sharp-ended, flat-bottomed bateau, sometimes equipped with sails, and formerly used on the northern Great Lakes.

Mackinaw cloth A heavy-napped woolen fabric, or one having cotton or rayon mixed in the yarns: the two sides may be different colors, sometimes in plaids: used for lumbermen's jackets, sport clothes, windbreakers, etc.

Mackinaw coat A thick, short, double-breasted coat with a plaid pattern.

Mackinaw trout See NAMAYCUSH.

mack·in·tosh (mak'ən·tosh) *n.* **1** A waterproof overgarment or cloak. **2** Thin rubber-coated cloth. Also *macintosh.* [after Charles *Macintosh,* 1766–1843, Scottish chemist, inventor of the cloth]

mack·le (mak'əl) *n.* A spot or blemish; also, a blurred impression. —*v.t.* & *v.i.* **mack·led, mack·ling** To print with a blurred or double image; blur; blot. Also spelled *macule.* [<F *macule* <L *macula* a spot]

Mac·lar·en (mə·klar'ən), **Ian** Pseudonym of John Watson, 1850–1907, Scottish author.

Mac·Lau·rin (mə·klôr'in), **trisectrix of** See TRISECTRIX OF MACLAURIN.

mac·le (mak'əl) *n.* **1** A twin crystal, especially of a diamond. **2** Chiastolite. **3** A mackle. **4** Mascle. [<F <OF *mascle* <Med. L *mascula* mesh of net <L *macula* spot]

Mac·Leish (mək·lēsh'), **Archibald,** born 1892, U.S. poet.

Mac·leod (mə·kloud'), **Fiona** Pseudonym of William Sharp.

—**John James Rickard,** 1876–1935, Scottish physiologist.

Ma·clu·ra (mə·klŏŏr'ə) *n.* The Osage orange. [<NL, after Wm. *Maclure,* 1763–1840, U.S. geologist born in Scotland]

Mac-Ma·hon (måk·må·ôn'), **Marie Edmé Patrice Maurice de,** 1808–93, Duke of Magenta, French marshal; president of France 1873–79.

Mac·Mil·lan (mək·mil'ən), **Donald Baxter,** born 1874, U.S. Arctic explorer.

Mac·mil·lan (mək·mil'ən), **Harold,** born 1894, British statesman; prime minister 1957–.

Mac·Mon·nies (mək·mon'ēz), **Frederick William,** 1863–1937, U.S. sculptor.

Ma·con (mā'kən) A city in central Georgia.

Mâ·con (må·kôn') *n.* A wine produced in the neighborhood of Mâcon, France.

Mac·Pher·son (mək·fûr'sən), **James,** 1736–1796, Scottish writer. See OSSIAN.

Mac·quar·ie River (mə·kwôr'ē, -kwor'ē) A river in central New South Wales, Australia, flowing 590 miles NW to the Darling River.

mac·ra·mé (mak'rə·mā) *n.* A fringe, lace, or trimming of knotted thread or cord; knotted work. [Appar. <Turkish *maqramah* a towel <Arabic *miqramah* a veil]

Mac·rea·dy (mə·krē'dē), **William Charles,** 1793–1873, English tragedian.

mac·ren·ceph·a·ly (mak'ren·sef'ə·lē) *n. Pathol.* Hypertrophy of the brain. [<MACR(O)- + ENCEPHAL(O)- + -Y[1]] —**mac'ren·ce·phal'ic** (-sə·fal'ik), **mac'ren·ceph'a·lous** *adj.*

macro- *combining form* Large or long in size or duration: *macrocephaly, macrobiosis.* Also, before vowels, **macr-.** [<Gk. *makros* large]

mac·ro·bi·o·sis (mak'rō·bī·ō'sis) *n.* Longevity. [<NL <Gk. *makros* long + *bios* life] —**mac'·ro·bi·ot'ic** (-ot'ik) *adj.*

mac·ro·bi·ot·ics (mak'rō·bī·ot'iks) *n.pl.* (*construed as sing.*) A dietetic regimen advocating the use of whole-grain cereals, the avoidance of meat, etc. [<MACRO- + BIOTIC]

mac·ro·ceph·a·ly (mak'rō·sef'ə·lē) *n.* Excessive size of the head. [<MACRO- + Gk. *kephalē* head] —**mac'ro·ce·phal'ic** (-sə·fal'ik) *adj.* & *n.* —**mac'ro·ceph'a·lous** *adj.*

mac·ro·chem·is·try (mak'rō·kem'is·trē) *n.* The chemistry of large-scale operations or of reactions visible to the naked eye. —**mac'·ro·chem'i·cal** (-i·kəl) *adj.*

mac·ro·cli·mate (mak'rō·klī'mit) *n. Meteorol.* The general climate prevailing over a large area considered as a unit. Compare MICROCLIMATE. —**mac'ro·cli·mat'ic** (-klī·mat'ik) *adj.*

mac·ro·cosm (mak'rə·koz'əm) *n.* **1** The great world; the universe: opposed to *microcosm.* **2** The whole of any sphere or department of nature or knowledge to which man is related. [<OF *macrocosme* <Med. L *macrocosmus* <Gk. *makros* long, great + *kosmos* world] —**mac'ro·cos'mic** *adj.*

mac·ro·cyst (mak'rə·sist) *n. Biol.* **1** An enlarged cyst. **2** *Bot.* A large reproductive cell in certain fungi.

mac·ro·cyte (mak'rə·sīt) *n.* An abnormally large erythrocyte. [<MACRO- + (ERYTHRO)-CYTE]

mac·ro·dome (mak'rə·dōm) See under DOME.

mac·ro·e·co·nom·ics (mak'rō·ē'kə·nom'iks, -ek'ə-) *n.* Economics studied in terms of large aggregates of data whose mutual relationships are interpreted with reference to the behavior of the system as a whole: developed by John Maynard Keynes. —**mac'ro·e'co·nom'ic** *adj.*

mac·ro·ga·mete (mak'rō·gə·mēt', -gam'ēt) *n. Biol.* The female of two conjugating gametes: so called from its being the larger. Compare MICROGAMETE. [<MACRO- + GAMETE]

ma·crog·a·my (mə·krog'ə·mē) *n. Biol.* Conjugation between gametes similar in structure to the original vegetative cells.

mac·ro·graph (mak'rə·graf, -gräf) *n.* A drawing or illustration of an object as seen with the unaided eye.

ma·crog·ra·phy (mə·krog'rə·fē) *n.* **1** Examination with the unaided eye. **2** Extremely large writing: contrasted with *micrography.*

ma·crom·e·ter (mə·krom′ə·tər) *n.* A range-finding instrument similar to a sextant, for measuring distant objects.

mac·ro·me·te·or·ol·o·gy (mak′rō·mē′tē·ə·rol′ə·jē) *n.* The meteorology of large areas; world meteorology; also, the study of climatic phenomena over extended periods of time. Compare MICROMETEOROLOGY.

mac·ro·mol·e·cule (mak′rə·mol′ə·kyōōl) *n.* A giant molecule, as that of a protein, rubber, cellulose, starch, etc. —**mac′ro·mo·lec′u·lar** (-yə·lər) *adj.*

mac·ro·mor·phol·o·gy (mak′rō·môr·fol′ə·jē) *n.* The gross anatomy of plants.

ma·cron (mā′krən, -kron) *n.* A straight line (-) over a vowel to show that it has a long sound, as, ā: opposed to *breve* (˘). [<Gk. *makron,* neut. of *makros* long]

mac·ro·nu·cle·us (mak′rō·nōō′klē·əs, -nyōō′-) *n. pl.* **·cle·i** (-klē·ī) *Biol.* The larger of two nuclei in certain protozoans, as *Paramecium.*

mac·ro·nu·tri·ent (mak′rō·nōō′trē·ənt, -nyōō′-) *n.* A chemical nutrient required in large amounts for plant growth and vitality.

mac·ro·phys·ics (mak′rō·fiz′iks) *n.* The physics of masses, or of large bodies. —**mac′ro·phys′i·cal** *adj.*

mac·ro·po·di·an (mak′rə·pō′dē·ən) *n.* Any of a family *(Macropodidae)* of marsupials, especially those having six sharp upper incisors and two larger lower ones, enlarged saltatorial hind legs, and long tail: including wallabies and kangaroos. —*adj.* Of or pertaining to the *Macropodidae*: also **ma·crop·o·dine** (mə·krop′ə·din, -dīn), [<NL <Gk. *makropous, -podos* long-footed <*makros* long + *pous, podos* a foot]

mac·rop·si·a (mə·krop′sē·ə) *n. Pathol.* A condition of the eyes in which objects appear larger than they really are: often called *megalopsia.* Also **ma·cro′pi·a** (-krō′pē·ə). [<NL <Gk. *makros* large + *ōps, ōpos* eye]

mac·ro·scop·ic (mak′rə·skop′ik) *adj.* Visible to the naked eye. Also **mac′ro·scop′i·cal.**

mac·ro·spe·cies (mak′rə·spē′shēz) *n. Biol.* A species of which the members exhibit a large range of variation. Compare MICROSPECIES.

mac·ro·spo·ran·gi·um (mak′rō·spə·ran′jē·əm) See MEGASPORANGIUM.

mac·ro·spore (mak′rə·spôr, -spōr) *n.* **1** *Bot.* A megaspore. **2** *Biol.* One of the larger of the two kinds of anisospores in ameboid protozoans.

mac·ro·struc·ture (mak′rə·struk′chər) *n.* The structure of metal as observed with the naked eye or under low magnification on a polished or etched surface. —**mac′ro·struc′tur·al** *adj.*

mac·ro·therm (mak′rə·thûrm) *n.* A tropical plant, or one requiring much heat and moisture for survival: also called *megatherm.*

ma·cru·ran (mə·krŏŏr′ən) *n.* One of a suborder *(Macrura)* of crustaceans with well-developed, elongated abdomens, including shrimps, prawns, lobsters, and crayfishes. [<NL <Gk. *makros* long + *oura* tail] —**ma·cru′ral, ma·cru′roid, ma·cru′rous** *adj.*

mac·ta·tion (mak·tā′shən) *n.* The killing of a sacrificial victim. [<L *mactatio, -onis* < *mactatus,* pp. of *mactare* kill]

mac·u·la (mak′yə·lə) *n. pl.* **·lae** (-lē) **1** A spot, as of color on the skin. **2** *Astron.* A dark spot on the sun's surface. **3** A fleck; blotch. [<L, a spot]

mac·u·late (mak′yə·lāt) *v.t.* **·lat·ed, ·lat·ing** To spot or blemish; stain. —*adj.* (-lit) Spotted; stained. [<L *maculatus,* pp. of *maculare* < *macula* a spot]

mac·u·la·tion (mak′yə·lā′shən) *n.* **1** The act of spotting, or a spotty condition. **2** The marking of a spotted animal or plant. **3** A soiling; defilement.

mac·ule (mak′yōōl) See MACKLE.

mad (mad) *adj.* **mad·der, mad·dest 1** Mentally deranged; insane. **2** Subject to an overpowering emotion; excited intensely or beyond self-control: *mad* with jealousy or grief. **3** *Colloq.* Angry; furious; enraged. **4** Rabid; having hydrophobia; hence, uncontrollable. **5** Proceeding from or indicating a disordered mind; rash: a *mad* project. **6** Tumultuous or uncontrollable in movement or action: said of things: a *mad* torrent. **7** Reckless; heedless. —*n. Slang* Anger; a fit of temper. —**to have a mad on** *Slang* To be angry. [Aphetic var. of OE *gemǣd, gemǣded,* pp. of *gemǣdan* make mad <*gemād* insane] —**mad′ly** *adv.* —**mad′·ness** *n.*

Mad·a·gas·car A country off the east coast of Africa, and the world's fourth largest island, in the Indian Ocean; land that was originally rainforest, now deforested; 227,600 square miles; capital, Antananarivo; pop.13,000,000. French **Grande-Ile. Grande-Terre.** Formerly **Malagasy Republic.** —*adj. & n.* **Madagascan, Malagasy.**

mad·am (mad′əm) *n. pl.* **mes·dames** (mā·däm′, *Fr.* mā·dȧm′) *for def.* **1**; **mad·ams** *for def.* **2. 1** My lady; mistress: a title of courtesy originally addressed to a woman of rank or high position, but now used to any woman, as at the beginning of a letter. Compare SIR. See MA'AM. **2** The mistress of a brothel. [<OF *ma dame* <*ma* my (<L *meus*) + *dame* lady <L *domina.* Doublet of MADONNA, MADAME.]

mad·ame (mad′əm, *Fr.* mȧ·dȧm′) *n. pl.* **mes·dames** (mā·däm′, *Fr.* mā·dȧm′) The French title of courtesy for a married woman, equivalent to the English *Mrs.*: abbreviated *Mme.*; often used in English, especially in the plural. [<F <OF *ma dame.* Doublet of MADAM, MADONNA.]

Ma·da·ria·ga y Ro·jo (mä′thä·ryä′gä ē rō′hō), **Salvador de,** born 1886, Spanish writer and diplomat.

mad·cap (mad′kap′) *adj.* Wild; rattle-brained. —*n.* One who acts wildly or rashly.

mad·den (mad′n) *v.t. & v.i.* To make or become mad or insane; inflame with anger; enrage. —**mad′den·ing** *adj.* —**mad′den·ing·ly** *adv.*

mad·der[1] (mad′ər) Comparative of MAD.

mad·der[2] (mad′ər) *n.* **1** Any plant of the genus *Rubia* (family *Rubiaceae*); especially, an Old World shrubby, perennial, hairy herb *(R. tinctorum),* resembling the common bedstraw. **2** A brilliant red tinctorial extract from the root of the madder plant, used in dyeing and as a pigment in many lakes: the coloring principle, alizarin, is now made also synthetically. —*v.t.* To dye with madder. [OE *mædere, mæddre*]

madder lake A pigment and dyestuff formerly made from the root of the madder plant, now largely replaced by alizarin.

mad·ding (mad′ing) *adj.* Being or growing mad; delirious; raging.

mad·dish (mad′ish) *adj.* Rather mad.

mad-dog skullcap (mad′dôg′, -dog′) A common American plant *(Scutellaria lateriflora)* having blue flowers: formerly believed to cure hydrophobia.

made (mād) Past tense and past participle of MAKE. —*adj.* **1** Fabricated; produced, especially artificially. **2** Assured of fortune. **3** Filled in: *made* land.

Ma·dei·ra (mə·dir′ə, *Pg.* mə·thā′rə) *n.* A fortified wine made in the Madeira islands.

Ma·dei·ra (mə·dir′ə, *Pg.* mə·thā′rə) **1** An archipelago west of Morocco, including Madeira, Porto Santo, and the Desertas and Selvagens islands, comprising an administrative district *(Funchal)* of Portugal; 305 square miles; capital, Funchal, on Madeira. **2** A river in NW Brazil, the most important tributary of the Amazon, flowing 2,100 miles NE. —**Ma·dei′ran** *adj.*

Madeira vine A vine *(Boussingaultia baselloides)* having a bulbous root, shiny leaves, and clusters of white flowers.

Mad·e·leine (mad′ə·lin, -lān, *Fr.* mȧ·dlen′) A feminine personal name. See MAGDALENE. Also **Mad′e·line** (-lin, -līn), **Mad·e·lon** (mad′ə·lon, *Fr.* mȧ·dlôn′).

mad·e·moi·selle (mad′ə·mə·zel′, *Fr.* mȧd·mwȧ·zel′) *n. pl.* **mad·e·moi·selles,** *Fr.* **mes·de·moi·selles** (mād·mwȧ·zel′) **1** The French title of courtesy for unmarried women, equivalent to the English *Miss*: abbreviated *Mlle.* **2** A French nurse or governess. [<F <*ma* my + *demoiselle.* See DEMOISELLE.]

Ma·de·ro (mä·thā′rō), **Francisco Indalecio,** 1873–1913, president of Mexico 1911–13.

made-up (mād′up′) *adj.* **1** Artificial; fictitious. **2** Complete; finished. **3** With make-up or cosmetics applied.

mad·house (mad′hous′) *n.* **1** A lunatic asylum. **2** A place of confusion, turmoil, and uproar; bedlam.

Ma·dhya Bha·rat (mu′dyə bä′rət) A former constituent state in west central India, formed in 1948 by merger of Gwalior and the states of Central India, most of which became merged into Madhya Pradesh, November 1, 1956; 46,710 square miles; capitals, Lashkar and Indore.

Ma·dhya Pra·desh (mu′dyə prə·dāsh′) A constituent State in central India on the northern Deccan Plateau; 171,201 square miles; capital, Bhopal: formerly *Central Provinces and Behar.*

Mad·i·son (mad′ə·sən) The capital of Wisconsin.

Mad·i·son (mad′ə·sən), **Dolly,** 1768–1849, *née* Payne, wife of James; celebrated as a hostess. —**James,** 1751–1836, president of the United States 1809–17.

Madison Avenue 1 A street running north and south through Manhattan borough of New York City, center of a commercial district containing many advertising agencies and offices of mass media. **2** The world of American advertising and mass media, its power, influence, policies, etc.

Madison's War The War of 1812.

mad·man (mad′man′, -mən) *n. pl.* **·men** (-men′, -mən) A lunatic; maniac.

Ma·doe·ra (mə·dōō′rä) The Dutch spelling of MADURA.

Ma·don·na (mə·don′ə) *n.* **1** My lady; madam: an Italian title of respect now replaced by *Signora.* **2** The Virgin Mary; also, a painting or statue of the Virgin Mary. [<Ital. <*ma* my (<L *meus*) + *donna* lady <L *domina.* Doublet of MADAM, MADAME.]

ma·dras (mə·dras′, -dräs′, mad′rəs) *n.* **1** A kind of cotton cloth, with thick strands at intervals throughout its weave, giving either a striped, corded, or checked effect. **2** A large, brightly colored kerchief, formerly worn as a headdress by Negroes. [from *Madras,* India, because originally made there]

Ma·dras (mə·dras′, -dräs′, mad′rəs) **1** A constituent state in southern India; 50,110 square miles. **2** Its capital, a port on the Bay of Bengal.

Madras hemp Sunn.

ma·dre (*Ital.* mä′drā, *Pg., Sp.* mä′thrā) Italian, Portuguese, and Spanish form of MOTHER.

Ma·dre de Dios (mä′thrā thā dyōs′) A river in the Amazon basin of Peru and Bolivia, flowing 700 miles NE to the Beni.

mad·re·po·rar·i·an (mad′rə·pô·râr′ē·ən) *n.* One of a suborder *(Madreporaria)* of anthozoans with a calcareous skeleton secreted by cells; one of the reef-forming stony corals of tropical seas. —*adj.* Of or pertaining to the *Madreporaria*: also **mad′re·po′ral** (-pôr′əl, -pō′rəl). [<NL <Ital. *madrepora* MADREPORE]

mad·re·pore (mad′rə·pôr, -pōr) *n.* **1** A branched reef coral (family *Acroporidae*); also, any perforate stone coral. **2** The animal which produces madrepore coral. **3** Limestone consisting of fossil madrepores. Also **mad′re·po′ra** (-pôr′ə, -pō′rə). [<F <Ital. *madrepora,* lit., mother stone <*madre* mother (<L *mater*) +*poro,* ? calcareous stone <L *porus* <Gk. *pōros*] —**mad′re·por′ic** (-pôr′·ik, -por′ik) *adj.*

mad·re·po·rite (mad′rə·pô·rīt′) *n. Zool.* In starfishes and certain other echinoderms, the circular perforated plate by which the internal ambulacral system communicates with the outside. Also **madreporic plate.** [<MADREPOR(E) + -ITE[1]

Ma·drid (mə·drid′, *Sp.* mä·thrēth′) The capital of Spain, in the central part.

mad·ri·gal (mad′rə·gəl) *n.* **1** A short lyric poem, usually dealing with a pastoral or amatory subject. **2** A musical setting for such a poem; an a capella part song characterized by elaborate rhythm and contrapuntal imitation. **3** Any part song **4** Any song. [<Ital. *madrigale, mandrigale* <LL *matricale* original, chief <L *matrix* womb; infl. in form by Ital. *mandra* aflock <L, a herd <Gk., a stable, fold]

mad·ri·gal·ist (mad′rə·gəl·ist) *n.* One who writes, or performs in, madrigals.

ma·dri·lène (mad′rə·len′, *Fr.* mȧ·drē·len′) *n.* A consommé flavored with tomato and served hot or cold. [<F <Sp. *Madrileño* of Madrid]

Mad·ri·le·ño (mä′dri·lā′nyō) *n. pl.* **-ños.** One who was born or lives in Madrid.

ma·dro·ña (mə·drō′nyə) *n.* A large evergreen tree *(Arbutus menziesii)* of northern California with shining oval or oblong leaves, dense racemes of white flowers, and dry, yellow, edible berries, called **madroña apples.** Also **ma·dro′ño** (-nyō). [<Sp. *madroño*]

mad·stone (mad′stōn′) *n.* A stone formerly believed to cure hydrophobia.

Ma·du·ra (mä·dōō′rä) An Indonesian island in the Java Sea; 2,112 square miles including offshore islands: Dutch *Madoera.*

Madura foot Mycetoma.

Ma·du·rai (maj′o͝o·rī, mə·do͝or′i) A city in southern Madras State, India: also *Mathurai.* Formerly **Ma·du·ra** (maj′o͝o·rə, mə·do͝or′ə).

Mad·u·rese (maj′o͝o·rēz′, -rēS′) *adj.* Of or pertaining to Madurai, its people, or their language. —*n. pl.* **·rese 1** A native or inhabitant of Madurai and eastern Java. **2** The Indonesian language of the Madurese.

Ma·du·ro (mə·do͞o′r′ō) *adj.* Matured; that is, of full strength and color: said of cigars. —*n.* Such a cigar. [<Sp. <L *maturus*]

mad·wom·an (mad′wo͝om′ən) *n. pl.* **·wom·en** (-wim′in) An insane woman; lunatic.

mad·wort (mad′wûrt′) *n.* Any of various shrubs or herbs of the mustard family (genera *Alyssum* or *Lobularia*) with small alternate leaves and small yellow or white flowers in terminal racemes or clusters. [? Trans. of NL *Alyssum*, genus name <L <Gk. *alysson* <*a-* not + *lyssa* rabies]

mae (mā) *adj.* & *adv. Scot.* More.

Mae·an·der (mē·an′dər) See MEANDER. Also Mæ·an′der.

Mae·ce·nas (mi·sē′nəs), **Gaius Cilnius,** 73?-8 B.C., Roman statesman; friend and patron of Horace and Vergil; hence, any patron of the arts.

mael·strom (māl′strəm) *n.* Any irresistible movement or influence: from the **Maelstrom,** a whirlpool or current off the NW coast of Norway. [<Du. *maelstrom, maalstroom* <*malen* grind, whirl round + *stroom* a stream]

mae·nad (mē′nad) *n.* **1** A female votary or priestess of Dionysius; a bacchante. **2** Any woman beside herself with frenzy or excitement. Also spelled *menad.* [<L *Maenas, -adis* <Gk. *mainas* frenzied <*mainesthai* rave] —**mae·nad′ic** *adj.*

Mae Nam (ma′ näm′) See CHAO PHRAYA.

ma·es·to·so (mäs′es·tō′sō) *adj.* & *adv. Music* With majesty; stately. [<Ital., majestic <L *majestas* greatness]

Maes·tricht (mäs′trikht) A city in southern Netherlands, capital of Limburg province: also *Maastricht.*

ma·es·tro (mä·es′trō, mī′strō) *n.* A master in any art, especially in music. [<Ital., a master <L *magister*]

Mae·ter·linck (mā′tər·lingk), **Maurice,** 1862–1949, Belgian poet, dramatist, and essayist.

Mae West (mā) An inflatable vestlike life preserver used by aviators downed at sea in World War II. [after *Mae West,* born 1892, U.S. actress]

Maf·e·king (maf′ə·king) A town in Northwest province, Republic of South Africa.

maf·fick (maf′ik) *v.i. Brit.* To celebrate uproariously. [Back formation <*mafficking* <MAFEKING, taken as a ppr.; from the extravagant celebration of the relief of the British garrison at Mafeking, May 17, 1900]

Ma·fi·a (mä′fē·ä, maf′ē·ə) *n.* A Sicilian secret society, characterized by hostility to and deliberate flouting of the law and its representatives; also, any similar organization of Italians and Sicilians believed to exist in other countries; Black Hand. Also **Maf′fi·a.** Compare CAMORRA. [<Ital. *maffia*; ult. origin uncertain]

ma·fi·o·so (mä′fē·ō′sō, -zō, maf′ē-) *n. pl.* **·si** (-sē, -zē) *Sometimes cap.* A member of the Mafia. [<Ital. <MAFIA]

ma foi (ma fwä′) *French* My faith; upon my word: an interjection.

mag (mag) *n. Brit. Slang* A halfpenny. [<dial. E *make* a halfpenny; infl. in form by *meg,* orig. a guinea]

Mag (mag) Diminutive of MARGARET.

Ma·gal·la·nes (mä′gä·yä′näs) See PUNTA ARENAS.

mag·a·zine (mag′ə·zēn′, mag′ə·zēn) *n.* **1** A house, room, or receptacle in which anything is stored; a depot; warehouse; specifically, a strong building for storing gunpowder and other military stores; also, a storeroom for gunpowder and shells aboard ship. **2** A receptacle in which the supply of reserve cartridges of a repeating rifle is placed; also, a case in which cartridges are carried. **3** A periodical publication containing sketches, stories, essays, etc. **4** A reservoir or supply chamber in a battery, camera, or the like. —*v.t.* **·zined, ·zin·ing** To store up for future use. [<MF *magasin* <OF *magazin* <Arabic *makhāzin, pl.* of *makhzan* a storehouse <khazana store up]

magazine gun A quick-firing small arm fitted with a case carrying a supply of reserve cartridges. See MAGAZINE (def. 2). Also **magazine pistol** or **rifle.**

mag·a·zin·ist (mag′ə·zē′nist) *n.* A contributor to or editor of a magazine. —**mag′a·zin′ism** *n.*

mag·da·len (mag′də·lin) *n.* A reformed prostitute. Also **mag′da·lene** (-lēn). [after *Mary Magdalene*]

Mag·da·le·na (mäg′dä·lā′nä) A river in Colombia, flowing 1,060 miles north to the Caribbean Sea.

Mag·da·lene (mag′də·lēn, *Ger.* mäg′dä·lā′nə) A feminine personal name. Also **Mag′da·len, Mag·da·le·na** (mag′də·lē′nə, *Du., Pg., Sp., Sw.* mäg′dä·lā′nä). [<LL <Gk. *Magdalēnē,* lit., of Magdala <*Magdala* Magdala, a town on the Sea of Galilee] —**the Magdalene** Mary Magdalene.

Mag·da·le·ni·an (mag′də·lē′nē·ən) *adj. Anthrophol.* Describing an advanced culture stage of the upper Paleolithic in western Europe, immediately preceding the Mesolithic period: it is noted especially for its delicate carvings in bone and ivory and for the brilliant realism of its polychrome cave paintings. [<F *magdalenien,* from *La Madeleine* in west central France, where artifacts were found]

Mag·da·len Islands (mag′də·lin) An island group in the Gulf of Saint Lawrence, eastern Quebec province, Canada; total, 102 square miles. *French* **Iles Ma·de·leine** (ēl mȧ·dlen′).

Mag·de·burg (mag′də·bûrg, *Ger.* mäg′də·bo͝orkh) A city in central Germany, on the Elbe.

mage (māj) *n.* A magician. [<F <L *magus.* See MAGI.]

Ma·ge·lang (mä′gə·läng′) A town in central Java.

Ma·gel·lan (mə·jel′ən), **Fernando,** 1480–1521, Portuguese navigator in the Spanish service. —**Mag·el·lan·ic** (maj′ə·lan′ik) *adj.*

Magellan, Strait of The channel between the Atlantic and the Pacific separating the South American mainland from Tierra del Fuego.

Magellanic clouds *Astron.* Two aggregations of star clusters and nebulae near the south pole of the heavens, looking like detached fragments of the Milky Way. See under COAL-SACK.

Ma·gen·die (mȧ·zhäṅ·dē′), **François,** 1783–1855, French physician and physiologist.

ma·gen·ta (mə·jen′tə) *n.* **1** A somewhat glaring red coal-tar dyestuff derived from aniline: also called *aniline red* and *fuchsia.* **2** The color given by the pigment, a strong purplish-rose or purplish-red. [from *Magenta;* so called because discovered just after the French victory (1859)]

Ma·gen·ta (mä·jen′tä) A town in Lombardy, northern Italy; scene of a French victory over Austrian forces, 1859.

Ma·gers·fon·tein (mä′gərs·fôn·tān′) A locality of Northern Cape Province, Republic of South Africa; scene of a Boer victory in the South African War.

Mag·gio·re (mäd·jō′rā), **Lago** A lake in northern Italy and Switzerland; 65 square miles.

mag·got (mag′ət) *n.* **1** The larva of a fly; a footless insect larva; a grub. **2** A whim; fancy. [Prob. alter. of ME *maddock, mathek* <ON *mathkr* a worm]

mag·got·y (mag′ət·ē) *adj.* **1** Infested with maggots; flyblown. **2** Whimsical.

Ma·gi (mā′jī) *n. pl.* of **Ma·gus** (mā′gəs) **1** The priestly caste of the Medes and Persians. **2** Specifically, the three 'wise men' who came 'from the east' to Bethlehem to pay homage to the infant Jesus. *Matt.* ii 1. [<L, pl. of *magus* <Gk. *magos* <Persian *magu* a priest, a magician] —**Ma′gi·an** *adj.* & *n.*

Ma·gi·an·ism (mā′jē·ən·iz′əm) *n.* The creed and cult of the Magi.

mag·ic (maj′ik) *n.* **1** Any supernatural art; sorcery; necromancy. **2** Sleight of hand. **3** Any agency that works with wonderful effect. See synonyms under SORCERY. —**black magic** Any of the branches of magic which invoke the aid of demons or spirits, as witchcraft or diabolism. —**like magic** As if by magic; instantly. — *adj.* **1** Of the nature of magic; used in magic; possessing supernatural powers; sorcerous. **2** Acting like magic. [<OF *magique* <LL *magica (ars)* magic (art) <Gk. *magikē (technē)* <*magikos* of the Magi]

mag·i·cal (maj′i·kəl) *adj.* Pertaining to or produced by or as by magic. ◆ The adjective *magic* is applied more commonly to the powers, influences, or practices, while *magical* is more frequently used of the effects of magic: *magic* arts, a *magic* wand, but *magical* effect, a *magical* result. —**mag′i·cal·ly** *adv.*

ma·gi·cian (mə·jish′ən) *n.* An expert in magic arts; sorcerer; wizard.

magic lantern A device for throwing magnified pictures upon a screen in a darkened room by means of a light placed behind a lens or lenses.

ma·gilp (mə·gilp′) *n.* A mixture used as a vehicle for oil colors, usually composed of a pale drying oil and a turpentine varnish, such as mastic: also spelled *megilp.* Also **ma·gilph′** (-gilf′). [? after *McGilp,* a surname]

Ma·gi·not line (mazh′ə·nō, *Fr.* mȧ·zhē·nō′) A system of French fortifications along the German frontier, built during 1925–1935. [after André *Maginot,* 1877–1932, French statesman]

mag·is·te·ri·al (maj′is·tir′ē·əl) *adj.* **1** Of or pertaining to a magistrate or magistracy; like or befitting a master; commanding; authoritative. **2** Hence, having an air of authority; dictatorial. **3** Domineering; pompous. **4** Pertaining to a chemist's or alchemist's magistery. See synonyms under DOGMATIC. [<Med. L *magisterialis* <LL *magisterius* <L *magister* a master] —**mag′is·te′ri·al·ly** *adv.* —**mag′is·te′ri·al·ness** *n.*

mag·is·te·ri·um (maj′is·tir′ē·əm) *n.* The authority of the church to teach dogmatically: a Roman Catholic usage. [<L, the office of a master <*magister* a master]

mag·is·ter·y (maj′is·ter′ē, -tər·ē) *n. pl.* **·ter·ies 1** An authoritative statement or exposition; a magisterial decree. **2** A fundamental master principle of nature; also, a panacea. **3** In alchemy, the power to transmute metals or the product of transmutation. **4** A compound, as a precipitate, formed when two liquids are mixed, and differing in character from either: a term used by the older chemists and preserved in the phrase *magistery of bismuth.* [<Med. L *magisterium* the philosopher's stone <L. See MAGISTERIUM.]

mag·is·tra·cy (maj′is·trə·sē) *n. pl.* **·cies 1** The office or dignity of a magistrate. **2** The district under a magistrate's jurisdiction. **3** Magistrates collectively.

mag·is·tral (maj′is·trəl) *adj.* **1** Like a magistrate; imperious or pedagogical; magisterial. **2** In pharmacy, specially compounded or prescribed; not kept in stock. **3** Having sovereign power as a medicine. **4** Chief; main: the *magistral* line. —*n. Mil.* The line from which the positions of the various members of a fortification are determined: also **magistral line.** [<F <L *magistralis* <*magister* a master]

mag·is·trate (maj′is·trāt, -trit) *n.* **1** One clothed with public civil authority; an executive or judicial officer. **2** Usually, when unqualified, a minor local justice. [<L *magistratus* magisterial office <L *magister* a master]

mag·is·tra·ture (maj′is·trə·cho͝or) *n.* **1** Magistracy; government. **2** The term of a magistrate's office. **3** Magistrates collectively. [<F <*magistrat* <L *magistratus.* See MAGISTRATE.]

Mag·le·mo·si·an (mä′glə·mō′zē·ən) *adj.* Of or

relating to the special phases or aspects of the Mesolithic forest culture of northern Europe as indicated by discoveries at Maglemose, Denmark.

mag·ma (mag′mə) *n. pl.* **·ma·ta** (-mə·tə) **1** Any soft, doughy mixture of organic and mineral materials. **2** *Geol.* The molten mass from which igneous rocks are formed. **3** The residue obtained after expressing the juice from fruits. [<L <Gk. < root of *massein* knead] **— mag·mat·ic** (mag·mat′ik) *adj.*

Mag·na Car·ta (mag′nə kär′tə) **1** The Great Charter of English liberties, delivered June 19, 1215, by King John, at Runnymede, on the demand of the English barons: first document of the English constitution. **2** Any fundamental constitution that secures personal liberty and civil rights. Also **Mag′na Char′ta,** the erroneous but common form. [<Med. L, lit., Great Charter]

mag·na cum lau·de (mag′nə kum lô′dē, mäg′·nä kŏŏm lou′də) See under CUM LAUDE.

mag·na·flux test (mag′nə·fluks) A method for the detection of defects in metals and in engine parts by noting the arrangement of the particles of a magnetic powder scattered over the magnetized surface. [<MAGN(ETIC) + *-a-* + FLUX]

Magna Grae·ci·a (grē′shē·ə) See GRAECIA MAGNA. Also **Mag′na Græ′ci·a.**

mag·na·nim·i·ty (mag′nə·nim′ə·tē) *n. pl.* **·ties** **1** The quality of being magnanimous; greatness of soul; generosity in sentiment or conduct toward others; exaltation above mean or petty motives. **2** A magnanimous deed.

mag·nan·i·mous (mag·nan′ə·məs) *adj.* **1** Elevated in soul; scorning what is mean or base. **2** Dictated by magnanimity; unselfish: *magnanimous* candor. See synonyms under GENEROUS. [<L *magnanimus* < *magnus* great + *animus* mind, soul] **— mag·nan′i·mous·ly** *adv.* **— mag·nan′i·mous·ness** *n.*

mag·nate (mag′nāt) *n.* A person of rank or importance; a noble or grandee; one notable or powerful in any sphere: an industrial *magnate.* [<LL *magnas, -atis* < *magnus* great]

mag·ne·sia (mag·nē′zhə, -shə, -zē·ə) *n. Chem.* Magnesium oxide, MgO, a light, white, earthy powder, used in medicine as an antacid laxative, in glassmaking, etc. It can be made by burning magnesium or by igniting certain of the magnesium salts. **— milk of magnesia** A milk-white aqueous suspension of magnesium hydroxide, $Mg(OH)_2$: used as a laxative and antacid. [<Med. L <Gk. *Magnēsia (lithos)* (stone) of Magnesia <*Magnēsia* Magnesia (def. 2)] **— mag·ne′sian, mag·ne′sic** *adj.*

Mag·ne·sia (mag·nē′zhə, -shə) **1** An ancient city of Lydia, western Asia Minor, on the site of modern Manissa; scene of the defeat of Antiochus the Great by the two Scipios, 190 B.C. Also **Magnesia ad Si·py·lum** (ad sip′ə·lum). **2** In classical geography, the coastal district of Thessaly south of the Vale of Tempe, part of which forms a nome of modern Greece.

mag·ne·site (mag′nə·sīt) *n.* A massive, granular carbonate of magnesium, $MgCO_3$. [<MAGNES(IA) (ALBA) + -ITE[1]]

mag·ne·si·um (mag·nē′zē·əm, -zhē-, -shē-) *n.* A light, malleable, ductile, silver-white, metallic element (symbol Mg), used to produce a brilliant light by its combustion, and also as an alloy metal. It occurs abundantly in combination, as in magnesite and dolomite. See ELEMENT. [<NL, magnesia]

magnesium light A brilliant and intense light obtained by the combustion of magnesium: used in signaling, pyrotechnics, etc.

mag·net (mag′nit) *n.* **1** A lodestone. **2** Any mass of a material capable of attracting magnetic or magnetized bodies. Magnets are natural when, like lodestones, they are found already magnetized, or artificial when magnetism has been given to them by placing them in the field of another magnet or in that caused by an electric current. See ELECTROMAGNET. **3** Figuratively, a person or thing exercising a strong attraction. [<OF *magnete* <L *magnes, magnetis* <Gk. *Magnēs (lithos)* Magnesian (stone), i.e., a magnet <*Magnēsia* Magnesia (def. 2)]

mag·net·ic (mag·net′ik) *adj.* **1** Pertaining to a magnet or magnetism. **2** Able to attract or be attracted by a lodestone. **3** Capable of exerting or responding to magnetic force. **4** Pertaining to terrestrial magnetism. **5** Possessing personal attractiveness or magnetism. **—** *n.* A substance that has or may be given a magnetic field, as iron, steel, nickel, cobalt. **— mag·net′i·cal·ly** *adv.*

magnetic chart A chart indicating the variations in the earth's magnetic field for a given area.

magnetic equator An irregular, unstable line on the earth's surface, encircling it nearly midway between the magnetic poles, where a free magnetic needle has no tendency to dip; the aclinic line. It coincides nearly with the terrestrial equator. See ACLINIC.

magnetic field That region in the neighborhood of a magnet or current-carrying body in which magnetic forces are observable.

magnetic flux *Physics* The flux of magnetic intensity through a surface: expressed in maxwells or webers.

magnetic head *Electronics* A device for recording and playback by which magnetized particles on a moving tape are impressed with a pattern analogous to that of incident sound waves.

magnetic hysteresis That property of a magnetic material by virtue of which the magnetic induction depends upon the previous conditions of magnetization.

magnetic induction *Physics* The magnetic flux per unit of area at a point on a surface: expressed in gauss or in webers per square meter.

magnetic latitude Latitude as measured from the magnetic equator.

magnetic lens *Physics* An assembly of coils and electromagnets so arranged as to produce a magnetic field which will constrain a stream of charged particles to follow a prescribed path.

magnetic meridian A grid line indicating any of the horizontal components of the earth's magnetic field and which passes through the magnetic poles.

magnetic mine An underwater mine containing a sensitive device which, in the presence of any large mass of magnetic material, as a ship, senses the change in the magnetic field and actuates an electrical circuit which detonates the mine.

magnetic moment A measure of the magnetizing force exerted by a magnetized body or electric current.

magnetic needle A freely movable, needle-shaped piece of magnetized material which tends to point to the north and south (magnetic) poles of the earth.

magnetic north That direction on the earth's surface toward which one end of the magnetic needle tends to point.

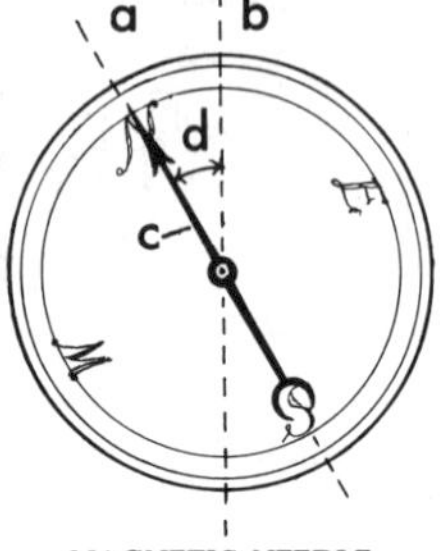

MAGNETIC NEEDLE
a. Magnetic north.
b. True north.
c. Magnetic needle.
d. Angle of variation.

magnetic pole **1** Either of the poles of a magnet; more specifically, those points on the earth's surface where the lines of magnetic force are vertical, called the **North** and **South Magnetic Poles.** These slowly change position and do not coincide with the geographical poles. **2** A pole of a magnet.

magnetic pyrites See PYRRHOTITE.

mag·net·ics (mag·net′iks) *n. pl. (construed as singular)* The science of magnetism.

magnetic signature The specific magnetic susceptibility of a material, product, or structure: said especially of the change of field in the neighborhood of ships exposed to the danger of sensitive magnetic mines.

magnetic speaker A loudspeaker.

magnetic storm A sudden disturbance of the magnetic field surrounding the earth, occurring simultaneously over areas of the earth and apparently connected with sunspots.

magnetic tape *Electronics* A thin ribbon of paper or plastic, one side of which is coated with particles of iron oxide which form magnetic patterns corresponding to the electromagnetic impulses of a tape recorder.

mag·net·ism (mag′nə·tiz′əm) *n.* **1** The specific properties of a magnet, regarded as an effect of molecular interaction. **2** The science that treats of the laws and conditions of magnetic phenomena: also *magnetics.* **3** The amount of magnetic moment in a magnetized body. **4** The sympathetic personal quality that attracts or interests. **5** Mesmerism. Compare ANIMAL MAGNETISM.

mag·net·ite (mag′nə·tīt) *n.* A massive, granular, isometric, black iron oxide, Fe_3O_4; lodestone; an important ore of iron. [<MAGNET + -ITE[1]] **— mag′net·it′ic** (-tit′ik) *adj.*

mag·net·i·za·tion (mag′nə·tə·zā′shən) *n.* The amount of magnetism in or the magnetic moment of a material.

mag·net·ize (mag′nə·tīz) *v.t.* **·ized, ·iz·ing** **1** To communicate magnetic properties to. **2** To attract by strong personal influence; captivate. **3** *Obs.* To hypnotize. Also *Brit.,* **mag′·net·ise.** **— mag′net·iz′a·bil′i·ty** *n.* **— mag′net·iz′a·ble** *adj.* **— mag′net·iz′er** *n.*

magnetizing force A vector quantity that measures the capacity of magnetized bodies or electric currents to produce magnetic induction. Symbol, H.

mag·ne·to (mag·nē′to) *n. pl.* **·tos** Any magnetoelectric machine in which the rotation of a coil of wire between the poles of a permanent magnet induces a current of electricity in the coil; especially, a type of alternator, widely used as a means of igniting the explosive mixtures used in internal-combustion engines, as in automobiles. Also **mag·ne·to·dy·na·mo** (mag·nē′tō·dī′nə·mō), **mag·ne·to·gen·er·a·tor** (mag·nē′tō·jen′ə·rā′tər). [Short for *magnetoelectric machine*]

magneto– *combining form* Magnetic; magnetism: *magnetomotive.*

mag·ne·to·chem·is·try (mag·nē′tō·kem′is·trē) *n.* The science which treats of the interrelations between magnetic and chemical phenomena. **— mag·ne′to·chem′i·cal** *adj.*

mag·ne·to·e·lec·tric·i·ty (mag·nē′tō·i·lek·tris′·ə·tē) *n.* **1** Electricity generated by the inductive action of a magnet. **2** The science that treats of the principles and phenomena of such electricity. **— mag·ne′to·e·lec′tric, mag·ne′to·e·lec′tri·cal** *adj.*

mag·ne·to·graph (mag·nē′tə·graf, -gräf) *n.* A recording magnetometer.

mag·ne·to·hy·dro·dy·nam·ic (mag·nē′tō·hī′·drō·dī·nam′ik) *adj. Physics* Of, pertaining to, or characterized by the interaction of electromagnetic, mechanical, thermal, and hydrodynamic forces, as by an electric arc in the generation of a plasma jet.

mag·ne·tol·y·sis (mag′nə·tol′ə·sis) *n.* Chemical action in a substance placed in a magnetic field: analogous to electrolysis. [<MAGNETO- + -LYSIS] **— mag·net·o·lyt·ic** (mag·net′ə·lit′ik) *adj.*

mag·ne·tom·e·ter (mag′nə·tom′ə·tər) *n.* An instrument for measuring the intensity and direction of magnetic forces. **— mag′ne·tom′·e·try** *n.*

mag·ne·to·mo·tive (mag·nē′tō·mō′tiv, mag′·nə·tō-) *adj.* **1** Acting magnetically. **2** Characterizing a force producing magnetic flux: distinguished from *electromotive.*

mag·ne·ton (mag′nə·ton) *n. Physics* A unit of magnetic moment: The Bohr magneton has the value of 9.27×10^{-21} erg $gauss^{-1}$.

mag·ne·to–op·tics (mag·nē′tō·op′tiks) *n.* The study of the behavior of light waves in a magnetic field. **— mag·ne′to–op′tic, mag·ne′to–op′ti·cal** *adj.*

mag·ne·to·scope (mag·nē′tə·skōp, -net′ə-) *n.* An instrument designed to indicate the presence of magnetic force lines without measuring them.

mag·ne·to·sphere (mag·nē′tə·sfir) *n.* A region of the atmosphere extending beyond the exosphere to about 40,000 miles and forming a continuous band of ionized particles trapped by the earth's magnetic field. Compare VAN ALLEN RADIATION.

mag·ne·to·stric·tion (mag·nē′tō·strik′shən) *n. Physics* The mechanical deformation produced in certain materials when subjected to the action of a magnetic field.

mag·ne·tron (mag′nə·tron) *n. Electronics* A vacuum tube in which the flow of electrons is subject to the control of an external magnetic field. [<MAGNET + (ELEC)TRON]

magni– *combining form* **1** Great; large: *magnirostrate,* large-beaked. **2** *Zool.* Long: *magnicaudate,* long-tailed. [<L *magnus* great]

mag·nif·ic (mag·nif′ik) *adj.* **1** Illustrious; magnificent; sumptuous. **2** Strikingly vast or dignified; imposing. **3** Of language, exalted; sublime; also, pompous; grandiloquent. Also **mag·nif′i·cal.** [<F *magnifique* <L *magnificus* <*magnus* great + *fic-*, stem of *facere* make] — **mag·nif′i·cal·ly** *adv.*

Mag·nif·i·cat (mag·nif′ə·kat) *n.* The hymn or canticle of the Virgin Mary, beginning with the word *Magnificat* in the Latin version. *Luke* i 46–55. [<L, it magnifies]

mag·ni·fi·ca·tion (mag′nə·fə·kā′shən) *n.* **1** The act, process, or degree of magnifying. **2** The state of being magnified. **3** Magnifying power. **4** The act of extolling or glorifying. [<L *magnificatio, -onis* <*magnificare* <*magnificus.* See MAGNIFIC.]

mag·nif·i·cence (mag·nif′ə·səns) *n.* **1** The state or quality of being magnificent; the exhibition of greatness of action, character, intellect, wealth, or power; brilliant or imposing appearance; display of splendor. **2** A title of courtesy in medieval Rome. [<OF <L *magnificentia* <*magnificus* noble. See MAGNIFIC.]

mag·nif·i·cent (mag·nif′ə·sənt) *adj.* **1** Grand or majestic in appearance, quality, character, or action; extremely fine or good; befitting the great, as in deeds, manners, or surroundings; great in effect, promise, or import: a *magnificent* prospect, pearl, plan, etc.; also, exalted; imposing: *magnificent* language. **2** Exhibiting magnificence; characterized by splendor: sometimes used as a title: Suleiman the *Magnificent.* See synonyms under GRAND, IMPERIAL, SUBLIME. [<OF <LL *magnificens,* var. of *magnificus.* See MAGNIFIC.] — **mag·nif′i·cent·ly** *adv.*

mag·nif·i·co (mag·nif′ə·kō) *n. pl.* **·coes 1** A noble of the Venetian republic: an old title. **2** A lordly personage; one who affects state or splendor. [<Ital. <L *magnificus.* See MAGNIFICENCE.]

mag·ni·fy (mag′nə·fī) *v.t.* **·fied, ·fy·ing 1** To increase the apparent size of, as by a microscope. **2** To increase the size of; enlarge. **3** To cause to seem greater or more important. **4** *Archaic* To extol; exalt. See synonyms under AGGRAVATE, INCREASE, PRAISE. [<OF *magnifier* <L *magnificare* <*magnificus.* See MAGNIFICENCE.] — **mag′ni·fi′a·ble** *adj.* — **mag′ni·fi′er** *n.*

mag·nil·o·quent (mag·nil′ə·kwənt) *adj.* Of bombastic, pompous style; vainglorious. [<L *magnus* great + *loquens, -entis,* ppr. of *loqui* speak] — **mag·nil′o·quence** *n.* — **mag·nil′o·quent·ly** *adv.*

Mag·ni·to·gorsk (mäg·nē′tô·gôrsk′) A city on the Ural in Russian S.F.S.R.

mag·ni·tude (mag′nə·to͞od, -tyo͞od) *n.* **1** Great size or extent; grandeur; importance. **2** *Math.* That which is conceived of as measurable. **3** The property of having size or extent. **4** *Astron.* A measure of the relative brightness of a star, ranging from one for the brightest to six for those just visible to the naked eye. The standard of reference is the polestar, with a brightness 2.512 times greater than the one next below it; magnitudes greater than one on the scale are expressed as minus quantities. Compare LIGHT RATIO. **5** Largeness in respect to relation or effect. [<L *magnitudo* <*magnus* large]

Synonyms: bigness, bulk, dimension, extent, greatness, hugeness, immensity, largeness, size, vastness. *Antonyms*: diminutiveness, littleness, pettiness, slightness, smallness.

mag·no·li·a (mag·nō′lē·ə, -nōl′yə) *n.* **1** Any of a genus *(Magnolia)* of trees or shrubs with large, fragrant, and often showy flowers. **2** The blossom of the evergreen magnolia *(M. grandiflora),* the State flower of Louisiana and of Mississippi. [<NL, genus name, after Pierre *Magnol,* 1638–1715, French botanist]

mag·no·li·a·ceous (mag·nō′lē·ā′shəs) *adj.* Of or pertaining to a family *(Magnoliaceae)* of polypetalous trees or shrubs, the magnolia family, often aromatic, with alternate, undivided, feather-veined leaves, and large, solitary, axillary or terminal flowers with calyx and corolla colored alike, in three or more rows of three each. [<NL *Magnoliaceae,* family name <*Magnolia* MAGNOLIA]

magnolia warbler The black-and-yellow warbler *(Dendroica magnolia)* of North America.

mag·num (mag′nəm) *n.* A wine bottle of twice the ordinary size, holding about two quarts; also, the quantity such a bottle will hold. [<L, neut of *magnus* great]

magnum o·pus (ō′pəs) *Latin* The chief work of an artist; a masterpiece; literally, great work.

Mag·nus effect (mag′nəs) *Physics* The deflecting effect upon the normal path of a rotating cylinder or sphere caused by the transverse forces of wind or air currents circulating around it. [after H. G. *Magnus,* 1802–70, German physicist]

mag·nus hitch (mag′nəs) A knot used to fasten a rope to a spar, etc., similar to a clove-hitch but having one more turn. [Prob. <L *magnus* large]

Ma·gog (mā′gog) See GOG AND MAGOG.

ma·got (mà·gō′) *n.* The Barbary ape. [<F, ? <*Magog* MAGOG]

Mag·ot·ty-bay bean (mag′ə·tē·bā′) A leguminous vine *(Chamaecrista fasciculata)* common on eastern American shores. [? from *Magothy* River, Maryland]

mag·pie (mag′pī) *n.* **1** A corvine bird (genus *Pica*), having a long, graduated tail. The common **European magpie** *(P. pica* or *caudata)* has iridescent black plumage with white scapulars, belly, sides, flanks, and inner web of flight feathers: often tamed and taught to speak words, and noted for its thievishness. The **American magpie** *(P. hudsonia)* is a variety of the European magpie. *P. nuttali* is the **yellow-billed magpie** of California. **2** An Australian crow shrike resembling a magpie. **3** A chatterbox; a garrulous gossip. [<*Mag,* diminutive of MARGARET, + PIE[2]]

Mag·say·say (mäg·sī′sī), **Ramón,** 1907–57, president of the Philippines 1953–57.

mag·uey (mag′wā, *Sp.* mä·gā′ē) *n.* **1** Any of various Mexican agave plants with fleshy leaves and edible cabbage-like heads, especially the century plant *(Agave americana)* and the pulque agave *(A. atrovirens).* **2** A fiber plant (genus *Furcraea)* related to the agave. **3** The fiber of these plants. [<Sp., prob. <Taino]

MAGUEY
(Leaves up to 6 feet long; 8 to 10 inches broad)

Ma·gus (mā′gəs) Singular of MAGI.

Mag·yar (mag′yär, *Hungarian* mud′yär) *n.* **1** One of a people who invaded and conquered Hungary at the end of the ninth century; a Hungarian. **2** The Finno-Ugric language of Hungary. — *adj.* Of or pertaining to the Magyars or their language.

Mag·yar·or·szág (mud′yär·ôr′säg) The Hungarian name for HUNGARY.

Ma·ha·bha·ra·ta (mə·hä′bä′rə·tə) An ancient Hindu epic, written in Sanskrit and thought to date from 300 B.C., recounting the dynastic wars of two related families over a kingdom in northern India. This large work, probably the longest in the world, and the *Râmâyana* are the two great epics of ancient India. Also **Ma·ha′bha′ra·tam.** [<Skt. *Mahābhārata,* lit., the great story]

ma·hal·a (mə·hal′ə) *n.* In the western United States and Canada, an Indian squaw. [<N. Am. Ind. *muk'ela*]

Ma·hal·la el Ku·bra (mə·hal′ə el ko͞o′brə) A city in the Nile delta. Also **Ma·hal′la.**

Ma·han (mə·han′), **Alfred Thayer,** 1840–1914, U. S. admiral and naval historian.

Ma·ha·na·di (mə·hä′nə·dē) A river in eastern India, flowing 512 miles to the Bay of Bengal.

ma·ha·ra·ja (mä′hə·rä′jə, *Hind.* mə·hä′rä′jə) *n.* **1** A great Hindu prince; the title of some native rulers. **2** A prominent religious teacher of the Hindus. Also **ma′ha·ra′jah.** [<Hind. <Skt. *mahārāja* <*maha* great + *rājā* a king]

ma·ha·ra·ni (mä′hə·rä′nē, *Hind.* mə·hä′rä′nē) *n.* A Hindu princess; the wife of a maharaja. Also **ma′ha·ra′nee.** [<Hind. <*maha* great + *rānī* a queen]

ma·hat·ma (mə·hat′mə, -hät′-) *n.* In theosophy or esoteric Buddhism, an adept of the highest order; literally, great-souled one: a title of respect. [<Skt. *mahātman* <*maha* great + *ātman* soul] — **ma·hat′ma·ism** *n.*

Mah·di (mä′dē) *n.* The Moslem messiah, or one claiming the title; specifically, Mohammed Ahmed, 1843–85, who led a revolt in the Sudan, 1883. [<Arabic *mahdīy,* lit., he who is guided aright, pp. of *hadā* lead rightly] — **Mah′dism** *n.* — **Mah′dist** *adj.* & *n.*

Ma·hé (mä·hā′) A free city and former French settlement in SW Madras, India, on the Arabian Sea; 23 square miles.

Mahé Island The principal island in the Seychelles group in the western Indian Ocean; 56 square miles.

Ma·hi·can (mə·hē′kən) *n.* One of a tribe of North American Indians of Algonquian linguistic stock formerly occupying the territory from the Hudson River to Lake Champlain; later, one of an Algonquian tribe between the Hudson River and Narragansett Bay, dialectally divided into the *Mohegans* of the Thames and lower Connecticut rivers, and the *Mohicans,* occupying both banks of the Hudson. [<Algonquian, lit., a wolf]

mah jong (mä′jong′, jông′) A game of Chinese origin, usually for four persons, played with 144 tiles marked in suits, dice, and counters. Also **mah jongg.** [<dial. Chinese <Chinese *ma ch'iao,* lit., a house sparrow; from the design on one of the tiles]

Mah·ler (mä′lər), **Gustav,** 1860–1911, Austrian composer and conductor.

mahl·stick (mäl′stik′, môl′-) *n.* A staff with a ball at one end, used by painters to steady the hand while using the brush. Also spelled *maulstick.* [<Du. *maalstok* <*malen* paint + *stok* a stick]

Mah·moud (mä·mo͞od′, mä′mo͞od) Persian form of MOHAMMED. Also **Mah·mud′.**
— **Mahmoud II,** 1785–1839, sultan of Turkey; defeated (1829) in Greek war for independence.

ma·hog·a·ny (mə·hog′ə·nē) *n.* **1** A large tropical American tree (genus *Swietenia*), with fine-grained, hard, reddish wood much used for cabinetwork. **2** The wood itself. **3** One of various trees yielding a similar wood, as African mahogany *(Khaya ivorensis)*; also its wood. **4** Acajou. **5** Any of the various shades of brownish-red or reddish-brown of the finished wood. — *adj.* **1** Of or pertaining to, or consisting of mahogany. **2** Of a mahogany color. [<obs. Sp. *mahogani.* prob. <Arawakan]

Ma·hom·et (mə·hom′it) See MOHAMMED.

Ma·hom·e·tan (mə·hom′ə·tən), etc. See MOHAMMEDAN, etc.

Ma·hón (mə·hōn′, *Sp.* mä·ōn′) The chief city and port of Minorca, Balearic Islands: formerly *Port Mahón.*

Ma·hound (mə·hound′, -ho͞ond′) *n.* **1** The prophet Mohammed. **2** *Scot.* Satan; an evil spirit. [<OF *Mahon, Mahum* <*Mahomet* Mohammed]

ma·hout (mə·hout′) *n.* The keeper and driver of an elephant. [<Hind. *mahāut, mahāvat* <Skt. *mahāmātra,* lit., great in measure]

Mah·rat·i (mə·rat′ē) See MARATHI.

Mah·rat·ta (mə·rat′ə) *n.* One of a Hindu people of SW and central India. Also spelled *Maratha.* [<Hind. *Marhaṭa* <Marathi *Maraṭhi* <Skt. *Mahārāṣṭra,* lit., great country]

Mäh·ren (mā′rən) The German name for MORAVIA.

Mäh·risch-Os·trau (mā′rish·ôs′trou) The German name for MORAVSKÁ OSTRAVA.

ma huang (mä hwäng′) A Chinese species of joint fir. [<Chinese]

Mai·a (mā′yə, mī′ə) **1** In Greek mythology, the eldest of the Pleiades, mother by Zeus of Hermes. **2** In Roman mythology, a goddess of growth and spring: identified with the Greek *Maia* and the *Bona Dea.* Also **Maia Ma·jes·ta** (mə·jes′tə).

maid (mād) *n.* **1** Any unmarried woman; virgin; girl; lass. **2** A female servant: also **maidservant.** [Short for MAIDEN]

mai·dan (mī·dän′) *n.* In Persia and India, a public plaza or parade ground; hence, an open space. [<Persian *maidān*]

Mai·da·nek (mī′də·nek) During World War II,

a Nazi concentration and extermination camp near Lublin, Poland.

maid•en (mād'n) *n.* **1** An unmarried woman, especially if young; a maid; virgin. **2** Something untried or unused, as a race horse that has never won an event. **3** A rude kind of beheading machine used in Scotland in the 16th and 17th centuries. —*adj.* **1** Pertaining to or suitable for a maiden. **2** Virgin; unmarried. **3** Initiatory; unused; untried. **4** Of or pertaining to the first use or experience: a *maiden* voyage. **5** Pure; sinless. [OE *mægden,* prob. dim. of *mægeth* a virgin] —**maid'en•li•ness** *n.* —**maid'en•ly** *adj. & adv.*

maid•en•hair (mād'n•hâr') *n.* A very delicate and graceful fern (genus *Adiantum*) with an erect black stem, common in damp, rocky woods. Also **maidenhair fern.**

maidenhair tree The ginkgo.

maid•en•head (mād'n•hed') *n.* **1** The hymen. **2** Maidenhood; virginity.

maid•en•hood (mād'n•ho͝od) *n.* The state of being a maiden; freshness; purity; virginity. Also **maid'hood.**

maiden name A woman's surname before marriage.

Maid Marian **1** The sweetheart and companion of Robin Hood. **2** A character in morris dances and other ancient sports: at first a May queen, later a grotesque buffoon, often impersonated by a boy.

maid of honor **1** An unmarried lady attendant upon an empress, queen, or princess: usually of noble birth. **2** The chief unmarried attendant of a bride at a wedding ceremony.

maid•ser•vant (mād'sûr'vənt) *n.* A female servant.

Maid•stone (mād'stən, -stōn) The county town of Kent, England.

Mai•du•gu•ri (mī•do͞o'go͝or•ē) A city in NE Nigeria, capital of Bornu province.

ma•ieu•tic (mā•yo͞o'tik) *adj.* Helping to bring forth ideas and truths from the mind of a pupil by a series of pertinent questions: said of the Socratic method. Also **ma•ieu'ti•cal.** [< Gk. *maieutikos,* lit., obstetric <*maieuesthai* act as a midwife <*maia* a midwife]

mai•gre (mā'gər) *adj.* Not consisting of flesh or its juices: said of dishes used by Roman Catholics on days of abstinence; hence, of or appropriate for a fast. —*n.* A large marine food fish, the European *Sciaena aquila.* [<OF. See MEAGER.]

mai•hem (mā'hem) See MAYHEM.

Mai•kop (mī'kôp) A city in the NW Caucasus mountains, Russian S.F.S.R. Also **May'kop.**

mail[1] (māl) *n.* **1** The governmental system for handling letters, etc., by post. **2** Letters, magazines and other printed matter, parcels, etc., consigned and sent from place to place under a governmental post-office system. **3** The collection or delivery of postal matter at a specified time: My letter missed the *mail.* **4** Letters, papers, etc., received by, or for, a person: Your *mail* is on the table. **5** A conveyance, as a train, plane, etc., for carrying postal matter. —*adj.* Pertaining to or used in the process of conveying or handling mail. —*v.t.* To send by mail, as letters; deposit in a mailbox or at a post office; post. ◆ Homophone: *male.* [<OF *male* <OHG *malha* a wallet] —**mail'a•ble** *adj.*

mail[2] (māl) *n.* **1** Armor of chains, rings, or scales: often called **chain mail. 2** Any strong covering or defense, as the shell of a turtle. —**coat of mail** A hauberk. —*v.t.* To cover with or as with mail. ◆ Homophone: *male.* [<OF *maille* <L *macula* spot, mesh of a net]

CHAIN MAIL ARMOR

mail[3] (māl) *n. Scot. & Brit. Dial.* That which is paid; rent; wages. Also **maill.** ◆ Homophone: *male.* [OE *māl* <ON, speech, agreement; infl. in sense by ON *māle* contract, stipend]

mail•bag (māl'bag') *n.* A bag or pack in which mail is transported.

mail•box (māl'boks') *n.* **1** A box in which letters, etc., are posted for collection. **2** A box into which private mail is put when delivered. Also **mail box.**

mail car A railroad car for carrying mail.

mail•catch•er (māl'kach'ər) *n.* A mechanical device for transferring mailbags to or from a moving train.

mailed (māld) *adj.* **1** Covered or armed with mail. **2** *Zool.* Having a defensive armor, as scales. [<MAIL[2]]

mailed fist Menace of attack or violence; especially, menace of aggressive war.

mail•er (mā'lər) *n.* **1** A mail boat. **2** An addressing machine: also **mailing machine. 3** One who mails a letter.

mail•gram (māl'gram') *n. U.S.* A message transmitted electronically between place of origin and destination, converted to written form, and delivered in the next scheduled distribution of mail. [<MAIL + (TELE)GRAM]

mail•ing (mā'ling) *n.* **1** The act of sending mail. **2** The mail sent at one time. **3** *Scot.* A rented piece of ground; farm; homestead: also **mail'en.**

mailing list A list of names, as of individuals, organizations, etc., to which advertising circulars, announcements, solicitations, and the like, are sent.

Mail•lol (mȧ•yôl'), **Aristide,** 1861–1944, French sculptor.

mail•lot (mī•yō') *n.* A tightly fitting garment which covers the torso, used by dancers, acrobats, and swimmers. [<F, dim. of *maille* knitted material, lit., mail[2]]

mail•man (māl'man', -mən) *n. pl.* **•men** (-men', -mən) A letter-carrier; postman.

mail order An order for goods, sent and filled through the agency of the mail. —**mail-or•der** (ôr'dər) *adj.*

mail train **1** A railway train that carries mail. **2** A train of wagons that formerly carried mail in the western United States.

maim (mām) *v.t.* To deprive of the use of a bodily part; mutilate; disable. —*n. Rare* A crippling; mutilation; maiming. See MAYHEM. [<OF *mahaigner, mayner;* ult. origin uncertain] —**maim'er** *n.*

Mai•mon•ides (mī•mon'ə•dēz), 1135–1204, Spanish rabbi, theologian, and philosopher: also called *Moses ben Maimon.*

main[1] (mān) *n.* **1** A chief conduit or conductor, as for conveying gas, water, etc. **2** The mainland. **3** *Poetic* The ocean. **4** Violent effort; strength: chiefly in the phrase *with might and main.* **5** The chief part; the most important point. —**in** (or **for**) **the main** For the most part; on the whole. —*adj.* **1** First or chief in size, rank, importance, strength, extent, etc.; principal; chief; leading: the *main* building, the *main* line of a railroad, with which branch lines connect. **2** undivided; unqualified; full: by *main* force. **3** Designating any broad extent or expanse, as of land or sea. **4** *Naut.* Near or connected with the mainsail or mainmast. **5** *Brit. Dial.* Considerable; remarkable. **6** *Obs.* Vast; mighty; powerful. —*adv. Brit. Dial.* Very; greatly; extremely. ◆ Homophone: *mane.* [OE *mægen*] —**main'ly** *adv.*

main[2] (mān) *n.* **1** A match of several battles at cockfighting. **2** A hand or throw of dice; also, a number selected by the caster before he throws the dice in games of hazard and craps. ◆ Homophone: *mane.* [? <MAIN[1], as in *main chance*]

main[3] (mān) *Scot. v.i.* To moan. —*n.* A moan. ◆ Homophone: *mane.*

Main (mān, *Ger.* mīn) A river in western Germany, flowing 305 miles west to the Rhine.

main deck *Naut.* The chief deck of a vessel; on a warship, the topmost deck stretching from stem to stern; on a merchantman, the deck between and below the poop and forecastle decks.

main drag *U.S. Slang* The principal street or section of a city.

Maine (mān), **Sir Henry James,** 1822–88, English jurist.

Maine (mān) **1** A State of the NE United States bordering on Canada and the Atlantic; 32,562 square miles; capital, Augusta; entered the Union March 15, 1820; nickname, *Pine-Tree State:* abbr. ME **2** An ancient province of western France.

Maine (mān) A U.S. battleship, blown up in Havana harbor, Feb. 15, 1898, with the loss of 260 lives: one of the events precipitating the Spanish-American War.

Main•fran•ken (mīn'fräng'kən) The former name of Lower Franconia, 1938–45.

main•land (mān'land', -lənd) *n.* A principal body of land; a continent, as distinguished from an island. —**main'land'er** *n.*

Main•land (mān'lənd) **1** Pomona Island. **2** The largest of the Shetland Islands, Scotland; 406 square miles.

main•line (mān'līn') *n.* A main road, railroad line, etc. —*v.t. & v.i.* **•lined, •lin•ing** *Slang* To inject (a narcotic drug, especially heroin) directly into a vein. —**main'lin'er** *n.*

Main Line A traditionally wealthy and fashionable residential district outside of Philadelphia.

main•mast (mān'məst, -mast', -mäst') *n. Naut.* The principal mast of a vessel: ordinarily, the second mast from the bow.

main•sail (mān'səl, -sāl') *n. Naut.* A sail bent to the main yard, or one carried on the mainmast: in a square-rigged vessel, called the **main course.**

main sequence *Astron.* The area of the Hertzsprung-Russell diagram that includes the sun and the majority of stars.

main•sheet (mān'shēt') *n. Naut.* The sheet by which the mainsail is trimmed and set.

main•spring (mān'spring') *n.* **1** The principal spring of a mechanism, as of a watch. **2** The most efficient cause or motive.

main•stay (mān'stā') *n.* **1** *Naut.* The rope from the mainmast head forward, used to steady the mast in that direction. **2** A chief support or dependence.

main•stream (mān'strēm') *n.* The main or middle course or direction: in the *mainstream* of American political thought.

Main Street The principal business street of a small town: a symbol of its manners, customs, culture, typical thinking, etc.

main•tain (mān•tān') *v.t.* **1** To carry on or continue; engage in, as a correspondence. **2** To keep unimpaired or in proper condition: to *maintain* roads; to *maintain* a reputation. **3** To supply with food or livelihood; support; pay for. **4** To uphold; claim to be true. **5** To assert or state; affirm. **6** To hold or defend, as against attack. See synonyms under AFFIRM, ALLEGE, ASSERT, JUSTIFY, KEEP, PRESERVE, RETAIN, SUPPORT. [<OF *maintenir* < L *manu tenere,* lit., hold in one's hand < *manu,* ablative of *manus* hand + *tenere* hold]

main•te•nance (mān'tə•nəns) *n.* **1** The act of maintaining. **2** Means of support. **3** *Law* The officious intermeddling in a suit, by assisting or maintaining either party, with money or otherwise. [<OF *maintenance* < *maintenir* MAINTAIN]

Main•te•non (maṅt•nôṅ'), **Marquise de,** 1635–1719, Françoise d'Aubigné; second wife of Louis XIV of France.

main•top (mān'top') *n. Naut.* A platform at the head of the lower section of the mainmast.

main•top•gal•lant•mast (mān'tə•gal'ənt•məst, mast', -mäst', -top-) *n. Naut.* On a square-rigged vessel, the mast next above the mainmast.

main•top•mast (mān'top'məst) *n. Naut.* **1** On a square-rigged vessel, the mast next above the maintopgallantmast. **2** On a fore-and-aft-rigged ship, the mast next above the mainmast.

main yard *Naut.* The lower yard on the mainmast.

Mainz (mīnts) A city on the Rhine, capital of Rhineland-Palatinate, West Germany: French *Mayence.*

ma•iol•i•ca (mä•yol'ē•kä) See MAJOLICA.

mai•o•sis (mī•ō'sis) See MEIOSIS (def. 1).

mair (mâr) *adj. & n. Scot.* More.

maist (māst) *adj., n., & adv. Scot.* Most.

mais•ter (mās'tər) *n. Scot.* Master.

Mai•sur (mī•so͝or') See MYSORE.

Mait•land (māt'lənd), **Frederic William,** 1850–1906, English jurist and historian.

maî•tre (me'tr') *n. French* Master.

maî•tre d' (mā'trə dē') *pl.* **maî•tre d's** (dēz) A headwaiter. [Short for MAÎTRE D'HOTEL]

maître d'hô•tel (dō•tel') *French* **1** The proprietor or manager of a hotel. **2** A headwaiter; steward. **3** A sauce of melted butter, parsley, and lemon juice or vinegar.

maize (māz) *n.* **1** A tall, stout food and forage plant *(Zea mays).* **2** Its grain; Indian corn. **3** A light, soft shade of yellow; any of the various yellow tints of ripe corn. ◆ Homophone: *maze.* [<Sp. *maíz* <Taino *mahiz*]

maize•bird (māz'bûrd') *n.* A bird that feeds on Indian corn, as the red-winged blackbird.

ma·jes·tic (mə·jes′tik) *adj.* Having or exhibiting majesty; stately; royal, august. Also **ma·jes′ti·cal.** See synonyms under AWFUL, GRAND, IMPERIAL, KINGLY, SUBLIME. —**ma·jes′ti·cal·ly** *adv.* —**ma·jes′ti·cal·ness** *n.*

maj·es·ty (maj′is·tē) *n. pl.* **·ties** Exalted dignity; stateliness; grandeur; especially, **His, Her,** or **Your Majesty,** a title given to monarchs. [<OF *majesté* <L *majestas, -tatis* (related to *majus,* neut. compar. of *magnus* great)]

ma·jol·i·ca (mə·jol′i·kə, -yol′-) *n.* A kind of Italian pottery, glazed and decorated, usually in rich colors and Renaissance designs; any glazed Italian pottery; faience. Also spelled *maiolica.* [<Ital. *maiolica,* prob. < *Majolica,* early name of MAJORCA, where formerly made]

ma·jor (mā′jər) *adj.* **1** Greater in number, quantity, or extent. **2** Greater in dignity or importance; of primary consideration; principal; leading. **3** *Music* **a** Designating a chord or interval greater by a half-step than the preceding minor. **b** Containing a major third, sixth, and seventh. See INTERVAL. **4** *Logic* Designating the first premise of a syllogism, or the premise containing the first proposition. **5** *Law* Being of legal age. —*n.* **1** An officer in the U. S. Army, Air Force, or Marine Corps ranking next above a captain and next below a lieutenant colonel. **2** *Law* One who is of legal age. **3** *Music* A major key, chord, or interval. **4** *U. S.* The specialized course of study in a definite field which a college or university student follows to obtain his degree. **5** *U. S.* A student who follows a (specified) course of study: an English *major.* —*v.i.* To pursue a definite field of study: with *in*: to *major* in history. [<L, compar. of *magnus* great. Doublet of MAYOR.]

Ma·jor·ca (mə·jôr′kə) The largest of the Balearic Islands; 1,352 square miles; capital, Palma: Spanish *Mallorca.* —**Ma·jor′can** *adj.* & *n.*

ma·jor·do·mo (mā′jər·dō′mō) *n. pl.* **·mos** **1** The chief steward of a royal household. **2** A butler. **3** *SW U.S.* The overseer of a ranch. [<Sp. *mayordomo* <Med. L *major domus* chief of a house < *major* an elder (<L, greater) + *domus* a house]

major general See under GENERAL.

ma·jor·i·ty (mə·jôr′ə·tē, -jor′-) *n. pl.* **·ties** **1** More than half of a given number or group; the greater part. **2** The amount or number by which one group of things exceeds another group; excess. **3** The age at which the laws of a country permit a person to manage his or her own affairs: in most States of the United States, the age of 21 years. **4** The rank or commission of a major. **5** In U. S. politics, more than half of the people; more than half of the votes cast. **6** The number of votes cast for a candidate over and above the number cast for his nearest opponent; a plurality. **7** The party having the most power in a legislature. [<MF *majorité* <L *majoritas, -tatis* < *major.* See MAJOR.]

major key *Music* A key based on the tones of a major scale, the intervals being a half-step larger than minor intervals.

major league In baseball, either of the two main groups of professional teams in the United States. —**ma′jor–league′** *adj.*

major mode See under MODE.

major scale See under SCALE.

major suit In bridge, either of the sets of spades and hearts: so called from their higher point value.

major term See under TERM.

ma·jus·cule (mə·jus′kyōōl) *n.* A capital letter; especially, a large initial letter, as in old manuscripts. [<F <L *majuscula (littera),* fem. of *majusculus* somewhat larger, dim. of *major.* See MAJOR.] —**ma·jus′cu·lar** *adj.*

MAJUSCULE

mak (mak) *v.t.* & *v.i. Scot.* To make.

Ma·kas·sar (mə·kas′ər) See MACASSAR.

Ma·ka·te·a (mä′kä·tā′ə) An island dependency of Tahiti in the Society Islands.

make[1] (māk) *v.* **made, mak·ing** *v.t.* **1** To bring about the existence of by the shaping or combining of materials; produce; build; construct; fashion. **2** To bring about; cause: Don't *make* trouble. **3** To bring to some state or condition; cause to be: The wind *made* him cold. **4** To appoint or assign; elect: They *made* him captain. **5** To form or create in the mind, as a plan. **6** To compose or create, as a poem or piece of music. **7** To understand or infer to be the meaning or significance; interpret; think: What do you *make* of it? **8** To put forward; advance: to *make* an offer. **9** To present, as for record; utter or express: to *make* a declaration. **10** To obtain for oneself; earn; accumulate: to *make* a fortune. **11** To amount to; add up to: Four quarts *make* a gallon. **12** To bring the total to: That *makes* five attempts. **13** To develop into; become: He *made* a good soldier. **14** To accomplish; effect or form: to *make* an agreement. **15** To estimate to be; reckon: He *made* the height twenty feet. **16** To induce or force; compel: He *made* me do it! **17** To draw up, enact, or frame, as laws, testaments, etc. **18** To prepare for use, as a bed. **19** To afford or provide: This brandy *makes* good drinking. **20** To be the essential element or determinant of: Stone walls do not a prison *make.* **21** To cause the success of: His speech *made* him politically. **22** To traverse; cover: to *make* fifty miles before noon. **23** To travel at the rate of: to *make* fifty miles per hour. **24** To arrive at; reach: to *make* Boston. **25** To board before departure: to *make* a train. **26** To earn so as to count on a score: to *make* a touchdown. **27** *Electr.* To complete (a circuit). **28** *Colloq.* To win a place on: to *make* the team. **29** In card games: **a** To declare as trump. **b** To capture a trick with (a card). **c** To shuffle: to *make* the deck. **30** In bridge, to win (a bid). **31** *U. S. Slang.* To seduce. —*v.i.* **32** To cause something to assume a specified condition: to *make* ready; to *make* fast. **33** To act or behave in a certain manner: to *make* merry. **34** To start: They *made* to go. **35** To go or extend in some direction: with *to* or *toward.* **36** To flow, as the tide; rise, as water. —**to make as if** (or **as though**) To pretend. —**to make away with** **1** To carry off; steal. **2** To get rid of; destroy. —**to make believe** To pretend. —**to make do** To get along with what is available, especially with an inferior substitute. —**to make for** **1** To go toward. **2** To attack; assail. **3** To have effect on; contribute to. —**to make heavy weather** *Naut.* To roll and pitch, as a ship in a storm. —**to make it** To succeed in doing something. —**to make off** To leave suddenly; run away. —**to make off with** To steal. —**to make out** **1** To see; discern. **2** To comprehend; understand. **3** To establish by evidence. **4** To fill out; draw up, as a bank draft. **5** To be successful; manage. —**to make over** **1** To put into new form; renovate. **2** To transfer title or possession of. —**to make up** **1** To compose; compound, as a prescription. **2** To be the parts of; comprise: These elements *make up* the structure. **3** To settle differences and become friendly again: to kiss and *make up.* **4** To devise; invent; fabricate: to *make up* an answer. **5** To supply what is lacking in. **6** To compensate for; atone for. **7** To settle; decide: to *make up* one's mind. **8** *Printing* To arrange, as lines, into columns or pages. **9** To put cosmetics on (the face). **10** In education, to repeat (an examination or course one has failed), or take (an examination) one has missed. —**to make up to** *Colloq.* To make a show of friendliness and affection toward; flatter. —*n.* **1** The manner in which parts or qualities are grouped to constitute a whole; constitution; structure; shape. **2** The operation or product of manufacture; brand: a new *make* of automobile. **3** The amount produced; yield. **4** The closing or completion of an electrical circuit. **5** A declaration (def. 3). —**on the make** *Slang* **1** Greedy for profit; interested only in making money. **2** Eager for amorous conquest. [OE *macian*]

Synonyms (verb): become, cause, compel, compose, constitute, constrain, construct, create, do, effect, establish, execute, fabricate, fashion, force, frame, get, manufacture, occasion, perform, reach, require, shape. *Make* is essentially causative; to the idea of cause all its various senses may be traced (compare synonyms for CAUSE *noun*). To *make* is to *cause* to exist, or to *cause* to exist in a certain form or in certain relations; it thus includes the idea of *create. Make* includes also the idea of *compose, constitute*; as, The parts *make* up the whole. Similarly, to *cause* a voluntary agent to do a certain act is to *make* him do it, or *compel* him to do it, *compel* fixing the attention more on the process, *make* on the accomplished fact. See COMPEL, GET, PRODUCE, REACH. *Antonyms*: see synonyms for ABOLISH, BREAK, DEMOLISH.

make[2] (māk) *n. Obs.* A mate. [OE *gemaca*]

make–and–break (māk′ənd·brāk′) *n. Electr.* A device for making and breaking an electrical circuit.

make–be·lieve (māk′bi·lēv′) *adj.* Pretended; unreal. —*n.* A mere pretense; sham. Also **make′–be·lief′** (-lēf′).

make–fast (māk′fast′, -fäst′) *n. Naut.* An iron ring or other object to which a boat is made fast.

make·less (māk′lis) *adj. Obs.* **1** Without a mate. **2** Matchless. [<MAKE[2] + -LESS]

make·peace (māk′pēs′) *n.* A peacemaker.

mak·er (mā′kər) *n.* **1** One who makes. **2** A manufacturer. **3** *Law* One who signs a promissory note. **4** *Archaic* A poet.

Mak·er (mā′kər) *n.* God, as the creator of the universe.

-maker *combining form* One who or that which produces: *glassmaker.* [<MAKE]

make–read·y (māk′red′ē) *n. Printing* The operation of leveling up and adjusting a type form on a press so that all parts of it will give a clear, clean, and uniform impression when printed.

make·shift (māk′shift′) *adj.* Having the character of or being a temporary resource: also **make′shift′y.** —*n.* Something adopted as a temporary contrivance in any emergency.

make–up (māk′up′) *n.* **1** The arrangement or combination of the parts of which anything is composed; an aggregate of qualities. **2** *Printing* The arrangement of composed type in pages, columns, or forms, as in imposition. **3** The costumes, wigs, cosmetics, etc., used to assume a theatrical role; also, the art of applying or assuming them. **4** Lipstick, powder, rouge, etc., applied to a woman's face.

make·weight (māk′wāt′) *n.* **1** That which is thrown into a scale to increase weight. **2** Any person or thing made use of to fill up a deficiency.

Ma·ke·yev·ka A city in the Donbas, eastern Ukraine.

Ma·khach·ka·la A port on the Caspian Sea, capital of Dagestan in Russia.

Ma·kin (mā′kin, mug′in) See BUTARITARI.

mak·ing (mā′king) *n.* **1** The act of causing, fashioning, or constructing; workmanship. **2** That which contributes to improvement or success: He has the *making* of a fine character. **3** A quantity of anything made at one time; batch. **4** *Often pl.* The materials or ingredients required to make something. **5** Composition; structure; make.

-making *combining form* Act of causing or producing; creating or causing to be: *paper-making.* [<MAKE]

mal– *prefix* Bad; ill; evil; wrong; defective; imperfect; uneven: signifying also simple negation, and forming words directly from Latin and mediately through French: opposed to *bene–, eu–.* [<F *mal-* <L *male-* < *malus* bad]

Many words containing the prefix *mal–* are self-explaining, the prefix simply adding the meaning defective or evil:

maladaptation	**malconstruction**
maladjustment	**malexecution**
maladminister	**malinfluence**
malconformation	**malnutrition**

Mal·a·bar (mal′ə·bär) A district of SW India extending 450 miles NW from Cape Comorin to the Madras–Bombay border. Also **Malabar Coast.**

Ma·lac·ca (mə·lak′ə) A port on the Strait of Malacca and the capital of the **Settlement of**

Malacca, a State of Malaya, formerly under British protection; 633 square miles. *Malay* **Ma·lak′a.**

Malacca, Strait of A channel between the Malay Peninsula and Sumatra connecting the Andaman Sea and the South China Sea.

Malacca cane A walking stick made from the wood of an Asian rattan palm *(Calamus rotang).* [from *Malacca*]

ma·la·ceous (mə·lā′shəs) *adj.* Designating a family *(Malaceae)* of trees, including the apple, pear, quince, etc. See POMACEOUS. [<NL, family name <L *malum* an apple <Gk. *mēlon*]

Mal·a·chi (mal′ə·kī) A masculine personal name. [<Hebrew *malākhī,* lit., my messenger] —**Malachi** A minor Hebrew prophet of the fifth century B.C.; also, the book containing his prophecies.

mal·a·chite (mal′ə·kīt) *n.* A green basic cupric carbonate, $CuCO_3 \cdot Cu(OH)_2$, found usually massive, rarely in crystals, and sometimes as an incrustation. It is one of the ores of copper. [<OF *melochite,* ult. <L *malache* a mallow <Gk. *malachē;* so called because resembling mallow leaves in color]

malachite green A pigment made of malachite, having an intense bluish–green color. Compare BICE GREEN.

malaco– *combining form* Soft; mucilaginous: *malacopterous.* Also, before vowels, **malac–.** [<Gk. *malakos* soft]

mal·a·coid (mal′ə·koid) *adj.* Having a soft texture.[<MALAC(O)- + -OID]

mal·a·col·o·gy (mal′ə·kol′ə·jē) *n.* The branch of zoology that treats of mollusks. [MALACO- + -LOGY]

mal·a·cop·ter·ous (mal′ə·kop′tər·əs) *adj.* Having soft fins, as certain fishes. [<MALACO- + -PTEROUS]

mal·a·cos·tra·can (mal′·ə·kos′trə·kən) *n.* Any of a division or subclass *(Malacostraca)* of crustaceans, embracing crabs, lobsters, crayfish, etc. —*adj.* Of or pertaining to the *Malacostraca:* also **mal′a·cos′tra·cous.** [<NL *Malacostraca,* subclass name <Gk. *malakostrakos* soft–shelled <*malakos* soft + *ostrakon* a shell]

mal·ad·dress (mal′ə·dres′) *n.* Awkwardness or rudeness in speech or manner; lack of politeness or tact. [<F *maladresse* <*maladroit* MALADROIT]

mal·ad·just·ed (mal′ə·jus′tid) *adj.* **1** Imperfectly adjusted. **2** *Psychol.* Poorly adapted to one's environment through conflict between personal desires and external circumstances. —**mal′ad·just′ment** *n.*

mal·ad·min·is·ter (mal′əd·min′is·tər) *v.t.* To administer badly or dishonestly.

mal·ad·min·is·tra·tion (mal′əd·min′is·trā′shən) *n.* Bad management, as of public affairs.

mal·a·droit (mal′ə·droit′) *adj.* Clumsy or blundering. See synonyms under AWKWARD. [<F <*mal-* MAL- +*adroit* clever] —**mal′a·droit′ly** *adv.* —**mal′a·droit′ness** *n.*

mal·a·dy (mal′ə·dē) *n. pl.* **·dies 1** A disease, especially when chronic or deep–seated; sickness; illness. **2** Any disordered condition. See synonyms under DISEASE. [<OF *maladie* <LL *male habitus* <L *male* ill + *habitus,* pp. of *habere* have]

ma·la fi·de (mā′lə fī′dē) *Latin* In bad faith.

Mal·a·ga (mal′ə·gə) *n.* **1** A rich, sweet white wine made in Málaga, Spain. **2** A white, sweet grape of the muscat variety, grown in Spain and California.

Mál·a·ga (mal′ə·gə, *Sp.* mä′lä·gä) A port on the Mediterranean in Andalusia, southern Spain.

Mal·a·gas·y (mal′ə·gas′ē) *adj.* Of or pertaining to Madagascar, its inhabitants, or their language. —*n.* **1** A native of Madagascar. **2** The Indonesian language of Madagascar.

Malagasy Republic The former name of Madagascar (1958–1974); comprising the island of Madagascar; 227,602 square miles; capital, Tananarive.

ESKIMO MALAMUTE (From 22 to 25 inches high at the shoulder)

mal·aise (mal·āz′, *Fr.* má·lez′) *n.* Uneasiness; indisposition. [<F <*mal* ill + *aise* EASE]

Ma·lai·ta (mə·lā′tə) One of the British Solomon Islands; 2,500 miles.

ma·la·mute (mä′lə·myōōt, mal′ə-) *n.* A large sled dog of Alaska, having a compact body, a thick, long coat, usually gray or black–and–white, a broad head, straight, big–boned forelegs, and well–cushioned feet. Also spelled *malemute, malemiut.* [Orig., name of an Innuit tribe, alter. of Eskimo (Malamute) *Mahlemut* <*Mahle,* the tribe's name +*mut* a village]

Ma·lan (mə·län′), **Daniel François,** 1874–1959, South African prime minister 1948–54.

mal·an·ders (mal′ən·dərz) *n. pl.* A scaly disease on the hock and at the bend of the knee of the foreleg of a horse: also spelled *mallenders.* Compare SALLENDERS. [<OF *malandre* a sore in a horse's knee <L *malandria*]

Ma·lang (mä·läng′) A city in eastern Java.

mal·a·pert (mal′ə·pûrt) *adj.* Bold or forward; impudent; saucy. —*n.* A saucy person. [<OF <*mal-* MAL-+ *apert, espert* clever, able <L *expertus.* See EXPERT.] —**mal′a·pert′ly** *adv.* —**mal′a·pert′ness** *n.*

mal·ap·por·tion·ment (mal′ə·pôr′shən·mənt, -pōr′-) *n.* Unfair apportionment of representatives in a legislature.

Mal·a·prop (mal′ə·prop), **Mrs.** A character in Sheridan's *The Rivals,* who uses words inappropriately. [<MALAPROPOS]

mal·a·prop·ism (mal′ə·prop·iz′əm) *n.* The incorrect or inappropriate use of a word; a verbal blunder. [after Mrs. *Malaprop*] —**mal′a·pro′pi·an** (-prō′pē·ən) *adj.*

mal·ap·ro·pos (mal′ap·rə·pō′) *adj.* Out of place; not appropriate. [<F *mal à propos* not to the point <*mal* ill + *à* to + *propos* purpose] —**mal′ap·ro·po′ism** *n.*

ma·lar (mā′lər) *adj. Anat.* Relating to or being in or near the cheek. —*n.* The cheek bone. [<NL *malaris* <L *mala* jaw, cheek]

ma·lar·i·a (mə·lâr′ē·ə) *n.* **1** *Pathol.* A disease caused by any of certain animal parasites (genus *Plasmodium*), which are introduced into the system by the bite of the infected anopheles mosquito and invade the red corpuscles of the blood, causing intermittent chills and fever. **2** Any foul or unwholesome air, as from decomposition; miasma; mephitis. [<Ital. *mal'aria, mala aria,* lit., bad air] —**ma·lar′i·al, ma·lar′i·an, ma·lar′i·ous** *adj.*

ma·lar·i·o·ther·a·py (mə·lâr′ē·ō·ther′ə·pē) *n. Med.* The treatment of cerebrospinal syphilis by inoculation with the parasite causing tertian malaria. [MALARI(A) + *-o-* +THERAPY]

ma·lar·ky (mə·lär′kē) *n. Slang* Insincere or senseless talk; bunk. Also **ma·lar′key.** [? <an Irish personal name]

mal·as·sim·i·la·tion (mal′ə·sim′ə·lā′shən) *n.* Imperfect or faulty assimilation.

mal·ate (mal′āt, mā′lāt) *n. Chem.* A salt or ester of malic acid. [<MAL(IC) + -ATE[3]]

Ma·la·wi (mä′lä·wē) An independent member of the Commonwealth of Nations in SE Africa; 49,177 square miles; capital, Zomba: formerly *Nyasaland.*

Ma·lay (mā′lā, mə·lā′) *n.* **1** A member of the dominant race in Malaysia; a Malayan. **2** The language spoken on the Malay Peninsula and widely used as a lingua franca throughout the East Indies, belonging to the Indonesian subfamily of Austronesian languages. **3** A variety of domestic fowl. —*adj.* Of or pertaining to the Malays; Malayan.

Ma·lay·a (mə·lā′ə) A federation of eleven states in the Commonwealth of Nations, now incorporated in Malaysia, including the former Federated Malay States and Unfederated Malay States, the two settlements of Malacca and Penang on the southern Malay Peninsula, and adjacent islands; 50,600 square miles; capital, Kuala Lumpur: formerly **Malayan Union.** Also **Malaya.**

Mal·a·ya·lam (mal′ə·yä′ləm) *n.* The language of the Malabar coast, India, related to Tamil, and belonging to the Dravidian family of languages.

Ma·lay·an (mə·lā′ən) *adj.* **1** Malay. **2** Indonesian. —*n.* **1** A Malay (def. 1). **2** An Indonesian. **3** The Indonesian subfamily of Austronesian languages.

Malay Archipelago An island group in the Indian and Pacific oceans SE of Asia, including Java, Borneo, Sumatra, Celebes, Timor, the Lesser Sunda Islands, and the Philippines; about 773,000 square miles: also the *East Indies, Malaysia.*

Ma·lay·o-Pol·y·ne·sian (mə·lā′ō·pol′ə·nē′zhən, -shən) *adj.* **1** Of or pertaining to the brown peoples of the Indian and Pacific oceans, including Malays and Polynesians. **2** Designating the languages of these peoples. —*n.* The Austronesian family of languages. [<MALAY + *-o-* + POLYNESIAN]

Malay Peninsula The southernmost peninsula of Asia, including the Federation of Malaya and part of Thailand.

Ma·lay·sia (mə·lā′zhə, -shə) **1** A federation of fourteen states in the Commonwealth of Nations, including Malaya, Sabah, and Sarawak; 127,334 square miles; capital, Kuala Lumpur. **2** The Malay Archipelago. —**Ma·lay′sian** *adj.* & *n.*

Mal·colm (mal′kəm) A masculine personal name. [<Celtic, servant of (St.) Columba]

Mal·colm X (mal′kəm eks) Name adopted by *Malcolm Little,* 1925–65, U.S. political and religious leader, active in the Black Muslim movement; assassinated.

mal·con·tent (mal′kən·tent) *adj.* Discontented, as with a government or economic system; dissatisfied; uneasy. —*n.* A person dissatisfied with the existing state of affairs; one rebellious against authority. [<OF <*mal-* MAL- + *content* CONTENT]

mal de dents (mál də däṅ′) *French* Toothache.

mal de mer (mál də mâr′) *French* Seasickness.

mal·dis·tri·bu·tion (mal′dis·trə·byōō′shən) *n.* Unfair or uneven distribution of people or goods.

Mal·dive Islands (môl′dīv, mal′-) An independent republic in the Indian Ocean; 12 islands SW of Sri Lanka; 115 square miles; capital, Malé.

mal du pays (mál dü pā·ē′) *French* Homesickness.

male (māl) *adj.* **1** Pertaining to the sex that begets young; masculine. **2** Made up of men or boys. **3** *Bot.* Having stamens, but no pistil; also, adapted to fertilize, but not to produce fruit, as stamens. **4** Denoting some implement or object, as a gage or plug, which fits into a corresponding part known as *female.* **5** Indicating superiority of strength and quality of anything. See synonyms under MASCULINE. —*n.* **1** An organism that produces sperm cells; a male person or animal. **2** *Bot.* A plant with only staminate flowers. ◆ Homophone: *mail.* [<OF *male, mascle* <L *masculus.* Doublet of MASCULINE.]

Ma·le·a (mə·lē′ə), **Cape 1** The SE extremity of Lesbos Island. **2** The SE extremity of Peloponnesus, Greece, on the Aegean.

mal·e·dict (mal′ə·dikt) *adj. Obs.* Accursed.

mal·e·dic·tion (mal′ə·dik′shən) *n.* **1** An invocation of evil; a cursing: opposed to *benediction.* **2** Slander. **3** The state of being reviled. See synonyms under IMPRECATION, OATH. [<L *maledictio, -onis* <*maledictus,* pp. of *maledicere* <*male* ill +*dicere* speak] —**mal′e·dic′to·ry** *adj.*

mal·e·fac·tor (mal′ə·fak′tər) *n.* One who commits a crime. [<L <*malefactus,* pp. of *malefacere* <*male* ill + *facere* do] —**mal′e·fac′tion** *n.* —**mal′e·fac′tress** *n. fem.*

male fern A fern *(Dryopteris filixmas)* used in medicine as a vermifuge.

ma·lef·ic (mə·lef′ik) *adj.* Occasioning evil or disaster. [<L *maleficus* <*malefacere.* See MALEFACTOR.]

ma·lef·i·cent (mə·lef′ə·sənt) *adj.* Causing or doing evil or mischief; harmful: opposed to *beneficent.*[<L *maleficus* MALEFIC]

ma·le·ic (mə·lē′ik) *adj. Chem.* Pertaining to or designating a white, crystalline, astringent acid, $C_4H_4O_4$, prepared by the catalytic oxidation of benzene: used as a dye for fabrics, etc. [<F *maléique* < *malique* MALIC]

Ma·lé Island (ma′lā) The capital of the Maldive Islands.

Ma·le·ku·la (mal′ə·kōō′lə) An island of the New Hebrides group; 980 square miles.

ma·le·mute (mä′lə·myōōt, mal′ə-), **ma·le·miut** See MALAMUTE.

Mal·en·kov (mal′ən·kôv, mə·len′-; *Russian* mä′·lyin·kôf), **Georgi,** born 1902, U.S.S.R. leader; premier 1953–55.

mal·en·ten·du (mál·äṅ·täṅ·dü′) *n. French* Misunderstanding.

Mal·e·ven·tum (mal′ə·ven′təm) The ancient name for BENEVENTO.

ma·lev·o·lent (mə·lev′ə·lənt) *adj.* Having an evil disposition toward others; ill–disposed. See synonyms under MALICIOUS. [<OF <L *malevolens, -entis* <*male* ill + *volens, -entis,* ppr. of *velle* wish, will] —**ma·lev′o·lence** *n.* —**ma·lev′o·lent·ly** *adv.*

mal·fea·sance (mal·fē′zəns) *n. Law* The performance of some act which is unlawful or wrongful or which one has specifically contracted not to perform: said usually of official misconduct. Compare MISFEASANCE, NONFEASANCE. [<AF *malfaisance* <OF *malfaisant* < *mal* ill + *faisant*, ppr. of *faire* do <L *facere*]

mal·fea·sant (mal·fē′zənt) *adj.* Guilty of malfeasance. —*n.* A person guilty of malfeasance.

mal·for·ma·tion (mal′fôr·mā′shən) *n.* Any irregularity, anomaly, or abnormal deformation in the structure of an organism. [<MAL- + FORMATION]

mal·formed (mal·fôrmd′) *adj.* Badly formed or made; deformed.

mal·func·tion (mal·fungk′shən) *n. Physiol.* Impairment or disturbance of any bodily function; dysfunction.

Mal·gache (mȧl·gȧsh′) *n.* & *adj. French* Madagascan.

mal·gré (mȧl·grā′) *prep. French* In spite of; notwithstanding. Also, *Obs., maugre.*

malgré lui (lwē) *French* In spite of himself or herself.

Mal·herbe (mȧ·lerb′), **François de,** 1555–1628, French poet.

Ma·li (mä′lē) A landlocked, independent republic in west Africa; 464,873 miles; capital, Bamako; formerly French Sudan, an overseas territory. —**Ma′li** *adj.* & *n.*

mal·ic (mal′ik, mā′lik) *adj.* 1 Of, pertaining to, or obtained from apples. 2 *Chem.* Pertaining to or designating a deliquescent crystalline acid, $C_4H_6O_5$, with a pleasant taste: contained in the juice of many sour fruits and some plants, and also made synthetically. [< F *malique* <L *malum* an apple]

mal·ice (mal′is) *n.* 1 A disposition to injure another; evil intent; spite; ill will. 2 *Law* A wilfully formed design to do another an injury: also **malice aforethought.** See synonyms under ENMITY, HATRED. [<OF <L *malitia*< *malus* bad]

ma·li·cious (mə·lish′əs) *adj.* 1 Harboring malice, ill will, or enmity; spiteful. 2 Resulting from or prompted by malice. [<OF *malicios* <L *malitiosus* <*malitia* MALICE] —**ma·li′·cious·ly** *adv.* —**ma·li′cious·ness** *n.*

Synonyms: bitter, evil–disposed, evil–minded, hostile, ill–disposed, ill–natured, invidious, malevolent, malign, malignant, mischievous, rancorous, resentful, spiteful, venomous, virulent. The *malevolent* person wishes ill to another; the *malicious* person has the desire and intent to do evil, if possible, to another. The *malign* or *malignant* spirit has a deep, intense, and insatiable hostility, such as is indicated by *rancorous* or *venomous*, with or without active desire or intent to injure. *Spiteful* is a feeble word indicating the desire or intent to inflict petty, exasperating annoyance or injury. Compare ACRIMONY, BITTER, ENMITY, HATRED. *Antonyms*: amiable, amicable, beneficent, benevolent, benign, benignant, friendly, good–natured, kind, kind–hearted, kindly, sympathetic, tender, well–disposed.

ma·lign (mə·līn′) *v.t.* To speak slander of. See synonyms under ABUSE, ASPERSE, REVILE. —*adj.* 1 Having an evil disposition toward others; ill–disposed; malevolent: opposed to *benign.* 2 Tending to injure; pernicious. See synonyms under MALICIOUS. [<OF *malignier, maliner* plot, deceive <L *malignare* contrive maliciously <*malignus* evil–disposed <*malus* evil] —**ma·lign′ly** *adv.* —**ma·lign′er** *n.*

ma·lig·nant (mə·lig′nənt) *adj.* 1 Having or manifesting extreme malevolence or enmity. 2 Evil in nature, or tending to do great harm; also, malcontent. 3 *Pathol.* So aggravated as to threaten life: opposed to *benign*: a *malignant* tumor. 4 Boding ill; baleful; threatening. —*n.* A person of extreme enmity or evil intentions. [<L *malignans, -antis*, ppr. of *malignare.* See MALIGN.] —**ma·lig′nance, ma·lig′nan·cy** *n.* —**ma·lig′nant·ly** *adv.*

ma·lig·ni·ty (mə·lig′nə·tē) *n. pl.* **·ties** 1 The state or quality of being malign; violent animosity. 2 Destructive tendency; virulence. 3 *Often pl.* An evil thing or event. See synonyms under ACRIMONY, ENMITY, HATRED.

ma·lines (mə·lēn′, *Fr.* mȧ·lēn′) *n.* 1 Lace made in Mechlin, Belgium: also called *Mechlin lace.* 2 A gauzelike veiling for trimming hats: also **ma·line′.** [<F, from *Malines* Mechlin]

Ma·lines (mȧ·lēn′) The French name for MECHLIN.

ma·lin·ger (mə·ling′gər) *v.i.* To feign sickness or incapacity, especially so as to avoid work or duty. [<F *malingre* sickly <*mal* bad (<L *malus*) + OF *heingre* lean] —**ma·lin′ ger·er** *n.*

Ma·li·now·ski (mä′li·nôf′skē), **Bronislaw Kasper,** 1884–1942, U.S. anthropologist born in Poland.

mal·i·son (mal′ə·zən, -sən) *n. Archaic* A malediction; curse. [<OF <L *maledictio* MALEDICTION]

mal·kin (mô′kin, môl′-, mal′-) *n. Obs.* 1 A kitchenmaid; a slattern. 2 A scarecrow representing a woman. 3 A cat. 4 *Scot.* A hare. Also spelled *maukin.* [Dim. of MATILDA, MAUD]

mall[1] (môl, mal) *n.* 1 A maul. 2 A war hammer. —*v.t.* To maul. [Var. of MAUL]

mall[2] (môl, mal, mel) *n.* 1 The game pall–mall, or a place in which it is played. 2 A level, shaded walk. [Short for PALL–MALL]

mal·lard (mal′ərd) *n.* 1 The common wild duck *(Anas platyrhynchos)*, or, formerly, its drake. 2 Any wild duck. 3 *Obs.* The domesticated duck. [<OF *malart* <*masle* MALE]

Mal·lar·mé (mȧ·lȧr·mā′), **Stéphane,** 1842–98, French poet.

mal·le·a·ble (mal′ē·ə·bəl) *adj.* 1 Capable of being hammered or rolled out without breaking; ductile. 2 Hence, susceptible to the shaping power of surrounding influences; pliant. [<OF <L *malleare* MALLEATE] —**mal′le·a·bil′i·ty, mal′le·a·ble·ness** *n.* —**mal′le·a·bly** *adv.*

malleable iron 1 Cast iron that has been rendered tough and malleable by long–continued high heating and slow cooling. 2 Wrought iron; forged iron.

mal·le·ate (mal′ē·āt) *v.t.* **·at·ed, ·at·ing** To shape into a plate or leaf by beating; hammer. [<L *malleatus*, pp. of *malleare* <*malleus* a hammer] —**mal′le·a′tion** *n.*

mal·lee (mal′ē) *n. Austral.* 1 Any one of several scrubby species of eucalyptus of South Australia and Victoria; especially, *Eucalyptus dumosa* and *E. oleosa.* 2 Brushwood composed of such trees.

mal·le·in (mal′ē·in) *n. Biochem.* A poisonous, yellowish–white compound, obtained from the active metabolic products of the bacillus of glanders, used for the diagnosis of that disease. Also **mal′le·ine** (-in, -ēn). [<L *malle(us)* glanders + -IN]

mal·le·muck (mal′ə·muk) *n.* The southern albatross, fulmar, petrel, or other closely related bird. [<Du. *mallemok* <*mol* foolish + *mok* a gull]

mal·len·ders (mal′ən·dərz) See MALANDERS.

mal·le·o·lus (mə·lē′ə·ləs) *n. pl.* **·o·li** (-ə·lī) *Anat.* A hammer–shaped bony process on each side of the ankle. [<L, dim. of *malleus* a hammer] —**mal·le′o·lar** *adj.*

mal·let (mal′it) *n.* 1 A wooden hammer or light maul. 2 A light hammer, frequently of metal. 3 A long–handled wooden hammer used in the game of croquet. 4 A wooden–headed Malacca cane or stick used in the game of polo. [<OF *maillet*, dim. of *mail* a MAUL]

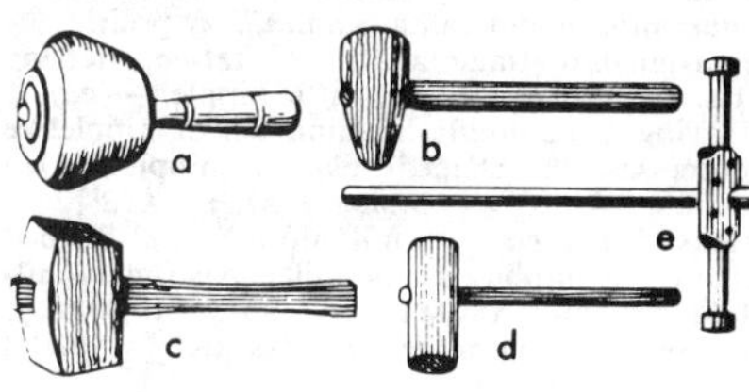

MALLETS
a. Mason's mallet. *b.* Bossing mallet.
c. Carpenter's mallet. *d.* Tinsmith's mallet.
e. Calking mallet.

mal·le·us (mal′ē·əs) *n. pl.* **·le·i** (-lē·ī) *Anat.* The club–shaped outermost ossicle of the middle ear, articulating with the incus. See illustration under EAR. [<L, a hammer]

Mal·lor·ca (mä·lyôr′kä) The Spanish spelling of MAJORCA.

mal·low (mal′ō) *n.* 1 Any plant of the genus *Malva.* The most common in the United States is the **running** or **dwarf mallow** *(M. rotundifolia)*, a spreading herb with roundish leaves, small, pale–pink flowers, and flat, disklike fruit: the leaves are used in brewing a medicinal tea. 2 Any plant of the mallow family: Indian *mallow.* [OE *mealuwe* <L *malva.* Double of MAUVE.]

mallow rose See ROSEMALLOW.

malm (mäm) *n.* 1 A soft, friable, whitish limestone. 2 A whitish calcareous loam occurring in the southern counties of England; marl. [OE *mealm(stan)* sandstone or limestone]

Mal·mé·dy (mȧl·mā·dē′) A town on the Belgian–German frontier; awarded to Belgium under the Versailles Treaty.

Malmes·bur·y (mämz′bər·ē), **William of,** 1095?–1143?, English monk and historian.

Mal·mö (mal′mō, *Sw.* mäl′mœ) A port in SW Sweden.

malm·sey (mäm′zē) *n.* A rich sweet wine made in the Canary Islands, Madeira, Spain, and Greece. [<Med. L *malmasia* <Gk. *Monembasia* Monemvasia, Greece, a small Laconian coastal town formerly exporting wine]

mal·nu·tri·tion (mal′nōō·trish′ən, -nyōō-) *n.* Faulty or inadequate nutrition.

ma·lo (mä′lō) *n.* A loin cloth or girdle worn by Hawaiian men, formerly made of tapa, now of brightly dyed cotton fabrics. [<Hawaiian, cloth]

mal·oc·clu·sion (mal′ə·klōō′zhən) *n. Dent.* Faulty closure of the upper and lower teeth. [<MAL- + OCCLUSION]

mal·o·dor (mal·ō′dər) *n.* An offensive odor.

mal·o·dor·ous (mal·ō′dər·əs) *adj.* Having a disagreeable smell, literally or figuratively; obnoxious. —**mal·o′dor·ous·ly** *adv.* —**mal·o′·dor·ous·ness** *n.*

ma·lon·ic (mə·lon′ik, -lō′nik) *adj. Chem.* Of, pertaining to, or designating a white, crystalline acid, $CH_2(CO_2H)_2$ obtained chiefly by oxidizing malic acid. [<F *malonique* <*malique* MALIC]

mal·o·nyl·u·re·a (mal′ə·nil·yŏŏr′ē·ə) *n.* Barbituric acid. [<MALON(IC) + -YL +UREA]

Mal·o·ry (mal′ər·ē), **Sir Thomas,** died 1470?, English author and translator; compiled the *Morte d'Arthur*, a collection of stories about King Arthur translated from the French.

mal·pais (mal′pīs) *n. SW U.S.* Bad land; specifically, land having an under layer of basaltic lava. [<Sp. *mal, malo* bad (<L *malus*) + *país* a country <L *patria*]

Mal·pi·ghi (mäl·pē′gē), **Marcello,** 1628–94, Italian anatomist. —**Mal·pigh′i·an** (-pig′ē·ən) *adj.*

mal·pigh·i·a·ceous (mal·pig′ē·ā′shəs) *adj.* Of or pertaining to a family *(Malpighiaceae)* of trees, shrubs, or, more rarely, herbs, with hermaphrodite flowers, mostly native to the tropics. [<NL *Malpighiaceae*, family name < *Malpighia*, genus name, after Marcello *Malpighi*]

Malpighian bodies *Anat.* A tuft of blood vessels at the commencement of the uriniferous tubules in the kidney. Also **Malpighian capsules** or **corpuscles.** [after Marcello *Malpighi*]

Malpighian layer *Anat.* The deeper, softer layer of the epidermis, comprising the active cells.

Malpighian tubes *Entomol.* The tubular portions of the excretory organ of an insect. Also **Malpighian vessels.**

Mal·pla·quet (mȧl·plȧ·ke′) A village in northern France; scene of Marlborough's victory over the French, 1709.

mal·po·si·tion (mal′pə·zish′ən) *n. Pathol.* A wrong or faulty position, as of the fetus. —**mal·posed** (-pōzd′) *adj.*

mal·prac·tice (mal·prak′tis) *n.* 1 Improper or illegal practice, as in medicine or surgery. 2 Improper or immoral conduct. —**mal·prac·ti·tion·er** (mal′prak·tish′ən·ər) *n.*

Mal·raux (mȧl·rō′), **André,** 1901–1976, French novelist and art critic.

malt (môlt) *n.* 1 Grain, usually barley, softened by water, artificially germinated and then dried: rich in carbohydrates and proteins and essential in brewing and as a nutrient. 2 *Slang* Malt liquor; beer or ale. —*v.t.* 1 To cause (grain) to germinate artificially, by moisture and heat, and become malt. 2 To treat with malt, or extract of malt. —*v.i.* **3** To be changed into or become malt: said of grain. **4** To convert grain into malt. [OE *mealt.* Akin to MELT.]

Mal·ta (môl′tə) **1** A republic in the Mediterranean, comprising the **Maltese Islands;** Malta, Gozo, and Comino; 122 square miles; capital, Valletta. **2** The largest of these islands; 95 square miles: ancient *Melita.*

Malta fever Undulant fever.

mal·tase (môl′tās) *n. Biochem.* A digestive enzyme which hydrolyzes maltose into dextrose. [<MALT + -ASE]

malted milk 1 A powder made of dehydrated milk and malted cereals, soluble in milk or water. **2** The beverage made with this powder.

Mal·tese (môl·tēz′, -tēs′) *adj.* Of or pertaining to Malta, its inhabitants, or their language, or to the Knights of Malta. —*n. pl.* **·tese 1** A native of Malta; the people of Malta collectively. **2** The language of Malta, a dialectal Arabic with elements of Italian. **3** A Maltese cat or dog.

Maltese cat A domestic cat with long, silky, bluish–gray hair.

Maltese cross See under CROSS.

Maltese dog An ancient breed of toy spaniel, originating in Malta, with a long, silky, white coat.

mal·tha (mal′thə) *n.* **1** A thick mineral pitch, formed by drying petroleum. **2** A variety of ozocerite. **3** Any similar preparation used as a cement, stucco, or mortar. [<L <Gk., a mixture of wax and pitch]

malt house A building in which grains are malted and other preparations made for use in the brewer's trade.

Mal·thus (mal′thəs), **Thomas Robert,** 1766–1834, English political economist.

Mal·thu·si·an (mal·thōō′zē·ən, -zhən) *adj.* Of or pertaining to the theory of T. R. Malthus that population increases faster than the means of support and, unless checked by sexual restraint, is restricted only by famine, pestilence, war, etc. —*n.* A believer in the theories of Malthus. —**Mal·thu′si·an·ism** *n.*

malt liquor A fermented liquor, esp. beer or ale made from malt.

malt·ose (môl′tōs) *n. Biochem.* A hard, white, dextrorotatory, crystalline sugar, $C_{12}H_{22}O_{11} \cdot H_2O$, formed by the action of amylase on starch. [<MALT + -OSE[2]]

mal·treat (mal·trēt′) *v.t.* To treat badly or unkindly; abuse. See synonyms under ABUSE. [<F *maltraiter* <*mal-* MAL- + *traiter* <OF *traitier* TREAT] —**mal·treat′ment** *n.*

malt·ster (môlt′stər) *n.* A maker of or dealer in malt.

malt·y (môl′tē) *adj.* **malt·i·er, malt·i·est** Of, pertaining to, containing, or resembling malt.

mal·va·ceous (mal·vā′shəs) *adj.* Pertaining or belonging to the mallow family *(Malvaceae)* of herbs, shrubs, or trees, with alternate palmately nerved leaves and regular flowers, including althea, cotton, okra, etc. [<LL *malvaceus* < *malva* a mallow]

mal·va·si·a (mal′və·sē′ə) *n.* Malmsey wine; also, the kind of grape from which malmsey wine is made. [<Ital. *Malvasia,* alter. of Gk. *Monembasia.* See MALMSEY.] —**mal′va·si′an** *adj.*

Mal·vern Hill (mal′vərn) A plateau near Richmond, Virginia; scene of a Confederate defeat in the Civil War, 1862.

Malvern Hills A range in western England on the Worcester–Hereford border; highest point, 1,307 feet.

mal·ver·sa·tion (mal′vər·sā′shən) *n.* Evil or corrupt conduct; misconduct, as in public office. [<MF <*malverser* <L *male versari* < *male* wrongly, ill + *versari* behave, passive freq. of *vertere* turn]

mal·voi·sie (mal′voi·zē, -və-) *n.* Malmsey. [<OF *malvesia* <Ital. *malvasia* MALVASIA; refashioned after F *malvoisie*]

Mal·vo·li·o (mal·vō′lē·ō) In Shakespeare's *Twelfth Night,* the pompous majordomo of Olivia.

ma·ma (mä′mə, mə·mä′) *n.* Mother: a term of familiar address and endearment. Also **mam′·ma.** [Repetition of infantile syllable *ma*]

mam·ba (mäm′bə) *n.* Any of certain long, venomous, arboreal snakes (genus *Dendraspis*) of southern Africa; especially, the common olive-green or black mamba *(D. angusticeps).* [< Zulu *in–amba*]

mam·bo (mäm′bō) *n. pl.* **·bos** A form of popular music, derived from Cuban Negro styles, achieving its effects by syncopation of a four–beat rhythmic pattern, with accents on the second and fourth beats.

ma·melle (ma·mel′) *n.* In western United States, a rounded hillock. [F, breast]

mam·e·luke (mam′ə·lōōk) *n.* In Moslem countries, a male slave. [<F *mameluk* <Arabic *mamlūk* a slave, orig. pp. of *malaka* possess]

Mam·e·luke (mam′ə·lōōk) *n.* A member of a famous military caste, originally composed of slaves, which dominated Egypt from 1254 to 1811. Also **Mam′a·luke.**

ma·mey (mä·mā′, -mē′) *n.* **1** A tropical American tree *(Mamea americana)* bearing edible, yellow fruits resembling the pomelo in size and shape: also **mamey de Santo Domingo. 2** A fruit of this tree: also **mamey apple. 3** The sapodilla or marmalade tree. Also **mam·mee** (mä·mā′, -mē′). [<Sp.<Taino]

mam·ma (mam′ə) *n. pl.* **·mae** (-ē) The milk–secreting organ of a mammal; a breast, udder, or bag. [<L, breast]

mam·mal (mam′əl) *n.* A vertebrate animal whose female suckles its young. [< MAMMALIA]

Mam·ma·li·a (ma·mā′lē·ə) *n. pl.* A class of vertebrates whose females have milk–secreting mammae to nourish their young, including man, all warm–blooded quadrupeds, seals, cetaceans, and sirenians. [<NL <LL *mammalis* of the breast <L *mamma* breast]

mam·ma·lif·er·ous (mam′ə·lif′ər·əs) *adj.* Containing remains of mammals, as geological strata. [<MAMMALI(A) + -FEROUS]

mam·mal·o·gy (ma·mal′ə·jē) *n.* The branch of zoology that treats of the *Mammalia.* [< MAMMAL + -LOGY]

mam·ma·ry (mam′ər·ē) *adj.* Of, pertaining to, or of the nature of a mamma or breast, or the mammae.

mammary gland The milk gland, which in a female forms the bulk of the breast or mamma. The mammary glands occur in both the male and female in all mammals, but are rudimentary in the male.

mam·mate (mam′āt) *adj.* Having mammae or breasts. Also **mam′me·at′ed** (-ē·ā′tid). [<L *mammatus* <*mamma* breast]

mam·ma·tus (ma·mā′təs) *n. Meteorol.* A cloud form characterized by pouchlike protuberances along the lower surface: noted especially in stratocumulus and cumulonimbus clouds. [< L. See MAMMATE.]

mam·mer (mam′ər) *v.i. Brit. Dial.* To stammer; hesitate; be confused. [Prob. imit.]

mam·mer·ing (mam′ər·ing) *n.* A state of doubt or perplexity.

mam·met (mam′it) See MAUMET.

mam·mie (mam′ē) See MAMMY.

mam·mif·er·ous (ma·mif′ər·əs) *adj.* Having mammae or breasts; mammalian. [<MAMM(A) + -(I)FEROUS]

mam·mil·la (ma·mil′ə) *n. pl.* **·lae** (-ē) *Anat.* A nipple or teat, or some nipplelike or teat–shaped structure or protuberance. [<L *mamilla, mammilla,* dim. of *mamma* breast]

mam·mil·lar·y (mam′ə·ler′ē) *adj.* **1** Of, pertaining to, or resembling a mammilla or a mamma. **2** Studded with or composed of breast–shaped or rounded protuberances: a *mammillary* mineral, a *mammillary* prairie.

mam·mil·late (mam′ə·lāt) *v.t.* **·lat·ed, ·lat·ing** To shape like a breast or a nipple. —*adj.* **1** Having a mammilla, mammillae, or nipplelike processes. **2** Shaped like a nipple. Also **mam′mil·lat′ed.** [<MAMMILL(A) + -ATE[1]]

mam·mil·li·form (ma·mil′ə·fôrm) *adj.* Shaped like or resembling a mammilla. Also **mam·mil·loid** (mam′ə·loid). [MAMMILL(A) + -(I)FORM]

mam·mi·tis (ma·mī′tis) *n.* Mastitis. [<MAMM(A) + -ITIS]

mam·mock (mam′ək) *n. Archaic* A fragment; scrap. [<dial. E; ult. origin uncertain]

mam·mo·gram (mam′ə·gram) *n.* An X–ray photograph of the breast or breasts.

mam·mog·ra·phy (mə·mog′rə·fē) *n.* X–ray examination of the breast or breasts. [<L *mamma* breast + Gk. *graphein* write]

mam·mol·o·gy (ma·mol′ə·jē) *n.* Mammalogy. [<MAMM(ALIA) + -(O)LOGY]

mam·mon (mam′ən) *n.* **1** Riches; wealth. **2** Worldliness; avarice. *Matt.* vi 24; *Luke* xvi 9. [<LL <Gk. *mammōnas* <Aramaic *māmōnā* riches, prob. ult. < *'āman* trust]

Mam·mon (mam′ən) **1** The personification of riches, avarice, and worldly gain. **2** In Milton's *Paradise Lost,* one of the fallen angels.

mam·mon·ism (mam′ən·iz′əm) *n.* Devotion to the acquisition of wealth; worldliness. —**mam′·mon·ist, mam′mon·ite** *n.*

mam·moth (mam′·əth) *n.* **1** A large, once very abundant, extinct northern elephant *(Mammuthus primigenius)* of the Pleistocene, closely resembling the Indian elephant, with coarse outer hair, close woolly under hair, and enormous, usually curved tusks: its remains have been found in Alaska and Siberia. **2** The extinct imperial elephant *(M. imperator)* which ranged west of the Mississippi River. —*adj.* Huge; colossal. [<Russian *mammot, mamant*]

WOOLLY MAMMOTH
(About 9 feet high at the shoulder)

Mammoth Cave National Park A series of underground caverns in SW Kentucky, noted for their remarkable onyx formations; 79 square miles; established, 1936.

mam·my (mam′ē) *n. pl.* **·mies 1** Mother; mama. **2** A Negro nurse or foster mother of white children, especially in the Southern U.S. Also spelled *mammie.* [Dim. of MAMA]

man (man) *n. pl.* **men** (men) **1** A member of the genus *Homo* (family *Hominidae,* class *Mammalia*), the most highly developed of the primates, differing from other animals in having erect posture, extraordinary development of the brain, and the power of articulate language: only existing species, *Homo sapiens.* Earlier forms include the following: CRO–MAGNON MAN, GRIMALDI MAN, HEIDELBERG MAN, MIDLAND MAN, MODJOKERTO MAN, NEANDERTHAL MAN, RHODESIAN MAN, SOLO MAN, WADJAK MAN. **2** The human race. **3** Any one, indefinitely. **4** An adult male of the human kind: distinguished from *woman, boy,* and *youth.* **5** The male part of the race collectively. **6** A male person who is manly; also, manhood. **7** An adult male servant, dependent, or vassal. **8** A piece, figure, disk, etc., used in playing certain games, as chess or checkers. **9** A ship or vessel: used in composition: a *man*–of–war; an *Indiaman.* **10** A husband; lover; *man* and wife; Her *man* is dead. **11** Fellow: used in direct address: Hey, *man,* look at this! —**the Man** *U.S. Slang* A white man regarded as a representative of the establishment, as a police officer or a boss. —**to a man** Every one. —**to be one's own man** To be independent. —*v.t.* **manned, man·ning 1** To supply with men: to *man* a fort. **2** To take stations at, on, or in for work, defense, etc.: *Man* the pumps! —**to man oneself** To prepare or brace oneself, as for an ordeal. [OE *mann*]

Man may appear as a combining form in hyphemes or in solidemes, meaning "of, by, for, or like a man":

man–baiting	**man–hating**
man–bodied	**man–high**
man–born	**man–hunt**
man–catching	**man–hunting**
man–changed	**mankiller**
man–created	**mankilling**
man–degrading	**man–made**
man–destroyer	**man–minded**
man–destroying	**man–ridden**
man–devised	**man–shaped**
man–eating	**man–size**
man–enslaved	**man–stealing**
man–fearing	**man–taught**
man–grown	**mantrap**
man–hater	**man–worthy**

Man (man), **Isle of** One of the British Isles in the Irish Sea between Northern Ireland and England; 220 square miles; capital Douglas: ancient *Mona*: a native of the island is known as a *Manxman.*

ma·na (mä′nə) *n.* Among Pacific islanders, the supernatural power or force that works through a person or an inanimate object.

man–a·bout–town (man′ə·bout′toun′) *n.* A man who frequents night clubs, theaters, restaurants, bars, etc.; hence, a sophisticate.

man·a·cle (man′ə·kəl) *n.* **1** *Usually pl.* One of a connected pair of metallic instruments for confining or restraining the hands; a handcuff. **2** Anything that constrains or fetters. —*v.t.* **·cled, ·cling 1** To put manacles on. **2** To hamper; constrain. [<OF *manicle* <L *manicula,* dim. of *manus* hand]

man·age (man′ij) *v.* **·aged, ·ag·ing** *v.t.* **1** To direct or conduct the affairs or interests of: to *manage* a business. **2** To control the direction, operation, etc., of, as a machine. **3** To cause to do one's bidding, as by persuasion or flattery. **4** To bring about or contrive: to *manage* to do something. **5** To handle or wield, as a weapon or implement. **6** To train (a horse) in the exercises of a manège. —*v.i.* **7** To carry on or conduct business or affairs. **8** to contrive to get along: I'll *manage.* See synonyms under GOVERN, REGULATE. —*n. Obs.* **1** Management. **2** Behavior. **3** Manège; a riding school. [<Ital. *maneggiare* handle, train horses, ult. <L *manus* a hand]

man·age·a·ble (man′ij·ə·bəl) *adj.* Capable of being managed; tractable; docile. See synonyms under DOCILE. —**man′age·a·bil′i·ty, man′age·a·ble·ness** *n.* —**man′age·a·bly** *adv.*

man·age·ment (man′ij·mənt) *n.* **1** The act, art, or manner of managing, controlling, or conducting. **2** The skilful use of means to accomplish a purpose. **3** Managers or directors collectively. See synonyms under CARE, OVERSIGHT.

man·ag·er (man′ij·ər) *n.* **1** One who manages; especially, one who has the control of a business or a business establishment; a director. **2** An adroit schemer; intriguer. See synonyms under MASTER, SUPERINTENDENT. —**man′ag·er·ship** *n.*

man·ag·er·ess (man′ij·ər·is, -ij·ris; *Brit.* man′ij·ər·es′) *n.* Chiefly Brit. A female manager.

man·a·ge·ri·al (man′ə·jir′ē·əl) *adj.* Of, pertaining to, or characteristic of a manager or management. —**man′a·ge′ri·al·ly** *adv.*

Ma·na·gua (mä·nä′gwä) The capital of Nicaragua, on **Lake Managua,** a lake in SW Nicaragua (390 square miles).

man·a·kin (man′ə·kin) *n.* **1** Any of numerous small tropical American birds (family *Pipridae*) of brilliant plumage. **2** A manikin. [Orig. var. of MANIKIN]

Ma·na·ma (mä·nä′mä) The capital of the Bahrein Islands, on Bahrein.

ma·ña·na (mä·nyä′nä) *n.* & *adv. Spanish* Tomorrow. —**land of mañana** Land of perpetual procrastination.

Man·a·sa·ro·war (man′ə·sə·rō′ər) A lake in SW Tibet; 200 square miles.

Ma·nas·sas (mə·nas′əs) A town in NE Virginia; scene of two battles of Bull Run in the Civil War, July 21, 1861, and Aug. 29–30, 1862.

Ma·nas·seh (mə·nas′ə) A masculine personal name. [<Hebrew, causing to forget] —**Manasseh** A son of Joseph (*Gen.* xli 51); also, a tribe of Israel descended from him. —**Manasseh** King of Judah, in the seventh century B.C.; restored idol-worship.

man-at-arms (man′ət·ärmz′) *n. pl.* **men-at-arms** (men′-) A soldier; especially, a heavily armed soldier of medieval times.

man·a·tee (man′ə·tē′) *n.* A sirenian (genus *Trichechus*) of the tropical Atlantic shores and rivers; a sea cow. [<Sp. *manati* <Cariban *manattoui*]

MANATEE
(From 8 to 12 feet in length over—all)

Ma·naus (mä·nous′) A city on the Rio Negro in NW Brazil, capital of Amazonas. Formerly **Ma·ná·os** (mä·nä′ōs).

ma·nav·e·lins (mə·nav′ə ·linz) *n. pl. Naut. Slang* Odds and ends; leftover scraps. Also **ma·nav′i·lins.** [Var. of nautical slang *manarvelings* <*manarvel* steal small stores]

Man·ches·ter (man′ches·tər, -chis-) **1** A county borough and city in Lancashire, England. A native of Manchester is known as a *Mancunian.* **2** A city in southern New Hampshire.

man·chet (man′chit) *n. Archaic* A small loaf of fine white bread. [ME *manchett,* ? dim. <OF *(painde)maine* <L *panis dominicus,* lit., lord's bread]

man-child (man′chīld′) *n. pl.* **·chil·dren** (-chil′·drən) A male child.

man·chi·neel (man′chi·nēl′) *n.* A tropical American tree *(Hippomane mancinella)* having an acrid, milky, poisonous sap. [<F *mancenille* <Sp. *manzanilla,* dim. of *manzana* an apple <L *(mala) matiana* (apples) of Matius <*Matius,* a Roman culinary author]

Man·chu (man·chōō′, man′chōō) *n.* **1** One of a Mongoloid people that conquered China in 1643 and established the dynasty overthrown in 1912. **2** The language of this people, belonging to the Manchu-Tungusic subfamily of Altaic languages. —*adj.* Of or pertaining to Manchuria, its people, or its language. Also **Man·choo′.** [< Manchu, lit., pure] —**Man·chu′ri·an** (-chŏŏr′ē·ən) *adj.* & *n.*

Man·chu·kuo (man′chōō′kwō′, *Chinese* män′·jō′kwō′) A former empire in NE Asia, 1932–45, established under Japanese auspices; comprising Manchuria and the Chinese province of Jehol and part of Chahar in Inner Mongolia; about 503,013 square miles; capital, Hsinking. Also **Man′chou′kuo′.**

Man·chu·ri·a (man·chŏŏr′ē·ə) A major division of NE China; 585,000 square miles; capital, Mukden. See MANCHUKUO. —**Man·chu′ri·an** *adj.* & *n.*

Man·chu-Tun·gus·ic (man·chōō′tōōn·gōōz′ik) *n.* A subfamily of the Altaic languages, consisting of Manchu and Tungus.

man·cip·i·um (man·sip′ē·əm) *n.* In ancient Roman law, the legal status of a person conveyed by the paterfamilias to another by the ceremony of mancipation. If emancipated from the mancipium, the person became again subject to paternal power and so remained, unless sold three times, when the authority of the paterfamilias ceased. [<L <*manceps* a buyer < *manus* a hand + *capere* take]

man·ci·ple (man′sə·pəl) *n.* A steward, as of an English college. [<OF *manciple, mancipe* <L *mancipium* MANCIPIUM]

Man·cu·ni·an (man·kyōō′nē·ən) *n.* A native of Manchester, England. [< Med. L *Mancunium* Manchester]

man·cus (mang′kəs) *n.* An Anglo-Saxon monetary unit worth thirty pence. [OE]

-mancy *combining form* Divining, foretelling, or discovering by means of: *necromancy.* [<Gk. *manteia* power of divination]

Man·da·lay (man′də·lā, man′də·lā′) A city on the Irrawaddy in central Burma.

man·da·mus (man·dā′məs) *n.* Law A writ originally (in England) of royal prerogative, now a writ of right, issued by courts of superior jurisdiction and directed to subordinate courts, corporations, or the like, commanding them to do something therein specified: modified by statute from the ordinary common law form in jurisdiction. —*v.t. Colloq.* To command by or serve with a mandamus. [<L, we command < *mandare.* See MANDATE.]

Man·dan (man′dan) *n.* **1** One of a tribe of North American Indians of Siouan stock, of the NW United States. **2** The Siouan language of this tribe.

man·da·rin (man′də·rin) *n.* **1** An official of the Chinese Empire, either civil or military: a title used by foreigners indiscriminately. The recognized official grades under the Empire were nine, each rank being distinguished by its official specific regalia, a conspicuous part of which is the **mandarin button. 2** Any of certain small Chinese oranges, having a loose skin and very sweet pulp; a tangerine. **3** An orange or reddish-yellow dye. [<Pg. *mandarim* <Malay *mantrī* a minister of state <Hind. <Skt. *mantrin* a counselor <*mantra* counsel]

Man·da·rin (man′də·rin) *n.* **1** The Chinese language of north China, in the Peking dialect now the official language of the country. **2** Formerly, the court language of the Chinese Empire.

mandarin duck A crested duck *(Aix galericulata)* , with variously colored plumage.

man·da·tar·y (man′də·ter′ē) *n. pl.* **·tar·ies** One to whom a charge is given; an agent. See MANDATE (def. 2).

man·date (man′dāt, -dit) *n.* **1** An authoritative requirement, as of a sovereign; a command; order; charge. **2** A charge to a nation, authorizing the government, administration, and development of conquered territory, given by a congress or league of nations, to which the grantee is responsible; also, the territory given in charge. **3** A judicial command directed to an officer of the court to enforce an order of that court; a precept from an appellate court directing what a subordinate court shall do in an appealed case. **4** A rescript of the pope ordering that the person named shall have the first vacant benefice in the gift of the person addressed. **5** An instruction from an electorate to the legislative body, or its representative, to follow a certain course of action. See synonyms under LAW. —*v.t.* (-dāt) **·dat·ed, ·dat·ing** To assign (a colony or other territory) to a specific nation under a mandate. [<L *mandatum,* pp. neut. of *mandare* command <*manus* hand + *dare* give (to)]

man·da·tor (man·dā′tər) *n.* One who gives a mandate; a director. [<L < *mandatus,* pp. of *mandare.* See MANDATE.]

man·da·to·ry (man′də·tôr′ē, -tō′rē) *adj.* Expressive of positive command; obligatory. —*n. pl.* **·ries 1** A mandatary. **2** A mandate.

Man·de·an (man·dē′ən) *n.* **1** A member of an ancient sect of Gnostics, Christians of St. John, still existing in Mesopotamia, who combine Judaism, Mohammedanism, and Christianity with the ancient Babylonian worship. **2** The Aramaic dialect used in the writings of the Mandeans. —*adj.* Of or pertaining to the Mandeans or their doctrines. Also **Man·dae′an.** [<Mandean *mandayyā,* lit., having knowledge (<*mandā* knowledge), trans. of Gk. *gnostikoi* Gnostics] —**Man·de′ism** *n.*

Man·dela (man·de′lə) **Nelson Rolihlahla,** 1918–, first black president of Republic of South Africa (1994–).

man·del·ic (man·del′ik) *adj.* Pertaining to or designating a white crystalline acid, $C_8H_8O_3$, used in medicine as a urinary antiseptic. [<G *mandel* an almond]

Man·de·ville (man′də·vil), **Bernard,** 1670?–1733, English author born in Holland. —**Sir John,** 1300?–72, pseudonym of a reputed English traveler whose *Narrative of Travels* appeared in Latin and French, 1357–71, and in English in the 15th century.

man·di·ble (man′də·bəl) *n. Biol.* **1** The lower jaw bone, or its equivalent. **2** Either the upper or the lower part of the beak of a bird, or of the beak of a cephalopod. **3** Either one of the upper or outer pair of jaws in an insect. **4** The operculum of a polyzoan. [<LL *mandibula* jaw <L *mandere* chew]

man·dib·u·lar (man·dib′yə·lər) *adj.* Of, pertaining to, or formed by a mandible: the *mandibular* arch of the fetal skull. Also **man·dib′u·lar′y** (-ler′ē). — *n.* The lower jaw, or mandible. [<LL *mandibul(a)* MANDIBLE + -AR]

man·dib·u·late (man·dib′yə·lit, -lāt) *adj.* Having mandibles adapted for biting and chewing: said of certain insects. —*n.* Any insect having chewing jaws.

Man·din·go (man·ding′gō) *n. pl.* **·gos** or **·goes 1** One of a Negroid people of western Sudan, Africa. **2** Any of the Sudanic languages of the Mandingos. —**Man·din′gan** *adj.* & *n.*

man·do·la (man·dō′lə) *n.* A large mandolin. [<Ital. *mandola, mandora* <L *pandura.* See BANDORE.]

man·do·lin (man′də·lin, man′də·lin′) *n.* A stringed musical instrument with an almond-shaped body and metal strings arranged like those of a violin. [<F *mandoline* <Ital. *mandolino,* dim. of *mandola* MANDOLA] —**man′·do·lin′ist** *n.*

man·drake (man′drāk) *n.* **1** A short-stemmed Old World plant *(Mandragora officinarum)* of the nightshade family, with narcotic properties. **2** Its fleshy roots, sometimes having a fancied resemblance to the human form. **3** The May apple. Also **man·drag·o·ra** (man·drag′ ə·rə). [Alter. of ME *mandrag(g)e,* <OE *mandragora* <LL <L *mandragoras* <Gk.; infl. in form by folk etymology <MAN + DRAKE[2] a dragon]

man·drel (man′drəl) *n. Mech.* **1** A shaft or spindle on which an object may be fixed for rotation. **2** A smooth, hard, cylindrical or conical core about which wire may be coiled or metal or glass forged. **3** A pattern or form against which metalwork is pressed in spinning. Also **man′dril.** [Prob. alter. of F *mandrin* a lathe]

man·drill (man′dril) *n.* A large, ferocious West African baboon (genus *Papio*), having large canine teeth and bony prominences on the cheeks striped with blue and scarlet. [<MAN + DRILL[3]]

MANDRILL
(About 30 inches at the shoulder: length 3 to 4 feet)

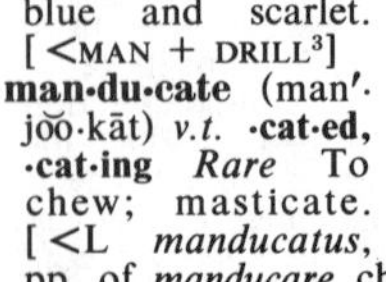

man·du·cate (man′jōō·kāt) *v.t.* **·cat·ed, ·cat·ing** *Rare* To chew; masticate. [<L *manducatus*, pp. of *manducare* chew]

Man·dy (man′dē) Diminutive of AMANDA.

mane (mān) *n.* The long hair growing on and about the neck of some animals, as the horse, lion, etc. ◆ Homophone: *main.* [OE *manu*] **— maned** *adj.* **— mane′less** *adj.*

man–eat·er (man′ē′tər) *n.* **1** A cannibal. **2** An animal that devours, likes to devour, or is supposed to devour human flesh; especially, a tiger or a lion. **3** A large shark with trenchant teeth; especially, *Carcharodon carcharias.*

ma·nège (ma·nezh′) *n.* **1** The art of training and riding horses. **2** A school of horsemanship; riding school; also, a school for the training of horses. **3** The style and movements of a trained horse. Also **ma·nege′.** [<F <Ital. *maneggio* < *maneggiare.* See MANAGE.]

ma·nes (mā′nēz) *n. pl.* **1** In ancient Roman religion, the spirits of the dead; especially, the spirits of dead ancestors. **2** Deified ancestral spirits collectively. [<L, ? orig. pl. of *manis* good]

Ma·nes (mā′nēz), 216?–276?, Persian prophet; founder of Manicheism: also called *Manicheus.*

Ma·net (ma·nā′, *Fr.* mà·ne′), **Édouard,** 1832–1883, French painter.

Man·e·tho (man′ə·thō) An Egyptian priest and writer of the third century B.C.

ma·neu·ver (mə·nōō′vər, -nyōō′-) *n.* **1** A movement or change of position, as of troops or war vessels. **2** Any dexterous or artful proceeding. **—** *v.t.* **1** To put, as troops, through a maneuver or maneuvers. **2** To put, bring, make, etc., by a maneuver or maneuvers. **3** To manipulate; conduct adroitly. **—** *v.i.* **4** To perform a maneuver or maneuvers. **5** To use tricks or stratagems; manage adroitly. Also spelled *manoeuver, manoeuvre.* [<F *manoeuvre* <OF *maneuvre* <LL *manopera* < *manoperare* <L *manu operari* work with the hand < *manus* hand + *operari.* See OPERATE. Doublet of MAINOR, MANURE.] **— ma·neu′ver·a·bil′i·ty** or **·vra·bil′i·ty** *n.* **— ma·neu′ver·a·ble** or **·vra·ble** *adj.* **— ma·neu′ver·er** *n.*

ma·neu·vers (mə·nōō′vərz, -nyōō′-) *n. pl.* Large-scale military exercises involving the use of great numbers of troops under conditions simulating actual battle conditions; war games.

man·fash·ion (man′fash′ən) *adv.* **1** In a manly, confident, straightforward way. **2** Astride: to ride *manfashion.*

man Friday A person devoted or subservient to another, like Robinson Crusoe's servant of that name; a factotum.

man·ful (man′fəl) *adj.* Having a manly spirit; characterized by courage and perseverance; sturdy. See synonyms under MANLY, MASCULINE. **— man′ful·ly** *adv.* **— man′ful·ness** *n.*

mang (mang) *prep. Scot.* Among.

Man·ga·lore (mang′gə·lôr′, -lōr′) A port of western Madras, SW India.

Man·gan (mang′gən), **James Clarence,** 1803–1849, Irish poet.

man·ga·nate (mang′gə·nāt) *n. Chem.* A salt of manganic acid, such as those of sodium, potassium, and barium. [<MANGAN(IC) + -ATE[3]]

man·ga·nese (mang′gə·nēs, -nēz) *n. Chem.* A hard, brittle, metallic element (symbol Mn). In color, it is grayish-white tinged with red; it rusts like iron, but is not magnetic; it is widely distributed (in combination) in nature, and forms an important component of certain alloys, such as manganese steel. See ELEMENT. [<F *manganèse* <Ital. *manganese,* alter. of Med. L *magnesia* MAGNESIA]

manganese dioxide Pyrolusite.

manganese spar 1 Rhodonite. **2** Rhodochrosite.

manganese steel A very hard, ductile steel containing from 12 to 14 percent of manganese.

man·gan·ic (mang·gan′ik) *adj. Chem.* Of, pertaining to, containing, or obtained from manganese in its highest valence, as manganic acid, H_2MnO_4, known chiefly by its salts. [<MANGAN(ESE) + -IC]

man·ga·nite (mang′gə·nīt) *n.* **1** A dark, steel-gray to iron-black orthorhombic manganese hydroxide, MnO(OH). **2** *Chem.* Any salt obtained from certain hydroxides of manganese, and regarded as an acid.

man·ga·nous (mang′gə·nəs) *adj.* Of, pertaining to, or containing manganese in its lowest valence.

Man·ga·re·va (mäng′ä·rā′vä) **1** Largest of the Gambier Islands. **2** The Gambier Islands.

mange (mānj) *n.* An itching skin disease of dogs and other domestic animals, caused by burrowing parasitic mites. Also **the mange.** [<OF *manjue* an itch, eating < *manjuer, mangier.* See MANGER.]

man·gel-wur·zel (mang′gəl·wûr′zəl, -wûrt′səl) *n.* A large-rooted European beet *(Beta vulgaris)*, fed to cattle. Also **man′gel.** [<G < *mangoldwurzel* < *mangold* a beet + *wurzel* a root]

man·ger (mān′jər) *n.* A trough or box, for feeding horses or cattle. [<OF *mangeoire, mangeure* < *mangier* eat <L *manducare* chew]

man·gle[1] (mang′gəl) *v.t.* **·gled, ·gling 1** To disfigure or mutilate, as by cutting, bruising, or crushing; lacerate. **2** To mar or ruin; spoil: to *mangle* a word. See synonyms under REND. [<AF *mangler, mahangler,* appar. freq. of OF *mahaigher* MAIM]

man·gle[2] (mang′gəl) *n.* A machine for smoothing fabrics by pressing them between rollers. **—** *v.t.* **·gled, ·gling** To smooth with a mangle. [<Du. *mangel* <MDu. *mange* <Ital. *mangano* <LL *manganum* <Gk. *manganon* a pulley, a war machine. Doublet of MANGONEL.]

man·gler (mang′glər) *n.* One who or that which mangles.

man·go (mang′gō) *n. pl.* **·goes** or **·gos 1** The edible, fleshy fruit of a tropical tree allied to the sumac. **2** The tree *(Mangifera indica,* family *Anacardiaceae)* producing the fruit. **3** A pickled green muskmelon. [<Pg. *manga* <Malay *mañga* <Tamil *mān-kāy* < *mān* a mango tree + *kāy* a fruit]

man·go·nel (mang′gə·nel) *n.* A military engine formerly used for throwing stones and other missiles. [<OF, dim. of LL *manganum.* Doublet of MANGLE[2].]

man·go·steen (mang′gə·stēn) *n.* **1** The reddish-brown fruit of an East Indian tree, about the size of an apple, having a thick, fleshy rind, and a white, juicy pulp. **2** The tree *(Garcinia mangostana)* producing this fruit. [<Malay *mangustan*]

man·grove (mang′grōv, man′-) *n.* **1** A tropical tree (genus *Rhizophora,* especially *R. mangle*) which throws out many aerial roots from the lower branches and stem, forming dense thickets. **2** A shrub of the vervain family, as the **black mangrove** *(Avicennia marina).* [<Sp. *mangle* <Taino; infl. in form by GROVE]

mangrove cuckoo A cuckoo *(Coccyzus minor)* frequenting mangroves of the West Indies, Florida, etc.

man·gy (mān′jē) *adj.* **·gi·er, ·gi·est 1** Affected with the mange. **2** Figuratively, poverty-stricken; squalid. **— man′gi·ly** *adv.* **— man′gi·ness** *n.*

man·han·dle (man′han′dəl) *v.t.* **·dled, ·dling 1** To move by manpower without mechanical aids. **2** To handle with roughness, as in anger.

Man·hat·tan (mən·hat′ən, man-) *n.* **1** A cocktail made of whisky and vermouth, often with a dash of bitters and a cherry. **2** One of a tribe of Algonquian North American Indians, formerly inhabiting Manhattan Island.

Man·hat·tan Island (mən·hat′ən, man-) An island in SE New York at the mouth of the Hudson River; 22 square miles; comprising **Manhattan** borough of New York City.

man·hole (man′hōl′) *n.* An opening through which a man may enter a boiler, conduit, sewer, etc., for making repairs.

man·hood (man′hŏŏd) *n.* **1** Manly qualities collectively; manliness; courage. **2** The state of being of age; man's estate. **3** The state of being a man, or a human being as distinguished from other animals or beings. **4** Men collectively: the *manhood* of the nation.

man–hour (man′our′) *n.* A unit of measure equal to the amount of work one man can do in one hour.

ma·ni·a (mā′nē·ə, mān′yə) *n.* **1** Madness. **2** *Psychiatry* Exaggerated melancholia alternating periodically with an exaggerated sense of well-being, accompanied by excessive activity (both mental and physical): also called *manic-depressive psychosis.* **3** A strong, ungovernable desire; also, colloquially, a craze: a *mania* for rare books. See synonyms under FRENZY, INSANITY. [<L <Gk., madness < *mainesthai* rage. Akin to MANTIC.]

-mania *combining form* An exaggerated, persistent, or irrational craving for or infatuation with. [<Gk. *mania* madness] Below are some examples.

agromania	open country
bibliomania	books
cratomania	power
dipsomania	alcohol
kleptomania	stealing
megalomania	greatness, fame
mythomania	telling lies
nostomania	one's home
nymphomania	men
plutomania	wealth
pyromania	setting fires
toxicomania	poisons

ma·ni·ac (mā′nē·ak) *adj.* Having a mania; raving. See synonyms under INSANE. **—** *n.* A person wildly or violently insane; a madman. [<LL *maniacus* <L *mania* MANIA] **— ma·ni·a·cal** (mə·nī′ə·kəl) *adj.* **— ma·ni′a·cal·ly** *adv.*

-maniac *combining form* Forming adjectives (often used as nouns) from nouns in *-mania*: *kleptomaniac.*

man·ic (man′ik, mā′nik) *adj.* Pertaining to, like, or affected by mania. [<MAN(IA) + -IC]

man·ic-de·pres·sive (man′ik·di·pres′iv) *adj. Psychiatry* Denoting a mental disorder characterized by sudden fluctuations of depression and excitement. **—** *n.* One who suffers from this disorder.

Man·i·chee (man′ə·kē) *n.* A follower of the Persian Manes. [<LL *Manichaeus* <LGk. *Manichaios* Manes]

Man·i·che·ism (man′ə·kē′iz·əm) *n.* A dualistic religious philosophy developed by the Persian Manes and his followers in which goodness, typified as light, God, or the soul, is represented as in conflict with evil, typified by darkness, Satan, or the body: taught from the third to the seventh century. Also **Man′i·chae′ism. — Man′i·che′an, Man′i·chae′an** *adj.* & *n.*

man·i·cure (man′ə·kyŏŏr) *n.* **1** The care or treatment of the hands and fingernails. **2** *Obs.* A manicurist. **—** *v.t.* & *v.i.* **·cured, ·cur·ing** To take care of or treat (the hands and nails). [<F <L *manus* hand + *cura* care]

man·i·cur·ist (man′ə·kyŏŏr′ist) *n.* One who cares for or treats the hands and fingernails.

man·i·fest (man′ə·fest) *n.* **1** In shipping and transportation: **a** An itemized account of a carrier's cargo, showing ports of lading, consignees, etc. **b** The list of passengers, cargo, etc., for an airplane flight. **c** A detailed list of the cars of a train. **d** A fast freight train, or perishable goods on it. **2** *Obs.* A manifesto. **—** *v.t.* **1** To make plain to sight or understanding; reveal; display. **2** To prove; be evidence of. **3** To show the manifest of (a shipment). **—** *adj.* Plainly apparent to sight or understanding; evident; plain. [<L *manifestus* evident, lit., struck by the hand] **— man′i·fest′ly** *adv.*

Synonyms (adj.): apparent, bare, clear, conspicuous, distinct, evident, glaring, indubitable, obvious, open, overt, palpable, patent, plain, transparent, unmistakable, visible. See CLEAR, EVIDENT, NOTORIOUS, OVERT. *Antonyms*: concealed, covert, dark, hidden, impalpable, impenetrable, imperceptible, invisible, latent, obscure, occult, secret, undiscovered, unimagined, unknown, unseen.

man·i·fes·ta·tion (man′ə·fes·tā′shən) *n.* **1** The act of manifesting or making plain; the state or fact of being manifested; disclosure or display; a revelation. **2** Hence, a public or collective act by a government or party in order to emphasize its power, determination, or special views. 3 A revealing agency. 4 In spiritualism, the materialization of a spirit. See synonyms under MARK[1], SIGN. — **man'i·fes'tant** *n.*

man·i·fes·to (man'ə·fes'tō) *n. pl.* **·toes** A public, official, and authoritative declaration making announcement or explanation of intentions, motives, or principles of actions. [<Ital. <L *manifestus.* See MANIFEST.]

man·i·fold (man'ə·fōld) *v.t.* 1 To make more than one copy of at once, as with carbon paper on a typewriter. 2 To multiply. —*adj.* 1 Of great variety; numerous. 2 Manifested in many ways, or including many acts or elements; complex; being so in many ways or for many reasons. 3 Existing in great abundance. 4 Comprising or uniting several parts or channels of the same kind, as a pipe with several outlets. See synonyms under COMPLEX, MANY. —*n.* 1 A copy made by manifolding. 2 *Math.* A number of objects related under one system. 3 A tube with one or more inlets and two or more outlets; a T branch, as the pipe between carburetor and engine, in internal-combustion engines with more than one cylinder. [OE *manigfeald* varied, numerous] — **man'i·fold·ly** *adv.* — **man'i·fold·ness** *n.*

man·i·fold·er (man'ə·fōl'dər) *n.* 1 One who or that which manifolds. 2 A machine or apparatus for making manifold copies, as of a document.

Ma·ni·hi·ki (mä'nē·hē'kē) An island of the South Pacific administered by New Zealand with the Cook Islands: also *Humphrey Island.*

man·i·hot (man'ē·hot) *n.* Any of a large genus (*Manihot*) of tropical American, mainly Brazilian, herbs or woody plants of the spurge family. Brazilian or Ceará rubber is the product of *M. glaziovi.* [<NL <F <Tupian *mandioca* manioc root]

man·i·kin (man'ə·kin) *n.* 1 A model of the human body, showing its structure. 2 A dressmaker's assistant or lay figure wearing new costumes so as to display them for sale: also spelled *mannequin.* 3 A little man; dwarf. Also spelled *manakin, mannikin.* [<Du. *manneken,* dim. of *man* man]

ma·nil·a (mə·nil'ə) *n.* 1 A cheroot made in Manila. 2 The fiber of the abaca (*Musa textilis*), a tall, perennial herb of the same genus as the banana: also **Manila hemp, ma·nil'la.**

Ma·nil·a (mə·nil'ə, *Sp.* mä·nē'lä) A port on SW Luzon; former capital of the Philippines.

Manila Bay A landlocked inlet of the China Sea in SW Luzon, Philippines.

Manila paper A heavy, light-brown paper originally made of Manila hemp, now made of various fibers.

Manila rope Rope made of Manila hemp.

man·i·oc (man'ē·ok, mā'nē-) *n.* The bitter or sweet cassava. [<F <Tupian *mandioca* manioc root]

man·i·ple (man'ə·pəl) *n.* 1 *Eccl.* A band worn on the left arm as a vestment by the clergy of the Roman Catholic and sometimes of the Anglican Church. 2 A subdivision of the Roman legion containing 60 or 120 men. [<OF *maniple, manipule* <L *manipulus* a handful <*manus* hand + base of *plere* fill]

ma·nip·u·lar (mə·nip'yə·lər) *adj.* 1 Pertaining to manipulation or handling. 2 Pertaining to a maniple. [<L *manipularis* <*manipulus* a MANIPLE; infl. in sense by MANIPULATION]

ma·nip·u·late (mə·nip'yə·lāt) *v.t.* **·lat·ed, ·lat·ing** 1 To handle, operate, or use with or as with the hands, especially with skill. 2 To influence or control artfully or deceptively: to *manipulate* stocks. 3 To change or alter (figures, accounts, etc.), usually fraudulently. [Back formation <MANIPULATION <F, ult. <L *manipulus* a MANIPLE] — **ma·nip'u·la'tion** *n.* — **ma·nip'u·la'tive, ma·nip'u·la·to'ry** *adj.* — **ma·nip'u·la'tor** *n.*

Ma·ni·pur (mun'i·po͝or) A Union Territory of NE India, bordering on Burma; 8,628 square miles; capital, Imphal.

Man·i·pu·ri (mun'i·po͝or'ē) *n.* A native or inhabitant of Manipur.

ma·nis (mā'nis) *n.* A pangolin. [<NL, sing. <L *manes* MANES]

Ma·nis·sa (mä'nē·sä', mä'nē·sä) A city in eastern Turkey in Asia, on the site of ancient Magnesia. Also **Ma'ni·sa'.**

man·i·to (man'ə·tō) *n.* Among the Algonquian Indians, the unfathomable spirit or power behind life and the universe. See WAKANDA. Also **man·i·tou** (man'ə·to͞o), **man'i·tu.** — **Kitchi Manito** Great Spirit. [<Algonquian (Massachuset) *manitto* he is a god]

Man·i·to·ba (man'ə·tō'bə, -tō·bä') A province in central Canada; 246,512 square miles; capital, Winnipeg. — **Man'i·to'ban** *adj.* & *n.*

Manitoba, Lake A lake in SW Manitoba; 67 square miles.

Manitoba maple *Canadian* The box elder.

Man·i·tou·lin Island (man'ə·to͞o'lin) A Canadian island in Lake Huron, south central Ontario; 1,600 square miles.

Ma·ni·za·les (mä'nē·sä'lās) A city in west central Colombia.

man·kind (man'kīnd', man'kīnd') *n.* 1 The whole human species. 2 (man'kīnd') Men collectively as distinguished from women.

Synonyms: humanity, humankind, man, men. See HUMANITY.

man·like (man'līk') *adj.* Like a man; having the qualities proper to the human race, to the male sex, to manly character. See synonyms under MANLY, MASCULINE.

man·ly (man'lē) *adj.* **·li·er, ·li·est** Possessing the characteristics of a true man, as strength, frankness, and intrepidity. —*adv. Archaic* In a manner befitting a man. — **man'li·ly** *adv.* — **man'li·ness** *n.*

Synonyms: manful, manlike, mannish. *Manlike* may mean only having the outward appearance or semblance of a man, or it may be substantially equivalent to *manly. Manly* refers to all the qualities and traits worthy of a man; *manful* especially to the valor and prowess that become a man; we speak of a *manful* struggle; *manly* decision; we say *manly* gentleness, or tenderness; we could not say *manful* tenderness. *Mannish* is a depreciatory word referring to the mimicry or parade of some superficial qualities of manhood; as, a *mannish* woman. See MASCULINE.

Mann (man), **Horace,** 1796–1859, U. S. educator.

Mann (män), **Heinrich,** 1871–1950, German novelist active in the United States. — **Thomas,** 1875–1955, German novelist active in the United States; brother of the preceding.

man·na (man'ə) *n.* 1 The miraculously supplied food on which the Israelites subsisted in the wilderness. *Exodus* xvi 14–36. 2 Divine or spiritual nourishment. 3 A sweetish substance obtained from incisions in the stems of various trees or shrubs, especially the stems of the flowering ash (*Fraxinus ornus* and *F. rotundifolia*) of southern Europe. It is a mild laxative. [OE <LL <Gk. <Aramaic *mannā* <Hebrew *mān*]

Mann Act (man) A bill prohibiting the interstate transportation of women and girls for immoral purposes, enacted by Congress in June, 1910: also called *White-slave Act.* [after James Robert *Mann,* 1856–1922, U. S. congressman]

Man·nar (mə·när'), **Gulf of** An inlet of the Indian Ocean between southern Madras and Ceylon.

man·ne·quin (man'ə·kin) See MANIKIN (def. 2).

man·ner (man'ər) *n.* 1 The way of doing anything; method of procedure; mode. 2 The demeanor or bearing peculiar to one; personal carriage; mien; address. 3 *pl.* General modes of life or conduct; especially, social behavior. 4 *pl.* Polite, civil, or well-bred behavior. 5 Usual or ordinary practice; habit; custom; also, characteristic style in literature or art. 6 Sort or kind. 7 Character; guise. — **to the manner born** Familiar with something from birth. ◆ Homophone: *manor.* [<AF *manere,* OF *maniere,* ult. <L *manuarius* of the hand <*manus* hand]

Synonyms: appearance, aspect, carriage, demeanor, deportment, fashion, habit, look, mien, mode, practice, style, way. See ADDRESS, AIR, BEHAVIOR, CUSTOM, SYSTEM.

man·nered (man'ərd) *adj.* 1 Having (specified) manners: often used in combination: ill-*mannered.* 2 Affected.

Man·ner·heim (män'ər·hīm), **Baron Carl Gustaf Emil von,** 1867–1951, Finnish soldier and statesman.

man·ner·ism (man'ər·iz'əm) *n.* 1 Characteristic or marked adherence to an unusual or affected manner, style, or peculiarity. 2 A peculiarity of manner, as in behavior or speech.

man·ner·ist (man'ər·ist) *n.* A person addicted to mannerism; an imitator; specifically, an artist or writer whose work is marked by a persistent or extreme adherence to some style, manner, etc., as one of the school of painters of the 16th and 17th centuries who unduly emphasized and imitated the style of Michelangelo and other Italian painters.

man·ner·less (man'ər·lis) *adj.* Lacking manners; ill-mannered.

man·ner·ly (man'ər·lē) *adj.* Well-behaved; polite. —*adv.* With good manners; politely. — **man'ner·li·ness** *n.*

man·ners-bit (man'ərz·bit') *n.* A small amount left on a plate by a guest at table, for the sake of good manners, as indicating that the serving was abundant.

Mann·heim (män'hīm) A city on the Rhine in NW Baden-Württemberg, West Germany.

man·ni·kin (man'ə·kin) See MANIKIN.

Man·ning (man'ing), **Henry Edward,** 1808–92, English Roman Catholic cardinal and writer. — **William Thomas,** 1866–1949, U. S. Episcopalian divine; bishop of New York 1921–46.

man·nish (man'ish) *adj.* Resembling, characteristic of, or suitable to a man; aping manhood; masculine. See synonyms under MANLY, MASCULINE. [OE *menisc*] — **man'nish·ly** *adv.* — **man'nish·ness** *n.*

man·ni·tol (man'ə·tōl, -tol) *n. Biochem.* A slightly sweet crystalline alcohol, $C_6H_{14}O_6$, found widely distributed in nature, as in celery, sponges, sea grasses, and especially in the dried sap of the flowering ash. Also **man'nite** (-īt). [<MANNA (def. 3) + -ITE[3] + -OL[1]] — **man·nit·ic** (mə·nit'ik) *adj.*

man·nose (man'ōs) *n.* A hexose, $C_6H_{12}O_6$, obtained by the oxidation of mannitol. [< MANN(ITOL) + -OSE]

man·o·cry·om·e·ter (man'ō·krī·om'ə·tər) *n.* An instrument for determining the variations in the freezing or melting point of substances with changes in pressure. [<Gk. *manos* thin, rare + *kryos* an icy cold + -METER]

Ma·no·el (mä'nō·el') Portuguese form of EMMANUEL.

ma·noeu·ver (mə·no͞o'vər, -nyo͞o'-), **ma·noeu·vre** See MANEUVER.

Man of Destiny Napoleon I: so regarded by himself.

man of God 1 A saint, prophet, etc.; a holy man. 2 A clergyman.

Man of Sorrows A name supposed to allude to the Messiah (*Isa.* liii 3); hence, Jesus Christ.

man of straw One put forward as an irresponsible tool or as a fraudulent surety.

man-of-war (man'əv·wôr', man'ə-) *n. pl.* **men-of-war** (men'-) 1 A naval vessel armed for active hostilities. 2 The Portuguese man-of-war. Also **man'-o'-war'.**

man-of-war bird or **hawk** A frigate bird.

ma·nom·e·ter (mə·nom'ə·tər) *n.* An instrument for measuring pressure, as of gases and vapors; usually, a U-tube. [<Gk. *manos* thin, rare + -METER] — **man·o·met·ric** (man'ə·met'rik) or **·ri·cal** *adj.*

Ma·non Les·caut (mȧ·nôn' les·kō') Promiscuous heroine of Prévost's novel *Histoire du Chevalier Des Grieux et de Manon Lescaut.*

man·or (man'ər) *n.* 1 *Brit.* A nobleman's or gentleman's landed estate. 2 In old English law, a tract or district of land granted by the king to one as lord, with authority to exercise jurisdiction over it by a court-baron. 3 In Anglo-Saxon times, a thane's or lord's estate, composed of the land and of a part of the agricultural capital employed to till it, as well as the laborers, beasts, implements, etc., and having on it a community of serfs or villeins; later, an estate complying with the minimum requirements entitling the lord of the manor to hold a court-baron. 4 *U.S.* A tract of land originally granted as a manor and let by the proprietor to tenants in perpetuity or for a long term. See synonyms under HOUSE. ◆ Homophone: *manner.* [<OF *manoir* a

dwelling, orig. a verb <L *manere* remain] —**ma·no·ri·al** (mə·nôr′ē·əl, -nō′rē-) *adj.*
man·or-house (man′ər·hous′) *n.* The residence of the lord of the manor. Also **man′ or-seat′** (-sēt′).
man·pow·er (man′pou′ər) *n.* **1** Power supplied by the physical strength of a man or men. **2** The normal rate at which a man can work, generally equal to 1/10 horsepower. **3** The strength of all the men available for any service; specifically, the warpower of a nation in terms of the number of men available for military service, industry, agriculture, etc.
man·qué (män·kā′) *adj. French* Defective; falling short of what is intended. —**man·quée′** *adj.* fem.
man·rope (man′rōp′) *n. Naut.* A rope serving as a hand railing to a gangway, ladder, etc., on board ship.
man·sard (man′särd) *n.* **1** A roof with a double pitch on all sides; also **mansard roof. 2** A room within such a roof; an attic. [<F *mansarde,* after François *Mansard,* 1598–1666, French architect who revived it]
manse (mans) *n.* **1** A clergyman's house, especially a Scottish Presbyterian minister's house; a parsonage. **2** A landholder's residence. [<Med. L *mansa, mansus.* See MANSION.]
man·ser·vant (man′sûr′vənt) *n.* An adult male servant.
Mans·field (manz′fēld, mans′-) A municipal borough of Nottinghamshire, England.
Mans·field (manz′fēld, mans′-), **Katherine** Pseudonym of Kathleen Beauchamp Murry, 1888–1923, British author born in New Zealand. —**Richard,** 1854–1907, U.S. actor born in England.
Mans·field (manz′fēld, mans′-), **Mount** The highest peak of the Green Mountains, Vermont; 4,393 feet.
Man·ship (man′ship), **Paul,** Born 1885, U.S. sculptor.
man·sion (man′shən) *n.* **1** A large or handsome dwelling; specifically, the house of the lord of a manor; a manor-house. **2** In astrology, one of the 12 divisions of the heavens; a house. **3** According to Oriental and medieval astronomers, one of the 28 divisions of the heavens occupied by the moon on successive days. **4** *Archaic* Any place of abode. **5** A small compartment, abode, or dwelling in a larger house or enclosure. **6** *pl. Brit.* An apartment house. See synonyms under HOUSE. [<OF <L *mansio, -onis* a dwelling < *mansus,* pp. of *manere* remain, dwell. Doublet of MENAGE.]
man-sized (man′sīzd′) *adj. Colloq.* Of a size appropriate for a man; large.
man·slaugh·ter (man′slô′tər) *n.* The killing of man by man; especially, such killing without malice.
man·slay·er (man′slā′ər) *n.* One who commits homicide. —**man′slay′ing** *n.*
man·sue·tude (man′swə·to͞od, -tyo͞od) *n.* Accustomed gentleness or mildness; tameness. [<L *mansuetudo, -inis* <*mansuetus,* pp. of *mansuesere* tame <*manus* hand + *suescere* accustom]
man·swear (man′swâr′) *v.i.* **·swore, ·sworn, ·swear·ing** *Obs.* To swear falsely. [OE *mānswerian* <*mān* wickedness + *swerian* swear]
mant (mänt) *v.t. & v.i. Scot.* To stammer. —**mant′er** *n.*
man·ta (man′tə) *n.* **1** A coarse cotton cloth used by the lower classes of Spanish America for clothing; specifically, a woman's shawl or other article of clothing made of such material. **2** In the Rocky Mountains, the canvas covering of the load of a pack-animal. **3** A devilfish. **4** *Obs.* A mantelet. [<Sp., a blanket <LL *mantum* a cloak, back formation <L *mantellum.* See MANTLE.]
man·teau (man′tō, *Fr.* mä ṅ·tō′) *n. pl.* **·teaus** (-tōz) or **·teaux** (*Fr.* -tō′) **1** A cloak or mantle worn by women; any mantle. **2** *Obs.* A woman's gown; a mantua. [<F <OF *mantel* MANTLE]
man·tel (man′təl) *n.* The facing about a fireplace, including the shelf above it; also, the shelf. ◆Homophone: *mantle.* [Var. of MANTLE; infl. in meaning by F *manteau* a mantelpiece]
man·tel·et (man′təl·,et, mant′lit) *n.* **1** A small mantle or short cloak. **2** *Mil.* A screen or shield, as in an embrasure, to protect the defenders; a movable roof to protect a besieging party; also, a shield or protection, made of metal, rope, or wood, placed at openings, portholes, etc., to protect the gunner from bullets or smoke. **3** In target-shooting, a bulletproof enclosure for observation. **4** A movable shelter used by hunters. Also spelled *mantlet.* [<OF, dim. of *mantel.* See MANTLE.]
man·tel·let·ta (man′tə·let′ ə) *n.* In the Roman Catholic Church, a sleeveless vestment reaching almost to the knees, worn by bishops and various church dignitaries. [<Ital., dim. of *mantello* <L *mantellum.* See MANTLE.]
man·tel·piece (man′təl·pēs′) *n.* A mantel shelf.
man·tel·tree (man′təl·trē′) *n.* A wooden mantel; also, the arch of a mantel.
man·tic (man′tik) *adj.* Relating to divination, soothsaying, or the supposed inspired condition of a soothsayer; prophetic: *mantic* frenzy. [<Gk. *mantikos* <*mantis* a prophet. Akin to MANIA.]
-mantic *combining form* Used to form adjectives corresponding to nouns ending in *-mancy*: *necromantic.* [<Gk. *mantikos* prophetic < *manteia* divination]
man·til·la (man·til′ə) *n.* **1** A woman's light scarf or head covering of lace, as worn in Spain, Mexico, Italy, etc. **2** Any short mantle. [<Sp., dim. of *manta* MANTA]
man·tis (man′tis) *n. pl.* **·tis·es** or **·tes** (-tēz) A carnivorous, orthopterous, long-bodied insect (family *Mantidae*) with large eyes and movable head, which assumes a position with its forelegs folded as if in prayer. Also called *praying mantis.* For illustration see INSECTS (beneficial). [<Gk., a prophet, also a kind of insect]
man·tis·sa (man·tis′ə) *n. Math.* The decimal or fractional part of a logarithm: so named as being added to the integral part or characteristic. [<L, a makeweight, trifling addition, ? <Etruscan]
mantis shrimp A squill. Also **mantis crab.**
man·tle (man′təl) *n.* **1** A loose garment, usually without sleeves, worn over the other garments; a cloak. **2** Anything that clothes or envelops; hence, whatever covers or conceals; a *mantle* of darkness. **3** *Zool.* **a** The variously modified flap or folds of the membranous covering of a mollusk. It secretes the shell. **b** The back, scapulars, and folded wings of a bird, when distinguished by color, as in gulls. **c** The soft external body-wall in the tunic of ascidians. **4** The outer covering of a wall. **5** The outer masonry of a blast furnace. **6** A sheath of clay laid over a wax model, forming a mold when the wax is melted out. **7** A mantel. **8** A hood of network fabric, generally cylindrical, of the salts of certain rare refractory earths with high radiating power, as cerium oxide, intended to give light by incandescence, as in the flame of a Bunsen burner, or in the Welsbach burner. —*v.* **·tled, ·tling** *v.t.* **1** To cover with or as with a mantle; conceal. —*v.i.* **2** To overspread or cover the surface of something. **3** To be or become covered, overspread, or suffused. **4** To spread out one wing at a time over the corresponding outstretched leg: said of hawks. ◆Homophone: *mantel.* [Fusion of OE *mentel* and OF *mantel,* both <L *mantellum, mantelum* a cloak, cloth, towel]
mant·let (mant′lit) See MANTELET.
man·tu·a (man′cho͞o·ə, -to͞o·ə) *n.* A woman's loose cloak, worn about 1700. [Alter. of *manteau* ; infl. in form by *Mantua*]
Man·tu·a (man′cho͞o·ə, -to͞o·ə) A city on the Mincio, Lombardy, Italy; birthplace of Vergil. *Italian* **Man·to·va** (män′tō·vä). —**Man′tu·an** *n. & adj.*
Ma·nu·a Islands (mä·no͞o′ä) An island group in American Samoa; 22 square miles.
man·u·al (man′yo͞o·əl) *adj.* **1** Done, made, or used by the hand; of, relating to, or affecting the hand; *manual* employments. **2** *Law* Actually possessed; in one's own hands. **3** Resembling a manual; designed to be retained for reference: said of a book. — *n.* **1** A compact volume; handbook of instruction or directions. **2** A keyboard, as of an organ. **3** A systematic exercise in the handling of some military weapon. [<OF *manuel* <L *manualis* <L *manus* hand] —**man′u·al·ly** *adv.*
manual alphabet A series of manual signs or gestures representing the letters of the written alphabet, used by the deaf as a substitute for vocal speech. See illustration.
manual training In U.S. schools, training of pupils in carpentry, woodworking, etc.
ma·nu·bri·um (mə·no͞o′brē ·əm, -nyo͞o′-) *n. pl.* **·bri·a** (-brē·ə) **1** *Anat.* Some part or process like or likened to a handle; especially, the an-

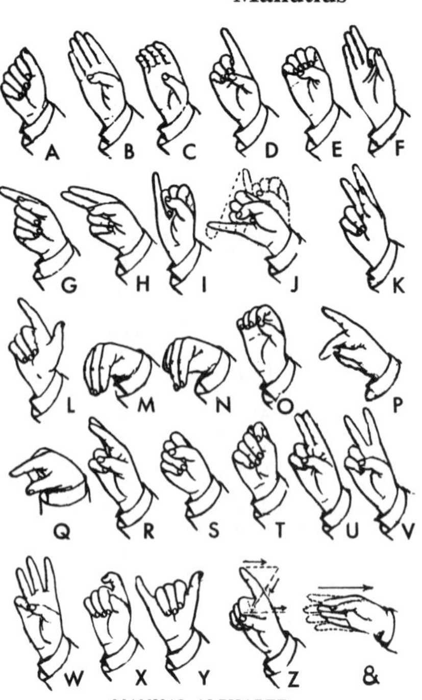

MANUAL ALPHABET

terior part of the sternum in man and many mammals: also called *episternum.* **2** *Mech.* A handle or haft, as of an organ stop. [<L, a handle, <*manus* hand] —**ma·nu′bri·al** *adj.*
Ma·nu·el (mä′no͞o·el′) Portuguese and Spanish form of EMMANUEL.
man·u·fac·to·ry (man′yə·fak′tər·ē) *n. pl.* **·ries** A place or establishment where anything is manufactured; a factory. [<MANUFACTURE; on analogy with FACTORY]
man·u·fac·ture (man′yə·fak′chər) *v.t.* **·tured, ·tur·ing 1** To make or fashion by hand or machinery, especially in large quantities. **2** To work into useful form, as wool or steel. **3** To create by artifice; invent falsely; concoct. **4** To produce in a mechanical way, as art, poetry, etc. See synonyms under MAKE[1], PRODUCE. —*n.* **1** The production of goods by hand or by industrial art or processes. **2** Anything made by industrial art or processes; manufactured articles collectively. **3** The making or contriving of anything. [<MF <Med. L *manufactura* <L *manus* hand + *factura* a making <*factus,* pp. of *facere* make] —**man′u·fac′tur·er** *n.* —**man′u·fac′tur·ing** *adj.*
man·u·mit (man′yə·mit′) *v.t.* **·mit·ted, ·mit·ting** To free from bondage, as a slave; emancipate; liberate. [<L *manumittere* <*manu emittere,* lit., send forth from one's hand <*manus* hand + *emittere* <*ex* away from + *mittere* send] —**man′u·mis′sion** (-mish′ən) *n.*
ma·nure (mə·no͝or′, -nyo͝or′) *n.* Any substance, as dung, decaying animal or vegetable matter, or certain minerals, applied to fertilize soil. —*v.t.* **·nured, ·nur·ing** To apply manure or other fertilizer to, as soil. [<AF *maynoverer* work with the hands, OF *manouvrer* < LL *manoperare.* Doublet of MANEUVER, MAINOR.] —**ma·nur′er** *n.*
ma·nus (mā′nəs) *n. pl.* **ma·nus 1** *Anat.* The hand, or the corresponding terminal part of a limb in vertebrates, as a forefoot, claw, hoof, or the like. **2** In ancient Roman law, authoritative control: said of persons rather than of things, as of the wife or children being *in manu* (literally, in the hand) of the husband or father. [<L, hand]
Ma·nus (mä′no͞os) Largest of the Admiralty Islands; 633 square miles.
man·u·script (man′yə·skript) *n.* **1** Matter written by hand with a pen or the like; a composition in handwriting or typewriting, as distinguished from a printed one. Abbr. *MS.,* plural *MSS.* **2** A roll or book written before the invention of printing. —*adj.* Written by hand. [<Med. L *manuscriptus* <L *manus* hand + *scriptus,* pp. of *scribere* write]
Ma·nu·ti·us (mə·no͞o′shē·əs, -shəs, -nyo͞o′-),

Aldus, 1450–1515, Italian printer; inventor of italic letters.

man•ward (man′wərd) *adv.* To or toward man. Also **man′wards.**

man•wise (man′wīz′) *adv.* After the manner of a man or of men.

Manx (mangks) *adj.* Pertaining to the Isle of Man, its people, or their language. —*n.* **1** The people of the Isle of Man collectively: with *the.* **2** The Gaelic language of the Manx, virtually extinct. [<ON *manskr* of the Isle of Man, ult. <Celtic]

Manx cat (mangks) A variety of domestic cat having no tail.

Manx•man (mangks′-mən) *n. pl.* **•men** (-mən) A native of the Isle of Man.

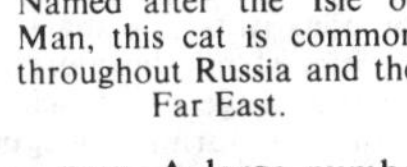

MANX CAT
Named after the Isle of Man, this cat is common throughout Russia and the Far East.

man•y (men′ē) *adj.* **more, most** Constituting a large number; numerous. —*n.* **1** A large number: *Many* of those present left early. **2** The masses; crowd; multitude: with *the.* —*pron.* A large number of persons or things. [OE *manig*]

◆ *Many* followed by *a, an,* or *another* indicates a great number thought of singly: *Many a* man has had to find this out for himself. The phrase *a great many* is idiomatic; it resembles a collective noun, but takes only a plural verb: *A great many* are involved.

Synonyms (adj.): divers, frequent, manifold, multifarious, multiplied, multitudinous, numerous, sundry, various. *Antonyms:* few, infrequent, rare, scarce, uncommon.

man•y•plies (men′i·plīz′) *n. Zool.* The third stomach of a ruminant, whose lining membrane is raised into many closely set, longitudinal folds; omasum. [<MANY + *plies,* pl. of PLY[1], *n.*]

Man•za•na•res (män′thä·nä′räs) A river in central Spain, flowing 55 miles SE past Madrid to a tributary of the Tagus.

man•za•nil•la (man′zə·nil′ə, *Sp.* män′thä·nē′lyä) *n.* **1** A pale, dry sherry with low alcoholic content. **2** A bitter olive usually stuffed with pimentos. [<Sp., orig. name of several carduaceous plants, dim. of *manzana* an apple. See MANCHINEEL.]

Man•za•nil•lo (män′sä·nē′yō) A port in SE Cuba.

man•za•ni•ta (man′zə·nē′tə, *Sp.* män′sä·nē′tä) *n.* Any one of several shrubs or small trees (genus *Arctostaphylos*) of the western United States, including the bearberry. [<Sp., dim. of *manzana* an apple. See MANCHINEEL.]

Man•zi•kert (man′zi·kûrt) A village in eastern Turkey NW of Lake Van; scene of the decisive defeat of the Byzantine Empire by the Seljuk Turks, 1071.

Man•zo•ni (män·dzō′nē), **Alessandro,** 1785–1873, Italian novelist and poet.

Mao•ism (mou′iz′əm) *n.* The militant communist doctrines or practices of Mao Tse-tung, characterized especially by a rejection of the possibility of coexistence with capitalistic states. —**Mao′ist** *n.*

Ma•o•ri (mä′ō·rē, mou′rē) *n.* **1** One of an aboriginal, light-brown people of New Zealand, chiefly Polynesian, mixed somewhat with Melanesian. **2** The Polynesian language of these people. —*adj.* Of or pertaining to the Maoris or their language.

Mao Tse-tung (mou′ dzu′dŏŏng′), 1893–1976, Chinese Communist leader; chairman of the People's Republic of China 1949–59.

map (map) *n.* **1** A representation on a plane surface of any region, as of the earth's surface; a chart. **2** Figuratively, any exact delineation. **3** *Slang* The face. —**off the map** Out of existence; out of the running. —*v.t.* **mapped, map•ping 1** To make a map of. **2** To plan in detail: often with *out.* [<OF *mappe-(monde)* <Med. L *mappa (mundi)* map (of the world) <L, cloth, napkin]

Map (map), **Walter,** 1140?–1209?, Welsh author: also called **Ma•pes** (mā′pēz).

ma•ple (mā′pəl) *n.* **1** Any of a large genus *(Acer)* of deciduous trees of the north temperate zone, with opposite leaves and a fruit of two joined samaras. **2** Its wood, which is hard, light in color, and of close grain. **3** The amber-yellow color of the finished wood. **4** The flavor of the sap of the sugar maple. —**hard maple 1** The sugar maple. **2** The black maple *(A. nigrum).* [OE *mapel(trēow), mapul(der)* a maple (tree)]

ma•qui (mä′kē) *n.* An ornamental evergreen shrub *(Aristotelia macqui),* used in Chile in making musical instruments. A medicinal wine is made from its purple acid berries. [< Sp. <Araucan]

ma•quis (mä·kē′) *n.* A zone of shrubby, mostly evergreen plants in the Mediterranean region, transitional between steppe and forest growths: known as cover for game or bandits: also called *macchia.* [<F <Ital. *macchia* a thicket, orig. a spot <L *macula* a spot]

Ma•quis (mȧ·kē′) *n. pl.* **•quis** The military branch of the French Underground, originally guerrilla bands, named for the maquis, chaparral-like brush of the Mediterranean coasts where they were first organized; by extension, the whole French Forces of the Interior, or French Underground, which developed after the fall of France in World War II.

mar (mär) *v.t.* **marred, mar•ring 1** To do harm to; impair or ruin. **2** To injure so as to deface; disfigure. See synonyms under HURT. —*n.* A disfiguring mark; blemish; injury. [OE *merran, mierran* hinder, injure] —**mar′•rer** *n.*

Mar (mär), **Earl of,** 1675–1732, John Erskine, Scottish politician and rebel, defeated by Argyle at Dunblane, 1715.

mar•a•bou (mar′ə·bōō) *n.* **1** A stork of the genus *Leptoptilos,* especially the **African marabou** *(L. crumeniferus),* whose soft, white, lower tail and wing feathers are used in millinery. **2** The adjutant bird. **3** A plume from the marabou. **4** A delicate white silk that can be dyed without being freed from gum. Also **mar′a•bout** (-bōōt). [<F *marabou, marabout.* See MARABOUT.]

MARABOU
(From 3 to 4 feet high at the shoulder)

Mar•a•bout (mar′ə·bōōt) *n.* A Moslem hermit or holy man of northern Africa, revered as a saint by the Berbers. [<F <Arabic *murābit* a hermit]

ma•ra•ca (mə·rä′kə, *Pg.* mä·rä′kä) *n.* A percussion instrument made of a gourd or gourd-shaped rattle with beans or beads inside it. [< Pg. *maracá* <Tupian]

Ma•ra•cai•bo (mä′rä·kī′bō) A port and the second largest city of Venezuela, on the narrows between **Lake Maracaibo** (5,000 square miles) in NW Venezuela and the **Gulf of Maracaibo** (also *Gulf of Venezuela*), an inlet of the Caribbean in Venezuela and Colombia.

Mar•a•can•da (mar′ə·kan′də) Ancient name for SAMARKAND.

Ma•ra•cay (mä′rä·kī′) A city in northern Venezuela.

Ma•rah (mā′rə, mâr′ə) *n.* Bitter water: used in allusion to the meaning in *Exodus* xv 23. [< Hebrew *mārāh,* fem. of *mar* bitter]

mar•a•na•tha (mar′ə·nath′ə) See ANATHEMA MARANATHA.

Ma•ran•hão (mä′rə·nyoun′) A state of NE Brazil on the Atlantic; 129,270 square miles; capital, São Luis de Maranhão.

Ma•ra•ñón (mä′rä·nyōn′) One of the main sources of the Amazon in Peru, flowing 1,000 miles north.

ma•ran•ta (mə·ran′tə) *n.* Starch from arrowroot. [after Bartolommeo *Maranta,* died 1554, Italian physician and botanist]

ma•ras•ca (mə·ras′kə) *n.* A small, wild cherry *(Prunus cerasus marasca)* of the Dalmatian mountains. [<Ital., aphetic var. of *amarasca* < *amaro* bitter <L *amarus*]

mar•a•schi•no (mar′ə·skē′nō) *n.* A cordial distilled from the fermented juice of the marasca and flavored with the cracked pits. [<Ital. < *marasca* MARASCA]

maraschino cherries Cherries preserved in maraschino liqueur.

ma•ras•mus (mə·raz′məs) *n. Pathol.* A gradual and continuous wasting away of the body; emaciation, especially in infants and the aged. [<NL <Gk. *marasmos* <*marainein* waste]—**ma•ras′mic** *adj.*

Ma•rat (mȧ·rȧ′), **Jean Paul,** 1743–93, French revolutionary leader; killed by Charlotte Corday.

Ma•ra•tha (mə·rä′tə) See MAHRATTA.

Ma•ra•thi (mə·rä′tē) *n.* The Indic language of the Mahratta of India: also spelled *Mahrati.*

mar•a•thon (mar′ə·thon) *n.* **1** A footrace of 26 miles, 385 yards: a feature of the Olympic games: so called from a messenger's legendary run from Marathon to Athens to announce the Athenian victory over the Persians, 490 B.C. **2** Any endurance contest.

Mar•a•thon (mar′ə·thon) A plain in Attica, Greece, on the Aegean; scene of decisive victory of the Athenians over the Persians, 490 B.C.

ma•raud (mə·rôd′) *v.i.* To rove in search of plunder; make raids for booty. —*v.t.* To invade for plunder; raid. —*n.* A foray. [<F *marauder* <*maraud* a rogue]—**ma•raud′er** *n.*

mar•a•ve•di (mar′ə·vā′dē) *n.* A former Spanish coin of little value. [<Sp. *maravedí* <Arabic *murābitīn,* a Moorish dynasty of Spain, 1087–1147]

mar•ble (mär′bəl) *n.* **1** A compact, granular, partly crystallized limestone, occurring in many colors, valuable for building or ornamental purposes. ◆ Collateral adjective: *marmoreal.* **2** A sculptured or inscribed piece of this stone. **3** A small ball made of this stone, or of baked clay, glass, or porcelain. **4** *pl.* A boys' game played with such balls. **5** Marbling (def. 1). —*v.t.* **•bled, •bling** To color or vein in imitation of marble, as book edges.—*adj.* **1** Made of or like marble. **2** Without feeling; cold. See synonyms under PALE[2]. [<OF *marble, marbre* <L *marmor* < Gk. *marmaros,* lit., sparkling-stone, orig. stone; infl. in sense by *marmairein* sparkle]

marble cake A cake made of light and dark batter mixed to give a marblelike appearance.

mar•bled (mär′bəld) *adj.* Veined, clouded, or variegated like marble.

mar•ble•ize (mär′bəl·īz) *v.t.* **•ized,•iz•ing** *U.S.* To marble.

mar•ble•wood (mär′bəl·wŏŏd′) *n.* **1** A large East Indian tree *(Diospyros marmorata)* of the ebony family, yielding a variegated wood. **2** Its wood.

mar•bling (mär′bling) *n.* **1** A marking, mottling, or coloring resembling that of marble. **2** The act or method of imitating marble.

mar•bly (mär′blē) *adj.* **1** Resembling or containing marble. **2** Still or rigid like marble.

Mar•burg (mär′bûrg, *Ger.* mär′bŏŏrkh) A city in west central Hesse, West Germany. Also **Mar′burg an der Lahn** (än der län′).

marc (märk) *n.* **1** Solid refuse remaining from grapes or other fruit after pressing. **2** A brandy distilled from this. **3** Any insoluble residue after a substance has been treated with a solvent. [<F, prob. <*marcher* tread, press (grapes). See MARCH[1].]

Marc (märk), **Franz,** 1880–1916, German painter.

mar•ca•site (mär′kə·sīt) *n.* **1** A pale, bronze-yellow, orthorhombic iron disulfide, FeS_2; white iron pyrites. It is a dimorphous form of pyrites. **2** An ornament made of crystallized white pyrites or of highly polished steel. [<Med. L *marcasita,* prob. <Arabic *marqashītā*<Aramaic]

mar•cel (mär·sel′) *v.t.* **•celled, •cel•ling** To dress (the hair) in even, continuous waves by means of special irons. [after M. *Marcel,* 19th c. French hairdresser] —**mar•cel′ler** *n.*

marcel wave In hairdressing, a style of dressing the hair in tiers of even, continuous waves.

Mar•cel•la (mär·sel′ə) A feminine personal name.

Mar•cel•lus (mär·sel′əs) A masculine personal

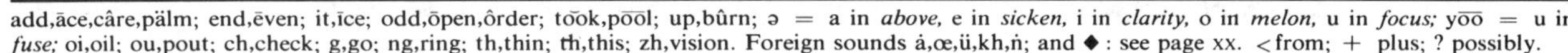

name; diminutive of MARCUS. Also *Fr.* **Mar·cel** (mȧr·sel′), *Ital.* **Mar·cel·lo** (mär·chel′lō). —**Marcellus, Marcus Claudius,** 268?–208 B.C., Roman general in the Second Punic War.

mar·ces·cent (mär·ses′ənt) *adj.* **1** Withering; withered. **2** *Bot.* Withering without falling off, as the corollas of heaths, etc. [<L *marcescens, -entis,* ppr. of *marcescere,* inceptive of *marcere* be faint, languid] —**mar·ces′cence** *n.*

march[1] (märch) *n.* **1** Movement together on foot and in time, as of soldiers; a stately, dignified walk. **2** A movement, as of soldiers, from one stopping place to another. **3** The distance thus passed over. **4** Onward progress: the *march* of events. **5** A piece of music suitable for regulating the movements of persons marching. —*v.i.* **1** To move with measured, regular steps, as a soldier; proceed in steps, as troops. **2** To walk in a solemn or dignified manner. **3** To proceed steadily; advance. —*v.t.* **4** To cause to march. [<MF*marche* < *marcher* walk, orig. trample, ult. <LL *marcus* a hammer <L *marculus*] —**march′er** *n.*

march[2] (märch) *n.* **1** A region or district lying along a boundary line; frontier. **2** *pl.* The border regions of England and Wales, or of England and Scotland. **3** *Scot.* The boundary or boundary marks between lands or estates. See synonyms under BOUNDARY. [<OF *marche* < Gmc. Akin to MARK[1], MARGIN.]

March The third month of the year, containing 31 days. [<AF *marche,* OF *marz* <L *Martius (mensis)* (month) of Mars <*Mars* the god Mars]

March (märkh) A river in Czechoslovakia forming part of the boundary between Czechoslovakia and Austria and flowing 180 miles NW to the Danube: Czech *Morava.*

Marche (mȧrsh) A region and former province of central France.

Mär·chen (mer′khən) *n. pl.* **Mär·chen** *German* A story; especially, a fairy tale or folk tale.

march·er (mär′chər) *n.* **1** An officer who defended a march. **2** One who resides in a march. [<MARCH[2]]

Mar·ches (mär′chiz), **The** A region of central Italy; 3,741 square miles; capital, Ancona. *Italian* **Le Mar·che** (lā mär′kā).

mar·che·sa (mär·kā′zä) *n. pl.* **·che·se** (-kā′zā) *Italian* A marchioness.

mar·che·se (mär·kā′zā) *n. pl.* **·che·si** (-kā′zē) *Italian* A nobleman of the rank of a marquis.

Mar·ches·van (mär·khesh′vən) See HESHWAN.

March hare A hare in the breeding season: regarded as a symbol of madness from the supposed wildness of hares at this time.

mar·chion·ess (mär′shən·is) *n.* **1** The wife or widow of a marquis. **2** A woman having in her own right the rank corresponding to that of a marquis. [<Med. L *marchionissa,* fem. of *marchio, -onis* a captain of the marches < *marca* march[2] <Gmc.]

march·land (märch′land′) *n.* Land along the boundaries of adjacent countries; borderland. [<MARCH[2] + LAND]

march·pane (märch′pān) *n.* Marzipan. [<MF *marcepain* <Ital. *marzapane* MARZIPAN]

Mar·ci·a (mär′shē·ə, -shə) A feminine personal name.

Mar·co Po·lo (mär′kō pō′lō) See POLO, MARCO.

Mar·co·ni (mär·kō′nē) *adj.* Pertaining to or designating the system of wireless telegraphy, developed by Guglielmo Marconi.

Mar·co·ni (mär·kō′nē), **Guglielmo,** 1874–1937, Italian inventor of wireless telegraphy.

Marconi rig In yachting, a type of rig consisting of a triangular sail mounted on a tall mast and having no gaff and a relatively short boom: so called from the resemblance of the mast and its stays to a radio mast. Compare GAFF RIG.

mar·cot·tage (mär′kō·täzh′) *n.* A method for the vegetative propagation of plants in which a part of the stem or branch is packed with moss until roots have formed and the treated part is ready for independent growth. [<F < *marcotter* plant layers <*marcotte* a layer (def. 3) <L *mergus* a vine layer, a diver <*mergere* dip, bury]

Mar·cus (mär′kəs) See MARK. Also *Fr.* **Marc** (mȧrk), *Ital.* **Mar·co** (mär′kō). [<L, of MARS]

—**Marcus Antonius** See ANTONY, MARK.

—**Marcus Aurelius** See under AURELIUS.

Mar·cus Island (mär′kəs) A North Pacific island east of the Volcano Islands, administered by the United States; one square mile; held (1899–1945) by Japan as **Mi·na·mi To·ri Shi·ma** (mē·nä·mē tō·rē shē·mä).

Mar del Pla·ta (mär thel plä′tä) A city in SE Buenos Aires province, Argentina.

Mar·di gras (mär′dē grä′) Shrove Tuesday; last day before Lent: celebrated as a carnival in certain cities. [<F., lit., fat Tuesday]

Mar·duk (mär′dook) In Babylonian mythology, the chief deity, originally a local sun-god.

mare[1] (mâr) *n.* The female of the horse and other equine animals. [OE *mēre,* fem. of *mearh* a horse]

mare[2] (mâr) *n.* A hag or goblin supposed to produce nightmare; also, nightmare. [OE. Akin to MAR.]

mar·e[3] (mâr′ē) *n. pl.* **mar·i·a** (mâr′ē·ə) Any of a number of dark, seemingly flat areas of the moon's surface. [<L, sea; because of their resemblance to seas]

ma·re clau·sum (mâr′ē klô′səm) *Latin* A closed sea; a sea subject to one nation: distinguished from an *open sea,* which is free to all.

Mare Island (mâr) An island in San Pablo Bay, north California; site of U.S. Navy yard.

ma·rem·ma (mə·rem′ə) *n. pl.* **·me** (-ē) **1** A fertile, marshy, but unhealthful piedmont region near the sea, as in Tuscany, Italy. **2** The miasmatic exhalations of such a region. [<Ital.< L *maritimus* MARITIME]

Ma·ren·go (mə·reng′gō) A village in Piedmont, NW Italy; scene of Napoleon's defeat of the Austrians, 1800.

ma·re nos·trum (mâr′ē nos′trəm) *Latin* Our sea: the Roman name for the Mediterranean.

mare's-nest (mârz′nest′) *n.* A seemingly important discovery that proves worthless, imaginary, or false.

mare's-tail (mârz′tāl′) *n.* **1** *Meteorol.* Long, fibrous, cirrus clouds, supposed to indicate rain. **2** A perennial aquatic herb *(Hippuris vulgaris)* with entire lineal leaves in whorls.

Mar·ga·ret (mär′gə·rət) **1** A feminine personal name. Also **Mar·ger·y** (mär′jər·ē), *Lat.* **Mar·ga·re·ta** (mär′gə·rē′tə), *Du.* **Mar·ga·re·tha** (mär′·gä·rē′tä), *Ger.* **Mar·ga·re·the** (mär′gə·rā′tə), *Pg.* **Mar·ga·ri·da** (mär′gə·rē′thə) *Lat., Ital.* **Mar·ga·ri·ta** (mär′gä·rē′tä), *Ital.* **Mar·ghe·ri·ta** (mär′ge·rē′tä), *Fr.* **Mar·gue·rite** (mȧr·gə·rēt′). [<Gk., pearl] **2** In Goethe's *Faust,* Margarethe, the heroine: also *Gretchen.*

—**Margaret of Anjou,** 1430–82, wife of Henry VI of England; a leader of the Lancastrians in the Wars of the Roses.

—**Margaret of Navarre,** 1492–1549, queen of Navarre, 1544–49.

—**Margaret of Valois,** 1553–1615, wife of Henry of Navarre; divorced: also known as *Margaret of France.*

mar·gar·ic (mär·gar′ik, -gär′-) *adj.* Of, pertaining to, or resembling pearl; pearly. Also **mar·ga·rit·ic** (mär′gə·rit′ik). [<F *margarique* <Gk. *margaron* a pearl]

margaric acid A white, crystalline, fatty acid, $C_{17}H_{34}O_2$, obtained from the wax of lichens or made synthetically. [<F *margarique* MARGARIC; with ref. to the pearly luster of its crystals]

mar·ga·rine (mär′jə·rin, -rēn, -gə-) *n.* A blend of refined, edible vegetable oil or meat fat, or a combination of both, churned with cultured skim milk to the consistency of butter. Also called *oleomargarine.* [<the early mistaken belief that it contained a derivative of margaric acid]

mar·ga·ri·ta (mar′gə·rē′tə) *n.* A cocktail made of tequila, lime or lemon juice, and an orange liqueur.

mar·ga·rite (mär′gə·rīt) *n.* **1** A hydrated silicate of calcium and aluminum. **2** Minute spherical crystals arranged as a beadlike pattern in glassy igneous rocks. **3** *Obs.* A pearl. [<OF <L *margarita* a pearl. See MARGARET.]

Mar·gate (mär′git) A municipal borough, port, and resort in NE Kent, England.

mar·gay (mär′gā) *n.* One of various South and Central American striped and spotted wild cats; especially, the long-tailed *Felis tigrina* [<F <*margaia* <Pg. *maracajá* <Tupian *mbaracaïa*]

marge[1] (märj) *n. Archaic* A margin. [<MF < L *margo* a margin]

marge[2] (märj) *n. Brit. Colloq.* Margarine.

mar·gin (mär′jin) *n.* **1** A bounding line; border; verge; brink; edge. **2** An allowance, provision, or reservation for contingencies or changes, as of time or money. **3** Range or scope; provision for increase or progress. **4** The difference between the cost of an article and its selling price. **5** A sum of money or other security deposited with a broker to protect him against loss in buying and selling for his principal; also, the difference in value between the security and the loan. **6** The difference between price and cost of production; in the adjustment of the relations of capital and labor, the minimum profit which will enable an undertaking to continue active. **7** The part of a page left blank around the body of printed or written text. —*v.t.* **1** To furnish with a margin; form a margin or border to; border. **2** To enter, place, or specify on the margin of a page, as a note or comment. **3** In commerce, to deposit a margin upon; hold by giving an addition to or a deposit upon a margin. [<L *margo, -inis.* Akin to MARK[1], MARCH[2].]

Synonyms (noun): beach, border, boundary, brim, brink, confines, edge, limit, lip, marge, shore, skirt, verge. See BANK, BOUNDARY.

mar·gi·nal (mär′jə·nəl) *adj.* **1** Pertaining to or constituting a margin. **2** Written, printed, or placed on the margin. **3** *Psychol.* Relating to the fringe of consciousness. **4** *Econ.* Operating or furnishing goods at a rate barely meeting the costs of production. **5** Of a nature that barely qualifies as useful, productive, or necessary. —**mar′gi·nal·ly** *adv.*

mar·gi·na·li·a (mär′jə·nā′lē·ə, nāl′yə) *n. pl.* **1** Marginal notes. **2** *Zool.* Spicules forming a collar around the osculum of a sponge. [< NL, neut. pl. of *marginalis* marginal <L *margo, -inis* a margin]

mar·gi·nate (mär′jə·nāt) *v.t.* **·nat·ed, ·nat·ing** To provide with a margin or margins. —*adj. Biol.* Having a margin, especially one of a distinct character, appearance, or color: also **mar′·gi·nat′ed.** [<L *marginatus,* pp. of *marginare* <*margo, -inis* a margin] —**mar′gi·na′·tion** *n.*

mar·grave (mär′grāv) *n.* **1** A hereditary German title of nobility, corresponding to *marquis.* **2** Formerly, the lord or governor of a German mark, march, or border. **3** A hereditary title of certain princes of the Holy Roman Empire. [<MDu. *markgrave* < MHG *marcgrave* <*mark* a march[2] + *graf* a count]

mar·gra·vi·ate (mär·grā′vē·it) *n.* The territory of a margrave. Also **mar·gra·vate** (mär′grə·vāt). [<Med. L *margravius,* ? <MHG *marcgrave* a margrave]

mar·gra·vine (mär′grə·vēn) *n.* The wife or widow of a margrave. [<Du. *markgravin,* fem. of *markgraaf* <MDu. *markgrave* a margrave]

mar·gue·rite (mär′gə·rēt′) *n.* A flower of the composite family, as the common garden daisy and the oxeye daisy of the fields; also, a chrysanthemum, *Chrysanthemum frutescens.* [<F, a pearl, daisy, from a proper name. See MARGARET.]

Ma·ri·a (mə·rī′ə, -rē′ə; *Du., Ger., Ital., Sp., Sw.* mä·rē′ä; *Hungarian* mä′rē·ä) A feminine personal name. See also MARY. Also **Mar·i·an** (mar′ē·ən), **Ma·rie** (mə·rē′; *Dan.* mä·rē′e, *Fr.* mȧ·rē′), **Mar·i·on** (mar′ē·ən). [See MARY]

—**Maria de 'Medici,** 1573–1642, wife of Henry IV of France. Also *Marie de Médicis.*

—**Maria Theresa,** 1717–80, wife of Francis I, Holy Roman Emperor.

—**Marie Antoinette,** 1755–93, wife of Louis XVI of France; guillotined.

—**Marie Louise,** 1791–1847, wife of Napoleon I; empress of the French.

ma·ri·a·chi (mär·ē·ä′chē) *n.* **1** A wandering band of Mexican street musicians. **2** The musicians, usually made up of singers and guitarists. **3** The music they play. [<Mexican Sp.]

ma·ri·age de con·ve·nance (mȧ·ryȧzh′ də kôṅ·näṅs) *French* A marriage of convenience; an advantageous marriage; not a love match.

Mar·i·an (mâr′ē·ən) *n.* **1** A worshiper or devotee of the Virgin Mary. **2** An adherent of Mary I, queen of England, or a defender of Mary Queen of Scots. —*adj.* **1** Of or pertaining to the Virgin Mary, or characterized by a special devotion to her. **2** Pertaining to Queen Mary of England, or to Mary Queen of Scots.

Mar·i·an (mar′ē·ən) A feminine personal name. See MARIA.

Ma·ria·na·o (mä′ryä·nä′ō) A city in western Cuba.
Ma·ri·a·nas Islands (mä′rē·ä′näs) An archipelago in the western Pacific Ocean, including Guam, Saipan, Tinian, and Rota; comprising part of the United Nations Trust Territory of the Pacific Islands (excluding Guam); total, 450 square miles; Japanese mandate, 1919–1944: formerly *Ladrones.* Also **Ma′ri·a′na** or **Ma′ri·an′ne Islands** (-rē·än′ə).
Ma·ri·anne (mâr′ē·an′) **1** A feminine personal name. **2** The French Republic, as personified on coins, etc.
Ma·ri·a Ther·e·si·o·pel (mä·rē′ä ter·ā′zē·ō′pel) A German name for SUBOTICA.
Ma·ri Autonomous S.S.R. (mä′rē) An administrative division of central European Russian S.F.S.R.; 8,900 square miles; capital, Ioshkar-Ola.
Ma·rie (mə·rē′) See MARIA.
Ma·rie Ga·lante (mà·rē′ gà·länt′) An island dependency of Guadeloupe; 60 square miles. Also **Ma·rie′-Ga·lante′.**
Ma·ri·gna·no (mä′rē·nyä′nō) A former name for MELEGNANO.
mar·i·gold (mar′ə·gōld) *n.* **1** A plant of the composite family (genus *Tagetes*), with golden-yellow flowers; especially, the French marigold *(T. patula)*, and the Aztec or African marigold *(T. erecta)*. **2** The calendula. **3** The marsh marigold. [<MARY, prob. with ref. to the Virgin Mary + GOLD]
marigold yellow The bright orange-yellow color of various marigolds.
mar·i·hua·na (mar′ə·wä′nə, *Sp.* mä′rē·hwä′nä) *n.* The hemp plant *(Cannabis sativa)*, whose dried leaves and flower tops yield a narcotic smoked in cigarettes. Also **ma′ri·jua′na.** [<Am. Sp. *marihuana, mariguana,* ? blend of N. Am. Ind. name and Sp. *Maria Juana* Mary Jane, a personal name]

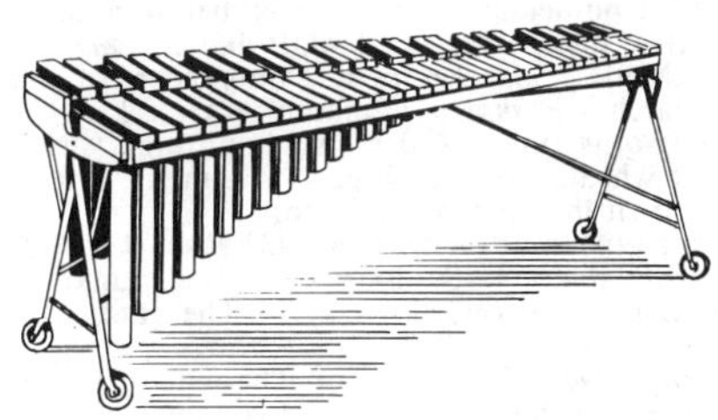

MODERN MARIMBA

ma·rim·ba (mə·rim′bə) *n.* A form of xylophone sometimes having calabash resonators. [< Bantu *marimba, malimba,* pl. of *limba,* a kind of musical instrument]
Ma·rin (mä′rin), **John,** 1870–1953, U.S. painter.
ma·ri·na (mə·rē′nə) *n. Naut.* A basin or safe anchorage for small vessels; especially, one at which provisions, supplies, etc., may be obtained. [<Ital., a seacoast <L *marinus* MARINE]
Ma·ri·na (mä·rē′nä) See ESPÍRITO SANTO.
mar·i·nade (mar′ə·nād′) *n.* **1** A brine pickle sometimes flavored with wine, spices, and herbs, in which meat or fish are placed before cooking, to improve their flavor. **2** Pickled meat or fish. [<F <Sp. *marinada* <*marinar* pickle in brine <*marino* marine <L *marinus* MARINE]
mar·i·nate (mar′ə·nāt) *v.t.* **·nat·ed, ·nat·ing** **1** To soak in oil and vinegar or brine preparatory to cooking; prepare with marinade. **2** To allow, as salad, to soak in French dressing before serving. [<MARIN(ADE) + -ATE[1]]
Ma·rin·du·que (mä′rin·do͞o′kä) An island of the Philippines south of Luzon; 346 square miles.
ma·rine (mə·rēn′) *adj.* **1** Of or pertaining to the sea or matters connected with the sea; maritime. **2** Native to, existing in, or formed by the sea. **3** Intended for use at sea or in navigation; nautical; naval: *marine* currents, *marine* law, a *marine* almanac. **4** Employed on shipboard. See synonyms under NAUTICAL. — *n.* **1** A soldier trained for service at sea and on land; a member of the Marine Corps: also **Marine. 2** Shipping, or shipping interests generally. See MERCHANT MARINE. **3** A picture or painting of the sea. [<OF *marin* <L *marinus* <*mare, maris* a sea]
Marine Corps A branch of the U.S. Navy made up of combat troops, air forces, etc., under their own officers: the oldest organized military or naval body in the United States, authorized 1775: officially, the *United States Marine Corps.*
mar·i·ner (mar′ə·nər) *n.* One who navigates or assists in navigating a ship; a sailor. [<AF <L *marinus* marine]
Mariner's Medal A medal awarded to any seaman who is wounded or suffers from exposure owing to enemy action while serving on a ship during a war.
Ma·ri·nism (mä·rē′nə·niz′əm) *n.* An ornate and flamboyant literary style, of the type cultivated by the Italian poet **Giambattista Ma·ri·ni** (mä·rē′nē), 1569–1625.
Mar·i·ol·a·try (mâr′ē·ol′ə·trē) *n.* Worship of the Virgin Mary: an opprobrious term: also spelled *Maryolatry.* [<*Mario-* (<MARY) + -LATRY] — **Mar′i·ol′a·trous** *adj.*
Mar·i·ol·o·gy (mâr′ē·ol′ə·jē) *n.* The whole body of religious belief and dogma relating to the Virgin Mary. Also spelled *Maryology.* [< *Mario-* (<MARY) + -LOGY]
Mar·i·on (mar′ē·ən) A masculine or feminine personal name. [<F, dim. of *Marie* MARY]
Mar·i·on (mar′ē·ən), **Francis,** 1732–95, American Revolutionary general: called "the Swamp Fox."
mar·i·o·nette (mar′ē·ə·net′) *n.* A puppet moved by strings. [<F *marionnette,* dim. of *Marion,* dim. of *Marie* MARY; prob. orig. a small image of the Virgin Mary]
Mar·i·po·sa (mar′ə·pō′zə) A county in central California, containing Yosemite Valley; 1,455 square miles.
Mariposa lily Any of a genus *(Calochortus)* of showy, colorful, liliaceous Mexican and Californian plants. Also **Mariposa tulip.**
mar·ish (mar′ish) *Obs. adj.* Marshy; boggy; growing in marshes, as plants. — *n.* A marsh; fen. [<OF *marais, mareis* <Med. L *mariscus* a marsh <Gmc.]
Mar·ist (mâr′ist) *adj.* **1** Of, pertaining to, or dedicated to the Virgin Mary. **2** Of or pertaining to the Marist Fathers, or to institutions founded by them. — *n.* A member of a Roman Catholic order devoted specifically to instruction and foreign missions: also **Marist Fathers.** [<(the VIRGIN) MAR(Y) + -IST]
Ma·ri·tain (mà·rē·tăn′), **Jacques,** 1882–1973, French philosopher.
mar·i·tal (mar′ə·təl) *adj.* **1** Of or pertaining to marriage. **2** Of or pertaining to a husband. [<L *maritalis* <*maritus* a husband, orig. married] — **mar′i·tal·ly** *adv.*
mar·i·time (mar′ə·tīm) *adj.* **1** Situated on or near the sea. **2** Pertaining to the sea or matters connected with the sea; marine. **3** Characterized by pursuits, interests, or power at sea; nautical. See synonyms under NAUTICAL. [<F <L *maritimus* <*mare, maris* a sea]
Maritime Alps The part of the Alps between France and Italy, extending to the Mediterranean coast.
Maritime Provinces The provinces of New Brunswick, Nova Scotia, and Prince Edward Island on the Atlantic seaboard of eastern Canada.
Ma·ri·tza (mä·rē′tsä) A river in SE Europe, flowing 300 miles SE to the Aegean. Also **Ma·ri′tsa.** *Turkish* **Me·riç** (me·rēch′), *Greek* **Év·ros** (ev′ros).
Mar·itz·burg (mar′its·bûrg) A popular name for PIETERMARITZBURG.
Ma·riu·pol (mä·ryo͞o′pôl) The former name for ZHDANOV.
Mar·i·us (mâr′ē·əs), **Gaius,** 157–86 B.C., Roman general and consul.
Ma·ri·vaux (mà·rē·vō′), **Pierre Carlet de Chamblain de,** 1688–1763, French dramatist and novelist.
mar·jo·ram (mär′jər·əm) *n.* Any of several perennial herbs of the mint family (genus *Majorana*), with nearly entire leaves, dense oblong spikes of flowers, and colored bracts. *M. hortensis* is the **sweet marjoram,** used for seasoning in cookery. [<OF *majorane* <Med. L *majorana,* ? ult. <L *amaracus* <Gk. *amarakos*]
mark[1] (märk) *n.* **1** A visible trace, impression, or sign produced or left on any substance, as a line, scratch, dot, scar, spot, stain, or blemish; any physical peculiarity produced by drawing, indenting, stamping, or other process or agency. **2** A symbol or character, as a stamp, brand, or device, made on or attached to something to identify, distinguish, or call attention; a trademark. **3** A cross or other character made instead of a signature by one who cannot write. **4** A letter of the alphabet, number, or character by which excellence, defect, or quality is registered, as on a student's paper or record. **5** A symbol, written or printed: a *mark* of interrogation. **6** An object serving to guide, direct, or point out, as a boundary, a course, or a place in a book. **7** That which indicates the presence or existence of something; a characteristic; an evidence; a symptom. **8** That which is aimed at, or toward which effort is directed; something shot, fired, or thrown at, as a target; that which one strives to attain or achieve; a goal. **9** A proper bound or limit; standard. **10** Distinction; eminence: a person of *mark.* **11** A license to make reprisals. See LETTER OF MARQUE. **12** A person easily duped: an easy *mark.* **13** *Naut.* A strip of cloth or the like knotted or twisted into a lead line at intervals to indicate fathoms of depth. **14** An observing or noting; heed. **15** In medieval times, a piece of land held in common by a body of kindred freemen. **16** *Archaic* A boundary; limit. — **beside the mark** Pointless. — **bless the mark! save the mark!** Ejaculations of deprecation, irony, scorn, or humorous surprise: used originally of a good, then ironically of a bad, marksman. — **to make one's mark** To succeed. — **of mark** Famous; noteworthy; important. — **up to the mark** Up to standard; in good health or condition, etc. — *v.t.* **1** To make a mark or marks on. **2** To trace the boundaries of; limit. **3** To indicate by a mark or sign: X *marks* the spot. **4** To make or produce by writing, drawing, etc. **5** To be a characteristic of; typify. **6** To designate as if by marking; destine: He was *marked* for death. **7** To pay attention to; notice; remark. **8** To make known; manifest; show: to *mark* displeasure with a frown. **9** To apply a price, identification, etc., to. **10** To give marks or grades to; grade. — *v.i.* **11** To take notice; pay attention. **12** To keep score or count. **13** To make a mark or marks. See synonyms under INSCRIBE. Compare CIRCUMSCRIBE. — **to mark down 1** To note down by writing or making marks. **2** To put a lower price on, as for a sale. — **to mark time 1** To keep time by moving the feet but not advancing. **2** To pause in action or progress temporarily, as while awaiting developments. — **to mark up 1** To make marks on; scar. **2** To increase the price of. [OE *mearc,* orig. boundary. Akin to MARGIN, MARCH[2].]

Synonyms (noun): badge, characteristic, fingerprint, footprint, impress, impression, indication, line, manifestation, print, sign, stamp, symbol, token, trace, track, vestige. See AIM, CHARACTERISTIC, LETTER, SIGN, TRACE.
mark[2] (märk) *n.* **1** The former monetary unit of Germany, a silver coin equivalent to 100 pfennige and valued at 23.8 cents: superseded in 1924 by the **reichs·mark** (rīkhs′märk′) and, after World War II, by the **deut·sche·mark** (doi′chə·märk′) in West Germany and the **ost·mark** (ôst′märk′) in East Germany. **2** A former silver coin of Scotland and England, worth 13*s.* 4*d.* **3** A former European unit of weight, equal to 256.27 grains. **4** A markka. [OE *marc* a unit of weight, prob. <LL *marca,* ? <Gmc. ? Akin to MARK[1].]
Mark (märk) A masculine personal name. Also *Greek* **Mar·kos** (mär′kos), *Ger., Sw.* **Mar·kus** (mär′ko͝os). [<L, of Mars]
— **Mark** The evangelist who wrote the second of the gospel narratives in the New Testament; also, the Gospel by him. Also **Saint Mark.**
— **Mark Antony** See under ANTONY.
marked (märkt) *adj.* Brought prominently to

notice; distinguished; prominent. — **mark·ed·ly** (mär′kid·lē) *adv.* — **mark′ed·ness** *n.*

marked man One who is singled out by others, as for suspicion, vengeance, etc.

mark·er (mär′kər) *n.* **1** That which marks; specifically, a bookmark, a milestone, a gravestone, etc. **2** A scorekeeper. **3** A device for tracing the lines of a tennis court or other playing ground. **4** *Slang* A written promise to pay a specified amount, used as currency in gambling, speculation, etc.

mar·ket (mär′kit) *n.* **1** A place where merchandise is exposed for sale; specifically, an open space or a large building in a town or city, generally with stalls or designated positions occupied by different dealers, especially such a place for the sale of provisions: also **market place.** **2** A private store for the sale of provisions: a meat *market.* **3** The state of trade as determined by prices, supply, and demand; traffic: a brisk *market.* **4** A locality or country where anything can be bought or sold; a place where any commodity is in demand: the South American *markets.* **5** A gathering of people for selling and buying, especially of a particular commodity: the wheat *market.* **6** The value of a thing as determined by the price it will bring; value in general; worth. — *v.t.* **1** To take or send to market for sale; sell. — *v.i.* **2** To deal in a market; sell or buy. **3** To buy food. [OE <AF <L *mercatus,* orig. pp. of *mercari* trade < *merx, mercis* merchandise. Doublet of MART[1].]

mar·ket·a·ble (mär′kit·ə·bəl) *adj.* **1** Suitable for sale; in demand. **2** Current in markets. **3** Of or pertaining to trading. — **mar′ket·a·bil′i·ty** *n.*

mar·ket·er (mär′kit·ər) *n.* One who buys or sells in a market.

market order An order to a broker to buy or sell at the current market price.

market price See under PRICE.

mar·ket–ripe (mär′kit·rīp′) *adj.* Not quite ripe: said of slightly unripe fruits picked to reach the market in salable condition.

market value The price which may be expected for a given commodity, security, or service under the conditions of a given market: distinguished from *normal value,* which is the average of values over a long period.

Mark·ham (mär′kəm), **(Charles) Edwin,** 1852–1940, U. S. poet.

Markham, Mount An Antarctic peak on the west edge of Ross Shelf Ice; 15,100 feet.

mark·ing (mär′king) *n.* **1** A mark or an arrangement of marks; characteristic coloring. **2** The act of making a mark.

mark·ka (märk′kä) *n.* The monetary unit of Finland. [<Finnish <Sw. *mark* <ON *mörk.* Akin to MARK[2].]

marks·man (märks′mən) *n. pl.* **·men** (-mən) **1** One skilled in hitting the mark, as with a rifle or other weapon. **2** In the U. S. Army, the lowest of three grades for skill in the use of small arms. **3** The soldier having this grade. Compare SHARPSHOOTER, EXPERT. — **marks′man·ship** *n.* — **marks′wom′an** *n. fem.*

Mark Twain (märk twān) Pseudonym of Samuel Langhorne Clemens, 1835–1910, U. S. humorist and novelist.

mark–up (märk′up′) *n.* **1** A raising of price. **2** The amount of price increase. **3** The sum added to cost, in computing selling price, to cover overhead and profit. **4** *Printing* The placement on copy of editorial directions for the printer or engraver.

marl[1] (märl) *v.t. Naut.* To wrap with marline, tying each turn with a hitch. [<Du. *marlen,* appar. freq. <MDu. *merren* tie]

marl[2] (märl) *n.* **1** An earthy deposit containing lime, clay, and sand, used as fertilizer. **2** A soft, earthy, crumbling stratum of varying composition. — *v.t.* To fertilize or spread with marl. [<OF *marle* <LL *margila,* dim. of L *marga,* ? <Celtic]

Marl·bor·ough (märl′bûr·ō, -bər·ə) A municipal borough in eastern Wiltshire, England.

Marl·bor·ough (märl′bûr·ō, -bər·ə), **Duke of,** 1650–1722, John Churchill; English general who defeated the French at Blenheim, Aug. 13, 1704.

marled (märld) *adj. Scot.* Variegated; marbled; mottled.

mar·lin[1] (mär′lin) *n.* Any of various deep–sea game fishes of the genus *Makaira;* especially, *M. ampla* of the Atlantic and the black or striped marlins of the Pacific. [<MARLINE(SPIKE); so called because of its shape]

mar·lin[2] (mär′lin) *n. U.S. Dial.* A curlew. [Alter. of obs. *marling,* var. of MERLIN]

mar·line (mär′lin) *n. Naut.* A small rope of two strands loosely twisted together: used for winding ropes, cables, etc. [<Prob. fusion of Du. *marlijn* (< *marren* tie + *lijn* a line) and E *marling* a binding <Du. <*marlen,* freq. of *marren*]

mar·line·spike (mär′lin·spīk′) *n. Naut.* A sharp–pointed iron pin used in splicing ropes. Also **mar′lin·spike′, mar′ling·spike′** (-ling-).

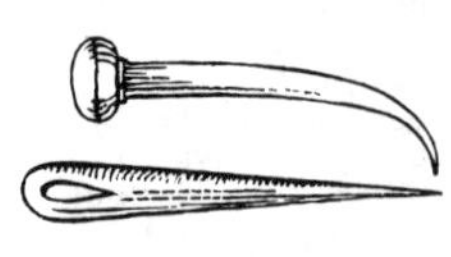
MARLINESPIKES

marl·ite (märl′īt) *n.* A variety of marl that differs from common marl by remaining solid on exposure to air. [<MARL[2] + -ITE[1]] — **mar·lit·ic** (mär·lit′ik) *adj.*

Mar·lowe (mär′lō), **Christopher,** 1564–93, English dramatist. — **Julia** Stage name of *Sarah Frost Sothern,* 1866–1950, U. S. actress born in England; wife of E. H. Sothern.

marl·y (mär′lē) *adj.* Resembling or of the nature of marl; abounding in marl. Also **mar·la·ceous** (mär·lā′shəs).

mar·ma·lade (mär′mə·lād) *n.* A preserve made by boiling the pulp and part of the rind or skin of fruits, usually citrus fruits, with sugar to the consistency of jam. [<MF *marmelade* <Pg. *marmelada* < *marmelo* a quince <L *melimelum* <Gk. *melimēlon* < *meli* honey + *mēlon* an apple]

marmalade tree A tall, tropical American, sapotaceous evergreen tree *(Achras zapota).* It bears plumlike fruits used chiefly for preserving. Also called *sapodilla.*

Mar·ma·ra (mär′mə·rə), **Sea of** A sea between Europe and Asia, leading by the Bosporus to the Black Sea, and by the Dardanelles to the Aegean: ancient *Propontis.* Also **Mar·mo·ra** (mär′mə·rə, mär·môr′ə, -mō′rə).

Mar·mi·on (mär′mē·ən), **Lord** The hero of *Marmion, A Tale of Flodden Field,* a romantic poem by Sir Walter Scott.

mar·mite (mär·mēt′) *n.* A small, lidded ceramic or enameled cooking pot. [<F, a pot, kettle]

Mar·mo·la·da (mär′mō·lä′dä) The highest mountain in the Dolomites, northern Italy; 10,964 feet.

mar·mo·re·al (mär·môr′ē·əl, -mō′rē-) *adj.* Pertaining to, made of, or resembling marble. Also **mar·mo′re·an** (-môr′ē-, -mō′rē-). [<L *marmoreus* < *marmor* MARBLE]

mar·mo·set (mär′mə·zet) *n.* **1** A small Central and South American monkey (family *Callithricidae*) with soft, woolly hair and a long hairy tail. **2** A related species, Goeldi's marmoset *(Callimico goeldii).* **3** The tamarin. **4** The ouistiti. [<OF *marmouset* a grotesque figure, prob. ult. <Gk. *mormō, -ous* a she–monster, bogey; with ref. to its appearance]

MARMOSET
(About the size of a large squirrel)

mar·mot (mär′mət) *n.* **1** A stout, short–tailed, burrowing rodent of mountain regions (genus *Marmota*). The species found in North America is known as a *woodchuck* or *ground hog.* **2** A related rodent, as the prairie dog. [<F *marmotte,* fusion of OF *marmotte* a monkey and Romansch *murmont* a marmot <L *mus, muris* a mouse + *mons, montis* a mountain]

Marne (märn) A river in NE France, flowing 325 miles NW to the Seine; scene of two decisive battles of World War I, 1914, 1918.

Ma·roc (mȧ·rôk′) The French name for MOROCCO.

Ma·ro·ni (mə·rō′nē) A river in the Guianas, flowing 450 miles north to the Atlantic. *Dutch* **Ma·ro·wij·ne** (mä′rō·wī′nə).

ma·roon[1] (mə·ro͞on′) *v.t.* **1** To put ashore and abandon on a desolate island or coast. **2** To abandon; leave helpless. [< *n.* (def. 1)] — *n.* **1** One of a class of Negroes, chiefly fugitive slaves or their descendants, living wild in the mountains of some West Indies islands and of Guiana. **2** *Rare* A person left alone on an island; a marooned person. [<F *marron* a maroon (def. 1) <Sp. *cimarron* wild]

ma·roon[2] (mə·ro͞on′) *n.* **1** A dull, dark–red color. **2** A coal–tar dyestuff. — *adj.* Having a dull, dark–red color. [<F *marron* a chestnut, chestnut color <Ital. *marrone*]

Ma·ros (mô·rōsh′) The Hungarian name for the MURES.

mar·plot (mär′plot′) *n.* One who, by meddling, mars or frustrates a design or plan.

marque (märk) *n.* A license of reprisal upon an enemy, as at sea in wartime: chiefly in the phrase *letter of marque.* [<F, mark, imprint, stamp <Provençal *marca* seizure < *marcar* seize as a pledge < *marc* a pledge <Gmc. Akin to MARK[1].]

mar·quee (mär·kē′) *n.* **1** A large field tent, especially one for an officer, or one used at lawn entertainments. **2** An awning or rooflike structure over the entrance to a hotel, theater, or other building. [<MARQUISE a canopy, mistaken as pl. <F]

Mar·que·san (mär·kā′sən) *adj.* Of the Marquesas Islands, the inhabitants, or their language. — *n.* **1** A native of the Marquesas Islands. **2** Their Polynesian language.

Mar·que·sas Islands (mär·kā′säs) A group of islands in French Oceania, in the South Pacific north of the Tuamotu group; 480 square miles. Also **Mar·que′zas Islands.** *French* **Îles Mar·quises** (ēl mȧr·kēz′).

Marquesas Keys A group of Florida islets west of Key West.

mar·quess (mär′kwis) See MARQUIS.

mar·que·try (mär′kə·trē) *n.* Inlaid work of wood often interspersed with stones, ivory, etc., especially as used in the decoration of furniture. Also **mar′que·te·rie.** [<MF *marqueterie* < *marqueter* variegate, inlay < *marque* a mark[1], ult. <Gmc.]

Mar·quette (mȧr·ket′), **Jacques,** 1636–75, French Jesuit priest and missionary who explored Canada: called "Père Marquette."

mar·quis (mär′kwis, *Fr.* mȧr·kē′) *n.* The title of a nobleman next in rank below a duke. Also, *Brit., marquess.* [<OF *marchis, marquis* <Med. L *marchensis* a commander of the marches < *marca* a march[2] <Gmc.]

Mar·quis (mär′kwis) *n.* An important variety of wheat, first developed in Canada, widely grown in the United States.

Mar·quis (mär′kwis), **Don(ald) Robert Perry,** 1878–1937, U. S. journalist and humorist.

mar·quis·ate (mär′kwiz·it) *n.* The rank of a marquis.

mar·quise (mär·kēz′) *n.* **1** The wife or widow of a French marquis. **2** An ornamental hood over a door; a marquee. **3** In gem–cutting, a pointed oval form, especially for diamonds. **4** A ring set with an oval cluster of gemstones. [<F, fem. of *marquis* a marquis]

MARQUISE

mar·qui·sette (mär′ki·zet′, -kwi-) *n.* A lightweight, open–mesh fabric of cotton, silk, rayon, or nylon, or a combination of these, used for curtains and women's and children's garments. [<F, dim. of *marquise* a marquise]

Marquis of Queensberry Rules A widely observed boxing code devised in 1869 by John Sholto Douglas (1844–1900), eighth Marquis of Queensberry.

Mar·ra·kesh (mä·rä′kesh) **1** A city in SW Morocco: formerly *Morocco.* **2** A region of SW Morocco; 45,725 square miles. Also **Mar·ra′kech.**

mar·ram (mar′əm) *n.* **1** Beachgrass. **2** A dune overgrown and bound together by this grass. [<ON *maralmr* < *marr* a sea + *halmr* haulm]

mar·riage (mar′ij) *n.* **1** The act of marrying, or the state of being married; specifically, a compact entered into by a man and a woman, to live together as husband and wife; wedlock. ◆ Collateral adjectives: *hymeneal, marital.* **2** A wedding; a nuptial celebration: with *of* or *between.* **3** Figuratively, any close union. **4** In pinochle, the king and queen of any suit. [<OF *mariage,* ult. <L *maritus* a husband]
Synonyms: matrimony, nuptials, union, wedding, wedlock. *Matrimony* denotes the state of those united in the *marriage* relation; *marriage* denotes primarily the act of so uniting, but is much used also for the state. *Wedlock,* a word of specific legal use, is the Saxon term for the state or relation denoted by *matrimony. Wedding* denotes the ceremony, with any attendant festivities, by which two persons are united as husband and wife, *nuptials* being the more formal and stately term to express the same idea. *Antonyms*: bachelorhood, celibacy, divorce, maidenhood, virginity, widowhood.

mar·riage·a·ble (mar′ij·ə·bəl) *adj.* Fitted by age, physical condition, etc., for marriage; nubile. **— mar′riage·a·bil′i·ty, mar′riage·a·ble·ness** *n.*

marriage lines *Brit.* A marriage certificate.

mar·ried (mar′ēd) *adj.* **1** Pertaining to marriage; connubial; conjugal: the *married* state. **2** Having a spouse; united by or as by matrimony; wedded: a *married* man.

mar·ron (mar′ən, *Fr.* må·rôn′) *n.* A chestnut, especially when used as food and in confectionery. [<F. See MAROON[2].]

marron gla·cé (glå·sā′) *French* A candied chestnut.

mar·row[1] (mar′ō) *n.* **1** A soft vascular tissue found in the central cavities of bones. **2** The interior substance of anything; essence; pith. [OE *mearg, mearh*] **— mar′row·y** *adj.*

mar·row[2] (mar′ō) *v.t.* & *v.i. Scot.* & *Brit. Dial.* To associate; marry. [? <Scand. Cf. ON *margr* friendly, lit., many.]

mar·row·bone (mar′ō·bōn′) *n.* **1** A bone containing marrow. **2** *pl.* One's knees: used humorously. **3** *pl.* Crossbones, the piratical emblem.

mar·row·fat (mar′ō·fat′) *n.* A large, rich pea. Also **marrow pea.**

marrow squash A variety of squash having an ovoid, fine-grained body; vegetable marrow.

Mar·rue·cos (mär·rwā′kōs) The Spanish name for MOROCCO.

mar·ry[1] (mar′ē) *v.* **·ried, ·ry·ing** *v.t.* **1** To join as husband and wife in marriage. **2** To take in marriage. **3** To give in marriage. **4** To unite closely. **5** *Naut.* To fasten end to end, as ropes, without increasing the diameter. — *v.i.* **6** To take a husband or wife. [<OF *marier* <L *maritare* <*maritus* a husband, married] **— mar′ri·er** *n.*

mar·ry[2] (mar′ē) *interj. Archaic* An exclamation of surprise or asseveration: a euphemistic variant of *Mary!* or *by Mary!* [Alter. of MARY; with ref. to the Virgin Mary]

Mar·ry·at (mar′ē·it, -at), **Frederick,** 1792–1848, English naval captain and novelist.

Mars (märz) *n. Obs.* In medieval alchemy, iron. [after *Mars,* the planet]

Mars (märz) **1** In Roman mythology, the god of war: identified with the Greek *Ares*: formerly called *Mavors.* **2** *Astron.* The fourth planet in order of distance from the sun, from which its mean distance is 141,500,000 miles, its least distance from the earth being about 35,000,000 miles. Mars has two satellites, a diameter of about 4,230 miles, a diurnal rotation of 24 hours, 37 minutes, 22.67 seconds, and a year of 686.9 days.

Mar·sa·la (mär·sä′lä) *n.* A light, sweet white wine originally made in Marsala.

Mar·sa·la (mär·sä′lä) A port of western Sicily.

Marse (märs) *n. U.S. Dial.* Master: formerly used by Negro slaves. Also **Mars.** [Alter. of MASTER]

Mar·seil·lais (mär′sə·lāz′, *Fr.* mår·sā·ye′) *adj.* Of or pertaining to Marseille, or to its inhabitants. — *n.* A native or inhabitant of Marseille. [<F <*Marseille* Marseille] — **Mar·seil·laise** (mär′sə·lāz′, *Fr.* mår·sā·yez′) *n.* & *adj. fem.*

Marseillaise The national anthem of the French Republic, written in 1792 by Rouget de Lisle. [<F, fem. of *Marseillais* MARSEILLAIS]

mar·seille (mär·sāl′) *n.* A thick cotton fabric having a raised weave, similar to piqué. Also **mar·seilles**(mär·sālz′). [from *Marseille,* France]

Mar·seille (mår·sā′y′) A port on the Gulf of the Lion; the second largest city in France. Also **Mar·seilles** (mär·sā′, -sālz′).

marsh (märsh) *n.* A tract of low, wet land; swamp. ◆ Collateral adjective: *paludal.* [OE *mersc, merisc.* Akin to MORASS.] **— marsh′y** *adj.* **— marsh′i·ness** *n.*

Marsh (märsh), **Othniel Charles,** 1831–1899, U. S. paleontologist.

mar·shal (mär′shəl) *n.* **1** An officer authorized to regulate ceremonies, preserve order, etc. **2** An official of the United States courts; also, the head of the police force or fire department in some cities. **3** In some European countries, a military officer of high rank; a field marshal. **4** In medieval times, a groom or master of the horse; later, as an officer of the king, a judge in courts of chivalry, etc. — *v.t.* **·shaled** or **·shalled, ·shal·ing** or **·shal·ling 1** To arrange or dispose in order, as facts. **2** To array or draw up, as troops for battle. **3** To lead; usher. ◆ Homophone: *martial.* [<OF *mareschal* <Med. L *mariscalcus* <OHG *marahscalh,* lit., a horse-servant <*marah* a horse + *scalh* a servant] **— mar′shal·cy, mar′shal·ship** *n.* **— mar′shal·er, mar′shal·ler** *n.*

Mar·shall (mär′shəl), **Alfred,** 1842–1924, English economist. **— George Catlett,** 1880–1959, chief of staff of U. S. Army in World War II; secretary of state 1947–49. **— John,** 1755–1835, U.S. statesman; jurist; secretary of state 1800–01; chief justice of United States 1801–1835.

Mar·shall Islands (mär′shəl) An island group in the NW Pacific, including Bikini, Eniwetok, Kwajalein, Jaluit, and other islands, comprising part of the United Nations Trust Territory of the Pacific Islands; total, 65 square miles; capital, Jaluit; Japanese mandate, 1920–1944.

Marshall Plan A post-World War II recovery program of U. S. financial aid to certain European countries, initiated June, 1947.

Mar·shal·sea (mär′shəl·sē) *Brit.* **1** The court (abolished 1849) held by the marshal of the royal household, originally to administer justice to the sovereign's domestic servants. **2** A debtors' prison in Southwark, abolished in 1842. [Var. of *marshalcy* <AF *mareschalcie* <Med. L *marisalcia* <*mariscalcus* a marshal]

marsh bluebill A ring-necked duck.

marsh elder 1 Any of a genus *(Iva)* of American salt-marsh plants, especially the high-water shrub *(I. frutescens)* of the SE United States: also called *sumpweed.* **2** The guelder-rose.

marsh frog A pickerel frog.

marsh gas Methane.

marsh hare In Louisiana, the muskrat.

marsh harrier An Old World hawk *(Circus aeruginosus)* with a yellowish head and predominantly dark-brown plumage: it nests on swampy ground and feeds largely on frogs, snakes, and small waterfowl.

marsh hawk An American hawk *(Circus hudsonius)* inhabiting marshes where it preys on snakes, frogs, etc.

marsh hen 1 The northern clapper rail *(Rallus longirostris crepitans),* which inhabits salt-water marshes along the American Atlantic coast. **2** The American coot *(Fulica americana).*

marsh·mal·low (marsh′mal′ō, -mel′ō) *n.* **1** A plant of the mallow family *(Althaea officinalis)* growing in marshy places. **2** A sweetmeat formerly made from the root of this plant; now a confection made of starch, corn sirup, and gelatin, coated with powdered sugar.

marsh marigold A showy swamp plant *(Caltha palustris)* of the crowfoot family, having bright-yellow flowers, found in swamps and wet meadows: also called *cowslip.*

marsh poisoning Impaludism.

marsh rosemary 1 A seaside perennial herb *(Limonium carolinianum),* with a strongly astringent root: used medicinally. **2** The moorwort.

Mar·si·an (mär′sē·ən) *adj.* Of or pertaining to the **Mar·si** (mär′sī), a people of ancient Italy. — *n.* **1** One of the Marsi. **2** Their language, belonging to the Sabellian branch of the Italic languages.

Mar·si·van (mär′sē·vän′) See MERZIFON.

Mar·ston (mär′stən), **John,** 1575?–1634, English dramatist and satirist.

Mar·ston Moor (mär′stən) An area in central Yorkshire, England, where Cromwell defeated the Royalists July 2, 1644.

mar·su·pi·al (mär·sōō′pē·əl) *n.* Any member of an order *(Marsupialia)* of mammals, as the kangaroos, opossums, wombats, etc., whose females typically lack a placenta, carrying their young in a marsupium. — *adj.* **1** Having a marsupium. **2** Of or pertaining to the *Marsupialia,* or of the nature of a marsupium or pouch. [<NL *marsupialis* <L *marsupium.* See MARSUPIUM.] **— mar·su′pi·a′li·an** (-ā′lē·ən), **mar·su′pi·an** *adj.* & *n.*

marsupial mouse Any of several small marsupials of Australia, as the **fat-tailed marsupial mouse** *(Sminthopsis crassicaudata),* or the **yellow-footed marsupial mouse** *(Antechinus flavipes).*

mar·su·pi·um (mär·sōō′pē·əm) *n. pl.* **·pi·a** (-pē·ə) A pouchlike invagination; specifically, a brood pouch or external receptacle for carrying young, as on the abdomen of marsupials. [<L, a pouch, purse <Gk. *marsypion,* dim. of *marsipos*]

Mars yellow A pigment consisting chiefly of hydrous oxide of iron and aluminum; iron yellow. Other pigments in the same group are **Mars orange, Mars red, Mars violet.**

Mar·sy·as (mär′sē·əs) In Greek mythology, a satyr and flute-player, who was defeated in a musical contest and flayed alive by Apollo.

mart[1] (märt) *n.* **1** A market. **2** *Archaic* A fair; also, traffic; trading. [<MDu. *markt, mart* <L *mercatus.* Doublet of MARKET.]

mart[2] (märt) *n. Scot.* An animal slaughtered at Martinmas.

Mar·ta (mär′tä) Italian and Spanish form of MARTHA.

Mar·ta·ban (mär′tə·bän′) A triangular inlet of the Andaman Sea in SE Burma.

mar·ta·gon (mär′tə·gon) See under LILY.

mar·tel·lo tower (mär·tel′ō) A circular tower of masonry, formerly erected on coasts for defense against invasion. Also **mar·tel′lo.** [from Cape *Mortella,* in Corsica, where such a tower was erected; infl. in form by Ital. *martello* a hammer]

mar·ten (mär′tən) *n.* **1** A weasel-like, fur-bearing carnivorous mammal (genus *Martes)* having arboreal habits, as the American pine marten *(M. americana),* and the large, sturdy fisher marten *(M. pennanti).* **2** The fur of a marten, often dyed and sold as an inferior sable. [<OF *martrine* of the marten <*martre* a marten <WGmc.]

MARTEN
(Species vary from 1 1/2 to 2 1/2 feet in body size)

mar·tens·ite (mär′tənz·īt) *n. Metall.* A constituent of rapidly quenched steel, consisting of iron and up to two percent of carbon. [after Prof. A. *Martens,* German metallurgist + -ITE[1]] **— mar′ten·sit′ic** (-tən·zit′ik) *adj.*

Mar·tha (mär′thə, *Dan., Du., Ger., Sw.* mär′tä) A feminine personal name. Also *Fr.* **Marthe** (mårt). [<Aramaic, a lady]
— Martha Friend of Jesus, and sister of Lazarus and Mary, who served Jesus at Bethany (*Luke* x 40); hence, figuratively, a houseworker.

Martha's Vineyard An island off SE Massachusetts; 20 miles long.

mar·tial (mär′shəl) *adj.* **1** Pertaining to, connected with, or suggestive of war or military operations: opposed to *civil*: court *martial.* **2** Warlike; brave; characteristic of a warlike person. See synonyms under WARLIKE. ◆ Homophone: *marshal.* [<OF <L *martialis* pertaining to Mars <*Mars, Martis* Mars] **— mar′tial·ism** *n.* **— mar′tial·ist** *n.* **— mar′tial·ly** *adv.*

Mar·tial (mär′shəl) *adj.* **1** Pertaining to the god

Mars. 2 In astrology, under the evil influence of the planet Mars. 3 *Astron.* Martian.

Mar•tial (mär′shəl), 40?–100?, Latin epigrammatist: full name *Marcus Valerius Martialis.*

martial law Military jurisdiction exercised by a government temporarily governing the civil population of a locality through its military forces, without the authority of written law, as necessity may require.

Mar•tian (mär′shən) *adj.* 1 *Astron.* Pertaining to the planet Mars. 2 Martial (defs. 1 and 2). —*n.* One of the supposed inhabitants of Mars. [<L *Martius* <*Mars, Martis* Mars]

mar•tin (mär′tən) *n.* 1 Any of certain birds of the swallow family, having a tail less forked than the common swallows; specifically, the **purple martin** *(Progne subis),* the **sand martin** or bank swallow *(Riparia riparia),* etc. 2 Some bird likened to a true martin, as a kingbird or chimney swift. [<F, prob. <*Martin* MARTIN]

Mar•tin (mär′tən; *Fr.* mȧr·taṅ′, *Ger.* mär′tēn) A masculine personal name. Also **Mar•tyn** (mär′tən), *Du.* **Mar•tijn** (mär′tīn), *Pg.* **Mar•ti•nho** (mär·tē′nyoo), *Ital., Sp.* **Mar•ti•no** (mär·tē′nō), *Lat.* **Mar•ti•nus** (mär·tī′nəs). [<L *Martinus* warlike]

—**Martin, Saint,** 315?–399?, bishop of Tours. See MARTINMAS.

Mar•tin (mär′tən), **Homer Dodge,** 1836–97, U.S. painter.

Mar•tin du Gard (mȧr·taṅ′ dü gȧr′), **Roger,** 1881–1958, French novelist.

Mar•ti•neau (mär′tə·nō), **Harriet,** 1802–76, English writer. —**James,** 1805–1900, English theologian and writer; brother of the preceding.

mar•ti•net (mär′tə·net′) *n.* A strict disciplinarian, especially military or naval: often used in derogatory sense. [after General *Martinet,* 17th c. French drillmaster]

Mar•ti•net (mȧr·tē·ne′), **André,** born 1908, French linguist.

mar•tin•gale (mär′tən·gāl) *n.* 1 A forked strap for holding down a horse's head by connecting the head gear with the bellyband. 2 *Naut.* A vertical spar under the bowsprit used in guying the stays. Also **mar′tin•gal** (-gal). [<F <Provençal *martengalo,* appar. fem. of *martengo* an inhabitant of Martigues, a town in Provence; ? with ref. to tight hose or breeches worn there]

mar•ti•ni (mär·tē′nē) *n.* A cocktail made of gin and dry vermouth, usually served with a green olive or a twist of lemon peel. [after *Martini* and Rossi, a company making vermouth]

Mar•ti•ni (mär·tē′nē), **Simone di,** 1283–1344, Sienese painter.

Mar•ti•nique (mär′ti·nēk′) An island in the Lesser Antilles, comprising an overseas department of France; 427 square miles; capital, Fort-de-France.

Mar•tin•mas (mär′tən·məs) *n.* The feast of St. Martin, November 11. [<Saint *Martin* + -MAS]

mart•let (märt′lit) *n.* 1 A martin. 2 *Her.* A martin or swallow without feet: used as a bearing, crest, or mark of cadency. [<F *martelet,* alter. of *martinet,* dim. of *martin* a martin; ? infl. in form by *roitelet* a wren]

mar•ton•ite (mär′tən·īt) *n.* Bromacetone.

mar•tyr (mär′tər) *n.* 1 One who submits to death rather than forswear his religion; specifically, one of the early Christians who suffered death for their religious principles. 2 One who dies or suffers for principles, or sacrifices all for a cause: a *martyr* to science. 3 One who suffers much or long, as from ill health or misfortune: a *martyr* to rheumatism. —*v.t.* 1 To put to death as a martyr. 2 To torture; persecute or torment. [OE <LL < Gk. *martyr,* Aeolic form of *martys, martyros* a witness]

mar•tyr•dom (mär′tər·dəm) *n.* 1 The condition or fate of a martyr. 2 Protracted or extreme suffering. [OE *martyrdōm*]

mar•tyr•ize (mär′tər·īz) *v.* **•ized, •iz•ing** *v.t.* To make a martyr of. —*v.i.* To become a martyr. —**mar′tyr•i•za′tion** *n.* —**mar′tyr•iz′er** *n.*

mar•tyr•ol•o•gy (mär′tə·rol′ə·jē) *n. pl.* **•gies** A historical record of martyrs. [<Med. L *martyrologium* <LGk. *martyrologion* <*martyr* martyr + Gk. *logos* word, account] —**mar•tyr•o•log•ic** (mär′tər·ə·loj′ik) or **•i•cal** *adj.* —**mar′tyr•ol′o•gist** *n.*

mar•vel (mär′vəl) *v.* **•veled** or **•velled, •vel•ing** or **•vel•ling** *v.i.* To be filled with wonder, surprise, etc.: We *marveled* at the young pianist's precocious brilliance. —*v.t.* To wonder at or about: with a clause as object. —*n.* 1 That which excites wonder; a prodigy. 2 The emotion of wonder. 3 A miracle. See synonyms under PRODIGY. [<OF *merveillier* <*merveille* a wonder <L *mirabilia,* neut. pl. of *mirabilis* wonderful <*mirari* wonder at]

Mar•vell (mär′vəl), **Andrew,** 1621–78, English poet and satirist.

mar•vel–of–Pe•ru (mär′vəl·əv·pə·rōō′) *n.* The four-o'clock.

mar•vel•ous (mär′vəl·əs) *adj.* 1 Exciting astonishment; singular; wonderful. 2 Pertaining to the supernatural; miraculous. Also **mar′vel•lous.** See synonyms under EXTRAORDINARY. —**mar′vel•ous•ly, mar′vel•lous•ly** *adv.* —**mar′•vel•ous•ness, mar′vel•lous•ness** *n.*

Mar•war (mär′wär) See JODHPUR.

Marx (märks), **Karl,** 1818–83, German socialist, revolutionary leader and writer on economics; author of *Das Kapital.* —**Marx′i•an** *adj.* & *n.*

Marx•ism (märk′siz·əm) *n.* The body of doctrine formulated by Karl Marx and Friedrich Engels in systematic form, including economic determinism, class conflicts leading inevitably to revolution in the transition from feudalism to capitalism and thence to communism under the dictatorship of the proletariat, and the predicted ultimate triumph of world communism as a result of destructive rivalries among the capitalist-imperialist powers.

Marx•ism–Len•in•ism (märk′siz·əm·len′in·iz′əm) *n.* The philosophy of history and politics based upon the works of Karl Marx and Nikolai Lenin, stressing Lenin's recension of Marxism in order to make it applicable to backward agrarian countries. —**Marx′ist–Len′in•ist** *n.*

Marx•ist (märk′sist) *adj.* 1 Of or pertaining to Karl Marx or his theories; Marxian. 2 Like or developed from the theories of Karl Marx: *Marxist* socialism. —*n.* A follower of Karl Marx; specifically, an adherent of Marxist socialism.

Mar•y (mâr′ē) A feminine personal name. Also *Polish* **Mar•ya** (mär′yä). See also MARIA. [< Hebrew, bitter]

—**Mary** The mother of Jesus: also *Virgin Mary.*

—**Mary** The sister of Lazarus and Martha.

—**Mary I,** 1516–58, queen of England, 1553–1558: known as *Mary Tudor* or *Bloody Mary.*

—**Mary II,** 1662–94, queen of England 1689–1694, ruling jointly with her husband, William III.

—**Mary Magdalene** A disciple from Magdala out of whom Jesus cast seven devils. *Luke* viii 2. She is often identified with the penitent sinner whom Jesus forgave. *Luke* vii 36–50.

—**Mary Queen of Scots,** 1542–87, queen of Scotland 1542–67; beheaded: also *Mary Stuart.*

Mary Jane (jān) 1 A low-heeled, usually patent-leather slipper with an ankle strap, worn especially by young girls. 2 *Slang* Marihuana. [def. 2 <folk etymology]

Mar•y•land (mâr′i·lənd, mer′i-) An eastern State of the United States, on Chesapeake Bay; 12,327 square miles; capital, Annapolis; entered the Union April 28, 1788, one of the original thirteen States; nickname, *Cockade State* or *Old Line State*: abbr. MD

Maryland yellowthroat See under YELLOWTHROAT.

Mar•y•le•bone (mâr′i·lə·bōn′, mâr′lə·bən, *Brit.* mal′ə·bōn′) A metropolitan borough of NW London, England: also *St. Marylebone.*

Mar•y•ol•a•try (mâr′ē·ol′ə·trē), **Mar•y•ol•o•gy** (-ol′ə·jē) See MARIOLATRY, etc.

mar•zi•pan (mär′zə·pan) *n.* A confection of grated almonds, sugar, and white of eggs, usually made into a paste and molded into various shapes: formerly known as *marchpane.* [<G <Ital. *marzapane,* orig. a small box, a dry measure, a weight <Med. L *matapanus* a Venetian coin stamped with an enthroned Christ <Arabic *mauthabān* a seated king, a coin <*wathaba* sit]

-mas *combining form* Mass; a (specified) festival or its celebration: *Christmas.* [<MASS[2]]

Ma•sac•cio (mä·sät′chō), 1402–28, Florentine painter: real name *Tommaso Guidi.*

Ma•san (mä·sän) A port in southern Korea. Formerly **Ma•sam•po** (mä·säm·pō).

Ma•sa•ryk (mä′sä·rik), **Jan,** 1886–1948, Czechoslovak diplomat and politician. — **Tomás,** 1850–1937, philosopher; first president of Czechoslovakia 1918–35; father of the preceding.

Mas•ba•te (mäz·bä′tā) One of the Visayan Islands, Philippines; 1,262 square miles.

Mas•ca•gni (mäs·kä′nyē), **Pietro,** 1863–1945, Italian composer.

mas•ca•longe (mas′kə·lonj) See MUSKELLUNGE.

mas•car•a (mas·kar′ə) *n.* A cosmetic preparation used to darken the eyelashes, usually black, brown, or blue. [<Sp. *máscara* a mask <Arabic *maskharah* a buffoon]

Mas•ca•rene Islands (mas′kə·rēn) An island group, including Réunion and Mauritius, in the Indian Ocean.

mas•cle (mas′kəl) *n.* 1 A lozenge-shaped plate used in scale armor. 2 *Her.* A lozenge voided. Also spelled *macle.* [<OF. See MACLE.]

mas•con (mas′kon, mäs-) *n.* Any of the dense concentrations of mass in the moon's lithosphere which cause irregularities in the gravitational field surrounding the moon. [<MAS(S) + CON(CENTRATION)]

mas•cot (mas′kot, -kət) *n.* 1 A person, animal, or thing thought to bring good luck. 2 *Brit.* An ornament on the radiator of an automobile. [<F *mascotte* <Provençal *mascot,* dim. of *masco* a sorcerer, lit., a mask]

mas•cu•line (mas′kyə·liṅ) *adj.* 1 Having the distinguishing qualities of the male sex, or pertaining to males; specially suitable for men; manly: opposed to *feminine.* 2 *Gram.* Being of the male gender. 3 *Bot.* Male; staminate. —*n.* 1 A male person; that which is of the male sex. 2 *Gram.* The masculine gender or a word of this gender: opposed to *feminine* and *neuter.* [<OF *masculin* <L *masculinus* <*masculus* male <*mas.* Doublet of MALE.] —**mas′cu•line•ly** *adv.* —**mas′cu•lin′i•ty, mas′•cu•line•ness** *n.*

Synonyms (adj.): male, manful, manlike, manly, mannish, virile. *Male* is applied to the sex, *masculine* to the qualities, especially to the stronger, hardier, and more imperious qualities that distinguish the *male* sex; as applied to women, *masculine* has often the depreciatory sense of unwomanly, rude, or harsh; as, a *masculine* face or voice, or the like; still one may say in a commendatory way, she acted with *masculine* courage or decision. *Masculine* may apply to the distinctive qualities of the *male* sex at any age; *virile* applies to the distinctive qualities of mature manhood only, as opposed not only to *feminine* or *womanly* but to *childish,* and is thus an emphatic word for *sturdy, intrepid,* etc. See also under MANLY. *Antonyms*: see synonyms for FEMININE.

Mase•field (mās′fēld), **John,** 1878–1967, English poet, novelist, and dramatist; poet laureate 1930–1967.

ma•ser (mā′zər) *n. Physics* Any of various devices that generate electromagnetic waves of precise frequency or that amplify such waves while maintaining frequency and phase, by using the excess energy of a resonant atomic or molecular system. [Acronym derived from *m(icrowave) a(mplification by) s(timulated) e(mission of) r(adiation)*]

mash (mash) *n.* 1 A soft, pulpy mass. 2 A mixture of meal, bran, etc., and water, fed warm to cattle. 3 Crushed or ground grain or malt, infused in hot water to produce wort. 4 In winemaking, the crushed grapes before fermentation begins. —*v.t.* 1 To crush or beat into a mash or pulp. 2 To convert into mash, as malt or grain, by infusing in hot water. [OE *māsc(wyrt)* mashwort, infused malt]

mash•er (mash′ər) *n.* 1 One who or that which mashes. 2 *Slang* A man who persistently annoys women unacquainted with him, as by attempting familiarities, etc.

Mash•er•brum (mush′ər·broom) A peak in the Karakoram mountain system, Kashmir; 25,600 feet. Also **Mash′ar•brum.**

Mash•had (mȧsh·hȧd′) See MESHED.

mash•ie (mash′ē) *n.* An iron golf club with a deep, short blade and much loft: used in approaching. See illustration under GOLF CLUB. Also **mash′y.** [? Alter. of F *massue* a club < LL *mattiuca* (assumed), prob. <Celtic]

mash·lin (mash′lin) *n. Scot.* Mixed grain.

Ma·sho·na·land (mə·shō′nə·land) A region of Southern Rhodesia; 80,344 square miles.

Mas·i·nis·sa (mas′ə·nis′ə), 238–148 B.C., king of Numidia; ally of Scipio against the Carthaginians.

mas·jid (mus′jid) *n. Arabic* A Moslem mosque.

mask[1] (mask, mäsk) *n.* **1** A cover or disguise, as for the features; a protective appliance for the face or head: a gas *mask.* **2** A subterfuge. **3** A cast of the face taken just after death. **4** A play or dramatic performance, in vogue in the 16th and 17th centuries, in which the actors were masked and represented allegorical or mythological subjects, originally in dumb show, but later in dialog, poetry, and song; also, a dramatic composition written for such a play: also spelled *masque.* **5** A masquerade: also spelled *masque.* **6** A masker. **7** An artistic covering for the face, used by Greek and Roman actors in comedy and tragedy. **8** *Archit.* A reproduction of a face or a face and neck, used as a gargoyle, a keystone of an arch, etc. **9** *Mil.* A screen of brush or the like for hiding a battery or any military operation from the enemy; camouflage. **10** *Zool.* Any formation about the head suggesting a mask; specifically, the enlarged lower lip of a larval dragonfly. **11** A fox's or dog's head. See synonyms under PRETENSE. —*v.t.* **1** To cover (the face, head, etc.) with a mask. **2** To hide or conceal with or as with a mask; disguise. —*v.i.* **3** To put on a mask; assume a disguise. [<F *masque* <Ital. *maschera, mascara* <Arabic *maskharah* a buffoon]

Synonyms (verb): cloak, conceal, cover, disguise, dissemble, hide, masquerade, pretend, screen, shroud, veil. See HIDE. *Antonyms:* betray, communicate, declare, disclose, divulge, exhibit, expose, publish, reveal, show, tell.

MASKS
a. Greek tragedy. *c.* Tibetan ceremonial.
b. Greek comedy. *d.* Ancient Shinto.
e. Domino.

mask[2] (mask, mäsk) *v.t. & v.i. Brit. Dial.* To infuse or be infused. [Var. of MASH]

masked (maskt, mäskt) *adj.* **1** Having the face covered with or as with a mask; disguised. **2** Personate. **3** *Zool.* Having markings resembling a mask, as various pupae of insects.

masked or **mask ball** A ball at which the dancers wear masks or dominos.

masked hunter The kissing bug.

mas·keg (mas′keg) See MUSKEG.

mask·er (mas′kər, mäs′-) *n.* One who wears a mask: also spelled *masquer.*

mask·ing (mas′king, mäs′-) *n. Scot.* A crushing into a mash.

masking tape An adhesive tape used to protect those parts of a surface not to be painted, sprayed, or otherwise treated.

mas·ki·nonge (mas′kə·nonj) See MUSKELLUNGE.

mas·lin (maz′lin) *n. Brit. Dial.* **1** Mixed grain, especially wheat and rye. **2** Bread made from such mixture. **3** A mixture; potpourri. [<OF *mesteillon* <LL *mistilio, -onis,* ult. <L *mixtus,* pp. of *miscere* mix]

mas·o·chism (mas′ə·kiz′əm) *n. Psychiatry* A condition in which sexual gratification depends on being dominated, cruelly treated, beaten, etc. [after Leopold von Sacher-*Masoch,* 1835–95, Austrian novelist, who described this condition] —**mas′o·chist** *n.* —**mas′o·chis′tic** *adj.*

ma·son (mā′sən) *n.* One who lays brick and stone in building; also, a stonecutter. —*v.t.* To build of masonry. [<OF *masson, maçon* <Med. L *matio, macio, -onis,* prob. <Gmc.]

Ma·son (mā′sən) *n.* A member of the order of Freemasons. —**Ma·son·ic** (mə·son′ik) *adj.*

Ma·son (mā′sən), **James Murray,** 1798–1871, Confederate statesman; with John Slidell, seized on board the British steamer *Trent,* 1861. —**Walt,** 1862–1939, U.S. humorist and poet.

mason bee A solitary bee *(Chalicodoma muraria)* of southern Europe which builds its nest of sand, clay, etc.

Ma·son–Dix·on line (mā′sən·dik′sən) The boundary between Pennsylvania and Maryland as surveyed by the Englishmen Charles Mason and Jeremiah Dixon in 1763–67: before the Civil War it was regarded as dividing Slave States from Free States, and is still used to distinguish the North from the South. Also **Mason and Dixon's line.**

Ma·son·ite (mā′sən·īt) *n.* A tough, dense, moisture-resistant fiberboard made from wood fibers exploded under high steam pressure: widely used as a building and construction material: a trade name.

Mason jar A glass jar having a tightly fitting screw top, used for canning and preserving: patented by John L. Mason of New York in 1857.

ma·son·ry (mā′sən·rē) *n. pl.* **·ries 1** The art or work of building with brick or stone. **2** That which is built by masons or of materials which masons use.

Ma·son·ry (mā′sən·rē) *n.* Freemasonry.

Ma·so·ra (mə·sō′rə) *n.* **1** A collection of criticisms and marginal notes to the Old Testament, made by Jewish writers before the tenth century. **2** The tradition relied on by the Jews to preserve the Old Testament text from corruption. Also **Ma·so′rah.** [<Hebrew (modern) *māsōrah* <Hebrew *māsōreth* tradition, orig., bond (of the covenant)] —**Mas·o·ret·ic** (mas′ə·ret′ik) or **·i·cal,** *adj.* —**Mas′o·rete** (-rēt), **Mas′o·rite** (-rīt) *n.*

Mas·pe·ro (mäs′pə·rō, *Fr.* mås·pə·rō′), **Gaston Camille Charles,** 1846–1916, French Egyptologist.

Mas·qat (mus′kat, mäs′kät) See MUSCAT.

masque (mask, mäsk), **mas·quer** (mas′kər, mäs′-) See MASK[1] (defs. 4 and 5), MASKER.

mas·quer·ade (mas′kə·rād′, mäs′-) *n.* **1** A social party composed of persons masked and costumed; also, the costumes and disguises worn on such an occasion. **2** A false show or disguise. **3** Formerly, a form of dramatic representation. —*v.i.* **·ad·ed, ·ad·ing 1** To take part in a masquerade. **2** To wear a mask or disguise. **3** To disguise one's true character; assume a false appearance. See synonyms under MASK[1]. [Alter. of F *mascarade* <Sp. *mascarada* <*máscara* a mask. See MASCARA.] —**mas′quer·ad′er** *n.*

mass[1] (mas, mäs) *n.* **1** An assemblage of things that collectively make one quantity. **2** A body of concrete matter; a lump. **3** The principal part of anything. **4** Extent of volume; bulk; size. **5** *Physics* The measure or expression of the inertia of a body, as indicated by the acceleration imparted to it when acted upon by a given force: it is the quotient of the weight of a body divided by the acceleration due to gravity. —*adj.* **1** Of, for, or consisting of the public in general. **2** Done on a large scale: *mass* production. —**the masses** The common people. See synonyms under MOB[1]. —*v.t. & v.i.* To form into a mass; assemble. [<OF *masse* <L *massa,* prob. <Gk. *maza* a barley cake]

Synonyms (noun): aggregate, body, bulk, heap, lump, matter, substance, total, totality, whole. See AGGREGATE, HEAP, THRONG.

mass[2] (mas, mäs) *n. Eccl.* **1** The eucharistic liturgy in the Roman Catholic and some Anglican churches, regarded as a commemoration or repetition of Christ's sacrifice on Calvary. **2** A celebration of this. See HIGH MASS, LOW MASS. **3** A musical setting for the fixed portions of this liturgy, as the Credo, Sanctus, Kyrie eleison, etc. Also **Mass.** —**black mass 1** A mass for the dead: so called because the celebrant wears black vestments. **2** A ceremony performed in so-called worship of Satan as a burlesque of the Christian mass. [OE *mæsse* <LL *messa* dismissal <L *missa,* pp. fem. of *mittere* send, dismiss < *ite, missa est* go, you are dismissed; said by the priest after the Eucharist is ended]

Mas·sa·chu·set (mas′ə·chōō′sit) *n.* **1** One of a large and important tribe of North American Indians of Algonquian linguistic stock, formerly inhabiting the region around Massachusetts Bay. **2** The language of this tribe. Also **Mas′sa·chu′sett.** [<Algonquian (Massachuset) *Massa-adchu-es-et,* lit., at the big hill <*massa* big + *wadchu* hill + *es,* dim. suffix + *et* at the]

Mas·sa·chu·setts (mas′ə·chōō′sits) A NE State of the United States on the Atlantic; 8,266 square miles; capital, Boston; entered the Union Feb. 6, 1788, one of the thirteen original States; nickname, *Bay State*: abbr. MA

Massachusetts Bay A wide inlet of the Atlantic on the eastern coast of Massachusetts, extending from Cape Ann to Cape Cod.

mas·sa·cre (mas′ə·kər) *n.* The indiscriminate killing of human beings, as in savage warfare; slaughter. —*v.t.* **·cred** (-kərd), **·cring** To kill indiscriminately or in great numbers; slaughter. [<MF <OF *maçacre, macecle,* ? < *mache-col* butcher <*macher* smash + *col* neck <L *collum*] —**mas′sa·crer** *n.*

Synonyms (noun): butchery, carnage, havoc, slaughter. A *massacre* is the indiscriminate killing in numbers of the unresisting or defenseless; *butchery* is the killing of men rudely and ruthlessly as cattle are killed in the shambles. *Havoc* may not be so complete as *massacre,* nor so coldly brutal as *butchery,* but is more widely spread and furious; it is destruction let loose, and may be applied to organizations, interests, etc., as well as to human life. *Carnage* refers to widely scattered or heaped up corpses of the slain; *slaughter* is similar in meaning, but refers more to the process, and *carnage* to the result.

mas·sage (mə·säzh′) *n.* A system of remedial treatment consisting of kneading, rubbing, and otherwise manipulating a part or the whole of the body with the hands. —*v.t.* **·saged, ·sag·ing** To treat by massage. [<F *masser* massage <*masse* mass <L *massa,* ? < Gk. *massein* knead] —**mas·sag′er, mas·sag′ist** *n.* —**mas·sa·geuse** (mas′ə·zhœz′) *n. fem.*

mas·sa·sau·ga (mas′ə·sô′gə) *n.* The pigmy rattlesnake *(Sistrurus miliarius)* of the southern United States, seldom exceeding 20 inches in length, and living in dry, warm areas: also called *ground rattlesnake.* [<Ojibwa name of a river in Ontario, Canada]

Mas·sa·soit (mas′ə·soit), died 1661, American Indian chief of Massachusetts; friendly with the Pilgrims of Plymouth Colony.

Mas·sa·wa (mäs·sä′wä) The chief port of Eritrea, on the Red Sea; former capital of Eritrea. Formerly **Mas·so′wa.**

mass bell The Sanctus bell.

mass communication The simultaneous dissemination of a single item of information, advertising, propaganda, etc., to the largest possible audience by the use of mass media.

mass defect *Physics* The difference between the mass number of a nuclide and its nucleon mass.

mas·sé (ma·sā′) *n.* In billiards, a stroke with a cue held perpendicularly, causing the cue ball to return in a straight line or to describe a curve. Also **massé shot.** [<F <*masser* make a massé shot <*masse* billiard cue, lit., a mace]

Mas·sé·na (må·sā·nå′), **André,** Prince d'Essling, 1758–1817, French marshal under Napoleon I.

Mas·se·net (mas′nā′, *Fr.* mås·ne′), **Jules Émile Frédéric,** 1842–1912, French composer.

mas·se·ter (ma·sē′tər) *n. Anat.* A masticatory muscle connected with the lower jaw. [<NL <Gk. *masētēr* chewer <*masasthai* chew] —**mas·se·ter·ic** (mas′ə·ter′ik), **mas′se·ter′ine** (-ēn, -īn) *adj.*

mas·seur (ma·sûr′, *Fr.* må·sœr′) *n. French* A man who practices or gives massage. —**mas·seuse** (ma·sōōz′, -sōōs′; *Fr.* må·sœz′) *n. fem.*

mas·si·cot (mas′ə·kot) *n.* **1** Lead monoxide: a rare mineral associated with galena. **2** A yellowish paint pigment similar to litharge. [< F <Sp. *mexacote* <Arabic *shabb qubṭi* Coptic alum]

mas·sif (mas′if, *Fr.* må·sēf′) *n. Geol.* **1** The dominant, central mass of a mountain ridge more or less defined by longitudinal or transverse valleys. **2** A diastrophic block of the earth's crust, isolated by boundary faults. [<F]

Mas·sif Cen·tral (mȧ·sēf′ säṅ·trȧl′) A plateau region of central France, covering one sixth of the country's surface.

Mas·si·mi·lia·no (mäs′sē·mē·lyä′nō) Italian form of MAXIMILIAN.

Mas·sine (mä·sēn′), **Léonide,** born 1896, Russian ballet dancer and choreographer.

Mas·sin·ger (mas′ən·jər), **Philip,** 1583–1640, English dramatist.

mas·sive (mas′iv) *adj.* **1** Constituting a large mass; ponderous; large: a *massive* forehead. **2** Belonging to the total mass of anything. **3** Being without definite form, as a mineral; amorphous. **4** *Geol.* Homogeneous: said of certain rock formations. **5** Figuratively, imposing in scope or degree; having considerable magnitude. See synonyms under LARGE. [<F *massif*] **— mas′sive·ly** *adv.* **— mas′sive·ness** *n.*

Massive Mount The second highest peak in the Rocky Mountains, in central Colorado; 14,418 feet. Also **Massive Mountain.**

mass media Newspapers, magazines, paperbound books, radio, television, and motion pictures, considered as means of reaching a very wide public audience.

mass meeting A large public gathering for the discussion of some topic, usually political.

mass number *Physics* **1** The whole number nearest the mass of any isotope of an element: 3 and 4 are *mass numbers* of the isotopes of helium. **2** The number of protons and neutrons in an atom: distinguished from *atomic number.*

mas·so·ther·a·py (mas′ō·ther′ə·pē) *n.* Treatment by massage. [<Gk. *massein* knead + THERAPY] **— mas′so·ther′a·peu′tic** (-ther′ə·pyōō′tik) *adj.*

mass–pro·duce (mas′prə·dōōs′, -dyōōs′) *v.t.* **·duced, ·duc·ing** To manufacture or produce by machinery (goods or articles) in great numbers or quantities. **— mass production**

mass ratio The ratio of the total mass of a rocket to its mass after the expenditure of fuel, calculated at approximately 2.72 to 1 for a rocket designed to travel at the exhaust velocity of its fuel.

mass spectrograph *Physics* An instrument for determining the relative masses of electrically charged particles by passing a stream of them through a magnetic field and noting the variable deflections from a straight path.

mass·y (mas′ē) *adj.* **mass·i·er, mass·i·est** Consisting of a mass or masses; big; bulky. **— mass′i·ness** *n.*

mast[1] (mast, mäst) *n.* **1** *Naut.* A pole or spar of round timber or tubular iron or steel, set upright in a sailing vessel to sustain the yards, sails, etc. **2** The upright pole of a derrick. **3** Any large, upright pole. **—before the mast** Occupying the position of, or serving as, a common sailor: from the fact that common sailors were quartered forward of the foremast. **—** *v.t.* To furnish with a mast or masts. [OE *mæst*] **— mast′less** *adj.*

mast[2] (mast, mäst) *n.* The fruit of the oak, beech, and other trees; acorns, etc. [OE *mæst* mast, fodder]

mast– Var. of MASTO–.

mas·ta·ba (mas′tə·bə) *n.* In ancient Egypt, an oblong building used as a mortuary chapel and place of offerings, with sloping sides and flat top, covering the mouth of a sepulchral pit. Also **mas′ta·bah.** [<Arabic *maṣṭabah* bench]

MASTABA
Of solid masonry, except for a small chapel and (unconnected) shaft to the mummy chamber.

mas·tax (mas′taks) *n. Zool.* The pharynx or gizzard of a rotifer. [<Gk., mouth, jaws <*masasthai* chew]

mas·tec·to·my (mas·tek′tə·mē) *n. Surg.* The operation of removing the breast. [<MAST- + -ECTOMY]

mas·ter (mas′tər, mäs′-) *n.* **1** A male person who has authority over others, as the principal of a school, an employer, the head of a household, the owner of a domestic animal, etc. **2** One who has control or disposal of something; an owner. **3** In the U.S. merchant marine, the captain of a vessel. **4** One who is familiar with all the details of an art, profession, science, or trade. **5** One who has charge of some special thing, place, or business. **6** A young gentleman. **7** An honorary title; specifically, **Master,** a scholastic title and rank between bachelor and doctor. **8** *Law* Any of various officers of the court who assist the judges by hearing evidence, reporting, etc.: a *master* in chancery. **9** *Scot.* The courtesy title of a viscount's (or baron's) eldest son. **10** One who has disciples or followers; a religious leader. **11** One who gains the victory; a victor. **— the** (or **our**) **Master** Christ. **—** *v.t.* **1** To overcome or subdue; bring under control; defeat. **2** To become expert in: to *master* Greek. **3** To control or govern as a master. See synonyms under CONQUER, GAIN, LEARN, SUBDUE. **—** *adj.* Having the mastery; chief; controlling. [Fusion of OE *magister* and OF *maistre,* both <L *magister,* orig. a double compar. of *magnus* great] **— mas′ter·dom** *n.* **— mas′ter·hood** *n.* **— mas′·ter·less** *adj.*

Synonyms (noun): boss, captain, chief, commander, despot, director, employer, foreman, governor, head, leader, lord, manager, monarch, overseer, owner, prince, principal, proprietor, schoolmaster, sovereign, teacher. See CHIEF, SUPERINTENDENT, VICTOR. *Antonyms*: assistant, attendant, dependent, drudge, inferior, menial, retainer, serf, servant, servitor, slave, subaltern, subordinate, valet, waiter.

mas·ter–at–arms (mas′tər·ət·ärmz′, mäs′-) *n. pl.* **mas·ters–at–arms** A petty officer who maintains discipline and order on a naval vessel.

master builder **1** A contractor who employs men to build. **2** One who has charge of building operations; a foreman or architect.

mas·ter·ful (mas′tər·fəl, mäs′-) *adj.* **1** Having the power or characteristics of a master; domineering; arbitrary. **2** Showing mastery, as of an art, science, situation, etc. **— mas′ter·ful·ly** *adv.* **— mas′ter·ful·ness** *n.*

master hand **1** One skilled in his craft; an expert. **2** Great skill; expertness.

master key A key that will unlock two or more locks each of which has its own key that fits no other lock.

mas·ter·ly (mas′tər·lē, mäs′-) *adj.* Characteristic of a master; befitting a master. **—** *adv.* In a masterly manner; as befits a master. **— mas′ter·li·ness** *n.*

master mason A skilled mason.

Master Mason A Freemason of the third degree.

mas·ter·mind (mas′tər·mīnd′, mäs′-) *n.* A person of great intelligence and executive ability. **—** *v.t.* To plan and direct (a project) skilfully: to *mastermind* a plot.

Master of Arts **1** A degree given by a college or university to a person who has completed a prescribed course of graduate study in the humanities, social sciences, etc. **2** A person who has received this degree. Abbr. *M.A., A.M.*

master of ceremonies A person presiding over an entertainment or dinner and introducing the performers or speakers: also, *emcee.*

Master of Science **1** A degree given by a college or university to a person who has completed a prescribed course of graduate study in science. **2** A person who has received this degree. Abbr. *M.S., M.Sc.*

mas·ter·piece (mas′tər·pēs′, mäs′-) *n.* A work or piece of art or literature done with consummate skill or showing the hand of a master; a supreme accomplishment; chef–d'oeuvre. [after G *meisterstück*]

Mas·ters (mas′tərz, mäs′-), **Edgar Lee,** 1869–1950, U. S. poet.

mas·ter·ship (mas′tər·ship, mäs′-) *n.* **1** The state, personality, or character of a master; also, mastery. **2** Masterly skill; preeminence.

mas·ter·sing·er (mas′tər·sing′ər, mäs′-) See MEISTERSINGER.

mas·ter·stroke (mas′tər·strōk′, mäs′-) *n.* A masterly or decisive action or achievement.

mas·ter·work (mas′tər·wûrk′, mäs′-) *n.* A masterpiece.

mas·ter·work·man (mas′tər·wûrk′mən, mäs′-) *n. pl.* **·men** (-mən) A skilled workman, craftsman, or artist; also, a foreman or overseer over workmen.

mas·ter·wort (mas′tər·wûrt′, mäs′-) *n.* **1** Any of several herbs of the parsley family, especially those of the genus *Astrantia.* **2** A European plant (*Peucedanum ostruthium*), formerly used as a pot herb.

mas·ter·y (mas′tər·ē, mäs′-) *n.* **1** The condition of having power and control; dominion. **2** The knowledge or skill of a master. **3** Superiority in a contest; victory. See synonyms under VICTORY.

mast·head (mast′hed′, mäst′-) *n.* **1** *Naut.* **a** The top of a lower mast. **b** The head or top of a mast to which a flag is raised. **c** A sailor acting as look–out at the masthead. **2** That section of a newspaper or other periodical, published in each edition, stating the ownership, officers, and staff conducting it, the advertising, editorial, and publishing offices, etc. **—** *v.t.* **1** To raise to or display at the masthead, as a flag. **2** To send to a masthead for punishment.

mas·tic (mas′tik) *n.* **1** A small Mediterranean evergreen tree (*Pistacia lentiscus*) of the cashew family. **2** The aromatic resin obtained from this tree, used as a varnish and in medicine as a styptic. **3** A quick–drying cement. [<F <LL *mastichum* <Gk. *mastichē*]

mas·ti·cate (mas′tə·kāt) *v.t.* **·cat·ed, ·cat·ing** **1** To crush or grind (food) for swallowing; chew. **2** To reduce, as rubber, to a pulp by crushing or kneading. [<LL *masticatus,* pp. of *masticare* chew <Gk. *mastichaein* gnash the teeth <*mastax* jaw] **— mas′ti·ca′tion** *n.* **— mas′ti·ca′tor** *n.*

mas·ti·ca·to·ry (mas′tə·kə·tôr′ē, -tō′rē) *adj.* **1** Of, pertaining to, or used in mastication. **2** Adapted for chewing: the *masticatory* mouth of a bee. **—** *n. pl.* **·ries** A substance chewed to increase the secretion of saliva.

mas·tiff (mas′tif, mäs′-) *n.* One of an old English breed of large hunting dogs, with a thick–set, heavy body, straight forelegs, a broad skull, drooping ears, and pendulous lips. [<OF *mastin* <L *mansuetus* gentle < pp. of *mansuescere* tame <*manus* hand; infl. in form by OF *mestif* mongrel]

MASTIFF
(About 30 inches high at the shoulder)

mas·ti·goph·o·ran (mas′ti·gof′ər·ən) *n.* Any one of a class of protozoa (*Mastigophora*), many of which are parasitic in man and other animals, characterized by the presence of one or more whiplike organs of locomotion called flagellae. **—** *adj.* Of or pertaining to the *Mastigophora.* [<Gk. *mastix, mastigos* whip + *phoros* bearing <*pherein* bear]

mas·ti·tis (mas·tī′tis) *n.* **1** *Pathol.* Inflammation of the mammary gland. **2** Garget. [< MAST- + -ITIS]

masto– *combining form Med.* The breast or the mammary gland. Also, before vowels, *mast–,* as in *mastitis.* [<Gk. *mastos* the breast]

mas·to·don (mas′tə·don) *n.* A primitive elephantlike mammal (order *Proboscidea*), distinguished from elephants and mammoths chiefly by its molar teeth; especially, the extinct, shaggy–haired *Mammut americanus* once common in North America. [< NL <MAST- + Gk. *odous, odontos* tooth; from the nipple–shaped projections on its teeth]

MASTODON
(About 9 feet high at the shoulder)

mas·toid (mas′toid) *adj. Anat.* **1** Designating a process of the temporal bone behind the ear for the attachment of muscles. **2** Pertaining to or situated near this process. **3** Nipplelike; breastlike. **—** *n.* The mastoid process. [<Gk. *mastoeidēs* <*mastos* breast + *eidos* form]

mas·toid·ec·to·my (mas′toid·ek′tə·mē) *n. Surg.* Excision of mastoid cells or of the mastoid process. [<MASTOID + -ECTOMY]

mas·toid·i·tis (mas′toid·ī′tis) *n. Pathol.* Inflammation of the mastoid process. [<MASTOID + -ITIS]

mas·tur·bate (mas′tər·bāt) *v.i.* **·bat·ed, ·bat·ing** To perform masturbation. [<L *masturbatus,* pp. of *masturbari*; ult. origin uncertain]

mas·tur·ba·tion (mas′tər·bā′shən) *n.* Sexual

self-gratification; onanism: also called *self-abuse.* [<L *masturbatio, -onis*] **—mas′tur·ba′tor** *n.*

Ma·su·ri·a (mə·zŏŏr′ē·ə, -sŏŏr′-) A region of NE Poland on the U. S. S. R. border, containing the many **Masurian Lakes:** Polish *Mazury.* *German* **Ma·su·ren·land** (mä·zōō′rən·länt).

ma·su·ri·um (mə·sŏŏr′ē·əm) *n.* A supposed metallic element whose place in the periodic table is now occupied by technetium. [from *Masuria,* where first found]

mat[1] (mat) *n.* **1** A flat article, woven or plaited, or made of some perforated or corrugated material, to be laid on a floor, and on which to wipe one's shoes or feet. **2** Any flat piece of lace, plaited straw, leather, etc., used as a floor covering, table protection, ornament, etc. **3** Any dense or twisted growth, as of hair or rushes. *—v.* **mat·ted, mat·ting** *v.t.* **1** To cover with or as with mats. **2** To knot or entangle into a mat. *—v.i.* **3** To become knotted or entangled together. [OE *matt(e)* <LL *matta*]

mat[2] (mat) *n.* **1** A lusterless, dull, or roughened surface; also, a tool for producing such a surface. **2** *Printing* A sheet of papier-mâché or wood fiber for recording the impression of type or cuts in stereotyping; a matrix. **3** A border of white cardboard, serving as the frame, or part of the frame, of a picture. *—v.t.* **mat·ted, mat·ting** To produce a dull surface on, as metal or glass. *—adj.* Presenting a lusterless surface. Also *matte.* [OF, defeated, overcome <Arabic *māt*]

Mat·a·be·le (mat′ə·bē′lē) *n. pl.* ·be·le or ·be·les (-bē′lēz) One of a Zulu people who were driven across the Vaal by the Boers in 1837 and occupied the region north of the Limpopo, later known as Matabeleland.

Mat·a·be·le·land (mat′ə·bē′lē·land′) A region in southwest Zimbabwe between the Limpopo and Zambezi rivers; 69,989 square miles.

mat·a·dor (mat′ə·dôr) *n.* **1** In bullfighting, the man who kills the bull with a thrust of a sword. **2** In various card games, one of the highest trumps. [<Sp., killer <*matar* slay]

Ma·ta·mo·ros (mä′tä·mō′rōs) A city near the mouth of the Rio Grande in NE Mexico.

Mat·a·nus·ka Valley (mat′ə·nōōs′kə) A region of southern Alaska, site of an experimental colonization project by the United States government in 1935.

Ma·tan·zas (mä·tän′säs) **1** A province in western Cuba; 3,260 square miles. **2** Its capital, a port.

Ma·ta·pan (mä′tä·pän′), **Cape** The southernmost point of the Greek mainland: also *Cape Tainaron.*

match[1] (mach) *n.* **1** One similar or equal in appearance, position, quality, or character; a suitable or fit associate; also a possible mate. **2** A person or thing that is the equal of another in ability, strength, character, position, etc.; one able to cope with or oppose another; a peer. **3** A contest of skill, strength, etc., between persons or animals. **4** A counterpart; facsimile; also, either of two things harmonizing or corresponding. **5** A marriage or mating, or an agreement to marry or pair; a pairing or coupling. *—v.t.* **1** To be similar to or in accord with in quality, degree, etc.: His looks *match* his mood; The hat *matches* the coat. **2** to make or select as equals or as suitable for one another: to *match* pearls. **3** To place together as mates or companions; marry. **4** To cause to correspond: adapt: *Match your efforts to your salary.* **5** To compare so as to decide superiority; test: to *match* wits. **6** to set (equal opponents) in opposition: to *match* boxers. **7** To equal; oppose successfully: No one could *match* him. *—v.i.* **8** To be equal, similar, or corresponding; suit. **9** To be married; mate. [OE *gemæcca* companion] **—match′a·ble** *adj.* **—match′er** *n.*

match[2] (mach) *n.* **1** Any article manufactured for the purpose of starting or communicating a fire; specifically, a splinter of soft wood or a piece of waxed thread or cardboard tipped with a combustible composition that ignites by friction. **2** A fuse of cotton wicking prepared to burn quickly or slowly, and used for firing cannon. [<OF *mesche* wick, prob. <L *myxa* wick of a candle]

match·board (mach′bôrd′, -bōrd′) *n.* A board, specially cut with a groove along one edge and a tongue along the other, for close joining on floors, ceilings, etc.

match·book (match′bŏŏk′) *n.* A small paper folder containing safety matches, with a strip of specially prepared surface at one end for striking them.

match·box (mach′boks′) *n.* a small box for containing matches.

matched (macht) *adj.* Having a tongue on one edge and a groove on the other: said of boards.

match·less (mach′lis) *adj.* That cannot be matched or equaled; peerless. **—match′less·ly** *adv.* **—match′less·ness** *n.*

match·lock (mach′lok′) *n.* **1** An old type of musket fired by placing a lighted match against the powder in the pan. **2** The gunlock on such a musket.

match·maker[1] (mach′mā′kər) *n.* One who makes plans, or schemes, to bring about a marriage. **2** One who arranges matched games or contests. **—match′mak′ing** *adj. & n.*

match·maker[2] (mach′mā′kər) *n.* One who makes matches for lighting. **—match′mak′ing** *adj. & n.*

match·mark (mach′märk′) *n.* A distinguishing mark placed on separable parts of machinery as a guide for assembling. *—v.t.* To put a matchmark upon.

match play In golf, a form of competitive play in which the score is computed by totaling the number of holes won or lost by each side.

match player A golfer who competes in match play.

match point In tennis and similar games, the final point needed to win a match.

match·stick (mach′stik′)′ *n.* A piece of wood tipped with sulfur and used as a match.

match·wood (mach′wŏŏd′) *n.* **1** Wood suitable for making matches; also, splinters. **2** *Obs.* A combustible substance used as tinder; touchwood.

mate[1] (māt) *n.* **1** A companion or associate; comrade. **2** One that is paired or coupled with another, as in matrimony; also, the male or female of animals paired for propagation. **3** An equal in a contest; a match. **4** An officer of a merchant vessel, ranking next below the captain. **5** *Nav.* An assistant to a warrant officer; a petty officer: the boatswain's *mate.* See synonyms under ASSOCIATE, *—v.* **mat·ed, mat·ing** *v.t.* **1** To join as mates or a pair; match; marry. **2** To pair for breeding, as animals. **3** To associate; couple. *—v.i.* **4** To match; marry. **5** To pair. **6** To consort; associate. [<MLG <*gemate* <*ge* together + *mat* meat, food. Prob. akin to MEAT.] **—mate′less** *adj.*

mate[2] (māt) *v.t.* **mat·ed, mat·ing** **1** In chess, to checkmate. **2** To defeat or confound. *—n.* A checkmate. *—Interj.* Checkmate. [<CHECKMATE]

ma·té (mä′tā, mat′ā) *n.* **1** An infusion of the leaves of a Brazilian holly *(Ilex paraguariensis),* much used as a beverage in South America: also called *Paraguay tea, yerba.* **2** The Paraguay tea plant. [<Sp. <Quechua *mati* calabash (in which it was steeped)]

mat·e·lote (mat′ə·lōt) *n.* A Stew of fish in wine and oil, with herb seasoning. Also **mat′e·lotte** (-lot). [<F <*matelot* sailor]

Ma·te·o (mä·tā′ō) Spanish form of MATTHEW.

ma·ter (mā′tər, mä′-) *n. Latin* Mother.

mater do·lo·ro·sa (dō′lə·rō′sə) *Latin* Sorrowful mother: in art or music, the Virgin Mary as the sorrowing mother.

ma·ter·fa·mil·i·as (mā′tər·fə·mil′ē·əs) *n. Latin* The mother of a family; a matron.

ma·te·ri·al (mə·tir′ē·əl) *n.* **1** That of which anything is composed or may be constructed; matter considered as a component part of something. **2** Collected facts, impressions, ideas, or notes containing them, and sketches, etc., that may be used in completing a literary or an artistic production. **3** Matter regarded as the amorphous substratum of reality. **4** The tools, instruments, articles, etc., for doing something. See also MATERIEL. **5** A cloth or fabric. *—adj.* **1** Pertaining to matter; having a corporeal existence; physical. **2** Pertaining to matter in a corporeal relation; affecting the physical nature; also, pertaining to the body or the appetites; corporeal; sensuous; sensual. **3** Pertaining to the subject matter; essential; important. **4** Pertaining to matter as opposed to form. **5** Consisting of, relating to, or composed of matter regarded as the primary substance of the physical universe. **6** Replete with matter or good sense. See synonyms under IMPORTANT, PHYSICAL. [<LL *materialis* <L *materia* matter, stuff]

ma·te·ri·al·ism (mə·tir′ē·əl·iz′əm) *n.* **1** The doctrine that the facts of experience are all to be explained by reference to the reality, activities, and laws of physical or material substance. **2** Undue regard for material interests.

ma·te·ri·al·ist (mə·tir′ē·əl·ist) *n.* **1** A believer in the doctrine of materialism; also, a believer in the existence of matter. **2** One who takes interest exclusively, chiefly, or excessively in the material or bodily necessities and comforts of life. **—ma·te′ri·al·is′tic** *adj.* **—ma·te′·ri·al·is′ti·cal·ly** *adv.*

ma·te·ri·al·i·ty (mə·tir′ē·al′ə·tē) *n. pl.* **·ties** **1** The quality or state of being material; physical as distinguished from psychical being. **2** Substance; matter; a material thing; a body. Also **ma·te′ri·al·ness.**

ma·te·ri·al·ize (mə·tir′ē·əl·īz′) *v.* **·ized, ·iz·ing** *v.t.* **1** To give material or actual form to; represent as material. **2** To cause (a spirit, etc.) to appear in visible form. **3** To make materialistic. *—v.i.* **4** To assume material or visible form; appear. **5** To take form or shape; be realized: Our plans never *materialized.* **—ma·te′ri·al·i·za′tion** *n.* **—ma·te′ri·al·iz′er** *n.*

ma·te·ri·al·ly (mə·tir′ē·əl·ē) *adv.* **1** In a material and important manner. **2** In essence or substance. **3** From a physical point of view; physically.

ma·te·ri·a med·i·ca (mə·tir′ē·ə med′i·kə) *Med.* **1** The branch of medical science that relates to medicinal substances, their nature, uses, effects, etc. **2** The substances employed as remedial agents. [<Med. L <*materia* matter + *medica,* fem. of *medicus* medical]

ma·te·ri·el (mə·tir′ē·el′) *n. Mil.* **1** All nonexpendable ordnance, transport, and equipment of an army. **2** All material things of an army except personnel. Also *French* **ma·té·riel** (mȧ·tā·ryel′). [<F, material]

ma·te·ri·es mor·bi (mə·tir′i·ēz môr′bī) *Latin* The morbid substances, organisms, etc., which cause disease.

ma·ter·nal (mə·tûr′nəl) *adj.* **1** Pertaining to a mother; motherly. **2** Connected with or inherited from one's mother; coming through the relationship of a mother. [<F *maternel* <L *maternus* <*mater* a mother] **—ma·ter′·nal·ly** *adv.*

ma·ter·nal·ize (mə·tûr′nəl·īz) *v.t.* **·ized, ·iz·ing** To make maternal.

ma·ter·ni·ty (mə·tûr′nə·tē) *n. pl.* **·ties** **1** The condition of being a mother. **2** The qualities of a mother; motherliness. [<F *maternité* <L *maternitas*]

maternity hospital A hospital for the care of women during childbirth and of newborn babies; lying-in hospital.

mate·ship (māt′ship) *n.* **1** The state or condition of being a mate or companion. **2** The position or authority of one holding the office of mate.

ma·tey (mā′tē) *Brit. Colloq. adj.* Friendly; chummy. *—n.* Friend; chum.

math[1] (math) *n.* A mowing, or that obtained by mowing: now rare except in *aftermath.* [OE *mǣth*]

math[2] (math) *n. Colloq.* Mathematics.

math·e·mat·i·cal (math′ə·mat′i·kəl) *adj.* **1** Pertaining to or of the nature of mathematics. **2** Rigidly exact or precise. Also **math′e·mat′ic.** [<L *mathematicus* <Gk. *mathēmatikos* disposed to learn, mathematical <*mathēma* learning <*manthanein* learn] **—math′e·mat′·i·cal·ly** *adv.*

mathematical expectation *Stat.* The probability of the occurrence of a given event multiplied by the amount of money offered or wagered on its occurrence.

mathematical logic Symbolic logic.

math·e·ma·ti·cian (math′ə·mə·tish′ən) *n.* One versed in mathematics.

math·e·mat·ics (math′ə·mat′iks) *n.* The logical study of quantity, form, arrangement, and magnitude; especially, the methods for disclosing, by the use of rigorously defined concepts and self-consistent symbols, the properties and exact relations of quantities and magnitudes, whether in the abstract, **pure mathematics,** or in their practical connections, **applied mathematics.**

mat·i·née (mat′ə·nā′) *n.* An entertainment or reception held in the daytime; specifically, a theatrical or cinematic performance given in the afternoon. Also **mat′i·nee′.** [<F <*matin* morning. See MATIN.]

mat·ing (mā′ting) *n.* The act of pairing or matching.

Ma·tisse (mà·tēs′), **Henri,** 1869–1954, French painter.

MATHEMATICAL SYMBOLS

Symbol	Meaning	Symbol	Meaning
$+$	Plus or positive; sign of addition	$\int$	Integral of
$-$	Minus or negative; sign of subtraction	$\int_b^a$	Integral between limits of *a* and *b*
$\pm$	Plus or minus	$\doteq$ or $\rightarrow$	Approaches as a limit
$\mp$	Minus or plus	$f(x), F(x), \phi(x)$	Function of *x*
$\times$ or $\cdot$	Multiplied by	Δ	Increment of, as Δy
$\div$ or $:$	Divided by	d	Differential, as *dy*
$=$ or $::$	Equals; is equal to; as	$\frac{dy}{dx}$, or $f'(x)$	Derivative of $y = f(x)$ with respect to *x*
$\neq$ or $\ne$	Does not equal	δ	Variation, as δy
$\cong$	Approximately equal; congruent	π	pi; ratio of circumference of circle to diameter
$>$	Greater than	$n!$ or $\lfloor n$	Factorial *n* or *n* factorial
$<$	Less than	$\angle$, $\angle$s	Angle, angles
$\geqq$	Greater than or equal to	$\perp$, $\perp$s	Perpendicular to, perpendiculars
$\leqq$	Less than or equal to	$\parallel$, $\parallel$s	Parallel to, parallels
$\backsim$	Similar to; equivalent	$\triangle$, $\triangle$s	Triangle, triangles
$\therefore$	Therefore	$\llcorner$, $\llcorner$s	Right angle, right angles
$\because$	Since or because	$\square$, $\square$s	Parallelogram, parallelograms
$\equiv$	Identical; identically equal to		
$\propto$	Directly proportional to; varies directly as	$\square$, $\square$s	Rectangle, rectangles
∞	Infinity	$\square$, $\square$s	Square, squares
$\surd$	Square root	$\bigcirc$ or $\odot$	Circle, circumference
$\sqrt[n]{\ }$	*n*th root	$'$	Minutes of arc; prime; minutes of time; feet
e or ϵ	Base (2.718···) of natural system of logarithms	$''$	Seconds of arc; double prime; seconds of time; inches
Σ	Summation of		

Math·er (math′ər), **Cotton,** 1663?–1728?, American clergyman and writer. **— Increase,** 1639–1723, American clergyman and writer; father of Cotton.

Ma·thi·as (mä·tē′äs) German form of MATTHIAS. Also *Sp.* **Ma·tí·as** (mä·tē′äs).

Ma·thieu (mà·tyœ′) French form of MATTHEW.

Ma·thu·ra (mu′tŏŏr·ə) A city in western Uttar Pradesh, India, sacred to Hindus as the birthplace of Krishna: formerly *Muttra.*

Ma·thu·rai (mə·tŏŏr′ī) See MADURAI.

ma·ti·co (mə·tē′kō) *n.* A tropical American shrub *(Piper angustifolium)* of the pepper family: its hairy leaves yield a volatile oil having stimulant and hemostatic properties. [<Sp., dim. of *Mateo* Matthew]

Ma·til·da (mə·til′də; *Ital.* mä·tēl′dä, *Sw.* mä·til′dä) A feminine personal name. Also **Ma·thil·da** (mə·til′də, *Du.* ma·til′dä), **Ma·thil·de** (*Dan.* mä·til′de, *Fr.* mà·tēld′), **Ma·til·de** (*Ger.* mä·tēl′də, *Sp.* mä·tēl′dä). [<Gmc., mighty in battle]
— Matilda, 1102–67, daughter of Henry I of England; disputed the English throne with Stephen of Blois: known as *Maud.*
— Matilda of Flanders, died 1083, wife of William the Conqueror.

mat·in (mat′in) *n.* **1** *pl. Eccl.* The first of the canonical hours, usually said at midnight. **2** *pl.* In the Anglican Church, Morning Prayer. **3** Figuratively, any morning song, as of a bird. **4** *Obs.* Morning. **—** *adj.* Of or belonging to the morning: also **mat′in·al.** Also spelled *mattin.* [<OF *matin* early <L *matutinus (tempus)* (time) of the morning, appar. <*Matuta* goddess of morning]

mat-knife (mat′nīf′) *n. pl.* **-knives** (-nīvz′) A knife having the edge ground at an angle, used for cutting engravings, heavy paper, artist's matboard, etc. See illustration under KNIFE.

Ma·to Gros·so (mat′ə grō′sō, *Pg.* mä′tŏŏ grō′·sŏŏ) A state of central and western Brazil, the second largest state in Brazil; 487,489 square miles; capital, Cuiabá: formerly *Matto Grosso.*

mat·rass (mat′rəs) *n.* **1** A long-necked, round-bodied glass vessel for distilling and digesting. See BOLTHEAD (def. 1). **2** A thin, hard glass tube used in blowpipe analysis. Also spelled *mattrass.* [<F *matras* bolt]

matri- *combining form* Mother: *matricide.* [<L *mater, matris* mother]

ma·tri·arch (mā′trē·ärk) *n.* A woman holding the position corresponding to that of a patriarch in her family or tribe. [<MATRI- + (PATRI)ARCH] **— ma′tri·ar′chal** *adj.* **— ma′tri·ar′chal·ism** *n.*

ma·tri·ar·chate (mā′trē·är′kit) *n.* Matriarchal government; a system of matriarchalism. [< MATRIARCH + -ATE[2]]

ma·tri·ar·chy (mā′trē·är′kē) *n. pl.* **·chies** A social organization having the mother as the head of the family, in which descent, kinship, and succession are reckoned through the mother, instead of the father; also, government by women. **— ma′tri·ar′chic** *adj.*

ma·tri·ces (mā′trə·sēz, mat′rə-) Plural of MATRIX.

mat·ri·cide (mat′rə·sīd) *n.* **1** The killing of one's mother. **2** One who kills his mother. [<L *matricidium* <*mater, matris* mother + *caedere* kill; def. 2 <L *matricida*] **— mat′ri·ci′dal** *adj.*

mat·ri·cli·nous (mat′rə·klī′nəs) *adj. Biol.* Showing hereditary characteristics inclined to the maternal side: opposed to *patriclinous.* Also **mat′ro·cli′nous, mat′ro·cli′nal.**

ma·tric·u·lant (mə·trik′yə·lənt) *n.* A candidate or applicant for matriculation.

ma·tric·u·late (mə·trik′yə·lāt) *v.t.* & *v.i.* **·lat·ed, ·lat·ing** To enrol in a college or university as a candidate for a degree. **—** *n.* One who is so enrolled. [<Med. L *matriculatus,* pp. of *matriculare* enrol <*matricula,* dim. of *matrix* womb, origin, public roll <*mater* mother] **— ma·tric′u·la′tion** *n.* **— ma·tric′u·la′tor** *n.*

mat·ri·lin·e·al (mat′rə·lin′ē·əl) *adj.* Pertaining to or describing descent or derivation through the female line. Compare PATRILINEAL.

mat·ri·lo·cal (mat′rə·lō′kəl) *adj. Anthropol.* Denoting residence of a married couple in the wife's community, as in certain clan societies. Compare PATRILOCAL.

mat·ri·mo·ni·al (mat′rə·mō′nē·əl) *adj.* Pertaining to matrimony. **— mat′ri·mo′ni·al·ly** *adv.*
Synonyms: bridal, conjugal, connubial, hymeneal, hymenean, nuptial, sponsal, spousal. *Antonyms:* celibate, single, unespoused, unwedded.

mat·ri·mo·ny (mat′rə·mō′nē) *n. pl.* **·nies** **1** The union of a man and a woman in marriage; wedlock. **2** A card game played by any number of persons; also, a combination of king and queen in this and certain other games. See synonyms under MARRIAGE. [<L *matrimonium* <*mater, matris* mother]

matrimony vine The boxthorn.

ma·trix (mā′triks) *n. pl.* **ma·tri·ces** (mā′trə·sēz, mat′rə-) **1** That which contains and gives shape or form to anything. **2** The womb. **3** *Biol.* Intercellular substance; hence, the formative cells from which a structure grows. **4** A mold in which anything is cast or shaped, or that which encloses like a mold. **5** *Printing* A papier-mâché, plaster, or other impression of a form, from which a plate for printing may be made. **6** *Geol.* The impression or mold of the exterior of a crystal or other mineral left in the containing rock when the object is removed, or the mass in which a fossil, gemstone, mineral, etc., is embedded. **7** *Math.* A rectangular array of symbols or terms enclosed between parentheses or double vertical bars to facilitate the study of relationships. **8** The material used as a filler between the fragments of a shrapnel projectile. [<L, womb, breeding animal <*mater, matris* mother]

ma·tron (mā′trən) *n.* **1** A married woman; mother; also, a woman of established age and dignity. **2** A housekeeper, or a female superintendent, as of an institution. [<OF *matrone* <L *matrona* <*mater, matris* mother] **— ma′·tron·al** *adj.* **— ma′tron·like′** *adj.*

ma·tron·age (mā′trən·ij) *n.* **1** The condition of being a matron. **2** Matronly attention or care. **3** Matrons collectively.

ma·tron·ize (mā′trən·īz) *v.t.* **·ized, ·iz·ing** **1** To render matronlike. **2** To chaperon.

ma·tron·ly (mā′trən·lē) *adj.* Of or like a matron; elderly. **—** *adv.* In a matronly manner. **— ma′tron·li·ness** *n.*

matron of honor A married woman acting as chief attendant to a bride at her wedding. See MAID OF HONOR.

mat·ro·nym·ic (mat′rō·nim′ik) See METRONYMIC.

Ma·trûh (mə·trōō′) A Mediterranean port of western Egypt: also *Mersa Matrûh.*

Ma·tsu·ya·ma (mä·tsōō·yä·mä) A port on NW Shikoku island, Japan.

Matt (mat) Diminutive of MATTHEW.

matte[1] (mat) *n. Metall.* An impure metallic product containing sulfur, obtained in smelting sulfide ores, as of copper, lead, etc. [<F]

matte[2] (mat) See MAT[2].

mat·ted (mat′id) *adj.* **1** Covered with mats or matting. **2** Tangled like the fibers of a mat. **— mat′ted·ly** *adv.* **— mat′ted·ness** *n.*

mat·ter (mat′ər) *n.* **1** That which makes up the substance of anything, especially of material things. **2** The material of which a thing is composed. **3** *Physics* That aspect of reality conceived as existing prior to and independently of the mind and to have characteristics susceptible to precise measurement in terms of extension, force, mass, radiation, and energy. **4** That which constitutes the essence or substance of a particular thing. **5** Something not exactly conceived or stated; an indefinite, often a comparatively small, amount. **6** A subject for discussion or feeling. **7** Something of moment and importance. **8** A condition of affairs, especially if unpleasant or unfortunate; case; difficulty; trouble: What's the *matter*? **9** The thought, or material of thought. **10** Pus. **11** *Philos.* The as yet undifferentiated substratum of those properties and changes of which the human senses take cognizance and which, by their differentiation and combination in an infinite variety of forms, constitute the separate existences and characteristic qualities of physical things. **12** *Printing* Type that is set or composed; also, material to be set up; copy. **13** Written or printed documents sent by mail. See synonyms under MASS[1], TOPIC. — *v.i.* **1** To be of concern or importance; signify. **2** To form or discharge pus; suppurate. [<F *matière* <L *materia* stuff]

Mat·ter·horn (mat′ər·hôrn, *Ger.* mä′ter·hôrn) A mountain in the Alps on the Swiss-Italian border: 14,780 feet: French *Mont Cervin.*

mat·ter-of-course (mat′ər·əv·kôrs′, -kōrs′) *adj.* Following or accepting as an expected conclusion or as a natural or logical result.

mat·ter-of-fact (mat′ər·əv·fakt′) *adj.* Closely adhering to facts; straightforward.

mat·ter-of-fact·ly (mat′ər·əv·fakt′lē) *adv.* In a matter-of-fact manner; straightforwardly. — **mat′ter-of-fact′ness** *n.*

Mat·thew (math′yo͞o) A masculine personal name. Also *Lat.* **Mat·thae·us** (mə·thē′əs, *Dan.* mä·tā′əs), *Ger., Sw.* **Mat·thä·us** (mä·tā′o͞os), *Du.* **Mat·the·us** (mä·tā′əs), *Ital.* **Mat·te·o** (mät·tā′ō). [<Hebrew, gift of God]

— **Matthew** One of the Twelve Apostles, author of the first Gospel; also, the Gospel by him. Also **Saint Matthew.**

— **Matthew of Paris,** 1200–59?, English monk and chronicler.

Mat·thews (math′yo͞oz), **(James) Brander,** 1852–1929, U. S. scholar, author, and educator.

Mat·thi·as (mə·thī′əs, *Fr.* mà·tē·às′) A masculine personal name. Also *Du.* **Mat·thijs** (mä·tīs′). [See MATTHEW]

— **Matthias** The apostle chosen by lot to succeed Judas Iscariot. *Acts* i 23–26.

mat·tin (mat′in) See MATIN.

mat·ting (mat′ing) *n.* **1** A woven fabric of fiber, straw, etc., used as a floor covering, etc. **2** The act or process of making mats. **3** A dull, flat surface effect, as in gilding, etc.

mat·tock (mat′ək) *n.* A pickaxlike tool for digging and grubbing, having blades instead of points. [OE *mattuc*]

MATTOCK

Mat·to Gros·so (mat′ə grō′sō, *Pg.* mä′to͞o grō′so͞o) A former spelling of MATO GROSSO.

mat·toid (mat′oid) *n.* A person mentally unbalanced in one way or on one subject. [<Ital. *mattoide* <*matto* mad <L *mattus* intoxicated]

mat·trass (mat′rəs) See MATRASS.

mat·tress (mat′rəs) *n.* **1** A casing of ticking or other strong fabric filled with hair, cotton, or rubber, and used as a bed. **2** A mat woven of brush, poles, etc., used in protecting embankments, forming dikes, jetties, etc. [<OF *materas* <Ital. *materasso* <Arabic *maṭraḥ* place where something is thrown]

mat·u·rate (mach′o͞o·rāt, mat′yo͞o-) *v.i.* **·rat·ed, ·rat·ing** **1** To ripen or mature. **2** *Med.* To suppurate; form pus. [<L *maturatus,* pp. of *maturare* ripen <*maturus* ripe, fully developed] — **mat′u·ra′tive** *adj.*

mat·u·ra·tion (mach′o͞o·rā′shən, mat′yo͞o-) *n.* **1** *Med.* The formation of pus. **2** The process of ripening or coming to maturity; ripeness. **3** *Biol.* The final stages in the preparation of gametes for fertilization, during which reduction to one half in the number of chromosomes in the germ cells occurs; meiosis.

ma·ture (mə·cho͝or′, -to͝or′, -tyo͝or′) *adj.* **1** Completely developed; perfectly ripe: *mature* grain; as applied to persons, fully developed in character and powers: a *mature* thinker. **2** Highly developed; approaching perfection. **3** Thoroughly elaborated or arranged; fully digested or considered; complete in detail: a *mature* scheme. **4** Due and payable; having reached its time limit: a *mature* bond. **5** *Geol.* Designating the maximum complexity and diversity of earth features, as achieved by the forces of erosion at full vigor; also, adjusted to local surroundings, as the course of a river. See synonyms under RIPE. — *v.* **·tured, ·tur·ing** *v.t.* **1** To cause to ripen or come to maturity; bring to full development. **2** To perfect; complete. — *v.i.* **3** To come to maturity or full development; ripen. **4** To become due, as a note. [<L *maturus* of full age] — **ma·ture′ly** *adv.*

ma·tur·i·ty (mə·cho͝or′ə·tē, -to͝or′-, -tyo͝or′-) *n.* **1** The state or condition of being mature: also **ma·ture′ness.** **2** Full development, as of the body. **3** The time at which a thing matures: a note payable at *maturity.* [<F *maturité* <L *maturitas*]

ma·tu·ti·nal (mə·to͞o′tə·nəl, -tyo͞o′-) *adj.* Pertaining to morning; before noon; early. [<L *matutinalis* <*matutinus* early in the morning <*Matuta,* goddess of morning] — **ma·tu′ti·nal·ly** *adv.*

mat·zo (mät′sə, -sō) *n. pl.* **mat·zoth** (mät′sōth, -sōs) or **mat·zos** (-səs, -səz) **1** Unleavened bread in the form of wafers, eaten by Jews at Passover. **2** A wafer of unleavened bread. [<Hebrew *matstsōth,* pl. of *matstsāh* unleavened]

mat·zoon (mat·so͞on′) See YOGURT.

Mau·beuge (mō·bœzh′) A city in northern France.

Maud (môd) A feminine personal name; also, diminutive of MAGDALENE and MATILDA. Also **Maude.**

maud·lin (môd′lin) *adj.* **1** Made foolish by liquor. **2** Foolishly and tearfully affectionate. [<*Maudlin* <OF *Maudelene, Madeleine* (Mary) Magdalen, who was often depicted with eyes swollen from weeping]

Maugham (môm), **(William) Somerset,** 1874–1965, English novelist and dramatist.

mau·gre (mô′gər) *prep.* Obsolete form of MALGRÉ. [<OF]

Mau·i (mou′ē) The second largest of the Hawaiian Islands; 728 square miles.

mau·kin (mô′kin) See MALKIN.

maul (môl) *n.* A heavy mallet for driving wedges, piles, etc. — *v.t.* **1** To beat and bruise; batter. **2** To handle roughly; manhandle; abuse. **3** *U.S.* To split by means of a maul and wedges, as logs or rails. Also spelled *mall.* [<OF *mail* <L *malleus* hammer. ? Akin to L *molere* grind into pieces, crush.] — **maul′er** *n.*

STEEL FENCE-POST MAUL

Maul·main (môl·mān′) See MOULMEIN.

maul·stick (môl′stik′) See MAHLSTICK.

Mau Mau (mou′ mou′) *pl.* **Mau Mau** or **Mau Maus** A member of a secret organization of Kikuyu tribesmen, active from 1952 in terrorist activities directed against European colonists in Kenya, Africa. [<native name]

mau·met (mô′mit) *n.* **1** *Obs.* An idol: from the early belief that the Moslems worshiped images of Mohammed. **2** *Brit. Dial.* A scarecrow; a doll. Also spelled *mammet.* [Contraction of MAHOMET] — **mau′met·ry** *n.*

maun (môn) *v.i. Scot.* Must.

mau·na (mô′nə) *Scot.* Must not. Also **maun′na.**

Mau·na Ke·a (mou′nä kā′ä) An extinct volcano on Hawaii; highest mountain in the Hawaiian Islands; 13,825 feet.

Mau·na Lo·a (mou′nä lō′ä) An active volcano on Hawaii; 13,675 feet.

maund (mônd) *n.* A unit of weight used in India, varying from 24.7 to 82.28 lbs. avoirdupois. [<Hind. *man*]

maun·der (môn′dər) *v.i.* **1** To talk in a wandering or incoherent manner; drivel. **2** To move dreamily or idly. [? Freq. of obs. *maund* beg; infl. in meaning by MEANDER] — **maun′der·er** *n.*

maun·dy (môn′dē) *n.* The religious ceremony of washing the feet of others, especially of inferiors: in commemoration of the washing of the disciples' feet by Christ; hence, **Maundy,** the service connected with such ceremony. [<OF *mandé* <L *mandatum* command; from the use of *mandatum* at the beginning of the ceremony. See MANDATE.]

Maundy Thursday The day before Good Friday, commemorating the Last Supper of Christ with his disciples, at which he washed their feet. [See MAUNDY]

Mau·pas·sant (mō·pà·säṅ′), **(Henri René Albert) Guy de,** 1850–93, French writer.

Mau·re·ta·ni·a (môr′ə·tā′nē·ə) An ancient country of North Africa, including the northern part of modern Morocco and the western part of Algeria.

Mau·re·ta·ni·an (môr′ə·tā′nē·ən) *adj.* Pertaining to ancient Mauretania or its inhabitants. — *n.* **1** One of the ancient people of Mauretania. **2** The Libyan dialect spoken by these people.

Mau·riac (mô·ryàk′), **François,** 1885–1970, French novelist.

Mau·rice (mə·rēs′, môr′is, mor′is; *Fr.* mô·rēs′) A masculine personal name. Also *Sp.* **Mau·ri·cio** (mou·rē′thyō), *Ital.* **Mau·ri·sio** (mou·rē′syō) or **Mau·ri·zio** (mou·rē′tsyō), **Mau·ri·ti·us** (*Du.* mou·rē′sē·əs, *Lat.* mou·rish′əs), *Du.* **Mau·rits** (mou′rits). [<L, Moorish]

— **Maurice,** 1521–53, Elector of Saxony; secured religious freedom in Germany.

— **Maurice of Nassau,** 1567–1625, Prince of Orange; Dutch general; son of William the Silent.

Mau·ri·ta·ni·a (môr′ə·tā′nē·ə), **Islamic Republic of** An independent republic of the French Community, on the coast of west Africa; 418,120 square miles; capital, Nouakchott; formerly a French overseas territory. — **Mau′·ri·ta′ni·an** *adj.* & *n.*

Mau·ri·ti·us (mô·rish′ē·əs) An island in the Indian Ocean east of Madagascar; 720 square miles; comprising with its dependencies a British crown colony (804 square miles); capital, Port Louis. *French* **Mau·rice** (mô·rēs′). — **Mau·ri′ti·an** *adj.* & *n.*

Mau·rois (mô·rwà′), **André** Pseudonym of Émile Herzog, 1885–1967, French biographer and novelist.

Mau·ry (mô′rē), **Matthew Fontaine,** 1806–1873, U. S. naval officer and oceanographer.

Maur·ya (mour′yə) An Indian dynasty, 325?–184? B.C., founded by *Chandragupta I.*

Mau·ser (mou′zər) *n.* A magazine rifle having great range and high muzzle velocity; also, a type of automatic pistol: a trade name. [after P. P. *Mauser,* 1838–1914, German inventor]

mau·so·le·um (mô′sə·lē′əm) *n. pl.* **·le·ums** or **·le·a** (-lē′ə) A large, stately tomb. [<L <Gk. *Mausōleion,* tomb of King Mausolus of Caria, erected by Queen Artemisia at Halicarnassus about 350 B.C. See SEVEN WONDERS OF THE WORLD.] — **mau′so·le′an** *adj.*

mauve (mōv) *n.* **1** A purple pigment and dye derived from mauvein. **2** Any of various purplish-rose shades. [<F, mallow <L *malva.* Doublet of MALLOW.]

mauve·in (mō′vin) *n. Chem.* A coal-tar violet dyestuff, $C_{27}H_{24}N_4$, obtained by oxidizing aniline: the first aniline dye of commerce. Also **mauve·ine** (mō′vin, -vēn). [<MAUVE]

mav·er·ick (mav′ər·ik) *n.* **1** *U.S.* An unbranded or orphaned animal, particularly a calf, legitimately belonging to the first one to brand it. **2** *Colloq.* A person with no attachments or affiliations, especially political ones. [after Samuel A. *Maverick,* 1803–1870, Texas lawyer, who did not brand his cattle]

ma·vis (mā′vis) *n.* The European song thrush or throstle (genus *Turdus*). [<F *mauvis*]

Ma·vors (mā′vôrz) An early name for Mars, the Roman god of war.

ma·vour·neen (mə·vo͝or′nēn, -vôr′-) *n.* My darling: an expression of affection. Also **ma·vour′nin.** [<Irish *mo muirnīn*]

maw[1] (mô) *n.* **1** The craw of a bird. **2** The stomach. **3** The air bladder of a fish. **4** The gullet, jaws, or mouth of a voracious mammal or fish. [OE *maga* stomach]

maw[2] (mô) *v.t. Scot.* To mow, as hay.

mawk·ish (mô′kish) *adj.* **1** Productive of disgust or loathing; sickening or insipid. **2** Char-

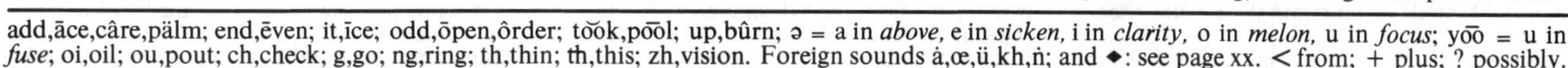

acterized by false or feeble sentimentality; lacking in strength or vigor. See synonyms under FLAT. [<obs. *mawk* a maggot] — **mawk′ish·ly** *adv.* — **mawk′ish·ness** *n.*

Maw·son (mô′sən), **Sir Douglas,** 1882–1958, Australian explorer.

Max (maks) A masculine personal name; originally a diminutive of MAXIMILIAN.

max·i (maks′ē) *n.* *pl.* **max·is** A long skirt or coat, usually reaching to the ankle.

max·il·la (mak·sil′ə) *n.* *pl.* **·lae** (-ē) **1** *Anat.* The upper jaw bone in vertebrates. **2** *Zool.* One of the pair or pairs of jaws behind the mandibles of an arthropod. [<L, dim. of *mala* jaw]

max·il·lar·y (mak′sə·ler′ē, mak·sil′ər·ē) *adj.* Of, pertaining to, or situated near the jaw or a maxilla: a *maxillary* artery. — *n.* *pl.* **·lar·ies** A maxilla or jaw bone.

max·il·li·ped (mak·sil′ə·ped) *n. Zool.* **1** One of the limbs of certain crustaceans, modified to serve as masticatory organs, and situated behind the maxillae. **2** One of a pair of poisonous claws situated near the mouth of a centipede. [<L *maxilla* jaw bone + -PED]

max·im (mak′sim) *n.* A brief statement of a practical principle or proposition; a proverbial saying. See synonyms under ADAGE, RULE. [<F *maxime* <L *maxima (sententia, propositio)* greatest (authority, premise), fem. of *maximus.* See MAXIMUM.]

Max·im (mak′sim), **Hiram Percy,** 1869–1936, U. S. inventor, son of Sir Hiram. — **Sir Hiram Stevens,** 1840–1916, U.S. inventor, civil, mechanical, and electrical engineer; became a British subject. — **Hudson,** 1853–1927, U.S. mechanical engineer and inventor; brother of Sir Hiram.

max·i·mal (mak′sə·məl) *adj.* Greatest; highest. See MAXIMUM.

Max·i·mal·ist (mak′sə·məl·ist) *n.* One of a former party or faction of extremist Russian revolutionists: distinguished from *Minimalist.*

Maxim gun A water-cooled machine-gun which utilizes the recoil of each shot to fire the next: invented by Sir Hiram S. Maxim.

Max·i·mil·ian (mak′sə·mil′yən, *Ger., Sw.* mäk′·si·mē′lē·än) A masculine personal name. Also *Sp.* **Max·i·mi·li·a·no** (mäk′sē·mē′lē·ä′nō), **Max·i·mi·li·a·nus** (*Du.* mäk′si·mē′lē·ä′nəs, *Lat.* mak′si·mil′ē·ā′nəs), *Pg.* **Max·i·mi·li·ão** (mäk′·si·mē′lē·oun′), *Fr.* **Max·i·mi·lien** (màk·sē·mē·lyaṅ′). [<L, greatest Aemilius]

— **Maximilian I,** 1459–1519, Holy Roman Emperor 1493–1519.

— **Maximilian II,** 1527–76, Holy Roman Emperor 1564–76.

— **Maximilian (Ferdinand Joseph),** 1832–67, archduke of Austria; emperor of Mexico 1864–67; executed.

max·im·ite (mak′sim·īt) *n.* A picric-acid high explosive used as a bursting charge for projectiles: invented by Hudson Maxim.

max·i·mize (mak′sə·mīz) *v.t.* **·mized, ·miz·ing** To make as great as possible; increase to the maximum; intensify. — **max′i·mi·za′tion** *n.*

max·i·mum (mak′sə·məm) *n.* *pl.* **·ma** (-mə) **1** The greatest quantity, amount, degree, or magnitude that can be assigned. **2** *Math.* **a** A value of a varying quantity that is greater than any neighboring value. **b** The highest possible of all the values which a variable or a function can express; the point at which a varying quantity ceases to increase and begins to decrease. **3** *Astron.* The moment of greatest brightness in a variable star, or its magnitude at such time. — *adj.* **1** As large or great as possible. **2** Pertaining to a maximum: *maximum* weight. [<L *maximus,* superl. of *magnus* great]

ma·xi·xe (mə·shē′shā, màk·sēks′) *n.* A Brazilian dance to the two-step. [<Brazilian Pg.]

Max Mül·ler (mäks mül′ər), **Friedrich** See MÜLLER.

max·well (maks′wel) *n.* The practical cgs unit of magnetic flux, equal to the flux through one square centimeter normal to a magnetic field with an intensity of one gauss. [after James Clerk *Maxwell*]

Max·well (maks′wel), **James Clerk,** 1831–79, Scottish physicist.

Maxwell's demon *Physics* An imaginary being of molecular proportions, devised by James Clerk Maxwell to illustrate the kinetic theory of gases.

may[1] (mā) *v.* Present: *sing.* **may, may** (*Archaic* **may·est** or **mayst), may,** *pl.* **may;** past: **might** A defective verb now used only in the present and past tenses as an auxiliary followed by the infinitive without *to,* or elliptically with the infinitive understood, to express: **1** Permission or allowance: *May* I go? You *may.* **2** Desire or wish: *May* your tribe increase! **3** Contingency, especially in clauses of result, concession, purpose, etc.: He died that we *might* live. **4** Possibility: You *may* be right. **5** *Law* Obligation or duty: the equivalent of *must* or *shall.* **6** *Obs.* Ability; power: now usually *can.* ◆ See usage note under CAN. [OE *mæg*]

may[2] (mā) *n.* The English hawthorn *(Crataegus oxyacantha),* with white, rose, or crimson flowers. Also **may′bush′** (-bŏŏsh′). [<MAY, because it blooms in this month]

May (mā) **1** The fifth month of the year, containing 31 days. **2** The prime of life; youth. **3** May Day festivities. [<OF *mai* <L *(mensis) Maius* (month of) May, prob. <*Maia,* goddess of growth; so called because regarded as a month of growth]

May (mā) A feminine personal name: contraction of MARY.

May (mā), **Cape** The southernmost point in New Jersey between the Atlantic and Delaware Bay.

Ma·ya (mä′yə) **1** In Hindu religion, Devi, mother of the world; the personified active will of the Creator. **2** In Hindu philosophy, illusion, often personified as a maiden. [<Skt. *māyā* illusion]

Ma·ya (mä′yə) *n.* **1** One of a tribe of Central American Indians, the most important tribe of the Mayan linguistic stock, still comprising a large percentage of the population of Yucatán, northern Guatemala, and British Honduras. They were the first Indians to develop writing and an accurate astronomical calendar. **2** The language of the Mayas, in its historical and modern forms. — *adj.* Of or pertaining to the Mayas, their culture, or their language.

Ma·ya·güez (mä′yä·gwās′) A port in western Puerto Rico.

Ma·yan (mä′yən) *adj.* Of the Mayas, their culture, or their language. — *n.* **1** A Maya. **2** A family of Central American Indian languages, including Maya and Quiché.

May apple **1** The ovoid, oblong, yellowish fruit of a North American herb *(Podophyllum peltatum).* **2** The herb itself, of which the rhizomes yield podophyllin. Also called *mandrake root.*

MAY APPLE
a. Flower.
b. Fruit.

Ma·ya·ri iron (mä·yä′rē) An iron made from Cuban ores, containing small percentages of chromium, vanadium, nickel, titanium, and certain other elements: used in high-grade machine castings. [from *Mayari,* a Cuban town]

May basket A little basket of flowers left at the door of a friend as a May Day token.

may·be (mā′bē) *adv.* Perhaps; possibly. [<*(it) may be*]

May·bird (mā′bûrd′) *n.* **1** In the southern United States, the bobolink. **2** In the eastern United States, the redbreast (def. 3).

May·bug (mā′bug′) *n.* **1** The cockchafer. **2** The June beetle. Also **May′bee′tle** (-bēt′l).

May·day (mā′dā′) *n.* The international radiotelephone call for immediate help sent out by an aircraft or ship in distress. [<F *m'aidez* help me]

May Day The first day of May, traditionally celebrated as a spring festival by crowning a May Queen, dancing around a Maypole, etc.: commemorated in many countries as a labor holiday.

Ma·yence (mà·yäṅs′) The French name for MAINZ.

Ma·yenne (mà·yen′), **Duc de,** 1554–1611, Charles of Lorraine; French general; defeated by Henry IV.

May·er (mī′ər), **Julius Robert von,** 1814–78, German physicist.

may·est (mā′ist) May: obsolescent or poetic second person singular, present tense of MAY: with *thou.* Also spelled *mayst.*

May·fair (mā′fâr) A fashionable residential district of the West End, London.

may·flow·er (mā′flou′ər) *n.* **1** The trailing arbutus, State flower of Massachusetts. **2** *Brit.* The hawthorn or may; also, the marsh marigold. **3** Any of various other plants which blossom in the spring.

Mayflower The ship on which the Pilgrims came to America in 1620.

may·fly (mā′flī′) *n.* *pl.* **·flies** **1** An ephemerid insect, which in the nymphal state inhabits water and is long-lived, and in the adult state merely propagates its kind and then dies. **2** An artificial fly in imitation of this insect. **3** *Brit.* A caddis fly.

may·hap (mā′hap) *adv. Archaic* It may chance or happen; very likely; peradventure; perhaps. Also **may′hap′pen** (-ən). [<*(it) may hap(pen)*]

may·hem (mā′hem) *n.* **1** *Law* The offense of depriving a person by violence of any limb, member, or organ, or causing any mutilation of the body. Also spelled *maihem.* **2** Egregious disorder or damage. [<OF *mehaing, mahaigne.* Related to MAIM.]

May·ing (mā′ing) *n.* The celebration of May Day.

May·kop (mī·kôp′) See MAIKOP.

May·o (mā′ō) A maritime county of western Connacht, Ireland; 2,084 square miles; county town, Castlebar.

May·o (mā′ō), **Charles Horace,** 1865–1939, U. S. surgeon. — **William James,** 1861–1939, surgeon, brother of the preceding.

Ma·yon (mä·yôn′) An active volcano in SE Luzon, Philippines; 7,916 feet.

may·on·naise (mā′ə·nāz′, mī′-) *n.* A sauce or dressing made by beating together raw egg yolk, butter or olive oil, lemon juice or vinegar, and condiments. [<F, ? <*Mahón,* Balearic port]

may·or (mā′ər, mâr) *n.* The chief magistrate of a city, borough, or municipal corporation. [<F *maire* <L *major* greater. Doublet of MAJOR.] — **may′or·al** *adj.*

may·or·al·ty (mā′ər·əl·tē, mâr′əl-) *n.* *pl.* **·ties** The office or term of a mayor. [<OF *mairalté*]

Ma·yotte (mà·yôt′) Easternmost of the Comoro Islands, NW of Madagascar; 140 square miles.

May·pole (mā′pōl′) *n.* A pole decorated with flowers and ribbons, around which dancing takes place on May Day.

may·pop (mā′pop) *n.* **1** The passionflower *(Passiflora incarnata)* of the southern United States. **2** The small yellow fruit of this plant. [Alter. of N. Am. Ind. *maracock.* Cf. Tupian *maracujá.*]

May Queen A young girl crowned with flowers in May Day festivities.

mayst (māst) See MAYEST.

May·thorn (mā′thôrn′) *n.* The hawthorn.

May·time (mā′tīm′) *n.* The month of May. Also **May′tide′** (-tīd′).

may·weed (mā′wēd′) *n.* A strong-scented, acrid weed *(Anthemis cotula)* of the composite family, bearing white-rayed flowers on a yellow disk; stinking camomile. [Alter. of *maidweed* <*maytheweed* <OE *magothe* + WEED]

May wine Any still, white wine flavored with steeped orange and pineapple slices and woodruff: named for the month of May, in which the woodruff flowers.

Maz·a·gan (maz′ə·gan′) A port in western Morocco.

maz·ard (maz′ərd) *n. Obs.* **1** A mazer. **2** The skull; the head. Also **maz′zard.** [Var. of MAZER]

Maz·a·rin (maz′ə·rin, *Fr.* mà·zà·raṅ′), **Jules,** 1602–61, French cardinal and statesman; prime minister under Louis XIV: real name *Giulio Mazzarini.*

Maz·a·rine (maz′ə·rēn) *adj.* Of or pertaining to Cardinal Mazarin, or named from him.

Mazarine blue A deep, rich blue: named after Cardinal Mazarin.

Maz·a·ru·ni (maz′ə·rōō′nē) A river in northern British Guiana, flowing 350 miles NE to the Essequibo.

Ma·za·tlán (mä′sä·tlän′) A port in NW Mexico, on the Gulf of California.

Maz·da·ism (maz′də·iz′əm) *n.* Zoroastrianism. Also **Maz′de·ism.** [<OPersian *Aura mazda* the principle of good]

maze (māz) *n.* **1** An intricate network of paths or passages; a labyrinth. **2** Embarrassment; uncertainty; perplexity. — *v.t. Archaic* To daze or stupefy; bewilder. ◆ Homophone: *maize.* [<AMAZE] — **maz′y** *adj.* — **maz′i·ly** *adv.* — **maz′i·ness** *n.*

Ma·zep·pa (mə·zep′ə), **Ivan Stephanovich,**

1644–1709, a Cossack chief; hero of a poem by Byron.

ma·zer (mā′zər) *n.* A bowl, goblet, or drinking cup made of hard wood. Also *mazard.* [<OF *masere* maple wood <Gmc.] .

ma·zu·ma (mə·zōō′mə) *n. U.S. Slang* Money. [<Yiddish *m'zumon* "the ready necessary"]

ma·zur·ka (mə·zûr′kə, -zōōr′-) *n.* **1** A lively Polish round dance resembling the polka. **2** The music for such a dance. Also **ma·zour′·ka.** [<Polish, woman from Mazovia, a province in Poland]

Ma·zu·ry (mä·zōō′rē) The Polish name for MSURIA.

ma·zut (mə·zōōt′) *n.* The residue from the distillation of Russian petroleum: used as a fuel oil. Also **ma·zout′.** [<Russian]

maz·zard cherry (maz′ərd) The fruit of the European wild sweet cherry *(Prunus avium)* . [Earlier *mazer* maple wood; appar. from the hardness of the wood]

Maz·zi·ni (mät·tsē′nē), **Giuseppe,** 1805–72, Italian patriot and revolutionary; aided Garibaldi to unite Italy.

Mba·ba·ne (mbä·bä′nā) The capital of Swaziland.

M'bo·mu (mbō′mōō) See BOMU.

Mc– See also MAC-.

Mc·A·doo (mak′ə·dōō), **William Gibbs,** 1863–1941, U.S. lawyer and statesman; secretary of the treasury 1913–18.

Mc·Car·thy·ism (mə·kär′thē·iz′əm) *n.* **1** The practice of making public and sensational accusations of disloyalty or corruption, usually with little or no proof or with doubtful evidence. **2** The practice of conducting sensational inquisitorial investigations, ostensibly to expose subversion, especially pro-Communist activity. [after Joseph *McCarthy,* 1909–1957, U.S. Senator]

Mc·Clel·lan (mə·klel′ən), **George Brinton,** 1826–85, Union general in the Civil War.

Mc·Col·lum (mə·kol′əm), **Elmer Verner,** 1879–1967, American physiological chemist.

Mc·Cor·mack (mə·kôr′mik), **John,** 1884–1945, U.S. tenor born in Ireland.

Mc·Cor·mick (mə·kôr′mik), **Cyrus Hall,** 1809–1884, U.S. inventor of the reaping machine. **—Joseph Medill,** 1877–1925, U.S. newspaper publisher.

Mc·Coy (mə·koi′), **the (real)** *U.S. Slang* The authenic person or thing. [Appar. from an episode, existing in many versions, in which a celebrated American boxer, Kid McCoy, spectacularly established his identity]

Mc·Dou·gal (mək·dōō′gəl), **William,** 1871–1938, U.S. psychologist born in England.

Mc·Guf·fey (mə·guf′ē), **William Holmes,** 1800–1873, U.S. educator; author of a series of children's readers.

Mc·In·tire (mak′ən·tīr) *adj.* Pertaining to or naming the finely carved furniture and architectural embellishments in the neo-classic taste by Samuel McIntire, 1757–1811, woodcarver of Salem, Mass.

Mc·In·tosh (mak′ən·tosh) *n.* A red variety of early autumn apple. Also **McIntosh red.** [after John *McIntosh* of Ontario, who discovered it in the 18th century]

Mc·Kin·ley (mə·kin′lē), **Mount** A peak in central Alaska, highest in North America, 20,300 feet.

Mc·Kin·ley (mə·kin′lē), **William,** 1843–1901, president of the United States, 1897–1901; assassinated.

Mc·Mas·ter (mək·mas′tər, -mäs′-), **John Bach,**1852–1932, U.S. historian.

M–Day (em′dā′) *n.* Mil. Mobilization day; the day the Department of Defense orders mobilization for war.

Mdi·na (mə·dē′nə) The Maltese name for CITTÀ VECCHIA.

me (mē) *pron.* The objective case of *I.*

◆ **It's me, etc.** Anyone who answers the question "Who's there?" by saying "It's me" is using acceptable colloquial idiom. Here *It is I* would seem stilted, although at the formal level of writing it is expected: They have warned me that *it is I,* and not he, who will have to bear the brunt of the criticism. After a finite impersonal form of the verb *to be,* as *it is, it was,* etc., a personal pronoun should, according to prescriptive grammar, be in the same case as the subject: the nominative; accordingly, at the formal level, we find *It is he, It is we, It is they,* etc. Since only the personal and relative pronouns retain different inflected forms for the nominative and objective cases, the rule might appear to be invented to cover this one exceptional situation. The normal subject-verb-object order of the English sentence creates a strong expectation that what follows the verb will be in the objective case, and perhaps for this reason popular usage has long favored *It's me* over the formal *It is I.* British and American playwrights in recent years have also represented their characters, and not only the uneducated speakers among them, as saying *It's him, It's her, It's them,* etc. In spite of the exact parallel in construction with *It's me,* these expressions are not yet condoned to the same extent, even at the colloquial level.

me·a cul·pa (mē′ə kul′pə) *Latin* My fault; my blame.

mead[1] (mēd) *n.* A liquor of fermented honey and water to which malt, yeast, and spices are added; metheglin. See HYDROMEL. ◆ Homophone: *meed.* [OE *meodu*]

mead[2] (mēd) *n. Poetic* A meadow. ◆ Homophone: *meed.* [OE *mæd*]

Mead (mēd), **Lake** A reservoir formed by Hoover Dam in Boulder Canyon of the Colorado River in Arizona and Nevada; 246 square miles; largest artificial lake in the world. See BLACK CANYON.

Mead (mēd), **Margaret,** 1901–1978, U.S. anthropologist.

Meade (mēd), **George Gordon,** 1815–72, Union general in the Civil War, born in Spain.

mead·ow (med′ō) *n.* A tract of low or level land, producing grass for hay. [OE *mæ dwe,* oblique case of *moed*] **—mead′ ow·y** *adj.*

mead·ow·beau·ty (med′ō·byōō ′tē) *n. pl.* **·ties** Any of a genus *(Rhexia)* of low-growing herbs, usually with four-parted purple flowers; especially, the common species *(R. virginica).*

meadow bird The bobolink.

meadow hen The American bittern.

mead·ow·lark (med′ō·lärk′) *n.* An American songbird (genus *Sturnella)* related to the blackbird; especially, the southern meadowlark *(S. magna),* brownish or grayish above, marked with black and yellow beneath.

meadow lily The Canada lily.

meadow mouse The field mouse.

meadow rue Any species of the genus *Thalictrum* of the crowfoot family, having leaves like those of rue.

mead·ow·sweet (med′ō·swēt′) *n.* **1** A shrub of the rose family (genus *Spiraea*); especially, *S. salicifolia,* having alternate simple or pinnate leaves and white or rose-colored flowers: also **meadow queen. 2** Any plant of a related genus *(Filipendula).*

meadow weed Wild oat (def. 1).

mea·ger (mē′gər) *adj.* **1** Deficient or destitute of quantity or quality; scanty; inadequate. **2** Deficient in or scantily supplied with fertility, strength, or richness. **3** Wanting in flesh; thin; emaciated. Also **mea′gre.** [<OF *maigre* <L *macer* lean] **—mea′ ger·ly** *adv.* **—mea′ger·ness** *n.*

Synonyms: barren, emaciated, feeble, gaunt, jejune, lank, lean, poor, skinny, spare, starved, starveling, tame, thin. See GAUNT. *Antonyms.*: bonny, bouncing, burly, chubby, corpulent, fat, fleshy, hearty, obese, plump, portly, stout.

meal[1] (mēl) *n.* **1** Comparatively coarsely ground grain. **2** Unbolted wheat flour; chop. **3** A powder produced by grinding; any powdery, meal-like material: sulfur *meal.* [OE *melu*]

meal[2] (mēl) *n.* **1** The portion of food taken at one time; a repast. **2** Its occasion or time. ◆ Collateral adjective: *prandial.* [OE *mæl* measure, time, meal]

–meal *suffix* The quantity taken at one time or the unit of measurement: now obsolete except in *piecemeal.* [OE *-mælum,* oblique case of *mæl* measure, time]

meal·ie (mē′lē) *n.* **1** An ear of maize. **2** *pl.* Maize; Indian corn. [<Afrikaans *mielie* <Pg. *milho* millet <L *milium*]

meal·time (mēl′tīm′) *n.* The habitual time for eating a meal.

meal·worm (mēl′wûrm′) *n.* **1** The larva of a beetle *(Tenebrio molitor)* destructive to flour, meal, etc. **2** A meal-bred grub prepared as bait for ground fishing.

meal·y (mē′lē) *adj.* **meal·i·er, meal·i·est 1** Having a resemblance to or the qualities or taste of meal; farinaceous. **2** Overspread or besprinkled with or as with meal; pale-colored; of anemic appearance. **3** Having the appearance of being covered with meal; farinose. **4** Mealy-mouthed. **5** Friable; floury: said of the endosperm of malt. **6** Flecked with white spots: said of cattle. **7** Smooth-flavored; harsh to the taste: said of tea. **—meal′i·ness** *n.*

meal·y·bug (mē′lē·bug′) *n.* Any of a large cosmopolitan family *(Pseudococcidae)* of coccids whose soft, oval bodies are usually covered with a mealy wax secretion: they include many of the most destructive plant pests.

meal·y–mouthed (mē′lē·moutht′, -mouth′) *adj.* Unwilling to express adverse opinions plainly; euphemistic; insincere.

mean[1] (mēn) *v.* **meant, mean·ing** *v.t.* **1** To have in mind as a purpose or intent: I *meant* to visit him. **2** To intend or design for some purpose, destination, etc.: Was that remark *meant* for me? **3** To intend to express or convey: That's not what I *meant.* **4** To have as the particular sense or significance; denote; portend: Those clouds *mean* snow. —*v.i.* **5** To have disposition or intention; be disposed: He *means* well. **6** To be of specified importance or influence: Her beauty *means* everything to her. See synonyms under IMPORT, PURPOSE. ◆ Homophone: *mien.* [OE *mænan* tell, wish, intend]

mean[2] (mēn) *adj.* **1** Low in grade, quality, or condition; of humble antecedents; lowly; also, indicative of or suited to low rank; poor; inferior; shabby. **2** *Colloq.* Disagreeable; unpleasant; unkind; wicked. **3** Ignoble in mind, character, and spirit; lacking magnanimity or honor; base; petty; also, miserly; stingy. **4** Worthy of no respect; slight or contemptible. **5** Of little value or efficiency. **6** Not fit for cultivation: said of land. **7** Vicious or unmanageable: said of horses. **8** *Colloq.* Irritable; ashamed; paltry; also, ill: to feel *mean.* See synonyms under BAD, BASE, COMMON, INSIGNIFICANT, LITTLE, SMALL, VULGAR. ◆ Homophone: *mien.* [OE *(ge)mæne* common, ordinary] **—mean′ly** *adv.* **—mean′ness** *n.*

mean[3] (mēn) *n.* **1** The middle state between two extremes; hence, moderation; avoidance of excess; medium: the happy *mean.* **2** *Math.* A quantity having an intermediate value between two extremes, or between several quantities: the arithmetical *mean.* **3** *pl.* The medium through which anything is done; instrumentality: used often with singular construction: a *means* to an end. **4** *pl.* Money or property as a procuring medium; wealth. **5** A plan of procedure. **6** *Logic* The middle term in a syllogism. **7** *Obs.* An intermediary; mediator. See synonyms under AGENT. **—arithmetical mean** The quotient of the sum of two or more quantities divided by the number of quantities; the average. **—by all means** Without hesitation; certainly. **—by any means 1** In any manner possible; somehow; at all. **2** By all means. **—by no manner of means** Most certainly not; not for any consideration; on no account whatever: also **by no means. —geometric** (or **geometrical) mean** The square root of the product of two given numbers. **—golden mean** A wise moderation; the avoidance of extremes. —*adj.* **1** Intermediate as to position between extremes. **2** Intermediate as to size, degree, or quality; medium; average. **3** Intermediate as to time; intervening. **4** Having an intermediate value between two extremes or among several values; average: the *mean* distance covered daily. ◆ Homophone: *mien.* [<OF *meien* <L *medianus* <*medius* middle. Doublet of MEDIAN, MESNE, MIZZEN.]

me·an·der (mē·an′dər) *v.i.* **1** To wind and turn in a course. **2** To wander aimlessly. —*n.* **1** A tortuous or winding course; hence, a maze; perplexity. **2** The Greek key or fret pattern. [<MEANDER] **—me·an′der·er** *n.* **—me·an′der·ing, me·an′drous** *adj.*

Me·an·der (mē·an′dər) The ancient name for

the MENDERES, proverbial for its windings: also *Maeander.*

mean·ing (mē′ning) *n.* **1** That which is intended; object; intention; aim. **2** That which is signified; significance; sense; acceptation; import; connotation. See synonyms under PURPOSE. — *adj.* **1** Having purpose or intention: usually in combination: well-*meaning.* **2** Significant; suggestive. — **mean′ing·ful** *adj.* — **mean′ing·ful·ly** *adv.* — **mean′ing·less** *adj.* — **mean′ing·less·ly** *adv.* — **mean′ing·less·ness** *n.* — **mean′ing·ly** *adv.*

mean latitude Middle latitude.

mean sun *Astron.* A fictitious sun considered to be moving uniformly with respect to the equator: a concept used to facilitate the computation of time.

meant (ment) Past tense and past participle of MEAN[1].

mean·time (mēn′tīm′) *n.* Intervening time or occasion. — *adv.* In or during the meantime.

mean time See under TIME. Also **mean solar time.**

mean·while (mēn′hwīl′) *n.* & *adv.* Meantime.

Mearns (mûrnz), **The** See KINCARDINE.

mea·sle (mē′zəl) *n.* **1** The larva *(Cysticercus)* of a certain tapeworm (genus *Taenia*) found in meat and generally producing measles in swine. **2** Any excrescence upon a plant or tree. [See MEASLES]

mea·sled (mē′zəld) *adj.* Affected with measles.

mea·sles (mē′zəlz) *n.* **1** An acute, highly contagious, generally self-immunizing virus disease affecting children and sometimes adults: it is characterized by chills, fever, severe coryza, and an extensive eruption of small red macules; rubeola. **2** Any of various eruptive diseases of a similar character: used with a qualifying adjective: French *measles.* **3** A disease affecting swine and cattle, caused by the presence of larval tapeworms in the flesh. — **French measles, German measles** Rubella. [ME *maseles,* pl. of *masel* a blister <LG. Cf. MDu. *masel* spot on the skin.]

mea·sly (mēz′lē) *adj.* **·sli·er, ·sli·est** **1** Affected with measles. **2** Containing tapeworm larvae: said of meat. **3** *Slang* Not fit to be touched; beneath contempt; also, mean; skimpy; stingy; scanty.

meas·ur·a·ble (mezh′ər·ə·bəl) *adj.* **1** Capable of being measured or of computation. **2** Limited; moderate: *measurable* severity. — **meas′·ur·a·bil′i·ty, meas′ur·a·ble·ness** *n.* — **meas′·ur·a·bly** *adv.*

meas·ure (mezh′ər) *n.* **1** The extent or dimensions of anything. **2** A standard of measurement. **3** Hence, any standard of criticism, comparison, judgment, or award. **4** A series of measure units; a system of measurements: dry *measure.* See WEIGHT. **5** An instrument or vessel of measurement. **6** The act of measuring; measurement. **7** A quantity measured, or regarded as measured. **8** Reasonable limits; moderation: beyond *measure*; also, degree; reasonable proportion: A *measure* of allowance should be made. **9** A certain proportion; relative extent. **10** A specific act or course; transaction; specifically, a legislative bill. **11** That which makes up a sum or total. **12** Any quantity regarded as a unit and standard of comparison with other quantities; a quantity of which some other given quantity forms an exact multiple. **13** *Music* **a** That division of time by which melody and rhythm are regulated; rate of movement; time. **b** The portion of music contained between two bar lines; bar. **14** In prosody, meter; a rhythmical period. **15** A slow and stately dance or dance movement. **16** *pl. Geol.* A series of related rock strata, having some common feature. — *v.* **·ured, ·ur·ing** *v.t.* **1** To take or ascertain the dimensions, quantity, capacity, etc., of, especially by means of a measure. **2** To set apart, mark off, etc., by measuring: often with *off* or *out.* **3** To estimate by comparison; judge; weigh: to *measure* a risk. **4** To serve as the measure of. **5** To bring into competition or comparison. **6** To traverse as if measuring; travel over. **7** To adjust; regulate: *Measure* your actions to your aspirations. — *v.i.* **8** To make or take measurements. **9** To yield a specified measurement: The table *measures* six by four feet. **10** To admit measurement. — **to measure one's length** To fall prostrate at full length. — **to measure out** To distribute or allot by measure. — **to measure swords** **1** To fight with swords. **2** To fight or contend as in a debate. — **to measure up to** To fulfil, as expectations. [<F *mesure* <L *mensura* < *metiri* measure] — **meas′ur·er** *n.*

meas·ured (mezh′ərd) *adj.* **1** Ascertained, adjusted, or proportioned by rule. **2** Uniform; slow and stately; rhythmical; deliberate. **3** In moderation; held in restraint; guarded. — **meas′ured·ly** *adv.* — **meas′ured·ness** *n.*

meas·ure·less (mezh′ər·lis) *adj.* Incapable of measurement; unlimited; immense. See synonyms under INFINITE.

meas·ure·ment (mezh′ər·mənt) *n.* **1** The process or result of measuring anything; mensuration. **2** The amount, capacity, or extent determined by measuring. **3** A system of measuring units.

measuring worm A geometrid.

meat (mēt) *n.* **1** The flesh of animals used as food: sometimes limited to the flesh of mammals, as opposed to fish or fowl; also, any animal killed for food: to hunt one's *meat.* **2** Anything eaten for nourishment; victuals; hence, that which nourishes. **3** The edible part of anything. **4** A meal; especially, dinner; the main meal. **5** The essence, gist, or pith: the *meat* of an essay. **6** *Slang* Anything one does with special ease or pleasure; forte. ◆ Homophones: *meet, mete.* [OE *mete*] — **meat′less** *adj.*

Meath (mēth, mēth) A county of NE Leinster province, Ireland; 903 square miles; county town, Trim.

meat packing *U.S.* The commercial slaughtering of meat-producing animals and the processing, packaging, and distribution of meat and meat products. — **meat packer**

me·a·tus (mē·ā′təs) *n. pl.* **·tus** or **·tus·es** *Anat.* A conspicuous passage or canal: the auditory *meatus.* [<L, a passage < *meare* go]

meat·y (mē′tē) *adj.* **meat·i·er, meat·i·est** **1** Full of or resembling meat. **2** Having strength; nourishing. **3** Significant; pithy. — **meat′i·ness** *n.*

Meaux (mō) A city in north central France.

me·ca·te (mā·kä′tā) *n. SW U.S.* A rope made of maguey fiber, or sometimes of plaited horsehair: used for tying horses. [<Sp. < Nahuatl]

mec·ca (mek′ə) *n.* **1** A place visited by many people; any attraction. **2** The object of one's aspiration, yearning, or effort. [from *Mecca*]

Mec·ca (mek′ə) The capital of Hejaz and one of the capitals of Saudi Arabia; birthplace of Mohammed and a holy city of Islam to which Moslems make pilgrimages: also *Mekka.*

me·chan·ic (mə·kan′ik) *n.* **1** One engaged in mechanical employment; an artisan; handicraftsman. **2** *Obs.* A mean or lowly fellow. See synonyms under ARTIST. — *adj.* **1** Pertaining to mechanics; mechanical. **2** Involving manual labor or skill. [<L *mechanicus* <Gk. *mēchanikos* < *mēchanē* a machine]

me·chan·i·cal (mə·kan′i·kəl) *adj.* **1** Pertaining to mechanics; in accordance with the laws of mechanics. **2** Produced by a machine. **3** Operated by mechanism. **4** Operating as if by a machine or machinery. **5** Doing or done involuntarily, by mere force of habit. **6** Automatic; not instinct with life; artificial. **7** Failing to show independence of thought; slavish. **8** Skilled in the use of tools and mechanisms. — **me·chan′i·cal·ly** *adv.* — **me·chan′i·cal·ness** *n.*

mech·a·ni·cian (mek′ə·nish′ən) *n.* One who understands the science of mechanics; a designer of machinery.

me·chan·ics (mə·kan′iks) *n. pl.* **1** The branch of physics that treats of the phenomena caused by the action of forces on material bodies, including statics and kinetics: construed as singular. **2** The science of machinery and of its practical applications: construed as singular. **3** The mechanical or technical aspects: construed as plural.

Me·chan·ics·ville (mə·kan′iks·vil) A hamlet 7 miles NE of Richmond, Virginia; site of a battle (June 26, 1862) in the Civil War.

mech·a·nism (mek′ə·niz′əm) *n.* **1** The parts of a machine collectively; machinery in general. **2** A system which constitutes a working agency. **3** Technique; mechanical execution or action. **4** The theory that the forces that produce organic growth are the same physical and chemical agencies that operate in the inorganic world, differing from them only in degree: opposed to *vitalism.* **5** *Psychol.* The mental processes, conscious or unconscious, by which certain actions are effected. See synonyms under TOOL. — **mech′·a·nis′tic** *adj.* — **mech′a·nis′ti·cal·ly** *adv.*

mech·a·nist (mek′ə·nist) *n.* **1** A mechanician. **2** A believer in philosophical mechanism.

mech·a·ni·za·tion (mek′ə·nə·zā′shən, -nī-) *n.* **1** The act or process of applying machinery to the performance of specified operations. **2** The aggregate results of such application. **3** *Mil.* The maximum coordinated utilization of power-driven equipment, mechanized armament, and automatic weapons in the service of the combat personnel.

mech·a·nize (mek′ə·nīz) *v.t.* **·nized, ·niz·ing** **1** To make mechanical. **2** To convert (an industry, etc.) to machine production. **3** *Mil.* To equip with tanks, trucks, etc. — **mech′a·nized** *adj.*

mech·a·no·ther·a·py (mek′ə·nō·ther′ə·pē) *n. Med.* The treatment of disease by mechanical means, as massage. [< *mechano-* (<MECHANIC) + THERAPY]

Mech·lin (mek′lin) *n.* A lace with bobbin ground and designs outlined by thread or flat cord, made in Malines (Mechlin), Belgium: also called *malines.*

Mech·lin (mek′lin) A town of north central Belgium: French *Malines. Flemish* **Mech·e·len** (mekh′ə·lən).

Meck·len·burg (mek′lən·bûrg, *Ger.* mek′lən·bŏŏrkh) A former state of northern Germany on the Baltic, comprising the former grand duchies of **Meck′len·burg-Schwe·rin′** (-shvā·rēn′), **Meck′len·burg-Stre′litz** (-shtrā′lits), and western Pomerania; 8,856 square miles; capital, Schwerin; divided, July 1952, into several districts of East Germany.

mec·on·ism (mek′ə·niz′əm, mē′kə-) *n. Pathol.* Addiction to opium; poisoning by opium. [<Gk. *mēkōn* a poppy]

me·cop·ter·ous (mə·kop′tər·əs) *adj.* Of, pertaining or belonging to an order *(Mecoptera)* of slender, predacious insects with biting mouth parts and long, narrow wings. [<NL <Gk. *mēkos* length + *pteron* wing]

med·al (med′l) *n.* A small piece of metal, bearing a device, usually commemorative of some event or deed of bravery, scientific research, or literary production, etc. — *v.t.* **·aled** or **·alled, ·al·ing** or **·al·ling** To confer a medal upon. ◆ Homophone: *meddle.* [<F *médaille* <Ital. *medaglia,* ult. <L *metallum.* Doublet of METAL.] — **me·dal·lic** (mə·dal′ik) *adj.*

Medal for Merit A medal awarded by the United States to civilians for exceptional services in times of peace or war.

med·al·ist (med′l·ist) *n.* **1** A collector, engraver, or designer of medals. **2** The recipient of a medal awarded for services or merit. **3** In golf, the winner at medal play. Also **med′·al·list.**

me·dal·lion (mə·dal′yən) *n.* **1** A large medal; also, a subject painted, engraved, etc., and set in a circular or oval frame or design: used as decorative elements in carpets, lace, etc. **2** Any one of several ancient Greek silver coins. [<F *médaillon* <Ital. *medaglione,* aug. of *medaglia* MEDAL] — **me·dal′lion·ist** *n.*

Medal of Honor The highest U. S. decoration, awarded to a member of the armed forces who risked his life in action beyond the call of duty. It is awarded in the name of Congress and usually presented personally by the president. Also called *Congressional Medal of Honor.*

medal play In golf, a form of competitive play in which the score is computed by counting only the total number of strokes played by each competitor in playing the designated number of holes.

Me·dan (me·dän′) A town in NE Sumatra.

med·dle (med′l) *v.i.* **·dled, ·dling** **1** To take part in or concern oneself with something without need or request: often with *in* or *with.* **2** *Obs.* To mix; mingle. See synonyms under INTERPOSE, MIX. ◆ Homophone: *medal.* [<OF *medler, mesdler,* var. of *mesler,* ult. <L *miscere* mix] — **med′dler** *n.* — **med′dling** *adj.* & *n.*

med·dle·some (med′l·səm) *adj.* Given to meddling; officiously inclined; interfering; intrusive. — **med′dle·some·ly** *adv.* — **med′dle·some·ness** *n.*

Synonyms: impertinent, intrusive, meddling, obtrusive, officious. The *meddlesome* person interferes unasked in the affairs of others; the *intrusive* person thrusts himself uninvited into their company or conversation; the *obtrusive* person thrusts himself or his opinions conceitedly and undesirably upon their notice; the *officious* person thrusts his services, unasked and undesired, upon others. Compare ACTIVE, INQUISITIVE, INTERPOSE. *Antonyms*: modest, reserved, retiring, shy, unassuming, unobtrusive.

Mede (mēd) *n.* One of an ancient Asiatic people who flourished in Media in the sixth century B.C.

Me·de·a (mə·dē'ə) In Greek legend, a sorceress of Colchis who aided Jason to obtain the Golden Fleece and, when deserted by him for Creusa, killed her rival and her own children and fled to Athens.

Me·del·lín (mā'thā·yēn') A city in NW Colombia.

med·e·vac (med'ə·vak') *n.* The evacuation of the wounded, as from battle sites, usually by helicopter. [< *med(ical) evac(uation)*]

me·di·a (mē'dē·ə) *n. pl. of* **medium** 1 Means of disseminating information, entertainment, etc., such as books, newspapers, radio, television, motion pictures, and magazines. 2 In advertising, all means of communication that carry advertisements, including billboards, direct mail, catalogs, radio, etc.

Me·di·a (mē'dē·ə) An ancient country of SW Asia, corresponding to the NW Iranian plateau. — **Me'di·an** *adj.* & *n.*

me·di·a·cy (mē'dē·ə·sē) *n.* 1 The state or quality of being mediate. 2 Mediation.

me·di·ae·val (mē'dē·ē'vəl, med'ē-), **me·di·ae·val·ism,** etc. See MEDIEVAL, etc

me·di·al (mē'dē·əl) *adj.* 1 Of or pertaining to the middle, in position or character or in calculation; mean. 2 Nearer the median plane of a body: opposed to *lateral.* 3 Designating a letter neither initial nor final. — *n. Phonet.* Any of a group of voiced stops (b, d, g), conceived as intermediate between the voiceless stops (p, t, k) and the rough or aspirate group (bh, dh, gh, ph, th, kh). [<LL *medialis* <L *medius* middle] — **me'di·al·ly** *adv.*

me·di·an (mē'dē·ən) *adj.* 1 Pertaining to the middle, or situated in the median plane. 2 *Stat.* Of, pertaining to, or designating that point in a series of values which divides the series into two groups, each containing the same number of entries: 8 is the *median* point of the series 2, 5, 8, 10, 13. [<L *medianus* < *medius* middle. Doublet of MEAN[3], MESNE, MIZZEN.] — **me'di·an·ly** *adv.*

median plane That plane that divides a body longitudinally into symmetrical halves.

me·di·as·ti·num (mē'dē·as·tī'nəm) *n. pl.* **·na** (-nə) *Anat.* 1 A median partition or septum separating two cavities of the body. 2 The partition between the two pleural sacs of the chest, extending from the sternum to the thoracic vertebrae and downward to the diaphragm. [<NL <Med. L *mediastinus* medial < *medius*] — **me'di·as·ti'nal** *adj.*

me·di·ate (mē'dē·āt) *v.* **·at·ed, ·at·ing** *v.t.* 1 To settle or reconcile by mediation, as differences. 2 To bring about or effect by mediation. 3 To serve as the medium for effecting (a result) or conveying (an object, information, etc.). — *v.i.* 4 To act between disputing parties in order to bring about a settlement, compromise, etc. 5 To occur or be in an intermediate relation or position. See synonyms under INTERPOSE. — *adj.* (-it) 1 Acting as an intervening agency; indirect. 2 Occurring or effected as a result of indirect or median agency. 3 Intermediate. [<LL *mediatus*, pp. of *mediare* stand between, mediate] — **me'·di·ate·ly** *adv.* — **me'di·ate·ness** *n.* — **me'di·a'·tive** *adj.* — **me'di·a'tor** *n.* — **me'di·a·to'ri·al** (-tôr'ē·əl, -tō'rē·əl), **me'di·a·to'ry** *adj.*

me·di·a·tion (mē'dē·ā'shən) *n.* 1 The act of mediating; intercession; interposition. 2 A friendly intervention in the disputes of others, with their consent, for the purpose of adjusting differences. See CONCILIATION.

med·ic[1] (med'ik) *n.* Any one of several plants of the bean family (genus *Medicago*), especially the lucerne or alfalfa. [<L *medicus* <Gk. *Mēdikē (poa)* Median (grass) <*Mēdos* a Mede]

med·ic[2] (med'ik) *n. Colloq.* 1 A doctor, physician, or intern. 2 A medical corpsman.

med·i·ca·ble (med'ə·kə·bəl) *adj.* Capable of relief by medicine; curable.

Med·i·caid (med'i·kād') *n. U.S.* A tax-supported health insurance program for low-income people.

med·i·cal (med'i·kəl) *adj.* 1 Pertaining to medicine or its practice. 2 Having curative properties. [<F *médicale* <LL *medicalis* <L *medicus* a physician] — **med'i·cal·ly** *adv.*

medical examiner 1 *Law* An official legally designated to examine the bodies of those dead as a result of violence or crime, to perform autopsies, and to establish the proximate cause and circumstances of the death. 2 A doctor authorized by a life insurance company to determine the physical fitness of a prospective insurant.

medical jurisprudence The branch of medicine and related sciences which deals with questions involving the applications of the civil and criminal law; forensic medicine. See under JURISPRUDENCE.

med·i·ca·ment (med'ə·kə·mənt, mə·dik'ə-) *n.* 1 Any substance for the alleviation of disease or wounds. 2 A healing agency. [<L *medicamentum* < *medicare.* See MEDICATE.] — **med'i·ca·men'tal** *adj.*

med·i·care (med'i·kâr') *n. Often cap. U.S.* A health insurance program supported in part by government funds, serving especially the aged.

med·i·cate (med'ə·kāt) *v.t.* **·cat·ed, ·cat·ing** 1 To treat medicinally. 2 To tincture or impregnate with medicine. [<L *medicatus*, pp. of *medicare* heal < *medicus* a physician] — **med'i·ca'tive, med'i·ca·to'ry** (-kə·tôr'ē, -tō'rē) *adj.*

med·i·ca·tion (med'ə·kā'shən) *n.* 1 Any substance used to treat disease, heal wounds, etc.; a medicine. 2 The act or process of medicating.

Med·i·ce·an (med'ə·sē'ən, -chē'-) *adj.* Of or pertaining to the Medici.

Med·i·ci (med'ə·chē, *Ital.* mā'dē·chē) A family of Florentine bankers who became rulers of Tuscany, patrons of the arts, literature, etc. Among its members were **Catherine de' Medici,** 1519–89, queen of Henry II of France, who planned the St. Bartholomew's Day Massacre; **Cosimo (Cosmo) de' Medici,** 1389–1464; **Cosimo (Cosmo) de' Medici,** 1519–74, first Grand Duke of Tuscany: called "Cosimo the Great"; **Lorenzo de' Medici,** 1448?–92, prince of Florence, statesman, educator, patron of art, literature, and printing: known as *Lorenzo the Magnificent*; **Maria de' Medici** (see under MARIA); **Giovanni de' Medici** (see LEO X).

me·dic·i·nal (mə·dis'ə·nəl) *adj.* Adapted to cure or mitigate disease. — **me·dic'i·nal·ly** *adv.*

med·i·cine (med'ə·sin) *n.* 1 A substance possessing, or reputed to possess, curative or remedial properties. 2 The healing art; the science of the preservation of health and of treating disease for the purpose of cure, specifically, as distinguished from surgery or obstetrics. 3 Among North American Indians, any agent or influence used to prevent or cure ills or to invoke supernatural protection or aid, varying from actual remedies (cinchona, etc.) to fetishes, prayers, and symbolic rites (**medicine dance, medicine song,** etc.); specifically, among the Algonquians, any mystery. See MANITO. 4 *Colloq.* Something distasteful or unpleasant: to give someone a dose of his own *medicine.* 5 *Obs.* Something used for other than healing purposes, as the philosopher's stone, elixirs, poisons, love philters, etc. — **to take one's medicine** To endure necessary hardship, discomfort, or punishment, or to do something unpleasant but required. [<L *medicina* < *medicus* physician < *mederi* heal]

medicine ball A large, heavy, leather-covered ball, thrown and caught for physical exercise.

medicine lodge A lodge in a North American Indian village, used for ritualistic, religious ceremonies.

medicine man Among North American Indians, one professing supernatural powers of healing and of invoking the spirits; a shaman.

med·i·co (med'ə·kō) *n. pl.* **·cos** *Colloq.* A doctor or a medical student. [<Ital., a physician]

medico- *combining form* Pertaining to medical science and: *medico-legal.* Also, before vowels, **medic-.** [<L *medicus* a physician]

me·di·e·val (mē'dē·ē'vəl, med'ē-) *adj.* Belonging to or descriptive or characteristic of the Middle Ages: also spelled *mediaeval.* [<L *medius* middle + *aevum* age] — **me'di·e'val·ly** *adv.*

Medieval Greek See under GREEK.

me·di·e·val·ism (mē'dē·ē'vəl·iz'əm, med'ē-) *n.* The spirit or practices of the Middle Ages; the flavor or general tone of medieval life; devotion to the institutions, ideas, or traits of the Middle Ages; also, any custom, idea, etc., surviving from the Middle Ages. — **me'di·e'val·ist** *n.*

Medieval Latin See under LATIN.

Me·di·na (mə·dē'nə) A Moslem holy city in Hejaz, western Saudi Arabia; goal of Mohammed's Hegira and the place of his tomb.

medio- *combining form* Middle. Also, before vowels, **medi-.** [<L *medius* middle]

me·di·o·cre (mē'dē·ō'kər, mē'dē·ō'kər) *adj.* Of only middle quality; ordinary; commonplace. [<L *mediocris* < *medius* middle]

me·di·oc·ri·ty (mē'dē·ok'rə·tē) *n. pl.* **·ties** 1 Commonplace ability or condition. 2 A commonplace person.

med·i·tate (med'ə·tāt) *v.* **·tat·ed, ·tat·ing** *v.i.* To engage in continuous and contemplative thought; muse; cogitate. — *v.t.* To think about doing; plan; intend: to *meditate* mischief. See synonyms under CONSIDER, DELIBERATE, MUSE. [<L *meditatus*, pp. of *meditari* muse, ponder] — **med'i·tat'er, med'i·ta'tor** *n.* — **med'i·ta'tive** *adj.* — **med'i·ta'tive·ly** *adv.*

med·i·ta·tion (med'ə·tā'shən) *n.* The act of meditating; the turning or revolving of a subject in the mind; continuous thought; contemplation. See synonyms under REFLECTION, THOUGHT.

med·i·ter·ra·ne·an (med'ə·tə·rā'nē·ən) *adj.* Enclosed nearly or wholly by land, as a sea or other large body of water; landlocked. [<L *medius* middle + *terra* earth]

Med·i·ter·ra·ne·an (med'ə·tə·rā'nē·ən) *adj.* 1 Of or pertaining to the Mediterranean Sea. 2 Inhabiting the shores of the Mediterranean. — *n.* 1 The Mediterranean Sea. 2 One who lives in a Mediterranean country, or belongs to the Mediterranean race. — **Key of the Mediterranean** Gibraltar.

Mediterranean fever Undulant fever.

Mediterranean race A subdivision of the Caucasoid race, regarded as designating the peoples inhabiting the shores of the Mediterranean Sea, including the ancient Iberian, Ligurian, Pelasgian, and Hamitic stocks and their modern descendants.

Mediterranean Sea An arm of the Atlantic Ocean comprising a great inland sea between Europe, Asia Minor, and Africa; 965,000 square miles.

me·di·um (mē'dē·əm) *n. pl.* **·di·ums** *(always for def 5)* or **me·di·a** (-dē·ə) 1 An intermediate quality, degree, or condition; mean. 2 A surrounding or enveloping element; condition of life; environment. 3 Any substance, as air, through or in which something may move or an effect be produced: Air is a *medium* of sound. 4 An intermediate means or agency; instrument: Radio is an advertising *medium.* 5 A person believed to be in communication with or controlled by the personality of someone deceased. 6 In painting, a liquid which gives fluency to the pigment. 7 A mathematical mean. 8 *Bacteriol.* A substance sterilized by heat in which bacteria, viruses, and other micro-organisms are developed: also **culture medium.** 9 A size of paper, usually 18 x 23 inches, between demy and royal. — **circulating medium** A money currency. — *adj.* 1 Intermediate in quantity, quality, position, size, or degree; middle. 2 Mediocre. [<L, orig. neut. sing. of *medius* middle]

medium bomber See under BOMBER.

me·di·um·is·tic (mē'dē·əm·is'tik) *adj.* Of or pertaining to spiritualist mediums or to their practices.

me·dji·di·e (me·jē'dē·e) *n.* 1 A modern Turkish silver coin equivalent to 19 piasters. 2 A Turkish gold coin, the lira. [<Turkish *mejīdī*]

med·lar (med'lər) *n.* 1 A small, European tree *(Mespilus germanica)* of the rose family. 2 Its edible fruit, hard and bitter when ripe, but agreeably acid when it begins to decay. [<OF *medler,* var. of *meslier* < *mesle* fruit of the medlar <L *mespila* <Gk. *mespilē*]

med·ley (med′lē) *n.* **1** A mingled and confused mass of ingredients, usually incongruous; a heterogeneous group; jumble. **2** A composition of different songs or parts of songs arranged to run as a continuous whole. **3** A cloth woven from yarn of mingled colors: properly including blue and black. **4** In sports, a relay race in which all legs are not the same, as in distance or in swimming stroke used. —*adj.* **1** Mixed; confused. **2** Of mixed colors; motley. [<OF *medlee,* orig. fem. pp. of *medler.* See MEDDLE.]

Mé·doc (mā·dôk′) *n.* A red wine originally made in Médoc, France.

Mé·doc (mā·dôk′) A region of SW France.

me·dul·la (mə·dul′ə) *n. pl.* **·lae** (-ē) **1** *Anat.* **a** The inner portion of an organ or part, distinguished from the cortex. **b** The marrow of long bones. **c** The pith of a hair. **d** The spinal cord: also **medulla spi·na·lis** (spī·nā′lis). **2** The ganglion of the brain which, connecting with the spinal cord, controls breathing, swallowing, circulation, etc.: also **medulla ob·lon·ga·ta** (ob′lông·gä′tə). **3** *Bot.* The inner central columnar mass of parenchymatous tissue in the stems and roots of certain plants; also, in lichens, the middle layer of tissue composing the thallus, and in fungi proper, the central tissue within the rind of the fungus body. [< L <*medius* middle] —**med·ul·lar·y** (med′ə·ler′ē, mi·dul′ər·ē), **me·dul′lar** *adj.*

medullary rays 1 *Anat.* Extensions of the tubules of the kidney into the cortical substance. **2** *Bot.* The vertical bands or plates of cellular (parenchymatous) tissue, proceeding from the pith to the surface, and characteristic of the species of exogenous plants.

medullary sheath Myelin. See illustration under EXOGEN.

med·ul·lat·ed (med′ə·lā′tid, mi·dul′ā·tid) *adj.* Provided with a medullary sheath: said of nerve fibers.

me·du·sa (mə·dōō′sə, -zə, -dyōō′-) *n. pl.* **·sas** or **·sae** (-sē, -zē) A jellyfish. [<L] —**me·du′·san** *adj.*

Me·du·sa (mə·dōō′sə, -zə, -dyōō′-) One of the Gorgons, killed by Perseus who gave her head to Athena.

me·du·soid (mə·dōō′soid, -zoid, -dyōō′-) *adj.* Resembling a medusa or jellyfish. —*n.* **1** A medusa-shaped gonophore of a hydrozoan. **2** Any medusa.

Med·way (med′wā) A river rising in SE Surrey and NE Sussex, England, and flowing 70 miles NE through western Kent to the Thames estuary at Sheerness.

meed (mēd) *n. Archaic* **1** A well-deserved reward; recompense. **2** A present, gift, or bribe. ◆ Homophone: *mead.* [OE *mēd*]

meek (mēk) *adj.* **1** Of gentle and long-suffering disposition. **2** Submissive; compliant; lacking spirit or backbone. **3** Humble; lowly. **4** *Obs.* Gentle; indulgent; kind; compassionate. See synonyms under HUMBLE, PACIFIC. —*adv.* Meekly. [<ON *miukr* gentle, soft] —**meek′ly** *adv.* —**meek′ness** *n.*

meer (mir) *n. Scot.* Mare.

meer·schaum (mir′shəm, -shôm, -shoum) *n.* **1** A soft, light, compact, heat-resisting magnesium silicate, $H_4Mg_2Si_3O_{10}$, used for carving into tobacco pipes, cigar holders, and the like; sepiolite. It is closely related to talc. **2** A pipe made from this material. [<G <*meer* sea + *schaum* foam]

Mee·rut (mē′rət) A city in NW Uttar Pradesh, India.

meet[1] (mēt) *v.* **met, meet·ing** *v.t.* **1** To come upon; encounter. **2** To make the acquaintance of; be introduced to. **3** To be at the place of arrival of: We *met* him at the station. **4** To come into contact, conjunction, or intersection with; join: where the path *meets* the road. **5** To keep an appointment with. **6** To come into the view, hearing, etc., of: A ghastly sight *met* our eyes. **7** To experience; undergo: to *meet* bad weather. **8** To oppose in battle; fight with. **9** To face or counter: to *meet* a blow with a blow. **10** To deal with; refute or cope with: to *meet* an accusation. **11** To comply with; act or result in conformity with, as expectations or wishes. **12** To pay, as a bill. —*v.i.* **13** To come together, as from opposite or different directions. **14** To come together in contact, conjunction, or intersection; join. **15** To assemble. **16** To make acquaintance or be introduced. **17** To come together in conflict or opposition; contend. **18** To agree. —**to meet up with** *U.S. Colloq.* **1** To encounter. **2** To experience; undergo. —**to meet with 1** To come upon; encounter. **2** To deal or confer with. **3** To experience. **4** To be the subject or recipient of. —*n.* **1** An assembling together of huntsmen; also, the company or rendezvous. **2** An athletic contest: a track *meet.* ◆ Homophones: *meat, mete.* [OE *mētan*]

meet[2] (mēt) *adj.* Suitable, as to an occasion; adapted; fit. See synonyms under APPROPRIATE, BECOMING. —*adv. Obs.* Meetly; suitably. ◆ Homophones: *meat, mete.* [OE *gemǣte*] —**meet′ly** *adv.* —**meet′ness** *n.*

meet·ing (mē′ting) *n.* **1** A coming together. **2** An assembly of persons; specifically, a congregation of the Friends or Quakers; also, their meeting house. See synonyms under ASSEMBLY, COLLISION, COMPANY.

meeting house 1 A house used for public meetings, especially for public worship. **2** A place of worship used by the Friends.

mega– *combining form* **1** Great; large; powerful: *megaphone.* **2** In the metric system, electricity, etc., a million, or a million times, as in the following:

megabar	**mega–erg**	**megampere**
megacycle	**megafarad**	**megavolt**
megadyne	**megameter**	**megohm**

Also, before vowels, **meg–.** [<Gk. *megas* large]

meg·a·ce·phal·ic (meg′ə·sə·fal′ik) *adj.* Large-headed; specifically, having a cranial capacity above the average. Also **meg′a·ceph′a·lous** (-sef′ə·ləs).

meg·a·death (meg′ə·deth) *n.* The death of one million persons: a term used in reference to nuclear warfare. [<MEGA- + DEATH]

Me·gae·ra (mə·jir′ə) In Greek mythology, one of the three Furies. Also **Me·gæ′ra.** [<L < Gk. *Megaira* < *magairein* grudge]

meg·a·ga·mete (meg′ə·gə·mēt′, -gam′ēt) *n.* A macrogamete.

meg·a·hertz (meg′ə·hûrtz′) *n.* A unit of frequency equal to one million cycles per second.

meg·a·lith (meg′ə·lith) *n. Archeol.* A huge stone, especially one used in prehistoric monuments. —**meg′a·lith′ic** *adj.*

megalo– *combining form* Big; indicating excessive or abnormal size: *megalocephalic.* Also, before vowels, **megal–.** [<Gk. *megas, megalou* big]

meg·a·lo·car·di·a (meg′ə·lō·kär′dē·ə) *n. Pathol.* Morbid enlargement of the heart. [<MEGALO- + Gk. *kardia* heart]

meg·a·lo·ceph·a·ly (meg′ə·lō·sef′ə·lē) *n.* **1** Unusual largeness of the head. **2** *Pathol.* Progressive enlargement of the cranium. Also **meg′a·lo·ce·pha′li·a** (-sə·fā′lē·ə). [<MEGALO- + Gk. *kephalē* head] —**meg′a·lo·ce·phal′ic** (-sə·fal′ik), **meg′a·lo·ceph′a·lous** *adj.*

meg·a·lo·ma·ni·a (meg′ə·lō·mā′nē·ə, -mān′yə) *n.* **1** *Psychiatry* A mental disorder in which the subject thinks himself great or exalted; delusions of grandeur, power, etc. **2** A tendency to magnify and exaggerate. —**meg′a·lo·ma′ni·ac** *adj. & n.* —**meg′a·lo·ma·ni′a·cal** (-mə·nī′ə·kəl) *adj.*

meg·a·lop·o·lis (meg′ə·lop′ə·lis) *n.* A densely populated urban area including one or more major cities. [<MEGALO- + Gk. *polis* city] —**meg·a·lo·pol·i·tan** (meg′ə·lō·pol′ə·tən) *n.*

meg·a·lop·si·a (meg′ə·lop′sē·ə) *n.* Macropsia.

Meg·a·lop·ter·a (meg′ə·lop′tər·ə) *n. pl.* An order of soft-bodied insects with large wings, long antennae, chewing mouth parts, and aquatic larvae; alderflies and hellgrammites or dobson flies. [<MEGALO- + Gk. *pteron* wing] —**meg′a·lop′ter·ous** *adj.*

meg·a·lo·saur (meg′ə·lə·sôr) *n. Paleontol.* A gigantic, terrestrial, carnivorous dinosaur (genus *Megalosaurus*) of the suborder *Therapoda.* [< MEGALO- + Gk. *sauros* lizard] —**meg′a·lo·saur′i·an** *adj. & n.*

Meg·an·thro·pus (meg·an′thrə·pəs) *n. Zool.* An extinct giant hominoid primate of the Pleistocene, represented by massive fossile jawbones found in 1939 and 1941 in central Java. [<NL <Gk. *megas* great + *anthrōpos* man]

meg·a·phone (meg′ə·fōn) *n.* A funnel-shaped device for amplifying or directing sound. —*v.t. & v.i.* **·phoned, ·phon·ing** To address or speak through a megaphone.

meg·a·pod (meg′ə·pod) *adj.* Having large feet, as certain Australian jungle birds.

Meg·a·ra (meg′ər·ə) An ancient city in east central Greece, capital of Megaris. —**Me·gar·i·an** (mə·gâr′ē·ən), **Me·gar·ic** (mə·gar′ik) *adj.*

Meg·a·ris (meg′ə·ris) A mountainous region of ancient Greece on the isthmus between the Peloponnesus and northern Greece.

meg·a·spo·ran·gi·um (meg′ə·spə·ran′jē·əm) *n. pl.* **·gi·a** (-jē·ə) *Bot.* A sporangium which bears only megaspores: also called *macrosporangium.*

meg·a·spore (meg′ə·spôr, -spōr) *n. Bot.* A large, asexual spore developed by certain seed plants, and giving rise always to a female gamete; the embryo sac of a seed plant: also called *macrospore.*

meg·a·spo·ro·phyll (meg′ə·spôr′ə·fil, -spō′rə-) *n. Bot.* A leaf or sporophyll which produces only megasporangia.

me·gass (mə·gas′, -gäs′) *n.* Bagasse. Also **me·gasse′.**

meg·a·there (meg′ə·thir) *n. Paleontol.* A gigantic, extinct, slothlike edentate (genus *Megatherium*), associated with the Pleistocene in North America. [<MEGA- + Gk. *thērion* wild animal]

MEGATHERE
(Fossils indicate length up to 20 feet)

meg·a·therm (meg′ə·thûrm) *n.* A macrotherm.

meg·a·ton (meg′ə·tun′) *n.* A unit of nuclear explosive power equal to one million tons of TNT.

meg·a·tron (meg′ə·tron) *n.* A compact, sturdy type of vacuum tube designed to increase the range of wave frequencies and power in radio, television, and other electronic fields. [<MEGA- + (ELEC)TRON]

meg·a·vi·ta·min (meg′ə·vī′tə·min) *adj.* Pertaining to the treatment of disease by the administering of very large vitamin dosage: *megavitamin therapy.*

Megh·na (meg′nə) A river in East Pakistan, flowing 132 miles SW to the Bay of Bengal.

Me·gid·do (mə·gid′ō) An ancient city of NW Palestine at the western edge of the Plain of Jezreel.

me·gilp (mə·gilp′) See MAGILP.

me·grim (mē′grim) *n.* **1** A headache confined to one side of the head, characterized by nausea and vomiting; migraine. **2** *pl.* Dulness; depression of spirits. **3** A whim or fad. [< F *migraine*]

Me·hem·et A·li (mə·hem′et ä′lē, me·met′), 1769–1849, viceroy of Egypt 1805–48. Also known as *Mohammed Ali.*

Mei·ji (mā·jē) *n.* The reign, 1867–1912, of the Emperor Mutsuhito, 1852–1912, of Japan, regarded as a historic era. [<Japanese, lit., enlightened peace]

mei·kle (mē′kəl) See MICKLE.

Meik·le·john (mik′əl·jon), **Alexander,** 1872–1964, U.S. educator born in England.

Mei·ning·en (mī′ning·ən) A town in the former state of Thuringia, SW East Germany.

Mein Kampf (min kämpf′) A book by Adolf Hitler, outlining his political philosophy and personal history, and setting forth his plans for the German domination of Europe. [<G, my battle]

mei·ny (mā′nē) *n.* **1** *Obs.* An army or retinue; attendants; household; crew. **2** *Scot.* A multitude or throng. Also **mei′nie.** [<OF *mesnee, meyné,* ult. <L *mansio* a dwelling. See MANSION.]

mei·o·sis (mī·ō′sis) *n.* **1** *Biol.* That process in the division of germ cells by which the number of chromosomes is reduced from the double or *diploid* number typical of somatic cells to the halved or *haploid* number characteristic of gametes: distinguished from *mitosis*: also spelled *maiosis*. **2** In rhetoric, understatement, often giving the effect of irony or humor, by representing a fact, thing, deed, etc., as being smaller than it really is: also spelled *miosis*. [<Gk. *meiōsis* lessening] **— mei·ot′ic** (-ot′ik) *adj.*

Meis·sen (mī′sən) A city on the Elbe in SE East Germany in the former state of Saxony.

Meissen ware A kind of porcelain or chinaware made in Meissen, Germany.

Meis·so·nier (mā·sô·nyā′), **Jean Louis Ernest,** 1815–91, French painter.

Meis·ter·sing·er (mīs′tər·sing′ər, *Ger.* mīs′tər·zing′ər) *n. pl.* **·sing·er** *German* One of the burgher poets and musicians of Germany in the 14th, 15th, and 16th centuries, the successors of the minnesingers: often called *mastersinger*. **— Die Meistersinger von Nürnberg** Title of a comic opera by Richard Wagner.

Meit·ner (mīt′nər), **Lise,** 1878–1968, German physicist.

Mé·ji·co (mā′hē·kō) The Spanish name for MEXICO.

Mek·ka (mek′ə) See MECCA.

Mek·nès (mek·nes′) A city in NW Morocco: formerly *Mequinez*.

Me·kong (mā·kong′) A river in SE Asia, flowing 2,600 miles south to the China Sea: Chinese *Lantsang*.

mel (mel) *n.* Honey; especially the pure, clarified honey used in the preparation of certain drugs. [<L]

mel·a·mine (mel′ə·mēn, -min) *n. Chem.* A transparent, colorless, crystalline compound, $C_3N_2(NH_2)_3$, the amide of cyanuric acid: combined with cellulose pulp and formaldehyde, it produces a synthetic resin of good qualities. [< *mel(am)*, a chemical compound + AMINE]

melan– Var. of MELANO–.

mel·an·cho·li·a (mel′ən·kō′lē·ə) *n. Psychiatry* Mental disorder characterized by excessive brooding and depression of spirits: typical of manic-depressive psychoses. [<L. See MELANCHOLY.] **— mel′an·cho′li·ac** *adj. & n.*

mel·an·chol·y (mel′ən·kol′ē) *adj.* **1** Morbidly gloomy; sad; dejected. **2** Suggesting or promoting sadness. **3** Somberly thoughtful; pensive. **—** *n.* **1** Low spirits; despondency; depression. **2** Melancholia. **3** Pensive contemplation; serious and sober reflection. **4** *Archaic* The dark, acrid, and viscous substance once believed to be secreted by the kidneys and to be responsible for gloomy dejection of spirits; one of the humors. [<F *melancolie* <L *melancholia* <Gk. < *melas, -anos* black + *cholē* bile] **— mel′an·chol′ic** *adj.* **— mel′an·chol′i·cal·ly** *adv.*

Me·lanch·thon (mə·langk′thən), **Philipp,** Grecized name of Philipp Schwarzert, 1497–1560, religious reformer and scholar; associate of Luther. Also **Me·lanc′thon.**

mel·a·ne·mi·a (mel′ə·nē′mē·ə) *n. Pathol.* A morbid excess of black pigment in the blood: noted chiefly in pernicious anemia. Also **mel′·a·nae′mi·a.** [<MELAN- + Gk. *haima* blood] **— mel′a·ne′mic** *adj.*

Mel·a·ne·sia (mel′ə·nē′zhə, -shə) The islands of the western Pacific south of the Equator, comprising one of the three main divisions of the Pacific Islands; total, 60,000 square miles.

Mel·a·ne·sian (mel′ə·nē′zhən, -shən) *n.* **1** One of the native people of Melanesia, having dark skins and thick, kinky beards and hair: believed to be a mixture of Papuan, Polynesian, and Malay stocks. **2** A branch of the Oceanic subfamily of the Austronesian family of languages, including the languages spoken in the Solomon, Loyalty, and Admiralty islands, Fiji, the New Hebrides, New Caledonia, etc., and the Micronesian group of the Caroline, Gilbert, and Marshall islands. **—** *adj.* Of or pertaining to Melanesia, its native inhabitants, or their languages.

mé·lange (mā·länzh′) *n. French* A mixture or medley; also, a literary miscellany.

me·la·ni·an (mə·lā′nē·ən) *adj. Anthropol.* Having dark or black pigmentation: said of Negroes, Melanesians, etc. [<F *mélanien* <Gk. *melas, -anos* black]

me·lan·ic (mə·lan′ik) *adj.* **1** Relating to or resembling melanosis or melanism; melanoid. **2** Black; melanian.

mel·a·nin (mel′ə·nin) *n. Biochem.* The brownish-black pigment contained in animal tissues, as the skin and hair, formed by the action of the enzyme tyrosinase upon tyrosine.

mel·a·nism (mel′ə·niz′əm) *n.* **1** Abnormal development of dark coloring matter in the skin, feathers, etc.: opposed to *albinism*. **2** Excessive darkness, as of the eyes, hair, skin, etc., due to extreme pigmentation. **— mel′a·nis′tic** *adj.*

mel·a·nite (mel′ə·nīt) *n.* A black variety of garnet.

melano– *combining form* Black; dark-colored: *melanosis*. Also, before vowels, *melan–*. [< Gk. *melas, melanos* black]

Mel·a·noch·ro·i (mel′ə·nok′rō·ī) *n. pl.* Caucasians having fair skins and dark hair. [< MELAN- + Gk. *ōchros* pale] **— Mel′a·noch′·roid** *adj.*

mel·an·o·crat·ic (mel′ən·ō·krat′ik) *adj. Geol.* Of or pertaining to those igneous rocks characterized by a predominance of dark or ferromagnesian minerals: opposed to *leucocratic*.

mel·a·noid (mel′ə·noid) *adj.* **1** Looking black or having a dark appearance. **2** Of the nature of melanosis.

mel·a·no·ma (mel′ə·nō′mə) *n. Pathol.* A black-pigmented tumor. [<MELAN- + -OMA]

mel·a·no·sis (mel′ə·nō′sis) *n. Pathol.* An organic disease in which pigment is deposited in the skin and other tissues; black degeneration. **— mel′a·not′ic** (-not′ik) *adj.*

mel·a·nous (mel′ə·nəs) *adj.* Having dark or black skin and hair: opposed to *xanthous*.

mel·an·tha·ceous (mel′ən·thā′shəs) *adj.* Of or pertaining to a former family *(Melanthaceae)* of monocotyledonous plants in the lily order, distinguished from lilies by the absence of bulbs: it included plants of the genera *Colchicum* and *Veratrum*. [<NL <Gk. *melas, -anos* black + *anthos* flower]

mel·a·phyre (mel′ə·fīr) *n.* Any igneous porphyry with a dark groundmass. [<F <Gk. *melas* black + F *(por)phyre* porphyry]

Mel·ba (mel′bə), **Dame Nellie,** 1861–1931, Australian operatic soprano: real name *Helen Mitchell Armstrong*.

Melba toast Thinly sliced bread toasted until brown and crisp.

Mel·bourne (mel′bərn) A port and capital of Victoria, Australia.

Mel·bourne (mel′bərn), **Viscount,** 1779–1848, William Lamb, English statesman; prime minister 1834, 1835–41.

Mel·chi·or (mel′kē·ôr) One of the three Magi.

Mel·chis·e·dec (mel·kiz′ə·dek) **1** In Old Testament history, a priest; king of Salem. *Gen.* xiv 18. **2** Of or denoting the greater priesthood of the Mormon Church. Also **Mel·chiz′·e·dek.**

meld (meld) *v.t. & v.i.* In pinochle and other card games, to announce or declare (a combination of cards in the hand), for inclusion in one's total score. **—** *n.* A group of cards to be declared, or the act of declaring them. [<G *melden* announce]

mel·der (mel′dər) *n. Scot.* The quantity of grain ground at one time; a grist.

Mel·e·a·ger (mel′ē·ā′jər) In Greek mythology, the son of Oeneus and Althaea, who slew the Calydonian boar and in a quarrel over the spoils killed his mother's brothers: Althaea took revenge by burning the log she had removed from the hearth at his birth, when it had been prophesied that her son would die after it was consumed.

mê·lée (mā′lā, mā·lā′; *Fr.* me·lā′) *n.* A general hand-to-hand fight; an affray. [<F <OF *meslee*, var. of *medlee*. See MEDLEY.]

Me·le·gna·no (mā′lā·nyä′nō) A town in northern Italy SE of Milan; scene of French victory over Swiss, 1515: formerly *Marignano*.

me·li·a·ceous (mē′lē·ā′shəs) *adj.* Of or pertaining to a family *(Meliaceae)* of trees and shrubs of the order *Geraniales*, mainly native to the warm portions of Asia and America; the mahogany family, including the Spanish cedar (genus *Cedrela*). [<NL <Gk. *melia* an ash tree]

mel·ic (mel′ik) *adj.* Suitable for singing, or meant to be sung: said of poetry. In ancient Greek poetry it is the successor of the elegiac and iambic forms of verse and includes the Aeolian or single-voice lyric, and the Dorian or choral lyric. **—** *n.* Melic poetry. Compare ELEGIAC and IAMBIC. [<Gk. *melikos* < *melos* song]

Me·lil·la (mā·lē′lyä) A Spanish possession on the NW coast of Africa, constituting a port and enclave in eastern Morocco.

mel·i·lot (mel′ə·lot) *n.* Any one of several sweet-smelling, cloverlike herbs of the genus *Melilotus*, especially the **sweet clover** *(M. officinalis)* and the **Bokhara clover** *(M. alba)*. [<OF *melilot* <LL *melilotos* <Gk. *melilōtos* < *meli* honey + *lōtos* a lotus]

mel·i·nite (mel′ə·nīt) *n.* An explosive of great power and similar to lyddite, yielded by combining guncotton with picric acid. [<Gk. *mēlinos* yellow]

mel·io·rate (mēl′yə·rāt) *v.t. & v.i.* **·rat·ed, ·rat·ing** To improve, as in quality or condition; ameliorate. See synonyms under AMEND. [<LL *melioratus*, pp. of *meliorare* improve < *melior* better] **— mel′io·ra·ble** *adj.* **— mel′·io·ra′tive** *adj.* **— mel′io·ra′tor** *n.*

mel·io·ra·tion (mēl′yə·rā′shən) *n.* **1** A betterment. **2** *Ling.* An improvement or elevation in the meaning of a word, as in *nice* (formerly "foolish"): opposed to *pejoration*.

mel·io·rism (mēl′yə·riz′əm) *n.* **1** The improvement of society by bettering man's physical being and environment instead of by ethical or religious means. **2** A modified optimism, teaching that the world is neither the best nor the worst possible, but is susceptible of improvement through the increase of good as man evolves. Compare OPTIMISM and PESSIMISM. [<L *melior* better] **— mel′io·rist** *adj. & n.* **— mel′io·ris′tic** *adj.*

mel·ior·i·ty (mēl·yôr′ə·tē, -yor′-) *n.* The state of being better; superiority.

mel·is·mat·ic (mel′is·mat′ik) *adj. Music* Florid and ornate in phrasing. [<NL *melisma* song <Gk.]

Me·lis·sa (mə·lis′ə, *Ital.* mā·lēs′sä) A feminine personal name. Also *Fr.* **Mé·lisse** (mā·lēs′) or **Mé·lite** (mā·lēt′). [<Gk., bee]

Mel·i·ta (mel′ə·tə) The ancient name for MALTA.

Mel·i·to·pol (mel′ə·tô′pəl) A city in southern Ukrainian S.S.R.

mell (mel) *v.t. & v.i. Obs.* **1** To mix; mingle. **2** To meddle. [<OF *meller*, var. of *mesler*. See MEDDLE.]

mel·lif·er·ous (mə·lif′ər·əs) *adj.* Producing or bearing honey. Also **mel·lif′ic.** [<L *mellifer* honey-bearing < *mel* honey + *ferre* bear]

mel·lif·lu·ous (mə·lif′lo͞o·əs) *adj.* **1** Sweetly or smoothly flowing; dulcet; honeyed. **2** Flowing like or as with honey. Also **mel·lif′lu·ent.** [<L *mellifluus* < *mel* honey + *fluere* flow] **— mel·lif′lu·ence, mel·lif′lu·ous·ness** *n.* **— mel·lif′lu·ous·ly, mel·lif′lu·ent·ly** *adv.*

mel·liph·a·gous (mə·lif′ə·gəs) *adj.* Feeding on honey, as certain animals and birds: often **mel·liv′o·rous** (-liv′ər·əs). Also **me·liph′a·gous.** [<Gk. *meli* honey + *phagein* to eat]

mel·lite (mel′īt) *n.* **1** Any medicated preparation containing honey. **2** The mineral honeystone. [<L *mel* honey + -ITE[1]]

Mel·lon (mel′ən), **Andrew William,** 1855–1937, U. S. banker, secretary of the treasury 1921–1932.

mel·lo·phone (mel′ō·fōn) *n.* A circular althorn. [<MELLOW + -PHONE]

mel·low (mel′ō) *adj.* **1** Soft by reason of ripeness; well-matured; not bitter or acid: *mellow* fruit; *mellow* wine. **2** Of a rich or delicate quality: *mellow* tints; *mellow* tones. **3** Companionable; jolly. **4** Made jovial by liquor. **5** Soft and friable, as soil. See synonyms under RIPE. **—** *v.t. & v.i.* To make or become mellow; ripen; soften. [ME *melwe*, ? <OE *melu* meal. Akin to Flemish *meluw* soft, tender.] **— mel′low·ly** *adv.* **— mel′low·ness** *n.*

me·lo·de·on (mə·lō′dē·ən) *n.* A small reed organ or harmonium. [<Gk. *melōdia* melody]

me·lo·di·a (mə·lō′dē·ə) *n.* An organ stop having wood pipes and a tone nearly like the clarabella; a stopped diapason. [<LL]

me·lod·ic (mə·lod′ik) *adj.* Pertaining to or containing melody; melodious. **— me·lod′i·cal·ly** *adv.*

me·lod·ics (mə·lod′iks) *n. pl.* *(construed as singular)* The branch of musical science relating to the pitch of tones and the principles of melody.

me·lo·di·ous (mə·lō′dē·əs) *adj.* Agreeable to the ear; producing or characterized by melody; tuneful. **— me·lo′di·ous·ly** *adv.* **— me·lo′di·ous·ness** *n.*

mel·o·dize (mel′ə·dīz) *v.* **·dized, ·diz·ing** *v.t.* **1** To make melodious. **2** To compose melody for. **—** *v.i.* **3** To make melody or melodies. **— mel′o·diz′er, mel′o·dist** *n.*

mel·o·dra·ma (mel′ə·drä′mə, -dram′ə) *n.* **1** Originally, a drama with a romantic story or plot, sensational incidents, and usually including some music and song. **2** Any sensational and emotional drama, usually having a happy ending. **3** Behavior or language of a theatrical nature. [<F *mélodrame* <Gk. *melos* song + *drama* drama] **— mel′o·dram′a·tist** *n.*

mel·o·dra·mat·ic (mel′ə·drə·mat′ik) *adj.* Of, pertaining to, or like melodrama; sensational. **— mel′o·dra·mat′i·cal·ly** *adv.*

mel·o·dra·mat·ics (mel′ə·drə·mat′iks) *n. pl.* Melodramatic behavior.

mel·o·dy (mel′ə·dē) *n. pl.* **·dies** **1** Pleasing sounds or an agreeable succession of such sounds. **2** Musical sounds or quality, as in the words of a poem. **3** A poem written or suitable for being set to music. **4** *Music* **a** A succession of simple tones, usually in the same key, constituting, in combination, a rhythmic whole: distinguished as a formal element from *harmony* and *rhythm.* **b** The chief part or voice in a harmonic composition; the air. [<OF *melodie* <LL *melodia* <Gk. *melōidia* choral song <*melōidos* melodious <*melos* song + *aoidos* singer]

Synonyms: harmony, music, symphony, unison. *Harmony* is simultaneous; *melody* is successive; *harmony* is the correspondence of two or more notes sounded at once, *melody* the succession of a number of notes continuously following one another. A *melody* may be wholly in one part; *harmony* must be of two or more parts. Accordant notes of different pitch sounded simultaneously produce *harmony*; *unison* is the simultaneous sounding of two or more notes of the same pitch. Tones sounded at the interval of an octave are also said to be in *unison,* but this is not literally exact. *Music* may denote the simplest *melody* or the most complex and perfect *harmony.* A *symphony* (apart from its technical orchestral sense) is any pleasing consonance of musical sounds, vocal or instrumental. Compare METER², SONG, TUNE. *Antonyms*: discord, dissonance.

Me·lo·i·dae (mə·lō′ə·dē) *n. pl.* A family of coleopterous insects with plump cylindrical bodies; the blister beetles. [<NL <*meloē* oil beetle; ult. origin unknown] **— mel·oid** (mel′·oid) *adj.* & *n.*

Mel·o·lon·thi·nae (mel′ə·lon·thī′nē) *n. pl.* A subfamily of beetles (family *Scarabaeidae*) including the cockchafers and June beetles. [<NL <Gk. *mēlolonthē* cockchafer] **— mel′o·lon′thine** (-thīn, -thin) *adj.* & *n.*

mel·o·ma·ni·a (mel′ə·mā′nē·ə, -mān′yə) *n.* An excessive or morbid fondness for music. [<Gk. *melos* song + -MANIA] **— mel′o·ma′·ni·ac** *n.*

mel·on (mel′ən) *n.* A trailing plant of the gourd family, or its fruit. There are two genera, the muskmelon and the watermelon, each with numerous varieties. [<F <LL *melo, melonis* <L *melopepo* <Gk. *mēlopepōn* apple-shaped melon <*mēlon* apple + *pepōn* melon]

mel·on·ite (mel′ən·īt) *n.* A reddish-white, granular nickel telluride, Ni_2Te_3; tellurnickel. [from *Melones* mine, Calif., where found]

Me·los (mē′los) See MILO.

Mel·pom·e·ne (mel·pom′ə·nē) The Muse of tragedy. [<Gk. *Melpomenē,* lit., the songstress <*melpein* sing]

Mel·rose (mel′rōz) A burgh of SE Scotland; site of a ruined Cistercian abbey, founded 1136.

melt (melt) *v.t.* & *v.i.* **melt·ed, melt·ed** (*Archaic* **mol·ten**), **melt·ing** **1** To reduce or change from a solid to a liquid state by heat; fuse. **2** To dissolve, as in water. **3** To disappear or cause to disappear; dissipate: often with *away.* **4** To blend by imperceptible degrees; merge. **5** To make or become softened in feeling or attitude. **—** *n.* **1** Something melted. **2** A single operation of fusing. **3** The amount of a single fusing. [OE *meltian.* Akin to MALT.] **— melt′·a·ble** *adj.* **— melt′a·bil′i·ty** *n.* **— melt′er** *n.*

Synonyms (verb): dissolve, fuse, liquefy, thaw. *Antonyms*: congeal, freeze, harden, indurate, solidify.

melt·age (mel′tij) *n.* **1** The process of melting. **2** The amount resulting from melting.

melting point The temperature at which a specified solid substance becomes liquid.

melting pot **1** A vessel in which things are melted; crucible. **2** A country, city, or region in which immigrants of various racial and cultural backgrounds are assimilated.

mel·ton (mel′tən) *n.* A heavy woolen cloth with a short nap: used for overcoats. [after *Melton* Mowbray, England]

melt·wa·ter (melt′wô′tər, -wot′ər) *n.* The whitish water from melting glaciers.

Me·lun·geon (mə·lun′jən) *n.* One of a dark-skinned people of mixed white, Negro, and Indian stock, living in the mountains of Tennessee. [? <F *mélange* mixture]

mel·vie (mel′vē) *v.t. Scot.* To cover with meal.

Mel·ville (mel′vil), **Herman,** 1819–91, U.S. novelist and poet.

Melville Bay An inlet of Baffin Bay in NW Greenland.

Melville Island **1** The largest of the Parry Islands, in the Arctic Ocean, Northwest Territories, Canada; 16,503 square miles. **2** An Australian island comprising part of Northern Territory, Australia; 2,400 square miles.

Melville Lake A lake in SE Labrador; 120 miles long.

Melville Peninsula A peninsula in Northwest Territories, Canada, between the Gulf of Boothia and Foxe Basin; 24,156 square miles; 250 miles long.

Mel·vin (mel′vin) A masculine personal name. [OE, high protector]

mem (mem) *n.* The thirteenth Hebrew letter. See ALPHABET. [<Hebrew *mēm,* lit., water]

mem·ber (mem′bər) *n.* **1** A person belonging to an incorporated or organized body, society, etc.: a *Member* of Congress, a *member* of a club. **2** A limb or other functional organ of an animal body. **3** A part or element of a structural or composite whole, distinguishable from other parts or elements, as a part of a sentence, syllogism, period, or discourse, or any necessary part of a structural framework, as a tie rod, post, or strut in the truss of a bridge. **4** A subordinate classificatory part: A species is a *member* of a genus. **5** *Bot.* A part of a plant considered with reference to position and structure, but regardless of function. **6** *Math.* **a** Either side of an equation. **b** A set of figures or symbols forming part of a formula or number. **c** Any one of the items forming a series. See synonyms under PART, TERM. [<OF *membre* <L *membrum* limb]

mem·ber·ship (mem′bər·ship) *n.* **1** The state of being a member. **2** The members of an organization, collectively.

mem·brane (mem′brān) *n.* **1** A thin, pliable, sheetlike layer of animal or vegetable tissue serving as a cover, connection, or lining. **2** A piece of parchment. [<L *membrana,* lit., limb coating <*membrum* member] **— mem′bra·nous** (-brə·nəs), **mem′bra·na′ceous** (-nā′shəs) *adj.*

membrane bone *Anat.* A bone developed in membrane, as one of those of the vault of the skull.

Mem·el (mem′əl, *Ger.* mā′məl) **1** A territory of western Lithuanian S.S.R.; 1,026 square miles. **2** Its capital, a port on the Baltic Sea: Lithuanian *Klaipeda.* **3** The German name for the NEMAN.

me·men·to (mə·men′tō) *n. pl.* **·toes** or **·tos** **1** A hint or reminder to awaken memory; souvenir; memorial. **2** *Eccl.* Either of the two prayers in the canon of the mass in which the living and the departed are respectively mentioned. [<L, remember, imperative of *meminisse* remember]

memento mo·ri (môr′ī) *Latin* An emblem or reminder of death, as a skull, etc.: literally, remember that you must die.

Mem·ling (mem′ling), **Hans,** 1430–95, Flemish painter. Also **Mem·linc** (mem′lingk).

Mem·non (mem′non) **1** In Greek legend, a king of the Ethiopians killed by Achilles and made immortal by Zeus. **2** A statue of Amenhotep III at Thebes, Egypt, associated with Memnon by the Greeks and said to emit a musical note when touched by the sun at dawn. **— Mem·no·ni·an** (mem·nō′nē·ən) *adj.*

mem·o (mem′ō) *n. pl.* **mem·os** *Colloq.* A memorandum.

mem·oir (mem′wär) *n.* **1** An account of something deemed worthy of record; especially, one addressed to a public institution or scientific society. **2** *pl.* The reminiscences of a person, either general or relating to a particular period, published together. **3** A biographic memorial. See synonyms under HISTORY. [<F *mémoire* <L *memoria* memory. Doublet of MEMORY.] **— mem′oir·ist** *n.*

mem·o·ra·bil·i·a (mem′ə·rə·bil′ē·ə) *n. pl.* Things worthy of memory, or an account of them. [<L, neut. pl. of *memorabilis* memorable]

mem·o·ra·ble (mem′ər·ə·bəl) *adj.* Worthy to be remembered; noteworthy. [<L *memorabilis*] **— mem′o·ra·bil′i·ty, mem′o·ra·ble·ness** *n.* **— mem′o·ra·bly** *adv.*

mem·o·ran·dum (mem′ə·ran′dəm) *n. pl.* **·dums** or **·da** (-də) **1** Something to be remembered; hence, a brief note of a thing or things to be remembered. **2** *Law* A brief written outline of the terms of a transaction. **3** An informal letter. **4** A statement of goods sent from a consignor to a consignee. See synonyms under RECORD. [<L, a thing to be remembered]

me·mo·ri·al (mə·môr′ē·əl, -mō′rē-) *adj.* **1** Commemorating the memory of a deceased person or of any event. **2** Contained within one's memory: distinguished from *immemorial.* **—** *n.* **1** Something designed to keep in remembrance a person, event, etc. **2** A summary or presentation of facts usually made the ground of a petition or remonstrance. **3** *Law* A memorandum filed for record. See synonyms under HISTORY, RECORD, TRACE. [<OF <L *memorialis*]

Memorial Day Decoration Day.

me·mo·ri·al·ist (mə·môr′ē·əl·ist, -mō′rē-) *n.* **1** One who writes memoirs. **2** One who writes, signs, or presents a memorial.

me·mo·ri·al·ize (mə·môr′ē·əl·īz′, -mō′rē-) *v.t.* **·ized, ·iz·ing** **1** To commemorate. **2** To present a memorial to. Also *Brit.* **me·mo′ri·al·ise′.** **— me·mo′ri·al·i·za′tion** *n.*

mem·o·rize (mem′ə·rīz) *v.t.* **·rized, ·riz·ing** To commit to memory; learn by heart. See synonyms under LEARN. **— mem′o·ri·za′tion** *n.* **— mem′o·riz′er** *n.*

mem·o·ry (mem′ər·ē) *n. pl.* **·ries** **1** The mental process or faculty of representing in consciousness an act, experience, or impression, with recognition that it belongs to time past. **2** The experiences of the mind taken in the aggregate, and considered as influencing present and future behavior. **3** The accuracy and ease with which a person can retain and recall past experiences. **4** That which is remembered, as an act, event, person, or thing. **5** The period of time covered by the faculty of remembrance: beyond the *memory* of man. **6** The state of being remembered; posthumous reputation: The *memory* of Washington will endure. **7** That which reminds; a memorial; a memento. **8** The information storage unit of a computer. [<OF *memorie* <L *memoria* <*memor* mindful. Doublet of MEMOIR.]

Synonyms: recollection, remembrance, reminiscence, retrospect, retrospection. *Memory* is the faculty by which knowledge is retained or recalled; *memory* is a retention of knowledge within the grasp of the mind, while *remembrance* is the having what is known consciously before the mind. Either may be voluntary or involuntary. *Recollection* involves volition, the mind making a distinct effort to recall something, or fixing the attention actively upon it when recalled. *Reminiscence* is a half-dreamy *memory* of scenes or events long past; *retrospection* is a distinct turning of the mind back upon the past, bringing long periods under survey. *Antonyms*: forgetfulness, oblivion, obliviousness.

Mem·phi·an (mem′fē·ən) *adj.* Of or pertaining to ancient Memphis, Egypt, or to its inhabitants.

Mem·phis (mem′fis) **1** A port on the Mississippi River in SW Tennessee. **2** The ancient capital of Egypt on the Nile above the apex of its delta.

Mem·phre·ma·gog (mem′frə·mā′gog), **Lake** A lake in northern Vermont and southern Quebec; 30 miles long.

mem·sah·ib (mem′sä·ib) *n. Anglo-Indian* A

European lady or mistress: a name given by native servants. [< MA'AM + Arabic *sāhib* master]

men[1] (men) *v.t. & v.i. Scot.* To mend.

men[2] (men) Plural of MAN.

men·ace (men′is) *v.* **·aced, ·ac·ing** *v.t.* **1** To threaten with evil or harm. **2** To make threats of. —*v.i.* **3** To make threats; appear threatening. See synonyms under THREATEN. —*n.* A threat; something which threatens; an impending evil. [< OF *manace* < L *minacia* < *minax, -acis* threatening < *minari* threaten] —**men′ac·er** *n.* —**men′ac·ing·ly** *adv.*

me·nac·me (mə·nak′mē) *n. Physiol.* The reproductive period of a woman's life, during which menstruation occurs. [< Gk. *mēn* month + *akmē* peak]

me·nad (mē′nad), **me·nad·ic** (mə·nad′ik) See MAENAD, etc.

mé·nage (mā·näzh′, *Fr.* mā·nȧzh′) *n.* **1** The persons of a household, collectively; a domestic establishment. **2** Household management. Also **me·nage′.** [< F < L *mansio, -onis* house. Doublet of MANSION.]

me·nag·er·ie (mə·naj′ər·ē) *n.* **1** A collection of wild animals kept for exhibition. **2** The enclosure in which they are kept. [< F]

Men·ai Strait (men′ī) A channel between the island of Anglesey and the mainland in NW Wales.

Me·nam (me·näm′) See CHAO PHRAYA.

Me·nan·der (mə·nan′dər), 343?–291? B.C., Greek comic dramatist.

me·nar·che (mə·när′kē) *n. Physiol.* The commencement of menstrual function in women. [< Gk. *mēn* month + *archē* beginning]

Men·cius (men′shəs), 372?–289? B.C., Chinese philosopher: Latin form of Chinese *Meng-tse.*

Menck·en (meng′kən), **H(enry) L(ouis),** 1880–1956, U.S. author and editor.

mend (mend) *v.t.* **1** To make sound or serviceable again by repairing; patch. **2** To correct errors or faults in; reform; improve: *Mend* your ways. **3** To correct (some defect). —*v.i.* **4** To become better, as in health; improve. —*n.* **1** The act of repairing or patching. **2** A mended portion of a garment. —**on the mend** Recovering health; recuperating; convalescing. [Aphetic form of AMEND] —**mend′a·ble** *adj.* —**mend′er** *n.*

men·da·cious (men·dā′shəs) *adj.* **1** Addicted to lying; falsifying. **2** Characterized by deceit; false. [< L *mendax, -acis* lying] —**men·da′·ci·ous·ly** *adv.* —**men·da′cious·ness** *n.*

men·dac·i·ty (men·das′ə·tē) *n.* Lying; falsity. [< L *mendacitas, -tatis*]

Men·del (men′dəl), **Gregor Johann,** 1822–1884, Austrian monk and botanist; founder of the science of genetics.

Men·de·ley·ev (men′də·lā′əf), **Dmitri Ivanovich,** 1834–1907, Russian chemist; discovered the periodic law. Also **Men′de·lej′eff.**

men·de·le·vi·um (men′də·lē′vē·əm) *n. Chem.* The short-lived radioactive element (symbol Md) of atomic number 101 and mass number 256. [after Dmitri Ivanovich *Mendeleyev*]

Men·de·li·an (men·dē′lē·ən) *adj.* **1** Of or pertaining to Gregor Mendel. **2** Relating to or in accordance with Mendel's laws.

Men·del·ism (men′dəl·iz′əm) *n.* The theory of heredity as put forth by Mendel. Also **Men·de′li·an·ism.**

Mendel's laws *Genetics* Principles formulated by Gregor Mendel as a result of experiments in breeding garden peas. They state that certain contrasting characters of cross-bred parents, as color height, etc., are inherited by the hybrid offspring through determining factors which act as units, and that subsequent cross-bred generations manifest these characters in varying combinations from dominant to recessive, each combination being present in a definite proportion of the total number of offspring.

Men·dels·sohn (men′dəl·sən, *Ger.* men′dəl·zōn), **Moses,** 1729–86, German Jewish theologian and philosopher.

Men·dels·sohn-Bar·thol·dy (men′dəl·sən·bär·tōl′dē, *Ger.* men′dəl·zōn·bär·tôl′dē), **Felix,** 1809–47, German composer and musician; grandson of Moses Mendelssohn. Also **Men′dels·sohn.**

Men·de·res (men′də·res′) **1** A river in western Turkey in Asia, flowing SW to the Aegean: ancient *Meander.* **2** A river in NW Turkey in Asia, flowing NW across the plain of ancient Troy to the Dardanelles: ancient *Scamander.*

men·di·cant (men′də·kənt) *adj.* **1** Begging; depending on alms for a living. **2** Pertaining to or like a beggar. —*n.* **1** A beggar. **2** A begging friar. [< L *mendicans, -antis,* ppr. of *mendicare* beg < *mendicus* needy] —**men′di·can·cy, men·dic·i·ty** (men·dis′ə·tē) *n.*

men·di·go (men′di·gō) The splake.

mend·ing (men′ding) *n.* Articles to be mended.

Men·do·ci·no (men′də·sē′nō), **Cape** The westernmost point of California.

Men·do·za (men·dō′sä) A province of western Argentina; 58,239 square miles; capital, Mendoza.

Men·do·za (men·dō′thä), **Pedro de,** 1487?–1537, Spanish explorer who founded Buenos Aires and Asunción.

mends (mendz) *n. pl. Brit. Dial.* Amends. —**to the mends** *Brit. Dial.* Over and above.

Men·e·la·us (men′ə·lā′əs) In Greek legend, a son of Atreus, brother of Agamemnon, and a king of Sparta; after his wife Helen was abducted by Paris, Menelaus led the Greek princes against Troy, where he defeated Paris; reconciled with Helen, after eight years of wandering, he returned with her to Sparta.

Men·e·lik II (men′e·lik), 1844–1913, emperor of Abyssinia 1889–1910; defeated Italians at Aduwa, 1896.

me·ne, me·ne, tek·el, u·phar·sin (mē′nēmē′ nētek′əl yōō·fär′sin) *Aramaic* Numbered, numbered, weighed, (and) divided: in the Bible, the words that appeared on the wall at Belshazzar's feast, and which Daniel interpreted to mean that God had judged and doomed Belshazzar's kingdom. *Dan.* vi 24–28.

Me·nén·dez de A·vi·les (mā·nen′dāth thää·vē′lās), **Pedro,** 1519–74. Spanish captain, founder of St. Augustine, Florida.

Me·nes (mē′nēz) Traditionally the first Egyptian king; founder of the first dynasty of Egypt in the fifth millennium B.C. Also **Me·ni** (mē′nē).

Meng-tse (mung′dzu′) See MENCIUS.

Meng·tze (mung′dzu′) A city in SE Yunnan province, China.

men·ha·den (men·hād′n) *n.* A herringlike fish *(Brevoortia tyrannus)* found along the North Atlantic coast of the United States: it is the source of **menhaden oil,** used in industry, and of fertilizer. [Alter. of Algonquian *munnawhat* fertilizer]

men·hir (men′hir) *n.* A prehistoric sepulchral or battle monument consisting of a single tall stone, usually left rough. [< F < Celtic (Breton) *men* stone + *hir* long]

me·ni·al (mē′nē·əl, mēn′yəl) *adj.* **1** Pertaining or appropriate to servants. **2** Servile. See synonyms under BASE[2] —*n.* **1** One doing servile work: generally in contempt. **2** Figuratively, a person of low or servile nature. [< AF < OF *meisniee, maisnie* household < LL *mansionata* < L *mansio* house] —**me′·ni·al·ly** *adv.*

Mé·nière's disease (mā·nyârz′) *Pathol.* Progressive deafness of one ear, with vertigo, tinnitus, nausea, and vomiting. [after Prosper *Ménière,* 1799–1862, French physician]

me·nin·ges (mə·nin′jez) *n. pl.* of **me·ninx** (mē′ ningks) *Anat.* The membranes (the dura mater, pia mater, and arachnoid) enveloping the brain and spinal cord. [< NL < Gk. *mēninx, mēningos* membrane] —**me·nin′·ge·al** *adj.*

men·in·gi·tis (men′ən·jī′tis) *n. Pathol.* Inflammation of the enveloping membranes of an organ, especially those of the brain and spinal cord. Certain forms are caused by infection with diplococcus bacterium *(Neisseria intracellularis).* —**men′in·git′ic** (-jit′ik) *adj.*

me·nis·cus (mə·nis′kəs) *n. pl.* **·nis·cus·es** or **·nis·ci** (-nis′ī) **1** Any crescent-shaped body. **2** *Optics* A lens convex on one side and concave on the other. **3** *Anat.* A disklike body of fibro-cartilage found in some joints of the body exposed to concussion. **4** *Physics* The surface or upper part of a liquid column made convex or concave by capillarity. [< L < Gk. *mēniskos* crescent, dim. of *mēnē* the moon]

MENISCUS LENSES

men·i·sper·ma·ceous (men′ē·spər·mā′shəs) *adj.* Designating a family (*Menispermaceae*) of mostly tropical, woody or herbaceous climbing plants having alternate leaves and small dioecious flowers, and yielding substances of narcotic and toxic properties; the moonseed family. [< NL *menispermaceae* < Gk. *mēnē* moon + *sperma* seed]

Men·non·ite (men′ən·īt) *n.* A member of a Protestant denomination that grew out of the Anabaptist movement in the 16th century, and still flourishes in Europe and the United States: named after Menno Simons, 1496?–1561, a leader of the sect in the Netherlands. They are opposed to the taking of oaths, the holding of public office, and military service.

me·no (mā′nō) *adv. Music* Less. [< Ital. < L *minus*]

me·nol·o·gy (mə·nol′ə·jē) *n.* **1** A calendar of the months; especially, one having a record of events by month. **2** A register or collection of lives of the saints arranged according to months and days of the month, as in the Greek Church. [< Gk. *mēn* month + -LOGY]

me·nom·i·nee (mə·nom′ə·nē) *n. Canadian* Wild rice. [< Algonquian (Cree)]

men·o·pause (men′ə·pôz) *n. Physiol.* Final cessation of the menses; change of life: opposed to *menarche.* [< Gk. *mēn* month + *pauein* cause to cease]

Me·nor·ca (mā·nôr′kä) The Spanish name for MINORCA.

men·or·rha·gi·a (men′ə·rā′jē·ə) *n. Pathol.* Excessive menstruation [< Gk. *mēn* month + -RRHAGIA]

Me·not·ti (mə·not′ē), **Gian Carlo,** born 1911, U.S. composer and librettist.

Men·sa (men′sə) A southern constellation. See CONSTELLATION.

men·sal[1] (men′səl) *adj.* Belonging to or used at the table. [< L *mensalis* < *mensa* table]

men·sal[2] (men′səl) *adj.* Monthly. [< L *mensis* month]

mensch (mensh) *n. pl.* **men·schen** *Colloq.* A genuine, respected, honored person. [< Yiddish < Ger., person]

mense (mens) *n. Scot. & Brit. Dial.* Dignified conduct or manner; decorum. [OE *mensk* < ON *mennska* humanity] —**mense′ful** *adj.*

men·ses (men′sēz) *n. pl. Physiol.* A periodical bloody flow from the uterus of a female mammal, resulting when an ovum is not fertilized, and occuring in women about once every lunar month; the menstrual flow. [< L, pl. of *mensis* month]

Men·she·vik (men′shə·vik) *n. pl.* **·vi·ki** (-vē′kē) or **·viks** A member of the conservative element in the Russian Social Democratic Party. Compare BOLSHEVIK, MAXIMALIST. Also **Men′she·vist.** [< **Russian** *menshe* smaller, minority] —**Men′ she·vism** *n.*

mens le·gis (menz lē′jis) *Latin* The spirit of the law.

mens sa·na in cor·po·re sa·no (menz sā′nəin kôr′pə·rēsā′nō) *Latin* A sound mind in a sound body.

men·stru·al (men′strōō·əl) *adj.* **1** *Physiol.* Pertaining to the menses or to a menstruum. **2** Continuing a month; occurring monthly. Also **men′stru·ous.**

men·stru·ate (men′strōō·āt) *v.i.* **·at·ed, ·at·ing** To discharge the menses. [< L *menstruatus,* pp. of *menstruare menstruus* monthy < *mensis* month] —**men′stru·a′tion** *n.*

men·stru·um (men′strōō·əm) *n. pl.* **·stru·ums** or **·stru·a** (-strōō·ə) The medium in which a substance is dissolved; a solvent.

men·su·ra·ble (men′shər·ə·bəl) *adj.* **1** That can be measured. **2** Mensural. [< LL *mensurabilis* < *mensurare* measure < *mensura.* See MEASURE.] —**men′su·ra·bil′i·ty** *n.*

men·su·ral (men′shər·əl) *adj.* **1** Pertaining to measure. **2** *Music* Characterized by a fixed rhythm and measure.

men·su·rate (men′shə·rāt) *v.t.* **·rat·ed, ·rat·ing** *Rare* To measure the dimensions or quantity of. [< L *mensuratus,* pp. of *mensurare* < *mensura.* See MEASURE.]

men·su·ra·tion (men′shə·rā′shən) *n.* **1** The act, art, or process of measuring. **2** The branch of mathematical science that has to do with measurement, as of lines, surfaces, or volume. **3** The result of measuring; measure.

[<LL *mensuratio, -onis*] — **men′su·ra′tive** *adj.*

-ment *suffix of nouns* **1** The concrete result of; a thing produced by: *achievement.* **2** The instrument or means of: *atonement.* **3** The process or action of: *government.* **4** The quality, condition, or state of being: *astonishment.* [<F <L *-mentum*]

men·tal[1] (men′təl) *adj.* **1** Pertaining to the mind: contrasted with *corporeal.* **2** Effected by or due to the mind, especially without the aid of written symbols. [<F <LL *mentalis* <L *mens, mentis* mind] — **men′tal·ly** *adv.*

men·tal[2] (men′təl) *adj.* Of, pertaining to, or situated near the chin: the *mental* point. — *n.* A plate or scale of the chin, as in snakes. [<L *mentum* chin]

mental age See under AGE.

mental blindness A mental condition in which images conveyed by the optic nerves are not properly recognized: also called *mind-blindness, psychic blindness.*

mental deafness A form of deafness in which sounds and words are heard but cannot be interpreted: also called *mind-deafness, psychic deafness.*

mental deficiency *Psychiatry* Lack of one or more mental capacities and functions present in the normal individual, usually to the point of disqualifying from full participation in ordinary life; feeble-mindedness. The principal types, in order of increasing deficiency, are moronism, imbecility, and idiotism.

mental healing The curing of any disorder, ailment, or disease by concentrating the mind either directly on the healing forces in nature, or on the denial of the discomforts experienced.

mental hygiene The scientific study and rational application of all methods that will restore, preserve, promote, and improve mental health, especially in relation to the normal functioning of the personality as a whole.

men·tal·i·ty (men·tal′ə·tē) *n. pl.* **·ties** **1** The sum of the mental faculties or powers; mental activity. **2** Cast or habit of mind.

Mental Science New Thought.

Men·ta·wai Islands (men·tä′wī) An Indonesian island group off the west coast of Sumatra; 2,354 square miles. Also **Men·ta′·wei** (-wā).

men·tha·ceous (men·thā′shəs) *adj.* Designating or pertaining to a genus *(Mentha)* of odorous perennial herbs of the mint family, with opposite leaves and small flowers, including the peppermint, spearmint, etc. [<L *mentha* mint + -ACEOUS]

men·thane (men′thān) *n. Chem.* Any one of three isomeric, saturated hydrocarbons, $C_{10}H_{20}$, corresponding to cymenes: parent substance for several of the terpenes. [<MENTHOL + -ANE[2]]

men·thene (men′thēn) *n. Chem.* A colorless, liquid, oily hydrocarbon, $C_{10}H_{18}$, derived from the oil of peppermint. [<L *mentha* mint + -ENE]

men·thol (men′thôl, -thōl, -thol) *n. Chem.* A white, waxy, crystalline alcohol, $C_{10}H_{19}OH$, obtained from and having the odor of oil of peppermint: used as a flavoring agent, in perfumery, and in medicine as an anodyne for neuralgia and similar ailments. [<L *mentha* mint + -OL[1]]

men·tho·lat·ed (men′thə·lā′tid) *adj.* Treated with, containing, or impregnated with menthol.

men·ti·cide (men′tə·sīd) *n.* The undermining and destruction of a person's mental powers by deliberate intent and with the use of all available psychological means. [<L *mens, mentis* mind + -CIDE]

men·tion (men′shən) *v.t.* To speak of incidentally or briefly; refer to in passing; specify or name. See synonyms under ALLUDE, INFORM. — *n.* The act of mentioning; casual allusion; notice: used especially in the phrase *to make mention of.* [<OF <L *mentio, -onis* <*mens, mentis* mind] — **men′tion·a·ble** *adj.* — **men′tion·er** *n.*

Men·ton (mäṅ·tôṅ′) A resort town on the Italian border of the French Riviera. *Italian* **Men·to·ne** (män·tō′nā).

men·tor (men′tər, -tôr) *n.* A wise and trusted teacher, guide, and friend; an elderly monitor or adviser. [<MENTOR] — **men·to′ri·al** (-tôr′ē·əl, -tō′rē-) *adj.*

Men·tor (men′tər, -tōr) In the *Odyssey,* the sage guardian of Telemachus, appointed by Odysseus before he departed for the Trojan War. [<Gk., lit., adviser]

men·tum (men′təm) *n.* **1** The chin. **2** *Entomol.* The distal sclerite of the labium or lower lip of insects.

men·u (men′yōō, mān′-; *Fr.* mə·nü′) *n.* A bill of fare or the dishes included in it. [<F, small, detailed <L *minutus.* See MINUTE[2].]

Men·u·hin (men′yōō·in), **Yehudi,** born 1917, U. S. violinist.

me·ow (mē·ou′, myou) See MEW[2]. [Imit.]

me·per·i·dine hydrochloride (mə·per′ə·dēn, -din) A white, odorless, crystalline compound, $C_{15}H_{22}ClO_2$, used in medicine as an analgesic and sedative; Demerol.

Me·phis·to·phe·le·an (mə·fis′tə·fē′lē·ən) *adj.* Of, pertaining to, or like Mephistopheles; cynical; crafty; sardonic; fiendish. Also **Me·phis′to·phe′li·an.**

Meph·is·toph·e·les (mef′is·tof′ə·lēz) **1** In medieval legend, a devil to whom Faust sold his soul for wisdom and power. **2** A crafty, sardonic fiend; a diabolical person. Also **Me·phis·to** (mə·fis′tō).

me·phit·ic (mə·fit′ik) *adj.* Poisonous; pestilential; foul; noxious. Also **me·phit′i·cal.**

me·phi·tis (mə·fī′tis) *n.* **1** A noxious exhalation caused by the decomposition of organic remains. **2** A pestilential or deadly gas, as from a cave or mine. Also **me·phi′tism.** [<L]

Me·qui·nez (mā′kē·nāth′) The former name for MEKNÈS.

mer- Var. of MERO-.

Me·rak (mē′rak) The star Beta in the constellation Ursa Major; the smaller of the two stars composing the Pointers toward the polestar.

mer·can·tile (mûr′kən·til, -tīl) *adj.* **1** Pertaining to or characteristic of merchants. **2** Conducted or acting on business principles; commercial. [<F <Ital. <L *mercans, -antis,* pp. of *mercari* traffic. See MERCHANT.]

mercantile agency An institution which collects, records, and furnishes to regular clients full information about the financial standing, credit ratings, etc., of individuals and firms.

mercantile paper Negotiable instruments for the payment of money, given in course of business, as bills of exchange, promissory notes, etc.: also called *commercial paper.*

mercantile system A theory in political economy that wealth consists not in labor and its products, but in the quantity of silver and gold in a country, and hence that mining, the exportation of goods, and the importation of gold should be encouraged by the state.

mer·can·til·ism (mûr′kən·til·iz′əm) *n.* **1** The spirit or theory of mercantile life or trade in general. **2** The mercantile system. — **mer′can·til·ist** *n.* & *adj.* — **mer′can·til·is′tic** *adj.*

mer·cap·tan (mər·kap′tan) *n.* Thiol. [<G <Med. L *mer(curium) captan(s)* seizing mercury]

mer·cap·tide (mər·kap′tīd) *n.* The metal salt of a mercaptan or thiol, obtained by replacing the sulfur hydrogen constituent with a metal.

mer·cap·to (mər·kap′tō) *n.* Sulfhydryl. [See MERCAPTAN]

Mer·ca·tor (mər·kā′tər, *Flemish* mer·kä′tôr), **Gerhard,** 1512–94, Flemish geographer and cartographer.

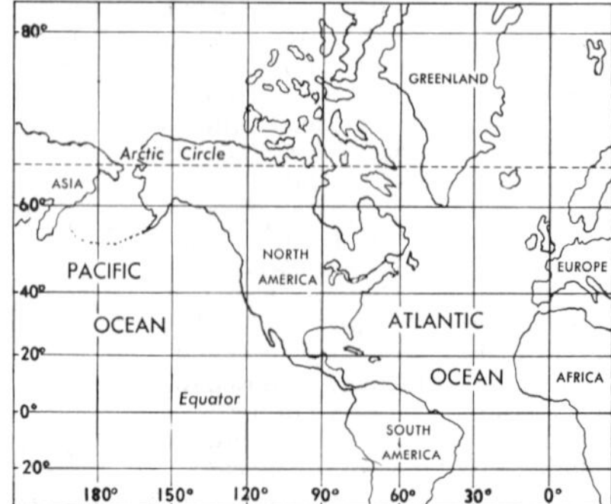

MERCATOR'S PROJECTION

Mercator's projection A system of making maps in which the meridians are represented by parallel straight lines, and the parallels of latitude by lines perpendicular to the meridians, and at increasing intervals, so as to preserve the actual ratio between the increments of longitude and latitude at every point. It is accurate at the equator, but areas become increasingly distorted toward the poles.

Mer·ced River (mər·sed′) A river in central California, flowing 150 miles SW to the San Joaquin.

mer·ce·nar·y (mûr′sə·ner′ē) *adj.* **1** Influenced by desire for gain or reward; greedy; venal. **2** Serving for pay or profit; hired: *mercenary* soldiers. **3** Pertaining to or resulting from sordidness. See synonyms under VENAL[1]. — *n. pl.* **·nar·ies** A person working or serving only or chiefly for pay; a hired soldier in foreign service. See synonyms under AUXILIARY. [<L *mercenarius* <*merces* reward, hire] — **mer′ce·nar′i·ly** *adv.* — **mer′ce·nar′i·ness** *n.*

mer·cer (mûr′sər) *n. Brit.* **1** Formerly, a dealer in small wares. **2** A dealer in cloth or silks. [<F *mercier* <L *merx, mercis* wares]

mer·cer·ize (mûr′sə·rīz) *v.t.* **·ized, ·iz·ing** To treat (cotton fabrics) with caustic soda or potash, so as to increase their color-absorbing qualities and impart a silky gloss. [after John *Mercer,* 1791–1866, English inventor] — **mer·cer·i·za·tion** (mûr′sər·ə·zā′shən, -ī·zā′shən) *n.*

mer·cer·y (mûr′sər·ē) *n. pl.* **·cer·ies** *Brit.* A mercer's wares or place of business. [<OF *mercerie*]

mer·chan·dise (mûr′chən·dīz, -dīs) *n.* **1** Anything movable customarily bought and sold for profit. **2** *Obs.* Mercantile dealings; commerce; trade: hence, gain or advantage. — *v.t.* & *v.i.* **·dised, ·dis·ing** To barter; trade; buy and sell. **2** To promote the sale of (an article) through advertising, etc. Also **mer′chan·dize.** [<F *marchandise.* See MERCHANT.] — **mer′chan·dis′er** *n.*

mer·chant (mûr′chənt) *n.* **1** A person who buys and sells commodities as a business or for profit; a trader. **2** A shopkeeper; storekeeper. — *adj.* Of or pertaining to merchants or merchandise; commercial. [<OF *marchant* <L *mercari* traffic, buy <*merx, mercis* wares]

mer·chant·a·ble (mûr′chən·tə·bəl) *adj.* That can be bought or sold.

merchant iron Wrought iron converted into marketable bars or rods of various sizes and shapes: often used for making hooks, chains, and rivets, and in reinforcing concrete.

mer·chant·man (mûr′chənt·mən) *n. pl.* **·men** (-mən) **1** A trading or merchant vessel. **2** *Archaic* A merchant.

merchant marine **1** All the vessels of a nation, collectively, both publicly and privately owned, engaged in commerce and trade. **2** The officers and men employed on these vessels.

mer·ci (mer·sē′) *interj. French* Thank you.

Mer·ci·a (mûr′shē·ə, -shə) An ancient Anglo-Saxon kingdom of central England, later annexed to Wessex.

Mer·ci·an (mûr′shē·ən, -shən) *adj.* Of or pertaining to Mercia, its people, or their dialect. — *n.* **1** An inhabitant of Mercia. **2** The dialect of Old English spoken in Mercia: the forerunner of the Midland dialects.

mer·ci beau·coup (mer·sē′ bō·kōō′) *French* Thank (you) very much.

Mer·cier (mer·syā′), **Désiré Joseph,** 1851–1926, Belgian cardinal.

mer·ci·ful (mûr′sə·fəl) *adj.* **1** Full of mercy; compassionate. **2** Characterized by or indicating mercy. — **mer′ci·ful·ly** *adv.* — **mer′ci·ful·ness** *n.*

Synonyms: benignant, clement, compassionate, forgiving, gentle, gracious, humane, pitiful, pitying, tender, tender-hearted. The *merciful* man is disposed to withhold or mitigate the suffering even of the guilty; the *compassionate* man sympathizes with and desires to relieve actual suffering, while one who is *humane* would forestall and prevent the suffering which he sees to be possible. See CHARITABLE, GOOD, HUMANE, PROPITIOUS.

mer·ci·less (mûr′sə·lis) *adj.* Having or showing no mercy. See synonyms under BARBAROUS, IMPLACABLE. — **mer′ci·less·ly** *adv.* — **mer′ci·less·ness** *n.*

mer·cu·ri·al (mər·kyŏŏr′ē·əl) *adj.* **1** Pertaining to the god Mercury; hence, lively; volatile. **2** Of or relating to quicksilver. — *n.* A preparation containing mercury. [<L *mercurialis*

<*Mercurius* Mercury] **—mer·cu′ri·al·ly** *adv.* **— mer·cu′ri·al·ness** *n.*

mer·cu·ri·al·ism (mər·kyŏŏr′ē·əl·iz′əm) *n.* *Pathol.* The condition produced by excessive use of medicines containing mercury; mercury poisoning.

mer·cu·ri·al·ize (mər·kyŏŏr′ē·əl·īz′) *v.t.* **·ized, ·iz·ing 1** To make mercurial. **2** To treat with mercury. **— mer·cu′ri·al·i·za′tion** *n.*

mer·cu·ric (mər·kyŏŏr′ik) *adj. Chem.* Of, pertaining to, or containing mercury in its highest valence.

mercuric chloride Corrosive sublimate. Also **mercury chloride.**

mercuric oxide *Chem.* A compound, HgO, obtained from mercuric nitrate by heat, forming both red and yellow powders which, with lard, are used in making ointments for certain skin diseases.

mercuric sulfide *Chem.* A compound, HgS, found native as cinnabar, or artificially produced as a black or a vermilion powder by the action of hydrogen sulfide on mercury salts.

Mer·cu·ro·chrome (mər·kyŏŏr′ə·krōm) *n.* Proprietary name of an iridescent, green, crystalline mercury compound, $C_{20}H_8Br_2Na_2$-Hg, turning red in an aqueous solution, which is used as a germicide and as a moderately active local antiseptic. [<MERCURY + -CHROME]

mer·cu·rous (mər·kyŏŏr′əs) *adj. Chem.* Of, pertaining to, or containing mercury in its lowest valence: *mercurous* chloride, *mercurous* oxide, etc.

mer·cu·ry (mûr′kyə·rē) *n. pl.* **·ries 1** A heavy, silver-white metallic element (symbol Hg), liquid at ordinary temperatures; quicksilver. See ELEMENT. **2** The quicksilver in a thermometer or barometer, as indicating temperature, etc. **3** A messenger. **4** An Old World plant (genus *Mercurialis*), especially *M. annua,* the **annual** or **French mercury,** used in medicine, and *M. perennis,* the **perennial** (or **dog's**) **mercury,** which is poisonous.

Mer·cu·ry (mûr′kyə·rē) **1** In Roman mythology, the herald and messenger of the gods, god of commerce, eloquence, and skill, and patron of messengers, travelers, merchants, and thieves: identified with the Greek *Hermes.* **2** *Astron.* The planet of the solar system nearest the sun, from which its mean distance is about 36,000,000 miles. It is the smallest of the major planets, having a diameter of about 3,000 miles, and revolving about the sun in 88 of our days.

mer·cu·ry-va·por lamp (mûr′kyə·rē·vā′pər) A glass tube or bulb containing mercury vapor made luminous by the passage of an electric discharge. Its light is a source of ultraviolet rays.

Mer·cu·ti·o (mər·kyōō′shē·ō) In Shakespeare's *Romeo and Juliet,* a witty and brave young nobleman; friend of Romeo.

mer·cy (mûr′sē) *n. pl.* **·cies 1** The act of treating an offender with less severity than he deserves; also, forbearance to injure others when one has power to do so. **2** The act of relieving suffering, or the disposition to relieve it; compassion. **3** A providential blessing. [<OF <L *merces, mercedis* hire, payment, reward; with ref. to the heavenly reward for compassion]

Synonyms: benevolence, benignity, blessing, clemency, compassion, favor, forbearance, forgiveness, gentleness, grace, kindness, lenience, leniency, lenity, mildness, pardon, pity, tenderness. *Mercy* is the exercise of less severity than one deserves, or in a more extended sense, the granting of *kindness* or *favor* beyond what one may rightly claim. *Clemency* is a colder word than *mercy* signifying *mildness* and moderation in the use of power where severity would have legal sanction; it often denotes a habitual *mildness* of disposition on the part of the powerful, and is a matter rather of good nature or policy than of principle. *Leniency* or *lenity* denotes an easy-going avoidance of severity; these words are more general and less magisterial than *clemency. Grace* is *favor, kindness,* or *blessing* shown to the undeserving; *forgiveness, mercy,* and *pardon* are exercised toward the ill-deserving. *Pardon* remits the outward penalty which the offender deserves; *forgiveness* dismisses resentment or displeasure from the heart of the one offended. *Mercy* is also used in the wider sense of refraining from harshness or cruelty toward those who are in one's power without fault of their own; as, They besought the robber to have *mercy.* See LENITY, PITY. *Antonyms*: cruelty, hardness, harshness, implacability, justice, penalty, punishment, revenge, rigor, severity, sternness, vengeance.

mercy killing Euthanasia.

mercy seat 1 In ancient Jewish ritual, the golden lid of the ark of the covenant whence God gave his oracles to the high priest, and upon which was sprinkled the blood of the yearly atonement. **2** Figuratively, the throne of God.

mere[1] (mir) *adj.* **1** Such as is mentioned and no more; nothing but. **2** *Obs.* Absolute; entire; unqualified. See synonyms under PURE. [<L *merus* unmixed, bare]

mere[2] (mir) *n.* **1** A pond; pool. **2** *Scot.* The sea. [OE *mere*]

mere[3] (mir) *n. Brit.* A boundary line. [OE *gemǣre*]

-mere *combining form Zool.* A part or division: *blastomere.* [<Gk. *meros* part]

Mer·e·dith (mer′ə·dith), **George,** 1828–1909, English novelist and poet. **— Owen** See LYTTON.

mere·ly (mir′lē) *adv.* **1** Without including anything else; only; solely. **2** *Obs.* Absolutely; wholly. See synonyms under BUT[1].

mer·e·tri·cious (mer′ə·trish′əs) *adj.* **1** Deceitfully or artificially attractive; vulgar; tawdry. **2** Pertaining to a harlot; wanton. [<L *meretricius* <*meretrix, -icis* prostitute <*merere* earn, gain] **— mer′e·tri′cious·ly** *adv.* **— mer′e·tri′cious·ness** *n.*

Me·rezh·kov·ski (mi′rish·kôf′skē), **Dmitri,** 1865–1941, Russian novelist and critic. Also **Me′rej·kow′ski.**

mer·gan·ser (mər·gan′sər) *n.* A fish-eating duck (subfamily *Merginae*), with toothlike processes along the upper edge of the bill, and the head usually crested, as the hooded merganser *(Lophodytes cucullatus)* of North America. [<NL <L *mergus* diver <*mergere* plunge + *anser* goose]

merge (mûrj) *v.t.* & *v.i.* **merged, merg·ing** To combine or be combined so as to lose separate identity; blend. See synonyms under UNITE. [<L *mergere* dip, immerse] **— mer′gence** *n.*

Mer·gen·tha·ler (mûr′gən·thä′lər, *Ger.* mer′·gən·tä′lər), **Ottmar,** 1854–99, U.S. inventor of the Linotype, born in Germany.

merg·er (mûr′jər) *n.* **1** *Law* The extinguishment of a lesser estate, right, or liability in a greater one. **2** One who or that which merges. **3** A combination of a number of commercial interests or companies in one.

Mer·gui Archipelago (mər·gwē′) An island group in the Andaman Sea off the Tenasserim coast of Lower Burma, to which they belong.

Mé·ri·da (mā′rē·thä) A city in SE Mexico, capital of Yucatán state.

me·rid·i·an (mə·rid′ē·ən) *n.* **1** *Obs.* Noontime; midday. **2** The highest or culminating point of anything; the zenith: the *meridian* of life. **3** *Astron.* A great circle passing through the poles and zenith of the celestial sphere at any point; the celestial meridian. **4** *Geog.* **a** A great circle drawn from any point on the earth's surface and passing through both poles. **b** The half-circle so drawn between the poles, called a meridian of longitude, or geographic meridian. **5** A line on a surface of revolution in the same plane as its axis. **—** *adj.* **1** Of or pertaining to noonday: *meridian* heat. **2** Pertaining to or at the highest or culminating point; brightest: *meridian* fame. **3** Of or pertaining to a meridian. [<OF *meridien* <L *meridianus* <*meridies* noon, south <*medidies* <*medius* middle + *dies* day]

me·rid·i·o·nal (mə·rid′ē·ə·nəl) *adj.* **1** Of or pertaining to the meridian. **2** Relating to southern climates or people: *meridional* customs. **3** Approximating a direction north and south. **4** Situated or lying in the south; southerly. **—** *n.* An inhabitant of a southern country; specifically, a resident of southern France. [<OF <LL *meridionalis* southern] **— me·rid′·i·o·nal′i·ty** *n.* **— me·rid′i·o·nal·ly** *adv.*

Mé·ri·mée (mā·rē·mā′), **Prosper,** 1803–70, French novelist and historian.

me·ringue (mə·rang′) *n.* The beaten white of eggs sweetened, baked, and used to garnish pastry; also, pastry so garnished. [<F <G *meringe,* lit., cake of Mehringen (in Germany)]

me·ri·no (mə·rē′nō) *n. pl.* **·nos 1** A superior breed of sheep, originating in Spain, and having very fine, closely set, silky wool. See SHEEP. Also **Merino sheep. 2** The wool of this sheep. **3** A fabric made of merino wool. **4** A kind of knitted goods used for underwear. **—** *adj.* **1** Pertaining to merino sheep or their wool. **2** Made of merino wool. [<Sp.]

Mer·i·on·eth·shire (mer′ē·on′ith·shir) A county of NW Wales; 660 square miles; county town, Dolgelley. Also **Mer′i·on′eth.**

mer·i·stem (mer′ə·stem) *n. Bot.* Plant tissue in process of formation; vegetable cells in a state of active division and growth, as those at the apex of growing stems and roots. [<Gk. *meristos* divided <*merizein* divide <*meros* part] **— mer′i·ste·mat′ic** (-stə·mat′ik) *adj.*

me·ris·tic (mə·ris′tik) *adj.* Divided into parts; segmented. [<Gk. *meristos*]

mer·it (mer′it) *n.* **1** *Often pl.* The quality or fact of deserving, especially of deserving well; desert: Does his *merit* justify the reward? **2** Worth or excellence; quality: A man of *merit.* **3** That which deserves esteem, praise, or reward; a commendable act or quality: the *merit* of silence. **4** *pl.* The actual rights or wrongs of a matter considered exclusively of extraneous details or technicalities: to decide a case on its *merits.* **5** Reward, recompense, or, sometimes, punishment received or deserved; a token or award of excellence. See synonyms under WORTH. **—** *v.t.* To earn as a reward or punishment; deserve. [<OF *merite* <L *meritum* <*meritus,* pp. of *merere* deserve] **— mer′it·ed** *adj.* **— mer′it·ed·ly** *adv.*

mer·i·toc·ra·cy (mer′ə·tok′rə·sē) *n. pl.* **·ra·cies 1** A system or society in which talent, intellectual achievements, and excellence of performance are considered worthier of reward than race, sex, social status, or wealth. **2** The leaders produced by such a system or society. **— mer·i·to·crat** (mer′ə·tə·krat′) *n.* **— mer·i·to·crat·ic** (mer′ə·tə·krat′ik) *adj.*

mer·i·to·ri·ous (mer′ə·tôr′ē·əs, -tō′rē-) *adj.* Deserving of reward; praiseworthy. **— mer′i·to′ri·ous·ly** *adv.* **— mer′i·to′ri·ous·ness** *n.*

merit system A system adopted in the U.S. Civil Service whereby appointments and promotions are made on the basis of the merit and fitness of the appointee, ascertained through qualifying examinations.

merle (mûrl) *n.* The European blackbird *(Turdus merula).* Also **merl.** [<F <L *merula* blackbird]

mer·lin (mûr′lin) *n.* A small European falcon *(Falco columbarius aesalon)*; also, a related American species, the pigeon hawk *(F. columbarius).* [<OF *esmerillon,* dim. of *esmeril*]

Mer·lin (mûr′lin) In the Arthurian cycle and other medieval legends, a magician and prophet who built the Round Table for King Arthur. [<Med. L *Merlinus* <Welsh *Myrrdin,* lit., sea fortress]

mer·lon (mûr′lən) *n. Mil.* The solid part of a battlement, between the embrasures. See illustration under BATTLEMENT. [<F <Ital. *merlone,* aug. of *merlo* battlement]

mer·maid (mûr′mād′) *n.* A legendary marine creature having as its upper part the head and body of a lovely woman and as its lower part the scaled body and tail of a fish. Also **mer′·maid′en.** [<MERE[2] + MAID]

mer·man (mûr′man′) *n. pl.* **·men** (-men′) A legendary marine creature, having as its upper part the head and body of a man and as its lower part the scaled body and tail of a fish. [<MERE[2] + MAN]

mero- *combining form* Part; partial; incomplete: *meroplankton.* Also, before vowels, *mer-.* [<Gk. *meros* a part, division]

mer·o·blast (mer′ə·blast) *n.* A meroblastic ovum. [<MERO- + Gk. *blastos* sprout]

mer·o·blas·tic (mer′ə·blas′tik) *adj. Biol.* Undergoing partial or incomplete segmentation, with formation of food yolk, as in the eggs of birds: opposed to *holoblastic.* **— mer′o·blas′ti·cal·ly** *adv.*

Mer·o·ë (mer′ō·ē) The ancient capital of Ethiopia on the Nile in northern Sudan; an archeological site of extensive ruins and groups of pyramids partly excavated.

mer·o·gen·e·sis (mer′ə·jen′ə·sis) *n. Biol.* Segmentation; reproduction by the formation of parts. [<MERO- + GENESIS] —**mer′o·ge·net′ic** (-jə·net′ik) *adj.*

Me·rom (mē′rəm), **Waters of** See LAKE HULA.

Mer·o·pe (mer′ə·pē) In Greek mythology, one of the Pleiades, not seen by the naked eye with the other six among the stars, supposedly having hidden herself from shame for loving a mortal: called the *lost Pleiad.*

mer·o·plank·ton (mer′ə·plangk′tən) *n. Biol.* Plankton found only at certain times or in certain seasons of the year.

-merous *suffix Zool.* Having (a specified number or kind of) parts: *trimerous, pentamerous* (often written *3-merous, 5-merous,* etc.). [<Gk. *meros* a part, division]

Mer·o·vin·gi·an (mer′ə·vin′jē·ən, -jən) *adj.* Designating or pertaining to the first royal Frankish dynasty, founded by Clovis I in 486, and lasting until 751. —*n.* A member of the Merovingian dynasty. Also **Mer′o·win′gi·an.** [<L *Merovingi,* descendants of Merovaeus, a legendary Frankish king]

mer·o·zo·ite (mer′ə·zō′īt) *n. Zool.* One of the mature spores liberated in the sporulating stage of certain protozoa, as the parasite causing malaria *(Plasmodium).* [<MERO- + (SPORO)-ZO(A) + -ITE[1]]

Mer·ri·am (mer′ē·əm), **John Campbell,** 1869–1945, U. S. paleontologist.

Mer·ri·mack (mer′ə·mak) *n.* The U. S. first armored warship, a Confederate vessel; fought the *Monitor* at Hampton Roads, 1862: Confederate name *Virginia.*

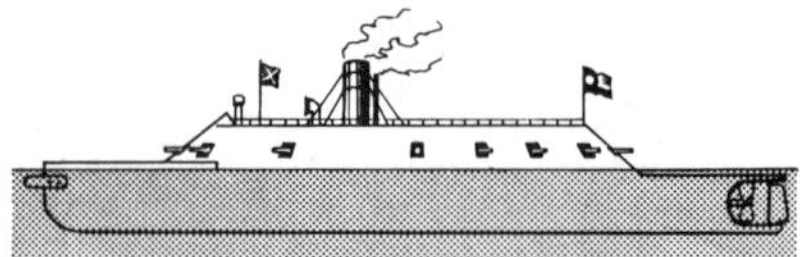

THE MERRIMACK: 4,636 TONS; DRAFT 23 FEET
Originally the U.S.S. *Merrimack,* later renamed C.S.S. *Virginia.*

Mer·ri·mac River (mer′ə·mak) A river in New Hampshire and Massachusetts, flowing 110 miles to the Atlantic. Also **Mer′ri·mack.**

mer·ri·ment (mer′i·mənt) *n.* The act of making merry; mirth; celebration. See synonyms under ENTERTAINMENT, HAPPINESS, LAUGHTER, SPORT.

mer·ry (mer′ē) *adj.* **·ri·er, ·ri·est 1** Inclined to mirth and laughter; full of fun; lively. **2** Of or pertaining to mirth or scenes of mirth; jovial and sportive; mirthful. **3** Inciting to mirth, cheerfulness, and gay spirits; fitted or calculated to enliven; exhilarating; bracing. **4** *Colloq.* Slightly tipsy; high. **5** *Obs.* Jibing; sarcastic. [OE *myrige* pleasant] —**mer′ri·ly** *adv.* —**mer′ri·ness** *n.*

Synonyms: blithe, blithesome, facetious, frolicsome, gay, glad, gladsome, gleeful, hilarious, jocose, jocund, jolly, jovial, joyous, lighthearted, lively, mirthful, sportive. See CHEERFUL, HAPPY, JOCOSE, VIVACIOUS, WANTON. *Antonyms*: see synonyms for SAD.

mer·ry-an·drew (mer′ē·an′drōō) *n.* A clown or buffoon.

Mer·ry del Val (mer′rē thel väl′), **Alfonso Marquis de,** 1864–1943, Spanish diplomat born in London. —**Rafael,** 1865–1930, cardinal; papal secretary of state 1903–1914: born in London.

mer·ry-go-round (mer′ē·gō·round′) *n.* **1** A revolving platform fitted with wooden horses, boatlike vehicles, etc., on which people ride for amusement, usually to music; a carousel. **2** A whirl, as of pleasure.

mer·ry·mak·ing (mer′ē·mā′king) *adj.* Frolicking. —*n.* Festivity; frolic. See synonyms under FROLIC, REVEL, SPORT. —**mer′ry·mak′er** *n.*

mer·ry·thought (mer′ē·thôt′) *n. Brit.* The wishbone of a fowl's breast.

Mer·sa Ma·trûh (mər·sa′ mə·trōō′) See MATRÛH.

Mer·sey (mûr′zē) A river between Cheshire and Lancashire, NW England, flowing 70 miles NW to the Irish Sea: its estuary is 16 miles long and forms Liverpool harbor.

Mer·sin (mər·sēn′) See IÇEL.

Mer·thyr Tyd·fil (mûr′thər tid′vil) A county borough in NE Glamorganshire, Wales.

Mer·zi·fon (mer′zē·fôn′) A town in north central Turkey in Asia: also *Marsivan.* Also **Mer′si·van′** (-vän′).

mes- Var. of MESO-.

me·sa (mā′sə, *Sp.* mā′sä) *n.* A high, broad, and flat tableland with sharp, usually rocky, slopes descending to the surrounding plain, common in the SW United States. [<Sp. <L *mensa* table]

Me·sa·bi Range (mə·sa′bē) A long, narrow range of iron-ore-producing hills in NE Minnesota.

mé·sal·li·ance (mā·zal′ē·əns, *Fr.* mā·zà·lyäṅs′) *n.* A marriage with one of inferior position; misalliance. [<F]

Mesa Verde National Park (mā′sə vûrd′) An area in SW Colorado containing ruins of prehistoric cliff-dwellings; 80 square miles; established as a national park in 1906.

mes·cal (mes·kal′) *n.* **1** A spineless cactus *(Lophophora williamsii),* native to the SW United States and northern Mexico. Its tops, which are often called **mescal buttons,** grow but little above the ground, contain a narcotic stimulating substance, and are chewed by the Indians, especially during the performance of religious ceremonies. **2** A mescal maguey. **3** An intoxicating liquor distilled from pulque. [<Sp. *mezcal* <Nahuatl *mexcalli*]

mes·ca·line (mes′kə·lēn, -lin) *n. Chem.* A white, crystalline alkaloid, $C_{11}H_{17}O_3N$, extracted from mescal buttons. It has narcotic and tetanic properties, and induces powerful color hallucinations: also spelled *mezcaline.* [<MESCAL]

mescal maguey Any plant from which the liquor mescal is obtained, especially the pulque agave *(Agave atrovirens).*

mes·dames (mā·däm′, *Fr.* mā·dȧm′) Plural of MADAME.

mes·de·moi·selles (mād·mwȧ·zel′) *French* Plural of MADEMOISELLE.

me·seems (mē·sēmz′) *v., impersonal Archaic* It seems to me.

mes·en·ceph·a·lon (mes′en·sef′ə·lon) *n. Anat.* The central division of the brain; the midbrain. [<NL <MES- + ENCEPHALON] —**mes·en·ce·phal·ic** (mes·en′sə·fal′ik) *adj.*

mes·en·chyme (mes′eng·kim) *n. Biol.* The portion of the mesoderm that produces the connective tissues of the body, the blood vessels, lymphatic system, and heart. It is cellular in structure, and in some of the lower forms of life is the same as *mesoblast.* Also **mes·en·chy·ma** (mes·eng′kə·mə). [<NL *mesenchyma* <MES- + Gk. *en-* in + *chein* pour] —**mes·en′chy·mal, mes′en·chym′a·tous** (-kim′ə·təs) *adj.*

mes·en·ter·i·tis (mes·en′tə·rī′tis) *n. Pathol.* Inflammation of the mesentery. [<MESENTER(ON) + -ITIS]

mes·en·ter·on (mes·en′tər·on) *n. pl.* **·ter·a** (-tər·ə) *Biol.* **1** The middle portion of the primitive intestinal cavity, lined with endoderm: distinguished from the buccal and anal parts, which are lined with ectoderm. **2** The midgut. [<MES- + ENTERON] —**mes·en′ter·on′ic** (-tə·ron′ik) *adj.*

mes·en·ter·y (mes′ən·ter′ē) *n. pl.* **·ter·ies** *Anat.* A fold of the peritoneum that invests an intestine and connects it with the abdominal wall; especially, the fold investing the small intestine. Also **mes′en·te′ri·um** (-tir′ē·əm). [<Med. L *mesenterium* <Gk. *mesenterion* <*mesos* middle + *enteron* intestine] —**mes′·en·ter′ic** *adj.*

Me·se·ta (mā·sā′tä) The entire interior of Spain, covering almost three fourths of the country and comprising an immense plateau with Madrid at its center.

mesh (mesh) *n.* **1** One of the open spaces between the cords of a net or the wires of a sieve: often expressed numerically in terms of a unit area: a 100-*mesh* screen. **2** *pl.* Such cords or wires collectively. **3** Anything that entangles or involves. **4** *Mech.* The engagement of gear teeth. —*v.t.* & *v.i.* **1** To make or become entangled, as in a net. **2** To make or become engaged, as gear teeth. [Cf. OE *max* a net and MDu. *maesche* a mesh] —**mesh′y** *adj.*

Me·shach (mē′shak) Babylonian captive. *Dan.* iii. See SHADRACH.

Me·shed (me·shed′) A walled city and Moslem shrine in NE Iran: also *Mashhad.* Also **Mesh·hed** (mesh·hed′).

mesh·work (mesh′wûrk′) *n.* A combination of meshes; network.

me·si·al (mē′zē·əl, mes′ē·əl) *adj.* Situated in or directed toward the middle: the *mesial* plane of the body. Also **me′si·an.** [<Gk. *mesos* middle] —**me′si·al·ly** *adv.*

mes·ic[1] (mes′ik, mē′zik) *adj. Bot.* Pertaining to or characterized by a medium moisture supply, as in certain plants. [<Gk. *mesos* middle]

mes·ic[2] (mes′ik, mē′sik) *adj. Physics* Of, pertaining to, characteristic of, or produced by mesons. [<MESON[2]]

me·sit·y·lene (mə·sit′ə·lēn, -lin) *n. Chem.* A colorless, liquid hydrocarbon, C_9H_{12}, made by heating acetone with concentrated sulfuric acid. [<*mesityl* a hypothetical organic radical (<Gk. *mesitēs* mediator + -YL) + -ENE]

mes·i·tyl oxide (mes′i·təl) *Chem.* A colorless hydrocarbon, $C_6H_{10}O$, used as a solvent for nitrocellulose and certain gums and resins. [See MESITYLENE]

mes·mer·ism (mes′mə·riz′əm, mez′-) *n.* **1** The theory, as exemplified by Franz Anton Mesmer, 1733–1815, that one person can produce in another an abnormal condition resembling sleep, during which the mind of the subject is passively responsive to the will of the operator: now identified with hypnotism. Compare ANIMAL MAGNETISM. **2** Personal magnetism. —**mes·mer·ic** (mes·mer′ik, mez-), **mes·mer′i·cal** *adj.* —**mes·mer′i·cal·ly** *adv.* —**mes′mer·ist** *n.*

mes·mer·ize (mes′mə·rīz, mez′-) *v.t.* **·ized, ·iz·ing** To hypnotize. Also *Brit.* **mes′mer·ise.** —**mes′mer·i·za′tion** *n.* —**mes′mer·iz′er** *n.*

mesn·al·ty (mē′nəl·tē) *n.* The estate of a mesne lord. Also **mesn·al·i·ty** (mē·nal′ə·tē). [<MF *mesnalte*]

mesne (mēn) *adj. Law* Being between two periods or extremes; intermediate; intervening. [<MF. alter. of AF *meen* <L *medianus* mean. Doublet of MEAN[3], MEDIAN, MIZZEN.]

mesne lord One holding lands as an intermediate between a superior lord and a subordinate tenant.

meso- *combining form* **1** Situated in the middle: *mesocarp.* **2** Intermediate in size or degree: *mesognathous.* Also, before vowels, *mes-.* [<Gk. *mesos* middle]

mes·o·blast (mes′ə·blast, mē′sə-) *n. Biol.* The middle germinal layer of the embryo. See MESENCHYME. [<MESO- + Gk. *blastos* sprout] —**mes′o·blas′tic** *adj.*

mes·o·carp (mes′ə·kärp, mē′sə-) *n. Bot.* The middle layer of a pericarp.

mes·o·ce·phal·ic (mes′ō·sə·fal′ik, mē′sō-) *adj. Anat.* **1** Intermediate in head form, having a cephalic index of from 76.0 to 80.9. **2** Having a medium cranial capacity. **3** Of or pertaining to the mesocephalon. Also **mes′o·ceph′a·lous** (-sef′ə·ləs). —**mes′o·ceph′a·ly** *n.*

mes·o·ceph·a·lon (mes′ə·sef′ə·lon, mē′sə-) *n.* The pons Varolii.

mes·o·crat·ic (mes′ə·krat′ik, mē′sə-) *adj. Geol.* Having the dark constituents slightly in excess of the light ones: said of certain igneous rocks.

mes·o·derm (mes′ə·dûrm, mē′sə-) *n.* **1** *Biol.* The middle germ layer of the embryo, from which are developed the muscular, vascular, and osseous systems. **2** *Bot.* The middle layer of the wall of a moss and capsule. —**mes′o·der′mal, mes′o·der′mic** *adj.*

mes·o·gas·tri·um (mes′ə·gas′trē·əm, mē′sə-) *n. Biol.* One of the two mesenteries in the stomach of an embryo; also, the region of the umbilicus. [<MESO- + Gk. *gastēr* belly] —**mes′o·gas′tric** *adj.*

me·sog·na·thous (mə·sog′nə·thəs) *adj.* Having moderately projecting jaws; also, having a facial profile angle of 98° to 103°. Also **mes·og·nath·ic** (mes′əg·nath′ik). [<MESO- + -GNATHOUS] —**me·sog′na·thism, me·sog′na·thy** *n.*

mes·o·kur·to·sis (mes′ō·kər·tō′sis, mē′sō-) *n. Stat.* The symmetrical kurtosis characterizing the region near the mode of a normal probability curve. —**mes′o·kur′tic** (-kûr′tik) *adj.*

Mes·o·lith·ic (mes′ə·lith′ik, mē′sə-) *adj. Anthropol.* Pertaining to or describing that period of human culture immediately following the Magdalenian stage of the Paleolithic, characterized by small, delicately worked microliths and an economy transitional between food gathering and a settled agriculture. Also called *Epipaleolithic, Miolithic.* [<MESO- + LITH(O)- + -IC]

me·sol·o·gy (mə·sol′ə·jē) *n.* The study of the environment in its relations to organisms;

ecology. [<MESO- + -LOGY] —**mes′o·log′ic, mes′o·log′i·cal** (mes′ə·loj′i·kəl) *adj.*

Mes·o·lon·ghi (mes′ō·lông′gē) See MISSOLONGHI.

mes·o·mor·phic (mes′ə·môr′fik, mē′sə-) *adj.* **1** *Physics* Of or pertaining to a state of matter intermediate between the true liquid and the crystal; liquo-crystalline: also **mes′o·mor′·phous. 2** Designating a physical type developed predominantly from the mesodermal layer of the embryo; the muscular or athletic type. Compare ECTOMORPHIC, ENDOMORPHIC.

mes·on[1] (mes′on, mē′son) *n.* **1** The plane that divides the body longitudinally into two halves; the median or mesial plane. **2** *Music* Loosely, a tetrachord. [<NL <Gk. *mesos* middle]

mes·on[2] (mes′on, mē′son) *n. Physics* Any of a group of short-lived, unstable atomic particles having a mass intermediate between that of the electron and the proton. They are believed to be a product of cosmic-ray disintegration and may be electrically neutral or carry either a positive or negative charge. The principal types are the mu-meson and pi-meson. [< Gk. *mesos* middle]

mes·o·neph·ros (mes′ə·nef′rəs, mē′sə-) *n. Biol.* The middle of three tubular organs found in connection with the primitive genitourinary apparatus, and formed later than the pronephros; the mid-kidney or Wolffian body. It is the permanent kidney in some animals, as amphibians. [<NL <MESO-+ Gk. *nephros* kidney] —**mes′o·neph′ric** *adj.*

mes·o·pause (mez′ō·pôz) *n.* A transition zone between the mesosphere and the ionosphere, beginning at a height of about 50 miles.

mes·o·phyll (mes′ə·fil, mē′sə-) *n. Bot.* The soft, inner, parenchymatous tissue of a leaf; the cellular portion lying between the upper and lower epidermis. Also **mes′o·phyl, mes′o·phyl′·lum.** [<MESO- + Gk. *phyllon* leaf]

mes·o·phyte (mes′ə·fīt, mē′sə-) *n. Bot.* A plant requiring medium conditions of moisture and dryness, intermediate between a hydrophyte and a xerophyte. —**mes′o·phyt′ic** (-fit′ik) *adj.*

mes·o·plast (mes′ə·plast, mē′sə-) *n. Biol.* A cell nucleus. [<MESO- + Gk. *plastos* formed] —**mes′o·plas′tic** *adj.*

Mes·o·po·ta·mi·a (mes′ə·pə·tā′mē·ə) An ancient country of Asia comprising the region about the lower Tigris and the lower Euphrates, included in modern Iraq. [<Gk. <*mesos* middle +*potamos* river] —**Mes′o·po·ta′mi·an** *n. & adj.*

mes·or·rhine (mes′ə·rīn, -rin, mē′sə-) *adj.* Having a relatively broad, high-bridged nose. [< MESO- +Gk. *rhis, rhinos* nose]

mes·o·sere (mes′ə·sir, mē′sə-) *n. Bot.* The flora and major plant development of the Mesozoic era. [<MESO- +L *serere* sow, plant]

mes·o·sphere (mes′ō·sfir) *n.* A layer of the atmosphere lying between the stratopause and mesopause.

mes·o·the·li·um (mes′ə·thē′lē·əm, mē′sə-) *n. Biol.* **1** The portion of the mesoderm and the tissues derived from it that in vertebrates forms two principal layers, visceral and parietal, and produces the epithelium of the peritoneum and pleurae, the striated muscles, etc. **2** Epithelium when mesoblastic in origin. [< NL <MESO-+ (EPI)THELIUM] —**mes′o·the′·li·al** *adj.*

mes·o·ther·mal (mes′ə·thûr′məl, mē′sə-) *adj.* Possessing or pertaining to medium warmth. Also **mes′o·ther′mic.**

mes·o·tho·rax (mes′ə·thôr′aks, -thō′raks, mē′ sə-) *n. Entomol.* The middle one of the three segments of the thorax in insects, bearing the anterior wings and the middle legs. —**mes′o·tho·rac′ic** (-thô·ras′ik, -thō·ras′ik) *adj.*

mes·o·tho·ri·um (mes′ə·thôr′ē·əm, -thō′rē-, mē′sə-) *n. Physics* Either of two isotopes resulting from the radioactive disintegration of thorium, intermediate between thorium and radiothorium.

mes·o·tron (mes′ə·tron, mē′sə-) *n. Physics* Meson. [<MESO- + (ELEC)TRON]

Mes·o·zo·ic (mes′ə·zō′ik, mē′sə-) *n. Geol.* The era between the Paleozoic and the Cenozoic, including the Triassic, Jurassic, and Cretaceous periods: characterized by the dominance of the reptiles, the rise of flowering plants, and the beginnings of archaic mammals. —*adj.* Of or pertaining to this era. [<MESO- + -ZOIC]

mes·quite (mes·kēt′, mes′kēt) *n.* Either of two spiny, deep-rooted shrubs or small trees of the pea family, found in the southwestern United States, and extending southward to Peru. The **honey mesquite** *(Prosopis glandulosa* or *juliflora)* yields sweet algarroba pods used for cattle fodder; the **screw-pod mesquite** *(Strombocarpa odorata),* or screwbean, has edible spiral pods. Also spelled *mezquite, muskit.* Also **mes·quit′.** [< Sp. *mezquite* <Nahuatl *mizquitl*]

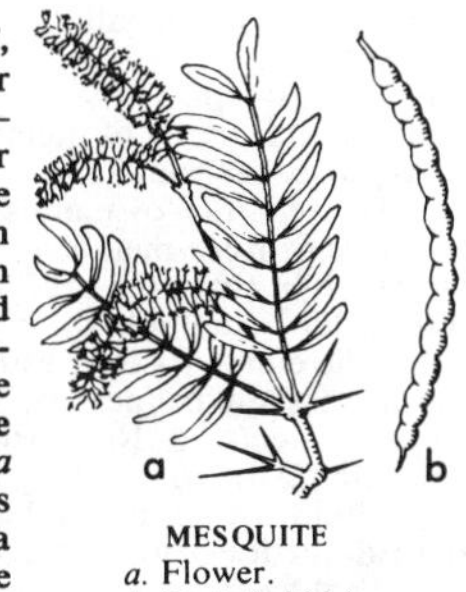

MESQUITE
a. Flower.
b. Fruit (edible).

mess (mes) *n.* **1** A quantity of food sufficient for one meal or for a particular occasion: a *mess* of beans; also, a portion of soft, partly liquid food, as pottage. **2** A number of persons who habitually take their meals together, as on board ship or in military units; also, a meal taken by them. **3** The sum or total of a haul of fish. **4** A state of disorder; especially, a condition of unclean confusion. **5** A confusing and embarrassing situation. **6** An unpleasant or unclean concoction; confused jumble. —*v.i.* **1** To busy oneself; dabble: often with *around* or *about.* **2** To make a mess; bungle: often with *up.* **3** To interfere; meddle: often with *around.* **4** To eat with a mess (def. 2). —*v.t.* **5** To make a mess of; muddle; botch: often with *up.* **6** To make dirty; be foul: often with *up.* **7** To provide meals for. [<OF *mes* <L *missus* course at a meal, orig. pp. of *mittere* send] —**mess′y** *adj.* —**mess′i·ly** *adv.* —**mess′i·ness** *n.*

mes·sage (mes′ij) *n.* **1** A communication, as of information, sent in any way. **2** A formal communication from a chief executive to a legislative body, not delivered in person: a *message* from the president to Congress. **3** An errand; the carrying out of a mission; a messenger's business. **4** An utterance divinely inspired; hence, any important communication embodying a truth, principle, or advice. **5** A television or radio commercial. [<OF < Med. L *missaticum* <*missus,* pp. of *mittere*]

message center *Mil.* An agency attached to a headquarters or command post, and charged with the receipt, transmission, and delivery of messages.

Mes·sa·li·na (mes′ə·lī′nə), **Valeria,** executed A.D. 48, third wife of Emperor Claudius; notorious for profligacy.

mes·sa·line (mes′ə·lēn′, mes′ə·lēn) *n.* A lightweight, lustrous, twilled silk fabric.

Mes·sa·pi·an (mə·sā′pē·ən) *n.* **1** A member of an ancient people inhabiting SE Italy. **2** The Indo-European language of the Messapians, possibly related to ancient Illyrian. —*adj.* Of or pertaining to the Messapians or their language.

Mes·se·ne (me·sē′nē) A town in SW Peloponnesus, Greece, capital of ancient Messenia. Also **Mes·si′ni.**

mes·sen·ger (mes′ən·jər) *n.* **1** One sent with a message or on an errand; one employed to carry messages; specifically, a bearer of official dispatches. **2** A forerunner; herald. [ME *messanger, messanger* <OF *messagier* <*message* MESSAGE: the *n* is non-historic]

Mes·se·ni·a (me·sē′nē·ə) A region of SW Peloponnesus, Greece, on the Ionian Sea, comprising an ancient country. Also **Mes·si′·ni·a.**

Mes·ser·schmitt (mes′ər·shmit), **Wilhelm,** 1898–1978, German aircraft designer.

mess hall A building or room where meals are regularly eaten, as by a military group.

Mes·si·ah (mə·sī′ə) *n.* **1** The Anointed One; the Christ: the name for the promised deliverer of the Hebrews, assumed by Jesus, and given to him by Christians: with *the.* **2** Loosely, a looked-for liberator of a country or people. Also **Mes·si′as.** [<LL *Messias* <Gk. <Aramaic *mĕshīhā,* Hebrew *māshīah* anointed] —**Mes·si′ah·ship** *n.* —**Mes·si·an·ic** (mes′ē·an′ik) *adj.*

Mes·si·dor (me·sē·dôr′) See under CALENDAR (Republican).

mes·sieurs (mes′ərz, *Fr.* mā·syœ′) *n. pl.* of *Fr.* **mon·sieur** (mə·syœ′) Sirs; gentlemen: in English in the contracted form *Messrs.,* used as plural of *Mr.*

mes·sin (mes′in) *n. Scot.* A lap dog; hence, an insignificant person. Also **mes′san.**

Mes·si·na (mə·sē′nə, *Ital.* mās·sē′nä) A port in NE Sicily on the **Strait of Messina,** the channel between Italy and Sicily, two miles wide at its narrowest point.

Mes·sines (me·sēn′) A village in western Belgium, scene of two battles in World War I, 1914 and 1917.

mess jacket A man's short, tailored jacket, usually white and terminating exactly at the waistline: worn on semiformal occasions.

mess kit A small, compactly arranged unit containing cooking and eating utensils: used by soldiers and campers.

mess·mate (mes′māt′) *n.* An associate at a mess, especially onboard ship.

mes·suage (mes′wij) *n. Law* A dwelling house with its belongings, outhouses, garden, etc. [< OF *mesuage,* prob. alter. of *mesnage.* See MÉNAGE.]

Mes·ta (mes′tä) A river in SW Bulgaria and NE Greece, flowing 150 miles SE to the Aegean. *Greek* **Nes·tos** (nes′tos).

mes·tee (mes·tē′) *n.* The offspring of a white person and a quadroon; an octoroon: also spelled *mustee.* [<Sp. *mestizo* mongrel, hybrid]

mes·ti·zo (mes·tē′zō) *n. pl.* **·zos** or **·zoes** Any one of mixed blood; in Mexico and the western United States, a person of Spanish and Indian blood. Also **mes·te′so, mes·ti′no** (-nō). [<Sp. <LL *mixticius* <L *mixtus,* pp. of *miscere* mix] —**mes·ti′za** (-zə) *n. fem.*

Meš·tro·vić (mesh′trô·vich), **Ivan,** 1883–1962, Yugoslav sculptor.

met (met) Past tense and past participle of MEET[1].

met– Var. of META–.

meta– *prefix* **1** Changed in place or form; reversed; altered: *metamorphosis.* **2** *Anat. & Zool.* Behind; after; on the farther side of; later: often equivalent to *post–* or *dorso–*: *metathorax, metaplasis.* **3** With; alongside: *metabiosis.* **4** Beyond; over; transcending: *metaphysics, metapsychology.* **5** *Chem.* **a** A modification, usually polymeric, of. **b** A derivative of: *metaprotein.* **c** A derivative of an acid anhydride, formed by withdrawal of one or more water molecules: distinguished from *ortho–*: *metaphosphoric* acid. **d** A benzene derivative in which the substituted atoms or radicals occupy the positions 1, 3: abbr. *m–*. Compare ORTHO–, PARA–. See BENZENE RING. Also, before vowels and *h, met–.* [<Gk. < *meta* after, beside, with]

met·a·bi·o·sis (met′ə·bī·ō′sis) *n. Biol.* The condition of dependence of one organism upon another. [<META- + Gk. *bios* life] —**met′a·bi·ot′ic** (-ot′ik) *adj.*

met·a·bol·ic (met′ə·bol′ik) *adj.* **1** Of, pertaining, to, or exhibiting metabolism: *metabolic* processes. **2** Pertaining to or undergoing change, transformation, or metamorphosis. Also **met′a·bol′i·cal.** [<Gk. *metabolikos*]

me·tab·o·lism (mə·tab′ə·liz′əm) *n. Biol.* The aggregate of all physical and chemical processes constantly taking place in living organisms, including those which use energy to build up assimilated materials (anabolism) and those which release energy by breaking them down (catabolism). Also **me·tab′o·ly** (-ə·lē). [<Gk. *metabolē* <*meta-* beyond + *ballein* throw]

me·tab·o·lite (mə·tab′ə·līt) *n.* A chemical product of metabolism.

me·tab·o·lize (mə·tab′ə·līz) *v.t. & v.i.* **·lized, ·liz·ing** To subject to or change by metabolism.

met·a·car·pal (met′ə·kär′pəl) *adj.* Of or pertaining to the metacarpus. —*n.* One of the bones of the metacarpus.

met·a·car·pus (met′ə·kär′pəs) *n. Anat.* The part of the fore- or thoracic limb between the carpus or wrist and the phalanges or bones of the finger. It consists in man of five bones. [< NL <Gk. *metakarpion* <*meta-* beyond + *karpos* wrist]

met·a·cen·ter (met′ə·sen′tər) *n. Physics* That point in a floating body slightly displaced from equilibrium through which the resultant upward pressure of the fluid always passes; the center of gravity of the unsubmerged portion of a floating body. Also **met′a·cen′tre.** — **met′a·cen′tric** *adj.*

met·a·chem·is·try (met′ə·kem′is·trē) *n.* The chemistry of elements and compounds which yield exceptionally large amounts of energy in relation to their mass. — **met′a·chem′i·cal** *adj.*

met·a·chro·ma·tism (met′ə·krō′mə·tiz′əm) *n.* An alteration in color; specifically, such alteration due to heating or cooling. — **met′a·chro·mat′ic** (-krō·mat′ik) *adj.*

Met·a·com·et (met′ə·kom′it) Indian name of American Indian chief, King Philip.

met·a·gal·ax·y (met′ə·gal′ək·sē) *n. pl.* **·ax·ies** *Astron.* The entire material universe, regarded especially as a system including all the galaxies.

met·age (mē′tij) *n.* **1** Measurement. **2** The price charged for measurement. **3** A general term for the tolls formerly exacted by the corporation of London over a part of the Thames above and below the city. [<METE[1]]

met·a·gen·e·sis (met′ə·jen′ə·sis) *n. Biol.* A type of reproduction in which a series of generations of unlike forms comes between the egg and the parent type; alternation of generations. — **met′a·ge·net′ic** (-jə·net′ik) *adj.*

me·tag·na·thous (mə·tag′nə·thəs) *adj. Ornithol.* Having the points of the mandibles crossing each other, as in the crossbill. [< META- + -GNATHOUS] — **me·tag′na·thism** *n.*

met·ag·nos·tic (met′ag·nos′tik) *adj.* Beyond the knowledge, whether of the sense or the understanding, of man as he is at present constituted; metaphysical. — *n.* A person holding a belief in the existence of a Supreme Being who transcends human knowledge. [<META- + Gk. *gnōstikos* knowing] — **met′ag·nos′ti·cism** *n.*

met·al (met′l) *n.* **1** An element that forms a base by combining with a hydroxyl group or groups. It is usually hard, heavy, lustrous, malleable, ductile, tenacious, and a good conductor of heat and electricity. **2** A composition of some metallic element; also, an alloy: generally with a qualifying word. **3** Cast iron while melted. **4** Broken stone for road surfaces or for railway ballast: also called **road metal. 5** *Her.* Gold *(or)* or silver *(argent)* tincture. **6** Molten glass. **7** The weight of the projectiles that a warship's guns can throw at once. **8** *Printing* Type metal; also, composed type. **9** The constituent material of anything; essential quality. — **noble metal** A metal that does not readily oxidize in the open air, as gold, silver, and platinum. — **white metal** Any one of the various white alloys, such as pewter, used for making ornaments, small castings, etc; specifically, a soft, smooth, malleable, copper-zinc alloy of exceptional antifrictional properties used to form the bearing surface in the crankshaft and connecting-rod bearings in most internal-combustion engines. — *adj.* Consisting of or pertaining to metal. — *v.t.* **·aled** or **·alled, ·al·ing** or **·al·ling** To furnish or cover with metal. ◆ Homophone: *mettle.* [<OF <L *metallum* mine <Gk. *metallon.* Doublet of MEDAL.]

met·a·lin·guis·tics (met′ə·ling·gwis′tiks) *n.* An area of linguistic study concerned with the interrelationship of the structure and meaning of the language of a society and other aspects of its culture, such as the social system.

met·al·ist (met′l·ist) *n.* **1** One who works with or has special knowledge of metals. **2** An advocate of metallic money as against a paper currency. Also **met′al·list.**

met·al·ize (met′l·īz) *v.t.* **·ized, ·iz·ing** To turn into or treat with metal. Also **met′al·lize,** *Brit.* **met′al·ise.**

me·tal·lic (mə·tal′ik) *adj.* **1** Being, containing, yielding, or having the characteristics of a metal: a *metallic* voice; *metallic* luster. **2** Pertaining to a metal. — **me·tal′li·cal·ly** *adv.*

metallic soap A soapy, waxlike material made by combining the salts of certain metals, as lead or aluminum, with various fatty acids: used in the textile, varnish, and paint industries.

met·al·lif·er·ous (met′ə·lif′ər·əs) *adj.* Yielding or containing metal.

met·al·line (met′ə·lin, -līn) *adj.* **1** Relating to, having the properties of, or resembling metal. **2** Impregnated with metals or metallic salts.

met·al·log·ra·phy (met′ə·log′rə·fē) *n.* **1** The science that treats of metallic substances; also, a treatise on metals. **2** Microscopic study of the structure of metals and alloys. [<Gk. *metallon* mine, metal + -GRAPHY] — **me·tal·lo·graph·ic** (mə·tal′ə·graf′ik) *adj.*

met·al·loid (met′ə·loid) *n.* One of those nonmetallic elements that resemble the metals in some of their properties, as arsenic and antimony. — *adj.* **1** Resembling a metal. **2** Of, pertaining to, or having the properties of a metalloid. Also **met′al·loi′dal.**

me·tal·lo·ther·a·py (mə·tal′ō·ther′ə·pē) *n.* Medical treatment by the use of metals, especially metal salts. [<Gk. *metallon* mine, metal + THERAPY]

met·al·lur·gy (met′ə·lûr′jē) *n.* The art or science of extracting a metal or metals from ores, as by smelting, reducing, refining, alloying, electrolysis, etc. [<NL *metallurgia* <Gk. *metallourgos* working in mines <*metallon* mine + *-ergos* working] — **met′al·lur′gic** or **·gi·cal** *adj.* — **met′al·lur′gi·cal·ly** *adv.* — **met′·al·lur′gist** *n.*

met·al·work (met′l·wûrk′) *n.* **1** Articles made of metal. **2** Metalworking.

met·al·work·ing (met′l·wûr′king) *n.* The making or the business of making things out of metal. — **met′al·work′er** *n.*

met·a·math·e·mat·ics (met′ə·math′ə·mat′iks) *n.* That branch of mathematics which is concerned with the formalized and rigorously logical treatment of pure symbols, having regard only to internal consistency and the establishment of absolute proofs of the validity of a given set of axioms, postulates, theorems, etc., within a mathematical system. — **met′a·math′e·mat′i·cal** *adj.*

met·a·mer (met′ə·mər) *n. Chem.* A compound or substance exhibiting metamerism. [<META- + Gk. *meros* part] — **met′a·mer′ic** (-mer′ik) *adj.*

met·a·mere (met′ə·mir) *n. Biol.* One of the series of homologous segments that form the body of a chordate or articulate animal, as a worm; a somite. Also **me·tam·er·on** (mə·tam′·ər·on). [<META- + -MERE] — **met′a·mer′ic, me·tam′er·al** *adj.* — **met′a·mer′i·cal·ly** *adv.*

me·tam·er·ism (mə·tam′ə·riz′əm) *n.* **1** *Chem.* A variety of isomerism in which the compounds have not only the same percentage of composition, but also the same molecular weight. **2** *Biol.* Disposition in metameres; the state of being a metamere; also, an example of this. Also **me·tam′er·y.**

met·a·mor·phic (met′ə·môr′fik) *adj.* **1** Producing metamorphism. **2** Pertaining to, caused by, or exhibiting metamorphism. Also **met′a·mor′phous.**

met·a·mor·phism (met′ə·môr′fiz·əm) *n.* **1** *Geol.* The changes in the composition and texture of rocks caused by earth forces accompanied by heat, pressure, moisture, etc. **2** Any metamorphosis. [See METAMORPHOSIS]

met·a·mor·phop·si·a (met′ə·môr·fop′sē·ə) *n. Pathol.* A defect in vision which makes objects appear distorted. [<NL <Gk. *metamorphōsis* transformation + *ōps* eye]

met·a·mor·phose (met′ə·môr′fōz) *v.t.* **·phosed, ·phos·ing 1** To change the form of; transmute. **2** To change by metamorphism. Also **met′a·mor′phize.** See synonyms under CHANGE. [<F *métamorphoser*]

met·a·mor·pho·sis (met′ə·môr′fə·sis) *n. pl.* **·pho·ses** (-fə·sēz) **1** A passing from one form or shape into another; transformation with or without change of nature: especially applied to change by means of witchcraft, sorcery, etc. **2** Complete transformation of character, purpose, circumstances, etc.; also, a person or thing metamorphosed. **3** *Biol.* A change in form, structure, or function in an organism resulting from development; transformation; specifically, the series of marked external changes through which an individual passes after leaving the egg and before attaining sexual maturity, as the larva, pupa, and imago of an insect. Compare METAGENESIS. **4** *Bot.* The varied development of plant organs of the same morphological value, such development resulting from their adaptations of different functions: also **met′a·mor′phy. 5** *Pathol.* A morbid change of the elements of tissues into another form of structure. **6** The changes in form going on in living tissues, blood corpuscles, etc. [<L <Gk. *metamorphōsis* < *metamorphoein* transform < *meta-* beyond + *morphē* form]

met·a·neph·ros (met′ə·nef′ros) *n. Biol.* The posterior one of three similar tubular organs in connection with the genitourinary apparatus. It develops into the permanent kidney. [<NL <META- + Gk. *nephros* kidney]

met·a·phase (met′ə·fāz) *n. Biol.* The middle stage of mitotic cell division, during which the chromosomes split along the equatorial plane between the two poles of the spindle. [<META- + -PHASE]

met·a·phor (met′ə·fôr, -fər) *n.* A figure of speech in which one object is likened to another by speaking of it as if it were that other: distinguished from *simile* by not employing any word of comparison, such as "like" or "as." See synonyms under ALLEGORY, SIMILE. — **mixed metaphor** Figurative language in which incongruous, and often contradictory, metaphors are used; confusion of figurative with plain statement. [<F *métaphore* <L *metaphora* <Gk. <*metapherein* <*meta-* beyond, over + *pherein* carry] — **met′a·phor′·ic** (-fôr′ik, -for′ik) or **·i·cal** *adj.* — **met′a·phor′·i·cal·ly** *adv.*

met·a·phos·phate (met′ə·fos′fāt) *n. Chem.* A salt of metaphosphoric acid.

met·a·phos·phor·ic acid (met′ə·fos·fôr′ik,-for′·ik) *Chem.* The glacial phosphoric acid of commerce, HPO_3, usually sold in the form of transparent sticks. It is obtained by heating orthophosphoric acid.

met·a·phrase (met′ə·frāz) *v.t.* **·phrased, ·phras·ing 1** To translate word for word. **2** To alter the wording of. — *n.* **1** A literal translation. **2** A phrase in response; retort. **3** A school exercise consisting in the rendering of a piece of poetry into prose or of prose into verse. [<Gk. *metaphrasis* <*metaphrazein* paraphrase <*meta-* beyond + *phrazein* phrase]

met·a·phrast (met′ə·frast) *n.* One who renders poetry into prose or prose into poetry, or changes the meter of verse. [<Gk. *metaphrastēs*] — **met′a·phras′tic** or **·ti·cal** *adj.*

met·a·phys·ic (met′ə·fiz′ik) *n.* Metaphysics. — *adj.* Metaphysical.

met·a·phys·i·cal (met′ə·fiz′i·kəl) *adj.* **1** Of or pertaining to metaphysics. **2** Treating of or versed in metaphysics. **3** Beyond or above the physical or experiential; pertaining to or being of the essential nature of reality; transcendental. **4** Dealing with abstractions; apart from, or opposed to, the practical. **5** Designating certain poets of the 17th century, notably Cowley and Donne, whose verses were characterized by complex, intellectualized imagery: term originating with Dr. Samuel Johnson. [See METAPHYSICS] — **met′a·phys′i·cal·ly** *adv.*

metaphysical healing Christian Science.

met·a·phy·si·cian (met′ə·fi·zish′ən) *n.* One skilled or versed in metaphysics. Also **met′a·phys′i·cist.**

met·a·phys·ics (met′ə·fiz′iks) *n. pl. (construed as singular)* **1** The systematic study or science of the first principles of being and of knowledge; the doctrine of the essential nature and fundamental relations of all that is real. **2** Speculative philosophy in the wide sense. **3** The principles of philosophy as applied to the methodology of any particular science. **4** Mental science in general; psychology. **5** In popular use, abstruse and bewildering discussion. Also *metaphysic.* [<Med. L *metaphysica* <Med. Gk. < *ta meta ta physika* the (works) after the physics; in ref. to Aristotle's ontological treatises, which came after his *Physics*]

met·a·pla·si·a (met′ə·plā′zhē·ə) *n. Biol.* The direct transformation of one kind of tissue into another, as cartilage into bone. [<NL <Gk. *meta-* beyond + *plassein* mold]

me·tap·la·sis (mə·tap′lə·sis) *n. Biol.* The period of completed growth in the life cycle of an organism; maturity. [<NL]

met·a·plasm (met′ə·plaz′əm) *n.* **1** *Biol.* The lifeless, non-protoplasmic material of a cell, as inclusions of fats and carbohydrates. **2** A reversal or change in the order of the letters or syllables of a word. [<L *metaplasmus* <Gk. *metaplasmos* < *meta-* beyond + *plassein* mold] — **met′a·plas′mic** *adj.*

met·a·po·di·um (met′ə·pō′dē·əm) *n. pl.* **·di·a** (-dē·ə) **1** The posterior part of the foot in gastropods and pteropods. 2 The metacarpus and metatarsus of quadrupeds. Also **met′a·pode** (-pōd), **met′a·pod** (-pod).

met·a·pro·te·in (met′ə·prō′tē·in, -tēn) *n. Biochem.* A protein resulting from the action of acids and alkalis and soluble in weak solutions of either but not in solutions of neutral salts.

met·a·psy·chics (met′ə·sī′kiks) *n.* Parapsychology.

met·a·psy·chol·o·gy (met′ə·sī·kol′ə·jē) *n.* 1 Psychology restricted to philosophical speculations on the origin, structure, function, purpose, etc., of the mind. 2 *Psychoanal.* The investigation and study of mental processes from three points of view: the dynamic, topographical, and economic. — **met′a·psy′·cho·log′i·cal** (-sī′kə·loj′i·kəl) *adj.*

met·a·psy·cho·sis (met′ə·sī·kō′sis) *n.* Interchange of mental influence or action without a recognized physical medium.

met·a·so·ma·to·sis (met′ə·sō′mə·tō′sis) *n. Geol.* That form of metamorphism by means of which a rock or mineral undergoes chemical change through the action of external materials. Also **met′a·so′ma·tism** (-sō′mə·tiz′əm). [<META- + SOMAT(O)- + -OSIS]

met·a·some (met′ə·sōm) *n. Geol.* A mineral which has developed individually within another mineral. [<META- + -SOME[2]]

met·a·sta·ble (met′ə·stā′bəl) *adj. Physics & Chem.* Denoting an apparent state of equilibrium, as in supersaturated solutions. — **met′a·sta·bil′i·ty** (-stə·bil′ə·tē) *n.*

me·tas·ta·sis (mə·tas′tə·sis) *n. pl.* **·ses** (-sēz) 1 Change of one thing into another. 2 Metabolism. 3 *Pathol.* The transfer of a disease or of its manifestations from one part of the body to another. 4 In rhetoric, a rapid change from one point to another. [<L <Gk. <*methistanai* place differently, change < *meta-* after + *histanai* place] — **met·a·stat′ic** (-stat′·ik) *adj.* — **met′a·stat′i·cal·ly** *adv.*

tive changes, but without localized external lesions. 2 Parasyphilis. — **met′a·syph′i·lit′ic** (-sif′ə·lit′ik) *adj.*

met·a·tar·sal (met′ə·tär′səl) *adj.* Of or pertaining to the metatarsus. — *n.* One of the bones of the metatarsus. See illustration under FOOT.

met·a·tar·sal·gi·a (met′ə·tär·sal′jē·ə) *n. Pathol.* Neuralgia in the middle of the foot. [<METATARS(US) + -ALGIA]

met·a·tar·sus (met′ə·tär′səs) *n. pl.* **·si** (-sī) *Anat.* The part of the hind or pelvic limb between the tarsus or ankle and the phalanges or bones of the toe. In man it consists of five bones. [<NL <META- + TARSUS]

met·a·the·ri·an (met′ə·thir′ē·ən) *n.* Any one of a subclass *(Metatheria)* of mammals whose young are born immature and are carried in a pouch until fully developed; one of the marsupials, as a kangaroo, opossum, or bandicoot. — *adj.* Of or pertaining to the *Metatheria.* [<META- + Gk. *thērion* beast]

me·tath·e·sis (mə·tath′ə·sis) *n. pl.* **·ses** (-sēz) 1 The transposition of letters, syllables, or sounds in a word. 2 *Chem.* A substitution, as the replacing or exchange of one or more radicals or groups in a compound; double decomposition or mutual exchange. 3 *Surg.* The operation of removing a morbific substance from one place to another for relief, as by pushing a calculus lodged in the urethra back into the bladder. 4 Any change or reversal of conditions. [<LL <Gk. < *metatithenai* transpose < *meta-* over + *tithenai* place] — **met·a·thet·ic** (met′ə·thet′ik) or **·i·cal** *adj.*

met·a·tho·rax (met′ə·thôr′aks, -thō′raks) *n. Entomol.* The hindmost of the three segments of the thorax in insects, bearing the hind wings and the third pair of legs. — **met′a·tho·rac′ic** (-thô·ras′ik, -thō-) *adj.*

met·a·troph·ic (met′ə·trof′ik) *adj.* Saprophytic. [<META- + Gk. *trophikos* feeding, nursing]

me·tat·ro·phy (mə·tat′rə·fē) *n. Pathol.* A wasting away because of disordered nutrition. Also **met·a·tro·phi·a** (met′ə·trō′fē·ə). [<MET- + ATROPHY]

METEOROLOGY SYMBOLS

Symbol	Meaning	Symbol	Meaning
,	Drizzle		Duststorm; Sandstorm
•	Rain		Lightning
✱	Snow	⌒	Rainbow
≡	Fog		Smoke
⌴	Frost	∞	Haze
▽	Showers	∧	Squalls
	Thunderstorms	0	Exceptional visibility
↔	Ice crystals or ice needles		Signs of tropical storm
▲	Sleet	○	Cloudless sky
	Aurora		Partly cloudy sky
	Lunar corona		Cloudy sky
⦶	Solar corona		Overcast sky
	Dew		

WIND DIRECTION

↓	North	↑	South
↓↙	NNE	↑↖	SSE
↙	NE	↖	SE
↘	NW	↗	SW
↓↘	NNW	↑↗	SSW
←	East	→	West
←↖	ESE	→↗	WSW
←↙	ENE	→↘	WNW

me·tas·ta·size (mə·tas′tə·sīz) *v.i.* **·sized, ·siz·ing** *Pathol.* To shift or spread from one part of the body to another: said specifically of malignant growths.

met·as·then·ic (met′əs·then′ik) *adj. Biol.* Having the posterior or lower part of the body well developed, as a kangaroo. [<META- + STHENIC]

met·a·syph·i·lis (met′ə·sif′ə·ləs) *n. Pathol.* 1 Congenital syphilis, with typical degenera-

Me·tau·ro (mā·tou′rō) A river in central Italy, flowing 207 miles NE to the Adriatic; at its delta the Romans defeated the Carthaginians under Hasdrubal, 207 B.C. Ancient **Me·tau·rus** (me·tô′rus).

Me·tax·as (mə·tak′səs, *Greek* me′täk·säs′), **Joannes,** 1871–1941, Greek soldier and statesman.

met·a·xy·lem (met′ə·zī′ləm) *n. Bot.* The thick-walled cell portion in the woody tissues of plants, developed outside the primary xylem. [<META- + XYLEM]

met·a·zo·an (met′ə·zō′ən) *n.* Any member of a primary division *(Metazoa)* of the animal kingdom, whose cells become differentiated into at least an outer and an inner wall, including all animals higher than protozoans. Also **met′a·zo′on.** — *adj.* Of or pertaining to the metazoans: also **met′a·zo′ic.** [<META- + Gk. *zōion* animal]

Metch·ni·koff (mech′ni·kôf), **Elie,** 1845–1916, Russian physiologist and bacteriologist: also known as *Ilya Ilich Metchnikoff.*

mete[1] (mēt) *v.t.* **met·ed, met·ing** 1 To allot or distribute by measure; apportion: usually with *out.* 2 *Obs.* To measure. — *n. Obs.* Measure. ◆ Homophones: *meat, meet.* [OE *metan* measure]

mete[2] (mēt) *n. Obs.* A boundary line; limit; confine: usually in the phrase *metes and bounds.* ◆ Homophones: *meat, meet.* [<OF <L *meta* goal, boundary]

met·em·pir·i·cal (met′em·pir′i·kəl) *adj.* Lying beyond the bounds of experience, as intuitive principles; not derived from experience; transcendental; a priori: opposed to *empirical.* Also **met′em·pir′ic.**

met·em·pir·i·cism (met′em·pir′ə·siz′əm) *n.* The science of pure reason; metaphysics proper; hence, with some, transcendental philosophy. Also **met′em·pir′ics.**

me·tem·psy·cho·sis (mə·temp′sə·kō′sis, met′·əm·sī-) *n.* Transmigration of souls from body to body. [<LL <Gk. *metempsychōsis* < *metempsychoein* < *meta-* over + *empsychoein* animate < *en-* in + *psychē* soul, life]

met·en·ceph·a·lon (met′ən·sef′ə·lən) *n. pl.* **·la** (-lə) *Anat.* 1 The fifth cerebral vesicle of the brain and the parts derived therefrom, comprising the medulla oblongata and the posterior part of the roof of the fourth ventricle. 2 The part of the brain consisting of the cerebellum and pons Varolii. [<NL <MET- + ENCEPHALON] — **met′en·ce·phal′ic** (-sə·fal′·ik) *adj.*

me·te·or (mē′tē·ər, -ôr) *n.* 1 *Astron.* A luminous phenomenon, produced by a small mass of matter from the celestial spaces which strikes the earth's atmosphere with great velocity and is dissipated by heat: when not very brilliant, called a *shooting star.* 2 A meteoroid. 3 *Obs.* Any phenomenon of the atmosphere: **aerial meteors** (winds, hurricanes, etc.), **aqueous meteors** (rain, snow, etc.), **igneous meteors** (lightning, shooting stars, etc.), **luminous meteors** (aurora, rainbow, etc.). [<Med. L *meteorum* <Gk. *meteōron* thing in the air < *meteōros* high in the air < *meta-* beyond + *eōra* suspension]

Meteor Crater A depression caused by a meteor in central Arizona; 600 feet deep, 4,000 feet in diameter: also *Diablo Crater.*

me·te·or·ic (mē′tē·ôr′ik, -or′ik) *adj.* 1 Relating to meteors. 2 Meteorological. 3 Transitorily brilliant: a *meteoric* career. Also **me′·te·or′i·cal.** — **me′te·or′i·cal·ly** *adv.*

me·te·or·ite (mē′tē·ə·rīt′) *n.* 1 A fallen meteor; a mass of stone or iron that has fallen upon the earth from outer space. 2 A meteoroid. — **me′te·or·it′ic** (-ə·rit′ik) *adj.*

me·te·or·o·graph (mē′tē·ər·ə·graf′, -gräf′, mē′·tē·ôr′ə-, -or′ə-) *n.* A self-recording instrument, frequently attached to a kite or balloon, by which several meteorological elements are plotted in the form of a diagram. [<F *météorographe*]

me·te·or·oid (mē′tē·ə·roid) *n. Astron.* One of innumerable small particles of matter moving through the celestial spaces, which, when they encounter the earth's atmosphere, form meteors or shooting stars.

me·te·or·ol·o·gy (mē′tē·ə·rol′ə·jē) *n.* 1 The science that treats of atmospheric phenomena, especially those that relate to weather. 2 The character of the weather and of atmospheric changes of any particular place. [<Gk. *meteōrologia* < *meteōros* high in the air + *logos* discourse] — **me′te·or′o·log′ic** (-ôr′ə·loj′ik), **me′te·or′o·log′i·cal** *adj.* — **me′te·or′o·log′i·cal·ly** *adv.* — **me′te·or·ol′o·gist** *n.*

meteor shower *Astron.* The apparent passage of a group of meteors upon entering the earth's atmosphere.

me·ter[1] (mē′tər) *n.* **1** An instrument, apparatus, or machine for measuring fluids, gases, electric currents, grain, etc., and recording the results obtained. **2** Any person or thing that measures; specifically, one of several officers appointed to measure certain commodities, as for tolls. —*v.t.* To measure or test by means of a meter. [< METE[1]]

me·ter[2] (mē′tər) *n.* **1** The fundamental unit of length in the metric system, originally defined as one ten-millionth of the distance on the earth's surface from the pole to the equator; 39.37 inches. In practice, it is the distance between two fiducial lines marked on the platinum-iridium International Prototype Meter deposited at Sèvres, France. See METRIC SYSTEM. **2** A measured verbal rhythm, the structure of verse; a definite arrangement of groups of syllables in a line, having a time unit and a regular beat; also, a specific arrangement of words, or a specific sequence of such lines in a stanza. **3** The character of a musical composition as being divisible into measures equal in time and length, and similar in rhythmic pattern. Also spelled *metre.* [< F *mètre* < L *metrum* measure < Gk. *metron*]

Synonyms : euphony, measure, rhythm, verse. *Euphony* is agreeable linguistic sound, however produced; *meter, measure,* and *rhythm* denote agreeable succession of sounds in the utterance of connected words; *euphony* may apply to a single word or even a single syllable; the other words apply to lines, sentences, paragraphs, etc.; *rhythm* and *meter* may be produced by accent only, as in English, or by accent and quantity combined, as in Greek or Italian; *rhythm* or *measure* may apply either to prose or to poetry, or to music, dancing, etc.; *meter* is more precise than *rhythm,* applies only to poetry, and denotes a measured *rhythm.* A *verse* is strictly a metrical line, but the word is often used as synonymous with stanza. *Verse,* in the general sense, denotes metrical writing; as, prose and *verse.* Compare MELODY, POETRY.

-meter *combining form* **1** That (instrument or unit) by which a thing is measured: *calorimeter.* **2** Measure according to or containing (the main element): *hexameter.* [< L *metrum* < Gk. *metron* measure]

me·ter·age (mē′tər·ij) *n.* **1** The act or result of measuring. **2** The charge for measurement.

met·es·trus (met·es′trəs) *n. Biol.* The period of sexual quiescence following estrus in female mammals: often spelled *metoestrus, metoestrum.* Also **met·es′trum.** [< NL < MET- + ESTRUS] —**met·es′trous** *adj.*

meth·ac·ry·late (meth·ak′rə·lāt) *n. Chem.* An ester of methacrylic acid.

meth·a·cryl·ic acid (meth′ə·kril′ik) *Chem.* A colorless acid, $C_4H_6O_2$, the esters of which are extensively used in the making of plastics. [< METH(YL) + ACRYLIC]

meth·a·done (meth′ə·dōn) *n.* A synthetic opiate used as an analgesic and experimentally as a substitute for heroin in the treatment of addicts. Also **meth′a·don** (-don). [< *(di)meth(yl) a(mino) d(iphenylheptan)one*]

meth·am·phet·a·mine (meth′am·fet′ə·mēn,-min) *n. Chem.* A compound, $C_{10}H_{15}N{\cdot}HCl$, related to the amphetamines, that allays hunger and stimulates the central nervous system. [< METH- + AMPHETAMINE]

meth·ane (meth′ān) *n. Chem.* A colorless, inflammable gas, CH_4, the simplest of the saturated hydrocarbons, formed by decomposition of vegetable matter, or artificially by dry distillation of certain organic matter, or by chemical treatment of certain metal compounds, as aluminum carbide. It is an important component of illuminating gas: often called *marsh gas.* [< METH(YL) + -ANE[2]]

methane series *Chem.* A group of saturated aliphatic hydrocarbons having the general formula C_nH_{2n+2}, and identified by the ending *-ane* : also called *alkanes.*

meth·a·nol (meth′ə·nōl, -nol) *n. Chem.* Methyl alcohol; a colorless, volatile, inflammable liquid, CH_3OH, obtained by the destructive distillation of wood or by catalytic treatment of hydrogen and carbon monoxide: highly toxic and widely used in industry and the arts: also called *carbinol, wood alcohol.* [< METHANE + -OL[1]]

meth·a·qua·lone (meth′ə·kwā′lōn) *n.* An addictive drug, $C_{16}H_{14}N_2O$, used as a sedative; Quaalude.

Meth·e·drine (meth′ə·drēn) *n.* Proprietary name for a brand of methamphetamine.

me·theg·lin (mə·theg′lin) *n.* A fermented drink made of water and honey; mead. [< Welsh *meddyglyn* < *meddyg* doctor (< L *medicus*) + *llyn* juice, liquor]

met·he·mo·glo·bin (met·hē′mə·glō′bin, -hem′ə-) *n. Biochem.* A stable, brown-red, crystalline compound formed by the decomposition of blood and by oxidation of hemoglobin. Also **met·haé·mo·glo′bin.** [< MET- + HEMOGLOBIN]

me·the·na·mine (mə·thē′nə·mēn, -min) *n. Chem.* An organic compound, $C_6H_{12}N_4$, crystallized from a mixture of formalin and ammonia: used in the vulcanization of rubber, in making synthetic resins, and as an antiseptic: also called *Urotropin, hexamethylenamine, hexamethylenetetramine.* [< *methene* (< METHYL + -ENE) + AMINE]

me·thinks (mē·thingks′) *v., impersonal Obs.* It seems to me; I think. [OE *me thyncth* < *thyncan* seem]

me·thi·o·nine (mə·thī′ə·nēn, -nin) *n. Biochem.* An amino acid, $C_5H_{11}O_2NS$, containing sulfur and closely related to cystine: obtained from various proteins. [< ME(THYL) + THIO- + -INE[2]]

metho- *combining form Chem.* Used to indicate the presence of a methyl group in a compound. Also, before vowels, **meth-,** as in *methane.* [< METHYL]

meth·od (meth′əd) *n.* **1** A general or established way or order of doing anything, or the means or manner by which it is presented or taught. **2** Orderly and systematic arrangement, as of ideas and topics, etc.; the design or plan of a speaker or of an author. **3** The arrangement of natural bodies according to their common characteristics. See synonyms under MANNER, RULE, SYSTEM. [< F *méthode* < L *methodus* < Gk. *methodos* < *meta-* after + *hodos* way]

me·thod·i·cal (mə·thod′i·kəl) *adj.* **1** Given to or characterized by orderly arrangement. **2** Arranged with method. Also **me·thod′ic.** —**me·thod′i·cal·ly** *adv.* —**me·thod′i·cal·ness** *n.*

meth·od·ist (meth′əd·ist) *n.* An observer of method or order. —**meth′od·ism** *n.* —**meth′od·is′tic, meth′od·is′ti·cal** *adj.*

Meth·od·ist (meth′əd·ist) *n.* A member of any one of the Protestant churches that have grown out of the religious movement begun at Oxford University in the first half of the 18th century, in which John Wesley as a leader was associated with Charles Wesley, George Whitefield, and others. The largest Methodist body in the United States is the **Methodist Church,** formed by the union of the **Methodist Episcopal Church,** the **Methodist Episcopal Church, South,** and the **Methodist Protestant Church.** —*adj.* Pertaining to, belonging to, like, or typical of this church or its doctrines. [< METHOD + -IST] —**Meth′od·ism** *n.* —**Meth′od·is′tic, Meth′od·is′ti·cal** *adj.*

meth·od·ize (meth′əd·īz) *v.t.* **·ized, ·iz·ing** To reduce or subject to method; systematize. Also *Brit.* **meth′od·ise.** See synonyms under REGULATE. —**meth′od·i·za′tion** *n.*

meth·od·ol·o·gy (meth′ə·dol′ə·jē) *n.* **1** The science of method or of arranging in due order. **2** The division of pure logic that treats of the methods of directing the means of thinking to the end of clear and connected thinking. [< Gk. *methodos* method + -LOGY]

me·thought (mē·thôt′) *v., impersonal Obs.* It seemed to me; I thought.

Me·thu·se·lah (mə·thōō′zə·lə) The son of Enoch; a Hebrew patriarch reputed to have lived 969 years. *Gen.* v 27.

meth·yl (meth′əl) *n. Chem.* An organic radical, CH_3, existing only in combination, as in methyl alcohol, etc. It is univalent, and forms esters with acids. [< METHYLENE] —**me·thyl·ic** (mə·thil′ik) *adj.*

methyl acetate *Chem.* A liquid product, $CH_3CO_2CH_3$, of wood alcohol or wood vinegar, used as a solvent or a flavoring material.

meth·yl·al (meth′əl·al) *n. Chem.* A colorless, volatile, inflammable liquid, $C_3H_8O_2$, with a pungent taste and the odor of chloroform, used in medicine and in the making of perfumery and artificial resins: also called *formal.* [< METHYL + AL(COHOL)]

methyl alcohol Methanol.

meth·yl·am·ine (meth′əl·am′ēn, -in) *n. Chem.* A colorless, gaseous, inflammable amine, CH_3NH_2, with a strong fishy odor, contained in the products of the decomposition of certain organic compounds, and also made synthetically from ammonia by replacement of hydrogen by methyl. [< METHYL + AMINE]

meth·yl·ate (meth′əl·āt) *v.t.* **·at·ed, ·at·ing** *Chem.* To mix or saturate with methyl or methanol. —*n.* A compound derived from methanol by replacing the hydrogen of the hydroxyl group with an element or radical of equal valence: potassium *methylate.* [< METHYL + -ATE] —**meth′yl·a′tion** *n.*

methylated spirit *Chem.* A mixture of ethyl alcohol with ten percent of methanol: used in the arts, unfit for drinking.

methyl chloride *Chem.* A gas, CH_3Cl, which on compression becomes a colorless liquid of ethereal odor yielding a poisonous vapor: used as a refrigerant and fire extinguisher.

meth·yl·cho·lan·threne (meth′əl·kō·lan′thrēn) *n. Biochem.* A yellow, crystalline hydrocarbon, $C_{21}H_{16}$, extracted from bile acids and also prepared synthetically: believed to be strongly carcinogenic. [< METHYL + CHOL(E)- + ANTHR(ACINE) + -ENE]

meth·yl·di·chlor·ar·sine (meth′əl·dī′klôr·är′·sēn, -sin) *n. Chem.* A colorless liquid compound, CH_3AsCl_2, adapted for chemical warfare as a vesicant and lung irritant. [< METHYL + DI- + CHLOR- + ARSINE]

meth·yl·ene (meth′əl·ēn) *n. Chem.* A bivalent organic radical, CH_2, derived from methane. [< F *méthyline* < Gk. *methyl* wine + *hylē* wood]

methylene blue *Chem.* A dark, blue-green aniline dye, $C_{16}H_{18}N_3ClS{\cdot}3H_2O$, having medicinal properties in the treatment of diphtheria, malaria, etc., and as an antidote in cyanide poisoning: used also as a chemical indicator and bacteriological stain.

meth·yl·gua·ni·dine (meth′əl·gwä′nə·dēn, -din) *n. Biochem.* A ptomaine, $C_2H_7N_3$, derived from creatinine and from certain foods, as spoiled fish. [< METHYL + GUANADINE]

methyl methacrylate *Chem.* A polymerized methacrylate forming transparent thermosetting plastics resembling glass in their optical properties. [See METHACRYLIC]

meth·yl·naph·tha·lene (meth′əl·naf′thə·lēn) *n. Chem.* A methyl compound, $C_{10}H_7CH_3$, occurring in two isomeric forms, one of which is used in the determination of cetane numbers. [< METHYL + NAPHTHALENE]

methyl orange *Chem.* An azo dyestuff used chiefly as an indicator in alkalimetry; a brilliant orange-yellow powder, readily soluble in water, colored red on the addition of acids.

meth·yl·ros·an·i·line (meth′əl·roz·an′ə·lēn, -lin) *n.* Gentian violet. [< METHYL + ROSANILINE]

me·tic·u·lous (mə·tik′yə·ləs) *adj.* Careful about trivial matters; finical; particular. [< F *méticuleux* < L *meticolosus* fearful < *metus* fear] —**me·tic′u·los′i·ty** (-los′ə·tē) *n.* —**me·tic′u·lous·ly** *adv.*

mé·tier (mā·tyā′) *n. French* Trade; profession.

mé·tif (mā·tēf′) *n. pl.* **·tifs** (-tēfs′) or **·tis** (-tēs′) *French* A person of mixed blood; especially, a person half French and half American Indian. Also **me·tiff′.**

met·o·chy (met′ə·kē) *n. Entomol.* The relationship of mutual tolerance without mutual aid existing between ants and their neutral insect guests. [< Gk. *metochē* sharing < *metochein* share in]

met·o·don·ti·a·sis (met′ō·don·tī′ə·sis) *n. Dent.* **1** Abnormal or imperfect dentition. **2** Faulty teething. [< NL < MET- + Gk. *odontiaein* cut teeth + -IASIS]

met·oes·trus (met·es′trəs), **met·oes·trum** See METESTRUS.

Me·ton·ic cycle (mə·ton′ik) A period of 19 Julian years, amounting to nearly 235 lunar revolutions, at the conclusion of which the phases of the moon recur at the same time of the year. [after *Meton,* Athenian astronomer of the fifth century B.C.]

met·o·nym (met′ə·nim) *n.* A word used as a substitute for another. [See METONYMY]

me·ton·y·my (mə·ton′ə·mē) *n.* A figure of speech that consists in the naming of a thing by one of its attributes, as "the crown prefers" for "the king prefers." [< L *metonymia* < Gk. *metōnymia* < *meta-* altered + *onyma* name] —**met·o·nym·ic** (met′ə·nim′ik), **met′o·nym′i·cal** *adj.* —**met′o·nym′i·cal·ly** *adv.*

me–too·ism (mē′tōō′iz′əm) *n.* The practice of representing as one's own the popular or successful policies of another, especially a political rival. — **me′–too′er** *n.*
met·o·pe[1] (met′ə·pē) *n. Archit.* **1** A square slab, sculptured or plain, between triglyphs in a Doric frieze. **2** Originally, the opening supposed to have been left by primitive Greek builders between the ends of adjoining ceiling beams. [<L *metopa* <Gk. *metopē* < *meta-* between + *opē* opening]
met·o·pe[2] (met′ə·pē) *n. Anat.* The face, forehead, or frontal surface. [Gk. *metōpon* forehead < *meta-* between + *ōps* eye] — **me·top·ic** (mə·top′ik) *adj.*
me·tox·e·ny (mə·tok′sə·nē) *n.* Heteroecism. [<Gk. *meta-* among, after + *xenos* host]
metr– Var. of METRO–.
me·tral·gi·a (mə·tral′jē·ə) *n. Pathol.* Pain in the womb. [<METR(O)-[1] + -ALGIA]
Met·ra·zol (met′rə·zōl, -zol) *n.* Proprietary name of a synthetic drug, $C_6H_{10}N_4$, used in medicine as a heart stimulant and in the shock treatment of certain nervous and mental disorders.
me·tre (mē′tər) See METER[2].
met·ric (met′rik) *adj.* **1** Pertaining to the meter as a unit of measurement or to the metric system. **2** Metrical (def. 1). [<L *metricus* <Gk. *metrikos*]
met·ri·cal (met′ri·kəl) *adj.* **1** Relating to meter or versification; composed in poetic measures; rhythmical. **2** Metric (def. 1). — **met′ri·cal·ly** *adv.*
metrical stress The emphasis required by the meter of a poem: opposed to *rhetorical stress.*
metric centner A quintal.
metric hundredweight A weight of 50 kilograms.
me·tri·cian (mə·trish′ən) *n.* **1** One versed in metrics. **2** A composer of verse.
met·rics (met′riks) *n. pl. (construed as singular)* **1** The mathematical theory of measurement. **2** The art of metrical composition.
metric system A decimal system of weights and measures having as fundamental units the gram and the meter. From the *gram* are derived measures of weight, and from the *meter* measures of length; measures of surface are based on the *square meter* and measures of capacity on the *liter*. The table shown above gives the basic and derived units of the metric system, together with abbreviations and a list of equivalent values in customary U. S. standards; originating in a report to the French Academy (1791) it was legalized in France, Nov. 2, 1801; now universally used in scientific measurement.
metric ton A unit of weight, equal to 1,000 kilograms, 0.984 long ton, or 1.023 short tons.
met·ri·fi·ca·tion (met′rə·fə·kā′shən) *n.* The adoption of the metric system or the conversion to metric units from those of another system. Also *Brit.* **met·ri·ca·tion** (met′rə·kā′shən).
met·ri·fy (met′rə·fī) *v.t.* & *v.i.* **·fied, ·fy·ing** **1** To write in meter, versify. **2** To convert to the metric system or metric units.
me·trist (mē′trist, met′rist) *n.* One versed in meters or skilled in metrical composition; a versemaker. [<Med. L *metrista*]
me·tri·tis (mə·trī′tis) *n. Pathol.* Inflammation of the womb. — **me·trit′ic** (-trit′ik) *adj.*
met·ro (met′rō) *n. pl.* **·ros** *Often cap.* In European countries, an underground railway; subway. [<F *métro* < *chemin de fer) métro-(politain)* metro(politan railroad); in England <METRO(POLITAN DISTRICT RAILWAY)]
metro–[1] *combining form* The uterus; pertaining to the uterus: *metropathic.* Also, before vowels, **metr–**. [<Gk. *metra* the uterus]
metro–[2] *combining form* Measure: *metrology.* Also, before vowels, **metr–**. [<Gk. *metron* a measure]
me·trol·o·gy (mə·trol′ə·jē) *n.* The science that treats of systems of weights and measures or of measure. [<METRO-[2] + -LOGY] — **met·ro·log·i·cal** (met′rə·loj′i·kəl) *adj.* — **me·trol′o·gist** *n*
met·ro·nome (met′rə·nōm) *n.* An instrument for indicating and marking exact time in music, consisting usually of a reversed pendulum whose period of vibration is regulated by a shifting weight. [<METRO-[2] + Gk. *nomos* law] — **met′ro·nom′ic** (-nom′ik) *adj.*

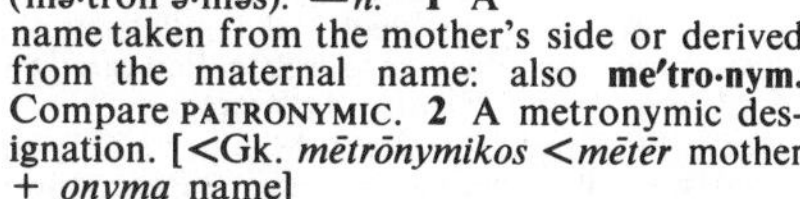
METRONOME

me·tro·nym·ic (mē′trə·nim′ik, met′rə-) *adj.* Pertaining to or derived from the name of one's mother or female ancestors: also **me·tron·y·mous** (mə·tron′ə·məs). — *n.* **1** A name taken from the mother's side or derived from the maternal name: also **me′tro·nym.** Compare PATRONYMIC. **2** A metronymic designation. [<Gk. *mētrōnymikos* <*mētēr* mother + *onyma* name]
met·ro·path·ic (met′rə·path′ik) *adj. Pathol.* Of or pertaining to disorders of the uterus. [< METRO-[1] + Gk. *pathos* suffering] — **me·trop·a·thy** (mə·trop′ə·thē) *n.*
me·trop·o·lis (mə·trop′ə·lis) *n.* **1** A chief city, either the capital or the largest or most important city of a state or country. **2** The seat of a metropolitan bishop. **3** In ancient Greece, the mother city of a colony. [<Gk. *mētropolis* city <*mētēr* mother + *polis* city]
met·ro·pol·i·tan (met′rə·pol′ə·tən) *n.* **1** An archbishop who exercises a limited authority over the bishops of the same ecclesiastical province. **2** A citizen of the mother city, as opposed to a colonist. **3** One who lives in a metropolis; also, one who has the manners and the ideas, or practices the customs, of a metropolis. — *adj.* Pertaining to a metropolis or to a metropolitan. [<LL *metropolitanus*]
me·tror·rha·gi·a (mē′trə·rā′jē·ə, met′rə-) *n. Pathol.* Uterine hemorrhage, especially when not menstrual. [<METRO-[1] + -RRHAGIA]
–metry *combining form* The process, science, or art of measuring: *geometry.* [<Gk. *metria* < *metron* a measure]
Met·su (met′sü), **Gabriel,** 1630–67, Dutch painter. Also **Met′zu.**
Met·ter·nich (met′ər·nikh), **Prince,** 1773–1859, Klemens Wenzel Nepomuk Lothar von Metternich, Austrian statesman and diplomat.
met·tle (met′l) *n.* The stuff or material of which a thing is composed; especially, constitutional temperament or disposition; specifically, courage; ardor. See synonyms under COURAGE. — **on one's mettle** Aroused to one's utmost or best efforts. ◆ Homophone: *metal.* [Var. of METAL]
met·tle·some (met′l·səm) *adj.* Having courage or spirit; ardent; fiery. Also **met′tled.**
me·tump (mə·tump′) *n. Canadian* A tumpline.
Metz (mets, *Fr.* mes) A city in NE France on the Moselle.
me·um (mē′əm) *pron. Latin* Mine; belonging to me: used in the phrase **meum and tuum,** mine and thine.
Meurthe (mûrt) A river in NE France, flowing 105 miles NW to the Moselle.
Meuse (myōōz, *Fr.* mœz) A river in western Europe, flowing 580 miles north from France to the North Sea: Dutch *Maas.*
mew[1] (myōō) *n.* **1** A cage for molting birds; an enclosure; pen for fattening or breeding; also, any place of concealment. **2** *pl.* A stable; specifically, the stables in London in which the royal horses are kept: so called because built on the site of the *mews* or cages of the royal hawks. — *v.t.* **1** To confine in or as in a mew; immure or conceal: often with *up.* **2** *Obs.* To change (feathers); molt. — *v.i.* **3** *Obs.* To molt. [<OF *muer* change <L *mutare*]
mew[2] (myōō) *v.i.* To cry as a cat. — *n.* The ordinary plaintive cry of a cat. Also spelled *miaou, miaow, meow.* [Imit.]
mew[3] (myōō) *n.* A European sea gull. Also **mew gull.** [OE *mæw*; imit.]
Me·war (mā·wär′) See UDAIPUR (def. 1).
mewl (myōōl) *v.i.* To cry, as an infant. — *n.* An infant's cry or crying. [Freq. of MEW[2]]
Mex·i·can (mek′sə·kən) *n.* **1** A native or inhabitant of Mexico. The inhabitants are chiefly of mestizo and native Indian blood, with a minority of white persons of Spanish ancestry. **2** The Nahuatl or Aztec language. — *adj.* Pertaining to Mexico, its inhabitants, or their language.
Mexican bean beetle A ladybird (*Epilachna varivestis*) with spotted wings, which feeds on the leaves and green pods of beans. For illustration see INSECTS (injurious).
Mexican broomroot Zacatón.
Mexican chickpea A leguminous herb of western Asia and tropical America (*Cicer*

METRIC SYSTEM

Length		Equivalents				Weight or Mass		Equivalents				Capacity		Equivalents			
		Metric		U.S.				Metric		U. S.				Metric		U. S.	
millimeter	(mm)	.001	m	.03937	in.	milligram	(mg)	.001	g	.0154	gr.	milliliter	(ml)	.001	l	.033	fl. oz.
centimeter	(cm)	.01	m	.3937	in.	centigram	(cg)	.01	g	.1543	gr.	centiliter	(cl)	.01	l	.338	fl. oz.
decimeter	(dm)	.1	m	3.937	in.	decigram	(dg)	.1	g	1.543	gr.	deciliter	(dl)	.1	l	3.38	fl. oz.
METER	(m)	1	m	39.37	in.	GRAM	(g)	1	g	15.43	gr.	LITER	(l)	1	l	1.056	li. qts.
dekameter	(dkm)	10	m	10.93	yds.	dekagram	(dkg)	10	g	.3527	oz. av.	dekaliter	(dkl)	10	l	.283	bu.
hectometer	(hm)	100	m	328.08	ft.	hectogram	(hg)	100	g	3.527	oz. av.	hectoliter	(hl)	100	l	2.837	bu.
kilometer	(km)	1000	m	.6213	mi.	kilogram	(kg)	1000	g	2.2	lbs. av.	kiloliter	(kl)	1000	l	264.18	gal.

Area		Equivalents				Volume		Equivalents			
		Metric		U. S.				Metric		U. S.	
sq. millimeter	(mm^2)	.000001	ca	.00155	sq. in.	cu. millimeter	(mm^3)	.001	cm^3	.016	minim
sq. centimeter	(cm^2)	.0001	ca	.155	sq. in.	cu.centimeter	(cc, cm^3)	.001	dm^3	.061	cu. in.
sq. decimeter	(dm^2)	.01	ca	15.5	sq. in.	cu. decimeter	(dm^3)	.001	m^3	61.023	cu. in.
CENTARE	(ca, m^2)	1	m^2	10.76	sq. ft.	STERE	(s, m^3)	1	m^3	1.307	cu. yds.
sq. dekameter	(dkm^2)	100	ca	.0247	acre	cu. dekameter	(dkm^3)	1000	m^3	1307.942	cu. yds.
Also are	(a)			2.47	acres	cu. hectometer	(hm^3)	1,000,000	m^3	1,307,942.8	cu. yds.
sq. hectometer	(hm^2)	10,000	ca	.386	sq. mi.	cu. kilometer	(km^3)	1,000,000,000	m^3	0.24	cu. mile
Also hectare	(ha)										
sq. kilometer	(km^2)	1,000,000	ca								

Other prefixes occasionally used are: MICRO—one millionth; MYRIA—10,000 times; MEGA—1,000,000 times *arietinum)* with short inflated pods containing seeds used as food and in coffee blends: also called *garbanzo.*

Mexican hairless An ancient breed of small dog found in Mexico, hairless excepting a tuft on the head and a fuzzy growth toward the end of the tail: also called *biche.*

MEXICAN HAIRLESS (From 11 to 13 inches high at the shoulder)

Mexican saddle A heavy leather saddle, having a high pommel and cantle and, usually, wooden stirrups.

Mexican War See table under WAR.

Mex·i·co (mek′sə·kō) **1** A republic in southern North America between the Pacific and the Caribbean and the Gulf of Mexico, administratively divided into 29 states; 760,373 square miles. **2** Its capital, the largest city in the republic and capital of the **Federal District of Mexico** (573 square miles) in the center of the country: also **Mexico City. 3** A state in central Republic of Mexico; 8,267 square miles; capital, Toluca. Spanish *Méjico.*

Mexico, Gulf of An arm of the Atlantic; nearly enclosed by the United States, Mexico, and Cuba; 700,000 square miles.

Mey·er (mī′ər), **Adolf,** 1866–1950, U.S. psychiatrist. **—Kuno,** 1858–1919, German Celtic scholar.

Mey·er·beer (mī′ər·bār), **Jakob,** 1791–1864, German composer.

Mey·er·hof (mī′ər·hōf), **Otto,** 1884–1951, German physiologist.

Meyn·ell (men′əl), **Alice,** *née* Thompson, 1847–1922, English poet and essayist.

mez·ca·line (mez′kə·lēn, -lin) See MESCALINE.

me·ze·re·on (mə·zir′ē·ən) *n.* **1** A low, Old World shrub *(Daphne mezereum)* with clusters of sweet-smelling, lilac-purple flowers: cultivated in the United States. **2** Mezereum (def. 1). [< Med. L < Arabic *māzariyān* camellia]

me·ze·re·um (mə·zir′ē·əm) *n.* **1** The dried bark of any of the *Daphne* species: used in medicine as an irritant and vesicant, and in the treatment of syphilis, rheumatism, and various skin diseases. **2** Mezereon (def. 1).

mez·qui·te (mes·kē′tā) See MESQUITE.

me·zu·zah (mə·zo͞o′zə, me·zo͞o′zä) *n. pl.* **·zoth** (-zōth) In Judaism, a parchment inscribed with the passages *Deut.* vi 4–9 and xi 13–21, to be rolled up in a case or tube and affixed to the doorpost of a dwelling, as the passages command. Also **me·zu′za.** [< Hebrew *mezūzāh* doorpost]

mez·za·nine (mez′ə·nēn, -nin) *n. Archit.* **1** A low-ceilinged story between two main ones, especially between the ground floor and the one above it. Also **mezzanine floor, mezzanine story. 2** In a theater, the first balcony or the front rows of the first balcony. [< F < Ital. *mezzanino,* dim. of *mezzano* middle < L *medianus*]

mez·zo (met′sō, med′zō, mez′ō) *adj.* Half; medium; moderate. [< Ital. < L *medius* middle]

mez·zo-re·lie·vo (met′sō·ri·lē′vō) *n. pl.* **·vos** Half relief; a piece of sculpture in which the rounded figures project half-way from the background material; demi-relief. See RELIEF. [< Ital. *mezzo rilievo.* See MEZZO and RELIEF.]

mez·zo-ri·lie·vo (med′zō·rē·lyā′vō) *n. pl.* **mez·zi-ri·lie·vi** (-vē) *Italian* Mezzo-relievo.

mezzo soprano A voice lower than a soprano and higher than a contralto; also, a person possessing, or a part written for, such a voice.

mez·zo·tint (met′sō·tint′, med′zō-, mez′ō-) *n.* **1** A method of copperplate engraving, producing an even gradation of tones, like a photograph. **2** An impression so produced. *—v.t.* To engrave in or represent by mezzotint. [< Ital. *mezzotinto* < *mezzo* middle + *tinto* painted] **—mez′zo·tint′er** *n.*

mho (mō) *n.* The practical unit of electrical conductance, being the reciprocal of the ohm. [< OHM reversed]

mi (mē) *n. Music* **1** The third note of the diatonic scale. **2** The note E. [< Ital. See GAMUT.]

Mi·am·i (mī·am′ē) *n.* A member of an Algonquian tribe of North American Indians formerly located between the Miami and Wabash rivers. [< N. Am. Ind.]

Miami A city on Biscayne Bay, southern Florida.

Miami Beach A resort city on an island between the Atlantic and Biscayne Bay, southern Florida.

Miami River A river in SW Ohio, flowing 160 miles SW to the Ohio River: also *Great Miami River.*

mi·a·na bug (mē·ä′nə) The tampan. [from *Miana,* an Iranian town]

mi·aou, mi·aow (mē·ou′) See MEW².

mi·ar·o·lit·ic (mī·ar′ə·lit′ik) *adj. Geol.* Of, pertaining to, or designating a form of igneous rock containing small cavities into which fully developed crystals have projected. [< Ital. *miarola* a granite found near Baveno, Italy + Gk. *lithos* stone]

mi·as·ma (mī·az′mə, mē-) *n. pl.* **·mas** or **·ma·ta** (-mə·tə) Polluting exhalations; the poisonous effluvium once supposed to rise from putrid matter, swamps, and marshy ground, especially at night. Also **mi′asm.** [< NL < Gk., pollution < *miainein* stain, defile] **—mi·as′mal, mi·as·mat·ic** (mī′az·mat′ik), **mi·as′mic** *adj.*

mi·aul (mē·ôl′, -oul′) *v.i.* To cry as a cat; mew. *— n.* The mewing of a cat. [Imit.]

mib (mib) *n.* **1** A marble. **2** *pl.* The game of marbles. [? Alter. of MARBLE]

mi·ca (mī′kə) *n.* Any of a class of silicates, crystallizing in the monoclinic system and having eminently perfect basal cleavage, affording thin, tough laminae or scales, colorless to jet-black, transparent to translucent, and of widely varying chemical composition. The better grades are extensively used for electrical insulation; the transparent varieties are loosely called *isinglass.* [< L, crumb; infl. by *micare* glitter]

mi·ca·ceous (mī·kā′shəs) *adj.* **1** Of, pertaining to, consisting of, or containing mica. **2** Resembling mica; laminated; sparkling: also used figuratively: a *micaceous* literary style.

mica diorite A variety of diorite in which mica replaces hornblende.

Mi·cah (mī′kə) A masculine personal name. [< Hebrew, like Jehovah]
—Micah A Hebrew prophet of the eighth century B.C.; also, the book of the Old Testament bearing his name.

Mi·caw·ber (mə·kô′bər), **Wilkins** In Dickens's *David Copperfield,* an improvident family man, always waiting for "something to turn up."

mice (mīs) Plural of MOUSE.

mi·celle (mi·sel′) **1** *Biol.* One of the theoretical structural units which are said to make up organized bodies. **2** *Chem.* The structural unit of a colloid, composed of an aggregate of molecules having crystalline properties and able to change in size without chemical alteration. Also **mi·cell′, mi·cel′la** (-sel′ə). [< NL *micella,* dim. of L *mica* crumb, grain] **—mi·cel′lar** *adj.*

Mi·chael (mī′kəl; *Ger.* mi′khä·el, *Lat.* mī′kə·el) A masculine personal name. Also *Polish* **Mi·chal** (mē′khäl), *Russian* **Mi·cha·il** (mē·kä·ēl), *Fr.* **Mi·chel** (mē·shel′), *Ital.* **Mi·che·le** (mē·kā′·lā). [< Hebrew, who is like God]
—Michael An archangel. *Rev.* xii 7. In Milton's *Paradise Lost,* he expels Adam and Eve from Paradise. In Moslem mythology, one of the four archangels, called the champion of the faith.
—Michael I, born 1921, king of Rumania 1927–30, 1940–47.

Mich·ael·mas (mik′əl·məs) The feast of St. Michael, Sept. 29; a quarterly rent day in England. [< MICHAEL + -MAS]

Michaelmas daisy 1 A European blue aster *(Aster tripolium).* **2** Any of several North American asters, wild and cultivated.

Mi·chel·an·ge·lo (mī′kəl·an′jə·lō), 1475–1564, Italian sculptor, painter, architect, and poet. Also **Mi′chael An′ge·lo**: full name **Mi·chel·an·ge·lo Buo·nar·ro·ti** (mē′kel·än′je·lō bwô′·när·rô′tē).

Miche·let (mēsh·le′), **Jules,** 1798–1874, French historian.

Mi·chel·son (mī′kəl·sən), **Albert Abraham,** 1852–1931, U.S. physicist born in Germany.

Mich·i·gan (mish′ə·gən) A north central State of the United States: 57,980 square miles; capital, Lansing; entered the Union Jan. 26, 1837; nickname, *Wolverine State* : abbr. MI **—Mich′i·gan·ite′** (-īt′), **Mich′i·gan′der** (-gan′dər) *n.*

Michigan, Lake The only one of the Great Lakes entirely within the United States, lying between Michigan and Wisconsin; 22,400 square miles.

Mi·cho·a·cán (mē′chō·ä·kän′) A maritime state of SW Mexico; 23,200 square miles; capital, Morelia.

Mick (mik) *n. Slang* An Irishman: a contemptuous usage. [< MICHAEL]

mick·ey finn (mik′ē fin′) *Slang* A drugged drink. Also **mick′ey, Mick′ey Finn.** [Origin unknown]

mick·le (mik′əl) *Obs.* or *Scot. adj.* **1** Large; great. **2** Much; many. *—n.* **1** A large amount or quantity; abundance. **2** By corruption, a small amount or quantity. Also spelled *meikle.* [OE *micel*]

Mic·mac (mik′mak) *n. pl.* **·mac** or **·macs** One of a tribe of North American Indians of Algonquian linguistic stock located in Nova Scotia, New Brunswick, and Newfoundland. [< N. Am. Ind., lit., allies]

mi·cra (mī′krə) Plural of MICRON.

mi·cri·fy (mī′krə·fī) *v.t.* **·fied, ·fy·ing** To make small or insignificant. [< MICR(O)- + -(I)FY]

micro- *combining form* **1** In the metric and other systems of measurement, the one-millionth part of (the specified unit):

microampere **microfarad** **micromho**
microangstrom **microhenry** **micromicron**
microbar **microhm** **microphot**
microcoulomb **microjoule** **microvolt**
microcurie **microlux** **microwatt**

2 An apparatus or instrument which enlarges in size or volume: *microphone.* **3** Exceptionally or abnormally small: *micro-organism.* **4** Microscopic; using or requiring a microscope:

microbotany **micropathology**
microgeology **micropetrography**
microhistology **micropetrology**
micromechanics **microphysiography**
micrometallurgy **microphysiology**
micromineralogy **microzoology**

Also, before vowels, sometimes **micr-.** [< Gk. *mikros* small]

mi·cro·a·nal·y·sis (mī′krō·ə·nal′ə·sis) *n.* The chemical analysis and identification of minute quantities. **—mi′cro·an′a·lyst** *n.* **—mi′cro·an′a·lyt′i·cal** (-an′ə·lit′i·kəl) *adj.* **—mi′cro·an′a·lyt′i·cal·ly** *adv.*

mi·cro·bar·o·graph (mī′krō·bar′ə·graf, -gräf) *n. Meteorol.* An instrument which records the lesser fluctuations of atmospheric pressure.

mi·crobe (mī′krōb) *n.* A microscopic organism; especially, a pathogenic bacterium. Also **mi·cro·bi·on** (mī·krō′bē·on). [< F < Gk. *mikros* small + *bios* life] **—mi·cro′bi·al, mi·cro′bi·an, mi·cro′bic** *adj.*

mi·cro·bi·cide (mī·krō′bə·sīd) *n.* Any substance or agent that destroys microbes; a germ-killer. [< MICROBE + -CIDE] **—mi·cro′bi·ci′dal** *adj.*

mi·cro·bi·ol·o·gy (mī′krō·bī·ol′ə·jē) *n.* The scientific study of the structure, development, function, and mode of action of micro-organisms, as bacteria, viruses, molds, etc., especially with regard to their significance in health and disease. **—mi·cro·bi·o·log·i·cal** (mī′·krō·bī′ə·loj′i·kəl) *adj.* **—mi′cro·bi·ol′o·gist** *n.*

mi·cro·bi·o·ta (mī′krō·bī·ō′tə) *n. pl. Ecol.* The microscopic plant and animal organisms of a region. [< NL < MICRO- + BIOTA] **—mi′cro·bi·ot′tic** (-ot′ik) *adj.*

mi·cro·ceph·a·ly (mī′krō·sef′ə·lē) *n.* Abnormal smallness of the head; imperfect development of the cranium. Also **mi′cro·ce·pha′li·a** (-sə·fā′lē·ə). [< MICRO- + Gk. *kephalē* head] **—mi′cro·ce·phal·ic** (-sə·fal′ik), **mi′cro·ceph′a·lous** *adj.*

mi·cro·chem·is·try (mī′krō·kem′is·trē) *n.* The chemistry of very small objects or quantities, especially those requiring the use of the microscope. **—mi′cro·chem′i·cal** *adj.*

mi·cro·chip (mī′krō·chip′) *n.* A chip (def. 8).

mi·cro·cir·cuit (mī′krō·sûr′kət) *n.* An electronic circuit made up of very tiny components.

mi·cro·cli·mate (mī′krō·klī′mit) *n. Meteorol.* The climate of a very small area, as of a forest, meadow, lake, wheat field, etc., with special reference to local variations from the general climate of a region. Compare MACRO-

CLIMATE. —**mi·cro·cli·mat·ic** (mī′krō·klī·mat′·ik) *adj.*

mi·cro·cline (mī′krə·klīn) *n.* A grayish, reddish, greenish, or green translucent potash feldspar, $KAlSi_3O_8$, crystallizing in the triclinic system. See FELDSPAR.

mi·cro·coc·cus (mī′krə·kok′əs) *n. pl.* **·coc·ci** (-kok′sī) Any member of a genus *(Micrococcus)* of spherical bacteria occurring in irregular masses or in plates. They are generally Gram–positive, and feed either on living or on dead matter. [<NL]

mi·cro·cop·y (mī′krə·kop′ē) *n. pl.* **·cop·ies** A reduced photographic copy, as of a letter, manuscript, etc.

mi·cro·cosm (mī′krə·koz′əm) *n.* **1** A little world; the world or universe on a small scale; hence, man, as if combining in himself all the elements of the great world: opposed to *macrocosm.* **2** A little community. Also **mi′·cro·cos′mos** (-koz′məs), **mi′cro·cos′mus.** [<F *microcosme* <LL *microcosmus* <Gk. *mikros kosmos,* lit., little world] —**mi′cro·cos′mic, mi′cro·cos′mi·cal, mi′cro·cos′mi·an** *adj.*

microcosmic salt *Chem.* A white crystalline salt, sodium ammonium hydrogen phosphate, $Na(NH_4)HPO_4 \cdot 4H_2O$, used to identify metallic oxides in lead tests.

mi·cro·crys·tal·line (mī′krō·kris′tə·lin, -lēn) *adj.* **1** Cryptocrystalline. **2** Having a crystalline structure visible only under a microscope.

mi·cro·cyte (mī′krə·sīt) *n. Pathol.* A small red blood corpuscle found in cases of anemia.

mi·cro·dis·sec·tion (mī′krō·di·sek′shən) *n.* Dissection, as of tissue, under the microscope.

mi·cro·dont (mī′krə·dont) *adj.* Having unusually small teeth. Also **mi′cro·don′tous.** [<MICR(O) + Gk. *odous, odontos* tooth]

mi·cro·e·co·nom·ics (mī′krō·ē′kə·nom′iks, -ek′·ə-) *n.* Economics studied in terms of individual areas of the economy, esp. a company or a family.

mi·cro·e·lec·tron·ics (mī′krō·i·lek′tron′iks) *n.* Branch of electronics that deals with the miniaturization of circuits and components.

mi·cro·fiche (mī′krō·fēsh′) *n.* A sheet of microfilm. [<F <MICRO- + *fiche* card]

mi·cro·film (mī′krə·film) *n.* **1** A photograph, as of a printed page, document, or other object, highly reduced for ease in transmission and storage, and capable of reenlargement or reading by suitable optical devices. **2** A microphotograph. —**mi′cro·film′ing** *n.*

mi·cro·form (mī′krō·fôrm′) *n.* A method of reproducing images greatly reduced in size, as on microfilm.

mi·cro·fos·sil (mī′krə·fos′əl) *n.* The fossilized remains of an extremely minute organism, usually of submarine origin and of value in the study of early geological conditions and biological development.

mi·cro·ga·mete (mī′krō·gə·mēt′, -gam′ēt) *n. Biol.* The male of two conjugating gametes: so called from its being the smaller one. Compare MACROGAMETE.

mi·cro·gram (mī′krə·gram) *n.* A unit of weight in the metric system, equal to one thousandth of a milligram. Also **mi′cro·gramme.**

mi·cro·graph (mī′krə·graf, -gräf) *n.***1** A pantograph instrument for minute writing, drawing, or engraving. **2** A picture of an object as seen through a microscope. **3** An instrument for recording and photographically magnifying very small movements, as those of a diaphragm. —**mi′cro·graph′ic** *adj.*

mi·crog·ra·phy (mī·krog′rə·fē) *n.* **1** The description or study of microscopic objects. **2** The art or habit of writing very minutely. **3** Very minute handwriting. Contrasted with *macrography.*

mi·cro·groove (mī′krə·grōōv) *n.* **1** A fine groove or channel, especially as cut in the surface of a long–playing phonograph record. **2** A phonograph record having such grooves. —*adj.* Having microgrooves.

mi·cro·in·cin·er·a·tion (mī′krō·in·sin′ə·rā′shən) *n.* A method for the study of the inorganic constituents of cells and tissues by burning the organic materials and examining the residue under the microscope.

mi·cro·lec·i·thal (mī′krə·les′ə·thəl) *adj.* Alecithal. [<MICRO- + Gk. *lekithos* yolk]

mi·cro·li·ter (mī′krə·lē′tər) *n.* A metric unit of capacity, equal to one thousandth of a milliliter. Also **mi′cro·li′tre.**

mi·cro·lith (mī′krə·lith) *n. Anthropol.* A small, flint implement of the late Paleolithic, Mesolithic, and Neolithic culture periods. —**mi′cro·lith′ic** *adj.*

mi·crol·o·gy (mī·krol′ə·jē) *n.* **1** The branch of science that treats of microscopic objects or is dependent on microscopic investigations. **2** Undue attention to minute and unimportant matters. [<MICRO- + -LOGY]

mi·cro·me·te·or·ol·o·gy (mī′krō·mē′tē·ə·rol′ə·jē) *n.* The study of climatic conditions in very small areas or localities. Compare MACROMETEOROLOGY.

mi·crom·e·ter (mī·krom′ə·tər) *n.* **1** An instrument for measuring very small distances or dimensions. **2** A caliper or gage arranged to allow of minute measurements. [<MICRO- + METER] —**mi·cro·met·ri·cal** (mī′krə·met′ri·kəl), **mi′·cro·met′ric** *adj.* —**mi′cro·met′ri·cal·ly** *adv.* —**mi·crom′e·try** *n.*

MICROMETER

micrometer caliper A caliper or gage having a micrometer screw.

micrometer screw A screw with fine and very accurately cut threads, and a circular, graduated head, which shows the amount of advancement or retraction of the screw: used in making fine measurements, often to .0001 of an inch.

mi·cro·mil·li·me·ter (mī′krō·mil′ə·mē′tər) *n.* **1** The one–millionth part of a millimeter, or the one–billionth part of a meter (1 × 10^{-9} m.). **2** One millimicron.

mi·cro·min·i·a·tur·ize (mī′krō·min′ē·ə·chər·īz, -min′ə-) *v.t.* **-ized, -iz·ing.** To reduce the size of, as the parts of electronic circuits, to a scale smaller than miniature. —**mi′cro·min′i·a·tur′i·za′tion** *n.*

mi·cron (mī′kron) *n. pl.* **·cra** (-krə) The one–thousandth part of a millimeter, or the one–millionth part of a meter (symbol μ). Also spelled *mikron.* [<NL <Gk. *mikron,* neut. of *mikros* small]

Mi·cro·ne·sia (mī′krə·nē′zhə, -shə) One of the three main divisions of Pacific islands, in the western Pacific north of the equator.

Mi·cro·ne·sian (mī′krə·nē′zhən, -shən) *n.* **1** A native of Micronesia. The Micronesians are a mixed race of Melanesian, Polynesian, and Malay stocks, but have shorter stature and darker skins than the Polynesians. **2** A group of Melanesian languages of the Austronesian family, spoken in the Caroline, Gilbert, and Marshall islands. —*adj.* Of or pertaining to Micronesia, its people, or their languages.

mi·cron·ize (mī′krən·īz) *v.t.* **·ized, ·iz·ing** To comminute (a substance) into particles not more than a few microns in diameter. [<MICRON + -IZE] —**mi′cron·i·za′tion** *n.*

mi·cro·nu·cle·us (mī′krō·nōō′klē·əs,-nyōō′-) *n. pl.* **·cle·i** (-klē·ī) *Biol.* A small nucleus, especially the smaller of two nuclei, as in infusorians.

mi·cro·nu·tri·ent (mī′krō·nōō′trē·ənt, -nyōō′-) *n.* A substance essential in the nourishment of animals and plants but only in small amounts or in low concentration, as certain minerals. —*adj.* Of or pertaining to such a substance.

mi·cro–or·gan·ism (mī′krō·ôr′gən·iz′əm) *n.* Any extremely small plant or animal organism, especially one visible only in an optical or electron microscope, as a bacterium, protozoan, or virus.

mi·cro·pa·le·on·tol·o·gy (mī′krō·pā′lē·ən·tol′·ə·jē) *n.* The study of microscopic fossils in relation to their geologic and ecological environment, especially those forms found in core samples from submarine depths. —**mi′cro·pa′le·on′to·log′ic** (-pā′lē·on′tə·loj′ik) or **·i·cal** *adj.* —**mi′cro·pa′le·on·tol′o·gist** *n.*

mi·cro·par·a·site (mī′krō·par′ə·sīt) *n.* A parasitic micro–organism.

mi·cro·phone (mī′krə·fōn) *n.* A device for amplifying sounds by the electromagnetic conyersion of sound waves impinging upon a sensitive diaphragm. It forms the principal element of a telephone transmitter, and is the first component of any sound–reproducing system, as in radio broadcasting, sound films, etc. —**mi′cro·phon′ic** (-fon′ik) *adj.*

mi·cro·pho·to·graph (mī′krō·fō′tə·graf, -gräf) *n.* **1** A microscopic photograph of any object, as a writing, picture, etc. Compare PHOTOMICROGRAPH. **2** Microfilm. —**mi′cro·pho′to·graph′ic** *adj.* —**mi′cro·pho·tog′ra·phy** (-fə·tog′·rə·fē) *n.*

mi·cro·pho·tom·e·ter (mī′krō·fō·tom′ə·tər) *n.* An instrument for the measurement of very small luminous intensities, and for the comparative study of spectral lines. —**mi′cro·pho′·to·met′ric** (-fō′tə·met′rik) *adj.* —**mi′cro·pho·tom′e·try** *n.*

mi·cro·phys·ics (mī′krə·fiz′iks) *n.* **1** That branch of physics which investigates the structure, characteristics, and behavior of microscopic particles of matter. **2** Nucleonics.

mi·cro·phyte (mī′krə·fīt) *n.* A microscopic plant, generally parasitic. —**mi′cro·phy′tal, mi′·cro·phyt′ic** (-fit′ik) *adj.*

mi·cro·pla·si·a (mī′krə·plā′zhē·ə, -zē·ə) *n. Pathol.* A condition of arrested development; dwarfism.

mi·cro·print (mī′krə·print) *n.* A microphotograph reproduced in a print that may be examined or read by means of a magnifying glass.

mi·cro·proc·ess·or (mī′krō·pros′əs·ər) *n.* Electronic processor located in a quarter–inch square silicon chip, which can carry out the functions of an ordinary computer or processor.

mi·crop·si·a (mī·krop′sē·ə) *n. Pathol.* A defect in vision causing objects to appear unusually small. Also **mi·cro′pi·a** (-krō′pē·ə). [<NL < MICR(O)- + -OPSIS] —**mi·crop′tic** (-tik) *adj.*

mi·cro·pyle (mī′krə·pīl) *n.* **1** *Bot.* The aperture in the coats of a plant ovule through which the pollen tube penetrates. **2** *Biol.* An aperture in the vitelline membrane of the ovum, serving to admit a spermatozoon. [<MICRO- + Gk. *pylē* gate] —**mi′cro·py′lar** *adj.*

mi·cro·py·rom·e·ter (mī′krō·pī·rom′ə·tər) *n.* An optical instrument for observing the temperature, etc., of minute light– or heat–radiating bodies.

mi·cro·rock·et (mī′krō·rok′it) *n.* A miniature rocket used for testing a proposed full–scale model.

mi·cro·scope (mī′krə·skōp) *n.* An optical instrument consisting of a single lens or a combination of lenses for magnifying objects too small to be seen or clearly observed by the naked eye. [<NL *microscopium*]

mi·cro·scop·ic (mī′krə·skop′ik) *adj.* **1** Pertaining to a microscope or to microscopy. **2** Made with or as with a microscope. **3** Exceedingly minute; visible only under the microscope: opposed to *macroscopic.* See synonyms under LITTLE. Also **mi′cro·scop′i·cal.** —**mi′cro·scop′i·cal·ly** *adv.*

Mi·cro·sco·pi·um (mī′krə·skō′pē·əm) A southern constellation. See CONSTELLATION. [<NL]

mi·cros·co·py (mī·kros′kə·pē, mī′krə·skō′pē) *n.* The art or practice of examining objects with a microscope. —**mi·cros′co·pist** *n.*

mi·cro·sec·ond (mī′krə·sek′ənd) *n.* One millionth of a second: used especially in timing the action of subatomic particles in nuclear physics.

mi·cro·seism (mī′krə·sīz′əm) *Geol.* A very slight tremor or vibration of the earth's crust, detectable only by a microseismometer. [<MICRO- + Gk. *seisma* shaking] —**mi′cro·seis′·mic, mi′cro·seis′mi·cal** *adj.*

mi·cro·seis·mom·e·ter (mī′krō·sīz·mom′ə·tər, -sīs-) *n.* An apparatus for indicating the direction, duration, and intensity of microseisms. Also **mi′cro·seis′mo·graph** (-sīz′mə·graf, -gräf, -sīs′-). [<MICROSEISM + (O)METER]

mi·cro·some (mī′krə·sōm) *n. Biol.* A minute corpuscle embedded in the protoplasm of an active cell. The great number of these corpuscles contributes to the granular appearance of protoplasm. Also **mi′cro·so′ma** (-sō′mə).

mi·cro·spe·cies (mī′krə·spē′shēz) *n. Biol.* A species having definite but slight variability; also, a species distributed within the confines of a limited area.

mi·cro·spec·tro·scope (mī′krō·spek′trə·skōp) *n.* A combination of the microscope and spectroscope for observing the absorptive spectrum of a minute body.

mi·cro·spo·ran·gi·um (mī′krō·spə·ran′jē·əm)

n. pl. **·gi·a** (-jē·ə) *Bot.* A sporangium producing or containing microspores, as in the pollen sac of the anther in seed plants.

mi·cro·spore (mī′krə·spôr, -spōr) *n. Bot.* A small, asexually produced spore in seed plants, male in function.

mi·cro·spo·ro·phyll (mī′krə·spôr′ə·fil, -spō′rə-) *n. Bot.* A sporophyll producing microsporangia.

mi·cros·to·mous (mī·kros′tə·məs) *adj.* Having an unusually small mouth. Also **mi·cro·stom·a·tous** (mī′krō·stom′ə·təs). [<MICRO- + -STOMOUS]

mi·cro·tome (mī′krə·tōm) *n.* An instrument for making very thin sections for microscopic observations. — **mi′cro·tom′ic** (-tom′ik) or **·i·cal** *adj.* — **mi·crot·o·mist** (mī·krot′ə·mist) *n.* — **mi·crot′o·my** *n.*

mi·cro·wave (mī′krə·wāv) *n.* A high-frequency electromagnetic wave having a wavelength of from 1 millimeter to about 30 centimeters.

mi·crur·gy (mī′krûr·jē) *n.* A highly refined precision technique for the microdissection, study, and investigation of living protoplasm, usually in the form of single cells, as bacteria, amebae, etc. [<MICR(O)- + -URGY] — **mi·crur·gic** (mī·krûr′jik) or **·gi·cal** *adj.* — **mi′crur·gist** *n.*

mic·tu·rate (mik′chə·rāt) *v.i.* **·rat·ed, ·rat·ing** To urinate. [<MICTURITION; an erroneous formation]

mic·tu·ri·tion (mik′chə·rish′ən) *n.* The act of urination. [<L *micturitus,* pp. of *micturire,* desiderative of *mingere* pass water]

mid[1] (mid) *adj.* **1** Middle. **2** *Phonet.* Produced with the tongue in a relatively midway position between high and low: said of certain vowels, as (ō) in *boat.* — *n. Archaic* The middle. [OE *midd*]

mid[2] (mid) *prep.* Amid; among: a poetical usage.

mid- *combining form* Middle; middle point or part of:

mid-act
mid-African
midafternoon
mid-April
mid-arctic
mid-Asian
mid-August
midautumn
midaxillary
mid-block
mid-breast
mid-Cambrian
mid-career
midcarpal
mid-century
mid-channel
mid-chest
mid-continent
mid-course
mid-court
mid-crowd
mid-current
mid-December
mid-diastolic
mid-dish
middorsal
mid-eighteenth
mid-Empire
mid-European
midevening
midfacial
mid-February
mid-field
mid-flight
midforenoon
mid-forty
midfrontal
mid-hour
mid-ice
mid-incisor
mid-Italian
mid-January
mid-July
mid-June
mid-lake
midleg
mid-length
mid-life
mid-line
mid-link
mid-lobe
midmandibular
mid-March
mid-May
midmonth
midmonthly
midmorning
mid-mouth
mid-movement
mid-nineteenth
mid-November
mid-ocean
mid-October
mid-oestral
mid-orbital
mid-Pacific
mid-part
mid-period
mid-periphery
mid-pillar
midpit
mid-Pleistocene
mid-position
midrange
mid-refrain
mid-region
mid-Renaissance
mid-river
mid-road
mid-sea
midseason
midsentence
mid-September
mid-Siberian
mid-side
mid-sky
mid-slope
mid-sole
midspace
mid-span
midstory
midstout
midstreet
mid-stride
mid-styled
mid-sun
mid-swing
mid-tap
midtarsal
mid-Tertiary
mid-thigh
mid-thoracic
mid-tide
mid-time
mid-totality
mid-tow
mid-town
mid-value
midventral
mid-volley
mid-walk
mid-wall
mid-watch
mid-water
midwintry
mid-world
midyear
mid-zone

mid-air (mid′âr′) *n.* The middle or midst of the air.

Mi·das (mī′dəs) In Greek legend, a king of Phrygia to whom Dionysus granted the power of turning whatever he touched into gold; when his food and even his daughter were thus transmuted, he prayed to have the power taken back.

mid-At·lan·tic (mid′ət·lan′tik) *n.* The middle part of the Atlantic Ocean.

mid-brain (mid′brān′) *n.* The mesencephalon.

mid-Can·a·da line (mid′kan′ə·də) A chain of radar stations in Canada along the 55th and 56th parallels, maintained by the Canadian government.

mid·day (mid′dā′) *n.* Noon.

mid·den (mid′n) *n.* **1** A kitchen midden. **2** *Brit. Dial.* A dunghill or heap of refuse. [ME *midding* <Scand. Cf. Dan. *mödding* < *mög* dung, muck + *dynge* heap (of dung).]

mid·dle (mid′l) *adj.* **1** Occupying a position equally distant from the extremes; mean. **2** Occupying any intermediate position. **3** *Gram.* In Greek and Sanskrit, designating a voice of the verb which indicates action by the subject for his own sake. See VOICE. — *n.* **1** The part or point equally distant from the extremities. ◆ Collateral adjective: *median.* **2** Something that is intermediate. **3** The middle voice. See synonyms under CENTER. — *v.t.* **·dled, ·dling** *Naut.* To fold or double in the middle. [OE *middel*]

middle age The time of life between youth and old age, commonly between 40 and 60. — **mid′dle-aged′** (-ājd′) *adj.*

Middle Ages The period in European history between classical antiquity and the Renaissance: usually regarded as extending from the downfall of Rome, in 476, to about 1450.

Middle America That part of Latin America north of South America and south of the United States; specifically, the six Central American states as well as Mexico, Cuba, Haiti, and the Dominican Republic.

Middle Atlantic States New York, New Jersey, and Pennsylvania.

mid·dle-break·er (mid′l·brā′kər) *n. Agric.* A lister. Also **mid′dle-bust′er** (-bus′tər).

mid·dle·brow (mid′l·brou′) *n.* A person who has conventional or middle-class tastes, interests, opinions, etc.

middle C *Music* The note written on the first leger line above the bass staff and the first leger line below the treble staff; also, the corresponding tone or key.

middle class The class of a society that occupies a position between the laboring class and the very wealthy or the nobility. — **mid′dle-class′** (-klas′, -kläs′) *adj.*

Middle Congo See CONGO REPUBLIC.

Middle Dutch See under DUTCH.

middle ear *Anat.* The tympanum: occasionally applied to the tympanum, the mastoid cells, and the Eustachian tube.

Middle East See under EAST.

Middle English See under ENGLISH.

Middle French See under FRENCH.

Middle High German See under GERMAN.

Middle Kingdom **1** The former Chinese Empire, regarded as occupying the center of the world: later considered as the 18 provinces of China proper. **2** A kingdom of ancient Egypt, 2400–1580 B.C., having first Heracleopolis, then Thebes, for its capital: also **Middle Empire.**

Middle Latin See MEDIEVAL LATIN under LATIN.

middle latitude The latitude midway between two places on the same hemisphere: also called *mean latitude.*

Middle Low German See under GERMAN.

mid·dle·man (mid′l·man′) *n. pl.* **·men** (-men′) **1** One who acts as an agent; one who buys in bulk from producers and resells. **2** The actor in the middle of a line of minstrel performers who propounds questions to the endmen; the interlocutor. **3** Any intermediary.

mid·dle·most (mid′l·mōst′) *adj.* **1** Situated exactly in the middle. **2** Being in the midst of; hence, very intimate. Also *midmost.*

mid·dle-of-the-road (mid′l·əv·thə·rōd′) *adj.* Tending toward neither side or extreme; moderate, especially in politics. Also **mid·dle-road·ing** (mid′l·rō′ding).

middle of the road A moderate position.

mid·dle-of-the-road·er (mid′l·əv·thə·rō′dər) *n.* One who endorses a moderate course, especially in politics. Also **mid′dle-road′er.**

mid·dle·piece (mid′l·pēs′) *n. Biol.* The part lying between the nucleus and the flagellum of a spermatozoon.

Middle Persian See under PERSIAN.

Mid·dles·brough (mid′lz·brə) A port and county borough in NE Yorkshire, England.

Mid·dle·sex (mid′l·seks) A county of SE England, comprising the NW part of London; 232 square miles.

Middle States The eastern States of the United States between New England and the South: New York, New Jersey, Pennsylvania, Delaware, and Maryland.

Middle Temple See INNS OF COURT.

Mid·dle·ton (mid′l·tən), **Arthur,** 1742–87, South Carolina patriot; signer of Declaration of Independence. — **Thomas,** 1570?–1627, English dramatist.

mid·dle·weight (mid′l·wāt′) *n.* A boxer or wrestler weighing between 147 and 160 pounds.

Middle West That section of the United States between the Rockies and the Alleghenies and north of the Ohio River and the southern borders of Kansas and Missouri: also *Midwest.* Also **middle west.** — **Middle Western**

mid·dling (mid′ling) *adj.* **1** Of middle rank, condition, size, or quality. **2** In tolerable but not good health; in fair health. — *n.* **1** *pl.* The coarser part of ground wheat, as distinguished from flour and bran: formerly used only for feed, but now manufactured into the best brand of flour, since it contains most gluten. **2** Pork or bacon cut from between the shoulder and ham of a hog. **3** A quality of cotton on which prices are based. [<MID + -LING[2]]

mid·dling·ly (mid′ling·lē) *adj.* Tolerably. Also **mid′dling.**

mid·dy (mid′ē) *n. pl.* **·dies** *Colloq.* A midshipman.

middy blouse A woman's or child's blouse not closely fitted and having a wide collar similar to that of a sailor's blouse.

Mid·gard (mid′gärd) In Norse mythology, the earth, middlemost of several worlds, and girdled by a great serpent: also spelled *Mithgarthr.* Also **Mid′garth** (-gärth). [<ON *Mithgarther* < *mithr* mid + *garthr* yard, house]

midge (mij) *n.* **1** A gnat or small fly; especially, a small, long-legged, dipterous insect of the family *Ceratopogonidae* that does not bite and has aquatic larvae. For illustration see INSECTS (injurious). **2** A small person; dwarf. [OE *mycge*]

midg·et (mij′it) *n.* **1** An extremely small person. **2** Anything very small of its kind. — *adj.* Small; diminutive. [Dim. of MIDGE]

mid·gut (mid′gut′) *n. Anat.* The primitive intestinal cavity, formed by the closure of the body walls of the embryo.

mid·i (mid′ē) *n. pl.* **mid·is** A shirt, dress, or coat with a hemline at mid-calf. [< MIDDLE]

Mi·di (mē·dē′) *French* Southern France.

Mid·i·an·ite (mid′ē·ən·īt′) *n.* One of an ancient nomadic tribe of NW Arabia, descended from **Midian,** a son of Abraham. *Gen.* xxv 2. [< Hebrew *Midhyān* name of a son of Abraham] — **Mid′i·an·it′ish** *adj.*

mi·di·nette (mē′dē·net′) *n. fem. French* A young working girl, so called because she leaves the shop at noon for lunch.

mid-i·ron (mid′ī′ərn) *n.* An iron golf club with a loft intermediate between that of the cleek and that of the mashie.

mid·land (mid′lənd) *adj.* **1** In the interior country. **2** Surrounded by the land; mediterranean. — *n.* The interior of a country.

Mid·land (mid′lənd) *n.* The dialects of Middle English spoken in London and the Midland counties of England; especially, **East Midland,** the direct predecessor of Modern English.

Mid·lands (mid′ləndz) *n. pl.* A region comprising the middle counties of England, generally coextensive with Anglo-Saxon Mercia.

Mid·lo·thi·an (mid·lō′thē·ən) A county in SE Scotland; 366 square miles; county town, Edinburgh.

mid·most (mid′mōst′) *adj.* Middlemost. — *n.*

The midmost part of anything. —*adv.* In the midst or middle. [OE *mydmest*]

mid·night (mid′nīt′) *n.* Twelve o'clock at night; the middle of the night. —*adj.* Pertaining to, occurring in, or like the middle of the night; dark.

midnight blue A very dark blue, almost black.

midnight sun The sun visible at midnight as a result of the fact that the latitude of the place from which it is viewed is greater than the polar distance of the sun, or above 66 degrees.

mid·noon (mid′no͞on′) *n.* The middle of the day; noon.

mid-point (mid′point′) *n.* A point at the middle.

Mid·rash (mid′rash, -räsh) *n. pl.* **Mid·rash·im** (mid·rash′im, -räsh′-) or **Mid·rash·oth** (mid·rash′ōth, -räsh′-) Jewish exegetical treatises on the Old Testament, dating from the 4th to the 12th century; specifically, the Haggadah. [< Hebrew, explanation]

mid·rib (mid′rib′) *n. Bot.* The primary vein, or rib, of a leaf, usually running from apex to base.

mid·riff (mid′rif) *n.* The diaphragm. [OE *midhrif* < *midd* mid + *hrif* belly]

mid·ship (mid′ship′) *adj. Naut.* At or pertaining to the middle of a vessel's hull.

mid·ship·man (mid′ship′mən) *n. pl.* **·men** (-mən) **1** A student training at the United States Naval Academy for commissioning as an officer. **2** *Brit.* In the Royal Navy: **a** An officer ranking between a naval cadet and the lowest commissioned officer. **b** Formerly, one of a class of youths performing minor duties on shipboard as training for commissioning as officers. [<*amidshipman*; so called from being amidships when on duty]

mid·ships (mid′ships) *adv.* Amidships. —*n. pl.* The midship timbers.

midst (midst) *n.* The central part; middle: often with the implication of being surrounded, beset, or hard pressed: in the *midst* of duties or dangers. See synonyms under CENTER. Compare synonyms for AMID. —**in our, your,** or **their midst** In the midst of, or among, us, you, or them. —*prep.* Amidst. —*adv.* In the middle. [OE *midd* + adverbial *-s* + intrusive or superlative *-t*]

mid·stream (mid′strēm′) *n.* The middle of a stream.

mid·sum·mer (mid′sum′ər) *n.* **1** The middle of summer. **2** Popularly, the time of the summer solstice, about June 21. —*adj.* Like, or occurring in, the middle of the summer.

mid-term (mid′tûrm′) *adj.* & *adv.* In the middle of the term. —*n.* **1** The middle of the term. **2** *Colloq.* A mid-term examination, as at a college.

mid-Vic·to·ri·an (mid′vik·tôr′ē·ən, -tō′rē-) *adj.* Of or characteristic of the middle period of Queen Victoria's reign in England, or the period approximately 1850–80. —*n.* **1** A British person belonging to this era. **2** A person of markedly Victorian ideas or tastes.

mid·way (mid′wā′, -wā′) *adj.* Being in the middle of the way or distance. —*n.* (mid′wā′) **1** The middle or the middle course. **2** The space, at a fair or exposition, assigned for the display of exhibits and along which the various amusements are situated. —*adv.* Half-way. [OE *midweg*]

Midway Islands Two islets in the North Pacific NW of Honolulu, belonging to the United States and under jurisdiction of the U.S. Navy; 2 square miles; scene of one of the decisive battles of World War II, June, 1942.

mid·week (mid′wēk′) *n.* The middle of the week. —*adj.* In the middle of the week. —**mid′week′ly** *adv.*

Mid·week (mid′wēk′) *n.* In the Society of Friends, Wednesday.

Mid·west (mid′west′) *n.* The Middle West. —**Mid′west′ern** *adj.*

Mid·west·ern·er (mid′wes′tər·nər) *n.* A person from the Middle West.

mid·wife (mid′wīf′) *n. pl.* **·wives** (-wīvz′) A woman who assists women in childbirth. [OE *mid* with + *wif* wife]

mid·wife·ry (mid′wī′fər·ē, -wif′rē) *n.* Obstetrics.

mid·win·ter (mid′win′tər) *n.* **1** The middle of winter. **2** Popularly, the winter solstice, about Dec. 21.

mid·years (mid′yirz′) *n. pl.* Examinations given in the middle of a school or college year.

mien (mēn) *n.* The external appearance or manner of a person; carriage; bearing. See synonyms under AIR[1], MANNER. ◆ Homophone: *mean.* [? Aphetic form of DEMEAN; infl. by F *mine* <Celtic (Breton) *min* beak, muzzle]

miff (mif) *Colloq. v.t.* To cause to be irritated or offended. —*v.i.* To take offense. —*n.* A huff. [Origin uncertain. Cf. G *muffen* sulk.]

mif·fy (mif′ē) *adj. Colloq.* **1** Supersensitive; easily offended. **2** Delicate: said of plants. —**mif′fi·ness** *n.*

Mig (mig) *n.* A type of jet fighter plane of the Soviet air force. [< *Mi(koyan)* and *G(urevich)*, Soviet aircraft designers] Also **MIG.**

might[1] (mīt) Past tense of MAY[1]. Both *may* and *might* are now considered subjunctives with present or future sense, the difference between the two being one of degree rather than of time. *May* implies a greater probability than *might*, the latter indicating possibility but less likelihood: He *might* be on time, but don't depend on it. As a request for permission, *might* is felt to be more hesitant in approach: *Might* we expect your reply by Tuesday? *Might* I come to dinner some evening?

might[2] (mīt) *n.* **1** Ability to do anything requiring force or power; strength. **2** The possession of great resources; intensity of will; ability. See synonyms under POWER. —**with might and main** With utmost endeavor; with one's whole strength. ◆ Homophone: *mite.* [OE *meaht, miht*]

might·i·ly (mī′tə·lē) *adv.* **1** With might; with great force, energy, or earnestness. **2** To a great degree; greatly; very much: I wanted *mightily* to go.

might·i·ness (mī′tē·nis) *n.* The state or quality of being mighty or powerful.

might·y (mī′tē) *adj.* **might·i·er, might·i·est** **1** Possessed of might; powerful; strong. **2** Of unusual bulk, consequence, etc. **3** Momentous; wonderful: a *mighty* host. See synonyms under POWERFUL. —*adv. Colloq.* Very; to a great degree; very much: a *mighty* fine person.

mi·gnon (min′yon, *Fr.* mē·nyôn′) *adj.* Delicately small; dainty. [<F <Gmc. Cf. OHG *minna* love. Doublet of MINION.] —**mi·gnonne** (min′yon, *Fr.* mē·nyôn′) *adj. fem.*

mi·gnon·ette (min′yən·et′) *n.* A North African annual plant (*Reseda odorata*) having wedge-shaped leaves, greenish, fragrant flowers with fringed petals, and bladdery seed vessels open at the top. [<F]

mi·graine (mī′grān) *n.* A form of recurrent paroxysmal headache, usually confined to one side of the head, and associated with various gastric and nervous disturbances. See MEGRIM. [<F <LL *hemicrania* <Gk. *hēmikrania* < *hēmi* half + *kranion* skull]

mi·grant (mī′grənt) *adj.* Migratory. —*n.* A migratory bird or other animal or person. [<L *migrans, -antis*, ppr. of *migrare* roam]

mi·grate (mī′grāt) *v.i.* **·grat·ed, ·grat·ing** **1** To move from one country, region, etc., to settle in another. **2** To move periodically from one region or climate to another, as birds or fish. See synonyms under EMIGRATE. [<L *migratus*, pp. of *migrare*] —**mi′gra·tor** *n.*

mi·gra·tion (mī·grā′shən) *n.* **1** The act of migrating. **2** The totality of persons or animals migrating, or the time occupied in migrating. **3** *Chem.* The removal or shifting of one or more atoms from one position in the molecule to another. **4** *Physics* The drift or movement of ions, under the influence of electromotive force, toward one or the other electrode. [<L *migratio, -onis*] —**mi·gra′tion·al** *adj.* —**mi·gra′tion·ist** *n.*

mi·gra·to·ry (mī′grə·tôr′ē, -tō′rē) *adj.* **1** Pertaining to migration. **2** Given to migrating. **3** Roving; nomadic.

Mi·guel (mē·gel′) Portuguese and Spanish form of MICHAEL. Also *Hungarian* **Mi·ha·ly** (mē′·hä·lē), *Sw.* **Mi·ka·el** (mē′kä·äl).

mi·ka·do (mi·kä′dō) *n.* The sovereign of Japan: a title used chiefly by foreigners. [<Japanese *mi* august + *kado* door]

mike (mīk) *n. Colloq.* A microphone. [Short for MICROPHONE]

Mike (mīk) Diminutive of MICHAEL.

Mi·khai·lo·vić (mē·khī′lô·vich), **Draja,** 1893–1946, Serb guerrilla leader in Yugoslavia in World War II; executed.

Mi·klós (mē′klōsh) Hungarian form of NICHOLAS.

mi·kron (mī′kron) See MICRON.

mil (mil) *n.* **1** A unit of length or diameter, equal to one thousandth of an inch or to 25.4001 microns. **2** A milliliter, or one cubic centimeter. **3** *Mil.* **a** A unit of angular measure equal to 1/6400 of a circle, or about 0.0560 degree. **b** A unit of angular measure equal to 0.001 radian. **4** A former monetary unit of Palestine, equal to one thousandth of a pound; also, the coin having this value. [<L *mille* thousand]

mi·la·dy (mi·lā′dē) *n.* An English noblewoman; a gentlewoman: a Continental term used of such a woman. Also **mi·la′di.** [<F <E *my lady*]

mil·age (mī′lij) See MILEAGE.

Mi·lan (mi·lan′, -län′, mil′ən) The second largest city of Italy, in Lombardy. *Italian* **Mi·la·no** (mē·lä′nō).

Mil·an·ese (mil′ən·ēz′, -ēs′) *adj.* Pertaining to Milan, in Italy. —*n. pl.* **·ese** A native or inhabitant of Milan; the people of Milan.

Mi·laz·zo (mē·lät′sō) A port in NE Sicily: site of ancient *Mylae.*

milch (milch) *adj.* Giving milk, as a cow. [OE *milc, meolc* milk]

milch·y (mil′chē) *adj.* Milky.

mild (mīld) *adj.* **1** Moderate in action or disposition. **2** Expressing kindness; calm. **3** Moderate in effect or degree. **4** Not of strong flavor. **5** *Metall.* Designating strong and tough but malleable steel containing only a small percentage of carbon. See synonyms under BLAND, CHARITABLE, PACIFIC. [OE *milde*] —**mild′ly** *adv.* —**mild′ness** *n.*

mild·en (mīl′dən) *v.t.* & *v.i.* To make or become mild.

mil·dew (mil′do͞o, -dyo͞o) *n.* **1** Any of a family (*Erysiphaceae*) of ascomycetous parasitic fungi that attack a great variety of plants, as hops, cherries, roses, etc. **2** A fungous disease of plants, particularly one caused by a fungus that makes a superficial downy coating on the diseased part of the host plant. **3** Any mold on walls, food, clothing, etc. —*v.t.* & *v.i.* To affect or be affected with mildew. [OE *mildēaw* honeydew] —**mil′dew·y** *adj.*

Mil·dred (mil′drid) A feminine personal name. [OE, moderate power]

mile (mīl) *n.* A measure of distance (see STATUTE MILE below) in the United States, Great Britain, and Ireland, and in all British possessions; remotely derived from the ancient Roman mile, which was about 1,620 yards or 4,860 feet. —**air mile** A nautical mile by air. —**geographical, nautical,** or **sea mile** One sixtieth of a degree of the earth's equator, or 6,080.2 feet. That of the United States is now the international nautical mile, equal to 6,076.103 feet or 1,852 meters. —**statute mile** The legal mile of the United States, Great Britain, etc., 5,280 feet, or 1,609.35 meters. [OE *mīl* <LL *milia, millia* <L *mille passuum* thousand paces]

mile·age (mī′lij) *n.* **1** The entire length or amount of anything that is or may be measured in miles, especially when stated in miles; aggregate number of miles of track, wire, etc., traversed, made, or used. **2** Compensation reckoned at so much a mile, allowed in lieu of expenses of travel. **3** The rate a mile paid by one traveling in a car, or using a car for any purpose. **4** Number of miles traveled by an automobile, etc., as estimated for each gallon of fuel used. **5** Length of service, quality of performance, etc.; use. Also spelled *milage.*

mileage ticket A ticket entitling the holder to transportation for a specific number of miles.

mil·er (mī′lər) *n.* A person or horse trained to race a mile.

Miles (mīlz) A masculine personal name. [< Gmc., warrior, or L, soldier]

Mi·le·sian (mī·lē′zhən, -shən) *adj.* Of Miletus. —*n.* A native or citizen of Miletus.

Mi·le·sian (mī·lē′zhən, -shən) *n.* **1** In ancient Irish legend, one of the sons or people of Miledh, the mythical ancestor of all the Irish, who migrated from Asia Minor and wandered, via Spain, to Ireland; hence, one of the first Celtic settlers of Ireland. **2** An Irishman.

mile·stone (mīl′stōn′) *n.* **1** A post, pillar, or stone set up to indicate distance in miles from a given point: also **mile′post′** (-pōst′). **2** An important event or turning point in a person's life.

MILESTONE
A 17th century stone, Brooklyn, N. Y.

Mi·le·tus (mī·lē′təs) An ancient port in western Asia Minor.

mil·foil (mil′foil) *n.* Yarrow. [< OF <L *millefolium* < *mille* thousand + *folium* leaf]

Mil·ford Ha·ven (mil′fərd hā′vən) A port in southern Pembroke, Wales.

Mil·haud (mē·yō′), **Darius,** 1892–1974, French composer.

mil·i·ar·i·a (mil′ē·âr′ē·ə) *n. Pathol.* An acute inflammatory disease of the sweat glands marked by an eruption of vesicles and papulae of the size of a pinpoint or larger; miliary fever; the millet-seed rash. [< NL, fem. of L *miliarius.* See MILIARY.]

mil·i·a·ri·sion (mil′ē·ə·rizh′ən) *n.* A silver coin introduced by Constantine and valued at one thousandth of the gold pound; the chief silver coin of the early Middle Ages. Also **mil′i·a·rense′** (-rens′), **mil′i·a·ren′sis** (-ren′sis). [<L *milia,* pl. of *mille* thousand]

mil·i·ar·y (mil′ē·er′ē, mil′yə·rē) *adj.* **1** Like millet seeds. **2** Accompanied by a rash of pimples the size of a millet seed. **3** *Pathol.* Designating a form of tuberculosis caused by the discharge into one or more organs of minute bacillary tubercles originating elsewhere in the body. [<L *miliarius* < *milium* millet]

Mil·i·cent (mil′ə·sənt) A feminine personal name. Also **Mil′li·cent.** [<Gmc., power to work]

mi·lieu (mē·lyœ′) *n.* Surroundings; environment. [<F <OF *mi* middle (<L *medius*) + *lieu* place <L *locus*]

mil·i·tant (mil′ə·tənt) *adj.* **1** Pertaining to conflict with opposing powers or influences. **2** Of a warlike or combative tendency; aggressive. —*n.* A combative person; a soldier. [<L *militans, -antis,* ppr. of *militare* be a soldier] —**mil′i·tan·cy** *n.* —**mil′i·tant·ly** *adv.*

mil·i·ta·rism (mil′ə·tə·riz′əm) *n.* **1** A system emphasizing and aggrandizing the military spirit and the need of constant preparation for war. **2** A desire to foster the maintenance of a powerful military position. —**mil′i·ta·rist** *n.* —**mil′i·ta·ris′tic** *adj.* —**mil′i·ta·ris′ti·cal·ly** *adv.*

mil·i·ta·rize (mil′ə·tə·rīz′) *v.t.* **·rized, ·riz·ing** **1** To imbue with militarism. **2** To convert to a military system. —**mil′i·ta·ri·za′tion** (-rə·zā′shən, -rī-) *n.*

mil·i·tar·y (mil′ə·ter′ē) *adj.* **1** Pertaining to armed forces or to warfare; martial; warlike. **2** Done or carried on by force of arms: distinguished from *civil.* See synonyms under WARLIKE. —*n.* A body of armed men or soldiers; soldiery. See synonyms under ARMY. [<F *militaire* <L *militaris* < *miles, militis* soldier] —**mil′i·tar′i·ly** *adv.*

military academy A school for boys or young men combining military training and academic education; specifically, the U. S. Military Academy at West Point, New York.

military attaché An army officer attached to his country's embassy or legation in a foreign country.

military governor An army or navy officer serving (usually temporarily) as the civil governor of a state or territory under martial law.

military intelligence **1** Information, of whatever character and however obtained, that is of military value to a country in peace or war. **2** The branch or division of a government engaged in obtaining, interpreting, and using such information.

military mast A strong mastlike structure on a warship, designed to carry a turret, observation tower, etc.

military police *Mil.* A body of soldiers charged with police duties among troops.

mil·i·tate (mil′ə·tāt) *v.i.* **·tat·ed, ·tat·ing** To have influence: with *against,* or, more rarely, *for.* [<L *militatus,* pp. of *militare* be a soldier < *miles, militis*]

mi·li·tia (mə·lish′ə) *n.* **1** A body of citizens enrolled and drilled in military organizations other than the regular military forces, and called out only in emergencies. **2** *U.S.* All able-bodied male citizens between eighteen and forty-five years of age not members of the regular military forces. —**organized militia** *U.S.* The National Guard, Organized Reserves, the Naval Reserve, and the Marine Corps Reserve. [<L, military service < *miles, militis*] —**mi·li′tia·man** (-mən) *n.*

mil·i·um (mil′ē·əm) *n. Pathol.* A skin disease characterized by small yellowish globules. [<L, millet; after the resemblance of the globules to millet seed]

Mil·i·um (mil′ē·əm) *n.* A genus of millet grass. [<NL]

milk (milk) *n.* **1** The opaque, whitish liquid secreted by the mammary glands of female mammals for the nourishment of their young; especially, cow's milk, drunk or used by human beings. ◆ Collateral adjectives: *galactic, lacteal.* **2** The sap of certain plants. **3** Any one of various emulsions. —*v.t.* **1** To draw milk from the mammary glands of. **2** To draw (milk). **3** To draw off as if by milking; extract: to *milk* sap from a tree. **4** To draw or extract something from: to *milk* someone of information. **5** To exploit; take advantage of. —*v.i.* **6** To yield milk. [OE *meolc, milc*]

milk adder The house snake.

milk-and-wa·ter (milk′ən·wô′tər, -wot′ər) *adj.* **1** Weak and vacillating; namby-pamby. **2** Mawkish; sentimental.

milk·ber·ry (milk′ber′ē) *n.* The snowberry.

milk·er (mil′kər) *n.* **1** One who or that which milks; specifically, a mechanical device for milking cows. **2** A domestic animal, especially a cow, that is milked or that gives milk.

milk fever **1** *Pathol.* A fever attending the secretion of milk about the third day after childbirth. **2** A similar disease of milk cows.

milk·fish (milk′fish′) *n. pl.* **·fish** or **·fish·es** A large, toothless, silvery fish (genus *Chanos*) allied to the herring, especially *C. chanos* of South Pacific waters.

milk leg **1** *Pathol.* A painful white swelling of the leg of a parturient woman. **2** A chronic swelling of a horse's leg, caused by inflammation of the lymphatic vessels.

milk-liv·ered (milk′liv′ərd) *adj.* Cowardly; timorous.

milk·maid (milk′mād′) *n.* A dairymaid.

milk·man (milk′man′) *n. pl.* **·men** (-men′) **1** One who delivers milk from door to door. **2** A man who milks cows.

milk of magnesia See under MAGNESIA.

Milk River A river in Canada and Montana, flowing 625 miles east to the Missouri.

milk run *U.S. Slang* In the air force, a regularly repeated mission.

milk shake A drink made of chilled, flavored milk, and sometimes ice-cream, shaken or whipped until frothy.

milk sickness *Pathol.* A disease caused by drinking the milk or eating the dairy products of cows that have fed on certain poisonous plants: marked by vomiting, intestinal disturbances, and trembling.

milk snake The house snake. Also called *milk adder.*

milk·sop (milk′sop′) *n.* An effeminate man; a sissy.

milk·stone (milk′stōn′) See GALALITH.

milk sugar The sugar contained in milk; lactose.

milk tooth A tooth of the deciduous or first dentition.

milk·vetch (milk′vech′) *n.* The ground plum: so called from the supposed increase in the secretion of milk by goats feeding upon it.

milk·weed (milk′wēd′) *n.* **1** One of a genus *(Asclepias)* of plants having a milky juice. **2** Any of several similar or related plants.

milkweed butterfly The monarch butterfly.

milk white A bluish-white color, like the color of skimmed milk.

milk·wort (milk′wûrt′) *n.* **1** Any of a genus *(Polygala)* of plants with varicolored, showy flowers: so called from the fancied property of increasing the secretion of milk in nursing women; specifically, the **orange milkwort** *(P. lutea)* of the SE United States. **2** The sea milkwort.

milk·y (mil′kē) *adj.* **milk·i·er, milk·i·est** **1** Containing or like milk. **2** Yielding milk. **3** Very mild; spiritless. **4** Containing young or spawn: said of oysters. Also spelled *milchy.* —**milk′i·ly** *adv.* —**milk′i·ness** *n.*

Milky Way *Astron.* A luminous band encircling the heavens, composed of distant stars and nebulae not separately distinguishable to the naked eye; the Galaxy.

mill[1] (mil) *n.* **1** A machine by means of which grain is ground for food. **2** Any one of various kinds of machines that transform raw material by other processes than grinding: often in combination: a *sawmill;* planing *mill.* **3** A machine for reducing to small or smaller proportions hard substances of any kind. **4** A building fitted up with the machinery requisite for a factory: often in combination: *powdermill.* **5** A hardened steel roller, bearing a design in relief, by which a printing plate or a die may be made by pressure. **6** A milling cutter. **7** *Slang* A pugilistic combat; set-to. **8** A raised or ridged edge or surface made by milling. **9** A machine for crushing or grinding vegetable substances in order to express the juice. —**to go through the mill** To receive or undergo the experiences or hardships needed to acquire a certain degree of skill or wisdom. —*v.t.* **1** To grind, shape, polish, roll, etc., in or with a mill. **2** To raise and indent the edge of (a coin). **3** To cause to move with a circular motion. **4** To beat or whip to a froth, as chocolate. **5** *Slang* To strike or thrash; beat. —*v.i.* **6** To move slowly in a circle, as cattle. **7** *Slang* To fight or box. [OE *myln, mylen* <LL *molina* <L *mola* millstone]

mill[2] (mil) *n.* **1** A thousandth part. **2** *U.S.* The thousandth part of a dollar, or the tenth part of a cent. [<L *mille* thousand]

Mill (mil), **James,** 1773–1836, Scottish historian, philosopher, and political economist. —**John Stuart,** 1806–73, English philosopher; political economist; son of the preceding.

Mil·lais (mi·lā′), **Sir John Everett,** 1829–96, English painter.

Mil·lay (mi·lā′), **Edna St. Vincent,** 1892–1950, U. S. poet.

mill·board (mil′bôrd′, -bōrd′) *n.* Heavy pasteboard used for the covers of books; imitation pressboard.

mill·cake (mil′kāk′) *n.* **1** The by-product left after the oil has been extracted from linseed. **2** The cake formed by mixing and pressing together the materials of gunpowder previous to granulation.

mill car A railroad flat car upon which heavy hoisting apparatus is mounted.

mill cinder The slag from the puddling furnaces of a steel-rolling mill.

mill·dam (mil′dam′) *n.* **1** A barrier thrown across a watercourse to raise its level sufficiently to turn a millwheel. **2** The pond formed by such a barrier.

milled (mild) *adj.* **1** Passed through, cut by, or mixed in a mill. **2** Having the edges fluted or grooved: said of coins.

mil·le·fi·o·ri (mil′ə·fē·ôr′ē, -ō′rē) *n. Italian* An ancient mosaic glass, later made in Venice, having a flowerlike pattern; literally, a thousand flowers.

mil·le·nar·i·an (mil′ə·nâr′ē·ən) *adj.* Of or pertaining to a thousand; specifically, relating to the millennium. —*n.* One who believes in the millennium. —**mil′le·nar′i·an·ism** *n.*

mil·le·nar·y (mil′ə·ner′ē) *adj.* Of or pertaining to a thousand; millenarian; millennial. —*n. pl.* **·nar·ies** **1** The space of a thousand years; the millennium. **2** A millenarian. [<LL *millenarius* <L *milleni* a thousand each < *mille* thousand]

mil·len·ni·al (mi·len′ē·əl) *adj.* Of or pertaining to the millennium or to any period of a thousand years. —*n.* A thousandth anniversary. —**mil·len′ni·al·ist** *n.* —**mil·len′ni·al·ly** *adv.*

mil·len·ni·um (mi·len′ē·əm) *n. pl.* **·ni·a** (-ē·ə) **1** A period of a thousand years. **2** The thousand years of the kingdom of Christ on earth. *Rev.* xx 1–5. **3** Hence, by extension, any period of happiness, beneficial government or the like. [<NL < *mille* thousand + *annus* year]

mil·le·ped (mil′ə·ped), **mil·le·pede** (mil′ə·pēd) See MILLIPEDE.

mil·le·pore (mil′ə·pôr, -pōr) *n. Zool.* A coral-like hydrozoan (genus *Millepora*) with numerous cavities in the enclosing and often bulky limestone structure. Also **mil·lep·o·ra** (mə·lep′ər·ə). [<F *millépore* < *mille* thousand + *pore* pore]

mill·er (mil′ər) *n.* **1** One who keeps or tends a mill, particularly a gristmill. **2** A milling machine. **3** A mothmiller.

Mil·ler (mil′ər), **Arthur,** born 1915, U. S. playwright. — **Henry,** born 1891, U. S. author. — **Joaquin** Pseudonym of Cincinnatus Heine Miller, 1839–1913, U. S. poet. — **Joe,** 1684–1738, English comedian: real name *Josias Miller.* — **William,** 1782–1849, U. S. Adventist; founder of the Millerites.

Mille·rand (mēl·räṅ′), **Alexandre,** 1859–1943, French statesman; president 1920–24.

mil·ler·ite (mil′ər·īt) *n.* A metallic, brass-yellow, brittle nickel sulfide, NiS, crystallizing in the hexagonal system. [after W. H. *Miller,* 1801–80, English mineralogist]

Mil·ler·ite (mil′ər·īt) *n.* A follower of William Miller, who announced in 1831 that Christ's second coming and the end of the world would be in 1843. — **Mil′ler·ism** *n.*

miller's thumb A small, fresh-water fish (family *Cottidae*) with broad, flattened head and spiny fins.

Mil·les (mil′əs), **Carl,** 1875–1955, Swedish sculptor active in the United States.

mil·les·i·mal (mi·les′ə·məl) *adj.* Pertaining to thousandths. — *n.* A thousandth. [<L *millesimus* < *mille* thousand]

mil·let (mil′it) *n.* **1** A grass *(Panicum miliaceum),* or its seed, cultivated in the United States for forage, but in the Old World from earliest times, and still in some parts of Europe, as a cereal. **2** One of various other grasses, or their seed, as the **foxtail** or **Italian millet** *(Setaria italica),* **pearl millet** *(Pennisetum glaucum),* etc. [<F, dim. of *mil* <L *milium*]

Mil·let (mē·le′), **Jean François,** 1814–75, French artist.

mill finish A surface finish produced on sheet and plate steel characteristic of the ground finish that is present on the rollers used in fabrication.

mill·hand (mil′hand′) *n.* A worker in a mill.

milli– *combining form* **1** A thousand: *millipede.* **2** In the metric and other systems of measurement, the thousandth part of (a specified unit):

milliampere	**millicurie**	**millilux**
milliangstrom	**millifarad**	**milliphot**
milliare	**millihenry**	**millistere**
millibar	**millilambert**	**millivolt**

[<L *mille* a thousand]

mil·liard (mil′yərd) *n.* A thousand millions; usually, in the United States, called a billion. [<F <Pg. *milhar* thousand]

mil·li·ar·y (mil′ē·er′ē) *adj.* Pertaining to a Roman mile. — *n. pl.* **·ar·ies** A Roman milestone, set up at intervals of 1,000 paces. [<L *milliarius*]

mil·lier (mē·lyā′) *n.* A metric ton, 1,000 kilograms. [<F]

mil·li·gram (mil′ə·gram) *n.* The thousandth part of a gram. See METRIC SYSTEM. Also **mil′·li·gramme.** [<F *milligramme*]

Mil·li·kan (mil′ə·kən), **Robert Andrews,** 1868–1955, U. S. physicist.

mil·li·li·ter (mil′ə·lē′tər) *n.* The thousandth part of a liter. See METRIC SYSTEM. Also **mil′·li·li′tre.** [<F *millilitre*]

mil·li·me·ter (mil′ə·mē′tər) *n.* The thousandth part of a meter. See METRIC SYSTEM. Also **mil′·li·me′tre.** [<F *millimètre*]

mil·li·mi·cron (mil′ə·mī′kron) *n.* A thousandth of a micron, or a millionth of a millimeter; also, ten angstroms (symbol m, also μ).

mil·li·mol (mil′ə·mol) *n.* The thousandth part of a mol. Also **mil′li·mole** (-mōl). [<MILLI- + MOL]

mil·line (mil·līn′) *n.* The rate of cost for placing an advertisement of one agate line before a million readers. [<MILL(ION) + LINE]

mil·li·ner (mil′ə·nər) *n.* **1** A person employed in making, trimming, or selling bonnets, women's hats, etc. **2** *Obs.* A dealer in small wares: a haberdasher. [<*Milaner* an inhabitant of Milan, in Italy; hence, a man from Milan who imported silks and the like]

mil·li·ner·y (mil′ə·ner′ē, -nər·ē) *n.* **1** The articles made or sold by milliners. **2** The occupation or establishment of a milliner. [<MILLINER]

mill·ing (mil′ing) *n.* **1** The operating of a mill or mills, as in the grinding of meal or metals, the preparation of cloth, etc. **2** A milled surface, as of a coin, or the act or process of producing it: distinguished from *reeding.* **3** The slow, round-and-round motion of or as of a herd of cattle. [<MILL, *v.*]

mil·lion (mil′yən) *n.* **1** The cardinal number equivalent to ten hundred thousand or to a thousand thousand, or the symbols (1,000,000) representing it; ten to the sixth power. **2** Elliptically, a thousand thousand of the ordinary units of account, as dollars, francs, or pounds: He is worth a *million.* **3** An indefinitely great number. — **the million** The common people. [<OF <Ital. *millione* (now *milione*), aug. of *mille* thousand]

mil·lion·aire (mil′yən·âr′) *n.* One whose possessions are valued at a million or more, as of dollars, pounds, etc. Also **mil′lion·naire′.** [<F *millionaire*]

mil·lion·fold (mil′yən·fōld′) *adj.* A million times the quantity. — *adv.* In a millionfold proportion; a million times in amount: with the indefinite article *a,* construed as a plural.

mil·lionth (mil′yənth) *adj.* **1** Being last in a series of a million: an ordinal numeral. **2** Being one of a million equal parts: a *millionth* part. — *n.* One part in a million equal parts; one divided by one million.

mil·li·pede (mil′ə·pēd) *n.* A herbivorous, slow-moving arthropod (class *Diplopoda*) having a rounded body marked by numerous segments, from nearly all of which issue two pairs of appendages: also spelled *milleped, millepede.* Also **mil′li·ped** (-ped). [<L *millepeda* < *mille* thousand + *pes, pedis* foot]

mill·pond (mil′pond′) *n.* **1** A body of water dammed up to run a mill. **2** A body of water adjoining a sawmill where logs are floated until sawn.

mill·race (mil′rās′) *n.* The sluice through which the water runs to a millwheel.

mill·run (mil′run′) *n.* **1** A millrace. **2** A certain amount of ore tested for content or quality by the process of milling. **3** The mineral yielded by the test.

mill-run (mil′run′) *adj.* Average; just as it comes from the mill; not selected: also *run-of-the-mill.*

Mills bomb (milz) A highly explosive grenade weighing about 1 1/2 pounds and usually thrown by hand. Also **Mills grenade.** [after Sir Wm. *Mills,* 1856–1932, British inventor]

mill·stone (mil′stōn′) *n.* **1** One of a pair of thick, heavy, stone disks for grinding something, as grain. **2** That which pulverizes or bears down. **3** A heavy or burdensome weight. *Matt.* xvii 6.

mill town A town whose center of activity is a mill or group of mills, and whose population is employed, for the most part, in the mill or mills.

mill·wheel (mil′hwēl′) *n.* The waterwheel that drives a mill.

mill·work (mil′wûrk′) *n.* Carpentry work delivered from a mill ready for installation or use.

mill·wright (mil′rīt′) *n.* One who plans, builds, or fits out mills; also, a machinist who sets up shafting, etc.

Milne (miln), **A(lan) A(lexander),** 1882–1956, English playwright, novelist, and writer of children's books.

Mil·ner (mil′nər), **Sir Alfred,** 1854–1925, first Viscount Milner; British administrator in South Africa.

mi·lo (mī′lō) *n.* A non-saccharin sorghum similar to millet. [<Bantu *maili*]

Mi·lo (mī′lō) A renowned Greek athlete, about 520 B.C.

Mi·lo (mē′lō) The southwesternmost island in the Cyclades group; 61 square miles: also *Melos.* Also **Mi′los** (-lôs).

mil·o·maize (mil′ō·māz) *n.* See MILO.

mi·lord (mi·lôrd′) *n.* An English nobleman; a gentleman: a Continental term used of such a man. [<F <E *my lord*]

Milque·toast (milk′tōst) See CASPAR MILQUETOAST.

mil·reis (mil′rās) *n.* **1** A former Brazilian monetary unit, equivalent to 1,000 reis. **2** A former Portuguese monetary unit, superseded in 1911 by the escudo. [<Pg., lit., a thousand reis]

milt[1] (milt) *n.* The spleen. [OE *milte* spleen]

milt[2] (milt) *n.* **1** The sperm of a fish. **2** The spermatic organs of a fish when filled with seminal fluid; the soft roe. — *v.t.* To impregnate (fish roe) with milt. [OE *milte*]

milt·er (mil′tər) *n.* **1** A male fish. **2** The milt of a fish.

Mil·ti·a·des (mil·tī′ə·dēz) Athenian general; defeated the Persians at Marathon, 490 B.C.

Mil·ton (mil′tən), **John,** 1608–74, English poet.

Mil·ton·ic (mil·ton′ik) *adj.* Of, pertaining to, or like the poet Milton or his works or style; sublime; majestic. Also **Mil·to′ni·an** (-tō′nē·ən).

Mil·town (mil′toun) *n.* Proprietary name for a synthetic drug used in pill form as a tranquilizer.

Mil·wau·kee (mil·wô′kē) A port on Lake Michigan in SE Wisconsin.

Mil·yu·kov (mē·lyo͞o′kôf), **Pavel Nikolaevich,** 1859–1943, Russian politician and historian.

mim (mim) *Brit. Dial.* Demure; precise. [Imit.]

mime (mīm) *n.* **1** A mimic play or farce or the dialog for this; a dramatic representation, akin to comedy, mimicking real persons or events: a favorite amusement among the Greeks and Romans. **2** An actor in a mime; hence, a mimic; clown, buffoon. — *v.* **mimed, mim·ing** *v.t.* To mimic; imitate. — *v.i.* To play the mimic; play a part with gestures and usually without words. [<L *mimus* <Gk. *mimos*] — **mim′er** *n.*

Mim·e·o·graph (mim′ē·ə·graf′, -gräf′) *n.* An apparatus in which a thin fibrous paper coated with paraffin is used as a stencil for reproducing copies of written or typewritten matter: a trade name. — *v.t.* To reproduce by means of a Mimeograph. [<Gk. *mimeisthai* imitate + -GRAPH]

mi·me·sis (mi·mē′sis, mī-) *n.* **1** Imitation or representation of the supposed speech, characteristic dialect, carriage, or gestures of an individual or a people, as in art and literature. **2** *Biol.* Mimicry. [<NL <Gk. *mimēsis* imitation]

mi·met·ic (mi·met′ik, mī-) *adj.* **1** Quick to mimic; imitative. **2** Relating to mimicry or mimesis. **3** Mimic (*adj.* def. 1). Also **mi·met′i·cal.** [<Gk. *mimētikos*] — **mi·met′i·cal·ly** *adv.*

mim·ic (mim′ik) *v.t.* **·icked, ·ick·ing** **1** To imitate the speech or actions of, as in ridicule. **2** To copy closely; ape. **3** To have or assume the color, shape, etc., of; simulate: Some insects *mimic* leaves. See synonyms under IMITATE. — *n.* **1** One who is given to mimicry; a mimic actor; buffoon. **2** A copy; imitation. — *adj.* **1** Of the nature of mimicry; imitative; mimetic: a *mimic* gesture. **2** Copying the real; simulated; mock: a *mimic* court. [<L *mimicus* <Gk. *mimikos* < *mimos* mime] — **mim′i·cal** *adj.* — **mim′ick·er** *n.*

mim·ic·ry (mim′ik·rē) *n. pl.* **·ries** **1** The act of imitating, especially for sport; also, a thing produced as a copy. **2** *Zool.* An imitative superficial resemblance in one animal to another or to its immediate environment, for purposes of concealment or protection. Compare PROTECTIVE COLORATION. See synonyms under CARICATURE.

Mi·mir (mē′mir) In Norse mythology, the giant who kept the **Mi·mis·brun·nen** (mē′mis·bro͝on′·ən), or well of wisdom, flowing from the root of Ygdrasil, and for a draft from which Odin bartered his eye. Also **Mi′mer.**

mi·mo·sa (mi·mō′sə, -zə) *n.* **1** Any plant of a large genus *(Mimosa)* of tropical herbs, shrubs, or trees of the bean family, with feathery, bipinnate foliage, and clusters of small flowers; especially, the sensitive plant. **2** A light yellow: the color of certain varieties of mimosa. [<NL <L *mimus* mime; from its supposed mimicry of animal life] — **mim·o·sa·ceous** (mim′ō·sā′shəs, mī′mō-) *adj.*

Min (min) **1** A river in Fukien province, China, flowing 350 miles SE to the China Sea. **2** A river in Szechwan province, China, flowing 500 miles south to the Yangtze.

min′ (mīn) *v.* & *n. Scot.* Mind.

mi·na[1] (mī′nə) *n. pl.* **·nae** (-nē) or **·nas** An ancient Greek and Asian weight or sum of money, equal to 100 drachmas. [<L <Gk. *mna*]

mi·na[2] (mī′nə) See MYNA. Also **mi′nah.**

mi·na·cious (mi·nā′shəs) *adj.* Threatening; of a menacing character. [<L *minax, minacis.* See MENACE.] — **mi·na′cious·ly** *adv.* — **mi·na′·cious·ness, mi·nac·i·ty** (mi·nas′ə·tē) *n.*

min·a·ret (min′ə·ret′) *n.* A high, slender tower attached to a Moslem mosque, surrounded by one or more balconies, from which is sounded the stated summons to prayer. [<Sp. *minarete* <Turkish *manārat* <Arabic *manārah* lamp, lighthouse <*minār* candlestick]

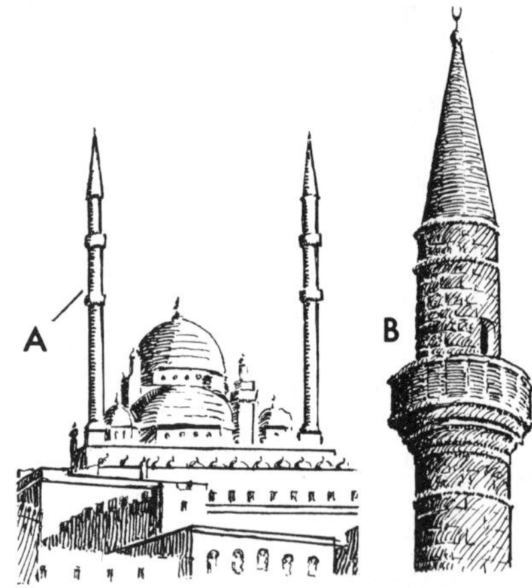

MINARET
A. Shown in relation to mosque.
B. Detail showing the balcony.

Mi·nas Basin (mī′nəs) The NE arm of the Bay of Fundy, Nova Scotia; connected by the **Minas Channel** (24 miles long) with the Bay of Fundy.

Mi·nas de Rí·o·tin·to (mē′näs thā rē′ō·tēn′tō) A town in SW Spain; site of copper mines since Roman times: also **Ríotinto.**

Mi·nas Ge·rais (mē′nəzh zhə·rīs′) An inland state in eastern Brazil; 224,701 square miles; capital, Bello Horizonte. Formerly **Minas Geraes.**

min·a·to·ry (min′ə·tôr′ē, -tō′rē) *adj.* Threatening, as with destruction or punishment. Also **min′a·to′ri·al.** [<OF *minatoire* <LL *minatorius* <*minatus,* pp. of *minari* threaten] — **min′a·to′ri·al·ly, min′a·to′ri·ly** *adv.*

mince (mins) *v.* **minced, minc·ing** *v.t.* **1** To cut or chop into small bits, as meat. **2** To subdivide minutely. **3** To diminish the force or strength of; moderate: He didn't *mince* words with her. **4** To say or do with affected primness or elegance. — *v.i.* **5** To walk with short steps or affected daintiness. **6** To speak or behave with affected primness. — *n.* **1** Mincemeat. **2** *Rare* An affectation. [<OF *mincier*; ult. <L *minuere* lessen, make smaller] — **minc′er** *n.* — **minc′ing·ly** *adv.*

minced oath (minst) A mild or weak oath: "Egad" is a *minced oath.*

mince·meat (mins′mēt′) *n.* **1** Meat chopped very fine. **2** A mixture of chopped meat, fruit, spices, etc., used in mince pie.

mince pie A pie made of mincemeat.

minc·ing-horse (min′sing·hôrs′) *n.* A heavy block of hardwood usually mounted on legs, used for chopping meats or vegetables.

minc·ing-spade (min′sing·spād′) *n.* A knife-edged spade used in whaling, for chopping or mincing blubber.

Min·cio (mēn′chō) A river in northern Italy, flowing 115 miles from Lake Garda to the Po. Ancient **Min·cius** (min′shəs).

mind (mīnd) *n.* **1** The aggregate of all conscious and unconscious processes originating in and associated with the brain, especially those pertaining to cognition, intelligence, and intellect. **2** Memory; remembrance: to bear in *mind.* **3** Opinion; way of thinking: to change one's *mind.* **4** Desire; inclination: to have a *mind* to leave. **5** Mental disposition, character, or temper: a liberal *mind*; a cheerful *mind.* **6** Intellectual power or capacity. **7** The faculty of cognition and intellect, as opposed to the will and emotions: a noble heart and a cultivated *mind.* **8** A person, regarded as having intellect: the great *minds* of our time. **9** Sanity; sound mentality: to lose one's *mind.* **10** *Philos.* The spirit of intelligence pervading the universe: opposed to *matter.* **11** In Christian Science, God: also **Divine Mind.** — **a month's mind** The monthly commemoration, usually the first, of a person's death. — **on one's mind** Occupying one's thoughts. — **to speak one's mind** To declare one's opinions freely or candidly. — **to take one's mind off** To turn one's thoughts from. — *v.t.* **1** To pay attention to; occupy oneself with: *Mind* your own business. **2** To be careful or wary concerning: *Mind* your step. **3** To give heed to, as commands; obey. **4** To care for; tend. **5** To be concerned about; regard with annoyance; dislike: Do you *mind* the noise? **6** To be aware of; notice; perceive. **7** *Colloq.* To remember: sometimes used reflexively. **8** *Archaic* To remind. **9** *Obs.* To intend; purpose. — *v.i.* **10** To pay attention; take notice; watch. **11** To be obedient. **12** To be concerned; care: I don't *mind.* **13** To be careful. [OE *gemynd*] — **mind′er** *n.*

Synonyms (noun): brain, consciousness, disposition, instinct, intellect, intelligence, reason, sense, soul, spirit, thought, understanding. *Mind* includes all the powers of sentient being apart from the physical factors in bodily faculties and activities; in a limited sense, *mind* is nearly synonymous with *intellect,* but includes *disposition,* or the tendency toward action, as appears in the phrase "to have a *mind* to work." The *intellect* is that assemblage of faculties which is concerned with knowledge, as distinguished from emotion and volition. *Understanding* is chiefly used of the reasoning powers: the *understanding* is distinguished by many philosophers from *reason* in that *reason* is the faculty of the high cognitions or a priori truth. *Thought,* the act, process, or power of thinking, is often used to denote the thinking faculty, and especially the *reason.* The *instinct* of animals is held to be of the same nature as the *intellect* of man, but inferior and limited; yet the apparent difference is very great. Human *instincts* denote tendencies independent of reasoning or instruction. As the seat of mental activity, *brain* is often used as a synonym for *mind, intellect, intelligence. Sense* is used as denoting clear mental action, good judgment, acumen; as, He is a man of *sense,* or, he showed good *sense. Consciousness* includes all that a sentient being perceives, knows, thinks, or feels, from whatever source. See GENIUS, SOUL, UNDERSTANDING. *Antonyms*: body, brawn, matter.

Min·da·na·o (min′də·nä′ō) The southernmost and second largest island in the Philippines; 36,537 square miles.

Mindanao Sea Part of the Pacific bounded by Mindanao to the south and by Leyte, Bohol, Cebu, and Negros to the north.

mind-blind·ness (mīnd′blīnd′nis) *n.* Mental blindness.

mind-cure (mīnd′kyŏŏr′) *n.* **1** The treatment and cure of disease, especially of neuroses, by direct influence upon the mind of the patient and without the use of drugs. **2** Psychotherapy.

mind-deaf·ness (mīnd′def′nis) *n.* Mental deafness.

mind·ed (mīn′did) *adj.* **1** Disposed. **2** Having a specified kind of mind: evil-*minded.*

Min·del (min′dəl) See GLACIAL EPOCH.

mind·ful (mīnd′fəl) *adj.* Keeping in mind; heeding; having knowledge (of); aware. See synonyms under THOUGHTFUL. — **mind′ful·ly** *adv.* — **mind′ful·ness** *n.*

mind·less (mīnd′lis) *adj.* **1** Devoid of intelligence. **2** Not giving heed or attention; careless. — **mind′less·ly** *adv.* — **mind′less·ness** *n.*

Min·do·ro (min·dō′rō) An island in the central Philippines; 3,759 square miles.

mind-read·ing (mīnd′rē′ding) *n.* **1** The ascertaining of the thoughts or purpose of some other mind by the interpretation of voluntary or involuntary muscle movements or facial expressions. **2** Telepathy. — **mind′-read′er** *n.*

Mind·szen·ty (mind′sen·tē) **Joseph,** born 1892, Hungarian Roman Catholic cardinal, imprisoned by the Nazis in 1944 and by the Communist regime in Hungary 1948–56.

mine[1] (mīn) *n.* **1** An excavation for digging out some useful product, as ore or coal. **2** Any deposit of such material suitable for excavation. **3** An underground tunnel dug beneath an enemy's fortifications, as for the placement of an explosive charge. **4** A case containing such a charge buried in the earth, or floating on or near, or anchored beneath, the surface of the water. **5** Any productive source of supply. **6** A burrow made by an insect. — **bounding mine** A land mine set just beneath the surface of the ground and designed to rise a few feet in the air before exploding its charge of shrapnel and fragments. — **land mine** A high-explosive or chemical mine, actuated by the weight of a person, troops, or vehicles. — *v.* **mined, min·ing** *v.t.* **1** To dig (coal, ores, etc.) from the earth. **2** To dig into (the earth, etc.) for coal, ores, etc. **3** To make by digging, as a tunnel; burrow. **4** To dig a tunnel under, as for placing an explosive mine; sap. **5** To attack or destroy by slow or secret means; undermine. **6** To place an explosive mine or mines in or under: to *mine* a harbor. — *v.i.* **7** To dig in a mine for coal, ores, etc.; work in a mine. **8** To make a tunnel, etc., by digging; burrow. **9** To place explosive mines. [<OF <Celtic. Cf. Irish *mein* vein of metal.] — **min′er** *n.*

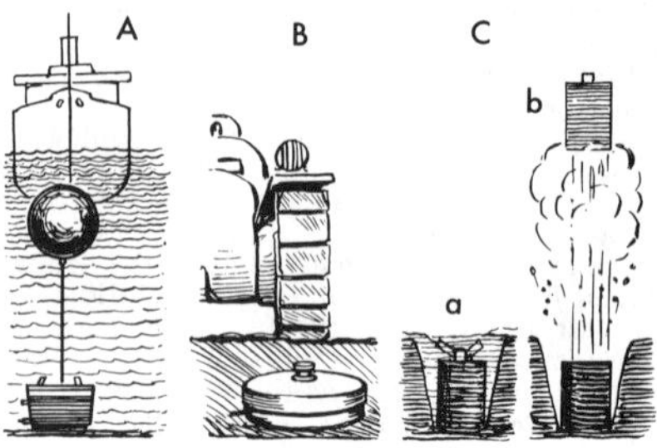

MINES
A. Marine mine anchored in harbor entrance.
B. Buried anti-tank mine.
C. Anti-personnel mine (*a*); inner canister rises and explodes (*b*).

mine[2] (mīn) *pron.* **1** The possessive case of *I* employed predicatively; belonging or pertaining to me: That book is *mine.* **2** The things or persons belonging or pertaining to me: His work is better than *mine*; Fortune has been good to me and *mine.* — **of mine** Belonging or relating to me; my: the double possessive. — *pronominal adj. Archaic* My: *mine* eyes. [OE *mīn*]

mine detector An electromagnetic instrument for detecting the presence and locating the position of mines.

mine field An area in water or on land systematically planted with mines.

mine layer An auxiliary naval vessel, of submarine or surface type, provided with special equipment for the laying of mines.

min·er·al (min′ər·əl) *n.* **1** A naturally occurring, homogeneous substance or material formed by inorganic processes and having a characteristic set of physical properties, a definite range of chemical composition, and a molecular structure usually expressed in crystalline forms. **2** Any inorganic substance, as ore, a rock, or a fossil. — **accessory minerals** Those components or minerals forming so small a part of a rock or occurring so rarely as not to be included in its description. — *adj.* **1** Pertaining to, consisting of, or resembling minerals. **2** Impregnated with mineral constituents. [<OF <Med. L *minerale,* neut. sing. of *mineralis* of a mine <*minera* a mine]

mineral butter *Chem.* Antimony trichloride, $SbCl_3$, a colorless, translucent, poisonous, crystalline substance: used as a mordant and reagent, and in the manufacture of certain dyes.

mineral carbon Graphite.

mineral charcoal A pulverulent substance showing patterned traces of vegetable origin but consisting mainly of carbon: it occurs in thin layers in bituminous coal.

min·er·al·ize (min′ər·əl·īz′) *v.* **·ized, ·iz·ing** *v.t.* **1** To convert from a metal to a mineral, as iron to rust. **2** To convert to a mineral substance; petrify. **3** To impregnate with minerals or other inorganic substances. — *v.i.* **4** To observe, study, and collect minerals. Also **min·er·al·o·gize** (min′ə·ral′ə·jīz), *Brit.* **min′er·al·ise′.** — **min′er·al·i·za′tion** *n.*

min·er·al·iz·er (min′ər·əl·īz′ər) *n.* **1** An element that combines with a metal to form an ore, as sulfur. **2** A volatile or other substance, as boron or water, that facilitates the recrystallization of rocks.

mineral jelly See PETROLATUM.

mineral kingdom The great division of nature

which comprises all inorganic and non-living materials, as rocks, metals, minerals, etc. Compare ANIMAL KINGDOM, VEGETABLE KINGDOM.

min·er·al·o·gy (min′ə·ral′ə·jē) *n.* The science of minerals. **—min′er·a·log′i·cal** (-ər·ə·loj′i·kəl) *adj.* **—min′er·a·log′i·cal·ly** *adv.* **—min′·er·al′o·gist** *n.*

mineral oil Any of various oils derived from inorganic matter, especially petroleum and its products: used as a fuel, in medicine as a laxative, etc.

mineral pitch Asphalt.

mineral tar Maltha.

mineral water Any natural water containing one or more minerals in solution, especially one impregnated with salts or gases having therapeutic properties.

mineral wax Ozocerite.

mineral wool A fibrous, fluffy material resembling wool in appearance, and made by subjecting molten silicate, molten slag, or other similar materials to a steam blast and cooling rapidly to prevent crystallization: used as packing and as an insulator: also called *rock wool, slag wool.* Compare GLASSWOOL.

Mi·ner·va (mi·nûr′və) In Roman mythology, the goddess of wisdom, handicraft, and technical dexterity: identified with Greek *Athena.*

min·e·stro·ne (min′ə·strō′nē) *n.* A thick vegetable soup containing vermicelli, barley, etc., in a meat broth.

mine sweeper 1 A naval vessel equipped for the detection, destruction, and removal of marine mines. **2** A heavy roller attached to the front of a tank for exploding land mines.

mine thrower A trench mortar.

Ming (ming) *n.* In Chinese history, the last ruling dynasty (1368–1644) of truly Chinese origin: noted for the artistic works, as porcelains, produced during its rule. [<Chinese, lit., luminous]

min·gle (ming′gəl) *v.* **min·gled, min·gling** *v.t.* **1** To mix or unite together; blend. **2** To join or combine; bring into close relation. *—v.i.* **3** To be or become mixed, united, or closely joined. **4** To enter into company; mix or associate, as with a crowd. **5** To take part; become involved, as in a dispute. See synonyms under MIX. [<Freq. of OE *mengan*] **—min′gler** *n.*

Min·how (min′hō′) A former name for FOOCHOW.

min·i (min′ē) *n. pl.* **min·is 1** A miniskirt. **2** *Colloq.* Anything smaller or shorter than others of its class. *—adj.* **·i·er, ·i·est** Very small or miniaturized. [<MINI-]

mini- *combining form* Small; tiny: *miniskirt.* [<L *minimus* least, smallest]

min·i·a·ture (min′ē·ə·chər, min′ə·chər) *n.* **1** A painting of small dimensions and delicate workmanship, usually a portrait, or the art of executing such paintings on ivory, metal, or vellum, in water-colors or oils. **2** A portrayal of anything on a small scale; hence, reduced dimensions or extent. **3** *Obs.* Lettering in red; rubrication, as of medieval manuscripts. See synonyms under PICTURE. *—adj.* Much smaller than reality; very small. [<F <Ital. *miniatura* <Med. L <L *miniare* paint red <*minium* red lead, ? <Iberian; later infl. in meaning by L *minuere* lessen]

min·i·a·tur·ize (min′ē·ə·chər·īz′, min′ə·chər·īz′) *v.t.* **·ized, ·iz·ing** To reduce the size of, as the parts of an instrument or machine. **—min′·i·a·tur′i·za′tion** *n.*

min·i·bike (min′ē·bīk′) *n.* A small motorcycle with a single seat.

min·i·cam (min′ə·kam) *n.* A small, portable camera, usually one using 35-mm. film.

min·i·com·put·er (min′ē·kəm·pyōō′tər) *n.* A small, inexpensive electronic computer.

Min·i·é ball (min′ē·ā, min′ē; *Fr.* mē·nyā′) A conical rifle ball with hollow base and a plug driven in by the explosion of the charge to expand the lead and fill the grooves of the rifling: formerly used in the **Minié rifle,** specially designed for it. [after Capt. Claude Etienne *Minié,* 1814–79, French inventor]

min·i·fy (min′ə·fī) *v.t.* **·fied, ·fy·ing 1** To make small or less. **2** To lessen the worth or importance of. [<L *minor* less + -FY]

min·i·kin (min′ə·kin) *adj. Obs.* Of small size or delicate form. *—n. Rare* Something very minute or delicate, as the smallest size of pin. [<Du. *minneken,* dim. of *minne* love]

min·im (min′im) *n.* **1** An apothecaries' fluid measure; roughly, one drop, or one sixtieth of a fluid dram: in the United States, 0.06 cubic centimeter; in England, 0.059 cubic centimeter. **2** *Music* A half note. **3** An extremely small creature; a pigmy. **4** A down-stroke in writing, as in forming the letter *n.* **5** *Printing* A size of type, about 7-point, between nonpareil and brevier. — *adj.* Extremely small. [<F *minime* <L *minimus* least, smallest. Doublet of MINIMUM.] — **min′i·mal** *adj.*

Min·i·mal·ist (min′ə·məl·ist) *n.* One belonging to the more conservative branch of the former Russian Social Democrats: distinguished from *Maximalist.*

min·i·mize (min′ə·mīz) *v.t.* **·mized, ·miz·ing 1** To reduce to the smallest possible amount or degree. **2** To regard or represent at a minimum. Also *Brit.* **min′i·mise. —min′i·miz′er** *n.* — **min′i·mi·za′tion** *n.*

min·i·mum (min′ə·məm) *adj.* Consisting of or showing the least possible amount or degree; being a minimum. *—n. pl.* **·ma** (-mə) or **·mums 1** The least possible quantity, amount, or degree. **2** A value of a function that is less than any value which immediately precedes and follows it. **3** The lowest degree, variation, etc., as of temperature, recorded. [<L, neut. of *minimus.* Doublet of MINIM.] **—min′i·mal** *adj.*

minimum wage 1 A wage fixed by law or agreement as the smallest amount an employer may offer an employee in a specific group. **2** A living wage.

min·ing (mī′ning) *n.* **1** The act, process, or business of extracting coal, ores, etc., from mines. **2** The act of laying explosive mines.

mining camp A temporary settlement around or near a mine.

min·ion (min′yən) *n.* **1** A servile favorite or follower: a term of contempt. **2** *Printing* A size of type, about 7-point. **3** A saucy girl or woman; minx. **4** *Obs.* One who is beloved; a paramour. — *adj. Rare* Dainty; delicate; fine. [<F *mignon.* Doublet of MIGNON.]

min·i·scule (min′əs·kyōōl) *adj.* Minuscule.

min·ish (min′ish) *v.t.* & *v.i. Obs.* To make or become less; diminish. [<F *menuisier* make small <L *minutus,* pp. of *minuere* lessen]

min·i·skirt (min′i·skûrt′) *n.* A short skirt worn by women with the hemline well above the knee. Also **min′i-skirt′.** [<MINI- + SKIRT]

min·is·ter (min′is·tər) *n.* **1** The chief of an executive department of a government. **2** One commissioned to represent his government in diplomatic intercourse with another government. **3** One who is authorized to preach the gospel and administer the ordinances of the church; a clergyman. **4** One who acts in subservience to the will of another; a servant; agent. **5** One who promotes or dispenses. *—v.i.* **1** To give attendance or aid; provide for the wants or needs of someone. **2** To be conducive; contribute. *—v.t.* **3** To administer or apply. **4** *Archaic* To supply; furnish. See synonyms under SERVE. [<OF *ministre* <L *minister* an attendant <*minor* less; after L *magister* master <*magis* greater]

min·is·te·ri·al (min′is·tir′ē·əl) *adj.* **1** Of or pertaining to a minister of the gospel or the ministry; clerical. **2** Of or pertaining to a minister or executive staff in civil government. **3** *Law* Pertaining to an act or duty performed according to the mandate of legal authority, so that the agent is not accountable for its propriety or consequences: opposed to *judicial.* **4** Instrumental; causative. [<F *ministériel*] **—min′is·te′ri·al·ly** *adv.*

min·is·te·ri·al·ist (min′is·tir′ē·əl·ist) *n.* In English politics, one who supports the ministry.

minister plenipotentiary See PLENIPOTENTIARY.

minister resident See under RESIDENT.

min·is·trant (min′is·trənt) *adj.* Ministering. *—n.* One who ministers. [<L *ministrans, -antis,* ppr. of *ministrare* serve]

min·is·tra·tion (min′is·trā′shən) *n.* **1** The act of performing service as a minister. **2** Any religious ceremonial. [<L *ministratio, -onis*] — **min′is·tra′tive** *adj.*

min·is·try (min′is·trē) *n. pl.* **·tries 1** The body of officials in charge of the administration of the departments of a government. In the United States it is selected by the president with the advice and consent of the Senate, and is called the *Cabinet.* **2** An executive department of government. **3** Ministers of the gospel collectively, or their office. **4** The act of ministering, or the state or office of a minister; ministration; service. [<L *ministerium*]

Min·i·track (min′i·trak′) *n.* A sensitive electronic system for tracking the paths of earth satellites by the timing of radio signals received by ground stations: a trade name.

min·i·um (min′ē·əm) *n.* **1** A vivid opaque red lead oxide, Pb_3O_4: used chiefly as a pigment. **2** Cinnabar. [<L]

min·i·ver (min′ə·vər) *n.* **1** A fur or mixture of furs used in the Middle Ages for trimming. **2** Any white fur, as ermine. [<OF *menu vair,* lit., little spotted (fur)]

mink (mingk) *n.* **1** An amphibious, slender-bodied, carnivorous mammal (genus *Mustela*), related to the weasel and valued for its soft, thick, glossy, brown fur. **2** The fur of this mammal. [<Scand. Cf. Sw. *menk.*]

Min·kow·ski (ming·kôf′skē), **Hermann,** 1864–1909, Russian mathematician.

Min·ne·ap·o·lis (min′ē·ap′ə·lis) A city on the Mississippi in SE central Minnesota.

Min·ne·ha·ha (min′ē·hä′hä) In Longfellow's *The Song of Hiawatha,* a Dakota Indian maiden, the wife of Hiawatha.

min·ne·sing·er (min′ə·sing′ər) *n.* A lyric poet of medieval Germany. Compare TROUBADOUR. [<G <*minne* love + *singer* singer]

Min·ne·so·ta (min′ə·sō′tə) A State in the north central United States bordering on Canada and Lake Superior; 84,682 square miles; capital, St. Paul; entered the Union May 11, 1858; nickname, *Gopher State*: abbr. MN **—Min′ne·so′tan** *n.* & *adj.*

Min·ne·wit (min′ə·wit), **Peter** See MINUIT, PETER.

Min·nie (min′ē) A feminine personal name. [<G, love]

min·now (min′ō) *n.* **1** A small European cyprinoid fish *(Phoxinus phoxinus).* **2** One of various other small fishes; especially, in the United States, a fish of the carp family. **3** The young of various fishes. Also **min′nie.** [OE *myne* small fish; prob. infl. in meaning by F *menu* small]

Mi·no·an (mi·nō′ən) *adj.* **1** Of or pertaining to an advanced Bronze Age civilization that flourished in Crete from about 3000 to 1100 B.C. **2** Denoting two types of linear script using pictographic and syllabic signs, found on clay tablets at Minos's palace at Cnossus, Nestor's palace at Pylos, and other Greek and Cretan sites, and dating from the 17th to 13th centuries B.C.: **Linear A** is thought to be Akkadian on the basis of a tentative decipherment made in 1957; **Linear B,** deciphered in 1952, is an Achaean dialect of Greek.

mi·nor (mī′nər) *adj.* **1** Less in number, quantity, or extent: opposed to *major.* **2** Of secondary consideration. **3** *Music* **a** Higher than the corresponding major interval by a semitone. **b** Characterized by minor intervals, scales, or tones. **c** In a minor key; sad; plaintive. **4** *Logic* Designating a minor term. *—n.* **1** One below the age when full civil and personal rights can be exercised. **2** *Logic* A minor term or minor premise. See SYLLOGISM. **3** *Music* A minor key, interval, etc. **4** Hence, a pathetic or plaintive quality, as in literature or art. **5** *U.S.* A branch of study for degree candidates in colleges and universities, usually related to but requiring less time than a major; a secondary subject of study. **6** In English public schools, the younger of two namesakes; junior. ◆ Homophone: *miner.* [<L]

Mi·nor·ca (mi·nôr′kə) *n.* One of a breed of domestic fowls resembling Leghorns. [from *Minorca*]

Mi·nor·ca (mi·nôr′kə) Second largest of the Balearic islands; 264 square miles. Spanish *Menorca.*

Mi·nor·can (mi·nôr′kən) *n.* A native or inhabitant of Minorca. *—adj.* Of or pertaining to Minorca or its people.

Mi·nor·ite (mī′nə·rīt) *n.* A Franciscan. Also

Mi′nor·ist. [< Med. L *(Fratres) Minores* Lesser (Brethren), original name of the order]
mi·nor·i·ty (mə·nôr′ə·tē, -nor′-, mī-) *n. pl.* **·ties 1** The smaller in number of two parts or parties: opposed to *majority.* **2** The state of being a minor; legal infancy. **3** A group comprising less than half of a population and differing from the others and especially from a larger predominant group, as in race, religion, political affiliation, etc.: also **minority group.** [< F *minorité*]
minor key *Music* A key or mode based on the minor scale and characterized by the use of the minor third, and producing a plaintive or mournful effect. See THIRD *n.*
minor league Any professional sports league not having the standing of a major league. **—mi′nor-league′** *adj.*
minor mode See under MODE.
minor scale See under SCALE.
minor suit In bridge, diamonds or clubs.
minor term *Logic* The subject of both the minor premise and the conclusion of a syllogism.
Mi·nos (mī′nəs, -nos) In Greek mythology, a king of Crete, son of Zeus and husband of Pasiphae, who became a judge of the lower world after his death. [< Gk. *Minōs*]
Min·o·taur (min′ə·tôr) In Greek mythology, the offspring, half man and half bull, of Pasiphae and a white bull sent by Poseidon to Minos, who confined it in the Labyrinth where it was annually fed human flesh until killed by Theseus. See ANDROGEUS. [< L *Minotaurus* < Gk. *Minōtauros* < *Minōs* Minos + *tauros* bull]
Minsk 1 The capital of the Republic of Belarus, in Eastern Europe: pop. 900,000; **2** the central and largest province in Belarus.
min·ster (min′stər) *n.* A monastery church; in Great Britain, often a cathedral: often used in combination: *Axminster.* [OE *mynster* < LL *monasterium.* Doublet of MONASTERY.]
min·strel (min′strəl) *n.* **1** Originally, in the Middle Ages, a retainer whose business it was to play musical instruments for the entertainment of his lord. **2** A wandering musician who composed and sang to the harp; one of a class of vagrant musicians and mountebanks, repressed by Henry IV. **3** A performer in a minstrel show. **4** *Poetic* A poet; singer; musician. See synonyms under POET. [< OF *menestrel* < LL *ministerialis* servant, jester < L *minister* attendant]
minstrel show A comic variety show of songs, dances, jokes, etc., given by a company of performers in blackface.
min·strel·sy (min′strəl·sē) *n. pl.* **·sies 1** The occupation of a minstrel. **2** Ballads or lyrics collectively. **3** A troupe of minstrels. [< AF *menestralcie,* OF *menestralsie*]
mint[1] (mint) *n.* **1** A place where the coin of a country is manufactured. **2** Figuratively, an abundant supply of anything: used especially of money. **3** Figuratively, the source of a fabrication or invention. *—v.t.* **1** To make (money) by stamping; coin. **2** To invent or fabricate, as a word. *—adj.* Unused; in original condition: a *mint* stamp. [OE *mynet* coin < L *moneta* mint < *Moneta* epithet of Juno, whose temple at Rome was used as a mint. Doublet of MONEY.] **—mint′er** *n.*
mint[2] (mint) *n.* Any one of several aromatic herbs of the genus *Mentha,* of the family *Labiatae;* especially, spearmint and peppermint, used medicinally. [OE *minte* < L *menta, mentha* < Gk. *mintha*]
mint[3] (mint) *v.t. Scot.* To hint; intend.
mint·age (min′tij) *n.* **1** The act of minting, or that which is minted; coinage; also, figuratively, the act of fabricating or coining. **2** The duty paid for coining. **3** The authorized impression placed upon a coin.
mint julep A drink made of brandy or whisky mixed with crushed ice and sugar and flavored with fresh mint.
min·u·end (min′yo͞o·end) *n.* The number from which another is to be subtracted: opposed to *subtrahend.* [< L *minuendus* to be lessened, gerundive of *minuere* lessen]
min·u·et (min′yo͞o·et′) *n.* **1** A slow, stately dance for couples in triple measure: introduced in France in the 17th century. **2** A musical composition suited to this dance: often as a movement in a sonata or symphony. [< F *menuet,* dim. of *menu* small < L *minutus*]
Min·u·it (min′yo͞o·it), **Peter,** 1580?–1641, third governor of New Netherlands (New York): originally known as *Peter Minnewit.*
mi·nus (mī′nəs) *prep.* **1** Lessened, or requiring to be lessened by; less: 10 *minus* 5. **2** *Colloq.* Deprived of; lacking: *minus* a hat. *—adj.* **1** Lying or reckoned in that one of two opposite directions arbitrarily assumed as negative. **2** Negative: A debt may be treated as a *minus* quantity. *—n.* **1** A minus sign. **2** A minus quantity. [< L, neut. of *minor*]
mi·nus·cule (mi·nus′kyo͞ol) *n.* **1** A semi-uncial cursive script, developed by the monks out of the uncial in the 7th–9th centuries and forming the basis of the modern small Roman and Greek letters; hence, any small or lower-case letter. **2** Any very small thing. *—adj.* **1** Of, pertaining to, like, or composed of minuscules. **2** Very small; miniature. [< L *minusculus,* dim. of *minor* less]
minus sign A sign (−) denoting subtraction, or reckoning or measuring in the negative direction.
min·ute[1] (min′it) *n.* **1** The 60th part of an hour; also, a moment; hence, any short, indefinite period of time. **2** The 60th part of a degree: a unit of angular measure indicated by the sign(′), and called a *minute* of arc. **3** A brief note or summary in writing of something to be remembered; memorandum; specifically, in the plural, an official record of the proceedings of any deliberative body. *—v.t.* **·ut·ed, ·ut·ing 1** To make a minute or brief note of; record. **2** To time to the minute. [< F < Med. L *minuta (pars)* small (part), minute < L *minutus* small]
mi·nute[2] (mī·no͞ot′, -nyo͞ot′, mi-) *adj.* **1** Exceedingly small; hence, unimportant; trifling. **2** Attending to small things; critically careful; very exact. [< L *minutus* small, little, orig. pp. of *minuere* lessen] **—mi·nute′ness** *n.*
Synonyms: circumstantial, comminuted, critical, detailed, diminutive, exact, fine, little, particular, precise, slender, tiny. That is *minute* which is of exceedingly limited dimensions, as a grain of dust. That which is broken up into *minute* particles is said to be *comminuted*; things may be termed *fine* which would not be termed *comminuted*; as, *fine* sand; *fine* gravel; but, in using an adverb, we say a substance is finely *comminuted.* An account extended to very *minute* particulars is *circumstantial, detailed, particular,* and examination so extended is *critical, exact, precise.* See FINE, LITTLE, PRECISE, SMALL. *Antonyms*: see synonyms for LARGE.
min·ute gun (min′it) A gun fired at intervals of a minute as a sign of distress, or of mourning as at a funeral.
min·ute hand (min′it) The hand of a timepiece that marks the minutes.
min·ute·ly[1] (min′it·lē) *adj. & adv.* At intervals of a minute.
mi·nute·ly[2] (mī·no͞ot′lē, -nyo͞ot′-, mi-) *adv.* In a minute manner; very finely, closely, or exactly.
min·ute·man (min′it·man′) *n. pl.* **·men** (-men′) A man ready for service at a minute's notice: specifically applied to certain militiamen and armed citizens in the American Revolution.
min·u·the·sis (min′yə·thē′sis) *n. Physiol.* Diminished response of a sense organ due to continuous stimulation. [< LL < Gk. *minythēsis* a lessening < *minytheein* decrease]
mi·nu·ti·a (mi·no͞o′shē·ə, -shə, -nyo͞o′-) *n. pl.* **·ti·ae** (-shi·ē) *Chiefly pl.* Small or unimportant details. [< L]
minx (mingks) *n.* A saucy, forward girl or woman. [Prob. < LG *minsk* impudent woman]
mi·o·car·di·a (mī′ə·kär′dē·ə) *n. Physiol.* Contraction of the heart; systole. [< NL < Gk. *meiōn* less + *kardia* heart]
Mi·o·cene (mī′ə·sēn) *adj.* Pertaining to or designating a geological epoch near the end of the Tertiary period, associated with a great development of modern mammals: also **Mi′o·cen′ic** (-sen′ik), See chart under GEOLOGY. *—n.* The Miocene epoch or series. [< Gk. *meiōn* less + *kainos* recent]
Mi·o·lith·ic (mī′ə·lith′ik) *adj. Anthropol.* Mesolithic. [< Gk. *meiōn* less + -LITH[1] + -IC]
mi·o·sis (mī·ō′sis) *n.* **1** *Pathol.* **a** The period in the course of a disease when the symptoms begin to diminish. **b** Excessive contraction of the pupil of the eye: also spelled *myosis.* **2** Meiosis. [< Gk. *myein* close + -OSIS] **—mi·ot′ic** (-ot′ik) *adj.*
mi·o·ther·mic (mī′ə·thûr′mik) *adj.* Of or pertaining to those temperature conditions now prevailing on earth, especially as compared with past geological periods. [< Gk. *meiōn* less + *thermē* heat]
miq·ue·let (mik′ə·let) *n.* **1** A Spanish infantryman detailed for escort duty. **2** *Obs.* A partisan; a bandit of the Pyrenees. [< F < Sp. *miquelete*]
Mi·que·lon (mik′ə·lon, *Fr.* mē·kə·lôṅ′) An island off southern Newfoundland; 83 square miles. See under SAINT PIERRE.
mir (mir) *n.* A Russian local community, with common land apportioned by lot. [< Russian]
Mi·ra·beau (mē·rà·bō′), **Comte de,** 1749–91, Gabriel Honoré de Riquetti, French Revolutionary orator, writer, and statesman.
mi·ra·bi·le dic·tu (mi·rab′ə·lē dik′to͞o, -tyo͞o) *Latin* Wonderful to relate.
mir·a·bil·i·a (mir′ə·bil′ē·ə) *n. pl. Latin* Miracles; wonders.
mir·a·cle (mir′ə·kəl) *n.* **1** Any wonderful or amazing thing, fact, or event; a wonder. **2** An event in the natural world, but out of its established order, possible only by the intervention of divine power. **3** A medieval dramatic representation of religious subjects: also **miracle play:** see MYSTERY[1] (def. 10). See synonyms under PRODIGY. [< F < L *miraculum* < *mirari* wonder < *mirus* wonderful]
mi·rac·u·lous (mi·rak′yə·ləs) *adj.* **1** Effected by direct divine agency; supernatural. **2** Surpassingly strange; wonderful. **3** Possessing the power to work miracles; wonder-working. See synonyms under SUPERNATURAL. [< F *miraculeux* < Med. L *miraculosus* < L *miraculum*] **—mi·rac′u·lous·ly** *adv.* **—mi·rac′u·lous·ness** *n.*
mir·a·dor (mir′ə·dôr′, -dōr′-) *n. Archit.* A balcony or oriel window. [< Sp. < *mirar* behold < L *mirari* wonder]
Mir·a·flo·res Lake (mir′ə·flôr′əs, -flō′rəs) An artificial lake in southern Canal Zone, linking Gaillard Cut with the Pacific section through **Miraflores Locks.**
mi·rage (mi·räzh′) *n.* **1** An optical illusion, as of an oasis or a sheet of water in the desert, or ships seen inverted in the air. It occurs when the lower strata of air are at a very different temperature from the higher strata, so that images are seen as by reflection. **2** Anything that falsely appears to be real. [< F < *se mirer* be reflected, look at oneself < L *mirari* wonder at]
Mi·ran·da (mi·ran′də) A feminine personal name. [< L, admirable]
—Miranda In Shakespeare's *Tempest,* the heroine; daughter of Prospero.
mir·bane oil (mûr′bān) Nitrobenzene. [Prob. a fanciful formation]
mire (mīr) *n.* Wet, yielding earth; swampy ground; deep mud or slush. *—v.* **mired, mir·ing** *v.t.* **1** To cause to sink or become stuck in or as in mire. **2** To defile; soil. *—v.i.* **3** To sink in mire; bog down. [< ON *mȳrr* swampy ground] **— mir′y** *adj.* **—mir′i·ness** *n.*
mir·ex (mir′eks) *n.* A persistent, toxic chlorinated hydrocarbon, $C_{10}Cl_{12}$, formerly used widely as a pesticide against fire ants. Also **Mir′ex.**
Mir·i·am (mir′ē·əm) A feminine personal name. [< Hebrew, bitter]
—Miriam Sister of Moses and Aaron. *Ex.* xv 20.
mirk[1] (mûrk), **mirk·i·ly,** etc. See MURK, etc.
mirk[2] (mûrk) *Scot. adj.* Dark, gloomy. *—n.* Darkness.
mir·mil·lon (mir·mil′ən) *n.* One of a class of ancient Roman gladiators armed with sword and shield and characterized by the figure of a fish on the helmet. See illustration under GLADIATOR. [< L *mirmillo* < Gk. *mormyros* sea fish]
Mi·ró (mē·rō′), **Joan,** born 1893, Spanish painter.
mir·ror (mir′ər) *n.* **1** An object having a nearly perfect reflecting surface; a looking-glass. **2** *Optics* A speculum. **3** Whatever reflects or clearly represents; an exemplar. **4** A crystal used by diviners. *—v.t.* To reflect or show an image of, as in a mirror. [< OF *mirour* < LL *mirare* look at < L *mirari* wonder at, admire]
mir·ror·scope (mir′ər·skōp) *n.* **1** A mirror used to reflect a design so as to permit of rapid reproduction, as by artists. **2** A projector (def. 3).

mir•ror•stone (mir′ər·stōn′) *n.* Mica, especially of the muscovite variety.

mirth (mûrth) *n.* 1 Pleasurable feelings, or gaiety of spirits, manifested in jesting and laughter; social merriment; jollity. 2 *Obs.* Pleasure; joy. See synonyms under HAPPINESS, LAUGHTER, SPORT. [OE *myrth, myrgth* < *myrig* pleasant, merry]

mirth•ful (mûrth′fəl) *adj.* Merry. See synonyms under CHEERFUL, HAPPY, MERRY, VIVACIOUS. — **mirth′ful·ly** *adv.* — **mirth′ful·ness** *n.*

mirth•less (mûrth′lis) *adj.* Lacking mirth or merriment; joyless. — **mirth′less·ly** *adv.* — **mirth′less·ness** *n.*

mir•za (mir′zä) *n.* A Persian title, placed before a name to denote a scholar and after a name to denote a prince. [<Persian, contraction of *mīrzādah* < *mīr* prince (<Arabic *amīr* ruler) + *zādah* son of]

mis–[1] *prefix* Bad; amiss; wrongly. [OE *mis-* wrong; infl. in meaning by ME *mes-* MIS-[2]] *Mis-* may appear as a prefix in hyphemes or solidemes; for examples, see the list of self–explanatory words at the foot of the page.

mis–[2] *prefix* Bad; amiss; not: found with negative or depreciatory force in words borrowed from Old French; *misadventure, miscreant.* [<OF *mes-* <L *minus* less]

mis–[3] Var. of MISO–.

mis•ad•ven•ture (mis′əd·ven′chər) *n.* An unlucky chance; misfortune. See synonyms under ACCIDENT, MISFORTUNE. [<OF *mesaventure*]

mis•ad•ven•tured (mis′əd·ven′chərd) *adj. Obs.* Unfortunate.

mis•al•li•ance (mis′ə·lī′əns) *n.* An undesirable alliance, as marriage with one of inferior station or character. [<F *mésalliance*]

mis•an•thrope (mis′ən·thrōp, miz′-) *n.* One who entertains aversion to or distrust of his fellow men. Also **mis•an•thro•pist** (mis·an′thrə·pist). [<Gk. *misanthrōpos* hating mankind < *misein* hate + *anthrōpos* a man] — **mis′an·throp′ic** (-throp′ik) or **·i·cal** *adj.* — **mis′an·throp′i·cal·ly** *adv.*

mis•an•thro•py (mis·an′thrə·pē) *n.* Hatred or distrust of mankind.

mis•ap•ply (mis′ə·plī′) *v.t.* **·plied, ·ply·ing** 1 To use or apply incorrectly or inefficiently. 2 To use or apply wrongfully or dishonestly.

mis•ap•pro•pri•ate (mis′ə·prō′prē·āt) *v.t.* **·at·ed, ·at·ing** To use or take improperly or dishonestly; misapply. — **mis′ap·pro′pri·a′tion** *n.*

mis•be•come (mis′bi·kum′) *v.t.* **·came, ·come, ·com·ing** To be unbecoming or not befitting to.

mis•brand (mis·brand′) *v.t.* To label or brand incorrectly or falsely.

mis•call (mis·kôl′) *v.t.* 1 To call by a wrong name; misname. 2 *Brit. Dial.* To revile; abuse.

mis•car•riage (mis·kar′ij) *n.* 1 *Med.* A premature delivery of a non–viable fetus; abortion. 2 Failure to reach or to bring to an expected result, destination, or conclusion.

mis•car•ry (mis·kar′ē) *v.i.* **·ried, ·ry·ing** 1 To fail of an intended effect; go wrong. 2 To bring forth a fetus prematurely; have a miscarriage; abort.

mis•ce•ge•na•tion (mis′i·jə·nā′shən) *n. Biol.* Interbreeding of races, especially intermarriage or interbreeding between white and Negro or white and Oriental races. [<L *miscere* mix + *genus* race] — **mis′ce·ge·net′ic** (-jə·net′ik) *adj.*

mis•cel•la•ne•a (mis′ə·lā′nē·ə) *n. pl.* A miscellaneous collection; especially, literary miscellanies. [<L]

mis•cel•la•ne•ous (mis′ə·lā′nē·əs) *adj.* Consisting of several kinds; variously mixed; also, many–sided; promiscuous; varied. See synonyms under HETEROGENEOUS. [<L *miscellaneus* < *miscellus* mixed < *miscere* mix] — **mis′cel·la′ne·ous·ly** *adv.* — **mis′cel·la′ne·ous·ness** *n.*

mis•cel•la•nist (mis′ə·lā′nist, -lə·nist) *n.* A composer of miscellanies.

mis•cel•la•ny (mis′ə·lā′nē) *n. pl.* **·nies** 1 *Often pl.* A collection of literary compositions on various subjects. 2 Any miscellaneous collection. [Anglicized var. of MISCELLANEA]

mis•chance (mis·chans′, -chäns′) *n.* An instance of ill–luck; a mishap. See synonyms under CATASTROPHE, MISFORTUNE. [<OF *mescheance*]

mis•chief (mis′chif) *n.* 1 Any occurrence attended with evil or injury; troublesome or damaging action or its result; damage; vexation. 2 Any annoying or vexatious action or course of conduct; a prank; also, the spirit or mood leading to such acts. 3 A prankish person. See synonyms under INJURY. [<OF *meschef* bad result < *meschever* come to grief < *mes-* mis- (<L *minus* less) + *chief* head, end <L *caput* head]

mis•chief-mak•er (mis′chif·mā′kər) *n.* One who causes mischief, especially by instigating ill–feeling between others. — **mis′chief-mak′·ing** *adj.* & *n.*

mis•chie•vous (mis′chi·vəs) *adj.* 1 Inclined to mischief; of a prankish nature. 2 Injurious. See synonyms under BAD, MALICIOUS, NOISOME, PERNICIOUS. — **mis′chie·vous·ly** *adv.* — **mis′·chie·vous·ness** *n.* [<AF *meschevous*]

mis•ci•ble (mis′i·bəl) *adj.* 1 Capable of being mixed. 2 Suitable for mixing. [<L *miscere* mix] — **mis′ci·bil′i·ty** *n.*

mis•col•late (mis′kə·lāt′) *v.t.* **·lat·ed, ·lat·ing** In bookbinding, to assemble (sheets or signatures) in wrong sequence. — **mis′col·la′tion** *n.*

mis•col•or (mis·kul′ər) *v.t.* 1 To give a wrong color to. 2 To misrepresent. Also *Brit.* **mis·col′our.**

mis•con•ceive (mis′kən·sēv′) *v.t.* & *v.i.* **·ceived, ·ceiv·ing** To conceive wrongly; misunderstand. — **mis′con·ceiv′er** *n.* — **mis′con·cep′tion** (-sep′·shən) *n.*

mis•con•duct (mis′kən·dukt′) *v.t.* 1 To behave (oneself) improperly. 2 To mismanage. —*n.* (mis·kon′dukt) 1 Improper conduct; bad behavior. 2 *Law* Adultery. 3 Mismanagement.

mis•con•stru•al (mis′kən·strōō′əl) *n.* 1 An erroneous interpretation. 2 The act of putting a false meaning upon something said or done by another. 3 Misunderstanding or the result of a misunderstanding.

mis•con•strue (mis′kən·strōō′) *v.t.* **·strued, ·stru·ing** To interpret erroneously; put a false or unwarranted meaning to; misunderstand. — **mis′con·struc′tion** (-struk′shən) *n.*

mis•cre•ance (mis′krē·əns) *n. Archaic* The condition or quality of adhering to a false faith; heresy. [<OF *mescreant* disbelieving, ppr. of *mescroire* < *mes-* mis- (<L *minus* less) + *croire* believe <L *credere*]

mis•cre•an•cy (mis′krē·ən·sē) *n. Archaic* 1 The condition or act of a miscreant; villainy. 2 Miscreance.

mis•cre•ant (mis′krē·ənt) *n.* 1 A vile wretch; an evil–doer. 2 *Archaic* An unbeliever; infidel. —*adj.* 1 Villainous; conscienceless. 2 *Archaic* Unbelieving; infidel. [<OF *mescreant* unbelieving]

mis•cue (mis·kyōō′) *n.* In billiards, a stroke spoiled in effect by a slipping of the cue. —*v.i.* **·cued, ·cu·ing** 1 To make a miscue. 2 In the theater, to miss one's cue; to answer another's cue.

mis•deed (mis·dēd′) *n.* A wrong or improper act. See synonyms under OFFENSE, SIN. [OE *misdǣd*]

mis•de•mean•ant (mis′di·mē′nənt) *n.* One who is guilty of a misdemeanor or misconduct. — **first-class misdemeanant** In English law, one of a class of prisoners guilty of misdemeanor, but not subjected to the same prison regulations as a criminal, nor considered as a person convicted of a crime.

mis•de•mean•or (mis′di·mē′nər) *n.* 1 Misbehavior; a misdeed. 2 *Law* Any offense less than a felony. In England the distinction between a felony and a misdemeanor is still maintained. In the United States this distinction has, in most States, either been abolished or is treated in a manner that makes it of no practical value. Compare FELONY. Also *Brit.* **mis′de·mean′our.** See synonyms under OFFENSE.

mis•do (mis·dōō′) *v.t.* & *v.i.* **·did, ·done, ·do·ing** To do wrongly; bungle. [OE *misdon*] — **mis·do′er** *n.* — **mis·do′ing** *n.*

mis•doubt (mis·dout′) *v.t. Archaic* 1 To doubt; call in question. 2 To fear; suspect. —*v.i.* 3 To be in doubt; suspect. —*n.* 1 Doubt; wavering; irresolution. 2 Suspicion; apprehension.

mise (mīz) *n.* 1 *Law* The issue pleaded in a writ of right. 2 *Law* Expenses; specifically, the costs and charges in an action. 3 The adjustment of a dispute by arbitration or compromise. [<AF <OF *mis* put, laid out, pp. of *mettre* <L *mittere* send]

mise en scène (mēz äṅ sen′) *French* The setting of a play on the stage; hence, general or visible surroundings.

Mi•se•no (mē·zā′nō), **Cape** A promontory in southern Italy between the Bay of Naples and the Gulf of Gaeta. Ancient **Mi·se·num** (mī·sē′nəm).

mi•ser (mī′zər) *n.* One who saves and hoards avariciously. [<L *miser* wretched]

mis•er•a•ble (miz′ər·ə·bəl, miz′rə-) *adj.* 1 Wretchedly unhappy. 2 Of mean quality; bad; valueless: sometimes expressing contempt. 3 Producing, proceeding from, or exhibiting misery; pitiable: *miserable* weather; a *miserable* groan. See synonyms under PITIFUL, SAD. —*n. Obs.* A miserable person. [<OF <L *miserabilis* pitiable < *miserari* pity < *miser* wretched] — **mis′er·a·ble·ness** *n.* — **mis′er·a·bly** *adv.*

mis•e•re•re (miz′ə·râr′ē, -rir′ē) *n.* In church stalls, a small wooden bracket affixed perpendicularly to the bottom of the seat and designed to afford support to the worshiper when the seat is turned up: also called *misericorde.*

Mis•e•re•re (miz′ə·râr′ē, -rir′ē) *n.* 1 The 51st psalm, so called from the opening words in the Latin version. 2 A musical setting of this psalm. [<L, imperative of *misereri* have mercy]

mis•er•i•corde (miz′ər·i·kôrd′, mi·zer′i·kôrd) *n.* 1 A small dagger used in the Middle Ages to give the death stroke to a fallen knight. 2 Formerly, a dispensation from fasting given to a member of a monastic order. 3 An apartment in a monastery serving as a refectory for monks who had received such dispensation. 4 Miserere. Also **mis′er·i·cord′.** [<OF <L *misericordia* < *misereri* have pity + *cor, cordis* heart]

mis•e•ri•cor•di•a (miz′ə·ri·kôr′dē·ə) *Latin* Pity; compassion; mercy.

mi•ser•ly (mī′zər·lē) *adj.* Of or like a miser; grasping; mean. See synonyms under AVARICIOUS. — **mi′ser·li·ness** *n.*

mis•er•y (miz′ər·ē) *n. pl.* **·er·ies** 1 Extreme distress or suffering, especially as a result of poverty; wretchedness; also, a cause of wretchedness. 2 *Dial.* A cause of pain: a

misaccent	**misadvise**	**misanalyze**	**misassay**	**misbandage**	**mischaracterization**	**miscoinage**
misaccentuation	**misaffection**	**misanswer**	**misassent**	**misbegin**	**mischaracterize**	**miscollocation**
misachievement	**misaffirm**	**misapparel**	**misassert**	**misbelove**	**mischarge**	**miscommand**
misacknowledge	**misagent**	**misappear**	**misassign**	**misbestow**	**mischristen**	**miscommit**
misact	**misaim**	**misappearance**	**misassociate**	**misbetide**	**miscipher**	**miscommunicate**
misadapt	**misalienate**	**misappellation**	**misassociation**	**misbias**	**miscitation**	**miscompare**
misadaptation	**misalinement**	**misappoint**	**misatone**	**misbill**	**miscite**	**miscomplain**
misadd	**misallegation**	**misappointment**	**misattribute**	**misbind**	**misclaim**	**miscomplaint**
misaddress	**misallege**	**misappraise**	**misattribution**	**misbuild**	**misclaiming**	**miscompose**
misadjust	**misallotment**	**misappraisement**	**misauthorization**	**miscanonize**	**misclass**	**miscomputation**
misadmeasurement	**misallowance**	**misapprehensible**	**misauthorize**	**miscensure**	**misclassification**	**miscompute**
misadministration	**misalphabetize**	**misascribe**	**misaver**	**miscenter**	**misclassify**	**miscon**
misadvice	**misalter**	**misascription**	**misaward**	**mischallenge**	**miscoin**	**misconclusion**

add,āce,câre,pälm; end,ēven; it,īce; odd,ōpen,ôrder; tŏŏk,pōōl; up,bûrn; ə = a in *above,* e in *sicken,* i in *clarity,* o in *melon,* u in *focus;* yōō = u in *fuse;* oi,oil; ou,pout; ch,check; g,go; ng,ring; th,thin; th,this; zh,vision. Foreign sounds à,œ,ü,kh,ṅ; and ◆: see page xx. < from; + plus; ? possibly.

misery in the back. See synonyms under MISFORTUNE, PAIN. [<OF *miserie* <L *miseria* < *miser* wretched]

mis·fea·sance (mis·fē′zəns) *n. Law* The performance of a lawful act in an unlawful or culpably negligent manner. Compare MALFEASANCE, NONFEASANCE. [<OF *mesfaisance* < *mesfaire* do wrong < *mes-* mis- + *faire* do <L *facere*] — **mis·fea′sor** *n.*

mis·fire (mis·fīr′) *n.* The failure to discharge or explode when desired: said of a firearm, explosive, or internal-combustion engine. —*v.i.* **·fired, ·fir·ing** To fail to explode or be fired.

mis·fit (mis·fit′) *v.t.* & *v.i.* **·fit·ted, ·fit·ting** To fail to fit or make fit. —*n.* **1** Something that fits badly. **2** (mis′fit′) A person who does not adjust or adapt himself readily to his surroundings. **3** The act or condition of fitting badly.

mis·for·tune (mis·fôr′chən) *n.* **1** Adverse or ill fortune. **2** An unlucky chance or occurrence; calamity.

Synonyms: adversity, affliction, bereavement, blow, calamity, chastening, chastisement, disappointment, disaster, distress, failure, hardship, harm, ill, misadventure, mischance, misery, mishap, reverse, ruin, sorrow, stroke, trial, tribulation, trouble, visitation. *Misfortune* is usually of lingering character or consequences, and such as the sufferer is not deemed directly responsible for; as, He had the *misfortune* to be born blind. Any considerable *disappointment, failure,* or *misfortune,* as regards outward circumstances, as loss of fortune, position, and the like, when long continued or attended with enduring consequences, constitutes *adversity*. For the loss of friends by death we commonly use *affliction* or *bereavement*. *Calamity* and *disaster* are used of sudden and severe *misfortunes*. We speak of the *misery* of the poor, the *hardships* of the soldier. *Affliction, chastening, trial,* and *tribulation* all suggest some disciplinary purpose of God with beneficent design. *Affliction* may be keen and bitter, but brief; *tribulation* is long and wearing. Compare ACCIDENT, ADVERSITY, BLOW, CATASTROPHE, LOSS. *Antonyms*: blessing, boon, comfort, consolation, gratification, happiness, joy, pleasure, prosperity, relief, success, triumph.

mis·give (mis·giv′) *v.* **·gave, ·giv·ing** *v.t.* To make fearful, suspicious, or doubtful: My heart *misgives* me. —*v.i.* To be apprehensive.

mis·giv·ing (mis·giv′ing) *n.* A feeling of doubt, premonition, or apprehension. See synonyms under ANXIETY, DOUBT, FEAR.

mis·guide (mis·gīd′) *v.t.* **·guid·ed, ·guid·ing** To guide wrongly in action or thought; mislead. — **mis·guid′ance** *n.* — **mis·guid′er** *n.*

mi·shan·ter (mi·shan′tər) *n. Scot.* Misfortune; ill-luck; misadventure.

mis·hap (mis′hap, mis·hap′) *n.* An unfortunate accident; slight misfortune. See synonyms under ACCIDENT, CATASTROPHE, MISFORTUNE. [<MIS-[1] + HAP]

mish·mash (mish′mash′, -mosh′) *n.* A medley; hotch-potch. —*v.t.* To make a hotch-potch of; jumble. Also **mish′-mash′**. [Reduplication of MASH]

Mish·na (mish′nə) *n. pl.* **Mish·na·yoth** (mish′·nä·yōth′) **1** The first part of the Talmud, consisting of a collection of traditions and decisions made by Rabbi Juda, called the Holy (born about A.D. 150), summing up all previous rabbinical labors. **2** A paragraph of this collection. **3** The opinion of any notable expounder of the Jewish law; also, the sum and substance of his teachings. Also **Mish′nah.** [<Hebrew *mishnāh* repetition, oral law < *shānāh* repeat, teach] — **Mish·na·ic** (mish·nā′ik), **Mish′nic** or **·ni·cal** *adj.*

mis·in·form (mis′in·fôrm′) *v.t.* To give false or erroneous information to. — **mis′in·for·ma′tion** *n.* — **mis′in·form′er, mis′in·form′ant** *n.*

mis·in·ter·pret (mis′in·tûr′prit) *v.t.* To interpret wrongly; misunderstand. — **mis′in·ter′pre·ta′tion** *n.* — **mis′in·ter′pret·er** *n.*

Mi·sio·nes (mē·syō′nās) A national territory in NE Argentina; 11,514 square miles; capital, Posadas.

mis·join·der (mis·join′dər) *n. Law* The uniting of things or persons that should not be united: the *misjoinder* of parties in action: contrasted with *non-joinder*.

mis·kal (mis·käl′) *n.* An Oriental weight equivalent to 4.7 grams in Persia, and to 4.8 grams in Turkey. [<Arabic *mithqāl* weight]

Mis·kolc (mēsh′kōlts) A city in NE Hungary. Formerly **Mis′kolcz.**

mis·lay (mis·lā′) *v.t.* **·laid, ·lay·ing** To lay in a place not remembered; misplace. See synonyms under DISPLACE. — **mis·lay′er** *n.*

mis·lead (mis·lēd′) *v.t.* **·led, ·lead·ing** To direct wrongly; lead astray or into error. — **mis·lead′er** *n.* — **mis·lead′ing** *adj.* — **mis·lead′·ing·ly** *adv.*

mis·leared (mis·lird′) *adj. Scot.* Ill-bred or ill-taught.

mis·like (mis·līk′) *v.t.* **1** To dislike. **2** To displease. —*n.* Dislike; aversion; disapproval. — **mis·lik′er** *n.* — **mis·lik′ing** *n.* — **mis·lik′·ing·ly** *adv.*

mis·man·age (mis·man′ij) *v.t.* & *v.i.* **·aged, ·ag·ing** To manage badly or improperly. — **mis·man′age·ment** *n.* — **mis·man′ag·er** *n.*

mis·mar·riage (mis·mar′ij) *n.* An unhappy, incongruous, or inharmonious marriage.

mis·no·mer (mis·nō′mər) *n.* **1** A name wrongly applied; an inapplicable designation. **2** A misnaming; specifically, the giving of a wrong name to a person in a legal document. [<AF <OF *mesnommer* call by the wrong name < *mes-* wrongly + *nomer* <L *nominare* name]

miso- *combining form* Hating: *misogynist.* Also, before vowels, *mis-*. [<Gk. *misein* hate]

mis·og·a·my (mis·og′ə·mē) *n.* Hatred of marriage. [<MISO- + -GAMY] — **mis·og′a·mist** *n.*

mis·og·y·ny (mis·oj′ə·nē) *n.* Hatred of woman: opposed to *philogyny*. [<Gk. *misogynia* < *misein* hate + *gynē* woman] — **mis·og′y·nist** *n.* — **mis·og′y·nous** *adj.*

mis·ol·o·gy (mis·ol′ə·jē) *n.* Hatred of discussion or inquiry; aversion to enlightenment. [<Gk. *misologia* < *misein* hate + *logos* discourse] — **mis·ol′o·gist** *n.*

mis·o·ne·ism (mis′ō·nē′iz·əm, mī′sō-) *n.* Hatred of change, innovation or novelty. [<MISO- + Gk. *neos* new] — **mis′o·ne′ist** *n.*

mis·pick·el (mis′pik·əl) *n.* Arsenopyrite. [<G; ult. origin unknown]

mis·play (mis·plā′) *n.* In games, a wrong play; hence, any bad move.

mis·plead (mis·plēd′) *v.t.* & *v.i.* **·plead·ed** or **·pled, ·plead·ing** *Law* To plead erroneously.

mis·print (mis·print′) *v.t.* To print incorrectly. —*n.* (mis′print′, mis·print′) An error in printing.

mis·pri·sion (mis·prizh′ən) *n.* **1** *Law* Concealment of a crime, especially of treason or felony; also, loosely, contempt or high misdemeanor. **2** *Archaic* Misconception; misunderstanding. [<OF *mesprision* mistake < *mesprendre* do wrong, take amiss < *mes-* mis- + *prendre* take <L *prehendere*]

mis·rep·re·sent (mis′rep·ri·zent′) *v.t.* To give an incorrect or false representation of. See synonyms under PERVERT. — **mis′rep·re·sen·ta′tion** *n.* — **mis′rep·re·sen′ta·tive** *adj.* & *n.*

mis·rule (mis·ro͞ol′) *v.t.* **·ruled, ·rul·ing** To rule unwisely or unjustly; misgovern. —*n.* **1** Bad or unjust rule or government. **2** Disorder or confusion.

miss[1] (mis) *n.* **1** A young girl: chiefly colloquial, or in trade use: clothing for *misses*. **2** *Often cap.* A title used in speaking to an unmarried woman or girl: used without the name. [Contraction from MISTRESS]

miss[2] (mis) *v.t.* **1** To fail to hit or strike. **2** To fail to meet, catch, obtain, accomplish, see, hear, perceive, etc.: to *miss* the point. **3** To fail to attend, keep, perform, etc.: to *miss* church. **4** To overlook or fail to take advantage of, as an opportunity. **5** To discover or feel the loss or absence of. **6** To escape; avoid: He just *missed* being wounded. —*v.i.* **7** To fail to hit; strike wide of the mark. **8** To be unsuccessful; fail. —**to miss fire 1** To fail to discharge: said of firearms. **2** To be unsuccessful; fail. —*n.* **1** The act of missing; a failure to hit, find, attain, succeed, etc. **2** *Obs.* Loss; want. [OE *missan*]

Miss (mis) *n.* A title of address used with the name of a girl or an unmarried woman.

mis·sal (mis′əl) *n.* **1** The book containing the service for the celebration of mass throughout the year; a mass book. **2** Loosely, an illuminated black-letter or manuscript book of early date resembling the old mass books. ◆ Homophone: *missile.* [<Med. L *missale,* neut. of *missalis (liber)* mass (book) <LL *missa* mass]

mis·say (mis·sā′) *v.t.* & *v.i.* **·said, ·say·ing** *Archaic* To say (something) wrongly or incorrectly.

mis·sel thrush (mis′əl) A large European thrush (*Turdus viscivorus*) that feeds largely on mistletoe berries. Also **mis′sel.** [OE *mistel* mistletoe]

mis·shape (mis·shāp′) *v.t.* **·shaped, ·shaped** or **·shap·en, ·shap·ing** To shape badly; deform.

mis·shap·en (mis·shā′pən) *adj.* Shaped badly; deformed.

mis·sile (mis′əl) *n.* **1** Any object, especially a weapon, intended to be thrown or discharged; a projectile. **2** A guided missile. —*adj.* Such as may be thrown or hurled. ◆ Homophone: *missal.* [<L *missilis* < *missus,* pp. of *mittere* send]

mis·sile·man (mis′əl·mən) *n. pl.* **·men** (-mən) One who is skilled in the practical details of missilery, rocketry, and spacemanship.

mis·sile·ry (mis′əl·rē) *n.* The science and art of missiles, their design, construction, launching, range, and destructive capacities.

miss·ing (mis′ing) *adj.* Absent from the proper or accustomed place; lost; gone: said specifically of soldiers who are absent but whose fate has not been definitely ascertained. —**to turn up missing** To be absent; fail to arrive or be found.

missing link 1 Something lacking to make complete a chain or series. **2** *Biol.* A hypothetical form of life assumed to be intermediate in development between man and the anthropoid apes.

mis·sion (mish′ən) *n.* **1** The act of sending, or the state of being sent, as on some errand. **2** The sending forth of men with authority to preach or spread the gospel; authority so given by God or the church. **3** The business or service on which one is sent. **4** That which one is or feels destined to accomplish; the destined or chosen end of one's efforts. **5** An effort to spread, or the work of spreading, religious teaching. **6** A single field or locality covered by missionary work; the body of missionaries there established; a missionary station; also, any educational, religious, or welfare center for the underprivileged in a city. **7** *Eccl.* A regularly organized church and congregation not having the status of a parish in canon law; a quasi-parish. **8** The office of a foreign ambassador or envoy. **9** The persons sent on any errand or service. **10** *Mil.* A definite task assigned to an individual or unit of the armed services. **11** *Aeron.* A flight operation of a single aircraft or formation.

misconfer
misconfident
misconfiguration
misconjecture
misconjugate
misconjugation
misconjunction
misconsecrate
misconsequence
miscook
miscookery
miscopy
miscredulity
miscultivated
misculture
miscurvature
miscut
misdaub
misdecide
misdecision
misdeclaration
misdeclare
misdefine
misdeliver
misdelivery
misdentition
misdesire
misdetermine
misdevise
misdevoted
misdevotion
misdiet
misdispose
misdisposition
misdistinguish
misdistribute
misdistribution
misdivide
misdower
misdraw
misdrive
miseat
misecclesiastic
misedit
miseducate
miseducation
miseducative
miseffect
misencourage
misendeavor
misenforce
misengrave
misenjoy
misenrol
misenter
misentitle
misentry
misenunciation
misevent
misexample
misexecute
misexecution
misexpectation
misexpend
misexpenditure
misexplain
misexplanation
misexplication
misexposition
misexpound
misexpress
misexpression
misexpressive
misfashion
misfather
misfault
misfield
misfile
misfond
misform
misformation
misframe
misgage
misgesture
misgraft
misgrave
misground
misgrow
misgrown
misguess
mis-hallowed

—*adj.* **1** Pertaining to or belonging to a mission. **2** Like the early Spanish architecture and simple furniture of the missions of the SW United States. —*v.t.* **1** To send on a mission. **2** To establish a mission in. [<L *missio, -onis* <*missus,* pp. of *mittere* send] — **mis′ sion·al** *adj.*

mis·sion·ar·y (mish′ən·er′ē) *n. pl.* **·ar·ies** **1** A person sent to propagate religion or to do educational or charitable work in some place where his church has no self-supporting local organization; hence, one who spreads any new system or doctrine. **2** A person sent on a mission; a messenger; ambassador. —*adj.* Pertaining to missions.

Missionary Baptist A Baptist who believes in or contributes to missionary work: opposed to *Primitive Baptist.*

Missionary Ridge A ridge of hills about 1,000 feet high in Tennessee and Georgia; a Civil War battleground, 1863.

Mis·sis·sip·pi (mis′ə·sip′ē) A State in the south central United States on the Gulf of Mexico; 47,716 square miles; capital, Jackson; entered the Union Dec. 10, 1817: nickname *Bayou State.* Abbr. MS

Mis·sis·sip·pi·an (mis′ə·sip′ē·ən) *adj.* **1** Relating to the Mississippi River or to the State. **2** *Geol.* Relating to the earlier of the two geological periods or systems in the American Carboniferous division of the Paleozoic era. See chart under GEOLOGY. —*n.* **1** One born or residing in Mississippi. **2** The Lower Carboniferous or Mississippian geological formation.

Mississippi River A river in the central United States, flowing 2,350 miles south to the Gulf of Mexico; from the headwaters of the Missouri River, flowing 3,892 miles to the Gulf of Mexico.

Mississippi scheme A plan formulated by the Scottish economist, John Law, in which a company was formed to exploit and monopolize all the land drained by the Mississippi, the Ohio, and the Missouri rivers. Subsequent mismanagement of minting rights which were granted the company led to wild speculation, panic, and inflation, causing the failure of the company in 1720. Also called **Mississippi bubble.**

Mississippi Sound An arm of the Gulf of Mexico bordering Louisiana, Mississippi, and Alabama.

mis·sive (mis′iv) *n.* That which is sent; especially a letter; a message in writing. —*adj.* Sent or designed to be sent. [<Med. L *missivus* <L *missus,* pp. of *mittere* send]

miss–lick (mis′lik) *n. Colloq.* A cut made by an ax or knife off the true line; hence, any mistake.

Mis·so·lon·ghi (mis′ə·lông′gē) A port in west central Greece; here Byron died, April 29, 1824, during the Greek struggle for independence from Turkish rule: Greek *Mesolonghi.*

Mis·sou·ri (mi·zo͝or′ē) *n. pl.* **·ri** One of a tribe of North American Indians of the Siouan family, formerly inhabiting northern Missouri, now in Oklahoma with the Otoe.

Mis·sou·ri (mi·zo͝or′ē, -zo͝or′ə) A State in the west central United States west of the Mississippi; 69,674 square miles; capital, Jefferson City; entered the Union Aug. 10, 1821: nickname, *Ozark State* or *Show Me State*: abbr. MO —**to be from Missouri** To be on the alert against deception; be skeptical. —**Mis·sou′ri·an** *adj. & n.*

Missouri River The longest river of the United States and chief tributary of the Mississippi, flowing 2,714 miles from the Rocky Mountains to the Mississippi River near St. Louis.

Missouri skylark A pipit of the North American plains *(Anthus spraguei)*: also called *Sprague's pipit.*

Missouri Synod A leading conservative Lutheran body in the Lutheran Synodical Conference, first organized in 1847 and characterized by a strict adherence to traditional Lutheran doctrines: officially called *The Lutheran Church–Missouri Synod.*

mis·spell (mis·spel′) *v.t. & v.i.* **·spelled** or **·spelt, ·spell·ing** To spell incorrectly.

mis·state (mis·stāt′) *v.t.* **·stat·ed, ·stat·ing** To state wrongly or falsely.

mis·step (mis·step′) *n.* A false or wrong step; error.

mis·sus (mis′əz) *n. Colloq.* Mistress; wife. Also **mis′sis.** [Alter. of MISTRESS]

miss·y (mis′ē) *n. pl.* **miss·ies** Miss: a colloquial or diminutive form.

mist (mist) *n.* **1** An aggregation of fine drops of water in the atmosphere at or near the earth's surface, floating or falling very slowly: used either synonymously with *fog* or distinguished from it, as being less dense, or as consisting of drops large enough to fall perceptibly but slowly. **2** *Meteorol.* A very thin fog in which the horizontal visibility is greater than 1,100 yards. **3** Water vapor condensed on and dimming a surface. **4** Any colloidal suspension of a liquid in a gas. **5** Anything that dims or darkens; that which obscures physical or mental vision. —*v.i.* **1** To be or become dim or misty; blur. **2** To rain in very fine drops. —*v.t.* **3** To make dim or misty; blur. [OE]

mis·take (mis·tāk′) *n.* An error in action, judgment, perception, or impression; a blunder. See synonyms under ERROR. —*v.* **·took, ·tak·en, ·tak·ing** *v.t.* **1** To understand wrongly; acquire a wrong conception of; misinterpret. **2** To take (a person or thing) to be another; fail to identify correctly: to *mistake* friends for enemies. —*v.i.* **3** To make a mistake. [<ON *mistaka*] —**mis·tak′a·ble** *adj.*

mis·tak·en (mis·tā′kən) *adj.* **1** Characterized by mistake; incorrect; wrong. **2** Being in error; wrong in opinion or judgment. See synonyms under ABSURD. —**mis·tak′en·ly** *adv.* —**mis·tak′en·ness** *n.*

Mis·tas·si·ni Lake (mis′tä·sē′nē) A lake in central Quebec, Canada; 840 square miles.

Mis·ter (mis′tər) *n.* **1** Master: a title of address prefixed to the name and to some official titles of a man: commonly written *Mr.*: *Mr.* Darwin; *Mr.* Chairman. **2** Official salutation in addressing a warrant officer, flight officer, or a cadet in the U.S. Military Academy at West Point, and, in some practice, officers below the rank of captain. In the Navy it is directed to those of all ranks below that of commander; in the Maritime Service it is applicable to all ranks below the captain of the ship. [Var. MASTER]

mist·flow·er (mist′flou′ər) *n.* A tall perennial herb *(Eupatorium coelestinum)* of the composite family, with coarsely toothed leaves and clusters of light-blue or violet flowers.

Mis·ti (mēs′tē), **El** See EL MISTI.

mis·tle·toe (mis′əl·tō) *n.* **1** A European evergreen parasitic shrub *(Viscum album)* with yellowish-green leaves and inconspicuous flowers, succeeded by glutinous white berries: found on various deciduous trees. **2** An American plant *(Phoradendron flavescens)* related to this shrub: the State flower of Oklahoma. [OE *misteltan* mistletoe twig]

MISTLETOE

mis·took (mis·to͝ok′) Past tense of MISTAKE. Also *Scot.* **mis·teuk** (-tyo͞ok′).

mis·tral (mis′trəl, *Fr.* mēs·träl′) *n.* **1** A cold, dry, and violent northwest Alpine wind blowing from the Ebro to the Gulf of Genoa and also through the southern provinces of France. **2** A worsted dress fabric with twisted warp and weft threads woven to give a nubbed effect. [<F, lit., master wind <L *magistralis* <*magister* master]

Mis·tral (mēs·träl′), **Frédéric Joseph Étienne,** 1830–1914, Provençal poet and lexicographer. —**Gabriela,** 1889–1957, Chilean poet; real name *Lucila Godoy de Alcavaga.*

mis·treat (mis·trēt′) *v.t.* To treat badly or unkindly; abuse. —**mis·treat′ment** *n.*

mis·tress (mis′tris) *n.* **1** A woman in authority or control, or to whom service is rendered; a female head, chief, or owner, as of a country household, an institution, or an estate; also a female schoolteacher. **2** A woman who unlawfully, or without marriage, fills the place of a wife; also, a woman beloved and courted; a sweetheart. **3** A woman who is well skilled in or has mastered anything. **4** *Scot.* A married woman or wife. [<OF *maistresse,* fem. of *maistre.* See MASTER.]

Mis·tress (mis′tris) *n.* A title of address formerly applied to both married and unmarried women: now generally supplanted by *Mrs.* for married and *Miss* for unmarried women.

Mistress of the Adriatic Venice.

Mistress of the Seas Great Britain.

Mistress of the World Rome: when its empire embraced the known world.

mis·tri·al (mis·trī′əl) *n.* A trial of a lawsuit that is void because of errors; also, a trial of a lawsuit in which the jury cannot agree on a verdict.

mis·trust (mis·trust′) *n.* Lack of trust or confidence. —*v.t. & v.i.* To regard (someone or something) with suspicion or doubt; distrust. See synonyms under DOUBT, SUSPECT. —**mis·trust′er** *n.* —**mis·trust′ful** *adj.* —**mis·trust′ful·ly** *adv.* —**mis·trust′ful·ness** *n.*

mis·tryst (mis·trist′) *v.t. Scot.* **1** To fail to keep an engagement with. **2** To perplex.

mist·y (mis′tē) *adj.* **mist·i·er, mist·i·est** **1** Containing, characterized by, or accompanied by mist. **2** Dimmed or obscured by or as by mist; hence, lacking clearness or perspicuity; confused; indistinct; vague. See synonyms

mis–hear	**misincite**	**misinter**	**mislive**	**misnatured**	**mispagination**	**misphrase**
mis–hearer	**misinclination**	**misinterment**	**mislocate**	**misnavigation**	**mispaint**	**mispoint**
mis–heed	**misincline**	**misintimation**	**mislocation**	**misnumber**	**misparse**	**mispoise**
mis–hit	**misinfer**	**misjoin**	**mislodge**	**misnurture**	**mispart**	**mispolicy**
mis–hold	**misinference**	**miskeep**	**mismark**	**misnutrition**	**mispassion**	**misposition**
mishumility	**misinflame**	**miskindle**	**mismeasure**	**misobservance**	**mispatch**	**mispossessed**
misidentification	**misingenuity**	**mislabel**	**mismeasurement**	**misobserve**	**mispen**	**mispractice**
misidentify	**misinspired**	**mislabor**	**mismeet**	**misoccupy**	**misperceive**	**misprejudiced**
misimagination	**misinstruct**	**mislanguage**	**mismenstruation**	**misopinion**	**misperception**	**mispresent**
misimagine	**misinstruction**	**mislearn**	**misminded**	**misordination**	**misperform**	**misprincipled**
misimpression	**misinstructive**	**mislie**	**mismingle**	**misorganization**	**misperformance**	**misproceeding**
misimputation	**misintend**	**mislight**	**mismotion**	**misorganize**	**mispersuade**	**misproduce**
misimpute	**misintention**	**mislikeness**	**misnarrate**	**mispage**	**misperuse**	**mispronounce**

under THICK. — **mist'i·ly** *adv.* — **mist'i·ness** *n.*

mis·un·der·stand (mis'un·dər·stand', mis·un'-) *v.t.* & *v.i.* **·stood, ·stand·ing** To understand wrongly; misinterpret.

mis·un·der·stand·ing (mis'un·dər·stan'ding, mis·un'-) *n.* **1** A misapprehension; mistake as to meaning or motive. **2** A disagreement; dissension. See synonyms under QUARREL.

mis·un·der·stood (mis'un·dər·stŏŏd', mis·un'-) *adj.* **1** Not comprehended; wrongly interpreted. **2** Not appreciated at true worth.

mis·use (mis·yōōs') *n.* **1** Ill-treatment; violence; abuse. **2** Erroneous or improper use; misapplication. Also **mis·us'age.** — *v.t.* (mis·yōōz') **·used, ·us·ing 1** To use or apply wrongly or improperly. **2** To subject to ill-treatment; abuse; maltreat. See synonyms under ABUSE.

mis·us·er (mis·yōō'zər) *n.* **1** One who misuses. **2** *Law* Such a misuse or abuse of a privilege or franchise as should cause its forfeiture.

mis·ven·ture (mis·ven'chər) *n.* An ill venture; a misadventure.

Mi·tau (mē'tou) The German name for JELGAVA. *Russian* **Mi·ta·va** (mē'tə·və).

Mitch·ell (mich'əl), **John,** 1870–1919, U. S. labor leader. — **Maria,** 1818–89, U. S. astronomer. — **Silas Weir,** 1829–1914, U. S. physician and novelist. — **William,** 1879–1936, U. S. general; advocate of air power; called "Billy Mitchell."

Mitch·ell (mich'əl), **Mount** A peak in the Black Mountains, NW North Carolina; the highest point in the United States east of the Mississippi; 6,684 feet.

mite[1] (mīt) *n.* Any of various small arachnids (order *Acarina*) of both terrestrial and aquatic habits: many of them are parasitic on men, animals, plants, and stored grain, as the *itch mite, cheese mite,* etc. ◆ Homophone: *might.* [OE *mīte*] — **mit'y** *adj.*

mite[2] (mīt) *n.* **1** A very small amount or particle. **2** Any very small coin or sum of money: the widow's *mite. Mark* xii 42. See synonyms under PARTICLE. ◆ Homophone: *might.* [<Du. *mijt*]

mi·ter (mī'tər) *n.* **1** A headdress worn by various church dignitaries, as popes, archbishops, bishops, and abbots: a tall ornamental cap terminating in two peaks; hence, the office or dignity of a bishop, etc. **2** The official headdress of the ancient Jewish high priest. **3** A headdress resembling a bishop's miter, worn in the 15th century by women. **4** The junction of two bodies at an equally divided angle, as at the corner of a picture frame: also **miter joint.** — *v.t.* **1** To confer a miter upon; raise to the rank of bishop. **2** To make or join with a miter joint. Also *mitre.* [<OF *mitre* <L *mitra* <Gk., belt, turban] — **mi'·ter·er** *n.*

ECCLESIASTICAL MITER

miter box A box having a bottom and sides, but no top or ends, the sides having kerfs or sawguides in which wooden strips may be sawed to accurate miters.

mi·ter·wort (mī'tər·wûrt') *n.* Any of a genus *(Mitella)* of low, slender, mainly North American perennial herbs of the saxifrage family, having small miter-shaped flowers. Also **mi'tre·wort'.**

Mit·ford (mit'fərd), **Mary Russell,** 1787–1855, English author.

mith·er (mith'ər) *n. Scot.* Mother.

Mith·gar·thr (mith'gär·thər) See MIDGARD.

Mith·ra (mith'rə) **1** The ancient Persian god of light and truth. **2** In the Zoroastrian belief, a god often acting as the mediator between the Supreme God and man. Also **Mith'ras** (-rəs). [<L <Gk. *Mithras* <OPersian *Mithra*] — **Mith·ra·ic** (mith·rā'ik) *adj.* — **Mith·ra'i·cism** *n.* — **Mith'ra·ism** *n.* — **Mith'·ra·is'tic** *adj.*

Mith·ri·da·tes VI (mith'rə·dā'tēz), 132?–63 B.C., king of Pontus; defeated by Pompey: known as *Mithridates the Great.*

Mith·ri·dat·ic (mith'rə·dat'ik) *adj.* Of or pertaining to any of several kings of Pontus named Mithridates, especially Mithridates VI.

mith·ri·dat·ism (mith'rə·dā'tiz·əm) *n.* Immunity against poisons secured by the administration of gradually increasing doses: so called from King Mithridates VI of Pontus, who is said to have immunized himself by this method. [<obs. *mithridiate* an antidote against poison <LL *mithridatium* <*Mithridateus* of Mithridates] — **mith'ri·dat'ic** (-dat'ik) *adj.*

mi·ti·cide (mī'tə·sīd) *n.* A chemical agent destructive of mites: also called *acaricide.* [<*miti-* (<MITE[1]) + -CIDE]

mit·i·gate (mit'ə·gāt) *v.t.* & *v.i.* **·gat·ed, ·gat·ing** To make or become milder, less harsh, or less severe; moderate. See synonyms under ABATE, ALLAY, ALLEVIATE, AMEND, PALLIATE, RELAX. [<L *mitigatus,* pp. of *mitigare* <*mitis* mild + *agere* do, drive] — **mit'i·ga·ble** *adj.* — **mit'·i·gant** *adj.* & *n.* — **mit'i·ga'tion** *n.* — **mit'i·ga'·tive** *adj.* — **mit'i·ga'tor** *n.* — **mit'i·ga·to'ry** (-gə·tôr'ē, -tō'rē) *adj.* & *n.*

mi·tis casting (mī'tis, mē'-) **1** The process of making castings of wrought iron of which the melting point has been lowered by the addition of a small amount of aluminum. **2** A casting so made. [<L *mitis* mild + CASTING]

mi·to·chon·dri·a (mī'tə·kon'drē·ə) *n.* Chondriosome. [<NL <Gk. *mitos* thread + *chondros* cartilage, granule]

mi·to·sis (mī·tō'sis) *n. Biol.* The series of changes in indirect cell division by which the chromatin of the nucleus is modified into a double set of chromosomes that splits longitudinally, one set going to each nuclear pole of the spindle before final division into two fully mature daughter cells. Compare MEIOSIS. [<NL <Gk. *mitos* thread + -OSIS] — **mi·tot·ic** (mī·tot'ik) *adj.* — **mi·tot'i·cal·ly** *adv.*

mi·trail·leur (mē·trà·yœr') *n.* **1** A soldier who operates a mitrailleuse. **2** A mitrailleuse. [<F <*mitrailler* fire grapeshot <*mitraille* grapeshot, small coins <OF *mitre, mite* small coin]

mi·trail·leuse (mē·trà·yœz') *n.* **1** A kind of breechloading machine-gun of grouped barrels for the rapid firing of small missiles. **2** Any machine-gun. [<F]

mi·tral (mī'trəl) *adj.* **1** Pertaining to or resembling a miter. **2** Of or pertaining to the mitral valve.

mitral valve *Anat.* A membranous valve between the left auricle and the left ventricle of the heart: it prevents the flow of blood into the auricle.

mi·tre (mī'tər) See MITER.

mitt (mit) *n.* **1** A glove, often of lace or knitwork, that does not extend over the fingers. **2** A mitten; specifically, in baseball, a heavy padded mitten used by the catcher and the first baseman. **3** *pl. Slang* The hands. [<MITTEN]

mit·ten (mit'n) *n.* **1** A covering for the hand, encasing the four fingers together and the thumb separately. **2** A mitt. **3** *pl. Slang* The hands; also, boxing gloves. [<F *mitaine*]

mit·ti·mus (mit'ə·məs) *n.* **1** *Law* An order by a magistrate committing a prisoner to jail. **2** A dismissal. [<L, we send <*mittere* send]

mitz·vah (mits'vä) *n. pl.* **·voth** (-vōth) A command of God; hence, the fulfilment of such a command, regarded as a special privilege; especially, a function of the synagog ceremonial or an act promoting the welfare of the Jews. Also **mits'vah.** [<Hebrew *mitzwah* commandment]

Mi·vart (mī'vərt, miv'ərt), **St. George Jackson,** 1827–1900, English biologist.

mix (miks) *v.* **mixed** or **mixt, mix·ing** *v.t.* **1** To put together in one mass or compound; blend. **2** To make by combining ingredients: to *mix* dough. **3** To combine or join: to *mix* business with pleasure. **4** To cause to associate or mingle: to *mix* social classes together. **5** To crossbreed. — *v.i.* **6** To be mixed or blended. **7** To associate; get along. **8** To take part; become involved. — **to mix up 1** To blend thoroughly. **2** To confuse; bewilder. **3** To implicate or involve. — *n.* **1** The act or effect of mixing. **2** A mixture, expecially a commercial mixture of prepared ingredients: a cake *mix.* **3** A proportion, as of things that make up a mixture; specifically, the proportion of certain substances or raw materials before their subjection to a fabricating or manufacturing process: a *mix* of cement. **3** *Telecom.* The correct blending of the sound input of two or more microphones. **4** A combination of various elements; mixture: a movie providing a heady *mix* of violence, sex, and glamour. [Back formation <MIXED] — **mix'a·ble, mix'i·ble** *adj.*

Synonyms (verb): amalgamate, associate, blend, combine, commingle, commix, compound, confuse, fuse, incorporate, join, meddle, mingle, unite. Compare COMPLEX, HETEROGENEOUS.

mixed (mikst) *adj.* **1** Mingled in a body or mass; joined together; associated; blended: generally of different or even incongruous elements: a *mixed* metaphor. **2** Containing persons of both sexes: a *mixed* school, *mixed* foursome, etc. **3** Mentally confused, as with liquor. **4** *Law* Designating statutes which concern both persons and property; also, designating property which is not altogether real nor personal, but a compound of both. **5** *Bot.* Denoting inflorescence which combines cymose and racemose. [<F *mixte* <L *mixtus,* pp. of *miscere* mix]

mixed bag A mixture or assortment of miscellaneous elements.

mixed economy A combination of laissez-faire with governmentally planned and/or controlled economy.

mixed marriage Marriage between persons of different religions or races.

mixed number See under NUMBER.

mixed train A train transporting both passengers and freight.

mixed-up (mikst'up') *adj.* Confused or disordered.

mix·en (mik'sən) *n. Archaic* A dunghill; compost heap. [OE *mixen* <*meox* dung]

mix·er (mik'sər) *n.* **1** One who or that which mixes; a machine or device for mixing. **2** *Colloq.* A person with reference to his ability to mix socially or get along well in groups.

mix·o·troph·ic (mik'sə·trof'ik) *adj. Biol.* Pertaining to or designating plants and animals capable of feeding on both inorganic and dead organic material, as certain flagellate protozoa. [<Gk. *mixis* mingling + *trophē* food]

mix·ture (miks'chər) *n.* **1** The act of mixing. **2** Something resulting from mixing; admixture. **3** Something added as an ingredient. **4** A pharmaceutical preparation consisting of an aqueous solution in which is suspended an insoluble compound: intended for internal use. **5** A commingling of two or more substances in varying proportions, in which the ingredients retain their individual chemical properties, and from which they may be separated, unaltered, by mechanical means. Compare COMPOUND. [<F <L *mixtura* <*miscere* mix]

misproportion	**misrate**	**misreform**	**misresemblance**	**mis-sheathed**	**misstroke**	**misthread**
misproposal	**misread**	**misregulate**	**misresolved**	**mis-ship**	**misstyle**	**misthrive**
mispropose	**misrealize**	**misrehearsal**	**misresult**	**misshod**	**missuggestion**	**misthrow**
misprovide	**misreason**	**misrehearse**	**misreward**	**mis-sing**	**missuit**	**mistitle**
misprovidence	**misreceive**	**misrelate**	**misrime**	**missolution**	**missummation**	**mistouch**
misprovoke	**misrecital**	**misrelation**	**misseason**	**missort**	**missuppose**	**mistranscribe**
mispunctuate	**misrecite**	**misreliance**	**misseat**	**missound**	**mis-sway**	**mistranscription**
mispunctuation	**misrecognition**	**misrely**	**mis-see**	**misspace**	**misswear**	**mistranslate**
mispurchase	**misrecognize**	**misrender**	**mis-seed**	**misspeak**	**missyllabication**	**mistranslation**
mispursuit	**misrecollect**	**misrepeat**	**missemblance**	**misstart**	**missyllabify**	**mistune**
misqualify	**misrefer**	**misreposed**	**mis-send**	**missteer**	**mistaught**	**mistutor**
misquote	**misreference**	**misreprint**	**mis-sense**	**misstop**	**mistend**	**misunion**
misraise	**misreflect**	**misrepute**	**missentence**	**misstrike**	**misterm**	**misyoke**

mix-up (miks′up′) *n.* 1 A confusion; muddle. 2 *Colloq.* A fight.

Mi·ya·za·ki (mē·yä·zä ·kē) A city on SE Kyushu island, Japan.

Mi·zar (mī′zər, mē′-) The star Zeta, second from the end in the handle of the Dipper, constellation of Ursa Major: the faint star close to it is *Alcor.* [<Arabic *mi'zar* veil, cloak]

miz·zen (miz′ən) *n. Naut.* 1 A mizzenmast. 2 A triangular sail set on the mizzen. —*adj.* Of or pertaining to the mizzen or mizzenmast. Also **miz′en.** [<F *misaine* <Ital. *mezzana,* fem. of *mezzano* middle < L *medianus.* Doublet of MEIDIAN, MEAN,[3] MESNE.]

miz·zen·mast (miz′ən·məst, -mast′, -mäst′) *n. Naut.* 1 The mast next abaft the mainmast. 2 The shorter of the two masts of a ketch or yawl.

Mjol·nir (myol′nir) *n.* In Norse mythology, Thor's terrible hammer. Also **Mjoll′nir, Mjöll·nir** (myœl′nir), **Mjol′ner.**

mks The meter-kilogram-second system of units for the measurement of physical quantities. It differs from the cgs system in using the international standards of length and mass instead of their submultiples, the centimeter and the gram.

mne·me (nē′mē) *n.* A hypothetical unit of memory assumed to exist in all animal cells. [<Gk. *'mnēmē* memory]

mne·mon·ic (ni·mon′ik) *adj.* Pertaining to, aiding, or designed to aid the memory. Also **mne·mon′i·cal.** [<Gk. *mnēmonikos* <*mnēmōn* mindful <*mnasthai* remember]

mne·mon·ics (ni·mon′iks) *n.* The science of memory improvement. Also **mne·mo·tech·nics** (nē′mō·tek′niks).

Mne·mos·y·ne (nē·mos′ə·nē, -moz′-) In Greek mythology, the goddess of memory and mother (by Zeus) of the Muses. [<L <Gk. *mnēmosynē* memory <*mnasthai* remember]

-mo *suffix Printing* Folded into a (specified) number of leaves: said of a sheet of paper: 12 *mo* or *duodecimo.* Also shown by the symbol (°), as in 12°. [<L *-mo,* as in the phrase *induodecimo* twelvefold]

mo·a (mō′ə) *n.* A large, flightless, extinct bird (family *Dinornithiformes*) of New Zealand, having enormous legs with at least three toes; especially, the largest species *(Dinornis robustus).* [<native name]

MOA
(Thought to have ranged from 4 to 12 feet in height)

Mo·ab (mō′ab) An ancient country in the upland area east of the Dead Sea.

Mo·ab·ite (mō′əb·īt) *n.* One of the descendants of Moab, son of Lot. *Gen.* xix 37. —**Mo·ab·it·ess** (mō′əb·īt′is) *n.* fem.

Moabite Stone A stone slab with a Moabite inscription, dating from 850 B.C.; discovered, 1868.

moan (mōn) *n.* 1 A low mournful sound indicative of grief or pain. 2 A similar sound: the *moan* of the wind. 3 *Obs.* Lamentation; complaint. —*v.i.* 1 To utter moans of grief or pain. 2 To make a low, mournful sound, as wind in trees. —*v.t.* 3 To lament; bewail. [Cf. OE *mænan* lament, moan]

moat (mōt) *n.* A defensive ditch on the outside of a fortress wall. —*v.t.* To surround with or as with a moat. ◆Homophone: *mote.* [<OF *mote* embankment]

mob[1] (mob) *n.* 1 A turbulent or lawless crowd or throng; a rabble. 2 The lowest class of people; the masses; populace. 3 *Austral.* A herd, as of sheep or cattle. 4 *Slang* A gang, as of thieves. —*v.t.* **mobbed, mob·bing** 1 To attack in a mob; crowd around and annoy. 2 To crowd into, as a hall. [<L *mob(ile vulgus)* movable crowd] —**mob′ber** *n.* —**mob′bish** *adj.* —**mob′bish·ly** *adv.*

Synonyms (noun): canaille, crowd, masses, people, populace, rabble.

mob[2] (mob) *n.* A cap or headdress formerly worn by women and girls and usually tied under the chin. Also **mob′cap′.** [<Du. *mop* coif, cap]

mo·bile (mō′bəl, -bēl) *adj.* 1 Characterized by freedom of movement; movable. 2 Changing easily in expression or in state of mind; changeable. 3 Moving or flowing freely. 4 That can be easily and quickly moved, as military units. 5 Designating a mobile. —*n.* (mō′bēl) A form of sculpture arranged so that its movable parts, suspended or balanced on rods, wires, etc., describe kinetic rather than static patterns. [<F <L *mobilis* movable] —**mo·bil·i·ty** (mō·bil′ə·tē) *n.*

Synonyms: changeable, changing, expressive, fickle, movable, sensitive, variable, volatile. See ACTIVE. *Antonyms*: dull, fixed, immovable, still, stolid, unchanging, unvarying.

Mo·bile (mō·bēl′) A port of Alabama, on **Mobile Bay,** an arm of the Gulf of Mexico in SW Alabama.

mobile home *U.S.* A movable living unit, originally conceived of as a trailer but now designed more like a ranch house, which can be connected to utilities and is often put on a foundation as a permanent dwelling.

Mobile River A river in SW Alabama flowing 45 miles south from the confluence of the Tombigbee and Alabama rivers to Mobile Bay at Mobile.

mo·bi·lize (mō′bə·līz) *v.* **·lized, ·liz·ing** *v.t.* 1 To make ready for war, as an army, industry, etc. 2 To assemble for use; organize. 3 To make mobile; put into circulation or use. —*v.i.* 4 To get ready for war. Also *Brit.* **mo′bi·lise.** [<F *mobiliser*] —**mo′bi·li·za′ tion** (-lə·zā′shən, -lī·zā′-) *n.*

Mö·bi·us surface (mœ′bē·o͞os) *Geom.* A surface both sides of which may be completely traversed without crossing either edge: made by joining the half-twisted ends of a rectangular strip of paper or other flexible material. Also **Möbius strip.** [after August Ferdinand *Möbius,* 1790–1868, German mathematician and astronomer]

mob law Lynch law.

mob·le (mob′əl) *v.t. Archaic* To cover with a cap or mob. [<MOB[2]]

mob·oc·ra·cy (mob·ok′rə·sē) *n. pl.* **·cies** 1 Lawless control of public affairs by the mob or populace. 2 The mob considered as the dominant class. [<MOB[1] + -(O)CRACY]

mob·o·crat (mob′ə·krat) *n.* One who favors mobocracy; a demagog. —**mob′o·crat′ic, mob′o·crat′i·cal** *adj.*

mob·ster (mob′stər) *n. Slang* A gangster.

moc·ca·sin (mok′ə·sin) *n.* 1 A foot covering made of soft leather or buckskin: worn by North American Indians; also, a soft shoe or slipper. 2 A dark-colored, obscurely blotched, venomous snake (genus *Agkistrodon*) of the southern United States. *A. piscivorus* is the **water moccasin.** [<Algonquian *mohkisson*]

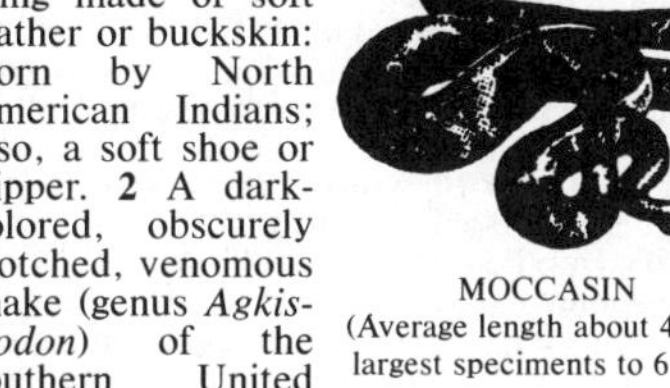

MOCCASIN
(Average length about 4 feet; largest speciments to 6 feet)

moccasin flower Any one of certain orchids of the genus *Cypripedium,* common in the United States, especially the showy ladyslipper *(C. reginae),* State flower of Minnesota.

mo·cha (mō′kə) *n.* 1 A choice coffee, originally grown in Arabia. 2 A rich, coffee-flavored icing, or a cake flavored with it. 3 A fine sheepskin leather used for making gloves. 4 A dark, dull, grayish-brown color. [from *Mocha*]

Mo·cha (mō′kə) A port of Yemen, in SW Arabia: also *Mokha.*

mock (mok) *v.t.* 1 To treat or address scornfully or derisively; hold up to ridicule. 2 To ridicule by imitation of action or speech; mimic derisively. 3 To deceive; delude. 4 To defy; make futile. 5 *Poetic* To imitate; counterfeit. —*v.i.* 6 To express or show ridicule, scorn, or contempt; scoff. —*adj.* Merely imitating the reality; sham. —*n.* An act of mocking; a jeer; mockery. [<OF *mocquer*] —**mock′er** *n.* —**mock′ing·ly** *adv.*

Synonyms (verb): banter, chaff, deride, flout, gibe, insult, jeer, taunt. See IMITATE, MISLEAD, SCOFF. Compare COUNTERFEIT.

mock·er·y (mok′ər·ē) *n. pl.* **·er·ies** 1 Derisive or contemptuous mimicry. 2 A false show; sham. 3 A butt of ridicule. 4 Labor in vain. See synonyms under BANTER, SCORN.

mock-he·ro·ic (mok′hi·rō′ik) *adj.* Imitating or satirizing the heroic manner, style, attitude, or character. —*n.* 1 Any writing using the grand style as a comic expedient. 2 *pl.* Affectation of the grand manner in expressing trivialities.

mock·ing·bird (mok′ing·bûrd′) *n.* 1 A bird *(Mimus polyglottos)* common in the southern and eastern United States, noted for its rich song and powers of imitating the calls of other birds. 2 One of various other birds that mock, as the catbird.

mocking thrush The thrasher.

mocking wren 1 The Carolina wren. 2 Bewick's wren. See under WREN.

mock moon A paraselene.

mock orange Any of a genus *(Philadelphus)* of ornamental shrubs of the saxifrage family: also called *syringa.*

mock sun A parhelion.

mock title See HALF-TITLE.

mock-tur·tle soup (mok′tûr′təl) Soup prepared from calf's head or other meat, and somewhat resembling green-turtle soup.

mock·up (mok′up′) *n.* 1 A model, usually full-scale, of a proposed structure, machine, apparatus, etc. 2 An airplane, etc., constructed for purposes of study, testing, or training of personnel.

Moc·te·zu·ma (môk′tā·so͞o ′mä) See MONTEZUMA.

mod (mod) *adj.* Bold, flamboyant, and unconventional, as in dress or behavior. —*n. Sometimes cap.* One who dresses or behaves in a flamboyant or unconventional manner. [<MODERN]

mo·dal (mōd′l) *adj.* 1 Of or denoting a mode or manner, especially a mode of grammar, a mode in music, or a mode of logical statement. 2 Characterized by form or manner without reference to matter or substance. 3 Pertaining to or designating a statistical mode. —**mo′dal·ly** *adv.*

mo·dal·i·ty (mō·dal′ə·tē) *n. pl.* **·ties** 1 Modal character; the fact or quality of being modal. 2 *Logic* The character of a proposition as expressing or asserting a sequence of necessity (including impossibility) or of contingency (including probability and possibility).

Mod·der (mod′ər) A river in Orange Free State Province, Republic of South Africa, flowing 225 miles NW to the Riet.

mode (mōd) *n.* 1 Manner of being, doing, etc.; way; method. 2 Prevailing style; common fashion. 3 *Gram.* Mood. 4 *Music* A method of dividing an octave by placing the steps and half-steps of which it is composed in certain arbitrary relations. In the **major mode,** tones are arranged as given in the major scale; in the **minor mode,** as in the minor scale. 5 *Psychol.* A faculty or phenomenon of mind considered as a state of consciousness. 6 *Philos.* The manner of a thing's existence so far as it is not essential. 7 *Logic* **a** The style of the connection between the antecedent and the consequent of a proposition. **b** The arrangement of the propositions of a syllogism according to their quantity and quality. 8 *Stat.* That value, magnitude, or score which occurs the greatest number of times in a given series of observations: also called *norm.* 9 *Geol.* The actual mineral composition of a rock, expressed in percentages by weight: distinguished from *norm.* 10 A light bluish-gray color. 11 *Physics* One of a set of forms of motion of a dynamic system, having the properties that the variation with time is either harmonic or exponential and that any form of motion of the system can be represented as a superposition of members of the set. See synonyms under MANNER, SYSTEM. [< L *modus* measure, manner]

mod·el (mod′l) *n.* 1 An object, usually in miniature, representing accurately something to be made or already existing; more rarely, a plan or drawing: a *model* of a building. 2 A person who poses for painters, sculptors, etc. 3 A thing or person to be imitated or patterned after; that which is taken as a pattern or an example. **4** A person employed to wear articles of clothing to display them to customers. **5** That which strikingly resembles something else; an approximate copy or image. —*v.* **·eled** or **·elled, ·el·ing** or **·el·ling** *v.t.* **1** To plan or fashion after a model or pattern. **2** To make a model of. **3** To fashion; make. **4** To display by wearing, as a coat or hat. —*v.i.* **5** To make a model or models. **6** To pose or serve as a model (defs. 2 and 4). **7** To assume the appearance of natural form. —*adj.* Serving or used as a model; suitable for a model; worthy to be imitated. [<F *modèle* <Ital. *modello*, dim. of *modo* <L *modus* measure, manner] —**mod'el·er, mod'el·ler** *n.*

Synonyms (noun): archetype, copy, design, ectype, example, facsimile, image, imitation, mold, original, pattern, prototype, replica, representation, type. A *pattern* must be closely followed in its minutest particulars by a faithful copyist; a *model* may allow a great degree of freedom. A sculptor may idealize his living *model*; his workmen must exactly copy in marble or metal the *model* he has made in clay. The *archetype* is the original form, actual or ideal, in accordance with which existing things are made; a *prototype* is either the original or an authenticated copy that has the authority of the original. See EXAMPLE, IDEA, IDEAL.

Model T An early model of automobile manufactured by Henry Ford in great numbers: also called *tin lizzie*.

Mo·de·na (mō'dā·nä) A city in north central Italy.

mod·er·ate (mod'ər·it) *adj.* **1** Keeping or kept within reasonable limits; not extreme, excessive, or radical; also, mild; temperate; calm; reasonable; gentle. **2** Not strongly partisan: said of political and religious parties, and their tenets or views. **3** Medium; fair; also, mediocre. **4** Slow in thought, speech, or action. **5** *Meteorol.* Designating a breeze (No. 4) or a gale (No. 7) on the Beaufort scale. See synonyms under GRADUAL, MODEST, SLOW, SOBER. —*n.* A person of moderate views, opinions, or practices; especially, a member of a political or religious party which is not strongly partisan. —*v.* (mod'ə·rāt) **·at·ed, ·at·ing** *v.t.* **1** To reduce the violence, severity, etc., of; make less extreme; restrain. **2** To preside over. —*v.i.* **3** To become less intense or violent; abate. **4** To act as moderator. See synonyms under ABATE, ALLAY, ALLEVIATE, TEMPER, TRANQUILIZE. [<L *moderatus*, pp. of *moderare* regulate < *modus* measure] —**mod'er·ate·ly** *adv.* —**mod'er·ate·ness** *n.* —**mod'er·a'tion** *n.*

mod·e·ra·to (mod'ə·rä'tō) *adj.* & *adv. Music* In moderate time; moderately. [<Ital.]

mod·er·a·tor (mod'ə·rā'tər) *n.* **1** One who restrains or regulates. **2** The presiding officer of a meeting; also, the presiding officer in Presbyterian and Congregational courts. **3** *Physics* A substance, as graphite or beryllium, used to control the rate of a nuclear chain reaction in an atomic-energy reactor. —**mod'er·a'tor·ship** *n.*

mod·ern (mod'ərn) *adj.* **1** Pertaining to the present or recent period; not ancient. **2** *Obs.* Commonplace; common; trite. —*n.* **1** A person of modern times, or modern views or characteristics: also **mod'ern·er.** **2** *Printing* A style of type face characterized by contrasting heavy down-strokes and thin cross-strokes. [<LL *modernus* recent <L *modo* just now] —**mod'ern·ly** *adv.* —**mo·der·ni·ty** (mo·dûr'nə·tē), **mod'ern·ness** *n.*

Synonyms (adj.): fresh, late, new, novel, recent. *Modern* history pertains to any period since the Middle Ages; *modern* literature, *modern* architecture, etc., are not strikingly remote from the styles and types prevalent today. That which is *late* is somewhat removed from the present, but not far enough to be called old. That which is *recent* is very close to the present, but not quite so sharply distinguished from the past as *new*. See NEW.

mod·ern·ism (mod'ərn·iz'əm) *n.* **1** Something characteristic of modern as distinguished from former or classical times; a modern idiom or practice. **2** Modern character, methods, or mental attitude. **3** The humanistic tendency in religious thought to supplement old theological creeds and dogmas by new scientific and philosophical learning and thus to place emphasis on practical ethics and world-wide social justice: distinguished from *fundamentalism*. —**mod'ern·ist** *n.* —**mod'ern·is'tic** *adj.*

mod·ern·ize (mod'ərn·īz) *v.t.* & *v.i.* **·ized, ·iz·ing** To make or become modern in ideas, standards, methods, etc. —**mod'ern·i·za'tion** *n.* —**mod'ern·iz'er** *n.*

mod·est (mod'ist) *adj.* **1** Restrained by a sense of propriety or humility. **2** Characterized by reserve, propriety, or purity; decorous; chaste. **3** Free from excess; moderate. [<F *modeste* <L *modestus* moderate < *modus* measure] —**mod'est·ly** *adv.*

Synonyms: chaste, decent, decorous, humble, moderate, proper, pure, retiring, unassuming, unobtrusive, unostentatious, unpretending, unpretentious, virtuous. See HUMBLE.

mod·es·ty (mod'is·tē) *n.* Decent reserve and propriety; delicacy; decorum.

Synonyms: backwardness, bashfulness, coldness, constraint, coyness, diffidence, reserve, shyness, timidity, unobtrusiveness. *Bashfulness* is a shrinking from notice without assignable reason. *Coyness* is a half encouragement, half avoidance of offered attention, and may be real or affected. *Diffidence* is self-distrust; *modesty*, a humble estimate of oneself in comparison with others or with the demands of some undertaking. *Modesty* has also the specific meaning of a sensitive shrinking from anything indelicate. *Shyness* is a tendency to shrink from observation; *timidity*, a distinct fear of criticism, error, or failure. *Reserve* is holding oneself aloof from others, or holding back one's feelings from expression, or one's affairs from communication to others. Compare ABASH, PRIDE, RESERVE, TACITURN. *Antonyms*: abandon, arrogance, assumption, assurance, boldness, conceit, confidence, egotism, forwardness, frankness, freedom, haughtiness, impudence, indiscretion, loquaciousness, loquacity, pertness, sauciness, self-conceit, self-sufficiency, sociability.

mod·i·cum (mod'i·kəm) *n. pl.* **·cums** or **·ca** (-kə) **1** A moderate amount; a little. **2** A small thing or person. [<L < *modus* measure]

mod·i·fi·ca·tion (mod'ə·fə·kā'shən) *n.* **1** The act of modifying, or the state of being modified. **2** *Biol.* Variation in plants and animals, specifically by localized changes in an organism due to external influences and not inheritable. Compare MUTATION. **3** That which results from modifying. —**mod·i·fi·ca·to·ry** (mod'ə·fə·kā'tər·ē) *adj.*

mod·i·fi·er (mod'ə·fī'ər) *n.* **1** One who or that which qualifies, changes, limits, or varies. **2** *Gram.* A word, phrase, or clause that alters, restricts, or varies the application of another word or group of words, as an adjective or adverb. See also UNIT MODIFIER.

mod·i·fy (mod'ə·fī) *v.* **·fied, ·fy·ing** *v.t.* **1** To make somewhat different in form, character, etc.; vary. **2** To reduce in degree or extent; moderate. **3** *Gram.* To qualify the meaning of; restrict; limit. **4** *Ling.* To alter (a vowel) by umlaut. —*v.i.* **5** To be or become modified; change. See synonyms under CHANGE, TEMPER. [<F *modifier* <L *modificare* < *modus* measure + *facere* make] —**mod'i·fi'a·ble** *adj.*

Mo·di·glia·ni (mō'dē·lyä'nē), **Amedeo**, 1884–1920, Italian painter and sculptor.

mo·dil·lion (mō·dil'yən) *n. Archit.* An enriched block or horizontal bracket used in series under a Corinthian or Composite cornice: sometimes, with less ornament, under one of the Roman Ionic order. [<F *modillon* <Ital. *modiglione*]

mo·di·o·lus (mō·dī'ə·ləs) *n. pl.* **·li** (-lī) *Anat.* The central stem round which wind the passages of the cochlea of the internal ear. [<L, bucket on a water wheel < *modus* measure]

mod·ish (mō'dish) *adj.* Conformable to the current mode, fashion, or usage; stylish. —**mod'ish·ly** *adv.* —**mod'ish·ness** *n.*

mo·diste (mō·dēst') *n.* A woman who makes or deals in fashionable articles, especially of women's dress or millinery. [<F]

Mo·djes·ka (mō·jes'kə), **Helena**, 1840–1909, Polish actress active in the United States.

Mo·djo·ker·to Man (mō'jō·kâr'tō) A primitive hominid identified from the fossil skull of an infant found in 1931 in Pleistocene deposits near Modjokerto, Java: it bears anatomical resemblances both to Pithecanthropus and to Neanderthal man.

Mo·doc (mō'dok) *n.* A North American Indian of a small, nearly extinct tribe of Lutuamian linguistic stock, formerly living in California, now on reservations in Oregon and Oklahoma. See LUTUAMIAN.

mo·do et for·ma (mō'dō et fôr'mə) *Latin* In manner and form.

Mo·dred (mō'drid) In Arthurian legend, King Arthur's treacherous nephew (or son). During Arthur's absence Modred usurped the throne: after Arthur's return they killed each other in battle.

mod·u·lar (moj'ŏŏ·lər) *adj.* **1** Of, like, or pertaining to a module or modulus. **2** Composed of modules: *modular* homes.

mod·u·late (moj'ŏŏ·lāt) *v.* **·lat·ed, ·lat·ing** *v.t.* **1** To vary the tone, inflection, or pitch of. **2** To regulate or adjust; temper; soften. **3** *Music* To change or cause to change to a different key. **4** To intone or sing. **5** *Electronics* To alter the frequency or amplitude of (a radio carrier wave). —*v.i.* **6** *Electronics* To alter the frequency or amplitude of a carrier wave. **7** *Music* To change from one key to another by using a transitional chord common to both. [<L *modulatus*, pp. of *modulari* regulate < *modulus* MODULE] —**mod'u·la·to'ry** (-lə·tôr'ē, -tō'rē) *adj.*

mod·u·la·tion (moj'ŏŏ·lā'shən) *n.* **1** The act of modulating, or the state of being modulated; specifically, a musical inflection of the voice; change in pitch. **2** *Music* A change from one key to another by the use of a transitional chord common to both. **3** *Telecom.* The process of varying the frequency, amplitude, intensity, or phase of a carrier wave so as to conform with a transmitted signal wave.

mod·u·la·tor (moj'ŏŏ·lā'tər) *n.* **1** One who or that which modulates. **2** *Telecom.* A tube or valve for effecting modulation. **3** A musical chart showing the relations of tones and scales.

mod·ule (moj'ŏŏl) *n.* **1** A standard or unit of measurement. **2** *Archit.* A measure of proportion among the parts of a classical order, the size of the diameter or semidiameter of the base of a column shaft usually being taken as a unit. **3** A standard structural component repeatedly used, as in a building, computer, etc.: cubic *modules* used in the design of a table. **4** A preassembled, self-contained unit, often a component or subassembly of a larger structure: a housing *module*; a lunar *module*. **5** *Obs.* A mere image. [<L *modulus* < *modus* measure. Doublet of MOLD[1].]

mod·u·lor (moj'ŏŏ·lôr) *n.* A system of industrial design based upon the ideal proportions of the human body: units derived from the basic dimensions can be assembled to secure maximum harmony and utility. —*adj.* Of or characterized by such design.

mod·u·lus (moj'ŏŏ·ləs) *n. pl.* **·li** (-lī) **1** *Physics* A number, coefficient, or quantity that measures a force, function, or effect: *modulus* of elasticity: sometimes abbreviated to M or μ. See CONGRUENT. **2** *Math.* The logarithm of e to the base 10 ($\log_{10}e$): Napierian logarithms are multiplied by this factor to convert them to logarithms to the base 10. [<L, dim. of *modus* a measure]

mo·dus (mō'dəs) *n. Latin* Mode; manner.

modus op·er·an·di (op'ə·ran'dī) *Latin* A manner of operation.

modus vi·ven·di (vi·ven'dī) *Latin* A manner of living; especially, a temporary arrangement pending a final settlement.

moe (mō) *adj.* & *adv. Obs.* More.

mo·el·lon (mō'əl·on) *n.* **1** A form of rubble masonry used as a filling in the facing walls of a structure. **2** Dégras (def. 1). [<F, alter. of OF *moilon*; ? infl. by F *moelle* pith]

Moe·rae (mē'rē) See MOIRAI. Also **Mœ'ræ.**

Moe·ro (mwe·rō') The French spelling of MWERU.

Moe·si·a (mē'shē·ə) An ancient country and former Roman province in SE Europe south of the Danube. Also **Mœ'si·a.**

Moe·so·goth (mē'sə·goth) *n.* A member of the Gothic tribe that settled in Moesia. —**Moe'so·goth'ic** *adj.*

mo·fette (mō·fet') *n.* **1** A noxious emanation of gas from a fissure; a gas spring. **2** An opening in the earth from which noxious gas escapes, as from a volcano. Also **mof·fette'.** [<F <Ital. *mofetta* < *muffare* decay <G *muff* mold]

mo·fus·sil (mə·fus'əl) *n. Anglo-Indian* The

country as distinguished from the residencies and the towns.

Mog·a·di·shu (mog′ə·dish′ōō) The chief port and capital of Somalia, on the Indian Ocean. *Italian* **Mo·ga·di·scio** (mō′gä·dē′shō).

Mog·a·dor (mog′ə·dôr′, -dōr′; *Fr.* mô·gȧ·dôr′) A port on the Atlantic coast of SW Morocco.

mo·gen Da·vid (mō′gən dä′vid, duv′id) A mystic device formed by the intertwining of two equilateral triangles; the six-pointed star: used as a symbol of Judaism. Also called *star of David, shield of David, Solomon's seal.* [<Hebrew, star of David]

Mo·gi·lev (mō′gi·lef, *Russian* mô′gē·lyôf′) A city in SW Belorussian S.S.R., on the Dnieper. Also **Mo·hi·lev** (mô′hē·lyôf′).

mo·gul (mō′gul, mō·gul′) *n.* **1** Any great or pretentious personage; autocrat: also **great mogul. 2** A type of freight locomotive with three pairs of coupled drivers and one pair of leading truck wheels.

Mo·gul (mō′gul, mō·gul′) *n.* A Mongol; Mongolian; specifically, one of the Mongol conquerors of Hindustan, or a follower of Genghis Khan in the 13th century. Also **Mo·ghul′.** — **the Great** or **Grand Mogul** The former Mongol emperor of Delhi. [<Persian *mugal* a Mongol]

Mo·hács (mō′häch) A city on the Danube in southern Hungary; scene of a decisive Turkish victory over the Hungarians, 1526.

mo·hair (mō′hâr) *n.* **1** The hair of the Angora goat. **2** A smooth, wiry fabric made of mohair filling and cotton warp: often called *brilliantine.* **3** A fabric of cut or uncut loops with cotton or wool back and mohair pile: used chiefly for upholstery. [Earlier *mocayare* <Arabic *mukhayyar;* infl. in form by *hair*]

Mo·ham·med (mō·ham′id), 570–632, Arabian religious and military leader; founder of Islam and author of the *Koran*: also spelled *Mahomet.* Also **Mo·hom′ed.**
— **Mohammed II,** 1430?–81, sultan of Turkey 1451–81; captured Constantinople, 1453.

Mohammed Ali See MEHEMET ALI.

Mo·ham·me·dan (mō·ham′ə·dən) *adj.* Pertaining to Mohammed or to his religion and institutions. — *n.* A follower of Mohammed or believer in Islam; a Muslim. Also *Mahometan, Muhammadan.*

Mo·ham·me·dan·ism (mō·ham′ə·dən·iz′əm) *n.* The religion founded by Mohammed; Islam.

mo·har·ra (mə·här′ə) See MOJARRA.

Mo·har·ran (mə·här′ən) See MUHARRAM.

Mo·ha·ve (mō·hä′vē) *n.* A member of a tribe of North American Indians of Yuman linguistic stock, formerly living along the Colorado River. — *adj.* Of or pertaining to this tribe. Also spelled *Mojave.*

Mohave Desert See MOJAVE DESERT.

Mo·hawk (mō′hôk) *n.* **1** One of a tribe of North American Indians of Iroquoian stock, one of the original tribes of the Five Nations, formerly ranging from the Mohawk River Valley, New York, to the St. Lawrence: now in Canada, New York, and Wisconsin. **2** The Iroquoian language of this tribe. **3** A Mohock. [<N. Am. Ind. Cf. Narragansett *mohowaicuck,* lit., they eat animate things, hence, eaters of human flesh; so named by enemy tribes.]

Mohawk River A river in central New York, flowing 140 miles SE to the Hudson.

Mo·he·gan (mō·hē′gən) *n.* One of a tribe of North American Indians of Algonquian linguistic stock, the eastern branch of the Mahican group: formerly occupying the region from the lower Connecticut and Thames rivers northward to Massachusetts. See MAHICAN. [<Algonquian *maingan* wolf]

Mo·hen·jo-Da·ro (mō·hen′jō·dä′rō) A site of Indus Valley civilization in NW Sind, West Pakistan.

Mo·hi·can (mō·hē′kən) *n.* One of a warlike tribe of North American Indians belonging to the Algonquian linguistic stock, and formerly dwelling along both banks of the Hudson. See MAHICAN.

Mo·hock (mō′hok, -hôk) *n.* One of a band of lawless rowdies, often aristocratic rakes, who frequented the streets of London early in the 18th century. Also **Mo′hawk.** [Var. of MOHAWK]

Mo·hole (mō′hōl′) *n.* A hole drilled or to be drilled through the ocean floor to the Mohorovicic discontinuity.

Mo·hor·o·vic·ic discontinuity (mə·hôr′ə·vis′ik, -vich′ik) *n. Geol.* A rock layer forming a boundary between the earth's crust and mantle about 6 to 25 miles deep. Also **Mo·ho** (mō′·hō′). [after Andrija *Mohorović*, Yugoslavian scientist]

Mohs scale (mōz) *Mineral.* A qualitative scale in which the hardness of a mineral is determined by its ability to scratch, or be scratched by, any one of 10 standard minerals arranged in the following increasing order of hardness: 1, talc; 2, gypsum; 3, calcite; 4, fluorite; 5, apatite; 6, feldspar; 7, quartz; 8, topaz; 9, corundum; 10, diamond. [after Friedrich *Mohs,* 1773–1839, German mineralogist who conceived it]

moi·dore (moi′dôr, -dōr) *n.* A former Portuguese or Brazilian gold coin. [Pg. *moeda d'ouro* coin of gold <L *moneta* money + *aurum* gold]

moi·e·ty (moi′ə·tē) *n. pl.* **·ties 1** A half. **2** A small portion. [<F *moitié* <L *medietas* < *medius* half]

moil (moil) *v.i.* To work hard; toil; drudge. — *n.* **1** A soiling; defilement; spot. **2** Confusion; vexation; trouble. **3** *Scot.* Toil; drudgery. [<OF *moillier, muiller* wet <L *mollis* soft; infl. in meaning by *toil*] — **moil′er** *n.* — **moil′ing·ly** *adv.*

Moi·rai (moi′rī) In Greek mythology, the three birth goddesses, identified with the Fates: also spelled *Moerae.*

moi·ré (mwä·rā′) *adj.* Having a wavelike or watered appearance, as certain fabrics. — *n.* **1** A corded silk or rayon fabric, having a wavy or watered pattern produced by passing the fabric between engraved cylinders which press the design into the material: also **moire** (mwär). **2** The finish or effect of this process on certain fabrics. [<F < *moirer* water silk < *moire* watered silk <MOHAIR]

Mo·ïse (mō·ēz′) French form of MOSES. Also *Ital.* **Mo·i·se** (mō′ē·zā′), *Sp.* **Mo·i·ses** (mō′ē·sās′, *Pg.* mō·ē·zesh′).

Mois·san (mwä·säṅ′), **Henri,** 1852–1907, French chemist.

moist (moist) *adj.* **1** Having slight sensible wetness; damp; humid. **2** Tearful: *moist* eyes. **3** Marked by the presence of pus, phlegm, etc. [<OF *moiste* <a fusion of L *musteus* dew + *mucidus* moldy < *mucus* mucus] — **moist′ly** *adv.* — **moist′ness** *n.*

mois·ten (mois′ən) *v.t.* & *v.i.* To make or become moist. — **mois′ten·er** *n.*

mois·ture (mois′chər) *n.* Slight sensible wetness; a small amount of liquid exuding from, diffused through, or resting on a substance; dampness. [<OF *moisteur*]

mo·jar·ra (mə·här′ə) *n.* A large salt-water fish (genus *Gerres*), similar to a bass, inhabiting mostly tropical waters: also spelled *moharra.* [<Sp.]

Mo·ja·ve (mō·hä′vē) See MOHAVE.

Mojave Desert An arid region comprising part of the Great Basin in southern California; 15,000 square miles: also *Mohave Desert.*

Mo·ji (mō·jē) A port on northern Kyushu island, Japan.

Mo·kha (mō′kə) See MOCHA.

Mo·ki (mō′kē) See MOQUI.

Mok·po (mōk·pō) A port of SW Korea. *Japanese* **Mop·po** (mop·pō).

mol (mōl) *n. Chem.* The gram-molecule; that weight of a substance, expressed in grams, which is equal numerically to its molecular weight: also spelled *mole.* [<G]

mo·la (mō′lə) *n. pl.* **·lae** (-lē) Mole[4]. [<L]

mo·lal (mō′ləl) *adj. Chem.* **1** Pertaining to the mol or gram-molecule. **2** Designating a solution which has a concentration equivalent to one mol of the solute in 1,000 grams of the solvent. Compare MOLAR[1]. [<MOL + -AL] — **mo·lal·i·ty** (mō·lal′ə·tē) *n.*

mo·lar[1] (mō′lər) *adj.* **1** *Physics* Pertaining to a mass; acting on or exerted by a mass, as force. **2** *Chem.* Having or containing a gram-molecular weight or mol; specifically, denoting a solution containing one mol of solute to the liter. Compare MOLAL. [<MOL + -AR] — **mo·lar·i·ty** (mō·lar′ə·tē) *n.*

mo·lar[2] (mō′lər) *n.* A grinding tooth with flattened crown, situated behind the canine and incisor teeth. — *adj.* **1** Grinding, or adapted for grinding. **2** Pertaining to a molar. [<L *molaris* < *mola* mill]

mo·las·ses (mə·las′iz) *n.* A viscid, dark-colored liquor drained off from raw cane or beet sugar; treacle. [<Pg. *melaco* <L *mellaceus* honeylike < *mel* honey]

mold[1] (mōld) *v.t.* **1** To work into a particular shape or form; model; shape. **2** To shape or cast in or as in a mold; make on a mold. **3** In founding, to form a mold of or from. **4** To ornament with molding. See synonyms under BEND, GOVERN, INFLUENCE. [<*n.*] — *n.* **1** A matrix for shaping anything in a fluid or plastic condition: distinguished from *cast.* **2** Hence, that after which something else is patterned, or the thing that is molded. **3** Form; nature; also, kind; character. **4** The physical form; shape: now applied to the human form. **5** A molding, or number of moldings. See synonyms under MODEL. Also spelled *mould.* [<OF *modle* <L *modulus* < *modus* measure, limit. Doublet of MODULE.] — **mold′a·ble** *adj.* — **mold′er** *n.*

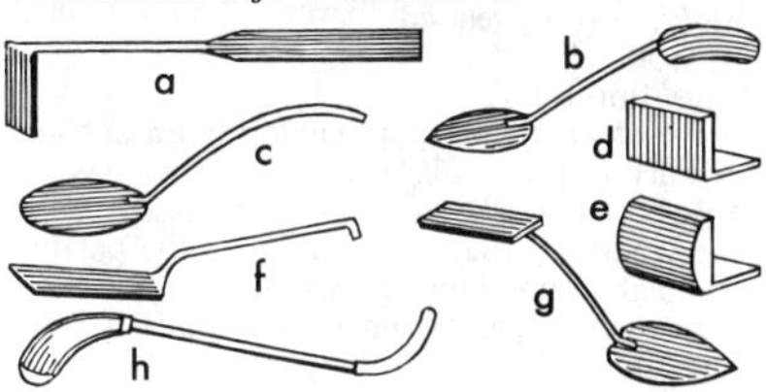

IRON-MOLDER'S TOOLS
a. Lifter. *b.* Taper and square. *c.* Oval or dog-tail. *d.* Square corner. *e.* Half-round corner. *f.* Yankee. *g.* Heart and square. *h.* Flange and bead.

mold[2] (mōld) *n.* **1** Any fungous growth on food, clothing, walls, etc., especially such growths as form a woolly or furry coating on decaying vegetable matter or in moist, warm places. **2** Any of various fungi producing such growths. **3** Mustiness; decay. — *v.t.* & *v.i.* To become or cause to become moldy. Also spelled *mould.* [< obs. *moul* grow moldy <Scand. Cf. Dan. *mugle* grow moldy.]

mold[3] (mōld) *n.* **1** Earth that is fine and soft, and rich in organic matter. **2** The constituent material of anything; earthy material; matter. **3** The earth; ground; hence, a grave. — *v.t.* To cover with mold. Also spelled *mould.* [OE *molde* earth]

Mold (mōld) County town of Flintshire, Wales.

Mol·dau (môl′dou) The German name for the VLTAVA.

Mol·da·vi·a (mol·dā′vē·ə) A historical province of eastern Rumania; 14,690 square miles. Also **Mol·do·va** (môl·dō′vä).

Mol·da·vi·an (mol·dā′vē·ən) *adj.* Of or relating to Moldavia. — *n.* **1** A native or naturalized inhabitant of Moldavia. **2** The Rumanian language of the Moldavians.

Moldavian Soviet Socialist Republic A constituent republic of SW European U.S.S.R.; 13,000 square miles; capital, Kishinev.

mol·da·vite (mol′də·vīt) *n.* **1** A dull-green natural glass resembling obsidian and thought to be of meteoritic origin. **2** A variety of ozocerite found in Moravia. [from the *Moldau,* near which it is found]

mold·board (mōld′bôrd′, -bōrd′) *n.* **1** *Agric.* The curved metal plate of a plow, by which the earth is turned over and pulverized. **2** A similar part of a machine for building roads: also spelled *mouldboard.* [<MOLD[3] + BOARD]

mold·er (mōl′dər) *v.i.* To decay gradually and turn to dust; crumble; waste away. — *v.t.* To cause to crumble. Also spelled *moulder.* See synonyms under DECAY. [Freq. of obs. *mold* crumble]

-mol·der *combining form* One who molds or fashions (a specific thing): *glass-molder, iron-molder.* [<MOLD[1]]

mold fungus A fungus which causes mold; specifically, any of an order (*Mucorales*) of phycomycetous fungi, as the common bread mold (*Rhizopus nigricans*).

mold·ing (mōl′ding) *n.* **1** The act of shaping with or as with a mold. **2** Anything made in or as in a mold. **3** *Archit.* **a** A more or less ornamental strip on some part of a structure.

b A cornice or other depressed or projecting decorative member on a surface or angle of any part of a building. Also spelled *moulding.*

mold·warp (mōld′wôrp) *n. Brit. Dial.* The European mole. Also spelled *molewarp, mouldwarp.* [OE *molde* soil + *weorpan* throw up]

mold·y (mōl′dē) *adj.* **mold·i·er, mold·i·est** Covered with mold; hence, old; musty: also spelled *mouldy.* **—mold′i·ness** *n.*

mole[1] (mōl) *n.* **1** A small permanent spot on the skin; a birthmark. **2** A stain or spot, as in a garment. [OE *māl*]

mole[2] (mōl) *n.* A small, insectivorous mammal (family *Talpidae*) with velvety fur, minute eyes, and very broad forefeet adapted for digging and forming extensive underground excavations. [ME *molle* <MLG. Cf. MDu. *molle.* Prob. related to MOLD[3].]

COMMON MOLE (About 5 1/2 inches long, with tail an inch long)

mole[3] (mōl) *n.* A jetty or breakwater, partially enclosing an anchorage or harbor. [<F *môle* <L *moles* great mass]

mole[4] (mōl) *n. Pathol.* A morbid mass formed in the womb by the degeneration of the partly developed ovum, and giving rise to false pregnancy: also spelled *mola.* [<F *môle* <L *mola* millstone, false conception]

mole[5] (mōl) See MOL.

Mo·lech (mō′lek) See MOLOCH.

mole cricket 1 A burrowing cricket (family *Gryllotalpidae*) with a soft, cylindrical body and broad, stout, molelike front legs, found in some sandy soils. For illustration see INSECTS (injurious). **2** Any of several related species.

mo·lec·u·lar (mə·lek′yə·lər) *adj.* **1** Of, pertaining to, or consisting of molecules. **2** Resulting from the action of molecules: *molecular* changes. [<NL *molecularis*]

molecular film A layer of a substance having a thickness of one molecule: also called *monolayer.*

molecular volume *Chem.* The molecular weight of a substance divided by its density under specified conditions, usually the boiling point and normal atmospheric pressure.

molecular weight *Chem.* The sum of the weights of the constituent atoms of a molecule; specifically, the weight of a molecule of any gas or vapor as compared with some standard gas, such as oxygen.

mol·e·cule (mol′ə·kyōōl) *n.* **1** *Physics* The smallest part of an element, substance, or compound that can exist freely in the solid, liquid, or gaseous state and still retain its composition and properties. **2** Any small particle. See synonyms under PARTICLE. [<F *molécule* <NL *molecula,* dim. of L *moles* mass]

mole·hill (mōl′hil′) *n.* A small heap or ridge of earth raised by a burrowing mole.

mole·skin (mōl′skin′) *n.* **1** The skin of a mole. **2** A heavy, twill fabric, usually cotton, having a thick, soft nap resembling moleskin: used chiefly for coats, jackets, etc.

mo·lest (mə·lest′) *v.t.* To annoy or harm by interference; disturb injuriously. See synonyms under ABUSE, PERSECUTE. [<OF *molester* <L *molestare* <*molestus* troublesome <*moles* mass, burden] **—mo·les·ta·tion** (mō′les·tā′shən, mol′es·tā′shən) *n.* **—mo·lest′er** *n.*

mole·warp (mōl′wôrp) See MOLDWARP.

Mol·fet·ta (môl·fet′tä) A port in Apulia, SE Italy, on the Adriatic.

Mo·lière (mô·lyâr′) Pseudonym of Jean Baptiste Poquelin, 1622–73, French dramatist.

moll (mol) *n. Slang* **1** A girl; a sweetheart. **2** The mistress of a thief or vagrant. **3** A prostitute. [<MOLL]

Moll (mol) Diminutive of Mary. [<*Molly,* dim. of MARY]

mol·lah (mol′ə) *n.* A Moslem complimentary title of address given to religious dignitaries; also, a judge. Also spelled *moolah, mullah.* [<Turkish *mulla* <Arabic *mawla* master, sir]

mol·le (mō·lā′) *n.* The sharp, astringent condiment extracted from the drupes of a tropical American pepper tree *(Schinus molle).*

mol·les·cent (mə·les′ənt) *adj.* Producing softness; softening. [<L *mollescens, -entis*] **—mol·les′cence** *n.*

Moll Flan·ders (flan′dərz) The heroine of Daniel Defoe's novel *Moll Flanders* (1722), one of the first English fictional works to express a note of social criticism.

mol·lient (mol′yənt) See EMOLLIENT.

mol·li·fy (mol′ə·fī) *v.t.* **·fied, ·fy·ing 1** To make less angry; soothe; pacify; appease. **2** To reduce the violence or intensity of. See synonyms under ALLAY, TEMPER. [<F *mollifier* <LL *mollificare* <L *mollis* soft + *facere* make] **—mol′li·fi′a·ble** *adj.* **—mol′li·fi·ca′tion** *n.* **—mol′li·fi′er** *n.* **—mol′li·fy′ing·ly** *adv.*

mol·li·ti·es (mə·lish′i·ēz) *n. Pathol.* A softening of an organ or tissue. [<L]

mol·lus·cum (mə·lus′kəm) *n. Pathol.* Any of various skin diseases, especially, **molluscum con·ta·gi·o·sum** (kən·tā′jē·ō′səm), caused by a filtrable virus and characterized by the formation of hard skin tubercles, usually on the face. [<NL]

mol·lusk (mol′əsk) *n.* Any member of a large phylum *(Mollusca)* of mostly marine invertebrates having a soft, unsegmented body protected usually by a calcareous shell and including snails, oysters, cuttlefish, squids, whelks, limpets, etc. Also mol lusc. [<F. *mollusque* <L *molluscus (nux)* soft, thin-shelled (nut) <*mollis* soft] **—mol·lus·can** (mə·lus′kən) *adj.* & *n.* **—mol·lus′cous** *adj.*

mol·ly·cod·dle (mol′ē·kod′l) *n.* Any excessively pampered or protected person; one who is coddled or coddles himself; a sissy. *—v.t.* **·dled, ·dling** To pamper; coddle. [<*Molly,* dim. of MARY, + CODDLE] **—mol′ly·cod′dler** *n.*

Mol·ly Ma·guire (mol′ē mə·gwīr′) **1** One of a secret society that terrorized inhabitants of the coal regions of eastern Pennsylvania (1867–77). **2** Originally, one of a secret society in Ireland organized (1843) to prevent evictions by terrorizing officers of the law. [So called because the members were often disguised as women]

Mol·nár (mōl′när), **Ferenc,** 1878–1952, Hungarian playwright.

mo·loch (mō′lok) *n.* A spiny Australian lizard (genus *Moloch*), resembling the horned toad. [<NL *Moloch,* genus name <MOLOCH]

Mo·loch (mō′lok) **1** In the Bible, a god of the Ammonites and Phoenicians to whom human sacrifices were offered. **2** Any system or principle involving merciless sacrifice: also spelled *Molech.* [<LL <Gk. <Hebrew *Mōlekh* a king]

Mo·lo·kai (mō′lə·kī′) An island in the central Hawaiian Islands; 260 square miles.

Mo·lo·tov (mô′lə·tôf) A former name for PERM.

Mo·lo·tov (mô′lə·tôf), **Vyacheslav Mikhailovich,** born 1890, U.S.S.R. statesman: original name *Skryabin.*

Molotov breadbasket A container filled with small incendiary bombs which are designed to scatter over a large area when dropped from aircraft.

Molotov cocktail See FRANGIBLE GRENADE under GRENADE.

molt (mōlt) *v.t.* & *v.i.* To cast off or shed (feathers, horns, skin, etc.) in preparation for replacement by new growth. *—n.* The molting process or season. Also spelled *moult.* [ME *mouten,* OE *bimūtian* exchange for <L *mutare* change] **—emolt′er** *n.*

mol·ten (mōl′tən) Archaic past participle of MELT. *—adj.* **1** Reduced to fluid by heat; melted. **2** Made by molding; cast.

molten sea See BRAZEN SEA.

Molt·ke (môlt′kə), **Count Helmuth Karl Bernhard von,** 1800–91, Prussian field marshal. **—Helmuth Johannes Ludwig von,** 1848–1916, German general in World War I; nephew of preceding.

mol·to (môl′tō) *adv. Music* Much; very: *molto* adagio. [<Ital. <L *multum* much]

Mo·luc·ca Islands (mə·luk′ə) A widely scattered island group, comprising a province of Indonesia, between Celebes and New Guinea: 33,315 square miles: formerly *Spice Islands. Malay* **Ma·lu·ku** (mä·lōō′kōō). Also **Mo·luc′cas.**

mo·ly (mō′lē) *n. pl.* **·lies 1** A mythical plant of magic virtues, with a white flower and a black root: mentioned in the *Odyssey.* **2** A European wild garlic. **3** Molybdenum. [<L <Gk. *mōly*]

mo·lyb·date (mə·lib′dāt) *n. Chem.* A salt of molybdic acid.

mo·lyb·de·nite (mə·lib′də·nīt) *n.* A scaly, metallic, lead-gray, soft molybdenum disulfide, MoS_2: an important ore of molybdenum.

mo·lyb·de·num (mə·lib′də·nəm, mol′ib·dē′·nəm) *n.* A silvery-white, very hard metallic element (symbol Mo, atomic number 42) widely distributed in various minerals, used in alloys and essential in trace amounts to plant nutrition. See PERIODIC TABLE. [<NL <L. *molybdaena* lead, galena <Gk. *molybdaina* <*molybdos* lead]

mo·lyb·dic (mə·lib′dik) *adj. Chem.* Of, pertaining to, or containing molybdenum. especially in its higher valence.

mo·lyb·dous (mə·lib′dəs) *adj. Chem.* Of or pertaining to molybdenum, especially in its lower valence.

mom (mom) *n. U.S. Colloq.* Mother. [<MAMA]

Mom·ba·sa (mom·bä′sə, -bas′ə) A port in SE Kenya on **Mombasa Island** (7 square miles), separated from the mainland by Mombasa harbor.

mome (mōm) *n. Obs.* A stupid fellow; also, a buffoon. [? <MUM[1]]

mo·ment (mō′mənt) *n.* **1** A very short period of time; an instant; also, a point of time; definite period. **2** The present time. **3** Consequence or importance, as in influencing judgment or action. **4** *Stat.* The arithmetic mean of the deviations in a frequency distribution, each deviation being raised to the same power. **5** *Physics* **a** The product of a quantity and its distance to some significant related point: *moment* of area, *moment* of mass, etc. **b** The measure of a force with reference to its effect in producing rotation: also called *torque.* **6** The thing originating or causing; principle of movement or development; a moving force. See synonyms under WEIGHT. [<F <L *momentum* movement. Doublet of MOMENTUM.]

mo·men·tar·i·ly (mō′mən·ter′ə·lē, mō′mən·ter′·ə·lē) *adv.* **1** For a moment. **2** From moment to moment. **3** At any moment. Also **mo′ment·ly.**

mo·men·tar·y (mō′mən·ter′ē) *adj.* Lasting but a moment. **—mo′men·tar′i·ness** *n.*

mo·men·tous (mō·men′təs) *adj.* Of great importance; weighty. See synonyms under IMPORTANT, SERIOUS. **—mo·men′tous·ly** *adv.* **—mo·men′tous·ness** *n.*

mo·men·tum (mō·men′təm) *n. pl.* **·ta** (-tə) or **·tums 1** *Mech.* The impetus of a moving body. **2** *Physics* The quantity of motion in a body as measured by the product of its mass and velocity. **3** An essential or constituent element. **4** *Music* An eighth rest. [<L. Doublet of MOMENT.] **—mo·men′tal** *adj.*

mom·ism (mom′iz·əm) *n.* Dominance of feminine values in a society, attributed to undue prolongation of maternal influence: a derogatory term. [<MOM + -ISM; coined by Philip Wylie, 1902–1971, U.S. author]

Momm·sen (mom′sən, -zən; *Ger.* mom′zən), **Theodor,** 1817–1903, German historian.

Mom·son lung (mom′sən) A respiratory device to aid persons to escape from a sunken submarine: invented by Rear Admiral Charles B. Momson, born 1896, U.S. Navy.

Mo·mus (mō′məs) In Greek mythology, the god of blame and mockery. [<L <Gk. *mōmos* blame, ridicule]

mon (mon) *n. Scot.* Man.

Mon (mōn) *n.* **1** One of the dominant native peoples of the Pegu region in Burma. **2** The Austro-Asiatic language of the Mons. Also *Peguan.*

mon- *combining form* Var. of MONO-.

Mo·na (mō′nə) The ancient name for the ISLE OF MAN. Also **Mo·na·pi·a** (mō·nä′pē·ə).

mon·ac·e·tin (mon·as′ə·tin) *n.* A colorless or pale-yellow, hygroscopic liquid, $C_5H_{10}O_4$, obtained by heating glycerol with glacial acetic acid: it is used as a solvent for basic dyes, and in making certain explosives: also spelled *monoacetin.* [<MON- + *acetin* a liquid ester of acetic acid]

mon·a·chism (mon′ə·kiz′əm) *n.* The monastic manner of life; monasticism. [<L *monachus* monk + -ISM] **—mon′a·chal** (-kəl) *adj.*

mon·ac·id (mon·as′id) See MONOACID.

Mon·a·co (mon′ə·kō, mə·nä′kō; *Fr.* mô·nà·kō′) An independent principality on the Mediterranean in SE France; 370 acres. **—Mon′a·can** *adj.*

mon·ad (mon′ad, mō′nad) *n.* **1** An indestructible unit; a simple and indivisible substance. **2** A minute, simple, single-celled organism, especially a flagellate infusorian. **3** In metaphysics, the one inseparable spirit in mankind manifesting itself in each person; also, the one inseparable spirit in nature. —*adj.* Of, pertaining to, or consisting of a monad: also **mo·nad′ic** or **·i·cal.** [< LL *monas, monadis* < Gk. *monas* a unit < *monos* alone]

mon·a·del·phous (mon′ə·del′fəs) *adj. Bot.* Having the stamens united by their filaments into a single set or tube, as in plants of the mallow family. Also **mon′a·del′phi·an.** [< MON- + Gk. *adelphos* brother]

mon·ad·ism (mon′ad·iz′əm, mō′nad-) *n.* A theory of monads in philosophy or physics. —**mon′ad·is′tic** *adj.*

mo·nad·nock (mə·nad′nok) *n. Geog.* An isolated hill or mass of rock rising above a peneplain. [from Mt. *Monadnock*]

Mo·nad·nock (mə·nad′nok), **Mount** An isolated peak in SW New Hampshire; 3,165 feet.

Mon·a·ghan (mon′ə·gən, -hən) A county of Ulster province, Ireland; 498 square miles; county seat, Monaghan.

Mo·na Li·sa (mō′nə lē′zə) A portrait by Leonardo da Vinci of a Neapolitan woman: also called *La Gioconda.*

mon a·mi (môṅ nà·mē′) *French* My friend.

mo·nan·drous (mə·nan′drəs) *adj.* **1** Having one male or husband at a time. **2** *Bot.* Having one stamen to the flower. [< Gk. *monandros* < *mono-* single + *anēr, andros* male, man]

mo·nan·dry (mə·nan′-drē) *n.* **1** The custom or practice of having only one husband at a time. **2** *Bot.* The condition of possessing only one perfect stamen, as in certain orchids. [< Gk. *monandria.* See MONANDROUS.]

mo·nan·thous (mə·nan′thəs) *adj. Bot.* Having but one flower: said of a peduncle or a whole plant. [< MON- + Gk. *anthos* flower]

mon·arch (mon′ərk) *n.* **1** A sovereign, as a king or emperor; in modern times, usually, a hereditary constitutional sovereign; originally, the sole ruler of a nation. **2** One who or that which surpasses others of the same kind. **3** A large, orange-brown butterfly *(Danaus menippe)* whose larva feeds on milkweed: also called *milkweed butterfly.* See synonyms under MASTER. [< LL *monarcha* < Gk. *monarchēs* < *monarchos* ruling alone < *monos* alone + *archein* rule] —**mo·nar·chal** (mə·när′kəl) *adj.* —**mo·nar′chal·ly** *adv.*

mo·nar·chi·an·ism (mə·när′kē·ən·iz′əm) *n.* A heretical doctrine of the second and third centuries which denied any real distinction between the persons of the Trinity. [< LL *monarchianus* < *monarchia* sovereignty of a single person < *monarcha* MONARCH] —**mo·nar′chi·an·is′tic** *adj.*

mo·nar·chi·cal (mə·när′ki·kəl) *adj.* Pertaining to, governed by, or favoring a monarch or monarchy. Also **mo·nar′chi·al, mo·nar′chic.** —**mo·nar′chi·cal·ly** *adv.*

mon·arch·ism (mon′ərk·iz′əm) *n.* Monarchical preferences or principles. —**mon′arch·ist** *n.* —**mon′arch·is′tic** *adj.*

mon·ar·chy (mon′ər·kē) *n. pl.* **·chies 1** Government by a monarch; sovereign control. **2** A government or territory ruled by a monarch. —**absolute monarchy** A government in which the will of the monarch is positive law; a despotism. —**constitutional** or **limited monarchy** A monarchy in which the power and prerogative of the sovereign are limited by constitutional provisions. [< LL *monarchia* < Gk.]

Mo·nar·da (mə·när′də) *n.* A genus of aromatic American herbs of the mint family, with toothed leaves and large flowers in showy clusters; including the horsemint and Oswego tea. [< NL, after N. *Monardes,* 1493–1588, Spanish botanist]

mon·as (mon′əs, mō′nəs) *n.* A monad. [< Gk.]

mon·as·ter·y (mon′əs·ter′ē) *n. pl.* **·ter·ies** A dwelling place occupied in common by persons, especially monks, under religious vows of seclusion; also, the community of persons living in such a place. See synonyms under CLOISTER. [< LL *monasterium* < Gk. *monastērion* < *monastēs* a monk < *monazein* be alone < *monos* alone. Doublet of MINSTER.]

mo·nas·tic (mə·nas′tik) *adj.* **1** Pertaining to religious seclusion. **2** Characteristic of monasteries or their inhabitants; monkish. Also **mon·as·te·ri·al** (mon′əs·tir′ē·əl), **mo·nas′ti·cal.** —*n.* A monk or other religious recluse. [< F *monastique* < Med. L *monasticus* < Gk. *monastikos*] —**mo·nas′ti·cal·ly** *adv.*

mo·nas·ti·cism (mə·nas′tə·siz′əm) *n.* The monastic life; asceticism.

mon·a·tom·ic (mon′ə·tom′ik) *adj. Chem.* **1** Consisting of a single atom, as the molecules of certain elements. **2** Containing one replaceable or reactive atom. **3** Monovalent.

mon·au·ral (män′ôr·əl, mōn′-) *adj.* **1** Pertaining to, designed for, or characterized by the perception of sound by one ear only. **2** Designating the transmission or reproduction of sound through a single channel.

mon·ax·i·al (mon·ak′sē·əl) *adj.* Having but one axis; uniaxial.

mon·a·zite (mon′ə·zīt) *n.* A resinous, brownish-red or brown phosphate of the rare-earth metals, chiefly cerium, lanthanum, and didymium: an important source of thorium. [< G *monazit* < Gk. *monazein* be alone < *monos* alone]

mon cher (môṅ shâr′) *French* My dear. —**ma chère** (mà shâr′) *fem.*

Monck (mungk), **George** See MONK, GEORGE.

Monc·ton (mungk′tən) A city in SE New Brunswick, Canada.

Mon·day (mun′dē, -dā) *n.* The second day of the week. [OE *mōn(an)dæg* day of the moon; trans. of L *lunae dies*]

monde (mônd) *n. French* The world; society. [< F < L *mundus* world]

Mond process (mond) *Metall.* A method for obtaining pure nickel by passing a stream of carbon monoxide over powdered nickel oxide and separating it from the resulting nickel-carbonyl vapor. [after Ludwig *Mond,* 1839–1909, English chemist born in Germany]

Mon·dri·an (môn′drē·än), **Piet,** 1872–1944, Dutch painter.

mo·ne·cious (mə·nē′shəs, mō-) See MONOECIOUS.

Mo·né·gasque (mō′nə·gask, *Fr.* mô·nā·gàsk′) *French* A citizen of Monaco.

Mo·nel metal (mō·nel′) A corrosion-resistant nickel alloy of copper, iron, and manganese, reduced from ore of the same composition: used for industrial equipment, machine parts, etc.: a trade name. [after Ambrose *Monel,* d. 1921, U.S. manufacturer]

mo·ner·on (mə·nir′ən) *n. pl.* **·a** An organism that lacks a cellular nucleus, including bacteria and blue-green algae. [< NL < GK. *monos* alone]

Mo·net (mō·ne′), **Claude,** 1840–1926, French painter.

mon·e·tar·ism (mon′ə·tə·riz′əm, mun′-) *n.* The theory that the economy of a country is determined chiefly by the amount of money available. **-mon′é·tar·ist** *adj., n.*

mon·e·tar·y (mon′ə·ter′ē, mun′-) *adj.* Pertaining to money, finance, or currency; consisting of money; pecuniary. See synonyms under FINANCIAL.[< L *monetarius* of a mint < *moneta* mint. See MINT.] —**mon′e·tar′i·ly** *adv.*

mon·e·tize (mon′ə·tīz, mun′-) *v.t.* **·tized, ·tiz·ing 1** To legalize as money. **2** To give a standard value to (a metal) as currency. **3** To coin into money. Also *Brit.* **mon′e·tise.** [< L *moneta* mint, money] —**mon′e·ti·za′tion** *n.*

mon·ey (mun′ē) *n. pl.* **mon·eys** or **mon·ies 1** Anything that serves as a common medium of exchange in trade, as coin or notes. ◆Collateral adjective: *pecuniary.* **2** Legal tender for debts. **3** Purchasing power; credit; bank deposits, etc.; a denomination of value or unit of account. **4** Wealth; property. **5** *pl.* Cash payments or receipts. **6** A system of coinage. —**call money** Money loaned on security, or deposited in a bank, subject to repayment on demand of the lender. —**hard money** Metallic currency or specie. [< OF *moneie* < L *moneta.* Doublet of MINT.]

Synonyms : bills, bullion, capital, cash, coin, currency, funds, gold, notes, property, silver, specie. Money is the authorized medium of exchange; coined *money* is called *coin* or *specie.* What are termed in England *banknotes* are in the United States commonly called *bills* : a five-dollar *bill. Cash* is *specie* or *money* in hand, or paid in hand: the *cash* account; the *cash* price. In the legal sense, *property* is not *money,* and *money* is not *property;* for *property* is that which has inherent value, while *money,* as such, has but representative value, and may or may not have intrinsic value. *Bullion* is either *gold* or *silver* uncoined or the coined metal considered without reference to its coinage, but simply as merchandise, when its value as *bullion* may be very different from its value as *money.* The word *capital* is used chiefly of accumulated *property* or *money* invested in productive enterprises or available for such investment. Compare PROPERTY, WEALTH.

mon·ey·bags (mun′ē·bagz′) *n. Slang* **1** A rich man. **2** Wealth.

mon·ey·chang·er (mun′ē·chān′jər) *n.* A person who changes money at a prescribed rate. Also **mon′ey-deal′er** (-dē′lər), **mon′ey-job′ ber** (-job′ər).

money cowry See COWRY.

mon·eyed (mun′ēd) *adj.* **1** Possessed of money; wealthy. **2** In the form of money. Also spelled *monied.*

mon·ey·lend·er (mun′ē·len′dər) *n.* A person whose business is the lending of money at interest.

mon·ey·mak·ing (mun′ē·mā′king) *adj.* **1** Bent upon and successful in accumulating wealth. **2** Likely to bring in money; profitable. —*n.* The acquisition or procurement of money or wealth. —**mon′ey·mak′er** *n.*

money market The market in which money is the commodity bought and sold; the sphere of financial operations.

money of account A monetary denomination used in keeping accounts, but not represented by a coin, as the mill of the United States.

money order An order for the payment of a specified sum of money; specifically, such an order issued at one post office or telegraph office and payable at another.

mon·ey·wort (mun′ē·wûrt′) *n.* A trailing herb *(Lysimachia nummularia)* of the primrose family with solitary yellow flowers and rounded leaves. [< MONEY + WORT; trans. of NL *Nummularia* < *nummus* a coin]

mon·ger (mung′gər, mong′-) *n.* **1** *Brit.* A dealer or trader: chiefly in compounds: *fishmonger.* **2** One who engages in discreditable matters: chiefly in compounds: a *scandalmonger.* [OE *mangere* < *mangian* traffic]

Mon·gol (mong′gəl, -gol, -gōl,) *adj.* Of or pertaining to Mongolia or its inhabitants. —*n.* **1** A member of any of the native tribes of Mongolia; specifically, a Mongol (eastern Mongolia), a Buriat (Siberia), or an Eleut or Kalmuck (western Mongolia). **2** The Mongolian language of any of these peoples. **3** Any member of the Mongoloid race. [< Mongolian *mong* brave]

Mon·go·lia (mong·gō′lē·ə, mon-) A region of east central Asia south of Asiatic Russian S.F.S.R., east and north of China's Sinkiang-Uigur Autonomous Region, west of most of former Manchuria and the rest of NE China, and north of central China; about 1,000,000 square miles; divided into: (1) the **Mongolian People's Republic** (formerly *Outer Mongolia*), an independent country in the northern and western part; 590,966 square miles; capital, Ulan Bator; (2) *Inner Mongolia,* a region of northern China, including the former provinces of Ningsia, Suiyuan, Chahar, and Jehol and western (former) Manchuria, most of which region now comprises: (3) the *Inner Mongolian Autonomous Region,* an autonomous division of central northern China, including parts of western (former) Manchuria, and former Chahar and Jehol provinces and all of former Suiyuan province; over 400,000 square miles; capital, Huhehot (formerly *Kweisui*).

Mon·go·li·an (mong·gō′lē·ən, -gōl′yən, mon-) *adj.* **1** Of or pertaining to Mongolia, its people, or their languages; Mongol. **2** Exhibiting Mongolism. —*n.* **1** A native of Mongolia. **2** A subfamily of the Altaic languages, including the languages of the Mongols.

Mon·gol·ic (mong·gol′ik, mon-) *adj.* Of or peculiar to the Mongols; Mongolian. —*n.* Any of the Mongolian languages.

Mon·gol·ism (mong′gəl·iz′əm) *n.* Down syndrome.

Mon·go·loid (mong′gə·loid) *adj.* **1** *Anthropol.* Of or pertaining to the racial group native to Asia and North America, including Malaysians, Eskimos, and some Native Americans.

Characteristics include broad noses, high cheek bones, and dark eyes with marked epicanthic folds. 2 Resembling a Mongol or a Mongolian. 3 Characterized by Mongolism. —*n.* A member of the Mongoloid race.

mon·goose (mong′gōōs, mung′-) *n. pl.* **·goos·es** A small, ferretlike mammal (family *Viverridae*) which fearlessly attacks and kills venomous snakes; especially, the **Indian mongoose** *(Herpestes nyula)*: often written *mungoose.* [< Marathi *mungūs*]

MONGOOSE

mon·grel (mung′grəl, mong′-) *n.* 1 The progeny of crossed breeding; sometimes restricted to the progeny of artificial varieties: distinguished from a *hybrid;* specifically, a dog of mixed breed. 2 Any incongruous mixture. —*adj.* Of mixed breed or origin; specifically, of a word or language made up of other words or languages: often a term of contempt. [< obs. *mong* mixture < OE *gemang* + *-rel,* dim. suffix]

mon·grel·ize (mung′grə·līz′, mong′-) *v.t.* **·ized, ·iz·ing** To mix, esp. racial characteristics.

'mongst (mungst) *prep.* Amongst: an aphetic form.

mon·ied (mun′ēd) See MONEYED.

Mon·i·er–Wil·liams (mun′ē·ər·wil′yəmz, mon′-), **Sir Monier,** 1819–99, English Sanskrit scholar.

mon·i·ker (mon′ə·kər) *n. Slang* 1 A name; a signature. 2 A tramp's initials or other mark of identification. Also **mon′ick·er.** [Prob. blend of MONOGRAM and MARKER]

mon·i·li·a·sis (mon′ə·lī′ə·sis) *n. Pathol.* A disease caused by infection with any of various gas-forming fungi (family *Moniliaceae*). Also **mon′i·li′o·sis.** [< NL < L *monile* necklace + -IASIS; from the alternating swellings and constrictions caused by it]

mo·nil·i·form (mō·nil′ə·fôrm) *adj. Biol.* Resembling a string of beads; contracted or jointed at regular intervals so as to resemble a necklace. [< L *monile* necklace + -FORM]

mon·ish (mon′ish) *v.t. Obs.* To admonish. [See ADMONISH.]

mon·ism (mon′iz·əm, mō′niz·əm) *n.* 1 The doctrine of cosmology that attempts to explain the phenomena of the cosmos by one principle of being or ultimate substance: opposed to philosophical *dualism* and *pluralism.* 2 Any theory that refers many different facts to a single principle. 3 See MONOGENESIS (Def. 1). [< NL *monismus* < Gk. *monos* single] —**mon′ist** *n.* —**mo·nis′tic** or **·ti·cal** *adj.* —**mo·nis′ti·cal·ly** *adv.*

mo·ni·tion (mō·nish′ən) *n.* 1 Friendly counsel given by way of warning and implying caution or reproof; admonition. 2 Indication; notice. 3 *Law* A summons or citation in civil law and admiralty practice. [< F < L *monitio, -onis* < *monitus,* pp. of *monere* warn] —**mon·i·tive** (mon′ə·tiv) *adj.*

mon·i·tor (mon′ə·tər) *n.* 1 One who advises or cautions. 2 A senior pupil placed in charge of a dormitory or class. 3 Something that warns or advises; a reminder. 4 *Nav.* An ironclad vessel having a low, flat deck and low freeboard, and fitted with a blister and with one or more turrets carrying heavy guns; specifically, the first vessel of the type, **"The Monitor."** See MERRIMAC. 5 *Zool.* Any of several large carnivorous lizards (family *Varanidae*) of the Old World tropics; especially, the East Indian kabara-goya *(Varanus salvator),* which reaches a length of seven feet. 6 *Mining* A contrivance, consisting of nozzle and holder, whereby the direction of a stream can be readily changed. 7 *Telecom.* **a** A high-fidelity loudspeaker in the control-room of a radio studio, used to insure adequate sound transmission. **b** A receiver for listening to a station's broadcasts to check on quality and frequency of transmission, compliance with laws, material transmited, etc. —*v.t.* 1 *Telecom.* To listen to (a station, broadcast, etc.) with or as with a monitor. 2 To have charge of (a person or group) as a monitor. 3 To keep watch over or check as a means of control: to *monitor* tax returns. [< L < *monitus.* See MONITION.]

mon·i·to·ri·al (mon′ə·tôr′ē·əl, -tō′rē-) *adj.* 1 Pertaining to a monitor or to instruction by monitors. 2 Monitory.

mon·i·to·ry (mon′ə·tôr′ē, -tō′rē) *adj.* Conveying monition; admonitory: a *monitory* look. —*n.* An ecclesiastical monition. [< L *monitorius.* See MONITION]

monitory letter A papal letter of monition.

monk (mungk) *n.* 1 Formerly, a religious hermit. 2 One of a company of men vowed to separation from the world and to poverty, celibacy, and religious duties; a member of a monastic order. 3 *Printing* An area on a printed page or sheet containing too much ink: opposed to *friar.* [OE *munuc* < LL *monachus* < Gk. *monachos* < *monos* alone] —**monk′ish** *adj.* —**monk′ish·ly** *adv.*

Monk (mungk), **George,** 1608–70, Duke of Albemarle; English soldier. Also spelled *Monck.*

monk·er·y (mungk′ər·ē) *n. pl.* **·er·ies** 1 Monastic life, ways, or beliefs: generally used opprobriously. 2 A monastery or its inmates.

mon·key (mung′kē) *n.* 1 Any of a group of primates (suborder *Anthropoidea*) having elongate limbs, hands and feet adapted for grasping, and a highly developed nervous system, including marmosets, baboons, and macaques, but not the anthropoid apes. 2 Any primate below man, especially the smaller arboreal forms, as lemurs and tarsiers. 3 A person regarded as a monkey, as a mischievous child. 4 One of various small articles or contrivances; especially, an iron block or ram with a catch, used in pile-driving by hoisting and dropping. —*v.t.* To play or trifle; fool; meddle: often with *with* or *around with.* [? < MLG *Moneke,* name of the son of Martin the Ape in *Reynard the Fox.* Cf. MF *monne,* Sp. *mona* a female ape.]

monkey bread See BAOBAB.

monkey business *Slang* Foolish tricks; deceitful or mischievous behavior; folly.

monkey chatter In electronics slang, garbled speech, music, or other sound signals in radio reception, caused by interference of adjoining frequencies with the carrier wave of the desired channel.

monkey cup An East Indian pitcherplant; any species of the genus *Nepenthes.*

monkey flower Any one of various figworts of the genus *Mimulus,* especially the cultivated species, *M. luteus* with yellow flowers, and *M. cardinalis* with red: so called from the gaping or grimacing appearance of the corolla.

monkey gaff *Naut.* A gaff attached to the mizzentopmast of a vessel for the display of signals.

monkey jacket 1 A short jacket of coarse material, worn especially by sailors. 2 *Slang* A dinner jacket.

monkey jar A large, undecorated earthenware jar, used for cooling drinking water.

monkey pot 1 The hard, woody, pot- or urn-shaped fruit of several tropical American trees of the family *Lecythidaceae,* especially *Lecythis ollaria* and *L. zabucajo;* also, the plant, the fruit of which has a circular lid which, when the nut-like seeds are ripe, separates with a cracking sound. 2 A barrel-shaped melting pot used in making flint glass.

monkey puzzle A large Chilean tree *(Araucaria araucana)* yielding a hard, durable, yellowish-white wood and edible seeds.

mon·key·shines (mung′kē·shīnz′) *n. pl. U.S. Slang* Frolicsome tricks like a monkey's; pranks. [< MONKEY + SHINE, *n.* (def. 4)]

monkey wrench A wrench having an adjustable jaw for grasping a nut, bolt, or the like.

monk·fish (mungk′fish′) *n. pl.* **·fish** or **·fish·es** 1 The angelfish. 2 The angler. [So called from a hoodlike protuberance suggesting a monk's cowl]

Mon-Khmer (mōn′kmer′) *n.* A subfamily of the Austro–Asiatic family of languages, spoken chiefly in Indochina, including Mon, Khmer, and the Annamese dialects.

monk·hood (mungk′hŏŏd) *n.* 1 The character or condition of a monk. 2 Monks collectively. [OE *munukhade*]

monks·hood (mungks′hŏŏd′) *n.* 1 A plant of the genus *Aconitum,* especially the poisonous *A. napellus,* having the upper sepal arched at the back like a hood. 2 Aconite.

MONKSHOOD (Plants from 1 to 6 feet tall, varying with species)

Mon·mouth (mon′məth) 1 A county in western England on the border of Wales; 546 square miles; county town, Monmouth. Also **Mon′mouth·shire** (-shir). 2 A county in east central New Jersey; site of the Revolutionary War battle of **Monmouth Courthouse,** June 28, 1778.

Mon·mouth (mon′məth), **Duke of,** 1649–85, James Scott, an illegitimate son of Charles II of England, who claimed the throne and led an insurrection against James II; beheaded.

mon·o (mon′ō) *adj.* Monophonic (def. 1). —*n.* Mononucleosis.

mono- *combining form* 1 Single; one. 2 *Chem.* Denoting the presence in a compound of a single atom, or an equivalent of the element or radical to the name of which it is prefixed: *monobasic.* Also, before vowels, **mon-.** [< Gk. < *monos* single, alone]

mon·o·ac·e·tin (mon′ō·as′ə·tin) See MONACETIN.

mon·o·ac·id (mon′ō·as′id) *adj. Chem.* Possessing one hydroxyl group that can replace the hydrogen of an acid: said of bases: also spelled *monacid.* Also **mon′o·a·cid′ic** (-ə·sid′ik).

mon·o·ba·sic (mon′ə·bā′sik) *adj. Chem.* Possessing but a single hydrogen atom replaceable by a metal or positive radical: applied to acids.

Mo·noc·a·cy River (mə·nok′ə·sē) A river in Pennsylvania and northern Maryland which rises near Gettysburg and flows 60 miles SW to the Potomac; scene of Civil War battle in 1864 near Frederick, Maryland.

mon·o·carp (mon′ə·kärp) *n. Bot.* A plant that yields fruit only once before dying.

mon·o·car·pel·lar·y (mon′ə·kär′pə·ler′ē) *adj. Bot.* Consisting of a single carpel.

mon·o·car·pous (mon′ə·kär′pəs) *adj. Bot.* Having a gynoecium composed of a single carpel.

Mo·noc·er·os (mə·nos′ər·əs) A southern constellation, the Unicorn. See CONSTELLATION. [< NL < Gk. *mono-* single + *keras* horn]

mon·o·chā·si·um (mon′ə·kā′ze·əm, -zhē-) *n. Bot.* A uniparous cyme; a cyme having only one lateral axis. [< NL < Gk. *mono-* single + *chasis* division] —**mon′o·cha′si·al** *adj.*

mon·o·chlo·ride (mon′ə·klôr′īd, -klō′rīd) *n. Chem.* A chloride which contains one chlorine atom in each molecule.

mon·o·chord (mon′ə·kôrd) *n.* 1 A single chord or string on which intervals can be marked in mathematical ratios, the vibrations giving the notes in the musical scale. 2 An acoustical instrument with one string and a movable bridge, used for measuring intervals. [< Med. L *monochordus* < Gk. *mono-* single *chordē* string]

mon·o·chro·mat·ic (mon′ə·krō·mat′ik) *adj.* Of one color. Also **mon′o·chro′ic.** [< Gk. *monochrōmatikos*] —**mon′o·chro·mat′i·cal·ly** *adv.*

mon·o·chrome (mon′ə·krōm) *n.* A painting or the art of painting in a single color, or different shades of a single color. —*adj.* Monochromatic. [< Gk. *monochrōmos*] —**mon′o·chro′mic, mon′o·chro′mi·cal** *adj.*

mon·o·cle (mon′ə·kəl) *n.* An eyeglass for one eye. [< F < LL *monoculus* one-eyed < Gk. *monos* single + L *oculus* eye] —**mon′o·cled** *adj.*

mon·o·cli·nal (mon′ə·klī′nəl) *adj. Geol.* Having an inclination in only one direction, or composed of rock strata so inclined. —*n.* A monocline. —**mon′o·cli′nal·ly** *adv.*

mon·o·cline (mon′ə·klīn) *n. Geol.* A stratum or fold of rocks inclined in only one direction. [< MONO- + Gk. *klinein* incline]

mon·o·clin·ic (mon′ə·klin′ik) *adj.* Pertaining to or designating a crystal system having two oblique axes and a third perpendicular to both.

mon·o·cli·nous (mon′ə·klī′nəs) *adj. Bot.* Containing both androecium and gynoecium in the same flower; bisexual; hermaphrodite.

mon·o·clo·nal antibody (mon′ō·clō′nəl) An antibody produced by cloning a specific hybridoma.

mo·no·coque (mô·nô·kôk′) *n. French Aeron.* An airplane construction having a shell-shaped fuselage or nacelle in which the skin carries the main stresses.

mon·o·cot·y·le·don (mon′ə·kot′ə·lēd′n) *n.* Any of a great subclass *(Monocotyledones)* of seed plants *(Angiospermae)* bearing one cotyledon in the embryo, including palms, orchids, lilies, and grasses. Compare DICOTYLEDON. Also **mon′·o·cot. —mon′o·cot′y·le′do·nous** *adj.*

mon·o·crat (mon′ə·krat) *n.* A person in favor of rule by a monarch: term used by Thomas Jefferson about 1790 to mean a Federalist sympathizer with England in the war between England and France. **—mon′o·crat′ic** *adj.***—mo·noc·ra·cy** (mo·nok′rə·sē) *n.*

mo·noc·u·lar (mə·nok′yə·lər) *adj.* **1** One-eyed. **2** Of or pertaining to one eye. Also **mo·noc′·u·lous.** [See MONOCLE]

mon·o·cul·ture (mon′ə·kul′chər) *n. Agric.* The use of a given tract of land for the intensive cultivation of only one crop or product, as cotton, wool, tobacco, etc.

mon·o·cy·cle (mon′·ə·sī′kəl) *n.* A one-wheeled vehicle.

MONOCYCLE

mon·o·cyte (mon′ə·sīt) *n. Physiol.* A large, white blood corpuscle with a horseshoe-shaped nucleus surrounded by clear cytoplasm.

mon·o·dac·ty·lous (mon′ə · dak′tə · ləs) *adj. Zool.* Having only one toe, finger, or claw. Also **mon′o·dac′tyl.** [< Gk. *monodaktylos* < *monos* single + *daktylos* finger]

Mon·o·del·phi·a (mon′ə·del′fē·ə) See EUTHERIA.

mon·o·dra·ma (mon′ə·drä′mə, -dram′ə) *n.* A drama written for or acted by a single performer.

mon·o·dy (mon′ə·dē) *n. pl.* **·dies 1** Any melancholy literary composition with a single emotional motive; especially, a poem on the death of a friend. Compare THRENODY. **2** In Greek tragedy, the lyric solo, usually of a somber character; hence, a dirge. **3** *Music* **a** A composition in which one vocal part predominates, or the style of such a composition; homophony: opposed to *polyphony.* **b** A song for a single voice, with instrumental accompaniment. **4** A monotonous sound; unvarying tone: the *monody* of waves. [< LL *monodia* < Gk. *monōidia* < *monōidos* singing alone < *monos* alone + *aedein* sing] **—mo·nod·ic** (mə·nod′ik), **mo·nod′i·cal** *adj.* **—mo·nod′i·cal·ly** *adv.* **—mon′o·dist** *n.*

mo·noe·cious (mə·nē′shəs) *adj. Bot.* Having male and female organs in the same individual, as stamens and pistils in separate blossoms on the same plant. Also spelled *monecious, monoicous.* Also **mo·ne′cian.** [< MON- + Gk. *oikos* house]

mo·nog·a·mist (mə·nog′ə·mist) *n.* **1** One who has only one living spouse: opposed to *bigamist* and *polygamist.* **2** One who does not practice or believe in second marriage after the death of the first spouse: opposed to *digamist.* **—mo·nog′a·mis′tic** *adj.*

mo·nog·a·mous (mə·nog′ə·məs) *adj.* **1** Pertaining to monogamy: *monogamous* practices. **2** Having only one spouse; holding to monogamy. **3** Having or paired with but one mate, as certain birds. **4** *Biol.* Having flowers with the anthers united. [< LL *monogamus*] **—mo·nog′a·mous·ly** *adv.*

mo·nog·a·my (mə·nog′ə·mē) *n.* **1** The principle or practice of single marriage: opposed to *bigamy* and *polygamy,* and to *digamy.* **2** The habit of pairing with or having but one mate. [< F *monogamie* < LL *monogamia* < Gk. < *monos* single + *gamos* marriage]

mon·o·gen·e·sis (mon′ə·jen′ə·sis) *n. Biol.* **1** Oneness of origin; the doctrine of the descent of all living organisms from a single cell. Compare POLYGENESIS. **2** Asexual reproduction. **3** Direct development of an ovum into an organism which resembles the parent. **4** Monogenism. [< NL]

mon·o·ge·net·ic (mon′ə·jə·net′ik) *adj.* **1** Pertaining to or exhibiting monogenesis or monogenism. **2** Asexual. **3** *Geol.* Resulting from one genetic process, as a group of mountains. **4** Giving only one color to textile fabrics: said of dyestuffs.

mon·o·gen·ic (mon′ə·jen′ik) *adj.* **1** *Biol.* Having but one method of reproduction, specifically asexual reproduction. **2** *Geol.* Having parts all of the same nature: said of certain rocks.

mo·nog·e·nism (mə·noj′ə·niz′əm) *n.* The doctrine that the whole human race is of one blood or species. [< MONO- + -GEN + -ISM] **—mo·nog′e·nist** *n.*

mo·nog·e·nous (mə·noj′ə·nəs) *adj.* Asexual. [< MONO- + -GENOUS]

mo·nog·e·ny (mə·noj′ə·nē) *n.* **1** Monogenesis. **2** Monogenism. ◆ Homophone: *monogyny.*

mon·o·gram (mon′ə·gram) *n.* **1** A character consisting of two or more letters interwoven into one, as the initials of several names. **2** A single character in writing, or a mark representing a word. [< LL *monogramma* < Gk. *monos* single + *gramma* letter] **—mon′o·gram·mat′ic** (-grə·mat′ik) *adj.*

mon·o·graph (mon′ə·graf, -gräf) *n.* A description or systematic exposition of one thing or class of things; a dissertation or treatise written in great detail. **—mo·nog·ra·pher** (mə·nog′rə·fər) *n.* **—mon′o·graph′ic** *adj.* **—mo·nog′ra·phy** *n.*

mo·nog·y·ny (mə·noj′ə·nē) *n.* The custom or practice of having only one wife at a time. Compare MONANDRY. ◆ Homophone: *monogeny.* [< MONO- + Gk. *gynē* woman] **—mo·nog′y·nist** *n.* **—mo·nog′y·nous** *adj.*

mon·o·hy·brid (mon′ō·hī′brid) *n. Biol.* A hybrid offspring of parents differing in one characteristic.

mon·o·hy·drate (mon′ō·hī′drāt) *n. Chem.* The union of a single molecule of water with an element or a compound.

mon·o·hy·dric (mon′ō·hī′drik) *adj. Chem.* Possessing a single hydroxyl radical.

mo·noi·cous (mə·noi′kəs) See MONOECIOUS.

mo·nol·a·try (mə·nol′ə·trē) *n.* Worship of some one of several gods: distinguished from *monotheism.* [< MONO- + -LATRY] **—mo·nol′a·ter, mo·nol′a·trist** *n.* **—mo·nol′a·trous** *adj.*

mon·o·lay·er (mon′ō·lā′ər) *n.* A molecular film.

mon·o·lith (mon′ə·lith) *n.* **1** A single piece or block of stone fashioned or placed by art, particularly one notable for its size. **2** Something like a monolith, as in size, structure, aspect, or quality.

mon·o·lith·ic (mon′ə·lith′ik) *adj.* **1** Of or resembling a monolith. **2** Single in character, as a political movement or ideology; marked by uniformity.

mon·o·log (mon′ə·lôg, -log) *n.* **1** That which is spoken by one person alone; especially, a dramatic soliloquy, or a story or drama told or performed by one person; also, a lengthy speech by one person, occurring in the course of conversation. **2** A literary composition, or a poem, written as a soliloquy. Also **mon′o·logue.** [< F *monologue* < Gk. *monologos* speaking alone < *monos* alone + *logos* discourse] **—mon′o·log′ic** (-loj′ik) or **·i·cal** *adj.* **—mo·nol·o·gist** (mə·nol′ə·jist) *n.*

mon·o·ma·ni·a (mon′ə·mā′nē·ə, -mān′yə) *n.* **1** A mental disorder characterized by obsession with one idea. **2** The unreasonable pursuit of one idea; a craze. [< NL] **—mon′o·ma′ni·ac** *n.* **—mon′o·ma·ni′a·cal** (-mə·nī′ə·kəl) *adj.*

mon·o·mer (mon′ə·mər) *n. Chem.* The structural unit of a polymer: either a single molecule or a substance consisting of identical molecules. [< MONO- + Gk. *meros* part]

mon·o·mer·ic (mon′ə·mer′ik) *adj.* **1** Having or consisting of a single piece. **2** *Zool.* Derived from one segment or part. [< MONOMER]

mo·nom·er·ous (mə·nom′ər·əs) *adj. Bot.* Having a single member in each whorl or circular series: said of a flower. Sometimes written *1-merous.* [< MONO- + -MEROUS]

mon·o·met·al·ism (mon′ō·met′əl·iz′əm) *n.* The theory or system of a single metallic standard in coinage. Also **mon′o·met′al·lism. —mon′o·met′·al·ist** *n.*

mon·o·me·tal·lic (mon′ō·mə·tal′ik) *adj.* **1** Consisting of a single metal: a *monometallic* currency. **2** Of or pertaining to monometalism.

mo·nom·e·ter (mə·nom′ə·tər) *n.* **1** A line of verse having one metrical foot. **2** Verse consisting of monometers. [< MONO- + METER²]

mon·o·met·ric (mon′ə·met′rik) *adj.* Isometric.

mo·no·mi·al (mō·nō′mē·əl) *adj.* Consisting of a single term: a *monomial* expression. *—n. Math.* An expression consisting of a single term. [< MONO- + *-nomial,* as in *binomial;* an irregular formation]

mon·o·mo·lec·u·lar (mon′ō·mə·lek′yə·lər) *adj. Chem.* Having a thickness of one molecule.

mon·o·mor·phic (mon′ə·môr′fik) *adj.* **1** *Biol.* Of the same or an essentially similar type of structure; also, having the same form throughout successive stages of development. **2** *Bot.* Forming similar spores: said of fungi. Also **mon′o·mor′·phous.**

Mo·non·ga·he·la River (mə·nong′gə·hē′lə) A river in West Virginia and western Pennsylvania, flowing 128 miles NE to the Allegheny River at Pittsburgh.

mon·o·nu·cle·o·sis (mon′ō·nōō′klē·ō′sis,-nyōō′-) *n. Pathol.* See INFECTIOUS MONONUCLEOSIS. [< NL < MONO- + NUCLE(US) + -OSIS]

mon·o·pet·al·ous (mon′ə·pet′əl·əs) *adj. Bot.* **1** Gamopetalous. **2** Having corollas actually consisting of a single laterally placed petal: applicable to a few flowers.

mo·noph·a·gous (mə·nof′ə·gəs) *adj.* Monotrophic. [< MONO- + -PHAGOUS]

mon·o·pho·bi·a (mon′ə·fō′bē·ə) *n. Psychiatry* Morbid fear of solitude.

mon·o·phon·ic (mon′ə·fon′ik) *adj.* **1** Of, pertaining to, or functioning in the reproduction of sound through a single channel. **2** *Music* Of or pertaining to a monody.

mon·oph·thong (mon′əf·thông, -thong) *n. Phonet.* **1** A vowel, or single vowel sound. **2** A vowel digraph, or two written vowels with a simple sound. [< MONO- + Gk. *phthongos* sound] **—mon′oph·thon′gal** *adj.*

mon·o·phy·let·ic (mon′ō·fī·let′ik) *adj.* **1** *Zool.* Of or pertaining to a single phylum. **2** *Biol.* Derived from one parent form.

mon·o·phyl·lous (mon′ə·fil′əs) *adj. Bot.* Having or composed of one leaf.

Mo·noph·y·site (mə·nof′ə·sīt) *n.* One of a Christian sect originating in the fifth century which affirms that Christ had but one nature, the divine alone or a single compounded nature, and not two natures so united as to preserve their distinctness. [< LGk. *monophysitēs* < *monos* single + *physis* nature] **—Mon·o·phy·sit·ic** (mon′ō·fi·sit′ik) *adj.* **—Mo·noph′y·sit′ism** *n.*

mon·o·plane (mon′ə·plān) *n. Aeron.* An airplane with only one supporting surface: distinguished from *biplane* and *triplane.*

mon·o·ple·gi·a (mon′ə·plē′jē·ə) *n. Pathol.* Paralysis of one part of the body. [< NL] **—mon′o·ple′gic** *adj.*

mon·o·pode (mon′ə·pōd) *n.* **1** Anything sustained by one foot; particularly, one of a fabulous Ethiopian race with only one leg. **2** A monopodium. *—adj.* One-footed: also **mo·nop·o·dous** (mə·nop′ə·dəs). [< LL *monopodius* < Gk. *monos* single + *pous, podos* foot]

mon·o·po·di·al (mon′ə·pō′dē·əl) *adj.* **1** Of or pertaining to a monopode. **2** *Bot.* Having but one main or primary axis, as ordinary plants. **—mon′o·po′di·al·ly** *adv.*

mon·o·po·di·um (mon′ə·pō′dē·əm) *n. pl.* **·di·a** (-dē·ə) *Bot.* A stem or axis of growth, as in the pine and other conifers, formed by the continued development of a terminal bud, all branches originating as lateral appendages.

mon·o·pole (mon′ə·pōl) *n. Physics.* A hypothetical particle carrying a single magnetic pole and representing the basic unit of magnetism.

mo·nop·o·lize (mə·nop′ə·līz) *v.t.* **·lized, ·liz·ing 1** To obtain or exercise a monopoly of. **2** To assume exclusive possession or control of: to *monopolize* one's time. Also *Brit.* **mo·nop′o·lise. —mo·nop′o·liz′er** *n.*

of a commodity, as allows prices to be raised. **2** A combination or company controlling a monopoly. **3** Exclusive possession or control of anything. **4** That which is the subject of a monopoly. **5** *Law* An exclusive license from the government for buying, selling, making, or using anything, and now granted only in case of patents and copyrights. [< L *monopolium* < Gk. *monopōlion* < *monos* alone + *pōlein* sell] — **mo·nop′o·lism** *n.* —**mo·nop′o·list** *n.* & *adj.* — **mo·nop′o·lis′tic** *adj.*

mon·o·pro·pel·lant (mon′ō·prə·pel′ənt) *n.* A liquid rocket propellant consisting of fuel and oxidizer mixed and ready for ignition in the combustion chamber: applied also to solid fuels.

mo·nop·so·ny (mə·nop′sə·nē) *n. Econ.* A condition of the market in which there is only one buyer for the product of a number of sellers. [< MON- + Gk. *opson* market]

mon·o·rail (mon′ō·rāl) *n.* **1** A single rail serving as a track for cars either suspended from it or balanced upon it by means of gyroscopes. **2** A railway using such a track.

mon·o·sac·cha·ride (mon′ə·sak′ə·rīd, -rid) *n. Biochem.* Any of a class of simple sugars which cannot be decomposed by hydrolysis, as glucose and fructose.

mon·o·sep·a·lous (mon′ə·sep′ə·ləs) *adj. Bot.* Having the sepals more or less united by their edges into a tube: also, more properly, *gamosepalous*: applied also to those rare cases in which the calyx actually consists of a single laterally placed sepal.

mon·o·sil·ane (mon′ə·sil′ān) *n. Chem.* Silane.

mon·o·so·di·um glu·ta·mate (gloo͞′tə·māt) The sodium salt of glutamic acid $C_5H_8O_4NaN$, sometimes used in cooking as a flavor enhancer.

mon·o·some (mon′ə·sōm) *n. Genetics* The unpaired sex or X-chromosome.

mon·o·sper·mous (mon′ə·spûr′məs) *adj. Bot.* One-seeded. Also **mon′o·sper′mal.**

mon·o·stich (mon′ə·stik) *n.* A composition of one verse; especially, an epigram.

mon·o·stome (mon′ə·stōm) *adj. Zool.* Having a single sucker or mouth: also **mo·nos·to·mous** (mə·nos′tə·məs). —*n.* An animal with but a single mouth or sucker.

mo·nos·tro·phe (mə·nos′trə·fē) *n.* A metrical composition containing only one kind of strophe. [< MONO- + STROPHE] —**mon·o·stroph·ic** (mon′ə·strof′ik) *adj.*

mon·o·stroph·ics (mon′ə·strof′iks) *n. pl.* Monostrophic verses.

mon·o·sty·lous (mon′ə·stī′ləs) *adj. Bot.* Having only one style. [< MONO- + Gk. *stylos* pillar]

mon·o·syl·la·bism (mon′ə·sil′ə·biz′əm) *n.* The state or quality of being monosyllabic; addiction to the use of words having but one syllable.

mon·o·syl·la·ble (mon′ə·sil′ə·bəl) *n.* A word of one syllable. —**mon′o·syl·lab′ic** (-si·lab′ik) *adj.* — **mon′o·syl·lab′i·cal·ly** *adv.*

mon·o·the·ism (mon′ə·thē·iz′əm) *n.* The doctrine that there is but one God. [< MONO- + Gk. *theos* god] —**mon′o·the′ist** *n.* —**mon′o·the·is′tic** or **·ti·cal** *adj.* —**mon′o·the·is′ti·cal·ly** *adv.*

mon·o·ther·mi·a (mon′ə·thûr′mē·ə) *n. Med.* A condition of uniform temperature, as in the body. [< NL < Gk. *monos* single + *thermē* heat] —**mon′o·ther′mic** *adj.*

mon·o·tint (mon′ə·tint) *n.* A monochrome.

mon·o·tone (mon′ə·tōn) *n.* **1** Sameness of utterance or tone; monotony in the style of composition or speech, or something composed in such style. **2** A single musical tone unvaried in pitch or key; also, a chant in such a tone; an intoning.

mo·not·o·nous (mə·not′ə·nəs) *adj.* **1** Not varied in inflection, cadence, or pitch. **2** Tiresomely uniform. See synonyms under TEDIOUS. [< Gk. *monotonos*] —**mo·not′o·nous·ly** *adv.* —**mo·not′o·nous·ness** *n.*

mo·not·o·ny (mə·not′ə·nē) *n.* **1** The state or quality of being monotonous; irksome uniformity or lack of variety; also, sameness of tone; want of variety in cadence or inflection. **2** *Math.* **a** Continual increase or decrease of a quantity, function, etc. **b** Absence of either increase or decrease. [< Gk. *monotonia* < *monos* single + *tonos* tone] —**mon·o·ton·ic** (mon′ə·ton′ik) *adj.*

mon·o·treme (mon′ə·trēm) *n.* Any member of the lowest order of mammals *(Monotremata)*, without true teeth in the adult stage and having a single opening for the genitourinary and digestive organs, as in duckbills and echidnas. [< MONO- + Gk. *trēma* hole] —**mon′o·trem′a·tous** (-trem′ə·təs), **mon′o·tre′mous** *adj.*

mo·not·ri·chous (mə·not′rə·kəs) *adj.* Having only one polar flagellum, as certain bacteria: also **mon·o·trich·ic** (mon′ə·trik′ik). [< MONO- + Gk. *thrix, trichos* hair]

mon·o·troph·ic (mon′ə·trof′ik) *adj.* Subsisting on or requiring only one kind of food; monophagous. [< MONO- + Gk. *trophē* food]

mo·not·ro·py (mə·not′rə·pē) *n.* The property, possessed by certain substances, tissues, or organs, of occurring in only one stable form. [< MONO- + -TROPY] —**mon·o·trop′ic** (mon′ə·trop′ik) *adj.*

mon·o·type (mon′ə·tīp) *n.* **1** *Biol.* The only representative of its kind, as a species of a genus or the like. **2** *Printing* A print from a metal plate on which a design, painting, etc., has been made.

Mon·o·type (mon′ə·tīp) *n. Printing* A machine which automatically casts and sets type in single characters or units: a trade name. Compare LINOTYPE.

mon·o·typ·ic (mon′ə·tip′ik) *adj.* **1** Containing but one representative; having only one type: a *monotypic* genus. **2** Being a monotype.

mon·o·va·lence (mon′ə·vā′ləns) *n. Chem.* Univalence. Also **mon′o·va′len·cy.** —**mon′o·va′lent** *adj.*

mon·ox·ide (mon·ok′sīd, mə·nok′-) *n. Chem.* A compound containing a single atom of oxygen in each molecule.

Mon·roe (mən·rō′), **James,** 1758–1831, president of the United States 1817–25.

Monroe Doctrine The doctrine, essentially formulated by President Monroe in his message to Congress (December 2, 1823), that any attempt by European powers to interfere in the affairs of the American countries or to acquire territory on the American continents would be regarded by the United States as an unfriendly act.

Mon·ro·vi·a (mən·rō′vē·ə) The capital of Liberia, a port on the Atlantic.

mons (monz) *n. pl.* **mon·tes** (mon′tēz) *Anat.* The rounded fatty eminence at the lower part of the abdomen, covered with hair in the adult: the **mons pu·bis** (pyoo͞′bis) of the male, or the **mons ven·er·is** (ven′ər·is) of the female. [< L, hill, mountain]

Mons (môns) A city in SW Belgium, capital of Hainaut province.

mon·sei·gneur (mon′sen·yûr′, mon·sēn′yər; *Fr.* môn·se·nyœr′) *n. pl.* **mes·sei·gneurs** (me·se·nyœr′) My lord: a title given to princes of the church and formerly to the higher nobility of France. [< F < *mon* my + *seigneur* lord < L *senior* older. See SENIOR.]

mon·sieur (mə·syûr′, *Fr.* mə·syœ′) *n. pl.* **mes·sieurs** (mes′ərz, *Fr.* me·syœ′) **1** The French title of courtesy for men, equivalent to *Mr.* and *sir*; abbreviated, M., *pl.* MM. It is capitalized when used with a proper name. **2** A Frenchman. [< F < *mon* + *sieur,* short for *seigneur.* See MONSEIGNEUR.]

mon·si·gnor (mon·sēn′yər, *Ital.* môn′sē·nyōr′) *n. pl.* **·gnors** or *Ital.* **·gno·ri** (-nyō′rē) A title of honor of certain prelates and Roman Catholic officials, as of the papal court: abbreviated *Mgr.* Also **mon·si·gno·re** (môn′sē·nyō′rā). [< Ital. *monsignore* < F *monseigneur.* See MONSEIGNEUR.]

mon·soon (mon·soo͞n′) *n. Meteorol.* **1** A wind that blows more or less steadily along the Asiatic coast of the Pacific, in winter from the northeast **(dry monsoon)**, in summer from the southwest **(wet monsoon). 2** A trade wind. [< MDu. *monssoen* < Pg. *monção* < Arabic *mausim* season]

mon·ster (mon′stər) *n.* **1** A fabulous animal, compounded of various brute forms. **2** A being that is greatly malformed; anything hideous or abnormal in structure and appearance; a teratism. **3** One abhorred because of his unnatural or inhuman character. **4** A very large person, animal, or thing. See synonyms under PRODIGY. —*adj.* Extraordinary or enormous in size or numbers; huge. [< OF *monstre* < L *monstrum* divine omen, monster < *monere* warn]

mon·strance (mon′strəns) *n.* In Roman Catholic ritual, a sacred vessel in which the consecrated Host is exposed for adoration: also called *ostensorium, ostensory.* [< OF < Med. L *monstrantia* < L *monstrare* show]

mon·stros·i·ty (mon·stros′ə·tē) *n. pl.* **·ties 1** Anything unnaturally huge, malformed, or distorted. **2** The character of being monstrous.

mon·strous (mon′strəs) *adj.* **1** Deviating greatly from the natural or normal; unnatural in form or structure. **2** Of extraordinary size or number; excessive; huge: a *monstrous* beast or multitude. **3** Inspiring abhorrence, hate, incredulity, etc., in a remarkable degree; hateful; hideous; incredible; intolerable: a *monstrous* cruelty. See synonyms under ABSURD, EXTRAORDINARY, FLAGRANT. —*adv. Archaic* Extremely. [< OF *monstreux* < L *monstrosus* < *monstrum.* See MONSTER.] —**mon′strous·ly** *adv.* —**mon′strous·ness** *n.*

mon·tage (mon·täzh′) *n.* **1** A picture made by superimposing several different pictures so as to blend into one another, or so as to show figures upon a desired background; a composite picture; also, the process of composing such a picture. **2** In motion pictures, a swiftly run sequence of images or pictures illustrating a sequence of associated ideas; the dizzy revolving of several images around a central, focused image or picture to signify the passage of time or the like. **3** The section of a motion picture using this method. [< F]

Mon·ta·gu (mon′tə·gyoo͞), **Lady Mary Wortley,** 1689–1762, English writer.

Mon·ta·gue (mon′tə·gyoo͞) The family of Romeo, in Shakespeare's *Romeo and Juliet.*

Mon·taigne (mon·tān′, *Fr.* môn·ten′y′), **Michel Eyquem de,** 1533–92, French essayist.

Mon·tan·a (mon·tan′ə) A State in the NW United States bordering on Canada; 147,138 square miles; capital, Helena; entered the Union Nov. 8, 1889; nickname, *Treasure State*: abbr. MT —**Mon·tan′an** *adj.* & *n.*

mon·tan·ic (mon·tan′ik) *adj.* Of or pertaining to mountains; mountainous. Also **mon·tane** (mon′tān). [< L *montan(us)* + -IC]

Mon·ta·nism (mon′tə·niz′əm) *n.* The doctrine of an ascetic Christian sect of the second century, founded by Montanus of Phrygia. —**Mon′ta·nist** *n.* —**Mon′ta·nis′tic** or **·ti·cal** *adj.*

mon·tan wax (mon′tən) A hydrocarbon wax of high melting point extracted from lignite, used as insulation and in making polishes, candles, phonograph records, etc. [< L *montanus* of the mountain]

Mon·tauk Point (mon′tôk) The easternmost point of New York, a promontory at the tip of the southern peninsula of Long Island.

Mont Blanc (mont blangk′, *Fr.* môn blän′) The highest mountain of the Alps, on the French-Italian border; 15,780 feet.

Mont·calm (mont·käm′, *Fr.* môn·kälm′), **Joseph Louis,** 1712–59, Marquis de Saint Véran, French general; fell in defense of Quebec against the British under Wolfe.

mont-de-pié·té (môn·də·pyā·tā′) *n. French* A pawnshop authorized and controlled by the state to lend money to the poor; literally, mount of piety: originated in Italy in the 15th century. Also *Italian* **mon·te di pie·tà** (môn′tā dē pyā·tä′).

mon·te (mon′tē) *n.* **1** A Spanish gambling game of cards. **2** A table on which, or a place where, monte is played. **3** The money stacked in front of the dealer to pay off stakes: also **monte bank** [< Sp., lit., mountain; in ref. to the pile of unplayed cards]

Mon·te Car·lo (mon′tē kär′lō, *Ital.* môn′tā kär′lō) A resort town in Monaco, on the Mediterranean.

Monte Cassino See CASSINO.

mon·teith (mon·tēth′) *n.* An ornamental punch bowl. [from *Monteigh,* a surname]

Mon·te·mez·zi (môn′tā·med′dzē), **Italo,** 1875–1952, Italian composer.

Mon·te·ne·gro (mon′tə·nē′grō) A constituent republic of southern Yugoslavia; formerly a kingdom; 5,343 square miles; capital, Titograd. *Serbo-Croatian* **Cr·na Go·ra** (tsûr′nä gō′rä). — **Mon′te·ne′grin** *adj.* & *n.*

Mon·te·rey (mon′tə·rā′) A city in western California on **Monterey Bay,** an inlet of the Pacific south of San Francisco.

Mon·ter·rey (mon′tə·rā′, *Sp.* mōn′ter·rā′) A city in NE Mexico, capital of Nuevo León state; captured by United States troops (September, 1846) in the Mexican War.

Mon·tes·pan (mon′tə·span′, *Fr.* môn·tes·pän′),

Marquise de, 1641–1707, Françoise Athénaïs de Rochechouart, mistress of Louis XIV of France.
Mon·tes·quieu (mon′təs·kyo͞o′, *Fr.* môn·tes·ky′), **Baron de la Brède et de,** 1689–1755, Charles Louis de Secondat, French jurist and philosophical writer on history and government.
Mon·tes·so·ri (mon′tə·sôr′ē, sō′rē; *Ital.* môn′·tes·sō′rē), **Maria,** 1870–1952, Italian educator.
Montessori method A system of teaching small children by training their sense perceptions, and by guiding rather than controlling their activity.
Mon·teux (môn·tü′), **Pierre,** 1875–1964, French conductor.
Mon·te·ver·di (mon′tə·vûr′dē, *Ital.* môn′tā·ver′·dē), **Claudio,** 1567–1643, Italian composer.
Mon·te·vid·e·o (mon′tə·vi·dā′ō, -vid′ē·ō; *Sp.* mōn′tā·vē·thā′ō) A port on the Rio de la Plata, capital of Uruguay.
Mon·te·zu·ma (mon′tə·zo͞o′mə), 1479?–1520, last Aztec emperor of Mexico; dethroned by Cortez: also *Moctezuma.*
Mont·fort (mont′fərt, *Fr.* môn·fôr′), **Simon de,**1160?–1218, French crusader. **—Simon de,** 1208?–65, Earl of Leicester, English general and statesman; son of the preceding.
mont·gol·fi·er (mont·gol′fē·ər) *n.* A hot-air balloon. [after the *Montgolfier* brothers]
Mont·gol·fi·er (mont·gol′fē·ər, *Fr.* môn·gôl·fyā′), **Jacques Étienne,** 1745–99, and **Joseph Michel,** 1740–1810, french inventors, brothers, whose hot-air balloon was the first to make a successful ascent (1783).
Mont·gom·er·y (mont·gum′ər·ē) **1** The capital of Alabama, in the east central part of the State on the Alabama River. **2** A county in central Wales; 797 square miles; county town, Montgomery: also **Mont·gom′er·y·shire** (-shir).
Mont·gom·er·y (mont·gum′ər·ē, mən-), **Sir Bernard Law,**1887–1976, first Viscount Montgomery of Alamein, English field marshal in World War II. **—Richard,** 1736?–75, general in the Continental Army; killed at Quebec.
month (munth) *n.* **1** A unit of time, originally equal to the interval between two new moons, afterward called a **lunar month,** and equal on the average to 29.53 days. **2** One of the 12 parts into which the calendar year is divided, called a **calendar month;** loosely, thirty days or four weeks. **3** The twelfth part of a solar year: also **solar month.** ◆ **Collateral adjective:** *mensal.* [OE *mōnath.* Akin to MOON.]
month·ly (munth′lē) *adj.* **1** Continuing a month, or done in a month. **2** Happening once a month. **3** Pertaining to the menses. —*adv.* Once a month. —*n. pl.* **·lies 1** A periodical published once a month. **2** *pl.* The menses.
monthly meeting In the Society of Friends, a meeting held once a month, by two or more neighboring congregations, for worship and business; also, the organized unit composed of these congregations.
Mon·ti·cel·lo (mon′tə·sel′ō, -chel′ō) The estate and residence of Thomas Jefferson about 3 miles east of Charlottesville, Virginia.
Mont·mar·tre (môn·mär′tr′) A northern district of Paris, famous for its night clubs.
Mont·mo·ren·cy River (mont′mə·ren′sē) A river in southern Quebec, Canada, flowing 60 miles south to the St. Lawrence River; near its mouth is **Montmorency Falls,** 275 feet high.
Mont·pel·ier (mont·pēl′yər) The capital of Vermont.
Mont·pel·lier (môn·pe·lyā ′) A city in southern France.
Mon·tre·al (mon′trē·ôl′) A city in southern Quebec, Canada, on **Montreal Island** at the confluence of the St. Lawrence and Ottawa rivers. *French* **Mont·ré·al** (môn·rā·äl′).
Mon·treux (môn·tr′) A resort in western Switzerland on the eastern shore of Lake Geneva.
Mon·trose (mon·trōz′, mont·rōz′,) **Marquis of,** 1612–50, James Graham, Scottish royalist leader; executed.
Mont Saint Mi·chel (môn san mē·shel′) A rocky islet, site of a famous ancient fortress and abbey, in **Mont Saint Michel Bay,** an inlet of the Gulf of Saint Malo in NW France.
Mont·ser·rat (mont′sə·rat′) **1** An island in the Leeward Islands, a British colony, member of The West Indies; 37.5 square miles. **2** A mountain in NE Spain, 4,054 feet; site of the 11th century Benedictine **Montserrat Monastery.**
mon·u·ment (mon′yə·mənt) *n.* **1** Something erected to perpetuate the memory of a person or of an event. **2** A notable structure, deed, production, etc., worthy to be considered as a memorial of the past, or of some event of person. **3** A stone or other permanent mark serving to indicate an angle or boundary. **4** A tomb. **5** *Obs.* A statue; effigy. [<F <L *monumentum* <L *monere* remind]
mon·u·men·tal (mon′yə·men′təl) *adj.* **1** Pertaining to or like a monument. **2** Serving as a monument; memorial; impressive; conspicuous; enduring. **3** Spectacular; excessive: a *monumental* fraud. [<L *monumentalis*] **—mon′u·men′tal·ly** *adv.*
mon·u·men·tal·ize (mon′yə·men′təl·īz) *v.t.* **·ized, ·iz·ing** To establish a lasting record or memorial of.
mon·y (mon′ē) *adj. Scot.* Many. Also **mon′ie.**
-mony *suffix* of nouns The condition, state, or thing resulting from: *parsimony.* [<L *-monia, -monium*]
Mon·za (môn′tsä) A city in Lombardy, Italy.
mon·zo·nite (mon′zə·nīt) *n.* A coarse-grained, igneous rock containing approximately equal amounts of orthoclase and plagioclase, with inclusions of colored silicates. [from Mount *Monzoni,* in the Tirol] **—mon′zo·nit′ic** (-nit′·ik) *adj.*
moo (mo͞o) *v.i.* To low as or like a cow. —*n.* The lowing noise made by a cow. [Imit.]
mooch (mo͞och) *Slang v.t.* **1** To obtain without paying; beg; cadge: to *mooch* a drink. **2** To steal. —*v.i.* **3** To loiter about; skulk; sneak. Also spelled *mouch.* [Var. of dial. *miche* pilfer <OF *muchier* hide, skulk] **—mooch′er** *n.*
mood[1] (mo͞od) *n.* **1** Temporary or capricious state of mind in regard to passion or feeling; humor; disposition. **2** *pl.* Fits of morose or sullen behavior; the state of being moody: to have *moods.* **3** *Obs.* Anger. See synonyms under FANCY, TEMPER. [OE *mō d*]
mood[2] (mo͞od) *n.* **1** *Gram.* The manner in which the action or condition expressed by a verb is stated, whether as actual, doubtful, commanded, etc. The English moods proper are the indicative, subjunctive, and imperative. The infinitive is sometimes also classed as a mood. Certain verb-phrases are likewise loosely called moods, as those formed by *may, might, can, could* (potential), *should, would* (conditional), *must, ought* (obligative). Also *mode.* **2** *Logic* Mode. **3** *Music* Mode. [Var. of MODE]
mood·y (mo͞o′dē) *adj.* **mood·i·er, mood·i·est 1** Given to or expressive of capricious moods. **2** Petulant; sullen; melancholy. See synonyms under MOROSE. **— mood′i·ly** *adv.* **—mood′i·ness** *n.*
Mood·y (mo͞o′dē), **Dwight Lyman,** 1837–99, U.S. evangelist. **—William Vaughn,** 1869–1910, U.S. poet and dramatist.
mool (mo͞ol) *Scot. n.* **1** Dirt; dust. **2** The grave. —*v.t.* **1** To crumble. **2** To bury.
moo·lah (mo͞o′lə) See MOLLAH.
moo·ley (mo͞o′lē) *n.* A cow without horns. See MULEY.

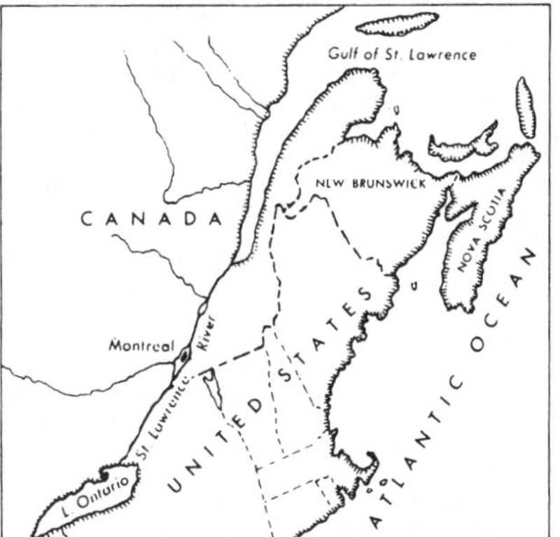

moon (mo͞on) *n.* **1** A celestial body revolving around the earth from west to east in a lunar month of 29.53 days or a sidereal month of 27.33 days; mean diameter, 2,160 miles; mean distance from the earth, 238,900 miles. In mass, the earth is 81.5 times greater than the moon; in volume, 49 times greater. **2** A satellite revolving about any planet. See under PLANET. **3** A lunar month. **4** Something resembling a moon or crescent. **5** Moonlight. **—dark of the moon** That period of time between the full moon and the new moon. —man in the moon The fancied appearance of a face in the disk of the full moon, caused by the shadows, lines, spots, etc., on its surface. —*v.i.* Colloq. To stare or wander about in an abstracted or listless manner. —*v.t.* To pass (time) thus. [OE *mōna.* Akin to MONTH.]

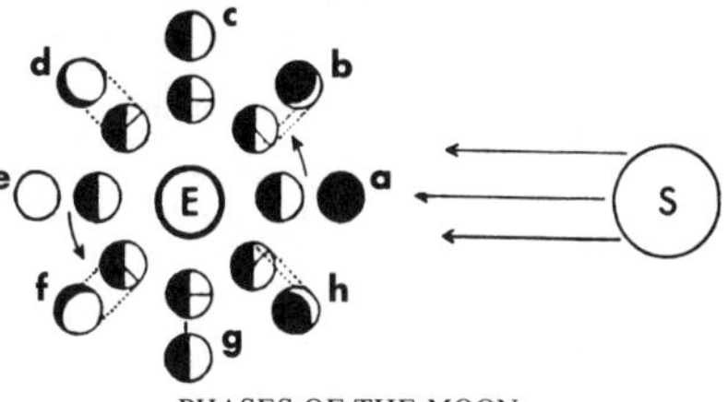

PHASES OF THE MOON
E. Earth. *S.* Sun.
a. New. *b.* Crescent. *c.* 1st Quarter.
d. Gibbous. *e.* Full. *f.* Gibbous.
g. 3rd Quarter. *h.* Crescent.

Moon, Mountains of the See RUWENZORI.
moon·beam (mo͞on′bēm′) *n.* A ray of moonlight.
moon·blind (mo͞on′blīnd′) *adv.* **1** Purblind; feeble-sighted. **2** Moon-struck. **3** Affected with moonblindness.
moon·blind·ness (mo͞on′blīnd′nis) *n.* **1** A form of blindness erroneously attributed to moonlight; nyctalopia. **2** A periodic inflammation of the eyes of a horse.
moon·calf (mo͞on′kaf′, -käf′) *n.* **1** A stupid person; dolt; idiot. **2** A monster; deformity. [With ref. to the supposed bad influence of the moon]
moon·craft (mo͞on′kraft′, -kräft′) *n.* A spacecraft designed to travel to the moon.
moon-eye (mo͞on′ī′) *n.* **1** An eye affected with moonblindness. **2** Moonblindness.
moon-eyed (mo͞on′īd′) *adj.* **1** Having moon-eyes. **2** Moonblind (def. 3). **3** Having eyes wide open, as with amazement, awe, etc.
moon·fish (mo͞on′fish′) *n. pl.* **·fish** or **·fish·es 1** Any of various carangoid fishes found on either coast of the western hemisphere, having a silvery or yellowish, much compressed body, especially *Vomer setipinnis* : also called *horsefish.* **2** The opah. **3** The Mexican top minnow *(Platypoecilus maculatus).*
moon·flow·er (mo͞on′flou′ər) *n.* Any of a genus *(Calonyction)* of perennial climbing herbs of the morning-glory family; especially, *C. aculeatum* (formerly genus *Ipomoea*), bearing fragrant, white flowers which open at night.
moon·glade (mo͞on′glād′) *n.* The silvery reflection of moonlight on water.
moon·light (mo͞on′līt′) *n.* The light of the moon. —*adj.* Pertaining to or illuminated by moonlight. —*v.i. Colloq.* To work at a job in addition to one's regular job. **—moon′ light′·er, moon′light′ing** *n.*
moon·lit (mo͞on′lit′) *adj.* Lighted by the moon.
moon·quake (mo͞on′kwāk′) *n.* A trembling or shaking of the moon's surface analogous to an earthquake. [<MOON + (EARTH)QUAKE]
moon·rise (mo͞on′rīz′) *n.* The appearing of the moon above the horizon, or the time when it appears.
moon·seed (mo͞on′sēd′) *n.* A North American climbing plant of the genus *Menispermum,* of the family *Menispermaceae*: so called from its crescent-shaped seeds.
moon·set (mo͞on′set′) *n.* The setting, or the time of setting, of the moon; specifically, the

moment at which it passes below the horizon.

moon·shine (mo͞on′shīn′) *n.* **1** Moonlight. **2** Something visionary or unreal; pretence; nonsense. **3** *Colloq.* Smuggled or illicitly distilled spirits. **—moon′shin′y** *adj.*

moon·shin·er (mo͞on′shī′nər) *n. Colloq.* An illicit distiller; smuggler.

moon·stone (mo͞on′stōn′) *n.* A whitish, cloudy feldspar, valued as a gemstone.

moon–struck (mo͞on′struk′) *adj.* Affected by or as by the moon; lunatic; deranged. Also **moon′–strick′en** (-strik′ən).

moon·wort (mo͞on′wûrt′) *n.* **1** The herb honesty. **2** Any fern of the genus *Botrychium,* especially *B. lunaria.* [Trans. of Med. L *lunaria* <L *luna* moon]

moon·y (mo͞o′nē) *adj.* **moon·i·er, moon·i·est 1** Moon–struck. **2** Moonlit. **3** Like moonlight, or giving out light resembling moonlight. **4** Round or crescent–shaped. **5** Absent–minded; dreaming; vacant.

moop (mo͞op) *v.i. Scot.* To live or associate: with *with.*

moor[1] (mo͝or) *v.t.* **1** To secure (a ship, etc.) in one place by means of cables attached to shore, anchors, etc. **2** To secure in place; fix. *—v.i.* **3** To secure a ship in position; anchor. **4** To be secured by chains or cables. [Cf. OE *mǣrels* mooring rope]

moor[2] (mo͝or) *n.* **1** A tract of wasteland sometimes covered with heath, often elevated and frequently marshy and abounding in peat. **2** A tract of land on which game is preserved for shooting. [OE *mōr*] **—moor′ish** *adj.*

Moor (mo͝or) *n.* **1** A person of mixed Berber and Arab blood, inhabiting Morocco and the southern Mediterranean coast. **2** Any North African native; specifically, a Saracen or a Spanish descendant of the Saracens. **3** A Mohammedan of India. [<F *more, maure* < L *Maurus* Moor, Mauritanian <Gk. *Mauros*] **—Moor′ish** *adj.*

moor·age (mo͝or′ij) *n.* A mooring place.

moor·cock (moor′kok′) *n.* The male of the red grouse.

Moore (mo͝or, môr, mōr), **George,** 1852–1933, Irish novelist, critic, and dramatist. **—Henry,** 1898–1978, English sculptor.**—John Bassett,** 1860–1947, U.S. jurist. **—Marianne Craig,** 1887–1972, U.S. poet. **—Thomas,** 1779–1852, Irish poet.

Mo·o·re·a (mō′ō·rā′ə) The second largest island in the Windward group of the Society Islands; 50 square miles.

moor·fowl (mo͝or′foul′) *n.* The red grouse.

moor·hen (mo͝or′hen′) *n.* **1** The female of the moorfowl. **2** The water hen *(Gallinula chloropus).* **3** The American coot.

moor·ing (mo͝or′ing) *n.* **1** The act of securing a vessel. **2** *Chiefly pl.* The place where a vessel is moored. **3** *Chiefly pl.* Anything by which an object is fastened.

mooring mast The tower to which a dirigible or blimp is secured when not in flight: also **mooring tower.**

moor·land (mo͝or′land′) *n.* A moor or marsh. *—adj.* Having marshy properties. **—moor′·land′er** *n.*

moor·wort (mo͝or′wûrt′) *n.* A low, smooth shrub *(Andromeda polifolia)* of the heath family, with narrow, thick, evergreen leaves, growing in wet bogs.

moor·y (mo͝or′ē) *adj.* **moor·i·er, moor·i·est** Of the nature of moorland; marshy.

moose (mo͞os) *n. pl.* **moose 1** A large, heavily built mammal *(Alces americana)* of the deer family, found in northern North America: the male bears huge, palmate antlers. **2** The northern European elk. [<Algonquian (Massachuset) *moos* he strips off; because it eats the bark of trees]

MOOSE
(Up to nearly 7 feet high at the shoulder; weight to 1,000 pounds)

moose·bird (mo͞os′·bûrd′) *n.* The Canada jay.

moose·call (mo͞os′kôl′) *n.* A small horn or trumpet made of birch bark or other materials, used by hunters to lure moose within shooting distance. Also **moose horn.**

moose·flow·er (mo͞os′flou′ər) *n.* Trillium: also called *wakerobin.*

moose·grass (mo͞os′gras′, -gräs′) *n.* Ground hemlock.

Moose·head Lake (mo͞os′hed) The largest lake in Maine, source of the Kennebec River; 36 miles long; 120 square miles.

moose·wood (mo͞os′wo͝od′) *n.* Leatherwood.

moot (mo͞ot) *n.* **1** In Anglo–Saxon times, the meeting of freemen and farmers for the discussion or debate of local affairs. **2** Hence, discussion or argument; especially, in modern usage, discussion of a mock lawsuit for the sake of practice. **3** The place where a meeting is held. *—v.t.* **1** To debate; discuss. **2** To argue (a case) in a moot court. *—adj.* Still open to discussion; intended for discussion: a *moot* point. [OE *mōt* assembly, court] **—moot′er** *n.*

moot court A court for the trial of a fictitious suit by law students.

mop[1] (mop) *n.* **1** A piece of cloth, or the like, attached to a handle: used for washing floors. **2** Any loosely tangled bunch or mass, as of hair. *—v.t.* **mopped, mop·ping** To rub or wipe with or as with a mop. **—to mop up 1** To take up with or as with a mop. **2** *Mil.* To wipe out remnants of enemy resistance in (captured areas). **—to mop (up) the floor with** *Slang* To defeat easily and decisively. [Origin uncertain. Cf. F. *mappe* napkin <L mappa.]

mop[2] (mop) *n.* **1** A wry mouth; grimace. **2** A pouting or petted young person; a young girl. [<*v.*] *—v.i.* To make a wry face; grimace. [Cf. Du. *moppen* pout]

mope (mōp) *v.* **moped, mop·ing** *v.i.* To be gloomy, listless, or dispirited. *—v.t.* To make gloomy or dispirited.*—n.* **1** One who mopes. **2** *pl.* Dejection; depression. [Prob. <Scand. Cf. Sw. *mopa* sulk, Dan. *maabe* be stupid, unaware.] **—mop′er** *n.* **—mop′ish** *adj.* **—mop′·ish·ly** *adv.* **—mop′ish·ness** *n.*

mo·ped (mō′ped) *n.* A heavy–duty bicycle equipped with an engine. [<*mo(tor)* +*ped (al)*]

mop·pet (mop′it) *n.* **1** A rag doll or one made of cloth. **2** A child; youngster. [Dim. of ME *moppe* rag doll, ? <L *mappa* napkin]

mop–up (mop′up′) *n. Colloq.* An ending or wiping out.

mo·quette (mō·ket′) *n.* A woolen fabric with a velvety pile, used for carpets and upholstery. [<F; ult. origin uncertain]

Mo·qui (mō′kē) *n.* A Hopi Indian: also spelled *Moki.*

mo·ra (môr′ə, mō′rə) *n. pl.* **mo·rae** (môr′ē, mō′rē) or **mo·ras 1** In civil law, delay, especially if unjustifiable; default. **2** In prosody, a unit of meter, the common short foot, usually indicated by the breve. [<L, delay]

mo·ra·ceous (mô·rā′shəs, mō-) *adj.* Denoting or belonging to a family *(Moraceae)* of mostly tropical herbs, shrubs, and trees of the order *Urticales,* including the mulberry, common fig, hop, hemp, etc. [<L *morus* mulberry]

Mo·rad·a·bad (mō·rad′ə·bad, mō·rad′ä·bäd′) A city in north central Uttar Pradesh State, northern India.

mo·raine (mə·rān′, mō-) *n. Geol.* A ridge or heap of earth, stones, etc., carried by a glacier and deposited on adjacent ground, either along the course or at the edges of the glacier, as a **medial** or **lateral moraine,** or at its lower terminus, as a **terminal moraine.** [<dial. F] **—mo·rain′al, mo·rain′ic** *adj.*

mor·al (môr′əl, mor′-) *adj.* **1** Pertaining to character and behavior from the point of view of right and wrong, and obligation of duty; pertaining to rightness and duty in conduct. **2** Conforming to right conduct; actuated by a sense of the good, true, and right; good; righteous; virtuous. **3** Concerned with the principles of right and wrong; ethical: *moral* philosophy; *moral* values. **4** Acting or suited to act through man's intellect or sense of right: often opposed to *physical*: *moral* support. **5** *Logic* Probable as opposed to demonstrative: *moral* proof. **6** Of or pertaining to the science or doctrine of human nature as fitted for conduct. Most writers on modern philosophy use the term to cover the entire sphere of human conduct which comes under the distinctions of right and wrong. **7** Attempting or serving to inculcate or convey a moral; moralizing: a *moral* writer. **8** Of or influencing morals or morale: *moral* force. **9** Capable of understanding the difference between right and wrong: a *moral* agent. *—n.* **1** The lesson taught by a fable or the like. **2** *pl.* Conduct or behavior; ethics. [<F <L *moralis* <*mos, moris* custom; in the pl., manners, morals] **—mor′al·ly** *adv.*

Synonyms (adj.): dutiful, ethical, excellent, faithful, good, honest, honorable, incorruptible, just, pious, religious, right, righteous, true, upright, virtuous, worthy. *Antonyms*: see synonyms for IMMORAL.

mo·rale (mə·ral′, -räl′, mô-) *n.* **1** State of mind with reference to confidence, courage, hope, etc.: used especially of a number of persons associated in some enterprise, as troops, workers, etc. **2** Obs. Morality. [<F. See MORAL.]

moral hazard In insurance, a risk resulting from doubt as to the honesty of the person insured.

moral insanity Mental deficiency amounting to the incapacity to distinguish between right and wrong, or characterized by compulsions to perform unsocial, irresponsible, or criminal acts: a legal term variously interpreted in different statutes.

mor·al·ism (môr′əl·iz′əm, mor′-) *n.* The belief in a morality divested of all religious character.

mor·al·ist (môr′əl·ist, mor′-) *n.* **1** A teacher of morals. **2** One who practices morality without religion. **—mor′al·is′tic** *adj.*

mo·ral·i·ty (mə·ral′ə·tē, mô-) *n. pl.* **·ties 1** The doctrine of man's moral duties; ethics. **2** Virtuous conduct; rectitude; chastity. **3** The quality of being morally right. **4** A lesson inferred; a moral. **5** Conformity, or degree of conformity, to conventional rules, without or apart from inspiration and guidance by religion or other spiritual influences. **6** A form of allegorical drama of the 15th and 16th centuries in which the characters were personified virtues, vices, mental attributes, etc. See synonyms under VIRTUE. [<L *moralitas, -tatis* <*moralis.* See MORAL.]

mor·al·ize (môr′əl·īz, mor′-) *v.* **·ized, ·iz·ing** *v.i.* **1** To make moral reflections; talk about morality. *—v.t.* **2** To explain in a moral sense; derive a moral from. **3** To improve the morals of. Also *Brit.* **mor′al·ise. —mor′al·i·za′tion** *n.* **—mor′al·iz′er** *n.*

moral philosophy Ethics.

moral victory A defeat that is accounted a victory on the moral level, as when the righteousness of a defeated cause has been clearly established.

mo·rass (mə·ras′, mô-, mō-) *n.* A tract of low–lying, soft, wet ground; marsh. [<Du. *moeras,* earlier *marasch* <OF *maresc* <Med. L *mariscus* <Gmc. Ult. akin to MARSH.]

mor·a·to·ri·um (môr′ə·tôr′ē·əm, -tō′rē-, mor′-) *n. pl.* **·ri·a** (-ē·ə) or **·ri·ums** *Law* An emergency act of legislation or a government edict authorizing a debtor or bank to suspend payments for a given period; also, the period during which it is, or is to be, in force. [<NL <LL *moratorius.* See MORATORY.]

mor·a·to·ry (môr′ə·tôr′ē, -tō′rē, mor′-) *adj.* Pertaining or intended to delay: particularly applied to legislation in the nature of a moratorium. [<LL *moratorius* <L *morari* delay <*mora* delay]

Mo·ra·va (mô′rä·vä) **1** The Czech name for the river MARCH. **2** The Czech name for MORAVIA.

Mo·ra·vi·a (mô·rā′vē·ə, mō-) A central region of Czechoslovakia; 8,219 square miles; a former Austrian crownland: German *Mähren,* Czech *Morava.*

Mo·ra·vi·an (mô·rā′vē·ən, mō-) *adj.* Pertaining to Moravia or the Moravians. *—n.* **1** A native of Moravia. **2** One of a Christian sect founded by disciples of John Huss in Moravia (15th century), and now in Germany, Britain, and America. The sect is also known as the *Renewed Church of the United Brethren* or *Unity of the Brethren.*

Moravian Gap A mountain pass between the Carpathians and the Sudeten in central Europe.

Mo·rav·ská O·stra·va (mô′räf·skä ôs′trä·vä) A city of northern Moravia, Czechoslovakia: German *Mährisch–Ostrau*: also *Ostrava.*

mo·ray (môr′ā, mō·rā′) *n.* A brightly colored, voracious, savage eel of the family *Muraenidae,* inhabiting tropical and subtropical waters, especially among coral reefs: also called *murry.* The Mediterranean moray *(Muraena helena)* is esteemed as a food fish.

A related species is the **banded moray** *(Gymnothorax waialuoe)* of Hawaiian waters. [? <Pg. *moreia* <L *muraena*]

Mor·ay (mûr′ē, *Scot.* mûr′ā) A county of NE Scotland; 476 square miles; county town, Elgin. Formerly *Elgin.* Also **Mor′ay·shire** (-shir).

mor·bid (môr′bid) *adj.* **1** Being in a diseased or abnormal state. **2** Caused by or denoting a diseased condition of body or mind. **3** Taking an excessive interest in matters of a gruesome or unwholesome nature; also, apprehensive; suspicious. **4** Grisly; gruesome: a *morbid* story. **5** Of or pertaining to disease; pathological: *morbid* anatomy. [<L *morbidus* <*morbus* disease] **—mor′bid·ly** *adv.* **—mor′bid·ness** *n.*

mor·bi·dez·za (môr′bē·ded′dzä) *n. Italian* In painting, delicacy or softness of flesh tints.

mor·bid·i·ty (môr·bid′ə·tē) *n.* **1** The condition of being morbid or diseased. **2** The rate of disease or proportion of diseased persons in a community: compare MORTALITY (def. 3).

mor·bif·ic (môr·bif′ik) *adj.* Producing disease. Also **mor·bif′i·cal.** **—mor·bif′i·cal·ly** *adv.*

mor·bil·li (môr·bil′ī) *n. pl.* The measles. [<Med. L, pl. of *morbillus,* dim. of *morbus* disease]

mor·bil·li·form (môr·bil′ə·fôrm) *adj.* Resembling measles. [<MORBILLI + -FORM]

mor·bil·lous (môr·bil′əs) *adj.* Relating to or affected with measles.

mor·ceau (môr·sō′) *n. pl.* **·ceaux** (sō′) *French* A small bit or fragment; also, a short composition, as of music or poetry.

mor·da·cious (môr·dā′shəs) *adj.* Biting, or given to biting; hence, sarcastic. [<L *mordax, -acis* <*mordere* bite] **—mor·da′cious·ly** *adv.* **—mor·dac′i·ty** (-das′ə·tē) *n.*

mor·dan·cy (môr′dən·sē) *n.* Pungency; the quality of being biting or sarcastic. **2** Acting as a mordant. —*v.t.* To treat or imbue with a mordant. [<OF]

mor·dant (môr′dənt) *n.* **1** Any substance, such as tannic acid or aluminum hydroxide, which, by combining with a dyestuff to form an insoluble compound (lake), serves to produce a fixed color in a textile fiber. **2** The corrosive used in etching. —*adj.* **1** Biting; pungent; sarcastic. **2** Acting as a mordant. —*v.t.* To treat or imbue with a mordant. [<OF]

Mor·de·cai (môr′də·kī) In the Old Testament, Esther's cousin, instrumental in saving the Jews from extermination. *Esth.* ii 15.

mor·dent (môr′dənt) *n. Music* The rapid alternation of a tone with the tone immediately below it or the character indicating it: a form of trill. Also **mor·den·te** (môr·den′tā). **—inverted mordent** The rapid alternation of a note with one above it: a pralltriller. [<G <Ital. *mordente,* ppr. of *mordere* bite <L]

Mor·dred (môr′drid) See MODRED.

Mord·vin·i·an Autonomous Soviet Socialist Republic (môrd·vin′ē·ən) An administrative division of central European Russian S.F.S.R.; 10,080 square miles; capital, Saransk: also **Mor·do·vi·an Autonomous S.S.R.** (môr·dō′vē·ən).

more (môr, mōr) *adj. superlative* **most** **1** Greater in amount, extent, or degree: comparative of *much*: *more* water. **2** Greater in number: comparative of *many.* **3** Greater in rank or dignity. **4** Added to some former number; extra. —*n.* **1** A greater quantity, amount, etc. **2** Something that exceeds something else. —*adv.* **1** To a greater extent or degree. **2** In addition; further; again: usually qualified by *any, never,* a numeral, etc.: I cannot walk any *more.* [OE *māra*]

More (môr, mōr), **Hannah,** 1745–1833, English religious writer. **—Paul Elmer,** 1864–1937, U.S. critic and essayist. **—Sir Thomas,** 1478?–1535, lord chancellor of England; author; beheaded; canonized, 1935.

Mo·re·a (mō·rē′ə, mō-) A former name for PELOPONNESUS.

Mo·reau (mō·rō′), **Jean Victor,** 1761–1813, French Republican general.

mo·reen (mə·rēn′) *n.* A sturdy, ribbed, cotton, wool, or wool and cotton fabric, often with a watered or embossed finish, used for hangings and upholstery. [Prob. <MOIRE + *-een,* as in *velveteen*]

mo·rel[1] (mə·rel′) *n.* An edible mushroom of the genus *Morchella,* somewhat resembling a sponge on the end of a stalk. [<MF *morille,* ult. <Gmc. Cf. OHG *morhila* little carrot.]

mo·rel[2] (mə·rel′) *n.* The black nightshade *(Solanum nigrum).* Also **mo·relle′.** [<OF *morele* <Med. L *morella,* ? <LL *maurella,* a kind of plant]

Mo·re·lia (mō·rā′lyä) A city of south central Mexico, capital of Michoacán state.

mo·rel·lo (mə·rel′ō) *n.* A variety of cultivated cherry, with a dark-red skin, flesh, and juice: used in cooking and preserving. [<Flemish *marelle,* aphetic var. of *amarelle* <Ital. *amarello,* dim. of *amaro* bitter <L *amarus*]

Mo·re·los (mō·rā′lōs) A state in southern Mexico; 1,916 square miles; capital, Cuernavaca.

more·o·ver (môr·ō′vər, mōr-) *adv.* Beyond what has been said; further; besides; likewise.

mo·res (môr′ēz, mō′rēz) *n. pl. Sociol.* **1** Those established, traditional customs or folkways regarded by a social group as essential to its preservation and welfare. **2** The accepted conventions of a group or community. [<L, pl. of *mos, moris* custom]

Mo·res·net (mō·rez·ne′) A mining district on the Belgian–German frontier; ceded to Belgium under the Treaty of Versailles, 1919.

Mo·resque (mō·resk′, mə-) *adj.* Moorish; decorated in the style of the Moors. —*n.* Decorative work, by means of interlacings, relief, etc., highly colored and gilded. Compare MORISCO (def. 3). [<F <Ital. *moresco* <L *Maurus* Mauritanian]

MORESQUE PANEL DECORATION

Mor·gain (môr′gān, -gən) See MORGAN LE FAY.

Mor·gan (môr′gən), **Daniel,** 1736–1802, American Revolutionary general. **—Sir Henry,** 1635?–88, Welsh leader of American buccaneers. **—John Hunt,** 1825–64, American Confederate cavalry leader. **—John Pierpont,** 1837–1913, U.S. banker, financier, and art collector. **—Thomas Hunt,** 1866–1945, U.S. zoologist.

mor·ga·nat·ic (môr′gə·nat′ik) *adj.* Designating a legitimate marriage between a male member of certain royal families of Europe and a woman of inferior rank, in which the titles and estates of the husband are not shared by the wife or their children. Also **mor′ga·nat′i·cal.** [<NL *morganaticus* <LL *(matrimonium ad) morganaticum* (wedding with) morning gift <OHG *morgengeba* morning gift (in lieu of a share in the estate)] **—mor′ga·nat′i·cal·ly** *adv.*

Morgan horse A breed of horse of Arabian strain descendent from the stallion *Justin Morgan* (died 1821): noted for its powerful frame, gentle disposition, and versatility. [after Justin *Morgan,* owner of the original horse]

mor·gan·ite (môr′gən·īt) *n.* A rose–pink variety of beryl, used as a semiprecious gemstone. [after John Pierpont *Morgan*]

Morgan le Fay (lə fā′) In Arthurian legend, the fairy half–sister of Arthur. She appears in Carlovingian romance as *Fata Morgana.* [<OF *Morgain la fée* Morgan the fairy]

mor·gen (môr′gən) *n. pl.* **·gen** or **·gens** A land measure formerly used by the Dutch, and still employed in South Africa: equal to about two acres. [<Du. & G, morning; hence, area plowed in one morning]

Mor·gen·thau (môr′gən·thô), **Henry,** 1891–1967, U.S. secretary of the Treasury 1934–1945.

morgue (môrg) *n.* **1** A place where bodies of the dead are kept until identified or claimed. **2** In a newspaper editorial office, the department in charge of filed items and biographical material: used for obituary notices, etc. [<F, orig., the name of the Paris building used for this purpose]

Mo·ri·ah (mə·rī′ə) A hill in Jerusalem; site of Solomon's temple. II *Chron.* iii 1.

mor·i·bund (môr′ə·bund, -bənd, mor′-) *adj.* Dying; at the point of death. [<L *moribundus* <*mori* die] **—mor′i·bun′di·ty** *n.* **—mor′i·bund·ly** *adv.*

mo·rin (môr′in, mō′rin) *n.* A crystalline compound, $C_{15}H_{10}O_7$, obtained from old fustic: used as a yellow dyestuff and as a reagent for aluminum. [<F *morine* <L *morum* mulberry]

mo·ri·on[1] (môr′ē·on, mō′rē-) *n.* A kind of open helmet without vizor worn by men–at–arms: also spelled *morrion.* [<OF <Sp. *morrión* <*morra* crown of the head]

mo·ri·on[2] (môr′ē·on, mō′rē-) *n.* A dark, sometimes nearly black, variety of smoky quartz. [<F <LL, a misreading of L mormorion]

Mo·ris·co (mə·ris′kō) *adj.* Moorish. —*n. pl.* **·cos** or **·coes** **1** One of the Moors who remained in Spain after the conquest of Granada in 1492; a Moor. **2** A morris dance or dancer. **3** The Moresque style of architecture or decoration. [<Sp. <*Moro* Moor]

Mo·ri·son (môr′ə·sən, mor′-), **Samuel Eliot,** 1887–1976, U.S. historian.

mo·ri·tu·ri te sa·lu·ta·mus (môr′i·tyŏŏr′ē tē sal′yŏŏ·tā′məs) *Latin* We (who are) about to die salute thee: salutation of the gladiators to the Roman emperor.

Mo·ritz (mō′rits) Danish, Swedish, and German form of MAURICE.

Mor·land (môr′lənd), **George,** 1763–1804, English painter.

Mor·ley (môr′lē), **Christopher,** 1890–1957, U.S. writer. **— John,** 1838 – 1923, first Viscount Morley of Blackburn, English statesman and man of letters.

Mor·mon (môr′mən) *n.* **1** A member of a religious sect officially styled "The Church of Jesus Christ of Latter–day Saints," founded in the U.S. by Joseph Smith in 1830: also **Mor′mon·ist, Mor′mon·ite.** **2** In Mormon belief, a prophet and sacred historian of the fourth century A.D. who wrote, on golden tablets, a history of an early American people. The tablets, called the **Book of Mormon,** one of the holy books of the Mormon faith, were found by Joseph Smith near Palmyra, New York, and translated and published by him in 1830. **—Mor′mon·ism** *n.*

Mormon Bible The Book of Mormon. See under MORMON.

Mormon Church The Church of Jesus Christ of Latter–day Saints.

Mormon State Nickname of UTAH.

Mormon trail The trail taken by the Mormons, 1847, from Iowa to Utah.

morn (môrn) *n. Poetic* The morning. [OE *morgen*]

Mor·nay (môr·nā′), **Philippe de,** 1549–1623, Seigneur du Plessis, French Huguenot leader; minister of Henry IV: also known as *Duplessis–Mornay.*

morn·ing (môr′ning) *n.* **1** The early part of the day; the time from midnight to noon, or from sunrise to noon; hence, any early stage. **2** The dawn: often personified as **Morning,** the goddess Eos or Aurora. —*adj.* Pertaining to or occurring in the early part of the day. ◆ Collateral adjective: *matutinal.* [<MORN; by analogy with EVENING]

morn·ing-glo·ry (môr′ning·glôr′ē, -glō′rē) *n. pl.* **·ries** **1** A twining plant (genus *Ipomoea*) with funnel–shaped flowers of various colors. **2** Any one of many convolvulaceous plants.

morning gun A gun fired at reveille on military posts as a signal for raising the flag.

Morning Prayer In the Anglican church, the order for public worship in the morning.

morning sickness Vomiting and nausea in the morning, common in early pregnancy.

morn·ing–star (môr′ning·stär′) *n.* A weapon made of a metal ball set with spikes and chained to a handle; a mace.

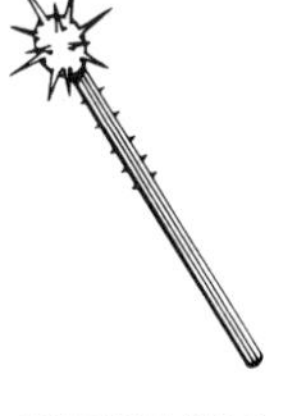

MORNING–STAR

morning star Any of the planets Jupiter, Mars, Saturn, Mercury, or especially Venus, when rising shortly before the sun.

Mo·ro (môr′ō, mō′rō) *n. pl.* **·ros** **1** A member of one of the Moslem tribes of the southern Philippines. **2** The Indonesian language of the Moros. [<Sp., a Moor]

Mo·roc·co (mə·rok′ō) **1** A kingdom on the Atlantic and Mediterranean coasts of NW

Africa; 160,000 square miles; capital, Rabat: French *Maroc,* Spanish *Marruecos.* **2** A former name for MARRAKESH. *Arabic* **El Maghreb el Ag·sa** (al mä′greb al äg′sä). **—Mo·roc′can** *adj.* & *n.*

morocco leather A fine leather made from goatskin tanned with sumac. Also **mo·roc′co.**

Mo·ro Gulf (môr′ō, mō′rō) A large northern inlet of the Celebes Sea in SW Mindanao.

mo·ron (môr′on, mō′ron) *n.* A person whose mental capacity has been arrested during development and who represents mentally the condition of a child of from 8 to 12 years of age. [<Gk. *mōron,* neut. of *mōros* dull, sluggish] **—mo·ron·ic** (mô·ron′ik, mō-) *adj.* **—mo·ron′i·cal·ly** *adv.*

mo·ron·ism (môr′on·iz′əm, mō′ron-) *n.* The mildest degree of feeble-mindedness, rated above imbecility and idiocy. Also **mo·ron·i·ty** (mô·ron′ə·tē, mō-).

Mor·o·pus (môr′ə·pəs, mor′-) *n. Paleontol.* A genus of extinct North American chalicotheres of the Tertiary period having a skull similar to that of the horse, slender legs, and hoofs modified into three large claws. [<NL <Gk. *mōros* sluggish + *pous* foot]

mo·rose (mə·rōs′) *adj.* Having a surly temper; sullen; gloomy. [<L *morosus* <*mos, moris* manner, habit] **—mo·rose′ly** *adv.* **—mo·rose′·ness, mo·ros·i·ty** (-ros′ə·tē) *n.*

Synonyms (adj.): acrimonious, bitter, churlish, crabbed, crusty, dogged, gloomy, gruff, ill-humored, ill-natured, moody, severe, sour, splenetic, sulky, sullen, surly. The *sullen* and *sulky* are discontented and resentful; *sullen* denotes more of pride, *sulky* more of resentful obstinacy. The *morose* are bitterly dissatisfied with the world in general, and disposed to vent their ill nature upon others. The *sullen* and *sulky* are for the most part silent; the *morose* growl out bitter speeches. A *surly* person is in a state of latent anger, resenting approach as intrusion, and ready to take offense at anything. See AUSTERE. Compare ACRIMONY. *Antonyms*: amiable, benignant, bland, complaisant, friendly, genial, gentle, good-natured, indulgent, kind, mild, pleasant, sympathetic, tender.

mor·phal·lax·is (môr′fə·lak′sis) *n. Biol.* The regeneration of parts of a living organism by the gradual transformation of other parts. [<Gk. *morphē* form + *allaxis* exchange]

mor·pheme (môr′fēm) *n. Ling.* The smallest lexical unit of a language, as a word, root, affix, or inflectional ending. *Man, run, pro-, -ess, -ing, ouch,* etc., are morphemes. [<F *morphème* <Gk. *morphē* form]

Mor·phe·us (môr′fē·əs, -fyōōs) In Greek mythology, the god of dreams, son of Hypnos, god of sleep. [<L <Gk. *morphē* form; from the shapes he calls up in dreams] **—Mor′·phe·an** *adj.*

mor·phic (môr′fik) *adj.* Morphologic.

-morphic *combining form* Having the form or shape of: *anthropomorphic.* [<Gk. *morphē* form]

mor·phine (môr′fēn) *n. Chem.* A bitter, white, crystalline, narcotic alkaloid, $C_{17}H_{19}NO_3 \cdot H_2O$, contained in opium and used for alleviating pain. Also **mor′phi·a** (-fē·ə). [<F <L *Morpheus* god of sleep]

mor·phin·ism (môr′fin·iz′əm) *n. Pathol.* A morbid condition of the system produced by an excessive dose or habitual use of morphine.

morpho- *combining form* Form; shape: *morpholysis.* Also, before vowels, **morph-.** [<Gk. *morphē* form]

mor·pho·gen·e·sis (môr′fō·jen′ə·sis) *n. Biol.* **1** The evolution of forms of structure. **2** The development of organic forms. Also **mor·phog·e·ny** (môr·foj′ə·nē). **—mor′pho·ge·net′ic** (-jə·net′ik) *adj.*

mor·phol·o·gy (môr·fol′ə·jē) *n.* **1** That branch of biology which treats of the form and structure of plants and animals. **2** The form of an organism considered apart from function. **3** *Geog.* The study of the forms of earth features. **4** *Ling.* **a** The branch of linguistics which deals with morphemes, their arrangement in words, and the changes they undergo in various grammatical constructions. **b** The arrangement, composition, and inflection of the morphemes of a language. [<MORPHO- + -LOGY] **—mor·pho·log·ic** (môr′·fə·loj′ik) or **·i·cal** *adj.* **—mor′pho·log′i·cal·ly** *adv.* **—mor·phol′o·gist** *n.*

mor·phol·y·sis (môr·fol′ə·sis) *n.* The breakdown of form or structure. [<MORPHO- + -LYSIS]

mor·pho·sis (môr·fō′sis) *n. Biol.* The order or mode of formation of an organ or organism. [<Gk. *morphōsis* shaping <*morphē* form] **—mor·phot′ic** (-fot′ik) *adj.*

-morphous *combining form* Having a (specified) form: often equivalent to *-morphic*: *anthropomorphous.* [<Gk. *morphē* form]

Mor·rig·u (môr′ē·ōō) In Old Irish mythology, a war goddess, described as attending the battlefield in the form of a demoniacal raven. She helped the Tuatha De Danann defeat the Fomorians. Also **Mor·ri·gan** (môr′ē·ən).

mor·ri·on (môr′ē·on, mō′rē-) See MORION[1].

mor·ris (môr′is, mor′-) *n.* **1** An old English rustic dance, in which the performers took the part of Robin Hood and other characters in English folklore. **2** A dance by a single dancer with castanets. Also **mor′rice, morris dance.** [Earlier *morys, morish* Moorish]

Mor·ris (môr′is, mor′-), **Gouverneur,** 1752–1816, American statesman; financier. **—Robert,** 1734–1806, American statesman, financier, and philanthropist; signer of the Declaration of Independence. **—William,** 1834–96, English painter, craftsman, poet, and socialist; invented the **Morris chair,** an armchair with an adjustable back.

Mor·ris Jes·up (môr′is jes′əp, mor′is), **Cape** The world's northernmost point of land, at the northern extremity of Greenland; 440 miles from the North Pole.

Mor·ri·son (môr′ə·sən, mor′-), **Herbert Stanley,** 1888–1965, English Labour party leader and politician.

Mor·ri·son (môr′ə·sən, mor′-), **Mount** The highest mountain of Taiwan; 13,599 feet. *Chinese* **Sin·kao** (shin′kou′), *Japanese* **Ni·i·ta·ka** (nē·ē·tä·kä).

mor·ro (môr′ō, mor′ō; *Sp.* môr′rō) *n. pl.* **mor·ros** (môr′ōz, mor′-; *Sp.* môr′rōs) A round hill. [<Sp.]

Morro Castle A fort defending the entrance to Havana harbor, Cuba; bombarded, 1898.

mor·row (môr′ō, mor′ō) *n.* **1** The first day after the present or after a day specified; hence, any time following immediately after a specified event. **2** Formerly, morning: good *morrow.* **—*adj.*** Next succeeding, as a day. [OE *morgen* morning]

Mors (môrs) In Roman mythology, the god of death: identified with the Greek *Thanatos.* [<L, death]

Morse (môrs), **Philip McCord,** born 1903, U.S. physicist. **—Samuel Finley Breese,** 1791–1872, U.S. artist and inventor; constructed (1832–35) the first practical telegraph.

INTERNATIONAL MORSE CODE

LETTERS

a	•–	**j**	•–––	**s**	•••
b	–•••	**k**	–•–	**t**	–
c	–•–•	**l**	•–••	**u**	••–
d	–••	**m**	––	**v**	•••–
e	•	**n**	–•	**w**	•––
f	••–•	**o**	–––	**x**	–••–
g	––•	**p**	•––•	**y**	–•––
h	••••	**q**	––•–	**z**	––••
i	••	**r**	•–•		

NUMERALS

1	•––––	**4**	••••–	**8**	–––••
2	••–––	**5**	•••••	**9**	––––•
3	•••––	**6**	–••••	**0**	–––––
		7	––•••		

PUNCTUATION

Period	•–•–•–
Comma	––••––
Semicolon	–•–•–•
Question mark	••––••
Exclamation	–––•
Colon	–––•••
Apostrophe	•––––•
Hyphen	–••••–
Fraction bar	–••–•
Parenthesis	–•––•–
Quotation marks	•–••–•
Double dash	–•••–

Morse code **1** A system of telegraphic signals invented by S. F. B. Morse, comprised of dots and dashes or short and long flashes representing the letters of the alphabet and used in transmitting messages. **2** International Morse code. Also **Morse alphabet.**

mor·sel (môr′səl) *n.* **1** A bit of food; bite. **2** A small piece of anything. [<OF, dim. of *mors* bite <L *morsus* <*mordere*]

Morse telegraph A telegraph employing the dot-and-dash or Morse code, recording the signals on a continuous paper strip. The first commercial system was set up between Baltimore and Washington in 1844.

mort[1] (môrt) *n.* **1** *Obs.* Death. **2** A flourish on the hunting horn, announcing the death of game. Also **morte.** [<F *mort* <L *mors, mortis* <*mori* die]

mort[2] (môrt) *n. Brit. Dial.* A great quantity or number. [? <*mortal* (def. 6)]

mort[3] (môrt) *n. Brit. Dial.* A salmon in its third year. [Orig. unknown]

mor·tal (môr′təl) *adj.* **1** Subject to death; hence, pertaining to humanity; human. **2** Causing, or that may or will cause, death; fatal. **3** *Theol.* Incurring the penalty of eternal death, as a sin: opposed to *venial.* **4** Marking the end of life. **5** Subject to fatal injury, as a vital organ. **6** *Colloq.* Extreme: a *mortal* fright; also, long and tedious. **7** Deadly in malice or purpose; inveterate: a *mortal* foe. **—*n.*** Whatever is mortal or subject to death; a human being. **—*adv. Colloq.*** Very; exceedingly: *mortal* tired. [<OF <L *mortalis* <*mors, mortis* death]

mor·tal·i·ty (môr·tal′ə·tē) *n.* **1** The quality of being mortal. **2** Death. **3** Frequency of death; the proportion of deaths in a specified number of the population; the death rate. **4** Humanity; mankind. [<OF *mortalité* <L *mortalitas*]

mortality table A life table.

mor·tal·ly (môr′təl·ē) *adv.* **1** Fatally. **2** After the manner of a mortal. **3** Extremely.

mortal mind In Christian Science, nothing, claiming to be something, for Mind is immortal; a belief that life, substance, and intelligence are in and of matter: the opposite of Spirit and therefore the opposite of God, or good.

mor·tar[1] (môr′tər) *n.* **1** A strong bowl-like vessel in which substances are crushed or pounded with a pestle. **2** *Mil.* A piece of ordnance with a large bore for firing heavy shells at low muzzle velocity and great angles of elevation that they may drop upon the object aimed at. **3** *Mining* A tublike cast-iron receptacle with grated sides, in which ore is stamped. **4** Any of several devices for hurling pyrotechnic shells or bombs and also life lines. [OE *mortere* <L *mortarium*]

mor·tar[2] (môr′tər) *n.* **1** A building material prepared by mixing lime, plaster of Paris, or cement, with sand, water, and sometimes other materials. It is used in masonry, plastering, etc. **2** Loosely, a cement. **—*v.t.*** To plaster or join with mortar. [<OF *mortier* <L *mortarium*]

mor·tar·board (môr′tər·bôrd′, -bōrd′) *n.* **1** A square board with a handle, on which a mason holds mortar. **2** The academic cap: so called from the four-cornered piece forming its crown.

mortar hoe A hoe with openings in the blade, used for mixing mortar, cement, etc. See illustration under HOE.

mort·gage (môr′gij) *n.* **1** *Law* An estate in land created by conveyance coupled with a condition of defeasance on the performance of some stipulated condition, as the payment of money. **2** A lien upon land or other property as security for the performance of some obligation, to become void on such performance. **3** The act of conveying, or the instrument effecting the conveyance. **4** A state or condition of being pledged as security for a debt like that of a mortgage of property. **—first mortgage** A mortgage having precedence as a lien over all other mortgages. **—*v.t.* ·gaged, ·gag·ing 1** To make over or pledge (property) by mortgage. **2** To pledge. [<F, dead pledge]

mort·ga·gee (môr′gi·jē′) *n.* The person to whom a mortgage is given; the holder of a mortgage.

mort·ga·gor (môr′gi·jər) *n.* A person who mortgages his property to another as security for a loan. Also **mort′gag·er.**

mor·tice (môr′tis) See MORTISE.

mor·ti·cian (môr·tish′ən) *n.* A funeral director; undertaker. [<L *mors, mortis* death + -ICIAN]

mor·ti·fi·ca·tion (môr′tə·fə·kā′shən) *n.* **1** The state of being humbled or depressed by disappointment or chagrin. **2** *Pathol.* The death of one part of an animal body, as from gangrene, while the rest is still alive. **3** In religion, the act of subduing the passions and appetites by fasting, penance, or painful severities inflicted on the body. **4** That which mortifies or causes humiliation. See synonyms under CHAGRIN. [<LL *mortificatio, -onis*]

mor·ti·fy (môr′tə·fī) *v.* **·fied, ·fy·ing** *v.t.* **1** To affect with humiliation, shame, or chagrin; humiliate. **2** To discipline or punish (the body, passions, etc.) by fasting, penance, or other ascetic practices. **3** *Pathol.* To cause mortification in (a part of the body). —*v.i.* **4** To practice ascetic self-discipline. **5** *Pathol.* To undergo mortification; become gangrenous. [<OF *mortifier* <LL *mortificare* <L *mors, mortis* death + *facere* make] — **mor′ti·fi′er** *n.* —**mor′ti·fy′ing·ly** *adv.*

Mor·ti·mer (môr′tə·mər), **Roger de,** 1287?–1330, Earl of March; Welsh rebel, favorite of Isabella, queen of Edward II of England.

mor·tise (môr′tis) *n.* **1** A space hollowed out, as in a timber, to receive a tenon or the like. **2** Figuratively, adhering power; firmness. —*v.t.* **·tised, ·tis·ing 1** To cut or make a mortise in. **2** To join by a tenon and mortise. Also spelled *mortice.* [<OF *mortaise* < Arabic *murtazza* joined, fixed in]

MORTISE AND TENON
a. Mortise.
b. Tenon.

mort·main (môrt′mān) *n. Law* The state of lands and tenements held by one that cannot alienate them, as a religious corporation; inalienable tenure or possession. The term is applied in some of the United States to statutes restricting the right of religious corporations to hold land. [<OF *mortemain* <Med. L *mortua manus* dead hand]

Mor·ton (môr′tən), **William Thomas Green,** 1819–68, U. S. dentist; pioneer in use of ether as an anesthetic.

mor·tu·ar·y (môr′chōō·er′ē) *adj.* Pertaining to the burial of the dead; also, relating to or reminiscent of the dead. —*n. pl.* **·ar·ies 1** In old English law, a gift claimed by or given to a parish minister on the death of a parishioner. **2** A place for the temporary reception of the dead; dead house. [<L *mortuarius* belonging to the dead]

mor·u·la (môr′yōō·lə, -ōō-) *n. pl.* **·lae** (-lē) *Biol.* The compact, spherical mass of cells formed by an ovum in the early stages of its development; the mulberry body. [<NL, dim. of L *morum* mulberry] —**mor′u·lar** *adj.*

mo·sa·ic (mō·zā′ik) *n.* **1** Inlaid work composed of bits of stone, glass, etc., forming a pattern or picture. **2** A piece of inlaid work of this kind, or anything resembling such work. **3** *Phot.* An assemblage of aerial photographs pieced together and joined at the margins so as to form a single, continuous picture of a terrain. **4** The plate covered with minute, photosensitive granules which is mounted in the image-scanning element of an electron television camera. —*adj.* Of, pertaining to, or resembling mosaic; tessellated; inlaid. —*v.t.* **·icked, ·ick·ing 1** To make as if by combining in a mosaic. **2** To decorate with mosaic. [<OF *mosaicq* <Med. L *musaicus* <Gk. *mouseios* of the Muses, artistic <*Mousa* Muse] —**mo·sa·i·cist** (mō·zā′ə·sist) *n.*

Mo·sa·ic (mō·zā′ik) *adj.* Of or pertaining to Moses or his laws. Also **Mo·sa′i·cal.** [<NL *Mosaicus* <L *Moses* Moses]

mosaic disease One of several destructive and infectious diseases of plants caused by a filtrable virus and characterized by a pale, mottled appearance of the foliage: tobacco *mosaic*; potato *mosaic.*

mosaic gold 1 An alloy of copper and zinc; ormolu varnish. **2** Stannic sulfide.

Mo·san·der (mōō·sän′dər), **Carl Gustav,** 1797–1858, Swedish chemist.

Mos·by (mōz′bē), **John Singleton,** 1833–1916, American Confederate soldier and author.

mos·ca·tel (mos′kə·tel′) See MUSCATEL (def. 2).

mos·chate (mos′kāt, -kit) *adj.* Having the odor of musk. [<NL *moschatus* <Med. L *moschus* musk]

mos·cha·tel (mos′kə·tel′, mos′kə·tel) *n.* A low perennial herb (*Adoxa moschatellina*) with greenish flowers and having a musky odor; muskroot. [<F *moscatelle* <Ital. *moscatella*]

Mos·cow The capital of Russia; pop. 9,000,000. The former capital of the Soviet Union. *Russian* **Mos·kva** (mos·kvä′).

Mose·ley (mōz′lē), **Henry Gwyn–Jeffreys,** 1887–1915, English physicist.

Mo·selle (mō·zel′) *n.* A light, dry wine made in the valley of the Moselle, chiefly in the region from Trier to Traben–Trarbach.

Mo·selle (mō·zel′) A river in NE France, Luxemburg, and western Germany, flowing 320 miles NE to the Rhine at Coblenz. *German* **Mo·sel** (mō′zəl).

Mo·ses (mō′zis, -ziz; *Ger., Sw.* mō′ses) A masculine personal name. [<Egyptian, child, son] —**Moses** In the Old Testament, the younger son of Amram and Jochebed, who led the Israelites out of Egypt into the Promised Land, received the Ten Commandments from God, and gave laws to the people; hence, a leader; legislator.

Moses (mō′zis, -ziz), **Anna Mary,** 1860–1961, U. S. painter: called "Grandma Moses."

mo·sey (mō′zē) *v.i. U. S. Slang* **1** To saunter, or stroll; shuffle along. **2** To go away; move off. [? <VAMOOSE]

Mos·kva A river in Russia, flowing 315 miles to the Oka.

Mos·lem (moz′ləm, mos′-) *n. pl.* **·lems** or **·lem** A Muslim. —*adj.* Muslim. —**Mos′lem·ism** *n.*

Mos·ley (mōz′lē), **Sir Oswald,** born 1896, English politician.

mosque (mosk) *n.* A Muslim temple of worship. Also **mosk.** [<F *mosquée* <Ital. *moschea* <Arabic *masjid* < *sajada* prostrate oneself, pray]

mos·qui·to (məs·kē′tō) *n. pl.* **·toes** or **·tos 1** A two-winged, dipterous insect (family *Culicidae*), having (in the female) a long proboscis capable of puncturing the skin for extracting blood. The infections of malaria and yellow fever are spread by the bite of certain species. For illustration see INSECTS (injurious). **2** Any of various other gnats or flies inflicting a similar puncture. Also spelled *musquito.* [<Sp., dim. of *mosca* fly <L *musca*] —**mos·qui′tal** *adj.*

mosquito boat A patrol torpedo boat.

mosquito fleet *Naut. Slang* An assemblage of small craft.

mosquito hawk 1 A nighthawk. **2** A dragonfly.

mosquito net A fine netting or gauze placed in windows, over beds, etc., to keep out mosquitoes.

mosquito netting A coarsely meshed fabric used to make mosquito nets.

moss[1] (môs, mos) *n.* **1** A delicate, bryophytic plant (class *Musci*), growing on the ground, decaying wood, rocks, trees, etc., having a stem and distinct leaves, and producing capsules which open by an operculum and contain spores unmixed with elaters. **2** Any of several other cryptogamous plants, as certain lichens, clubmosses, etc. —*v.t.* To cover with moss. [<MOSS[2]] —**moss′y** *adj.* — **moss′i·ness** *n.*

moss[2] (môs, mos) *n.* A bog; peat bog. [OE *mos*]

moss agate A variety of quartz containing mineral oxides, as manganese dioxide, arranged in mosslike forms.

moss·back (môs′bak′, mos′-) *n.* **1** An old fish or turtle on whose back is a growth of algae or the like. **2** One who is out of touch with the progress of the times; a conservative or reactionary person; especially, an extreme conservative in politics. **3** During the American Civil War, in the South, one who avoided conscription by hiding.

moss–backed (môs′bakt′, mos′-) *adj.* **1** Having moss or mosslike growth on the back. **2** Behind the times; reactionary.

Möss·bau·er effect (mœs′bou′ər) The absorption of gamma rays emitted from a radioactive isotope by nuclei of the same isotope, with resonance between the emitting and absorbing nuclei, both of which are anchored in crystals. It is used in the exact determination of wavelengths, time intervals, the red shift, and in testing various concepts of relativity and quantum theory. [after Rudolf L. *Mössbauer,* born 1929, U.S. physicist born in Germany]

moss·board (môs′bôrd′, -bōrd′, mos′-) *n.* A type of pasteboard made principally of peat moss and used in the preparation of surgical dressings.

moss·bunk·er (môs′bungk·ər, mos′-) *n.* The menhaden. Also **moss′bank·er.** [Alter. of Du. *marskanker*]

moss green Any of various shades of dull yellowish green.

moss·grown (môs′grōn′, mos′-) *adj.* Overgrown with moss; hence, very ancient.

moss hag *Scot.* A pit or slough in a moss or bog, where the moss or peat has been cut away.

mos·so (môs′sō) *adj. Music* Rapid; literally, moved. [<Ital., pp. of *movere* move <L]

moss pink A plant (*Phlox subulata*) of the eastern United States, occurring in several varieties which form mats close to the ground and have white, pink, or purplish flowers. Also **moss phlox.**

moss rose 1 A cultivated variety of the rose (*Rosa centifolia muscosa*) with a mossy calyx and stem. **2** Portulaca.

moss starch Lichenin.

moss–troop·er (môs′trōō′pər, mos′-) *n.* One of the marauders who infested the mossy marshes between Scotland and England prior to the union of the two kingdoms; hence, a bandit or undisciplined soldier.

most (mōst) *adj.* **1** Consisting of the greatest number: superlative of *many.* **2** Consisting of the greatest amount or quantity: superlative of *much.* **3** *Obs.* Greatest in size, rank, or age. —*n.* **1** The greater number; the larger part: the *most* of my belongings. **2** Greatest amount, value, or advantage; utmost degree, extent, or effect. —*adv.* **1** In the highest degree, or in the greatest number or quantity. **2** *Dial.* Almost. **3** Greatest, as in amount or degree: used with adjectives and adverbs to form the superlative degree. [OE *mǣst*]

-most *suffix* Most: added to adjectives, adverbs, and prepositions to form superlatives: *outmost.* [OE *-mest* < *-ma* + *-est,* superlative suffixes]

Mos·tar A city in central Bosnia and Herzegovina; an historic region of Herzogovina, named for the Stari Most bridge that spanned the Neretva River from 1566 until it was destroyed during the civil war in Yugoslavia in 1993.

most·ly (mōst′lē) *adv.* For the most part; principally.

Mo·sul (mō·sōōl′) The second largest city of Iraq, on the Tigris opposite the site of ancient Nineveh. Also **Mos·sul′.**

Mosz·kow·ski (môsh·kôf′skē), **Moritz,** 1854–1925, Polish composer born in Germany.

mot[1] (mō) *n.* A witty or pithy saying; bon mot. [<F, word <LL *muttum* uttered sound < *muttire* murmur]

mot[2] (mot) *n.* A bugle note, or its mark in music. [<OF]

mote[1] (mōt) *v.* **1** *Archaic* May; might. **2** *Obs.* Must. ◆ Homophone: *moat.* [OE *mōt* it is permitted]

mote[2] (mōt) *n.* A minute particle; speck. ◆ Homophone: *moat.* [OE *mot* atom]

mo·tel (mō·tel′) *n.* A hotel for motorists, usually comprising private cabins and garage or parking facilities. [<MO(TOR) + (HO)TEL]

mo·tet (mō·tet′) *n. Music* A contrapuntal, polyphonic song of a sacred nature, usually unaccompanied. Also **mo·tet′to.** [<OF, dim. of *mot* word. See MOT[1].]

moth (môth, moth) *n. pl.* **moths** (môthz, môths, mothz, moths) Any of various typically nocturnal, lepidopterous insects (division *Heterocera*), distinguished from butterflies by their stout bodies and smaller, usually dull-colored wings, which fold laterally across the abdomen. The larvae of the gipsy moth, silkworm, etc., feed on plants; those of the clothes moth (family *Tineidae*) feed on textiles, clothing, and furs. [OE *moththe*]

moth ball A ball of camphor or naphthalene, for the protection of clothing, etc., from moths. —**in moth balls** In protective storage.

moth-ball (môth′bôl′, moth′-) *Mil. & Nav. adj.* Designating ships or military equipment laid up in reserve and covered or coated with protective materials. — *v.t.* To put in reserve and protective storage.

moth-eat·en (môth′ēt′n, moth′-) *adj.* Eaten by moths; hence, used up or worn out: also *mothy.*

moth·er[1] (muth′ər) *n.* **1** A female parent. **2** That which has produced or given birth to anything. **3** An abbess or other nun of rank or dignity. **4** An elderly woman or matron: a familiar title. — *v.t.* **1** To care for as a mother. **2** To bring forth as a mother; produce. **3** To admit or claim parentage, authorship, etc., of. — *adj.* **1** Native: *mother* tongue. **2** Holding a maternal relation. [OE *mōdor*]

moth·er[2] (muth′ər) *n.* **1** A slimy film composed of bacteria and yeast cells that forms on the surface of fermenting liquids and is active in the production of vinegar: also called *mother-of-vinegar.* **2** Dregs; lees. — *v.i.* To become mothery, as vinegar. [Special use of MOTHER[1]] — **moth′er·y** *adj.*

Mother Car·ey's chicken (kâr′ēz) The petrel; especially, the storm petrel. [Alter. of L *mater cara* dear mother, an epithet of the Virgin Mary]

mother cell A cell which by division produces other cells.

Mother Goose **1** The imaginary narrator of a volume of folk tales, compiled in French by Charles Perrault in 1697. **2** The imaginary compiler of a collection of nursery rimes of English folk origin, first published in London about 1760 by John Newbery.

moth·er·hood (muth′ər·hŏŏd) *n.* The state of being a mother.

Mother Hub·bard (hub′ard) **1** The main character in an old nursery rime. **2** A woman's loose, flowing gown, unconfined at the waist.

moth·er-in-law (muth′ər·in·lô′) *n. pl.* **moth·ers-in-law** **1** The mother of one's spouse. **2** *Brit. Dial.* A stepmother.

moth·er·land (muth′ər·land′) *n.* The land of one's ancestors; native land; mother country.

moth·er·less (muth′ər·lis) *adj.* Having no mother.

mother liquor The liquid remaining after the substances in solution have been deposited by crystallization or precipitation.

mother lode *Mining* **1** *Cap.* The great gold-bearing quartz vein in California, traced by its outcrop from Mariposa to Amador. **2** Any principal vein in a mining region.

moth·er·ly (muth′ər·lē) *adj.* **1** Resembling a mother: a *motherly* woman. **2** Pertaining to or becoming to a mother: *motherly* authority, *motherly* care. — *adv.* In the manner of a mother. — **moth′er·li·ness** *n.*

Mother of God A title officially given to the Virgin Mary at the Council of Ephesus in 431.

moth·er-of-pearl (muth′ər·əv·pûrl′) *n.* The hard, iridescent internal layer of certain shells, as of pearl oysters, abalones, and mussels; nacre.

Mother of the Gods Rhea.

moth·er-of-vin·e·gar (muth′ər·əv·vin′ə·gər) See MOTHER[2].

Mother's Day A memorial day in honor of mothers, observed annually in the United States on the second Sunday in May. See FATHER'S DAY.

mother tongue **1** One's native language. **2** A language from which another language has sprung.

Moth·er·well and Wish·aw (muth′ər·wel ənd wish′ô) A burgh on the Clyde in Lanarkshire, Scotland; formerly two towns.

mother wit Inherent, natural, or native intelligence; common sense.

moth·er·wort (muth′ər·wûrt′) *n.* An Old World herb (*Leonurus cardiaca*) of the mint family, with lanceolate, toothed leaves, and small, purplish flowers: now common in the U. S. [So called because once thought to be valuable in the treatment of diseases of the womb]

moth·mill·er (môth′mil′ər, moth′-) *n.* **1** A pale moth with floury wings; a miller. **2** *Colloq.* Any moth.

moth·proof (môth′prōōf′, moth′-) *adj.* Resistant to the attack of moths. — *v.t.* **·proofed, ·proof·ing** To render (textiles) resistant to moths.

moth·y (môth′ē, moth′ē) *adj.* **moth·i·er, moth·i·est** Moth-eaten.

mo·tif (mō·tēf′) *n.* **1** The underlying idea or main feature or element in literary, musical, or artistic work. **2** In the decorative arts, a distinctive element of design. Also **mo·tive** (mō′tiv). [<F]

mo·tile (mō′til) *adj.* **1** *Biol.* Having the power of spontaneous motion, as certain minute organisms. **2** Causing motion. [<L *motus,* pp. of *movere* move] — **mo·til′i·ty** *n.*

mo·tion (mō′shən) *n.* **1** Change of position in reference to an assumed point or center; a shifting movement. **2** The interaction of parts in a mechanism to produce a particular result. **3** A formal proposition in a deliberative assembly. **4** A significant movement of the limbs, eyes, etc.; a gesture: She made *motions* to him. **5** An impulse to action; incentive. **6** *Music* Melodic progression. **7** *Law* An application to a court to obtain an order or rule directing some act to be done. **8** A mechanism. **9** *Obs.* A puppet or puppet show. — **perpetual motion** Continuous mechanical motion, especially as applied to machines which are claimed to do useful work without the expenditure of equivalent amounts of work upon them. — *v.i.* To make a gesture of direction or intent, as with the hand. — *v.t.* To direct or guide by a gesture. [<F <L *motio, -onis* < *motus,* pp. of *movere* move] — **mo′tion·al** *adj.* — **mo′tion·less** *adj.* — **mo′tion·less·ly** *adv.*

Synonyms (noun): act, action, change, move, movement, passage, transit, transition. *Motion* may be either abstract or concrete, more frequently the former; *movement* is always concrete, that is, considered in connection with the thing that moves or is moved; thus we speak of the *movements* of the planets, but of the laws of planetary *motion*; of military *movements,* but of perpetual *motion. Motion* is *change* of place or position in space; *transition* is a passing from one point or position in space to another. *Move* is used chiefly of contests or competition, as in chess or politics: as, It is your *move*; a shrewd *move* of the opposition. We speak of mental or spiritual *acts* or processes, or of the laws of mental *action,* but a formal proposal of *action* in a deliberative assembly is termed a *motion. Action* is a more comprehensive word than *motion.* See ACT, TOPIC. *Antonyms*: quiescence, quiet, repose, rest.

motion picture **1** A sequence of pictures, each slightly different from the last, photographed by a special camera on a single strip of film, for projection on a screen, giving the optical illusion of continuous, ordered movement: also called *cinema, movie, moving picture.* **2** A photoplay. — **mo′tion-pic′ture** *adj.*

motion sickness Nausea and sometimes vomiting caused by the effect of certain complex movements on the semicircular canals of the inner ear, typically experienced in a moving vehicle, ship, or airplane.

motion study The detailed observation and analysis of the different movements involved in the performance of a given repetitive task, with a view to lessening the fatigue and increasing the efficiency of the workers.

mo·ti·vate (mō′tə·vāt) *v.t.* **·vat·ed, ·vat·ing** To provide with a motive; instigate; induce.

mo·ti·va·tion (mō′tə·vā′shən) *n.* Causative factor; incentive; drive. — **mo′ti·va′tion·al** *adj.*

motivation research The use of psychological or other social-science concepts and techniques in marketing, advertising, and public-opinion research to investigate the conscious or subliminal causes of consumer behavior, and the motives that lead to a favorable or unfavorable response.

mo·tive (mō′tiv) *n.* **1** That which incites to motion or action. **2** A predominant idea; design. — *adj.* **1** Having power to move; causing motion. **2** Relating to a motive or motives. — *v.t.* **·tived, ·tiv·ing** **1** To motivate; prompt. **2** To relate to the leading idea or motif in a work of art, etc. [<OF *motif* <Med. L *motivus* < *motus,* pp. of *movere* move]

Synonyms (noun): consideration, ground, incentive, incitement, inducement, influence, reason. *Motive* may signify either a mental impulse, or something external that is an object of desire, and so an *inducement* or *incitement* to action. Compare CAUSE, IMPULSE, PURPOSE, REASON.

motive power **1** The power, or means of generating power, by which motion is imparted to an object, machine, etc. **2** Figuratively, an impelling force.

mo·tiv·i·ty (mō·tiv′ə·tē) *n.* The power of producing motion; motive energy.

mot juste (mō zhüst′) *French* The precise word; exactly the right expression.

mot·ley (mot′lē) *adj.* **1** Variegated in color; parti-colored. **2** Composed of heterogeneous elements. **3** Clothed in varicolored garments. — *n.* **1** A dress of various colors, such as was formerly worn by court jesters. **2** A jester or fool in motley garments. **3** A medley, as of colors. [ME *motteley*; origin uncertain]

MOTLEY (*n. def. 1*)

Mot·ley (mot′lē), **John Lothrop,** 1814–77, U. S. historian.

mot·mot (mot′mot) *n.* One of a family of birds, the *Momotidae,* of the warmer parts of America, related to the kingfishers; a sawbill. The middle pair of tail feathers is usually elongated and racket-shaped. [Imit. of its note]

mo·to·fa·cient (mō′tə·fā′shənt) *adj. Physiol.* Producing motion: said especially of muscles whose contraction results in a definite movement. [<L *motus* motion, moving < *movere* move + *faciens, -entis,* ppr. of *facere* make, cause]

mo·tor (mō′tər) *n.* **1** One who or that which produces motion, as a machine, nerve, etc. **2** An internal-combustion engine, especially one operating on gasoline. **3** A motorcar or motorcycle. **4** An electric motor. — **rotary motor** An internal-combustion engine having multiple radial cylinders rotating about a fixed crankshaft. — *adj.* **1** Causing, producing, or imparting motion. **2** Transmitting impulses from the nerve centers to the muscles. **3** Pertaining to consciousness of motion. — *v.i.* To travel or ride in an automobile. [<L < *motus,* pp. of *movere*] — **mo′tor·ing** *adj. & n.*

mo·tor·boat (mō′tər·bōt′) *n.* A boat propelled by an internal-combustion engine, or by an electric motor.

mo·tor·bus (mō′tər·bus′) *n.* A power-driven omnibus. Also **motor coach.**

mo·tor·cade (mō′tər·kād) *n.* A procession of motorcycles or automobiles. [<MOTOR + (CAVAL)CADE]

mo·tor·car (mō′tər·kär′) *n.* An automobile.

mo·tor·cy·cle (mō′tər·sī′kəl) *n.* A two-wheeled vehicle, sometimes having an attached sidecar with a third wheel, propelled by an internal-combustion engine. — *v.i.* **·cled, ·cling** To travel or ride on a motorcycle. — **mo′tor·cy′clist** *n.*

motor drive A power unit consisting of an electric motor and auxiliaries, used to operate a machine or group of machines.

mo·tor·drome (mō′tər·drōm) *n.* An enclosure, course, or track where motor-driven vehicles of various kinds are tested in competition or otherwise.

motor generator A device for transforming electrical power by permanently connecting, usually on a common bedplate, a motor and a generator; a dynamotor.

motor home *U.S.* An automotive vehicle equipped with living accommodations and resembling a trailer but built on a single chassis.

mo·tor·ist (mō′tər·ist) *n.* One who drives an automobile; one who travels by automobile.

mo·to·ri·um (mō·tôr′ē·əm, -tō′rē-) *n. Physiol.* **1** That portion of the nervous system which controls the motor apparatus. **2** Any center of a motor function. [<NL <L *motor* a mover]

mo·tor·ize (mō′tər·īz) *v.t.* **·ized, ·iz·ing** **1** To equip with a motor or motors. **2** To equip with motor-propelled vehicles in place of horses and horse-drawn vehicles. — **mo′tor·i·za′tion** *n.*

mo·tor·man (mō′tər·mən) *n. pl.* **·men** (-mən) One who operates a motor, as on a street car or an electric locomotive.

motor oil A high-grade lubricating oil, designed for the exacting requirements of internal-combustion engines.

motor scooter See SCOOTER (def. 2).

mo·tor·ship (mō′tər·ship′) *n.* A vessel, as a

passenger ship, of which the principal motive power is derived from an internal-combustion oil or gas engine.
motor spirit Any fuel adapted for spark-ignition, internal-combustion engines; specifically, coal or petroleum distillates blended with suitable additions, as alcohol.
motor transport *Mil.* Any motor vehicle used for transport only: distinguished from *combat vehicle.*
motor vehicle 1 Any vehicle operated by a motor or engine. 2 A vehicle adapted to be pulled by another, as a trailer.
Mott (mot), **John Raleigh,** 1865–1955, U. S. clergyman and leader in the Y.M.C.A. — **Lucretia,** 1793–1880, *née* Coffin, U. S. social reformer.
Mot·ta (môt′tä), **Giuseppi,** 1871–1940, Swiss lawyer and statesman.
motte (mot) *n. Dial.* A small growth of trees on a prairie. Also **mott.** [<Sp. *mata* clump, grove]
mot·tet·to (môt·tet′tō) *n. Italian* Motet.
Mot·teux (mô·tœ′), **Peter Anthony,** 1663–1718, English dramatist and translator, born in France.
mot·tle (mot′l) *v.t.* **·tled, ·tling** To mark with spots or streaks of different colors or shades; blotch. — *n.* 1 The spotted, blotched, or variegated appearance of any mottled surface, as of wood or marble. 2 One of a number of spots or blotches on any surface. [<MOTLEY]
mot·tled (mot′ld) *adj.* Marked with spots of different color or shades of color; blotched; variegated.
mot·to (mot′ō) *n. pl.* **·toes** or **·tos** 1 An expressive word or pithy sentence enunciating some guiding principle, rule of conduct, or the like; a phrase inscribed on something or prefixed to a literary composition as somehow indicative of its qualities. 2 A piece of paper printed with a motto or sentiment and wrapped around a small piece of candy; also, the piece of candy enclosed. See synonyms under ADAGE. [<Ital. <F *mot.* See MOT.]
mot·ty (mot′ē) *adj. Scot.* Abounding in motes. Also **mot′tie.**
mou' (mo͞o) *n. Scot.* The mouth.
mouch (mo͞och) See MOOCH.
mou·choir (mo͞o·shwär′) *n. French* A pocket handkerchief.
mou·die (mou′dē) *n. Scot.* A mole; also, a molecatcher. Also **mou′di·wort** (-wûrt).
moue (mo͞o) *n.* A pouting grimace expressive of disdain or distaste. [<F]
mouf·lon (mo͞of′lon) *n.* A hairy wild sheep; specifically, *Ovis musimon* of the mountains of Corsica and Sardinia, the males with very large and curved horns. Also **mouf′flon.** [<F <dial. Ital. *muffolo* <*muffione* <LL *mufro, -onis*]
mouil·lé (mo͞o·yā′) *adj.* Given a palatalized pronunciation, as *ll* in the French name *Villon.* [<F, pp. of *mouiller* moisten]
mou·jik (mo͞o·zhēk′) See MUZHIK.
Mouk·den (mo͝ok′den′, mo͝ok′dən, mo͝ok′-) See MUKDEN.
moul (mo͞ol) *v.t.* & *v.i. Obs.* or *Brit. Dial.* To make or become moldy.
mou·lage (mo͞o·läzh′) *n.* 1 A cast, in plaster of Paris or other similar material, of an object or of its impressed outlines on a surface: frequently used in criminal identification, as of footprints, tire marks, etc. 2 A synthetic, rubberlike, plastic material used in making casts. [<F]
mould (mōld), **moult** (mōlt), etc. See MOLD, etc.
mould goose The musk duck.
mould·warp (mōld′wôrp) See MOLDWARP.
mou·lin (mo͞o·laṅ′) *n.* A nearly vertical shaft in a glacier, formed by the surface water trickling through a crevice. [<F, mill <LL *molina.* See MILL.]
mou·line (mo͞o·lēn′) *n.* 1 The circular swing of a saber. 2 The drum of a winch, capstan, or the like; a windlass mechanism. 3 A form of turnstile. Also **mou·li·net** (mo͞o′lē·net). [<F, dim. of *moulin* mill]
Mou·lins (mo͞o·laṅ′) The capital of Allier department, central France.
Moul·mein (mo͞ol·mān′) A port on the Andaman Sea in Lower Burma, chief town of Tenasserim: also *Maulmain.*
mouls (mo͞olz) *Scot.* See MOOLS.
moult (mōlt), **moult·ing,** etc. *Brit.* Molt, etc.
Moul·ton (mōl′tən), **Forest Ray,** 1872–1952, U. S. astronomer.
Moul·trie (mo͞ol′trē, mo͞o′-, mōl′-), **William,** 1730–1805, American Revolutionary general; builder and defender (1776) of Fort Moultrie, Charleston Harbor, South Carolina.
mound[1] (mound) *n.* 1 A heap or pile of earth, either natural or artificial; hillock. 2 One of the earthworks built by the Mound Builders for burial or fortification. 3 In baseball, the slightly raised ground from which the pitcher pitches the ball. See synonyms under RAMPART. — *v.t.* 1 To fortify or enclose with a mound. 2 To heap up in a mound. [Origin uncertain]
mound[2] (mound) *n.* A jeweled ball or globe, often surmounted by a cross, forming part of the regalia of a king or emperor: an emblem of sovereignty; an orb. [<F *monde* <L *mundus* world]

MOUND[2]

Mound Builder One of the aboriginal people who built the burial mounds and fortifications found in the Mississippi basin and adjoining regions: the ancestors of the North American Indians dwelling in that region at the time of the first European explorers.
Mounds·ville (moundz′vil) A city in NW West Virginia; site of a conical Indian mound.
mount[1] (mount) *v.t.* 1 To ascend by climbing; go up, as stairs. 2 To climb upon; ascend and seat oneself on, as a horse. 3 To put on horseback. 4 To furnish with a horse or horses. 5 To set or place in an elevated position: to *mount* a plaque on a wall. 6 To place in position for use or operation, as a cannon or engine. 7 To put in or on a support, frame, etc., as for exhibition: to *mount* a butterfly. 8 To furnish, as a play, with scenery, costumes, etc. 9 To copulate with a female: said of male animals. 10 In microscopy: **a** To place or fix (a sample) on a slide. **b** To prepare (a slide) for examination. 11 *Mil.* & *Nav.* To carry or be equipped with: a ship *mounting* thirty-two guns. 12 To put on (clothing), especially for display. 13 *Mil.* To stand or post (guard). 14 *Mil.* To prepare for and begin: to *mount* an offensive. — *v.i.* 15 To rise or ascend; go up. 16 To increase in number, amount, or degree: often with *up*: The bills *mounted* up. 17 To get on horseback. 18 To get up on or on top of something. — *n.* 1 That upon or by which anything is prepared or equipped for use, exhibition, ornament, preservation, or examination. 2 The card, etc., upon which a drawing or photograph is mounted. 3 The parts and appliances by which a gun is attached to its carriage. 4 The glass slide and its adjuncts upon which a microscopic subject is secured for examination. 5 A saddle horse or other animal used for riding: by extension, a bicycle. 6 The act of riding a horse in a race; also, the privilege or opportunity of doing so. 7 A style of mounting. [<OF *monter* <L *mons, montis* mountain] — **mount′a·ble** *adj.* — **mount′er** *n.*
mount[2] (mount) *n.* 1 An elevation of the earth's surface; a mountain; a hill. When used as part of a proper name it usually precedes the specific application: *Mount* Washington. 2 *Obs.* A raised fortification commanding the surrounding country. 3 In palmistry, one of seven fleshy protuberances in the palm of the hand. [OE *munt* <L *mons* mountain]
moun·tain (moun′tən) *n.* 1 A natural elevation of the earth's surface, rising more or less abruptly to a small summit area, attaining an elevation greater than that of a hill, and standing either in a single mass or forming part of a series. 2 Any large heap or pile resembling this. 3 Something of great magnitude. — **the Mountain** A name given to the ultra-revolutionary party of the French National Assembly or Convention in 1793, from the fact that its members occupied the highest seats in the chamber. — *adj.* 1 Of, pertaining to, or living or growing on mountains. 2 Like or suggesting a mountain or mountains. [<OF *montaigne* <L *montanus* mountainous <*mons, montis* mountain]
mountain ape *Paleontol.* Oreopithecus.
mountain ash 1 Any of various American deciduous shrubs (genus *Sorbus*), having alternate simple or pinnate leaves, white flowers, and vivid red fruit, especially *S. americana.* 2 The rowan.
mountain avens A small evergreen plant (*Dryas octopetala*) of the rose family, growing in arctic and alpine regions.
mountain cat 1 The cougar. 2 The bobcat.
mountain chain A series of mountains connected and having some common characteristics.
mountain cork A variety of asbestos occurring in light, flexible sheets which will float on water. Also **mountain leather.**
mountain cranberry The mountain cowberry (*Vaccinium vitis-idaea minus*), having edible red berries, evergreen leaves, and pink or red flowers.
mountain dew *Slang* Illicitly distilled whiskey.
moun·tain·eer (moun′tən·ir′) *n.* 1 An inhabitant of a mountainous district. 2 One who climbs mountains. — *v.i.* To climb mountains.
mountain goat The Rocky Mountain goat; a goat antelope.

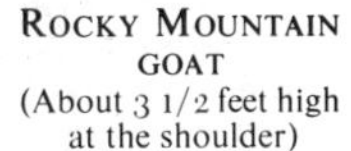
ROCKY MOUNTAIN GOAT
(About 3 1/2 feet high at the shoulder)

mountain laurel In the eastern United States, the low-growing calicobush (*Kalmia latifolia*), an evergreen shrub with white or pink flowers; State flower of Connecticut and Pennsylvania. The foliage is poisonous to livestock.
mountain lion The puma or cougar.
moun·tain·ous (moun′tən·əs) *adj.* 1 Full of mountains. 2 Huge. — **moun′tain·ous·ly** *adv.*
mountain range 1 One of the components of a mountain chain, usually a group of more or less parallel ridges of similar origin, structure, etc. 2 A land area dominated by such a group of mountains, characterized by great variations in elevation above sea level.
mountain rat A pack rat.
mountain sheep The bighorn.
mountain sickness *Pathol.* A form of anoxemia accompanied by nausea, due to insufficient oxygen consumption at high altitudes, especially on mountains.
Mountains of the Moon See RUWENZORI.
mountain specter The specter of the Brocken.
Mountain Standard Time See STANDARD TIME. Abbr. **M.S.T.**
Mount·bat·ten (mount·bat′n), **Lord Louis,** born 1900, English admiral in World War II: originally *Prince Louis Francis Battenberg.*
Mount Des·ert (dez′ərt, di·zûrt′) An island in Acadia National Park off the SE coast of Maine; 100 square miles.
moun·te·bank (moun′tə·bangk) *n.* 1 A vendor of quack medicines at fairs, who usually mounts a platform or wagon to sell his wares. 2 Hence, a charlatan. See synonyms under QUACK. — *v.i.* To play the mountebank. [<Ital. *montimbanco* <*monta* mount + *in* on + *banco* bench]
mount·ed (moun′tid) *adj.* Elevated on or equipped with horses: *mounted* police.
Mount·ie (moun′tē) See MOUNTY.
mount·ing (moun′ting) *n.* 1 The act of mounting; elevation. 2 A mount, as of a picture. 3 The act of preparing for use, etc.
Mount McKinley National Park A region in south central Alaska; 3,030 square miles; established as a national park in 1917.
Mount Rainier National Park A region in the Cascade Mountains of west central Washington; 378 square miles; established as a national park in 1899.
Mount Rob·son Provincial Park (rob′sən) A national park in eastern British Columbia, Canada, near the Alberta border; 65 miles long, 10 to 20 miles wide.
Mount Ver·non (vûr′nən) The home and burial place of George Washington; 15 miles below

Washington, D.C., on the Potomac River.

Moun·ty (moun′tē) *n. pl.* **·ties** *Colloq.* A member of the Royal Canadian Mounted Police: also spelled *Mountie.*

mourn (môrn, mōrn) *v.i.* **1** To feel or express grief or sorrow. **2** To display the conventional signs of grief after someone's death; wear mourning. —*v.t.* **3** To grieve or sorrow for (someone dead). **4** To grieve over or lament (misfortune, failure, etc.); bewail; deplore. **5** To utter in a sorrowful manner. [OE *murnan*]

Synonyms: bemoan, bewail, deplore, grieve, lament, regret, rue, sorrow. Mourning is thought of as prolonged; grief or regret may be transient. One may *grieve* or *mourn, regret, rue,* or *sorrow* without a sound; he *bemoans* with suppressed and often inarticulate sounds of grief; *bewails* with passionate utterance, whether of inarticulate cries or of spoken words; he *laments* in plaintive or pathetic words.

mourn·er (môr′nər, mōr′-) *n.* **1** One who mourns; specifically, one who attends a funeral. **2** A penitent at a revival meeting.

mourner's bench *U.S.* A bench near the preacher reserved for penitents at a revival meeting: also called *anxious seat.*

mourn·ful (môrn′fəl, mōrn′-) *adj.* **1** Indicating or expressing grief. **2** Oppressed with grief. **3** Exciting sorrow. See synonyms under PITIFUL, SAD. **—mourn′ful·ly** *adv.* **—mourn′ful·ness** *n.*

mourn·ing (môr′ning, mōr′-) *n.* **1** The act of sorrowing or expressing grief; lamentation; sorrow. **2** The symbols or outward manifestations of grief, as the use of symbolical colors in dress, the draping of buildings or doors, and the half-masting of flags. —*adj.* Relating to or expressive of mourning. **—mourn′ing·ly** *adv.*

mourning cloak A brownish-black butterfly *(Nymphalis antiopa)* widely distributed in temperate regions: it has a row of dark spots just inside the yellow border on the upper side of the wings: also called *Camberwell beauty.*

mourning dove The Carolina turtledove *(Zenaidura macroura),* common in North America: so called for its plaintive note.

mourning warbler A warbler of the eastern United States *(Oporonis philadelphia)* also called for its plaintive note.

mouse (mous) *n. pl.* **mice** (mīs) **1** One of various small rodents frequenting human habitations throughout the world, as the common **house mouse** *(Mus musculus).* ◆ Collateral adjective: *murine.* **2** Any of various similar animals, as the American **harvest mouse** (genus *Reithrodontomys*), or the **lemming mouse** (genus *Synaptomys*). **3** *Slang* A young woman. **4** *Slang* A discolored swelling of the eye, caused by a blow or bruise. **5** *Naut.* A swelling worked on a rope to prevent its slipping; also, a mousing. —*v.* (mouz) **moused, mous·ing** *v.i.* **1** To hunt or catch mice. **2** To hunt for something cautiously and softly; prowl. —*v.t.* **3** To hunt for, as a cat hunts mice. **4** *Naut.* To secure (a hook) with mousing. **5** *Obs.* To rend as a cat does a mouse. [OE *mūs,* pl. *mȳs.*]

mouse·bane (mous′bān′) *n.* Aconite.

mouse·bird (mous′bûrd′) *n.* **1** An African bird (genus *Colius*) with a conical bill, long medial tail feathers, and soft plumage. **2** A shrike.

mouse-ear (mous′ir′) *n.* **1** Any one of various plants whose leaves resemble the ears of a mouse; especially, the European hawkweed *(Hieracium pilosella).* **2** The forget-me-not.

mouse gray A medium shade of gray, the color of the fur of the common house mouse.

mous·er (mou′zər) *n.* **1** An animal that catches mice; especially, a cat. **2** A person who goes about stealthily.

mouse·tail (mous′tāl′) *n.* One of a genus *(Myosurus)* of plants of the crowfoot family: so called from its slender spike.

mouse·trap (mous′trap′) *n.* A trap for catching mice.

mous·ing (mou′zing) *n.* **1** The act of hunting mice. **2** *Naut.* A lashing or shackle passed around the shank and point of a hook, to prevent its spreading or unhooking. —*adj.* **1** Given to catching mice; prowling. **2** Thorough; careful; patient, as a cat hunting a mouse.

mous·que·taire (mo͞os′kə·târ′) *n.* **1** A member of one of the two companies of mounted musketeers forming the bodyguard of the French kings between 1622 and 1786. **2** A woman's cloth cloak with large buttons: in fashion about 1855. **3** A long glove of kid or silk, loose about the wrist: worn by women [<F, musketeer]

mous·sa·ka (mo͞o′sə·kä′) *n.* A baked dish of the Middle East made of alternating layers of ground meat and eggplant, served with a cheese sauce.

mousse (mo͞os) *n.* A light, frozen dessert made of whipped cream, white of egg, sugar, and flavoring extract, sometimes with the beaten yolks of eggs and gelatin; also, a similar dish made with finely ground meat, fish, or vegetables: lobster *mousse.* [<F]

mousse·line (mo͞os·lēn′) *n.* **1** Fine French muslin. **2** A thin glass blown to resemble lace. [<F. See MUSLIN.]

mousse·line-de-soie (mo͞os·lēn′də·swȧ′) *n. French* A plain-weave silk chiffon fabric, often figured; silk muslin.

Mous·sorg·sky (mo͞o·sôrg′skē), **Modest Petrovich,** 1835–81, Russian composer: also *Mussorgsky.*

mous·tache (məs·tash′, mus′tash) See MUSTACHE.

Mous·te·ri·an (mo͞o·stir′ē·ən) *adj. Anthropol.* Pertaining to or describing the culture stage of the Middle Paleolithic, represented in western Europe by artifacts of stone and other materials believed to indicate the social forms of the Neanderthal race of hunters. [<F *moustérien* <*Le Moustier,* a village in France where such remains were found]

mous·y (mou′sē, -zē) *adj.* **mous·i·er, mous·i·est** **1** Infested with or inhabited by mice. **2** Of, pertaining to, or like a mouse; having the color or smell of a mouse. **3** Like a mouse in appearance or manner; pallid; timid. Also **mous′ey.**

mouth (mouth) *n. pl.* **mouths** (mouthz) **1** The orifice at which food is taken into the body; the entrance to the alimentary canal; the cavity between the lips and throat. ◆ Collateral adjective: *oral.* **2** The human mouth as the channel of speech. **3** A wry face; grimace. **4** That part of a stream where its waters are discharged; also, the entrance to a harbor. **5** The opening for discharge in the muzzle of a firearm. **6** The slit in an organ pipe, from which the wind passes against the lip; also, the edge of the opening in a flute or similar instrument, against which the performer's breath is directed. **7** The opening of a vessel by which it is emptied or filled. **8** The entrance or opening into a cavity, mine, etc. **9** The space or opening between the jaws of a vice. **—down in** (or **at**) **the mouth** Disconsolate; dejected. **—to fix one's mouth for** To get ready for. —*v.t.* (mouth) **1** To utter in a forced or affected manner; declaim. **2** To seize or take in the mouth. **3** To caress or fondle with the mouth. **4** To accustom (a horse) to the bit. —*v.i.* **5** To speak in a forced or affected manner. **6** To distort the mouth; grimace. [OE *mūth*] **—mouth′er** (mou′thər) *n.*

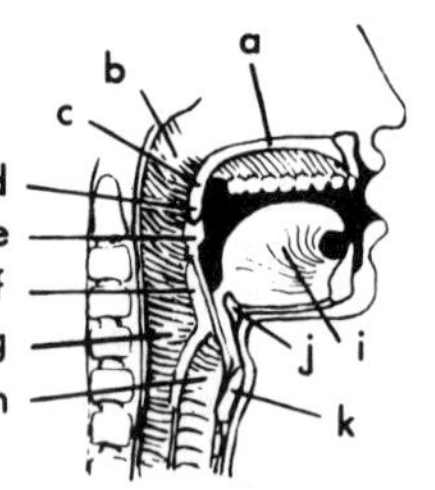

HUMAN MOUTH
a. Hard palate.
b. Pharynx.
c. Soft palate.
d. Uvula.
e. Tonsil.
f. Epiglottis.
g. Esophagus.
h. Trachea
i. Tongue.
j. Hyoid bone.
k. Larynx.

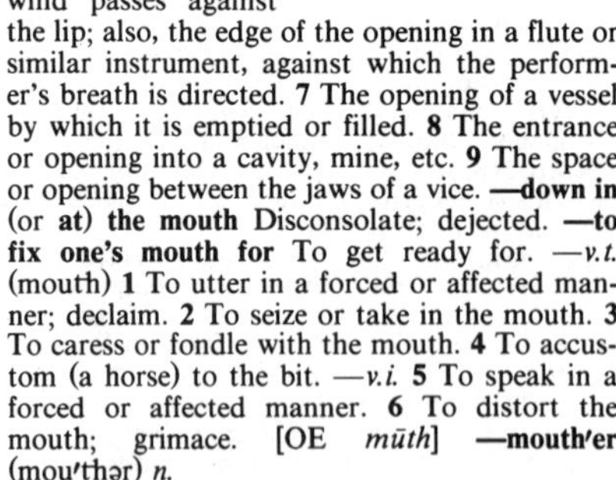

mouthed (mouthd, moutht) *adj.* **1** Having a mouth: used in composition, to denote a characteristic of the mouth or of speech: a hard-*mouthed* horse. **2** Provided with a mouth.

mouth·ful (mouth′fo͝ol′) *n. pl.* **·fuls** (-fo͝olz′) **1** As much as can be or is usually put into or held in the mouth at one time. **2** A small quantity.

mouth organ **1** A harmonica. **2** A set of panpipes.

mouth·piece (mouth′pēs′) *n.* **1** That part of any instrument, tool, etc., that is applied to the mouth. **2** One who speaks for others. **3** *Slang* A criminal lawyer.

mouth-to-mouth (mouth′tə·mouth′) *adj.* Pertaining to or designating a first-aid technique in which the lungs of a nonbreathing subject are repeatedly and forcibly filled with air from the mouth of the operator, which is closely applied to the mouth of the subject at each insufflation.

mouth·y (mou′thē, -thē) *adj.* **mouth·i·er, mouth·i·est** **1** Garrulous. **2** Addicted to grimaces in speaking. **—mouth′i·ly** *adv.* **—mouth′i·ness** *n.*

mou·ton (mo͞o′ton) *n.* Processed lambskin or sheepskin used in various types of apparel, especially coats. [<F, sheep]

mou·ton·née (mo͞o′tə·nā′) *French adj. Geog.* Having the form of a sheep's back: said of rocks, etc. Also **mou′ton·néed′.**

mov·a·ble (mo͞o′və·bəl) *adj.* **1** Capable of being moved in any way, as from one place, position, or posture to another; susceptible of transposition: *movable* property. **2** Capable of being moved in respect of time; recurring at varying intervals. See synonyms under MOBILE. —*n.* **1** Anything that can be moved; especially, anything that may be readily moved or is adapted for moving. **2** *pl.* House furniture of a movable nature; also, personal property, as distinguished from real or fixed property. Also **move′a·ble.** **—mov′a·ble·ness, mov′a·bil′i·ty** *n.* **—mov′a·bly** *adv.*

movable kidney A floating kidney.

move (mo͞ov) *v.* **moved, mov·ing** *v.i.* **1** To change place or position; pass or go from one place to another. **2** To change one's residence. **3** To make progress; advance; proceed. **4** To live or associate; be active: to *move* in cultivated circles. **5** To operate or revolve; work: said of machines, etc. **6** *Colloq.* To depart; go or start: often with *on.* **7** To take action; begin to act. **8** To be disposed of by sale. **9** To make an application, appeal, or proposal: to *move* for adjournment. **10** To evacuate: said of the bowels. **11** In chess, checkers, etc., to make a move. —*v.t.* **12** To change the place or position of; carry, push, or pull from one place to another. **13** To set or keep in motion; stir or shake. **14** To rouse, influence, or impel to some action; prompt; actuate. **15** To affect with passion, sympathy, etc.; stir; excite. **16** To offer for consideration, action, etc.; propose, especially formally. **17** To cause (the bowels) to evacuate. See synonyms under ACTUATE, CARRY, CONVEY, INFLUENCE, PERSUADE, STIR[1]. —*n.* **1** The act of moving; movement. **2** An act in the carrying out of a plan. **3** In games, the changing of the place of a piece. **—to get a move on** To hurry; get going. See synonyms under MOTION. [<AF *mover,* OF *moveir* <L *movere*]

move·ment (mo͞ov′mənt) *n.* **1** The act of changing place or of moving in any way; any change of position. **2** A series of actions, incidents, or ethical impulses tending toward some end: the temperance *movement.* **3** An effect resembling motion, as in a picture. **4** *Mech.* A particular arrangement of related parts accomplishing a motion: the *movement* of a watch. **5** *Music* **a** The pace or speed at which a piece or section of music sounds best. **b** One of the sections of a larger work, as of a symphony. **c** Melodic progression. **6** Rhythm; meter. **7** The act of emptying the bowels; also, the state of being or the matter so emptied. **8** An elemental part of action in military or naval evolution or maneuver. See synonyms under ACT, MOTION.

mov·er (mo͞o′vər) *n.* **1** One who or that which moves; specifically, one engaged in the business of moving household goods and other possessions. **2** A tenant farmer who moves away as soon as the soil is exhausted.

mov·ie (mo͞o′vē) *n. Colloq.* **1** A motion picture. **2** A motion-picture theater. **3** *pl.* The motion-picture industry. **4** *pl.* A showing of motion pictures. [Contraction of *moving picture*]

mov·ie-go·er (mo͞o′vē·gō′ər) *n. Colloq.* One who attends motion-picture showings regularly or frequently. **—mov′ie-go′ing** *n.*

mov·ing (mo͞o′ving) *adj.* **1** Causing to move; impelling to act; influencing; instigating; persuading. **2** Exciting the susceptibilities; affecting; touching. **—mov′ing·ly** *adv.* **—mov′ing·ness** *n.*

moving picture A motion picture.

moving platform A platform operated by an endless belt or several such side by side, moving at graduated speeds, carrying along passengers or merchandise. Also **moving sidewalk.**

moving staircase An escalator.

mow[1] (mō) *v.* **mowed, mowed** or **mown, mowing** *v.t.* **1** To cut down, as grain, with a scythe or machine. **2** To cut the grain or grass of, as a field or lawn. **3** To cut down or kill rapidly or indiscriminately: with *down.* —*v.i.* **4** To cut down grass or grain. [OE *māwan*] —**mow′er** *n.*

mow[2] (mō, mou) *v.i.* To make faces; grimace. [< *n.*] —*n.* A grimace. [< OF *moue*]

mow[3] (mou) *n.* Hay or grain stored in a barn; also, the place of storage. —*v.t.* To store in a mow. [OE *mūga*]

mown (mōn) *adj.* Cut down, as by mowing.

mox·a (mok′sə) *n.* **1** A cottony material, used, when ignited, as a counterirritant or cautery, prepared in China and Japan from certain species of *Artemisia,* especially *A. moxa.* **2** A substance for similar use obtained from other sources. **3** Any of the plants producing this material. [< Japanese *mogusa* a caustic < *moe kusa* burning herb]

moy·en âge (mwȧ·yen äzh′) *French* The Middle Ages.

Moy·zesz (moi′zesh) Polish form of MOSES. Also **Mo·zes** (*Dan.* mō′zes, *Hungarian* mō′·zesh).

Mo·zam·bique (mō′zam·bēk′) **1** A Portuguese overseas province in SE Africa; 297,731 square miles; capital, Lourenço Marques: also *Portuguese East Africa.* **2** A port of northern Mozambique, on **Mozambique Channel,** a strait of the Indian Ocean between Madagascar and SE Africa. *Portuguese* **Mo·cam·bi·que** (mōō′səm·bē′kə).

Moz·ar·ab (mōz·âr′əb) *n.* A member of a Christian congregation in Spain that maintained a modified form of its religion after the Moslem conquest. [< Sp. *Mozárabe* < Arabic *musta′rib* would-be Arab]

Mo·zart (mō′tsärt, -zärt), **Wolfgang Amadeus,** 1756–91, Austrian composer.

mo·zet·ta (mō·zet′ə) *n.* A hooded jacket worn by the prelates of the Roman Catholic Church. Also **moz·zet′ta.** [< Ital.]

Moz·za·rel·la (môd′dzä·rel′lä) *n.* A soft Italian curd cheese, originally made of buffalo's milk: used mainly in cooking. [< Ital.]

Mr. (mis′tər) *n. pl.* **Messrs.** (mes′ərz) A title prefixed to the name of a man: a contracted form of *Mister.*

Mrs. (mis′iz) *n. pl.* **Mmes.** (mā·däm′) A title prefixed to the name of a married woman: a contracted form of *Mistress.*

Ms. (miz) *n. pl.* **Ms.'s** (miz′əz) A title prefixed to the name of a woman: a contracted form of *Mistress.*

MSG (em′es′jē′) *n.* Monosodium glutamate.

mu (myōō, mōō) *n.* **1** The twelfth letter in the Greek alphabet (M, μ): equivalent to *m.* As a numeral it denotes 40. **2** The micron (symbol μ).

muc- Var. of MUCO-.

much (much) *adj.* **more, most 1** Great in quantity or amount. **2** *Obs.* Many in number. —*n.* **1** A considerable quantity. **2** A remarkable or important thing. —*adv.* **1** In a great degree. **2** For the most part; nearly. [ME *muchel,* OE *mycel*] —**much′ness** *n.*

mu·cic (myōō′sik) *adj. Chem.* Of, pertaining to, or designating a crystalline acid, $C_6H_{10}O_8$, formed by the oxidation of milk sugar, various gums, etc. [< F *mucique* < L *mucus* mucus]

mu·cid (myōō′sid) *adj.* Moldy; also, slimy; mucilaginous. [< L *mucidus* < *mucere* be moldy] —**mu′cid·ness** *n.*

mu·ci·lage (myōō′sə·lij) *n.* **1** A gummy or slimy substance obtained from the seeds, bark, or roots of various plants by infusion in water. **2** A solution of vegetable gum or mucus in water, especially when intended as an adhesive. [< F < LL *mucilago* < *mucere* be moldy, musty < *mucus* mucus]

mu·ci·lag·i·nous (myōō′si·laj′ə·nəs) *adj.* **1** Of, pertaining to, or like mucilage; soft, slimy, and viscid. **2** Producing mucilage, as glands. [< F *mucilagineux*] —**mu′ci·lag′i·nous·ness** *n.*

mu·cin (myōō′sin) *n. Biochem.* A glycoprotein secreted by the mucous membranes. [< F *mucine* mucus] —**mu′cin·ous** *adj.*

muck (muk) *n.* **1** Moist manure containing decomposed vegetable matter. **2** A nasty mess; filth. **3** Vegetable mold combined with earth. —*v.t.* **1** To fertilize with manure. **2** *Colloq.* To make dirty; pollute. **3** To remove muck from. [ME *muk* < Scand. Cf. ON *myki* dung, *moka* shovel manure.]

Muck (mo͝ok), **Karl,** 1859–1940, German conductor, active in the United States.

muck·er (muk′ər) *n. Brit. Slang* A coarse, rude person. [Cf. G *mucker* a low person]

muck·le (muk′əl) *Scot. adj.* Much. —*n.* A large quantity.

muck·rake (muk′rāk′) *v.i.* **·raked, ·rak·ing** To search for or expose real or alleged corruption on the part of political officials, businessmen, etc. [Back formation < MUCKRAKER, used in 1906 by President Theodore Roosevelt, in allusion to the "man with the muckrake" in Bunyan's *Pilgrim's Progress*] —**muck′rak′er** *n.* —**muck′rak′ing** *n.*

muck rake A rake used in collecting muck or dung.

muck·worm (muk′wûrm′) *n.* **1** The larva of a beetle *(Ligyrus gibbosus)* common in dung heaps. **2** *Slang* A miser.

muck·y (muk′ē) *adj.* **muck·i·er, muck·i·est** Foul; nasty. —**muck′i·ly** *adv.* —**muck′i·ness** *n.*

muco- *combining form* Mucus; mucus and: *mucopurulent*: also, before vowels, *muc-.* Also **muci-.** [< L *mucus* mucus]

mu·coid (myōō′koid) *adj.* Like mucus. —*n. Biochem.* A compound glycoprotein similar to mucin, found in connective tissue, in cysts, in the vitreous humor, etc. [< MUC- + -OID]

mu·co·pro·te·in (myōō′kō·prō′tē·in, -tēn) *n. Biochem.* A glycoprotein combining a protein with a carbohydrate group.

mu·co·pu·ru·lent (myōō′kō·pyōōr′ə·lənt, -yə·lənt) *adj.* Relating to or consisting of both mucus and purulent matter.

Mu·co·ra·les (myōō′kō·rā′lēz) *n. pl.* An order of fungi (class *Phycomycetes*) which includes several mold species, as the common bread mold. [< NL]

mu·co·sa (myōō·kō′sə) *n. pl.* **·sae** (-sē) *Anat.* A mucous membrane. [< NL, fem. of L *mucosus* mucous] —**mu·co′sal** *adj.*

mu·cous (myōō′kəs) *adj.* **1** Secreting mucus. **2** Pertaining to or resembling mucus. Also **mu′cose** (-kōs). [< L *mucosus* slimy < *mucus*] —**mu·cos′i·ty** (-kos′ə·tē) *n.*

mucous membrane *Anat.* A membrane secreting or producing mucus, that lines passages communicating with the exterior, as the alimentary canal, air passages, etc.

mu·cro (myōō′krō) *n. pl.* **mu·cro·nes** (myōō·krō′nēz) *Biol.* A small, sharp process or part, as the point of a leaf; a spine. [< NL < L, point of a sword]

mu·cro·nate (myōō′krə·nāt) *adj. Biol.* Having a short, straight point, as a leaf, feather, etc.: also **mu′cro·nat′ed.** [< L *mucronatus* < *mucro* point of a sword]

mu·cus (myōō′kəs) *n.* **1** *Biol.* A viscid animal substance, as that secreted by the mucous membranes. **2** *Bot.* A gummy substance in plants. [< L]

mud (mud) *n.* **1** Wet and sticky earth; mire. **2** *Colloq.* Slander; abuse; detraction of character: to sling *mud* at someone. —*v.t.* **mud·ded, mud·ding** To soil or cover with mud. [? < MLG *mudde*]

mud boat 1 A scow or barge used in dredging: also **mud scow. 2** A kind of low sledge with wide runners used for hauling logs over swampy ground.

mud·cap (mud′kap′) *v.t.* **·capped, ·cap·ping 1** To cap with mud. **2** To cover (a charge of high explosive) with mud before detonating it above an exposed mass of rock. —**mud′cap′ping** *n.*

mud·cat (mud′kat′) *n.* A large catfish of the Mississippi valley.

mud dauber 1 Any of various wasps (family *Sphecidae*) that build mud cells in which their larvae develop. For illustration see INSECTS (beneficial). **2** A swallow that builds a nest of mud.

mud·dle (mud′l) *v.* **·dled, ·dling** *v.t.* **1** To mix in confusion; jumble. **2** To confuse mentally; bewilder. **3** To make muddy or turbid; roil. **4** To stir or mix, as a drink. —*v.i.* **5** To act in a confused or ineffective manner. —**to muddle through** *Brit.* To achieve one's object despite one's own confusion and mistakes; succeed despite oneself. —*n.* **1** A muddy or dirty condition. **2** A mixed or confused condition, as of the mind; a mess. [< MUD + freq. suffix]

mud·dle-head·ed (mud′l·hed′id) *adj.* Mentally confused; addle-brained.

mud·dler (mud′lər) *n.* **1** A stick for churning or stirring liquids. **2** One who muddles.

mud drum An enclosed container placed at the bottom of any manufacturing or power apparatus, as a boiler, for the purpose of collecting insoluble waste matter, sludge, etc.

mud·dy (mud′ē) *adj.* **·di·er, ·di·est 1** Bespattered with mud; turbid. **2** Mentally confused. **3** Consisting of mud; earthy; gross; impure. **4** Dull; cloudy: a *muddy* complexion, *muddy* weather. See synonyms under FOUL, THICK. —*v.t.* & *v.i.* **·died, ·dy·ing** To become or cause to become muddy. —**mud′di·ly** *adv.* —**mud′di·ness** *n.*

mud eel An eel-shaped amphibian having very small forelegs and no hind legs, that buries itself in the mud; especially, *Siren lacertina* of the swamps of the southern United States: also called *congo* and *siren.*

mud·fish (mud′fish′) *n. pl.* **·fish** or **·fish·es** Any of various fishes that inhabit stagnant or muddy water, as the bowfin, killifish, etc.

mud flat A low-lying strip of ground covered with mud, especially one between high and low tide.

mud·guard (mud′gärd′) *n.* A guard over the wheel of a vehicle to protect from splashing mud.

mud hen 1 The American coot *(Fulica americana).* **2** The Florida gallinule *(Gallenula chloropus).* **3** The clapper rail. See under RAIL[2].

mud·lark (mud′lärk′) *n. Brit. Colloq.* One who works or dabbles in mud; a street urchin.

mud·pot (mud′pot′) *n.* A geyser which ejects mud. Also **mud geyser.**

mud·pup·py (mud′·pup′ē) *n. pl.* **·pies 1** The hellbender. **2** A tailed amphibian with bushy, persistent, external gills, especially *Necturus maculosus,* found in the large lakes of North America.

MUDPUPPY
(From 12 to 17 inches long)

mud·sill (mud′sil′) *n.* **1** The foundation timber of a structure placed directly on the ground. **2** *U.S. Dial.* A person of low social state or condition.

mud·sling·ing (mud′sling′ing) *n.* The practice of casting malicious slurs at an opponent, especially in a political campaign. —**mud′sling′er** *n.*

mud·stone (mud′stōn′) *n.* A gray, sandy shale that readily decomposes into mud.

mud·suck·er (mud′suk′ər) *n.* A California fish related to the goby *(Gillichthys mirabilis),* much used as bait.

mud turtle Any of various turtles inhabiting muddy rivers in different parts of the world, especially the small common variety of the United States (genus *Kinosternon).*

mu·ez·zin (myōō·ez′in) *n.* In Moslem countries, a crier from a minaret or other part of the mosque who calls the faithful to prayer. Also **mu·ed′din** (-ed′in). [< Arabic *mu′adhdhin* < *adhana* call]

muff[1] (muf) *v.t.* & *v.i.* **1** To perform (some act) clumsily; blunder. **2** In baseball, to fail to hold (the ball) in attempting a catch. —*n.* **1** A bungling action; in baseball, etc., a failure to catch the ball. **2** A bungler. **3** A stupid fellow; dolt. [Origin unknown]

muff[2] (muf) *n.* A covering of fur or cloth, usually cylindrical, into which the hands are thrust from opposite ends to keep them warm. [< Du. *mof* < F *moufle*]

muf·fin (muf′in) *n.* A light, quick bread, baked in small cup-shaped tins, and usually eaten hot with butter; also, a small, flat yeast bread: also called *English muffin.* [Origin uncertain. Cf. OF *moufflet* soft (bread).]

add, āce, câre, pälm; end, ēven; it, īce; odd, ōpen, ôrder; to͝ok, pōōl; up, bûrn; ə = a in *above,* e in *sicken,* i in *clarity,* o in *melon,* u in *focus*; yōō = u in *fuse,* oi, oil; ou, pout; ch, check; g, go; ng, ring; th, thin; th, this; zh, vision. Foreign sounds ȧ, œ, ü, kh, ṅ; and ◆: see page xx. < from; + plus; ? possibly.

muf·fin·eer (muf′in·ir′) **1** A metal cruet with a perforated top for sprinkling salt or sugar on muffins. **2** A covered dish to keep muffins, etc., hot.

muffin stand A small tiered stand used in tea service for holding and passing cakes, sandwiches, etc.

muf·fle (muf′əl) *v.t.* **·fled, ·fling 1** To wrap up in a blanket, scarf, etc., as for warmth or concealment. **2** To prevent from seeing, hearing, or speaking by wrapping the head. **3** To deaden the sound of by or as by wrapping: to *muffle* a cry. **4** To deaden (a sound). — *n.* **1** Something used for muffling. **2** A clay oven for firing pottery without direct exposure to flame. **3** The naked upper lip and nose of ruminants and certain other mammals. [<OF *moufle* heavy leather or fur mitten]

muf·fler (muf′lər) *n.* **1** Anything used for wrapping up or muffling; specifically, a scarf worn about the neck; also, a veil or scarf worn by women. **2** A device to reduce noise, as from the exhaust of an internal-combustion engine. **3** A mitten. [<MUFFLE]

muf·ti[1] (muf′tē) *n.* In Moslem countries, an expounder of religious law. [<Arabic <*āftā* expound the law]

muf·ti[2] (muf′tē) *n.* Civilian dress; plain clothes, especially when worn by one who normally wears a uniform. [<MUFTI[1]; prob. from the fact that a mufti is a civil official]

mug[1] (mug) *n.* **1** A drinking cup, usually cylindrical, with a handle and no lip. **2** That which is contained in a mug. [Cf. Sw. *mugg*, Norw. *mugga*]

mug[2] (mug) *Slang n.* **1** The human face or mouth. **2** A grimace. **3** A photograph of the face of a suspect: also **mug shot. 4** A criminal. — *v.* **mugged, mug·ging** *v.t.* **1** To photograph (someone), especially for official purposes. **2** To assault, usually with the intent to rob. — *v.i.* **3** To make faces; grimace. [<MUG[1]; prob. from the fact that drinking mugs were often shaped to resemble a face] — **mug′ger** *n.*

mug·ger (mug′ər) *n.* A crocodile (*Crocodilus palustris*) of India and the East Indies, with a broad snout: it grows to a length of about 12 feet. Also **mug′gar, mug′gur.** [<Hind. *magar* <Skt. *makara* sea monster]

mug·ging (mug′ing) *n. Slang* Assault, often with the intention of robbery, usually by attacking the victim from behind and locking an arm around his throat. [<MUG[2]]

mug·gins (mug′inz) *n.* **1** One of several card games in which exposed cards are matched or suits are built. **2** A variant in the game of dominoes. **3** *Brit. Slang* A foolish person. [Prob. < *Muggins*, a surname used in arbitrary allusion to *mug* (slang) a card-sharper's dupe]

mug·gy (mug′ē) *adj.* **·gi·er, ·gi·est** Warm, moist, and close; sultry. [< dial. E *mug* drizzle, prob. <ON *mugga* drizzling mist] — **mug′gi·ness** *n.*

mug·wort (mug′wûrt′) *n.* An aromatic bitter herb (*Artemisia vulgaris*) of the composite family, sometimes used in folk medicine as a diaphoretic and emmenagog.

mug·wump (mug′wump) *n. U.S.* **1** A Republican who bolted the party candidate, James G. Blaine, in the presidential election of 1884. **2** Anyone who claims the right of independent action, especially in politics; an independent. [<Algonquian *mugquomp* great man, chief] — **mug′wump·er·y, mug′wump·ism** *n.*

Mu·ham·ma·dan (mo͝o·ham′ə·dən), etc. See MOHAMMEDAN, etc.

Mu·har·ram (mo͝o·har′əm) *n.* A Mohammedan month; also, the first ten days of the month, a period of lamentation. See CALENDAR (Mohammedan). Also spelled *Moharran.* [<Arabic *muḥarram* sacred, the first month of the year]

Mühl·bach (mül′bäkh), **Luise** Pen name of *Klara Mundt*, 1814–73, German novelist.

Muh·len·berg (myo͞o′lən·bûrg), **Frederick Augustus Conrad,** 1750–1801, American politician and clergyman; member of the Continental Congress. — **John Peter,** 1746–1807, American Revolutionary general.

Müh·len·berg (myo͞o′lən·bûrg, *Ger.* mü′lən·berkh), **Heinrich,** 1711–87, German clergyman, chief founder of Lutheranism in the United States.

muh·ly grass (myo͞o′lē) Any of a genus (*Muhlenbergia*) of mostly perennial, wiry grasses growing in the SW United States and Mexico, as the **ring muhly** (*M. torreyi*), and **spike muhly** (*M. wrightii*), valued as forage plants for livestock. [after Dr. G. H. E. *Muhlenberg*, 1753–1815, American botanist]

Mu·hu (mo͞o′ho͞o) An Estonian island in the Baltic; 79 square miles. Also *Russian* **Mu·khu** (mo͞o′kho͞o).

muir (myo͝or) *n. Scot.* A moor; heath.

Muir (myo͝or), **John,** 1838–1914, U.S. naturalist.

mu·i·ra·pu·a·ma (mo͞o·ē′rä·po͞o·ä′mä) *n.* The dried stems and roots of a Brazilian plant (*Liriosma ovata*), reputed to have properties as a nerve stimulant and aphrodisiac. [<Pg. <Tupian]

Muir Glacier (myo͝or) A glacier in the St. Elias Mountains, Alaska; 350 square miles.

mu·jik (mo͞o·zhēk′, mo͞o′zhik) See MUZHIK.

Muk·den (mo͝ok′den′, mo͝ok′dən, mo͝ok′-) Former name of SHENYANG.

Mu·ker·ji (mo͞o′ker·jē′), **Dhan Gopal,** 1890–1936, East Indian writer, active in the United States.

muk·luk (muk′luk) *n.* **1** An Alaskan Eskimo boot of seal or other animal skin, made so that the fur is inside. **2** *pl.* Sport or lounging shoes of the soft moccasin type. [<Alaskan Eskimo *makliak*, *muklok* large seal]

mu·la·da (mo͞o·lä′thä) *n. SW U.S.* A drove of mules.

mu·lat·to (mə·lat′ō, myo͞o-, -lä′tō) *n. pl.* **·toes** A person having one white and one Negro parent; loosely, anyone having white and Negro blood. — *adj.* **1** Of or pertaining to a person of such descent. **2** Of a light-brown color. [<Sp. *mulato* of mixed breed < *mulo* mule <L *mulus*]

mul·ber·ry (mul′ber′ē, -bər·ē) *n. pl.* **·ries 1** The edible, berrylike fruit of a tree (genus *Morus*) whose leaves are valued for silkworm culture, especially the white mulberry (*M. alba*). **2** A deep purplish-red, the color of a mulberry. [ME *mulberie*, dissimilated var. of *murberie*, OE *morberie* <L *morum* mulberry + OE *berie* a berry]

mulberry body The morula.

mulch (mulch) *n.* Any loose material, as straw, placed about the stalks of plants to protect their roots. — *v.t.* To cover with mulch. [ME *molsh*. Cf. dial. G *molsch* soft, decaying.]

mulct (mulkt) *v.t.* **1** To punish (a person) by a fine or penalty. **2** To deprive of something fraudulently or deceitfully; cheat. — *n.* A fine, or similar penalty. [<L *mulctare* < *mulcta*, *multa* a fine]

mule[1] (myo͞ol) *n.* **1** A hybrid between the ass and horse, especially between a jackass and a mare, as distinguished from a hinny. **2** Any hybrid or cross, especially one that is sterile. **3** A spinning machine which draws, stretches, and twists at one operation: also called *spinning mule, jenny, spinning jenny*: also **mule′-jen′ny** (-jen′ē). **4** A person having the stubborn qualities of a mule. **5** A small electric engine or tractor for towing canal boats. [<F <L *mulus*]

mule[2] (myo͞ol) *n.* A backless lounging slipper. [<MF <L *mulleus* red slipper]

mule deer The black-tailed deer (genus *Odocoileus*), of the western United States, having long ears.

mule-driv·er (myo͞ol′drī′vər) *n.* One who drives mules.

mule-skin·ner (myo͞ol′skin′ər) *n. U.S. Colloq.* A mule-driver.

mu·le·teer (myo͞o′lə·tir′) *n.* A mule-driver. [<F *muletier* < *mulet* mule]

mule train A train of mules carrying packs; also, a train of heavy freight wagons drawn by mules.

mu·ley (myo͞o′lē, mo͝ol′ē, mo͞o′lē) *adj.* Hornless: said of cattle. — *n.* A hornless cow. Also spelled *mooley, mulley.* [<Irish *maol, moile* hornless, dismantled]

Mul·ha·cén (mo͞o′lä·thān′) A mountain in SE Spain, in the Sierra Nevada; the highest peak in Spain; 11,411 feet. Also **Mu·ley-Ha·cén** (mo͞o·lā′ä·thān′).

Mül·heim-an-der-Ruhr (mül′hīm·än·dər·ro͞or′) A city on the Ruhr in western North Rhine-Westphalia, West Germany. Also **Mül′heim.**

Mul·house (mül·o͞oz′) A city in eastern France near the German border. *German* **Mül·hau·sen** (mül′hou·zən).

mu·li·eb·ri·ty (myo͞o′lē·eb′rə·tē) *n.* The state of being a woman; womanliness. [<LL *muliebris* womanly < *mulier* woman]

mul·ish (myo͞o′lish) *adj.* Resembling a mule; stubborn. See synonyms under OBSTINATE. — **mul′ish·ly** *adv.* — **mul′ish·ness** *n.*

mull[1] (mul) *v.t.* To heat and spice, as wine or beer. [<MULSE]

mull[2] (mul) *v.t.* To ponder; cogitate: usually with *over.* [< obs. *mull* grind, OE *myl* dust]

mull[3] (mul) *n.* **1** A thin, soft, cotton, rayon, or silk dress goods. **2** A variety of soft, thin muslin used as a base for medicated ointments, as mulla. [Short for *mulmull* <Hind. *malmal*]

mull[4] (mul) *n.* A horn snuffbox. [Var. of *mill* (in a Scottish use); orig., a snuffbox in which tobacco could be ground to a powder by a mechanism]

Mull (mul) An island in NW Argyllshire, Scotland, the largest of the Inner Hebrides; 351 square miles.

mul·la (mul′ə) *n. Med.* An ointment having a base of lard and salt, spread on a piece of mull.

mul·lah (mul′ə, mo͝ol′ə) See MOLLAH.

mul·len (mul′ən) *n.* **1** A tall, stout, woolly herb (*Verbascum thapsus*) of the figwort family, the **great mullen. 2** Any plant of the same genus, as the **moth mullen** (*V. blattaria*). Also **mul′lein.** [<AF *moleine* <OF *mol* soft <L *mollis*]

mull·er (mul′ər) *n.* **1** A pestlelike implement with which to mix paints. **2** A mechanical pulverizer or grinder. [<obs. *mull* pulverize, OE *myl* dust]

Mul·ler (mul′ər), **Hermann Joseph,** born 1890, U. S. geneticist.

Mül·ler (mül′ər), **(Friedrich) Max,** 1823–1900, English philologist and Orientalist born in Germany. — **Johannes Peter,** 1801–58, German physiologist.

mul·let[1] (mul′it) *n. pl.* **·lets** or **·let 1** A food fish (family *Mugilidae*), usually greenish or copper-colored, with silvery sides, found on warm coasts. *Mugil cephalus* is the **striped mullet** of both coasts of the Atlantic. **2** A food fish (family *Mullidae*): often called *surmullet. Mullus barbatus* is the highly esteemed European **red mullet.** [<OF *mulet* <L *mullus* red mullet]

mul·let[2] (mul′it) *n. Her.* A star of five or more points. [<OF *molette* rowel]

mul·let·head (mul′it·hed′) *n.* A fresh-water fish having a flat head.

mul·let-head·ed (mul′it·hed′id) *adj. Slang* Stupid.

mul·ley (mo͝ol′ē, mo͞o′lē) See MULEY.

mul·li·gan (mul′i·gən) *n. Slang* **1** A stew, originally made by tramps, composed of odds and ends of food: also **mulligan stew. 2** In golf, an extra shot, especially a tee shot, after an inept first shot. [< *Mulligan*, Irish surname]

mul·li·ga·taw·ny (mul′i·gə·tô′nē) *n.* A strongly flavored soup of meat and curry. [<Tamil *milagu-tannīr* pepper water]

mul·li·grubs (mul′ə·grubz) *n. Slang* An acute colicky pain; colic; hence, the blues. [A grotesque arbitrary formation]

Mul·lin·gar (mul′in·gär′) The county town of Westmeath, Ireland.

mul·lion (mul′yən) *n. Archit.* A vertical dividing piece between window lights or panels. — *v.t.* To furnish with or divide by means of mullions. [Prob. metathetic var. of earlier *monial* <OF *moinel, monial;* ult. origin unknown] — **mul′lioned** *adj.*

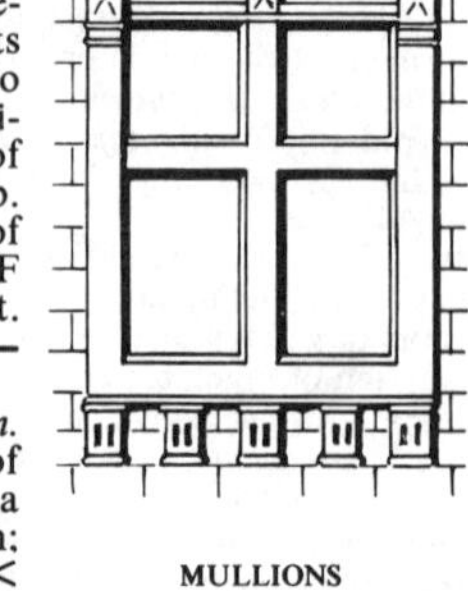
MULLIONS

mul·lock (mul′ək) *n.* An accumulation of waste rock about a mine; refuse earth; a waste dump. [< obs. *mull* dust + -OCK] — **mul′lock·y** *adj.*

Mu·lock (myo͞o′lok), **Miss** See CRAIK, DINAH MARIA.

mulse (muls) *n.* Wine heated and sweetened. [<L *mulsum*, pp. of *mulcere* sweeten]

Mul·tan (mo͞ol·tän′) A city in southern Punjab, West Pakistan.

multi– *combining form* 1 Much; many; consisting of many; as in:

multiangular
multiareolate
multiarticulate
multiarticulated
multiaxial
multiblade
multibladed
multibranchiate
multicamerate
multicapital
multicapitate
multicapsular
multicarinate
multicellular
multicentral
multicentric
multicharge
multichord
multichrome
multiciliate
multiciliated
multicircuit
multicoil
multicolor
multiconductor
multicore
multicourse
multicrystalline
multidenominational
multidentate
multidenticulate
multidenticulated
multidigitate
multidimensional
multidirectional
multidisciplinary
multiethnic
multifaced
multifaceted
multifactorial
multiflagellate
multiflorous
multiflue
multifocal
multifoliate
multifurcate
multigranulate
multigyrate
multihead
multihearth
multihued
multi–infection
multijet
multilamellar
multilaminar
multilaminate
multilaminated
multilevel
multilighted
multilineal
multilinear
multilingual
multilobar
multilobate
multilobed
multilobular
multilobulate
multimedial
multimetallic
multimillion
multimolecular
multination
multinational
multinervate
multinodal
multinodous
multinodular
multiovular
multiovulate
multipartisan
multiperforate
multiperforated
multipersonal
multipinnate
multipointed
multipolar
multiracial
multiradial
multiradiate
multiradicate
multiramified
multiramose
multiramous
multirate
multireflex
multirooted
multisaccate
multisacculate
multisegmental
multisensitivity
multiseptate
multiserial
multiserially
multiseriate
multishot
multispermous
multispicular
multispiculate
multispindle
multispinous
multispiral
multispired
multistaminate
multistoried
multistratified
multistriate
multisulcate
multisulcated
multisyllable
multiterminal
multititular
multitoed
multituberculate
multituberculated
multitubular
multivaned
multivoiced
multivolumed

2 Having more than two (or sometimes, more than one); as in:

multicostate
multicuspid
multicuspidate
multicylinder
multielectrode
multiengine
multiexhaust
multiflow
multimammae
multimammate
multimotor
multinuclear
multinucleate
multinucleolar
multinucleolate
multispeed

3 Many times over: *multimillionare.* 4 *Med.* Affecting many; as in:

multiarticular
multifamilial
multiganglionic
multiglandular

Also, before vowels, sometimes **mult–.** [<L *multus* much]

mul·ti·cip·i·tal (mul′ti·sip′ə·təl) *adj. Bot.* Many–headed: said of plants with many stems from one root. [<MULTI- + L *caput* head]

mul·ti–col·ored (mul′ti·kul′ərd) *adj.* Exhibiting or made up of many colors.

mul·ti·far·i·ous (mul′tə·fâr′ē·əs) *adj.* Having great diversity or variety. [<L *multifarius*] **— mul′ti·far′i·ous·ly** *adv.* **— mul′ti·far′i·ous·ness** *n.*

mul·ti·fid (mul′tə·fid) *adj. Bot.* Cut into many lobes or segments, as a leaf. Also **mul·tif·i·dous** (mul·tif′ə·dəs). [<MULTI- + -FID]

mul·ti·foil (mul′tə·foil) *n. Geom.* A plane figure made of the congruent arcs of circles which are symmetrically arranged along the sides of a regular polygon.

mul·ti·fold (mul′tə·fōld) *adj.* Many times doubled; manifold.

mul·ti·form (mul′tə·fôrm) *adj.* Having many forms, shapes, or appearances. See synonyms under COMPLEX. [<L *multiformis*] **— mul′ti·form′i·ty** *n.*

Mul·ti·graph (mul′tə·graf, -gräf) *n.* A typesetting and printing machine in which the type is moved from a typesetting drum to a printing drum: a trade name.

mul·ti·lat·er·al (mul′ti·lat′ər·əl) *adj.* 1 Having many sides. 2 *Govt.* Involving more than two nations: a *multilateral* trade agreement.

mul·ti·me·di·a (mul′ti·mē′dē·ə) *adj.* Relating to or using two or more media, especially a combination apprehended by different senses, as sight and hearing.

mul·ti·mil·lion·aire (mul′ti·mil′yən·âr′) *n.* A person having a fortune of several or many millions of dollars, pounds, francs, etc.

mul·ti·no·mi·al (mul′ti·nō′mē·əl) *adj.* Polynomial. [<MULTI- + (BI)NOMIAL]

mul·tip·a·ra (mul·tip′ə·rə) *n. pl.* **·rae** (-rē) A woman who has borne more than one child, or who is parturient the second time. [<NL <L *multiparus*]

mul·tip·a·rous (mul·tip′ə·rəs) *adj.* 1 Giving birth to many at one time. 2 Having borne more than one child. [<MULTI- + -PAROUS]

mul·ti·par·tite (mul′ti·pär′tīt) *adj.* 1 Divided into many parts. 2 *Govt.* Multilateral (def. 2).

mul·ti·pede (mul′tə·pēd) *n.* A many–footed animal or insect. *— adj.* Having many feet. Also **mul′ti·ped** (-ped).

mul·ti·phase (mul′tə·fāz) *adj.* Polyphase.

mul·ti·plane (mul′tə·plān) *n. Aeron.* An airplane with two or more supporting surfaces, one above another.

mul·ti·ple (mul′tə·pəl) *adj.* 1 Containing or consisting of more than one; repeated more than once; manifold. 2 *Electr.* Having two or more conductors or pieces of apparatus, such as lamps, connected in parallel: a *multiple* circuit. *— n. Math.* The product of a given number and its factor. **— common multiple** Any number which is exactly divisible by two or more numbers, not including itself. **— lowest common multiple** The smallest number divisible by each of two or more numbers: 12 is the *least common multiple* of 2, 3, 4, and 6: often abbr. *L.C.M.* Also **least common multiple.** [<F <L *multiplex*]

multiple allele *Genetics* One of three or more alleles, only two of which may pass from the parents to a normal diploid offspring.

multiple factors *Genetics* Two or more distinct genes which are believed to act as a unit or with cumulative effect in the transmission of certain plant and animal characteristics, as size, pigmentation, color of eyes, etc.

multiple fruit *Bot.* A fruit consisting of numerous smaller fruits, each developed from a single flower, as the pineapple: also called *collective fruit.*

multiple myeloma *Pathol.* A malignant tumor of the bone marrow occurring at numerous sites.

multiple neuritis *Pathol.* Neuritis involving several nerves simultaneously.

multiple sclerosis *Pathol.* Sclerosis occurring in patches in the brain or spinal cord or both, and characterized by tremors, failure of coordination, and various nervous and mental symptoms.

multiple star *Astron.* A system of three or more stars revolving around a common gravitational center.

mul·ti·plet (mul′tə·plit) *n. Physics* Two or more spectral lines very close together in an atomic spectrum and associated with different energy characteristics of the atom. [<MULTIPLE]

mul·ti·plex (mul′tə·pleks) *adj.* 1 Multiple; manifold. 2 *Telecom.* Designating a system for the simultaneous transmission of two or more messages in either or both directions over the same wire, as in telegraphy or telephony. 3 *Phot.* Designating a method based upon the stereoscopic principle: three cameras are used, together with auxiliary equipment designed to facilitate the construction of accurate maps. *— v.t. & v.i. Telecom.* To send (two or more messages) at the same time over the same wire. [<L <*multus* much + stem of *plicare* fold]

mul·ti·pli·cand (mul′tə·plə·kand′) *n.* A number multiplied, or to be multiplied, by another. [<L *multiplicandus* to be multiplied, gerundive of *multiplicare.* See MULTIPLY.]

mul·ti·pli·cate (mul′tə·plə·kāt) *adj.* Consisting of or being many or more than one. [<L *multiplicatus,* pp. of *multiplicare* multiply]

mul·ti·pli·ca·tion (mul′tə·plə·kā′shən) *n.* 1 The process of multiplying. 2 The process of finding the sum (the *product*) of a number (the *multiplicand*) repeated a given number of times (the *multiplier*). Opposed to *division.* [<OF <L *multiplicatio, -onis*]

mul·ti·pli·ca·tive (mul′tə·plə·kā′tiv) *adj.* Tending to multiply; indicating multiplication. **— mul′ti·pli·ca′tive·ly** *adv.*

mul·ti·plic·i·ty (mul′tə·plis′ə·tē) *n.* The condition of being manifold or various; hence, a large number. [<LL *multiplicitas, -tatis* <L *multiplex*]

mul·ti·pli·er (mul′tə·plī′ər) *n.* 1 One who or that which multiplies or increases in quantity, or causes something else to multiply or increase. 2 *Math.* The number by which a quantity is multiplied. 3 *Physics* An instrument or mechanical device for increasing or intensifying an effect. 4 *Electr.* An open spiral coil in a wireless telegraph receiver which has the effect of exalting the potential oscillations.

mul·ti·ply (mul′tə·plī) *v.* **·plied, ·ply·ing** *v.t.* 1 To increase the quantity, amount, or degree of; make more numerous. 2 *Math.* To perform the operation of multiplication upon. *— v.i.* 3 To become more in number, amount, or degree; increase. 4 *Math.* To perform the operation of multiplication. See synonyms under PROPAGATE. *— adv.* So as to be numerous; in many ways. [<OF *multiplier* <L *multiplicare* < *multiplex.* See MULTIPLEX.] **— mul′ti·pli′a·ble** *adj.*

mul·ti·pro·pel·lant (mul′ti·prə·pel′ənt) *n.* A rocket propellant consisting of two or more chemicals separately fed into the combustion chamber. *— adj.* Of or pertaining to such a propellant.

mul·ti·pur·pose (mul′ti·pûr′pəs) *adj.* Adapted to more than one use or type of service.

mul·ti·range (mul′tə·rānj) *adj.* Having a wide range of operations or performance, as certain precision instruments.

mul·ti·sec·tion (mul′ti·sek′shən) *adj.* Having or occupying more than one section.

mul·ti·stage (mul′tə·stāj) *adj.* 1 Having or characterized by a number of definite stages in the completion of a process or action. 2 Having several sections, each of which fulfils a given task before burnout: said especially of a rocket or ballistic missile.

mul·ti·tude (mul′tə·tōōd, -tyōōd) *n.* 1 The state of being many or numerous. 2 A large gathering; concourse. 3 A large number of things. See synonyms under ARMY, ASSEMBLY, COMPANY, THRONG. **— the multitude** The common people. [<OF <L *multitudo* < *multus* much, many]

mul·ti·tu·di·nous (mul′tə·tōō′də·nəs, -tyōō′-) *adj.* Consisting of a vast number. See synonyms under MANY. [<L *multitudo, -inis* a crowd + -OUS] **— mul′ti·tu′di·nous·ly** *adv.* **— mul′ti·tu′di·nous·ness** *n.*

mul·ti·va·lent (mul′ti·vā′lənt) *adj. Chem.* Having three or more valences. **— mul′ti·va′lence** *n.*

mul·ti·valve (mul′tə·valv) *n.* A shell with many valves. *— adv.* Having many valves. **— mul′·ti·val′vu·lar** (-val′vyə·lər) *adj.*

mul·ti·verse (mul′tə·vûrs) *n. Philos.* The plurality of worlds as conceived in or projected by the mind: contrasted with *universe.* [<MULTI- + (UNI)VERSE]

mul·ti·ver·si·ty (mul′ti·vûr′sə·tē) *n. pl.* **·ties** A very large university with a student enrollment of many thousands, offering instruction and graduate study in many fields and often on a number of campuses. [<MULTI- + (UNI)VERSITY]

mul·tiv·o·cal (mul·tiv′ə·kəl) *adj.* Having various meanings. —*n.* A word that has more than one signification. [< MULTI- + VOCAL]

mul·ti·vol·tine (mul′ti·vol′tin, -tēn) *adj. Entomol.* Having many broods of offspring in a year, as certain insects. [< MULTI- + Ital. *volta* turn]

Mult·no·mah Falls (mult·nō′mə) A waterfall in NW Oregon in a small tributary of the Columbia River; about 850 feet high.

mul·toc·u·lar (mul·tok′yə·lər) *adj.* **1** Having two or more eyes. **2** Having eyes divisible, like those of a fly, into facets. [< MULT(I)- + OCULAR]

mul·tum in par·vo (mul′təm in pär′vō) *Latin* Much in little.

mul·ture (mul′chər) *n.* **1** A grinding of grain. **2** The grain ground or the toll paid for the grinding. [< OF *moulture* < Med. L *molitura* < L *molere* grind]

mum[1] (mum) *v.i.* **mummed, mum·ming** *Obs.* To be silent. —*adj.* Silent; saying nothing. —*n.* Silence: *Mum's* the word. —*interj.* Hush! Be quiet! [Imit.]

mum[2] (mum) *v.i.* **mummed, mum·ming** To play or act in a mask, as at Christmas; be a mummer. Also **mumm.** [< MUM[1]. Cf. MDu. *mommen* mask, OF *momer* act in a dumb show.]

mum[3] (mum) *n.* A strong sweet beer, first brewed in Germany by Christian Mumme, 1492.

mum[4] (mum) Corruption of MADAM, MA'AM.

mum[5] (mum) *n. Colloq.* A chrysanthemum.

mum·ble (mum′bəl) *v.t.* & *v.i.* **·bled, ·bling 1** To speak or utter in low, indistinct tones; mutter. **2** *Rare* To chew slowly and ineffectively, as with toothless gums. —*n.* A low, mumbling speech; mutter. [ME *momelen,* freq. of obs. *mum* make inarticulate sounds. Cf. G *mummeln.*] —**mum′bler** *n.* —**mum′bling** *adj.* —**mum′bling·ly** *adv.*

mum·ble-the-peg (mum′bəl·thə·peg′) *n.* A boy's game played with a jackknife, which is tossed and flipped in various ways so as to stick into the ground: so called because the player who failed was originally required to draw a peg out of the ground with his teeth. Also **mum′ble-peg′, mum·ble·ty-peg** (mum′bəl·tē·peg′). [< MUMBLE, *v.* (def. 2) + PEG]

mum·bo jum·bo (mum′bō jum′bō) **1** Any object of superstitious homage; a fetish. **2** Incantation. [< MUMBO JUMBO]

Mum·bo Jum·bo (mum′bō jum′bō) Among certain tribes of the western Sudan, a village god or presiding genius, who protects the village from evil and terrifies the women and keeps them in subjection. [< Mandingo *mama dyambo*]

mu·mes·on (myo͞o′mes′on, -mē′son) *n. Physics.* A muon. [< MU + MESON]

mum·mer (mum′ər) *n.* **1** One who acts or makes sport in a mask. **2** An actor.

mum·mer·y (mum′ər·ē) *n. pl.* **·mer·ies 1** A masked performance. **2** Hypocritical parade of ritual. [< MF *mommerie* dumb show]

mum·mi·fy (mum′ə·fī) *v.* **·fied, ·fy·ing** *v.t.* To make a mummy of; preserve by drying. —*v.i.* To dry up; shrivel. Also *mummy.* [< F *momifier*] —**mum′mi·fi·ca′tion** *n.*

mum·my (mum′ē) *n. pl.* **·mies 1** A body embalmed in the ancient Egyptian manner; also, any dead body which is very well preserved. **2** A person or thing that is dried up and withered. **3** *Obs.* The dried flesh of mummies; dead meat. —*v.t.* & *v.i.* **·mied, ·my·ing** To mummify. [< F *momie* < Med. L *mumia* < Arabic *mūmiyā* < Persian *mūm* wax] —**mum′mi·form** *adj.*

mummy cloth 1 The fabric in which a mummy is enwrapped. **2** A crêpelike fabric of cotton, silk, rayon, or wool.

mump·ish (mum′pish) *adj.* Sullen; sulky; morose; petulant. [< obs. *mump* mutter, ? < Du. *mompelen* mumble]

mumps (mumps) *n. pl. (construed as singular) Pathol.* An acute, contagious, febrile disease of viral origin, characterized by inflammation and swelling of the facial glands, and occasionally of the ovaries and testicles: also called *parotitis.* [Pl. of obs. *mump* grimace]

mun[1] (mun) *n. Brit. Dial.* Man.

mun[2] (mun, mo͞on) *v. Scot.* & *Brit. Dial.* Must.

Mu·na (mo͞o′nə) An Indonesian island SE of Celebes; 659 square miles. *Dutch* **Moe·na** (mo͞o′nə).

munch (munch) *v.t.* & *v.i.* To chew steadily and noisily. [ME *monchen, manchen.* Prob. ult. imit.] —**munch′er** *n.*

Mun·chau·sen (mun·chô′zən, mun′chou′zən), **Baron,** 1720–97, Hanoverian nobleman, whose extravagant stories of his exploits formed the basis of the *Tales of Munchausen,* collected by Rudolf Erich Raspe. Also **Münch·hau·sen** (münkh′hou′zən). —**Mun·chau′sen·ism** *n.*

Mün·chen-Glad·bach (mün′khən gläd′bäkh) A city in central western North Rhine-Westphalia, West Germany; the twin city of Rheydt.

Mun·cie (mun′sē) A city in central Indiana.

Mun·da (mo͞on′də) *n.* A subfamily of the Austro-Asiatic family of languages, spoken in central India and along the southern slope of the Himalayas.

mun·dane (mun′dān, mun·dān′) *adj.* Pertaining to the world; worldly. [< F *mondain* < L *mundanus* < *mundus* world] —**mun′dane·ly** *adv.* —**mun′dane·ness** *n.*

Mun·de·lein (mun′də·līn), **George William,** 1872–1939, U.S. cardinal.

mun·dic (mun′dik) *n. Brit. Dial.* Pyrite. [? < Celtic (Cornish) *maen tag* pretty stone]

mun·dun·go (mun·dung′gō) *n. Archaic* A black malodorous tobacco. Also **mun·dun′gus.** [Jocular alter. of Sp. *mondongo* tripe]

mun·go (mung′gō) *n.* The waste produced from hard-spun or felted cloth. Compare SHODDY. [? < *mung,* var. of obs. *mong* mixture]

mun·goose (mung′go͞os) See MONGOOSE.

Mu·nich (myo͞o′nik) A city on the Isar, capital of Bavaria, SE West Germany. *German* **Mün·chen** (mün′khən).

mu·nic·i·pal (myo͞o·nis′ə·pəl) *adj.* **1** Pertaining to a town or city or its local government; also, having local self-government. **2** Pertaining to the internal government of a state or nation. [< L *municipalis* < *municipium* town possessing right of self-government < *municeps* free citizens < *munia* official duties + *capere* take] —**mu·nic′i·pal·ly** *adv.*

municipal borough See under BOROUGH.

municipal corporation An incorporated town.

mu·nic·i·pal·ism (myo͞o·nis′ə·pəl·iz′əm) *n.* Municipal government as opposed to central government; also, the theory of this.—**mu·nic′i·pal·ist** *n.*

mu·nic·i·pal·i·ty (myo͞o·nis′ə·pal′ə·tē) *n. pl.* **·ties 1** An incorporated borough, town, or city. **2** In Cuba and some other Latin-American countries, an administrative area somewhat like a county. [< F *municipalité*]

mu·nic·i·pal·ize (myo͞o·nis′ə·pəl·īz) *v.t.* **·ized, ·iz·ing 1** To place within municipal authority or transfer to municipal ownership. **2** To make a municipality of. —**mu·nic′i·pal′i·za′·tion** *n.*

municipal ownership Ownership by a municipality: said especially of public services, as electricity, waterworks, etc.

mu·nif·i·cent (myo͞o·nif′ə·sənt) *adj.* Extraordinarily generous or bountiful; liberal. See synonyms under GENEROUS. [< L *munificens, -entis* < *munificus* < *munus* gift + *facere* make] —**mu·nif′i·cence, mu·nif′i·cen·cy** *n.* —**mu·nif′i·cent·ly** *adv.*

mu·ni·ment (myo͞o′nə·mənt) *n.* **1** That which supports or defends. **2** *Law* Any deed, record, or instrument by which title to property may be defended or evidenced: usually in the plural. **3** Any means of defending. [< OF < L *munimentum* fortification, support < *munire* fortify]

mu·ni·tion (myo͞o·nish′ən) *n.* **1** Ammunition and all necessary war materiel: usually in the plural. **2** The requisites for any undertaking. **3** *Obs.* A fort; stronghold. —*v.t.* To furnish with munitions. [< F < L *munitio, -onis* < *munire* fortify]

mun·nion (mun′yən) *n.* A mullion.

Mun·ro (mun·rō′), **Hector Hugh** See SAKI.

Mun·sell color system (mun·sel′) A system for the classification and identification of colors by means of reference to the three standard factors of hue, chroma (saturation), and value (lightness). [after Albert H. *Munsell,* 1858–1918, U.S. artist]

Mun·sey (mun′sē), **Frank Andrews,** 1854–1925, U.S. publisher.

Mun·ster (mun′stər) A province in southern Ireland; 9,317 square miles.

Mün·ster (mün′stər) A city in northern North Rhine-Westphalia, western West Germany. Also **Münster-in-West·fa·len** (-ēn·vest·fä′lən).

Mün·ster·berg (mün′stər·berkh), **Hugo,** 1863–1916, U.S. philosopher and psychologist born in Germany.

munt (munt) *v.t.* & *v.i. Scot.* To mount.

Mun·te·ni·a (mun·tē′nē·ə, *Rumanian* mo͞on·tä′nyä) The eastern region of Walachia, Rumania; 20,070 square miles: also *Greater Walachia.*

Mun·the (mun′te), **Axel,** 1857–1949, Swedish physician and writer.

munt·jac (munt′jak) *n.* Any of various small, short-legged deer (genus *Muntiacus*) of east Asia, the males having short, two-pronged horns on long pedicles; especially, *M. muntjak* of Java. Also **munt′iak.** [< Javanese *mĕnjaṅan*]

mu·on (myo͞o′on) *n. Physics* An unstable subatomic particle bearing an electric charge and having a mass approximately 210 times that of an electron.

Muo·nio (mwô′nyô) A river rising in Lapland near the meeting point of the Norwegian, Swedish, and Finnish borders and flowing 180 miles SE and south along the Swedish-Finnish border, to its confluence with the Torne.

Mur (mo͝or) A river in Austria, Hungary, and Yugoslavia, flowing 300 miles east to the Drava. *Hungarian* **Mu·ra** (mo͞o′rä).

mu·rae·na (myo͞o·rē′nə) *n.* An eel; moray. [< L *muraena,* a fish < Gk. *myraina* sea eel, lamprey]

mu·ral (myo͝or′əl) *adj.* **1** Pertaining to or supported by a wall. **2** Resembling a wall. —*n.* A painting or decoration on a wall. [< L *muralis* < *murus* wall]

mu·ral·ist (myo͝or′əl·ist) *n.* A painter of murals.

Mu·ra·sa·ki (mo͞o·rä·sä·kē), **Lady,** Japanese novelist and poet of the eleventh century.

Mu·rat (mo͞o·rät′) A river in east central Turkey, flowing 380 miles west to the Euphrates. Also **Mu·rad** (-räd′).

Mu·rat (mü·rȧ′), **Joachim,** 1771–1815, French general; marshal of France 1804; king of Naples 1808–15; brother-in-law of Napoleon.

Mur·chi·son Falls (mûr′chə·sən) A series of three waterfalls in the lower Victoria Nile; 400 feet high.

Mur·chi·son River (mûr′chə·sən) A river in Western Australia, flowing 440 miles SW to the Indian Ocean.

Mur·cia (mûr′shə, mo͝or′-; *Sp.* mo͞or′thyä) **1** A region and former kingdom of southern Spain; 10,108 square miles. **2** Its former capital, a city in SE Spain.

mur·der (mûr′dər) *v.t.* **1** To kill (a human being) with premeditated malice. **2** To kill in a barbarous or inhuman manner; slaughter. **3** To spoil by bad performance, etc.; mangle; butcher. See synonyms under KILL. —*n.* The unlawful and intentional killing of one human being by another. —**murder will out** Murder cannot be concealed. [Fusion of OE *morthor* + OF *murdre,* both < Gmc.] —**mur′der·er** *n.* —**mur′der·ess** *n. fem.*

mur·der·ous (mûr′dər·əs) *adj.* **1** Pertaining to murder; destructive. **2** Given to murder. **3** Characterized by murder. See synonyms under SANGUINARY. —**mur′der·ous·ly** *adv.* —**mur′·der·ous·ness** *n.*

mure (myo͝or) *v.t.* **mured, mur·ing** To immure; confine. —*n. Obs.* A wall. [< F *murer,* ult. < L *murus* wall]

Mu·res (mo͞o′resh) A river of NW Rumania and SE Hungary, flowing 550 miles from the Carpathians to the Tisza: Hungarian *Maros.* Also **Mu′resh.**

mu·rex (myo͝or′eks) *n. pl.* **mu·ri·ces** (myo͝or′ə·sēz) or **·rex·es** A rough-shelled marine gastropod (genus *Murex*) of warm seas, especially *M. trunculus* and *M. brandaris,* from whose large mucus gland a purple dye was obtained in ancient times. [< L, purple fish]

mu·rex·ide (myo͞o·rek′sīd) *n. Chem.* The ammonium hydrogen salt, $C_8H_8O_6N_6 \cdot H_2O$, of purpuric acid: formerly used to produce pink, purple, or red dyes, now displaced by aniline colors. [< MUREX + -IDE]

Mur·free (mûr′frē), **Mary Noailles** See CRADDOCK.

Mur·frees·bor·o (mûr′frēz·bûr′ō) A city in central Tennessee; site of the Civil War battle of Stones River, December 31, 1862, and January 2, 1863.

mur·geon (mûr′jən) *n. Scot.* A smirk; a grimace.

mu·ri·ate (myŏŏr′ē·āt) Former name for CHLORIDE.
mu·ri·at·ed (myŏŏr′ē·ā′tid) *adj.* 1 Salted; pickled. 2 *Archaic* Treated with or containing a chloride or hydrochloric acid.
mu·ri·at·ic (myŏŏr′ē·at′ik) *adj.* Hydrochloric. [<L *muriaticus* pickled < *muria* brine]
mu·ri·cate (myŏŏr′ə·kit) *adj. Biol.* Rough, with short, hard, tubercular excrescences. [<L *muricatus* murex-shaped, pointed < *murex*]
Mu·ri·el (myŏŏr′ē·əl) A feminine personal name. [<Gk., myrrh]
mu·ri·form (myŏŏr′ə·fôrm) *adj. Bot.* Regularly arranged like bricks in a wall: said of cells in plants. Also **mu′rine** (-ēn). [<L *murus* wall + -FORM]
Mu·ril·lo (myŏŏ·ril′ō, *Sp.* mōō·rē′lyō), **Bartolomé Esteban,** 1618–82, Spanish painter.
mu·rine (myŏŏr′īn, -in) *adj.* Of or pertaining to a family *(Muridae)* or a subfamily *(Murinae)* of rodents, embracing true mice and rats. — *n.* One of the *Murinae* or *Muridae.* [<L *murinus* < *mus, muris* a mouse]
murk (mûrk) *adj.* Murky; dark. — *n.* Darkness; gloom. Also spelled *mirk.* [<ON *myrkr* darkness] — **murk′ly** *adv.*
murk·y (mûr′kē) *adj.* **murk·i·er, murk·i·est** Darkened, thickened, or obscured; hazy; gloomy; obscure: also spelled *mirky.* See synonyms under DARK. — **murk′i·ly** *adv.* — **murk′i·ness** *n.*
Mur·man Coast (mŏŏr·män′) The Arctic coast of the Kola Peninsula in NW U.S.S.R.: also *Norman Coast.*
Mur·mansk (mŏŏr·mänsk′) A port of the western Murman Coast; world's largest city north of the Arctic Circle.
mur·mur (mûr′mər) *n.* 1 A low sound continually repeated. 2 A complaint uttered in a half-articulate voice. 3 An abnormal, rasping sound heard in certain morbid conditions: a *heart* murmur. — *v.i.* 1 To make a murmur. 2 To complain in a low tone; mutter. — *v.t.* 3 To utter in a low tone. See synonyms under BABBLE, COMPLAIN. [<OF <L] — **mur′mur·er** *n.* — **mur′mur·ing** *adj.* — **mur′mur·ing·ly** *adv.*
mur·mur·ous (mûr′mər·əs) *adj.* Characterized or accompanied by murmurs. — **mur′mur·ous·ly** *adv.* — **mur′mur·ous·ness** *n.*
Mu·ro·ran (mōō·rō·rän) A port on SW Hokkaido island, Japan.
mur·phy (mûr′fē) *n. pl.* **·phies** *Slang* A potato. [from an Irish surname]
Mur·phy (mûr′fē), **Frank,** 1890–1949, U. S. jurist, associate justice of the Supreme Court 1940–49. — **William Parry,** born 1892, U. S. physician.
mur·ra (mûr′ə) *n. Latin* A material of ancient Rome which has been variously supposed to be Chinese jade, porcelain, iridescent glass, or artificially colored chalcedony. Also **mur′rha.**
mur·rain (mûr′in) *n.* 1 A malignant contagious fever affecting domestic animals, as anthrax. 2 Any plague or pestilence. See RINDERPEST. — *adj.* Affected with murrain. [<OF *morine* <L *mori* die]
Mur·ray (mûr′ē), **Gilbert,** 1866–1957, English classical scholar. — **Sir James Augustus Henry,** 1837–1915, Scottish philologist and lexicographer. — **John,** 1778–1843, English publisher; first published works of Byron, Jane Austen, etc. — **Lindley,** 1745–1826, U. S. grammarian. — **Philip,** 1866–1952, U. S. labor leader. — **William,** 1705–93, Earl of Mansfield; English jurist.
Murray River The principal river of Australia, forming part of the boundary between Victoria and New South Wales and flowing 1,600 miles to the Indian Ocean.
murre (mûr) *n. pl.* **murres** or **murre** 1 The foolish guillemot. 2 The razor-billed auk. Also **murr.** [Origin uncertain]
murre·let (mûr′lit) *n.* Any of certain small sea birds (family *Alcidae*) of the islands of the North Pacific. [Dim. of MURRE]
mur·rey (mûr′ē) *adj.* Of a purplish-red or mulberry color. — *n.* 1 *Her.* The tincture sanguine. 2 A dark purplish red. [<OF *moree* <L *morum* mulberry]
mur·rine (mûr′in, -īn) *adj.* Of, pertaining to, or consisting of murra. Also **mur′rhine.** [<L *murrinus*]
murrine glass Glassware having a transparent ground with embedded flowers, ribbons, etc., of colored glass.
Mur·rum·bid·gee (mûr′əm·bij′ē) A river in New South Wales, Australia, rising in the Great Dividing Range and flowing 1,050 miles north to the Murray River.
mur·ry (mûr′ē) See MORAY.
Mur·vie·dro (mŏŏr·vyā′thrō) A former name for SAGUNTO.
mu·sa·ceous (myōō·zā′shəs) *adj.* Pertaining to or designating a family *(Musaceae)* of monocotyledonous plants including the common banana, proceeding from rootstocks, with stems composed of sheathing leafstalks and flowers bursting through spathes. [<NL *Musaceae* < *Musa,* genus name < Arabic *mawzah* banana]
Mus Al·lah (mōōs′ ä·lä′) See STALIN PEAK (def. 3).
mus·ca (mus′kə) *n. pl.* **mus·cae** (mus′sē) A fly; any of a genus *(Musca)* of dipterous insects of the family *Muscidae,* including the housefly. [<L, fly] — **mus·cid** (mus′id) *adj.* & *n.*
Mus·ca (mus′kə) A southern constellation, the Fly. See CONSTELLATION. [<NL]
mus·ca·dine (mus′kə·din, -dīn) *n.* The fox grape or scuppernong *(Vitis* or *Muscadinia rotundifolia)* of the southern United States. [<Provençal *muscade,* fem. of *muscat.* See MUSCAT.]
mus·cae vol·i·tan·tes (mus′sē vol′ə·tan′tēz) Minute specks or motes apparently moving before the eye, caused by defects or impurities in the vitreous humor of the eye, etc. [<L, flying flies]
mus·ca·rine (mus′kə·rēn, -rin) *n. Chem.* A deliquescent, extremely poisonous, white, crystalline alkaloid, $C_8H_{13}O_3N$, found in certain fungi, as the fly agaric, and in putrefying fish. [<NL *muscarius* of flies <L *musca* fly]
mus·cat (mus′kat, -kət) *n.* 1 One of several varieties of musk-flavored Old World grapes. 2 A sweet, white wine made from such grapes. [<F <Provençal <Ital. *moscato* <LL *muscus* musk]
Mus·cat (mus·kat′) A port on the Gulf of Oman, capital of Muscat and Oman: also *Masqat.*
Muscat and Oman An independent sultanate of SE Arabia on the Gulf of Oman; 82,000 square miles; capital, Muscat: also *Oman.*
mus·ca·tel (mus′kə·tel′) *n.* 1 A rich, sweet wine made from the muscat grape. 2 The muscat grape: also spelled *moscatel.* Also **mus′ca·del′** (-del′). [<OF, dim. of *muscat.* See MUSCAT.]
mus·cle (mus′əl) *n.* 1 *Anat.* An organ composed of tissue arranged in bundles of fibers, by whose contraction bodily movements are effected. Two principal types are known: *striated* (striped), involved in voluntary movements, and *smooth* (unstriped), acting independently of the will. The heart muscle belongs anatomically between the two. 2 The tissue of the muscular organs. 3 Muscular strength. — *v.i.* **·cled, ·cling** To push in or ahead by sheer physical strength. ◆ Homophone: *mussel.* [<F <L *musculus,* lit., little mouse, dim. of *mus.* Doublet of MUSSEL.]
mus·cle-bound (mus′əl·bound′) *adj.* Affected with a form of muscular hypertrophy characterized by lack of elasticity in a muscle: caused by excessive exercise in training.
mus·cled (mus′əld) *adj.* Having or supplied with muscles.
muscle fiber *Physiol.* A muscle cell consisting of a soft contractile substance enclosed in a tubular sheath.
muscle plasma *Physiol.* The liquid that can be expressed from muscle tissue: it clots spontaneously and is sometimes injected intravenously as a restorative and stimulant.
muscle sense *Physiol.* The perception of muscular movement derived from the functioning of afferent nerves connected with muscle tissue, skin, joints, and tendons.
Muscle Shoals Rapids in the Tennessee River, NW Alabama; site of the Wilson Dam.
muscle spindle *Anat.* One of various groups of muscle fibers enclosed in a sheath of connective tissue and terminating in sensory organs.
muscle sugar Inositol.
mus·coid (mus′koid) *adj.* Mosslike. — *n.* A mosslike plant. [<L *muscus* moss + -OID]
mus·co·va·do (mus′kə·vā′dō) *n.* A raw brown sugar obtained by evaporating the juice of sugarcane and draining off the molasses. Also **mus′ca·va′da** (-də), **mus′co·vade** (-vād). [<Sp. *mascabado* unrefined, pp. of *mascabar* diminish, var. of *menoscabar* < *menos* (<L *minus*) + *cabo* head (<L *caput*)]
mus·co·vite (mus′kə·vīt) *n.* The most common and important white or potash mica, $KAl_2(OH)_2AlSi_3O_{10}$. [<earlier *Muscovy glass*]
Mus·co·vite (mus′kə·vīt) *n.* An inhabitant of Muscovy or ancient Russia; hence, a Russian. — *adj.* Of or pertaining to Muscovy or to Russia; Russian. — **Mus′co·vit′ic** (-vit′ik) *adj.*
mus·co·vy (mus′kə·vē) *n. pl.* **·vies** A large greenish-black duck *(Cairina moschata)* of America from Mexico to Brazil, now widely domesticated. Also **muscovy duck.** [Alter. of MUSK DUCK]
Mus·co·vy (mus′kə·vē) *Archaic* Russia.
mus·cu·lar (mus′kyə·lər) *adj.* 1 Pertaining to or depending upon muscles. 2 Possessing strong muscles; powerful. 3 Accomplished by muscle or muscles. — **mus′cu·lar′i·ty** (-lar′ə·tē) *n.* — **mus′cu·lar·ly** *adv.*
muscular dystrophy *Pathol.* One of various diseases of undetermined cause, characterized by wasting of muscles and often terminating in physical helplessness.
mus·cu·la·ture (mus′kyə·lə·chŏŏr) *n.* 1 The disposition or arrangement of muscles in a part or organ. 2 The muscle system as a whole. Also **mus′cu·la′tion.** [<F]
muse[1] (myōōz) *n.* Something regarded as the source of artistic inspiration; the inspiring power of a poet or of poetry. [<MUSE]
muse[2] (myōōz) *v.t.* & *v.i.* **mused, mus·ing** To consider thoughtfully or at length; ponder; meditate. — *n.* 1 The act or state of musing; reverie. 2 Wonder. [<OF *muser*] — **mus′er** *n.* — **muse′ful** *adj.*
Synonyms (verb): brood, cogitate, consider, contemplate, deliberate, dream, meditate, ponder, reflect, ruminate, stew, study, think. Compare REFLECTION.

THE MUSES—FROM A SARCOPHAGUS IN THE LOUVRE, PARIS

A. Clio. *B.* Thalia. *C.* Erato. *D.* Euterpe. *E.* Polyhymnia. *F.* Calliope. *G.* Terpsichore. *H.* Urania. *I.* Melpomene.

Muse (myōōz) In Greek mythology, any of the nine goddesses presiding over poetry, the arts, sciences, etc.: Calliope, Clio, Erato,

Euterpe, Melpomene, Polyhymnia, Terpsichore, Thalia, and Urania. [<F <L *Musa* <Gk. *Mousa* a Muse, eloquence, music]

mu·sette (myo͞o·zet′) *n.* **1** Any melody of soft, pastoral character written in imitation of bagpipe airs. **2** A small bagpipe formerly popular in France. **3** A variety of small oboe. **4** A small leather or canvas knapsack or wallet, used especially by soldiers, and carried by a strap worn over the shoulder: also **musette bag.** [<F, dim. of *muse* a bagpipe]

mu·se·um (myo͞o·zē′əm) *n.* **1** A place preserving and exhibiting works of nature, art, curiosities, etc.; also, any collection of such objects. **2** Any place where curiosities, freaks, monstrosities, etc., are exhibited. [<L <Gk. *mouseion* temple of the Muses < *Mousa*]

mush[1] (mush) *n.* **1** Thick porridge, made by boiling meal or flour in water or milk. **2** Anything soft and pulpy. **3** *Colloq.* Sentimentality. [Var. of MASH]

mush[2] (mush) *v.i.* In Alaska and the Canadian Arctic, to travel on foot, especially over snow with a dog sled. —*interj.* Get along! a call of the drivers of a dog team. [Prob. <*mush on,* alter. of F (Canadian) *marchons,* the cry of voyageurs and trappers to their dogs] —**mush′er** *n.*

mush·mel·on (mush′·mel′ən) See MUSKMELON.

mush·room (mush′·ro͝om, -ro͞om) *n.* **1** A large, rapidly growing fungus of the order *Agaricales,* consisting of an erect stalk and a caplike expansion: certain poisonous varieties are called *toadstools,* but the distinction is not scientifically correct. The best-known edible mushrooms are of the genus *Agaricus,* especially the **field mushroom,** *A. campestris.* **2** An object or excrescence of similar shape. —*v.i.* **1** To grow or spread rapidly, like a mushroom: The town *mushroomed* overnight. **2** To expand at one end into a mushroomlike shape: said of bullets. —*adj.* **1** Pertaining to or made of mushrooms. **2** Sudden in growth and rapid in decay; ephemeral; upstart. [<OF *mouscheron* < *mousse* moss]

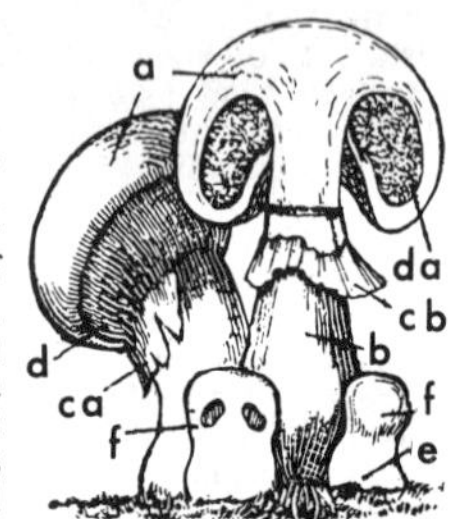

AGARIC MUSHROOM
a. Pileus, entire and cut.
b. Stipe in velum.
ca. Ruptured velum.
d. Gills.
cb. Velum forming ring.
da. Cross-section of gill.
e. Mycelium.
f.f. Young mushrooms.

mush·y (mush′ē) *adj.* **mush·i·er, mush·i·est** **1** Soft; pulpy. **2** *Colloq.* Sentimental; romantic. —**mush′i·ly** *adv.* —**mush′i·ness** *n.*

mu·sic (myo͞o′zik) *n.* **1** The science and art of the rhythmic combination of tones, vocal or instrumental, embracing melody and harmony. **2** A composition, or mass of compositions, conceived or executed according to musical rule or spirit. **3** Any rhythmic succession or combination of sounds, especially if pleasing to the ear; also, the sensations or emotions thus produced. **4** A band of musicians; an orchestra. See synonyms under MELODY. —**absolute music** Pure or abstract music wholly self-sufficient without representation or dependence on title, program, etc.: opposed to the pictorial or descriptive **program music.** —**to face the music** To take the consequences courageously and without complaint; accept facts. [<F *musique* <L *musica* <Gk. *mousikē* (*technē*) musical (art) < *Mousa* a Muse]

mu·si·cal (myo͞o′zi·kəl) *adj.* **1** Pertaining to music. **2** Capable of producing or appreciating music; fond of music. **3** Melodious. —*n.* **1** A musical comedy. **2** *Colloq.* A musicale. —**mu′si·cal·ly** *adv.* —**mu′si·cal·ness** *n.*

musical chairs A marching game played to music, in which the contestants circle around a row of opposite-facing chairs, one less than the number of players. When the music stops, each marcher rushes for a chair, one person for whom there is no chair being eliminated. On each round, a chair is removed until finally only one remains, the contestant reaching it first being declared the winner. Also called "Going to Jerusalem."

musical comedy A kind of theatrical performance, characterized by music, songs, dances, jokes, and elaborate costumes, staging, and settings, usually based on a tenuous plot: also *musical.*

mu·si·cale (myo͞o′zə·kal′, *Fr.* mü·zē·kȧl′) *n.* An informal concert or private recital: also *musical.* [<F]

music box A case containing a mechanism that reproduces melodies.

music hall **1** A public hall or building devoted to musical entertainments. **2** *Brit.* A vaudeville house.

music house A firm that publishes music.

mu·si·cian (myo͞o·zish′ən) *n.* One skilled in music; especially, a professional performer. [<OF *musicien*]

mu·si·cian·ly (myo͞o·zish′ən·lē) *adj.* Exhibiting musical taste, learning, or skill.

music of the spheres The harmony produced by the movements of the celestial spheres: a conception of Pythagorean philosophy.

mu·si·col·o·gist (myo͞o′zə·kol′ə·jist) *n.* One engaged in or versed in musicology.

mu·si·col·o·gy (myo͞o′zə·kol′ə·jē) *n.* The scientific and historical study of music as an art and as a craft.

music stand **1** A rack to hold sheet music for a performer. **2** A bandstand.

mus·ing (myo͞o′zing) *adj.* Thoughtful; dreamy; preoccupied. —**mus′ing·ly** *adv.*

musk (musk) *n.* **1** A soft, reddish-brown, powdery secretion of a penetrating odor, obtained from the preputial follicles or **musk bag** of the male musk deer. It is used by perfumers and in medicine. **2** A similar substance from some other animals, as the muskrat or civet. **3** *Chem.* Any of several organic compounds used to replace natural musk. **4** Muskroot. **5** The odor of musk. [<OF *musc* <LL *muscus* <Gk. *moschos* <Persian *mushk* (prob. akin to Skt. *mushka* testicle, dim. of *mus* a mouse)]

musk beaver The muskrat.

musk beetle A large European beetle (*Aromia moschata*) of a bronze-green color, and having a musky odor suggesting roses.

musk cat **1** A civet. **2** *Obs.* A perfumed, effeminate man; a dandy.

musk deer A small hornless deer (*Moschus moschiferus*) of central and eastern Asia, of which the male has a musk-secreting gland.

MUSK DEER
(From 17 to 20 inches high; color brown speckled with gray or buff)

musk duck **1** A muscovy. **2** An Australian duck (*Biziura lobata*), with a disklike appendage on the chin, and having a musky odor in the breeding season: also called *mould goose.*

mus·keg (mus′keg) *n.* **1** A rocky basin filled by successive deposits of unstable material, as leaves, muck, and moss, incapable of sustaining much weight. **2** A swamp. Also spelled *maskeg.* [<Chippewa *muskig* grassy bog]

muskeg moss An absorbent, sterilized swamp moss (genus *Sphagnum*) used as a surgical dressing.

mus·kel·lunge (mus′kə·lunj) *n. pl.* **·lunge** *n.* A large North American pike (*Esox masquinongy*), valued as a game fish: also spelled *mascalonge, maskinonge.* [<Algonquian *maskinonge* < *mas* great + *kinonge* pike]

mus·ket (mus′kit) *n.* A smoothbore military hand gun; specifically, a hand gun for infantry, now superseded by the rifle. [<OF *mosquet* gun, hawk <Ital. *moschetto* hawk <L *musca* fly]

mus·ket·eer (mus′kə·tir′) *n.* A soldier armed with a musket; hence, a foot soldier. [<F *mousquetaire*]

mus·ket·ry (mus′kit·rē) *n.* **1** Muskets collectively. **2** The science of the operation of small arms.

Mus·kho·ge·an (mus·kō′gē·ən, mus′kō·gē′ən) *n.* One of the principal North American Indian linguistic stocks, well advanced in culture, including the Chickasaw, Choctaw, Creek, and Seminole tribes, formerly inhabiting the Gulf region of the SE United States. Also **Mus·ko·gi·an** (mus·kō′gē·ən).

mus·kit (mus·kēt′) See MESQUITE.

musk·mel·on (musk′mel′ən) *n.* **1** The juicy, edible, gourdlike fruit of a trailing herb (*Cucumis melo*) of the melon family; cantaloup. **2** The plant bearing this fruit. Also, *Colloq., mushmelon.*

musk ox A shaggy, hollow-horned ruminant (*Ovibos moschatus*) combining the characteristics of the sheep and ox and emitting a strong odor of musk: now restricted to Greenland and the North American continent.

MUSK OX
(About 4 feet high at the shoulder)

musk·rat (musk′rat′) *n. pl.* **·rats** or **·rat** A North American aquatic rodent (*Ondatra zibethica*) yielding a valuable fur and secreting a substance with a musky odor: sometimes called *musquash.*

MUSKRAT
(About 22 inches over-all in length)

musk·root (musk′ro͞ot′, -ro͝ot′) *n.* The musky, spongy root of a plant (*Ferula sumbul*) of the parsley family, from Russian Turkestan: employed medicinally as a stimulant and anti-spasmodic. Also called *sumbul.*

musk rose A cultivated climbing rose (*Rosa moschata*) from Europe, with large white flowers in panicled clusters.

musk turtle A small turtle (*Sternotherus odoratus*) of the eastern United States and Canada, distinguished by bright-yellow lines on each side of the head.

musk·y (mus′kē) *adj.* **musk·i·er, musk·i·est** Like musk; smelling of musk. —**musk′i·ly** *adv.* —**musk′i·ness** *n.*

Mus·lim (muz′lim, mo͝oz′-, mo͞os′-) *n. pl.* **·lims** or **·lim** A believer in Islam; Mohammedan. —*adj.* Of or pertaining to Islam or the Muslims. Also called *Moslem*: also **Mus′lem.** [< Arabic, one who submits < *aslama* surrender (to God)] —**Mus′lim·ism** *n.*

mus·lin (muz′lin) *n.* Any of several varieties of plain-weave cotton cloth ranging from thin batiste and nainsook to heavy sheetings such as longcloth and percale. [<F *mousseline* <Ital. *mussolino,* dim. of *mussolo* muslin < *Mussolo* Mosul, city in Iraq where made.

mus·lin-kail (muz′lin·kāl′) *n. Scot.* A thin broth containing greens and shelled barley.

mus·quash (mus′kwosh) *n.* The muskrat. [<N. Am. Ind., it is red]

mus·qui·to (mus·kē′tō) See MOSQUITO.

muss (mus) *v.t. U.S. Colloq.* To make messy or untidy; rumple; crumple: often with *up.* —*n. Colloq.* **1** A state of disorder or disturbance; mess. **2** Confused struggle or tumult; squabble. [Alter. of MESS]

mus·sel (mus′əl) *n.* **1** A small bivalve mollusk, especially the common edible mussel (*Mytilus edulis*). **2** One of several other fresh-water mollusks, of the genera *Anodonta, Unio,* and others, whose shells are made into buttons, etc. ◆ Homophone: *muscle.* [OE *musle* <L *musculus,* dim. of *mus* mouse. Doublet of MUSCLE.]

Mus·sel·shell River (mus′əl·shel) A river in central Montana, flowing 292 miles NE to the Missouri.

Mus·set (mü·se′), **(Louis Charles) Alfred de,** 1810–57, French poet, dramatist, and novelist.

Mus·so·li·ni (mo͞os′ə·lē′nē, *Ital.* mo͞os′sō·lē′nē), **Benito,** 1883–1945, Italian Fascist leader; premier 1922–43; executed: called "Il Duce" (the leader).

Mus·sul·man (mus′əl·mən) *n. pl.* **·mans** (-mənz) or **·men** (-mən) A Muslim; Mohammedan. —*adj.* Belonging or relating to the Moslems. [<Persian & Turkish *musulmān* <Arabic *muslimūn,* pl. of *muslim*]

muss·y (mus′ē) *U.S. Colloq. adj.* **muss·i·er, muss·i·est** Disarranged; rumpled; slightly soiled. —**muss′i·ly** *adv.* —**muss′i·ness** *n.*

must[1] (must) *v.* A defective verb now used only as an auxiliary followed by the infinitive without *to,* or elliptically with the infinitive understood, to express: **1** Obligation or compulsion: *Must* you go? I *must.* **2** Requirement: You *must* be healthy to be accepted. **3** Probability or supposition: You *must* be tired. **4** Conviction or certainty: War *must* follow. ◆ A past conditional is formed by placing the following verb in the perfect infinitive: *He must have gone.* —*n.* **1** Anything that is required or vital. **2** A news item or other material that must be printed: usually marked *must.* —*adj.* Important and essential: a *must* book. [OE *moste,* pt. of *mōtan* may]

must[2] (must) *n.* Mustiness; mold. —*v.t.* & *v.i. Obs.* To make or become musty. [Back formation < MUSTY[1]]

must[3] (must) *n.* **1** The expressed unfermented juice of the grape. **2** Unfermented potato pulp. [OE < L *mustum (vinum)* new wine]

must[4] (must) *n.* **1** A state of dangerous frenzy, related to sexual excitement, associated with adult male animals, especially elephants. **2** An elephant in this condition. —*adj.* Being in a state of must. Also spelled *musth.* [< Hind. *mast* drunk, lustful]

must[5] (must) *n. Scot.* Musk, especially in the form of hair powder.

mus·tache (məs·tash′, mus′tash) *n.* **1** The growth of hair on the upper lip of men: occasionally used in the plural, in reference to its two parts. **2** The hair or bristles growing near the mouth of an animal. **3** An old soldier: a brave old *mustache*: a gallicism. Also **mus·ta′chio** (-tä′shō): sometimes spelled *moustache.* [< F *moustache* < Ital. *mostaccio* face < Med. L *mustacia* < Gk. *mystax* upper lip < *mastax* mouth, jaws] — **mus·tached** (məs·tasht′) *adj.*

Mus·ta·fa (mōōs′tä·fä), **Kemal Pasha** See KEMAL.

Mus·tagh (mōōs·tä′) See KARAKORAM.

mus·tang (mus′tang) *n.* **1** The wild horse of the American plains. **2** One of these horses broken to the saddle; a cow pony. [< Sp. *mesteño,* obs. *mestengo,* lit., belonging to a cattlemen's association, wild < *mesta* association, group < L *mixtus,* pp. of *miscere* mix]

mustang grape A vine *(Vitis candicans)* of the SW United States, having light-colored pungent berries or grapes.

mus·tard (mus′tərd) *n.* **1** Either of two species of *Brassica,* **white mustard** *(B. hirta)* and **black mustard** *(B. nigra),* both annual herbs with yellow flowers and pods of roundish seeds. **2** The pungent seed of the mustard, crushed and adapted for use as a condiment or as a medicinal rubefacient and diuretic. **3** A strong, dark-yellow color, the color of ground mustard. [< OF *moustarde* < L *mustum* must[3]; from once having been prepared with must]

mustard gas *Chem.* An oily amber liquid, dichlorethyl sulfide, $C_4H_8Cl_2S$, having an odor of mustard or garlic, and used in warfare because of its powerful blistering effect.

mustard oil A fixed oil of unpleasant odor extracted from mustard seeds and used in making soap, as a lubricant, etc.

mustard plaster A plaster of powdered mustard and flour used as a counterirritant and rubefacient.

mus·tee (mus·tē′, mus′tē) See MESTEE.

mus·te·line (mus′tə·lin, -līn) *adj.* Pertaining to a family *(Mustelidae)* of fur-bearing, predacious mammals which includes weasels, skunks, badgers, otters, wolverines, and martens. [< L *mustelinus* < *mustela* weasel]

mus·ter (mus′tər) *v.t.* **1** To summon or assemble (troops, etc.), as for service, review, or roll call. **2** To collect or summon: often with *up*: to *muster* up one's courage. —*v.i.* **3** To come together or assemble, as troops for service, review, etc. **—to muster in** To enrol as military recruits. **—to muster out** To collect or assemble, as troops, for discharge from military service. See synonyms under CONVOKE. —*n.* **1** An assemblage, especially of troops for parade or review. **2** A muster roll. **3** A specimen; pattern; sample. **4** An imposing gathering; array. **—to pass muster** To pass inspection; hence, to be acceptable or accepted. [< OF *mostrer* exhibit < L *monstrare* show]

mus·ter-mas·ter (mus′tər·mas′tər, -mäs′-) *n.* An officer who inspects troops, their equipment, etc.

muster roll The official list or roll of officers and men in a military troop or a ship's crew.

musth (must) See MUST[4].

must·y[1] (mus′tē) *adj.* **must·i·er, must·i·est 1** Having a moldy odor; ill-flavored; fetid; stale. **2** Without life, sparkle, or flavor. **3** Without life or energy; listless; apathetic. See synonyms under TRITE. [? Alter. of earlier *moisty* < MOIST] — **must′i·ly** *adv.* **—must′i·ness** *n.*

must·y[2] (mus′tē) *n.* Formerly, a cheap quality of snuff having a musty flavor.

mu·ta·ble (myōō′tə·bəl) *adj.* Capable of changing; liable to change; hence, fickle; unstable. See synonyms under FICKLE. [< L *mutabilis* < *mutare* change] **—mu′ta·ble·ness, mu′ta·bil′i·ty** *n.* — **mu′ta·bly** *adv.*

mu·ta·gen (myōō′tə·jən) *n.* Any agent that increases the incidence of mutation in germ plasm. [< L *mutare* change + -GEN] **—mu·ta·gen·ic** (myōō′tə·jen′ik) *adj.*

mu·ta·gen·e·sis (myōō′tə·jen′ə·sis) *n.* The initiation of mutation.

Mu·tan·kiang (mōō′dän′jyäng′) A city in eastern Manchuria.

mu·tant (myōō′tənt) *n.* **1** That which admits of or undergoes mutation or change. **2** *Biol.* A plant or animal organism differing from its parents in one or more characteristics that are inheritable; a sport. [< L *mutans, -antis,* ppr. of *mutare* change]

mu·tate (myōō′tāt) *v.t.* & *v.i.* **·tat·ed, ·tat·ing** To undergo or subject to change, especially by mutation. [< L *mutatus,* pp. of *mutare* change] — **mu′ta·tive** *adj.*

mu·ta·tion (myōō·tā′shən) *n.* **1** The act or process of change; alteration; variation. **2** Modification of one vowel by another; umlaut. See UMLAUT. **3** *Biol.* A sudden, well-marked, transmissible variation in the organism of a plant or animal, especially as resulting from new combinations of genes and chromosomes and as distinguishable from cumulative evolutionary changes over a long period. **4** Change; hence, succession and serial succession; consecutive order. See synonyms under CHANGE. [< L *mutatio, -onis*] **—mu·ta′tion·al** *adj.*

mu·ta·tis mu·tan·dis (myōō·tā′tis myōō·tan′dis) *Latin* The necessary changes having been made.

mutch (much) *n. Scot.* A woman's close-fitting cap; also, a man's nightcap; a child's cap.

mutch·kin (much′kin) *n. Scot.* A liquid measure containing three quarters of one imperial pint.

mute (myōōt) *adj.* **1** Uttering no word or sound; silent. **2** *Law* Refusing to plead upon arraignment. **3** Lacking the power of speech; dumb. **4** *Phonet.* Of or pertaining to a stop consonant. See synonyms under TACITURN. —*n.* **1** One who is silent; especially, a person who refuses or is unable to speak; a person who is dumb by reason of deafness or other infirmity: also called *deaf-mute.* **2** An undertaker's assistant. **3** *Law* A prisoner who refuses to plead on arraignment. **4** *Phonet.* A stop consonant, as (b), (p), (t), (d). **5** A device to silence, muffle, or deaden the tone of a musical instrument. —*v.t.* **mut·ed, mut·ing** To deaden or muffle the sound of (a musical instrument). [< L *mutus* dumb] **—mute′ly** *adv.* **—mute′ness** *n.*

mu·ti·cous (myōō′tə·kəs) *adj. Biol.* Without a point; unarmed; defenseless: said especially of certain plants and animals. Also **mu′tic, mu′ti·cate** (-kāt). [< L *muticus,* var. of *mutilus* docked, curtailed. See MUTILATE.]

mu·ti·late (myōō′tə·lāt) *v.t.* **·lat·ed, ·lat·ing 1** To deprive (a person, animal, etc.) of a limb or essential part; maim. **2** To damage or injure by the removal of an important part or parts: to *mutilate* a speech. [< L *mutilatus,* pp. of *mutilare* maim < *mutilus* docked, maimed] **—mu′ti·la′tion** *n.* **—mu′ti·la′tive** *adj.* **—mu′ti·la′tor** *n.*

mu·ti·neer (myōō′tə·nir′) *n.* One who takes part in mutiny: also *Obs.* **mu·tine** (myōō′tin). —*v.i.* To mutiny. [< MF *mutinier* < *mutin.* See MUTINY.]

mu·ti·nous (myōō′tə·nəs) *adj.* Disposed to mutiny; seditious. See synonyms under REBELLIOUS, RESTIVE, TURBULENT. **—mu′ti·nous·ly** *adv.* — **mu′ti·nous·ness** *n.*

mu·ti·ny (myōō′tə·nē) *n. pl.* **·nies 1** Rebellion against constituted authority; insubordination; especially, a revolt of soldiers or sailors against their officers or commander. **2** *Obs.* Tumult; discord; strife. See synonyms under REVOLUTION. —*v.i.* **·nied, ·ny·ing** To revolt against constituted authority, as in the army or navy; take part in a mutiny. [< F *mutiner* rebel < OF *mutin, meutin* riotous < *muete* riot < L *motus,* pp. of *movere*]

mut·ism (myōō′tiz·əm) *n.* **1** Inability or refusal to utter articulate sounds: often associated with certain mental disorders. **2** Muteness. [< F *mutisme*]

Mu·tsu·hi·to (mōō·tsōō·hē·tō), 1852–1912, emperor of Japan 1867–1912.

mutt (mut) *n. Slang* **1** A cur; mongrel dog. **2** A stupid person; blockhead. Also **mut.** [< MUTT(ONHEAD)]

mut·ter (mut′ər) *v.i.* **1** To speak in a low, indistinct tone and with compressed lips, as in complaining or talking to oneself. **2** To complain; grumble. **3** To make a low, rumbling sound. — *v.t.* **4** To say in a low, indistinct tone. —*n.* An imperfect utterance; murmur. [Prob. imit. Cf. dial. G *muttern* and L *muttire.*] **—mut′ter·er** *n.* **—mut′ter·ing** *n.* & *adj.* **—mut′ter·ing·ly** *adv.*

mut·ton (mut′n) *n.* **1** The flesh of sheep as food. **2** Humorously, a sheep. [< F *mouton* < Celtic. Cf. O Irish *molt* ram, Welsh *mollt* Breton *maout.*] **—mut′ton·y** *adj.*

mutton chop 1 A piece of mutton from the rib for broiling or frying. **2** *Printing* An em quad or em rule. **—mut′ton-chop′** (-chop′) *adj.*

mut·ton·chops (mut′n·chops′) *n. pl.* Burnsides or side whiskers shaped like mutton chops.

mut·ton·fish (mut′n·fish′) *n. pl.* **·fish** or **·fish·es 1** The eelpout. **2** An abalone *(Haliotis iris)* said to taste like mutton. **3** The pargo or other snapper found from Florida to Brazil. **4** The mojarra.

mutton ham *Naut.* A small sail shaped like a leg of mutton, used on small fishing boats: also *mutton-leg.*

mut·ton·head (mut′n·hed′) *n. Slang* A stupid, dense person. [< MUTTON (def. 2) + HEAD; from the traditional stupidity of sheep] **—mut′ton·head′ed** (-hed′id) *adj.*

mut·ton-leg (mut′n·leg′) *n.* **1** A woman's dress sleeve, very full at the top: so called because shaped like a leg of mutton. **2** Mutton ham.

Mut·tra (mu′trə) The former name for MATHURA.

mu·tu·al (myōō′chōō·əl) *adj.* **1** Pertaining reciprocally to both of two; reciprocally related or bound; reciprocal in action or effect. **2** Shared or experienced alike; common. [< F *mutuel* < LL *mutualis* < L *mutuus* < *mutare* change] — **mu′tu·al·ly** *adv.* **—mu′tu·al′i·ty** *n.*

Synonyms: common, correlative, interchangeable, joint, reciprocal. That is *common* to which two or more persons have the same or equal claims, or in which they have equal interest or participation; that is *mutual* which is freely interchanged; that is *reciprocal* in respect to which one act or movement is met by a corresponding act or movement in return. *Antonyms*: detached, disconnected, dissociated, distinct, disunited, separate, separated, severed, sundered, unconnected, unreciprocated, unshared.

mutual fund An investment company which provides diversification and professional management for the pooled capital of the investors, paying out to its shareholders as mutual owners virtually all earnings including realized capital gains except for management fees and administrative costs, thus remaining tax free in its own operations. The shares of an **open-end mutual fund** are redeemable at the option of the stockholder at the net asset value of the portfolio calculated daily, and its shares are generally sold continually with a distribution charge on purchase. The shares are not listed on the stock exchange. A **closed-end mutual fund** has fixed capitalization, the shares not being offered or redeemable.

mutual insurance 1 A method of insurance based upon a reciprocal contract whereby various persons engage to indemnify each other against certain designated losses. **2** Popularly, the system of a company in which policyholders receive a certain share of the profits: also **mutual plan.**

mu·tu·al·ism (myōō′chōō·əl·iz′əm) *n. Biol.* Symbiosis advantageous to both or all parties concerned.

mu·tu·al·ize (myōō′chōō·əl·īz) *v.t.* & *v.i.* **·ized, ·iz·ing 1** To make or become mutual. **2** To put (a firm or corporation) on the basis of majority employee or consumer ownership of common stock. **—mu′tu·al·i·za′tion** *n.*

mu·tule (myōō′chōōl) *n. Archit.* One of a series of rectangular blocks under a Doric corona, with dependent droplike ornaments called guttae. [< F < L *mutulus* modillion]

muu·muu (mōō′mōō′) *n.* A long, loose gown for women, originally worn in Hawaii. [< Hawaiian]

mu·zhik (mōō·zhēk′, mōō′zhēk) *n.* A Russian peasant in Czarist times: also spelled *moujik, mujik.* Also **mu·zjik′.** [< Russian]

Muz·zey (muz′ē), **David Saville,** 1870–1965, U.S. historian.

muz·zle (muz′əl) *n.* **1** The projecting snout of an animal. **2** A guard or covering for an animal's snout to prevent biting or eating. **3** The front end of a firearm. *—v.t.* **·zled, ·zling 1** To put a muzzle on. **2** To restrain from speaking, expressing opinions, etc.; gag. [< OF *musel* < Med. L *musellum,* dim. of LL *musus* snout] **—muz′zler** *n.*

muz·zle·load·er (muz′əl·lō′dər) *n.* A firearm loaded through the muzzle. **—muz′zle·load′ing** *adj.*

muzzle velocity The velocity of a bullet or projectile at the instant of leaving the muzzle of a gun.

muz·zy (muz′ē) *adj. Colloq.* Muddled; hence, stupid.

MVD The secret police of Soviet Russia. [< Russian < *M(inisterstvo) V(nutrennikh) D(el)* Ministry of Internal Affairs]

Mwe·ru (mwā′rōō) A lake between SE Belgian Congo and Northern Rhodesia; 173 square miles: French *Moero.*

my (mī) *pronominal adj.* **1** The possessive case of the pronoun *I* employed attributively; belonging or pertaining to me: *my* house. **2** An adjective used in forms of address in customary phrases: *my* lord; also used in expressions of endearment: *my* boy. *—interj.* An exclamation of surprise: oh *my*! [OE *mīn*]

my- Var. of MYO-.

my·al·gi·a (mī·al′jē·ə) *n. Pathol.* Pain in a muscle; cramp. [< NL < MY- + -ALGIA] **—my·al′gic** *adj.*

my·a·sis (mī′ə·sis) See MYIASIS.

my·as·the·ni·a (mī′əs·thē′nē·ə) *n. Pathol.* Muscular debility, accompanied by general and usually progressive exhaustion but without marked sensory disturbance or atrophy. [< NL < MY- + ASTHENIA]

Myc·a·le (mik′ə·lē), **Mount** A peak in SW Turkey on the mainland opposite Samos; scene of a Greek naval victory over the Persians, 479 B.C.

my·ce·li·um (mī·sē′lē·əm) *n. Bot.* The thallus or vegetative portion of a fungus, consisting of threadlike tubes, or hyphae. See illustration under MUSHROOM. Also **my′cele** (-sēl). [< NL < Gk. *mykēs* mushroom] **—my·ce′li·al, my·ce′li·an** *adj.* **—my·ce′li·oid, my·ce·loid** (mī′sə·loid) *adj.*

My·ce·nae (mī·sē′nē) An ancient city in NE Peloponnesus, Greece; excavated 1876–77. Also **My·ce′næ.**

My·ce·nae·an (mī′sə·nē′ən) *adj.* Of or pertaining to Mycenae or to a civilization of which it was the center, existing in parts of Greece, Asia Minor, Sicily, and neighboring countries before the advance of the Hellenes, and thought to have been at its height about 1400 B.C.

-mycete *combining form Bot.* A member of a class of fungi: corresponding in use to class names in *-mycetes*: *Basidiomycete.* See -MYCETES]

-mycetes *combining form Bot.* Used to form class names of fungi: *Basidiomycetes.* [< Gk. *mykēs, mykētos* fungus]

my·ce·to·gen·ic (mī·sē′tō·jen′ik) *adj.* Produced or caused by a fungus. Also **my·ce′to·ge·net′ic** (-jə·net′ik), **my′ce·tog′e·nous** (-toj′ə·nəs). [< Gk. *mykēs, mykētos* mushroom + -GENIC]

my·ce·to·ma (mī′sə·tō′mə) *n. pl.* **·to·ma·ta** (-tō′mə·tə) *Pathol.* A tumor or tumorlike growth caused by a fungus, as Madura foot. [< Gk. *mykēs, mykētos* fungus + -OMA]

my·ce·to·zo·an (mī·sē′tō·zō′ən) A myxomycete. [< Gk. *mykēs, mykētos* fungus + -ZOA]

myco- *combining form* Fungus: *mycology.* Also before vowels, **myc-.** [< Gk. *mykēs* fungus]

my·co·bac·te·ri·um (mī′kō·bak·tir′ē·əm) *n. pl.* **·ri·a** (-ē·ə) One of a genus *(Mycobacterium)* of slender, typically aerobic bacteria difficult to stain, including the bacterium of tuberculosis and that of leprosy. [< MYCO- + BACTERIUM]

my·col·o·gy (mī·kol′ə·jē) *n.* **1** The science of fungi. **2** The fungous life of a region. [< MYCO- + -LOGY] **—my·co·log·ic** (mī′kə·loj′ik) or **·i·cal** *adj.* **—my·col′o·gist** *n.*

my·cor·rhi·za (mī′kə·rī′zə) *n. Bot.* A subterranean hyphal mass or mycelium often found on the roots of certain trees, especially of the oak, heath, and pine families. Also **my′co·rhi′za.** [< MYCO- + Gk. *rhiza* root] **—my′cor·rhi′zic** *adj.*

my·co·sis (mī·kō′sis) *n. Pathol.* **1** A fungous growth within the body. **2** A disease or morbid condition caused by a fungous growth, as ringworm. [< MYC(O) + -OSIS] **—my·cot′ic** (-kot′ik) *adj.*

my·co·tro·phism (mī′kō·trō′fiz·əm) *n. Bot.* The nutrition of the higher plants by the aid of fungi on their roots and in their leaves; nourishment by mycorrhiza. [< MYCO- + Gk. *trophē* nutrition] **—my′co·tro′phic** *adj.*

my·dri·a·sis (mi·drī′ə·sis, mī-) *n. Pathol.* An abnormal or prolonged dilation of the pupil of the eye. [< LL < Gk.]

myd·ri·at·ic (mid′rē·at′ik) *adj. Med.* Relating to or causing dilation of the pupil. *—n.* A drug that dilates the pupil, as belladonna.

my·e·len·ceph·a·lon (mī′ə·len·sef′ə·lon) *n. Anat.* The afterbrain; the posterior part of the rhombencephalon or that portion of the medulla oblongata lying behind the pons Varolii and cerebellum. [< MYEL(O) + ENCEPHALON]

my·e·lin (mī′ə·lin) *n. Biochem.* A semisolid, fatlike substance that surrounds the axillary portion of medullated nerve fibers; the medullary sheath. Also **my′e·line** (-lēn, -lin). [< Gk. *myelos* marrow]

my·e·li·tis (mī′ə·lī′tis) *n. Pathol.* **1** Inflammation of the spinal cord. **2** Inflammation of the bone marrow. [< MYEL(O) + -ITIS]

myelo- *combining form Anat.* **1** The bone marrow. **2** The spinal cord. Also, before vowels, **myel-.** [< Gk. *myelon* marrow]

my·e·loid (mī′ə·loid) *adj. Anat.* **1** Pertaining to, from, or resembling marrow. **2** Of or pertaining to the spinal cord. [< MYEL(O)- + -OID]

my·e·lo·ma (mī′ə·lō′mə) *n. pl.* **·mas** or **·ma·ta** (-mə·tə) *Pathol.* A tumor composed of bone marrow cells. [< MYEL- + -OMA]

My·ers (mī′ərz), **F(rederic) W(illiam) H(enry),** 1843–1901, English philosopher and writer.

my·ia·sis (mī′yə·sis) *n. Pathol.* Any of various diseases caused by flies or maggots. [< NL < Gk. *myia* fly + -(O)SIS]

Myit·kyi·na The capital of Kachin State, Myanmar.

My·lae (mī′lē) The ancient name for MILAZZO; scene of a Roman naval victory over Carthage, 260 B.C. Also **My′læ.**

my·lo·nite (mī′lə·nīt) *n. Geol.* A hard, compact rock having a banded or streaky appearance, produced by the crushing and reforming of earth material under extreme pressure. [< Gk. *mylōn* mill]

my·na (mī′nə) *n.* One of various Oriental, starlinglike birds of the genera *Acridotheres* and *Eulabes. Eulabes religiosa,* the common myna of India, is often tamed and taught to speak words: sometimes spelled *mina, minah.* Also **my′nah.** [< Hind. *mainā*]

MYNA (About 9 inches over all)

myn·heer (mīn·hâr′, -hir′) *n.* Sir; Mr.: a Dutch title of address; hence, a Dutchman. [< Du. *mijn heer,* lit., my lord]

myo- *combining form* Muscle; of or pertaining to muscle: *myology.* Also, before vowels, *my-.* [< Gk. *mys, myos* a muscle]

my·o·car·di·al (mī′ō·kär′dē·əl) *adj. Anat.* Of or pertaining to the heart muscle. [< MYO- + Gk. *kardia* heart]

my·o·car·di·o·gram (mī′ō·kär′dē·ə·gram) *n.* The record made by a myocardiograph.

my·o·car·di·o·graph (mī′ō·kär′dē·ə·graf, -gräf) *n.* An instrument for registering the muscular action of the heart.

my·o·car·di·tis (mī′ō·kär·dī′tis) *n. Pathol.* Inflammation of the myocardium. [< NL] **—my′o·car·dit′ic** (-dit′ik) *adj.*

my·o·car·di·um (mī′ō·kär′dē·əm) *n. Anat.* The muscular tissue of the heart. [< NL < MYO- + Gk. *kardia* heart]

my·o·ge·net·ic (mī′ō·jə·net′ik) *adj. Physiol.* Originating in muscle or in muscle tissue. Also **my′o·gen′ic, my·og·e·nous** (mī·oj′ə·nəs).

my·o·gram (mī′ə·gram) *n.* The record made by a myograph.

my·o·graph (mī′ə·graf, -gräf) *n.* An instrument for recording and showing muscular movement.

my·og·ra·phy (mī·og′rə·fē) *n.* A scientific description of muscles.

my·oid (mī′oid) *adj.* Resembling a muscle or muscle tissue.

my·ol·o·gy (mī·ol′ə·jē) *n.* The study of the structure, functions, and diseases of the muscles. [< MYO- + -LOGY] **—my·o·log·ic** (mī′ə·loj′ik) or **·i·cal** *adj.* **—my·ol′o·gist** *n.*

my·o·ma (mī·ō′mə) *n. pl.* **·ma·ta** (-mə·tə) *Pathol.* A muscular tumor. [< MY- + -OMA] **—my·om′a·tous** (-om′ə·təs) *adj.*

my·o·mec·to·my (mī′ō·mek′tə·mē). *n. Surg.* The removal of a myoma. [< MYOMA + -ECTOMY]

my·op·a·thy (mī·op′ə·thē) *n. Pathol.* Disease of a muscle. Also **my·o·path·i·a** (mī′ō·path′ē·ə) [< MYO- + -PATHY] **—my′o·path′ic** *adj.*

my·ope (mī′ōp) *n.* One who is near-sighted. Also **my′ops** (-ops). [< F < LL *myops* < Gk. *myōps* < *myein* close + *ōps* an eye]

my·o·pi·a (mī·ō′pē·ə) *n. Pathol.* Defect in vision so that objects can be seen distinctly only when very near the eye; near-sightedness due to focusing of images in front of instead of on the retina. Also **my·o·py** (mī′ə·pē). [< NL] **—my·op′ic** (-op′ik) *adj.*

my·o·scope (mī′ə·skōp) *n. Med.* An instrument for observing the contraction of muscles.

my·o·sin (mī′ə·sin) *n.* A globulin constituting about half of the protein in muscle and combining with actin to form actomyosin. [< Gk. *mys, myos* muscle]

my·o·sis (mī·ō′sis) See MIOSIS.

my·o·so·tis (mī′ə·sō′tis) *n.* Any of a genus of plants *(Myosotis)* of the borage family; especially, *M. scorpioides,* having branched racemes of blue or pink flowers. Also **my′o·sote** (-sōt). [< NL < Gk., lit., mouse ear < *mys, myos* a mouse + *ous, ōtos* ear]

my·ot·ic (mī·ot′ik) *adj.* Of, pertaining to, or having miosis. *—n.* A drug causing contraction of the pupil of the eye.

My·ra (mī′rə) An ancient city of Lycia, Asia Minor, *Acts* xxvii 5.

myria- *combining form* **1** Very many; of great number: *myriapod.* **2** In the metric system, ten thousand: *myriagram.* Also, before vowels, **myri-.** [< Gk. *myrios* < *myrioi* ten thousand]

myr·i·ad (mir′ē·əd) *adj.* Composed of a very large indefinite number; innumerable. *—n.* **1** A vast indefinite number. **2** Ten thousand. [< Gk. *myrias, myriados* < *myrois* numberless]

myr·i·a·gram (mir′ē·ə·gram′), **myr·i·a·li·ter** (-lē′tər), **myr·i·a·me·ter** (mē′tər) *n.* In the metric system, 10,000 grams, liters, or meters.

myr·i·a·pod (mir′ē·ə·pod) *n.* One of a class of arthropods *(Myriapoda)* whose bodies are made up of a varying number of segments, each of which bears one or two pairs of jointed appendages: includes the centipedes and millipedes. **—myr·i·ap·o·dan** (mir′ē·ap′ə·dən) *adj.* & *n.* **—myr′i·ap′o·dous** *adj.*

my·ri·ca (mi·rī′kə) *n.* The dried bark of the wax-myrtle root, used in medicine as an alterative and emetic. [< L < Gk. *myrikē* tamarisk]

my·ris·tic (mi·ris′tik) *adj.* **1** Of, pertaining to, or containing the principle of nutmeg. **2** *Chem.* Designating a white crystalline acid, $C_{14}H_{28}O_2$, contained in nutmeg butter and similar vegetable sources. [< NL *nux myristica* nutmeg genus < Gk. *myrizein* anoint]

myrmeco- *combining form* Ant; pertaining to ants: *myrmecophagous.* Also, before vowels, **myrmec-.** [< Gk. *myrmēx, myrmēkos* ant]

myr·me·col·o·gy (mûr′mə·kol′ə·jē) *n.* The department of entomology that treats of ants. [< MYRMECO- + -LOGY] **—myr′me·co·log′i·cal** (-kə·loj′i·kəl) *adj.* **—myr′me·col′o·gist** *n.*

myr·me·coph·a·gous (mûr′mə·kof′ə·gəs) *adj.* Feeding on ants. [< MYRMECO- + -PHAGOUS]

myr·mi·don (mûr′mə·don, -dən) *n.* A faithful adherent; also, a follower or underling of rough or desperate character, who executes the commands of his master without question or scruple; especially, a petty officer of the law. [<MYRMIDON]

Myr·mi·don (mûr′mə·don, -dən) *n.* One of a warlike people of ancient Thessaly, represented as followers of Achilles in the Trojan War. [<Gk. *Myrmidones*] —**Myr′mi·do′ni·an** (-dō′nē·ən) *adj.*

my·rob·a·lan (mī·rob′ə·lən, mi-) *n.* **1** Any of the prunelike fruits of several tropical plants (genus *Terminalia*), formerly much used by tanners and calico printers. **2** The weeping plum of the western Mediterranean region *(Phyllanthus emblica).* **3** The myrobalan plum of SW Asia *(Prunus cerasifera),* having a sweet, very juicy fruit. [<F <L *myrobalanum* <Gk. *myrobalanos* <*myron* juice, ointment + *balanos* nut]

My·ron (mī′rən) A Greek sculptor of the fifth century B.C. —**My·ron′ic** (-ron′ik) *adj.*

my·ro·sin (mī′rə·sin, mir′ə·sin) *n. Biochem.* An enzyme found in the seeds of black and white mustard: it hydrolyzes the glycosides. [<Gk. *myron* ointment]

myrrh (mûr) *n.* **1** An aromatic gum resin that exudes from several trees or shrubs of Arabia and Abyssinia: used in medicine. **2** Any shrub or tree that yields this gum, especially *Commiphora myrrha* and *C. abyssinica.* [OE *murra* <L *myrrha* <Gk. <Semitic. Cf. Arabic *myrr,* Hebrew *mōr.*]

myr·rhin (mûr′in, mir′-) *n. Biochem.* A resinous principle found in myrrh. Also **myr′rhine.**

myr·ta·ceous (mûr·tā′shəs) *adj.* Pertaining to or designating a family *(Myrtaceae)* of trees or shrubs, the myrtle family, widely distributed in tropical and semitropical countries, and including many valuable aromatic resin- and timber-producing genera, as *Pimenta, Eucalyptus, Caryophyllus,* etc. [<NL *Myrtaceae* <L *myrtus* a myrtle tree]

myr·tle (mûr′təl) *n.* **1** A tree or shrub of the genus *Myrtus;* especially, *M. communis* of southern Europe, originally from Asia. It is a bushy shrub or small tree with glossy evergreen leaves, fragrant white or rose-colored flowers, and black berries. **2** One of various other plants like the common myrtle. Among the ancients it was sacred to Venus. **3** The periwinkle *(Vinca minor);* also, the California laurel *(Umbellularia californica).* [<F *myrtille* bilberry <Med. L *myrtillus* myrtle, dim. of L *myrtus* <Gk. *myrtos* <Semitic. Cf. Persian *mūrd.*]

Myr·tle (mûr′təl) A feminine personal name. [<MYRTLE]

myrtle warbler A small insectivorous bird *(Dendroica coronata)* of North America, with blue-gray or black-and-yellow back.

my·sel (mī·sel′) *pron. Scot.* Myself; by myself. Also **my·sell′.**

my·self (mī·self′) *pron.* **1** I; me: the emphatic form of *I* and *me,* and reflexive of *me:* used in the nominative with *I* in apposition: I *myself* will see to it; I'll write it *myself;* also, in poetical nominative use as a simple subject: *Myself* hath often heard; also used as the object of a verb either direct or indirect: I deceived *myself* (reflexive); She invited Helen, Jeff, and *myself* (compound object); I got it for *myself* (object of a preposition). **2** Normal condition of mind or body: I feel *myself* again. [OE *mē sylf*]

My·si·a (mish′ē·ə) An ancient region of NW Asia Minor on the Aegean and the Sea of Marmara.

My·sore (mī·sôr′, -sōr′) **1** A constituent State of southern India on the southern Deccan Plateau; 74,326 square miles; capital, Bangalore. **2** The former dynastic capital of Mysore State. Also *Maisur.*

mys·ta·gog (mis′tə·gôg, -gog) *n.* An interpreter of religious mysteries; an initiator into mysteries; teacher. Also **mys′ta·gogue.** [<F <L *mystagogus* <Gk. *mystagōgos* <*mystēs* an initiate + *agōgos* leader <*agein.* See MYSTERY.] —**mys′ta·gog′ic** (-goj′ik) *adj.* —**mys′ta·go′gy** (-gō′jē) *n.*

mys·te·ri·ous (mis·tir′ē·əs) *adj.* Involved in or implying mystery; unexplained; obscure. [<L *mysterium*] —**mys·te′ri·ous·ly** *adv.* —**mys·te′ri·ous·ness** *n.*

Synonyms: abstruse, cabalistic, dark, enigmatic, hidden, incomprehensible, inexplicable, inscrutable, mystic, mystical, obscure, occult, recondite, secret, transcendental, unfathomable, unfathomed, unknown. That is *mysterious* in the true sense which is beyond human comprehension; that is *mystic* or *mystical* which has associated with it some *hidden* or *recondite* meaning. See DARK, SECRET. *Antonyms:* see synonyms for CLEAR.

mys·ter·y[1] (mis′tər·ē) *n. pl.* **·ter·ies** **1** Something unknown or incomprehensible in its nature; an inexplicable phenomenon. **2** Secrecy or obscurity: an event wrapped in *mystery.* **3** A secret: the *mysteries* of freemasonry. **4** Any affair or event so concealed or unexplained as to excite awe or curiosity: a murder *mystery.* **5** A literary or dramatic piece relating such an affair. **6** *Theol.* A truth known only through faith or revelation and incomprehensible to the human reason. **7** *Eccl.* **a** A sacrament, especially the Eucharist. **b** *pl.* The eucharistic elements. **8** *pl.* In classical antiquity, certain religious rites to which only selected worshipers were admitted. **9** *pl.* A cult practicing such rites. **10** A medieval dramatic performance based on Scriptural events or characters: also **mystery play.** [<L *mysterium* <Gk. *mystērion* secret worship, secret thing <*mystēs* an initiate into the mysteries <*myein* shut, shut the eyes]

mys·ter·y[2] (mis′tər·ē) *n. pl.* **·ter·ies** *Archaic* A trade; occupation. [<Med. L *misterium* <L *ministerium* service, office; infl. in form by L *mysterium*]

mys·tic (mis′tik) *adj.* **1** Pertaining to a mystery of the faith. **2** Spiritually symbolic. **3** Of or designating an occult or esoteric rite, practice, etc. **4** Of mysterious meaning or character; mysterious. —*n.* **1** One who professes a knowledge of spiritual truth or a feeling of union with the divine, reached through contemplation or intuition. **2** A practicer of occult or mystical rites. [<L *mysticus* <Gk. *mystikos* pertaining to secret rites <*mystēs* an initiate]

mys·ti·cal (mis′ti·kəl) *adj.* **1** Having a spiritual character or reality beyond the comprehension of human reason. **2** Relating to mystics or mysticism. **3** Mystic (defs. 2 and 3).

mys·ti·cism (mis′tə·siz′əm) *n.* **1** The belief that knowledge of divine truth or the soul's union with the divine is attainable by spiritual insight or ecstatic contemplation without the medium of the senses or reason. **2** Any theory advancing intense meditative and intuitive methods of thought or conduct. **3** Vague or obscure speculation involving confused or fanciful thinking.

mys·ti·fy (mis′tə·fī) *v.t.* **·fied, ·fy·ing** **1** To confuse, especially deliberately; perplex or bewilder; hoax. **2** To treat as obscure or mysterious. See synonyms under PERPLEX. [<F *mystifier*] —**mys′ti·fi·ca′tion** *n.* —**mys′ti·fi′er** *n.*—**mys′ti·fy′ing** *adj.* —**mys′ti·fy′ing·ly** *adv.*

mys·tique (mis·tēk′) *n. French* The mythical and enigmatic character of a person, idea, or thing, as a focus of popular veneration: the *mystique* of Stalin.

myth (mith) *n.* **1** A story, presented as historical, dealing with the cosmological and supernatural traditions of a people, their gods, culture, heroes, religious beliefs, etc. **2** A popular fable or folk tale. **3** A parable; allegory. See synonyms under FICTION. [<LL *mythos* <Gk., word, speech, story]

myth·i·cal (mith′i·kəl) *adj.* **1** Pertaining to myth; legendary. **2** Fictitious. Also **myth′ic.** —**myth′i·cal·ly** *adv.*

myth·i·cize (mith′ə·sīz) *v.t.* **·cized, ·ciz·ing** To convert into or explain as a myth.

mytho- *combining form* Myth; myth and: *mythography.* Also, before vowels, **myth-.** [<Gk. *mythos* a legend]

my·thog·ra·phy (mi·thog′rə·fē) *n.* **1** The collecting of myths; descriptive mythology. **2** Expression of mythic characters or ideas in art form. [<MYTHO- + -GRAPHY] —**my·thog′ra·pher** *n.*

my·thol·o·gize (mi·thol′ə·jīz) *v.* **·gized, ·giz·ing** *v.i.* To narrate, classify, or explain myths. —*v.t.* To mythicize. Also *Brit.* **my·thol′o·gise.** [<F *mythologiser*] —**my·thol′o·gist, my·thol′o·giz′er** *n.*

my·thol·o·gy (mi·thol′ə·jē) *n. pl.* **·gies** **1** The myths and legends of a people concerning creation, gods, and heroes. **2** The scientific collection and study of myths; study of the beliefs of mankind; also, a volume of myths. [<LL *mythologia* <Gk., telling of tales <*mythos* legend + *logos* discourse] —**myth·o·log·i·cal** (mith′ə·loj′i·kəl), **myth′o·log′ic** *adj.* —**myth′o·log′i·cal·ly** *adv.*

myth·o·ma·ni·a (mith′ə·mā′nē·ə, -mān′yə) *n.* A compulsive tendency to tell lies.

myth·o·pe·ic (mith′ə·pē′ik) *adj.* Mythmaking; relating to a supposed stage of human culture when all natural phenomena are explained by myths. Also **myth′o·poe′ic.** [<Gk. *mythopoios* <*mythos* legend + *poieein* make] —**myth′o·pe′ist** *n.*

Myt·i·le·ne (mit′ə·lē′nē) **1** Lesbos. **2** A seaport on SE Lesbos, capital of the Aegean Islands division of Greece: formerly *Kastro.* Also **Myt′i·li′ni.**

myx·e·de·ma (mik′sə·dē′mə) *n. Pathol.* A disease associated with hypotrophy of the thyroid gland and characterized by dryness and wrinkling of the skin, swelling of the face, and progressive mental deterioration. Also **myx′oe·de′ma.** [<NL <MYX(O)- + EDEMA] —**myx′e·dem′ic** (-dem′ik), **myx′e·dem′a·tous** (-dem′ə·təs) *adj.*

myxo- *combining form* Slimy; like mucus. Also, before vowels, **myx-.** [<Gk. *myxa* mucus]

myx·o·ma (mik·sō′mə) *n. pl.* **·ma·ta** (-mə·tə) *Pathol.* A soft, elastic tumor composed of mucous tissue. [<NL <MYX(O)- + -OMA] —**myx·om·a·tous** (mik·som′ə·təs) *adj.*

myx·o·my·cete (mik′sō·mī·sēt′) *n.* One of the slime molds *(Myxomycetes),* a class of fungi exhibiting both plant and animal characteristics and classified by some authorities as *Mycetozoa.* They consist of masses of naked protoplasm with ameboid movements, and are chiefly saprophytic, living on dead and decaying matter. [<MYXO- + -MYCETE] —**myx′o·my·ce′tous** *adj.*

N

n, N (en) *n. pl.* **n's, N's** or **ns, Ns, ens** (enz) **1** The 14th letter of the English alphabet: from Phoenician *nun,* Greek *nu,* Roman *N.* **2** The sound of the letter *n,* a voiced, alveolar nasal. See ALPHABET. —*symbol* **1** *Printing* An en: see EN. **2** *Chem.* Nitrogen (symbol N). **3** *Math.* An indefinite number.

Na *Chem.* Sodium (symbol Na). [<NL *natrium*]

nab[1] (nab) *v.t.* **nabbed, nab·bing** *Colloq.* **1** To catch or arrest, as a criminal. **2** To take or seize suddenly. [Cf. Norw., Sw. *nappa* snatch]

nab[2] (nab) *n.* **1** *Geog.* A projecting part of a hill or rock; a peak, promontory, or summit. **2** *Mech.* A projection or spur on the bolt of a lock. [<ON *nabbi* a knoll]

Nab·a·te·an (nab′ə·tē′ən) *n.* **1** One of an ancient Arabic people dwelling east and southeast of Palestine, independent from 312 B.C. to A.D. 106, when they submitted to Roman rule. **2** The language of these people, belonging to the Aramaic subgroup of the Northwest Semitic languages.

Na·blus (nä·blo͞os′) The chief town of Samaria, western Jordan, on the site of ancient *Sechem*, rebuilt by Hadrian as *Neapolis*.

na·bob (nā′bob) *n.* **1** A European who has become rich in India; hence, any rich man. **2** A nawab, viceroy, or governor in India under the old Mogul empire. [<Hind. *nawwāb* <Arabic *nuwwab*, pl. of *nā'ib* a deputy] **—na′bob·er·y** *n.* **—na′bob·ish** *adj.*

Na·both (nā′both) In the Bible, the owner of a vineyard which Ahab coveted and, with the aid of Jezebel, unlawfully procured. I *Kings* xxi.

nac·a·rat (nak′ə·rat) *n.* **1** Bright red-orange color. **2** A fine linen or crêpe fabric dyed this color. [<F, appar. <Sp. *nacarado* <*nacar* nacre]

na·celle (nə·sel′) *n.* Aeron. **1** The basket suspended from a balloon. **2** The framework below the envelope of a dirigible balloon, which carries the motor, passengers, etc. **3** An enclosed shelter for housing the cargo or power plant and sometimes the personnel of an airplane. [<F]

na·cho (nä′chō) *n. pl.* **-chos** A tortilla chip covered with beans, hot peppers, etc., then sprinkled with cheese. [<Sp.]

na·cre (nā′kər) *n.* Mother-of-pearl. [<F]

na·cre·ous (nā′krē·əs) *adj.* **1** Of, like, or producing nacre. **2** Iridescent; pearly.

na·da (nä′də) *n.* In East Indian music, the term for a esthetically agreeable sound, as distinct from noise, grinding, clanging, etc.

na·dir (nā′dər, -dir) *n.* **1** The point of the celestial sphere directly beneath the place where one stands: opposed to *zenith*. **2** Figuratively, the lowest possible point: the *nadir* of melancholy. [<F <Arabic *nadir (es-semt)* opposite (the zenith)]

nae (nā) *adj. Scot.* No; none.

nae·thing (nā′thing) *n. Scot.* Nothing.

nae·void (nē′void), **nae·vus** (nē′vəs) See NEVOID, NEVUS.

Na·fud (na·fo͞od′) A desert area in northern Saudi Arabia: also *Nefud*.

nag[1] (nag) *v.* **nagged, nag·ging** *v.t.* To torment with constant faultfinding, scolding, and urging. *—v.i.* To scold, find fault, or urge continually. *—n.* One who nags, especially a woman. [<Scand. Cf. Sw. *nagga* vex.] **—nag′·ger** *n.* **—nag′ging** *adj.* **—nag′ging·ly** *adv.*

nag[2] (nag) *n.* **1** A pony or small horse. **2** An old or inferior horse. **3** *Archaic* A worthless person; jade. [ME *nagge;* origin uncertain]

Na·ga Hills (nä′gə) A series of hill ranges between NE India and western Burma.

na·ga·na (nə·gä′nə) *n.* A disease of cattle and horses caused by trypanosomes introduced into the blood by the tsetse fly. [<Zulu]

Na·ga·ri (nä′gə·rē) *n.* **1** Any one of a group of vernacular alphabets in India. **2** Devanagari.

Na·ga·sa·ki (nä·gä·sä·kē) A port on western Kyushu island, Japan; largely destroyed by an atomic bomb dropped by U.S. airmen on August 9, 1945.

Nä·ge·li (nā′gə·lē), **Karl Wilhelm von,** 1817–1891, Swiss botanist.

Na·gor·no-Ka·ra·bakh Autonomous Region (nä·gôr′nə·kä′rä·bäkh′) An administrative division of SW Azerbaijan S.S.R.; 1,700 square miles.

Na·go·ya (nä·gō·yä) A city on southern Honshu island, Japan, on Ise Bay.

Nag·pur (näg′po͝or) A city in NE Bombay State, India, former capital of Madhya Pradesh State.

Nag·y·va·rad (nôd′y′·vä ′rôd) Hungarian name for ORADEA.

Na·ha (nä·hä) Chief city of Okinawa island and headquarters of the U.S. military government of the Ryukyu Islands.

Na·hua (nä′wä) *n. pl.* **Na·hua** One of a group of civilized Indian peoples of Mexico and Central America belonging to the Uto-Aztecan linguistic stock, including the Aztecs, Toltecs, etc.

Na·hua·tl (nä′wät′l) *n.* The Uto-Aztecan language of the Aztecs, including many dialects. *—adj.* Designating or pertaining to this language.

Na·hua·tlan (nä′wät·lən) *n.* A branch of the Uto-Aztecan linguistic family of North American Indians, including the Aztec dialects. — *adj.* Of or pertaining to this linguistic branch.

Na·huel Hua·pí (nä·wel′ wä ·pē′) A lake on the eastern slope of the Andes in western Argentina near the Chilean border; 210 square miles.

Na·hum (nā′əm, -hum) A Hebrew prophet; also, the book of the Old Testament containing his prophecies. [<Hebrew, consolation]

nai·ad (nā′ad, nī′-) *n. pl.* **·ads** or **·a·des** (-ə·dēz) **1** In classical mythology, one of the water nymphs who were believed to dwell in and preside over fountains, lakes, brooks, and wells. **2** *Bot.* A plant of the pondweed family (genus *Naias*). **3** The nymph stage in the life cycle of certain insects: applied especially to aquatic forms. [<Gk. *Naias, -ados.* Related to Gk. *naein* flow.]

nai·ant (nā′ənt) See NATANT.

Na·i·du (nä′i·do͞o), **Sarojini,** 1879–1949, Hindu poet and reformer.

na·if (nä·ēf′) *adj. French* Masculine form of NAIVE. Also **na·ïf′.**

naig (nāg) *n. Scot.* A nag; riding horse. Also **naig′ ie.**

nail (nāl) *n.* **1** A thin horny plate on the end of a finger or toe. **2** A claw, talon, or hoof. **3** A slender piece of metal having a point and a head, and used for driving into or through wood, etc., as for fastening pieces together. **4** A measure of length, 2 1/4 inches. **5** A callosity on the inner side of a horse's leg. **—on the nail** *Colloq.* **1** Right away; immediately. **2** At the exact spot or moment. **3** Of immediate interest or importance; under discussion. — *v.t.* **1** To fasten or fix in place with a nail or nails. **2** To close up or shut in by means of nails. **3** To secure by decisive or prompt action: to *nail* a contract. **4** To fix firmly or immovably: Terror *nailed* him to the spot. **5** To succeed in hitting or striking. **6** *Colloq.* To catch or seize; intercept. **7** *Colloq.* To detect and expose, as a lie or liar. [OE *nægel*]

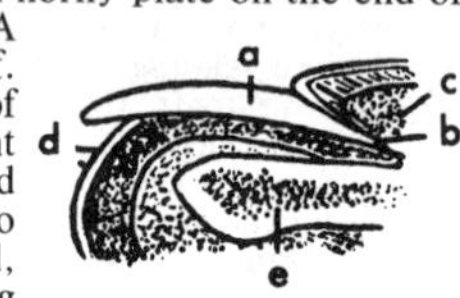

HUMAN FINGERNAIL
Longitudinal section
a. Nail.
b. Matrix.
c. Nailfold.
d. Epidermis.
e. Phalanx.

nail bed *Anat.* That portion of the true skin upon which the nail rests.

nail·brush (nāl ′brush′) *n.* A brush with stiff bristles, used for cleaning the hands and fingernails.

nail file A fine, flat file used for manicuring the fingernails.

nail·fold (nāl′fōld′) *n. Anat.* The duplication of the skin that surrounds the edges of a nail; cuticle.

nail polish A lacquer applied to the nails to give a glossy finish, made from soluble cotton treated with various organic compounds, as toluene, ethyl acetate, ethanol, etc., and usually colored by the addition of dyes. Also **nail enamel.**

nain·sook (nān′so͝ok, nan′-) *n.* A soft, lightweight cotton fabric, heavier than batiste: used for lingerie and infants' wear. [<Hind. *nainsukh*, lit., pleasure of the eye]

Nai·paul (nī′pôl;), **V.S.,** born 1932, West Indian novelist, educated in Trinidad and England. Full name, **Vidiadhar Surajprasad Naipaul.**

Nairn (nârn) A county in NE Scotland; 163 square miles; county town, Nairn. Also **Nairn·shire** (nârn′shir, -shər).

Nai·ro·bi (nī·rō′bē) The capital of Kenya in eastern Africa.

na·ive (nä·ēv′) *adj.* **1** Ingenuous; artless; without sophistication. **2** Not consciously logical; uncritical. Also **na·ïve′.** See synonyms under CANDID. [<F, fem. of *naïf* <L *nativus* natural. Doublet of NATIVE.] **—na·ive′ly** *adv.* **—na·ive′ness** *n.*

na·ive·té (nä·ēv′tā′, nä·ēv′tā) *n.* The state or quality of being naive. Also **na·ïve′té′, na·ive·ty** (nä·ēv′tē).

Najd (näjd) See NEJD.

Na·jin (nä·jēn) A port of Northern Korea. *Japanese* **Ra·shin** (rä·shēn).

na·ked (nā′kid) *adj.* **1** Having no clothes or garments on; nude. **2** Having no covering, or lacking the usual covering. **3** Unsheathed; bare, as a sword. **4** Unsaddled, as a horse. **5** Having no defense or protection; exposed. **6** Being without means of sustenance, etc.; destitute; bare; also, stripped. **7** Being without concealment or excuse. **8** Without addition or adornment; plain; evident; mere. **9** Without some accessory, qualification, belonging, etc., which is customary or natural. **10** *Law* Having no consideration or inducement; unconfirmed; not validated. **11** *Bot.* **a** Not enclosed in an ovary or case. **b** Without a pericarp: said of seeds. **c** Destitute of leaves: said of stalks. **d** Having no hairs; smooth: said of leaves. **12** *Zool.* Lacking fur, hair, scales, or feathers. [OE *nacod*] **—na′ked·ly** *adv.* **—na′ked·ness** *n.*

naked eye The eye unaided by optical instruments.

Na·khi·che·van Autonomous S.S.R. (nä ′·khē·che·vän′) **1** A republic forming part of the Azerbaijan S.S.R.; 2,100 square miles. **2** Its capital and chief city, on the Araxes.

Nak·tong (näk·tông) The largest river of Korea, flowing 326 miles to Korea Strait near Pusan.

Nal·chik (näl′chik) The capital of Kabardian Autonomous S.S.R.

nam (näm, nam) Past tense of NIM.

nam·a·ble (nā′mə·bəl) *adj.* **1** Capable of being named. **2** Memorable; worthy of being mentioned. Also **name′a·ble. —nam′a·bil′i·ty, name′a·bil′i·ty** *n.*

Na·man·gan (nä′män·gän′) A city in eastern Uzbek S.S.R.

Na·ma·qua·land (nə·mä′ kwə·land) A coastal region of SW Africa, divided by the Orange River into **Great Namaqualand** in Namibia and **Little Namaqualand** in Northern Cape Province, Republic of South Africa. Also **Na′ma·land.**

nam·ay·cush (nam′ə·kush, -ā -) *n.* The great lake trout *(Cristivomer namaycush)* of North America; the Mackinaw trout: also spelled *naymacush*. [<Algonquian (Cree) *namekus* trout]

nam·by-pam·by (nam′bē·pam′bē) *adj.* Weakly sentimental; insipid; inane. — *n. pl.* **-pam·bies** **1** Writing, talk, or action of a feebly sentimental or finical character. **2** A person given to such talk or action. [<nickname of Ambrose Philips, 1671–1749, English poet; with ref. to his feeble, sentimental verse]

name (nām) *n.* **1** The distinctive appellation by which a person or thing is known. **2** A descriptive or arbitrary appellation; designation; title. **3** General reputation; eminence; fame. **4** A person, cause, thing, or class, or the claims of authority thereof, as represented by the name. **5** An opprobrious appellation. **6** A race or family, as having a common descent and patronymic. **7** A memorable person, character, or thing: great *names* in music. **8** Mere sound or simulation, in distinction from substance or reality: a wife in *name* only. **—by the name of** Named. *—v.t.* **named, nam·ing** **1** To give a name to; entitle; style; term. **2** To mention or refer to by name; cite. **3** To designate for some particular purpose or office; nominate; appoint. **4** To give the name of; identify: *Name* the capital of Peru. **5** To set or specify, as a price or requirement. [OE *nama*] **—nam′er** *n.*

Synonyms (noun) : agnomen, appellation, cognomen, denomination, designation, epithet, style, title. *Name* in the most general sense includes all other words of this group; in the more limited sense a *name* is personal, an *appellation* is descriptive, a *title* is official. In the phrase William the Conqueror, king of England, William is the man's *name*, which belongs to him personally; Conqueror is the *appellation* which he won by his acquistion of England; king is the *title* denoting his royal rank. An *epithet* is given to mark some assumed characteristic, good or bad. *Designation* may be used in the sense of *appellation*, but is far broader and more general in meaning. One's personal *name*, as John or Mary, is given in infancy, and is often called the given or Christian, or first *name*. The *cognomen* is the family *name* which belongs to one by right of birth or marriage. In modern use, *style* is the legal *designation* by which a person or house is known in official or business